# HARRAP'S
# GIANT PAPERBACK

# SPANISH
# DICTIONARY

## SPANISH-ENGLISH
## ENGLISH-SPANISH

*First published in Great Britain as*
*Harrap Concise Spanish Dictionary 1998*
by Chambers Harrap Publishers Ltd
7 Hopetoun Crescent, Edinburgh EH7 4AY

© Chambers Harrap Publishers 1998

ISBN 0-02-862375-4

Macmillan General Reference
A Simon and Schuster Macmillan Company
1633 Broadway
New York, NY 10019-6785

MACMILLAN is a registered trademark
of Macmillan Inc.

Printed in the United States of America

iii

**Trademarks**

Words considered to be trademarks have been designated in this dictionary by the symbol ®. However, no judgement is implied concerning the legal status of any trademark by virtue of the presence or absence of such a symbol.

**Marcas Registradas**

Las palabras consideradas marcas registradas vienen señaladas en este diccionario con una ®. Sin embargo, la presencia o la ausencia de tal distintivo no implica juicio alguno acerca de la situación legal de la marca registrada.

# Contents
# Contenido

# Preface

Harrap's *Giant Paperback Spanish Dictionary* is the result of several years' work by a team of British and Spanish lexicographers based in Harrap's Edinburgh offices, with the assistance of specialists in Latin-American Spanish and American English. The English side has been enriched by neologisms collected as part of our sister company Chambers' *Wordtrack* programme to ensure that this dictionary is as up-to-date as possible. The result is an easy-to-use guide to modern English and Spanish, in both European and American varieties, with accurate, reliable translations.

As the dictionary will have a wide variety of users, and will find a place in school and workplace alike, it contains a broad range of vocabulary. In addition to good coverage of the Spanish and English spoken today, including slang (an important feature of all Harrap dictionaries), technical terms from computing, finance, education, the media and business will be found alongside encyclopedic information such as geographical names and cultural items. Within both the English-Spanish and Spanish-English sides of the dictionary the user will find usage panels which give help on particular points of grammatical difficulty.

The growth of the Internet and the information super-highway is taking communication between the peoples of the world into a new era. Harrap has responded to the challenge this represents. Terms such as **Web site**, **browser**, **newsgroup** and **navegar por Internet**, **ciberespacio**, **internauta**, which are now commonplace, will all be found in these pages.

# Prefacio

El diccionario *Giant Paperback Spanish Dictionary* de Harrap's es el resultado
de varios años de trabajo llevado a cabo en nuestra sede de Edimburgo por
un equipo de lexicógrafos británicos y españoles con la colaboración de
especialistas en español de América e inglés norteamericano. La inclusión
de neologismos procedentes de la base de datos del programa *Wordtrack* de la
editorial asociada Chambers garantiza una lista de términos lo más
actualizada posible. El resultado es un manual del inglés y del español
modernos, en sus variedades europea y americana, claro y fácil de usar
que ofrece al usuario unas traducciones fieles y precisas.

Este diccionario va dirigido a un público muy amplio y gracias a la variedad
del vocabulario que contiene resultará de utilidad tanto en la escuela como
en la oficina. Además de la extensa cobertura del español y el inglés
actuales, incluidos términos de argot (uno de los puntos fuertes de la gama
de diccionarios Harrap's), el lector podrá encontrar términos técnicos
procedentes de los campos de la informática, del mundo financiero y de la
economía, de la educación y de los medios de comunicación, así como datos
enciclopédicos tales como topónimos y referencias culturales. Insertados
en el texto de las partes inglés-español y español-inglés se encuentran
cuadros que ilustran las dificultades gramaticales más comunes.

Ante el reto que supone la llegada de una nueva era en las comunicaciones
propiciada por el desarrollo de Internet, Harrap's no ha querido quedarse
atrás, por lo que hemos incluido los términos más avanzados de las nuevas
tecnologías, como **Web site**, **browser**, **newsgroup** o **navegar por Internet**,
**ciberespacio** e **internauta**.

# Structure of Entries

# Estructura de las Entradas

Field labels indicate senses belonging to a particular subject area
*Indicadores de campo semántico para los términos especializados*

**major** ['meɪdʒə(r)] **1** *n* (a) *Mil* comandante *m*; **m. general** general *m* de división (b) *US Univ (subject)* especialidad *f*
**2** *adj* (a) *(important)* importante, de primer orden; **of m. importance** de enorme importancia (b) *Mus* mayor
**3** *vi US Univ* **to m. in** *(subject)* especializarse en

American English senses indicated
*Se señalan las acepciones usadas en inglés americano*

Compounds placed under first element and listed in alphabetical order
*Las unidades formadas por más de una palabra aparecen en la entrada correspondiente al primer elemento y ordenadas alfabéticamente*

**management** ['mænɪdʒmənt] *n* (a) *(activity) (of company, project)* dirección *f*, gestión *f*; *(of economy, resources)* gestión *f*, administración *f*; **m. consultant** consultor(ora) *m,f* en administración de empresas; **m. studies** estudios *mpl* de gestión empresarial *or* administración de empresas; **m. style** estilo *m* de dirección
(b) *(managers, employers)* **the m.** la dirección; **under new m.** *(sign)* nuevos propietarios; **m. and unions** la patronal y los sindicatos; **m. buyout** = adquisición de una empresa por sus directivos; **m. team** equipo *m* de dirección

Headword abbreviated to first letter in examples
*En los ejemplos sólo aparece la inicial de la palabra de la entrada*

**managing director** ['mænɪdʒɪŋdaɪ'rektə(r)] *n* director(ora) *m,f* gerente

Phonetics shown in full for all headwords
*Todas las entradas llevan la transcripción fonética completa*

New grammatical category introduced by bold numeral, placed on new line
*Cada categoría gramatical aparece precedida por un número en negrita y en un nuevo párrafo*

**melt** [melt] **1** *vt* derretir, fundir; *Fig (sb's resistance)* vencer
**2** *vi* derretirse, fundirse; **it melts in the mouth** se funde en la boca; **to m. into thin air** esfumarse
▸**melt away** *vi (of snow)* derretirse; *(of crowd)* dispersarse, disgregarse; *(of objections, opposition)* disiparse, desvanecerse
▸**melt down** *vt sep (metal)* fundir

Gender of noun translations shown in italic
*El género de las traducciones se indica en letra cursiva*

Phrasal verbs introduced by ▸
*Los verbos con partícula vienen precedidos por el símbolo ▸*

**minute²** ['mɪnɪt] **1** *n* (a) *(of time)* minuto *m*; **it's ten minutes to three** son las tres menos diez; **it's ten minutes past three** son las tres y diez; **wait a m.!** ¡espera un momento!; **just a m.** un momento; **go downstairs this m.!** ¡baja ahora mismo!; **the m. my back was turned she...** en cuanto me di la vuelta, ella...; **he'll be here any m.** llegará en cualquier momento; **it'll be ready in a m.** estará listo en un minuto *or* momento; **I've just popped in for a m.** sólo me quedaré un momento; **until/at the last m.** hasta/en el último momento; **m. hand** *(of watch)* minutero *m*; **m. steak** filete *m* muy fino
(b) *(note)* nota *f*; **minutes** *(of meeting)* acta *f*, actas *fpl*
**2** *vt (make note of)* hacer constar en acta; **the meeting will be minuted** se levantará acta de la reunión

Superscript number marks homographs
*Las formas homógrafas aparecen*

Sense indicators shown in italic in brackets
*Los indicadores semánticos van entre paréntesis y en cursiva*

Feminine inflections shown consistently
*Se muestran todas las terminaciones femeninas*

**minute²** [maɪ'njuːt] *adj* (a) *(small)* diminuto(a), minúsculo(a); *(increase, improvement)* mínimo(a) (b) *(detailed) (examination)* minucioso(a)

This label means that the translation also works in a figurative sense
*La traducción también funciona en sentido figurado*

**mirage** ['mɪrɑːʒ] *n also Fig* espejismo *m*

American spelling variants shown
*Se da la ortografía americana cuando es diferente de la británica*

**MOD** [eməʊ'diː] *n Br (abbr* **Ministry of Defence)** Ministerio *m* de Defensa

Full form of all abbreviations given, with translation
*En las abreviaturas siempre se da la forma completa, así como una traducción*

**mollusc,** *US* **mollusk** ['mɒləsk] *n* molusco *m*

**AA EE** (*abrev de* **Asuntos Exteriores**) Ministerio de AA EE Ministry of Foreign Affairs, *Br* ≃ Foreign Office, *US* ≃ State Department

**abatible** *adj* **mesa a.** foldaway table; **asientos abatibles** (*en coche*) ≈ seats that tip forwards or fold flat

**abarcar** [61] *vt* (a) (*incluir*) to embrace, to cover; *Prov* **quien mucho abarca poco aprieta** don't bite off more than you can chew (b) (*ver*) to be able to see, to have a view of; **desde la torre se abarca todo el valle** you can see the whole valley from the tower

**abridor** *nm* (a) (*abrebotellas*) (bottle) opener (b) (*abrelatas*) *Br* (tin) opener, *US* (can) opener

**abril** *nm* April; **tiene 14 abriles** he is 14 (years of age); *Prov* **en a., aguas mil** March winds, April showers; *ver también* **septiembre**

**abstenerse** [67] *vpr* (a) (*guardarse*) to abstain (**de** from); **se abstuvo de mencionar su embarazo** she refrained from mentioning her pregnancy (b) (*en votación*) to abstain; **me abstuve en las últimas elecciones** I didn't vote in the last election

**abuso** *nm* (a) (*uso excesivo*) abuse (**de** of); **a. de confianza** breach of confidence; **a. de poder** abuse of power; **abusos deshonestos** sexual abuse (b) (*escándalo*) scandal, sin

**actualidad** *nf* (a) (*situación*) current situation; **en la a.** (*momento presente*) at the present time, nowadays; **estar de a.** (*ser de interés*) to be topical; **la a. política** the current political situation (b) (*noticia*) news (*singular*); **la a. informativa** the news; **la a. deportiva** the sports news; **ser a.** to be making the news (c) (*vigencia*) relevance to modern society; **sus libros siguen teniendo gran a.** her books are still very relevant today

**afiche** *nm Am* poster

**ají** *nm Andes, CSur* chilli (pepper)

**alberca** *nf* (a) (*depósito*) water tank (b) *Méx* (*piscina*) swimming pool

**albergar** [40] **1** *vt* (a) (*personas*) to accommodate, to put up (b) (*odio*) to harbour; (*esperanzas*) to cherish
**2 albergarse** *vpr* to stay; **¿en qué hotel se albergan?** what hotel are they staying in?

**albor** *nm* (a) *Literario* (*blancura*) whiteness (b) *Formal* (*luz del alba*) first light of day; *Fig* **albores** (*principio*) dawn, earliest days; **los albores de la civilización** the dawn of civilization

**antigualla** *nf Pey* (*cosa*) museum piece; (*persona*) old fogey, old fossil

**arrejuntarse** *vpr muy Fam* (*pareja*) to shack up together

**argüir** [9] **1** *vt* (a) *Formal* (*argumentar*) to argue (b) (*demostrar*) to prove, to demonstrate (c) (*deducir*) to deduce
**2** *vi* (*argumentar*) to argue

# Símbolos Fonéticos del Inglés

## Consonantes

[b]   but [bʌt]
[d]   dab [dæb]
[dʒ]  jam [dʒæm]; gem [dʒem]
[f]   fat [fæt]
[g]   go [gəʊ]
[h]   hat [hæt]
[j]   yet [jet]
[k]   cat [kæt]
[l]   lad [læd]
[m]   mat [mæt]
[n]   no [nəʊ]
[ŋ]   bang [bæŋ]
[p]   pat [pæt]
[r]   rat [ræt]
[(r)] *(se pronuncia únicamente cuando le sigue directamente un sonido vocálico)* far [fɑː(r)]
[s]   sat [sæt]
[ʃ]   sham [ʃæm]
[t]   tap [tæp]
[tʃ]  chat [tʃæt]
[θ]   thatch [θætʃ]
[ð]   that [ðæt]
[v]   vat [væt]
[w]   wall [wɔːl]
[z]   zinc [zɪŋk]
[ʒ]   pleasure ['pleʒə(r)]
[χ]   loch [lɒχ]

## Vocales

[æ]   at [bæt]
[ɑː]  art [ɑːt]
[e]   bet [bet]
[ɜː]  curl [kɜːl]
[ə]   amend [ə'mend]
[iː]  bee [biː]
[ɪ]   bit [bɪt]
[ɒ]   wad [wɒd]
[ɔː]  all [ɔːl]
[ʊ]   put [pʊt]
[uː]  shoe [ʃuː]
[ʌ]   cut [kʌt]

## Diptongos

[aɪ]  life [laɪf]
[aʊ]  house [haʊs]
[eə]  there [ðeə(r)]
[eɪ]  date [deɪt]
[əʊ]  low [ləʊ]
[ɪə]  beer [bɪə(r)]
[ɔɪ]  boil [bɔɪl]
[ʊə]  poor [pʊə(r)]

# Spanish Phonetic Symbols

## Consonants

[b]  bola ['bola], vaca ['baca]
[β]  abuelo [a'βuelo], novio ['noβjo] – *A very soft 'b' with the lips barely touching*
[tʃ]  chocar [tʃo'kar]
[k]  campo ['kampo], kilo ['kilo], queso ['keso]
[θ]  cereza [θe'reθa] – *Pronounced as [s] in Latin American Spanish*
[d]  decir [de'θir]
[ð]  adiós [a'ðjos] – *A very soft 'd'; the tip of the tongue barely touches the back of the teeth*
[f]  feroz [fe'roθ]
[g]  gato ['gato]
[ɣ]  agua ['aɣwa] – *A very soft 'g'; the back of the tongue barely touches the soft palate*
[x]  ajo ['axo] – *Like the Scottish 'ch' in* **loch**
[l]  luna ['luna]
[λ]  lluvia ['λuvia] – *Although considered the correct pronunciation of 'll', it is in practice substituted by the semivowel [j] except in some areas of Northern Spain*
[m]  mano ['mano]
[n]  no [no]
[ŋ]  anca ['aŋka]
[ɲ]  año ['aɲo] – *Nasal sound similar to 'ny' in* **canyon**
[p]  pan [pan]
[r]  cura ['kura]
[rr]  ahorro [a'orro] – *Strong 'r' trilled with the tip of the tongue, similar to Scottish 'r'*
[s]  sopa ['sopa]
[t]  tela ['tela]

*Note that the 'h' is not pronounced at all in Spanish (except when forming 'ch', which is pronounced [tʃ]).*

## Vowels

*The vowel sounds in Spanish are shorter than even the shortest English vowels but approximate equivalents are given below:*

| | | |
|---|---|---|
| [a] | casa ['kasa] | *first element of [aɪ] as in* **might** *or [aʊ] as in* **how** |
| [e] | elefante [ele'fante] | *first element of [eɪ] as in* **pay** |
| [i] | pila ['pila] | *[i:] as in* **see**, *but shorter* |
| [o] | oso ['oso] | *somewhere between [ɒ] as in* **lot** *and [ɔ:] as in* **caught** |
| [u] | cuna ['kuna] | *[u:] as in* **food**, *but shorter* |

## Diphthongs

*The pronunciation of the Spanish vowel pairs 'ai', 'au', 'ei', 'eu', 'oi', 'ou' presents no difficulties since these are merely combinations of the pure vowels above.*

## Semivowels

[j]  yo [jo], diente ['djente]
[w]  hueso ['weso]

# Abbreviations
## Abreviaturas

| | | |
|---|---|---|
| gloss | = | glosa |
| [introduces an explanation] | | [introduce una explicación] |
| cultural equivalent | ≃ | equivalente cultural |
| [introduces a translation which has a roughly equivalent status in the target language] | | [introduce una institución, un objeto, etc. equivalente en el idioma de destino] |
| abbreviation | *abbr, abrev* | abreviatura |
| adjective | *adj* | adjetivo |
| adverb | *adv* | adverbio |
| agriculture | *Agr* | agricultura |
| Latin American Spanish | *Am* | español de América |
| anatomy | *Anat* | anatomía |
| Andean Spanish (Bolivia, Chile, Colombia, Ecuador, Peru) | *Andes* | español andino (Bolivia, Chile, Colombia, Ecuador, Perú) |
| architecture | *Archit, Arquit* | arquitectura |
| Argentinian Spanish | *Arg* | español de Argentina |
| astronomy | *Astron* | astronomía |
| cars | *Aut* | automóvil |
| auxiliary | *aux* | auxiliar |
| aviation | *Av* | aviación |
| biology | *Biol* | biología |
| botany | *Bot* | botánica |
| British English | *Br* | inglés británico |
| Caribbean Spanish (Cuba, Puerto Rico, Dominican Republic, Venezuela) | *Carib* | español caribeño (Cuba, Puerto Rico, República Dominicana, Venezuela) |
| Central American Spanish | *CAm* | español centroamericano |
| chemistry | *Chem* | química |
| Chilean Spanish | *Chile* | español de Chile |
| cinema | *Cin, Cine* | cine |
| Colombian Spanish | *Col* | español de Colombia |
| commerce | *Com* | comercio |
| computing | *Comptr* | informática |
| conjunction | *conj* | conjunción |
| building industry | *Constr* | construcción |
| Cono Sur Spanish | *CSur* | español del Cono Sur |
| [note that although this geographical area covers Argentina, Uruguay, Paraguay and Chile, in this dictionary the Spanish spoken in Chile is treated separately] | | [aunque el área geográfica incluye a Argentina, Uruguay, Paraguay y Chile, a efectos de este diccionario el español de Chile se trata aparte] |
| Cuban Spanish | *Cuba* | español de Cuba |
| cooking | *Culin* | cocina |
| sport | *Dep* | deporte |
| law | *Der* | derecho |
| economics | *Econ* | economía |
| education | *Educ* | educación |
| electronics | *Elec* | electrónica |

| | | |
|---|---|---|
| euphemism | *Euph* | eufemismo |
| exclamation | *exclam* | interjección |
| feminine | *f* | femenino |
| familiar | *Fam* | familiar, coloquial |
| railways | *Ferroc* | ferrocarril |
| figurative | *Fig* | figurado |
| finance | *Fin* | finanzas |
| physics | *Fís* | física |
| photography | *Fot* | fotografía |
| geography | *Geog* | geografía |
| geology | *Geol* | geología |
| geometry | *Geom* | geometría |
| grammar | *Gram* | gramática |
| history | *Hist* | historia |
| humorous | *Hum* | humorístico |
| industry | *Ind* | industria |
| computing | *Informát* | informática |
| exclamation | *interj* | interjección |
| invariable | *inv* | invariable |
| [noun whose plural form is the same as the singular] | | [nombre cuya forma plural es igual a la forma singular] |
| ironic | *Ironic, Irón* | irónico |
| journalism | *Journ* | periodismo, prensa |
| linguistics | *Ling* | lingüística |
| literature | *Lit* | literatura |
| adjectival phrase | *loc adj* | locución adjetival |
| adverbial phrase | *loc adv* | locución adverbial |
| prepositional phrase | *loc prep* | locución preposicional |
| masculine | *m* | masculino |
| mathematics | *Math, Mat* | matemáticas |
| medicine | *Med* | medicina |
| weather | *Met* | meteorología |
| Mexican Spanish | *Méx* | español de México |
| military | *Mil* | militar |
| mining | *Min* | minería |
| mythology | *Mitol* | mitología |
| music | *Mus, Mús* | música |
| noun | *n* | nombre |
| ships | *Naut, Náut* | náutica |
| feminine noun | *nf* | nombre femenino |
| feminine plural noun | *nfpl* | nombre femenino plural |
| masculine noun | *nm* | nombre masculino |
| masculine plural noun | *nmpl* | nombre masculino plural |
| masculine and feminine noun [same form for both genders] | *nmf* | nombre masculino y femenino [formas idénticas] |
| masculine and feminine noun [different form in the feminine] | *nm,f* | nombre masculino y femenino [formas diferentes] |
| number | *núm* | número |
| parliament | *Parl* | parlamento |
| pejorative | *Pej, Pey* | peyorativo |
| Peruvian Spanish | *Perú* | español de Perú |

xiii

| | | |
|---|---|---|
| photography | *Phot* | fotografía |
| physics | *Phys* | física |
| plural | *pl* | plural |
| politics | *Pol* | política |
| past participle | *pp* | participio pasado |
| prefix | *pref* | prefijo |
| preposition | *prep* | preposición |
| pronoun | *pron* | pronombre |
| proverb | *Prov* | proverbio |
| psychology | *Psy, Psi* | psicología |
| past tense | *pt* | pretérito |
| chemistry | *Quím* | química |
| registered trademark | ® | marca registrada |
| radio | *Rad* | radio |
| railways | *Rail* | ferrocarril |
| religion | *Rel* | religión |
| relative | *relat* | relativo |
| somebody | *sb* | alguien |
| school | *Sch* | escuela |
| Scottish English | *Scot* | inglés de Escocia |
| something | *sth* | algo |
| suffix | *suf* | sufijo |
| bullfighting | *Taurom* | tauromaquia |
| technology | *Tech, Tec* | tecnología |
| telecommunications | *Tel* | telecomunicaciones |
| textiles | *Tex* | textil |
| theatre | *Th* | teatro |
| television | *TV* | televisión |
| printing | *Typ* | imprenta |
| university | *Univ* | universidad |
| American English | *US* | inglés norteamericano |
| verb | *v* | verbo |
| Venezuelan Spanish | *Ven* | español de Venezuela |
| intransitive verb | *vi* | verbo intransitivo |
| reflexive verb | *vpr* | verbo pronominal |
| transitive verb | *vt* | verbo transitivo |
| inseparable transitive verb [phrasal verb where the verb and the adverb or preposition cannot be separated, e.g. **look after** (cuidar); she **looked after** the children (cuidó a los niños)] | *vt insep* | verbo transitivo inseparable [verbo con preposición, entre cuyos elementos no se puede intercalar un objeto, p.ej.: **look after** (cuidar); she **looked after** the children (cuidó a los niños)] |
| separable transitive verb [phrasal verb where the verb and the adverb or preposition can be separated, e.g. **send back** (devolver); he **sent back** the present or he **sent** the present **back** (devolvió el regalo)] | *vt sep* | verbo transitivo separable [verbo con preposición, entre cuyos elementos se puede intercalar un objeto, p.ej.: **send back** (devolver); he **sent back** the present o he **sent** the present **back** (devolvió el regalo)] |
| vulgar | *Vulg* | vulgar |
| zoology | *Zool* | zoología |

# Spanish–English
## Español–Inglés

# A

**A¹** (*pl* **Aes**), **a** (*pl* **aes**) [a] *nf* (*letra*) A, a
**a²**

> **a** combines with the article **el** to form the contraction **al** (e.g. **al centro** to the centre).

*prep* (**a**) (*dirección*) to; **voy a Sevilla** I'm going to Seville; **me voy al extranjero** I'm going abroad; **llegó a Barcelona/a la fiesta** he arrived in Barcelona/at the party

(**b**) (*posición*) **está a la derecha/izquierda** it's on the right/left; **a orillas del mar** by the sea

(**c**) (*distancia*) **está a más de cien kilómetros** it's more than a hundred kilometres away; **de Segovia a Madrid** from Segovia to Madrid

(**d**) (*período de tiempo*) **a las pocas semanas** a few weeks later; **al mes de casados** a month after they were married; **al día siguiente** the following day

(**e**) (*momento preciso*) at; **a las siete** at seven o'clock; **a los 11 años** at the age of 11; **al caer la noche** at nightfall; **al oír la noticia se desmayó** on hearing the news, she fainted

(**f**) (*frecuencia*) per, every; **40 horas a la semana** 40 hours per *o* a week; **tres veces al día** three times a day

(**g**) (*con complemento indirecto*) to; **dáselo a Juan** give it to Juan; **dile a Juan que venga** tell Juan to come

(**h**) (*con complemento directo*) **quiere a sus hijos/su gato** she loves her children/her cat; **me cuidan como a un enfermo** they look after me as if I was an invalid

(**i**) (*cantidad, medida, precio*) **a cientos/miles/docenas** by the hundred/thousand/dozen; **la leche se vende a litros** milk is sold by the litre; **a ... kilómetros por hora a** ... kilometres per hour; **¿a cuánto están las peras?** how much are the pears?; **tiene las peras a cien pesetas** she's selling pears for *o* at a hundred pesetas; **ganaron tres a cero** they won three nil

(**j**) (*modo*) **lo hace a la antigua** he does it the old way; **a lo bestia** rudely; **a lo grande** in style; **a lo Mozart** after Mozart; **a escondidas** secretly; *Culin* **merluza a la vasca/gallega** Basque-style/Galician-style hake

(**k**) (*instrumento*) **escribir a máquina** to type; **a lápiz** in pencil; **a mano** by hand; **olla a presión** pressure cooker

(**l**) (*finalidad*) to; **entró a pagar** he came in to pay; **aprender a nadar** to learn to swim

(**m**) (*complemento de nombre*) **sueldo a convenir** salary to be agreed; **temas a tratar** matters to be discussed

(**n**) (*condición*) **a no ser por mí, hubieses fracasado** had it not been for me, you would have failed

(**o**) (*en oraciones imperativas*) **¡a la cama!** go to bed!; **¡a callar todo el mundo!** quiet, everyone!; **¡a bailar!** let's dance!; **¡a trabajar!** let's get to work!

(**p**) (*en busca de*) **ir a por pan** to go for bread

(**q**) (*indica desafío*) **¿a que no lo haces?** I bet you won't do it!

**AA 1** *nmpl* (*abrev de* **Alcohólicos Anónimos**) AA

 **2** *nfpl* (*abrev de* **Aerolíneas Argentinas**) = Argentinian state airline

**AA EE** (*abrev de* **Asuntos Exteriores**) **Ministerio de AA EE** Ministry of Foreign Affairs, *Br* ≃ Foreign Office, *US* ≃ State Department

**ABA** *nmpl* (*abrev de* **Agentes de Bolsa Asociados**) = Spanish association of stockbrokers

**ababol** *nm* poppy

**ábaco** *nm* abacus

**abad** *nm* abbot

**abadejo** *nm* cod

**abadesa** *nf* abbess

**abadía** *nf* abbey

**abajo 1** *adv* (**a**) (*posición*) (*en general*) below; (*en edificio*) downstairs; **de a.** bottom; **el estante de a.** the bottom shelf; **vive (en el piso de) a.** she lives downstairs; **está aquí/allí a.** it's down here/there; **a. del todo** right at the bottom; **más a.** further down; **la parte de a.** the bottom; *Am* **a. de** below, under

(**b**) (*dirección*) down; **ve a.** (*en edificio*) go downstairs; **hacia** *o* **para a.** down, downwards; **calle/escaleras a.** down the street/the stairs;

**río a.** downstream

(c) *(en un texto)* below

**2** *interj* **¡a...!** down with...!; **¡a. la dictadura!** down with the dictatorship!

**abalanzarse** [16] *vpr* **a. hacia** to rush towards; **a. sobre** to pounce on

**abalear** *vt Andes* to shoot

**abalorio** *nm* (a) *(cuenta)* glass bead (b) *(bisutería)* trinket

**abanderado** *nm también Fig* standard-bearer

**abandonado, -a** *adj* (a) *(desierto)* deserted (b) *(desamparado)* abandoned (c) *(descuidado)* *(persona)* unkempt; *(jardín, casa)* neglected

**abandonar 1** *vt (lugar, profesión, cónyuge)* to leave; *(hijo, proyecto)* to abandon; *(estudios)* to give up

**2 abandonarse** *vpr (de aspecto)* to neglect oneself, to let oneself go; **abandonarse a** *(desesperación, dolor)* to succumb to; *(placer, sentidos)* to abandon oneself to; *(vicio)* to give oneself over to

**abandono** *nm* (a) *(descuido) (de aspecto, jardín)* state of abandon; *(de estudios, obligaciones)* neglect (b) *(de lugar, profesión, cónyuge)* leaving; *(de hijo, proyecto)* abandonment; *Der* **a. de hogar** desertion *(of family, spouse)*; *Dep* **ganar por a.** to win by default

**abanicar** [61] **1** *vt* to fan

**2 abanicarse** *vpr* to fan oneself; **se abanicó la cara** she fanned her face

**abanico** *nm* (a) *(para abanicarse)* fan (b) *Fig (gama)* range; **hizo un a. con los naipes** he fanned out the cards

**abaratar 1** *vt (precio, coste)* to bring down, to reduce; *(artículo)* to reduce the price of

**2 abaratarse** *vpr* to go down in price, to become cheaper

**abarca** *nf* = type of sandal worn by country people

**abarcar** [61] *vt* (a) *(incluir)* to embrace, to cover; *Prov* **quien mucho abarca poco aprieta** don't bite off more than you can chew (b) *(ver)* to be able to see, to have a view of; **desde la torre se abarca todo el valle** you can see the whole valley from the tower

**abaritonado, -a** *adj Mús* baritone

**abarque** *etc ver* **abarcar**

**abarquillar 1** *vt (madera)* to warp

**2 abarquillarse** *vpr (madera)* to warp

**abarrotado, -a** *adj (teatro, autobús)* packed **(de** with); *(desván, baúl)* crammed **(de** with)

**abarrotar** *vt (teatro, autobús)* to pack **(de o con** with); *(desván, baúl)* to cram full **(de o con** of)

**abarrotería** *nf Am* grocer's (store)

**abarrotero, -a** *nm,f Am* grocer

**abarrotes** *nmpl Am* groceries; **tienda de a.** grocer's shop, *US* dry goods store

**abastecedor, -ora** *nm,f* supplier

**abastecer** [48] **1** *vt* to supply **(de** with); **a. de agua a la ciudad** to supply the city with water; **esa región nos abastece de materias primas** that region supplies o provides us with raw materials

**2 abastecerse** *vpr* to stock up **(de** on)

**abastecimiento** *nm* supplying; **se ha interrumpido el a.** they've cut off the supply; **a. de aguas** water supply

**abasto** *nm* **no dar a.** to be unable to cope; **no da a. con tanto trabajo** she can't cope with so much work

**abate** *nm* abbé *(title given to French or Italian priest)*

**abatible** *adj* **mesa a.** foldaway table; **asientos abatibles** *(en coche)* = seats that tip forwards or fold flat

**abatido, -a** *adj* dejected, downhearted

**abatimiento** *nm (desánimo)* low spirits, dejection

**abatir 1** *vt* (a) *(derribar) (muro)* to knock down; *(avión)* to shoot down (b) *(desanimar)* to depress, to dishearten

**2 abatirse** *vpr* (a) *(caer)* **abatirse sobre algo/alguien** to pounce on sth/sb (b) *(desanimarse)* to become dejected o disheartened

**abdicación** *nf (de monarca)* abdication

**abdicar** [61] **1** *vt* **a. el trono (en alguien)** to abdicate the throne (in favour of sb)

**2** *vi* to abdicate; *Fig* **a. de** *(principios, ideales)* to renounce

**abdomen** *nm (de persona, insecto)* abdomen

**abdominal 1** *adj* abdominal; **dolores abdominales** abdominal pains

**2 abdominales** *nmpl* sit-ups

**abductor** *nm Anat* abductor

**abecé** *nm también Fig* ABC

**abecedario** *nm* (a) *(alfabeto)* alphabet (b) *(libro)* spelling book

**abedul** *nm* birch (tree)

**abeja** *nf* bee; **a. obrera** worker bee; **a. reina** queen bee

**abejaruco** *nm* bee-eater

**abejorro** *nm* bumblebee

**aberración** *nf* (a) *(desviación de la norma)* **me parece una a.** I find it ridiculous; **echó gaseosa al champán, ¡qué a.!** he put lemonade in the champagne? that's sacrilege!; **a. sexual** sexual perversion (b) *Fot* aberration

**aberrante** *adj* (a) *(absurdo)* ridiculous, idiotic (b) *(perverso)* perverse

**abertura** *nf (agujero)* opening; *(ranura)* crack

**abertzale** [aβer'tʃale] *adj & nmf Pol* (radical) Basque nationalist

**abeto** *nm* fir

**abiertamente** *adv (claramente)* openly

**abierto, -a 1** *participio ver* **abrir**

**2** *adj* (a) *(puerta, boca, tienda)* open; **dejar el grifo a.** to leave the tap on *o* running; **bien** *o* **muy a.** wide open; **a. al público** open to the public (b) *Fig (liberal)* open-minded; **estar a. a cualquier sugerencia** to be open to suggestions

**abigarrado, -a** *adj* (a) *(mezclado)* **la habitación está a.** the room is a real jumble of different things (b) *(multicolor)* multi-coloured

**abisal** *adj* **fosa a.** ocean trough; **pez a.** abyssal fish

**abismal** *adj (diferencia, distancia)* vast, colossal

**abismar 1** *vt Formal* **a. a alguien en la desesperación** to plunge sb into despair

**2 abismarse** *vpr* **abismarse en** *(lectura)* to be engrossed in

**abismo** *nm* (a) *(profundidad)* abyss; *Fig* **estar al borde del a.** to be on the brink of ruin *o* disaster (b) *Fig (diferencia)* gulf; **entre su sueldo y el mío hay un a.** there's a huge difference between our salaries

**Abiyán** *n* Abidjan

**abjurar** *Formal* **1** *vt (fe, creencias)* to abjure, to renounce

**2** *vi* **a. de** *(fe, creencias)* to abjure, to renounce

**ablación** *nf Med (de tejido, órgano)* excision, surgical removal; **a. del clítoris** female circumcision

**ablandamiento** *nm también Fig* softening

**ablandar 1** *vt también Fig* to soften

**2 ablandarse** *vpr (material)* to soften, to become softer; *Fig (actitud, rigor)* to soften; **su padre se ablandó cuando la vio llorar** her father relented when he saw her cry

**ablativo** *nm Gram* ablative; **a. absoluto** ablative absolute

**ablución** *nf* **hizo sus abluciones** he performed his ablutions

**ablusado, -a** *adj (vestido, camisa)* loose, baggy

**abnegación** *nf* abnegation, self-denial

**abnegado, -a** *adj* selfless, unselfish

**abobado, -a** *adj Fam* (a) *(estupefacto)* blank, uncomprehending (b) *(estúpido)* stupid

**abocado, -a** *adj* destined (**a** to)

**abocar [61]** *vi* **a. en un fracaso** to end in failure

**abochornado, -a** *adj* embarrassed

**abochornar 1** *vt* to embarrass

**2 abochornarse** *vpr* to get embarrassed

**abofetear** *vt* to slap *(on the face)*

**abogacía** *nf* legal profession

**abogado, -a** *nm,f* (a) *Der* lawyer; **a. defensor** counsel for the defence; **a. del estado** public prosecutor; **a. laboralista** labour lawyer; **a. de oficio** legal aid lawyer (b) *Fig (intercesor)* intermediary; *(defensor)* advocate; **a. del diablo** devil's advocate

**abogar [40]** *vi* (a) *Der* **a. por alguien** to represent sb (b) *Fig (defender)* **a. por algo** to advocate sth; **a. por alguien** to stand up for sb, to defend sb

**abolengo** *nm* lineage; **de (rancio) a.** of noble lineage

**abolición** *nf* abolition

**abolicionismo** *nm Hist* abolitionism *(opposition to slavery)*

**abolicionista** *adj & nmf Hist* abolitionist

**abolir** *vt* to abolish

**abolladura** *nf* dent

**abollar 1** *vt* to dent

**2 abollarse** *vpr* to get dented

**abombado, -a** *adj (hacia fuera)* buckled; **la lata está un poco abombada** the tin has buckled slightly outwards

**abombar 1** *vt* to buckle (outwards)

**2 abombarse** *vpr* to buckle (outwards)

**abominable** *adj* abominable

**abominación** *nf* abomination

**abominar 1** *vt (detestar)* to abhor, to abominate

**2** *vi* **a. de** *(condenar)* to condemn, to criticize

**abonable** *adj Fin (pagadero)* payable

**abonado, -a** *nm,f (a telefónica, revista)* subscriber; *(al fútbol, teatro)* season-ticket holder

**abonar 1** *vt* (a) *(pagar) (factura, cuenta)* to pay; **a. algo en la cuenta de alguien** to credit sb's account with sth (b) *(tierra)* to fertilize

**2 abonarse** *vpr (a revista)* to subscribe (**a** to); *(al fútbol, teatro)* to buy a season ticket (**a** for)

**abono** *nm* (a) *(pase)* season ticket; **a. de diez viajes** a ten-journey ticket; **a. transporte** travel pass *(for bus, train and underground)* (b) *(fertilizante)* fertilizer (c) *(pago)* payment (d) *Com* credit entry (e) *Méx (plazo)* instalment; **pagar en abonos** to pay by instalments

**abordable** *adj (persona)* approachable; *(tema)* that can be tackled; *(tarea)* manageable

**abordaje** *nm Náut* boarding

**abordar** *vt* (a) *(barco)* to board *(in attack)* (b) *Fig (persona)* to approach (c) *Fig (tema, tarea)* to tackle

**aborigen** *adj (indígena)* indigenous; *(de Australia)* Aboriginal; **aborígenes** *(población indígena)* indigenous population; *(de Australia)* Aborígenes

**aborrecer [48]** *vt* to abhor, to loathe

**aborrecible** *adj* abhorrent, loathsome

**aborrecimiento** *nm* loathing, hatred

**aborregado, -a** *adj* (**a**) *Fam (adocenado)* **estar a.** to be like a sheep (**b**) **cielo a.** mackerel sky

**abortar 1** *vt (feto)* to abort; *Fig (hacer fracasar)* to foil

**2** *vi Med (espontáneamente)* to have a miscarriage, to miscarry; *(intencionadamente)* to have an abortion

**abortista** *adj & nmf* abortionist

**abortivo** *nm* abortifacient

**aborto** *nm* (**a**) *(espontáneo)* miscarriage; *(intencionado)* abortion; **a. clandestino** backstreet abortion (**b**) *muy Fam (persona fea)* freak; *(idiota)* moron

**abotargado, -a** *adj* (**a**) *(hinchado)* swollen; *(cara)* puffy (**b**) *(atontado)* **tengo la mente abotargada** my mind has gone fuzzy

**abotargarse** [40] *vpr* to swell (up)

**abotonar 1** *vt* to button up

**2 abotonarse** *vpr* to do one's buttons up; **abotonarse la camisa** to button one's shirt up

**abovedado, -a** *adj Arquit* vaulted

**abracadabra** *nm* abracadabra

**abrace** *etc ver* **abrazar**

**abrasador, -ora** *adj* burning

**abrasar 1** *vt (quemar) (casa, bosque)* to burn down; *(persona, mano, garganta)* to burn; *(desecar)* to scorch; **el sol abrasó los campos** the sun parched the fields

**2** *vi (café, sopa)* to be boiling hot; **este sol abrasa** the sun is really hot today

**3 abrasarse** *vpr (casa, bosque)* to burn down; *(persona)* to burn oneself; **me abrasé los brazos** I burnt my arms; **los campos se abrasaron con el calor** the heat parched the fields

**abrasión** *nf* (**a**) *(fricción)* abrasion (**b**) *Med (por fricción)* abrasion; *(por agente corrosivo)* burn

**abrasivo, -a 1** *adj* abrasive

**2** *nm* abrasive

**abrazadera** *nf Tec* brace, bracket; *(en carpintería)* clamp

**abrazar** [16] **1** *vt (rodear con los brazos)* to hug, to embrace; *Fig (doctrina)* to embrace; *Fig (profesión)* to go into

**2 abrazarse** *vpr* to hug, to embrace; **abrazarse a alguien** to hug sb, to cling to sb; **se abrazaron con pasión** they embraced passionately

**abrazo** *nm* embrace, hug; **un (fuerte) a.** *(en cartas)* Yours, Best wishes

**abrebotellas** *nm inv* bottle opener

**abrecartas** *nm inv* paper knife, letter opener

**abrelatas** *nm inv Br* tin opener, *US* can opener

**abrevadero** *nm (construido)* drinking trough; *(natural)* watering place

**abrevar** *vt* to water, to give water to

**abreviación** *nf (de texto)* abridgement

**abreviado, -a** *adj (texto)* abridged

**abreviar** [15] **1** *vt (proceso, explicación)* to shorten; *(texto)* to abridge; *(palabra)* to abbreviate; *(viaje, estancia)* to cut short

**2** *vi (darse prisa)* to hurry up; **para a.** *(al hacer algo)* to keep it quick; *(al narrar algo)* to cut a long story short

**abreviatura** *nf* abbreviation

**abridor** *nm* (**a**) *(abrebotellas)* (bottle) opener (**b**) *(abrelatas) Br* (tin) opener, *US* (can) opener

**abrigado, -a** *adj (persona)* well wrapped-up; *(jersey)* warm

**abrigar** [40] **1** *vt* (**a**) *(arropar)* to wrap up; *(calentar)* to keep warm (**b**) *Fig (albergar) (esperanza)* to cherish; *(sospechas, malas intenciones)* to harbour

**2** *vi (ropa, manta)* to be warm

**3 abrigarse** *vpr* (**a**) *(arroparse)* to wrap up (**b**) *(resguardarse)* to shelter (**de** from)

**abrigo** *nm* (**a**) *(prenda)* coat, overcoat; **a. de piel** fur coat (**b**) *(refugio)* shelter; **al a. de** *(peligro, ataque)* safe from; *(lluvia, viento)* sheltered from; *(ley)* under the protection of

**abrigue** *etc ver* **abrigar**

**abril** *nm* April; **tiene 14 abriles** he is 14 (years of age); *Prov* **en a., aguas mil** March winds, April showers; *ver también* **septiembre**

**abrillantador** *nm* polish

**abrillantar** *vt* to polish

**abrir 1** *vt* (**a**) *(en general)* to open; *(alas)* to spread; *(melón)* to cut open; *(grifo, agua, gas)* to turn on; *(cerradura)* to unlock, to open; *(cremallera)* to undo

(**b**) *(túnel)* to dig; *(canal, camino)* to build; *(agujero, surco)* to make

(**c**) *(negocio, colegio, hospital)* to open

(**d**) *(apetito)* to whet

(**e**) *(encabezar) (lista)* to head; *(manifestación)* to lead

(**f**) **a. fuego** (**sobre** *o* **contra**) to open fire (on)

**2** *vi* to open; **la tienda abre a las cinco** the shop opens at five (o'clock)

**3 abrirse** *vpr* (**a**) *(puerta, caja)* to open; **este bote no se abre** this jar won't open

(**b**) *(empezar) (película, función)* to begin, to begin

(**c**) *Fig (sincerarse)* to open up; **tienes que abrirte más a la gente** you should be more open with people

(**d**) *Fig (posibilidades)* to open up

(**e**) *(cielo)* to clear

(**f**) *muy Fam (irse)* to clear off

**(g)** *también Fig* **abrirse paso** *o* **camino** to make one's way

**abrochar 1** *vt (botones, camisa)* to do up; *(cinturón)* to fasten

**2 abrocharse** *vpr (botones, camisa)* to do up; *(cinturón)* to fasten; **abrocharse la camisa** to do up one's shirt; **¡abróchate!** *(el abrigo)* do your coat up!; **abróchense los cinturones de seguridad** fasten your seatbelts

**abrogar [40]** *vt Der* to abrogate, to repeal

**abroncar [61]** *vt* **(a)** *(reprender)* to tell off **(b)** *(abuchear)* to boo

**abrótano** *nm* southernwood

**abrumador, -ora** *adj* overwhelming

**abrumar** *vt (agobiar)* to overwhelm

**abrupto, -a** *adj (escarpado)* sheer; *(accidentado)* rugged

**ABS** *nm (abrev de* **antilock braking system)** ABS; **frenos A.** antilock brakes

**absceso** *nm Med* abscess

**abscisa** *nf Mat* x-axis

**absenta** *nf (bebida)* absinthe

**absentismo** *nm* **(a)** *(de terrateniente)* absentee landownership **(b)** *(de trabajador)* **a. laboral** *(justificado)* absence from work; *(injustificado)* absenteeism

**ábside** *nm Arquit* apse

**absolución** *nf* **(a)** *Der* acquittal **(b)** *Rel* absolution

**absolutismo** *nm* absolutism

**absolutista** *adj & nmf* absolutist

**absoluto, -a** *adj (no relativo)* absolute; *(completo)* total, absolute; **nada en a.** nothing at all; **no me gustó en a.** I didn't like it at all; **¿te gusta?/¿te importa? – en a.** do you like it?/ do you mind? – not at all

**absolver [43]** *vt* **(a)** *Der* to acquit **(b)** *Rel* to absolve

**absorbente** *adj (esponja, material)* absorbent; *Fig (persona, carácter)* demanding; *Fig (actividad)* absorbing

**absorber** *vt (líquido, gas)* to absorb; *Fig (consumir, gastar)* to soak up; **este trabajo me absorbe mucho** this job takes up a lot of my time; **su mujer le absorbe mucho** his wife is very demanding

**absorción** *nf (de líquido, gas)* absorption; *(de empresa)* takeover

**absorto, -a** *adj* absorbed **(en** in)

**abstemio, -a 1** *adj* teetotal

**2** *nm,f* teetotaller

**abstención** *nf* abstention; **hubo mucha a.** *(en elecciones)* there was a low turnout

**abstencionismo** *nm Pol* abstentionism

**abstenerse [67]** *vpr* **(a)** *(guardarse)* to abstain **(de** from); **se abstuvo de mencionar**

su embarazo she refrained from mentioning her pregnancy **(b)** *(en votación)* to abstain; **me abstuve en las últimas elecciones** I didn't vote in the last election

**abstinencia** *nf* abstinence

**abstracción** *nf* abstraction

**abstracto, -a 1** *adj* abstract

**2** *nm* **en a.** in the abstract

**abstraer [68] 1** *vt* to consider separately, to detach

**2 abstraerse** *vpr* to detach oneself **(de** from)

**abstraído, -a** *adj* lost in thought

**abstruso, -a** *adj* abstruse

**abstuviera** *etc ver* **abstenerse**

**absuelto, -a** *participio ver* **absolver**

**absuelvo** *etc ver* **absolver**

**absurdo, -a 1** *adj* absurd; **lo a. sería que no lo hicieras** it would be absurd for you not to do it

**2** *nm* **decir/hacer un a.** to say/do something ridiculous *o* idiotic; **reducción al a.** reductio ad absurdum

**abubilla** *nf* hoopoe

**abuchear** *vt* to boo

**abucheo** *nm* booing

**Abu Dabi** *n* Abu Dhabi

**abuelo, -a** *nm,f* **(a)** *(familiar)* grandfather, f grandmother; **abuelos** grandparents; *Fam* **¡cuéntaselo a tu abuela!** pull the other one!; *Fam* **éramos pocos y parió la abuela** that was all we needed; *Fam* **no necesitar abuela** to be full of oneself **(b)** *(anciano) (hombre)* old man, old person; *(mujer)* old woman, old person

**abuhardillado, -a** *adj* **habitación abuhardillada** attic room

**abulense 1** *adj* of/from Avila

**2** *nmf* person from Avila

**abulia** *nf* apathy, lethargy

**abúlico, -a 1** *adj* apathetic, lethargic

**2** *nm,f* apathetic *o* lethargic person

**abultado, -a** *adj (paquete)* bulky; *(labios)* thick; *(frente)* prominent; **estómago a.** pot belly; *Fig* **ganaron por una abultada mayoría** they won by a large majority

**abultamiento** *nm (bulto)* bulkiness

**abultar 1** *vt (hinchar) (mejillas)* to puff out; *Fig (cifras, consecuencias)* to exaggerate

**2** *vi (ocupar mucho espacio)* to be bulky; *(formar un bulto)* to bulge; **el equipaje abulta mucho** the luggage takes up a lot of room

**abundamiento** *nm Formal* **a mayor a., presenté las cifras** I provided the figures for further clarification

**abundancia** *nf* (a) *(gran cantidad)* abundance; **en a.** in abundance (b) *(riqueza)* plenty, prosperity; **nadar** *o* **vivir en la a.** to be filthy rich

**abundante** *adj* abundant

**abundar** *vi* (a) *(ser abundante)* to abound; **aquí abundan los camaleones** there are lots of chameleons here (b) *(estar de acuerdo)* **a. en** to agree completely with

**aburguesado, -a** *adj* bourgeois

**aburguesamiento** *nm* bourgeoisification

**aburguesarse** *vpr* to adopt middle-class ways; **se han aburguesado mucho desde que se casaron** they've become very bourgeois *o* middle-class since they married

**aburrido, -a 1** *adj* (a) *(harto, fastidiado)* bored; **estar a. de hacer algo** to be fed up with doing sth; *Fam* **estar a. como un hongo** to be bored stiff (b) *(que aburre)* boring

**2** *nm,f* bore; **¡eres un a.!** you're so boring!

**aburrimiento** *nm* boredom

**aburrir 1** *vt* to bore

**2 aburrirse** *vpr* to get bored; *(estar aburrido)* to be bored; *(hartarse)* to be bored sick (**de** of); *Fam* **aburrirse como una ostra** to be bored stiff

**abusado, -a** *adj Méx* astute, shrewd; **¡a!** look out!

**abusar** *vi (excederse)* to go too far; **a. de algo** to abuse sth; **a. del alcohol** to drink to excess; **a. de alguien** *(aprovecharse)* to take advantage of sb; *(forzar sexualmente)* to sexually abuse sb

**abusivo, -a** *adj (trato)* very bad, appalling; *(precio)* extortionate

**abuso** *nm* (a) *(uso excesivo)* abuse (**de** of); **a. de confianza** breach of confidence; **a. de poder** abuse of power; **abusos deshonestos** sexual abuse (b) *(escándalo)* scandal, sin

**abusón, -ona** *Fam* **1** *adj (caradura)* selfish; *(matón)* bullying

**2** *nm,f (caradura)* selfish person; *(matón)* bully

**abyección** *nf Formal (bajeza)* vileness; *(pobreza)* wretchedness

**abyecto, -a** *adj Formal (malo)* vile; *(pobre)* wretched

**a. C.** *(abrev de* **antes de Cristo***)* BC

**acá** *adv* (a) *(lugar)* here; **de a. para allá** back and forth; **más a.** closer; **¡ven a.!** come (over) here! (b) *(tiempo)* **de una semana a.** during the last week; **de un tiempo a.** recently

**acabado, -a 1** *adj* (a) *(terminado)* finished (b) *(completo)* perfect, consummate (c) *(fracasado)* finished, ruined

**2** *nm (de producto)* finish; *(de piso)* décor; **a. mate/satinado** matt/satin finish

**acabar 1** *vt (terminar)* to finish; *(consumir) (provisiones, dinero)* to use up; **hemos acabado el trabajo** we've finished the work; **acabó sus días en el exilio** he ended his days in exile

**2** *vi* (a) *(terminar)* to finish, to end; **el cuchillo acaba en punta** the knife ends in a point; **el asunto acabó mal** the affair finished *o* ended badly; **cuando acabes**, **avísame** tell me when you've finished; **a. de trabajar/comer** to finish working/eating; **ese acabará en la cárcel** he'll end up in jail; **a. con la paciencia de alguien** to exhaust sb's patience; **a. con algo** *(poner fin a)* to put an end to sth; *Fam* **¡acabáramos!** at last!, about time!

(b) *(haber hecho recientemente)* **a. de hacer algo** to have just done sth; **acabo de llegar** I've just arrived

(c) *(terminar por)* **a. por hacer algo** to end up doing sth

(d) *(destruir)* **a. con** *(enemigo)* to destroy; *(salud)* to ruin; **a. con alguien** *(matar)* to kill sb; *Fig* **ese niño va a a. conmigo** that boy will be the death of me!

(e) **no acabo de entenderlo** I can't quite understand it; **no acaba de parecerme bien** I don't really think it's a very good idea

**3 acabarse** *vpr* (a) *(agotarse)* to be used up, to be gone; **se nos ha acabado la gasolina** we're out of petrol; **se ha acabado la comida** there's no more food left

(b) *(terminar) (guerra, película)* to finish, to be over

(c) **¡se acabó!** *(¡basta ya!)* that's enough!; **¡cómprate uno nuevo y se acabó!** buy a new one and have done with it; **se acabó lo que se daba** that is/was the end of that

**acabóse** *nm* **¡es el a.!** it really is the limit!

**acacia** *nf* acacia

**academia** *nf* (a) *(colegio)* school, academy; **a. de idiomas** language school (b) *(sociedad)* academy

**academicismo** *nm* academicism

**académico, -a 1** *adj* academic

**2** *nm,f* academician

**acaecer** *vi* [48] *Formal* to take place, to occur

**acallar** *vt* to silence

**acalorado, -a** *adj* (a) *(por calor)* hot (b) *(por esfuerzo)* flushed (with effort) (c) *Fig (apasionado) (debate)* heated; *(persona)* hot under the collar; *(defensor)* fervent

**acalorar 1** *vt (dar calor)* to (make) warm; *Fig* **a. a alguien** *(excitar)* to make sb hot under the collar

**2 acalorarse** *vpr (coger calor)* to get hot; *Fig (excitarse)* to get hot under the collar

**acampada** *nf (acción)* camping; **ir/estar de a.** to go/be camping; **zona de a. libre** *(en letrero)* free campsite

**acampanado, -a** *adj (pantalones)* flared

**acampar** *vi* to camp

**acanalado, -a** *adj (columna)* fluted; *(tejido)* ribbed; *(hierro)* corrugated

**acanalar** *vt* (a) *(terreno)* to dig channels in (b) *(plancha)* to corrugate

**acantilado** *nm* cliff

**acanto** *nm* acanthus

**acantonamiento** *nm Mil (acción)* billeting; *(lugar)* billet

**acantonar** *Mil* **1** *vt* to billet
**2 acantonarse** *vpr* to be billeted

**acaparador, -ora 1** *adj* greedy
**2** *nm,f* hoarder

**acaparamiento** *nm (monopolio)* monopolization; *(en tiempo de escasez)* hoarding

**acaparar** *vt* (a) *(monopolizar)* to monopolize; *(mercado)* to corner; **acaparaba las miradas de todos** all eyes were upon her; **los atletas alemanes acapararon las medallas** the German athletes swept the board (b) *(aprovisionarse de)* to hoard

**acápite** *nm Am* paragraph

**acaramelado, -a** *adj* (a) *Fam Fig (pareja)* lovey-dovey (b) *Fam Fig (afectado)* sugary *(sweet)* (c) *(con caramelo)* covered in caramel

**acariciar** [15] **1** *vt* (a) *(persona)* to caress; *(animal, pelo, piel)* to stroke; **la brisa acariciaba su piel** the breeze caressed her skin (b) *Fig (idea, proyecto)* to cherish
**2 acariciarse** *vpr (mutuamente)* to caress *(each other)*; **se acarició el pelo** she stroked her hair

**ácaro** *nm* mite

**acarrear** *vt* (a) *(transportar)* to carry; *(carbón)* to haul (b) *Fig (ocasionar)* to bring, to give rise to

**acartonado, -a** *adj (persona, piel)* wizened

**acartonarse** *vpr* to become wizened

**acaso** *adv* perhaps; **¿a. no lo sabías?** are you trying to tell me you didn't know?; **por si a.** (just) in case; **¿te traigo algo? – si a., una botella de vino** can I get you anything? – you could get me a bottle of wine, if you like; **si a. lo vieras…** if you should see him…

**acatamiento** *nm* compliance (**de** with)

**acatar** *vt (normas)* to respect, to comply with; *(órdenes)* to obey

**acatarrado, -a** *adj* **estar a.** to have a cold

**acatarrarse** *vpr* to catch a cold

**acaudalado, -a** *adj* well-to-do, wealthy

**acaudillar** *vt también Fig* to lead

**acceder** *vi* (a) *(consentir)* to agree (**a algo/a hacer** to sth/to do sth); **a. a una petición** to grant a request (b) *(tener acceso)* **a. a algo** to enter sth, to gain entry to sth (c) *(alcanzar)* **a. al trono** to accede to the throne; **a. al poder** to come to power; **accedió al cargo de presidente** he became president

**accesible** *adj* (a) *(lugar)* accessible (b) *(persona)* approachable

**accésit** *nm inv* runners-up prize

**acceso** *nm* (a) *(entrada)* entrance (**a** to) (b) *(paso)* access (**a** to) (c) *(carretera)* access road (d) *Fig (ataque)* fit; *(de fiebre, gripe)* bout

**accesorio, -a 1** *adj* incidental, of secondary importance
**2** *nm (utensilio)* accessory; **accesorios** *(de moda, automóvil)* accessories

**accidentado, -a 1** *adj* (a) *(vida)* turbulent; *(viaje)* eventful (b) *(terreno, camino)* rough, rugged
**2** *nm,f* injured person, victim

**accidental** *adj* (a) *(no esencial)* incidental, of secondary importance (b) *(imprevisto)* chance, unforeseen

**accidentarse** *vpr* to be involved in *o* have an accident

**accidente** *nm* (a) *(suceso)* accident; **tener** *o* **sufrir un a.** to have an accident; **a. de avión/ de coche** plane/car crash; **a. de tráfico** road accident; **a. laboral** industrial accident; **a. mortal** fatal accident (b) *(irregularidad)* **a. geográfico** geographical feature; **los accidentes del terreno** the unevenness of the terrain

**acción** *nf* (a) *(efecto de hacer)* action; **entrar en a.** *(persona)* to go into action; **película de a.** action *Br* film *o US* movie (b) *(hecho)* deed, act; **una buena a.** a good deed; *Rel* **a. de gracias** thanksgiving (c) *Fin* share; **a. ordinaria/preferente** *Br* ordinary/preference share, *US* ordinary/preference stock; **acciones en cartera** *Br* shares *o US* stock in portfolio (d) *Der* **a. popular** action brought by the People

**accionamiento** *nm* activation

**accionar 1** *vt (mecanismo, palanca)* to activate
**2** *vi (gesticular)* to gesture, to gesticulate

**accionariado** *nm Fin Br* shareholders, *US* stockholders

**accionista** *nmf Fin Br* shareholder, *US* stockholder

**Accra** *n* Accra

**acebo** *nm (hojas)* holly; *(árbol)* holly bush *o* tree

**acebuche** *nm* wild olive tree

**acechanza** *nf* observation, surveillance

**acechar** *vt* to watch, to spy on; **el cazador acechaba a su presa** the hunter was stalking his prey

**acecho** *nm* observation, surveillance; **estar al a. de** to lie in wait for; *Fig* to be on the lookout for

**acedera** *nf* sorrel

**acéfalo, -a** *adj (estado, organización)* leaderless

**aceitar** vt *(motor)* to lubricate; *(comida)* to pour oil onto

**aceite** nm oil; **a. de colza/girasol/oliva** rapeseed/sunflower/olive oil; **a. de ricino/de hígado de bacalao** castor/cod-liver oil

**aceitera** nf oilcan; **aceiteras** cruet set *(for oil and vinegar)*

**aceitoso, -a** adj oily

**aceituna** nf olive; **a. rellena** stuffed olive

**aceitunado, -a** adj olive; **piel aceitunada** olive skin

**aceitunero, -a** nm,f (a) *(recogedor)* olive picker (b) *(vendedor)* olive merchant

**aceituno** nm olive tree

**aceleración** nf acceleration

**acelerado, -a** adj rapid, quick; *Fís* accelerated; *Fam Fig* **estar a.** to be hyper

**acelerador, -ora 1** adj accelerating

**2** nm *(de coche)* accelerator; **pisar el a.** to step on the accelerator; *Fig* to step on it; *Fís* **a. de partículas** particle accelerator

**acelerar 1** vt *(proceso)* to speed up; *(vehículo)* to accelerate; *(motor)* to gun

**2** vi *(conductor)* to accelerate

**3** **acelerarse** vpr *(proceso)* to speed up; *(motor)* to accelerate; *Fam Fig (persona)* to get hyper

**acelerón** nm *(de corredor, coche)* burst of speed; **dar un a.** *(conductor, coche)* to speed up; *Fig* to get a move on

**acelga** nf chard

**acendrado, -a** adj *Formal* untarnished, pure

**acendrar** vt *Formal (cualidad, sentimiento)* to refine

**acento** nm (a) *(entonación)* accent; **tener a. andaluz** to have an Andalusian accent (b) *(ortográfico)* accent (c) **poner el a. en algo** *(enfatizar)* to emphasize sth

**acentuación** nf (a) *(de palabra, sílaba)* accentuation (b) *(intensificación)* intensification; *(de problema)* worsening; **una a. de las actitudes racistas** a rise in racist attitudes

**acentuado, -a** adj (a) *(sílaba)* stressed; *(vocal)* *(con tilde)* accented (b) *(marcado)* marked, distinct

**acentuar [4] 1** vt (a) *(palabra, letra)* *(al escribir)* to accent, to put an accent on; *(al hablar)* to stress (b) *(intensificar)* to accentuate; **la inflación acentuó la crisis** inflation made the recession even worse (c) *(recalcar)* to stress, to emphasize; **a. la necesidad de hacer algo** to emphasize the need to do sth

**2** **acentuarse** vpr (a) *(intensificarse)* to deepen, to increase (b) *(llevar acento)* **las consonantes nunca se acentúan** consonants never have an accent

**acepción** nf *(de palabra, frase)* meaning, sense

**aceptable** adj acceptable

**aceptación** nf (a) *(aprobación)* acceptance (b) *(éxito)* success, popularity; **tener gran a.** to be very popular

**aceptar** vt to accept

**acequia** nf irrigation channel

**acera** nf (a) *(para peatones)* Br pavement, US sidewalk; *Fam* **ser de la otra a.** *(ser homosexual)* to be one of them (b) *(lado de la calle)* side of the street

**acerado, -a** adj (a) *(con acero)* containing steel (b) *Fig. (fuerte, resistente)* steely, tough (c) *Fig (mordaz)* cutting, biting

**acerar** vt (a) *(poner aceras)* to pave (b) *(convertir en acero)* to turn into steel

**acerbo, -a** adj *Formal* (a) *(áspero)* bitter (b) *Fig (mordaz)* caustic, cutting

**acerca** adv **a. de** about

**acercamiento** nm *(de personas, estados)* rapprochement; *(de suceso, fecha)* approach

**acercar [61] 1** vt to bring nearer; **¡acércame el pan!** could you pass me the bread?

**2** **acercarse** vpr (a) *(aproximarse)* to come closer, to approach; **acércate a ver esto** come and have a look at this; **no te acerques al precipicio** don't go near the edge (b) *(ir)* to go; *(venir)* to come; **se acercó a la tienda a por pan** she popped out to the shops for some bread; **acércate por aquí un día de estos** come over and see us some time (c) *(tiempo)* to draw nearer, to approach; **se acerca la Navidad** Christmas is coming; **nos acercamos al verano** it will soon be summer

**acería** nf steelworks *(singular)*

**acerico** nm pincushion

**acero** nm steel; **a. inoxidable** stainless steel

**acerque** etc ver **acercar**

**acérrimo, -a** adj *(defensor)* diehard, fervent; *(enemigo)* bitter

**acertado, -a** adj (a) *(certero)* *(respuesta)* correct; *(disparo)* on target; *(comentario)* appropriate (b) *(oportuno)* good, clever

**acertante 1** adj winning

**2** nmf winner; **los máximos acertantes** *(de quiniela, lotería)* the jackpot winners

**acertar [3] 1** vt (a) *(adivinar)* to guess (correctly); **acerté dos respuestas** I got two answers right (b) *(blanco)* to hit

**2** vi (a) *(al contestar, adivinar)* to be right; *(al escoger, decidir)* to make a good choice (b) *(conseguir)* **a. a hacer algo** to manage to do sth; *Fig* **acertaba a pasar por allí** she happened to pass that way (c) *(hallar)* **a. con** to find

**acertijo** nm riddle

**acervo** nm **a. cultural** *(de una nación, región)* cultural heritage; *Pol* **a. comunitario** acquis communautaire; **a. popular** popular culture

**acetato** *nm Quím* acetate

**acético, -a** *adj Quím* acetic

**acetileno** *nm Quím* acetylene

**acetona** *nf Quím* acetone; *(quitaesmaltes)* nail-polish remover

**achacable** *adj* attributable (**a** to)

**achacar** [61] *vt* to attribute (**a** to)

**achacoso, -a** *adj* (**a**) *(persona)* frail (**b**) *(cosa)* faulty, defective

**achampañado, -a** *adj* sparkling

**achantar 1** *vt Fam* to put the wind up
**2 achantarse** *vpr Fam* to get the wind up

**achaparrado, -a** *adj* squat

**achaque 1** *ver* **achacar**
**2** *nm* ailment, complaint

**achatado, -a** *adj* flattened; **la Tierra está achatada por los polos** the Earth is flattened at the poles

**achatar 1** *vt* to flatten
**2 achatarse** *vpr* to level out

**achicar** [61] **1** *vt* (**a**) *(empequeñecer)* to make smaller; *Fig (acobardar)* to intimidate (**b**) *(agua) (de barco)* to bale out; *(de mina)* to pump out
**2 achicarse** *vpr (acobardarse)* to be intimidated

**achicharrado, -a** *adj (quemado)* burnt to a crisp; *Fig (acalorado)* boiling (hot)

**achicharrante** *adj (calor, sol)* boiling

**achicharrar 1** *vt* (**a**) *(quemar)* to burn (**b**) *Fig (a preguntas)* to plague, to overwhelm (**a** with)
**2** *vi (sol, calor)* to be boiling
**3 achicharrarse** *vpr Fam (quemarse)* to fry, to get burnt; *Fig (de calor)* to be boiling (hot)

**achicoria** *nf* chicory

**achinado, -a** *adj* (**a**) *(ojos)* slanting (**b**) *(persona)* Chinese-looking (**c**) *CSur* Indian-looking

**achique 1** *ver* **achicar**
**2** *nm Náut* baling out

**achispado, -a** *adj Fam* tipsy

**achispar 1** *vt* to make tipsy
**2 achisparse** *vpr* to get tipsy

**achuchado, -a** *adj Fam* hard, tough; **la vida está muy achuchada** life is very hard, money is tight

**achuchar** *vt Fam* (**a**) *(abrazar)* to hug (**b**) *Fig (presionar)* to be on at, to badger

**achuchón** *nm Fam* (**a**) *(abrazo)* big hug (**b**) *(indisposición)* mild illness; **le dio un a.** he got sick

**achulado, -a** *adj* cocky

**achunchar** *CSur* **1** *vt (avergonzar)* to shame
**2 achuncharse** *vpr (avergonzarse)* to be ashamed

**aciago, -a** *adj Formal* black, fateful; **un día a.** a fateful day

**acicalado, -a** *adj* smart, neat and tidy

**acicalar 1** *vt* to do up
**2 acicalarse** *vpr* to do oneself up

**acicate** *nm* (**a**) *(espuela)* spur (**b**) *Fig (estímulo)* incentive

**acidez** *nf* acidity; **a. (de estómago)** heartburn

**ácido, -a 1** *adj (bebida, sabor, carácter)* acid, sour; *Quím* acidic
**2** *nm* (**a**) *Quím* acid; **á. desoxirribonucleico** deoxyribonucleic acid; **á. sulfúrico** sulphuric acid (**b**) *Fam (droga)* acid

**acierto 1** *ver* **acertar**
**2** *nm* (**a**) *(a pregunta)* correct answer (**b**) *(en quinielas)* = correct prediction of results in football pools entry (**c**) *(habilidad, tino)* good *o* sound judgement; **fue un a. vender las acciones** it was a good *o* smart idea to sell the shares

**ácimo** *adj (pan)* unleavened

**acimut** *(pl* **acimutes***) nm Astron* azimuth

**aclamación** *nf* acclamation, acclaim; **por a.** unanimously

**aclamar** *vt* to acclaim; **fue aclamado emperador** he was acclaimed emperor

**aclaración** *nf* explanation, clarification

**aclarado** *nm* rinsing; **dar un a. a algo** to rinse sth, to give sth a rinse

**aclarar 1** *vt* (**a**) *(enjuagar)* to rinse (**b**) *(explicar)* to clarify, to explain (**c**) *(color)* to make lighter (**d**) *(lo espeso) (chocolate, sopa)* to thin (down); *(bosque)* to thin out
**2** *v impersonal* **ya aclaraba** *(amanecía)* it was getting light; *(se despejaba)* the sky was clearing
**3 aclararse** *vpr* (**a**) *(entender)* to understand; **no me aclaro con este ordenador** I can't get the hang of this computer (**b**) *(explicarse)* **se aclaró la situación** the situation became clear (**c**) *(tener las cosas claras)* to know what one wants; **¡mi jefe no se aclara!** my boss doesn't know what he wants (**d**) **aclararse la garganta** to clear one's throat (**e**) **aclararse el pelo** *(de color)* to dye one's hair a lighter colour

**aclaratorio, -a** *adj* explanatory

**aclimatación** *nf* acclimatization

**aclimatar 1** *vt (planta, animal)* to acclimatize (**a** to)
**2 aclimatarse** *vpr (planta, animal)* to acclimatize (**a** to); *Fig (acostumbrarse)* to settle in; **aclimatarse a algo** to get used to sth

**acné** *nm Med* **a. (juvenil)** acne

**ACNUR** [ak'nur] *nf (abrev de* **Alta Comisaría de las Naciones Unidas para los Refugiados**) UNHCR

**acobardar 1** *vt* to frighten, to scare
**2 acobardarse** *vpr* to get frightened *o* scared; **acobardarse ante algo** to shrink back from sth

**acodado, -a** *adj* (**a**) *(persona)* leaning (on his/her elbows) (**b**) *(cañería)* elbowed

**acodarse** *vpr* to lean (**en** on)

**acogedor, -ora** *adj* *(país, persona)* friendly, welcoming; *(casa, ambiente)* cosy

**acoger** [54] 1 *vt* (**a**) *(recibir)* to welcome; *Fig (idea, noticia)* to receive (**b**) *(dar refugio a)* to take in; **que Dios lo/la acoja en su seno** God rest his/her soul

2 **acogerse** *vpr* **acogerse a** *(ley, derecho)* to take refuge in, to have recourse to

**acogida** *nf (de persona)* welcome, reception; *Fig (de idea, película)* reception; **tener buena/ mala a.** to be well/badly received, to go down well/badly

**acojo** *ver* **acoger**

**acojonado, -a** *adj Vulg* shit-scared

**acojonante** *adj Vulg* (**a**) *(impresionante)* bloody incredible (**b**) *(que da miedo)* bloody scary

**acojonar** *Vulg* 1 *vt* (**a**) *(asustar)* to scare shit-less (**b**) *(impresionar)* to gobsmack

2 *vi (asustar)* to be bloody scary

3 **acojonarse** *vpr* to get shit-scared

**acojono** *nm Vulg* **me entró un a. terrible** I started shitting myself

**acolchado, -a** *adj* padded

**acolchar** *vt* to pad

**acólito** *nm (monaguillo)* altar boy; *Fig* acolyte

**acometer 1** *vt* (**a**) *(atacar)* to attack; **le acometió el sueño** he was overcome by tiredness (**b**) *(emprender)* to undertake

2 *vi (embestir)* **a. contra** to hurtle into

**acometida** *nf (de ataque)* attack, charge (**b**) *(de luz, gas)* (mains) connection

**acomodadizo, -a** *adj* accommodating, easy-going

**acomodado, -a** *adj* (**a**) *(rico)* well-off, well-to-do (**b**) *(instalado)* ensconced

**acomodador, -ora** *nm,f Cine & Teatro* usher, *f* usherette

**acomodar 1** *vt* (**a**) *(instalar) (persona)* to seat, to instal; *(cosa)* to place (**b**) *(adaptar)* to fit

2 **acomodarse** *vpr* (**a**) *(instalarse)* to make oneself comfortable; **se acomodó en el sillón** he settled down in the armchair (**b**) *(adaptarse)* to adapt (**a** to); **el presupuesto deberá acomodarse a nuestras necesidades** our budget should meet our needs

**acomodaticio, -a** *adj (complaciente)* accommodating, easy-going

**acomodo** *nm (alojamiento)* accommodation; *Fig* **dar a. a algo** to allow for sth, to take sth into account

**acompañamiento** *nm* (**a**) *(comitiva) (en entierro)* cortege; *(de rey)* retinue (**b**) *Culin & Mús* accompaniment

**acompañante** *nmf* companion

**acompañar 1** *vt* (**a**) *(ir con)* to go with, to accompany; **a. a alguien a la puerta** to show sb out; **a. a alguien a casa** to walk sb home (**b**) *(hacer compañía)* **a. a alguien** to keep sb company; **la radio me acompaña mucho** I listen to the radio for company (**c**) *(compartir emociones con)* **a. en algo a alguien** to be with sb in sth; **le acompaño en el sentimiento** (you have) my condolences (**d**) *(adjuntar)* to enclose (**e**) *Mús* to accompany (**f**) *Culin* **a. la carne con verduras** to serve the meat with vegetables

2 *vi (hacer compañía)* to provide company

3 **acompañarse** *vpr Mús* **canta y se acompaña con el piano** she sings and accompanies herself on the piano

**acompasado, -a** *adj (crecimiento, desarrollo)* steady; *(pasos)* measured

**acompasar** *vt* **a. algo** to synchronize sth (**a** with)

**acomplejado, -a 1** *adj* **está a. por su calvicie** he has a complex about his bald patch

2 *nm,f* **es un a.** he has got a complex

**acomplejar 1** *vt* to give a complex

2 **acomplejarse** *vpr* to develop a complex

**Aconcagua** *nm* **el A.** Aconcagua

**acondicionado, -a** *adj* (**a**) *(equipado)* equipped; **estar bien/mal a.** to be in a fit/no fit state (**b**) **aire a.** air-conditioning

**acondicionador** *nm (de aire)* air-conditioner

**acondicionamiento** *nm (reforma)* conversion, upgrading

**acondicionar** *vt* (**a**) *(reformar)* to convert, to upgrade (**b**) *(preparar)* to prepare, to get ready

**aconfesional** *adj* secular

**acongojado, -a** *adj (apenado)* distressed, anguished

**acongojar 1** *vt* to distress, to cause anguish to

2 **acongojarse** *vpr* to be distressed

**aconsejable** *adj* advisable

**aconsejar** *vt* (**a**) *(dar consejos)* **a. a alguien (que haga algo)** to advise sb (to do sth) (**b**) *(hacer aconsejable)* to make advisable

**acontecer** [48] *vi* to take place, to happen

**acontecimiento** *nm* event; **adelantarse a los acontecimientos** *(precipitarse)* to jump the gun; *(prevenir)* to take preemptive measures

**acopiar** [15] *vt* to gather

**acopio** *nm* stock, store; **hacer a. de** *(existencias, comestibles)* to stock up on; *(valor, paciencia)* to summon up

**acoplable** *adj* attachable (**a** to)

**acoplamiento** *nm (de piezas)* attachment, connection; *(de módulo espacial)* docking

**acoplar 1** *vt (encajar)* to attach, to fit together; *Fig (adaptar)* to adapt, to fit

**2 acoplarse** *vpr* **(a)** *(adaptarse)* to adjust (**a** to); *(mutuamente)* to adjust to each other **(b)** *(encajar)* to fit together; **acoplarse a algo** to fit sth **(c)** *(micrófono)* to give feedback

**acoquinado, -a** *adj Fam* timid, nervous

**acoquinar** *Fam* **1** *vt* to put the wind up

**2 acoquinarse** *vpr* to get the wind up

**acorazado, -a 1** *adj* armour-plated

**2** *nm (buque de guerra)* battleship

**acorazar** [16] *vt* to armour-plate, to armour

**acordar** [65] **1** *vt* **a. algo/hacer algo** to agree on sth/to do sth

**2 acordarse** *vpr* **acordarse (de algo/de hacer algo)** to remember (sth/to do sth)

**acorde 1** *adj (conforme)* in agreement; **estar a. con** to be in keeping with

**2** *nm Mús* chord

**acordeón** *nm* accordion

**acordeonista** *nmf* accordionist

**acordonado, -a** *adj* cordoned off

**acordonar** *vt* **(a)** *(cercar)* to cordon off **(b)** *(atar)* to do *o* lace up

**acornear** *vt* to gore

**acorralamiento** *nm (de malhechor, animal de caza)* cornering

**acorralar** *vt también Fig* to corner

**acortar 1** *vt (longitud, cuerda)* to shorten; *(falda, pantalón)* to take up; *(reunión, viaje)* to cut short

**2** *vi* **por este camino acortaremos** we'll get there quicker this way

**3 acortarse** *vpr (días)* to get shorter

**acosado, -a** *adj* hounded, pursued

**acosador, -ora** *adj* relentless, persistent

**acosamiento** *nm* harassment

**acosar** *vt (perseguir)* to pursue relentlessly; *Fig (hostigar)* to harass

**acoso** *nm (persecución)* relentless pursuit; *Fig (hostigamiento)* harassment; **a. sexual** sexual harassment; **a. y derribo** = rural sport in which horsemen harry and bring down bulls; *Fig* constant harrying

**acostar** [65] **1** *vt* **(a)** *(en la cama)* to put to bed **(b)** *Náut* to lay alongside

**2 acostarse** *vpr (irse a la cama)* to go to bed; *(tumbarse)* to lie down; **suele acostarse tarde** he usually goes to bed late; *Fam* **acostarse con alguien** *(tener relaciones sexuales)* to sleep with sb

**acostumbrado, -a** *adj* **(a)** *(habitual)* usual **(b)** *(habituado)* **estamos acostumbrados** we're used to it; **estar a. a algo/a hacer algo** to be used to sth/to doing sth

**acostumbrar 1** *vt (habituar)* **a. a alguien a algo/a hacer algo** to get sb used to sth/to doing sth

**2** *vi (soler)* **a. a hacer algo** to be in the habit of doing sth; **acostumbra a trabajar los sábados** he usually works on Saturdays

**3 acostumbrarse** *vpr (habituarse)* **te acostumbrarás pronto** you'll soon get used to it; **acostumbrarse a algo/a hacer algo** to get used to sth/to doing sth

**acotación** *nf (nota)* note in the margin; *Teatro* stage direction

**acotado, -a** *adj* enclosed

**acotamiento** *nm* **(a)** *(de terreno, campo)* enclosing, demarcation **(b)** *Méx (arcén)* hard shoulder

**acotar** *vt* **(a)** *(terreno, campo)* to enclose, to demarcate; *Fig (tema, competencias)* to delimit **(b)** *(texto)* to write notes in the margin of

**acotejar** *vt Andes, Carib* to arrange

**ACP** *(abrev de* **África, el Caribe y el Pacífico***)* ACP; **países A.** ACP countries

**ácrata** *adj & nmf Pol* anarchist

**acre 1** *adj (olor)* acrid, pungent; *(sabor)* bitter; *Fig (brusco, desagradable)* caustic

**2** *nm* acre

**acrecentar** [3] **1** *vt* to increase

**2 acrecentarse** *vpr* to increase

**acreditación** *nf (de periodista)* press card; *(de diplomático)* credentials

**acreditado, -a** *adj* **(a)** *(médico, abogado)* distinguished; *(marca)* reputable **(b)** *(embajador, representante)* accredited

**acreditar** *vt* **(a)** *(certificar)* to certify; *(autorizar)* to authorize, to entitle **(b)** *(demostrar)* to prove, to confirm **(c)** *(dar fama a)* to do credit to **(d)** *(embajador)* to accredit **(e)** *Fin* to credit

**acreedor, -ora 1** *adj* **hacerse a. de algo** to earn sth

**2** *nm,f Fin* creditor

**acribillado, -a** *adj* **a. a balazos** riddled with bullets

**acribillar** *vt* to perforate, to pepper with holes; **a. a alguien a balazos** to riddle sb with bullets; **me han acribillado los mosquitos** the mosquitoes have bitten me all over; *Fig* **a. a alguien a preguntas** to fire questions at sb

**acrílico, -a 1** *adj* acrylic

**2** *nm Arte* painting done in acrylics

**acrimonia** *nf (aspereza)* acrimony

**acrisolado, -a** *adj* proven, tried and tested

**acristalado, -a** *adj (terraza, galería)* glazed

**acristalar** *vt* to glaze

**acrítico, -a** *adj* uncritical

**acritud** *nf (aspereza)* acrimony

**acrobacia** nf (a) (en circo) acrobatics (b) (de avión) aerobatic manoeuvre; Fig **hacer acrobacias con las cifras** to massage the figures

**acróbata** nmf acrobat

**acrobático, -a** adj (ejercicios, espectáculo) acrobatic

**acrónimo** nm acronym

**acrópolis** nf inv acropolis

**acróstico** nm acrostic

**acta** nf (a) **acta(s)** (de junta, reunión) minutes; (de congreso) proceedings; **constar en a.** to be recorded in the minutes; **levantar a.** to take the minutes (b) (certificado) certificate; **a. de defunción** death certificate; **a. notarial** affidavit; **a. (de nombramiento)** certificate of appointment

**actinia** nf sea anemone

**actitud** nf (a) (disposición de ánimo) attitude (b) (postura) posture, position

**activación** nf stimulation

**activar** vt (alarma, mecanismo) to activate; (explosivo) to detonate; (economía) to stimulate

**actividad** nf activity; **desplegar una gran a.** to be in a flurry of activity; **en a.** active; Educ **actividades extraescolares** extracurricular activities

**activismo** nm Pol activism

**activista** nmf Pol activist

**activo, -a 1** adj (a) (dinámico) también Gram active (b) (que trabaja) working; **en a.** (en funciones) on active service; Fam **hemos tratado por activa y por pasiva de...** we have tried everything to...
**2** nm Fin assets; **a. fijo** fixed assets; **a. financiero** financial assets; **a. líquido** liquid assets

**acto** nm (a) (acción) act; **hacer a. de presencia** to show one's face; también Fig **a. reflejo** reflex action; **a. sexual** sexual act; **a. de solidaridad** show of solidarity (b) (ceremonia) ceremony (c) Teatro act (d) (expresiones) **a. seguido** immediately after; **en el a.** on the spot, there and then; **reparaciones en el a.** repairs done while you wait

**actor** nm actor

**actriz** nf actress

**actuación** nf (a) (conducta, proceder) conduct, behaviour (b) (interpretación) performance (c) Der **actuaciones** proceedings

**actual** adj (a) (del momento presente) present, current (b) (de moda) modern, present-day (c) (de interés) topical; **el desempleo es un tema muy a.** unemployment is a very topical issue

**actualidad** nf (a) (situación) current situation; **en la a.** (momento presente) at the present time, nowadays; **estar de a.** (ser de interés) to be topical; **la a. política** the current political situation (b) (noticia) news (singular); **la a.**

**informativa** the news; **la a. deportiva** the sports news; **ser a.** to be making the news (c) (vigencia) relevance to modern society; **sus libros siguen teniendo gran a.** her books are still very relevant today

**actualización** nf (de información, datos) updating; (de tecnología, industria) modernization; Informát (de software, hardware) upgrade

**actualizar** [16] vt (información, datos) to update; (tecnología, industria) to modernize; Informát (nueva versión) to upgrade

**actualmente** adv (a) (en estos tiempos) these days, nowadays; **a. casi nadie viaja en burro** hardly anyone travels by donkey nowadays (b) (en este momento) at the (present) moment; **su padre está a. en paradero desconocido** his father's present whereabouts are unknown

**actuar** [4] vi (a) (obrar, producir efecto) to act; **actúa de o como escudo** it acts o serves as a shield; **este tranquilizante actúa directamente sobre los centros nerviosos** this tranquilizer acts directly on the nerve centres (b) Der to undertake proceedings (c) (en película, teatro) to perform, to act; **en esta película actúa Victoria Abril** Victoria Abril appears in this film

**actuario, -a** nm,f (a) Der clerk of the court (b) Fin **a. de seguros** actuary

**acuarela** nf (técnica, pintura) watercolour

**acuarelista** nmf (pintor) watercolourist

**acuario 1** nmf (persona) Aquarius
**2** nm (a) (edificio, pecera grande) aquarium; (pecera) fish-tank (b) (zodiaco) Aquarius; **ser a.** to be (an) Aquarius

**acuartelamiento** nm Mil (a) (acción) confinement to barracks (b) (lugar) barracks

**acuartelar** vt Mil (a) (alojar) to quarter (b) (retener) to confine to barracks

**acuático, -a** adj aquatic

**acuchillador** nm (de suelos) floor sander

**acuchillar** vt (a) (apuñalar) to stab (b) (suelo de madera) to sand

**acuciante** adj urgent, pressing

**acuciar** [15] vt (instar) to goad; Fig to press; **el deseo me acuciaba** I was driven by desire

**acuclillarse** vpr (agacharse) to squat (down)

**ACUDE** [a'kuðe] nf (abrev de **Asociación de Consumidores y Usuarios de España**) Br ≃ CA, US ≃ CAC, = Spanish consumer association

**acudir** vi (a) (ir) to go; (venir) to come; **a. a una cita/un mitin** to turn up for an appointment/at a rally; **nadie acudió a mi llamada de auxilio** no-one answered my cry for help; Fig **a. a la mente** to come to mind (b) (recurrir) **a. a alguien** to turn to sb; **si necesitáis**

**ayuda, podéis a. a mí** if you need help you can come to *o* ask me

**acueducto** *nm* aqueduct

**acuerdo 1** *ver* **acordar**

**2** *nm* agreement; **llegar a un a.** to reach (an) agreement; **de a.** all right; **de a. con** *(conforme a)* in accordance with; **estar de a. (con alguien/en hacer algo)** to agree (with sb/to do sth); **ponerse de a. (con alguien)** to agree (with sb), to come to an agreement (with sb); **de común a.** by common consent; **A. General sobre Aranceles y Comercio** General Agreement on Tariffs and Trade; *Ind* **a. marco** framework agreement; **a. tácito** tacit agreement

**acuesto** *etc ver* **acostar**

**acuicultivo** *nm* hydroponics *(singular)*

**acuífero** *nm* *Geol* aquifer

**acumulación** *nf* accumulation

**acumulador** *nm* *Elec* accumulator, storage battery

**acumular 1** *vt* to accumulate

**2 acumularse** *vpr* to accumulate, to build up

**acumulativo, -a** *adj* cumulative

**acunar** *vt (en cuna)* to rock; *(en brazos)* to cradle

**acuñar** *vt (moneda)* to mint; *Fig (palabra)* to coin

**acuoso, -a** *adj* **(a)** *(que contiene agua)* watery **(b)** *(jugoso)* juicy

**acupuntor, -ora** *nm,f* acupuncturist

**acupuntura** *nf* acupuncture

**acurrucarse** [61] *vpr* to crouch down; *(por frío)* to huddle up; *(por miedo)* to cower; **se acurrucó en un sillón** he curled up in an armchair

**acusación** *nf* **(a)** *(inculpación)* charge **(b)** *Der* **la a.** the prosecution; **a. particular** private action

**acusado, -a 1** *adj (marcado)* marked, distinct

**2** *nm,f (procesado)* accused, defendant

**acusador, -ora** *adj* accusing

**acusar 1** *vt* **(a)** *(culpar)* to accuse; *Der* to charge; **a. a alguien de algo** *(culpar)* to accuse sb of sth; *Der* to charge sb with sth **(b)** *(mostrar)* to show; **su rostro acusaba el paso del tiempo** his face showed the passage of time; **su espalda acusó el esfuerzo** the effort had taken its toll on his back **(c)** *(recibo)* to acknowledge

**2 acusarse** *vpr (mutuamente)* to blame one another **(de** for); *(uno mismo)* **acusarse de haber hecho algo** to confess to having done sth

**acusativo** *nm* *Gram* accusative

**acusatorio, -a** *adj* *Der* accusatory

**acuse** *nm* **a. de recibo** acknowledgement of receipt

**acusica** *nmf* *Fam* telltale

**acústica** *nf* **(a)** *(ciencia)* acoustics *(singular)* **(b)** *(de local)* acoustics

**acústico, -a** *adj* acoustic

**ADA** ['aða] *nf (abrev de* **Asociación de Ayuda al Automovilista)** *Br* ≃ AA, *US* ≃ AAA, = Spanish motoring association

**adagio** *nm* **(a)** *(sentencia breve)* adage **(b)** *Mús* adagio

**adalid** *nm* champion

**adaptable** *adj* adaptable

**adaptación** *nf* **(a)** *(acomodación)* adjustment **(a** to); **a. al medio** adaptation to the environment **(b)** *(modificación)* adaptation; **la película es una buena a. del libro** the film is a good adaptation of the book

**adaptado, -a** *adj* suited **(a** to)

**adaptador** *nm* *Elec* adapter

**adaptar 1** *vt* **(a)** *(acomodar, ajustar)* to adjust **(a** to) **(b)** *(modificar)* *(libro, obra de teatro)* to adapt

**2 adaptarse** *vpr* to adjust **(a** to)

**Addis Abeba** *n* Addis Ababa

**adecentar 1** *vt* to tidy up

**2 adecentarse** *vpr* to smarten oneself up

**ADECU** [a'ðeku] *nf (abrev de* **Asociación para la Defensa de los Consumidores y Usuarios)** *Br* ≃ CA, *US* ≃ CAC, = Spanish consumer association

**adecuación** *nf* *Formal (idoneidad, conveniencia)* suitability

**adecuado, -a** *adj* appropriate, suitable

**adecuar** [5] **1** *vt* to adapt

**2 adecuarse** *vpr (ser apropiado)* to be appropriate **(a** for); **las medidas se adecuan a las circunstancias** the measures are in keeping with the situation

**adefesio** *nm* *Fam* **(a)** *(persona)* fright, sight **(b)** *(cosa)* eyesore, monstrosity

**a. de JC.** *(abrev de* **antes de Jesucristo)** BC

**adelantado, -a** *adj* advanced; **llevo el reloj a.** my watch is fast; **por a.** in advance; **Galileo fue un hombre a. a su tiempo** Galileo was a man ahead of his time

**adelantamiento** *nm (en carretera)* overtaking

**adelantar 1** *vt* **(a)** *(vehículo, competidor)* to overtake **(b)** *(mover hacia adelante)* to move forward; *(pie, reloj)* to put forward **(c)** *(en el tiempo)* *(reunión, viaje)* to bring forward; *(dinero)* to pay in advance

**2** *vi* **(a)** *(progresar)* to make progress; **¿qué adelantas con eso?** what do you hope to gain *o* achieve by that? **(b)** *(reloj)* to be fast **(c)** *(en carretera)* to overtake; **prohibido a.** *(en señal)* no overtaking

**3 adelantarse** *vpr* **(a)** *(en el tiempo)* to be early; *(reloj)* to gain; **este año se ha adelanta-**

**do la primavera** spring has come early this year; **adelantarse a alguien** to beat sb to it; **se adelantó a mis deseos** she anticipated my wishes; **se adelantaron a la competencia** they stole a march on their rivals (**b**) *(en el espacio)* to go on ahead; **se adelantó unos pasos** he went on a few steps ahead

**adelante 1** *adv* forward, ahead; **(de ahora) en a.** from now on; **más a.** *(en el tiempo)* later (on); *(en el espacio)* further on; **sacar a.** *(proyecto, empresa)* to rescue; **salimos a.** we put our problems behind us

**2** *interj* **¡a.!** *(¡siga!)* go ahead!; *(¡pase!)* come in!

**adelanto** *nm (técnico, de dinero)* advance

**adelfa** *nf* oleander

**adelgazamiento** *nm* slimming

**adelgazante** *adj* slimming

**adelgazar** [16] **1** *vt (kilos)* to lose

**2** *vi* to lose weight, to slim

**ademán** *nm (gesto) (con las manos)* gesture; *(con la cara)* face, expression; **hizo a. de decir algo/huir** he made as if to say sth/run away

**además** *adv* moreover, besides; **a. de** as well as; **es guapa y a. inteligente** she's beautiful, and clever too

**ADENA** [a'ðena] *nf (abrev de* **Asociación para la Defensa de la Naturaleza**) *Br* ≃ NCC, = Spanish nature conservancy organization

**adentrarse** *vpr* **a. en** *(jungla, barrio)* to go deep into; *(asunto)* to study in depth

**adentro** *adv* inside; **tierra a.** inland; **mar a.** out to sea; **para mis/tus/*etc* adentros** *(pensar, decir)* to myself/yourself/*etc*; **sonrió para sus adentros** he smiled to himself

**adepto, -a 1** *adj (partidario)* supporting; **ser a. a** to be a follower of

**2** *nm,f* follower **(a** *o* de of**)**

**aderezar** [16] *vt (sazonar) (ensalada)* to dress; *(comida)* to season; *Fig (conversación)* to liven up, to spice up

**aderezo** *nm (aliño) (de ensalada)* dressing; *(de comida)* seasoning; *Fig (adorno)* adornment

**adeudar 1** *vt* (**a**) *(deber)* to owe (**b**) *Com* to debit; **a. 5.000 pts a una cuenta** to debit 5,000 pesetas to an account

**2** **adeudarse** *vpr* to get into debt

**adeudo** *nm Fin* debit

**adherencia** *nf* (**a**) *(de sustancia, superficie)* stickiness, adhesion; *Aut (de ruedas)* road-holding (**b**) *(parte añadida)* appendage

**adherente** *adj* adhesive, sticky

**adherir** [64] **1** *vt* to stick

**2** **adherirse** *vpr (pegarse)* to stick; *Fig* **adherirse a** *(opinión, idea)* to adhere to; *(partido, asociación)* to join

**adhesión** *nf* (**a**) *(a opinión, idea)* support (**a** of) (**b**) *(a una organización)* entry (**a** into)

**adhesivo, -a 1** *adj* adhesive

**2** *nm* (**a**) *(pegatina)* sticker (**b**) *(sustancia)* adhesive

**adhiero** *etc ver* **adherir**

**adhiriera** *etc ver* **adherir**

**adicción** *nf* addiction (**a** to)

**adición** *nf* addition

**adicional** *adj* additional

**adictivo, -a** *adj* addictive

**adicto, -a 1** *adj* addicted (**a** to)

**2** *nm,f* addict; **un a. a la heroína/al tabaco** a heroin/nicotine addict

**adiestramiento** *nm* training

**adiestrar** *vt* to train; **a. a alguien en algo/para hacer algo** to train sb in sth/to do sth

**adinerado, -a** *adj* wealthy

**adiós** ( *pl* **adioses**) **1** *interj* goodbye; *Fig* **decirle a. a algo** to wave *o* kiss sth goodbye

**2** *interj* **¡a.!** goodbye!; *(al cruzarse con alguien)* hello!

**adiposidad** *nf Med* fattiness

**adiposo, -a** *adj Med* fatty

**aditamento** *nm (complemento)* accessory; *(cosa añadida)* addition

**aditivo** *nm* additive

**adivinador, -ora** *nm,f* fortune-teller

**adivinanza** *nf* riddle

**adivinar 1** *vt* (**a**) *(predecir)* to foretell; *(el futuro)* to tell (**b**) *(acertar)* to guess (correctly) (**c**) *(intuir)* to suspect (**d**) *(vislumbrar)* to spot, to make out

**2** **adivinarse** *vpr (vislumbrarse)* to be visible

**adivino, -a** *nm,f* fortune-teller; *Fig* **no soy a.** I'm not psychic

**adjetivar** *vt Gram* to use adjectivally

**adjetivo, -a 1** *adj* adjectival

**2** *nm Gram* adjective; **a. calificativo** qualifying adjective; **a. demostrativo** demonstrative adjective; **a. numeral** quantitative adjective

**adjudicación** *nf* awarding

**adjudicar** [61] **1** *vt (asignar)* to award

**2** **adjudicarse** *vpr (apropiarse)* to take for oneself

**adjuntar** *vt* to enclose *(in letter)*

**adjunto, -a 1** *adj* (**a**) *(incluido)* enclosed; **a. le remito...** please find enclosed... (**b**) *(auxiliar)* assistant; **profesor a.** assistant lecturer

**2** *nm,f (auxiliar)* assistant

**adminículo** *nm* gadget

**administración** *nf* (**a**) *(de empresa)* administration, management; **a. de recursos** resource management (**b**) *(oficina)* manager's office; **la A.** *(Gobierno) Br* the Government, *US* the Administration; **a. de justicia** legal system; **a. local** local government; **a. pública** civil service (**c**) *(de medicamentos)* administering

**administrador, -ora** *nm,f (de empresa)* manager; *(de bienes ajenos)* administrator

**administrar 1** *vt* (**a**) *(empresa, finca)* to manage, to run; *(casa)* to run; *(país)* to govern, to run; *(recursos)* to manage (**b**) *(medicamento, sacramentos)* to administer

**2 administrarse** *vpr (organizar dinero)* to manage one's finances

**administrativo, -a 1** *adj* administrative

**2** *nm,f* white-collar worker

**admirable** *adj* admirable

**admiración** *nf* (**a**) *(sentimiento)* admiration (**b**) *(signo ortográfico)* Br exclamation mark, US exclamation point

**admirador, -ora** *nm,f* admirer

**admirar 1** *vt* (**a**) *(personaje, obra de arte)* to admire; **lo admiro por su honradez** I admire his honesty; **ser de a.** to be admirable (**b**) *(sorprender)* to amaze; **me admira su descaro** I can't believe his cheek

**2 admirarse** *vpr* to be amazed (**de** by)

**admisibilidad** *nf* acceptability

**admisible** *adj* acceptable

**admisión** *nf (de persona)* admission; *(de solicitudes)* acceptance; **reservado el derecho de a.** *(en letrero)* the management reserves the right to refuse admission

**admitir** *vt* (**a**) *(dejar entrar)* to admit, to allow in; **a. a alguien en** to admit sb to (**b**) *(reconocer)* to admit; **admito que estaba equivocado** I admit I was wrong (**c**) *(aceptar)* to accept; **se admiten propinas** *(en letrero)* gratuities at your discretion (**d**) *(permitir, tolerar)* to allow, to permit; **no admite ni un error** he won't stand for a single mistake

**admón.** *(abrev de* **administración***)* admin.

**admonición** *nf Formal* warning

**ADN** *nm* (*abrev de* **ácido desoxirribonucleico**) DNA

**adobado, -a** *adj* marinated

**adobar** *vt* to marinate

**adobe** *nm* adobe

**adobo** *nm (acción)* marinating; *(salsa)* marinade; **en a.** marinated

**adocenado, -a** *adj* mediocre, run-of-the-mill

**adocenarse** *vpr* to lapse into mediocrity

**adoctrinamiento** *nm (de ideas)* indoctrination; *(enseñanza)* instruction

**adoctrinar** *vt (inculcar ideas)* to indoctrinate; *(enseñar)* to instruct

**adolecer** [48] *vi* **a. de** *(enfermedad)* to suffer from; *(defecto)* to be guilty of

**adolescencia** *nf* adolescence

**adolescente** *adj & nmf* adolescent

**adonde 1** *adv* where; **la ciudad a. vamos** the city we are going to

**2** *prep Fam (a casa de)* **vamos a. la abuela** we're going to granny's

**adónde** *ver* **dónde**

**adondequiera** *adv* wherever

**adonis** *nm inv Fig* Adonis, handsome young man

**adopción** *nf (de hijo, moda, decisión)* adoption; **Uruguay es mi país de a.** Uruguay is my adopted country

**adoptar** *vt (hijo, moda, decisión)* to adopt

**adoptivo, -a** *adj (hijo, país)* adopted; *(padre)* adoptive

**adoquín** *nm* (**a**) *(piedra)* cobblestone (**b**) *Fam (persona)* blockhead

**adoquinado, -a 1** *adj* cobbled

**2** *nm* (**a**) *(suelo)* cobbles (**b**) *(acción)* cobbling

**adoquinar** *vt* to cobble

**adorable** *adj (persona)* adorable; *(lugar, película)* wonderful

**adoración** *nf* adoration; **sentir a. por alguien** to worship sb; *Rel* **la A. de los Reyes Magos** Epiphany

**adorar** *vt (Dios, ídolo)* to worship; *(persona, comida)* to adore

**adormecer** [48] **1** *vt (producir sueño)* to lull to sleep; *Fig (aplacar) (miedo, ira)* to calm; *(pena, dolor)* to alleviate, to lessen

**2 adormecerse** *vpr* to nod off, to drop off

**adormidera** *nf* poppy

**adormilado, -a** *adj (dormido)* dozing; *(con sueño)* sleepy

**adormilarse** *vpr* to doze

**adornado, -a** *adj* decorated

**adornar 1** *vt* to decorate

**2** *vi* to serve as decoration

**adorno** *nm* decoration; **de a.** *(árbol, figura)* decorative; *Fam Fig* **estar de a.** *(persona)* to be a waste of space

**adosado, -a** *adj (casa)* semi-detached

**adosar** *vt* **a. algo a algo** to push sth up against sth

**adquirir** [6] *vt* (**a**) *(comprar)* to acquire, to purchase (**b**) *(conseguir) (conocimientos, hábito, cultura)* to acquire; *(éxito, popularidad)* to achieve

**adquisición** *nf* (**a**) *(compra, cosa comprada)* purchase; **ser una buena/mala a.** to be a good/bad buy (**b**) *(de conocimiento, hábito)* acquisition

**adquisitivo, -a** *adj* **poder a.** purchasing power

**adrede** *adv* on purpose, deliberately

**adrenalina** *nf Med* adrenalin

**Adriático** *nm* el (mar) A. the Adriatic (Sea)

**adscribir 1** *vt* (a) *(asignar)* to assign (b) *(destinar)* to appoint

**2 adscribirse** *vpr* adscribirse a *(grupo, partido)* to become a member of; *(ideología)* to subscribe to

**adscrito, -a 1** *participio ver* **adscribir**

**2** *adj* assigned

**aduana** *nf* customs; **derechos de a.** customs duty; **pasar por la a.** to go through customs

**aducir** [20] *vt (motivo, pretexto)* to give, to furnish; "**estaba muy cansado**" – **adujo** "I was very tired," he explained

**adueñarse** *vpr* a. de *(apoderarse de)* to take over, to take control of; *Fig (dominar)* to take hold of; **el pánico se adueñó de ellos** panic took hold of them

**adujera** *etc ver* **aducir**

**adulación** *nf* flattery

**adulador, -ora 1** *adj* flattering

**2** *nm,f* flatterer

**adular** *vt* to flatter

**adulón, -ona** *nm,f* toady

**adulteración** *nf* adulteration

**adulterar** *vt* (a) *(alimento)* to adulterate (b) *(falsear)* to doctor, to distort

**adulterio** *nm* adultery

**adúltero, -a 1** *adj* adulterous

**2** *nm,f* adulterer, *f* adulteress

**adulto, -a** *adj & nm,f* adult

**adusto, -a** *adj* dour

**aduzco** *ver* **aducir**

**advenedizo, -a** *adj & nm,f* upstart

**advenimiento** *nm (llegada)* advent; *(ascenso al trono)* accession

**adverbial** *adj Gram* adverbial

**adverbio** *nm Gram* adverb; **a. de cantidad/ lugar/modo/tiempo** adverb of degree/place/ manner/time

**adversario, -a** *nm,f* adversary

**adversidad** *nf* adversity

**adverso, -a** *adj (condiciones)* adverse; *(destino)* unkind; *(suerte)* bad; *(viento)* unfavourable

**advertencia** *nf* warning; **servir de a.** to serve as a warning

**advertir** [64] *vt* (a) *(notar)* to notice (b) *(prevenir, avisar)* to warn; **me advirtió del peligro** he warned me of the danger; **te advierto que no me sorprende** mind you, it doesn't surprise me

**adviento** *nm Rel* Advent

**advierto** *etc ver* **advertir**

**advirtiera** *etc ver* **advertir**

**adyacente** *adj* adjacent

**AEE** *nf (abrev de* **Agencia Espacial Europea**) ESA

**Aenor** *nf (abrev de* **Asociación Española para la Normalización y Certificación**) *Br* ≃ BSI, *US* ≃ MBS

**Aeorma** *nf (abrev de* **Asociación Española para la Ordenación del Medio Ambiente**) *US* ≃ EPA, = Spanish association for the protection of the environment

**aeración** *nf* aeration

**aéreo, -a** *adj (del aire)* aerial; *(de la aviación)* air; **base aérea** airbase; **controlador a.** air-traffic controller

**aerobic, aeróbic** *nm* aerobics *(singular)*

**aerobio, -a** *adj Biol* aerobic

**aeroclub** *(pl* aeroclubes) *nm* flying club

**aerodeslizador** *nm* hovercraft

**aerodinámica** *nf* aerodynamics *(singular)*

**aerodinámico, -a** *adj* (a) *Fís* aerodynamic (b) *(forma, línea)* streamlined

**aeródromo** *nm Av* airfield, aerodrome

**aeroespacial** *adj Av* aerospace

**aerofaro** *nm Av* beacon

**aerógrafo** *nm Arte* airbrush

**aerolínea** *nf Av* airline

**aerolito** *nm* aerolite

**aeromodelismo** *nm* airplane modelling

**aeromoza** *nf Am* air hostess

**aeronauta** *nmf* aeronaut

**aeronáutica** *nf* aeronautics *(singular)*

**aeronáutico, -a** *adj* aeronautic

**aeronaval** *adj* **fuerzas aeronavales** air and sea forces

**aeronave** *nf Av (avión, helicóptero)* aircraft; *(dirigible)* airship

**aeroplano** *nm* aeroplane

**aeropuerto** *nm* airport

**aerosol** *nm* aerosol

**aerostático, -a** *adj* **globo a.** hot-air balloon

**aeróstato, aerostato** *nm* hot-air balloon

**aerotaxi** *nm Av* light aircraft *(for hire)*

**aerotransportado, -a** *adj (tropas, polen)* airborne

**AES** ['aes] *nm (abrev de* **acuerdo económico y social**) = agreement between Spanish government and trade unions on social and economic issues

**afabilidad** *nf* affability

**afable** *adj* affable

**afamado, -a** *adj* famous

**afán** *nm* (a) *(esfuerzo)* hard work; **con a.** energetically, enthusiastically (b) *(anhelo)* urge (c) **lo único que le mueve es el a. de lucro** he's only interested in money; **sin a. de lucro** profit-making

**afanador, -ora** *nm,f Méx* cleaner

**afanar** *Fam* **1** *vt (robar)* to pinch, to swipe

**2 afanarse** *vpr (esforzarse)* to do everything one can

**afanoso, -a** *adj (trabajador, diligente)* keen, eager

**afasia** *nf Psi* aphasia

**afear** *vt* to make ugly, to scar; *Fig* **a. a alguien su conducta** *(criticar)* to condemn sb's behaviour

**afección** *nf* complaint, disease; **a. cutánea/ del riñón** skin/kidney complaint

**afectación** *nf* affectation

**afectado, -a** **1** *adj* (a) *(amanerado)* affected (b) *(afligido)* upset, badly affected

**2** *nm,f* victim; **los afectados por las inundaciones serán indemnizados** the people affected by the floods will receive compensation

**afectar** *vt* (a) *(influir)* to affect (b) *(afligir)* to upset, to affect badly (c) *(simular)* to affect, to feign; **afectó enfado** he feigned *o* affected anger

**afectísimo, -a** *adj (en carta)* **suyo a.** Best wishes

**afectividad** *nf* emotions; **la a. en el niño** the emotional world of the child

**afectivo, -a** *adj (emocional)* emotional; **tener problemas afectivos** to have emotional problems

**afecto** *nm* affection, fondness; **sentir a. por alguien** to be fond of sb

**afectuosamente** *adv (en carta)* (yours) affectionately

**afectuoso, -a** *adj* affectionate, loving

**afeitado** *nm* (a) *(del pelo)* shave (b) *Taurom* = blunting of the bull's horns for safety reasons

**afeitar** **1** *vt* (a) *(barba, pelo, persona)* to shave (b) *Taurom* = to blunt the bull's horns for safety reasons

**2 afeitarse** *vpr (uno mismo)* to shave; **se afeitó las piernas** she shaved her legs

**afeite** *nm Anticuado (cosmético)* make-up; **no usa afeites** she doesn't use any make-up

**afelpado, -a** *adj* plush

**afeminado, -a** **1** *adj* effeminate

**2** *nm* effeminate man

**afeminarse** *vpr* to become effeminate

**aferrar** *vt* to grab (hold of)

**2 aferrarse** *vpr también Fig* **aferrarse a algo** to cling to sth

**affaire** [a'fer] *nm* affair

**Afganistán** *n* Afghanistan

**afgano, -a** *adj & nm,f* Afghan

**afianzamiento** *nm (de construcción)* reinforcement; *Fig* consolidation

**afianzar** [16] **1** *vt (construcción)* to reinforce; *Fig* to consolidate

**2 afianzarse** *vpr* to steady oneself; **se afianzó en su opinión** he became more convinced of his opinion; **afianzarse en una posición** to establish oneself in a position

**afiche** *nm Am* poster

**afición** *nf* (a) *(inclinación)* fondness, liking; **por a.** as a hobby; **tener a. a algo** to be keen on sth (b) *(aficionados)* fans; **la a. futbolística** football fans; **la a. taurina** followers of bullfighting

**aficionado, -a 1** *adj* (a) *(interesado)* keen; **ser a. a algo** to be keen on sth (b) *(no profesional)* amateur

**2** *nm,f* (a) *(interesado)* fan; **a. al cine** film buff (b) *(no profesional)* amateur; **un trabajo de aficionados** an amateurish piece of work

**aficionar 1** *vt* **a. a alguien a algo** to make sb keen on sth

**2 aficionarse** *vpr* to become keen (**a** on)

**afijo, -a 1** *adj* affixed

**2** *nm Gram* affix

**afilado, -a 1** *adj* (a) *(cuchillo, punta)* sharp (b) *Fig (dedos, rasgos)* pointed (c) *Fig (comentario, crítica)* cutting

**2** *nm* sharpening

**afilador, -ora 1** *adj* sharpening

**2** *nm,f (persona)* knifegrinder

**3** *nm (objeto)* sharpener; **a. de cuchillos** knife sharpener

**afilalápices** *nm inv* pencil sharpener

**afilar 1** *vt (cuchillo, lápiz)* to sharpen; **piedra de a.** whetstone, grindstone

**2 afilarse** *vpr Fig* to become pointed, to taper

**afiliación** *nf* (a) *(acción)* joining (b) *(efecto)* membership

**afiliado, -a** *nm,f* member (**a** of)

**afiliarse** [15] *vpr* **a. a un partido** to join a party

**afín** *adj* similar; **su postura es a. a la nuestra** his opinion is close to ours

**afinar 1** *vt* (a) *Mús (instrumento)* to tune; **a. la voz** to sing in tune (b) *(perfeccionar, mejorar)* to fine-tune; **a. la puntería** to improve one's aim (c) *(pulir)* to refine

**2** *vi (cantar)* to sing in tune

**afincarse** [61] *vpr* to settle (**en** in)

**afinidad** *nf* (a) *también Quím* affinity (b) *(parentesco)* **por a.** by marriage

**afinque** *etc ver* **afincarse**

**afirmación** *nf* statement, assertion

**afirmar 1** *vt* (a) *(decir)* to say, to declare; **afirmó que...** he stated that... (b) *Constr* to reinforce

**2** *vi (asentir)* to agree, to consent; **a. con la cabeza** to nod (in agreement)

**3 afirmarse** *vpr* (a) *(asegurarse)* **afirmarse en los estribos** to steady oneself in the stirrups (b) *(ratificarse)* **afirmarse en algo** to re-affirm sth

**afirmativa** *nf* affirmative

**afirmativo, -a** *adj* affirmative

**aflautado, -a** *adj* high-pitched

**aflicción** *nf* suffering, sorrow

**afligir** [26] **1** *vt (causar daño)* to afflict; *(causar pena)* to distress

**2 afligirse** *vpr* to be distressed (**por** by)

**aflojar 1** *vt* (a) *(presión, tensión)* to reduce; *(cinturón, corbata)* to loosen; *(cuerda)* to slacken (b) *Fam (dinero)* to fork out

**2** *vi* (a) *(disminuir)* to abate, to die down (b) *Fig (ceder)* to ease off

**3 aflojarse** *vpr (presión, cinturón)* to come loose; *(cuerda)* to slacken

**afloramiento** *nm (de mineral)* outcrop

**aflorar** *vi* (a) *Fig (surgir)* to (come to the) surface, to show; **a. a la superficie** to come to the surface (b) *(mineral)* to outcrop

**afluencia** *nf* (a) *(concurrencia)* influx; **hubo una gran a. de público** the attendance was high (b) *(abundancia)* abundance

**afluente** *nm* tributary

**afluir** [36] *vi (gente)* to flock (**a** to); *(río)* to flow (**a** into); *(sangre, fluido)* to flow (**a** to)

**afluyo** *etc ver* **afluir**

**afmo., -a.** *(abrev de* **afectísimo, -a)** *(en carta)* **suyo a.** Best wishes

**afonía** *nf* **tener a.** to have lost one's voice

**afónico, -a** *adj* **quedarse a.** to lose one's voice

**aforado, -a** *nm,f Der (parlamentario)* = person enjoying parliamentary immunity

**aforar** *vt Tec* to gauge

**aforismo** *nm* aphorism

**aforo** *nm (de teatro, plaza de toros)* seating capacity

**afortunadamente** *adv* fortunately, luckily

**afortunado, -a 1** *adj* (a) *(persona)* lucky, fortunate (b) *(coincidencia, frase)* happy, felicitous

**2** *nm,f (persona)* lucky person; *(en lotería)* lucky winner

**afrancesado, -a 1** *adj* Frenchified

**2** *nm,f Hist* = supporter of the French during the Peninsular War

**afrenta** *nf (ofensa, agravio)* affront

**afrentar** *vt (ofender)* to affront

**África** *n* Africa

**africada** *nf Ling* affricate

**africado, -a** *adj Ling* affricative

**africanismo** *nm* Africanism

**africano, -a** *adj & nm,f* African

**afrikaans** *nm (idioma)* Afrikaans

**afrikáner** *adj & nmf* Afrikaner

**afro** *adj inv* afro; **un peinado a.** an afro (hairstyle)

**afrodisíaco, -a, afrodisiaco, -a** *adj & nm* aphrodisiac

**afrontar** *vt (hacer frente a)* to face; **a. las consecuencias** to face (up to) the consequences

**afrutado, -a** *adj* fruity

**afta** *nf Med* mouth ulcer

**after shave** ['after seif] *nm* aftershave

**afuera 1** *adv* outside; **por (la parte de) a.** on the outside

**2** *nfpl* **las afueras** the outskirts; **en las afueras** on the outskirts

**agachadiza** *nf* snipe

**agachar 1** *vt* to lower; **a. la cabeza** *(inclinar)* to stoop; *(repentinamente)* to duck

**2 agacharse** *vpr (acuclillarse)* to crouch down; **se agachó a recoger el pañuelo** she bent down to pick up the handkerchief

**agalla** *nf* (a) *(de pez)* gill (b) *(de árbol)* gall (c) *Fig* **agallas** guts, pluck; **tener agallas para hacer algo** to have the guts to do sth

**ágape** *nm* banquet, feast

**agarrada** *nf Fam* row, bust-up

**agarradero** *nm* (a) *(asa)* hold (b) *Fam Fig (pretexto)* pretext, excuse

**agarrado, -a 1** *adj* (a) *(asido)* **me tenía a. de un brazo/del cuello** he had me by the arm/throat; **agarrados del brazo** arm in arm; **agarrados de la mano** hand in hand (b) *Fam (tacaño)* tight, stingy

**2** *nm Fam (baile)* slow dance

**agarrar 1** *vt* (a) *(asir)* to grab (b) *(pillar) (ladrón, enfermedad)* to catch; *Am (tomar)* to take; **¡si la agarro, la mato!** if I catch her I'll kill her!; **me agarró desprevenido** he caught me off guard (c) *(expresiones)* **agarrarla, a. una buena** to get sloshed; **esto no hay por dónde agarrarlo** this is a mess!

**2** *vi (tinte)* to take; *(planta)* to take root

**3 agarrarse** *vpr* (a) *(sujetarse)* to hold on; **agarrarse de** to hold on to; *Fam Fig* **¡agárrate!** guess what! (b) *(pegarse)* to stick; **el arroz se ha agarrado a la cazuela** the rice has stuck to the pot (c) *Fam Fig (pelearse)* to scrap, to have a fight; *Am* **agarrarse a golpes** to get into a fistfight (d) *Fig (pretextar)* **agarrarse a algo** to use sth as an excuse

**agarrón** *nm* (a) *(tirón)* pull, tug (b) *Fam (altercado)* scrap, fight

**agarrotar 1** *vt* (a) *(parte del cuerpo)* to cut off the circulation in (b) *(ejecutar con garrote)* to garotte

**2 agarrotarse** *vpr (parte del cuerpo)* to go numb; *(mecanismo)* to seize up

**agasajar** *vt* to lavish attention on, to treat like a king; **a. a alguien con algo** to lavish sth upon sb

**agasajo** *nm* lavish attention

**ágata** *nf* agate

**agazapado, -a** *adj* crouching

**agazaparse** *vpr (ocultarse)* to crouch (down)

**agencia** *nf* (a) *(empresa)* agency; **a. de aduanas** customs agent's; **a. inmobiliaria** *Br* estate agent's, *US* real estate office; **a. matrimonial** marriage bureau; **a. de noticias** news agency; **a. de publicidad** advertising agency; **a. de seguros** insurance company; **a. de viajes** travel agency (b) *(sucursal)* branch

**agenciar** [15] 1 *vt* **a. algo a alguien** to fix sb up with sth

2 **agenciarse** *vpr* to get hold of, to fix oneself up with

**agenda** *nf* (a) *(de notas, fechas)* diary; *(de anillas)* Filofax®; *(de teléfonos, direcciones)* address book; **a. electrónica** electronic personal organizer (b) *(de trabajo, reunión)* agenda

**agente** 1 *nmf* (a) *(persona)* agent; **a. de aduanas** customs officer; **a. de cambio (y bolsa)** stockbroker; **a. comercial** broker; **a. de policía** policeman, *f* policewoman; **a. secreto** secret agent (b) *Econ* **agentes económicos** social partners

2 *nm (causa activa)* agent

**agigantar** *vt* to blow up, to magnify

**ágil** *adj (movimiento, persona)* agile; *(estilo, lenguaje)* fluent; *(respuesta, mente)* nimble, sharp

**agilidad** *nf* agility; **a. mental** mental agility

**agilipollado, -a** *adj muy Fam* **estar a.** *(estúpido)* to be daft, *US* to be dumb; *(atontado)* to be out of it

**agilizar** [16] *vt* to speed up

**agio** *nm Econ* agio

**agiotaje** *nm Econ* agiotage, speculation

**agitación** *nf* (a) *(de las aguas)* choppiness (b) *(intranquilidad)* restlessness, agitation (c) *(jaleo)* racket, commotion (d) *(conflicto)* unrest

**agitado, -a** *adj (persona)* upset, agitated; *(mar)* rough, choppy

**agitador, -ora** *nm,f* agitator

**agitanado, -a** *adj* gypsy-like

**agitar** 1 *vt* (a) *(sacudir)* to shake; *(remover)* to stir; **a. los brazos/un pañuelo** to wave one's arms/a handkerchief; **agítese antes de usar** shake before use (b) *(inquietar)* to worry, to upset (c) *(masas, pueblo)* to stir up

2 **agitarse** *vpr* (a) *(moverse)* to move, shake (b) *(inquietarse)* to become agitated

**aglomeración** *nf (de objetos, sustancia)* build-up; *(de gente)* crowd; **a. urbana** urban sprawl

**aglomerar** 1 *vt* to bring together

2 **aglomerarse** *vpr* to amass

**aglutinante** *adj* (a) *(sustancia)* binding (b) *Ling* agglutinative

2 *nm* binding agent

**aglutinar** 1 *vt* *(aunar, reunir)* *(personas)* to unite, to bring together; *(ideas, esfuerzos)* to pool

2 **aglutinarse** *vpr (pegarse)* to bind (together); *Fig (agruparse)* to gather, to come together

**agnosticismo** *nm* agnosticism

**agnóstico, -a** *adj & nm,f* agnostic

**agobiado, -a** *adj (trabajo)* snowed under (**de** with); *(problemas)* weighed down (**de** with)

**agobiante** *adj (presión, trabajo, persona)* overwhelming; *(calor)* oppressive

**agobiar** [15] 1 *vt* to overwhelm

2 **agobiarse** *vpr* to feel overwhelmed; **¡no te agobies!** don't worry!

**agobio** *nm* (a) *(físico)* choking, suffocation; **¡qué a.!** it's stifling! (b) *(psíquico)* pressure; **¡qué a.!** this is murder *o* a nightmare!

**agolparse** *vpr (gente)* to crowd round; *(sangre)* to rush; *Fig (problemas)* to come to a head

**agonía** *nf (del moribundo)* death throes; *Fig (decadencia)* decline, dying days; *Fig (pena)* agony

**agónico, -a** *adj también Fig* dying

**agonizante** *adj también Fig* dying

**agonizar** [16] *vi (expirar)* to be dying; *Fig (extinguirse)* to fizzle out; *Fig (sufrir)* to be in agony

**agorafobia** *nf Psi* agoraphobia

**agorero, -a** *nm,f* prophet of doom

**agostado, -a** *adj* parched

**agosto** *nm (mes)* August; *Fig (cosecha)* harvest (time); **hacer el a.** to line one's pockets; *ver también* **septiembre**

**agotado, -a** *adj* (a) *(persona, animal)* exhausted; **estar a. de hacer algo** to be tired out from doing sth (b) *(producto)* out of stock, sold out (c) *(pila, batería)* flat

**agotador, -ora** *adj* exhausting

**agotamiento** *nm* (a) *(cansancio)* exhaustion (b) *(de producto)* selling-out; *(de reservas)* exhaustion

**agotar** 1 *vt* (a) *(cansar)* to exhaust (b) *(producto)* to sell out of; *(agua)* to drain; *(recursos)* to exhaust, to use up; **este niño me agota** this child tires me out

2 **agotarse** *vpr* (a) *(cansarse)* to tire oneself out (b) *(acabarse)* to run out; *(libro, disco, entradas)* to sell out; *(pila, batería)* to go flat; **las entradas se agotaron en seguida** the tickets sold out almost immediately

**agraciado, -a** 1 *adj* (a) *(atractivo)* attractive, fetching (b) *(afortunado)* **a. con algo** lucky enough to win sth

**2** *nm,f (afortunado)* lucky winner

**agraciar** [15] *vt* (**a**) *(embellecer)* to make more attractive (**b**) *(conceder una gracia)* to pardon (**c**) *Formal (premiar)* to reward

**agradable** *adj* pleasant

**agradar 1** *vi* to be pleasant; **siempre trata de a.** she always tries to please

**2** *vt* to please; **me agradó recibir tu carta** I was pleased to receive your card

**agradecer** [48] *vt* (**a**) *(sujeto: persona)* **a. algo a alguien** *(dar las gracias)* to thank sb for sth; *(estar agradecido)* to be grateful to sb for sth (**b**) *(sujeto: cosa)* to be thankful for; **esa pared agradecería una mano de pintura** that wall could do with a lick of paint; **se agradece el interés mostrado** we are grateful for the interest you have shown

**agradecido, -a** *adj* grateful; **estar muy a. (por algo)** to be very grateful (for sth); **ser muy a.** *(cosa)* to be very pleasing

**agradecimiento** *nm* gratitude

**agrado** *nm (gusto)* pleasure; **esto no es de mi a.** this is not to my liking

**agrandar 1** *vt (en general)* to make bigger; *(imagen)* to magnify

**2 agrandarse** *vpr* to get bigger

**agrario, -a** *adj (reforma)* agrarian; *(producto, política)* agricultural

**agravación** *nf*, **agravamiento** *nm* worsening, exacerbation

**agravante 1** *adj* aggravating

**2** *nm o nf (problema)* additional problem; *Der* aggravating circumstance

**agravar 1** *vt (situación, enfermedad)* to aggravate

**2 agravarse** *vpr* to get worse, to worsen

**agraviado, -a** *adj* offended; **sentirse a. (por algo)** to feel offended (by sth)

**agraviar** [15] *vt* to offend

**agravio** *nm* (**a**) *(ofensa)* offence, insult (**b**) *(perjuicio)* wrong; **a. comparativo** unequal treatment

**agredido, -a** *nm,f* victim

**agredir** *vt* to attack

**agregación** *nf* addition

**agregado, -a 1** *adj (añadido)* added on

**2** *nm,f* (**a**) *Educ* assistant teacher (**b**) *(de embajada)* attaché; **a. cultural** cultural attaché

**3** *nm* (**a**) *(conjunto)* aggregate; *(añadido)* addition (**b**) *Econ* aggregate

**agregar** [40] *vt* to add (**a** to)

**agresión** *nf (ataque)* act of aggression, attack; **sufrir una a.** to be the victim of an attack

**agresividad** *nf* aggression

**agresivo, -a** *adj también Fig* aggressive

**agresor, -ora** *nm,f* attacker, assailant

**agreste** *adj (abrupto, rocoso)* rough, rugged; *Fig (basto, rudo)* coarse, uncouth

**agriar** [34] **1** *vt (vino, leche)* to (turn) sour; *Fig (carácter)* to sour, to embitter

**2 agriarse** *vpr también Fig* to turn sour

**agrícola** *adj (sector, política)* agricultural; **región a.** farming region

**agricultor, -ora** *nm,f* farmer

**agricultura** *nf* agriculture; **a. extensiva/intensiva** extensive/intensive farming

**agridulce** *adj* bittersweet; *Culin* sweet-and-sour

**agrietado, -a** *adj (muro, tierra, plato)* cracked, covered with cracks; *(labios, piel)* chapped

**agrietar 1** *vt (muro, tierra, plato)* to crack; *(labios, piel)* to chap

**2 agrietarse** *vpr (muro, tierra, plato)* to crack; *(labios, piel)* to chap

**agrimensor, -ora** *nm,f* surveyor

**agrio, -a 1** *adj (ácido)* sour; *Fig (áspero)* acerbic, bitter

**2** *nmpl* **agrios** citrus fruits

**agriparse** *vpr Chile, Col, Méx* to catch the flu

**agro** *nm* agricultural sector; **el a. español** Spanish agriculture

**agroalimentario, -a** *adj* **sector a.** food-processing industry

**agronomía** *nf* agronomy

**agrónomo, -a** *nm,f* agronomist

**agropecuario, -a** *adj* **sector a.** farming and livestock sector

**agrupación** *nf* (**a**) *(asociación)* group, association (**b**) *(agrupamiento)* grouping

**agrupamiento** *nm (concentración)* grouping

**agrupar 1** *vt* to group (together)

**2** *vpr* **agruparse** *(congregarse)* to gather (**en torno a** round); *(unirse)* to form a group

**agua** *nf* (**a**) *(líquido elemento)* water; *Náut* **hacer a.** to leak; *Fig* to go under; *Fig* **la empresa está haciendo a.** the company is going under; **claro como el a.** as clear as day; **estar con el a. al cuello** to be up to one's neck (in it); **venir como a. de mayo** to be a godsend; **quedar en a. de borrajas** to come to nothing; **nadar entre dos aguas** to sit on the fence; **ha roto aguas** her waters have broken; **eso es a. pasada** that's water under the bridge; **a. bendita** holy water; **a. de colonia** eau de cologne; **a. destilada** distilled water; **a. dulce** fresh water; **a. mineral sin gas/con gas** still/sparkling mineral water; **a. oxigenada** hydrogen peroxide; **a. potable** drinking water; **aguas menores** urine; **aguas residuales** sewage; **aguas termales** thermal spring waters; **aguas territoriales** territorial waters (**b**) *(vertiente de tejado)* slope; **un tejado de dos**

**aguas** a ridged roof
 (**c**) **aguas** *(en diamante, tela)* water

**aguacate** *nm (fruto)* avocado (pear); *(árbol)* avocado (tree)

**aguacero** *nm* shower

**aguachirle** *nf Fam* **este café es un a.** this coffee tastes like dishwater

**aguada** *nf Arte* gouache

**aguadilla** *nf Fam* ducking

**aguado, -a** *adj (con demasiada agua)* watery; *(diluido a propósito)* watered-down

**aguafiestas** *nmf inv* spoilsport

**aguafuerte** *nm Arte* etching

**aguamanil** *nm* ewer and basin

**aguamarina** *nf* aquamarine

**aguamiel** = water mixed with honey or, in Mexico, cane syrup; *Méx* = sap of the agave cactus used to make alcoholic drinks

**aguanieve** *nf* sleet; **está cayendo a.** it's sleeting

**aguantar 1** *vt* (**a**) *(sostener)* to hold (**b**) *(peso)* to bear (**c**) *(tolerar, soportar)* to bear, to stand; **no aguanto más** I can't bear it any longer; **no sé cómo la aguantas** I don't know how you put up with her; **no sabe a. una broma** he doesn't know how to take a joke (**d**) *(contener) (risa)* to contain; *(respiración)* to hold (**e**) *(tiempo)* to hold out for, to wait for
 **2 aguantarse** *vpr* (**a**) *(contenerse)* to restrain oneself, to hold oneself back (**b**) *(resignarse)* **no quiere aguantarse** he refuses to put up with it; **no quiero – ¡pues te aguantas!** I don't want to – too bad, you'll just have to!

**aguante** *nm* (**a**) *(paciencia)* self-restraint, tolerance (**b**) *(resistencia)* strength; *(de persona)* stamina

**aguar** [12] **1** *vt (mezclar con agua)* to water down; *Fig (estropear)* to spoil, to ruin; **a. el vino** to water the wine; **la noticia nos aguó la fiesta** the news spoiled our enjoyment
 **2 aguarse** *vpr* to be spoiled

**aguardar** *vt* to wait for, to await

**aguardiente** *nm* spirit, liquor

**aguarrás** *nm* turpentine

**aguce** *etc ver* **aguzar**

**aguda** *nf* word stressed on the last syllable

**agudeza** *nf* (**a**) *(de filo, punta)* sharpness; *(de vista, olfato)* keenness; *Fig (dicho ingenioso)* witticism

**agudizar** [16] **1** *vt (afilar)* to sharpen; *Fig (acentuar)* to exacerbate, to make worse; **a. el ingenio** to sharpen one's wits
 **2 agudizarse** *vpr* (**a**) *(crisis)* to get worse (**b**) *(ingenio)* to get sharper

**agudo, -a** *adj* (**a**) *(filo, punta)* sharp; *(vista, olfato)* keen; *(crisis, problema, enfermedad)* serious, acute; *Fig (perspicaz)* keen, sharp; *Fig (ingenioso)*

witty (**b**) *Gram (palabra)* stressed on the last syllable (**c**) *Mús (sonido)* high, high-pitched

**agüe** *etc ver* **aguar**

**agüero** *nm* **de buen/mal a.** that bodes well/ ill

**aguerrido, -a** *adj (valiente)* battle-hardened; *Fig (experimentado)* veteran

**aguijar** *vt (caballo)* to spur; *(buey)* to goad

**aguijón** *nm* (**a**) *(de insecto, escorpión)* sting (**b**) *(vara afilada)* goad; *Fig (estímulo)* spur, stimulus

**aguijonear** *vt (animal)* to goad on; *Fig (estimular)* to drive on; **a. a alguien para que haga algo** to spur sb on to do sth

**águila** *nf (ave)* eagle; *Fig* **ser un á.** *(ser vivo, listo)* to be sharp *o* perceptive; **á. imperial** *Zool* Spanish imperial eagle; **á. real** golden eagle

**aguileño, -a** *adj* aquiline

**aguilucho** *nm* (**a**) *(polluelo de águila)* eaglet (**b**) *(ave rapaz)* harrier

**aguinaldo** *nm* Christmas box

**aguja** *nf* (**a**) *(de coser, jeringuilla)* needle; *(de hacer punto)* knitting needle; *(de tocadiscos)* stylus, needle; **es como buscar una a. en un pajar** it's like looking for a needle in a haystack; **a. hipodérmica** hypodermic needle (**b**) *(de reloj)* hand; *(de brújula)* pointer; *(de iglesia)* spire (**c**) *(de conífera)* needle (**d**) *Ferroc* point (**e**) **agujas** *(de res)* ribs

**agujerear 1** *vt* to make a hole/holes in
 **2 agujerearse** *vpr* **se me han agujereado los pantalones** I've got a hole in my trousers

**agujero** *nm* (**a**) *(hole)* hole; *Astron* **a. negro** black hole (**b**) *(deuda)* deficit; **hay un a. de cien millones** a hundred million pesetas are unaccounted for

**agujetas** *nfpl* (**a**) *(en los músculos)* **tener a.** to feel stiff (**b**) *Méx* shoelaces

**agustino, -a** *adj & nm,f Rel* Augustinian

**aguzar** [16] *vt (afilar)* to sharpen; *Fig (apetito)* to whet; *Fig (ingenio, oído)* to sharpen

**ah** *interj (admiración)* ooh!; *(sorpresa)* oh!; *(pena)* ah!; *(al caer en la cuenta de algo)* ah, I see!

**ahí** *adv* there; **vino por a.** he came that way; **la solución está a.** that's where the solution lies; **¡a. tienes!** here *o* there you are!; **de a. que** *(por eso)* and consequently; **está por a.** *(en lugar indefinido)* she is around *(somewhere)*; *(en la calle)* she is out; *Fig* **por a.** something like that; **por a. va la cosa** you're not too far wrong

**ahijado, -a** *nm,f (de padrinos)* godson, *f* goddaughter; *Fig (protegido)* protégé, *f* protégée

**ahijar** *vt* to adopt

**ahínco** *nm* enthusiasm, devotion; **con a.** *(estudiar, trabajar)* hard, enthusiastically; *(solicitar)* insistently

**ahíto, -a** *adj (saciado)* **estar a.** to be full; *Fig (harto)* to be fed up (**de** with)

**ahogadilla** *nf* ducking

**ahogado, -a 1** *adj* **(a)** *(en el agua)* drowned **(b)** *(falto de aliento) (respiración)* laboured; *(grito)* muffled; *(persona)* out of breath; *Fig (agobiado)* overwhelmed, swamped

 **2** *nm,f* drowned person

**ahogar [40] 1** *vt* **(a)** *(asfixiar) (en el agua)* to drown; *(cubriendo la boca y nariz)* to smother, to suffocate **(b)** *(estrangular)* to strangle **(c)** *(extinguir)* to extinguish, to put out; *Fig (dominar) (levantamiento)* to put down, to quell; *Fig (pena)* to hold back, to contain

 **2 ahogarse** *vpr (en el agua)* to drown; *(asfixiarse)* to suffocate; *Fig (de calor)* to be stifled; **ahogarse en un vaso de agua** to make heavy weather of it

**ahogo** *nm (asfixia)* breathlessness, difficulty in breathing; *Fig (angustia)* anguish, distress; *Fig (económico)* financial difficulty

**ahogue** *etc ver* **ahogar**

**ahondar 1** *vt (hoyo, túnel)* to deepen

 **2** *vi Fig* **a. en** *(penetrar)* to penetrate deep into; *(profundizar)* to study in depth

**ahora** *adv* **(a)** *(en el presente)* now; **a. mismo** right now; **se acaban de marchar a. mismo** they just left a few moments ago, they've just left; **por a.** for the time being

 **(b)** *(pronto)* in a second

 **2** *conj* **(a)** *(ya… ya)* **a. habla, a. canta** one minute she's talking, the next she's singing

 **(b)** *(pero)* but, however; **a. bien** but; **a. que** but

**ahorcado, -a** *nm,f* hanged man, *f* hanged woman

**ahorcamiento** *nm* hanging

**ahorcar [61] 1** *vt* to hang; **a. los hábitos** to give up the cloth, to leave the clergy

 **2 ahorcarse** *vpr* to hang oneself

**ahorita, ahoritita** *adv Am Fam* right now

**ahorque** *etc ver* **ahorcar**

**ahorrador, -ora 1** *adj* thrifty, careful with money

 **2** *nm,f* thrifty person

**ahorrar 1** *vt (guardar)* to save; *(evitar)* **ahórrame los detalles** spare me the details

 **2 ahorrarse** *vpr* **ahorrarse la molestia (de hacer algo)** to save oneself the trouble (of doing sth); **me ahorré un viaje** I saved myself a journey

**ahorrativo, -a** *adj (persona)* thrifty; *(medida)* money-saving

**ahorro** *nm* saving; **ahorros** savings

**ahuecar [61] 1** *vt* **(a)** *(poner hueco) (manos)* to cup; *(tronco)* to hollow out **(b)** *(mullir) (colchón)* to plump up; *(tierra)* to hoe; *muy Fam*

**a. el ala** to clear off

 **2** *vi muy Fam (irse)* to clear off

 **3 ahuecarse** *vpr Fig* to puff up *(with pride)*

**ahuevado, -a** *adj CAm Fam (tonto)* daft

**ahumado, -a 1** *adj (alimento, cristal)* smoked

 **2** *nm* smoking

**ahumar 1** *vt* **(a)** *(jamón, pescado)* to smoke **(b)** *(lugar)* to fill with smoke

 **2 ahumarse** *vpr (ennegrecerse de humo)* to become blackened with smoke

**ahuyentar** *vt (espantar, asustar)* to scare away; *Fig (apartar)* to drive away; **el elevado precio ahuyentó a los compradores** the high price put buyers off

**AI** *nf (abrev de* **Amnistía Internacional**) AI

**AID** *nf (abrev de* **Asociación Internacional de Desarrollo**) IDA

**AIEA** *nf (abrev de* **Agencia Internacional de Energía Atómica**) IAEA

**aikido** *nm* aikido

**aimara** *adj & nmf* Aymara

**aindiado, -a** *adj* Indian *(used of American Indians)*

**airado, -a** *adj* angry

**airar 1** *vt* to anger, to make angry

 **2 airarse** *vpr* to get angry

**airbag** ['erβay] *(pl* **airbags**) *nf (en coche)* airbag

**aire** *nm* **(a)** *(fluido)* air; **al a. libre** in the open air; **con el pecho al a.** bare-chested; **cambiar de aires** to have a change of scene; **dejar algo en el a.** to leave sth up in the air; **estar en el a.** to be in the air; **saltar** *o* **volar por los aires** to be blown sky high; **tomar el a.** to go for a breath of fresh air; **a mi a.** in my own way; **a. acondicionado** air-conditioning; **a. comprimido** compressed air; **a. puro** fresh air

 **(b)** *(viento)* wind; *(corriente)* draught; **hoy hace mucho a.** it's very windy today

 **(c)** *(aspecto)* air, appearance; *(parecido)* **tiene un a. a su madre** she has something of her mother; **aires** *(vanidad)* airs (and graces); **darse aires (de algo)** to put on airs (about sth)

**aireación** *nf* ventilation

**aireado, -a** *adj* airy

**airear 1** *vt (ventilar)* to air; *Fig (contar)* to air *(publicly)*

 **2 airearse** *vpr* to get a breath of fresh air

**airoso, -a** *adj* **(a)** *(garboso)* graceful, elegant **(b)** *(triunfante)* **salir a. de algo** to come out of sth with flying colours

**aislacionismo** *nm Pol* isolationism

**aislado, -a** *adj* **(a)** *(lugar, suceso)* isolated **(b)** *(cable, pared)* insulated

**aislamiento** *nm* **(a)** *(de lugar, persona)* isolation **(b)** *(de cable, vivienda)* insulation

**aislante 1** *adj* insulating
 **2** *nm* insulating material

**aislar 1** *vt* (a) *(persona)* to isolate (b) *(cable, pared)* to insulate
 **2 aislarse** *vpr* to isolate oneself, to cut oneself off (**de** from)

**aizkolari** *nm* = competitor in the rural Basque sport of chopping felled tree-trunks

**ajá** *interj* ¡a.! *(sorpresa)* aha!

**ajado, -a** *adj (flor)* withered; *(persona)* wizened

**ajar 1** *vt (flores)* to wither, to cause to fade; *(piel)* to wrinkle; *(colores)* to cause to fade; *(ropa)* to wear out
 **2 ajarse** *vpr (flores)* to fade, to wither; *(piel)* to wrinkle, to become wrinkled; *(belleza, juventud)* to fade

**ajardinado, -a** *adj* landscaped

**a. JC.** *(abrev de* **antes de Jesucristo***)* BC

**ajedrea** *nf* savory *(plant)*

**ajedrecista** *nmf* chess player

**ajedrez** *nm inv* chess

**ajenjo** *nm* (a) *(planta)* wormwood, absinthe (b) *(licor)* absinthe

**ajeno, -a** *adj* (a) *(de otro)* of others; **jugar en campo a.** to play away from home (b) *(no relacionado)* **es un problema a. a la sociedad de hoy** it's a problem that no longer exists in today's society; **esto es a. a nuestro departamento** our department doesn't deal with that; **por causas ajenas a nuestra voluntad** for reasons beyond our control; **era ajena a lo que estaba ocurriendo** she had no knowledge of what was happening

**ajete** *nm* = green stalk of young garlic plant; **revuelto de ajetes** = dish of scrambled egg with garlic stalks

**ajetreado, -a** *adj* busy; **he tenido un día muy a.** I've had a very busy day

**ajetreo** *nm (gestiones, molestias)* running around, hard work; *(actividad)* (hustle and) bustle

**ají** *nm Andes, CSur* chilli (pepper)

**ajiaceite** *nm* = sauce made from garlic and olive oil

**ajiaco** *nm Andes (estofado)* = spicy stew with a lot of chilli

**ajillo** *nm* **al a.** = in a sauce made with oil, garlic and sometimes chilli

**ajo** *nm* garlic; *Culin* **a. blanco** cold garlic soup; **a. tierno** = green stalk of young garlic plant; *muy Fam* **¡a. y agua!** too bad!, tough!; *Fig* **andar** *o* **estar en el a.** to be in on it

**ajuar** *nm* (a) *(de casa)* furnishings (b) *(de novia)* trousseau

**ajuntar** *Fam* **1** *vt (lenguaje infantil)* **¿me ajuntas?** will you be my friend again?
 **2 ajuntarse** *vpr (irse a vivir juntos)* to move in together

**ajustable** *adj* adjustable; **sábana a.** fitted sheet

**ajustado, -a 1** *adj* (a) *(ceñido) (ropa)* tight-fitting; *(tuerca, pieza)* tight; *(resultado, final)* close (b) *(justo)* correct, right; *(precio)* reasonable
 **2** *nm* fitting

**ajustador, -ora 1** *adj* adjusting
 **2** *nm,f Imprenta* typesetter

**ajustar 1** *vt* (a) *(arreglar)* to adjust (b) *(apretar)* to tighten (c) *(encajar) (piezas de motor)* to fit; *(puerta, ventana)* to push to (d) *(pactar) (matrimonio)* to arrange; *(pleito)* to settle; *(paz)* to negotiate; *(precio)* to fix, to agree
 **2** *vi (venir justo)* to fit properly, to be a good fit; **la ventana no ajusta bien** the window won't close properly
 **3 ajustarse** *vpr* (a) *(adaptarse)* to adapt (**a** to) (b) *(conformarse)* to fit in (**a** with)

**ajuste** *nm (de pieza)* fitting; *(de mecanismo)* adjustment; *(de salario)* agreement; *Fig* **a. de cuentas** settling of scores

**ajusticiar** *vt* to execute

**al** *ver* **a, el**

**Alá** *nm* Allah

**ala 1** *nf* (a) *(de ave)* wing; *Fig (de edificio, partido)* wing; **cortar las alas a alguien** to clip sb's wings; *Dep* **a. delta** *(aparato)* hang glider (b) *(parte lateral) (de tejado)* eaves; *(de sombrero)* brim; *(de nariz)* side; *(de mesa)* leaf
 **2** *nmf Dep* winger, wing

**alabanza** *nf* praise

**alabar 1** *vt* to praise; *Fam* **¡alabado sea (el Señor)!** thank heavens!
 **2 alabarse** *vpr* to boast; **se alaba de valiente** he is always boasting about how brave he is

**alabarda** *nf* halberd

**alabardero** *nm* halberdier

**alabastro** *nm* alabaster

**alabear 1** *vt* to warp
 **2 alabearse** *vpr* to warp

**alacena** *nf* kitchen cupboard

**alacrán** *nm* scorpion

**alado, -a** *adj (con alas)* winged; *Fig (ligero)* swift, fleet

**ALALC** *nf (abrev de* **Asociación Latinoamericana de Libre Comercio***)* LAFTA

**alambicado, -a** *adj* elaborate, involved

**alambicar** [61] *vt (destilar)* to distil; *Fig (complicar)* to over-complicate

**alambique** *nm* still

**alambrada** *nf* wire fence

**alambrar** *vt* to fence with wire

**alambre** *nm* wire; **a. de espino** barbed wire

**alameda** *nf* (a) *(sitio con álamos)* poplar grove (b) *(paseo)* tree-lined avenue

**álamo** *nm* poplar

**alano** *nm* (perro) mastiff

**alante** *adv Fam* = **adelante**

**alarde** *nm* show *o* display (**de** of); **hacer a. de algo** to show sth off, to flaunt sth

**alardear** *vi* **a. de** to show off about

**alargadera** *nf* extension lead

**alargado, -a** *adj* long

**alargador** *nm* extension lead

**alargamiento** *nm* extension, lengthening

**alargar** [40] **1** *vt* (a) *(ropa)* to lengthen (b) *(viaje, visita, plazo)* to extend; *(conversación)* to spin out (c) *(brazo, mano)* to stretch out; **a. el brazo** to stretch out one's arm (d) *(pasar)* **a. algo a alguien** to pass sth (over) to sb

**2 alargarse** *vpr (hacerse más largo) (días)* to get longer; *(reunión)* to be prolonged; *Fig (hacerse muy largo)* to go on for ages

**alarido** *nm* shriek, howl

**alarma** *nf* alarm; *Mil* call to arms; **dar la a.** to raise the alarm; **cundió la a.** panic spread

**alarmante** *adj* alarming

**alarmar 1** *vt (avisar)* to alert; *Fig (asustar)* to alarm

**2 alarmarse** *vpr (inquietarse)* to be alarmed

**alarmista** *nmf* alarmist

**Alaska** *n* Alaska

**alavés, -esa 1** *adj* of/from Alava

**2** *nm,f* person from Alava

**alazán, -ana 1** *adj* chestnut

**2** *nm,f* chestnut (horse)

**alba** *nf* (a) *(amanecer)* dawn, daybreak; **al a.** at dawn (b) *(vestidura)* alb

**albacea** *nmf Der* executor, *f* executrix

**albaceteño, -a 1** *adj* of/from Albacete

**2** *nm,f* person from Albacete

**albahaca** *nf* basil

**albanés, -esa 1** *adj & nm,f* Albanian

**2** *nm (lengua)* Albanian

**Albania** *n* Albania

**albañil** *nm* bricklayer

**albañilería** *nf* (a) *(oficio)* bricklaying (b) *(obra)* brickwork

**albarán** *nm Com* delivery note

**albaricoque** *nm* apricot

**albaricoquero** *nm* apricot tree

**albatros** *nm inv* albatross

**albedrío** *nm (antojo, elección)* fancy, whim; **a su a.** as takes his/her fancy; *Filosofía* **libre a.** free will; **a su libre a.** of his/her own free will

**alberca** *nf* (a) *(depósito)* water tank (b) *Méx (piscina)* swimming pool

**albergar** [40] **1** *vt* (a) *(personas)* to accommodate, to put up (b) *(odio)* to harbour; *(esperanzas)* to cherish

**2 albergarse** *vpr* to stay; **¿en qué hotel se albergan?** what hotel are they staying in?

**albergue** *nm* accommodation, lodgings; *(de montaña)* shelter, refuge; **a. de juventud** *o* **juvenil** youth hostel; *Am* **a. transitorio** hourly hotel

**albino, -a** *adj & nm,f* albino

**albo, -a** *adj Literario* white

**albóndiga** *nf* meatball

**albor** *nm* (a) *Literario (blancura)* whiteness (b) *Formal (luz del alba)* first light of day; *Fig* **albores** *(principio)* dawn, earliest days; **los albores de la civilización** the dawn of civilization

**alborada** *nf* (a) *(amanecer)* dawn, daybreak (b) *Mús* = popular song sung at dawn (c) *Mil* reveille

**alborear** *v impersonal* **empezaba a a.** dawn was breaking

**albornoz** *nm* bathrobe

**alborotado, -a** *adj (agitado)* rowdy; *(pelo)* messed up, tousled; **los niños están alborotados con la excursión** the children are all excited about the trip; **los ánimos están alborotados** feelings are running high

**alborotador, -ora 1** *adj* rowdy

**2** *nm,f* troublemaker

**alborotar 1** *vt (perturbar)* to disturb, to unsettle; *(amotinar)* to stir up, to rouse; *(desordenar)* to mess up; **el viento le alborotó el pelo** the wind messed up her hair

**2** *vi* to be rowdy; **¡niños, no alborotéis!** calm down, children!

**3 alborotarse** *vpr (perturbarse)* to get worked up

**alboroto** *nm* (a) *(ruido)* din (b) *(jaleo)* fuss, to-do

**alborozado, -a** *adj* overjoyed, delighted

**alborozar** [16] *vt* to delight

**alborozo** *nm* delight, joy

**albricias** *interj* **¡a.!** great!, fantastic!

**albufera** *nf* lagoon

**álbum** *(pl* **álbumes)** *nm* album; **á. de fotos/sellos** photo/stamp album

**albúmina** *nf Quím* albumin

**albuminoide** *adj Quím* albuminoid

**alcachofa** *nf* (a) *(planta)* artichoke (b) *(pieza) (de regadera)* rose, sprinkler; *(de ducha)* shower head

**alcahuete, -a** *nm,f* (a) *(mediador)* go-between (b) *(chismoso)* gossipmonger

**alcaide** *nm* prison governor

**alcalde, -esa** *nm,f* mayor, *f* mayoress

**alcaldía** *nf* (a) *(cargo)* mayoralty (b) *(sede)* mayor's office (c) *(término municipal)* municipality

**álcali** *nm Quím* alkali

**alcalino, -a** *adj Quím* alkaline

**alcaloide** *nm Quím* alkaloid

**alcance** *nm* (a) *(de arma, misil, emisora)* range; **de corto/largo a.** short-/long-range; *(de persona)* **a mi a.** within my reach; **al a. de la mano** within arm's reach; **al a. de la vista** within sight; **dar a. a alguien** to catch up with sb; **fuera del a. de** beyond the reach of (b) *(de reformas, medidas)* scope, extent; **de a.** important (c) *Fig (inteligencia)* **de pocos alcances** slow, dim-witted

**alcancía** *nf* money box

**alcanfor** *nm* camphor

**alcantarilla** *nf (conducto)* sewer; *(boca)* drain

**alcantarillado** *nm* sewers

**alcanzar** [16] **1** *vt* (a) *(igualarse con)* to catch up with; **¿a que no me alcanzas?** bet you can't catch me!
 (b) *(llegar a)* to reach; **a. la meta** to reach the finishing line; **a. la fama/el éxito** to achieve fame/success; **a. el autobús** to catch the bus; **la epidemia no les alcanzó** they were unaffected by the epidemic
 (c) *(entregar)* to pass; **alcánzame la sal** could you pass me the salt?
 (d) *(golpear, dar)* to hit; **le alcanzaron dos disparos** he was hit by two shots

**2** *vi* (a) *(ser suficiente)* **a. para algo/alguien** to be enough for sth/sb; **a. para hacer algo** to be enough to do sth; **no sé si alcanzará para todos** I don't know if there'll be enough for everyone
 (b) *(poder)* **a. a hacer algo** to be able to do sth; **alcancé a verlo unos segundos** I managed to see him for a few seconds; **no alcanzo a comprender por qué** I can't begin to understand why

**alcaparra** *nf* caper

**alcatraz** *nm* gannet

**alcaucil** *nm (alcachofa)* artichoke

**alcayata** *nf* hook

**alcazaba** *nf* citadel

**alcázar** *nm* fortress

**alce 1** *ver* **alzar**
 **2** *nm* elk, moose

**alcista** *adj Fin* **mercado a.** bull market

**alcoba** *nf* bedroom

**alcohol** *nm* alcohol; *Quím* **a. etílico** ethyl alcohol; **a. de quemar** methylated spirits

**alcoholemia** *nf* blood alcohol level; **test de a.** Breathalyzer® test

**alcohólico, -a** *adj & nm,f* alcoholic

**alcoholímetro** *nm* (a) *(para bebida)* alcoholometer (b) *(para la sangre) Br* Breathalyzer®, *US* drunkometer

**alcoholismo** *nm* alcoholism

**alcoholizar** [16] **1** *vt* to turn into an alcoholic
 **2 alcoholizarse** *vpr* to become an alcoholic

**alcornoque** *nm (árbol)* cork oak; *(madera)* cork, corkwood; *Fig (persona)* idiot, fool

**alcotán** *nm* hobby *(bird)*

**alcurnia** *nf* lineage, descent

**aldaba** *nf* (a) *(llamador)* doorknocker (b) *(pestillo)* latch

**aldabonazo** *nm* loud knock *(with doorknocker)*; *Fig* **ser un a.** to be a bombshell

**aldea** *nf* small village

**aldeano, -a 1** *adj (pueblerino, rústico)* rustic
 **2** *nm,f* villager

**aldehído** *nm Quím* aldehyde

**ale** *interj* **¡a.!** come on!

**aleación** *nf* (a) *(acción)* alloying (b) *(producto)* alloy

**alear** *vt* to alloy

**aleatorio, -a** *adj* random

**alebrestarse** *vpr Col* (a) *(rebelarse)* to rebel (b) *(ponerse nervioso)* to get worked up

**aleccionador, -ora** *adj* (a) *(instructivo)* instructive (b) *(ejemplar)* exemplary

**aleccionar** *vt* to instruct, to teach

**aledaño, -a 1** *adj* adjacent
 **2** *nmpl* **aledaños** surrounding area; **en los aledaños del estadio** in the vicinity of the stadium

**alegación** *nf* allegation

**alegar** [40] **1** *vt (motivos, pruebas)* to put forward; **a. que** to claim (that)
 **2** *vi Am (quejarse)* to complain

**alegato** *nm Der* plea; *Fig* **hacer un a. a favor de/en contra de** to make a case for/against

**alegoría** *nf* allegory

**alegórico, -a** *adj* allegorical

**alegrar 1** *vt (persona)* to cheer up, to make happy; *(fiesta)* to liven up; *Fig (habitación, decoración)* to brighten up; *Fig (emborrachar)* to make tipsy; **me alegró el día** it made my day
 **2 alegrarse** *vpr* (a) *(sentir alegría)* to be pleased **(de algo/por alguien** about sth/for sb); **me alegro de que me hagas esa pregunta** I'm glad you asked me that; **me alegro!** good! (b) *Fig (emborracharse)* to get tipsy

**alegre** *adj (contento)* happy; *(que da alegría)* cheerful, bright; *Fig (irreflexivo)* happy-go-lucky;

*Fig (borracho)* tipsy; *Fig* **una mujer de vida a.** a loose woman

**alegremente** *adv (con alegría)* happily, joyfully; *(irreflexivamente)* blithely

**alegría** *nf (gozo)* happiness, joy; *(motivo de gozo)* joy; *Fig (irresponsabilidad)* rashness, recklessness; **gastaron el dinero con demasiada a.** they spent the money too freely

**alegro** *adv & nm Mús* allegro

**alegrón** *nm* pleasant surprise

**alegue** *etc ver* **alegar**

**alejado, -a** *adj* distant (**de** from)

**alejamiento** *nm* (**a**) *(lejanía)* remoteness (**b**) *(distancia)* distance (**c**) *(separación) (de objetos)* separation; *(entre personas)* estrangement

**Alejandría** *n* Alexandria

**alejar 1** *vt (poner más lejos)* to move away; *Fig (ahuyentar) (sospechas, temores)* to allay

**2 alejarse** *vpr (ponerse más lejos)* to go away (**de** from); *(retirarse)* to leave; **se alejaron demasiado del refugio** they strayed too far from the shelter; **¡aléjate de mí!** go away!

**alelado, -a** *adj* stupid

**alelar** *vt* to daze, to stupefy

**aleluya 1** *nm o nf* hallelujah

**2** *interj* **¡a.!** hallelujah!

**alemán, -ana 1** *adj & nm,f* German

**2** *nm (lengua)* German

**Alemania** *n* Germany; *Antes* **A. Occidental/Oriental** West/East Germany

**alentador, -ora** *adj* encouraging

**alentar** [3] *vt* to encourage

**alerce** *nm* larch

**alergia** *nf también Fig* allergy; **tener a. a algo** to be allergic to sth; **a. a la primavera** *o* **al polen** hayfever

**alérgico, -a** *adj también Fig* allergic (**a** to)

**alero** *nm* (**a**) *(del tejado)* eaves (**b**) *Dep* winger, wing (**c**) *Aut* wing

**alerón** *nm* (**a**) *Av* aileron (**b**) *muy Fam (axila)* armpit

**alerta 1** *adj inv & adv* alert

**2** *nf* alert; **a. roja** red alert

**3** *interj* **¡a.!** watch *o* look out!

**alertar** *vt* to alert (**de** about, to)

**aleta** *nf* (**a**) *(de pez)* fin (**b**) *(de buzo, foca)* flipper (**c**) *(de coche)* wing (**d**) *(de nariz)* flared part

**aletargar** [40] **1** *vt* to make drowsy, to send to sleep

**2 aletargarse** *vpr (adormecerse)* to become drowsy; *(hibernar)* to hibernate

**aletear** *vi (ave)* to flap its wings

**aleteo** *nm* flapping (of wings)

**alevín** *nm* (**a**) *(cría de pez)* fry, young fish (**b**) *Fig (persona)* novice, beginner (**c**) *Dep* alevines colts *(youngest category of players)*

**alevosía** *nf* (**a**) *(premeditación)* premeditation; **con premeditación y a.** with malice aforethought (**b**) *(traición)* treachery

**alevoso, -a** *adj* (**a**) *(premeditado)* premeditated (**b**) *(traidor)* treacherous

**alfa** *nf Fís & Mat* alpha; **a. y omega** beginning and end

**alfabético, -a** *adj* alphabetical

**alfabetización** *nf* (**a**) *(de personas) (acción)* teaching to read and write; *(estado)* literacy (**b**) *(de palabras, letras)* alphabetization

**alfabetizar** [16] *vt* (**a**) *(personas)* to teach to read and write (**b**) *(palabras, letras)* to put into alphabetical order

**alfabeto** *nm* alphabet; **a. Morse** Morse code

**alfajor** *nm* (**a**) *(de ajonjolí)* = crumbly shortbread, flavoured with sesame seeds (**b**) *(en Argentina)* = small sponge cake filled with creamy toffee

**alfalfa** *nf* alfalfa, lucerne

**alfanumérico, -a** *adj Informát* alphanumeric

**alfaque** *nm* sandbank, bar

**alfarería** *nf* (**a**) *(técnica)* pottery (**b**) *(lugar)* potter's, pottery shop

**alfarero, -a** *nm,f* potter

**alféizar** *nm* window-sill

**alfeñique** *nm Fig (persona)* weakling

**alférez** *nm Mil* second lieutenant

**alfil** *nm (pieza de ajedrez)* bishop

**alfiler** *nm* (**a**) *(para coser)* pin; *CSur* **a. de gancho** safety pin; **no cabe ni un a.** it's jam-packed; *Fig* **prendido con alfileres** sketchy (**b**) *(joya)* brooch, pin; **a. de corbata** tie-pin

**alfiletero** *nm* pin box

**alfombra** *nf (grande)* carpet; *(pequeña)* rug; **a. voladora** magic carpet

**alfombrar** *vt también Fig* to carpet

**alfombrilla** *nf (alfombra pequeña)* rug; *(felpudo)* doormat; *(del baño)* bathmat; *Informát (para ratón)* mouse mat

**alforja** *nf* (**a**) *(de persona)* knapsack (**b**) *(de caballo)* saddlebag

**alga** *nf* algas *(plantas de mar)* seaweed; *Biol (microscópicas)* algae; **un a.** a piece of seaweed

**algarabía** *nf* (**a**) *(habla confusa)* gibberish (**b**) *(alboroto)* racket

**algarada** *nf* racket, din

**algarroba** *nf* (**a**) *(planta)* vetch (**b**) *(fruto)* carob *o* locust bean

**algarrobo** *nm* carob *o* locust tree

**algazara** *nf* racket, uproar

**álgebra** *nf* algebra

**algebraico, -a** *adj* algebraic

**álgido, -a** *adj (culminante)* critical; **en el punto á. del conflicto** at the height of the conflict

**algo 1** *pron* (a) *(alguna cosa)* something; *(en interrogativas)* anything; **¿te pasa a.?** is anything the matter?; **a. es a.** something is better than nothing; **a. así, a. por el estilo** something like that; **a. así como...** something like...; **por a. lo habrá dicho** he must have said it for a reason

(b) *(cantidad pequeña)* a bit, a little; **a. de** some

(c) *Fam (ataque)* **te va a dar a. como sigas trabajando así** you'll make yourself ill if you go on working like that; **¡a mí me va a dar a.!** *(de risa)* I'm going to do myself an injury (laughing)!; *(de enfado)* this is going to drive me mad!

(d) *Fig (cosa importante)* something; **se cree que es a.** he thinks he's something (special)

**2** *adv (un poco)* a bit; **es a. más grande** it's a bit bigger

**algodón** *nm* cotton; **a. (hidrófilo)** *Br* cotton wool, *US* absorbent cotton; **una camisa de a.** a cotton shirt; *Fig* **criado entre algodones** pampered

**algodonero, -a** *adj* cotton; **la industria algodonera** the cotton industry

**algodonoso, -a** *adj* fluffy; **nubes algodonosas** cotton-wool clouds

**algoritmo** *nm Informát* algorithm

**alguacil** *nm* (a) *(del ayuntamiento)* mayor's assistant (b) *(del juzgado)* bailiff

**alguacilillo** *nm Taurom* = mounted official at bullfight

**alguien** *pron* (a) *(alguna persona)* someone, somebody; *(en interrogativas)* anyone, anybody; **¿hay a. ahí?** is anyone there?

(b) *Fig (persona de importancia)* somebody; **se cree a.** she thinks she's somebody (special)

**alguno, -a**

> **algún** is used instead of **alguno** before masculine singular nouns (e.g. **algún día** some day).

**1** *adj* (a) *(indeterminado)* some; *(en interrogativas)* any; **¿tienes algún libro?** do you have any books?; **algún día** some *o* one day; **compró algunas cosas** he bought some things; **ha surgido algún (que otro) problema** the odd problem has come up

(b) *(ninguno)* any; **no tengo interés a. (en hacerlo)** I'm not in the least (bit) interested (in doing it)

**2** *pron* (a) *(persona)* someone, somebody; *(plural)* some people; *(en interrogativas)* anyone, anybody; **¿conocisteis a algunos?** did you get to know any?; **algunos de** some *o* a few of

(b) *(cosa)* the odd one; *(plural)* some, a few; *(en interrogativas)* any; **me salió mal a.** I got the odd one wrong; **algunos de** some *o* a few of

**alhaja** *nf (joya)* jewel; *(objeto de valor)* treasure; *Fig (persona)* gem; *Irón* **¡menuda a.!** he's a right one!

**alharaca** *nf* fuss; **hacer alharacas** to kick up a fuss

**alhelí** (*pl* **alhelíes**) *nm* wallflower

**alheña** *nf* privet

**aliado, -a** **1** *adj* allied

**2** *nm,f* ally; *Hist* **los Aliados** the Allies

**alianza** *nf* (a) *(pacto, parentesco)* alliance (b) *(anillo)* wedding ring

**aliar [34] 1** *vt (naciones)* to ally (**con** with); *(cualidades)* to combine

**2 aliarse** *vpr* to form an alliance (**con** with)

**alias** *adv & nm inv también Informát* alias

**alicaído, -a** *adj* (a) *(triste)* depressed (b) *Fig (débil)* weak

**alicantino, -a 1** *adj* of/from Alicante

**2** *nm,f* person from Alicante

**alicatado, -a 1** *adj* tiling

**alicatar** *vt* to tile

**alicates** *nmpl* pliers

**aliciente** *nm* (a) *(incentivo)* incentive (b) *(atractivo)* attraction

**alícuota** *adj Mat* aliquot

**alienación** *nf* (a) *(sentimiento)* alienation (b) *(trastorno psíquico)* derangement, madness

**alienado, -a 1** *adj* insane

**2** *nm,f* insane person, lunatic

**alienante** *adj* alienating

**alienar** *vt* (a) *(enajenar)* to derange, to drive mad (b) *Filosofía* to alienate

**alienígena** *nmf* alien

**aliento 1** *ver* **alentar**

**2** *nm* (a) *(respiración)* breath; **cobrar a.** to catch one's breath; **sin a.** breathless (b) *Fig (ánimo)* strength

**aligerar 1** *vt* (a) *(peso)* to lighten; *Fig (pena)* to relieve, to ease (b) *(ritmo)* to speed up; **a. el paso** to quicken one's pace

**2** *vi (darse prisa)* to hurry up; **aligera, que llegamos tarde** hurry up, or we'll be late

**alijo** *nm* contraband; **a. de drogas** consignment of drugs

**alimaña** *nf* pest *(animal)*

**alimentación** *nf* (a) *(acción)* feeding (b) *(comida)* food; **el sector de la a.** the food industry (c) *(régimen alimenticio)* diet; **una a. equilibrada** a balanced diet (d) *Tec* feed, input

**alimentador, -ora 1** *adj Tec* feeding

**2** *nm Tec* feed, feeder; *Informát* **a. de papel** paper feed

**alimentar 1** *vt (dar comida, energía, material)* to feed; *(motor, coche)* to fuel; **la lectura alimenta el espíritu** reading improves your mind

**2** *vi (nutrir)* to be nourishing; **los garbanzos**

**alimentan mucho** chickpeas are very nutritious

**3 alimentarse** *vpr (comer)* **alimentarse de** to live on

**alimentario, -a** *adj* food; **la industria alimentaria** the food industry

**alimenticio, -a** *adj* nourishing; **productos alimenticios** foodstuffs

**alimento** *nm* food; *Fig* **la lectura es un a. para el espíritu** reading improves your mind

**alimoche** *nm* Egyptian vulture

**alimón** *nm* **al a.** jointly, together

**alineación** *nf* (a) *(colocación en línea)* alignment (b) *Dep (composición de equipo)* line-up

**alineado, -a** *adj* (a) *(en línea recta)* lined up (b) *Dep (en equipo)* selected (c) *Pol* **países no alineados** non-aligned countries

**alineamiento** *nm* alignment; *Pol* **no a.** non-alignment

**alinear 1** *vt* (a) *(colocar en línea)* to line up (b) *Dep (seleccionar)* to select

**2 alinearse** *vpr Pol* to align

**aliñar** *vt (ensalada)* to dress; *(carne)* to season

**aliño** *nm (para ensalada)* dressing; *(para carne)* seasoning

**alioli** *nm* garlic mayonnaise

**alirón** *interj* ¡a.! hooray!

**alisar** *vt* to smooth (down)

**alisio** *Met* **1** *adj* **vientos alisios** trade winds

**2** *nm* trade wind

**aliso** *nm* alder

**alistamiento** *nm Mil* enlistment

**alistarse** *vpr Mil* to enlist

**aliteración** *nf* alliteration

**aliviar** [15] *vt* (a) *(atenuar)* to soothe (b) *(aligerar) (persona)* to relieve; *(carga)* to lighten

**alivio** *nm* relief; **de a.** *(terrible)* dreadful

**aljibe** *nm* (a) *(de agua)* cistern (b) *Náut* tanker

**allá** *adv* (a) *(espacio)* over there; **a. abajo/arriba** down/up there; **hacer a.** to move over *o* along; **hacia a.** that way, in that direction; **más a.** further on; **más a. de** beyond; **échate para a.** move over

(b) *(tiempo)* **a. por los años cincuenta** back in the 50s; **a. para el mes de agosto** around August some time

(c) *(expresiones)* **a. él/ella** that's his/her problem; **a. tú, a. te las compongas** that's your problem; **el más a.** the great beyond; **no ser muy a.** to be nothing special

**allanamiento** *nm* forceful entry; *Der* **a. de morada** breaking and entering

**allanar** *vt* (a) *(terreno)* to flatten, to level; *Fig (dificultad)* to overcome; **allanarle el camino a alguien** to smooth the way for sb (b) *(irrumpir en)* to break into; *Am (hacer una redada en)*

to raid; **las tropas allanaron las viviendas de los campesinos** the troops sacked the peasants' houses

**allegado, -a 1** *adj* close

**2** *nm,f* (a) *(familiar)* relative (b) *(amigo)* close friend

**allende** *prep Literario* beyond; **a. los mares** across the seas

**allí** *adv* there; **a. abajo/arriba** down/up there; **a. mismo** right there; **está por a.** it's around there somewhere

**alma** *nf* (a) *(espíritu)* soul; **sentir algo en el a.** to be truly sorry about sth; **agradecer algo en el a.** to be deeply grateful for sth; **lo que dijo me llegó al a.** her words really struck home; **se le cayó el a. a los pies** his heart sank; **como a. en pena** like a lost soul; **como a. que lleva el diablo** like a bat out of hell; *Fig* **el a. de la fiesta** the life and soul of the party; *Fig* **el a. del proyecto** the driving force behind the project

(b) *(persona)* soul; **un pueblo de doce mil almas** a town of twelve thousand people; **no se ve un a.** there isn't a soul to be seen

(c) *(de cañón)* bore

**almacén** *nm* warehouse; **(grandes) almacenes** department store

**almacenaje** *nm* storage

**almacenamiento** *nm también Informát* storage

**almacenar** *vt* (a) *(guardar) también Informát* to store (b) *(reunir)* to collect

**almanaque** *nm* (a) *(calendario)* calendar (b) *(publicación anual)* almanac

**almeja** *nf* clam

**almena** *nf* **almenas** battlements

**almendra** *nf* almond

**almendrado, -a 1** *adj* almond-shaped; **ojos almendrados** almond eyes

**2** *nm Culin* almond paste

**almendro** *nm* almond (tree)

**almeriense 1** *adj* of/from Almería

**2** *nm,f* person from Almería

**almíbar** *nm* syrup

**almibarado, -a** *adj* (a) *(con almíbar)* covered in syrup (b) *Fig (afectado)* sugary, sugary

**almibarar** *vt* to cover in syrup

**almidón** *nm* starch

**almidonado, -a 1** *adj* starched

**2** *nm* starching

**almidonar** *vt* to starch

**alminar** *nm* minaret

**almirantazgo** *nm* (a) *(dignidad)* admiralty (b) *(de la Armada)* Admiralty

**almirante** *nm* admiral

**almirez** *nm* mortar

**almizcle** *nm* musk

**almizclero** *nm* musk deer

**almohada** *nf* pillow; *Fig* **consultarlo con la a.** to sleep on it

**almohadilla** *nf* (a) *(cojín)* small cushion (b) *(de animal)* pad

**almohadillado, -a** *adj* padded

**almohadón** *nm* cushion

**almoneda** *nf* (a) *(subasta)* auction (b) *(local)* discount store

**almorávide** *adj & nmf* Almoravid

**almorranas** *nfpl* piles

**almorzar** [33] **1** *vt (a mediodía)* to have for lunch; *(a media mañana)* to have as a mid-morning snack; **los viernes almuerzan pescado** on Fridays they have fish for lunch

**2** *vi (a mediodía)* to have lunch; *(a media mañana)* to have a mid-morning snack

**almuerzo** *nm (a mediodía)* lunch; *(a media mañana)* mid-morning snack; **a. de trabajo** working lunch

**aló** *interj CSur (al teléfono)* hello

**alocado, -a 1** *adj* crazy

**2** *nm,f* **es un a.** he's crazy

**alocución** *nf* address, speech

**alojamiento** *nm* accommodation; **dar a. a** to put up

**alojar 1** *vt* to put up

**2 alojarse** *vpr* (a) *(hospedarse)* to stay (b) *(introducirse)* to lodge; **la bala se alojó en el pulmón derecho** the bullet lodged in her right lung

**alondra** *nf* lark

**alopecia** *nf Med* alopecia

**alpaca** *nf* alpaca

**alpargata** *nf* espadrille

**Alpes** *nmpl* **los A.** the Alps

**alpinismo** *nm* mountaineering

**alpinista** *nmf* mountaineer

**alpino, -a** *adj* Alpine

**alpiste** *nm* (a) *(planta)* canary grass (b) *(semilla)* birdseed

**alquería** *nf* farmstead

**alquilado, -a** *adj (casa)* rented; *(coche, traje)* hired

**alquilar 1** *vt (casa, televisión, oficina)* to rent; *(coche)* to hire

**2 alquilarse** *vpr (casa, televisión, oficina)* to be for rent; *(coche)* to be for hire; **se alquila** *(en letrero)* to let

**alquiler** *nm* (a) *(acción) (de casa, televisión, oficina)* renting; *(de coche)* hiring; **de a.** *(casa)* rented; **coche de a.** hire car; **tenemos pisos de a.** we have *Br* flats *o US* apartments to let (b) *(precio) (de casa, oficina)* rent; *(de televisión)* rental; *(de coche)* hire charge

**alquimia** *nf* alchemy

**alquimista** *nmf* alchemist

**alquitrán** *nm* tar

**alquitranar** *vt* to tar

**alrededor 1** *adv* (a) *(en torno)* around; **a. de** around; **de a.** surrounding (b) *(aproximadamente)* **a. de** around

**2** *nm* **miré a mi a.** I looked around (me); **alrededores** surrounding area

**Alsacia** *nf* Alsace

**alsaciano, -a** *adj & nm,f* Alsatian

**alta** *nf* (a) *(del hospital)* **a. (médica)** discharge; **dar de a. a alguien** to discharge sb (from hospital) (b) *(documento)* certificate of discharge (c) *(en una asociación)* membership; **darse de a.** to become a member

**altanería** *nf* haughtiness

**altanero, -a** *adj* haughty

**altar** *nm* altar; **a. mayor** high altar; *Fig* **conducir** *o* **llevar a alguien al a.** to lead sb down the aisle

**altavoz** *nm (para anuncios)* loudspeaker; *(de tocadiscos)* speaker

**alteración** *nf* (a) *(cambio)* alteration (b) *(excitación)* agitation (c) *(alboroto)* disturbance; **a. del orden público** breach of the peace

**alterar 1** *vt* (a) *(cambiar)* to alter; **a. el orden de las palabras** to change the order of the words; **esto altera nuestros planes** that changes our plans (b) *(perturbar) (persona)* to agitate, to fluster; *(orden público)* to disrupt; **le alteran mucho los cambios** the changes upset him a lot (c) *(estropear)* **el calor alteró los alimentos** the heat made the food go off

**2 alterarse** *vpr* (a) *(perturbarse)* to get agitated *o* flustered (b) *(estropearse)* to go off

**altercado** *nm* argument, row

**álter ego** *nm* alter ego

**alternador** *nm Elec* alternator

**alternancia** *nf* alternation

**alternar 1** *vt* to alternate

**2** *vi* (a) *(relacionarse)* to mix (con with), to socialize (con with) (b) *(sucederse)* **a. con** to alternate with

**3 alternarse** *vpr* (a) *(en el tiempo)* to take turns; **se alternan para cuidar al niño** they take turns in looking after the child (b) *(en el espacio)* to alternate

**alternativa** *nf* (a) *(opción)* alternative; **a. de poder** alternative party of government (b) *Taurom* = ceremony in which bullfighter shares the kill with his novice, accepting him as a professional; **tomar la a.** to become a professional bullfighter

**alternativamente** *adv* alternately

**alternativo, -a** *adj* (a) *(movimiento)* alternating (b) *(posibilidad)* alternative (c) *(cine, teatro)* alternative

**alterne** *nm* **bar de a.** = bar where women encourage people to drink in return for a commission

**alterno, -a** *adj* alternate; *Elec* alternating

**alteza** *nf Fig (de sentimientos)* loftiness; **A.** *(tratamiento)* Highness; **Su A. Real** His/Her Royal Highness

**altibajos** *nmpl (del terreno)* unevenness; *Fig (de la vida)* ups and downs

**altillo** *nm* (a) *(desván)* attic, loft (b) *(armario)* = small storage cupboard above head height, usually above another cupboard (c) *(cerro)* hillock

**altímetro** *nm* altimeter

**altiplanicie** *nf*, **altiplano** *nm* high plateau

**Altísimo** *nm* **el A.** *Rel* the Most High

**altisonante** *adj* high-sounding

**altitud** *nf* altitude

**altivez** *nf* haughtiness

**altivo, -a** *adj* haughty

**alto, -a 1** *adj* (a) *(posición, lugar)* high; *(piso)* top, upper
(b) *(persona, árbol, edificio)* tall
(c) *(sonido, voz)* loud
(d) *Geog* upper, northern; **el A. Egipto** Upper Egypt
(e) *(hora)* late; **a altas horas de la noche** late at night

**2** *nm* (a) *(altura)* height; **mide dos metros de a.** *(cosa)* it's two metres high; *(persona)* he's two metres tall
(b) *(lugar elevado)* height; **en lo a. de** at the top of; **los Altos del Golán** the Golan Heights
(c) *(detención)* stop; **hacer un a.** to make a stop; **a. el fuego** ceasefire; **dar el a. a alguien** to challenge sb; **¡a.! ¿quién va?** halt! who goes there?; **¡a. ahí!** *(en discusión)* hold on a minute!; *(a un fugitivo)* stop!
(d) **pasar algo por a.** to pass over sth; **hacer algo por todo lo a.** to do sth in (great) style; **una boda por todo lo a.** a sumptuous wedding

**3** *adv* (a) *(arriba)* high (up)
(b) *(hablar)* loud

**altozano** *nm* hillock

**altramuz** *nm* lupin

**altruismo** *nm* altruism

**altruista 1** *adj* altruistic
**2** *nmf* altruist

**altura** *nf* (a) *(posición, talla)* height; **volar a gran a.** to fly at altitude; **tiene dos metros de a.** *(cosa)* it's two metres high; *(persona)* he's two metres tall; **Viella está a 1.000 m de a.** Viella is 1,000 metres above sea level; *Fig* **las**

**alturas** *(el cielo)* Heaven
(b) *(nivel)* level; **está a la a. del ayuntamiento** it's next to the town hall
(c) *(latitud)* latitude
(d) *Fig (de persona)* stature; *Fig (de sentimientos, espíritu)* loftiness; **estar a la a. de las circunstancias** to be equal to the occasion
(e) *Fig (tiempo)* **a estas alturas** this far on; **si a estas alturas no te has decidido...** if you haven't decided by now...

**alubia** *nf* bean; **a. blanca** cannellini bean; **a. roja** kidney bean

**alucinación** *nf* hallucination

**alucinado, -a** *adj* (a) *Med* hallucinating (b) *Fam (sorprendido)* gobsmacked

**alucinante** *adj* (a) *Med* hallucinatory (b) *Fam (extraordinario)* amazing

**alucinar 1** *vi* (a) *Med* to hallucinate (b) *Fam* **¡tú alucinas!** you must be dreaming!; **¡yo alucino!** I can't believe it!

**2** *vt Fam Fig* (a) *(seducir)* to hypnotize, to captivate (b) *(gustar)* **le alucinan las motos** he's crazy about motorbikes

**alucine** *nm Fam* **¡qué a.!** bloody hell!, *Br* well stone me!; **un a. de moto** a humdinger of a bike, a bloody amazing bike

**alucinógeno, -a 1** *adj* hallucinogenic
**2** *nm* hallucinogen

**alud** *nm también Fig* avalanche

**aludido, -a** *nm,f* **el a.** the aforesaid; **darse por a.** *(ofenderse)* to take it personally; *(reaccionar)* to take the hint

**aludir** *vi* **a. a algo** *(sin mencionar)* to allude to sth; *(mencionando)* to refer to sth

**alumbrado** *nm* lighting; **a. público** street lighting

**alumbramiento** *nm* (a) *(con luz)* lighting (b) *(parto)* delivery

**alumbrar 1** *vt* (a) *(iluminar)* to light up (b) *(dar a luz)* to give birth to
**2** *vi (iluminar)* to give light

**aluminio** *nm* aluminium

**aluminosis** *nf inv Constr* = structural weakness of buildings as a result of inadequate building materials containing aluminium

**alumnado** *nm (de escuela)* pupils; *(de universidad)* students

**alumno, -a** *nm,f (de escuela, profesor particular)* pupil; *(de universidad)* student

**alunizaje** *nm* landing on the moon

**alunizar [16]** *vi* to land on the moon

**alusión** *nf (sin mencionar)* allusion; *(mencionando)* reference; **hacer a. a** *(sin mencionar)* to allude to; *(mencionando)* to refer to

**alusivo, -a** *adj* allusive

**aluvión** *nm* (a) *(de agua)* flood; **un a. de insultos** a torrent of abuse (b) *Geol (sedimento)* alluvium; **tierras de a.** alluvial deposits

**alveolo, alvéolo** *nm* (a) *(de panal)* cell (b) *Anat* alveolus

**alza** *nf* (a) *(subida)* rise; **en a.** *Fin* rising; *Fig* gaining in popularity; **jugar al a.** *Fin* to bull the market (b) *(de zapato)* raised insole

**alzacuello** *nm* *(en traje eclesiástico)* dog collar

**alzada** *nf* (a) *(de caballo)* height (b) *Der* appeal

**alzado, -a 1** *adj* (a) *(sublevado)* raised (b) *(precio)* fixed; **a tanto a.** *(modo de pago)* in a single payment
**2** *nm (dibujo técnico)* elevation

**alzamiento** *nm* uprising, revolt; *Hist* **el A. Nacional** = Francoist term for the 1936 rebellion against the Spanish Republican Government

**alzar** [16] **1** *vt* (a) *(levantar)* to lift, to raise; *(voz)* to raise; *(cuello de abrigo)* to turn up (b) *(aumentar)* to raise (c) *(construir)* to erect (d) *(sublevar)* to stir up, to raise
**2 alzarse** *vpr* (a) *(levantarse)* to rise (b) *(sublevarse)* to rise up, to revolt; **alzarse en armas** to take up arms (c) *(conseguir)* **alzarse con la victoria** to win, to be victorious; **los ladrones se alzaron con un cuantioso botín** the thieves made off with a large sum

**Alzheimer** *nm* **(mal** *o* **enfermedad de) A.** Alzheimer's (disease)

**AM** *(abrev de* **amplitude modulation)** AM

**a.m.** *(abrev de* **ante meridiem)** a.m.

**ama** *nf* (a) *(dueña)* owner (b) *(de criado)* mistress; **a. de casa** housewife; **a. de cría** wet nurse; **a. de llaves** housekeeper

**amabilidad** *nf* kindness; **¿tendría la a. de…?** would you be so kind as to…?

**amabilísimo, -a** *superlativo ver* **amable**

**amable** *adj* kind; **¿sería tan a. de…?** would you be so kind as to…?

**amado, -a 1** *adj* **mis seres amados** my loved ones
**2** *nm,f* loved one

**amaestrado, -a** *adj (animal)* trained; *(en circo)* performing

**amaestrar** *vt* to train

**amagar** [40] **1** *vt* (a) **le amagó un golpe** he made as if to hit him; **amagó una sonrisa** she gave a hint of a smile (b) *(dar indicios de)* to show signs of
**2** *vi (tormenta)* to be imminent, to threaten

**amago** *nm* (a) *(en boxeo)* feint; **hizo a. de darle un puñetazo** she made as if to punch him; **hizo a. de salir corriendo** he made as if to run off (b) *(indicio)* sign, hint; **tuve un a. de gripe** I felt like I had a bout of flu coming on

**amague** *etc ver* **amagar**

**amainar 1** *vt Náut* to take in
**2** *vi también Fig* to abate, to die down

**amalgama** *nf también Fig* amalgam

**amalgamar** *vt también Fig* to amalgamate

**amamantar** *vt (animal)* to suckle; *(bebé)* to breastfeed

**amancebamiento** *nm* living together, cohabitation

**amancebarse** *vpr* to live together, to cohabit

**amanecer** [48] **1** *nm* dawn
**2** *v impersonal* **amaneció a las siete** dawn broke at seven
**3** *vi (en un lugar)* to see in the dawn; **amanecimos en Estambul** we arrived in Istanbul at dawn; *Am* **¿cómo amaneciste?** how did you sleep?

**amanerado, -a** *adj* (a) *(afeminado)* effeminate (b) *(afectado)* mannered, affected

**amaneramiento** *nm* (a) *(afeminamiento)* effeminacy (b) *(afectación)* affectation

**amanerarse** *vpr* (a) *(afeminarse)* to become effeminate (b) *(volverse afectado)* to become affected

**amanita** *nf* amanita

**amansar 1** *vt (animal)* to tame; *Fig (persona)* to calm down; *Fig (pasiones)* to calm; *Prov* **la música amansa a las fieras** music hath charms to soothe the savage breast
**2 amansarse** *vpr* to calm down

**amante** *nmf* (a) *(querido)* lover (b) *(aficionado)* **ser a. de algo/de hacer algo** to be keen on sth/doing sth; **los amantes del arte** art lovers

**amanuense** *nmf* scribe

**amañado, -a** *adj (elecciones, resultado)* rigged

**amañar 1** *vt (elecciones, resultado)* to rig; *(documento)* to doctor
**2 amañarse** *vpr* to manage

**amaño** *nm (treta)* ruse, trick

**amapola** *nf* poppy

**amar** *vt* to love; **ama a tu prójimo como a ti mismo** love thy neighbour as thyself

**amaraje** *nm (de hidroavión)* landing at sea; *(de vehículo espacial)* splashdown

**amaranto** *nm* amaranth

**amarar** *vi (hidroavión)* to land at sea; *(vehículo espacial)* to splash down

**amargado, -a 1** *adj (resentido)* bitter
**2** *nm,f* bitter person; **estar a. de la vida** to be bitter and twisted

**amargar** [40] **1** *vt (alimento)* to make bitter; *Fig (día, vacaciones)* to spoil, to ruin; **a. la vida a alguien** to make sb's life hell
**2 amargarse** *vpr también Fig* to become bitter

**amargo, -a** adj también Fig bitter

**amargor** nm (sabor) bitterness

**amargue** etc ver **amargar**

**amargura** nf (disgusto) sorrow

**amariconado, -a** Fam Pey **1** adj poofy
**2** nm pansy

**amarillear 1** vt to turn yellow
**2** vi to (turn) yellow

**amarillento, -a** adj yellowish

**amarillismo** nm Prensa sensationalism

**amarillo, -a 1** adj (a) (color) yellow (b) Prensa sensationalist (c) Ind **sindicato a.** = union controlled by the employers
**2** nm (color) yellow

**amariposado, -a** adj Fam (afeminado) effeminate

**amarra** nf Náut mooring rope; **largar** o **soltar amarras** to cast off; Fig **tener amarras** (contactos) to have connections, to have friends in high places

**amarrar** vt (a) Náut to moor (b) (atar) to tie (up); **a. algo/a alguien a algo** to tie sth/sb to sth

**amarre** nm Náut mooring

**amarrete** Chile, CSur Fam **1** adj mean, tight
**2** nmf mean person, miser

**amartelado, -a** adj (ojos, mirada) adoring; **están amartelados** they are very much in love

**amartillar** vt (arma) to cock

**amasar** vt (a) (masa) to knead; (yeso) to mix (b) Fig (riquezas) to amass

**amasijo** nm Fig (mezcla) hotchpotch

**amateur** [ama'ter] (pl **amateurs**) adj & nmf amateur

**amatista** nf amethyst

**amazacotado, -a** adj (comida) stodgy

**amazona** nf (a) (jinete) horsewoman (b) Mitol Amazon

**Amazonia** nf **la A.** the Amazon

**Amazonas** nm **el A.** the Amazon

**amazónico, -a** adj (selva, región) Amazon; (tribu, cultura) Amazonian

**ambages** nmpl **sin a.** without beating about the bush

**ámbar** nm amber

**ambarino, -a** adj amber

**Amberes** n Antwerp

**ambición** nf ambition

**ambicionar** vt to have as one's ambition; **ambiciona el puesto de presidente** it is his ambition to become president

**ambicioso, -a 1** adj ambitious
**2** nm,f ambitious person

**ambidextro, -a, ambidiestro, -a 1** adj ambidextrous
**2** nm,f ambidextrous person

**ambientación** nf (a) Cine, Lit & Teatro setting (b) Rad sound effects

**ambientador** nm (de aire) air-freshener

**ambiental** adj (a) (físico, atmosférico) ambient (b) (del medio ambiente) environmental

**ambientar 1** vt (a) **la película/historia está ambientada en...** the film/story is set in... (b) (iluminar) to light; (decorar) to decorate
**2 ambientarse** vpr (acostumbrarse) to settle down (in new place, job)

**ambiente 1** adj ambient
**2** nm (a) (aire) air, atmosphere (b) (circunstancias) environment (c) (ámbito) world, circles (d) (animación) life, atmosphere

**ambigüedad** nf ambiguity

**ambiguo, -a** adj (a) ambiguous (b) Gram **sustantivo a.** noun that may be either masculine or feminine

**ámbito** nm (a) (espacio, límites) confines, scope; **una ley de á. provincial** a law which is applicable at provincial level; **dentro del á. de** within the scope of; **fuera del á. de** outside the realm of (b) (ambiente) world, circles

**ambivalencia** nf ambivalence

**ambivalente** adj ambivalent

**ambos, -as 1** adj pl both
**2** pron pl both (of them)

**ambrosía** nf Mitol ambrosia

**ambulancia** nf ambulance

**ambulante** adj travelling; **vendedor a.** pedlar, hawker; **prohibida la venta a.** (en letrero) no hawking

**ambulatorio, -a 1** adj **tratamiento a.** outpatient treatment
**2** nm clinic, health centre

**ameba** nf amoeba

**amedrentar 1** vt to scare, to frighten
**2 amedrentarse** vpr to get scared o frightened

**amén** interj amen; Fig **en un decir a.** in the twinkling of an eye; Fig **decir a. a** to accept unquestioningly; **a. de** (además de) in addition to

**amenaza** nf threat; **a. de bomba** bomb scare; **a. de muerte** death threat

**amenazador, -ora** adj threatening, menacing

**amenazante** adj threatening, menacing

**amenazar** [16] vt to threaten; **a. a alguien con hacerle algo** to threaten to do sth to sb; **a. a alguien con hacer algo** to threaten sb with doing sth; **a. a alguien con el despido/de muerte** to threaten to sack/kill sb; **amenaza lluvia** it's threatening to rain

**amenidad** nf (a) (entretenimiento) entertaining qualities (b) (agrado) pleasantness

**amenizar** [16] *vt Fig* to liven up

**ameno, -a** *adj* (a) *(entretenido)* entertaining (b) *(placentero)* pleasant

**amenorrea** *nf Med* amenorrhea

**América** *n (continente)* America; *Am (Latinoamérica)* Latin America; **A. Central** Central America; **A. del Sur/Norte** South/North America

**americana** *nf (chaqueta)* jacket

**americanada** *nf Fam Pey (película)* typical Hollywood film

**americanismo** *nm* (a) *(carácter)* American character (b) *Ling* Americanism

**americanizar** [16] **1** *vt* to Americanize

**2 americanizarse** *vpr* to become Americanized

**americano, -a** *adj & nm,f* American

**amerindio, -a** *adj & nm,f* American Indian, Amerindian

**ameritar** *vt Am* to deserve

**amerizaje** *nm Av (de hidroavión)* landing at sea; *(de vehículo espacial)* splashdown

**amerizar** [16] *vi Av (hidroavión)* to land at sea; *(vehículo espacial)* to splash down

**ametralladora** *nf* machinegun

**ametrallar** *vt* (a) *(con ametralladora)* to machinegun (b) *(con metralla)* to shower with shrapnel

**amianto** *nm* asbestos

**amigable** *adj* amicable

**amígdala** *nf* tonsil

**amigdalitis** *nf inv Med* tonsillitis

**amigo, -a 1** *adj* (a) *(no enemigo)* friendly (b) *(aficionado)* **a. de algo/hacer algo** keen on sth/doing sth; **a. de la buena mesa** partial to good food

**2** *nm,f* (a) *(persona)* friend; **hacerse a. de** to make friends with; **hacerse amigos** to become friends (b) *Fam (compañero, novio)* partner; *(amante)* lover (c) *(tratamiento)* (my) friend; **¡a., eso es otra cuestión!** that's another matter, my friend!

**amigote, amiguete** *nm Fam* pal, *Br* mate

**amiguismo** *nm* **hay mucho a.** there are always jobs for the boys

**amilanar 1** *vt* (a) *(intimidar)* to intimidate (b) *(desanimar)* to discourage

**2 amilanarse** *vpr (acobardarse)* to be discouraged, to lose heart

**aminoácido** *nm Biol* amino acid

**aminorar 1** *vt* to reduce

**2** *vi* to decrease, to diminish

**amistad** *nf* friendship; **hacer** *o* **trabar a. (con)** to make friends (with); **amistades** friends

**amistoso, -a 1** *adj* friendly; *Dep* **un partido a.** a friendly

**2** *nm Dep* friendly

**amnesia** *nf Psi* amnesia

**amnésico, -a** *Psi* **1** *adj* amnesic, amnesiac

**2** *nm,f* amnesiac

**amniótico, -a** *adj Med* amniotic; **líquido a.** amniotic fluid

**amnistía** *nf* amnesty; **a. fiscal** = amnesty during which people guilty of tax evasion may pay what they owe without being prosecuted; **A. Internacional** Amnesty International

**amnistiar** [34] *vt* to grant amnesty to

**amo** *nm* (a) *(dueño)* owner (b) *(de criado)* master; *Fam* **ser el a. del cotarro** to rule the roost

**amodorrado, -a** *adj* drowsy

**amodorrarse** *vpr* to get drowsy

**amoldable** *adj* adaptable; **ser a. a** to be able to adapt to

**amoldar 1** *vt (adaptar)* to adapt (a to)

**2 amoldarse** *vpr (adaptarse)* to adapt (a to)

**amonal** *nm* ammonal

**amonestación** *nf* (a) *(reprimenda)* reprimand (b) *Dep* warning (c) **amonestaciones** *(para matrimonio)* banns

**amonestar** *vt* (a) *(reprender)* to reprimand (b) *Dep* to warn, to caution (c) *(para matrimonio)* to publish the banns of

**amoníaco, amoniaco** *nm (gas)* ammonia; *(líquido)* liquid ammonia

**amontillado 1** *adj* **vino a.** amontillado, = medium-dry sherry

**2** *nm* amontillado, = medium-dry sherry

**amontonar 1** *vt (apilar)* to pile up; *Fig (reunir)* to accumulate

**2 amontonarse** *vpr (personas)* to form a crowd; *(problemas, trabajo)* to pile up; *(ideas, solicitudes)* to come thick and fast

**amor** *nm* love; **hacer algo con a.** to do sth lovingly, to do sth with loving care; **hacer el a.** to make love; **de mil amores** with pleasure; **por a. al arte** for the love of it; **¡por el a. de Dios!** for God's sake!; **al a. de la lumbre** *o* **del fuego** by the fireside; **a. libre** free love; **a. platónico** platonic love; **a. propio** pride

**amoral** *adj* amoral

**amoralidad** *nf* amorality

**amoratado, -a** *adj (de frío)* blue; *(por golpes)* black and blue

**amoratarse** *vpr (por el frío)* to turn blue; *(por golpes)* to turn black and blue

**amordazar** [16] *vt (persona)* to gag; *(perro)* to muzzle; **a. a la prensa** to gag the press

**amorfo, -a** *adj* (a) *(sin forma)* amorphous (b) *Fig (persona)* lacking in character

**amorío** *nm* fling

**amoroso, -a** *adj (trato, sentimiento)* loving; **carta/relación amorosa** love letter/affair

**amortajar** *vt (difunto)* to shroud

**amortiguación** *nf* (a) *(de ruido)* muffling; *(de golpe)* softening, cushioning (b) *Aut* suspension, shock absorbers

**amortiguador, -ora 1** *adj (de ruido)* muffling; *(de golpe)* softening, cushioning
  **2** *nm Aut* shock absorber

**amortiguar** [12] **1** *vt (ruido)* to muffle; *(golpe)* to soften, to cushion
  **2 amortiguarse** *vpr (ruido)* to die away; *(golpe)* to be cushioned

**amortizable** *adj Fin (bonos, acciones)* redeemable

**amortización** *nf Fin (de deuda, préstamo)* amortization, paying-off; *(de inversión, capital)* recouping; *(de bonos, acciones)* redemption; *(de bienes de equipo)* depreciation

**amortizar** [16] *vt* (a) *(sacar provecho)* to get one's money's worth out of (b) *Fin (deuda, préstamo)* to amortize, to pay off; *(inversión, capital)* to recoup; *(bonos, acciones)* to redeem; *(bienes de equipo)* to depreciate (c) *(puesto de trabajo)* to abolish, to do away with

**amoscarse** [61] *vpr Fam* to get in a huff

**amotinado, -a** *adj & nm,f* rebel, insurgent

**amotinamiento** *nm (de subordinados)* rebellion, uprising; *(de marineros)* mutiny

**amotinar 1** *vt (a subordinados)* to incite to riot; *(a marineros)* to incite to mutiny
  **2 amotinarse** *vpr (subordinados)* to riot; *(marineros)* to mutiny

**amovible** *adj (cargo)* revocable

**amparar 1** *vt (proteger)* to protect; *(dar cobijo a)* to give shelter to, to take in; **ese derecho lo ampara la Constitución** that right is enshrined in the Constitution
  **2 ampararse** *vpr (cobijarse)* **ampararse de** to (take) shelter from; **ampararse en una ley** to have recourse to a law; **se ampara en la excusa de que no sabía nada** she uses her ignorance as an excuse

**amparo** *nm* protection; **al a. de** *(persona, caridad)* with the help of; *(ley)* under the protection of

**amperaje** *nm Elec* amperage

**amperímetro** *nm Elec* ammeter

**amperio** *nm Elec* amp, ampere

**ampliable** *adj (plazo)* extendible; *Informát* expandable

**ampliación** *nf* (a) *(aumento)* expansion; *(de edificio, plazo)* extension; *Econ* **a. de capital** share issue (b) *Fot* enlargement

**ampliadora** *nf Fot* enlarger

**ampliar** [34] *vt* (a) *(agrandar)* to expand; *(local, vivienda)* to add an extension to; *(plazo)* to extend (b) *Fot* to enlarge, to blow up (c) *(estudios)* to further, to continue

**amplificación** *nf* amplification

**amplificador** *nm Elec* amplifier

**amplificar** [61] *vt* to amplify

**amplio, -a** *adj* (a) *(sala, maletero)* roomy, spacious; *(avenida, gama)* wide (b) *(ropa)* loose (c) *(explicación, cobertura)* comprehensive; **en el sentido más a. de la palabra** in the broadest sense of the word (d) **de amplias miras** broadminded

**amplitud** *nf* (a) *(espaciosidad)* roominess, spaciousness; *(de avenida)* wideness (b) *(de ropa)* looseness (c) *Fig (extensión)* extent, comprehensiveness; **a. de miras** broadmindedness (d) *Fís* **a. de onda** amplitude

**ampolla** *nf* (a) *(en piel)* blister; *Fig* **levantar ampollas** to create bad feeling (b) *(para inyecciones)* ampoule; *(frasco)* phial

**ampollarse** *vpr* to blister; **se me han ampollado los pies** I've got blisters on my feet

**ampulosidad** *nf* pomposity

**ampuloso, -a** *adj* pompous

**amputación** *nf* amputation

**amputar** *vt* to amputate

**Amsterdam** *n* Amsterdam

**amueblado 1** *adj (piso)* furnished
  **2** *nm CSur* room hired for sex

**amueblar** *vt* to furnish

**amuermar** *Fam* **1** *vt (aburrir)* to bore senseless
  **2 amuermarse** *vpr (aburrirse)* to get bored senseless; *(adormilarse)* to get sleepy

**amuleto** *nm* amulet

**amurallado, -a** *adj* walled

**amurallar** *vt* to build a wall around

**anabaptista** *adj & nmf* Anabaptist

**anabolizante 1** *adj* anabolic
  **2** *nm* anabolic steroid

**anacarado, -a** *adj* pearly

**anacardo** *nm* cashew nut

**anaconda** *nf* anaconda

**anacoreta** *nmf* anchorite, hermit

**anacrónico, -a** *adj* anachronistic

**anacronismo** *nm* anachronism

**ánade** *nm* duck

**anaerobio, -a** *adj Biol* anaerobic

**anagrama** *nm* anagram

**anal** *adj Anat* anal

**anales** *nmpl también Fig* annals

**analfabetismo** *nm* illiteracy

**analfabeto, -a** *adj & nm,f* illiterate

**analgésico, -a** *adj & nm* analgesic

**análisis** *nm inv* analysis; **a. clínico** (clinical) test; **a. gramatical** sentence analysis; **a. de mercado** market analysis; **a. de orina** urine analysis; **a. de sangre** blood test

**analista** *nmf* analyst; *Informát* (computer) analyst; **a. de mercado** market analyst; **a. de sistemas** systems analyst

**analítica** *nf Med* clinical testing

**analítico, -a** *adj* analytical

**analizar [16]** *vt* to analyse

**analogía** *nf* similarity; **por a.** by analogy

**analógico, -a** *adj* (**a**) *(análogo)* analogous, similar (**b**) *Informát & Tec* analogue, analog

**análogo, -a** *adj* analogous *o* similar (**a** to)

**ananá, ananás** *nm CSur* pineapple

**anaquel** *nm* shelf

**anaranjado, -a** *adj* orange

**anarco** *Fam* **1** *adj* anarchistic

**2** *nmf* anarchist

**anarcosindicalismo** *nm Pol* anarcho-syndicalism

**anarcosindicalista** *adj & nmf Pol* anarchosyndicalist

**anarquía** *nf Pol* (**a**) *(falta de gobierno)* anarchy (**b**) *(doctrina política)* anarchism (**c**) *Fig (desorden)* chaos, anarchy

**anárquico, -a** *adj* anarchic

**anarquismo** *nm Pol* anarchism

**anarquista** *adj & nmf* anarchist

**anatema** *nm Rel* curse, anathema; *Fig* curse

**anatematizar** *vt Fig* to condemn

**anatomía** *nf* anatomy

**anatómico, -a** *adj* (**a**) *Anat* anatomical (**b**) *(asiento)* anatomically-shaped; *(calzado)* orthopaedic

**anca** *nf* haunch; **ancas de rana** frogs' legs

**ancestral** *adj (costumbre)* age-old

**ancestro** *nm* ancestor

**ancho, -a 1** *adj (abertura, carretera, río)* wide; *(ropa)* loose-fitting; **te va** *o* **está a.** it's too big for you; *Fig* **a mis/tus anchas** at ease; **quedarse tan a.** not to care less; **lo dijo delante de todos y se quedó tan a.** he said it in front of everyone, just like that

**2** *nm* width; **a lo a.** crosswise; **tener cinco metros de a.** to be five metres wide; **a lo a. de** across (the width of); *Ferroc* **a. de vía** gauge; *Informát* **a. de banda** bandwidth

**anchoa** *nf* anchovy

**anchura** *nf* width

**anciano, -a 1** *adj* old

**2** *nm,f (hombre)* old man, old person; *(mujer)* old woman, old person; **los ancianos** the elderly

**3** *nm (de tribu)* elder

**ancla** *nf* anchor; **echar/levar anclas** to drop/weigh anchor

**anclado, -a** *adj Fig* **una aldea anclada en el pasado** a village stuck in the past

**anclaje** *nm Náut* anchoring; *Tec* **los anclajes de una grúa** the moorings of a crane

**anclar** *vi* to (drop) anchor

**áncora** *nf* anchor

**anda** *interj* (**a**) *(indica sorpresa)* **¡a.!** gosh!; **¡a. la osa!** good grief! (**b**) *(por favor)* go on! (**c**) *(venga)* come on! (**d**) **¡a. ya!** *(negativa despectiva)* get away!, come off it!

**andadas** *nfpl Fam* **volver a las a.** to return to one's evil ways

**andaderas** *nfpl* baby-walker

**andador, -ora 1** *adj* fond of walking

**2** *nm (tacataca)* babywalker; *(para adultos)* Zimmer frame®

**andadura** *nf Fig* **la a. de un país** the evolution of a country; **su a. por Europa** his travels through Europe

**ándale** *interj CAm, Méx Fam* **¡á.!** come on!

**Andalucía** *n* Andalusia

**andalucismo** *nm* (**a**) *Pol (doctrina)* = doctrine favouring Andalusian autonomy (**b**) *(palabra)* = Andalusian word or expression

**andaluz, -uza** *adj & nm,f* Andalusian

**andamiaje** *nm* scaffolding; *Fig* structure, framework

**andamio** *nm* scaffold

**andanada** *nf* (**a**) *también Mil* broadside (**b**) *Taurom* = covered stand in a bullring

**andando** *interj* **¡a.!** come on!, let's get a move on!

**andante** *adj* (**a**) *(que anda)* walking (**b**) *Mús* andante

**andanza** *nf (aventura)* adventure

**andar** **[8] 1** *vt* (**a**) *(recorrer)* to go, to travel; **anduvimos 15 kilómetros** we walked (for) 15 kilometres

(**b**) *CAm (llevar puesto)* to wear

(**c**) *CAm (llevar)* to carry

**2** *vi* (**a**) *(caminar)* to walk; *(moverse)* to move; **a. por la calle** to walk in the street

(**b**) *(funcionar)* to work, to go; **el reloj no anda** the clock has stopped; **las cosas andan mal** things are going badly

(**c**) *(estar)* to be; **a. preocupado** to be worried; **a. mal de dinero** to be short of money; **creo que anda por el almacén** I think he's somewhere in the warehouse; *Fig* **a. tras algo/alguien** to be after sth/sb; **a. haciendo algo** to be doing sth; **anda echando broncas a todos** he's going round telling everybody off; **anda explicando sus aventuras** he's talking about his adventures; **de a. por casa** *(bata, zapatillas)* for wearing around the house; *Fig (explicación, método)* basic, rough and ready; *Prov* **quien mal anda mal acaba** everyone gets their just deserts

(**d**) *(ocuparse)* **a. en** *(asuntos, líos)* to be involved in; *(papeleos, negocios)* to be busy with

(**e**) *(hurgar)* **a. en** to rummage around in; **¿quién ha andado en mis papeles?** who has been messing around with my papers?

(**f**) *(expresa acción)* **en ese país andan a tiros** in that country they go round shooting one another; **andan a voces todo el día** they spend the whole day shouting at each other; **a. a vueltas con algo** to be having trouble with sth

(**g**) *(alcanzar, rondar)* **a. por** to be about; **anda por los 60** he's about sixty

(**h**) *Fam (enredar)* **a. con algo** to play with sth

**3 andarse** *vpr* (**a**) *(obrar)* **andarse con cuidado/misterios** to be careful/secretive; **andarse con rodeos, andarse por las ramas** to beat about the bush

(**b**) **todo se andará** all in good time

**4** *nm* gait, walk; **andares** *(de persona)* gait; **tener andares de** to walk like

**andarín, -ina** *adj* fond of walking

**andas** *nfpl* **llevar a alguien en a.** to give sb a chair-lift

**ándele** *interj CAm, Méx Fam* **¡á.!** come on!

**andén** *nm* (**a**) *Ferroc* platform (**b**) *Andes, CAm (acera) Br* pavement, *US* sidewalk

**Andes** *nmpl* **los A.** the Andes

**andinismo** *nm Am* mountaineering

**andinista** *nmf Am* mountaineer

**andino, -a** *adj & nm,f* Andean

**Andorra** *n* Andorra

**andorrano, -a** *adj & nm,f* Andorran

**andrajo** *nm (harapo)* rag

**andrajoso, -a 1** *adj* ragged

**2** *nm,f* person dressed in rags

**andrógino, -a 1** *adj* androgynous

**2** *nm* hermaphrodite

**androide** *nm (autómata)* android

**andurriales** *nmpl* remote place; **¿qué haces por estos a.?** what are you doing as far off the beaten track as this?

**anduviera** *etc ver* **andar**

**anea** *nf* (bul)rush; **silla de a.** chair with a wickerwork seat

**anécdota** *nf* anecdote

**anecdotario** *nm* collection of anecdotes

**anecdótico, -a** *adj* (**a**) *(con historietas)* anecdotal (**b**) *(no esencial)* incidental

**anegar** [40] **1** *vt* (**a**) *(inundar)* to flood (**b**) *(ahogar) (planta)* to drown

**2 anegarse** *vpr* (**a**) *(inundarse)* to flood; **sus ojos se anegaron de lágrimas** tears welled up in his eyes (**b**) *(ahogarse)* to drown

**anejo, -a 1** *adj (edificio)* connected (**a** to); *(documento)* attached (**a** to)

**2** *nm* annexe

**anemia** *nf Med* anaemia

**anémico, -a** *adj Med* **1** *adj* anaemic

**2** *nm,f* anaemia sufferer

**anemómetro** *nm* wind gauge, *Tec* anemometer

**anémona** *nf (planta)* anemone; *(actinia)* sea anemone

**anestesia** *nf Med* anaesthesia; **a. general/local** general/local anaesthesia

**anestesiar** [15] *vt Med* to anaesthetize, to place under anaesthetic

**anestésico, -a** *adj & nm Med* anaesthetic

**anestesista** *nmf* anaesthetist

**Aneto** *nm* **el A.** Aneto

**aneurisma** *nm Med* aneurysm

**anexar** *vt (documento)* to attach

**anexión** *nf* annexation

**anexionar** *vt* to annex

**anexionista** *nmf Pol* annexationist

**anexo, -a 1** *adj (edificio)* connected; *(documento)* attached

**2** *nm* annexe

**anfeta** *nf muy Fam* tab of speed

**anfetamina** *nf* amphetamine

**anfibio, -a 1** *adj también Fig* amphibious

**2** *nm* amphibian

**anfiteatro** *nm* (**a**) *(en teatro)* circle; *(en cine)* balcony (**b**) *(romano)* amphitheatre

**anfitrión, -ona 1** *adj* host; **país a.** host country

**2** *nm,f* host, *f* hostess

**ánfora** *nf (cántaro)* amphora

**ángel** *nm* angel; **á. custodio** *o* **de la guarda** guardian angel; **tener á.** to have something special; **¡eres un á.!** you're an angel!

**angelical** *adj* angelic

**ángelus** *nm inv Rel* angelus

**angina** *nf* (**a**) **anginas** *(amigdalitis)* sore throat; **tener anginas** to have a sore throat (**b**) **a. de pecho** angina (pectoris)

**anglicanismo** *nm Rel* Anglicanism

**anglicano, -a** *adj & nm,f Rel* Anglican

**anglicismo** *nm* anglicism

**angloamericano, -a** *adj & nm,f* Anglo-American

**anglófilo, -a** *adj & nm,f* anglophile

**anglófobo, -a** *adj & nm,f* anglophobe

**anglófono, -a, angloparlante 1** *adj* English-speaking, anglophone

**2** *nm,f* English speaker, anglophone

**anglosajón, -ona** *adj & nm,f* Anglo-Saxon

**Angola** *n* Angola

**angoleño, -a, angolano, -a** *adj & nm,f* Angolan

**angora** *nf (de conejo)* angora; *(de cabra)* mohair

**angosto, -a** *adj* narrow

**angostura** *nf* (a) *(estrechez)* narrowness (b) *(extracto)* angostura

**ángstrom** (*pl* **ángstroms**) *nm Fís* angstrom

**anguila** *nf* eel; **a. de mar** conger eel

**angula** *nf* elver

**angular 1** *adj* angular

**2** *nm Fot* **gran a.** wide-angle lens

**ángulo** *nm* (a) *(figura geométrica)* angle; **á. agudo/obtuso/recto** acute/obtuse/right angle; *Mil* **á. de mira** line of sight; *Mil* **á. de tiro** elevation (b) *(rincón)* corner

**anguloso, -a** *adj* angular

**angustia** *nf* (a) *(aflicción)* anxiety (b) *Psi* distress

**angustiado, -a** *adj* anguished, distressed

**angustiar** [15] **1** *vt* to distress

**2 angustiarse** *vpr (agobiarse)* to get worried (**por** about)

**angustioso, -a** *adj (espera, momentos)* anxious; *(situación, noticia)* distressing

**anhelante** *adj* longing (**por algo/por hacer algo** for sth/to do sth)

**anhelar** *vt* to long *o* wish for; **a. hacer algo** to long to do sth

**anhelo** *nm* longing

**anhídrido** *nm Quím* anhydride; **a. carbónico** carbon dioxide

**anidar** *vi* (a) *(pájaro)* to nest (b) *Fig (sentimiento)* **a. en** to find a place in

**anilina** *nf Quím* aniline

**anilla** *nf* ring; **anillas** *Dep* rings

**anillo** *nm* (a) *también Astron* ring; **a. de boda** wedding ring; *Fam Fig* **me viene como a. al dedo** *(cosa)* it's just what I needed; **me vienes como a. al dedo, necesitaba un fontanero** how lucky that you should have come, I was looking for a plumber!; *Fam Fig* **no se me van a caer los anillos** it won't hurt me (to do it) (b) *Zool* annulus

**ánima** *nf* soul; **á. bendita** soul in purgatory

**animación** *nf* (a) *(alegría)* liveliness (b) *(bullicio)* hustle and bustle, activity (c) *Cine* animation

**animado, -a** *adj* (a) *(con buen ánimo)* cheerful (b) *(divertido)* lively (c) *Cine* animated

**animador, -ora** *nm,f* (a) *(en espectáculo)* compere (b) *(en fiesta de niños)* children's entertainer (c) *(en deporte)* cheerleader

**animadversión** *nf* animosity

**animal 1** *adj* (a) *(instintos, funciones)* animal; **el reino a.** the animal kingdom (b) *(persona) (basto)* rough; *(ignorante)* ignorant

**2** *nm* animal; **a. doméstico** *(de granja)* farm animal; *(de compañía)* pet; **a. de carga** beast of burden

**3** *nmf (persona)* animal, brute

**animalada** *nf Fig* **decir/hacer una a.** to say/do something crazy

**animar 1** *vt* (a) *(estimular)* to encourage; **a. a alguien a hacer algo** to encourage sb to do sth (b) *(alegrar) (persona)* to cheer up; *Fig (fuego, diálogo, fiesta)* to liven up

**2 animarse** *vpr* (a) *(persona)* to cheer up; *(fiesta, ambiente)* to liven up (b) *(decidir)* to finally decide (**a hacer algo** to do sth)

**anímico, -a** *adj* **estado a.** state of mind

**animismo** *nm* animism

**ánimo 1** *nm* (a) *(valor)* courage (b) *(aliento)* encouragement; **dar ánimos a alguien** to encourage sb (c) *(intención)* **con/sin á. de** with/without the intention of; **lo hice sin á. de ofenderte** I didn't mean to offend you (d) *(humor)* disposition; **no tiene ánimos para nada** she doesn't feel like doing anything (e) *(alma)* mind

**2** *interj* **¡á.!** *(¡adelante!)* come on!; *(¡anímate!)* cheer up!

**animosidad** *nf* animosity

**animoso, -a** *adj (valiente)* courageous; *(decidido)* undaunted

**aniñado, -a** *adj (comportamiento)* childish; *(voz, rostro)* childlike

**aniquilación** *nf* annihilation

**aniquilar** *vt* to annihilate, to wipe out

**anís** (*pl* **anises**) *nm* (a) *(planta)* anise (b) *(grano)* aniseed (c) *(licor)* anisette

**anisete** *nm* anisette

**aniversario** *nm (de muerte, fundación, suceso)* anniversary; *(cumpleaños)* birthday; **a. de boda** wedding anniversary

**Ankara** *n* Ankara

**ano** *nm* anus

**anoche** *adv* last night, yesterday evening; **antes de a.** the night before last

**anochecer** [48] **1** *nm* dusk, nightfall; **al a.** at dusk

**2** *v impersonal* to get dark; **anochecía** it was getting dark

**3** *vi* **a. en algún sitio** to be somewhere at nightfall

**anodino, -a** *adj (persona, libro)* dull; *(comida)* bland, insipid

**ánodo** *nm Elec* anode

**anomalía** *nf* anomaly

**anómalo, -a** *adj* anomalous

**anonadado, -a** *adj* (a) *(sorprendido)* astonished, bewildered (b) *(abatido)* stunned

**anonadar 1** *vt* (a) *(sorprender)* to astonish, to bewilder (b) *(abatir)* to stun

**2 anonadarse** *vpr* (a) *(sorprenderse)* to be astonished, to be bewildered (b) *(abatirse)* to be stunned

**anonimato** *nm* anonymity; **permanecer en el a.** to remain nameless; **vivir en el a.** to live out of the public eye; **salir del a.** to reveal one's identity

**anónimo, -a 1** *adj* anonymous
**2** *nm* anonymous letter

**anorak** (*pl* **anoraks**) *nm* anorak

**anorexia** *nf Psi* anorexia

**anoréxico, -a** *adj & nm,f* anorexic

**anormal 1** *adj* (a) (*anómalo*) abnormal (b) (*subnormal*) subnormal; (*como insulto*) moronic
**2** *nmf* (*persona*) subnormal person; (*como insulto*) moron

**anormalidad** *nf* (a) (*anomalía*) abnormality (b) (*defecto físico o psíquico*) handicap, disability

**anotación** *nf* (*nota escrita*) note; (*en registro*) entry; *Com* **a. contable** book entry

**anotar** *vt* (a) (*escribir*) to note down, to make a note of (b) (*tantos*) to notch up

**anovulatorio, -a 1** *adj* (*anticonceptivo*) anovulatory
**2** *nm* (*anticonceptivo*) anovulant

**anquilosamiento** *nm Med* paralysis; *Fig* (*estancamiento*) stagnation

**anquilosarse** *vpr Med* to become paralysed; (*estancarse*) to stagnate

**ánsar** *nm* goose

**ansarón** *nm* gosling

**ansia** *nf* (a) (*afán*) longing, yearning (**de** for) (b) (*ansiedad*) anxiousness; (*angustia*) anguish; **ansias** (*náuseas*) sickness, nausea

**ansiar** [34] *vt* **a. algo** to long for sth; **a. hacer algo** to long to do sth

**ansiedad** *nf* (a) (*inquietud*) anxiety; **con a.** anxiously (b) *Psi* nervous tension

**ansiolítico, -a** *adj & nm Med* sedative

**ansioso, -a** *adj* (a) (*impaciente*) impatient; **estar a. por** *o* **de hacer algo** to be impatient to do sth (b) (*angustiado*) in anguish

**antagónico, -a** *adj* antagonistic

**antagonismo** *nm* antagonism

**antagonista** *nmf* opponent

**antaño** *adv* in days gone by

**antártico, -a 1** *adj* Antarctic
**2** *nm* **el A.** the Antarctic; **el océano Glacial A.** the Antarctic Ocean

**Antártida** *nf* **la A.** the Antarctic

**ante¹** *nm* (a) (*piel*) suede (b) (*animal*) elk, moose

**ante²** *prep* (a) (*delante de, en presencia de*) before (b) (*frente a*) (*hecho, circunstancia*) in the face of (c) (*respecto de*) compared to; **su opinión prevaleció a. la mía** his opinion prevailed over mine; **a. todo** (*sobre todo*) above all; (*en primer lugar*) first of all

**anteanoche** *adv* the night before last

**anteayer** *adv* the day before yesterday

**antebrazo** *nm* forearm

**antecámara** *nf* antechamber

**antecedente 1** *adj* preceding, previous
**2** *nm* (a) (*precedente*) precedent (b) *Gram & Mat* antecedent; **antecedentes** (*de asunto*) background; **poner a alguien en antecedentes de** (*informar*) to fill sb in on; **antecedentes penales** criminal record

**anteceder** *vt* to come before, to precede

**antecesor, -ora** *nm,f* (*predecesor*) predecessor; **antecesores** (*antepasados*) ancestors

**antedicho, -a** *adj* aforementioned

**antediluviano, -a** *adj también Fig* antediluvian

**antelación** *nf* **con a.** in advance; **con dos horas de a.** two hours in advance

**antemano** *adv* **de a.** beforehand, in advance

**antena** *nf* (a) *Rad & TV* aerial, antenna; **estar/salir en a.** to be/go on the air; **a. colectiva** = aerial shared by all the inhabitants of a block of flats; **a. parabólica** satellite dish (b) (*de animal*) antenna

**anteojeras** *nfpl Br* blinkers, *US* blinders

**anteojos** *nmpl* (a) *Anticuado o Am* (*gafas*) spectacles (b) (*prismáticos*) binoculars

**antepasado, -a** *nm,f* ancestor

**antepecho** *nm* (*de puente*) parapet; (*de ventana*) sill

**antepenúltimo, -a** *adj & nm,f* last but two

**anteponer** [52] **1** *vt* **a. algo a algo** to put sth before sth
**2** **anteponerse** *vpr* **anteponerse a algo** to come before sth

**anteproyecto** *nm* draft; *Pol* **a. de ley** draft bill

**antepuesto, -a** *participio ver* **anteponer**

**anterior** *adj* (a) (*previo*) previous (**a** to) (b) (*delantero*) front

**anterioridad** *nf* **con a.** beforehand; **con a.** a before, prior to

**anteriormente** *adv* previously

**antes** *adv* (a) (*en el tiempo*) before; **no importa si venís a.** it doesn't matter if you come earlier; **ya no nado como a.** I can't swim as I used to; **mucho/poco a.** long/shortly before; **lo a. posible** as soon as possible; **a. de (que)** before; **a. de hacer algo** before doing sth; **a. de nada** first of all, before anything else; **a. de que llegarais** before you arrived (b) (*primero*) first; **esta señora está a.** this lady is first (c) (*expresa preferencia*) **a.... que** rather... than; **prefiero la sierra a. que el mar** I like the mountains better than the sea; **iría a la cárcel a. que mentir** I'd rather go to prison than lie; **a. que nada** above all, first and foremost; **a. bien, a. al contrario** on the contrary

**antesala** *nf* anteroom; *Fig* **estar en la a. de** to be on the verge of; **hacer a.** *(esperar)* to wait

**antevíspera** *nf* day before yesterday; **la a. de…** two days before…

**antiabortista 1** *adj* anti-abortion, pro-life
**2** *nmf* anti-abortion *o* pro-life campaigner

**antiácido, -a** *adj & nm (medicamento)* antacid

**antiadherente** *adj* nonstick

**antiaéreo, -a** *adj* anti-aircraft

**antiarrugas** *adj inv* anti-wrinkle

**antibalas, antibala** *adj inv* bullet-proof

**antibiótico, -a** *adj & nm* antibiotic

**anticancerígeno** *nm* cancer drug

**antichoque** *adj* shockproof

**anticiclón** *nm Met* anticyclone

**anticipación** *nf* earliness; **con a.** in advance; **con un mes de a.** a month in advance; **con a.** prior to

**anticipado, -a** *adj (elecciones)* early; *(pago)* advance; **por a.** in advance

**anticipar 1** *vt* **(a)** *(prever)* to anticipate **(b)** *(adelantar)* to bring forward **(c)** *(pago)* to pay in advance **(d)** *(información)* **no te puedo a. nada** I can't tell you anything just now
**2 anticiparse** *vpr* **(a)** *(suceder antes)* to arrive early; **se anticipó a su tiempo** he was ahead of his time **(b)** *(adelantarse)* **anticiparse a alguien** to beat sb to it

**anticipo** *nm* **(a)** *(de dinero)* advance **(b)** *(presagio)* foretaste

**anticlerical** *adj* anticlerical

**anticlericalismo** *nm* anticlericalism

**anticoagulante** *adj & nm Med* anticoagulant

**anticomunismo** *nm* anti-communism

**anticomunista** *adj & nmf* anti-communist

**anticoncepción** *nf* contraception

**anticonceptivo, -a** *adj & nm* contraceptive

**anticonformismo** *nm* non-conformism

**anticongelante** *adj & nm* antifreeze

**anticonstitucional** *adj Der* unconstitutional

**anticonstitucionalidad** *nf Der* unconstitutional nature

**anticorrosivo, -a 1** *adj* anticorrosive
**2** *nm* anticorrosive substance

**anticristo** *nm* Antichrist

**anticuado, -a** *adj* old-fashioned

**anticuario, -a 1** *nm,f (comerciante)* antique dealer; *(experto)* antiquarian
**2** *nm (establecimiento)* antique shop

**anticuerpo** *nm Med* antibody

**antidemocrático, -a** *adj* undemocratic

**antideportivo, -a** *adj* unsporting, unsportsmanlike

**antidepresivo, -a 1** *adj* antidepressant
**2** *nm* antidepressant (drug)

**antideslizante** *adj Aut (ruedas)* non-skid

**antideslumbrante** *adj* anti-dazzle

**antidisturbios 1** *adj inv* riot; **material a.** riot gear
**2** *nmpl (policía)* riot police

**antidopaje** *nm Dep* dope tests

**antidoping** [anti'ðopiŋ] *adj Dep* doping; **prueba a.** doping test

**antídoto** *nm* antidote

**antier** *adv Am Fam* the day before yesterday

**antiestético, -a** *adj* unsightly

**antifascista** *adj & nmf* anti-fascist

**antifaz** *nm* mask

**antigás** *adj inv* gas; **careta a.** gas mask

**antígeno** *nm Med* antigen

**antigripal 1** *adj* designed to combat flu
**2** *nm* flu remedy

**antigualla** *nf Pey (cosa)* museum piece; *(persona)* old fogey, old fossil

**antiguamente** *adv (hace mucho)* long ago; *(previamente)* formerly

**Antigua y Barbuda** *n* Antigua and Barbuda

**antigubernamental** *adj* anti-government

**antigüedad** *nf* **(a)** *(edad)* antiquity; *(veteranía)* seniority; *Hist* **la A. (clásica)** (Classical) Antiquity **(b) antigüedades** *(objetos)* antiques

**antiguo, -a 1** *adj* **(a)** *(viejo)* old; *(inmemorial)* ancient **(b)** *(anterior, previo)* former; **el a. régimen** the former regime; *Hist* the ancien régime **(c)** *(veterano)* senior **(d)** *(pasado de moda)* old-fashioned; **a la antigua** in an old-fashioned way
**2** *nmpl* **antiguos** *Hist* ancients

**antihéroe** *nm* antihero

**antihielo** *nm* de-icer

**antihigiénico, -a** *adj* unhygienic

**antihistamínico** *nm (medicamento)* antihistamine

**antiinflacionista** *adj Econ* anti-inflationary

**antiinflamatorio, -a 1** *adj* anti-inflammatory
**2** *nm* anti-inflammatory drug

**antillano, -a 1** *adj* West Indian, of/from the Caribbean
**2** *nm,f* West Indian, person from the Caribbean

**Antillas** *nfpl* **las A.** the West Indies

**antílope** *nm* antelope

**antimateria** *nf Fís* antimatter

**antimilitarismo** *nm* antimilitarism

**antimilitarista** *adj & nmf* antimilitarist

**antimisil** *nm Mil* antimissile

**antimonio** *nm Quím* antimony

**antimonopolio** *adj inv Econ* antitrust

**antinatural** *adj* unnatural

**antiniebla** *adj inv Aut* **faros a.** fog lamps

**antioxidante 1** *adj (contra el óxido)* anti-rust; *(contra la oxidación)* antioxidant

**2** *nm (contra el óxido)* rustproofing agent; *(contra la oxidación)* antioxidant

**antipapa** *nm* antipope

**antiparasitario, -a 1** *adj (para perro, gato)* **collar a.** flea collar; **pastillas antiparasitarias** worming tablets

**2** *nm* (a) *(para perro, gato) (collar)* flea collar; *(pastilla)* worming tablet (b) *Tel* suppressor

**antiparras** *nfpl Fam* specs

**antipatía** *nf* dislike; **tener a. a alguien** to dislike sb

**antipático, -a 1** *adj* unpleasant

**2** *nm,f* unpleasant person

**antipirético, -a** *adj & nm (medicamento)* antipyretic

**antípodas** *nfpl* **las a.** the Antipodes

**antiquísimo, -a** *superlativo ver* **antiguo**

**antirreflectante** *adj* non-reflective

**antirreglamentario, -a** *adj* against the rules; **un procedimiento a.** a procedure which contravenes the rules

**antirrobo 1** *adj inv* antitheft; **dispositivo a.** antitheft device

**2** *nm (en coche)* antitheft device; *(en edificio)* burglar alarm

**antisemita 1** *adj* anti-Semitic

**2** *nmf* anti-Semite

**antisemitismo** *nm* anti-Semitism

**antiséptico, -a** *adj & nm* antiseptic

**antisocial** *adj* antisocial

**antiterrorismo** *nm* fight against terrorism

**antiterrorista** *adj* anti-terrorist

**antítesis** *nf inv* antithesis

**antitetánico, -a** *adj* anti-tetanus

**antitético, -a** *adj Formal* antithetical

**antivirus** *nm inv Informát* antivirus system

**antojadizo, -a** *adj* capricious

**antojarse** *vpr* (a) *(capricho)* **se le antojaron esos zapatos** she fancied those shoes; **se le ha antojado ir al cine** he felt like going to the cinema; **cuando se me antoje** when I feel like it (b) *(posibilidad)* **se me antoja que...** I have a feeling that...

**antojitos** *nmpl Andes* snacks, tapas

**antojo** *nm* (a) *(capricho)* whim; *(de embarazada)* craving; **a mi/tu a.** my/your (own) way (b) *(lunar)* birthmark

**antología** *nf* anthology; **de a.** memorable, unforgettable

**antológico, -a** *adj* (a) *(recopilador)* anthological (b) *(inolvidable)* memorable, unforgettable

**antónimo** *nm* antonym

**antonomasia** *nf* **por a.** par excellence

**antorcha** *nf* torch; **a. olímpica** Olympic torch

**antracita** *nf* anthracite

**ántrax** *nm inv Med* anthrax

**antro** *nm Fam Pey* dive, dump

**antropocentrismo** *nm* anthropocentrism

**antropofagia** *nf* anthropophagy, cannibalism

**antropófago, -a 1** *adj* anthropophagous

**2** *nm,f* cannibal

**antropología** *nf* anthropology

**antropólogo, -a** *nm,f* anthropologist

**antropomórfico, -a** *adj* anthropomorphic

**anual** *adj* annual

**anualidad** *nf* annuity, yearly payment

**anuario** *nm* yearbook

**anudar 1** *vt* to knot, to tie in a knot

**2 anudarse** *vpr (atarse)* to get into a knot; **anudarse los cordones** to tie one's (shoe)-laces

**anuencia** *nf Formal* consent, approval

**anulación** *nf* (a) *(cancelación)* cancellation; *(de ley)* repeal; *(de matrimonio, contrato)* annulment (b) *Dep (de un partido)* calling-off; *(de un gol)* disallowing; *(de un resultado)* declaration as void

**anular¹ 1** *adj (en forma de anillo)* ring-shaped; **dedo a.** ring finger

**2** *nm (dedo)* ring finger

**anular² ** *vt* (a) *(cancelar)* to cancel; *(ley)* to repeal; *(matrimonio, contrato)* to annul (b) *Dep (partido)* to call off; *(gol)* to disallow; *(resultado)* to declare void (c) *(reprimir)* to repress

**anunciación** *nf* announcement; *Rel* **A.** Annunciation

**anunciante 1** *adj* advertising

**2** *nmf* advertiser

**anunciar [15] 1** *vt* (a) *(notificar)* to announce; **hoy anuncian los resultados** the results are announced today (b) *(hacer publicidad de)* to advertise (c) *(presagiar)* to herald; **esas nubes anuncian tormenta** by the look of those clouds, it's going to rain

**2 anunciarse** *vpr* to advertise (**en** in)

**anuncio** *nm* (a) *(notificación)* announcement; *(cartel, aviso)* notice; *(póster)* poster (b) **a. (publicitario)** advertisement, advert; **anuncios por palabras** classified adverts (c) *(presagio)* sign, herald

**anverso** *nm (de moneda)* head, obverse; *(de hoja)* front

**anzuelo** *nm* (fish) hook; *Fam Fig* bait; **tragarse el a.** to take the bait

**añadido, -a 1** *adj* added (**a** to)
**2** *nm* addition

**añadidura** *nf* addition; **por a.** in addition

**añadir** *vt* to add

**añagaza** *nf* trick, ruse

**añejo, -a** *adj* (**a**) *(vino, licor)* mature (**b**) *(costumbre)* long-established

**añicos** *nmpl* **hacer algo a.** to smash sth to pieces, to shatter sth; **hacerse a.** to shatter

**añil** *adj & nm* indigo

**año** *nm* year; **en el a. 1939** in 1939; **los años 30** the thirties; **a. académico/escolar/fiscal** academic/school/tax year; **a. bisiesto/solar** leap/solar year; **a. nuevo** New Year; **¡feliz a. nuevo!** Happy New Year!; **a. sabático** sabbatical; *Fam* **el a. de la nana** *o* **pera** the year dot; **años** *(edad)* age; **¿cuántos años tienes?** how old are you?; **cumplir años** to have one's birthday; **cumplo años el 25** it's my birthday on the 25th; **estar entrado en años** to be getting on; **te has quitado años de encima** *(rejuvenecer)* you look much younger; *Astron* **a. luz** light year; *Fig* **estar a años luz de** to be light years away from

**añojo** *nm (animal)* yearling; *(carne)* veal *(from a yearling calf)*

**añoranza** *nf (persona, pasado)* nostalgia (**de** for); *(hogar, país)* homesickness (**de** for)

**añorar** *vt* to miss

**aorta** *nf Anat* aorta

**aovado, -a** *adj* egg-shaped

**aovar** *vi (aves, reptiles)* to lay eggs; *(peces)* to spawn

**AP** *nm (abrev de* **Alianza Popular**) = former name of PP, Spanish party to the right of the political spectrum

**APA** ['apa] *nf (abrev de* **Asociación de Padres de Alumnos**) ≃ PTA, = Spanish association for parents of schoolchildren

**apabullante** *adj* overwhelming

**apabullar 1** *vt* to overwhelm
**2 apabullarse** *vpr* to be overwhelmed

**apacentar** [3] *vt* to graze

**apache** *adj & nmf* Apache

**apachurrar** *vt Fam* to squash, to crush

**apacible** *adj (temperamento, trato)* mild, gentle; *(lugar, ambiente)* pleasant

**apaciento** *etc ver* **apacentar**

**apaciguador, -ora** *adj* calming

**apaciguamiento** *nm* calming; *Pol* appeasement

**apaciguar** [12] **1** *vt (tranquilizar)* to calm down; *(dolor)* to soothe
**2 apaciguarse** *vpr (tranquilizarse)* to calm down; *(dolor)* to abate

**apadrinar** *vt* (**a**) *(niño)* to act as a godparent to (**b**) *(artista)* to sponsor

**apagado, -a** *adj* (**a**) *(luz, fuego)* out; *(aparato)* off (**b**) *(color, persona)* subdued (**c**) *(sonido)* dull, muffled; *(voz)* low, quiet

**apagar** [40] **1** *vt* (**a**) *(fuego)* to put out; *(luz)* to switch off; *(vela)* to extinguish; *(aparato)* to turn *o* switch off; **a. el fuego de la cocina** to turn *o* switch off the cooker (**b**) *Fig (reducir)* (sed) to quench; *(dolor)* to get rid of; *(color)* to soften; *(sonido)* to muffle; *Fam* **¡apaga y vámonos!** we have nothing more to talk about
**2 apagarse** *vpr (extinguirse)* (fuego, vela, luz) to go out; *(dolor, rencor)* to die down; *(ilusión)* to die, to be extinguished; *(sonido)* to die away

**apagón** *nm* power cut

**apague** *etc ver* **apagar**

**apaisado, -a** *adj Informát* landscape; **un cuadro/espejo a.** a painting/mirror which is wider than it is high

**apalabrar** *vt (concertar)* to make a verbal agreement regarding; *(contratar)* to engage on the basis of a verbal agreement

**Apalaches** *nmpl* **los A.** the Appalachians

**apalancamiento** *nm* (**a**) *Econ* leverage (**b**) *muy Fam* lounging (about)

**apalancar** [61] **1** *vt (para abrir)* to lever open; *(para mover)* to lever; *muy Fam* **se pasó la tarde apalancada delante del televisor** she spent the afternoon lounging in front of the television
**2 apalancarse** *vpr muy Fam (apoltronarse)* to install oneself

**apalear** *vt* to beat up

**apañado, -a** *adj Fam (hábil, mañoso)* clever, resourceful; **estar a.** to have had it; **¡estamos apañados!** we've had it!

**apañar** *Fam* **1** *vt* (**a**) *(reparar)* to mend (**b**) *(amañar)* to fix, to arrange
**2 apañarse** *vpr* to cope, to manage; **se apaña con muy poco dinero** she gets by on very little money; **apañárselas (para hacer algo)** tó manage (to do sth)

**apaño** *nm Fam* (**a**) *(reparación)* patch (**b**) *(chanchullo)* fix, shady deal (**c**) *(acuerdo)* compromise

**apapachado, -a** *adj Méx* pampered, spoilt

**apapachador, -ora** *adj Méx* comforting

**apapachar** *vt Méx* to cuddle

**apapachos** *nmpl Méx* cuddles

**aparador** *nm* (**a**) *(mueble)* sideboard (**b**) *(escaparate)* shop window

**aparato** *nm* (**a**) *(máquina)* machine; *(electrodoméstico)* appliance; **aparatos de laboratorio** laboratory apparatus (**b**) *(dispositivo)* device (**c**) *(teléfono)* **¿quién está al a.?** who's speaking? **(d)** *(avión)* plane **(e)** *Med (prótesis)* aid; *(para dientes)* brace **(f)** *Anat* system **(g)** *Pol* machinery **(h)** *(ostentación)* pomp, ostentation

**aparatoso, -a** *adj* **(a)** *(ostentoso)* ostentatious, showy **(b)** *(espectacular)* spectacular

**aparcacoches** *nmf inv (en hotel, discoteca)* parking valet

**aparcamiento** *nm (estacionamiento) Br* car park, *US* parking lot; *(hueco)* parking place; **a. subterráneo** underground car park

**aparcar** [61] **1** *vt (estacionar)* to park; *Fig (posponer)* to shelve

**2** *vi* to park

**aparcero, -a** *nm,f* sharecropper

**apareamiento** *nm* mating

**aparear 1** *vt (animales)* to mate

**2 aparearse** *vpr (animales)* to mate

**aparecer** [48] **1** *vi (ante la vista)* to appear; *(algo perdido)* to turn up; **a. por** *(lugar)* to turn up at

**2 aparecerse** *vpr* to appear; **se le apareció la Virgen** the Virgin Mary appeared to him; *Fig* he had a real stroke of luck

**aparecido, -a** *nm,f* ghost

**aparejado, -a** *adj* **llevar** *o* **traer a.** *(conllevar)* to entail

**aparejador, -ora** *nm,f* quantity surveyor

**aparejar** *vt* **(a)** *(preparar)* to get ready, to prepare **(b)** *(caballerías)* to harness **(c)** *Náut* to rig (out)

**aparejo** *nm* **(a)** *(de caballerías)* harness **(b)** *(de pesca)* tackle **(c)** *Tec* block and tackle **(d)** *Náut* rigging; **aparejos** equipment

**aparentar 1** *vt* **(a)** *(parecer)* to look, to seem; **no aparenta más de treinta** she doesn't look more than thirty **(b)** *(fingir)* to feign; **aparentó estar enfadado** he pretended to be angry, he feigned anger

**2** *vi (presumir)* to show off; **viste así sólo para a.** she just dresses like that to show off

**aparente** *adj* **(a)** *(falso, supuesto)* apparent **(b)** *(visible)* visible **(c)** *(llamativo)* striking

**aparentemente** *adv* apparently, seemingly

**aparición** *nf (de persona, cosa)* appearance; *(de ser sobrenatural)* apparition

**apariencia** *nf* **(a)** *(aspecto)* appearance; **en a.** apparently; **guardar las apariencias** to keep up appearances; **las apariencias engañan** appearances can be deceptive **(b)** *(falsedad)* illusion

**aparque** *etc ver* **aparcar**

**apartado, -a 1** *adj* **(a)** *(separado)* **a. de** away from **(b)** *(alejado)* remote

**2** *nm (párrafo)* paragraph; *(sección)* section; **a. de correos** PO Box

**apartamento** *nm* apartment

**apartar 1** *vt* **(a)** *(alejar)* to move away; *(quitar)* to remove **(b)** *(separar)* to separate **(c)** *(escoger)* to take, to select

**2 apartarse** *vpr* **(a)** *(hacerse a un lado)* to move to one side, to move out of the way; **se apartó para dejarme pasar** he stood aside to let me pass **(b)** *(separarse)* to separate, to move away from each other; **apartarse de** *(grupo, lugar)* to move away from; *(tema)* to get away from; *(mundo, sociedad)* to cut oneself off from; **nos apartamos de la carretera** we left the road

**aparte 1** *adv* **(a)** *(en otro lugar, a un lado)* aside, to one side; **bromas a.** joking apart **(b)** *(además)* besides; **a. de feo...** besides being ugly... **(c)** *(por separado)* separately; **a. de** *(excepto)* apart from, except from

**2** *adj inv* separate; **ser caso a.** to be a different matter

**3** *nm* **(a)** *(párrafo)* new paragraph **(b)** *Teatro* aside

**apartheid** [apar'xeið] *(pl* **apartheids)** *nm Pol* apartheid

**apartotel, aparthotel** *nm* hotel apartments

**apasionado, -a 1** *adj* passionate

**2** *nm,f* lover, enthusiast

**apasionante** *adj* fascinating

**apasionar 1** *vt* to fascinate; **le apasiona la música** he's mad about music

**2 apasionarse** *vpr* to get excited; **apasionarse por** to be mad about

**apatía** *nf* apathy

**apático, -a 1** *adj* apathetic

**2** *nm,f* apathetic person

**apátrida 1** *adj* stateless

**2** *nmf* stateless person

**apdo.** *(abrev de* **apartado)** PO Box; **a. de correos 8000** PO Box 8000

**apeadero** *nm (de tren)* halt

**apear 1** *vt* **(a)** *(bajar)* to take down **(b)** *Fam (disuadir)* **a. a alguien de** to talk sb out of; **no pudimos apearle de su idea** we couldn't get him to give up his idea

**2 apearse** *vpr* **(a)** *(bajarse)* **apearse (de)** *(tren)* to alight (from), to get off; *(coche, autobús)* to get out (of); *(caballo)* to dismount (from) **(b)** *Fam* **apearse de** *(abandonar)* *(idea)* to give up; *Fam Fig* **apearse del burro** to back down

**apechugar** [40] *vi Fam* **a. con** to put up with

**apedrear** *vt (persona)* to stone; *(cosa)* to throw stones at

**apegarse** [40] *vpr* **a. a** to become fond of

**apego** *nm* fondness, attachment; **tener/tomar a. a** to be/become fond of

**apelación** *nf* appeal

**apelar** *vi* (a) *Der* to (lodge an) appeal; **a. ante/contra** to appeal to/against (b) *(recurrir)* **a. a** *(persona)* to go to; *(sentido común, bondad)* to appeal to; *(violencia)* to resort to

**apelativo** *nm* name

**apellidarse** *vpr* **se apellida Suárez** her surname is Suárez

**apellido** *nm* surname

**apelmazado, -a** *adj* *(pelo)* matted; *(arroz, bizcocho)* stodgy; **el jersey está todo a.** the jumper has lost its fluffiness

**apelmazar** [16] **1** *vt* *(jersey, pelo)* to matt; *(arroz, bizcocho)* to make stodgy

**2 apelmazarse** *vpr* *(jersey, pelo)* to get matted; *(arroz, bizcocho)* to go stodgy

**apelotonar 1** *vt* to bundle up

**2 apelotonarse** *vpr* *(gente)* to crowd together

**apenado, -a** *adj* (a) *(entristecido)* sad (b) *Méx (avergonzado)* ashamed, embarrassed

**apenar 1** *vt (entristecer)* to sadden

**2 apenarse** *vpr* (a) *(entristecerse)* to be saddened (b) *CAm, Méx (avergonzarse)* to be ashamed, to be embarrassed

**apenas** *adv* (a) *(casi no)* scarcely, hardly; **a. me puedo mover** I can hardly move (b) *(tan sólo)* only; **hace a. dos minutos** only two minutes ago (c) *(tan pronto como)* as soon as; **a. llegó, sonó el teléfono** no sooner had he arrived than the phone rang

**apencar** [61] *vi* *Fam* **a. con** *(trabajo)* to take on; *(responsabilidad)* to shoulder; *(consecuencias, dificultad)* to live with

**apéndice** *nm también Anat* appendix

**apendicitis** *nf inv Med* appendicitis

**Apeninos** *nmpl* **los A.** the Appenines

**apercibir 1** *vt* *(reprender, advertir)* to reprimand, to give a warning to; *Der* to issue with a warning

**2 apercibirse** *vpr* **apercibirse de algo** to notice sth; **no se apercibió de mi llegada** he didn't notice my arrival

**apergaminado, -a** *adj* *(piel, papel)* parchment-like

**apergaminarse** *vpr* *(piel)* to become parchment-like

**aperitivo** *nm* *(bebida)* aperitif; *(comida)* appetizer

**apero** *nm* tool; **aperos (de labranza)** farming implements

**apertura** *nf* (a) *(acción de abrir)* opening; *(de año académico, temporada)* start (b) *Dep (en rugby)* kick-off; *(en ajedrez)* opening (move) (c) *Pol (liberalización)* liberalization

**aperturismo** *nm* *Pol* progressive policies

**aperturista** *adj & nmf* *Pol* progressive

**apesadumbrado, -a** *adj* *(apenado)* grieving, sorrowful

**apesadumbrar 1** *vt* to sadden

**2 apesadumbrarse** *vpr* to be saddened

**apestar 1** *vi* to stink (**a** of); **huele que apesta** it stinks to high heaven

**2** *vt* (a) *(hacer que huela mal)* to infest, to stink out (b) *(contagiar la peste)* to infect with the plague

**apestoso, -a** *adj* foul

**apetecer** [48] **1** *vi* **¿te apetece un café?** do you fancy a coffee?; **me apetece salir** I feel like going out

**2** *vt* **tenían todo cuanto apetecían** they had everything they wanted

**apetecible** *adj* *(comida)* appetizing, tempting; *(vacaciones)* desirable

**apetito** *nm* appetite; **abrir el a.** to whet one's appetite; **perder el a.** to lose one's appetite; **tener a.** to be hungry

**apetitoso, -a** *adj* (a) *(comida)* appetizing (b) *(oferta, empleo)* tempting

**apiadar 1** *vt* to earn the pity of

**2 apiadarse** *vpr* to show compassion; **apiadarse de** to take pity on

**ápice** *nm* (a) *(vértice)* (de montaña) peak; *(de hoja, lengua)* tip (b) *Fig (punto culminante)* peak, height (c) *Fig (pizca)* iota; **ni un á.** not a single bit; **no cedió un á.** he didn't budge an inch

**apicultor, -ora** *nm,f* beekeeper

**apicultura** *nf* beekeeping

**apilar 1** *vt* to pile up

**2 apilarse** *vpr* to pile up

**apiñado, -a** *adj* *(apretado)* packed, crammed

**apiñar 1** *vt* to pack

**2 apiñarse** *vpr* *(agolparse)* to crowd together; *(para protegerse, por miedo)* to huddle together; **apiñarse en torno a alguien/algo** to huddle round sb/sth

**apio** *nm* celery

**apisonadora** *nf* steamroller

**apisonar** *vt* *(con vehículo apisonadora)* to roll; *(con apisonadora manual)* to tamp down

**aplacar** [61] **1** *vt* *(persona, ánimos)* to placate; *(hambre)* to satisfy; *(sed)* to quench; *(dolor)* to ease

**2 aplacarse** *vpr* *(persona, ánimos)* to calm down; *(dolor)* to abate

**aplace** *etc ver* **aplazar**

**aplanar** *vt* to level

**aplaque** *etc ver* **aplacar**

**aplastamiento** *nm* squashing, crushing

**aplastante** *adj* *Fig (apabullante)* overwhelming, devastating

**aplastar** vt (por el peso) to squash, to crush; Fig (derrotar) to crush

**aplatanado, -a** adj Fam listless

**aplatanar** Fam **1** vt to make listless; **este calor me aplatana** this heat makes me feel listless

**2 aplatanarse** vpr to become listless

**aplaudir 1** vt to applaud; **aplaudo su propuesta** I applaud your proposal

**2** vi to applaud, to clap

**aplauso** nm (ovación) round of applause; Fig (alabanza) applause; **aplausos** applause

**aplazamiento** nm postponement

**aplazar** [16] vt to postpone

**aplicable** adj applicable (**a** to)

**aplicación** nf (a) (uso, utilidad) application, use; Informát application (b) (al estudio) application (c) (decoración) appliqué

**aplicado, -a** adj (a) (estudioso) diligent (b) (ciencia) applied

**aplicar** [61] **1** vt (técnica, pintura, teoría) to apply; (nombre, calificativo) to give, to apply

**2 aplicarse** vpr (a) (esmerarse) to apply oneself (**en algo** to sth) (b) (concernir) **aplicarse a** to apply to

**aplique** nm wall lamp

**aplomo** nm composure; **perder el a.** to lose one's composure

**apocado, -a** adj timid

**apocalipsis** nm inv calamity; **A.** Apocalypse

**apocalíptico, -a** adj apocalyptic

**apocamiento** nm timidity

**apocarse** [61] vpr (intimidarse) to be frightened; (humillarse) to humble oneself

**apocopar** vt Gram to apocopate

**apócope** nf Gram apocopation

**apócrifo, -a** adj apocryphal

**apodar 1** vt to nickname

**2 apodarse** vpr to be nicknamed

**apoderado, -a** nm,f (a) Der (official) representative (b) Taurom agent, manager

**apoderar 1** vt (autorizar) to authorize, to empower; Der to grant power of attorney to

**2 apoderarse** vpr **apoderarse de** (adueñarse de) to seize; Fig (dominar) to take hold of, to grip

**apodo** nm nickname

**apogeo** nm height, apogee; **está en (pleno) a.** it is at its height

**apolillado, -a** adj también Fig moth-eaten

**apolillar 1** vt to eat holes in

**2 apolillarse** vpr to get moth-eaten

**apolítico, -a** adj apolitical

**apología** nf apology, eulogy; Der **a. del terrorismo** defence of terrorism

**apoltronarse** vpr (a) (hacerse sedentario) to become less active; **desde que se casaron se han apoltronado mucho** they've been going out a lot less since they got married (b) (acomodarse) **a. en** to lounge in

**apoplejía** nf Med apoplexy

**apoquinar** vt & vi Fam to fork out

**aporrear** vt to bang

**aportación** nf (a) (suministro) provision (b) (contribución) contribution; **hacer una a.** to contribute

**aportar** vt (a) (proporcionar) to provide (b) (contribuir con) to contribute

**aporte** nm contribution; **a. vitamínico** vitamin content

**aposentar 1** vt to put up, to lodge

**2 aposentarse** vpr to take up lodgings

**aposento** nm (a) (habitación) room; Anticuado & Hum **se retiró a sus aposentos** she withdrew (to her chamber) (b) (alojamiento) lodgings

**aposición** nf Gram apposition

**apósito** nm dressing

**aposta** adv on purpose, intentionally

**apostante** nmf person who places a bet

**apostar** [65] **1** vt (a) (jugarse) to bet; **te apuesto una cena a que gana el Madrid** I bet you the price of a dinner that Madrid will win (b) (emplazar) to post

**2** vi to bet (**por** on); **apuesto a que no viene** I bet he doesn't come

**3 apostarse** vpr (a) (jugarse) to bet; **apostarse algo con alguien** to bet sb sth (b) (colocarse) to post oneself

**apóstata** nmf apostate

**a posteriori** adv with hindsight; **habrá que juzgarlo a.** we'll have to judge it after the event

**apostilla** nf (nota) note; (comentario) comment

**apostillar** vt (anotar) to annotate; (añadir) to add

**apóstol** nm también Fig apostle

**apostolado** nm Rel (a) (de apóstol) apostolate (b) (de ideales) mission

**apostólico, -a** adj Rel apostolic

**apóstrofe** nm o nf apostrophe

**apóstrofo** nm Gram apostrophe

**apostura** nf dashing appearance

**apoteósico, -a** adj tremendous

**apoteosis** nf inv (final) grand finale

**apoyabrazos** nm inv armrest

**apoyacabezas** nm inv headrest

**apoyar 1** vt (a) (inclinar) to lean, to rest; **apoya la cabeza en mi hombro** rest your head on my shoulder (b) (respaldar) to support

**2 apoyarse** *vpr* (a) *(sostenerse)* **apoyarse en** to lean on; **la anciana se apoyaba en un bastón** the old woman was leaning on a walking stick (b) *Fig (basarse)* **apoyarse en** *(sujeto: tesis, conclusiones)* to be based on; *(sujeto: persona)* to base one's arguments on (c) *(respaldarse mutuamente)* to support one another

**apoyo** *nm también Fig* support

**APRA** ['apra] *nf (abrev de* **Alianza Popular Revolucionaria Americana)** = Peruvian political party to the centre-right of the political spectrum

**apreciable** *adj* (a) *(perceptible)* appreciable, significant (b) *Fig (estimable)* worthy

**apreciación** *nf* (a) *(estimación)* evaluation, assessment (b) *Fin (de moneda)* appreciation

**apreciado, -a** *adj* (a) *(querido)* esteemed, highly regarded (b) *(valorado)* prized (**por** by)

**apreciar** [15] **1** *vt* (a) *(valorar)* to appreciate; *(sopesar)* to appraise, to evaluate (b) *(sentir afecto por)* to think highly of (c) *(percibir)* to tell, to make out

**2 apreciarse** *vpr Fin (moneda)* to appreciate

**aprecio** *nm* esteem; **sentir a. por alguien** to think highly of sb

**aprehender** *vt* (a) *(coger) (persona)* to apprehend; *(alijo, mercancía)* to seize (b) *(comprender)* to take in

**aprehensión** *nf (de persona)* arrest, capture; *(de alijo, mercancía)* seizure

**apremiante** *adj* pressing, urgent

**apremiar** [15] **1** *vt* (a) *(meter prisa)* **a. a alguien para que haga algo** to urge sb to do sth (b) *(obligar)* **a. a alguien a hacer algo** to compel sb to do sth

**2** *vi (ser urgente)* to be pressing; **¡el tiempo apremia!** we're running out of time, time is short

**apremio** *nm* (a) *(urgencia)* urgency (b) *Der* writ

**aprender 1** *vt (adquirir conocimientos de)* to learn; *(memorizar)* to memorize; *Fig* **aprendieron la lección** they learned their lesson

**2** *vi* to learn (**a hacer algo** to do sth); **¡para que aprendas!** that'll teach you!

**3 aprenderse** *vpr (adquirir conocimientos de)* to learn; *(memorizar)* to memorize; **aprenderse algo de memoria** to learn sth by heart

**aprendiz, -iza** *nm,f* (a) *(ayudante)* apprentice, trainee (b) *(novato)* beginner

**aprendizaje** *nm* (a) *(adquisición de conocimientos)* learning (b) *(tiempo, situación)* apprenticeship

**aprensión** *nf (miedo)* apprehension (**por** about); *(escrúpulo)* squeamishness (**por** about)

**aprensivo, -a** *adj* (a) *(miedoso)* apprehensive (b) *(escrupuloso)* squeamish (c) *(hipocondríaco)* hypochondriac

**apresar** *vt (presa)* to catch; *(delincuente)* to catch, to capture

**aprestar 1** *vt* (a) *(preparar)* to prepare, to get ready (b) *(tela)* to size

**2 aprestarse** *vpr* **aprestarse a hacer algo** to get ready to do sth

**apresto** *nm (rigidez de la tela)* stiffness; *(sustancia)* size; **el almidón da a. a las telas** starch is used to stiffen cloth

**apresurado, -a** *adj* hasty, hurried

**apresuramiento** *nm* haste

**apresurar 1** *vt* to hurry along, to speed up; **a. a alguien para que haga algo** to try to make sb do sth more quickly

**2 apresurarse** *vpr* to hurry; **apresurarse a hacer algo** to rush to do sth; **se apresuró a aclarar que no sabía nada** she was quick to point out that she knew nothing

**apretado, -a** *adj* (a) *(ropa)* tight; *(triunfo)* narrow; *(esprint)* close; *(caligrafía)* cramped (b) *(estrujado)* packed; **íbamos un poco apretados en el coche** it was a bit of a squeeze in the car

**apretar** [3] **1** *vt* (a) *(oprimir) (botón, tecla)* to press; *(gatillo)* to pull, to squeeze; *(nudo, tuerca, cinturón)* to tighten; **el zapato me aprieta** my shoe is pinching (b) *(estrechar)* to squeeze (c) *(juntar) (dientes)* to grit; *(labios)* to press together (d) *Fig (presionar)* to press (e) **a. el paso** to quicken one's pace

**2** *vi (calor, lluvia)* to get worse; *Fam* **a. a correr** to run off

**3 apretarse** *vpr (agolparse)* to crowd together; *(acercarse)* to squeeze up; *Fig* **apretarse el cinturón** to tighten one's belt

**apretón** *nm (estrechamiento)* squeeze; **a. de manos** handshake; **apretones** crush; **hubo apretones para entrar** there was a crush to get in

**apretujar 1** *vt (aplastar)* to squash; *(hacer una bola con)* to screw up

**2 apretujarse** *vpr (en banco, autobús)* to squeeze together; *(por frío)* to huddle up

**apretujón** *nm (abrazo)* bearhug; **hubo apretujones para entrar en el cine** there was a crush to get into the cinema

**apretura** *nf (estrechez)* crush; *Fig* **pasar apreturas** to be hard up

**aprieta** *etc ver* **apretar**

**aprieto** *nm Fig* fix, difficult situation; **poner en un a. a alguien** to put sb in a difficult position; **estar en un a.** to be in a fix

**a priori** *adv* in advance, a priori

**aprisa** *adv* quickly

**aprisionar** *vt* (a) *(encarcelar)* to imprison (b) *(inmovilizar)* **a. a alguien con cadenas** to put sb in chains; **quedaron aprisionados bajo los escombros** they were trapped under the rubble

**aprobación** *nf* approval

**aprobado, -a 1** *adj (aceptado)* approved
**2** *nm Educ* pass

**aprobar** [65] *vt* (a) *(proyecto, moción, medida)* to approve; *(ley)* to pass (b) *(examen, asignatura)* to pass (c) *(comportamiento)* to approve of

**aprobatorio, -a** *adj (gesto, mirada)* approving

**apropiación** *nf (incautación, ocupación)* appropriation; *(robo)* theft; *Der* **a. indebida** embezzlement

**apropiado, -a** *adj* suitable, appropriate

**apropiar** [15] **1** *vt* to adapt (**a** to)
**2 apropiarse** *vpr* **apropiarse de** *(tomar posesión de)* to appropriate; *(robar)* to steal

**aprovechable** *adj* usable

**aprovechado, -a 1** *adj* (a) *(caradura)* **es muy a.** he's always sponging off other people (b) *(bien empleado) (tiempo)* well-spent; *(espacio)* well-planned (c) *(aplicado)* diligent
**2** *nm,f (caradura)* sponger

**aprovechamiento** *nm* (a) *(utilización)* use (b) *(en el estudio)* progress, improvement

**aprovechar 1** *vt* (a) *(tiempo, dinero)* to make the most of; *(oferta, ocasión)* to take advantage of; *(conocimientos, experiencia)* to use, to make use of; **a. que...** to make the most of the fact that... (b) *(lo inservible)* to put to good use
**2** *vi (ser provechoso)* to be beneficial; **¡que aproveche!** enjoy your meal!
**3 aprovecharse** *vpr* to take advantage (**de** of)

**aprovisionamiento** *nm* supplying

**aprovisionar 1** *vt* to supply
**2 aprovisionarse** *vpr* **aprovisionarse de algo** to stock up on sth

**aprox.** *(abrev de* **aproximadamente***)* approx.

**aproximación** *nf* (a) *(acercamiento)* approach; *(en cálculo)* approximation; *Fig (de países)* rapprochement; *(de puntos de vista)* converging (b) *(en lotería)* = consolation prize given to numbers immediately before and after the winning number

**aproximadamente** *adv* approximately

**aproximado, -a** *adj* approximate

**aproximar 1** *vt* to move closer
**2 aproximarse** *vpr* to come closer; **se aproximan las vacaciones** the holidays are getting nearer

**apruebo** *etc ver* **aprobar**

**aptitud** *nf* ability, aptitude; **tener a. para algo** to have an aptitude for sth

**apto, -a** *adj (adecuado, conveniente)* suitable (**para** for); *(capacitado) (intelectualmente)* capable, able; *(físicamente)* fit; *Cine* **a./no a. para menores** suitable/unsuitable for children

**apuesta 1** *ver* **apostar**
**2** *nf* bet

**apuesto, -a** *adj* dashing

**apunar** *Andes* **1** *vt* to cause to have altitude sickness
**2 apunarse** *vpr* to get altitude sickness

**apuntador, -ora** *nm,f Teatro* prompter

**apuntalamiento** *nm también Fig* underpinning

**apuntalar** *vt también Fig* to underpin

**apuntar 1** *vt* (a) *(anotar)* to make a note of, to note down; **a. a alguien** *(en lista)* to put sb down; **apúntamelo (en la cuenta)** put it on my account
(b) *(dirigir) (dedo)* to point; *(arma)* to aim; **a. a alguien** *(con el dedo)* to point at sb; *(con un arma)* to aim at sb
(c) *Teatro* to prompt
(d) *Fig (sugerir)* to hint at; *(indicar)* to point out
**2** *vi* (a) *(vislumbrarse)* to appear; *(día)* to break
(b) *Fig (indicar)* **a.** a to point to; **todo apunta a que ganará Brasil** everything points to a win for Brazil
**3 apuntarse** *vpr* (a) *(en lista)* to put one's name down; *(en curso)* to enrol
(b) *(participar)* to join in (**a hacer algo** doing sth); **yo me apunto** I'm in; *Fam* **ese se apunta a un bombardeo** he's game for anything
(c) *(tantos, éxitos)* to score, to notch up; *Fam* **¡apúntate diez!** *(al acertar)* bingo!, bang on!

**apunte** *nm* (a) *(nota)* note (b) *(boceto)* sketch (c) *Com* entry (d) *Teatro* prompt; **apuntes** *(en colegio, universidad)* notes; **tomar apuntes** to take notes

**apuñalamiento** *nm* stabbing

**apuñalar** *vt* to stab

**apurado, -a** *adj (necesitado)* in need; **a. de** short of (b) *(avergonzado)* embarrassed (c) *(difícil)* awkward, difficult; **una situación apurada** a tricky situation

**apurar 1** *vt* (a) *(agotar)* to finish off; *(existencias, la paciencia)* to exhaust (b) *(meter prisa)* to hurry (c) *(preocupar)* to trouble (d) *(avergonzar)* to embarrass
**2 apurarse** *vpr* (a) *(preocuparse)* to worry (**por** about) (b) *(darse prisa)* to hurry

**apuro** *nm* (a) *(dificultad)* fix, difficult situation; **estar en un a.** to be in a tight spot (b) *(penuria)* **pasar apuros** to undergo *o* experience hardship (c) *(vergüenza)* embarrassment; **me da a.**

**(decírselo)** I'm embarrassed (to tell her) **(d)** *Am (prisa)* **tener a.** to be in a hurry

**aquejado, -a** *adj* **a. de** suffering from

**aquejar** *vt* to afflict; **le aquejan varias enfermedades** he suffers from a number of illnesses

**aquel, aquella** (*pl* **aquellos, -ellas**) *adj demostrativo* that; *(plural)* those

**aquél, -élla** (*pl* **aquéllos, -éllas**)

---

Note that **aquél** and its various forms can be written without an accent when there is no risk of confusion with the adjective.

---

*pron demostrativo* **(a)** *(ese)* that (one); *(plural)* those (ones); **este cuadro me gusta pero a. del fondo no** I like this picture, but I don't like that one at the back; **a. fue mi último día en Londres** that was my last day in London

**(b)** *(nombrado antes)* the former; **teníamos un coche y una moto, ésta estropeada y a. sin gasolina** we had a car and a motorbike, the former was out of petrol, the latter had broken down

**(c)** *(con oraciones relativas)* whoever, anyone who; **a. que quiera hablar que levante la mano** whoever wishes *o* anyone wishing to speak should raise their hand; **aquéllos que...** those who...

**aquelarre** *nm* coven

**aquella** *ver* **aquel**

**aquélla** *ver* **aquél**

**aquello** *pron demostrativo* that; **no consiguió saber si a. lo dijo en serio** he never found out whether she meant those words *o* that seriously; **a. de su mujer es una mentira** all that about his wife is a lie

**aquellos, -ellas** *ver* **aquel**

**aquéllos, -éllas** *ver* **aquél**

**aquí** *adv* **(a)** *(indica lugar)* here; **a. abajo/arriba** down/up here; **a. dentro/fuera** in/out here; **a. mismo** right here; **a. y allá** here and there; **de a. para allá** *(de un lado a otro)* to and fro; **por a.** over here

**(b)** *(ahora)* now; **de a. a mañana** between now and tomorrow; **de a. a poco** shortly, soon; **de a. a un mes** a month from now, in a month

**(c)** *(en tiempo pasado)* **a. empezaron los problemas** that was when the problems started

**(d)** **de a. que** *(por eso)* hence, therefore

**aquiescencia** *nf Formal* approval

**aquietar 1** *vt* to calm down

**2 aquietarse** *vpr* to calm down

**aquilatar** *vt (metales, joyas)* to assay; *Fig (examinar)* to assess

**aquilino, -a** *adj (nariz)* aquiline

**ara** *nf Formal (losa)* altar stone; *(altar)* altar; **en aras de** for the sake of

**árabe 1** *adj* Arab, Arabian

**2** *nmf (persona)* Arab

**3** *nm (lengua)* Arabic

**arabesco** *nm* arabesque

**Arabia Saudí, Arabia Saudita** *n* Saudi Arabia

**arábigo, -a** *adj (de Arabia)* Arab, Arabian; *(numeración)* Arabic

**arácnido** *nm* arachnid

**arado** *nm* plough; *Fam* **es más bruto** *o* **bestia que un a.** he's a complete Neanderthal

**Aragón** *n* Aragon

**aragonés, -esa** *adj & nm,f* Aragonese

**Aral** *nm* **el mar de A.** the Aral Sea

**arameo** *nm (lengua)* Aramaic

**arancel** *nm Com* tariff; **a. aduanero** customs duty

**arancelario, -a** *adj Com* tariff; **barreras (no) arancelarias** (non) tariff barriers

**arándano** *nm* bilberry, blueberry

**arandela** *nf (pieza)* washer

**araña** *nf* **(a)** *(animal)* spider; **a. de mar** spider crab **(b)** *(lámpara)* chandelier

**arañar** *vt (raspar)* to scratch; *Fig (reunir)* to scrape together

**arañazo** *nm* scratch

**arar** *vt* to plough

**araucaria** *nf* monkey-puzzle tree

**araucano, -a** *adj & nm,f* Araucanian

**arbitraje** *nm* **(a)** *Dep (en fútbol, baloncesto)* refereeing; *(en tenis, voleibol)* umpiring **(b)** *Der* arbitration

**arbitral** *adj* **(a)** *Dep* **una polémica decisión a.** a controversial decision by the referee **(b)** *Der* **procedimiento a.** arbitration process

**arbitrar 1** *vt* **(a)** *Dep (en fútbol, baloncesto)* to referee; *(en tenis, voleibol)* to umpire **(b)** *(medidas, recursos)* to bring together **(c)** *Der* to arbitrate

**2** *vi* **(a)** *Dep (en fútbol, baloncesto)* to referee; *(en tenis, voleibol)* to umpire **(b)** *Der* to arbitrate

**arbitrariedad** *nf* **(a)** *(cualidad)* arbitrariness **(b)** *(acción)* arbitrary action

**arbitrario, -a** *adj* arbitrary

**arbitrio** *nm (decisión)* judgment; **dejar algo al a. de alguien** to leave sth to sb's discretion; **arbitrios** *(impuestos)* taxes

**árbitro, -a** *nm,f* **(a)** *Dep* referee; *(en tenis, críquet)* umpire **(b)** *Der* arbitrator

**árbol** *nm* **(a)** tree; **á. de Navidad** Christmas tree; **á. genealógico** family tree **(b)** *Tec* shaft; **á. de levas** camshaft **(c)** *Náut* mast

**arbolado, -a 1** *adj* **(a)** *(terreno)* wooded; *(calle)* tree-lined **(b)** *(mar)* tempestuous

**2** *nm* woodland

**arboladura** *nf Náut* masts and spars

**arboleda** *nf* wood

**arbotante** *nm Arquit* flying buttress

**arbusto** *nm* bush, shrub

**arca** *nf* (a) *(arcón)* chest; *Fig* **arcas** *(fondos)* coffers; *Fig* **las arcas públicas** the Treasury (b) *(barco)* **a. de Noé** Noah's Ark

**arcabuz** *nm* arquebus

**arcada** *nf* (a) *(de estómago)* **me dieron arcadas** I retched (b) *Arquit (arcos)* arcade; *(de puente)* arch

**arcaico, -a** *adj* archaic

**arcaísmo** *nm* archaism

**arcángel** *nm* archangel

**arcano, -a 1** *adj* arcane
**2** *nm (misterio)* mystery

**arce** *nm* maple

**arcén** *nm (de autopista)* hard shoulder; *(de carretera)* verge

**archiconocido, -a** *adj* very well-known

**archiduque, -esa** *nm,f* archduke, *f* archduchess

**archimillonario, -a** *nm,f* multimillionaire

**archipiélago** *nm* archipelago

**archisabido, -a** *adj* very well-known

**archivador, -ora 1** *nm,f* archivist
**2** *nm (mueble)* filing cabinet

**archivar** *vt también Informát* to file; *Fig (olvidar)* to push to the back of one's mind

**archivo** *nm* (a) *(lugar)* archive; *(documentos)* archives; *TV* **imágenes de a.** library pictures (b) *(informe, ficha)* file (c) *Informát* file

**arcilla** *nf* clay

**arcipreste** *nm* archpriest

**arco** *nm* (a) *también Arquit (forma)* arch; **a. de herradura/de medio punto/apuntado** horseshoe/semicircular/Gothic arch; **a. triunfal** triumphal arch; **a. iris** rainbow (b) *Dep, Mil & Mús* bow (c) *Mat* arc (d) *Dep (portería)* goal, goalmouth

**arcón** *nm* large chest

**arder** *vi (con llama)* to burn; *(sin llama)* to smoulder; *Fig* **a. de** to burn with; *Fig* **está que arde** *(persona)* he's fuming; *(reunión)* it's getting pretty heated; *Fig* **a. en deseos de hacer algo** to be dying to do sth; **la ciudad ardía en fiestas** the city was one great party

**ardid** *nm* ruse, trick

**ardiente** *adj (en llamas)* burning; *(líquido)* scalding; *Fig (deseo)* burning; *Fig (admirador, defensor)* ardent

**ardilla** *nf* squirrel

**ardite** *nm* **no vale un a.** it isn't worth a brass farthing

**ardor** *nm (calor)* heat; *(quemazón)* burning (sensation); *Fig (entusiasmo)* fervour; **a. de estómago** heartburn

**arduo, -a** *adj* arduous

**área** *nf* (a) *(superficie, zona, ámbito)* area; **á. metropolitana/de servicio** metropolitan/service area; *Econ* **á. de libre cambio** free exchange area (b) *(medida)* are, = 100 square metres (c) *Dep* **á. (de penalty o castigo)** (penalty) area

**arena** *nf* (a) *(de playa)* sand; **arenas movedizas** quicksand (b) *(escenario de la lucha)* arena; **la a. política** the political arena (c) *Taurom* bullring

**arenal** *nm* area of sandy ground

**arenga** *nf* harangue

**arengar** [40] *vt* to harangue

**arenilla** *nf (polvo)* dust; **arenillas** *(cálculos de la vejiga)* bladder stones

**arenisca** *nf* sandstone

**arenoso, -a** *adj* sandy

**arenque** *nm* herring

**arepa** *nf Am* = pancake made of maize flour

**arete** *nm Andes, Méx* earring

**argamasa** *nf* mortar

**Argel** *n* Algiers

**Argelia** *n* Algeria

**argelino, -a** *adj & nm,f* Algerian

**argentífero, -a** *adj* silver-bearing

**Argentina** *nf* **(la) A.** Argentina

**argentinismo** *nm* = word peculiar to Argentinian Spanish

**argentino, -a** *adj & nm,f* Argentinian

**argolla** *nf* (a) *(aro)* (large) ring (b) *Am (alianza)* wedding ring

**argonauta** *nm* Argonaut

**argot** ( *pl* **argots**) *nm (popular)* slang; *(técnico)* jargon

**argucia** *nf* sophism

**argüir** [9] **1** *vt* (a) *Formal (argumentar)* to argue (b) *(demostrar)* to prove, to demonstrate (c) *(deducir)* to deduce
**2** *vi (argumentar)* to argue

**argumentación** *nf* line of argument

**argumentar 1** *vt (alegar)* to argue (**que** that); **no argumentó bien su hipótesis** he didn't argue his theory very well
**2** *vi (discutir)* to argue

**argumento** *nm* (a) *(razonamiento)* argument (b) *(trama)* plot

**argüya** *ver* **argüir**

**argüyera** *ver* **argüir**

**aria** *nf (de ópera)* aria

**aridez** *nf (de terreno, clima)* aridity, dryness

**árido, -a 1** *adj (terreno, clima)* arid, dry; *Fig (libro, tema)* dry
  **2** *nmpl* **áridos** dry goods

**aries 1** *nm inv* Aries; **ser a.** to be (an) Aries
  **2** *nmf inv (persona)* Aries

**ariete** *nm Hist & Mil* battering ram; *Fig Dep* centre forward

**ario, -a** *adj & nm,f* Aryan

**arisco, -a** *adj* surly

**arista** *nf* edge

**aristocracia** *nf* aristocracy

**aristócrata** *nmf* aristocrat

**aristocrático, -a** *adj* aristocratic

**aristotélico, -a** *adj & nm,f Filosofía* Aristotelian

**aritmética** *nf* arithmetic; **a. parlamentaria** parliamentary arithmetic

**aritmético, -a** *adj* arithmetic(al)

**arlequín** *nm* harlequin

**arma** *nf (instrumento)* arm, weapon; *Fig (medio)* weapon; **presentar/rendir armas** to present/surrender arms; **a. arrojadiza** = hand-hurled projectile such as spear or stone; **alzarse en armas** to rise up in arms; *Fig* **a. de doble filo** double-edged sword; *Fig* **ser de armas tomar** to be someone to be reckoned with; **las armas** *(profesión)* the military career, the Army; **a. blanca** blade *(weapon with a sharp blade)*; **a. de fuego** firearm; **a. homicida** murder weapon; **a. nuclear** nuclear weapon; **a. química** chemical weapon

**armada** *nf (marina)* navy; *(escuadra)* fleet; **la A.** the Navy; *Hist* **la A. Invencible** the Spanish Armada

**armadillo** *nm* armadillo

**armado, -a** *adj* **(a)** *(con armas)* armed **(b)** *(con armazón)* reinforced

**armador, -ora** *nm,f (dueño)* shipowner; *(constructor)* shipbuilder

**armadura** *nf* **(a)** *(de guerrero)* armour **(b)** *(de barco, tejado)* framework

**armamentista, armamentístico, -a** *adj* arms; **carrera armamentista** arms race

**armamento** *nm* **(a)** *(armas)* arms **(b)** *(acción)* arming

**armar 1** *vt* **(a)** *(montar) (mueble, modelo)* to assemble; *(tienda)* to pitch **(b)** *(ejército, personas)* to arm **(c)** *(fusil, pistola)* to load **(d)** *Fig (lío, escándalo)* to cause; **armarla** to cause trouble
  **2 armarse** *vpr* **(a)** *(con armas)* to arm oneself; *Fig* **armarse de** *(valor, paciencia)* to summon up **(b)** *(organizarse)* **se armó un gran escándalo** there was a huge fuss; *Fam* **se armó la gorda** *o* **la de Troya** all hell broke loose

**armario** *nm (para objetos)* cupboard; *(para ropa)* wardrobe; **a. empotrado** fitted cupboard/wardrobe

**armatoste** *nm (mueble, objeto)* unwieldy object; *(máquina)* contraption

**armazón** *nf (estructura)* framework, frame; *(de avión, coche)* chassis; *(de edificio)* skeleton

**Armenia** *n* Armenia

**armenio, -a** *adj & nm,f* Armenian

**armería** *nf* **(a)** *(depósito)* armoury **(b)** *(tienda)* gunsmith's (shop) **(c)** *(arte)* gunsmith's craft

**armero** *nm (fabricante)* gunsmith; *Mil* armourer

**armiño** *nm (piel)* ermine; *(animal)* stoat

**armisticio** *nm* armistice

**armonía** *nf* harmony

**armónica** *nf* harmonica

**armónico, -a 1** *adj* harmonic
  **2** *nm Mús* harmonic

**armonio** *nm* harmonium

**armonioso, -a** *adj* harmonious

**armonización** *nf* harmonization

**armonizar [16] 1** *vt* **(a)** *(concordar)* to match; **a. las políticas de los Estados miembros** to harmonize the policies of the member states **(b)** *Mús* to harmonize
  **2** *vi (concordar)* **a. con** to match

**ARN** *nm (abrev de* **ácido ribonucleico***)* RNA

**arnés** *(pl* **arneses***) nm* armour; **arneses** *(de animales)* trappings, harness

**árnica** *nf* arnica

**aro** *nm* **(a)** *(círculo)* hoop; *Tec* ring; **los aros olímpicos** the Olympic rings; *Fig* **pasar por el a.** to knuckle under; **un sostén de aros** an underwired bra **(b)** *Am (pendiente)* earring

**aroma** *nm (olor)* aroma; *(de vino)* bouquet; **a. artificial** artificial flavouring

**aromático, -a** *adj* aromatic

**aromatizante** *nm* flavouring

**aromatizar [16]** *vt (con perfume)* to perfume; *(comida)* to flavour

**arpa** *nf* harp; **a. de boca** Jew's harp

**arpegio** *nm Mús* arpeggio

**arpía** *nf Mitol* harpy; *Fig* old hag

**arpillera** *nf* sackcloth, hessian

**arpón** *nm* harpoon

**arponear** *vt* to harpoon

**arquear 1** *vt (madera)* to warp; *(vara, fusta)* to flex; *(cejas, espalda)* to arch; **el gato arqueó el lomo** the cat arched its back
  **2 arquearse** *vpr* to warp

**arqueo** *nm* **(a)** *(de cejas, espalda, lomo)* arching **(b)** *Com* cashing up **(c)** *Náut* registered tonnage

**arqueología** *nf* archeology

**arqueológico, -a** *adj* archeological

**arqueólogo, -a** *nm,f* archeologist

**arquero** *nm* (a) *Dep & Mil* archer (b) *(tesorero)* treasurer (c) *Dep (portero)* goalkeeper

**arquetípico, -a** *adj* archetypal

**arquetipo** *nm* archetype

**arquitecto, -a** *nm,f* architect

**arquitectónico, -a** *adj* architectural

**arquitectura** *nf también Informát* architecture

**arquitrabe** *nm Arquit* architrave

**arquivolta** *nf Arquit* archivolt

**arrabal** *nm (barrio pobre)* slum; *(barrio periférico)* outlying district

**arrabalero, -a 1** *adj* (a) *(periférico)* outlying (b) *(barriobajero)* rough, coarse

  **2** *nm,f (barriobajero)* rough o coarse person

**arracimarse** *vpr* to cluster together

**arraigado, -a** *adj (costumbre, idea)* deeply rooted; *(persona)* established

**arraigar** [40] **1** *vt* to establish

  **2** *vi también Fig* to take root

  **3 arraigarse** *vpr (establecerse)* to settle down

**arraigo** *nm* roots; **tener mucho a.** to be deeply rooted

**arrancada** *nf* sudden start

**arrancar** [61] **1** *vt* (a) *(sacar de su sitio) (árbol)* to uproot; *(malas hierbas, flor)* to pull up; *(cable, página, pelo)* to tear out; *(cartel, cortinas)* to tear down; *(muela)* to pull out, to extract; *(ojos)* to gouge out; *Fig* **a. a alguien de un sitio** to shift sb from somewhere

  (b) *(arrebatar)* **a. algo a alguien** to grab o snatch sth from sb

  (c) *(poner en marcha) (coche, máquina)* to start; *Informát* to start up, to boot (up)

  (d) *Fig (obtener)* **a. algo a alguien** *(confesión, promesa, secreto)* to extract sth from sb; *(sonrisa, dinero, ovación)* to get sth out of sb; *(suspiro, carcajada)* to bring sth from sb

  **2** *vi* (a) *(partir)* to set off

  (b) *(máquina, coche)* to start

  (c) *(provenir)* **a. de** to stem from

  **3 arrancarse** *vpr (salir corriendo)* to rush off

**arranque** *nm* (a) *(comienzo)* start (b) *Aut* starter motor (c) *Fig (arrebato)* fit; **en un a. de ira/generosidad** in a fit of anger/generosity

**arras** *nfpl* (a) *(fianza)* deposit (b) *(en boda)* = coins given by the bridegroom to the bride

**arrasar** *vt* to destroy, to devastate

**arrastrado, -a** *adj Fig* miserable, wretched

**arrastrar 1** *vt* (a) *(objeto, pies) también Informát* to drag; *(carro, vagón)* to pull; **el viento arrastró las hojas** the wind blew the leaves along; *Informát* **a. y soltar** to drag and drop

  (b) *Fig (convencer)* to win over, to sway; **a. a alguien a algo/a hacer algo** to lead sb into sth/to do sth; **dejarse a. por algo/alguien** to

allow oneself to be swayed by sth/sb

  (c) *Fig (producir)* to bring

  (d) *Fig (soportar)* **arrastra una vida miserable** she leads a miserable life; **arrastra muchas deudas/muchos problemas** he has a lot of debts/problems hanging over him

  **2** *vi (rozar el suelo)* to drag along the ground; **te arrastra el vestido** your dress is dragging on the ground

  **3 arrastrarse** *vpr* to crawl; *Fig* to grovel

**arrastre** *nm* (a) *(acarreo)* dragging; *Fam Fig* **estar para el a.** to have had it (b) *(pesca)* trawling

**arrayán** *nm* myrtle

**arre** *interj* **¡a.!** gee up!

**arrear** *vt* (a) *(azuzar)* to gee up (b) *(propinar)* to give; **a. una bofetada a alguien** to give sb a thump (c) *(poner arreos)* to harness

**arrebatado, -a** *adj* (a) *(impetuoso)* impulsive, impetuous (b) *(iracundo)* enraged

**arrebatador, -ora** *adj* captivating

**arrebatar 1** *vt* (a) *(quitar)* **a. algo a alguien** to snatch sth from sb (b) *Fig (cautivar)* to captivate

  **2 arrebatarse** *vpr (enfurecerse)* to get furious

**arrebato** *nm* (a) *(arranque)* fit, outburst; **un a. de amor** a crush (b) *(furia)* rage, fury

**arrebolado, -a** *adj* blushing

**arrebujar 1** *vt* (a) *(amontonar)* to bundle (up) (b) *(arropar)* to wrap up (warmly)

  **2 arrebujarse** *vpr (arroparse)* to wrap oneself up; *(encogerse)* to huddle up

**arrechar** *CAm, Méx muy Fam* **1** *vt* to make horny, to turn on

  **2 arrecharse** *vpr* to get horny

**arrecho, -a** *adj CAm, Méx Vulg* horny, randy

**arrechucho** *nm Fam* **me dio un a.** I was ill, I wasn't feeling too well

**arreciar** [15] **1** *vi (temporal, lluvia)* to get worse; *Fig (críticas)* to intensify

  **2 arreciarse** *vpr* to intensify; *Am* **se arrecia el viento** the wind is growing stronger

**arrecife** *nm* reef

**arredrar 1** *vt* to put off, to frighten off; **no le arredra nada** nothing puts him off

  **2 arredrarse** *vpr* **arredrarse ante** to be put o frightened off by

**arreglado, -a** *adj* (a) *(reparado)* fixed, repaired; *(ropa)* mended (b) *(ordenado)* tidy (c) *(bien vestido)* smart (d) *(solucionado)* sorted out; **¡y asunto a.!** that's that!; *Fig* **estamos arreglados** we're really done for (e) *Fig (precio)* reasonable

**arreglar 1** *vt* (a) *(reparar)* to fix, to repair; *(ropa) (estrechar)* to take in; *(agrandar)* to let out (b) *(ordenar)* to tidy (up) (c) *(solucionar)* to sort out (d) *Mús* to arrange (e) *(acicalar)* to smarten up; (cabello) to do (**f**) (adornar) to decorate (**g**) Fam (escarmentar) **¡ya te arreglaré yo!** I'm going to sort you out!

**2 arreglarse** vpr (**a**) (asunto, problema) to sort itself out; (apañarse) to make do (**con algo** with sth); **arreglárselas (para hacer algo)** to manage (to do sth) (**b**) (acicalarse) to smarten up

**arreglista** nmf Mús (musical) arranger

**arreglo** nm (**a**) (reparación) mending, repair; (de ropa) **hacer un a. a** (estrechar) to take in; (agrandar) to let out (**b**) (solución) settlement (**c**) (acuerdo) agreement; **llegar a un a.** to reach agreement; **con a. a** in accordance with; **un a. pacífico de las diferencias** an amicable settlement of differences (**d**) Mús **arreglos musicales** musical arrangements

**arrejuntarse** vpr muy Fam (pareja) to shack up together

**arrellanarse** vpr to settle back

**arremangado, -a** adj rolled-up

**arremangar** [40] Fam **1** vt to roll up

**2 arremangarse** vpr to roll up one's sleeves

**arremeter** vi **a. contra** to attack

**arremetida** nf attack

**arremolinarse** vpr (agua, hojas) to swirl (about); Fig (personas) **a. alrededor de** o **en torno a** to mill round about, to crowd round

**arrendador, -ora** nm,f Der lessor

**arrendamiento** nm Der (**a**) (acción) renting, leasing; **contrato de a.** lease (**b**) (precio) rent

**arrendar** [3] vt Der (**a**) (dar en arriendo) to let, to lease (**b**) (tomar en arriendo) to rent, to lease; Am **se arrienda** (en letrero) for o to rent

**arrendatario, -a** Der **1** adj leasing

**2** nm,f leaseholder, tenant

**arreos** nmpl harness

**arrepanchigarse** [40] vpr Fam to stretch out, to sprawl

**arrepentido, -a 1** adj repentant

**2** nm,f (**a**) Rel penitent (**b**) Pol = person who renounces terrorist activities

**arrepentimiento** nm (de pecado, crimen) repentance

**arrepentirse** [64] vpr (**a**) (lamentar) (de acción) to regret it; (de pecado, crimen) to repent; **a. de algo/de haber hecho algo** (acción) to regret sth/having done sth; (pecado, crimen) to repent (of) sth/having done sth; **ven a Escocia, no te arrepentirás** come to Scotland, you won't regret it (**b**) (volverse atrás) **al final, me arrepentí y no fui** in the end, I decided not to go; **no te arrepientas en el último momento** don't change your mind at the last minute

**arrestado, -a 1** adj under arrest

**2** nm,f detainee, person under arrest

**arrestar** vt to arrest

**arresto** nm (**a**) (detención) arrest; Der **a. domiciliario** house arrest (**b**) **arrestos** courage; **tener arrestos para hacer algo** to have the courage to do sth

**arriar** [34] vt (velas) to lower

**arriate** nm (flower) bed

**arriba 1** adv (**a**) (posición) (en general) above; (en edificio) upstairs; **vive (en el piso de) a.** she lives upstairs; **está aquí/allí a.** it's up here/there; **a. del todo** right at the top; **más a.** further up; Am **a. de** above

(**b**) (dirección) up; **ve a.** (en edificio) go upstairs; **hacia/para a.** up; **calle/escaleras a.** up the street/stairs; **río a.** upstream

(**c**) (en un texto) above; **el a. mencionado…** the above-mentioned…

(**d**) (expresiones) **a. de** more than; **de a.** top; **el estante de a.** the top shelf; **de a. abajo** (cosa) from top to bottom; (persona) from head to toe; **mirar a alguien de a. abajo** (con desdén) to look sb up and down

**2** prep Am **a. (de)** (encima de) on top of

**3** interj **¡a. …!** up (with)…!; **¡a. los mineros!** up (with) the miners!; **¡a. las manos!** hands up!

**arribar** vi to arrive; Náut to reach port

**arribista** adj & nmf arriviste

**arriende** etc ver **arrendar**

**arriendo** nm Der (**a**) (acción) leasing (**b**) (precio) rent

**arriero, -a** nm,f muleteer

**arriesgado, -a** adj (**a**) (peligroso) risky (**b**) (osado) daring

**arriesgar** [40] **1** vt (exponer a peligro) to risk; (proponer) to venture, to suggest

**2 arriesgarse** vpr to take risks/a risk; **no quiero arriesgarme** I don't want to risk it

**arrimar 1** vt (**a**) (acercar) to move o bring closer; **a. algo a algo** (pared, mesa) to move sth up against sth; Fam Fig **a. el hombro** to lend a hand, to muck in (**b**) Fig (arrinconar) to put away

**2 arrimarse** vpr (**a**) (acercarse) to come closer; **arrimaos que no cabemos** move up or we won't all fit in; **arrimarse a algo** (acercándose) to move closer to sth; (apoyándose) to lean on sth (**b**) Fig (ampararse) **arrimarse a alguien** to seek sb's protection; Prov **quien a buen árbol se arrima (buena sombra le cobija)** it pays to have friends in high places

**arrinconado, -a** adj (acorralado) cornered; (abandonado) discarded, forgotten

**arrinconar** vt (**a**) (apartar) to put in a corner; Fig (persona) (dar de lado) to cold-shoulder (**b**) (abandonar) to discard, to put away (**c**) (acorralar) to (back into a) corner

**arritmia** nf Med arrhythmia

**arrítmico, -a** *adj* arrythmic

**arroba** *nf* (a) *(peso)* = 11.5 kg; *Fig* **por arrobas** by the sackful (b) *Informát (en dirección de correo electrónico)* at, @ symbol

**arrobado, -a** *adj* enraptured

**arrobamiento** *nm* rapture

**arrobar 1** *vt* to captivate

**2 arrobarse** *vpr* to go into raptures

**arrobo** *nm* rapture

**arrocero, -a 1** *adj* rice; **una región arrocera** a rice-growing region

**2** *nm,f* rice grower

**arrodillarse** *vpr* to kneel down; *Fig* to go down on one's knees, to grovel

**arrogancia** *nf* arrogance

**arrogante** *adj* arrogant

**arrogarse** [40] *vpr* to assume, to claim for oneself

**arrojado, -a** *adj* bold, fearless

**arrojar 1** *vt* (a) *(lanzar)* to throw; *(con violencia)* to hurl, to fling (b) *(despedir) (humo)* to send out; *(olor)* to give off; *(lava)* to spew out (c) *(echar)* **a. a alguien de** to throw sb out of (d) *(resultado)* to produce, to yield (e) *(vomitar)* to throw up

**2 arrojarse** *vpr* to hurl oneself; **arrojarse en los brazos de alguien** to fling *o* throw oneself at sb

**arrojo** *nm* courage, fearlessness

**arrollador, -ora** *adj* *(victoria, superioridad)* overwhelming; *(belleza, personalidad)* dazzling

**arrollar** *vt* (a) *(enrollar)* to roll (up) (b) *(atropellar)* to knock down, to run over (c) *(tirar) (sujeto: agua, viento)* to sweep away (d) *(vencer)* to crush

**arropar 1** *vt* *(con ropa)* to wrap up; *(en cama)* to tuck up; *Fig (proteger)* to protect

**2 arroparse** *vpr* to wrap oneself up

**arrostrar** *vt* to face up to

**arroyo** *nm* (a) *(riachuelo)* stream (b) *(de la calle)* gutter; *Fig* **sacar a alguien del a.** to drag sb out of the gutter

**arroz** *nm* rice; **a. blanco** boiled rice; **a. integral** brown rice; **a. con leche** rice pudding; *Fig* **¡que si quieres a., Catalina!** for all the good that did!

**arrozal** *nm* paddy field

**arruga** *nf* *(en ropa, papel)* crease; *(en piel)* wrinkle, line

**arrugar** [40] **1** *vt (ropa, papel)* to crease, to crumple; *(piel)* to wrinkle

**2 arrugarse** *vpr* (a) *(ropa)* to get creased; *(piel)* to get wrinkled (b) *Fam Fig (acobardarse)* to be intimidated; **no se arrugaron** they were undaunted

**arruinado, -a** *adj* ruined

**arruinar 1** *vt también Fig* to ruin

**2 arruinarse** *vpr* to go bankrupt, to be ruined

**arrullar 1** *vt* to lull to sleep

**2 arrullarse** *vpr (animales)* to coo; *Fam Fig (personas)* to whisper sweet nothings

**arrullo** *nm (de palomas)* cooing; *(nana)* lullaby; *Fig (de agua, olas)* murmur

**arrumaco** *nm Fam* **hacerse arrumacos** *(amantes)* to be lovey-dovey; **hacer arrumacos a** *(bebé)* to coo at

**arrumbar** *vt* to put away

**arrume** *nm Col* pile

**arsenal** *nm* (a) *(de barcos)* shipyard (b) *(de armas)* arsenal (c) *Fig (de cosas, pruebas)* array

**arsénico** *nm Quím* arsenic

**art.** *(abrev de* **artículo***)* art.

**arte** *nm o nf* (a) *(creación estética)* art; **a. abstracto/figurativo** abstract/figurative art; **a. dramático** drama

(b) *(habilidad)* artistry

(c) *(astucia)* artfulness, cunning; **malas artes** trickery

(d) *(expresiones)* **no tener a. ni parte en** to have nothing whatsoever to do with; **como por a. de birlibirloque** *o* **de magia** as if by magic; **artes gráficas/plásticas** graphic/plastic arts; **artes liberales** liberal arts; **artes marciales** martial arts; **(escuela de) artes y oficios** technical college; **bellas artes** fine arts

**artefacto** *nm (aparato)* device; *(máquina)* machine; **a. explosivo** explosive device

**arteria** *nf también Fig* artery

**arterial** *adj* arterial

**arterioesclerosis, arteriosclerosis** *nf inv Med* arteriosclerosis

**artero, -a** *adj* cunning, sly

**artesa** *nf* trough

**artesanal** *adj (hecho a mano)* handmade

**artesanía** *nf* craftsmanship; **de a.** *(producto)* handmade

**artesano, -a** *nm,f* craftsman, *f* craftswoman

**artesonado** *nm Arquit* coffered ceiling

**ártico, -a 1** *adj* arctic; **el océano Glacial Á.** the Arctic Ocean

**2** *nm* **el Á.** the Arctic

**articulación** *nf* (a) *Anat & Tec* joint (b) *Ling* articulation (c) *(estructuración)* coordination

**articulado, -a** *adj* articulated

**articular** *vt* (a) *(palabras, piezas)* to articulate (b) *(ley, contrato)* to break down into separate articles (c) *(plan, proyecto)* to coordinate

**articulista** *nmf* journalist

**artículo** *nm* (a) *Gram* article; **a. definido** definite article; **a. indefinido** indefinite article (b) *(periodístico)* article; *(de diccionario)* entry; **a.**

**de fondo** editorial (**c**) *Com* article, item; **a. básico** basic product; **a. de importación** import; **a. líder** product leader; **a. de primera necesidad** basic commodity (**d**) *Rel & Fig* **a. de fe** article of faith; **tomar algo como a. de fe** to take sth as gospel

**artifice** *nmf Fig* architect

**artificial** *adj* artificial

**artificiero** *nm (desactivador)* bomb disposal expert

**artificio** *nm* (**a**) *(aparato)* device (**b**) *Fig (falsedad)* artifice; *(artimaña)* trick

**artificioso, -a** *adj Fig (engañoso)* deceptive

**artillería** *nf Mil* artillery

**artillero** *nm Mil* artilleryman

**artilugio** *nm* gadget, contrivance

**artimaña** *nf* trick, ruse

**artista** *nmf (creador)* artist; *(de espectáculos)* artiste; *Fig* **es una a. en la cocina** she is a superb cook

**artístico, -a** *adj* artistic

**artritis** *nf inv Med* arthritis

**artrópodo** *nm Zool* arthropod

**artrosis** *nf inv Med* arthrosis

**arveja** *nf Andes, CSur* pea

**arzobispado** *nm* archbishopric

**arzobispo** *nm* archbishop

**as** *nm* (**a**) *(carta, dado)* ace (**b**) *(campeón)* **un a. del volante** an ace driver; **ser un a.** to be brilliant

**asa** *nf* handle

**asado** *nm* roast

**asador** *nm* (**a**) *(aparato)* roaster (**b**) *(varilla)* spit (**c**) *(restaurante)* grill, grillroom

**asaduras** *nfpl (de cordero, ternera)* offal; *(de pollo, pavo)* giblets

**asaetear** *vt (disparar)* to shoot arrows at; *(matar)* to kill with arrows

**asalariado, -a** *nm,f* salaried employee

**asalariar** [15] *vt* to take on

**asalmonado, -a** *adj* salmon (pink)

**asaltante** *nmf (agresor)* attacker; *(atracador)* robber

**asaltar** *vt* (**a**) *(atacar)* to attack; *(castillo, ciudad)* to storm (**b**) *(robar)* to rob (**c**) *Fig (sujeto: dudas)* to assail (**d**) *(importunar)* to plague

**asalto** *nm* (**a**) *(ataque)* attack; *(de castillo, ciudad)* storming; **tomar algo por a.** to storm sth (**b**) *(robo)* robbery (**c**) *Dep (en boxeo)* round

**asamblea** *nf (reunión)* assembly; *Pol* mass meeting; **a. de trabajadores** works meeting

**asambleario, -a** *adj* reunión **asambleario, -a** *adj* reunión asamblearia full meeting; **decisión asamblearia** decision taken by a meeting

**asar 1** *vt (alimentos) (al horno)* to roast; *(a la parrilla)* to grill; *Fam Fig (importunar)* **a. a al-**

**guien a preguntas** to plague sb with questions

**2 asarse** *vpr Fig* to be boiling hot

**asaz** *adv Anticuado & Hum* very, exceedingly

**ascendencia** *nf (linaje)* descent; *(extracción social)* extraction; *Fig (influencia)* ascendancy

**ascendente 1** *adj* rising

**2** *nm (en astrología)* ascendant

**ascender** [66] **1** *vi* (**a**) *(subir)* to go up, to climb (**b**) *(aumentar, elevarse)* to rise, to go up (**c**) *(en empleo, deportes)* to be promoted (**a** to) (**d**) **a. a** *(totalizar)* to come o amount to

**2** *vt* **a. a alguien** (**a**) *(en empleo, deportes)* to promote sb (to)

**ascendiente 1** *nmf (antepasado)* ancestor

**2** *nm (influencia)* influence

**ascensión** *nf* ascent; *Rel* **A.** Ascension

**ascenso** *nm* (**a**) *(en empleo, deportes)* promotion (**b**) *(a montaña)* ascent

**ascensor** *nm Br* lift, *US* elevator

**ascensorista** *nmf Br* lift attendant, *US* elevator attendant

**asceta** *nmf* ascetic

**ascético, -a** *adj* ascetic

**ascetismo** *nm* asceticism

**ASCII** ['asθi] *nm Informát (abrev de* **American Standard Code for Information Interchange**) ASCII

**asco** *nm (sensación)* revulsion; **siento a.** I feel sick; **¡qué a. de tiempo!** what foul weather!; **me da a.** I find it disgusting; **¡qué a.!** how disgusting!; **tener a. a algo** to find sth disgusting; **hacer ascos a** to turn one's nose up at; *Fam* **estar hecho un a.** *(cosa)* to be filthy; *(persona)* to be a real sight; *Fam* **ser un a.** to be the pits

**ascua** *nf* ember; **siempre quieren arrimar el a. a su sardina** they always put themselves first; **tener a alguien en ascuas** to keep sb on tenterhooks

**aseado, -a** *adj (limpio)* clean; *(arreglado)* smart

**ASEAN** [ase'an] *(abrev de* **asociación de naciones del sudeste asiático)** ASEAN

**asear 1** *vt* to clean

**2 asearse** *vpr* to get washed and dressed

**asechanza** *nf* snare

**asediar** [15] *vt Mil* to lay siege to; *Fig* to pester, to badger

**asedio** *nm Mil* siege; *Fig* pestering, badgering

**asegurado, -a** *nm,f* policy-holder

**asegurador, -ora 1** *adj* insurance; **compañía aseguradora** insurance company

**2** *nm,f* insurer

**asegurar 1** *vt* (**a**) *(fijar)* to secure (**b**) *(garantizar)* to assure; **te lo aseguro** I assure you; **a. a alguien que...** to assure sb that... (**c**) *(contra* *riesgos*) to insure (**contra** against); **a. algo en** (*cantidad*) to insure sth for

**2 asegurarse** *vpr* (**a**) (*cerciorarse*) **asegurarse de que...** to make sure that...; **asegúrate de cerrar la puerta** make sure you close the door (**b**) *Com* to insure oneself, to take out an insurance policy

**asemejar 1** *vi* **a. a** to be similar to, to be like

**2 asemejarse** *vpr* to be similar; **asemejarse a** to be similar to

**asentado, -a** *adj Fig* (*establecido*) settled, established

**asentamiento** *nm* (*de población*) settlement

**asentar** [3] **1** *vt* (**a**) (*instalar*) (*empresa, campamento*) to set up; (*comunidad, pueblo*) to settle (**b**) (*asegurar*) to secure; (*cimientos*) to lay

**2 asentarse** *vpr* (**a**) (*instalarse*) to settle down (**b**) (*sedimentarse*) to settle

**asentimiento** *nm* approval, assent

**asentir** [64] *vi* (**a**) (*estar conforme*) to agree (a to) (**b**) (*afirmar con la cabeza*) to nod

**aseo** *nm* (**a**) (*limpieza*) (*acción*) cleaning; (*cualidad*) cleanliness (**b**) (*habitación*) bathroom; **aseos** *Br* toilets, *US* restroom

**asepsia** *nf Med* asepsis; *Fig* (*indiferencia*) detachment

**aséptico, -a** *adj Med* aseptic; *Fig* (*indiferente*) detached

**asequible** *adj* (**a**) (*accesible, comprensible*) accessible (**b**) (*razonable*) (*precio, producto*) affordable

**aserción** *nf* assertion

**aserradero** *nm* sawmill

**aserrar** [3] *vt* to saw

**aserto** *nm* assertion

**asesinar** *vt* (*persona*) to murder; (*rey, jefe de Estado*) to assassinate

**asesinato** *nm* (*de persona*) murder; (*de rey, jefe de Estado*) assassination

**asesino, -a 1** *adj también Fig* murderous

**2** *nm,f* (*de persona*) murderer, *f* murderess; (*de rey, jefe de Estado*) assassin; **a. a sueldo** hired killer; **a. profesional** professional killer

**asesor, -ora** *nm,f* adviser; *Fin* consultant; **a. de imagen** image consultant; **a. fiscal** tax adviser

**asesoramiento** *nm* advice; *Fin* consultancy

**asesorar 1** *vt* to advise; *Fin* to provide with consultancy services

**2 asesorarse** *vpr* to seek advice; **asesorarse de o con** to consult

**asesoría** *nf* (**a**) (*oficio*) consultancy (**b**) (*oficina*) consultant's office; **a. fiscal** (*oficina*) financial adviser's office

**asestar** *vt* (*golpe*) to deal; (*tiro*) to fire

**aseveración** *nf* assertion

**aseverar** *vt* to assert

**asexuado, -a** *adj* asexual

**asexual** *adj* asexual

**asfaltado** *nm* (*acción*) asphalting, surfacing; (*asfalto*) asphalt, (road) surface

**asfaltadora** *nf* (road) surfacer

**asfaltar** *vt* to asphalt, to surface

**asfalto** *nm* asphalt

**asfixia** *nf* asphyxiation, suffocation

**asfixiante** *adj* asphyxiating; *Fig* (*calor*) stifling

**asfixiar** [15] **1** *vt* (*ahogar*) to asphyxiate, to suffocate; *Fig* (*agobiar*) to overwhelm

**2 asfixiarse** *vpr* (*ahogarse*) to asphyxiate, to suffocate; *Fig* (*agobiarse*) to be overwhelmed; **¡aquí me asfixio!** (*de calor*) I'm suffocating in here!

**así 1** *adv* (*de este modo*) in this way, like this; (*de ese modo*) in that way, like that; **era así de largo** it was this/that long; **a. es/era/fue como...** that is/was how...; **a. a. a.** (*no muy bien*) so so; **algo a.** (*algo parecido*) something like that; **algo a. como** (*algo igual a*) something like; **a. es** (*para asentir*) that is correct; **y a. todos los días** and the same thing happens day after day; **a. como** (*también*) as well as; (*tal como*) just as; **¡no puedes marcharte a. como a.!** you can't leave just like that!; **a. y todo, aun a.** even so

**2** *conj* (**a**) (*de esa manera*) **a. (es) que**, so; **a. pues** so, therefore

(**b**) (*tan pronto como*) **a. que** as soon as

(**c**) (*aunque*) although

(**d**) *Am* (*aun si*) even if

**3** *adj inv* (*como éste*) like this; (*como ése*) like that

**Asia** *n* Asia

**asiático, -a** *adj & nm,f* Asian, Asiatic

**asidero** *nm* (*agarradero*) handle; *Fig* (*apoyo*) support

**asiduidad** *nf* frequency

**asiduo, -a** *adj & nm,f* regular

**asienta** (**a**) *ver* **asentar** (**b**) *ver* **asentir**

**asiento** *nm* (**a**) (*silla, butaca*) seat; **tomar a.** to sit down; **a. abatible** seat that can be tipped forward (**b**) (*base*) bottom (**c**) (*excavación arqueológica*) site (**d**) *Com* entry; **a. contable** book entry

**asierre** *ver* **aserrar**

**asignación** *nf* (**a**) (*atribución*) allocation (**b**) (*sueldo*) salary

**asignar** *vt* (**a**) (*atribuir*) **a. algo a alguien** to assign *o* allocate sth to sb (**b**) (*destinar*) **a. a alguien a** to send sb to

**asignatura** *nf Educ* subject; **a. pendiente** subject which a pupil has to resit; *Fig* unresolved matter

**asilado, -a** *nm,f* person living in an old people's home, convalescent home etc; **a. político** political refugee

**asilar** *vt (huérfano, anciano)* to put into a home; *(refugiado político)* to grant political asylum to

**asilo** *nm* (a) *(hospicio)* home; **a. de ancianos** old people's home (b) *(refugio)* refuge, sanctuary; *Fig (amparo)* asylum; **a. político** political asylum

**asimetría** *nf* asymmetry

**asimétrico, -a** *adj* asymmetric(al)

**asimilación** *nf* (a) *también Ling* assimilation (b) *(comparación)* comparison (c) *(equiparación)* granting of equal rights

**asimilar 1** *vt* (a) *(idea, conocimientos, alimentos)* to assimilate (b) *(comparar)* to compare (c) *(equiparar)* to grant equal rights to

**2 asimilarse** *vpr* Ling to become assimilated; *(parecerse)* **asimilarse a algo** to resemble sth

**asimismo** *adv (también)* also, as well; *(a principio de frase)* likewise

**asíncrono, -a** *adj Informát* asynchronous

**asintiera** *ver* **asentir**

**asir** [10] **1** *vt* to grasp, to take hold of

**2 asirse** *vpr también Fig* to cling (**a** to)

**asirio, -a** *adj & nm,f* Hist Assyrian

**asistencia** *nf* (a) *(ayuda)* assistance; **a. letrada** *o* **jurídica** legal advice; **a. médica** medical attention; **a. pública** social security; **a. sanitaria** health care; **a. social** social work; **a. técnica** technical assistance (b) *(presencia) (acción)* attendance; *(hecho)* presence (c) *(afluencia)* audience (d) *Dep* assist

**asistencial** *adj Med* healthcare; **servicios asistenciales** healthcare services

**asistenta** *nf* cleaning lady

**asistente** *nmf* (a) *(ayudante)* assistant, helper; **a. social** social worker (b) *(presente)* person present; **los asistentes** *(el público)* the audience

**asistido, -a** *adj Aut* power; *Informát* computer-assisted; **dirección asistida** power steering

**asistir 1** *vt* (a) *(ayudar)* to attend to; **le asiste el doctor Jiménez** he is being treated by Dr Jiménez (b) *(acompañar)* to accompany

**2** *vi* to attend; **a. a un acto** to attend an event

**asma** *nf Med* asthma

**asmático, -a** *adj & nm,f* asthmatic

**asno** *nm también Fig* ass

**asociación** *nf* association; **a. de consumidores** consumer association; **a. de ideas** association of ideas; **a. de vecinos** residents' association

**asociado, -a 1** *adj* (a) *(relacionado)* associated (b) *(miembro)* associate

**2** *nm,f* (a) *(miembro)* associate, partner (b) *Educ* associate lecturer

**asocial** *adj* asocial

**asociar** [15] **1** *vt* (a) *(relacionar)* to associate (b) *Com* to take into partnership

**2 asociarse** *vpr* to form a partnership

**asociativo, -a** *adj* associative

**asolado, -a** *adj* devastated

**asolar** [65] *vt* to devastate

**asolearse** *vpr* to bask in the sun

**asomar 1** *vt* to stick; **a. la cabeza por la ventana** to stick one's head out of the window

**2** *vi (sobresalir)* to peep up; *(del interior de algo)* to peep out

**3 asomarse** *vpr* **asomarse a la ventana** to stick one's head out of the window; **asomarse al balcón** to go out onto the balcony, to appear on the balcony

**asombrar 1** *vt (causar admiración)* to amaze; *(causar sorpresa)* to surprise

**2 asombrarse** *vpr (sentir admiración)* to be amazed (**de** at); *(sentir sorpresa)* to be surprised (**de** at)

**asombro** *nm (admiración)* amazement; *(sorpresa)* surprise

**asombroso, -a** *adj (sensacional)* amazing; *(sorprendente)* surprising

**asomo** *nm (indicio)* trace, hint; *(de esperanza)* glimmer; **ni por a.** not under any circumstances

**asonancia** *nf (en poesía)* assonance

**asonante** *adj (rima)* assonant

**asorochar** *Andes* **1** *vt* to cause to have altitude sickness

**2 asorocharse** *vpr* to get altitude sickness

**aspa** *nf (figura)* X-shaped cross; *(de molino)* arm

**aspaviento** *nm* furious gesticulations

**aspecto** *nm* (a) *(apariencia)* appearance; **tener buen/mal a.** *(persona)* to look well/awful; *(cosa)* to look nice/horrible (b) *(faceta)* aspect; **bajo este a.** from this angle; **en todos los aspectos** in every respect

**aspereza** *nf* roughness; *Fig* sharpness, sourness; **limar asperezas** to smooth things over

**áspero, -a** *adj (rugoso)* rough; *Fig (desagradable) (sabor)* sharp, sour; *(persona, carácter)* sour, unpleasant; **una áspera disputa** *(entre grupos)* a bitter dispute

**aspersión** *nf (de jardín)* sprinkling; *(de cultivos)* spraying; **riego por a.** spraying *(of garden or field with sprinkler)*

**aspersor** *nm (para jardín)* sprinkler; *(para cultivos)* sprayer

**áspid** *nm* asp

**aspiración** *nf* (a) *(pretensión)* aspiration (b) *(de aire) (por una persona)* breathing in; *(por una máquina)* suction

**aspirador** *nm*, **aspiradora** *nf* vacuum cleaner

**aspirante 1** *adj (persona)* aspiring

**2** *nmf* candidate (**a** for); *(en deportes, concursos)* contender (**a** for)

**aspirar 1** *vt* (a) *(aire) (sujeto: persona)* to breathe in, to inhale; *(sujeto: máquina)* to suck in (b) *Ling* to aspirate

**2** *vi* **a. a algo** *(ansiar)* to aspire to sth

**aspirina** *nf* aspirin

**asquear** *vt* to disgust, to make sick

**asquerosidad** *nf* disgusting *o* revolting thing

**asqueroso, -a** *adj* disgusting, revolting

**asta** *nf* (a) *(de bandera)* flagpole, mast; **a media a.** at half-mast (b) *(de lanza)* shaft; *(de brocha)* handle (c) *(de toro)* horn

**astado** *nm Taurom* bull

**astenia** *nf (debilidad)* fatigue, *Med* asthenia

**asténico, -a** *adj (débil)* easily fatigued, *Med* asthenic

**asterisco** *nm* asterisk

**asteroide** *nm Astron* asteroid

**astigmatismo** *nm Med* astigmatism

**astil** *nm (de hacha, pico)* haft; *(de azada)* handle

**astilla** *nf* splinter; *Fig* **hacer astillas** to smash to smithereens

**astillar 1** *vt (mueble)* to splinter; *(tronco)* to chop up

**2 astillarse** *vpr* to splinter

**astillero** *nm* shipyard

**astracán** *nm* astrakhan

**astracanada** *nf Fam* farce

**astrágalo** *nm* (a) *Anat* astragalus (b) *Arquit* astragal

**astral** *adj* astral

**astringente** *adj* astringent

**astro** *nm Astron* heavenly body; *Fig* star

**astrofísica** *nf* astrophysics *(singular)*

**astrolabio** *nm* astrolabe

**astrología** *nf* astrology

**astrólogo, -a** *nm,f* astrologer

**astronauta** *nmf* astronaut

**astronáutica** *nf* astronautics *(singular)*

**astronave** *nf* spacecraft, spaceship

**astronomía** *nf* astronomy

**astronómico, -a** *adj también Fig* astronomical

**astrónomo, -a** *nm,f* astronomer

**astroso, -a** *adj (andrajoso)* shabby, ragged

**astucia** *nf (trampas)* cunning; *(sagacidad)* astuteness

**asturiano, -a** *adj & nm,f* Asturian

**Asturias** *n* Asturias

**astuto, -a** *adj (ladino, tramposo)* cunning; *(sagaz, listo)* astute

**asuelo** *etc ver* **asolar**

**asueto** *nm* break, rest; **unos días de a.** a few days off

**asumir** *vt* (a) *(adoptar)* to assume; **el descontento asumió caracteres alarmantes** the discontent began to take on alarming proportions (b) *(aceptar)* to accept; **a. la responsabilidad de algo** to take on responsibility for sth

**asunceño, -a 1** *adj* of/from Asunción

**2** *nm,f* person from Asunción

**Asunción** *n* Asunción

**asunción** *nf* assumption; *Rel* **la A.** the Assumption

**asunto** *nm* (a) *(tema) (general)* subject; *(específico)* matter; *(de obra, libro)* theme; **asuntos a tratar** agenda (b) *(cuestión, problema)* issue; **¡...y a. concluido!** and that's that!; **no es a. tuyo** it's none of your business; *Pol* **asuntos exteriores** foreign affairs (c) *(romance)* affair

**asustadizo, -a** *adj* easily frightened

**asustado, -a** *adj* frightened, scared

**asustar 1** *vt* to frighten, to scare; **¡me has asustado!** you gave me a fright!

**2 asustarse** *vpr* to be frightened (**de** of); **me asusté al verlo** I got a shock when I saw him

**Atacama** *nm* **el (desierto de) A.** the Atacama (Desert)

**atacante 1** *adj* attacking

**2** *nmf (agresor)* attacker

**3** *nm Dep* forward

**atacar [61]** *vt* (a) *(acometer)* to attack; *Fig* **le atacó la risa/fiebre** he had a fit of laughter/a bout of fever; *Fig* **me ataca los nervios** it gets on my nerves (b) *(corroer)* to corrode

**atado** *nm* bundle

**atadura** *nf también Fig* tie

**atajar 1** *vi (acortar)* to take a short cut (**por** through)

**2** *vt (contener)* to put a stop to; *(hemorragia, inundación)* to stem; *Fig (interrumpir)* to cut short

**atajo** *nm* (a) *(camino corto, medio rápido)* short cut; **coger** *o* **tomar un a.** to take a short cut (b) *Pey (panda)* bunch

**atalaya** *nf (torre)* watchtower; *(altura)* vantage point

**atañer** *vi* (a) *(concernir)* **a. a** to concern; **en lo que atañe a este asunto** as far as this subject is concerned (b) *(corresponder)* **a. a** to be the responsibility of

**ataque 1** *ver* **atacar**

**2** *nm* (a) *(acometida) también Dep* attack (b) *Fig (acceso)* fit, bout; **a. cardíaco** heart attack

**atar 1** *vt* (**a**) *(unir)* to tie (up) (**b**) *Fig (relacionar)* to link together; **a. cabos** to put two and two together (**c**) *Fig (constreñir)* to tie down; **a. corto a alguien** to keep a tight rein on sb; **su trabajo le ata mucho** her work takes up a lot of her time

**2 atarse** *vpr* to tie oneself down

**atarazana** *nf* shipyard

**atardecer** [48] **1** *nm* dusk

**2** *v impersonal* to get dark; **está atardeciendo** it's getting dark

**atareado, -a** *adj* busy

**atascar** [61] **1** *vt* to block (up)

**2 atascarse** *vpr (obstruirse)* to get blocked up; *Fig (detenerse)* to get stuck; *(al hablar)* to dry up

**atasco** *nm (obstrucción)* blockage; *(de vehículos)* traffic jam

**atasque** *etc ver* **atascar**

**ataúd** *nm* coffin

**ataviar** [34] **1** *vt* to dress up

**2 ataviarse** *vpr* to dress up

**atávico, -a** *adj* atavistic

**atavío** *nm* (**a**) *(adorno)* adornment (**b**) *(indumentaria)* attire; **llevaba sus mejores atavíos** she was wearing her finest attire

**ate** *nm Méx* jelly

**ateísmo** *nm* atheism

**atemorizado, -a** *adj* frightened

**atemorizar** [16] **1** *vt* to frighten

**2 atemorizarse** *vpr* to get frightened

**atemperar** *vt (críticas, protestas)* to temper, to tone down; *(ánimos, nervios)* to calm

**Atenas** *n* Athens

**atenazar** [16] *vt* (**a**) *(sujetar)* to clench (**b**) *Fig* **el miedo la atenazaba** she was gripped by fear

**atención 1** *nf* (**a**) *(interés)* attention; **a la a. de** for the attention of; **llamar la a.** *(atraer)* to attract attention; **llamar la a. a alguien** *(amonestar)* to tell sb off; **poner** *o* **prestar a.** to pay attention (**b**) *(cortesía)* attentiveness; **atenciones** attentions, attentiveness; **nos colmaron de atenciones** they waited on us hand and foot; **en a. a** *(teniendo en cuenta)* out of consideration for; *(en honor a)* in honour of

**2** *interj* **¡a.!** *(en aeropuerto, conferencia)* your attention please!

**atender** [66] **1** *vt* (**a**) *(satisfacer) (petición, ruego)* to attend to; *(consejo, instrucciones)* to heed; *(propuesta)* to agree to (**b**) *(cuidar de) (necesitados, invitados)* to look after; *(enfermo)* to care for; *(cliente)* to serve; **¿le atienden?** are you being served?

**2** *vi* (**a**) *(estar atento)* to pay attention (**a** to) (**b**) *(considerar)* **atendiendo a…** taking into

account… (**c**) *(llamarse) (animales)* **a. por** to answer to the name of

**ateneo** *nm* athenaeum

**atenerse** [67] *vpr* (**a**) *(promesa, orden)* to stick to; *(ley, normas)* to observe, to abide by (**b**) **a. a** *(consecuencias)* to bear in mind

**ateniense** *adj & nmf* Athenian

**atentado** *nm* **a. contra alguien** attempt on sb's life; **a. contra algo** crime against sth; **a. terrorista** terrorist attack; **sufrir un a.** to be attacked

**atentamente** *adv* (**a**) *(con atención, cortesía)* attentively; **mire a.** watch carefully (**b**) *(en cartas)* Yours sincerely/faithfully

**atentar** *vi* **a. contra (la vida de) alguien** to make an attempt on sb's life; **a. contra algo** *(principio)* to be a crime against sth

**atento, -a** *adj* (**a**) *(pendiente)* attentive; **estar a. a** *(explicación, programa, lección)* to pay attention to; *(ruido, sonido)* to listen out for; *(acontecimientos, cambios, avances)* to keep up with (**b**) *(cortés)* considerate, thoughtful

**atenuación** *nf (de dolor)* easing, alleviation; *(de sonido, luz)* attenuation

**atenuante** *nm Der* extenuating circumstance

**atenuar** [4] **1** *vt (disminuir, suavizar)* to diminish; *(dolor)* to ease, to alleviate; *(sonido, luz)* to attenuate

**2 atenuarse** *vpr (disminuir, suavizarse)* to lessen, to diminish

**ateo, -a 1** *adj* atheistic

**2** *nm,f* atheist

**aterciopelado, -a** *adj* velvety

**aterido, -a** *adj* freezing; **a. de frío** shaking *o* shivering with cold

**aterirse** *vpr* to be freezing

**aterrador, -ora** *adj* terrifying

**aterrar 1** *vt* to terrify

**2 aterrarse** *vpr* to be terrified

**aterrizaje** *nm (de avión)* landing; **a. forzoso** emergency landing

**aterrizar** [16] *vi (avión)* to land; *Fig (persona)* to turn up; *Fig Hum (objeto)* to land; **el tapón aterrizó en mi plato** the cork landed on my plate

**aterrorizado, -a** *adj* terrified, terrorized

**aterrorizar** [16] **1** *vt* to terrify; **me aterrorizan las arañas** I'm terrified of spiders; **el atracador aterrorizaba a sus víctimas** the robber terrorized his victims

**2 aterrorizarse** *vpr* to be terrified

**atesorar** *vt (riquezas)* to amass; *Fig (virtudes)* to be blessed with

**atestado** *nm* official report

**atestar** *vt* (**a**) *(llenar)* to pack, to cram (**b**) *Der* to testify to

**atestiguar** [12] *vt* to testify to

**atezado, -a** *adj* tanned

**atiborrar** *Fam* **1** *vt* to stuff full

**2 atiborrarse** *vpr* to stuff one's face (**de** with)

**atice** *etc ver* **atizar**

**ático** *nm* penthouse

**atiendo** *etc ver* **atender**

**atigrado, -a** *adj* (*gato*) tabby

**atildado, -a** *adj* smart, spruce

**atildar** **1** *vt* (*acicalar*) to smarten up

**2 atildarse** *vpr* to smarten oneself up

**atinado, -a** *adj* (**a**) (*respuesta*) correct; (*comentario*) appropriate (**b**) (*oportuno*) good, clever

**atinar** *vi* (*adivinar*) to guess correctly; (*dar en el blanco*) to hit the target; **a. a hacer algo** to succeed in doing sth; **a. con** to hit upon

**atípico, -a** *adj* atypical

**atiplado, -a** *adj* shrill

**atisbar** *vt* (**a**) (*divisar, prever*) to make out (**b**) (*acechar*) to observe, spy on

**atisbo** *nm* (*indicio*) trace, hint; (*de esperanza*) glimmer

**atizador** *nm* poker

**atizar** [16] **1** *vt* (**a**) (*fuego*) to poke, to stir (**b**) *Fig* (*sospechas, discordias*) to fan (**c**) (*puñetazo, patada*) to land, to deal; **me atizó bien fuerte** he hit me really hard

**2 atizarse** *vpr Fam* (*comida, bebida*) to guzzle

**atlante** *nm Arquit* atlas, telamon

**atlántico, -a** **1** *adj* Atlantic; **el océano A.** the Atlantic (Ocean)

**2** *nm* **el A.** the Atlantic (Ocean)

**atlantismo** *nm Pol* pro-NATO stance

**atlas** *nm inv* atlas

**atleta** *nmf* athlete

**atlético, -a** *adj* athletic

**atletismo** *nm* athletics (*singular*)

**atmósfera** *nf también Fig* atmosphere

**atmosférico, -a** *adj* atmospheric

**atole** *nm CAm, Méx* = drink made of cornflour

**atolladero** *nm* (*apuro*) fix, jam; **meter en/sacar de un a. a alguien** to put sb in/get sb out of a tight spot

**atolón** *nm* atoll

**atolondrado, -a** **1** *adj* (**a**) (*precipitado*) hasty, disorganized (**b**) (*aturdido*) bewildered

**2** *nm,f* (*precipitado*) hasty o disorganized person

**atolondramiento** *nm* (**a**) (*precipitación*) haste, disorganization (**b**) (*aturdimiento*) bewilderment

**atolondrar** **1** *vt* to bewilder; **me atolondra tanto griterío** all this shouting is making my head spin

**2 atolondrarse** *vpr* (*por golpe*) to be stunned;

(*por griterío, confusión*) to be bewildered; **se atolondró con el golpe** she was stunned by the blow

**atómico, -a** *adj* (*energía, armas*) atomic, nuclear; (*central*) nuclear; **núcleo a.** (atomic) nucleus

**atomizador** *nm* atomizer, spray

**átomo** *nm también Fig* atom; **á. gramo** gram atom

**atonía** *nf* (*de mercado, economía*) sluggishness

**atónito, -a** *adj* astonished, astounded

**átono, -a** *adj* atonic

**atontado, -a** **1** *adj* (**a**) (*aturdido*) dazed, stunned (**b**) (*tonto*) stupid

**2** *nm,f* idiot, half-wit

**atontar** *vt* (**a**) (*aturdir*) to daze, to stun (**b**) (*volver tonto*) to dull the mind of

**atorarse** *vpr Am* (**a**) (*atascarse*) to get caught (**b**) (*meterse en un lío*) to get into a mess

**atormentado, -a** *adj* tormented

**atormentar** *vt* to torture; *Fig* to torment

**atornillar** *vt* to screw

**atorrante** *CSur* **1** *adj* lazy

**2** *nmf* layabout

**atosigar** [40] *vt Fig* to harass

**atrabiliario, -a** *adj* foul-tempered, bilious

**atracadero** *nm* landing stage

**atracador, -ora** *nm,f* (*de banco*) armed robber; (*en la calle*) mugger

**atracar** [61] **1** *vt* (*banco*) to rob; (*persona*) to mug

**2** *vi Náut* to dock (**en** at)

**3 atracarse** *vpr* to eat one's fill (**de** of)

**atracción** *nf* (**a**) (*gravitatoria, magnética*) attraction (**b**) (*atractivo*) attractiveness, charm (**c**) (*espectáculo*) act (**d**) *Fig* (*centro de atención*) centre of attention (**e**) (*diversión infantil*) fairground attraction

**atraco** *nm* robbery; **a. a mano armada** armed robbery; *Fig* **¿cinco mil pesetas por eso? ¡menudo a.!** five thousand pesetas for that? that's daylight robbery!

**atracón** *nm Fam* feast; **darse un a. de algo** (*comida*) to stuff one's face with sth; *Fig* (*películas, televisión*) to overdose on sth

**atractivo, -a** **1** *adj* attractive

**2** *nm* (*de persona*) attractiveness, charm; (*de cosa*) attraction

**atraer** [68] *vt* (**a**) (*causar acercamiento*) to attract; (*atención*) to attract, to draw; **lo atrajo hacia sí tirándole de la corbata** she pulled him towards her by his tie (**b**) (*gustar*) to attract; **no me atrae mucho la comida china** I'm not too keen on Chinese food; **la miel atrae a las moscas** honey attracts flies

**atragantarse** *vpr* to choke (**con** on); *Fig* **se me ha atragantado este libro/tipo** I can't stand that book/guy

**atraiga** *etc ver* **atraer**

**atrajera** *etc ver* **atraer**

**atrancar** [61] **1** *vt* (**a**) *(cerrar)* to bar (**b**) *(obstruir)* to block

**2 atrancarse** *vpr* (**a**) *(encerrarse)* to lock oneself in (**b**) *(atascarse)* to get blocked (**c**) *Fig (al hablar, escribir)* to dry up

**atrapar** *vt (agarrar, alcanzar)* to catch

**atraque** *ver* **atracar**

**atrás 1** *adv* (**a**) *(detrás) (posición)* behind, at the back; *(movimiento)* backwards; **el asiento de a.** the back seat; *Am* **a. de** behind; **dejar a alguien a.** to leave sb behind; **echarse para a.** to move backwards; **dar un paso a.** to take a step backwards; **hacia a.** backwards; **la falda es más larga por a.** the skirt is longer at the back; **quedarse a.** to fall behind

(**b**) *(antes)* earlier, before; **años a.** *(desde ahora)* years ago; *(desde el pasado)* years before *o* previously

**2** *interj* **¡a.!** get back!

**atrasado, -a** *adj* (**a**) *(en el tiempo)* delayed; *(reloj)* slow; *(pago)* overdue, late; **número a.** back number (**b**) *(en evolución, capacidad)* backward

**atrasar 1** *vt (retrasar) (cita, reloj)* to put back; *(poner más atrás)* to move (further) back

**2** *vi (reloj)* to be slow

**3 atrasarse** *vpr* (**a**) *(demorarse)* to be late (**b**) *(quedarse atrás)* to fall behind

**atraso** *nm* (**a**) *(del reloj)* slowness (**b**) *(de evolución)* backwardness (**c**) *Fin* **atrasos** arrears

**atravesar** [3] **1** *vt* (**a**) *(interponer)* to put across (**b**) *(cruzar)* to cross; **atravesó el río a nado** he swam across the river; **atravesó la calle corriendo** he ran across the street (**c**) *(traspasar)* to pass *o* go through (**d**) *Fig (pasar)* to go through, to experience; **a. una mala racha** to be going through a bad patch

**2 atravesarse** *vpr (interponerse)* to be in the way; *Fig* **se me ha atravesado la vecina** I can't stand my neighbour

**atrayente** *adj* attractive

**atrechar** *vi Am Fam* to take a short cut

**atreverse** *vpr* to dare (**a hacer algo** to do sth); **a. a algo** to be bold enough for sth; **a. con alguien** to take sb on; **¡atrévete y verás!** just you dare and see what happens!

**atrevido, -a 1** *adj (osado)* daring; *(caradura)* cheeky

**2** *nm,f (osado)* daring person; *(caradura)* cheeky person

**atrevimiento** *nm* (**a**) *(osadía)* daring (**b**) *(insolencia)* cheek

**atrezo** *nm Teatro & Cine* props

**atribución** *nf* (**a**) *(imputación)* attribution (**b**) *(competencia)* responsibility, duty

**atribuir** [36] **1** *vt (imputar)* **a. algo a** to attribute sth to; **un cuadro atribuido a Goya** a painting attributed to Goya

**2 atribuirse** *vpr (méritos)* to claim to have; *(poderes)* to assume for oneself

**atribulado, -a** *adj* distressed

**atribular** *Formal* **1** *vt* to distress

**2 atribularse** *vpr* to be distressed

**atributivo, -a** *adj Gram* attributive

**atributo** *nm* attribute

**atril** *nm (para libros)* lectern; *(para partituras)* music stand

**atrincherado, -a** *adj* entrenched, dug in; *Fig (en una postura)* entrenched

**atrincherarse** *vpr* (**a**) *Mil* to entrench oneself, to dig oneself in (**b**) *Fig* **se atrincheró en su oposición a la propuesta** he persisted in his opposition to the proposal; **se atrincheraron en su postura** *(en negociación)* they dug their heels in and refused to give up their position

**atrio** *nm* (**a**) *(pórtico)* portico (**b**) *(claustro)* cloister

**atrocidad** *nf (crueldad)* atrocity; *Fig* **decir/ hacer una a.** *(necedad)* to say/do something stupid

**atrofia** *nf Med* atrophy; *Fig* deterioration

**atrofiado, -a** *adj también Fig* atrophied

**atrofiar** [15] **1** *vt Med* to atrophy; *Fig* to weaken

**2 atrofiarse** *vpr Med* to atrophy; *Fig* to deteriorate, to become atrophied

**atronador, -ora** *adj* deafening

**atropellado, -a** *adj* hasty

**atropellar 1** *vt* (**a**) *(sujeto: vehículo)* to run over; **le atropelló un coche** he was knocked down *o* run over by a car (**b**) *también Fig (sujeto: persona)* to trample on

**2 atropellarse** *vpr (al hablar)* to trip over one's words

**atropello** *nm* (**a**) *(por vehículo)* running over (**b**) *Fig (moral)* abuse (**c**) *Fig (precipitación)* **con a.** hastily

**atroz** *adj* terrible, awful; **hace un frío a.** it's terribly *o* awfully cold

**ATS** *nmf (abrev de* **ayudante técnico sanitario**) qualified nurse

**attaché** [ataˈtʃe] *nm* attaché case

**atte.** *(abrev de* **atentamente**) Yours faithfully/sincerely

**atuendo** *nm* attire

**atufar** *Fam* **1** *vi* to stink; **¡huele que atufa!** it really stinks!

**2** *vt (persona)* to overpower

**atún** *nm* tuna

**aturdido, -a** *adj* dazed

**aturdimiento** *nm* (a) *(desconcierto)* bewilderment, confusion (b) *(torpeza mental)* slowness

**aturdir** **1** *vt (sujeto: golpe, noticia)* to stun; *(sujeto: alcohol)* to fuddle; *(sujeto: ruido, luz)* to confuse, to bewilder

**2 aturdirse** *vpr (por golpe, noticia)* to be stunned; *(por alcohol)* to get fuddled; *(con ruido, luz)* to get confused

**aturullar** *Fam* **1** *vt* to fluster

**2 aturrullarse** *vpr* to get flustered

**atusarse** *vpr* to preen oneself; **a. el bigote/pelo** to straighten out one's moustache/hair

**audacia** *nf (valentía)* daring, boldness; *(descaro)* gall, cheek

**audaz** *adj* daring, bold

**audible** *adj* audible

**audición** *nf* (a) *(acción de oír)* hearing (b) *Mús & Teatro* audition

**audiencia** *nf* (a) *(público, recepción)* audience; **dar a.** to grant an audience (b) *Der (juicio)* hearing; *(tribunal, edificio)* court; **a. provincial** provincial court; **A. Nacional** = court in Madrid dealing with cases that cannot be dealt with at regional level; **a. pública** public hearing

**audífono** *nm* hearing aid

**audiómetro** *nm* audiometer

**audiovisual** *adj* audiovisual

**auditar** *vt Fin* to audit

**auditivo, -a** *adj Anat* **pabellón a.** (outer) ear

**auditor, -ora** *nm,f Fin* auditor

**auditoría** *nf Fin* (a) *(profesión)* auditing (b) *(despacho)* auditor's, auditing company (c) *(balance)* audit; **a. externa/interna** external/internal audit

**auditorio** *nm* (a) *(público)* audience (b) *(lugar)* auditorium

**auge** *nm también Econ* boom; **estar en (pleno) a.** to be booming

**augurar** *vt (sujeto: persona)* to predict; *(sujeto: suceso)* to augur

**augurio** *nm* omen, sign

**augusto, -a** *adj* august

**aula** *nf (de escuela)* classroom; *(de universidad)* lecture room; **a. magna** great hall

**aulaga** *nf* gorse

**aullar** *vi* to howl

**aullido** *nm* howl

**aumentar** **1** *vt* to increase; **a. la producción** to increase production; **la lente aumenta la imagen** the lens magnifies the image; **me han aumentado el sueldo** my salary has been raised; **aumentó casi diez kilos** he put on almost ten kilos

**2** *vi* to increase, to rise

**aumentativo, -a** *adj & nm* augmentative

**aumento** *nm* (a) *(incremento)* increase; *(de sueldo, precios)* rise; **ir en a.** to be on the increase; **a. lineal** across-the-board pay rise (b) *(en óptica)* **una lente de 20 aumentos** a lens of magnification × 20

**aun** **1** *adv* even

**2** *conj* even; **a. estando cansado, lo hizo** even though he was tired, he did it; **ni a. puesta de puntillas logra ver** she can't see, even on tiptoe; **a. cuando** *(a pesar de que)* even though, although; *(incluso si)* even if; **a. así** even so

**aún** *adv* (a) *(todavía)* still; *(con negativo)* yet, still; **a. no** not yet; **a. no lo he recibido** I still haven't got it, I haven't got it yet; **están a. aquí** they are still here (b) *(incluso)* even; **a. más** even more

**aunar** **1** *vt* to join, to pool; **a. esfuerzos** to join forces

**2 aunarse** *vpr (aliarse)* to unite

**aunque** *conj* (a) *(a pesar de que)* even though, although; *(incluso si)* even if; **tendrás que venir a. no quieras** you'll have to come, even if you don't want to; **a. es caro, me lo voy a comprar** although it's expensive I'm going to buy it, I'm going to buy it even though it's expensive (b) *(pero)* although; **es lista, a. un poco perezosa** she's clever, although *o* if a little lazy

**aúpa** *interj* (a) **¡a.!** *(¡levántate!)* get up!; *(al coger a un niño en brazos)* up you come!, up we go! (b) *(¡viva!)* **¡a. (el) Atleti!** up the Athletic! (c) *Fam* **una comida de a.** a brilliant meal; *Fam* **un susto de a.** a hell of a fright

**au pair** [o'per] *(pl* **au pairs)** *nf* au pair

**aupar** **1** *vt (subir)* to help up; *(coger en brazos)* to lift up in one's arms; *Fig (animar)* to cheer on

**2 auparse** *vpr* to climb up

**aura** *nf* (a) *(halo) también Med* aura (b) *(viento)* gentle breeze

**áureo, -a** *adj* golden

**aureola** *nf Astron & Rel* halo; *Fig (fama)* aura

**aurícula** *nf Anat (del corazón)* auricle, atrium

**auricular** **1** *adj* auricular

**2** *nm (de teléfono)* receiver; **auriculares** *(cascos)* headphones

**aurífero** *adj* gold-bearing

**aurora** *nf* first light of dawn; **al despuntar** *o* **romper la a.** at dawn; **a. boreal** aurora borealis, northern lights

**auscultar** *vt Med* to listen to *(with a stethoscope)*

**ausencia** *nf* absence; **brillar por su a.** to be conspicuous by one's/its absence; **en a. de** in the absence of; **si llama alguien en mi a., toma el recado** if anyone calls while I'm out, take a message

**ausentarse** *vpr* to go away

**ausente 1** *adj* (**a**) *(no presente)* absent; **estará a. todo el día** he'll be away all day (**b**) *(distraído)* absent-minded

**2** *nmf* (**a**) *(no presente)* **hay varios ausentes** there are a number of absentees; **criticó a los ausentes** she criticized the people who weren't there (**b**) *Der* missing person

**auspiciar** [15] *vt (apoyar)* to back

**auspicio** *nm (protección)* protection; **bajo los auspicios de** under the auspices of; **auspicios** *(señales)* omens

**austeridad** *nf* austerity

**austero, -a** *adj* austere; **adoptar un presupuesto a.** to limit budgetary expenditure

**austral 1** *adj* southern

**2** *nm Antes (moneda)* austral

**Australia** *n* Australia

**australiano, -a** *adj & nm,f* Australian

**Austria** *n* Austria

**austriaco, -a** *adj & nm,f* Austrian

**autarquía** *nf* (**a**) *Econ* autarky, self-sufficiency (**b**) *Pol* autarchy

**autárquico, -a** *adj* (**a**) *Econ* autarkic, self-sufficient (**b**) *Pol* autarchical

**autenticar** *vt Der (firma, documento)* to authenticate

**autenticidad** *nf* authenticity

**auténtico, -a** *adj* genuine, real; **ser a.** to be genuine; **un a. imbécil** a real idiot

**autentificar** [61] *vt* to authenticate

**autismo** *nm Psi* autism

**autista** *Psi* **1** *adj* autistic

**2** *nmf* autistic person

**auto** *nm* (**a**) *Am (coche)* car; **autos de choque** Dodgems®, bumper cars (**b**) *Der* **a. (judicial)** judicial decree; **a. de procesamiento** indictment; **autos** case documents; **constar en autos** to be recorded in the case documents; **la noche de autos** the night of the crime (**c**) *Hist* **a. de fe** auto-da-fé *(public punishment of heretics by the Inquisition)* (**d**) *Lit* (mystery) play

**autoabastecerse** *vpr (ser autosuficiente)* to be self-sufficient (**de** in)

**autoabastecimiento** *nm* self-sufficiency

**autoadhesivo, -a** *adj* self-adhesive

**autoafirmación** *nf* assertiveness

**autoalimentación** *nf Informát* automatic paper feed

**autobanco** *nm* drive-in cash machine

**autobiografía** *nf* autobiography

**autobiográfico, -a** *adj* autobiographical

**autobombo** *nm Fam* **darse a.** to blow one's own trumpet

**autobús** ( *pl* **autobuses**) *nm* bus

**autocar** *nm* coach

**autocartera** *nf* = shares in a company held by that same company

**autocensura** *nf* self-censorship

**autocine** *nm* drive-in (cinema)

**autoclave** *nm Med* autoclave, sterilizing unit

**autocomplacencia** *nf* self-satisfaction

**autocomplaciente** *adj* self-satisfied

**autocontrol** *nm* self-control

**autocracia** *nf Pol* autocracy

**autócrata** *nmf Pol* autocrat

**autocrítica** *nf* self-criticism

**autóctono, -a** *adj* indigenous, native

**2** *nm,f* native

**autodefensa** *nf* self-defence

**autodestrucción** *nf* self-destruction

**autodeterminación** *nf Pol* self-determination

**autodiagnóstico** *nm Informát* self-test

**autodidacta 1** *adj* self-taught

**2** *nmf* self-taught person

**autodirigido, -a** *adj* guided

**autodisciplina** *nf* self-discipline

**autodominio** *nm* self-control

**autódromo** *nm* motor racing circuit

**autoedición** *nf Informát* desktop publishing

**autoempleo** *nm* self-employment

**autoencendido** *nm Aut* automatic ignition

**autoescuela** *nf* driving school

**autoestima** *nf* self-esteem

**autoestop** *nm* hitch-hiking; **hacer a.** to hitch-hike

**autoestopista** *nmf* hitch-hiker

**autoexec** [auto'eksek] *nm Informát* autoexec file

**autofinanciación** *nf Fin* self-financing

**autofocus** *nm inv* autofocus

**autogestión** *nf* self-management

**autogobierno** *nm Pol* self-government, self-rule

**autógrafo** *nm* autograph

**autómata** *nm también Fig* automaton, robot

**automático, -a 1** *adj* automatic

**2** *nm (cierre)* press-stud

**automatismo** *nm* automatism

**automatización** *nf* automation

**automatizar** [16] *vt* to automate

**automedicarse** [61] *vpr* to self-administer medicine

**automotor, -triz** *adj* self-propelled

**automóvil** *nm* car, *US* automobile

**automovilismo** *nm* motoring; *Dep* motor racing

**automovilista** *nmf* motorist, driver

**automovilístico, -a** *adj* motor; *Dep* motor-racing; **industria automovilística** motor industry

**autonomía** *nf* (a) *Pol (facultad)* autonomy; *(territorio)* autonomous region (b) *(de persona)* independence (c) *(de vehículo)* range; *(de videocámara)* recording time; **a. de vuelo** range

**autonómico, -a** *adj Pol* autonomous

**autonomismo** *nm Pol* autonomy movement

**autonomista** *adj & nmf Pol* autonomist

**autónomo, -a 1** *adj* (a) *Pol* autonomous (b) *(trabajador)* self-employed; *(traductor, periodista)* freelance

2 *nm,f (trabajador)* self-employed person; *(traductor, periodista)* freelance(r)

**autopista** *nf Br* motorway, *US* freeway; **a. de peaje** *Br* toll motorway, *US* turnpike; *Fig* **a. de información** information superhighway

**autopropulsado, -a** *adj* self-propelled

**autopropulsión** *nf* self-propulsion

**autopsia** *nf Med* autopsy, post-mortem

**autor, -ora** *nm,f (de libro)* author; *(de cuadro)* painter; *(de canción)* writer; *(de sinfonía)* composer; *(de crimen, fechoría)* perpetrator; *(de gol)* scorer; *Der* **a. material del hecho** actual perpetrator of the crime

**autoría** *nf (de obra)* authorship; *(de crimen)* perpetration

**autoridad** *nf* authority; **la a.** the authorities; **impusieron su a.** they imposed their authority; **es una a. en historia** he is an authority on history

**autoritario, -a** *adj & nm,f* authoritarian

**autoritarismo** *nm Pol* authoritarianism

**autorización** *nf* authorization; **dar a. a alguien (para hacer algo)** to authorize sb (to do sth)

**autorizado, -a** *adj* (a) *(permitido a)* authorized (b) *(digno de crédito)* authoritative

**autorizar** [16] *vt* (a) *(dar permiso a)* to allow; *(en situaciones oficiales)* to authorize; **a. la publicación de un informe** to authorize the publication of a report (b) *(capacitar)* to allow, to entitle; **este título nos autoriza para ejercer en la UE** this qualification allows us to practise in the EU

**autorradio** *nm o nf* car radio

**autorretrato** *nm* self-portrait

**autoservicio** *nm* (a) *(restaurante)* self-service restaurant (b) *(supermercado)* self-service shop

**autostop** *nm* hitch-hiking; **hacer a.** to hitch-hike

**autostopista** *nmf* hitch-hiker

**autosuficiencia** *nf* self-sufficiency

**autosuficiente** *adj* self-sufficient

**autosugestión** *nf* autosuggestion

**autosugestionarse** *vpr* to convince oneself *(de* of)

**autovacuna** *nf Med* autoinoculation

**autovía** *nf Br* dual carriageway, *US* divided road

**auxiliar** [15] **1** *adj también Gram* auxiliary

2 *nmf* assistant; **a. administrativo** office clerk; **a. de vuelo** air steward(ess)

3 *vt* to assist, to help

**auxilio** *nm* assistance, help; **pedir/prestar a.** to call for/give help; **primeros auxilios** first aid

**av.** *(abrev de* **avenida)** Ave

**aval** *nm* (a) *(persona)* guarantor (b) *(documento)* guarantee, reference; **a. bancario** banker's reference

**avalancha** *nf también Fig* avalanche

**avalar** *vt (préstamo, crédito)* to guarantee; **su reputación lo avala** his reputation is guarantee enough

**avalista** *nmf* guarantor

**avance 1** *ver* **avanzar**

2 *nm* (a) *(movimiento hacia delante)* advance; *Fig* **avances científicos** scientific advances (b) *Fin (anticipo)* advance payment (c) *Rad & TV (de futura programación)* preview; **a. informativo** news in brief

**avanzada** *nf Mil* advance patrol

**avanzadilla** *nf* advance party; *Mil* advance patrol

**avanzado, -a 1** *adj (adelantado)* advanced; *Fig (progresista)* progressive

2 *nm,f* person ahead of his/her time

**avanzar** [16] **1** *vi* to advance; **el tiempo avanza muy deprisa** time passes quickly

2 *vt* (a) *(adelantar)* to move forward (b) *(noticias)* **a. algo a alguien** to inform sb of sth in advance

**avaricia** *nf* greed, avarice; **la a. rompe el saco** greed doesn't pay; *Fam* **ser feo/pesado con a.** to be ugly/boring in the extreme

**avaricioso, -a 1** *adj* avaricious, miserly

2 *nm,f* miser

**avariento, -a 1** *adj* avaricious, miserly

2 *nm,f* miser

**avaro, -a 1** *adj* miserly, mean

2 *nm,f* miser

**avasallador, -ora 1** *adj* overwhelming

2 *nm,f* slave driver

**avasallar** *vi* **va por la vida avasallando** she barges her way through life

**avatar** *nm* vagary, sudden change; **los avatares de la vida** the ups and downs of life

**Avda, avda.** (*abrev de* **avenida**) Ave

**AVE** *nm* (*abrev de* **alta velocidad española**) = Spanish high-speed train

**ave 1** *nf* (*animal*) bird; *Am* (*pollo*) chicken; **a. del Paraíso** bird of paradise; **a. rapaz** *o* **rapiña** bird of prey; *también Fig* **el A. Fénix** the phoenix; *Fig* **ser un a. de paso** to be a rolling stone

**2** *interj* **¡A. María Purísima!** (*indica sorpresa*) saints preserve us!

**avecinarse** *vpr* to be on the way; **¡la que se nos avecina!** are we in for it!

**avefría** *nf* lapwing

**avejentado, -a** *adj* (*persona, cuero*) aged

**avejentar 1** *vt* to age, to put years on

**2 avejentarse** *vpr* to age

**avellana** *nf* hazelnut

**avellano** *nm* hazel (tree)

**avemaría** *nf* (*oración*) Hail Mary

**avena** *nf* (**a**) (*planta*) oat (**b**) (*grano*) oats

**avenencia** *nf* (*acuerdo*) compromise

**avenida** *nf* (**a**) (*calle*) avenue (**b**) (*crecida de río*) flood

**avenido, -a** *adj* **bien/mal avenidos** on good/bad terms

**avenirse** [71] *vpr* (**a**) (*llevarse bien*) to get on (well) (**b**) (*ponerse de acuerdo*) to come to an agreement; **a. a algo/a hacer algo** to agree on sth/to do sth

**aventajado, -a** *adj* (*adelantado*) outstanding

**aventajar** *vt* (*rebasar*) to overtake; (*estar por delante de*) to be ahead of; **a. a alguien en algo** to surpass sb in sth

**aventar** [3] *vt* (**a**) (*abanicar*) to fan (**b**) (*trigo*) to winnow (**c**) *Andes, CAm, Méx* (*tirar*) to throw

**aventón** *nm Am* **pedir/dar a.** to hitch/give a lift

**aventura** *nf* (**a**) (*suceso, empresa*) adventure; **embarcarse en una a.** to set off on an adventure (**b**) (*relación amorosa*) affair

**aventurado, -a** *adj* risky

**aventurar 1** *vt* (*opinión*) to venture, to hazard

**2 aventurarse** *vpr* to take a risk/risks; **aventurarse a hacer algo** to dare to do sth

**aventurero, -a 1** *adj* adventurous

**2** *nm,f* adventurer, *f* adventuress

**avergonzado, -a** *adj* (*humillado, dolido*) ashamed; (*abochornado*) embarrassed

**avergonzar** [11] **1** *vt* (*deshonrar, humillar*) to shame; (*abochornar*) to embarrass

**2 avergonzarse** *vpr* (*por remordimiento*) to be ashamed (**de** of); (*por timidez*) to be embarrassed (**de** about)

**avería** *nf* (*de máquina*) fault; (*de coche*) breakdown; **llamar a averías** (*para coche*) to call the garage; (*para aparato*) to call the repair service; *Fam* **hacerse una a.** (*herida*) to hurt oneself

**averiado, -a** *adj* (*máquina*) out of order; (*coche*) broken down

**averiar** [34] **1** *vt* to damage

**2 averiarse** *vpr* (*máquina, coche*) to break down

**averiguación** *nf* investigation; **hacer averiguaciones** to make inquiries

**averiguar** [12] *vt* to find out

**aversión** *nf* aversion; **tener a. a** to feel aversion towards

**avestruz** *nm* ostrich; **la política/táctica del a.** burying one's head in the sand

**avezado, -a** *adj* accustomed (**a** to)

**aviación** *nf* (**a**) (*navegación*) aviation (**b**) (*ejército*) airforce

**aviador, -ora** *nm,f* aviator

**aviar** [34] **1** *vt* (*comida*) to prepare; *Fam* **estar aviado** to be in a mess

**2 aviarse** *vpr Fam* (*manejarse*) to manage; **se las avía muy bien solo** he manages very well on his own

**avícola** *adj* poultry; **granja a.** poultry farm

**avicultura** *nf* poultry farming

**avidez** *nf* eagerness

**ávido, -a** *adj* eager (**de** for)

**aviento** *etc ver* **aventar**

**avieso, -a** *adj* (*malo*) evil, twisted

**avinagrado, -a** *adj también Fig* sour

**avinagrarse** *vpr* to go sour; *Fig* **se le avinagró el carácter** she became bitter

**avío** *nm* (**a**) (*preparativo*) preparation (**b**) (*víveres*) provisions; *Fam* **avíos** (*equipo*) things, kit

**avión** *nm* (**a**) (*aeronave*) plane; **en a.** by plane; **por a.** (*en un sobre*) airmail; **a. nodriza** supply plane; **a. a reacción** jet (**b**) (*pájaro*) house-martin

**avioneta** *nf* light aircraft

**avisar** *vt* (**a**) (*informar*) **a. a alguien de algo** to let sb know sth, to tell sb sth (**b**) (*advertir*) to warn (**de** of) (**c**) (*llamar*) to call, to send for

**aviso** *nm* (**a**) (*advertencia, amenaza*) warning; **andar sobre a.** to be on the alert; **estar sobre a.** to be forewarned; **poner sobre a. a alguien** to warn sb; **a. de bomba** bomb warning (**b**) (*notificación*) notice; (*en teatros, aeropuertos*) call; **hasta nuevo a.** until further notice; **sin previo a.** without notice; **Com a. de vencimiento** due-date reminder (**c**) *Taurom* = warning to matador not to delay the kill any longer

**avispa** *nf* wasp

**avispado, -a** *adj Fam* sharp, quick-witted

**avispero** *nm* (**a**) *(nido)* wasp's nest (**b**) *Fam Fig (lío)* mess; **meterse en un a.** to get into a mess

**avistar** *vt* to sight, to make out

**avitaminosis** *nf inv Med* vitamin deficiency

**avituallamiento** *nm* provisioning

**avituallar** *vt* to provide with food

**avivar 1** *vt (sentimiento)* to rekindle; *(color)* to brighten; *(fuego)* to stoke up

**2 avivarse** *vpr (sentimiento)* to be rekindled; *(color)* to brighten; *(fuego)* to flare up

**avizor** *adj* **estar ojo a.** to be on the lookout

**avutarda** *nf* great bustard

**axial** *adj* axial

**axila** *nf* armpit

**axioma** *nm* axiom

**axiomático, -a** *adj* axiomatic

**ay** *(pl* **ayes) 1** *nm* groan

**2** *interj* **¡ay!** *(dolor físico)* ouch!; *(sorpresa, pena)* oh!; **¡ay de ti si te cojo!** Heaven help you if I catch you!

**aya** *nf* governess

**ayatola, ayatolá** *nm* ayatollah

**ayer 1** *adv* yesterday; *Fig* in the past; **a. (por la) noche** last night; **a. por la mañana** yesterday morning

**2** *nm Fig* yesteryear

**ayo** *nm (tutor)* tutor

**ayuda** *nf* help, assistance; *Pol & Econ* aid; **acudir en a. de alguien** to go to sb's assistance; **a. en carretera** breakdown service; **a. humanitaria** humanitarian aid

**ayudante** *adj & nmf* assistant

**ayudar 1** *vt* to help; **a. a alguien a hacer algo** to help sb (to) do sth; **¿en qué puedo ayudarle?** how can I help you?

**2 ayudarse** *vpr* **ayudarse de** *o* **con** to make use of

**ayunar** *vi* to fast

**ayunas** *nfpl* **estar en a.** *(sin comer)* not to have eaten; *Fig (sin enterarse)* to be in the dark

**ayuno** *nm* fast; **hacer a.** to fast

**ayuntamiento** *nm* (**a**) *(corporación)* town council (**b**) *(edificio)* town hall

**azabache** *nm* jet; **negro como el a.** jet-black

**azada** *nf* hoe

**azadón** *nm* (large) hoe

**azafata** *nf* **a. (de vuelo)** air stewardess, *Br* air hostess; **a. de exposiciones y congresos** hostess; **a. de tierra** stewardess

**azafrán** *nm (condimento)* saffron

**azahar** *nm (del naranjo)* orange blossom; *(del limonero)* lemon blossom

**azalea** *nf* azalea

**azar** *nm* chance, fate; **al a.** at random; **por (puro) a.** by (pure) chance

**azarar 1** *vt (avergonzar)* to embarrass, to fluster; **a. a alguien** *(ruborizar)* to make sb blush

**2 azararse** *vpr (avergonzarse)* to be embarrassed, to be flustered; *(ruborizarse)* to blush

**azaroso, -a** *adj (vida, viaje)* eventful

**Azerbaiyán** *n* Azerbaijan

**azerbaiyano, -a** *adj & nm,f* Azerbaijani

**azeri** *adj & nm* Azerbaijani

**ázimo** *adj (pan)* unleavened

**azimut** *(pl* **azimutes)** *nm Astron* azimuth

**azogue** *nm Anticuado* quicksilver, mercury

**azor** *nm* goshawk

**azorado, -a** *adj* embarrassed, flustered

**azoramiento** *nm* embarrassment

**azorar 1** *vt* to embarrass

**2 azorarse** *vpr* to be embarrassed

**Azores** *nfpl* **las A.** the Azores

**azotaina** *nf Fam* **dar una a. a alguien** to give sb a good smacking

**azotar** *vt (pegar, golpear)* to beat; *(en el trasero)* to smack, to slap; *(con látigo)* to whip; *Fig* **la epidemia azotó la región** the region was devastated by the epidemic

**azote** *nm* (**a**) *(utensilio para golpear)* whip, scourge (**b**) *(latigazo)* lash; *(golpe)* blow; *(en el trasero)* smack, slap; *Fig (calamidad)* scourge

**azotea** *nf (de edificio)* terraced roof; *Fam Fig* **estar mal de la a.** to be funny in the head

**azteca 1** *adj* Aztec; *Fam* **el equipo a.** the Mexican team

**2** *nmf* Aztec

**3** *nm (lengua)* Nahuatl, Aztec

**azúcar** *nm o nf* sugar; **a. blanquilla/moreno** refined/brown sugar; **a. cande** sugar candy; **a. glas** *o* **de lustre** icing sugar

**azucarado, -a** *adj* sweet, sugary

**azucarera** *nf (fábrica)* sugar refinery; *(recipiente)* sugar bowl

**azucarero, -a 1** *adj* sugar; **la industria azucarera** the sugar industry

**2** *nm* sugar bowl

**azucarillo** *nm* (**a**) *(Culin* lemon candy (**b**) *(terrón)* sugar lump

**azuce** *etc ver* **azuzar**

**azucena** *nf* white lily

**azufre** *nm* sulphur

**azul** *adj & nm* blue; **a. celeste/marino/eléctrico** sky/navy/electric blue; **a. turquesa** turquoise

**azulado, -a** *adj* bluish

**azulejo** *nm* (glazed) tile

**azulete** *nm (para lavar)* blue

**azulgrana** *adj inv Dep* = relating to Barcelona football club

**azuzar** [16] *vt (animal)* to set on; *Fig (persona)* to egg on

# B

**B, b** [be] *nf (letra)* B, b

**baba** *nf* (a) *(saliva) (de niño)* dribble; *(de adulto)* spittle, saliva; *(de animal)* slobber (b) *(de caracol)* slime (c) *Fam* **se le cae la b. con su hija** she drools over her daughter; *Fam* **tener mala b.** to be bad-tempered

**babear** *vi* (a) *(niño)* to dribble (b) *(adulto, animal)* to slobber (c) *Fig* to drool

**babel** *nm o nf Fam Fig* **el debate se convirtió en una b.** the debate degenerated into noisy chaos

**babero** *nm* bib

**babi** *nm Fam* = child's overall

**Babia** *nf* **estar** *o* **quedarse en B.** to have one's head in the clouds

**Babilonia** *n Hist* Babylon

**babilónico, -a** *adj* (a) *Hist* Babylonian (b) *(fastuoso)* lavish

**bable** *nm* = Asturian dialect

**babor** *nm* port; **a b.** to port

**babosa** *nf Zool* slug

**babosada** *nf CAm, Méx Fam (disparate)* daft thing; **no digas babosadas** don't talk rubbish!

**babosear** *vt* to slobber on *o* all over

**baboso, -a 1** *adj* (a) *(niño)* dribbling; *(adulto, animal)* slobbering (b) *Am Fam (tonto)* daft, stupid (c) *Fam (despreciable)* slimy

**2** *nm,f Fam* (a) *(persona despreciable)* creep (b) *Am (tonto)* twit, idiot

**babucha** *nf (zapatilla)* slipper; *(árabe)* Moorish slipper

**baca** *nf* roof rack

**bacaladero, -a 1** *adj* cod-fishing; **la flota bacaladera** the cod-fishing fleet

**2** *nm* cod-fishing boat

**bacaladilla** *nf* blue whiting

**bacalao** *nm* cod; *Culin* **b. a la vizcaína** = Basque dish of salt cod cooked in a tomato and red pepper sauce; *Culin* **b. al pil-pil** = Basque dish of salt cod cooked with olive oil and garlic; **b. salado** salt cod; *Fam Fig* **partir** *o* **cortar el b.** to be the boss

**bacán** *CSur* **1** *adj* fine

**2** *nm* toff; **como un b.** like a real gentleman

**bacanal** *nf* orgy

**bacarrá, bacará** *nm* baccarat

**bache** *nm* (a) *(en carretera)* pothole (b) *(en un vuelo)* air pocket (c) *Fig (dificultades)* bad patch

**bachiller** *nmf* = person who has passed the "bachillerato"

**bachillerato** *nm* = Spanish course of secondary studies for academically orientated 16-18-year-olds

**bacilo** *nm* bacillus; **b. de Koch** tubercle bacillus, Koch's bacillus

**bacín** *nm*, **bacinilla** *nf* chamber pot

**bacinica** *nf Am* chamber pot

**bacon** ['beikon] *nm inv* bacon

**bacteria** *nf* germ; **bacterias** germs, bacteria

**bacteriano, -a** *adj* bacterial

**bactericida 1** *adj Med* bactericidal

**2** *nm* bactericide

**bacteriología** *nf* bacteriology

**bacteriológico, -a** *adj* **guerra bacteriológica** germ *o* bacteriological warfare

**bacteriólogo, -a** *nm,f* bacteriologist

**báculo** *nm* (a) *(de obispo)* crosier (b) *Fig (sostén)* support; **ella será el b. de mi vejez** she'll comfort me in my old age

**badajo** *nm* clapper *(of bell)*

**badajocense 1** *adj* of/from Badajoz

**2** *nm,f* person from Badajoz

**badana** *nf (de sombrero)* hatband; *Fam* **zurrarle a alguien la b.** to tan sb's hide

**badén** *nm* (a) *(de carretera)* ditch (b) *(cauce)* channel

**bádminton** *nm inv* badminton

**bafle** *(pl* **bafles***)*, **baffle** *(pl* **baffles***) nm* loudspeaker

**bagaje** *nm* background; **b. cultural** cultural baggage

**bagatela** *nf* trifle

**Bagdad** *n* Baghdad

**Bahamas** *nfpl* **las B.** the Bahamas

**bahía** *nf* bay

**Bahrain** *n* Bahrain

**Baikal** *nm* **el (lago) B.** Lake Baikal

**bailable** *adj* danceable; **música b.** music you can dance to

**bailaor, -ora** *nm,f* flamenco dancer

**bailar 1** vt to dance; **b. una rumba** to dance a rumba; *Fam* **que me quiten lo bailado** no one can take away the good times

**2** vi (a) (*danzar*) to dance; *Fam* **es otro que tal baila** he's just the same, he's no different (b) (*no encajar*) to be loose; **le baila un diente** he has a loose tooth; **los pies me bailan (en los zapatos)** my shoes are too big

**bailarín, -ina** nm,f dancer; (*de ballet*) ballet dancer

**baile** nm (a) (*pieza, arte*) dance; **b. clásico** ballet; **¿me concede este b.?** may I have the pleasure of this dance? (b) (*fiesta*) ball (c) (*en contabilidad*) **b. de cifras** number transposition (d) *Med* **b. de San Vito** St Vitus' dance

**bailongo** nm *Fam* bop, boogie

**bailotear** vi *Fam* to bop, to boogie

**bailoteo** nm *Fam* bopping

**baja** nf (a) (*descenso*) drop, fall; *Fin* **jugar a la b.** to bear the market (b) (*cese*) **dar de b. a alguien** (*en una empresa*) to lay sb off; (*en un club, sindicato*) to expel sb; **darse de b.** (d) (*dimitir*) to resign (from); (*salirse*) to drop out (of) (c) (*por enfermedad*) (*permiso*) sick leave; (*documento*) sick note, doctor's certificate; **estar/darse de b.** to be on/take sick leave (d) *Mil* loss, casualty

**bajada** nf (a) (*descenso*) descent; **cuando veníamos de b.** on our way (back) down; **b. de bandera** (*de taxi*) minimum fare (b) (*pendiente*) (downward) slope (c) (*disminución*) decrease, drop; **b. de los precios** (*caída*) drop *o* fall in prices; (*rebaja*) reduction in prices

**bajamar** nf low tide

**bajante** nmf (*tubería*) drainpipe

**bajar 1** vt (a) (*poner abajo*) (*libro, cuadro*) to take/bring down; (*telón, ventanilla, mano*) to lower

(b) (*descender*) (*montaña, escaleras*) to go/come down

(c) (*precios, inflación, hinchazón*) to reduce; (*música, volumen, radio*) to turn down; (*fiebre*) to bring down; **b. el fuego (de la cocina)** to reduce the heat

(d) (*ojos, cabeza, voz*) to lower

(e) *Fam Informát* to download

**2** vi (a) (*descender*) to go/come down; **b. en ascensor** to go/come down in the lift; **b. por la escalera** to go/come down the stairs; **b. (a) por algo** to go out and get sth; **b. corriendo** to run down

(b) (*disminuir*) to fall, to drop; (*fiebre, hinchazón*) to go/come down; **bajó la Bolsa** share prices fell; **las acciones de C & C han bajado** C & C share prices have fallen

**3 bajarse** vpr (a) *Fam* (*ir, venir*) to come/go down; **bájate a la playa conmigo** come

down to the beach with me

(b) (*de coche*) to get out (**de** of); (*de moto, tren, avión*) to get off; (*de árbol, escalera, silla*) to get/come down (**de** from)

**bajel** nm *Lit* vessel, ship

**bajero, -a** adj lower; (*sábana*) bottom

**bajeza** nf (a) (*cualidad*) baseness (b) (*acción*) vile deed

**bajial** nm *Perú* lowland

**bajío** nm sandbank

**bajista 1** adj *Fin* bearish; **mercado b.** bear market

**2** nmf *Mús* bassist

**bajo, -a 1** adj (a) (*objeto, cifra*) low; (*persona, estatura*) short; (*sonido*) soft, faint; **planta baja** ground floor; **me lo dijo por lo b.** he said it to me under his breath; **tirando por lo b.** at least, at the minimum

(b) (*territorio, época*) lower; **el b. Amazonas** the lower Amazon; **la baja Edad Media** the late Middle Ages

(c) (*pobre*) lower-class

(d) (*vil*) base

**2** nm (a) (*dobladillo*) hem

(b) (*piso*) *Br* ground floor flat, *US* first floor apartment; **los bajos** *Br* the ground floor, *US* the first floor

(c) *Mús* (*instrumento, cantante*) bass; (*instrumentista*) bassist

(d) *Aut* (*de vehículo*) underside

**3** adv (a) (*caer*) low

(b) (*hablar*) quietly, softly

**4** prep (a) (*debajo de*) under; **b. cero** below zero; *Fig* **b. cuerda** *o* **mano** secretly, in an underhand manner

(b) (*sometido a*) **prohibido aparcar b. multa de 5.000 pts.** no parking – penalty 5,000 pesetas

**bajón** nm slump; **dar un b.** to slump

**bajonazo** nm **dar un b.** (*salud*) to get worse; (*ventas*) to decline

**bajorrelieve** nm bas-relief

**bajura** nf **pesca de b.** coastal fishing

**bakalao** *Fam* **1** adj rave

**2** nm (*música*) rave music; **la ruta del b.** = originally, string of rave clubs along the Madrid-Valencia road, now also the rave scene in general

**bala** nf (a) (*proyectil*) bullet; *Fam Fig* **b. perdida** good-for-nothing (b) (*fardo*) bale

**balacear** vt *Am* (*tirotear*) to shoot

**balacera** nf *Am* shootout

**balada** nf ballad

**baladí** ( pl **baladíes**) adj trivial

**baladrón, -ona** nm,f braggart

**baladronada** nf boast

**balance** *nm* (a) *Com (operación)* balance; *(documento)* balance sheet; **b. consolidado** consolidated balance sheet (b) *(resultado)* outcome; **hacer b. (de)** to take stock (of); **el accidente tuvo un b. de seis heridos** a total of six people were wounded in the accident

**balancear 1** *vt (cuna)* to rock; *(columpio)* to swing

 **2 balancearse** *vpr (en columpio, hamaca)* to swing; *(de pie)* to sway; *(en cuna, mecedora)* to rock; *(barco)* to roll

**balanceo** *nm* (a) *(de columpio, hamaca)* swinging; *(de cuna, mecedora)* rocking; *(de barco)* roll (b) *Am Aut* wheel balance

**balancín** *nm* (a) *(mecedora)* rocking chair; *(en el jardín)* swing hammock (b) *(columpio)* seesaw (c) *Aut* rocker arm

**balandrista** *nmf* yachtsman, *f* yachtswoman

**balandro** *nm* yacht

**balanza** *nf* (a) *(báscula)* scales; **b. de cocina** kitchen scales; **b. de precisión** precision balance; **la b. se inclinó a nuestro favor** the balance *o* scales tipped in our favour (b) *Com* **b. comercial/de pagos** balance of trade/payments

**balar** *vi* to bleat

**balarrasa** *nm Fam* good-for-nothing

**balaustrada** *nf* balustrade; *(de escalera)* banister

**balazo** *nm (disparo)* shot; *(herida)* bullet wound

**balbucear, balbucir** *vi & vt* to babble

**balbuceo** *nm* babbling

**Balcanes** *nmpl* **los B.** the Balkans

**balcánico, -a** *adj* Balkan

**balcón** *nm* (a) *(terraza)* balcony (b) *(mirador)* vantage point

**balconada** *nf (balcón corrido)* long balcony *(running across building)*

**balda** *nf* shelf

**baldado, -a** *adj* (a) *(tullido)* crippled (b) *Fam (exhausto)* shattered

**baldar 1** *vt* to cripple

 **2 baldarse** *vpr* to injure oneself

**balde** *nm* pail, bucket; **de b.** free (of charge); **estar de b.** *(estar sin hacer nada)* to be hanging around doing nothing; **en b.** in vain

**baldear** *vt* to sluice down

**baldío, -a** *adj* (a) *(sin cultivar)* uncultivated; *(no cultivable)* barren; **un terreno b.** an area of wasteland (b) *(inútil)* fruitless

**baldón** *nm* **ser un b. para** to bring shame upon

**baldosa** *nf (en casa, edificio)* floor tile; *(en la acera)* paving stone

**baldosín** *nm* tile

**balear 1** *vt Am* to shoot

 **2** *adj* Balearic; **el archipiélago b.** the Balearic Islands

 **3** *nmf* = person from the Balearic Islands

**Baleares** *nfpl* **las B.** the Balearic Islands

**baleárico, -a** *adj* Balearic

**balero** *nm* (a) *(juego) CSur, Méx* cup and ball (b) *Méx (articulación)* bearing

**Bali** *n* Bali

**balido** *nm* bleat, bleating

**balín** *nm* pellet

**balística** *nf* ballistics *(singular)*

**balístico, -a** *adj* ballistic

**baliza** *nf Náut* marker buoy; *Av* beacon; *Aut* warning light *(for roadworks)*

**balizar** *vt Náut* to mark out with buoys; *Av* to mark out with beacons; *Aut* to mark out with warning lights

**balizamiento** *nm Náut* marker buoys; *Av* beacons; *Aut* warning lights *(for roadworks)*

**ballena** *nf* (a) *(animal)* whale (b) *(varilla) (de corsé)* stay

**ballenato** *nm* whale calf

**ballenero, -a 1** *adj* whaling; **barco b.** whaler, whaling ship

 **2** *nm (barco)* whaler, whaling ship

**ballesta** *nf* (a) *Hist* crossbow (b) *Aut (suspension)* spring

**ballet** [ba'le] *(pl* **ballets***) nm* ballet

**balneario** *nm* spa

**balompié** *nm Br* football, *US* soccer

**balón** *nm (pelota)* ball; **echar balones fuera** to evade the issue; **b. de oxígeno** oxygen bag; *Fig* shot in the arm

**balonazo** *nm* **rompió la ventana de un b.** he smashed the window with the football; **me dio un b. en la cara** he hit me right in the face with the ball

**baloncestista** *nmf* basketball player

**baloncesto** *nm* basketball

**balonmano** *nm* handball

**balonvolea** *nm* volleyball

**balotaje** *nm Am* run-off, = second round of voting

**balsa** *nf* (a) *(embarcación)* raft (b) *(estanque)* pond, pool; *Fig* **ser una b. de aceite** *(mar)* to be as calm as a millpond; *(reunión)* to go smoothly

**balsámico, -a** *adj* balsamic

**bálsamo** *nm* (a) *Med* balsam (b) *(alivio)* balm

**balsero, -a** *nm,f* = refugee fleeing Cuba on a raft

**báltico 1** *adj (país, mar)* Baltic

 **2** *nm* **el B.** the Baltic (Sea)

**baluarte** nm (a) (fortificación) bulwark (b) Fig (bastión) bastion, stronghold

**bamba** nf (a) (bollo) cream bun (b) **bambas** (zapatillas de deporte) Br sandshoes, plimsolls, US sneakers

**bambalina** nf backdrop; Fig **entre bambalinas** backstage

**bambolear 1** vt to shake

**2 bambolearse** vpr (árbol, persona) to sway; (mesa, silla) to wobble; (tren, autobús) to judder

**bamboleo** nm (de árbol, persona) swaying; (de mesa, silla) wobbling; (de tren, autobús) juddering

**bambú** (pl **bambúes** o **bambús**) nm bamboo

**banal** adj banal

**banalidad** nf banality

**banalizar** [16] vt to trivialize

**banana** nf banana

**bananero, -a 1** adj banana; **república bananera** banana republic
**2** nm (árbol) banana tree

**banano** nm banana tree

**banca** nf (a) (actividad) banking; **b. electrónica** electronic banking (b) (institución) **la b.** the banks (c) (en juegos) bank; **hacer saltar la b.** to break the bank (d) (asiento) bench

**bancal** nm Agr (terraza) terrace; (parcela) plot

**bancario, -a** adj banking; **crédito b.** bank loan; **sector b.** banking sector

**bancarrota** nf bankruptcy; **estar en b.** to be bankrupt; **ir a la b.** to go bankrupt

**banco** nm (a) (asiento) bench; (de iglesia) pew; Pol **b. azul** = seats in Spanish parliament where government ministers sit
(b) Fin bank; **b. central/comercial/emisor/industrial** central/commercial/issuing/industrial bank; **el B. Mundial** the World Bank
(c) (de peces) shoal
(d) (de sangre, semen) bank; Informát **b. de datos** data bank
(e) (de carpintero, artesano) workbench
(f) Tec **b. de pruebas** test bench; Fig testing ground
(g) **b. de arena** sandbank

**banda** nf (a) (cuadrilla) gang; **b. armada** terrorist organization
(b) Mús band
(c) (faja) sash
(d) (cinta) ribbon; **b. magnética** magnetic strip; **b. sonora** (de película) soundtrack
(e) (franja) stripe; **b. sonora** (en carretera) rumble strip
(f) Rad waveband; **b. de frecuencias** frequency (band)
(g) (en fútbol) **línea de b.** touchline; **saque de b.** throw-in; **avanzar por la b.** to come/go

down the wing
(h) (en billar) cushion
(i) **cerrarse en b.** to dig one's heels in

**bandada** nf (de aves) flock; (de peces) shoal

**bandazo** nm (del barco) lurch; **dar bandazos** (barco, borracho) to lurch; Fig (ir sin rumbo) to chop and change; **dar un b.** (con el volante) to swerve violently

**bandear 1** vt to buffet
**2 bandearse** vpr to look after oneself, to cope

**bandeja** nf tray; Fig **servir o poner algo a alguien en b.** to hand sth to sb on a plate

**bandera** nf flag; **jurar b.** to swear allegiance (to the flag); **la b. pirata** the Jolly Roger; **b. blanca** white flag; Fam **de b.** (magnífico) fantastic, terrific

**banderilla** nf (a) Taurom banderilla, = barbed dart thrust into bull's back
(b) (aperitivo) = hors d'œuvre of pickles and olives on a cocktail stick

**banderillear** vi Taurom to stick "banderillas" in the bull's back

**banderillero, -a** nm,f Taurom banderillero, = bullfighter's assistant who sticks "banderillas" into the bull

**banderín** nm (a) (bandera) pennant (b) Mil pennant-bearer

**banderola** nf pennant

**bandidaje** nm banditry

**bandido, -a** nm,f (delincuente) bandit; (granuja) rascal, scamp; **ese tendero es un b.** that shopkeeper is a shark

**bando** nm (a) (facción) side; **pasarse al otro b.** to change sides (b) (edicto) (de alcalde) edict

**bandolera** nf (correa) bandoleer; **en b.** slung across one's chest

**bandolerismo** nm banditry

**bandolero, -a** nm,f bandit

**bandurria** nf = small 12-stringed guitar

**Bangkok** n Bangkok

**Bangladesh** [bangla'ðeʃ] n Bangladesh

**Bangui** n Bangui

**banjo** nm ['banjo] banjo

**Banjul** n [ban'jul] Banjul

**banquero, -a** nm,f banker

**banqueta** nf (a) (asiento) stool (b) CAm (acera) Br pavement, US sidewalk

**banquete** nm (comida) banquet; **b. de boda** wedding breakfast; **b. eucarístico** holy communion

**banquillo** nm (asiento) low stool; Dep bench; Der **b. de los acusados** dock

**bañado, -a** adj (a) **b. en oro/plata** gold-/silver-plated (b) **b. en sudor** bathed in sweat

**bañador** *nm (de mujer)* swimsuit; *(de hombre)* swimming trunks

**bañar 1** *vt* (a) *(asear)* to bath; *Med* to bathe (b) *(remojar)* to soak (c) *(revestir)* to coat (d) *(sujeto: río)* to flow through; *(sujeto: mar)* to wash the coast of (e) *(sujeto: sol, luz)* to bathe

**2 bañarse** *vpr* (a) *(en el baño)* to have *o* take a bath; *Am (ducharse)* to have a shower (b) *(en playa, piscina)* to go for a swim

**bañera** *nf* bathtub, bath

**bañista** *nmf* bather

**baño** *nm* (a) *(acción)* *(en bañera)* bath; *(en playa, piscina)* swim; **darse un b.** *(en bañera)* to have *o* take a bath; *(en playa, piscina)* to go for a swim; *Fig* **dar un b. a alguien** to run rings round sb; **b. de asiento** hip bath; **b. María** bain Marie; **baños de sol** sunbathing (b) *(bañera)* bathtub, bath (c) *(cuarto de aseo)* bathroom (d) **baños** *(balneario)* spa (e) *(vahos)* inhalation (f) *(capa)* coat

**baobab** *nm* baobab (tree)

**baptista** *adj & nmf* Baptist

**baptisterio** *nm* baptistry

**baquelita** *nf* Bakelite®

**baqueta** *nf* (a) *(de fusil)* ramrod; *Fig* **tratar** *o* **llevar a la b.** to treat harshly (b) *Mús* drumstick

**baqueteado, -a** *adj Fam* **estar muy b.** to have been to the school of hard knocks

**bar** *nm* bar; **ir de bares** to go out drinking, to go on a pub crawl

**barahúnda** *nf* racket, din

**baraja** *nf* pack (of cards); *Fig* **jugar con dos barajas** to play a double game

**barajar** *vt* (a) *(cartas)* to shuffle (b) *(considerar)* *(nombres, posibilidades)* to consider; *(datos, cifras)* to mention

**baranda, barandilla** *nf* handrail

**baratija** *nf* trinket, knick-knack

**baratillo** *nm* (a) *(género)* junk (b) *(tienda)* junkshop; *(mercadillo)* flea market

**barato, -a 1** *adj* cheap

**2** *adv* cheap, cheaply; **vender algo b.** to sell sth cheaply

**barba** *nf* beard; **b. incipiente** stubble; **apurarse la b.** to shave close; **dejarse b.** to grow a beard; **por b.** *(cada uno)* per head; **lo hizo en sus (propias) barbas** he did it right under her nose; **reírse de alguien en sus propias barbas** to laugh in sb's face; **un hombre con toda la b.** a real man; **barbas** *(de persona)* beard; *(de pez)* barbel

**barbacoa** *nf* barbecue; **hacer una b.** to have a barbecue

**Barbados** *n* Barbados

**barbaridad** *nf* (a) *(cualidad)* cruelty (b) *(disparate)* stupid thing; **¡qué b.!** that's ridiculous! (c) *(montón)* **una b. (de)** tons (of); **se gastó una b.** she spent a fortune

**barbarie** *nf* (a) *(crueldad)* *(cualidad)* cruelty, savagery; *(acción)* atrocity (b) *(incultura)* barbarism

**barbarismo** *nm* (a) *(extranjerismo)* foreign word (b) *(incorrección)* substandard usage

**bárbaro, -a 1** *adj* (a) *Hist* barbarian (b) *(cruel)* barbaric, cruel (c) *(bruto)* uncouth, coarse (d) *Fam (extraordinario)* brilliant, great

**2** *nm,f Hist* barbarian

**3** *adv Fam (magníficamente)* **pasarlo b.** to have a wild time

**barbecho** *nm* fallow (land); *(retirada de tierras)* land set aside

**barbería** *nf* barber's (shop)

**barbero** *nm* barber

**barbilampiño, -a 1** *adj* smooth-faced, beardless

**2** *nm* beardless man

**barbilla** *nf* chin

**barbitúrico** *nm* barbiturate

**barbo** *nm* barbel; **b. de mar** red mullet

**barboquejo** *nm* chinstrap

**barbotar** *vi & vt* to mutter

**barbudo, -a 1** *adj* bearded; **la mujer barbuda** *(en circo)* the bearded woman

**2** *nm* man with a beard

**barbullar** *vi* to jabber

**barca** *nf* dinghy, small boat; **b. de remos** rowing boat

**barcarola** *nf* barcarole, gondolier's song

**barcaza** *nf* barge, lighter

**Barcelona** *n* Barcelona

**barcelonés, -esa 1** *adj* of/from Barcelona

**2** *nm,f* person from Barcelona

**barco** *nm* (a) *(más pequeño)* boat; *(de gran tamaño)* ship; **en b.** by boat; **b. cisterna** tanker; **b. de guerra** warship; **b. mercante** cargo ship; **b. de pesca** *o* **pesquero** fishing boat; **b. de vapor** steamer, steamboat; **b. de vela** sailing ship

**bardo** *nm* bard

**baremo** *nm* *(escala)* scale; *(norma)* yardstick

**bario** *nm* barium

**barítono** *nm* baritone

**barlovento** *nm* windward (side)

**barman** *(pl* **barmans)** *nm* barman

**Barna.** *abrev de* **Barcelona**

**barniz** *nm* *(para madera)* varnish; *(para cerámica)* glaze

**barnizado, -a 1** *adj* *(madera)* varnished; *(cerámica)* glazed

**2** *nm* *(acción)* *(de madera)* varnishing; *(de cerámica)* glazing

**barnizador, -ora** *nm,f* French polisher

**barnizar** [16] *vt (madera)* to varnish; *(cerámica)* to glaze

**barómetro** *nm* barometer

**barón** *nm* baron

**baronesa** *nf* baroness

**barquero, -a** *nm,f* boatman, *f* boatwoman

**barquilla** *nf (de globo)* basket

**barquillo** *nm (plano)* wafer; *(cono)* cornet, cone; *(enrollado)* rolled wafer

**barra** *nf* **(a)** *(pieza alargada)* bar; *(de hielo)* block; *(para cortinas)* rod; *(de bicicleta)* crossbar; **la b.** *(de tribunal)* the bar; **b. de labios** lipstick; **b. de pan** baguette, French stick
 **(b)** *(de bar, café)* bar *(counter)*; **b. americana** = bar where hostesses chat with clients; **b. libre** =unlimited drink for a fixed price
 **(c)** *(para bailarines)* barre
 **(d)** *Dep* **b. fija** horizontal bar; **barras paralelas** parallel bars
 **(e)** *(signo gráfico)* slash, oblique stroke
 **(f) no se paró en barras** he stopped at nothing to get what he wanted

**barrabasada** *nf Fam* **hacer barrabasadas** to get up to mischief; **aquello fue una b.** that was a really mischievous thing to do

**barraca** *nf* **(a)** *(chabola)* shack **(b)** *(caseta de feria)* stall **(c)** *(en Valencia y Murcia)* thatched farmhouse

**barracón** *nm* large hut

**barragana** *nf (concubina)* concubine

**barranco** *nm* **(a)** *(precipicio)* precipice **(b)** *(cauce)* ravine

**barrena** *nf* **(a)** *(herramienta)* drill **(b) entrar en b.** *Av* to go into a spin; *Fig (persona, gobierno)* to totter

**barrenar** *vt* **(a)** *(taladrar)* to drill **(b)** *(frustrar)* to scupper

**barrendero, -a** *nm,f* street sweeper

**barreno** *nm* **(a)** *(instrumento)* large drill **(b)** *(agujero para explosiones)* blast hole

**barreño** *nm* washing-up bowl

**barrer 1** *vt* **(a)** *(con escoba)* to sweep **(b)** *(sujeto: viento, olas)* to sweep away; **el huracán barrió todo a su paso** the hurricane destroyed everything in its path **(c)** *Informát & Med (con escáner)* to scan **(d)** *Fam (derrotar)* to thrash, to annihilate
 **2** *vi* **b. con** *(llevarse)* to finish off, to make short work of; *Fig* **b. hacia** *o* **para adentro** to look after number one

**barrera** *nf* **(a)** *(obstáculo)* barrier; *Ferroc* crossing gate; *(de campo, casa)* fence; *Fig* **poner barreras a algo** to erect barriers against sth, to hinder sth; **barreras arancelarias** tariff barriers; **b. del sonido** sound barrier **(b)** *Taurom* = barrier around the edge of a bullring **(c)** *Dep (de jugadores)* wall

**barriada** *nf (barrio)* neighbourhood, area; *Am* shanty town

**barrica** *nf* keg

**barricada** *nf* barricade

**barrida** *nf* **dar una b. a algo** to give sth a sweep

**barrido** *nm* **(a)** *(con escoba)* **dar un b. (a algo)** to sweep (sth); **servir** *o* **valer tanto para un b. como para un fregado** *(persona)* to be a jack-of-all-trades **(b)** *Informát & Med* scan, scanning **(c)** *Cine* pan, panning

**barriga** *nf* belly; **echar b.** to get a paunch; *Fig* **rascarse** *o* **tocarse la b.** to twiddle one's thumbs, to laze around

**barrigazo** *nm Fam* **darse un b.** to fall flat on one's face

**barrigón, -ona, barrigudo, -a** *Fam* **1** *adj* paunchy
 **2** *nm,f (persona)* portly person
 **3** *nm (barriga)* big belly

**barril** *nm* barrel; **de b.** *(bebida)* draught

**barrilete** *nm* **(a)** *(de revólver)* chamber **(b)** *CSur (cometa)* kite

**barrillo** *nm (granito)* blackhead

**barrio** *nm* area, district, *US* neighborhood; **los barrios bajos** the rough parts of town; **b. comercial/periférico** shopping/outlying district; **b. chino** red light district; **b. latino** Latin Quarter; **de b.** *(cine, tienda)* local; *Fam Fig* **mandar a alguien al otro b.** to do sb in, to kill sb

**barriobajero, -a** *Pey* **1** *adj* **un chico b.** a lout, *Br* a yob; **ese acento es muy b.** that accent is very common *o* vulgar
 **2** *nm,f* lout, *Br* yob, *f* rough girl

**barrizal** *nm* mire

**barro** *nm* **(a)** *(fango)* mud **(b)** *(arcilla)* clay; **una figurita de b.** a clay figure **(c)** *(grano)* blackhead **(d) arrastrarse por el b.** to abase oneself

**barroco, -a 1** *adj* **(a)** *Arte* baroque **(b)** *(recargado)* ornate
 **2** *nm Arte* baroque

**barroquismo** *nm Arte* baroque style

**barrote** *nm* bar; **estar entre barrotes** *(en prisión)* to be behind bars

**barruntar** *vt (presentir)* to suspect

**barrunto** *nm* **(a)** *(presentimiento)* suspicion **(b)** *(indicio)* sign, indication

**bartola** *nf Fam* **tumbarse a la b.** to lounge around

**bártulos** *nmpl* things, bits and pieces; *Fam Fig* **liar los b.** to pack one's bags

**barullo** *nm Fam* **(a)** *(ruido)* din, racket; **armar b.** to raise hell **(b)** *(desorden)* mess

**basa** *nf Arquit* base

**basalto** *nm* basalt

**basamento** *nm Arquit* base, plinth

**basar 1** *vt* **b. algo en** to base sth on

**2 basarse** *vpr* **basarse en** *(persona)* to base one's argument on; *(teoría, obra)* to be based on; **¿en qué te basas (para decir eso)?** what basis do you have for saying that?

**basca** *nf* (a) *muy Fam (de amigos)* pals, mates; **vino toda la b.** the whole crew came along (b) *(náusea)* nausea

**báscula** *nf* scales; **b. de baño/de precisión** bathroom/precision scales

**basculador** *nm* dumper truck

**bascular** *vi* to tilt

**base** *nf* (a) *(parte inferior) & Mat & Mil* base; *(de edificio)* foundations; **b. aérea** air base; **b. espacial** space station; **b. de lanzamiento** launch site; **b. de operaciones** operational base
(b) *(fundamento, origen)* basis; **sentar las bases para** to lay the foundations of; **ese argumento se cae por su b.** that argument is built on sand
(c) *(de partido, sindicato)* **las bases** the grass roots, the rank and file; **militante/afiliado de b.** grassroots member
(d) *Quím* base
(e) **a b. de** by (means of); **me alimento a b. de verduras** I live on vegetables; **a b. de bien** extremely well
(f) *Informát* **b. de datos** database; **b. de datos documental/relacional** documentary/relational database
(g) *Fin* **b. imponible** taxable income

**BASIC, basic** ['beisik] *nm Informát* BASIC

**básico, -a** *adj también Quím* basic; **lo b. de** the basics of

**Basilea** *n* Basle, Basel

**basílica** *nf* basilica

**basilisco** *nm Fam Fig* **ponerse hecho un b.** to go mad, to fly into a rage

**básquet, basket** *nm* basketball

**basset** *nm* basset hound

**basta** *interj* **¡b.!** that's enough!; **¡b. de chistes/tonterías!** that's enough jokes/of this nonsense!

**bastante 1** *adj* (a) *(suficiente)* enough; **no tengo dinero b.** I haven't got enough money (b) *(mucho)* **tengo b. frío** I'm quite *o* pretty cold; **bastantes libros** quite a lot of books, a fair number of books
**2** *adv* (a) *(suficientemente)* **es lo b. lista para...** she's smart enough to... (b) *(considerablemente)* quite, pretty; **es b. fácil** it's pretty *o* quite easy; **b. mejor** quite a lot better; **me gustó b.** I enjoyed it quite a lot (c) *Am (muy)* very

**3** *pron* **éramos bastantes** there were quite a few *o* a lot of us

**bastar 1** *vi* to be enough; **basta con que se lo digas** it's enough for you to tell her; **con ocho basta** eight will be enough

**2 bastarse** *vpr* to be self-sufficient; **él solo se basta para terminar el trabajo** he'll be able to finish the work himself

**bastardía** *nf* bastardy

**bastardilla** *nf* **letra b.** italics

**bastardo, -a** *adj (hijo)* bastard

**2** *nm,f* (a) *(hijo)* bastard (b) *muy Fam Pey* bastard, swine

**bastedad** *nf* coarseness

**bastidor** *nm* (a) *(armazón)* frame; *(para bordar)* embroidery frame (b) *Aut* chassis (c) *Náut* screw propeller's frame (d) *Teatro* **bastidores** wings; *Fig* **entre bastidores** behind the scenes

**bastilla** *nf* *(dobladillo)* hem

**bastión** *nm también Fig* bastion

**basto, -a 1** *adj* coarse

**2** *nmpl* **bastos** *(naipes)* = suit in Spanish deck of cards, with the symbol of a wooden club

**bastón** *nm* (a) *(para andar)* walking stick; **usar b.** to walk with a stick (b) *(de mando)* baton; *Fig* **empuñar el b.** to take the helm (c) *(para esquiar)* ski stick

**bastonazo** *nm* blow (with a stick)

**bastoncillo** *nm (para los oídos) Br* cotton bud, *US* Q-tip®

**basura** *nf también Fig Br* rubbish, *US* garbage, **tirar algo a la b.** to throw sth away; **este artículo es una b.** this article is *Br* a load of rubbish *o US* trash; **b. orgánica** organic waste

**basurero** *nm* (a) *(persona) Br* dustman, *US* garbage man (b) *(vertedero) Br* rubbish dump, *US* garbage dump

**bata** *nf* (a) *(de casa)* housecoat; *(para baño, al levantarse)* dressing gown (b) *(de trabajo)* overall; *(de médico)* white coat; *(de laboratorio)* lab coat

**batacazo** *nm* bump, bang

**batahola** *nf* row, rumpus

**batalla** *nf* battle; **b. campal** pitched battle; **de b.** *(de uso diario)* everyday

**batallador, -ora** *adj* battling; **es muy b.** he's a real fighter

**batallar** *vi* (a) *(con armas)* to fight (b) *Fig (por una cosa)* to battle

**batallón** *nm* (a) *Mil* battalion (b) *Fig (grupo numeroso)* crowd

**batata** *nf* sweet potato

**bate** *nm Dep* bat

**bateador, -ora** *nm,f Dep* batsman, *f* batswoman

**batear** *Dep* **1** *vt* to hit
**2** *vi* to bat

**batel** *nm* small boat

**batería 1** *nf* (a) *Elec & Mil* battery; **b. solar** solar cell (b) *Mús* drums (c) *Teatro* floodlights (d) *(conjunto)* set; *(de preguntas)* barrage; **b. de cocina** pots and pans (e) **aparcado en b.** parked at an angle to the pavement
  **2** *nmf* drummer

**batiborrillo, batiburrillo** *nm* jumble

**batida** *nf* (a) *(de caza)* beat (b) *(de policía)* combing, search

**batido, -a 1** *adj* (a) *(nata)* whipped; *(claras)* whisked (b) *(senda, camino)* well-trodden
  **2** *nm* (a) *(acción de batir)* beating (b) *(bebida)* milkshake

**batidor** *nm* (a) *(aparato manual)* whisk (b) *(en caza)* beater (c) *Mil* scout

**batidora** *nf* *(eléctrica)* mixer

**batiente** *nm* (a) *(de puerta)* jamb; *(de ventana)* frame (b) *(costa)* shoreline

**batín** *nm* dressing gown

**batir 1** *vt* (a) *(mezclar)* *(huevos, mezcla líquida)* to beat, to whisk; *(nata)* to whip (b) *(golpear)* to beat against; **las olas batían las rocas** the waves beat against the rocks; **el viento batía las ventanas** the windows were banging in the wind (c) *(derrotar)* to beat; *(récord)* to break (d) *(explorar)* to comb, to search
  **2** *vi* *(sol, lluvia)* to beat down
  **3 batirse** *vpr* (a) *(luchar)* to fight; **batirse en duelo** to fight a duel (b) *(puerta)* to slam shut (c) *también Fig* **batirse en retirada** to beat a retreat

**batiscafo** *nm* bathyscaphe

**batista** *nf* batiste, cambric

**batracio** *nm* amphibian

**baturro, -a 1** *adj* Aragonese
  **2** *nm,f* Aragonese peasant

**batuta** *nf* baton; *Fig* **llevar la b.** to call the tune

**baudio** *nm* *Informát* baud

**baúl** *nm* (a) *(cofre)* trunk (b) *CSur (maletero) Br* boot, *US* trunk

**bauprés** ( *pl* **baupreses**) *nm* *Náut* bowsprit

**bautismal** *adj* baptismal

**bautismo** *nm* baptism

**Bautista** *nm* *Rel* **el B.** John the Baptist

**bautizar** [16] *vt* (a) *Rel* to baptize, to christen (b) *Fig (denominar, poner mote a)* to christen (c) *Fam Fig (aguar)* to dilute

**bautizo** *nm* *(ceremonia)* baptism, christening; *(fiesta)* christening party

**bauxita** *nf* bauxite

**bávaro, -a** *adj & nm,f* Bavarian

**Baviera** *n* Bavaria

**baya** *nf* berry

**bayeta** *nf* (a) *(tejido)* flannel (b) *(para limpiar)* kitchen cloth; **b. de gamuza** chamois

**bayonesa** *nf* *(bollo)* = pastry filled with strands of crystallized pumpkin

**bayoneta** *nf* (a) *(arma)* bayonet (b) **bombilla de b.** light bulb with bayonet fitting

**baza** *nf* (a) *(en naipes)* trick (b) *(ventaja)* advantage (c) **meter b. en algo** to butt in on sth; **no pude meter b. (en la conversación)** I couldn't get a word in edgeways

**bazar** *nm* bazaar

**bazo** *nm* spleen

**bazofia** *nf* (a) *(comida)* pigswill (b) *Fig (libro, película)* **ser (una) b.** to be *Br* rubbish *o US* garbage

**bazuca, bazooka** *nm* bazooka

**BBS** *nf* *Informát (abrev de* **Bulletin Board Service)** BBS

**bearnesa** *nf* *Culin* **salsa b.** bearnaise sauce

**beatería** *nf* devoutness

**beatificación** *nf* beatification

**beatificar** [61] *vt* to beatify

**beatitud** *nf* beatitude

**beato, -a 1** *adj* (a) *(beatificado)* blessed (b) *(piadoso)* devout (c) *Fig (santurrón)* sanctimonious
  **2** *nm,f* (a) *Rel* beatified person (b) *(piadoso)* devout person (c) *Fig (santurrón)* sanctimonious person

**bebe, -a** *nm,f* *CSur Fam* baby

**bebé** *nm* baby; **b. probeta** test-tube baby

**bebedero** *nm* (a) *(de jaula)* water dish (b) *(abrevadero)* drinking trough

**bebedizo** *nm* potion; *(de amor)* love potion

**bebedor, -ora** *nm,f* *(borrachín)* heavy drinker

**beber 1** *vt* (a) *(líquido)* to drink (b) *Fig (absorber)* *(palabras, consejos)* to lap up; *(sabiduría, información)* to draw, to acquire
  **2** *vi* (a) *(tomar líquido)* to drink; **b. de una fuente** to drink from a fountain (b) *Fig (emborracharse)* to drink (heavily); **bebí más de la cuenta** I had one too many (c) *(brindar)* **b. a la salud de alguien** to drink to sb's health; **b. por algo** to drink to sth

**bebida** *nf* drink; **darse** *o* **entregarse a la b.** to take to drink *o* the bottle; **el problema de la b.** the problem of alcoholism *o* drinking

**bebido, -a** *adj* drunk

**beca** *nf* *(del gobierno)* grant; *(de organización privada)* scholarship; **b. de investigación** research grant/scholarship

**becada** *nf* woodcock

**becar** [61] *vt* *(sujeto: gobierno)* to award a grant to; *(sujeto: organización privada)* to award a scholarship to

**becario, -a** *nm,f (del gobierno)* grant holder; *(de organización privada)* scholarship holder

**becerrada** *nf* = bullfight with young bulls

**becerro, -a** *nm,f* calf

**bechamel** *nf* béchamel sauce

**bedel** *nm* janitor

**beduino, -a** *adj & nm,f* Bedouin

**befa** *nf* jeer; **hacer b. de** to jeer at

**begonia** *nf* begonia

**beicon** *nm* bacon

**beige** [beis] *(pl* **beiges)** *adj & nm,* **beis** *adj inv & nm inv* beige

**Beirut** *n* Beirut

**béisbol** *nm* baseball

**bel canto** *nm inv* bel canto

**beldad** *nf Formal Hum* fairness, beauty

**Belén** *n* Bethlehem

**belén** *nm* **(a)** *(de Navidad)* crib, Nativity scene **(b)** *Fam (desorden)* bedlam **(c)** *Fig (embrollo)* mess; **meterse en belenes** to get mixed up in trouble

**belfos** *nmpl* horse's lips

**belga** *adj & nmf* Belgian

**Bélgica** *n* Belgium

**Belgrado** *n* Belgrade

**Belice** *n* Belize

**beliceño, -a** *adj & nm,f* Belizean

**belicismo** *nm* warmongering

**belicista 1** *adj* belligerent
**2** *nmf* warmonger

**bélico, -a** *adj* **conflicto b.** military conflict; **esfuerzo b.** war effort; **espiral bélica** spiral towards war

**belicosidad** *nf* bellicosity

**belicoso, -a** *adj* bellicose; *Fig* aggressive

**beligerancia** *nf* belligerence

**beligerante** *adj & nmf* belligerent

**bellaco, -a** *nm,f* villain, scoundrel

**belladona** *nf* belladonna, deadly nightshade

**bellaquería** *nf* wickedness, roguery; **ser una b.** to be a wicked thing to do

**belleza** *nf* beauty

**bello, -a** *adj* beautiful; **bellas artes** fine arts; **el b. sexo** the fair sex

**bellota** *nf* acorn

**bemol** *Mús* **1** *adj* flat
**2** *nm* flat; **doble b.** double flat; *Fig* **tener (muchos) bemoles** *(ser difícil)* to be tricky; *(tener valor)* to have guts; *(ser un abuso)* to be a bit rich o much

**benceno** *nm Quím* benzene

**bencina** *nf* **(a)** *Quím* benzine **(b)** *Andes (gasolina)* petrol

**bendecir** [53] *vt* to bless; **b. la mesa** to say grace

**bendición** *nf* blessing; **ser una b. de Dios** to be wonderful; *Rel* **bendiciones (nupciales)** *(boda)* wedding

**bendigo** *ver* **bendecir**

**bendijera** *etc ver* **bendecir**

**bendito, -a 1** *adj* **(a)** *(santo)* holy; *(alma)* blessed; *Fam Fig* **¡b. sea Dios!** thank goodness! **(b)** *(dichoso)* lucky **(c)** *(para enfatizar)* damned
**2** *nm,f* simple soul; **dormir como un b.** to sleep like a baby

**benedictino, -a** *adj & nm,f Rel* Benedictine

**benefactor, -ora 1** *adj* beneficent
**2** *nm,f* benefactor, *f* benefactress

**beneficencia** *nf* charity

**beneficiar** [15] **1** *vt* to benefit
**2 beneficiarse** *vpr* to benefit; **beneficiarse de algo** to do well out of sth; *muy Fam* **beneficiarse a alguien** to lay sb, to sleep with sb

**beneficiario, -a** *nm,f (de seguro)* beneficiary; *(de cheque)* payee

**beneficio** *nm* **(a)** *(bien)* benefit; **a b. de** *(gala, concierto)* in aid of; **en b. de** for the good of; **en b. de todos** in everyone's interest; **en b. propio** for one's own good **(b)** *(ganancia)* profit; **b. bruto/neto** gross/net profit

**beneficioso, -a** *adj* beneficial **(para** to)

**benéfico, -a** *adj* **(a)** *(favorable)* beneficial **(b)** *(de caridad)* charity; **rifa benéfica** charity raffle; **organización benéfica** charity, charitable organisation

**Benelux** *nm (abrev de* **Belgïe-Nederland-Luxembourg)** **el B.** Benelux

**benemérito, -a 1** *adj* worthy
**2** *nf* **la Benemérita** = name given to the "Guardia Civil"

**beneplácito** *nm* consent

**benevolencia** *nf* benevolence

**benevolente, benévolo, -a** *adj* benevolent

**bengala** *nf* **(a)** *(de señalización)* flare **(b)** *(de fiesta)* sparkler

**bengalí** *adj & nmf* Bengali

**benignidad** *nf* **(a)** *(de persona, carácter, enfermedad)* benign nature **(b)** *(de clima, temperatura)* mildness

**benigno, -a** *adj* **(a)** *(persona, carácter, enfermedad)* benign **(b)** *(clima, temperatura)* mild

**Benín** *n* Benin

**benjamín, -ina** *nm,f* youngest child

**benzol** *nm Quím* benzol

**beodo, -a** *adj & nm,f* drunk

**beque** *etc ver* **becar**

**berberecho** *nm* cockle

**berbiquí** *nm* brace and bit

**bereber 1** *adj & nmf* Berber
**2** *nm (lengua)* Berber

**berenjena** *nf Br* aubergine, *US* eggplant

**berenjenal** *nm Fam (enredo)* mess; **meterse en un b.** to get oneself into a right mess

**bergamota** *nf* bergamot

**bergantín** *nm* brigantine

**beriberi** *nm Med* beriberi

**berilio** *nm Quím* beryllium

**Berlín** *n* Berlin

**berlina** *nf* four-door saloon

**berlinés, -esa 1** *adj* of/from Berlin

**2** *nm,f* Berliner

**bermejo, -a** *adj* reddish

**bermellón** *adj inv & nm* vermilion

**Bermudas** *nfpl* **las B.** Bermuda

**bermudas** *nfpl* Bermuda shorts

**Berna** *n* Berne

**berrear** *vi* (a) *(animal)* to bellow; *(niño)* to howl (b) *Fam (cantar mal)* to screech, to howl

**berrido** *nm* (a) **dar berridos/un b.** *(animal)* to bellow; *(niño)* to howl (b) *Fam (cantar mal)* **dar berridos** to screech

**berrinche** *nm Fam* tantrum; **coger** *o* **agarrarse un b.** to throw a tantrum

**berro** *nm* watercress

**berza** *nf* cabbage; *muy Fam* **hoy está con la b.** *(atontado)* he's not with it today

**berzas, berzotas** *nmf inv Fam* thickhead

**besamel** *nf* béchamel sauce

**besar 1** *vt* to kiss

**2 besarse** *vpr* to kiss

**beso** *nm* kiss; **comerse a besos a alguien** to smother sb with kisses

**bestia 1** *adj* (a) *(ignorante)* thick, stupid (b) *(torpe)* clumsy (c) *(maleducado)* rude (d) *Fam* **comer a lo b.** to stuff one's face; **cerró la puerta a lo b.** he slammed the door

**2** *nmf* (a) *(ignorante, torpe)* brute (b) *(maleducado)* rude person

**3** *nf (animal)* beast; **b. de carga** beast of burden

**bestiada** *nf Fam* (a) *(barbaridad)* **decir/hacer una b.** to say/do something stupid (b) **una b. de** *(muchos)* tons *o* stacks of

**bestial** *adj* (a) *(brutal)* animal, brutal; *(apetito)* tremendous (b) *Fam (formidable)* terrific

**bestialidad** *nf* (a) *(brutalidad)* brutality (b) *Fam (barbaridad)* **decir/hacer una b.** to say/do something stupid (c) *Fam (montón)* **una b. de** tons *o* stacks of

**bestiario** *nm Lit* bestiary

**best-séller** [bes'seler] ( *pl* **best-sellers**) *nm* best-seller

**besucón, -ona** *Fam* **1** *adj* kissy

**2** *nm,f* kissy person

**besugo** *nm (pescado)* sea bream; *Fam (persona)* idiot

**besuquear** *Fam* **1** *vt* to smother with kisses

**2 besuquearse** *vpr* to smooch

**besuqueo** *nm Fam* smooching

**bético, -a** *adj* (a) *(andaluz)* Andalusian (b) *Dep* = relating to Real Betis Football Club

**betún** *nm* (a) *(para calzado)* shoe polish (b) *Quím* bitumen; **b. de Judea** asphalt

**bi-** *prefijo* bi-

**bianual** *adj* (a) *(dos veces al año)* biannual, twice-yearly (b) *(cada dos años)* biennial

**biberón** *nm* (baby's) bottle; **dar el b. a** to bottle-feed

**Biblia** *nf* Bible; *Fam* **ser la B. en verso** to be endless

**bíblico, -a** *adj* biblical

**bibliobús** ( *pl* **bibliobuses**) *nm* mobile library

**bibliófilo, -a** *nm,f* (a) *(coleccionista)* book collector (b) *(lector)* book lover

**bibliografía** *nf* bibliography

**bibliográfico, -a** *adj* bibliographic

**bibliorato** *nm CSur* file

**biblioteca** *nf* (a) *(lugar, conjunto de libros)* library; **b. ambulante/pública** mobile/public library (b) *(mueble)* bookcase

**bibliotecario, -a** *nm,f* librarian

**biblioteconomía** *nf* librarianship, library science

**bicameral** *adj Pol* bicameral, two-chamber; **sistema b.** two-chamber *o* bicameral system

**bicarbonato** *nm* (a) *(medicamento)* bicarbonate of soda (b) *Quím* bicarbonate

**bicentenario** *nm* bicentenary

**bíceps** *nm inv* biceps

**bicha** *nf Fam* snake

**bicharraco** *nm Fam* (a) *(animal)* disgusting creature (b) *(persona mala)* nasty piece of work

**bicho** *nm Fam* (a) *(animal)* beast, animal; *(insecto)* bug (b) *(persona mala)* **(mal) b.** nasty piece of work; **b. raro** weirdo; **todo b. viviente** every Tom, Dick and Harry (c) *(pillo)* little terror

**bici** *nf Fam* bike

**bicicleta** *nf* bicycle

**bicoca** *nf Fam (compra, alquiler)* bargain; *(trabajo)* cushy number

**bidé, bidet** *nm* bidet

**bidimensional** *adj* two-dimensional

**bidón** *nm (barril)* drum; *(lata)* (jerry) can; *(de plástico)* plastic jerry can, = large water container with handle

**biela** *nf* connecting rod

**Bielorrusia** *n* Belarus

**bielorruso, -a** *adj & nm,f* Belorussian, Byelorussian

**bien 1** *adj inv (respetable)* **una familia b.** a good family; *Pey* **niño b.** rich kid

**2** *nm* good; **el b. y el mal** good and evil; **hacer el b.** to do good (deeds); **esto te hará b.** this will do you good; **por el b. de** for the sake of; **lo hice por tu b.** I did it for your own good

**3** *nmpl* **bienes (a)** *(patrimonio)* property; **bienes inmuebles** *o* **raíces** real estate; **bienes gananciales** shared possessions; **bienes muebles** personal property

**(b)** *(productos)* goods; **bienes de consumo** consumer goods; **bienes de equipo** capital goods; **bienes de producción** industrial goods

**4** *adv* **(a)** *(debidamente, adecuadamente)* well; **hacer algo b.** to do sth well; **has hecho b.** you did the right thing; **¡b. hecho!** well done!; **habla inglés b.** she speaks English well; **cierra b. la puerta** shut the door properly; **hiciste b. en decírmelo** you were right to tell me

**(b)** *(expresa opinión favorable)* **estar b.** *(de aspecto)* to be nice; *(de salud)* to be *o* feel well; *(de calidad)* to be good; *(de comodidad)* to be comfortable; **está b. que te vayas, pero antes despídete** it's all right for you to go, but say goodbye first; **oler/saber b.** to smell/taste nice *o* good; **pasarlo b.** to have a good time; **sentar b. a alguien** *(ropa)* to suit sb; *(comida)* to agree with sb; *(comentario)* to please sb

**(c)** *(muy, bastante)* very; **hoy me he levantado b. temprano** I got up nice and early today; **quiero un vaso de agua b. fría** I'd like a nice cold glass of water

**(d)** *(vale, de acuerdo)* all right, OK; **¿nos vamos? – b.** shall we go? – all right

**(e)** *(de buena gana, fácilmente)* quite happily; **ella b. que lo haría, pero no le dejan** she'd be happy to do it, but they won't let her

**(f)** *(expresiones)* **¡b. por...!** three cheers for...!; **¡está b.!** *(bueno, vale)* all right then!; *(es suficiente)* that's enough; **¡ya está b.!** that's enough!; **estar a b. con alguien** to be on good terms with sb; **más b.** rather; **no estoy contento, más b. estupefacto** I'm not so much happy as stunned; **¡muy b.!** very good!, excellent!; **no b.** no sooner, as soon as; **no b. me había marchado cuando empezaron a...** no sooner had I gone than they started...; **¡pues (sí que) estamos b.!** that's all we needed!; **si b.** although, even though; **tener a b. hacer algo** to be good enough to do sth

**5** *conj* **b.... b.** either... or; **dáselo b. a mi hermano, b. a mi padre** either give it to my brother or to my father

**bienal 1** *adj* biennial

**2** *nf* biennial exhibition

**bienaventurado, -a** *nm,f Rel* blessed person

**bienaventuranza** *nf* **(a)** *Rel* divine vision; **bienaventuranzas** Beatitudes **(b)** *(felicidad)* happiness

**bienestar** *nm* wellbeing

**bienhechor, -ora 1** *adj* beneficial

**2** *nm,f* benefactor, *f* benefactress

**bienintencionado, -a** *adj* well-intentioned

**bienio** *nm* **(a)** *(periodo)* two years **(b)** *(aumento de sueldo)* two-yearly increment

**bienvenida** *nf* welcome; **dar la b. a alguien** to welcome sb

**bienvenido, -a** *adj* welcome; **¡b.!** welcome!

**bies** *nm inv* bias binding; **al b.** *(costura)* on the bias

**bifásico, -a** *adj Elec* two-phase; **sistema b.** AC system

**bife** *nm Andes, CSur* steak

**bífido, -a** *adj* forked

**bifocal 1** *adj* bifocal

**2** *nfpl* **bifocales** *(gafas)* bifocals

**bifurcación** *nf* fork; *Tel* bifurcation

**bifurcarse** [61] *vpr* to fork

**bigamia** *nf* bigamy

**bígamo, -a 1** *adj* bigamous

**2** *nm,f* bigamist

**bígaro** *nm* winkle

**bigote** *nm* moustache; *Fig* **de bigotes** fantastic

**bigotudo, -a** *adj* with a big moustache

**bigudí** *( pl* **bigudís** *o* **bigudíes** *) nm* curler

**bikini** *nm (bañador)* bikini

**bilateral** *adj* bilateral

**bilbaíno, -a 1** *adj* of/from Bilbao

**2** *nm,f* person from Bilbao

**biliar** *adj Anat* bile; **conducto b.** bile duct; **vesícula b.** gall bladder

**bilingüe** *adj* bilingual

**bilingüismo** *nm* bilingualism

**bilioso, -a** *adj también Fig* bilious

**bilis** *nf inv también Fig* bile; *Fig* **tragar b.** to grin and bear it

**billar** *nm* **(a)** *(juego)* billiards *(singular)*; **b. americano** pool; **b. romano** bar billiards **(b)** *(mesa)* billiard table **(c)** *(sala)* billiard hall

**billete** *nm* **(a)** *(de banco) Br* note, *US* bill **(b)** *(de rifa, transporte)* ticket; *Teatro* **no hay billetes** *(en letrero)* sold out; **b. de ida y vuelta** *Br* return (ticket), *US* round-trip (ticket); **b. kilométrico** = ticket to travel a set distance; **b. de lotería** lottery ticket; **b. sencillo** *Br* single (ticket), *US* one-way (ticket)

**billetera** *nf*, **billetero** *nm* wallet

**billón** *núm Br* billion, *US* trillion; *ver también* **seis**

**bimensual** *adj* twice-monthly

**bimestral** *adj* two-monthly

**bimestre** *nm* two months

**bimotor 1** *adj* twin-engine(d); **avión b.** twin-engine(d) plane
 **2** *nm* twin-engine(d) plane

**binario, -a** *adj también Informát* binary

**bingo** *nm* (**a**) *(juego)* bingo (**b**) *(sala)* bingo hall (**c**) *(premio)* (full) house

**binoculares** *nmpl (prismáticos)* binoculars; *(de ópera, teatro)* opera glasses

**binomio** *nm* (**a**) *Mat* binomial (**b**) *Fig (de personas)* duo

**biodegradable** *adj* biodegradable

**biofísica** *nf* biophysics *(singular)*

**biofísico, -a** *adj* biophysical

**biografía** *nf* biography

**biográfico, -a** *adj* biographical

**biógrafo, -a** *nm,f (persona)* biographer

**bioingeniería** *nf* bioengineering

**biología** *nf* biology

**biológico, -a** *adj* biological

**biólogo, -a** *nm,f* biologist

**biomasa** *nf Biol* biomass

**biombo** *nm* (folding) screen

**biopsia** *nf* biopsy

**bioquímica** *nf (ciencia)* biochemistry

**bioquímico, -a 1** *adj* biochemical
 **2** *nm,f (persona)* biochemist

**biorritmo** *nm* biorhythm

**biosfera** *nf* biosphere

**bióxido** *nm Quím* dioxide; **b. de carbono** carbon dioxide

**bipartidismo** *nm Pol* two-party system

**bipartidista** *adj Pol* **sistema b.** two-party system

**bipartito, -a** *adj* bipartite

**bípedo, -a 1** *adj* two-legged
 **2** *nm,f* biped

**biplano** *nm* biplane

**biplaza 1** *adj* **vehículo b.** two-seater
 **2** *nm* two-seater

**bipolar** *adj* bipolar

**biquini** *nm (bañador)* bikini

**birlar** *vt Fam* to pinch, to nick

**birlibirloque** *nm* **como por arte de b.** as if by magic

**Birmania** *n* Burma

**birmano, -a 1** *adj & nm,f* Burmese
 **2** *nm (lengua)* Burmese

**birome** *nm o nf CSur* Biro®

**birra** *nf muy Fam* beer

**birrete** *nm* (**a**) *(de clérigo)* biretta (**b**) *(de catedrático)* mortarboard (**c**) *(de abogados, jueces)* = cap worn by judges and lawyers

**birria** *nf Fam (persona)* drip; **una b. de jugador** a useless player; **esta película es una b.** this film is a load of rubbish

**birriático, -a, birrioso, -a** *adj Fam (malo)* pathetic; *(escaso)* measly

**biruji** *nm Fam* **¡qué b. hace!** it's freezing cold!

**bis** (*pl* **bises**) **1** *adj inv* **viven en el 150 b.** they live at 150a
 **2** *nm* encore
 **3** *adv Mús (para repetir)* bis

**bisabuelo, -a** *nm,f* great-grandfather, *f* great-grandmother; **bisabuelos** great-grandparents

**bisagra** *nf* hinge

**bisbisar, bisbisear** *vt Fam* to mutter

**bisbiseo** *nm* muttering

**biscote** *nm* rusk

**bisección** *nf Mat* bisection

**bisectriz** *nf Mat* bisector

**bisel** *nm* bevel

**biselado, -a 1** *adj* bevelled
 **2** *nm* bevelling

**biselar** *vt* to bevel

**bisemanal** *adj* twice-weekly

**bisexual** *adj & nmf* bisexual

**bisiesto** *adj* **año b.** leap year

**bisílabo, -a** *adj* two-syllabled

**bismuto** *nm Quím* bismuth

**bisnieto, -a** *nm,f (varón)* great-grandson, great-grandchild; *(hembra)* great-granddaughter, great-grandchild; **bisnietos** great-grandchildren

**bisonte** *nm* bison

**bisoñé** *nm* toupee

**bisoño, -a** *nm,f* novice

**Bissau** *n* Bissau

**bistec** *nm* steak

**bisturí** (*pl* **bisturíes**) *nm* scalpel

**bisutería** *nf* imitation jewellery

**bit** [bit] (*pl* **bits**) *nm Informát* bit

**bitácora** *nf Náut* binnacle

**bíter, bitter** *nm* bitters *(singular)*

**bituminoso, -a** *adj* bituminous

**bizantino, -a 1** *adj* (**a**) *Hist* Byzantine (**b**) *(discusión, razonamiento)* hair-splitting
 **2** *nm,f* Byzantine

**bizarría** *nf* (**a**) *(valor)* bravery (**b**) *(generosidad)* generosity

**bizarro, -a** *adj* (**a**) *(valiente)* brave, valiant (**b**) *(generoso)* generous

**bizco, -a 1** *adj* cross-eyed
 **2** *nm,f* cross-eyed person

**bizcocho** *nm (de repostería)* sponge

**bizquear** *vi* to squint

**bizquera** *nf* squint

**blablablá** *nm Fam* blah, blahblah

**blanca** *nf Mús* minim; *Fig* **estar** *o* **quedarse sin b.** to be flat broke

**blanco, -a 1** *adj* white; **en b.** *(página, cuaderno)* blank; **se quedó con la mente en b.** his mind went blank; **una noche en b.** a sleepless night

**2** *nm,f (persona)* white

**3** *nm* **(a)** *(color)* white; **b. del ojo** white of the eye

**(b)** *(diana)* target; **dar en el b.** to hit the target; *Fig* to hit the nail on the head

**(c)** *Fig (objetivo)* target; *(de miradas)* object

**(d)** *(espacio vacío)* blank (space)

**(e)** *(vino)* white wine

**blancura** *nf* whiteness

**blancuzco, -a** *adj* off-white

**blandengue** *adj también Fig* weak

**blandir** *vt* to brandish

**blando, -a** *adj* **(a)** *(suave, mullido)* soft **(b)** *Fig (persona) (débil)* weak; *(indulgente)* lenient, soft

**blandura** *nf* **(a)** *(calidad de suave, mullido)* softness **(b)** *Fig (debilidad)* weakness; *(indulgencia)* leniency

**blanqueador, -ora 1** *adj* **líquido b.** whitener

**2** *nm (líquido)* whitener

**blanquear** *vt* **(a)** *(ropa)* to whiten; *(con lejía)* to bleach; *Fig (dinero)* to launder **(b)** *(con cal)* to whitewash

**blanquecino, -a** *adj* off-white

**blanqueo** *nm* **(a)** *(de ropa)* whitening; *(con lejía)* bleaching; *Fig* **b. de dinero** money laundering **(b)** *(encalado)* whitewashing

**blanquillo** *nm* **(a)** *CAm, Méx* egg **(b)** *Andes* white peach

**blasfemar** *vi* **(a)** *Rel* to blaspheme **(contra** against) **(b)** *(maldecir)* to swear, to curse

**blasfemia** *nf* **(a)** *Rel* blasphemy **(b)** *(palabrota)* curse **(c)** *Fig (injuria)* **es una b. hablar así de…** it's sacrilege to talk like that about…

**blasfemo, -a 1** *adj* blasphemous

**2** *nm,f* blasphemer

**blasón** *nm (escudo)* coat of arms; *Fig (orgullo)* honour, glory

**blaugrana** *adj inv Dep* = relating to Barcelona football club

**bledo** *nm Fam* **me importa un b. (lo que diga)** I don't give a damn (about what he says)

**blenorragia, blenorrea** *nf Med* gonorrhoea

**blindado, -a 1** *adj (puerta)* armour-plated; **coche b.** bullet-proof car; *Mil* **vehículo b.**

armoured vehicle; *Mil* **columna blindada** armoured column

**2** *nm Mil (vehículo)* armoured vehicle

**blindaje** *nm (de puerta)* armour-plating; *(de coche)* armour

**blindar** *vt* to armour-plate

**bloc** *(pl blocs)* *nm* pad; **b. de dibujo** sketchpad; **b. de notas** notepad

**blocar [61]** *vt Dep* to block

**blonda** *nf (encaje)* lace trim

**bloque 1** *ver* **blocar**

**2** *nm* **(a)** *(edificio, pieza) & Informát* block **(b)** *Pol* bloc; **en b.** en masse **(c)** *Tec* cylinder block

**bloquear 1** *vt* **(a)** *también Dep* to block **(b)** *(con ejército, barcos)* to blockade; *(por nieve, inundación)* to cut off **(c)** *Fin* to freeze **(d)** *Aut* to lock

**2 bloquearse** *vpr (atascarse)* to be stuck; *Fig (persona)* to have a mental block

**bloqueo** *nm* **(a)** *también Dep* blocking; **b. mental** mental block **(b)** *Econ & Mil* blockade **(c)** *Fin* freeze, freezing **(d)** *Aut* locking

**blues** [blus] *nm inv Mús* blues

**blusa** *nf* blouse

**blusón** *nm* smock

**bluyín** *nm,* **bluyines** *nmpl Am* jeans

**BNG** *nm (abrev de* **Bloque Nacionalista Gallego)** = Galician nationalist party

**boa 1** *nf (serpiente)* boa; **b. constrictor** boa constrictor

**2** *nm (prenda)* (feather) boa

**boato** *nm* show, ostentation

**bobada** *nf* **decir/hacer una b.** to say/do something stupid; **decir bobadas** to talk nonsense; **hacer bobadas** to mess about

**bobalicón, -ona** *Fam* **1** *adj* simple

**2** *nm,f* simpleton

**bóbilis** *adv Fam* **de b. b.** *(de balde)* for free, for nothing

**bobina** *nf* **(a)** *(de cordel, cable, papel)* reel; *(en máquina de coser)* bobbin **(b)** *Elec* coil

**bobinar** *vt* to wind

**bobo, -a 1** *adj* **(a)** *(tonto)* stupid, daft **(b)** *(ingenuo)* naive, simple

**2** *nm,f* **(a)** *(tonto)* fool, idiot **(b)** *(ingenuo)* simpleton

**boca** *nf* **(a)** *(de persona, animal)* mouth; **b. arriba/abajo** face up/down; **abrir** *o* **hacer b.** to whet one's appetite; **andar** *o* **ir de b. en b.** to be on everyone's lips; **a pedir de b.** perfectly; **cerrar la b. a alguien** to make sb shut up; **se fue de la b.** he let the cat out of the bag; **me lo has quitado de la b.** you took the words right out of my mouth; **meterse en la b. del lobo** to put one's head into the lion's mouth; **no decir esta b. es mía** not to open one's mouth; **por la b. muere el pez** silence is golden; **quedarse con la b. abierta** to be left speechless; **se me hace la b. agua** it makes my mouth water; **tapar la b. a alguien** to silence sb; **(respiración) b. a b.** mouth-to-mouth resuscitation

(**b**) *Fig (entrada)* opening; *(de cañón)* muzzle; **b. del estómago** pit of the stomach; **b. de metro** *Br* tube *o* underground entrance, *US* subway entrance; **b. de riego** hydrant; **a b. de jarro** point-blank

**bocacalle** *nf (entrada)* entrance *(to a street)*; *(calle)* side street; **gire en la tercera b.** take the third turning

**bocadillo** *nm* (a) *(comida)* sandwich (b) *(en cómic)* speech bubble, balloon

**bocado** *nm* (a) *(comida)* mouthful; **no probar b.** *(por desgana)* not to touch one's food; **no he probado b. en todo el día** I haven't had a bite to eat all day (b) *(mordisco)* bite (c) **b. de Adán** Adam's apple

**bocajarro** *nm* **a b.** point-blank; **se lo dije a b.** I told him to his face

**bocamanga** *nf* cuff

**bocanada** *nf (de líquido)* mouthful; *(de humo)* puff; *(de viento)* gust

**bocata** *nm Fam* sandwich, *Br* sarnie

**bocazas** *nmf inv Fam Pey* big mouth, blabbermouth

**boceto** *nm* sketch, rough outline

**bocha** *nf (bolo)* bowl; **bochas** *(juego)* bowls *(singular)*

**bochinche** *nm Fam* commotion, uproar

**bochorno** *nm* (a) *(calor)* stifling *o* muggy heat (b) *(vergüenza)* embarrassment

**bochornoso, -a** *adj* (a) *(tiempo)* stifling, muggy (b) *(vergonzoso)* embarrassing

**bocina** *nf* (a) *Aut & Mús* horn (b) *(megáfono)* megaphone, loudhailer

**bocinazo** *nm Aut* hoot

**bocio** *nm Med* goitre

**bock** *(pl* **bocks)** *nm* stein

**boda** *nf* wedding; **bodas de diamante/oro/plata** diamond/golden/silver wedding

**bodega** *nf* (a) *(cava)* wine cellar (b) *(tienda)* wine shop; *(taberna)* bar *(mainly selling wine)* (c) *(en buque, avión)* hold (d) *Am (colmado)* small grocery store (e) *Méx (almacén)* store

**bodegón** *nm* (a) *Arte* still life (b) *(taberna)* tavern, inn

**bodeguero, -a** *nm,f (dueño)* = owner of a wine cellar

**bodrio** *nm muy Fam Pey (comida)* slop, pigswill; **ser un b.** *(película, novela, cuadro)* to be rubbish; **¡qué b.!** what a load of rubbish!

**body** ['boði] *(pl* **bodies)** *nm* body *(garment)*

**BOE** ['boe] *nm (abrev de* **Boletín Oficial del Estado)** official Spanish gazette, = daily state publication, giving details of legislation, etc

**bóer** *nmf* Boer

**bofe** *nm Fam* **echar el b.** *o* **los bofes** to puff and pant

**bofetada** *nf* slap (in the face); **dar una b. a alguien** to slap sb (in the face); *Fig* **darse de bofetadas con algo** *(no armonizar)* to clash with sth

**bofetón** *nm* hard slap (in the face)

**bofia** *nf muy Fam* **la b.** the cops

**boga** *nf* **estar en b.** to be in vogue

**bogar** [40] *vi* (a) *(remar)* to row (b) *(navegar)* to sail

**bogavante** *nm* lobster

**Bogotá** *n* Bogota

**bogue** *etc ver* **bogar**

**Bohemia** *n* Bohemia

**bohemia** *nf* bohemian lifestyle

**bohemio, -a 1** *adj* (a) *(aspecto, vida, barrio)* bohemian (b) *(de Bohemia)* Bohemian

**2** *nm,f* (a) *(artista, vividor)* bohemian (b) *(de Bohemia)* Bohemian

**bohío** *nm Carib* hut

**boicot** *(pl* **boicots)** *nm* boycott

**boicotear** *vt* to boycott

**boicoteo** *nm* boycotting

**boina** *nf* beret

**boîte** [bwat] *(pl* **boîtes)** *nf* nightclub

**boj** *(pl* **bojes)** *nm* (a) *(árbol)* box (b) *(madera)* boxwood

**bol** *(pl* **boles)** *nm* bowl

**bola** *nf* (a) *(esfera)* ball; *(canica)* marble; **b. de cristal** crystal ball; **b. de nieve** snowball; **bolas de naftalina** *o* **alcanfor** mothballs; *Fig* **convertirse en una b. de nieve** to snowball (b) *Fam (mentira)* fib (c) *Am (rumor)* rumour (d) *(expresiones)* **en bolas** stark-naked, *Br* starkers; **no rascar b.** to get everything wrong

**bolada** *nf CSur Fam* opportunity

**bolchevique** *adj & nmf* Bolshevik

**bolchevismo** *nm* Bolshevism

**boldo** *nm (infusión)* = type of herbal tea

**bolea** *nf Dep* volley

**boleador** *nm Am* shoe shine boy

**boleadoras** *nfpl* bolas, = set of three ropes, weighted at the ends, used by Argentinian gauchos for capturing cattle by entangling their legs

**bolear** *vt Méx* to shine, to polish

**bolera** *nf* bowling alley

**bolero** *nm* bolero

**boletería** *nf Am* box office, ticket office

**boletín** *nm* journal, periodical; **b. de noticias** *o* **informativo** news bulletin; **b.**

**meteorológico** weather forecast; **b. de prensa** press release; **b. de suscripción** subscription form; **Boletín Oficial del Estado** official Spanish gazette, = daily state publication, giving details of legislation, etc

**boleto** *nm* (a) *(de lotería, rifa)* ticket; *(de quinielas)* coupon; **b. de apuestas** betting slip (b) *Am (billete)* ticket

**boli** *nm Fam* Biro®

**boliche** *nm* (a) *(en petanca)* jack (b) *(bolos)* tenpin bowling (c) *(bolera)* bowling alley (d) *CSur (tienda)* small grocery store

**bólido** *nm* racing car; *Fig* **ir como un b.** to go like the clappers

**bolígrafo** *nm* ballpoint pen, Biro®

**bolillo** *nm* (a) *(en costura)* bobbin (b) *Méx (panecillo)* bread roll

**bolinga** *muy Fam* **1** *adj (borracho)* plastered, *Br* pissed

**2** *nm (persona)* boozer, *Br* piss artist

**3** *nf* **agarrar una b.** to get plastered

**bolitas** *nfpl CSur* marbles

**bolívar** *nm* bolivar

**Bolivia** *n* Bolivia

**boliviano, -a** *adj & nm,f* Bolivian

**bollera** *nf muy Fam* dyke

**bollería** *nf* (a) *(tienda)* cake shop (b) *(productos)* cakes

**bollo** *nm* (a) *(para comer) (de pan)* (bread) roll; *(dulce)* bun (b) *(abolladura)* dent; *(abultamiento)* bump (c) *Fam Fig (persona atractiva)* dish, gorgeous guy/woman; **ser un b.** to be a bit of all right

**bolo** *nm* (a) *Dep (pieza)* skittle, bowling pin; **el juego de los bolos** skittles, bowling (b) *CAm (borracho)* drunk

**bolsa** *nf* (a) *(recipiente)* bag; **b. de aire** air pocket; **b. de basura** bin liner; **b. de deportes** holdall, sports bag; *CSur* **b. de dormir** sleeping bag; **b. de plástico** *(en tiendas)* carrier *o* plastic bag; *Fig* **b. de pobreza** deprived area; **b. de viaje** travel bag

(b) *Fin* **b. (de valores)** stock exchange, stock market; **la b. ha subido/bajado** share prices have gone up/down; **jugar a la b.** to speculate on the stock market

(c) *(de dinero)* **¡la b. o la vida!** your money or your life!

(d) **b. de trabajo** *(en universidad, organización)* = list of job vacancies and situations wanted; *(en periódico)* appointments section

(e) *Min* pocket

(f) *Anat* sac

**bolsillo** *nm* pocket; **calculadora de b.** pocket calculator; **edición de b.** pocket edition; **lo pagué de mi b.** I paid for it out of my own pocket; **meterse** *o* **tener a alguien en el b.** to

have sb eating out of one's hand; *Fam* **rascarse el b.** to fork out

**bolso** *nm* bag; *(de mujer)* handbag

**boludo, -a** *nm,f CSur muy Fam Br* prat, *US* jerk

**bomba 1** *nf* (a) *(explosivo)* bomb; **b. atómica** atom *o* nuclear bomb; **b. H** *o* **de hidrógeno** H *o* hydrogen bomb; **b. lacrimógena** tear gas grenade; **b. de mano** (hand) grenade; **b. de neutrones** neutron bomb; **b. de relojería** time-bomb

(b) *(de agua, de bicicleta)* pump; *(en gasolinera) Br* petrol pump, *US* gas pump; *Med* **b. de cobalto** cobalt bomb; **b. hidráulica** hydraulic pump

(c) *Fig (acontecimiento)* bombshell; **caer como una b.** to be a bombshell

(d) *Am (gasolinera) Br* petrol station, *US* gas station

(e) *Fam* **pasarlo b.** to have a great time; **la fiesta de anoche fue la b.** the party last night was something else

**2** *adj inv Fam* astounding

**bombacha** *nf CSur* loose trousers; **bombachas** knickers

**bombachos** *nmpl* baggy trousers

**bombardear** *vt también Fig* to bombard

**bombardeo** *nm* bombardment; **b. aéreo** air raid; *Fís* **b. atómico** bombardment in a particle accelerator

**bombardero** *nm (avión)* bomber

**bombazo** *nm (explosión)* explosion, blast; *Fig (noticia)* bombshell

**bombear** *vt también Dep* to pump

**bombeo** *nm* (a) *(de líquido)* pumping (b) *(abombamiento)* bulge

**bombero, -a** *nm,f* (a) *(de incendios)* fireman, *f* firewoman; **tener ideas de b.** to have crazy ideas (b) *Andes (de gasolinera) Br* petrol-pump *o US* gas-pump attendant

**bombilla** *nf* light bulb

**bombillo** *nm Andes, CAm* light bulb

**bombín** *nm* bowler (hat)

**bombo** *nm* (a) *Mús* bass drum; *Fam* **tengo la cabeza como un b.** my head is throbbing; *muy Fam* **estar con b.** to be in the club, to be up the duff (b) *Fam (elogio)* hype; **a b. y platillo** with a lot of hype; **le están dando mucho b. a la nueva película** the new film is getting a lot of hype (c) *Tec* drum

**bombón** *nm* (a) *(golosina)* chocolate (b) *Fam Fig (mujer)* **ser un b.** to be a bit of all right

**bombona** *nf* cylinder; **b. de butano** (butane) gas cylinder

**bonachón, -ona 1** *adj* kindly

**2** *nm,f* kindly person

**bonaerense 1** *adj* of/from Buenos Aires

**2** *nmf* person from Buenos Aires

**bonancible** *adj (tiempo)* fair; *(mar)* calm

**bonanza** *nf (de tiempo)* fair weather; *(de mar)* calm at sea; *Fig (prosperidad)* prosperity

**bondad** *nf (cualidad)* goodness; *(inclinación)* kindness; **tener la b. de hacer algo** to be kind enough to do sth

**bondadoso, -a** *adj* kind, good-natured

**bonete** *nm (eclesiástico)* biretta; *(universitario)* mortarboard

**bongó** *nm* bongo (drum)

**boniato** *nm* sweet potato

**bonificación** *nf* (a) *(oferta especial)* bonus; *(descuento)* discount (b) *(mejora)* improvement

**bonificar** [61] *vt* (a) *(descontar)* to give a discount of (b) *(mejorar)* to improve

**bonito, -a 1** *adj* (a) *(lindo)* pretty; *(agradable)* nice (b) *Irón* **¡muy b.!** great!, wonderful!; **¿te parece b. lo que has hecho?** are you proud of what you've done, then?

**2** *nm* bonito *(type of tuna)*

**Bonn** *n* Bonn

**bono** *nm* (a) *(vale)* voucher (b) *Com* bond; **b. basura/de caja** junk/short-term bond; **b. del Estado/del tesoro** government/treasury bond

**bonobús** (*pl* **bonobuses**) *nm* = multiple-journey bus ticket

**bonoloto** *nm* = Spanish state-run lottery

**bonotrén** *nm* multiple-journey railway ticket

**bonsái** *nm* bonsai

**bonzo** *nm* (a) *(budista)* Buddhist monk, bonze (b) **quemarse a lo b.** to set oneself alight

**boñiga** *nf* cowpat

**boom** *nm* boom

**boqueada** *nf* **dar las (últimas) boqueadas** to breathe one's last

**boquear** *vi* to breathe one's last

**boquera** *nf* = cracked lip in the corner of one's mouth

**boquerón** *nm* (fresh) anchovy; **boquerones en vinagre** pickled anchovy fillets

**boquete** *nm* hole

**boquiabierto, -a** *adj* open-mouthed; *Fig* astounded, speechless

**boquilla** *nf* (a) *(para fumar)* cigarette holder (b) *(de pipa, instrumento musical)* mouthpiece (c) *(de tubo, aparato)* nozzle (d) *Fam* **es todo de b.** it's all hot air

**borbónico, -a** *adj* Bourbon

**borbotear, borbotar** *vi* to bubble

**borboteo** *nm* bubbling

**borbotón** *nm* **salir a borbotones** to gush out

**borda** *nf Náut* gunwale; *Fig* **tirar** *o* **echar algo por la b.** to throw sth overboard; **un**

**fuera b.** *(barco)* an outboard motorboat; *(motor)* an outboard motor

**bordado, -a 1** *adj* embroidered; *Fig* **el discurso/examen le salió b.** his speech/the exam went like a dream

**2** *nm* embroidery

**bordar** *vt (coser)* to embroider; *Fig (hacer bien)* to do excellently; **la actriz borda el papel de Cleopatra** the actress is outstanding in the role of Cleopatra

**borde 1** *adj muy Fam (antipático)* miserable, *Br* stroppy

**2** *nmf muy Fam (antipático)* miserable *o Br* stroppy person

**3** *nm (límite)* edge; *(de carretera)* side; *(de río)* bank; *(de vaso, botella)* rim; *Fig* **al b. de** on the verge *o* brink of

**bordeado, -a** *adj* **b. de** lined with; **un camino b. de árboles** a tree-lined path

**bordear** *vt* (a) *(estar alrededor de)* to border; *(moverse alrededor de)* to skirt (round) (b) *Fig (rozar)* to be close to

**bordillo** *nm* kerb

**bordo** *nm Náut & Av* **a b.** on board; **bienvenidos a b.** welcome aboard

**boreal** *adj* northern

**borgoña** *nm* burgundy

**bórico** *adj* boric

**borla** *nf (de flecos)* tassel; *(pompón)* pompom

**borne** *nm Elec* terminal

**Borneo** *n* Borneo

**boro** *nm Quím* boron

**borra** *nf (lana basta)* flock

**borrachera** *nf (embriaguez)* drunkenness; *Fig (emoción)* intoxication; **tener/cogerse una b.** to be/get drunk

**borrachín, -ina** *nm,f Fam* boozer

**borracho, -a 1** *adj (ebrio)* drunk; *Fig* **b. de** *(emocionado)* drunk *o* intoxicated with

**2** *nm,f (persona)* drunk

**3** *nm (bizcocho)* $\simeq$ rum baba, = sponge cake soaked in alcohol

**borrador** *nm* (a) *(escrito)* rough draft (b) *(para pizarra)* board duster; *(goma de borrar) Br* rubber, *US* eraser

**borraja** *nf* borage

**borrar 1** *vt* (a) *(hacer desaparecer) (con goma) Br* to rub out, *US* to erase; *(en ordenador)* to delete; *(en casete)* to erase; *Fig* **b. a alguien/algo del mapa** to wipe sb/sth off the map (b) *(tachar)* to cross out; *Fig (de lista)* to take off; **me he borrado de las clases** I've stopped going to those classes (c) *(la pizarra)* to wipe, to dust (d) *Fig (olvidar)* to erase

**2 borrarse** *vpr* (a) *(desaparecer)* to disappear; *Fig* **se borró del mapa** he dropped out of sight, he disappeared from circulation (b) *Fig*

*(olvidarse)* to be wiped away; **se le borró de la mente** he forgot all about it

**borrasca** *nf (tormenta)* thunderstorm; *Met (baja presión)* area of low pressure

**borrascoso, -a** *adj (tiempo)* stormy; *Fig (vida, reunión, relación)* stormy, tempestuous

**borrego, -a** *nm,f* (a) *(animal)* lamb (b) *Fam Pey (persona)* **todos le siguen como borregos** they all follow him like sheep

**borrico, -a 1** *adj* dimwitted, dim
 **2** *nm,f* donkey; *Fig* dimwit, dunce

**borriquero** *adj* **cardo b.** cotton thistle

**borriqueta** *nf* trestle

**borrón** *nm (de tinta)* blot; *Fig* blemish; **hacer b. y cuenta nueva** to wipe the slate clean

**borronear** *vt* (a) *(garabatear)* to scribble on (b) *(escribir deprisa)* to scribble

**borroso, -a** *adj (foto, visión)* blurred; *(escritura, texto)* smudgy

**Bósforo** *nm* **el B.** the Bosphorus

**Bosnia** *n* Bosnia

**Bosnia(-Herzegóvina)** *n* Bosnia (-Herzegovina)

**bosnio, -a** *adj & nm,f* Bosnian

**bosque** *nm (pequeño)* wood; *(grande)* forest

**bosquejar** *vt (esbozar)* to sketch (out); *Fig (dar una idea de)* to give a rough outline of

**bosquejo** *nm (esbozo)* sketch; *Fig (de idea, tema, situación)* rough outline

**bosquimano, -a** *nm,f* Bushman

**bossa-nova** *nf* bossa nova

**bosta** *nf* cow dung

**bostezar** [16] *vi* to yawn

**bostezo** *nm* yawn

**bota** *nf* (a) *(calzado)* boot; **botas camperas/ de montar** cowboy/riding boots; **botas de agua** *o* **de lluvia** wellingtons; *Fig* **morir con las botas puestas** to die with one's boots on; *Fam Fig* **ponerse las botas** *(comiendo)* to stuff one's face (b) *(de vino)* = small leather container in which wine is kept

**botadura** *nf* launching

**botana** *nf Am* snack, tapa

**botánica** *nf (ciencia)* botany

**botánico, -a 1** *adj* botanical
 **2** *nm,f (persona)* botanist

**botanista** *nmf* botanist

**botar 1** *vt* (a) *(pelota)* to bounce (b) *(barco)* to launch (c) *Fam (despedir)* to throw *o* kick out (d) *Dep (córner)* to take (e) *Am (tirar)* to throw away
 **2** *vi* (a) *(saltar)* to jump; *Fam Fig* **está que bota** he is hopping mad (b) *(pelota)* to bounce

**botarate** *nm Fam* madcap

**botavara** *nf Náut* boom

**bote** *nm* (a) *(envase)* *(tarro)* jar; *(lata)* tin, can; *(de champú, pastillas)* bottle; *Am* **b. de la basura**

*Br* rubbish bin, *US* garbage can; **b. de humo** smoke canister
 (b) *(barca)* boat; **b. salvavidas** lifeboat
 (c) *(propinas)* tips; **para el b.** as a tip
 (d) *(salto)* jump; **dar botes** *(saltar)* to jump up and down; *(tren, coche)* to bump up and down; **pegar un b.** *(de susto)* to jump, to give a start
 (e) *(de pelota)* bounce; **dar botes** to bounce; *Dep* **a b. pronto** on the rebound
 (f) *(expresiones)* **chupar del b.** to feather one's nest; **tener en el b. a alguien** to have sb eating out of one's hand; **a b. pronto** *(sin pensar)* off the top of one's head; **de b. en b.** chock-ablock

**botella** *nf* bottle; **b. de oxígeno** oxygen cylinder

**botellazo** *nm* blow with a bottle

**botellero** *nm* wine rack

**botellín** *nm (de cerveza)* small bottle *(0.2 litre)*

**botica** *nf Anticuado* pharmacy, *Br* chemist's (shop)

**boticario, -a** *nm,f Anticuado* pharmacist, *Br* chemist

**botijo** *nm* = earthenware vessel with a spout used for drinking water

**botín** *nm* (a) *(de guerra, atraco)* plunder, loot; **repartirse el b.** to share out the spoils (b) *(calzado)* ankle boot

**botiquín** *nm (caja)* first-aid kit; *(mueble)* first-aid cupboard; *(enfermería)* sick bay

**botón** *nm (para abrochar, de aparato)* button; *(de timbre)* buzzer; *Fig* **b. de muestra** sample; **botones** *(de hotel)* bellboy, *US* bellhop; *(de oficina)* errand boy

**botonadura** *nf* buttons

**Botsuana** *n* Botswana

**botulismo** *nm* botulism

**bouquet** [bu'ke] *(pl* bouquets*)* *nm* bouquet

**bourbon** ['burβon] *(pl* bourbons*)* *nm* bourbon

**boutique** [bu'tik] *nf* boutique

**bóveda** *nf Arquit* vault; **b. celeste** firmament; **b. craneal** cranial vault

**bovino, -a** *adj* bovine; **ganado b.** cattle

**box** *(pl* boxes*)* *nm* (a) *(de caballo)* stall (b) *(de coches)* pit; **entrar en boxes** to make a pit stop (c) *Am (boxeo)* boxing

**boxeador, -ora** *nm,f* boxer

**boxear** *vi* to box

**boxeo** *nm* boxing

**bóxer** *(pl* bóxers*)* *nm* (a) *(perro)* boxer (b) *(calzoncillo)* boxer shorts

**boya** *nf* (a) *(en el mar)* buoy (b) *(de una red)* float

**boyante** adj (a) (feliz) happy (b) (próspero) (empresa, negocio) prosperous; (economía, comercio) buoyant

**boy scout** [bojes'kaut] (pl **boy scouts**) nm boy scout

**bozal** nm (a) (para perro) muzzle (b) Am (cabestro) halter

**bozo** nm (bigote) down (on upper lip)

**bracear** vi (a) (mover los brazos) to wave one's arms about (b) (nadar) to swim

**bracero** nm (a) (jornalero) day labourer (b) Am wetback, = illegal Mexican immigrant in the US

**braga** nf knickers; **una b., unas bragas** a pair of knickers; **muy Fam estar hecho una b.** to be whacked; **muy Fam coger** o **pillar a alguien en bragas** to catch sb unprepared; **¿la capital de Chad? ¡me pillas en bragas!** the capital of Chad? you've got me there!

**bragado, -a** adj (persona) gutsy

**bragazas** nm inv Fam Pey henpecked man

**braguero** nm truss

**bragueta** nf Br flies, US zipper

**braguetazo** nm Fam marriage for money

**brahmán, bramán** nm Brahman

**brahmanismo, bramanismo** nm Brahmanism

**braille** ['braile] nm Braille

**brainstorming** [brein'stormin] (pl **brainstormings**) nm brainstorming session

**bramante** nm cord

**bramar** vi (a) (animal) to bellow (b) (persona) (de dolor) to groan; (de ira) to roar

**bramido** nm (a) (de animal) bellow (b) (de persona) (de dolor) groan; (de ira) roar

**brandy** nm brandy

**branquias** nfpl gills

**brasa** nf ember; Culin **a la b.** barbecued

**brasear** vt to barbecue

**brasero** nm brazier

**brasier** nm Am bra

**Brasil** nm (el) B. Brazil

**brasileño, -a** adj & nm,f Brazilian

**brasilero, -a** adj & nm,f CSur Brazilian

**Brasilia** n Brasilia

**brassier** nm Am bra

**Bratislava** n Bratislava

**bravatas** nfpl (a) (amenazas) threats (b) (fanfarronería) bravado

**braveza** nf (de persona) bravery; (del viento, mar) fierceness, fury

**bravío, -a** adj (caballo, toro) spirited; (persona) free-spirited; (mar) choppy, rough

**bravo, -a1** adj (a) (valiente) brave (b) (violento) fierce (c) (animal, planta) wild (d) (mar) rough
**2** interj ¡b.! bravo!

**bravucón, -ona1** adj swaggering
**2** nm,f braggart

**bravuconada** nf show of bravado

**bravuconear** vi to brag

**bravuconería** nf bravado

**bravura** nf (a) (de persona) bravery (b) (de animal) ferocity

**braza** nf (a) Dep breaststroke; **nadar a b.** to do the breaststroke (b) (medida) fathom

**brazada** nf stroke

**brazalete** nm (a) (en la muñeca) bracelet (b) (en el brazo, para nadar) armband

**brazo** nm (a) (de persona, sillón) arm; (de animal) foreleg; **cogidos del b.** arm in arm; **en brazos** in one's arms; Fig **echarse en brazos de alguien** to throw oneself at sb; **luchar a b. partido** (con empeño) to fight tooth and nail; **con los brazos abiertos** with open arms; Fig **quedarse de brazos cruzados** to sit back and do nothing; **no dio su b. a torcer** he didn't budge an inch, he didn't allow himself to be persuaded; **ser el b. derecho de alguien** to be sb's right-hand man (f woman); **el b. político de ETA** the political wing of ETA; **b. de gitano** Br swiss roll, US jelly roll; Geog **b. de mar** arm (of the sea)
(b) (de árbol, río, candelabro) branch; (de grúa) boom, jib
(c) Fig (trabajador) hand

**Brazzaville** [bratsa'βil] n Brazzaville

**brea** nf (sustancia) tar; (para barco) pitch

**break** nm Dep **punto de b.** break point

**brear** vt Fam Fig (a palos) to bash in; **b. a preguntas** to bombard with questions

**brebaje** nm concoction, foul drink

**brecha** nf (a) (abertura) hole, opening (b) Mil breach (c) Fig (impresión) impression (d) **seguir en la b.** to keep at it

**brécol** nm broccoli

**brega** nf (lucha) struggle, fight

**bregar** [40] vi (a) (luchar) to struggle, to fight (b) (trabajar) to work hard (c) (reñir) to quarrel

**breña** nf scrub

**Bretaña** n Brittany

**brete** nm fix, difficulty; **estar en un b.** to be in a fix; **poner a alguien en un b.** to put sb in a difficult position

**breteles** nmpl inv CSur braces

**bretón, -ona1** adj & nm,f Breton
**2** nm (lengua) Breton

**breva** nf (a) (fruta) early fig (b) (cigarro) flat cigar (c) Fam ¡**no caerá esa b.!** some chance (of that happening!)

**breve1** adj brief; **en b.** (pronto) shortly; (en pocas palabras) in short
**2** nf Mús breve

**brevedad** *nf* shortness; **a** *o* **con la mayor b.** as soon as possible

**breviario** *nm* (**a**) *Rel* breviary (**b**) *(compendio)* compendium

**brezal** *nm* moorland, moors

**brezo** *nm* heather

**bribón, -ona** *nm,f* scoundrel, rogue

**bribonada** *nf* **ser una b.** to be a roguish thing to do; **bribonadas** roguery

**bricolaje** *nm* D.I.Y., do-it-yourself

**brida** *nf* (**a**) *(de caballo)* bridle (**b**) *(de tubo)* bracket, collar (**c**) *Med* adhesion

**bridge** [britʃ] *nm* bridge

**brigada 1** *nm Mil* warrant officer

  **2** *nf* (**a**) *Mil* brigade (**b**) *(equipo)* squad, team; **b. antidisturbios/antidroga** riot/drug squad

**brigadier** *nm* brigadier

**brigadista** *nmf Hist* = member or veteran of the International Brigades during the Spanish Civil War

**brillante 1** *adj* (**a**) *(reluciente) (luz, astro)* shining; *(metal, zapatos, pelo)* shiny; *(ojos, sonrisa, diamante)* sparkling (**b**) *(magnífico)* brilliant; **el pianista estuvo b.** the pianist was outstanding

  **2** *nm* diamond

**brillantez** *nf Fig* brilliance; **hacer algo con b.** to do sth outstandingly

**brillantina** *nf* hair cream, Brylcreem®

**brillar** *vi también Fig* to shine; **b. por su ausencia** to be conspicuous by its/one's absence; **b. con luz propia** to be outstanding

**brillo** *nm* (**a**) *(resplandor) (de luz)* brilliance; *(de estrellas)* shining; *(de zapatos)* shine; **sacar b. a** to polish, to shine (**b**) *(lucimiento)* splendour, brilliance

**brilloso, -a** *adj Am* shining

**brincar** [61] *vi (saltar)* to skip (about); **b. de alegría** to jump for joy; *Fig* **está que brinca** *(enfadado)* he's hopping mad

**brinco** *nm* jump; *Fig* **en un b.** in a second, quickly; **pegar un b.** to jump, to give a start

**brindar 1** *vi* to drink a toast; **b. por algo/alguien** to drink to sth/sb; **b. a la salud de alguien** to drink to sb's health

  **2** *vt* to offer; **b. el triunfo a alguien** to dedicate one's victory to sb; **su visita me brindó la ocasión de conocerlo mejor** his visit gave me the opportunity to get to know him better

  **3 brindarse** *vpr* **brindarse a hacer algo** to offer to do sth

**brindis** *nm inv* toast

**brinque** *etc ver* **brincar**

**brío** *nm (energía, decisión)* spirit, verve

**brioso, -a** *adj* spirited, lively

**brisa** *nf* breeze; **b. marina** sea breeze

**brisca** *nf* = card game where each player gets three cards and one suit is trumps

**británico, -a 1** *adj* British

  **2** *nm,f* British person, Briton; **los británicos** the British

**brizna** *nf (filamento) (de hierba)* blade; *(de tabaco)* strand; *Fig (un poco)* trace, bit

**broca** *nf* (drill) bit

**brocado** *nm* brocade

**brocal** *nm* curb, parapet

**brocha** *nf* brush; **b. de afeitar** shaving brush

**brochazo** *nm* brushstroke

**broche** *nm* (**a**) *(cierre)* clasp, fastener (**b**) *(joya)* brooch; *Fig* **b. de oro** final flourish

**brocheta** *nf Culin* shish kebab; *(aguja)* skewer

**brócoli** *nm* broccoli

**bróker** *nmf* broker

**broma** *nf (ocurrencia, chiste)* joke; *(jugarreta)* prank, practical joke; **en** *o* **de b.** as a joke; **fuera de b.** joking apart; **gastar una b. a alguien** to play a joke *o* prank on sb; **tomar algo a b.** not to take sth seriously; **b. de mal gusto** bad joke; **b. pesada** nasty practical joke; **ni en** *o* **de b.** no way, not on your life; *Fam* **me salió la b. por 80.000 pts** it cost me the tidy sum of 80,000 pesetas

**bromear** *vi* to joke; **con la religión no se bromea** religion isn't something to be taken lightly

**bromista 1** *adj* **ser muy b.** to be a real joker

  **2** *nmf* joker

**bromo** *nm Quím* bromine

**bromuro** *nm Quím* bromide

**bronca** *nf* (**a**) *(jaleo)* row; **armar (una) b.** to kick up a row; **buscar b.** to look for trouble (**b**) *(regañina)* scolding, telling-off; **echar una b. a alguien** to give sb a row, to tell sb off (**c**) *CSur (enfado)* **me da b.** it makes me mad

**bronce** *nm* (**a**) *(aleación)* bronze; **Bulgaria se llevó el b.** Bulgaria won (the) bronze (**b**) *(estatua)* bronze (statue)

**bronceado, -a 1** *adj* tanned

  **2** *nm* tan

**bronceador, -ora 1** *adj* **crema bronceadora** suntan cream

  **2** *nm (loción)* suntan lotion; *(crema)* suntan cream

**broncear 1** *vt* to tan

  **2 broncearse** *vpr* to get a tan

**bronco, -a** *adj* (**a**) *(grave) (voz)* harsh; *(tos)* throaty (**b**) *Fig (brusco)* gruff, surly (**c**) *(tosco)* rough; *(paisaje, peñascos)* rugged

**bronquial** *adj* bronchial

**bronquio** *nm* bronchial tube

**bronquitis** *nf inv* bronchitis

**broquel** *nm (escudo)* small shield; *Fig (amparo)* shield

**brotar** *vi* (a) *(planta)* to sprout, to bud (b) *(agua, sangre) (suavemente)* to flow; *(con violencia)* to spout; **b. de** to well up out of; **brotaba humo de la chimenea** smoke billowed from the chimney (c) *Fig (esperanza, sospechas, pasiones)* to stir (d) *(en la piel)* **le brotó un sarpullido** he broke out in a rash

**brote** *nm (de planta)* bud, shoot; *Fig (inicio)* sign, hint; *(de enfermedad)* outbreak; **brotes de soja** beansprouts

**broza** *nf* (a) *(maleza)* brush, scrub (b) *Fig (relleno)* waffle

**bruces** *nfpl* **de b.** face down; **se cayó de b.** he fell headlong, he fell flat on his face; *Fig* **darse de b. con alguien/algo** to find oneself face-to-face with sb/sth

**bruja** *nf (hechicera)* witch, sorceress; *Fam (mujer fea)* hag; *Fam (mujer mala)* (old) witch; *Carib, Méx Fam* **estar b.** *(sin dinero)* to be broke o skint

**Brujas** *n* Bruges

**brujería** *nf* witchcraft, sorcery

**brujo, -a 1** *adj (hechicero)* enchanting, captivating
 **2** *nm* wizard, sorcerer

**brújula** *nf* compass

**bruma** *nf (niebla)* mist; *(en el mar)* sea mist

**brumoso, -a** *adj* misty

**Brunei** *n* Brunei

**bruñido** *nm* polishing

**bruñir** *vt* to polish

**brusco, -a 1** *adj* (a) *(repentino, imprevisto)* sudden, abrupt (b) *(tosco, grosero)* brusque
 **2** *nm,f* brusque person

**Bruselas** *n* Brussels

**bruselense 1** *adj* of/from Brussels
 **2** *nmf* person from Brussels

**brusquedad** *nf* (a) *(imprevisión)* suddenness, abruptness (b) *(grosería)* brusqueness

**brut** *nm inv* brut

**brutal** *adj* (a) *(violento)* brutal (b) *Fam (extraordinario)* tremendous

**brutalidad** *nf* (a) *(cualidad)* brutality (b) *(acción)* brutal act

**bruto, -a 1** *adj* (a) *(violento)* rough; *(torpe)* clumsy; *(ignorante)* thick, stupid; *(maleducado)* rude (b) *(sin tratar)* **en b.** *(diamante)* uncut; *(petróleo)* crude (c) *(sueldo, peso)* gross; **gana 300.000 ptas brutas al mes** she earns 300,000 pesetas a month gross
 **2** *nm,f* brute

**Bs.As.** *(abrev de* **Buenos Aires**) Buenos Aires

**bubónica** *adj Med* **peste b.** bubonic plague

**bucal** *adj* oral

**bucanero** *nm* buccaneer

**Bucarest** *n* Bucharest

**buceador, -ora** *nm,f* (underwater) diver

**bucear** *vi* (a) *(en agua)* to swim underwater, to dive (b) *Fig (investigar)* **b. en** to delve into

**buceo** *nm* (underwater) diving

**buche** *nm* (a) *(de ave)* crop (b) *(de animal)* maw (c) *Fam (de persona)* belly; **llenar el b.** to fill one's belly (d) *(trago)* **tomó un b. de agua** he took o drank a mouthful of water

**bucle** *nm* (a) *(de pelo)* curl, ringlet (b) *Aut & Informát* loop

**bucólico, -a** *adj* (a) *(campestre)* **un paisaje b.** a charmingly rural landscape (b) *Lit* bucolic

**Budapest** *n* Budapest

**budín** *nm (pastel)* pudding; *Am* bread pudding

**budismo** *nm* Buddhism

**budista** *adj & nmf* Buddhist

**buen** *adj ver* **bueno**

**buenamente** *adv* **hice lo que b. pude** I did what I could, I did as much as I could

**buenas** *interj ver* **bueno**

**buenaventura** *nf* (a) *(adivinación)* fortune; **leer** o **decir la b. a alguien** to tell sb's fortune (b) *(suerte)* good luck

**bueno, -a**

> **buen** is used instead of **bueno** before masculine singular nouns (e.g. **buen hombre** good man). The comparative form of **bueno** is **mejor** (better), and the superlative form is **el mejor** (masculine) or **la mejor** (feminine) (the best).

**1** *adj* (a) *(en general)* good
 (b) *(bondadoso)* kind, good; **ser b. con alguien** to be good to sb
 (c) *(curado, sano)* well, all right; **ponerse b.** to get well
 (d) *(apacible)* nice, fine; **buen tiempo** good o fine weather
 (e) *(aprovechable)* all right; *(comida)* fresh
 (f) *(uso enfático)* **ese buen hombre** that good man; **un buen día** one fine day
 (g) *(expresiones)* **¡buenas!** hello!; **de buen ver** good-looking, attractive; **de buenas a primeras** *(de repente)* all of a sudden; *(a simple vista)* at first sight, on the face of it; *Fam* **estar b.** *(persona)* to be a bit of all right, to be tasty; **estar de buenas** to be in a good mood; *Irón* **estaría b.** that would really cap it all; **librarse de una buena** to have a narrow escape; **lo b. es que...** the best thing about it is that...; *Fig* **poner b. a alguien** to criticize sb harshly; **por las buenas** willingly
 **2** *nm,f Cine* **el b.** the goody

**3** *adv* (**a**) *(vale, de acuerdo)* all right, O.K. (**b**) *(pues)* well

**4** *interj Méx (al teléfono)* ¡**b**.! hello

**Buenos Aires** *n* Buenos Aires

**buey** (*pl* **bueyes**) *nm* (**a**) *(mamífero)* ox (**b**) *(crustáceo)* = type of large crab

**bueyada** *nf Am* drove of oxen

**búfalo** *nm* buffalo

**bufanda** *nf* scarf, muffler

**bufar** *vi (toro, caballo)* to snort; *(gato)* to hiss; *Fig (persona)* **está que bufa** he's furious

**bufé** (*pl* **bufés**) *nm* (**a**) *(en restaurante)* buffet (**b**) *(mueble)* sideboard

**búfer, buffer** ['bafer] (*pl* **buffers**) *nm Informát* buffer

**bufete** *nm* lawyer's practice

**bufido** *nm* (**a**) *(de toro, caballo)* snort; *(de gato)* hiss (**b**) *Fam (de persona)* snarl of anger

**bufo, -a** *adj también Mús* comic

**bufón** *nm* buffoon, jester

**bufonada** *nf* jape; **bufonadas** buffoonery

**bug** [buy] (*pl* **bugs**) *nm Informát* bug

**buga** *nm muy Fam (coche)* wheels, *Br* motor

**buganvilla** *nf* bougainvillea

**buhardilla** *nf* (**a**) *(habitación)* attic (**b**) *(ventana)* dormer (window)

**búho** *nm* owl

**buhonero, -a** *nm,f* hawker, pedlar

**buitre 1** *nm* (**a**) *(ave) & Fig* vulture (**b**) *CAm* buzzard

**2** *adj Fam* **es muy b.** *(con la comida)* he's a greedy pig; *(con las chicas)* he's a real womanizer *o Br* lech

**bujía** *nf Aut* spark plug

**bula** *nf (documento)* (papal) bull

**bulbo** *nm Anat & Bot* bulb; **b. raquídeo** medulla oblongata, rachidian bulb

**buldog** (*pl* **buldogs**) *nm* bulldog

**buldózer** (*pl* **buldozers**) *nm* bulldozer

**bulerías** *nfpl* = popular Andalusian song and dance

**bulevar** (*pl* **bulevares**) *nm* boulevard

**Bulgaria** *n* Bulgaria

**búlgaro, -a 1** *adj & nm,f* Bulgarian

**2** *nm (lengua)* Bulgarian

**bulimia** *nf* bulimia

**bulímico, -a** *adj* bulimic

**bulín** *nm CSur* bachelor flat

**bulla** *nf Fam* (**a**) *(ruido)* racket, uproar; **armar b.** to kick up a racket (**b**) *(prisa)* **meter b. a alguien** to hurry sb up

**bullabesa** *nf Culin* bouillabaisse

**bullanga** *nf* merrymaking

**bullanguero, -a** *adj* **ser muy b.** to love a good time, to love partying

**bulldog** [bul'doy] (*pl* **bulldogs**) *nm* bulldog

**bulldozer** [bul'doθer] (*pl* **bulldozers**) *nm* bulldozer

**bullicio** *nm (de ciudad, mercado)* hustle and bustle; *(de multitud)* hubbub

**bullicioso, -a 1** *adj* (**a**) *(agitado) (reunión, multitud)* noisy; *(calle, mercado)* busy, bustling (**b**) *(inquieto)* rowdy, boisterous

**2** *nm,f* boisterous person

**bullir** *vi* (**a**) *(hervir)* to boil; *(burbujear)* to bubble (**b**) *Fig (multitud)* to bustle; *(ratas, hormigas)* to swarm; *(mar)* to boil; **b. de** to seethe with; **la calle bullía de gente** the street was swarming with people

**bulo** *nm* false rumour

**bulto** *nm* (**a**) *(volumen)* bulk, size; **a b.** approximately, roughly; **hacer mucho b.** to take up a lot of space; *Fig* **de b.** glaringly obvious; *Fig* **escurrir el b.** *(trabajo)* to shirk; *(cuestión)* to evade the issue (**b**) *(abombamiento) (en rodilla, superficie)* bump; *(en maleta, bolsillo)* bulge; **me ha salido un b. en el brazo** I've got a lump on my arm (**c**) *(forma imprecisa)* blurred shape (**d**) *(paquete)* package; *(maleta)* item of luggage; *(fardo)* bundle; **b. de mano** piece *o* item of hand luggage

**bumerán** (*pl* **bumeranes**) *nm* boomerang

**bungaló** (*pl* **bungalós**), **bungalow** [buŋga'lo] (*pl* **bungalows**) *nm* bungalow

**búnker** (*pl* **bunkeres**) *nm* (**a**) *(refugio)* bunker (**b**) *Pol* reactionary forces

**buñuelo** *nm Culin (dulce)* doughnut; *(de bacalao)* dumpling; **b. de viento** doughnut

**BUP** [bup] *nm (abrev de Bachillerato Unificado Polivalente)* = academically orientated Spanish secondary school course for pupils aged 14-17

**buque** *nm* ship; **b. de carga** cargo ship; **b. de guerra** warship; **b. nodriza** supply ship; **b. de pasajeros** passenger ship, liner

**buqué** *nm* bouquet

**burbuja** *nf* bubble; **hacer burbujas** to bubble

**burbujear** *vi* to bubble

**burbujeo** *nm* bubbling

**burdel** *nm* brothel

**Burdeos** *n* Bordeaux

**burdeos 1** *adj inv* maroon

**2** *nm inv* Bordeaux

**burdo, -a** *adj (lenguaje, modales)* crude, coarse; *(tela)* coarse

**burgalés, -esa 1** *adj* of/from Burgos

**2** *nm,f* person from Burgos

**búrger, burguer** ['buryer] *nm Fam* burger bar *o* restaurant

**burgués, -esa1** adj middle-class, bourgeois
**2** nm,f member of the middle class; Hist & Pol member of the bourgeoisie

**burguesía** nf middle class; Hist & Pol bourgeoisie; **alta b.** upper middle class; Hist & Pol haute bourgeoisie

**Burkina Faso** n Burkina Faso

**burla** nf (a) (mofa) taunt; **hacer b. de** to mock (b) (broma) joke (c) (engaño) trick

**burladero** nm Taurom = wooden board behind which the bullfighter can hide from the bull

**burlador** nm Casanova, Don Juan

**burlar** 1 vt (esquivar) to evade; (ley) to flout; **consiguió b. a sus perseguidores** she managed to outwit her pursuers; Fig **burla burlando** without anyone noticing
**2 burlarse** vpr to mock; **burlarse de algo/ alguien** to mock sth/sb, to make fun of sth/sb; **burlarse de las leyes** to flout the law

**burlesco, -a** adj (tono) jocular; Lit burlesque

**burlete** nm draught excluder

**burlón, -ona** adj (a) (bromista) waggish, fond of telling jokes (b) (sarcástico) mocking

**buró** nm (a) (escritorio) bureau, writing desk (b) Pol executive committee (c) Méx (mesa de noche) bedside table

**burocracia** nf bureaucracy; **ya no hay tanta b. para sacarse el pasaporte** there isn't so much red tape involved in getting a passport any more

**burócrata** nmf bureaucrat

**burocrático, -a** adj bureaucratic

**burocratizar** [16] vt to bureaucratize

**burrada** nf (a) (tontería) decir/hacer una b. to say/do something stupid; **decir burradas** to talk nonsense; **hacer burradas** to act stupidly (b) Fam (cantidad) **una b. (de)** tons (of), masses (of)

**burro, -a1** adj (necio) stupid, dim
**2** nm,f (a) (animal) donkey; Fam **no ver tres en un b.** to be as blind as a bat (b) Fam (necio) ass, dimwit (c) Fam (trabajador) **b. (de carga)** workhorse; **trabaja como una burra** she works like a slave

**bursátil** adj **mercado b.** stock market

**Burundi** n Burundi

**bus** (pl **buses**) nm (a) Informát bus (b) Fam (autobús) bus; **en b.** by bus

**busca** 1 nf search; (**ir**) **en b. de** (to go) in search of; **orden de b. y captura** arrest warrant; **en b. y captura** on the run (from the police)
**2** nm (buscapersonas) pager

**buscador, -ora** nm,f (a) (en general) hunter; **b. de oro** gold prospector (b) Informát (en Internet) search engine

**buscapersonas** nm inv bleeper, pager

**buscapiés** nm inv firecracker, jumping jack

**buscapleitos** nmf inv troubleseeker

**buscar** [61] **1** vt (a) (para encontrar) to look for; (provecho, beneficio propio) to seek; **voy a b. el periódico** I'm going for the paper o to get the paper; **ir a b. a alguien** (ir a recoger) to pick sb up; **se fue a b. fortuna a América** he went to seek his fortune in America (b) (en diccionario, índice, horario) to look up (c) Informát to search for (d) Fam (provocar) to push, to try the patience of
**2** vi to look
**3 buscarse** vpr (a) (castigo, desgracia) **buscársela** to be asking for it (b) Fam **buscarse la vida** (ganarse el sustento) to seek one's fortune; Fig (arreglárselas uno solo) to look after oneself (c) **se busca camarero** (en letrero) waiter wanted

**buscavidas** nmf inv Fam (a) (ambicioso) go-getter (b) (entrometido) nosy person, Br nosy parker

**buscón, -ona** nm,f (estafador) swindler

**buscona** nf Fam (prostituta) whore

**buseta** nf Andes minibus

**busque** etc ver **buscar**

**búsqueda** nf search

**busto** nm (a) (pecho) chest; (de mujer) bust (b) (escultura) bust

**butaca** nf (a) (mueble) armchair (b) (localidad) seat

**butacón** nm large easy chair

**Bután** n Bhutan

**butanero, -a** nm,f = person who delivers gas cylinders

**butano** nm butane (gas)

**buten: de buten** loc adv muy Fam wicked, terrific

**butifarra** nf = type of Catalan pork sausage

**butrón** nm Fam **método del b.** = method of carrying out a robbery involving gaining access via a hole made in the adjoining building

**buzo** nm (a) (persona) diver (b) CSur (chandal) tracksuit

**buzón** nm (a) letterbox; **echar algo al b.** to post sth (b) Informát (de correo electrónico) (electronic) mailbox, e-mail address

**buzoneo** nm leafleting

**bypass** [bai'pas] (pl **bypasses**) nm Med heart bypass operation

**byte** [bait] (pl **bytes**) nm Informát byte

# C

**C, c** [θe] *nf (letra)* C, c

**c., c/** *(abrev de* **calle***)* St.

**c/** *(abrev de* **cuenta***)* a/c

**cabal 1** *adj* (a) *(honrado)* upright, honest (b) *(exacto)* exact; *(completo)* complete; **a los nueve meses cabales** at exactly nine months

**2** *nmpl* **no estar en sus cabales** not to be in one's right mind

**cábala** *nf (doctrina)* cabbala; *Fig* **hacer cábalas** *(conjeturas)* to speculate, to guess

**cabalgadura** *nf* mount

**cabalgar** [40] *vi* to ride

**cabalgata** *nf* cavalcade, procession; **la c. de los Reyes Magos** = procession to celebrate the journey of the Three Kings, on 5th January

**cabalístico, -a** *adj (de cábala)* cabbalistic; *Fig (oculto)* mysterious

**caballa** *nf* mackerel

**caballar** *adj* equine, horse; *Agr* **ganado c.** horses

**caballeresco, -a** *adj (persona, modales)* chivalrous; *(literatura)* chivalric

**caballería** *nf* (a) *(animal)* mount, horse (b) *(cuerpo militar)* cavalry (c) **novela de c.** courtly romance

**caballeriza** *nf* stable

**caballerizo** *nm* groom, stable lad

**caballero 1** *adj (cortés)* gentlemanly

**2** *nm* (a) *(señor)* gentleman; *(al dirigir la palabra)* sir; **ser todo un c.** to be a real gentleman; **caballeros** *(en letrero) (en aseos)* gents; *(en grandes almacenes)* menswear (b) *(miembro de una orden)* knight; **armar c. a alguien** to knight sb; **c. andante** knight errant (c) *(noble)* nobleman

**caballerosidad** *nf* gentlemanliness

**caballeroso, -a** *adj* chivalrous, gentlemanly

**caballete** *nm* (a) *(de pintor)* easel (b) *(de mesa)* trestle (c) *(de nariz)* bridge (d) *(de tejado)* ridge

**caballito** *nm* small horse, pony; **llevar a alguien a c.** to give sb a piggy-back; **caballitos** *(de feria)* merry-go-round; **c. de mar** seahorse; **c. del diablo** dragonfly

**caballo** *nm* (a) *(animal)* horse; **montar a c.** to ride; **a c.** on horseback; *Fig* **estar a c. entre dos cosas** to be halfway between two things;

*Fig* **vive a c. entre Madrid y Bruselas** she lives part of the time in Madrid and part of the time in Brussels; *Prov* **a c. regalado no le mires el diente** don't look a gift horse in the mouth; **c. de batalla** *(dificultad, escollo)* bone of contention; *(objetivo, obsesión)* hobbyhorse

(b) *(pieza de ajedrez)* knight

(c) *(naipe)* = card in Spanish deck with a picture of a knight, equivalent to queen in standard deck

(d) *Tec* **c. (de fuerza** *o* **de vapor)** horsepower

(e) *muy Fam (heroína)* smack, horse

**cabaña** *nf* (a) *(choza)* hut, cabin (b) *(ganado)* livestock; **la c. bovina de Gales** the national herd of Welsh cattle

**cabaré, cabaret** *(pl* cabarets*)* *nm* cabaret

**cabaretera** *nf* cabaret girl

**cabás** *(pl* cabases*)* *nm* = plastic/metal case with handle used by schoolgirls for carrying lunch, etc

**cabecear** *vi* (a) *(dormitar)* to nod (off) (b) *(persona) (negando)* to shake one's head (c) *(caballo)* to toss its head (d) *(en fútbol)* to head the ball (e) *(balancearse) (barco)* to pitch

**cabeceo** *nm (con sueño)* nodding; *(de caballo)* tossing

**cabecera** *nf* (a) *(de fila, de mesa)* head; *(de cama)* headboard (b) *(de texto)* heading; *(de periódico)* headline (c) *(de río)* headwaters

**cabecilla** *nmf* ringleader

**cabellera** *nf* head of hair; **cortar la c. a** to scalp

**cabello** *nm* hair; *Culin* **c. de ángel** = preserve made of strands of pumpkin in syrup

**cabelludo, -a** *adj* hairy

**caber** [13] *vi* (a) *(entrar, pasar)* to fit (en *in* o *into*); **c. por** to go through; **caben cinco personas** there is room for five people; **no cabía ni un alfiler** the place was packed out; **no me cabe en el dedo** it won't fit (on) my finger

(b) *Mat* **nueve entre tres caben a tres** three into nine goes three (times)

(c) *(ser posible)* to be possible; **cabe destacar que...** it's worth pointing out that...; **cabe preguntarse si...** one might ask whether...

**(d)** *(expresiones)* **dentro de lo que cabe** *(en cierto modo)* up to a point, to some extent; **no c. en sí de alegría** to be beside oneself with joy

**cabestrante** *nm* capstan

**cabestrillo** *nm* **en c.** in a sling

**cabestro** *nm* **(a)** *(cuerda)* halter **(b)** *(animal)* leading ox

**cabeza 1** *nf* **(a)** *(de persona, animal)* head; **lavarse la c.** to wash one's hair; **me duele la c.** I've got a headache; **por c.** per head; **tirarse de c. (al agua)** to dive (into the water); **c. de ajo** head of garlic; *también Informát* **c. (lectora)** head

**(b)** *(población)* **c. de partido** *Br* ≃ county town, *US* ≃ county seat

**(c)** *(expresiones)* **c. abajo** upside down; **c. arriba** the right way up; **a la** *o* **en c.** *(en competición)* in front, in the lead; *(en lista)* at the top *o* head; **alzar** *o* **levantar c.** to get back on one's feet, to recover; **andar** *o* **estar mal de la c.** to be funny in the head; **no me cabe en la c.** I simply can't understand it; *Fam* **calentar** *o* **hinchar la c. a alguien** to drive sb mad; **de c.** at once, without thinking twice; **con la c. (bien) alta** with one's head held high; **ir de c. a** to head straight for; **meterle algo en la c. a alguien** to get sth into sb's head; **se le ha metido en la c. que…** he has got it into his head that…; **obrar con c.** to use one's head; **se me pasó por la c.** it crossed my mind; **perder la c.** to lose one's head; **romperse la c.** to rack one's brains; **sentar la c.** to settle down; **se le subió a la c.** it went to his head; **tener la c. llena de pájaros** to have one's head in the clouds; **esa chica tiene mucha c.** that girl has got brains; **traer de c. a alguien** to drive sb mad; **venir a la c.** to come to mind

**2** *nmf Fam* **c. de chorlito** scatterbrain; **c. de familia** head of the family; *Pol* **c. de lista** = person who heads a party's list of candidates; **c. rapada** skinhead; **c. de turco** scapegoat

**cabezada** *nf* **(a)** *(de sueño)* **dar cabezadas** to nod off; **echar** *o* **dar una c.** to have a nap **(b)** *(golpe)* headbutt

**cabezal** *nm* **(a)** *(de aparato)* head **(b)** *(almohada)* bolster

**cabezazo** *nm* *(golpe)* *(con la cabeza)* headbutt; *(en la cabeza)* blow *o* bump on the head; *Dep* header

**cabezón, -ona 1** *adj* **(a)** *(persona)* *(de cabeza grande)* **ser c.** to have a big head; *Fig* *(terco)* to be pigheaded *o* stubborn **(b)** *Fam* *(vino)* rough; **este vino es muy c.** this wine gives you a headache

**2** *nm,f* *(terco)* pigheaded *o* stubborn person

**cabezonería** *nf* *Fam* pigheadedness, stubbornness

**cabezota** *Fam* **1** *adj* pigheaded, stubborn

**2** *nmf* pigheaded *o* stubborn person

**cabezudo, -a 1** *adj* *Fam* pigheaded, stubborn

**2** *nm,f Fam* pigheaded *o* stubborn person

**3** *nmpl* **cabezudos** *(en fiesta)* = giant-headed carnival figures

**cabida** *nf* capacity; **dar c. a, tener c. para** to hold, to have room for; *Fig* **dar c. a** to allow

**cabildo** *nm* **(a)** *(municipio)* ≃ district council **(b)** *(de eclesiásticos)* chapter **(c)** *(sala)* chapterhouse

**cabina** *nf* *(cuartito)* booth, cabin; *(de avión)* *(del piloto)* cockpit; *(de los pasajeros)* (passenger) cabin; *(de camión)* cab; **c. de proyección** projection room; **c. telefónica** *(con puerta)* phone box, *US* phone booth

**cabinera** *nf Col* air hostess

**cabizbajo, -a** *adj* crestfallen, downcast

**cable** *nm* **(a)** *Elec* *(para conectar)* cable, lead; *(dentro de aparato)* wire; *Fam Fig* **echar un c.** to help out, to lend a hand; *Fam Fig* **se le cruzaron los cables** *(se confundió)* he got mixed up; **se le cruzaron los cables y la pegó** in a moment of madness, he hit her **(b)** *(de puente)* cable

**cableado, -a** *Informát* **1** *adj* hardwired

**2** *nm* hardwiring

**cablegrafiar** [34] *vt* to cable

**cablegrama** *nm* cablegram, cable

**cablevisión** *nf* cable television

**cabo** *nm* **(a)** *(cuerda)* rope

**(b)** *Mil* corporal; **c. primero** = military rank between corporal and sergeant

**(c)** *Geog* cape

**(d)** *(trozo)* bit, piece; *(trozo final)* stub, stump; *(de cuerda)* end

**(e)** *(expresiones)* **al c. de una semana** after a week, a week later; **al fin y al c.** after all; **atar cabos** to put two and two together; **c. suelto** loose end; **de c. a rabo** from beginning to end; **estar al c. de la calle** to be well-informed; **llevar algo a c.** to carry sth out; **no dejar ningún c. suelto** to tie up all the loose ends

**cabotaje** *nm* coastal shipping

**Cabo Verde** *n* Cape Verde

**caboverdiano, -a** *adj & nm,f* Cape Verdean

**cabra** *nf* goat; **c. montés** wild goat; **pie** *o* **pata de c.** crowbar; *Br* jemmy, *US* jimmy; *Fam* **estar como una c.** to be off one's head; *Prov* **la c. siempre tira al monte** you can't make a leopard change his spots

**cabrales** *nm inv* = Asturian cheese similar to Roquefort

**cabré** *etc ver* **caber**

**cabrear** *muy Fam* **1** *vt* **c. a alguien** to get sb's goat, to annoy sb

**2 cabrearse** *vpr* to get really *Br* narked *o US* pissed (**con** with)

**cabreo** *nm muy Fam* rage, fit; **cogerse** *o* **cogerse un c.** to get really *Br* narked *o US* pissed

**cabrero, -a** *nm,f* goatherd

**cabrestante** *nm* capstan

**cabría** *etc ver* **caber**

**cabrío** *adj* **macho c.** billy-goat

**cabriola** *nf* prance; **hacer cabriolas** to prance about

**cabritas** *nfpl Chile* popcorn

**cabritilla** *nf* kid, kidskin

**cabrito** *nm* (**a**) *(animal)* kid (goat) (**b**) *muy Fam (cabrón)* bastard

**cabro, -a** *nm,f Andes, CSur Fam* kid

**cabrón, -ona** **1** *Vulg adj* **¡qué c. eres!** you bastard!

**2** *Vulg nm,f (insulto)* bastard, *f* bitch

**3** *nm* (**a**) *Vulg (cornudo)* cuckold (**b**) *(animal)* billy-goat

**cabronada** *nf Vulg* **hacerle una c. a alguien** to be a bastard to sb

**cabronazo** *nm Vulg* bastard

**cabuya** *nf CAm* rope

**caca** *nf Fam (excremento)* pooh; *Fig (cosa sucia)* nasty *o* dirty thing; **hacer c.** to do a pooh; **una c. de vaca** a cow pat; *Fig* **el partido fue una c. (muy malo)** the match was crap

**cacahuate** *nm Méx* peanut

**cacahuete** *nm* (**a**) *(fruto)* peanut (**b**) *(planta)* groundnut

**cacao** *nm* (**a**) *(bebida) (caliente)* cocoa; *(fría)* chocolate milk (**b**) *(semilla)* cocoa bean (**c**) *(árbol)* cacao (**d**) *(para labios)* lip salve (**e**) *Fam (confusión)* chaos, mess; *(jaleo)* fuss, rumpus; **c. mental** mental confusion; **tener un c. mental** to be at sixes and sevens

**cacarear** **1** *vt Fam* (**a**) *(jactarse de)* to boast about (**b**) *(pregonar)* to blab about

**2** *vi (gallo)* to cluck, to cackle

**cacareo** *nm* clucking

**cacatúa** *nf* (**a**) *(ave)* cockatoo (**b**) *Fam (mujer vieja)* old bat

**cace** *etc ver* **cazar**

**cacería** *nf (a caballo)* hunt; *(con fusiles)* shoot

**cacereño, -a** **1** *adj* of/from Cáceres

**2** *nm,f* person from Cáceres

**Cáceres** *n* Cáceres

**cacerola** *nf* pot, pan

**cacha** **1** *nf* (**a**) *Fam (muslo)* thigh (**b**) *(mango) (de cuchillo)* handle; *(de pistola)* butt

**2** *nm inv Fam* **cachas** *(hombre fuerte)* he-man, strong man; **estar cachas** to be well-built

**cachalote** *nm* sperm whale

**cacharrazo** *nm Fam* thump; **pegarse un c.** *(al caer)* to bang oneself; *(en coche)* to have a smash

**cacharro** *nm* (**a**) *(recipiente)* pot; **fregar los cacharros** to do the dishes (**b**) *Fam (trasto)* piece of junk; **tendremos que tirar todos estos cacharros** we'll have to throw all this junk *o* rubbish out (**c**) *Fam (máquina)* crock; *(coche)* banger

**cachaza** *nf Fam* **tener c.** to be laid-back

**caché, cachet** [ka'tʃe] *(pl* cachets*) nm* (**a**) *(tarifa de artista)* fee (**b**) *(distinción)* cachet (**c**) *Informát* **(memoria) c.** cache memory

**cachear** *vt* to frisk

**cachemir** *nm,* **cachemira** *nf* cashmere

**cacheo** *nm* **someter a alguien a un c.** to frisk sb

**cachetada** *nf Am Fam* smack

**cachete** *nm* (**a**) *(moflete)* chubby cheek (**b**) *(bofetada)* slap

**cachetear** *vt* to slap

**cachimba** *nf* pipe

**cachiporra** *nf Fam (garrote)* club, cudgel; *(de policía)* truncheon

**cachirulo** *nm* (**a**) *(chisme)* thingamajig (**b**) *(pañuelo)* = headscarf worn by men as part of traditional Aragonese costume

**cachivache** *nm Fam* knick-knack

**cacho** *nm* (**a**) *Fam (pedazo)* piece, bit (**b**) *Am (asta)* horn

**cachondearse** *vpr Fam* to take the mickey (**de** out of)

**cachondeo** *nm Fam* (**a**) *(diversión)* **ser un c.** to be a laugh; **irse de c.** to go out on the town (**b**) *Pey (cosa poco seria)* joke; **tomarse algo a c.** to treat sth as a joke

**cachondo, -a** **1** *adj* (**a**) *Fam (divertido)* **ser c.** to be funny (**b**) *muy Fam (excitado)* **estar c.** to be randy; **poner c.** to turn on; **ponerse c.** to get randy *o* turned on

**2** *nm,f Fam* **es un c. (mental)** he's always pissing around

**cachorro, -a** *nm,f (de perro)* pup, puppy; *(de gato)* kitten; *(de león, lobo, oso)* cub

**cacique** *nm* (**a**) *(jefe local)* cacique, local political boss; *Fig Pey (déspota)* petty tyrant (**b**) *(jefe indio)* chief, cacique

**caciquil** *adj Fig Pey* despotic

**caciquismo** *nm* caciquism

**caco** *nm Fam* thief

**cacofonía** *nf* cacophony

**cacofónico, -a** *adj* cacophonous

**cacto** *nm,* **cactus** *nm inv* cactus

**cacumen** *nm Fam (ingenio)* brains, wits

**CAD** [kað] *nm (abrev de* **computer aided design***)* CAD

**cada** *adj inv* (**a**) *(en general)* each; *(con números, tiempo)* every; **c. dos meses** every two months; **c. cosa a su tiempo** one thing at a time; **c. cual** each one, everyone; **c. uno de** each of; **c. uno** *o* **cual a lo suyo** everyone should get on with their own business

(**b**) *(valor progresivo)* **c. vez más** more and more; **c. vez más largo** longer and longer; **c. día más** more and more each day

(**c**) *(valor enfático)* such; **¡se pone c. sombrero!** she wears such hats!

**cadalso** *nm* scaffold

**cadáver** *nm* corpse, (dead) body; **por encima de mi c.** over my dead body

**cadavérico, -a** *adj* cadaverous; *(pálido)* deathly pale

**caddy** ( *pl* **caddies**) *nm* caddie

**cadena** *nf* (**a**) *(de eslabones)* chain; **tirar de la c.** to pull the chain, to flush the toilet; **c. alimenticia** food chain; **c. de tiendas** chain of stores; **c. perpetua** life imprisonment; **reacción en c.** chain reaction; *Fig* **rompió sus cadenas** he broke out of his chains; *Aut* **cadenas** (tyre) chains (**b**) *TV* channel; *Rad* station (**c**) *(de proceso industrial)* line; **c. de montaje** assembly line (**d**) *(aparato de música)* sound system

**cadencia** *nf* rhythm, cadence

**cadencioso, -a** *adj* rhythmical

**cadeneta** *nf* chain stitch

**cadera** *nf* hip

**cadete** *nm* cadet

**cadie** *nm* caddie

**cadmio** *nm Quím* cadmium

**caducado, -a** *adj (carné, pasaporte)* out-of-date; *(alimento, medicamento)* past its use-by date

**caducar** [61] *vi (carné, ley, pasaporte)* to expire; *(alimento, medicamento)* to pass its use-by date

**caducidad** *nf* expiry; **fecha de c.** *(de carné, pasaporte)* expiry date; *(de alimento, medicamento)* use-by date

**caducifolio, -a** *adj* deciduous

**caduco, -a** *adj* (**a**) *(persona)* decrepit; *(idea, moda)* outmoded; *(perecedero)* perishable (**b**) *Bot* **de hoja caduca** deciduous

**caduque** *etc ver* **caducar**

**caer** [14] **1** *vi* (**a**) *(hacia abajo)* to fall; **c. de un tejado/árbol** to fall from a roof/tree; **c. rodando por la escalera** to fall down the stairs; **dejar c. algo** *(objeto)* to drop sth; **dejar c. que** *(comentar)* to let drop that; **tropezó y cayó al suelo** she tripped and fell (over *o* down)

(**b**) *(estar, quedar)* **cae cerca de aquí** it's not far from here; **eso cae fuera de mis competencias** that is *o* falls outside my remit

(**c**) *(darse cuenta)* **c. en la cuenta** *(entender)* to realize, to understand; **c. (en algo)** *(recordar)* to be able to remember (sth); **no dije nada porque no caí** I didn't say anything because it didn't occur to me to do so; **¡ahora caigo!** *(lo entiendo)* I see it now!; *(lo recuerdo)* now I remember!; **no caigo** I give up, I don't know

(**d**) *(coincidir)* *(fecha)* **c. en** to fall on; **cae en domingo** it falls on a Sunday

(**e**) *(picar)* *(en trampa, broma)* to fall for it

(**f**) *Am (visitar)* to drop in

(**g**) *(expresiones)* **c. (muy) bajo** to sink (very) low; **c. bien/mal** *(comentario, noticia)* to go down well/badly; **me cae bien/mal** *(persona)* I like/don't like him; **c. sobre alguien** *(ladrón)* to pounce *o* fall upon sb; **la desgracia cayó sobre él** he was overtaken by misfortune; **se proseguirá con la investigación caiga quien caiga** the investigation will proceed no matter who might be implicated *o* even if it means that heads will roll; **dejarse c. por casa de alguien** to drop by sb's house; **estar al c.** to be about to arrive

**2 caerse** *vpr* (**a**) *(persona)* to fall over *o* down; **caerse de algo** to fall from sth; *Fig* **caerse de ingenuo/listo** to be incredibly naive/clever

(**b**) *(objeto)* to drop, to fall; *(árbol)* to fall

(**c**) *(diente, pelo)* to fall out; **se me ha caído un diente** one of my teeth has fallen out; *(botón)* to fall off; *(cuadro)* to fall down

(**d**) *(falda, pantalones)* to fall down; **se te caen los pantalones** your trousers are falling down

(**e**) *Fam Informát (red de ordenadores)* to go down; **la red se ha caído** the network is down

**café 1** *nm* (**a**) *(bebida)* coffee; **c. americano** large weak black coffee; **c. cortado** coffee with a dash of milk; **c. expreso** expresso; **c. instantáneo** *o* **soluble** instant coffee; **c. irlandés** Irish coffee; **c. con leche** white coffee; **c. molido** ground coffee; *Andes* **c. perfumado** coffee with alcohol; **c. solo** *o* *Andes* **tinto** black coffee (**b**) *(establecimiento)* cafe

**2** *adj inv (color)* coffee-coloured

**cafeína** *nf* caffeine

**cafetal** *nm* coffee plantation

**cafetera** *nf* (**a**) *(italiana)* = screw-together stove-top coffee percolator with metal filter; *(eléctrica)* (filter) coffee machine; *(en bares)* expresso machine; **c. de émbolo** cafetiere (**b**) *Fam Fig (aparato viejo)* old crock

**cafetería** *nf* cafe

**cafetero, -a 1** *adj* (**a**) *(de café)* coffee; *(país)* coffee-producing; **producción cafetera** coffee production (**b**) *(bebedor de café)* fond of coffee

**2** *nm,f (cultivador)* coffee grower; *(comerciante)* coffee merchant

**cafeto** *nm* coffee bush

**cafiche** *nm CSur, Perú Fam* pimp

**cafre 1** *adj* brutish

**2** *nmf* brute

**cagada** *nf* (a) *(equivocación) Br* cock-up, *US* foul-up (b) *(excremento)* shit

**cagado, -a** *muy Fam nm,f (cobarde)* yellow-belly, chicken

**cagalera** *nf Fam (diarrea)* the runs

**cagar** [40] **1** *vi Fam (defecar)* to shit, to crap

**2** *vt muy Fam Fig* **cagarla** *(estropear)* to balls *o Br* cock up; **¡la has cagado!** *(estás en un lío)* you're in deep shit *o* up shit creek

**3 cagarse** *vpr Fam también Fig* to shit oneself; *Vulg* **¡me cago en la hostia!** fucking hell!; **¡me cago en diez!** bleeding hell!; *Vulg* **hace un frío que te cagas ahí fuera** it's bloody freezing out there!

**cagarruta** *nf* dropping

**cagón, -ona** *adj Fam* (a) *(que caga)* shitty (b) *(miedica)* chicken, cowardly

**cague 1** *ver* **cagar**

**2** *nm Fam (miedo)* **¡me entró un c.!** I was shit-scared!

**cagueta** *Fam* **1** *adj* chicken, cowardly

**2** *nmf* chicken, coward

**caída** *nf* (a) *(de hojas, persona, imperio)* fall; *(de diente, pelo)* loss; **a la caída de la tarde** at nightfall (b) *(de paro, precios, terreno)* drop (**de** in) (c) *(de tela, vestido)* drape (d) *Fam Informát (de red de ordenadores)* crash

**caído, -a 1** *adj* (a) *(árbol, hoja)* fallen (b) *(decaído)* low

**2** *nmpl* **los caídos** the fallen

**caigo** *ver* **caer**

**caimán** *nm* alligator, cayman

**Cairo** *nm* **El C.** Cairo

**caja** *nf* (a) *(recipiente)* box; *(para transporte, embalaje)* crate; **una c. de cervezas** a crate of beer; **c. de cambios** gearbox; **c. de música** music box; **c. torácica** thorax; *Fig* **la c. de Pandora** Pandora's box; *Fam Fig* **la c. tonta** the box, the telly (b) *(para el dinero)* cash box; *(en tienda, supermercado)* till; *(en banco)* cashier's desk; **c. de ahorros** savings bank; **c. fuerte** *o* **de caudales** safe, strongbox; **c. registradora** cash register; *Com* **hacer c.** to cash up (c) *(ataúd)* coffin (d) *(de instrumento musical)* body

**cajero, -a 1** *nm,f (en tienda)* cashier; *(en banco)* teller

**2** *nm* **c. (automático)** cash machine, cash dispenser

**cajetilla** *nf (de cigarrillos)* packet

**cajista** *nmf Imprenta* typesetter

**cajón** *nm (de mueble)* drawer; *Fig* **c. de sastre** muddle, jumble; *Fam Fig* **eso es de c.** that goes without saying

**cajonera** *nf* chest of drawers

**cajuela** *nf Méx (maletero) Br* boot, *US* trunk

**cal** *nf* *(pintura)* whitewash (b) *(en polvo)* lime; **el agua tiene mucha c.** the water is very hard; **c. viva** quicklime; **cerrar a c. y canto** to shut tight *o* firmly; **con este hombre, es una de c. y otra de arena** you never know with that man, he's nice one minute and horrible the next

**cala** *nf* (a) *(bahía pequeña)* cove (b) *(del barco)* hold (c) *(de fruta)* sample slice (d) *Bot* arum lily (e) *Fam (dinero)* peseta

**calabacín** *nm Br* courgette, *US* zucchini

**calabaza** *nf* pumpkin, gourd; *Fam Fig* **dar calabazas a alguien** *(a pretendiente)* to turn sb down; *(en exámenes)* to fail sb

**calabobos** *nm inv* drizzle

**calabozo** *nm* cell

**calada** *nf* (a) *(inmersión)* soaking (b) *(de cigarrillo)* drag; **dar una c.** to take a drag

**caladero** *nm* fishing grounds, fishery

**calado, -a 1** *adj* (a) *(empapado)* soaked; **c. hasta los huesos** soaked to the skin (b) *(en costura)* embroidered *(with openwork)*

**2** *nm* (a) *Náut* draught (b) *(bordado)* openwork

**calafatear** *vt* to caulk

**calamar** *nm* squid; **calamares en su tinta** squid cooked in its own ink; **calamares a la romana** squid rings fried in batter

**calambre** *nm* (a) *(descarga eléctrica)* (electric) shock (b) *(contracción muscular)* cramp; **me dio un c. en la pierna** I got cramp in my leg

**calamidad** *nf* calamity; **pasar calamidades** to suffer great hardship; *Fig* **ser una c.** to be a dead loss

**calamitoso, -a** *adj* calamitous

**calandria** *nf (pájaro)* calandra lark

**calaña** *nf Pey* **de esa c.** of that ilk

**calar 1** *vt* (a) *(empapar)* to soak (b) *Fig (persona)* to see through (c) *(gorro, sombrero)* to jam on (d) *(fruta)* to cut a sample of (e) *(perforar)* to perforate, to pierce

**2** *vi* (a) *Náut* to draw (b) *(ser permeable)* **estos zapatos calan** these shoes let in water; *Fig* **c. (hondo) en** *(penetrar)* to have a (great) impact on

**3 calarse** *vpr* (a) *(empaparse)* to get soaked (b) *(motor)* to stall

**calato, -a** *adj Andes, CSur (desnudo)* naked

**calavera 1** *nf* (a) *(cráneo)* skull (b) *Méx Aut* **calaveras** rear lights (c) *Méx (dulce)* sugar skull

**2** *nm Fig (libertino)* rake

**calcado, -a** *adj* traced; **ser c. a alguien** to be the spitting image of sb

**calcamonía** *nf Fam* transfer

**calcañal, calcañar** *nm* heel

**calcar** [61] *vt* (a) *(dibujo)* to trace (b) *(imitar)* to copy

**calcáreo, -a** *adj (terreno)* chalky; **aguas calcáreas** hard water

**calce 1** *ver* **calzar**
2 *nm (cuña)* wedge

**calceta** *nf* stocking; **hacer c.** to knit

**calcetar** *vi* to knit

**calcetín** *nm* sock

**calcificarse** [61] *vpr* to calcify

**calcinación** *nf* burning

**calcinado, -a** *adj* charred, burnt

**calcinar** *vt* to burn, to char

**calcio** *nm Quím* calcium

**calco** *nm* (a) *(reproducción)* tracing; *Fig (imitación)* carbon copy; **papel de c.** carbon paper (b) *Ling* calque, loan translation

**calcografía** *nf* chalcography

**calcomanía** *nf* transfer

**calculador, -ora** *adj también Fig* calculating

**calculadora** *nf* calculator; **c. de bolsillo** pocket calculator

**calcular** *vt* (a) *(cantidades)* to calculate; **c. mal** to miscalculate (b) *(suponer)* to reckon; **le calculo sesenta años** I reckon he's about sixty

**cálculo** *nm* (a) *(operación)* calculation; **hacer cálculos mentales** to do mental arithmetic; **hacer cálculos** to do some calculations (b) *(ciencia)* calculus; **c. diferencial/infinitesimal/integral** differential/infinitesimal/integral calculus (c) *(evaluación)* estimate; **c. de probabilidades** probability theory (d) *Med* stone, calculus; **c. biliar** gallstone; **c. renal** kidney stone

**caldas** *nfpl* hot springs

**caldear** *vt* (a) *(calentar)* to heat (up) (b) *Fig (excitar)* to warm up, to liven up

**caldera** *nf* boiler; **c. de vapor** steam boiler

**caldereta** *nf (de pescado)* fish stew; *(de carne)* meat stew

**calderilla** *nf* small change

**caldero** *nm* cauldron

**calderón** *nm Mús* pause

**caldo** *nm* (a) *(para cocinar)* stock; *(sopa)* broth (b) *(vino)* wine (c) *Biol* **c. de cultivo** culture medium; *Fig (condición idónea)* breeding ground

**caldoso, -a** *adj (comida)* with lots of stock; **estar demasiado c.** to be watery

**calé** *adj & nmf* gypsy

**calefacción** *nf* heating; **c. central** central heating

**calefactor** *nm* heater

**caleidoscopio** *nm* kaleidoscope

**calendario** *nm* calendar; **c. escolar/laboral** school/working year

**caléndula** *nf* calendula, pot marigold

**calentador** *nm* (a) *(aparato)* heater (b) *(prenda)* **calentadores** legwarmers

**calentamiento** *nm* (a) *(subida de temperatura)* heating; **c. global** global warming (b) *(ejercicios)* warm-up

**calentar** [3] **1** *vt* (a) *(subir la temperatura de)* to heat (up), to warm (up) (b) *Fig (animar)* to liven up (c) *Fig (pegar)* to hit, to strike; **¡te voy a c.!** you'll feel the back of my hand! (d) *Fam Fig (sexualmente)* to turn on
2 *vi* (a) *(dar calor)* to give off heat (b) *(entrenarse)* to warm up
3 **calentarse** *vpr* (a) *(por calor) (persona)* to warm oneself, to get warm; *(cosa)* to heat up (b) *Fam Fig (sexualmente)* to get randy o horny

**calentón** *nm* **dar un c. al arroz** to heat up the rice

**calentura** *nf* (a) *(fiebre)* fever, temperature (b) *(herida)* cold sore

**calenturiento, -a** *adj* feverish; *Fig* **tener una imaginación calenturienta** *(incontrolada)* to have a wild imagination; *(sexualmente)* to have a dirty mind

**calesa** *nf* calash

**calesitas** *nfpl CSur* merry-go-round

**calibrado** *nm,* **calibración** *nf* (a) *(medida)* calibration (b) *(de arma)* boring

**calibrador** *nm* callipers

**calibrar** *vt* (a) *(medir)* to calibrate, to gauge (b) *(dar calibre a) (arma)* to bore (c) *Fig (juzgar)* to gauge

**calibre** *nm* (a) *(diámetro) (de pistola)* calibre; *(de alambre)* gauge; *(de tubo)* bore (b) *(instrumento)* gauge (c) *Fig (tamaño)* size; *(importancia)* importance, significance

**calidad** *nf* (a) *(de producto, servicio)* quality; **un género de (buena) c.** a quality product; **c. de vida** quality of life; **la relación c.-precio** value (for money) (b) *(clase)* class (c) *(condición)* **en c. de** in one's capacity as

**cálido, -a** *adj* warm

**calidoscopio** *nm* kaleidoscope

**calientapiernas** *nmpl inv* legwarmers

**calientapiés** *nm inv* foot warmer

**calientaplatos** *nm inv* hotplate

**calientapollas** *nf inv Vulg* prickteaser

**caliente 1** *ver* **calentar**
2 *adj* (a) *(a alta temperatura)* hot; *(templado)* warm; *Fig* **en c.** in the heat of the moment (b) *Fig (acalorado)* heated (c) *Fam (excitado)* horny, *Br* randy

**caliento** *etc ver* **calentar**

**califa** *nm* caliph

**califato** *nm* caliphate

**calificación** *nf Educ* mark

**calificado, -a** *adj* (a) *(importante)* eminent (b) *(apto)* qualified

**calificar** [61] *vt* (a) *(denominar)* **c. a alguien de algo** to call sb sth, to describe sb as sth (b) *Educ* to mark (c) *Gram* to qualify

**calificativo, -a 1** *adj* qualifying
**2** *nm* epithet

**caligrafía** *nf* (a) *(arte)* calligraphy (b) *(letra)* handwriting

**calígrafo, -a** *nm,f* calligrapher

**calima, calina** *nf* haze, mist

**calipso** *nm* calypso

**cáliz** *nm* (a) *Rel* chalice (b) *Bot* calyx

**caliza** *nf* limestone

**calizo, -a** *adj* chalky

**callado, -a** *adj* **estar c.** to be quiet *o* silent; **ser c.** to be quiet *o* reserved

**callampa** *nf Chile (seta)* mushroom

**callampas** *nfpl CSur* shanty town

**callandito** *adv Fam* on the quiet

**callar 1** *vi* (a) *(no hablar)* to keep quiet, to be silent; **quien calla otorga** silence signifies consent
(b) *(dejar de hablar)* to be quiet, to stop talking; **mandar c. a alguien** to tell sb to shut up; **¡calla, si eso me lo dijo a mí también!** guess what, he said that to me, too!
**2** *vt* (a) *(ocultar)* to keep quiet about
(b) *(acallar)* to silence

**3 callarse** *vpr* (a) *(no hablar)* to keep quiet, to be silent
(b) *(dejar de hablar)* to be quiet, to stop talking; **¡cállate!** shut up!
(c) *(ocultar)* to keep quiet about; **esa no se calla nada** she always says what she thinks

**calle** *nf* (a) *(en población)* street, road; **salir a la c.** to go out; **¿qué se opina en la c.?** what does the man in the street think?; **el lenguaje de la c.** everyday language; **c. arriba/abajo** up/down the street; **c. de dirección única** one-way street; **c. peatonal** pedestrian precinct
(b) *Dep* lane
(c) *(expresiones)* **dejar a alguien en la c.** to put sb out of a job; **echar a alguien a la c.** *(de un trabajo)* to sack sb; *(de un lugar público)* to kick *o* throw sb out; **echarse a la c.** *(manifestarse)* to take to the streets; **hacer la c.** *(prostituta)* to walk the streets; **llevarse a alguien de c.** to win sb over; **traer** *o* **llevar a uno por la c. de la amargura** to drive sb mad

**calleja** *nf* sidestreet, alley

**callejear** *vi* to wander the streets

**callejero, -a 1** *adj* **hace mucha vida callejera** he likes going out a lot; **disturbios callejeros** street riot; **perro c.** stray dog
**2** *nm (guía)* street map

**callejón** *nm* alley; **c. sin salida** cul-de-sac; *Fig* blind alley, impasse

**callejuela** *nf* backstreet, sidestreet

**callista** *nmf* chiropodist

**callo** *nm (dureza)* callus; *(en el pie)* corn; *Fam Fig (persona fea)* sight, fright; *Fam Fig* **dar el c.** to slog; *Culin* **callos** tripe; **callos a la madrileña** = tripe cooked with ham, pork sausage, onion and peppers

**callosidad** *nf* callus; **callosidades** calluses, hard skin

**calloso, -a** *adj* calloused

**calma** *nf* (a) *(sin ruido o movimiento)* calm; **en c.** calm; **c. chicha** dead calm (b) *(sosiego)* tranquility; **perder la c.** to lose one's composure; **tener c.** *(tener paciencia)* to be patient; **tómatelo con c.** take it easy

**calmante 1** *adj* sedative, soothing
**2** *nm* sedative

**calmar 1** *vt* (a) *(mitigar)* to relieve (b) *(tranquilizar)* to calm, to soothe
**2 calmarse** *vpr (persona, ánimos)* to calm down; *(dolor, tempestad)* to abate

**calmoso, -a** *adj* calm

**caló** *nm* gypsy dialect

**calor** *nm* (a) *(temperatura alta)* heat; *(tibieza)* warmth; **al c. de la lumbre** by the fireside; **entrar en c.** to get warm; *Fig (público, deportista)* to warm up; **hace c.** it's warm *o* hot; **tener c.** to be warm *o* hot; **c. animal** body heat; *Fís* **c. específico** specific heat (b) *Fig (afecto, entusiasmo)* warmth

**caloría** *nf* calorie

**calórico, -a** *adj* caloric

**calorífero, -a** *adj (que da calor)* heat-producing

**calorífico, -a** *adj* calorific

**calostro** *nm* colostrum

**calque** *etc ver* **calcar**

**calumnia** *nf (oral)* slander; *(escrita)* libel

**calumniar** *vt (oralmente)* to slander; *(por escrito)* to libel

**calumnioso, -a** *adj (de palabra)* slanderous; *(por escrito)* libellous

**caluroso, -a** *adj* (a) *(excesivamente)* hot; *(agradablemente)* warm (b) *Fig (afectuoso)* warm (c) *Fam* **es muy c.** he doesn't feel the cold

**calva** *nf (en la cabeza)* bald patch; *Fig (en tejido, terreno)* bare patch

**calvados** *nm inv* Calvados

**calvario** *nm (vía crucis)* Calvary, stations of the Cross; *Fig (sufrimiento)* ordeal

**calvicie** *nf* baldness

**calvinismo** *nm* Calvinism

**calvinista** *adj* Calvinist

**calvo, -a 1** *adj* bald; **ni tanto ni tan c.** neither one extreme nor the other
**2** *nm,f* bald person
**calza** *nf* (a) *(cuña)* wedge, block (b) *Anticuado (media)* stocking (c) *Col (empaste)* filling *(in tooth)*
**calzada** *nf* road (surface)
**calzado, -a 1** *adj (con zapatos)* shod
**2** *nm* footwear
**calzador** *nm* shoehorn
**calzar [16] 1** *vt (calzado)* to wear; **calzaba zapatos de ante** she was wearing suede shoes; **¿qué número calza?** what size (shoe) do you take? (b) *(poner cuña a)* to wedge, to block (c) *Col (empastar)* to fill *(a tooth)*
**2 calzarse** *vpr* to put one's shoes on; **se calzó las botas** he put on his boots; **¡cálzate!** put your shoes on!
**calzo** *nm (cuña)* wedge
**calzón** *nm Dep* shorts; *Perú* **calzones** *(bragas)* knickers
**calzonazos** *nm inv Fam* henpecked husband
**calzoncillo** *nm,* **calzoncillos** *nmpl* underpants
**CAM** [kam] (a) *nm (abrev de* **computer aided manufacturing)** CAM (b) *(abrev de* **Comunidad Autónoma de Madrid)** autonomous region of Madrid
**cama** *nf* bed; **estar en** *o* **guardar c.** to be confined to bed; **hacer la c.** to make the bed; **c. de agua** water bed; **c. individual/de matrimonio** single/double bed; **c. nido** pull-out bed *(under other bed)*; **c. turca** divan bed; *Fig* **hacerle** *o* **ponerle la c. a alguien** to plot against sb
**camada** *nf* litter
**camafeo** *nm* cameo
**camaleón** *nm también Fig* chameleon
**camaleónico, -a** *adj Fig* fickle
**cámara 1** *nf* (a) *(sala)* chamber; **c. frigorífica** cold-storage room; **c. mortuoria** funeral chamber (b) *Pol & Com* chamber; **c. alta/baja** upper/lower house; **c. de Comercio** Chamber of Commerce; **c. de compensación** clearing house (c) *(de fotos, cine)* camera; *también Fig* **a c. lenta** in slow motion; **c. oscura** camera obscura (d) *(receptáculo)* chamber; **c. de aire/gas** air/gas chamber; **c. de combustión** combustion chamber (e) *(de balón, neumático)* inner tube
**2** *nmf (persona)* cameraman, *f* camerawoman
**camarada** *nmf* (a) *Pol* comrade (b) *(compañero)* colleague
**camaradería** *nf* camaraderie
**camarera** *nf Am (azafata)* air hostess
**camarero, -a** *nm,f* (a) *(de restaurante)* waiter, *f* waitress; *(de hotel)* steward, *f* chambermaid (b) *(de rey)* chamberlain, *f* lady-in-waiting

**camarilla** *nf* clique; *Pol* lobby, pressure group
**camarón** *nm* shrimp
**camarote** *nm* cabin
**camastro** *nm* ramshackle bed
**cambalache** *nm Fam* (a) *(trueque)* swap (b) *CSur (tienda)* junk shop
**cambiante** *adj* changeable
**cambiar [15] 1** *vt* to change; **c. algo (por algo)** to exchange sth (for sth); **c. libras en pesetas** to change pounds into pesetas; **c. un artículo defectuoso** to exchange a faulty item; **he cambiado mi turno con un compañero** I swapped shifts with a colleague
**2** *vi (alterarse)* to change; **c. de** to change; **c. de casa** to move (house); **c. de trabajo** to move *o* change jobs (b) *Aut (de marchas)* to change gear
**3 cambiarse** *vpr* **cambiarse (de ropa)** to change (one's clothes); **cambiarse de casa** to move (house); **no me cambiaría por él** I wouldn't be in his shoes!
**cambiazo** *nm Fam* (a) *(cambio grande)* radical change (b) *(sustitución)* switch *(in order to steal bag, etc)*; *Fig* **dar el c.** to do a switch
**cambio** *nm* (a) *(alteración)* change; **a las primeras de c.** at the first opportunity; **en c.** *(por otra parte)* on the other hand, however; *(en su lugar)* instead; **c. climático** *(calentamiento global)* global warming, climate change; **c. de gobierno** change of government; **c. de rasante** brow of a hill; **c. de sentido** U-turn
(b) *(trueque)* exchange; *(en letrero)* bureau de change; **a c. (de)** in exchange *o* return (for)
(c) *(monedas)* change; **¿tiene c. de cinco mil?** have you got change of *o* for five thousand?; **quédese con el c.** keep the change
(d) *Fin (de acciones)* price; *(de divisas)* exchange rate; **c. base** base rate; **libre c.** *Econ* free trade; *(de divisas)* floating exchange rates
(e) *Aut* **c. automático** automatic transmission; **c. de marchas** *o* **velocidades** gear change
**cambista** *nmf* money changer
**Camboya** *n* Cambodia
**camboyano, -a** *adj & nm,f* Cambodian
**cámbrico, -a** *adj & nm Geol* Cambrian
**cambur** *nm Am* (a) *(empleo)* job (b) *(empleado)* clerk (c) *(plátano)* banana
**camelar** *vt Fam* (a) *(convencer)* to butter up, to win over (b) *(enamorar)* to flirt with
**camelia** *nf* camellia
**camello, -a** *nm,f* (a) *(animal)* camel (b) *Fam (traficante)* drug pusher *o* dealer
**camellón** *nm Col, Méx (en avenida)* Br central reservation, *US* median
**camelo** *nm Fam* (a) *(engaño)* **es puro c.** it's just humbug (b) *(noticia falsa)* hoax

**camembert** ['kamember] (*pl* **camemberts**) *nm* camembert

**camerino** *nm Teatro* dressing room

**Camerún** *nm* (**el**) C. Cameroon

**camerunés, -esa 1** *adj* Cameroon, of/ from Cameroon
 **2** *nm,f* Cameroonian

**camilla 1** *nf* stretcher
 **2** *adj inv* **mesa c.** = round table with heater underneath

**camillero, -a** *nm,f* stretcher-bearer

**caminante** *nmf* walker

**caminar 1** *vi* (a) (*andar*) to walk; *Fig* **c. hacia** to head for (b) *Am* (*funcionar*) to work
 **2** *vt* (*una distancia*) to travel, to cover

**caminata** *nf* long walk

**camino** *nm* (a) (*sendero*) path, track; (*carretera*) road
 (b) (*ruta, vía*) way; **por este c.** this way
 (c) **C. de Santiago** *Astron* Milky Way; *Rel* = pilgrimage route to Santiago de Compostela
 (d) **caminos** (*ingeniería*) civil engineering
 (e) (*expresiones*) **abrir c. a** to clear the way for; **abrirse c.** to get on *o* ahead; **fueron cada cual por su c.** they went their separate ways; **a medio c.** halfway; **estar a medio c.** to be halfway there; **quedarse a medio c.** to stop halfway through; **c. de** on the way to; *Fig* **van c. del desastre/éxito** they're on the road to disaster/success; **en el** *o* **de c.** on the way; **ponerse en c.** to set off; **c. trillado** well-trodden path

**camión** *nm* (a) (*de mercancías*) truck, *Br* lorry; **c. de la basura** *Br* dustcart, *US* garbage truck; **c. cisterna** tanker; *Fam Fig* **estar como un c.** to be gorgeous (b) *CAm, Méx* (*autobús*) bus

**camionero, -a** *nm,f Br* lorry driver, *US* trucker

**camioneta** *nf* van

**camisa** *nf* (a) (*prenda*) shirt; **c. de fuerza** straitjacket (b) (*de serpiente*) slough, skin (c) *Tec* lining (d) (*expresiones*) **jugarse hasta la c.** to stake everything; **meterse en c. de once varas** to complicate matters unnecessarily; **mudar** *o* **cambiar de c.** to change sides; **no le llega la c. al cuerpo** she's scared stiff

**camisería** *nf* (*tienda*) shirt shop, outfitter's

**camisero, -a** *nm,f* (a) (*fabricante*) shirtmaker (b) (*vendedor*) outfitter

**camiseta** *nf* (a) (*ropa interior*) vest (b) (*de manga corta*) T-shirt (c) *Dep* (*de tirantes*) vest; (*con mangas*) shirt

**camisola** *nf* (a) (*prenda interior*) camisole (b) *Dep* sports shirt

**camisón** *nm* nightdress

**camomila** *nf* camomile

**camorra** *nf* trouble; **buscar c.** to look for trouble

**camorrista 1** *adj* belligerent, quarrelsome
 **2** *nmf* troublemaker

**camote** *nm Am* sweet potato

**camp** [kamp] *adj inv* (*estilo, moda*) retro

**campal** *adj también Fig* **batalla c.** pitched battle

**campamento** *nm* camp

**campana** *nf* bell; *Fig* **echar las campanas al vuelo** to jump for joy; *Fam Fig* **oír campanas y no saber dónde** not to know what one is talking about; **c. de buzo** *o* **de salvamento** diving bell; **c. extractora (de humos)** extractor hood

**campanada** *nf* (a) (*de campana*) peal (b) (*de reloj*) stroke (c) *Fig* (*suceso*) sensation; **dar la c.** to make a big splash, to cause a sensation

**campanario** *nm* belfry, bell tower

**campanero, -a** *nm,f* bell-ringer

**campanilla** *nf* (a) (*de la puerta*) (small) bell; (*con mango*) handbell (b) *Anat* uvula (c) (*flor*) campanula, bellflower

**campanilleo** *nm* tinkle, tinkling sound

**campante** *adj Fam* **estar** *o* **quedarse tan c.** to be quite unruffled

**campaña** *nf* (a) (*acción organizada*) campaign; **hacer c. (de/contra)** to campaign (for/against); **c. electoral** election campaign; **c. publicitaria** advertising campaign (b) (*período de pesca*) fishing season; **la c. del atún** the tuna-fishing season (c) (*campo llano*) open countryside (d) *Mil* **hospital de c.** field hospital; **uniforme de c.** combat uniform

**campar** *vi* **campa por sus respetos** he follows his own rules, he does things his own way

**campechanía** *nf* geniality, good-natured character

**campechano, -a** *adj* genial, good-natured

**campeón, -ona** *nm,f* champion

**campeonato** *nm* championship; *Fig* **de c.** (*bueno*) terrific, great; (*malo*) terrible

**campera** *nf* (a) *CSur* (*chaqueta*) short leather jacket (b) **camperas** cowboy boots

**campero, -a 1** *adj* **botas camperas** cowboy boots
 **2** *nm Am* Jeep®

**campesinado** *nm* peasants, peasantry

**campesino, -a 1** *adj* (*del campo*) rural, country; (*en el pasado, en países pobres*) peasant; **las labores campesinas** farmwork
 **2** *nm,f* (*persona del campo*) country person; (*en el pasado, en países pobres*) peasant

**campestre** *adj* country; **comida c.** picnic; **fiesta c.** open-air country festival

**cámping** ['kampin] (*pl* **cámpings**) *nm* (**a**) *(actividad)* camping; **ir de c.** to go camping; **c. gas** portable gas stove (**b**) *(terreno)* campsite

**campiña** *nf* countryside

**campista** *nmf* camper

**campo** *nm* (**a**) *(terreno, área) también Informát* field; *Fig* **dejar el c. libre** to leave the field open; **c. de aviación** airfield; **c. de batalla** battlefield; **c. de concentración** concentration camp; **Fís c. magnético** magnetic field; **c. de refugiados** refugee camp; **c. de tiro** firing range; **c. de trabajo** *(de vacaciones)* work camp; *(para prisioneros)* labour camp; **c. visual** field of vision

(**b**) *(campiña)* country, countryside; **en mitad del c.** in the middle of the country *o* countryside; **c. abierto** open countryside; **a c. traviesa** cross country

(**c**) *Dep (de fútbol)* pitch; *(de tenis)* court; *(de golf)* course; **jugar en c. propio/contrario** to play at home/away (from home)

**camposanto** *nm* cemetery

**campus** *nm inv* campus

**camuflado, -a** *adj Mil* camouflaged; *(oculto)* hidden; **un coche c. de la policía** an unmarked police car

**camuflaje** *nm* camouflage

**camuflar** *vt* to camouflage

**can** *nm* hound, dog

**cana** *nf* grey hair; *Fam* **echar una c. al aire** to let one's hair down; *Fam* **peinar canas** to be getting on, to be old

**Canadá** *nm* (**el**) **C.** Canada

**canadiense** *adj & nmf* Canadian

**canal 1** *nm* (**a**) *(cauce artificial)* canal; **c. de riego** irrigation channel

(**b**) *Geog (estrecho)* channel, strait; **el C. de la Mancha** the (English) Channel; **el C. de Suez/Panamá** the Suez/Panama Canal

(**c**) *Rad & TV* channel

(**d**) *Anat* canal, duct

(**e**) *Fig (medio, vía)* channel; *Econ* **c. de comercialización** distribution channel

(**f**) *(res)* carcass; **abrir en c.** to slit open; *Fig* to tear apart

**2** *nm o nf (de un tejado)* (valley) gutter

**canalé** *nm* ribbed knitwear

**canalización** *nf* (**a**) *(de agua)* piping; **todavía no tienen c. de agua** they're not yet connected to the water mains (**b**) *Fig (orientación)* channelling

**canalizar** [16] *vt* (**a**) *(territorio)* to canalize; *(agua)* to channel (**b**) *(cauce)* to deepen the course of (**c**) *Fig (orientar)* to channel

**canalla** *nmf* swine, dog

**canallada** *nf* dirty trick

**canallesco, -a** *adj (acción, intención)* despicable, vile; *(sonrisa)* wicked, evil

**canalón** *nm (de tejado)* gutter; *(en la pared)* drainpipe

**canana** *nf* cartridge belt

**canapé** *nm* (**a**) *Culin* canapé (**b**) *(sofá)* sofa, couch

**Canarias** *nfpl* **las (islas) C.** the Canary Islands, the Canaries

**canario, -a 1** *adj* of/from the Canary Islands, Canary

**2** *nm,f (persona)* Canary Islander

**3** *nm (pájaro)* canary

**canasta** *nf* (**a**) *(cesto) también Dep* basket (**b**) *(juego de naipes)* canasta

**canastero, -a** *nm,f* basket weaver

**canastilla** *nf* (**a**) *(cesto pequeño)* basket (**b**) *(de bebé)* layette

**canasto** *nm* large basket; *Anticuado o Hum* **¡canastos!** *(expresa enfado)* for Heaven's sake!; *(expresa sorpresa)* good heavens!

**Canberra** *n* Canberra

**cancán** *nm (baile)* cancan

**cancela** *nf* wrought-iron gate

**cancelación** *nf* (**a**) *(anulación)* cancellation (**b**) *(de deuda)* payment, settlement

**cancelar** *vt* (**a**) *(anular)* to cancel (**b**) *(deuda)* to pay, to settle

**cáncer 1** *nmf (persona)* Cancer, Cancerian

**2** *nm* (**a**) *Med & Fig* cancer (**b**) *(zodiaco)* Cancer; **ser c.** to be (a) Cancer

**cancerbero** *nm (en fútbol)* goalkeeper

**cancerígeno, -a** *adj Med* carcinogenic

**cancerología** *nf Med* oncology

**cancerológico, -a** *adj Med* oncological

**cancerólogo, -a** *nm,f Med* cancer specialist, oncologist

**canceroso, -a** *Med* **1** *adj (úlcera, tejido)* cancerous; *(enfermo)* suffering from cancer

**2** *nm,f (enfermo)* cancer patient

**cancha** *nf (de tenis, baloncesto)* court; *Am (de fútbol)* pitch

**canciller** *nm Pol* (**a**) *(de gobierno, embajada)* chancellor (**b**) *(de asuntos exteriores)* foreign minister

**cancillería** *nf Pol* (**a**) *(de Gobierno)* chancellorship (**b**) *(de embajada)* chancellery (**c**) *(de Asuntos Exteriores)* foreign ministry

**canción** *nf* song; **c. de cuna** lullaby; *Fig* **la misma c.** the same old story

**cancionero** *nm* songbook

**cancro** *nm Med* cancer

**candado** *nm* padlock

**candeal** *adj* **pan c.** white bread *(of high quality, made from durum wheat)*

**candela** *nf* (a) *(vela)* candle; *Fam Fig (lumbre)* light (b) *(fuego)* fire

**candelabro** *nm* candelabra

**candelero** *nm* candlestick; *Fig* **estar en el c.** to be in the limelight

**candente** *adj* (a) *(incandescente)* red-hot (b) *Fig (actual)* highly topical; **de c. actualidad** highly topical; **tema c.** burning issue

**candidato, -a** *nm,f* candidate

**candidatura** *nf* (a) *(para un cargo)* candidacy; **presentar uno su c.** to put oneself forward as a candidate for (b) *(lista)* list of candidates

**candidez** *nf* ingenuousness

**cándido, -a** *adj* ingenuous, simple

**candil** *nm (lámpara)* oil lamp

**candilejas** *nfpl* footlights

**candombe, candomblé** *nm (danza)* = South American carnival dance of African origin; *(tambor)* = drum used in the "candombe" dance

**candor** *nm* ingenuousness

**candoroso, -a** *adj* ingenuous, simple

**caneca** *nf Col (para basura) Br* rubbish bin, *US* trashcan

**caneco** *nm (petaca)* hip flask

**canela** *nf* cinnamon; *Fig* **ser c. fina** to be sheer class

**canelo, -a 1** *adj (caballo, perro)* golden brown

**2** *nm Fam* **hemos hecho el c.** we've been had!

**canelones** *nmpl Culin* cannelloni

**canesú** *(pl* **canesús***) nm* (a) *(de vestido)* bodice (b) *(de blusa)* yoke

**cangrejo** *nm* crab; **c. de río** crayfish

**canguelo** *nm Fam* **le entró c.** she got the wind up

**canguro 1** *nm (animal)* kangaroo

**2** *nmf Fam (persona)* babysitter; **hacer de c.** to babysit

**caníbal 1** *adj* cannibalistic

**2** *nmf* cannibal

**canibalismo** *nm* cannibalism

**canica** *nf* marble; **las canicas** *(juego)* marbles; **jugar a las canicas** to play marbles

**caniche** *nm* poodle

**canicie** *nf* grey hair

**canícula** *nf* dog days, high summer

**canicular** *adj* **calor c.** blistering heat

**canijo, -a 1** *adj (pequeño)* tiny; *(enfermizo)* sickly

**2** *nm,f* small, sickly person

**canilla** *nf* (a) *(espinilla)* shinbone (b) *(bobina)* bobbin (c) *CSur (grifo)* tap (d) *CSur (pierna)* leg

**canillita** *nm Am* newspaper vendor

**canino, -a 1** *adj* canine

**2** *nm (diente)* canine (tooth)

**canje** *nm* exchange

**canjeable** *adj* exchangeable

**canjear** *vt* to exchange

**cannabis** *nm inv* cannabis

**cano, -a** *adj* grey *(hair)*

**canoa** *nf* canoe

**canódromo** *nm* greyhound track

**canon** *nm* (a) *(norma)* canon (b) *(modelo)* ideal (c) *(impuesto)* tax (d) *Mús* canon; *Der* **cánones** canon law

**canónico, -a** *adj* canonical; *Der* **derecho c.** canon law

**canónigo** *nm* canon

**canonizar** [16] *vt* to canonize

**canoso, -a** *adj (persona)* grey-haired

**canotier** [kano'tije] *(pl* **canotiers***) nm (sombrero)* straw boater

**cansado, -a** *adj* (a) *(fatigado)* tired; **estar c. de algo/de hacer algo** to be tired of sth/of doing sth (b) *(pesado, cargante)* tiring

**cansador, -ora** *adj CSur* boring

**cansancio** *nm* (a) *(fatiga)* tiredness (b) *(hastío)* boredom

**cansar 1** *vt* to tire (out)

**2** *vi* to be tiring

**3 cansarse** *vpr también Fig* to get tired **(de** of)

**cansino, -a** *adj* lethargic

**Cantabria** *n* Cantabria

**cantábrico, -a 1** *adj* **la cordillera cantábrica** the Cantabrian Mountains **2** *nm* **el (mar) C.** the Cantabrian Sea

**cántabro, -a** *adj & nm,f* Cantabrian

**cantado, -a** *adj* **el resultado está c.** the result is a foregone conclusion

**cantaleta** *nf Am* nagging

**cantamañanas** *nmf inv* unreliable person

**cantante 1** *adj* singing

**2** *nmf* singer

**cantaor, -ora** *nm,f* flamenco singer

**cantar 1** *vt* (a) *(canción)* to sing (b) *(bingo, línea, el gordo)* to call (out)

**2** *vi* (a) *(persona, ave)* to sing; *(gallo)* to crow; *(insecto)* to chirp (b) *Fam Fig (confesar)* to talk (c) *muy Fam Fig (apestar)* to stink; **le cantan los pies** he has smelly feet (d) *Fam Fig (desentonar)* to stick out like a sore thumb (e) *Fig (alabar)* **c. a** to sing the praises of

**3** *nm Lit* poem; *Fam Fig* **eso es otro c.** that's another story

**cántaro** *nm* large pitcher; **a cántaros** in torrents; **llover a cántaros** to rain cats and dogs

**cantata** *nf* cantata

**cantautor, -ora** *nm,f* singer-songwriter

**cante** *nm* c. **(jondo** *o* **hondo)** flamenco singing; *muy Fam* **dar el c.** to call attention to oneself

**cantegril** *nm Urug* shanty town

**cantera** *nf (de piedra)* quarry; *Fig (de jóvenes promesas)* young blood; **un jugador de la c.** a home-grown *o* local player

**cantero** *nm CSur, Cuba* flowerbed

**cántico** *nm* canticle

**cantidad 1** *nf* **(a)** *(medida)* quantity **(b)** *(abundancia)* abundance, large number; **c. de** lots of; **en c.** in abundance **(c)** *(número)* number **(d)** *(suma de dinero)* sum (of money)

**2** *adv muy Fam* really; **me gusta c.** I really like it a lot

**cantiga, cántiga** *nf* ballad

**cantilena** *nf Fig* **la misma c.** the same old story

**cantimplora** *nf* water bottle

**cantina** *nf (de soldados)* mess; *(en fábrica)* canteen; *(en estación de tren)* buffet

**cantinela** *nf Fig* **la misma c.** the same old story

**cantinero, -a** *nm,f* canteen manager, *f* canteen manageress

**canto** *nm* **(a)** *(acción, arte)* singing; *(canción)* song; *Fig* **c. del cisne** swansong; **c. fúnebre** funeral chant; *Fig* **c. del gallo** daybreak; **c. gregoriano** Gregorian chant; **c. guerrero** war song; *Fig* **c. de sirena** wheedling **(b)** *(lado, borde)* edge; *(de cuchillo)* blunt edge; **de c.** edgeways; *Fam Fig* **por el c. de un duro** by a hair's breadth *(de bota)* pebble; *Fig* **darse con un c. en los dientes** to consider oneself lucky; **c. rodado** pebble

**cantón** *nm (territorio)* canton

**cantonera** *nf (de esquina, libro)* corner piece

**cantor, -ora 1** *adj* singing; **ave cantora** songbird

**2** *nm,f* singer

**cantoral** *nm* choir book

**canturrear** *vt & vi Fam* to sing softly

**canturreo** *nm Fam* humming, quiet singing

**cánula** *nf Med* cannula

**canutas** *nfpl Fam* **pasarlas c.** to have a rough time

**canuto** *nm* **(a)** *(tubo)* tube; *Fam* **no sabe hacer la o con un c.** he is as thick as two short planks **(b)** *muy Fam (porro)* joint

**caña** *nf* **(a)** *(planta)* cane; *(de río, de estanque)* reed; **c. de azúcar** sugarcane **(b)** *(de cerveza)* small glass of beer **(c)** **c. (de pescar)** fishing rod **(d)** *(de bota)* leg **(e)** *(tuétano)* bone marrow **(f)** *Fam* **darle** *o* **meterle c. a algo** to get a move on with sth; **meter c. al coche** to step on it

**cañabrava** *nf Am* = kind of reed

**cañada** *nf* **(a)** *(desfiladero)* gorge, ravine **(b)** *(camino para ganado)* cattle track

**cáñamo** *nm* hemp

**cañamón** *nm* hempseed

**cañaveral** *nm* reedbed

**cañería** *nf* pipe

**cañizo** *nm* wattle

**caño** *nm (de fuente)* jet

**cañón** *nm* **(a)** *(arma)* gun; *Hist* cannon **(b)** *(de fusil, pistola)* barrel; *(de chimenea)* flue; *(de órgano)* pipe **(c)** *Geog* canyon; **el (Gran) C. del Colorado** the Grand Canyon **(d)** *Fam* **estar c.** to be gorgeous

**cañonazo** *nm* **(a)** *(disparo de cañón)* gunshot **(b)** *Fam (en fútbol)* powerful shot

**cañonear** *vt* to shell

**cañonera** *nf* gunboat

**caoba** *nf* mahogany

**caos** *nm inv* chaos; **ser un c.** to be in chaos

**caótico, -a** *adj* chaotic

**CAP** [kap] *nm (abrev de* **Certificado de Aptitud Pedagógica)** = Spanish teaching certificate needed to teach in secondary education

**cap.** *(abrev de* **capítulo)** ch.

**capa** *nf* **(a)** *(manto)* cloak, cape; *Fam* **andar de c. caída** *(persona)* to be in a bad way; *(negocio)* to be struggling; **defender algo a c. y espada** to defend sth tooth and nail; **hacer de su c. un sayo** to do as one pleases **(b)** *(baño) (de barniz, pintura)* coat; *(de chocolate)* coating **(c)** *(estrato)* layer; *Geol* stratum, layer; **c. atmosférica** atmosphere; **c. de ozono** ozone layer; **c. terrestre** Earth's surface **(d)** *(grupo social)* stratum, class **(e)** *Taurom* cape

**capacho** *nm* wicker basket

**capacidad** *nf* **(a)** *(cabida)* capacity; **con c. para 500 personas** with a capacity of 500; **c. máxima** *(en ascensor)* maximum load **(b)** *(aptitud, talento)* ability; **no tener c. para algo/para hacer algo** to be no good at sth/ at doing sth

**capacitación** *nf* training

**capacitar** *vt* **c. a alguien para hacer algo** *(habilitar)* to entitle sb to do sth; *(formar)* to train sb to do sth

**capado** *adj* castrated, gelded

**capar** *vt* to castrate, to geld

**caparazón** *nm también Fig* shell

**capataz, -aza** *nm,f* foreman, *f* forewoman

**capaz** *adj* **(a)** *(apto)* capable; **c. de algo/de hacer algo** capable of sth/of doing sth; **es muy c. de robarle a su propia madre** she would be quite capable of stealing from her own mother; **¡no serás c. de dejarme sola!** surely you wouldn't leave me all alone! **(b)** *(espacioso)* **muy/poco c.** with a large/small capacity **(c)** *Der* competent

**capazo** *nm* large wicker basket

**capcioso, -a** *adj* disingenuous; **pregunta capciosa** trick question

**capea** *nf Taurom* = amateur bullfight with young bulls

**capear** *vt Fig (eludir)* to get out of; **c. el temporal** to ride out *o* weather the storm

**capellán** *nm* chaplain

**capelo** *nm* **c. (cardenalicio)** cardinal's hat

**Caperucita Roja** *nf* Little Red Riding Hood

**caperuza** *nf* **(a)** *(gorro)* hood **(b)** *(capuchón)* top, cap

**capicúa 1** *adj inv* reversible
**2** *nm inv* reversible number

**capilar 1** *adj* **(a)** *(del cabello)* hair; **loción c.** hair lotion **(b)** *Anat & Fís* capillary
**2** *nm Anat* capillary

**capilaridad** *nf Fís* capillarity, capillary action

**capilla** *nf* chapel; **c. ardiente** funeral chapel; *Fig* **estar en c.** *(condenado a muerte)* to be awaiting execution; *Fam (en ascuas)* to be on tenterhooks

**capirotazo** *nm* flick

**capirote** *nm* **(a)** *(gorro)* hood **(b)** *Fam* **ser un tonto de c.** to be a complete idiot

**cápita** *nf* **per c.** per capita

**capital 1** *adj* **(a)** *(importante)* supreme **(b)** *(principal)* main **(c)** *Rel (pecado)* deadly
**2** *nm Econ* capital; **c. circulante/fijo/social** working/fixed/share capital; **c. escriturado** declared capital, capital stock; **c. líquido** liquid assets; **c. bajo riesgo** sum at risk; **c. de riesgo** venture capital
**3** *nf (ciudad)* capital

**capitalidad** *nf Formal* **ostentar la c. de** to be the capital of

**capitalino, -a** *adj* of the capital (city), capital; **la vida capitalina** life in the capital (city)

**capitalismo** *nm* capitalism

**capitalista** *adj & nmf* capitalist

**capitalización** *nf* capitalization

**capitalizar** [16] *vt* **(a)** *Econ* to capitalize **(b)** *Fig (sacar provecho de)* to capitalize on

**capitán, -ana** *nm,f* captain; *Mil* **c. general** *Br* field marshal, *US* general of the army

**capitana** *nf Náut* flagship

**capitanear** *vt* **(a)** *Dep & Mil* to captain **(b)** *(dirigir)* to head, to lead

**capitanía** *nf Mil* **(a)** *(empleo)* captaincy **(b)** *(oficina)* military headquarters; **c. general** Captaincy General

**capitel** *nm Arquit* capital

**capitolio** *nm* **(a)** *(edificio)* capitol; **el C.** *(en Estados Unidos)* the Capitol **(b)** *(acrópolis)* acropolis

**capitoste** *nmf Fam* big wheel, big boss

**capitulación** *nf* capitulation, surrender; **capitulaciones matrimoniales** marriage contract

**capitular** *vi* to capitulate, to surrender

**capítulo** *nm* **(a)** *(sección, división)* chapter **(b)** *Fig (tema)* subject; **ser c. aparte** to be another matter (altogether)

**capo** *nm (de la mafia)* mafia boss, capo

**capó** *nm Br* bonnet, *US* hood

**capón** *nm* **(a)** *(animal)* capon **(b)** *Fam (golpe)* rap on the head

**caporal** *nm Mil* corporal

**capota** *nf Br* hood, *US* top

**capotazo** *nm Taurom* = pass with the cape

**capote** *nm* **(a)** *(capa)* cape with sleeves; *(militar)* greatcoat **(b)** *Taurom* cape **(c)** *Fig* **echar un c. a alguien** to give sb a (helping) hand

**caprichoso, -a** *adj* capricious

**capricornio 1** *nmf (persona)* Capricorn
**2** *nm (zodiaco)* Capricorn; **ser c.** to be (a) Capricorn

**cápsula** *nf* **(a)** *también Anat* capsule **(b)** *(tapón)* cap

**captación** *nf (de adeptos)* recruitment; **c. de fondos** fundraising

**captar 1** *vt* **(a)** *(atraer) (simpatía)* to win; *(interés)* to gain, to capture **(b)** *(entender)* to grasp **(c)** *(sintonizar)* to pick up, to receive
**2** **captarse** *vpr (atraer)* to win, to attract

**captor, -ora** *adj & nm,f* captor

**captura** *nf* capture

**capturar** *vt* to capture

**capucha** *nf* hood

**capuchino, -a 1** *adj* Capuchin
**2** *nm* **(a)** *(fraile)* Capuchin **(b)** *(café)* cappuccino

**capuchón** *nm* **(a)** *(de prenda)* hood **(b)** *(de bolígrafo, pluma)* top, cap

**capullo, -a 1** *adj muy Fam* bloody stupid
**2** *nm (de flor)* bud **(b)** *(de gusano)* cocoon **(c)** *Vulg (prepucio)* foreskin
**3** *nm,f muy Fam (persona despreciable) Br* prat, *US* jerk

**caqui 1** *adj inv (color)* khaki
**2** *nm* **(a)** *(fruto)* kaki **(b)** *(color)* khaki

**cara** *nf* (**a**) *(rostro)* face
(**b**) *(lado)* side; *Geom* face
(**c**) *(de moneda)* heads; **c. o cruz** heads or tails; **echar algo a c. o cruz** to toss (a coin) for sth
(**d**) *Fam (desvergüenza)* cheek; **tener (mucha) c., tener la c. muy dura** to have a cheek
(**e**) *(parte frontal)* front
(**f**) *(expresiones)* **a c. descubierta** openly; **c. a** *(frente a)* facing; **c. a c.** face to face; **se le cayó la c. de vergüenza** she blushed with shame; **cruzar la c. a alguien** to slap sb in the face; **dar la c. por alguien** to make excuses for sb; **de c.** *(sol, viento)* in one's face; **de c. a** with a view to; **decir algo a alguien en** *o* **a la c.** to say sth to sb's face; **echar en c. algo a alguien** to reproach sb for sth; **hacer c. a** to stand up to; **poner c. de tonto** to pull a stupid face; **por su linda c., por su c. bonita** because his/her face fits; **romper** *o* **partir la c. a alguien** to smash sb's face in; **tener buena/mala c.** *(persona)* to look well/awful; **tener c. de enfadado** to look angry; **tiene c. de ponerse a llover** it looks as if it's going to rain; **tener dos caras** to be two-faced; **verse las caras** *(pelearse)* to have it out; *(enfrentarse)* to fight it out

**carabela** *nf* caravel

**carabina** *nf* (**a**) *(arma)* carbine, rifle (**b**) *Fam Fig (mujer)* chaperone

**carabinero** *nm* (**a**) *(en España)* customs policeman (**b**) *(en Italia)* carabiniere (**c**) *Am (policía)* armed policeman

**Caracas** *n* Caracas

**caracol** *nm* (**a**) *(animal)* snail (**b**) *(concha)* shell (**c**) *(del oído)* cochlea (**d**) *(rizo)* curl
   **2** *interj* **¡caracoles!** good grief!

**caracola** *nf* conch

**caracolada** *nf Culin* = stew made with snails

**caracolear** *vi (caballo)* to prance about

**carácter** *(pl* **caracteres)** *nm* character; **tener buen/mal c.** to be good-natured/bad-tempered; **una reunión de c. privado/oficial** a private/official meeting; **caracteres de imprenta** typeface

**característica** *nf* characteristic

**característico, -a** *adj* characteristic

**caracterización** *nf* (**a**) *(de personaje)* characterization (**b**) *(maquillaje)* make-up

**caracterizar** [16] **1** *vt* (**a**) *(definir)* to characterize (**b**) *(representar)* to portray (**c**) *(maquillar)* to make up
   **2 caracterizarse** *vpr* to be characterized (**por** by)

**caradura** *Fam* **1** *adj* cheeky
   **2** *nmf* cheeky person

**carajillo** *nm* coffee with a dash of liqueur

**carajo** *muy Fam* **1** *nm* **me importa un c.** I couldn't give a monkey's; **irse al c.** to go down the tubes; **¡vete al c.!** go to hell!
   **2** *interj* **¡c.!** damn it!

**caramba** *interj* **¡c.!** *(sorpresa)* good heavens!; *(enfado)* for heaven's sake!

**carámbano** *nm* icicle; *Fam Fig* **estar hecho un c.** to be frozen stiff

**carambola** *nf* cannon *(in billiards)*; *Fig* **de** *o* **por c.** by a (lucky) fluke; **¡carambolas!** good heavens!

**caramelo** *nm* (**a**) *(golosina)* sweet (**b**) *(azúcar fundido)* caramel; *Fig* **de c.** great

**caramillo** *nm* shepherd's flute

**carantoñas** *nfpl* **hacer c. a alguien** to butter sb up

**caraota** *nf Ven* bean

**caraqueño, -a** **1** *adj* of/from Caracas
   **2** *nm,f* person from Caracas

**cárate** *nm* karate

**carátula** *nf* (**a**) *(de libro)* front cover; *(de disco)* sleeve (**b**) *(máscara)* mask

**caravana** *nf* (**a**) *(remolque)* caravan (**b**) *(de camellos)* caravan; *(de carromatos)* wagon train (**c**) *(de coches)* tailback (**d**) *CSur* **caravanas** *(pendientes)* earrings

**caravaning** [kara'βanin] *(pl* **caravanings)** *nm* caravanning

**caray** *interj* **¡c.!** *(sorpresa)* good heavens!; *(enfado)* damn it!

**carbón** *nm* (**a**) *(para quemar)* coal; **negro como el c.** *(negro)* black as coal; *(bronceado)* brown as a berry; **c. de leña** *o* **vegetal** charcoal; **c. mineral** *o* **de piedra** coal (**b**) *(para dibujar)* charcoal

**carbonatado, -a** *adj* carbonated

**carbonato** *nm Quím* carbonate

**carboncillo** *nm* charcoal

**carbonera** *nf* coal bunker

**carbonero, -a** **1** *adj* coal; **industria carbonera** coal industry
   **2** *nm,f (persona)* coal merchant; *Fig* **la fe del c.** blind faith

**carbónico, -a** *adj* carbonic

**carbonífero, -a** *adj & nm Geol (era)* Carboniferous

**carbonilla** *nf* (**a**) *(ceniza)* cinder (**b**) *(carbón pequeño)* small coal

**carbonizado, -a** *adj* charred

**carbonizar** [16] **1** *vt* to char, to carbonize; **morir carbonizado** to burn to death
   **2 carbonizarse** *vpr* to be charred

**carbono** *nm* carbon; **c. 14** carbon 14

**carburación** *nf Aut* carburation

**carburador** *nm* carburettor

**carburante** *nm* fuel

**carburar 1** *vt* to carburate

**2** *vi Fam* to function

**carburo** *nm* carbide

**carca** *Fam Pey* **1** *adj* old-fashioned

**2** *nmf* old fogey

**carcaj** (*pl* **carcajes**) *nm* quiver

**carcajada** *nf* guffaw; **reír a carcajadas** to roar with laughter

**carcajearse** *vpr* to roar with laughter

**carcajeo** *nm* roars of laughter

**carcamal** *nmf Fam Pey* old crock

**cárcel** *nf* prison; **meter a alguien en la c.** to put sb in prison; **c. de alta seguridad** top security prison

**carcelario, -a** *adj* prison; **la vida carcelaria** prison life; **régimen c.** prison conditions

**carcelero, -a** *nm,f* warder, jailer

**carcinoma** *nm Med* carcinoma, cancerous tumour

**carcoma** *nf* (a) (*insecto*) woodworm (b) (*polvo*) wood dust

**carcomer 1** *vt también Fig* to eat away at

**2 carcomerse** *vpr Fig* (*consumirse*) to be eaten up *o* consumed

**carcomido, -a** *adj* (*madera*) wormeaten

**cardado, -a 1** *adj* (*lana*) carded; (*pelo*) backcombed

**2** *nm* (*de lana*) carding; (*del pelo*) backcombing

**cardador, -ora** *nm,f* carder

**cardamomo** *nm* cardamom

**cardán** *nm* cardan joint

**cardar** *vt* (*lana*) to card; (*pelo*) to backcomb

**cardenal** *nm* (a) *Rel* cardinal (b) (*hematoma*) bruise

**cardenalicio, -a** *adj* **colegio c.** college of cardinals (*group*); **manto c.** cardinal's robe

**cardenillo** *nm* verdigris

**cárdeno, -a** *adj* purple

**cardiaco, -a, cardíaco, -a** *adj* cardiac; **paro c.** cardiac arrest; **insuficiencia cardiaca** heart failure

**cárdigan** *nm* cardigan

**cardinal** *adj* cardinal

**cardiograma** *nm* electrocardiogram

**cardiología** *nf* cardiology

**cardiólogo, -a** *nm,f* cardiologist

**cardiopatía** *nf* heart condition

**cardiovascular** *adj* cardiovascular

**cardo** *nm* (a) (*planta*) thistle; **c. borriquero** cotton thistle (b) *Fam Fig* (*persona*) (*fea*) ugly mug; (*arisca*) prickly customer

**carear** *vt* (*testigos, acusados*) to bring face to face

**carecer** [48] *vi* **c. de algo** to lack sth

**carenado** *nm* (*de moto*) fairing

**carencia** *nf* (*ausencia*) lack; (*defecto*) deficiency; **sufrir carencias afectivas** to be deprived of love and affection; **sufrir muchas carencias** to suffer great need

**carente** *adj* **c. de** lacking (in)

**careo** *nm* (*de testigos, acusados*) confrontation; **someter a un c.** to bring face to face

**carero, -a** *Fam* **1** *adj* pricey

**2** *nm,f* (*tendero*) = shopkeeper who charges high prices; **el pescadero es un c.** the fishmonger is a bit pricey

**carestía** *nf* (*alto precio*) **la c. de la vida** the high cost of living

**careta** *nf* (*máscara*) mask; **c. antigás** gas mask

**careto** *nm muy Fam* (*cara*) mug

**carey** *nm* (*material*) tortoiseshell; (*tortuga*) sea turtle

**carga** *nf* (a) (*acción*) loading; **zona de c. y descarga** loading bay

(b) (*cargamento*) (*de avión, barco*) cargo; (*de tren*) freight

(c) (*peso*) load; *Fig* (*sufrimiento*) burden; **representa una enorme c. para sus hijos** she is a great burden on her children

(d) (*ataque, explosivo*) charge; **¡a la c.!** charge!; *Fig* **volver a la c.** (*insistir*) to insist; (*atacar de nuevo*) to go back on the offensive; *Mil* **c. de profundidad** depth charge

(e) (*de mechero, bolígrafo*) refill

(f) (*impuesto*) tax; **cargas fiscales** taxes; **c. tributaria** levy

(g) (*eléctrica*) charge

**cargado, -a** *adj* (a) (*lleno*) loaded (**de** with); (*arma*) loaded; *Fig* **estar c. de** to have loads of (b) (*bebida*) strong (c) (*bochornoso*) (*habitación*) stuffy; (*tiempo*) sultry, close; (*cielo*) overcast (d) *Fís* (*eléctricamente*) charged

**cargador** *nm* (a) (*de arma*) chamber (b) (*persona*) loader; **c. de muelle** docker, stevedore (c) (*de baterías*) charger

**cargamento** *nm* cargo

**cargante** *adj Fam Fig* annoying

**cargar** [40] **1** *vt* (a) (*llenar*) to load; (*pluma, mechero*) to refill; **c. las tintas** to exaggerate, to lay it on thick

(b) (*peso encima*) to throw over one's shoulder

(c) *Elec* to charge

(d) *Fam Fig* (*molestar*) to annoy; **me carga su pedantería** I find his pedantry irritating

(e) (*adeudar*) (*importe, factura, deuda*) to charge (**a** to); **c. un impuesto a algo/alguien** to tax sth/sb

**2** *vi* (a) **c. con** (*paquete, bulto*) to carry away; *Fig* (*coste, responsabilidad*) to bear; *Fig* (*consecuencias*) to accept; *Fig* (*culpa*) to get

(b) (*atacar*) **c. (contra)** to charge

**3 cargarse** *vpr* (a) *Fam (romper)* to break; **se cargó el jarrón** she broke the vase

(b) *Fam (suspender)* to fail; **el profesor se cargó a la mitad de la clase** the teacher failed half the class

(c) *Fam (matar) (persona)* to bump off; *(animal)* to kill

(d) *(por el humo)* to get stuffy

(e) **cargarse de deudas** to get up to one's neck in debt

(f) *Fam* **¡te la vas a c.!** you're in for it!

**cargo** *nm* (a) *(cuidado)* charge; **estar a c. de algo,** **tener algo a c. de uno** to be in charge of sth; **hacerse c. de** *(asumir el control de)* to take charge of; *(ocuparse de)* to take care of; *(comprender)* to understand

(b) *(empleo)* post, position; *Pol* **alto c.** high-ranking official

(c) *Econ* charge; **con c. a** charged to; **correr a c. de** to be borne by

(d) *Der (acusación)* charge; *Fig* **me da c. de conciencia dejarle pagar** I feel bad about letting him pay

**cargosear** *vt Chile, CSur* to annoy, to pester

**cargoso, -a** *adj Chile, CSur* annoying

**carguero** *nm* cargo boat

**cariacontecido, -a** *adj* crestfallen

**cariado, -a** *adj* decayed

**cariarse** [15] *vpr* to decay

**cariátide** *nf* caryatid

**Caribe 1** *adj* **el mar C.** the Caribbean (Sea)
  **2** *nm* **el C.** the Caribbean (Sea)

**caribeño, -a 1** *adj* Caribbean
  **2** *nm,f* person from the Caribbean

**caricatura** *nf* caricature

**caricaturesco, -a** *adj* caricature; **un retrato c. de la situación** a caricature of the situation

**caricaturista** *nmf* caricaturist

**caricaturizar** [16] *vt* to caricature

**caricia** *nf (a persona)* caress, stroke; *(a animal)* stroke; **hacer caricias/una c. a alguien** to caress sb

**Caricom** *nf (abrev de* **comunidad (económica) del Caribe)** Caricom

**caridad** *nf* charity

**caries** *nf inv* tooth decay; **tengo tres c.** I have three cavities

**carillón** *nm* carillon

**cariñena** *nm* = wine from Cariñena, in the province of Zaragoza

**cariño** *nm* (a) *(afecto)* affection; **tener c. a** to be fond of; **tomar c. a** to grow fond of (b) *(cuidado)* loving care (c) *(apelativo)* love, dear

**cariñoso, -a** *adj* affectionate

**carioca 1** *adj* of/from Rio de Janeiro
  **2** *nmf* person from Rio de Janeiro

**carisma** *nm* charisma

**carismático, -a** *adj* charismatic

**Cáritas** *nf* = charitable organization run by the Catholic Church

**caritativo, -a** *adj* charitable

**cariz** *nm* look, appearance; **tomar mal/buen c.** to take a turn for the worse/better

**carlinga** *nf Av (para piloto)* cockpit; *(para pasajeros)* cabin

**carlismo** *nm Hist* Carlism

**carlista** *adj & nmf* Carlist

**carmelita** *adj & nmf* Carmelite

**carmesí** *(pl* **carmesíes)** *adj & nm* crimson

**carmín 1** *adj (color)* carmine
  **2** *nm* (a) *(color)* carmine (b) *(lápiz de labios)* lipstick

**carnada** *nf también Fig* bait

**carnal** *adj* (a) *(de la carne)* carnal (b) *(parientes)* **primo c.** first cousin; **tío c.** uncle *(not by marriage)*

**carnaval** *nm* (a) *(fiesta)* carnival (b) *Rel* Shrovetide

**carnavalada** *nf Fam* farce

**carnavalesco, -a** *adj* carnival; **ambiente c.** carnival atmosphere

**carnaza** *nf también Fig* bait

**carne** *nf* (a) *(de persona, fruta)* flesh; **en c. viva** raw; **entrado o metido en carnes** plump (b) *(alimento)* meat; **c. de cerdo** *o Am* **chancho** pork; **c. de cordero** lamb; **c. picada** *Br* mince, *US* mincemeat; *Am* **c. de res** beef; **c. roja** red meat; **c. de ternera** veal; **c. de vaca** beef (c) *(sensualidad)* flesh; **los placeres de la c.** the pleasures of the flesh (d) *(expresiones)* **c. de cañón** cannon fodder; **c. de gallina** gooseflesh; **en c. y hueso** in person; **poner toda la c. en el asador** to go for broke; **ser de c. y hueso** to be human

**carné** *(pl* **carnés), carnet** *(pl* **carnets)** *nm* (a) *(documento)* card; **c. de conducir** *Br* driving licence, *US* driver's license; **c. de identidad** identity card (b) *(agenda)* notebook

**carnear** *vt CSur* to slaughter, to butcher

**carnero** *nm* ram

**carnicería** *nf* (a) *(tienda)* butcher's (b) *Fig (masacre)* massacre, bloodbath; **fue una c.** it was carnage

**carnicero, -a 1** *adj (animal)* carnivorous
  **2** *nm,f también Fig (persona)* butcher

**cárnico, -a** *adj* meat; **industrias cárnicas** meat industry; **productos cárnicos** meat products

**carnitas** *nfpl Am* barbecued pork

**carnívoro, -a 1** *adj* carnivorous

**2** *nm* carnivore

**carnosidad** *nf* fleshy part

**carnoso, -a** *adj (persona, rodillas)* fleshy; *(labios)* full

**caro, -a 1** *adj* **(a)** *(costoso)* expensive **(b)** *Formal (querido)* cherished

**2** *adv* **costar c.** to be expensive; *Fig* **pagar c. algo** to pay dearly for sth; *Fig* **un día te va a salir cara tu conducta** you'll pay dearly for this behaviour one day; **vender c. algo** to sell sth at a high price; *Fig* not to give sth up easily

**carolingio, -a** *adj & nm,f* Carolingian

**carota** *nmf Fam* cheeky so-and-so

**carótida** *adj & nf* carotid

**carozo** *nm Am* stone *(of fruit)*

**carpa** *nf* **(a)** *(pez)* carp **(b)** *(de circo)* big top; *(en parque, la calle)* marquee **(c)** *Am (tienda de campaña)* tent

**Cárpatos** *nmpl* **los C.** the Carpathians

**carpeta** *nf* file, folder

**carpetazo** *nm* **dar c. a algo** to shelve sth

**carpetovetónico, -a** *adj* deeply Spanish

**carpintería** *nf* **(a)** *(de muebles y utensilios)* carpentry; *(de puertas y ventanas)* joinery **(b)** *(taller)* carpenter's/joiner's shop

**carpintero, -a** *nm,f* **(a)** *(de muebles y utensilios)* carpenter; *(de puertas y ventanas)* joiner

**carraca** *nf* *(instrumento)* rattle; *Fig (cosa vieja)* old crock

**carraspear** *vi* to clear one's throat

**carraspeo** *nm* cough, clearing of one's throat

**carraspera** *nf* **tener c.** to have a frog in one's throat

**carrera** *nf* **(a)** *(acción de correr)* **a la c.** running, at a run; *Fig* in a rush; **ir a un sitio de una c.** to run somewhere; **tuve que dar una c. para coger el autobús** I had to run to catch the bus **(b)** *Dep & Fig* race; **¿echamos una c.?** shall we race each other?; **c. armamentística** *o* **de armamentos** arms race; **c. contrarreloj** race against the clock; **c. de coches** motor race; **c. de obstáculos** steeplechase **(c)** *(estudios)* university course; **hacer la c. de derecho/físicas** to study law/physics (at university) **(d)** *(profesión)* career; **hacer c.** *(triunfar)* to succeed (in life) **(e)** *Fam* **hacer la c.** *(prostituirse)* to walk the streets **(f)** *(trayecto)* route **(g)** *(de taxi)* ride **(h)** *(en medias)* *Br* ladder, *US* run **(i)** *(calle)* = name of certain Spanish streets

**carrerilla** *nf* **coger** *o* **tomar c.** to take a run-up; **decir algo de c.** to reel sth off

**carreta** *nf* cart

**carrete** *nm* **(a)** *(de hilo)* bobbin, reel; *(de alambre)* coil; *(de pesca)* reel **(b)** *Fot* roll *(of film)* **(c)** **dar c. a alguien** to draw sb out

**carretera** *nf* road; **c. de circunvalación** ring road; **c. comarcal** minor road; **c. de peaje** *o Am* **cuota** toll road; **c. nacional** *Br* ≃ A road, *US* ≃ state highway

**carretero** *nm Fig* **fumar como un c.** to smoke like a chimney

**carretilla** *nf* wheelbarrow

**carricoche** *nm Anticuado* jalopy, *Br* old banger

**carril** *nm* **(a)** *(de carretera)* lane; **c. de aceleración** slip road; **c. bici** *Br* cycle lane, *US* bikeway; **c. bus** bus lane **(b)** *(de vía de tren)* rail **(c)** *(de ruedas)* rut

**carrillo** *nm* cheek; *Fig* **comer a dos carrillos** to cram one's face with food

**carrito** *nm* trolley, *US* cart

**carrizal** *nm* reedbed

**carrizo** *nm* reed

**carro** *nm* **(a)** *(vehículo)* cart; *Mil* **c. de combate** tank; **¡para el c.!** *(espera un momento)* hang on a minute!; **aguantar carros y carretas** to put up with a lot **(b)** *(carrito)* trolley; *(de bebé)* pram; **c. de la compra** shopping trolley *(two-wheeled)* **(c)** *(de máquina de escribir)* carriage **(d)** *Am (coche)* car; **c. comedor** dining car; **c. dormitorio** sleeper

**carrocería** *nf* bodywork

**carromato** *nm (carro)* wagon

**carroña** *nf* carrion

**carroñero, -a** *adj (animal)* carrion-eating

**carroza 1** *nf (coche)* carriage

**2** *nmf Fam (viejo)* old fogey

**carruaje** *nm* carriage

**carrusel** *nm* **(a)** *(tiovivo)* carousel, merry-go-round **(b)** *(de caballos)* dressage, display of horsemanship

**carta** *nf* **(a)** *(escrito)* letter; **echar una c.** to post a letter; **c. certificada/urgente** registered/express letter; **c. de recomendación** reference (letter) **(b)** *(naipe)* (playing) card; **echar las cartas a alguien** to tell sb's fortune *(with cards)*; **jugar a las cartas** to play cards **(c)** *(menú)* menu; **c. de vinos** wine list; **comer a la c.** to eat à la carte **(d)** *(mapa)* map; *Náut* chart; **c. astral** star chart **(e)** *(documento)* charter; *Com* **c. de crédito** letter of credit; **c. de naturaleza** naturalization papers; *Com* **c. de pago** receipt; **c. de trabajo** work permit; **c. verde** green card; **cartas credenciales** letters of credence **(f)** *TV* **c. de ajuste** *Br* test card, *US* test pattern

**(g)** *(expresiones)* **a c. cabal** through and through; **dar c. blanca a alguien** to give sb carte blanche *o* a free hand; **jugarse la última c.** to play one's last card; **jugarse todo a una c.** to put all one's eggs in one basket; **no saber a qué c. quedarse** to be unsure; **poner las cartas boca arriba** *o* **sobre la mesa** to put one's cards on the table; **tomar cartas en un asunto** to intervene in a matter

**cartabón** *nm* set square

**cartaginés, -esa** *adj & nm,f Hist* Carthaginian

**cartapacio** *nm* **(a)** *(carpeta)* folder **(b)** *(cuaderno)* notebook

**cartearse** *vpr* to correspond; **nos seguimos carteando** we still write to each other

**cartel** *nm* **(a)** *(anuncio)* poster; **prohibido fijar carteles** *(en letrero)* billposters will be prosecuted **(b)** *Fig (fama)* **tener buen/mal c.** to be popular/unpopular

**cártel** *nm* cartel

**cartelera** *nf* **(a)** *(tablón)* hoarding, billboard **(b)** *Prensa* entertainments page; **estar en c.** to be showing; **lleva un año en c.** it has been running for a year

**cartelero, -a** *adj* popular, big-name

**cartelista** *nmf* poster artist

**carteo** *nm* correspondence

**cárter** *nm Aut* housing

**cartera** *nf* **(a)** *(para dinero)* wallet **(b)** *(para documentos)* briefcase; *(sin asa)* portfolio; *(de colegial)* satchel; *Fig* **tener algo en c.** to have sth in the pipeline **(c)** *Com, Fin & Pol* portfolio; **c. de pedidos** *(pedidos pendientes)* orders in hand; *(pedidos atrasados)* backlog; **c. de valores** portfolio **(d)** *Am (bolso)* bag

**carterista** *nmf* pickpocket

**cartero, -a** *nm,f* postman, *f* postwoman

**cartesiano, -a** *adj & nm,f Filosofía* Cartesian

**cartilaginoso, -a** *adj* cartilaginous

**cartílago** *nm* cartilage

**cartilla** *nf* **(a)** *(documento)* book; **c. (de ahorros)** savings book; **c. militar** = booklet to say one has completed one's military service; **c. del paro** *Br* ≃ UB40, = registration card .issued to the unemployed; **c. de la seguridad social** = social security card **(b)** *(para aprender a leer)* primer; *Fig* **leerle la c. a alguien** to read sb the riot act

**cartografía** *nf* cartography

**cartógrafo, -a** *nm,f* cartographer

**cartomancia** *nf* cartomancy, fortune-telling *(with cards)*

**cartón** *nm* **(a)** *(material)* cardboard; **c. piedra** papier mâché **(b)** *(de cigarrillos)* carton **(c)** *(de leche, zumo)* carton

**cartoné** *nm* **en c.** bound in boards

**cartuchera** *nf* cartridge belt

**cartucho** *nm* **(a)** *(de arma, tinta)* cartridge; *Fig* **quemar el último c.** to play one's last card **(b)** *(envoltorio) (de monedas)* roll; *(cucurucho)* paper cone

**cartuja** *nf* charterhouse

**cartujo, -a 1** *adj* Carthusian

**2** *nm* **(a)** *(religioso)* Carthusian **(b)** *Fig (persona retraída)* hermit

**cartulina** *nf* card, thin cardboard; **una carpeta de c.** a cardboard folder

**casa** *nf* **(a)** *(edificio)* house; *(piso) Br* flat, *US* apartment; **c. adosada** semi-detached house; **c. de campo** country house; **c. solariega** ancestral home, family seat; **c. unifamiliar** = house (usually detached) on an estate; **una mentira como una c.** a whopping great lie; **se le cae la c. encima** *(se deprime)* it's the end of the world for him; **echar** *o* **tirar la c. por la ventana** to spare no expense; **empezar la c. por el tejado** to put the cart before the horse; **ser de andar por c.** *(sencillo)* to be simple *o* basic; *Prov* **en c. del herrero cuchillo de palo** the shoemaker's wife is always worst shod

**(b)** *(hogar)* home; **buscar c.** to look for somewhere to live; **en c.** at home; **ir a c.** to go home; **pásate por mi c.** come round to my place

**(c)** *(familia)* family; *(linaje)* house; *Hist* **la c. de Austria** the Hapsburgs; *Hist* **la c. de Borbón** the Bourbons

**(d)** *(establecimiento)* company; **c. de empeño** *o* **préstamo** pawnshop; **c. de citas** brothel; **c. de comidas** = cheap restaurant serving simple meals; **c. discográfica** record company; **c. de huéspedes** guesthouse; *Fig* **¡esto es una c. de locos!** this place is a madhouse!; *Com* **c. matriz** *(de empresa)* head office; *(de grupo de empresas)* parent company; **c. de socorro** first-aid post

**Casablanca** *n* Casablanca

**casaca** *nf* *(de chaqué)* frock coat; *(chaquetón)* jacket

**casación** *nf Der* annulment

**casadero, -a** *adj* marriageable

**casado, -a 1** *adj* married **(con** to**)**

**2** *nm,f* married man, *f* married woman; **los recién casados** the newly-weds

**casamentero, -a 1** *adj* matchmaking

**2** *nm,f* matchmaker

**casamiento** *nm* wedding, marriage

**casanova** *nm* Casanova

**casar 1** *vt* (**a**) *(en matrimonio)* to marry (**b**) *(unir)* to fit together

**2** *vi* to match

**3 casarse** *vpr* to get married (**con** to); **casarse por la iglesia/lo civil** to have a church/civil wedding; *Fig* **no se casa con nadie** he doesn't take sides

**cascabel** *nm* (small) bell; *Fig* **poner el c. al gato** to bell the cat, to dare to go ahead

**cascabeleo** *nm* tinkle, jingle

**cascada** *nf (de agua)* waterfall; **en c.** one after another

**cascado, -a** *adj* (**a**) *Fam (estropeado)* bust; *(persona, ropa)* worn-out (**b**) *(ronco)* rasping

**cascajo** *nm* rubble; *Fam Fig* **estar hecho un c.** to be a wreck

**cascanueces** *nm inv* nutcracker

**cascar** [61] **1** *vt* (**a**) *(romper)* to crack; **c. un huevo** to crack an egg (**b**) *Fam (dañar)* to damage, to harm; *Fig* **cascarla** to kick the bucket (**c**) *Fam (la voz)* to make croaky (**d**) *Fam (pegar)* to thump

**2** *vi Fam (hablar)* to witter on

**3 cascarse** *vpr* (**a**) *(romperse)* to crack (**b**) *Fam* **se le cascó la voz** his voice went croaky

**cáscara** *nf (de almendra, huevo)* shell; *(de limón, naranja)* peel

**cascarilla** *nf* husk

**cascarón** *nm* eggshell; *Fig* **salir del c.** *(independizarse)* to leave the nest; *(abrirse)* to come out of one's shell

**cascarrabias** *nmf inv* grouch, misery guts

**casco 1** *nm* (**a**) *(para la cabeza)* helmet; *(de motorista)* crash helmet; **cascos azules** U.N. peacekeeping troops, blue berets (**b**) *(de barco)* hull (**c**) *(de ciudad)* **c. antiguo** old (part of) town; **c. urbano** city centre (**d**) *(de caballo)* hoof (**e**) *(envase)* empty bottle (**f**) *(pedazo)* fragment, piece

**2** *nmpl* **cascos** (**a**) *Fam (auriculares)* headphones (**b**) *(expresiones)* **calentarse o romperse los cascos** to rack one's brains; **ser alegre o ligero de cascos** *(irresponsable)* to be irresponsible; *(mujer)* to be flighty

**cascote** *nm* piece of rubble

**caserío** *nm* (**a**) *(aldea)* hamlet (**b**) *(casa de campo)* country house

**casero, -a 1** *adj* (**a**) *(de casa) (comida)* homemade; *(trabajos)* domestic; *(celebración)* family (**b**) *(hogareño)* home-loving

**2** *nm,f* (**a**) *(propietario)* landlord, *f* landlady (**b**) *(encargado)* house agent

**caserón** *nm* large, rambling house

**caseta** *nf* (**a**) *(casa pequeña)* hut (**b**) *(en la playa)* bathing hut (**c**) *(de feria)* stall, booth (**d**) *(para perro)* kennel

**casete 1** *nf (cinta)* cassette

**2** *nm (magnetófono)* cassette *o* tape recorder

**casi** *adv* almost; **c. me muero** I almost *o* nearly died; **c. no dormí** I hardly slept at all; **c., c.** almost, just about; **c. nunca** hardly ever; **¿qué te pasa? – ¡c. nada! que me ha dejado mi mujer** what's up? – my wife only went and left me

**casilla** *nf* (**a**) *(taquilla)* box office (**b**) *(de caja, armario)* compartment; *(para cartas)* pigeonhole; *Andes, CSur* **c. de correos** PO Box (**c**) *(en un impreso)* box (**d**) *(de tablero de juego)* square (**e**) **sacar a alguien de sus casillas** to drive sb mad; **salir *o* salirse de sus casillas** to fly off the handle

**casillero** *nm* (**a**) *(mueble)* set of pigeonholes (**b**) *(casilla)* pigeonhole

**casino** *nm* (**a**) *(para jugar)* casino (**b**) *(asociación)* (social) club

**casís** *nm inv* (**a**) *(arbusto)* blackcurrant bush (**b**) *(fruto)* blackcurrant (**c**) *(licor)* cassis

**caso** *nm* case; **el c. es que** the thing is (that); **el c. Dreyfus** the Dreyfus affair; **en c. de** in the event of; **en c. de que** if; **(en) c. de que venga** should she come; **en cualquier *o* todo c.** in any event *o* case; **en el mejor/peor de los casos** at best/worst; **en tal *o* ese c.** in that case; **en último c.** as a last resort; **hacer c. a** to pay attention to; **hacer c. omiso de** to ignore; **ir al c.** to get to the point; **se lo dije, pero ella, ni c.** I told her but she didn't take any notice; **tú, ni c.** don't take any notice; **no me hace ni c.** she doesn't pay a blind bit of attention to me; **no hacer *o* venir al c.** to be irrelevant; **pongamos por c. que...** let's suppose (that)...; *Fam* **ser un c.** to be a case, to be a right one; **c. de conciencia** matter of conscience; **fue un c. de fuerza mayor** it was due to force of circumstances; **ser un c. perdido** to be a lost cause

**caspa** *nf* dandruff

**Caspio 1** *adj* **el mar C.** the Caspian Sea

**2** *nm* **el C.** the Caspian Sea

**cáspita** *interj Anticuado o Hum* **¡c.!** *(sorpresa)* my word!; *(enfado)* dash it!

**casposo, -a** *adj Fam Pey (asqueroso)* disgusting

**casque** *etc ver* **cascar**

**casquería** *nf (tienda)* = shop selling offal; *(productos)* offal; *Fam Fig* **en esa película sale demasiada c.** that film is too gory

**casquete** *nm* (**a**) *(gorro)* skullcap (**b**) **c. esférico** segment of a sphere; **c. polar** polar icecap (**c**) *muy Fam* **echar un c.** to have a screw *o* *Br* shag

**casquillo** *nm* (**a**) *(de bala)* case (**b**) *(de lámpara)* socket, lampholder

**casquivano, -a** *adj Fam (irresponsable)* irresponsible; *(mujer)* flighty

**cassette** [ka'sete, ka'set] **1** *nf (cinta)* cassette
**2** *nm (magnetófono)* cassette *o* tape recorder

**casta** *nf* (a) *(linaje)* stock, lineage; **de c. le viene al galgo** it runs in the family (b) *(especie, calidad)* breed (c) *(en la India)* caste

**castaña** *nf* (a) *(fruto)* chestnut; *Fam* **sacarle a alguien las castañas del fuego** to get sb out of trouble (b) *Fam (golpe)* bash (c) *Fam (borrachera)* **agarrarse una c.** to get legless (d) *Fam (cosa aburrida)* bore; **este libro es una c.** this book is boring

**castañazo** *nm Fam* bash; **darse un c.** *(golpe)* to bump oneself; *(con el coche)* to have a crash

**castañeta** *nf Taurom* = bullfighter's ornamental pigtail

**castañetear** *vi (dientes)* to chatter; **me castañetean las rodillas** my knees are knocking

**castañeteo** *nm (de castañuelas)* clacking; *(de dientes)* chattering

**castaño, -a 1** *adj (color)* chestnut
**2** *nm* (a) *(color)* chestnut; *Fig* **pasar de c. oscuro** to be beyond a joke (b) *(árbol)* chestnut (tree); **c. de Indias** horse chestnut (tree) (c) *(madera)* chestnut

**castañuela** *nf* castanet; *Fig* **estar como unas castañuelas** to be over the moon

**castellanizar** [16] *vt* to hispanicize

**castellano, -a 1** *adj & nm,f* Castilian
**2** *nm (lengua)* (Castilian) Spanish

**castellanohablante, castellanoparlante 1** *adj* Spanish-speaking
**2** *nmf* Spanish speaker

**castellano-leonés, -esa 1** *adj* of/from Castilla y León
**2** *nm,f* person from Castilla y León

**castellano-manchego, -a 1** *adj* of/from Castilla-La Mancha
**2** *nm,f* person from Castilla-La Mancha

**castellonense 1** *adj* of/from Castellón
**2** *nm,f* person from Castellón

**casticismo** *nm* purism

**castidad** *nf* chastity

**castigador, -ora** *adj Fam* **1** *adj* seductive
**2** *nm,f* ladykiller, *f* man-eater

**castigar** [40] *vt* (a) *(imponer castigo a)* to punish (b) *Dep* to penalize (c) *(piel, salud)* to damage; *(sujeto: sol, viento, epidemia)* to devastate; **una zona castigada por las inundaciones** a region severely hit by the floods (d) *Fig (enamorar)* to seduce

**castigo** *nm* (a) *(sanción)* punishment; **c. ejemplar** exemplary punishment (b) *(daño)* damage; **infligir un duro c. a** to inflict severe damage on (c) *Fam (persona)* **¡qué c. de niño/hombre!** what a pain that child/man is! (d)

*Dep* **máximo c.** penalty; **el árbitro señaló el máximo c.** the referee pointed to the spot

**Castilla** *n* Castile; **C. la Nueva/la Vieja** New/Old Castile

**Castilla-La Mancha** *n* Castile and La Mancha

**Castilla y León** *n* Castile and León

**castillo** *nm* (a) *(edificio)* castle; **castillos en el aire** *o* **de naipes** *Fig* castles in the air (b) *Náut* **c. de popa** quarterdeck; **c. de proa** forecastle

**casting** *nm Cine & Teatro* casting; **hacer un c.** to hold an audition

**castizo, -a** *adj (lenguaje, palabra)* = derived from popular usage and considered linguistically pure; *(barrio, taberna)* typical; **un andaluz c.** a typical Andalusian

**casto, -a** *adj* chaste

**castor** *nm* beaver

**castración** *nf* castration

**castrador, -ora** *adj Fig* **una madre castradora** a strong *o* dominant mother

**castrar** *vt* (a) *(animal, persona)* to castrate; *(gato)* to neuter (b) *Fig (debilitar)* to sap, to impair

**castrense** *adj* military

**castrismo** *nm* Castroism

**castrista** *adj & nmf* Castroist

**casual** *adj* accidental; **un encuentro c.** a chance encounter

**casualidad** *nf* coincidence; **la c. hizo que nos encontráramos** chance brought us together; **dio la c. de que...** it so happened that...; **por c.** by chance; **¡qué c.!** what a coincidence!

**casualmente** *adv* by chance

**casucha** *nf Pey* hovel, dump

**casuística** *nf Der* case law

**casuístico, -a** *adj Formal* casuistic

**casulla** *nf* chasuble

**cata** *nf* tasting

**catabolismo** *nm* catabolism

**cataclismo** *nm* cataclysm

**catacumbas** *nfpl* catacombs

**catador, -ora** *nm,f* taster

**catadura** *nf Fig* look, appearance

**catafalco** *nm* catafalque

**catalán, -ana 1** *adj & nm,f* Catalan, Catalonian
**2** *nm (lengua)* Catalan

**catalanismo** *nm* (a) *(palabra)* Catalanism (b) *Pol* Catalan nationalism

**catalanista** *adj & nmf* Catalan nationalist

**catalejo** *nm* telescope

**catalepsia** *nf* catalepsy

**cataléptico, -a** *adj Med* cataleptic; *Fam Fig* half asleep

**catalítico, -a** *adj Quím* catalytic

**catalizador, -ora 1** *adj* (a) *Quím* catalytic (b) *Fig* **el principio c. del cambio** *(impulsor)* the catalyst of change

**2** *nm* (a) *Quím & Fig* catalyst (b) *Aut* catalytic converter

**catalizar** [16] *vt Quím* to catalyse; *Fig (impulsar)* to provoke

**catalogación** *nf* cataloguing; **no admitir c.** *(ser extraordinario)* to be hard to categorize

**catalogar** [40] *vt* (a) *(en catálogo)* to catalogue (b) *(clasificar)* **c. a alguien (de)** to class sb (as)

**catálogo** *nm* catalogue

**Cataluña** *n* Catalonia

**catamarán** *nm* catamaran

**cataplasma** *nf* (a) *Med* poultice (b) *Fam Fig (pesado)* bore

**cataplines** *nmpl Fam (testículos)* nuts, *Br* goolies

**catapulta** *nf* catapult

**catapultar** *vt* to catapult

**catapún** *interj Fam* ¡c.! *(en lenguaje infantil)* crash!, bang!; **abrí la puerta y ¡c.! me encontré con Juanita** I opened the door and who should I see but Juanita; **en el año c.** ages ago; **es del año c.** it's ancient

**catar** *vt* to taste

**catarata** *nf* (a) *(de agua)* waterfall; **las cataratas del Iguazú** the Iguaçu Falls; **las cataratas del Niágara** the Niagara Falls (b) *Med* cataract

**catarro** *nm* cold

**catarsis** *nf inv (purificación)* catharsis

**catártico, -a** *adj* cathartic

**catastro** *nm* land registry

**catástrofe** *nf* catastrophe; *(accidente de avión, tren)* disaster

**catastrófico, -a** *adj* catastrophic

**catastrofismo** *nm* *(pesimismo)* scaremongering, alarmism

**catastrofista** *adj & nmf* alarmist

**catavino** *nm* wine tasting glass

**catavinos** *nmf inv* wine taster

**cate** *nm Fam* fail

**catear** *vt Fam* to fail; **he cateado** *o* **me han cateado la física** I failed physics

**catecismo** *nm* catechism

**cátedra** *nf* (a) *(cargo)* *(en universidad)* chair; *(en instituto)* post of head of department (b) *(departamento)* department (c) **sentar c.** to lay down the law

**catedral** *nf* cathedral; **una mentira como una c.** a whopping great lie

**catedralicio, -a** *adj* cathedral; **ciudad catedralicia** cathedral city

**catedrático, -a** *nm,f (de universidad)* professor; *(de instituto)* head of department

**categoría** *nf* (a) *(clase)* category (b) *(posición social)* standing; **de c.** important (c) *(calidad)* quality; **de (primera) c.** first-class

**categórico, -a** *adj* categorical

**catequesis** *nf inv* catechesis, ≃ Sunday school

**catequizar** [16] *vt* (a) *(enseñar religión)* to instruct in Christian doctrine (b) *Fig (adoctrinar)* to convert

**cátering** *nm* catering

**caterva** *nf* host, multitude

**catéter** *nm Med* catheter

**cateto, -a 1** *adj Pey* uncultured, uncouth

**2** *nm,f Pey* country bumpkin

**3** *nm Geom* cathetus

**catire, -a** *adj Andes, Cuba* blond(e)

**cátodo** *nm* cathode

**catolicismo** *nm* Catholicism

**católico, -a 1** *adj* Catholic; *Fam Fig* **no estar muy c.** to be under the weather

**2** *nm,f* Catholic

**catorce** *núm* fourteen; *ver también* **seis**

**catorceavo, -a, catorzavo, -a** *núm (fracción)* fourteenth; **la catorceava parte** a fourteenth

**catre** *nm (cama)* camp bed; *Fam* **irse al c.** to hit the sack

**caucásico, -a** *adj & nm,f* Caucasian

**Cáucaso** *nm* **el C.** the Caucasus

**cauce** *nm* (a) *Agr & Fig* channel (b) *(de río)* river-bed; **volver a su c.** to return to normal

**caucho** *nm* (a) *(sustancia)* rubber; **c. vulcanizado** vulcanized rubber (b) *(planta)* rubber tree

**caudal** *nm* (a) *(cantidad de agua)* flow, volume (b) *(capital, abundancia)* wealth

**caudaloso, -a** *adj* (a) *(río)* with a large flow (b) *(persona)* wealthy, rich

**caudillaje** *nm* leadership

**caudillo** *nm (en la guerra)* leader, head; *Hist* **el C.** = title used to refer to Franco

**causa** *nf* (a) *(origen, ideal)* cause; **dieron su vida por la c.** they gave their lives for the cause (b) *(razón)* reason; **a** *o* **por c. de** because of; **por c. mayor** for reasons beyond my/our *etc* control (c) *Der* case

**causal** *adj* causal

**causalidad** *nf* causality

**causante 1** *adj* **la razón c.** the cause

**2** *nm* cause; **el c. del accidente** the person responsible for the accident

**causar** *vt (originar)* to cause; *(impresión)* to make; *(placer)* to give

**causticidad** *nf también Fig* causticity

**cáustico, -a** *adj también Fig* caustic

**cautela** *nf* caution, cautiousness; **con c.** cautiously

**cautelar** *adj* precautionary, preventive

**cauteloso, -a 1** *adj* cautious, careful
**2** *nm,f* cautious person

**cauterizar** [16] *vt* to cauterize

**cautivador, -ora 1** *adj* captivating, enchanting
**2** *nm,f* charmer

**cautivar** *vt* (a) *(apresar)* to capture (b) *(seducir)* to captivate, to enchant

**cautiverio** *nm* captivity

**cautividad** *nf* captivity; **vivir en c.** to live in captivity

**cautivo, -a** *adj & nm,f* captive

**cauto, -a** *adj* cautious, careful

**cava 1** *nm (bebida)* = Spanish champagne-type wine
**2** *nf (bodega)* wine cellar

**cavar 1** *vt (hoyo)* to dig; *(con azada)* to hoe; *Fig* **está cavando su propia tumba** she is digging her own grave
**2** *vi (hacer hoyo)* to dig; *(con azada)* to hoe

**caverna** *nf (cueva)* cave; *(más grande)* cavern

**cavernícola** *nmf* caveman, *f* cavewoman

**cavernoso, -a** *adj (voz, tos)* hollow

**caviar** *nm* caviar

**cavidad** *nf* cavity; **la c. bucal** the buccal *o* oral cavity

**cavilación** *nf* deep thought, pondering

**cavilar** *vi* to think deeply, to ponder

**caviloso, -a** *adj* thoughtful, pensive

**cayado** *nm* (a) *(de pastor)* crook (b) *(de obispo)* crozier

**cayena** *nf (especia)* Cayenne pepper

**cayera** *etc ver* **caer**

**caza 1** *nf* (a) *(acción de cazar)* hunting; **ir de c.** to go hunting; *Fig* **dar c. a** to hunt down; *Fig* **c. de brujas** witch-hunt (b) *(animales, carne)* game; **c. mayor** big game; **c. menor** small game
**2** *nm (avión)* fighter (plane)

**cazabombardero** *nm* fighter-bomber

**cazador, -ora 1** *adj* hunting
**2** *nm,f (persona)* hunter; **c. furtivo** poacher

**cazadora** *nf (prenda)* bomber jacket

**cazadotes** *nm inv* fortune hunter

**cazalla** *nf (bebida)* = aniseed-flavoured spirit

**cazar** [16] *vt* (a) *(animales)* to hunt (b) *Fam (pillar, atrapar)* to catch; *(en matrimonio)* to trap; *Fig* **cazarlas al vuelo** to be quick on the uptake

**cazo** *nm* (a) *(cacerola)* saucepan; *(cucharón)* ladle (b) *Fam (persona fea)* ugly mug

**cazoleta** *nf* (a) *(recipiente)* pot (b) *(de pipa)* bowl

**cazuela** *nf* (a) *(recipiente)* pot, saucepan; *(de barro)* earthenware cooking pot (b) *(guiso)* casserole, stew; **a la c.** casseroled

**cazurro, -a 1** *adj (bruto)* stupid
**2** *nm,f (bruto)* idiot, fool

**CC** *nm* (a) *(abrev de* **código civil***)* civil code (b) *(abrev de* **código de circulación***)* highway code (c) *(abrev de* **cuerpo consular***)* consular staff

**cc** *(abrev de* **centímetros cúbicos***)* cc

**c/c** *(abrev de* **cuenta corriente***)* a/c

**CC OO** *nfpl (abrev de* **Comisiones Obreras***)* = Spanish left-wing trade union

**CD** *nm* (a) *(abrev de* **club deportivo***)* sports club; *(en fútbol)* FC (b) *(abrev de* **cuerpo diplomático***)* CD (c) *(abrev de* **compact disc***)* CD

**CD-ROM** ['θeðe'rrom] *nm* CD-ROM

**CE 1** *nm (abrev de* **Consejo de Europa***)* CE
**2** *nf (abrev de* **Comunidad Europea***)* EC

**ce** *nf Fig* **ce por be** in great detail

**cebada** *nf* barley

**cebador** *nm* (a) *(de fluorescente)* ballast (b) *(de pólvora)* primer

**cebar 1** *vt* (a) *(engordar)* to fatten (up) (b) *(fuego, caldera)* to stoke, to fuel; *(máquina, arma)* to prime (c) *(anzuelo)* to bait
**2 cebarse** *vpr Fig* **cebarse en** *(ensañarse)* to be merciless with

**cebo** *nm también Fig* bait

**cebolla** *nf (planta)* onion; *Fam (cabeza)* nut, head

**cebolleta** *nf* (a) *(planta)* spring onion (b) *(en vinagre)* small pickled onion

**cebollino** *nm* (a) *(planta)* chive; *(cebolleta)* spring onion (b) *Fam (necio)* idiot

**cebón, -ona 1** *adj* fattened
**2** *nm* pig

**cebra** *nf* zebra; **paso de c.** zebra crossing

**cebú** *(pl* **cebúes***) nm* zebu

**CECA** ['θeka] *nf (abrev de* **Comunidad Europea del Carbón y del Acero***)* ECSC

**ceca** *nf* mint; *Fam* **ir de la C. a la Meca** to go here, there and everywhere

**cecear** *vi* to lisp

**ceceo** *nm* lisp

**cecina** *nf* dried, salted meat

**cedazo** *nm* sieve

**ceder 1** *vt* (a) *(traspasar, transferir)* to hand over (b) *(conceder)* to give up
**2** *vi* (a) *(venirse abajo)* to give way; **la puerta finalmente cedió** the door finally gave way (b) *(destensarse)* to give, to become loose; **ha cedido el jersey** the jersey has gone baggy

**(c)** *(disminuir)* to abate **(d)** *(rendirse)* to give up; **c. a** to give in to; **c. en** to give up on

**cedilla** *nf* cedilla

**cedro** *nm* cedar

**cédula** *nf* document; **c. de citación** summons *(singular)*; **c. de habitabilidad** = certificate stating that a place is habitable; **c. hipotecaria** mortgage bond; *Am* **c. (de identidad)** identity card; **c. de vecindad** identity card

**CEE** *nf Antes (abrev de* **Comunidad Económica Europea***)* EEC

**cefalea** *nf Med* headache

**cefalópodo** *nm Zool* cephalopod

**cegador, -ora** *adj* blinding

**cegar** [45] **1** *vt* **(a)** *también Fig* to blind **(b)** *(tapar) (ventana)* to block off; *(tubo)* to block up

**2** *vi* to be blinding

**3 cegarse** *vpr también Fig* to be blinded

**cegato, -a** *Fam* **1** *adj* short-sighted

**2** *nm,f* short-sighted person

**cegesimal** *adj* = of or relating to cgs units

**cegué** *etc ver* **cegar**

**ceguera** *nf también Fig* blindness

**CEI** *nf (abrev de* **Confederación de Estados Independientes***)* CIS

**Ceilán** *n Antes* Ceylon

**ceja** *nf* **(a)** *(en la cara)* eyebrow; *Fam Fig* quemarse las cejas to burn the midnight oil; *Fam* se le metió entre c. y c. que... he got it into his head that...; *Fam* tener a alguien entre c. y c. not to be able to stand the sight of sb **(b)** *(de instrumento de cuerda) (puente)* bridge; *(cejilla)* capo

**cejar** *vi* **c. en** to give up on; **no cejaremos en nuestro empeño (de...)** we will not flag in our efforts (to...)

**cejijunto, -a** *adj* **(a)** *(persona)* bushy-eyebrowed **(b)** *(gesto)* frowning

**cejilla** *nf (de guitarra)* capo

**celada** *nf* **(a)** *(pieza de armadura)* helmet **(b)** *(emboscada)* ambush; *Fig* trick, trap

**celador, -ora** *nm,f (de colegio, hospital)* watchman, *f* watchwoman; *(de prisión)* warder; *(de museo)* attendant

**celda** *nf también Informát* cell; **c. de castigo** solitary confinement cell

**celdilla** *nf (de panal)* cell

**celebérrimo, -a** *adj* extremely famous

**celebración** *nf* **(a)** *(festejo)* celebration **(b)** *(de ceremonia, reunión)* holding

**celebrar** **1** *vt* **(a)** *(festejar)* to celebrate **(b)** *(llevar a cabo)* to hold; *(oficio religioso)* to celebrate **(c)** *(alegrarse de)* to be delighted with **(d)** *(alabar)* to praise, to applaud

**2 celebrarse** *vpr* **(a)** *(festejarse)* to be

celebrated; **esa fiesta se celebra el 25 de Julio** that holiday falls on 25 July **(b)** *(llevarse a cabo)* to take place, to be held

**célebre** *adj* famous, celebrated

**celebridad** *nf* **(a)** *(fama)* fame **(b)** *(persona famosa)* celebrity

**celeridad** *nf* speed; **con c.** rapidly

**celeste** *adj (del cielo)* celestial, heavenly; **(azul) c.** sky blue

**celestial** *adj* celestial, heavenly

**celestina** *nf* lovers' go-between

**celibato** *nm* celibacy

**célibe** *adj & nmf* celibate

**celo** *nm* **(a)** *(esmero)* zeal, keenness **(b)** *(devoción)* devotion **(c)** *(de animal)* heat; **en c.** *Br* on heat, *US* in heat **(d)** *(cinta adhesiva)* Sellotape® **(e)** *(celos)* jealousy; **dar celos a alguien** to make sb jealous; **tener celos de alguien** to be jealous of sb

**celofán** *nm* cellophane

**celosía** *nf* lattice window, jalousie

**celoso, -a 1** *adj* **(a)** *(con celos)* jealous **(b)** *(cumplidor)* keen, eager

**2** *nm,f (con celos)* jealous person

**celta 1** *adj* Celtic

**2** *nmf (persona)* Celt

**3** *nm (lengua)* Celtic

**celtíbero, -a, celtibero, -a** *adj & nm,f* Celtiberian

**céltico, -a** *adj* Celtic

**célula** *nf* cell; **c. fotoeléctrica** photoelectric cell, electric eye; **c. fotovoltaica** photovoltaic cell

**celular** *adj Biol* cellular

**celulitis** *nf inv* cellulite

**celuloide** *nm* **(a)** *Quím* celluloid **(b)** *(película)* film

**celulosa** *nf* cellulose

**cementerio** *nm (de muertos)* cemetery; **c. de automóviles** *o* **coches** scrapyard; **c. nuclear** *o* **radiactivo** nuclear dumping ground

**cemento** *nm (material)* cement; *(hormigón)* concrete; **c. armado** reinforced concrete

**cena** *nf* dinner, evening meal; **dar una c.** to give a dinner party; **c. de despedida** farewell dinner; *Rel* **la última c.** the Last Supper

**cenáculo** *nm Formal Fig (grupo)* circle

**cenador** *nm* arbour, bower

**cenagal** *nm* bog, marsh

**cenagoso, -a** *adj* muddy

**cenar 1** *vt* to have for dinner

**2** *vi* to have dinner; **c. fuera** to eat out, to go out for dinner

**cencerro** *nm* cowbell; *Fam* **estar como un c.** to be as mad as a hatter

**cenefa** *nf (en vestido)* border; *(en pared)* frieze

**cenetista 1** *adj* = relating to the CNT
**2** *nmf* member of the CNT

**cenicero** *nm* ashtray

**ceniciento, -a 1** *adj* ashen, ash-grey
**2** *nf* **(la) Cenicienta** Cinderella

**cenit** *nm también* Fig zenith

**cenital** *adj* **luz c.** light from above

**ceniza** *nf* ash; **cenizas** *(de cadáver)* ashes

**cenizo, -a 1** *adj* ashen, ash-grey
**2** *nm,f* Fam *(gafe)* jinxed person; **ser un c.** to be jinxed

**censar** *vt* to take a census of

**censo** *nm* (a) *(padrón)* census; **c. electoral** electoral roll (b) *(tributo)* tax (c) *Der* lease

**censor, -ora** *nm,f* (a) *(funcionario)* censor (b) *(crítico)* critic (c) *Econ* **c. (jurado) de cuentas** auditor

**censura** *nf* (a) *(prohibición)* censorship (b) *(organismo)* censors (c) *(reprobación)* censure, severe criticism (d) *Econ* **c. de cuentas** inspection of accounts, audit

**censurable** *adj* censurable

**censurar** *vt* (a) *(prohibir)* to censor (b) *(reprobar)* to criticize severely, to censure

**centauro** *nm* centaur

**centavo, -a 1** *núm* hundredth; **la centava parte** a hundredth
**2** *nm* *(moneda)* *(en países anglosajones)* cent; *(en países latinoamericanos)* centavo; **sin un c.** penniless

**centella** *nf* (a) *(rayo)* flash (b) *(chispa)* spark (c) Fig *(cosa, persona)* **es una c.** he's like lightning; **rápido como una c.** quick as a flash

**centellear** *vi* *(luz)* to sparkle; *(estrella)* to twinkle

**centelleo** *nm* *(de joya)* sparkle; **el c. de las estrellas/luces** the twinkle o twinkling of the stars/lights

**centena** *nf* hundred; **una c. de coches** a hundred cars

**centenar** *nm* hundred; **un c. de** a hundred; **a centenares** by the hundred

**centenario, -a 1** *adj* *(persona)* in his/her hundreds; *(institución, edificio)* century-old
**2** *nm* centenary; **quinto c.** five hundredth anniversary

**centeno** *nm* rye

**centésimo, -a** *núm* hundredth

**centígrado, -a** *adj* Centigrade; **veinte grados centígrados** twenty degrees Centigrade

**centigramo** *nm* centigram

**centilitro** *nm* centilitre

**centímetro** *nm* (a) *(medida)* centimetre (b) *(cinta)* measuring tape

**céntimo** *nm* *(moneda)* cent; Fig **estar sin un c.** to be flat broke

**centinela** *nm* sentry

**centollo** *nm* spider crab

**centrado, -a** *adj* (a) *(basado)* **c. en** based on (b) *(equilibrado)* stable, steady (c) *(rueda, cuadro)* centred

**central 1** *adj* central
**2** *nf* (a) *(oficina)* headquarters, head office; *(de correos, comunicaciones)* main office; **c. telefónica** telephone exchange (b) *(de energía)* power station; **c. eólica** wind farm; **c. hidroeléctrica** o **hidráulica** hydroelectric power station; **c. nuclear** nuclear power station; **c. térmica** thermal power station
**3** *nm* Dep central defender

**centralismo** *nm* Pol centralism

**centralista** *adj & nmf* Pol centralist

**centralita** *nf* switchboard

**centralización** *nf* centralization

**centralizar** [16] *vt* to centralize

**centrar 1** *vt* (a) *también* Dep to centre (b) *(persona)* to steady, to make stable (c) *(atraer)* to be the centre of; **centraba todas las miradas** all eyes were on her
**2 centrarse** *vpr* (a) *(concentrarse)* **centrarse en** to concentrate o focus on (b) *(equilibrarse)* to find one's feet

**céntrico, -a** *adj* central

**centrifugadora** *nf* (a) *(máquina)* centrifuge (b) *(para secar ropa)* spin-dryer

**centrifugar** [40] *vt* (a) Tec to centrifuge (b) *(ropa)* to spin-dry

**centrífugo, -a** *adj* centrifugal

**centrípeto, -a** *adj* centripetal

**centrismo** *nm* Pol centrism

**centrista 1** *adj* Pol centre, centrist; **un partido c.** a party of the centre
**2** *nmf* centrist; **los centristas propusieron una reforma** the centre proposed a reform

**centro** *nm también* Fig centre; *(de ciudad)* town centre; Pol **ser de c.** to be at the centre of the political spectrum; **me voy al c.** I'm going to town; **c. de atracción** centre of attraction; **c. de cálculo** computer centre; **c. comercial** shopping centre o US plaza; **c. de desintoxicación** detoxification centre o clinic; **c. docente** o **de enseñanza** educational institution; **c. de gravedad** centre of gravity; **c. de mesa** centrepiece; **c. nervioso/óptico** nerve/optic centre; **c. de planificación familiar** family planning clinic; **c. social** community centre

**centroafricano, -a** *adj & nm,f* central African

**Centroamérica** *n* Central America

**centroamericano, -a** *adj & nm,f* Central American

**centrocampista** *nmf* Dep midfielder

**centuplicar** [61] *vt* to increase a hundred-fold

**centuria** *nf (siglo, en el ejército romano)* century

**centurión** *nm Hist* centurion

**cenutrio, -a** *nm,f Fam (estúpido)* idiot, fool

**ceñido, -a** *adj* tight

**ceñidor** *nm* belt

**ceñir** [49] **1** *vt* (a) *(apretar)* to be tight on (b) *(abrazar)* to embrace (c) *Fig (amoldar)* **c. a** to keep o restrict to

**2 ceñirse** *vpr* (a) *(apretarse)* to tighten (b) *(limitarse)* **ceñirse a** to keep o stick to

**ceño** *nm* frown, scowl; **fruncir el c.** to frown, to knit one's brow

**ceñudo, -a** *adj* frowning, scowling

**CEOE** *nf (abrev de* **Confederación Española de Organizaciones Empresariales)** *Br* ≃ CBI, = Spanish employers' organization

**cepa** *nf* (a) *(vid)* vine (b) *(de vino)* variety (c) *Fig (linaje)* stock; **de pura c.** *(auténtico)* real, genuine; *(de pura sangre)* thoroughbred

**CEPAL** [θe'pal] *nf (abrev de* **Comisión Económica para América Latina)** ECL

**cepillar 1** *vt* (a) *(ropa, pelo)* to brush (b) *(madera)* to plane (c) *Fam (robar)* to pinch; **c. algo a alguien** to pinch sth off sb (d) *Fam (adular)* to butter up, to flatter

**2 cepillarse** *vpr* (a) *(pelo, ropa)* to brush; **cepillarse el pelo** to brush one's hair (b) *Fam (comida, trabajo)* to polish off (c) *(suspender)* to fail; **se lo cepillaron** they failed him (d) *muy Fam* **cepillarse a alguien** *(copular)* to screw sb; *(matar)* to bump sb off

**cepillo** *nm* (a) *(para limpiar)* brush; **c. de dientes** toothbrush; **c. del pelo** hairbrush; **c. de uñas** nailbrush (b) *(de carpintero)* plane (c) *(de donativos)* collection box, poor box

**cepo** *nm* (a) *(para cazar)* trap (b) *(para vehículos)* wheel clamp (c) *(para sujetar)* clamp (d) *(para presos)* stocks

**ceporro** *nm Fam* idiot, blockhead

**CEPYME** [θe'pime] *nf (abrev de* **Confederación Española de la Pequeña y Mediana Empresa)** = Spanish confederation of SMEs

**cera** *nf* wax; **c. de abeja** beeswax; **c. depilatoria** hair-removing wax

**cerámica** *nf* (a) *(arte)* ceramics *(singular)*, pottery (b) *(objeto)* piece of pottery

**ceramista** *nmf* potter

**cerbatana** *nf* blowpipe

**cerca 1** *nf (valla)* fence; *(muro)* wall

**2** *adv* close, near; **por aquí c.** nearby; **c. de** *(en el espacio)* near, close to; *(aproximadamente)* nearly, about; **de c.** *(examinar, mirar)* closely; *(afectar)* deeply; *(vivir)* first-hand; **ver algo/a alguien de cerca** to see sth/sb close up

**cercado** *nm* (a) *(valla)* fence (b) *(lugar)* enclosure

**cercanía** *nf* *(cualidad)* nearness, closeness; **cercanías** *(lugar)* outskirts, suburbs; **en las cercanías de** on the outskirts of; **tren de cercanías** local train

**cercano, -a** *adj* (a) *(pueblo, lugar)* nearby (b) *(tiempo)* near (c) *(pariente, fuente de información)* close (a to)

**cercar** [61] *vt* (a) *(vallar)* to fence (off) (b) *(rodear, acorralar)* to surround

**cercenar** *vt* (a) *(extremidad)* to amputate (b) *Fig (restringir)* to cut back, to curtail

**cerciorarse** *vpr* to make sure (de of)

**cerco** *nm* (a) *(marca)* circle, ring; **el vaso ha dejado un c. en la mesa** the glass has left a ring on the table (b) *(de astro)* halo (c) *(asedio)* siege; **poner c. a** to lay siege to

**cerda** *nf (pelo) (de cerdo, jabalí)* bristle; *(de caballo)* horsehair

**cerdada** *nf Fam* dirty trick

**Cerdeña** *n* Sardinia

**cerdo, -a 1** *nm,f* (a) *(animal)* pig, *f* sow (b) *Fam Fig (persona)* pig, swine

**2** *nm (carne)* pork

**cereal** *nm* cereal; **cereales** *(breakfast)* cereal

**cerealista** *adj (región)* cereal-growing

**cerebelo** *nm Anat* cerebellum

**cerebral** *adj Anat & Fig* cerebral; **lesión c.** cerebral lesion

**cerebro** *nm* (a) *(órgano)* brain; **c. electrónico** electronic brain (b) *Fig (cabecilla)* brains *(singular)*; *Fig (inteligencia)* brains

**ceremonia** *nf* ceremony

**ceremonial** *adj & nm* ceremonial

**ceremonioso, -a** *adj* ceremonious

**cereza** *nf* cherry

**cerezo** *nm* (a) *(árbol)* cherry tree (b) *(madera)* cherry (wood)

**cerilla** *nf* match

**cerillo** *nm Méx* match

**cerner** [66], **cernir** [27] **1** *vt* to sieve, to sift

**2 cernerse** *vpr (ave, avión)* to hover; *Fig (amenaza, peligro)* to loom

**cernícalo** *nm* (a) *(ave)* kestrel (b) *Fam (bruto)* brute

**cero 1** *adj inv* zero

**2** *núm* zero; *ver también* **seis**

**3** *nm* (a) *(signo)* nought, zero (b) *(cantidad)* nothing; *(en fútbol)* nil; *(en tenis)* love (c) *(temperatura)* zero; **sobre/bajo c.** above/below zero; **c. absoluto** absolute zero (d) *(expresiones)* **cortarse el pelo al c.** to shave one's head, to cut all one's hair off; **partir de c.** to start from scratch; *Fig* **ser un c. a la izquierda** *(un inútil)* to be useless; *(un don nadie)* to be a nobody

**cerque** *etc ver* **cercar**

**cerquillo** *nm Am* fringe

**cerquita** *adv* very near

**cerrado, -a** *adj* **(a)** *(al exterior)* closed, shut; *(con llave, pestillo)* locked **(b)** *(tiempo, cielo)* overcast; *(noche)* dark **(c)** *(mentalidad, sociedad)* closed **(a** to) **(d)** *(rodeado)* surrounded; *(por montañas)* walled in **(e)** *(circuito)* closed **(f)** *(curva)* sharp, tight **(g)** *(vocal)* close **(h)** *(acento)* broad, thick

**cerradura** *nf* lock

**cerrajería** *nf* **(a)** *(oficio)* locksmithery **(b)** *(local)* locksmith's (shop)

**cerrajero, -a** *nm,f* locksmith

**cerrar 1** *vt* **(a)** *(en general)* to close; *(puerta, cajón, boca, tienda)* to shut, to close; *(puños)* to clench; *(con llave)* to lock; *(botella, tarro)* to put the lid *o* top on

 **(b)** *(empresa, fábrica)* to close down

 **(c)** *(grifo, llave de gas)* to turn off

 **(d)** *(carretera, calle)* to block; **la policía cerró la calle** the police closed off the street; **c. el paso a alguien** to block sb's way

 **(e)** *(agujero, hueco)* to fill, to block (up)

 **(f)** *(cercar)* to fence (off), to enclose

 **(g)** *(cicatrizar)* to heal, to close up

 **(h)** *(terminar)* to close; **c. la marcha** *(ir en última posición)* to bring up the rear

 **2** *vi* **(a)** *(en general)* to close; *(tienda)* to close, to shut; *(con llave, pestillo)* to lock up

 **(b)** *(definitivamente)* to close down

 **3 cerrarse** *vpr* **(a)** *(al exterior)* to close, to shut

 **(b)** *(incomunicarse)* to clam up; **cerrarse a** to close one's mind to

 **(c)** *(herida)* to heal, to close up

 **(d)** *(acto, debate, discusión)* to (come to a) close

**cerrazón** *nf Fig (obstinación)* stubbornness, obstinacy

**cerril** *adj* **(a)** *(animal)* wild **(b)** *(obstinado)* stubborn, obstinate; *(tosco, grosero)* coarse

**cerro** *nm* hill; *Fam Fig* **irse por los cerros de Úbeda** to go off at a tangent, to stray from the point

**cerrojazo** *nm* **dar c. a** *(puerta)* to bolt shut; *Fig (conversación, reunión)* to bring to a halt

**cerrojo** *nm* bolt; **echar el c.** to bolt the door

**certamen** *nm* competition, contest

**certero, -a** *adj* **(a)** *(tiro)* accurate **(b)** *(opinión, respuesta)* correct

**certeza** *nf* certainty; **tener la c. de que** to be certain (that)

**certidumbre** *nf* certainty

**certificación** *nf* **(a)** *(hecho)* certification **(b)** *(documento)* certificate

**certificado, -a 1** *adj (documento)* certified; *(carta, paquete)* registered

 **2** *nm* certificate; **c. de calidad** quality guarantee; *Fin* **c. de depósito** certificate of deposit; **c. médico** medical certificate; *Com* **c. de origen** certificate of origin

**certificar** [61] *vt* **(a)** *(constatar)* to certify **(b)** *(en correos)* to register **(c)** *Fig (sospechas, inocencia)* to confirm

**cerumen** *nm* earwax

**cerval** *adj* **miedo c.** terror

**cervantino, -a** *adj* Cervantine

**cervatillo** *nm* (small) fawn

**cervato** *nm* fawn

**cervecera** *nf* brewery

**cervecería** *nf* **(a)** *(fábrica)* brewery **(b)** *(bar)* bar

**cervecero, -a 1** *adj* brewing; **fábrica cervecera** brewery; **industria cervecera** brewing industry

 **2** *nm,f (que hace cerveza)* brewer

**cerveza** *nf* beer; **c. de barril** draught beer; **c. negra** stout; **c. sin alcohol** alcohol-free beer, non-alcoholic beer

**cervical 1** *adj* **(a)** *(del útero)* cervical **(b)** *(del cuello)* neck; **lesión c.** neck injury; **vértebra c.** cervical vertebra

 **2** *nfpl* **cervicales** neck vertebrae

**cerviz** *nf Anat* nape, back of the neck; *Fig* **bajar** *o* **doblar la c.** *(humillarse)* to bow down, to submit

**cesante 1** *adj* **(a)** *(destituido)* dismissed, sacked **(b)** *Am (parado)* unemployed

 **2** *nmf* dismissed civil servant *(after change of government)*

**cesantear** *vt Chile, CSur* to make redundant

**cesantía** *nf* **(a)** *(destitución)* sacking **(b)** *Chile, CSur (desempleo)* unemployment

**cesar 1** *vt (destituir)* to sack; *(alto cargo)* to remove from office

 **2** *vi (parar)* to stop *o* cease **(de hacer algo** doing sth); **sin c.** non-stop, incessantly

**césar** *nm Hist* Caesar

**cesárea** *nf Med* caesarean (section)

**cese** *nm* **(a)** *(detención, paro)* stopping, ceasing **(b)** *(destitución)* sacking; *(de alto cargo)* removal from office

**Cesid** *nm (abrev de* **Centro Superior de Investigación de la Defensa)** = Spanish military intelligence and espionage service

**cesio** *nm* caesium

**cesión** *nf* cession, transfer; *Der* **c. de bienes** surrender of property

**césped** *nm* **(a)** *(hierba)* lawn, grass; **cortar el c.** to mow the lawn, to cut the grass; **prohibi-**

**do pisar el c.** *(en letrero)* keep off the grass **(b)** *Dep* field, pitch

**cesta** *nf* **(a)** *(canasta)* basket; *Fig* **c. de la compra** cost of living **(b)** *Dep* **c. punta** jai alai, = type of pelota

**cestería** *nf* **(a)** *(oficio)* basket-making **(b)** *(tienda)* basket shop

**cestero, -a** *nm,f* basket weaver

**cesto** *nm* **(a)** *(cesta)* (large) basket **(b)** *Dep (canasta)* basket

**cesura** *nf* caesura

**cetáceo** *nm Zool* cetacean

**cetme** *nm* = light automatic rifle used by Spanish army

**cetrería** *nf* falconry

**cetrino, -a** *adj Formal* sallow

**cetro** *nm* **(a)** *(vara)* sceptre; *Fig (reinado)* reign **(b)** *Fig (superioridad)* **ostentar el c. de** to hold the crown of

**Ceuta** *n* Ceuta

**ceutí** *(pl* **ceutíes)** **1** *adj* of/from Ceuta
**2** *nmf* person from Ceuta

**ceviche** *nm Am* = raw fish salad

**cf., cfr.** *(abrev de* **confróntese)** cf

**cg** *(abrev de* **centigramo)** cg

**CGPJ** *nm (abrev de* **Consejo General del Poder Judicial)** = governing body of the Spanish judiciary, elected by the Spanish parliament

**Ch, ch** *nf* [tʃe] Ch, ch

**ch/** *(abrev de* **cheque)** cheque

**chabacanada** *nf* vulgar thing; **ser una c.** to be vulgar

**chabacanería** *nf* **(a)** *(acción, comentario)* **lo que hizo/dijo fue una c.** what he did/said was vulgar **(b)** *(cualidad)* vulgarity

**chabacano, -a 1** *adj* vulgar
**2** *nm Méx* apricot

**chabola** *nf* shack; **barrios de chabolas** shanty town

**chabolismo** *nm* **erradicar el c.** to deal with the shanty-town problem; **el crecimiento del c.** the growing number of people living in shanty towns

**chabolista** *nmf* shanty town dweller

**chacal** *nm* jackal

**chacarero, -a** *nm,f Andes, CSur* farmer

**chacha** *nf Fam* maid

**chachachá** *nm* cha-cha

**cháchara** *nf Fam* chatter, nattering; **estar de c.** to have a natter

**chachi** *adj inv Fam* cool, neat

**chacina** *nf* cured o prepared pork

**chacinería** *nf (tienda)* pork butcher's

**chacinero, -a** *nm,f* pork butcher

**chacolí** *(pl* **chacolís)** *nm* = light wine from the Basque Country

**chacota** *nf* **tomar algo a c.** to take sth as a joke

**chacra** *nf Am (terreno)* piece of land, plot; *Andes, CSur* farm

**Chad** *nm* **el C.** Chad

**chador** *nm* chador

**chafar 1** *vt* **(a)** *(aplastar)* to flatten **(b)** *(arrugar)* to crease **(c)** *Fam Fig (estropear)* to spoil, to ruin; **el robo nos chafó las vacaciones** the robbery ruined our holiday
**2 chafarse** *vpr Fam Fig (estropearse)* to be ruined

**chaflán** *nm* **(a)** *(de edificio)* corner **(b)** *Geom* bevel

**chal** *nm* shawl

**chalado, -a** *Fam* **1** *adj* crazy, mad; *Fig* **estar c. por algo/alguien** to be crazy about sth/sb
**2** *nm,f* loony

**chaladura** *nf Fam* **(a)** *(locura)* craziness, madness **(b)** *(enamoramiento)* crazy infatuation

**chalán, -ana** *nm,f (comerciante)* horse-dealer; *Fig* shark, wheeler-dealer

**chalana** *nf Náut* barge

**chalaneo** *nm (comercio)* horse-dealing; *Fig* horse-trading

**chalar** *Fam* **1** *vt* to drive round the bend
**2 chalarse** *vpr* **chalarse por** to be crazy about

**chalé** *(pl* **chalés)**, **chalet** *(pl* **chalets)** *nm* *(casa)* detached house (with garden); *(en el campo)* cottage; *(de alta montaña)* chalet; **c. adosado** semi-detached house

**chaleco** *nm* waistcoat, *US* vest; *(de punto)* tank top; **c. antibalas** bullet-proof vest; **c. salvavidas** life-jacket

**chalupa** *nf Náut* small boat

**chamaco, -a** *nm,f Méx Fam (niño)* nipper, lad; *(niña)* nipper, lass

**chamán** *nm* shaman

**chamanismo** *nm* shamanism

**chamarileo** *nm* dealing in second-hand goods

**chamarilero, -a** *nm,f* rag-and-bone-man

**chamarra** *nf* jacket

**chambelán** *nm* chamberlain

**chambergo** *nm (chaquetón)* short coat

**chamizo** *nm (choza)* thatched hut; *Fam Pey (lugar)* hovel, dive

**champa** *nf CAm* **(a)** *(tienda de campaña)* tent **(b)** *(cobertizo)* shed

**champán, champaña** *nm* champagne

**champiñón** *nm* mushroom

**champú** *(pl* **champús** o **champúes)** *nm* shampoo

**chamuscado, -a** *adj (pelo, plumas)* singed; *(tela, papel)* scorched; *(tostada)* burnt

**chamuscar [61] 1** *vt (pelo, plumas)* to singe; *(tela, papel)* to scorch; *(tostada)* to burn

**2 chamuscarse** *vpr (pelo, plumas)* to get singed; *(tela, papel)* to get scorched; *(tostada)* to burn, to get burnt

**chamusquina** *nf Fam Fig* **me huele a c.** it smells a bit fishy to me, I don't like the look of this

**chance** *nf Am* opportunity; **¿me das chance?** can I have a go?

**chanchada** *nf Am* dirty trick

**chancho** *nm Am* pig

**chanchullero, -a** *Fam* **1** *adj* crooked, dodgy
**2** *nm,f* trickster, crook

**chanchullo** *nm Fam* fiddle, racket

**chancla, chancleta** *nf (sandalia)* backless sandal; *(para la playa)* flip-flop, *US* thong

**chanclo** *nm* (a) *(de madera)* clog (b) *(de plástico)* galosh

**chándal** *( pl* **chandals)** *nm* tracksuit

**changarro** *nm Méx* small shop

**chango** *nm Méx* monkey

**changurro** *nm* = typical Basque dish of dressed crab

**chanquete** *nm* = small translucent fish eaten like whitebait

**chantaje** *nm* blackmail; **hacer c. a alguien** to blackmail sb; **c. emocional** emotional blackmail

**chantajear** *vt* to blackmail

**chantajista** *nmf* blackmailer

**chantillí** *nm* whipped cream

**chanza** *nf* joke

**chao** *interj Fam* **¡c.!** bye!, see you!

**chapa** *nf* (a) *(lámina) (de metal)* sheet, plate; *(de madera)* board; *Aut* bodywork; **taller de c. y pintura** body shop (b) *(de botella)* top, cap; **juego de las chapas** = children's game played with bottle tops (c) *(insignia)* badge (d) *Am (cerradura)* lock

**chapado, -a** *adj* (a) *(recubierto) (con metal)* plated; *(con madera)* veneered; **c. en oro** gold-plated; *Fig* **c. a la antigua** stuck in the past, old-fashioned (b) *muy Fam (cerrado)* shut, closed

**chapar 1** *vt* (a) *(recubrir) (con metal)* to plate; *(con madera)* to veneer (b) *muy Fam (cerrar)* to shut, to close
**2** *vi muy Fam (cerrar)* to shut, to close

**chaparro, -a 1** *adj* short and squat
**2** *nm,f (persona)* short, squat person
**3** *nm Bot* dwarf oak

**chaparrón** *nm* downpour; *Fam Fig (gran cantidad)* torrent

**chapear** *vt (con metal)* to plate; *(con madera)* to veneer

**chapela** *nf* beret

**chapero** *nm muy Fam* rent boy

**chapista** *nmf Aut* panel beater

**chapó** *interj* **¡c.!** *(¡bien hecho!)* well done!, bravo!

**chapopote** *nm Carib, Méx* bitumen, pitch

**chapotear** *vi* to splash about

**chapoteo** *nm* splashing

**chapucear** *vt* to botch (up)

**chapucería** *nf* botch (job)

**chapucero, -a 1** *adj (trabajo)* shoddy, sloppy; *(persona)* bungling
**2** *nm,f* bungler

**chapulín** *nm CAm, Méx* grasshopper

**chapurrar, chapurrear** *vt* to speak badly

**chapurreo** *nm* jabbering

**chapuza** *nf* (a) *(trabajo mal hecho)* botch (job) (b) *(trabajo ocasional)* odd job

**chapuzón** *nm* dip; **darse un c.** to go for a dip

**chaqué** *nm* morning coat

**chaqueta** *nf (de traje)* jacket; *(de punto)* cardigan; *Fig* **cambiarse de c.** to change sides

**chaqueteo** *nm* changing sides

**chaquetero, -a** *adj & nm,f Fam* turncoat

**chaquetilla** *nf* short jacket

**chaquetón** *nm* heavy jacket, short coat

**charada** *nf* = newspaper puzzle in which a word must be guessed, with its meaning and certain syllables given as clues

**charanga** *nf* (a) *(banda)* brass band (b) *Fam (fiesta)* party

**charango** *nm* = small South American guitar, often made from armadillo shell

**charca** *nf* pool, pond

**charco** *nm* puddle; *Fam Fig* **cruzar el c.** to cross the pond *o* Atlantic

**charcutería** *nf* (a) *(tienda)* ≃ delicatessen, = shop selling cold meats and cheeses (b) *(productos)* cold cuts and cheese

**charcutero, -a** *nm,f* = seller of "charcutería"

**charla** *nf* (a) *(conversación)* chat (b) *(conferencia)* talk

**charlar** *vi* to chat (**sobre** about); **c. con alguien** to chat with sb, to have a chat with sb

**charlatán, -ana 1** *adj* talkative
**2** *nm,f* (a) *(hablador)* chatterbox (b) *Pey (mentiroso)* trickster, charlatan (c) *(vendedor)* travelling salesman, *f* travelling saleswoman

**charlatanería** *nf* (a) *Pey (palabrería)* spiel (b) *(locuacidad)* talkativeness

**charlestón** *nm* charleston

**charlotada** nf Fam (a) (payasada) **charlota-das** clowning around (b) Taurom slapstick bull-fight

**charlotear** vi to chat

**charloteo** nm chatting; **estar de c.** to be chatting o having a chat

**charnego, -a** nm,f = pejorative term refer-ring to immigrant to Catalonia from another part of Spain

**charol** nm (piel) patent leather

**charola** nf Andes tray

**charretera** nf epaulette

**charro, -a 1** adj (a) (salmantino) Salamancan (b) Fig (recargado) gaudy, showy
   **2** nm,f (a) (salmantino) Salamancan (b) Méx (jinete) horseman (c) Méx (líder sindical) (cor-rupt) trade union leader

**charrúa** adj inv & nmf inv CSur Uruguayan

**chárter 1** adj inv **vuelo c.** charter flight
   **2** nm charter flight

**chasca** nf (a) Fam (hoguera) camp fire (b) Andes mop of hair

**chascar** [61] **1** vt (lengua) to click; (dedos) to snap; (látigo) to crack
   **2** vi (lengua) to click

**chascarrillo** nm Fam funny story

**chasco** nm (a) (decepción) disappointment; **llevarse un c.** to be disappointed (b) (burla) trick; **dar un c. a alguien** to play a trick on sb

**chasis** nm inv (a) Aut chassis (b) Fot plate-holder (c) Fam (esqueleto) body

**chasque** etc ver **chascar**

**chasquear 1** vt (a) (látigo) to crack (b) (len-gua) to click (c) Fig (engañar) to play a trick on
   **2** vi (madera) to crack

**chasquido** nm (de látigo, madera, hueso) crack; (de lengua, arma) click; (de dedos) snap

**chasquillas** nfpl Chile (flequillo) Br fringe, US bangs

**chata** nf (orinal) bedpan

**chatarra** nf (a) (metal) scrap (metal) (b) (obje-tos, piezas) junk (c) Fam (joyas) cheap and nasty jewellery; (condecoraciones) brass, medals (d) Fam (monedas) small change

**chatarrería** nf scrapyard

**chatarrero, -a** nm,f scrap (metal) dealer

**chatear** vi Fam to go out drinking, to go on a pub-crawl

**chateo** nm Fam **ir de c.** to go out drinking, to go on a pub-crawl

**chato, -a 1** adj (nariz) snub; (persona) snub-nosed; (superficie, objeto) flat
   **2** nm,f (a) (persona) snub-nosed person (b) Fam (apelativo) love, dear
   **3** nm Fam = small glass of wine

**chau, chaucito** interj Andes, CSur Fam **¡c.!** see you later!

**chaucha** nf (a) Andes, CSur (moneda) coin of little value (b) CSur (haba) early bean (c) Andes (patata) early potato

**chauvinismo** [tʃoβi'nismo] nm chauvinism

**chauvinista** [tʃoβi'nista] **1** adj chauvinistic
   **2** nmf chauvinist

**chaval, -a** nm,f (niño) kid, lad; (niña) kid, girl

**chavalería** nf kids

**chavalo, -a** nm,f CAm Fam lad, f girl

**chaveta** nf (a) (clavija) cotter pin (b) Fam (cabeza) nut, head; Fig **perder la c.** to go off one's rocker (c) Andes (navaja) penknife

**chavo** nm Fam (a) (dinero) **no tener un c.** to be penniless (b) Méx (hombre) guy

**chayote** nm Am chayote

**ché, che** interj **¡c.!** (¡oye!) hey!; **¡pero qué hacés, c.!** what do you think you're doing?

**checo, -a 1** adj & nm,f Czech
   **2** nm (lengua) Czech

**checoslovaco, -a** adj & nm,f Antes Czechoslovakian, Czechoslovak

**Checoslovaquia** n Antes Czechoslovakia

**chef** (pl **chefs**) [tʃef] nm chef

**cheli** nm Fam = slang typical of Madrid

**chelín** nm shilling

**chelo** nm cello

**chepa** nf Fam hump

**cheposo, -a, chepudo, -a** Fam **1** adj hunchbacked
   **2** nm,f hunchback

**cheque** nm Br cheque, US check; **extender un c.** to make out a cheque; también Fig **c. en blanco** blank cheque; **c. cruzado** o **barrado** crossed cheque; **c. sin fondos** bad cheque; **c. (de) gasolina** petrol voucher; **c. nominativo** = cheque in favour of a specific person; **c. al portador** cheque payable to the bearer; **c. de ventanilla** US ≃ counter check, = check writ-ten by bank teller to be drawn on customer's account; **c. de viaje** traveller's cheque

**chequear** vt (a) Med **c. a alguien** to exam-ine sb, to give sb a checkup (b) (comprobar) to check

**chequeo** nm (a) Med checkup; **hacerse un c.** to have a checkup (b) (comprobación) check; **hacer un c. (de algo)** to check (sth)

**chequera** nf Br chequebook, US checkbook

**chévere** adj Andes, Carib Fam great, fantastic

**cheviot** (pl **cheviots**) nm cheviot

**chic** adj inv chic

**chica** nf (a) (joven) girl; **mira, c., haz lo que quieras** look, dear o darling, you can do what you want; **c. de alterne** = girl who works in bars encouraging customers to drink in return for a commission (**b**) *(criada)* maid

**chicano, -a 1** *adj & nm,f* Chicano, Mexican-American

**2** *nm (lengua)* Chicano

**chicarrón, -ona** *nm,f Fam* strapping lad, *f* strapping girl

**chicha** *nf* (**a**) *Fam (para comer)* meat (**b**) *Fam (de persona)* flesh (**c**) *Fam* **no ser ni c. ni limonada** *o* **limoná** to be neither one thing nor the other, to be neither fish nor fowl (**d**) *Andes =* alcoholic drink made from fermented maize

**chícharo** *nm CAm, Méx* pea

**chicharra** *nf* (**a**) *Zool* cicada (**b**) *Méx (timbre)* electric buzzer

**chicharro** *nm (pez)* horse mackerel

**chicharro** *nm Am (guisante)* pea

**chicharrón** *nm (frito)* pork crackling; **chicharrones** *(embutido) =* cold processed meat made from pork

**chiche** *Chile, CSur* **1** *nm (adorno)* adornment

**2** *nf CAm, Méx muy Fam (pecho de mujer)* tit

**chichón** *nm* bump

**chichonera** *nf (para niños) =* protective headband to prevent toddlers hurting themselves when they bang into sth; *(para ciclistas) =* track helmet, soft protective headgear for cyclists

**chicle** *nm* chewing gum

**chiclé, chicler** *nm Aut* jet

**chico, -a 1** *adj (pequeño)* small

**2** *nm* (**a**) *(joven)* boy (**b**) *(tratamiento)* sonny, mate (**c**) **c. (de los recados)** *(en oficina)* office-boy; *(en tienda)* errand-boy

**chicote** *nm Am* whip

**chifa** *adj & nmf Andes* Chinese

**chifla** *nf Fam* **tomarse algo a c.** to treat sth as a joke; **tomarse las cosas a c.** to treat everything as a joke

**chiflado, -a** *Fam* **1** *adj* crazy, mad

**2** *nm,f* loony

**chifladura** *nf (locura)* madness; **su última c. son las motos** his latest craze is for motorbikes

**chiflar 1** *vt Fam (encantar)* **me chiflan las patatas fritas** I'm mad about chips

**2** *vi (silbar)* to whistle

**chiflido** *nm Am* whistling

**chifonier** *nm (mueble)* tallboy

**chigüín** *nm CAm* kid, nipper

**chihuahua** *nm* chihuahua

**chií, chiíta** *adj & nmf* Shi'ite

**chilaba** *nf* jellaba

**Chile** *n* Chile

**chile** *nm* chilli

**chileno, -a** *adj & nm,f* Chilean

**chilindrón** *nm Culin =* seasoning made of tomatoes and peppers

**chillar 1** *vi* (**a**) *(gritar) (personas)* to scream, to yell; *(aves, monos)* to screech; *(cerdo)* to squeal; *(ratón)* to squeak (**b**) *(chirriar)* to screech; *(puerta, madera)* to creak; *(bisagras)* to squeak

**2** *vt Fam (reñir)* to yell at

**chillido** *nm (de persona)* scream, yell; *(de ave, mono)* screech; *(de cerdo)* squeal; *(de ratón)* squeak

**chillón, -ona 1** *adj* (**a**) *(voz)* piercing (**b**) *(persona)* noisy, screeching (**c**) *(color)* loud, gaudy

**2** *nm,f* noisy person

**chilpayate, -a** *nm,f Méx* kid

**chimenea** *nf* (**a**) *(hogar)* fireplace (**b**) *(tubo)* chimney

**chimpancé** *nm* chimpanzee

**China** *nf* (**la**) C. China

**china** *nf* (**a**) *(piedra)* small stone, pebble; *Fam* **le tocó la c.** he drew the short straw (**b**) *muy Fam (droga)* deal *(small amount of hash)* (**c**) *Am (india)* Indian woman (**d**) *Arg, Chile (criada)* maid

**chinchar** *Fam* **1** *vt* to pester, to bug

**2 chincharse** *vpr* to put up with it; **¡tú no tienes, para que te chinches!** I've got one and you haven't, so there!

**chinche 1** *adj Fam Fig* annoying

**2** *nf* (**a**) *(insecto)* bedbug (**b**) *Am (chincheta)* drawing pin, *US* thumbtack

**3** *nmf Fam Fig (persona)* pest, pain

**chincheta** *nf Br* drawing pin, *US* thumbtack

**chinchilla** *nf* chinchilla

**chinchín** *nm* (**a**) *(ruido)* noise of a brass band (**b**) *(brindis)* toast; **¡c.!** cheers!

**chinchón** *nm* (**a**) *(bebida) =* aniseed liquor (**b**) *(juego de cartas) =* card game where players aim to collect two sets of three cards

**chinchorro** *nm* (**a**) *Méx (red)* net (**b**) *Chile, Ven (hamaca)* hammock

**chinchoso, -a 1** *adj Fam* annoying

**2** *nm,f* pest, pain

**chinero** *nm china o* glass cabinet

**chingada** *nf Méx Vulg* **¡vete a la c.!** fuck off!

**chingado, -a** *adj* (**a**) *muy Fam (estropeado)* bust, *Br* knackered (**b**) *Méx Vulg* fucking

**chingar [40] 1** *vt* (**a**) *muy Fam (estropear)* to bust, *Br* to knacker (**b**) *Vulg (copular)* to fuck; *Méx* **¡chinga tu madre!** fuck you!

**2** *vi Vulg (copular)* to screw, to fuck

**3 chingarse** *vpr muy Fam (estropearse)* to pack in, to conk out

**chinita** *nf* (**a**) *Am (criada)* maid (**b**) *Chile (animal)* ladybird

**chino, -a 1** *adj* Chinese

**2** *nm,f* Chinese (man/woman); *Fig* **trabajar**

**como un c.** to slave away

**3** *nm* **(a)** *(lengua)* Chinese; *Fam* **me suena a c.** *(no lo conozco)* I've never heard of it; *(no lo entiendo)* it's all Greek to me **(b) chinos** *(juego)* = game in which each player must guess the number of coins or pebbles in the other's hand **(c)** *(pasapuré)* sieve

**chip** *(pl* **chips)** *nm Informát* chip

**chipé, chipén** *adj inv Fam* brilliant, terrific; **ser de c.** to be brilliant *o* terrific

**chipirón** *nm* baby squid

**Chipre** *n* Cyprus

**chipriota** *adj & nmf* Cypriot

**chiquero** *nm Taurom* bull-pen

**chiquilicuatro** *nm* insignificant person, nobody

**chiquilín, -ina** *nm,f* small boy, *f* small girl

**chiquillada** *nf (cosa de niños)* childish thing; *(travesura)* childish prank; **hacer una c. (a alguien)** to play a childish prank (on sb)

**chiquillería** *nf* kids

**chiquillo, -a** *nm,f* kid

**chiquitín, -ina 1** *adj* tiny

**2** *nm,f* tiny tot

**chiquito, -a 1** *adj* tiny

**2** *nm (de vino)* = small glass of wine

**3** *nfpl Fig* **no andarse con chiquitas** not to mess about

**chiribita** *nf (chispa)* spark; *Fam* **ver chiribitas** to see spots in front of one's eyes; **le hacían chiribitas los ojos al verlo** her eyes lit up when she saw him

**chirigota** *nf Fam* joke

**chirimbolo** *nm Fam* thingamajig, whatsit

**chirimía** *nf Mús* shawm

**chirimoya** *nf* custard apple

**chiringuito** *nm* **(a)** *(bar)* refreshment stall **(b)** *Fam (negocio)* **montarse un c.** to set up a little business

**chiripa** *nf Fam Fig* fluke; **de** *o* **por c.** by luck

**chirivía** *nf Bot* parsnip

**chirla** *nf* small clam

**chirona** *nf Fam* clink, slammer; **en c.** in the clink

**chirriar** [34] *vi (sonar)* to screech; *(puerta, madera)* to creak; *(bisagra, muelles)* to squeak

**chirrido** *nm (ruido)* screech; *(de puerta, madera)* creak; *(de bisagra, muelles)* squeak

**chis** *interj* ¡c.! ssh!

**chisme** *nm* **(a)** *(cotilleo)* rumour, piece of gossip **(b)** *Fam (cosa)* thingamajig, thingy

**chismorrear** *vi* to spread rumours, to gossip

**chismorreo** *nm* gossip

**chismoso, -a 1** *adj* gossipy

**2** *nm,f* gossip, scandalmonger

**chispa** *nf* **(a)** *(de fuego, electricidad)* spark; *Fam Fig* **echar chispas** to be hopping mad **(b)** *Fig (pizca)* bit **(c)** *Fig (agudeza, gracia)* sparkle; **esa novela tiene c.** that novel has really got something

**chispazo** *nm también Fig* spark

**chispeante** *adj* **(a)** *(que chispea)* that gives off sparks **(b)** *Fig (conversación, discurso, mirada)* sparkling

**chispear 1** *vi* **(a)** *(chisporrotear)* to spark **(b)** *(relucir)* to sparkle

**2** *v impersonal (llover)* to spit (with rain); **empezó a c.** a few spots of rain started to fall

**chisporrotear** *vi (fuego, leña)* to crackle; *(aceite)* to splutter; *(comida)* to sizzle

**chisporroteo** *nm (de fuego, leña)* crackling; *(de aceite)* spluttering; *(de comida)* sizzling

**chisquero** *nm (cigarette)* lighter

**chist** *interj* ¡c.! ssh!

**chistar** *vi* **sin c.** without a word (of protest)

**chiste** *nm* joke; **contar chistes** to tell jokes; **c. verde** dirty joke; *Fig* **no tiene ningún c.** there's nothing special about it

**chistera** *nf (sombrero)* top hat

**chistorra** *nf* = type of cured pork sausage typical of Aragon and Navarre

**chistoso, -a 1** *adj* funny

**2** *nm,f* amusing *o* funny person

**chistu** *nm* Basque flute

**chistulari** *nmf* "chistu" player

**chita** *nf Fam* **a la c. callando** quietly, on the quiet

**chitón** *interj* ¡c.! quiet!

**chivar** *Fam* **1** *vt* to whisper, to tell secretly

**2 chivarse** *vpr (niños)* to tell **(de** on), *Br* to split **(de** on); *(delincuentes)* to squeal **(de** on), *Br* to grass **(de** on)

**chivatazo** *nm Fam* tip-off; **dar el c.** to squeal, *Br* to grass

**chivato, -a 1** *nm,f Fam (delator)* informer, *Br* grass; *(acusica)* telltale

**2** *nm* **(a)** *(luz)* warning light; *(alarma)* alarm bell **(b)** *Ven Fam (pez gordo)* big cheese

**chivo, -a** *nm,f* kid, young goat; *Fig* **ser el c. expiatorio** to be the scapegoat

**chocante** *adj* puzzling

**chocar** [61] **1** *vi* **(a)** *(colisionar)* to crash **(contra** into), to collide **(contra** with); **c. de frente con** to have a head-on collision with **(b)** *Fig (enfrentarse)* to clash; **mis ideas siempre han chocado con las suyas** he and I have always had different ideas about things

**2** *vt* **(a)** *(manos)* to shake; *Fam* **¡chócala!**, **¡choca esos cinco!** put it there! **(b)** *(copas, vasos)* to clink **(c)** *Fig (extrañar)* to puzzle

**chochear** vi (a) (viejo) to be senile (b) Fam Fig (de cariño) **c. por alguien** to dote on sb

**chochez** nf (a) (vejez) senility (b) (dicho, hecho) **decir/hacer chocheces** to say/do senile things

**chocho, -a 1** adj (a) (viejo) senile (b) Fam Fig (encariñado) soft, doting

**2** nm (a) Vulg (vulva) cunt (b) Fam (altramuz) lupin seed (for eating)

**choclo** nm Andes, CSur (maíz) Br maize, US corn

**choclón** nm Chile Fam crowd

**choco** nm (sepia) cuttlefish

**chocolatada** nf = afternoon party where people drink thick drinking chocolate

**chocolate** nm (a) (para comer) chocolate; (para beber) **c. (a la taza)** thick drinking chocolate; **c. blanco** white chocolate; **c. con leche** milk chocolate (b) muy Fam (hachís) hash

**chocolatería** nf (a) (fábrica) chocolate factory (b) (establecimiento) = café where drinking chocolate is served

**chocolatero, -a 1** adj **ser muy c.** to love chocolate

**2** nm,f (a) (aficionado al chocolate) chocoholic, person fond of chocolate (b) (oficio) chocolate maker/seller

**chocolatina** nf chocolate bar

**chofer** (pl chóferes) nmf Am chauffeur

**chófer** (pl chóferes) nmf chauffeur

**chollo** nm Fam (a) (producto, compra) bargain (b) (trabajo, situación) cushy number

**cholo, -a** nm,f CAm educated indian

**chomba, chompa** nf Andes, CSur sweater, jumper

**chompa** nf CAm dried potatoes

**chompipe** nm CAm = species of turkey

**chonchón** nm Chile lamp

**chongo** nm Méx (a) (moño) bun (b) (dulce) = dessert made from milk curds, served in syrup

**chóped** nm = type of luncheon meat

**chopera** nf poplar grove

**chopito** nm baby squid

**chopo** nm poplar

**choque 1** ver **chocar**

**2** nm (a) (impacto) impact; (de coche, avión) crash; **c. frontal** head-on collision (b) Fig (enfrentamiento) clash (c) (impresión) shock

**chorbo, -a** nm,f muy Fam (chico) lad, f girl, Br lass; (adulto) guy, Br bloke, f woman

**chorico** nm Fam (robo) robbery; (timo) rip-off

**chorizar** [16] vt Fam to swipe, to pinch

**chorizo** nm (a) (embutido) = cured pork sausage, flavoured with paprika (b) Fam (ladrón) thief

**chorlito** nm (a) Zool plover (b) Fam **cabeza de c.** scatterbrain

**choro** nm Andes mussel

**chorra** Fam **1** nmf (tonto) Br wally, US jerk; **hacer el c.** to muck about

**2** nf (suerte) luck

**chorrada** nf Fam rubbish; **decir chorradas** to talk rubbish; **decir una c.** to say something stupid

**chorrear 1** vi (a) (gotear) (gota a gota) to drip; (en un hilo) to trickle; **estar chorreando** (estar empapado) to be soaking o wringing wet (b) (brotar) to spurt o gush (out)

**2** vt (sujeto: prenda) to drip; (sujeto: persona) to drip with

**chorreo** nm (a) (goteo) (gota a gota) dripping; (en un hilo) trickling; Fig **un c. de dinero** a steady drain on funds (b) (brote) spurting, gushing

**chorreras** nfpl frill

**chorretón** nm (a) (chorro) spurt; **le caían chorretones de helado por la barbilla** he'd got ice cream all over his chin (b) (mancha) stain

**chorro** nm (a) (de líquido) (borbotón) jet, spurt; (hilo) trickle; **salir a chorros** to spurt o gush out; Fam Fig **como los chorros del oro** as clean as a new pin (b) Fig (de luz, gente, preguntas) stream; **tiene un c. de dinero** she has loads of money

**chotearse** vpr Fam to make fun (**de** of)

**choteo** nm Fam joking, kidding; **estar de c.** to be kidding

**chotis** nm inv = dance typical of Madrid

**choto, -a** nm,f (a) (cabrito) kid, young goat; Fam **estar como una chota** to be crazy, to be off one's rocker (b) (ternero) calf

**chovinismo** nm chauvinism

**chovinista 1** adj chauvinistic

**2** nmf chauvinist

**choza** nf hut

**christmas** ['krismas] nm inv Christmas card

**chubasco** nm (lluvia) shower

**chubasquero** nm raincoat, Br mac

**chúcaro, -a** adj Am Fam wild

**chuchería** nf (a) (golosina) sweet (b) (objeto) trinket

**chucho** nm Fam mutt, dog

**chueco, -a** adj Am twisted

**chufa** nf (a) (planta) chufa (b) (tubérculo) tiger nut

**chufla** nf Fam joke; **estar de c.** to be kidding; **tomarse las cosas a c.** to treat everything as a joke, not to take things seriously

**chulada** nf (a) (bravuconada) piece of bravado; **chuladas** bravado (b) Fam (cosa bonita) delight, gorgeous thing

**chulapo, -a, chulapón, -ona** *nm,f* = lower-class native of 18th-19th century Madrid

**chulear** *Fam* **1** *vt* **c. a una mujer** to live off a woman

**2 chulearse** *vpr (fanfarronear)* to be cocky (**de** about); **se está chuleando de que aprobó el examen** he's showing off about having passed the exam

**chulería** *nf* (a) *(bravuconería)* cockiness (b) *(salero)* charm, winning ways

**chulesco, -a** *adj* = relating to lower-class Madrid life of the 18th-19th centuries

**chuleta 1** *nf* (a) *(de carne)* chop (b) *(en exámenes)* crib note

**2** *nmf Fam (chulo)* cocky person

**3** *adj Fam (chulo)* cocky

**chuletada** *nf* barbecue

**chulo, -a 1** *adj* (a) *(descarado)* cocky; **ponerse c.** to get cocky (b) *Fam (bonito)* lovely

**2** *nm,f* (a) *(descarado)* cocky person (b) *(madrileño)* = lower-class native of 18th-19th century Madrid

**3** *nm (proxeneta)* pimp

**chumba** *adj* **higuera c.** prickly pear

**chumbera** *nf* prickly pear cactus

**chumbo** *nm* **higo c.** prickly pear

**chuminada** *nf Fam* silly thing, trifle

**chumino** *nm Vulg* cunt; **no me sale del c.** I can't be bloody well bothered, *Br* I can't be arsed

**chungo, -a** *muy Fam* **1** *adj (persona)* horrible, nasty; *(cosa)* lousy; **la cosa está chunga** it's really difficult, it's a real bitch

**2** *nf* **tomarse algo a chunga** to take sth as a joke, not to take sth seriously

**chupa** *nf Fam* coat

**chupachups®** *nm inv* lollipop

**chupacirios** *nmf inv Fam Pey* holy Joe

**chupada** *nf (de helado) (con la lengua)* lick; *(con los labios)* suck; *(de cigarrillo)* puff, drag

**chupado, -a** *adj* (a) *(delgado)* skinny (b) *Fam (fácil)* **estar c.** to be dead easy *o* a piece of cake

**chupar 1** *vt* (a) *(succionar)* to suck; *(lamer)* to lick; *(fumar)* to puff at (b) *(absorber)* to soak up (c) *Fig (quitar)* **chuparle algo a alguien** to milk sb for sth; **esa mujer le está chupando la sangre** that woman is bleeding him dry

**2 chuparse** *vpr* (a) *(adelgazar)* to get thinner (b) *Fam (aguantar)* to put up with (c) *Fam* **¡chúpate esa!** take that!

**chupatintas** *nmf inv Pey* pen-pusher

**chupe** *nm Andes, Arg* stew

**chupete** *nm Br* dummy, *US* pacifier

**chupetear** *vt* to suck on, to suck away at

**chupetón** *nm* (a) *(con la lengua)* lick; *(con los labios)* suck; **dar un c. a algo** to lick sth (b) *Fam (moradura en la piel)* lovebite, *US* hickey

**chupi** *adj Fam* great, brill

**chupinazo** *nm* (a) *(cañonazo)* cannon shot (b) *Fam Dep (patada)* hard kick; *(a puerta)* screamer, hard shot

**chupito** *nm* shot

**chupón, -ona 1** *nm,f Fam (gorrón)* sponger, cadger

**2** *nm Méx (chupete) Br* dummy, *US* pacifier

**chupóptero, -a** *nm,f Fam* parasite

**churrasco** *nm* barbecued *o* grilled meat

**churrería** *nf* = shop or stall selling "churros"

**churrero, -a** *nm,f* "churros" seller

**churrete** *nm (chorro)* spurt; *(mancha)* stain

**churrigueresco, -a** *adj Arte* churrigueresque

**churro** *nm* (a) *(para comer)* = dough formed into sticks or rings and fried in oil (b) *Fam (fracaso)* botch; **ese dibujo es un c.** that drawing is awful

**churruscado, -a** *adj (quemado)* burnt; *Fam (crujiente)* crispy

**churruscar** *vt* to burn

**churrusco** *nm Fam (pan)* piece of burnt toast; **¡esto no es una chuleta, es un c.!** this chop is burnt to a cinder!

**churumbel** *nm Fam* kid

**chusco, -a 1** *adj* funny

**2** *nm Fam* crust of stale bread

**chusma** *nf* rabble, mob

**chut** *(pl* **chuts)** *nm Dep (patada)* kick; *(a puerta)* shot

**chutar 1** *vi* (a) *(lanzar la pelota)* to kick the ball; *(a puerta)* to shoot (b) *Fam (funcionar)* to work; **esto va que chuta** it's going great; **con eso va que chuta** that's plenty *o* more than enough

**2 chutarse** *vpr muy Fam* to shoot up

**chute** *nm muy Fam* fix

**chuzo** *nm Fig* **llover a chuzos, caer chuzos de punta** to rain cats and dogs

**CI** *nm (abrev de* **cociente de inteligencia)** IQ

**CIA** ['θia] *nf (abrev de* **Central Intelligence Agency)** CIA

**cía., Cía.** *(abrev de* **compañía)** Co

**cianuro** *nm* cyanide

**ciática** *nf* sciatica

**ciático, -a** *adj* sciatic

**cibercafé** *nm* cybercafe

**ciberespacio** *nm* cyberspace

**cibernauta** *nmf* Nettie, Net user

**cibernética** *nf* cybernetics *(singular)*

**cibernético, -a** *adj* cybernetic

**cibersexo** *nm* cybersex

**cicatería** *nf* stinginess, meanness

**cicatero, -a 1** *adj* stingy, mean

**2** *nm,f* skinflint, miser

**cicatriz** *nf también Fig* scar

**cicatrización** *nf* scarring

**cicatrizante 1** *adj* healing

**2** *nm* healing substance

**cicatrizar** [16] **1** *vi* to form a scar, to heal (up)

**2** *vt* to heal

**cicerón** *nm* eloquent speaker, orator

**cicerone** *nmf* guide

**ciclamen** *nm* cyclamen

**cíclico, -a** *adj* cyclical

**ciclismo** *nm* cycling

**ciclista 1** *adj* cycling; **equipo c.** cycling team; **prueba c.** cycle race

**2** *nmf* cyclist

**ciclo** *nm* (**a**) *(período) también Econ* cycle (**b**) *(de conferencias, actos)* series

**ciclocross** *nm* cyclo-cross

**ciclomotor** *nm* moped

**ciclón** *nm* cyclone

**cíclope** *nm* Cyclops

**ciclópeo, -a** *adj Fig (enorme)* colossal, massive

**ciclostil, ciclostilo** *nm* cyclostyle

**cicloturismo** *nm* bicycle touring

**cicloturista** *nmf* = person on cycling holiday

**CICR** *nm (abrev de* **Comité Internacional de la Cruz Roja**) IRCC

**cicuta** *nf* hemlock

**ciego, -a 1** *ver* **cegar**

**2** *adj* (**a**) *también Fig* blind; **a ciegas** blindly; **quedarse c.** to go blind (**b**) *Fig (enloquecido)* blinded (**de** by) (**c**) *(pozo, tubería)* blocked (up) (**d**) *muy Fam (borracho)* blind drunk, *Br* pissed; *(drogado)* stoned

**3** *nm,f (invidente)* blind person; **los ciegos** the blind

**4** *nm* (**a**) *Anat* caecum (**b**) *muy Fam (de droga)* trip; **tener/cogerse un c.** *(de alcohol)* to be/get blind drunk *o Br* pissed (**c**) **los ciegos** *(sorteo de la ONCE)* = lottery organized by Spanish association for the blind

**ciegue** *etc ver* **cegar**

**cielo** *nm* (**a**) *(atmósfera)* sky; *Min* **a c. abierto** opencast

(**b**) *Rel* heaven; **¡c. santo!, ¡cielos!** good heavens!

(**c**) *(nombre cariñoso)* my love, my dear

(**d**) *(parte superior)* **c. del paladar** roof of the mouth; **c. raso** ceiling

(**e**) *(expresiones)* **me viene bajado del c.** it's a godsend (to me); **como llovido del c.** *(inesperadamente)* out of the blue; *(oportunamente)* at

just the right moment; **estar en el séptimo c.** to be in seventh heaven; **se le juntó el c. con la tierra** he lost his nerve; **mover c. y tierra** to move heaven and earth; **ser un c.** to be an angel; **ver el c. abierto** to see one's way out

**ciempiés** *nm inv* centipede

**cien** *núm* a *o* one hundred; **c. mil** a *o* one hundred thousand; **por c.** per cent; **c. por c.** a hundred per cent; *ver también* **seis**

**ciénaga** *nf* marsh, bog

**ciencia** *nf* (**a**) *(método, estudio)* science; **a c. cierta** for certain; *Fam* **tener poca c.** to be straightforward; *Educ* **ciencias** science; **ciencias económicas** economics *(singular)*; **ciencias exactas** mathematics *(singular)*; **ciencias naturales/sociales** natural/social sciences; **c. ficción** science fiction (**b**) *(sabiduría)* learning, knowledge

**cieno** *nm* mud, sludge

**cientificismo** *nm* = over-emphasis on scientific ideas

**científico, -a 1** *adj* scientific

**2** *nm,f* scientist

**cientista** *nmf Arg, Chile* **c. social** sociologist

**ciento** *núm* a *o* one hundred; **c. cincuenta** a *o* one hundred and fifty; **cientos de** hundreds of; **por c.** per cent; *Fam Fig* **darle c. y raya a alguien** to run rings around sb; *Fam Fig* **eran c. y la madre** everybody and his dog was there; *ver también* **seis**

**ciernes** *nmpl* **estar en c.** to be in its infancy; **una campeona en c.** a budding champion; **tenemos un viaje en c.** we're planning a journey

**cierno** *etc ver* **cerner**

**cierre** *nm* (**a**) *(acción de cerrar)* closing, shutting; *(de fábrica)* shutdown; *Rad & TV* closedown; *Ind* **c. patronal** lockout (**b**) *(mecanismo)* fastener; *Aut* **c. centralizado** central locking; **c. metálico** *(de tienda)* metal shutter; *Am* **c. relámpago** *(cremallera) Br* zip, *US* zipper

**cierto, -a 1** *adj* (**a**) *(verdadero)* true; **estar en lo c.** to be right; **lo c. es que...** the fact is that... (**b**) *(seguro)* certain, definite (**c**) *(algún)* certain; **c. hombre** a certain man; **en cierta ocasión** once, on one occasion

**2** *adv* right, certainly; **por c.** by the way

**ciervo, -a** *nm,f (macho)* deer, stag; *(hembra)* deer, hind

**cierzo** *nm* north wind

**CIF** [θif] *nm (abrev de* **código de identificación fiscal**) = number identifying company for tax purposes

**cifra** *nf* (**a**) *(signo)* figure; **un código de cuatro cifras** a four-digit code (**b**) *(cantidad)* number, total; *(de dinero)* sum; **ingresó la c. de un**

**millón de pesetas** he deposited the sum of one million pesetas; *Econ* **c. de negocios** turnover (**c**) *(código)* **en c.** in code

**cifrado, -a** *adj* coded, in code

**cifrar 1** *vt* (**a**) *(codificar)* to code (**b**) *Fig (resumir, reducir)* to summarize

**2 cifrarse en** *vpr* (**a**) *(ascender a)* to come to, to amount to (**b**) *Fig (resumirse en)* to be summarized by

**cigala** *nf* Dublin Bay prawn

**cigarra** *nf* cicada

**cigarrera** *nf (caja)* cigar case

**cigarrero, -a** *nm,f (persona)* cigar maker

**cigarrillo** *nm* cigarette

**cigarro** *nm* (**a**) *(puro)* cigar (**b**) *(cigarrillo)* cigarette

**cigüeña** *nf* stork

**cigüeñal** *nm* crankshaft

**cilantro** *nm* coriander

**cilicio** *nm (faja, cordón)* spiked belt *(of penitent)*; *(vestidura)* hair shirt

**cilindrada** *nf* cylinder capacity

**cilíndrico, -a** *adj* cylindrical

**cilindro** *nm* cylinder; *(de imprenta)* roller

**cima** *nf (cúspide) (de montaña)* peak, summit; *(de árbol)* top; *Fig (apogeo)* peak, high point; **dar c. a** *(negociaciones, acuerdo)* to conclude

**cimarrón, -ona 1** *adj (animal)* feral

**2** *nm,f Am (esclavo)* runaway slave

**címbalo** *nm* cymbal

**cimborrio** *nm Arquit* cupola

**cimbreante** *adj* swaying

**cimbrear 1** *vt* (**a**) *(vara)* to wave about (**b**) *(caderas)* to sway

**2 cimbrearse** *vpr* to sway

**cimentación** *nf* (**a**) *(acción)* laying of the foundations (**b**) *(cimientos)* foundations

**cimentar** [3] *vt (edificio)* to lay the foundations of; *(ciudad)* to found, to build; *Fig (idea, paz, fama)* to cement, to consolidate

**cimero, -a** *adj (alto)* topmost; *Fig (sobresaliente)* foremost, most outstanding

**cimiento** *etc ver* **cimentar**

**cimientos** *nmpl* (**a**) *Constr* foundation; *también Fig* **echar los c.** to lay the foundations (**b**) *Fig (base)* basis *singular*

**cimitarra** *nf* scimitar

**cinabrio** *nm* cinnabar

**cinc** *nm* zinc

**cincel** *nm* chisel

**cincelar** *vt* to chisel

**cincha** *nf* girth

**cincho** *nm* (**a**) *(cinturón)* belt (**b**) *(aro de hierro)* hoop

**cinco** *núm* five; *Fam* **¡choca esos c.!** put it there!; *ver también* **seis**

**cincuenta** *núm* fifty; **los (años) c.** the fifties; *ver también* **seis**

**cincuentena** *nf* fifty; **andará por la c.** he must be about fifty; **una c. de persones** fifty people

**cincuentenario** *nm* fiftieth anniversary

**cincuentón, -ona** *nm,f Fam* person in his/her fifties

**cine** *nm* cinema; **hacer c.** to make films; **c. de estreno/de verano** first-run/open-air cinema; **c. fórum** film with discussion group; **c. mudo** silent films; **c. sonoro** talking pictures, talkies

**cineasta** *nmf* film maker *o* director

**cineclub** *nm* (**a**) *(asociación)* film society (**b**) *(sala)* club cinema

**cinéfilo, -a** *nm,f* film buff

**cinegético, -a 1** *adj* hunting; **asociación cinegética** hunting club; **deporte c.** hunting, blood sports

**2** *nf* **cinegética** hunting

**cinemascope**® *nm* cinemascope®

**cinemateca** *nf* film library

**cinemática** *nf Fís* kinematics *(singular)*

**cinematografía** *nf* cinematography, filmmaking

**cinematográfico, -a** *adj* film; **guión c.** film script

**cinematógrafo** *nm* (**a**) *(aparato)* film projector (**b**) *(local)* cinema

**cinerama**® *nm* Cinerama®

**cinética** *nf* kinetics *(singular)*

**cinético, -a** *adj* kinetic

**cingalés, -esa** *adj & nm,f* Sinhalese

**cíngaro, -a** *adj & nm,f* Tzigane

**cínico, -a 1** *adj (desvergonzado)* shameless

**2** *nm,f (desvergonzado)* shameless person

**cinismo** *nm (desvergüenza)* shamelessness

**cinta** *nf* (**a**) *(de plástico, papel)* strip, band; *(de tela)* ribbon; **c. adhesiva** *o* **autoadhesiva** adhesive *o* sticky tape; **c. aislante** insulating tape; **c. de impresora** printer ribbon; **c. métrica** tape measure; **c. perforada** punched tape (**b**) *(de imagen, sonido, ordenadores)* tape; **c. digital/ magnética** digital/magnetic tape; **c. magnetofónica** recording tape; **c. de vídeo** videotape (**c**) *(mecanismo)* belt; **c. transportadora** conveyor belt (**d**) *(película)* film

**cinto** *nm* belt

**cintura** *nf* waist; *Fam Fig* **meter en c.** to bring under control

**cinturilla** *nf* waistband

**cinturón** *nm* (**a**) *(cinto)* belt; *Fig* **apretarse el c.** to tighten one's belt; *Dep* **c. negro** black belt (**b**) *(área circundante)* belt; **c. industrial/verde** industrial/green belt (**c**) *Aut* ring road (**d**) *(en coche, avión)* **c. de seguridad** seat *o* safety belt

**ciñera** *etc ver* **ceñir**

**ciño** *etc ver* **ceñir**

**cipote¹** *nm* (a) *Fam (bobo)* dimwit, moron (b) *Vulg (pene)* prick, cock

**cipote²**, **-a** *nm,f CAm* kid

**ciprés** (*pl* **cipreses**) *nm* cypress

**CIR** *nm* (*abrev de* **Centro de Instrucción de Reclutas**) = Spanish training centre for new army recruits

**circense** *adj* circus; **artista c.** circus performer; **espectáculo c.** circus show

**circo** *nm* (a) *(espectáculo)* circus (b) *Geog* cirque, corrie

**circuito** *nm* (a) *Dep & Elec* circuit; **c. cerrado** closed circuit; **c. impreso/integrado** printed/integrated circuit (b) *(contorno)* belt (c) *(viaje)* tour

**circulación** *nf* (a) *(movimiento) también Fin* circulation; **tiene problemas de c.** *(de la sangre)* he has bad circulation; *Fin* **c. fiduciaria** *o* **monetaria** paper currency (b) *(tráfico)* traffic

**circulante** *adj Fin* **capital c.** working capital

**circular 1** *adj & nf* circular

**2** *vi* (a) *(líquido)* to flow *o* circulate (**por** through); *(persona)* to move *o* walk (**por** around); *(vehículos)* to drive (**por** along); **este autobús no circula hoy** this bus doesn't run today (b) *(de mano en mano)* to circulate; *(moneda)* to be in circulation (c) *(difundirse)* to go round

**circulatorio**, **-a** *adj* (a) *Anat* circulatory (b) *(del tráfico)* traffic; **caos c.** traffic chaos

**círculo** *nm también Fig* circle; **círculos económicos/políticos** economic/political circles; **el c. polar antártico/ártico** the Antarctic/Arctic Circle; **c. vicioso** vicious circle

**circuncidar** *vt* to circumcise

**circuncisión** *nf* circumcision

**circunciso** *adj* circumcised

**circundante** *adj* surrounding

**circundar** *vt* to surround

**circunferencia** *nf* circumference

**circunflejo** *adj* **acento c.** circumflex

**circunlocución** *nf*, **circunloquio** *nm* circumlocution

**circunnavegar** [40] *vt* to circumnavigate, to sail round

**circunscribir 1** *vt* (a) *(limitar)* to restrict, to confine (b) *Geom* to circumscribe

**2 circunscribirse** *vpr* to confine oneself (**a** to)

**circunscripción** *nf* (a) *(limitación)* limitation (b) *(distrito)* district; *Mil* division; *Pol* constituency

**circunscrito**, **-a 1** *participio ver* **circunscribir**

**2** *adj* restricted, limited

**circunspección** *nf Formal* (a) *(comedimiento)* circumspection (b) *(seriedad)* graveness, seriousness

**circunspecto**, **-a** *adj Formal* (a) *(comedido)* circumspect (b) *(serio)* grave, serious

**circunstancia** *nf* circumstance; **en estas circunstancias** under the circumstances; **poner cara de circunstancias** to put on a brave face; *Der* **c. agravante/atenuante/eximente** aggravating/extenuating/exonerating circumstance

**circunstancial** *adj* (a) *(del momento)* chance; **un hecho c.** a chance occurrence; **una decisión c.** an ad hoc decision (b) *Gram* **complemento c.** adjunct

**circunvalación** *nf* (a) *(acción)* going round (b) *(carretera)* ring road

**circunvalar** *vt* to go round

**cirílico**, **-a** *adj* Cyrillic

**cirio** *nm* (a) *(vela)* (wax) candle; **c. pascual** paschal candle (b) *Fam (alboroto)* row, rumpus; **montar un c.** to kick up a row

**cirrosis** *nf inv Med* cirrhosis

**cirrótico**, **-a** *adj Med* cirrhotic; *Fam Fig* **estar c.** to be an alcoholic

**ciruela** *nf* plum; **c. claudia** greengage; **c. pasa** prune

**ciruelo** *nm* plum tree

**cirugía** *nf* surgery; **c. estética/plástica** cosmetic/plastic surgery

**cirujano**, **-a** *nm,f* surgeon

**cisco** *nm* (a) *(carbón)* slack; *Fig* **hecho c.** shattered (b) *Fam (alboroto)* row, rumpus

**Cisjordania** *nf* the West Bank

**cisma** *nm Rel* schism; *Fig (escisión)* split

**cismático**, **-a** *adj & nm,f* schismatic

**cisne** *nm* swan

**cisterciense** *adj & nmf* Cistercian

**cisterna** *nf* (a) *(de retrete)* cistern (b) *(aljibe, tanque)* tank

**cistitis** *nf inv Med* cystitis

**cita** *nf* (a) *(entrevista)* appointment; *(de novios)* date; **darse c.** to meet; **tener una c.** to have an appointment (b) *(referencia)* quotation

**citación** *nf Der* summons *(singular)*

**citar 1** *vt* (a) *(convocar)* to make an appointment with (b) *(aludir)* to mention; *(textualmente)* to quote (c) *Der* to summons

**2 citarse** *vpr* **citarse (con alguien)** to arrange to meet (sb)

**cítara** *nf* zither

**citología** *nf* (a) *Med (análisis ginecológico)* smear test; **hacerse una c.** to have a smear test (b) *Biol* cytology

**citoplasma** *nm Biol* cytoplasm

**cítrico, -a 1** *adj* citric
**2 cítricos** *nmpl* citrus fruits

**CiU** [θiu] *nf* (*abrev de* **Convergència i Unió**) = Catalan coalition party to the right of the political spectrum

**ciudad** *nf* (a) *(localidad) (grande)* city; *(pequeña)* town; **C. del Cabo** Cape Town; **c. dormitorio/satélite** commuter/satellite town; **c. jardín** garden city; **C. de México** Mexico City; **C. del Vaticano** Vatican City; **la C. Eterna** the Eternal City; **la C. Santa** the Holy City (b) *(instalaciones)* complex; **c. sanitaria** hospital complex; **c. universitaria** university campus

**ciudadanía** *nf* (a) *(nacionalidad)* citizenship (b) *(población)* public, citizens

**ciudadano, -a 1** *adj (deberes, conciencia)* civic; *(urbano)* city; **vida c.** city life
**2** *nm,f* citizen; **el c. de a pie** the man in the street

**ciudadela** *nf* citadel, fortress

**ciudadrealeño, -a 1** *adj* of/from Ciudad Real
**2** *nm,f* person from Ciudad Real

**cívico, -a** *adj (deberes, conciencia)* civic; *(conducta)* public-spirited

**civil 1** *adj también Fig* civil
**2** *nmf (no militar)* civilian (b) *Fam (Guardia Civil)* = member of the "Guardia Civil"

**civilización** *nf* civilization

**civilizado, -a** *adj* civilized

**civilizar** [16] **1** *vt* to civilize
**2 civilizarse** *vpr* to become civilized

**civismo** *nm* (a) *(urbanidad)* community spirit (b) *(cortesía)* civility, politeness

**cizalla** *nf* (a) *(herramienta)* shears, metal cutters; *(guillotina)* guillotine (b) *(recortes)* metal cuttings

**cizaña** *nf Bot* darnel; *Fig* **meter *o* sembrar c.** to sow discord; *Fig* **separar la c. del buen grano** to separate the wheat from the chaff

**cl** *(abrev de* **centilitro***)* cl

**clamar 1** *vt (exigir)* to cry out for; **c. justicia** to cry out for justice
**2** *vi* (a) *(implorar)* to appeal (b) *(protestar)* to cry out; *Fig* **es como c. en el desierto** it's like talking to a brick wall

**clamor** *nm* clamour

**clamoroso, -a** *adj* (a) *(victoria, éxito)* resounding (b) *(protesta, llanto)* loud, clamorous

**clan** *nm* (a) *(tribu, familia)* clan (b) *(banda)* faction

**clandestinidad** *nf* secrecy; **en la c.** underground

**clandestino, -a** *adj* clandestine; *Pol* underground

**claque** *nf* claque

**claqué** *nm* tap dancing

**claqueta** *nf* clapperboard

**clara** *nf* (a) *(de huevo)* white (b) *Fam (bebida)* shandy

**claraboya** *nf* skylight

**clarear 1** *vt* to light up
**2** *v impersonal* (a) *(amanecer)* **empezaba a c.** dawn was breaking (b) *(despejarse)* to clear up, to brighten up; **saldremos cuando claree** we'll go out when it clears up
**3 clarearse** *vpr (transparentarse)* to be see-through

**clarete 1** *adj* **vino c.** light red wine
**2** *nm* light red wine

**claridad** *nf* (a) *(transparencia)* clearness, clarity (b) *(luz)* light (c) *(franqueza)* candidness; **ser de una c. meridiana** to be crystal clear (d) *(lucidez)* clarity

**clarificación** *nf* clarification

**clarificador, -ora** *adj* clarifying

**clarificar** [61] *vt* (a) *(aclarar)* to clarify; *(misterio)* to clear up (b) *(purificar)* to refine

**clarín 1** *nm (instrumento)* bugle
**2** *nmf (persona)* bugler

**clarinete 1** *nm (instrumento)* clarinet
**2** *nmf (persona)* clarinettist

**clarinetista** *nmf* clarinettist

**clarividencia** *nf* farsightedness, perception

**clarividente 1** *adj* farsighted, perceptive
**2** *nmf* perceptive person

**claro, -a 1** *adj* (a) *(en general)* clear; **está c. que...** of course...; **¿está c.?** is that clear?; **dejar algo c.** to make sth clear; **a las claras** clearly; **está más c. que el agua** it's perfectly *o* crystal clear; *Fig* **pasar una noche en c.** to have a sleepless night; **poner algo en c.** to get sth clear, to clear sth up; **sacar algo en c. (de)** to make sth out (from)
(b) *(luminoso)* bright
(c) *(color)* light
(d) *(diluido, té, café)* weak; *(salsa)* thin
(e) *(poco tupido)* thin, sparse
**2** *nm* (a) *(en bosque)* clearing; *(en multitud)* space, gap; *(en cielo nublado)* break in the clouds; **se esperan nubes y claros** it will be cloudy with some bright spells
(b) **c. de luna** moonlight
**3** *adv* **claro** clearly; **¡c.!** of course!; **¡c. que sí!** of course!; **¡c. que no!** of course not!; **hablar c.** to speak clearly

**claroscuro** *nm* chiaroscuro

**clase** *nf* (**a**) *(grupo, categoría)* class; **c. alta/media** upper/middle class; **c. obrera** *o* **trabajadora** working class; **clases pasivas** = pensioners and people on benefit; **c. preferente/turista** club/tourist class; **primera c.** first class

(**b**) *(tipo)* sort, kind; **toda c. de** all sorts *o* kinds of

(**c**) *Educ (asignatura, alumnos)* class; *(aula)* classroom; **dar clases** *(en un colegio)* to teach; *(en una universidad)* to lecture; **faltar a c.** to miss school; **hoy tengo c.** *(en colegio)* I have to go to school today; *(en universidad)* I've got lectures today; **clases de conducir** driving lessons; **clases particulares** private tuition

(**d**) *(estilo)* **tener c.** to have class

**clasicismo** *nm* (**a**) *Arte & Lit* classicism (**b**) *(carácter de obra, autor)* classical nature

**clásico, -a 1** *adj* (**a**) *(de la Antigüedad)* classical (**b**) *(ejemplar, prototípico)* classic (**c**) *(peinado, estilo, música)* classical (**d**) *(habitual)* customary (**e**) *(peculiar)* **c. de** typical of

**2** *nm,f (escritor)* classic

**clasificación** *nf* classification; *Dep (liga)* (league) table

**clasificador, -ora 1** *adj* classifying

**2** *nm (mueble)* filing cabinet

**clasificadora** *nf (máquina)* sorter

**clasificar** [61] **1** *vt* to classify

**2 clasificarse** *vpr* (**a**) *(ganar acceso)* to qualify (**para** for); *Dep* to get through (**para** to) (**b**) *(llegar)* **se clasificó en segundo lugar** she came second

**clasismo** *nm* class discrimination

**clasista 1** *adj* class-conscious; *Pey* snobbish

**2** *nmf* class-conscious person; *Pey* snob

**claudia** *adj* **ciruela c.** greengage

**claudicación** *nf Formal (cesión, rendición)* capitulation, surrender

**claudicar** [61] *vi Formal (ceder, rendirse)* to capitulate, to give up

**claustro** *nm* (**a**) *Arquit* cloister (**b**) *(en universidad)* senate (**c**) *(en instituto, colegio) (profesores)* teaching staff; *(reunión)* ≃ staff meeting (**d**) **c. materno** *(matriz)* womb

**claustrofobia** *nf* claustrophobia

**claustrofóbico, -a** *adj* claustrophobic

**cláusula** *nf* clause

**clausura** *nf* (**a**) *(acto solemne)* closing ceremony (**b**) *(cierre)* closing down (**c**) *(aislamiento)* enclosed life, enclosure; *Rel* **convento/monja de c.** convent/nun of an enclosed order

**clausurar** *vt* (**a**) *(acto)* to close, to conclude (**b**) *(local)* to close down

**clavadista** *nmf CAm, Méx* diver

**clavado, -a 1** *adj* (**a**) *(con clavos)* nailed (**b**) *(en punto)* **a las cuatro clavadas** at four o'clock

on the dot (**c**) *(a la medida)* just right (**d**) *(parecido)* almost identical; **ser c. a alguien** to be the spitting image of sb (**e**) *(fijo)* fixed

**2** *nf* **clavada** *Fam (precio abusivo)* rip-off

**clavar 1** *vt* (**a**) *(clavo, estaca)* to drive; *(cuchillo)* to thrust; *(chincheta, alfiler)* to stick (**b**) *(letrero, placa)* to nail, to fix (**c**) *Fig (mirada, atención)* to fix, to rivet; **c. los ojos en** to stare at (**d**) *Fam (cobrar)* **me han clavado mil pesetas** they stung me for a thousand pesetas; **en esa tienda te clavan** they charge you an arm and a leg in that shop

**2 clavarse** *vpr (hincarse)* **me clavé una astilla en el pie** I got a splinter in my foot

**clave 1** *adj inv* key

**2** *nm Mús* harpsichord

**3** *nf* (**a**) *(código)* code; **en c.** in code; **c. de acceso** access code (**b**) *Fig (solución)* key (**c**) *Mús* clef; **c. de sol/fa** treble/bass clef (**d**) *Informát* key

**clavecín** *nm* spinet

**clavel** *nm* carnation

**clavellina** *nf* small carnation, pink

**claveteado** *nm* studding

**clavetear** *vt* (**a**) *(adornar con clavos)* to stud (with nails) (**b**) *(poner clavos)* to nail *(roughly)*

**clavicémbalo** *nm* harpsichord

**clavicordio** *nm* clavichord

**clavícula** *nf* collar bone

**clavija** *nf* (**a**) *Elec* pin; *(de auriculares, teléfono)* jack (**b**) *Mús* peg (**c**) *Fam Fig* **apretar las clavijas a alguien** to put the screws on sb

**clavo** *nm* (**a**) *(pieza metálica)* nail; *Fam Fig* **agarrarse a un c. ardiendo** to clutch at straws; **estaré allí como un c.** I'll be there on the dot; *Fam* **dar en el c.** to hit the nail on the head (**b**) *(especia)* clove (**c**) *Fam (precio abusivo)* rip-off (**d**) *Med (para huesos)* pin

**claxon** *(pl* **cláxones***) nm* horn; **tocar el c.** to sound the horn

**clemencia** *nf* mercy, clemency

**clemente** *adj (persona)* merciful, clement; *Fig (invierno)* mild

**clementina** *nf* clementine

**cleptomanía** *nf* kleptomania

**cleptómano, -a** *nm,f* kleptomaniac

**clerecía** *nf* (**a**) *(clero)* clergy (**b**) *(oficio)* priesthood

**clerical 1** *adj* clerical

**2** *nmf* clericalist

**clérigo** *nm (católico)* priest; *(anglicano)* clergyman

**clero** *nm* clergy

**clic, click** *nm Informát* click; **hacer c.** to click; **hacer doble c.** to double click

**cliché** nm (a) Fot negative (b) Imprenta plate (c) Fig (tópico) cliché

**cliente, -a** nm,f (de tienda, garaje, bar) customer; (de banco, abogado) también Informát client; (de hotel) guest; **el c. siempre tiene razón** the customer is always right

**clientela** nf (de tienda, garaje) customers; (de banco, abogado) clients; (de hotel) guests; (de bar, restaurante) clientele

**clientelismo** nm Pol = practice of giving preferential treatment to a particular interest group in exchange for its support

**clima** nm también Fig climate

**climaterio** nm Med menopause

**climático, -a** adj climatic

**climatización** nf air conditioning

**climatizado, -a** adj air-conditioned; **piscina climatizada** heated swimming pool

**climatizar** [16] vt to air-condition

**climatología** nf (a) (tiempo) climate (b) (ciencia) climatology

**climatológico, -a** adj climatological

**clímax** nm inv climax

**clínica** nf clinic

**clínico, -a 1** adj clinical

**2** nm,f doctor

**clip** nm (a) (para papel) paper clip (b) (para el pelo) hairclip (c) (videoclip) (video) clip

**clíper** nm clipper

**clisé** nm (a) Fot negative (b) Imprenta plate (c) Fig (tópico) cliché

**clítoris** nm inv clitoris

**cloaca** nf sewer

**clon** nm clone

**clonación** nf cloning

**clonar** vt to clone

**clónico, -a 1** adj cloned

**2** nm Informát (ordenador) clone

**cloquear** vi to cluck

**cloración** nf chlorination

**clorar** vt to chlorinate

**clorato** nm Quím chlorate

**clorhídrico** adj Quím **ácido c.** hydrochloric acid

**clórico, -a** adj Quím chloric

**cloro** nm Quím chlorine

**clorofila** nf Bot chlorophyll

**cloroformo** nm Quím chloroform

**cloruro** nm Quím chloride; **c. de cal** bleaching powder; **c. de sodio** o **sódico** sodium chloride

**clown** (pl clowns) nm clown

**club** (pl clubs o clubes) nm (a) (sociedad) club; **c. de fans** fan club; **c. náutico** yacht club (b) (local de alterne) = roadside bar and brothel

**clueca** adj broody

**cm** (abrev de **centímetro**) cm

**CNT** nf (abrev de **Confederación Nacional del Trabajo**) = Spanish anarchist trade union federation created in 1911

**Co.** (abrev de **compañía**) Co.

**coacción** nf coercion

**coaccionar** vt to coerce

**coactivo, -a** adj coercive

**coadyuvar** vi Formal **c. en algo/a hacer algo** to contribute to sth/to doing sth

**coagulación** nf Med clotting, coagulation

**coagulante** Med **1** adj clotting

**2** nm clotting agent

**coagular 1** vt (sangre) to clot, to coagulate; (líquido) to coagulate

**2 coagularse** vpr (sangre) to clot; (líquido) to coagulate

**coágulo** nm Med clot

**coalición** nf coalition

**coaligar** [40] **1** vt to ally, to unite

**2 coligarse** vpr to unite, to join together

**coartada** nf alibi

**coartar** vt to limit, to restrict

**coaseguro** nm coinsurance

**coautor, -ora** nm,f coauthor

**coaxial** adj coaxial

**coba** nf Fam (halago) flattery; **dar c. a alguien** (hacer la pelota) to suck up o crawl to sb; (aplacar) to soft-soap sb

**cobalto** nm cobalt

**cobarde 1** adj cowardly

**2** nmf coward

**cobardía** nf cowardice

**cobaya** nmf también Fig guinea pig

**cobertizo** nm (a) (tejado adosado) lean-to (b) (caseta) shed

**cobertor** nm bedspread

**cobertura** nf (a) (cubierta) cover (b) (de un servicio) coverage; **c. informativa** news coverage; **c. nacional/regional** national/regional coverage (c) (de un seguro) cover

**cobija** nf Am blanket

**cobijar 1** vt (a) (albergar) to house (b) (proteger) to shelter

**2 cobijarse** vpr to take shelter

**cobijo** nm shelter; Fig (protección) protection, shelter; **dar c. a alguien** to give shelter to sb, to take sb in

**cobista** nmf Fam creep

**Cobol** nm Informát COBOL

**cobra** nf cobra

**cobrador, -ora** nm,f (del autobús) conductor, f conductress; (de deudas, recibos) collector

**cobrar 1** vt (a) Com (dinero) to charge; (cheque) to cash; (deuda) to collect; **cantidades por c.**

amounts due; **¿me** o **se cobra, por favor?** how much do I owe you?; **me cobró de más** he overcharged me **(b)** *(en el trabajo)* to earn, to be paid **(c)** *(adquirir)* to take on, to acquire; **c. fama** to become famous **(d)** *(sentir)* **cobrarle afecto** o **cariño a alguien** to take a liking to sb

**2** *vi* **(a)** *(en el trabajo)* to get paid **(b)** *Fam (recibir una paliza)* **¡vas a c.!** you'll catch it!

**3 cobrarse** *vpr* **el accidente se cobró nueve vidas** nine people were killed in the crash

**cobre** *nm* copper; *Am* **no tener un c.** to be flat broke

**cobrizo, -a** *adj (pelo, piel)* copper

**cobro** *nm (de talón)* cashing; *(de pago)* collection; **llamar a c. revertido a alguien** *Br* to make a reverse-charge call to sb, *US* to call sb collect

**coca** *nf* **(a)** *(planta)* coca **(b)** *Fam (cocaína)* coke

**Coca-Cola**® *nf* Coca-Cola®, Coke®

**cocaína** *nf* cocaine

**cocainómano, -a** *nm,f* cocaine addict

**cocción** *nf (de alimentos)* cooking; *(en agua)* boiling; *(en horno)* baking

**cóccix** *nm inv* coccyx

**cocear** *vi* to kick

**cocer** [17] **1** *vt* **(a)** *(alimentos)* to cook; *(hervir)* to boil; *(en horno)* to bake **(b)** *(cerámica, ladrillos)* to fire

**2 cocerse** *vpr (alimentos)* to cook; *(hervir)* to boil; *(en horno)* to bake; *Prov* **en todas partes cuecen habas** it's the same wherever you go; *Fig* **¿qué se cuece por aquí?** what's cooking?, what's going on here?

**cochambre** *nf Fam (suciedad)* filth; *(basura)* rubbish

**cochambroso, -a** *adj Fam* filthy

**cochayuyo** *nm Andes* seaweed

**coche** *nm* **(a)** *(automóvil)* car, *US* automobile; **ir en c.** to drive; **viajar en c.** to travel by car; *Fam Fig* **ir en el c. de San Fernando** to go on foot; **c. bomba** car bomb; **c. de bomberos** fire engine; **c. de carreras** racing car; **c. celular** police van; **c. deportivo** sports car; **c. familiar** estate car; **c. fúnebre** hearse; **c. grúa** *Br* breakdown truck, *US* tow truck; **c. patrulla** patrol car; **coches de choque** Dodgems®, bumper cars

**(b)** *(de caballos)* carriage

**(c)** *(de niño) Br* pram, *US* baby carriage

**(d)** *(de tren)* coach, *Br* carriage, *US* car; **c. cama** sleeping car, sleeper; **c. restaurante** restaurant o dining car

**cochecito** *nm (de niño) Br* pram, *US* baby carriage

**cochera** *nf (para coches)* garage; *(de autobuses, tranvías)* depot

**cochero** *nm* coachman

**cochinada** *nf* **(a)** *(cosa sucia)* filthy thing; **es una c.** it's filthy; *Fig* **hacer cochinadas** *(porquerías)* to be disgusting; *(sexuales)* to be naughty **(b)** *Fig (grosería)* obscenity, dirty word **(c)** *Fig (mala jugada)* dirty trick

**cochinilla** *nf* **(a)** *(crustáceo)* woodlouse **(b)** *(insecto)* cochineal

**cochinillo** *nm* suckling pig

**cochino, -a 1** *adj (sucio)* filthy; *Fam (maldito)* bloody; **¡está obsesionado con el c. dinero!** with him it's always money, money, money!

**2** *nm,f (animal)* pig, *f* sow

**cocido 1** *adj (a) (alimentos)* cooked; *(hervido)* boiled **(b)** *(barro)* fired

**2** *nm Culin* stew; **c. madrileño** = chickpea stew, containing meat, sausage and potatoes

**cociente** *nm* quotient; **c. intelectual** IQ

**cocina** *nf* **(a)** *(habitación)* kitchen **(b)** *(electrodoméstico)* cooker, stove; **c. eléctrica/de gas** electric/gas cooker **(c)** *(arte)* cooking; **c. española** Spanish cuisine o cooking; **libro/clase de c.** cookery book/class

**cocinar 1** *vt* to cook; **¿qué se cocina por aquí?** what's cooking?, what's going on here?

**2** *vi* to cook

**cocinero, -a** *nm,f* cook; *Fig* **ha sido c. antes que fraile** he's got experience on the subject

**cocker** ['koker] *(pl* cockers) *nm* cocker spaniel

**coco** *nm* **(a)** *(fruto)* coconut **(b)** *Fam (cabeza)* nut, head; **comerse el c.** to worry (one's head); **comerle el c. a alguien** *(convencer)* to brainwash sb **(c)** *Fam (fantasma)* bogeyman **(d)** *Biol (bacteria)* coccus

**cococha** *nf* barbel

**cocodrilo** *nm* crocodile

**cocotero** *nm* coconut palm

**cóctel, coctel** *nm* **(a)** *(bebida, comida)* cocktail **(b)** *(reunión)* cocktail party **(c)** **c. molotov** petrol bomb, Molotov cocktail

**coctelera** *nf* cocktail shaker

**coda** *nf Mús* coda

**codazo** *nm (suave)* nudge; *(fuerte)* jab *(with one's elbow)*; **abrirse paso a codazos** to elbow one's way through; **dar un c. a alguien** to nudge/elbow sb

**codearse** *vpr* to rub shoulders **(con** with)

**codeína** *nf* codeine

**codera** *nf* elbow patch

**códice** *nm* codex

**codicia** *nf* **(a)** *(de riqueza)* greed **(b)** *Fig (de aprender, saber)* thirst **(de** for)

**codiciar** [15] *vt* to covet

**codicioso, -a** *adj* greedy

**codificación** *nf* (a) *(de norma, ley)* codification (b) *(de mensaje en clave)* encoding (c) *Informát* coding

**codificado, -a** *adj (emisión de TV)* scrambled

**codificador, -ora 1** *adj* codifying
**2** *nm (aparato)* scrambler *(for pay TV)*

**codificar** [61] *vt* (a) *(ley)* to codify (b) *(un mensaje)* to encode (c) *Informát* to code

**código** *nm también Informát* code; **c. ASCII** ASCII (code); **c. de barras/de señales** bar/signal code; **c. de circulación** highway code; **c. civil/penal** civil/penal code; *Informát* **códigos de fusión** merge codes; **c. máquina** machine code; **c. mercantil** *o* **de comercio** commercial law; **c. Morse** Morse code; **c. postal** *Br* post code, *US* zip code; **c. territorial** *Br* dialling code, *US* area code

**codillo** *nm* (a) *(en un cuadrúpedo)* upper foreleg; *Culin* knuckle of pork (b) *(de jamón)* shoulder (c) *(de un tubo)* elbow, bend

**codirector, -ora** *nm,f* co-director

**codo** *nm* (a) *(en brazo)* elbow; **tenía los codos sobre la mesa** she was leaning (with her elbows) on the table; **c. con c., c. a c.** side by side; *Fam* **empinar el c.** to booze; *Fam Fig* **hablar por los codos** to talk nineteen to the dozen, to be a chatterbox; *Fam* **hincar** *o* **romperse los codos** *(estudiar)* to study hard (b) *(en tubería)* bend; *(pieza)* elbow joint (c) *(medida)* cubit

**codorniz** *nf* quail

**COE** ['koe] *nm (abrev de* **Comité Olímpico Español**) Spanish Olympic Committee

**COEs** ['koes] *nfpl (abrev de* **Compañía de Operaciones Especiales**) = crack army force trained for special operations

**coedición** *nf* joint publication

**coeditar** *vt* to publish jointly

**coeficiente** *nm (índice)* rate; *Mat & Fís* coefficient; *Fin* **c. de caja** cash ratio; **c. intelectual** *o* **de inteligencia** IQ

**coercer** [42] *vt* to restrict, to constrain

**coerción** *nf* coercion

**coercitivo, -a** *adj* coercive

**coetáneo, -a** *adj & nm,f* contemporary

**coexistencia** *nf* coexistence; **c. pacífica** peaceful coexistence

**coexistente** *adj* coexisting

**coexistir** *vi* to coexist

**cofia** *nf (de enfermera, camarera)* cap; *(de monja)* coif

**cofrade** *nmf (de cofradía religiosa)* brother, *f* sister; *(de cofradía no religiosa)* member

**cofradía** *nf (religiosa)* brotherhood, *f* sisterhood; *(profesional)* guild

**cofre** *nm* (a) *(arca)* chest, trunk (b) *(para joyas)* jewel box

**coger** [54] **1** *vt* (a) *(tomar, agarrar)* to take; **c. a alguien de la mano** to take sb by the hand (b) *(atrapar)* (ladrón, pez, pájaro) to catch; **¿a que no me coges?** bet you can't catch me! (c) *(alcanzar)* (persona, vehículo) to catch up with (d) *(recoger)* (frutos, flores) to pick (e) *(quedarse con)* (propina, empleo, piso) to take; **llegaremos pronto para c. buen sitio** we'll get there early to get a good seat (f) *(contratar)* (personal) to take on (g) *(quitar)* (quitar) (c. a alguien from sb); **¿quién me ha cogido el lápiz?** who's taken my pencil? (h) *(tren, autobús)* to take, to catch; **no me gusta c. el avión** I don't like flying (i) *(contraer)* (gripe, resfriado) to catch, to get; **c. una borrachera** to get drunk; **c. frío** to get cold (j) *(sentir)* (manía, odio, afecto) to start to feel; **c. cariño/miedo a** to become fond/scared of (k) *(cobrar)* (fuerzas) to build up one's strength; **c. velocidad** to gather speed (l) *(sujeto: vehículo)* to knock over, to run over; *(sujeto: toro)* to gore (m) *(oír)* to catch; *(entender)* to get; **no cogió el chiste** he didn't get the joke (n) *(sorprender, encontrar)* **c. a alguien haciendo algo** to catch sb doing sth; **c. a alguien desprevenido** to take sb by surprise (o) *(sintonizar)* (canal, emisora) to get, to receive (p) *(abarcar)* (espacio) to cover, to take up (q) *Am Vulg* to screw, to fuck

**2** *vi* (a) *(situarse)* to be; **coge muy cerca de aquí** it's not very far from here (b) *(dirigirse)* **c. a la derecha/la izquierda** to turn right/left (c) **cogió y se fue** he upped and went; **de pronto cogió y me insultó** she turned round and insulted me

**3 cogerse** *vpr* (a) *(asirse)* **cogerse de** *o* **a algo** to cling to *o* clutch sth (b) *(pillarse)* **cogerse los dedos/la falda con la puerta** to catch one's fingers/skirt in the door; *Fam* **cogerse un cabreo** to throw a fit; **cogerse una gripe** to catch the flu

**cogestión** *nf* joint management, comanagement

**cogida** *nf (de torero)* goring

**cognac** [ko'nak] *(pl* **cognacs**) *nm* brandy, cognac

**cogollo** *nm* (a) *(de lechuga)* heart (b) *(brote)* shoot

**cogorza** *nf Fam* **agarrar una c.** to get smashed, to get blind drunk

**cogotazo** *nm* rabbit punch

**cogote** *nm* nape, back of the neck

**cogulla** *nf Rel* habit

**cohabitación** *nf* cohabitation

**cohabitar** *vi* to cohabit, to live together

**cohecho** *nm* bribery

**coherencia** *nf (de conducta, estilo)* consistency; *(de razonamiento)* coherence

**coherente** *adj (conducta, estilo)* consistent; *(razonamiento)* coherent

**cohesión** *nf* cohesion; **la c. del partido** party unity

**cohesivo, -a** *adj* cohesive

**cohete** *nm* rocket; **cohetes** *(fuegos artificiales)* fireworks

**cohibición** *nf* inhibition

**cohibido, -a** *adj* inhibited

**cohibir 1** *vt* to inhibit

**2 cohibirse** *vpr* to become inhibited

**cohorte** *nf* cohort

**COI** ['koi] *nm (abrev de* **Comité Olímpico Internacional)** IOC

**coima** *nf Andes, CSur Fam* bribe

**coincidencia** *nf* coincidence

**coincidir** *vi* **(a)** *(superficies, versiones, gustos)* to coincide **(b)** *(estar de acuerdo)* to agree; **coincidimos en opinar que...** we both agreed that... **(c)** *(en un sitio)* **coincidimos en la fiesta** we were both at the party

**coito** *nm* (sexual) intercourse

**coitus interruptus** *nm inv* coitus interruptus

**cojear** *vi* **(a)** *(persona)* to limp; *Fam Fig* **ya sé de qué pie cojea María** I know Maria's weak points **(b)** *(mueble)* to wobble **(c)** *Fig (argumento)* to be faulty

**cojera** *nf (acción)* limp; *(estado)* lameness

**cojín** *nm* cushion

**cojinete** *nm (en eje)* bearing; *(en un riel de ferrocarril)* chair

**cojo, -a 1** *ver* **coger**

**2** *adj* **(a)** *(persona)* lame **(b)** *(mueble)* wobbly **(c)** *Fig (razonamiento, frase)* faulty

**3** *nm,f* cripple

**cojones** *nmpl Vulg* balls; **¡ahora lo vas a hacer por c.!** you bloody well are going to do it!; **es bueno/malo de c.** it's fucking marvellous/awful; **¡no me sale de los c.!** I can't be fucking bothered!, *Br* I can't be arsed!; **tener c.** to have balls *o* guts; **¡c.!** *(enfado)* for fuck's sake!

**cojonudo, -a** *adj muy Fam* bloody brilliant

**cojudear** *vt Andes, CSur Fam* **(a)** *(hacer tonterías)* to piss about, to muck about **(b)** *(engañar)* to trick

**cojudez** *nf Andes, CSur muy Fam* rubbish, stupidity; **decir cojudeces** to talk nonsense

**cojudo, -a** *adj Andes, CSur muy Fam* bloody stupid

**col** *nf* cabbage; **coles de Bruselas** Brussels sprouts; **c. lombarda** red cabbage

**cola** *nf* **(a)** *(de animal, avión)* tail

**(b)** *(de vestido de novia)* train

**(c)** *(fila) Br* queue, *US* line; **hacer c.** *Br* to queue (up), *US* to stand in line; **¡a la c.!** go to the back of the *Br* queue *o US* line!; *Informát* **c. de impresión** printing queue

**(d)** *(pegamento)* glue; *Fam Fig* **no pegan ni con c.** they don't match at all

**(e)** *(de clase, lista)* bottom; *(de desfile)* end; **ir a la c. del pelotón** to be one of the backmarkers; *Fam Fig* **tener** *o* **traer c.** to have serious consequences *o* repercussions

**(f)** *(bebida)* cola

**(g)** *(peinado)* **c. (de caballo)** ponytail

**(h)** *Fam (pene)* willy

**colaboración** *nf* **(a)** *(cooperación)* collaboration; **hacer algo en c. con alguien** to do sth in collaboration with sb **(b)** *(de prensa)* contribution, article

**colaboracionismo** *nm Pol* collaborationism

**colaboracionista** *Pol* **1** *adj* collaborationist

**2** *nmf* collaborator

**colaborador, -ora 1** *adj* cooperative

**2** *nm,f (compañero)* associate, colleague; *(de prensa)* contributor, writer; **c. externo** freelancer

**colaborar** *vi* **(a)** *(ayudar)* to collaborate **(b)** *(en prensa)* **c. en** *o* **con** to write for, to work for **(c)** *(contribuir)* to contribute

**colación** *nf* **(a)** *(para comer)* snack **(b)** *Fam* **sacar** *o* **traer algo a c.** *(tema)* to bring sth up

**colada** *nf (ropa)* laundry; **hacer la c.** to do the washing

**coladero** *nm Fam* easy way through

**colado, -a** *adj* **(a)** *(líquido)* strained **(b)** *Fam (enamorado)* **estar c. por alguien** to have a crush on sb

**colador** *nm (para líquidos)* strainer, sieve; *(para verdura)* colander

**colágeno** *nm* collagen

**colapsar 1** *vt* to bring to a halt, to stop; **el tráfico ha colapsado las calles** traffic has blocked the streets

**2 colapsarse** *vpr (mercado)* to collapse; **se ha colapsado el tráfico** traffic has ground to a halt

**colapso** *nm* **(a)** *Med* collapse, breakdown **(b)** *(de actividad)* stoppage; *(de tráfico)* traffic jam, hold-up

**colar** [65] **1** *vt* (**a**) *(leche, té)* to strain; *(café)* to filter (**b**) *Fam (dinero falso)* to pass off as genuine; *(mentira)* to slip through (**c**) *(en cola)* **me coló** he let me jump the *Br* queue *o US* line (**d**) *(en fiesta)* **nos coló en la fiesta** he got us into the party (**e**) *(introducir)* to slip, to squeeze (**por** through)

**2** *vi Fam (pasar por bueno)* **esto no colará** this won't wash

**3 colarse** *vpr* (**a**) *(líquido)* **colarse por** to seep through (**b**) *(persona) (en un sitio)* to slip, to sneak; *(en una cola)* to jump the *Br* queue *o US* line; **colarse en una fiesta** to gatecrash a party; **¡eh, no te cueles!** oi, don't jump the queue! (**c**) *Fam (equivocarse)* to slip up

**colateral** *adj* on either side

**colcha** *nf* bedspread

**colchón** *nm* (**a**) *(de cama)* mattress; **c. inflable** *o* **hinchable** air bed (**b**) *Informát* buffer

**colchonero, -a 1** *nm,f* upholsterer, mattress-maker

**2** *adj Dep* = relating to Atlético de Madrid Football Club

**colchoneta** *nf (de playa)* beach mat; *(en gimnasio)* mat

**cole** *nm Fam* school

**colear** *vi* (**a**) *(animal)* to wag its tail (**b**) *Fig (asunto, problema)* to drag on

**colección** *nf también Fig* collection

**coleccionable 1** *adj* collectable

**2** *nm* = special supplement in serialized form

**coleccionar** *vt* to collect

**coleccionista** *nmf* collector

**colecta** *nf* collection; **hacer una c.** to collect money, to organize a collection

**colectividad** *nf* community

**colectivismo** *nm* collectivism

**colectivización** *nf* collectivization

**colectivizar** [16] *vt* to collectivize

**colectivo, -a 1** *adj* collective

**2** *nm* (**a**) *(grupo)* group (**b**) *Am (taxi)* taxi; *(autobús)* minibus

**colector, -ora 1** *adj* collecting

**2** *nm,f (persona)* collector

**3** *nm* (**a**) *(sumidero)* sewer; **c. de basuras** chute (**b**) *Tec (de motor)* manifold (**c**) *(de transistor)* collector

**colega** *nmf* (**a**) *(compañero profesional)* colleague (**b**) *(homólogo)* counterpart, opposite number (**c**) *Fam (amigo)* mate

**colegiado, -a 1** *adj* = who belongs to a professional association

**2** *nm,f Dep* referee

**colegial, -ala** *nm,f* schoolboy, *f* schoolgirl; **cartera/uniforme de c.** school bag/uniform

**colegiarse** [15] *vpr* = to join a professional association

**colegiata** *nf* collegiate church

**colegio** *nm* (**a**) *(escuela)* school; **c. nacional** state primary school; **c. de pago** fee-paying *o* private school (**b**) *(de profesionales)* **c. (profesional)** professional association (**c**) *Pol* **c. electoral** *(lugar)* polling station; *(votantes)* ward (**d**) **c. mayor** hall of residence

**colegir** [57] *vt* to infer (**de** from), to gather (**de** from); **de ahí se puede c. que** it can thus be inferred that

**colegislador, -ora** *adj (asamblea)* joint legislative

**coleóptero** *nm* beetle

**cólera 1** *nm Med* cholera

**2** *nf (ira)* anger, rage; **montar en c.** to get angry, to lose one's temper

**colérico, -a** *adj (furioso)* furious; *(irritable)* bad-tempered; **estar c.** to be furious

**colesterol** *nm* cholesterol

**coleta** *nf* pigtail; *Fig* **cortarse la c.** to call it a day, to retire

**coletazo** *nm* flick *o* swish of the tail; *Fig* **está dando (los últimos) coletazos** it's in its death throes

**coletilla** *nf (de discurso, escrito)* closing comment

**colgado, -a** *adj* (**a**) *(cuadro, jamón)* hanging (**de** from) (**b**) *(teléfono)* on the hook (**c**) *Fam (atontado, loco)* crazy, daft (**d**) *Fam Fig (abandonado)* **dejar c. a alguien** to leave sb in the lurch (**e**) *Fam (enganchado)* **quedarse c. (con)** to get hooked (on) (**f**) *Fam* **tengo c. el inglés del curso pasado** I flunked my English exam last year

**colgador** *nm (percha)* hanger, coathanger; *(gancho)* hook

**colgajo** *nm* (**a**) *(tela)* hanging piece of material; *(hilo)* loose thread (**b**) *(de piel)* flap

**colgante 1** *adj* hanging

**2** *nm* pendant

**colgar** [18] **1** *vt* (**a**) *(suspender, ahorcar)* to hang (**b**) *(teléfono)* **c. el teléfono** to hang up; **me colgó en mitad de la frase** she hung up on me when I was in mid-sentence (**c**) *(imputar)* **c. algo a alguien** to pin the blame for sth on sb (**d**) *(abandonar)* to give up; **c. los hábitos** to leave the priesthood, to give up the cloth; *Fig (renunciar)* to give up one's job; **c. los estudios** to abandon one's studies

**2** *vi* (**a**) *(pender)* to hang (**de** from) (**b**) *(hablando por teléfono)* to hang up, to put the phone down

**3 colgarse** *vpr (suspenderse)* to hang (**de** from); *(ahorcarse)* to hang oneself

**colibrí** *nm* hummingbird

**cólico** nm upset stomach; Med colic; **c. hepático** biliary colic; **c. nefrítico** o **renal** renal colic

**coliflor** nf cauliflower

**coligar** [40] **1** vt to ally, to unite

**2 coligarse** vpr to unite, to join together

**colijo** ver **colegir**

**colilla** nf cigarette butt o stub

**colimba** nf Arg Fam military service

**colín** nm breadstick

**colina** nf hill

**colindante** adj neighbouring, adjacent

**colindar** vi to be adjacent, to adjoin

**colirio** nm eyewash, eyedrops

**coliseo** nm coliseum

**colisión** nf (de vehículos) collision, crash; (de ideas, intereses) clash; **c. múltiple** pileup

**colisionar** vi (a) (coche) to collide (**contra** with), to crash (**contra** into) (b) Fig (ideas) to clash

**colista** nmf (en liga de fútbol) bottom team; (en carreras) tailender

**colitis** nf inv (diarrea) stomach infection

**collado** nm (colina) hill

**collage** [ko'laʃ] nm collage

**collar** nm (a) (para personas) necklace (b) (para animales) collar (c) (abrazadera) collar, ring

**collarín** nm surgical collar

**collera** nf Chile cufflink

**collie** nm collie

**colmado, -a 1** adj full to the brim (**de** with); **está c. de problemas** he is loaded down with problems

**2** nm grocer's (shop)

**colmar** vt (recipiente) to fill (to the brim); Fig (aspiración, deseo) to fulfil; **c. a alguien de regalos/elogios** to shower gifts/praise on sb

**colmena** nf beehive

**colmenar** nm apiary

**colmillo** nm (de persona) canine, eye-tooth; (de perro) fang; (de elefante) tusk; Fig **enseñar los colmillos** to show one's teeth

**colmo** nm height; **el c. de la estupidez** the height of stupidity; **es el c. de la locura** it's sheer madness; **para c. de desgracias** to crown it all; **¡eso es el c.!** that's the last straw!

**colocación** nf (a) (acción) placing, positioning; (situación) place, position (b) (empleo) position, job

**colocado, -a** adj (a) (en lugar) placed; (en empleo) **estar muy bien c.** to have a very good job (b) Fam (drogado) high, stoned; (borracho) blind drunk, smashed

**colocar** [61] **1** vt (a) (en un sitio) to place, to put

(b) (en una posición) **c. los brazos en alto** to raise one's arms

(c) (en un empleo) to find a job for

(d) (casar) to marry off

(e) (invertir) to place, to invest

(f) Fam (sujeto: droga) to give a high to; **¿a ti te coloca la marihuana?** does marihuana give you a high?

**2** vi Fam (droga, alcohol) **este costo coloca cantidad** this hash gives you a real high; **este ponche coloca mucho** this punch is strong stuff

**3 colocarse** vpr (a) (en una posición, en un lugar) (de pie) to stand; (sentado) to sit

(b) (en un trabajo) to get a job

(c) Fam (emborracharse) to get blind drunk o smashed; (drogarse) to get high o stoned

**colofón** nm (a) (remate, fin) climax, culmination (b) (de libro) colophon

**coloide** adj colloid

**Colombia** n Colombia

**colombianismo** nm Colombian expression

**colombiano, -a** adj & nm,f Colombian

**colombino, -a** adj = relating to Christopher Columbus

**Colombo** n Colombo

**colombofilia** nf pigeon-fancying

**colon** nm colon

**colón** nm colon (unit of currency in Costa Rica and El Salvador)

**Colonia** n Cologne

**colonia** nf (a) (estado dependiente) colony (b) (de niños) **c. (de verano)** (summer) camp; **ir de colonias** to go on a summer camp (c) (perfume) eau de cologne; **me gusta la c. que usa tu novio** I like your boyfriend's aftershave (d) (barrio) district; Méx **c. proletaria** shanty town, slum area

**colonial** adj colonial

**colonialismo** nm colonialism

**colonialista** adj & nmf colonialist

**colonización** nf colonization

**colonizador, -ora 1** adj colonizing

**2** nm,f colonizer, colonist

**colonizar** [16] vt to colonize

**colono** nm settler, colonist

**coloque** etc ver **colocar**

**coloquial** adj colloquial

**coloquio** nm (a) (conversación) conversation (b) (debate) discussion, debate

**color** nm (a) (que se ve) colour; **¿de qué c.?** what colour?; **de c.** (persona) coloured; **es de c. azul** it's blue; **de colores** colourful; **televisión en c.** colour television; **c. azul** blue; **c. rojo** red; **c. local** local colour; **c. primario** primary colour; **colores complementarios**

complementary colours; *Fig* **defender los colores del Barça** *(el equipo)* to play for Barcelona

**(b)** *Fig (aspecto)* tone; **no tienes muy buen c.** you look a bit off-colour

**(c)** *(para pintar)* paint; **colores** *(lápices)* coloured pencils

**(d)** *(en los naipes)* suit

**(e)** *(expresiones)* **dar c. a algo** to colour sth in; *Fig* to brighten *o* liven sth up; **no hay c.** it's no contest; **sacarle** *o* **salirle a alguien los colores (a la cara)** to make sb blush; **ver las cosas de c. de rosa** to see things through rose-coloured *o* rose-tinted spectacles

**colorado, -a 1** *adj (color)* red; **ponerse c.** to blush, to go red

**2** *nm (color)* red

**colorante** *nm* colouring

**colorear** *vt* to colour (in)

**colorete** *nm (maquillaje)* rouge, blusher; *Andes (de labios)* lipstick; **tener coloretes** to be red in the face

**colorido** *nm* colourfulness; *Fig* **una fiesta de gran c.** a very colourful local festival

**colorín** *nm* bright colour; **de colorines** brightly coloured; **c. colorado, este cuento se ha acabado** and they all lived happily ever after

**colorista** *adj* colouristic

**colosal** *adj* **(a)** *(estatura, tamaño)* colossal **(b)** *(extraordinario)* great, enormous

**coloso** *nm (estatua)* colossus; *Fig (cosa, persona)* giant

**colt®** [kolt] *nm* Colt®; **un c. del 45** a Colt 45

**columna** *nf (en edificio, de soldados, de texto)* column; *Fig (pilar)* pillar; **c. vertebral** spinal column; **quinta c.** fifth column

**columnata** *nf* colonnade

**columnista** *nmf* columnist

**columpiar** [15] **1** *vt* to swing

**2 columpiarse** *vpr* to swing

**columpio** *nm* swing; **los columpios** *nm* children's playground

**colza** *nf* rape; **aceite de c.** rapeseed oil

**coma 1** *nm Med* coma; **en c.** in a coma

**2** *nf* **(a)** *Gram* comma; *Fig* **sin faltar una c.** word for word **(b)** *Mat* ≃ decimal point

**comadre** *nf (mujer chismosa)* gossip, gossipmonger; *(vecina)* neighbour

**comadrear** *vi* to gossip

**comadreja** *nf* weasel

**comadreo** *nm* gossip

**comadrona** *nf* midwife

**comandancia** *nf* **(a)** *(rango)* command **(b)** *(edificio)* command headquarters

**comandante** *nm Mil (rango)* major; *(de un puesto)* commander, commandant; *(de avión)* captain; **c. en jefe** commander-in-chief

**comandar** *vt Mil* to command

**comando** *nm* **(a)** *Mil* commando; **c. suicida** suicide squad; **c. terrorista** terrorist cell **(b)** *Informát* command

**comarca** *nf* area, district; **una c. arrocera** a rice-growing region *o* area

**comarcal** *adj* local; **un problema de ámbito c.** a local problem

**comatoso, -a** *adj* comatose

**comba** *nf* **(a)** *(juego)* skipping; **jugar a la c.** to skip, *US* to jump rope **(b)** *(cuerda)* skipping rope

**combado, -a** *adj* warped

**combadura** *nf (de alambre, barra)* bend; *(de pared)* bulge; *(de viga)* sag

**combar 1** *vt* to warp

**2 combarse** *vpr* to warp

**combate** *nm (lucha)* fight; *(batalla)* battle; *también Fig* **dejar a alguien fuera de c.** to knock sb out

**combatiente** *nmf* combatant, fighter

**combatir 1** *vt* to combat, to fight; **un producto para c. la caries** a product which fights tooth decay

**2** *vi* to fight **(contra** against)

**combatividad** *nf* fighting spirit

**combativo, -a** *adj* aggressive, combative

**combi** *nm* **(a)** *(frigorífico)* fridge-freezer **(b)** *Am (autobús)* minibus

**combinación** *nf* **(a)** *(unión)* combination; **una c. explosiva** an explosive combination **(b)** *(de bebidas)* cocktail **(c)** *(de caja fuerte)* combination **(d)** *Quím* compound **(e)** *(prenda)* slip **(f)** *(plan)* scheme **(g)** *(de medios de transporte)* connections; **no hay buena c. para ir de aquí allí** there's no easy way of getting there from here

**combinado 1** *adj (con distintos elementos)* combined

**2** *nm* **(a)** *(bebida)* cocktail **(b)** *Dep* combined team

**combinar** *vt* **(a)** *(mezclar)* to combine **(b)** *(bebidas)* to mix **(c)** *(colores)* to match **(d)** *(planificar)* to arrange, to organize

**combinatoria** *nf Mat* combinatorial analysis

**combustible 1** *adj* combustible

**2** *nm* fuel

**combustión** *nf* combustion

**comecocos** *nm inv* **(a)** *Fam (para convencer)* **este panfleto es un c.** this pamphlet is designed to brainwash you **(b)** *Fam (cosa difícil de* *comprender)* mind-bending problem *o* puzzle (**c**) *(juego)* pac-man®

**comedero** *nm* trough

**comedia** *nf* comedy; *Fig (engaño)* farce; **c. musical** musical (comedy)

**comediante, -a** *nm,f* actor, *f* actress; *Fig (farsante)* fraud

**comedido, -a** *adj* moderate, restrained

**comedimiento** *nm* moderation, restraint

**comediógrafo, -a** *nm,f* playwright, dramatist

**comedirse** [49] *vpr* to be restrained

**comedor** *nm* (**a**) *(habitación) (de casa)* dining room; *(de fábrica)* canteen (**b**) *(muebles)* dining-room suite

**comendadora** *nf* mother superior

**comensal** *nmf* fellow diner; **los comensales charlaban animadamente** the diners were having a lively conversation

**comentar** *vt (opinar sobre)* to comment on; *(hablar de)* to discuss

**comentario** *nm* (**a**) *(observación)* comment, remark; **sin comentarios** no comment (**b**) *(crítica)* commentary (**c**) **comentarios** *(murmuraciones)* gossip

**comentarista** *nmf* commentator; **c. deportivo** (sports) commentator

**comenzar** [19] **1** *vt* to start, to begin; **c. diciendo que...** to start *o* begin by saying that...

**2** *vi* to start, to begin; **c. a hacer algo** to start doing *o* to do sth; **c. por hacer algo** to begin by doing sth; **el partido comenzó tarde** the game started late

**comer 1** *vt* (**a**) *(alimentos)* to eat; *(al mediodía)* to have for lunch; **no come carne casi nunca** she hardly ever eats meat; **¿qué tenemos hoy de c.?** what's for lunch today?

(**b**) *(en los juegos de tablero)* to take, to capture; **me comió un alfil** he took one of my bishops (**c**) *Fig (consumir)* to eat up; **les come la envidia** they're eaten up with envy; **eso me come mucho tiempo** that takes up a lot of my time (**d**) *(expresiones)* **ni come ni deja c.** he's a dog in the manger; **sin comerlo ni beberlo** *(algo bueno)* through no credit of one's own; *(algo malo)* through no fault of one's own

**2** *vi (ingerir alimentos)* to eat; *(al mediodía)* to have lunch; **c. fuera** to go out for lunch; **dar de c.** to feed

**3 comerse** *vpr* (**a**) *(alimentos)* to eat; **se comió los tres platos** he had all three courses; **comerse las uñas** to bite one's nails; *Fig* **comerse a alguien con los ojos** *o* **con la mirada** to be unable to keep one's eyes off sb; *Fig* **¿y eso cómo se come?** and what are we/am I supposed to make of that?

(**b**) *(desgastar) (recursos)* to eat up; *(metal)* to corrode; **el sol se comió los colores de la ropa** the sun made the clothes fade

(**c**) *(en los juegos de tablero)* to take, to capture

(**d**) *Fam Fig* **se va a c. sus palabras** she'll have to eat her words

**comercial 1** *adj (de empresas)* commercial; *(internacional)* trade; **relaciones comerciales** trade relations

**2** *nmf (vendedor, representante)* sales rep

**comercialización** *nf* marketing

**comercializar** [16] *vt* to market

**comerciante** *nmf* tradesman, *f* tradeswoman; *(tendero)* shopkeeper; **pequeños comerciantes** small businessmen

**comerciar** [15] *vi* to trade, to do business; **c. con armas/pieles** to deal *o* trade in arms/furs

**comercio** *nm* (**a**) *(de productos)* trade; **c. exterior/interior** foreign/domestic trade; **c. justo** fair trade; **libre c.** free trade (**b**) *(actividad)* business, commerce (**c**) *(tienda)* shop

**comestible 1** *adj* edible, eatable

**2** *nmpl* **comestibles** food; **tienda de comestibles** grocer's (shop)

**cometa 1** *nm Astron* comet

**2** *nf* kite

**cometer** *vt (crimen)* to commit; *(error)* to make

**cometido** *nm* (**a**) *(objetivo)* mission, task (**b**) *(deber)* duty

**comezón** *nf* (**a**) *(picor)* **tener c.** to have an itch; **tengo c. en la nariz** I've got an itchy nose (**b**) *Fig (remordimiento)* twinge; *(deseo)* urge, itch

**cómic** *(pl* **cómics)**, **comic** *(pl* **comics)** *nm* (adult) comic

**comicidad** *nf* humorousness

**comicios** *nmpl Pol* elections

**cómico, -a 1** *adj* (**a**) *(de la comedia)* comedy, comic; **actor c.** comedy actor (**b**) *(gracioso)* comic, comical

**2** *nm,f (actor de teatro)* actor, *f* actress; *(humorista)* comedian, comic, *f* comedienne

**comida** *nf* (**a**) *(alimento)* food; **c. casera** home cooking; *Am* **c. corrida** *o* **corriente** set meal (**b**) *(almuerzo, cena)* meal; *(al mediodía)* lunch

**comidilla** *nf Fam* **ser/convertirse en la c.** to be/become the talk of the town

**comidió** *etc ver* **comedirse**

**comienzo 1** *ver* **comenzar**

**2** *nm* start, beginning; **a comienzos del siglo XX** at the beginning of the twentieth century; **dar c. (a algo)** to start (sth), to begin (sth)

**comillas** *nfpl* inverted commas, quotation marks; **entre c.** in inverted commas

**comilón, -ona** *Fam* **1** *adj* greedy

**2** *nm,f (persona)* greedy pig, glutton

**comilona** *nf (festín)* blow-out

**comino** *nm (planta)* cumin, cummin; *Fam Fig* **me importa un c.** I don't give a damn; *Fam Fig* **no vale un c.** it isn't worth tuppence

**comisaría** *nf* police station, *US* precinct

**comisario, -a** *nm,f* **(a) (c. de policía)** police superintendent **(b)** *(delegado)* commissioner; **c. europeo** European Commissioner; **c. político** political commissar

**comisión** *nf* **(a)** *(delegación)* committee, commission; **C. Europea** European Commission; **c. investigadora** committee of inquiry; **c. parlamentaria** parliamentary committee; **c. permanente** standing committee; **c. de servicio** special assignment; **Comisiones Obreras** = Spanish left-wing trade union **(b)** *Com* commission; **(trabajar) a c.** (to work) on a commission basis; *Econ* **c. fija** flat fee; **cobro de comisiones** *(delito)* acceptance of bribes **(c)** *(de un delito)* perpetration

**comisionado, -a** *nm,f* committee member

**comisionar** *vt* to commission

**comisionista** *nmf* commission agent

**comisura** *nf* corner *(of mouth, eyes)*

**comité** *nm* committee; **c. ejecutivo** executive committee; *Ind* **c. de empresa** works council

**comitiva** *nf* retinue

**como** *adv* **(a)** *(comparativo)* **tan... c....** as... as...; **es (tan)** negro como el carbón it's as black as coal; **ser c. algo** to be like sth; **vive c. un rey** he lives like a king; **lo que dijo fue c. para ruborizarse** his words were enough to make you blush

**(b)** *(de la manera que)* as; **lo he hecho c. es debido** I did it as *o* the way it should be done; **me encanta c. bailas** I love the way you dance

**(c)** *(según)* as; **c. te decía ayer...** as I was telling you yesterday...

**(d)** *(en calidad de)* as; **trabaja c. bombero** he works as a fireman; **dieron el dinero c. anticipo** they gave the money as an advance

**(e)** *(aproximadamente)* about; **me quedan c. mil pesetas** I've got about a thousand pesetas left; **estamos c. a mitad de camino** we're about half-way there; **tiene un sabor c. a naranja** it tastes a bit like an orange

**2** *conj* **(a)** *(ya que)* as, since; **c. no llegabas, nos fuimos** as *o* since you didn't arrive, we left

**(b)** *(si)* if; **c. no me hagas caso, lo pasarás mal** if you don't listen to me, there will be trouble

**(c)** *(que)* that; **después de tantas veces c. te lo he explicado** after all the times (that) I've explained it to you

**(d)** *(expresiones)* **le pareció c. que lloraban** it seemed to him (that) they were crying; **pareces cansado – c. que he trabajado toda la noche** you seem tired – well, I've been up all night working; **¡c. que te voy a creer a ti que eres un mentiroso!** as if I'd believe a liar like you!; **c. quiera** *(de cualquier modo)* anyway, anyhow; *(dado que)* since, given that; **c. quiera que** *(de cualquier modo que)* whichever way, however; **c. quiera que sea** whatever the case may be; **c. si** as if

**cómo 1** *adv* **(a)** *(de qué modo, por qué motivo)* how; **¿c. lo has hecho?** how did you do it?; **¿c. son?** what are they like?; **no sé c. has podido decir eso** I don't know how you could say that; **¿c. que no la has visto nunca?** what do you mean you've never seen her?; **¿a c. están los tomates?** how much are the tomatoes?; **¿c.?** *(¿qué dices?)* sorry?, what?; *Fam* **¿c. es eso?** *(¿por qué?)* how come?

**(b)** *(exclamativo)* how; **¡c. pasan los años!** how time flies!; **¡c. no!** of course!; **¡c.! ¿no te has enterado?** what! you mean you haven't heard?; **está lloviendo, ¡y c.!** it's raining like crazy, *Br* it isn't half raining!

**2** *nm* **el c. y el porqué** the whys and wherefores

**cómoda** *nf* chest of drawers

**comodidad** *nf (estado, cualidad)* comfort; *(conveniencia)* convenience; **para su c.** for your convenience; **comodidades** comforts; **el equipo ganó con c.** the team won comfortably *o* easily

**comodín** *nm (naipe)* joker; *Fig (excusa)* well-worn excuse; *Informát* wild card

**cómodo, -a** *adj* **(a)** *(confortable)* comfortable; **estar c.** to feel comfortable **(b)** *(conveniente)* convenient *(c)* *(oportuno, fácil)* easy

**comodón, -ona 1** *adj (amante de la comodidad)* comfort-loving; *(vago)* laid-back; **no seas c.** don't be so lazy

**2** *nm,f (amante de la comodidad)* comfort-lover; *(vago)* laid-back person

**comodoro** *nm* commodore

**comoquiera** *adv* **c. que** *(de cualquier manera que)* whichever way, however; *(dado que)* since, seeing as

**Comores** *nfpl* **las (Islas) C.** the Comoros (Islands)

**compa** *nmf Fam* mate, buddy

**compacto, compact** ['kompak] *(pl compacts) nm* **(a)** *(aparato)* compact disc player **(b)** *(disco)* compact disc, CD

**compactación** *nf Informát* compression; **c. de ficheros** zipping

**compactar** *vt* to compress

**compact disk, compact disc**
['kompak'ðis(k)] (*pl* **compact disks, discs**)
*nm* compact disc

**compacto, -a 1** *adj* compact

**2** *nm (disco)* compact disc, CD

**compadecer** [48] **1** *vt* to pity, to feel sorry
for

**2 compadecerse** *vpr* **compadecerse de**
to pity, to feel sorry for

**compadrazgo** *nm Am* kinship

**compadre** *nm Fam (amigo)* friend, mate

**compadrear** *vi Am* to brag, to boast

**compadreo** *nm Fam (amistad)* friendship

**compaginación** *nf* (a) *(combinación)* rec-
onciling (b) *(en imprenta)* page make-up

**compaginar 1** *vt* (a) *(combinar)* to reconcile
(b) *(en imprenta)* to make up

**2 compaginarse** *vpr* **compaginarse con**
to square with, to go together with

**compañerismo** *nm* comradeship

**compañero, -a** *nm,f* (a) *(acompañante)*
companion (b) *(colega)* colleague; **c. de clase**
classmate; **c. de piso** flatmate (c) *(par)* **el c. de
este guante** the glove that goes with this one

**compañía** *nf también Com* company; **en c.
de** accompanied by, in the company of; **hacer
c. a alguien** to keep sb company

**comparación** *nf* comparison; **en c. con** in
comparison with, compared to; **las c. son
odiosas** comparisons are odious

**comparado, -a** *adj* **c. con** compared to;
**gramática comparada** comparative grammar

**comparar** *vt* to compare (**con** to)

**comparativo, -a** *adj & nm* comparative

**comparecencia** *nf (ante el juez, la prensa)*
appearance

**comparecer** [48] *vi* to appear

**comparsa 1** *nf* (a) *Teatro* extras (b) *(en carnaval)* = group of people at carnival in same
costume and with masks

**2** *nmf* (a) *Teatro* extra (b) *Fig (en carreras, competiciones)* also-ran; **no es más que un c.** he's
just there to make up the numbers

**compartimentar** *vt* to compartmentalize

**compartimento, compartimiento**
*nm* compartment; **c. estanco** watertight compartment

**compartir** *vt* (a) *(ganancias)* to share (out)
(b) *(piso, ideas)* to share

**compás** (*pl* **compases**) *nm* (a) *(instrumento)*
pair of compasses (b) *Náut (brújula)* compass
(c) *Mús (periodo)* bar; *(ritmo)* rhythm, beat; **al c.
(de la música)** in time (with the music); **llevar el c.** to keep time; **perder el c.** to lose the
beat (d) *Fig* **c. de espera** pause, interlude; **las**

**negociaciones se hallan en un c. de
espera** negotiations have been temporarily
suspended

**compasión** *nf* compassion, pity

**compasivo, -a** *adj* compassionate, sympathetic

**compatibilidad** *nf también Informát* compatibility

**compatibilizar** [16] *vt* to make compatible

**compatible** *adj también Informát* compatible

**compatriota** *nmf (hombre)* compatriot, fellow countryman; *(mujer)* compatriot, fellow
countrywoman

**compeler** *vt* to compel, to force

**compendiar** [15] *vt* (a) *(cualidades, características)* to epitomize (b) *(libro, historia)* to
abridge

**compendio** *nm* (a) *(libro)* compendium (b)
*Fig (síntesis)* epitome, essence

**compenetración** *nf* mutual understanding

**compenetrarse** *vpr* to understand each
other

**compensación** *nf también Fin* compensation; **en c. (por)** in return (for); **c. bancaria**
bank clearing

**compensar 1** *vt* (a) *(valer la pena)* to make up
for; **no me compensa (perder tanto tiem-
po)** it's not worth my while (wasting all that
time) (b) *(indemnizar)* **c. a alguien (de o por)**
to compensate sb (for)

**2** *vi* **no compensa** it's not worth it

**competencia** *nf* (a) *(entre personas, empresas)* competition; *Com* **c. desleal** unfair competition, dumping; **la c.** the competition; **hacer
la c. a alguien** to compete with sb (b) *(incumbencia)* field, province; **no es de mi c.** it's not
my responsibility (c) *(atribuciones)* **competencias** powers (d) *(aptitud)* competence

**competente** *adj* competent; **c. en materia
de** responsible for

**competer** *vi* **c. a** *(incumbir)* to be up to, to be
the responsibility of; *(a una autoridad)* to come
under the jurisdiction of

**competición** *nf* competition

**competidor, -ora 1** *adj* rival, competing

**2** *nm,f* competitor

**competir** [49] *vi* to compete (**con/por**
with/for)

**competitividad** *nf* competitiveness

**competitivo, -a** *adj* competitive

**compilación** *nf (acción)* compiling; *(colección)* compilation

**compilador, -ora 1** *adj* compiling

**2** *nm,f (persona)* compiler

**3** *nm Informát* compiler

**compilar** vt también Informát to compile

**compincharse** vpr c. para hacer algo to plot to do sth

**compinche** nmf crony

**compitiera** etc ver **competir**

**compito** etc ver **competir**

**complacencia** nf pleasure, satisfaction

**complacer** [44] **1** vt to please; **me complace anunciar...** I am pleased to announce...

**2 complacerse** vpr **complacerse en hacer algo** to take pleasure in doing sth

**complaciente** adj (amable) obliging, helpful (b) (indulgente) indulgent

**complejidad** nf complexity

**complejo, -a 1** adj complex

**2** nm (a) Psi complex; **c. de Edipo/de inferioridad** Oedipus/inferiority complex (b) (zona construida) complex; **c. deportivo** sports complex; **c. industrial** industrial park; **c. residencial** private housing estate

**complementar 1** vt to complement

**2 complementarse** vpr to complement each other

**complementario, -a** adj complementary

**complemento** nm (a) (añadido) complement (b) Gram object, complement; **c. agente** agent; **c. circunstancial** adjunct; **c. directo/indirecto** direct/indirect object (c) **complementos** (accesorios) accessories

**completamente** adv completely, totally

**completar 1** vt to complete

**2 completarse** vpr to be completed

**completo, -a** adj (a) (entero, perfecto) complete; **por c.** completely; **un deportista muy c.** an all-round sportsman (b) (lleno) full

**complexión** nf build

**complicación** nf (a) (dificultad) complication (b) (complejidad) complexity

**complicado, -a** adj complicated

**complicar** [61] **1** vt (dificultar) to complicate

**2 complicarse** vpr (problema) to become complicated; (enfermedad) to get worse; **¡no te compliques la vida!** don't complicate matters (unnecessarily)!

**cómplice** nmf accomplice

**complicidad** nf complicity

**complot, compló** nm plot, conspiracy

**componenda** nf shady deal

**componente 1** adj component, constituent

**2** nm también Elec component; (persona) member

**3** nf viento de c. Este easterly wind

**componer** [52] **1** vt (a) (formar, ser parte de) to make up (b) (música, versos) to compose (c) (reparar) to repair (d) (adornar) (cosa) to deck out, to adorn; (persona) to dress up (e) (en imprenta) to set, to compose

**2 componerse** vpr (a) (estar formado) **componerse de** to be made up of, to consist of (b) (engalanarse) to dress up (c) **allá se las compongan** that's their problem; **componérselas (para hacer algo)** to manage (to do sth)

**comportamiento** nm behaviour

**comportar 1** vt to involve, to entail

**2 comportarse** vpr to behave

**composición** nf composition; **hacerse una c. de lugar** to size up the situation

**compositor, -ora** nm,f composer

**compostelano, -a 1** adj of/from Santiago de Compostela

**2** nm,f person from Santiago de Compostela

**compostura** nf (a) (reparación) repair (b) (de persona, rostro) composure (c) (en comportamiento) restraint; **guardar la c.** to show restraint

**compota** nf Culin compote, stewed fruit

**compra** nf purchase; **hacer la c.** to do the shopping; **ir de compras** to go shopping; **c. a plazos** hire purchase

**comprador, -ora 1** adj buying, purchasing

**2** nm,f (adquiriente) buyer, purchaser; (en una tienda) shopper, customer

**comprar** vt (a) (adquirir) to buy, to purchase; **c. algo a alguien** to buy sth from sb (b) (sobornar) to buy (off), to bribe

**compraventa** nf trading (de in); **c. de armas** arms dealing

**comprender 1** vt (a) (incluir) to include, to comprise (b) (entender) to understand

**2 comprenderse** vpr (personas) to understand each other

**comprensible** adj understandable, comprehensible

**comprensión** nf understanding

**comprensivo, -a** adj understanding

**compresa** nf (a) (femenina) Br sanitary towel, US sanitary napkin (b) (para herida) compress

**compresión** nf compression

**compresor, -ora 1** adj compressing

**2** nm compressor

**comprimido, -a 1** adj compressed

**2** nm pill, tablet

**comprimir** vt también Informát to compress; **c. un archivo** to zip a file

**comprobación** nf checking

**comprobante** nm (documento) supporting document, proof; (recibo) receipt

**comprobar** [65] vt (averiguar) to check; (demostrar) to prove

**comprometedor, -ora** adj compromising

**comprometer 1** *vt* **(a)** *(poner en peligro)* *(éxito, posibilidades)* to jeopardize; *(persona, inversión)* to compromise **(b)** *(avergonzar)* to embarrass **(c)** *(hacer responsable)* **c. a alguien (a hacer algo)** to oblige *o* compel sb (to do sth)

**2 comprometerse** *vpr* **(a)** *(hacerse responsable)* to commit oneself **(a hacer algo** to doing sth) **(b)** *(ideológicamente, moralmente)* to become involved **(en** in)

**comprometido, -a** *adj* **(a)** *(con una idea)* committed **(con** to) **(b)** *(situación)* compromising, awkward

**compromisario** *nm Pol* delegate, representative *(in an election)*

**compromiso** *nm* **(a)** *(obligación)* commitment; *(acuerdo)* agreement **(b)** *(cita)* engagement; **c. matrimonial** engagement **(c)** *(dificultad)* compromising *o* difficult situation; **poner a alguien en un c.** to put sb in a difficult *o* awkward position

**compuerta** *nf* sluice, floodgate

**compuesto, -a 1** *participio ver* **componer**

**2** *adj* **(a)** *(formado)* **c. de** composed of, made up of **(b)** *(múltiple)* compound; **interés c.** compound interest; **ojo c.** compound eye **(c)** *(acicalado)* dressed up

**3** *nm Gram & Quím* compound

**compulsar** *vt* to check against the original

**compulsivo, -a** *adj* compulsive, urgent

**compungido, -a** *adj* contrite, remorseful

**compusiera** *etc ver* **componer**

**computable** *adj* **gastos computables a efectos fiscales** expenditure taken into account for tax purposes

**computador** *nm*, **computadora** *nf* computer

**computar** *vt* **(a)** *(calcular)* to compute, to calculate **(b)** *(considerar)* to count, to regard as valid

**computarizar, computerizar** [16] *vt* to computerize

**cómputo** *nm* *(recuento)* calculation; *(de votos)* count

**comulgar** [40] *vi* **(a)** *Rel* to take communion **(b)** *Fig (estar de acuerdo)* **c. con algo** to share sth

**común** *adj* **(a)** *(habitual)* common; **poco c.** unusual; **por lo c.** generally **(b)** *(compartido)* *(amigo, interés)* mutual; *(bienes, pastos)* communal; **hacer algo en c.** to do sth together; **tener algo en c.** to have sth in common **(c)** *(ordinario, normal)* ordinary, average

**comuna** *nf* commune

**comunal** *adj* communal

**comunicación** *nf* **(a)** *(contacto, intercambio de información)* communication; **ponerse en c.**

**con alguien** to get in touch with sb; **medios de c. de masas** mass media; **comunicaciones** communications; *Telecom* **se cortó la c. mientras hablábamos** we were cut off **(b)** *(escrito oficial)* communiqué

**comunicado, -a 1** *adj* **bien c.** *(lugar)* well-served, with good connections

**2** *nm* announcement, statement; **c. oficial** official communiqué; **c. a la prensa** press release

**comunicante 1** *adj* communicating

**2** *nmf* informant

**comunicar** [61] **1** *vt* **(a)** *(transmitir)* *(sentimientos, ideas)* to convey; *(movimiento, virus)* to transmit **(b)** *(información)* **c. algo a alguien** to inform sb of sth, to tell sb sth **(c)** *(conectar)* to connect; **esta carretera comunica los dos pueblos** this road connects the two towns

**2** *vi* **(a)** *(estar conectado)* **c. con** to lead to; **nuestras habitaciones comunican** there's a door between our two rooms **(b)** *Telecom (teléfono)* *Br* to be engaged, *US* to be busy; *(hablar)* to get through; **está comunicando** the line's *Br* engaged *o US* busy; **no consigo c. con él** I can't get through to him

**3** **comunicarse** *vpr* **(a)** *(hablarse)* to communicate (with each other) **(b)** *(dos lugares)* to be connected **(c)** *(propagarse)* to spread

**comunicativo, -a** *adj* communicative, open

**comunidad** *nf* **(a)** *(grupo)* community; *Pol* **c. autónoma** autonomous region, = largest administrative division in Spain, with its own Parliament and a number of devolved powers; *Antes* **C. Económica Europea** European Economic Community; **c. de propietarios** *o* **de vecinos** residents' association **(b)** *(cualidad de común)* *(de ideas, bienes)* communion; **c. de bienes** co-ownership *(between spouses)*

**comunión** *nf también Fig* communion; *Rel* **hacer la primera c.** to take one's First Communion

**comunismo** *nm Pol* communism

**comunista** *adj & nmf Pol* communist

**comunitario, -a** *adj* **(a)** *(de la comunidad)* community; **espíritu c.** community spirit **(b)** *(de la UE)* Community, of the European Union; **política comunitaria** EU *o* Community policy

**con** *prep* **(a)** *(en general)* with; **¿c. quién vas?** who are you going with?; **lo ha conseguido c. su esfuerzo** he has achieved it through his own efforts; **una cartera c. varios documentos** a briefcase containing several documents; **c. el tiempo lo olvidé** in time I forgot it

**(b)** *(a pesar de)* in spite of; **c. todo** despite everything; **c. lo estudioso que es, le**

**suspendieron** for all his hard work, they still failed him

**(c)** *(hacia)* **para c.** towards; **es amable para c. todos** she is friendly towards *o* with everyone

**(d)** *(seguido de infinitivo) (para introducir una condición)* by; **c. hacerlo así** by doing it this way; **c. salir a las diez es suficiente** if we leave at ten, we'll have plenty of time

**(e)** *(a condición de que)* **c. (tal) que** *(seguido de subjuntivo)* as long as; **c. que llegue a tiempo me conformo** I don't mind as long as he arrives on time

**(f)** *(para expresar queja o decepción)* **mira que perder ¡c. lo bien que jugaste!** it's bad luck you lost, you played really well!

**conato** *nm* attempt; **c. de robo** attempted robbery; **un c. de incendio** the beginnings of a fire

**concatenación** *nf* succession

**concatenar, concadenar** *vt* to link together

**concavidad** *nf* **(a)** *(cualidad)* concavity **(b)** *(lugar)* hollow

**cóncavo, -a** *adj* concave

**concebir** [49] **1** *vt* **(a)** *(plan, hijo)* to conceive; *(imaginar)* to imagine

**2** *vi* to conceive

**conceder** *vt* **(a)** *(dar)* to grant; *(premio)* to award **(b)** *(asentir)* to admit, to concede

**concejal, -ala** *nm,f* (town) councillor

**concejalía** *nf* seat on the town council

**concejo** *nm* **(a)** *(ayuntamiento)* (town) council **(b)** *(municipio)* municipality

**concelebrar** *vt Rel* to concelebrate

**concentración** *nf* **(a)** *(mental)* concentration **(b)** *(densidad) también Quím* concentration; *Econ* **c. parcelaria** land consolidation; **c. urbana** conurbation **(c)** *(reunión)* gathering **(d)** *Dep* training camp

**concentrado** *nm* concentrate

**concentrar 1** *vt* **(a)** *(atención, esfuerzos)* to concentrate **(b)** *(gente)* to bring together; *(tropas)* to assemble; **esta zona concentra el 80% de los casos** 80% of the cases occurred in this region

**2 concentrarse** *vpr* **(a)** *(mentalmente)* to concentrate **(b)** *(disolución)* to become more concentrated **(c)** *(reunirse)* to gather, to congregate

**concéntrico, -a** *adj* concentric

**concepción** *nf* conception

**concepto** *nm* **(a)** *(idea)* concept **(b)** *(opinión)* opinion; **tener buen c. de alguien** to have a high opinion of sb **(c)** *(motivo)* **bajo ningún c.** under no circumstances **(d)** *(de una cuenta)* heading, item; **pagar algo en c. de adelanto** to pay sth in advance

**conceptual** *adj* conceptual

**conceptualismo** *nm* conceptualism

**conceptualista 1** *adj* conceptualistic

**2** *nmf* conceptualist

**concerniente** *adj* **c. a** concerning, regarding

**concernir** [27] *v impersonal* to concern; **en lo que concierne a** as regards; **por lo que a mí concierne** as far as I'm concerned

**concertación** *nf* settlement; *Ind* **c. social** *Br* ≃ social contract, = process of employer-trade-union negotiations

**concertar** [3] **1** *vt* *(precio)* to agree on; *(cita)* to arrange; *(pacto)* to reach

**2** *vi* *(concordar)* to tally **(con** with), to fit in **(con** with)

**concertina** *nf* concertina

**concertino** *nm* first violin

**concertista** *nmf* soloist

**concesión** *nf* **(a)** *(de préstamo, licencia)* granting; *(de premio)* awarding **(b)** *(cesión) también Com* concession; **sin hacer concesiones (a)** without making concessions (to)

**concesionario, -a** *Com* **1** *adj* concessionary

**2** *nm,f* *(persona con derecho exclusivo de venta)* licensed dealer; *(titular de una concesión)* concessionaire, licensee; **c. de automóviles** car dealer *(of particular make)*

**concha 1** *nf* **(a)** *(de molusco)* shell **(b)** *(carey)* tortoiseshell **(c)** *CSur Vulg (vulva)* cunt

**2** *nmf CSur Vulg* **c. de su madre** fucker

**conchabarse** *vpr Fam* to gang up **(contra** on)

**conchudo, -a** *adj CSur, Perú Vulg* bloody stupid

**concibiera** *etc ver* **concebir**

**concibo** *etc ver* **concebir**

**conciencia, consciencia** *nf* **(a)** *(conocimiento)* consciousness, awareness; **tener/tomar c. de** to be/become aware of **(b)** *(moral, integridad)* conscience; **en c.** in all honesty; **me remuerde la c.** I have a guilty conscience; **hacer algo a c.** *(con esmero)* to do sth conscientiously

**concienciar** [15] **1** *vt* **c. a alguien de algo** to make sb aware of sth

**2 concienciarse** *vpr* to become aware **(de** of)

**concienzudo, -a** *adj* conscientious

**concierna** *etc ver* **concernir**

**concierto** **1** *ver* **concertar**

**2** *nm* **(a)** *(actuación)* concert **(b)** *(composición)* concerto; **c. para viola/piano** viola/piano

**concerto** (**C**) *(acuerdo)* agreement; *Fin* **c. económico** economic agreement *o* accord (**d**) *(orden)* order

**conciliación** *nf (en un litigio)* reconciliation; *(en un conflicto laboral)* conciliation

**conciliar** [15] **1** *adj* conciliar

  **2** *vt* to reconcile; **c. el sueño** to get to sleep

**concilio** *nm* council; *Rel* **c. ecuménico** ecumenical council; *Rel* **C. Vaticano II** Second Vatican Council

**concisión** *nf* conciseness

**conciso, -a** *adj* concise

**concitar** *vt Formal* to stir up, to arouse

**conciudadano, -a** *nm,f* fellow citizen

**cónclave, conclave** *nm Rel* conclave; *Fig (reunión)* meeting

**concluir** [36] **1** *vt* to conclude; **c. haciendo** *o* **por hacer algo** to end up doing sth

  **2** *vi* to (come to an) end

**conclusión** *nf* conclusion; **en c.** in conclusion; **llegar a una c.** to come to *o* reach a conclusion; **sacar conclusiones** to draw conclusions

**concluyente** *adj* conclusive

**concomerse** *vpr* **c. de** *(envidia)* to be green with; *(arrepentimiento)* to be consumed with; *(impaciencia)* to be itching with

**concomitancia** *nf* concomitance

**concomitante** *adj* concomitant

**concordancia** *nf también Gram* agreement

**concordar** [65] **1** *vt* to reconcile

  **2** *vi (estar de acuerdo)* to agree *o* tally (**con** with); *Gram* to agree (**con** with)

**concordato** *nm* concordat

**concordia** *nf* harmony

**concreción** *nf* (**a**) *(de idea, medida)* specificity (**b**) *(de partículas)* concretion

**concretar 1** *vt* (**a**) *(precisar)* to specify, to state exactly (**b**) *(reducir a lo esencial)* to summarize

  **2 concretarse** *vpr* (**a**) *(limitarse)* **concretarse a hacer algo** to confine *o* limit oneself to doing sth (**b**) *(materializarse)* to take shape

**concreto, -a 1** *adj* specific, particular; **en c.** *(en resumen)* in short; *(específicamente)* specifically; **nada en c.** nothing definite

  **2** *nm Am* **c. armado** concrete

**concubina** *nf* concubine

**concubinato** *nm* concubinage

**concuerdo** *ver* **concordar**

**conculcar** [61] *vt Formal* to infringe, to break

**concuñado, -a** *nm,f (hermano del cuñado)* = brother or sister of one's brother-in-law or sister-in-law; *(cónyuge del cuñado)* = spouse of one's brother-in-law or sister-in-law

**concupiscencia** *nf* concupiscence, lustfulness

**concurrencia** *nf* (**a**) *(asistencia)* attendance; *(espectadores)* crowd, audience (**b**) *(de sucesos)* concurrence (**c**) *Com* competition; *Der* **no c.** non-competition clause

**concurrente 1** *adj* concurrent

  **2** *nmf* person present

**concurrido, -a** *adj (bar, calle)* crowded, busy; *(espectáculo)* well-attended

**concurrir** *vi* (**a**) *(reunirse)* **c. a algo** to go to sth, to attend (**b**) *(influir)* to contribute (**a** to) (**c**) *(participar)* **c. a** *(concurso)* to take part in, to compete in; *(examen)* to take, *Br* to sit

**concursante** *nmf (en concurso)* competitor, contestant; *(en oposiciones)* candidate

**concursar** *vi (competir)* to compete, to participate; *(en oposiciones)* to be a candidate

**concurso** *nm* (**a**) *(prueba) (literaria, deportiva)* competition; *(de televisión)* game show; **c. de belleza** beauty contest (**b**) *(para una obra)* tender; **salir a c. público** to be put out to tender (**c**) *(ayuda)* cooperation

**condado** *nm (territorio)* county

**condal** *adj* **la ciudad c.** Barcelona

**conde, -esa** *nm,f* count, *f* countess

**condecoración** *nf también Mil* decoration

**condecorar** *vt* to decorate

**condena** *nf* (**a**) *(judicial)* sentence; **cumplir c.** to serve a sentence (**b**) *(reprobación)* condemnation (**por** of)

**condenable** *adj* condemnable

**condenado, -a 1** *adj* (**a**) *(a una pena)* sentenced; *(a un sufrimiento)* condemned (**b**) *Fam (maldito)* damned, wretched

  **2** *nm,f (a una pena)* convicted person; *(a muerte)* condemned person; *Fam Fig* **correr como un c.** to run like the blazes *o Br* the clappers; *Fam Fig* **trabajar como un c.** to work like a slave

**condenar 1** *vt* (**a**) *(declarar culpable)* to convict (**b**) *(castigar)* **c. a alguien a algo** to sentence sb to sth (**c**) *(predestinar)* **estar condenado a** to be doomed to (**d**) *(reprobar)* to condemn

  **2 condenarse** *vpr* to be damned

**condensación** *nf* condensation

**condensado, -a** *adj* condensed

**condensador, -ora 1** *adj* condensing

  **2** *nm* condenser

**condensar** *vt también Fig* to condense

**condescendencia** *nf (benevolencia)* graciousness, kindness; *(altivez)* condescension

**condescender** [66] *vi* **c. a** *(con amabilidad)* to consent to, to accede to; *(con desprecio)* to deign to, to condescend to

**condescendiente** *adj* obliging

**condestable** *nm Hist* constable

**condición** *nf* (a) *(término, estipulación)* condition; **con la** *o* **a c. de que** on condition that; **con una sola c.** on one condition; **las condiciones de un contrato** the terms of a contract; **poner condiciones** to set conditions; **sin condiciones** unconditional

(b) **condiciones** *(circunstancias)* conditions; **condiciones atmosféricas** weather conditions; **condiciones de vida** living conditions

(c) *(estado)* condition; **estar en condiciones de** *o* **para hacer algo** *(físicamente)* to be in a fit state to do sth; *(por la situación)* to be in a position to do sth; **no estar en condiciones** *(carne, pescado)* to be off; *(vivienda)* to be unfit for living in; *(instalaciones)* to be unfit for use

(d) *(naturaleza)* nature; *(clase social)* social class; **de c. humilde** of humble circumstances; **mi c. de mujer...** the fact that I am a woman...

(e) *(aptitud)* **tener condiciones para algo/para hacer algo** to have the ability *o* capacity for sth/to do sth

**condicionado, -a** *adj* conditioned

**condicional** *adj & nm* conditional

**condicionamiento** *nm* conditioning

**condicionante** *nm* determinant

**condicionar** *vt* **c. algo a algo** to make sth dependent on sth

**condimentación** *nf* seasoning

**condimentar** *vt* to season

**condimento** *nm* seasoning; **añadir condimentos** to add seasoning

**condiscípulo, -a** *nm,f* schoolmate

**condolencia** *nf* condolence; **expresó sus condolencias a la viuda** he offered his condolences to the widow

**condolerse** [43] *vpr* to feel pity (**de** for)

**condominio** *nm Der* (*de un territorio*) condominium; (*de una cosa*) joint ownership

**condón** *nm* condom

**condonar** *vt* (a) *(deuda, pena)* to remit (b) *(violencia, terrorismo)* to condone

**cóndor** *nm* condor

**conducción** *nf* (a) *(de vehículo)* driving (b) *(por tubería)* piping; *(por cable)* wiring (c) *(conducto)* *(de agua, gas)* pipe; *(de electricidad)* cable (d) *Fig (dirección)* management, running

**conducir** [20] **1** *vt* (a) *(vehículo)* to drive (b) *(dirigir)* *(empresa)* to manage, to run; *(ejército)* to lead; *(asunto)* to handle (c) *(persona)* to lead (d) *(por tubería, cable)* *(calor)* to conduct; *(líquido)* to convey; *(electricidad)* to carry

**2** *vi* (a) *(en vehículo)* to drive (b) *(a sitio, situación)* **c. a** to lead to

**3 conducirse** *vpr* to behave

**conducta** *nf* behaviour, conduct

**conductismo** *nm Psi* behaviourism

**conductividad** *nf Fís* conductivity

**conducto** *nm* (a) *(de fluido)* pipe (b) *Fig (vía)* channel; **por c. de** through (c) *Anat* duct

**conductor, -ora 1** *adj Fís* conductive

**2** *nm,f* *(de vehículo)* driver

**3** *nm Fís* conductor

**conectado, -a** *adj* (a) *Elec* connected (**a** to) (b) *Informát* on-line

**conectar 1** *vt* to connect sth (**a** *o* **con** to *o* up to)

**2** *vi* **c. con** *Rad & TV* to go over to; *(persona)* to contact

**conectividad** *nf Informát* number of ports

**conector** *nm* *(cable)* cable, lead

**conejera** *nf* *(madriguera)* (rabbit) warren; *(conejar)* rabbit hutch

**conejillo** *nm* **c. de Indias** guinea pig

**conejo, -a 1** *nm,f* rabbit, *f* doe; *Culin* **c. a la cazadora** = rabbit cooked in olive oil with chopped onion, garlic and parsley

**2** *nm Vulg (vulva) Br* twat, *US* muff

**conexión** *nf* (a) *(vínculo)* connection (b) *Rad & TV* link-up; **c. vía satélite** satellite link (c) *Fig* **tener conexiones** *(amistades influyentes)* to have connections

**conexo, -a** *adj* related, connected

**confabulación** *nf* conspiracy

**confabularse** *vpr* to plot, to conspire

**confección** *nf* (a) *(de ropa)* tailoring, dressmaking; **de c.** off-the-peg (b) *(de comida)* preparation, making; *(de lista)* drawing up

**confeccionar** *vt* (a) *(ropa)* to make (up) (b) *(lista)* to draw up; *(plato)* to prepare

**confederación** *nf* confederation; **la C. Helvética** Switzerland

**confederado, -a 1** *adj* confederate

**2** *nm Hist* Confederate

**confederarse** *vpr* to confederate, to form a confederation

**conferencia** *nf* (a) *(charla)* lecture; **dar una c.** to give a talk *o* lecture; **c. de prensa** press conference (b) *(reunión)* conference (c) *(por teléfono)* (long-distance) call

**conferenciante** *nmf* speaker

**conferenciar** [15] *vi* to have a discussion

**conferir** [64] *vt* *(cualidad)* to give, to lend; **c. algo a alguien** *(honor, dignidad)* to confer *o* bestow sth upon sb; *(responsabilidades)* to give sth to sb

**confesar** [3] **1** *vt también Rel* to confess (to); **le confesó antes de morir** he heard his confession before he died; **confieso que te mentí** I admit I lied to you

**2 confesarse** *vpr Rel* **c. (de algo)** to confess (sth)

**confesión** *nf* (a) *(de pecado, crimen)* confession (b) *(credo)* religion, (religious) persuasion

**confesional** *adj* denominational; **Estado c.** = country with an official state religion

**confesionario** *nm* confessional

**confeso, -a** *adj* self-confessed

**confesor** *nm* confessor

**confeti** *nm* confetti

**confiado, -a** *adj* (seguro) (over) confident; *(crédulo)* trusting

**confianza** *nf* (a) *(seguridad)* confidence (**en** in); **c. en uno mismo** self-confidence (b) *(fe)* trust; **de c.** trustworthy (**c**) *(familiaridad)* familiarity; **amigo de c.** close *o* intimate friend; **en c.** in confidence; *Fam* **donde hay c. da asco** familiarity breeds contempt; **tengo mucha c. con él** I am very close to him

**confiar** [34] **1** *vt* (a) *(secreto)* to confide (b) *(responsabilidad, persona, asunto)* **c. algo a alguien** to entrust sth to sb

**2** *vi* (a) *(tener fe)* **c. en** to trust; **c. en la suerte** to trust to luck (b) *(suponer)* **c. en que** to be confident that

**3 confiarse** *vpr* (a) *(despreocuparse)* to be too sure (of oneself), to be overconfident (b) *(sincerarse)* **confiarse a** to confide in

**confidencia** *nf* confidence, secret

**confidencial** *adj* confidential

**confidencialidad** *nf* confidentiality

**confidente** *nmf* (a) *(amigo)* confidant, *f* confidante (b) *(soplón)* informer

**confiero** *etc ver* **conferir**

**confieso** *etc ver* **confesar**

**configuración** *nf* (disposición) también *Informát* configuration; *(del terreno)* lie; *(de la costa)* outline, shape; *(de ciudad)* layout

**configurar** *vt* (a) *(formar)* to shape, to form (b) *Informát* to configure

**confín** *nm* (a) *(límite)* border, boundary (b) *(extremo)* *(del reino, universo)* outer reaches; **en los confines de** on the very edge of

**confinamiento** *nm* (a) *(de un detenido)* confinement (**en** to) (b) *(de un desterrado)* banishment (a *o* en to)

**confinar** *vt* (a) *(detener)* to confine (**en** to) (b) *(desterrar)* to banish (a *o* en to)

**confiriera** *etc ver* **conferir**

**confirmación** *nf* también *Rel* confirmation

**confirmar** *vt* to confirm

**confiscar** [61] *vt* to confiscate

**confitado, -a** *adj* candied; **frutas confitadas** crystallized fruit

**confitar** *vt* to candy

**confite** *nm* *Br* sweet, *US* candy

**confitería** *nf* (a) *(tienda)* sweetshop, confectioner's (b) *CSur (café)* cafe

**confitero, -a** *nm,f* confectioner

**confitura** *nf* preserve, jam

**conflagración** *nf* conflict, war

**conflictividad** *nf* conflict; **c. laboral** industrial unrest

**conflictivo, -a** *adj* (asunto) controversial; *(situación)* troubled; *(persona)* difficult

**conflicto** *nm* (desacuerdo, lucha) conflict; *(de intereses, opiniones)* clash; **conflictos** conflict; **c. armado** armed conflict; **c. laboral** industrial dispute; **entrar en c. con** to be in conflict with

**confluencia** *nf* confluence; **la c. de las dos calles** the place where the two roads meet

**confluir** [36] *vi* (a) *(corriente, cauce)* to converge, to meet (**en** at) (b) *(personas)* to come together, to gather (**en** in)

**conformar 1** *vt* (configurar) to shape

**2 conformarse con** *vpr* (suerte, destino) to resign oneself to; *(apañárselas con)* to make do with; *(contentarse con)* to settle for

**conforme 1** *adj* (a) *(acorde)* **c. a** in accordance with; **c. al reglamento** in accordance with the rules (b) *(de acuerdo)* in agreement (**con** with); **si no estás c., protesta** if you don't agree, say so (**c**) *(contento)* happy (**con** with)

**2** *adv* (a) *(a medida que)* as; **c. envejecía** as he got older (b) *(como)* exactly as; **te lo cuento c. lo vi** I'm telling you exactly what I saw (**c**) *(en cuanto)* as soon as; **c. amanezca, me iré** I'll leave as soon as it gets light

**conformidad** *nf* (aprobación) approval; **dio su c.** she gave her consent; **de c. con** in accordance with

**conformismo** *nm* conformity

**conformista** *adj & nmf* conformist

**confort** *( pl* **conforts***) nm* comfort; **todo c.** *(en anuncio)* all mod cons

**confortable** *adj* comfortable

**confortar** *vt* to console, to comfort

**confraternidad** *nf* brotherhood

**confraternizar** [16] *vi* to get along (like brothers)

**confrontación** *nf* (a) *(enfrentamiento)* confrontation (b) *(comparación)* comparison

**confrontar** *vt* (a) *(enfrentar)* to confront (b) *(comparar)* to compare

**confucianismo, confucionismo** *nm* Confucianism

**confundir 1** *vt* (a) *(trastocar)* **c. una cosa con otra** to mistake one thing for another; **c. dos cosas** to get two things mixed up; *Fam Fig* **confundir el tocino con la velocidad** to mix up two completely different things

(b) *(liar)* to confuse; **me confundes con tanta información** you're confusing me with all that information

**(c)** *(mezclar)* to mix up

**(d)** *(abrumar)* to confound

**2 confundirse** *vpr* **(a)** *(equivocarse)* to make a mistake; **confundirse de piso/tren** to get the wrong floor/train; **se ha confundido** *(al teléfono)* (you've got the) wrong number; **no te confundas: yo no soy un mentiroso** don't get the wrong idea – I'm no liar

**(b)** *(liarse)* to get confused; **me confundo con tanta información** I get confused by all that information

**(c)** *(mezclarse) (colores, siluetas)* to merge **(en** into); *(personas)* **confundirse entre la gente** to lose oneself in the crowd

**confusión** *nf* **(a)** *(desorden, lío)* confusion; **hubo una gran c.** there was great confusion **(b)** *(error)* mix-up; **ha habido una c.** there has been a bit of a mix-up

**confusionismo** *nm* confusion

**confuso, -a** *adj* **(a)** *(explicación)* confused **(b)** *(poco claro) (clamor, griterío)* confused; *(contorno, forma)* blurred **(c)** *(turbado)* confused, bewildered

**conga** *nf* conga

**congelación** *nf* *(de alimentos)* freezing; *Fig Econ (de precios, salarios)* freeze

**congelador** *nm* freezer

**congelados** *nmpl* frozen foods

**congelar 1** *vt también Econ* to freeze

**2 congelarse** *vpr* to freeze; **¡me congelo de frío!** I'm freezing!

**congénere** *nmf* **me avergüenzo de mis congéneres** I am ashamed of my own kind

**congeniar** [15] *vi* to get on **(con** with)

**congénito, -a** *adj* *(enfermedad)* congenital; *(talento, estupidez)* innate

**congestión** *nf* congestion; **tengo c. nasal** I've got a blocked nose

**congestionado, -a** *adj* *(cara)* flushed; *(calle)* congested; *(nariz)* blocked; **tener la nariz congestionada** to have a blocked nose

**congestionar 1** *vt* to block

**2 congestionarse** *vpr* **(a)** *(calle)* to become congested **(b)** *(cara)* to flush, to turn purple

**conglomerado** *nm Geol & Tec* conglomerate; *Fig (mezcla)* combination

**conglomerar** *vt Tec* to conglomerate; *Fig (intereses, tendencias)* to unite

**Congo** *nm* **el C.** (the) Congo

**congoja** *nf* anguish

**congoleño, -a** *adj & nm,f* Congolese

**congraciarse** [15] *vpr* **c. con alguien** to win sb over, to get on sb's good side

**congratulación** *nf Formal* **congratulaciones** congratulations; **recibió la c. del ministro** he received the minister's congratulations

**congratular** *Formal* **1** *vt* to congratulate **(por** on)

**2 congratularse** *vpr* to be pleased **(por** about)

**congregación** *nf* congregation

**congregar** [40] **1** *vt* to assemble, to bring together

**2 congregarse** *vpr* to assemble, to gather

**congresista** *nmf* **(a)** *(en un congreso)* delegate **(b)** *(político)* congressman, *f* congresswoman

**congreso** *nm* **(a)** *(de una especialidad)* conference, congress **(b)** *(asamblea nacional)* **C. (de los Diputados)** *(en España) Br* ≃ House of Commons, *US* ≃ House of Representatives, = lower house of Spanish Parliament; **el C.** *(en Estados Unidos)* Congress **(c)** *(edificio)* parliament building

**congrio** *nm* conger eel

**congruencia** *nf* consistency

**congruente** *adj* consistent, coherent

**cónico, -a** *adj* conical

**conífera** *nf* conifer

**conjetura** *nf* conjecture; **hacer conjeturas, hacerse una c.** to conjecture

**conjeturar** *vt* to conjecture about, to make predictions about

**conjugación** *nf* **(a)** *Gram* conjugation **(b)** *(combinación)* combination; *(de esfuerzos, ideas)* pooling

**conjugar** [40] *vt* **(a)** *Gram* to conjugate **(b)** *(combinar)* to combine

**conjunción** *nf* **(a)** *Astron & Gram* conjunction **(b)** *(de circunstancias, hechos)* combination

**conjuntado, -a** *adj* coordinated

**conjuntar** *vt* to coordinate

**conjuntiva** *nf Anat* conjunctiva

**conjuntivitis** *nf inv* conjunctivitis

**conjuntivo, -a** *adj* conjunctive

**conjunto, -a 1** *adj (acción, esfuerzo)* joint; **cuenta conjunta** joint account

**2** *nm* **(a)** *(agrupación)* collection, group; **un c. de circunstancias** a number of factors **(b)** *(de ropa)* outfit **(c)** *(de música)* group, band **(d)** *(totalidad)* whole; **en c.** overall, as a whole **(e)** *Mat* set

**conjura** *nf* conspiracy, plot

**conjurado, -a** *nm,f* plotter, conspirator

**conjurar 1** *vt* **(a)** *(exorcizar)* to exorcize; *Fig* **sus palabras conjuraron mi miedo** his words dispelled my fears **(b)** *(un peligro)* to ward off, to avert

**2** *vi (conspirar)* to conspire, to plot

**3 conjurarse** *vpr (conspirar)* to conspire, to plot

**conjuro** *nm (encantamiento)* spell, incantation; *(exorcismo)* exorcism

**conllevar** *vt* (a) *(implicar)* to involve, to entail (b) *(soportar)* to bear

**conmemoración** *nf* commemoration; **en c. de** in commemoration of

**conmemorar** *vt* to commemorate

**conmemorativo, -a** *adj* commemorative

**conmensurable** *adj Fig* quantifiable

**conmigo** *pron personal* with me; **c. mismo/misma** with myself; **llevo siempre el pasaporte c.** I always carry my passport on me; **estaba hablando c. mismo** I was talking to myself

**conminación** *nf* threat

**conminar** *vt* (a) *(forzar)* **c. a alguien a hacer algo** to instruct *o* order sb to do sth (b) *(amenazar)* **c. a alguien (con hacer algo)** to threaten sb (with doing sth)

**conmiseración** *nf* compassion, pity

**conmoción** *nf* (a) *(física o psíquica)* shock; **c. cerebral** concussion (b) *Fig (trastorno, disturbio)* upheaval

**conmocionar** *vt* (a) *(psíquicamente)* to shock, to stun (b) *(físicamente)* to concuss

**conmovedor, -ora** *adj* moving, touching

**conmover** [43] **1** *vt* (a) *(emocionar)* to move, to touch (b) *(sacudir)* to shake

**2 conmoverse** *vpr* (a) *(emocionarse)* to be moved, to be touched (b) *(sacudirse)* to be shaken

**conmutación** *nf Der* commutation

**conmutador** *nm* (a) *Elec* switch (b) *Am (centralita)* switchboard

**conmutar** *vt Der* to commute

**connatural** *adj* innate

**connivencia** *nf* **en c.** in collusion

**connotación** *nf* connotation; **una c. irónica** a hint of irony

**connotar** *vt* to suggest, to have connotations of

**cono** *nm* cone; **el C. Sur** = Chile, Argentina, Paraguay and Uruguay

**conocedor, -ora** *nm,f* expert; **es un gran c. de los vinos franceses** he is a connoisseur of French wine

**conocer** [21] **1** *vt* (a) *(saber cosas acerca de)* to know; **darse a c.** to make oneself known; **c. bien un tema** to know a lot about a subject (b) *(lugar, país) (descubrir)* to get to know, to visit for the first time; *(desde hace tiempo)* to know (c) *(a una persona) (por primera vez)* to meet; *(desde hace tiempo)* to know; **c. a alguien de vista** to know sb by sight; **c. a alguien de oídas** to have heard of sb

(d) *(reconocer)* **c. a alguien (por algo)** to recognize sb (by sth)

**2 conocerse** *vpr* (a) *(a uno mismo)* to know oneself (b) *(dos o más personas) (por primera vez)* to meet, to get to know each other; *(desde hace tiempo)* to know each other

**3** *v impersonal (parecer)* **se conoce que...** apparently...

**conocido, -a 1** *adj* well-known

**2** *nm,f* acquaintance

**conocimiento** *nm* (a) *(saber)* knowledge; **hablar/actuar con c. de causa** to know what one is talking about/doing; **tener c. de algo** to be aware of sth; **conocimientos** knowledge; **tener muchos conocimientos (acerca de)** to be very knowledgeable (about) (b) *Med (sentido)* consciousness; **perder/recobrar el c.** to lose/regain consciousness

**conozco** *ver* **conocer**

**conque** *conj* so; **¿c. te has cansado?** so you're tired, are you?; **¿c. esas tenemos?** so that's what you're up to?

**conquense 1** *adj* of/from Cuenca

**2** *nmf* person from Cuenca

**conquista** *nf (de tierras, persona)* conquest; *Fig (de libertad, derecho)* winning

**conquistador, -ora 1** *adj (seductor)* seductive

**2** *nm,f* (a) *(de tierras)* conqueror (b) *Hist* conquistador

**3** *nm (seductor)* Casanova, ladykiller

**conquistar** *vt* (a) *(tierras)* to conquer (b) *Fig (libertad, derechos, simpatía)* to win (c) *(seducir)* to win the heart of

**consabido, -a** *adj (conocido)* well-known; *(habitual)* usual

**consagración** *nf* (a) *Rel* consecration (b) *(dedicación)* dedication (c) *(reconocimiento)* recognition; **esta obra supuso la c. del joven escritor** this work gained recognition for the young writer

**consagrado, -a** *adj* (a) *Rel* consecrated (b) *(dedicado)* dedicated (c) *(reconocido)* recognized, established

**consagrar 1** *vt* (a) *Rel* to consecrate (b) *(dedicar) (tiempo, espacio)* to devote; *(monumento, lápida)* to dedicate; **consagró su vida a la literatura** he devoted *o* dedicated his life to literature (c) *(acreditar, confirmar)* to confirm, to establish

**2 consagrarse** *vpr* (a) *(dedicarse)* to devote *o* dedicate oneself (a to) (b) *(alcanzar reconocimiento)* to establish oneself

**consanguíneo, -a** *adj* related by blood; **hermano c.** half-brother *(of same father)*

**consanguinidad** *nf* blood relationship

**consciencia** *nf* = **conciencia**

**consciente** *adj* conscious; **estar c.** *(estar despierto)* to be conscious; **ser c. de** to be aware of

**consecución** *nf (de un deseo)* realization; *(de un objetivo)* attainment; *(de un premio)* winning

**consecuencia** *nf* **(a)** *(resultado)* consequence; **a** *o* **como c. de** as a consequence *o* result of; **en c.** consequently; **tener consecuencias** to have consequences **(b)** *(coherencia)* consistency; **actuar en c.** to act accordingly; **cuando supo que estaba embarazada actuó en c.** when he found out that she was pregnant he did the decent thing

**consecuente** *adj (coherente)* consistent; **una persona c.** a person of principle

**consecutivo, -a** *adj* consecutive; **tres victorias consecutivas** three consecutive victories, three victories in a row; **siete semanas consecutivas** seven consecutive weeks, seven weeks on end

**conseguir** [63] *vt (obtener)* to obtain, to get; *(un objetivo)* to achieve; **c. hacer algo** to manage to do sth

**consejería** *nf (de comunidad autónoma)* department

**consejero, -a** *nm,f* **(a)** *(en asuntos personales)* counsellor; *(en asuntos técnicos)* adviser, consultant **(b)** *(de un consejo de administración)* member; *Pol* councillor

**consejo** *nm* **(a)** *(advertencia)* advice; **dar un c.** to give some advice *o* a piece of advice; **dar consejos** to give (some) advice; **pedir c. a alguien** to ask sb for advice, to ask (for) sb's advice **(b)** *(organismo)* council; *(reunión)* meeting; **c. de administración** board of directors; *(reunión)* board meeting; **c. de ministros** cabinet; *(reunión)* cabinet meeting **(c) c. de guerra** court martial

**consenso** *nm (acuerdo)* consensus; *(consentimiento)* consent

**consensuado, -a** *adj* approved by consensus

**consensual** *adj* consensual

**consensuar** [4] *vt* to approve by consensus

**consentido, -a 1** *adj* spoilt

**2** *nm,f* spoilt brat

**consentimiento** *nm* consent

**consentir** [64] **1** *vt* **(a)** *(tolerar)* to allow, to permit **(b)** *(mimar)* to spoil; **le consienten demasiado** they let him have his own way too much

**2** *vi* **c. en algo/en hacer algo** to agree to sth/ to do sth; **consintió en que se quedaran** he agreed to let them stay

**conserje** *nmf (portero)* porter; *(encargado)* caretaker

**conserjería** *nf* porter's lodge

**conserva** *nf* **conservas** canned food, *Br* tinned food; **c. de carne** tinned meat; **en c.** canned, *Br* tinned

**conservación** *nf* **(a)** *(de costumbres, patrimonio)* conservation; *(de alimentos)* preservation; **en buen estado de c.** in good condition **(b)** *(mantenimiento)* maintenance

**conservador, -ora 1** *adj (tradicionalista)* conservative; *(del partido conservador)* Conservative

**2** *nm,f* **(a)** *(tradicionalista)* conservative; *(miembro del partido conservador)* Conservative **(b)** *(de museo)* curator

**conservadurismo** *nm* conservatism

**conservante** *nm* preservative

**conservar 1** *vt* **(a)** *(mantener) también Culin* to preserve; *(amistad)* to sustain, to keep up; *(salud)* to look after; *(calor)* to retain **(b)** *(guardar) (libros, cartas, secreto)* to keep

**2 conservarse** *vpr* to keep; **se conserva bien** he's keeping well

**conservatorio** *nm* conservatoire

**conservero, -a** *adj* canning; **la industria conservera** the canning industry

**considerable** *adj (grande)* considerable; *(importante, eminente)* notable

**consideración** *nf* **(a)** *(reflexión)* consideration, factor; **debemos tener en cuenta estas consideraciones** we must take these factors into consideration; **tomar en c.** to take into consideration *o* account **(b)** *(respeto)* respect; **en c. a algo** in recognition of sth; **tratar a alguien con c.** to be nice to sb **(c)** *(importancia)* **de c.** serious; **hubo varios heridos de c.** several people were seriously injured

**considerado, -a** *adj (atento)* considerate, thoughtful; *(respetado)* respected, highly-regarded

**considerar** *vt* **(a)** *(valorar, pensar en)* to consider **(b)** *(juzgar, estimar)* to think **(c)** *(respetar)* to esteem, to treat with respect

**consiento** *etc ver* **consentir**

**consigna** *nf* **(a)** *(órdenes)* instructions **(b)** *(para el equipaje) Br* left-luggage office, *US* baggage room

**consignar** *vt* **(a)** *(poner por escrito)* to record, to write down **(b)** *(asignar)* to allocate **(c)** *(mercancía)* to consign, to dispatch **(d)** *(equipaje)* to deposit in the *Br* left-luggage office *o US* baggage room

**consignatario, -a** *nm,f* **(a)** *(de una mercancía)* consignee **(b)** *(representante)* **c. de buques** shipping agent

**consigo 1** *ver* **conseguir**

**2** *pron personal (singular)* with him/her; *(plural)* with them; *(con usted)* with you; *(con uno mismo)* with oneself; **c. mismo/misma** with himself/

herself; **lleva siempre el pasaporte c.** she always carries her passport on her; **hablar c. mismo** to talk to oneself

**consiguiente** *adj* resulting; **con la c. decepción** with the resulting disappointment; **por c.** consequently, therefore

**consiguiera** *etc ver* **conseguir**

**consintiera** *etc ver* **consentir**

**consistencia** *nf también Fig* consistency

**consistente** *adj* (a) *(sólido) (material)* solid (b) *(coherente) (argumento)* sound, convincing (c) *(compuesto)* **c. en** consisting of

**consistir** *vi* (a) **c. en** *(ser, componerse de)* to consist of; **¿en qué consiste su problema?** what exactly is your problem? (b) **c. en** *(basarse en)* to lie in, to be based on

**consistorial** *adj* of the town council; **casa c.** town hall

**consistorio** *nm* town council

**consola** *nf* (a) *Informát & Tec* console; **c. de videojuegos** video console (b) *(mesa)* console table

**consolación** *nf* consolation

**consolador, -ora** *adj* consoling, comforting

**consolar** [65] **1** *vt* to console; **me consuela pensar que podría haber sido peor** it's some consolation to reflect that it could have been worse

**2 consolarse** *vpr* to console oneself, to take comfort; **¡consuélate! al menos no has suspendido** look on the bright side! at least you didn't fail

**consolidación** *nf* consolidation

**consolidar** *vt* to consolidate

**consomé** *nm* consommé

**consonancia** *nf* harmony; **en c. con** in keeping with

**consonante** *nf* consonant

**consonántico, -a** *adj* consonant, consonantal

**consorcio** *nm* consortium; **c. bancario** bankers' consortium

**consorte** *nmf* *(cónyuge)* spouse; *(príncipe)* consort

**conspicuo, -a** *adj* *(evidente)* conspicuous; *(ilustre)* eminent

**conspiración** *nf* plot, conspiracy

**conspirador, -ora** *nm,f* conspirator, plotter

**conspirar** *vi* to conspire, to plot

**constancia** *nf* (a) *(perseverancia) (en una empresa)* perseverance; *(en las ideas, opiniones)* steadfastness; **hacer algo con c.** to persevere with sth (b) *(testimonio)* record; **dejar c. de**

**algo** *(registrar)* to put sth on record; *(probar)* to demonstrate sth

**constante 1** *adj* (a) *(persona) (en una empresa)* persistent; *(en ideas, opiniones)* steadfast (b) *(acción)* constant

**2** *nf* constant; *Med* **constantes vitales** signs of life; *Med* **mantener las constantes vitales de alguien** to keep sb alive

**constar** *vi* (a) *(una información)* to appear (**en** in), to figure (**en** in); **constarle a alguien** to be clear to sb; **hacer c.** to put on record; **me consta que...** I am quite sure that...; **que conste que...** let it be clearly understood that..., let there be no doubt that... (b) *(estar constituido por)* **c. de** to consist of

**constatación** *nf* confirmation

**constatar** *vt* *(observar)* to confirm; *(comprobar)* to check

**constelación** *nf* constellation

**consternación** *nf* consternation, dismay

**consternado, -a** *adj* dismayed, extremely upset

**consternar** *vt* to dismay, to upset

**constipado, -a 1** *adj* **estar c.** to have a cold

**2** *nm* cold

**constiparse** *vpr* to catch a cold

**constitución** *nf* (a) constitution; **tener una c. fuerte/débil** to have a strong/weak constitution (b) **C.** *(de un Estado)* Constitution (c) *(creación)* creation, forming (d) *(composición)* composition, make-up

**constitucional** *adj* constitutional

**constitucionalidad** *nf* constitutionality

**constituir** [36] *vt* (a) *(componer)* to make up (b) *(ser)* to be (c) *(crear)* to set up, to constitute

**constitutivo, -a** *adj* constituent; **elemento c.** constituent element; **ser c. de algo** to constitute sth

**constituyente** *adj & nm* constituent

**constreñir** *vt* (a) *(obligar)* **c. a alguien a hacer algo** to compel *o* force sb to do sth (b) *(oprimir, limitar)* to restrict

**construcción** *nf* (a) *(acción) también Gram* construction; **en c.** under construction (b) *(edificio)* building

**constructivo, -a** *adj* constructive

**constructor, -ora 1** *adj* building, construction; **empresa constructora** construction firm, building company

**2** *nm (de edificios)* builder

**construir** [36] *vt* *(edificio, barco, muro)* to build; *(aviones, coches)* to manufacture; *(frase, teoría)* to construct

**consubstancial** *adj* **ser c. a algo** to be an integral part of sth

**consuegro, -a** *nm,f* = father-in-law/mother-in-law of one's son or daughter

**consuelo 1** *ver* **consolar**

**2** *nm* consolation, solace

**consuetudinario, -a** *adj* customary; **derecho c.** common law

**cónsul** *nm* consul

**consulado** *nm (oficina)* consulate; *(cargo)* consulship

**consular** *adj* consular

**consulta** *nf* (a) *(sobre un problema) (acción)* consultation; *(pregunta)* query, enquiry; **hacer una c. a alguien** to seek sb's advice (b) *(despacho de médico)* consulting room; **horas de c.** surgery hours; **pasar c.** to hold a surgery

**consultar 1** *vt (dato, fecha)* to look up; *(libro, persona)* to consult; **me consultó antes de hacerlo** *(me pidió consejo)* he consulted me before doing it; *(me pidió permiso)* he asked me before he did it

**2** *vi* **c. con** to consult, to seek advice from

**consultivo, -a** *adj* consultative, advisory

**consultor, -ora** *nm,f* consultant

**consultoría** *nf* consultancy firm

**consultorio** *nm* (a) *(de un médico)* consulting room (b) *(en periódico)* problem page; *(en radio)* = programme answering listeners' questions; **c. sentimental** *(en radio)* = phone-in where people get advice on their personal problems (c) *(asesoría)* advice bureau

**consumación** *nf (de matrimonio, proyecto)* consummation; *(de un crimen)* perpetration

**consumado, -a** *adj* consummate, perfect; **es un granuja c.** he's a real rascal

**consumar** *vt (realizar completamente)* to complete; *(un crimen)* to perpetrate; *(el matrimonio)* to consummate

**consumición** *nf* (a) *(acción)* consumption (b) *(bebida)* drink; *(comida)* food; **son 1.000 ptas la entrada con c.** it costs 1,000 pesetas to get in, including the first drink

**consumido, -a** *adj (flaco)* emaciated

**consumidor, -ora** *nm,f (de producto)* consumer; *(en bar, restaurante)* patron

**consumir 1** *vt* (a) *(producto)* to consume; **c. preferentemente antes de…** best before…; **mi coche consume cinco litros a los cien** my car does twenty kilometres to the litre; **en casa consumimos mucho aceite de oliva** we use a lot of olive oil at home (b) *(destruir) (sujeto: fuego)* to destroy; *(sujeto: enfermedad)* to eat away at; *Fig* **le consumen los celos** he is eaten up by *o* consumed with jealousy

**2** *vi* to consume

**3 consumirse** *vpr* (a) *(persona)* to waste away (b) *(fuego)* to burn out

**consumismo** *nm* consumerism

**consumista** *adj* consumerist, materialistic

**consumo** *nm* consumption; **bienes/sociedad de c.** consumer goods/society; **c. de drogas** drug-taking; **se ha disparado el c. de agua mineral** sales of mineral water have shot up

**consustancial** *adj* **ser c. a algo** to be an integral part of sth

**contabilidad** *nf* (a) *(oficio)* accountancy (b) *(de persona, empresa)* bookkeeping, accounting; **llevar la c.** to do the accounts; **doble c.** double-entry bookkeeping

**contabilización** *nf Com* entering

**contabilizar** [16] *vt Com* to enter

**contable** *nmf* accountant

**contactar 1** *vt (comunicarse con)* to contact

**2** *vi* **c. con** to contact

**contacto** *nm* (a) *(entre dos cosas, personas)* contact; **perder el c.** to lose touch; **ponerse en c. con** to get in touch with (b) *Aut* ignition (c) *Elec* **hacer c.** to make contact

**contactólogo, -a** *nm,f* contact lens specialist

**contado, -a** *adj* (a) *(raro)* rare, infrequent; **en contadas ocasiones** very rarely, on very few occasions (b) **pagar al c.** to pay (in) cash (c) **había diez personas mal contadas** there were no more than ten people

**contador, -ora 1** *nm,f Am (persona)* accountant

**2** *nm (aparato)* meter; **el c. del gas/de la luz** the gas/electricity meter

**contaduría** *nf (oficina)* accountant's office; *(departamento)* accounts office

**contagiar** [15] **1** *vt (persona)* to infect; *(enfermedad)* to transmit; **me has contagiado el resfriado** you've given me your cold

**2 contagiarse** *vpr (enfermedad, risa)* to be contagious; *(persona)* to become infected

**contagio** *nm* infection, contagion

**contagioso, -a** *adj (enfermedad)* contagious, infectious; *(risa)* infectious

**contáiner** *nm (para mercancías)* container

**contaminación** *nf (acción)* contamination; *(del medio ambiente)* pollution; **c. acústica** noise pollution

**contaminado, -a** *adj (alimento)* contaminated; *(medio ambiente)* polluted

**contaminante 1** *adj* contaminating, polluting

**2** *nmpl* **contaminantes** pollutants

**contaminar** *vt* (a) *(envenenar)* to contaminate; *(el medio ambiente)* to pollute (b) *Fig (pervertir)* to corrupt

**contante** *adj Fam* **con dinero c. y sonante** in hard cash

**contar** [65] **1** vt (a) *(enumerar, incluir)* to count; **somos 57 sin c. a los niños** there are 57 of us, not counting the children; **un perro, dos gatos y para de c.** a dog, two cats and that's it; **se pueden c. con los dedos de una mano** you can count them on (the fingers of) one hand (b) *(narrar)* to tell; *Fam* **¿qué (te) cuentas?** how are you doing?

**2** vi to count; **c. con** *(confiar en)* to count on; *(tener, poseer)* to have; *(tener en cuenta)* to take into account; **con esto no contaba** I hadn't reckoned with that; **cuenta con dos horas para hacerlo** she has two hours to do it

**contemplación** nf (a) *(meditación)* contemplation (b) *(consideración)* **contemplaciones** consideration; **tratar a alguien sin contemplaciones** not to take into account sb's feelings; **nos echaron sin contemplaciones** they threw us out unceremoniously

**contemplar** vt (a) *(opción, posibilidad)* to contemplate, to consider (b) *(paisaje, monumento)* to look at, to contemplate

**contemplativo, -a** adj contemplative

**contemporáneo, -a** adj & nm,f contemporary

**contemporizar** [16] vi to be accommodating

**contención** nf (a) *Constr* **muro de c.** retaining wall (b) *(moderación)* restraint, self-restraint

**contencioso, -a 1** adj (a) *(tema, cuestión)* contentious (b) *Der* litigious
**2** nm dispute, conflict

**contender** [66] vi *(competir)* to contend; *(pelear)* to fight

**contendiente 1** adj *(en una competición)* competing; **las partes contendientes** *(en una guerra)* the warring factions; **los ejércitos contendientes** the opposing armies
**2** nmf *(en una competición)* contender; *(en una guerra)* warring faction

**contenedor, -ora 1** adj containing
**2** nm *(recipiente grande)* container; *(para escombros)* skip; **c. de basura** = large wheeled bin for collecting rubbish from blocks of flats etc; **c. de vidrio** bottle bank

**contener** [67] **1** vt (a) *(encerrar)* to contain; **¿qué contiene esa maleta?** what's in this suitcase?; **la novela contiene elementos diversos** the novel has many different aspects (b) *(detener, reprimir)* to restrain, to hold back; **no pudo c. la risa/el llanto** he couldn't help laughing/crying
**2 contenerse** vpr to restrain oneself, to hold oneself back

**contengo** ver **contener**

**contenido** nm *(de recipiente, libro)* contents; *(de discurso, redacción)* content

**contentar 1** vt to please, to keep happy
**2 contentarse** vpr **contentarse con** to make do with, to be satisfied with

**contento, -a 1** adj *(alegre)* happy; *(satisfecho)* pleased
**2** nm happiness, joy; **no caber en sí de c.** to be beside oneself with joy

**conteo** nm counting-up

**contertulio, -a** nm,f companion *(at a social gathering)*

**contestación** nf answer

**contestador** nm **c. (automático)** answering machine

**contestar** vt (a) *(responder)* to answer (b) *(con insolencia)* to answer back; **¡no contestes a tu madre!** don't answer back to your mother!

**contestatario, -a** adj anti-establishment

**contestón, -ona** adj cheeky; **es muy c.** he's always answering back

**contexto** nm context

**contextualizar** [16] vt *(problema, situación)* to put into perspective o context

**contextura** nf *(estructura)* structure; *(complexión)* build

**contienda 1** ver **contender**
**2** nf *(competición, combate)* contest; *(guerra)* conflict, war

**contiene** ver **contener**

**contigo** pron personal with you; **c. mismo/misma** with yourself; **¿estás hablando c. mismo?** are you talking to yourself?

**contigüidad** nf adjacency

**contiguo, -a** adj adjacent

**continencia** nf continence, self-restraint

**continental** adj continental

**continente** nm (a) *Geog* continent (b) *(recipiente)* container

**contingencia** nf *(eventualidad)* eventuality; *Formal (posibilidad)* possibility

**contingente 1** adj *Formal* possible; **es un hecho c.** it's not impossible
**2** nm (a) *(grupo)* contingent (b) *Com* quota

**continuación** nf *(de acción, estado)* continuation; *(de novela, película)* sequel; **a c.** next; **¡a c., para todos ustedes, la gran cantante...!** and now, we bring you the great singer...!

**continuar** [4] **1** vt to continue, to carry on with
**2** vi to continue, to go on; **c. haciendo algo** to continue doing o to do sth; **continúa lloviendo** it's still raining; **continuará** *(historia, programa)* to be continued

**continuidad** *nf (en una sucesión)* continuity; *(permanencia)* continuation; *Formal* **sin solución de c.** without stopping

**continuista** *nmf Pol* supporter of the status quo

**continuo, -a** *adj* (a) *(ininterrumpido)* continuous; **las continuas lluvias obligaron a suspender el partido** the constant *o* continual rain forced them to call off the match (b) *(perseverante)* continual; **me irritan sus continuas preguntas** her continual questioning irritates me

**contonearse** *vpr (hombre)* to swagger; *(mujer)* to swing one's hips

**contoneo** *nm (de hombre)* swagger; *(de mujer)* sway of the hips

**contornear** *vt (seguir el contorno de)* to go round; *(perfilar)* to outline

**contorno** *nm* (a) *Mat* contour; *(línea)* outline; **c. de cintura** waist (measurement); **c. de pecho** bust (measurement); **el c. accidentado de la isla** the ragged coastline of the island (b) **contornos** *(vecindad)* neighbourhood; *(de una ciudad)* outskirts

**contorsión** *nf* contortion

**contorsionarse** *vpr (retorcerse)* to do contortions; *(de dolor)* to writhe

**contorsionista** *nmf* contortionist

**contra 1** *prep* against; **un jarabe c. la tos** a cough syrup; **en c.** against; **estar en c. de algo, estar c. algo** to be opposed to sth; **en c. de** *(a diferencia de)* contrary to; **eso va c. el reglamento** that's against regulations
**2** *nm* **los pros y los contras** the pros and cons

**contraalmirante** *nm Mil* rear admiral

**contraatacar** [61] *vt* to counterattack

**contraataque** *nm* counterattack

**contrabajo 1** *nm (instrumento)* double-bass
**2** *nmf (instrumentista)* double-bass player

**contrabandista** *nmf* smuggler

**contrabando** *nm (acto)* smuggling; *(mercancías)* contraband; **pasar algo de c.** to smuggle sth in; **c. de armas** gunrunning; **tabaco de c.** contraband cigarettes

**contracción** *nf también Ling & Med* contraction

**contracepción** *nf* contraception

**contraceptivo, -a** *adj* contraceptive

**contrachapado, -a 1** *adj* (made of) plywood
**2** *nm* plywood

**contracorriente** *nf* crosscurrent; **ir a c.** to go against the current *o* tide

**contráctil** *adj* contractile

**contractual** *adj* contractual

**contracultura** *nf* counter-culture

**contracultural** *adj* counter-culture; **una corriente c.** a counter-culture movement

**contradecir** [53] **1** *vt* to contradict
**2 contradecirse** *vpr* to contradict oneself

**contradicción** *nf* contradiction; **estar en c. con** to be in (direct) contradiction to

**contradicho, -a** *participio ver* **contradecir**

**contradictorio, -a** *adj* contradictory

**contraer** [68] **1** *vt* (a) *(encoger)* to contract (b) *(vicio, costumbre)* to acquire (c) *(enfermedad)* to catch (d) **c. matrimonio (con)** to get married (to)
**2 contraerse** *vpr* to contract

**contraespionaje** *nm* counterespionage

**contrafuerte** *nm* (a) *Arquit* buttress (b) *(del calzado)* heel reinforcement (c) *Geog* foothill

**contragolpe** *nm* counter-attack

**contrahecho, -a** *adj* deformed

**contraindicación** *nf (en medicamento)* **contraindicaciones: embarazo, diabetes** not to be taken during pregnancy or by diabetics

**contraindicado, -a** *adj* **está c. beber alcohol durante el embarazo** alcohol should be avoided during pregnancy

**contraindicar** *vt (médico)* to advise against

**contralor** *nm Chile, Méx* = inspector of public spending

**contraloría** *nf Chile, Méx* = office controlling public spending

**contralto 1** *nm (voz)* contralto
**2** *nmf (cantante)* counter tenor, *f* contralto

**contraluz** *nm* back lighting; **a c.** against the light

**contramaestre** *nm* (a) *Náut* boatswain; *Mil* warrant officer (b) *(capataz)* foreman

**contramano: a contramano** *loc adv (en sentido contrario)* the wrong way

**contraofensiva** *nf* counteroffensive

**contraorden** *nf* countermand

**contrapartida** *nf* compensation; **como c.** to make up for it

**contrapelo: a contrapelo** *loc adv (acariciar)* the wrong way; **su intervención iba a c. del resto** his remarks went against the general opinion; **vivir a c.** to have an unconventional lifestyle

**contrapesar** *vt (físicamente)* to counterbalance; *Fig (contrarrestar)* to compensate for

**contrapeso** *nm (en ascensores, poleas)* counterweight; *Fig (fuerza que iguala)* counterbalance

**contraponer** [52] **1** *vt* (a) *(oponer)* **a su postura intransigente contrapusimos una más flexible** we responded to his

intransigence by suggesting greater flexibility
(**b**) *(cotejar)* to compare

**2 contraponerse** *vpr* to be opposed

**contraportada** *nf (de periódico, revista)* back
page; *(de libro, disco)* back cover

**contraposición** *nf* (**a**) *(oposición)* conflict
(**b**) *(comparación)* comparison

**contraproducente** *adj* counterproductive

**contraprogramación** *nf* = competitive
TV scheduling

**contrapuesto, -a 1** *participio ver* **contraponer**

**2** *adj* conflicting

**contrapunto** *nm Mús* counterpoint; *Fig (contraste)* contrast

**contrariado, -a** *adj* upset

**contrariar** [34] *vt* (**a**) *(contradecir)* to go
against (**b**) *(disgustar)* to upset

**contrariedad** *nf* (**a**) *(dificultad)* setback (**b**)
*(disgusto)* annoyance (**c**) *(oposición)* contrary *o*
opposing nature

**contrario, -a 1** *adj* (**a**) *(opuesto) (dirección,
sentido, idea)* opposite; *(parte)* opposing; **ser c.
a algo** to be opposed to sth (**b**) *(desfavorable)* **es
c. a nuestros intereses** it goes against our
interests

**2** *nm,f (rival)* opponent

**3** *nm (opuesto)* opposite; **al c., por el c.** on the
contrary; **de lo c.** otherwise; **todo lo c.** quite
the contrary

**4** *nf* **llevar la contraria** to be awkward *o*
contrary; **¡siempre me está llevando la contraria!** *(verbalmente)* she's always contradicting
me!; *(con acciones)* she always does the opposite
of what I tell her!

**contrarreembolso** *nm* cash on delivery

**Contrarreforma** *nf* *Hist* Counter-
Reformation

**contrarreloj 1** *adj inv Dep* **etapa c.** time
trial; *Fig* **trabajar a c.** to work against the clock

**2** *nf Dep* time trial

**contrarrembolso** *nm* cash on delivery

**contrarréplica** *nf* reply; **en su c., el ministro dijo que…** the minister countered
that…

**contrarrestar** *vt (neutralizar)* to counteract

**contrarrevolución** *nf* counterrevolution

**contrarrevolucionario, -a** *adj & nm,f*
counterrevolutionary

**contrasentido** *nm* **hacer/decir eso es un
c.** it doesn't make sense to do/say that

**contraseña** *nf* password

**contrastar 1** *vi* to contrast (**con** with)

**2** *vt (comprobar)* to check, to verify

**contraste** *nm* contrast; **en c. con** *(a diferencia de)* in contrast with *o* to; *(comparado con)* in
comparison with

**contrata** *nf Der* (fixed price) contract

**contratación** *nf (de personal)* hiring

**contratante** *nmf* contracting party

**contratar** *vt* (**a**) *(obreros, personal, detective)* to
hire; *(deportista)* to sign (**b**) *(servicio, obra, mercancía)* **c. algo a alguien** to contract for sth with
sb

**contraterrorismo** *nm* counterterrorism

**contraterrorista** *adj* counterterrorist

**contratiempo** *nm (accidente)* mishap; *(dificultad)* setback

**contratista** *nmf* contractor; **c. de obras**
building contractor

**contrato** *nm Com* contract; **c. administrativo** administrative contract; **c. de arrendamiento** lease; **c. basura** short-term contract
*(with poor conditions)*; **c. de compraventa** contract of sale; **c. fijo** *o* **indefinido** permanent
contract; **c. laboral** *o* **de trabajo** work contract; **c. mercantil** commercial contract; **c.
temporal** temporary *o* short-term contract; **c.
verbal** oral contract

**contraveneno** *nm* antidote

**contravenir** [71] *vi* **c. a** to contravene

**contraventana** *nf* shutter

**contrayente** *nmf Formal* **los contrayentes**
the bride and groom

**contribución** *nf* (**a**) *(aporte)* contribution
(**b**) *(impuesto)* tax; **c. directa/indirecta** di-
rect/indirect tax; **c. urbana** *Br* ≃ council tax,
= tax for local services

**contribuir** [36] *vi* (**a**) *(aportar)* to contribute
(**a** to); **c. con algo para** to contribute sth towards (**b**) *(pagar impuestos)* to pay taxes

**contribuyente** *nmf* taxpayer

**contrición** *nf* contrition

**contrincante** *nmf* rival, opponent

**contrito, -a** *adj* (**a**) *(arrepentido)* contrite (**b**)
*(triste, compungido)* downcast

**control** *nm* (**a**) *(dominio, mando)* control; **bajo
c.** under control; **perder el c.** to lose one's
temper; *Econ* **c. de cambios** foreign exchange
regulation; **c. de la natalidad** birth control; **c.
remoto** remote control (**b**) *(verificación)* examination, inspection; **(bajo) c. médico** (under) medical supervision; **c. antidoping**
dope *o* drugs test; **c. de calidad** quality control (**c**) *(de policía)* checkpoint

**controlador, -ora** *nm,f* controller; **c.
aéreo** air-traffic controller

**controlar 1** *vt* (**a**) *(dominar)* to control (**b**)
*(comprobar)* to check (**c**) *(vigilar)* to watch, to
keep an eye on

**2 controlarse** *vpr* to control oneself, to restrain oneself

**controversia** *nf* controversy

**contubernio** *nm Fig* conspiracy

**contumacia** *nf* obstinacy, stubbornness

**contumaz** *adj* stubborn, obstinate

**contundencia** *nf (de golpes)* force; *Fig (de palabras, argumentos)* forcefulness

**contundente** *adj (arma, objeto)* blunt; *(golpe)* thudding; *Fig (razonamiento, argumento)* forceful

**conturbar** *vt Formal* to trouble, to perturb

**contusión** *nf* bruise

**contusionar** *vt* to bruise

**contuviera** *etc ver* **contener**

**conurbación** *nf* conurbation

**convalecencia** *nf* convalescence

**convalecer** [48] *vi* to convalesce **(de** after)

**convaleciente** *adj* convalescent

**convalidación** *nf Educ (de estudios)* recognition; *(de asignaturas)* validation

**convalidar** *vt Educ (estudios)* to recognize; *(asignaturas)* to validate

**convección** *nf Fís* convection

**convector** *nm* convector; **c. de aire caliente** convection heater

**convencer** [42] **1** *vt* to convince; **c. a alguien de algo** to convince sb of sth

**2 convencerse** *vpr* **convencerse de** to become convinced of

**convencimiento** *nm (certeza)* conviction; *(acción)* convincing

**convención** *nf* convention

**convencional** *adj* conventional

**convencionalismo** *nm* conventionality

**conveniencia** *nf* **(a)** *(utilidad)* usefulness; *(oportunidad)* suitability **(b)** *(interés)* convenience; **sólo mira su c.** he only looks after his own interests

**conveniente** *adj (útil)* useful; *(oportuno)* suitable, appropriate; *(lugar, hora)* convenient; *(aconsejable)* advisable; **sería c. asistir** it would be a good idea to go

**convenio** *nm* agreement; *Ind* **c. colectivo** collective agreement; **c. salarial** wage agreement *o* settlement

**convenir** [71] **1** *vi* **(a)** *(venir bien)* to be suitable; **no te conviene hacerlo** you shouldn't do it **(b)** *(acordar)* **c. en** to agree on

**2** *vt* to agree on

**3** *v impersonal* **conviene analizar la situación** it would be a good idea to analyse the situation

**convento** *nm (de monjas)* convent; *(de monjes)* monastery

**conventual** *adj* **la vida c.** *(de monjas)* convent life; *(de monjes)* monastic life

**convergencia** *nf* convergence

**convergente** *adj* converging, convergent

**converger** [54] *vi* to converge

**conversación** *nf* conversation; **dar c. a alguien** to keep sb talking; **conversaciones** *(contactos)* talks

**conversada** *nf Am* chat

**conversador, -ora 1** *adj* talkative

**2** *nm,f* conversationalist

**conversar** *vi* to talk, to converse

**conversión** *nf* conversion

**converso, -a 1** *adj* converted

**2** *nm,f* convert

**convertibilidad** *nf Econ* convertibility

**convertible** *adj* convertible

**convertir** [27] **1** *vt* **(a)** *Rel* to convert **(b)** *(transformar)* **c. algo/a alguien en** to convert sth/sb into, to turn sth/sb into

**2 convertirse** *vpr* **(a)** *Rel* to convert **(a** to) **(b)** *(transformarse)* **convertirse en** to become, to turn into

**convexidad** *nf* convexity

**convexo, -a** *adj* convex

**convicción** *nf* conviction; **tener la c. de que** to be convinced that

**convicto, -a** *adj* convicted

**convidado, -a** *nm,f* guest; *Fig* **estuvo en la cena como el c. de piedra** he sat through the whole meal without saying a word

**convidar 1** *vt (invitar)* to invite; **c. a alguien a una copa** to stand *o* buy sb a drink; **me convidaron a comer en su casa** they invited me round for a meal

**2** *vi Fig (mover, incitar)* **el buen tiempo convida a salir** this good weather makes you want to get out

**conviene** *ver* **convenir**

**convierta** *etc ver* **convertir**

**convincente** *adj* convincing

**conviniera** *etc ver* **convenir**

**convite** *nm* **(a)** *(invitación)* invitation **(b)** *(fiesta)* banquet

**convivencia** *nf* living together

**convivir** *vi* to live together; **c. con** to live with

**convocar** [61] *vt (reunión)* to convene; *(huelga, elecciones)* to call

**convocatoria** *nf* **(a)** *(anuncio, escrito)* notice; **c. de huelga** strike (action); **llamar a c.** to summon **(b)** *(de examen)* **tengo el inglés en cuarta c.** this is the fourth time I've had to sit this exam

**convoy** *(pl* **convoyes***) nm* **(a)** *(de barcos, camiones)* convoy **(b)** *(tren)* train

**convulsión** *nf* **(a)** *(de músculos)* convulsion **(b)** *(de tierra)* tremor **(c)** *Fig (política, social)* **un**

**período de convulsiones** a period of upheaval

**convulsionar** vt Fig to throw into upheaval

**convulsivo, -a** adj convulsive

**convulso, -a** adj convulsed

**conyugal** adj conjugal; **vida c.** married life

**cónyuge** nmf spouse; **los cónyuges** husband and wife

**coña** nf muy Fam (a) (guasa) joke; **está de c.** she's joking; **¡ni de c.!** no way!, not on your life! (b) (casualidad) **acertó de c.** he got it right by chance (c) (molestia) drag, pain

**coñá, coñac** (pl coñacs) nm brandy, cognac

**coñazo** nm muy Fam pain, drag; **dar el c.** to be a pain; **ser un c.** (aburrido) to be really boring; (pesado) to be a pain

**coño** Vulg **1** nm (a) (vulva) cunt; **no me sale del c.** I can't be fucking bothered, Br I can't be arsed (b) (para enfatizar) **¿dónde/qué c....?** where/what the fuck...?; **en el quinto c.** in the back of beyond

**2** interj (a) (enfado) **¡c.!** for fuck's sake! (b) (sorpresa) **¡c.!** fucking hell!

**cooperación** nf cooperation

**cooperador, -ora** adj cooperative

**cooperante 1** adj cooperating

**2** nmf (overseas) volunteer worker

**cooperar** vi to cooperate (**con alguien en algo** with sb in sth)

**cooperativa** nf cooperative; **c. agrícola** farming cooperative; **c. de viviendas** housing cooperative

**cooperativismo** nm cooperative movement

**cooperativo, -a** adj cooperative

**coordenadas** nfpl coordinates; Mat **c. cartesianas** Cartesian coordinates

**coordinación** nf coordination

**coordinado, -a** adj coordinated

**coordinador, -ora 1** adj coordinating

**2** nm,f coordinator

**coordinadora** nf (organización) grouping

**coordinar** vt (a) (movimientos, gestos) to coordinate (b) (esfuerzos, medios) to combine, to pool

**copa** nf (a) (vaso) glass; **beber una c. de más** to have a drink too many; **ir de copas** to go out drinking; **¿quieres (tomar) una c.?** would you like (to have) a drink? (b) (de árbol) top; Fig **una mentira como la c. de un pino** a whopper (of a lie); **un penalti como la c. de un pino** a blatant penalty (c) (de sombrero) crown (d) (trofeo, competición) cup (e) **copas** (naipes) = suit in Spanish deck of cards, with the symbol of a goblet

**copar** vt Fig to monopolize

**copartícipe** nmf (en empresa) partner; (en actividad) participant

**copear** vi to have a few drinks

**Copenhague** n Copenhagen

**copeo** nm drinking; **ir de c.** to go out drinking

**copero, -a** adj Dep **un equipo c.** a good cup team; **partido c.** cup tie

**copete** nm (a) (de ave) crest (b) (de pelo) tuft (c) Fam **de alto c.** posh

**copetín** nm CSur cocktail

**copia** nf (a) (reproducción) copy; Informát **c. de seguridad** backup (b) (acción) copying (c) (persona) (spitting) image

**copiador, -ora** adj copying

**copiadora** nf (máquina) photocopier

**copiar** [15] **1** vt también Informát to copy; **copió lo que yo iba diciendo** he took down what I was saying

**2** vi (en examen) to cheat, to copy

**copiloto** nmf copilot

**copión, -ona** nm,f Fam (imitador) copycat; (en examen) cheat

**copiosamente** adv (llover) heavily; **llorar c.** to cry one's eyes out

**copioso, -a** adj abundant

**copista** nmf copyist

**copistería** nf (tienda) copy shop

**copla** nf (a) (canción) folksong, popular song; Fig **ya está otra vez con la misma c.** he's back on his hobbyhorse (b) (estrofa) verse, stanza

**copo** nm (a) (de nieve, cereales) flake; **copos de avena** rolled oats (b) (de algodón) ball

**copón** nm muy Fam **un lío del c.** a hell of a mess; **nos lo pasamos del c.** we had a hell of a good time

**coprocesador** nm Informát coprocessor; **c. matemático** maths coprocessor

**coproducción** nf coproduction

**copropiedad** nf timesharing

**copropietario, -a** nm,f co-owner, joint owner

**cópula** nf (a) (sexual) copulation (b) Gram copula

**copulación** nf también Gram copulation

**copular** vi to copulate

**copulativo, -a** adj Gram copulative

**copyright** [kopi'rrait] nm copyright

**coque** nm coke

**coqueta** nf (tocador) dressing table

**coquetear** vi también Fig to flirt

**coquetería** nf coquetry

**coqueto, -a** adj (a) (persona) (que flirtea) flirtatious; (que se arregla mucho) concerned with one's appearance (**b**) *(cosa)* charming, delightful

**coraje** *nm* (**a**) *(valor)* courage (**b**) *(rabia)* anger; **me da mucho c.** it makes me furious

**coral 1** *adj* choral

**2** *nm* coral

**3** *nf* (**a**) *(coro)* choir (**b**) *(composición)* chorale

**coralino, -a** *adj* coral

**Corán** *nm Rel* **el C.** the Koran

**coránico, -a** *adj Rel* Koranic

**coraza** *nf* (**a**) *(de soldado)* cuirasse (**b**) *(de tortuga)* shell (**c**) *Fig (protección)* shield

**corazón** *nm* (**a**) *también Fig* heart; *Fig* **con el c. en la mano** frankly, openly; **de buen c.** kindhearted; **de (todo) c.** from the bottom of one's heart, quite sincerely; **no tener c.** to have no heart, to be heartless; **se me encoge el c. al ver...** it breaks my heart to see...; **romper** *o* **partir el c. a alguien** to break sb's heart (**b**) *(de frutas)* core (**c**) *Rel* **Sagrado C.** Sacred Heart

**corazonada** *nf* (**a**) *(presentimiento)* feeling, hunch (**b**) *(impulso)* sudden impulse

**corbata** *nf* tie; **c. de pajarita** bow tie

**corbeta** *nf Mil* corvette

**Córcega** *n* Corsica

**corcel** *nm* steed

**corchea** *nf Mús Br* quaver, *US* eighth note

**corchera** *nf* lane marker *(in swimming pool)*

**corchete** *nm* (**a**) *(broche)* hook and eye (**b**) *(signo ortográfico)* square bracket (**c**) *Chile (grapa)* staple

**corchetera** *nf · Chile* stapler

**corcho** *nm* cork

**corcholata** *nf Méx* metal bottle top

**córcholis** *interj (para expresar sorpresa)* ¡**c**.! good heavens!

**corcova** *nf* hump

**corcovado, -a** *nm,f* hunchback

**cordada** *nf* = roped party of mountaineers

**cordaje** *nm* (**a**) *(de guitarra, raqueta)* strings (**b**) *Náut* rigging

**cordel** *nm* cord; **a c.** in a straight line

**cordelería** *nf (tienda)* = shop selling rope, string etc

**cordero, -a** *nm,f también Fig* lamb

**cordial** *adj* cordial

**cordialidad** *nf* cordiality

**cordillera** *nf* mountain range; **la C. Cantábrica** the Cantabrian Mountains; *CSur* **la C.** the southern Andes

**cordobés, -esa 1** *adj* of/from Córdoba

**2** *nm,f* person from Córdoba

**cordón** *nm* (**a**) *(cuerda) también Anat* cord; *(de zapato)* lace; **c. umbilical** umbilical cord (**b**) *(cable eléctrico)* flex (**c**) *Fig (para protección, vigilancia)* cordon; **c. sanitario** cordon sanitaire (**d**)

*CSur, Chile, Cuba (de la acera)* kerb; **aparcar en c.** to park end-to-end

**cordura** *nf (juicio)* sanity; *(sensatez)* sense

**Corea** *n* **C. del Norte/del Sur** North/South Korea

**coreana** *nf (abrigo)* parka, snorkel jacket

**coreano, -a** *adj & nm,f* Korean

**corear** *vt (exclamando)* to chorus; *(cantando)* to sing

**coreografía** *nf* choreography

**coreógrafo, -a** *nm,f* choreographer

**corintio, -a** *adj & nm,f* Corinthian

**corista 1** *nmf (en coro)* chorus singer

**2** *nf (en cabaret)* chorus girl

**cormorán** *nm* cormorant

**cornada** *nf Taurom* = wound from bull's horns; **el torero recibió tres cornadas** the bullfighter was gored three times

**cornamenta** *nf* (**a**) *(de toro)* horns; *(de ciervo)* antlers (**b**) *Fam Fig (de marido engañado)* cuckold's horns

**cornamusa** *nf* (**a**) *(trompeta)* hunting horn (**b**) *(gaita)* bagpipes

**córnea** *nf* cornea

**cornear** *vt* to gore

**corneja** *nf* crow

**córner** *( pl* **córners)** *nm Dep* corner (kick)

**corneta 1** *nf (instrumento)* bugle

**2** *nmf (persona)* bugler

**cornete** *nm* (**a**) *Anat* turbinate bone (**b**) *(helado)* cornet, cone

**cornetín 1** *nm (instrumento)* cornet

**2** *nmf (persona)* cornet player

**cornflakes®** ['konfleiks] *nmpl* Cornflakes®

**cornisa** *nf* (**a**) *Arquit* cornice (**b**) *Geog* **la c. cantábrica** the Cantabrian coast

**Cornualles** *n* Cornwall

**cornucopia** *nf* (**a**) *(espejo)* = small decorative mirror (**b**) *(cuerno)* cornucopia, horn of plenty

**cornudo, -a 1** *adj* (**a**) *(animal)* horned (**b**) *Fam Fig (marido)* cuckolded

**2** *nm Fam Fig* cuckold

**coro** *nm* (**a**) *(grupo de voces, parte de iglesia)* choir; **contestar a c.** to answer all at once (**b**) *(de obra musical)* chorus

**corola** *nf* corolla

**corolario** *nm* corollary

**corona** *nf* (**a**) *(de monarca)* crown (**b**) *(de flores)* garland; **c. fúnebre/de laurel** funeral/laurel wreath (**c**) *(de santos)* halo

**coronación** *nf* (**a**) *(de monarca)* coronation (**b**) *Fig (remate, colmo)* culmination

**coronamiento** *nm* (**a**) *Fig (remate, fin)* culmination (**b**) *Arquit* crown

**coronar** vt (a) (persona) to crown (b) Fig (terminar) to complete; (culminar) to crown, to cap (c) Fig (cima) to reach

**coronario, -a** adj Anat coronary

**coronel** nm Mil colonel

**coronilla** nf crown (of the head); Fam **estar hasta la c. (de)** to be sick and tired (of)

**corotos** nmpl Carib things, whatnots

**corpachón** nm big body, big frame

**corpiño** nm bodice

**corporación** nf corporation; **corporaciones locales** local authorities

**corporal** adj corporal

**corporativismo** nm Pol = self-interested behaviour, especially of professional groups

**corporativo, -a** adj corporate

**corpóreo, -a** adj corporeal

**corpulencia** nf corpulence

**corpulento, -a** adj corpulent

**Corpus Christi** ['korpus 'kristi] nm Rel Corpus Christi

**corpúsculo** nm corpuscle

**corral** nm (a) (para aves) run; (para cerdos, ovejas) pen (b) Hist (para teatro) = open-air theatre in courtyard

**corrala** nf = building with several floors of small flats on running balconies round a central courtyard

**corralito** nm (para niños) playpen

**correa** nf (a) (de bolso, reloj) strap; (cinturón) belt; (de perro) lead, leash (b) Tec belt; **c. del ventilador** fan belt

**correaje** nm (de caballo) harness; (de soldado) equipment belts

**corrección** nf (a) (de error) correction; (de examen) marking; (de texto) revision; **c. de pruebas** proofreading (b) (perfección) correctness (c) (de comportamiento) correctness, courtesy (d) (reprimenda) reprimand

**correccional** nm reformatory, reform school

**correctivo, -a 1** adj corrective
**2** nm punishment

**correcto, -a** adj (a) (resultado, texto, respuesta) correct (b) (persona) polite; (conducta) proper

**corrector, -ora 1** adj corrective
**2** nm,f **c. (de pruebas)** proofreader
**3** nm Informát **c. de estilo** stylechecker; **c. ortográfico** spellchecker

**corredera** nf (ranura) runner; **puerta de c.** sliding door

**corredizo, -a** adj sliding

**corredor, -ora 1** adj running; **ave corredora** large flightless bird
**2** nm,f (a) (deportista) runner; **c. de fondo** long-distance runner; Fig **ser un c. de fondo** to have staying power (b) Fin & Com (intermediario) **c. de bolsa** stockbroker; **c. de comercio** registered broker; **c. de fincas** land agent; **c. de seguros** insurance broker
**3** nm (pasillo) corridor, passage

**correduría** nf Com **c. de seguros** (oficina) insurance broker's

**corregidor, -ora** nm,f Hist = magistrate appointed by the king, especially in former Spanish colonies

**corregir** [57] **1** vt (a) (error) to correct; (examen) to mark (b) (reprender) to reprimand
**2 corregirse** vpr to change for the better

**correlación** nf correlation

**correlacionar** vt to correlate

**correlativo, -a** adj correlative

**correligionario, -a** nm,f (en política, ideología) person of the same ideological persuasion; (en religión) fellow believer; **Churchill y sus correligionarios** Churchill and his fellow conservatives

**correo 1** adj **tren c.** mail train
**2** nm post, mail; **a vuelta de c.** by return (of post); **echar algo al c.** to post sth; **mandar algo por c.** to send sth by post; **Correos** (organismo) the post office; **c. aéreo** airmail; **c. certificado** registered post o mail; **c. comercial** direct mail; **c. electrónico** electronic mail, e-mail; **c. urgente** special delivery

**correoso, -a** adj (carne) leathery, tough; (pan) chewy

**correr 1** vi (a) (persona, animal) to run; **a todo c.** at full speed o pelt; Fam **corre que se las pela** she runs like the wind
(b) (conductor) to drive fast
(c) (río) to flow; (camino, agua del grifo) to run
(d) (el tiempo, las horas) to pass, to go by
(e) (noticia) to spread; **corre el rumor de que…** there's a rumour that…
(f) **c. con los gastos (de algo)** to bear the cost (of sth); **c. a cargo de** to be taken care of by
**2** vt (a) (recorrer) (una distancia) to cover; **corrió los 100 metros** he ran the 100 metres
(b) (mover) (mesa, silla) to move o pull up
(c) (cerrar) **c. las cortinas** to draw the curtains; **c. el pestillo** to bolt the door; Fig **corramos un tupido velo (sobre ese asunto)** let's draw a veil over that
(d) (experimentar) **c. aventuras** to have adventures; **c. peligro** to be in danger; **c. el riesgo de (hacer) algo** to run the risk of (doing) sth
(e) Fam Informát (programa, aplicación) to run
**3 correrse** vpr (a) (desplazarse) (persona) to move over; (cosa) to slide
(b) (pintura, colores) to run; **se me ha corrido el rímel** my mascara has run

**(c)** *Vulg (tener un orgasmo)* to come; *Fig* **correrse de gusto (con algo)** *(disfrutar)* to get off (on sth)

**correría** *nf* foray

**correspondencia** *nf* **(a)** *(relación, correo)* correspondence **(b)** *(de metro, tren)* connection; **próxima estación, Sol, c. con línea tres** next stop Sol, change here for line three

**corresponder 1** *vi* **(a)** *(compensar)* **c. (con algo) a alguien/algo** to repay sb/sth (with sth) **(b)** *(pertenecer)* to belong **(c)** *(coincidir)* to correspond **(a/con** to/with**) (d)** *(competer)* **corresponderle a alguien hacer algo** to be sb's responsibility to do sth

**2** *vt (sentimiento)* to repay; **ella no le corresponde** she didn't feel the same way about him; **amor no correspondido** unrequited love

**3 corresponderse** *vpr* **(a)** *(escribirse)* to correspond **(b)** *(amarse)* to love each other

**correspondiente** *adj* **(a)** *(perteneciente, relativo)* corresponding **(a** to**) (b)** *(respectivo)* respective

**corresponsal** *nmf* **(a)** *Prensa* correspondent **(b)** *Com* agent

**corresponsalía** *nf* post of correspondent

**corretaje** *nm Com* brokerage

**corretear** *vi* **(a)** *(correr)* to run about **(b)** *Fam (vagar)* to hang about **(c)** *Méx (adelantar)* to overtake

**correveidile** *nmf* gossip

**corrida** *nf* **(a)** *Taurom* bullfight **(b)** *(acción de correr)* run

**corrido, -a 1** *adj* **(a)** *(cortinas)* drawn **(b)** *(avergonzado)* embarrassed **(c)** *(continuo)* continuous; **balcón c.** long balcony *(running across building)*; **banco c.** long bench; *Fig* **de c.** by heart; **recitar algo de c.** to recite sth parrot-fashion

**2** *nm (canción mejicana)* Mexican ballad

**corriente 1** *adj* **(a)** *(normal)* ordinary, normal; *Fam* **c. y moliente** run-of-the-mill **(b)** *(agua)* running **(c)** *(mes, año, cuenta)* current

**2** *nf* **(a)** *(de río, electricidad)* current; *Elec* **c. alterna/continua** alternating/direct current **(b)** *(de aire)* draught **(c)** *Fig (tendencia)* trend, current; *(de opinión)* tide **(d)** *(expresiones)* **dejarse llevar de o por la c.** to follow the crowd; **estar al c. de** to be up to date with; **ir contra c.** to go against the tide

**corrigió** *ver* **corregir**

**corrijo** *ver* **corregir**

**corrillo** *nm* knot *o* small group of people; **formar corrillos** to go into huddles

**corrimiento** *nm* shift, slipping; **c. de tierras** landslide

**corro** *nm* **(a)** *(círculo)* circle, ring; **en c.** in a circle; **hacer c.** to form a circle **(b)** *Fin (cotizaciones)* stocks

**corroboración** *nf* corroboration

**corroborar** *vt* to corroborate

**corroer** [59] *vt* **(a)** *(desgastar)* to corrode; *Geol* to erode **(b)** *Fig (consumir)* to consume, to eat away at; **le corroe la envidia** he's consumed with envy

**corromper 1** *vt* **(a)** *(madera)* to rot; *(alimentos)* to turn bad, to spoil **(b)** *(pervertir)* to corrupt **(c)** *(sobornar)* to bribe

**2 corromperse** *vpr* **(a)** *(pudrirse)* to rot **(b)** *(pervertirse)* to become corrupted

**corrosión** *nf* **(a)** *(desgaste)* corrosion; *(de un metal)* rust; *Geol* erosion

**corrosivo, -a** *adj también Fig* corrosive

**corrupción** *nf* **(a)** *(delito, decadencia)* corruption; *Der* **c. de menores** corruption of minors **(b)** *(soborno)* bribery **(c)** *(de una sustancia)* decay

**corruptela** *nf* corruption

**corrupto, -a** *adj* corrupt

**corruptor, -ora 1** *adj* corrupting

**2** *nm,f* corrupter; *Der* **c. de menores** corruptor of minors

**corrusco** *nm* hard crust

**corsario, -a 1** *adj* pirate; **un buque c.** a pirate ship

**2** *nm* corsair, pirate

**corsé** *nm* corset

**corsetería** *nf* ladies' underwear shop

**corso, -a 1** *adj & nm,f* Corsican

**2** *nm (dialecto)* Corsican

**cortacésped** *(pl* **cortacéspedes)** *nm* lawnmower

**cortacircuitos** *nm inv* circuit breaker

**cortado, -a 1** *adj* **(a)** *(labios, manos)* chapped **(b)** *(leche)* sour, off; *(mayonesa)* off **(c)** *Fam (persona)* **estar c.** to be inhibited; **quedarse c.** to be left speechless; **ser c.** to be shy

**2** *nm (café)* = small coffee with just a little milk **(b)** *Fam (persona)* **ser un c.** to be shy

**cortador, -ora 1** *adj* cutting

**2** *nm (de césped)* lawnmower

**cortadora** *nf* cutter; **c. de césped** lawnmower

**cortadura** *nf* cut

**cortafuego** *nm* firebreak

**cortante** *adj* **(a)** *(afilado)* sharp **(b)** *Fig (tajante)* *(frase, estilo)* cutting; *(viento)* biting; *(frío)* bitter

**cortapisa** *nf* limitation, restriction

**cortaplumas** *nm inv* penknife

**cortapuros** *nm inv* cigar cutter

**cortar 1** *vt* **(a)** *(seccionar)* to cut; *(en pedazos)* to cut up; *(escindir)* *(rama, brazo, cabeza)* to cut off;

*(talar)* to cut down; **c. una rebanada de pan** to cut a slice of bread

**(b)** *(recortar)* *(tela, figura de papel)* to cut out

**(c)** *(interrumpir)* *(retirada, luz, teléfono)* to cut off; *(carretera)* to block (off); *(hemorragia)* to stop, to staunch; *(discurso, conversación)* to interrupt

**(d)** *(atravesar)* *(calle, territorio)* to cut across

**(e)** *(labios, piel)* to crack, to chap

**(f)** *(hender)* *(aire, olas)* to slice through

**(g)** *(baraja)* to cut

**(h)** *(leche)* to curdle

**(i)** *(recortar)* *(gastos)* to cut back

**(j)** *(poner fin a)* *(beca)* to cut; *(abusos)* to put a stop to; **c. un problema de raíz** *(impedirlo)* to nip a problem in the bud; *(erradicarlo)* to root a problem out

**(k)** *(avergonzar)* **este hombre me corta un poco** I find it hard to be myself when that man's around

**(l)** *(censurar)* to censor; *(película)* to cut

**(m)** *Informát* **c. y pegar** cut and paste

**2** *vi* **(a)** *(producir un corte)* to cut; *Fig* **c. por lo sano** *(aplicar una solución drástica)* to resort to drastic measures; *(para evitar más pérdidas)* to cut one's losses

**(b)** *(atajar)* to take a short cut (**por** through)

**(c)** *(terminar una relación)* to split up (con with)

**3 cortarse** *vpr* **(a)** *(herirse)* to cut oneself; **cortarse el pelo** to have a haircut; **cortarse (en) la cara** to cut one's face

**(b)** *(labios, piel)* to become chapped *o* cracked

**(c)** *(leche)* to curdle

**(d)** *(interrumpirse)* **se cortó la comunicación** I was/we were *etc* cut off; **se te va a c. la digestión** you'll get stomach cramps

**(e)** *Fam* *(turbarse)* to become tongue-tied; **no se corta a la hora de criticar** he doesn't mince his words *o* hold back when he has criticisms to make

**cortaúñas** *nm inv* nail clippers

**corte 1** *nm* **(a)** *(raja)* cut; **c. y confección** *(para mujeres)* dressmaking; *(para hombres)* tailoring

**(b)** *(retal de tela)* length

**(c)** *(contorno)* shape

**(d)** *(interrupción)* **c. de luz** power cut; **c. de digestión** stomach cramps

**(e)** *(sección)* section

**(f)** *(concepción, estilo)* style

**(g)** *(pausa)* break

**(h)** *(filo)* (cutting) edge

**(i)** *Fam* *(vergüenza)* embarrassment; **dar c. a alguien** to embarrass sb; **me da c. decírselo** I feel embarrassed to tell him

**(j)** *Fam* *(respuesta ingeniosa)* put-down; **dar** *o* **pegar un c. a alguien** to cut sb dead

**(k)** **c. de mangas** = obscene gesture involving raising one arm with a clenched fist

and placing one's other hand in the crook of one's elbow; *Fig* **hacer un c. de mangas a alguien** to stick two fingers up at sb

**2** *nf* **(a)** *(del Rey)* court; **las Cortes** *Pol* the Spanish parliament

**(b)** *Fig* **hacer la c. a alguien** to court sb

**cortedad** *nf* **(a)** *(de longitud)* shortness; *(de duración)* shortness, brevity **(b)** *Fig (timidez)* shyness; **c. de miras** shortsightedness

**cortejar** *vt* to court

**cortejo** *nm* retinue; **c. fúnebre** funeral cortège *o* procession

**cortés** ( *pl* **corteses**) *adj* polite, courteous

**cortesana** *nf* *(prostituta)* courtesan

**cortesano, -a 1** *adj* *(modales)* courtly; **la vida cortesana** life at court

**2** *nm,f* *(personaje de la corte)* courtier

**cortesía** *nf* courtesy; **de c.** courtesy; **por c. de** courtesy of; **una visita de c.** a courtesy call

**corteza** *nf* **(a)** *(del árbol)* bark **(b)** *(de pan)* crust; *(de queso, tocino, limón)* rind; *(de naranja)* peel; **cortezas de cerdo** pork scratchings **(c)** *Geol (terrestre)* crust **(d)** *Anat* cortex

**cortical** *adj* cortical

**corticoide** *nm* corticoid

**cortijo** *nm (finca)* farm *(typical of Andalusia and Extremadura)*; *(casa)* farmhouse

**cortina** *nf* *(de tela)* curtain; *Fig* **c. de agua** sheet of water; *Fig* **c. de humo** smokescreen

**cortinaje** *nm* curtains

**cortisona** *nf* cortisone

**corto, -a 1** *adj* **(a)** *(de poca longitud, duración)* short **(b)** *(escaso)* *(raciones)* small, meagre; *(disparo)* short of the target; **c. de** *(dinero)* short of; *Fig* **c. de miras** short-sighted; **c. de vista** short-sighted **(c)** *Fig (tonto)* **c. (de alcances)** dim, simple **(d)** *(expresiones)* **ni c. ni perezoso** just like that; **quedarse c.** *(al calcular)* to underestimate; **decir que es bueno es quedarse c.** it's an understatement to call it good

**2** *nf* **a la corta o a la larga** sooner or later

**3** *nm Cine* short (film)

**cortocircuito** *nm* short circuit

**cortometraje** *nm* short (film)

**coruñés, -esa 1** *adj* of/from La Coruña

**2** *nm,f* person from La Coruña

**corva** *nf* back of the knee

**corvo, -a** *adj (curvado)* curved; *(nariz)* hooked

**corzo, -a** *nm,f* roe buck, f roe deer

**cosa** *nf* **(a)** *(objeto, idea)* thing; **¿queréis alguna c.?** is there anything you want?; **no es gran c.** it's not important, it's no big deal; **poca c.** nothing much; **eso es c. fácil** that's easy

**(b)** *(asunto)* matter; **la c. se pone fea** things are getting ugly, there's trouble brewing; **eso es**

**c. mía** that's my affair o business; **no era c. de presentarse sin avisar** you couldn't just turn up without warning

(**c**) *(ocurrencia)* funny remark; **¡qué cosas tienes!** you do say some funny things!; **son cosas de mamá** that's just the way Mum is, that's just one of Mum's little idiosyncrasies

(**d**) *Fam (reparo)* **me da c. decírselo** I'd rather not tell him

(**e**) *(expresiones)* **se presentó al examen a c. hecha** he sat the exam although he knew he was certain to pass; **hacer algo como quien no quiere la c.** *(disimuladamente)* to do sth innocently; *(sin querer)* to do sth almost without realizing it; **como si tal c.** as if nothing had happened; **c. de** about; **tardará c. de tres semanas** it'll take about three weeks; **las cosas como son, nunca vas a aprobar ese examen** let's face it, you're never going to pass that exam; **entre unas cosas y otras** what with one thing and another; **no sea c. que** just in case; **tendrá treinta años o c. así** he must be thirty or thereabouts; **¡qué c.!** how strange!; **y cosas así** and so on

**cosaco, -a 1** *adj* Cossack
**2** *nm,f* Cossack; **beber como un c.** to drink like a fish

**coscorrón** *nm* bump on the head; **se dio un c.** he bumped his head

**cosecante** *nf Mat* cosecant

**cosecha** *nf* (**a**) *Agr* harvest; *Fam Fig* **ser de la (propia) c. de alguien** to be made up o invented by sb (**b**) *(del vino)* vintage

**cosechadora** *nf* combine harvester

**cosechar 1** *vt* (**a**) *(cultivar)* to grow (**b**) *(recolectar)* to harvest (**c**) *Fig (obtener)* to win, to reap; **su última novela ha cosechado muchos éxitos** his latest novel has been a great success
**2** *vi* to (bring in the) harvest

**cosechero, -a** *nm,f (de cereales)* harvester, reaper; *(de frutos)* picker

**coseno** *nm Mat* cosine

**coser 1** *vt* (**a**) *(con hilo)* to sew; **c. un botón** to sew on a button (**b**) *(con grapas)* to staple (together) (**c**) *(expresiones)* **c. a alguien a balazos** to riddle sb with bullets; **c. a cuchilladas** to stab repeatedly
**2** *vi* to sew; *Fam Fig* **ser c. y cantar** to be child's play o a piece of cake

**cosido** *nm* stitching

**cosmética** *nf* cosmetics *(singular)*

**cosmético, -a 1** *adj* cosmetic; **productos cosméticos** cosmetics
**2** *nm* cosmetic

**cósmico, -a** *adj* cosmic

**cosmogonía** *nf* cosmogony

**cosmografía** *nf* cosmography

**cosmología** *nf* cosmology

**cosmonauta** *nmf* cosmonaut

**cosmopolita** *adj & nmf* cosmopolitan

**cosmos** *nm inv* cosmos

**coso** *nm* (**a**) *Taurom (plaza)* bullring (**b**) *Chile, CSur (chisme)* whatnot, thing

**cosquillas** *nfpl* **hacer c.** to tickle; **tener c.** to be ticklish; *Fig* **buscarle las c. a alguien** to wind sb up, to irritate sb

**cosquilleo** *nm* tickling sensation

**costa** *nf* (**a**) *Geog* coast; **la C. Azul** the Côte d'Azur; **la C. Brava** the Costa Brava (**b**) *(coste)* **a c. de** at the expense of; **lo hizo a c. de grandes esfuerzos** he did it by dint of much effort; **aún vive a c. de sus padres** he's still living off his parents; **a toda c.** at all costs; *Der* **costas (judiciales)** (legal) costs

**Costa de Marfil** *n* Ivory Coast

**costado** *nm* side; **de c.** sideways

**costal 1** *adj Med* rib, costal; **tiene una fractura c.** he has a fractured rib
**2** *nm* sack

**costalada** *nf,* **costalazo** *nm* heavy fall *(backwards)*; **darse una c.** to fall over backwards

**costanera** *nf Chile, CSur* seaside promenade

**costar** [65] *vi* (**a**) *(dinero)* to cost; **¿cuánto cuesta?** how much is it?; *Fig* **c. un ojo de la cara** o **un riñón** to cost an arm and a leg
(**b**) *(tiempo)* to take; **nos costó seis horas llegar** it took us six hours to get there
(**c**) *(ser difícil, penoso)* **me costó decírselo** I found it difficult to tell him; **no le habría costado nada ayudarme** it wouldn't have cost him anything to help me; **c. trabajo** to be difficult, to take a lot of work; **me costó (trabajo) acostumbrarme** it took me a while to get used to it; **cuesta (trabajo) abrir esa puerta** this door is difficult to open
(**d**) *(expresiones)* **c. caro a alguien** to cost sb dear; **cueste lo que cueste** whatever the cost; **le costó la vida** it cost him his life

**Costa Rica** *n* Costa Rica

**costarricense, costarriqueño, -a** *adj & nm,f* Costa Rican

**coste** *nm (de producción)* cost; *(de un objeto)* price; **c. de la vida** cost of living; *Econ* **c. unitario** unit cost

**costear 1** *vt* (**a**) *(pagar)* to pay for (**b**) *Náut (la costa)* to hug, to keep close to
**2** *costearse vpr (pagarse)* **algo** *(pagarse)* to pay for sth oneself; **trabaja para costearse los estudios** she's working to pay for her studies

**costeño, -a, costero, -a 1** *adj* coastal; **un pueblo c.** a seaside town

**2** *nm,f Am* = person from the coast

**costilla** *nf* (a) *Anat & Náut* rib; *Fam* **costillas** *(espalda)* back (b) *Culin* cutlet (c) *Fam Fig (cónyuge)* better half

**costillar** *nm (de persona)* ribs, ribcage; *(de carne)* side

**costo** *nm* (a) *(de una mercancía)* price; *(de un producto, de la vida)* cost (b) *muy Fam (hachís)* hash

**costoso, -a** *adj (operación, maquinaria)* expensive; *Fig (trabajo)* exhausting; *(triunfo)* costly

**costra** *nf (de suciedad, de tierra)* layer, crust; *(de pan)* crust; *(de herida)* scab

**costumbre** *nf* habit, custom; **tomar/perder la c. de hacer algo** to get into/out of the habit of doing sth; **como de c.** as usual; **tener la c. de** *o* **tener por c. hacer algo** to be in the habit of doing sth; **costumbres** *(de país, cultura)* customs; *(de persona)* habits

**costumbrista** *adj (novela)* = describing the customs of a country or region

**costura** *nf* (a) *(labor)* sewing, needlework (b) *(en tela)* seam (c) *(oficio)* dressmaking; **alta c.** haute couture (d) *(cicatriz)* scar

**costurera** *nf* dressmaker, seamstress

**costurero** *nm (caja)* sewing box

**cota** *nf* (a) *(altura)* altitude, height above sea level (b) *(armadura)* **c. de mallas** coat of mail (c) *Fig* **alcanzar altas cotas de popularidad** to become very popular

**cotangente** *nf Mat* cotangent

**cotarro** *nm Fam* riotous gathering; **dirigir el c.** to rule the roost, to be the boss

**cotejar** *vt* to compare

**cotejo** *nm* comparison

**cotice** *etc ver* **cotizar**

**cotidianidad** *nf (vida cotidiana)* everyday life; *(frecuencia)* commonness

**cotidiano, -a** *adj* daily; **el trabajo c.** day-to-day tasks; **ser algo c.** to be an everyday occurrence

**cotiledón** *nm* cotyledon

**cotilla** *Fam* **1** *adj* gossipy

**2** *nmf* gossip, busybody

**cotillear** *vi Fam* to gossip

**cotilleo** *nm Fam* gossip, tittle-tattle; **tengo que contarte un c.** I've got a bit of gossip to tell you

**cotillón** *nm* = party on New Year's Eve or 5th of January

**cotizable** *adj* quotable

**cotización** *nf* (a) *(valor)* value (b) *(en Bolsa)* quotation, price (c) *(a la seguridad social)* contribution

**cotizado, -a** *adj* (a) *(en Bolsa)* quoted (b) *(persona)* sought-after

**cotizar** **[16] 1** *vt* (a) *(valorar)* to quote, to price (b) *(pagar)* to pay

**2** *vi Com (pagar)* to contribute; **los trabajadores tienen que c. a la seguridad social** employees have to pay Social Security contributions

**3 cotizarse** *vpr* (a) *(estimarse)* to be valued *o* prized; **el conocimiento de idiomas se cotiza mucho** a knowledge of foreign languages is considered extremely important (b) **cotizarse a mil pesetas** *(producto)* to sell for a thousand pesetas, to fetch a thousand pesetas; *(bonos, valores)* to be quoted at a thousand pesetas

**coto** *nm* preserve; **c. de caza** game preserve; *Fig* **poner c. a** to put a stop to

**cotorra** *nf* (a) *(ave)* parrot (b) *Fam Fig (persona)* chatterbox; **hablar como una c.** to talk nineteen to the dozen

**cotorrear** *vi Fam* to chatter

**coturno** *nm* buskin

**COU** [kou] *nm (abrev de* **curso de orientación universitaria***)* = one-year course which prepares pupils aged 17-18 for Spanish university entrance examinations

**country** ['kauntri] **1** *adj* **estilo c.** country (and western) style

**2** *nm* country (and western) music

**covacha** *nf* hovel

**coxal** *adj* hip; **fractura c.** hip fracture

**coxis** *nm inv* coccyx

**coyote** *nm* coyote

**coyuntura** *nf* (a) *(situación)* moment; **la c. económica** the economic situation (b) *(articulación)* joint

**coyuntural** *adj* temporary, provisional

**coz** *nf* kick; *Fam Fig* **tratar a alguien a coces** to treat sb like dirt

**CPS** *Informát (abrev de* **caracteres por segundo***)* CPS

**CPU** *nf Informát (abrev de* **Central Processing Unit***)* CPU

**crac** *(pl* **cracs***) nm Fin* crash

**crack** [krak] *(pl* **cracks***) nm* (a) *Fig (estrella)* star, superstar (b) *Fin* crash (c) *(droga)* crack

**cracker** *nmf Fam Informát* cracker

**crampón** *nm* crampon

**craneal** *adj* cranial

**cráneo** *nm* cranium, skull; *Fam* **ir de c.** to be doing badly

**crápula** *nmf* libertine

**craso, -a** *adj* (a) *Fig (grave) (error)* serious; *(ignorancia)* astonishing (b) *(grueso)* fat

**cráter** *nm* crater

**creación** *nf* creation

**creador, -ora 1** *adj* creative

**2** *nm,f* creator; **c. gráfico** creator *(of cartoon etc)*; **el C.** the Creator

**crear 1** *vt* **(a)** *(hacer, producir, originar)* to create; **me crea muchos problemas** it gives me a lot of trouble, it causes me a lot of problems; **Picasso creó escuela** Picasso's works have had a seminal influence **(b)** *(inventar)* to invent **(c)** *(fundar)* to found

**2 crearse** *vpr (inventarse)* **se ha creado un mundo de fantasía** he lives in his own little world; **se crea problemas él solo** he imagines problems where there aren't any

**creatividad** *nf* creativity

**creativo, -a 1** *adj* creative

**2** *nm,f (en publicidad)* ideas man, *f* ideas woman

**crecepelo** *nm* hair tonic *o* restorer

**crecer** [48] **1** *vi* **(a)** *(persona, planta)* to grow **(b)** *(días, noches)* to grow longer **(c)** *(río, marea)* to rise **(d)** *(aumentar) (desempleo, valor)* to grow, to increase; *(rumores)* to spread **(e)** *(la luna)* to wax

**2 crecerse** *vpr* to become more self-confident; **crecerse ante las dificultades** to thrive in the face of adversity

**creces** *nmpl* **con c.** with interest; **los italianos nos superan con c.** the Italians are a lot better than us

**crecida** *nf* spate, flood

**crecido, -a** *adj (cantidad)* large; *(hijo)* grown-up

**creciente** *adj (seguridad, confianza)* growing; *(luna)* crescent, waxing

**crecimiento** *nm (desarrollo)* growth; *(de precios)* rise; **c. económico** economic growth; **c. sostenible** sustainable growth

**credencial 1** *adj* accrediting

**2** *nf (de acceso a un lugar)* pass; **credenciales (diplomáticas)** credentials

**credibilidad** *nf* credibility

**crediticio, -a** *adj* credit; **entidad crediticia** credit institution, lender

**crédito** *nm* **(a)** *Econ (préstamo)* loan; **(comprar algo) a c.** (to buy sth) on credit; **c. bancario** bank loan; **c. blando** soft loan; **c. al consumo** consumer credit; **c. a la exportación** export credit; **c. hipotecario** mortgage (loan); **c. oficial** official credit; **c. personal** personal loan **(b)** *(plazo de préstamo)* credit **(c)** *(confianza)* trust, belief; **digno de c.** trustworthy; **dar c. a algo** to believe sth; **¡no doy c. a mis oídos!** I can't believe my ears! **(d)** *(fama)* standing, reputation **(e)** *(en universidad)* credit **(f)** *Cine* **títulos de c.** credits

**credo** *nm* **(a)** *(religioso)* creed **(b)** *(ideológico, político)* credo

**credulidad** *nf* credulity

**crédulo, -a 1** *adj* credulous, gullible

**2** *nm,f* credulous *o* gullible person

**creencia** *nf* belief; **cada cual es libre de tener sus creencias** everyone is entitled to their own opinion; **es una c. popular** it's a commonly held belief

**creer** [39] **1** *vt* **(a)** *(estar convencido de)* to believe; **¡ya lo creo!** of course! **(b)** *(suponer)* to think; **no creo** I don't think so; **creo que sí** I think so; **c. a alguien capaz de hacer algo** to believe sb to be capable of doing sth

**2** *vi* to believe **(en** in)

**3 creerse** *vpr* **(a)** *(considerarse)* to believe oneself to be; **pero ¿tú quién te has creído que eres?** just who do you think you are? **(b)** *(dar por cierto)* to believe completely

**creíble** *adj* credible, believable

**creído, -a** *adj (presumido)* conceited

**crema 1** *nf (de leche, hidratante)* cream; **c. de espárragos** cream of asparagus soup; **c. de marisco** seafood bisque; **c. pastelera** (confectioner's) custard; **c. para zapatos** shoe polish

**2** *adj* cream; **color c.** cream(-coloured)

**cremación** *nf* cremation

**cremallera** *nf* **(a)** *(para cerrar)* Br zip (fastener), *US* zipper **(b)** *Tec* rack

**crematístico, -a** *adj* financial

**crematorio, -a 1** *adj* **horno c.** cremator

**2** *nm* crematorium

**cremoso, -a** *adj* creamy

**crepe** *nf* crepe

**crepé** *nm (tejido)* crepe

**crepitar** *vi* to crackle

**crepuscular** *adj* crepuscular, twilight; **luz c.** twilight

**crepúsculo** *nm (al amanecer)* first light; *(al anochecer)* twilight, dusk; *Fig* **en el c. de su vida** in his twilight years

**crescendo** [kres'tʃendo] *nm Mús & Fig* crescendo; **in c.** growing

**creso, -a** *adj Fam* **rico y c.** filthy rich

**crespo, -a** *adj* tightly curled, frizzy

**crespón** *nm* crepe

**cresta** *nf* **(a)** *(de gallo)* comb; *(de punk)* Mohican **(b)** *(de ola, montaña)* crest; **estar en la c. (de la ola)** to be riding high

**Creta** *n* Crete

**creta** *nf* chalk

**cretense** *adj & nmf* Cretan

**cretino, -a** *nm,f* cretin

**cretona** *nf* cretonne

**creyente 1** *adj* **ser c.** to be a believer

**2** *nmf* believer

**creyera** etc ver **creer**

**crezca** etc ver **crecer**

**cría** nf (a) (hijo del animal) young (b) (crianza) (de animales) breeding; (de plantas) growing

**criadero** nm (a) (de animales) farm (breeding place); (de árboles, plantas) nursery (b) (de mineral) seam

**criadillas** nfpl Culin bull's testicles

**criado, -a 1** adj brought up; **niño mal c.** spoilt child
**2** nm,f servant, f maid

**criador, -ora 1** adj producing
**2** nm,f (de animales) breeder; (de vinos) grower

**crianza** nf (a) (de bebé) nursing, breastfeeding (b) (de animales) breeding, rearing (c) (del vino) vintage; **vino de c.** vintage wine (d) (educación) breeding

**criar** [34] **1** vt (a) (amamantar) (sujeto: mujer) to breastfeed; (sujeto: animal) to suckle (b) (animales) to breed, to rear; (flores, árboles) to grow (c) (vino) to mature (d) (educar) to bring up
**2** **criarse** vpr (a) (crecer) to grow up; (educarse) to be educated (b) (reproducirse) to breed

**criatura** nf (a) (niño) child; (bebé) baby (b) (ser vivo) creature

**criba** nf (a) (tamiz) sieve (b) (selección) screening

**cribar** vt (a) (con tamiz) to sieve (b) (seleccionar) to screen out, to select

**Crimea** n Crimea

**crimen** nm crime; **cometer un c.** to commit a crime; **c. de guerra** war crime; **c. pasional** crime of passion, crime passionnel

**criminal** adj & nmf criminal

**criminalidad** nf (a) (cualidad) criminality (b) (índice de) **c.** crime rate

**criminalista 1** adj criminal; **abogado c.** criminal lawyer
**2** nmf criminal lawyer

**criminología** nf criminology

**crin** nf mane; **cepillo de c.** horsehair brush

**crío, -a** nm,f (niño) kid

**criollo, -a 1** adj (a) (persona) = native to Latin America (b) (comida, lengua) creole
**2** nm,f (persona) = person (black or white) born in Latin America
**3** nm (idioma) creole

**cripta** nf crypt

**críptico, -a** adj cryptic

**criptografía** nf cryptography

**criptograma** nm cryptogram

**criptón** nm Quím krypton

**críquet** nm cricket

**crisálida** nf chrysalis

**crisantemo** nm chrysanthemum

**crisis** nf inv (situación difícil) crisis; **c. económica** recession; **c. nerviosa** nervous breakdown; **estar en c.** to be in crisis

**crisma¹** nf Fam nut, Br bonce; **romperle la c. a alguien** to smash sb's head in; **romperse la c.** to bash one's head

**crisma²** nm inv Christmas card

**crisol** nm (de metales) crucible; Fig (lugar donde se mezclan cosas) melting pot

**crispado, -a** adj tense

**crispación** nf (de nervios) tension; (de músculos) tenseness

**crispar 1** vt (los nervios) to set on edge; (los músculos) to tense; (las manos) to clench; **este trabajo me crispa los nervios** this work sets my nerves on edge
**2** **crisparse** vpr to become tense

**cristal** nm (a) (material) glass; (vidrio fino) crystal; **el suelo está lleno de cristales** there's glass all over the floor; **c. tintado** tinted glass (b) (de ventana) (window) pane; (de gafas) lens (c) Min crystal (d) Fig (espejo) mirror

**cristalera** nf (puerta) French window; (ventana) large window

**cristalería** nf (a) (objetos) glassware; **les regalamos una c.** we gave them a set of glassware (b) (tienda) glazier's (shop); (fábrica) glassworks (singular)

**cristalero, -a** nm,f glazier

**cristalino, -a 1** adj crystalline
**2** nm crystalline lens

**cristalización** nf también Fig crystallization

**cristalizar** [16] **1** vi también Fig to crystallize
**2** **cristalizarse** vpr to crystallize; Fig **cristalizarse en** to develop into

**cristiandad** nf Christianity

**cristianismo** nm Christianity

**cristianización** nf Christianization, conversion to Christianity

**cristianizar** [16] vt to Christianize, to convert to Christianity

**cristiano, -a 1** adj & nm,f Christian
**2** nm Fam Fig **hablar en c.** (en castellano) to speak (proper) Spanish; (en lenguaje comprensible) to speak clearly

**cristo** nm crucifix; **C.** Christ; **armar un C.** to kick up a fuss; Fam Fig **donde C. dio las tres voces/perdió el gorro** in the back of beyond

**criterio** nm (a) (norma) criterion (b) (juicio) taste, discernment (c) (opinión) opinion

**crítica** nf (a) (juicio, análisis) review; **c. literaria** literary criticism (b) (conjunto de críticos) **la c.** the critics (c) (ataque) criticism

**criticable** adj censurable, open to criticism

**criticar** [61] **1** *vt* (a) *(censurar)* to criticize (b) *(enjuiciar)* *(literatura, arte)* to review
**2** *vi* to gossip

**crítico, -a 1** *adj* critical
**2** *nm,f (persona)* critic

**criticón, -ona 1** *adj* nit-picking, over-critical
**2** *nm,f* nit-picker

**Croacia** *n* Croatia

**croar 1** *vi* to croak
**2** *nm* croaking

**croata 1** *adj* Croatian
**2** *nmf* Croat, Croatian

**crocanti** *nm (helado)* = ice-cream covered in chocolate and nuts

**croché, crochet** [kro'tʃe] *(pl* **crochets)** *nm* (a) *(labor)* crochet; **hacer c.** to crochet; **una colcha de c.** a crocheted bedspread (b) *(en boxeo)* hook

**croissant** [krwa'san] *(pl* **croissants)** *nm* croissant

**croissantería** [krwasante'ria] *nf* = shop selling filled croissants

**crol** *nm Dep* crawl; **nadar a c.** to do the crawl

**cromado** *nm* chromium-plating

**cromar** *vt* to chrome, to chromium-plate

**cromático, -a** *adj* chromatic

**cromatismo** *nm* colouring

**cromo** *nm* (a) *(metal)* chrome (b) *(estampa)* picture card; **c. repetido** swap

**cromosoma** *nm* chromosome

**cromosómico, -a** *adj* chromosomal

**crónica** *nf* (a) *(de la historia)* chronicle (b) *(de un periódico)* column; *(de la televisión)* feature, programme; **la c. deportiva** the sports news o roundup

**crónico, -a** *adj* chronic

**cronicón** *nm* = brief, usually anonymous, chronicle

**cronista** *nmf (historiador)* chronicler; *(periodista) (en televisión)* reporter; *(en periódico)* writer

**crono** *nm Dep* time

**cronología** *nf* chronology

**cronológico, -a** *adj* chronological

**cronometrador, -ora** *nm,f* timekeeper

**cronometraje** *nm* timing

**cronometrar** *vt* to time

**cronómetro** *nm Dep* stopwatch; *Tec* chronometer

**cróquet** *nm* croquet

**croqueta** *nf* croquette

**croquis** *nm inv* sketch

**cross** *nm inv Dep (carrera)* cross-country race; *(deporte)* cross-country (running)

**crótalo** *nm* rattlesnake

**croupier** [kru'pjer] *nm* croupier

**cruasán** *nm* croissant

**cruce 1** *ver* **cruzar**
**2** *nm* (a) *(de líneas)* crossing, intersection; *(de carreteras)* crossroads; **gira a la derecha en el próximo c.** turn right at the next junction (b) *(de animales)* cross; **un c. de fox-terrier y chihuahua** a cross between a fox terrier and a chihuahua (c) *(de teléfono)* crossed line

**crucero** *nm* (a) *(viaje)* cruise (b) *(barco)* cruiser (c) *(de iglesias)* transept

**cruceta** *nf* (a) *(de una cruz)* crosspiece (b) *(en fútbol)* angle *(of crossbar and goalpost)*

**crucial** *adj* crucial

**crucificar** [61] *vt* (a) *(en una cruz)* to crucify (b) *Fig (atormentar)* to torment

**crucifijo** *nm* crucifix

**crucifixión** *nf* crucifixion

**crucigrama** *nm* crossword (puzzle)

**cruda** *nf Méx* hangover

**crudeza** *nf* (a) *(de clima)* harshness (b) *(de descripción, imágenes)* brutality, harsh realism

**crudo, -a 1** *adj* (a) *(natural)* raw; *(petróleo)* crude (b) *(sin cocer completamente)* undercooked (c) *(realidad, clima, tiempo)* harsh; *(novela)* harshly realistic, hard-hitting (d) *(cruel)* cruel (e) *(color)* beige
**2** *nm* crude (oil)

**cruel** *adj (persona, acción)* cruel; *(dolor)* excruciating, terrible; *(clima)* harsh

**crueldad** *nf* (a) *(de persona, acción)* cruelty; *(del clima)* harshness (b) *(acción cruel)* act of cruelty

**cruento, -a** *adj* bloody

**crujido** *nm (de madera)* creaking; *(de hojas secas)* crackling; **un c.** *(de madera)* a creak; *(de hojas secas)* a crackle; **el c. de sus pisadas** the crunch of his footsteps

**crujiente** *adj (patatas fritas)* crunchy; *(madera)* creaky; *(hojas secas)* rustling; *(pan)* crusty

**crujir** *vi (patatas fritas, nieve)* to crunch; *(madera)* to creak; *(hojas secas)* to crackle; *(dientes)* to grind

**crupier** *nm* croupier

**crustáceo** *nm* crustacean

**cruz** *nf* (a) *(forma)* cross; **c. gamada** swastika; **la C. Roja** the Red Cross (b) *(de una moneda)* tails *(singular)* (c) *Fig (aflicción)* burden, torment; **¡qué c.!** what a life! (d) *Fam Fig* **hacer c. y raya** to break off relations

**cruza** *nf Am* cross, crossbreed

**cruzada** *nf también Fig* crusade

**cruzado, -a 1** *adj* (a) *(cheque, piernas, brazos)* crossed (b) *(atravesado)* **c. en la carretera** blocking the road (c) *(animal)* crossbred (d) *(abrigo, chaqueta)* double-breasted
**2** *nm* crusader

**cruzar** [16] **1** *vt* (**a**) *(calle, río, animales)* to cross (**b**) *(unas palabras)* to exchange (**c**) *Fam Fig* **cruzarle la cara a alguien** *(pegarle)* to slap sb across the face

**2 cruzarse** *vpr* (**a**) *(atravesarse)* to cross; **la A1 no se cruza con la A6** the A1 doesn't meet the A6 at any point; **cruzarse de brazos** to fold one's arms; *Fig* to stand back and do nothing (**b**) *(personas)* **cruzarse con alguien** to pass sb (**c**) *Fam Fig* **se le han cruzado los cables** he went mad

**CSCE** *nf* (*abrev de* **Conferencia de Seguridad y Cooperación Europeas**) CSCE

**CSD** *nm* (*abrev de* **Consejo Superior de Deportes**) = Spanish national sports council

**CSIC** [θe'sik] *nm* (*abrev de* **Consejo Superior de Investigaciones Científicas**) = Spanish council for scientific research

**CSN** *nm* (*abrev de* **Consejo de Seguridad Nuclear**) = Spanish nuclear safety council

**cta.** (*abrev de* **cuenta**) a/c

**cte.** (*abrev de* **corriente**) inst.

**c/u** (*abrev de* **cada uno**) per item

**cuaderna** *nf* *Náut* rib

**cuaderno** *nm* (*libreta*) notebook; *(de colegial)* exercise book; **c. de anillas** ring binder; *Náut* **c. de bitácora** logbook

**cuadra** *nf* (**a**) *(de caballos)* stable; *Fam Fig (lugar sucio)* pigsty (**b**) *Am (manzana)* block

**cuadrado, -a 1** *adj* (**a**) *(figura)* también *Mat* square (**b**) *(persona)* square-built, stocky

**2** *nm* también *Mat* square

**cuadragésimo, -a** *núm* fortieth

**cuadrangular** *adj* quadrangular

**cuadrángulo** *nm* quadrangle

**cuadrante** *nm* (**a**) *(de círculo)* quadrant (**b**) *(reloj de sol)* sundial

**cuadrar 1** *vi* (**a**) *(información, hechos)* to square, to agree (**con** with) (**b**) *(números, cuentas)* to tally, to add up

**2** *vt (dar forma de cuadrado)* to make square, to square off

**3 cuadrarse** *vpr Mil* to stand to attention

**cuadratura** *nf* *Geom* quadrature; *Fig* **la c. del círculo** squaring the circle

**cuádriceps** *nm inv* quadriceps

**cuadrícula** *nf* grid

**cuadriculado, -a** *adj* squared; *Fam Fig* **ser muy c.** *(rígido)* to have a very rigid mentality

**cuadricular** *vt* to divide into squares

**cuadriga, cuádriga** *nf* *Hist* four-in-hand

**cuadrilátero** *nm* (**a**) *Geom* quadrilateral (**b**) *Dep* ring

**cuadrilla** *nf* (**a**) *(de amigos, trabajadores)* group; *(de maleantes)* gang (**b**) *(de torero)* team of helpers

**cuadro** *nm* (**a**) *(pintura)* painting (**b**) *(escena)* scene, spectacle (**c**) *(descripción)* portrait (**d**) *(cuadrado)* square; *(de flores)* bed; **una camisa a cuadros** a check shirt (**e**) *(equipo)* team; **c. flamenco** flamenco group (**f**) *(gráfico)* chart, diagram; **c. sinóptico** tree diagram (**g**) *(de bicicleta)* frame (**h**) *(de aparato)* **c. de distribución** switchboard; **c. de mandos** control panel (**i**) *Teatro* scene

**cuadrúpedo** *nm* quadruped

**cuádruple** *nm* quadruple

**cuadruplicar** [61] *vt* to quadruple

**cuádruplo** *nm* quadruple

**cuajada** *nf* curd (cheese)

**cuajado, -a** *adj* (**a**) *(leche)* curdled (**b**) *(lleno)* **c. de** full of

**cuajar 1** *vt* (**a**) *(solidificar)* *(leche)* to curdle; *(sangre)* to clot, to coagulate (**b**) **c. de** *(llenar)* to fill with; *(cubrir)* to cover with

**2** *vi Fig* (**a**) *(lograrse)* *(acuerdo)* to be settled; *(negocio)* to take off, to get going (**b**) *(ser aceptado)* *(persona)* to fit in; *(moda)* to catch on (**c**) *(nieve)* to settle

**3 cuajarse** *vpr* (**a**) *(leche)* to curdle; *(sangre)* to clot, to coagulate (**b**) *(llenarse)* **cuajarse de** to fill (up) with

**cuajo** *nm* (**a**) *(fermento)* rennet (**b**) **arrancar de c.** *(árbol)* to uproot; *(brazo, cabeza)* to tear right off

**cual** *pron relat* **el/la c.** *(de persona)* *(sujeto)* who; *(complemento)* whom; *(de cosa)* which; **lo c.** which; **conoció a una española, la c. vivía en Buenos Aires** he met a Spanish girl who lived in Buenos Aires; **está muy enfadada, lo c. es comprensible** she's very angry, which is understandable; **todo lo c.** all of which; **sea c. sea** *o* **fuere su decisión** whatever his decision (may be); **los tres son a c. más inteligente** all three are equally intelligent

**cuál** *pron* (**a**) *(interrogativo)* what; *(en concreto, especificando)* which one; **¿c. es tu nombre?** what is your name?; **¿c. es la diferencia?** what's the difference?; **no sé cuáles son mejores** I don't know which are best; **¿c. prefieres?** which one do you prefer?

(**b**) *(en oraciones distributivas)* **todos contribuyeron, c. más, c. menos** everyone contributed, although some more than others

**cualesquiera** *ver* **cualquiera**

**cualidad** *nf* quality

**cualificación** *nf* degree of skill *(of a worker)*; **debemos mejorar la c. de los obreros** we have to get a more highly skilled workforce

**cualificado, -a** *adj* skilled

**cualificar** [61] *vt* to qualify

**cualitativo, -a** *adj* qualitative

**cualquier** *ver* **cualquiera**

**cualquiera** (*pl* **cualesquiera**)

> **cualquier** is used before singular nouns (e.g. **cualquier hombre** any man).

**1** *adj* any; **no es un escritor c.** he's no ordinary writer; **cualquier día vendré a visitarte** I'll drop by one of these days; **en cualquier momento** at any time; **en cualquier lugar** anywhere

**2** *pron* anyone; **c. te lo dirá** anyone will tell you; **c. que** (*persona*) anyone who; (*cosa*) whatever; **c. que te vea se reiría** anyone who saw you would laugh; **c. que sea la razón** whatever the reason (may be); **cualesquiera que sean las razones** whatever the reasons (may be)

**3** *nmf* (*don nadie*) nobody

**4** *nf Fam* (*prostituta*) tart

**cuan** *adv* (*todo lo que*) **se desplomó c. largo era** he fell flat on the ground

**cuán** *adv* how

**cuando 1** *adv* when; **de c. en c., de vez en c.** from time to time, now and again; **c. más** at the most; **c. menos** at least

**2** *conj* (a) (*de tiempo*) when; **c. llegue el verano iremos de viaje** when summer comes we'll go travelling; **c. quiera que** whenever

(b) (*si*) if; **c. tú lo dices será verdad** it must be true if you say so

(c) (*después de 'aun'*) (*aunque*) **no mentiría aun c. le fuera en ello la vida** she wouldn't lie even if her life depended on it

**cuándo 1** *adv* when; **¿c. vas a venir?** when are you coming?; **quisiera saber c. sale el tren** I'd like to know when *o* at what time the train leaves

**2** *nm* **ignorará el cómo y el c. de la operación** he won't know how or when the operation will take place

**cuantía** *nf* (*suma*) amount, quantity; (*alcance*) extent

**cuántica** *nf* quantum mechanics (*singular*)

**cuántico, -a** *Fís adj* quantum; **mecánica/teoría cuántica** quantum mechanics/theory

**cuantificable** *adj* quantifiable

**cuantificar** [61] *vt* to quantify

**cuantioso, -a** *adj* large, substantial

**cuantitativo, -a** *adj* quantitative

**cuanto, -a 1** *adj* (a) (*todo*) **despilfarra c. dinero gana** he squanders all the money he earns; **soporté todas cuantas críticas me hizo** I put up with every single criticism he made of me

(b) (*algunos*) **unos cuantos chicos** some *o* a few boys

(c) (*antes de adv*) (*compara cantidades*) **cuantas más mentiras digas, menos te creerán** the more you lie, the less people will believe you

**2** *pron relat* (a) (*todo lo que*) everything, as much as; **come c. quieras** eat as much as you like; **comprendo c. dice** I understand everything he says; **todo c.** everything

(b) (*compara cantidades*) **c. más se tiene, más se quiere** the more you have, the more you want

**3** *adv* (a) (*compara cantidades*) **c. más come, más gordo está** the more he eats, the fatter he gets; **c. antes** as soon as possible

(b) (*en calidad de*) as; **en c. cabeza de familia** as head of the family

(c) (*expresiones*) **en c.** (*tan pronto como*) as soon as; **en c. acabe** as soon as I've finished; **en c. a** as regards; **en c. a tu petición** as regards your request, as far as your request is concerned

**4** *pron relat pl* **cuantos** (a) (*todos*) (*personas*) everyone who; (*cosas*) everything (that); **cuantos fueron alabaron el espectáculo** everyone who went said the show was excellent; **dio las gracias a todos cuantos le ayudaron** he thanked everyone who helped him

(b) (*algunos*) **unos cuantos** some, a few

**cuánto, -a 1** *adj* (a) (*interrogativo*) (*singular*) how much; (*plural*) how many; **¿cuántas manzanas tienes?** how many apples do you have?; **¿c. pan quieres?** how much bread do you want?; **no sé cuántos hombres había** I don't know how many men were there

(b) (*exclamativo*) what a lot of; **¡cuánta gente (había)!** what a lot of people (were there)!

**2** *pron* (a) (*interrogativo*) (*singular*) how much; (*plural*) how many; **¿c. quieres?** how much do you want?; **¿a c. están los tomates?** how much are the tomatoes?; **me gustaría saber c. te costarán** I'd like to know how much they'll cost you; **¿cuántos han venido?** how many came?; **dime cuántas quieres** tell me how many you want

(b) (*exclamativo*) **¡c. han cambiado las cosas!** how things have changed!; **¡c. me gusta!** I really like it!; **¡cuántos han venido!** so many people have come!

**cuáquero, -a** *nm,f Rel* Quaker

**cuarenta** *núm* forty; **los (años) c.** the forties; **Fam Fig cantar a alguien las c.** to give sb a piece of one's mind; *ver también* **seis**

**cuarentena** *nf* (a) (*por epidemia*) quarantine; **poner en c.** (*enfermos*) to (put in) quarantine; (*noticia*) to put on hold (b) (*cuarenta unidades*) forty; **andará por la c.** he must be about forty; **una c. de...** (*unos cuarenta*) about forty...; (*cuarenta*) forty...

**cuarentón, -ona** *nm,f Fam* person in his/her forties

**cuaresma** *nf Rel* Lent

**cuarta** *nf (palmo)* span

**cuarteamiento** *nm (resquebrajamiento)* cracking

**cuartear 1** *vt* to cut *o* chop up

**2 cuartearse** *vpr* to crack

**cuartel** *nm* (a) *Mil* barracks; **c. general** headquarters (b) *Fig (buen trato)* **guerra sin c.** all-out war; **lucha sin c.** fight to the death

**cuartelada** *nf* minor military uprising

**cuartelazo** *nm* military uprising, revolt

**cuartelero, -a** *adj* (a) *Mil* barracks; **vida cuartelera** life in barracks (b) *Fig (lenguaje)* vulgar, coarse

**cuartelillo** *nm (de la Guardia Civil)* = post of the Guardia Civil

**cuarteto** *nm* quartet; **c. de cuerda** string quartet

**cuartilla** *nf* sheet of quarto

**cuarto, -a 1** *núm* fourth; **la cuarta parte** a quarter; **el c. poder** *(la prensa)* the Fourth Estate

**2** *nm* (a) *(parte)* quarter; **un c. de hora** a quarter of an hour; **son las dos y c.** it's a quarter *Br* past *o US* after two; *Fam* **ser tres cuartos de lo mismo** to be exactly the same *o* no different; **c. creciente/menguante** first/last quarter

(b) *(habitación)* room; **c. de aseo** washroom, small bathroom; **c. de baño** bathroom; **c. de estar** living room

(c) *(dinero)* **estar sin un c.** to be skint; *Fam* **cuartos** dough, cash

(d) *Dep* **cuartos de final** quarter finals

**cuarzo** *nm* quartz

**cuate** *nmf inv CAm, Méx (amigo)* friend

**cuaternario, -a** *Geol* **1** *adj* Quaternary

**2** *nm* **el C.** the Quaternary (era)

**cuatrero, -a** *nm,f (de caballos)* horse thief; *(de ganado)* cattle rustler

**cuatrillizo, -a** *nm,f* quadruplet, quad

**cuatrimestral** *adj* (a) *(en frecuencia)* four-monthly (b) *(en duración)* four-month, lasting four months; *Educ* **asignatura c.** = four-month course in a given subject

**cuatrimestre** *nm* (period of) four months

**cuatrimotor** *nm* four-engined plane

**cuatripartito, -a** *adj* four-part

**cuatro 1** *núm* four; *ver también* **seis**

**2** *adj Fig (poco)* a few; **hace c. días** a few days ago; *Fam* **Fig c. gatos** hardly a soul; **éramos c. gatos** there were only a handful of us

**3** *nm Carib* = four- or five-stringed guitar

**cuatrocientos, -as** *núm* four hundred; *ver también* **seis**

**Cuba** *n* Cuba

**cuba** *nf* barrel, cask; *Fam* **estar como una c.** to be legless *o* blind drunk

**cubalibre** *nm* rum and Coke®

**cubano, -a** *adj & nm,f* Cuban

**cubata** *nm Fam (combinado)* long drink; *(ron con coca-cola)* rum and Coke®

**cubero** *nm* **a ojo de buen c.** roughly

**cubertería** *nf* (set of) cutlery

**cubeta** *nf (cuba pequeña)* bucket, pail; *(de barómetro)* bulb; *Fot* tray

**cubicaje** *nm Aut* capacity

**cúbico, -a** *adj* cubic

**cubierta** *nf* (a) *(de libro, cama)* cover (b) *(de neumático)* carcass, body (c) *(de barco)* deck

**cubierto, -a 1** *participio ver* **cubrir**

**2** *adj* (a) *(tapado, recubierto)* covered (**de** with); **estar a c.** *(protegido)* to be under cover; *(con saldo acreedor)* to be in the black; **ponerse a c.** to take cover (b) *(cielo)* overcast (c) *(vacante)* filled

**3** *nm* (a) *(pieza de cubertería)* piece of cutlery (b) *(juego de cubertería)* set of cutlery (c) *(para cada persona)* place setting (d) *(comida)* set menu

**cubil** *nm (de animales)* den, lair; *Fig (de personas)* poky room

**cubilete** *nm (en juegos)* cup; *(molde)* mould

**cubismo** *nm Arte* cubism

**cubista** *adj & nmf Arte* cubist

**cubito** *nm (de hielo)* ice cube

**cúbito** *nm Anat* ulna

**cubo** *nm* (a) *(recipiente)* bucket; **c. de la basura** *Br* rubbish bin, *US* garbage can (b) *Geom & Mat* cube; **elevar al c.** to cube (c) *(de rueda)* hub

**cubrecama** *nm* bedspread

**cubrir 1** *vt* (a) *(tapar, recubrir, recorrer)* to cover (b) *(proteger)* to protect (c) *(ocultar)* to cover up, to hide (d) *(puesto, vacante)* to fill (e) *(noticia)* to cover (f) *(el macho a la hembra)* **c. a** to mate with (g) *Fig* **c. a alguien de insultos/alabanzas** to heap insults/praise on sb

**2 cubrirse** *vpr* (a) *(taparse)* to become covered (**de** with) (b) *(protegerse)* to shelter (**de** from) (c) *(con sombrero)* to put one's hat on (d) *(con ropa)* to cover oneself (**de** with) (e) *(cielo)* to cloud over (f) *Fig* **cubrirse de gloria** *(triunfar)* to cover oneself in *o* with glory; *Irón* to land oneself in it

**cuca** *nf Fam* peseta

**cucaña** *nf* greasy pole

**cucaracha** *nf* cockroach

**cuchara** *nf* (a) *(para comer)* spoon (b) *(cucharada)* spoonful

**cucharada** *nf* spoonful

**cucharilla** *nf* teaspoon

**cucharón** *nm* ladle

**cuchichear** *vi* to whisper

**cuchicheo** *nm* whispering

**cuchilla** *nf* blade; **c. de afeitar** razor blade

**cuchillada** *nf* *(golpe)* stab; *(herida)* stab wound

**cuchillo** *nm* knife; **pasar a c.** to put to the sword; **c. eléctrico** electric carving knife; **c. de monte** hunting knife

**cuchipanda** *nf* *Fam* party, *Br* knees-up

**cuchitril** *nm* hovel

**cuchufleta** *nf* *Fam* joke; **estar de c.** to be joking

**cuclillas** *nfpl* **en c.** squatting; **ponerse en c.** to squat (down)

**cuclillo** *nm* cuckoo

**cuco, -a 1** *adj Fam* **(a)** *(bonito)* pretty **(b)** *(astuto)* shrewd, canny

**2** *nm* cuckoo

**cucú** *nm* **(a)** *(canto)* cuckoo **(b)** *(reloj)* cuckoo clock

**cucurucho** *nm* **(a)** *(de papel)* paper cone **(b)** *(para helado)* cornet, cone **(c)** *(gorro)* pointed hat

**cuece** *ver* **cocer**

**cuelgo** *etc ver* **colgar**

**cuello** *nm* **(a)** *(de persona, animal, botella)* neck **(b)** *(de prendas)* collar; **c. de cisne** *o* **vuelto** polo neck; **c. de pico** V-neck **(c)** *Anat* **c. uterino** *o* **del útero** cervix

**cuelo** *etc ver* **colar**

**cuenca** *nf* **(a)** *(de río)* basin **(b)** *(del ojo)* (eye) socket **(c)** *(región minera)* coalfield

**cuenco** *nm* earthenware bowl

**cuenta 1** *ver* **contar**

**2** *nf* **(a)** *(acción de contar)* count; **echar cuentas** to reckon up; **llevar/perder la c. de** to keep/lose count of; **c. atrás** countdown

**(b)** *(cálculo)* sum; *Fam* **c. de la vieja** counting on one's fingers

**(c)** *Fin, Com & Informát* account; **abonar/cargar algo en c. a alguien** to credit/debit sth to sb's account; **abrir una c.** to open an account; **llevar las cuentas** to keep the books; **pagar mil pesetas a c.** to pay a thousand pesetas down; **c. de ahorros** savings account; **c. de ahorro vivienda** home loan; **c. bancaria** bank account; **c. de correo (electrónico)** e-mail account; **c. corriente** current account; **c. de crédito** current account with an overdraft facility; **c. deudora** overdrawn account; **c. de explotación** operating statement; **c. a plazo fijo** deposit account

**(d)** *(factura)* bill; **domiciliar una c.** to pay an account by direct debit; **pasar la c.** to send the bill; **c. por cobrar/pagar** account receivable/payable

**(e)** *(obligación, cuidado)* responsibility; **déjalo de mi c.** leave it to me; **trabajar por c. propia/ajena** to be self-employed/an employee

**(f)** *(de collar, rosario)* bead

**(g)** *(expresiones)* **a fin de cuentas** in the end; **ajustarle a alguien las cuentas** to settle an account *o* a score with sb; **caer en la c. de algo** to realize sth; **dar c. de algo** *(comunicar)* to report sth; *(terminar)* to account for sth, to finish sth off; **darse c. de algo** to realize sth; **en resumidas cuentas** in short; **más de la c.** too much; **pedir cuentas a alguien** to call sb to account; **por mi/tu c.** on my/your own; **salir de cuentas** to be due to give birth; **tener en c. algo** to bear sth in mind

**cuentagotas** *nm inv* dropper; *Fig* **a** *o* **con c.** in dribs and drabs

**cuentakilómetros** *nm inv Aut (de distancia recorrida)* ≃ mileometer; *(de velocidad)* speedometer

**cuentarrevoluciones** *nm inv Aut* tachometer, rev counter

**cuentista** *nmf* **(a)** *(escritor)* short story writer **(b)** *Fam (mentiroso)* fibber, story-teller

**cuento** *nm* **(a)** *(fábula)* tale; **c. de hadas** fairy tale; *Fam* **el c. de la lechera** wishful thinking **(b)** *(narración)* short story **(c)** *Fam (mentira, exageración)* story, lie; **c. chino** story, lie **(d)** *(expresiones)* **quitarse** *o* **dejarse de cuentos** to stop beating about the bush; **ser el c. de nunca acabar** to be the same old story; **ese tiene mucho c.** he's always putting it on; **venir a c.** to be relevant; **venir con cuentos** to tell fibs *o* stories; **vivir del c.** to live by one's wits

**cuerda** *nf* **(a)** *(para atar) (fina)* string; *(más gruesa)* rope; **c. floja** tightrope **(b)** *(de instrumento)* string **(c)** *(de reloj)* spring; **dar c. a** *(reloj)* to wind up **(d)** *Geom* chord **(e)** *Anat* **cuerdas vocales** vocal cords **(f)** *(expresiones)* **bajo c.** secretly, in an underhand manner; **estar en la c. floja** to be hanging by a thread; **este conferenciante todavía tiene c. para rato** this speaker looks like he's going to go on for a while yet; **tirar de la c.** to go too far, to push it

**cuerdo, -a 1** *adj* **(a)** *(sano de juicio)* sane **(b)** *(sensato)* sensible

**2** *nm,f* sane person

**cueriza** *nf Am* beating

**cuerno** *nm (de animal)* horn; *(de ciervo)* antler; *Fam* **mandar al c. a alguien** to send sb packing; *Fam* **poner cuernos a alguien** to be unfaithful to sb; *(a un hombre)* to cuckold sb; *Geog* **el C. de África** the Horn of Africa

**cuero** *nm* **(a)** *(material)* leather; **una chamarra de c.** a leather jacket **(b)** *(piel de animal)* skin; *(piel curtida)* hide; **c. cabelludo** scalp; **en cueros (vivos)** stark-naked

**cuerpo** nm (a) (en general) body; **c. extraño** foreign body; **de c. entero** (persona) complete, consummate; (retrato, espejo) full-length; **a c.** without a coat on; **en c. y alma** body and soul; **luchar c. a c.** to fight hand-to-hand; **tomar c.** to take shape; **vivir a c. de rey** to live like a king

(b) (tronco) trunk

(c) (parte principal) main body

(d) (espesura) thickness

(e) (cadáver) corpse; **de c. presente** (lying) in state

(f) (corporación consular, militar) corps; **c. de bomberos** fire brigade; **c. diplomático** diplomatic corps; **c. de policía** police force

(g) (parte de armario, edificio) section

(h) Der **c. del delito** = evidence of a crime or means of perpetrating it

**cuervo** nm raven

**cuesco** nm Fam (pedo) loud fart

**cuesta** 1 ver **costar**

2 nf slope; **c. arriba** uphill; **c. abajo** downhill; **a cuestas** on one's back, over one's shoulders; Fam Fig **trabajar los viernes se me hace muy c. arriba** I find working on Fridays heavy going

**cuestación** nf collection (for charity)

**cuestión** nf (a) (pregunta) question (b) (problema) problem (c) (asunto) matter, issue; **en c.** in question; **en c. de** (en materia de) as regards; **en c. de una hora** in no more than an hour

**cuestionable** adj questionable, debatable

**cuestionar** 1 vt to question

2 **cuestionarse** vpr to (call into) question

**cuestionario** nm questionnaire

**cuesto** etc ver **costar**

**cueva** nf cave

**cuezo** ver **cocer**

**cuicos** nmpl Méx Fam cops

**cuidado** 1 nm care; **el c. de la piel/del cabello** skin/hair care; **de c.** (peligroso) dangerous; **fue un accidente/una fiesta de (mucho) c.** (tremendo) it was some accident/ party; **estar al c. de** to be in charge of; **tener c. con** to be careful with; **eso me tiene o trae sin c.** I couldn't care less about that; **c. con el perro** (en letrero) beware of the dog; **c. con el escalón** (en letrero) mind the step; Med **cuidados intensivos** intensive care

2 interj **¡c.!** careful!, look out!

**cuidador, -ora** nm,f Dep trainer

**cuidadoso, -a** adj careful

**cuidar** 1 vt (enfermo, niño, casa) to look after; (aspecto, ropa) to take care over; (detalles) to pay attention to

2 vi **c. de** to look after; **cuida de que no lo haga** make sure she doesn't do it

3 **cuidarse** vpr to take care of o to look after oneself; **se cuidó mucho de que no la vieran** she took great care to ensure that no-one saw her

**cuita** nf trouble, worry

**culata** nf (a) (de arma) butt (b) (de animal) hindquarters (c) (de motor) cylinder head

**culatazo** nm (golpe) blow with the butt of a rifle; (retroceso) recoil, kick

**culé** adj Fam Dep = relating to Barcelona Football Club

**culebra** nf snake

**culebrón** nm Fam soap opera

**culinario, -a** adj culinary

**culmen** nm high point

**culminación** nf culmination

**culminante** adj culminating; **punto c.** high point

**culminar** 1 vt to crown (**con** with)

2 vi to finish, to culminate

**culo** nm Fam (a) (de persona) Br bum, US butt; muy Fam **ir de c.** (negocio, país) to be going down the tubes; muy Fam **con esa estrategia vas de c.** you'll never get anywhere that way; Vulg **¡que te den por c.!**, **¡vete a tomar por c.!** fuck off!; Fig **ser un c. inquieto** o **de mal asiento** (enredador) to be fidgety; (errante) to be a restless soul (b) (de vaso, botella) bottom (c) (líquido) **queda un c. de vino** there's a drop (or two) of wine left in the bottom

**culpa** nf (a) (responsabilidad) fault; **echar la c. a alguien (de)** to blame sb (for); **por c. de** because of; **tener la c. de algo** to be to blame for sth (b) Rel **culpas** sins

**culpabilidad** nf guilt

**culpabilizar** [16] 1 vt to blame

2 **culpabilizarse** vpr to accept the blame (**de** for)

**culpable** 1 adj guilty (**de** of); **declarar c. a alguien** to find sb guilty; **declararse c.** to plead guilty

2 nmf Der guilty party; **tú eres el c.** you're to blame

**culpar** vt **c. a alguien (de)** (atribuir la culpa) to blame sb (for); (acusar) to accuse sb (of)

**culteranismo** nm Lit Gongorism

**culterano, -a** Lit 1 adj Gongoristic

2 nm,f Gongorist

**cultismo** nm literary o learned word

**cultivable** adj cultivable, arable

**cultivado, -a** adj cultivated

**cultivador, -ora** nm,f grower

**cultivar** 1 vt (a) (tierra) to farm, to cultivate; (plantas) to grow (b) (amistad, inteligencia) to cultivate (c) (arte) to practise (d) (germen) to culture

**2 cultivarse** *vpr (persona)* to improve oneself

**cultivo** *nm* (a) *(de tierra)* farming; *(de plantas)* growing (b) *(plantación)* crop (c) *(de gérmenes)* culture

**culto, -a 1** *adj (persona)* cultured, educated; *(estilo)* refined; *(palabra)* literary, learned

**2** *nm (devoción)* worship; **rendir c. a** *(dios)* to worship; *(persona, valentía)* to pay homage o tribute to (b) *(religión)* cult

**cultura** *nf* (a) *(de sociedad)* culture (b) *(sabiduría)* learning, knowledge

**cultural** *adj* cultural

**culturismo** *nm* body-building

**culturista** *nmf* body-builder

**culturizar** [16] *vt* to educate

**cumbia** *nf* = type of Colombian dance

**cumbre 1** *adj* greatest

**2** *nf* (a) *(de montaña)* summit (b) *Fig (punto culminante)* peak, pinnacle (c) *Pol* summit (conference)

**cumpleaños** *nm inv* birthday

**cumplido, -a 1** *adj* (a) *(orden)* carried out; *(promesa)* kept; *(deber, profecía)* fulfilled; *(plazo)* expired (b) *(completo, lleno)* full, complete (c) *(cortés)* courteous

**2** *nm* compliment

**cumplidor, -ora 1** *adj* reliable, dependable

**2** *nm,f* reliable o dependable person

**cumplimentar** *vt* (a) *(saludar)* to greet (b) *(felicitar)* to congratulate (c) *(cumplir)* *(orden)* to carry out; *(contrato)* to fulfil

**cumplimiento** *nm (de un deber)* performance; *(de contrato, promesa)* fulfilment; *(de la ley)* observance; *(de órdenes)* carrying out; *(de condena)* completion; *(de plazo)* expiry

**cumplir 1** *vt* (a) *(orden)* to carry out; *(promesa)* to keep; *(ley)* to observe; *(contrato)* to fulfil (b) *(años)* to reach; **mañana cumplo 20 años** I'm 20 o it's my 20th birthday tomorrow (c) *(condena)* to serve; *(servicio militar)* to do

**2** *vi* (a) *(plazo, garantía)* to expire (b) *(realizar el deber)* to do one's duty; **c. con alguien** to do one's duty by sb; **para** o **por c.** out of politeness; **c. con el deber** to do one's duty; **c. con la palabra** to keep one's word

**cúmulo** *nm* (a) *(de objetos)* pile, heap (b) *(nube)* cumulus (c) *Fig (de circunstancias, asuntos)* accumulation, series

**cuna** *nf* (a) *(de niño)* cot, cradle (b) *Fig (de movimiento, civilización)* cradle; *(de persona)* birthplace

**cundir** *vi* (a) *(propagarse)* to spread (b) *(dar de sí)* *(comida, reservas)* to go a long way; *(trabajo, estudio)* to go well; **me cundió mucho el tiempo** I got a lot done

**cuneiforme** *adj* cuneiform

**cuneta** *nf (de una carretera)* ditch; *(de una calle)* gutter

**cunilingus** *nm inv* cunnilingus

**cuña** *nf* (a) *(pieza)* wedge (b) *(de publicidad)* commercial break (c) *(orinal)* bedpan (d) *Am (enchufe)* **tener c.** to have friends in high places

**cuñado, -a** *nm,f* brother-in-law, *f* sister-in-law

**cuño** *nm* (a) *(troquel)* die (b) *(sello, impresión)* stamp (c) *Fig* **ser de nuevo c.** to be a new coinage

**cuota** *nf* (a) *(contribución)* *(a entidad, club)* membership fee, subscription; *(a Hacienda)* tax (payment) (b) *(precio, gasto)* fee, cost (c) *(cupo)* quota; *Econ* **c. de mercado** market share

**cupé** *nm* coupé

**cupido** *nm (representación del amor)* cupid

**cupiera** *etc ver* **caber**

**cuplé** *nm* popular song

**cupletista** *nmf* "cuplé" singer

**cupo 1** *ver* **caber**

**2** *nm* (a) *(cantidad máxima)* quota (b) *(cantidad proporcional)* share; *(de una cosa racionada)* ration

**cupón** *nm (vale)* coupon; *(de lotería, rifa)* ticket

**cúprico, -a** *adj Quím* copper; **óxido/sulfato c.** copper oxide/sulphate

**cúpula** *nf* (a) *Arquit* dome, cupola (b) *Fig (mandos)* leaders

**cura 1** *nm* priest

**2** *nf* (a) *(curación)* recovery (b) *(tratamiento)* treatment, cure; **necesitar una c. de sueño** to need a good sleep (c) **no tener c.** *(ser incurable)* to be incurable; *Fam (ser incorregible)* to be incorrigible

**curación** *nf* (a) *(de un enfermo)* *(recuperación)* recovery; *(tratamiento)* treatment; *(de una herida)* healing (b) *(de alimento)* curing

**curado, -a 1** *adj (alimento)* cured; *(pieles)* tanned; *Fam* **estar c. de espanto** to be unshockable

**2** *nm (de alimentos)* curing; *(de pieles)* tanning

**curandería** *nf* quackery

**curandero, -a** *nm,f* quack

**curanto** *nm CSur* = stew of meat and shellfish

**curar 1** *vt* (a) *(sanar)* to cure (b) *(herida)* to dress (c) *(alimentos)* to cure (d) *(pieles)* to tan

**2** *vi (enfermo)* to get well, to recover; *(herida)* to heal up

**3 curarse** *vpr* (a) *(sanar)* to recover (**de** from); **curarse en salud** to play safe (b) *(alimento)* to cure

**curare** *nm* curare

**curasao** *nm* curaçao

**curativo, -a** *adj* curative

**curazao** [kura'sao] *nm* curaçao

**curcuncho** *nm Andes* (**a**) *(joroba)* hump (**b**) *(jorobado)* hunchback

**curda** *nf Fam* **coger** *o* **agarrar una c.** to get plastered

**curdo, -a 1** *adj* Kurdish

**2** *nm,f (persona)* Kurd

**3** *nm (lengua)* Kurdish

**curia** *nf* (**a**) *Hist & Rel* curia (**b**) *Der (abogacía)* legal profession

**curiosear 1** *vi (fisgonear)* to nose around; *(en tienda)* to browse round

**2** *vt (libros, revistas)* to browse through

**curiosidad** *nf* (**a**) *(deseo de saber)* curiosity; **sentir** *o* **tener c. por** to be curious about (**b**) *(limpieza)* neatness, tidiness

**curioso, -a 1** *adj (por saber, averiguar)* curious, inquisitive (**b**) *(raro)* odd, strange (**c**) *(limpio)* neat, tidy; *(cuidadoso)* careful

**2** *nm,f* onlooker

**curita** *nf Am* sticking plaster

**currante** *Fam* **1** *adj* hard-working

**2** *nmf* worker

**currar** *vi Fam* to work

**curre** *nm Fam* work

**currelar** *vi Fam* to work

**currelo** *nm Fam* work

**currículum (vitae)** [ku'rrikulum ('bite)] *(pl* **currícula** *o* **currículums (vitae))**, **currículo** *nm* curriculum vitae, CV

**curro** *nm Fam* work

**currusco** *nm Fam* crust (of bread)

**curry** *nm* curry; **pollo al c.** chicken curry

**cursar** *vt* (**a**) *(estudiar)* to study; **c. estudios de medicina** to study medicine; **cursaba segundo** she was in her second year (**b**) *(enviar)* to send (**c**) *(ordenar)* to give, to issue (**d**) *(tramitar)* to submit

**cursi 1** *adj (vestido, canción)* tacky, *Br* naff; *(modales, persona)* affected

**2** *nmf* affected person

**cursilada** *nf* **ser una c.** *(acto, comportamiento)* to be affected; *(comentario)* to be stupid *o Br* naff; *(decoración, objeto)* to be tacky

**cursilería** *nf* (**a**) **ser una c.** *(acto, comportamiento)* to be affected; *(comentario)* to be stupid *o Br* naff; *(decoración, objeto)* to be tacky (**b**) *(cualidad)* tackiness *o Br* naffness

**cursillo** *nm* (**a**) *(curso)* short course (**b**) *(conferencias)* series of lectures

**cursiva 1** *adj (letra)* italic

**2** *nf* italics

**curso** *nm* (**a**) *(año académico)* year (**b**) *(lecciones)* course; **c. intensivo** crash course (**c**) *(texto, manual)* textbook (**d**) *(dirección) (de río, acontecimientos)* course; *(de la economía)* trend; **dar c. a algo** *(dar rienda suelta)* to give free rein to sth; *(tramitar)* to pro-

cess *o* deal with sth; **en el c. de** during (the course of); **en c.** *(mes, año)* current; *(trabajo)* in progress; **seguir su c.** to go on, to continue (**e**) *(circulación)* **moneda de c. legal** legal tender

**cursor** *nm Informát* cursor

**curtido, -a 1** *adj* (**a**) *(piel, cuero)* tanned (**b**) *Fig (experimentado)* seasoned

**2** *nm* tanning

**curtir 1** *vt* (**a**) *(piel)* to tan (**b**) *Fig (persona)* to harden

**2 curtirse** *vpr* (**a**) *(piel)* to tan (**b**) *Fig (persona)* to become hardened

**curva** *nf (gráfico, línea, forma)* curve; *(de carretera, río)* bend; *Fam* **Fig c. de la felicidad** *(barriga)* paunch; **c. de nivel** contour line

**curvado, -a** *adj (forma)* curved; *(espalda)* bent

**curvar 1** *vt (doblar)* to bend; *(espalda, cejas)* to arch

**2 curvarse** *vpr* to become bent

**curvatura** *nf* curvature

**curvilíneo, -a** *adj (en geometría)* curved; *(silueta del cuerpo)* curvaceous

**curvo, -a** *adj (forma)* curved; *(doblado)* bent

**cuscurro** *nm (pan frito)* crouton; *(punta de pan)* end *(of baguette)*

**cuscús** *nm inv* couscous

**cúspide** *nf* (**a**) *(de montaña)* summit, top (**b**) *Fig (apogeo)* peak, height (**c**) *Geom* apex

**custodia** *nf* (**a**) *(de cosas)* safekeeping (**b**) *(de personas)* custody; **estar bajo la c. de** to be in the custody of (**c**) *Rel* monstrance

**custodiar** [15] *vt* (**a**) *(vigilar)* to guard (**b**) *(proteger)* to look after

**custodio** *nm* guard

**cutáneo, -a** *adj* skin; **enfermedad cutánea** skin disease; **erupción cutánea** rash

**cúter** *nm (cuchilla)* Stanley knife®

**cutícula** *nf* cuticle

**cutis** *nm inv* skin, complexion

**cutre** *adj Fam* (**a**) *(de bajo precio, calidad)* cheap and nasty (**b**) *(sórdido)* shabby, dingy (**c**) *(tacaño)* tight, stingy

**cutrería, cutrez** *nf Fam* shabbiness, dinginess; **este hotel es una c.** this hotel is a dump; **me regaló una c.** he gave me a cheap and nasty present

**cuyo, -a** *adj (posesión) (por parte de personas)* whose; *(por parte de cosas)* of which, whose; **ésos son los amigos en cuya casa nos hospedamos** those are the friends in whose house we spent the night; **ese señor, c. hijo conociste ayer** that man, whose son you met yesterday; **un equipo cuya principal estrella...** a team, the star player of which *o* whose star player...; **en c. caso** in which case

**CV** *nm (abrev de* **currículum vitae**) CV

# D

**D, d** [de] *nf (letra)* D, d

**D.** *(abrev de* **don)** ≃ Mr; *ver* **don**

**Dacca** *n* Dacca

**dactilar** *adj* **huella d.** fingerprint

**dactilografía** *nf* typing

**dadá, dadaísmo** *nm Arte* Dada, Dadaism

**dádiva** *nf (regalo)* gift; *(donativo)* donation

**dadivoso, -a** *adj* generous

**dado, -a1** *adj* given; **en un momento d.** *(en el tiempo)* at a certain point; **ser d. a** to be inclined *o* given to; **d. que** since, seeing as

**2** *nm* dice, die

**dador, -ora** *nm,f* **(a)** *(de letra de cambio)* drawer **(b)** *(de carta)* bearer

**daga** *nf* dagger

**daguerrotipo** *nm* daguerreotype

**daiquiri** *nm* daiquiri

**Dakar** *n* Dakar

**dalai-lama** *nm* Dalai Lama

**dale** *interj* **¡d.! ¡otra vez con lo mismo!** there you go again!; **te digo que pares y tú ¡d. (que d.)!** I've told you to stop, but you just carry on and on!

**dalia** *nf* dahlia

**dálmata** *adj & nmf* **(a)** *(persona)* Dalmatian **(b)** *(perro)* Dalmatian

**daltónico, -a1** *adj* colour-blind

**2** *nm,f* person with colour blindness

**daltonismo** *nm* colour blindness

**dama** *nf* **(a)** *(mujer)* lady; **d. de honor** *(de novia)* bridesmaid; *(de reina)* lady-in-waiting; *Teatro* **primera d.** leading lady; *US Pol* first lady **(b)** *(en juego de damas)* king; *(en ajedrez, naipes)* queen; **damas** *(juego)* draughts *(singular)*

**damajuana** *nf* demijohn

**Damasco** *n* Damascus

**damasco** *nm* **(a)** *(tela)* damask **(b)** *Am (albaricoque)* apricot

**damasquinado** *nm* damascene

**damero** *nm* draughts board

**damisela** *nf Anticuado* damsel

**damnificado, -a1** *adj* affected, damaged

**2** *nm,f* victim

**damnificar** [61] *vt (cosa)* to damage; *(persona)* to harm, to injure

**dance** *etc ver* **danzar**

**dandi, dandy** *nm* dandy

**danés, -esa1** *adj* Danish

**2** *nm,f (persona)* Dane

**3** *nm (lengua)* Danish

**dantesco, -a** *adj también Fig* Dantesque

**Danubio** *nm* **el D.** the (River) Danube

**danza** *nf (actividad)* dancing; *(baile)* dance; **d. clásica** classical ballet; **d. española** Spanish dance; **estar siempre en d.** to be always on the go *o* doing sth; **estar metido en d.** to be up to no good

**danzar** [16] *vi (bailar)* to dance; *Fig (ir de un sitio a otro)* to run about

**danzarín, -ina1** *adj* active, lively

**2** *nm,f* dancer

**dañar 1** *vt (vista, cosecha)* to harm, to damage; *(persona)* to hurt; *(pieza, objeto)* to damage

**2 dañarse** *vpr (persona)* to hurt oneself; *(cosa)* to become damaged

**dañino, -a, dañoso, -a** *adj* harmful

**daño** *nm* **(a)** *(dolor)* pain, hurt; **hacer d. a alguien** to hurt sb; **hacerse d.** to hurt oneself; **me hacen d. los zapatos** my shoes are hurting me **(b)** *(perjuicio) (a algo)* damage; *(a alguien)* harm; **daños y perjuicios** damages; **los daños se calculan en un millón de pesetas** the damage is estimated to be about a million pesetas

**dar** [22] **1** *vt* **(a)** *(entregar, otorgar)* to give; *(proporcionar)* to give, to provide with; *(naipes)* to deal; **d. algo a alguien** to give sth to sb, to give sb sth

**(b)** *(producir)* to give, to produce; *(frutos, flores)* to bear; *(beneficios, intereses)* to yield

**(c)** *(fiesta, cena)* to have, to hold; **d. una cena en honor de alguien** to hold *o* give a dinner in someone's honour

**(d)** *(luz, agua, gas) (encender)* to turn *o* switch on; *(suministrar por primera vez)* to connect; *(suministrar tras un corte)* to turn back on

**(e)** *Cine, Teatro & TV* to show; *(concierto, interpretación)* to give

**(f)** *(mostrar)* to show; **d. muestras de sensatez** to show good sense

**(g)** *(untar con, aplicar)* to apply; **d. barniz a**

**una silla** to varnish a chair

(h) *(provocar)* to give; **le dio un infarto** he had a heart attack; **me da vergüenza/pena** it makes me ashamed/sad; **me da risa** it makes me laugh; **me da miedo** it frightens me; *Fam* **si no se calla me va a d. algo** if he doesn't shut up soon, I'll go mad; *Fam* **si sigues trabajando así te va a d. algo** you can't go on working like that

(i) *(enseñar)* to teach; **d. inglés/historia** to teach English/history

(j) *(expresa acción)* **d. un grito** to give a cry; **d. un vistazo a** to have a look at; **darle un golpe/una puñalada a alguien** to hit/stab sb; **voy a d. un paseo** I'm going (to go) for a walk

(k) *(considerar)* **d. algo por** to consider sth as; **eso lo doy por hecho** I take that for granted; **d. a alguien por muerto** to give sb up for dead

(l) *(expresiones)* **donde las dan las toman** you get what you deserve; **el reloj ha dado las doce** the clock struck twelve; **es tan pesado que me dio la tarde** he's so boring that he ruined the afternoon for me; **no d. una** to get everything wrong

**2** *vi* (a) *(repartir)* *(en naipes)* to deal

(b) *(horas)* to strike; **han dado las tres en el reloj** three o'clock struck

(c) *(golpear)* **le dieron en la cabeza** they hit him on the head; **la piedra dio contra el cristal** the stone hit the window

(d) *(accionar)* **d. a** *(llave de paso)* to turn; *(botón, timbre)* to press

(e) *(estar orientado)* **d. a** *(sujeto: ventana, balcón)* to look out onto, to overlook; *(sujeto: pasillo, puerta)* to lead to; *(sujeto: casa, fachada)* to face

(f) *(encontrar)* **d. con algo/alguien** to find sth/sb; **he dado con la solución** I've hit upon the solution

(g) *(proporcionar)* **d. de beber a alguien** to give sb sth to drink; **da de mamar a su hijo** she breast-feeds her son

(h) *(ser suficiente)* **d. para** to be enough for

(i) *(motivar)* **d. que hablar** to set people talking; **aquello me dio que pensar** that made me think

(j) *(expresa repetición)* **le dieron de palos** they beat him repeatedly with a stick

(k) *(tomar costumbre)* **darle a uno por hacer algo** to get it into one's head to do sth; **le ha dado por la gimnasia** she's taken it into her head to start gymnastics

(l) *(expresiones)* **d. de sí** *(ropa, calzado)* to give, to stretch; **no d. más de sí** *o* **para más** *(persona, animal)* not to be up to much any more

**3 darse** *vpr* (a) *(suceder)* to occur, to happen; **se da pocas veces** it rarely happens

(b) *(entregarse)* **darse a la bebida** to take

to drink

(c) *(golpearse)* **darse contra** *o* **con** to hit; **se dieron contra una farola** they crashed into *o* hit a lamppost

(d) *(tener aptitud)* **se me da bien/mal el latín** I'm good/bad at Latin

(e) *(considerarse)* **darse por** to consider oneself (to be); **darse por vencido** to give in

(f) *(expresiones)* **dársela a alguien** *(engañar)* to take sb in; **se las da de intelectual/elegante** he fancies himself as an intellectual/a dandy

**dardo** *nm* dart

**dársena** *nf* dock

**darvinismo** *nm* Darwinism

**datación** *nf* *(de restos arqueológicos)* dating

**datar 1** *vt* to date

**2** *vi* **datar de** to date back to, to date from

**dátil** *nm* (a) *Bot & Culin* date (b) *Fam* **dátiles** *(dedos)* fingers (c) *(animal)* **d. (de mar)** date mussel

**dativo** *nm* *Gram* dative

**dato** *nm* *(hecho, cifra)* piece of information, fact; **datos** *(información)* information, data; *Informát* data; **datos (personales)** (personal) details

**dcha.** *(abrev de* **derecha***)* rt.

**d. de JC., d. JC.** *(abrev de* **después de Jesucristo***)* AD

**de**

> **de** combines with the article **el** to form the contraction **del** (e.g. **del hombre** of the man).

*prep* (a) *(posesión, pertenencia)* of; **el coche de mi padre/mis padres** my father's/parents' car; **es de ella** it's hers; **la pata de la mesa** the table leg

(b) *(procedencia, distancia)* from; **salir de casa** to leave home; **soy de Bilbao** I'm from Bilbao; **de la playa al apartamento hay 100 metros** it's 100 metres from the beach to the apartment

(c) *(materia)* (made) of; **un vaso de plástico** a plastic cup; **un reloj de oro** a gold watch

(d) *(contenido)* **un vaso de agua** a glass of water

(e) *(en descripciones)* **una película de terror** a horror film; **de fácil manejo** user-friendly; **la señora de verde** the lady in green; **el chico de la coleta** the boy with the ponytail; **he comprado las peras de 100 ptas el kilo** I bought the pears that were 100 pesetas a kilo; **un sello de 50 ptas** a 50 peseta stamp

(f) *(asunto)* about; **hablábamos de ti** we were talking about you; **libros de historia** history books

(g) *(uso)* **una bici de carreras** a racer; **ropa**

**de deporte** sportswear

(**h**) *(en calidad de)* as; **trabaja de bombero** he works as a fireman

(**i**) *(tiempo) (desde)* from; *(durante)* in; **trabaja de nueve a cinco** she works from nine to five; **de madrugada** early in the morning; **a las cuatro de la tarde** at four in the afternoon; **trabaja de noche y duerme de día** he works at night and sleeps during the day

(**j**) *(causa, modo)* with; **morirse de hambre** to die of hunger; **llorar de alegría** to cry with joy; **de una patada** with a kick; **de una sola vez** in one go; **de tres en tres** three at a time

(**k**) *(con superlativos)* **el mejor de todos** the best of all; **el más importante del mundo** the most important in the world

(**l**) *(en comparaciones)* **más/menos de...** more/less than...

(**m**) *(antes de infin) (condición)* if; **de querer ayudarme, lo haría** if she wanted to help me, she'd do it; **de no ser por ti, me hubiese hundido** if it hadn't been for you, I wouldn't have made it

(**n**) *(después de adj y antes de sust) (enfatiza cualidad)* **el idiota de tu hermano** your stupid brother

(**o**) *(después de adj y antes de infin)* **es difícil de creer** it's hard to believe

**dé** *ver* **dar**

**deambular** *vi* to wander (about)

**deán** *nm* dean

**debacle** *nf* debacle

**debajo** *adv* underneath; **d. de** underneath, under; **el de d.** the one underneath; **el vecino/oficina de d.** the neighbour/office downstairs; **por d. de lo normal** below normal; **pasamos por d. del puente** we went under the bridge; **llevo una camiseta por d.** I've got a vest on underneath

**debate** *nm* debate

**debatir 1** *vt* to debate

**2 debatirse** *vpr (luchar)* to struggle; **debatirse entre la vida y la muerte** to hover between life and death

**debe** *nm* debit (side); **d. y haber** debit and credit

**deber 1** *nm (obligación)* duty; **deberes** *(trabajo escolar)* homework; **hacer los deberes** to do one's homework

**2** *vt (adeudar)* to owe; **d. algo a alguien** to owe sb sth, to owe sth to sb; **¿qué o cuánto le debo?** how much is that?

**3** *vi* (**a**) *(antes de infin) (expresa obligación)* **debo hacerlo** I have to do it, I must do it; **deberían abolir esa ley** they ought to *o* should abolish that law; **debes dominar tus impulsos** you must *o* should control your impulses

(**b**) *(expresa posibilidad)* **el tren debe de llegar alrededor de las diez** the train should arrive at about ten; **deben de ser las diez** it must be ten o'clock; **no debe de ser muy mayor** she can't be very old

**4 deberse a** *vpr* (**a**) *(ser consecuencia de)* to be due to; **y eso, ¿a qué se debe?** and what's the reason for that?

(**b**) *(dedicarse a)* to have a responsibility towards

**debidamente** *adv* properly

**debido, -a** *adj* (**a**) *(adeudado)* owing, owed (**b**) *(justo, conveniente)* due, proper; **como es d.** properly (**c**) **d. a su enfermedad** owing to *o* because of his illness; **esto es d. a la falta de previsión** this is due to lack of foresight

**débil 1** *adj* (**a**) *(persona) (sin fuerzas)* weak; *(condescendiente)* lax, lenient; **de constitución d.** prone to illness, sickly; **d. de carácter** of weak character (**b**) *(voz, sonido)* faint; *(luz)* dim; **una d. mejoría** a slight improvement; **una d. brisa movía la cortinas** a slight breeze moved the curtains

**2** *nmf* weak person

**debilidad** *nf* (**a**) *(flojedad)* weakness; **tener d. por** to have a soft spot for; **el chocolate es su d.** he has a weakness for chocolate (**b**) *(condescendencia)* laxness

**debilitación** *nf*, **debilitamiento** *nm* weakening

**debilitante** *adj* debilitating

**debilitar 1** *vt* to weaken

**2 debilitarse** *vpr* to become *o* grow weak

**débito** *nm (debe)* debit; *(deuda)* debt

**debut** *nm (de persona)* debut; *(de obra)* premiere; **su d. en sociedad fue brillante** her entry into society was impressive

**debutante** *nmf* = person making his/her debut

**debutar** *vi (actor, cantante)* to make one's debut; **la obra debuta en Madrid el día 4** the play opens in Madrid on the fourth

**década** *nf* decade

**decadencia** *nf* decadence; **en d.** *(moda)* on the way out; *(cultura, sociedad)* in decline; **la d. del imperio** the decline of the empire

**decadente** *adj (ambiente)* decadent; *(economía)* in decline

**decaedro** *nm* decahedron

**decaer** [14] *vi (debilitarse)* to decline; *(enfermo)* to get weaker; *(salud)* to fail; *(entusiasmo)* to flag; *(empresa)* to go downhill; **¡que no decaiga!** don't lose heart!; **su belleza no ha decaído con los años** her beauty has not faded with the age

**decágono** *nm* decagon

**decaído, -a** adj (desalentado) gloomy, downhearted; (débil) frail

**decaigo** ver **decaer**

**decaimiento** nm (desaliento) gloominess; (decadencia) decline; (falta de fuerzas) weakness

**decalitro** nm decalitre

**decálogo** nm Rel Decalogue; Fig (normas) golden o basic rules

**decámetro** nm decametre

**decanato** nm (a) (cargo) deanship (b) (despacho) dean's office

**decano, -a** nm,f (a) (de corporación, facultad) dean (b) (veterano) (hombre) senior member, doyen; (mujer) senior member, doyenne

**decantar 1** vt to decant

**2 decantarse** vpr (a) (inclinarse) to lean (towards) (b) **decantarse por** (optar por) to opt for

**decapante 1** adj **líquido d.** paint-stripper
**2** nm paint-stripper

**decapar** vt to strip the paint from

**decapitación** nf decapitation, beheading

**decapitar** vt to decapitate, to behead

**decatlón** nm decathlon

**decayera** etc ver **decaer**

**deceleración** nf deceleration

**decelerar** vt & vi to decelerate, to slow down

**decena** nf ten; **una d. de...** (unas diez) about ten...; (diez) ten...

**decencia** nf (a) (decoro) decency; (en el vestir) modesty (b) (dignidad) dignity

**decenio** nm decade

**decente** adj (a) (digno) decent; **un sueldo d.** a decent salary o wage (b) (en el comportamiento) proper; (en el vestir) modest; **este es un establecimiento d.** this is a respectable establishment (c) (limpio) clean

**decepción** nf disappointment

**decepcionante** adj disappointing

**decepcionar** vt to disappoint

**deceso** nm decease, death

**dechado** nm **ser un d. de virtudes** to be a paragon of virtue

**decibelio** nm decibel

**decididamente** adv (a) (con decisión) resolutely, with determination (b) (sin duda) definitely; **d., es buena idea** it's definitely a good idea

**decidido, -a** adj determined

**decidir 1** vt (a) (tomar una decisión) to decide; **d. hacer algo** to decide to do sth (b) (determinar) to determine
**2** vi to decide, to choose
**3 decidirse** vpr to decide, to make up one's mind; **decidirse a hacer algo** to decide to do sth; **si te decides a venir, llámame** if you

decide to come, give me a ring; **decidirse por** to decide on, to choose

**decigramo** nm decigram

**decilitro** nm decilitre

**décima** nf (en medidas) tenth; **tiene unas décimas de fiebre** she has a slight fever; **una d. de segundo** a tenth of a second; **ganó por décimas de segundo** he won by tenths of a second

**decimal** adj & nm decimal

**decímetro** nm decimetre

**décimo, -a 1** núm tenth; **la décima parte** a tenth
**2** nm (a) (fracción) tenth (b) (en lotería) = ticket giving a tenth share in a number entered in the Spanish "Lotería Nacional"

**decimoctavo, -a** núm eighteenth

**decimocuarto, -a** núm fourteenth

**decimonónico, -a** adj (a) (del siglo XIX) nineteenth-century (b) (anticuado) old-fashioned

**decimonoveno, -a** núm nineteenth

**decimoquinto, -a** núm fifteenth

**decimoséptimo, -a** núm seventeenth

**decimosexto, -a** núm sixteenth

**decimotercero, -a** núm thirteenth

**decir** [23] **1** vt (a) (en general) to say; **d. que sí/no** to say yes/no; **dice que no viene** she says (that) she is not coming; **¿cómo se dice "estación" en inglés?** how do you say "estación" in English?; **¿diga?, ¿dígame?** (al teléfono) hello?

(b) (contar, ordenar) to tell; **d. a alguien que haga algo** to tell sb to do sth; **se dice que** they o people say (that); **d. la verdad** to tell the truth

(c) (recitar) to recite, to read

(d) Fig (revelar) to tell, to show; **eso lo dice todo** that says it all

(e) (llamar) to call

(f) (expresiones) **como quien no dice nada** as if it were nothing; **como quien dice, como si dijéramos** so to speak; **d. para sí** to say to oneself; **decirle a alguien cuatro verdades** to tell sb a few home truths; **preocuparse por el qué dirán** to worry about what people will say; **es d.** that is, that's to say; **ni que d. tiene** needless to say; **¡no me digas!** no!, never!; **¡no me digas que no te gusta!** don't tell me you don't like it!; **no me dice nada el tenis** tennis doesn't do anything for me; **no hay más que d.** that's all there is to it, that's that; **(o) mejor dicho** or rather; **por decirlo así, por así decirlo** in other words, so to speak; **no está lloviendo mucho que digamos** it's not exactly raining; **querer d.** to mean; **¿qué quieres d. con eso?** what do you mean by that?; **¡y que lo digas!** you can say that again!

**2 decirse** *vpr Fam (reflexionar)* to say to oneself

**3** *nm* **es un d.** it's not strictly true

**decisión** *nf* (a) *(dictamen, resolución)* decision; **tomar una d.** to make *o* take a decision (b) *(empeño, tesón)* determination, resolve; *(seguridad, resolución)* decisiveness; **actuar con d.** to act decisively

**decisivo, -a** *adj* decisive

**decisorio, -a** *adj* decision-making

**declamar** *vt & vi* to declaim, to recite

**declaración** *nf* (a) *(manifestación)* statement; *(de amor, impuestos, guerra)* declaration; **prestar d.** to give evidence; **tomar d. (a)** to take a statement (from); **d. del impuesto sobre la renta** income tax return; **en sus declaraciones a la prensa, el ministro dijo que...** in his statement to the press, the minister said that... (b) *(comienzo) (de incendio)* outbreak

**declarado, -a** *adj (manifiesto)* open, professed; **es un homosexual d.** he is openly gay; **hay un odio d. entre ellos** there is open hostility between them

**declarante** *nmf* witness

**declarar 1** *vt (manifestar)* to declare; *(afirmar)* to state, to say; **d. la verdad** to tell the truth; **d. culpable/inocente a alguien** to find sb guilty/not guilty; **¿algo que declarar?** *(en aduana)* anything to declare?

**2** *vi Der* to testify, to give evidence; **lo llamaron a d.** he was called to give evidence

**3 declararse** *vpr* (a) *(incendio, epidemia)* to break out (b) *(confesar el amor)* to declare one's feelings *o* love; **se le ha declarado Fernando** Fernando has declared his love to her (c) *(dar una opinión)* **declararse a favor de algo** to say that one supports sth; **declararse en contra de algo** to say one is opposed to sth; **declararse culpable/inocente** to plead guilty/not guilty

**declinación** *nf* (a) *(caída)* decline (b) *Gram* declension

**declinar 1** *vt también Gram* to decline; *(responsabilidad)* to disclaim; **declinó amablemente la invitación** he politely declined the invitation

**2** *vi (día, tarde)* to draw to a close; *(fiebre)* to subside, to abate; *(economía)* to decline; **su interés por la caza ha declinado** his interest in hunting has declined

**declive** *nm* (a) *(decadencia)* decline, fall; **en d.** in decline (b) *(pendiente)* slope; **un terreno en d.** an area of sloping ground

**decolaje** *nm Andes* take-off

**decolar** *vi Andes* to take off

**decolorante 1** *adj* bleaching

**2** *nm* bleaching agent

**decolorar 1** *vt* to bleach

**2 decolorarse** *vpr* to fade; **decolorarse el pelo** to bleach one's hair

**decomisar** *vt* to confiscate, to seize

**decomiso** *nm (acción)* confiscation *(by customs)*; **tienda de decomisos** = shop selling goods (such as cameras and radios) confiscated by customs

**decoración** *nf* (a) *(acción)* decoration; *(efecto)* décor (b) *(adorno)* decorations

**decorado** *nm Cine & Teatro* set; **decorados** sets, scenery

**decorador, -ora** *nm,f* interior designer; *Cine & Teatro* set designer

**decorar 1** *vt* to decorate

**2** *vi* to be decorative

**decorativo, -a** *adj* decorative

**decoro** *nm* (a) *(pudor)* decency, decorum (b) *(dignidad)* dignity; **vivir con d.** to live decently

**decoroso, -a** *adj (decente)* decent; *(correcto)* seemly, proper

**decrecer** [48] *vi (disminuir)* to decrease, to decline; *(caudal del río)* to go down; **el paro decreció en un 2%** unemployment has fallen by 2%; **la luna está decreciendo** the moon is on the wane

**decreciente** *adj* declining, decreasing

**decrépito, -a** *adj Pey (anciano)* decrepit; *(civilización)* decadent, declining

**decrepitud** *nf Pey (de un anciano)* decrepitude; *(de una civilización)* decline

**decretar** *vt* to decree

**decreto** *nm* decree; **por real d.** by royal decree; **d. ley** decree, *Br* order in council

**decúbito** *nm* horizontal position

**dedal** *nm* thimble

**dédalo** *nm Fig* labyrinth, maze

**dedicación** *nf* dedication; **con d. (en) exclusiva** full-time; **trabaja con d.** he works with real dedication

**dedicar** [61] **1** *vt* (a) *(tiempo, dinero, energía)* to devote (b) *(libro, monumento)* to dedicate

**2 dedicarse a** *vpr* (a) *(a una profesión)* **¿a qué se dedica usted?** what do you do for a living?; **se dedica a la enseñanza** she works as a teacher (b) *(a una actividad, persona)* to spend time on; **los domingos me dedico al estudio** I spend Sundays studying; **se dedica a perder el tiempo** he spends his time doing nothing useful

**dedicatoria** *nf* dedication

**dedillo** *nm Fam* **saber algo al d.** to know sth inside out

**dedique** *etc ver* **dedicar**

**dedo** nm (a) *(de la mano)* finger; **dos dedos de whisky** two fingers of whisky; **d. anular** ring finger; **d. corazón** o **medio** middle finger; **d. gordo** o **pulgar** thumb; **d. índice/meñique** index/little finger

(b) *(del pie)* toe; **d. gordo/pequeño** big/little toe

(c) *(expresiones)* **escaparse de entre los dedos** to slip through one's fingers; **estar para chuparse los dedos** to be mouthwatering; *Fam* **hacer a., ir a d.** to hitchhike; *Fig* **mamarse** o **chuparse el d.** to be a fool; **no creas que me chupo el d.** I wasn't born yesterday, you know; **nombrar a alguien a d.** to handpick sb; **no tener dos dedos de frente** to be as thick as two short planks; **pillarse** o **cogerse los dedos** to get one's fingers burnt; **poner el d. en la llaga** to put one's finger on it; **señalar a alguien con el d.** *(criticar a alguien)* to criticize sb

**dedocracia** nf = situation where appointments are made at the whim of those in power

**deducción** nf deduction; *Econ* **d. fiscal** tax-deductible expenditure

**deducible** adj (a) *(idea)* deducible (b) *(dinero)* deductible

**deducir** [20] vt (a) *(inferir)* to guess, to deduce; **por la luz dedujo que debía de ser tarde** he could tell by the light that it must be late; **dedujo quién era el asesino** he worked out who the killer was (b) *(descontar)* to deduct; **me deducen del sueldo la seguridad social** national insurance is deducted from my salary

**deductivo, -a** adj deductive

**dedujera** etc ver **deducir**

**deduzco** ver **deducir**

**de facto** adj de facto

**defecación** nf defecation

**defecar** [61] vi to defecate

**defección** nf defection, desertion

**defectivo, -a** adj defective

**defecto** nm *(físico)* defect; *(moral)* fault, shortcoming; **d. de fabricación** defect in manufacturing; **d. de forma** administrative error; **d. de pronunciación** speech defect; **por d.** by default

**defectuoso, -a** adj *(mercancía)* defective, faulty; *(trabajo)* inaccurate

**defender** [66] 1 vt (a) *(país, reo)* to defend; *(amigo)* to stand up for; **d. los intereses de alguien** to defend sb's interests; **defendió su teoría con sólidos argumentos** he supported his theory with sound arguments (b) *(proteger)* *(del frío, calor)* to protect (**de** against)

2 **defenderse** vpr (a) *(protegerse)* to defend oneself (**de** against) (b) *Fig (apañarse)* to get by;

**se defiende bien en su trabajo** he's getting along okay at work; **se defiende en inglés** he can get by in English

**defendible** adj defensible

**defendido, -a** nm,f *(de abogado)* client *(of defence counsel)*

**defenestración** nf *Fig* sacking, unceremonious removal

**defenestrar** vt *Fig* to sack, to get rid of

**defensa** 1 nf (a) *(protección)* defence; **en d. de** in defence of; **la d. del medio ambiente** the protection of the environment (b) *Der* **la d.** *(parte en un juicio)* the defence; *(acción)* **en d. propia, en legítima d.** in self-defence; **basó su d. en la falta de pruebas** he based his defence on the lack of evidence

2 nmf *Dep* defender; **d. central** centre-back

**defensiva** nf defensive; **ponerse/estar a la d.** to go/be on the defensive

**defensivo, -a** adj defensive; **estrategia defensiva** defensive strategy

**defensor, -ora** 1 adj **abogado d.** counsel for the defence

2 nm,f *(de ideal, persona)* defender; *(abogado)* counsel for the defence; *(adalid)* champion; **un gran d. de la paz** a great campaigner for peace; **d. del pueblo** ombudsman; **d. del soldado** = public body created to defend soldiers' rights, especially young soldiers doing military service

**deferencia** nf deference; **por d. a** in deference to

**deferente** adj *(cortés)* deferential

**deferir** [64] 1 vt *Der* to refer

2 vi to defer (**a** to)

**deficiencia** nf *(defecto)* deficiency, shortcoming; *(insuficiencia)* lack

**deficiente** 1 adj (a) *(defectuoso)* *(producto, cantidad, persona)* deficient; *(audición, vista)* defective; (b) *(mediocre)* poor, unsatisfactory

2 nmf **d. (mental)** mentally handicapped person

3 nm *Educ* **muy d.** very poor, E

**déficit** *(pl* **déficits)** nm (a) *Econ* deficit (b) *(falta)* lack, shortage

**deficitario, -a** adj *(empresa, operación)* loss-making; *(balance)* negative, showing a deficit

**defiendo** etc ver **defender**

**definición** nf (a) *(explicación)* definition; **por d.** by definition (b) *(descripción)* description (c) *(en televisión)* resolution; **alta d.** high resolution

**definido, -a** adj (a) *(límite, idea)* (clearly) defined (b) *Gram* **artículo d.** definite article

**definir** 1 vt (a) *(explicar, precisar)* to define (b) *(describir)* to describe

2 **definirse** vpr to take a clear stance; **no se definió por ninguno de los dos bandos** he

took neither side; **el plan no acababa de definirse** the plan had not yet taken any definite shape

**definitivamente** *adv* (a) *(sin duda)* definitely (b) *(para siempre)* for good

**definitivo, -a** *adj* final; **la versión definitiva** *(de un texto)* the definitive version; **en definitiva** in short, anyway

**deflación** *nf Econ* deflation

**deflacionario, -a** *adj Econ* deflationary

**defoliación** *nf* defoliation

**deforestación** *nf* deforestation

**deforestar** *vt* to deforest

**deformación** *nf (de huesos, objetos)* deformation; *Fig (de la verdad)* distortion; **d. física** *(physical)* deformity; **tener d. profesional** to be always acting as if one were still at work

**deformar 1** *vt (huesos, objetos)* to deform; *Fig (la verdad)* to distort

**2 deformarse** *vpr* to go out of shape; **se me ha deformado el jersey al lavarlo** my jumper lost its shape when I washed it

**deforme** *adj (cuerpo)* deformed, disfigured; *(imagen)* distorted; *(objeto)* misshapen

**deformidad** *nf* deformity

**defraudación** *nf (fraude fiscal)* tax evasion

**defraudador, -ora 1** *adj (a hacienda)* tax-evading

**2** *nm,f (a hacienda)* tax evader

**defraudar** *vt* (a) *(decepcionar)* to disappoint (b) *(estafar)* to defraud; **d. a Hacienda** to practise tax evasion

**defunción** *nf* decease, death; **cerrado por d.** *(en letrero)* closed due to bereavement

**degeneración** *nf* degeneration

**degenerado, -a** *adj & nm,f* degenerate

**degenerar** *vi* to degenerate (**en** into)

**degenerativo, -a** *adj (proceso, enfermedad)* degenerative

**deglución** *nf* swallowing

**deglutir** *vt & vi* to swallow

**degolladero** *nm* slaughterhouse

**degollar** [65] *vt (cortar la garganta)* to cut o slit the throat of; *(decapitar)* to behead; *Fig* **¡como lo pille, lo degüello!** I'll kill him if I catch him!

**degradación** *nf* (a) *(de moral, naturaleza)* degradation (b) *(de un cargo)* demotion

**degradante** *adj* degrading

**degradar 1** *vt* (a) *(moralmente)* to degrade, to debase (b) *(de un cargo)* to demote

**2 degradarse** *vpr* to degrade o lower oneself

**degüello 1** *ver* **degollar**

**2** *nm (decapitación)* beheading; *(degolladura)* slaughter; *Fig* **entrar a d.** to storm in ruthlessly

**degustación** *nf* tasting *(of wines, food)*

**degustar** *vt* to taste *(wines, food)*

**dehesa** *nf* meadow

**deidad** *nf* deity

**deificar** [61] *vt* to deify

**dejada** *nf (en tenis)* drop shot

**dejadez** *nf (abandono)* neglect; *(en aspecto)* slovenliness; *(pereza)* laziness; **no lo hizo por d.** he didn't do it because he couldn't be bothered

**dejado, -a 1** *adj* careless; *(aspecto)* slovenly

**2** *nm,f (persona)* slovenly person

**dejar 1** *vt* (a) *(poner)* to leave, to put; **dejó los papeles en la mesa** he put o left the papers on the table; **deja el abrigo en la percha** put your coat on the hanger

(b) *(encomendar)* **dejarle algo a alguien** to leave sth with sb; **le dejé los niños a mi madre** I left the children with my mother

(c) *(prestar)* **d. algo a alguien** to lend sb sth, to lend sth to sb; **¿me dejas un paraguas?** could you lend me an umbrella?

(d) *(abandonar) (casa, trabajo, país)* to leave; *(tabaco, estudios)* to give up; *(familia)* to abandon; **d. a alguien en algún sitio** *(con el coche)* to drop sb off somewhere; **d. algo por imposible** to give sth up as a lost cause; **d. a alguien atrás** to leave sb behind; **su marido la ha dejado** her husband has left her

(e) *(permitir)* **d. a alguien hacer algo** to let sb do sth, to allow sb to do sth; **sus gritos no me dejaron dormir** his cries prevented me from sleeping; **déjame a mí** let me do it, let me; **deja que tu hijo venga con nosotros** let your son come with us; **¿me dejas ir?** will you let me go?, can I go?; *Fig* **d. correr algo** to leave sth be; **déjalo estar** leave it as it is, let it be; **dejó pasar tres semanas** he let three weeks go by

(f) *(reservar)* **deja algo de café para mí** leave some coffee for me

(g) *(omitir)* to leave out; **d. algo por o sin hacer** to fail to do sth; **dejó lo más importante por resolver** he left the most important question unresolved

(h) *(en imperativo) (olvidar)* to forget (about); **déjalo, no importa** forget it, it doesn't matter

(i) *(en imperativo) (no molestar)* to leave alone o in peace; **¡déjame, que tengo trabajo!** leave me alone, I'm busy!; **déjame tranquilo o en paz** leave me alone o in peace

(j) *(indica resultado)* **d. algo hecho** to get sth done; **d. algo como nuevo** to leave something as good as new; **el examen me dejó agotado** I was left exhausted by the exam

(k) *(esperar)* **d. que** to wait until; **dejó que acabara de llover para salir** he waited until it had stopped raining before going out

**2** vi (a) *(parar)* **d. de hacer algo** to stop doing sth; **no deja de venir ni un solo día** he never fails to come; **poco a poco dejaron de llamarse** they gradually stopped phoning one another

(b) *(expresando promesa)* **no d. de** to be sure to; **¡no dejes de escribirme!** be sure to write to me!

(c) **d. (mucho o bastante) que desear** to leave a lot to be desired

**3 dejarse** vpr (a) *(olvidar)* **dejarse algo en algún sitio** to leave sth somewhere

(b) *(permitir)* **dejarse engañar** to allow oneself to be taken in

(c) *(cesar)* **dejarse de hacer algo** to stop doing sth; **¡déjate de tonterías!** don't talk nonsense!

(d) *(descuidarse)* to let oneself go

(e) **dejarse llevar (por algo)** to get carried away (with sth)

**deje** nm *(acento)* accent

**dejo** nm (a) *(acento)* accent (b) *(sabor)* aftertaste

**del** ver **de**

**delación** nf denunciation

**delantal** nm apron

**delante** adv (a) *(en primer lugar, en la parte delantera)* in front (**de** of); **el de d.** the one in front; **el asiento de d.** the seat in front

(b) *(enfrente)* opposite; **lo tienes d. de las narices** it's in front of your nose

(c) *(presente)* present

**delantera** nf (a) Dep forwards, attack (b) Fam *(de una mujer)* bust (c) *(expresiones)* **coger o tomar la d.** to take the lead; **coger o tomar la d. a alguien** to beat sb to it; **llevar la d.** to be in the lead

**delantero, -a 1** adj front

**2** nm,f Dep forward; **d. centro** centre forward

**delatar 1** vt to denounce; Fig *(sujeto: sonrisa, ojos)* to give away; **lo delaté a la policía** I reported him to the police

**2 delatarse** vpr to give oneself away

**delator, -ora** nm,f informer

**delco** nm Aut distributor

**delectación** nf Formal delight, great pleasure; **con d.** with delight, delightedly

**delegación** nf (a) *(autorización, comisión)* delegation; **d. de poderes** devolution (of power) (b) *(sucursal)* branch; **D. del Gobierno** = office representing central government in each province (c) *(oficina pública)* local office

**delegado, -a** nm,f (a) *(representante)* delegate; **d. de curso** class representative (b) Com representative

**delegar** [40] vt **d. algo en alguien** to delegate sth to sb

**deleitar 1** vt to delight

**2 deleitarse** vpr **deleitarse con o en algo** to take pleasure in sth; **deleitarse haciendo algo** to take pleasure in o enjoy doing sth

**deleite** nm delight

**deletrear** vt to spell (out)

**deleznable** adj Fig *(malo)* *(clima, libro, actuación)* appalling; *(excusa, razón)* contemptible

**delfín** nm (a) *(animal)* dolphin (b) Hist dauphin; Fig successor

**delgadez** nf *(en general)* thinness; *(esbeltez)* slimness

**delgado, -a** adj *(en general)* thin; *(esbelto)* slim, slender

**deliberación** nf deliberation

**deliberado, -a** adj deliberate

**deliberar** vi to deliberate

**delicadeza** nf (a) *(miramiento)* *(con cosas)* care; *(con personas)* kindness, attentiveness; **le dio la noticia con d.** he broke the news to her tactfully (b) *(finura)* *(de perfume, rostro)* delicacy; *(de persona)* sensitivity (c) *(de un asunto, situación)* delicacy

**delicado, -a** adj (a) *(objeto, perfume, gusto)* delicate; **una situación delicada** a delicate o tricky situation (b) *(persona)* *(sensible)* sensitive; *(muy exigente)* fussy; *(educado)* polite; **estar d. de salud** to be in poor health

**delicia** nf delight; **hacer las delicias de alguien** to delight sb

**delicioso, -a** adj *(comida)* delicious; *(persona, lugar, clima)* lovely, delightful

**delictivo, -a** adj criminal

**delimitación** nf *(de terreno)* fixing of the boundaries; *(de funciones)* delimitation

**delimitar** vt *(terreno)* to set out the boundaries of; *(funciones)* to define

**delincuencia** nf crime; **d. juvenil** juvenile delinquency

**delincuente** nmf criminal; **d. habitual** habitual offender

**delineante** nmf draughtsman, f draughtswoman

**delinear** vt to draw; Fig to outline

**delinquir** [24] vi to commit a crime

**delirante** adj (a) *(persona)* delirious (b) *(idea, fiesta)* wild, crazy

**delirar** vi *(un enfermo, un borracho)* to be delirious; Fig *(decir disparates)* to talk nonsense

**delirio** nm *(por fiebre, borrachera)* delirium; *(de un enfermo mental)* ravings; **delirios de grandeza** delusions of grandeur

**delírium tremens** nm inv delirium tremens

**delito** nm crime, offence; **cometer un d.** to commit a crime o an offence; **d. fiscal** tax offence

**delta** *nm & nf* delta

**demacrado, -a** *adj* gaunt, haggard

**demacrar 1** *vt* to make gaunt *o* haggard

**2 demacrarse** *vpr* to become gaunt *o* haggard

**demagogia** *nf* demagoguery

**demagógico, -a** *adj* demagogic

**demagogo, -a** *nm,f* demagogue

**demanda** *nf* (a) *(petición)* request; *(reivindicación)* demand; **d. salarial** wage claim; **en d. de** asking for (b) *Econ* demand (c) *Der* lawsuit; *(por daños y perjuicios)* claim; **presentar una d. contra** to take legal action against

**demandado, -a** *nm,f* defendant

**demandante** *nmf* plaintiff

**demandar** *vt* (a) *Der* **d. a alguien (por)** to sue sb (for) (b) *(pedir)* to ask for, to seek

**demarcación** *nf* (a) *(señalización)* demarcation (b) *(territorio)* area; *(jurisdicción)* district

**demarcar** *vt* to demarcate, to mark out

**demás 1** *adj* other; **los d. invitados** the other *o* the remaining guests

**2** *pron* **lo d.** the rest; **todo lo d.** everything else; **los/las d.** the others, the rest; **por lo d.** apart from that, otherwise; **y d.** and so on

**demasía: en demasía** *loc adv* in excess, too much

**demasiado, -a 1** *adj* too much; *(plural)* too many; **demasiada comida** too much food; **demasiados niños** too many children

**2** *adv* too much; *(antes de adj o adv)* too; **habla d.** she talks too much; **iba d. rápido** he was going too fast

**3** *pron* **éramos demasiados** there were too many of us

**demencia** *nf* madness, insanity; **d. senil** senile dementia

**demencial** *adj* *(disparatado)* crazy, mad

**demente 1** *adj* mad

**2** *nmf* *Med* mental patient; *(loco)* lunatic

**demérito** *nm* *Formal (desventaja)* disadvantage; **los méritos y deméritos de algo** the merits and demerits of sth

**demiurgo** *nm* demiurge

**democracia** *nf* democracy; *Pol* **d. popular** people's democracy

**demócrata 1** *adj* democratic

**2** *nmf* democrat

**democratacristiano, -a** *adj & nm,f* *Pol* Christian Democrat

**democrático, -a** *adj* democratic

**democratización** *nf* democratization

**democratizar [16]** *vt* to democratize

**democristiano, -a** *adj & nm,f* *Pol* Christian Democrat

**demografía** *nf* demography

**demográfico, -a** *adj* *(estudio, instituto)* demographic; **crecimiento d.** population increase; **explosión demográfica** population explosion

**demoledor, -ora** *adj* *(huracán, críticas)* devastating; *Fig (argumento)* overwhelming, crushing

**demoler [43]** *vt* *(edificio)* to demolish, to pull down; *Fig* to destroy

**demolición** *nf también Fig* demolition

**demoniaco, -a, demoníaco, -a** *adj* devilish, diabolic

**demonio** *nm* (a) *también Fig* devil; *Fam* **saber/oler a demonios** to taste/smell disgusting; **se lo llevaban todos los demonios** *(estaba muy enfadado)* he was hopping mad (b) *(para enfatizar)* **¿qué/dónde demonios…?** what/where the hell…?; **¡demonios!** damn (it)!

**demora** *nf* delay; **sin d.** without delay, immediately

**demorar 1** *vt* to delay

**2 demorarse** *vpr* (a) *(retrasarse)* to be delayed (b) *(detenerse)* to stop (somewhere) (c) *Am (llegar tarde)* to be late

**demostración** *nf* (a) *(muestra)* demonstration; **hacer una d.** *(de cómo funciona algo)* to demonstrate, to give a demonstration; **me hizo una d. de cómo preparar una paella** he showed me how to make a paella (b) *(matemática)* proof (c) *(exhibición)* display

**demostrar [65]** *vt* (a) *(mostrar, exhibir)* to show, to display; **demuestra tener mucho interés (en)** he shows a lot of interest (in) (b) *(probar)* to demonstrate, to prove (c) *(funcionamiento, procedimiento)* to demonstrate, to show

**demostrativo, -a** *adj* (a) *(representativo)* representative (b) *Gram* demonstrative

**demudado, -a** *adj* tenía el rostro d. his face was pale; **estaba completamente demudada** *(angustiada)* she looked grief-stricken

**demudar 1** *vt* to change, to alter

**2 demudarse** *vpr* *(tejido)* to change colour; *(persona, rostro)* to change expression

**demuelo** *etc ver* **demoler**

**demuestro** *etc ver* **demostrar**

**denegación** *nf* refusal, rejection

**denegar [45]** *vt* to turn down, to reject

**denigrante** *adj* *(humillante)* degrading; *(insultante)* insulting

**denigrar** *vt* *(humillar)* to denigrate, to vilify; *(insultar)* to insult

**denodado, -a** *adj* *Formal (decidido)* determined; *(valiente)* brave, intrepid

**denominación** *nf* naming; **d. de origen** = guarantee of region of origin of a wine or other product

**denominador** *nm* denominator; *Mat & Fig* **d. común** common denominator

**denominar 1** *vt* to call

**2 denominarse** *vpr* to be called

**denostar** [65] *vt Formal* to insult

**denotar** *vt* to indicate, to show

**densidad** *nf también Informát* density; **d. de población** population density; *Informát* **alta/ doble d.** high/double density

**denso, -a** *adj (vegetación, humo)* dense; *(líquido, material)* thick; *(tráfico)* heavy; *(libro, película)* difficult to follow, involved

**dentado, -a** *adj (rueda)* cogged, toothed; *(filo, cuchillo)* serrated; *(sello)* perforated; *(hojas)* dentate

**dentadura** *nf* teeth; **d. postiza** false teeth, dentures

**dental** *adj* dental; **hilo o seda d.** dental floss

**dentellada** *nf (mordisco)* bite; *(herida, marca)* toothmark

**dentera** *nf* **dar d. a alguien** to set sb's teeth on edge

**dentición** *nf* (a) *(proceso)* teething (b) *(conjunto)* teeth

**dentífrico, -a 1** *adj* **pasta dentífrica** toothpaste

**2** *nm* toothpaste

**dentista** *nmf* dentist

**dentistería** *nf Col,Ven* dental surgery

**dentística** *nf Chile* dentistry

**dentro** *adv* inside; **está ahí d.** it's in there; **d. de** in; **d. del coche** in o inside the car; **d. de poco/un año** in a while/a year; **dentro de los próximos meses** within the next few months; **d. de lo posible** as far as possible; **de d.** inside; **el bolsillo de d.** the inside pocket; **hacia/para d.** inwards; **por d.** (on the) inside; *Fig* inside, deep down

**denuedo** *nm (valor)* courage; *(esfuerzo)* resolve

**denuncia** *nf (acusación)* accusation; *(condena)* denunciation; *(a la policía)* complaint; **presentar una d. contra** to file a complaint against

**denunciante** *nmf* = person who reports a crime

**denunciar** [15] *vt (acusar, reprobar)* to denounce; *(delito)* to report

**deontología** *nf* deontology

**deparar** *vt* (a) *(traer)* ¿**qué nos deparará el futuro?** what will the future bring?, what does the future have in store for us? (b) *(ofrecer)* **d. la ocasión de hacer algo** to provide the opportunity to do sth

**departamental** *adj* departmental

**departamento** *nm* (a) *(en oficina, organización, universidad)* department; *(ministerio)* ministry o department (b) *(división territorial)* administrative district; *(en Francia)* department (c) *(compartimento)* compartment (d) *Am (apartamento)* flat, *US* apartment

**departir** *vi* to chat, to talk

**depauperación** *nf* (a) *(física)* weakening, enfeeblement (b) *(económica)* impoverishment

**depauperado, -a** *adj* (a) *(físicamente)* enfeebled, debilitated (b) *(económicamente)* impoverished

**depauperar** *vt* (a) *(físicamente) (persona)* to debilitate, to weaken; *(salud)* to undermine (b) *(económicamente)* to impoverish

**dependencia** *nf* (a) *(de una persona)* dependence; *(de drogas)* dependency (b) *(departamento)* section; *(sucursal)* branch; **dependencias** *(instalaciones)* outbuildings; **en dependencias policiales** on police premises

**depender** *vi* to depend; **d. de algo** to depend on sth; **d. de alguien** to be dependent on sb; **depende…** it depends…; **depende de ti** it's up to you

**dependiente, -a 1** *adj* dependent

**2** *nm,f* shop assistant

**depilación** *nf* hair removal; **d. eléctrica** electrolysis; **d. a la cera** waxing

**depilar 1** *vt (piernas, axilas)* to remove the hair from; *(cejas)* to pluck; *(con cera)* to wax

**2 depilarse** *vpr* **depilarse las piernas/axilas** *(con maquinilla)* to shave one's legs/armpits; *(con cera)* to wax one's legs/armpits; **depilarse las cejas** to pluck one's eyebrows

**depilatorio, -a 1** *adj* hair-removing

**2** *nm* hair-remover

**deplorable** *adj (suceso, comportamiento)* deplorable; *(aspecto)* sorry, pitiful

**deplorar** *vt* to regret deeply

**deponer** [52] *vt* (a) *(abandonar) (actitud)* to drop, to set aside; *(armas)* to lay down (b) *(destituir) (ministro, secretario)* to remove from office; *(líder, rey)* to depose; **d. a alguien de su cargo** to strip sb of his/her office

**deportación** *nf* deportation

**deportado, -a 1** *adj* deported

**2** *nm,f* deportee

**deportar** *vt* to deport

**deporte** *nm* sport; **hacer d.** to do o practise sports; **practicar un d.** to do a sport; **hacer algo por d.** to do sth as a hobby

**deportista 1** *adj* sporty, sports-loving

**2** *nmf* sportsman, *f* sportswoman

**deportividad** *nf* sportsmanship

**deportivo, -a 1** *adj (conducta, espíritu)* sportsmanlike; **coche d.** sports car; **instalaciones deportivas** sports complex; **periódico d.** sports paper

**2** *nm* sports car

**deposición** *nf* (a) *(destitución) (de ministro, secretario)* removal from office; *(de líder, rey)* overthrow (b) *Med* **deposiciones** *(heces)* stools

**depositar 1** *vt* (a) *(dejar, colocar)* to place; **depositaron su confianza en ella** they placed their trust in her; **había depositado sus ilusiones en su hijo** he had placed all his hopes on his son (b) *(en el banco)* to deposit
  **2 depositarse** *vpr (asentarse)* to settle

**depositario, -a** *nm,f* (a) *(de dinero)* trustee (b) *(de confianza)* repository (c) *(de mercancías)* depositary

**depósito** *nm* (a) *(almacén) (de mercancías)* store, warehouse; *(de armas)* dump, arsenal; **d. de cadáveres** morgue, mortuary (b) *(recipiente)* tank (c) *(de dinero)* deposit (d) *(de polvo, sedimento)* deposit; **d. legal** = copy of a publication legally required to be sent to the authorities

**depravación** *nf* depravity

**depravado, -a 1** *adj* depraved
  **2** *nm,f* depraved person; **ser un d.** to be depraved *o* degenerate

**depravar 1** *vt* to corrupt, to deprave
  **2 depravarse** *vpr* to become depraved

**depre** *Fam* **1** *adj* **estar d.** to be feeling down
  **2** *nf* **tener la d.** to be feeling down

**depreciación** *nf* depreciation

**depreciar** [15] **1** *vt* to (cause to) depreciate
  **2 depreciarse** *vpr* to depreciate

**depredación** *nf* (a) *(entre animales)* hunting, preying on (b) *Fig (daño)* depredation, pillaging

**depredador, -ora 1** *adj* predatory
  **2** *nm,f* predator

**depredar** *vt (animal)* to prey on; *(piratas, invasores)* to pillage

**depresión** *nf* (a) *(económica, anímica)* depression; **d. nerviosa** nervous breakdown (b) *(en superficie, terreno)* hollow, depression

**depresivo, -a 1** *adj (propenso a la depresión)* depressive; *(deprimente)* depressing
  **2** *nm,f (propenso a la depresión)* depressive

**deprimente** *adj* depressing

**deprimido, -a** *adj* depressed

**deprimir 1** *vt* to depress
  **2 deprimirse** *vpr* to get depressed

**deprisa** *adv* fast, quickly; **¡d.!** quick!

**depuesto, -a 1** *participio ver* **deponer**
  **2** *adj (destituido) (ministro, secretario)* removed from office; *(líder, rey)* deposed

**depuración** *nf (de agua, metal, gas)* purification; *Fig (de organismo, sociedad)* purge

**depurado, -a** *adj (estilo)* refined, polished; *(diseño, líneas)* sleek, elegant

**depurador, -ora 1** *adj* purifying
  **2** *nm* purifier

**depuradora** *nf* purifier; **d. de aguas** water purification plant

**depurar** *vt (agua, metal, gas)* to purify; *Fig (organismo, sociedad)* to purge; *Fig (estilo, gusto)* to refine; *Informát* to debug

**depusiera** *etc ver* **deponer**

**derby** *nm (en hípica)* derby; *(en fútbol)* (local) derby

**derecha** *nf* (a) *(contrario de izquierda)* right, right-hand side; **a la d. (de)** to the right (of); **a mi/vuestra d.** on my/your right(-hand side); **girar a la d.** to turn right (b) *Pol* right (wing); **ser de derechas** to be right-wing (c) **no hacer nada a derechas** to do nothing right

**derechazo** *nm (en boxeo)* right

**derechista 1** *adj* right-wing
  **2** *nmf* right-winger

**derecho, -a 1** *adj* (a) *(vertical)* upright
  (b) *(recto)* straight
  (c) *(de la derecha)* right; **mano/pierna derecha** right hand/leg
  **2** *nm* (a) *(leyes, estudio)* law; **d. administrativo** administrative law; **d. canónico** canon law; **d. civil** civil law; **d. internacional** international law; **d. laboral** *o* **del trabajo** labour law; **d. mercantil** mercantile law; **d. natural** natural law; **d. penal** criminal law
  (b) *(prerrogativa)* right; **tener d. a algo** to have a right to sth; **tener d. a hacer algo** to have the right to do sth; **el d. al voto** the right to vote; **reservado el d. de admisión** the management reserves the right of admission; **¡no hay d.!** it's not fair!; **me queda el d. al pataleo** all I can do now is complain; **derechos de autor** *(potestad)* copyright; **derechos civiles** civil rights; **derechos humanos** human rights
  (c) *(impuesto, tarifa)* **derechos de aduana** customs duty; **derechos de autor** *(dinero)* royalties; **derechos de inscripción** membership fee; *Econ* **d. de retención** right of retention; **derechos reales** death duty
  (d) *(contrario de revés)* right side; **del d.** right side out
  **3** *adv* (a) *(en posición vertical)* upright
  (b) *(directamente)* straight; **ir d. a** to go straight to
  (c) *Am (de frente)* straight on, straight ahead

**deriva** *nf* drift; **a la d.** adrift; **ir a la d.** to drift; *Geol* **d. continental** continental drift

**derivación** *nf* (a) *(cable, canal, carretera)* branch (b) *Elec* shunt (c) *Gram* derivation

**derivada** *nf Mat* derivative

**derivado, -a 1** *adj Gram* derived
  **2** *nm* (a) *(producto)* by-product (b) *Quím* derivative

**derivar 1** *vt* **(a)** *(desviar)* to divert **(b)** *Mat* to derive

**2** *vi* **(a)** *(desviarse)* to change direction, to drift **(b)** *(proceder)* **d. de** to derive from; *Gram* to be derived from

**dermatología** *nf Med* dermatology

**dermatológico, -a** *adj Med* dermatological

**dermatólogo, -a** *nm,f Med* dermatologist

**dermis** *nf inv Anat* dermis

**derogación** *nf Der* repeal

**derogar** [40] *vt Der (ley)* to repeal

**derramamiento** *nm* spilling; **d. de sangre** bloodshed

**derramar 1** *vt (por accidente)* to spill; *(verter)* to pour; **d. lágrimas/sangre** to shed tears/blood

**2 derramarse** *vpr (por accidente)* to spill

**derrame** *nm* **(a)** *Med* discharge; **d. cerebral** stroke; **d. sinovial** water on the knee **(b)** *(de líquido)* spilling; *(de sangre)* shedding

**derrapar** *vi* to skid; *Fam* **le derrapan las neuronas** he's gone crazy

**derrape** *nm* skid

**derrengado, -a** *adj Fam (agotado)* exhausted

**derrengar** *vt Fig (agotar)* to exhaust, to tire out

**derretir** [49] **1** *vt (licuar)* to melt; *(nieve)* to thaw

**2 derretirse** *vpr* **(a)** *(metal, mantequilla)* to melt; *(hielo, nieve)* to thaw **(b)** *Fam Fig (enamorarse)* to be madly in love **(por** with); *(emocionarse)* **se derrite cada vez que ella lo mira** his heart misses a beat whenever she looks at him

**derribar** *vt (construcción)* to knock down, to demolish; *(hacer caer) (árbol)* to cut down, to fell; *(avión)* to bring down; *Fig (gobierno, gobernante)* to overthrow

**derribo** *nm (de edificio)* demolition; *(de árbol)* felling; *(de avión)* bringing down; *Fig (de gobierno, gobernante)* overthrow; **material de d.** rubble

**derritiera** *etc ver* **derretir**

**derrito** *etc ver* **derretir**

**derrocamiento** *nm (de gobierno)* toppling, overthrow; *(de rey)* overthrow

**derrocar** [61] *vt (gobierno)* to topple, to overthrow; *(rey)* to oust

**derrochador, -ora 1** *adj* wasteful

**2** *nm,f* spendthrift

**derrochar** *vt (malgastar)* to squander; *Fig (rebosar de)* to ooze, to be full of

**derroche** *nm (despilfarro)* waste, squandering; *Fig (abundancia)* profusion

**derrota** *nf* **(a)** *(fracaso)* defeat **(b)** *Náut rumbo)* course

**derrotado, -a** *adj* defeated

**derrotar** *vt* to defeat

**derrotero** *nm* **(a)** *(camino)* direction; **tomar diferentes derroteros** to follow a different course **(b)** *Náut* course

**derrotismo** *nm* defeatism

**derrotista** *adj & nmf* defeatist

**derruir** [36] *vt* to demolish, to knock down

**derrumbamiento** *nm (de puente, edificio) (por accidente)* collapse; *(intencionado)* demolition; *Fig (de imperio)* fall; *Fig (de empresa)* collapse; *Fig (de persona)* devastation

**derrumbar 1** *vt (puente, edificio)* to demolish; *Fig (moralmente)* to destroy, to devastate

**2 derrumbarse** *vpr (puente, edificio)* to collapse; *(techo)* to fall in, to cave in; *Fig* to be devastated; *Fig (esperanzas)* to be shattered

**derrumbe** *nm* collapse

**desabastecido, -a** *adj* without supplies; **d. de** short *o* out of

**desaborido, -a** *Fam* **1** *adj* boring, dull

**2** *nm,f* bore

**desabotonar 1** *vt* to unbutton

**2 desabotonarse** *vpr (persona)* to undo one's buttons; *(ropa)* to come undone

**desabrido, -a** *adj (tiempo)* unpleasant, bad; *(persona)* surly; *(tono)* harsh

**desabrigarse** *vpr* **(a)** *(en la calle)* **¡no te desabrigues!** make sure you wrap up warmly! **(b)** *(en la cama)* to throw off the covers

**desabrochar 1** *vt* to undo

**2 desabrocharse** *vpr (persona)* to undo one's buttons; *(ropa)* to come undone; **se desabrochó el cuello de la camisa** he unbuttoned his shirtcollar; **se te ha desabrochado la bragueta** your fly has come undone

**desacatar** *vt (ley, regla)* to disobey; *(costumbre, persona)* not to respect

**desacato** *nm* **(a)** *(falta de respeto)* lack of respect **(a** for), disrespect **(a** for) **(b)** *Der (al juez, tribunal)* contempt of court; **d. a la autoridad** = refusal to obey an offical

**desacertado, -a** *adj (inoportuno)* unwise, ill-considered; *(erróneo)* mistaken, wrong

**desacierto** *nm (error)* error

**desaconsejar** *vt* **d. algo (a alguien)** to advise (sb) against sth; **d. a alguien que haga algo** to advise sb not to do sth

**desacoplar** *vt Elec* to disconnect; *Tec* to uncouple

**desacorde** *adj (opiniones)* differing, conflicting

**desacostumbrado, -a** *adj* unusual, uncommon

**desacreditar 1** *vt* to discredit

**2 desacreditarse** *vpr* to become discredited

**desactivar** *vt* to defuse

**desacuerdo** nm disagreement; **estar en d. (con)** to disagree (with)

**desafiante** adj defiant

**desafiar** [34] vt (a) (persona) to challenge; **d. a alguien a algo/a que haga algo** to challenge sb to sth/to do sth (b) (peligro, ley) to defy

**desafinado, -a** adj (instrumento) out of tune

**desafinar** vi (instrumento) to be out of tune; (persona) to sing out of tune

**desafío** nm challenge

**desaforadamente** adv (a) (excesivamente) to excess (b) (con furia) furiously

**desaforado, -a** adj (a) (excesivo) uncontrolled (b) (furioso) furious, wild

**desafortunadamente** adv unfortunately

**desafortunado, -a 1** adj (a) (desgraciado) unfortunate (b) (sin suerte) unlucky
  **2** nm,f unlucky person

**desafuero** nm outrage, atrocity

**desagradable 1** adj unpleasant
  **2** nmf **son unos desagradables** they're unpleasant people

**desagradar** vi to displease; **me desagrada su actitud** I don't like her attitude

**desagradecido, -a** nm,f ungrateful person

**desagrado** nm displeasure; **con d.** reluctantly

**desagraviar** [15] vt **d. a alguien por algo** (por una ofensa) to make amends to sb for sth; (por un perjuicio) to compensate sb for sth

**desagravio** nm **en señal de d.** (in order) to make amends

**desaguadero** nm drain

**desaguar** [12] vi (a) (bañera, agua) to drain (b) (río) **d. en** to flow into

**desagüe** nm (cañería) drainpipe

**desaguisado** nm (destrozo, desorden) **hacer un d.** to make a mess; **la inauguración fue un verdadero d.** the opening was a disaster

**desahogado, -a** adj (de espacio) spacious, roomy; (de dinero) well-off, comfortable

**desahogar** [40] **1** vt (ira) to vent; (pena) to relieve, to ease
  **2 desahogarse** vpr (contar penas) **desahogarse con alguien** to pour out one's woes o to tell one's troubles to sb; (desfogarse) to let off steam

**desahogo** nm (alivio) relief, release; (de espacio) space, room; (económico) ease; **vivir con d.** to be comfortably off

**desahuciar** [15] vt (a) (inquilino) to evict (b) (enfermo) **d. a alguien** to give up all hope of saving sb

**desahucio** nm eviction

**desairado, -a** adj (a) (poco airoso) (actuación) unimpressive, unsuccessful (b) (humillado) spurned

**desairar** vt (persona) to snub, to slight; (cosa) not to think much of, to be unimpressed by

**desaire** nm snub, slight; **hacer un d. a alguien** to snub sb

**desajustar 1** vt (piezas) to disturb, to knock out of place
  **2 desajustarse** vpr **el mecanismo se ha desajustado** the mechanism isn't working properly

**desajuste** nm (a) (de piezas) misalignment; (de máquina) malfunction, fault (b) (de declaraciones, versiones) inconsistency; (económico) imbalance

**desalentar** [3] **1** vt to dishearten, to discourage
  **2 desalentarse** vpr to be discouraged, to lose heart

**desaliento** nm dismay, dejection

**desalinearse** vpr to go out of line

**desaliñado, -a** adj (persona, aspecto) scruffy

**desaliño** nm (de persona, aspecto) scruffiness

**desalmado, -a 1** adj heartless
  **2** nm,f heartless person

**desalojar** vt (a) (por emergencia) (edificio, personas) to evacuate (b) (por la fuerza) (ocupantes) to eject, to remove; (inquilinos) to evict (c) (por propia voluntad) to abandon, to move out of

**desalojo** nm (a) (por emergencia) (edificio, personas) evacuation (b) (por la fuerza) (ocupantes) ejection, removal; (inquilinos) eviction

**desamarrar** vt to cast off

**desamor** nm (falta de afecto) indifference, coldness; (odio) dislike

**desamortización** nf (de propiedades) disentailment, alienation

**desamortizar** [16] vt (propiedades) to disentail, to alienate

**desamparado, -a 1** adj (persona) helpless; (lugar) desolate, forsaken
  **2** nm,f helpless person

**desamparar** vt (persona) to abandon

**desamparo** nm (abandono) abandonment; (aflicción) helplessness

**desandar** [8] vt (camino) to go back over; **d. lo andado** to retrace one's steps; Fig to go back to square one

**desangelado, -a** adj (casa, habitación) drab; (acto, celebración) dull, uninspiring

**desangrar 1** vt (animal, persona) to bleed; Fig (económicamente) to bleed dry
  **2 desangrarse** vpr to lose a lot of blood; **murió desangrado** he bled to death

**desanimado, -a** adj (a) (persona) downhearted (b) (fiesta, lugar) quiet, lifeless

**desanimar 1** vt to discourage
**2 desanimarse** vpr to get downhearted o discouraged

**desánimo** nm (desaliento) dejection

**desanudar** vt to untie

**desapacible** adj unpleasant

**desaparecer** [48] **1** vi (a) (de la vista) to disappear; **d. de la faz de la tierra** to vanish from the face of the earth (b) (en guerra, accidente) to go missing
**2** vt Am (persona) to kidnap and take away

**desaparecido, -a** nm,f missing person

**desaparición** nf disappearance

**desapasionado, -a** adj dispassionate

**desapego** nm indifference

**desapercibido, -a** adj unnoticed; **pasar d.** to go unnoticed

**desaprensión** nf unscrupulousness

**desaprensivo, -a** nm,f unscrupulous person

**desaprobación** nf disapproval

**desaprobar** [65] vt (mostrar disconformidad) to disapprove of; (propuesta, plan) to reject

**desaprovechado, -a** adj (tiempo, ocasión, talento) wasted; (espacio, recursos, terreno) not put to the best use

**desaprovechamiento** nm (de tiempo, ocasión, talento) waste; (de espacio, recursos, terreno) failure to exploit fully

**desaprovechar** vt (tiempo, ocasión, talento) to waste; (espacio, recursos, terreno) to underuse, to fail to exploit fully

**desarmador** nm Méx screwdriver

**desarmar** vt (a) (quitar las armas) to disarm (b) (desmontar) to take apart, to dismantle

**desarme** nm Mil & Pol disarmament; **d. nuclear** nuclear disarmament

**desarraigado, -a** adj (persona) uprooted, rootless

**desarraigar** [40] vt (vicio, costumbre) to root out; (persona, pueblo) to banish, to drive (out)

**desarraigo** nm (de vicio, costumbre) rooting out; (de persona, pueblo) banishment

**desarreglado, -a** adj (cuarto, armario, persona) untidy; (vida) disorganized

**desarreglar** vt (armario, pelo) to mess up; (planes, horario) to upset

**desarreglo** nm (de cuarto, persona) untidiness; (de vida) disorder; **me siento rara, debo de tener un d. hormonal** I'm feeling a bit funny, it must be my hormones

**desarrollado, -a** adj developed

**desarrollador, -ora** nm,f Informát developer; **d. de software** software developer

**desarrollar 1** vt (a) (mejorar) (crecimiento, país) to develop (b) (exponer) (teoría, tema, fórmula) to expound, to explain (c) (realizar) (actividad, trabajo) to carry out (d) Mat to expand
**2 desarrollarse** vpr (a) (crecer, mejorar) to develop (b) (suceder) (reunión) to take place; (película) to be set

**desarrollismo** nm = policy of development at all costs

**desarrollo** nm (a) (mejora) development (b) (crecimiento) growth

**desarrugar** [40] vt (alisar) to smooth out; (planchar) to iron out the creases in

**desarticulación** nf (de huesos) dislocation; Fig (de organización, banda) breaking up

**desarticular** vt (huesos) to dislocate; Fig (organización, banda) to break up; Fig (plan) to foil

**desaseado, -a** adj (sucio) dirty; (desarreglado) untidy

**desasosegar** [45] **1** vt to disturb, to make uneasy
**2 desasosegarse** vpr to become uneasy

**desasosiego** nm (a) (inquietud) unease, anxiety (b) (nerviosismo) nervousness

**desastrado, -a** adj (desaseado) scruffy; (sucio) dirty

**desastre** nm disaster; **su madre es un d.** her mother is hopeless; **¡vaya d.!** what a shambles!

**desastroso, -a** adj disastrous

**desatar 1** vt (a) (nudo, lazo) to untie; (paquete) to undo; (animal) to unleash (b) Fig (tormenta, iras, pasión) to unleash; (entusiasmo) to arouse; (lengua) to loosen
**2 desatarse** vpr (a) (nudo, lazo) to come undone (b) Fig (desencadenarse) (tormenta) to break; (ira, cólera) to erupt

**desatascador** nm (sink) plunger

**desatascar** [61] vt to unblock

**desatención** nf (falta de atención) lack of attention; (descortesía) discourtesy, impoliteness

**desatender** [66] vt (obligación, persona) to neglect; (ruegos, consejos) to ignore

**desatento, -a** adj (distraído) inattentive; (descortés) impolite

**desatinar** vi (al actuar) to act foolishly; (al hablar) to say stupid things

**desatino** nm (a) (estupidez) (al actuar) foolish action; (al hablar) foolish remark (b) (desacierto) mistake

**desatornillar** vt to unscrew

**desatrancar** [61] vt (puerta, ventana) to unbolt; (tubería) to unblock

**desautorizar** [16] vt (a) (desmentir) (noticia) to deny (b) (prohibir) (manifestación, huelga) to ban (c) (desacreditar) to discredit

**desavenencia** *nf (desacuerdo)* friction, tension; *(riña)* quarrel

**desavenirse** [71] *vpr* to fall out

**desayunar 1** *vi* to have breakfast
**2** *vt* to have for breakfast
**3 desayunarse** *vpr* **se desayunaron con café y tostadas** they had coffee and toast for breakfast

**desayuno** *nm* breakfast

**desazón** *nf (ansiedad)* unease, anxiety; *(molestia)* annoyance

**desazonar** *vt (causar ansiedad)* to worry, to cause anxiety to; *(causar molestia)* to annoy, to upset

**desbancar** [61] *vt Fig (ocupar el puesto de)* to oust, to replace

**desbandada** *nf* breaking up, scattering; **en d.** in great disorder

**desbandarse** *vpr* to scatter

**desbarajuste** *nm* disorder, confusion; **¡vaya d.!** what a mess!

**desbaratar** *vt* to ruin, to wreck

**desbarrar** *vi* to talk nonsense

**desbloquear** *vt (cuenta)* to unfreeze; *(país)* to lift the blockade on; *(negociación)* to end the deadlock in

**desbocado, -a** *adj (caballo)* runaway

**desbocarse** [61] *vpr (caballo)* to bolt

**desbordamiento** *nm (de río)* overflowing; *Fig (de sentimiento)* loss of control

**desbordar** *vt (a)* *(cauce, ribera)* to overflow, to burst *(b)* *(límites, previsiones, capacidad)* to exceed; *(paciencia)* to push beyond the limit *(c)* *(contrario, defensa)* to get past, to pass
**2** *vi* **d. de** to overflow with
**3 desbordarse** *vpr (río)* to flood, to burst its banks; *(bañera)* to overflow; *Fig (pasión, sentimiento)* to erupt

**descabalgar** [40] *vi* to dismount

**descabellado, -a** *adj* crazy

**descabellar** *vt Taurom* to give the coup de grâce to

**descabello** *nm Taurom* coup de grâce

**descabezar** [16] *vt (a)* *(quitar la cabeza)* *(persona)* to behead; *(cosa)* to break the head off *(b)* *(quitar la punta)* *(planta, árbol)* to top

**descacharrado, -a** *adj Fam* clapped-out

**descacharrante** *adj Fam* hilarious

**descacharrar** *vt Fam* to smash up

**descafeinado, -a1** *adj (a)* *(sin cafeína)* decaffeinated *(b)* *Fig (sin fuerza)* watered down
**2** *nm* decaffeinated coffee

**descafeinar** *vt (a)* *(quitar cafeína)* to decaffeinate *(b)* *Fig (quitar fuerza a)* to water down

**descalabrar1** *vt (herir)* to wound in the head; *Fam Fig (perjudicar)* to do serious damage to

**2 descalabrarse** *vpr* to hurt one's head; *Fam Fig* to brain oneself

**descalabro** *nm* major setback, disaster

**descalcificación** *nf Med* loss of calcium

**descalcificarse** [61] *vpr Med* to decalcify, to lose calcium

**descalificación** *nf (a)* *(de competición)* disqualification *(b)* *(ofensa)* dismissive insult; **una guerra de descalificaciones** a slanging match

**descalificar** [61] *vt (a)* *(en una competición)* to disqualify *(b)* *(desprestigiar)* to discredit; **descalificó con saña a su oponente** he viciously attacked his opponent

**descalzar** [16] **1** *vt* **d. a alguien** to take sb's shoes off
**2 descalzarse** *vpr* to take off one's shoes

**descalzo, -a** *adj* barefoot

**descamación** *nf (de la piel)* flaking

**descamarse** *vpr (piel)* to flake

**descaminado, -a** *adj Fig (equivocado)* **andar** *o* **ir d.** to be on the wrong track; *(caminante, excursionista)* to be heading in the wrong direction

**descaminar 1** *vt (sujeto: malas compañías)* to lead astray; *(sujeto: guía)* to take the wrong way
**2 descaminarse** *vpr (por malas compañías)* to go astray; *(en una excursión)* to go the wrong way

**descamisado, -a1** *adj (a)* *(sin camisa)* barechested *(b)* *Fig (pobre)* wretched
**2** *nm,f* poor wretch

**descampado** *nm* open country; **juegan al fútbol en un d.** they play football on an area of waste ground

**descansado, -a** *adj (actividad)* restful; **estar d.** to be rested *o* refreshed

**descansar** *vi (a)* *(reposar)* to rest; **que en paz descanse** may he/she rest in peace; **descansó un rato antes de seguir** he rested for a while before continuing *(b)* *(dormir)* to sleep; **¡que descanses!** sleep well! *(c)* *Fig (viga, teoría)* **d. en** to rest on *(d)* *Mil* **¡descanso!** at ease!

**descansillo** *nm* landing

**descanso** *nm (a)* *(reposo)* rest; **tomarse un d.** to take a rest; **día de d.** day off *(b)* *(pausa)* break; *Cine & Teatro* interval; *Dep* half-time, interval *(c)* *Fig (alivio)* relief *(d)* *Mil* **adoptar la posición de d.** to stand at ease

**descapitalización** *nf Com* undercapitalization

**descapitalizar** [16] **1** *vt Com* to undercapitalize
**2 descapitalizarse** *vpr* to be undercapitalized

**descapotable** *adj & nm* convertible

**descarado, -a 1** *adj* (**a**) *(desvergonzado) (persona)* cheeky, impertinent (**b**) *(flagrante)* barefaced, blatant; **¡es un robo d.!** it's daylight robbery! (**c**) *muy Fam (por supuesto, seguro)* **¡d.!** you bet!

**2** *nm,f* cheeky devil

**descarga** *nf* (**a**) *(de mercancías)* unloading (**b**) *(de electricidad)* shock (**c**) *(disparo)* firing, shots

**descargador, -ora** *nm,f* *(en mercado)* porter; *(en puerto)* docker

**descargar** [40] **1** *vt* (**a**) *(vaciar)* to unload; *Fig* **descargó su cólera sobre mí** he took his anger out on me; **descargó su conciencia en mí** he unburdened his conscience on me (**b**) *(disparar)* to fire (**sobre** at) (**c**) *(puntapié, puñetazo)* to deal, to land (**d**) *Elec (pila, batería)* to run down (**e**) *(exonerar)* **d. a alguien de algo** to free *o* release sb from sth (**f**) *Der (absolver)* **d. a alguien de algo** to clear sb of sth

**2** *vi* to burst; *(tormenta)* to break

**3 descargarse** *vpr* (**a**) *(desahogarse)* **descargarse con** *o* **en alguien** to take it out on sb (**b**) *Der* to clear oneself (**de** of) (**c**) *Elec (pila, batería)* to go flat

**descargo** *nm* (**a**) *(excusa)* **d. a** argument against (**b**) *Der* defence; **en su d.** in his/her defence (**c**) *Com (de deuda)* discharge; *(recibo)* receipt

**descarnado, -a** *adj* (**a**) *(descripción)* brutal (**b**) *(persona, animal)* scrawny

**descaro** *nm* cheek, impertinence

**descarriado, -a** *adj (animal)* stray; *Fig* **una mujer descarriada** a fallen woman

**descarriarse** [34] *vpr (ovejas, ganado)* to stray; *Fig (pervertirse)* to lose one's way, to go astray

**descarrilamiento** *nm* derailment

**descarrilar** *vi* to be derailed

**descartar 1** *vt (ayuda)* to refuse, to reject; *(posibilidad)* to rule out

**2 descartarse** *vpr* **descartarse (de)** to discard

**descarte** *nm (de naipes)* discard

**descascarillado, -a** *adj (desconchado)* chipped

**descascarillar 1** *vt (pelar)* to hull

**2 descascarillarse** *vpr (desconcharse)* to chip; **la pared se está descascarillando** the paint is flaking off the wall

**descastado, -a** *nm,f Fig* ungrateful person

**descendencia** *nf* (**a**) *(hijos)* offspring; *(hijos, nietos)* descendants; **morir sin d.** to die without issue (**b**) *(linaje)* lineage, descent

**descendente** *adj (número, temperatura)* falling; *(movimiento, dirección)* downward, descending

**descender** [66] *vi* (**a**) *(en estimación)* to go down; **d. a segunda** to be relegated to the second division (**b**) *(valor, temperatura, nivel)* to fall, to drop; **d. de un avión** to get off a plane; **d. de un coche** to get out of a car; **desciendo de Cristóbal Colón** I am descended from Christopher Columbus

**descendiente** *nmf* descendant

**descenso** *nm* (**a**) *(en el espacio)* descent (**b**) *(de valor, temperatura, nivel)* drop; **ir en d.** to be decreasing *o* on the decline (**c**) *(de esquí)* downhill (**d**) *(en fútbol)* relegation

**descentrado, -a** *adj* (**a**) *(geométricamente)* off-centre (**b**) *(mentalmente)* unsettled, disorientated

**descentralización** *nf* decentralization

**descentralizar** [16] *vt* to decentralize

**descentrar** *vt (geométricamente)* to knock off-centre; *Fig (desconcentrar)* to distract

**descerrajar** *vt (disparo)* to fire

**desciendo** *etc ver* **descender**

**descifrable** *adj (mensaje, jeroglífico)* decipherable; *(letra)* legible

**descifrar** *vt* (**a**) *(clave, mensaje)* to decipher; **¿has descifrado las instrucciones?** have you managed to make sense of the instructions? (**b**) *(motivos, intenciones)* to work out; *(misterio)* to solve; *(problemas)* to puzzle out

**desclasificar** *vt* to declassify

**desclavar** *vt* to unnail

**descocado, -a** *adj Fam (persona)* carried away; **anoche estaba completamente d.** he was completely over the top last night; **un vestido d.** a provocative dress

**descocarse** *vpr* to get carried away, to go a bit wild

**descoco** *nm* **¡qué d.!** how shameless!

**descodificador** *nm* decoder

**descodificar** [61] *vt* to decode

**descojonante** *adj Vulg* **ser d.** to be a scream, to make one wet oneself

**descojonarse** *vpr Vulg* to piss oneself laughing (**de** at)

**descojono, descojone** *nm Vulg* **ser un d.** to be a scream, to make one wet oneself

**descolgar** [18] **1** *vt* (**a**) *(una cosa colgada)* to take down; **d. la ropa** to take down the washing (**b**) *(teléfono)* to pick up, to take off the hook

**2 descolgarse** *vpr (bajar)* **descolgarse (por algo)** to let oneself down *o* to slide down (sth) (**b**) *Dep* **descolgarse de** to break away from (**c**) *muy Fam (mencionar)* **descolgarse con que** to come out with the idea that

**descollar** *vi Fig (sobresalir)* to stand out

**descolocado, -a** *adj (objeto)* out of place; *Fam Fig (confuso)* disorientated, confused

**descolocar** *vt (objeto)* to put out of place, to disturb; *Fam Fig (persona)* to confuse; **me descolocó totalmente con esa pregunta** I didn't know what to say in reply to his question

**descolonización** *nf* decolonization

**descolonizar** [16] *vt* to decolonize

**descolorar** *vt* to fade

**descolorido, -a** *adj* faded

**descomedido, -a** *adj* excessive, uncontrollable

**descompasado, -a** *adj* excessive, uncontrollable

**descompensación** *nf* imbalance

**descompensado, -a** *adj* unbalanced

**descompensar** *vt* to unbalance

**descomponer** [52] **1** *vt* **(a)** *(pudrir) (fruta)* to rot; *(cadáver)* to decompose **(b)** *(dividir)* to break down; **d. algo en** to break sth down into **(c)** *(desordenar)* to mess up **(d)** *(estropear)* to damage, to break; **la cena le descompuso el vientre** the dinner gave him an upset stomach **(e)** *Fig (enojar)* to annoy

**2 descomponerse** *vpr* **(a)** *(pudrirse) (fruta)* to rot; *(cadáver)* to decompose **(b)** *(turbarse, alterarse)* **se le descompuso el rostro** he looked distraught **(c)** *Fig (irritarse)* to get (visibly) annoyed **(d)** *Méx (averiarse)* to break down

**descomposición** *nf* **(a)** *(de elementos)* decomposition **(b)** *(putrefacción) (de fruta)* rotting; *(de cadáver)* decomposition; **en avanzado estado de d.** in an advanced state of decomposition **(c)** *(alteración)* distortion **(d)** *(diarrea)* diarrhoea

**descompostura** *nf* **(a)** *(falta de mesura)* lack of respect, rudeness **(b)** *Méx (avería)* breakdown

**descompresión** *nf* decompression

**descompuesto, -a** **1** *participio ver* **descomponer**

**2** *adj* **(a)** *(putrefacto) (fruta)* rotten; *(cadáver)* decomposed **(b)** *(alterado) (rostro)* distorted, twisted **(c)** *(con diarrea)* **estar d.** to have an upset stomach

**descomunal** *adj* tremendous, enormous

**desconcentrar 1** *vt* to distract

**2 desconcentrarse** *vpr* to get distracted

**desconcertado, -a** *adj* disconcerted; **estar d.** to be disconcerted *o* thrown

**desconcertante** *adj* disconcerting

**desconcertar** [3] **1** *vt* to disconcert, to throw

**2 desconcertarse** *vpr* to be thrown *o* bewildered

**desconchado, desconchón** *nm* **la pared tenía varios desconchados** the plaster had come off the wall in several places; **el plato tenía un d.** the plate was chipped

**desconchar 1** *vt* to chip

**2 desconcharse** *vpr (pintura)* to flake off; *(loza)* to chip; **la pared se había desconchado en varios sitios** the plaster had come off the wall in several places

**desconcierto** *nm (desorden)* disorder; *(desorientación, confusión)* confusion

**desconectado, -a** *adj (aparato)* unplugged; *Fig* **está muy d. de su familia** he isn't in touch with his family very often

**desconectar 1** *vt (aparato)* to switch off; *(línea)* to disconnect; *(desenchufar)* to unplug

**2** *vi Fam (persona)* to switch off; **d. de la realidad** to cut oneself off from one's surroundings

**3 desconectarse** *vpr Fig (aislarse, olvidarse)* to forget about one's worries; **desconectarse de algo** to shut sth out, to forget (about) sth

**desconfiado, -a 1** *adj* distrustful

**2** *nm,f* distrustful person

**desconfianza** *nf* distrust

**desconfiar** [34] *vi* **(a)** **d. de** *(sospechar de)* to distrust; **desconfío de él** I don't trust him **(b)** **d. de** *(no confiar en)* to have no faith in; **desconfío de que venga** I doubt whether he'll come

**descongelar** *vt* **(a)** *(producto)* to thaw; *(nevera)* to defrost **(b)** *Fig (precios)* to free; *(créditos, salarios)* to unfreeze

**descongestión** *nf* **(a)** *(nasal)* clearing, decongestion **(b)** **d. del tráfico** clearing up of traffic congestion

**descongestionar** *vt* **(a)** *Med* to clear **(b)** *Fig (calle, centro de ciudad)* to make less congested; **d. el tráfico** to reduce congestion

**desconocedor, -ora** *adj* unaware (**de** of)

**desconocer** [21] *vt (ignorar)* not to know

**desconocido, -a 1** *adj* **(a)** *(no conocido)* unknown **(b)** *(muy cambiado)* **estar d.** to have changed beyond all recognition

**2** *nm,f* stranger

**desconocimiento** *nm* ignorance, lack of knowledge

**desconsideración** *nf* thoughtlessness; **me parece una d. por su parte** I think it is rather thoughtless of them

**desconsiderado, -a 1** *adj* thoughtless, inconsiderate

**2** *nm,f* thoughtless *o* inconsiderate person

**desconsolado, -a** *adj* disconsolate

**desconsolar** [65] *vt* to distress

**desconsuelo** *nm* distress, grief

**descontado, -a** *adj* discounted; **por d.** obviously, needless to say; **dar algo por d.** to take sth for granted

**descontaminar** *vt* to decontaminate

**descontar** [65] *vt* **(a)** *(una cantidad)* to deduct; **siete, descontando a los profesores**

seven, not counting the teachers **(b)** *Com* to discount

**descontentar** *vt* to upset, to make unhappy

**descontento, -a 1** *adj* unhappy, dissatisfied

**2** *nm* dissatisfaction

**descontrol** *nm* lack of control; *Fam* **la fiesta fue un d.** the party was rather wild; *Fam* **su vida es un d.** he leads a very disorganized life

**descontrolado, -a** *adj* **estar d.** to be out of control

**descontrolar 1** *vt Fam* to confuse; **¡no me descontroles!** stop confusing me!; **el cambio de horario me ha descontrolado** the change in timetable has got me all mixed up

**2** *vi Fam* **ese tío descontrola mucho** that guy is pretty wild

**3 descontrolarse** *vpr (coche, inflación)* to go out of control; *(persona)* to lose control; *Fam (desmadrarse)* to go wild, to go over the top

**desconvocar** *[61] vt* to cancel, to call off

**descorazonador, -ora** *adj* discouraging

**descorazonamiento** *nm* discouragement

**descorazonar 1** *vt* to discourage

**2 descorazonarse** *vpr* to be discouraged, to lose heart

**descorchar** *vt* to uncork

**descorrer** *vt* **(a)** *(cortinas)* to draw back, to open **(b)** *(cerrojo, pestillo)* to draw back

**descortés** *(pl* descorteses, *f inv) adj* rude, discourteous

**descortesía** *nf* discourtesy

**descortezar** *vt (árbol)* to strip the bark from; *(pan)* to take the crust off

**descoser 1** *vt* to unstitch

**2 descoserse** *vpr* to come unstitched

**descosido, -a 1** *adj* unstitched

**2** *nm (roto)* burst seam; **como un d.** *(hablar)* endlessly, non-stop; *(beber, comer)* to excess; *(gritar)* wildly

**descoyuntar 1** *vt* to dislocate; *Fam Fig* **no hagas eso, que te vas a d.** don't do that – you'll do yourself an injury *o* a mischief

**2 descoyuntarse** *vpr* to dislocate

**descrédito** *nm* discredit; **ir en d. de algo/alguien** to count against sth/sb; **estar en d.** to be discredited

**descreído, -a** *nm,f* non-believer, disbeliever

**descreimiento** *nm* unbelief

**descremado, -a** *adj* skimmed

**descremar** *vt* to skim

**describir** *vt* to describe

**descripción** *nf* description; **una d. de los hechos** an account of what happened

**descriptivo, -a** *adj* descriptive

**descrito, -a** *participio ver* **describir**

**descuajar** *vt* **(a)** *(derretir)* to melt **(b)** *(arrancar)* to uproot

**descuajaringado, -a, descuajeringado, -a** *adj Fam (coche, aparato)* falling to bits

**descuajaringar, descuajeringar** *[40] Fam* **1** *vt* to break into pieces

**2 descuajaringarse, descuajeringarse** *vpr (descomponerse)* to fall apart *o* to pieces **(b)** *(troncharse de risa)* to fall about laughing

**descuartizamiento** *nm (de persona)* dismemberment; *(de res)* carving up, quartering

**descuartizar** *[16] vt (persona)* to dismember; *(res)* to carve up, to quarter

**descubierto, -a 1** *participio ver* **descubrir**

**2** *adj* **(a)** *(sin cubrir)* uncovered; *(coche)* open; **decir/hacer algo a cara descubierta** to say/do sth openly **(b)** *(cielo)* clear **(c)** *(sin sombrero)* bareheaded

**3** *nm* **(a)** *Fin (de empresa)* deficit; *(de cuenta bancaria)* overdraft; **al** *o* **en descubierto** overdrawn **(b)** *(expresiones)* **al descubierto** *(al raso)* in the open; **quedar al d.** to be exposed *o* uncovered; **poner al d.** to reveal

**descubridor, -ora** *nm,f* discoverer

**descubrimiento** *nm* **(a)** *(de nuevas tierras, invenciones)* discovery **(b)** *(de placa, busto)* unveiling **(c)** *(de complot)* uncovering; *(de asesinos)* detection

**descubrir 1** *vt* **(a)** *(hallar)* to discover; *(petróleo)* to strike **(b)** *(destapar) (estatua, placa)* to unveil; *(complot, parte del cuerpo)* to uncover; **d. el pastel** to let the cat out of the bag; to give the game away; **la entrevista nos descubrió otra faceta de su personalidad** the interview revealed another aspect of his character **(c)** *(vislumbrar)* to spot, to spy **(d)** *(delatar)* to give away

**2 descubrirse** *vpr* **(a)** *(quitarse el sombrero)* to take one's hat off; *Fig* **descubrirse ante algo** to take one's hat off to sth **(b)** *(cielo, horizonte)* to clear

**descuelgo** *ver* **descolgar**

**descuento 1** *ver* **descontar**

**2** *nm* discount; **hacer d.** to give a discount; **con d.** at a discount; **un d. del 10%** 10% off

**descuerar** *vt Chile* to slam, to criticize

**descuidado, -a** *adj* **(a)** *(desaseado) (persona, aspecto)* untidy; *(jardín)* neglected **(b)** *(negligente)* careless; **es muy d. con sus cosas** he's very careless with his things **(c)** *(distraído)* **estaba d.** he wasn't paying attention

**descuidar 1** *vt (desatender)* to neglect

**2** *vi (no preocuparse)* not to worry; **descuida, que yo me encargo** don't worry, I'll take care of it

**3 descuidarse** *vpr* (**a**) *(abandonarse)* to neglect one's appearance; **descuidarse de algo/de hacer algo** to neglect sth/to do sth (**b**) *(despistarse)* not to be careful, to be careless; **no te puedes d. ni un momento** you've got to be alert all the time (**c**) *(expresiones)* **en cuanto te descuidas, se pone a llover** it rains all the time; **en cuanto te descuidas se pone a cantar** he'll break into song at the drop of a hat

**descuido** *nm* (**a**) *(falta de aseo)* carelessness (**b**) *(olvido)* oversight; *(error)* slip; **al menor d.** if you let your attention wander for even a moment; **en un d., borré el fichero** I deleted the file by mistake

**desde** *prep* (**a**) *(tiempo)* since; **no lo veo d. el mes pasado/d. ayer** I haven't seen him since last month/yesterday; **d. ahora** from now on; **d. hace mucho/un mes** for ages/a month; **d.... hasta...** from... until...; **d. el lunes hasta el viernes** from Monday till Friday; **d. entonces** since then; **d. que** since; **d. que murió mi madre** since my mother died; **d. ya** *(inmediatamente)* right now
(**b**) *(espacio)* from; **d.... hasta...** from... to...; **d. aquí hasta el centro** from here to the centre
(**c**) *(cantidad)* from; **d. 100.000 pts** from 100.000 pesetas
(**d**) *(expresiones)* **¡d. luego (que sí)!** of course!; **d. luego** *(en tono de reproche)* for goodness' sake!; **¡d. luego, tienes cada idea!** you really come out with some funny ideas!

**desdecir** [53] **1** *vi* **d. de** *(desmerecer)* to be unworthy of; *(no cuadrar con)* not to go with, to clash with

**2 desdecirse** *vpr* to go back on one's word; **desdecirse de** to go back on

**desdén** *nm* disdain, contempt

**desdentado, -a** *adj* toothless

**desdeñable** *adj* contemptible; **una cantidad nada d.** a considerable amount

**desdeñar** *vt* to scorn

**desdeñoso, -a** *adj* scornful, disdainful

**desdibujado, -a** *adj* blurred

**desdibujarse** *vpr* to blur, to become blurred

**desdice** *ver* **desdecir**

**desdicha** *nf* *(desgracia) (situación)* misery; *(suceso)* misfortune; **por d.** unfortunately

**desdichado, -a 1** *adj (decisión, situación)* unfortunate; *(persona) (sin suerte)* unlucky; *(sin felicidad)* unhappy
**2** *nm,f* poor wretch

**desdicho, -a** *participio ver* **desdecir**

**desdigo** *ver* **desdecir**

**desdijera** *etc ver* **desdecir**

**desdoblamiento** *nm* (**a**) *(de objeto)* unfolding (**b**) *(de imagen, personalidad)* splitting

**desdoblar 1** *vt* (**a**) *(servilleta, papel)* to unfold; *(alambre)* to straighten out (**b**) *Fig (dividir)* to split

**2 desdoblarse** *vpr* (**a**) *(servilleta, papel)* to unfold (**b**) *Fam Fig (multiplicarse)* to be in two places at once

**desdoro** *nm Formal* disgrace, cause of shame

**desdramatizar** [16] *vt* to play down

**deseable** *adj* desirable

**desear** *vt* (**a**) *(querer)* to want; *(anhelar)* to wish; **¿qué desea?** *(en tienda)* what can I do for you?; **desearía estar allí** I wish I was there; **estoy deseando que llegue** I can't wait for her to arrive; **dejar mucho/no dejar nada que d.** to leave much/nothing to be desired; **es de d. que las negociaciones terminen pronto** a quick end to the negotiations would be desirable; **me deseó lo mejor/un buen viaje** he wished my all the best/a pleasant journey; **me deseó buenas noches** he said good night (to me) (**b**) *(sexualmente)* to desire

**desecar** [61] **1** *vt* to dry out

**2 desecarse** *vpr* to dry out

**desechable** *adj (pañal, jeringuilla)* disposable; *(plan, opción)* provisional

**desechar** *vt* (**a**) *(tirar)* to throw out, to discard (**b**) *(rechazar) (ayuda, oferta)* to refuse, to turn down; *(idea)* to reject; *(plan, proyecto)* to drop (**c**) *(despreciar)* to ignore, to take no notice of

**desecho** *nm* (**a**) *(objeto usado)* unwanted object; *(ropa)* castoff; **material de d.** *(residuos)* waste products; *(metal)* scrap (**b**) *(escoria)* dregs; **desechos** *(basura)* rubbish; *(residuos)* waste products

**desembalar** *vt* to unpack

**desembarazar** [16] **1** *vt (habitación, camino)* to clear; **d. a alguien de algo** to rid sb of sth

**2 desembarazarse** *vpr* **desembarazarse de** to get rid of

**desembarazo** *nm* ease

**desembarcadero** *nm* pier, landing stage

**desembarcar** [61] **1** *vt (pasajeros)* to disembark; *(mercancías)* to unload

**2** *vi* (**a**) *(de barco, avión)* to disembark (**b**) *Am (de autobús, tren)* to get off

**3 desembarcarse** *vpr Am* to get off

**desembarco** *nm* (**a**) *(de pasajeros)* disembarkation (**b**) *Mil* landing

**desembarque** *nm (de mercancías)* unloading

**desembarrancar** [61] *vt* to refloat

**desembocadura** *nf* *(de río)* mouth; *(de calle)* opening

**desembocar** [61] *vi* **d. en** *(río)* to flow into; *(calle)* to lead onto; *Fig (asunto)* to lead to, to result in

**desembolsar** *vt* to pay out

**desembolso** *nm* payment; **d. inicial** down payment; **la operación supuso un d. de 100 millones** the operation cost 100 million

**desembozar** [16] *vt* (a) *(rostro)* to unmask, to uncover (b) *(cañería)* to unblock

**desembragar** [40] *vi Aut* to disengage the clutch, to declutch

**desembrollar** *vt Fam (lío, malentendido)* to straighten out; *(ovillo)* to disentangle

**desembuchar** *vi Fam Fig* to spit it out

**desempacar** [61] *vt* to unpack

**desempalmar** *vt* to disconnect

**desempañar** *vt (quitar el vaho a) (con trapo)* to wipe the steam off; *(electrónicamente)* to demist

**desempaquetar** *vt (paquete)* to unwrap; *(caja)* to unpack

**desempatar** *vi* **todavía no han desempatado** it's still a draw; **jugar para d.** to have a play-off

**desempate** *nm* **el d. llegó en el minuto treinta con un gol del Barcelona** Barcelona took the lead in the thirtieth minute; **partido de d.** decider

**desempeñar 1** *vt* (a) *(función, misión)* to carry out; *(cargo, puesto)* to hold (b) *(papel)* to play (c) *(joyas)* to redeem

  **2 desempeñarse** *vpr* to get oneself out of debt

**desempeño** *nm* (a) *(de función)* carrying out (b) *(de papel)* performance (c) *(de objeto)* redemption

**desempleado, -a 1** *adj* unemployed

  **2** *nm,f* unemployed person

**desempleo** *nm* unemployment; **d. de larga duración** long-term unemployment

**desempolvar** *vt (mueble, jarrón)* to dust; *Fig (recuerdos)* to revive; *Fig* **un día decidió d. su violín** one day he decided to take up the violin again

**desenamorarse** *vpr* to fall out of love **(de** with)

**desencadenar 1** *vt* (a) *(preso, perro)* to unchain (b) *Fig (suceso, polémica)* to give rise to, to spark off; *(pasión, furia)* to unleash; **la medida desencadenó fuertes protestas** the measure provoked furious protests

  **2 desencadenarse** *vpr* (a) *(pasiones, odios, conflicto)* to erupt; *(guerra)* to break out (b) *(viento)* to blow up; *(tormenta)* to burst; *(terremoto)* to strike

**desencajado, -a** *adj* (a) *(mueble)* broken; **la puerta está desencajada** the door won't shut properly (b) *(rostro)* contorted

**desencajar 1** *vt* (a) *(mecanismo, piezas) (sin querer)* to knock out of place; *(intencionadamente)* to take apart (b) *(cajón, puerta)* to unjam (c)

*(rostro)* **el terror le desencajó el rostro** his face was contorted with fear

  **2 desencajarse** *vpr* (a) *(piezas)* to come apart (b) *(rostro)* to distort, to become distorted (c) *(hueso)* to dislocate; **se le ha desencajado la mandíbula** he's dislocated his jaw

**desencajonar** *vt* to take out of a box

**desencantar 1** *vt* (a) *(decepcionar)* to disappoint (b) *(romper el hechizo)* to disenchant

  **2 desencantarse** *vpr* to be disappointed

**desencanto** *nm* disappointment

**desenchufar** *vt (quitar el enchufe)* to unplug; *(apagar)* to switch off

**desencuentro** *nm (en una cita)* failure to meet up; *Fig (desacuerdo)* disagreement

**desenfadado, -a** *adj (persona, conducta)* relaxed, easy-going; *(comedia, programa de TV)* light-hearted; *(estilo)* light; *(en el vestir)* casual

**desenfadar** *vt* to pacify, to appease

**desenfado** *nm (desenvoltura)* ease; *(desparpajo)* forwardness, uninhibited nature

**desenfocado, -a** *adj (imagen)* out of focus; *(visión)* blurred; **ver d.** to have blurred vision

**desenfocar** [61] *vt (objeto)* to focus incorrectly; *(foto)* to take out of focus

**desenfrenado, -a** *adj (ritmo, baile)* frantic, frenzied; *(comportamiento)* uncontrolled; *(apetito)* insatiable

**desenfrenar 1** *vt (coche)* to take the brake off; *(caballo)* to unbridle

  **2 desenfrenarse** *vpr (persona)* to lose one's self-control

**desenfreno** *nm* (a) *(descontrol)* lack of restraint (b) *(vicio)* debauchery

**desenfundar** *vt (pistola)* to draw; *(mueble)* to uncover; **desenfundó el violín** he took the violin out of its case

**desenganchar 1** *vt* (a) *(vagón)* to uncouple (b) *(caballo)* to unhitch (c) *(pelo, jersey)* to free

  **2 desengancharse** *vpr Fam (de un vicio)* to kick the habit

**desengañado, -a 1** *adj* disillusioned **(de** with)

  **2** *nm,f* person who has been disillusioned *(with life or love)*

**desengañar 1** *vt* (a) *(a una persona equivocada)* **d. a alguien** to reveal the truth to sb (b) *(a una persona esperanzada)* to disillusion

  **2 desengañarse** *vpr* to become disillusioned **(de** with); **desengáñate** stop kidding yourself

**desengaño** *nm* disappointment; **llevarse** *o* **sufrir un d. con alguien** to be disappointed in sb; **d. amoroso** unhappy affair

**desengarzar** [16] *vt (perlas)* to unstring; *(diamante)* to remove from its setting

**desengrasar** *vt* to remove the grease from

**desenlace** nm denouement, ending

**desenlazar** [16] vt (nudo) to undo; (brazos) to unlink; **desenlazó las manos** he unclasped his hands

**desenmarañar** vt (a) (ovillo, pelo) to untangle (b) Fig (asunto) to sort out; (problema) to resolve

**desenmascarar** vt (descubrir) to unmask

**desenredar 1** vt (a) (hilos, pelo) to untangle (b) Fig (asunto) to sort out; (problema) to resolve
**2 desenredarse** vpr to extricate oneself (**de algo** from sth); **desenredarse el pelo** to unknot one's hair

**desenrollar** vt (hilo, cinta) to unwind; (persiana) to roll down; (pergamino, papel) to unroll

**desenroscar** [61] vt to unscrew

**desensillar** vt to unsaddle

**desentenderse** [66] vpr to pretend not to hear/know; **d. de** to refuse to have anything to do with

**desentendido, -a** adj **hacerse el d.** to pretend one hasn't noticed/heard sth

**desenterrar** [3] vt (a) (cadáver) to disinter; (tesoro, escultura) to dig up (b) Fig (recordar) to recall, to revive (**de** from) (c) Fig (sacar a la luz) **d. viejos rencores** to rake up old quarrels

**desentonar** vi (a) Mús (cantante) to sing out of tune; (instrumento) to be out of tune (b) (color, cortinas, edificio) to clash (**con** with) (c) (persona, modales) to be out of place

**desentrañar** vt to unravel, to figure out

**desentrenado, -a** adj (bajo de forma) out of training; (falto de práctica) out of practice

**desentrenarse** vpr (bajar de forma) to get out of training

**desentubar** vt Fam **d. a un enfermo** (sacar tubos) to remove a tube/tubes from a patient

**desentumecer** [48] **1** vt to stretch
**2 desentumecerse** vpr to loosen up

**desenvainar** vt (espada) to draw

**desenvoltura** nf (al moverse, comportarse) ease; (al hablar) fluency

**desenvolver** [43] **1** vt to unwrap
**2 desenvolverse** vpr (a) (asunto, proceso) to progress; (trama) to unfold; (entrevista) to pass off (b) (persona) to cope, to manage; **se desenvuelve muy bien en su nuevo trabajo** he's getting along fine in his new job

**desenvuelto, -a 1** participio ver **desenvolver**
**2** adj (comportamiento, movimiento) natural, easy; (al hablar) fluent

**desenzarzar** [16] vt (prenda) to untangle

**deseo** nm (a) (pasión) desire; **arder en deseos de hacer algo** to be burning with desire to do sth (b) (anhelo) wish; **buenos deseos**

good intentions; **pedir/conceder un d.** to ask for/grant a wish

**deseoso, -a** adj **estar d. de algo/de hacer algo** to long for sth/to do sth

**deseque** etc ver **desecar**

**desequilibrado, -a 1** adj (a) (persona) unbalanced (b) (balanza, eje) off-centre
**2** nm,f madman, f madwoman

**desequilibrar** vt (a) (persona, mente) to unbalance (b) (objeto) to knock off balance; (economía) to upset

**desequilibrio** nm (a) (mecánico, en la dieta) lack of balance (b) (mental) mental instability (c) (en la economía) imbalance

**deserción** nf desertion

**desertar** vi (soldado) to desert; Fig **d. de** to abandon; **desertó de sus obligaciones** to neglect one's duties

**desértico, -a** adj (a) (del desierto) desert; **clima d.** desert climate (b) (despoblado) deserted

**desertificación** nf desertification

**desertización** nf (del terreno) desertification; (de la población) depopulation

**desertizar 1** vt to turn into a desert
**2 desertizarse** vpr to turn into a desert

**desertor, -ora** nm,f deserter

**desesperación** nf (a) (falta de esperanza) despair, desperation; **con d.** in despair (b) Fig (enojo) **es una d. lo lento que van los trenes** it's maddening how slowly the trains go

**desesperado, -a** adj (persona, intento) desperate; (estado, situación) hopeless; (esfuerzo) furious; (hacer algo) **a la desesperada** (to do sth) in desperation

**desesperante** adj infuriating

**desesperanza** nf lack of hope; **cuando la vio besar a Rodrigo, la d. se apoderó de él** when he saw her kiss Rodrigo he gave up hope

**desesperanzar** [16] **1** vt to cause to lose hope
**2 desesperanzarse** vpr to lose hope

**desesperar 1** vt (a) (quitar la esperanza a) to drive to despair (b) (irritar, enojar) to exasperate, to drive mad
**2** vi **d. de hacer algo** to lose all hope of doing sth
**3 desesperarse** vpr (a) (perder la esperanza) to be driven to despair (b) (irritarse, enojarse) to get mad o exasperated

**desestabilización** nf destabilization

**desestabilizador, -ora** adj destabilizing

**desestabilizar** [16] vt to destabilize

**desestimar** vt (a) (rechazar) to turn down (b) (despreciar) to turn one's nose up at

**desfachatez** nf cheek

**desfalcar** [61] vt to embezzle

**desfalco** *nm* embezzlement

**desfallecer** [48] *vi* (a) *(debilitarse)* to be exhausted; **d. de** to feel faint from (b) *(desmayarse)* to faint

**desfallecimiento** *nm* (a) *(desmayo)* fainting fit (b) *(debilidad)* faintness

**desfasado, -a** *adj (persona)* out of touch; *(libro, moda)* out of date; **estar d.** to be out of touch

**desfasar** *vt Elec* to phase out

**desfase** *nm (diferencia)* gap; **llevamos un d. de diez años con respecto a Suecia** we are ten years behind Sweden

**desfavorable** *adj* unfavourable

**desfavorecer** [48] *vt* (a) *(perjudicar)* to go against the interest of (b) *(sentar mal)* not to suit

**desfiguración** *nf (de rostro, cuerpo)* disfigurement; *Fig (de la verdad)* distortion

**desfigurado, -a** *adj* disfigured

**desfigurar** *vt (rostro, cuerpo)* to disfigure; *Fig (la verdad)* to distort

**desfiladero** *nm* narrow mountain pass

**desfilar** *vi* (a) *también Mil* to parade (b) *Fig (marcharse)* to head off, to leave

**desfile** *nm* (a) *Mil* parade (b) *(de carrozas)* procession; **d. de modelos** fashion show

**desflorar** *vt* to deflower

**desfogar** [40] **1** *vt* to vent

**2 desfogarse** *vpr* to let off steam

**desfogue** *nm* letting off of steam

**desfondar 1** *vt* (a) *(caja, bolsa)* to knock the bottom out of; **vas a d. la caja si la llenas más** the bottom will fall out of that box if you put any more in it (b) *(agotar)* to wear out

**2 desfondarse** *vpr (persona)* to become completely exhausted

**desforestación** *nf* deforestation

**desforestar** *vt* to deforest

**desgajar 1** *vt (página)* to tear out; *(rama)* to break off; *(libro, periódico)* to rip up; *(naranja)* to split into segments

**2 desgajarse** *vpr (rama)* to break off; *(hoja)* to fall

**desgana** *nf* (a) *(falta de apetito)* lack of appetite (b) *(falta de ánimo)* lack of enthusiasm; **con d.** unenthusiastically

**desganado, -a** *adj* (a) *(sin apetito)* **estar d.** to be off one's food (b) *(sin ganas)* listless, apathetic

**desgañitarse** *vpr* to scream oneself hoarse

**desgarbado, -a** *adj* clumsy, ungainly

**desgarrador, -ora** *adj* harrowing

**desgarrar 1** *vt* to rip; **d. el corazón** to break one's heart

**2 desgarrarse** *vpr* to rip

**desgarro** *nm* tear

**desgarrón** *nm* big tear

**desgastar 1** *vt* to wear out

**2 desgastarse** *vpr* to become worn

**desgaste** *nm* (a) *(de tela, muebles)* wear and tear; *(de roca)* erosion; *(de pilas)* running down; *(de cuerdas)* fraying; **el d. de las ruedas** the wear on the tyres (b) *(de persona)* wear and tear; *(de dirigentes)* losing of one's touch; **el d. de los años** the wear and tear of the years

**desglosar** *vt* to break down

**desglose** *nm* breakdown

**desgobernar** [3] *vt (país)* to govern badly

**desgobierno** *nm (de país)* misgovernment, misrule

**desgracia** *nf* (a) *(mala suerte)* misfortune; **por d.** unfortunately (b) *(catástrofe)* disaster; **desgracias personales** casualties; **es una d. que...** it's a terrible shame that... (c) *(expresiones)* **caer en d.** to fall into disgrace; **es la d. de la familia** he's the shame of the family

**desgraciadamente** *adv* unfortunately

**desgraciado, -a 1** *adj* (a) *(afectado)* unfortunate (b) *(sin suerte)* unlucky (c) *(infeliz)* unhappy

**2** *nm,f* (a) *(persona sin suerte)* born loser (b) *Fig (pobre infeliz)* miserable wretch (c) *(canalla)* **el muy d. me robó el ordenador** the swine stole my computer

**desgraciar** [15] **1** *vt* (a) *(cosa)* to spoil (b) *(persona) (deshonrar)* to demean; *(herir)* to injure seriously

**2 desgraciarse** *vpr (plan, proyecto)* to be a complete disaster, to fall through

**desgranar** *vt* (a) *(insultos, oraciones)* to spout, to come out with (b) *(maíz, trigo)* to thresh

**desgravable** *adj* tax-deductible

**desgravación** *nf* deduction; **d. fiscal** tax relief

**desgravar 1** *vt* to deduct from one's tax bill

**2** *vi* to be tax deductible

**desgreñado, -a** *adj* dishevelled

**desguace** *nm* (a) *(acción) (de coches)* scrapping; *(de buques)* breaking (b) *(depósito)* scrap yard

**desguarnecer** [48] *vt* (a) *(quitar los adornos)* to strip (b) *Mil* to leave unprotected *o* without troops

**desguazar** [16] *vt (coche)* to scrap; *(buque)* to break up

**deshabillé** *nm* negligée

**deshabitado, -a** *adj (casa)* empty, uninhabited; *(región)* uninhabited

**deshabitar** *vt* (a) *(casa)* to leave (b) *(territorio)* to depopulate, to empty of people

**deshabituar** [4] **1** *vt* **d. a alguien (de)** to get sb out of the habit (of)

**2 deshabituarse** *vpr* to break the habit (**a** of)

**deshacer** [35] **1** *vt* (**a**) *(nudo, paquete) también Informát* to undo; *(tarta, castillo de arena)* to destroy; **d. las maletas** to unpack one's suitcases *o* bags

(**b**) *(disolver) (helado, mantequilla)* to melt; *(pastilla, terrón de azúcar)* to dissolve

(**c**) *(despedazar) (libro)* to tear up; *(res, carne)* to cut up

(**d**) *(poner fin a) (contrato, negocio)* to cancel; *(pacto, tratado)* to break; *(plan, intriga)* to foil; *(organización)* to dissolve; **tenemos que d. este lío** we have to sort this problem out

(**e**) *(destruir) (enemigo)* to rout; *(matrimonio)* to ruin

(**f**) *Fig (afligir)* to devastate

**2 deshacerse** *vpr* (**a**) *(desvanecerse)* to disappear

(**b**) *(afligirse)* to go to pieces; **se deshizo en lágrimas al enterarse** he dissolved into tears when he found out

(**c**) *Fig (librarse)* **deshacerse de** to get rid of

(**d**) *Fig* **deshacerse en elogios (con** *o* **hacia alguien)** to lavish praise (on sb)

(**e**) *Fig* **deshacerse por alguien** *(desvivirse)* to bend over backwards for sb; *(estar enamorado)* to be madly in love with sb

**desharrapado, -a 1** *adj* ragged

**2** *nm,f* person dressed in rags

**deshecho, -a 1** *participio ver* **deshacer**

**2** *adj* (**a**) *(nudo, paquete)* undone; *(cama)* unmade; *(maleta)* unpacked

(**b**) *(enemigo)* destroyed; *(tarta, matrimonio)* ruined

(**c**) *(derretido) (pastilla, terrón de azúcar)* dissolved; *(helado, mantequilla)* melted

(**d**) *(anulado) (contrato, negocio)* cancelled; *(pacto, tratado)* broken; *(plan, intriga)* foiled; *(organización)* dissolved

(**e**) *(afligido)* devastated; **d. en lágrimas** in floods of tears

(**f**) *(cansado)* tired out; **la carrera le dejó d.** the run left him exhausted; **vengo d.** I'm wrecked *o* exhausted

**deshelar** [3] **1** *vt* (*nieve, lago, hielo*) to thaw, to melt; *(parabrisas)* to de-ice

**2 deshelarse** *vpr* to thaw, to melt

**desheredado, -a 1** *adj (excluido de herencia)* disinherited; *Fig (indigente)* underprivileged

**2** *nm,f (indigente)* deprived person; **los desheredados** the underprivileged

**desheredar** *vt* to disinherit

**deshice** *etc ver* **deshacer**

**deshidratación** *nf* dehydration

**deshidratado, -a** *adj* dehydrated

**deshidratar 1** *vt* to dehydrate

**2 deshidratarse** *vpr* to become dehydrated

**deshiela** *ver* **deshelar**

**deshielo** *nm* thaw

**deshilachar 1** *vt* to unravel

**2 deshilacharse** *vpr* to fray

**deshilar** *vt* to unravel

**deshilvanado, -a** *adj* (**a**) *(tela)* untacked (**b**) *Fig (discurso, guión)* disjointed

**deshilvanar** *vt* to untack

**deshinchar 1** *vt* (**a**) *(globo, rueda)* to let down, to deflate (**b**) *(hinchazón)* to reduce the swelling in

**2 deshincharse** *vpr* (**a**) *(globo, hinchazón)* to go down; *(neumático)* to go flat (**b**) *Fig (desanimarse)* to get off one's high horse

**deshizo** *ver* **deshacer**

**deshojar 1** *vt* (*árbol*) to strip the leaves off; *(flor)* to pull the petals off; *(libro)* to pull the pages out of; **d. una margarita** = to pull the petals off a daisy saying "she loves me, she loves me not"

**2 deshojarse** *vpr* (*árbol*) to shed its leaves; *(flor)* to drop its petals

**deshollinador, -ora** *nm,f* chimney sweep

**deshollinar** *vt* to sweep

**deshonestidad** *nf* dishonesty

**deshonesto, -a** *adj (sin honradez)* dishonest; *(sin pudor)* indecent; **proposiciones deshonestas** indecent proposals

**deshonor** *nm*, **deshonra** *nf* dishonour

**deshonrar** *vt* to dishonour; **con su conducta deshonra a toda la familia** he is dishonouring the entire family with his conduct

**deshonroso, -a** *adj* dishonourable, shameful

**deshora** *nf* **a d., a deshoras** *(en momento inoportuno)* at a bad time; *(en horas poco habituales)* at an unearthly hour

**deshuesar** *vt (carne)* to bone; *(fruto)* to stone

**deshumanizar** [16] **1** *vt* to dehumanize

**2 deshumanizarse** *vpr (relaciones)* to become dehumanized; *(persona)* to lose one's humanity

**desiderátum** *nm inv* greatest wish

**desidia** *nf (en el trabajo)* carelessness; *(en el aspecto)* slovenliness

**desidioso, -a** *adj (en el trabajo)* careless; *(en el aspecto)* slovenly

**desierto, -a 1** *adj* (**a**) *(vacío)* deserted, empty; **una isla desierta** a desert island (**b**) *(vacante) (concurso)* void; *(premio)* deferred

**2** *nm* desert; **el d. de Gobi** the Gobi Desert

**designación** *nf* (**a**) *(nombre)* designation (**b**) *(nombramiento)* appointment

**designar** vt (**a**) *(nombrar)* to appoint; **han designado a Gómez para el cargo** Gómez has been appointed to the post (**b**) *(fijar, determinar)* to name, to fix; **d. medidas contra la corrupción** to draw up measures against corruption

**designio** nm intention, plan

**desigual** adj (**a**) *(diferente)* different; *(terreno)* uneven (**b**) *(tiempo, persona, humor)* changeable; *(alumno, actuación)* inconsistent; *(lucha)* unevenly matched, unequal; *(tratamiento)* unfair, unequal

**desigualdad** nf *(económica, social, racial)* inequality; *(diferencia)* difference; *(del terreno)* roughness; *(de carácter)* changeability; *(de actuación, rendimiento)* inconsistency; **acabar con las desigualdades regionales** to put an end to inequalities between the regions

**desilusión** nf *(chasco)* disappointment; *(estado de ánimo)* disillusionment; **llevarse** o **sufrir una d.** to be disappointed; **caer en la d.** to become disillusioned

**desilusionar 1** vt *(desengañar)* to reveal the truth to; *(decepcionar)* to disappoint, to disillusion

**2 desilusionarse** vpr *(decepcionarse)* to be disappointed o disillusioned; *(desengañarse)* to realize the truth

**desincrustar** vt *(tuberías)* to descale

**desinencia** nf *Gram* ending

**desinfección** nf disinfection

**desinfectante** adj & nm *(para objetos)* disinfectant; *(para heridas)* antiseptic

**desinfectar** vt to disinfect

**desinflamar 1** vt to reduce the inflammation in

**2 desinflamarse** vpr to become less inflamed

**desinflar 1** vt (**a**) *(quitar aire)* to let down, to deflate (**b**) *Fig (quitar importancia)* to play down (**c**) *(desanimar)* to depress

**2 desinflarse** vpr (**a**) *(perder aire)* (balón) to go down; *(neumático)* to go flat (**b**) *(desanimarse)* to get depressed (**c**) *(achicarse)* to become discouraged, to lose heart

**desinformación** nf misinformation

**desinformar** vt to misinform

**desinhibición** nf lack of inhibition

**desinhibido, -a** adj uninhibited

**desinhibir 1** vt to free from inhibitions

**2 desinhibirse** vpr to lose one's inhibitions

**desintegración** nf (**a**) *(de objetos)* disintegration; *Fís* **d. nuclear** nuclear decay (**b**) *(de grupos, organizaciones)* breaking up

**desintegrar 1** vt (**a**) *(objetos)* to disintegrate; *(átomo)* to split (**b**) *(grupos, organizaciones)* to break up

**2 desintegrarse** vpr (**a**) *(objetos)* to disintegrate (**b**) *(grupos, organizaciones)* to break up

**desinterés** *(pl desintereses)* nm (**a**) *(indiferencia)* disinterest, lack of interest (**b**) *(generosidad)* unselfishness

**desinteresado, -a** adj (**a**) *(generoso)* unselfish (**b**) *(indiferente)* uninterested

**desinteresarse** vpr to lose interest (**de** in)

**desintoxicación** nf detoxification; **clínica o d.** *(para alcohólicos)* drying-out clinic

**desintoxicar** [61] **1** vt to detoxify

**2 desintoxicarse** vpr *(dejar de beber)* to dry out; *Fig* **se fue al campo para desintoxicarse de la ciudad** he went to the country to get the city out of his system

**desistimiento** nm giving up; *Der* abandonment

**desistir** vi to give up, to stop (**de hacer algo** doing sth)

**deslavazado, -a** adj *(discurso)* disconnected, rambling

**desleal** adj disloyal (**a** o **con** to); **competencia d.** unfair competition

**deslealtad** nf disloyalty

**desleír** [58] vt to dissolve

**deslenguado, -a** adj *Fig* foul-mouthed

**desliar** [34] vt to unwrap

**desligar** [40] **1** vt (**a**) *(desatar)* to untie (**b**) *Fig (separar)* to separate (**de** from)

**2 desligarse** vpr (**a**) *(desatarse)* to untie oneself (**b**) *Fig (separarse)* to become separated (**de** from); *(distanciarse)* to distance oneself (**de** from)

**deslindar** vt *(limitar)* to mark out (the boundaries of); *Fig (separar)* to define

**deslió** ver **desleír**

**deslío** etc ver **desleír**

**desliz** nm slip, error; **tener** o **cometer un d.** *(error)* to slip up; *(infidelidad conyugal)* to be unfaithful

**deslizante** adj slippery

**deslizar** [16] **1** vt (**a**) *(mano, objeto)* **d. algo en** to slip sth into; **d. algo por algo** to slide sth along sth; **deslizó la mano por la barandilla** he ran his hand down the banister (**b**) *(indirecta, comentario)* to let slip in

**2 deslizarse** vpr (**a**) *(resbalar)* **deslizarse por** to slide along; **el barco se deslizaba por la superficie** the boat slid along the surface (**b**) *(introducirse)* **deslizarse en** *(persona)* to slip into; *(error)* to creep into (**c**) *(sujeto: tiempo, vida)* to slip away o by

**deslomar 1** vt *(a golpes)* to thrash

**2 deslomarse** vpr *Fam Fig* to break one's back, to wear oneself out

**deslucido, -a** *adj* (a) *(sin brillo)* faded; *(plata)* tarnished (b) *(sin gracia)* *(acto, ceremonia)* dull; *(actuación)* lacklustre, uninspired

**deslucir** [41] *vt* *(espectáculo)* to spoil, to ruin

**deslumbrante** *adj* *(luz)* dazzling; *Fig* *(atractivo)* **María estaba d.** María looked stunning

**deslumbrar** *vt también Fig* to dazzle

**deslustrar** *vt también Fig* to take the shine off

**desmadejar** *vt* to wear o tire out

**desmadrarse** *vpr Fam* to go wild

**desmadre** *nm Fam* (a) *(caos)* chaos, utter confusion (b) *(desenfreno)* rave-up

**desmán** *nm* (a) *(exceso)* excess; **con sus desmanes ahuyenta a mis amigos** his outrageous behaviour scares off my friends (b) *(abuso de poder)* abuse (of power)

**desmandado, -a** *adj* *(desobediente)* unruly

**desmandarse** *vpr* (a) *(desobedecer)* to be disobedient (b) *(insubordinarse)* to get out of hand

**desmano** *nf* **a d.** *(fuera de alcance)* out of reach; *(fuera del camino seguido)* out of the way

**desmantelado, -a** *adj* dismantled

**desmantelamiento** *nm* *(de casa, fábrica)* stripping; *(de organización)* disbanding; *(de arsenal, andamiaje)* dismantling; *(de barco)* unrigging; **el d. de todas las bases americanas** the closing of all American bases

**desmantelar** *vt* *(casa, fábrica)* to clear out, to strip; *(organización)* to disband; *(arsenal, andamio)* to dismantle; *(barco)* to unrig

**desmañado, -a** *adj* clumsy, awkward

**desmaquillador** *nm* make-up remover

**desmaquillar 1** *vt* to remove the make-up from
**2 desmaquillarse** *vpr* to take one's make-up off

**desmarcar 1** *vt Dep* to draw the marker away from
**2 desmarcarse** *vpr Dep* to lose one's marker; *Fig (escabullirse)* to make oneself scarce

**desmayado, -a** *adj* (a) *(persona)* unconscious; **caer d.** to faint (b) *(color)* pale; *(voz)* faint, weak

**desmayar 1** *vi* to lose heart
**2 desmayarse** *vpr* to faint

**desmayo** *nm* (a) *(físico)* fainting fit; **sufrir un d.** to faint (b) *(moral)* loss of heart; **sin d.** unfalteringly; **con d.** feebly

**desmedido, -a** *adj* excessive, disproportionate

**desmedirse** [49] *vpr* to go too far, to go over the top

**desmejorar 1** *vt* to spoil
**2** *vi* to go downhill, to deteriorate
**3 desmejorarse** *vpr* to go downhill, to deteriorate

**desmelenado, -a** *adj* (a) *(persona)* reckless, wild (b) *(cabello)* tousled, dishevelled

**desmelenar 1** *vt* *(cabello)* to dishevel
**2 desmelenarse** *vpr* to go wild

**desmembramiento** *nm* *(de cuerpo)* dismemberment; *(de miembro, extremidad)* loss; *(de estados, partidos)* breaking up

**desmembrar** [3] **1** *vt* (a) *(trocear)* *(cuerpo)* to dismember; *(miembro, extremidad)* to cut off (b) *(disgregar)* to break up
**2 desmembrarse** *vpr* to break up; **el Estado se está desmembrando** the State is breaking up o falling apart

**desmemoriado, -a 1** *adj* forgetful
**2** *nm,f* forgetful person

**desmentido** *nm* denial

**desmentir** [64] *vt* (a) *(negar)* to deny; **desmintió la noticia** he denied the report (b) *(no corresponder)* to belie

**desmenuzar** [16] **1** *vt* (a) *(trocear)* *(pan, pastel, roca)* to crumble; *(carne)* to chop up; *(papel)* to tear up into little pieces (b) *Fig (examinar, analizar)* to scrutinize
**2 desmenuzarse** *vpr* *(pan, pastel, roca)* to crumble

**desmerecer** [48] **1** *vt* not to deserve, to be unworthy of
**2** *vi* to lose value; **d. (en algo) de alguien** to be inferior to sb (in sth); **ganó el equipo visitante, pero el Bétis no desmereció** the visiting team won, but Bétis gave a good account of themselves

**desmesurado, -a** *adj* *(excesivo)* excessive, disproportionate; *(enorme)* enormous

**desmidiera** *etc ver* **desmedirse**

**desmido** *etc ver* **desmedirse**

**desmiembro** *ver* **desmembrar**

**desmiento** *ver* **desmentir**

**desmigajar 1** *vt* to crumble
**2 desmigajarse** *vpr* to crumble

**desmilitarización** *nf* *(de país, zona)* demilitarization

**desmilitarizar** [16] *vt* to demilitarize

**desmintiera** *etc ver* **desmentir**

**desmitificación** *nf* demythologizing

**desmitificar** [61] *vt* **d. algo/a alguien** to stop idealizing sth/sb; **el escándalo desmitificó al presidente** the scandal showed the president had feet of clay

**desmochado, -a** *adj* *(árbol)* polled

**desmochar** *vt* *(árbol)* to poll

**desmontable** *adj* that can be dismantled; **una librería d.** a self-assembly bookcase

**desmontar 1** *vt* (a) *(desarmar)* *(máquina)* to take apart o to pieces; *(motor)* to strip down; *(piezas)* to dismantle; *(rueda)* to remove, to take off; *(tienda de campaña)* to take down; *(arma)* to uncock (**b**) *(de caballo, moto, bicicleta)* to unseat; **el caballo desmontó al jinete** the horse threw its rider; **desmontó al niño de la bicicleta** he took the boy off the bicycle

**2** *vi* **d. de** *(caballo)* to dismount from; *(moto, bicicleta)* to get off; *(coche)* to get out of

**3 desmontarse** *vpr* **desmontarse de** *(caballo)* to dismount from; *(moto, bicicleta)* to get off; *(coche)* to get out of

**desmonte** *nm* (**a**) *(terreno)* **un d.** an area of levelled ground (**b**) *(allanamiento)* levelling (**c**) *(de bosque)* clearing

**desmoralización** *nf* demoralization

**desmoralizador, -ora, desmoralizante** *adj* demoralizing

**desmoralizar** [16] **1** *vt* to demoralize

**2 desmoralizarse** *vpr* to become demoralized

**desmoronamiento** *nm (de edificio, roca, ideales)* crumbling; *(de imperio)* fall

**desmoronar 1** *vt (edificio, roca)* to cause to crumble

**2 desmoronarse** *vpr* (**a**) *(edificio, roca, ideales)* to crumble, to fall to pieces (**b**) *Fig (persona)* to go to pieces; *(imperio)* to fall apart

**desmotivar** *vt* to demotivate

**desmovilizar** [16] *vt* to demobilize

**desnacionalizar** [16] *vt* to denationalize, to privatize

**desnatado, -a** *adj (leche)* skimmed

**desnatar** *vt* to skim

**desnaturalizado, -a** *adj (sustancia)* adulterated; *(alcohol)* denatured

**desnaturalizar** [16] *vt* (**a**) *(sustancia)* to adulterate (**b**) *(persona)* to deny the natural rights of

**desnivel** *nm* (**a**) *(cultural, social)* inequality, gap (**b**) *(del terreno)* drop; **había un d. de 500 metros** there was a drop of 500 metres

**desnivelar 1** *vt* to make uneven; *(balanza)* to tip

**2 desnivelarse** *vpr* to become uneven

**desnucar** [61] **1** *vt* to break the neck of

**2 desnucarse** *vpr* to break one's neck

**desnuclearización** *nf (de armas)* nuclear disarmament; *(de centrales nucleares)* = getting rid of nuclear power

**desnuclearizar** [16] *vt* to make nuclear-free

**desnudar 1** *vt* (**a**) *(persona)* to undress (**b**) *Fig (cosa)* to strip (**de** of); **desnudó su discurso de toda floritura** he avoided all ornament in his speech

**2 desnudarse** *vpr* to undress, to get undressed

**desnudez** *nf (de persona)* nakedness, nudity; *(de cosa)* bareness

**desnudismo** *nm* nudism

**desnudo, -a1** *adj* (**a**) *(persona, cuerpo)* naked (**b**) *Fig (salón, hombro, árbol)* bare; *(verdad)* plain; *(paisaje)* bare, barren

**2** *nm* nude; **pintar un d.** to paint a nude

**desnutrición** *nf* malnutrition

**desnutrido, -a** *adj* undernourished

**desnutrirse** *vpr* to become malnourished

**desobedecer** [48] *vt* to disobey

**desobediencia** *nf* disobedience

**desobediente** *adj* disobedient

**desocupado, -a** *adj* (**a**) *(persona) (ocioso)* free, unoccupied; *(sin empleo)* unemployed (**b**) *(asiento, cargo)* vacant, unoccupied (**c**) *(tiempo)* free

**desocupar** *vt (edificio)* to vacate; *(habitación, mesa)* to leave; **si consigo d. una tarde, te llamo** if I can free up an afternoon, I'll call you; **desocupó su silla para cedérsela a la anciana** he gave (up) his seat to the old lady

**desodorante 1** *adj* deodorant, deodorizing

**2** *nm* deodorant; **d. de barra/de spray** deodorant stick/spray

**desodorizar** [16] *vt* to deodorize

**desoír** *vt* not to listen to, to take no notice of; **d. los consejos de alguien** to ignore sb's advice

**desolación** *nf (destrucción)* desolation; *(desconsuelo)* distress, grief; **sumir en la d.** to devastate

**desolado, -a** *adj (paraje)* desolate; *(persona)* devastated

**desolador, -ora** *adj (imagen, espectáculo)* desolate; *(noticia)* devastating

**desolar 1** *vt* (**a**) *(destruir)* to devastate, to lay waste (**b**) *(afligir)* to cause anguish to; **la muerte del padre desoló a la familia** the father's death devastated the family

**2 desolarse** *vpr* to be devastated

**desollar** [65] *vt* to skin; *Fig* **si lo pillo, lo desuello** if I catch him I'll skin him alive

**desorbitado, -a** *adj (exagerado)* disproportionate; *(precio)* exorbitant (**b**) **con los ojos desorbitados** pop-eyed

**desorbitar 1** *vt Fig (exagerar)* to exaggerate, to blow out of proportion; **la inflación ha desorbitado los precios** inflation has sent prices sky-high

**2 desorbitarse** *vpr* **la inflación se ha desorbitado** inflation has gone out of control *o* through the roof

**desorden** *nm* (**a**) *(confusión)* disorder, chaos; *(falta de orden)* mess (**b**) *(disturbio)* disturbance (**c**) *(vida desenfrenada)* excess

**desordenado, -a 1** *adj* (**a**) *(habitación, persona)* untidy, messy; *(documentos, fichas)* jumbled (up) (**b**) *Fig (vida, comportamiento)* disorganized, messy

**2** *nm,f* untidy person; **es una desordenada** she's very untidy

**desordenar** *vt (habitación, cajón)* to mess up; *(documentos, fichas)* to jumble up; *(pelo)* to ruffle

**desorganización** *nf* disorganization

**desorganizar** [16] *vt* to disrupt, to disorganize

**desorientación** *nf* (a) *(en el espacio)* disorientation (b) *Fig (en la mente)* confusion

**desorientado, -a** *adj (en el espacio)* lost; *(confuso)* confused; **tiene 98 años y anda ya algo d.** he's 98 and he's a bit confused

**desorientar 1** *vt* (a) *(en el espacio)* to disorientate, to mislead (b) *Fig (en la mente)* to confuse

**2 desorientarse** *vpr* to lose one's way *o* bearings

**desovar** *vi (peces, anfibios)* to spawn; *(insectos)* to lay eggs

**desoxirribonucleico** *adj Quím* **ácido d.** deoxyribonucleic acid

**despabilado, -a** *adj* (a) *(despierto)* wide-awake (b) *(listo)* smart, quick

**despabilar 1** *vt* (a) *(despertar)* to wake up (b) *(hacer más avispado)* to make streetwise

**2 despabilarse** *vpr* (a) *(despertarse)* to wake up (b) *(darse prisa)* to hurry up

**despachar 1** *vt* (a) *(mercancía)* to dispatch (b) *(en tienda) (cliente)* to serve; *(entradas, bebidas)* to sell; **¿le despachan?** are you being served? (c) *Fam Fig (terminar) (trabajo, discurso)* to finish off; *(comida)* to polish off (d) *(del trabajo)* **d. a alguien (de)** to dismiss *o* sack sb (from) (e) *(asunto, negocio)* to settle (f) *Am (facturar)* to check in

**2** *vi* (a) *(sobre un asunto)* to do business (b) *(en una tienda)* to serve

**3 despacharse** *vpr* (a) *(hablar francamente)* **despacharse con alguien** to give sb a piece of one's mind (b) *(desembarazarse)* **despacharse de** to get rid of

**despacho** *nm* (a) *(oficina)* office; *(en casa)* study (b) *(muebles)* set of office furniture (c) *(comunicación oficial)* dispatch (d) *(venta)* sale; *(lugar de venta)* **d. de billetes/localidades** ticket/box office

**despachurrar** *vt Fam* to squash

**despacio 1** *adv* slowly

**2** *interj* **¡d.!** take it easy!

**despampanante** *adj* stunning; **una rubia d.** a stunning blonde

**despanzurrar 1** *vt Fam* to cause to burst open

**2 despanzurrarse** *vpr* to burst (open); **se ha despanzurrado el sofá** the stuffing is coming out of the sofa

**desparejado, -a** *adj (calcetín, guante)* odd

**desparejar** *vt* to mix up

**desparpajo** *nm Fam* forwardness, self-assurance; **con d.** with assurance, confidently

**desparramar 1** *vt* (a) *(líquido)* to spill; *(objetos)* to spread, to scatter (b) *Fig (dinero)* to squander

**2 desparramarse** *vpr (líquido)* to spill; *(objetos, personas)* to scatter, to spread out

**despatarrarse** *vpr Fam* to open one's legs wide; **se despatarró en el sofá y se quedó dormido** he sprawled out on the sofa and fell asleep

**despavorido, -a** *adj* terrified; **salir d.** to rush out in terror

**despavorir** *vt* to terrify

**despecharse** *vpr* to get angry

**despecho** *nm (rencor, venganza)* spite; *(desengaño)* bitterness; **(hacer algo) por d.** (to do sth) out of spite; **a d. de** in spite of, despite

**despechugarse** [40] *vpr Fam Fig* to bare one's breast

**despectivo, -a** *adj* (a) *(despreciativo)* scornful, contemptuous (b) *Gram* pejorative

**despedazar** [16] *vt* (a) *(físicamente)* to tear apart (b) *Fig (moralmente)* to shatter

**despedida** *nf* (a) *(adiós)* goodbye, farewell (b) *(fiesta)* farewell party; **d. de soltero/de soltera** stag/hen party

**despedir** [49] **1** *vt* (a) *(decir adiós)* to say goodbye to; **fuimos a despedirle a la estación** we went to see him off at the station (b) *(echar) (de un empleo)* to dismiss, to sack; *(de un club)* to throw out (c) *(lanzar, arrojar)* to fling; **salir despedido de/por/hacia algo** to fly out of/through/towards sth (d) *Fig (difundir, desprender)* to give off; **despide un olor insoportable** it gives off an unbearable smell

**2 despedirse** *vpr* to say goodbye (**de** to)

**despegado, -a** *adj Fig* cold, detached

**despegar** [40] **1** *vt* to unstick

**2** *vi (avión)* to take off

**3 despegarse** *vpr (etiqueta, pegatina, sello)* to come unstuck; *Fig (persona)* **despegarse de alguien** to break away *o* withdraw from sb; **no se despegó de su novia ni un minuto** he didn't leave his girlfriend's side for a minute

**despego** *nm* detachment, indifference

**despegue** *nm* takeoff; *Fig* **d. económico** economic takeoff

**despeinar 1** *vt (pelo)* to ruffle; **d. a alguien** to mess up sb's hair; **el viento la había despeinado** the wind had ruffled her hair

**2 despeinarse** *vpr* to get one's hair messed up

**despejado, -a** *adj* (a) *(tiempo, día)* clear (b) *Fig (persona, mente)* alert (c) *(espacio) (ancho)* spacious; *(sin estorbos)* clear, uncluttered

**despejar 1** vt (a) *(habitación, mente)* to clear (b) *(misterio, incógnita)* to clear up; to put an end to

**2** v impersonal to clear up

**3 despejarse** vpr (a) *(persona)* *(espabilarse)* to clear one's head; *(despertarse)* to wake oneself up (b) *(tiempo)* to clear up; *(cielo)* to clear

**despeje** nm Dep clearance

**despellejar 1** vt (a) *(animal)* to skin (b) Fig *(criticar)* to pull to pieces

**2 despellejarse** vpr to peel; **se te está despellejando la nariz** your nose is peeling

**despelotarse** vpr Fam (a) *(desnudarse)* to strip off (b) *(mondarse)* **d. (de risa)** to laugh one's head off

**despelote** nm Fam (a) *(caos)* chaos; **se armó un d.** chaos broke out; **ser un d.** *(proyecto, reunión)* to be chaotic (b) *(cachondeo)* **tu primo es un d.** your cousin is a good laugh; **esa película es un d.** that film is a great laugh o a scream

**despeluchado, -a** adj *(despeinado)* with dishevelled hair

**despeluchar 1** vt *(despeinar)* to mess o dishevel sb's hair

**2 despelucharse** vpr *(despeinarse)* to get one's hair messed up o dishevelled; *(pelarse)* to be/get worn bare; **la alfombra se ha despeluchado por el uso** the carpet has been worn bare with use

**despenalización** nf decriminalization

**despenalizar** [16] vt to decriminalize; **d. las drogas blandas** to decriminalize soft drugs

**dependolarse** vpr Fam to go wild

**dependole** nm loss of control; **la fiesta fue un d.** the party was a rave-up

**despensa** nf larder, pantry

**despeñadero** nm precipice

**despeñar 1** vt to throw over a cliff

**2 despeñarse** vpr to fall over a cliff

**desperdiciar** [15] vt *(tiempo, comida)* to waste; *(dinero)* to squander; *(ocasión)* to throw away

**desperdicio** nm (a) *(acción)* waste (b) *(residuo)* **desperdicios** scraps (c) **no tener d.** to be excellent from start to finish

**desperdigar** [40] **1** vt to scatter, to disperse

**2 desperdigarse** vpr to scatter

**desperezarse** [16] vpr to stretch

**desperfecto** nm *(deterioro)* damage; *(defecto)* flaw, imperfection; **pagar los desperfectos ocasionados** to pay for the damage caused; **sufrir desperfectos** to get damaged

**despersonalizar** [16] vt to depersonalize

**despertador** nm alarm clock; **d. telefónico** alarm call service

**despertar** [3] **1** vt (a) *(persona, animal)* to wake (up) (b) Fig *(reacción)* to arouse; **d. odio/pasión** to arouse hatred/passion (c) Fig *(recuerdo)* to revive, to awaken

**2** vi to wake up

**3** nm awakening

**4 despertarse** vpr to wake up

**despiadado, -a** adj pitiless, merciless

**despidiera** etc ver **despedir**

**despido 1** ver **despedir**

**2** nm dismissal, sacking; **d. improcedente** wrongful dismissal

**despiece** nm cutting-up

**despierto** etc ver **despertar**

**despierto, -a** adj (a) *(sin dormir)* awake (b) Fig *(espabilado, listo)* bright, sharp

**despilfarrador, -ora 1** adj wasteful, spendthrift

**2** nm,f spendthrift, squanderer

**despilfarrar** vt *(dinero)* to squander; *(energía, agua)* to waste

**despilfarro** nm *(de dinero)* squandering; *(de energía, agua)* waste

**despintar** vt to take the paint off

**despiojar** vt to delouse

**despiole** nm Arg Fam rumpus, shindy

**despiporre** nm Fam **fue el d.** it was something else

**despistado, -a 1** adj absent-minded; **en ese momento estaba d. y no la vi** I was distracted at the time and didn't see her

**2** nm,f scatterbrain

**despistar 1** vt (a) *(dar esquinazo)* to throw off the scent; **despistaron a sus perseguidores** they shook off their pursuers (b) Fig *(confundir)* to mislead; *(distraer)* to distract; **el ruido me despista** the noise is distracting me

**2 despistarse** vpr (a) *(perderse)* to lose one's way, to get lost (b) Fig *(distraerse)* to get confused

**despiste** nm (a) *(distracción)* absent-mindedness; *(error)* mistake, slip (b) *(persona)* **Marta es un d.** Marta is very absent-minded

**desplante** nm rude remark; **hacer un d. a alguien** *(con acciones)* to do sth rude to sb; *(con palabras)* to be rude to sb

**desplazado, -a** adj Fig *(persona)* out of place

**desplazamiento** nm (a) *(viaje)* journey; *(traslado)* move (b) Náut displacement

**desplazar** [16] **1** vt (a) *(trasladar)* to move (a to); **d. algo/a alguien de** to remove sb/sth from (b) *(tomar el lugar de)* to take the place of (c) Náut to displace

**2 desplazarse** vpr *(viajar)* to travel; *(moverse)* to move

**desplegar** [45] *vt* (**a**) *(tela, periódico, mapa)* to unfold; *(alas)* to spread, to open; *(bandera)* to unfurl (**b**) *(cualidad)* to display (**c**) *Mil* to deploy

**despliegue** *nm* (**a**) *(de cualidad)* display (**b**) *Mil* deployment; **d. de misiles** missile deployment

**desplomarse** *vpr (caer)* to collapse; *(techo)* to fall in; *Fig* **se desplomó agotado en el sillón** he collapsed exhausted into the chair

**desplome** *nm* collapse

**desplumar** *vt (ave)* to pluck; *Fam Fig (estafar)* to fleece

**despoblación** *nf* depopulation

**despoblado, -a 1** *adj* unpopulated, deserted
**2** *nm* deserted spot

**despoblar 1** *vt* to depopulate
**2 despoblarse** *vpr* to become depopulated

**despojar 1** *vt* **d. a alguien de algo** to strip sb of sth
**2 despojarse** *vpr* **despojarse de algo** *(bienes, alimentos)* to give sth up; *(ropa, adornos)* to take sth off

**despojo** *nm* (**a**) *(acción)* stripping, plundering (**b**) **despojos** *(de animales)* offal (**c**) *(cadáver)* hallaron los despojos del héroe they found the hero's mortal remains; *Fig* **es un d. humano** he's a (physical/mental) wreck

**despolitizar** [16] *vt* to depoliticize

**desposado, -a** *nm,f (hombre)* groom; *(mujer)* bride; **los desposados** the newlyweds

**desposar 1** *vt* to marry
**2 desposarse** *vpr* to get married, to marry

**desposeer** [39] *vt* to dispossess

**desposeído, -a 1** *adj (pobre)* poor, dispossessed (**de** of); **un hombre d. de todos sus bienes** a man deprived of all his possessions (**b**) **d. de** *(carente)* lacking (in)
**2** *nm,f* **los desposeídos** the have-nots, the wretched

**desposorios** *nmpl Formal* (**a**) *(compromiso)* betrothal (**b**) *(matrimonio)* marriage, wedding

**déspota** *nmf* despot; **es un d. con sus hijos** he's a tyrant with his children

**despótico, -a** *adj* despotic

**despotismo** *nm* despotism; *Hist* **d. ilustrado** enlightened despotism

**despotricar** [61] *vi* to rant on (**contra** at)

**despreciable 1** *adj (indigno)* contemptible; *(de poca importancia)* negligible
**2** *nmf* contemptible person, wretch

**despreciar** [15] *vt* (**a**) *(desdeñar)* to scorn (**b**) *(rechazar)* to spurn

**desprecio** *nm* scorn, contempt; **hacer un d. a alguien** to snub sb; **con d.** contemptuously, with contempt

**desprender 1** *vt* (**a**) *(lo que estaba fijo)* to remove, to detach (**b**) *(olor, luz, calor)* to give off
**2 desprenderse** *vpr* (**a**) *(soltarse)* to come o fall off (**b**) *Fig (deducirse)* **de sus palabras se desprende que...** from his words it is clear o it can be seen that... (**c**) *(librarse)* **desprenderse de** to get rid of (**d**) *(renunciar)* **desprenderse de algo** to part with sth, to give sth up

**desprendido, -a** *adj (generoso)* generous

**desprendimiento** *nm* (**a**) *(separación)* detachment; **d. de tierras** landslide; *Med* **d. de retina** detachment of the retina (**b**) *Fig (generosidad)* generosity

**despreocupación** *nf* lack of concern o worry; **con d.** in a carefree manner

**despreocupadamente** *adv* in a carefree manner

**despreocupado, -a 1** *adj (libre de preocupaciones)* unworried, unconcerned; **es demasiado d.** he's too laid-back, he doesn't take things seriously enough
**2** *nm,f* = person who doesn't take things too seriously

**despreocuparse** *vpr* **d. de** *(asunto)* to stop worrying about; *(persona)* to be neglectful of

**desprestigiar** [15] *vt* to discredit

**desprestigio** *nm* discredit

**despresurización** *nf* depressurization; **en caso de d. de la cabina** *(en avión)* if there is a sudden fall in cabin pressure

**desprevenido, -a** *adj* unprepared; **pillar d. a alguien** to catch sb unawares, to take sb by surprise

**desproporción** *nf* disproportion

**desproporcionado, -a** *adj* disproportionate

**despropósito** *nm* stupid remark; **fue un d.** it was a stupid thing to say; **decir despropósitos** to say stupid things, to talk nonsense

**desprovisto, -a** *adj* **d. de** lacking in, devoid of

**después** *adv* (**a**) *(en el tiempo) (más tarde)* afterwards, later; *(entonces)* then; *(justo lo siguiente)* next; **poco d.** soon after; **años d.** years later; **ellos llegaron d.** they arrived later; **llamé primero y d. entré** I knocked first and then I went in; **yo voy d.** it's my turn next; **d. de (que)** after; **d. de hacer algo** after doing sth; **d. de que amanezca** after dawn; **d. de que te fueras a la cama** after you went to bed; *Fig* **d. de todo** after all
(**b**) *(en el espacio)* next, after; **¿qué viene d.?** what comes next o after?; **hay una farmacia y d. está mi casa** there's a chemist's and then there's my house; **varias manzanas d.** several blocks further on
(**c**) *(en una lista)* further down **d. de** after;

**llegó d. de ti** she arrived after you; **d. de él, nadie lo ha conseguido** since he did it, no one else has

**despuntar 1** vt (romper la punta) to break the point off; (desgastar la punta) to blunt

**2** vi (a) (flor, capullo) to bud; (planta) to sprout (b) Fig (persona) to excel, to stand out (c) (alba) to break; (día) to dawn

**desquiciado, -a** adj deranged, unhinged

**desquiciar [15]** vt (a) (puerta, ventana) to unhinge (b) (persona) (desequilibrar) to derange, to disturb mentally; (poner nervioso) to drive mad

**desquitarse** vpr to get one's own back (**de algo/alguien** for sth/on sb)

**desquite** nm revenge

**desratización** nf rodent extermination

**desratizar [16]** vt to clear of rodents

**desriñonarse** vpr Fam Fig (esforzarse) to break one's back

**destacado, -a** adj (persona) distinguished, prominent; (acto) outstanding

**destacamento** nm Mil detachment

**destacar [61] 1** vt (a) (poner de relieve) to emphasize, to highlight; **cabe d. que...** it is important to point out that... (b) Mil to detach, to detail

**2** vi (sobresalir) to stand out

**3 destacarse** vpr to stand out (**de/por** from/because of)

**destajo** nm piecework; **trabajar a d.** (por trabajo hecho) to do piecework; Fig (mucho) to work flat out

**destapar 1** vt (a) (caja, botella) to open; (olla) to take the lid off (b) (descubrir) to uncover

**2 destaparse** vpr (a) (desabrigarse) to lose the covers (b) Fig (revelarse) to open up

**destape** nm (en revistas) nude photos; (en películas, teatro) striptease

**destartalado, -a** adj (viejo, deteriorado) dilapidated; (desordenado) untidy

**destellar** vi (diamante, ojos) to sparkle; (estrellas) to twinkle

**destello** nm (a) (de luz) sparkle; (de estrella) twinkle (b) Fig (manifestación momentánea) glimmer; **un d. de ironía** a hint of irony

**destemplado, -a** adj (a) (persona) **me siento un poco d.** I'm feeling a bit cold (b) (instrumento) out of tune (c) (tiempo, clima) unpleasant (d) (carácter, actitud) irritable (e) (voz) sharp

**destemplarse** vpr (a) (enfriarse) to catch a chill (b) (irritarse) to get upset (c) (instrumento musical) to get out of tune

**destensar 1** vt (músculo) to relax; (cuerda, cable) to slacken

**2 destensarse** vpr (cuerda, cable) to slacken, to sag

**desteñido, -a** adj (descolorido) faded; (manchado) discoloured

**desteñir 1** vt (decolorar) to fade, to bleach; (manchar) to discolour

**2** vi to run, not to be colour fast; **estos pantalones destiñen** the colour in these trousers runs

**3 desteñirse** vpr to fade

**desternillante** adj hysterically funny

**desternillarse** vpr **d. de risa** to split one's sides laughing o with laughter

**desterrar [3]** vt (a) (persona) to banish, to exile (b) Fig (idea) to dismiss; (costumbre, hábito) to do away with

**destetar** vt to wean

**destete** nm weaning

**destiempo: a destiempo** loc adv at the wrong time

**destierro 1** ver **desterrar**

**2** nm (fuera del país) exile; (dentro del país) internal exile; **en el d.** in exile

**destilación** nf distillation

**destilar 1** vt (a) (agua, alcohol) to distil (b) (sangre, pus) to ooze (c) Fig (cualidad, sentimiento) to exude, to ooze

**2** vi (gotear) to trickle, to drip

**destilería** nf distillery

**destinar** vt (a) **d. algo** a o **para** (cantidad, edificio) to set sth aside for; (empleo, cargo) to assign sth to; (carta) to address sth to; (medidas, programa, publicación) to aim sth at (b) **d. a alguien a** (cargo, empleo) to appoint sb to; (plaza, lugar) to post sb to; **estar destinado al éxito/ fracaso** to be destined for success/failure

**destinatario, -a** nm,f addressee

**destino** nm (a) (sino) destiny, fate (b) (rumbo) destination; (ir) **con d. a** (to be) bound for o going to; **un vuelo con d. a...** a flight to... (c) (empleo, plaza) position, post (d) (finalidad) use, function

**destitución** nf dismissal

**destituir [36]** vt to dismiss

**destornillador** nm (a) (herramienta) screwdriver (b) Fam (bebida) screwdriver

**destornillar** vt to unscrew

**destreza** nf skill, dexterity

**destripar** vt (a) (sacar las tripas a) (animal, persona) to disembowel; (pescado) to gut (b) Fig (despanzurrar) to rip open

**destronar** vt (rey) to dethrone, to depose; Fig (rival) to unseat, to replace at the top

**destrozado, -a** adj (a) (mueble) broken, ruined (b) (persona) (emocionalmente) shattered, devastated; (físicamente) shattered

**destrozar** [16] *vt* (a) *(físicamente) (romper)* to smash; *(estropear)* to ruin (b) *(emocionalmente) (persona)* to shatter, to devastate; *(vida)* to ruin

**destrozo** *nm* damage; **alguien tendrá que pagar los destrozos** someone will have to pay for the damage

**destrozón, -ona** *Fam* **1** *adj* **ese niño es muy d.** that child is always breaking things; **d. con la ropa** hard on one's clothes

**2** *nm,f* **ese niño es un d.** that child is always breaking things

**destrucción** *nf* destruction

**destructivo, -a** *adj* destructive

**destructor, -ora 1** *adj* destructive

**2** *nm Mil* destroyer

**destruir** [36] *vt (deshacer)* to destroy; *(casa, argumento)* to demolish; *(proyecto)* to ruin, to wreck; *(ilusión)* to dash

**desubicar** *vt Am* to lose, to misplace

**desunión** *nf* (a) *(separación)* separation (b) *(división, discordia)* disunity

**desunir** *vt* (a) *(separar)* to separate (b) *(enemistar) (grupos)* to divide, to cause a rift between

**desusado, -a** *adj* (a) *(pasado de moda)* old-fashioned, obsolete (b) *(desacostumbrado)* unusual

**desuso** *nm* disuse; **caer en d.** to become obsolete, to fall into disuse

**desvaído, -a** *adj (color)* pale, washed-out; *(forma, contorno)* blurred; *(mirada)* vague

**desvalido, -a 1** *adj* needy, destitute

**2** *nm,f* needy *o* destitute person

**desvalijador, -ora** *nm,f (de casas)* burglar

**desvalijamiento** *nm (de casa)* burglary; *(de persona)* robbery

**desvalijar** *vt (casa)* to burgle; *(persona)* to rob; *Fig* **mis nietos me han desvalijado la nevera** my grandchildren have cleaned out my fridge

**desvalimiento** *nm Formal* destitution

**desvalorizar** [16] *vt* to devalue

**desván** *nm* attic, loft

**desvanecer** [48] **1** *vt* (a) *(humo, nubes)* to dissipate, to disperse (b) *(sospechas, temores)* to dispel

**2 desvanecerse** *vpr* (a) *(desmayarse)* to faint (b) *(humo, nubes, color)* to clear, to disappear; *(sonido, sospechas, temores)* to fade away

**desvanecimiento** *nm (desmayo)* fainting fit

**desvariar** [34] *vi (delirar)* to be delirious; *Fam (decir tonterías)* to talk nonsense, to rave; **¡no desvaríes!** don't talk nonsense *o* rubbish!

**desvarío** *nm* (a) *(dicho)* raving; *(hecho)* act of madness (b) *(delirio)* delirium

**desvelar 1** *vt* (a) *(quitar el sueño)* to keep awake (b) *(noticia, secreto)* to reveal, to tell

**2 desvelarse** *vpr* **desvelarse por hacer algo** to make every effort to do sth

**desvelo** *nm* (a) *(insomnio)* sleeplessness, insomnia (b) *(esfuerzo, cuidado)* **a pesar de nuestros desvelos...** despite all our care and effort...

**desvencijado, -a** *adj (silla, mesa)* rickety; *(camión, coche)* battered

**desvencijar** *vt (romper)* to break; *(desencajar)* to cause to come apart

**desventaja** *nf* disadvantage; **estar en d.** to be at a disadvantage

**desventura** *nf* misfortune

**desventurado, -a 1** *adj* unfortunate

**2** *nm,f* poor wretch

**desvergonzado, -a 1** *adj* shameless, insolent

**2** *nm,f* shameless person; **¡habráse visto el d.!** what a bad-mannered lout!

**desvergüenza** *nf* (a) *(atrevimiento, frescura)* shamelessness (b) *(dicho)* shameless remark; *(hecho)* shameless act

**desvestir** [49] **1** *vt* to undress

**2 desvestirse** *vpr* to undress (oneself)

**desviación** *nf* (a) *(de dirección, cauce, norma)* deviation (b) *(en la carretera)* diversion, detour; *Med* **d. de columna** curvature of the spine

**desviar** [34] **1** *vt (tráfico, río)* to divert; *(dirección)* to change; *(golpe)* to parry; *(pelota, disparo)* to deflect; *(pregunta)* to evade; *(conversación)* to change the direction of; *(mirada, ojos)* to avert

**2 desviarse** *vpr* (a) *(cambiar de dirección) (conductor)* to take a detour; *(vehículo)* to go off course; **desviarse de** to turn off (b) *(cambiar)* **desviarse de** *(tema)* to wander *o* digress from; *(propósito, idea)* to lose sight of

**desvincular 1** *vt Der (bienes, propiedades)* to disentail

**2 desvincularse** *vpr* to disassociate oneself (**de** from)

**desvío** *nm* diversion, detour

**desvirgar** [40] *vt* to deflower

**desvirtuar** [4] *vt (estropear)* to spoil; *(distorsionar)* to distort; **su victoria quedó totalmente desvirtuada** his victory was rendered meaningless; **esta actuación desvirtúa el espíritu del acuerdo** this action violates the spirit of the agreement

**desvistiera** *etc ver* **desvestir**

**desvisto** *etc ver* **desvestir**

**desvivirse** *vpr (desvelarse)* to do everything one can (**por** for); **d. por hacer algo** to bend over backwards to *o* do sth

**detalladamente** *adv* in (great) detail

**detallado, -a** *adj* detailed, thorough

**detallar** *vt (historia, hechos)* to detail, to give a rundown of; *(cuenta, gastos)* to itemize

**detalle** nm (a) (pormenor, rasgo) detail; **con d.** in detail; **entrar en detalles** to go into detail; **dar detalles** to give details (b) (atención) kind gesture o thought; **tener un d. (con alguien)** to be considerate (to sb); **es todo un d.** how courteous o considerate (c) Com **al d.** retail

**detallista 1** adj (meticuloso) painstaking; (atento) thoughtful

  **2** nmf Com retailer

**detección** nf detection

**detectar** vt to detect

**detective** nmf detective; **d. privado** private detective

**detectivesco, -a** adj **labor detectivesca** detective work; **novela detectivesca** detective novel

**detector, -ora 1** adj **aparato d.** detecting equipment

  **2** nm detector; **d. de mentiras/de incendios** lie/fire detector

**detención** nf (a) (parada) stopping, holding-up (b) (arresto) arrest

**detener** [67] **1** vt (a) (parar) to stop; (retrasar) to hold up (b) (arrestar) to arrest (c) (entretener) to keep, to delay

  **2 detenerse** vpr (a) (pararse) to stop; **detenerse a hacer algo** to stop to do sth (b) (demorarse) to hang about, to linger

**detenidamente** adv carefully, thoroughly

**detenido, -a 1** adj (a) (detallado) careful, thorough; **un examen d.** a careful, detailed examination (b) (arrestado) **(estar) d.** (to be) under arrest

  **2** nm,f prisoner, person under arrest

**detenimiento** nm **con d.** carefully, thoroughly

**detentar** vt to hold unlawfully; **los militares que detentan el poder en...** the military in power in...

**detergente** nm detergent

**deteriorar 1** vt to damage, to spoil

  **2 deteriorarse** vpr (estropearse) to deteriorate; Fig (empeorar) to deteriorate, to get worse

**deterioro** nm (daño) damage; (empeoramiento) deterioration; **el d. de la situación** the worsening of o deterioration in the situation

**determinación** nf (a) (de precio, fecha) settling, fixing (b) (resolución) determination, resolution (c) (decisión) **tomar una d.** to take a decision

**determinado, -a** adj (a) (concreto) specific; (en general) particular (b) (resuelto) determined (c) Gram definite

**determinante 1** adj decisive, determining

  **2** nm (a) Gram determiner (b) Mat determinant

**determinar 1** vt (a) (fijar) (fecha, precio) to settle, to fix (b) (averiguar) to determine; **d. las causas de la muerte** to establish the cause of death (c) (motivar) to cause, to bring about; **aquello determinó su decisión** that led to his decision (d) (decidir) to decide; **d. hacer algo** to decide to do sth

  **2 determinarse** vpr **determinarse a hacer algo** to make up one's mind to do sth

**determinismo** nm determinism

**detestable** adj detestable

**detestar** vt to detest

**detiene** ver **detener**

**detonación** nf (acción) detonation; (sonido) explosion

**detonador** nm detonator

**detonante 1** adj explosive

  **2** nm (explosivo) explosive; Fig (desencadenante) **ser el d. de algo** to spark sth off

**detonar** vi to detonate, to explode

**detractor, -ora 1** adj disparaging (de about)

  **2** nm,f detractor

**detrás** adv (a) (en el espacio) behind; **d. de** behind; **d. de alguien** behind sb's back; **deja un espacio d. de la coma** leave a space after the comma; **por d.** at the back; **hablar de alguien por d.** to talk about sb behind his/her back; **tus amigos vienen d.** your friends are coming on behind; **el interruptor está d.** the switch is at the back

  (b) (en el orden) then, afterwards; **Portugal y d. Puerto Rico** Portugal and then Puerto Rico

**detrimento** nm damage; **en d. de** to the detriment of

**detrito** nm, **detritus** nm inv Biol detritus; **detritos** (residuos) waste

**detuviera** etc ver **detener**

**deuce** [djus] nm Dep deuce

**deuda** nf debt; **contraer una d.** to get into debt; Fig **estar en d. con alguien** to be indebted to sb; Econ **d. exterior** foreign debt; Econ **d. pública** Br national debt, US public debt

**deudo, -a** nm,f relative, relation

**deudor, -ora 1** adj Fin **saldo d.** debit balance

  **2** nm,f debtor

**devaluación** nf devaluation

**devaluado, -a** adj (moneda) devalued

**devaluar** [4] **1** vt to devalue

  **2 devaluarse** vpr to go down in value

**devanar 1** vt to wind

  **2 devanarse** vpr Fam **devanarse los sesos** to wrack one's brains

**devaneo** nm (a) (distracción) idle pursuit (b) (coqueteo) **tener un d. con alguien** (amoroso) to have an affair with sb; **me contó sus devaneos con Juan** she told me about her flirtation with Juan; *Fig* **en su juventud tuvo sus devaneos con la ultraderecha** he flirted with the far right when he was young

**devastador, -ora** *adj* devastating

**devastar** *vt* to devastate

**devengar** [40] *vt (intereses)* to yield, to earn; *(sueldo)* to earn

**devenir** [71] **1** *nm* transformation; **la vida es un continuo d.** life is a continual process of change

**2** *vi (convertirse)* to become, to turn into

**devoción** *nf* devotion; **tener d. por alguien** to be devoted to sb; **tener d. por algo** to have a passion for sth

**devocionario** *nm Rel* prayer book

**devolución** *nf (de objeto)* return; *(de dinero)* refund; *Fin* **d. fiscal** tax rebate *o* refund

**devolver** [43] **1** *vt* (a) *(restituir) (coche, dinero)* to give back (**a** to); *(producto defectuoso, carta)* to return (**a** to) (b) *(restablecer, colocar en su sitio)* **d. algo a** to return sth to (c) *(favor, agravio)* to pay back for; *(visita)* to return (d) *(vomitar)* to bring *o* throw up

**2** *vi* to throw up

**3 devolverse** *vpr Am* to come back

**devorar** *vt también Fig* to devour; **le devoraban los celos** he was consumed by jealousy

**devoto, -a 1** *adj* (a) *(piadoso)* devout; **ser d. de** to have a devotion for (b) *(admirador)* devoted (**de** to) (c) *(imagen, templo, lugar)* devotional

**2** *nm,f* (a) *(beato)* **los devotos** the faithful (b) *(admirador)* devotee

**devuelto, -a 1** *participio ver* **devolver**

**2** *nm Fam (vómito)* sick

**devuelvo** *etc ver* **devolver**

**deyección** *nf Geol (de una montaña)* debris *(singular)*; *(de un volcán)* ejecta *(plural)*; *Med* **deyecciones** stools, faeces

**DF** *nm (abrev de* **Distrito Federal**) *(en México)* Mexico City; *(en Venezuela)* Caracas

**dg** *(abrev de* **decigramo**) dg

**DGS** *nf Antes (abrev de* **Dirección General de Seguridad**) = Spanish police headquarters

**di** (a) *ver* **dar** (b) *ver* **decir**

**día** *nm* (a) *(período de tiempo)* day; **me voy el d. ocho** I'm going on the eighth; **¿a qué d. estamos?** what day is it today?; **¿qué tal d. hace?** what's the weather like today?; **todos los días** every day; **un d. sí y otro no** every other day; *Fam* **un d. sí y otro también** every blessed day; **el d. que se entere nos mata** when he finds out, he'll kill us; **de d. en d.** from day to day, day by day; **del d.** fresh; **en su d.** in due course; **hoy (en) d.** nowadays; **todo el (santo) d.** all day long; **el d. de mañana** in the future; **al d. siguiente** (on) the following day; *Com* **d. de deuda** pay-by date; **d. festivo** (public) holiday; **d. hábil** *o* **laborable** *o* **de trabajo** working day; **el D. del Juicio Final** Judgement Day; *Fam* **hasta el d. del juicio** until doomsday; **d. lectivo** school *o* teaching day; **d. libre** day off; **un d. martes** one Tuesday; **d. de pago** payday

(b) *(luz diurna)* daytime, day; **es de d.** it's daytime; **hacer algo de d.** to do sth in the daytime *o* during the day; **d. y noche** day and night; **en pleno d., a plena luz del d.** in broad daylight

(c) *(expresiones)* **dar el d. a alguien** to ruin sb's day (for them); **mañana será otro d.** tomorrow is another day; **no pasar los días para alguien** not to look one's age; **tener un buen/mal d.** to have a good/bad day; **un d. es un d.** this is a special occasion; **el d. menos pensado...** when you least expect it ...; **estar/ponerse al d. (de)** to be/get up to date (with); **poner algo/a alguien al d.** to update sth/sb; **vivir al d.** to live from hand to mouth; **terminó sus días en la pobreza** he ended his days in poverty; **en mis días** in my day; **en aquellos días** in those days; *Am* **¡buen d.!** good morning!; **¡buenos días!** good morning!

**diabetes** *nf inv Med* diabetes *(singular)*

**diabético, -a** *adj & nm,f* *Med* diabetic

**diablo** *nm también Fig* devil; **pobre d.** poor devil; **tener el d. en el cuerpo, ser la piel del d.** to be a little devil; **mandar al d. a alguien** to send sb packing; **más sabe el d. por viejo que por d.** experience is what really counts; *Fam* **¿dónde/cómo diablos...?** where/how the hell...?; **¡diablos!** damn it!

**diablura** *nf* prank

**diabólico, -a** *adj* (a) *(del diablo)* diabolic (b) *Fig (muy malo, difícil)* diabolical

**diábolo** *nm* diabolo

**diácono** *nm Rel* deacon

**diacrónico, -a** *adj* diachronic

**diadema** *nf (joya)* tiara; *(para el pelo)* hairband

**diáfano, -a** *adj (transparente)* transparent, diaphanous; *Fig (claro)* clear

**diafragma** *nm* diaphragm

**diagnosis** *nf inv* diagnosis

**diagnosticar** [61] *vt* to diagnose; **le diagnosticaron cáncer** he was diagnosed as having cancer

**diagnóstico** *nm* diagnosis

**diagonal** *adj & nf* diagonal; **en d.** diagonally

**diagrama** *nm* diagram; **d. de barras** bar chart; **d. de flujo** flow diagram *o* chart

**dial** *nm* dial

**dialectal** *adj* **variante/expresión d.** dialect variant/expression

**dialéctica** *nf* dialectics *(singular)*

**dialéctico, -a** *adj* dialectic(al)

**dialecto** *nm* dialect

**diálisis** *nf inv Med* dialysis

**dialogante** *adj* **ser una persona d.** to be open to dialogue

**dialogar** [40] *vi (hablar)* to have a conversation **(con** with), to talk **(con** to); *(negociar)* to hold a dialogue *o* talks **(con** with)

**diálogo** *nm (conversación)* conversation; *Lit & Pol* dialogue; *Fam* **d. de besugos** half-witted conversation; **fue un d. de sordos** nobody listened to anyone else; **los diálogos** *(en película, serie)* the dialogue

**diamante** *nm (gema)* diamond; **diamantes** *(en naipes)* diamonds; **d. en bruto** uncut diamond; *Fig* **ser un d. en bruto** to have a lot of potential

**diametralmente** *adv* diametrically; **d. opuesto a** diametrically opposed to

**diámetro** *nm* diameter

**diana** *nf* (a) *(de dardos)* dartboard; **hacer d.** to hit the bull's-eye; **¡d.!** bullseye! (b) *(toque de corneta)* reveille; **tocar d.** to sound the reveille

**diantre** *interj* **¡d.!** dash it!

**diapasón** *nm Mús* tuning fork

**diapositiva** *nf* slide, transparency

**diario, -a 1** *adj* daily; **a d.** every day; **ropa de d.** everyday clothes

**2** *nm* (a) *(periódico)* newspaper, daily; **d. hablado** radio news (bulletin) (b) *(relación día a día)* diary; **d. íntimo** (personal) diary; **d. de navegación** logbook; **d. de sesiones** parliamentary report

**diarrea** *nf Med* diarrhoea; *Fam* **tener una d. mental** not to be thinking straight

**diáspora** *nf* diaspora

**diástole** *nf* diastole, dilation of the heart

**diatriba** *nf* diatribe

**dibujante** *nmf (artista)* drawer, sketcher; *(de dibujos animados, tebeos)* cartoonist; *(de dibujo técnico)* draughtsman, *f* draughtswoman

**dibujar 1** *vt & vi* to draw, to sketch

**2 dibujarse** *vpr* (a) *(mostrarse, verse)* to be outlined; **la montaña se dibujaba en el horizonte** the mountain was outlined on the horizon (b) *(revelarse)* **Fuster se está dibujando como un futuro campeón** Fuster is beginning to look like a future champion

**dibujo** *nm* (a) *(técnica, obra)* drawing; **d. a lápiz/al carboncillo** pencil/charcoal drawing; **d. anatómico** anatomical drawing; *Educ* **d. lineal** = drawing of geometrical figures;

**d. técnico** technical drawing; **dibujos animados** cartoons (b) *(en tela, prenda)* pattern

**dicción** *nf* diction

**diccionario** *nm* dictionary; **d. de sinónimos** thesaurus

**dice** *ver* **decir**

**dicha** *nf (felicidad)* joy

**dicharachero, -a** *adj Fam* talkative

**dicho, -a 1** *participio ver* **decir**

**2** *adj* said, aforementioned; **dichos individuos...** the said *o* aforesaid individuals...; **lo d. no significa que...** having said this, it does not mean (that)...; **¡lo d.!** that's settled then!; **mejor d.** or rather; **d. y hecho** no sooner said than done

**3** *nm* saying; **del d. al hecho hay un gran** *o* **mucho trecho** it's easier said than done

**dichoso, -a** *adj* (a) *(feliz)* happy (b) *Fam (para enfatizar)* blessed, confounded; **¡siempre está con la dichosa tele puesta!** he always has that blasted TV on!; **no vamos a resolver nunca este d. asunto** we'll never get to the bottom of this blessed business

**diciembre** *nm* December; *ver también* **septiembre**

**dicotomía** *nf* dichotomy

**dictado** *nm* dictation; **escribir al d.** to take dictation; **obedecer al d. de** to follow the dictates of; **dictados** *(órdenes)* dictates

**dictador, -ora** *nm,f* dictator

**dictadura** *nf Pol* dictatorship; **d. del proletariado** dictatorship of the proletariat

**dictáfono** *nm* Dictaphone

**dictamen** *nm (opinión)* opinion, judgement; *(informe)* report

**dictaminar** *vt* **los expertos dictaminaron que no había peligro** the experts stated that there was no danger; **todavía no se han dictaminado las causas de la enfermedad** the cause of the illness has still not been found *o* determined

**dictar** *vt* (a) *(texto)* to dictate (b) *(emitir) (sentencia, fallo)* to pronounce, to pass; *(ley)* to enact; *(decreto)* to issue

**dictatorial** *adj* dictatorial

**didáctica** *nf* didactics *(singular)*

**didáctico, -a** *adj* didactic

**diecinueve** *núm* nineteen; *ver también* **seis**

**diecinueveavo, -a** *núm (fracción)* nineteenth; **la diecinueveava parte** a nineteenth

**dieciocho** *núm* eighteen; *ver también* **seis**

**dieciochoavo, -a** *núm (fracción)* eighteenth; **la dieciochoava parte** an eighteenth

**dieciséis** *núm* sixteen; *ver también* **seis**

**dieciseisavo, -a** *núm (fracción)* sixteenth; **la dieciseisava parte** a sixteenth

**diecisiete** *núm* seventeen; *ver también* **seis**

**diecisieteavo, -a** *núm (fracción)* seventeenth; **la diecisieteava parte** a seventeenth

**diente** *nm* tooth; **armado hasta los dientes** armed to the teeth; **enseñar los dientes** to bare one's teeth; **hablar entre dientes** to mumble, to mutter; **hincar el d. a algo** to sink one's teeth into sth; *Fig* to get one's teeth into sth; **ponerle a alguien los dientes largos** to turn sb green with envy; **me hace rechinar los dientes** it sets my teeth on edge; **d. de ajo** clove of garlic; **d. incisivo** incisor; **d. de leche** milk tooth; **d. de león** *(planta)* dandelion

**diera** *ver* **dar**

**diéresis** *nf inv* diaeresis

**dieron** *ver* **dar**

**diesel, diésel** *adj* diesel

**diestra** *nf* right hand; **a la d.** on the right *o* right-hand side

**diestro, -a 1** *adj* **(a)** *(mano derecha)* right; *(persona)* right-handed; *Fig* **a d. y siniestro** left, right and centre, all over the place **(b)** *(hábil)* skilful (**en** at)
  **2** *nm Taurom* matador

**dieta** *nf* diet; **estar a d.** to be on a diet; **poner alguien a d.** to put sb on a diet; *Com* **dietas** *(dinero para gastos)* daily allowance for travelling expenses

**dietario** *nm* housekeeping book

**dietética** *nf* dietetics *(singular)*

**dietético, -a** *adj* dietetic, dietary

**dietista** *nmf Chile, Méx* dietician

**diez 1** *núm* ten; *Fam* **una chica d.** a stunning woman, a ten; *ver también* **seis**
  **2** *nm (nota)* A, top marks

**diezmar** *vt* to decimate

**diezmo** *nm Hist* tithe

**difamación** *nf (verbal)* slander; *(escrita)* libel

**difamar** *vt (verbalmente)* to slander; *(por escrito)* to libel

**difamatorio, -a** *adj (declaraciones, críticas)* defamatory; *(texto, carta, escrito)* libellous

**diferencia** *nf* difference; **a d. de** unlike; **establecer** *o* **hacer una d. entre** to make a distinction between; **el mejor/peor con d.** by far the best/worst; **tuvieron sus diferencias** they had their differences; **limar diferencias** to settle one's differences

**diferencial 1** *adj* distinguishing
  **2** *nm Tec* differential
  **3** *nf Mat* differential

**diferenciar [15] 1** *vt* to distinguish (**de** from)
  **2** *vi* to distinguish, to differentiate
  **3 diferenciarse** *vpr* **(a)** *(diferir)* to differ, to

be different (**de/en** from/in) **(b)** *(descollar)* **diferenciarse de** to stand out from

**diferente 1** *adj* different (**de** *o* **a** from *o* to)
  **2** *adv* differently

**diferido** *nm TV* **en d.** recorded

**diferir [64] 1** *vt (posponer)* to postpone, to put off
  **2** *vi (diferenciarse)* to differ, to be different; **d. de alguien en algo** to differ from sb in sth

**difícil** *adj* difficult; **d. de hacer** difficult to do; **es d. que ganen** they are unlikely to win; **no me lo pongas d.** don't make things difficult for me; **tener un carácter d.** to be an awkward person, to be difficult to get on with

**dificultad** *nf* **(a)** *(calidad de difícil)* difficulty **(b)** *(obstáculo)* problem; **poner dificultades** to raise objections; **encontrar dificultades** to run into trouble *o* problems; **pasar por dificultades** to suffer hardship

**dificultar** *vt (estorbar)* to hinder; *(obstruir)* to obstruct

**dificultoso, -a** *adj* hard, fraught with difficulties

**difiero** *etc ver* **diferir**

**difiriera** *etc ver* **diferir**

**difteria** *nf Med* diphtheria

**difuminar** *vt* to blur

**difundir 1** *vt (noticia, doctrina, epidemia)* to spread; *(luz, calor)* to diffuse; *(emisión radiofónica)* to broadcast
  **2 difundirse** *vpr (noticia, doctrina, epidemia)* to spread; *(luz, calor)* to be diffused

**difunto, -a 1** *adj* deceased, dead; **el d. Sr. Pérez** the late Mr Pérez
  **2** *nm,f* **el d.** the deceased

**difusión** *nf (de cultura, noticia, doctrina)* dissemination; *(de luz, calor, ondas)* diffusion; *(de programa)* broadcasting

**difuso, -a** *adj (luz)* diffuse; *(estilo, explicación)* wordy

**difusor, -ora 1** *adj (medio, agencia)* broadcasting
  **2** *nm,f* propagator

**diga** *ver* **decir**

**digerir [64]** *vt* to digest; *Fig (hechos)* to assimilate, to take in

**digestión** *nf* digestion

**digestivo, -a 1** *adj* digestive
  **2** *nm* digestive (drink)

**digiero** *etc ver* **digerir**

**digiriera** *etc ver* **digerir**

**digital 1** *adj* **(a)** *(del dedo)* **huellas digitales** fingerprints **(b)** *Informát & Tec* digital
  **2** *nf (planta)* foxglove

**digitalización** *nf Informát* digitizing

**digitalizar** *vt Informát* to digitize

**dígito** *nm Mat* digit

**dignarse** *vpr* **d. (a)** to deign to; **no se dignó (a) contestarme** he didn't deign to reply

**dignatario, -a** *nm,f* dignitary

**dignidad** *nf* **(a)** *(cualidad)* dignity **(b)** *(cargo)* office **(c)** *(personalidad)* dignitary

**dignificar** [61] *vt* to dignify

**digno, -a** *adj* **(a)** *(actitud, respuesta)* dignified; *(persona)* honourable, noble **(b)** *(merecedor)* **d. de** worthy of; **d. de elogio** praiseworthy; **d. de mención/de ver** worth mentioning/seeing **(c)** *(adecuado)* **d. de** appropriate for, fitting for **(d)** *(decente) (sueldo, actuación)* decent, good

**digo** *ver* **decir**

**digresión** *nf* digression

**dije** *adj Chile* nice, pleasant

**dijera** *etc ver* **decir**

**dilación** *nf* delay; **sin d.** without delay, at once

**dilapidar** *vt* to squander, to waste

**dilatación** *nf* *(de sólido, gas)* expansion; *(de pupila, cuello del útero)* dilation

**dilatar 1** *vt* **(a)** *(sólido, gas)* to expand; *(pupila, cuello del útero)* to dilate; **el calor dilata los cuerpos** heat causes bodies to expand **(b)** *(prolongar)* to prolong **(c)** *(demorar)* to delay

**2 dilatarse** *vpr* **(a)** *(extenderse)* to expand; *(pupila, cuello de útero)* to dilate; **los cuerpos se dilatan con el calor** bodies expand when heated **(b)** *(prolongarse)* to be prolonged, to go on; **la reunión se dilató hasta el amanecer** the meeting went on until dawn **(c)** *(demorarse)* to be delayed

**dilema** *nm* dilemma

**diletante** *adj & nmf* dilettante

**diligencia** *nf* **(a)** *(prontitud)* speed; **actuar con d.** to act speedily **(b)** *(trámite, gestión)* **diligencias** formalities, official paperwork **(c)** *(vehículo)* stagecoach **(d)** *Der* **diligencias** proceedings; **instruir diligencias** to start proceedings

**diligente** *adj* *(persona)* efficient, swift; *(respuesta)* prompt

**dilucidar** *vt* to elucidate

**diluir** [36] **1** *vt* to dilute

**2 diluirse** *vpr* to dissolve

**diluviar** [15] *v impersonal* to pour with rain

**diluvio** *nm también Fig* flood; **el D. Universal** the Flood

**diluyera** *etc ver* **diluir**

**diluyo** *etc ver* **diluir**

**dimanar** *vi* **d. de** *(alegría)* to emanate from; *(medidas, consecuencias)* to arise from

**dimensión** *nf* dimension; **una habitación de grandes dimensiones** a large room; **una película en tres dimensiones** a 3-D film; *Fig*

**las dimensiones de la tragedia** the extent of the tragedy

**diminutivo** *nm* diminutive

**diminuto, -a** *adj* tiny, minute

**dimisión** *nf* resignation; **presentar la d.** to hand in one's resignation

**dimitir** *vi* to resign **(de** from)

**dimos** *ver* **dar**

**Dinamarca** *n* Denmark

**dinámica** *nf también Fís* dynamics *(singular)*; **entramos en una d. de desarrollo económico** we are beginning a process of economic development

**dinámico, -a** *adj* dynamic

**dinamismo** *nm* dynamism

**dinamita** *nf* dynamite; *Fig* **ese cóctel/jugador es pura d.** that cocktail/player is dynamite

**dinamitar** *vt* to dynamite

**dinamizar** [16] *vt* to speed up

**dinamo, dínamo** *nf* dynamo

**dinar** *nm* dinar

**dinastía** *nf* dynasty

**dinástico, -a** *adj* dynastic

**dineral** *nm Fam* fortune

**dinero** *nm* money; **andar bien/mal de d.** to be well off for/short of money; **una familia de d.** a family of means; *Econ* **d. circulante** money in circulation; **d. de curso legal** legal tender; **d. en metálico** cash; **d. falso** counterfeit money; **d. negro** illegally obtained money; **d. contante (y sonante)** hard cash

**dinosaurio** *nm* dinosaur

**dintel** *nm Arquit* lintel

**diñar** *vt muy Fam* **diñarla** to snuff it

**dio** *ver* **dar**

**diócesis** *nf inv* diocese

**dioptría** *nf* dioptre

**dios, -osa 1** *nm,f* god, *f* goddess

**2** *nm* God; **¡a D. gracias!** thank heavens!; **a la buena de D.** any old how; **¡anda** *o* **ve con D.!** God be with you!; **armar la de D. es Cristo** to raise hell, to make an almighty racket; **como D. le da a entender** as best one can; **como D. manda** properly; **dejado de la mano de D.** godforsaken; **D. dirá** it's in the lap of the gods; **¡D. lo quiera!** let's hope so; *Prov* **D. los cría y ellos se juntan** birds of a feather flock together; **D. mediante, si D. quiere** God willing; **¡D. mío!** good God!, (oh) my God!; **D. sabe, sabe D.** God (alone) knows; **¡D. te oiga!** let's hope so!; **necesitar D. y ayuda** to have one's work cut out; **¡por D.!** for God's sake!; **que D. te lo pague** God bless you!; **sin encomendarse a D. ni al diablo** throwing caution to the winds; **¡vaya por D.!** for Heaven's sake!, honestly!

**dióxido** *nm Quím* dioxide

**diplodocus** *nm inv,* **diplodoco** *nm* diplodocus

**diploma** *nm* diploma

**diplomacia** *nf* (a) *(tacto)* diplomacy (b) *(carrera)* diplomatic service

**diplomado, -a 1** *adj* qualified
  **2** *nm,f* holder of a diploma

**diplomático, -a 1** *adj también Fig* diplomatic
  **2** *nm,f* diplomat

**diplomatura** *nf Educ* ≃ diploma, = qualification obtained after three years of university study

**dipsomanía** *nf* dipsomania

**diptongo** *nm* diphthong

**diputación** *nf* (comisión) committee; *(de comunidad autónoma)* = government and administrative body in certain autonomous regions; **d. permanente** standing committee; **d. provincial** *Br* ≃ county council, = governing body of each province in Spain

**diputado, -a** *nm,f Br* ≃ Member of Parliament, MP, *US* ≃ representative; **d. por Cádiz** ≃ the MP for Cadiz

**dirá** *ver* **decir**

**dirección** *nf* (a) *(sentido, rumbo)* direction; **calle de d. única** one-way street; **en d. a** towards, in the direction of; **en d. contraria** in the opposite direction; **se fue en d. sur** he went south
  (b) *(domicilio)* address; *Informát* **d. de correo electrónico** e-mail address; **d. web** web address
  (c) *(mando) (de empresa, hospital)* management; *(de partido)* leadership; *(de colegio)* headship; *(de periódico)* editorship; *(de una película)* direction; *(de una obra de teatro)* production; *(de una orquesta)* conducting; **estudia d. de cine** he's studying film directing
  (d) *(junta directiva)* management; **d. comercial** commercial department; **d. general** head office; **D. General de Tráfico** traffic department *(part of the Ministry of the Interior)*
  (e) *(de un vehículo)* steering; **d. asistida** power steering

**direccional 1** *adj* directional
  **2** *nm Méx Aut* indicator

**direccionamiento** *nm Informát* addressing

**direccionar** *vt Informát* to address

**directa** *nf Aut* top gear; **poner** *o* **meter la d.** to go into top gear; *Fig* to really get a move on

**directiva** *nf* (a) *(junta)* board (of directors) (b) *(ley de la UE)* directive

**directivo, -a 1** *adj* managerial
  **2** *nm,f (jefe)* manager

**directo, -a 1** *adj* direct
  **2** *nm* **en d.** *(retransmisión, concierto)* live
  **3** *adv* straight; **d. a** straight to

**director, -ora** *nm,f* (a) *(de empresa)* director; *(de hotel, hospital)* manager, *f* manageress; *(de periódico)* editor; *(de colegio)* headmaster, *f* headmistress; *(de cárcel)* governor; **d. espiritual** father confessor; **d. general** general manager; *Dep* **d. técnico** trainer; **d. de tesis** supervisor (b) *(de obra artística)* **d. de cine** film director; **d. de escena** producer, stage manager; **d. de orquesta** conductor

**directorio** *nm también Informát* directory; *Informát* **d. raíz** root directory

**directriz** *nf también Mat* directrix; **directrices** *(normas)* guidelines

**dirham** *nm* dirham

**diría** *ver* **decir**

**dirigente 1** *adj (en partido)* leading; *(en empresa)* management; **la clase d.** the ruling class
  **2** *nmf (de partido político)* leader; *(de empresa)* manager; **el máximo d. del partido** the leader of the party

**dirigible** *nm* airship

**dirigir** [26] **1** *vt* (a) *(conducir) (coche, barco)* to steer; *(avión)* to pilot
  (b) *(llevar) (empresa, hotel, hospital)* to manage; *(colegio, cárcel, periódico)* to run; *(partido, revuelta)* to lead; *(expedición)* to head, to lead; *(tesis)* to supervise
  (c) *(película, obra de teatro)* to direct; *(orquesta)* to conduct
  (d) *(apuntar, encaminar)* **dirigió la mirada hacia la puerta** he looked towards the door; **dirigió sus pasos hacia la casa** he headed towards the house
  (e) *(carta, paquete)* to address
  (f) *(guiar) (persona)* to guide
  (g) *(dedicar)* **d. algo a** to aim sth at; **d. unas palabras a alguien** to speak to sb, to address sb; **no me dirigen la palabra** they don't speak to me
  **2 dirigirse** *vpr* (a) *(encaminarse)* **dirigirse a** *o* **hacia** to head for
  (b) *(hablar)* **dirigirse a** to address, to speak to
  (c) *(escribir)* **dirigirse a** to write to

**dirigismo** *nm* state control

**dirijo** *ver* **dirigir**

**dirimir** *vt* (a) *(resolver)* to resolve (b) *(disolver)* to annul, to dissolve

**discapacidad** *nf* disability, handicap

**discapacitado, -a 1** *adj* disabled, handicapped
**2** *nm,f* handicapped person

**discar** [61] *vt Andes, CSur* to dial

**discernimiento** *nm* discernment

**discernir** [27] *vt* to discern, to distinguish; **d. algo de algo** to distinguish sth from sth

**disciplina** *nf* discipline

**disciplinado, -a** *adj* disciplined

**disciplinar** *vt* to discipline

**disciplinario, -a** *adj* disciplinary

**discípulo, -a** *nm,f* disciple

**disc-jockey** [dis'jokei] *nmf* disc jockey

**disco 1** *nm* **(a)** *(Anat, Astron & Geom)* disc; **d. solar** the sun
**(b)** *(de música)* record; **d. compacto** compact disc; **d. de larga duración** LP, long-playing record; *Fam Fig* **ser como un d. rayado** to go on like a cracked record
**(c)** *(semáforo)* (traffic) light
**(d)** *Dep* discus
**(e)** *Informát* disk; **d. de arranque/del sistema** startup/system disk; **d. duro/flexible** hard/floppy disk; **d. magnético** magnetic disk; **d. óptico** optical disk; **d. removible/rígido** removable/hard disk; **d. virtual** virtual disk
**(f)** *(del teléfono)* dial
**2** *nf Fam (discoteca)* disco

**discografía** *nf* records previously released *(by an artist or group)*

**discográfico, -a** *adj* record; **casa discográfica** record company; **la industria discográfica** the recording *o* music industry

**díscolo, -a** *adj* disobedient, rebellious

**disconforme** *adj* in disagreement; **estar d. con** to disagree with

**disconformidad** *nf* disagreement

**discontinuidad** *nf* lack of continuity; **una d. en el crecimiento** a change in the rate of growth

**discontinuo, -a** *adj (intermitente)* intermittent; **línea discontinua** broken *o* dotted line

**discordancia** *nf (de sonidos)* discord; *(de colores)* clash; *(de opiniones)* clash, conflict; **una d. entre los planes y el resultado final** a discrepancy between the plans and the final result

**discordante** *adj (sonidos)* discordant; *(colores)* clashing; *(opiniones)* conflicting

**discordar** [65] *vi* **(a)** *(desentonar) (colores, opiniones)* to clash; *(instrumentos)* to be out of tune **(b)** *(discrepar)* **d. de alguien (en)** to disagree with sb (on *o* about)

**discorde** *adj (colores, opiniones)* clashing; *Mús* discordant

**discordia** *nf* discord

**discoteca** *nf* **(a)** *(local)* disco, discotheque **(b)** *(colección)* record collection

**discotequero, -a 1** *adj* disco; **música discotequera** disco music
**2** *nm,f* nightclubber

**discreción** *nf* **(a)** *(reserva)* discretion; **tuvo la d. de no mencionarlo** he had the tact not to mention it **(b)** *(voluntad)* **a d.** as much as one wants, freely; **lo dejo a tu d.** I leave it to your discretion; **fuego a d.** fire at will

**discrecional** *adj (cantidad)* according to taste; *(poderes)* discretionary; **parada d.** *(en autobús)* request stop

**discrepancia** *nf (diferencia)* difference, discrepancy; *(desacuerdo)* disagreement

**discrepar** *vi (diferenciarse)* to differ (**de** from); *(disentir)* to disagree (**de** with)

**discreto, -a** *adj* **(a)** *(prudente, reservado)* discreet **(b)** *(cantidad)* moderate, modest **(c)** *(no extravagante)* modest; **ropa discreta** inconspicuous clothes **(d)** *(normal) (actuación)* fair, reasonable

**discriminación** *nf* discrimination; **d. racial** racial discrimination

**discriminar** *vt* **(a)** *(distinguir)* **d. algo de** to discriminate *o* distinguish sth from **(b)** *(marginar)* to discriminate against

**discriminatorio, -a** *adj* discriminatory

**disculpa** *nf (pretexto)* excuse; *(excusa, perdón)* apology; **dar disculpas** to make excuses; **pedir disculpas a alguien (por)** to apologize to sb (for)

**disculpar 1** *vt* to excuse; **disculpen la tardanza** I'm sorry for being late; **d. a alguien (de** *o* **por algo)** to forgive sb (for sth); **discúlpame por haber olvidado tu cumpleaños** please forgive me for forgetting your birthday
**2 disculparse** *vpr* to apologize (**de** *o* **por** for)

**discurrir 1** *vi* **(a)** *(pasar) (personas)* to wander, to walk; *(tiempo, vida, sesión)* to go by, to pass; *(río, tráfico)* to flow **(b)** *(pensar)* to think, to reflect
**2** *vt* to come up with

**discurso** *nm* speech

**discusión** *nf (conversación)* discussion; *(pelea)* argument; **eso no admite d.** there's no denying it

**discutible** *adj* debatable

**discutidor, -a 1** *adj* argumentative
**2** *nm,f* argumentative person

**discutir 1** *vi* **(a)** *(hablar)* to discuss **(b)** *(pelear)* to argue (**de** *o* **sobre** about)
**2** *vt (hablar)* to discuss; *(contradecir)* to dispute; **no te discuto que tengas razón** I don't dispute that you're right

**disecar** [61] *vt (cadáver)* to dissect; *(animal)* to stuff; *(planta)* to dry

**disección** *nf (de cadáver)* dissection

**diseminar** *vt (semillas)* to scatter; *(ideas)* to disseminate

**disensión** *nf* disagreement, dissension

**disentería** *nf* dysentery

**disentir** [64] *vi* to disagree (**de/en** with/on)

**diseñador, -ora** *nm,f* designer; **d. gráfico** graphic designer; **d. de modas** fashion designer

**diseñar** *vt* to design

**diseño** *nm* design; **bar de d.** trendy bar; **ropa de d.** designer clothes; *Informát* **d. asistido por ordenador** computer-aided design; **d. gráfico** graphic design

**diseque** *etc ver* **disecar**

**disertación** *nf (oral)* lecture, discourse; *(escrita)* dissertation

**disertar** *vi* to speak (**sobre** on), to lecture (**sobre** on)

**disfraz** *nm* llevar un d. *(para camuflarse)* to wear a disguise; *(para baile, fiesta)* to wear fancy dress; **un d. de bruja/gorila** a witch/gorilla costume

**disfrazar** [16] **1** *vt* to disguise; **d. a alguien de** to dress sb up as

**2 disfrazarse** *vpr* to disguise oneself; **disfrazarse de princesa** to dress up as a princess

**disfrutar 1** *vi* (a) *(sentir placer)* to enjoy oneself; **d. de lo lindo** to enjoy oneself very much, to have a great time; **disfruté mucho con el concierto** I enjoyed the concert a lot (b) *(disponer de)* **d. de algo** to enjoy sth

**2** *vt* to enjoy; **¡que lo disfrutes con salud!** I hope you enjoy it!

**disfrute** *nm* (a) *(placer)* enjoyment (b) *(provecho)* benefit, use

**disfunción** *nf* malfunction

**disgregar** [40] **1** *vt* (a) *(multitud, manifestación)* to disperse, to break up (b) *(roca, imperio, Estado)* to break up; *(átomo)* to split

**2 disgregarse** *vpr* (a) *(multitud, manifestación)* to disperse, to break up (b) *(roca, imperio, estado)* to break up

**disgustar 1** *vt* (a) *(desagradar)* **ese sombrero no me disgusta** that hat's not bad (b) *(consternar)* to upset; **le disgustó que olvidáramos su cumpleaños** he was upset that we forgot his birthday

**2 disgustarse** *vpr (sentir enfado)* to get upset (**con alguien/por algo** with sb/about sth); *(enemistarse)* to fall out (with sb/over sth)

**disgusto** *nm* (a) *(enfado)* annoyance; *(pesadumbre)* sorrow, grief; **dar un d. a alguien** to upset sb; **casi nos da un d.** we almost had a tragedy on our hands; **llevarse un d.** to be

upset; **matar a alguien a disgustos** to worry sb to death (b) *(desinterés, incomodidad)* **hacer algo a d.** to do sth unwillingly *o* reluctantly; **estar a d.** to feel uncomfortable *o* uneasy (c) *(pelea)* **tener un d. con alguien** to have a quarrel with sb

**disidencia** *nf (política, religiosa)* dissidence; *(desacuerdo)* disagreement

**disidente 1** *adj (en política)* dissident; *(en religión)* dissenting

**2** *nmf (político)* dissident; *(religioso)* dissenter; **un d. soviético** a Soviet dissident

**disiento** *etc ver* **disentir**

**disimulado, -a** *adj* hidden, concealed; **hacerse el d.** to pretend not to notice

**disimular 1** *vt* to hide, to conceal

**2** *vi* to pretend; **lo disimulas muy mal** you're not very good at hiding it

**disimulo** *nm* pretence, concealment; **con d.** furtively

**disimulón, -ona** *Fam* **1** *adj* sneaky, shifty

**2** *nm,f* sneaky *o* shifty person

**disintiera** *etc ver* **disentir**

**disipar 1** *vt* (a) *(dudas, sospechas)* to dispel; *(ilusiones)* to shatter (b) *(fortuna, herencia)* to squander, to throw away (c) *(niebla, humo, vapor)* to drive *o* blow away

**2 disiparse** *vpr* (a) *(dudas, sospechas)* to be dispelled; *(ilusiones)* to be shattered (b) *(niebla, humo, vapor)* to vanish

**diskette** [dis'kete, dis'ket] *nm Informát* diskette, floppy disk

**dislate** *nm* piece of nonsense *o* absurdity; **su plan es un d.** her plan is absurd

**dislexia** *nf* dyslexia

**disléxico, -a** *adj & nm,f* dyslexic

**dislocación** *nf* dislocation

**dislocar** [61] **1** *vt* to dislocate

**2 dislocarse** *vpr* (a) **se me ha dislocado un codo** I've dislocated an elbow (b) *Fam Fig* to go wild

**disminución** *nf* decrease, drop

**disminuido, -a 1** *adj* handicapped

**2** *nm,f* handicapped person; **un d. físico/psíquico** a physically/mentally handicapped person

**disminuir** [36] **1** *vt* to reduce, to decrease

**2** *vi (decrecer)* to decrease; *(precios, temperatura)* to drop, to fall; *(vista, memoria)* to fail; *(días)* to get shorter; *(beneficios)* to fall off

**disnea** *nf* dyspnoea, difficulty in breathing

**disociación** *nf* dissociation

**disociar** [15] *vt* to dissociate (**de** from)

**disolución** *nf* (a) *(acción)* dissolving (b) *(de matrimonio, sociedad, partido)* dissolution (c) *(mezcla)* solution

**disoluto, -a 1** *adj* dissolute

**2** *nm,f* dissolute person

**disolvente** *adj & nm* solvent

**disolver** [43] **1** *vt* (a) *(en líquido)* to dissolve; **d. en leche agitando constantemente** dissolve it in milk, stirring continuously; **d. un caramelo en la boca** to suck a sweet (b) *(reunión, manifestación, familia)* to break up

**2 disolverse** *vpr* (a) *(en líquido)* to dissolve (b) *(reunión, manifestación, familia)* to break up

**dispar** *adj* disparate, dissimilar

**disparadero** *nm* **poner a alguien en el d.** to push sb too far

**disparado, -a** *adj* **salir/entrar d.** to shoot out/in

**disparador** *nm* (a) *(de armas)* trigger (b) *Fot* shutter release

**disparar 1** *vt* to shoot; *(pedrada)* to throw

**2** *vi (con arma)* to shoot, to fire; *(con cámara)* to shoot, to take a photograph

**3 dispararse** *vpr* (a) *(arma)* to go off (b) *(precipitarse) (persona)* to rush off; *(caballo)* to bolt (c) *(perder los estribos)* to get carried away (d) *(precios, inflación)* to shoot up

**disparatado, -a** *adj* absurd, crazy

**disparatar** *vi (decir tonterías)* to talk nonsense; *(hacer tonterías)* to behave foolishly

**disparate** *nm* (a) *(comentario, acción)* silly thing; *(idea)* crazy idea; **¡no digas disparates!** don't talk nonsense!; **hacer un d.** to do something crazy (b) *(precio)* **gastar/costar un d.** to spend/cost a ridiculous amount

**disparidad** *nf* difference, disparity

**disparo** *nm* shot

**dispendio** *nm* extravagance, spending on luxuries

**dispendioso, -a** *adj* costly, expensive

**dispensa** *nf (de examen)* exemption; *(para casarse)* dispensation

**dispensar** *vt* (a) *(disculpar)* to excuse, to forgive; **¡dispense!** excuse me!, pardon me!, I beg your pardon! (b) *(rendir) (honores)* to confer (**a alguien** upon sb); *(bienvenida, ayuda)* to give sth (to sb) (c) *(eximir)* to excuse (**de** from), to exempt (**de** from)

**dispensario** *nm* dispensary

**dispepsia** *nf* dyspepsia

**dispersar 1** *vt* (a) *(esparcir) (objetos)* to scatter (b) *(disolver) (gentío)* to disperse; *(manifestación)* to break up; *(esfuerzos)* to dissipate

**2 dispersarse** *vpr* to scatter; *(distraerse)* to let one's attention wander

**dispersión** *nf (de objetos, gente, luz)* scattering; *(de manifestación)* breaking up

**disperso, -a** *adj* scattered; **chubascos dispersos** scattered showers

**display** [dis'plei] *nm Informát* display

**displicencia** *nf* (a) *(desagrado)* contempt (b) *(negligencia)* carelessness; *(desgana)* lack of enthusiasm

**displicente** *adj* (a) *(desagradable)* contemptuous (b) *(negligente)* careless; *(desganado)* unenthusiastic

**disponer** [52] **1** *vt* (a) *(arreglar)* to arrange; **dispuso todo para el viaje** he got everything ready for the journey (b) *(cena, comida)* to lay on (c) *(decidir) (sujeto: persona)* to decide; *(sujeto: ley)* to stipulate

**2** *vi* (a) *(poseer)* **d. de** to have (b) *(usar)* **d. de** to make use of; **dispón de mi casa siempre que quieras** you're welcome in my house whenever you like

**3 disponerse** *vpr* **disponerse a hacer algo** to prepare *o* get ready to do sth

**disponibilidad** *nf* (a) *(de plazas, producto)* availability (b) *(a ayudar)* readiness to help (c) **disponibilidades** *(medios)* financial resources

**disponible** *adj* available; **no tengo mucho tiempo d.** I don't have much free time

**disposición** *nf* (a) *(colocación)* arrangement, layout (b) *(estado)* **estar** *o* **hallarse en d. de hacer algo** to be prepared *o* ready to do sth (c) *(orden)* order; *(de ley)* provision (d) *(uso)* **a d. de** at the disposal of; **poner algo a la d. de alguien** to put sth at sb's disposal (e) *(aptitud)* talent; **tiene buena d. para la pintura** he has a natural gift for painting

**dispositivo** *nm* device; **d. intrauterino** intrauterine device, IUD

**dispuesto, -a 1** *participio ver* **disponer**

**2** *adj* (a) *(preparado)* ready; **estar d. a hacer algo** to be prepared to do sth; **está d. a todo con tal de conseguir lo que quiere** he's prepared to do anything to get what he wants (b) *(capaz)* capable; *(a ayudar)* ready to help

**dispusiera** *etc ver* **disponer**

**disputa** *nf* dispute

**disputar** *vt* (a) *(cuestión, tema)* to argue about (b) *(trofeo, puesto)* to compete for, to dispute; *(carrera, partido)* to compete in; **mañana se disputará la final** the final will take place tomorrow

**disquete** *nm Informát* diskette, floppy disk

**disquetera** *nf Informát* disk drive

**disquisición** *nf (exposición)* disquisition **disquisiciones** *(digresiones)* digressions

**distancia** *nf* (a) *(espacio)* distance; **a d.** from a distance; **mantener a d.** to keep at a distance; **d. de seguridad** safe distance; **mantenerse a una d. prudencial de** to keep at a safe distance from (b) *(en el tiempo)* gap, space (c) *(diferencia)* difference (d) *(expresiones)* **acortar las distancias** to come closer (to an agreement); **guardar las distancias** to keep one's distance; **salvando las distancias** only up to a point

**distanciamiento** *nm (afectivo)* distance, coldness; *(de opiniones, posturas)* distancing

**distanciar** [15] 1 *vt (alejar)* to drive apart; *(rival)* to forge ahead of; **con el tiempo se fueron distanciando** they grew o drifted apart as time went on

2 **distanciarse** *vpr (alejarse) (afectivamente)* to grow apart; *(físicamente)* to distance oneself

**distante** *adj* (a) *(en el espacio)* far away (**de** from) (b) *(en el trato)* distant; **estaba d., con la mirada perdida** he was distant, staring into space

**distar** *vi* (a) *(hallarse a)* **ese sitio dista varios kilómetros de aquí** that place is several kilometres away from here (b) *Fig (diferenciarse)* **d. de** to be far from

**diste** *ver* **dar**

**distender** [66] *vt (situación, relaciones)* to ease; *(cuerda)* to slacken

**distendido, -a** *adj (informal)* relaxed, informal

**distensión** *nf* (a) *(entre países)* détente; *(entre personas)* easing of tension (b) *(de arco, cuerda)* slackening (c) *Med (muscular)* strain

**distiendo** *etc ver* **distender**

**distinción** *nf* (a) *(diferencia)* distinction; **a d. de** in contrast to, unlike; **sin d.** alike; **sin d. de sexo, raza o religión** without distinction of sex, race or religion; **hacer distinciones en el trato** not to treat everyone the same (b) *(privilegio)* privilege (c) *(modales, elegancia)* refinement, elegance

**distingo** *nm* reservation; **no hacer distingos** to make no distinctions

**distinguido, -a** *adj* (a) *(notable)* distinguished (b) *(elegante)* refined

**distinguir** [28] 1 *vt* (a) *(diferenciar)* to distinguish; **d. algo de algo** to tell sth from sth (b) *(separar)* to pick out (c) *(caracterizar)* to characterize (d) *(premiar)* to honour (e) *(vislumbrar)* to make out

2 **distinguirse** *vpr* (a) *(destacarse)* to stand out; **se distingue por su elegancia** she is noted for her elegance (b) *(caracterizarse)* to be characterized (**por** by) (c) *(vislumbrarse)* to be visible

**distintivo, -a 1** *adj* distinctive; *(señal)* distinguishing

2 *nm* badge

**distinto, -a** *adj* (a) *(diferente)* different (**de** o **a** from o to); **hay distintos libros sobre el tema** there are various books on the subject (b) *(claro)* clear; **claro y d.** perfectly clear

**distorsión** *nf (de imágenes, sonidos, palabras)* distortion

**distorsionar** *vt* to distort

**distracción** *nf* (a) *(entretenimiento)* entertainment; *(pasatiempo)* hobby, pastime (b) *(despiste)* slip; *(falta de atención)* absent-mindedness

**distraer** [68] 1 *vt* (a) *(divertir)* to amuse, to entertain (b) *(despistar)* to distract

2 **distraerse** *vpr* (a) *(divertirse)* to enjoy oneself; *(pasar el tiempo)* to pass the time; **trata de distraerte** try to take your mind off things (b) *(despistarse)* to let one's mind wander; **este niño se distrae con una mosca** this child can't concentrate for two seconds

**distraído, -a 1** *adj* (a) *(entretenido) (libro)* readable; *(programa de TV, película)* watchable; **una tarde/conversación distraída** quite a nice afternoon/conversation (b) *(despistado)* absent-minded

2 *nm,f* daydreamer, absent-minded person

**distribución** *nf* (a) *(reparto, división)* distribution; **d. de premios** prizegiving; **d. de la riqueza** distribution of wealth; **d. de tareas** assignment of duties (b) *(de mercancías)* delivery; **d. comercial** commercial distribution (c) *(de casa, habitaciones)* layout

**distribuidor, -ora 1** *adj (entidad)* wholesale; **una red distribuidora** a distribution network

2 *nm,f (repartidor)* deliveryman, *f* deliverywoman; *(vendedor)* sales representative

3 *nm (máquina de tabaco, bebidas)* vending machine; *(cajero automático)* cash dispenser o machine

**distribuidora** *nf (firma)* wholesaler, supplier; *(de películas)* distributor

**distribuir** [36] 1 *vt* (a) *(repartir)* to distribute; *(carga, trabajo)* to spread; *(pastel, ganancias)* to divide up; *(correo)* to deliver; *Com (mercancías)* to distribute; **d. las tareas** to divide up o share out the tasks (b) *(casa, habitaciones)* to arrange

2 **distribuirse** *vpr* (a) *(repartirse)* **nos distribuimos las tareas domésticas** we share the household chores; **las ganancias se distribuirán entre los accionistas** the profits will be divided up among the shareholders (b) *(colocarse)* to spread out; **los alumnos se distribuyeron en pequeños grupos** the pupils got themselves into small groups

**distributivo, -a** *adj* distributive

**distrito** *nm* district; **d. electoral** constituency; **d. postal** *(número)* postal code

**disturbio** *nm* disturbance; *(violento)* riot; **disturbios callejeros** street disturbances, rioting

**disuadir** *vt* to dissuade (**de** from)

**disuasión** *nf* deterrence

**disuasivo, -a, disuasorio, -a** *adj* deterrent; **elemento d.** deterring factor

**disuelto, -a** *participio ver* **disolver**

**disuelva** *etc ver* **disolver**

**disyuntiva** *nf* straight choice

**disyuntivo, -a** *adj Gram* disjunctive

**DIU** [diu] *nm (abrev de* **dispositivo intrauterino)** IUD, coil; **llevar un D.** to have *o* use an IUD; **ponerse un D.** to have an IUD inserted

**diurético, -a** *adj & nm* diuretic

**diurno, -a** *adj (de día)* daytime; *(planta, animal)* diurnal; **horas diurnas** daytime *o* daylight hours

**diva** *nf Mús* diva, prima donna

**divagación** *nf* digression

**divagar** [40] *vi* to digress

**diván** *nm* divan; *(de psiquiatra)* couch

**divergencia** *nf (de líneas)* divergence; *Fig (de opinión)* difference of opinion

**divergente** *adj también Fig* divergent, diverging

**divergir** [26] *vi (calles, líneas)* to diverge; *Fig (opiniones)* to differ (**en** on)

**diversidad** *nf* diversity; **d. de opiniones** variety of opinions

**diversificación** *nf* diversification

**diversificar** [61] **1** *vt* to diversify

**2 diversificarse** *vpr* to become more varied, to diversify

**diversión** *nf* entertainment, amusement

**diverso, -a 1** *adj (diferente)* different

**2** *adj pl* **diversos, -as** *(varios)* several, various

**divertido, -a** *adj* **(a)** *(entretenido)* (película, libro) entertaining; *(fiesta)* enjoyable **(b)** *(que hace reír)* funny

**divertimento** *nm Mús* divertimento; *(novela, película)* entertainment, divertissement

**divertir** [64] **1** *vt* to entertain, to amuse

**2 divertirse** *vpr* to enjoy oneself

**dividendo** *nm Fin & Mat* dividend; **d. a cuenta** interim dividend

**dividir 1** *vt* to divide (**en/entre** into/between); *Mat* to divide by; **nos dividimos las tareas domésticas** we shared the household chores between us

**2 dividirse** *vpr* to divide (**en** into)

**divierto** *etc ver* **divertir**

**divinidad** *nf (dios)* divinity, god

**divino, -a** *adj también Fig* divine; **habló de lo d. y lo humano** he talked about everything under the sun

**divirtiera** *etc ver* **divertir**

**divisa** *nf* **(a)** *(moneda)* foreign currency; **d. convertible** convertible currency; **una d.**

**fuerte** a strong currency **(b)** *(distintivo)* emblem

**divisar** *vt* to spy, to make out; **divisó un barco en la lejanía** he could make out a ship in the distance

**división** *nf (repartición)* division; *(partición)* splitting up; **d. acorazada** armoured division; **d. del trabajo** division of labour; *Dep* **primera/segunda d.** first/second division

**divisor** *nm Mat* divisor; **máximo común d.** highest common factor

**divisorio, -a** *adj* dividing

**divo, -a** *nm,f* **(a)** *Mús (mujer)* diva, prima donna; *(hombre)* opera singer **(b)** *(celebridad)* star; *Fam* **ir de d.** to give oneself airs

**divorciado, -a 1** *adj* divorced

**2** *nm,f* divorcé, *f* divorcée

**divorciar** [15] **1** *vt también Fig* to divorce

**2 divorciarse** *vpr* to get divorced; **sus padres se han divorciado hace poco** his parents (got) divorced recently

**divorcio** *nm* **(a)** *Der* divorce **(b)** *Fig (diferencia)* difference, inconsistency

**divulgación** *nf (de noticia, secreto)* revelation; *(de rumor)* spreading; *(de cultura, ciencia, doctrina)* popularization; **una obra de d. científica** a work of popular science

**divulgar** [40] *vt (noticia, secreto)* to reveal; *(rumor)* to spread; *(cultura, ciencia, doctrina)* to popularize

**divulgativo, -a** *adj* popularizing

**dizque** *adv Am* apparently

**dl** *(abrev de* **decilitro)** dl

**dm** *(abrev de* **decímetro)** dm

**DNI** *nm (abrev de* **documento nacional de identidad)** ID card

**Dña.** *(abrev de* **doña)** ≃ Mrs

**do** *nm Mús* C; *(en solfeo)* doh; *Fam Fig* **dar el do de pecho** to give one's all

**dóberman** *nm* Doberman (pinscher)

**dobladillo** *nm (de traje, vestido)* hem; *(de pantalón) Br* turn-up, *US* cuff

**doblado, -a** *adj* **(a)** *(papel, camisa)* folded **(b)** *(voz, película)* dubbed

**doblaje** *nm* dubbing; **actor de d.** = actor who dubs voices in a foreign-language film

**doblar 1** *vt* **(a)** *(duplicar)* to double; **dobló la apuesta** he doubled the bet **(b)** *(plegar)* to fold **(c)** *(torcer)* to bend **(d)** *(esquina)* to turn, to go round **(e)** *Fig* **d. el espinazo** *(someterse)* to bend the knee **(f)** *(voz, actor)* to dub

**2** *vi* **(a)** *(girar)* to turn; **dobla en la primera a la derecha** take the first right **(b)** *(campanas)* to toll

**3 doblarse** *vpr (someterse)* **doblarse a** to give in to

**doble 1** *adj* double; **tiene d. número de habitantes** it has double o twice the number of inhabitants; **es d. de ancho** it's twice as wide; **una frase de d. sentido** a phrase with a double meaning; **una calle de d. sentido** a two-way street

**2** *nmf (persona parecida)* double; *Cine* stand-in; **buscan a un d. de Groucho Marx** they're looking for a Groucho Marx lookalike; **esa chica es tu d.** that girl is your double

**3** *nm* **(a)** *(duplo)* **el d.** twice as much; **gana el d. que yo** she earns twice as much as I do, she earns double what I do; **el d. de gente** twice as many people

**(b)** *Fam (de cerveza)* = tall glass of beer

**(c) dobles** *Dep* doubles

**4** *adv* double; **trabajar d.** to work twice as hard

**doblegar [40] 1** *vt (someter)* to bend, to cause to give in

**2 doblegarse** *vpr* to give in **(ante** to), to yield **(ante** to)

**doblete** *nm* **hacer d.** to have a second job; **hace d. de panadero por las noches** he has a second job as a baker at night

**doblez 1** *nm (pliegue)* fold, crease

**2** *nm o nf Fig (falsedad)* deceit

**doblón** *nm* doubloon

**doc.** *(abrev de* **documento***)* doc.

**doce** *núm* twelve; **las d. campanadas** the bells *(at New Year)*; *ver también* **seis**

**doceavo, -a** *núm (fracción)* twelfth; **la doceava parte** a twelfth

**docena** *nf* dozen; **a docenas** by the dozen; **media d. de niños** half a dozen children

**docencia** *nf* teaching

**docente 1** *adj* teaching; **personal d.** teaching staff

**2** *nmf* teacher

**dócil** *adj (niño, animal)* obedient; *(persona)* docile, tractable

**docilidad** *nf* obedience

**docto, -a** *adj* learned

**doctor, -ora** *nm,f* **(a)** *(de universidad)* doctor **(en** of*)*; **ser d. honoris causa** to have an honorary doctorate **(b)** *(médico)* doctor; **la doctora Piñán le atenderá enseguida** Dr Piñán will see you in a minute

**doctorado** *nm* doctorate

**doctoral** *adj* doctoral

**doctorar 1** *vt* to confer a doctorate on

**2 doctorarse** *vpr* to get one's doctorate **(en** in*)*

**doctrina** *nf* doctrine

**doctrinal** *adj* doctrinal

**documentación** *nf* **(a)** *(ciencia, manuales de uso)* documentation **(b)** *(identificación personal)* papers

**documentado, -a** *adj* **(a)** *(informado) (informe, estudio)* researched; *(persona)* informed **(b)** *(con papeles encima)* having identification

**documental** *adj & nm* documentary

**documentalista** *nmf* archivist

**documentar 1** *vt* **(a)** *(evidenciar)* to document **(b)** *(informar)* to brief

**2 documentarse** *vpr* to do research

**documento** *nm* **(a)** *(escrito)* document; **d. nacional de identidad** identity card **(b)** *(testimonio)* record

**dodecaedro** *nm* dodecahedron

**dogma** *nm Rel & Fig* dogma; **d. de fe** article of faith

**dogmático, -a** *adj* dogmatic

**dogmatismo** *nm* dogmatism

**dogmatizar** *vi* to express oneself dogmatically, to pontificate

**dogo** *nmf* bull mastiff

**dólar** *nm* dollar

**dolencia** *nf* complaint, ailment

**doler [43] 1** *vi* to hurt; **me duele la pierna** my leg hurts; **me duele la garganta** I have a sore throat; **me duele la cabeza** I have a headache; **¿te duele?** does it hurt?; **me duele ver tanta injusticia** it pains me to see so much injustice; **le dolió en el alma** it upset her terribly; *Fam Fig* **¡ahí le duele!** that has really got to him!

**2 dolerse** *vpr* **dolerse de** o **por algo** *(quejarse)* to complain about sth; *(arrepentirse)* to be sorry about sth

**dolido, -a** *adj* hurt, upset; **estar/sentirse d.** to be/feel hurt

**doliente** *adj (enfermo)* ill; *(afligido)* grieving

**dolmen** *nm* dolmen

**dolo** *nm Der* **hacer algo con d.** to do sth with premeditation o wittingly

**dolor** *nm* **(a)** *(físico)* pain; **siento un d. en el costado** I have a pain in my side; **(tener) d. de cabeza** (to have a) headache; **d. de estómago** stomachache; **d. de muelas** toothache **(b)** *(moral)* grief, sorrow

**dolorido, -a** *adj* **(a)** *(físicamente)* sore; **tener la pierna/espalda dolorida** to have a sore leg/back **(b)** *(moralmente)* grieving, sorrowing; **estar d.** to be grieving/sorrowing

**doloroso, -a** *adj (físicamente)* painful; *(moralmente)* distressing

**doma** *nf* taming; **d. de caballos** breaking-in of horses

**domador, -ora** *nm,f (de caballos)* breaker; *(de leones)* lion tamer

**domar** *vt (fiera)* to tame; *(caballo)* to break in; *Fig (personas, pasiones)* to control

**domesticar** [61] *vt también Fig* to tame

**doméstico, -a** *adj* domestic

**domiciliación** *nf Fin* **pagar mediante d. (bancaria)** to pay by direct debit

**domiciliar** [15] **1** *vt Fin (pago)* to pay by direct debit *o* standing order

**2 domiciliarse** *vpr (persona)* to establish residence

**domiciliario, -a** *adj Der* **arresto d.** house arrest; **asistente d.** home help

**domicilio** *nm* **(a)** *(vivienda)* residence, home; **servicio a d.** home delivery; **vender a d.** to sell door-to-door **(b)** *(dirección)* address; **sin d. fijo** of no fixed abode; **d. fiscal** registered office; **d. social** head office **(c)** *(localidad)* residence

**dominación** *nf* rule, dominion

**dominador, -ora** *adj* dominating

**dominante 1** *adj* **(a)** *(nación, religión, tendencia)* dominant; *(vientos)* prevailing **(b)** *(persona)* domineering

**2** *nf* predominant feature

**dominar 1** *vt* **(a)** *(controlar) (país, territorio)* to dominate, to rule (over); *(pasión, nervios, caballo)* to control; *(situación)* to be in control of; *(incendio)* to bring under control; *(rebelión)* to put down **(b)** *(divisar)* to overlook; **desde aquí se domina todo Bilbao** you can see the whole of Bilbao from here **(c)** *(conocer) (técnica, tema)* to master; *(lengua)* to be fluent in

**2** *vi (predominar)* to predominate

**3 dominarse** *vpr* to control oneself

**domingo** *nm* Sunday; *Rel* **D. de Ramos** Palm Sunday; *Rel* **D. de Resurrección** *o* **de Pascua** Easter Sunday; *ver también* **sábado**

**dominguero, -a** *nm,f Fam Pey (conductor)* Sunday driver; *(en campo, playa)* day tripper

**Dominica** *n* Dominica

**dominical** *adj* **excursión/suplemento d.** Sunday outing/supplement

**dominicano, -a** *adj & nm,f* Dominican

**dominico, -a** *adj & nm,f Rel* Dominican

**dominio** *nm* **(a)** *(dominación, posesión)* control **(sobre** over) **(b)** *(autoridad)* authority, power **(c)** *Fig (territorio)* domain; *(ámbito)* realm; **dominios** *(territorio)* dominions **(d)** *(conocimiento) (de arte, técnica)* mastery; *(de idiomas)* command **(e)** **ser del d. público** to be public knowledge **(f)** *Informát* domain

**dominó** *nm* **(a)** *(juego)* dominoes *(singular)* **(b)** *(fichas)* set of dominoes

**don** *nm* **(a)** *(tratamiento)* **d. Andrés Iturbe** Mr Andrés Iturbe; *(en cartas)* Andrés Iturbe Esquire; **d. Andrés** Mr Iturbe **(b)** *(habilidad)* gift; **d. de mando** leadership qualities; **tener el d. de la**

**palabra** *(cualidad humana)* to have the gift of speech; *(de orador)* to be a gifted speaker; **tener d. de gentes** to have a way with people

**donación** *nf* donation

**donaire** *nm (al expresarse)* wit; *(al andar, moverse)* grace

**donante** *nmf* donor; **d. de sangre** blood donor

**donar** *vt* to donate; **d. sangre** to give blood

**donativo** *nm* donation

**doncel** *nm Hist* page

**doncella** *nf* maid

**donde**

> **donde** combines with the preposition **a** to form **adonde** when following a noun, pronoun or adverb expressing location (e.g. **el sitio adonde vamos** the place where we're going; **es allí adonde iban** that's where they were going).

**1** *adv* where; **el bolso está d. lo dejaste** the bag is where you left it; **puedes ir d. quieras** you can go wherever you want; **hasta d.** as far as, up to where; **llegaré hasta d. pueda** I'll get as far as I can; **por d.** wherever; **iré por d. me manden** I'll go wherever they send me

**2** *pron* where; **la casa d. nací** the house where I was born; **la ciudad de d. viene** the town (where) she comes from, the town from which she comes; **hacia d.** towards where, towards which; **hasta d.** as far as where, as far as which; **de d.** *(de lo cual)* from which

**3** *prep (en casa de)* **fui d. mi madre** I went to my mother's

**dónde**

> **dónde** can combine with the preposition **a** to form **adónde** (e.g. **¿adónde vamos?** where are we going?).

*adv (interrogativo)* where; **¿d. está el niño?** where's the child?; **no sé d. se habrá metido** I don't know where she can be; **¿adónde vas?** where are you going?; **¿de d. eres?** where are you from?; **¿hacia d. vas?** where are you heading?; **¿por d.?** whereabouts?; **¿por d. se va al teatro?** how do you get to the theatre from here?

**dondequiera** *adv* **d. que** wherever

**donjuán, don Juan** *nm Fam* ladykiller, Casanova

**donostiarra 1** *adj* of/from San Sebastian

**2** *nmf* person from San Sebastian

**dónut®** *nm* doughnut

**doña** *nf* **d. María Rey** Mrs María Rey; **d. María** Mrs Rey

**dopado, -a** *adj (deportista)* = having taken performance-enhancing drugs

**dopaje** *nm Dep* drug-taking

**dopar 1** *vt* to dope

**2 doparse** *vpr* to take artificial stimulants

**doping** ['dopin] (*pl* **dopings**) *nm* doping

**doquier** *adv* **por d.** everywhere

**dorada** *nf* (*pez*) gilthead

**dorado, -a 1** *adj también Fig* golden

**2** *nm* (*parte dorada*) gilt; **limpiar los dorados** to clean the brass fittings

**dorador, -ora** *nm,f* gilder

**dorar 1** *vt* (**a**) (*cubrir con oro*) to gild; *Fam Fig* **d. la píldora** (**a alguien**) to sweeten the pill (for sb) (**b**) (*alimento*) to brown (**c**) (*piel*) to turn golden brown

**2 dorarse** *vpr* (**a**) (*comida*) to brown (**b**) (*piel*) to tan

**dórico, -a** *adj* Doric

**dormilón, -ona** *Fam* **1** *adj* fond of sleeping

**2** *nm,f* (*persona*) sleepyhead

**dormir** [29] **1** *vt* (*niño*) to get off to sleep; **d. la siesta** to have an afternoon nap; *Fam* **dormirla, d. la mona** to sleep it off

**2** *vi* to sleep

**3 dormirse** *vpr* (**a**) (*persona*) to fall asleep (**b**) (*brazo, mano*) to go to sleep; **se me ha dormido la pierna** my leg has gone to sleep (**c**) *Fig* (*despistarse*) to be slow to react; **¡no te duermas y haz algo!** don't just stand there – do something!

**dormitar** *vi* to doze

**dormitorio** *nm* (**a**) (*de casa*) bedroom; (*de colegio*) dormitory (**b**) (*muebles*) bedroom suite

**dorsal 1** *adj* dorsal

**2** *nm Dep* number (*on player's back*)

**dorso** *nm* back; **al d., en el d.** on the back; **véase al d.** see overleaf; **el d. de la mano** the back of the hand

**DOS** [dos] *nm* (*abrev de* **disk operating system**) DOS

**dos** *núm* two; **de d. en d.** in twos, two by two; **en un d. por tres** in no time at all; **cada d. por tres** every five minutes; *ver también* **seis**

**doscientos, -as** *núm* two hundred; *ver también* **seis**

**dosel** *nm* canopy

**dosificador** *nm* dispenser

**dosificar** [61] *vt* (**a**) *Quím* to measure out (**b**) *Fig* (*fuerzas, alimentos*) to use sparingly

**dosis** *nf inv también Fig* dose

**dossier** [do'sjer] *nm inv* dossier, file

**dotación** *nf* (**a**) (*de dinero, armas, medios*) amount granted (**b**) (*personal*) staff, personnel; (*tripulantes*) crew; (*patrulla*) squad

**dotado, -a** *adj* gifted; **d. de** (*persona*) blessed with; (*edificio, instalación, aparato*) equipped with

**dotar** *vt* (**a**) (*proveer*) **d. algo de** to provide sth with (**b**) (*tripular*) **d. algo de** to man sth with (**c**) *Fig* (*conferir*) **d. a algo/alguien de** to endow sth/sb with; **la naturaleza le dotó de una gran inteligencia** nature had endowed him with great intelligence (**d**) (*dar una dote*) to give a dowry to

**dote** *nf* (*en boda*) dowry; **dotes** (*aptitud*) qualities; **tener dotes de algo** to have a talent for sth; **dotes de mando** leadership qualities

**doy** *ver* **dar**

**DPI** (*abrev de* **dots per inch**) DPI

**dpto.** (*abrev de* **departamento**) dept; **d. de personal** personnel dept

**Dr.** (*abrev de* **doctor**) Dr.

**Dra.** (*abrev de* **doctora**) Dr.

**dracma** *nf* drachma

**draconiano, -a** *adj Fig* draconian

**DRAE** ['drae] *nm* (*abrev de* **Diccionario de la Real Academia Española**) = dictionary of the Spanish Royal Academy

**draga** *nf* (*máquina*) dredge; (*barco*) dredger

**dragado** *nm* dredging

**dragaminas** *nm inv* minesweeper

**dragar** [40] *vt* to dredge

**drago** *nm* dragon tree

**dragón** *nm* dragon

**drague** *etc ver* **dragar**

**drama** *nm* (*obra*) play; *Fig* (*desgracia*) drama; *Fam Fig* **hacer un d.** (**de algo**) to make a drama (out of sth)

**dramático, -a** *adj* dramatic

**dramatismo** *nm* dramatic nature, drama; **con d.** dramatically

**dramatizar** [16] *vt* to dramatize; *Fam* **¡no hay que d.!** there's no need for melodrama!, don't exaggerate!

**dramaturgo, -a** *nm,f* playwright, dramatist

**dramón** *nm Fam* melodrama

**drástico, -a** *adj* drastic

**drenaje** *nm* drainage

**drenar** *vt* to drain

**dribbling** ['driβlin] (*pl* **dribblings**) *nm Dep* (*habilidad*) dribbling; (*regate*) dribble

**driblar** *vt Dep* to dribble

**dril** *nm* drill

**drive** [draif] *nm* (**a**) *Informát* drive (**b**) (*en tenis, golf*) drive

**droga** *nf* drug; **la d.** drugs; **d. blanda/dura** soft/hard drug; **drogas sintéticas** *o* **de diseño** designer drugs

**drogadicción** *nf* drug addiction

**drogadicto, -a 1** *adj* addicted to drugs

**2** *nm,f* drug addict

**drogar** [40] **1** vt to drug
 **2 drogarse** vpr to take drugs

**drogata, drogota** adj & nmf Fam junkie

**drogodependencia** nf drug dependence, drug addiction

**drogodependiente** nmf drug addict

**drogue** etc ver **drogar**

**droguería** nf = shop selling paint, cleaning materials, etc

**droguero, -a** nm,f = owner of a "droguería"

**dromedario** nm dromedary

**drugstore** ['druʏstor] nm = establishment comprising late-night shop and bar

**druida** nm, **druidesa** nf druid, f druidess

**dto.** (abrev de **descuento**) discount

**dual** adj dual

**dualidad** nf duality

**dualismo** nm dualism

**dubitativo, -a** adj hesitant

**Dublín** n Dublin

**dublinés, -esa 1** adj of/from Dublin
 **2** nm,f Dubliner

**ducado** nm (a) (tierras) duchy (b) (moneda) ducat

**ducal** adj ducal

**ducha** nf shower; **tomar** o **darse una d.** to have o take a shower; Fam Fig **una d. de agua fría** a bucket of cold water

**duchar 1** vt (dar una ducha) to shower; Fam (mojar) to soak; **¡me has duchado entero con tu gaseosa!** you've soaked me with your lemonade!
 **2 ducharse** vpr to have a shower

**ducho, -a** adj **ser d. en** (entendido) to know a lot about; (diestro) to be skilled at

**dúctil** adj (a) (metal) ductile (b) (persona) malleable

**ductilidad** nf (a) (de metal) ductility (b) (de persona) malleability

**duda** nf doubt; **poner algo en d.** to call sth into question; **sacar a alguien de la d.** to remove sb's doubts; **salir de dudas** to set one's mind at rest; **sin d.** doubtless; **tengo mis dudas** I have my doubts; **¡la d. ofende!** how could you doubt me!; **no cabe d.** there is no doubt about it; **no te quepa d.** don't doubt it, make no mistake about it

**dudar 1** vi (a) (desconfiar) **d. de algo/alguien** to have one's doubts about sth/sb (b) (no estar seguro) **d. sobre algo** to be unsure about sth (c) (vacilar) to hesitate; **d. entre hacer una cosa u otra** to be unsure whether to do one thing or another
 **2** vt to doubt; **lo dudo mucho** I very much doubt it

**dudoso, -a** adj (a) (improbable) **ser d. (que)** to be doubtful (whether); to be unlikely (that) (b) (vacilante) hesitant, indecisive (c) (sospechoso) questionable, suspect; **una broma de gusto d.** a joke in questionable taste

**duela** etc ver **doler**

**duelo** nm (a) (combate) duel (b) (sentimiento) grief, sorrow; **en señal de d.** as a sign of mourning

**duende** nm (a) (personaje) imp, goblin (b) Fig (encanto) charm

**dueño, -a** nm,f (propietario) owner; (de piso alquilado) landlord, f landlady; **hacerse d. de algo** to take control of sth; **ser d. de sí mismo** to be self-possessed; **ser muy d. de hacer algo** to be free to do sth

**duermevela** nm snooze; **en d.** snoozing

**duermo** etc ver **dormir**

**Duero** nm **el D.** the Douro

**dueto** nm duet

**dulce 1** adj (a) (sabor) sweet (b) (agua) fresh (c) (mirada) tender
 **2** nm (caramelo, postre) sweet; (pastel) cake, pastry; Fig **a nadie le amarga un d.** anything's better than nothing; **d. de membrillo** quince jelly

**dulcificar** [61] vt (a) (endulzar) to sweeten (b) Fig (suavizar) to soften

**dulzaina** nf = musical instrument similar to a clarinet, but smaller and higher-pitched, used in folk music

**dulzón, -ona** adj sickly-sweet

**dulzura** nf (suavidad) sweetness; Fam **ven aquí, d.** come here, darling o sweetheart

**duna** nf dune

**dúo** nm (a) Mús duet (b) (pareja) duo; **a d.** together

**duodécimo, -a** núm twelfth

**duodeno** nm Anat duodenum

**dúplex** nm inv (a) (piso) duplex (b) Elec linkup

**duplicado, -a 1** adj in duplicate
 **2** nm duplicate, copy
 **3** adv (por) **d.** (in) duplicate

**duplicar** [61] **1** vt (a) (cantidad) to double (b) (documento) to duplicate
 **2 duplicarse** vpr to double

**duplicidad** nf (a) (repetición) duplication (b) (falsedad) duplicity

**duplo, -a** adj & nm double

**duque, -esa** nm,f duke, f duchess

**duración** nf length

**duradero, -a** adj (que permanece) lasting; (ropa, zapatos) hard-wearing

**duralex**® nm = heat-resistant glass

**durante** *prep* during; **d. las vacaciones** during the holidays; **d. una hora** for an hour; **d. toda la semana** all week

**durar** *vi (continuar siendo)* to last; *(permanecer, subsistir)* to remain, to stay; *(ropa)* to wear well; **¿cuánto dura la película?** how long is the film?; **aún dura la fiesta** the party's still going on

**durazno** *nm Am* peach

**durex** *nm Méx* Scotch® tape

**dureza** *nf* (a) *(de objeto, metal)* hardness (b) *(de clima, persona)* harshness (c) *(callosidad)* callus, patch of hard skin

**durmiente** *adj* sleeping; **la Bella D.** Sleeping Beauty

**durmiera** *etc ver* **dormir**

**duro, -a 1** *adj* (a) *(material, superficie)* hard; *(carne)* tough (b) *(resistente)* tough (c) *(palabras, clima)* harsh (d) *(expresiones)* **estar a las duras y a las maduras** *(sin rendirse)* to be there through thick and thin; *(sin quejarse)* to take the rough with the smooth; **ser d. de pelar** to be a hard nut to crack

**2** *nm* (a) *(moneda)* five-peseta coin; **me debes mil duros** you owe me five thousand pesetas; **cinco duros** *(moneda)* twenty-five peseta coin; **estar sin un d.** to be flat broke (b) *(persona)* tough guy

**3** *adv* hard

**duty free** ['djuti'fri] ( *pl* **duty frees**) *nm* duty free shop

**d/v** *(abrev de* **días vista**) 15 d. within 15 days

# E

**E, e** [e] *nf (letra)* E, e

**e** *conj* and

> e is used instead of **y** in front of words beginning with "i" or "hi" (e.g. **apoyo e interés** support and interest; **corazón e hígado** heart and liver).

**EAU** *nmpl (abrev de* **Emiratos Árabes Unidos)** UAE

**ebanista** *nmf* cabinet-maker

**ebanistería** *nf* . **(a)** *(oficio)* cabinet-making **(b)** *(taller)* cabinet-maker's

**ébano** *nm* ebony

**ebonita** *nf* ebonite, vulcanite

**ebrio, -a** *adj* **(a)** *(borracho)* drunk **(b)** *Fig (ofuscado)* **e. de** blind with

**Ebro** *nm* **el E.** the Ebro

**ebullición** *nf* **en e.** boiling; *Fig* in a state of excitement

**eccema** *nm Med* eczema

**ECG** *nm (abrev de* **electrocardiograma)** ECG

**echar 1** *vt* **(a)** *(tirar)* to throw; *(red)* to cast; **e. algo a la basura** to throw sth in the bin

**(b)** *(meter)* to put

**(c)** *(añadir) (vino, agua)* to pour **(a** *o* **en** into); *(sal, azúcar)* to add sth **(a** *o* **en** to)

**(d)** *(decir) (discurso)* to give; *(reprimenda)* to dish out

**(e)** *(carta, postal)* to post; **e. al correo** to put in the post

**(f)** *(humo, vapor, chispas)* to give off, to emit; *Fam Fig* **está que echa humo** she's fuming

**(g)** *(hojas, flores)* to sprout, to shoot

**(h)** *(expulsar)* **e. a alguien (de)** to throw sb out (of); **le han echado del partido** he's been expelled from the party

**(i)** *(despedir)* **e. a alguien (de)** to sack sb (from); **¡que lo echen!** sack him!, kick him out!

**(j)** *(accionar)* **e. la llave/el cerrojo** to lock/bolt the door; **e. el freno** to brake, to put the brakes on

**(k)** *(acostar)* to lie (down)

**(l)** *(calcular)* **¿cuántos años le echas?** how old do you reckon he is?

**(m)** *Fam* **le echaron diez años** *(de cárcel)* he got ten years; **¿qué echan esta noche en la tele?** what's on telly tonight?

**(n)** *(buenaventura)* to tell; **e. las cartas (a alguien)** to read sb's fortune *(in cards)*

**(o)** *(expresiones)* **e. abajo** *(edificio)* to pull down, to demolish; *(gobierno)* to bring down; *(proyecto)* to ruin; **e. a perder** *(vestido, alimentos, plan)* to ruin; *(ocasión)* to waste; **e. de menos** to miss

**2** *vi* **(a)** *(encaminarse)* **e. por la calle arriba** to go *o* head up the street

**(b)** *(empezar)* **e. a andar** to set off; **e. a correr** to break into a run; **e. a llorar** to burst into tears; **e. a reír** to burst out laughing

**3 echarse** *vpr* **(a)** *(lanzarse)* **echarse al suelo** to throw oneself on the floor; **se echó a sus brazos** she threw herself into his arms

**(b)** *(acostarse)* to lie down; **me voy a e. un rato** I'm going to have a nap

**(c)** *(empezar)* **echarse a hacer algo** to begin to do sth, to start doing sth; **se echó a cantar/reír** he burst into song/laughter

**(d)** *(apartarse)* **echarse a un lado** to move aside; *Fig* **echarse atrás** to back out

**(e)** *(obtener)* **echarse (un) novio** to get oneself a boyfriend

**(f)** **echarse a perder** *(comida)* to go off, to spoil; *(plan)* to fall through

**echarpe** *nm* shawl

**eclecticismo** *nm* eclecticism

**ecléctico, -a** *adj & nm,f* eclectic

**eclesiástico, -a 1** *adj* ecclesiastical
**2** *nm* clergyman

**eclipsar 1** *vt también Fig* to eclipse
**2 eclipsarse** *vpr* to go into eclipse; *Fig* to drop out of the limelight

**eclipse** *nm* eclipse; **e. de sol/luna** eclipse of the sun/moon

**eclosión** *nf* emergence

**eco 1** *nm* **(a)** *(de sonido)* echo; *Fig* **hacerse e. de algo** *(dar noticia)* to report sth; *(repetir)* to echo sth; *Fig* **tener e.** to arouse interest **(b)** *(rumor)* rumour; **el e. lejano de los tambores** the distant sound of the drums; **ecos**

**de sociedad** society column

**2** *nf Fam (ecografía)* (ultrasound) scan

**ecografía** *nf Med (técnica)* ultrasound scanning; *(imagen)* ultrasound (image)

**ecología** *nf* ecology

**ecológico, -a** *adj (medioambiental)* ecological; *(alimentos)* organic; *(detergente)* environmentally-friendly

**ecologismo** *nm* Green movement

**ecologista 1** *adj* environmental, ecological

**2** *nmf* environmentalist, ecologist

**economato** *nm* company cooperative shop

**econometría** *nf Econ* econometrics *(singular)*

**economía** *nf* **(a)** *(actividad productiva)* economy; **e. doméstica** housekeeping; **e. de libre mercado** free-market economy; **e. de mercado** market economy; **e. mixta** mixed economy; **e. planificada** planned economy; **e. sumergida** black economy *o* market **(b)** *(estudio)* economics *(singular)*; **e. aplicada** applied economics; **e. política** political economy **(c)** *(ahorro)* saving; **hacer economías** to save

**económico, -a** *adj* **(a)** *(asunto, doctrina)* economic **(b)** *(barato)* cheap, low-cost **(c)** *(que gasta poco) (motor, aparato)* economical; *(persona)* thrifty

**economista** *nmf* economist

**economizar** [16] *vt también Fig* to save

**ecosistema** *nm* ecosystem

**ecotasa** *nf (impuesto)* ecotax

**ecu** *nm (abrev de* **unidad de cuenta europea)** ecu

**ecuación** *nf Mat* equation; **e. de segundo grado** quadratic equation

**Ecuador** *n* Ecuador

**ecuador** *nm* equator; *Fig* **pasar el e.** to pass the half-way point

**ecualizador** *nm* equalizer

**ecuánime** *adj* **(a)** *(en el ánimo)* level-headed **(b)** *(en el juicio)* impartial, fair

**ecuanimidad** *nf* **(a)** *(del ánimo)* equanimity, composure **(b)** *(del juicio)* impartiality, fairness

**ecuatorial** *adj* equatorial

**ecuatoriano, -a** *adj & nm,f* Ecuadorian, Ecuadoran

**ecuestre** *adj* equestrian

**ecuménico, -a** *adj* ecumenical

**ed.** **(a)** *(abrev de* **editor)** ed. **(b)** *(abrev de* **edición)** edit.

**edad** *nf* age; **¿qué e. tienes?** how old are you?; **tiene 25 años de e.** she's 25 years old; **una persona de e.** an elderly person; **¡son cosas de la e.!** it's (just) his/her/their age!; **estar en e. de merecer** to be of marriageable age; **e. del juicio** *o* **de la razón** age of reason; **e. escolar** school age; **E. Media** Middle Ages; *Fig* **e. de oro** golden age; *Fam* **e. del pavo** awkward age; **e. de piedra** Stone Age; **la tercera e.** *(ancianos)* senior citizens

**edelweiss** ['eðelweis] *nm inv* edelweiss

**edema** *nm Med* oedema

**edén** *nm Rel* Eden; *Fig* paradise

**edición** *nf* **(a)** *(acción) Imprenta* publication; *Informát, Rad & TV* editing; **e. de Jorge Urrutia** *(en libro)* edited by Jorge Urrutia **(b)** *(ejemplares)* edition; **e. de bolsillo/de lujo** pocket/deluxe edition; **e. crítica/pirata/príncipe** critical/pirate/first edition **(c)** *(celebración periódica)* **la e. de los Oscars/del Mundial de 1998** the 1998 Oscars/World Cup

**edicto** *nm* edict

**edificación** *nf* building

**edificante** *adj (conducta)* exemplary; *(libro, discurso)* edifying

**edificar** [61] *vt* **(a)** *(construir)* to build **(b)** *(aleccionar)* to edify

**edificio** *nm* building; **e. inteligente** intelligent building

**edil** *nm (town)* councillor

**Edimburgo** *n* Edinburgh

**editar** *vt* **(a)** *(libro, periódico)* to publish; *(disco)* to release **(b)** *Informát, Rad & TV* to edit

**editor, -ora 1** *adj* publishing; **empresa editora** publishing company

**2** *nm,f* **(a)** *(de libro, periódico)* publisher **(b)** *Rad & TV* editor

**3** *nm Informát* editor; **e. de textos** text editor

**editorial 1** *adj* **empresa e.** publishing house *o* company

**2** *nm Prensa* editorial, leader

**3** *nf* publisher, publishing house

**editorialista** *nmf Prensa* leader writer

**edredón** *nm* duvet, eiderdown

**educación** *nf* **(a)** *(enseñanza)* education; **escuela de e. especial** special school; **e. física/sexual** physical/sex education; **e. primaria/secundaria** primary/secondary education **(b)** *(modales)* good manners; **¡qué poca e.!** how rude!; **¡un poco de e.!** do you mind!; **mala e.** bad manners

**educado, -a** *adj* polite, well-mannered; **mal e.** rude, ill-mannered

**educador, -ora** *nm,f* teacher

**educar** [61] *vt* **(a)** *(enseñar)* to educate **(b)** *(criar)* to bring up **(c)** *(cuerpo, voz, oído)* to train

**educativo, -a** *adj* educational; **sistema e.** education system

**edulcorante 1** *adj* **sustancia e.** sweetener

**2** *nm* sweetener

**edulcorar** *vt* to sweeten

**eduque** *etc ver* **educar**

**EEE** *nm* (*abrev de* **espacio económico europeo**) EEA

**EE UU** *nmpl* (*abrev de* **Estados Unidos**) USA

**efebo** *nm* Adonis

**efectista** *adj* designed for effect, dramatic

**efectivamente** *adv* (*en respuestas*) precisely, exactly

**efectividad** *nf* effectiveness

**efectivo, -a 1** *adj* (*real*) actual, true; **hacer e.** (*realizar*) to carry out; (*promesa*) to keep; (*dinero, crédito*) to pay; (*cheque*) to cash

**2** *nm* (*dinero*) cash; **en e.** in cash; *Mil* **efectivos** forces

**efecto** *nm* (a) (*consecuencia, resultado*) effect; **en e.** indeed; **hacer** *o* **surtir e.** to have the desired effect; **tener e.** (*vigencia*) to come into *o* take effect; **efectos especiales** special effects; **e. invernadero** greenhouse effect; **e. óptico** optical illusion; **efectos secundarios** side effects; **efectos sonoros/visuales** sound/visual effects

(b) (*finalidad*) aim, purpose; **a tal e.** to that end; **a efectos** *o* **para los efectos de algo** as far as sth is concerned

(c) (*impresión*) impression; **producir buen/mal e.** to make a good/bad impression

(d) (*de balón, bola*) spin; **dar e. a** to put spin on

(e) *Com* (*documento*) bill; **e. de comercio** commercial paper; **e. de favor** accommodation bill

(f) (*posesiones*) **efectos personales** personal possessions *o* effects

**efectuar** [4] **1** *vt* (*realizar*) to carry out; (*compra, pago, viaje*) to make

**2 efectuarse** *vpr* to take place

**efeméride** *nf* (*suceso*) major event; (*conmemoración*) anniversary; *Prensa* **efemérides** = list of the day's anniversaries published in a newspaper

**efervescencia** *nf* (a) (*de líquido*) effervescence; (*de bebida*) fizziness (b) *Fig* (*agitación, inquietud*) unrest; **estar en plena e.** to be buzzing *o* humming with activity

**efervescente** *adj* (*bebida*) fizzy; **aspirina/comprimido e.** soluble aspirin/tablet

**eficacia** *nf* (*de persona*) efficiency; (*de medicamento, medida*) effectiveness

**eficaz** *adj* (*persona*) efficient; (*medicamento, medida*) effective

**eficiencia** *nf* efficiency

**eficiente** *adj* efficient

**efigie** *nf* (*imagen*) effigy; (*en monedas*) image, picture

**efímero, -a** *adj* ephemeral

**efluvio** *nm* (*emanación*) vapour; (*aroma*) scent; *Fig* (*de alegría, simpatía*) aura; **los efluvios de su perfume** the smell of her perfume

**EFTA** ['efta] *nf* (*abrev de* **European Free Trade Association**) EFTA

**efusión** *nf* (*cordialidad*) effusiveness, warmth

**efusividad** *nf* effusiveness

**efusivo, -a** *adj* effusive

**EGB** *nf* *Antes* (*abrev de* **educación general básica**) = stage of Spanish education system for pupils aged 6-14

**Egeo** *nm* **el (mar) E.** the Aegean (Sea)

**egipcio, -a** *adj & nm,f* Egyptian

**Egipto** *n* Egypt

**ego** *nm* ego

**egocéntrico, -a 1** *adj* egocentric, self-centred

**2** *nm,f* egocentric *o* self-centred person

**egocentrismo** *nm* egocentricity

**egoísmo** *nm* selfishness, egoism

**egoísta 1** *adj* egoistic, selfish

**2** *nmf* egoist, selfish person

**ególatra 1** *adj* egotistical

**2** *nmf* egotist

**egolatría** *nf* egotism

**egregio, -a** *adj* *Formal* illustrious

**egresado, -a** *nm,f* *Am* (a) (*de escuela*) student who has completed a course (b) (*de universidad*) graduate

**egresar** *vi* *Am* (a) (*de escuela*) to leave school after graduation (b) (*de universidad*) to graduate

**egreso** *nm* *Am* (*de universidad*) graduation

**eh** *interj* ¡eh! hey!

**Eire** *n* *Hist* Eire

**ej.** (*abrev de* **ejemplo**) example, ex.

**eje** *nm* (a) (*de rueda*) axle; (*de máquina*) shaft (b) *Mat* axis; **ejes de coordenadas** Cartesian coordinate axes (c) *Fig* (*idea central*) central idea, basis (d) *Hist* **el E.** the Axis

**ejecución** *nf* (a) (*realización*) carrying out; **tuvimos problemas durante la e. de la tarea** we had problems while carrying out the task; **la e. del tenista fue brillante** the tennis player's performance was outstanding (b) (*de condenado*) execution (c) (*de concierto*) performance, rendition (d) *Informát* (*de un programa*) execution, running

**ejecutar** *vt* (a) (*realizar*) to carry out; **e. las órdenes de alguien** to carry out sb's orders (b) (*condenado*) to execute (c) (*concierto*) to perform (d) *Informát* (*programa*) to execute, to run

**ejecutiva** *nf* (*junta*) executive; **la e. del partido socialista** the executive of the socialist party

**ejecutivo, -a 1** *adj* executive

**2** *nm,f* (*persona*) executive; **e. agresivo** thrusting executive; **e. de cuentas** account administrator

**3** *nm* *Pol* **el E.** the government

**ejecutor, -ora** *nm,f* (a) *Der* executor (b) *(verdugo)* executioner

**ejecutorio, -a** *adj Der* final

**ejem** *interj* ¡e.! hum!, ahem!

**ejemplar 1** *adj* exemplary; **castigo e.** exemplary punishment

**2** *nm (de libro)* copy; *(de revista)* issue; *(de moneda)* example; *(de especie, raza)* specimen; **pescó un e. de 200 kilos** he caught one weighing 200 kilos

**ejemplaridad** *nf* exemplary nature

**ejemplificar** [61] *vt* to exemplify

**ejemplo** *nm* example; **por e.** for example; **dar e.** to set an example; **no des mal e. a los niños** don't set the children a bad example; **predicar con el e.** to practise what one preaches; **poner de e.** to give as an example

**ejercer** [42] **1** *vt* (a) *(profesión)* to practise; *(cargo)* to hold (b) *(poder, derecho)* to exercise; *(influencia, dominio)* to exert; **e. presión sobre** to put pressure on; **e. influencia (en)** to have an effect *o* influence (on)

**2** *vi* to practise (one's profession); **e. de** to practise *o* work as; *Fig* **ejerce mucho de jefe** he acts like he's the boss

**ejercicio** *nm* (a) *(tarea, deporte)* exercise; *Mil* drill; **hacer e.** to (do) exercise; *Rel* **ejercicios espirituales** retreat (b) *(de profesión)* practising; *(de cargo, funciones)* carrying out (c) *(de poder, derecho)* exercising (d) *Econ* financial year; **e. económico/fiscal** financial/tax year

**ejercitar 1** *vt* (a) *(derecho)* to exercise (b) *(idioma)* to practise

**2 ejercitarse** *vpr* to train (**en** in)

**ejército** *nm Mil & Fig* army; **E. de Tierra** army *(as opposed to navy and airforce)*; **el E. de Salvación** the Salvation Army

**ejerzo** *ver* **ejercer**

**ejote** *nm CAm, Méx* green bean

**el** *( f* **la,** *mpl* **los,** *fpl* **las)**

> **el** is used instead of **la** before feminine nouns which are stressed on the first syllable and begin with "a" or "ha" (e.g. **el agua, el hacha**).
>
> Note that **el** combines with the prepositions **a** and **de** to produce the contracted forms **al** and **del**.

*artículo* (a) *(en general)* the; **el coche** the car; **la casa** the house; **los niños** the children; **el agua/hacha/águila** the water/axe/eagle; **fui a recoger a los niños** I went to pick up the children

(b) *(con sustantivo abstracto o sentido genérico)* **el amor** love; **la vida** life; **el hombre** Man, human beings; **los niños imitan a los adultos** children copy adults

(c) *(indica posesión, pertenencia)* **se partió la pierna** he broke his leg; **se quitó los zapatos** she took her shoes off; **tiene el pelo oscuro** he has dark hair; **se dieron la mano** they shook hands

(d) *(con días de la semana)* **vuelven el sábado** they're coming back on Saturday

(e) *(con nombres propios geográficos)* **el Sena** the (River) Seine; **el Everest** (Mount) Everest; **la España de la postguerra** post-war Spain

(f) *Fam (con nombre propio de persona)* **llama a la María** call Maria

(g) *(con complemento de nombre, especificativo)* **el de** the one; **he perdido el tren, cogeré el de las nueve** I've missed the train, I'll get the nine o'clock one; **el de azul** the one in blue; **el de aquí** this one here

(h) *(con complemento de nombre, posesivo)* **mi hermano y el de Juan** my brother and Juan's

(i) *(antes de frase)* **el que** *(cosa)* the one, whichever; *(persona)* whoever; **coge el que quieras** take whichever you like; **el que más corra** whoever runs fastest

(j) *(antes de adjetivo)* **prefiero el rojo al azul** I prefer the red one to the blue one

**él, ella** *pron personal* (a) *(sujeto, predicado) (persona)* he, *f* she; *(animal, cosa)* it; **mi hermana es ella** she's the one who is my sister

(b) *(después de prep) (complemento)* him, *f* her; **de él** his; **de ella** hers; **voy a ir de vacaciones con ella** I'm going on holiday with her; **díselo a ella** tell it to her; **este regalo es para él** this present is for him

**elaboración** *nf (de producto)* manufacture; *(de idea)* working out; *(de plan, informe)* drawing up; **de e. casera** home-made; **proceso de e.** *(industrial)* manufacturing process

**elaborar** *vt (producto)* to make, to manufacture; *(idea)* to work out; *(plan, informe)* to draw up

**elasticidad** *nf (de un cuerpo)* elasticity; *Fig (de horario, interpretación)* flexibility

**elástico, -a 1** *adj (cuerpo)* elastic; *Fig (horario, interpretación)* flexible

**2** *nm (cinta)* elastic; *(goma elástica)* rubber band; *(de pantalón, falda)* elasticated waistband

**Elba** *nm* **el E.** the Elbe

**elección** *nf* (a) *(nombramiento)* election; **la e. del árbito no llevó mucho tiempo** it didn't take a long time to choose the referee

(b) *(opción)* choice; **no tenemos e.** we have no choice; **un regalo de su e.** a gift of his own choosing

(c) *Pol* **elecciones** election; **elecciones autonómicas** elections to the regional parliament; **elecciones generales** general election; **elecciones municipales** local elections

**electo, -a** *adj* elect; **el presidente e.** the president elect

**elector, -ora** *nm,f* voter, elector

**electorado** *nm* electorate

**electoral** *adj* electoral

**electoralismo** *nm* electioneering

**electoralista** *adj* electioneering; **una medida e.** a vote-catching measure

**electricidad** *nf* electricity; **e. estática** static electricity

**electricista 1** *adj* electrical

**2** *nmf* electrician

**eléctrico, -a** *adj* electric

**electrificación** *nf* electrification

**electrificar** [61] *vt* to electrify

**electrizar** [16] *vt Fig (exaltar)* to electrify

**electrocardiograma** *nm* electrocardiogram, ECG; **el e. mostró que tenía problemas de corazón** the ECG revealed that there were problems with his heart

**electrochoque** *nm* electric shock therapy

**electrocución** *nf* electrocution

**electrocutar 1** *vt* to electrocute

**2 electrocutarse** *vpr* to electrocute oneself

**electrodo** *nm* electrode

**electrodoméstico** *nm* electrical household appliance

**electroencefalógrafo** *nm* electroencephalograph

**electroencefalograma** *nm* electroencephalogram

**electrógeno, -a** *adj* **1 grupo e.** generator

**2** *nm* generator

**electrólisis** *nf inv* electrolysis

**electrólito** *nm* electrolyte

**electromagnético, -a** *adj* electromagnetic

**electromagnetismo** *nm* electromagnetism

**electrón** *nm* electron

**electrónica** *nf* electronics *(singular)*

**electrónico, -a** *adj* electronic; **microscopio e.** electron microscope

**electroshock** [elektro'ʃok] *nm (terapia)* electric shock therapy

**electrostática** *nf* electrostatics *(singular)*

**electrostático, -a** *adj* electrostatic

**elefante, -a 1** *nm,f* elephant

**2 e. marino** elephant seal

**elefantiasis** *nf inv* elephantiasis

**elegancia** *nf* elegance

**elegante** *adj* elegant, smart

**elegantoso, -a** *adj Am* elegant

**elegía** *nf* elegy

**elegiaco, -a, elegíaco, -a** *adj* elegiac

**elegible** *adj* eligible

**elegido, -a 1** *adj (escogido)* selected, chosen; *Pol* elected

**2** *nm,f* person elected/chosen; *Fig* **los elegidos** the chosen few

**elegir** [57] *vt (escoger)* to choose, to select; *(por votación)* to elect

**elemental** *adj* **(a)** *(básico)* basic **(b)** *(obvio)* obvious

**elemento** *nm* **(a)** *(sustancia)* element; **e. químico** chemical element; **estar (uno) en su e.** to be in one's element **(b)** *(factor)* factor; **el e. sorpresa** the surprise factor **(c)** *(en equipo, colectivo) (persona)* individual; *(objeto, característica)* element **(d) elementos** *(fundamentos)* rudiments **(e)** *Fam (persona) Br* chap, *US* guy; **un e. de cuidado** a bad lot

**elenco** *nm* **(a)** *(reparto)* cast **(b)** *(catálogo)* list, index

**elepé** *nm* LP *(record)*

**elevación** *nf* **(a)** *(de pesos, objetos)* lifting; *(de nivel, altura, precios)* rise **(b)** *(de terreno)* elevation, rise

**elevado, -a** *adj (alto)* high; *Fig (sublime)* lofty

**elevador** *nm* **(a)** *(montacargas)* hoist **(b)** *Am (ascensor) Br* lift, *US* elevator

**elevadorista** *nmf Am Br* lift operator, *US* elevator operator

**elevalunas** *nm inv* window winder; **e. eléctrico** electric window

**elevar 1** *vt* **(a)** *también Mat* to raise; *(peso, objeto)* to lift; **e. x al cuadrado/al cubo** to square/cube x; **diez elevado a quince** ten to the fifteenth (power) **(b)** *(subir)* to elevate **(a** to); **lo elevaron a la categoría de héroe** they made him into a hero **(c)** *Fig (propuesta, quejas)* to present

**2 elevarse** *vpr (subir)* to rise; *(edificio, montaña)* to rise up; **elevarse a** *(altura)* to reach; *(gastos, daños)* to amount *o* come to

**elidir** *vt* to elide

**eligió** *ver* **elegir**

**elijo** *ver* **elegir**

**eliminación** *nf* elimination; **e. de residuos** waste disposal

**eliminar** *vt (en juego, deporte)* to eliminate; *(matar)* to eliminate, to get rid of; *(contaminación, enfermedad)* to get rid of

**eliminatoria** *nf (primera fase)* qualifying round; *(en atletismo)* heat

**eliminatorio, -a** *adj* qualifying; **prueba eliminatoria** *(examen)* selection test; *(en deporte)* qualifying heat

**elipse** *nf* ellipse

**elipsis** *nf inv* ellipsis

**elipsoide** *nm* ellipsoid

**elíptico, -a** *adj* elliptical

**élite, elite** *nf* elite; **deportista de é.** top-class sportsman/sportswoman

**elitismo** *nm* elitism

**elitista** *adj & nmf* elitist

**elixir** *nm* *(remedio milagroso)* elixir; **el e. de la eterna juventud** the elixir of eternal youth; **e. bucal** mouthwash

**ella** *ver* **él**

**ellas** *ver* **ellos**

**ello** *pron personal (neutro)* it; **no nos llevamos bien, pero e. no nos impide formar un buen equipo** we don't get on very well, but it o that doesn't stop us making a good team; **no quiero hablar de e.** I don't want to talk about it; **por e.** for that reason

**ellos, ellas** *pron personal* **(a)** *(sujeto, predicado)* they; **los invitados son e.** they are the guests, it is they who are the guests

 **(b)** *(después de prep) (complemento)* them; **de e.** theirs; **me voy al bar con ellas** I'm going with them to the bar; **díselo a e.** tell it to them

**elocuencia** *nf* eloquence

**elocuente** *adj* eloquent; **se hizo un silencio e.** there was an eloquent silence; **una mirada e.** a meaningful look

**elogiar** [15] *vt* to praise

**elogio** *nm* praise

**elogioso, -a** *adj* appreciative, eulogistic

**elongación** *nf* elongation

**El Salvador** *nm* El Salvador

**elucidar** *vt* to elucidate, to throw light upon

**elucubración** *nf* *(reflexión)* reflection, meditation; *Fig* **eso no son más que elucubraciones suyas** it's all just a lot of crazy ideas he's dreamed up

**elucubrar** *vt* *(reflexionar)* to reflect o meditate upon; *Fig* *(teorías, fantasías)* to dream up

**eludir** *vt* *(evitar)* to avoid; *(perseguidores)* to escape; **e. a la prensa** to avoid the press

**emanación** *nf* emanation, emission

**emanar 1** *vt* *(olor, humo)* to emanate, to give off; *(hostilidad)* to emanate; *(alegría, confianza)* to exude, to radiate; **emanaba tristeza por todos los poros** she exuded sadness from every pore

 **2** *vi* to emanate **(de** from)

**emancipación** *nf* *(de mujeres, esclavos)* emancipation; *(de menores de edad)* coming of age; *(de países)* obtaining of independence

**emancipar 1** *vt* *(liberar)* to emancipate, to free; *(países)* to grant independence (to)

 **2 emanciparse** *vpr* to free oneself, to become independent; **se emancipó (de su familia) a los 17 años** she became independent from her family at 17

**embadurnado, -a** *adj* smeared **(de** with)

**embadurnar 1** *vt* to smear **(de** with)

 **2 embadurnarse** *vpr* **embadurnarse de** to smear oneself with

**embajada** *nf* **(a)** *(edificio)* embassy **(b)** *(cargo)* ambassadorship **(c)** *(empleados)* embassy staff

**embajador, -ora** *nm,f* ambassador

**embalaje** *nm* **(a)** *(acción)* packing **(b)** *(material)* packaging

**embalar 1** *vt* to wrap up, to pack

 **2 embalarse** *vpr* *(corredor)* to race away; *(vehículo)* to pick up speed; *Fig (entusiasmarse)* to get carried away; **cuando se embala a hablar no hay quien lo pare** once he gets into his stride you can't shut him up

**embaldosar** *vt* *(piso)* to tile

**embalsamamiento** *nm* embalming

**embalsamar** *vt* to embalm

**embalsar 1** *vt* to dam (up)

 **2 embalsarse** *vpr* to collect, to form puddles

**embalse** *nm* reservoir

**embarazada** *nf* pregnant woman

**embarazado, -a** *adj* pregnant; **dejar embarazada a alguien** to get sb pregnant; **estar embarazada de ocho meses** to be eight months pregnant; **quedarse embarazada** to get pregnant

**embarazar** [16] *vt* **(a)** *(preñar)* to get pregnant **(b)** *(impedir)* to restrict **(c)** *(avergonzar)* to inhibit

**embarazo** *nm* **(a)** *(preñez)* pregnancy; **e. psicológico** phantom pregnancy **(b)** *(timidez)* embarrassment **(c)** *(impedimento)* obstacle

**embarazoso, -a** *adj* awkward, embarrassing

**embarcación** *nf* boat, vessel

**embarcadero** *nm* jetty

**embarcar** [61] **1** *vt* **(a)** *(personas)* to board; *(mercancías)* to ship **(b)** *Fig (involucrar)* **e. a alguien en algo** to involve sb in sth

 **2** *vi* to board

 **3 embarcarse** *vpr* **(a)** *(para viajar)* to board **(b)** *Fig (aventurarse)* **embarcarse en algo** to get oneself involved in sth

**embargado, -a** *adj* **e. por la pena/la alegría** overcome with grief/joy

**embargar** [40] *vt* **(a)** *Der* to seize, to distrain; **le han embargado todos sus bienes** his property has been seized **(b)** *(sujeto: emoción)* to overcome

**embargo** *nm* **(a)** *Der* seizure **(b)** *Econ* embargo **(c)** *conj* **sin e.** however, nevertheless

**embarque** *nm* *(de personas)* boarding; *(de mercancías)* embarkation; **el e. se realizará por la puerta G** the flight will board at gate G

**embarrancar** [61] **1** *vi* to run aground

**2 embarrancarse** *vpr (barco)* to run aground; *(coche)* to get stuck

**embarrar 1** *vt* to cover with mud

**2 embarrarse** *vpr* to get covered in mud

**embarullar** *Fam* **1** *vt* to mess up

**2 embarullarse** *vpr* to get into a muddle

**embate** *nm (del mar)* pounding; *Fig (del destino)* blow; **el e. de las olas** the pounding of the waves

**embaucador, -ora 1** *adj* deceitful

**2** *nm,f* swindler, confidence trickster

**embaucar** [61] *vt* to deceive, to take in; **no te dejes e.** don't (let yourself) be taken in; **e. a alguien en algo** to talk sb into sth

**embeber** *vt* **1** to soak up

**2 embeberse** *vpr Fig (ensimismarse)* to become absorbed (**en** in); **se embebió en sus fantasías** he lost himself in his dream world; **me embebí de la poesía de Lorca** I immersed *o* steeped myself in Lorca's poetry

**embelesar 1** *vt* to captivate; **su belleza lo embelesó** he was enchanted *o* captivated by her beauty

**2 embelesarse** *vpr* to be captivated

**embellecedor** *nm (moldura)* go-faster stripes; *(tapacubos)* hubcap

**embellecer** [48] *vt* to adorn, to embellish

**embellecimiento** *nm* embellishment

**embestida** *nf (ataque)* attack; *(de toro)* charge; **derribó la puerta de una e.** he broke down the door with a single charge

**embestir** [49] **1** *vt (lanzarse contra)* to attack; *(toro)* to charge; **el coche embistió al árbol** the car smashed into the tree

**2** *vi (lanzarse)* to attack; *(toro)* to charge; **el coche embistió contra el árbol** the car smashed into the tree

**emblanquecer** [48] *vt* to whiten

**emblema** *nm* **(a)** *(divisa, distintivo)* emblem, badge **(b)** *(símbolo)* symbol

**embobar 1** *vt* to absorb, to fascinate; **esa mujer lo tiene embobado** he's crazy *o* potty about that woman

**2 embobarse** *vpr* to be captivated *o* fascinated (**con** by)

**embocadura** *nf* **(a)** *(de río, puerto)* mouth **(b)** *(de instrumento)* mouthpiece

**embocar** [61] *vt* to enter *(a narrow space),* to squeeze into

**embolado** *nm Fam* **(a)** *(mentira)* fib **(b)** *(follón)* jam, mess

**embolia** *nf* clot, embolism

**émbolo** *nm Aut* piston

**embolsarse** *vpr (ganar)* to make, to earn

**embonar** *vt Méx Fam* to suit

**emborrachar 1** *vt* to make drunk; *Fig* **la alegría lo emborrachaba** he was drunk with joy

**2 emborracharse** *vpr* to get drunk

**emborrascarse** [61] *vpr* to cloud over, to turn black

**emborronar** *vt* **(a)** *(garabatear)* to scribble on; *(manchar)* to smudge **(b)** *(escribir de prisa)* to scribble

**emboscada** *nf también Fig* ambush; **caer en/tender una e.** to walk into/to lay an ambush

**emboscar** [61] *vt* to ambush

**embotamiento** *nm* dullness

**embotar** *vt (sentidos)* to dull; **tenía la mente embotada de tanto estudiar** his mind had been dulled by so much studying

**embotellado, -a 1** *adj* bottled

**2** *nm* bottling

**embotellamiento** *nm* **(a)** *(de tráfico)* traffic jam **(b)** *(de líquidos)* bottling

**embotellar** *vt* **(a)** *(tráfico)* to block **(b)** *(líquido)* to bottle

**embozar** [16] **1** *vt (rostro)* to cover (up)

**2 embozarse** *vpr (persona)* to cover one's face

**embozo** *nm (de sábana)* turnover

**embragar** [40] *vi* to engage the clutch

**embrague** *nm* clutch

**embravecer** [48] **1** *vt* to enrage

**2 embravecerse** *vpr* **(a)** *(animal, persona)* to become enraged **(b)** *(mar)* to become rough

**embriagador, -ora** *adj* intoxicating, heady

**embriagar** [40] **1** *vt* **(a)** *(extasiar)* to intoxicate **(b)** *(emborrachar)* to make drunk

**2 embriagarse** *vpr* **(a)** *(extasiarse)* to become drunk (**de** with) **(b)** *(emborracharse)* to get drunk (**con** on)

**embriaguez** *nf* **(a)** *(borrachera)* drunkenness **(b)** *(éxtasis)* intoxication

**embriología** *nf* embryology

**embrión** *nm* embryo

**embrionario, -a** *adj también Fig* embryonic

**embrollar 1** *vt (asunto)* to confuse, to complicate; *(hilos)* to tangle up

**2 embrollarse** *vpr* to get muddled up *o* confused

**embrollo** *nm (de hilos)* tangle; *Fig (lío)* mess; *(mentira)* lie

**embromado, -a** *adj Am Fam* tricky

**embromar** *vt* **(a)** *(burlarse de)* to tease **(b)** *Am Fam (fastidiar)* to annoy

**embrujar** *vt también Fig* to bewitch

**embrujo** *nm (maleficio)* curse, spell; *Fig (de ciudad, ojos)* charm, magic

**embrutecer** [48] **1** vt to stultify, to make dull

**2 embrutecerse** vpr to become stultified

**embrutecimiento** nm (acción) stultification

**embuchado, -a** adj **carne embuchada** cured cold meat

**embuchar** vt (a) Fam (comer) to wolf down, to gobble up (b) (embutir) to process into sausages

**embudo** nm funnel

**embuste** nm lie

**embustero, -a 1** adj lying

**2** nm,f liar

**embutido** nm (a) (comida) cold cured meat (b) (acción) sausage-making, stuffing

**embutir** vt to stuff; Fig **se embutió en unos pantalones de cuero** he squeezed himself into a pair of leather trousers

**eme** nf Fam (mierda) **¡vete a la e.!** bog off!

**emergencia** nf (a) (urgencia) emergency; **en caso de e.** in case of emergency (b) (brote) emergence

**emergente** adj emerging

**emerger** [54] vi (salir del agua) to emerge; (aparecer) to come into view, to appear

**emérito, -a** adj emeritus

**emerjo** ver **emerger**

**emigración** nf (a) (de personas) emigration; (de aves) migration (b) (grupo de personas) emigrant community

**emigrado, -a** nm,f emigrant

**emigrante** adj & nmf emigrant

**emigrar** vi (persona) to emigrate; (ave) to migrate

**eminencia** nf (persona) eminent figure, leading light; (excelencia) excellence; **la e. de su obra** the outstanding nature of his work; **e. gris** éminence grise; **Su E.** His Eminence

**eminente** adj (a) (excelente) eminent (b) (elevado) high

**emir** nm emir

**emirato** nm emirate

**Emiratos Árabes Unidos** nmpl **los E.** the United Arab Emirates

**emisario, -a** nm,f emissary

**emisión** nf (a) (de energía, rayos) emission (b) (de bonos, sellos, monedas) issue; Com **e. de obligaciones** debentures issue (c) Rad & TV (transmisión) broadcasting; (programa) programme, broadcast

**emisor, -ora 1** adj (a) (de radio, TV) transmitting, broadcasting; **una fuente emisora de calor** a heat source (b) (de dinero, bonos) issuing

**2** nm source; **un e. de ondas de radio** a source of radio waves

**emisora** nf (de radio) radio station

**emitir 1** vt (a) (rayos, calor, sonidos) to emit (b) (moneda, sellos, bonos) to issue (c) (expresar) (juicio, opinión) to express; (fallo) to pronounce (d) Rad & TV to broadcast

**2** vi to broadcast

**emoción** nf (a) (conmoción, sentimiento) emotion; **la e. le impedía hablar** he was so emotional he could hardly speak (b) (expectación) excitement; **¡qué e.!** how exciting!

**emocionado, -a** adj moved, excited

**emocional** adj emotional

**emocionante** adj (a) (conmovedor) moving, touching (b) (apasionante) exciting, thrilling

**emocionar 1** vt (a) (conmover) to move (b) (excitar, apasionar) to thrill, to excite

**2 emocionarse** vpr (a) (conmoverse) to be moved (b) (excitarse, apasionarse) to get excited

**emolumento** nm emolument

**emotividad** nf emotional impact, emotiveness

**emotivo, -a** adj (persona) emotional; (escena, palabras) moving

**empacar** [61] vt to pack

**empachar 1** vt to give indigestion to

**2 empacharse** vpr (comer demasiado) to stuff oneself (**de** with); Fam Fig to overdose (**de** on); (sufrir indigestión) to get indigestion

**empacho** nm (a) (indigestión) indigestion (b) Fam Fig (hartura) **tener un e. de** to have had enough o one's fill of; **se dio un e. de televisión** he overdosed on television

**empadronamiento** nm registration on the electoral roll

**empadronar 1** vt to register on the electoral roll

**2 empadronarse** vpr to register on the electoral roll; **me he empadronado en Madrid** I've got my name on the electoral roll in Madrid

**empalagar** [40] **1** vt **los bombones me empalagan** I find chocolates sickly; **me empalaga con tanta cortesía** I find his excessive politeness rather cloying

**2 empalagarse** vpr **empalagarse de** o **con** to get sick of

**empalago** nm cloying taste

**empalagoso, -a** adj (pastel) sickly-sweet, cloying; (persona) smarmy; (discurso) syrupy

**empalizada** nf (cerca) fence; Mil stockade

**empalmar 1** vt (a) (tubos, cables) to connect, to join (b) (planes, ideas) to link (c) (en fútbol) to volley

**2** vi (a) (autocares, trenes) to connect (b) (carreteras) to link o join (up) (c) (sucederse) to follow on (**con** from)

**3 empalmarse** vpr Vulg to get a hard-on

**empalme** *nm* (a) *(entre cables, tubos)* joint, connection (b) *(de líneas férreas, carreteras)* junction

**empanada** *nf* pasty; **e. gallega** = pie typical of Galicia, filled with seafood or meat; *Fam* **tener una e. mental** to be in a real muddle, not to be able to think straight

**empanadilla** *nf* small pasty

**empanado, -a** *adj* breaded, covered in breadcrumbs

**empanar** *vt Culin* to coat in breadcrumbs

**empantanado, -a** *adj* (a) *(inundado)* flooded (b) *Fig* bogged down

**empantanar 1** *vt* to flood
**2 empantanarse** *vpr* (a) *(inundarse)* to be flooded *o* waterlogged (b) *Fig (atascarse)* to get bogged down

**empañado, -a** *adj* (a) *(cristal)* misted *o* steamed up; *(metal)* tarnished; **tenía los ojos empañados por las lágrimas** his eyes were misted over with tears (b) *Fig (reputación)* tarnished

**empañar 1** *vt* (a) *(cristal)* to mist up, to steam up (b) *Fig (reputación)* to tarnish; *(felicidad)* to spoil, to cloud
**2 empañarse** *vpr* to mist up, to steam up

**empapar 1** *vt* (a) *(humedecer)* to soak (b) *(absorber)* to soak up
**2 empaparse** *vpr* (persona, traje) to get soaked; *Fam* **¡para que te empapes!** so there!, stick that in your pipe and smoke it!

**empapelado** *nm* (a) *(acción)* papering (b) *(papel)* wallpaper

**empapelador, -ora** *nm,f* paperhanger

**empapelar** *vt* (a) *(pared)* to paper (b) *Fam Fig (procesar)* to have up (before the courts)

**empaque 1** *ver* **empacar**
**2** *nm (seriedad, solemnidad) (de ocasión)* solemnity; *(de persona)* presence

**empaquetar** *vt* (a) *(envolver)* to pack, to package (b) *Fam Fig (endilgar)* **empaquetarle algo a alguien** to lumber *o* land sb with sth; **me empaquetaron el trabajo** I was lumbered *o* landed with the job

**emparedado, -a 1** *adj* confined
**2** *nm* sandwich

**emparedamiento** *nm (como castigo)* walling up

**emparedar** *vt (como castigo)* to wall up

**emparejamiento** *nm* pairing

**emparejar 1** *vt* (a) *(juntar en pareja) (personas)* to pair off; *(zapatos, calcetines)* to match (up) (b) *(nivelar)* to make level
**2 emparejarse** *vpr (personas)* to find a partner

**emparentar** [3] *vi* **e. con** to marry into

**emparrado** *nm* = vines trained on an overhead frame to provide shade in a garden

**emparrar** *vt* to train

**empastar** *vt (diente)* to fill

**empaste** *nm (de diente)* filling

**empatar** *vi (en elecciones, competición)* to tie; *(en partido)* to draw; **e. a cero** to draw nil-nil; **e. a dos/tres (goles)** to draw two/three all

**empate** *nm (en elecciones, competición)* tie; *(en partido)* draw; **un e. a cero/dos** a goalless/ two-two draw

**empecé** *ver* **empezar**

**empecinado, -a** *adj* stubborn

**empecinamiento** *nm* stubbornness

**empecinarse** *vpr* to insist (**en hacer algo** on doing sth)

**empedernido, -a** *adj (bebedor, fumador)* heavy; *(criminal, jugador)* hardened

**empedrado** *nm* paving

**empedrar** [3] *vt* to pave

**empeine** *nm (de pie, zapato)* instep

**empellón** *nm* shove; **abrirse paso a empellones** to get through by pushing and shoving; **echar a alguien a empellones** to remove sb by force

**empeñado, -a** *adj* (a) *(en préstamo)* in pawn (b) *(obstinado)* determined; **estar e. en hacer algo** to be determined to do sth

**empeñar 1** *vt* (a) *(joyas, bienes)* to pawn (b) *(palabra)* to give
**2 empeñarse** *vpr* (a) *(obstinarse)* to insist; **empeñarse en hacer algo** *(obstinarse)* to insist on doing sth; *(persistir)* to persist in doing sth (b) *(endeudarse)* to get into debt

**empeño** *nm* (a) *(de joyas, bienes)* pawning; **casa de empeños** pawnshop (b) *(obstinación)* determination; **tener e. en hacer algo** to be determined to do sth; **poner e. en hacer algo** to make a great effort to do sth, to take pains to do sth; **morir en el e.** to die in the attempt

**empeoramiento** *nm* worsening, deterioration

**empeorar 1** *vi* to get worse, to deteriorate
**2** *vt* to make worse

**empequeñecer** [48] *vt (quitar importancia)* to diminish; *(en una comparación)* to overshadow, to dwarf

**emperador** *nm* (a) *(título)* emperor (b) *(pez)* swordfish

**emperatriz** *nf* empress

**emperifollado, -a** *adj Fam* dolled up, done up to the nines

**emperifollar** *Fam* **1** *vt* to doll *o* tart up
**2 emperifollarse** *vpr* to doll *o* tart oneself up

**empero** *conj Formal* but; *(sin embargo)* nevertheless

**emperrarse** *vpr* to insist (**en hacer algo** on doing sth)

**empezar** [19] **1** *vt* to begin, to start

**2** *vi* to begin, to start (**a hacer algo** to do sth; **por hacer algo** by doing sth); **para e.** to begin *o* start with

**empiece** *nm Fam* beginning, start

**empiezo** *etc ver* **empezar**

**empinado, -a** *adj* steep

**empinar 1** *vt* **(a)** *(inclinar)* to tip up **(b)** *(levantar)* to raise; *Fam* **e. el codo** to bend the elbow

**2 empinarse** *vpr* **(a)** *(animal)* to stand up on its hind legs **(b)** *(persona)* to stand on tiptoe

**empingorotado, -a** *adj* stuck-up, posh

**empírico, -a 1** *adj* empirical

**2** *nm,f* empiricist

**empirismo** *nm* empiricism

**emplasto** *nm* **(a)** *Med* poultice **(b)** *Fam (pegote, masa)* sticky *o* gooey mess

**emplazamiento** *nm* **(a)** *(ubicación)* location **(b)** *Der* summons

**emplazar** [16] *vt* **(a)** *(situar)* to locate; *Mil* to position **(b)** *(citar)* to summon; *Der* to summons

**empleado, -a** *nm,f (asalariado)* employee; *(de banco, oficina)* clerk; **empleada de hogar** maid

**empleador, -ora** *nm,f* employer

**emplear 1** *vt* **(a)** *(usar) (objetos, materiales)* to use; *(tiempo)* to spend; **e. algo en hacer algo** to use sth to do sth **(b)** *(contratar)* to employ **(c)** **le está bien empleado** he deserves it, it serves him right

**2 emplearse** *vpr* **(a)** *(colocarse)* to find a job **(b)** *(usarse)* to be used

**empleo** *nm* **(a)** *(uso)* use **(b)** *(trabajo)* employment; *(puesto)* job; **estar sin e.** to be out of work; **oficina de e.** ≃ job centre; **pleno e.** full employment; **e. comunitario** community service; **e. juvenil** youth employment

**emplomadura** *nf CSur (diente)* filling

**emplomar** *vt* **(a)** *(cubrir con plomo)* to lead **(b)** *CSur (diente)* to fill

**emplumar** *vt (como adorno)* to adorn with feathers; *(como castigo)* to tar and feather

**empobrecer** [48] **1** *vt* to impoverish

**2 empobrecerse** *vpr* to get poorer

**empobrecimiento** *nm* impoverishment

**empollar 1** *vt* **(a)** *(huevo)* to incubate **(b)** *Fam (estudiar)* to swot up (on)

**2** *vi Fam* to swot

**3 empollarse** *vpr Fam* to swot up (on)

**empollón, -ona** *Fam* **1** *adj* swotty

**2** *nm,f* swot

**empolvarse** *vpr* to powder one's face

**emponzoñar** *vt también Fig* to poison

**emporio** *nm* = centre of commerce, finance etc

**emporrado, -a** *adj muy Fam* stoned *(on cannabis)*

**emporrarse** *vpr muy Fam* to get stoned *(on cannabis)*

**empotrado, -a** *adj* fitted, built-in

**empotrar** *vt* to fit, to build in

**emprendedor, -ora** *adj* enterprising

**emprender** *vt (trabajo)* to start; *(viaje, marcha)* to set off on; **e. el vuelo** to fly off

**empresa** *nf* **(a)** *(sociedad)* company; **pequeña y mediana e.** small and medium-sized business; **e. filial** subsidiary; **e. libre, libre e.** free enterprise; **e. matriz** parent company; **e. mixta/privada** mixed/private company; **e. pública** public sector firm **(b)** *(acción)* enterprise, undertaking

**empresariado** *nm* employers

**empresarial 1** *adj* **estudios empresariales** management *o* business studies

**2** *nfpl* **empresariales** business studies

**empresario, -a** *nm,f (patrono)* employer; *(hombre, mujer de negocios)* businessman, f businesswoman; *(de teatro)* impresario; **pequeño e.** small businessman

**empréstito** *nm Fin* debenture loan

**empujar** *vt* to push; **e. a alguien a que haga algo** to push sb into doing sth; **verse empujado a hacer algo** to find oneself forced *o* having to do sth

**empuje** *nm* **(a)** *(presión)* pressure **(b)** *(energía)* energy, drive

**empujón** *nm* **(a)** *(empellón)* shove, push; **dar un e. a alguien** to give sb a shove *o* push; **abrirse paso a empujones** to shove *o* push one's way through **(b)** *Fig (impulso)* effort; **dar un último e. a** to make one last effort with

**empuñadura** *nf (de paraguas, bastón)* handle; *(de espada)* hilt

**empuñar** *vt* to take hold of, to grasp

**emulación** *nf también Informát* emulation

**emulador** *nm Informát* emulator

**emular** *vt también Informát* to emulate

**émulo, -a** *nm,f Formal* rival

**emulsión** *nf* emulsion

**en** *prep* **(a)** *(lugar) (en el interior de)* in; *(sobre la superficie de)* on; *(en un punto concreto de)* at; **viven en la capital** they live in the capital; **tiene el dinero en el banco** he keeps his money in the bank; **en la mesa/el plato** on the table/plate; **en casa/el trabajo** at home/work

**(b)** *(dirección)* into; **el avión cayó en el mar** the plane fell into the sea; **entraron en la**

**habitación** they came/went into the room (**c**) *(tiempo) (mes, año)* in; *(día)* on; **nació en 1953/marzo** she was born in 1953/March; **en Nochebuena** on Christmas Eve; **en Navidades** at Christmas; **en aquella época** at that time, in those days; **en un par de días** in a couple of days

(**d**) *(medio de transporte)* by; **ir en tren/coche/avión/barco** to go by train/car/plane/boat

(**e**) *(modo)* in; **en voz baja** in a low voice; **lo dijo en inglés** she said it in English; **pagar en libras** to pay in pounds; **la inflación aumentó en un 10%** inflation increased by 10%; **todo se lo gasta en ropa** he spends everything on clothes

(**f**) *(precio)* in; **las ganancias se calculan en millones** profits are calculated in millions; **te lo dejo en 5.000** I'll let you have it for 5,000

(**g**) *(tema)* **es un experto en la materia** he's an expert on the subject; **es doctor en medicina** he's a doctor of medicine

(**h**) *(causa)* from; **lo detecté en su forma de hablar** I could tell from the way he was speaking

(**i**) *(materia)* in, made of; **en seda** in silk

(**j**) *(cualidad)* in terms of; **le supera en inteligencia** she is more intelligent than he is

**enagua** *nf,* **enaguas** *nfpl* petticoat

**enajenación** *nf,* **enajenamiento** *nm* (**a**) *(locura)* mental derangement, insanity; *(éxtasis)* rapture (**b**) *Der (de una propiedad)* transfer of ownership, alienation

**enajenar** *vt* (**a**) *(volver loco)* to drive mad; *(extasiar)* to enrapture (**b**) *Der (propiedad)* to transfer ownership of, to alienate

**enaltecer** [48] *vt* to praise

**enamoradizo, -a 1** *adj* **es muy e.** he falls in love very easily
**2** *nm,f* person who falls in love easily

**enamorado, -a 1** *adj* in love (**de** with)
**2** *nm,f* lover

**enamoramiento** *nm* falling in love; **un e. pasajero** a brief infatuation

**enamorar 1** *vt* to win the heart of; **la enamoró** she fell in love with him
**2 enamorarse** *vpr* to fall in love (**de** with)

**enanismo** *nm Med* dwarfism

**enano, -a 1** *adj* dwarf
**2** *nm,f* dwarf; *Fam Fig (niño)* kid; *Fam* **me lo pasé como un e.** I got a real kick out of it

**enarbolar** *vt (bandera)* to raise, to hoist; *(pancarta)* to hold up; *(arma)* to brandish

**enarcar** [61] *vt* to arch

**enardecer** [48] **1** *vt (excitar)* to inflame; *(multitud)* to whip up, to inflame
**2 enardecerse** to become inflamed

**enarque** *etc ver* **enarcar**

**encabezamiento** *nm (de carta, escrito)* heading; *(en periódico)* headline; *(preámbulo)* foreword

**encabezar** [16] *vt* (**a**) *(artículo de periódico)* to headline; *(libro)* to write the foreword for (**b**) *(lista, carta)* to head (**c**) *(marcha, expedición)* to lead

**encabritarse** *vpr* (**a**) *(caballo, moto)* to rear up (**b**) *Fam (persona)* to get shirty

**encabronarse** *vpr Vulg* to get pissed off

**encadenado** *nm* (**a**) *Cine* fade, dissolve (**b**) *Constr* buttress

**encadenamiento** *nm* linking, stringing together

**encadenar** *vt* (**a**) *(atar)* to chain (up) (**b**) *Fig (enlazar)* to link (together); *(esclavizar)* to chain

**encajar 1** *vt* (**a**) *(meter ajustando)* to fit (**en** into) (**b**) *(meter con fuerza)* to push (**en** into) (**c**) *(hueso dislocado)* to set (**d**) *(golpe, noticia, críticas)* to take (**e**) *(soltar)* **e. algo a alguien** *(discurso)* to force sb to listen to *o* sit through sth; *(insultos)* to hurl sth at sb; **encajarle un golpe a alguien** to land sb a blow
**2** *vi* (**a**) *(piezas, objetos)* to fit (**b**) *(hechos, declaraciones, datos)* to match; **e. con algo** to match sth (**c**) *(ser oportuno, adecuado)* to fit nicely (**con** with)

**encaje** *nm* (**a**) *(ajuste)* insertion, fitting-in (**b**) *(tejido)* lace; **pañuelo/bragas de e.** lace handkerchief/knickers

**encajonar** *vt* (**a**) *(en cajas, cajones)* to pack, to put in boxes (**b**) *(en sitio estrecho)* **e. algo/a alguien (en)** to squeeze sth/sb (into)

**encalado, -a 1** *adj* whitewashed
**2** *nm* whitewash

**encalar** *vt* to whitewash

**encallar** *vi* (**a**) *(barco)* to run aground (**b**) *Fig (proceso, proyecto)* to founder

**encallecer** [48] **1** *vt (manos, piel)* to harden; *Fig (persona)* to harden, to make callous
**2 encallecerse** *vpr (manos, piel)* to become calloused *o* hard; *Fig (persona)* to become callous *o* hard

**encamarse** *vpr* (**a**) *(enfermo)* to take to one's bed (**b**) *muy Fam* **e. con alguien** *(acostarse)* to sleep with sb

**encaminar 1** *vt (persona, pasos)* to direct; *Fig* **estar encaminado a hacer algo** *(medidas, actividades)* to be aimed at doing sth
**2 encaminarse** *vpr* **encaminarse a/hacia** to set off for/towards

**encamotarse** *vpr Am Fam* to fall in love

**encandilado, -a** *adj* dazzled, fascinated

**encandilar 1** *vt* to dazzle, to impress greatly
**2 encandilarse** *vpr* to be dazzled

**encanecer** [48] **1** *vi* to go grey
**2 encanecerse** *vpr* to go grey

**encantado, -a** adj (**a**) (*contento*) delighted; **e. de conocerle** pleased to meet you (**b**) (*hechizado*) (*casa, lugar*) haunted; (*persona*) bewitched

**encantador, -ora 1** adj delightful, charming

**2** nm,f **e. de serpientes** snake charmer

**encantamiento** nm enchantment

**encantar** vt (**a**) (*gustar*) **encantarle a alguien algo/hacer algo** to love sth/doing sth; **¡me encanta!** I love it/him/her! (**b**) (*embrujar*) to bewitch, to cast a spell on

**encanto** nm (**a**) (*atractivo*) charm; **ser un e.** to be a treasure o delight (**b**) (*apelativo cariñoso*) darling (**c**) (*hechizo*) spell; **como por e.** as if by magic

**encañonar** vt (*persona*) to point a gun at

**encapotado, -a** adj overcast

**encapotarse** vpr to cloud over

**encapricharse** vpr (**a**) (*obstinarse*) **e. con algo/hacer algo** to set one's mind on sth/doing sth (**b**) (*sentirse atraído*) **e. de alguien** to become infatuated with sb; **e. de algo** to take a real liking to sth

**encapuchado, -a 1** adj hooded

**2** nm,f hooded person

**encapuchar 1** vt to put a hood on

**2 encapucharse** vpr to put one's hood on

**encaramar 1** vt to lift up

**2 encaramarse** vpr to climb up (**a** o **en** onto)

**encarar 1** vt (**a**) (*hacer frente a*) to confront, to face up to (**b**) (*poner frente a frente*) to bring face to face

**2 encararse** vpr (*enfrentarse*) **encararse a** o **con** to stand up to

**encarcelación** nf, **encarcelamiento** nm imprisonment

**encarcelar** vt to imprison

**encarecer** [48] **1** vt (**a**) (*productos, precios*) to make more expensive (**b**) (*alabar*) to praise

**2 encarecerse** vpr to become more expensive

**encarecidamente** adv earnestly

**encarecimiento** nm (**a**) (*de producto, coste*) increase in price (**b**) (*empeño*) **con e.** insistently

**encargado, -a 1** adj responsible (**de** for), in charge (**de** of)

**2** nm,f person in charge; *Com* manager, f manageress

**encargar** [40] **1** vt (**a**) (*poner al cargo*) **e. a alguien de algo** to put sb in charge of sth; **e. a alguien que haga algo** to tell sb to do sth (**b**) (*pedir*) to order

**2 encargarse** vpr (**a**) (*ocuparse*) **encargarse de** to be in charge of; **yo me encargaré de eso** I'll take care of o see to that (**b**) (*pedir*) to order

**encargo** nm (**a**) (*pedido*) order; **por e.** to order; **hecho de e.** tailor-made (**b**) (*recado*) errand (**c**) (*tarea*) task, assignment

**encariñarse** vpr **e. con** to become fond of

**encarnación** nf (*personificación*) (*cosa*) embodiment; (*persona*) personification; *Rel* **E.** Incarnation

**encarnado, -a 1** adj (**a**) (*personificado*) incarnate (**b**) (*color*) red

**2** nm red

**encarnar 1** vt (*ideal, doctrina*) to embody; (*personaje, papel*) to play

**2** vi *Rel* to become flesh

**encarnizado, -a** adj bloody, bitter

**encarnizarse** [16] vpr **e. con** (*presa*) to fall upon; (*prisionero, enemigo*) to treat savagely

**encarpetar** vt to file away

**encarrilar 1** vt (**a**) (*tren*) to put back on the rails (**b**) *Fig* (*negocio, situación*) to put on the right track, to point in the right direction

**2 encarrilarse** vpr to find out what one wants to do in life

**encarte** nm (*en naipes*) lead

**encasillado** nm grid

**encasillamiento** nm pigeonholing

**encasillar** vt (**a**) (*clasificar*) to pigeonhole; *Teatro* to typecast (**b**) (*poner en casillas*) to put in a box, to enter into a grid

**encasquetar 1** vt (**a**) (*gorro*) to pull on (**b**) *Fam Fig* (*inculcar*) **e. algo a alguien** (*idea, teoría*) to drum sth into sb; (*discurso, lección*) to force sb to sit through sth (**c**) *Fam Fig* (*endilgar*) **e. algo a alguien** to lumber sb with sth

**2 encasquetarse** vpr (*sombrero*) to pull on

**encasquillarse** vpr to get jammed

**encausar** vt *Der* to prosecute

**encauzar** [16] vt (*agua*) to channel; *Fig* (*orientar*) to direct

**encebollado, -a** *Culin* **1** adj cooked with onions

**2** nm stew of fish or meat and onions

**encebollar** vt *Culin* to add onions to

**encefálico, -a** adj *Anat* **masa encefálica** brain mass

**encéfalo** nm *Anat* brain

**encefalograma** nm *Med* encephalogram

**encendedor** nm lighter

**encender** [66] **1** vt (**a**) (*vela, cigarro, chimenea*) to light (**b**) (*aparato*) to switch on (**c**) *Fig* (*entusiasmo, ira*) to arouse; (*pasión, discusión*) to inflame

**2 encenderse** vpr (**a**) (*fuego, gas*) to ignite; (*luz, estufa*) to come on (**b**) *Fig* (*persona, rostro*) to go red, to blush; (*de ira*) to flare up

**encendido, -a 1** *adj* **(a)** *(luz, colilla)* burning; **la luz está encendida** the light is on **(b)** *Fig (deseos, mirada, palabras)* passionate, ardent **(c)** *(mejillas)* red, flushed

**2** *nm Aut* ignition

**encerado, -a 1** *adj* waxed, polished

**2** *nm* **(a)** *(acción)* waxing, polishing **(b)** *(pizarra)* blackboard; **salir al e.** to come/go out to the blackboard

**encerar** *vt* to wax, to polish

**encerrar [3] 1** *vt* **(a)** *(recluir)* to shut up *o* in; *(con llave)* to lock up *o* in; *(en la cárcel)* to lock away *o* up **(b)** *(contener)* to contain

**2 encerrarse** *vpr (recluirse)* to shut oneself away; *(con llave)* to lock oneself away

**encerrona** *nf (trampa)* trap

**encestar** *vt & vi Dep* to score *(in basketball)*

**enceste** *nm Dep* basket; **¡e. de Johnson!** Johnson scores!

**enchapado** *nm* veneer

**encharcado, -a** *adj (calle)* covered in puddles; *(campo de juego)* waterlogged

**encharcamiento** *nm* flooding, swamping

**encharcar [61] 1** *vt* to waterlog

**2 encharcarse** *vpr* **(a)** *(terreno)* to become waterlogged **(b)** *(pulmones)* to become flooded

**enchastrar** *vt CSur* to make dirty

**enchilada** *nf Am* = filled tortilla baked in chili sauce

**enchilarse** *vpr Méx Fam* to get angry

**enchinar** *vt Méx* to curl

**enchironar** *vt muy Fam* to bang up, to put away

**enchufado, -a** *Fam Fig* **1** *adj* **estar e.** = to have got where one is through connections

**2** *nm,f* = person who has got where they are through connections

**enchufar** *vt* **(a)** *(aparato)* to plug in **(b)** *Fam Fig (colocar en un trabajo)* to pull strings for

**enchufe** *nm* **(a)** *Elec (macho)* plug; *(hembra)* socket **(b)** *Fam Fig (recomendación)* connections; **tener e.** to have connections; **obtener algo por e.** to get sth by pulling strings *o* through one's connections

**enchufismo** *nm Fam* string-pulling

**encía** *nf* gum

**encíclica** *nf Rel* encyclical; **e. papal** papal encyclical

**enciclopedia** *nf* encyclopedia

**enciclopédico, -a** *adj* encyclopedic

**enciendo** *etc ver* **encender**

**encierro 1** *ver* **encerrar**

**2** *nm* **(a)** *(protesta)* sit-in **(b)** *Taurom* running of the bulls

**encima** *adv* **(a)** *(arriba)* on top; **yo vivo e.** I live upstairs; **e. de** *(en lugar superior que)* above;

*(sobre, en)* on (top of); **vivo e. de tu casa** I live upstairs from you; **el pan está e. de la nevera** the bread is on (top of) the fridge; *Fig* **estar e. de alguien** to be on at sb; **por e.** *(superficialmente)* superficially; **por e. de** over; *Fig* more than; **vive por e. de sus posibilidades** he lives beyond his means; **por e. de todo** more than anything else

**(b)** *(además)* on top of that; **e. de** on top of; **e. de ser tonto, es feo** on top of being stupid, he's also ugly

**(c)** *(sobre sí)* **lleva un abrigo e.** she has a coat on; **¿llevas dinero e.?** have you got any money on you?

**encimera** *nf (de cocina)* worktop; *(sábana)* top sheet

**encimero, -a** *adj* top

**encina** *nf* holm oak

**encinar** *nm* oak forest/grove

**encinta** *adj f* pregnant

**enclaustrar 1** *vt* to shut up in a convent

**2 enclaustrarse** *vpr* to shut oneself up in a convent; *Fig (encerrarse)* to lock oneself up in a room

**enclavado, -a** *adj* set, situated

**enclavar** *vt (clavar)* to nail

**enclave** *nm* enclave

**enclenque** *adj* sickly, frail

**encoger [54] 1** *vt* **(a)** *(ropa)* to shrink **(b)** *(miembro, músculo)* to contract

**2** *vi* to shrink

**3 encogerse** *vpr* **(a)** *(ropa)* to shrink; *(miembro, músculo)* to contract; **encogerse de hombros** to shrug one's shoulders **(b)** *Fig (apocarse)* to cringe

**encogido, -a** *adj Fig (tímido)* shy; *(pusilánime)* fearful, faint-hearted

**encojo** *ver* **encoger**

**encolado** *nm (de material, objeto)* glueing; *(de papel pintado)* pasting

**encolar** *vt (material, objeto)* to glue; *(papel pintado)* to paste

**encolerizar [16] 1** *vt* to infuriate, to enrage

**2 encolerizarse** *vpr* to get angry

**encomendar [3] 1** *vt* to entrust

**2 encomendarse** *vpr* **encomendarse a** *(persona)* to entrust oneself to; *(Dios, santos)* to put one's trust in; *Fam* **(hacer algo) sin encomendarse a Dios ni al diablo** (to do sth) entirely off one's own bat

**encomiable** *adj* laudable, praiseworthy

**encomiar [15]** *vt Formal* to praise, to extol

**encomienda** *nf* **(a)** *(encargo)* assignment, mission **(b)** *Hist* = area of land and its native inhabitants given to a conquistador

**encomio** *nm Formal* praise; **digno de e.** praiseworthy

**enconado, -a** *adj (lucha)* bitter; *(partidario)* passionate, ardent

**enconar 1** *vt* to inflame

**2 enconarse** *vpr* **(a)** *(persona)* to get angry **(b)** *(herida)* to become inflamed

**encono** *nm* rancour, animosity

**encontradizo, -a** *adj* **hacerse el e.** to contrive a meeting

**encontrado, -a** *adj (intereses, opiniones)* conflicting

**encontrar** [65] **1** *vt* **(a)** *(hallar)* to find **(b)** *(dificultades)* to encounter **(c)** *(persona)* to meet, to come across

**2 encontrarse** *vpr* **(a)** *(hallarse)* to be; **se encuentra en París** she's in Paris **(b)** *(coincidir)* **encontrarse (con alguien)** to meet (sb); **me encontré con Juan** I ran into *o* met Juan **(c)** *Fig (de ánimo)* to feel **(d)** *(chocar)* to collide

**encontronazo** *nm (golpe)* collision, crash

**encoñado, -a** *adj Vulg* **(a)** *(aburrido)* bored shitless **(b)** *(encaprichado)* **estar e. con algo/alguien** to be crazy *o* nuts about sth/sb

**encoñarse** *vpr Vulg* **(a)** *(aburrirse)* to be bored shitless **(b)** *(encapricharse)* **e. con** to go crazy *o* nuts about

**encopetado, -a** *adj* posh, upper-class

**encorsetar** *vt* to corset; *Fig (poner límites) to* straitjacket

**encorvar** *vt* **1** to bend

**2 encorvarse** *vpr* to bend down *o* over

**encrespar 1** *vt* **(a)** *(pelo)* to curl; *(mar)* to make choppy *o* rough **(b)** *(irritar)* to irritate

**2 encresparse** *vpr* **(a)** *(mar)* to get rough **(b)** *(persona)* to get irritated

**encriptación** *nf* encryption

**encrucijada** *nf* crossroads *(singular)*; *Fig* **en una e.** at a crossroads

**encuadernación** *nf (técnica)* binding; *(taller)* binder's, bookbinder's; **Encuadernaciones Olarte** *(empresa)* Olarte the Bookbinders

**encuadernador, -ora** *nm,f* bookbinder

**encuadernar** *vt* to bind

**encuadrar** *vt* **(a)** *(enmarcar) (cuadro, tema)* to frame **(b)** *(encerrar)* to contain **(c)** *(encajar)* to fit

**encuadre** *nm Fot* composition

**encubierto, -a** **1** *participio ver* **encubrir**

**2** *adj (intento)* covert; *(insulto, significado)* hidden

**encubridor, -ora 1** *adj* concealing; **no es más que una maniobra encubridora** it's just an attempt to conceal things

**2** *nm,f (de delito)* accessory **(de** to)

**encubrimiento** *nm (de delito)* concealment; *(de persona)* harbouring

**encubrir** *vt (delito)* to conceal; *(persona)* to harbour

**encuentro 1** *ver* **encontrar**

**2** *nm* **(a)** *(acción)* meeting, encounter; **salir al e. de alguien** *(para recibir)* to go to meet sb; *(para atacar)* to confront sb **(b)** *Dep* game, match **(c)** *(hallazgo)* find

**encuesta** *nf* **(a)** *(de opinión)* survey, opinion poll **(b)** *(investigación)* investigation, inquiry

**encuestado, -a** *nm,f* person polled

**encuestador, -ora** *nm,f* pollster

**encuestar** *vt* to poll

**encumbrado, -a** *adj* exalted, distinguished

**encumbramiento** *nm (acción)* rise; *(posición)* distinguished *o* exalted position

**encumbrar 1** *vt* to elevate *o* raise to a higher position

**2 encumbrarse** *vpr* to rise to a higher position

**encurtidos** *nmpl* pickles

**encurtir** *vt* to pickle

**endeble** *adj (persona, argumento)* weak, feeble; *(objeto)* fragile

**endemia** *nf Med* endemic disease

**endémico, -a** *adj Med & Fig* endemic

**endemoniado, -a 1** *adj* **(a)** *Fam Fig (molesto) (niño)* wicked; *(trabajo)* very tricky **(b)** *(desagradable)* terrible, foul **(c)** *(poseído)* possessed (by the devil)

**2** *nm,f* person possessed by the devil

**endenantes** *adv Am Fam* before

**enderezamiento** *nm (acción de poner derecho)* straightening; *(acción de poner vertical)* putting upright

**enderezar** [16] **1** *vt* **(a)** *(poner derecho)* to straighten; *(poner vertical)* to put upright **(b)** *Fig (corregir)* to set right, to straighten out

**2 enderezarse** *vpr (sentado)* to sit up straight; *(de pie)* to stand up straight

**endeudamiento** *nm* debt

**endeudarse** *vpr* to get into debt

**endiablado, -a** *adj (persona)* wicked; *(tiempo, genio)* foul; *(problema, crucigrama)* fiendishly difficult

**endibia** *nf* endive

**endilgar** [40] *vt Fam* **e. algo a alguien** *(sermón, bronca)* to dish sth out to sb; *(bulto, tarea)* to lumber sb with sth

**endiñar** *vt Fam* **e. algo a alguien** *(golpe)* to land *o* deal sb sth; *(tarea)* to lumber sb with sth

**endiosamiento** *nm* self-importance, conceit

**endiosarse** *vpr* to become conceited

**endivia** *nf* endive

**endocrino, -a** *Med* **1** *adj* **glándula endocrina** endocrine gland

**2** *nm,f* endocrinologist

**endocrinología** *nf Med* endocrinology

**endocrinólogo, -a** *Med nm,f* endocrinologist

**endogamia** *nf* endogamy

**endógeno, -a** *adj* endogenous

**endomingado, -a** *adj Fam* dressed-up, dolled-up

**endomingar** [40] *Fam* **1** *vt* to dress up, to doll up

**2 endomingarse** *vpr* to get dressed *o* dolled up in one's best clothes

**endorfina** *nf* endorphin

**endosar** *vt* (a) *Fig (tarea)* **e. algo a alguien** to lumber sb with sth (b) *Com* to endorse

**endosatario, -a** *nm,f Com* endorsee

**endoscopia** *nf Med* endoscopy

**endoscopio** *nm Med* endoscope

**endoso** *nm Com* endorsement

**endrogado, -a** *adj CAm, Méx* **estar e.** to be in debt

**endulzante** *nm* sweetener

**endulzar** [16] *vt (con azúcar)* to sweeten; *Fig (con dulzura)* to ease, to make more bearable

**endurecer** [48] *vt* (a) *(hacer más duro)* to harden (b) *(fortalecer)* to strengthen

**endurecimiento** *nm también Fig* hardening

**enebro** *nm* juniper

**enema** *nf* enema; **poner un e. a alguien** to give sb an enema

**enemigo, -a 1** *adj* enemy; **los ejércitos enemigos** the enemy armies; **ser e. de algo** to hate sth

**2** *nm,f* enemy

**enemistad** *nf* enmity; **su e. duraba ya años** they've been enemies for years; **siento una profunda e. hacia ellos** I feel intense hatred for them

**enemistar 1** *vt* to make enemies of; **el testamento enemistó a los hermanos** the will set the brothers against each other

**2 enemistarse** *vpr* to fall out (**con** with); **si Francia se enemistara con Alemania,...** if France were to fall out with Germany,...

**energética** *nf* energetics *(singular)*

**energético, -a** *adj* energy; **las legumbres proporcionan un alto aporte e.** pulses provide lots of energy

**energía** *nf* (a) *(para máquina)* energy; **energías alternativas** alternative energy sources; **e. atómica** *o* **nuclear** nuclear power; **e. eólica/hidráulica** wind/water power; **energías renovables** renewable forms of energy; **e. solar** solar energy *o* power (b) *Fig (de persona, respuesta)* strength; **respondió con e.** he responded energetically

**enérgico, -a** *adj (energético)* energetic; *(carácter)* forceful; *(gesto, medida)* vigorous; *(decisión, postura)* emphatic

**energúmeno, -a** *nm,f Fig* lunatic; **se puso hecho un e.** he went berserk *o* crazy

**enero** *nm* January; *ver también* **septiembre**

**enervante** *adj (debilitador)* draining; *(exasperante)* exasperating

**enervar** *vt* (a) *(debilitar)* to sap, to weaken (b) *(poner nervioso)* to exasperate

**enésimo, -a** *adj* (a) *Mat* nth (b) *Fig* umpteenth; **por enésima vez** for the umpteenth time

**enfadado, -a** *adj (molesto)* annoyed; *(enojado)* angry; **estar e. con alguien** to be annoyed/angry with sb; **están enfadados desde hace años** they fell out (with each other) years ago

**enfadar 1** *vt (molestar)* to annoy; *(enojar)* to anger

**2 enfadarse** *vpr* to get angry (**con** with); **se enfada por nada** he gets angry for no reason

**enfado** *nm* (a) *(irritación)* anger (b) *(enemistad)* hatred; **su e. dura ya años** *(recíproco)* they fell out years ago

**enfangar** [40] **1** *vt* to cover in mud

**2 enfangarse** *vpr* (a) *(con fango)* to get covered in mud (b) *Fam Fig* **enfangarse en un asunto sucio** to get mixed up in shady business

**énfasis** *nm inv* emphasis; **poner é. en algo** to emphasize sth

**enfático, -a** *adj* emphatic

**enfatizar** [16] *vt* to emphasize, to stress

**enfermar 1** *vt* (a) *(causar enfermedad a)* to make ill (b) *Fig (irritar)* **e. a alguien** to get on sb's nerves

**2** *vi* to fall ill

**3 enfermarse** *vpr* to fall ill

**enfermedad** *nf* (a) *(física)* illness; **e. infecciosa/venérea** infectious/venereal disease (b) *Fig (sentimiento)* sickness

**enfermera** *nf* nurse

**enfermería** *nf* sick bay

**enfermero** *nm* male nurse

**enfermizo, -a** *adj también Fig* unhealthy

**enfermo, -a 1** *adj* ill, sick; *Fig* **me pone e. su falta de puntualidad** his lack of punctuality gets on my nerves

**2** *nm,f (en general)* invalid, sick person; *(en el hospital)* patient

**enfervorizado, -a** *adj* wildly enthusiastic; **la multitud enfervorizada animaba a su equipo** the frenzied crowd cheered on their team

**enfervorizar** [16] *vt* to inflame, to rouse

**enfilado, -a** *adj* **tener a alguien e.** to have it in for sb

**enfilar 1** *vt* (a) *(camino)* to go o head straight along (b) *(arma)* to aim
  **2** *vi* **e. hacia** to go o head straight towards

**enfisema** *nm* emphysema

**enflaquecer** [48] **1** *vt* to make thin
  **2** *vi* to grow thin, to lose weight

**enfocar** [61] **1** *vt* (a) *(imagen, objetivo)* to focus (b) *(sujeto: luz, foco)* to shine on (c) *Fig (tema, asunto)* to approach, to look at
  **2** *vi* **e. hacia alguien/algo** *(cámara)* to focus on sb/sth; *(luz)* to shine on sb/sth

**enfoque** *nm* (a) *(de una imagen)* focus (b) *Fig (de un asunto)* approach, angle

**enfrascado, -a** *adj* **estar e. (en)** to be totally absorbed (in)

**enfrascar** [61] **1** *vt* to bottle
  **2** **enfrascarse** *vpr (riña)* to get embroiled (en in); *(lectura, conversación)* to become engrossed (en in)

**enfrentamiento** *nm* confrontation

**enfrentar 1** *vt* (a) *(hacer frente)* to confront, to face (b) *(poner frente a frente)* to bring face to face
  **2** **enfrentarse** *vpr* (a) *(luchar, encontrarse)* to meet, to clash; **nos enfrentamos al enemigo** we confronted the enemy (b) *(oponerse)* **enfrentarse con alguien** to confront sb

**enfrente** *adv* (a) *(delante)* opposite; **la tienda de e.** the shop across the road; **e. de** opposite, facing (b) *(en contra)* **tiene a todos e.** everyone's against her

**enfriamiento** *nm* (a) *(catarro)* cold (b) *(acción)* cooling; *Fig* **el e. de las relaciones entre Francia y Estados Unidos** the cooling of relations between France and the United States

**enfriar** [34] **1** *vt también Fig* to cool
  **2** *v impersonal* to get colder
  **3** **enfriarse** *vpr* (a) *(líquido, pasión, amistad)* to cool down (b) *(quedarse demasiado frío)* to go cold; **se te va a e. la sopa** your soup is going to get cold (c) *(resfriarse)* to catch a cold

**enfundar 1** *vt (espada)* to sheathe; *(pistola)* to put away
  **2** **enfundarse** *vpr* **enfundarse algo** to wrap oneself up in sth

**enfurecer** [48] **1** *vt* to infuriate, to madden
  **2** **enfurecerse** *vpr (enfadarse)* to get furious; *Fig (mar)* to become rough

**enfurecimiento** *nm* anger, fury

**enfurruñado, -a** *adj* **estar e.** to be sulking

**enfurruñarse** *vpr Fam* to sulk

**engalanado, -a** *adj (persona)* dressed up; *(ciudad, coche)* decked out (**con** with)

**engalanar 1** *vt* to decorate
  **2** **engalanarse** *vpr (persona)* to dress up; *(ciudad)* to be decked out (**con** with)

**enganchar 1** *vt* (a) *(agarrar) (vagones)* to couple; *(remolque, caballos)* to hitch up; *(pez)* to hook (b) *(colgar de un gancho)* to hang up (c) *Fam Fig (atraer)* **e. a alguien para que haga algo** to rope sb into doing sth (d) *(pillar) (empleo, marido)* to land (oneself)
  **2** *vi Fam (hacer adicto)* to be addictive
  **3** **engancharse** *vpr* (a) *(prenderse)* **engancharse algo con** o **en algo** to catch sth on sth; **se le enganchó la falda en las zarzas** she caught her skirt on the brambles (b) *(alistarse)* to enlist, to join up (c) *(hacerse adicto)* to get hooked (**a** on)

**enganche** *nm* (a) *(de trenes)* coupling (b) *(gancho)* hook (c) *(reclutamiento)* enlistment (d) *Méx (depósito)* deposit

**enganchón** *nm (de ropa, tela)* snag

**engañabobos** *nm inv Fam* (a) *(cosa)* con (trick) (b) *(persona)* con man, con artist

**engañar 1** *vt* (a) *(mentir)* to deceive; **engaña a su marido** she cheats on her husband; **a mí no me engañas, sé que tienes cincuenta años** you can't fool me, I know you're fifty (b) *(estafar)* to cheat, to swindle; **e. a alguien como a un chino** to take sb for a ride (c) *(hacer más llevadero)* to appease; **e. el hambre** to take the edge off one's hunger
  **2** **engañarse** *vpr* (a) *(hacerse ilusiones)* to delude oneself (b) *(equivocarse)* to be wrong

**engañifa** *nf Fam (mentira, broma)* trick; *(estafa)* swindle

**engaño** *nm (mentira, broma)* deceit; *(estafa)* swindle; **llamarse a e.** to claim one has been cheated

**engañoso, -a** *adj (persona, palabras)* deceitful; *(aspecto, apariencia)* deceptive

**engarce** *nm* setting

**engarzar** [16] *vt* (a) *(encadenar) (abalorios)* to thread; *(perlas)* to string (b) *(diamante)* to set (c) *(palabras)* to string together

**engatusador, -ora** *Fam* **1** *adj* coaxing, cajoling
  **2** *nm,f* coaxer

**engatusar** *vt Fam* to sweet-talk; **e. a alguien para que haga algo** to sweet-talk sb into doing sth

**engendrar** *vt* (a) *(hijo, idea)* to conceive (b) *(originar)* to give rise to; **la falta de cariño engendra inseguridad** lack of affection gives rise to insecurity

**engendro** *nm* (a) *(ser deforme)* freak, deformed creature; *(niño)* malformed child (b) *Fig (obra fea o mala)* monstrosity

**englobar** *vt* to include

**engolosinarse** *vpr* **e. con** to develop a taste for

**engomar** *vt* (**a**) *(dar goma)* to put glue on (**b**) *(dar apresto)* to size

**engominado, -a** *adj (pelo)* slicked-back

**engordar 1** *vt* (**a**) *(animal)* to fatten up (**b**) *Fig (aumentar)* to swell

**2** *vi* (**a**) *(persona)* to put on weight; **he engordado seis kilos** I've put on six kilos (**b**) *(comida, bebida)* to be fattening

**engorde** *nm* fattening (up)

**engorro** *nm* nuisance

**engorroso, -a** *adj (molesto)* bothersome; *(físicamente)* cumbersome

**engranaje** *nm* (**a**) *(acción)* gearing (**b**) **engranajes** *(de reloj, piñón)* cogs; *Aut* gears (**c**) *Fig (enlace) (de ideas)* chain, sequence (**d**) *(aparato) (político, burocrático)* machinery

**engranar** *vt* (**a**) *(piezas)* to engage (**b**) *Fig (ideas)* to link, to connect

**engrandecer** [48] *vt* (**a**) *Fig (enaltecer)* to exalt (**b**) *(aumentar)* to increase, to enlarge

**engrandecimiento** *nm* (**a**) *(ensalzamiento)* enhancement (**b**) *(aumento)* increase

**engrasar** *vt (motor)* to lubricate; *(bisagra, mecanismo)* to oil; *(eje)* to grease; *(molde de horno)* to grease, to oil

**engrase** *nm (de motor)* lubrication; *(de mecanismo)* oiling

**engreído, -a 1** *adj* conceited, full of one's own importance

**2** *nm,f* conceited person

**engrescar** [61] *vt* to egg on, to incite

**engrosar** [65] *vt Fig (aumentar)* to swell; **la herencia pasó a e. la fortuna familiar** the inheritance went to swell the family fortune

**engrudo** *nm* paste

**enguantarse** *vpr* to put one's gloves on

**engullir** *vt* to gobble up, to wolf down

**enharinar** *vt* to flour

**enhebrar** *vt* (**a**) *(aguja)* to thread; *(perlas)* to string (**b**) *Fig (palabras)* to string together

**enhiesto, -a** *adj (derecho)* erect, upright; *(bandera)* raised

**enhorabuena 1** *nf* congratulations; **dar la e. a alguien por algo** to congratulate sb on sth

**2** *adv* **¡e. (por…)!** congratulations (on…)!

**enigma** *nm* enigma

**enigmático, -a** *adj* enigmatic

**enjabonado, -a 1** *adj* soapy

**2** *nm* soaping

**enjabonar** *vt (con jabón)* to soap; *Fig (dar coba)* to soft-soap

**enjambre** *nm también Fig* swarm

**enjaulado, -a** *adj* caged; *Fig* **como un perro e.** like a caged animal

**enjaular** *vt (en jaula)* to cage; *Fam Fig (en prisión)* to jail, to lock up

**enjoyar 1** *vt* to adorn with jewels

**2 enjoyarse** *vpr* to put on (one's) jewels

**enjuagar** [40] **1** *vt* to rinse

**2 enjuagarse** *vpr* to rinse oneself/one's mouth/one's hands etc; **enjuagarse el pelo** to rinse one's hair

**enjuague** *nm* rinse; **e. bucal** *(acción)* rinsing of the mouth; *(líquido)* mouthwash

**enjugar** [40] *vt* (**a**) *(secar)* to dry, to wipe away; **enjugó sus lágrimas** he dried his tears (**b**) *Fig (pagar) (deuda)* to pay off; *(déficit)* to cancel out

**enjuiciamiento** *nm* (**a**) *Der* trial (**b**) *(opinión)* judgment

**enjuiciar** [15] *vt* (**a**) *Der* to try (**b**) *(opinar)* to judge

**enjuto, -a** *adj (delgado)* lean

**enlace 1** *ver* **enlazar**

**2** *nm* (**a**) *(conexión) también Informát* link (**b**) *(persona)* go-between; **e. sindical** shop steward (**c**) *Quím* bond (**d**) *(boda)* **e. (matrimonial)** marriage (**e**) *(de trenes)* connection; **estación de e.** junction; **vía de e.** crossover

**enladrillado** *nm* brick paving

**enladrillar** *vt* to pave with bricks

**enlatar** *vt* to can, to tin

**enlazar** [16] **1** *vt* **e. algo a** *(atar)* to tie sth up to; *(trabar, relacionar)* to link o connect sth with

**2** *vi (trenes)* to connect (**en** at)

**3 enlazarse** *vpr* to become linked

**enlodar** *vt* to cover in mud

**enloquecedor, -ora** *adj* maddening

**enloquecer** [48] **1** *vt* (**a**) *(volver loco)* to drive mad (**b**) *Fig (gustar mucho)* to drive wild o crazy; **le enloquece el esquí** she's mad o crazy about skiing

**2** *vi* to go mad

**enloquecimiento** *nm* madness

**enlosar** *vt* to pave

**enlutado, -a** *adj* in mourning

**enlutar** *vt* (**a**) *(vestir de luto)* to dress in mourning (**b**) *Fig (entristecer)* to cast a shadow over

**enmaderar** *vt (pared)* to panel; *(suelo)* to lay the floorboards of

**enmadrarse** *vpr* to become too tied to one's mother

**enmarañar 1** *vt* (**a**) *(enredar)* to tangle (up) (**b**) *(complicar)* to complicate, to confuse

**2 enmarañarse** *vpr* (**a**) *(enredarse)* to become tangled (**b**) *(complicarse)* to become confused o complicated

**enmarcar** [61] **1** *vt* (**a**) *(cuadro)* to frame (**b**) *(dar un contexto)* **enmarcan su política energética dentro del respeto al medio**

**ambiente** their energy policy is placed within a framework of respect for the environment

**2 enmarcarse** *vpr* **las medidas se enmarcan dentro de la nueva política conciliadora** the measures form part of the new policy of reconciliation; **esta actuación se enmarca dentro de la convención de Viena** this action falls within the provisions of the Vienna convention

**enmascarado, -a1** *adj* masked

**2** *nm,f* masked man, *f* masked woman

**enmascarar** *vt (rostro)* to mask; *Fig (encubrir)* to disguise

**enmendar** [3] **1** *vt (error)* to correct; *(ley, dictamen)* to amend; *(comportamiento)* to mend; *(daño, perjuicio)* to redress; **enmendarle la plana a alguien** *(corregir)* to find fault with what sb has done; *(superar)* to go one better than sb

**2 enmendarse** *vpr* to mend one's ways

**enmienda** *nf* **(a)** *(acción)* **hacer propósito de e.** to promise to mend one's ways **(b)** *(en un texto)* correction **(c)** *(de ley, contrato)* amendment

**enmiendo** *etc ver* **enmendar**

**enmohecer** [48] **1** *vt (con moho)* to turn mouldy; *(metal)* to rust

**2 enmohecerse** *vpr (con moho)* to grow mouldy; *(metal, conocimientos)* to go rusty

**enmohecido, -a** *adj (con moho)* mouldy; *(metal, conocimientos)* rusty

**enmoquetado, -a1** *adj* carpeted

**2** *nm* carpeting

**enmoquetar** *vt* to carpet

**enmudecer** [48] **1** *vt* to silence

**2** *vi (callarse)* to fall silent, to go quiet; *(perder el habla)* to be struck dumb

**enmudecimiento** *nm* silence

**ennegrecer** [48] **1** *vt (poner negro)* to blacken

**2** *vi* to darken

**3 ennegrecerse** *vpr (ponerse negro)* to become blackened; **el cielo se ennegreció de repente** the sky suddenly darkened *o* grew dark

**ennoblecer** [48] *vt* **(a)** *Fig (dignificar)* **estas acciones lo ennoblecen** these actions do him credit **(b)** *(dar un título)* to ennoble

**enojadizo, -a** *adj* irritable, touchy

**enojar 1** *vt (enfadar)* to anger; *(molestar)* to annoy

**2 enojarse** *vpr (enfadarse)* to get angry **(con** with); *(molestarse)* to get annoyed **(con** with)

**enojo** *nm (enfado)* anger; *(molestia)* annoyance

**enojoso, -a** *adj (molesto)* annoying; *(delicado, espinoso)* awkward

**enología** *nf* oenology, study of wine

**enólogo, -a** *nm,f* oenologist, wine expert

**enorgullecer** [48] **1** *vt* to fill with pride

**2 enorgullecerse** *vpr* to be proud **(de** of);

**me enorgullezco de pertenecer a esta familia** I am proud to be a member of this family

**enorme** *adj (en tamaño)* enormous, huge; *(en gravedad)* monstrous

**enormidad** *nf* **(a)** *(de tamaño)* enormity, hugeness; **me gustó una e.** I liked it enormously **(b)** *Fig (despropósito)* crass remark/mistake etc

**enquistado, -a** *adj Fig (odio, costumbre)* deeprooted, deeply entrenched

**enquistamiento** *nm Med* encystment

**enquistarse** *vpr* to develop into a cyst; *Fig (odio, costumbre)* to take root, to become entrenched; *(proceso)* to become bogged down

**enraizar** [16] *vi (árbol)* to take root; *(persona)* to put down roots

**enramada** *nf* **(a)** *(espesura)* branches, canopy **(b)** *(cobertizo)* bower

**enrarecer** [48] **1** *vt Fig (situación, ambiente)* to make strained

**2 enrarecerse** *vpr (atmósfera)* to become rarefied; *Fig (situación, ambiente)* to become strained

**enredadera** *nf* creeper

**enredador, -ora 1** *adj (travieso)* naughty, mischievous; *(chismoso)* gossiping

**2** *nm,f (travieso)* mischief-maker; *(chismoso)* gossip

**enredar 1** *vt* **(a)** *(madeja, pelo)* to tangle up; *(situación, asunto)* to complicate, to confuse **(b)** *Fig (implicar)* **e. a alguien (en)** to embroil sb (in), to involve sb (in) **(c)** *Fig (entretener)* to bother, to annoy

**2** *vi Fam* to get up to mischief; **e. con algo** to fiddle with *o* mess about with sth

**3 enredarse** *vpr* **(a)** *(plantas)* to climb; *(madeja, pelo)* to get tangled up; *(situación, asunto)* to become confused; **la cola de la cometa se enredó en unas ramas** the tail of the kite got tangled in some branches **(b)** *(meterse)* **enredarse en un asunto** to get mixed up *o* involved in something; **enredarse a hacer algo** to start doing sth **(c)** *Fam (sentimentalmente)* **enredarse con** to get involved *o* have an affair with

**enredo** *nm* **(a)** *(maraña)* tangle, knot **(b)** *(lío)* mess, complicated affair; *(asunto ilícito)* shady affair; *Teatro & Cine* **comedia de e.** farce **(c)** *(amoroso)* (love) affair

**enrejado** *nm* **(a)** *(barrotes) (de balcón, verja)* railings; *(de jaula, celda, ventana)* bars **(b)** *(de cañas)* trellis

**enrejar** *vt (ventanas)* to bar

**enrevesado, -a** *adj* complex, complicated

**enriquecedor, -ora** *adj* enriching

**enriquecer** [48] **1** *vt* **(a)** *(hacer rico)* to bring wealth to, to make rich **(b)** *Fig (sustancia)* to enrich

**2 enriquecerse** *vpr* to get rich

**enriquecimiento** *nm* enrichment

**enrojecer** [48] **1** *vt* to redden, to turn red
**2** *vi* (*por calor*) to flush; (*por turbación*) to blush
**3** **enrojecerse** *vpr* (*por calor*) to flush; (*por turbación*) to blush

**enrojecimiento** *nm* (a) (*de la piel*) redness, red mark (b) (*de las mejillas*) blushing

**enrolar 1** *vt* to enlist
**2** **enrolarse** *vpr* (*en la marina*) to enlist (**en** in); **enrolarse en un barco** to join a ship's crew

**enrollar 1** *vt* (a) (*arrollar*) to roll up (b) *muy Fam* (*gustar*) **me enrolla mucho** I love it, I think it's great
**2** **enrollarse** *vpr Fam* (a) (*tener relaciones*) to get involved *o* have an affair (**con** with); **está enrollado con una sueca** he's going out with a Swedish woman (b) (*hablar*) to go on (and on); **se enrolla como una persiana** he could talk the hind legs off a donkey

**enroque** *nm* (*en ajedrez*) castle

**enroscar** [61] *vt* (a) (*tuerca*) to screw in; (*tapa*) to screw on (b) (*enrollar*) to roll up; (*cuerpo, cola*) to curl up

**ensaimada** *nf* = cake made of sweet coiled pastry

**ensalada** *nf* (a) *Culin* salad (b) *Fam Fig (lío)* mishmash

**ensaladera** *nf* salad bowl

**ensaladilla** *nf* **e. (rusa)** Russian salad, = salad of boiled, diced potatoes and carrots or peas, in mayonnaise

**ensalmo** *nm* incantation, spell; **como por e.** as if by magic

**ensalzamiento** *nm* praise

**ensalzar** [16] *vt* to praise

**ensamblado, -a 1** *adj* (*mueble, piezas*) assembled
**2** *nm* assembly

**ensamblador, -ora 1** *nm,f* (*persona*) joiner
**2** *nm Informát* assembler

**ensambladura** *nf*, **ensamblaje** *nm* (*acción*) assembly; (*unión*) joint

**ensamblar** *vt también Informát* to assemble; (*madera*) to join

**ensanchamiento** *nm* (*de orificio, calle*) widening; (*de ropa*) letting out

**ensanchar 1** *vt* (*orificio, calle*) to widen; (*ropa*) to let out; (*ciudad*) to expand
**2** **ensancharse** *vpr* (*orificio, calle*) to widen, to open out

**ensanche** *nm* (a) (*de calle*) widening (b) (*en la ciudad*) new suburb

**ensangrentado, -a** *adj* bloodstained, covered in blood

**ensangrentar** [3] *vt* to cover with blood

**ensañamiento** *nm* viciousness, savagery

**ensañarse** *vpr* **e. con** to torment, to treat cruelly

**ensartado, -a** *adj* (*perlas*) strung; **trozos de carne ensartados en un pincho** pieces of meat threaded on a skewer

**ensartar** *vt* (a) (*perlas*) to string (b) (*atravesar*) (*torero*) to gore; (*puñal*) to plunge, to bury; **ensartó las verduras en pinchos** he threaded the vegetables on skewers

**ensayar** *vt* (a) (*experimentar*) to test (b) *Teatro* to rehearse

**ensayista** *nmf* essayist

**ensayo** *nm* (a) *Teatro* rehearsal; **e. general** dress rehearsal (b) (*prueba*) test; **le salió al primer e.** he got it at the first attempt (c) *Lit* essay (d) (*en rugby*) try

**enseguida** *adv* (*inmediatamente*) immediately, at once; (*pronto*) very soon; **llegará e.** he'll be here any minute now; **vino a las seis, pero se fue e.** he came at six, but he left soon after

**ensenada** *nf* cove, inlet

**enseña** *nf* ensign

**enseñante** *nmf* teacher

**enseñanza** *nf* (*educación*) education; (*instrucción*) teaching; **enseñanzas** (*de maestro*) teachings; **e. estatal** *o* **pública** state education; **e. media/primaria** secondary/primary education; **e. personificada** personal *o* individual tutoring; **e. privada** private (sector) education; **e. superior/universitaria** higher/university education

**enseñar** *vt* (a) (*instruir, aleccionar*) to teach; **e. a alguien a hacer algo** to teach sb (how) to do sth (b) (*mostrar*) to show; **enséñame tu vestido nuevo** show me your new dress; **va enseñando los hombros provocativamente** her shoulders are provocatively uncovered

**enseñorearse** *vpr* to take possession (**de** of)

**enseres** *nmpl* (a) (*efectos personales*) belongings (b) (*muebles, accesorios*) furnishings

**ensillado, -a** *adj* (*caballo*) saddled

**ensillar** *vt* (*caballo*) to saddle up

**ensimismado, -a** *adj* (*enfrascado*) absorbed; (*pensativo*) lost in thought

**ensimismamiento** *nm* self-absorption

**ensimismarse** *vpr* (*enfrascarse*) to become absorbed; (*abstraerse*) to lose oneself in thought

**ensoberbecer** [48] **1** *vt* to fill with pride
**2** **ensoberbecerse** *vpr* to become puffed up with pride

**ensombrecer** [48] **1** *vt también Fig* to cast a shadow over
**2** **ensombrecerse** *vpr* to darken

**ensoñación** *nf* daydream; **ni por e.** not even in one's wildest dreams

**ensopar** *vt Am* to soak

**ensordecedor, -ora** *adj* deafening

**ensordecer** [48] **1** *vt* (**a**) *(causar sordera)* to cause to go deaf (**b**) *(sujeto: sonido)* to deafen
**2** *vi* to go deaf

**ensordecimiento** *nm* deafness

**ensortijar** *vt* to curl

**ensuciar** [15] **1** *vt* to (make) dirty; *Fig (desprestigiar)* to sully, to tarnish; **e. el nombre de alguien** to sully sb's name *o* reputation
**2 ensuciarse** *vpr* to get dirty; **la alfombra se ha ensuciado de pintura** the carpet has got paint on it

**ensueño** *nm también Fig* dream; **de e.** dream, ideal; **tienen una casa de e.** they have a dream house

**entablado** *nm (armazón)* wooden platform; *(suelo)* floorboards

**entablar** *vt* (**a**) *(suelo)* to put down floorboards on (**b**) *(iniciar) (conversación, amistad)* to strike up; *(negocio)* to start up (**c**) *(entablillar)* to put in a splint

**entablillar** *vt* to put in a splint

**entallado, -a** *adj (vestido, chaqueta)* tailored

**entallar** *vt (prenda)* to take in at the waist

**entarimado** *nm (plataforma)* wooden platform; *(suelo)* floorboards

**entarimar** *vt (suelo)* to put down floorboards on

**ente** *nm* (**a**) *(ser)* being (**b**) *(corporación)* body, organization; **e. público** *(institución)* = state-owned body *o* institution; *(televisión)* = Spanish state broadcasting company (**c**) *Fam (personaje)* odd bod

**entelequia** *nf (fantasía)* pipe dream

**entendederas** *nfpl Fam* brains; **ser corto de e.** to be a bit dim

**entendedor, -ora** *nm,f Prov* **al buen e. le sobran las palabras** *o* **pocas palabras bastan** a word to the wise is sufficient

**entender** [66] **1** *vt* (**a**) *(comprender)* to understand; **¿tú qué entiendes por "amistad"?** what do you understand by "friendship"?; **dar a e. que...** to imply (that)...; **no te entiendo, habla más despacio** I don't understand you, could you speak more slowly?; **no entiendo cómo puede gustarte Arturo** I don't know what you see in Arturo
(**b**) *(darse cuenta)* to realize
(**c**) *(juzgar)* to think; **yo no lo entiendo así** I don't see it that way
**2** *vi* (**a**) *(comprender)* to understand
(**b**) *(saber)* **e. de algo** to know about sth; **e. poco/algo de** to know very little/a little about
**3** *nm* **a mi e....** the way I see it...

**4 entenderse** *vpr* (**a**) *(comprenderse) (uno mismo)* to know what one means; *(dos personas)* to understand each other
(**b**) *(llevarse bien)* to get on
(**c**) *(ponerse de acuerdo)* to reach an agreement
(**d**) *(comunicarse)* to communicate (with each other)
(**e**) *(amorosamente)* to have an affair (**con** with)

**entendido, -a 1** *adj* (**a**) *(comprendido)* understood; **¿e.?** (is that) understood?; **¡e.!** all right!, okay!; **no darse por e.** to pretend one hasn't heard (**b**) *(versado)* expert
**2** *nm,f* expert (**en** on)

**entendimiento** *nm (comprensión)* understanding; *(juicio)* judgment; *(inteligencia)* mind, intellect

**entente** *nf Pol* entente cordiale; *Com* agreement

**enterado, -a 1** *adj* well-informed (**en** about); **estar e. de algo** to be aware of sth; **darse por e.** to indicate that one is aware of sth; **no darse por e.** to turn a deaf ear
**2** *nm,f Irón* know-all

**enterar 1** *vt* **e. a alguien de algo** to inform sb about sth
**2 enterarse** *vpr* (**a**) *(descubrir, saber)* to find out (**de** about); **¿te has enterado de la noticia?** have you heard the news?; **¡entérate de una vez! ¡yo no soy tu criado!** get this straight – I'm not your servant! (**b**) *Fam (comprender)* to get it, to understand (**c**) *(darse cuenta)* **enterarse (de algo)** to realize (sth); **sus padres no se enteraron de nada** his parents never knew a thing about it (**d**) *(expresiones)* **¡para que te enteres!** I'll have you know!, as a matter of fact!; **¡te vas a e.!** you'll know all about it!, you'll catch it!

**entereza** *nf (serenidad)* composure, self-possession; *(honradez)* integrity; *(firmeza)* firmness

**enternecedor, -ora** *adj* touching, moving

**enternecer** [48] **1** *vt* to move, to touch
**2 enternecerse** *vpr* to be moved

**enternecimiento** *nm* **el desamparo de los refugiados consiguió su e.** he softened when he saw how helpless the refugees were

**entero, -a 1** *adj* (**a**) *(completo)* whole; **por e.** entirely, completely; **vi la película entera** I watched the whole film; **este cristal está e.** this pane is in one piece (**b**) *(sereno)* composed (**c**) *(honrado)* upright, honest
**2** *nm Fin* point

**enterrador, -ora** *nm,f* gravedigger

**enterramiento** *nm (acción, ceremonia)* burial; *(lugar)* burial site

**enterrar** [3] **1** *vt* (**a**) *(bajo tierra)* to bury (**b**) *Fig (olvidar)* to forget about

**2 enterrarse** *vpr Fig* **enterrarse en vida** to hide oneself away

**entibiar** [15] **1** *vt* (a) *(enfriar)* to cool (b) *(templar)* to warm

**2 entibiarse** *vpr* to cool; *Fig* **sus relaciones se entibiaron** *(de pareja)* their relationship lost its passion; *(diplomáticas, de amistad)* relations between them became more distant

**entidad** *nf* (a) *(corporación)* body; *(empresa)* firm, company; **e. bancaria** bank; **e. de crédito** lending institution (b) *(en filosofía)* entity (c) *(importancia)* importance; **de e.** of importance

**entiendo** *etc ver* **entender**

**entierro 1** *ver* **enterrar**

**2** *nm* *(acción)* burial; *(ceremonia)* funeral

**entlo.** *(abrev de* **entresuelo***)* mezzanine

**entoldado** *nm* *(toldo)* awning; *(para fiestas, bailes)* marquee

**entoldar** *vt* to cover with an awning

**entomología** *nf* entomology

**entomólogo, -a** *nm,f* entomologist

**entonación** *nf* intonation

**entonar 1** *vt* (a) *(cantar)* to sing (b) *(tonificar)* to pick up; **esta sopa te entonará** this soup will do you the world of good

**2** *vi* (a) *(al cantar)* to sing in tune (b) *(armonizar)* **e. (con algo)** to match (sth)

**3 entonarse** *vpr* to become tipsy *o* merry; **se entonó con una copa de oporto** he took a glass of port as a pick-me-up

**entonces** *adv* then; **desde e.** since then; **en** *o* **por aquel e.** at that time; **e., ¿vienes o no?** are you coming or not, then?

**entontecer** [48] *vt* **e. a alguien** to dull sb's brain

**entornado, -a** *adj* *(puerta, ventana)* ajar

**entornar** *vt* to half-close

**entorno** *nm* environment, surroundings

**entorpecer** [48] *vt* (a) *(debilitar)* *(movimientos)* to hinder; *(miembros)* to numb; *(mente)* to cloud (b) *(dificultar)* to obstruct, to hinder; *(tráfico)* to hold up, to slow down

**entorpecimiento** *nm* (a) *(debilitamiento)* *(físico)* numbness; *(mental)* haziness (b) *(dificultad)* hindrance; **el accidente provocó un e. del tráfico** the accident caused a hold-up in traffic

**entrada** *nf* (a) *(acción)* entry; *(llegada)* arrival; **prohibida la e.** *(en letrero)* no entry; **hizo una e. espectacular** she made a spectacular entrance

(b) *(lugar)* entrance; *(recibidor)* entrance hall; **e.** *(en letrero)* entrance, way in; **te espero a la e. del cine** I'll meet you outside the cinema

(c) *Tec* inlet, intake

(d) *(en espectáculos)* *(billete)* ticket; *(recaudación)* receipts, takings; **e. libre** *o* **gratuita** admission free; **sacar una e.** to buy a ticket; **no hay entradas** *(en letrero)* sold out

(e) *(público)* audience; *Dep* attendance

(f) *(pago inicial)* down payment

(g) *(en contabilidad)* income

(h) *(plato)* starter

(i) *(en la frente)* **tener entradas** to have a receding hairline

(j) *(en un diccionario)* entry

(k) *(principio)* beginning, start; **de e. no me gustó, pero...** at first I didn't like it, but...; **me di cuenta de e. de que algo andaba mal** I realized from the start that something was wrong

(l) *Informát* input

**entrado, -a** *adj* **e. el otoño** once we're into autumn; **entrada la noche** once night has set in; **e. en años** elderly; **e. en carnes** portly, rather large

**entramado** *nm* framework

**entramar** *vt* to make the framework of

**entrampado, -a** *adj Fam* *(endeudado)* **estar e.** to be up to one's neck in debt

**entrante 1** *adj* *(año, mes)* coming; *(presidente, gobierno)* incoming

**2** *nm* (a) *(plato)* starter (b) *(hueco)* recess

**entrañable** *adj* *(amigo)* very dear; *(reunión)* intimate

**entrañar** *vt* to involve

**entrañas** *nfpl* (a) *(vísceras)* entrails, insides; *Fig* **arrancarle a alguien las e.** to break sb's heart; *Fig* **no tener e.** to be heartless (b) *Fig* *(centro, esencia)* heart; **las e. de la Tierra** the bowels of the earth

**entrar 1** *vi* (a) *(introducirse)* *(viniendo)* to enter, to come in; *(yendo)* to enter, to go in; **e. en algo** to enter sth, to come/go into sth; **entré por la ventana** I got in through the window

(b) *(penetrar)* to go in; **e. en algo** to go into sth

(c) *(caber)* to fit *(en* in); **este anillo no me entra** I can't get this ring on my finger; **el pie no me entra en el zapato** I can't get this shoe on

(d) *(incorporarse)* **e. (en algo)** *(colegio, empresa)* to start (at sth); *(club, partido político)* to join (sth); **e. de** *(botones, ayudante)* to start off as

(e) *(empezar)* **e. a hacer algo** to start doing sth

(f) *(participar)* to join in; **e. en** *(discusión, polémica)* to join in; *(negocio)* to get in on; **no entremos en cuestiones morales** let's not get involved in moral issues; **yo ahí ni entro ni salgo** it has nothing to do with me

(g) *(estar incluido)* **e. en, e. dentro de** to be included in

(h) *(figurar)* **e. en** to belong to; **entro en el grupo de los disconformes** I number among the dissidents

**(i)** *(estado físico, de ánimo)* **le entraron ganas de hablar** he suddenly felt like talking; **me está entrando frío** I'm getting cold; **me entró mucha pena** I was filled with pity

**(j)** *(período de tiempo)* to start; **el verano entra el 21 de junio** summer starts on 21st June; **e. en** *(edad, vejez)* to reach; *(año nuevo)* to start

**(k)** *(cantidad)* **¿cuántos entran en un kilo?** how many do you get to the kilo?

**(l)** *(concepto, asignatura)* **no le entra la geometría** he can't get the hang of geometry

**(m)** *Aut* to engage; **no entra la tercera** it won't go into third gear

**2** *vt* **(a)** *(introducir)* to bring in

**(b)** *(prenda de vestir)* to take in

**(c)** *(acometer)* to approach, to deal with; **a ése no hay por donde entrarle** there's no way of getting through to him

**entre** *prep* **(a)** *(en medio de dos)* between; **e. nosotros** *(en confianza)* between you and me, between ourselves; **era un color e. verde y azul** the colour was somewhere between green and blue; **su estado de ánimo estaba e. la alegría y la emoción** his state of mind was somewhere between o was a mixture of joy and excitement; **e. una cosa y otra** what with one thing and another

**(b)** *(en medio de muchos)* among, amongst; **estaba e. los asistentes** she was among those present; **estuvo e. los mejores** he was one of o amongst the best; **e. hombres y mujeres somos más de cien** there are over a hundred of us, men and women together; **e. sí** amongst themselves; **discutían e. sí** they were arguing with each other

**entreabierto** *participio ver* **entreabrir**

**entreabrir** *vt* to half-open

**entreacto** *nm* interval

**entrecejo** *nm* = space between the eyebrows; **fruncir el e.** to frown

**entrecerrar** [3] *vt* to half-close

**entrechocar** [61] **1** *vt (espadas)* to clash

**2** *vi (dientes)* to chatter

**entrecomillado, -a 1** *adj* in quotation marks

**2** *nm* text in quotation marks

**entrecomillar** *vt* to put in quotation marks

**entrecortado, -a** *adj (voz, habla)* faltering; *(respiración)* laboured; *(señal, sonido)* intermittent

**entrecot, entrecote** *nm* entrecôte

**entrecruzar** [16] **1** *vt (entrelazar)* to interweave; *(dedos)* to link together

**2** **entrecruzarse** *vpr* to interweave; **sus destinos se entrecruzaban** their destinies were intertwined

**entredicho** *nm* **estar en e.** to be in doubt; **poner en e.** to question, to call into question

**entrega** *nf* **(a)** *(acto de entregar)* handing over; *(de pedido, paquete)* delivery; *(de premios)* presentation; **hacer e. de algo a alguien** to hand sth over to sb; **e. a domicilio** home delivery **(b)** *(dedicación)* devotion **(a** to) **(c)** *(fascículo)* **por entregas** in instalments

**entregar** [40] **1** *vt (dar)* to hand over; *(pedido, paquete)* to deliver; *(examen, informe)* to hand in; *(persona)* to turn over

**2** **entregarse** *vpr* **(a)** *(rendirse) (soldado, ejército)* to surrender; *(criminal)* to turn oneself in **(b)** **entregarse a** *(persona, trabajo)* to devote oneself to; *(vicio, pasión)* to give oneself over to

**entreguerras: de entreguerras** *loc adj* **período/literatura de e.** time/literature between the wars

**entrelazar** [16] *vt* to interlace, to interlink

**entrelínea** *nf* space between two lines

**entremedias, entremedio** *adv* in between

**entremés** *( pl* **entremeses)** *nm* **(a)** *Culin* entremeses hors d'œuvres **(b)** *Lit* = short, amusing one-act play

**entremeter 1** *vt* to insert, to put in

**2** **entremeterse** *vpr (inmiscuirse)* to meddle **(en** in)

**entremetido, -a 1** *adj* meddling

**2** *nm,f* meddler

**entremezclar 1** *vt* to mix up

**2** **entremezclarse** *vpr* to mix

**entrenador, -ora** *nm,f* coach; *(seleccionador)* manager

**entrenamiento** *nm* training

**entrenar 1** *vt & vi* to train

**2** **entrenarse** *vpr* to train

**entreoír** [46] *vt* to half-hear

**entrepierna** *nf* crotch; **muy** *Fam* **pasarse algo por la e.** to piss on sth from a great height

**entresacar** [61] *vt* to pick out

**entresijos** *nmpl* ins and outs

**entresuelo** *nm* mezzanine

**entretanto 1** *adv* meanwhile

**2** *nm* **en el e.** in the meantime

**entretecho** *nm* *Chile, Col* loft, attic

**entretejer** *vt* to interweave

**entretela** *nf (de ropa)* inner lining; *Fig* **entretelas** innermost heart

**entretención** *nf* *Am* entertainment

**entretener** [67] **1** *vt* **(a)** *(despistar)* to distract **(b)** *(retrasar)* to hold up, to keep **(c)** *(divertir)* to entertain **(d)** *(mantener)* to keep alive, to sustain

**2** **entretenerse** *vpr* **(a)** *(despistarse)* to get distracted **(b)** *(retrasarse)* to be held up **(c)** *(divertirse)* to amuse oneself

**entretenido, -a** *adj* entertaining, enjoyable

**entretenimiento** *nm* (a) *(acción)* entertainment (b) *(pasatiempo)* pastime

**entretiempo: de entretiempo** *loc adj* **ropa de e.** mild-weather clothes

**entrever** [72] **1** *vt* (a) *(vislumbrar)* to barely make out; *(por un instante)* to glimpse (b) *Fig (adivinar)* to see signs of

 **2 entreverse** *vpr* to be barely visible; *Fig* **no se entrevé una solución** there's no sign of a solution

**entreverar** *CSur* **1** *vt* to mix

 **2 entreverarse** *vpr* to get tangled

**entrevero** *nm CSur* tangle, mess

**entrevista** *nf* interview; **e. de trabajo** job interview

**entrevistado, -a** *nm,f* interviewee

**entrevistador, -ora** *nm,f* interviewer

**entrevistar 1** *vt* to interview

 **2 entrevistarse** *vpr* to have a meeting (**con** with)

**entrevisto** *participio ver* **entrever**

**entristecer** [48] **1** *vt* to make sad

 **2 entristecerse** *vpr* to become sad

**entristecimiento** *nm* sadness

**entrometerse** *vpr* to interfere (**en** in)

**entrometido, -a 1** *adj* interfering

 **2** *nm,f* meddler

**entrometimiento** *nm* meddling

**entromparse** *vpr Fam* to get legless

**entroncamiento** *nm (parentesco)* relationship, connection

**entroncar** [61] *vi* (a) *(emparentarse)* to become related (**con** to) (b) *(trenes)* to connect (c) *Fig (relacionarse)* to be related (**con** to)

**entronización** *nf* coronation, enthronement; *Fig* **sus películas son la e. del mal gusto** his films are the height of bad taste

**entronizar** [16] *vt* to crown, to enthrone; *Fig* to exalt, to praise to the skies

**entropía** *nf Fís* entropy

**entubar** *vt* to fit tubes to, to tube; *Med* to put tubes/a tube into

**entuerto** *nm* wrong, injustice; **deshacer entuertos** to right wrongs

**entumecer** [48] **1** *vt* to numb

 **2 entumecerse** *vpr* to become numb

**entumecido, -a** *adj* numb

**entumecimiento** *nm* numbness

**enturbiar** [15] *también Fig* **1** *vt* to cloud

 **2 enturbiarse** *vpr* to become cloudy

**entusiasmar 1** *vt* (a) *(animar)* to fill with enthusiasm (b) *(gustar)* **le entusiasma la música** he loves music

 **2 entusiasmarse** *vpr* to get excited (**con** about)

**entusiasmo** *nm* enthusiasm

**entusiasta 1** *adj* enthusiastic

 **2** *nmf* enthusiast

**entusiástico, -a** *adj* enthusiastic

**enumeración** *nf* enumeration, listing

**enumerar** *vt* to enumerate, to list

**enunciación** *nf*, **enunciado** *nm* formulation, enunciation

**enunciar** [15] *vt* to formulate, to enunciate

**envainar** *vt* to sheathe

**envalentonamiento** *nm* boldness

**envalentonar 1** *vt* to urge on, to fill with courage

 **2 envalentonarse** *vpr* to become daring

**envanecer** [48] **1** *vt* to make vain

 **2 envanecerse** *vpr* to become vain

**envanecimiento** *nm* vanity

**envarado, -a 1** *adj* stiff, formal

 **2** *nm,f* stiff *o* formal person

**envasado** *nm (en bolsas, cajas)* packing; *(en latas)* canning; *(en botellas)* bottling; **e. al vacío** vacuum packed

**envasar** *vt (en bolsas, cajas)* to package; *(en latas)* to can; *(en botellas)* to bottle

**envase** *nm* (a) *(envasado) (en bolsas, cajas)* packing; *(en latas)* canning; *(en botellas)* bottling (b) *(recipiente)* container; *(botella)* bottle; **e. desechable** disposable container; **e. sin retorno** non-returnable bottle; **e. (retornable)** returnable empty bottle

**envejecer** [48] **1** *vi (hacerse viejo)* to grow old; *(parecer viejo)* to age

 **2** *vt* to age

**envejecido, -a** *adj (de edad)* old; *(de aspecto)* aged

**envejecimiento** *nm* ageing

**envenenamiento** *nm* poisoning

**envenenar 1** *vt* to poison

 **2 envenenarse** *vpr* to poison oneself; *Fig (relación)* to become bitter

**envergadura** *nf* (a) *(importancia)* size, extent; *(complejidad)* complexity; **una reforma de gran e.** a wide-ranging reform (b) *(de ave, avión)* wingspan

**envés** (*pl* **enveses**) *nm (de hoja)* reverse (side), back; *(de tela)* wrong side

**enviado, -a** *nm,f* (a) *Pol* envoy (b) *Prensa* correspondent; **e. especial** special correspondent

**enviar** [34] *vt* to send

**enviciar** [15] **1** *vt* to addict, to get hooked

 **2 enviciarse** *vpr* to become addicted

**envidia** *nf* envy; **tener e. de** to envy

**envidiable** *adj* enviable

**envidiar** [15] *vt* to envy

**envidioso, -a 1** *adj* envious

 **2** *nm,f* envious person

**envilecer** [48] **1** *vt* to debase

**2 envilecerse** *vpr* to become debased

**envilecimiento** *nm* debasement

**envío** *nm* (a) *Com* dispatch; *(de correo)* delivery; *(de víveres, mercancías)* consignment (b) *(paquete)* package

**envite** *nm* (a) *(en el juego)* raise (b) *(ofrecimiento)* offer

**enviudar** *vi* to be widowed

**envoltorio** *nm,* **envoltura** *nf* wrapper, wrapping

**envolvente** *adj* enveloping

**envolver** [43] **1** *vt* (a) *(embalar)* to wrap (up) (b) *(enrollar)* to wind (c) *(implicar)* **e. a alguien en** to involve sb in (d) *Fig (dominar)* to envelop, to take over

**2 envolverse** *vpr* **envolverse en** *o* **con algo** to wrap oneself in sth

**envuelto** *participio ver* **envolver**

**envuelvo** *etc ver* **envolver**

**enyesar** *vt (brazo, pierna)* to put in plaster; *(pared)* to plaster

**enzarzar** [16] **1** *vt* to entangle, to embroil

**2 enzarzarse** *vpr* **enzarzarse en** to get entangled *o* embroiled in

**enzima** *nf* enzyme

**eólico, -a** *adj* **energía eólica** wind energy

**epatar** *vt* to shock

**e.p.d.** *(abrev de* **en paz descanse)** RIP

**épica** *nf* epic

**epicentro** *nm* epicentre

**épico, -a** *adj* epic

**epicureísmo** *nm* Epicureanism

**epicúreo, -a** *adj & nm,f* Epicurean

**epidemia** *nf* epidemic

**epidémico, -a** *adj* epidemic

**epidemiología** *nf Med* epidemiology

**epidérmico, -a** *adj Anat* epidermic

**epidermis** *nf inv Anat* epidermis

**epidural** *adj & nf Med* epidural

**Epifanía** *nf Rel* Epiphany

**epífisis** *nf inv Anat* pineal gland

**epiglotis** *nf inv Anat* epiglottis

**epígrafe** *nm* heading

**epigrafía** *nf* epigraphy

**epigrama** *nm* epigram

**epilepsia** *nf* epilepsy

**epiléptico, -a** *adj & nm,f* epileptic

**epílogo** *nm* epilogue

**episcopado** *nm Rel* (a) *(dignidad)* episcopate, episcopacy (b) *(territorio)* diocese

**episcopal** *adj* episcopal

**episodio** *nm* (a) *(de serie, libro)* episode (b) *(suceso)* event

**epistemología** *nf* epistemology

**epístola** *nf* (a) *Formal (carta)* epistle (b) *Rel* Epistle

**epistolar** *adj Formal* epistolary

**epistolario** *nm* collected letters

**epitafio** *nm* epitaph

**epitelio** *nm Anat* epithelium

**epíteto** *nm* epithet

**epítome** *nm* summary, synopsis

**e.p.m.** *(abrev de* **en propia mano)** by hand

**época** *nf (período)* period; *(estación)* season; **coche de é.** vintage car; **vestido de é.** period dress; **en aquella é.** at that time; **hacer é.** to become a symbol of its time

**epónimo, -a 1** *adj* eponymous

**2** *nm* eponym

**epopeya** *nf (poema)* epic; *Fig (hazaña)* feat

**épsilon** *nf* epsilon

**equidad** *nf* fairness

**equidistante** *adj* equidistant

**equidistar** *vi* to be equidistant (**de** from)

**equilátero, -a** *adj Geom* equilateral

**equilibrado, -a** *adj* (a) *(igualado)* balanced (b) *(sensato)* sensible

**equilibrar 1** *vt* to balance

**2 equilibrarse** *vpr* to balance

**equilibrio** *nm* balance; **mantener algo en e.** to balance sth; **mantener/perder el e.** to keep/lose one's balance; *Fig* **hacer equilibrios** to perform a balancing act; **e. ecológico** ecological balance

**equilibrismo** *nm (en trapecio)* trapeze; *(en cuerda)* tightrope walking

**equilibrista** *nmf (trapecista)* trapeze artist; *(en cuerda)* tightrope walker

**equino, -a** *adj* equine

**equinoccial** *adj* equinoctial

**equinoccio** *nm* equinox

**equipaje** *nm Br* luggage, *US* baggage; **hacer el e.** to pack; **e. de mano** hand luggage

**equipamiento** *nm (acción)* equipping; *(equipo)* equipment

**equipar 1** *vt* **e. a alguien (de** *o* **con)** *(de instrumentos, herramientas)* to equip sb (with); *(de ropa)* to fit sb out (with)

**2 equiparse** *vpr* to equip oneself (**de** *o* **con** with)

**equiparable** *adj* comparable (**a** to)

**equiparar 1** *vt* to compare

**2 equipararse** *vpr* to be compared

**equipo** *nm* (a) *(personas, jugadores)* team; **e. de rescate** rescue team; *Dep* **e. visitante** visiting team (b) *(equipamiento)* equipment; **e. de oficina** office equipment (c) *(de novia)* trousseau; *(de soldado)* kit; *(de colegial)* uniform (d) *(de música)* system; **e. de sonido** sound system

**equis 1** *adj* X; **un número e. de personas** x number of people

**2** *nf inv* **la letra e.** the letter x

**equitación** *nf* (*arte*) equestrianism; (*actividad*) horse riding

**equitativo, -a** *adj* fair, even-handed

**equivalencia** *nf* equivalence

**equivalente** *adj & nm* equivalent

**equivaler** [70] *vi* to be equivalent (**a** to); *Fig* (*significar*) to amount (**a** to)

**equivocación** *nf* mistake; **por e.** by mistake

**equivocado, -a** *adj* mistaken

**equivocar** [61] **1** *vt* **e. algo con algo** to mistake sth for sth; **e. el camino** to take the wrong road; **equivoqué la fecha** I got the date wrong

**2 equivocarse** *vpr* to be wrong; **equivocarse en algo** to make a mistake in sth; **se equivocó de nombre/puerta** he got the wrong name/door

**equívoco, -a1** *adj* (*ambiguo*) ambiguous, equivocal (**b**) (*sospechoso*) suspicious

**2** *nm* misunderstanding

**era 1** *ver* **ser**

**2** *nf* (**a**) (*período*) era; **e. cristiana/geológica** Christian/geological era (**b**) (*para trillar*) threshing floor

**erario** *nm* funds; **e. público** exchequer

**Erasmus** *nm inv* (*abrev de* **European Action Scheme for the Mobility of University Students**) Erasmus; **una beca/un estudiante E.** an Erasmus scholarship/student

**erección** *nf* erection

**eréctil** *adj* erectile

**erecto, -a** *adj* erect

**eremita** *nmf* hermit

**eres** *ver* **ser**

**ergonómico, -a** *adj* ergonomic

**erguir** [30] **1** *vt* to raise

**2 erguirse** *vpr* to rise up

**erial** *nm* uncultivated land

**erice** *etc ver* **erizar**

**erigir** [26] **1** *vt* (**a**) (*construir*) to erect, to build (**b**) (*nombrar*) to name

**2 erigirse** *vpr* **erigirse en** to set oneself up as

**eritema** *nm Med* skin rash

**Eritrea** *n* Eritrea

**erizado, -a** *adj* (**a**) (*pelo*) on end; (*con púas, espinas*) spiky (**b**) *Fig* (*lleno*) **e. de** plagued with

**erizar** [16] **1** *vt* to cause to stand on end

**2 erizarse** *vpr* (*pelo*) to stand on end; (*persona*) to stiffen

**erizo 1** *nm* (**a**) (*mamífero*) hedgehog (**b**) (*pez*) globefish; **e. de mar** sea urchin

**2** *adj* **pez e.** globefish

**ermita** *nf* hermitage

**ermitaño, -a** *nm,f* hermit

**erógeno, -a** *adj* erogenous

**eros** *nm inv* eros

**erosión** *nf* erosion

**erosionar 1** *vt* to erode

**2 erosionarse** *vpr* to erode

**erosivo, -a** *adj* erosive

**erótica** *nf* **la e. del poder** the thrill of power

**erótico, -a** *adj* erotic

**erotismo** *nm* eroticism

**erradicación** *nf* eradication

**erradicar** [61] *vt* to eradicate

**errado, -a** *adj* (*tiro*) wide of the mark, missed; (*razonamiento*) mistaken

**errante** *adj* wandering

**errar** [31] **1** *vt* (*vocación, camino*) to choose wrongly; (*tiro, golpe*) to miss

**2** *vi* (**a**) (*vagar*) to wander (**b**) (*equivocarse*) to make a mistake (**c**) (*al tirar*) to miss

**errata** *nf* misprint; **fe de erratas** errata *pl*

**errático, -a** *adj* wandering

**erre** *nf* **e. que e.** stubbornly

**erróneo, -a** *adj* mistaken

**error** *nm* mistake, error; **estar en un e.** to be mistaken; **por e.** by mistake; **salvo e. u omisión** errors and omissions excepted; **e. de imprenta** misprint

**ertzaina** [er'tʃaina] *nmf* = member of Basque regional police force

**Ertzaintza** [er'tʃaintʃa] *nf* = Basque regional police force

**eructar** *vi* to belch

**eructo** *nm* belch

**erudición** *nf* erudition

**erudito, -a 1** *adj* erudite

**2** *nm,f* scholar

**erupción** *nf* (**a**) *Geol* eruption; **en e.** erupting (**b**) *Med* **e. (cutánea)** rash

**eruptivo, -a** *adj* (*roca*) volcanic; (*volcán*) active

**es** *ver* **ser**

**esa** *ver* **ese**

**ésa** *ver* **ése**

**esbeltez** *nf* slenderness, slimness

**esbelto, -a** *adj* slender, slim

**esbirro** *nm* henchman

**esbozar** [16] *vt* to sketch, to outline; **e. una sonrisa** to give a hint of a smile

**esbozo** *nm* sketch, outline

**escabechado, -a** *Culin* **1** *adj* marinated

**2** *nm* marinade

**escabechar** *vt Culin* to marinate

**escabeche** *nm Culin* marinade; **en e.** marinaded

**escabechina** *nf Fam (destrozo)* destruction; *(en examen)* huge number of failures

**escabroso, -a** *adj* **(a)** *(abrupto)* rough **(b)** *(obsceno)* risqué **(c)** *(espinoso)* awkward, thorny

**escabullirse** *vpr* **(a)** *(desaparecer)* to slip away (**de** from) **(b)** *(escurrirse)* **se me escabulló** he slipped out of my hands

**escacharrado, -a** *adj Fam* clapped-out

**escacharrar** *Fam* **1** *vt* to knacker

  **2 escacharrarse** *vpr* to get knackered

**escafandra** *nf* diving suit; **e. espacial** spacesuit

**escafandrista** *nmf* diver

**escala** *nf* **(a)** *(para medir)* scale; *(de colores)* range; **a e.** *(reproducción)* to scale; **a e. mundial** on a worldwide scale; **a gran e.** on a large scale; **e. de popularidad** popularity stakes; **e. de valores** set of values **(b)** *(en un viaje)* stop-over; **hacer e.** to stop over **(c)** *(escalera)* ladder

**escalada** *nf* **(a)** *(de montaña)* climb **(b)** *(de violencia, precios)* escalation, rise (**de** in)

**escalador, -ora** *nm,f (alpinista, ciclista)* climber

**escalafón** *nm* scale, ladder

**escalar** *vt* to climb

**escaldado, -a** *adj* **(a)** *Culin* scalded **(b)** *Fig (receloso)* wary

**escaldar 1** *vt* to scald

  **2 escaldarse** *vpr* to get burned

**escaleno** *adj Geom* scalene

**escalera** *nf* **(a)** *(en edificio)* stairs, staircase; *(de mano)* ladder; **e. automática** *o* **mecánica** escalator; **e. de caracol** spiral staircase; **e. de incendios** fire escape; **e. de servicio** service stairs; **e. de tijera** step ladder **(b)** *(en naipes)* run; **e. de color** straight flush

**escalerilla** *nf (de avión)* stairs

**escalfado, -a** *adj (huevo)* poached

**escalfar** *vt* to poach

**escalinata** *nf* staircase

**escalofriante** *adj* spine-chilling

**escalofrío** *nm* shiver; **tener escalofríos** to be shivering; *Fig* **dar escalofríos a alguien** to give sb the shivers

**escalón** *nm* step; *Fig* grade

**escalonado, -a** *adj* **(a)** *(en el tiempo)* spread out **(b)** *(terreno)* terraced

**escalonar** *vt* **(a)** *(en el tiempo)* to spread out **(b)** *(terreno)* to terrace

**escalope** *nm* escalope

**escalpelo** *nm* scalpel

**escama** *nf* **(a)** *(de peces, reptiles)* scale **(b)** *(de jabón, piel)* flake

**escamado, -a** *adj Fam* suspicious, wary

**escamar 1** *vt* **(a)** *(pescado)* to scale **(b)** *Fam Fig (causar recelo a)* to make suspicious

  **2 escamarse** *vpr Fam* to smell a rat, to get suspicious

**escamotear** *vt* **e. algo a alguien** *(estafar)* to do *o* swindle sb out of sth; *(hurtar)* to rob sb of sth

**escampar** *v impersonal* to clear up, to stop raining

**escanciar** [15] *vt* to serve, to pour out

**escandalizar** [16] **1** *vt* to scandalize, to shock

  **2 escandalizarse** *vpr* to be shocked

**escándalo** *nm* **(a)** *(inmoralidad)* scandal; *(indignación)* outrage; **e. sexual** sex scandal **(b)** *(alboroto)* uproar, racket; **armar un e.** to kick up a fuss

**escandaloso, -a 1** *adj* **(a)** *(inmoral)* outrageous, shocking **(b)** *(ruidoso)* very noisy

  **2** *nm,f* very noisy *o* loud person

**Escandinavia** *n* Scandinavia

**escandinavo, -a** *adj & nm,f* Scandinavian

**escanear** *vt Informát & Med* to scan

**escáner** ( *pl* **escáneres**) *nm Informát & Med* scanner; *Med* **hacer un e. a alguien** to give sb a scan

**escaño** *nm* **(a)** *(cargo)* seat *(in parliament)* **(b)** *(asiento)* bench *(in parliament)*

**escapada** *nf* **(a)** *(huida)* escape, flight; *Dep* breakaway **(b)** *(viaje)* quick trip

**escapar 1** *vi* **(a)** *(huir)* to get away, to escape (**de** from) **(b)** *(quedar fuera del alcance)* **e. a alguien** to be beyond sb

  **2 escaparse** *vpr* **(a)** *(huir)* to get away, to escape (**de** from); **escaparse de casa** to run away from home **(b)** *(gas, agua)* to leak **(c)** *(perder)* **se me escapó la risa/un taco** I let out a laugh/an expletive; **se me escapó el tren** I missed the train; **se me escapó la ocasión** the opportunity slipped by

**escaparate** *nm (shop)* window

**escaparatista** *nmf* window dresser

**escapatoria** *nf* **(a)** *(fuga)* escape; **no tener e.** to have no way out **(b)** *Fam (evasiva)* way (of getting) out

**escape** *nm (de gas)* leak; *(de coche)* exhaust; *Fam Fig* **salir a e.** to leave in a rush, to rush off

**escapismo** *nm* escapism

**escapista** *adj* escapist

**escapulario** *nm Rel* scapular

**escaquearse** *vpr Fam* to duck out; **e. de (hacer) algo** to worm one's way out of (doing) sth; **¡no te escaquees!** don't skive off!

**escarabajo** *nm* beetle; **e. pelotero** dung beetle

**escaramuza** *nf Mil & Fig* skirmish

**escarapela** *nf* rosette, cockade

**escarbar** *vt* to scratch, to scrape

**escarceos** *nmpl* forays; **e. amorosos** flirtations

**escarcha** *nf* frost

**escarchado, -a** *adj (fruta)* candied

**escarchar** *v impersonal* to freeze (over)

**escardar** *vt* to weed

**escarlata** *adj & nm* scarlet

**escarlatina** *nf* scarlet fever

**escarmentar** [3] *vi* to learn (one's lesson)

**escarmiento** *nm* lesson; **dar un e. a alguien** to teach sb a lesson; **servir de e.** to serve as a lesson

**escarnecer** [48] *vt* to mock, to ridicule

**escarnecimiento** *nm* mockery, ridicule

**escarnio** *nm* mockery, ridicule

**escarola** *nf* (curly) endive

**escarpado, -a** *adj (inclinado)* steep; *(abrupto)* craggy

**escarpia** *nf* = L-shaped hook for hanging pictures etc

**escasear** *vi* to be scarce, to be in short supply

**escasez** *nf (insuficiencia)* shortage; *(pobreza)* poverty

**escaso, -a** *adj* **(a)** *(conocimientos, recursos)* limited, scant; *(tiempo)* short; *(cantidad, número)* low; *(víveres, trabajo)* scarce, in short supply; *(visibilidad, luz)* poor; **andar e. de** to be short of **(b)** *(casi completo)* **un metro e.** barely a metre

**escatimar** *vt (gastos, comida)* to be sparing with, to skimp on; *(esfuerzo, energías)* to use as little as possible; **no e. gastos** to spare no expense

**escatología** *nf (sobre excrementos)* scatology

**escatológico, -a** *adj (de excrementos)* scatological

**escay** *nm* Leatherette

**escayola** *nf Constr* plaster of Paris; *Med* plaster

**escayolado, -a** *adj (brazo, pierna)* in plaster

**escayolar** *vt* to put in plaster

**escayolista** *nmf* decorative plasterer

**escena** *nf* **(a)** *(escenario)* stage; **llevar a la e.** to dramatize; **poner en e.** to stage **(b)** *(suceso, acto)* scene; **hacer una e.** to make a scene

**escenario** *nm* **(a)** *(tablas, escena)* stage; *Cine & Teatro (lugar de la acción)* setting **(b)** *Fig (de suceso)* scene

**escénico, -a** *adj* scenic

**escenificación** *nf (de novela)* dramatization; *(de obra de teatro)* staging

**escenificar** [61] *vt (novela)* to dramatize; *(obra de teatro)* to stage

**escenografía** *nf* set design

**escenógrafo, -a** *nm,f* set designer

**escepticismo** *nm* scepticism

**escéptico, -a 1** *adj* **(a)** *(filósofo)* sceptic **(b)** *(incrédulo)* sceptical
 **2** *nm,f* sceptic

**escindir 1** *vt* to split
 **2 escindirse** *vpr* to split **(en** into)

**escisión** *nf (del átomo)* splitting; *(de partido político)* split

**esclarecedor, -ora** *adj* illuminating

**esclarecer** [48] *vt* to clear up, to shed light on; **e. los hechos** to establish the facts

**esclarecimiento** *nm* clearing up, elucidation

**esclava** *nf (pulsera)* = metal identity bracelet

**esclavina** *nf* short cape

**esclavismo** *nm* (system of) slavery

**esclavista 1** *adj* pro-slavery
 **2** *nmf* supporter of slavery

**esclavitud** *nf también Fig* slavery

**esclavizar** [16] *vt también Fig* to enslave

**esclavo, -a 1** *adj* enslaved
 **2** *nm,f también Fig* slave

**esclerosis** *nf inv Med* sclerosis; **e. múltiple** multiple sclerosis

**esclerótica** *nf* sclera, sclerotic

**esclusa** *nf (de canal)* lock; *(compuerta)* floodgate

**escoba** *nf* **(a)** *(para barrer)* broom **(b)** *(juego de cartas)* = type of card game

**escobazo** *nm* blow with a broom; *Fig* **echar a alguien a escobazos** to kick sb out

**escobilla** *nf* brush

**escobón** *nm* broom

**escocedura** *nf* **(a)** *(herida)* sore **(b)** *(sensación)* smarting, stinging

**escocer** [17] **1** *vi también Fig* to sting; **me escuecen los ojos** my eyes are stinging *o* smarting
 **2 escocerse** *vpr Fig* **escocerse de algo** to be hurt by sth

**escocés, -esa 1** *adj* Scottish; **tela escocesa** tartan; **whisky e.** scotch whisky
 **2** *nm,f (persona) (hombre)* Scot, Scotsman; *(mujer)* Scot, Scotswoman
 **3** *nm (lengua)* Scots *(singular)*

**Escocia** *n* Scotland

**escoger** [54] *vt* to choose

**escogido, -a** *adj (elegido)* selected, chosen; *(selecto)* choice, select

**escojo** *ver* **escoger**

**escolanía** *nf* choirboys

**escolapio, -a** *adj & nm,f* = member of the religious order of the Escuelas Pías

**escolar 1** *adj* **edad e.** school age

**2** *nmf (niño)* pupil, schoolboy; *(niña)* pupil, schoolgirl

**escolaridad** *nf* schooling

**escolarización** *nf* schooling

**escolarizar** [16] *vt* to provide with schools

**escolástica** *nf* scholasticism

**escolástico, -a** *adj* scholastic

**escollera** *nf* breakwater

**escollo** *nm (en el mar)* reef; *Fig (obstáculo)* stumbling block

**escolta 1** *nf (acompañamiento)* escort

**2** *nmf (para protección) (persona, grupo)* bodyguard

**escoltar** *vt* to escort

**escombrera** *nf (vertedero)* tip

**escombro** *nm,* **escombros** *nmpl* rubble, debris *(singular)*

**esconder 1** *vt* to hide, to conceal

**2 esconderse** *vpr* to hide **(de** from)

**escondido, -a** *adj (lugar)* secluded; **a escondidas** in secret

**escondite** *nm* **(a)** *(lugar)* hiding place **(b)** *(juego)* hide-and-seek

**escondrijo** *nm* hiding place

**escoñar** *muy Fam* **1** *vt* to knacker, to break

**2 escoñarse** *vpr* to get knackered

**escopeta** *nf* shotgun; **e. de aire comprimido** air gun; **e. de cañones recortados** sawn-off shotgun

**escopetado, -a** *adj* **salir e.** to shoot off

**escopetazo** *nm (disparo)* shotgun blast; *(herida)* shotgun wound

**escoplo** *nm* chisel

**escorar** *vi Náut* to list

**escorbuto** *nm* scurvy

**escoria** *nf Fig* dregs, scum

**escorpio 1** *nm (zodiaco)* Scorpio; **ser e.** to be (a) Scorpio

**2** *nmf (persona)* Scorpio

**escorpión** *nm* scorpion

**escotado, -a** *adj (vestido)* low-cut, low-necked

**escotar** *vt* to lower the neckline of

**escote** *nm (de prendas)* neckline; *(de persona)* cleavage; **pagar a e.** to go Dutch

**escotilla** *nf* hatch, hatchway

**escozor** *nm* stinging

**escriba** *nm* scribe

**escribanía** *nf (profesión)* clerkship; *(útiles de escribir)* inkstand

**escribano** *nm Hist* scrivener

**escribiente** *nmf* clerk

**escribir 1** *vt & vi* to write

**2 escribirse** *vpr* **(a)** *(personas)* to write to one another **(b)** *(palabras)* **se escribe con "h"** it is spelt with an "h"

**escrito, -a 1** *participio ver* **escribir**

**2** *adj* written; **por e.** in writing

**3** *nm (texto, composición)* text; *(documento)* document; *(obra literaria)* writing, work

**escritor, -ora** *nm,f* writer

**escritorio** *nm (mueble)* desk, bureau

**escritura** *nf* **(a)** *(técnica)* writing **(b)** *(sistema de signos)* script **(c)** *Der* **escrituras** deeds; **Sagrada E., Sagradas Escrituras** Holy Scripture

**escriturar** *vt Der* to execute by deed

**escroto** *nm* scrotum

**escrúpulo** *nm* **(a)** *(duda, recelo)* scruple; **sin escrúpulos** unscrupulous **(b)** *(minuciosidad)* scrupulousness, great care **(c)** *(aprensión)* qualm; **le da e.** he has qualms about it

**escrupuloso, -a** *adj* **(a)** *(minucioso)* scrupulous **(b)** *(aprensivo)* particular, fussy

**escrutar** *vt* **(a)** *(con la mirada)* to scrutinize, to examine **(b)** *(votos)* to count

**escrutinio** *nm* count *(of votes)*

**escuadra** *nf* **(a)** *(regla, plantilla)* set square **(b)** *(de buques)* squadron **(c)** *(de soldados)* squad

**escuadrilla** *nf (de buques, aviones)* squadron

**escuadrón** *nm (de aviones)* squadron; **e. de la muerte** death squad

**escuálido, -a** *adj* emaciated

**escualo** *nm (tiburón)* shark

**escucha** *nf* listening-in, monitoring; **estar o permanecer a la e.** to listen in; **escuchas telefónicas** telephone tapping

**escuchar 1** *vt* to listen to

**2** *vi* to listen

**escuchimizado, -a** *Fam* **1** *adj* skinny, thin as a rake

**2** *nm,f* skinny person

**escudar 1** *vt Fig* to shield

**2 escudarse** *vpr Fig* **escudarse en algo** to hide behind sth, to use sth as an excuse

**escudería** *nf* team *(in motor racing)*

**escudero** *nm* squire

**escudilla** *nf* deep bowl

**escudo** *nm* **(a)** *(arma)* shield **(b)** *(moneda)* escudo **(c)** *(emblema)* coat of arms

**escudriñar** *vt (examinar)* to scrutinize, to examine; *(otear)* to search

**escuece** *ver* **escocer**

**escuela** *nf* school; **hacer e.** to have a following; **ser de la vieja e.** to be of the old school; **e. pública** state school; **e. taurina** bullfighting school; **e. universitaria** = section of a university which awards diplomas in a vocational discipline (eg engineering, business) after three years of study

**escueto, -a** *adj (sucinto)* concise; *(sobrio)* plain, unadorned

**escueza** *etc ver* **escocer**

**escuincle, -a** *nm,f Méx* nipper, kid

**esculpir** *vt* to sculpt, to carve

**escultor, -ora** *nm,f* sculptor, *f* sculptress

**escultórico, -a** *adj* sculptural

**escultura** *nf* sculpture

**escultural** *adj* **(a)** *(en arte)* sculptural **(b)** *(persona)* statuesque

**escupidera** *nf* spittoon

**escupir 1** *vi* to spit

**2** *vt (sujeto: persona, animal)* to spit out; *(sujeto: volcán, chimenea)* to belch out

**escupitajo** *nm Fam* gob, spit

**escurreplatos** *nm inv* dish rack

**escurridero** *nm* draining board

**escurridizo, -a** *adj también Fig* slippery

**escurridor** *nm* colander

**escurrir 1** *vt (platos, verdura)* to drain; *(ropa)* to wring out; *Fam* **e. el bulto** to skive off

**2** *vi (gotear)* to drip

**3 escurrirse** *vpr* **(a)** *Fam (escabullirse)* to get away, to escape **(b)** *(resbalarse)* **se me escurrió de las manos** it slipped through my fingers

**escusado** *nm (retrete)* bathroom

**escúter** *(pl escúteres) nm (motor)* scooter

**esdrújula** *nf Gram* word stressed on the third-last syllable

**esdrújulo, -a** *adj Gram* stressed on the third-last syllable

**ese¹** *nf (figura)* zigzag; **hacer eses** *(en carretera)* to zigzag; *(al andar)* to stagger about

**ese², -a** *(pl esos, -as) adj demostrativo* **(a)** *(en general)* that, *pl* those

**(b)** *Fam Pey* **el hombre e. no me inspira confianza** I don't trust that guy

**ése, -a** *(pl ésos, -as)*

Note that **ése** and its various forms can be written without an accent when there is no risk of confusion with the adjective.

*pron demostrativo* **(a)** *(en general) (singular)* that one; *(plural)* those (ones); **ponte otro vestido, é. no te queda bien** put on another dress, that one doesn't suit you; **estos pasteles están muy buenos, pero ésos me gustan más** these cakes are very good but I like those ones better

**(b)** *Fam* **é. fue el que me pegó** that's the one who hit me

**(c)** *(expresiones)* **¡a é.!** stop that man!; **ni por ésas** not even then; **no me lo vendió ni por ésas** even then he wouldn't sell it me

**esencia** *nf* essence; **quinta e.** quintessence

**esencial** *adj* essential; **lo e.** the fundamental thing

**esfera** *nf* **(a)** *(figura)* sphere; **e. celeste** celestial sphere; **e. terrestre** (terrestrial) globe **(b)** *(de reloj)* face **(c)** *(círculo social)* circle; **las altas esferas de la política** high political circles

**esférico, -a 1** *adj* spherical

**2** *nm Dep* ball

**esfinge** *nf* sphinx

**esfínter** *(pl esfínteres) nm* sphincter

**esforzar [33] 1** *vt (voz, vista)* to strain; **tuve que e. la voz** I had to strain my voice

**2 esforzarse** *vpr* to make an effort; **esforzarse en o por hacer algo** to try very hard to do sth, to do one's best to do sth

**esfuerzo** *nm* effort; **sin e.** effortlessly

**esfumarse** *vpr* **(a)** *(esperanzas, posibilidades)* to fade away **(b)** *Fam (persona)* to vanish, to disappear; **¡esfúmate!** beat it!, get lost!

**esgrima** *nf* fencing

**esgrimir** *vt* **(a)** *(arma)* to brandish, to wield **(b)** *(argumento, datos)* to use, to employ

**esguince** *nm* sprain; **hacerse un e. en el tobillo** to sprain one's ankle

**eslabón** *nm (de cadena)* link; **el e. perdido** the missing link

**eslabonar** *vt también Fig* to link together

**eslalon** *(pl eslalons) nm Dep* slalom; **e. gigante** giant slalom

**eslavo, -a 1** *adj* slav, Slavonic

**2** *nm,f (persona)* Slav

**3** *nm (lengua)* Slavonic

**eslip** *(pl eslips) nm* briefs

**eslogan** *(pl eslóganes) nm* slogan

**eslora** *nf Náut* length

**eslovaco, -a 1** *adj & nm,f* Slovak, Slovakian

**2** *nm (lengua)* Slovak

**Eslovaquia** *n* Slovakia

**Eslovenia** *n* Slovenia

**esmaltado, -a 1** *adj* enamelled

**2** *nm* enamelling

**esmaltar** *vt* to enamel

**esmalte** *nm* **(a)** *(en dentadura, cerámica)* enamel; *(de uñas)* nail varnish o polish **(b)** *(objeto, joya)* enamel

**esmerado, -a** *adj (persona)* painstaking, careful; *(trabajo)* carefully done, polished

**esmeralda 1** *nf (piedra preciosa)* emerald

**2** *adj & nm inv* emerald

**esmerarse** *vpr (esforzarse)* to take great pains (en over)

**esmeril** *nm* emery

**esmerilado, -a** *adj (pulido)* polished with emery; *(translúcido)* ground

**esmerilar** *vt (pulir)* to polish with emery

**esmero** *nm* great care

**esmirriado, -a** *adj Fam* puny, weak

**esmoquin** (*pl* **esmóquines**) *nm Br* dinner jacket, *US* tuxedo

**esnifada** *nf muy Fam* sniff (*of a drug*)

**esnifar** *vt muy Fam* to sniff (*drugs*)

**esnob** (*pl* **esnobs**) **1** *adj* trying to be trendy
**2** *nmf* person who wants to be trendy

**esnobismo** *nm* desire to be trendy

**eso** *pron demostrativo (neutro)* that; **e. es la Torre Eiffel** that's the Eiffel Tower; **e. es lo que yo pienso** that's just what I think; **e. que propones es irrealizable** what you're proposing is impossible; **e. de vivir solo no me gusta** I don't like the idea of living on my own; **¡e., e.!** that's right!, yes!; **¡e. es!** that's it!; **¿cómo es e.?**, **¿y e.?** (*¿por qué?*) how come?; **para e. es mejor no ir** if that's all it is, you might as well not go; **por e. vine** that's why I came; **a e. de** (*at*) about *o* around; **en e.** just then, at that very moment; **y e. que** even though

**esófago** *nm* oesophagus

**esos, -as** *ver* **ese**

**ésos, -as** *ver* **ése**

**esotérico, -a** *adj* esoteric

**esoterismo** *nm* (**a**) (*impenetrabilidad*) esoteric nature (**b**) (*ciencias ocultas*) esotericism

**espabilado, -a** *adj* (*avispado*) quick-witted, on the ball

**espabilar 1** *vt* (**a**) (*despertar*) to wake up (**b**) (*avispar*) **e. a alguien** to sharpen sb's wits
**2 espabilarse** *vpr* (**a**) (*despertarse*) to wake up, to brighten up (**b**) (*darse prisa*) to get a move on (**c**) (*avisparse*) to sharpen one's wits

**espachurrar** *Fam* **1** *vt* to squash
**2 espachurrarse** *vpr* to get squashed

**espaciado, -a** *adj* at regular intervals

**espaciador** *nm* space bar

**espacial** *adj* **coordenadas espaciales** spatial coordinates; **cohete/lanzadera e.** space rocket/shuttle

**espaciar** [15] *vt* to space out

**espacio** *nm* (**a**) (*sitio, capacidad, extensión*) space; **no tengo mucho e.** I don't have much room; **a doble e.** double-spaced; **por e. de** over a period of; **e. aéreo** air space; **e. exterior** outer space; **e. verde** green area (*in town or city*); **e. vital** living space (**b**) *Rad & TV* programme; **e. publicitario** advertising spot

**espacioso, -a** *adj* spacious

**espada 1** *nf* (**a**) (*arma*) sword; **estar entre la e. y la pared** to be between the devil and the deep blue sea; **la e. de Damocles** the sword of Damocles (**b**) **espadas** (*en naipes*) = suit in Spanish deck of cards, with the symbol of a sword
**2** *nm Taurom* matador
**3** *adj* **pez e.** swordfish

**espadachín** *nm* swordsman

**espadaña** *nf* (**a**) (*planta*) bullrush (**b**) (*campanario*) bell gable

**espagueti** *nm* piece of spaghetti; **espaguetis** spaghetti (*singular*); *Fam Fig* **estar como un e.** to be skinny

**espalda** *nf* (**a**) (*del cuerpo*) back; **cargado de espaldas** round-shouldered; **de espaldas a alguien** with one's back turned on sb; **por la e.** from behind; *Fig* behind one's back; **cubrirse las espaldas** to cover oneself; *Fig* **echarse algo sobre las espaldas** to take sth on; **hablar de uno a sus espaldas** to talk about sb behind their back; **tener buenas espaldas** to be mentally tough; **tirar** *o* **tumbar de espaldas** to be amazing *o* stunning; **volver la e. a alguien** to turn one's back on sb (**b**) (*en natación*) backstroke

**espaldarazo** *nm* blow to the back; **eso le dio el e.** (**definitivo**) that finally earned her widespread recognition

**espalderas** *nfpl* wall bars

**espaldilla** *nf* shoulder (of lamb etc)

**espantada** *nf* **dar** *o* **pegar una e.** (*caballo*) to bolt; *Fam Fig* **dar la e.** to bolt, to take to one's heels

**espantadizo, -a** *adj* nervous, easily frightened

**espantajo** *nm* (**a**) (*espantapájaros*) scarecrow (**b**) (*persona fea*) fright, sight

**espantapájaros** *nm inv* scarecrow

**espantar 1** *vt* (**a**) (*ahuyentar*) to frighten *o* scare away (**b**) (*asustar*) to frighten, to scare
**2 espantarse** *vpr* to get frightened *o* scared

**espanto** *nm* fright; **¡qué e.!** how terrible!; **estar curado de espantos** to be unshockable

**espantoso, -a** *adj* (**a**) (*terrorífico*) horrific (**b**) (*enorme*) terrible (**c**) (*feísimo*) frightful, horrible

**España** *n* Spain

**español, -ola 1** *adj* Spanish
**2** *nm,f* (*persona*) Spaniard
**3** *nm* (*lengua*) Spanish

**españolada** *nf Pey* = exaggerated portrayal of Spain

**españolismo** *nm* (**a**) (*apego, afecto*) affinity for things Spanish (**b**) (*carácter, naturaleza*) Spanishness, Spanish character

**españolizar** [16] **1** *vt* to make Spanish, to hispanicize
**2 españolizarse** *vpr* to adopt Spanish ways

**esparadrapo** *nm* (sticking) plaster, *US* Band-Aid®

**esparcimiento** *nm* (**a**) (*diseminación*) scattering (**b**) (*ocio*) relaxation, time off

**esparcir** [74] **1** *vt* (*extender*) to spread; (*diseminar*) to scatter
**2 esparcirse** *vpr* to spread (out)

**espárrago** *nm* stalk of asparagus; **espárragos** asparagus; **espárragos trigueros** wild asparagus; *Fam Fig* ¡vete a freír espárragos! get lost!

**esparraguera** *nf* asparagus (plant)

**espartano, -a 1** *adj (de Esparta)* Spartan; *Fig (sobrio)* sober

  **2** *nm,f* Spartan

**esparto** *nm* esparto (grass)

**espasmo** *nm* spasm

**espasmódico, -a** *adj* spasmodic

**espatarrarse** *vpr Fam* to sprawl *(with one's legs wide open)*

**espátula** *nf* (a) *Culin & Med* spatula; *Arte* palette knife; *Constr* bricklayer's trowel; *(de empapelador)* stripping knife (b) *(ave)* spoonbill

**especia** *nf* spice

**especial 1** *adj* (a) *(adecuado)* special; **e. para** specially for (b) *(peculiar)* peculiar, strange

  **2** *adv* en e. especially, particularly; **¿alguno en e.?** any one in particular?

**especialidad** *nf* speciality; **e. de la casa** speciality of the house

**especialista 1** *adj* specializing **(en** in)

  **2** *nmf* (a) *(experto)* specialist **(en** in) (b) *Cine* stuntman, *f* stuntwoman

**especialización** *nf* specialization

**especializar [16] 1** *vt* to specialize

  **2 especializarse** *vpr* to specialize **(en** in)

**especie** *nf* (a) *(animal)* species *(singular)*; **e. protegida** protected species (b) *(clase)* kind, sort; **pagar en e.** *o* **especies** to pay in kind

**especiería** *nf* spice shop

**especificación** *nf* specification

**especificar [61]** *vt* to specify

**especificidad** *nf* specificity

**específico, -a 1** *adj* specific

  **2** *nmpl* **específicos** *Med* patent medicines

**espécimen** *(pl* **especímenes)** *nm* specimen

**espectacular** *adj* spectacular

**espectacularidad** *nf* spectacular nature

**espectáculo** *nm* (a) *(diversión)* entertainment; *(función)* show, performance; **e. de variedades** variety show; **el mundo del e.** (the world of) show business (b) *(suceso, escena)* sight; *Fam* **dar el e.** to cause a scene

**espectador** *nmf (de televisión)* viewer; *(de cine, teatro)* member of the audience; *(de espectáculo deportivo)* spectator; *(de suceso, discusión)* onlooker; **los espectadores** *(de cine, teatro)* the audience

**espectral** *adj* (a) *Fís* spectral (b) *Fig* ghostly

**espectro** *nm* (a) *Fís* spectrum (b) *(fantasma)* spectre, ghost

**especulación** *nf* speculation

**especulador, -ora 1** *adj* speculating

  **2** *nm,f* speculator

**especular** *vi* (a) *(reflexionar, formular hipótesis)* to speculate **(sobre** about) (b) **e. en** *(comerciar, traficar)* to speculate on

**especulativo, -a** *adj* speculative

**espejismo** *nm* mirage; *Fig* illusion

**espejo** *nm* mirror

**espeleología** *nf* potholing

**espeleólogo, -a** *nm,f* potholer

**espeluznante** *adj* hair-raising, lurid

**espera** *nf* wait; **en e. de, a la e.** de waiting for, awaiting; **seguimos a la e. de su respuesta** *(en cartas)* we await your reply; **sala de e.** waiting room

**esperanto** *nm* Esperanto

**esperanza** *nf (deseo, ganas)* hope; *(confianza, expectativas)* expectation; **perder la e.** to lose hope; **tener e. de hacer algo** to hope to be able to do sth; *Prov* **la e. es lo último que se pierde** where there's life there's hope; **e. de vida** life expectancy

**esperanzador, -ora** *adj* encouraging, hopeful

**esperanzar [16] 1** *vt* to give hope to, to encourage

  **2 esperanzarse** *vpr* to be encouraged

**esperar 1** *vt* (a) *(aguardar)* to wait for; **e. a que alguien haga algo** to wait for sb to do sth (b) *(tener esperanza de)* **e. que** to hope that; **espero que sí/no** I hope so/not; **e. hacer algo** to hope to do sth (c) *(tener confianza en)* to expect; **e. que** to expect (that); **e. algo de alguien** to expect sth from sb, to hope for sth from sb

  **2** *vi* (a) *(aguardar)* to wait; *Prov* **quien espera desespera** a watched pot never boils (b) *(ser inevitable)* to await, to be in store for; **le esperan dificultades** many difficulties await him; **como era de e.** as was to be expected

  **3 esperarse** *vpr* (a) *(imaginarse, figurarse)* to expect; **se esperaban lo peor** they expected *o* feared the worst (b) *(aguardar)* to wait; **esperarse a que alguien haga algo** to wait for sb to do sth

**esperma** *nm o nf (semen)* sperm

**espermatozoide, espermatozoo** *nm* sperm, spermatozoon

**espermicida 1** *adj* spermicidal

  **2** *nm* spermicide

**esperpéntico, -a** *adj* grotesque

**esperpento** *nm (persona)* grotesque sight; *(cosa)* absurdity, piece of nonsense

**espesar** *vt & vi* to thicken

**espeso, -a** *adj (crema, pintura, muro)* thick; *(bosque, niebla)* dense; *(nieve)* deep

**espesor** nm (a) *(grosor)* thickness; **tiene 2 metros de e.** it's 2 metres thick (b) *(densidad)* *(de niebla, bosque)* density; *(de nieve)* depth

**espesura** nf (a) *(vegetación)* thicket (b) *(grosor)* thickness; *(densidad)* density

**espetar** vt (a) *(palabras)* to blurt out, to tell straight out (b) *(carne)* to skewer

**espía** nmf spy; **avión e.** spy plane

**espiar** [34] vt to spy on

**espiga** nf (a) *(de cereal)* ear (b) *(en telas)* herringbone (c) *(pieza)* *(de madera)* peg; *(de hierro)* pin

**espigado, -a** adj (a) *(persona)* tall and slim (b) *(cereal)* ripe

**espigar** [40] **1** vt *(información)* to glean
  **2 espigarse** vpr (a) *(persona)* to shoot up (b) *(planta)* to go to seed

**espigón** nm breakwater

**espiguilla** nf herringbone

**espín** nm Fís spin

**espina** nf *(de pez)* bone; *(de planta)* thorn; **me da mala e.** it makes me uneasy, there's something fishy about it; **me da en la e. que…** I've got this funny feeling that…; Fig **sacarse una e.** *(desquitarse)* to settle an old score; *(desahogarse)* to relieve a long-standing frustration; **todavía tengo clavada la e. de no haber ido a la universidad** I still feel bad about not having gone to university; **e. dorsal** spine; Fig backbone

**espinaca** nf espinaca(s) spinach

**espinal** adj spinal

**espinazo** nm spine, backbone; Fig **doblar el e.** *(humillarse)* to kow-tow; *(trabajar duro)* to put one's back into it

**espinilla** nf (a) *(hueso)* shin, shinbone (b) *(grano)* blackhead

**espinillera** nf shin pad

**espino** nm (a) *(planta)* hawthorn (b) *(alambre)* barbed wire

**espinoso, -a** adj también Fig thorny

**espionaje** nm espionage; **e. industrial** industrial espionage

**espiración** nf exhalation, breathing out

**espiral** nf también Fig spiral; **en e.** *(escalera, forma)* spiral; Econ **e. inflacionaria** inflationary spiral

**espirar** vt & vi to exhale, to breathe out

**espiritismo** nm spiritualism

**espiritista** adj spiritualist

**espíritu** nm (a) *(mente, alma)* spirit; Rel soul; **E. Santo** Holy Ghost (b) *(fantasma)* ghost (c) *(modo de pensar)* attitudes; **e. deportivo** sporting spirit (d) *(ánimo)* **levantar el e. a alguien** to lift o raise sb's spirits

**espiritual** adj & nm spiritual

**espiritualidad** nf spirituality

**espita** nf spigot, tap, US faucet

**esplendidez** nf (a) *(generosidad)* generosity (b) *(magnificencia)* splendour

**espléndido, -a** adj (a) *(magnífico)* splendid, magnificent (b) *(generoso)* generous, lavish

**esplendor** nm (a) *(magnificencia)* splendour (b) *(apogeo)* greatness

**esplendoroso, -a** adj magnificent

**espliego** nm lavender

**espolear** vt también Fig to spur on

**espoleta** nf *(de proyectil)* fuse

**espolón** nm (a) *(de ave)* spur (b) Arquit buttress

**espolvorear** vt to dust, to sprinkle

**esponja** nf sponge; **beber como una e.** to drink like a fish

**esponjar** vt to fluff up

**esponjosidad** nf *(de toalla)* fluffiness; *(de bizcocho)* sponginess

**esponjoso, -a** adj *(toalla, jersey)* fluffy; *(bizcocho)* light, fluffy

**esponsales** nmpl betrothal

**esponsorizar** vt to sponsor

**espontaneidad** nf spontaneity

**espontáneo, -a 1** adj spontaneous
  **2** nm,f *(en los toros)* spectator who tries to join in a bullfight

**esporádico, -a** adj sporadic

**esposa** nf ver esposo

**esposado, -a** adj handcuffed

**esposar** vt to handcuff

**esposas** nfpl *(objeto)* handcuffs; **ponerle las e. a alguien** to handcuff sb

**esposo, -a** nm,f *(persona)* husband, f wife; **los esposos salieron de la iglesia** the couple o the newlyweds left the church

**espray** *(pl* esprays*)* nm spray

**esprint** *(pl* esprints*)* nm sprint

**esprínter** *(pl* esprínters*)* nmf sprinter

**ESPRIT** [es'prit] nm *(abrev de* **European Strategic Programme for Research and Development for Information Technology)** ESPRIT

**espuela** nf (a) *(en el talón)* spur (b) Fam *(última copa)* **tomar la e.** to have one for the road

**espuerta** nf *(recipiente)* basket; **a espuertas** by the sackful o bucket

**espuma** nf *(de cerveza)* head; *(de jabón)* lather; *(de olas)* surf; *(de un caldo)* scum; *(para pelo)* (styling) mousse; **e. de afeitar** shaving foam; **crecer como la e.** *(negocio)* to go from strength to strength

**espumadera** nf skimmer

**espumar** vt *(caldo)* to skim

**espumarajo** *nm* froth, foam; *también Fig* **echar espumarajos (por la boca)** to foam at the mouth; **el mar estaba lleno de espumarajos** there was lots of dirty foam on the sea

**espumillón** *nm* tinsel

**espumoso, -a 1** *adj (baño)* foamy, bubbly; *(cerveza)* frothy, foaming; *(vino)* sparkling; *(jabón)* lathery
**2** *nm* sparkling wine

**espurio, -a** *adj (bastardo)* illegitimate; *Fig (falso)* spurious, false

**esputar** *vi* to cough up *o* spit phlegm

**esputo** *nm (flema)* spittle; *Med* sputum

**esquech** *(pl* esqueches*)*, **esquetch** *(pl* esquetches*)* *nm* (comic) sketch

**esqueje** *nm* cutting *(of plant)*

**esquela** *nf* funeral notice *(in newspaper)*

**esquelético, -a** *adj Anat* skeletal; *Fam Fig (muy delgado)* skinny; **estar e.** to be extremely thin

**esqueleto** *nm* (a) *(de persona)* skeleton; *Fam* **menear** *o* **mover el e.** to boogie (on down); **estar como un e.** to be skin and bone (b) *(armazón)* framework; *(de novela, argumento)* outline

**esquema** *nm (gráfico)* diagram; *(resumen)* outline

**esquemático, -a** *adj* schematic; **muy e.** *(explicación, resumen)* concise

**esquí** *(pl* esquíes *o* esquís*)* *nm* (a) *(tabla)* ski (b) *(deporte)* skiing; **e. de fondo** *o* **nórdico** cross-country skiing; **e. náutico** *o* **acuático** water-skiing; **e. alpino** downhill skiing

**esquiador, -ora** *nm,f* skier

**esquiar** [34] *vi* to ski; **van a e. a los Alpes** they're going skiing in the Alps

**esquilador, -ora** *nm,f* sheepshearer

**esquilar** *vt* to shear

**esquilmar** *vt (recursos)* to overexploit

**esquimal 1** *adj & nmf* Eskimo
**2** *nm (lengua)* Eskimo

**esquina** *nf* corner; *también Fig* **a la vuelta de la e.** just round the corner; **doblar la e.** to turn the corner; **hacer e. (con)** to be on the corner (of)

**esquinado, -a** *adj* on the corner

**esquinazo** *nm* corner; **dar (el) e. a alguien** to give sb the slip

**esquirla** *nf (de loza, hueso)* splinter

**esquirol** *nm Pey* blackleg, scab

**esquivar** *vt (persona, discusión)* to avoid; *(golpe)* to dodge

**esquivez** *nf* shyness

**esquivo, -a** *adj* shy

**esquizofrenia** *nf* schizophrenia

**esquizofrénico, -a** *adj & nm,f* schizophrenic

**esquizoide** *adj* schizoid

**esta** *ver* **este**

**ésta** *ver* **éste**

**estabilidad** *nf* stability; **e. de precios** price stability

**estabilización** *nf* stabilization

**estabilizador, -ora 1** *adj* stabilizing
**2** *nm (de avión, barco)* stabilizer

**estabilizante** *nm (aditivo)* stabilizer

**estabilizar** [16] **1** *vt* to stabilize
**2 estabilizarse** *vpr* to stabilize, to become stable

**estable** *adj* (a) *(firme)* stable (b) *(permanente) (huésped)* permanent; *(cliente)* regular

**establecer** [48] **1** *vt* (a) *(en general)* to establish; *(récord)* to set (b) *(negocio, campamento)* to set up
**2 establecerse** *vpr* (a) *(instalarse)* to settle (b) *(poner un negocio)* to set up a business

**establecimiento** *nm* (a) *(tienda, organismo)* establishment; **e. de enseñanza** educational institution (b) *(de normas, hechos)* establishment; *(de récord)* setting (c) *(de negocio, colonia)* setting up (d) *(de emigrantes, colonos)* settlement

**establo** *nm (para caballos)* stable; *(para vacas)* cowshed

**estaca** *nf* (a) *(para clavar, delimitar)* stake; *(de tienda de campaña)* peg; **le clavó una e. en el corazón** she drove a stake through his heart (b) *(garrote)* cudgel

**estacada** *nf* **dejar a alguien en la e.** to leave sb in the lurch; **quedarse en la e.** to be left in the lurch

**estación** *nf* (a) *(edificio)* station; **e. de autocares/de tren** coach/railway station; **e. de esquí** ski resort; **e. meteorológica** weather station; **e. de servicio** service station; *Informát* **e. de trabajo** workstation (b) *(del año, temporada)* season

**estacionamiento** *nm Aut* parking; *(lugar) Br* car park, *US* parking lot; **e. indebido** parking offence

**estacionar 1** *vt (aparcar)* to park; **prohibido e.** *(en letrero)* no parking
**2 estacionarse** *vpr (aparcar)* to park

**estacionario, -a** *adj (inmóvil)* stationary; *Econ* stagnant

**estadio** *nm* (a) *Dep* stadium (b) *(fase)* stage

**estadista** *nmf* statesman, *f* stateswoman

**estadística** *nf* (a) *(ciencia)* statistics *(singular)* (b) *(dato)* statistic

**estadístico, -a 1** *adj* statistical
**2** *nm,f* statistician

**estado** nm (a) state; **su e. es grave** his condition is serious; **estar en buen/mal e.** (coche, terreno) to be in good/bad condition; (alimento, bebida) to be fresh/off; **en e. de guerra** at war; **estar en e. (de esperanza o buena esperanza)** to be expecting; **e. de ánimo** state of mind; **e. de bienestar** welfare state; **e. civil** marital status; **en e. de coma** in a coma; **e. de cuentas** statement of accounts; **e. de excepción o emergencia** state of emergency; **e. de salud** (state of) health; **e. de sitio** state of siege (b) **el E.** (Gobierno) the State; **Mil E. Mayor** general staff (c) **Estados Unidos de América** United States of America

**estadounidense 1** adj United States; **la política e.** United States o US politics
**2** nmf United States citizen

**estafa** nf (timo, robo) swindle; Com fraud
**estafador, -ora** nm,f swindler
**estafar** vt (timar, robar) to swindle; Com to defraud; **estafó cien millones a la empresa** he defrauded the company of a hundred million (pesetas)
**estafeta** nf sub-post office
**estafilococo** nm staphylococcus
**estalactita** nf stalactite
**estalagmita** nf stalagmite
**estalinismo** nm Stalinism
**estalinista** adj & nmf Stalinist
**estallar** vi (a) (reventar) (bomba) to explode; (neumático) to burst; (volcán) to erupt; (cristal) to shatter; (olas) to break, to crash (b) (sonar) (ovación) to break out; (látigo) to crack (c) Fig (guerra, epidemia) to break out; (tormenta) to break (d) Fig (persona) **e. en sollozos** to burst into tears; **e. en una carcajada** to burst out laughing
**estallido** nm (a) (de bomba) explosion; (de trueno) crash; (de látigo) crack (b) Fig (de guerra) outbreak
**Estambul** n Istanbul
**estamento** nm stratum, class; **el e. eclesiástico/intelectual** the clergy/the intelligentsia
**estampa** nf (a) (imagen, tarjeta) print (b) (aspecto) appearance (c) (retrato, ejemplo) image; Fig **es la viva e. de su madre** he's the (spitting) image of his mother!; **¡maldita sea su e.!** damn o curse him!
**estampado, -a 1** adj printed
**2** nm (a) (acción) printing (b) (dibujo) (cotton) print
**estampar** vt **1** (a) (imprimir) (en tela, papel) to print; (metal) to stamp (b) (escribir) **e. la firma** to sign one's name (c) Fig (arrojar) **e. algo/a alguien contra** to fling sth/sb against, to hurl sth/sb against (d) Fig (dar) (beso) to plant; (bofetada) to land

**2 estamparse** vpr (lanzarse, golpearse) **se estampó contra el muro** he crashed into the wall
**estampida** nf stampede; **de e.** suddenly, in a rush
**estampido** nm report, bang
**estampilla** nf (a) (para marcar) rubber stamp (b) Am (de correos) stamp
**estampillar** vt (sellar) to stamp; (documentos) to rubber-stamp
**estancado, -a** adj (agua) stagnant; (situación, proyecto) at a standstill
**estancamiento** nm stagnation
**estancarse** [61] vpr (situación, proceso) to come to a standstill
**estancia** nf (a) (tiempo) stay (b) (habitación) room (c) CSur (hacienda) cattle ranch
**estanciero** nm CSur ranch owner
**estanco, -a 1** adj watertight; **compartimento e.** watertight compartment
**2** nm tobacconist's
**estándar** (pl estándares) adj & nm standard
**estandarización** nf standardization
**estandarizar** [16] vt to standardize
**estandarte** nm standard, banner
**estanflación** nf Econ stagflation
**estanque** nm (a) (en parque, jardín) pond; (para riego) reservoir (b) Am (depósito) tank (of petrol)
**estanquero, -a** nm,f tobacconist
**estante** nm shelf
**estantería** nf (en general) shelves, shelving; (para libros) bookcase
**estañar** vt to tin-plate
**estaño** nm tin
**estar** [32] **1** vi (a) (hallarse) to be; **¿dónde está la llave?** where is the key?; **¿está María? – no, no está** is Maria there? – no, she's not here
(b) (con fechas) **¿a qué estamos hoy?** what's the date today?; **hoy estamos a martes/a 15 de julio** today is Tuesday/the 15th of July; **estábamos en octubre** it was October
(c) (quedarse) to stay, to be; **estaré un par de horas y me iré** I'll stay a couple of hours and then I'll go
(d) (antes de "a") (expresa valores, grados) **estamos a veinte grados** it's twenty degrees here; **el dólar está a 95 pesetas** the dollar is at 95 pesetas; **están a 100 ptas el kilo** they're 100 pesetas a kilo
(e) (hallarse listo) to be ready; **¿aún no está ese trabajo?** is that piece of work still not ready?
(f) (servir) **e. para** to be (there) for; **para eso**

**están los amigos** that's what friends are for; **para eso estoy** that's what I'm here for

(g) *(antes de gerundio)* *(expresa duración)* to be; **están golpeando la puerta** they're banging on the door

(h) *(antes de "sin" + infin)* *(expresa negación)* **estoy sin dormir desde ayer** I haven't slept since yesterday; **está sin acabar** it's not finished

(i) *(faltar)* **eso está aún por escribir** that has yet to be written; **eso está por ver** that remains to be seen

(j) *(hallarse a punto de)* **e. al llegar** *o* **caer** *(persona)* to be about to arrive; *(acontecimiento)* to be about to happen; **e. por hacer algo** to be on the verge of doing sth; **estuve por pegarle** I was on the verge of hitting him

(k) *(expresa disposición)* **e. para algo** to be in the mood for sth; **no estoy para bromas** I'm not in the mood for jokes

**2** *v copulativo* (a) *(antes de adj)* *(expresa cualidad, estado)* to be; **los pasteles están ricos** the cakes are delicious; **esta calle está sucia** this street is dirty

(b) *(antes de "con" o "sin" + sust)* *(expresa estado)* to be; **estamos sin agua** we have no water, we're without water

(c) *(expresa situación, acción)* **e. de vacaciones** to be on holiday; **e. de viaje** to be on a trip; **e. de mudanza** to be (in the process of) moving; **estamos de suerte** we're in luck; *Fig* **¡ya está bien!** that's enough (of that)!

(d) *(expresa permanencia)* **e. en uso** to be in use; **e. en guardia** to be on guard

(e) *(expresa apoyo, predilección)* **e. por** to be in favour of; **estoy con vosotros** I'm on your side

(f) *(expresa ocupación)* **e. como** *o* **de** to be; **está como cajera** she's a checkout girl

(g) *(consistir)* **estar en** to be, to lie in; **el problema está en la fecha** the problem is the date

(h) *(ropa)* **este traje te está bien** this suit looks good on you

(i) *(antes de "que" + verbo)* *(expresa actitud)* **está que muerde porque ha suspendido** he's furious because he failed

**3 estarse** *vpr (permanecer)* to stay; **te puedes e. con nosotros unos días** you can stay *o* spend a few days with us; **¡estate quieto!** keep still!

**estarcir** *vt* to stencil

**estárter** *(pl* **estárters)** *nm* choke

**estatal** *adj* state; **una empresa e.** a state-owned company; **la política e.** government policy

**estatalizar** [16] *vt* to nationalize

**estático, -a** *adj* (a) *Fís* static (b) *(inmóvil)* stock-still

**estatismo** *nm* (a) *Pol* statism, state interventionism (b) *(inmovilidad)* stillness

**estatua** *nf* statue

**estatura** *nf* height; *Fig* stature

**estatus** *nm inv* status

**estatutario, -a** *adj* statutory

**estatuto** *nm (norma)* statute; *(de empresa)* article (of association); *(de ciudad)* by-law; **e. de autonomía** = legislation devolving powers to an autonomous Spanish region

**este¹1** *adj (posición, parte)* east, eastern; *(dirección, viento)* easterly

**2** *nm* east; **viento del e.** east wind; **ir hacia el e.** to go east(wards); **está al e. de Madrid** it's (to the) east of Madrid; **los países del e.** the countries of Eastern Europe

**este², -a** *(pl* **estos, -as)** *adj demostrativo* (a) *(en general)* this; *(plural)* these

(b) *Fam Pey (singular)* that; *(plural)* those; **no soporto a la niña esta** I can't stand that girl

**éste, -a** *(pl* **éstos, -as)**

> Note that **éste** and its various forms can be written without an accent when there is no risk of confusion with the adjective.

*pron demostrativo* (a) *(en general)* this one; *(plural)* these (ones); **dame otro boli – é. no funciona** give me another pen – this one doesn't work; **aquellos cuadros no están mal, aunque éstos me gustan más** those paintings aren't bad, but I like these (ones) better; **ésta ha sido la semana más feliz de mi vida** this has been the happiest week of my life

(b) *(recién mencionado)* the latter; **entraron Juan y Pedro, é. con un abrigo verde** Juan and Pedro came in, the latter wearing a green coat

(c) *Fam (despectivo)* **e. es el que me pegó** this is the guy *or* the one who hit me; **éstos son los culpables de todo lo ocurrido** it's this lot who are to blame for everything

(d) *Fam* **en éstas** just then, at that very moment

**estela** *nf (de barco)* wake; *(de avión)* vapour trail; *Fig (de humo, olor)* trail

**estelar** *adj* (a) *Astron* stellar (b) *Cine & Teatro* star; **un reparto e.** a star-studded cast

**estenografía** *nf* shorthand

**estenotipia** *nf* (a) *(arte)* stenotypy (b) *(máquina)* Stenotype

**estenotipista** *nmf* stenotypist

**estenotipo** *nm* Stenotype

**estentóreo, -a** *adj Formal* stentorian

**estepa** *nf* steppe

**éster** *nm* ester

**estera** *nf* *(tejido)* matting; *(alfombrilla)* mat

**estercolero** *nm* dunghill; *Fig (lugar sucio)* pigsty

**estéreo** *adj inv & nm* stereo

**estereofonía** *nf* stereo

**estereofónico, -a** *adj* stereophonic, stereo; **sonido e.** stereo sound

**estereoscopio** *nm* stereoscope

**estereotipado, -a** *adj* stereotyped, stereotypical

**estereotipar** *vt* to stereotype

**estereotipo** *nm* stereotype

**estéril** *adj* **(a)** *(persona)* infertile, sterile; *(terreno)* barren, infertile **(b)** *(gasa)* sterilized **(c)** *Fig (inútil)* futile, fruitless

**esterilete** *nm* coil, IUD

**esterilidad** *nf* sterility

**esterilización** *nf* sterilization

**esterilizar** [16] *vt* to sterilize

**esterilla** *nf* beach mat

**esterlina** *adj* **libra e.** pound sterling

**esternón** *nm* breastbone, sternum

**esteroides** *nmpl* steroids

**estertor** *nm* death rattle

**esteta** *nmf* aesthete

**estética** *nf* **(a)** *(en filosofía)* aesthetics *(singular)* **(b)** *(belleza)* beauty **(c)** *(estilo)* style; **la e. de los años setenta** the style of the seventies

**esteticista** *nf* beautician

**estético, -a** *adj* aesthetic

**estetoscopio** *nm* stethoscope

**esthéticienne** [esteti'θjen] *nf* beautician

**estiba** *nf* stowage

**estibador, -ora** *nm,f* stevedore

**estibar** *vt* to stow

**estiércol** *nm* *(excrementos)* dung; *(abono)* manure

**estigma** *nm* **(a)** *(marca)* mark, scar **(b)** *Fig (deshonor)* stigma **(c)** *Rel* **estigmas** stigmata

**estigmatización** *nf* *(marca)* branding; *Fig (deshonra)* stigmatization

**estigmatizar** [16] *vt* *(marcar)* to scar; *(con hierro candente)* to brand; *Fig (deshonrar)* to stigmatize

**estilarse** *vpr Fam* to be in (fashion)

**estilete** *nm* *(daga)* stiletto

**estilismo** *nm* styling

**estilista** *nmf* **(a)** *(escritor)* stylist **(b)** *(de moda, accesorios)* stylist

**estilística** *nf* stylistics *(singular)*

**estilístico, -a** *adj* stylistic

**estilizado, -a** *adj* *(figura, cuerpo)* slim and elegant

**estilizar** [16] *vt* to stylize

**estilo** *nm* **(a)** *(manera, carácter)* style; **e. de vida** lifestyle; **esa chica tiene mucho e.** that girl has a lot of style **(b)** *(en natación)* stroke **(c)** *Gram* **e. directo/indirecto** direct/indirect speech **(d)** **algo por el e.** something of the sort; **ser por el e.** to be similar

**estilográfica** *nf* fountain pen

**estima** *nf* esteem, respect; **tener a alguien en gran** *o* **alta e.** to hold sb in high esteem

**estimable** *adj* **(a)** *(cantidad)* considerable **(b)** *(digno de estimación)* worthy of appreciation

**estimación** *nf* **(a)** *(aprecio)* esteem, respect **(b)** *(valoración)* valuation; *(cálculo aproximado)* estimate **(c)** *(en impuestos)* assessment

**estimado, -a** *adj* **(a)** *(querido)* esteemed, respected; **e. Señor** *(en carta)* Dear Sir **(b)** *(aproximado)* estimated

**estimar** **1** *vt* **(a)** *(apreciar)* to think highly of **(b)** *(evaluar)* to value; **e. el valor de algo** to estimate the value of sth **(c)** *(creer)* to consider, to think

**2 estimarse** *vpr (tener dignidad)* to have self-respect

**estimativo, -a** *adj* approximate, rough; **un juicio e. (sobre** *o* **de)** an evaluation (of)

**estimulador, -ora** *adj* encouraging

**estimulante** **1** *adj* **(a)** *(que anima)* encouraging **(b)** *(que excita)* stimulating

**2** *nm* stimulant

**estimular** *vt* **(a)** *(animar)* to encourage **(b)** *(excitar)* to stimulate

**estímulo** *nm* **(a)** *(aliciente)* incentive; *(ánimo)* encouragement **(b)** *(de un órgano)* stimulus

**estío** *nm* summer

**estipendio** *nm* remuneration

**estipulación** *nf* **(a)** *(acuerdo)* agreement **(b)** *Der* stipulation

**estipular** *vt* to stipulate

**estirado, -a** *adj* **(a)** *(persona)* *(altanero)* haughty; *(adusto)* uptight **(b)** *(brazos, piernas)* outstretched **(c)** *(jersey)* baggy, shapeless

**estiramiento** *nm* stretching

**estirar** **1** *vt* **(a)** *(alargar)* to stretch; **e. el cuello** to crane; *Fig* **e. las piernas** to stretch one's legs **(b)** *(desarrugar)* to straighten **(c)** *Fig (dinero)* to make last; *(discurso, tema)* to spin out

**2** *vi* **(a)** *(tirar)* **e. (de)** to pull **(b)** *(agrandarse)* **el jersey ha estirado al lavarlo** the jersey has gone baggy in the wash

**3 estirarse** *vpr* **(a)** *(desperezarse)* to stretch **(b)** *(tumbarse)* to stretch out **(c)** *(crecer)* to shoot up **(d)** *(agrandarse)* **el jersey se ha estirado al lavarlo** the jersey has gone baggy in the wash

**estirón** *nm* **(a)** *(acción)* tug, pull **(b)** *(al crecer)* **dar** *o* **pegar un e.** to shoot up suddenly

**estirpe** *nf* stock, lineage

**estival** *adj* summer; **vacaciones estivales** summer holidays

**esto** *pron demostrativo* this thing; **e. es tu regalo de cumpleaños** this is your birthday present; **e. que acabas de decir no tiene sentido** what you've just said doesn't make sense; **e. de trabajar de noche no me gusta** I don't like this business of working at night; **a todo e.** by the way; **e. es** that is (to say); **en e.** just then, at that very moment; **¿para e. me has hecho venir?** you got me to come here for THIS?; **por e.** that's why

**estocada** *nf (en esgrima)* stab; *Taurom (sword)* thrust

**Estocolmo** *n* Stockholm

**estofa** *nf* **de baja e.** *(gente)* low-class; *(cosas)* poor-quality

**estofado** *nm* stew

**estofar** *vt* to stew

**estoicismo** *nm* stoicism

**estoico, -a 1** *adj* stoic, stoical
  **2** *nm* stoic

**estola** *nf* stole

**estomacal 1** *adj (del estómago)* stomach; *(bebida)* digestive; **afección e.** stomach complaint
  **2** *nm (bebida)* digestive

**estómago** *nm* stomach

**Estonia** *n* Estonia

**estonio, -a** *adj & nm,f* Estonian

**estopa** *nf (fibra)* tow; *(tela)* burlap

**estoque** *nm* rapier

**estoquear** *vt* to stab

**estor** *nm* Venetian blind

**estorbar 1** *vt (obstaculizar)* to hinder; *(molestar)* to bother; **le estorba el flequillo para jugar al tenis** his fringe bothers him when he plays tennis
  **2** *vi (estar en medio)* to be in the way

**estorbo** *nm (obstáculo)* hindrance; *(molestia)* nuisance

**estornino** *nm* starling

**estornudar** *vi* to sneeze

**estornudo** *nm* sneeze

**estos, -as** *ver* **este**

**éstos, -as** *ver* **éste**

**estoy** *ver* **estar**

**estrábico, -a 1** *adj* squint-eyed
  **2** *nm,f* person with a squint

**estrabismo** *nm* squint

**estrado** *nm* platform; **subir al e.** *(orador)* to go up on to the platform; *(testigo)* to take the stand

**estrafalario** *adj* outlandish, eccentric

**estragón** *nm* tarragon

**estragos** *nmpl* **causar** *o* **hacer e. en** *(físicos)* to wreak havoc with; *(morales)* to destroy, to ruin

**estrambótico, -a** *adj* outlandish

**estramonio** *nm* thorn apple

**estrangulador, -ora** *nm,f* strangler

**estrangulamiento** *nm Med* strangulation

**estrangular 1** *vt* **(a)** *(ahogar)* to strangle **(b)** *(tubo, conducto)* to constrict; *Med* to strangulate **(c)** *(proyecto)* to stifle, to nip in the bud
  **2 estrangularse** *vpr* to strangle oneself

**estraperlista** *nmf* black marketeer

**estraperlo** *nm* black market; **productos de e.** black market goods

**Estrasburgo** *n* Strasbourg

**estratagema** *nf Mil* stratagem; *Fig (astucia)* artifice, trick

**estratega** *nmf* strategist

**estrategia** *nf* strategy

**estratégico, -a** *adj* strategic

**estratificación** *nf* stratification

**estratificado, -a** *adj* stratified

**estratificar** [61] **1** *vt* to stratify
  **2 estratificarse** *vpr Geol* to form strata; *(sociedad)* to become stratified

**estrato** *nm Geol, Meteo & Fig* stratum

**estratosfera** *nf* stratosphere

**estrechamiento** *nm* **(a)** *(de calle, tubo)* narrowing **(b)** *Fig* rapprochement

**estrechar 1** *vt* **(a)** *(hacer estrecho)* to narrow; *(ropa)* to take in **(b)** *Fig (relaciones)* to make closer **(c)** *(apretar)* to squeeze, to hug; **e. la mano a alguien** to shake sb's hand; **la estrechó entre sus brazos** he hugged *o* embraced her
  **2 estrecharse** *vpr* **(a)** *(hacerse estrecho)* to narrow **(b)** *(abrazarse)* to embrace **(c)** *(apretarse)* to squeeze up

**estrechez** *nf* **(a)** *(falta de anchura)* narrowness; *(falta de espacio)* lack of space; *(de ropa)* tightness; **e. de miras** narrow-mindedness **(b)** *Fig (falta de dinero)* hardship; **pasar estrecheces** to be hard up **(c)** *(intimidad)* closeness

**estrecho, -a 1** *adj* **(a)** *(no ancho)* narrow; *(ropa)* tight; **e. de miras** narrow-minded **(b)** *Fig (íntimo)* close
  **2** *nm,f Fam (persona)* prude
  **3** *nm Geog* strait

**estregar** [45] *vt* to rub

**estrella 1** *adj inv* star; **producto e.** star *o* flagship product
  **2** *nf* **(a)** *(astro, figura)* star; *Fig (suerte, destino)* fate; **e. fugaz** shooting star; **e. polar** Pole Star; **ver las estrellas** to see stars; **tener buena/mala e.** to be lucky/unlucky **(b)** **e. de mar** starfish

**estrellado, -a** *adj* (a) *(con estrellas)* starry (b) *(por la forma)* star-shaped (c) *(que ha chocado)* smashed; *Fig* **José ha nacido e.** José was born unlucky

**estrellar 1** *vt (arrojar)* to smash

**2 estrellarse** *vpr* (a) *(chocar) (persona, objeto)* to smash (**contra** against); *(avión, coche)* to crash (**contra** into) (b) *Fig (fracasar)* to come to nothing

**estrellato** *nm* stardom

**estremecer** [48] **1** *vt* to shake

**2 estremecerse** *vpr (de horror, miedo)* to tremble *o* shudder (**de** with); *(de frío)* to shiver (**de** with); **me estremezco sólo de pensarlo** I get the shivers just thinking about it

**estremecimiento** *nm (de miedo)* shudder; *(de frío)* shiver

**estrenar 1** *vt* (a) *(objeto)* to use for the first time; *(ropa)* to wear for the first time; *(piso)* to move into (b) *Cine* to release, to show for the first time; *Teatro* to premiere

**2 estrenarse** *vpr (persona)* to make one's debut, to start

**estreno** *nm* (a) *(de cosa)* first use (b) *(de espectáculo)* premiere, first night; *(de actor)* debut; **la noche del e.** the opening night

**estreñido, -a** *adj* constipated

**estreñimiento** *nm* constipation

**estreñir** *vt* to constipate

**estrépito** *nm (ruido)* racket, din; *Fig (ostentación)* fanfare

**estrepitoso, -a** *adj* (a) *(ruidoso)* noisy; *(aplausos)* deafening (b) *(derrota)* resounding; *(fracaso)* spectacular

**estreptomicina** *nf* streptomycin

**estrés** *nm inv* stress

**estresado, -a** *adj* suffering from stress; **estar e.** to be stressed

**estresante** *adj* stressful

**estresar** *vt* to cause stress to; **ese ruido me está estresando** that noise is getting on my nerves

**estría** *nf (surco)* groove; *(en la piel)* stretch mark

**estribaciones** *nfpl* foothills

**estribar** *vi* **e. en** to lie in, to consist in

**estribillo** *nm* (a) *Mús* chorus; *Lit* refrain (b) *Fam (coletilla)* pet word *o* phrase

**estribo** *nm* (a) *(de montura)* stirrup; **perder los estribos** to fly off the handle (b) *(de coche, tren)* step

**estribor** *nm* starboard; **a e.** (to) starboard

**estricnina** *nf* strychnine

**estricto, -a** *adj* strict

**estridencia** *nf (de ruido)* stridency, shrillness; *Fig (de colores, comportamiento)* loudness

**estridente** *adj (ruido)* strident, shrill; *Fig (color)* garish, loud; *Fig (persona, comportamiento)* loud

**estrofa** *nf* stanza, verse

**estrógeno, -a** *nm* oestrogen

**estroncio** *nm* strontium

**estropajo** *nm* scourer

**estropajoso, -a** *adj* (a) *(pelo)* coarse; *(textura)* fibrous; *(carne)* dry and chewy (b) *(lengua, boca)* dry and pasty

**estropeado, -a** (a) *adj (averiado)* broken (b) *(dañado)* damaged (c) *(echado a perder)* ruined, spoiled

**estropear 1** *vt* (a) *(averiar)* to break (b) *(dañar)* to damage; **el exceso de sol estropea la piel** too much sun is bad for the skin (c) *(echar a perder)* to ruin, to spoil

**2 estropearse** *vpr* (a) *(máquina)* to break down (b) *(comida)* to go off, to spoil; **María se ha estropeado mucho con los años** María hasn't aged well (c) *(plan)* to fall through

**estropicio** *nm* **hacer** *o* **causar un e.** to wreak havoc

**estructura** *nf* structure; **e. profunda/superficial** deep/surface structure

**estructuración** *nf* structuring, organization

**estructural** *adj* structural

**estructurar** *vt* to structure, to organize

**estruendo** *nm* (a) *(ruido)* din, roar; *(de trueno)* crash (b) *(alboroto)* uproar, tumult

**estrujar 1** *vt* (a) *(limón)* to squeeze; *(trapo, ropa)* to wring (out); *(papel)* to screw up; *(caja)* to crush (b) *(persona, mano)* to squeeze; **me estrujó un pie** he squashed my foot; **¡no me estrujes!** don't squash *o* crush me! (c) *Fig (sacar partido)* to bleed dry

**2 estrujarse** *vpr (apretujarse)* to huddle together

**estrujón** *nm* (a) *(abrazo)* bear hug (b) *(apretujón)* **hubo muchos estrujones** there was a lot of pushing and shoving

**estuario** *nm* estuary

**estucado** *nm* stucco, stuccowork

**estucar** [61] *vt* to stucco

**estuche** *nm (caja)* case; *(de joyas)* jewellery box; *(de gafas)* glasses case; *(de lápices)* pencil case

**estuco** *nm* stucco

**estudiado, -a** *adj* studied

**estudiante** *nmf (de universidad, secundaria)* student; *(de primaria)* schoolchild, pupil

**estudiantil** *adj* student; **protestas estudiantiles** student protests; **un bar con ambiente e.** a studenty bar

**estudiar** [15] **1** vt (a) *(carrera, libro)* to study; **estudia biológicas** he's studying biology; **estudia todas las tardes** he spends every afternoon studying (b) *(observar)* to observe

**2** vi to study; **e. para médico** to be studying to be a doctor; **¿estudias o trabajas?** do you work or are you a student?

**estudio** nm (a) *(actividad)* study; **estar en e.** to be under consideration; **e. de mercado** *(técnica)* market research; *(investigación)* market survey; **estudios** *(serie de cursos)* studies; **estudios primarios/secundarios** primary/secondary education; **no tiene estudios** he hasn't had much education (b) *(oficina)* study; *(de fotógrafo, pintor)* studio (c) *(apartamento)* studio flat (d) *Cine, Rad & TV* studio; **los estudios de la Metro** the Metro studios

**estudioso, -a 1** adj studious

**2** nm,f *(especialista)* specialist, expert; **un e. de la naturaleza humana** a student of human nature

**estufa** nf *(calefacción)* heater, fire; *Am (cocina)* stove

**estupa** nm muy Fam drug squad detective

**estupefacción** nf astonishment

**estupefaciente** nm narcotic, drug; **brigada de estupefacientes** drugs squad

**estupefacto, -a** adj astonished; **quedarse e.** to be speechless o flabbergasted

**estupendamente** adv wonderfully; **estoy e.** I feel wonderful

**estupendo, -a** adj wonderful, marvellous; **¡e.!** wonderful!, marvellous!

**estupidez** nf stupidity; **decir/hacer una e.** to say/do something stupid

**estúpido, -a 1** adj stupid

**2** nm,f idiot

**estupor** nm astonishment

**estupro** nm Der rape of a minor

**esturión** nm sturgeon

**estuviera** etc ver **estar**

**esvástica** nf swastika

**ETA** nf *(abrev de* **Euskadi Ta Askatasuna)** ETA, = terrorist Basque separatist organization

**etano** nm ethane

**etapa** nf stage; **por etapas** in stages; **quemar etapas** to come on in leaps and bounds, to progress rapidly; **está pasando una mala e.** he's going through a bad patch; **e. ciclista** stage *(of cycle race)*

**etarra 1** adj ETA; **el terrorismo e.** ETA terrorism

**2** nmf member of ETA

**ETB** nf *(abrev de* **Euskal Telebista)** = Basque television network

**etc.** *(abrev de* **etcétera)** etc.

**etcétera 1** adv etcetera

**2** nm **y un largo e. de…** and a long list of…

**éter** nm (a) *(gas)* ether (b) *Formal (cielo)* **el é.** the ether, the heavens

**etéreo, -a** adj ethereal

**eternidad** nf eternity; *Fam Fig* **hace una e. que no la veo** it's ages since I last saw her

**eternizar** [16] **1** vt **e. algo** to make sth last forever

**2 eternizarse** vpr **eternizarse (haciendo algo)** to spend absolutely ages (doing sth); **la reunión se eternizó** the meeting went on and on

**eterno, -a** adj *(perpetuo)* eternal; *Fam Fig (larguísimo)* never-ending, interminable; **la eterna canción** the same old story

**ética** nf (a) *(en filosofía)* ethics *(singular)* (b) *(moralidad)* ethics; **é. profesional** (professional) ethics

**ético, -a** adj ethical

**etileno** nm ethylene

**etílico, -a** adj *Quím* ethyl; **alcohol e.** ethyl alcohol; **intoxicación etílica** alcohol poisoning

**etilismo** nm intoxication

**etilo** nm ethyl

**etimología** nf etymology

**etimológico, -a** adj etymological

**etiología** nf *Med* etiology

**etíope** adj & nmf Ethiopian

**Etiopía** nf Ethiopia

**etiqueta** nf (a) *también Informát* label; *Fig* **colgarle a alguien la e. de…** to label sb as… (b) *(ceremonial)* etiquette; **de e.** formal

**etiquetado** nm labelling

**etiquetadora** nf pricing gun

**etiquetar** vt *también Fig* to label; **e. a alguien de algo** to label sb sth

**etiquetero, -a** adj ceremonious, formal

**etnia** nf ethnic group; **una persona de e. oriental** a person of Asian extraction

**étnico, -a** adj ethnic

**etnocentrismo** nm ethnocentrism

**etnografía** nf ethnography

**etnología** nf ethnology

**etnólogo, -a** nm,f ethnologist

**etrusco, -a** adj & nm,f Etruscan

**EUA** nmpl *(abrev de* **Estados Unidos de América)** USA

**eucalipto** nm eucalyptus

**eucaristía** nf **la e.** the Eucharist

**eucarístico, -a** adj Eucharistic

**eufemismo** nm euphemism

**euforia** nf euphoria, elation

**eufórico, -a** adj euphoric, elated

**Éufrates** *nm* el É. the Euphrates

**eunuco** *nm* eunuch

**Eurasia** *n* Eurasia

**EURATOM** [eura'tom] *nf* (*abrev de* **Comunidad Europea de la Energía Atómica**) EURATOM

**eureka** *interj* ¡e.! eureka!

**euro** *nm* (*moneda*) Euro

**euroasiático, -a** *adj & nm,f* Eurasian

**eurocámara** *nf* (*Parlamento Europeo*) European Parliament

**eurocheque** *nm* eurocheque

**eurocomunismo** *nm* Eurocommunism

**eurocomunista** *adj & nmf* Eurocommunist

**eurócrata** *adj & nmf* Eurocrat

**eurodiputado, -a** *nm,f* Euro-MP, MEP

**eurodivisa** *nf Fin* eurocurrency

**eurodólar** *nm Fin* Eurodollar

**Europa** *n* Europe

**europarlamentario, -a 1** *adj* of the European Parliament
   **2** *nm,f* Euro-MP, MEP

**europeidad** *nf* Europeanness

**europeísmo** *nm* Europeanism

**europeísta** *adj & nmf* pro-European

**europeización** *nf* Europeanization

**europeizar** [16] *vt* to Europeanize

**europeo, -a** *adj & nm,f* European

**eurovisión** *nf* Eurovision

**Euskadi** *n* the Basque Country

**euskera, euskara** *nm* Basque

**eutanasia** *nf* euthanasia

**evacuación** *nf* (*de zona, edificio, vientre*) evacuation

**evacuado, -a 1** *adj* evacuated
   **2** *nm,f* evacuee

**evacuar** [5] *vt* (*edificio, zona*) to evacuate; (*vientre*) to empty, to void

**evadido, -a 1** *adj* (*persona*) escaped; (*divisas, impuestos*) evaded
   **2** *nm,f* escapee, fugitive

**evadir 1** *vt* (*impuestos*) to evade; (*respuesta, peligro*) to avoid
   **2 evadirse** *vpr* to escape (**de** from)

**evaluable** *adj* calculable

**evaluación** *nf* (a) (*valoración*) evaluation; **hizo una e. positiva de la situación** he gave a positive assessment of the situation (b) *Educ* (*examen*) exam, test; (*período*) = division of school year, of which there may be three to five in total; **e. continua** continuous assessment

**evaluador, -ora** *adj* evaluating, evaluative

**evaluar** [4] *vt* to evaluate, to assess

**evanescencia** *nf Formal* evanescence

**evanescente** *adj Formal* evanescent

**evangélico, -a** *adj & nm,f* evangelical

**evangelio** *nm* (a) *Rel* gospel (b) *Fig* beliefs

**evangelista** *nm* Evangelist

**evangelización** *nf* evangelization, evangelizing

**evangelizar** [16] *vt* to evangelize

**evaporación** *nf* evaporation

**evaporar 1** *vt* to evaporate
   **2 evaporarse** *vpr* (a) (*líquido*) to evaporate (b) *Fam Fig* (*persona, fondos*) to disappear into thin air

**evasión** *nf* (a) (*huida*) escape (b) (*de dinero*) **e. de capitales** *o* **divisas** capital flight; **e. fiscal** tax evasion (c) *Fig* (*entretenimiento*) amusement, recreation; (*escapismo*) escapism; **literatura de e.** escapist literature

**evasiva** *nf* evasive answer; **responder con evasivas** not to give a straight answer

**evasivo, -a** *adj* evasive

**evasor, -ora 1** *adj* guilty of evasion
   **2** *nm,f* (*de la cárcel*) jailbreaker

**evento** *nm* event

**eventual** *adj* (a) (*no fijo*) (*trabajador*) temporary, casual; (*gastos*) incidental (b) (*posible*) possible

**eventualidad** *nf* (a) (*temporalidad*) temporariness (b) (*hecho incierto*) eventuality; (*posibilidad*) possibility; **en la e. de que viniera, lo recibiríamos** in the event of his coming, we would receive him

**Everest** *nm* el E. (Mount) Everest

**evidencia** *nf* (a) (*prueba*) evidence, proof (b) (*claridad*) obviousness; **poner algo en e.** to demonstrate sth; **poner a alguien en e.** to show sb up

**evidenciar** [15] **1** *vt* to show, to demonstrate
   **2 evidenciarse** *vpr* to be obvious *o* evident

**evidente** *adj* evident, obvious

**evitar** *vt* (*evadir*) to avoid; (*desastre, accidente*) to avert; **e. que alguien haga algo** to prevent sb from doing sth; **esto me evita tener que ir** this gets me out of going

**evocación** *nf* recollection, evocation

**evocador, -ora** *adj* evocative

**evocar** [61] *vt* (*recordar*) to evoke

**evolución** *nf* (a) (*de especies, proceso*) evolution; (*de enfermedad*) development, progress (b) *Mil* manoeuvre

**evolucionar** *vi* (a) (*progresar*) to evolve; (*enfermedad*) to develop, to progress; (*cambiar*) to change; **el paciente no evoluciona** the patient isn't making any progress (b) *Mil* to carry out manoeuvres

**evolucionismo** *nm* evolutionism

**evolucionista** *adj & nmf* evolutionist

**evolutivo, -a** *adj* evolutionary

**evoque** *etc ver* **evocar**

**ex 1** *nmf (cónyuge)* ex

**2** *prefijo* ex-; **el ex presidente** the ex-president, the former president

**exabrupto** *nm* sharp word *o* remark

**exacción** *nf (de impuestos, multas)* exaction, collection

**exacerbar** *vt* **(a)** *(agudizar)* to exacerbate, to aggravate **(b)** *(irritar)* to irritate, to infuriate

**exactamente** *adv* exactly, precisely

**exactas** *nfpl* mathematics *(singular)*

**exactitud** *nf (precisión)* accuracy, precision; *(puntualidad)* punctuality; **no lo sé con e.** I don't know exactly

**exacto, -a 1** *adj* **(a)** *(justo)* exact; **tres metros exactos** exactly three metres **(b)** *(preciso)* accurate, precise; *(correcto)* correct, right; **para ser exactos** to be precise **(c)** *(idéntico)* identical **(a** to**); es e. a su padre** he looks just like his father

**2** *interj* **¡e.!** exactly!, precisely!

**exageración** *nf* exaggeration; **este precio es una e.** that's a ridiculous price; **su reacción me pareció una e.** I thought his reaction was a bit over the top

**exagerado, -a** *adj (cifra, reacción, gesto)* exaggerated; *(precio)* exorbitant; **es muy e.** *(en cantidad, valoración)* he exaggerates a lot; *(en reacción)* he overreacts a lot

**exagerar** *vt & vi* to exaggerate

**exaltación** *nf* **(a)** *(júbilo)* elation, intense excitement; *(acaloramiento)* overexcitement **(b)** *(ensalzamiento)* exaltation

**exaltado, -a 1** *adj (jubiloso)* elated; *(acalorado)* *(persona)* worked up; *(discusión)* heated; *(excitable)* hotheaded

**2** *nm,f (fanático)* fanatic; *Pol* extremist

**exaltar 1** *vt* **(a)** *(elevar)* to promote, to raise **(b)** *(glorificar)* to exalt

**2 exaltarse** *vpr* to get excited *o* worked up **(por** about)

**examen** *nm* **(a)** *(ejercicio)* exam, examination; **aprobar/suspender un e.** to pass/fail an exam; **hacer un e.** to do *o* take an exam; **presentarse a un e.** to sit an exam; **e. de conducir** driving test; **e. de ingreso** entrance examination; **e. final/oral** final/oral (exam); **e. parcial** end-of-term exam **(b)** *(indagación)* consideration, examination; **hacer e. de conciencia** to take a good look at oneself; **e. médico** medical examination *o* check-up; **libre e.** personal interpretation

**examinador, -ora** *nm,f* examiner

**examinando, -a** *nm,f* examinee, candidate

**examinar 1** *vt* to examine

**2 examinarse** *vpr* to sit *o* take an exam

**exangüe** *adj Formal* exhausted

**exánime** *adj* **(a)** *(muerto)* dead **(b)** *(desmayado)* lifeless; *Fig (agotado)* exhausted, worn-out

**exasperación** *nf* exasperation

**exasperante** *adj* exasperating, infuriating

**exasperar 1** *vt* to exasperate, to infuriate

**2 exasperarse** *vpr* to get exasperated

**Exc.** *(abrev de* **Excelencia)** Excellency

**excarcelación** *nf* release (from prison)

**excarcelar** *vt* to release (from prison)

**excavación** *nf* **(a)** *(acción)* excavation **(b)** *(lugar)* dig, excavation; **e. arqueológica** archaeological dig

**excavador, -ora 1** *adj* excavating, digging

**2** *nm,f (persona)* excavator, digger

**excavadora** *nf (máquina)* digger

**excavar** *vt (cavar)* to dig; *(en arqueología)* to excavate

**excedencia** *nf* leave (of absence); *Educ* sabbatical; **un año de e.** a year's leave of absence; *Educ* a year's sabbatical

**excedentario, -a** *adj* surplus; **la balanza de pagos ha sido excedentaria** the balance of payments has been in surplus

**excedente 1** *adj* **(a)** *(producción)* surplus **(b)** *(funcionario)* on leave; *Educ* on sabbatical

**2** *nmf (persona)* person on leave; **e. de cupo =** person excused from military service because there are already enough new recruits

**3** *nm Com* surplus; **excedentes agrícolas** agricultural surpluses

**exceder 1** *vt* to exceed, to surpass

**2** *vi* to be greater; **e. a** *o* **de** to exceed

**3 excederse** *vpr* **(a)** *(propasarse)* to go too far *o* overstep the mark **(en** in**) (b)** *(rebasar el límite)* **se excede en el peso** it's too heavy

**excelencia 1** *nf (cualidad)* excellence; **por e.** par excellence

**2** *nmf* **Su E.** His Excellency, *f* Her Excellency

**excelente** *adj* excellent

**excelentísimo, -a** *adj* most excellent; **el e. ayuntamiento de Málaga** Malaga city council; **el e. embajador de...** his excellency the ambassador of...

**excelso, -a** *adj Formal* sublime, elevated

**excentricidad** *nf* eccentricity

**excéntrico, -a** *adj & nm,f* eccentric

**excepción** *nf* exception; **a** *o* **con e. de** with the exception of, except for; **de e.** exceptional; **e. hecha de Pérez** Pérez excepted; **hacer una e.** to make an exception; *Prov* **la e. confirma la regla** the exception proves the rule

**excepcional** *adj* exceptional

**excepto** *adv* except (for)

**exceptuar** [4] *vt* *(excluir)* to exclude (de from); *(eximir)* to exempt (de from); **exceptuando a...** excluding...; **se exceptúa a los menores de 16 años** children under the age of 16 are exempt

**excesivo, -a** *adj* excessive

**exceso** *nm* *(demasía)* excess; **cometer un e.** to go too far; **cometer un e. en la bebida/ comida** to drink/eat to excess; **en e.** excessively, to excess; **e. de equipaje** excess baggage; **e. de peso** *(obesidad)* excess weight; **e. de velocidad** speeding

**excipiente** *nm* excipient

**excisión** *nf Med* excision

**excitación** *nf* (a) *(nerviosismo)* agitation; *(por enfado, sexo)* arousal (b) *Biol & Elec* excitation

**excitado, -a** *adj* (a) *(nervioso)* agitated; *(por enfado, sexo)* aroused (b) *Biol & Elec* excited

**excitante** 1 *adj* *(emocionante)* exciting; *(sexualmente)* arousing; *(café, tabaco)* stimulating
  2 *nm* stimulant

**excitar** 1 *vt* (a) *(inquietar)* to upset, to agitate (b) *(estimular)* *(sentidos)* to stimulate; *(apetito)* to whet; *(curiosidad, interés)* to excite; *(sexualmente)* to arouse
  2 **excitarse** *vpr* (a) *(alterarse)* to get worked up *o* excited (**por** about) (b) *(sexualmente)* to become aroused

**exclamación** *nf* *(interjección)* exclamation; *(grito)* cry

**exclamar** *vt & vi* to exclaim

**exclamativo, -a** *adj* exclamatory

**excluir** [36] *vt* *(dejar fuera)* to exclude (de from); *(hipótesis, opción)* to rule out; *(hacer imposible)* to preclude

**exclusión** *nf* exclusion

**exclusiva** *nf* (a) *Prensa* exclusive (b) *Com* exclusive *o* sole right; **tenemos la distribución en España en e.** we are the sole distributor in Spain

**exclusividad** *nf* (a) *(de club, ambiente, producto)* exclusiveness (b) *Com* *(privilegio)* exclusive *o* sole right

**exclusivo, -a** *adj* *(club, ambiente, producto)* exclusive

**excluyente** *adj* excluding

**Excmo., Excma.** *(abrev de* **Excelentísimo, Excelentísima)** **el E. Ayto. de Málaga** Malaga City Council

**excombatiente** *nmf* Br ex-serviceman, f ex-servicewoman, *US* war veteran

**excomulgar** [40] *vt* to excommunicate

**excomunión** *nf* excommunication

**excrecencia** *nf* growth

**excremento** *nm* **un e. de perro** a piece of dog dirt; **excrementos** *(de ave, conejo, oveja)* droppings; *(de persona)* excrement

**excretar** 1 *vt* *(soltar)* to secrete
  2 *vi* *(evacuar)* to excrete

**excretorio, -a** *adj* excretory

**exculpación** *nf* exoneration; *Der* acquittal

**exculpar** 1 *vt* to exonerate; *Der* to acquit
  2 **exculparse** *vpr* to declare oneself innocent (**de** of)

**exculpatorio, -a** *adj* exonerative

**excursión** *nf* *(viaje)* excursion, trip; **ir de e.** to go on an outing *o* a trip

**excursionismo** *nm* *(en el campo)* rambling; *(de montaña)* hiking

**excursionista** *nmf* *(en el campo)* rambler; *(en la montaña)* hiker

**excusa** *nf* (a) *(pretexto, motivo)* excuse (b) *(petición de perdón)* apology; **presentó sus excusas** he apologized

**excusar** 1 *vt* (a) *(disculpar a)* to excuse; *(disculparse por)* to apologize for (b) *(evitar)* to avoid
  2 **excusarse** *vpr* to apologize, to excuse oneself

**execrable** *adj* abominable, execrable

**execrar** *vt Formal* to abhor

**exégesis** *nf inv* exegesis, explanation

**exención** *nf* exemption; *Fin* **e. fiscal** tax exemption

**exento, -a** *adj* exempt; **e. de** *(sin)* free from, without; *(eximido de)* exempt from

**exequias** *nfpl* funeral, funeral rites

**exfoliación** *nf* exfoliation

**exfoliante** 1 *adj* exfoliating
  2 *nm* exfoliating cream/lotion etc

**exhalación** *nf* *(emanación)* exhalation, vapour; *(suspiro)* breath (b) *Fam Fig* **como una e.** as quick as a flash

**exhalar** *vt* (a) *(aire)* to exhale, to breathe out; *(suspiros)* to heave; **e. el último suspiro** to breathe one's last (breath) (b) *(olor, vapor)* to give off

**exhaustivo, -a** *adj* exhaustive

**exhausto, -a** *adj* exhausted

**exhibición** *nf* (a) *(demostración)* show, display (b) *(deportiva, artística)* exhibition (c) *(de películas)* showing

**exhibicionismo** *nm* exhibitionism

**exhibicionista** *adj & nmf* *(que gusta de llamar la atención)* exhibitionist; *(pervertido sexual)* flasher

**exhibir** 1 *vt* (a) *(cuadros, fotografías)* to exhibit; *(modelos)* to show; *(productos)* to display (b) *(joyas, cualidades)* to show off (c) *(película)* to show, to screen
  2 **exhibirse** *vpr* *(alardear)* to show off

**exhortación** *nf* exhortation

**exhortar** *vt* e. a to exhort to

**exhumación** *nf* exhumation, disinterment

**exhumar** *vt* to exhume, to disinter

**exigencia** *nf* (a) *(requisito)* demand, requirement (b) *(petición)* demand; **venirle a alguien con exigencias** to make demands on sb

**exigente 1** *adj* demanding
   **2** *nmf* demanding person

**exigir** [26] **1** *vt* (a) *(pedir)* to demand; **e. algo de** *o* **a alguien** to demand sth from sb (b) *(requerir, necesitar)* to call for, to require
   **2** *vi* to be demanding

**exiguo, -a** *adj (escaso)* meagre, paltry; *(pequeño)* minute

**exijo** *ver* **exigir**

**exiliado, -a 1** *adj* exiled, in exile
   **2** *nm,f* exile

**exiliar** [15] **1** *vt* to exile
   **2** **exiliarse** *vpr* to go into exile

**exilio** *nm* exile; **en el e.** in exile

**eximente** *Der* **1** *adj* absolutory, absolving
   **2** *nf* case for acquittal

**eximio, -a** *adj Formal* eminent, illustrious

**eximir** *vt* to exempt (**de** from)

**existencia** *nf* existence; *Com* **existencias** stock; **en existencias** in stock

**existencial** *adj* existential

**existencialismo** *nm* existentialism

**existencialista** *adj & nmf* existentialist

**existente** *adj* existing, existent

**existir** *vi* to exist; **existe el riesgo de...** there is the risk that...

**éxito** *nm (logro, fama)* success; **con é.** successfully; **tener é.** to be successful; **ser un é. (de ventas)** *(libro)* to be a bestseller; *(canción)* to be a hit

**exitoso, -a** *adj* successful

**éxodo** *nm* exodus

**exonerar** *vt* e. a alguien (de) *(culpa, responsabilidad)* to exonerate sb (from); *(carga, obligación)* to free sb (from); *(empleo, cargo)* to dismiss *o* remove sb (from)

**exorbitante** *adj* exorbitant

**exorcismo** *nm* exorcism

**exorcista** *nmf* exorcist

**exorcizar** [16] *vt* to exorcize

**exótico, -a** *adj* exotic

**exotismo** *nm* exoticism

**expandir 1** *vt* to spread; *Fís* to expand
   **2 expandirse** *vpr* to spread; *Fís* to expand

**expansión** *nf (de economía)* growth; *(de gas)* expansion; *Fig (difusión)* spread, spreading; **en e.** expanding

**expansionarse** *vpr* (a) *(divertirse)* to relax, to let off steam (b) *(desarrollarse)* to expand

**expansionismo** *nm* expansionism

**expansionista** *adj* expansionist

**expansivo, -a** *adj (que se extiende)* expansive; *(persona)* open, frank

**expatriación** *nf* expatriation; *(exilio)* exile

**expatriado, -a 1** *adj* **los españoles expatriados** *(emigrantes)* expatriate Spaniards; *(exiliados)* Spanish exiles
   **2** *nm,f (emigrante)* expatriate; *(exiliado)* exile

**expatriar** [34] **1** *vt (expulsar)* to exile
   **2 expatriarse** *vpr (emigrar)* to leave one's country, to emigrate; *(exiliarse)* to go into exile

**expectación** *nf* expectancy, anticipation

**expectante** *adj* expectant

**expectativa** *nf (esperanza)* hope; *(perspectiva)* prospect; **contra toda e.** against all expectations; **estar a la e.** to wait and see; **estar a la e. de** *(atento)* to be on the lookout for; *(a la espera)* to be hoping for; **e. de vida** life expectancy

**expectoración** *nf Med* (a) *(acción)* expectoration (b) *(esputo)* sputum

**expectorante** *adj & nm* expectorant

**expectorar** *vi Med* to expectorate

**expedición** *nf (viaje, grupo)* expedition

**expedicionario, -a** *adj* expeditionary

**expedidor, -ora** *nm,f* sender, dispatcher

**expedientar** *vt (castigar)* to take disciplinary action against; *(llevar a juicio)* to start proceedings against

**expediente** *nm* (a) *(documentación)* documents; *(ficha)* file (b) *(historial)* record; **e. académico** academic record (c) *(investigación)* inquiry; **abrir e. a alguien** *(castigar)* to take disciplinary action against sb; *(llevar a juicio)* to start proceedings against sb (d) *Fam Fig* **cubrir el e.** to do the bare minimum

**expedir** [49] *vt (carta, pedido)* to send, to dispatch; *(pasaporte, decreto)* to issue; *(contrato, documento)* to draw up

**expeditivo, -a** *adj* expeditious; **utilizar métodos expeditivos** to adopt harsh measures

**expedito, -a** *adj* clear, free; *también Fig* **tener el paso** *o* **camino e.** to have one's way clear

**expeler** *vt* to emit

**expendedor, -ora 1** *adj* **máquina expendedora** vending machine
   **2** *nm,f (de mercancía)* dealer, retailer; *(de lotería)* seller, vendor

**expendeduría** *nf (estanco)* *Br* tobacconist's, *US* cigar store

**expender** *vt* to sell, to retail

**expensas** *nfpl (gastos)* expenses, costs; **a e. de** at the expense of

**experiencia** *nf* (a) *(veteranía, vivencia)* experience; **por (propia) e.** from (one's own) experience (b) *(experimento)* experiment

**experimentación** *nf* experimentation

**experimentado, -a** *adj (persona)* experienced; *(método)* tried and tested

**experimentador, -ora 1** *adj* experimenting
**2** *nm,f* experimenter

**experimental** *adj* experimental

**experimentar 1** *vt* (a) *(sensación, efecto)* to experience; *(derrota, pérdidas)* to suffer (b) *(probar)* to test; *(hacer experimentos con)* to experiment with *o* on
**2** *vi* **e. con** to experiment with *o* on

**experimento** *nm* experiment

**experto, -a** *adj & nm,f* expert

**expiación** *nf* atonement, expiation

**expiar** [34] *vt* to atone for, to expiate

**expiatorio, -a** *adj* expiatory

**expidiera** *etc ver* **expedir**

**expido** *etc ver* **expedir**

**expiración** *nf* expiry

**expirar** *vi* to expire

**explanación** *nf* (a) *(allanamiento)* levelling (b) *Formal (explicación)* explanation, explication

**explanada** *nf* area of flat *o* level ground

**explanar** *vt (terreno)* to level

**explayarse** *vpr* (a) *(divertirse)* to amuse oneself, to enjoy oneself (b) *(hablar mucho)* to talk at length (c) *(desahogarse)* to pour out one's heart (**con** to)

**explicación** *nf* explanation; **dar/pedir explicaciones** to give/demand an explanation

**explicar** [61] **1** *vt* (a) *(exponer, contar)* to explain; *(teoría)* to expound (b) *(enseñar)* to teach, to lecture in
**2 explicarse** *vpr* (a) *(comprender)* to understand; **no me lo explico** I can't understand it (b) *(dar explicaciones)* to explain oneself (c) *(expresarse)* to make oneself understood

**explicativo, -a** *adj* explanatory

**explícito, -a** *adj* explicit

**exploración** *nf* (a) *(de territorio)* exploration (b) *Med (interna)* exploration; *(externa)* examination (c) *Min* prospecting

**explorador, -ora** *nm,f (viajero)* explorer; *(scout)* boy scout, *f* girl guide; *Mil* scout

**explorar** *vt* (a) *(averiguar, reconocer)* to explore; *Mil* to scout (b) *Med (internamente)* to explore; *(externamente)* to examine (c) *Min* to prospect

**exploratorio, -a** *adj (instrumento, técnica)* exploratory; *Fig (conversaciones)* preliminary

**explosión** *nf también Fig* explosion; **hacer e.** to explode; **e. atómica** *o* **nuclear** atomic explosion; **e. demográfica** population explosion

**explosionar** *vt & vi* to explode, to blow up

**explosivo, -a 1** *adj* (a) *(sustancia, artefacto)* explosive (b) *Gram* plosive
**2** *nm* explosive

**explotación** *nf* (a) *(acción)* exploitation; *(de fábrica, negocio)* running; *(de yacimiento)* mining; *(agrícola)* farming; *(de petróleo)* drilling (b) *(instalaciones)* **e. agrícola** farm; **e. minera** mine; **e. petrolífera** oil field

**explotador, -ora 1** *adj* exploiting
**2** *nm,f* exploiter

**explotar 1** *vt (persona)* to exploit; *(fábrica)* to run, to operate; *(terreno)* to farm; *(mina)* to work
**2** *vi* to explode

**expoliación** *nf* pillaging, plundering

**expoliar** [15] *vt* to pillage, to plunder

**expolio** *nm* pillaging, plundering

**exponencial** *adj & nf* exponential

**exponente** *nm Mat & Fig* exponent

**exponer** [52] **1** *vt* (a) *(teoría)* to expound; *(ideas, propuesta)* to set out, to explain (b) *(cuadro, obra)* to exhibit; *(objetos en vitrinas)* to display (c) *(vida, prestigio)* to risk (d) *(parte del cuerpo)* to expose; **estar expuesto a** *(viento, lluvia, crítica)* to be exposed to
**2 exponerse** *vpr (a riesgo)* to run the risk (**a** of); *(a ataque, crítica)* to expose oneself (**a** to)

**exportación** *nf* (a) *(acción)* export (b) *(mercancías)* exports; *Com* **exportaciones invisibles** invisible exports

**exportador, -ora 1** *adj* **país e.** exporting country, exporter
**2** *nm,f* exporter

**exportar** *vt Com & Informát* to export

**exposición** *nf* (a) *también Fot* exposure (b) *(de arte)* exhibition; *(de objetos en vitrina)* display; **e. universal** world fair (c) *(de teoría)* exposition; *(de ideas, propuesta)* setting out, explanation

**exposímetro** *nm* exposure meter

**expositivo, -a** *adj* explanatory

**expósito, -a** *Anticuado* **1** *adj* **niño e.** foundling
**2** *nm,f* foundling

**expositor, -ora 1** *adj* exponent
**2** *nm,f (en feria)* exhibitor; *(de teoría)* exponent

**exprés** *adj inv* (a) *(carta)* ≃ first-class (b) *(café)* expresso

**expresado, -a** *adj (mencionado)* above-mentioned

**expresamente** *adv (a propósito)* expressly; *(explícitamente)* explicitly, specifically

**expresar 1** *vt (manifestar)* to express; *(mostrar)* to show
**2 expresarse** *vpr* to express oneself

**expresión** *nf* expression; **reducir a la mínima e.** to cut down to the bare minimum; **e. corporal** self-expression through movement; *Educ* **e. escrita** writing skills

**expresionismo** *nm* expressionism

**expresionista** *adj & nmf* expressionist

**expresividad** *nf* expressiveness

**expresivo, -a** *adj (vivaz, explícito)* expressive; *(cariñoso)* affectionate

**expreso, -a 1** *adj (explícito)* specific; *(deliberado)* express; *(claro)* clear

**2** *nm* (a) *(tren)* = slow overnight train (b) *(café)* expresso

**3** *adv* on purpose, expressly

**exprimelimones** *nm inv* lemon squeezer

**exprimidor** *nm* squeezer

**exprimir** *vt (fruta)* to squeeze; *(zumo)* to squeeze out; *Fig* to exploit

**ex profeso** *adv* intentionally, expressly

**expropiación** *nf* expropriation

**expropiar** [15] *vt* to expropriate

**expuesto, -a 1** *participio ver* **exponer**

**2** *adj* (a) *(desprotegido)* exposed (a to) (b) *(arriesgado)* dangerous, risky (c) *(dicho)* stated, expressed (d) *(exhibido)* on display

**expugnar** *vt Formal* to (take by) storm

**expulsar** *vt* (a) *(de local, organización)* to throw out; *(de clase)* to send out; *(de colegio, organización)* to expel (b) *Dep* to send off (c) *(humo)* to emit, to give off; *(objeto, sustancia)* to expel

**expulsión** *nf* (a) *(de colegio, organización)* expulsion (b) *Dep* sending-off (c) *(de objeto, sustancia)* expulsion

**expulsor** *nm (en arma de fuego)* ejector

**expurgar** [40] *vt (texto)* to expurgate

**expusiera** *etc ver* **exponer**

**exquisitez** *nf* (a) *(cualidad)* exquisiteness (b) *(cosa)* exquisite thing; *(comida)* delicacy

**exquisito, -a** *adj (refinado)* exquisite; *(comida)* delicious, sublime

**extasiarse** [34] *vpr* to go into ecstasies (ante *o* con over)

**éxtasis** *nm inv* ecstasy

**extemporáneo, -a** *adj* (a) *(clima)* unseasonable (b) *(inoportuno)* inopportune, untimely

**extender** [66] **1** *vt* (a) *(tela, plano, alas)* to spread (out); *(brazos, piernas)* to stretch out (b) *(mantequilla)* to spread; *(pintura)* to smear; *(objetos)* to spread out (c) *(ampliar)* to extend, to widen (d) *(documento)* to draw up; *(cheque)* to make out; *(certificado)* to issue

**2 extenderse** *vpr* (a) *(ocupar)* **extenderse por** to stretch *o* extend across (b) *(hablar mucho)* to enlarge, to expand (en on) (c) *(durar)* to extend, to last (d) *(difundirse)* to spread (por across) (e) *(tenderse)* to stretch out

**extensión** *nf* (a) *(superficie)* area, expanse (b) *(amplitud) (de país)* size; *(de conocimientos)* extent (c) *(duración)* duration, length (d) *(sentido)* range of meaning; **en toda la e. de la palabra** in every sense of the word; **por e.** by extension (e) *Informát & Telecom* extension

**extensivo, -a** *adj* extensive; **hacer algo e. a** to extend sth to

**extenso, -a** *adj (país)* vast; *(libro, película)* long

**extensor, -ora 1** *adj (músculo)* extensor

**2** *nm (aparato)* chest expander

**extenuación** *nf* severe exhaustion

**extenuado, -a** *adj* completely exhausted, drained

**extenuante** *adj* completely exhausting, draining

**extenuar** [4] **1** *vt* to exhaust completely, to drain

**2 extenuarse** *vpr* to exhaust oneself, to tire oneself out

**exterior 1** *adj* (a) *(de fuera)* outside; *(capa)* outer, exterior (b) *(visible)* outward (c) *(extranjero)* foreign

**2** *nm* (a) *(superficie)* outside; **en el e.** outside (b) *(extranjero)* **en el e.** abroad; **una apertura al e.** an opening to the outside world (c) *(aspecto)* appearance; *Cine* **exteriores** outside shots; **rodar los exteriores** to film the exteriors

**exterioridad** *nf* outward appearance

**exteriorización** *nf* outward demonstration, manifestation

**exteriorizar** [16] *vt* to show, to reveal

**exterminación** *nf* extermination

**exterminador, -ora** *adj* exterminating

**exterminar** *vt* (a) *(aniquilar)* to exterminate (b) *(devastar)* to destroy, to devastate

**exterminio** *nm* extermination

**externo, -a** *adj (de fuera)* external; *(parte, capa)* outer; *(influencia)* outside; *(signo, aspecto)* outward

**extiendo** *etc ver* **extender**

**extinción** *nf* (a) *(aniquilación)* extinction; *(de esperanzas)* loss (b) *(de plazos, obligaciones)* termination, end

**extinguir** [28] **1** *vt (incendio)* to put out, to extinguish; *(raza)* to wipe out; *(afecto, entusiasmo)* to put an end to

**2 extinguirse** *vpr (fuego, luz)* to go out; *(animal, raza)* to become extinct, to die out; *(ruido)* to die out; *(afecto)* to die

**extinto, -a** *adj (especie, volcán)* extinct; **el e. Pedro Bustamante** the late Pedro Bustamante

**extintor** *nm* fire extinguisher

**extirpación** *nf Med* removal; *Fig* eradication, stamping out

**extirpar** *vt (tumor)* to remove; *(muela)* to extract; *Fig* to eradicate, to stamp out

**extornar** *vt Com* to rebate

**extorno** *nm Com* rebate

**extorsión** *nf Der* extortion

**extorsionar** *vt Der* to extort

**extorsionista** *nmf Der* extortionist

**extra 1** *adj* (a) *(adicional)* extra (b) *(de gran calidad)* top quality, superior

 **2** *nmf Cine* extra

 **3** *nm (gasto)* extra

 **4** *nf Am (gasolina)* 4-star petrol, *US* premium gas

**extra-** *prefijo* extra-

**extracción** *nf* (a) *(de astilla, bala)* removal, extraction; *(de diente)* extraction; *(de carbón)* mining (b) *(en sorteos)* drawing (c) *(origen)* e. **social** social extraction

**extractar** *vt* to summarize, to shorten

**extracto** *nm* (a) *(resumen)* summary, résumé; **e. de cuentas** statement (of account) (b) *(concentrado)* extract

**extractor** *nm (de humos)* extractor fan

**extracurricular** *adj Educ* extracurricular

**extradición** *nf* extradition

**extraditar** *vt* to extradite

**extraer** [68] *vt (obtener, sacar)* to extract (**de** from); *(sangre)* to draw (**de** from); *(carbón)* to mine (**de** from); *(conclusiones)* to come to o draw (**de** from)

**extrafino, -a** *adj* top quality, de luxe

**extrajudicial** *adj* extrajudicial

**extralegal** *adj* extralegal

**extralimitación** *nf* abuse *(of power, authority)*

**extralimitarse** *vpr* to go too far

**extranjería** *nf* foreign status; *Der* **ley de e.** immigration legislation

**extranjerismo** *nm* foreign word

**extranjerizar** [16] *vt* to introduce foreign customs to

**extranjero, -a 1** *adj* foreign

 **2** *nm,f (persona)* foreigner

 **3** *nm (territorio)* foreign countries; **estar en el/ ir al e.** to be/go abroad

**extranjis: de extranjis** *loc adv Fam* on the quiet

**extrañamiento** *nm* banishment

**extrañar 1** *vt* (a) *(sorprender)* to surprise; **me extraña (que digas esto)** I'm surprised (that you should say that) (b) *(echar de menos)* to miss (c) *(desterrar)* to banish

 **2 extrañarse** *vpr (sorprenderse de)* to be surprised (**de** at)

**extrañeza** *nf* (a) *(sorpresa)* surprise (b) *(rareza)* strangeness

**extraño, -a** *adj* (a) *(raro)* strange (b) *(ajeno)* detached, uninvolved (c) *Med* foreign

 **2** *nm,f* stranger

**extraoficial** *adj* unofficial

**extraordinario, -a 1** *adj* (a) *(insólito)* extraordinary (b) *(gastos)* additional; *(edición, suplemento)* special

 **2** *nm* (a) *Prensa* special edition (b) *(correo)* special delivery

**extraparlamentario, -a** *adj* non-parliamentary

**extraplano, -a** *adj* super-slim, extra-thin

**extrapolación** *nf* generalization

**extrapolar** *vt* to generalize about, to jump to conclusions about

**extrarradio** *nm* outskirts, suburbs

**extrasensorial** *adj* extrasensory

**extraterrestre** *adj & nmf* extraterrestrial

**extraterritorial** *adj* extraterritorial

**extraterritorialidad** *nf* extraterritorial rights

**extravagancia** *nf* eccentricity

**extravagante** *adj* eccentric, outlandish

**extravasarse** *vpr* to flow out

**extraversión** *nf* extroversion

**extravertido, -a** *adj & nm,f* extrovert

**extraviado, -a** *adj* (a) *(perdido)* lost; *(animal)* stray (b) *Fig (descarriado)* debauched

**extraviar** [34] **1** *vt* (a) *(objeto)* to lose, to mislay; *(excursionista)* to mislead, to cause to lose one's way (b) *(mirada, vista)* to allow to wander

 **2 extraviarse** *vpr (persona)* to get lost; *(objeto)* to be mislaid, to go missing

**extravío** *nm* (a) *(pérdida)* loss, mislaying (b) *(desenfreno)* excess

**extremado, -a** *adj* extreme

**Extremadura** *n* Extremadura

**extremar 1** *vt (precaución, vigilancia)* to maximize

 **2 extremarse** *vpr* to take great pains o care

**extremaunción** *nf Rel* extreme unction

**extremeño, -a 1** *adj* of/from Extremadura

 **2** *nm,f* person from Extremadura

**extremidad** *nf (extremo)* end; **extremidades** *(del cuerpo)* extremities

**extremismo** *nm* extremism

**extremista** *adj & nmf* extremist

**extremo, -a 1** *adj (sumo)* extreme; *(en el espacio)* far

 **2** *nm* (a) *(punta)* end (b) *(límite)* extreme; **en último e.** as a last resort; **ir o pasar de un e. al otro** to go from one extreme to the other; **llegar a extremos ridículos/peligrosos** to

reach ridiculous/dangerous extremes (**c**) *Dep*
**e. derecho/izquierdo** outside right/left
**extremosidad** *nf (efusividad)* effusiveness
**extremoso, -a** *adj (efusivo)* effusive, gushing
**extrínseco, -a** *adj* extrinsic
**extroversión** *nf* extroversion
**extrovertido, -a** *adj & nm,f* extrovert
**exuberancia** *nf* exuberance
**exuberante** *adj* exuberant
**exudación** *nf* exudation
**exudar** *vt* to exude, to ooze

**exultación** *nf* exultation
**exultante** *adj* exultant
**exultar** *vi* to exult, to rejoice (**de** with)
**exvoto** *nm* votive offering, ex voto
**eyaculación** *nf* ejaculation; **e. precoz**
premature ejaculation
**eyacular** *vi* to ejaculate
**eyección** *nf* ejection, expulsion
**eyectar** *vt* to eject, to expel
**eyector** *nm (de armas)* ejector; *(de aire, gases)*
extractor

# F

**F, f** ['efe] *nf (letra)* F, f; **el 23 F** 23rd February, = day of the failed coup d'état in Spain in 1981

**f. (a)** *(abrev de* **factura)** inv. **(b)** *(abrev de* **folio)** f.

**fa** *nm Mús* F; *(en solfeo)* fa

**fabada** *nf* = Asturian stew made of beans, pork sausage and bacon

**fábrica** *nf* factory; **f. de papel** paper mill; **f. siderúrgica** iron and steelworks *(singular)*; **es así de f.** it was like that when I bought it

**fabricación** *nf* manufacture; **de f. casera** home-made; **f. en serie** mass production

**fabricante 1** *adj* manufacturing; **la empresa f.** the manufacturer
  **2** *nmf* manufacturer

**fabricar** [61] *vt (a) (producir)* to manufacture, to make **(b)** *(construir)* to build, to construct **(c)** *Fig (inventar)* to fabricate, to make up

**fábula** *nf (a) Lit* fable; *(leyenda)* legend, myth **(b)** *(rumor)* piece of gossip

**fabulación** *nf* invention, fantasy

**fabular** *vi* to make things up

**fabulista** *nmf* author of fables

**fabuloso, -a** *adj (a) (muy bueno)* fabulous, fantastic **(b)** *(ficticio)* mythical, fantastic

**facción** *nf (a) Pol* faction **(b) facciones** *(rasgos)* features

**faccioso, -a 1** *adj* factious, rebellious
  **2** *nm,f* rebel

**faceta** *nf* facet

**facha 1** *nf (a) (aspecto)* appearance, look **(b)** *(mamarracho)* mess; **vas hecho una f.** you look a mess
  **2** *nmf Fam Pey (fascista)* fascist

**fachada** *nf (a) Arquit* façade **(b)** *Fig (apariencia)* outward appearance; **es pura f.** it's just a show

**facial** *adj* facial

**fácil** *adj (a) (sencillo)* easy; **f. de hacer/decir** easy to do/say; **dinero f.** easy money **(b)** *(tratable)* easy-going **(c)** *(probable)* probable, likely

**facilidad** *nf (a) (simplicidad)* ease, easiness **(b)** *(aptitud)* aptitude; **tener f. para algo** to have a gift for sth; **tiene f. de palabra** he's good at expressing himself; **dar facilidades a alguien para hacer algo** to make it easy for

sb to do sth; **facilidades de pago** easy (payment) terms

**facilitar** *vt (a) (simplificar)* to facilitate, to make easy; *(posibilitar)* to make possible **(b)** *(proporcionar)* to provide

**fácilmente** *adv* easily; **tardará f. tres meses** it'll easily take three months

**facilón, -ona** *adj Fam (muy fácil)* dead easy; *(demasiado simple)* too simple

**facineroso, -a** *nm,f* miscreant, criminal

**facsímil, facsimile 1** *adj* facsimile; **edición f.** facsimile edition
  **2** *nm (a) (copia)* facsimile **(b)** *(fax)* facsimile, fax

**factible** *adj* feasible

**fáctico, -a** *adj* **los poderes fácticos** the powers that be, the forces of the establishment

**factor** *nm* factor; **f. (de protección) 8** *(de crema solar)* factor 8 (protection)

**factoría** *nf (a) (fábrica)* factory **(b)** *Com* outlet, agency

**factótum** *( pl* **factotums)** *nmf* factotum

**factura** *nf (a) (por mercancías, trabajo realizado)* invoice; *(de compra, luz, teléfono)* bill; *Com* **f. pro forma** *o* **proforma** pro forma invoice; *Fig* **pasar f.** *(los excesos, años)* to take their toll **(b)** *Arte (hechura)* **de buena/mala f.** well/badly made

**facturación** *nf (a) (de equipaje) (en aeropuerto)* checking-in; *(en estación)* registration; **mostrador de f.** check-in desk **(b)** *(ventas) Br* turnover, *US* net revenue **(c)** *(cobro)* invoicing

**facturar** *vt (a) (equipaje) (en aeropuerto)* to check in; *(en estación)* to register **(b)** *(vender)* to turn over; **facturaron 4.000 millones en 1996** they had a turnover of 4,000 million in 1996 **(c)** *(cobrar)* **facturarle a alguien algo** to invoice *o* bill sb for sth

**facultad** *nf (a) (capacidad)* faculty; **facultades (mentales)** (mental) faculties **(b)** *(universitaria)* faculty **(c)** *(poder)* power, right **(d)** *(propiedad)* property; **tiene la f. de ablandar la madera** it has the property of softening wood

**facultar** *vt* to authorize

**facultativo, -a 1** *adj* (a) *(voluntario)* optional (b) *(médico)* medical
  **2** *nm,f* doctor

**fado** *nm* = melancholy Portuguese folk song

**faena** *nf* (a) *(tarea)* task, work; **faenas domésticas** housework , household chores (b) *Fam (fastidio)* **hacerle una (mala) f. a alguien** to play a dirty trick on sb; **¡qué f.!** what a pain! (c) *Taurom* bullfighter's performance

**faenar** *vi (pescar)* to fish

**fagocitar** *vt Fig* to engulf, to swallow up

**fagocito** *nm* phagocyte

**fagot 1** *nm (instrumento)* bassoon
  **2** *nmf (músico)* bassoonist

**fair play** ['ferplei] *nm* fair play

**faisán** *nm* pheasant

**faja** *nf* (a) *(prenda de mujer, terapéutica)* corset; *(de esmoquin)* cummerbund; *(de campesino)* sash *(wrapped round waist)* (b) *(de terreno) (pequeña)* strip; *(grande)* belt (c) *(de libro)* band *(around new book)*

**fajar** *vt (periódico)* to put a wrapper on; *(libro)* to put a band on

**fajín** *nm* sash

**fajo** *nm (de billetes, papel)* wad; *(de leña, cañas)* bundle

**fakir** *nm* fakir

**falacia** *nf (mentira)* lie, untruth; *(concepción errónea)* fallacy; **eso es una f.** that's a lie, that's not true

**falange** *nf* (a) *Anat & Mil* phalanx (b) *Pol* **la F. (Española)** the Falange

**falangismo** *nm* Falangist movement

**falangista** *adj & nmf* Falangist

**falaz** *adj* false

**falda** *nf* (a) *(prenda)* skirt; **f. escocesa** kilt; **f. pantalón** culottes; *Fam Fig* **tener un lío de faldas** to have woman trouble (b) *(de montaña)* slope, mountainside (c) *(regazo)* lap (d) *(de mesa camilla)* cover

**faldero, -a** *adj* (a) *(dócil)* **perro f.** lapdog (b) *(mujeriego)* keen on women

**faldón** *nm* (a) *(de ropa)* tail; *(de cortina, mesa camilla)* folds (b) *(de tejado)* gable

**falibilidad** *nf* fallibility

**falible** *adj* fallible

**fálico, -a** *adj* phallic

**falla** *nf también Geol* fault; **las Fallas** *(fiesta)* = celebrations in Valencia during which giant papier mâché figures are burnt

**fallar 1** *vt* (a) *(equivocar) (respuesta)* to get wrong; *(tiro)* to miss (b) *(sentenciar)* to pass sentence on; *(premio)* to award
  **2** *vi* (a) *(equivocarse)* to get it wrong; *(no acertar)* to miss (b) *(fracasar, flaquear)* to fail; *(no funcionar)* to stop working; *(plan)* to go wrong; **me**

**fallaron los frenos** my brakes didn't work (c) *(decepcionar)* **fallarle a alguien** to let sb down (d) *(quebrarse, ceder)* to give way (e) *(sentenciar)* **f. a favor/en contra** to find in favour of/against

**fallecer** [48] *vi* to pass away, to die

**fallecimiento** *nm* decease, death

**fallero, -a** *adj* = relating to the celebrations in Valencia during which giant papier mâché figures are burnt

**fallido, -a** *adj (esfuerzo, intento)* unsuccessful, failed; *(esperanza)* vain; *(disparo)* missed

**fallo** *nm* (a) *(error)* mistake; *Dep* miss; **tener un f.** to make a mistake (b) *(defecto)* fault; **tener muchos fallos** to have lots of faults (c) *(veredicto)* verdict (d) *(opinión)* judgment

**fallutería** *nf CSur Fam* hypocrisy

**falluto, -a** *adj CSur Fam* phoney, hypocritical

**falo** *nm* phallus

**falocracia** *nf* male chauvinism

**falócrata** *nm* male chauvinist

**falsario, -a 1** *adj (persona)* untruthful
  **2** *nm,f* liar

**falsear** *vt (hechos, historia, datos)* to falsify, to distort; *(moneda, firma)* to forge

**falsedad** *nf* (a) *(falta de verdad, autenticidad)* falseness (b) *(mentira)* falsehood, lie

**falsete** *nm* falsetto; **voz de f.** falsetto voice

**falsificación** *nf* forgery

**falsificador, -ora** *nm,f* forger

**falsificar** [61] *vt* to forge

**falsilla** *nf* guide sheet *(for writing paper)*

**falso, -a** *adj* (a) *(afirmación, información, rumor)* false, untrue (b) *(dinero, firma, cuadro)* forged; *(joyas)* fake (c) *(hipócrita)* deceitful; **jurar en f.** to commit perjury; **dar f. testimonio** to give false evidence (d) *(inadecuado)* wrong, incorrect

**falta** *nf* (a) *(carencia)* lack; **hacer f.** to be necessary; **me hace f. suerte** I need some luck; **por f. de** for want o lack of
  (b) *(escasez)* shortage
  (c) *(ausencia)* absence; **a f. de** in the absence of; **echar en f. algo/a alguien** *(notar la ausencia de)* to notice that sth/sb is missing; *(echar de menos)* to miss sth/sb; **sin f.** without fail
  (d) *(imperfección)* fault; *(error)* mistake; **f. de educación** bad manners; **f. de ortografía** spelling mistake; **sacarle faltas a alguien/algo** to make nitpicking criticisms of sb/sth
  (e) *Dep* foul; *(en tenis)* fault; **f. libre directa** direct free kick offence; **f. personal** personal foul
  (f) *Der* offence
  (g) *(en la menstruación)* missed period

**faltar 1** *vi* (a) *(no haber)* to be lacking, to be needed; **falta aire** there's not enough air; **falta sal** it needs a bit of salt

**(b)** *(estar ausente)* to be absent *o* missing; **falta Elena** Elena is missing; **el día que yo falte** when I have passed on

**(c)** *(carecer)* **le faltan las fuerzas** he lacks *o* doesn't have the strength

**(d)** *(hacer falta)* to be necessary; **me falta tiempo** I need time; **para que su felicidad fuera completa sólo faltaba que viniera su hijo** all it needed to make her happiness complete was for her son to arrive; **¡lo que me faltaba!** that's all I needed!; **sólo le faltó ponerse a llorar** he did everything but burst into tears

**(e)** *(quedar)* **falta mucho por hacer** there is still a lot to be done; **sólo te falta firmar** all you have to do is sign

**(f)** *(expresiones)* **¡no faltaba** *o* **faltaría más!** *(asentimiento)* of course!; *(rechazo)* that tops it all!, that's a bit much!; **faltó a su palabra** she broke *o* didn't keep her word; **faltó a su obligación** he neglected his duty; **f. a una cita** not to turn up at an appointment; **¡no faltes (a la cita)!** I don't miss it!, be there!; **f. a alguien en algo** to offend sb in sth; **f. a alguien al respeto** to be disrespectful to sb

**2** *v impersonal (tiempo, distancia)* **falta un mes para las vacaciones** there's a month to go till the holidays; **¿cuánto falta para Leeds?** how much further is it to Leeds?; **falta poco para que llegue** it won't be long till he arrives; *Fig* **faltó poco para que le matase** I very nearly killed him

**falto, -a** *adj* **f. de** lacking in, short of; **f. de recursos/escrúpulos** lacking means/scruples

**fama** *nf* **(a)** *(renombre)* fame *o* *(reputación)* reputation; *Prov* **cría f. y échate a dormir** build yourself a good reputation, then you can rest on your laurels; **buena/mala f.** good/bad reputation; **tener f. de tacaño/generoso** to have a name for being mean/generous

**famélico, -a** *adj* starving, famished

**familia** *nf* family; **en f.** with one's family; *Fig* **estábamos en f.** there were only a few of us; *Fig* **no te dé vergüenza, que estamos en f.** don't be shy – you're among friends; **una f. numerosa** a large family

**familiar 1** *adj* **(a)** *(de familia)* family; **reunión f.** family gathering **(b)** *(en el trato) (agradable)* friendly; *(en demasía)* overly familiar **(c)** *(lenguaje, estilo)* informal, colloquial **(d)** *(conocido)* familiar; **su cara me es** *o* **me resulta f.** her face looks familiar

**2** *nmf* relative, relation

**familiaridad** *nf* *(en el trato)* familiarity

**familiarizado, -a** *adj* familiar, conversant **(con** with**)**; **estar f. con algo** to be familiar with sth

**familiarizar [16] 1** *vt* to familiarize **(con** with**)**

**2 familiarizarse** *vpr* **familiarizarse con** *(estudiar)* to familiarize oneself with; *(acostumbrarse a)* to get used to

**famoso, -a 1** *adj* famous; **es famosa por su belleza** she is famous for her beauty

**2** *nm,f* famous person, celebrity

**fan** *nmf* fan

**fanático, -a 1** *adj* fanatical

**2** *nm,f* *(exaltado)* fanatic; *Dep* fan

**fanatismo** *nm* fanaticism; **con f.** fanatically

**fanatizar [16]** *vt* to arouse fanaticism in

**fandango** *nm* *(baile)* fandango

**fandanguillo** *nm* type of fandango

**fané** *adj* *CSur* worn out

**fanega** *nf* = grain measure which varies from region to region

**fanfarria** *nf* **(a)** *Fam* *(ostentación)* show, razz(a)matazz; *(jactancia)* boasting, bragging **(b)** *(de música)* fanfare; *(banda)* brass band

**fanfarrón, -ona 1** *adj* boastful

**2** *nm,f* braggart, show-off

**fanfarronada** *nf* brag

**fanfarronear** *vi* to boast, to brag **(de** about**)**

**fanfarronería** *nf* showing-off, bragging

**fango** *nm* mud

**fangoso, -a** *adj* muddy

**fantasear 1** *vi* to fantasize

**2** *vt* to imagine, to fantasize about

**fantasía** *nf* **(a)** *(imaginación)* imagination; *(cosa imaginada)* fantasy; **bisutería de f.** costume jewellery; **ropa de f.** fancy clothes **(b)** *Mús* fantasia

**fantasioso, -a** *adj* imaginative

**fantasma 1** *adj* **pueblo/barco f.** ghost town/ship; *Fam* **es muy f.** *(persona)* he's a real show-off

**2** *nm* *(espectro)* ghost, phantom

**3** *nmf* *Fam* *(fanfarrón)* show-off

**fantasmada** *nf* *Fam* brag

**fantasmal** *adj* ghostly

**fantasmón, -ona** *nm,f* *Fam* show-off

**fantástico, -a** *adj* fantastic

**fantochada** *nf* crazy *o* mad thing

**fantoche** *nm* **(a)** *(títere)* puppet **(b)** *(mamarracho)* (ridiculous) sight

**FAO** [fao] *nf* *(abrev de* **Food and Agriculture Organization***)* FAO

**faquir** *nm* fakir

**faradio** *nm* farad

**farándula** *nf* **la f.** the theatre, the stage

**faraón** *nm* pharaoh

**faraónico, -a** *adj* pharaonic; *Fig* *(fastuoso)* lavish, magnificent

**fardada** *nf* *Fam* showing-off

**fardar** *vi Fam* f. de algo to show (sth) off

**fardo** *nm* bundle

**fardón, -ona** *Fam* **1** *adj* flashy
 **2** *nm,f* flash Harry

**farero, -a** *nm,f* lighthouse keeper

**farfullar** *vt & vi* to gabble, to splutter

**faringe** *nf* pharynx

**faringitis** *nf inv* sore throat

**fariseo, -a** *nm,f* (a) *Hist* Pharisee (b) *Fig (hipócrita)* hypocrite

**farmacéutico, -a** **1** *adj* pharmaceutical
 **2** *nm,f* chemist, pharmacist

**farmacia** *nf* (a) *(ciencia)* pharmacy (b) *(establecimiento) Br* chemist's (shop), pharmacy, *US* drugstore; **f. de turno** *o* **de guardia** duty chemist's

**fármaco** *nm* medicine, drug

**farmacología** *nf* pharmacology

**farmacopea** *nf* pharmacopoeia

**farmacoterapia** *nf* = treatment using course of drugs

**faro** *nm* (a) *(para barcos)* lighthouse (b) *(de coche)* headlight, headlamp; **f. antiniebla** foglamp

**farol** *nm* (a) *(farola)* street lamp *o* light; *(linterna)* lantern, lamp (b) *(en el juego)* bluff; **ir de f.** to be bluffing (c) *Fam (mentira)* fib, lie

**farola** *nf* *(farol)* street lamp *o* light; *(poste)* lamppost

**farolear** *vi Fam* to fib

**farolero, -a** **1** *adj Fam* boastful
 **2** *nm,f* (a) *(oficio)* lamplighter (b) *Fam (fanfarrón)* show-off

**farolillo** *nm* (a) *(de papel)* paper *o* Chinese lantern (b) *(planta)* Canterbury bell

**farra** *nf Fam* binge, spree; **ir de f.** to paint the town red

**farragoso, -a** *adj* confused, rambling

**farruco, -a** *adj (valiente)* cocky; **ponerse f.** to get cocky

**farsa** *nf también Fig* farce

**farsante** **1** *adj* deceitful
 **2** *nmf* deceitful person

**FAS** *nm inv (abrev de* **Fondo de Asistencia Social)** = Spanish social welfare fund

**fascículo** *nm (entrega)* part, instalment *(of publication)*; **por fascículos (semanales/mensuales)** in (weekly/monthly) instalments

**fascinación** *nf* fascination; **sentir f. por algo** to be fascinated by sth

**fascinante** *adj* fascinating

**fascinar** *vt* to fascinate; **me fascinan Klee y Kandinsky** I love *o* adore Klee and Kandinsky

**fascismo** *nm* fascism

**fascista** *adj & nmf* fascist

**fase** *nf* phase

**fastidiado, -a** *adj Fam* (a) *(de salud)* ill; **ando f. del estómago** I've got a bad stomach (b) *(estropeado)* **la máquina de café está fastidiada** *(no funciona)* the coffee machine is bust; *(funciona mal)* the coffee machine isn't working properly

**fastidiar** [15] **1** *vt* (a) *(estropear) (fiesta, vacaciones)* to spoil, to ruin; *(máquina, objeto)* to break (b) *(molestar)* to annoy, to bother
 **2** *vi* **¡no fastidies!** you're having me on!
 **3 fastidiarse** *vpr* (a) *(estropearse) (fiesta, vacaciones)* to be ruined; *(máquina)* to break down (b) *(aguantarse)* to put up with it

**fastidio** *nm* (a) *(molestia)* nuisance, bother (b) *(enfado)* annoyance (c) *(aburrimiento)* bore

**fastidioso, -a** *adj* (a) *(molesto)* annoying (b) *(aburrido)* boring, tedious

**fasto** *nm* pomp, extravagance

**fastuosidad** *nf* lavishness, sumptuousness

**fastuoso, -a** *adj* lavish, sumptuous

**fatal** **1** *adj* (a) *(mortal)* fatal (b) *(muy malo)* terrible, awful (c) *(inevitable)* inevitable (d) *(seductor)* **mujer f.** femme fatale
 **2** *adv* terribly; **sentirse f.** to feel terrible

**fatalidad** *nf* (a) *(destino)* fate, destiny (b) *(desgracia)* misfortune

**fatalismo** *nm* fatalism

**fatalista** **1** *adj* fatalistic
 **2** *nmf* fatalist

**fatídico, -a** *adj* fateful, ominous

**fatiga** *nf (cansancio)* tiredness, fatigue; **fatigas** *(penas)* troubles, hardships

**fatigado, -a** *adj* tired, weary

**fatigante** *adj* tiring

**fatigar** [40] **1** *vt* to tire, to weary
 **2 fatigarse** *vpr* to get tired

**fatigoso, -a** *adj* tiring, fatiguing

**fatigue** *etc ver* **fatigar**

**fatuidad** *nf* (a) *(necedad)* fatuousness, foolishness (b) *(vanidad)* conceit

**fatuo, -a** *adj* (a) *(necio)* fatuous, foolish (b) *(engreído)* conceited

**fauces** *nfpl* jaws

**fauna** *nf* fauna

**fauno** *nm* faun

**fausto, -a** *adj* happy, fortunate

**fauvismo** [fo'βismo] *nm* fauvism

**favor** *nm* favour; **estar a f. de** to be in favour of; **en f. de** to the benefit of; **hacerle un f. a alguien** *(ayudar a)* to do sb a favour; *Fam Fig (acostarse con)* to go to bed with sb; **hágame el f. de cerrar la puerta** would you mind shutting the door, please?; **pedir un f. a alguien** to ask sb a favour; **por f.** please; **tener a** *o* **en su f.**

**a alguien** to enjoy sb's support; **favores** (de una mujer) favours

**favorable** adj favourable; **ser f. a algo** to be in favour of sth

**favorecedor, -ora** adj flattering, becoming

**favorecer** [48] vt (a) (beneficiar) to favour; (ayudar) to help, to assist (b) (sentar bien) to suit

**favorecido, -a** adj **nación más favorecida** most favoured nation; **has salido muy favorecida** (en foto) you've come out really well

**favoritismo** nm favouritism

**favorito, -a** adj & nm,f favourite

**fax** nm (a) (aparato) fax (machine); **mandar algo por f.** to fax sth (b) (documento) fax

**faxear** vt Fam to fax

**fayuquero** nm CAm, Méx dealer in contraband

**faz** nf (a) Formal (cara) countenance, face (b) (del mundo, de la tierra) face

**FBI** nm (abrev de **Federal Bureau of Investigation**) FBI

**fe** nf (a) (creencia, confianza) faith; **hacer algo de buena f.** to do sth in good faith (b) (documento) certificate; **fe de erratas** errata (c) **dar fe de que** to testify that; **la fe mueve montañas** faith can move mountains

**fealdad** nf (a) (de rostro, paisaje, edificio) ugliness (b) (de conducta) unworthiness

**febrero** nm February; ver también **septiembre**

**febril** adj feverish; Fig (actividad) hectic

**fecal** adj faecal; **aguas fecales** sewage

**fecha** nf (día) date; (momento actual) current date; **en f. próxima** in the next few days; **fijar la f. de algo** to set a date for sth; **hasta la f.** to date, so far; **ocurrió por estas fechas** it happened around this time of year; **f. de caducidad** (de alimentos) sell-by date; (de carné, pasaporte) expiry date; (de medicamento) use before date; **f. tope o límite** deadline

**fechador** nm postmark

**fechar** vt to date

**fechoría** nf bad deed, misdemeanour; **cometer una f.** to do sth wicked

**fécula** nf starch (in food)

**fecundación** nf fertilization; **f. artificial o asistida** artificial insemination; **f. in vitro** in vitro fertilization

**fecundar** vt (a) (fertilizar) to fertilize (b) (hacer productivo) to make fertile

**fecundidad** nf (a) (fertilidad) fertility (b) (productividad) productiveness

**fecundo, -a** adj (tierra, mujer) fertile; (artista) prolific

**FEDER** ['feder] nm (abrev de **Fondo Europeo de Desarrollo Regional**) ERDF

**federación** nf federation

**federal** adj & nmf federal

**federalismo** nm federalism

**federalista** adj & nmf federalist

**federar** 1 vt to federate

**2 federarse** vpr (a) (formar federación) to become o form a federation (b) (ingresar en federación) to join a federation

**federativo, -a** 1 adj federative

**2** nm,f member of a federation

**feedback** ['fiðβak] (pl **feedbacks**) nm feedback

**fehaciente** adj irrefutable

**felación** nf fellatio

**feldespato** nm feldspar

**felicidad** nf happiness; ¡**felicidades!** (enhorabuena) congratulations!; (en cumpleaños) happy birthday!

**felicitación** nf (a) (acción) **felicitaciones** congratulations (b) (tarjeta) greetings card; **f. de Navidad** Christmas card

**felicitar** 1 vt to congratulate

**2 felicitarse** vpr to be pleased o glad (**por** about)

**félidos** nmpl felines, cats

**feligrés, -esa** nm,f parishioner

**felino, -a** 1 adj feline

**2** nm feline, cat

**feliz** adj (a) (dichoso, alegre) happy (b) (afortunado) lucky (c) (oportuno) timely

**felonía** nf (traición) treachery, betrayal; (infamia) vile deed

**felpa** nf (de seda) plush; (de algodón) towelling

**felpudo** nm doormat

**femenino, -a** 1 adj (de mujer) feminine; Bot & Zool female; **baloncesto f.** women's basketball

**2** nm Gram feminine

**fémina** nf woman, female

**feminidad, femineidad** nf femininity

**feminismo** nm feminism

**feminista** adj & nmf feminist

**feminizar** [16] vt to make feminine

**femoral** 1 adj femoral

**2** nf femoral artery

**fémur** (pl **fémures**) nm femur, thighbone

**fenecer** [48] vi Formal to pass away, to die

**fenicio, -a** 1 adj & nm,f Phoenician

**2** nm (lengua) Phoenician

**fénix** nm inv (ave) phoenix; **volvió como el ave f.** he rose like a phoenix from the ashes

**fenomenal** 1 adj (a) (magnífico) wonderful, fantastic (b) (enorme) phenomenal

**2** adv Fam wonderfully

**fenómeno** 1 nm (a) (suceso) phenomenon (b) (monstruo) freak; **es un f. jugando al tenis** she's an amazing tennis player

**2** *adv Fam* brilliantly, fantastically; **pasarlo f.** to have a great time

**3** *interj* **¡f.!** great!, terrific!

**fenomenología** *nf* phenomenology

**fenotipo** *nm* phenotype

**feo, -a 1** *adj* (a) *(persona)* ugly; **más f. que picio** as ugly as sin (b) *(aspecto, herida, conducta)* nasty; **es** *o* **está f. escupir** it's rude to spit; **ponerse f.** *(situación, tiempo)* to turn nasty (c) *(tiempo)* foul, horrible

**2** *nm,f (persona)* ugly person

**3** *nm (desaire)* slight, insult; **hacer un f. a alguien** to offend *o* slight sb

**féretro** *nm* coffin

**feria** *nf* (a) *(mercado, exhibición)* fair; **f. (de muestras)** trade fair (b) *(fiesta popular)* festival; *(de atracciones)* funfair (c) *Méx (monedas)* small change

**feriado, -a** *adj* **día f.** holiday

**ferial** *adj* fair; **recinto f.** showground, exhibition area

**feriante** *nmf (vendedor)* exhibitor *(at trade fair)*

**fermentación** *nf* fermentation

**fermentar** *vt & vi también Fig* to ferment

**fermento** *nm* ferment

**ferocidad** *nf* ferocity, fierceness

**Feroe** *nfpl* **las (Islas) F.** the Faeroes, the Faeroe Islands

**feromona** *nf* pheromone

**feroz** *adj* (a) *(animal, bestia)* fierce, ferocious (b) *Fig (criminal, asesino)* cruel, savage (c) *Fig (dolor, angustia)* terrible (d) *Fig (enorme)* massive

**férreo, -a** *adj también Fig* iron; **disciplina férrea** iron discipline

**ferretería** *nf Br* ironmonger's (shop), *US* hardware store

**ferretero, -a** *nm,f* ironmonger, hardware dealer

**férrico, -a** *adj* ferric

**ferrocarril** *nm (sistema, medio)* railway, *US* railroad; *(tren)* train; **por f.** by train

**ferroso, -a** *adj* ferrous

**ferroviario, -a 1** *adj* **línea ferroviaria** railway line; **red ferroviaria** rail(way) network

**2** *nm,f* railway worker

**ferry** *nm* ferry

**fértil** *adj también Fig* fertile

**fertilidad** *nf también Fig* fertility

**fertilización** *nf* fertilization; *Med* **f. in vitro** in vitro fertilization

**fertilizante 1** *adj* fertilizing

**2** *nm* fertilizer

**fertilizar** **[16]** *vt* to fertilize

**ferviente** *adj* fervent

**fervor** *nm* fervour

**fervoroso, -a** *adj* fervent

**festejar 1** *vt* (a) *(celebrar)* to celebrate (b) *(agasajar)* to entertain

**2 festejarse** *vpr (celebrarse)* to be celebrated

**festejo** *nm* (a) *(fiesta)* party; **festejos** *(celebraciones)* public festivities; **festejos taurinos** bullfights (b) *(agasajo)* entertaining

**festín** *nm* banquet, feast

**festival** *nm* festival

**festividad** *nf* festivity

**festivo, -a** *adj* (a) *(de fiesta)* festive; **día f.** (public) holiday (b) *(alegre)* cheerful, jolly; *(chistoso)* funny, witty

**festón** *nm (en costura)* scallop

**festonear** *vt (en costura)* to scallop

**fetal** *adj* foetal

**fetén** *adj inv Fam* brilliant, great

**fetiche** *nm* fetish

**fetichismo** *nm* fetishism

**fetichista 1** *adj* fetishistic

**2** *nmf* fetishist

**fétido, -a** *adj* fetid, foul-smelling

**feto** *nm (embrión)* foetus; *Fam Fig (persona fea)* ugly person, fright

**feudal** *adj* feudal

**feudalismo** *nm* feudalism

**feudo** *nm Hist* fief; *Fig (dominio)* domain, area of influence

**fez** *nm* fez

**FF AA** *nfpl (abrev de* **Fuerzas Armadas)** = Spanish armed forces

**fiabilidad** *nf* reliability

**fiable** *adj (máquina)* reliable; *(persona)* trustworthy

**fiador, -ora** *nm,f* guarantor, surety; **salir f. por** to vouch for

**fiambre** *nm (alimento) Br* cold meat, *US* cold cut; *Fam Fig (cadáver)* stiff, corpse

**fiambrera** *nf* lunch *o* sandwich box

**fianza** *nf* (a) *(depósito)* deposit (b) *Der* bail; **bajo f.** on bail (c) *(garantía)* security, bond

**fiar** **[34] 1** *vt Com* to sell on credit

**2** *vi Com* to sell on credit; *Fig* **ser de f.** to be trustworthy

**3 fiarse** *vpr* **¡no te fíes!** don't be too sure (about it)!; **fiarse de algo/alguien** to trust sth/sb

**fiasco** *nm* fiasco

**fibra** *nf* (a) *(de tela, alimenticia)* fibre; *(de madera)* grain; **f. de vidrio** fibreglass; *Tel* **f. óptica** optic fibre (b) *(energía)* character, vigour

**fibroma** *nm Med* fibroma

**fibrosis** *nf inv Med* fibrosis

**fibroso, -a** *adj (carne)* chewy, tough; *(persona)* lean; *Anat (tejido)* fibrous

**ficción** *nf* (a) *(invención)* fiction (b) *(simulación)* pretence, make-believe

**ficha** nf (a) *(tarjeta)* (index) card; *(con detalles personales)* file, record card (b) *(de guardarropa, aparcamiento)* ticket (c) *(de teléfono)* token (d) *(de juego)* counter; *(de ajedrez)* piece; *(de ruleta)* chip (e) *Dep (contrato)* contract (f) *Informát* card; **f. perforada** perforated card

**fichaje** nm *Dep (contratación)* signing (up); *(importe)* transfer fee

**fichar 1** vt (a) *(archivar)* to note down on an index card, to file (b) *(sujeto: policía)* to put on police files o records (c) *Dep* to sign up (d) *Fam (pillar)* to suss out, to see through

**2** vi (a) *(en el trabajo) (al entrar)* to clock in; *(al salir)* to clock out (b) *Dep* to sign up **(por** for)

**fichero** nm *también Informát* file

**ficticio, -a** adj (a) *(imaginario)* fictitious (b) *(convencional)* imaginary

**ficus** nm inv rubber plant

**fidedigno, -a** adj reliable

**fideicomisario, -a** nm,f trustee

**fideicomiso** nm *Der* trust

**fidelidad** nf (a) *(lealtad)* loyalty; *(de cónyuge, perro)* faithfulness (b) *(precisión)* accuracy; **alta f.** high fidelity

**fideo** nm noodle; **estar como un f.** to be as thin as a rake

**fiduciario, -a** adj & nm,f *Der & Econ* fiduciary

**fiebre** nf fever; **tener f.** to have a temperature; **f. amarilla/de Malta** yellow/Malta fever; **f. del heno** hay fever; **la f. del oro** gold rush

**fiel 1** adj (a) *(leal) (amigo, seguidor)* loyal; *(cónyuge, perro)* faithful (b) *(preciso)* accurate

**2** nm (a) *(de balanza)* needle, pointer (b) *Rel* **los fieles** the faithful

**fieltro** nm felt

**fiera** nf (a) *(animal)* wild animal (b) *Fig (persona) (genial)* demon; *(cruel)* brute; **estar/ponerse hecho una f.** to be/go wild with anger

**fiero, -a** adj savage, ferocious

**fierro** nm *Am* (a) *(hierro)* iron (b) *(navaja)* knife

**fiesta** nf (a) *(reunión)* party; *(de pueblo, barrio)* (local) festivities; **f. mayor** = local celebrations for the festival of a town's patron saint; **la f. nacional** bullfighting; **aguar la f. a alguien** to spoil sb's fun (b) *(día)* public holiday; **ser f.** to be a public holiday; **hacer f.** to be on holiday; **fiestas** *(vacaciones)* holidays (c) *Fig (alegría)* joy, delight

**FIFA** ['fifa] nf *(abrev de* **Federación Internacional de Fútbol Asociación)** FIFA

**figura** nf (a) *(objeto, de persona)* figure; *(forma)* shape (b) *(en naipes)* picture card

**figuraciones** nfpl imaginings; **son f. tuyas** it's all in your imagination

**figurado, -a** adj figurative

**figurante, -a** nm,f extra

**figurar 1** vi (a) *(aparecer)* to appear, to figure **(en** in) (b) *(ser importante)* to be prominent o important

**2** vt (a) *(representar)* to represent (b) *(simular)* to feign, to simulate

**3 figurarse** vpr *(imaginarse)* to imagine; **ya me lo figuraba yo** I thought as much

**figurativo, -a** adj *Arte* figurative

**figurín** nm fashion sketch; *Fig* **ir** o **estar hecho un f.** to be dressed up to the nines

**figurón** nm *Fam* (a) *(fanfarrón)* poseur (b) *(mangoneador)* = person who wants to be the centre of attention

**fijación** nf (a) *también Fot* fixing (b) *(obsesión)* fixation (c) **fijaciones** *(en esquí)* bindings

**fijador** nm *(líquido)* fixative; **f. de pelo** *(crema)* hair gel; *(espray)* hair spray

**fijar 1** vt (a) *(establecer)* to fix; *(asegurar)* to fix (a o en onto); *(cartel)* to stick up; *(sello)* to stick on (b) *(significado)* to establish; **f. el domicilio** to take up residence; **f. la mirada/la atención en** to fix one's gaze/attention on

**2 fijarse** vpr to pay attention; **fijarse en algo** *(darse cuenta)* to notice sth; *(prestar atención)* to pay attention to sth

**fijeza** nf firmness; **con f.** *(con seguridad)* definitely, for sure; *(con persistencia)* fixedly

**Fiji** [fiji] n Fiji

**fijo, -a 1** adj (a) *(no variable, inmóvil)* fixed; *(sujeto)* firmly attached; **no tienen fecha fija para la boda** they haven't set a date for the wedding (b) *(cliente)* regular (c) *(empleado, trabajo)* permanent

**2** adv *Fam* definitely; **f. que viene** he's definitely coming

**fila** nf (a) *(hilera)* line; *(de asientos)* row; **en f., en f. india** in line, in single file; **ponerse en f.** to line up (b) *Mil* rank; **filas** ranks; *Fig* **cerrar filas** to close ranks; **en filas** doing military service; **llamar a filas a alguien** to call sb up; **romper filas** to fall out

**filamento** nm filament

**filantropía** nf philanthropy

**filantrópico, -a** adj philanthropic

**filantropismo** nm philanthropy

**filántropo, -a** nm,f philanthropist

**filarmónica** nf philharmonic (orchestra)

**filarmónico, -a** adj philharmonic

**filatelia** nf philately

**filatélico, -a 1** adj philatelic

**2** nm,f philatelist

**filete** nm (a) *(grueso)* (fillet) steak; *(delgado)* fillet; *(solomillo)* sirloin (b) *(de tornillo)* thread

**filfa** *nf Fam* **¡menuda f.!** *(mentira)* what a whopper!; *(engaño)* what a swizz!

**filiación** *nf* (a) *(ficha militar, policial)* record, file (b) *Pol* affiliation (c) *(parentesco)* relationship

**filial 1** *adj* (a) *(de hijo)* filial (b) *(de empresa)* subsidiary
   **2** *nf* subsidiary

**filibustero** *nm* pirate

**filiforme** *adj* thread-like

**filigrana** *nf* (a) *(en orfebrería)* filigree (b) *Fig (habilidad)* skilful work (c) *(en billetes)* watermark

**Filipinas** *nfpl* **(las)** F. the Philippines *(singular)*

**filipino, -a 1** *adj & nm,f* Filipino
   **2** *nm (lengua)* Filipino

**filisteo, -a** *adj & nm,f* Philistine

**film** *(pl* **films)** *nm Br* film, *US* movie

**filmación** *nf* filming, shooting

**filmadora** *nf (cámara)* cine camera

**filmar** *vt* to film, to shoot

**filme** *nm Br* film, *US* movie

**filmografía** *nf* filmography

**filmoteca** *nf (archivo)* film library; *(sala de cine)* film institute; **la F. Nacional** the national film archive

**filo** *nm* (cutting) edge; *también Fig* **de doble f., de dos filos** double-edged; **al f. de** just before

**filología** *nf* (a) *(ciencia)* philology (b) *(carrera)* language and literature

**filológico, -a** *adj* philological

**filólogo, -a** *nm,f* philologist

**filón** *nm* (a) *(de carbón, oro)* seam (b) *Fig (mina)* gold mine

**filoso, -a** *adj* sharp

**filosofar** *vi* to philosophize

**filosofía** *nf* (a) *(estudio)* philosophy (b) *(resignación)* **tomarse algo con f.** to be philosophical about sth

**filosófico, -a** *adj* philosophical

**filósofo, -a** *nm,f* philosopher

**filoxera** *nf* phylloxera

**filtración** *nf* (a) *(de agua)* filtration (b) *Fig (de información)* leak

**filtrante** *adj* filtering

**filtrar 1** *vt* (a) *(tamizar)* to filter (b) *Fig (información)* to leak
   **2 filtrarse** *vpr* (a) *(penetrar)* to filter, to seep **(por** through) (b) *Fig (información)* to be leaked

**filtro** *nm* (a) *(de café, cigarrillo, aparato, cámara)* filter (b) *(pócima)* philtre

**filudo, -a** *adj Am* sharp

**fimosis** *nf inv Med* phimosis, = condition in which the foreskin is too tight to be retracted

**fin 1** *nm* (a) *(final)* end; **dar** *o* **poner f. a algo** to put an end to sth; **tocar a su f.** to come to a close; **a fines de** at the end of; **al** *o* **por f.** at last, finally; **a f. de cuentas** after all; **al f. y al cabo** after all; **sin f.** endless; **al f. del mundo** to the end of the earth (and back); **f. de fiesta** grand finale; **f. de semana** weekend (b) *(objetivo)* aim, goal
   **2** *adv* **a f. de** in order to; **en f.** anyway

**finado, -a** *nm,f* **el f.** the deceased

**final 1** *adj* final, end; **punto f.** end point
   **2** *nm* end; **f. feliz** happy ending; **a finales de** at the end of; **al f.** *(en conclusión)* in the end; **al f. de** at the end of
   **3** *nf* final

**finalidad** *nf* aim, purpose

**finalista 1** *adj* amongst the finalists
   **2** *nmf* finalist

**finalización** *nf (terminación)* end; *(de contrato)* termination

**finalizar** **[16] 1** *vt* to finish, to complete
   **2** *vi* to end, to finish **(con** in)

**financiación** *nf* financing

**financiar** **[15]** *vt* to finance

**financiera** *nf (firma)* finance company

**financiero, -a 1** *adj* financial
   **2** *nm,f (persona)* financier

**financista** *nmf Am* financier

**finanzas** *nfpl* finance

**finar** *vi Formal* to pass away

**finca** *nf (bien inmueble)* property; *(casa de campo)* country residence; *Der* **f. rústica/urbana** property (in the country/city)

**fineza** *nf* (a) *(cualidad)* (fine) quality (b) *(cortesía)* courtesy

**fingido, -a** *adj* feigned, apparent

**fingimiento** *nm* pretence

**fingir** **[26] 1** *vt* to feign
   **2** *vi* to pretend

**finiquitar** *vt Fin (deuda)* to settle; *(trabajador)* to pay off

**finiquito** *nm Fin (de deuda)* settlement; *(por despido)* redundancy settlement

**finito, -a** *adj* finite

**finjo** *ver* **fingir**

**finlandés, -esa 1** *adj* Finnish
   **2** *nm,f (persona)* Finn
   **3** *nm (lengua)* Finnish

**Finlandia** *n* Finland

**fino, -a 1** *adj* (a) *(de calidad) (tela, alimentos)* fine, high-quality (b) *(delgado)* thin; *(cintura)* slim (c) *(manos)* delicate; *(piel)* smooth; *(pelo)* fine (d) *(cortés)* refined (e) *(oído, olfato)* sharp, keen (f) *(gusto, humor, ironía)* refined
   **2** *nm* dry sherry

**finolis** *Fam* **1** *adj inv* affected

**2** *nmf inv* affected person

**finura** *nf* (a) *(buena calidad)* fineness (b) *(delgadez)* thinness (c) *(cortesía)* refinement (d) *(de oído, olfato)* sharpness, keenness (e) *(de gusto, humor, ironía)* refinement

**fiordo** *nm Geog* fiord

**firma** *nf* (a) *(rúbrica)* signature; *(acción)* signing; **estampar la f.** to sign, to write one's signature (b) *(empresa)* firm

**firmamento** *nm* firmament

**firmante 1** *adj* signatory

**2** *nmf* signatory; **el abajo f.** the undersigned

**firmar** *vt* to sign; *Fig* **f. algo en blanco** to rubber-stamp sth

**firme 1** *adj* (a) *(fuerte, sólido)* firm; *(andamio, construcción)* stable (b) *(argumento, base)* solid (c) *(carácter, actitud, paso)* resolute; **¡firmes!** *Mil* attention!

**2** *adv* hard; **mantenerse f. en** to hold fast to

**3** *nm* road surface

**firmeza** *nf* (a) *(fortaleza, solidez)* firmness; *(de construcción)* stability (b) *(de argumento)* solidity (c) *(de carácter, actitud)* resolution

**fiscal 1** *adj* fiscal; **año/asesor/fraude f.** tax year/adviser/fraud

**2** *nmf Der Br* ≃ public prosecutor, *US* ≃ district attorney; **F. General del Estado** *Br* ≃ Director of Public Prosecutions, *US* ≃ Attorney General

**fiscalía** *nf Der (cargo) Br* ≃ post of public prosecutor, *US* ≃ post of district attorney; *(oficina) Br* ≃ public prosecutor's office, *US* ≃ district attorney's office

**fiscalización** *nf* investigation, inquiry

**fiscalizador, -ora** *adj Formal* investigating, auditing; **órgano f.** auditing body; **función fiscalizadora** auditing function

**fiscalizar** [16] *vt* to inquire into *o* investigate the affairs of

**fisco** *nm* treasury, exchequer

**fisgar** [40] *vi Fam* to pry

**fisgón, -ona** *Fam* **1** *adj* nosey, prying

**2** *nm,f* busybody, nosy parker

**fisgonear** *vi Fam* to pry

**fisgoneo** *nm Fam* prying

**fisgue** *etc ver* **fisgar**

**física** *nf (ciencia)* physics

**físico, -a 1** *adj* physical

**2** *nm,f (persona)* physicist

**3** *nm (complexión)* physique

**fisiología** *nf* physiology

**fisiológico, -a** *adj* physiological

**fisión** *nf Fís* fission

**fisionomía** = **fisonomía**

**fisionomista** = **fisonomista**

**fisioterapeuta** *nmf Med* physiotherapist

**fisioterapia** *nf Med* physiotherapy

**fisonomía** *nf* features, appearance

**fisonomista** *nmf* **ser un buen/mal f.** to be good/bad at remembering faces

**fístula** *nf Med* fistula

**fisura** *nf (grieta)* fissure; *Fig* weakness, weak point

**fitología** *nf* botany

**flacidez, flaccidez** *nf* flabbiness

**flácido, -a, fláccido, -a** *adj* flaccid, flabby

**flaco, -a** *adj* thin, skinny; **hacer un f. servicio** *o* **favor a alguien** to do sb no favours, to be unhelpful to sb

**flagelación** *nf* flagellation

**flagelar 1** *vt* to flagellate

**2 flagelarse** *vpr* to flagellate oneself

**flagelo** *nm* (a) *(látigo)* whip (b) *Biol* flagellum

**flagrante** *adj* flagrant; *Der* **en f. delito** in flagrante delicto

**flamante** *adj (vistoso)* resplendent; *(nuevo)* brand-new

**flambear** *vt Culin* to flambé

**flamear** *vi* (a) *(fuego)* to blaze, to flare up (b) *(bandera, vela)* to flap

**flamenco, -a 1** *adj* (a) *(música, baile)* flamenco; **cante/espectáculo f.** flamenco singing/show (b) *(de Flandes)* Flemish

**2** *nm,f (de Flandes)* Fleming

**3** *nm* (a) *(ave)* flamingo (b) *(lengua)* Flemish (c) *(música, baile)* flamenco

**flamencología** *nf* study of flamenco

**flamencólogo, -a** *nm,f* expert in flamenco

**flan** *nm* crème caramel; **f. de huevo/vainilla** = crème caramel made with egg/vanilla; *Fam* **estar hecho un f., estar como un f.** to be shaking like a jelly, to be a bundle of nerves

**flanco** *nm* flank

**Flandes** *n* Flanders

**flanera** *nf* crème caramel mould

**flanquear** *vt* to flank

**flaquear** *vi (fuerzas)* to weaken; *(entusiasmo, equipo)* to flag

**flaqueza** *nf* weakness

**flash** [flaʃ, flas] *(pl flashes) nm* (a) *Fot* flash (b) *(informativo)* newsflash (c) *Fam (imagen mental)* flash of inspiration; **¡me llevé un f.!** I got a bit of a shock!

**flashback** ['flasβak] *(pl flashbacks) nm Cine* flashback

**flato** *nm* **tener f.** to have a stitch

**flatulencia** *nf* flatulence, wind

**flatulento, -a** *adj* flatulent

**flauta** *nf* (a) *Mús* flute; **f. dulce** recorder; **f. travesera** transverse flute (b) *Chile, CSur Fig*

**de la gran f.** tremendous; **¡(la gran) f.!** good grief!, good heavens!

**flautín** *nm* piccolo

**flautista** *nmf* flautist

**flebitis** *nf inv Med* phlebitis

**flebotomía** *nf Med* blood letting

**flecha** *nf* arrow; *Fig* **como una f.** like a shot

**flechazo** *nm* (a) *(con saeta)* arrow shot; *(herida)* arrow wound (b) *Fam Fig (amoroso)* **fue un f.** it was love at first sight

**fleco** *nm* (a) *(adorno)* fringe; **con flecos** fringed (b) *(de tela gastada)* frayed edge

**flema** *nf* phlegm

**flemático, -a** *adj (tranquilo)* phlegmatic

**flemón** *nm* gumboil

**flequillo** *nm* fringe

**fletamiento** *nm (de buque, avión)* charter, chartering

**fletar** *vt (buque, avión)* to charter

**flete** *nm* (a) *(precio)* freightage (b) *(carga)* cargo, freight

**flexibilidad** *nf* flexibility

**flexibilizar** [16] *vt* to make flexible

**flexible** *adj* flexible

**flexión** *nf* (a) *(de brazo, pierna)* bending; **flexiones de brazo** push-ups; **flexiones abdominales** sit-ups (b) *Gram* inflection

**flexionar** *vt* to bend

**flexo** *nm* adjustable table lamp *o* light

**flexor, -ora 1** *adj* flexional

  **2** *nm* flexor

**flipado, -a** *adj muy Fam (drogado)* stoned, high; *(asombrado)* gobsmacked

**flipante** *adj muy Fam* cool, wild

**flipar** *muy Fam* **1** *vi* (a) *(disfrutar)* to have a wild time (b) *(asombrarse)* to be gobsmacked (c) *(con una droga)* to be stoned *o* high

  **2** *vt (gustar a)* **me flipan los videojuegos** I'm wild about video games

  **3 fliparse** *vpr* (a) *(disfrutar)* to go wild (**con** about) (b) *(drogarse)* to get stoned *o* high

**flipe** *nm muy Fam* **¡qué f.!** what a gas!

**flipper** *nm* pinball machine

**flirtear** *vi* to flirt

**flirteo** *nm* flirtation, flirting

**flojear** *vi* (a) *(piernas, fuerzas)* to weaken; *(memoria)* to be failing; *(película, libro)* to flag; *(calor, trabajo)* to ease off; *(ventas)* to fall off; **me flojeaban las fuerzas** I was feeling weak; **le flojea la memoria** his memory is going *o* failing (b) *(no ser muy apto)* **f. en algo** to get worse at sth

**flojedad** *nf* weakness

**flojera** *nf Fam* lethargy, feeling of weakness

**flojo, -a** *adj* (a) *(suelto)* loose (b) *(persona, bebida)* weak; *(sonido)* faint; *(salud)* poor; *(viento)* light (c) *(sin calidad, aptitudes)* poor; **estar f. en algo** to be poor *o* weak at sth (d) *(mercado, negocio)* slack

**flor** *nf* (a) *Bot* flower; **en f.** in flower; *Fig* **f. de un día** flash in the pan; **echar flores a alguien** to pay sb compliments; **f. de lis** fleur-de-lis (b) *(lo mejor)* **la f. (y nata)** the crème de la crème, the cream; **en la f. de la edad** *o* **de la vida** in the prime of life (c) **a f. de agua/tierra** at water/ground level; *Fig* **a f. de piel** just below the surface

**flora** *nf* flora; *Med* **f. intestinal** intestinal flora

**floración** *nf* flowering, blossoming

**floral** *adj* floral

**floreado, -a** *adj* flowery

**florecer** [48] *vi* to flower; *Fig* to flourish

**floreciente** *adj Fig* flourishing

**florecimiento** *nm* flowering; *Fig* flourishing

**Florencia** *n* Florence

**florentino, -a** *adj & nm,f* Florentine

**florero** *nm* vase

**florete** *nm* fencing foil

**floricultor, -ora** *nm,f* flower grower

**floricultura** *nf* flower growing

**florido, -a** *adj (con flores)* flowery; *(estilo, lenguaje)* florid

**florín** *nm* florin

**florista** *nmf* florist

**floristería** *nf* florist's (shop)

**floritura** *nf* flourish

**flota** *nf* fleet; **f. pesquera** fishing fleet

**flotabilidad** *nf* (a) *(en el agua)* buoyancy (b) *Econ* floatability

**flotación** *nf también Econ* flotation

**flotador** *nm* (a) *(para nadar)* rubber ring (b) *(de caña de pescar)* float (c) *(de cisternas)* ballcock

**flotante** *adj también Econ* floating

**flotar** *vi también Econ* to float

**flote: a flote** *loc adv* afloat; **mantenerse a f.** to stay afloat; *Fig* **sacar algo a f.** to get sth back on its feet; *Fig* **salir a f.** to get back on one's feet

**flotilla** *nf* flotilla

**fluctuación** *nf* (a) *(variación)* fluctuation (b) *(vacilación)* wavering

**fluctuante** *adj* fluctuating

**fluctuar** [4] *vi* (a) *(variar)* to fluctuate (b) *(vacilar)* to waver

**fluidez** *nf* (a) *(de sustancia, líquido)* fluidity; *(del tráfico)* free flow (b) *(de relaciones)* smoothness (c) *Fig (en el lenguaje)* fluency

**fluido, -a 1** *adj* (a) *(sustancia)* fluid; *(tráfico)* free-flowing (b) *(relaciones)* smooth (c) *Fig (lenguaje)* fluent

**2** *nm* fluid; **f. eléctrico** electric current *o* power

**fluir** [36] *vi* to flow

**flujo** *nm* flow; *Com* **f. de caja** cash flow

**flúor** *nm* fluorine

**fluorescencia** *nf* fluorescence

**fluorescente 1** *adj* fluorescent

**2** *nm* strip light

**fluoruro** *nm Quím* fluoride

**fluvial** *adj* river; **cuenca f.** river basin

**fluya** *etc ver* **fluir**

**fluyera** *etc ver* **fluir**

**FM** *nf* (*abrev de* **frecuencia modulada**) FM

**FMI** *nm* (*abrev de* **Fondo Monetario Internacional**) IMF

**FMLN** *nm* (*abrev de* **Movimiento Farabundo Martí de Liberación Nacional**) FMLN

**FNMT** *nf* (*abrev de* **Fábrica Nacional de Moneda y Timbre**) = Spanish national mint

**fobia** *nf* phobia

**foca** *nf* seal; *Fam Fig* **está como una f.** (*está gorda*) she's like a whale

**focal** *adj* focal

**focalizar** [16] *vt* to focus

**foco** *nm* (a) *Fig* (*centro*) centre, focal point; (*de epidemia*) source, breeding ground; **un f. de miseria** a severely deprived area; **un f. de infecciones** a source of infection (b) (*lámpara*) (*para un punto*) spotlight; (*para una zona*) floodlight (c) *Fís & Geom* focus (d) *Am* (*bombilla*) light bulb (e) *Am* (*farola*) street light (f) *Am Aut* (*car*) headlight

**fofo, -a** *adj* flabby

**fogata** *nf* bonfire, fire

**fogón** *nm* (a) (*para cocinar*) stove (b) (*de máquina de vapor*) firebox

**fogonazo** *nm* flash

**fogonero, -a** *nm,f* stoker

**fogosidad** *nf* (*de persona*) passion; (*de caballo*) spirit

**fogoso, -a** *adj* (*persona*) passionate, intense; (*caballo*) spirited, lively

**fogueo** *nm* **de f.** blank

**foie-gras** [fwa'yras] *nm inv* (pâté de) foie-gras

**fol.** (*abrev de* **folio**) f.

**folclore, folclor** *nm* folklore

**folclórico, -a 1** *adj* traditional, popular

**2** *nm,f* flamenco singer

**folclorismo** *nm* folklore

**foliación** *nf* foliation

**folículo** *nm* follicle; **f. piloso** hair follicle

**folio** *nm* (*hoja*) leaf, sheet (*approximately A4 size*); **tamaño f.** ≃ A4-sized (*approximately*)

**folklor** *nm* folklore

**follaje** *nm* foliage

**follar** *vi Vulg* to fuck

**folletín** *nm* (*melodrama*) melodrama; **de f.** (*vida, incidente*) melodramatic

**folletinesco, -a** *adj* melodramatic

**folleto** *nm* (*turístico, publicitario*) brochure; (*explicativo, de instrucciones*) leaflet

**follón** *nm Fam* (a) (*discusión*) row; **se armó un f.** there was an almighty row (b) (*lío*) mess; **¡vaya f.!** what a mess!; **me hice un f. con las listas** I got into a real muddle *o* mess with the lists

**fomentar** *vt* to encourage, to foster

**fomento** *nm* encouragement, fostering; **Ministerio de F.** ministry of public works

**fonación** *nf* phonation

**fonda** *nf* boarding house; **hacer parada y f.** (*para comer*) to stop for something to eat; (*para dormir*) to make an overnight stop

**fondeadero** *nm* anchorage

**fondear 1** *vi* to anchor

**2** *vt* (*sondear*) to sound; (*registrar*) (*barco*) to search

**fondista** *nmf* (a) *Dep* (*corredor*) long-distance runner; (*nadador*) long-distance swimmer; (*esquiador*) cross-country skier (b) (*propietario de fonda*) landlord, f landlady

**fondo** *nm* (a) (*parte inferior*) bottom; *Fig* **bajos fondos** underworld; **doble f.** false bottom; **fondos** (*de embarcación*) bottom; **tocar f.** (*embarcación*) to scrape along the sea/river bed; *Fig* (*crisis*) to bottom out

(b) (*de habitación*) back; **al f. de** (*calle, pasillo*) at the end of; (*sala*) at the back of

(c) (*dimensión*) depth; **tener un metro de f.** to be one metre deep

(d) (*de cuadro, foto, tela*) background; **al f.** in the background

(e) (*de asunto, problema*) heart, bottom; **llegar al f. de** to get to the heart *o* bottom of; **el problema de f.** the underlying problem; **la cuestión de f.** the fundamental issue; **en el f.** (*en lo más íntimo*) deep down; (*en lo esencial*) basically

(f) (*de una persona*) **tener buen f.** to have a good heart

(g) (*de obra literaria*) substance

(h) (*de dinero*) fund; **a f. perdido** nonreturnable; **f. común** kitty; *Econ* **f. de amortización/de inversión/de pensiones** sinking/investment/pension fund; *Fin* **f. de garantía de depósito** deposit guarantee fund; **fondos** (*capital*) funds; **estar mal de fondos** (*persona*) to be badly off; (*empresa*) to be short of funds; **recaudar fondos** to raise funds

**(i)** *(fundamento)* reason, basis

**(j)** *(de biblioteca, archivo)* catalogue, collection; **f. editorial** collection of published works

**(k)** *Dep* stamina; **de f.** long-distance; **de medio f.** middle-distance

**(l)** *Col, Méx (combinación)* petticoat

**(m)** *(expresiones)* **hacer algo a f.** to do sth thoroughly; *Fig* **emplearse a f.** to do one's utmost

**fondue** [fon'di] *nf Culin (comida)* fondue; *(utensilios)* fondue set

**fonendoscopio** *nm* stethoscope

**fonética** *nf (ciencia)* phonetics *(singular)*

**fonético, -a** *adj* phonetic

**fonetista** *nmf* phonetician

**fónico, -a** *adj* phonic

**fono** *nm Andes, CSur* phone number

**fonógrafo** *nm* gramophone, *US* phonograph

**fonología** *nf* phonology

**fonometría** *nf* phonometry

**fonoteca** *nf* record library

**fontanería** *nf* plumbing

**fontanero, -a** *nm,f* plumber

**footing** ['futin] *nm* jogging; **hacer f.** to go jogging

**foque** *nm Náut* jib

**forajido, -a** *nm,f* outlaw

**foral** *adj* = relating to ancient regional laws still existing in some parts of Spain

**foráneo, -a** *adj* foreign

**forastero, -a** *nm,f* stranger

**forcé** *ver* **forzar**

**forcejear** *vi* to struggle

**forcejeo** *nm* struggle

**forcemos** *ver* **forzar**

**fórceps** *nm inv* forceps

**forense 1** *adj* forensic; **médico f.** pathologist

  **2** *nmf* pathologist

**forestal** *adj* forest; **incendio f.** forest fire; **repoblación f.** reforestation

**forfait** [for'fait, for'fe] *(pl* **forfaits)** *nm* **(a)** *Dep* default **(b)** *(para esquiar)* ski pass **(c)** *(precio invariable)* fixed rate; **a f.** fixed price

**forja** *nf (fragua)* forge; *también Fig (forjadura)* forging

**forjado, -a** *adj (hierro)* wrought

**forjador, -ora** *nm,f (metal)* forger

**forjar** *vt* **(a)** *(metal)* to forge **(b)** *Fig (persona, nación)* to create, to form; **las guerras forjan héroes** wars create heroes **(c)** *Fig (mentira)* to invent; *(plan)* to form

  **2 forjarse** *vpr* **(a)** *Fig (labrarse)* to carve out for oneself **(b)** *(imaginarse)* **forjarse demasiadas ilusiones** to build up false hopes (for oneself) **(c)** *(crearse, originarse)* to be forged; **la**

**revolución se forjó en las minas de carbón** the revolution was forged in the coal mines

**forma** *nf* **(a)** *(figura)* shape, form; **en f. de** in the shape of; **formas** *(silueta)* figure, curves; **tener f. ovalada** *o* **de óvalo** to be oval in shape

  **(b)** *(manera)* way, manner; **de cualquier f., de todas formas** anyway, in any case; **de esta f.** in this way; **de f. que** in such a way that, so that; **f. de pago** method of payment

  **(c) formas** *(modales)* manners, social conventions; *Fig* **guardar las formas** to keep up appearances

  **(d)** *(manifestación)* form; **la fotografía es una f. de arte** photography is an art form

  **(e)** *(condición física)* fitness; **estar en f.** to be fit; *también Fig* **estar en baja f.** to be in poor shape

  **(f)** *Rel* host

**formación** *nf* **(a)** *(creación)* formation **(b)** *(educación)* training; **f. profesional** vocational training **(c)** *(conjunto)* grouping; *Mil* formation; **f. política** political party

**formador, -ora** *adj* forming, constituting

**formal** *adj* **(a)** *(de la forma, legal)* formal; **ser novios formales** to be engaged **(b)** *(que se porta bien)* well-behaved, good **(c)** *(responsable, fiable)* reliable **(d)** *(serio)* serious, sober

**formalidad** *nf* **(a)** *(requisito)* formality; **es una mera f.** it's just a formality **(b)** *(educación)* (good) manners **(c)** *(fiabilidad)* reliability **(d)** *(seriedad)* seriousness

**formalismo** *nm* formalism

**formalista 1** *adj* formal

  **2** *nmf* formalist

**formalización** *nf* formalization

**formalizar** [16] *vt* to formalize

**formar 1** *vt* **(a)** *(hacer)* to form; **f. una bola con algo** to make sth into a ball; **f. un equipo** to make up a team **(b)** *(educar)* to train, to educate **(c)** *Mil* to form up

  **2** *vi Mil* to fall in

  **3 formarse** *vpr* **(a)** *(hacerse, crearse)* to form; **se formó espuma en la superficie** froth formed on the surface **(b)** *(educarse)* to be trained *o* educated

**formateado, -a** *Informát* **1** *adj* formatted

  **2** *nm (proceso)* formatting

**formatear** *vt Informát* to format

**formateo** *nm Informát* formatting

**formativo, -a** *adj* formative

**formato** *nm también Informát* format

**formica**® *nf* Formica®

**formidable** *adj (enorme)* tremendous; *(extraordinario)* amazing, fantastic

**formol** *nm* formalin

**fórmula** *nf* formula; **f. uno** formula one; **f. de cortesía** polite expression

**formulación** *nf* formulation

**formular 1** *vt* to formulate; **f. una pregunta** to ask a question; **formuló cuidadosamente su respuesta** she phrased her reply carefully
  **2** *vi* to write formulae

**formulario** *nm* form; **rellenar un f.** to fill in *o* out a form

**formulismo** *nm (apego) (a las formas)* formalism; *(a las normas)* sticking to the rules

**fornicación** *nf Formal* fornication

**fornicar** [61] *vi Formal* to fornicate

**fornido, -a** *adj* well-built

**foro** *nm* (a) *(tribunal)* court (of law) (b) *Teatro* back of the stage (c) *(lugar de discusión)* forum; **f. de debate** forum for debate; *Informát* **f. de discusión** discussion group

**forofo, -a** *nm,f Fam* fan, supporter

**forrado, -a** *adj (libro)* covered; *(ropa)* lined **(de** with); *(asiento)* upholstered; *Fam Fig* **estar f.** to be rolling in it

**forraje** *nm* fodder, fotage

**forrar 1** *vt (libro)* to cover; *(ropa)* to line **(de** with); *(asiento)* to uphoister
  **2 forrarse** *vpr Fam Fig* to make a packet

**forro** *nm (de libro)* cover; *(de ropa)* lining; *(de asiento)* upholstery; *Fam* **¡ni por el f.!** no way!; **tela de f.** lining material; **f. polar** fleece jacket

**fortachón, -ona** *adj* strapping, well-built

**fortalecer** [48] *vt* to strengthen

**fortalecimiento** *nm* strengthening

**fortaleza** *nf* (a) *(fuerza) (física)* strength; *(moral, mental)* strength, fortitude (b) *(recinto)* fortress

**fortificación** *nf* fortification

**fortificar** [61] *vt* to fortify

**fortín** *nm* small fort

**fortísimo, -a** *superlativo ver* **fuerte**

**FORTRAN** *nm Informát* FORTRAN

**fortuito, -a** *adj* chance; **encuentro f.** chance encounter

**fortuna** *nf* (a) *(suerte)* (good) luck; **por f.** fortunately, luckily; **probar f.** to try one's luck; **tuvo la mala f. de caerse** he had the misfortune *o* bad luck to fall (b) *(destino)* fortune, fate (c) *(riqueza)* fortune; **hacer f.** to make one's fortune

**forúnculo** *nm* boil

**forzado, -a** *adj* forced; **trabajos forzados** hard labour; **verse f. a hacer algo** to find oneself forced to do sth

**forzar** [33] *vt* (a) *(obligar, empujar)* to force; **f. a alguien a hacer algo** to force sb to do sth; **f. la vista** to strain one's eyes; **f. una cerradura** to force a lock (b) *(violar)* to rape

**forzoso, -a** *adj (obligatorio)* obligatory, compulsory; *(inevitable)* inevitable; *(necesario)* necessary

**forzudo, -a 1** *adj* strong
  **2** *nm,f* strong man, *f* strong woman

**fosa** *nf* (a) *(sepultura)* grave; **f. común** common grave (b) *Anat* cavity; **fosas nasales** nostrils (c) *(hoyo)* pit; **f. marina** ocean trough; **f. séptica** septic tank

**fosfatar** *vt (fertilizar)* to fertilize with phosphates

**fosfato** *nm* phosphate

**fosforescencia** *nf* phosphorescence

**fosforescente** *adj* phosphorescent

**fosforito** *adj Fam (color)* fluorescent

**fósforo** *nm* (a) *Quím* phosphorus (b) *(cerilla)* match

**fósil 1** *adj* fossil; **combustible f.** fossil fuel
  **2** *nm* fossil; *Fam Fig (viejo)* old fossil

**fosilización** *nf* fossilization

**fosilizarse** [16] *vpr (animal, hueso)* to fossilize; *Fig (persona)* to turn into an old fossil

**foso** *nm (hoyo)* ditch; *(de castillo)* moat; *(de garaje)* pit; *Dep & Teatro* pit

**foto** *nf* photo, picture; **le saqué una f.** I took a photo *o* picture of him

**fotocélula** *nf* photocell, photoelectric cell

**fotocomponer** *vt Imprenta* to typeset

**fotocomposición** *nf Imprenta* typesetting

**fotocopia** *nf* (a) *(objeto)* photocopy; **hacer una f.** to make *o* take a photocopy (b) *(procedimiento)* photocopying

**fotocopiadora** *nf (máquina)* photocopier; *(tienda)* copy shop

**fotocopiar** [15] *vt* to photocopy

**fotoeléctrico, -a** *adj* photoelectric

**fotofobia** *nf* photophobia

**fotogenia** *nf* photogenic qualities

**fotogénico, -a** *adj* photogenic

**fotograbado** *nm* photogravure

**fotografía** *nf* (a) *(arte)* photography (b) *(objeto)* photograph; **f. de carné** passport-sized photograph; **hacer** *o* **sacar una f. a alguien** to take a picture *o* photo of sb

**fotografiar** [34] *vt* to photograph, to take a photograph of

**fotográfico, -a** *adj* photographic

**fotógrafo, -a** *nm,f* photographer

**fotograma** *nm* still

**fotolito** *nm* photolithograph

**fotomatón** *nm* passport photo machine

**fotometría** *nf* photometry

**fotómetro** *nm* light meter

**fotomodelo** *nmf* photographic model

**fotomontaje** *nm* photomontage

**fotonovela** *nf* photo story

**fotosensible** *adj* photosensitive

**fotosíntesis** *nf inv* photosynthesis

**foulard** [fu'lar] (*pl* foulards) *nm* scarf

**foxterrier** [fokste'rrjer, foks'terrjer] (*pl* foxterriers) *nm* fox terrier

**foxtrot** *nm* foxtrot

**FP** *nf* (*abrev de* **formación profesional**) = vocationally orientated secondary education in Spain for pupils aged 14-18, currently being phased out

**fra.** (*abrev de* **factura**) inv

**frac** (*pl* fracs) *nm* tails, dress coat

**fracasado, -a 1** *adj* failed

  **2** *nm,f* failure

**fracasar** *vi* to fail (**en/como** at/as)

**fracaso** *nm* failure; **todo fue un f.** the whole thing was a disaster

**fracción** *nf* (a) (*parte, quebrado*) fraction; **f. decimal** decimal fraction (b) *Pol* faction

**fraccionadora** *nf Méx* estate agent

**fraccionamiento** *nm* (a) (*división*) division, breaking up (b) *Méx* (*urbanización*) housing estate

**fraccionar** *vt* to divide, to break up

**fraccionario, -a** *adj* fractional; **moneda fraccionaria** small change

**fractal** *nm* fractal

**fractura** *nf* fracture

**fracturar 1** *vt* to fracture

  **2 fracturarse** *vpr* to fracture; **fracturarse un brazo/una pierna** to fracture one's arm/leg

**fragancia** *nf* fragrance

**fragante** *adj* fragrant

**fragata** *nf* frigate

**frágil** *adj* (*objeto*) fragile; (*persona*) frail

**fragilidad** *nf* (*de objeto*) fragility; (*de persona*) frailty

**fragmentación** *nf* (*rotura*) fragmentation; (*división*) division

**fragmentar** *vt* (*romper*) to fragment; (*dividir*) to divide

**fragmentario, -a** *adj* (*incompleto*) fragmentary

**fragmento** *nm* fragment, piece; (*de obra*) excerpt

**fragor** *nm* (*de batalla*) clamour; (*de trueno*) crash

**fragua** *nf* forge

**fraguar** [12] **1** *vt* (a) (*forjar*) to forge (b) *Fig* (*idear*) to think up

  **2** *vi* to set, to harden

  **3 fraguarse** *vpr* (*tramarse*) to be in the offing; (*crearse, originarse*) to be hatched

**fraile** *nm* friar

**frailecillo** *nm* puffin

**frambuesa** *nf* raspberry

**francés, -esa 1** *adj* French

  **2** *nm,f* Frenchman, f Frenchwoman; **los franceses** the French; **marcharse** *o* **despedirse a la francesa** to leave without even saying goodbye

  **3** *nm* (*lengua*) French

**francesada** *nf Fam Pey* (*costumbre*) Frenchified habit; **¡es una f.!** (*película, libro*) it's typical French rubbish!

**Fráncfort** *n* Frankfurt

**franchute, -a** *nm,f Fam Pey* Frog, = pejorative term referring to a French person

**Francia** *n* France

**franciscano, -a** *adj & nm,f* Franciscan

**francmasón** *nm* Freemason

**francmasonería** *nf* Freemasonry

**francmasónico, -a** *adj* masonic

**franco, -a 1** *adj* (a) (*sincero*) frank, open; (*directo*) frank (b) (*sin obstáculos, gastos*) free; **puerto f.** free port (c) *Hist* Frankish

  **2** *nm,f Hist* Frank

  **3** *nm* (a) (*moneda*) franc (b) (*lengua*) Frankish

**francófono, -a 1** *adj* francophone

  **2** *nm,f* Francophone

**francotirador, -ora** *nm,f* (a) *Mil* sniper (b) *Fig* (*rebelde*) maverick

**franela** *nf* flannel

**franja** *nf* (*banda, tira*) strip; (*en bandera, uniforme*) stripe

**franquear** *vt* (a) (*paso, camino*) to clear (b) (*río, montañas*) to negotiate, to cross; *también Fig* **f. el umbral** to cross the threshold (c) (*correo*) to attach postage to

**franqueo** *nm* postage

**franqueza** *nf* (a) (*sinceridad*) frankness, openness (b) (*confianza*) familiarity

**franquicia** *nf* (a) (*tienda*) franchise (b) (*exención*) exemption; **f. postal** free postage

**franquismo** *nm* **el f.** (*régimen*) the Franco regime; (*doctrina*) Franco's doctrine

**franquista 1** *adj* pro-Franco, Francoist; **el régimen f.** the Franco regime

  **2** *nmf* supporter of Franco

**frasco** *nm* bottle

**frase** *nf* (a) (*oración*) sentence (b) (*locución*) expression; **f. hecha** (*modismo*) set phrase; (*tópico*) cliché

**fraseología** *nf* (a) (*estilo*) phraseology (b) (*palabrería*) verbiage

**fraternal** *adj* brotherly, fraternal

**fraternidad** *nf* brotherhood, fraternity

**fraternizar** [16] *vi* to get on like brothers

**fraterno, -a** *adj* brotherly, fraternal

**fratricida 1** *adj* fratricidal

  **2** *nmf* fratricide

**fratricidio** *nm* fratricide

**fraude** *nm* fraud; **f. fiscal** tax evasion

**fraudulento, -a** *adj* fraudulent

**fray** *nm* brother

**frazada** *nf Am* blanket; **f. eléctrica** electric blanket

**frecuencia** *nf* frequency; **con f.** often; **¿con qué f.?** how often?; **alta/baja f.** high/low frequency; **f. modulada, modulación de f.** frequency modulation

**frecuentación** *nf* frequenting

**frecuentado, -a** *adj* **una plaza muy frecuentada** a very busy square; **un lugar muy f. por estudiantes** a place which is very popular with students; **un sitio f. por carteristas** a place frequented by pickpockets

**frecuentar** *vt (lugar)* to frequent; *(persona)* to see, to visit

**frecuente** *adj (reiterado)* frequent; *(habitual)* common

**freelance, free lance** ['frilans] *adj* freelance

**Freetown** ['fritaun] *n* Freetown

**fregadero** *nm* (kitchen) sink

**fregado, -a 1** *adj Am Fam* troublesome, annoying
**2** *nm* **(a)** *(lavado) (de platos, suelo)* wash; *(frotando)* scrub **(b)** *Fam (lío)* mess **(c)** *Fam (discusión)* row, rumpus

**fregar** [45] *vt* **(a)** *(limpiar)* to wash; **f. los platos** to do the washing-up; **f. el suelo** to mop the floor **(b)** *(frotar)* to scrub **(c)** *Am Fam (molestar)* to bother, to pester

**fregona** *nf* **(a)** *(utensilio)* mop **(b)** *Fam Pey (criada)* skivvy

**fregotear** *vt Fam* to give a good wash to; **f. el suelo** to give the floor a good mop

**fregué** *ver* **fregar**

**freidora** *nf* deep fat fryer

**freiduría** *nf* = shop where fried food, especially fish, is cooked and served

**freír** [58] **1** *vt* **(a)** *Culin* to fry **(b)** *Fam Fig (molestar)* **f. a alguien a preguntas** to pester sb with questions **(c)** *Fam Fig (matar)* **f. a alguien (a tiros)** to gun sb down
**2 freírse** *vpr* to be frying

**frenado** *nm* braking

**frenar 1** *vt* **(a)** *Aut* to brake **(b)** *(contener)* to check; *(disminuir)* to curb, to slow down
**2** *vi Aut* to brake; *Fig* to slow down

**frenazo** *nm* **(a)** *Aut* **dar un f.** to brake hard **(b)** *Fig (parón)* sudden stop

**frenesí** *( pl frenesíes)* *nm* frenzy

**frenético, -a** *adj* **(a)** *(colérico)* furious, mad **(b)** *(enloquecido)* frenzied, frantic

**frenillo** *nm* fraenum

**freno** *nm* **(a)** *Aut* brake; **f. automático** automatic brake; **frenos ABS** ABS brakes; **frenos de disco** disc brakes **(b)** *(de caballerías)* bit **(c)** *Fig (contención)* check; *Fam* **¡echa el f.!** *(detente, cállate)* put a sock in it!, that's enough of that!; *(no te pases)* don't get carried away!; **poner f. a** to put a stop to

**frenopatía** *nf* psychiatry

**frenopático, -a 1** *adj* psychiatric
**2** *nm muy Fam (manicomio)* loony bin

**frente 1** *nf* forehead; **f. a f.** face to face
**2** *nm también Mil* front; **de f.** *(hacia delante)* forwards; **me encontré de f. con él** I found myself face to face with him; **estar al f. (de)** to be at the head (of); **f. a** *(enfrente de)* opposite; **estamos f. a una revolución científica** we are facing a scientific revolution; **hacer f. a** to face up to; *Meteo* **f. frío/cálido** cold/warm front

**fresa** *nf* **(a)** *(planta, fruto)* strawberry **(b)** *(herramienta) (de dentista)* drill; *(de orfebre)* milling cutter

**fresador, -ora** *nm,f (persona)* milling machine operator

**fresadora** *nf (máquina)* milling machine

**fresca** *nf* **(a)** *(insolencia)* **soltarle una f. o cuatro frescas a alguien** to tell sb a few home truths **(b)** *Pey (mujer)* loose woman

**fresco, -a 1** *adj* **(a)** *(reciente, no pasado)* fresh; *(temperatura, aire)* cool; *(pintura, tinta)* wet; **noticias frescas** fresh news; **un vestido f.** a cool dress **(b)** *(caradura)* cheeky; *Pey (mujer)* loose **(c)** **quedarse tan f.** not to bat an eyelid
**2** *nm,f (caradura)* cheeky person
**3** *nm* **(a)** *Arte* fresco; **al f.** in fresco **(b)** *(frescor)* coolness; **al f.** in a cool place; **hace f.** it's chilly; **tomar el f.** to get a breath of fresh air **(c)** *CAm* fruit pie

**frescor** *nm* coolness, freshness

**frescura** *nf* **(a)** *(de fruta, verdura)* freshness **(b)** *(espontaneidad)* freshness **(c)** *(descaro)* cheek, nerve; **¡qué f.!** what a cheek!

**fresno** *nm* ash (tree)

**fresón** *nm* large strawberry

**freudiano, -a** [froi'ðjano] *adj* Freudian

**fría 1** *ver* **freír**
**2** *ver* **frío**

**frialdad** *nf también Fig* coldness

**fricandó** *nm* fricandeau

**fricasé** *nm* fricassee

**fricativa** *nf* fricative

**fricativo, -a** *adj* fricative

**fricción** *nf* **(a)** *también Fig (roce)* friction **(b)** *(friega)* rub, massage

**friccionar** *vt* to rub, to massage

**fríe** *ver* **freír**

**friega 1** *ver* **fregar**

**2** *nf* massage; **dar friegas de alcohol a alguien** to give sb an alcohol rub

**friegaplatos** *nm inv* dishwasher

**friera** *etc ver* **freír**

**frigidez** *nf (sexual)* frigidity; *(de acogida, respuesta)* coldness

**frígido, -a** *adj (respuesta, mujer)* frigid

**frigorífico, -a 1** *adj (que produce frío)* **cámara frigorífica** cold store; **camión f.** refrigerated lorry

**2** *nm* refrigerator, *Br* fridge, *US* icebox

**frijol, fríjol** *nm Am* bean

**frió** *ver* **freír**

**frío, -a 1** *ver* **freír**

**2** *adj también Fig* cold; **dejar a alguien f.** to leave sb cold; **un recibimiento muy f.** a cold *o* unwelcoming reception

**3** *nm* cold; **coger f.** to catch a chill; *Fam* **¡hace un f. que pela!** it's freezing cold!; **pelarse de f.** to be freezing to death; **tener f.** to be cold; *Fig* **coger a alguien en f.** to catch sb on the hop; *Fig* **no darle a alguien ni f. ni calor** to leave sb cold

**friolento, -a** *adj Am* sensitive to the cold

**friolera** *nf Fam* **costó la f. de 20.000 pesetas** it cost a cool 20,000 pesetas

**friolero, -a 1** *adj* sensitive to the cold

**2** *nm,f* **mi padre es un f.** my father really feels the cold

**frisar** *vt* to be around, to be getting on for *(a certain age)*

**frisbee®** ['frisβi] *nm* frisbee®

**friso** *nm* **(a)** *Arquit* frieze **(b)** *(zócalo)* skirting board

**frisón, -ona** *adj & nm,f* Frisian

**fritada** *nf* fry-up, dish of fried food

**fritanga** *nf Fam* fry-up; **olor a f.** smell of frying

**frito, -a 1** *participio ver* **freír**

**2** *adj* **(a)** *(alimento)* fried **(b)** *Fam Fig (harto)* fed up (to the back teeth); **me tienen f. con tantas quejas** I'm sick (and tired) of all their complaining **(c)** *Fam Fig (dormido)* flaked out, asleep

**3** *nmpl* **fritos** fried food

**fritura** *nf* fry-up, dish of fried food

**frivolidad** *nf* frivolity

**frívolo, -a** *adj* frivolous

**frondosidad** *nf* leafiness

**frondoso, -a** *adj (planta, árbol)* leafy; *(bosque)* dense

**frontal** *adj (ataque)* frontal; *(colisión)* head-on; **la parte f.** the front, the front part

**frontera** *nf* border; *Fig (límite)* bounds

**fronterizo, -a** *adj* border; **ciudad fronteriza** border town; **conflicto f.** border dispute

**frontis** *nm inv* façade

**frontispicio** *nm* **(a)** *(de edificio) (fachada)* façade; *(remate)* pediment **(b)** *(de libro)* frontispiece

**frontón** *nm* **(a)** *(deporte)* pelota; *(cancha)* pelota court **(b)** *Arquit* pediment

**frotamiento** *nm* rubbing

**frotar 1** *vt (rozar, masajear)* to rub; *(al fregar)* to scrub

**2 frotarse** *vpr* **frotarse las manos** to rub one's hands

**fructífero, -a** *adj* fruitful

**fructificar** [61] *vi también Fig* to bear fruit

**fructosa** *nf* fructose

**fructuoso, -a** *adj* fruitful

**frugal** *adj* frugal

**frugalidad** *nf* frugality

**fruición** *nf* gusto, delight

**frunce** *nm (en tela)* gathering

**fruncido, -a 1** *adj* **(a)** *(tela)* gathered **(b)** **con el ceño f.** with a frown, frowning

**2** *nm (en tela)* gathering

**fruncir** [74] *vt* **(a)** *(tela)* to gather **(b)** *(labios)* to purse; **f. el ceño** to frown

**fruslería** *nf* triviality, trifle

**frustración** *nf* frustration

**frustrado, -a** *adj (persona)* frustrated; *(plan)* failed

**frustrante** *adj* frustrating

**frustrar 1** *vt* **(a)** *(persona)* to frustrate **(b)** *(posibilidades, ilusiones)* to thwart, to put paid to; *(plan)* to thwart

**2 frustrarse** *vpr* **(a)** *(persona)* to get frustrated **(b)** *(ilusiones)* to be thwarted; *(proyecto)* to fail

**fruta** *nf* fruit

**frutal 1** *adj* fruit; **árbol f.** fruit tree

**2** *nm* fruit tree

**frutería** *nf* fruit shop

**frutero, -a 1** *nm,f (persona)* fruiterer

**2** *nm (recipiente)* fruit bowl

**fruticultura** *nf* fruit farming

**frutilla** *nf Am* strawberry

**fruto** *nm* **(a)** *(naranja, plátano)* fruit; *(nuez, avellana)* nut; **frutos secos** dried fruit and nuts; *Fig* **f. prohibido** forbidden fruit **(b)** *(resultado)* fruit; **dar f.** to bear fruit; **sacar f. a** *o* **de algo** to profit from sth

**FSLN** *nm (abrev de* **Frente Sandinista de Liberación Nacional)** FSLN

**FTP** *Informát (abrev de* **file transfer protocol)** FTP

**fu:ni fu ni fa** *loc adv Fam* so-so

**fucsia 1** *nf (planta)* fuchsia

**2** *adj inv & nm inv (color)* fuchsia

**fue** *v* **(a)** *ver* **ir (b)** *ver* **ser**

**fuego** nm (a) *(incandescencia)* fire; *(de cocina, fogón)* ring, burner; *Culin* a f. **lento/vivo** over a low/high heat; **atizar el f.** to poke the fire; **hacer un f.** to make a fire; **pegar f. a algo** to set sth on fire, to set fire to sth; **pedir/dar f.** to ask for/give a light; **¿tiene f.?** have you got a light?; **f. fatuo** will-o'-the-wisp; **fuegos artificiales** fireworks; *Fig* **jugar con f.** to play with fire

(b) *(disparos)* fire; **abrir** o **hacer f.** to fire, to open fire; **f. cruzado** crossfire; *Fig* **estar entre dos fuegos** to be between the devil and the deep blue sea

(c) *Fig (apasionamiento)* passion, ardour

(d) *(sensación de ardor)* heat, burning

**fuel** nm fuel oil

**fuelle** nm (a) *(para soplar)* bellows (b) *(de maleta, bolso)* accordion pleats (c) *(entre vagones)* connecting corridor, concertina vestibule

**fuel-oil** nm fuel oil

**fuente** nf (a) *(construcción)* fountain (b) *(bandeja)* (serving) dish (c) *Fig (origen)* source; **fuentes oficiales** official sources; **f. de riqueza** source of wealth (d) *(manantial)* spring (e) *Elec* **f. de alimentación** feed source (f) *Imprenta & Informát* font

**fuera 1** v (a) *ver* **ir**
(b) *ver* **ser**
**2** adv (a) *(en el exterior)* outside; **f. de la casa** outside the house; **le echó f.** she threw him out; **hacia f.** outwards; **por f.** (on the) outside
(b) *(en otro lugar)* away; *(en el extranjero)* abroad; **de f.** *(extranjero)* from abroad
(c) *Fig (alejado)* **f. de** *(alcance, peligro)* out of; *(cálculos, competencia)* outside; **estar f. de sí** to be beside oneself (with rage); **f. de plazo** after the closing date
(d) *Dep* **f. de banda** out of play; **f. de combate** knocked out; *Fig* out of action; **f. de juego** offside
(e) *(expresiones)* **f. de** *(excepto)* except for, apart from; **f. de serie** exceptional, out of the ordinary; **ser un f. de serie** to be one of a kind
**3** interj **¡f.!** (get) out!; *(en el teatro)* (get) off!; **¡f. de aquí!** get out of my sight!

**fueraborda 1** adj inv outboard; **motor f.** outboard motor o engine; **lancha f.** outboard, boat with outboard motor
**2** nm inv *(motor)* outboard motor o engine
**3** nf inv *(lancha)* outboard, boat with outboard motor

**fuerce** ver **forzar**

**fuero** nm (a) *(ley local)* = ancient regional law still existing in some parts of Spain (b) *(jurisdicción)* code of laws (c) **en el f. interno de alguien** in sb's heart of hearts, deep down

**fuerte 1** adj (a) *(persona, viento)* strong; *(frío, dolor, color)* intense; *(lluvia)* heavy; *(ruido)* loud; *(golpe, pelea)* hard; **lenguaje f.** strong language
(b) *(comida) (pesado)* heavy; *(picante)* hot
(c) *(nudo)* tight
(d) *Fam (increíble)* astonishing, amazing; **¡qué f.!** *(fabuloso)* wow!, amazing!; *(terrible)* how awful!, oh no!
**2** adv (a) *(intensamente)* hard; *(abrazar, agarrar)* tight
(b) *(abundantemente)* a lot
(c) *(en voz alta)* loudly
**3** nm (a) *(fortificación)* fort
(b) *(punto fuerte)* strong point, forte

**fuerza 1** ver **forzar**
**2** nf (a) *(fortaleza)* strength; *(violencia)* force; *(de sonido)* loudness; *(de dolor)* intensity; **por f.** of necessity; **tener fuerzas para** to have the strength to; **a f. de** by dint of; **a la f.** *(contra la voluntad)* by force; *(por necesidad)* of necessity; **por la f.** by force; **sacar fuerzas de flaqueza** to screw up one's courage; *Der* **f. mayor** majeure; *(en seguros)* act of God; **no llegué por un caso de f. mayor** I didn't make it due to circumstances beyond my control; **f. de voluntad** willpower
(b) *Fís & Mil* force; **fuerzas** *(grupo)* forces; **Fuerzas Armadas** armed forces; **fuerzas del orden público** security forces; **fuerzas nacionalistas** *(partidos)* nationalist parties
(c) *Elec* power

**fuese** v (a) ver **ir** (b) ver **ser**

**fuet** nm *Culin* = type of cured pork sausage

**fuga** nf (a) *(huida)* escape; **darse a la f.** to take flight; **f. de cerebros** brain drain (b) *(escape)* leak (c) *Mús* fugue

**fugacidad** nf fleeting nature

**fugarse** [40] vpr to escape; **f. de casa** to run away from home; **f. con alguien** to run off with sb

**fugaz** adj fleeting; **una visita f.** a flying visit

**fugitivo, -a 1** adj (a) *(en fuga)* fleeing (b) *(fugaz)* fleeting
**2** nm,f fugitive

**fugue** etc ver **fugarse**

**führer** ['firer] *(pl* **führers)** nm führer

**fui** (a) ver **ir** (b) ver **ser**

**fulana** nf *(prostituta)* tart, whore

**fulano, -a** nm,f what's his/her name, so-and-so

**fular** nm scarf

**fulero, -a 1** adj (a) *(chapucero)* shoddy (b) *(tramposo)* dishonest
**2** nm,f trickster

**fulgor** nm shining; *(de disparo)* flash

**fulgurante** *adj (resplandeciente)* flashing; *Fig (rápido)* rapid; **un ascenso/éxito f.** a lightning rise/success

**fulgurar** *vi* to gleam; *(intermitentemente)* to flash

**fullero, -a 1** *adj* cheating, dishonest
**2** *nm,f* cheat

**fulminante** *adj* **(a)** *Fig (despido, muerte)* sudden; *(enfermedad)* devastating; *(mirada)* withering **(b)** *(explosivo)* fulminating

**fulminar** *vt (sujeto: enfermedad)* to strike down; **un rayo la fulminó** she was struck by lightning; **f. a alguien con la mirada** to look daggers at sb

**fumadero** *nm (de opio)* den

**fumador, -ora** *nm,f* smoker; **f. pasivo** passive smoker; **no f.** nonsmoker

**fumar 1** *vt* to smoke
**2** *vi* to smoke; **f. como un carretero** to smoke like a chimney

**fumeta** *nmf muy Fam* pot-head, pot smoker

**fumigación** *nf* fumigation

**fumigador** *nm* fumigator

**fumigar** [40] *vt* to fumigate

**funambulista** *nmf* tightrope walker

**función** *nf* **(a)** *(actividad, objetivo)* function; *(trabajo)* duty; **director en funciones** acting director; **entrar en funciones** to take up one's duties **(b)** *Teatro* show **(c)** **en f. de** depending on; **estar** *o* **ir en f. de** to depend on, to be dependent on **(d)** *Mat* function

**funcional** *adj* functional

**funcionalidad** *nf* functional qualities

**funcionalismo** *nm* functionalism

**funcionamiento** *nm* operation, functioning; **entrar/estar en f.** to come into/be in operation; **poner algo en f.** to start sth (working)

**funcionar** *vi* to work; **f. con gasolina** to run on petrol; **funciona a pilas** it works *o* runs off batteries; **no funciona** *(en letrero)* out of order

**funcionariado** *nm* civil service

**funcionario, -a** *nm,f* civil servant

**funda** *nf (de sofá, máquina de escribir)* cover; *(de almohada)* pillowcase; *(de disco)* sleeve; *(de gafas)* pouch

**fundación** *nf* foundation

**fundado, -a** *adj* **(a)** *(argumento, idea)* well-founded **(b)** *(creado, establecido)* founded

**fundador, -ora 1** *adj* founding
**2** *nm,f* founder

**fundamentación** *nf* foundation, basis

**fundamental** *adj* fundamental

**fundamentalismo** *nm* fundamentalism

**fundamentalista** *adj & nmf* fundamentalist

**fundamentar 1** *vt* **(a)** *(basar)* to base **(b)** *Constr* to lay the foundations of
**2 fundamentarse** *vpr Fig (basarse)* to be based *o* founded **(en** on)

**fundamento** *nm* **(a)** *(base)* foundation, basis **(b)** *(razón)* reason, grounds; **sin f.** unfounded, groundless; **fundamentos** *(principios)* basic principles; *(cimientos)* foundations

**fundar 1** *vt* **(a)** *(crear)* to found **(b)** *(basar)* to base **(en** on)
**2 fundarse** *vpr (basarse)* to be based **(en** on)

**fundición** *nf* **(a)** *(taller)* foundry **(b)** *(fusión)* smelting

**fundido** *nm Cine (apareciendo)* fade-in; *(desapareciendo)* fade-out; **f. en negro** fade-out (to black)

**fundir 1** *vt* **(a)** *(plomo)* to melt; *(hierro)* to smelt **(b)** *Elec* to fuse; *(fusible)* to blow **(c)** *Com & Fig* to merge
**2 fundirse** *vpr* **(a)** *Elec* to blow; **se han fundido los plomos** the fuses have gone; **se ha fundido la bombilla de la cocina** the light in the kitchen has gone **(b)** *(derretirse)* to melt; *Fig* **se fundieron en un abrazo** they fell into one another's arms **(c)** *Com & Fig* to merge

**fúnebre** *adj* funeral; *Fig (triste)* gloomy, funereal; **coche f.** hearse; **misa f.** funeral mass

**funeral** *nm (misa)* funeral (service *o* mass); *(entierro, cremación)* funeral

**funerala** *nf* **a la f.** *(ojo)* black

**funeraria** *nf Br* undertaker's, *US* mortician's

**funerario, -a** *adj* funeral; **rito f.** funeral *o* funerary rite

**funesto, -a** *adj* fateful, disastrous

**fungible** *adj* disposable

**fungicida 1** *adj* fungicidal
**2** *nm* fungicide

**fungir** [26] *vi Am* to act, to serve

**funicular 1** *adj* funicular
**2** *nm* **(a)** *(por tierra)* funicular **(b)** *(por aire)* cable car

**funky** ['fuŋki] **1** *adj* **música f.** funk
**2** *nm* funk

**furcia** *nf Pey* slag, whore

**furgón** *nm Aut* van; *Ferroc* wagon, van; **f. de equipajes** guard's van

**furgoneta** *nf* van

**furia** *nf* fury; **ponerse hecho una f.** to fly into a rage

**furibundo, -a** *adj* furious

**furioso, -a** *adj* furious

**furor** *nm* **(a)** *(enfado)* fury, rage **(b)** *(ímpetu)* fever, urge **(c)** **hacer f.** to be all the rage

**furtivo, -a 1** *adj (mirada, sonrisa)* furtive; **cazador f.** poacher
**2** *nm,f (cazador)* poacher

**furúnculo** *nm* boil

**fusa** *nf Mús* demisemiquaver

**fuseaux** [fu'so] *nm inv* ski pants

**fuselaje** *nm* fuselage

**fusible 1** *adj* fusible

 **2** *nm* fuse

**fusil** *nm* rifle

**fusilamiento** *nm* (a) *(ejecución)* execution by firing squad (b) *Fam (plagio)* plagiarism

**fusilar** *vt* (a) *(ejecutar)* to execute by firing squad, to shoot (b) *Fam (plagiar)* to plagiarize

**fusilero** *nm* fusilier, rifleman

**fusión** *nf* (a) *(agrupación)* merging; *(de empresas, bancos)* merger; *Informát* merge (b) *(de metal, hielo)* melting; *Fís* fusion; **f. nuclear** nuclear fusion

**fusionar 1** *vt también Econ* to merge

 **2 fusionarse** *vpr también Econ* to merge

**fusta** *nf* riding crop

**fustán** *nm Am* petticoat

**fuste** *nm* shaft

**fustigar** [40] *vt* (a) *(azotar)* to whip (b) *(censurar)* to criticize harshly

**fútbol** *nm* soccer, *Br* football; **f. sala** indoor five-a-side

**futbolero, -a** *Fam* **1** *adj* **es muy f.** he is soccer *o Br* football crazy

 **2** *nm,f* soccer fan, *Br* football fan

**futbolín** *nm* table football

**futbolista** *nmf* footballer

**futbolístico, -a** *adj* soccer, *Br* football; **campeonato f.** soccer *o Br* football championship

**fútil** *adj* trivial

**futilidad** *nf* triviality

**futón** *nm* futon

**futurible** *adj* potential

**futurista** *adj* futuristic

**futuro, -a 1** *adj* future

 **2** *nm también Gram* future; **f. perfecto** future perfect; **sin f.** with no future, without prospects; *Econ* **futuros** futures

**futurología** *nf* futurology

**futurólogo, -a** *nm,f* futurologist

# G

**G¹, g** [xe] *nf (letra)* G, g

**g²** *(abrev de* **gramo)** g

**gabacho, -a** *Fam Pey* **1** *adj* Froggy, = pejorative term meaning "French"

  **2** *nm,f* Frog, = pejorative term referring to a French person

**gabán** *nm* overcoat

**gabardina** *nf* **(a)** *(prenda)* raincoat, mac **(b)** *(tela)* gabardine

**gabinete** *nm* **(a)** *(gobierno)* cabinet **(b)** *(despacho)* office **(c)** *(sala)* study

**Gabón** *n* Gabon

**gacela** *nf* gazelle

**gaceta** *nf* gazette

**gacetillero, -a** *nm,f Fam Anticuado (periodista)* hack

**gachas** *nfpl Culin (corn)* porridge

**gachí** *nf Fam* bird, chick

**gacho, -a** *adj* drooping; **con la cabeza gacha** with head bowed, hanging one's head

**gachó** *nm Fam* guy, *Br* bloke

**gaditano, -a1** *adj* of/from Cadiz

  **2** *nm,f* person from Cadiz

**gaélico, -a1** *adj* Gaelic

  **2** *nm (lengua)* Gaelic

**gafado, -a** *adj Fam* **estar g.** to be jinxed

**gafar** *vt Fam* to jinx, to bring bad luck to

**gafas** *nfpl* glasses; *(protectoras, para nadar)* goggles; *(para submarinismo)* diving mask; **g. graduadas** prescription glasses; **g. de sol** sunglasses

**gafe 1** *adj* jinxed; **ser g.** to be jinxed

  **2** *nmf* jinxed person

  **3** *nm* **tener el g.** to be jinxed

**gag** *nm (broma)* gag

**gaita** *nf* **(a)** *(instrumento)* bagpipes **(b)** *Fam (pesadez)* drag, pain

**gaitero, -a** *nm,f* piper

**gaje** *nm* **gajes del oficio** occupational hazards

**gajo** *nm* **(a)** *(de naranja, limón)* segment **(b)** *(racimo)* bunch **(c)** *(rama)* broken-off branch

**GAL** [gal] *nmpl (abrev de* **Grupos Antiterroristas de Liberación)** = former Spanish terrorist group that directed its attacks against ETA

**gala** *nf* **(a)** *(fiesta)* gala; **cena de g.** black tie dinner, formal dinner; **traje de g.** formal dress; **uniforme de g.** dress uniform **(b)** *(ropa)* **se puso sus mejores galas** she put on her finery **(c)** *(actuación)* gala show o performance **(d)** *(expresiones)* **hacer g. de algo** *(preciarse de)* to be proud of sth; *(exhibir)* to demonstrate sth; **tener a g. algo** to be proud of sth

**galáctico, -a** *adj (de las galaxias)* galactic; *Fam Fig (moderno, futurista)* space-age

**galaico, -a** *adj Formal* Galician

**galán** *nm* **(a)** *(hombre atractivo)* attractive young man **(b)** *Teatro* leading man, lead

**galante** *adj* gallant

**galantear** *vt* to court, to woo

**galanteo** *nm* courting, wooing

**galantería** *nf* **(a)** *(cualidad)* politeness **(b)** *(acción)* gallantry, compliment

**galápago** *nm* turtle

**Galápagos** *nfpl* **las (islas) G.** the Galapagos Islands

**galardón** *nm* award, prize

**galardonado, -a** *adj* award-winning, prize-winning

**galardonar** *vt* to award a prize to

**galaxia** *nf* galaxy

**galbana** *nf Fam* laziness, sloth

**galena** *nf* galena, lead sulphide

**galeno** *nm Anticuado* doctor

**galeón** *nm* galleon

**galera** *nf* galley

**galerada** *nf* galley proof

**galería** *nf* **(a)** *(pasillo)* gallery; *(corredor descubierto)* verandah; **g. comercial** shopping arcade **(b)** *(para cortinas)* curtain rail **(c)** *Fig (vulgo)* masses; **hacer algo para la g.** to play to the gallery

**galerna** *nf* strong north-west wind

**Gales** *n* **(el país de) G.** Wales

**galés, -esa1** *adj* Welsh

  **2** *nm,f* Welshman, *f* Welshwoman; **los galeses** the Welsh

  **3** *nm (lengua)* Welsh

**galgo** *nm* greyhound; **carreras de galgos** greyhound races

**Galicia** *n* Galicia

**galicismo** *nm* gallicism

**galimatías** *nm inv* *(lenguaje)* gibberish; *(lío)* jumble

**gallardete** *nm* pennant

**gallardía** *nf* (a) *(valentía)* bravery (b) *(apostura)* noble bearing

**gallardo, -a** *adj* (a) *(valiente)* brave, dashing (b) *(bien parecido)* fine-looking, striking

**gallear** *vi* to strut about, to show off

**gallego, -a 1** *adj & nm,f* Galician; *CSur Fam* Spanish

**2** *nm (lengua)* Galician

**galleguismo** *nm (palabra, expresión)* Galician expression

**galleta** *nf* (a) *Culin* biscuit (b) *Fam (cachete)* slap, smack

**gallina 1** *nf* hen; **cría gallinas** *(gallinas, pollos y gallos)* he keeps chickens; *Fam* **la g. ciega** blind man's buff; *Fam Fig* **matar la g. de los huevos de oro** to kill the goose that lays the golden eggs

**2** *nmf Fam (persona)* chicken, coward

**gallináceo, -a** *adj* gallinaceous

**gallinazo** *nm Am* vulture

**gallinero** *nm* (a) *(corral)* henhouse (b) *Fam Teatro* gods *(singular)* (c) *Fam (alboroto)* madhouse

**gallito** *nm Fig* cock of the walk

**gallo** *nm* (a) *(ave)* cock, cockerel; **g. de pelea** fighting cock; *Fam Fig* **en menos que canta un g.** in no time at all; *Carib* **g. pinto** rice and beans (b) *(al cantar)* false note; *(al hablar)* squeak (c) *(pez)* John Dory (d) *Fig (mandón)* cock of the walk

**galo, -a 1** *adj Hist* Gallic; *(francés)* French

**2** *nm,f (persona)* Gaul

**galón** *nm* (a) *(adorno)* braid; *Mil* stripe (b) *(medida)* gallon

**galopada** *nf* gallop

**galopante** *adj Fig (inflación)* galloping

**galopar** *vi* to gallop

**galope** *nm* gallop; **al g.** at a gallop; *también Fig* **a g. tendido** at full gallop

**galpón** *nm Am* shed

**galvanización** *nf* galvanization

**galvanizar** [16] *vt* to galvanize

**gama** *nf (conjunto)* range; *(de colores, modelos)* range; *Mús* scale

**gamba** *nf* (a) *(animal)* prawn (b) *muy Fam* **meter la g.** to put one's foot in it

**gamberrada** *nf* act of vandalism

**gamberrismo** *nm* vandalism; *(en fútbol)* hooliganism

**gamberro, -a 1** *adj* loutish

**2** *nm,f (persona)* yob, lout; **hacer el g.** to muck about, to clown around

**Gambia** *n* The Gambia

**gameto** *nm* gamete

**gamín** *nm Col* child

**gamma** *nf* gamma

**gamo** *nm* fallow deer

**gamonal** *nm Andes, CAm* village chief

**gamuza** *nf* (a) *(tejido)* chamois (leather); *(trapo)* duster (b) *(animal)* chamois

**gana 1** *nf* (a) *(afán)* desire, wish (**de** to); **de buena g.** willingly; **de mala g.** unwillingly; *Fam* **porque me da la g.** because I bloody well want to; *Fam* **no me da la g.** I don't bloody want to; **hace/come todo lo que le viene en g.** she does/eats whatever she pleases (b) *(apetito)* appetite

**2** *nfpl* **tener ganas de (hacer) algo, sentir ganas de (hacer) algo** to feel like (doing) sth; **quedarse con (las) ganas de hacer algo** not to manage to do sth; **no tengo ganas de que me pongan una multa** I don't fancy getting a fine; **tenerle ganas a alguien** *(odiar)* to have it in for sb

**ganadería** *nf* (a) *(actividad)* livestock farming (b) *(ganado)* livestock (c) *(lugar)* livestock farm

**ganadero, -a 1** *adj* livestock-farming; **región ganadera** livestock-farming region

**2** *nm,f* livestock farmer

**ganado** *nm* livestock, stock; **g. ovino** sheep; **g. porcino** pigs; **g. vacuno** cattle

**ganador, -ora 1** *adj* winning

**2** *nm,f* winner

**ganancia** *nf (rendimiento)* profit; *(ingreso)* earnings; **ganancias y pérdidas** profit and loss; **g. líquida** net profit

**ganancial** *adj* **bienes gananciales** shared possessions

**ganapán** *nm* odd-job man

**ganar 1** *vt* (a) *(premio, competición)* to win (b) *(obtener) (sueldo, dinero)* to earn; *(peso, tiempo, terreno)* to gain; **¿qué gano yo con eso?** what's in it for me? (c) *(derrotar)* to beat; **te voy a g.** I'm going to beat you (d) *(aventajar)* **g. a alguien en algo** to be better than sb as regards sth (e) *(alcanzar)* to reach, to make it to (f) *(conquistar)* to take, to capture

**2** *vi* (a) *(vencer)* to win; **ganaron por tres a uno** they won three one (b) *(lograr dinero)* to earn money; **¿cuánto ganas?** how much do you earn?; *Fam Fig* **no gano para disgustos** I've more than enough worries *o* troubles (c) *(mejorar)* to benefit (**con** from); **gana mucho con la barba** he looks a lot better with a beard; **g. en algo** to gain in sth; **ha ganado en**

**amplitud** *(parece mayor)* it looks bigger

**3 ganarse** *vpr* (a) *(conquistar)* *(simpatía, respeto)* to earn; *(persona)* to win over (b) *(merecer)* to deserve

**ganchillo** *nm (aguja)* crochet hook; *(labor)* crochet; **hacer g.** to crochet

**ganchito** *nm* ≃ Wotsit®, = cheese-flavoured snack made from maize

**gancho** *nm* (a) *(garfio)* hook; *(de percha)* peg (b) *(cómplice)* *(de timador)* decoy; *(de vendedor)* person who attracts buyers (c) *Fam (atractivo)* charm, sex appeal; *(popularidad)* pulling power; **esa chica tiene mucho g.** that girl is quite something

**ganchudo, -a** *adj* hooked

**gandul, -ula 1** *adj* lazy
**2** *nm,f* lazybones, layabout

**gandulear** *vi* to loaf around

**gandulería** *nf* idleness

**ganga** *nf* snip, bargain

**Ganges** *nm* el G. the Ganges

**ganglio** *nm Anat* g. **(linfático)** lymph node *o* gland

**gangoso, -a 1** *adj (voz)* nasal *(caused by cleft palate)*
**2** *nm,f* = person with a nasal voice caused by a cleft palate

**gangrena** *nf* gangrene

**gangrenado, -a** *adj* gangrenous

**gangrenarse** *vpr* to become gangrenous

**gangrenoso, -a** *adj* gangrenous

**gángster** ['ganster] *(pl* **gángsters, gángsteres)** = **gánster**

**gangsterismo** [ganste'rismo] = **gansterismo**

**gansada** *nf Fam* silly thing

**ganso, -a 1** *nm,f* (a) *(ave)* *(hembra)* goose; *(macho)* gander (b) *Fam (tonto)* idiot, fool; **hacer el g.** to clown around
**2** *adj muy Fam (grande, alto)* tall

**gánster** ['ganster] *(pl* **gánsters, gánsteres)** *nm* gangster

**gansterismo** [ganste'rismo] *nm* gangsterism

**ganzúa** *nf* picklock

**gañido** *nm* yelp

**garabatear** *vi & vt* to scribble

**garabato** *nm* scribble; **hacer garabatos** to scribble

**garaje** *nm* garage *(for parking)*

**garante** *nmf* guarantor; **salir g.** to act as guarantor

**garantía** *nf* (a) *(seguro, promesa)* guarantee; **de g.** reliable, dependable; **ser g. de algo** to guarantee sth (b) *(fianza)* surety

**garantizado, -a** *adj* guaranteed

**garantizar** [16] *vt* (a) *(contra riesgo, deterioro)* to guarantee; **g. algo a alguien** to assure sb of sth (b) *(avalar)* to vouch for

**garbanzo** *nm* chickpea; *Fam Fig* **ser el g. negro** to be the black sheep

**garbeo** *nm Fam* stroll; **dar un g.** to go for *o* take a stroll

**garbo** *nm (de persona)* grace; *(de escritura)* stylishness, style

**garboso, -a** *adj (persona)* graceful; *(escritura)* stylish

**garceta** *nf* little egret

**gardenia** *nf* gardenia

**garduña** *nf* marten

**garete** *nm Fam* **ir** *o* **irse al g.** *(fracasar)* to go down the drain, to go to pot

**garfio** *nm* hook

**gargajo** *nm* phlegm

**garganta** *nf* (a) *Anat* throat; *Fig* **lo tengo atravesado en la g.** he/it sticks in my gullet (b) *(desfiladero)* gorge

**gargantilla** *nf* choker

**gargantúa** *nm* big eater, glutton

**gárgaras** *nfpl* gargling; **hacer g.** to gargle; *Fam* **mandar a alguien a hacer g.** to send sb packing; *Fam* **¡vete a hacer g.!** get lost!

**gárgola** *nf* gargoyle

**garita** *nf (de centinela)* sentry box; *(de conserje)* porter's lodge

**garito** *nm (casa de juego)* gambling den; *Fam (establecimiento)* dive

**garnacha** *nf (uva)* = purplish grape

**Garona** *nm* el G. the Garonne

**garra** *nf (de mamífero)* claw; *(de ave)* talon, claw; *Fig (de persona)* paw, hand; **caer en las garras de alguien** to fall into sb's clutches; *Fam* **tener g.** *(persona)* to have charisma; *(novela, canción)* to be gripping

**garrafa** *nf* carafe; *Fam* **de g.** *(bebida alcohólica)* cheap and nasty

**garrafal** *adj* monumental, enormous

**garrafón** *nm* demijohn

**garrapata** *nf* tick

**garrapiñado, -a** *adj* caramel-coated

**garrapiñar** *vt (fruta)* to candy; *(almendras)* to coat with caramelized sugar

**garrocha** *nf* pike, lance

**garrotazo** *nm* blow with a club *o* stick

**garrote** *nm* (a) *(estaca)* club, stick (b) *(instrumento de ejecución)* g. **(vil)** garotte; **dar g. a alguien** to garotte sb

**garrulo, -a** *Fam* **1** *adj* coarse, uncouth
**2** *nm,f* country bumpkin, yokel, *US* hick

**garúa** *nf Am* drizzle

**garza** *nf* heron; **g. real** grey heron

**garzón** *nm CSur* waiter

**gas** (*pl* gases) *nm* gas; *Aut* **dar g.** to step on the accelerator; *Fam* **a todo g.** flat out, at top speed; *Fam* **quedarse sin g.** to run out of steam; **g. butano** butane (gas); **g. ciudad** town gas; **g. lacrimógeno** tear gas; **g. natural** natural gas; *Quím* **g. noble** noble gas; **gases** (*en el estómago*) wind

**gasa** *nf* gauze

**gasear** *vt* to gas

**gaseoducto** *nm* gas pipeline

**gaseosa** *nf* lemonade

**gaseoso, -a** *adj* (*estado*) gaseous; (*bebida*) fizzy

**gásfiter, gasfitero** *nm Chile, Perú* plumber

**gasfitería** *nf Chile, Perú* plumber's (shop)

**gasificación** *nf* gasification

**gasificar** [61] *vt* (*convertir en gas*) to gasify; (*bebida*) to carbonate

**gasoducto** *nm* gas pipeline

**gasóleo, gasoil** *nm* diesel oil

**gasolina** *nf Br* petrol, *US* gas; **poner g.** to fill up (with *Br* petrol *o US* gas)

**gasolinera** *nf Br* petrol station, *US* gas station

**gastado, -a** *adj* (*objeto*) worn out; (*frase, tema*) hackneyed; (*persona*) broken, burnt out

**gastar 1** *vt* (a) (*consumir*) (*dinero, tiempo*) to spend; (*gasolina, electricidad*) to use (up); (*ropa, zapatos*) to wear out; (*malgastar*) to waste (b) (*tener, usar*) (*ropa*) to wear; (*número de zapatos*) to take; **g. mal genio** to have a bad temper; **g. una broma (a alguien)** to play a joke (on sb) (c) **gastarlas** to carry on, to behave; **¡no sabes cómo se las gastan allí!** you can't imagine how they carry on there!

**2** *vi* to spend (money)

**3 gastarse** *vpr* (a) (*deteriorarse, desgastarse*) to wear out (b) (*consumirse*) to run out

**gasto** *nm* (*empleo de dinero*) outlay, expenditure; (*coste*) expense; (*consumo*) consumption; (*despilfarro*) waste; **cubrir gastos** to cover costs, to break even; **no reparar en gastos** to spare no expense; *Econ* **g. amortizable** capitalized expense; *Econ* **g. deducible** tax-deductible expense; **g. público** public expenditure; *Com* **gastos fijos** fixed charges *o* costs; (*en una casa*) overheads; **gastos generales** overheads; **gastos de mantenimiento** maintenance costs; **gastos de representación** entertainment allowance

**gástrico, -a** *adj Anat* gastric

**gastritis** *nf inv Med* gastritis

**gastroenteritis** *nf inv Med* gastroenteritis

**gastrointestinal** *adj Anat* gastrointestinal

**gastronomía** *nf* gastronomy

**gastronómico, -a** *adj* gastronomic

**gastrónomo, -a** *nm,f* gourmet, gastronome

**gatas: a gatas** *loc adv Fam* on all fours

**gatear** *vi* to crawl

**gatera** *nf* cat flap *o* door

**gatillo** *nm* trigger

**gato, -a 1** *nm,f* cat; *Fam Fig* **dar g. por liebre a alguien** to swindle *o* cheat sb; *Fam* **buscar tres pies al g.** to overcomplicate matters; *Fam* **aquí hay g. encerrado** there's something fishy going on here; *Fam* **llevarse el g. al agua** to pull it off; *Fam Fig* **sólo había cuatro gatos** there was hardly a soul there; **g. montés** wildcat

**2** *nm Aut* jack

**GATT** [gat] *nm* (*abrev de* **General Agreement on Tariffs and Trade**) GATT

**gatuno, -a** *adj* catlike, feline

**gaucho, -a** *adj & nm,f* gaucho

**gavilán** *nm* sparrowhawk

**gavilla** *nf* sheaf

**gaviota** *nf* seagull

**gay** [gai, gei] *adj inv & nmf* gay

**gayumbos** *nmpl muy Fam* (*calzoncillos*) pants

**gazapo** *nm* (a) (*animal*) young rabbit (b) (*error*) misprint

**gazmoñería** *nf* sanctimoniousness

**gazmoño, -a** *adj* sanctimonious

**gaznate** *nm* gullet

**gazpacho** *nm* gazpacho, = Andalusian soup made from tomatoes, peppers, cucumbers and bread, served chilled

**GB** *nf* (*abrev de* **Gran Bretaña**) GB

**géiser** *nm* geyser

**geisha** ['geisa] *nf inv* geisha

**gel** *nm* gel

**gelatina** *nf* (*de carne*) gelatine; (*de fruta*) jelly

**gema** *nf* gem

**gemelo, -a 1** *adj* **hermano g.** twin brother, twin

**2** *nm,f* (*persona*) twin

**3** *nm* (*músculo*) calf

**4** *nmpl* **gemelos** (a) (*de camisa*) cufflinks (b) (*prismáticos*) binoculars; (*para teatro*) opera glasses

**gemido** *nm* (*de persona*) moan, groan; (*de animal*) whine

**géminis 1** *nm* (*zodiaco*) Gemini; **ser g.** to be (a) Gemini

**2** *nmf inv* (*persona*) Gemini

**gemir** [49] *vi* (a) (*persona*) to moan, to groan; (*animal*) to whine (b) (*viento*) to howl

**gemología** *nf* gemology

**gen** *nm* gene

**gendarme** *nmf* gendarme

**gendarmería** *nf* gendarmerie

**genealogía** *nf* genealogy

**genealógico, -a** *adj* genealogical

**generación** *nf* generation; **g. espontánea** spontaneous generation, autogenesis

**generacional** *adj* **conflicto g.** conflict between the generations, generation gap

**generador, -ora 1** *adj* generating

**2** *nm Elec* generator

**general 1** *adj* (*común*) general

**2** *nm Mil* general; **g. de brigada** *Br* brigadier, *US* brigadier general; **g. de división** major general

**3** *adv* **por lo g., en g.** in general, generally

**generala** *nf Mil* call to arms

**generalidad** *nf* (a) (*mayoría*) majority (b) (*vaguedad*) generalization; **generalidades** (*principios básicos*) basic principles

**generalísimo** *nm* supreme commander, generalissimo; *Hist* **el G.** = title given to Franco

**generalista** *adj* (*médico*) general

**Generalitat** [jenerali'tat] *nf* = autonomous government of the regions of Catalonia or Valencia

**generalización** *nf* (a) (*comentario*) generalization (b) (*extensión*) (*de conflicto*) escalation, widening; (*de prácticas, enseñanza*) spread

**generalizar** [16] **1** *vt* to spread, to make widespread

**2** *vi* to generalize

**3 generalizarse** *vpr* to become widespread

**generalmente** *adv* generally

**generar** *vt* (*originar, causar*) to generate; (*engendrar*) to create

**generatriz** *nf Geom* generatrix

**genérico, -a** *adj* (*común*) generic

**género** *nm* (a) (*clase*) kind, type

(b) *Gram* gender

(c) *Lit* genre

(d) *Biol* genus; **el g. humano** the human race

(e) *Mús* **g. chico** zarzuela, Spanish light opera; **g. lírico** opera

(f) (*productos*) merchandise, goods

(g) (*tejido*) cloth, material

**generosidad** *nf* generosity

**generoso, -a** *adj* generous

**génesis 1** *nf inv* genesis

**2** *nm inv Rel* **el G.** Genesis

**genética** *nf* genetics

**genético, -a** *adj* genetic

**genial** *adj* (a) (*artista, escritor*) of genius (b) *Fig* (*estupendo*) brilliant, great

**genialidad** *nf* (a) (*capacidad*) genius (b) (*acción*) stroke of genius

**genio** *nm* (a) (*talento*) genius (b) (*carácter*) nature, disposition (c) (*personalidad fuerte*) spirit (d) (*mal carácter*) bad temper; **estar de mal g.** to be in a mood; **tener mal g.** to be bad-tempered (e) (*ser mitológico*) genie

**genital 1** *adj* genital

**2** *nmpl* **genitales** genitals

**genitivo** *nm Gram* genitive

**genocidio** *nm* genocide

**genotipo** *nm* genotype

**Génova** *n* Genoa

**genovés, -esa** *adj & nm,f* Genoese

**gente** *nf* (a) (*personas*) people; **son buena g.** they're good people; **g. bien** well-to-do people; **g. guapa** beautiful people; **g. menuda** kids (b) *Fam* (*familia*) folks

**gentil 1** *adj* (*amable*) kind, nice

**2** *nmf Rel* gentile

**gentileza** *nf* courtesy, kindness; **¿tendría la g. de decirme...?** would you be so kind as to tell me...?; **por g. de** by courtesy of

**gentilhombre** *nm Hist* gentleman (*in the royal court*)

**gentilicio** *nm* = term referring to the natives or inhabitants of a particular place

**gentío** *nm* crowd

**gentuza** *nf Pey* riffraff, rabble

**genuflexión** *nf Rel* genuflection; **hacer una g.** to genuflect

**genuino, -a** *adj* genuine

**GEO** [xeo] *nm* (*abrev de* **Grupo Especial de Operaciones**) *Br* ≃ SAS, *US* ≃ SWAT, = specially trained police force; **los geos** = members of this group

**geodesia** *nf* geodesy

**geodinámica** *nf* geodynamics (*singular*)

**geofísica** *nf* (*ciencia*) geophysics (*singular*)

**geofísico, -a 1** *adj* geophysical

**2** *nm,f* (*persona*) geophysicist

**geografía** *nf* geography; **por toda la g. española** all over Spain; **g. humana** human geography

**geográfico, -a** *adj* geographical

**geógrafo, -a** *nm,f* geographer

**geología** *nf* geology

**geológico, -a** *adj* geological

**geólogo, -a** *nm,f* geologist

**geometría** *nf* geometry

**geométrico, -a** *adj* geometric

**geopolítica** *nf* geopolitics (*singular*)

**geopolítico, -a** *adj* geopolitical

**Georgia** *n* Georgia

**georgiano, -a 1** *adj & nm,f* Georgian

**2** *nm* (*lengua*) Georgian

**geranio** *nm* geranium

**gerencia** *nf* (a) *(dirección)* management (b) *(cargo)* post of manager (c) *(oficina)* manager's office

**gerente** *nmf* manager, director

**geriatra** *nmf Med* geriatrician

**geriatría** *nf Med* geriatrics *(singular)*

**geriátrico, -a 1** *adj* geriatric
**2** *nm (hospital)* geriatric hospital; *(residencia)* old folks' home

**gerifalte** *nm* (a) *(ave)* gerfalcon (b) *Fig (persona)* bigwig

**germanía** *nf Hist* thieves' slang

**germánico, -a 1** *adj (tribus, carácter)* Germanic, Teutonic
**2** *nm (lengua)* Germanic

**germanismo** *nm* Germanism

**germanista** *nmf* German scholar

**germano, -a 1** *adj (alemán)* German; *(tribus, carácter)* Germanic, Teutonic
**2** *nm,f (alemán)* German; *Hist* Teuton

**germen** *nm también Fig* germ

**germicida 1** *adj* germicidal
**2** *nm* germicide

**germinación** *nf* germination

**germinar** *vi también Fig* to germinate

**gerontocracia** *nf* gerontocracy

**gerontología** *nf Med* gerontology

**gerontólogo, -a** *nm,f Med* gerontologist

**gerundense 1** *adj* of/from Gerona
**2** *nmf* person from Gerona

**gerundio** *nm* gerund

**gesta** *nf* exploit, feat

**gestación** *nf también Fig* gestation

**gestar 1** *vi* to gestate
**2 gestarse** *vpr Fig* **se estaba gestando una nueva era** the seeds of a new era had been sown

**gesticulación** *nf (de manos, brazos)* gesticulation; *(de cara)* face-pulling

**gesticular** *vi (con manos, brazos)* to gesticulate; *(con la cara)* to pull faces

**gestión** *nf* (a) *(diligencia)* step, thing that has to be done; **tengo que hacer unas gestiones** I have a few things to do (b) *Com & Fin (administración)* management; **g. de cartera** portfolio management; **g. de personal** personnel management; **g. política** *(de gobierno, ministro)* conduct in government (c) *Informát* **g. de ficheros** file management

**gestionar** *vt* (a) *(tramitar)* to negotiate (b) *(administrar)* to manage

**gesto** *nm (expresión, ademán)* gesture; *(mueca)* face, grimace; **un g. de buena voluntad** a goodwill gesture, a gesture of goodwill; **hacer un g.** *(con las manos)* to gesture, to make a gesture; **hacer un g. de asentimiento** *(con la cabeza)* to nod; **torcer el g.** to pull a face *(expressing displeasure)*

**gestor, -ora** *nm,f* = person who carries out dealings with public bodies on behalf of private customers or companies, combining the roles of solicitor and accountant

**gestoría** *nf* = office of a "gestor"

**gestual** *adj* using gestures

**Ghana** *n* Ghana

**ghanés, -esa** *adj & nm,f* Ghanaian

**ghetto** ['geto] *nm* ghetto

**giba** *nf (de camello)* hump; *(de persona)* hunchback, hump

**giboso, -a 1** *adj* hunchbacked
**2** *nm,f* hunchback

**Gibraltar** *n* Gibraltar

**gibraltareño, -a** *adj & nm,f* Gibraltarian

**GIF** [gif] *nm Informát (abrev de* **graphics interchange format)** GIF

**gigabyte** [χiva'βait] *nm Informát* gigabyte

**giganta** *nf* giantess

**gigante 1** *adj* gigantic
**2** *nm* giant

**gigantesco, -a** *adj* gigantic

**gigantismo** *nm Med* gigantism

**gigoló** [jiγo'lo] *nm* gigolo

**gil, gila** *nm,f CSur Fam* twit, idiot

**gilí** *Fam* **1** *adj* stupid
**2** *nmf* pillock, prat

**gilipollada** *nf muy Fam* **hacer/decir una g.** to do/say something bloody stupid

**gilipollas, gilipuertas** *muy Fam* **1** *adj inv* daft, *US* dumb
**2** *nmf inv* pillock, prat

**gilipollez** *nf inv muy Fam* **hacer/decir una g.** to do/say something bloody stupid

**gima** *etc ver* **gemir**

**gimiera** *etc ver* **gemir**

**gimnasia** *nf (deporte)* gymnastics; *(ejercicio)* gymnastics; **confundir la g. con la magnesia** to get the wrong end of the stick; **g. correctiva** *o* **médica** *o* **terapéutica** physiotherapeutic exercises; **g. deportiva** gymnastics; **g. rítmica** rhythmic gymnastics; **g. sueca** free exercise, callisthenics

**gimnasio** *nm* gymnasium

**gimnasta** *nmf* gymnast

**gimnástico, -a** *adj* gymnastic

**gimo** *etc ver* **gemir**

**gimotear** *vi* to whine, to whimper

**gimoteo** *nm* whining, whimpering

**gincana** *nf (carrera de obstáculos)* gymkhana; *(de automóviles)* rally

**Ginebra** *n* Geneva

**ginebra** *nf* gin

**ginecología** *nf Med* gynaecology

**ginecológico, -a** *adj Med* gynaecological

**ginecólogo, -a** *nm,f Med* gynaecologist

**ginger ale** [jinje'reil] *nm inv* ginger ale

**gingivitis** *nf inv Med* gingivitis

**gintonic** [jin'tonik] *nm* gin and tonic

**gin-tonic** [jin'tonik] (*pl* **gin-tonics**) *nm* gin and tonic

**gira** *nf* tour; **estar de g.** to be on tour

**girar** 1 *vi* (a) (*dar vueltas*) to turn; (*rápidamente*) to spin (b) *Fig* (*centrarse*) **g. en torno a** o **alrededor de** to be centred around, to centre on (c) *Com* to remit payment

**2** *vt* (a) (*hacer dar vueltas a*) to turn; (*rápidamente*) to spin (b) *Com* to draw (c) (*dinero*) to transfer, to remit

**girasol** *nm* sunflower

**giratorio, -a** *adj* (*puerta*) revolving; (*silla*) swivel

**giro** *nm* (a) (*cambio de dirección*) turn; *Fig* **un g. de 180 grados** a U-turn (b) (*postal, telegráfico*) money order; **g. postal** postal order (c) (*de letras, órdenes de pago*) draft (d) (*expresión*) turn of phrase

**GIS** [χis] *nm inv Informát* (*abrev de* **geographical information system**) GIS

**gis** *nm Méx* chalk

**gitanería** *nf* (a) (*engaño*) wiliness, craftiness (b) (*gitanos*) gypsies

**gitano, -a** 1 *adj* (a) (*raza, persona*) gypsy (b) *Fig* wily, crafty

**2** *nm,f* gypsy

**glaciación** *nf* glaciation

**glacial** *adj* (*época*) glacial; (*viento, acogida*) icy

**glaciar** 1 *adj* glacial

**2** *nm* glacier

**gladiador** *nm* gladiator

**gladiolo, gladíolo** *nm* gladiolus

**glamour** [gla'mur] *nm* glamour

**glande** *nm Anat* glans (penis)

**glándula** *nf Anat* gland

**glasé** 1 *adj* glacé

**2** *nm* glacé silk

**glaseado, -a** 1 *adj* glacé

**2** *nm* glazing

**glasear** *vt* to glaze

**glicerina** *nf* glycerine

**global** *adj* global, overall

**globalización** *nf* (*mundialización*) globalization

**globalizar** [16] *vt* to give an overall view of

**globo** *nm* (a) (*Tierra*) globe, earth; **g. terráqueo** o **terrestre** globe (b) (*aeróstato, juguete*) balloon; **g. sonda** weather balloon (c) (*lámpara*) round glass lampshade (d) (*esfera*) sphere; *Anat* **g. ocular** eyeball

**glóbulo** *nm Med* corpuscle; **g. blanco/rojo** white/red corpuscle

**gloria** *nf* (a) (*en religión*) glory (b) (*celebridad*) celebrity, star (c) (*placer*) delight; **estar en la g.** to be in seventh heaven; **saber a g.** to taste divine o heavenly

**glorieta** *nf* (a) (*de jardín*) arbour (b) (*plazoleta*) square; (*plazoleta circular*) circus (c) (*rotonda*) *Br* roundabout, *US* traffic circle

**glorificación** *nf* glorification

**glorificar** [61] *vt* to glorify

**glorioso, -a** *adj* glorious

**glosa** *nf* marginal note

**glosador, -ora** *nm,f* commentator (*on text*)

**glosar** *vt* (a) (*anotar*) to annotate (b) (*comentar*) to comment on

**glosario** *nm* glossary

**glotis** *nf inv Anat* glottis

**glotón, -ona** 1 *adj* gluttonous, greedy

**2** *nm,f* glutton

**glotonería** *nf* gluttony, greed

**glucemia** *nf Med* glycaemia

**glúcido** *nm* carbohydrate

**glucosa** *nf* glucose

**gluten** *nm* gluten

**glúteo, -a** 1 *adj* gluteal

**2** *nm* gluteus

**gnomo** ['nomo] *nm* gnome

**gobernabilidad** *nf* governability

**gobernable** *adj* governable

**gobernación** *nf* (*gestión*) governing

**gobernador, -ora** 1 *adj* governing

**2** *nm,f* governor; *Antes* **g. civil** = person representing the central government in each province

**gobernanta** *nf* (*en hotel*) cleaning and laundry staff manageress

**gobernante** 1 *adj* ruling; **partido g.** governing party

**2** *nmf* ruler, leader

**gobernar** [3] 1 *vt* (a) (*regir, dirigir*) to govern, to rule; (*casa, negocio*) to run, to manage (b) (*barco*) to steer; (*avión*) to fly

**2** *vi Náut* to steer

**Gobi** *nm* **el desierto de G.** the Gobi Desert

**gobierno** *nm* (a) (*de país, región*) government; **g. autónomo/central** autonomous/central government; **g. civil** = body representing the central government in each province; **g. militar** = body representing the army in each province; **g. de transición** caretaker o interim government (b) (*edificio*) government buildings (c) (*administración, gestión*) running, management (d) (*control*) control

**goce** 1 *ver* **gozar**

**2** *nm* pleasure

**godo, -a 1** *adj* Gothic

**2** *nm,f Hist* Goth

**gofre** *nm* waffle

**gogó: a gogó** *loc adv* **hubo comida/bebida a g.** there was loads of food/drink

**gol** (*pl* **goles**) *nm* goal; *Fig* **meter un g. a alguien** to put one over on sb, to score an advantage over sb

**goleada** *nf* high score, cricket score; **ganar por g.** to win by an avalanche of goals

**goleador, -ora** *nm,f* goalscorer

**golear** *vt* to score a lot of goals against, to thrash

**goleta** *nf* schooner

**golf** *nm* golf

**golfa** *nf Fam* (*mujer promiscua*) tart, slag

**golfante** *nmf* scoundrel, rascal

**golfear** *vi Fam* (*hacer el golfo*) to hang out

**golfería** *nf* (**a**) (*golfos*) layabouts, good-for-nothings (**b**) (*actitud, comportamiento*) loutish behaviour

**golfista** *nmf* golfer

**golfo, -a 1** *adj* (*gamberro*) loutish, yobbish; (*pillo*) roguish

**2** *nm* (**a**) (*gamberro*) lout, yob; (*pillo*) rogue, wide boy (**b**) *Geog* gulf, bay; **el G. Pérsico** the Persian Gulf

**gollete** *nm* neck

**golondrina** *nf* swallow

**golondrino** *nm Med* boil in the armpit

**golosina** *nf* (*dulce*) sweet; (*exquisitez*) titbit, delicacy

**goloso, -a 1** *adj* sweet-toothed

**2** *nm,f* sweet-toothed person

**golpe** *nm* (**a**) (*impacto*) blow; (*bofetada*) smack; (*puñetazo*) punch; (*en puerta*) knock; (*en tenis, golf*) shot; (*entre coches*) bump, collision; **a golpes** by force; *Fig* in fits and starts; **moler a alguien a golpes** to beat sb up; *Dep* **un g. bajo** a blow below the belt; *Fig* a low blow; **g. de castigo** (*en rugby*) penalty (kick); **g. franco** free kick

(**b**) (*disgusto*) blow

(**c**) (*atraco*) raid, job, *US* heist; **dar un g.** to do a job

(**d**) *Pol* **g. (de Estado)** coup (d'état)

(**e**) (*ocurrencia*) witticism

(**f**) (*expresiones*) **errar** *o* **fallar el g.** to miss the mark; **no dar** *o* **pegar g.** not to lift a finger, not to do a stroke of work; **de g.** suddenly; *Fam* **de g. y porrazo** without warning, just like that; **de un g.** at one fell swoop, all at once; **g. de gracia** coup de grâce; **g. de suerte** stroke of luck; **g. de vista** glance; **al primer g. de vista** at a glance

**golpear 1** *vt & vi* (*pegar, impactar*) to hit; (*puerta*) to bang; (*con puño*) to punch

**2 golpearse** *vpr* to give oneself a bump *o* bang; **se golpeó en la cabeza** he bumped *o* banged his head

**golpeteo** *nm* (*de dedos, lluvia*) drumming; (*de puerta, persiana*) banging

**golpismo** *nm* tendency to military coups

**golpista 1** *adj* involved in a military coup; **una intentona g.** an attempted coup

**2** *nmf* = person involved in a military coup

**golpiza** *nf Am* beating

**goma** *nf* (**a**) (*sustancia*) gum; **g. arábiga** gum arabic; **g. de mascar** chewing gum (**b**) (*tira elástica*) rubber band, *Br* elastic band; **g. elástica** elastic (**c**) (*caucho*) rubber; **g. espuma** foam rubber; **g. de borrar** *Br* rubber, *US* eraser (**d**) *muy Fam* (*preservativo*) rubber

**gomaespuma** *nf* foam rubber

**gomero** *nm Am* (**a**) (*persona*) rubber plantation worker (**b**) (*árbol*) rubber tree

**gomina** *nf* hair gel

**gominola** *nf* = soft chewy gum-like sweet

**gomoso, -a** *adj* gummy

**gónada** *nf Anat* gonad

**góndola** *nf* (**a**) (*embarcación*) gondola (**b**) *Chile* (*autobús*) (long distance) bus

**gondolero** *nm* gondolier

**gong** *nm* gong

**gonorrea** *nf Med* gonorrhoea

**gordinflón, -ona** *Fam* **1** *adj* chubby, tubby

**2** *nm,f* fatty

**gordo, -a 1** *adj* (**a**) (*persona*) fat; *Fam* **me cae g.** I can't stand him (**b**) (*grueso*) thick (**c**) (*grande*) big (**d**) *Fam* (*problema, asunto*) big, serious

**2** *nm,f* (*persona obesa*) fat man, *f* fat woman; *Fig* **armar la gorda** to kick up a row *o* stink

**3** *nm* (*en lotería*) first prize, jackpot

**gordura** *nf* fatness, obesity

**gorgonzola** *nm* gorgonzola

**gorgorito** *nm* warble; *Fam* **hacer gorgoritos** (*cantar*) to warble

**gorgoteo** *nm* gurgle, gurgling

**gorila** *nm* (*animal*) gorilla; *Fig* (*guardaespaldas*) bodyguard; *Fig* (*en discoteca, pub*) bouncer

**gorjear** *vi* to chirp, to twitter

**gorjeo** *nm* chirping, twittering

**gorra** *nf* (*peaked*) cap; *Fam* **de g.** for free; *Fam* **vivir de g.** to scrounge; **g. de plato** peaked cap (*of officer*)

**gorrear** *vt & vi Fam* to sponge, to scrounge

**gorrinada** *nf* (**a**) (*guarrada*) (*acción*) disgusting behaviour; (*lugar*) pigsty (**b**) *Fig* (*mala pasada*) dirty trick

**gorrino, -a** *nm,f también Fig* pig

**gorrión** *nm* sparrow

**gorro** *nm* cap; *Fam* **estar hasta el g. (de)** to be fed up (with); **g. de ducha** shower cap; **g. de piscina** bathing o swimming cap

**gorrón, -ona** *Fam* **1** *adj* sponging, scrounging

  **2** *nm,f* sponger, scrounger

**gorronear** *vt & vi Fam* to sponge, to scrounge

**gorronería** *nf Fam* sponging, scrounging

**góspel** *nm Mús* gospel (music)

**gota** *nf* **(a)** *(de líquido)* drop; *(de sudor)* bead; **caer cuatro gotas** to spit (with rain); **ni g. (de)** not a drop (of); **no se veía ni g.** you couldn't see a thing; **no corre ni una g. de brisa** there isn't a breath of wind; **ni g. de sentido común** not an ounce of common sense; **como dos gotas de agua** like two peas in a pod; *Fam* **sudar la g. gorda** to sweat blood, to work very hard; *Med* **g. a g.** intravenous drip **(b)** *Meteo* **g. fría** = cold front that remains in one place for some time, causing continuous heavy rain **(c)** *Med* gout

**gotear** **1** *vi* *(líquido)* to drip; *(techo, depósito)* to leak; *Fig* to trickle through

  **2** *v impersonal (chispear)* to spit, to drizzle

**goteo** *nm* dripping; *Fig (de gente, información)* trickle

**gotera** *nf* **(a)** *(filtración)* leak **(b)** *(mancha)* stain *(left by leaking water)*

**gótico, -a 1** *adj* Gothic

  **2** *nm (arte)* Gothic

**gourmet** [gur'met] *(pl* **gourmets)** *nmf* gourmet

**goyesco, -a** *adj* = relating to or like Goya's paintings

**gozada** *nf Fam* absolute delight; **¡qué g. de coche/película!** what a wonderful car/film!

**gozar** [16] *vi* to enjoy oneself; **g. de algo** to enjoy sth; **g. de buena salud** to be in good health; **g. con** to take delight in

**gozne** *nm* hinge

**gozo** *nm* joy, pleasure; *Fam* **mi g. en un pozo** that's just my (bad) luck

**GP** *nm (abrev de* **gran premio)** GP

**g/p, g.p.** *(abrev de* **giro postal)** p.o.

**grabación** *nf* recording

**grabado** *nm (técnica, lámina)* engraving; **g. al agua fuerte** etching; **g. sobre madera** woodcut

**grabador, -ora** *nm,f (persona)* engraver

**grabadora** *nf (magnetófono)* tape recorder

**grabar** *vt* **(a)** *(en metal)* to record, to tape; **han grabado un nuevo disco** they've recorded a new album **(c)** *Fig (fijar)* **grabado en su memoria** imprinted o engraved on his memory; **¡que te quede bien grabado!** don't you forget it!

**(d)** *Informát* to save

  **2 grabarse** *vpr* **(a)** *(registrarse, reproducirse)* to be recorded **(b)** *Fig (fijarse)* **grabársele a alguien en la memoria** to become imprinted o engraved on sb's mind

**gracejo** *nm* **tener mucho g.** to be a good talker; **contar una historia con g.** to tell a story in an amusing way

**gracia 1** *nf* **(a)** *(humor, comicidad)* humour; **hacer g. a alguien** to amuse sb; **no me hizo g.** I didn't find it funny; **tener g.** *(ser divertido, curioso)* to be funny; **caer en g.** to be liked **(b)** *(arte, habilidad)* skill, natural ability **(c)** *(encanto)* grace, elegance **(d)** *(chiste)* joke **(e)** *(favor)* favour; *(indulto)* pardon

  **2** *nfpl* **gracias** thank you, thanks; **gracias a** thanks to; **dar las gracias a alguien (por)** to thank sb (for); **muchas gracias** thank you very much, thanks very much

**grácil** *adj (armonioso)* graceful; *(delicado)* delicate

**gracioso, -a 1** *adj* **(a)** *(divertido)* funny, amusing; **se cree muy g.** he thinks he's really smart **(b)** *(curioso)* funny; **es g. que...** it's funny how... **(c)** *(bonito, atractivo)* pretty

  **2** *nm,f* **(a)** *(persona divertida)* funny o amusing person; *Pey* smart alec, comedian **(b)** *Teatro* fool, clown

**grada** *nf* **(a)** *(peldaño)* step **(b)** *Teatro* row **(c)** *(en estadio)* **gradas** terraces

**graderío** *nm (gradas) Teatro* rows; *Dep* terraces; *Fig (público)* crowd

**grado** *nm* **(a)** *(unidad)* degree; **g. centígrado** degree centigrade **(b)** *(fase)* stage, level; *(índice, nivel)* extent, level; **en g. sumo** greatly **(c)** *(rango)* grade; *Mil* rank **(d)** *Educ* year, class, *US* grade **(e)** *(voluntad)* **hacer algo de buen/mal g.** to do sth willingly/unwillingly

**graduable** *adj* adjustable

**graduación** *nf* **(a)** *(acción)* grading; *(de la vista)* eye-test; *(de gafas)* strength **(b)** *Educ* graduation **(c)** *(de bebidas)* strength, proof; **bebidas de alta g.** spirits **(d)** *Mil* rank

**graduado, -a 1** *adj* **(a)** *(termómetro)* graduated; **gafas graduadas** prescription glasses; **recipiente g.** *(jarra)* measuring jug **(b)** *(universitario)* graduate

  **2** *nm,f (persona)* graduate

  **3** *nm Educ* **g. escolar** *(título)* = basic school-leaving certificate

**gradual** *adj* gradual

**graduar** [4] **1** *vt* **(a)** *(medir)* to gauge, to measure; *(regular)* to regulate; *(vista)* to test **(b)** *(escalonar)* to stagger **(c)** *Educ* to confer a degree on **(d)** *Mil* to confer a rank on, to commission

  **2 graduarse** *vpr* to graduate **(en** in)

**grafía** *nf* written symbol

**graffiti** *nm* piece of graffiti; **la pared estaba llena de graffitis** the wall was covered in graffiti

**gráfica** *nf* graph, chart

**gráfico, -a 1** *adj* graphic
　**2** *nm (figura)* graph, chart; *(dibujo)* diagram

**grafismo** *nm (diseño)* graphics

**grafista** *nmf* graphic artist *o* designer

**grafito** *nm* graphite

**grafología** *nf* graphology

**grafólogo, -a** *nm,f* graphologist

**gragea** *nf* **(a)** *(píldora)* pill, tablet **(b)** *(confite)* sugar-coated sweet

**graja** *nf*, **grajo** *nm* rook

**grajilla** *nf* jackdaw

**gral.** *(abrev de* **general)** gen.

**gramática** *nf (disciplina, libro)* grammar; *Fam* **tener g. parda** to be streetwise *o* worldly-wise

**gramatical** *adj* grammatical

**gramático, -a 1** *adj* grammatical
　**2** *nm,f (persona)* grammarian

**gramo** *nm* gram

**gramófono** *nm* gramophone

**gramola** *nf* gramophone

**grampa** *nf Am* staple

**gran** *adj ver* **grande**

**Granada** *n (a) (en España)* Granada **(b)** *(en las Antillas)* Grenada

**granada** *nf* **(a)** *(fruta)* pomegranate **(b)** *(proyectil)* grenade; **g. de mano** hand grenade

**granadina** *nf* **(a)** *(bebida)* grenadine **(b)** *(cante)* = type of flamenco from Granada

**granadino, -a** *adj* **(a)** *(en España)* of/from Granada **(b)** *(en las Antillas)* Grenadian

**granar** *vi* to seed

**granate 1** *nm* garnet
　**2** *adj inv* garnet-coloured

**Gran Barrera del Coral** *nf* **la G.** the Great Barrier Reef

**Gran Bretaña** *nf* Great Britain

**Gran Cañón** *nm* **el G.** the Grand Canyon

**grande**

---

**gran** is used instead of **grande** before masculine singular nouns (e.g. **gran hombre** great man).

---

**1** *adj* **(a)** *(de tamaño)* big, large; *(de altura)* tall; *(de intensidad, importancia)* great; **este traje me está g.** this suit is too big for me
　**(b)** *Fig & Irón (enojoso)* just great, a bit rich
　**(c)** *Am (fantástico)* great
　**(d)** *Am (de edad)* old
　**(e)** *Fam* **pasarlo en g.** to have a great time
　**2** *nm (noble)* grandee; **a lo g.** in a big way, in style; **en g.** on a large scale

**Grandes Lagos** *nmpl* **los G.** the Great Lakes

**grandeza** *nf* **(a)** *(de tamaño)* (great) size; *Fig (esplendor)* magnificence, grandeur; **en toda su g.** in all its splendour *o* grandeur **(b)** *(de sentimientos)* generosity, graciousness **(c)** *(aristocracia)* aristocracy, nobility

**grandilocuencia** *nf* grandiloquence

**grandilocuente** *adj* grandiloquent

**grandiosidad** *nf* grandeur

**grandioso, -a** *adj* grand, splendid

**grandullón, -ona** *Fam* **1** *adj* overgrown
　**2** *nm,f* big boy, *f* big girl

**granel** *nm* **a g.** *(sin envase)* loose; *(en gran cantidad)* in bulk; *(en abundancia)* in abundance; **vender/comprar vino a g.** to sell/buy wine from the barrel

**granero** *nm* granary

**granito** *nm* granite

**granizada** *nf* **(a)** *Meteo* hailstorm **(b)** *Fig (abundancia)* hail, shower

**granizado** *nm* = drink of flavoured crushed ice; **g. de limón/café** = lemon-/coffee-flavoured crushed ice

**granizar** [16] *v impersonal* to hail

**granizo** *nm* hail

**granja** *nf* farm; **g. avícola** poultry farm; **g. escuela** = farm which schoolchildren visit or stay at to learn about farming life and animals

**granjearse** *vpr* to gain, to earn

**granjero, -a** *nm,f* farmer

**grano** *nm* **(a)** *(de cereal, de uva)* grain; **g. de café** coffee bean; **g. de pimienta** peppercorn **(b)** *(partícula)* grain **(c)** *(en la piel)* spot, pimple **(d)** *(expresiones)* **aportar** *o* **poner uno su g. de arena** to do one's bit; **ir al g.** to get to the point

**granuja** *nmf (pillo)* rogue, scoundrel; *(canalla)* trickster, swindler

**granujada** *nf* dirty trick

**granulado, -a 1** *adj* granulated
　**2** *nm* granules

**granuloso, -a** *adj* bumpy

**grapa** *nf (para papeles)* staple; *(para heridas)* stitch, (wire) suture

**grapadora** *nf* stapler

**grapar** *vt* to staple

**GRAPO** ['grapo] *nmpl (abrev de* **Grupos de Resistencia Antifascista Primero de Octubre)** = left-wing Spanish terrorist group mainly active in the 70's and early 80's; **los grapos** = members of this group

**grasa** *nf* grasa **(a)** *(en comestibles)* fat; *(de cerdo)* lard; **g. vegetal** vegetable fat **(b)** *(lubricante)* grease, oil **(c)** *(suciedad)* grease

**grasiento, -a** *adj* greasy

**graso, -a** adj (mantecoso) greasy; (con alto contenido en grasas) fatty

**gratén** nm Culin gratin; **al g.** au gratin

**gratificación** nf (a) (moral) reward (b) (monetaria) bonus

**gratificante** adj rewarding

**gratificar** [61] vt (complacer) to reward; (retribuir) to give a bonus to; (dar propina a) to tip

**gratinado, -a** adj Culin au gratin

**gratinar** vt Culin to cook a dish au gratin

**gratis** adv free, for nothing; **ser g.** to be free; **me salió g. el viaje** the journey didn't cost me anything

**gratitud** nf gratitude

**grato, -a** adj pleasant; **nos es g. comunicarle que…** we are pleased to inform you that…

**gratuito, -a** adj (a) (sin dinero) free (b) (arbitrario) gratuitous; (infundado) unfair, uncalled for

**grava** nf gravel

**gravamen** nm (a) (impuesto) tax (b) (obligación moral) burden

**gravar** vt (a) (con impuestos) to tax (b) (agravar) to worsen

**grave 1** adj (a) (enfermedad, situación) serious; (estilo) formal; **estar g.** to be seriously ill (b) (sonido, voz) low, deep (c) Gram (palabra) stressed on the second-last syllable; (tilde) grave
**2** nf Gram word stressed on the second-last syllable

**gravedad** nf (a) (cualidad de grave) seriousness (b) Fís gravity

**gravidez** nf Formal pregnancy

**grávido, -a** adj Formal full

**gravilla** nf gravel

**gravitación** nf Fís gravitation

**gravitar** vi Fís to gravitate; Fig **g. sobre** (pender) to hang o loom over

**gravoso, -a** adj burdensome; (costoso) expensive, costly

**graznar** vi (cuervo) to caw; (ganso) to honk; (pato) to quack; Fig (persona) to squawk

**graznido** nm (de cuervo) caw, cawing; (de ganso) honk, honking; (de pato) quack, quacking; Fig (de personas) squawk, squawking

**Grecia** n Greece

**grecorromano, -a** adj Greco-Roman

**gregario, -a** adj gregarious; Fig incapable of independent thought

**gregoriano, -a** adj Gregorian

**grelo** nm turnip leaf

**gremial** adj Hist guild; **ordenanzas gremiales** guild statutes

**gremio** nm (a) Hist guild (b) (conjunto de profesionales) profession, trade (c) Fam (grupo) league, club

**greña** nf (a) (pelo enredado) tangle of hair; **greñas** (pelo largo) long hair (b) Fam **andar a la g. (con alguien)** to be at loggerheads (with sb)

**greñudo, -a** adj with dishevelled o unkempt hair

**gres** nm stoneware

**gresca** nf row; **se armó una g.** there was a fuss o row

**griego, -a 1** adj & nm,f Greek
**2** nm (lengua) Greek

**grieta** nf crack; (entre montañas) crevice; (que deja pasar luz) chink

**grifa** nf muy Fam marijuana

**grifería** nf taps

**grifero, -a** nm,f Perú Br petrol pump attendant, US gas pump attendant

**grifo** nm (a) (llave) Br tap, US faucet (b) Perú (gasolinera) Br petrol station, US gas station

**grill** [gril] (pl **grills**) nm grill

**grillado, -a** adj Fam crazy, loopy

**grillete** nm shackle

**grillo** nm (a) (insecto) cricket (b) **grillos** (grilletes) shackles

**grima** nf (a) (disgusto) annoyance; **me da g.** he/she/it gets on my nerves (b) (dentera) **me da g.** he/she/it sets my teeth on edge

**gringo, -a** adj & nm,f gringo

**gripa** nf Col, Méx flu

**gripe** nf flu

**griposo, -a** adj fluey

**gris** (pl **grises**) **1** adj grey; Fig (existencia) gloomy, miserable; Fig (discurso, persona) dull, characterless
**2** nm (a) grey; **g. marengo/perla** dark/pearl grey (b) Fam Antes **los grises** (la policía) the cops

**grisáceo, -a** adj greyish

**grisalla** nf Méx scrap metal

**grisear** vi to become grey

**grisú** (pl **grisúes**) nm Med firedamp

**gritar 1** vi (hablar alto) to shout; (chillar) to scream, to yell
**2** vt **g. algo a alguien** to shout sth at sb

**griterío** nm screaming, shouting

**grito** nm (chillido) shout; (de dolor, miedo) cry, scream; (de sorpresa, de animal) cry; **dar o pegar un g.** to shout o scream (out); Fam **a g. limpio** o **pelado** at the top of one's voice; Fig **pedir algo a gritos** to be crying out for sth; Fam **poner el g. en el cielo** to hit the roof; **ser el último g.** to be the latest fashion o craze, to be the in thing

**Groenlandia** *n* Greenland

**grog** *nm* grog

**grogui** *adj también Fig* groggy

**grosella** *nf* redcurrant; **g. negra** blackcurrant; **g. silvestre** gooseberry

**grosería** *nf (cualidad)* rudeness; *(acción)* rude thing; *(palabrota)* swear word

**grosero, -a 1** *adj* (a) *(maleducado)* rude, crude (b) *(tosco)* coarse, rough

 **2** *nm,f* rude person

**grosor** *nm* thickness

**grosso modo** *adv* roughly, in broad terms

**grotesco, -a** *adj* grotesque

**grúa** *nf* (a) *(máquina)* crane (b) *(vehículo)* breakdown truck

**grueso, -a 1** *adj* (a) *(espeso)* thick (b) *(corpulento)* thickset; *(obeso)* fat (c) *Meteo* **mar gruesa** stormy *o* heavy sea

 **2** *nm* (a) *(grosor)* thickness (b) *(parte mayor)* **el g. de** the bulk of

**grulla** *nf* crane; *Fam Pey* **una vieja g.** *(mujer)* an old trout

**grumete** *nm* cabin boy

**grumo** *nm (de líquido)* lump; *(de sangre)* clot

**grumoso, -a** *adj* lumpy

**grunge** [grunʃ] *nm* grunge

**gruñido** *nm (de perro)* growl; *(de cerdo)* grunt; *Fig (de persona)* grumble

**gruñir** *vi (perro)* to growl; *(cerdo)* to grunt; *Fig (persona)* to grumble

**gruñón, -ona 1** *adj* grumpy

 **2** *nm,f* old grump

**grupa** *nf* hindquarters

**grupo** *nm (conjunto)* group; *(de árboles)* cluster; *(de músicos)* group, band; *Tec* unit, set; **en g.** in a group; *Elec* **g. electrógeno** generator; *Econ* **g. de empresas** (corporate) group; *Informát* **g. de noticias** newsgroup; *Pol* **g. parlamentario** parliamentary group; *Pol* **g. de presión** pressure group, lobby; *Med* **g. sanguíneo** blood group

**grupúsculo** *nm* small group; *Pol* splinter group

**gruta** *nf* grotto

**gruyère** [gru'jer] **1** *adj* **queso g.** Gruyère cheese

 **2** *nm* Gruyère

**gta.** *abrev de* **glorieta**

**guacal** *nm CAm, Méx* (a) *(calabaza)* pumpkin (b) *(jaula)* cage

**guacamayo** *nm Am* parrot

**guacamole, guacamole** *nm* guacamole, avocado dip

**guachafita** *nf Col, Ven Fam* racket, uproar

**guachimán** *nm Am* night watchman

**guachinango** *nm Méx (pez)* red snapper

**guacho, -a** *nm,f Andes, CSur Fam* illegitimate child

**guadalajareño, -a 1** *adj* of/from Guadalajara

 **2** *nm,f* person from Guadalajara

**Guadalquivir** *nm* **el G.** the Guadalquivir

**guadaña** *nf* scythe

**Guadiana** *nm* **el G.** the Guadiana

**guagua** *nf* (a) *Carib (autobús)* bus (b) *Andes, CSur (niño)* baby

**guajiro, -a** *nm,f Col, Cuba Fam* peasant

**guajolote** *nm Am* turkey

**guampa** *nf CSur* horn

**guanábana** *nf Am* custard apple

**guanajo** *nm Carib* turkey

**guanche** *adj & nmf* = original inhabitant of the Canary islands

**guantazo** *nm Fam* slap

**guante** *nm* glove; **arrojar** *o* **tirar el g.** to throw down the gauntlet; **de g. blanco** gentlemanly; *Fam Fig* **echarle** *o* **la a algo/alguien** to get hold of sth/sb, to get one's hands on sth/sb; **estar más suave que un g.** to be as meek as a lamb; **g. de boxeo** boxing glove

**guantera** *nf (en coche)* glove compartment

**guaperas** *Fam* **1** *adj inv* pretty-pretty

 **2** *nm inv* (a) *(presumido)* pretty boy (b) *(artista, cantante)* heart-throb

**guapo, -a 1** *adj* (a) *(atractivo)* good-looking; *(hombre)* handsome; *(mujer)* pretty (b) *muy Fam (muy bueno)* cool, ace

 **2** *nm,f* (a) *(valiente)* **a ver quién es el g. que…** let's see who's brave enough to… (b) *(fanfarrón)* braggart

**guapura** *nf (de hombre)* handsomeness; *(de mujer)* prettiness

**guaraches** *nmpl Méx* sandals

**guarango, -a** *adj CSur* coarse, vulgar

**guaraní 1** *adj inv & nmf* Guarani

 **2** *nm* (a) *(lengua)* Guarani (b) *(moneda)* guarani

**guarda 1** *nmf (vigilante)* guard, keeper; **g. forestal** gamekeeper, forest ranger; **g. jurado** security guard

 **2** *nf* (a) *(tutela)* guardianship (b) *(de libros)* flyleaf

**guardabarrera** *nmf Ferroc* level crossing keeper

**guardabarros** *nm inv Br* mudguard, *US* fender

**guardabosque** *nmf* forest ranger

**guardacoches** *nmf inv* parking attendant

**guardacostas** *nm inv (barco)* coastguard boat

**guardador, -ora** *nm,f* keeper

**guardaespaldas** *nmf inv* bodyguard

**guardafrenos** *nmf inv Ferroc* brakeman, *f* brakewoman

**guardagujas** *nmf inv Ferroc* switchman, *f* switchwoman

**guardameta** *nmf* goalkeeper

**guardamuebles** *nm inv* furniture warehouse *(for storage)*

**guardapolvo** *nm* overalls

**guardar 1** *vt* (a) *(conservar)* to keep; *(poner en su sitio)* to put away (b) *(vigilar)* to keep watch over; *(proteger)* to guard (c) *(reservar, ahórrar)* to save (a o para alguien for sb) (d) *(cumplir) (ley)* to observe; *(secreto, promesa)* to keep (e) *Informát* to save (f) **g. cama** to stay in bed

**2 guardarse** *vpr* **guardarse de hacer algo** *(evitar)* to avoid doing sth; *(abstenerse de)* to be careful not to do sth; *Fam* **guardársela a alguien** to have it in for sb

**guardarropa** *nm* *(armario)* wardrobe; *(de cine, discoteca)* cloakroom; *Fig (ropa)* wardrobe

**guardarropía** *nf Teatro* wardrobe

**guardería** *nf* *(establecimiento)* nursery; *(en aeropuerto, supermercado)* crèche

**guardia 1** *nf* (a) *(conjunto de personas)* guard; **la vieja g.** the old guard; **G. Civil** Civil Guard, = armed Spanish police force who patrol rural areas and highways, guard public buildings in cities and police borders and coasts (b) *(vigilancia)* watch, guard; **en g.** on guard; **montar (la) g.** to mount guard; **aflojar o bajar la g.** to lower o drop one's guard (c) *(turno)* duty; **estar de g.** to be on duty

**2** *nmf (persona)* policeman, *f* policewoman; **g. civil** civil guard; **g. municipal** (local) policeman, *f* (local) policewoman; **g. de seguridad** security guard

**3** *nm* **g. marina** = sea cadet in final two years of training

**guardián, -ana** *nm,f (de persona)* guardian; *(de cosa)* watchman, keeper

**guarecer** [48] **1** *vt* to protect, to shelter (**de** from)

**2 guarecerse** *vpr* to shelter (**de** from)

**guarida** *nf* lair; *Fig* hideout

**guarismo** *nm* figure, number

**guarnecer** [48] *vt* (a) *(adornar)* to decorate; *(ropa)* to trim (b) *Culin (acompañar)* to garnish (c) *Mil (vigilar)* to be garrisoned in

**guarnición** *nf* (a) *(adorno)* decoration; *(de ropa)* trimming (b) *Culin* garnish (c) *Mil* garrison

**guarrada** *nf (cosa asquerosa)* filthy thing; *(mala pasada)* filthy o dirty trick

**guarrería** *nf (suciedad)* filth, muck; *(acción)* filthy thing

**guarro, -a 1** *adj* filthy

**2** *nm,f (animal)* pig; *Fig (persona)* filthy o dirty pig

**guarura** *nm Méx Fam* bodyguard

**guasa** *nf Fam* (a) *(gracia)* humour; *(ironía)* irony; **estar de g.** to be joking (b) *(pesadez)* **tener mucha g.** to be a pain in the neck

**guasca** *nf Chile, Perú* whip

**guasearse** *vpr Fam* to take the mickey (**de** out of)

**guasón, -ona 1** *adj* fond of teasing

**2** *nm,f* joker, tease

**guata** *nf* (a) *(de algodón)* cotton padding (b) *Am Fam (barriga)* belly

**guateado, -a** *adj* padded

**Guatemala** *n* (a) *(país)* Guatemala (b) *(ciudad)* Guatemala City

**guatemalteco, -a, guatemaltés, -esa** *adj & nm,f* Guatemalan

**guateque** *nm* private party

**guatón, -ona** *adj Am Fam* potbellied

**guau** *interj (ladrido)* woof

**guay** *adj, adv & interj Fam* cool, neat

**guayaba** *nf (fruta)* guava

**guayabera** *nf Am* = white shirt with pockets

**guayabo, -a** *nm (árbol)* guava tree

**guayín** *nm Méx Fam* van

**gubernamental** *adj* government; **política g.** government policy

**gubernativo, -a** *adj* government; **orden gubernativa** government decree

**guepardo** *nm* cheetah

**güero, -a** *adj Am Fam* blond, blonde

**guerra** *nf (conflicto)* war; *(pugna)* struggle, conflict; *(de intereses, ideas)* conflict; **declarar la g.** to declare war; **en g.** at war; **g. sin cuartel** all-out war; *Fig* **dar g.** to be a pain, to be annoying; *Fig* **le tiene la g. declarada a su hermano** he's at daggers drawn with his brother; **g. atómica o nuclear** nuclear war; **g. bacteriológica/química** germ/chemical warfare; **g. civil/mundial** civil/world war; **g. espacial o de las galaxias** star wars; **g. fría** cold war; **g. de guerrillas** guerrilla warfare; **g. de precios** price war; **g. santa** Holy War, crusade

**guerrear** *vi* to wage war (**contra** on o against)

**guerrera** *nf (prenda)* (military) jacket

**guerrero, -a 1** *adj (belicoso)* warlike; *(peleón)* argumentative, quarrelsome

**2** *nm,f* warrior

**guerrilla** *nf (grupo)* guerrilla group

**guerrillero, -a 1** *adj* guerrilla; **ataque g.** guerrilla attack

**2** *nm,f* guerrilla

**gueto** nm ghetto

**güevón** nm CSur Vulg bloody idiot

**guía 1** nmf (persona) guide; **g. espiritual** (persona, libro) spiritual guide; **g. turístico** tourist guide

**2** nf **(a)** (indicación) guidance **(b)** (libro) guide (book); **g. de ferrocarriles** train timetable; **g. telefónica** o **de teléfonos** telephone book o directory **(c)** (de bicicleta) handlebars **(d)** (para cortinas) rail

**guiar** [34] **1** vt **(a)** (indicar dirección) to guide, to lead; (aconsejar) to guide, to direct **(b)** Aut to drive; Náut to steer **(c)** (plantas, ramas) to train

**2 guiarse** vpr **guiarse por algo** to be guided by o to follow sth; **se guía por el instinto** he's guided by instinct

**guija** nf pebble

**guijarro** nm pebble

**guijarroso, -a** adj pebbly

**guillado, -a** adj crazy

**guilladura** nf craziness

**guillotina** nf guillotine

**guillotinar** vt to guillotine

**guinda** nf morello cherry; Fig **la g.** the finishing touch, the icing on the cake

**guindar** vt Fam **g. algo a alguien** to pinch o nick sth off sb

**guindilla** nf chilli (pepper)

**guindo** nm morello cherry tree

**guinea** nf guinea

**Guinea-Bissau** n Guinea-Bissau

**Guinea Ecuatorial** n Equatorial Guinea

**guineano, -a** adj & nm,f Guinean

**guiñapo** nm **(a)** (andrajo) rag **(b)** (persona) estar hecho un g. to be a wreck

**guiñar 1** vt to wink; **guiñarle un ojo a alguien** to wink at sb

**2 guiñarse** vpr to wink at each other

**guiño** nm wink

**guiñol** nm puppet theatre

**guiñolesco, -a** adj farcical

**guión** nm **(a)** (resumen) framework, outline **(b)** Cine & TV script; Fig **eso no estaba en el g.** that's not what was agreed on **(c)** Gram (signo) hyphen

**guionista** nmf scriptwriter

**guipuzcoano, -a 1** adj of/from Guipúzcoa

**2** nm,f person from Guipúzcoa

**guiri** Fam **1** adj foreign

**2** nmf foreigner

**guirigay** nm **(a)** Fam (jaleo) racket **(b)** (lenguaje ininteligible) gibberish

**guirlache** nm almond brittle

**guirnalda** nf garland

**guisa** nf way, manner; **a g. de** by way of, as; **de esta g.** in this way

**guisado** nm stew

**guisante** nm pea

**guisar** vt & vi to cook

**2 guisarse** vpr Fig to be cooking, to be going on

**guiso** nm stew

**güisqui** nm whisky

**guita** nf **(a)** Fam (dinero) dosh **(b)** (cuerda) twine, string

**guitarra 1** nf guitar; **chafar la g. a alguien** to mess things up for sb; **g. eléctrica** electric guitar

**2** nmf guitarist

**guitarrero, -a** nm,f guitar maker

**guitarrista** nmf guitarist

**gula** nf gluttony

**gulasch** [gu'las] nm inv goulash

**gulden** nm guilder, florin

**gurí, -isa** nm,f CSur Fam kid, child

**guripa** nm Fam cop

**gurú, guru** nm guru

**gusa** nf muy Fam **tener g.** (hambre) to be starving

**gusanillo** nm Fam **el g. de la conciencia** conscience; **entrarle a uno el g. del viaje** to be bitten by the travel bug; **matar el g.** (bebiendo) to have a drink on an empty stomach; (comiendo) to have a snack between meals; **sentir un g. en el estómago** to have butterflies (in one's stomach)

**gusano** nm también Fig worm; **g. de luz** glow worm; **g. de (la) seda** silkworm

**gusarapo, -a** nm,f creepy-crawly

**gustar 1** vi (agradar) to be pleasing; **me gusta esa chica/ir al cine** I like that girl/going to the cinema; **me gustan las novelas** I like novels; Formal **g. de hacer algo** to like o enjoy doing sth; **como guste** as you wish

**2** vt (saborear, probar) to taste, to try; **¿gustas?** (¿quieres?) would you like some?

**gustativo, -a** adj taste; **papila gustativa** taste bud

**gustazo** nm Fam great pleasure; **darse el g. de algo/hacer algo** to allow oneself the pleasure of sth/doing sth

**gustillo** nm **(a)** (sabor) aftertaste **(b)** (satisfacción) malicious sense of satisfaction

**gusto** nm **(a)** (estilo) taste; (sabor) taste, flavour; **una casa decorada con (buen) g.** a tastefully decorated house; **de buen/mal g.** in good/bad taste; **sobre gustos no hay nada escrito** there's no accounting for taste, each to his own; **tener buen/mal g.** to have good/bad taste

**(b)** (placer) pleasure; **con mucho g.** gladly,

with pleasure; **iría con (mucho) g., pero no puedo** I'd love to go but I can't; **da g. estar aquí** it's a real pleasure to be here; **mucho g. – el g. es mío** pleased to meet you – the pleasure's mine; **hacer algo a g.** *(de buena gana)* to do sth willingly *o* gladly; *(cómodamente)* to do sth comfortably; **mucho** *o* **tanto g.** pleased to meet you; **sentirse** *o* **encontrarse** *o* **estar a g.** to feel comfortable *o* at ease; **tomar g. a algo** to take a liking to sth

**gustoso, -a** *adj* **(a)** *(con placer)* **hacer algo** g. to do sth gladly *o* willingly; **lo habría hecho g., pero no pude** I'd gladly have done it, but I wasn't able to **(b)** *(sabroso)* tasty

**gutural** *adj* guttural

**Guyana** *nf* Guyana

**Guyana francesa** *nf* **la G.** French Guyana

**guyanés, -esa** *adj & nm,f* Guyanese

**gymkhana** [jin'kɑnɑ] *nf (carrera de obstáculos)* gymkhana; *(de automóviles)* rally

# H

**H¹, h** [ˈatʃe] *nf (letra)* H, h; *Fig* **por h o por b** for one reason or another

**H²** *(abrev de* **Hermano)** Br.

**h, h.** *(abrev de* **hora)** hr, h.

**ha 1** *ver* **haber**

**2** *nf (abrev de* **hectárea)** ha

**haba** *nf* broad bean

**habanera** *nf Mús* habanera

**habanero, -a** *adj* of/from Havana

**habano** *nm* Havana cigar

**habeas corpus** *nm inv* habeas corpus

**haber [1] 1** *v aux* **(a)** *(en tiempos compuestos)* to have; **lo he/había hecho** I have/had done it; **los niños ya han comido** the children have already eaten; **en el estreno ha habido mucha gente** there were a lot of people at the premiere

**(b)** *(expresa reproche)* **h. venido antes** you could have come a bit earlier; **¡haberlo dicho!** why didn't you say so?

**(c)** *(expresa obligación)* **h. de hacer algo** to have to do sth; **has de estudiar más** you have to study more

**2** *v impersonal* **(a)** *(existir, estar)* **hay** there is/are; **hay mucha gente en la calle** there are a lot of people in the street; **había/hubo muchos problemas** there were many problems; **habrá dos mil** *(expresa futuro)* there will be two thousand; *(expresa hipótesis)* there must be two thousand

**(b)** *(expresa obligación)* **hay que hacer más ejercicio** one *o* you should do more exercise; **habrá que soportar su mal humor** we'll have to put up with his bad mood

**(c)** *(expresiones)* **algo habrá** there must be something in it; **allá se las haya** that's his/her problem; **habérselas con alguien** to face *o* confront sb; **¡hay que ver!** well I never!; **lo habido y por h.** everything under the sun; **no hay de qué** don't mention it; *Fam* **¿qué hay?** *(saludo)* how are you doing?

**3** *nm* **(a)** *(bienes)* assets

**(b)** *(en cuentas, contabilidad)* credit (side); **haberes** *(sueldo)* remuneration

**habichuela** *nf* bean

**habido, -a** *adj* occurred; **los accidentes habidos este verano** the number of accidents this summer

**hábil** *adj* **(a)** *(diestro)* skilful; *(inteligente)* clever **(b)** *(utilizable)* *(lugar)* suitable, fit **(c)** *Der* **días hábiles** working days

**habilidad** *nf (destreza)* skill; *(inteligencia)* cleverness; **tener h. para algo** to be good at sth

**habilidoso, -a** *adj* skilful, clever

**habilitación** *nf* **(a)** *(acondicionamiento)* fitting out **(b)** *Der (autorización)* authorization, right

**habilitado, -a 1** *adj Der* authorized

**2** *nm,f* paymaster

**habilitar** *vt* **(a)** *(acondicionar)* to fit out, to equip; **habilitó el desván para cuarto de huéspedes** he fitted out the attic as a guest bedroom **(b)** *Der (autorizar)* to authorize **(c)** *(financiar)* to finance

**habiloso, -a** *adj Chile* shrewd, astute

**habitabilidad** *nf* habitability; **estar/no estar en condiciones de h.** to be fit/unfit for human habitation

**habitable** *adj* habitable, inhabitable

**habitación** *nf (cuarto)* room; *(dormitorio)* bedroom; **h. doble** *(con cama de matrimonio)* double room; *(con dos camas)* twin room; **h. individual** *o* **simple** single room

**habitáculo** *nm (casa)* dwelling; *(habitación)* room

**habitado, -a** *adj (región, casa)* inhabited

**habitante** *nm (de ciudad, país)* inhabitant; *(de barrio)* resident

**habitar 1** *vi* to live

**2** *vt* to live in, to inhabit

**hábitat** *(pl* **hábitats)** *nm* **(a)** *Biol* habitat; **h. marino/urbano** marine/urban habitat **(b)** *(vivienda)* housing conditions

**hábito** *nm* **(a)** *(costumbre)* habit; **tener el h. de hacer algo** to be in the habit of doing sth **(b)** *(de monje)* habit; **el h. no hace al monje** clothes maketh not the man

**habituación** *nf* **(a)** *(a drogas)* addiction **(b)** *(a situación)* **la h. al nuevo trabajo fue difícil** getting used to the new job was difficult

**habitual** *adj (costumbre, respuesta)* habitual; *(cliente, lector)* regular; **es h.** it's not uncommon, it's normal

**habituar** [4] **1** *vt* **h. a alguien a** to accustom sb to

**2 habituarse** *vpr* **habituarse a** *(acostumbrarse)* to get used *o* accustomed to; *(drogas)* to become addicted to

**habla** *nf* (a) *(idioma)* language; *(dialecto)* dialect; **el h. popular** the speech of ordinary people; **de h. española** Spanish-speaking (b) *(facultad)* speech; **quedarse sin h.** to be left speechless (c) *Ling* discourse (d) *(al teléfono)* **estar al h. con alguien** to be on the line to sb

**hablador, -ora 1** *adj* talkative

**2** *nm,f* chatterbox

**habladurías** *nfpl (rumores)* rumours; *(chismes)* gossip; **no son más que h.** it's all just idle gossip

**hablante 1** *adj* speaking

**2** *nmf* speaker

**hablar 1** *vi* to talk (con to), to speak (con to); **h. por h.** to talk for the sake of talking; **h. de** to talk about; **h. bien/mal de** to speak well/badly of; **h. claro** to speak clearly; **h. en voz alta/baja** to speak loudly/softly; **dar que h.** to make people talk; **¡ni h.!** no way!; **no me habla** he's not speaking to me

**2** *vt* (a) *(idioma)* to speak (b) *(asunto)* to discuss (con with)

**3 hablarse** *vpr* to speak (to each other); **no hablarse** not to be speaking, not to be on speaking terms; **se habla inglés** *(en letrero)* English spoken

**habón** *nm (roncha)* lump *(on skin)*

**habrá** *ver* **haber**

**hacedor, -ora** *nm,f* maker; **el H.** the Maker

**hacendado, -a** *nm,f* landowner

**hacendoso, -a** *adj* houseproud

**hacer** [35] **1** *vt* (a) *(elaborar, crear, cocinar)* to make; **h. una fiesta** to have a party; **h. un vestido/planes** to make a dress/plans; **h. un poema/una sinfonía** to write a poem/symphony; **para h. la carne...** to cook the meat...

(b) *(construir)* to build; **han hecho un edificio nuevo** they've put up a new building

(c) *(generar)* to produce; **el árbol hace sombra** the tree gives shade; **la carretera hace una curva** there's a bend in the road

(d) *(movimientos, sonidos, gestos)* to make; **le hice señas** I signalled to her; **el reloj hace tic-tac** the clock goes tick-tock; **h. ruido** to make a noise

(e) *(obtener)* *(fotocopia)* to make; *(retrato)* to paint; *(fotografía)* to take

(f) *(realizar)* *(trabajo, estudios)* to do; *(viaje)* to

make; *(comunión)* to take; **hoy hace guardia** she's on duty today; **estoy haciendo segundo** I'm in my second year

(g) *(practicar)* *(en general)* to do; *(tenis, fútbol)* to play; **debes h. deporte** you should start doing some sport

(h) *(arreglar)* *(casa, colada)* to do; *(cama)* to make

(i) *(dar aspecto a)* to cause to look *o* seem; **este espejo te hace gordo** that mirror makes you look *o* seem fat

(j) *(transformar en)* **h. a alguien feliz** to make sb happy; **la guerra no le hizo un hombre** the war didn't make him (into) a man; **hizo pedazos el papel** he tore the paper to pieces; **h. de algo/alguien algo** to make sth/sb into sth; **hizo de ella una buena cantante** he made a good singer of her

(k) *(comportarse como)* **h. el tonto** to act the fool; **h. el vándalo** to act like a hooligan

(l) *(causar)* **h. daño a alguien** to hurt sb; **me hizo gracia** I thought it was funny

(m) *Cine & Teatro (papel)* to play; **hace el papel de la hija del rey** she plays (the part of) the king's daughter

(n) *(suponer)* to think, to reckon; **a estas horas yo te hacía en París** I thought *o* reckoned you'd be in Paris by now

(o) *(ser causa de)* **h. que alguien haga algo** to make sb do sth; **me hizo reír** it made me laugh; **has hecho que se enfadara** you've made him angry

(p) *(mandar)* **h. que se haga algo** to have sth done; **voy a h. teñir este vestido** I'm going to have this dress dyed

**2** *vi* (a) *(intervenir)* **déjame h. a mí** let me do it

(b) *Cine & Teatro* **h. de** *(actuar)* to play; *(trabajar)* to act as

(c) *(aparentar)* **h. como si** to act as if; **haz como que no te importa** act as if you don't care

(d) *(procurar, intentar)* **h. por h. algo** to try to do sth; **haré por verle esta noche** I'll try to see him tonight

(e) **¿hace?** all right?

**3** *v impersonal* (a) *(tiempo meteorológico)* **hace frío/sol/viento** it's cold/sunny/windy; **hace un día precioso** it's a beautiful day

(b) *(tiempo transcurrido)* **hace diez años** ten years ago; **hace mucho/poco** a long time/not long ago; **hace un mes que llegué** it's a month since I arrived; **no la veo desde hace un año** I haven't seen her for a year

**4 hacerse** *vpr* (a) *(formarse)* to form

(b) *(desarrollarse, crecer)* to grow

(c) *(guisarse, cocerse)* to cook

(d) *(convertirse en)* to become; **hacerse musulmán** to become a Moslem

(e) *(resultar)* to get; **se hace muy pesado**

it gets very tedious

(**f**) *(crearse en la mente)* **hacerse ilusiones** to get one's hopes up; **hacerse una idea de algo** to imagine what sth is like

(**g**) *(mostrarse)* **se hace el gracioso/el simpático** he tries to act the comedian/the nice guy; **hacerse el distraído** to pretend to be miles away

**hacha** *nf* axe; *Fig* **desenterrar el h. de guerra** to sharpen one's sword; *Fam* **ser un h.** to be a whizz *o* an ace

**hachazo** *nm* blow of an axe, hack

**hache** *nf* = the letter "h"; **llamémosle h., llámale h.** call it what you like

**hachís** [ʃaˈtʃis] *nm* hashish

**hacia** *prep* (**a**) *(dirección, tendencia, sentimiento)* towards; **h. aquí/allí** this/that way; **h. abajo** downwards; **h. arriba** upwards; **h. atrás** backwards; **h. adelante** forwards (**b**) *(tiempo)* around, about; **h. las diez** around *o* about ten o'clock

**hacienda** *nf* (**a**) *(finca)* country estate *o* property (**b**) *(bienes)* property (**c**) *(del Estado)* **h. pública** public purse; **el Ministerio de H.** the Treasury; **pagar a H.** to pay one's taxes

**hacinamiento** *nm* *(de personas)* overcrowding; *(de objetos)* heaping, piling

**hacinar 1** *vt* to pile *o* heap (up)

**2 hacinarse** *vpr* *(gente)* to be crowded together; *(cosas)* to be piled *o* heaped (up)

**hacker** [ˈxaker] *nmf Fam Informát* hacker

**hada** *nf* fairy; **h. madrina** fairy godmother

**hado** *nm* fate, destiny

**hago** *ver* **hacer**

**Haití** *n* Haiti

**haitiano, -a** *adj & nm,f* Haitian

**hala** *interj* ¡**h.**! *(para dar ánimo, prisa)* come on!; *(para expresar incredulidad)* no!, you're joking!; *(para expresar admiración, sorpresa)* wow!

**halagador, -ora 1** *adj* flattering

**2** *nm,f* flatterer

**halagar** [40] *vt* to flatter

**halago** *nm* flattery

**halague** *etc ver* **halagar**

**halagüeño, -a** *adj* (**a**) *(halagador)* flattering (**b**) *(prometedor)* promising, encouraging

**halar** *vt Am Fam (tirar)* to pull

**halcón** *nm* *(ave)* falcon, hawk

**hale** *interj* ¡**h.**! come on!

**hálito** *nm* (**a**) *(aliento)* breath (**b**) *Fig (aire)* zephyr, gentle breeze

**halitosis** *nf inv* bad breath

**hall** [xol] *(pl* **halls**) *nm* entrance hall, foyer

**hallar 1** *vt (encontrar)* to find; *(averiguar)* to find out

**2 hallarse** *vpr* (**a**) *(en un lugar) (persona)* to be,

to find oneself; *(cosa, edificio)* to be (situated) (**b**) *(en una situación)* to be; **hallarse enfermo** to be ill

**hallazgo** *nm* (**a**) *(descubrimiento)* discovery (**b**) *(objeto)* find

**halo** *nm (de astros, santos)* halo; *(de objetos, personas)* aura

**halógeno, -a** *adj Quím* halogenous; **faros halógenos** halogen headlights; **lámpara halógena** halogen lamp

**halterofilia** *nf* weightlifting

**hamaca** *nf* (**a**) *(para colgar)* hammock (**b**) *(tumbona) (silla)* deckchair; *(canapé)* sunlounger

**hambre** *nf* (**a**) *(apetito)* hunger; *(inanición)* starvation; **tener h.** to be hungry; **h. canina** ravenous hunger; **matar el h.** to satisfy one's hunger (**b**) *(epidemia)* famine (**c**) *Fig (deseo)* **h. de hunger** *o* thirst for (**d**) *Prov* **a buen h. no hay pan duro** *(de comida)* hunger is the best sauce; *(de mujeres, placeres)* beggars can't be choosers; **se juntan el h. con las ganas de comer** it's one thing on top of another; **ser más listo que el h.** to be nobody's fool

**hambriento, -a 1** *adj* starving

**2** *nm,f* starving person; **los hambrientos** the hungry

**Hamburgo** *n* Hamburg

**hamburguesa** *nf* hamburger

**hamburguesería** *nf* hamburger joint

**hampa** *nf* underworld

**hampón** *nm* thug

**hámster** [ˈxamster] *(pl* **hámsters**) *nm* hamster

**hándicap** [ˈxandikap] *(pl* **hándicaps**) *nm* handicap

**hangar** *nm* hangar

**Hanoi** *n* Hanoi

**haragán, -ana 1** *adj* lazy, idle

**2** *nm,f* layabout, idler

**haraganear** *vi* to laze about, to lounge around

**haraganería** *nf* laziness, idleness

**harapiento, -a** *adj* ragged, tattered

**harapo** *nm* rag, tatter

**haraquiri, harakiri** [xaraˈkiri] *nm* harakiri

**Harare** *n* Harare

**hardware** [ˈxarwer] *nm Informát* hardware

**haré** *etc ver* **hacer**

**harén** *nm* harem

**harina** *nf* flour; *Fig* **ser h. de otro costal** to be a different kettle of fish

**harinoso, -a** *adj (consistencia, textura)* floury; *(manzana)* soft

**hartar 1** *vt* (**a**) *(atiborrar)* to stuff (full) (**b**) *(fastidiar, cansar)* **h. a alguien** to annoy sb, to get on sb's nerves; **me estás hartando con**

**tantas exigencias** I'm getting fed up with all your demands

**2 hartarse** *vpr* (a) *(atiborrarse)* to stuff *o* gorge oneself (b) *(cansarse)* to get fed up (**de** with) (c) *(no parar)* **hartarse de algo** to do sth non-stop

**hartazgo, hartón** *nm* fill; **darse un h.** (**de**) to have one's fill (of)

**harto, -a 1** *adj* (a) *(de comida)* full (b) *(cansado)* tired (**de** of), fed up (**de** with)

**2** *adv* (a) *(bastante)* somewhat, rather (b) *Am (muy)* very

**hash** [χaʃ, χas] *nm inv muy Fam* hashish

**hasta 1** *prep* (a) *(en el espacio)* as far as, up to; **desde aquí h. allí** from here to there; **¿h. dónde va este tren?** where does this train go? (b) *(en el tiempo)* until, till; **h. ahora** (up) until now, so far; **h. el final** right up until the end; **h. luego** *o* **pronto** *o* **la vista** see you (later); **h. que** until, till (c) *(con cantidades)* up to

**2** *adv (incluso)* even

**hastiar** [34] **1** *vt (aburrir)* to bore; *(asquear)* to sicken, to disgust

**2 hastiarse** *vpr* **hastiarse de** to tire of, to get fed up with

**hastío** *nm (tedio)* boredom; *(repugnancia)* disgust

**hatajo** *nm Pey* load, bunch; **un h. de** *(gamberros)* a bunch of; *(mentiras)* a pack of

**hatillo** *nm* bundle of clothes

**hato** *nm* (a) *(de ganado)* herd; *(de ovejas)* flock (b) *(de ropa)* bundle

**Hawai** [χa'wai] *n* Hawaii

**hawaiano, -a** [χawai'ano] *adj & nm,f* Hawaiian

**haya 1** *ver* **haber**

**2** *nf (árbol)* beech (tree); *(madera)* beech (wood)

**hayal** *nm* beech grove *o* wood

**haz 1** *ver* **hacer**

**2** *nm* (a) *(de leña)* bundle; *(de cereales)* sheaf (b) *(de luz)* beam

**hazaña** *nf* feat, exploit

**hazmerreír** *nm* laughing stock

**HB** *nf (abrev de* **Herri Batasuna)** = political wing of ETA

**he** *ver* **haber**

**heavy** ['χeβi] **1** *adj muy Fam* **¡qué h.!** *(increíble)* that's amazing *o* incredible!; *(terrible)* what a bummer!

**2** *nmf Fam (persona)* heavy metal fan

**3** *nm Mús* heavy metal; **h. metal** heavy metal

**hebdomadario, -a** *adj* weekly

**hebilla** *nf* buckle

**hebra** *nf (de hilo)* thread; *(de judías, puerros)* string; *(de tabaco)* strand (of tobacco); **pegar la h.** to start chatting

**hebreo, -a 1** *adj & nm,f* Hebrew

**2** *nm (lengua)* Hebrew

**hecatombe** *nf (desastre)* disaster; *Fig (partido, examen)* massacre; **la inundación causó una h.** the flood caused great loss of life

**hechicería** *nf* (a) *(arte)* witchcraft, sorcery (b) *(maleficio)* spell

**hechicero, -a 1** *adj* enchanting, bewitching

**2** *nm,f (hombre)* wizard, sorcerer; *(mujer)* witch, sorceress

**hechizar** [16] *vt* (a) to cast a spell on (b) *Fig* to bewitch, to captivate

**hechizo** *nm* (a) *(maleficio)* spell (b) *Fig (encanto)* magic, charm

**hecho, -a 1** *participio ver* **hacer**

**2** *adj* (a) *(llevado a cabo)* **lo h., h. está** what is done is done; **¡eso está h.!** it's a deal!, you're on!; **tú lo hiciste, así que a lo h., pecho** you did it, so you'll have to take the consequences (b) *(acabado)* mature; **una mujer hecha y derecha** a fully-grown woman; **estás h. un artista** you've become quite an artist (c) *(carne)* done; **muy h.** well done; **poco h.** rare

**3** *nm* (a) *(suceso)* event; **h. consumado** fait accompli; **de h.** in fact, actually *(de) (realidad, dato)* fact; **el h. es que...** the fact is that...

**hechura** *nf* (a) *(de traje)* cut (b) *(forma)* shape

**hectárea** *nf* hectare

**hectolitro** *nm* hectolitre

**hectómetro** *nm* hectometre

**heder** [66] *vi* (a) *(apestar)* to stink, to reek (b) *Fig (fastidiar)* to be annoying *o* irritating

**hediondez** *nf* stench, stink

**hediondo, -a** *adj (pestilente)* stinking, foul-smelling; *Fig (insoportable)* unbearable

**hedonismo** *nm* hedonism

**hedonista 1** *adj* hedonistic

**2** *nmf* hedonist

**hedor** *nm* stink, stench

**hegemonía** *nf (dominación)* dominance; *Pol* hegemony

**hegemónico, -a** *adj (dominante)* dominant; *(clase, partido)* ruling

**hégira, héjira** *nf* hegira

**helada** *nf* frost; **anoche cayó una h.** there was frost last night

**heladera** *nf CSur (nevera)* fridge

**heladería** *nf (tienda)* ice-cream parlour; *(puesto)* ice-cream stall

**heladero, -a** *nm,f* ice-cream seller

**helado, -a 1** *adj* (a) *(hecho hielo) (agua)* frozen; *(lago)* frozen over (b) *(muy frío) (manos, agua)* freezing (c) *Fig (atónito)* dumbfounded, speechless; **¡me dejas h.!** I don't know what to say!

**2** *nm* ice-cream

**helar** [3] **1** *vt* (a) *(líquido)* to freeze (b) *Fig (dejar atónito)* to dumbfound

**2** *v impersonal* **anoche heló** there was a frost last night

**3 helarse** *vpr (congelarse)* to freeze; *(plantas)* to be frostbitten

**helecho** *nm* fern, bracken

**helénico, -a** *adj* Hellenic, Greek

**helenismo** *nm* Hellenism

**helenista** *nmf* Hellenist

**heleno, -a** *adj* Hellenic, Greek

**hélice** *nf* (a) *Tec* propeller (b) *(espiral)* spiral, helix

**helicóptero** *nm* helicopter

**helio** *nm* helium

**helipuerto** *nm* heliport

**Helsinki** *n* Helsinki

**helvético, -a** *adj & nm,f* Swiss; **Confederación Helvética** *(Suiza)* Swiss Confederation

**hematíe** *nm* red blood cell

**hematología** *nf* haematology

**hematológico, -a** *adj* haematological

**hematólogo, -a** *nm,f* haematologist

**hematoma** *nm* bruise

**hembra** *nf* (a) *Biol* female; *(mujer)* woman; *(niña)* girl (b) *(del enchufe)* socket

**hembrilla** *nf (de corchete)* eye

**hemeroteca** *nf* newspaper library *o* archive

**hemiciclo** *nm* (a) *(semicírculo)* semicircle (b) *(en el parlamento)* floor

**hemiplejia, hemiplejía** *nf* hemiplegia

**hemipléjico, -a** *adj & nm,f* hemiplegic

**hemisférico, -a** *adj* hemispheric

**hemisferio** *nm* hemisphere

**hemodiálisis** *nf inv* kidney dialysis

**hemofilia** *nf* haemophilia

**hemofílico, -a** *adj & nm,f* haemophiliac

**hemoglobina** *nf* haemoglobin

**hemograma** *nm* blood test results

**hemopatía** *nf* blood disease *o* disorder

**hemorragia** *nf* haemorrhage; **h. nasal** nosebleed; **se puso un torniquete para detener la h.** he put on a tourniquet to stop the bleeding

**hemorrágico, -a** *adj* haemorrhagic

**hemorroides** *nfpl* haemorrhoids, piles

**henchido, -a** *adj* bloated; *Fig* **h. de orgullo** bursting with pride

**henchir** [49] **1** *vt* to fill (up)

**2 henchirse** *vpr* (a) *(hartarse)* to stuff oneself (b) *Fig (llenarse)* to be full (**de** of)

**hender** [66], **hendir** [64] *vt (carne, piel)* to carve open, to cleave; *(piedra, madera)* to crack open; *(aire, agua)* to cut *o* slice through

**hendido, -a** *adj* split (open)

**hendidura** *nf (en carne, piel)* cut, split; *(en piedra, madera)* crack

**heno** *nm* hay

**hepático, -a** *adj* liver; **afección hepática** liver complaint

**hepatitis** *nf inv* hepatitis

**heptagonal** *adj* heptagonal

**heptágono** *nm* heptagon

**heráldica** *nf* heraldry

**heráldico, -a** *adj* heraldic

**heraldo** *nm* herald

**herbario** *nm (colección)* herbarium

**herbicida** *nm* weedkiller

**herbívoro, -a 1** *adj* herbivorous

**2** *nm,f* herbivore

**herbolario, -a 1** *nm,f (persona)* herbalist

**2** *nm (tienda)* herbalist's (shop)

**herboristería** *nf* herbalist's (shop)

**hercio** *nm* hertz

**hercúleo, -a** *adj* very powerful, incredibly strong; *Fig* **un esfuerzo h.** a Herculean effort

**Hércules** *n* Hercules; **las Columnas de H.** *(el estrecho de Gibraltar)* the Pillars of Hercules

**hércules** *nm inv* ox, very strong man

**heredar** *vt (dinero, rasgos)* to inherit (**de** from); **ha heredado la nariz de su padre** he's got his father's nose

**heredero, -a** *nm,f* heir, *f* heiress; **el príncipe h.** the crown prince

**hereditario, -a** *adj* hereditary

**hereje** *nmf (renegado)* heretic; *Fig (irreverente)* iconoclast

**herejía** *nf (heterodoxia)* heresy; *Fig (insulto)* insult; *(disparate)* outrage

**herencia** *nf (de bienes)* inheritance; *(de características)* legacy; *Biol* heredity; **recibir una h.** to receive an inheritance

**herético, -a** *adj* heretical

**herida** *nf* (a) *(lesión)* injury; *(en lucha, atentado)* wound (b) *(ofensa)* injury, offence; *(pena)* hurt, pain

**herido, -a 1** *adj (dañado)* injured; *(en lucha, atentado)* wounded; *(sentimentalmente)* hurt, wounded; **resultaron heridos once civiles** eleven civilians were wounded; **se sintió h. en su amor propio** his pride was hurt

**2** *nm,f (persona)* injured person; *(en lucha, atentado)* wounded person; **no hubo heridos** there were no casualties; **los heridos** the wounded

**herir** [64] *vt* (a) *(físicamente)* to injure; *(en lucha, atentado)* to wound; *(vista)* to hurt; *(oído)* to pierce; **el nuevo edificio hiere la vista** the new building is an eyesore (b) *(sentimental-*

*mente)* to hurt; **me hiere que desconfíes de mí** I feel hurt that you don't trust me

**hermafrodita** *adj & nmf* hermaphrodite

**hermanado, -a** *adj (unido, ligado)* united (**con** with), joined (**con** to); *(ciudades)* twinned

**hermanamiento** *nm (unión)* union; *(de ciudades)* twinning

**hermanar 1** *vt (esfuerzos, personas)* to unite; *(ciudades)* to twin

**2 hermanarse** *vpr (ciudades)* to be twinned

**hermanastro, -a** *nm,f (medio hermano)* half brother, *f* half sister; *(hijo del padrastro/de la madrastra)* stepbrother, *f* stepsister

**hermandad** *nf* (a) *(asociación)* association; *Rel (de hombres)* brotherhood; *(de mujeres)* sisterhood (b) *(amistad)* intimacy, close friendship

**hermano, -a 1** *adj* related, connected

**2** *nm,f* brother, *f* sister; **hermanos gemelos** *o* **mellizos** twin brothers; **h. político** brother-in-law; **hermanos siameses** Siamese twins

**hermenéutica** *nf* hermeneutics *(singular)*

**hermenéutico, -a** *adj* hermeneutic

**hermético, -a** *adj* (a) *(al aire)* airtight, hermetic; *(al agua)* watertight, hermetic (b) *Fig (persona)* inscrutable, uncommunicative

**hermetismo** *nm (al aire)* airtightness; *(al agua)* watertightness (b) *Fig (de persona)* inscrutability, uncommunicativeness

**hermoso, -a** *adj* (a) *(bello) (paisaje, paseo, mujer)* beautiful, lovely; *(hombre)* handsome (b) *(excelente)* wonderful (c) *Fam (gordo, grande)* plump

**hermosura** *nf (belleza)* beauty; *(de hombre)* handsomeness

**hernia** *nf* hernia, rupture; **h. de hiato** hiatus hernia; **h. inguinal** inguinal hernia

**herniado, -a 1** *adj* ruptured

**2** *nm,f* person suffering from a hernia

**herniarse** [15] *vpr* (a) *Med* to rupture oneself (b) *Fam Irón* **¡cuidado, no te vayas a herniar!** careful! you don't want to strain yourself!

**héroe** *nm* hero

**heroicidad** *nf* (a) *(cualidad)* heroism (b) *(hecho)* heroic deed

**heroico, -a** *adj* heroic

**heroína** *nf* (a) *(mujer)* heroine (b) *(droga)* heroin

**heroinomanía** *nf* heroin addiction

**heroinómano, -a** *nm,f* heroin addict

**heroísmo** *nm* heroism

**herpes** *nm inv* herpes

**herradura** *nf* horseshoe

**herraje** *nm* iron fittings, ironwork

**herramienta** *nf* tool

**herrería** *nf* (a) *(taller)* smithy, forge (b) *(oficio)* smithery, blacksmith's trade

**herrerillo** *nm (carbonero)* great tit; *(común)* bluetit

**herrero** *nm* blacksmith, smith

**herrumbrarse** *vpr* to rust, to go rusty

**herrumbre** *nf* (a) *(óxido)* rust (b) *(sabor)* iron taste

**herrumbroso, -a** *adj* rusty

**hertz** [χerts] *(pl* **hertzs)** *nm* hertz

**hervidero** *nm* (a) *(de pasiones, intrigas)* hotbed (b) *(de gente) (muchedumbre)* swarm, throng; *(sitio)* place throbbing *o* swarming with people; **la sala era un h. de periodistas** the hall was swarming with journalists

**hervido, -a** *adj* boiled

**hervir** [64] **1** *vt* to boil

**2** *vi* (a) *(líquido)* to boil; **h. a borbotones** to be at a rolling boil (b) *Fig (lugar)* **h. de** to swarm with (c) *Fig (persona)* **h. en** to be burning with

**hervor** *nm* boiling; **dar un h. a algo** to blanch sth; **añadir las hierbas durante el h.** add the herbs while it's boiling

**heterodoxia** *nf* heterodoxy, unorthodox nature

**heterodoxo, -a 1** *adj* heterodox, unorthodox

**2** *nm,f* heterodox *o* unorthodox person

**heterogeneidad** *nf* heterogeneity

**heterogéneo, -a** *adj* heterogeneous

**heteromorfo, -a** *adj* heteromorphous

**heterosexual** *adj & nmf* heterosexual

**heterosexualidad** *nf* heterosexuality

**hexadecimal** *adj Informát* hexadecimal

**hexagonal** *adj* hexagonal

**hexágono** *nm* hexagon

**hez** *nf también Fig* dregs; **heces** *(excrementos)* faeces, excrement

**hg** *(abrev de* **hectogramo)** hg

**hiato** *nm Gram* hiatus

**hibernación** *nf (de animales)* hibernation

**hibernar** *vi* to hibernate

**hibridación** *nf* hybridization

**híbrido, -a 1** *adj también Fig* hybrid

**2** *nm (animal, planta)* hybrid; *Fig (mezcla)* cross

**hice** *etc ver* **hacer**

**hidalgo, -a 1** *adj* (a) *(noble)* noble (b) *Fig (caballeroso)* courteous, gentlemanly

**2** *nm f* nobleman, *f* noblewoman

**hidalguía** *nf* (a) *(aristocracia)* nobility (b) *Fig (caballerosidad)* courtesy, chivalry

**hidra** *nf* hydra

**hidratación** *nf (de la piel)* moisturizing; *(de persona)* rehydration; *(de sustancia)* hydration

**hidratado, -a** *adj (piel)* moist; *Quím* hydrated

**hidratante 1** *adj* moisturizing
  **2** *nm (crema, loción)* moisturizer

**hidratar** *vt (piel)* to moisturize; *Quím* to hydrate

**hidrato** *nm* hydrate; **h. de carbono** carbohydrate

**hidráulica** *nf* hydraulics *(singular)*

**hidráulico, -a** *adj* hydraulic

**hídrico, -a** *adj* hydric

**hidroavión** *nm* seaplane

**hidrocarburo** *nm* hydrocarbon

**hidrocefalia** *nf Med* water on the brain, hydrocephalus

**hidrodinámica** *nf* hydrodynamics *(singular)*

**hidrodinámico, -a** *adj* hydrodynamic

**hidroelectricidad** *nf* hydroelectricity

**hidroeléctrico, -a** *adj* hydroelectric; **central hidroeléctrica** hydroelectric power station

**hidrófilo, -a** *adj* absorbent; **algodón h.** *Br* cotton wool, *US* cotton

**hidrofobia** *nf* hydrophobia, rabies

**hidrófobo, -a** *adj* hydrophobic, rabid

**hidrófugo, -a** *adj (contra filtraciones)* waterproof; *(contra humedad)* damp-proof

**hidrogenar** *vt* to hydrogenate

**hidrógeno** *nm* hydrogen

**hidrografía** *nf* hydrography

**hidrográfico, -a** *adj* hydrographic

**hidrólisis** *nf inv* hydrolysis

**hidrolizado, -a** *adj* hydrolyzed

**hidromecánico, -a** *adj* hydrodynamic, water-powered

**hidrometría** *nf* hydrometry

**hidroplano** *nm* **(a)** *(barco)* hydrofoil **(b)** *(avión)* seaplane

**hidrosfera** *nf* hydrosphere

**hidrosoluble** *adj* water-soluble

**hidrostática** *nf* hydrostatics *(singular)*

**hidrostático, -a** *adj* hydrostatic

**hidroterapia** *nf* hydrotherapy

**hidróxido** *nm* hydroxide

**hidruro** *nm* hydride

**hiedra** *nf* ivy

**hiel** *nf* **(a)** *(bilis)* bile **(b)** *Fig (mala intención)* spleen, bitterness

**hiela** *ver* **helar**

**hielo** *nm* ice; *Fig* **quedarse de h.** to be stunned *o* speechless; *Fig* **romper el h.** to break the ice

**hiena** *nf* hyena

**hierático, -a** *adj (expresión, actitud)* solemn, impassive

**hierba, yerba** *nf* **(a)** *(planta)* herb; **mala h.** weed; **h. mate** maté; **hierbas medicinales** medicinal herbs **(b)** *(césped)* grass **(c)** *Fam (droga)* grass **(d)** *(expresiones)* **ser mala h.** to be a nasty piece of work; *Prov* **mala h. nunca muere** ill weeds grow apace; **y otras hierbas** and so on

**hierbabuena** *nf* mint

**hiero** *etc ver* **herir**

**hierro** *nm* **(a)** *(metal)* iron; *Fig* **tener una salud de h.** to have an iron constitution; **h. forjado/fundido** wrought/cast iron **(b)** *(de puñal)* blade; *(de flecha)* point; *Prov* **quien a h. mata a h. muere** he who lives by the sword dies by the sword

**hiervo** *etc ver* **hervir**

**hi-fi** ['ifi] *nf (abrev de* **high fidelity***)* hi-fi

**higadillo** *nm* **higadillos de pollo** chicken livers

**hígado** *nm* liver; **echar los hígados** to nearly kill oneself (with the effort); **tener hígados** to have guts

**higiene** *nf* hygiene; **h. mental** mental health

**higiénico, -a** *adj* hygienic

**higienista** *nmf* hygienist; **h. dental** dental hygienist

**higienización** *nf* sterilization

**higo** *nm* fig; **de higos a brevas** once in a blue moon; *Fam* **estar hecho un h.** *(persona)* to be wrecked; *(cosa)* to be falling apart; **h. chumbo** prickly pear

**higrometría** *nf* hygrometry

**higrómetro** *nm* hygrometer

**higuera** *nf* fig tree; *Fig* **estar en la h.** to live in a world of one's own; **h. chumba** prickly pear

**hijastro, -a** *nm,f* stepson, *f* stepdaughter

**hijo, -a 1** *nm,f* **(a)** *(descendiente)* son, *f* daughter; *Vulg* **h. de puta** *o Méx* **de la chingada** *Br* bastard, *US* mother-fucker; **h. ilegítimo** *o* **natural** illegitimate son; *Fam* **h. de papá** rich kid; **h. pródigo** prodigal son; **h. único** only son; *Fam Fig* **cualquier** *o* **todo h. de vecino** any Tom, Dick or Harry **(b)** *(natural)* native **(c)** *(como forma de dirigirse a alguien)* **¡h., no te pongas así!** don't be like that!; **¡pues h., podrías haber avisado!** you could at least have told me, couldn't you?; **¡hija mía, qué bruta eres!** God, you're stupid!
  **2** *nm (hijo o hija)* child; **hijos** children

**hilacha** *nf* loose thread

**hilada** *nf* row

**hilandería** *nf* **(a)** *(arte)* spinning **(b)** *(taller)* (spinning) mill

**hilandero, -a** *nm,f* spinner

**hilar** vt (hilo) to spin; (ideas, planes) to think up; Fig **h. delgado** o **muy fino** to split hairs

**hilarante** adj mirth-provoking; **gas h.** laughing gas

**hilaridad** nf hilarity

**hilatura** nf (actividad) spinning

**hilera** nf row; **en h.** in a row

**hilo** nm (a) (fibra, hebra) thread; **colgar** o **pender de un h.** to be hanging by a thread; **mover los hilos** to pull some strings; **h. dental** dental floss

(b) (tejido) linen

(c) (de metal, teléfono) wire

(d) (de agua, sangre) trickle; Fig **apenas le salía un h. de voz** he was barely able to speak

(e) Mús **h. musical** piped music

(f) Fig (de pensamiento) train; (de discurso, conversación) thread; **perder el h.** to lose the thread; **seguir el h.** to follow (the thread); **tomar** o **retomar el h. (de la conversación)** to pick up the thread (of the conversation); **esto viene al h. de lo que dijimos ayer** this relates to what we were saying yesterday

**hilván** nm (a) (costura) Br tacking, US basting

(b) (hilo) Br tacking stitch, US basting stitch

**hilvanado** nm Br tacking, US basting

**hilvanar** vt (a) (ropa) Br to tack, US to baste (b) Fig (coordinar) (ideas) to piece together (c) Fig (improvisar) to throw together

**Himalaya** nm **el H.** the Himalayas

**himen** nm hymen

**himeneo** nm Literario wedding

**himno** nm hymn; **h. nacional** national anthem

**hincapié** nm **hacer h. en** (insistir) to insist on; (subrayar) to emphasize, to stress

**hincar** [61] **1** vt **h. algo en** to stick sth into; Fig **hincarle el diente a algo** (empezar) to get to grips with sth, to get to work on sth

**2 hincarse** vpr **hincarse de rodillas** to fall to one's knees

**hincha 1** ver **henchir**

**2** nmf (seguidor) fan

**3** nf (rabia) **tener h. a alguien** to have it in for sb

**hinchada** nf fans

**hinchado, -a** adj (a) (rueda, globo) inflated; (cara, tobillo) swollen (b) Fig (persona) bigheaded, conceited; (lenguaje, estilo) bombastic

**hinchar 1** vt también Fig to blow up; Fam Fig **ya me está hinchando las narices** he's beginning to get up my nose

**2 hincharse** vpr (a) (pierna, mano) to swell (up) (b) Fig (persona) to become bigheaded (c) Fig (de comida) to stuff oneself (a o de with); **hincharse a hacer algo** to do sth a lot

**hinchazón** nf swelling; **ya está bajando la h.** the swelling is already going down

**hinchiera** etc ver **henchir**

**hincho** etc ver **henchir**

**hindi** nm Hindi

**hindú** (pl **hindúes**) adj & nmf (a) (de la India) Indian (b) Rel Hindu

**hinduismo** nm Hinduism

**hinojo** nm fennel

**hinque** etc ver **hincar**

**hip** interj ¡h.! (hipido) hic!; ¡h.! ¡h.! ¡hurra! hip, hip, hooray!

**hipar** vi to hiccup, to have hiccups

**híper** nm inv Fam hypermarket

**hiper-** prefijo Fam (muy) mega-; **me ha salido hipercaro** it was mega-expensive; **¡es hiperguapo!** he's a real dish!

**hiperactividad** nf hyperactivity

**hiperactivo, -a** adj hyperactive

**hipérbola** nf hyperbola

**hipérbole** nf hyperbole

**hiperbólico, -a** adj Mat & Lit hyperbolic

**hiperfunción** nf Med increase in normal rate of functioning

**hiperglucemia** nf hyperglycaemia

**hiperinflación** nf hyperinflation

**hipermercado** nm hypermarket

**hipermétrope 1** adj long-sighted

**2** nmf long-sighted person

**hipermetropía** nf long-sightedness

**hiperrealismo** nm = artistic movement concerned with almost photographic representation of reality

**hiperrealista 1** adj hyper-realistic; Arte hyper-realist

**2** nmf Arte hyper-realist

**hipersensibilidad** nf hypersensitivity (a to)

**hipersensible** adj hypersensitive

**hipersónico, -a** adj hypersonic

**hipertensión** nf high blood pressure

**hipertenso, -a 1** adj with high blood pressure

**2** nm,f person with high blood pressure

**hipertermia** nf hyperthermia

**hipertexto** nm Informát hypertext

**hipertrofia** nf hypertrophy; Fig overexpansion

**hip-hop** nm hip-hop

**hípica** nf (carreras de caballos) horseracing; (equitación) showjumping

**hípico, -a** adj **concurso h.** (de las carreras) horseraces; (de la equitación) showjumping

**hipido** nm hiccup, hiccough

**hipnosis** nf inv hypnosis

**hipnótico, -a 1** *adj* hypnotic
**2** *nm* hypnotic, narcotic

**hipnotismo** *nm* hypnotism

**hipnotizador, -ora 1** *adj* hypnotic; *Fig* spellbinding, mesmerizing
**2** *nm,f* hypnotist

**hipnotizar** [16] *vt* to hypnotize; *Fig* to mesmerize

**hipo** *nm* hiccups; **tener h.** to have (the) hiccups; *Fig* **quitar el h. a alguien** to take someone's breath away

**hipoalergénico, -a** *adj* hypoallergenic

**hipocalórico, -a** *adj (alimento, dieta)* low calorie

**hipocampo** *nm (caballito de mar)* seahorse

**hipocentro** *nm* hypocentre, focus

**hipocondría** *nf* hypochondria

**hipocondríaco, -a** *adj & nm,f* hypochondriac

**hipocrático, -a** *adj* **juramento h.** Hippocratic oath

**hipocresía** *nf* hypocrisy

**hipócrita 1** *adj* hypocritical
**2** *nmf* hypocrite

**hipodérmico, -a** *adj* hypodermic

**hipódromo** *nm* racecourse, racetrack

**hipófisis** *nf inv* pituitary gland

**hipofunción** *nf Med* decrease in normal rate of functioning

**hipoglucemia** *nf* hypoglycaemia

**hipopótamo** *nm* hippopotamus

**hipotálamo** *nm* hypothalamus

**hipoteca** *nf* mortgage; **levantar una h.** to pay off a mortgage

**hipotecable** *adj* mortgageable

**hipotecar** [61] *vt* **(a)** *(bienes)* to mortgage **(b)** *Fig (poner en peligro)* to compromise, to jeopardize

**hipotecario, -a** *adj* mortgage; **crédito h.** mortgage (loan)

**hipotensión** *nf* low blood pressure

**hipotenso, -a 1** *adj* with low blood pressure
**2** *nm,f* person with low blood pressure

**hipotensor** *nm* hypotensive drug

**hipotenusa** *nf* hypotenuse

**hipotermia** *nf* hypothermia

**hipótesis** *nf inv* hypothesis

**hipotético, -a** *adj* hypothetic, hypothetical

**hippy, hippie** ['χipi] *(pl* hippies) *adj & nmf* hippy

**hiriente** *adj (palabras)* hurtful, cutting

**hiriera** *etc ver* **herir**

**hirsuto, -a** *adj* **(a)** *(cabello)* wiry; *(brazo, pecho)* hairy **(b)** *Fig (persona)* gruff, surly

**hirviera** *etc ver* **hervir**

**hisopo** *nm* **(a)** *Rel* aspergillum, sprinkler **(b)** *Bot* hyssop

**hispalense** *adj & nmf* Sevillian

**hispánico, -a** *adj & nm,f (de España)* Hispanic; *(hispanohablante)* Spanish-speaking; **el mundo h.** the Spanish-speaking world

**hispanidad** *nf (cultura)* Spanishness; *(pueblos)* Spanish-speaking world

**hispanista** *nmf* Hispanist, student of Hispanic culture

**hispano, -a 1** *adj (español)* Spanish; *(hispanoamericano)* Spanish-American; *(en Estados Unidos)* Hispanic
**2** *nm,f (español)* Spaniard; *(estadounidense)* Hispanic

**hispanoamericano, -a 1** *adj* Spanish-American
**2** *nm,f* Spanish American

**hispanoárabe 1** *adj* Hispano-Arabic
**2** *nmf* Spanish Arab

**hispanohablante 1** *adj* Spanish-speaking
**2** *nmf* Spanish speaker

**hispanojudío, -a 1** *adj* Spanish-Jewish
**2** *nm,f* Spanish Jew

**histamina** *nf* histamine

**histerectomía** *nf* hysterectomy

**histeria** *nf Med & Fig* hysteria

**histérico, -a 1** *adj* hysterical; *Fam Fig* **estar h.** *(muy nervioso)* to be a bag *o* bundle of nerves; **ponerse h.** to go into hysterics; *Fam Fig* **ese ruido me pone h.** that noise really gets on my nerves
**2** *nm,f Med* hysteric; *Fam Fig* **es una histérica** the least thing sets her off

**histerismo** *nm Med & Fig* hysteria

**histerotomía** *nf* hysterotomy

**histograma** *nm* histogram

**histología** *nf* histology

**historia** *nf* **(a)** *(ciencia)* history; **pasar a la h.** to go down in history; **h. antigua/universal** ancient/world history; **h. del arte** art history; **h. natural** natural history **(b)** *(narración, chisme)* story; **¡déjate de historias!** that's enough of that!; **es siempre la misma h.** it's the same old story

**historiador, -ora** *nm,f* historian

**historial** *nm (ficha)* record; **h. médico** *o* **clínico** medical *o* case history

**historicidad** *nf* historicity, historical authenticity

**historicismo** *nm* historicism

**histórico, -a** *adj* **(a)** *(de la historia)* historical **(b)** *(verídico)* factual **(c)** *(importante)* historic

**historieta** *nf* **(a)** *(chiste)* funny story, anecdote **(b)** *(tira cómica)* comic strip

**historiografía** *nf* historiography

**historiógrafo, -a** *nm,f* historiographer

**histrión** *nm* (a) *(actor)* actor (b) *(persona afectada)* play-actor

**histriónico, -a** *adj* histrionic

**histrionismo** *nm* histrionics

**hit** [ʏit] *(pl* **hits)** *nm* hit

**hitita** *adj & nmf* Hittite

**hitleriano, -a** [ʏitle'rjano] *adj & nm,f* Hitlerite

**hito** *nm también Fig* milestone; **mirar a alguien de h. en h.** to stare at sb

**hizo** *ver* **hacer**

**hl** *(abrev de* **hectolitro)** hl

**hm** *(abrev de* **hectómetro)** hm

**hnos.** *(abrev de* **hermanos)** bros

**hobby** ['ʏoβi] *(pl* **hobbys)** *nm* hobby

**hocico** *nm* (a) *(de perro, zorro)* muzzle; *(de gato, ratón)* nose; *(de cerdo)* snout (b) *Fig (de personas) (boca)* rubber lips; *(cara)* mug; **meter los hocicos en un asunto** to stick one's nose into something

**hockey** ['ʏokei] *nm* hockey; **h. sobre hielo** *Br* ice hockey, *US* hockey; **h. sobre hierba** *Br* hockey, *US* field hockey; **h. sobre patines** roller hockey

**hogar** *nm* (a) *(de chimenea)* fireplace; *(de horno, cocina)* grate (b) *(domicilio)* home; **h. dulce h.** home sweet home

**hogareño, -a** *adj (persona)* home-loving, homely; *(tarea, economía)* domestic; *(ambiente)* family; **ambiente h.** family atmosphere; **la paz hogareña** domestic bliss

**hogaza** *nf* large loaf

**hoguera** *nf* bonfire; **morir en la h.** to be burned at the stake

**hoja** *nf* (a) *(de planta)* leaf; *(de hierba)* blade (b) *(de papel)* sheet (of paper); *(de libro)* page; **h. de servicios** record (of service), track record (c) *(de cuchillo)* blade; **h. de afeitar** razor blade (d) *(de puertas, ventanas)* leaf (e) *Informát* **h. de cálculo** spreadsheet

**hojalata** *nf* tinplate

**hojalatería** *nf* tinsmith's

**hojalatero** *nm* tinsmith

**hojaldre** *nm* puff pastry

**hojarasca** *nf* (a) *(hojas secas)* (dead) leaves; *(frondosidad)* tangle of leaves (b) *Fig (palabrería)* waffle

**hojear** *vt* to leaf through

**hola** *interj* (a) *(saludo)* ¡h.! hello! (b) *(expresión de sorpresa, admiración)* **¡h., menudo coche!** hey, that's some car!

**Holanda** *n* Holland

**holandés, -esa 1** *adj* Dutch

**2** *nm,f (persona)* Dutchman, *f* Dutchwoman

**3** *nm (lengua)* Dutch

**holandesa** *nf (hoja de papel)* = piece of paper measuring 22 × 28 cm

**holding** ['ʏoldin] *(pl* **holdings)** *nm Com* holding company

**holgado, -a** *adj* (a) *(ropa)* baggy, loose-fitting; *(habitación, espacio)* roomy (b) *(victoria, situación económica)* comfortable

**holganza** *nf* idleness

**holgar** [18] *vi* (a) *(estar ocioso)* to be idle, to be taking one's ease (b) *(sobrar)* to be unnecessary; **huelgan comentarios** one need say no more; **huelga decir que…** needless to say…

**holgazán, -ana 1** *adj* idle, good-for-nothing

**2** *nm,f* good-for-nothing

**holgazanear** *vi* to laze about

**holgazanería** *nf* idleness

**holgura** *nf* (a) *(de espacio)* room; *(de ropa)* bagginess, looseness; *(entre piezas)* play, give (b) *(bienestar)* comfort, affluence; **vivir con h.** to be comfortably off

**hollar** [65] *vt* to tread (on)

**hollejo** *nm* skin *(of grape, olive etc)*

**hollín** *nm* soot

**holocausto** *nm* holocaust

**holografía** *nf* holography

**holograma** *nm* hologram

**hombre 1** *nm* man; **un pobre h.** a nobody; **¡pobre h.!** poor *Br* chap *o US* guy!; **de h. a h.** man to man; **ser muy h.** to be a (real) man; **ser todo un h., ser un h. de pelo en pecho** to be a real man, to be every inch a man; **el h.** *(la humanidad)* man, mankind; **h. de acción** man of action; **el h. de la calle** *o* **de a pie** the man in the street; **h. de las cavernas** caveman; **h. lobo** werewolf; **h. de mundo** man of the world; **h. de negocios** businessman; **h. orquesta** one-man band; **h. de paja** front (man); **h. de palabra** man of his word; **h. rana** frogman; *Fam* **el h. del saco** the bogeyman

**2** *interj* **¡h.!** **¡qué alegría verte!** (hey,) how nice to see you!; **¡sí, h.!** sure!

**hombrear** *vi* to act the man

**hombrera** *nf (de traje, vestido)* shoulder pad; *(de uniforme)* epaulette

**hombría** *nf* manliness

**hombro** *nm* shoulder; **al h.** across one's shoulder; **a hombros** over one's shoulders; **encogerse de hombros** to shrug one's shoulders; **arrimar el h.** to lend a hand; **mirar por encima del h. a alguien** to look down one's nose at sb

**hombruno, -a** *adj* masculine, mannish

**homenaje** *nm (en honor de alguien)* tribute; *(al soberano)* homage; **partido (de) h.** testimonial (match); **en h. de** *o* **a** in honour of, as a tribute to; **rendir h. a** to pay tribute to

**homenajeado, -a 1** *adj* honoured

  **2** *nm,f* guest of honour

**homenajear** *vt* to pay tribute to, to honour

**homeópata** *nmf* homeopath

**homeopatía** *nf* homeopathy

**homeopático, -a** *adj* homeopathic

**homérico, -a** *adj Lit* Homeric

**homicida 1** *adj (agresión, mirada, intención)* murderous; **arma h.** murder weapon

  **2** *nmf* murderer

**homicidio** *nm* homicide, manslaughter

**homilía** *nf Rel* homily, sermon

**homínido** *nm* hominid

**homofobia** *nf* homophobia

**homófono, -a** *adj Ling* homophonic

**homogeneidad** *nf* homogeneity

**homogeneización** *nf* homogenization

**homogeneizador, -ora** *adj* homogenizing

**homogeneizar [16]** *vt* to homogenize

**homogéneo, -a** *adj* homogenous

**homógrafo, -a** *Ling* **1** *adj* homographic

  **2** *nm* homograph

**homologable** *adj* **h. (a)** comparable (to)

**homologación** *nf* **(a)** *(equiparación)* bringing into line **(b)** *(de un producto)* official authorization; *(de un récord)* official confirmation

**homologar [40]** *vt* **(a)** *(equiparar)* to bring into line **(con** with), to make comparable **(con** with) **(b)** *(producto)* to authorize officially; *(récord)* to confirm officially

**homólogo, -a 1** *adj* **(a)** *(semejante)* equivalent **(b)** *Quím* homologous

  **2** *nm,f* counterpart

**homonimia** *nf* homonymy

**homónimo, -a 1** *adj* homonymous

  **2** *nm,f (tocayo)* namesake

  **3** *nm Ling* homonym

**homosexual** *adj & nmf* homosexual

**homosexualidad** *nf* homosexuality

**honda** *nf* sling

**hondo, -a** *adj* **(a)** *también Fig (profundo)* deep; **lo h.** the depths; **calar h. en** to strike a chord with; **en lo más h. de** in the depths of **(b)** *cante* **h.** flamenco singing

**hondonada** *nf* hollow

**hondura** *nf* depth

**Honduras** *n* Honduras

**hondureño, -a** *adj & nm,f* Honduran

**honestamente** *adv (con honradez)* honestly; *(con decencia)* modestly, decently; *(con justicia)* fairly

**honestidad** *nf (honradez)* honesty; *(decencia)* modesty, decency; *(justicia)* fairness

**honesto, -a** *adj (honrado)* honest; *(decente)* modest, decent; *(justo)* fair

**hongo 1** *adj* **sombrero h.** *Br* bowler hat, *US* derby

  **2** *nm* **(a)** *(comestible)* mushroom; *(no comestible)* toadstool **(b)** *(enfermedad)* fungus **(c)** *(sombrero) Br* bowler (hat), *US* derby

**Honolulu** *n* Honolulu

**honor** *nm* honour; **en h. de** in honour of; **hacer h. a** to live up to; **en h. a la verdad** to be (quite) honest; **honores** *(ceremonial)* honours; *Fig* **hacer los honores de la casa** to do the honours, to look after the guests

**honorabilidad** *nf* honour

**honorable** *adj* honourable

**honorar** *vt* to honour

**honorario, -a 1** *adj* honorary

  **2** *nmpl* **honorarios** fees

**honorífico, -a** *adj* honorific

**honoris causa** *adj* honoris causa

**honra** *nf* honour; **ser la h. de** to be the pride of; **es la h. de su país** she's the pride *o* toast of her country; **tener algo a mucha h.** to be honoured by sth; **¡y a mucha h.!** and proud of it!; **honras fúnebres** funeral

**honradez** *nf* honesty

**honrado, -a** *adj* honest

**honrar 1** *vt* to honour

  **2 honrarse** *vpr* to be honoured **(con algo/de hacer algo** by sth/to do sth)

**honrilla** *nf* pride, concern about what people say

**honroso, -a** *adj (acto, gesto)* honourable

**hooligan** ['xulivan] *(pl* **hooligans)** *nmf* (football) hooligan

**hora** *nf* **(a)** *(del día)* hour; **a primera h.** first thing in the morning; **a última h.** *(al final del día)* at the end of the day; *(en el último momento)* at the last moment; **dar la h.** to strike the hour; **de última h.** *(noticia)* latest, up-to-the-minute; *(preparativos)* last-minute; *Prensa* **última h.** stop press; **(pagar) por horas** (to pay) by the hour; **poner el reloj en h.** to set one's watch *o* clock; **horas extraordinarias** overtime; **h. oficial** official time; **horas de oficina/trabajo** office/working hours; **h. punta** rush hour; **horas de visita** visiting times; **media h.** half an hour

  **(b)** *(momento determinado)* time; **¿a qué h. sale?** what time *o* when does it leave?; **es h. de irse** it's time to go; **a la h.** on time; **a su h.** when the time comes, at the appropriate time; **¿qué h. es?** what time is it?; **h.** H zero hour

  **(c)** *(cita)* appointment; **pedir/dar h.** to ask for/give an appointment; **tener h. en/con** to have an appointment at/with

  **(d)** *(muerte)* **llegó su h.** her time has come

**(e)** *(expresiones)* **a altas horas de la noche** in the small hours; *Fam* **¡a buenas horas (mangas verdes)!** that's a lot of good now!; **en mala h.** unluckily; **a la h. de la verdad** when it comes to the crunch; **tener las horas contadas** to have one's days numbered; **¡ya era h.!** and about time too!

**horadar** *vt (perforar)* to pierce; *(con máquina)* to bore through

**horario, -a 1** *adj* **aguja horaria** *(de reloj)* hour hand

**2** *nm* timetable; **h. comercial/laboral** opening/working hours; **h. flexible** flexitime; **h. intensivo** = working day without a long break for lunch; **h. partido** = working day with long (2-3 hour) lunch break, ending at 7-8pm; **h. de verano** summer opening hours; **h. de visitas** visiting hours

**horca** *nf* **(a)** *(patíbulo)* gallows **(b)** *(herramienta)* pitchfork

**horcajadas: a horcajadas** *loc adv* astride

**horchata** *nf* = cold drink made from ground tiger nuts, water and sugar

**horchatería** *nf* = milk bar where "horchata" is served

**horda** *nf* horde

**horizontal** *adj* horizontal

**horizontalidad** *nf* flatness

**horizonte** *nm* horizon

**horma** *nf (molde)* mould, pattern; *(de zapatos)* shoe tree; *(de sombrero)* hat block; *Fig* **encontrar alguien la h. de su zapato** to meet one's match

**hormiga** *nf* ant; *Fig* **ser una h.** to be hardworking and thrifty; **h. obrera/reina** worker/queen ant

**hormigón** *nm* concrete; **h. armado** reinforced concrete

**hormigonar** *vt* to construct with concrete

**hormigonera** *nf* concrete mixer

**hormiguear** *vi* **(a)** *(dar sensación de hormigueo)* **me hormiguean las piernas** I've got pins and needles in my legs **(b)** *(moverse, bullir)* to swarm

**hormigueo** *nm* **(a)** *(sensación)* pins and needles **(b)** *(movimiento)* bustle

**hormiguero 1** *adj* **oso h.** anteater

**2** *nm* ants' nest, anthill; *Fig* **Tokio es un h. humano** Tokyo is swarming with people

**hormiguita** *nf Fam Fig* = hard-working and thrifty person

**hormona** *nf* hormone

**hormonal** *adj* hormonal

**hornada** *nf también Fig* batch

**hornear** *vt* to bake

**hornillo** *nm (para cocinar)* camping *o* portable stove; *(de laboratorio)* small furnace

**horno** *nm Culin* oven; *Tec* furnace; *(de cerámica, ladrillos)* kiln; *Fam Fig* **no está el h. para bollos** the time is not right; **alto h.** blast furnace; **altos hornos** *(factoría)* iron and steelworks; **h. crematorio** crematorium; **h. eléctrico** electric oven; **h. microondas** microwave (oven)

**horóscopo** *nm* **(a)** *(signo zodiacal)* star sign **(b)** *(predicción)* horoscope

**horquilla** *nf* **(a)** *(para el pelo)* hairgrip, hairpin **(b)** *(herramienta)* wooden pitchfork

**horrendo, -a** *adj* **(a)** *(terrorífico)* horrifying, terrifying **(b)** *(muy malo)* terrible, awful **(c)** *(muy feo)* horrible, hideous

**hórreo** *nm* = raised granary typical of Asturias and Galicia

**horrible** *adj* **(a)** *(terrorífico)* horrifying, terrifying **(b)** *(muy malo)* terrible, awful **(c)** *(muy feo)* horrible, hideous

**horripilante** *adj* **(a)** *(terrorífico)* horrifying, spine-chilling **(b)** *(muy feo)* horrible, hideous

**horripilar** *vt* to terrify, to scare to death

**horror 1** *nm* **(a)** *(miedo)* terror, horror; **¡qué h.!** how awful **(b)** *(atrocidad)* atrocity; **los horrores de la guerra** the horrors of war

**2** *adv Fam* **horrores** terribly, an awful lot

**horrorizado, -a** *adj* terrified, horrified

**horrorizar** [16] **1** *vt* to terrify, to horrify

**2 horrorizarse** *vpr* to be terrified *o* horrified

**horroroso, -a** *adj* **(a)** *(terrorífico)* horrifying, terrifying **(b)** *(muy malo)* appalling, awful **(c)** *(muy feo)* horrible, hideous

**hortaliza** *nf (garden)* vegetable

**hortelano, -a** *nm,f* market gardener

**hortensia** *nf* hydrangea

**hortera** *Fam* **1** *adj* tasteless, tacky

**2** *nmf* person with no taste

**horterada** *nf Fam* tacky thing

**hortícola** *adj* horticultural

**horticultor, -ora** *nm,f* horticulturalist

**horticultura** *nf* horticulture

**hosco, -a** *adj (persona)* sullen, gruff; *(lugar)* grim, gloomy

**hospedaje** *nm* **(a)** *(alojamiento)* accommodation, lodgings **(b)** *(dinero)* (cost of) board and lodging

**hospedar 1** *vt* to put up

**2 hospedarse** *vpr* to stay

**hospedería** *nf (lugar de alojamiento)* guest house; *(de convento)* hospice

**hospiciano, -a** *nm,f* = resident of an orphanage

**hospicio** *nm (para niños)* orphanage, children's home; *(para pobres)* poorhouse

**hospital** *nm* hospital

**hospitalario, -a** *adj* (a) *(acogedor)* hospitable (b) *(de hospital)* hospital; **atención hospitalaria** hospital care

**hospitalidad** *nf* hospitality

**hospitalización** *nf* hospitalization

**hospitalizar** [16] *vt* to hospitalize, to take *o* send to hospital

**hosquedad** *nf* sullenness, gruffness

**host** [xost] (*pl* **hosts**) *nm* *Informát* host

**hostal** *nm* guesthouse

**hostelería** *nf* catering

**hostelero, -a1** *adj* catering; **sector h.** catering trade

  **2** *nm,f* landlord, *f* landlady

**hostería** *nf* guesthouse

**hostia** *nf* (a) *Rel* host (b) *Vulg (golpe)* bash, punch; *(accidente)* smash-up; **¡h.!, ¡hostias!** bloody hell!, damn it!; **¿para qué hostias…?** why the hell…?; **había la h. de gente** the place was heaving

**hostiar** [34] *vt* *Vulg* to bash

**hostigamiento** *nm* harassment

**hostigar** [40] *vt* (a) *(acosar)* to pester, to bother (b) *Mil* to harass

**hostil** *adj* hostile

**hostilidad** *nf* *(sentimiento)* hostility; *Mil* **hostilidades** hostilities

**hostilizar** [16] *vt* to harass

**hotel** *nm* hotel

**hotelero, -a 1** *adj* hotel; **hay escasez de plazas hoteleras** there is a shortage of hotel accommodation

  **2** *nm,f (hombre)* hotelier, hotel manager; *(mujer)* hotelier, hotel manageress

**hovercraft** *nm* hovercraft

**hoy** *adv* (a) *(en este día)* today; **de h. en adelante** from now on; **h. por ti y mañana por mí** you can do the same for me some time (b) *(en la actualidad)* nowadays, today; **h. día, h. en día** these days, nowadays; **h. por h.** at the present moment, as things are at the moment

**hoyo** *nm (concavidad)* hole, pit; *(de golf)* hole; *Fam (sepultura)* grave

**hoyuelo** *nm* dimple

**hoz** *nf* (a) *(herramienta)* sickle; **la h. y el martillo** the hammer and the sickle (b) *(barranco)* gorge, canyon

**HTML** *nm* *Informát* (*abrev de* **hypertext markup language**) HTML

**HTTP** *nm* *Informát* (*abrev de* **hypertext transfer protocol**) HTTP

**huacal** *nm* *Méx* (a) *(jaula)* cage (b) *(cajón)* drawer

**huachafería** *nf* *Perú Fam* (a) *(hecho)* tacky thing (b) *(dicho)* naff comment

**huachafo, -a** *adj* *Perú Fam* tacky

**huaso, -a** *nm,f* *Andes Fam* peasant

**hubiera** *etc ver* **haber**

**hucha** *nf* moneybox

**hueco, -a1** *adj* (a) *(vacío)* hollow (b) *(sonido)* resonant, hollow (c) *(sin ideas)* empty

  **2** *nm* (a) *(cavidad)* hole; *(en pared)* recess (b) *(rato libre)* spare moment (c) *(espacio libre)* space, gap; *(de escalera)* well; *(de ascensor)* shaft

**huela** *etc ver* **oler**

**huelga1** *ver* **holgar**

  **2** *nf* strike; **estar/declararse en h.** to be/to go on strike; **h. de brazos caídos** sit-down (strike); **h. de celo** work-to-rule; **h. general** general strike; **h. de hambre** hunger strike; **h. indefinida** indefinite strike; **h. salvaje** wildcat strike

**huelguista** *nmf* striker

**huella1** *ver* **hollar**

  **2** *nf* (a) *(de persona)* footprint; *(de animal, rueda)* track; **seguir las huellas de alguien** to follow in sb's footsteps; **h. digital** *o* **dactilar** fingerprint (b) *Fig (vestigio)* trace (c) *Fig (impresión profunda)* mark; **dejar h.** to leave one's mark

**huérfano, -a** *adj & nm,f* orphan

**huero, -a** *adj* hollow; *Fig* empty

**huerta** *nf* (a) *(huerto)* *Br* market garden, *US* truck farm (b) *(tierra de regadío)* = irrigated crop-growing region

**huertano, -a** *nm,f* (a) *(murciano)* Murcian (b) *(valenciano)* Valencian

**huertero, -a** *nm,f* market gardener

**huerto** *nm (de hortalizas)* vegetable garden; *(de frutales)* orchard; *Fam Fig* **llevarse a alguien al h.** to have (one's end away) and one's way with sb

**hueso** *nm* (a) *(del cuerpo)* bone; **acabar *o* dar con sus huesos en** to end up in; **estar en los huesos** to be all skin and bones; **no poder alguien con sus huesos** to be ready to drop, to be exhausted; **ser un h. duro de roer** to be a hard nut to crack; *Culin* **h. de santo** = small marzipan roll filled with egg yolk (b) *(de fruto)* *Br* stone, *US* pit (c) *Fam Fig (persona)* very strict person; *(asignatura)* difficult subject (d) *Méx Fam (enchufe)* contacts, influence; *(trabajo fácil)* cushy job

**huésped, -eda** *nm,f* guest

**hueste** *nf* *(ejército)* army; *Fig* **huestes** *(seguidores)* followers

**huesudo, -a** *adj* bony

**hueva** *nf* roe; **huevas de bacalao** cod roe

**huevada** *nf* *Arg, Chile Vulg* bollocks, crap

**huevear** *vi* *Am Fam* to muck about

**huevera** *nf* (a) *(para servir)* egg cup (b) *(para guardar)* egg box

**huevero, -a** *nm,f* egg seller

**huevo** *nm* **(a)** *(de animales)* egg; *Am* **h. a la copa** *o* **tibio** boiled egg; **h. duro** hard-boiled egg; **h. escalfado/frito** poached/fried egg; **h. pasado por agua** soft-boiled egg; **huevos al plato** = eggs cooked in the oven in an earthenware dish; **huevos revueltos** scrambled eggs **(b)** *Vulg* **huevos** *(testículos)* balls; **costar un h.** *(ser caro)* to cost a packet *o* bomb; *(ser difícil)* to be bloody hard; **saber un h.** to know a hell of a lot; **tener huevos** to have balls; **¡y un h.!** bollocks!, like hell!

**huevón, -ona** *Vulg* **1** *adj Am (vago)* lazy
**2** *nm CSur* stupid bastard

**hugonote, -a** *adj & nm,f* Huguenot

**huida** *nf* escape, flight

**huidizo, -a** *adj (esquivo)* shy, elusive; *(frente, mentón)* receding

**huir** [36] **1** *vi* **(a)** *(escapar) (de enemigo)* to flee **(de** from); *(de cárcel)* to escape **(de** from); **h. del país** to flee the country **(b) h. de algo** *(evitar)* to avoid sth, to keep away from sth
**2** *vt* to avoid

**huiro** *nm Chile* seaweed

**hule** *nm* oilskin

**hulla** *nf* soft coal

**hullero, -a** *adj* soft coal; **producción hullera** soft coal production

**humanidad** *nf* humanity; *Educ* **humanidades** humanities

**humanismo** *nm* humanism

**humanista 1** *adj* humanist, humanistic
**2** *nmf* humanist

**humanístico, -a** *adj* humanistic

**humanitario, -a** *adj* humanitarian

**humanitarismo** *nm* humanitarianism

**humanización** *nf* humanization, making more human

**humanizar** [16] **1** *vt* to humanize, to make more human
**2 humanizarse** *vpr* to become more human

**humano, -a 1** *adj* **(a)** *(del hombre)* human **(b)** *(compasivo)* humane
**2** *nm* human being; **los humanos** mankind

**humareda** *nf* cloud of smoke **¡qué h.!** what a lot of smoke!, it's so smoky!

**humazo** *nm* cloud of smoke

**humeante** *adj (que echa humo)* smoking; *(que echa vapor)* steaming

**humear** *vi (salir humo)* to (give off) smoke; *(salir vapor)* to steam

**humedad** *nf* **(a)** *(de suelo, tierra)* dampness; *(de pared, techo)* damp; *(de piel, ojos)* moistness; **hay mucha h. en la casa** the house is very damp **(b)** *(de atmósfera)* humidity

**humedecer** [48] **1** *vt* to moisten
**2 humedecerse** *vpr* to become moist; **humedecerse los labios** to moisten one's lips

**humedecimiento** *nm* moistening

**húmedo, -a** *adj* **(a)** *(suelo, tierra, casa)* damp; *(piel, ojos)* moist **(b)** *(aire, clima, atmósfera)* humid

**húmero** *nm Anat* humerus

**humidificador** *nm* humidifier

**humidificar** [61] *vt* to humidify

**humildad** *nf* humility

**humilde** *adj* humble

**humillación** *nf* humiliation

**humillado, -a** *adj* humiliated

**humillante** *adj* humiliating

**humillar 1** *vt* to humiliate
**2 humillarse** *vpr* to humble oneself; **humillarse a hacer algo** *(rebajarse)* to lower oneself to do sth, to stoop to doing sth

**humo** *nm (producto de combustión)* smoke; *(vapor)* steam; *(de vehículo)* fumes; *Fam* **bajarle a alguien los humos** to take sb down a peg or two; *Fam* **darse humos** to give oneself airs; *Fam Fig* **echar h.** to be fuming, to have smoke coming out of one's ears

**humor** *nm* **(a)** *(estado de ánimo)* mood; *(carácter)* temperament; **estar de buen/mal h.** to be in a good/bad mood; **estar de un h. de perros** to be in a filthy mood **(b)** *(gracia)* humour; **un programa de h.** a comedy programme; **h. negro** black humour **(c)** *(ganas)* mood; **no estoy de h.** I'm not in the mood **(d)** *Anat* humour

**humorismo** *nm (carácter burlón)* humour; *(en televisión, teatro)* comedy

**humorista** *nmf (persona burlona)* humorist; *(en televisión, teatro)* comedian, *f* comedienne

**humorístico, -a** *adj* humorous

**humoso, -a** *adj* smoky

**humus** *nm inv* humus

**hundimiento** *nm (de barco)* sinking; *Fig (ruina)* collapse

**hundir 1** *vt* **(a)** *(sumergir)* to sink; *Fig (esconder, introducir)* to bury; **hundió el cuchillo en su espalda** she buried the knife in his back; **hundió los dedos en su cabello** he ran his fingers through her hair **(b)** *Fig (afligir)* to devastate, to destroy **(c)** *Fig (hacer fracasar)* to ruin
**2 hundirse** *vpr* **(a)** *(sumergirse)* to sink; *(intencionadamente)* to dive **(b)** *(derrumbarse)* to collapse; *(techo)* to cave in **(c)** *Fig (fracasar)* to be ruined

**húngaro, -a 1** *adj & nm,f* Hungarian
**2** *nm (lengua)* Hungarian

**Hungría** *n* Hungary

**huno, -a 1** *adj* Hunnish
**2** *nm,f* Hun

**huracán** *nm* hurricane

**huracanado, -a** *adj Meteo (viento)* hurricane-force

**huraño, -a** *adj* unsociable

**hurgar** [40] **1** *vi (rebuscar)* to rummage around (**en** in); *(con dedo, palo)* to poke around (**en** in)

 **2 hurgarse** *vpr* **hurgarse la nariz** to pick one's nose; **hurgarse los bolsillos** to rummage around in one's pockets

**hurgón** *nm* poker

**hurgonear** *vt* to poke

**hurgue** *etc ver* **hurgar**

**Hurón** *nm* **lago H.** Lake Huron

**hurón** *nm* **(a)** *(animal)* ferret **(b)** *Fig (persona huraña)* unsociable person; *(persona fisgona)* nosey parker

**hurra** *interj* ¡h.! hurray!

**hurtadillas: a hurtadillas** *loc adv* on the sly, stealthily

**hurtar** *vt* to steal

**hurto** *nm* theft

**húsar** *nm Mil* hussar

**husmeador, -ora** *adj (perro)* sniffer; *(persona)* nosey, prying

**husmear 1** *vt (olfatear)* to sniff out, to scent

 **2** *vi (curiosear)* to nose around

**huso** *nm (para hilar)* spindle; *(en máquina)* bobbin; **h. horario** time zone

**huy** *interj* ¡h.! *(dolor)* ouch!; *(sorpresa)* gosh!

**huyera** *etc ver* **huir**

**huyo** *etc ver* **huir**

**I, i** [i] *nf (letra)* I, i

**IAE** *nm (abrev de* **Impuesto sobre Actividades Económicas**) = Spanish tax paid by professionals and shop owners

**ib.** *(abrev de* **ibídem**) ibid

**iba** *etc ver* **ir**

**ibérico, -a** *adj* Iberian

**íbero, -a** **1** *adj & nm,f* Iberian
  **2** *nm (lengua)* Iberian

**Iberoamérica** *n* Latin America

**iberoamericano, -a** *adj & nm,f* Latin American

**íbice** *nm* ibex

**ibicenco, -a** **1** *adj* of/from Ibiza
  **2** *nm,f* person from Ibiza

**ibíd.** *(abrev de* **ibídem**) ibid

**ibídem, ibidem** *adv* ibidem, ibid

**ibis** *nm inv* ibis

**ice** *etc ver* **izar**

**iceberg** [iθe'βer] *(pl* icebergs) *nm* iceberg

**ICI** *nm (abrev de* **Instituto de Cooperación Ibero-americana**) Institute for Latin American cooperation

**Icona** *nm (abrev de* **Instituto Nacional para la Conservación de la Naturaleza**) *Antes Br* ≃ NCC, = Spanish national institute for conservation

**icono** *nm* icon

**iconoclasta** **1** *adj* iconoclastic
  **2** *nmf* iconoclast

**iconografía** *nf* iconography

**iconográfico, -a** *adj* iconographical

**ictericia** *nf* jaundice

**ictiología** *nf* ichthyology

**I+D** ['imas'de] *(abrev de* **investigación y desarrollo**) R&D

**id** *ver* **ir**

**id.** *(abrev de* **ídem**) id., idem

**ida** *nf* outward journey; **a la i. fuimos en tren** we went by train on the way there; **(billete de) i. y vuelta** return (ticket); *Fig* **idas y venidas** comings and goings

**idea** *nf* **(a)** *(concepto, ocurrencia)* idea; *(propósito)* intention; **a mala i.** maliciously; **buena/mala i.** good/bad idea; **con la i. de** with the idea *o* intention of; **tener i. de hacer algo** to intend to do sth; **no tengo ni i. (de)** I don't have a clue (about); *Fig* **tener ideas de bombero** to have wild *o* crazy ideas; **tener una ligera i.** to have a vague idea; **i. fija** obsession; **ser una persona de ideas fijas** to be a person of fixed ideas; **i. brillante** brilliant idea, brainwave **(b)** *(opinión)* impression; **cambiar de i.** to change one's mind; **ideas** *(ideología)* ideas

**ideal** *adj & nm* ideal

**idealismo** *nm* idealism

**idealista** **1** *adj* idealistic
  **2** *nmf* idealist

**idealización** *nf* idealization

**idealizar** [16] *vt* to idealize

**idear** *vt* **(a)** *(planear)* to think up, to devise **(b)** *(inventar)* to invent

**ideario** *nm* ideology

**ídem** *pron* ditto; **i. de í.** *(lo mismo)* exactly the same; *(yo también)* same here

**idéntico, -a** *adj* identical (a to); **es i. a su abuelo** *(físicamente)* he's the image of his grandfather; *(en carácter)* he's exactly the same as his grandfather

**identidad** *nf* **(a)** *(de persona, pueblo)* identity **(b)** *(igualdad)* identical nature

**identificación** *nf* identification

**identificar** [61] **1** *vt* to identify
  **2 identificarse** *vpr* **identificarse con** *(persona, ideas)* to identify with; **¡identifíquese!** *(diga quién es)* identify yourself!; *(muestre una identificación)* show me some identification!

**ideograma** *nm* ideogram, ideograph

**ideología** *nf* ideology

**ideológico, -a** *adj* ideological

**ideólogo, -a** *nm,f* ideologist

**idílico, -a** *adj* idyllic

**idilio** *nm* love affair

**idioma** *nm* language

**idiomático, -a** *adj* idiomatic

**idiosincrasia** *nf* individual character

**idiosincrásico, -a** *adj* characteristic

**idiota 1** adj (a) (tonto) stupid (b) (enfermo) mentally deficient
  **2** nmf idiot

**idiotez** nf (a) (bobada) stupid thing, (bobería) stupidity (b) (enfermedad) mental deficiency

**idiotizar** [16] vt to turn into an idiot, to zombify

**ido, -a** adj mad, touched

**idólatra 1** adj también Fig idolatrous
  **2** nmf idolater, f idolatress; Fig idolizer

**idolatrar** vt to worship; Fig to idolize

**idolatría** nf también Fig idolatry

**ídolo** nm idol

**idoneidad** nf suitability

**idóneo, -a** adj suitable (**para** for)

**iglesia** nf church; **ir a la i.** to go to church; **con la i. hemos topado** now we're really up against it

**iglú** (pl **iglúes**) nm igloo

**ígneo, -a** adj igneous

**ignición** nf (de motor) ignition; **la chispa provocó la i. del combustible** the spark ignited the fuel

**ignífugo, -a** adj fireproof, flameproof

**ignominia** nf ignominy

**ignominioso, -a** adj ignominious

**ignorancia** nf ignorance; **i. supina** blind ignorance

**ignorante 1** adj ignorant; **i. de lo que ocurría** unaware of what was happening
  **2** nmf ignoramus

**ignorar** vt (a) (desconocer) not to know, to be ignorant of (b) (no tener en cuenta) to ignore

**ignoto, -a** adj unknown, undiscovered

**igual 1** adj (a) (idéntico) the same (**que** as); **llevan jerseys iguales** they're wearing the same jumper; **son iguales** they're the same (b) (parecido) similar (**que** to) (c) (equivalente) equal (**a** to) (d) (liso) even (e) (constante) (velocidad) constant; (clima, temperatura) even (f) Mat **A más B es i. a C** A plus B equals C
  **2** nmf equal; **sin i.** without equal, unrivalled
  **3** adv (a) (de la misma manera) the same; **yo pienso i.** I think the same, I think so too; **es muy alto, al i. que su padre** he's very tall, just like his father; **baila i. que la Pavlova** she dances just like Pavlova; **por i.** equally (b) (posiblemente) perhaps; **i. llueve** it could well rain (c) (expresiones) **dar** o **ser i. a alguien** to be all the same to sb; **es** o **da i.** it doesn't matter, it doesn't make any difference; Dep **van iguales** the scores are level

**igualación** nf (a) (de terreno) levelling; (de superficie) smoothing (b) (de cantidades) equalizing

**igualado, -a** adj (terreno) levelled, level; **de momento van igualados** they're level-pegging at the moment

**igualar 1** vt (a) (hacer igual) to make equal, to equalize; Dep to equalize; **i. algo a** o **con** to equate sth with (b) (persona) to be equal to; **nadie la iguala en generosidad** nobody is as generous as she is (c) (terreno) to level; (superficie) to smooth
  **2 igualarse** vpr (cosas diferentes) to become equal; **igualarse a** o **con** (otra persona, equipo) to become equal with, to match

**igualdad** nf (a) (equivalencia) equality; **en i. de condiciones** on equal terms; **i. de oportunidades** equal opportunities (b) (identidad) sameness

**igualitario, -a** adj egalitarian

**igualitarismo** nm egalitarianism

**igualmente** adv (a) (también) also, likewise (b) (fórmula de cortesía) the same to you, likewise

**iguana** nf iguana

**Iguazú** n (**las cataratas del**) **I.** the Iguaçu Falls

**ijada** nf, **ijar** nm flank, side

**ikastola** nf = primary school in the Basque country where classes are given entirely in Basque

**ikurriña** nf = Basque national flag

**ilación** nf cohesion

**ilegal** adj illegal

**ilegalidad** nf (a) (acción) unlawful act (b) (cualidad) illegality; **estar en la i.** to be illegal o outside the law

**ilegible** adj illegible

**ilegitimar** vt (logro) to invalidate; **su pasado lo ilegitima para ser alcalde** his past makes him unfit to be mayor; **sus infidelidades ilegitiman sus celos** her infidelities deny her the right to be jealous

**ilegitimidad** nf illegitimacy

**ilegítimo, -a** adj illegitimate; **hijo i.** illegitimate child

**ileso, -a** adj unhurt, unharmed; **salir** o **resultar i.** to escape unharmed

**iletrado, -a** adj & nm,f illiterate

**ilícito, -a** adj illicit

**ilimitado, -a** adj unlimited, limitless; **poder i.** absolute power

**ilógico, -a** adj illogical

**iluminación** nf (a) (luces) también Cine & Teatro lighting; (acción) illumination (b) Rel enlightenment

**iluminado, -a 1** adj (a) (con luz) lit (up) (b) Rel enlightened
  **2** nm,f Rel enlightened person

**iluminador, -ora 1** *adj* illuminating
**2** *nm,f* lighting technician

**iluminar 1** *vt* **(a)** *(dar luz a)* to illuminate, to light up **(b)** *Rel* to enlighten
**2** *vi* to give light; **la lámpara ilumina muy poco** the lamp doesn't give much light
**3 iluminarse** *vpr* **(a)** *(con luz)* to light up **(b)** *Rel* to become enlightened

**ilusión** *nf* **(a)** *(esperanza)* hope; *(infundada)* delusion, illusion; **hacerse** *o* **forjarse ilusiones** to build up one's hopes; **no te hagas demasiadas ilusiones** don't get your hopes up too much **(b)** *(emoción)* thrill, excitement; **¡qué i.!** how exciting!; **me hace mucha i.** I'm really looking forward to it **(c)** *(espejismo)* illusion

**ilusionar 1** *vt* **(a)** *(esperanzar)* **i. a alguien (con algo)** to build up sb's hopes (about sth) **(b)** *(emocionar)* to excite, to thrill
**2 ilusionarse** *vpr* **(a)** *(esperanzarse)* to get one's hopes up **(con** about) **(b)** *(emocionarse)* to get excited **(con** about)

**ilusionismo** *nm* conjuring, magic

**ilusionista** *nmf* conjurer, magician

**iluso, -a 1** *adj* naive
**2** *nm,f* naive person, dreamer

**ilusorio, -a** *adj* illusory; *(promesa)* empty

**ilustración** *nf* **(a)** *(estampa, dibujo)* illustration **(b)** *(cultura)* learning; **no tiene mucha i.** he doesn't have much education **(c)** *Hist* **la I.** the Enlightenment

**ilustrado, -a** *adj* **(a)** *(publicación)* illustrated **(b)** *(persona)* learned **(c)** *Hist* enlightened; **el despotismo i.** enlightened despotism

**ilustrador, -ora 1** *adj* illustrative
**2** *nm,f* illustrator

**ilustrar** *vt* **(a)** *(explicar)* to illustrate, to explain; **i. algo con un ejemplo** to illustrate sth with an example **(b)** *(publicación)* to illustrate **(c)** *(educar)* to enlighten

**ilustrativo, -a** *adj* illustrative

**ilustre** *adj* **(a)** *(distinguido)* illustrious, distinguished **(b)** *(título)* **el i. señor alcalde** his Worship, the mayor

**ilustrísimo, -a 1** *adj* **el i. ayuntamiento de Madrid** the City Council of Madrid
**2** *nf* **Su Ilustrísima** Your/His Grace, Your/His Worship

**imagen** *nf* *(figura)* image; *TV* picture; **a i. y semejanza** de identical to, exactly the same as; **imágenes del partido/de la catástrofe** pictures of the game/the disaster; **ser la viva i. de alguien** to be the spitting image of sb; **tener buena/mala i.** to have a good/bad image

**imaginable** *adj* imaginable, conceivable

**imaginación** *nf* **(a)** *(facultad)* imagination; **pasar por la i. de alguien** to occur to sb, to cross sb's mind; **no me pasó por la i.** it never occurred to me **(b)** *(idea falsa)* **imaginaciones** delusions, imaginings; **son imaginaciones tuyas** you're just imagining things, it's all in your mind

**imaginar 1** *vt* **(a)** *(figurarse)* to imagine **(b)** *(idear)* to think up, to invent
**2 imaginarse** *vpr* to imagine; **¡imagínate!** just think *o* imagine!; **me imagino que sí** I suppose so; *Fam* **¿te imaginas que viene?** what if he were to come?

**imaginaria** *nf* *(guardia)* sentry; **estar de imaginaria** to be on sentry duty

**imaginario, -a** *adj* imaginary

**imaginativo, -a** *adj* imaginative

**imaginería** *nf* religious image-making

**imán** *nm* **(a)** *(para atraer)* magnet **(b)** *(entre musulmanes)* imam

**imantación, imanación** *nf* magnetization

**imantar, imanar** *vt* to magnetize

**imbatible** *adj* unbeatable

**imbatido, -a** *adj* unbeaten

**imbebible** *adj* undrinkable

**imbécil 1** *adj* stupid
**2** *nmf* idiot

**imbecilidad** *nf* stupidity; **decir/hacer una i.** to say/do something stupid

**imberbe** *adj* beardless

**imborrable** *adj* *Fig* indelible; *(recuerdo)* unforgettable

**imbricación** *nf* overlap

**imbricado, -a** *adj* overlapping

**imbricar** **[61]** *vt* to make overlap

**imbuir** **[36]** *vt* to imbue **(de** with)

**imitación** *nf* imitation; *(de humorista)* impersonation; **a i. de** in imitation of; **piel de i.** imitation leather

**imitador, -ora** *nm,f* imitator; *(humorista)* impersonator

**imitamonas, imitamonos** *nmf inv Fam* copycat

**imitar** *vt* *(copiar)* to imitate, to copy; *(a personajes famosos)* to impersonate; *(producto, material)* to simulate

**imitativo, -a** *adj* imitative

**impaciencia** *nf* impatience

**impacientar 1** *vt* to make impatient, to exasperate
**2 impacientarse** *vpr* to grow impatient

**impaciente** *adj* impatient; **i. por hacer algo** impatient *o* anxious to do sth

**impactar 1** vt *(sujeto: noticia)* to have an impact on
**2** vi *(bala)* to hit

**impacto** nm (a) *(choque)* impact; *(de bala)* hit (b) *(señal)* (impact) mark; **i. de bala** bullethole; **i. ambiental** environmental impact (c) *Fig (impresión)* impact, strong impression; **causar un gran i. en alguien** to make a big impact o impression on sb

**impagable** adj invaluable

**impagado, -a 1** adj unpaid
**2** nm unpaid bill

**impago** nm non-payment

**impala** nm impala

**impalpable** adj impalpable

**impar** adj (a) *(número)* odd (b) *(sin igual)* unequalled

**imparable** adj unstoppable

**imparcial** adj impartial

**imparcialidad** nf impartiality

**impartir** vt to give; **i. clases** to teach

**impase, impasse** [im'pas] nm impasse

**impasibilidad** nf impassivity

**impasible** adj impassive

**impavidez** nf *(valor)* fearlessness, courage; *(impasibilidad)* impassivity

**impávido, -a** adj *(valeroso)* fearless, courageous; *(impasible)* impassive

**impecable** adj impeccable

**impedancia** nf impedance

**impedido, -a 1** adj disabled; **estar i. de un brazo** to have the use of only one arm
**2** nm,f disabled person

**impedimenta** nf baggage, appurtenances

**impedimento** nm *(obstáculo)* obstacle; *(para el matrimonio)* impediment; **no hay ningún i. para hacerlo** there's no reason why we shouldn't do it

**impedir** [49] vt (a) *(imposibilitar)* to prevent; **i. a alguien hacer algo** to prevent sb from doing sth; **impedirle el paso a alguien** to bar sb's way; **nada te impide hacerlo** there's nothing to stop you doing it (b) *(dificultar)* to hinder, to obstruct

**impeler** vt (a) *(hacer avanzar)* to propel (b) *(incitar)* **i. a alguien a algo/hacer algo** to drive sb to sth/to do sth

**impenetrabilidad** nf *también Fig* impenetrability

**impenetrable** adj *también Fig* impenetrable

**impenitencia** nf impenitence

**impenitente** adj unrepentant, impenitent; *Fig (incorregible)* inveterate

**impensable** adj unthinkable

**impensado, -a** adj unexpected

**impepinable** adj *Fam (argumento)* undeniable, unanswerable; **¡eso es i.!** that's for sure!

**imperante** adj prevailing

**imperar** vi to prevail

**imperativo, -a 1** adj (a) *también Gram* imperative (b) *(autoritario)* imperious
**2** nm *también Gram* imperative

**imperceptible** adj imperceptible

**imperdible** nm safety pin

**imperdonable** adj unforgivable

**imperecedero, -a** adj *(producto)* nonperishable; *Fig (eterno)* immortal, eternal

**imperfección** nf (a) *(cualidad)* imperfection (b) *(defecto)* flaw, defect

**imperfecto, -a 1** adj *(no perfecto)* imperfect; *(defectuoso)* faulty, defective; *Gram* **pretérito i.** (past) imperfect
**2** nm *Gram* imperfect

**imperial** adj imperial

**imperialismo** nm imperialism

**imperialista** adj & nmf imperialist

**impericia** nf *(torpeza)* lack of skill; *(inexperiencia)* inexperience

**imperio** nm (a) *(territorio)* empire (b) *(dominio)* rule; **valer un i.** to be worth a fortune (c) *(mandato)* emperorship

**imperioso, -a** adj (a) *(autoritario)* imperious (b) *(apremiante)* urgent, pressing

**impermeabilidad** nf impermeability

**impermeabilización** nf waterproofing

**impermeabilizante** adj waterproofing

**impermeabilizar** [16] vt to (make) waterproof

**impermeable 1** adj waterproof
**2** nm raincoat, *Br* mac

**impersonal** adj impersonal

**impertérrito, -a** adj *(impávido)* unperturbed, unmoved; *(ante peligros)* fearless

**impertinencia** nf (a) *(cualidad)* impertinence (b) *(comentario)* impertinent remark

**impertinente 1** adj impertinent; **ponerse i.** to be impertinent o rude
**2** nmf *(persona)* impertinent person
**3** nmpl **impertinentes** *(anteojos)* lorgnette

**imperturbabilidad** nf imperturbability

**imperturbable** adj imperturbable

**ímpetu** nm (a) *(brusquedad)* force (b) *(energía)* energy; **perder í.** to lose momentum

**impetuosidad** nf *(precipitación)* impetuosity

**impetuoso, -a 1** adj (a) *(olas, viento, ataque)* violent (b) *Fig (persona)* impulsive, impetuous
**2** nm,f impulsive person

**impidiera** etc ver **impedir**

**impido** etc ver **impedir**

**impío, -a** adj godless, impious

**implacable** *adj* implacable, relentless

**implantación** *nf* (a) *(establecimiento)* introduction (b) *Biol* implantation (c) *Med* insertion

**implantar1** *vt* (a) *(establecer)* to introduce (b) *Med* to insert

**2 implantarse** *vpr* (a) *(establecerse)* to be introduced (b) *Biol* to become implanted

**implante** *nm* implant

**implementar** *vt* to implement

**implemento** *nm* implement

**implicación** *nf* (a) *(participación)* involvement (b) **implicaciones** *(consecuencias)* implications

**implicar** [61] **1** *vt* (a) *(involucrar)* to involve (**en** in); *Der* to implicate (**en** in) (b) *(significar, suponer)* to mean, to imply

**2 implicarse** *vpr Der* to incriminate oneself; **implicarse en** to become involved in

**implícito, -a** *adj* implicit

**imploración** *nf* entreaty, plea

**implorar** *vt* to implore

**impoluto, -a** *adj* unpolluted, pure; *Fig* unblemished, untarnished

**imponderabilidad** *nf* imponderability

**imponderable 1** *adj* *(incalculable)* invaluable; *(imprevisible)* imponderable

**2** *nm* imponderable

**imponente** *adj* (a) *(impresionante)* imposing, impressive (b) *Fam (estupendo)* sensational, terrific; **¡la profesora está i.!** the teacher is a stunner!

**imponer** [52] **1** *vt* (a) **i. algo (a alguien)** *(forzar a aceptar)* to impose sth (on sb); **i. respeto** to command respect; **el profesor impuso silencio en la clase** the teacher silenced the class (b) *(moda)* to set; *(costumbre)* to introduce

**2** *vi* to be imposing

**3 imponerse** *vpr* (a) *(hacerse respetar)* to command respect, to show authority (b) *(prevalecer)* to prevail (c) *(asumir)* *(obligación, tarea)* to take on (d) *(ser necesario)* to be necessary (e) *Dep* to win, to prevail

**imponible** *adj* *Fin* **base i.** taxable income

**impopular** *adj* unpopular

**impopularidad** *nf* unpopularity

**importación** *nf* *(acción)* importing; *(artículo)* import; **de i.** imported

**importador, -ora 1** *adj* importing; **empresa importadora** importer, importing company

**2** *nm,f* importer

**importancia** *nf* importance; **dar i. a algo** to attach importance to sth; **darse i.** to give oneself airs; **de i.** important, of importance; **no tiene i.** *(no es importante)* it's not important; *(no pasa nada)* it doesn't matter; **sin i.** unimportant; **quitar i. a algo** to play sth down

**importante** *adj* (a) *(destacado, significativo)* important; *(lesión)* serious (b) *(cantidad)* considerable

**importar 1** *vt* (a) *(productos)* & *Informát* to import (b) *(sujeto: factura, coste)* to amount to, to come to

**2** *vi* (a) *(preocupar)* to matter; **no importa** it doesn't matter; *Fig* **¡no te importa!** it's none of your business!; **¿a mí qué me importa?** what's that to me?, what do I care?; **¿y a ti qué te importa?** what's it got to do with you?; *Fam* **me importa un bledo** *o* **comino** *o* **pito** I don't give a damn, I couldn't care less (b) *(en preguntas)* to mind; **¿le importa que me siente?** do you mind if I sit down?; **¿te importaría acompañarme?** would you mind coming with me?

**3** *v impersonal* to matter; **¡qué importa que llueva!** so what if it's raining?

**importe** *nm* *(precio)* price, cost; *(de factura)* total; **i. total** total cost

**importunar 1** *vt* to bother, to pester

**2** *vi* to be tiresome *o* a nuisance

**importuno, -a** *adj* (a) *(en mal momento)* inopportune, untimely (b) *(molesto)* inconvenient (c) *(inadecuado)* inappropriate

**imposibilidad** *nf* impossibility; **su i. para contestar la pregunta** his inability to answer the question; **i. física** physical impossibility

**imposibilitado, -a** *adj* disabled; **estar i. para hacer algo** to be unable to do sth

**imposibilitar** *vt* **i. a alguien (para) hacer algo** to make it impossible for sb to do sth, to prevent sb from doing sth

**imposible 1** *adj* (a) *(irrealizable)* impossible (b) *(insoportable)* unbearable, impossible

**2** *nm* **hacer lo i.** to do everything possible and more; **pedir imposibles** to ask for the impossible

**imposición** *nf* (a) *(obligación)* imposition (b) *(impuesto)* tax; **doble i.** double taxation (c) *Com* deposit; **hacer** *o* **efectuar una i.** to make a deposit (d) **i. de manos** laying on of hands

**impositivo, -a** *adj* tax; **política impositiva** tax *o* taxation policy

**impostar** *vt* *(la voz)* to make resonate

**impostergable** *adj* (extremely) urgent, impossible to postpone

**impostor, -ora 1** *adj* *(suplantador)* fraudulent

**2** *nm,f* *(suplantador)* impostor

**impostura** *nf* (a) *(suplantación)* fraud (b) *(calumnia)* slander

**impotencia** *nf* impotence

**impotente 1** *adj* impotent

**2** *nm* impotent man

**impracticable** *adj* (a) *(irrealizable)* impracticable (b) *(intransitable)* impassable

**imprecación** *nf* imprecation

**imprecar** [61] *vt* to imprecate

**imprecatorio, -a** *adj* imprecatory

**imprecisión** *nf* imprecision, vagueness; **contestó con imprecisiones** he gave vague answers

**impreciso, -a** *adj* imprecise, vague

**impredecible** *adj* *(inesperado)* unforeseeable; *(imprevisible)* unpredictable

**impregnar 1** *vt* to impregnate (**de** with)
**2 impregnarse** *vpr* to become impregnated (**de** with)

**impremeditación** *nf* lack of premeditation

**impremeditado, -a** *adj* unpremeditated

**imprenta** *nf* (a) *(máquina)* (printing) press (b) *(establecimiento)* printing house

**imprescindible** *adj* indispensable, essential

**impresentable 1** *adj* unpresentable
**2** *nmf* **es un i.** he's a disgrace

**impresión** *nf* (a) *(efecto)* impression; *(sensación física)* feeling; **causar (una) buena/mala i.** to make a good/bad impression; **dar la i. de** to give the impression of; **me causó mucha i. esa película** that film had a great effect on me; **tener la i. de que** to have the impression that (b) *(opinión)* **cambiar impresiones** to compare notes, to exchange views (c) *(huella)* imprint; **i. digital** *o* **dactilar** fingerprint (d) *Imprenta (acción)* printing; *(edición)* edition

**impresionable** *adj* impressionable

**impresionante** *adj* *(asombroso, extraordinario)* amazing, astonishing; *(maravilloso)* impressive; *(grande)* enormous

**impresionar 1** *vt* (a) *(maravillar)* to impress; *(emocionar)* to move; *(conmocionar, horrorizar)* to shock (b) *Fot* to expose
**2** *vi (maravillar)* to make an impression; *(emocionar)* to be moving; *(conmocionar, horrorizar)* to be shocking
**3 impresionarse** *vpr (maravillarse)* to be impressed; *(emocionarse)* to be moved; *(conmocionarse, horrorizarse)* to be shocked

**impresionismo** *nm* impressionism

**impresionista** *adj & nmf* impressionist

**impreso, -a 1** *participio ver* **imprimir**
**2** *adj* printed
**3** *nm* (a) *(texto)* printed sheet, printed matter (b) *(formulario)* form; **impresos (en sobre)** printed matter

**impresora** *nf Informát* printer; **i. láser/térmica** laser/thermal printer; **i. matricial** *o* **de agujas** dot-matrix printer; **i. de chorro de tinta** ink-jet printer

**impresor, -ora** *nm,f (persona)* printer

**imprevisible** *adj* *(inesperado)* unforeseeable; *(impredecible)* unpredictable; **el tiempo aquí es muy i.** the weather here is very unpredictable; **una persona i.** an unpredictable person

**imprevisión** *nf* lack of foresight

**imprevisto, -a 1** *adj* unexpected
**2** *nm (hecho)* unforeseen circumstance; **salvo imprevistos** barring accidents; **imprevistos** *(gastos)* unforeseen expenses

**imprimir 1** *vt* (a) *(libro, documento)* to print; *(huella, paso)* to leave, to make (b) *Fig* **i. algo a** to impart *o* bring sth to; **i. velocidad a algo** to speed sth up
**2** *vi* to print

**improbabilidad** *nf* improbability, unlikelihood

**improbable** *adj* improbable, unlikely

**improbo, -a** *adj Formal (trabajo, esfuerzo)* Herculean, strenuous

**improcedencia** *nf* (a) *(desacierto)* inappropriateness (b) *Der* inadmissibility

**improcedente** *adj* (a) *(inoportuno)* inappropriate (b) *Der* inadmissible

**improductivo, -a** *adj* unproductive

**impronta** *nf* mark, impression; **llevar la i. de** to have the hallmarks of

**impronunciable** *adj* unpronounceable

**improperio** *nm* insult; **lanzar improperios** to let fly insults

**impropiedad** *nf* impropriety

**impropio, -a** *adj* improper (**de** for), unbecoming (**de** to)

**improrrogable** *adj* *(plazo)* unextendable; **durante seis días improrrogables** for six days only; **la fecha es i.** the deadline is final

**improvisación** *nf* improvisation

**improvisado, -a** *adj* *(comida, actuación artística)* improvised; *(discurso)* impromptu; *(comentario)* ad-lib; *(cama, refugio)* makeshift

**improvisar 1** *vt (discurso, plan )* to improvise; *(comida)* to rustle up, to improvise; **i. una cama** to make (up) a makeshift bed
**2** *vi (músico, orador)* to improvise; *(actor)* to ad-lib

**improviso: de improviso** *loc adv* unexpectedly, suddenly; **coger a alguien de i.** to catch sb unawares

**imprudencia** *nf* (a) *(falta de prudencia) (en los actos)* carelessness, recklessness; *(en los comentarios)* indiscretion; *Der* **i. temeraria** criminal negligence (b) *(acción)* careless *o* reckless act, indiscretion; *(dicho indiscreto)* tactless remark, indiscretion; *(dicho desacertado)* foolish *o* reckless remark

**imprudente 1** adj (en los actos) careless, rash; (en los comentarios) indiscreet; **es muy i.** (al conducir) he's a reckless driver

**2** nmf (en los actos) rash o reckless person; (en los comentarios) indiscreet person

**impúber 1** adj pre-pubescent

**2** nmf pre-pubescent child

**impudicia** nf immodesty

**impúdico, -a** adj immodest, indecent

**impudor** nm immodesty

**impuesto, -a 1** participio ver **imponer**

**2** nm tax; **i. al consumo** tax on the consumer; **i. directo/indirecto** direct/indirect tax; **i. de lujo** luxury tax; **i. municipal** local tax; Fig **i. revolucionario** revolutionary tax, = protection money paid by businessmen to terrorists; **i. sobre el capital** capital tax; **i. sobre el valor añadido** value-added tax; **i. sobre la renta** income tax

**impugnable** adj contestable

**impugnación** nf contestation, challenge

**impugnar** vt to contest, to challenge

**impulsar** vt (a) (empujar) to propel, to drive (b) (incitar) **i. a alguien (a algo/a hacer algo)** to drive sb (to sth/to do sth) (c) (promocionar) (economía) to stimulate; (amistad) to foster

**impulsivo, -a 1** adj impulsive

**2** nm,f impulsive person, hothead

**impulso** nm (a) (progreso) stimulus, boost (b) (fuerza) momentum; **tomar i.** to take a run-up (c) (deseo, motivación) impulse, urge; **sentir el i. de hacer algo** to feel the urge to do sth

**impulsor, -ora 1** adj driving; **fuerza impulsora** driving force

**2** nm,f dynamic force; **él fue el i. del proyecto** he was the driving force behind the project

**impune** adj unpunished; **quedar i.** to go unpunished

**impunemente** adv with impunity

**impunidad** nf impunity

**impuntual** adj unpunctual

**impuntualidad** nf unpunctuality

**impureza** nf impurity

**impuro, -a** adj también Fig impure

**impusiera** etc ver **imponer**

**imputabilidad** nf imputability

**imputable** adj attributable (**a** to)

**imputación** nf accusation

**imputar** vt (a) (atribuir) **i. algo a alguien** (delito) to accuse sb of sth; (fracaso, error) to attribute sth to sb (b) Com to allocate, to assign

**inabarcable** adj unmanageable

**inabordable** adj inaccessible

**inacabable** adj interminable, endless

**inacabado, -a** adj unfinished

**inaccesible** adj inaccessible

**inacción** nf inaction, inactivity

**inaceptable** adj unacceptable

**inactividad** nf inactivity

**inactivo, -a** adj inactive

**inadaptación** nf maladjustment

**inadaptado, -a 1** adj maladjusted

**2** nm,f misfit

**inadecuado, -a** adj (inapropiado) unsuitable, inappropriate

**inadmisible** adj inadmissible

**inadvertido, -a** adj unnoticed; **pasar i.** to go unnoticed

**inagotable** adj inexhaustible

**inaguantable** adj unbearable

**inalámbrico, -a** adj cordless

**in albis** adv in the dark; **quedarse i.** to be left none the wiser

**inalcanzable** adj unattainable

**inalienable** adj inalienable

**inalterable** adj (a) (salud) stable; (amistad) undying; (principios) unshakeable; (decisión) final; **permanecer i.** to remain unchanged (b) (color) fast (c) (rostro, carácter) impassive (d) Dep **el marcador permanece i.** the score remains unchanged

**inamovible** adj immovable, fixed

**inane** adj Formal inane

**inanición** nf starvation; **morir de i.** to die of starvation, to starve to death

**inanimado, -a** adj inanimate

**inánime** adj lifeless

**inapagable** adj inextinguishable

**inapelable** adj (a) Der not open to appeal (b) Fig (inevitable) inevitable

**inapetencia** nf lack of appetite

**inapetente** adj lacking in appetite; **estar i.** to have no appetite

**inaplazable** adj (reunión, sesión) that cannot be postponed; (necesidad) urgent, pressing

**inaplicable** adj inapplicable, not applicable

**inapreciable** adj (a) (incalculable) invaluable, inestimable (b) (insignificante) imperceptible

**inapropiado, -a** adj inappropriate, unsuitable

**inarrugable** adj crease-resistant

**inasequible** adj (a) (por el precio) prohibitive (b) (inalcanzable) (meta, ambición) unattainable; (persona) unapproachable

**inatacable** adj unassailable; Fig irrefutable

**inaudible** adj inaudible

**inaudito, -a** adj unheard-of

**inauguración** nf (de edificio, puente, Juegos Olímpicos) official opening, opening (ceremony); (de congreso) opening session

**inaugural** adj opening, inaugural

**inaugurar** vt *(edificio, congreso)* to (officially) open; *(año académico, época)* to mark the beginning of, to inaugurate; *(estatua)* to unveil

**inca** adj & nmf Inca

**incaico, -a** adj Inca

**incalculable** adj incalculable; **de i. valor** priceless; *Fig* of inestimable value

**incalificable** adj unspeakable, indescribable

**incandescente** adj incandescent

**incansable** adj untiring, tireless

**incapacidad** nf **(a)** *(imposibilidad)* inability **(b)** *(falta de aptitud)* incompetence **(c)** *Der* incapacity; **i. laboral** industrial disablement *o* disability

**incapacitado, -a 1** adj *Der (para ejercer cargos, votar)* disqualified **(para** from); *(para testar, testificar)* incapacitated; *(para trabajar)* unfit
   **2** nm,f *Der* disqualified person, person declared unfit

**incapacitar** vt **(a)** *(sujeto: circunstancias) (para ejercer cargos, votar)* to disqualify **(para** from); *(para trabajar)* to render unfit **(para** for) **(b)** *(sujeto: juez) (para ejercer cargos, votar)* to disqualify **(para** from), to declare disqualified **(para** from); *(para trabajar)* to declare unfit **(para** for *or* to)

**incapaz** adj **(a)** *(no capaz)* incapable **(de** of); **es i. de hacer daño a nadie** he would never harm anyone **(b)** *(sin talento)* **i. para** incompetent at, no good at; **es i. de hacer una suma sin equivocarse** he can't do the simplest sum without making a mistake **(c)** *Der* **declarar i. a alguien** to declare sb incapable *o* unfit

**incautación** nf seizure, confiscation

**incautarse** vpr **(a)** *Der* **i. de** to seize, to confiscate **(b)** *(apoderarse)* **i. de** to grab

**incauto, -a 1** adj gullible, naive
   **2** nm,f gullible *o* naive person

**incendiar** [15] **1** vt to set fire to
   **2 incendiarse** vpr to catch fire; **se ha incendiado el bosque** the forest has caught fire *o* is on fire

**incendiario, -a 1** adj *(bomba)* incendiary; *Fig (artículo, libro)* inflammatory
   **2** nm,f arsonist, fire-raiser

**incendio** nm fire; **i. forestal** forest fire; **i. provocado** arson

**incensario** nm censer

**incentivar** vt to encourage

**incentivo** nm incentive

**incertidumbre** nf uncertainty

**incesante** adj incessant, ceaseless

**incesto** nm incest

**incestuoso, -a** adj incestuous

**incidencia** nf **(a)** *(repercusión)* impact, effect **(b)** *(suceso)* event; **el viaje transcurrió sin incidencias** the journey passed without incident

**incidental** adj incidental

**incidente 1** adj *(luz, rayo)* incident
   **2** nm incident; **el viaje transcurrió sin incidentes** the journey passed without incident

**incidir** vi **i. en (a)** *(incurrir en)* to fall into, to lapse into; *(insistir en)* to focus on; *(influir en)* to have an impact on, to affect

**incienso** nm incense; **oro, i. y mirra** gold, frankincense and myrrh

**incierto, -a** adj **(a)** *(dudoso)* uncertain **(b)** *(falso)* untrue

**incineración** nf *(de cadáver)* cremation; *(de basura)* incineration

**incinerador** nm *(de basura)* incinerator

**incinerar** vt *(cadáver)* to cremate; *(basura)* to incinerate

**incipiente** adj *(inicial)* incipient; **una democracia i.** a fledgling democracy; **una amistad i.** a budding friendship

**incisión** nf incision

**incisivo, -a 1** adj **(a)** *(instrumento)* sharp, cutting **(b)** *Fig (mordaz)* incisive **(c)** *(diente)* incisive
   **2** nm *(diente)* incisor

**inciso** nm *(corto)* comment, passing remark; *(más largo)* digression

**incitación** nf incitement

**incitante** adj *(insinuante)* provocative; *(interesante)* enticing

**incitar** vt *(a la violencia)* to incite; **el hambre le incitó a robar** hunger made him steal; **¿qué le incitó a hacerlo?** what made him do it?

**incivil** adj uncivil

**inclasificable** adj unclassifiable

**inclemencia** nf harshness, inclemency; **las inclemencias del tiempo** the inclemency of the weather

**inclemente** adj harsh, inclement

**inclinación** nf **(a)** *(desviación)* slant, inclination; *(de terreno)* slope **(b)** *Fig (afición)* penchant *o* propensity **(a** *o* **por** for); **tiene una i. natural por la música** she has a natural bent for music **(c)** *(cariño)* **i. hacia alguien** fondness towards sb **(d)** *(saludo)* bow; **nos saludó con una i. de cabeza** he greeted us with a nod

**inclinar 1** vt **(a)** *(doblar)* to bend; *(ladear)* to tilt; *Fig* **i. la balanza a favor de** to tip the balance in favour of **(b)** *(cabeza)* to bow **(c)** *(influir)* **i. a alguien a hacer algo** to persuade sb to do sth
   **2 inclinarse** vpr **(a)** *(doblarse)* to lean **(b)** *(para saludar)* to bow **(ante** before) **(c)** *(tender)* to be *o* feel inclined **(a** to); **me inclino a pensar que no** I'm rather inclined to think not **(d)**

*(preferir)* **inclinarse por** to favour, to lean towards

**incluir** [36] *vt (comprender)* to include; *(adjuntar)* to enclose

**inclusa** *nf* foundling hospital

**inclusión** *nf* inclusion

**inclusive** *adv* inclusive

**incluso** *adv & prep* even

**incógnita** *nf* (a) *Mat* unknown (quantity) (b) *(misterio)* mystery

**incógnito, -a** *adj* unknown; **viajar/estar de i.** to travel/be incognito

**incoherencia** *nf* (a) *(cualidad)* incoherence (b) *(comentario)* nonsensical remark

**incoherente** *adj* (a) *(inconexo)* incoherent (b) *(inconsecuente)* inconsistent

**incoloro, -a** *adj también Fig* colourless

**incólume** *adj Formal* unscathed

**incombustible** *adj* fire-resistant

**incomestible, incomible** *adj* inedible

**incomodar 1** *vt* (a) *(causar molestia)* to bother, to inconvenience (b) *(enfadar)* to annoy

**2 incomodarse** *vpr (enfadarse)* to get annoyed (**por** about)

**incomodidad** *nf* (a) *(de silla)* uncomfortableness (b) *(de situación, persona)* awkwardness, discomfort

**incómodo, -a** *adj* (a) *(silla, postura)* uncomfortable (b) *(situación)* awkward, uncomfortable; **sentirse i.** to feel awkward *o* uncomfortable

**incomparable** *adj* incomparable

**incomparecencia** *nf* failure to appear (in court)

**incompatibilidad** *nf* incompatibility; *Der* **i. de caracteres** incompatibility

**incompatible** *adj* incompatible (**con** with)

**incompetencia** *nf* incompetence

**incompetente** *adj* incompetent

**incompleto, -a** *adj* (a) *(falto de una parte)* incomplete (b) *(inacabado)* unfinished

**incomprendido, -a 1** *adj* misunderstood

**2** *nm,f* misunderstood person; **fue siempre un i.** no one ever understood him

**incomprensible** *adj* incomprehensible

**incomprensión** *nf* lack of understanding

**incomunicación** *nf* (a) *(falta de comunicación)* lack of communication (b) *(de detenido)* solitary confinement (c) *(de una localidad)* isolation

**incomunicado, -a** *adj* **estar i.** *(sin líneas de comunicación)* to be isolated; *(por la nieve)* to be cut off; *(preso)* to be in solitary confinement; *(detenido)* to be held incommunicado

**incomunicar** [61] *vt (dejar sin líneas de comunicación)* to keep isolated; *(sujeto: la nieve)* to cut off; *(preso)* to place in solitary confinement; *(detenido)* to hold incommunicado

**inconcebible** *adj* inconceivable

**inconcluso, -a** *adj* unfinished

**incondicional 1** *adj (rendición, perdón)* unconditional; *(ayuda)* wholehearted; *(seguidor)* staunch

**2** *nmf* staunch supporter

**inconexo, -a** *adj (parte)* unconnected; *(pensamiento, texto)* disjointed

**inconfesable** *adj* shameful

**inconformismo** *nm* nonconformism

**inconformista** *adj & nmf* nonconformist

**inconfundible** *adj* unmistakable

**incongruencia** *nf (cualidad)* inconsistency; **hacer/decir una i.** *(algo fuera de lugar)* to do/say sth incongruous; *(algo absurdo)* to do/say sth crazy *o* illogical; **lleno de incongruencias** *(relato, libro)* full of inconsistencies

**incongruente** *adj (fuera de lugar)* incongruous; *(desarticulado)* inconsistent; *(absurdo)* crazy, illogical

**inconmensurable** *adj (enorme)* vast, immense

**inconquistable** *adj* unassailable, impregnable

**inconsciencia** *nf* (a) *(aturdimiento, desmayo)* unconsciousness (b) *Fig (falta de juicio)* thoughtlessness

**inconsciente 1** *adj* (a) *(sin conocimiento)* unconscious; **estar i.** to be unconscious; **un acto i.** an unconscious action (b) *Fig (irreflexivo)* thoughtless, reckless

**2** *nmf* thoughtless *o* reckless person

**3** *nm Psi* **el i.** the unconscious

**inconscientemente** *adv (sin darse cuenta)* unconsciously, unwittingly

**inconsecuencia** *nf* inconsistency

**inconsecuente 1** *adj* inconsistent

**2** *nmf* inconsistent person

**inconsistencia** *nf* flimsiness

**inconsistente** *adj* flimsy, insubstantial

**inconsolable** *adj* disconsolate

**inconstancia** *nf* (a) *(en el trabajo, la conducta)* unreliability (b) *(de opinión, ideas)* changeability

**inconstante** *adj* (a) *(en el trabajo)* **es muy i.** he never sticks at anything (b) *(de opinión, ideas)* changeable, fickle

**inconstitucional** *adj* unconstitutional

**inconstitucionalidad** *nf* unconstitutionality

**incontable** *adj (innumerable)* countless, innumerable

**incontenible** adj (alegría) unbounded; (llanto) uncontrollable

**incontestable** adj indisputable, undeniable

**incontinencia** nf (a) (vicio) lack of restraint (b) Med incontinence

**incontinente** adj (a) (insaciable) lacking all restraint (b) Med incontinent

**incontrolable** adj uncontrollable

**incontrolado, -a** adj (velocidad) furious; (situación) out of hand; (comando) maverick, not controlled by the leadership; (aumento de precios) spiralling

**incontrovertible** adj incontrovertible, indisputable

**inconveniencia** nf (a) (inoportunidad) inappropriateness (b) (comentario) tactless remark; (acto) faux pas, mistake

**inconveniente 1** adj (a) (inoportuno) inappropriate (b) (descortés) rude

**2** nm (a) (dificultad) obstacle, problem; **no tener i. en hacer algo** to have no objection to doing sth (b) (desventaja) disadvantage, drawback

**incordiar** [15] vt Fam to bother, to pester

**incordio** nm Fam pain, nuisance

**incorporación** nf (unión, adición) incorporation (a into); **su i. tendrá lugar el día 31** (a un puesto) she starts work on the 31st

**incorporado, -a** adj Mec built-in; **llevar o tener algo i.** to have sth built in

**incorporar 1** vt (a) (añadir) to incorporate (a into); Culin to mix (a into); **incorporaron los territorios al imperio** the territories became part of the empire (b) (levantar) **i. a alguien** to sit sb up

**2 incorporarse** vpr (a) (unirse) (a equipo) to join; (a trabajo) to start; **incorporarse a filas** to start one's military service (b) (levantarse) to sit up

**incorpóreo, -a** adj incorporeal, intangible

**incorrección** nf (a) (falta de corrección) incorrectness; (error gramatical) mistake (b) (descortesía) lack of courtesy, rudeness

**incorrecto, -a** adj (a) (equivocado) incorrect, wrong (b) (descortés) rude, impolite

**incorregible** adj incorrigible

**incorruptible** adj (substancia) imperishable; Fig (persona) incorruptible

**incorrupto, -a** adj (cadáver) uncorrupted, not decomposed

**incredulidad** nf incredulity

**incrédulo, -a 1** adj sceptical, incredulous; Rel unbelieving

**2** nm,f unbeliever

**increíble** adj (difícil de creer) unconvincing, lacking credibility; Fig (extraordinario) incredible; Fig (inconcebible) unbelievable; **es i. que pasen cosas así** it's hard to believe that such things can happen

**incrementar 1** vt to increase

**2 incrementarse** vpr to increase

**incremento** nm (de precios, actividad) increase; (de temperatura) rise

**increpar** vt (a) (reprender) to reprimand (b) (insultar) to abuse, insult

**incriminación** nf accusation

**incriminar** vt to accuse

**incruento, -a** adj bloodless

**incrustación** nf inlay; **un marco con incrustaciones de oro** a frame with a gold inlay o inlaid with gold

**incrustado, -a** adj (a) (encajado) **i. en** fixed into (b) **con rubíes incrustados** inlaid with rubies

**incrustar 1** vt (introducir, empotrar) **i. nácar en la madera** to inlay the wood with mother of pearl; Fam Fig **me incrustó un codo en el costado** he jabbed o rammed his elbow into my ribs

**2 incrustarse** vpr (introducirse, empotrarse) **la bala se incrustó en el hueso/muro** the bullet embedded itself in the bone/wall; **el coche se incrustó en el muro** the car ploughed into the wall; **la cal se había incrustado en las tuberías** the pipes had become furred up

**incubación** nf (de huevos, enfermedad) incubation; **i. artificial** artificial incubation; **período de i.** (de enfermedad) incubation period

**incubadora** nf incubator

**incubar** vt (a) (huevo) to incubate (b) (enfermedad) to be sickening for

**incuestionable** adj (teoría, razón) irrefutable; (deber) bounden

**inculcar** [61] vt **i. algo a alguien** to instil sth into sb

**inculpación** nf accusation; Der charge

**inculpado, -a 1** adj accused; Der charged

**2** nm,f accused

**inculpar** vt (acusar) to accuse (de of); Der to charge (de with); **todas las pruebas le inculpan** all the evidence points to his guilt

**inculto, -a 1** adj (a) (persona) uneducated (b) (tierra) uncultivated

**2** nm,f ignoramus

**incultura** nf lack of education

**incumbencia** nf **es/no es de nuestra i.** it is/isn't a matter for us, it falls/doesn't fall within our area of responsibility; **no es asunto de tu i.** it's none of your business

**incumbir** *vi* **i. a alguien** to be a matter for sb, to be within sb's area of responsibility; **esto no te incumbe** this is none of your business

**incumplimiento** *nm (de deber)* failure to fulfil; *(de orden, ley)* non-compliance; *(de promesa)* failure to keep; **i. de contrato** breach of contract

**incumplir** *vt (deber)* to fail to fulfil, to neglect; *(orden, ley)* to fail to comply with; *(promesa)* to break; *(contrato)* to breach

**incunable 1** *adj* incunabular
   **2** *nm* incunabulum

**incurable** *adj también Fig* incurable

**incurrir** *vi* **i. en** *(delito, falta)* to commit; *(error)* to make; *(desprecio, castigo)* to incur

**incursión** *nf* incursion; *Fig* **hicieron una i. en la cocina** they raided the kitchen

**indagación** *nf* investigation, inquiry

**indagar** [40] **1** *vt* to investigate, to inquire into
   **2** *vi* to investigate, to inquire

**indebido, -a** *adj* **(a)** *(incorrecto)* improper **(b)** *(ilegal)* unlawful, illegal

**indecencia** *nf* **(a)** *(cualidad)* indecency **(b)** **¡es una i.!** *(es impúdico)* it's not decent!; *(es indignante)* it's outrageous!

**indecente** *adj* **(a)** *(impúdico)* indecent **(b)** *(indigno)* miserable, wretched

**indecible** *adj* indescribable, unspeakable

**indecisión** *nf* indecisiveness

**indeciso, -a** *adj* **(a)** *(persona) (inseguro)* indecisive; *(que está dudoso)* undecided, unsure; **estar i. sobre algo** to be undecided about sth **(b)** *(pregunta, respuesta)* hesitant; *(resultado)* undecided

**indecoroso, -a** *adj* unseemly

**indefectible** *adj Formal* unfailing

**indefensión** *nf* defencelessness

**indefenso, -a** *adj* defenceless

**indefinible** *adj* indefinable; **de edad i.** of indeterminate age

**indefinido, -a** *adj* **(a)** *(ilimitado) (tiempo)* indefinite; *(contrato)* open-ended **(b)** *(impreciso)* vague **(c)** *Gram* indefinite

**indeleble** *adj* indelible

**indemne** *adj* unhurt, unharmed; **salir i.** to escape unhurt

**indemnización** *nf (compensación) (por catástrofe)* compensation; *(por despido)* severance pay; *Der* **i. por daños y perjuicios** damages

**indemnizar** [16] *vt* **i. a alguien (por)** to compensate sb (for)

**indemostrable** *adj* unprovable

**independencia** *nf* independence; **con i. de** independently of

**independentismo** *nm* independence movement

**independentista 1** *adj* advocating independence
   **2** *nmf* supporter of independence

**independiente** *adj* **(a)** *(país, persona)* independent **(b)** *(aparte)* separate

**independizar** [16] **1** *vt* to grant independence to
   **2 independizarse** *vpr* to become independent **(de** of)

**indescifrable** *adj (código)* unbreakable; *(letra)* indecipherable; *(misterio)* inexplicable, impenetrable

**indescriptible** *adj* indescribable

**indeseable** *adj & nmf* undesirable

**indestructible** *adj* indestructible

**indeterminación** *nf (indecisión)* indecisiveness

**indeterminado, -a** *adj* **(a)** *(sin determinar)* indeterminate; **por tiempo i.** indefinitely **(b)** *(impreciso)* vague **(c)** *Gram* **artículo i.** indefinite article

**indexación** *nf también Informát* indexing

**indexar** *vt también Informát* to index

**India** *nf* **(la) I.** India

**indiano, -a 1** *adj* (Latin American) Indian
   **2** *nm,f* **(a)** *(indígena)* (Latin American) Indian **(b)** *(emigrante)* = Spanish emigrant to Latin America who returned to Spain having made his fortune

**indicación** *nf* **(a)** *(señal, gesto)* sign, signal **(b)** *(instrucción)* instruction; **pedir/dar indicaciones** *(para llegar a un sitio)* to ask for/give directions **(c)** *(nota, corrección)* note **(d)** *Med* **indicaciones** *(de medicamento)* uses

**indicado, -a** *adj* suitable, appropriate; **este jarabe está i. para la tos** this syrup is recommended for coughs

**indicador, -ora 1** *adj* indicating; **flecha indicadora** indicating arrow
   **2** *nm* **(a)** *(signo)* indicator; **i. económico** economic indicator **(b)** *Mec* gauge, meter

**indicar** [61] *vt* **(a)** *(señalar)* to indicate; *(sujeto: aguja, flecha)* to read **(b)** *(explicar)* to tell, to explain to **(c)** *(prescribir)* to prescribe

**indicativo, -a 1** *adj* indicative
   **2** *nm Gram* indicative

**índice** *nm* **(a)** *(indicador)* index; *(proporción)* level, rate; **i. bursátil** stock market index; **i. del coste de la vida** cost of living index; **i. de natalidad** birth rate; **i. de precios al consumo** retail price index **(b)** *(señal)* sign, indicator; **i. económico** economic indicator **(c)** *(lista, catálogo)* catalogue; *(de libro)* index; **i. (de contenidos)** (table of) contents **(d)** *(dedo)* index finger

**indicio** *nm (señal)* sign; *(pista)* clue; *(cantidad pequeña)* trace; **hay indicios de violencia** there are signs of violence

**Índico** *nm* **el (océano) Í.** the Indian Ocean

**indiferencia** *nf* indifference

**indiferente** *adj* indifferent; **me es i.** *(me da igual)* I don't mind, it's all the same to me; *(no me interesa)* I'm not interested in it

**indígena 1** *adj* indigenous, native
**2** *nmf* native

**indigencia** *nf* destitution, poverty

**indigente 1** *adj* destitute, poor
**2** *nmf* poor person

**indigestarse** *vpr* to get indigestion; **se me ha indigestado el guiso** the stew gave me indigestion; *Fam Fig* **se me ha indigestado esa chica** I can't stomach that girl

**indigestión** *nf* indigestion; **tener una i.** to have indigestion

**indigesto, -a** *adj* hard to digest, indigestible

**indignación** *nf* indignation

**indignante** *adj* shocking, outrageous

**indignar 1** *vt* to anger
**2 indignarse** *vpr* to get angry *o* indignant **(por)** about)

**indigno, -a** *adj* **(a)** *(impropio, no merecedor)* unworthy **(de** of), not worthy **(de** of); **soy i. de tal honor** I am not worthy of such an honour **(b)** *(degradante)* shameful, appalling

**indio, -a 1** *adj* Indian
**2** *nm,f* Indian; **hacer el i.** to play the fool

**indique** *etc ver* **indicar**

**indirecta** *nf* hint; **lanzar una i. a alguien** to drop a hint to sb

**indirecto, -a** *adj* indirect

**indisciplina** *nf* indiscipline

**indisciplinado, -a 1** *adj* undisciplined
**2** *nm,f* undisciplined person

**indiscreción** *nf* **(a)** *(cualidad)* indiscretion **(b)** *(comentario)* indiscreet remark; **si no es i.** if you don't mind my asking

**indiscreto, -a 1** *adj* indiscreet
**2** *nm,f* indiscreet person

**indiscriminado, -a** *adj* indiscriminate

**indiscutible** *adj* indisputable

**indisolubilidad** *nf* indissolubility

**indisoluble** *adj* **(a)** *(substancia)* insoluble **(b)** *(unión, ley)* indissoluble

**indispensable** *adj* indispensable, essential; **lo i.** the bare minimum, the (bare) essentials

**indisponer [52] 1** *vt* **(a)** *(enfermar)* to make ill, to upset **(b)** *(enemistar)* to set at odds
**2 indisponerse** *vpr* **(a)** *(enfermar)* to fall *o* become ill **(b)** *(enemistarse)* to fall out **(con** with)

**indisposición** *nf* **(a)** *(malestar)* indisposition **(b)** *(reticencia)* unwillingness

**indispuesto, -a 1** *participio ver* **indisponer**
**2** *adj* indisposed, unwell; **estar i.** to be unwell *o* indisposed

**indistintamente** *adj* **(a)** *(sin distinción)* equally, alike; **se refería a jóvenes y viejos i.** he was referring to young and old alike **(b)** *(sin claridad)* indistinctly

**indistinto, -a** *adj* **(a)** *(indiferente)* **es i.** it doesn't matter, it makes no difference **(b)** *(cuenta, cartilla)* joint **(c)** *(perfil, figura)* indistinct, blurred

**individual 1** *adj* **(a)** *(de uno solo)* individual; *(habitación, cama)* single; *(despacho)* personal; **los derechos individuales** the rights of the individual **(b)** *(prueba, competición)* singles; **competición i.** singles competition
**2** *nmpl* **individuales** *Dep* singles

**individualidad** *nf* individuality

**individualismo** *nm* individualism

**individualista 1** *adj* individualistic
**2** *nmf* individualist

**individualizado, -a** *adj* individualized

**individualizar [16]** *vt* **(a)** *(personalizar)* to individualize **(b)** *(caracterizar)* **su imaginación lo individualiza** his imagination singles him out

**individuo, -a** *nm,f* **(a)** *(persona)* person; *Pey* individual **(b)** *(de especie)* **algunos individuos de la especie** some members of the species; **cada i. ocupa un territorio** each animal occupies its own territory

**indivisibilidad** *nf* indivisibility

**indivisible** *adj* indivisible

**indiviso, -a** *adj* undivided

**Indochina** *n Antes* Indochina

**indochino, -a** *adj & nm,f* Indochinese

**indocumentado, -a 1** *adj* **(a)** *(sin documentación)* without identity papers; **estar i.** to have no (means of) identification **(b)** *Fam Fig (ignorante)* ignorant
**2** *nm,f Fam Fig (ignorante)* **es un i.** he doesn't know much

**indoeuropeo, -a 1** *adj* Indo-European
**2** *nm (lengua)* Indo-European

**índole** *nf* *(naturaleza)* nature; *(tipo)* type, kind; **de toda í.** of every kind

**indolencia** *nf* indolence, laziness

**indolente** *adj* indolent, lazy

**indoloro, -a** *adj* painless

**indomable** *adj* **(a)** *(animal)* untameable **(b)** *(carácter)* rebellious; *(pueblo)* unruly

**indómito, -a** *adj* **(a)** *(animal)* untameable **(b)** *(carácter)* rebellious; *(pueblo)* unruly

**Indonesia** *n* Indonesia

**indonesio, -a 1** *adj & nm,f* Indonesian
 **2** *nm (lengua)* Indonesian

**inducción** *nf* (a) *también Fís* induction (b) *Der* incitement (a to)

**inducir** [20] *vt* (a) *(incitar)* **i. a alguien a algo/a hacer algo** to lead sb into sth/into doing sth; **i. a error** to mislead (b) *(deducir)* to infer (c) *Fís* to induce

**inductor, -ora 1** *adj* instigating
 **2** *nm* inductor

**indudable** *adj* undoubted; **es i. que...** there is no doubt that...

**indujera** *etc ver* **inducir**

**indulgencia** *nf* indulgence; **i. plenaria** plenary indulgence

**indulgente** *adj* indulgent

**indultar** *vt* to pardon

**indulto** *nm Der* pardon; **otorgar** *o* **conceder el i. a alguien** to grant sb a pardon

**indumentaria** *nf* attire

**industria** *nf* (a) *(sector)* industry; **i. automotriz/pesada/punta** motor/heavy/sunrise industry (b) *(fábrica)* factory

**industrial 1** *adj* industrial
 **2** *nmf* industrialist

**industrialismo** *nm* industrialism

**industrialización** *nf* industrialization

**industrializado, -a** *adj* industrialized; **países industrializados** industrialized countries

**industrializar** [16] **1** *vt* to industrialize
 **2 industrializarse** *vpr* to become industrialized

**industrioso, -a** *adj* industrious

**induzca** *etc ver* **inducir**

**INE** ['ine] *nm (abrev de* **Instituto Nacional de Estadística)** *Br* ≃ HMSO, = organization that publishes official statistics about Spain

**inédito, -a** *adj* (a) *(no publicado)* unpublished (b) *(sorprendente)* unheard-of, unprecedented

**INEF** [i'nef] *nm (abrev de* **Instituto Nacional de Educación Física)** = Spanish training college for PE teachers

**inefable** *adj* indescribable

**ineficacia** *nf* (a) *(bajo rendimiento)* inefficiency (b) *(baja efectividad)* ineffectiveness

**ineficaz** *adj* (a) *(de bajo rendimiento)* inefficient (b) *(de baja efectividad)* ineffective

**ineficiencia** *nf* (a) *(bajo rendimiento)* inefficiency (b) *(baja efectividad)* ineffectiveness

**ineficiente** *adj* (a) *(de bajo rendimiento)* inefficient (b) *(de baja efectividad)* ineffective

**ineluctable** *adj Formal* inevitable, inescapable

**ineludible** *adj* unavoidable

**INEM** [i'nem] *nm (abrev de* **Instituto Nacional de Empleo)** = Spanish department of employment; **oficina del I.** job centre

**inenarrable** *adj* indescribable

**ineptitud** *nf* ineptitude

**inepto, -a 1** *adj* inept
 **2** *nm,f* inept person

**inequívoco, -a** *adj (apoyo, resultado)* unequivocal; *(señal, voz)* unmistakable

**inercia** *nf también Fig* inertia; **hacer algo por i.** to do sth out of inertia

**inerme** *adj (sin armas)* unarmed; *(sin defensa)* defenceless

**inerte** *adj* (a) *(materia)* inert (b) *(cuerpo, cadáver)* lifeless

**inescrutable** *adj* (a) *(persona, rostro)* inscrutable (b) *(misterio, verdad)* impenetrable

**inesperado, -a** *adj* unexpected

**inestabilidad** *nf* instability

**inestable** *adj* unstable; **tiempo i.** changeable weather

**inestimable** *adj* inestimable, invaluable

**inevitable** *adj* inevitable

**inexactitud** *nf* inaccuracy

**inexacto, -a** *adj* (a) *(impreciso)* inaccurate (b) *(erróneo)* incorrect, wrong

**inexcusable** *adj* (a) *(imperdonable)* inexcusable (b) *(ineludible)* unavoidable

**inexistencia** *nf* nonexistence

**inexistente** *adj* nonexistent

**inexorabilidad** *nf* inexorability

**inexorable** *adj (avance)* inexorable; *(persona)* pitiless, unforgiving

**inexperiencia** *nf* inexperience

**inexperto, -a 1** *adj* (a) *(falto de experiencia)* inexperienced (b) *(falto de habilidad)* unskilful, inexpert
 **2** *nm,f* person without experience

**inexplicable** *adj* inexplicable

**inexpresivo, -a** *adj (rostro)* expressionless; *(persona, carácter)* undemonstrative

**inexpugnable** *adj* unassailable, impregnable

**inextinguible** *adj (fuego)* unquenchable; *(sentimiento)* undying

**in extremis** *adv* right at the very last moment

**inextricable** *adj* intricate

**infalibilidad** *nf* infallibility

**infalible** *adj* infallible

**infamar** *vt Formal* to defame

**infame** *adj* vile, base

**infamia** *nf* (a) *(deshonra)* infamy, disgrace (b) *(mala acción)* vile *o* base deed

**infancia** *nf* (a) *(período)* childhood (b) *(todos los niños)* children *plural*; **la salud de la i.** children's health

**infante, -a1** *nm,f* (a) *(niño)* infant (b) *(hijo del rey) (niño)* infante, prince; *(niña)* infanta, princess

**2** *nm (soldado)* infantryman

**infantería** *nf* infantry; **i. de marina** marines; **i. ligera** light infantry

**infanticida 1** *adj* infanticidal

**2** *nmf* infanticide, child-murderer

**infanticidio** *nm* infanticide

**infantil** *adj* (a) *(para niños)* children's; **psicología i.** child psychology (b) *Fig (inmaduro)* infantile, childish

**infantilismo** *nm* infantilism

**infarto** *nm* **i. (de miocardio)** heart attack; **le dio un i.** he had a heart attack; *Fam Fig* **casi le dio un i.** she almost had a heart attack *o* a seizure

**infatigable** *adj* indefatigable, tireless

**infatuación** *nf* vanity

**infatuar** [4] *vt* to make conceited

**infausto, -a** *adj* ill-starred

**infección** *nf* infection

**infeccioso, -a** *adj* infectious

**infectar 1** *vt* to infect

**2 infectarse** *vpr* to become infected

**infecto, -a** *adj* (a) *(agua, carroña)* putrid (b) *(población, zona)* infected (c) *Fig (desagradable)* foul, terrible

**infecundidad** *nf* infertility

**infecundo, -a** *adj* infertile

**infelicidad** *nf* unhappiness

**infeliz 1** *adj (desgraciado)* unhappy; *Fig (ingenuo)* trusting

**2** *nmf (ingenuo)* **es un i.** he's a trusting soul; **un pobre i.** a poor wretch

**inferior 1** *adj (en espacio, cantidad)* lower (a than; *(de abajo)* bottom; *(en calidad)* inferior (a to); **una cifra i. a 100** a figure under *o* below 100

**2** *nmf* inferior

**inferioridad** *nf* inferiority; **estar en i. de condiciones** to be at a disadvantage

**inferir** [64] *vt* (a) *(deducir)* to deduce *(de* from), to infer *(de* from) (b) *(ocasionar) (herida)* to inflict; *(mal)* to cause

**infernal** *adj también Fig* infernal

**infestar** *vt* to infest; **durante el verano, los turistas infestan la ciudad** in summer the city is overrun by tourists

**infidelidad** *nf (conyugal)* infidelity; *(a la patria, un amigo)* unfaithfulness, disloyalty

**infiel 1** *adj* (a) *(desleal) (cónyuge)* unfaithful; *(amigo)* disloyal (b) *(inexacto)* inaccurate, unfaithful

**2** *nmf Rel* infidel

**infiernillo** *nm* portable stove

**infierno** *nm también Fig* hell; **en el quinto i.** in the middle of nowhere; **¡vete al i.!** go to hell!

**infiero** *etc ver* **inferir**

**infiltración** *nf* (a) *(de líquido)* seeping (b) *(de persona, ideas)* infiltration

**infiltrado, -a 1** *adj* infiltrated

**2** *nm,f* infiltrator

**infiltrar 1** *vt* (a) *(inyectar)* to inject (b) *Fig (ideas)* to infiltrate

**2 infiltrarse en** *vpr* to infiltrate

**ínfimo, -a** *adj (calidad, categoría)* extremely low; *(precio)* giveaway; *(importancia)* knockdown, minimal

**infinidad** *nf* **una i. de** an infinite number of; *Fig* masses of; **en i. de ocasiones** on countless occasions

**infinitesimal** *adj* infinitesimal

**infinitivo** *nm* infinitive

**infinito, -a1** *adj también Fig* infinite; **infinitas veces** hundreds of times

**2** *nm* infinity

**3** *adv (mucho)* extremely, infinitely

**infiriera** *etc ver* **inferir**

**inflación** *nf Econ* inflation

**inflacionario, -a, inflacionista** *adj* inflationary

**inflamable** *adj* inflammable, flammable

**inflamación** *nf Med* inflammation

**inflamar 1** *vt* (a) *Med & Fig* to inflame (b) *(encender)* to set alight

**2 inflamarse** *vpr (hincharse)* to become inflamed

**inflamatorio, -a** *adj* inflammatory

**inflar 1** *vt* (a) *(soplando)* to blow up, to inflate; *(con bomba)* to pump up (b) *Fig (exagerar)* to blow up, to exaggerate

**2 inflarse** *vpr (hartarse)* to stuff oneself (de with)

**inflexibilidad** *nf también Fig* inflexibility

**inflexible** *adj también Fig* inflexible

**inflexión** *nf* inflection

**infligir** [26] *vt* to inflict; *(castigo)* to impose

**influencia** *nf* influence

**influenciar** [15] *vt* to influence, to have an influence on

**influenza** *nf* influenza

**influir** [36] **1** *vt* to influence

**2** *vi* to have influence; **i. en** to influence, to have an influence on

**influjo** *nm* influence

**influyente** *adj* influential

**infografía** *nf (en periódico, revista)* graphics

**información** *nf* (a) *(conocimiento)* information; **para tu i.** for your information (b) *Prensa (noticias)* news *singular; (noticia)* report, piece of news; **i. deportiva** sports news; **i. meteorológica** weather report *o* forecast (c) *(oficina)* information office; *(mostrador)* information desk; **Sr. López, acuda a i.** would Mr. López please come to the information desk (d) *Telecom Br* directory enquiries, *US* directory assistance

**informador, -ora 1** *adj* informing, reporting
**2** *nm,f* reporter; **i. de la policía** police informer

**informal** *adj* (a) *(desenfadado, no solemne)* informal; **una reunión i.** an informal meeting; **vestido de manera i.** casually dressed (b) *(irresponsable)* unreliable

**informalidad** *nf* (a) *(desenfado, falta de formalismo)* informality (b) *(irresponsabilidad)* unreliability

**informante 1** *adj* informing
**2** *nmf* informant, informer

**informar 1** *vt* **i. a alguien (de)** to inform *o* tell sb (about)
**2** *vi* to inform; *Prensa* to report
**3 informarse** *vpr* to find out (details); **informarse de** to find out about

**informática** *nf (ciencia)* information technology, computing

**informático, -a 1** *adj* computer; **red informática** computer network
**2** *nm,f (persona)* computer expert

**informativo, -a 1** *adj* informative; **boletín i.** news bulletin; **folleto i.** information leaflet
**2** *nm* news (bulletin)

**informatización** *nf* computerization

**informatizar** [16] *vt* to computerize

**informe 1** *adj* shapeless
**2** *nm* (a) *(documento, estudio)* report (b) *Der* = oral summary of case given to the judge by counsel for defence or prosecution
**3** *nmpl* **informes** *(información)* information; *(sobre comportamiento)* report; *(para un empleo)* references

**infortunado, -a 1** *adj* unfortunate, unlucky; *(encuentro, conversación)* ill-fated
**2** *nm,f* unfortunate *o* unlucky person

**infortunio** *nm (hecho desgraciado)* calamity, misfortune; *(mala suerte)* misfortune, bad luck

**Infovía®** *nf Informát* = Spanish computer network providing access to Internet servers

**infracción** *nf (de reglamento)* infringement; **i. de circulación** driving offence

**infractor, -ora 1** *adj* offending
**2** *nm,f* offender

**infraestructura** *nf* (a) *(de organización, país)* infrastructure (b) *(de construcción)* foundations

**in fraganti** *adv* in flagrante; **coger a alguien i.** to catch sb red-handed *o* in the act

**infrahumano, -a** *adj* subhuman

**infranqueable** *adj* impassable; *Fig* insurmountable

**infrarrojo, -a** *adj* infrared

**infrautilización** *nf* underuse

**infrautilizar** [16] *vt* to underuse

**infravalorar 1** *vt* to undervalue, to underestimate
**2 infravalorarse** *vpr* to undervalue oneself

**infrecuente** *adj* infrequent; **no es i.** it's not uncommon *o* unusual

**infringir** [26] *vt (quebrantar)* to infringe, to break

**infructuoso, -a** *adj* fruitless, unsuccessful

**ínfulas** *nfpl* pretensions, presumption; **darse i.** to give oneself airs

**infumable** *adj* unsmokable; *Fam Fig* unbearable, intolerable

**infundado, -a** *adj* unfounded

**infundio** *nm Formal* untruth, lie

**infundir** *vt* **i. algo a alguien** to fill sb with sth, to inspire sth in sb; **i. miedo** to inspire fear

**infusión** *nf* herbal tea, infusion; **i. de manzanilla** camomile tea

**infuso, -a** *adj Hum* **por ciencia infusa** through divine inspiration

**ingeniar** [15] **1** *vt* to invent, to devise
**2 ingeniarse** *vpr* **ingeniárselas** to manage, to engineer it; **ingeniárselas para hacer algo** to manage *o* contrive to do sth

**ingeniería** *nf* engineering; **i. genética** genetic engineering; *Fig* **una obra de i.** a major operation

**ingeniero, -a** *nm,f* engineer; **i. agrónomo** agronomist; **i. de caminos, canales y puertos** civil engineer; **i. industrial/de telecomunicaciones** industrial/telecommunications engineer; **i. de sistemas/sonido** systems/sound engineer

**ingenio** *nm* (a) *(inteligencia)* ingenuity; **aguzar el i.** to sharpen one's wits (b) *(agudeza)* wit, wittiness (c) *(máquina)* device

**ingenioso, -a** *adj (inteligente)* ingenious, clever; *(agudo)* witty

**ingente** *adj* enormous, huge

**ingenuidad** *nf* ingenuousness, naivety

**ingenuo, -a 1** adj naive, ingenuous; **¡no seas i.!** don't be so naive!

**2** nm,f ingenuous o naive person; **hacerse el i.** to act the innocent

**ingerir** [64] vt to consume, to ingest

**ingestión** nf consumption; **en caso de i. accidental** if accidentally swallowed

**ingiero** etc ver **ingerir**

**ingiriera** etc ver **ingerir**

**Inglaterra** n England

**ingle** nf groin

**inglés, -esa 1** adj English

**2** nm,f (persona) Englishman, f Englishwoman; **los ingleses** the English

**3** nm (lengua) English

**ingobernable** adj (país) ungovernable; (niño) uncontrollable, unmanageable

**ingratitud** nf ingratitude, ungratefulness

**ingrato, -a** adj (persona) ungrateful; (trabajo) thankless

**ingravidez** nf weightlessness; **en estado de i.** in conditions of zero-gravity

**ingrávido, -a** adj weightless

**ingrediente** nm ingredient

**ingresar 1** vt (dinero) to deposit, to pay in

**2** vi **i. (en)** (asociación, ejército) to join; (hospital) to be admitted to); (convento, universidad) to enter; **i. cadáver** to be dead on arrival

**ingreso** nm (a) (entrada) entry, entrance; (en asociación, ejército) joining; (en hospital, universidad) admission; **examen de i.** entrance exam (b) Com deposit (c) **ingresos** (sueldo) income; (recaudación) revenue; **ingresos brutos/netos** gross/net income

**inhábil** adj (a) (torpe) clumsy, unskilful (b) (incapacitado) (por defecto físico) unfit; (por la edad) disqualified

**inhabilitación** nf (incapacitación) disqualification; (minusvalía) disablement

**inhabilitar** vt to disqualify (**para** from)

**inhabitable** adj uninhabitable

**inhalación** nf inhalation

**inhalador** nm inhaler

**inhalar** vt to inhale

**inherente** adj inherent; **ser i. a** to be inherent in o to, to be an inherent part of

**inhibición** nf inhibition

**inhibir 1** vt to inhibit

**2 inhibirse** vpr (a) (cortarse) to become inhibited o shy (b) **inhibirse de** to abstain from, to hold back from

**inhóspito, -a** adj inhospitable

**inhumación** nf burial

**inhumano, -a** adj (despiadado) inhuman; (desconsiderado) inhumane

**inhumar** vt to inter, to bury

**INI** ['ini] nm (abrev de **Instituto Nacional de Industria**) = Spanish governmental organization that promotes industry

**iniciación** nf (a) (ceremonia) initiation (b) (principio) start, beginning

**iniciado, -a 1** adj (a) (empezado) started (b) (neófito) initiated

**2** nm,f initiate

**inicial** adj & nf initial

**inicialización** nf Informát initialization

**inicializar** [16] vt Informát to initialize

**iniciar** [15] **1** vt (empezar) to start, to initiate; (debate, discusión) to start off; **i. a alguien en algo** to initiate sb into sth

**2 iniciarse** vpr (empezar) to start, to commence; **iniciarse en el estudio de algo** to begin one's studies in sth; **se inició en el piano a los sesenta años** he took up the piano at sixty

**iniciativa** nf (propuesta) proposal, initiative; (cualidad, capacidad) initiative; **tener i.** to have initiative; **tomar la i.** to take the initiative; **i. privada** private enterprise

**inicio** nm start, beginning

**inicuo, -a** adj iniquitous

**inigualable** adj unrivalled

**inigualado, -a** adj unequalled

**inimaginable** adj unimaginable

**inimitable** adj inimitable

**ininteligible** adj unintelligible

**ininterrumpido, -a** adj uninterrupted, continuous

**iniquidad** nf iniquity

**injerencia** nf interference, meddling

**injerir** [64] **1** vt to introduce, to insert

**2 injerirse** vpr (entrometerse) to interfere (**en** in), to meddle (**en** in)

**injertar** vt to graft

**injerto** nm graft; **i. de piel** skin graft

**injiero** etc ver **injerir**

**injiriera** etc ver **injerir**

**injuria** nf (insulto) insult; (agravio) offence; Der slander

**injuriar** [15] vt (insultar) to insult, to abuse; (agraviar) to offend; Der to slander

**injurioso, -a** adj insulting, abusive; Der slanderous

**injusticia** nf injustice; **¡es una i.!** (quejándose) it's not fair!; (con indignación) it's an outrage!

**injustificado, -a** adj unjustified

**injusto, -a** adj unfair, unjust

**Inmaculada** nf **la I.** the Virgin Mary

**inmaculado, -a** adj immaculate, spotless

**inmadurez** nf immaturity

**inmaduro, -a** adj (a) (fruta) unripe (b) (persona) immature

**inmaterial** adj immaterial

**inmediaciones** nfpl (de localidad) surrounding area; (de lugar, casa) vicinity; **en las i. del accidente** in the immediate vicinity of the accident

**inmediatamente** adv immediately, at once

**inmediatez** nf immediateness, immediacy

**inmediato, -a** adj (a) (instantáneo) immediate; **de i.** immediately, at once (b) (contiguo) next, adjoining

**inmejorable** adj unbeatable, that cannot be bettered

**inmemorial** adj immemorial; **desde tiempos inmemoriales** from time immemorial

**inmensidad** nf (a) (grandeza) immensity (b) (multitud) huge amount, sea

**inmenso, -a** adj (grande) immense; Fig (profundo) deep

**inmerecido, -a** adj undeserved

**inmersión** nf (de objeto) immersion; (de submarinista, submarino) dive

**inmerso, -a** adj también Fig immersed (**en** in)

**inmigración** nf (movimiento de personas) immigration; (oficina) Immigration

**inmigrante** adj & nmf immigrant

**inmigrar** vi to immigrate

**inminencia** nf imminence

**inminente** adj imminent, impending

**inmiscuirse** [36] vpr to interfere o meddle (**en** in)

**inmobiliaria** nf (a) (agencia) Br estate agency, US real estate agent (b) (constructora) construction company

**inmobiliario, -a** adj property, US real estate; **agente i.** estate agent; **propiedad inmobiliaria** real estate

**inmolación** nf immolation, sacrifice

**inmolar** vt to immolate, to sacrifice

**inmoral** adj immoral

**inmortal** adj immortal

**inmortalidad** nf immortality

**inmortalizar** [16] vt to immortalize

**inmóvil** adj (quieto) motionless, still; (coche, tren) stationary

**inmovilidad** nf immobility

**inmovilismo** nm defence of the status quo

**inmovilizado, -a 1** adj immobilized

**2** nm Econ fixed assets

**inmovilizar** [16] vt to immobilize

**inmueble 1** adj **bienes inmuebles** real estate

**2** nm (edificio) building

**inmundicia** nf (suciedad) filth, filthiness; (basura) rubbish

**inmundo, -a** adj filthy, dirty

**inmune** adj (a) Med & Fig immune; **ser i. a algo** to be immune to sth (b) (exento) exempt

**inmunidad** nf immunity; **i. diplomática/parlamentaria** diplomatic/parliamentary immunity

**inmunitario, -a** adj immune

**inmunizado, -a** adj Med immunized, inoculated; Fig immunized

**inmunizar** [16] vt to immunize (**contra** against)

**inmunodeficiencia** nf Med immunodeficiency

**inmunodepresor, -ora** adj immunosuppressant

**inmunología** nf immunology

**inmunoterapia** nf immunotherapy

**inmutabilidad** nf immutability

**inmutable** adj immutable, unchangeable

**inmutar 1** vt to upset, to perturb

**2 inmutarse** vpr to get upset, to be perturbed; **ni se inmutó** he didn't bat an eyelid

**innato, -a** adj innate; **es i. en él** it comes naturally to him

**innecesario, -a** adj unnecessary

**innegable** adj undeniable

**innegociable** adj unnegotiable, not negotiable

**innoble** adj ignoble

**innombrable** adj unmentionable

**innovación** nf innovation

**innovador, -ora 1** adj innovative, innovatory

**2** nm,f innovator

**innovar** vt (método, técnica) to improve on

**innumerable** adj countless, innumerable

**inobservancia** nf breaking, violation

**inocencia** nf innocence

**inocentada** nf practical joke, trick; **hacerle una i. a alguien** to play a trick o practical joke on sb

**inocente 1** adj (a) (no culpable) innocent (b) (ingenuo) naive, innocent (c) (sin maldad) harmless

**2** nmf (a) (no culpable) innocent person (b) (sin maldad) harmless person (c) **Día de los Inocentes** 28th December, ≃ April Fools' Day

**inocuidad** nf innocuousness, harmlessness

**inocular** vt to inoculate

**inocuo, -a** adj innocuous, harmless

**inodoro, -a 1** adj odourless

**2** nm toilet (bowl)

**inofensivo, -a** adj inoffensive, harmless

**inolvidable** adj unforgettable

**inoperancia** *nf* ineffectiveness

**inoperante** *adj* ineffective

**inopia** *nf* **estar en la i.** to be miles away, to be day-dreaming

**inopinado, -a** *adj* unexpected

**inoportuno, -a** *adj* (a) *(en mal momento)* inopportune, untimely (b) *(molesto)* inconvenient (c) *(inadecuado)* inappropriate

**inorgánico, -a** *adj* inorganic

**inoxidable** *adj* *(acero)* stainless

**input** ['imput] (*pl* **inputs**) *nm Informát* input

**inquebrantable** *adj* *(fe, amistad)* unshakeable; *(lealtad)* unswerving

**inquietante** *adj* worrying

**inquietar 1** *vt* to worry, to trouble
**2 inquietarse** *vpr* to worry, to get anxious

**inquieto, -a** *adj* (a) *(preocupado)* worried, anxious (**por** about) (b) *(agitado, emprendedor)* restless

**inquietud** *nf* *(preocupación)* worry, anxiety; **tener inquietudes** *(afán de saber)* to have an inquiring mind

**inquilino, -a** *nm,f* tenant

**inquina** *nf* antipathy, aversion; **tener i. a** to feel aversion towards

**inquirir** [6] *vt* to inquire into, to investigate

**inquisición** *nf* (a) *(indagación)* inquiry, investigation (b) **la I.** *(tribunal)* the Inquisition

**inquisidor, -ora 1** *adj* inquisitive, inquiring
**2** *nm* inquisitor

**inquisitivo, -a** *adj* inquisitive

**inri** *nm Fam Fig* **para más i.** to add insult to injury, to crown it all

**insaciable** *adj* *(apetito, curiosidad)* insatiable; *(sed)* unquenchable

**insalubre** *adj* insalubrious, unhealthy

**insalubridad** *nf* insalubrity, unhealthiness

**Insalud** *nm* (*abrev de* **Instituto Nacional de la Salud**) *Br* ≃ NHS, *US* ≃ Medicaid

**insano, -a** *adj* *(no saludable)* unhealthy; *(loco)* insane

**insatisfacción** *nf* (a) *(disgusto, descontento)* dissatisfaction (b) *(falta, carencia)* lack of fulfilment

**insatisfecho, -a** *adj* (a) *(descontento)* dissatisfied (**de** *o* **con** with) (b) *(no saciado)* not full, unsatisfied; **quedarse i.** to be left unsatisfied, to be left (still) wanting more

**inscribir 1** *vt* (a) *(grabar)* to engrave (**en** on), inscribe (**en** on) (b) *(apuntar)* **i. algo/a alguien (en)** to register sth/sb (on)
**2 inscribirse** *vpr* **inscribirse en** *(curso)* to enrol in; *(asociación, partido)* to join

**inscripción** *nf* (a) *Educ* registration, enrolment; *(en censo, registro)* registration; *(en concursos)* entry; **desde su i.** *(en asociación, partido)* since he joined; **está abierto el plazo de i.** now enrolling, registration now open (b) *(escrito)* inscription

**inscrito, -a** *participio ver* **inscribir**

**insecticida 1** *adj* insecticidal
**2** *nm* insecticide

**insectívoro, -a** *adj* insectivorous

**insecto** *nm* insect

**inseguridad** *nf* (a) *(falta de confianza)* insecurity (b) *(duda)* uncertainty (c) *(peligro)* lack of safety; **i. ciudadana** lack of law and order

**inseguro, -a** *adj* (a) *(sin confianza)* insecure (b) *(dudoso)* uncertain (**de** about), unsure (**de** of *o* about) (c) *(peligroso)* unsafe

**inseminación** *nf* insemination; **i. artificial** artificial insemination

**inseminar** *vt* to inseminate

**insensatez** *nf* foolishness, senselessness; **hacer/decir una i.** to do/say sth foolish

**insensato, -a 1** *adj* foolish, senseless
**2** *nm,f* foolish *o* senseless person, fool; **¡qué has hecho, i.!** what have you done, you fool *o* maniac?

**insensibilidad** *nf* *(emocional)* insensitivity; *(física)* numbness

**insensibilizar 1** *vt Med* to numb
**2 insensibilizarse** *vpr* *(emocionalmente)* to become desensitized (**a** to)

**insensible** *adj* (a) *(indiferente)* insensitive (**a** to) (b) *(entumecido)* numb (c) *(imperceptible)* imperceptible

**inseparable** *adj* inseparable

**insepulto, -a** *adj Formal* unburied

**inserción** *nf* insertion

**insertar** *vt también Informát* to insert (**en** into)

**inservible** *adj* useless, unserviceable

**insidia** *nf* (a) *(trampa)* trap, snare (b) *(mala acción)* malicious act

**insidioso, -a** *adj* malicious

**insigne** *adj* distinguished, illustrious

**insignia** *nf* (a) *(distintivo)* badge; *Mil* insignia (b) *(bandera)* flag, banner

**insignificancia** *nf* (a) *(cualidad)* insignificance (b) *(cosa, hecho)* trifle, insignificant thing

**insignificante** *adj* insignificant

**insinuación** *nf* hint, insinuation; **insinuaciones** *(amorosas)* innuendo

**insinuante** *adj* *(mirada, ropa)* suggestive; *(comentarios)* full of innuendo

**insinuar** [4] **1** *vt* to hint at, to insinuate; **¿qué insinuas?** what are you suggesting?

**2 insinuarse** *vpr* (a) *(amorosamente)* to make advances (**a** to) (b) *(notarse)* **empiezan a insinuarse problemas** it's beginning to look as if there might be problems

**insípido, -a** *adj también Fig* insipid

**insistencia** *nf* insistence

**insistente** *adj* insistent

**insistir** *vi* to insist (**en** on)

**in situ** *adj & adv* on the spot

**insobornable** *adj* incorruptible

**insociable** *adj* unsociable

**insolación** *nf Med* sunstroke

**insolencia** *nf* insolence; **hacer/decir una i.** to do/say sth insolent

**insolente 1** *adj (descarado)* insolent; *(orgulloso)* haughty

**2** *nmf* insolent person

**insolidaridad** *nf* lack of solidarity

**insolidario, -a 1** *adj* lacking in solidarity

**2** *nm,f* person lacking in solidarity

**insólito, -a** *adj* very unusual

**insoluble** *adj* insoluble

**insolvencia** *nf* insolvency

**insolvente** *adj* insolvent

**insomne** *adj & nmf* insomniac

**insomnio** *nm* insomnia, sleeplessness

**insondable** *adj también Fig* unfathomable

**insonorización** *nf* soundproofing

**insonorizado, -a** *adj* soundproof

**insonorizar** [16] *vt* to soundproof

**insoportable** *adj* unbearable, intolerable

**insoslayable** *adj* inevitable, unavoidable

**insospechable** *adj* impossible to tell, unforeseeable

**insospechado, -a** *adj* unexpected, unforeseen

**insostenible** *adj* untenable

**inspección** *nf (examen)* inspection; *(policial)* search; **i. de calidad** quality control inspection

**inspeccionar** *vt* to inspect; **la policía inspeccionó la zona** the police searched the area

**inspector, -ora** *nm,f* inspector; **i. de aduanas** customs official; **i. de Hacienda** tax inspector; **i. de policía** police inspector

**inspiración** *nf* (a) *(artística)* inspiration (b) *(respiración)* inhalation, breath

**inspirado, -a** *adj* inspired (**en** by)

**inspirar 1** *vt* (a) *(sentimientos, ideas)* to inspire (b) *(respirar)* to inhale, to breathe in

**2 inspirarse** *vpr* to be inspired (**en** by); **viajó al Caribe para inspirarse** he went to the Caribbean in search of inspiration

**instalación** *nf (de aparato)* installation; *(de local, puesto)* setting up; **i. eléctrica** wiring; **i. del gas** gas pipes; **instalaciones** *(deportivas, sanitarias)* facilities

**instalador, -ora 1** *adj* installing, fitting

**2** *nm,f* fitter

**instalar 1** *vt* (a) *(montar) (antena, aparato)* to instal, to fit; *(local, puesto)* to set up (b) *(situar) (objeto)* to place; *(gente)* to put up

**2 instalarse** *vpr (establecerse)* **instalarse en** to settle (down) in; *(nueva casa)* to move into; **a falta de dormitorios, se instalaron en el salón** as there were no bedrooms, they put themselves up in the living room

**instancia** *nf* (a) *(solicitud)* application (form) (b) *(ruego)* request; **a instancias de** at the request *o* bidding of; **en última i.** as a last resort (c) *Der* **juzgado de primera i.** court of first instance

**instantánea** *nf* snapshot, snap

**instantáneo, -a** *adj* (a) *(momentáneo)* momentary (b) *(rápido)* instantaneous; **provoca una reacción instantánea** it gets an immediate reaction (c) *(café)* instant

**instante** *nm* moment, instant; **a cada i.** all the time, constantly; **al i.** instantly, immediately; **en un i.** in a second

**instar** *vt* **i. a alguien a que haga algo** to urge *o* press sb to do sth

**instauración** *nf* establishment

**instaurar** *vt* to establish, to set up

**instigador, -ora 1** *adj* instigating

**2** *nm,f* instigator

**instigar** [40] *vt* **i. a alguien (a que haga algo)** to instigate sb (to do sth); **i. a algo** to incite to sth

**instintivo, -a** *adj* instinctive

**instinto** *nm* instinct; **i. maternal/de supervivencia** maternal/survival instinct; **por i.** instinctively

**institución** *nf* (a) *(organización, tradición)* institution; **i. benéfica** charitable organization; **i. pública** public institution; *Fig* **ser una i.** to be an institution (b) *(de ley, sistema)* introduction; *(de organismo)* establishment; *(de premio)* foundation

**institucional** *adj* institutional

**institucionalizar** [16] *vt* to institutionalize

**instituir** [36] *vt* (a) *(fundar) (Gobierno)* to establish; *(premio, sociedad)* to found; *(sistema, reglas)* to introduce (b) *(nombrar)* to appoint, to name

**instituto** *nm* (a) *(corporación)* institute (b) *Educ* **i. (de Bachillerato** *o* **Enseñanza Media)** state secondary school; **i. de Formación Profesional** technical college; **i. de belleza** beauty salon

**institutriz** *nf* governess

**instrucción** *nf* (a) *(conocimientos)* education; *(docencia)* instruction; **i. militar** military training (b) **instrucciones** *(de uso)* instructions (c) *Der (investigación)* preliminary investigation; *(curso del proceso)* proceedings

**instructivo, -a** *adj (experiencia, narración)* instructive; *(juguete, película)* educational

**instructor, -ora 1** *adj* training, instructing
**2** *nm,f* instructor, teacher

**instruido, -a** *adj* educated; **muy i.** well educated

**instruir** [36] *vt* (a) *(enseñar)* to instruct (b) *Der* to prepare

**instrumental 1** *adj* instrumental
**2** *nm* instruments; **i. médico** surgical instruments

**instrumentar** *vt* (a) *(composición musical)* to orchestrate, to score (b) *Fig* **i. medidas para hacer algo** to bring in measures to do sth

**instrumentista** *nmf* (a) *Mús* instrumentalist (b) *Med* surgeon's assistant

**instrumento** *nm* (a) *Mús & Fig* instrument; **i. de viento/de cuerda** wind/string instrument (b) *(herramienta)* tool, instrument; **i. de precisión** precision tool

**insubordinación** *nf* insubordination

**insubordinado, -a 1** *adj* insubordinate
**2** *nm,f* insubordinate (person), rebel

**insubordinar 1** *vt* to stir up, to incite to rebellion
**2 insubordinarse** *vpr* to rebel

**insubstancial** *adj* insubstantial

**insubstituible** *adj* irreplaceable

**insuficiencia** *nf* (a) *(escasez)* lack, shortage (b) *Med* failure, insufficiency; **i. cardiaca/renal** heart/kidney failure

**insuficiente 1** *adj* insufficient
**2** *nm (nota)* fail

**insufrible** *adj* intolerable, insufferable

**insula** *nf* island

**insular 1** *adj* insular, island; **el clima i.** the island climate
**2** *nmf* islander

**insulina** *nf* insulin

**insulinodependiente** *adj & nmf Med* insulin-dependent

**insulso, -a** *adj también Fig* bland, insipid

**insultante** *adj* insulting, offensive

**insultar** *vt* to insult

**insulto** *nm* insult; **proferir insultos** to hurl insults

**insumisión** *nf* (a) *Mil* = refusal to do military service or a civilian equivalent (b) *(rebeldía)* rebelliousness

**insumiso, -a 1** *adj* rebellious
**2** *nm,f* (a) *Mil* = person who refuses to do military service or a civilian equivalent (b) *(rebelde)* rebel

**insuperable** *adj* (a) *(inmejorable)* unsurpassable (b) *(sin solución)* insurmountable, insuperable

**insurgente** *adj* insurgent

**insurrección** *nf* insurrection, revolt

**insurrecto, -a** *adj & nm,f* insurgent, rebel

**insustancial** *adj* insubstantial

**insustituible** *adj* irreplaceable

**intachable** *adj* irreproachable

**intacto, -a** *adj* untouched; *Fig* intact

**intangible** *adj* intangible

**integración** *nf también Mat* integration; **i. racial** racial integration

**integral 1** *adj* (a) *(total)* total, complete (b) *(sin refinar) (pan, harina, pasta)* wholemeal; *(arroz)* brown (c) *(constituyente)* integral; **ser parte i. de algo** to be an integral part of sth (d) *Mat* **cálculo i.** integral calculus
**2** *nf Mat* integral

**integrante 1** *adj* integral, constituent; **Estado i. de la UE** member state of the EU; **ser parte i. de algo** to be an integral part of sth
**2** *nmf* member

**integrar 1** *vt* (a) *también Mat* to integrate (b) *(componer)* to make up
**2 integrarse** *vpr* to integrate; **integrarse en** to become integrated into

**integridad** *nf* (a) *(moral)* integrity (b) *(totalidad)* wholeness

**integrismo** *nm* (a) *Pol* reaction, traditionalism (b) *Rel* fundamentalism

**integrista** *adj & nmf* (a) *Pol* reactionary, traditionalist (b) *Rel* fundamentalist

**íntegro, -a** *adj* (a) *(completo)* whole, entire; **versión íntegra** *(de libro)* unabridged edition; *(de película)* uncut version (b) *(honrado)* upright, honourable

**intelecto** *nm* intellect

**intelectual** *adj & nmf* intellectual

**intelectualidad** *nf* intelligentsia, intellectuals

**intelectualizar** [16] *vt* to intellectualize

**inteligencia** *nf* intelligence; *Informát* **i. artificial** artificial intelligence

**inteligente** *adj también Informát* intelligent

**inteligibilidad** *nf* intelligibility

**inteligible** *adj* intelligible

**intelligentsia** *nf* intelligentsia

**intemperancia** *nf* intemperance, immoderation

**intemperie** *nf* **a la i.** in the open air

**intempestivo, -a** *adj (clima, comentario)* harsh; *(hora)* ungodly, unearthly; *(proposición, visita)* inopportune

**intemporal** *adj* timeless, independent of time

**intención** *nf* intention; **tener la i. de** to intend to; **buena/mala i., buenas/malas intenciones** good/bad intentions; **la i. es lo que cuenta** it's the thought that counts; **ya veo cuáles son tus intenciones** I see what you're up to now

**intencionado, -a** *adj* intentional, deliberate; **bien i.** *(acción)* well-meant; *(persona)* well-meaning; **mal i.** *(acción)* ill-meant, ill-intentioned; *(persona)* malevolent

**intencional** *adj* intentional, deliberate

**intencionalidad** *nf* intent

**intendencia** *nf* management, administration; **i. militar** service corps

**intendente** *nm (militar)* quartermaster

**intensidad** *nf (fuerza)* intensity; *(de lluvia)* heaviness; *(de luz, color)* brightness; *(de amor)* passion, strength; **de poca i.** *(luz)* dim, weak; **llovía con poca i.** light rain was falling; **i. de corriente** strength of current

**intensificación** *nf* intensification

**intensificar** [61] **1** *vt* to intensify

**2 intensificarse** *vpr* to intensify

**intensivo, -a** *adj* intensive; **curso i.** intensive course

**intenso, -a** *adj (mirada, calor)* intense; *(lluvia)* heavy; *(luz, color)* bright; *(amor)* passionate, strong; **poco i.** *(lluvia)* light; *(luz)* dim, weak

**intentar** *vt* **i. (hacer algo)** to try (to do sth)

**intento** *nm (tentativa)* attempt; *(intención)* intention; **i. de golpe/robo** attempted coup/robbery

**intentona** *nf Pol* **i. (golpista)** attempted coup

**interacción** *nf* interaction

**interaccionar** *vi* to interact

**interactividad** *nf* interactivity

**interactivo, -a** *adj* interactive

**intercalar** *vt* to insert, to put in

**intercambiable** *adj* interchangeable

**intercambiar** [15] *vt* to exchange; *(lugares, posiciones)* to change, to swap

**intercambio** *nm* exchange; **i. comercial** trade

**interceder** *vi* **i. (por alguien)** to intercede (on sb's behalf)

**interceptar** *vt* **(a)** *(detener)* to intercept **(b)** *(obstruir)* to block

**interceptor, -ora 1** *adj* intercepting

**2** *nm* interceptor

**intercesión** *nf* intercession

**intercesor, -ora 1** *adj* interceding

**2** *nm,f* interceder, intercessor

**interconexión** *nf* interconnection

**intercostal** *adj* intercostal, between the ribs

**interdicción** *nf* interdiction

**interés** (*pl* **intereses**) *nm* **(a)** *también Fin* interest; **de i.** interesting; **hacer algo por el i. de alguien, hacer algo en i. de alguien** to do sth in sb's interest; **poner i. en algo** to take a real interest in sth; **tener i. en** *o* **por** to be interested in; **tengo i. en que venga pronto** it's in my interest that he should come soon; **i. interbancario** interbank deposit rate; **i. preferencial** preferential interest rate; **i. simple/compuesto** simple/compound interest; **intereses creados** vested interests **(b)** *(egoísmo)* self-interest, selfishness; **por i.** out of selfishness; **casarse por (el) i.** to marry for money

**interesado, -a1** *adj* **(a)** *(preocupado, curioso)* interested (**en** *o* **por** in) **(b)** *(egoísta)* selfish, self-interested **(c)** *(implicado)* **las partes interesadas** the interested parties

**2** *nm,f* **(a)** *(deseoso, curioso)* interested person; **los interesados** those interested **(b)** *(involucrado)* person concerned; **los interesados** the parties concerned, those involved **(c)** *(egoísta)* selfish *o* self-interested person

**interesante** *adj* interesting; **¡eso suena muy i.!** that sounds really exciting!

**interesar 1** *vt* to interest; **le interesa el arte** she's interested in art; **me interesaría conocerla** I'd like to meet her; **por si te interesa** in case you're interested

**2 interesarse** *vpr* to take an interest (**en** *o* **por** in), to be interested (**en** *o* **por** in); **se interesó por ti/tu salud** she asked after you/your health

**interestatal** *adj* interstate

**interfaz** *nf Informát* interface

**interfecto, -a** *nm,f (víctima)* murder victim; *Hum (de quien se habla)* the body in question

**interferencia** *nf* interference

**interferir** [64] **1** *vt* **(a)** *Radio, Telecom & TV* to jam **(b)** *(interponerse)* to interfere with

**2** *vi* to interfere (**en** in)

**interfono** *nm* intercom

**interin** *nm inv Formal* interim; **en el í.** in the meantime

**interina** *nf (asistenta)* cleaning lady

**interinidad** *nf* **(a)** *(cualidad)* temporariness **(b)** *(período)* (period of) temporary employment

**interino, -a 1** *adj (provisional)* temporary; *(presidente, director)* acting; *(gobierno)* interim

**2** *nm,f (suplente)* stand-in, deputy; *(médico, juez)* locum; *(profesor)* teacher on temporary contract

**interior 1** *adj* (a) *(de dentro)* inside, inner; *(patio, jardín)* interior, inside; *(habitación, vida)* inner (b) *Pol* domestic (c) *Geog* inland

**2** *nm* (a) *(parte de dentro)* inside, interior (b) *Geog* interior, inland area (c) *(de una persona)* inner self, heart; **en mi i.** deep down (d) *Am (calzoncillos)* underpants

**interioridad** *nf (carácter)* inner self; **interioridades** *(asuntos)* private affairs

**interiorismo** *nm* interior design

**interiorista** *nmf* interior designer

**interiorización** *nf (de sentimientos, ideas)* internalization

**interiorizar** [16] *vt* (a) *(asumir, consolidar)* to internalize (b) *(no manifestar)* **interioriza sus emociones** he doesn't show his emotions

**interjección** *nf* interjection

**interlineado** *nm* spacing between the lines

**interlocutor, -ora** *nm,f (en negociación, debate)* participant; **su i.** the person she was speaking to

**interludio** *nm también Mús* interlude

**intermediar** [15] *vi* to mediate

**intermediario, -a 1** *adj* intermediary

**2** *nm,f* intermediary, go-between; *Com* middleman

**intermedio, -a 1** *adj* (a) *(etapa)* intermediate, halfway; *(calidad)* average; *(tamaño)* medium (b) *(tiempo)* intervening; *(espacio)* in between

**2** *nm también Teatro* interval; *Cine* intermission; *TV* break

**interminable** *adj* endless, interminable

**intermitencia** *nf* intermittence, intermittency

**intermitente 1** *adj* intermittent

**2** *nm* indicator

**Internacional** *nf Pol* International; **la I.** *(himno)* the Internationale

**internacional** *adj* international

**internacionalidad** *nf* internationality

**internacionalismo** *nm* internationalism

**internada** *nf Dep* break, breakaway

**internado, -a** *nm* (a) *(colegio)* boarding school (b) *(estancia)* (en manicomio) confinement; *(en colegio)* boarding

**internamiento** *nm (en manicomio)* confinement; *(en escuela)* boarding; *Pol* internment

**internar** *vt* (a) *(en escuela)* to send to boarding school (**en** at); *(en manicomio)* to commit (**en** to); *(en campo de concentración)* to intern (**en** in)

**2 internarse** *vpr (en un lugar)* to go o penetrate deep (**en** into); *(en un tema)* to become deeply involved (**en** in)

**internauta** *nmf* Net user, Nettie

**Internet** *nf* Internet; **está en I.** it's on the Internet

**internista** *adj & nmf* internist

**interno, -a 1** *adj* (a) *(de dentro)* internal; *Pol* domestic (b) *(alumno)* boarding (c) *Med* internal

**2** *nm,f* (a) *(alumno)* boarder (b) *(preso)* prisoner, inmate

**interparlamentario, -a** *adj* interparliamentary

**interpelación** *nf* formal question

**interpelar** *vt* to question

**interplanetario, -a** *adj* interplanetary

**Interpol** *nf (abrev de* **International Criminal Police Organization***)* Interpol

**interpolación** *nf* insertion, inclusion

**interpolar** *vt* to interpolate, to put in

**interponer** [52] **1** *vt* (a) *(entre dos cosas)* to put o place *(between two things)*, to interpose (b) *Der* to lodge, to make

**2 interponerse** *vpr* interponerse entre *(estar)* to be placed o situated between; *(ponerse)* to come o get between; **se interponía una barrera entre ellos** there was a barrier between them; **interponerse entre dos contendientes** to intervene between two opponents

**interposición** *nf* (a) *(entre dos contendientes)* mediation (b) *(entre dos cosas)* **la i. del panel evita que llegue el ruido** the panel serves as a barrier against noise (c) *Der* lodging *(of an appeal)*

**interpretación** *nf* (a) *(de ideas, significado)* interpretation (b) *(artística)* performance, interpretation; *(de obra musical)* performance, rendition; **estudia i. teatral** she's studying acting (c) *(traducción)* interpreting

**interpretar** *vt* (a) *(entender, explicar, traducir)* to interpret (b) *(artísticamente) (obra de teatro, sinfonía)* to perform; *(papel)* to play; *(canción)* to sing

**interpretativo, -a** *adj* (a) *(de la interpretación artística)* **tiene mucha capacidad interpretativa para los papeles cómicos** he's very good in comic roles; **el pianista tiene un gran estilo i.** he's a very stylish pianist (b) *(del significado)* interpretative

**intérprete** *nmf* (a) *(traductor) & Informát* interpreter (b) *(artista)* performer (c) *(comentarista)* commentator

**interpuesto, -a** *participio ver* **interponer**

**interregno** *nm* interregnum

**interrelación** *nf* interrelation

**interrelacionar 1** *vt* to interrelate

**2 interrelacionarse** *vpr* to be interrelated

**interrogación** *nf* (a) *(signo)* question mark (b) *(pregunta)* question (c) *(interrogatorio)* interrogation

**interrogador, -ora 1** *adj* questioning
  **2** *nm,f (que interroga)* questioner; *(con amenazas)* interrogator

**interrogante** *nm o nf* (a) *(incógnita)* question (b) *(signo de interrogación)* question mark

**interrogar** [40] *vt (preguntar)* to question; *(con amenazas)* to interrogate

**interrogativo, -a** *adj* interrogative

**interrogatorio** *nm (preguntas)* questioning; *(con amenazas)* interrogation

**interrumpir 1** *vt* (a) *(conversación, frase)* to interrupt (b) *(viaje, vacaciones)* to cut short; **interrumpió sus vacaciones el día 8** he ended his holiday early on the 8th (c) *(circulación)* to block
  **2 interrumpirse** *vpr* to be interrupted; *(tráfico)* to be blocked; **se interrumpió para beber agua** she paused to take a drink of water

**interrupción** *nf* (a) *(corte, parada)* interruption; **i. voluntaria del embarazo** termination of pregnancy (b) *(de discurso, trabajo)* breaking-off; *(de viaje, vacaciones)* cutting-short (c) *(de circulación)* blocking

**interruptor** *nm* switch; **i. general** mains switch

**intersección** *nf* intersection

**intersticio** *nm* crack, gap

**interurbano, -a** *adj* inter-city; *Telecom* long-distance

**intervalo** *nm también Mús* interval; **a intervalos** at intervals; **en el i. de un mes** in the space of a month

**intervención** *nf* (a) *(acción, participación)* intervention (b) *(discurso)* speech; *(pregunta, comentario)* contribution (**en** to) (c) *Com* auditing (d) *Med* operation (e) *Telecom* tapping

**intervencionismo** *nm* interventionism

**intervencionista** *adj & nmf* interventionist

**intervenir** [71] **1** *vt* (a) *Med* **i. (quirúrgicamente)** to operate on (b) *Telecom* to tap (c) *(incautarse de)* to seize (d) *Com* to audit
  **2** *vi* (a) *(participar)* to take part (**en** in); *(en discusión, debate)* to make a contribution (**en** to) (b) *(dar un discurso)* to make a speech (c) *(interferir, imponer el orden)* to intervene (**en** in) (d) *Med* **i. (quirúrgicamente)** to operate

**interventor, -ora** *nm,f* (a) *Com* auditor (b) *(de tren)* ticket collector (c) *(en elecciones)* scrutineer

**interviú** (*pl* **interviús**) *nf* interview

**intestado, -a** *adj & nm,f* intestate

**intestinal** *adj* intestinal

**intestino, -a 1** *adj* internecine
  **2** *nm* intestine; **i. delgado/grueso** small/large intestine

**intimar** *vi* to be/become close (**con** to)

**intimidación** *nf* intimidation

**intimidad** *nf* (a) *(vida privada)* private life; **en la i.** in private; **violar la i. de alguien** to invade sb's privacy (b) *(amistad)* intimacy (c) **intimidades** *(asuntos privados)* personal matters

**intimidar** *vt* to intimidate

**intimista** *adj* **pintor i.** painter of domestic scenes; **novela i.** novel of family life

**íntimo, -a 1** *adj* (a) *(vida, fiesta)* private; *(ambiente, restaurante)* intimate (b) *(relación, amistad)* close (c) *(sentimiento)* innermost; **en lo (más) í. de su corazón/alma** deep down in her heart/soul
  **2** *nm,f* close friend

**intitular** *vt* to entitle, to call

**intocable 1** *adj (persona, institución)* above criticism
  **2** *nmfpl* **intocables** *(en la India)* untouchables

**intolerable** *adj (inaceptable, indignante)* intolerable, unacceptable; *(dolor, ruido)* unbearable

**intolerancia** *nf* intolerance

**intolerante 1** *adj* intolerant
  **2** *nmf* intolerant person

**intoxicación** *nf* poisoning; **sufrió una i. alimentaria** he had a bout of food poisoning

**intoxicar** [61] **1** *vt* to poison
  **2 intoxicarse** *vpr* to poison oneself

**intraducible** *adj* untranslatable

**intramuros** *adv* within the city walls

**intramuscular** *adj* intramuscular

**intranet** *nf Informát* intranet

**intranquilidad** *nf* unease, anxiety

**intranquilizar** [16] **1** *vt* to worry, to make uneasy
  **2 intranquilizarse** *vpr* to get worried

**intranquilo, -a** *adj (preocupado)* worried, uneasy; *(nervioso)* restless

**intrascendencia** *nf* insignificance, unimportance

**intrascendente** *adj* insignificant, unimportant

**intransferible** *adj* non-transferable, untransferable

**intransigencia** *nf* intransigence

**intransigente** *adj* intransigent

**intransitable** *adj* impassable

**intransitivo, -a** *adj* intransitive

**intrascendencia** *nf* insignificance, unimportance

**intrascendente** *adj* insignificant, unimportant

**intratable** *adj* unsociable, difficult to get on with

**intrauterino, -a** *adj* intrauterine

**intravenoso, -a** *adj* intravenous

**intrépido, -a** *adj* intrepid

**intriga** *nf* (a) *(suspense)* curiosity; **película/novela de i.** thriller; **¡qué i.! ¿qué habrá pasado?** I'm dying to know what's happened! (b) *(maquinación)* intrigue (c) *(trama)* plot

**intrigado, -a** *adj* intrigued

**intrigante** 1 *adj* intriguing
  2 *nmf (maquinador)* schemer; *(chismoso)* stirrer

**intrigar** [40] *vt & vi* to intrigue

**intrincado, -a** *adj* (a) *(bosque)* thick, dense (b) *(problema)* intricate

**intrincar** [61] *vt* to complicate, to confuse

**intríngulis** *nm inv Fam (dificultad)* snag, catch; *(quid)* nub, crux

**intrínseco, -a** *adj* intrinsic

**intro** *nm Informát* enter (key), return (key); **darle al i.** to press enter *o* return

**introducción** *nf* introduction (a to)

**introducir** [20] 1 *vt* (a) *(meter)* *(llave, carta)* to put in, to insert (b) *(mercancías)* to bring in, to introduce (c) *(dar a conocer)* **i. a alguien en** to introduce sb to; **i. algo en** to introduce *o* bring sth to
  2 **introducirse** *vpr* **introducirse en** to get into; **se introdujo en la organización a los veinte años** she joined the organization at twenty

**introductor, -ora** 1 *adj* introductory; **el país i. de esta moda** the country that brought in this fashion
  2 *nm,f* introducer

**introductorio, -a** *adj* introductory

**intromisión** *nf* intrusion

**introspección** *nf* introspection

**introspectivo, -a** *adj* introspective

**introvertido, -a** *adj & nm,f* introvert

**intrusión** *nf* intrusion

**intrusismo** *nm* = illegal practice of a profession

**intruso, -a** *nm,f* intruder

**intubar** *vt* to intubate

**intuición** *nf* intuition

**intuir** [36] *vt* to know by intuition, to sense

**intuitivo, -a** *adj* intuitive

**intuyera** *etc ver* **intuir**

**intuyo** *etc ver* **intuir**

**inundación** *nf* flood, flooding

**inundar** 1 *vt* to flood; *Fig* to inundate, to swamp
  2 **inundarse** *vpr* to flood; *Fig* **inundarse de** to be inundated *o* swamped with

**inusitado, -a** *adj* uncommon, rare

**inusual** *adj* unusual

**inútil** 1 *adj* (a) *(objeto)* useless; *(intento, esfuerzo)* unsuccessful, vain; **sus intentos resultaron inútiles** his attempts were unsuccessful *o* in vain (b) *(inválido)* disabled (c) *(no apto)* unfit
  2 *nmf* hopeless case, useless person

**inutilidad** *nf* (a) *(falta de utilidad)* uselessness; *(falta de eficacia)* ineffectiveness; *(falta de sentido)* pointlessness (b) *(invalidez)* disablement

**inutilizar** [16] *vt (máquinas, dispositivos)* to disable, to put out of action; **esas cajas inutilizan la habitación de huéspedes** those boxes are stopping us from using the guest room

**invadir** *vt* to invade; **le invadió la tristeza** he was overcome by sadness

**invalidación** *nf* invalidation

**invalidar** *vt (sujeto: circunstancias)* to invalidate; *(sujeto: árbitro, juez)* to declare invalid

**invalidez** *nf* (a) *Med* disablement, disability; **i. permanente/temporal** permanent/temporary disability (b) *Der* invalidity

**inválido, -a** 1 *adj* (a) *Med* disabled (b) *Der* invalid
  2 *nm,f* invalid, disabled person; **los inválidos** the disabled

**invariable** *adj* invariable

**invasión** *nf* invasion

**invasor, -ora** 1 *adj* invading
  2 *nm,f* invader

**invectiva** *nf* invective

**invencible** *adj (ejército, enemigo)* invincible; *(timidez)* insurmountable, insuperable

**invención** *nf* invention

**invendible** *adj* unsaleable

**inventar** 1 *vt (máquina, sistema)* to invent; *(narración, falsedades)* to make up
  2 **inventarse** *vpr* to make up

**inventario** *nm* inventory; *Com* **hacer el i.** to do the stocktaking

**inventiva** *nf* inventiveness

**invento** *nm (invención)* invention; *(mentira)* lie, fib

**inventor, -ora** *nm,f* inventor

**invernadero** *nm* greenhouse

**invernal** *adj (de invierno)* winter; *(tiempo, paisaje)* wintry; **temporada i.** winter season

**invernar** [3] *vi (pasar el invierno)* to (spend the) winter; *(hibernar)* to hibernate

**inverosímil** *adj* improbable, implausible

**inverosimilitud** *nf* improbability, implausibility

**inversión** *nf* (a) *(del orden)* inversion (b) *(de dinero, tiempo)* investment; *Econ* **inversiones extranjeras** foreign investments

**inverso, -a** *adj* opposite; **a la inversa** the other way round; **en orden i.** in reverse o inverse order; **contar/escribir en orden i.** to count/write backwards; **traducción inversa** translation into a foreign language

**inversor, -ora 1** *adj* investing
**2** *nm,f Com & Fin* investor
**3** *nm Elec* inverter

**invertebrado, -a 1** *adj* (a) *Zool* invertebrate (b) *Fig (incoherente)* disjointed
**2** *nm* invertebrate

**invertido, -a 1** *adj* (a) *(al revés)* reversed, inverted; *(sentido, dirección)* opposite (b) *(dinero)* invested (c) *(homosexual)* homosexual
**2** *nm,f* homosexual

**invertir** [64] *vt* (a) *(orden)* to reverse; *(poner boca abajo)* to turn upside down, to invert (b) *(dinero, tiempo, esfuerzo)* to invest (c) *(tardar)* *(tiempo)* to spend

**investidura** *nf* investiture

**investigación** *nf* (a) *(estudio)* research; **i. y desarrollo** research and development (b) *(indagación)* investigation, inquiry

**investigador, -ora 1** *adj* (a) *(que estudia)* research; **capacidad investigadora** research capability (b) *(que indaga)* investigating
**2** *nm,f* (a) *(estudioso)* researcher (b) *(detective)* investigator; **i. privado** private investigator o detective

**investigar** [40] **1** *vt* (a) *(estudiar)* to research (b) *(indagar)* to investigate
**2** *vi* (a) *(estudiar)* to do research (b) *(indagar)* to investigate

**investir** [49] *vt* **i. a alguien de** o **con algo** to invest sb with sth

**inveterado, -a** *adj* deep-rooted

**inviabilidad** *nf* impracticability

**inviable** *adj* impractical, unviable

**invicto, -a** *adj* unconquered, unbeaten

**invidencia** *nf* blindness

**invidente 1** *adj* blind, sightless
**2** *nmf* blind o sightless person; **los invidentes** the blind

**invierno** *nm (estación)* winter; *Am (estación lluviosa)* rainy season

**invierta** *etc ver* **invertir**

**inviolabilidad** *nf* inviolability

**inviolable** *adj* inviolable

**invirtiera** *etc ver* **invertir**

**invisible** *adj* invisible

**invitación** *nf* invitation

**invitado, -a** *nm,f* guest

**invitar 1** *vt* (a) *(convidar)* **i. a alguien (a algo/a hacer algo)** to invite sb (to sth/to do sth); **me han invitado a una fiesta** I've been invited to a party (b) *(pagar)* **os invito** it's my treat, this one's on me; **i. a alguien a algo** to buy sb sth *(food, drink)*; **te invito a cenar fuera** I'll take you out for dinner
**2** *vi* to pay; **invita la casa** it's on the house; *Fig* **i. a algo** *(incitar)* to encourage sth; **este sol invita a salir** the sun makes you want to go out

**in vitro** *(de probeta)* in vitro; **fecundación i.** in vitro fertilization

**invocación** *nf* invocation

**invocar** [61] *vt* to invoke

**involución** *nf* regression, deterioration

**involucionar** *vi* to regress, to deteriorate

**involucionista 1** *adj* regressive, reactionary
**2** *nmf* reactionary

**involucrar 1** *vt* **i. a alguien (en)** to involve sb (in)
**2 involucrarse** *vpr* to get involved (**en** in)

**involuntario, -a** *adj (espontáneo)* involuntary; *(sin querer)* unintentional

**invoque** *etc ver* **invocar**

**invulnerabilidad** *nf* invulnerability

**invulnerable** *adj* immune (**a** to), invulnerable (**a** to)

**inyección** *nf* injection; **poner una i. a alguien** to give sb an injection

**inyectable 1** *adj* injectable
**2** *nm* injection

**inyectar 1** *vt* to inject
**2 inyectarse** *vpr (drogas)* to take drugs intravenously; **inyectarse algo** to inject oneself with sth

**iodo** *nm* iodine

**ion** *nm* ion

**iónico, -a** *adj* ionic

**ionizar** [16] *vt* to ionize

**ionosfera** *nf* ionosphere

**IPC** *nm (abrev de* **índice de precios al consumo**) = cost of living index

**ipso facto** *adv* immediately

**ir** [37] **1** *vi* (a) *(en general)* to go; **ir hacia el sur/al cine** to go south/to the cinema; **ir en autobús/coche** to go by bus/car; **ir andando** to go on foot, to walk; **¡vamos!** let's go!
(b) *(expresa duración gradual)* **ir haciendo algo** to be (gradually) doing sth; **va anocheciendo** it's getting dark; **voy mejorando mi estilo** I'm working on improving my style
(c) *(expresa intención, opinión)* **ir a hacer algo** to be going to do sth; **voy a decírselo**

**a tu padre** I'm going to tell your father; **te voy a echar de menos** I'm going to miss you

  **(d)** *(cambiar)* **ir a mejor/peor** to get better/worse

  **(e)** *(funcionar)* to work; **la manivela va floja** the crank is loose; **la televisión no va** the television isn't working

  **(f)** *(desenvolverse)* to go; **le va bien en su nuevo trabajo** things are going well for him in his new job; **su negocio va mal** his business is going badly; **¿cómo te va?** how are you doing?

  **(g)** *(corresponder)* to go; **estas tazas van con estos platos** these cups go with these saucers

  **(h)** *(colocarse)* to go, to belong; **esto no va ahí** that doesn't go *o* belong there

  **(i)** *(gustar, convenir)* **no me va el pop** I don't like pop music; **ni me va ni me viene** I don't care one way or the other

  **(j)** *(vestir)* **ir en/con** to wear; **iba en camisa y corbata** he was wearing a shirt and tie; **ir de azul/de uniforme** to be dressed in blue/in uniform; **iba hecho un pordiosero** he looked like a beggar

  **(k)** *(vacaciones, tratamiento)* **irle bien a alguien** to do sb good

  **(l)** *(ropa)* **irle (bien) a alguien** to suit sb; **ir con algo** to go with sth; **esta camisa no va con esos pantalones** this shirt doesn't go with these trousers

  **(m)** *(expresa apoyo)* **ir con** to support; **voy con el Real Madrid** I support Real Madrid

  **(n)** *(comentario, indirecta)* **ir con** *o* **por alguien** to be meant for sb, to be aimed at sb

  **(o)** *(película, novela)* **ir de** to be about

  **(p)** *Fam (persona)* **ir de** to think oneself; **va de listo** he thinks he's clever **¿de qué vas?** just who do you think you are?

  **(q)** *(buscar)* **ir (a) por algo/alguien** to go and get sth/sb, to go and fetch sth/sb

  **(r)** *(alcanzar)* **va por el cuarto vaso de vino** he's already on his fourth glass of wine; **vamos por la mitad de la asignatura** we covered about half the subject

  **(s)** *(expresiones)* **fue y dijo que…** he went and said that…; **ir a lo suyo** to look out for oneself, to look after number one; **¡qué va!** *(por supuesto que no)* not in the least!, not at all!; *(me temo que no)* I'm afraid not; *(no digas tonterías)* don't be ridiculous; **ser el no va más** to be the ultimate

  **2 irse** *vpr* **(a)** *(marcharse)* to go, to leave; **irse a** to go to; **¡vete!** go away!

  **(b)** *(gastarse, desaparecer)* to go; **se ha ido la luz** there's been a power cut

  **(c)** **irse abajo** *(edificio)* to fall down; *(negocio)* to collapse; *(planes)* to fall through

**IRA** ['ira] *nm (abrev de* **Irish Republican Army***)* IRA

**ira** *nf* anger, rage

**iracundo, -a** *adj (furioso)* angry, irate; *(irascible)* irascible

**Irán** *nm* (el) I. Iran

**iraní** *(pl* **iraníes**) **1** *adj & nmf* Iranian
  **2** *nm (lengua)* Iranian

**Iraq, Irak** *nm* (el) I. Iraq

**iraquí** *(pl* **iraquíes**), **iraki** *(pl* **irakíes**) *adj & nmf* Iraqi

**irascible** *adj* irascible

**iridiscencia** *nf* iridescence

**iridología** *nf* iridology

**iridólogo, -a** *nm,f Med* iridologist

**iris** *nm inv* iris

**Irlanda** *n* Ireland; **I. del Norte** Northern Ireland

**irlandés, -esa** **1** *adj* Irish
  **2** *nm,f (persona)* Irishman, *f* Irishwoman; **los irlandeses** the Irish
  **3** *nm (lengua)* Irish

**ironía** *nf* irony

**irónico, -a** *adj* ironic, ironical

**ironizar** [16] **1** *vt* to ridicule
  **2** *vi* to be ironical **(sobre** about)

**IRPF** *nm (abrev de* **Impuesto sobre la Renta de las Personas Físicas***)* = Spanish personal income tax

**irracional** *adj* irrational

**irracionalidad** *nf* irrationality

**irradiación** *nf* **(a)** *(de luz, calor)* radiation **(b)** *(de cultura, ideas)* dissemination, spreading **(c)** *(de alimentos)* irradiation

**irradiar** [15] *vt* **(a)** *(luz, calor) también Fig* to radiate **(b)** *(alimentos)* to irradiate

**irrazonable** *adj* unreasonable

**irreal** *adj* unreal

**irrealidad** *nf* unreality

**irrealizable** *adj (sueño, objetivo)* unattainable; *(plan)* impractical

**irrebatible** *adj* irrefutable, indisputable

**irreconciliable** *adj* irreconcilable

**irreconocible** *adj* unrecognizable

**irrecuperable** *adj* irretrievable

**irreductible** *adj & nmf* **(a)** *(fenómeno, fracción)* irreducible **(b)** *(país, pueblo)* unconquerable

**irreemplazable** *adj* irreplaceable

**irreflexión** *nf* rashness

**irreflexivo, -a** *adj* rash

**irrefrenable** *adj* irrepressible, uncontainable

**irrefutable** *adj* irrefutable

**irregular** *adj (verbo, situación)* irregular; *(terreno, superficie)* uneven

**irregularidad** nf (a) *(de verbo, de situación)* irregularity; *(de terreno, superficie)* unevenness (b) *(delito, falta)* irregularity

**irrelevancia** nf unimportance, insignificance

**irrelevante** adj unimportant, insignificant

**irremediable** adj unavoidable

**irremediablemente** adv inevitably

**irremisible** adj *(imperdonable)* unpardonable; *(irremediable)* irremediable

**irremplazable** adj irreplaceable

**irreparable** adj irreparable

**irrepetible** adj unique, unrepeatable

**irreprimible** adj irrepressible

**irreprochable** adj irreproachable

**irresistible** adj irresistible

**irresoluble** adj unsolvable

**irresoluto, -a 1** adj *Formal* irresolute
 **2** nm,f irresolute person

**irrespetuoso, -a** adj disrespectful

**irrespirable** adj unbreathable; *Fig* oppressive

**irresponsabilidad** nf irresponsibility

**irresponsable 1** adj irresponsible
 **2** nmf irresponsible person

**irreverente** adj irreverent

**irreversible** adj irreversible

**irrevocable** adj irrevocable

**irrigación** nf irrigation

**irrigador** nm *Med* irrigator

**irrigar** [40] vt to irrigate

**irrisorio, -a** adj *(excusa, historia)* laughable, risible; **nos ofrecieron un precio i.** we were offered a derisory sum; **una cantidad irrisoria** a ridiculously o ludicrously small amount

**irritabilidad** nf irritability

**irritable** adj irritable

**irritación** nf irritation

**irritante** adj irritating

**irritar 1** vt to irritate
 **2** irritarse vpr (a) *(enfadarse)* to get angry o annoyed (b) *(sujeto: piel)* to become irritated

**irrompible** adj unbreakable

**irrumpir** vi i. en *(lugar, vida)* to burst into; *(escena política, pantalla)* to burst onto

**irrupción** nf *(en lugar)* irruption (**en** into), bursting in; **su i. en la política** his sudden appearance on the political scene; **su i. en mi vida** his sudden entrance into my life

**isabelino, -a** adj *(en España)* Isabelline; *(en Inglaterra)* Elizabethan

**ISBN** nm *(abrev de* **International Standard Book Number***)* ISBN

**isla** nf island; **la i. de Pascua** Easter Island

**islam** nm Islam

**Islamabad** n Islamabad

**islámico, -a** adj Islamic

**islamismo** nm Islam

**islamizar** [16] **1** vt to Islamize, to convert to Islam
 **2** islamizarse vpr to convert to Islam

**islandés, -esa 1** adj Icelandic
 **2** nm,f *(persona)* Icelander
 **3** nm *(lengua)* Icelandic

**Islandia** n Iceland

**isleño, -a 1** adj island; **las costumbres isleñas** the island customs
 **2** nm,f islander

**isleta** nf *(en calle)* traffic island

**islote** nm small island

**ISO** ['iso] *(abrev de* **International Standards Organization***)* ISO

**isobara, isóbara** nf isobar

**isomorfo, -a** adj isomorphic

**isósceles** adj inv isosceles

**isótopo 1** adj isotopic
 **2** nm isotope

**Israel** n Israel

**israelí** *(pl* **israelíes***)* adj & nmf Israeli

**israelita** adj & nmf Israelite

**istmo** nm isthmus

**Italia** n Italy

**italianismo** nm Italianism

**italianizar** [16] vt to Italianize

**italiano, -a 1** adj & nm,f Italian
 **2** nm *(lengua)* Italian

**itálico, -a** adj & nm,f *Hist* Italic

**ítem** nm item

**itinerante** adj *(vida)* itinerant; *(exposición)* travelling; *(embajador)* roving

**itinerario** nm route, itinerary

**ITV** nf *(abrev de* **inspección técnica de vehículos***)* Br ≃ MOT, = annual technical inspection for motor vehicles of five years or more

**IU** nf *(abrev de* **Izquierda Unida***)* = Spanish left-wing coalition party

**IVA** ['iβa] nm *(abrev de* **impuesto sobre el valor añadido***)* VAT

**izar** [16] vt to raise, to hoist

**izda** *(abrev de* **izquierda***)* L, l

**izquierda** nf (a) *(lado)* left; **a la i. (de)** on o to the left (of); **girar a la i.** to turn left (b) *(mano)* left hand (c) *Pol* left (wing); **de izquierdas** left-wing (d) *(puerta)* **el segundo i.** the left-hand flat on the second floor

**izquierdismo** nm left-wing views

**izquierdista 1** adj left-wing
 **2** nmf left-winger

**izquierdo, -a** adj left; **a mano izquierda** on the left-hand side

**izquierdoso, -a** adj *Fam* leftish

# J

**J, j** ['xota] *nf (letra)* J, j

**ja** *interj* ¡ja! ha!

**jabalí** (*pl* jabalíes) *nm* wild boar

**jabalina** *nf Dep* javelin

**jabato, -a 1** *adj Fam (valiente)* brave
  **2** *nm* **(a)** *(animal)* young wild boar **(b)** *Fam (valiente)* daredevil

**jabón** *nm* soap; *Fam Fig* **dar j. a alguien** to soft-soap sb; **j. de afeitar** shaving soap; **j. líquido** liquid soap; **j. de tocador** toilet soap

**jabonar** *vt* to soap

**jaboncillo** *nm* tailor's chalk

**jabonera** *nf* soap dish

**jabonoso, -a** *adj* soapy

**jaca** *nf (caballo pequeño)* pony; *(yegua)* mare

**jacal** *nm Méx, Ven* hut

**jacinto** *nm* hyacinth

**jaco** *nm* **(a)** *(caballo)* nag **(b)** *muy Fam (heroína)* junk, heroin

**jacobeo, -a** *adj* of/relating to St James; **la ruta jacobea** = pilgrim's route to Santiago de Compostela

**jacobinismo** *nm Pol* Jacobinism

**jacobino, -a** *adj & nm,f Pol* Jacobin

**jactancia** *nf* boasting

**jactancioso, -a** *adj* boastful

**jactarse** *vpr* to boast (**de** about *o* of)

**jaculatoria** *nf Rel* short prayer

**jacuzzi** [ja'kusi] (*pl* jacuzzis) *nm* Jacuzzi®

**jade** *nm* jade

**jadeante** *adj* panting

**jadear** *vi* to pant

**jadeo** *nm* panting

**jaguar** *nm* jaguar

**jaiba** *nf Am (cangrejo de río)* crayfish

**jalar** *Fam* **1** *vt* **(a)** *Am (tirar)* to pull **(b)** *(comer)* to scoff
  **2** *vi* to stuff oneself, to scoff
  **3 jalarse** *vpr* to scoff (down)

**jalea** *nf* jelly; **j. real** royal jelly

**jalear** *vt* to cheer on

**jaleo** *nm Fam* **(a)** *(alboroto)* row, rumpus; **armar j.** to kick up a row *o* fuss **(b)** *(lío)* mess, confusion **(c)** *(aplausos, gritos)* cheering

**jalón** *nm (vara)* marker pole; *Fig (hito)* landmark, milestone

**jalonar** *vt* to stake *o* mark out; *Fig* to mark

**Jamaica** *n* Jamaica

**jamaicano, -a** *adj & nm,f* Jamaican

**jamás** *adv* never; **no lo he visto j.** I've never seen him; **la mejor novela que j. se haya escrito** the best novel ever written; *Fam* **¡j. de los jamases!** not in a million years!

**jamba** *nf* jamb, door post

**jamelgo** *nm Fam* nag

**jamón** *nm* ham; **j. (de) York** *o* **dulce** (boiled) ham; **j. serrano** cured ham, Parma ham; *Fam* **¡y un j. (con chorreras)!** you've got to be joking!, not on your life!

**jamona** *Fam* **1** *adj* well-stacked, buxom
  **2** *nf* buxom wench, well-stacked woman

**Japón** *nm* **(el)** J. Japan

**japonés, -esa 1** *adj & nm,f* Japanese
  **2** *nm (lengua)* Japanese

**jaque** *nm* **j. (al rey)** check; **j. mate** checkmate; *Fig* **tener en j. a alguien** to keep sb in a state of anxiety

**jaqueca** *nf* migraine; *Fam* **dar j. (a alguien)** to bother (sb), to pester (sb)

**jarabe** *nm* syrup; **j. para la tos** cough mixture *o* syrup; *Fam* **¡te voy a dar j. de palo!** I'll give you a clip round the ear!; *Fam* **tener mucho j. de pico** to have the gift of the gab, to be a smooth talker

**jarana** *nf Fam* **(a)** *(juerga)* **estar/irse de j.** to be/go out on the town **(b)** *(alboroto)* rumpus, shindy

**jaranero, -a** *Fam* **1** *adj* fond of partying
  **2** *nm,f* party animal

**jarcia** *nf Náut* rigging

**jardín** *nm* garden; **j. botánico** botanical garden; **j. de infancia** kindergarten, nursery school

**jardinera** *nf* flowerpot stand

**jardinería** *nf* gardening

**jardinero, -a** *nm,f* gardener; *Culin* **a la jardinera** garnished with vegetables

**jarra** *nf (para servir)* jug; *(para beber)* tankard; **con los brazos en jarras** *(postura)* hands on hips, with arms akimbo

**jarrear** *v impersonal Fam* **está jarreando** it's bucketing down, it's pouring

**jarrete** *nm* hock

**jarro** *nm* jug; *Fig* **fue como un j. de agua fría** it was a bolt from the blue; **llover a jarros** to be bucketing down

**jarrón** *nm* vase

**Jartúm** *n* Khartoum

**jaspe** *nm* jasper

**jaspeado, -a 1** *adj* mottled, speckled
   **2** *nm* mottling

**jaspear** *vt* to mottle, to speckle

**jauja** *nf Fam* paradise, heaven on earth; **ser j.** to be heaven on earth *o* paradise

**jaula** *nf* cage; *Fig* **j. de oro** gilded cage

**jauría** *nf* pack of dogs

**Java 1** *nm Informát* Java
   **2** *n* Java

**javanés, -esa** *adj & nm,f* Javanese

**jazmín** *nm* jasmine

**jazz** [jas] *nm inv* jazz

**JC** *(abrev de* **Jesucristo***)* JC

**je** *interj* ¡je! ha!

**jeans** [jins] *nmpl* jeans; **unos j.** a pair of jeans

**jeep** [jip] *(pl* **jeeps***) nm* jeep

**jefa** *nf ver* **jefe**

**jefatura** *nf* **(a)** *(cargo)* leadership **(b)** *(organismo)* headquarters, head office

**jefazo, -a** *nm,f Fam* big boss

**jefe, -a** *nm,f (persona al mando)* boss; *Com* manager, *f* manageress; *(líder)* leader; *(de tribu, ejército)* chief; *(de departamento)* head; *Fam (camarero, conductor)* guvnor, boss; *Mil* **en j.** in-chief; **j. de cocina** chef; **j. de estación** stationmaster; **j. de Estado** head of state; **j. de estudios** director of studies; **j. de producción/ventas** production/sales manager; **j. de redacción** editor-in-chief

**jemer** *nm* **jemeres rojos** Khmer Rouge

**jengibre** *nm* ginger

**jeque** *nm* sheikh

**jerarca** *nm* high-ranking person, leader

**jerarquía** *nf* hierarchy; **las altas jerarquías de la nación** the leaders of the nation

**jerárquico, -a** *adj* hierarchical

**jerarquizar** [16] *vt* to structure in a hierarchical manner

**jerez** *nm* sherry; **j. fino** dry sherry

**jerga** *nf* jargon

**jergón** *nm* straw mattress

**jerifalte** *nm* **(a)** *(ave)* gerfalcon **(b)** *Fig (persona)* bigwig

**jerigonza** *nf (galimatías)* gibberish; *(jerga)* jargon

**jeringa** *nf* syringe

**jeringar** *vt Fam (fastidiar)* to bother, to annoy

**jeringuilla** *nf* syringe; **j. hipodérmica** hypodermic syringe

**jeroglífico, -a 1** *adj* hieroglyphic
   **2** *nm* **(a)** *(inscripción)* hieroglyphic **(b)** *(pasatiempo)* rebus

**jersey** *(pl* **jerseys** *o* **jerséis***) nm* jumper, pullover

**Jerusalén** *n* Jerusalem

**jesuita** *adj & nm Rel* Jesuit

**jesuítico, -a** *adj Fig (ambiguo, disimulado)* jesuitical, devious

**jesús** *interj* ¡j.! *(sorpresa)* gosh!, good heavens!; *(tras estornudo)* bless you!; *Fam* **en un decir j.** in the blink of an eye

**jet** [jet] *(pl* **jets***)* **1** *nm* jet
   **2** *nf* jet set

**jeta** *Fam* **1** *nf (cara)* mug, face; **romperle la j. a alguien** to smash sb's face in; **tener (mucha) j.** to be a cheeky bugger
   **2** *nmf* cheeky bugger; **ser un j.** to be a cheeky bugger

**jet lag** *nm* jet lag

**jet-set** ['jetset] *nf* jet set

**jibia** *nf* cuttlefish

**jiennense 1** *adj* of/from Jaén
   **2** *nmf* person from Jaén

**jijona** *nm* = type of nougat made in Jijona

**jilguero** *nm* goldfinch

**jilipollada** *nf muy Fam* **hacer/decir una j.** to do/say something bloody stupid

**jilipollas** *muy Fam* **1** *adj inv* daft, *US* dumb
   **2** *nmf inv* pillock, prat

**jilipollez** *muy Fam nf inv* **hacer/decir una j.** to do/say something bloody stupid

**jineta** *nf* civet (cat)

**jinete** *nmf* horseman, *f* horsewoman; **el caballo derribó al j.** the horse threw its rider

**jiote** *nm Méx* rash

**jipioso, -a** *adj Fam (de estilo hippie)* hippy

**jirafa** *nf* **(a)** *Zool* giraffe **(b)** *Cine & TV* boom

**jirón** *nm* **(a)** *(andrajo)* shred, rag; **hecho jirones** in tatters **(b)** *Perú (calle)* street

**jitomate** *nm Méx* tomato

**jiu-jitsu** [jiu'jitsu] *nm* jujitsu

**JJ OO** *nmpl (abrev de* **Juegos Olímpicos***)* Olympic Games

**jo** *interj Fam* ¡jo! *(asombro, admiración)* wow!; ¡jo, mamá, yo quiero ir! but mum, I want to go!; ¡jo, déjame en paz! leave me alone, can't you?

**jockey** ['jokei] *(pl* **jockeys***) nm* jockey

**jocosidad** *nf* jocularity

**jocoso, -a** *adj* jocular

**jocundo, -a** *adj Formal* jovial, cheerful

**joder** *Vulg* **1** *vi* (a) *(copular)* to fuck (b) *(fastidiar)* to fuck about *o* around; **¡j.! fuck it!**, fucking hell!; **¡no jodas!** *(incredulidad, sorpresa)* well, fuck *o* bugger me!

**2** *vt* (a) *(fastidiar)* **j. a alguien** to fuck sb about *o* around (b) *(disgustar)* to fuck *o* piss off (c) *(estropear)* to fuck (up)

**3 joderse** *vpr* (a) *(aguantarse)* to fucking well put up with it; **¡que se joda!** he can fuck off!; **¡hay que joderse!** isn't that the fucking limit? (b) *(estropearse)* to get fucked (up)

**jodido, -a** *adj Vulg* (a) *(físicamente)* fucked; *(anímicamente)* fucked up (b) *(estropeado)* fucked (c) *(difícil)* fucking difficult (d) *(maldito)* fucking

**jodienda** *nf Vulg* fucking pain (in the arse)

**jofaina** *nf* washbasin

**jogging** ['joʝin] *nm* jogging

**Johannesburgo** *n* Johannesburg

**joker** ['joker] *(pl* jokers*) nm* joker *(in cards)*

**jolgorio** *nm* merrymaking

**jolín, jolines** *interj Fam* **¡j.!, ¡jolines!** *(fastidio)* sugar!, blast!; *(sorpresa)* gosh!, wow!

**jondo** *adj* **cante j.** = traditional flamenco singing

**jónico, -a** *adj* Ionic

**Jordania** *n* Jordan

**jordano, -a** *adj & nm,f* Jordanian

**jornada** *nf* (a) *(de trabajo)* working day; **j. intensiva** = working day from 8 am to 3 pm with only a short lunch break; **media j.** half day; **j. partida** = typical Spanish working day from 9 am to 1 pm and 5 to 8 pm; **j. de reflexión** = day immediately before elections when campaigning is forbidden; **jornadas (sobre)** *(congreso)* conference (on) (b) *(de viaje)* day's journey (c) *Dep* round of matches, programme

**jornal** *nm* day's wage

**jornalero, -a** *nm,f* day labourer

**joroba** *nf* hump

**jorobado, -a 1** *adj* (a) *(cheposo)* hunchbacked (b) *Fam (estropeado)* knackered; **tengo el estómago j.** I've got gut-rot

**2** *nm,f (cheposo)* hunchback

**jorobar 1** *vt Fam* (a) *(molestar)* to cheese off, to annoy (b) *(estropear)* to knacker, to ruin; **me ha jorobado las vacaciones** he/it has ruined my holiday

**2 jorobarse** *vpr Fam* (a) *(fastidiarse, aguantarse)* **¡pues te jorobas!** you can like it or lump it! (b) *(estropearse)* to get knackered

**jorongo** *nm Méx* (a) *(manta)* blanket (b) *(poncho)* poncho

**jota** *nf* (a) = lively folk song and dance, originally from Aragon (b) *Fam* **no entender ni j. (de)** *(no comprender)* not to understand a word (of); **no saber ni j. de algo** not to know the first thing about sth; **no ver ni j.** *(por mala vista)* to be as blind as a bat; *(por oscuridad)* not to be able to see a thing

**jotero, -a** *nm,f* jota dancer/singer

**joto** *nmf Méx Fam Pey Br* queer, *US* faggot

**joven 1** *adj* young; **de j.** as a young man/woman

**2** *nmf* young man, *f* young woman; **los jóvenes** young people

**jovenzuelo, -a** *nm,f* youngster

**jovial** *adj* jovial, cheerful

**jovialidad** *nf* joviality, cheerfulness

**joya** *nf* jewel; *Fig* gem

**joyería** *nf* (a) *(tienda)* jeweller's (shop) (b) *(arte, comercio)* jewellery

**joyero, -a 1** *nm,f (persona)* jeweller

**2** *nm (caja)* jewellery box

**joystick** ['joistik] *(pl* joysticks*) nm* joystick

**Jr.** *(abrev de* **júnior***)* Jr.

**juanete** *nm* bunion

**jubilación** *nf* (a) *(retiro)* retirement; **j. anticipada** early retirement (b) *(pensión)* pension

**jubilado, -a 1** *adj* retired

**2** *nm,f Br* pensioner, senior citizen; **club de jubilados** senior citizens' club

**jubilar 1** *vt* **j. a alguien (de)** to pension sb off *o* retire sb (from)

**2 jubilarse** *vpr* to retire

**jubileo** *nm Rel* jubilee

**júbilo** *nm* jubilation, joy

**jubiloso, -a** *adj* jubilant, joyous

**judaico, -a** *adj* Judaic, Jewish

**judaísmo** *nm Rel* Judaism

**judas** *nm inv* Judas, traitor

**judeocristiano, -a** *adj* Judaeo-Christian

**judeoespañol, -ola 1** *adj* Sephardic

**2** *nm,f (persona)* Sephardic Jew

**3** *nm (lengua)* Sephardi

**judería** *nf Hist* Jewish ghetto *o* quarter

**judía** *nf* bean; **j. blanca/verde** haricot/green bean

**judiada** *nf Fam* dirty trick

**judicatura** *nf* (a) *(cargo)* office of judge (b) *(institución)* judiciary

**judicial** *adj* judicial

**judío, -a 1** *adj* Jewish

**2** *nm,f* (a) *(hebreo)* Jew, *f* Jewess (b) *Fam (tacaño)* skinflint

**judo** ['juðo] *nm* judo

**judoka** [ju'ðoka] *nmf* judoist, judoka

**juego 1** *ver* **jugar**

**2** *nm* (a) *también Dep* game; *(acción)* play, playing; **estar/poner en j.** to be/put at stake; *Fig* **ser un j. de niños** to be child's play; **j. de azar** game of chance; **j. de manos** conjuring trick; **j. de mesa** board game; **j. de palabras** play on words, pun; **j. de prendas** game of forfeit; **j. sucio/limpio** foul/clean play; **descubrirle el j. a alguien** to see through sb; *Dep* **fuera de j.** offside; **juegos florales** poetry competition; **juegos malabares** juggling; *Fig* balancing act; **Juegos Olímpicos** Olympic Games

(b) *(con dinero)* gambling; **¡hagan su j.!** place your bets!

(c) *(mano) (de cartas)* hand; **me salió un buen j.** I was dealt a good hand

(d) *(conjunto de objetos)* set; **a j.** *(ropa)* matching; **hacer j. (con)** to match; **j. de herramientas** tool kit; **j. de llaves/sábanas** set of keys/sheets; **j. de té/café** tea/coffee service

**juegue** *etc ver* **jugar**

**juerga** *nf* rave-up, binge; **irse/estar de j.** to go/be out on the town; *Fam* **tomar algo a j.** to take sth as a joke

**juerguista 1** *adj* fond of partying

**2** *nmf* party-goer, reveller

**jueves** *nm inv* Thursday; *Fam* **no ser nada del otro j.** to be nothing out of this world; *Rel* **J. Santo** Maundy Thursday; *ver también* **sábado**

**juez** *nmf* (a) *Der* judge; **j. de instrucción, j. de primera instancia** examining magistrate; **j. de paz** Justice of the Peace (b) *Dep* *(árbitro)* referee; *(en atletismo)* official; **j. árbitro** referee; **j. de línea** *(fútbol)* linesman; *(rugby)* touch judge; **j. de salida** starter; **j. de silla** umpire

**jugada** *nf* (a) *Dep (en fútbol, rugby)* piece of play; *(en ajedrez)* move; *(en billar)* shot; **las mejores jugadas del partido** the highlights of the match (b) *(treta)* dirty trick; **hacer una mala j. a alguien** to play a dirty trick on sb

**jugador, -ora 1** *adj (en deporte)* playing; *(en casino, timba)* gambling

**2** *nm,f (en deporte)* player; *(en casino, timba)* gambler

**jugar** [38] **1** *vi* (a) *(practicar un deporte, juego)* to play; **j. al ajedrez/a las cartas** to play chess/cards; **j. en un equipo** to play for a team; **te toca j.** it's your turn o go; **j. limpio/sucio** to play clean/dirty; *Fig (ser desconsiderado)* **j. con** to play (around) with (b) *(con dinero)* to gamble (**a** on); **j. (en la Bolsa)** to speculate (on the Stock Exchange)

**2** *vt* (a) *(partido, juego)* to play; *(ficha, pieza)* to

move (b) *(dinero)* to gamble (**a** on)

**3 jugarse** *vpr* (a) *(apostarse)* to bet (b) *(arriesgar)* to risk (c) **jugársela a alguien** to play a dirty trick on sb

**jugarreta** *nf Fam* dirty trick

**juglar** *nm* minstrel

**juglaresco, -a** *adj* minstrel; **poesía juglaresca** troubadour poetry

**jugo** *nm* (a) *(líquido)* juice; *Am (de fruta)* fruit juice; **jugos gástricos** gastric juices (b) *Fam Fig (provecho, interés)* meat, substance; **sacar j. a algo/alguien** *(aprovechar)* to get the most out of sth/sb

**jugosidad** *nf* juiciness

**jugoso, -a** *adj* (a) *(con jugo)* juicy (b) *Fig (picante)* juicy; *(sustancioso)* meaty, substantial

**jugué** *etc ver* **jugar**

**juguete** *nm también Fig* toy; **una pistola/un coche de j.** a toy gun/car; **juguetes bélicos** war toys

**juguetear** *vi* to play (around); **j. con algo** to toy with sth

**juguetería** *nf* toy shop

**juguetón, -ona** *adj* playful

**juicio** *nm* (a) *Der* trial; **llevar a alguien a j.** to take sb to court; *Rel* **el J. Final** the Last Judgement (b) *(sensatez)* (sound) judgement; *(cordura)* sanity, reason; **estar/no estar en su (sano) j.** to be/not to be in one's right mind; **perder el j.** to lose one's reason, to go mad (c) *(opinión)* opinion; **a mi j.** in my opinion

**juicioso, -a** *adj* sensible, wise

**Jujem** *nf (abrev de* **Junta de Jefes de Estado Mayor)** = Spanish military joint chiefs of staff

**juliana** *nf Culin* = soup made with chopped vegetables and herbs; **en j.** julienne

**julio** *nm* (a) *(mes)* July; *ver también* **septiembre** (b) *Fís* joule

**jumbo** ['jumbo] *nm* jumbo (jet)

**juncal** *nm* bed of rushes

**junco** *nm* (a) *(planta)* rush, reed (b) *(embarcación)* junk

**jungla** *nf* jungle

**junio** *nm* June; *ver también* **septiembre**

**júnior** *(pl* **júniors) 1** *adj* (a) *Dep* under-21 (b) *(hijo)* junior

**2** *nmf Dep* under-21

**junta** *nf* (a) *(grupo, comité)* committee; *(de empresa, examinadores)* board; **j. directiva** board of directors; **j. de gobierno** = government and administrative body in certain autonomous regions; **j. militar** military junta (b) *(reunión)* meeting; **j. (general) de accionistas** shareholders' meeting (c) *(juntura)* joint; **j. de culata** gasket

**juntamente** *adv* **j. con** together with

**juntar 1** *vt* *(unir, reunir)* to put together; *(fondos)* to raise; *(personas)* to bring together

**2 juntarse** *vpr* (a) *(unirse) (personas)* to get together; *(ríos, caminos)* to meet (b) *(arrimarse)* to draw *o* move closer (c) *(convivir)* to live together

**junto, -a 1** *adj* (a) *(unido, reunido)* together (b) *(próximo, contiguo)* close together

**2** *adv* **j. a** next to; **j. con** together with; **hacer algo juntos** to do sth together

**juntura** *nf* joint

**Júpiter** *nm* Jupiter

**jura** *nf* *(promesa solemne)* oath; *(de un cargo)* swearing in; *Mil* **j. de bandera** oath of allegiance to the flag

**jurado, -a 1** *adj* *(declaración)* sworn; **enemigo j.** sworn enemy

**2** *nm* (a) *(tribunal)* jury (b) *(miembro)* member of the jury

**juramentar** *vt* to swear in

**juramento** *nm* (a) *(promesa solemne)* oath; **bajo j.** on *o* under oath; **prestar j.** to take the oath; **tomar j. a alguien** to swear sb in; *Med* **j. hipocrático** Hippocratic oath (b) *(blasfemia)* oath, curse

**jurar 1** *vt* *(prometer solemnemente)* to swear; *(constitución, bandera)* to pledge *o* swear allegiance to; **j. un cargo** to be sworn in; **j. que** to swear that; **j. por... to** swear by...; **te lo juro** I promise, I swear it

**2** *vi* *(blasfemar)* to swear; *Fam Fig* **j. en hebreo** *o* **arameo** to turn the air blue, to swear like a trooper

**jurásico, -a** *adj & nm* Jurassic

**jurel** *nm* scad, horse mackerel

**jurídico, -a** *adj* legal

**jurisconsulto, -a** *nm,f* jurist

**jurisdicción** *nf* jurisdiction

**jurisdiccional** *adj* jurisdictional; **aguas jurisdiccionales** territorial waters

**jurisprudencia** *nf* *(ciencia)* jurisprudence; *(casos previos)* case law; **sentar j.** to set a legal precedent

**jurista** *nmf* jurist

**justa** *nf Hist* joust

**justamente** *adv* (a) *(con justicia)* justly (b) *(exactamente)* exactly; **j., eso es lo que estaba pensando** exactly, that's just what I was thinking

**justicia** *nf* (a) *(derecho)* justice; *(equidad)* fairness, justice; **administrar j.** to administer justice; **en j.** in (all) fairness; **hacer j.** to do justice; **j. social** social justice; **ser de j.** to be only fair; **tomarse la j. por su mano** to take the law into one's own hands (b) *(sistema de leyes)* **la j.** the law (c) *(organización)* **la j. española** the Spanish legal system

**justiciero, -a** *adj* righteous; *Fig* **ángel j.** avenging angel

**justificable** *adj* justifiable

**justificación** *nf también Imprenta* justification; *Informát* **j. automática** automatic justification

**justificado, -a** *adj* justified

**justificante** *nm* written proof, documentary evidence

**justificar** [61] **1** *vt* (a) *también Imprenta* to justify (b) *(excusar)* **j. a alguien** to make excuses for sb

**2 justificarse** *vpr* (a) *(actitud, decisión)* to be justified (b) *(persona)* to justify *o* excuse oneself; **justificarse por algo** to excuse oneself for sth; **justificarse con alguien** to make one's excuses to sb

**justificativo, -a** *adj* providing evidence, supporting

**justiprecio** *nm* valuation

**justo, -a 1** *adj* (a) *(equitativo)* fair (b) *(merecido)* *(recompensa, victoria)* deserved; *(castigo)* just (c) *(exacto)* exact (d) *(idóneo)* right (e) *(apretado, ceñido)* tight; **estar** *o* **venir j.** to be a tight fit (f) *Rel* righteous

**2** *nm Rel* **los justos** the righteous; **pagarán justos por pecadores** the innocent will suffer instead of the guilty

**3** *adv* just; **j. ahora iba a llamarte** I was just about to ring you; **j. a tiempo** just in time, in the nick of time; **j. en medio** right in the middle

**juvenil 1** *adj* youthful; *Dep* **equipo j.** youth team

**2** *nmf Dep* **los juveniles** the youth team

**juventud** *nf* (a) *(edad, época)* youth (b) *(los jóvenes)* young people *(plural)*

**juzgado** *nm* (a) *(tribunal)* court; **j. municipal** magistrates' court; **j. de guardia** = court open during the night or at other times when ordinary courts are shut; *Fam* **ser de j. de guardia** to be criminal *o* a crime (b) *(jurisdicción)* jurisdiction

**juzgar** [40] *vt* (a) *Der* to try (b) *(enjuiciar)* to judge; *(estimar, considerar)* to consider, to judge; **j. mal a alguien** to misjudge sb; **a j. por (como)** judging by (how); **no tienes derecho a juzgarme** you have no right to judge me

# K

**K, k** [ka] *nf (letra)* K, k
**Kabul** *n* Kabul
**kafkiano, -a** *adj Fig* kafkaesque
**káiser** *(pl káisers) nm* kaiser
**kaki 1** *adj inv (color)* khaki
**2** *nm* **(a)** *(fruto)* kaki **(b)** *(color)* khaki
**Kalahari** *nm* el (desierto del) K. the Kalahari Desert
**kamikaze** *adj & nmf Mil & Fig* kamikaze
**Kampala** *n* Kampala
**Kampuchea** *n Antes* Kampuchea
**kantiano, -a** *adj & nm,f* Kantian
**karaoke** *nm* karaoke
**kárate** *nm* karate
**karateka** *nmf* karateka
**kart** *(pl karts) nm* go-kart
**KAS** [kas] *nf (abrev de* **Koordinadora Abertzale Sozialista**) = Basque left-wing nationalist political group which includes the terrorist organization ETA
**katiuscas, katiuskas** *nfpl* wellington boots, wellingtons
**Katmandú** *n* Katmandu
**kayak** *(pl kayaks) nm* kayak
**Kazajistán** *n* Kazak(h)stan
**kebab** *nm* kebab
**kéfir** *nm* kefir
**kelvin** *(pl kelvins) nm Fís* kelvin; **grados K.** degrees Kelvin
**Kenia** *n* Kenya
**keniano, -a, keniata** *adj & nmf* Kenyan
**kepis** *nm inv* kepi
**kermés** [ker'mes] *(pl kermeses)*, **kermesse** [ker'mes] *(pl kermesses) nf* fair, kermesse
**keroseno** *nm* kerosene
**ketchup** ['ketʃup] *(pl ketchups) nm* ketchup
**keynesianismo** *nm Econ* Keynesianism
**keynesiano, -a** *adj Econ* Keynesian
**kg** *(abrev de* **kilogramo**) kg
**KGB** *nm o nf Antes* KGB
**kibbutz** [ki'βuts] *nm inv* kibbutz
**Kiev** *n* Kiev
**kif** *nm* hashish

**kikiriki** *nm (canto del gallo)* cock-a-doodle-do
**kiko** *nm* kikos = toasted, salted maize kernels
**kilim** *nm* North African rug
**Kilimanjaro** *nm* el K. (Mount) Kilimanjaro
**kilo** *nm* **(a)** *(peso)* kilo, kilogram **(b)** *Fam (millón de pesetas)* million (pesetas)
**kilocaloría** *nf* kilocalorie
**kilogramo** *nm* kilogram
**kilohercio** *nm* kilohertz
**kilolitro** *nm* kilolitre
**kilometraje** *nm (de coche)* ≃ mileage; *(de carretera)* marking out of distance (in kilometres)
**kilometrar** *vt (carretera)* to mark out the distance (in kilometres)
**kilométrico, -a** *adj* **(a)** *(distancia)* kilometric **(b)** *Fig (largo)* very long
**kilómetro** *nm* kilometre; **k. cuadrado** square kilometre
**kilovatio** *nm* kilowatt; **k. hora** kilowatt hour
**kilovoltio** *nm* kilovolt
**kimono** *nm* kimono
**Kingston** *n* Kingston
**Kinshasa** *n* Kinshasa
**kioskero, -a** *nm,f* = person selling newspapers, drinks etc from a kiosk
**kiosko** *nm (tenderete)* kiosk; *(de periódicos)* newspaper stand; **k. de música** bandstand
**Kioto** *n* Kyoto
**Kirguizistán** *n* Kirg(h)izstan
**kirial** *nm Rel* plainsong book
**Kiribati** *n* Kiribati
**kirsch** [kirʃ] *nm* kirsch
**kit** *nm (conjunto)* kit, set; *(para montar)* kit
**kiwi** *(pl kiwis) nm* **(a)** *(ave)* kiwi **(b)** *(fruto)* kiwi (fruit)
**KKK** *nm (abrev de* **Ku-Klux-Klan**) KKK
**kleenex®** ['klines, 'klineks] *nm inv* paper hanky, (paper) tissue
**km** *(abrev de* **kilómetro**) km
**km/h** *(abrev de* **kilómetro por hora**) km/h
**knockout** [no'kaut] *(pl knockouts) nm* knockout

**KO** ['kao] *nm* (*abrev de* **knockout**) KO; *también Fig* **ganar por KO** to win by a knockout

**koala** *nm* koala (bear)

**kopek** (*pl* **kopeks**) *nm* kopeck

**Kremlin** *nm* **el K.** the Kremlin

**kril** *nm* krill

**Kuala Lumpur** *n* Kuala Lumpur

**Kurdistán** *nm* Kurdistan

**kurdo, -a 1** *adj* Kurdish
  **2** *nm,f* Kurd

**Kuwait** [ku'βait] *n* Kuwait

**kuwaití** [kuβai'ti] (*pl* **kuwaitíes**) *adj & nmf* Kuwaiti

**kv, kW** *nm* (*abrev de* **kilowatio**) kW

**kvh, kWh** *nm* (*abrev de* **kilowatio hora**) kWh

# L

**L, l** ['ele] *nf (letra)* L, l

**l** *(abrev de* **litro)** l

**la¹** *nm Mús* A; *(en solfeo)* lah

**la²** 1 *art ver* **el**

  2 *pron ver* **lo¹**

**laberíntico, -a** *adj también Fig* labyrinthine

**laberinto** *nm también Fig* labyrinth

**labia** *nf Fam* smooth talk; **tener mucha l.** to have the gift of the gab

**labial** 1 *adj* (a) *(de los labios)* lip; **protector l.** lip salve *o* balm (b) *Gram* labial

  2 *nf Gram* labial

**lábil** *adj (sustancia, estructura)* unstable; *(persona, situación)* volatile

**labio** *nm* (a) *Anat* lip; **l. leporino** harelip; **estar pendiente de los labios de alguien** to hang on sb's every word; **morderse los labios** to bite one's tongue; **no despegar los labios** not to utter a word (b) *(borde)* edge

**labiodental** *adj & nf* labiodental

**labor** *nf* (a) *(trabajo)* work; *(tarea)* task; **l. de equipo** teamwork; **labores domésticas** household chores; **ser de profesión sus labores** to be a housewife; **no estar por la l.** *(distraerse)* not to have one's mind on the job; *(ser reacio)* not to be keen on the idea (b) *(de costura)* needlework; *(de punto)* knitting (c) *Agr* **casa de l.** farm; **tierra de l.** agricultural land, arable land

**laborable** 1 *adj* **día l.** *(hábil)* working day; *(de semana)* weekday

  2 *nm* **este tren circula sólo los laborables** this train only runs on weekdays

**laboral** *adj (derecho)* labour; *(semana, condiciones)* working

**laboralista** 1 *adj* **abogado l.** labour lawyer

  2 *nmf* labour lawyer

**laboratorio** *nm* laboratory; **l. de idiomas** *o* **lenguas** language laboratory

**laboriosidad** *nf* (a) *(dedicación)* application, diligence (b) *(dificultad)* laboriousness

**laborioso, -a** *adj* (a) *(aplicado)* hard-working (b) *(difícil)* laborious, arduous

**laborismo** *nm* **el l.** *(ideología)* Labourism; *(movimiento)* the Labour Movement

**laborista** 1 *adj* Labour

  2 *nmf* Labour Party supporter *o* member; **los laboristas** Labour

**labrador, -ora** *nm,f* (a) *(agricultor)* farmer; *(trabajador)* farm worker (b) *(perro)* Labrador

**labranza** *nf Agr* **casa de l.** farm; **tierra de l.** agricultural land, arable land

**labrar** 1 *vt* (a) *(campo) (arar)* to plough; *(cultivar)* to cultivate (b) *(piedra, metal)* to work (c) *Fig (porvenir, fortuna)* to carve out

  2 **labrarse** *vpr* **labrarse un porvenir** to carve out a future for oneself

**labriego, -a** *nm,f* farmworker

**laca** *nf* (a) *(para muebles)* lacquer (b) *(para el pelo)* hairspray (c) **l. de uñas** nail varnish

**lacado** *nm* lacquering

**lacar** [61] *vt* to lacquer

**lacayo** *nm* footman; *Fig* lackey

**lacerante** *adj (dolor)* excruciating, stabbing; *(palabras)* hurtful, cutting; *(grito)* piercing

**lacerar** *vt* to lacerate; *Fig* to wound

**lacio, -a** *adj* (a) *(cabello) (liso)* straight; *(sin fuerza)* lank (b) *(planta)* wilted (c) *Fig (sin fuerza)* limp

**lacón** *nm* shoulder of pork

**lacónico, -a** *adj* laconic

**laconismo** *nm* terseness

**lacra** *nf* (a) *(secuela)* **la enfermedad le dejó como l. una cojera** he was left lame by the illness (b) *(defecto)* blight

**lacrar** *vt* to seal with sealing wax

**lacre** *nm* sealing wax

**lacrimal** *adj* lacrimal, tear; **conducto l.** tear duct

**lacrimógeno, -a** *adj* (a) *Fam (novela, película)* weepy, tear-jerking (b) **gas l.** tear gas

**lacrimoso, -a** *adj* (a) *(ojos)* tearful (b) *(historia)* weepy, tear-jerking

**lactancia** *nf* lactation; **l. artificial** bottle feeding; **l. materna** breastfeeding

**lactante** *nmf* baby *(not yet eating solid food)*

**lácteo, -a** *adj* (a) *(industria, productos)* dairy (b) *Fig (blanco)* milky; **de aspecto l.** milky

**láctico, -a** *adj* lactic

**lactosa** *nf* lactose

**lacustre** adj (animal, planta) lake-dwelling, lacustrine; **hábitat l.** lake habitat

**ladeado, -a** adj (torcido) tilted, at an angle; **métèlo l.** put it in sideways

**ladear 1** vt to tilt

**2 ladearse** vpr (cuadro) to tilt; (persona) to turn sideways

**ladera** nf slope, mountainside

**ladilla** nf crab (louse)

**ladino, -a 1** adj crafty

**2** nm (dialecto) Ladino

**lado** nm (a) (costado, cara, parte) side; **al l.** (cerca) nearby; **al l. de** (junto a) beside; **de al l.** next; **la casa de al l.** the house next door; **en el l. de arriba/abajo** on the top/bottom; **a ambos lados** on both sides; **estoy de su l.** I'm on her side; **ponerse del l. de alguien** to take o join sb's side; **de l.** (torcido) tilted, at an angle; **métèlo de l.** put it in sideways; **dormir de l.** to sleep on one's side; **viento de l.** crosswind; **atravesar algo de l. a l.** to cross sth from one side to the other; **echarse o hacerse a un l.** to move aside; **por un l.** on the one hand; **por otro l.** on the other hand; **por mi l.,...** as far as I'm concerned..., for my part...

(b) (lugar) place; **debe de estar en otro l.** it must be somewhere else; **de un l. para o a otro** to and fro; **por todos lados** everywhere, all around

(c) (expresiones) **dar de l. a alguien** to cold-shoulder sb; **dejar algo de l. o a un l.** (prescindir) to leave sth to one side; **mirar de l. a alguien** (despreciar) to look askance at sb

**ladrador, -ora** adj barking

**ladrar** vi también Fig to bark; **está que ladra** he is in a foul mood

**ladrido** nm también Fig bark, barking

**ladrillo** nm (a) Constr brick (b) Fam Fig (pesadez) drag, bore

**ladrón, -ona 1** adj thieving

**2** nm,f (persona) thief, robber; **l. de guante blanco** gentleman burglar o thief

**3** nm (para varios enchufes) adapter

**lagar** nm (de vino) winepress; (de aceite) oil press

**lagarta** nf Fam Fig (mujer) scheming woman

**lagartija** nf (small) lizard

**lagarto, -a** nm,f Zool lizard

**lago** nm lake

**Lagos** n Lagos

**lágrima** nf tear; **hacer saltar las lágrimas** to bring tears to the eyes; **llorar a l. viva** to cry buckets; Fig **lágrimas de cocodrilo** crocodile tears

**lagrimal 1** adj lacrimal, tear; **conducto l.** tear duct

**2** nm corner of the eye

**lagrimear** vi (persona) to weep; (ojos) to water

**laguna** nf (a) (lago) lagoon (b) Fig (en colección, memoria) gap; (en leyes, reglamento) loophole

**La Habana** n Havana

**La Haya** n The Hague

**laicismo** nm laicism

**laico, -a 1** adj lay, secular

**2** nm,f layman, f laywoman

**laísmo** nm = incorrect use of "la" and "las" instead of "le" and "les" as indirect objects

**lama** nm lama

**lambada** nf lambada

**lamé** nm lamé

**lameculos** nmf inv muy Fam brown-noser, arse-licker

**lamentable** adj (a) (triste) terribly sad (b) (malo) lamentable, deplorable

**lamentación** nf moaning

**lamentar 1** vt to regret, to be sorry about; **lo lamento** I'm very sorry; **lamentamos comunicarle...** we regret to inform you...

**2 lamentarse** vpr to complain (de o por about)

**lamento** nm moan, cry of pain

**lamer 1** vt to lick; muy Fam Fig **lamerle el culo a alguien** to lick sb's arse

**2 lamerse** vpr to lick oneself; Fig **lamerse las heridas** to lick one's wounds

**lametón, lametazo** nm (big) lick; **dar un l. a algo** to give sth a big lick

**lamida** nf lick; **dar una l. a algo** to lick sth, to give sth a lick

**lamido, -a** adj skinny

**lámina** nf (a) (plancha) sheet; (placa) plate (b) (rodaja) slice (c) (grabado) engraving (d) (dibujo) plate

**laminado, -a 1** adj (a) (cubierto por láminas) laminated (b) (reducido a láminas) rolled

**2** nm (a) (cubrir con láminas) lamination (b) (reducir a láminas) rolling

**laminador** nm, **laminadora** nf rolling mill

**laminar 1** adj laminar

**2** vt (a) (hacer láminas) to roll (b) (cubrir con láminas) to laminate

**lámpara** nf (a) (aparato) lamp; **l. de mesa** table lamp; **l. de pie** standard lamp (b) (bombilla) bulb (c) Mec valve

**lamparilla** nf small lamp

**lamparón** nm grease stain

**lampiño, -a** adj (sin barba) beardless, smooth-cheeked; (sin vello) hairless

**lamprea** nf lamprey

**lana 1** nf wool; **de l.** woollen; Prov **ir a por l. y volver trasquilado** to go for wool and come home shorn; **l. de vidrio** glass fibre

**2** nm Am Fam dosh, dough

**lanar** adj wool-bearing; **ganado l.** sheep

**lance 1** *ver* **lanzar**

**2** *nm* **(a)** *(en juegos, deportes)* incident; *(acontecimiento)* event **(b)** *(riña)* dispute

**lancero** *nm* lancer

**lanceta** *nf Am* sting

**lancha** *nf* **(a)** *(embarcación) (grande)* launch; *(pequeña)* boat; **l. motora** motor launch, motorboat; **l. neumática** rubber dinghy; **l. patrullera** patrol boat; **l. salvavidas** lifeboat **(b)** *(piedra)* slab

**lancinante** *adj* piercing, stabbing

**landa** *nf* moor

**landó** *(pl* **landós)** *nm* landau

**land rover**® [lan'rroβer] *(pl* **land rovers)** *nm* Land Rover®

**langosta** *nf* **(a)** *(crustáceo)* rock *o* spiny lobster **(b)** *(insecto)* locust

**langostino** *nm* king prawn

**languidecer** [48] *vi (persona)* to languish; *(conversación, entusiasmo)* to flag

**languidez** *nf (debilidad)* listlessness; *(falta de ánimo)* disinterest

**lánguido, -a** *adj (débil)* listless; *(falto de ánimo)* disinterested

**lanilla** *nf* **(a)** *(pelillo)* nap **(b)** *(tejido)* flannel

**lanolina** *nf* lanolin

**lanoso, -a, lanudo, -a** *adj* woolly

**lanza** *nf* **(a)** *(arma) (arrojadiza)* spear; *(en justas, torneos)* lance **(b)** *(de carruaje)* shaft

**lanzacohetes** *nm inv* rocket launcher

**lanzadera** *nf (de telar)* shuttle; **l. espacial** space shuttle

**lanzado, -a** *adj* **(a)** *(atrevido)* forward; *(valeroso)* fearless **(b)** *(rápido)* **ir l.** to hurtle along

**lanzador, -ora** *nm,f* thrower

**lanzagranadas** *nm inv* grenade launcher

**lanzallamas** *nm inv* flamethrower

**lanzamiento** *nm* **(a)** *(de objeto)* throwing; *(de cohete)* launching **(b)** *Dep (con la mano)* throw; *(con el pie)* kick; *(en béisbol)* pitch; **l. de disco** discus; **l. de jabalina** javelin; **l. de martillo** hammer; **l. de peso** shot put **(c)** *(de producto, artista)* launch; *(de disco)* release

**lanzamisiles** *nm inv* rocket launcher

**lanzaplatos** *nm inv Dep* (clay pigeon) trap

**lanzar** [16] **1** *vt* **(a)** *(tirar)* to throw; *(con fuerza)* to hurl, to fling; *(de una patada)* to kick; *(bomba)* to drop; *(flecha, misil)* to fire; *(cohete)* to launch **(b)** *(proferir)* to let out; *(acusación, insulto)* to hurl; *(suspiro)* to heave **(c)** *Com (producto, artista, periódico)* to launch; *(disco)* to release

**2 lanzarse** *vpr* **(a)** *(tirarse)* to throw oneself **(b)** *(abalanzarse)* to throw oneself **(sobre** upon) **(c)** *(empezar)* **lanzarse a hacer algo** to throw oneself into doing sth

**lanzatorpedos** *nm inv* torpedo tube

**Laos** *n* Laos

**laosiano, -a** *adj & nm,f* Laotian

**lapa** *nf* **(a)** *Zool* limpet **(b)** *Fam Fig (persona)* hanger-on, pest; **pegarse como una l.** to cling like a leech

**La Paz** *n* La Paz

**lapicera** *nf CSur, Chile (bolígrafo)* biro, pen

**lapicero** *nm* pencil

**lápida** *nf* memorial stone; **l. mortuoria** tombstone

**lapidación** *nf* stoning

**lapidar** *vt* to stone

**lapidario, -a** *adj (frase)* meaningful, oracular

**lapislázuli** *nm* lapis lazuli

**lápiz** *(pl* **lápices)** *nm* pencil; **l. de labios** lipstick; **l. de ojos** eyeliner; *Informát* **l. óptico** light pen

**lapo** *nm Fam* gob, spit

**lapón, -ona 1** *adj & nm,f* Lapp

**2** *nm (lengua)* Lapp

**Laponia** *n* Lapland

**lapso** *nm* space, interval; **en el l. de unas semanas** in the space of a few weeks

**lapsus** *nm inv* lapse, slip; **tener un l.** to make a slip of the tongue

**laquear** *vt* to lacquer

**lar 1** *nm* **(a)** *(lumbre)* hearth **(b)** *Mitol* household god

**2** *nmpl* **lares** *(hogar)* hearth and home; **¿qué haces tú por estos lares?** what are you doing in these parts?

**larga** *nf* **(a)** **a la l.** in the long run **(b)** **dar largas a algo** to put sth off; **siempre me está dando largas** he's always putting me off **(c)** *(luz)* full beam; **dar las largas** to put one's headlights on full beam

**largar** [40] **1** *vt* **(a)** *Fam (dar, decir)* to give; **le largué un bofetón** I gave him a smack **(b)** *(cuerda)* to pay out

**2** *vi muy Fam (hablar)* to rabbit on

**3 largarse** *vpr Fam* to clear off, to make oneself scarce; **¡me largo!** I'm off!

**largavistas** *nm inv Méx, CSur* binoculars

**largo, -a 1** *adj* **(a)** *(en espacio, tiempo)* long; **estarle l. a alguien** to be too long for sb; **vivió allí largos años** she lived there for many years; **estuvo enfermo l. tiempo** he was ill for a long time **(b)** *(alto)* tall **(c)** *(sobrado)* **media hora larga** a good half hour **(d)** *(generoso)* **l. en hacer algo** generous in doing sth

**2** *nm* **(a)** *(longitud)* length; **a lo l.** lengthways; **a lo l. de dos kilómetros** for 2 km; **a lo l. y (a lo) ancho de** right across, throughout; **tiene dos metros de l.** it's two metres long; **pasar de l.** to pass by; **vestirse de l.** to dress up, to dress formally **(b)** *(de piscina)* length; **hacerse**

**tres largos** to swim o do three lengths **(c)** *(mucho tiempo)* **la cosa va para l.** it's going to take a long time **(d)** *(largometraje)* feature

**3** *adv* at length; **l. y tendido** at great length

**4** *interj* **¡l. de aquí!** clear off!, get out of here!

**largometraje** *nm* feature film

**largue** *etc ver* **largar**

**larguero** *nm* **(a)** *Constr* main beam **(b)** *Dep* crossbar

**largueza** *nf (generosidad)* generosity

**larguirucho, -a** *adj Fam* lanky

**largura** *nf* length

**laringe** *nf* larynx

**laringitis** *nf inv* laryngitis

**laringología** *nf* laryngology

**laringólogo, -a** *nm,f* laryngologist

**La Rioja** *n* La Rioja

**larva** *nf* larva

**larvado, -a** *adj* latent

**las 1** *art ver* **el**

**2** *pron ver* **lo¹**

**lasaña** *nf* lasagne, lasagna

**lascivia** *nf* lasciviousness, lechery

**lascivo, -a 1** *adj* lascivious, lewd

**2** *nm,f* lascivious o lewd person

**láser 1** *adj inv* **rayo l.** laser beam

**2** *nm inv* laser

**laserterapia** *nf* laser therapy

**lasitud** *nf* lassitude

**laso, -a** *adj* **(a)** *(cansado)* weary **(b)** *(liso)* straight

**Las Palmas (de Gran Canaria)** *n* Las Palmas

**lástima** *nf* **(a)** *(compasión)* pity **(b)** *(pena)* shame, pity; **dar l.** to be a crying shame; **da l. ver gente así** it's sad to see people in that state; **¡qué l.!** what a shame o pity!; **quedarse hecho una l.** to be a sorry o pitiful sight

**lastimar 1** *vt* to hurt

**2 lastimarse** *vpr* to hurt oneself

**lastimoso, -a, lastimero, -a** *adj* pitiful, woeful

**lastrar** *vt* to ballast

**lastre** *nm (peso)* ballast; *Fig (estorbo)* burden; **soltar l.** to discharge ballast

**lata** *nf* **(a)** *(envase)* can, tin; *(de bebidas)* can; en l. tinned, canned **(b)** *Fam (fastidio)* pain; **¡qué l.!** what a pain!; **dar la l. a alguien** to pester sb

**latencia** *nf* latency; **período de l.** latent period

**latente** *adj* latent

**lateral 1** *adj* **(a)** *(del lado)* lateral; *(puerta, pared)* side **(b)** *(indirecto)* indirect

**2** *nm* **(a)** *(lado)* side **(b)** *Dep* **l. derecho/izquierdo** right/left back

**látex** *nm inv* latex

**latido** *nm (del corazón)* beat; *(en dedo, herida)* throb, throbbing

**latiente** *adj (corazón)* beating

**latifundio** *nm* large rural estate

**latifundismo** *nm* = system of land tenure characterized by the "latifundio"

**latigazo** *nm* **(a)** *(golpe)* lash **(b)** *(chasquido)* crack (of the whip) **(c)** *Fam (trago)* swig **(d)** *(dolor)* shooting pain

**látigo** *nm* whip

**latiguillo** *nm (palabra, frase)* verbal tic

**latín** *nm* Latin; **l. clásico/vulgar** Classical/Vulgar Latin; **l. de cocina** o **macarrónico** dog Latin; *Fig* **saber (mucho) l.** to be sharp, to be on the ball

**latinajo** *nm Fam Pey* = Latin word used in an attempt to sound academic

**latinismo** *nm* Latinism

**latinista** *nmf* Latinist

**latinizar** [16] *vt* to Latinize

**latino, -a** *adj & nm,f* Latin

**Latinoamérica** *n* Latin America

**latinoamericano, -a** *adj & nm,f* Latin American

**latir** *vi* to beat

**latitud** *nf Geog* latitude; **latitudes** *(parajes)* region, area

**lato, -a** *adj* **(a)** *(discurso)* extensive, lengthy **(b)** *(sentido)* broad

**latón** *nm* brass

**latoso, -a** *Fam* **1** *adj* tiresome

**2** *nm,f* pain (in the neck)

**latrocinio** *nm* larceny

**laúd** *nm* lute

**laudable** *adj* praiseworthy

**láudano** *nm* laudanum

**laudatorio, -a** *adj* laudatory

**laudo** *nm Der* = binding judgement in arbitration

**laureado, -a** *adj* prize-winning

**laurear** *vt* **l. a alguien (con)** to honour sb (with)

**laurel** *nm Bot* laurel; *Culin* bay leaf; *Fig* **laureles** *(honores)* laurels; *Fig* **dormirse en los laureles** to rest on one's laurels

**lava** *nf* lava

**lavable** *adj* washable

**lavabo** *nm* **(a)** *(objeto)* washbasin **(b)** *(habitación) Br* lavatory, *US* washroom

**lavacoches** *nmf inv* car washer

**lavadero** *nm (en casa)* laundry room; *(público)* washing place

**lavado** *nm* wash, washing; **l. de cerebro** brainwashing; **l. de estómago** stomach pumping; **l. y engrase** *(en garaje)* car wash and lubrication; **l. en seco** dry-cleaning

**lavadora** *nf* washing machine; **poner la l.** to do some washing (in the machine)

**lavafrutas** *nm inv* ≃ finger bowl

**La Valeta** *n* Valetta

**lavamanos** *nm inv* washbasin

**lavanda** *nf* lavender

**lavandería** *nf (en hospital, hotel)* laundry; *(automática)* launderette

**lavandero, -a** *nm* laundryman, *f* laundress

**lavaplatos 1** *nmf inv (persona)* dishwasher, washer-up

**2** *nm inv (aparato)* dishwasher

**lavar 1** *vt* **(a)** *(limpiar)* to wash; **l. y marcar** shampoo and set; **lavar en s.** to dry-clean **(b)** *Fig (honor)* to clear; *(ofensa)* to make up for

**2** *vi* **(a)** *(detergente)* to get things clean **(b)** *(hacer la colada)* to do the washing

**3 lavarse** *vpr* to wash (oneself); **lavarse las manos/la cara** to wash one's hands/face; **lavarse los dientes** to brush *o* clean one's teeth

**lavaseco** *nm Am* dry cleaner's

**lavativa** *nf* enema

**lavavajillas** *nm inv (aparato)* dishwasher; *(líquido)* washing-up liquid

**laxante 1** *adj* **(a)** *Med* laxative **(b)** *(relajante)* relaxing

**2** *nm Med* laxative

**laxar** *vt (vientre)* to loosen

**laxativo, -a** *adj & nm* laxative

**laxitud** *nf (de músculo, cable)* slackness; *(de moral)* laxity

**laxo, -a** *adj (músculo, cable)* slack; *(moral)* lax

**lazada** *nf* bow

**lazareto** *nm (leprosería)* leper hospital

**lazarillo** *nm (persona)* blind person's guide; **(perro) l.** guide dog

**lazo 1** *nm* **(a)** *(atadura)* bow **(b)** *(cinta)* ribbon **(c)** *(trampa)* snare; *(de vaquero)* lasso; *Fig* **echar el l. a alguien** to snare sb

**2** *nmpl* **lazos** *Fig (vínculos)* ties, bonds

**LCD** *(abrev de* **liquid crystal display)** LCD

**Lda.** *(abrev de* **licenciada)**

**Ldo.** *(abrev de* **licenciado)**

**le**

> **se** is used instead of **le** when it is used as an indirect object pronoun before "lo", "la", "los" or "las" (e.g. **se lo dije** I said it to him/her; **dáselos** give them to him/her).

*pron personal* **(a)** *(complemento indirecto) (hombre)* (to) him; *(mujer)* (to) her; *(cosa)* to it; *(usted)* to you; **le expliqué el motivo** I explained the reason to him/her; **le tengo miedo** I'm afraid of him/her; **ya le dije lo que pasaría** *(a usted)* I told you what would happen

**(b)** *(complemento directo)* him; *(usted)* you

**leal 1** *adj* loyal (**a** to)

**2** *nmf* loyal supporter (**a** of)

**lealtad** *nf* loyalty (**a** to)

**leasing** ['lisin] *(pl* **leasings)** *nm Fin* = system of leasing whereby the lessee has the option of purchasing the property after a certain time

**lebrel** *nm* whippet

**lección** *nf* lesson; **dar a alguien una l.** *(como castigo, advertencia)* to teach sb a lesson; *(como ejemplo)* to give sb a lesson; **servir de l.** to serve as a lesson; **l. magistral** *Mús* master class; *Educ =* lecture given by eminent academic to mark a special occasion

**lechal 1** *adj* sucking

**2** *nm* sucking lamb

**leche** *nf* **(a)** *(de mujer, hembra)* milk; **l. condensada** condensed milk; **l. en polvo** powdered milk; **l. descremada** *o* **desnatada** skimmed milk; **l. entera** full cream milk; **l. esterilizada/homogeneizada** sterilized/homogenized milk; **l. merengada** = drink made from milk, egg whites, sugar and cinnamon; **l. pasteurizada** pasteurized milk; **l. semidesnatada** semiskimmed milk

**(b)** *(loción)* **l. bronceadora** sun lotion; **l. hidratante** moisturizing lotion; **l. limpiadora** cleansing milk

**(c)** *muy Fam (golpe)* **dar** *o* **pegar una l. a alguien** to belt *o* clobber sb; **darse una l.** to come a cropper; **se dio una l. con el coche** he had a smash-up in his car

**(d)** *muy Fam (expresiones)* **estar de mala l.** to be in a bloody awful mood; **tener mala l.** *(mala intención)* to be a miserable git; **¡esto es la l.!** *(el colmo)* this is the absolute bloody end *o* limit!; **correr/trabajar a toda l.** *(muy rápido)* to run/work at full tilt *o* flat out; **¿cuándo/qué/por qué leches...?** when/what/why the hell *o* blazes...?

**lechera** *nf (para transportar)* milk churn; *(para servir)* milk jug

**lechería** *nf* dairy

**lechero, -a 1** *adj* milk, dairy; **producción lechera** milk production; **vaca lechera** dairy cow

**2** *nm,f (persona)* milkman, *f* milkwoman

**lecho** *nm* **(a)** *(cama)* bed; **ser un l. de rosas** to be a bed of roses **(b)** *(de río)* bed; *(de mar)* bed, floor **(c)** *Geol (capa)* layer

**lechón** *nm* sucking pig

**lechoso, -a** *adj* milky

**lechuga** *nf (planta)* lettuce; *Fam* **fresco como una l.** *(sano, lozano)* as fresh as a daisy

**lechuza** *nf* (barn) owl

**lecitina** *nf* lecithin

**lectivo, -a** *adj* school; **durante el horario l.** during school hours

**lector, -ora 1** *nm,f* **(a)** *(de libros)* reader **(b)** *Educ* language assistant

**2** *nm (de microfilmes)* reader, scanner; **l. óptico** optical scanner

**lectorado** *nm Educ* = post of language assistant; **hacer un l.** to work as a language assistant

**lectura** *nf* **(a)** *(de libros)* reading **(b)** *Educ (de tesis)* viva voce **(c)** *(escrito)* reading (matter) **(d)** *Fig (interpretación)* interpretation **(e)** *(de datos)* scanning; **l. óptica** optical scanning

**leer** [39] **1** *vt también Informát* to read

**2** *vi* to read; **l. en alto** to read aloud; *Fig* **l. entre líneas** to read between the lines

**legación** *nf* legation

**legado** *nm* **(a)** *(herencia)* legacy **(b)** *(representante) (cargo)* legation; *(persona)* legate

**legajo** *nm* file

**legal** *adj* **(a)** *(conforme a ley)* legal **(b)** *(forense)* forensic **(c)** *muy Fam (persona)* honest, decent; **es un tío muy l.** he's an OK bloke

**legalidad** *nf* legality

**legalismo** *nm* fine legal point, legalism

**legalista 1** *adj* legalistic

**2** *nmf* legalist

**legalización** *nf* **(a)** *(concesión de estatus legal)* legalization **(b)** *(certificado)* (certificate of) authentication

**legalizar** [16] *vt* **(a)** *(conceder estatus legal)* to legalize **(b)** *(certificar)* to authenticate

**legañas** *nfpl* sleep *(in the eyes)*

**legañoso, -a** *adj* full of sleep

**legar** [40] *vt* **(a)** *(dejar en herencia)* to bequeath **(b)** *(delegar)* to delegate

**legatario, -a** *nm,f Der* legatee

**legendario, -a** *adj* legendary

**legible** *adj* legible

**legión** *nf también Fig* legion

**legionario, -a 1** *adj* legionary

**2** *nm Hist* legionary; *Mil* legionnaire

**legislación** *nf* **(a)** *(leyes)* legislation **(b)** *(ciencia)* law

**legislador, -ora 1** *adj* legislative

**2** *nm,f* legislator

**legislar** *vi* to legislate

**legislativo, -a** *adj* legislative

**legislatura** *nf (período)* term of office

**legitimación** *nf* **(a)** *(legalización)* legitimation **(b)** *(certificación)* authentication

**legitimar** *vt* **(a)** *(justificar)* to legitimize **(b)** *(autentificar)* to authenticate

**legitimidad** *nf* legitimacy

**legítimo, -a** *adj* **(a)** *(lícito, justificado)* legitimate **(b)** *(auténtico)* real, genuine

**lego, -a 1** *adj* **(a)** *(profano, laico)* lay **(b)** *(ignorante)* ignorant; **ser l. en** to know nothing about

**2** *nm,f* **(a)** *(profano)* layman, *f* laywoman **(b)** *(ignorante)* ignorant person

**legua** *nf* league; **l. marina** marine league; *Fam Fig* **verse a la l.** to stand out a mile

**legue** *etc ver* **legar**

**leguleyo, -a** *nm,f Pey* bad lawyer

**legumbre** *nf* pulse, pod vegetable; **legumbres secas** dried pulses; **legumbres verdes** green vegetables

**leguminosa** *nf* pulse, legume

**lehendakari** [lenda'kari] *nm* = president of the autonomous Basque government

**leído, -a** *adj* **(a)** *(obra)* **muy/poco l.** much/ little read **(b)** *(persona)* well-read

**leísmo** *nm Gram* = incorrect use of "le" as direct object instead of "lo"

**leitmotiv** [leidmo'tif] *(pl* **leitmotivs)** *nm* leitmotiv

**lejanía** *nf* distance

**lejano, -a** *adj* distant

**lejía** *nf* bleach

**lejos** *adv* **(a)** *(en el espacio)* far (away); **¿está l.?** is it far?; **a lo l.** in the distance; **de** *o* **desde l.** from a distance

**(b)** *(en el pasado)* long ago; **eso queda ya l.** that happened a long time ago

**(c)** *(expresiones)* **l. de** far from; **l. de mejorar…** far from getting better…; *Fam* **no es el mejor ni de l.** he's not the best, or anything like *o* near it

**lelo, -a 1** *adj* stupid, slow

**2** *nm,f* idiot

**lema** *nm* **(a)** *(norma)* motto **(b)** *(eslogan político, publicitario)* slogan

**Leman** *nm* **el lago L.** Lake Geneva

**lempira** *nm* lempira

**lencería** *nf* **(a)** *(ropa interior)* lingerie; **departamento de l.** lingerie department **(b)** *(tienda)* lingerie shop **(c)** *(género de lienzo)* linen

**lengua** *nf* **(a)** *(órgano)* tongue; *Fam* **irse de la l.** to let the cat out of the bag; *Fam* **ir/llegar con la l. fuera** to go along/arrive puffing and panting; **morderse la l.** to bite one's tongue; **se le trabó la l.** she stumbled over her words; *Fam* **ser largo de l., tener la l. muy larga** to be a gossip; *Fam Fig* **tirar a alguien de la l.** to draw sb out; *Fig* **l. de víbora** *o* **viperina** malicious tongue; *Culin* **l. de gato** chocolate finger (biscuit) **(b)** *(idioma, lenguaje)* language; **l. materna** mother tongue; **l. muerta** dead language

**lenguado** *nm* sole

**lenguaje** *nm* language; **l. cifrado** code; **l. coloquial/comercial** colloquial/business language; **l. gestual** gestures; *Informát* **l. máquina** machine language; *Informát* **l. de alto nivel/de bajo nivel** high-level/low-level language; *Informát* **l. de programación** programming language

**lenguaraz** *adj* (a) *(malhablado)* foul-mouthed (b) *(charlatán)* talkative

**lengüeta** *nf (de instrumento musical, zapato)* tongue

**lengüetazo** *nm*, **lengüetada** *nf* lick

**lenidad** *nf Formal* leniency

**Leningrado** *n Antes* Leningrad

**leninismo** *nm Pol* Leninism

**leninista** *adj & nmf Pol* Leninist

**lenitivo, -a 1** *adj* soothing, lenitive
  **2** *nm* (a) *(físico)* lenitive (b) *(moral)* balm

**lenocinio** *nm Formal* procuring, pimping; **casa de l.** brothel

**lente 1** *nf* lens; **lentes de contacto** contact lenses
  **2** *nmpl* **lentes** *(gafas)* glasses

**lenteja** *nf* lentil

**lentejuela** *nf* sequin; **un vestido de lentejuelas** a sequined dress

**lenticular** *adj* lenticular

**lentilla** *nf* contact lens; **lentillas blandas/ duras** soft/hard lenses

**lentitud** *nf* slowness; **con l.** slowly

**lento, -a 1** *adj* (a) *(pausado)* slow; *(muerte, agonía)* lingering, long drawn out; **una película lenta** a slow film
  **2** *adv (pausadamente)* slowly

**leña** *nf* (a) *(madera)* firewood; *Fig* **echar l. al fuego** to add fuel to the flames *o* fire (b) *Fam (golpes)* beating; **dar l. a alguien** to beat sb up

**leñador, -ora** *nm,f* woodcutter

**leñazo** *nm Fam (golpe)* bang, bash; *(con el coche)* smash-up, crash

**leñe** *interj Fam* **¡l.!** for heaven's sake!

**leñera** *nf* woodshed

**leño** *nm* (a) *(de madera)* log; *Fam* **dormir como un l.** to sleep like a log (b) *Fam Fig (persona)* blockhead

**leñoso, -a** *adj* woody

**leo 1** *nm (signo del zodiaco)* Leo; **ser l.** to be (a) Leo
  **2** *nmf (persona)* Leo

**león** *nm (animal)* lion; *Fig (hombre)* fierce man; *Prov* **no es tan fiero el l. como lo pintan** he/ it/*etc* is not as bad as he/it/*etc* is made out to be; **l. marino** sea lion

**leona** *nf (animal)* lioness; *Fig (mujer) (valiente)* fierce woman, virago; *(exuberante)* brassy woman

**leonera** *nf (jaula)* lion's cage; *Fam Fig (cuarto sucio)* pigsty

**leonés, -esa 1** *adj* of/from León
  **2** *nm,f* person from León

**leonino, -a** *adj* (a) *(rostro, aspecto)* leonine (b) *(contrato, condiciones)* one-sided, unfair

**leopardo** *nm* leopard

**leotardos** *nmpl* (a) *(medias)* stockings, thick tights (b) *(de gimnasta)* leotard

**lépero, -a** *adj Am Fam* coarse, vulgar

**leporino** *adj* **labio l.** hare lip

**lepra** *nf* leprosy

**leprosería** *nf* leper colony

**leproso, -a 1** *adj* leprous
  **2** *nm,f* leper

**lerdo, -a** *Fam* **1** *adj (idiota)* dim, slow-witted; *(torpe)* useless, hopeless
  **2** *nm,f (idiota)* fool, idiot; *(torpe)* useless idiot

**leridano, -a 1** *adj* of/from Lérida
  **2** *nm,f* person from Lérida

**les**

> **se** is used instead of **les** when it is used as an indirect object pronoun before "lo", "la", "los", "las" (**se lo dije** I said it to them; **dáselo** give it to them).

*pron personal pl* (a) *(complemento indirecto)* (to) them; *(ustedes)* (to) you; **l. expliqué el motivo** I explained the reason to them; **l. tengo miedo** I'm afraid of them; **ya l. dije lo que pasaría** *(a ustedes)* I told you what would happen (b) *(complemento directo)* them; *(ustedes)* you (c) *ver* **se**

**lesbiana** *nf* lesbian

**lesbianismo** *nm* lesbianism

**lesbiano, -a, lésbico, -a** *adj* lesbian

**leseras** *nfpl Am* rubbish, nonsense

**lesión** *nf* (a) *(daño físico)* injury; *Der* **lesiones graves** grievous bodily harm (b) *Fig (perjuicio)* damage, harm

**lesionado, -a 1** *adj* injured
  **2** *nm,f* injured person

**lesionar 1** *vt* to injure; *Fig* to damage, to harm
  **2 lesionarse** *vpr* to injure oneself

**lesivo, -a** *adj Formal* damaging, harmful

**leso, -a** *adj Formal* **crimen de lesa humanidad** crime against humanity; **crimen de lesa patria** high treason

**Lesoto** *n* Lesotho

**letal** *adj* lethal

**letanía** *nf Rel & Fig* litany

**letárgico, -a** *adj* (a) *Med & Fig* lethargic (b) *Zool* hibernating

**letargo** *nm* (a) *Med & Fig* lethargy (b) *Zool* hibernation

**letón, -ona 1** *adj & nm,f* Latvian

**2** *nm (lengua)* Latvian

**Letonia** *n* Latvia

**letra** *nf* (a) *(signo)* letter

(b) *(escritura, caligrafía)* handwriting

(c) *(estilo)* script; *Imprenta* type, typeface; **l. cursiva** *o* **itálica** italic type, italics; **l. de imprenta** *o* **molde** *(impresa)* print; *(en formulario)* block capitals; **l. negrita** bold (face); *Fig* **leer la l. pequeña** to read the small print; **mandar cuatro letras a alguien** to drop sb a line

(d) *(texto de canción)* lyrics

(e) *Com* **l. (de cambio)** bill of exchange; **girar una l.** to draw a bill of exchange; **protestar una l.** to protest a bill; **l. avalada** guaranteed bill of exchange; **l. de cambio a la vista** sight bill

(f) *(sentido)* literal meaning; **seguir instrucciones al pie de la l.** to follow instructions to the letter

(g) *Educ* **letras** arts; *Fam* **ser de letras** to study an arts subject

**letrado, -a 1** *adj* learned

**2** *nm,f* lawyer

**letrero** *nm* sign

**letrina** *nf* latrine

**letrista** *nmf* lyricist

**leucemia** *nf Med* leukaemia

**leucocito** *nm Anat* leucocyte

**leva** *nf* (a) *Mil* levy (b) *Náut* weighing anchor (c) *Mec* cam

**levadizo, -a** *adj* **puente l.** drawbridge

**levadura** *nf* yeast, leaven; **l. de cerveza** brewer's yeast

**levantador, -ora 1** *adj* lifting

**2** *nm,f Dep* **l. de pesas** weightlifter

**levantamiento** *nm* (a) *(sublevación)* uprising (b) *(elevación)* raising; *Dep* **l. de pesas** weightlifting (c) *(supresión)* lifting, removal

**levantar 1** *vt* (a) *(alzar, elevar)* to raise; *(objeto pesado, capó, trampilla)* to lift (up); **l. la vista** *o* **mirada** to look up; *Fig* **no ha conseguido l. cabeza** he's still not back to his old self; *Fig* **l. el ánimo** to cheer up

(b) *(quitar)* *(pintura, venda, tapa)* to remove

(c) *(construir)* *(edificio, muro)* to build, to raise

(d) *(retirar)* *(campamento)* to strike; *(tienda de campaña, tenderete)* to take down

(e) *(provocar)* *(protestas, polémica)* to stir up; **l. a alguien contra** to stir sb up against

(f) *(suprimir)* *(embargo, prohibición)* to lift; *(pena, castigo)* to suspend

(g) *(sesión)* *(terminar)* to bring to an end; *(aplazar)* to adjourn; **si no hay más preguntas, se levanta la sesión** *(en reunión)* if there are no more questions, that ends the meeting

(h) *(redactar)* *(acta, atestado)* to draw up

(i) *muy Fam (robar)* to pinch, to swipe

**2 levantarse** *vpr* (a) *(ponerse de pie)* to stand up; *(de la cama)* to get up

(b) *(elevarse)* *(sol)* to climb in the sky; *(niebla)* to lift

(c) *(sublevarse)* to rise up

(d) *(viento, oleaje)* to get up, to rise

**levante** *nm* (a) *(este)* east; *(región)* east coast; *Geog* **L.** = the coastal provinces of Spain between Catalonia and Andalusia: Castellón, Valencia, Alicante and Murcia (b) *(viento)* east wind

**levantino, -a 1** *adj* of/from the Levante region of Spain

**2** *nm,f* person from the Levante region of Spain

**levar** *vt Náut* **l. el ancla** to weigh anchor; *Fam Fig (marcharse)* to sling one's hook

**leve** *adj* (a) *(suave, sutil)* light; *(olor, sabor, temblor)* slight, faint (b) *(pecado, falta, herida)* minor; *(enfermedad)* mild, slight

**levedad** *nf* (a) *(suavidad, sutileza)* lightness (b) *(de pecado, falta, herida)* minor nature; *(de enfermedad)* mildness

**levita** *nf* frock coat

**levitación** *nf* levitation

**levitar** *vi* to levitate

**lexema** *nm Ling* lexeme

**léxico, -a 1** *adj* lexical

**2** *nm (vocabulario)* vocabulary

**lexicografía** *nf* lexicography

**lexicográfico, -a** *adj* lexicographical

**lexicógrafo, -a** *nm,f* lexicographer

**lexicología** *nf* lexicology

**lexicólogo, -a** *nm,f* lexicologist

**ley** *nf* (a) *(norma, precepto)* law; *(parlamentaria)* act; **hecha la l., hecha la trampa** laws are made to be broken; *Fam* **ganaron con todas las de la l.** they won fair and square; **de buena l.** reliable, sterling; *Fam* **l. del embudo** one law for oneself and another for everyone else; *Dep* **l. de la ventaja** advantage (law); *Hist* **l. sálica** Salic law; **l. seca** prohibition law; **leyes** *(derecho)* law (b) *(de metal precioso)* **de l.** *(oro)* = containing the legal amount of gold; *(plata)* sterling

**leyenda** *nf* (a) *(narración)* legend (b) *(inscripción)* inscription, legend

**leyera** *etc ver* **leer**

**liante** *nmf Fam* (a) *(persuasivo)* patter merchant; **claro que me convenció, es un l.** of course he persuaded me, he could talk you into anything! (b) *(enredador)* stirrer, trouble-maker; **¡no seas l.!** don't complicate things!

**liar** [34] **1** *vt* (a) *(atar)* to tie up (b) *(cigarrillo)* to roll (c) *(envolver)* **l. algo en** *(papel)* to wrap sth up in (d) *(involucrar)* **l. a alguien (en)** to get sb mixed up (in) (e) *(complicar)* to confuse; **¡ya me has liado!** now you've really got me confused!
**2 liarse** *vpr* (a) *(enredarse)* to get muddled up (b) *(empezar)* to begin, to start; **liarse a hacer algo** to start *o* begin doing sth; **se liaron a puñetazos** they set about one another (c) *Fam (sentimentalmente)* to get involved (**con** with), to have an affair (**con** with)

**libación** *nf Literario* libation

**libanés, -esa** *adj & nm,f* Lebanese

**Líbano** *nm* **el L.** the Lebanon

**libar** *vt* to sip, to suck

**libelo** *nm* lampoon

**libélula** *nf* dragonfly

**liberación** *nf* (a) *(de ciudad, país)* liberation; *(de rehén, prisionero)* freeing; **l. de la mujer** women's liberation; **l. sexual** sexual liberation (b) *(de hipoteca)* redemption

**liberado, -a** *adj (ciudad, país)* liberated; *(rehén, prisionero)* freed

**liberal** *adj & nmf* liberal

**liberalidad** *nf* liberality

**liberalismo** *nm Pol* liberalism

**liberalización** *nf* liberalization; *Econ* deregulation

**liberalizar** [16] *vt* to liberalize; *Econ* to deregulate

**liberar** *también Fig* **1** *vt (ciudad, país)* to liberate; *(rehén, prisionero)* to free; **l. a alguien de algo** to free sb from sth
**2 liberarse** *vpr* to liberate oneself; **liberarse de algo** to free *o* liberate oneself from sth

**Liberia** *n* Liberia

**liberiano, -a** *adj & nm,f* Liberian

**libertad** *nf* freedom, liberty; **dejar** *o* **poner a alguien en l.** to set sb free, to release sb; **estar en l.** to be free; **tener l. para hacer algo** to be free to do sth; **tomarse la l. de hacer algo** to take the liberty of doing sth; **tomarse libertades (con)** to take liberties (with); *Econ* **l. de circulación de capitales/ trabajadores** free movement of capital/workers; **l. condicional** probation; **l. de expresión** freedom of speech; **l. de imprenta** *o* **prensa** freedom of the press; **l. provisional (bajo fianza)** bail; **l. provisional (bajo palabra)** parole

**libertador, -ora 1** *adj* liberating
**2** *nm,f* liberator

**libertar** *vt también Fig* to liberate

**libertario, -a** *adj & nm,f Pol* libertarian

**libertinaje** *nm* licentiousness

**libertino, -a 1** *adj* licentious
**2** *nm,f* libertine

**liberto, -a** *nm,f Hist* freedman, *f* freedwoman

**Libia** *n* Libya

**libidinoso, -a** *adj* libidinous, lewd

**libido** *nf* libido

**libio, -a** *adj & nm,f* Libyan

**libra 1** *nm (signo del zodiaco)* Libra; **ser l.** to be (a) Libra
**2** *nmf (persona)* Libran
**3** *nf* (a) *(unidad de peso, moneda)* pound; **l. esterlina** pound sterling (b) *muy Fam (cien pesetas)* = a hundred pesetas

**librado, -a 1** *nm,f Com* drawee
**2** *adj* **salir bien l.** to get off lightly; **salir mal l.** to come off badly

**librador, -ora** *nm,f Com* drawer

**libramiento** *nm,* **libranza** *nf Com* order of payment

**librar 1** *vt* (a) **l. a alguien (de algo/de hacer algo)** *(eximir)* to free sb (from sth/from doing sth); *(de pagos, impuestos)* to exempt sb (from sth/from doing sth) (b) *(entablar) (pelea, lucha)* to engage in; *(batalla, combate)* to join, to wage (c) *Com* to draw
**2** *vi (no trabajar)* to be off work
**3 librarse** *vpr* (a) *(salvarse)* **librarse (de hacer algo)** to escape (from doing sth); **de buena te libraste** you had a lucky escape (b) *(deshacerse)* **librarse de algo/alguien** to get rid of sth/sb

**libre** *adj* (a) *(no sujeto)* free; *(rato, tiempo)* spare; *(camino, vía)* clear; *(espacio, piso, retrete)* empty, vacant; *Dep* **200 metros libres** 200 metres freestyle; **l. de** *(sin)* free from; *(exento)* exempt from; **l. de franqueo** post-free; **l. de impuestos** tax-free; **ser l. de** *o* **para hacer algo** to be free to do sth; **ir por l.** to go it alone (b) *(alumno)* external; **estudiar por l.** to be an external student

**librea** *nf* livery

**librecambio** *nm* free trade

**librecambismo** *nm* (doctrine of) free trade

**librepensador, -ora 1** *adj* freethinking
**2** *nm,f* freethinker

**librepensamiento** *nm* freethinking

**librería** *nf* (a) *(tienda)* bookshop (b) *(mueble)* bookcase

**librero, -a 1** *nm,f (persona)* bookseller
**2** *nm Chile, Méx (mueble)* bookshelf

**libreta** *nf* (a) *(para escribir)* notebook (b) *(de banco)* **l. (de ahorros)** savings book

**libreto** *nm* (a) *Mús* libretto (b) *Am Cine* script

**libro** *nm* book; **llevar los libros** to keep the books; **hablar como un l.** to express oneself very clearly; *Pol* **l. blanco** white paper; **l. de bolsillo** (pocket-sized) paperback; **l. de cabecera** bedside book; *Com* **l. de caja** cashbook; **l. de cocina** cookery book; **l. de consulta** reference book; *Com* **l. de cuentas** *o* **contabilidad** accounts book; *Educ* **l. de escolaridad** school report; **l. de familia** = document containing personal details of the members of a family; **l. de reclamaciones** complaints book; **l. de registro (de entradas)** register; *Rel* **l. sagrado** Book *(in Bible)*; **l. de texto** textbook

**Lic.** *(abrev de* **licenciado)**

**licantropía** *nf* lycanthropy

**licántropo** *nm* werewolf

**licencia** *nf* (a) *(documento)* licence, permit; *(autorización)* permission; **l. de armas/caza** gun/hunting licence; **l. de exportación/importación** export/import licence; **l. de obras** planning permission; **l. fiscal** = official authorization to practise a profession; **l. poética** poetic licence (b) *Mil* discharge (c) *(confianza)* licence, freedom; **tomarse licencias con alguien** to take liberties with sb

**licenciado, -a 1** *adj Mil* discharged

**2** *nm,f* (a) *Educ* graduate; **l. en económicas/derecho** economics/law graduate (b) *Mil* discharged soldier

**licenciamiento** *nm Mil* discharge

**licenciar [15] 1** *vt Mil* to discharge

**2 licenciarse** *vpr* (a) *Educ* to graduate (**en** in) (b) *Mil* to be discharged

**licenciatura** *nf* degree (**en** *o* **de** in)

**licencioso, -a** *adj* licentious

**liceo** *nm* (a) *Educ* lycée (b) *(de recreo)* social club

**licitación** *nf* bid, bidding

**licitador, -ora** *nmf* bidder

**licitar** *vt* to bid for

**lícito, -a** *adj* (a) *(legal)* lawful (b) *(correcto)* right (c) *(justo)* fair

**licor** *nm* liquor

**licorera** *nf* (a) *(botella)* decanter (b) *(mueble)* cocktail cabinet

**licorería** *nf* (a) *(fábrica)* distillery (b) *(tienda)* off-licence

**licuado** *nm Am* milk shake

**licuadora** *nf* liquidizer, blender

**licuar [4]** *vt Culin* to liquidize

**licuefacción** *nf* liquefaction

**lid** *nf Anticuado* fight; *Fig* **en buena l.** in a fair contest; *Fig* **un experto en estas lides** an old hand in these matters

**líder 1** *adj* leading

**2** *nmf* leader

**liderar** *vt* to lead

**liderazgo, liderato** *nm* (a) *(primer puesto)* lead; *(en liga)* first place (b) *(dirección)* leadership

**lidia** *nf* (a) *(arte)* bullfighting (b) *(corrida)* bullfight

**lidiador, -ora** *nm,f Taurom* bullfighter

**lidiar [15] 1** *vi (luchar)* to struggle (**con** with)

**2** *vt Taurom* to fight

**liebre** *nf* (a) *(animal)* hare; *Fig* **correr como una l.** to run like a hare; *Fig* **levantar la l.** to let the cat out of the bag (b) *Chile (microbús)* minibus

**Liechtenstein** ['litʃenstein] *n* Liechtenstein

**liendre** *nf* nit

**lienzo** *nm* (a) *(tela)* (coarse) cloth; *(paño)* piece of cloth (b) *(para pintar)* canvas (c) *(cuadro)* painting

**lifting** ['liftin] *(pl* **liftings)** *nm* facelift

**liga** *nf* (a) *(confederación, agrupación)* & *Dep* league (b) *(para medias)* suspender

**ligadura** *nf* (a) *Med* & *Mús* ligature; *Med* **l. de trompas** tubal ligation (b) *(atadura)* bond, tie

**ligamento** *nm Anat* ligament; **rotura de ligamentos** torn ligaments

**ligar [40] 1** *vt* (a) *(unir, aglutinar)* to bind; *(atar)* to tie (up); *Med* to put a ligature on (b) *Mús* to slur

**2** *vi Fam (flirtear)* to flirt; **l. con alguien** *(entablar relaciones)* to get off with sb

**ligazón** *nf* link, connection

**ligereza** *nf* (a) *(levedad)* lightness; *(de dolor)* slightness (b) *(agilidad)* agility (c) *(rapidez)* speed (d) *(irreflexión)* rashness; **fue una l. decir eso** it was rash *o* reckless to say that

**ligero, -a** *adj* (a) *(leve)* light; *(dolor, rumor, descenso)* slight; *(traje, tela)* thin (b) *(ágil)* agile, nimble (c) *(rápido)* quick, swift (d) *(irreflexivo)* flippant; **hacer algo a la ligera** to do sth without much thought; **juzgar a la ligera** to be superficial in one's judgements

**light** [lait] *adj inv (comida)* low-calorie; *(refresco)* diet; *(cigarrillos)* light

**ligón, -ona** *Fam* **1** *adj* **es muy l.** he's always getting off with somebody or other

**2** *nm,f* goer, raver

**ligoteo** *nm Fam* **salir de l.** to go out on the pull

**ligue 1** *ver* **ligar**

**2** *nm Fam* (a) *(acción)* **ir de l.** to be on the pull (b) *(persona)* pick-up

**liguero, -a 1** *adj Dep* league; **partido l.** league game *o* match

**2** *nm Br* suspender belt, *US* garter belt

**liguilla** *nf Dep* mini-league, round-robin tournament

**lija** nf (a) (papel) sandpaper (b) (pez) dogfish

**lijadora** nf sander

**lijar** vt to sand down

**lila 1** nf (flor) lilac

**2** adj inv & nm (color) lilac

**liliputiense 1** adj dwarfish

**2** nmf midget

**Lima** n Lima

**lima** nf (a) (herramienta) file; **l. de uñas** nail file; Fam **comer como una l.** to eat like a horse (b) (fruto) lime

**limaco** nm slug

**limadora** nf polisher

**limar** vt (pulir) to file down; Fig (perfeccionar) to polish, to add the finishing touches to

**limbo** nm (a) Rel limbo; Fam **estar en el l.** to be miles away (b) Astron & Bot limb

**limeño, -a 1** adj of/from Lima

**2** nm,f person from Lima

**limitación** nf (a) (restricción) limitation, limit; **l. de velocidad** speed limit (b) (de distrito) boundaries

**limitado, -a** adj (restringido) limited; Fig (poco inteligente) dim-witted

**limitar 1** vt (a) (restringir) to limit (b) (terreno) to mark out (c) (atribuciones, derechos) to set out, to define

**2** vi to border (**con** on)

**3 limitarse** vpr **limitarse a** to limit oneself to

**límite 1** adj inv (a) (precio, velocidad, edad) maximum (b) (situación) extreme; (caso) borderline

**2** nm (a) (tope) limit; **dentro de un l.** within limits; **su pasión no tiene l.** her passion knows no bounds; **l. de velocidad** speed limit (b) (confín) boundary

**limítrofe** adj (país, territorio) bordering; (terreno, finca) neighbouring

**limo** nm mud (from bed of river, lake)

**limón** nm lemon

**limonada** nf = iced, sweetened lemon juice drink

**limonar** nm lemon grove

**limonero** nm lemon tree

**limosna** nf (a) Rel alms (b) (a mendigo) **dar l.** to give money; **pedir l.** to beg; Fig to ask for charity

**limosnear** vi to beg

**limpia** nmf Fam (limpiabotas) shoeshine, Br bootblack

**limpiabotas** nmf inv shoeshine, Br bootblack

**limpiacristales** nm inv window-cleaning fluid

**limpiador, -ora 1** adj cleaning

**2** nm,f cleaner

**limpiamente** adv (a) (con destreza) cleanly (b) (honradamente) honestly

**limpiametales** nm inv metal polish

**limpiaparabrisas** nm inv Br windscreen wiper, US windshield wiper

**limpiar** [15] vt (a) (quitar la suciedad) to clean; (con trapo) to wipe; (mancha) to wipe away; (zapatos) to polish (b) Fig (desembarazar) **l. algo de algo** to clear sth of sth (c) Fam (en el juego) to clean out (d) Fam (robar) to swipe, to pinch

**límpido, -a** adj Formal limpid

**limpieza** nf (a) (cualidad) cleanliness; Hist **l. de sangre** racial purity (b) (acción) cleaning; **hacer la l.** to do the cleaning; **l. en seco** dry cleaning; Fig **l. étnica** ethnic cleansing (c) Fig (destreza) skill, cleanness

**limpio, -a 1** adj (a) (sin suciedad) clean; (pulcro) neat; (cielo, imagen) clear (b) Fig (neto) (sueldo) net (c) Fig (honrado) honest; (intenciones) honourable; (juego) clean (d) Fig (sin culpa) **estar l.** to be in the clear; **l. de culpa/sospecha** free of blame/suspicion (e) Fam (sin dinero) broke, skint (f) (expresiones) **a puñetazo l.** with bare fists; **abrió la puerta a patada limpia** he kicked down the door

**2** adv cleanly, fair; **pasar a** o **poner en l.** to make a fair copy of, to write out neatly; **sacar algo en l. de** to make sth out from

**limusina** nf limousine

**linaje** nm lineage

**linaza** nf linseed

**lince** nm lynx; **ser un l. (para algo)** to be very sharp (at sth)

**linchamiento** nm lynching

**linchar** vt to lynch; **l. a alguien** to lynch sb

**lindante** adj **l. (con)** (espacio) bordering; (conceptos) bordering (on)

**lindar** vi **l. con** (terreno) to adjoin, to be next to; (conceptos, ideas) to border on

**linde** nm o nf boundary

**lindero** nm boundary

**lindeza** nf (a) (belleza) prettiness (b) **lindezas** Irón (insultos) insults

**lindo, -a** adj pretty, lovely; **de lo l.** a great deal

**línea** nf (a) también Dep & Telecom line; **cortar la l. (telefónica)** to cut off the phone; **l. aérea** airline; Dep **l. de banda** sideline, touchline; **l. de conducta** course of action; Aut **l. continua** solid white line; Com **l. de crédito/ de descubierto** credit/overdraft limit; **l. divisoria** dividing line; **l. de flotación** waterline; Dep **l. de meta** (en fútbol) goal line; (en carrera) finishing line; **l. de mira** o **tiro** line of fire; **l. punteada** o **de puntos** dotted line; Com **una nueva l. de productos** a new line of products; **l. recta** straight line; *Dep* **l. de saque** base line, service line

(**b**) *(silueta)* figure; **guardar la l.** to watch one's figure; **un coche de l. aerodinámica** a streamlined car

(**c**) *(estilo)* style; **de l. clásica** classical; **eso está muy en su l.** that's just his style

(**d**) *(categoría)* class, category; **de primera l.** first-rate

(**e**) *Informát* **en l.** on-line; **fuera de l.** off-line

(**f**) *(expresiones)* **en líneas generales** in broad terms; **en toda la l.** *(completamente)* all along the line; **leer entre líneas** to read between the lines

**lineal** *adj* (**a**) *(de la línea)* linear (**b**) *(aumento)* steady

**linfa** *nf* lymph

**linfático, -a** *adj* lymphatic; *Fig* lethargic

**linfocito** *nm Anat* lymphocyte

**lingotazo** *nm Fam* swig

**lingote** *nm* ingot

**lingüista** *nmf* linguist

**lingüística** *nf* linguistics *(singular)*

**lingüístico, -a** *adj* linguistic

**linier** [li'njer] (*pl* **liniers**) *nm* linesman

**linimento** *nm* liniment

**lino** *nm* (**a**) *(planta)* flax (**b**) *(tejido)* linen

**linóleo** *nm* linoleum

**linotipia** *nf* Linotype®

**linotipista** *nmf* linotypist

**linotipo** *nm* Linotype®

**linterna** *nf* (**a**) *(de pilas)* Br torch, US flashlight (**b**) *(farol)* lantern, lamp; **l. mágica** magic lantern

**lío** *nm* (**a**) *Fam (enredo)* mess; **hacerse un l.** to get muddled up; **meterse en líos** to get into trouble (**b**) *Fam (jaleo)* racket, row; **armar un l.** to kick up a fuss (**c**) *Fam (amorío)* affair; **tener un l. de faldas** to have woman trouble (**d**) *(paquete)* bundle

**liofilizado, -a** *adj* freeze-dried

**liofilizar** [16] *vt* to freeze-dry

**lioso, -a** *adj Fam* (**a**) *(complicado) (asunto)* complicated; *(explicación, historia)* convoluted, involved (**b**) *(persona)* troublemaking

**lípido** *nm* lipid

**liposoluble** *adj* soluble in fat

**liposoma** *nm* liposome

**liposucción** *nf* liposuction

**lipotimia** *nf* fainting fit

**liquen** *nm* lichen

**liquidación** *nf* (**a**) *(pago)* settlement, payment; *Com* **l. de bienes** liquidation of assets (**b**) *(rebaja)* clearance sale (**c**) *(final)* liquidation (**d**) *(finiquito)* redundancy settlement

**liquidar** *vt* (**a**) *(pagar) (deuda)* to pay; *(cuenta)* to settle (**b**) *(rebajar)* to sell off (**c**) *(malgastar)* to throw away (**d**) *(acabar) (asunto)* to settle; *(negocio, sociedad)* to wind up (**e**) *Fam (matar)* to liquidate

**liquidez** *nf Econ & Fís* liquidity

**líquido, -a 1** *adj* (**a**) *(estado)* liquid; **el l. elemento** water (**b**) *Econ (neto)* net

**2** *nm* (**a**) *(sustancia)* liquid (**b**) *Econ* liquid assets (**c**) *Med* fluid; **l. amniótico** amniotic fluid

**lira** *nf* (**a**) *Mús* lyre (**b**) *(moneda)* lira

**lírica** *nf* lyric poetry

**lírico, -a** *adj* (**a**) *Lit* lyric, lyrical (**b**) *(musical)* musical

**lirio** *nm* iris

**lirismo** *nm* lyricism

**lirón** *nm Zool* dormouse; *Fig* **dormir como un l.** to sleep like a log

**lis** *nf* (**flor de**) **l.** iris

**Lisboa** *n* Lisbon

**lisboeta 1** *adj* of/from Lisbon

**2** *nmf* person from Lisbon

**lisiado, -a 1** *adj* crippled

**2** *nm,f* cripple

**lisiar** [15] **1** *vt* to maim, to cripple

**2** **lisiarse** *vpr* to be maimed *o* crippled

**liso, -a 1** *adj* (**a**) *(llano)* flat; *(sin asperezas)* smooth; *(pelo)* straight; **los 400 metros lisos** the 400 metres; **lisa y llanamente** quite simply; **hablando lisa y llanamente** to put it plainly (**b**) *(no estampado)* plain

**2** *nm,f Arg, Perú* coarse *o* rude person

**lisonja** *nf* flattering remark

**lisonjear** *vt* to flatter

**lisonjero, -a** *adj* *(persona, comentario)* flattering; *(perspectiva)* promising

**lista** *nf* (**a**) *(enumeración)* list; **pasar l.** to call the register; **l. de boda/de espera/de precios** wedding/waiting/price list; **l. de la compra** shopping list; **l. de correos** poste restante; **l. negra** blacklist; *Informát* **l. de correo** mailing list (**b**) *(de tela, madera)* strip; *(de papel)* slip; *(de color)* stripe; **una camiseta a listas** a striped shirt

**listado, -a 1** *adj* striped

**2** *nm Informát* listing

**listar** *vt Informát* to list

**listillo, -a** *nm,f Fam Pey* a smart alec(k)

**listín** *nm* **l. (de teléfonos)** (telephone) directory

**listo, -a** *adj* (a) *(inteligente, hábil)* clever, smart; **dárselas de l.** to make oneself out to be clever; **pasarse de l.** to be too clever by half; **ser más l. que el hambre** to be nobody's fool (b) *(preparado)* ready; **¿estáis listos?** are you ready?; **estás** *o* **vas l. (si crees que...)** you've got another think coming (if you think that...); **¡l.!** (that's me) ready!, finished!

**listón** *nm (de madera)* lath; *Dep* bar; *Fig* **poner el l. muy alto** to set very high standards

**lisura** *nf Arg, Perú* rude remark, bad language

**litera** *nf* (a) *(cama)* bunk (bed); *(de barco)* berth; *(de tren)* couchette (b) *(vehículo)* litter

**literal** *adj* literal

**literario, -a** *adj* literary

**literato, -a** *nm,f* writer, author

**literatura** *nf* literature

**litigante** *adj & nmf* litigant

**litigar** [40] *vi* to go to law

**litigio** *nm Der* court case, law suit; *Fig* dispute; **en l.** in dispute

**litigue** *etc ver* **litigar**

**litio** *nm* lithium

**litografía** *nf* (a) *(arte)* lithography (b) *(grabado)* lithograph (c) *(taller)* lithographer's (workshop)

**litografiar** [34] *vt* to lithograph

**litoral 1** *adj* coastal

**2** *nm* coast

**litosfera** *nf* lithosphere

**litro** *nm* litre

**litrona** *nf muy Fam* = litre bottle of beer

**Lituania** *n* Lithuania

**lituano, -a 1** *adj & nm,f* Lithuanian

**2** *nm (lengua)* Lithuanian

**liturgia** *nf* liturgy

**litúrgico, -a** *adj* liturgical

**liviandad** *nf* (a) *(levedad)* lightness (b) *(frivolidad)* flightiness, frivolousness

**liviano, -a** *adj* (a) *(ligero) (blusa)* thin; *(carga)* light (b) *(sin importancia)* slight (c) *(superficial)* frivolous

**lividez** *nf (palidez)* pallor

**lívido, -a** *adj* (a) *(pálido)* very pale, white as a sheet (b) *(amoratado)* livid

**living** ['liβin] *(pl* **livings)** *nm* living room

**liza** *nf (lucha)* battle; **en l.** in opposition

**Ll, ll** ['eʎe, 'eʒe] *nf (letra)* Ll, ll

**llaga** *nf Med* sore, ulcer; *Fig* open wound

**llagar** [40] **1** *vt* to bring out in sores

**2 llagarse** *vpr* to become covered in sores

**llama** *nf* (a) *(de fuego, pasión)* flame; **en llamas** ablaze (b) *(animal)* llama

**llamada** *nf* (a) *(en general)* call; *(a la puerta)* knock; *(con timbre)* ring (b) *Telecom* telephone call; **hacer una l.** to make a phone call; **tienes dos llamadas en el contestador** you have two messages on your answering machine; **l. urbana/interurbana/a cobro revertido** local/long-distance/reverse-charge call (c) *(en un libro)* reference mark

**llamado, -a 1** *adj* so-called

**2** *nm Am (de teléfono)* call

**llamador** *nm (aldaba)* door knocker; *(timbre)* bell

**llamamiento** *nm* (a) *(apelación)* appeal, call; **hacer un l. a alguien para que haga algo** to call upon sb to do sth; **hacer un l. a la huelga** to call a strike (b) *Mil* call-up

**llamar 1** *vt* (a) *(en general )* to call; *(con gestos)* to beckon (b) *(por teléfono)* to phone, to call (c) *(dar nombre)* to call (d) *(convocar)* to summon, to call; *Mil* **l. (a filas)** to call up; **l. a la huelga** to call out on strike (e) *(atraer)* to attract, to call

**2** *vi* (a) *(a la puerta) (con golpes)* to knock; *(con timbre)* to ring; **están llamando** there's somebody at the door (b) *(por teléfono)* to phone

**3 llamarse** *vpr (tener por nombre)* to be called; **¿cómo te llamas?** what's your name?; **me llamo Patricia** my name's Patricia

**llamarada** *nf* (a) *(de fuego, ira)* blaze (b) *(de rubor)* flush

**llamativo, -a** *adj (color)* bright, gaudy; *(ropa)* showy

**llamear** *vi* to burn, to blaze

**llana** *nf* (a) *Gram* word stressed on the last syllable (b) *Constr* trowel

**llanear** *vi* to roam the plains

**llanero, -a 1** *adj* of the plainspeople

**2** *nm,f* plainsman, *f* plainswoman

**llaneza** *nf* naturalness, straightforwardness

**llanito, -a** *adj & nm,f Fam* Gibraltarian

**llano, -a 1** *adj* (a) *(campo, superficie)* flat (b) *(trato, persona)* natural, straightforward (c) *(pueblo, clase)* ordinary (d) *(lenguaje, expresión)* simple, plain (e) *Gram* stressed on the last syllable

**2** *nm (llanura)* plain; *Carib* **llanos** plains

**llanta** *nf* (a) *Aut* rim (a) *Am (cubierta)* tyre; *(rueda)* wheel

**llantera, llantina** *nf Fam* blubbing

**llanto** *nm* crying

**llanura** *nf* plain

**llave** *nf* (a) *(de cerradura)* key; **bajo l.** under lock and key; **echar la l., cerrar con l.** to lock up; **l. en mano** *(vivienda)* ready for immediate occupation; **l. de contacto** ignition key; **l. maestra** master key (b) *(grifo )* Br tap, US faucet; **l. de paso** stopcock; **cerrar la l. de paso** to turn the water/gas off at the mains (c) *(interruptor)* **l. de la luz** light switch (d) *(herramienta)* spanner; **l. allen** Allen key; **l. inglesa** monkey wrench **(e)** *(de judo)* hold, lock **(f)** *(signo ortográfico)* curly bracket

**llavero** *nm* keyring

**llavín** *nm* latchkey

**llegada** *nf* **(a)** *(acción)* arrival **(b)** *Dep* finish

**llegar** [40] **1** *vi* **(a)** *(a un sitio)* to arrive **(de** from); **l. a un hotel/una ciudad** to arrive at a hotel/in a city; **llegaré pronto** I'll be there early

**(b)** *(un tiempo, la noche)* to come; **ha llegado el invierno** winter has arrived

**(c)** *(durar)* **l. a** o **hasta** to last until

**(d)** *(alcanzar)* **l. a** to reach; **no llego al techo** I can't reach the ceiling; **l. hasta** to reach up to; **esta carretera sólo llega hasta Cádiz** this road only goes as far as Cadiz

**(e)** *(ser suficiente)* to be enough **(para** for)

**(f)** *(lograr)* **l. a (ser) algo** to get to be sth, to become sth; *Fig* **llegará lejos** she'll go far; **si llego a saberlo…** *(en el futuro)* if I happen to find out…; *(en el pasado)* if I had known…

**(g)** *(al extremo de)* **llegó a decirme…** he went as far as to say to me…; **hemos llegado a pagar 80.000 pts** at times we've had to pay as much as 80,000 pesetas

**2 llegarse** *vpr* **llegarse a** to go round to

**llenar 1** *vt* **(a)** *(ocupar) (vaso, hoyo, habitación)* to fill **(de** with); *(pared, suelo)* to cover **(de** with); **l. a alguien de alegría/tristeza** to fill sb with happiness/sadness; **l. el depósito** *(del coche)* to fill up the tank **(b)** *(satisfacer)* to satisfy **(c)** *(impreso)* to fill in o out

**2** *vi (comida)* to be filling

**3 llenarse** *vpr* **(a)** *(ocuparse)* to fill up **(b)** *(saciarse)* to be full **(c)** *(cubrirse)* **llenarse de** to become covered in

**llenazo** *nm* full house

**llenito, -a** *adj Fam (regordete)* chubby

**lleno, -a 1** *adj (recipiente, habitación)* full **(de** of); *(suelo, mesa, pared)* covered **(de** in o with); **l., por favor** *(en gasolinera)* fill her up, please

**2** *nm* **(a)** *(en teatro)* full house **(b)** **de l.** full in the face; **acertó de l.** he was bang on target

**llevadero, -a** *adj* bearable

**llevar 1** *vt* **(a)** *(en general)* to carry

**(b)** *(acompañar, coger y depositar)* to take; **l. algo/a alguien a** to take sth/sb to; **me llevó en coche** he drove me there

**(c)** *(prenda, objeto personal)* to wear; **llevo gafas** I wear glasses; **no llevo dinero** I haven't got any money on me

**(d)** *(problema, persona)* to handle

**(e)** *(conducir)* **l. a alguien a algo** to lead sb to sth; **l. a alguien a hacer algo** to lead o cause sb to do sth

**(f)** *(ocuparse de, dirigir)* to be in charge of; *(casa,*

*negocio)* to look after, to run; **lleva la contabilidad** she keeps the books

**(g)** *(hacer) (de alguna manera)* **lleva muy bien sus estudios** he's doing very well in his studies; *Fam* **¿cómo lo llevas?** how are you getting on?

**(h)** *(tener) (de alguna manera)* to have; **l. el pelo largo** to have long hair; **llevas las manos sucias** your hands are dirty

**(i)** *(soportar)* to deal o cope with; **l. algo bien/mal** to take sth well/badly

**(j)** *(mantener)* to keep; **l. el paso** to keep in step

**(k)** *(vida)* to lead; **lleva camino de ser famoso/rico** he's on the road to fame/riches; **l. las de perder** to be heading for defeat

**(l)** *(tiempo)* **lleva tres semanas sin venir** she hasn't come for three weeks now, it's three weeks since she was last here; **me llevó un día hacer este guiso** it took me a day to make this dish

**(m)** *(sobrepasar)* **te llevo seis puntos** I'm six points ahead of you; **me lleva dos centímetros** he's two centimetres taller than me

**(n)** **l. consigo** *(implicar)* to lead to, to bring about

**2** *vi* **(a)** *(conducir)* **l. a** to lead to; **esta carretera lleva al norte** this road leads north

**(b)** *(antes de participio)* *(tener, haber)* **llevo leída media novela** I'm halfway through the novel; **llevo dicho esto mismo docenas de veces** I've said the same thing over and over again

**(c)** *(antes de gerundio)* *(estar)* **l. mucho tiempo haciendo algo** to have been doing sth for a long time

**3 llevarse** *vpr* **(a)** *(coger)* to take; *(robar)* to steal; **alguien se ha llevado mi sombrero** someone has taken my hat

**(b)** *(conseguir)* to get; **se ha llevado el premio** she has carried off the prize; **yo me llevo siempre las culpas** I always get the blame

**(c)** *(recibir)* *(susto, sorpresa)* to get, to receive; **me llevé un disgusto** I was upset

**(d)** *(entenderse)* **llevarse bien/mal (con alguien)** to get on well/badly (with sb); **llevarse a matar con alguien** to be mortal enemies o at daggers drawn with sb

**(e)** *(estar de moda)* to be in (fashion); **este año se lleva el verde** green is in this year

**(f)** *Mat* **me llevo una** carry (the) one

**llorar 1** *vi* **(a)** *(con lágrimas)* to cry **(b)** *Fam (quejarse)* to whinge

**2** *vt* **l. la muerte de alguien** to mourn sb's death

**llorera** *nf Fam* crying fit

**llorica** *Fam Pey* **1** *adj* **ser l.** to be a crybaby

**2** *nmf* crybaby

**lloriquear** *vi* to whine, to snivel

**lloriqueo** *nm* whining, snivelling

**lloro** *nm* crying, tears

**llorón, -ona 1** *adj* who cries a lot

**2** *nm,f* crybaby

**lloroso, -a** *adj* tearful

**llover** [43] **1** *v impersonal* to rain; **está lloviendo** it's raining; *Fig* **llueve sobre mojado** it's just one thing after another; *Fig* **él, como quien oye l.** he wasn't paying a blind bit of attention; *Fig* **ha llovido mucho desde entonces** a lot of water has passed o gone under the bridge since then

**2** *vi Fig* **le llueven las ofertas** offers are raining down on him; *Fig* **el trabajo me cayó o llegó como llovido del cielo** the job fell into my lap

**llovizna** *nf* drizzle

**lloviznar** *v impersonal* to drizzle

**llueva** *ver* **llover**

**lluvia** *nf* (a) *Meteo* rain; **bajo la l.** in the rain; **l. ácida** acid rain; **l. radiactiva** (nuclear) fallout (b) *Fig (de panfletos, regalos)* shower; *(de preguntas)* barrage

**lluvioso, -a** *adj* rainy

**lo[1], -a** *(mpl* **los**, *fpl* **las)** *pron personal (complemento directo) (cosa)* it; *pl* them; *(persona)* him, f her; *pl* them; *(usted)* you

**lo[2] 1** *pron personal (neutro & predicado)* it; **su hermana es muy guapa pero él no lo es** his sister is very good-looking, but he isn't; **es muy bueno aunque no lo parezca** it's very good, even if it doesn't look it

**2** *art det (neutro)* **lo antiguo me gusta más que lo moderno** I like old things better than modern things; **lo mejor/peor** the best/worst part; **no me quiere ayudar, ¡con todo lo que yo he hecho por ella!** she doesn't want to help me – and after all I've done for her!; **no te imaginas lo grande que era** you can't imagine how big it was; **¿y lo de la fiesta?** what about the party, then?; **siento lo de ayer** I'm sorry about yesterday; **acepté lo que me ofrecieron** I accepted what they offered me

**loa** *nf* (a) *(alabanza)* praise (b) *Lit* eulogy

**loable** *adj* praiseworthy

**loar** *vt* to praise

**lobato** *nm* wolf cub

**lobby** ['loβi] *(pl* **lobbies**) *nm* lobby

**lobezno** *nm* wolf cub

**lobo, -a** *nm,f* wolf; **l. de mar** *(marinero)* sea dog; **l. marino** *(foca)* seal

**lobotomía** *nf* lobotomy

**lóbrego, -a** *adj* gloomy, murky

**lobulado, -a** *adj* lobulate

**lóbulo** *nm* lobe

**lobuno, -a** *adj* wolf-like

**local 1** *adj* local

**2** *nm (establecimiento)* (business) premises *(plural)*; **l. de ensayo** rehearsal space; **l. comercial** business premises

**localidad** *nf* (a) *(población)* place, town (b) *(asiento)* seat (c) *(entrada)* ticket; **no hay localidades** *(en letrero)* sold out

**localismo** *nm* (a) *(sentimiento)* parochialism (b) *Ling* localism

**localista** *adj* parochial

**localización** *nf* localization, tracking down

**localizar** [16] **1** *vt* (a) *(encontrar)* to locate, to track down (b) *(circunscribir)* to localize

**2 localizarse** *vpr* **la infección se localiza en el hígado** the infection is localized in the liver; **esta planta se localiza en los Alpes** this plant is only found in the Alps

**locatis** *Fam* **1** *adj inv* nutty

**2** *nmf inv* nutcase

**locativo** *nm* locative

**loc. cit.** *(abrev de* **loco citato***)* loc. cit.

**loción** *nf* lotion

**loco, -a 1** *adj* (a) *(demente)* & *Fig* mad, crazy; **estar l. de/por** to be mad with/about; **volver l. a alguien** to drive sb mad; **volverse l.** to go mad; **le vuelve l. el fútbol** he's mad about football; **l. de atar** o **remate** stark raving mad; **a lo l.** *(sin pensar)* hastily; *(temerariamente)* wildly; **¡ni l.!** (absolutely) no way!; **¡no lo haría ni l.!** there's no way you'd get me doing that! (b) *(extraordinario) (interés, ilusión)* tremendous; *(suerte, precio)* extraordinary; *(amor, alegría)* wild

**2** *nm,f también Fig (hombre)* lunatic, madman; *(mujer)* lunatic, madwoman; **hacerse el l.** to play dumb, to pretend not to understand

**3** *nf* **loca** *muy Fam (homosexual)* queen

**locomoción** *nf (transporte)* transport; *(de tren)* locomotion

**locomotor, -ora** o **-triz** *adj* locomotive

**locomotora** *nf* engine, locomotive

**locoto** *nm Andes* chilli

**locuacidad** *nf* loquacity, talkativeness

**locuaz** *adj* loquacious, talkative

**locución** *nf* phrase

**locura** *nf* (a) *(demencia)* madness (b) *(imprudencia)* folly; **hacer locuras** to do stupid o crazy things; **temía que hiciera una l.** I was afraid he might do something desperate (c) *(exageración)* **con l.** madly

**locutor, -ora** *nm,f Radio* & *TV (de noticias)* newsreader; *(de continuación)* announcer; *(de programa de radio)* presenter

**locutorio** *nm* (a) *(para visitas)* visiting room (b) *(telefónico)* = establishment containing a number of telephone booths for public use (c) *Radio* studio

**lodazal** *nm* quagmire

**loden** *nm* loden coat

**lodo** *nm también Fig* mud

**logarítmico, -a** *adj* logarithmic

**logaritmo** *nm* logarithm

**logia** *nf* (a) *(masónica)* lodge (b) *Arquit* loggia

**lógica** *nf* logic; **por l.** obviously; **tener l.** to make sense; **eso no tiene l.** that's absurd *o* ridiculous

**lógico, -a** *adj* logical; **es l. que se enfade** it stands to reason that he should get angry

**logística** *nf* logistics *(singular)*

**logístico, -a** *adj* logistic

**logopeda** *nmf* speech therapist

**logopedia** *nf* speech therapy

**logos** *nm inv* (a) *Filosofía* logos (b) *Rel* Logos, Word of God

**logotipo** *nm* logo

**logrado, -a** *adj (bien hecho)* accomplished

**lograr** *vt (objetivo)* to achieve; *(puesto, beca, divorcio)* to get, to obtain; *(resultado)* to obtain, to achieve; *(perfección)* to attain; *(victoria, premio)* to win; *(deseo, aspiración)* to fulfil; **¡lo logramos!** we did it!, we've done it!; **l. hacer algo** to manage to do sth; **l. que alguien haga algo** to manage to get sb to do sth; **no logro entender cómo lo hizo** I just can't see how he managed it

**logro** *nm* achievement

**logroñés, -esa 1** *adj* of/from Logroño
**2** *nm,f* person from Logroño

**Logroño** *n* Logroño

**LOGSE** [loχse] *nf (abrev de* **Ley Orgánica de Ordenación General del Sistema Educativo)** = Spanish Education Act

**Loira** *nm* el L. the (river) Loire

**loísmo** *nm* = incorrect use of "lo" as indirect object instead of "le"

**loma** *nf* hillock

**Lombardía** *n* Lombardy

**lombarda** *nf (verdura)* red cabbage

**lombardo, -a** *adj & nm,f (de Lombardía)* Lombard

**lombriz** *nf* **l. (de tierra)** worm, earthworm; **l. (intestinal)** worm, threadworm; **tener lombrices** to have worms

**Lomé** *n* Lomé

**lomo** *nm* (a) *(de animal)* back; **a lomos de** astride, riding (b) *(carne)* loin (c) *(de libro)* spine (d) *Fam (de persona)* loins, lower back (e) *(de cuchillo)* blunt edge

**lona** *nf* canvas; **una l.** a tarpaulin

**loncha** *nf* slice; *(de beicon)* rasher

**londinense 1** *adj* London; **las calles londinenses** the London streets, the streets of London
**2** *nmf* Londoner

**Londres** *n* London

**loneta** *nf* sailcloth

**longaniza** *nf* = type of spicy cold pork sausage

**longevidad** *nf* longevity

**longevo, -a** *adj* long-lived

**longitud** *nf* (a) *(dimensión)* length; *Fam (distancia)* distance; **tiene medio metro de l.** it's half a metre long; **l. de onda** wavelength (b) *Astron & Geog* longitude

**longitudinal** *adj* longitudinal, lengthways

**long play** ['lomplei] *(pl* **long plays)** *nm* LP, album

**longui, longuis** *nm muy Fam* **hacerse el l.** to act dumb, to pretend not to understand

**lonja** *nf* (a) *(loncha)* slice (b) *(edificio)* exchange; **l. de pescado** fish market

**lontananza** *nf* background; **en l.** in the distance

**look** [luk] *(pl* **looks)** *nm Fam* style

**loor** *nm* **fue recibido en l. de multitudes** he was welcomed by enraptured crowds

**loquero, -a** *nm,f Fam* **se lo llevaron los loqueros** the men in white coats took him away

**lord** *(pl* **lores)** *nm* lord

**loro** *nm* (a) *(animal)* parrot (b) *Fam Fig (charlatán)* chatterbox (c) *muy Fam (aparato de música)* sounds, = radio and/or cassette or CD player (d) *muy Fam* **estar al l.** *(alerta)* to keep one's ears *o* eyes open; *(enterado)* to be well up (on what's happening); **¡al l.!** get a load of this!

**los 1** *art ver* **el**
**2** *pron ver* **lo[1]**

**losa** *nf (piedra)* paving stone, flagstone; *(de tumba)* tombstone

**loseta** *nf* floor tile

**lote** *nm* (a) *(parte)* share (b) *(conjunto)* batch, lot; **un l. de libros** a set of books (c) *Fam* **darse** *o* **pegarse el l. (con)** to have a good snog (with)

**lotería** *nf* (a) *(sorteo)* lottery; **jugar a la l.** to play the lottery; **le tocó la l.** she won the lottery; **L. Nacional** = state-run lottery in which prizes are allocated to randomly chosen five-figure numbers; **l. primitiva** weekly state-run lottery, ≃ National Lottery (b) *(tienda)* place selling lottery tickets (c) *(juego de mesa)* lotto

**lotero, -a** *nm,f* seller of lottery tickets

**loto 1** *nf Fam* = weekly state-run lottery, ≃ National Lottery
**2** *nm (planta)* lotus

**loza** *nf* (a) *(material)* earthenware; *(porcelana)* china (b) *(objetos)* crockery

**lozanía** *nf* (a) *(de plantas)* luxuriance (b) *(de persona)* youthful vigour

**lozano, -a** *adj* (a) *(planta)* lush, luxuriant (b) *(persona)* youthfully vigorous

**LSD** *nm* LSD

**Luanda** *n* Luanda

**lubina** *nf* sea bass

**lubricación** *nf* lubrication

**lubricante, lubrificante 1** *adj* lubricating
**2** *nm* lubricant

**lubricar** [61], **lubrificar** [61] *vt* to lubricate

**lubricidad** *nf* lewdness

**lúbrico, -a** *adj* lewd, salacious

**lucense 1** *adj* of/from Lugo
**2** *nmf* person from Lugo

**lucero** *nm* bright star; **l. del alba/de la tarde** morning/evening star; **como un l.** as bright as a new pin

**lucha** *nf (combate)* fight; *Fig* struggle; **l. libre** all-in wrestling; **l. de clases** class struggle *o* war

**luchador, -ora 1** *adj* **ser muy l.** to be a fighter *o* battler
**2** *nm,f Dep* wrestler; *Fig* fighter

**luchar** *vi (combatir)* to fight; *Fig* to struggle; **l. contra** to fight (against); **l. por** to fight for

**lucidez** *nf* lucidity, clarity

**lucido, -a** *adj* splendid

**lúcido, -a** *adj* lucid

**luciérnaga** *nf* glow-worm

**Lucifer** *nm* Lucifer

**lucimiento** *nm (de ceremonia)* sparkle; *(de actriz)* brilliant performance

**lucio** *nm* pike

**lucir** [41] **1** *vi* (a) *(brillar)* to shine (b) *(rendir)* **no me lucían tantas horas de trabajo** I didn't have much to show for all those hours I worked (c) *(quedar bonito)* to look good (d) *Am (parecer)* to seem (e) *Am (tener)* to have (f) *Am (presumir)* to show off
**2** *vt (llevar)* to wear, to sport; *(exhibir)* to show off, to sport
**3** *lucirse vpr (destacar)* to shine (**en** at); *Irón* **te has lucido** you've excelled yourself!

**lucrarse** *vpr* to make money (for oneself)

**lucrativo, -a** *adj* lucrative; **no l.** non profit-making

**lucro** *nm* profit, gain

**luctuoso, -a** *adj* sorrowful, mournful

**lucubración** *nf* (a) *(reflexión)* cogitation (b) *(imaginación)* brainwave, harebrained idea; **no son más que lucubraciones suyas** it's just a lot of nonsense he's dreamed up

**lucubrar** *vt* to cogitate about, to consider deeply

**lúdico, -a** *adj* of enjoyment, of pleasure; **actividades lúdicas** leisure activities

**ludópata** *nmf* = pathological gambling addict

**ludopatía** *nf* = pathological addiction to gambling

**ludoteca** *nf* toy library

**luego 1** *adv* (a) *(a continuación)* then, next; **primero aquí y l. allí** first here and then there; **l. de** immediately after
(b) *(más tarde)* later; **hazlo l.** do it later
(c) *Am (pronto)* soon; **l. l.** right away
**2** *conj (así que, por lo tanto)* so, therefore

**lugar** *nm* (a) *(sitio)* place; *(localidad)* place, town; *(del crimen, accidente)* scene; *(para acampar, merendar)* spot; **en l. de** instead of; **yo en tu l.** if I were you; *Fig* **fuera de l.** out of place (b) *(puesto)* position; **en primer/segundo l.** in the first/second place, firstly/secondly (c) *(expresiones)* **dar l. a** to bring about, to cause; **sin l. a dudas** without the shadow of a doubt; **tener l.** to take place; **l. común** platitude, commonplace

**lugareño, -a 1** *adj* village; **vino l.** local wine
**2** *nm,f* villager

**lugarteniente** *nm* deputy

**lúgubre** *adj* gloomy, mournful

**lujo** *nm* luxury; *Fig* profusion; **a todo l.** with no expense spared; **de l.** luxury; **con todo l. de detalles** in great detail; **permitirse el l. de algo/de hacer algo** to be able to afford sth/to do sth; **l. asiático** undreamt of opulence *o* luxury

**lujoso, -a** *adj* luxurious

**lujuria** *nf* lust

**lujurioso, -a 1** *adj* lecherous
**2** *nm,f* lecher

**lumbago** *nm* lumbago

**lumbar** *adj* lumbar

**lumbre** *nf* fire; **dar l. a alguien** to give sb a light; **encender la l.** to light the fire

**lumbrera** *nf Fam* leading light

**lumínico, -a** *adj* light; **energía lumínica** light energy

**luminiscencia** *nf* luminescence

**luminosidad** *nf* brightness; *Fig* brilliance

**luminoso, -a** *adj* (a) *(con luz)* bright; **fuente luminosa** light source (b) *Fig (idea)* brilliant

**luminotecnia** *nf* lighting

**luminotécnico, -a** *nm,f* lighting specialist

**lumpen** *nm* **el l.** the underclass

**luna** *nf* (a) *(astro)* moon; **l. creciente** crescent moon *(when waxing)*; **l. llena/nueva** full/new moon; **l. menguante** crescent moon *(when waning)*; **media l.** half moon (b) *(cristal)* window (pane) (c) *(espejo)* mirror (d) **estar en la l.** to be miles away; **pedir la l.** to ask the impossible; **l. de miel** honeymoon

**lunar 1** *adj* lunar
 **2** *nm* (a) *(en la piel)* mole, beauty spot (b) *(en telas)* spot; **a lunares** spotted

**lunático, -a 1** *adj* crazy
 **2** *nm,f* lunatic

**lunch** [lantʃ] *(pl* **lunches)** *nm* buffet lunch

**lunes** *nm inv* Monday; *ver también* **sábado**

**luneta** *nf (de coche)* windscreen; **l. trasera** rear windscreen; **l. térmica** demister

**lunfardo** *nm* = Buenos Aires slang

**lupa** *nf* magnifying glass

**lupanar** *nm Formal* brothel

**lúpulo** *nm* hops

**Lusaka** *n* Lusaka

**lusitano, -a, luso, -a** *adj & nm,f* (a) *(de Lusitania)* Lusitanian (b) *(de Portugal)* Portuguese

**luso, -a** *adj & nm,f* Portuguese

**lustrabotas** *nm inv,* **lustrador** *nm Andes, CSur* bootblack

**lustrar** *vt* to polish

**lustre** *nm* (a) *(brillo)* shine; **dar l. a** to polish (b) *Fig (gloria)* glory

**lustro** *nm* five-year period

**lustroso, -a** *adj* shiny

**luteranismo** *nm Rel* Lutheranism

**luterano, -a** *adj & nm,f Rel* Lutheran

**luto** *nm* mourning; **estar de l.** to be in mourning

**luxación** *nf Med* dislocation

**Luxemburgo** *n* Luxembourg

**luxemburgués, -esa 1** *adj* Luxembourg; **costumbres luxemburguesas** Luxembourg customs
 **2** *nm,f* Luxembourger

**Luxor** *n* Luxor

**luz** *nf* (a) *(en general)* light; *(destello)* flash (of light); **apagar la l.** to switch off the light; **dar o encender la l.** to switch on the light; **se ha ido la l.** the lights have gone out; **a la l. de** in the light of; **a plena l. del día** in the full light of day; **arrojar l. sobre** to shed light on; **a todas luces** whichever way you look at it; **dar a l. (un niño)** to give birth (to a child); **dar l. verde** to give the green light *o* the go-ahead; **sacar a la l.** to bring to light; **l. natural** *(del sol)* natural light
 (b) *(electricidad)* electricity; **cortar la l.** to cut off the electricity supply; **pagar (el recibo de) la l.** to pay the electricity (bill)
 (c) *Aut* **luces** lights; **darle las luces a alguien** to flash (one's lights) at sb; **poner las luces de carretera** *o* **largas** to put (one's headlights) on full beam; **luces de cruce** *o* **cortas** dipped headlights; **luces de freno** brake lights; **luces de posición** *o* **situación** sidelights; **luces de tráfico** *o* **de señalización** traffic lights
 (d) *Hist* **las Luces** the Enlightenment
 (e) *(inteligencia)* **luces** intelligence; **de pocas luces** dim-witted

**luzca** *etc ver* **lucir**

**lycra®** *nf* Lycra®

**Lyon** *n* Lyons, Lyon

# M

**M¹, m** ['eme] *nf* (a) *(letra)* M, m (b) *Fam* **lo mandé a la m…** I told him where to go…

**m²** *(abrev de* **metro)** m

**maca** *nf* (a) *(de fruta)* bruise (b) *(de objetos)* flaw

**macabro, -a** *adj* macabre

**macana** *nf CSur, Carib Fam (disparate)* stupid thing

**macarra** *Fam* **1** *adj* loutish, yobbish
**2** *nm* (a) *(de prostitutas)* pimp (b) *(matón)* lout, yob

**macarrón** *nm* (a) **macarrones** *(pasta)* macaroni (b) *(dulce)* macaroon (c) *(tubo)* sheath *(of cable)*

**macarrónico, -a** *adj Fam* macaronic

**Macedonia** *n* Macedonia

**macedonia** *nf* **m. (de frutas)** fruit salad

**maceración** *nf Culin* soaking, maceration

**macerar** *vt Culin* to soak, to macerate

**maceta** *nf* (a) *(tiesto)* flowerpot (b) *(herramienta)* mallet

**macetero** *nm* flowerpot holder

**machaca** *nmf Fam* (a) *(pesado)* pain, bore (b) *(trabajador)* dogsbody

**machacador, -ora** **1** *adj* crushing
**2** *nf* **machacadora** crusher

**machacar** [61] **1** *vt* (a) *(desmenuzar)* to crush (b) *Fam (estudiar)* to swot up on
**2** *vi Fam (insistir)* to go on and on (**sobre** about)

**machacón, -ona** *Fam* **1** *adj* tiresome
**2** *nm,f* pain, bore

**machaconería** *nf Fam* annoying insistence; **su m. me tiene harto** I'm fed up with the way she just won't let it drop

**machada** *nf* act of bravado

**machamartillo: a machamartillo** *loc adv* very firmly; **creer algo a m.** to be firm in one's belief of sth

**machetazo** *nm (golpe)* machete blow; *(herida)* machete wound

**machete** *nm* machete

**machetear** *vt* to cut *o* strike (with a machete)

**machismo** *nm* machismo

**machista** *adj & nmf* male chauvinist

**macho 1** *adj Biol* male; *Fig (hombre)* macho; *Fam* **es muy m.** he's a real man
**2** *nm* (a) *Biol* male; *(mulo)* (male) mule; **m. cabrío** billy goat; *Fig (hombre)* macho man, he-man; *Fam* **¡oye, m.!** oy, mate! (b) *Elec (enchufe)* (male) plug, jack plug; *(pata de enchufe)* pin

**machote, -a** **1** *adj Fam* brave
**2** *nm,f Fam (niño)* big boy, *f* big girl
**3** *nm Am (modelo)* rough draft

**macilento, -a** *adj* wan

**macizo, -a** **1** *adj* solid; *Fam* **estar m.** *(hombre)* to be hunky; *(mujer)* to be gorgeous
**2** *nm* (a) *Geog* massif (b) *(de plantas)* flowerbed

**macramé** *nm* macramé

**macro** *nf Informát & Fot* macro

**macro-** *prefijo* macro-; **macrocárcel** super prison

**macrobiótico, -a** **1** *adj* macrobiotic
**2** *nf* **macrobiótica** macrobiotics

**macrocefalia** *nf Med* macrocephaly

**macroeconomía** *nf* macroeconomics

**mácula** *nf Formal* blemish

**macuto** *nm* backpack, knapsack

**Madagascar** *n* Madagascar

**Madeira** *n* Madeira

**madeja** *nf* hank, skein

**madera** *nf* (a) *(material)* wood; *Constr* timber; **de m.** wooden; *Fam Fig* **tocar m.** to touch wood; **m. contrachapada** plywood (b) *(tabla)* piece of wood (c) *Fig (cualidades)* **tener m. de algo** to have the makings of sth (d) *muy Fam (policía)* **la m.** the cops

**maderaje, maderamen** *nm Constr* timbers

**maderero, -a** *adj* timber; **industria maderera** timber industry

**madero** *nm* (a) *(tabla)* log (b) *Fig (necio)* half-wit (c) *muy Fam (agente de policía)* cop, pig

**madrás** *nm inv (tejido)* madras

**madrastra** *nf* stepmother

**madraza** *nf Fam* = indulgent *or* doting mother

**madrazo** *nm Méx* hard blow

**madre** *nf* (a) *(mujer, hembra)* mother; ¡m. mía! Jesus!, Christ!; *Fig* **la m. patria** the motherland; *Fam* **éramos ciento y la m.** there were hundreds of us there; *Méx* **dar a alguien en la m.** to beat sb up; *Méx* **mentarle la m. a alguien** to swear at o curse sb; *Méx Fig* **me vale m.** I couldn't care less; *Fam* **ser la m. del cordero** to be at the very root of the problem; **m. adoptiva** foster mother; **m. de alquiler** surrogate mother; **m. política** mother-in-law; **m. soltera** single mother; *Rel* **m. superiora** mother superior (b) *(cauce)* bed; **salirse de m.** *(río)* to burst its banks; *Fig (persona)* to go too far

**madreperla** *nf* *(ostra)* pearl oyster; *(nácar)* mother-of-pearl

**madreselva** *nf* honeysuckle

**Madrid** *n* Madrid

**madrigal** *nm Lit & Mús* madrigal

**madriguera** *nf* *(de animal) & Fig* den; *(de conejo)* burrow

**madrileño, -a 1** *adj* of/from Madrid
**2** *nm,f* person from Madrid

**madrina** *nf* *(de bautizo)* godmother; *(de boda)* bridesmaid; *(de barco)* = woman who launches ship

**madroño** *nm* *(árbol)* strawberry tree; *(fruto)* strawberry-tree berry

**madrugada** *nf* (a) *(amanecer)* dawn; **de m.** at dawn (b) *(noche)* early morning; **las tres de la m.** three in the morning

**madrugador, -ora 1** *adj* early-rising
**2** *nm,f* early riser

**madrugar** [40] *vi* to get up early; *Fig* to be quick off the mark; *Prov* **no por mucho m. amanece más temprano** time must take its course; *Prov* **al que madruga, Dios le ayuda** the early bird catches the worm

**madrugón** *nm Fam* early rise; **darse un m.** to get up very early

**madurar 1** *vt* (a) *(fruto)* to ripen (b) *(persona)* to mature (c) *(idea, proyecto)* to think through
**2** *vi* (a) *(fruto)* to ripen (b) *(persona)* to mature

**madurez** *nf* (a) *(de fruto)* ripeness (b) *(edad adulta)* adulthood (c) *(sensatez, juicio)* maturity

**maduro, -a** *adj* (a) *(fruto)* ripe (b) *(persona)* mature; **de edad madura** middle-aged

**maestra** *adj & nf ver* **maestro**

**maestranza** *nf Mil* arsenal

**maestrazgo** *nm Hist* = office and territory of the master of a military order

**maestría** *nf* (a) *(habilidad)* mastery, skill (b) *Méx* master's degree

**maestro, -a 1** *adj* (a) *(excelente)* masterly (b) *(principal)* main; **llave maestra** passkey, master key
**2** *nm,f* (a) *(profesor)* teacher (b) *(sabio)* master (c) *Mús* maestro (d) *(director)* **m. de ceremonias** master of ceremonies; **m. de obras** foreman (e) *Taurom* matador

**mafia** *nf* mafia

**mafioso, -a 1** *adj* mafia; **organización mafiosa** mafia organization
**2** *nm,f* mafioso

**magazine** [maɣaˈsin] *nm* magazine

**magdalena** *nf* fairy cake; **llorar como una m.** to cry one's eyes out

**magenta** *adj inv & nm* magenta

**magia** *nf* magic; **m. blanca/negra** white/black magic

**magiar 1** *adj & nmf* Magyar
**2** *nm (lengua)* Magyar

**mágico, -a** *adj* magic; *Fig* magical

**magisterio** *nm* (a) *(título)* teaching certificate (b) *(enseñanza)* teaching (c) *(profesión)* teaching profession

**magistrado, -a** *nm,f (juez)* judge

**magistral** *adj* (a) *(de maestro)* magisterial (b) *(excelente)* masterly

**magistratura** *nf Der* (a) *(oficio)* judgeship (b) *(jueces)* magistrature (c) *(tribunal)* tribunal; **m. de trabajo** industrial tribunal

**magma** *nm* magma

**magnanimidad** *nf* magnanimity

**magnánimo, -a** *adj* magnanimous

**magnate** *nm* magnate; **m. del petróleo/de la prensa** oil/press baron

**magnesia** *nf* magnesia

**magnesio** *nm Quím* magnesium

**magnético, -a** *adj también Fig* magnetic

**magnetismo** *nm también Fig* magnetism

**magnetizar** [16] *vt* to magnetize; *Fig* to mesmerize

**magnetofónico, -a** *adj (cinta)* magnetic

**magnetófono** *nm* tape recorder

**magnetoscopio** *nm* video recorder

**magnicida** *nmf* assassin *(of somebody important)*

**magnicidio** *nm* assassination *(of somebody important)*

**magnificar** [61] *vt (ensalzar)* to praise highly

**magnificencia** *nf* magnificence

**magnífico, -a** *adj* wonderful, magnificent

**magnitud** *nf* magnitude

**magno, -a** *adj* great

**magnolia** *nf* magnolia

**magnolio** *nm* magnolia (tree)

**mago, -a** *nm,f (prestidigitador)* magician; *(en cuentos, leyendas)* wizard

**magra** *nf* slice of ham

**magrear** *muy Fam* **1** *vt* to touch up

**2 magrearse** *vpr* to snog

**Magreb** *nm* **el M.** the Maghreb, = Morocco, Algeria and Tunisia

**magrebí** *adj & nmf* Maghrebi

**magreo** *nm muy Fam* touching up

**magro, -a 1** *adj* **(a)** *(sin grasa)* lean **(b)** *(pobre)* poor

**2** *nm* lean meat

**maguey** *nm Am* agave cactus

**magullado, -a** *adj* bruised

**magulladura** *nf* bruise

**magullar** *vt* to bruise

**maharaní** [mara'ni] *nf* maharani

**mahometano, -a** *adj & nm,f* Muslim

**mahonesa** *nf* mayonnaise

**maicena**® *nf Br* cornflour, *US* cornstarch

**mail** ['mail, 'meil] *nm Informát* e-mail message; **enviar un m. a alguien** to e-mail sb

**mailing** ['meiliŋ] *(pl* **mailings)** *nm Com* mailshot; **hacer un m.** to do a mailshot

**maillot** [ma'jot] *(pl* **maillots)** *nm* **(a)** *(prenda femenina)* maillot **(b)** *(en ciclismo)* jersey; **m. amarillo** yellow jersey

**maitines** *nmpl Rel* matins

**maître** ['meitre] *nm* maître

**maíz** *nm Br* maize, sweetcorn, *US* corn; **m. tostado** roasted maize kernels

**maizal** *nm* maize field

**maizena**® *nf Br* cornflour, *US* cornstarch

**majadería** *nf* idiocy

**majadero, -a** *nm,f* idiot

**majar** *vt (machacar)* to crush; *(moler)* to grind

**majareta** *Fam* **1** *adj* nutty

**2** *nmf* nutcase

**majestad** *nf* majesty; **Su M.** His/Her Majesty

**majestuosidad** *nf* majesty

**majestuoso, -a** *adj* majestic

**majo, -a 1** *adj Fam* **(a)** *(simpático)* nice **(b)** *(bonito)* pretty

**2** *nm,f Arte & Hist* Majo, *f* Maja

**majorette** [majo'ret] *nf* majorette

**mal 1** *adj ver* **malo**

**2** *nm* **(a)** *(maldad)* **el m.** evil; **m. de ojo** evil eye

**(b)** *(daño)* harm, damage

**(c)** *(enfermedad)* illness; **m. de altura** *o* **montaña** altitude *o* mountain sickness

**(d)** *(inconveniente)* bad thing; **un m. necesario** a necessary evil

**(e)** *(expresiones)* *Prov* **a grandes males, grandes remedios** drastic situations demand drastic action; **del m., el menos** it's the lesser of two evils; *Prov* **m. de muchos, consuelo de todos** at least I'm not the only one; *Prov* **no hay m. que por bien no venga** every cloud has a silver lining

**3** *adv* **(a)** *(incorrectamente)* wrong; **hacer algo m.** to do sth wrong; **has escrito m. esta palabra** you've spelt that word wrong; **hiciste m. en decírselo** it's was wrong of you to tell him

**(b)** *(inadecuadamente)* badly; **la conferencia/reunión salió m.** the talk/meeting went badly; **oigo/veo m.** I can't hear/see very well; **esta puerta cierra m.** this door doesn't shut properly

**(c)** *(expresa opinión desfavorable)* **estar m.** *(de salud)* to be *o* feel ill; *(de calidad)* to be bad; **está m. eso que has hecho** what you've done is wrong; **oler m.** to smell bad; *Fam Fig* **esto me huele m.** this smells fishy to me; **saber m.** to taste bad; *Fig* **me supo m. que no vinieses a despedirme** I was a bit put out that you didn't come to see me off; **pasarlo m.** to have a bad time; **sentar m. a alguien** *(ropa)* not to suit sb; *(comida)* to disagree with sb; *(comentario, actitud)* to upset sb

**(d)** *(difícilmente)* hardly; **m. puede saberlo si no se lo cuentas** he's hardly going to know it if you don't tell him

**(e)** *(expresiones)* **estar a m. con alguien** to have fallen out with sb; **ir de m. en peor** to go from bad to worse; **no estaría m. que...** it would be nice if...; **m. que** although, even though; **m. que te pese, las cosas están así** whether you like it or not, that's the way things are; **m. que bien** somehow or other; **tomar algo a m.** to take sth the wrong way

**malabar** *adj* **juegos malabares** juggling

**malabarismo** *nm también Fig* juggling; **hacer malabarismos** to juggle

**malabarista** *nmf* juggler

**malacostumbrado, -a** *adj* spoiled

**malacostumbrar** *vt* to spoil

**malagueño, -a 1** *adj* of/from Málaga

**2** *nm,f* person from Málaga

**malaleche** *nmf muy Fam (persona)* miserable sod

**malapata** *nmf muy Fam (persona)* clumsy oaf

**malaria** *nf* malaria

**malasangre** *nmf Fam (persona)* **ser un m.** to be a bit of a bastard

**Malasia** *n* Malaysia

**malasio, -a** *adj* Malaysian

**malasombra** *nmf Fam (persona)* pest

**Malaui** *n* Malawi

**malayo, -a 1** *adj & nm,f* Malay, Malayan

**2** *nm (lengua)* Malay, Malayan

**malcomer** *vi* to eat poorly

**malcriado, -a 1** *adj* spoiled

**2** *nm,f* spoilt brat

**malcriar [34]** *vt* to spoil

**maldad** *nf* (a) *(cualidad)* evil (b) *(acción)* evil thing

**maldecir [53] 1** *vt* to curse

**2** *vi* to curse; **m. de** to speak ill of

**maldición** *nf* curse

**maldiga** *etc ver* **maldecir**

**maldijera** *etc ver* **maldecir**

**maldito, -a** *adj* (a) *Rel & Fig (condenado)* cursed, damned (b) *Fam (para enfatizar)* damned; **¡maldita sea!** damn it!

**Maldivas** *nfpl* **las (Islas) M.** the Maldives

**maleable** *adj también Fig* malleable

**maleado, -a** *adj* gone to the bad, led astray

**maleante 1** *adj* wicked

**2** *nmf* crook

**malear** *vt* to corrupt

**malecón** *nm (muelle)* jetty

**maledicencia** *nf (difamación)* slander

**maleducado, -a 1** *adj* rude

**2** *nm,f* rude person

**maleficio** *nm* curse

**maléfico, -a** *adj* evil

**malentendido** *nm* misunderstanding

**malestar** *nm* (a) *(indisposición)* upset, discomfort; **sentir m. (general)** to feel unwell; **siento un m. en el estómago** I've got an upset stomach (b) *Fig (inquietud)* uneasiness, unrest

**maleta** *nf* suitcase; **hacer** *o* **preparar la m.** to pack (one's bags)

**maletera** *nf Am Br* boot, *US* trunk

**maletero** *nm Br* boot, *US* trunk

**maletilla** *nmf Taurom* apprentice bullfighter

**maletín** *nm* briefcase

**malevolencia** *nf* malevolence, wickedness

**malévolo, -a** *adj* malevolent, wicked

**maleza** *nf (arbustos)* undergrowth; *(malas hierbas)* weeds

**malformación** *nf Med* malformation

**malgache** *adj & nmf* Madagascan, Malagasy

**malgastar** *vt (dinero, tiempo)* to waste; *(salud)* to ruin

**malhablado, -a 1** *adj* foul-mouthed

**2** *nm,f* foul-mouthed person

**malhechor, -ora** *adj & nm,f* criminal

**malherir [64]** *vt* to injure seriously

**malhumor** *nm* bad mood

**malhumorado, -a** *adj (de mal carácter)* bad-tempered; *(enfadado)* in a bad mood

**Mali** *n* Mali

**malicia** *nf* (a) *(mala intención)* malice (b) *(agudeza)* sharpness, alertness

**malicioso, -a** *adj* (a) *(malintencionado)* malicious (b) *(avispado)* sharp, alert

**malignidad** *nf* malignance

**maligno, -a** *adj* malignant

**malintencionado, -a 1** *adj* ill-intentioned

**2** *nm,f* ill-intentioned person

**malinterpretar** *vt* to misinterpret, to misunderstand

**malla** *nf* (a) *(tejido)* mesh; **m. de alambre** wire mesh (b) *(red)* net; **las mallas** *(en fútbol)* the net (c) *CSur, Perú (traje de baño)* swimsuit (d) **mallas** *(de gimnasia)* leotard; *(de ballet)* tights

**Mallorca** *n* Majorca

**mallorquín, -ina** *adj & nm,f* Majorcan

**malnacido, -a 1** *adj* undesirable, nasty

**2** *nm,f* nasty type

**malnutrido, -a** *adj* undernourished

**malo, -a**

> **Mal** is used instead of **malo** before singular masculine nouns (e.g. **un mal ejemplo** a bad example). The comparative form of malo (= worse) is **peor**, the superlative forms (= the worst) are **el peor** (masculine) and **la peor** (feminine).

**1** *adj* (a) *(en general)* bad; *(calidad)* poor, bad; **lo m. es que...** the problem is (that)... (b) *(travieso)* naughty; *(malicioso, malvado)* wicked, evil (c) *(enfermo)* ill, sick; **estar/ponerse m.** to be/fall ill (d) *(molesto)* unpleasant; **mal tiempo** bad weather (e) *(podrido, pasado)* bad, off; **estar/ponerse m.** to be *o* go off (f) *(uso enfático)* **ni un mal trozo de pan** not even a crust of bread; **no había ni un mal bar en el pueblo** there wasn't even a spit-and-sawdust pub in the village

**2** *nm,f Cine* **el m.** the villain, the bad guy

**3** *nfpl* **ponerse a (las) malas con** to fall out with; **estar de malas** to be in a bad mood; **por las malas** by force

**malogrado, -a** *adj (desaprovechado)* wasted; **un actor/futbolista m.** *(muerto)* an actor/footballer who died before fulfilling their promise

**malograr 1** *vt* to waste

**2 malograrse** *vpr* (a) *(fracasar)* to fail (b) *(morir)* to die before one's time

**maloliente** *adj* smelly

**malparado, -a** *adj* **salir m. de algo** to come out of sth badly

**malpensado, -a 1** *adj* malicious, evil-minded

**2** *nm,f* evil-minded person

**malquerencia** *nf* dislike

**malsano, -a** *adj* unhealthy

**malsonante** *adj* rude

**Malta** *n* Malta

**malta** *nm* malt

**malteada** *nf Am* milk shake

**malteado, -a** *adj* malted

**maltés, -esa** *adj & nm,f* Maltese

**maltraer** [68] *vt (maltratar)* to ill-treat; **llevar** *o* **traer a m.** to cause headaches

**maltratar** *vt* (a) *(pegar, insultar)* to ill-treat (b) *(estropear)* to damage

**maltrato** *nm* ill-treatment

**maltrecho, -a** *adj* battered

**malva 1** *adj inv* mauve

**2** *nf* mallow; *Fam Fig* **criar malvas** to push up daisies

**3** *nm (color)* mauve

**malvado, -a 1** *adj* evil, wicked

**2** *nm,f* villain, evil person

**malvavisco** *nm* marshmallow

**malvender** *vt* to sell at a loss

**malversación** *nf* **m. (de fondos)** embezzlement (of funds)

**malversador, -ora** *nm,f* embezzler

**malversar** *vt* to embezzle

**Malvinas** *nfpl* **las (islas) M.** the Falkland Islands, the Falklands

**malvivir** *vi* to live badly, to scrape together an existence

**mama** *nf* (a) *(de mujer)* breast; *(de animal)* udder (b) *Fam (madre)* mum, mummy

**mamá** *nf Fam* mum, mummy; *Méx Fam* **m. grande** grandma

**mamadera** *nf Am* (baby's) bottle

**mamado, -a 1** *adj muy Fam* (a) *(borracho)* pissed (b) *(fácil)* **estar m.** to be piss easy

**2** *nf* **mamada** (a) *(de bebé)* (breast) feed, (breast) feeding (b) *Vulg* blowjob

**mamar 1** *vt* (a) *(leche)* to suckle; *Fig* **lo mamó desde pequeño** *(lo aprendió)* he was immersed in it as a child (b) *muy Fam (beber)* to knock back

**2** *vi* to suckle; **dar de m.** to breast-feed

**3** **mamarse** *vpr muy Fam (emborracharse)* to get plastered

**mamario, -a** *adj Anat* mammary

**mamarrachada** *nf Fam* stupid *o* idiotic thing

**mamarracho** *nm Fam* (a) *(fantoche)* sight, mess (b) *(imbécil)* idiot

**mambo** *nm* mambo

**mameluco** *nm* (a) *Hist* mameluke (b) *Fam (torpe, necio)* idiot

**mamífero, -a 1** *adj* mammal

**2** *nm* mammal

**mamografía** *nf Med* (a) *(técnica)* breast scanning, mammography (b) *(imagen)* breast scan

**mamón, -ona 1** *adj* (a) *(que mama)* unweaned (b) *muy Fam (idiota)* prattish

**2** *nm,f* (a) *(que mama)* unweaned baby (b) *muy Fam (idiota)* prat

**mamotreto** *nm* (a) *Fam (libro)* hefty volume (b) *(objeto grande)* unwieldy object

**mampara** *nf* screen

**mamporro** *nm Fam (golpe)* punch, clout; *(al caer)* bump

**mampostería** *nf* **muro de m.** dry-stone wall; **obra de m.** rubblework masonry

**mamut** ( *pl* **mamuts**) *nm* mammoth

**maná** *nm inv Rel* manna; *Fig* **como m. caído del cielo** like manna from heaven

**manada** *nf (rebaño)* herd; *(de lobos)* pack; *(de ovejas)* flock; *(de leones)* pride; *Fam Fig (de gente)* crowd, mob

**manager** ( *pl* **managers**) *nm* manager

**Managua** *n* Managua

**manantial** *nm* spring; *Fig* source

**manar** *vi también Fig* to flow (**de** from)

**manatí** *nm* manatee

**manazas** *Fam* **1** *adj inv* clumsy

**2** *nmf inv* clumsy person

**mancebo, -a 1** *nm,f* (a) *(mozo)* young man, *f* girl (b) *(en farmacia)* assistant

**2** *nf* **manceba** *Anticuado* concubine

**mancha** *nf* (a) *(de suciedad)* stain, spot; *(de tinta)* blot; *(de color)* spot, mark (b) *Astron* **m. solar** sun spot (c) *Fig (deshonra)* blemish

**manchado, -a** *adj (sucio)* dirty; *(con manchas)* stained; *(emborronado)* smudged

**manchar 1** *vt* (a) *(ensuciar)* to make dirty (**de** *o* **con** with); *(con manchas)* to stain (**de** *o* **con** with); *(emborronar)* to smudge (**de** *o* **con** with) (b) *Fig (deshonrar)* to tarnish

**2** **mancharse** *vpr (ensuciarse)* to get dirty

**manchego, -a 1** *adj* of/from La Mancha

**2** *nm,f* person from La Mancha

**3** *nm (queso)* = hard yellow cheese made in La Mancha

**mancillar** *vt Formal* to tarnish, to sully

**manco, -a** *adj* (a) *(sin una mano)* one-handed; *(sin un brazo)* one-armed; *Fig* **no ser m. para** *o* **en** to be a dab hand at (b) *Fig (incompleto)* imperfect, defective

**mancomunar 1** *vt* to pool (together)

**2** **mancomunarse** *vpr* to join together, to unite

**mancomunidad** *nf* association

**mancuernas** *nfpl* (a) *Am (gemelos)* cufflinks (b) *(pesas)* dumbbells

**mandado, -a 1** *nm,f (subordinado)* underling; *Fam* **yo sólo soy un m.** I'm only doing what I was told (to do)

**2** *nm (recado)* errand

**mandamás** (*pl* **mandamases**) *nmf Fam* bigwig, boss

**mandamiento** *nm* (**a**) *(orden)* order, command (**b**) *Der* writ (**c**) *Rel* **los diez mandamientos** the Ten Commandments

**mandanga** *nf* (**a**) *Fam* **mandangas** *(tonterías)* nonsense (**b**) *muy Fam (hachís)* dope, shit

**mandar 1** *vt* (**a**) *(dar órdenes a)* to order; **m. a alguien hacer algo** to order sb to do sth; **m. hacer algo** to have sth done (**b**) *(enviar)* to send (**c**) *(dirigir, gobernar)* to lead, to be in charge of; *(país)* to rule

**2** *vi* (**a**) *(dirigir)* to be in charge; *(jefe de estado)* to rule (**b**) *(dar órdenes)* to order people around

**mandarín** *nm* (**a**) *(título)* mandarin (**b**) *(dialecto)* Mandarin

**mandarina** *nf* mandarin

**mandarino** *nm* mandarin tree

**mandatario, -a** *nm,f* representative, agent; **primer m.** *(jefe de Estado)* head of state

**mandato** *nm* (**a**) *(orden, precepto)* order, command (**b**) *(poderes de representación, disposición)* mandate; *Der* **m. judicial** warrant (**c**) *Pol* term of office; *(reinado)* period of rule

**mandíbula** *nf* jaw; *Fam* **reír a m. batiente** to laugh one's head off

**mandil** *nm* apron

**mandioca** *nf* (**a**) *(planta)* cassava (**b**) *(fécula)* tapioca

**mando** *nm* (**a**) *(poder)* command, authority; **estar al m. (de)** to be in charge (of) (**b**) *Mil* **alto m.** high command; **los mandos** the command (**c**) *(dispositivo)* control; **m. automático/a distancia** automatic/remote control

**mandolina** *nf* mandolin

**mandón, -ona** *Fam* **1** *adj* bossy

**2** *nm,f* bossy-boots

**mandrágora** *nf* mandrake

**mandril** *nm* (**a**) *(animal)* mandrill (**b**) *(pieza)* mandrel

**manduca** *nf muy Fam* grub, scoff

**manducar** *vt & vi muy Fam* to scoff

**manecilla** *nf* (**a**) *(del reloj)* hand (**b**) *(cierre)* clasp

**manejable** *adj* *(persona, cosa)* manageable; *(herramienta)* easy to use; *(coche)* manoeuvrable

**manejar 1** *vt* (**a**) *(máquina, mandos)* to operate; *(caballo, bicicleta)* to handle; *(arma)* to wield (**b**) *(conocimientos, datos)* to use, to marshal (**c**) *(negocio)* to manage, to run; *(gente)* to handle (**d**) *Fig (dominar)* to boss about (**e**) *Am (conducir)* to drive

**2** *vi Am (conducir)* to drive

**3 manejarse** *vpr* (**a**) *(moverse)* to move o get about (**b**) *(desenvolverse)* to manage, to get by

**manejo** *nm* (**a**) *(de máquina, mandos)* operation; *(de armas, herramientas)* use; *(de caballo, bicicleta)* handling; **de fácil m.** user-friendly (**b**) *(de conocimientos, datos)* marshalling; *(de idiomas)* command (**c**) *(de negocio)* management, running (**d**) *Fig (intriga)* intrigue

**manera** *nf* (**a**) *(forma)* way, manner; **a m. de** *(como)* as, by way of; **a la m. de** in the style of, after the fashion of; **a mi m. de ver** the way I see it; **de cualquier m.** *(sin cuidado)* any old how; *(de todos modos)* anyway, in any case; **de mala m.** badly; **de esta m.** in this way; **de m. que** *(para)* so (that); **de ninguna m.,** *en absoluto* by no means, under no circumstances; *(respuesta exclamativa)* no way!, certainly not!; **de todas maneras** anyway; **de una m. o de otra** one way or another; **en cierta m.** in a way; **no hay m.** there is no way, it's impossible; **¡qué m. de llover!** just look at that rain!; **m. de ser** way of being, nature (**b**) **maneras** *(modales)* manners

**manga** *nf* (**a**) *(de prenda)* sleeve; **en mangas de camisa** in shirt sleeves; **m. corta/larga** short/long sleeve; **m. raglan** raglan sleeve; *Fam* **m. por hombro** topsy-turvy, higgledy-piggledy; *Fig* **ser de m. ancha, tener m. ancha** to be over-indulgent; *Fig* **tener** o **guardar algo en la m.** to have sth up one's sleeve (**b**) *(manguera)* hosepipe (**c**) *(filtro)* muslin strainer (**d**) *(medidor de viento)* wind sock (**e**) *(de pastelería)* forcing o piping bag (**f**) *Dep* stage, round

**manganeso** *nm* manganese

**mangante** *Fam* **1** *adj* (**a**) *(sinvergüenza)* good-for-nothing (**b**) *(ladrón)* thieving

**2** *nmf* (**a**) *(sinvergüenza)* good-for-nothing, layabout (**b**) *(ladrón)* thief

**mangar** [40] *vt Fam* to pinch, to nick; **m. algo a alguien** to pinch o nick sth from sb

**manglar** *nf* mangrove swamp

**mango** *nm* (**a**) *(asa)* handle (**b**) *(árbol)* mango tree; *(fruta)* mango (**c**) *Am Fam (dinero)* cash; **no tener un m.** not to have a bean, to be skint

**mangonear** *vi Fam* (**a**) *(entrometerse)* to meddle (**b**) *(mandar)* to push people around, to be bossy (**c**) *(manipular)* to fiddle about

**mangoneo** *nm Fam* (**a**) *(intromisión)* bossing o pushing around (**b**) *(manipulación)* fiddling

**mangosta** *nf* mongoose

**manguera** *nf* hosepipe; *(de bombero)* fire hose

**mangui** *muy Fam* **1** *adj* *(no fiable)* sneaky

**2** *nmf* (**a**) *(ladrón)* crook, thief (**b**) *(persona no fiable)* crook

**manguito** *nm* (**a**) *(para el frío)* muff (**b**) *(media manga)* protective sleeve, oversleeve

**maní** (*pl* **manises**) *nm Andes, CSur* peanut

**manía** *nf* (**a**) *(idea fija)* obsession; **m. persecutoria** persecution complex (**b**) *(peculiaridad)* idiosyncrasy (**c**) *(mala costumbre)* bad habit (**d**) *(afición exagerada)* mania, craze (**e**) *Fam (ojeriza)* dislike; **coger m. a alguien** to take a dislike to sb; **tener m. a alguien** not to be able to stand sb (**f**) *Psi* mania

**maníaco, -a, maníaco, -a 1** *adj* manic
**2** *nm,f* maniac; **m. sexual** sex maniac

**maniacodepresivo, -a** *adj & nm,f* manic-depressive

**maniatar** *vt* to tie the hands of

**maniático, -a 1** *adj* fussy
**2** *nm,f* fussy person; **es un m. del fútbol** he's football-crazy

**manicomio** *nm Br* mental *o* psychiatric hospital, *US* insane asylum

**manicura** *nf (técnica)* manicure; **hacerle la m. a alguien** to give sb a manicure

**manicuro, -a** *nm,f (persona)* manicurist

**manido, -a** *adj (tema)* hackneyed

**manierismo** *nm Arte* mannerism

**manifestación** *nf* (**a**) *(de alegría, dolor)* show, display; *(de opinión)* declaration, expression; *(indicio)* sign (**b**) *(por la calle)* demonstration

**manifestante** *nmf* demonstrator

**manifestar [3] 1** *vt* (**a**) *(alegría, dolor)* to show (**b**) *(opinión)* to express
**2 manifestarse** *vpr* (**a**) *(por la calle)* to demonstrate (**b**) *(hacerse evidente)* to become clear *o* apparent

**manifiesto, -a 1** *adj* clear, evident; **poner de m. algo** *(revelar)* to reveal sth; *(hacer patente)* to make sth clear; **ponerse de m.** *(descubrirse)* to become clear *o* obvious
**2** *nm* manifesto

**manija** *nf* handle

**Manila** *n* Manila

**manilargo, -a** *adj (generoso)* generous

**manileño, -a** *adj* of/from Manila

**manilla** *nf* (**a**) *(del reloj)* hand (**b**) *(grilletes)* manacle

**manillar** *nm* handlebars

**maniobra** *nf* (**a**) *(operación) & Mil* manoeuvre; **hacer maniobras** to manoeuvre (**b**) *Fig (treta)* trick

**maniobrar** *vi* to manoeuvre

**manipulación** *nf* (**a**) *(de objeto)* handling; **m. de alimentos** food handling (**b**) *(de persona, datos)* manipulation

**manipulador, -ora 1** *adj Pey (dominador)* manipulative
**2** *nm,f* (**a**) *(operario)* handler (**b**) *Pey (dominador)* manipulator

**manipular** *vt* (**a**) *(manejar)* to handle (**b**) *Pey (trastocar, dominar)* to manipulate

**maniqueísmo** *nm* (**a**) *(doctrina)* Manicheism (**b**) *(actitud)* seeing things in black and white

**maniqueo, -a 1** *adj* Manichean
**2** *nm,f* Manichee

**maniquí** (*pl* **maniquíes**) **1** *nm* dummy
**2** *nmf (modelo)* model

**manirroto, -a 1** *adj* extravagant
**2** *nm,f* spendthrift

**manitas** *Fam* **1** *adj inv* handy; **ser muy m.** to be very good with one's hands
**2** *nmf inv* handy person; **ser un m. (de plata)** to be (very) good with one's hands; **hacer m.** to canoodle

**manito** *nm Méx Fam* mate, chum

**manivela** *nf* crank

**manjar** *nm* **manjares** delicious food; **¡este queso es un m.!** this cheese is delicious!

**mano 1** *nf* (**a**) *(extremidad del brazo)* hand; **a m.** *(cerca)* to hand, handy; *(sin máquina)* by hand; **votación a m. alzada** show of hands; **a m. armada** armed; **dar** *o* **estrechar la m. a alguien** to shake hands with sb; **darse** *o* **estrecharse la m.** to shake hands; **lavarse las manos** to wash one's hands; **¡manos arriba!, ¡arriba las manos!** hands up!
(**b**) *Econ* **m. de obra** labour, workers; **la m. de obra barata atrae a los inversores** investors are attracted by the cheap labour costs; **m. de obra especializada** skilled labour *o* workers
(**c**) *Zool (en general)* forefoot; *(de perro, gato)* (front) paw; *(de cerdo)* (front) trotter
(**d**) *(lado)* **a m. derecha/izquierda** on the right/left
(**e**) *(de pintura)* coat
(**f**) *(influencia)* influence
(**g**) *(de mortero)* pestle
(**h**) *(partida de naipes)* game; **ser m.** to (be the) lead
(**i**) *Fig (serie, tanda)* series
(**j**) *Dep (falta)* handball
(**k**) *(expresiones)* **a manos de** at the hands of; **alzar la m. contra alguien** to raise one's hand to sb; **bajo m.** secretly; **caer en manos de alguien** to fall into sb's hands; **cargar la m.** to go over the top; **coger a alguien con las manos en la masa** to catch sb red-handed *o* in the act; **con una m. delante y otra detrás** without a penny to one's name, in the clothes one is standing up in; **de primera m.** *(coche)* brand new; *(noticias)* first-hand; **de segunda m.** second-hand; **dejar de la m.** to abandon; **dejar algo en manos de alguien** to leave sth in sb's hands; **echar m. de algo** to

make use of sth, to resort to sth; **echar/tender una m.** to give/offer a hand; **ensuciarse las manos** to get one's hands dirty; **escaparse de las manos a alguien** *(oportunidad)* to slip through sb's hands; *(control, proyecto)* to get out of hand for sb; **estar dejado de la m. de Dios** *(lugar)* to be godforsaken; *(persona)* to be a total failure; **ganar por la m. a alguien** to beat sb to it; **írsele a uno la m.** *(perder el control)* to lose control; *(exagerar)* to go too far; **se me fue la m. con la sal** I overdid the salt; **llevarse las manos a la cabeza** *(gesticular)* to throw one's hands in the air (in horror); *Fig* to be horrified; **m. a m.** tête-à-tête; **con m. dura** *o* **de hierro** with a firm hand; **¡yo me lavo las manos!** I wash my hands of it!; **m. sobre m.** sitting around doing nothing; **¡manos a la obra!** let's get down to it!; **meter m. a alguien** *(investigar)* to get onto sb, to start to investigate sb; *(sobar sin consentimiento)* to grope sb; *(sobar con consentimiento)* to touch sb up; **meter m. a algo** to tackle sth; **meter la m. en algo** *(intervenir)* to poke one's nose in(to) sth, to meddle in sth; **pedir la m. de una mujer** to ask for a woman's hand (in marriage); **ponerse en manos de alguien** to put oneself in sb's hands; **ser la m. derecha de alguien** to be sb's right hand man; **tener buena m. para algo** to have a knack for sth; **tener las manos largas** to be fond of a fight; **tener m. izquierda con algo** to know how to deal with sth; **traerse entre manos algo** to be up to sth; **venir** *o* **llegar a las manos** to come to blows

**2** *nm Méx Fam* mate, chum

**manojo** *nm* bunch; *Fig* **estar hecho un m. de nervios** to be a bundle of nerves; *Fig* **ser un m. de nervios** to be hyperactive

**manoletina** *nf* (a) *Taurom* = pass with the cape in bullfighting invented by the Spanish bullfighter, Manolete (b) *(zapato)* = type of open, low-heeled shoe, often with a bow

**manómetro** *nm* pressure gauge

**manopla** *nf* mitten

**manoseado, -a** *adj* shabby, worn

**manosear** *vt* (a) *(tocar)* to handle (roughly); *(papel, tela)* to rumple (b) *(persona)* to paw; *(sexualmente)* to grope

**manoseo** *nm* fingering, touching

**manotazo** *nm* slap

**mansalva: a mansalva** *loc adv (en abundancia)* in abundance

**mansarda** *nf* attic

**mansedumbre** *nf (tranquilidad)* calmness, gentleness; *(docilidad)* tameness

**mansión** *nf* mansion

**manso, -a** *adj (tranquilo)* calm; *(dócil)* docile; *(domesticado)* tame

**manta 1** *nf* (a) *(abrigo)* blanket; *Fig* **liarse la m. a la cabeza** to take the plunge; *Fig* **tirar de la m.** to let the cat out of the bag (b) *(pez)* **manta ray**

**2** *nmf Fam (persona)* hopeless *o* useless person

**mantear** *vt* to toss in a blanket

**manteca** *nf (grasa)* fat; *(mantequilla)* butter; **m. de cacao** cocoa butter; **m. de cerdo** lard

**mantecada** *nf (magdalena)* = small rectangular sponge cake

**mantecado** *nm* = very crumbly shortbread biscuit

**mantecoso, -a** *adj* fatty, greasy

**mantel** *nm* tablecloth

**mantelería** *nf* set of table linen

**manteleta** *nf* shawl

**mantener** [67] **1** *vt* (a) *(sustentar, aguantar)* to support (b) *(conservar)* to keep; *(en buen estado)* to maintain, to service; **m. una promesa** to keep a promise (c) *(tener)* *(relaciones, conversación)* to have (d) *(defender)* *(convicción)* to stick to; *(candidatura)* to refuse to withdraw; **mantiene que no la vió** he maintains that he didn't see her

**2 mantenerse** *vpr* (a) *(sustentarse)* to subsist, to support oneself (b) *(permanecer, continuar)* to remain; *(edificio)* to remain standing; **mantenerse aparte** *(en discusión)* to stay out of it; **mantenerse en pie** to remain standing

**mantengo** *ver* **mantener**

**mantenido, -a 1** *adj* sustained

**2** *nm,f (hombre)* gigolo; *(mujer)* kept woman

**mantenimiento** *nm* (a) *(sustento)* sustenance (b) *(conservación)* upkeep, maintenance; **clases de m.** *(gimnasia)* keep-fit classes

**mantequera** *nf* butter dish

**mantequería** *nf* (a) *(fábrica)* dairy, butter factory (b) *(tienda)* grocer's (shop)

**mantequilla** *nf* butter

**mantilla** *nf* (a) *(de mujer)* mantilla (b) *(de bebé)* shawl (c) **estar en mantillas** *(persona)* to be wet behind the ears; *(plan)* to be in its infancy

**mantis** *nf inv* mantis; **m. religiosa** praying mantis

**manto** *nm* (a) *(capa)* cloak; *Fig* mantle, layer (b) *Geol* mantle

**mantón** *nm* shawl; **m. de Manila** embroidered silk shawl

**mantuviera** *etc ver* **mantener**

**manual 1** *adj* manual; *Educ* **trabajos manuales** *(clase)* craftwork, handicraft

**2** *nm* manual; **m. de instrucciones** instruction manual

**manualidades** *nfpl (objetos)* craftwork, handicrafts

**manubrio** *nm* crank

**manufactura** *nf* (a) *(actividad)* manufacture (b) *Econ (producto)* manufacture, product (c) *(fábrica)* factory

**manufacturado, -a** *adj* manufactured

**manufacturar** *vt* to manufacture

**manumisión** *nf* liberation

**manuscrito, -a 1** *adj* handwritten
**2** *nm* manuscript

**manutención** *nf* (a) *(sustento)* support, maintenance (b) *(alimento)* food

**manzana** *nf* (a) *(fruta)* apple; *Fig* **m. de la discordia** bone of contention (b) *(grupo de casas)* block (of houses)

**manzanilla** *nf* (a) *(planta)* camomile (b) *(infusión)* camomile tea (c) *(vino)* manzanilla (sherry) (d) *(aceituna)* manzanilla, = type of small olive

**manzano** *nm* apple tree

**maña** *nf* (a) *(destreza)* skill; *Prov* **más vale m. que fuerza** brain is better than brawn (b) *(astucia)* wits, guile; **darse m. para hacer algo** to contrive to do sth (c) *(engaño)* ruse, trick

**mañana 1** *nf* morning; **(muy) de m.** (very) early in the morning; **a las dos de la m.** at two in the morning
**2** *nm* **el m.** tomorrow, the future
**3** *adv* tomorrow; **¡hasta m.!** see you tomorrow!; **m. por la m.** tomorrow morning; **pasado m.** the day after tomorrow

**mañanero, -a** *adj* (a) *(madrugador)* early rising (b) *(matutino)* morning; **paseo m.** morning walk

**mañanitas** *nfpl Méx* birthday song

**maño, -a** *adj & nm,f Fam* Aragonese

**mañoso, -a** *adj* skilful

**maoísmo** *nm* Maoism

**maoísta** *adj & nmf* Maoist

**maorí** *adj & nmf* Maori

**mapa** *nm* map; **m. físico/mudo/político** geographic/blank/political map; *Informát* **m. de bits** bit map; *Fam Fig* **desaparecer del m.** to vanish into thin air

**mapache** *nm* raccoon

**mapamundi** *nm* world map

**Maputo** *n* Maputo

**maqueta** *nf* (a) *(reproducción a escala)* (scale) model (b) *(de libro)* dummy (c) *(de disco)* demo (tape)

**maqui** *nmf inv* guerrilla

**maquiavélico, -a** *adj* Machiavellian

**maquiavelismo** *nm* Machiavellianism

**maquillador, -ora** *nm,f* make-up artist

**maquillaje** *nm* (a) *(producto)* make-up (b) *(acción)* making-up

**maquillar 1** *vt* (a) *(pintar)* to make up (b) *Fig (disimular)* to cover up, to disguise
**2 maquillarse** *vpr* to make oneself up; **se maquilla demasiado** she wears o uses too much make-up

**máquina** *nf* (a) *(aparato)* machine; **a toda m.** at full pelt; **escrito a m.** typewritten; **escribir a m.** to type; **hecho a m.** machine-made; **pasar algo a m.** to type sth out o up; *Fam Fig* **ser una m.** *(muy rápido, muy bueno)* to be a powerhouse; **m. de bebidas** drinks machine; **m. de café** (espresso) coffee machine; **m. de coser** sewing machine; **m. de escribir** typewriter; **m. de fotos** o **fotográfica** camera; **m. de marcianos** space invaders machine; **m. registradora** cash register; **m. de tabaco** cigarette machine; **m. tragaperras**, *CAm* **m. traganíqueles** slot machine, fruit machine (b) *(locomotora)* engine; **m. de vapor** steam engine (c) *(mecanismo)* mechanism (d) *Carib (coche)* car

**maquinación** *nf* machination

**maquinal** *adj* mechanical

**maquinar** *vt* to machinate, to plot; **m. algo contra alguien** to plot sth against sb

**maquinaria** *nf* (a) *(aparatos)* machinery (b) *(mecanismo) (de reloj, aparato)* mechanism; *Fig (de Estado, partido)* machinery

**maquinilla** *nf* **m. de afeitar** razor; **m. eléctrica** electric razor

**maquinismo** *nm* mechanization

**maquinista** *nmf (de tren) Br* engine driver, *US* engineer; *(de barco)* engineer

**maquinizar** [16] *vt* to mechanize

**maquis** *nmf inv* guerrilla

**mar** *nm* o *f también Fig* sea; **hacerse a la m.** to set sail, to put (out) to sea; **m. adentro** out to sea; **alta m.** high seas; *también Fig* **m. de fondo** groundswell; **m. gruesa** rough o stormy sea; **m. rizada** choppy sea; **a mares** a lot; **llover a mares** to rain buckets; **la m. de** really, very; **es la m. de inteligente** she's really intelligent; **el m. Muerto** the Dead Sea; **el m. del Norte** the North Sea; **el m. Negro/Rojo** the Black/Red Sea

**marabunta** *nf (de hormigas)* plague of ants; *Fig (muchedumbre)* crowd

**maraca** *nf* maraca

**marajá** *nm* maharajah; **vivir como un m.** to live in the lap of luxury

**maraña** *nf (maleza)* thicket; *Fig (enredo)* tangle

**marasmo** *nm* (a) *Med* marasmus, wasting (b) *Fig (de ánimo)* apathy; *(de negocio)* stagnation

**maratón** *nm también Fig* marathon

**maratoniano, -a** *adj* marathon

**maravilla** *nf* marvel, wonder; **es una m.** it's wonderful; **a las mil maravillas, de m.** wonderfully; **decir maravillas de alguien/algo** to praise sb/sth to the skies; **hacer maravillas** to do *o* work wonders; **una m. de niño/coche/carretera** a wonderful *o* marvellous child/car/road; **venir de m.** to be just the thing *o* ticket

**maravillar 1** *vt* to amaze

**2 maravillarse** *vpr* to be amazed (**con** by)

**maravilloso, -a** *adj* marvellous, wonderful

**marbellí 1** *adj* of/from Marbella

**2** *nm,f* person from Marbella

**marca** *nf* (**a**) *(señal)* mark; *(de rueda, animal)* track; *(en ganado)* brand; *(en papel)* watermark (**b**) *Com (de tabaco, café)* brand; *(de coche, ordenador)* make; **unos vaqueros de m.** a pair of designer jeans; **m. de fábrica** trademark; **m. registrada** registered trademark (**c**) *(etiqueta)* label (**d**) *Dep (tiempo)* time; *(plusmarca)* record (**e**) **de m. mayor** *(muy grande)* enormous; *(excelente)* outstanding

**marcado, -a 1** *adj (pronunciado)* marked

**2** *nm* (**a**) *(señalado)* marking (**b**) *(peinado)* set

**marcador, -ora 1** *adj* marking

**2** *nm* (**a**) *(tablero)* scoreboard (**b**) *Dep (jugador) (defensor)* marker; *(goleador)* scorer (**c**) *(para libros)* bookmark

**marcaje** *nm Dep* marking

**marcapasos** *nm inv* pacemaker

**marcar** [61] **1** *vt* (**a**) *(en general)* to mark (**b**) *(poner precio a)* to price (**c**) *(indicar)* to indicate (**d**) *(anotar)* to note down (**e**) *(destacar)* to emphasize (**f**) *(número de teléfono)* to dial (**g**) *(sujeto: termómetro, contador)* to read; *(sujeto: reloj)* to say (**h**) *Dep (tanto)* to score; *(a un jugador)* to mark (**i**) *(cabello)* to set

**2** *vi* (**a**) *(dejar secuelas)* to leave a mark (**b**) *Dep (anotar un tanto)* to score

**3 marcarse** *vpr Fam* **marcarse un detalle** to do something nice *o* kind; **marcarse un tanto** to earn a Brownie point

**marcha** *nf* (**a**) *(partida)* departure (**b**) *(transcurso)* course; *(progreso)* progress; **el tren detuvo su m.** the train stopped; **a marchas forzadas** *(contrarreloj)* against the clock; **a toda m.** at top speed; **en m.** *(motor)* running; *(plan)* underway; **poner en m.** *(empezar)* to start; *(dispositivo, alarma)* to activate; **hacer algo sobre la m.** to do sth as one goes along

(**c**) *Aut* gear; **cambiar de m.** to change gear; **m. atrás** reverse; **dar m. atrás** to reverse; *Fig* to back out

(**d**) *Mil & Pol* march; **abrir la m.** to head the procession; **cerrar la m.** to bring up the rear (**e**) *Mús* march; **m. fúnebre/nupcial** funeral/wedding march; **M. Real** Spanish national anthem

(**f**) *Dep* walk

(**g**) *Fam (animación)* liveliness, life; **hay mucha m.** there's a great atmosphere; **ir de m.** to go out on the town; **tener (mucha) m.** to be a (real) raver

**marchante, -a** *nm,f* dealer

**marchar 1** *vi* (**a**) *(andar)* to walk (**b**) *(partir)* to leave, to go (**c**) *(funcionar)* to work (**d**) *(desarrollarse)* to progress; **el negocio marcha** business is going well

**2 marcharse** *vpr* to leave, to go

**marchitar 1** *vt también Fig* to wither

**2 marchitarse** *vpr (planta)* to fade, to wither; *Fig (persona)* to languish, to fade away

**marchito, -a** *adj (planta)* faded; *Fig (persona)* worn

**marchoso, -a** *Fam* **1** *adj* lively

**2** *nm,f* livewire

**marcial** *adj* martial

**marcialidad** *nf* martial nature

**marcianitos** *nmpl (juego)* space invaders

**marciano, -a** *adj & nm,f* Martian

**marco** *nm* (**a**) *(de cuadro)* frame; *(de puerta)* doorframe; **m. de ventana** window frame (**b**) *Fig (ambiente, paisaje)* setting (**c**) *(ámbito)* framework; **acuerdo m.** general *o* framework agreement (**d**) *(moneda)* mark; **m. alemán** Deutschmark, German mark (**e**) *Dep (portería)* goalmouth

**marea** *nf* (**a**) *(del mar)* tide; **m. alta/baja** high/low tide; **m. negra** oil slick; **m. viva** spring tide; **está subiendo/bajando la m.** the tide is coming in/going out (**b**) *Fig (multitud)* flood

**mareado, -a** *adj* (**a**) *(con náuseas)* sick, queasy; *(en coche, avión)* travelsick; *(en barco)* seasick (**b**) *(aturdido)* dizzy (**c**) *Fam Fig (fastidiado)* fed up to the back teeth

**mareante 1** *adj* infuriating, irritating

**2** *nmf* pest, nuisance

**marear 1** *vt* (**a**) *(provocar náuseas)* to make sick; *(en coche, avión)* to make travelsick; *(en barco)* to make seasick (**b**) *(aturdir)* to make dizzy (**c**) *Fam Fig (fastidiar)* to annoy

**2 marearse** *vpr* (**a**) *(tener náuseas)* to get *o* become sick; *(en coche, avión)* to get travelsick; *(en barco)* to get seasick (**b**) *(aturdirse)* to get dizzy (**c**) *(emborracharse)* to get drunk

**marejada** *nf (mar agitada)* heavy sea; *Fig (agitación)* wave of discontent

**marejadilla** *nf* slight swell

**mare mágnum** *nm* jumble

**maremoto** *nm* tidal wave

**marengo** *adj* **gris m.** dark grey

**mareo** nm (a) (náuseas) sickness; (en coche, avión) travelsickness; (en barco) seasickness (b) (aturdimiento) dizziness, giddiness; **le dio un m.** he had a dizzy spell o turn, he felt dizzy (c) Fam Fig (fastidio) drag, pain

**marfil** nm ivory

**marfileño, -a** adj ivory; **piel marfileña** ivory skin

**marga** nf Geol marl

**margarina** nf margarine

**margarita 1** nf (a) (flor) daisy (b) Imprenta daisy wheel
  **2** nm (cóctel) margarita

**margen 1** nm (a) (de camino) side (b) (de página) margin (c) Com margin; **m. de beneficio** profit margin (d) (límites) leeway; **al m. de eso, hay otros factores** over and above this, there are other factors; **al m. de la ley** outside the law; **dejar al m.** to exclude; **estar al m. de** to have nothing to do with; **mantenerse al m. de** to keep out of; **m. de error** margin of error; **m. de seguridad** degree of certainty (e) (ocasión) **dar m. a alguien para hacer algo** to give sb the chance to do sth
  **2** nf (de río) bank

**marginación** nf exclusion; **m. social** exclusion from society

**marginado, -a 1** adj excluded
  **2** nm,f outcast

**marginal** adj (a) (nota) marginal; (tema) minor (b) Arte & Pol fringe

**marginalidad** nf **vivir en la m.** to live on the margins of society, to be a social outcast

**marginar** vt (a) (persona) (excluir) to exclude, to make an outcast; (dar de lado a) to give the cold shoulder to (b) (asunto, diferencias) to set aside, to set to one side

**maría** nf Fam (a) (marihuana) grass (b) (asignatura) easy subject, Mickey Mouse course (c) (mujer sencilla) (typical) housewife (d) Méx = migrant from country to urban areas

**mariachi** nm (a) (música) mariachi (music) (b) (orquesta) mariachi band; (músico) mariachi (musician)

**marianismo** nm Marianism

**mariano, -a** adj Marian

**marica** nm Fam queer, poof

**maricón, -ona 1** adj (a) Fam (homosexual) queer, poofy (b) muy Fam (insulto) **¡qué tío más m.!** what a bastard!
  **2** nm,f muy Fam (insulto) (cobarde) wimp; (odioso) bastard, git
  **3** nm Fam (homosexual) queer, poof

**mariconada** nf Fam (a) (dicho, hecho) **eso es una m.** that's really poofy (b) (mala jugada) dirty trick (c) (tontería) **no dice más que mariconadas** he talks through the back of his neck

**mariconear** vi Fam to camp it up

**mariconera** nf Fam (man's) clutch bag

**mariconería** nf Fam (a) (dicho, hecho) **eso es una m.** that's really poofy (b) (cualidad) campness

**marido** nm husband

**marihuana** nf marijuana

**marimacho** nm Fam (niña) tomboy; (mujer) butch woman

**marimba** nf CAm, Méx wooden xylophone

**marimandona** Fam **1** adj bossy
  **2** nf bossyboots

**marimorena** nf row; Fig **armar la m.** to kick up a row

**marina** nf (a) Mil **m. (de guerra)** navy; **m. mercante** merchant navy (b) Arte seascape

**marinar** vt to marinate

**marine** nm Mil marine

**marinería** nf (a) (profesión) sailoring (b) (marineros) crew, seamen

**marinero, -a 1** adj (de la marina, de los marineros) sea; (buque) seaworthy; **un pueblo m.** (nación) a seafaring nation; (población) a fishing village; **vestido m.** sailor suit
  **2** nm sailor

**marino, -a 1** adj sea, marine; **brisa marina** sea breeze
  **2** nm sailor

**marioneta** nf (muñeco) marionette, puppet; Fig puppet; **marionetas** (teatro) puppet show

**mariposa** nf (a) (insecto) butterfly (b) (tuerca) wing nut (c) (candela, luz) oil lamp (d) (en natación) **nadar a m.** to do the butterfly (stroke) (e) Fam **a otra cosa, m.** let's move on

**mariposear** vi (a) (ser inconstante) to flit about (b) (galantear) to flirt

**mariposón** nm Fam (a) (afeminado) fairy, pansy (b) (ligón) flirt, lounge lizard

**mariquita 1** nf (insecto) Br ladybird, US ladybug
  **2** nm Fam (homosexual) poof, queer

**marisabidilla** nf know-all

**mariscada** nf seafood meal

**mariscal** nm marshal; **m. de campo** field marshal

**marisco** nm seafood, shellfish

**marisma** nf salt marsh

**marismeño, -a** adj marshy

**marisquería** nf seafood restaurant

**marista** adj & nm Marist

**marital** adj marital

**marítimo, -a** *adj (del mar)* maritime; *(cercano al mar)* seaside; **pueblo m.** seaside town; **paseo m.** promenade

**marketing** ['marketin] (*pl* **marketings**) *nm* marketing

**marmita** *nf* pot

**mármol** *nm* marble; *Fig* **de m.** cold, insensitive

**marmóreo, -a** *adj Formal* marmoreal

**marmota** *nf* marmot; **dormir como una m.** to sleep like a log

**maroma** *nf* rope

**maromo** *nm Fam* bloke, guy

**maronita** *adj & nmf* Maronite

**marque** *etc ver* **marcar**

**marqués, -esa** *nm,f* marquis, *f* marchioness

**marquesina** *nf (cubierta)* canopy; *(parada de autobús)* bus-shelter

**marquetería** *nf* marquetry

**marranada** *nf Fam* **(a)** *(porquería)* filthy thing **(b)** *(mala jugada)* dirty trick

**marrano, -a** *nm,f* **(a)** *(animal)* pig **(b)** *Fam Fig (sucio)* (filthy) pig **(c)** *Fam Fig (sin escrúpulos)* swine

**Marraquech** *n* Marrakesh

**marras: de marras** *loc adj* **el perrito de m.** that blasted dog (I was telling you about); **el problema de m.** the same old problem

**marrón 1** *adj* brown

**2** *nm* **(a)** *(color)* brown **(b)** *muy Fam* **¡qué m.!** what a pain!; **pillar a alguien de m.** to catch sb in the act

**marrón glacé** [ma'rrongla'se] (*pl* **marrons glacés**) *nm* marron glacé

**marroquí** (*pl* **marroquíes**) *adj & nmf* Moroccan

**marroquinería** *nf* **(a)** *(arte)* leatherwork **(b)** *(artículos)* leather goods

**Marruecos** *n* Morocco

**marrullero, -a 1** *adj* sneaky, fly

**2** *nm,f* cheat

**Marsellesa** *nf* Marseillaise

**marsupial** *adj & nm* marsupial

**marta** *nf* (pine) marten; **m. cebellina** sable

**Marte** *nm* Mars

**martes** *nm inv* Tuesday; **M. de Carnaval** Shrove Tuesday; **m. y trece** ≃ Friday 13th; *ver también* **sábado**

**martillear, martillar** *vt* to hammer

**martillo** *nm* hammer; **m. neumático** *Br* pneumatic drill, *US* jackhammer

**martinete** *nm* heron

**Martinica** *n* Martinique

**martín pescador** *nm* kingfisher

**mártir** *nmf también Fig* martyr; **hacerse el m.** to act the martyr

**martirio** *nm Rel* martyrdom; *Fig (sufrimiento)* trial, torment

**martirizar** [16] *vt (torturar)* to martyr; *Fig (hacer sufrir)* to torment, to torture

**maruja** *nf Fam (mujer sencilla)* (typical) housewife

**marxismo** *nm* Marxism

**marxista** *adj & nmf* Marxist

**marzo** *nm* March; *ver también* **septiembre**

**mas** *conj* but

**más 1** *adv* **(a)** *(comparativo)* more; **Pepe es m. alto/ambicioso** Pepe is taller/more ambitious; **tener m. hambre** to be hungrier *o* more hungry; **m. de/que** more than; **m.... que...** more... than...; **Juan es m. alto que tú** Juan is taller than you; **de m.** *(en exceso)* too much; **me han cobrado 100 ptas. de m.** they've charged me 100 pesetas too much; **eso está de m.** that's not necessary

**(b)** *(superlativo)* **el/la/lo m.** the most; **el m. listo/ambicioso** the cleverest/most ambitious

**(c)** *(en frases negativas)* any more; **no necesito m. (trabajo)** I don't need any more (work)

**(d)** *(con pron interrogativos e indefinidos)* else; **¿qué/quién m.?** what/who else?; **nadie m.** vino nobody else came

**(e)** *(indica suma)* plus; **dos m. dos igual a cuatro** two plus two is four

**(f)** *(indica intensidad)* **no le aguanto, ¡es m. tonto!** I can't stand him, he's so stupid!; **¡qué día m. bonito!** what a lovely day!

**(g)** *(indica preferencia)* **m. vale que nos vayamos a casa** it would be better for us to go home

**(h)** *(expresiones)* **a m. de** *(además de)* in addition to, as well as; **ser de lo m. divertido** to be incredibly funny *o* amusing; **hoy está de lo m. amable** she's being really nice today; **el que m. y el que menos** everyone; **es m., m. aún** indeed, what is more; **lo que es m.** moreover; **m. bien** rather; **m. o menos** more or less; **¿qué m. da?** what difference does it make?; **por m. que** however much; **por m. que lo intente no lo conseguirá** however much *o* hard she tries, she'll never manage it; **sin m. (ni más)** just like that

**2** *nm inv Mat* plus (sign); **tiene sus m. y sus menos** it has its good points and its bad points

**masa** *nf* **(a)** *(en general)* mass; **m. atómica** atomic mass; **m. salarial** total wages bill **(b)** *(multitud)* throng; **en m.** en masse; **las masas** the masses **(c)** *(mezcla, pasta)* mixture; *Culin* dough **(d)** *Elec* earth **(e)** *CSur (pastelito)* shortcake biscuit

**masacrar** *vt* to massacre

**masacre** *nf* massacre

**masaje** *nm* massage

**masajear** *vt* to massage, to rub

**masajista** *nmf* masseur, *f* masseuse

**mascar** [61] *vt & vi* to chew

**máscara** *nf* mask; *Fig* front, pretence; **m. antigás** gas mask; *Fig* **quitar la m. a alguien** to unmask sb; *Fig* **quitarse la m.** to reveal oneself

**mascarada** *nf* (*fiesta*) masquerade; *Fig* (*farsa*) farce

**mascarilla** *nf* (a) (*de protección, de oxígeno*) mask (b) (*cosmética*) face pack

**mascarón** *nm Arquit* grotesque head; **m. de proa** figurehead

**mascota** *nf* mascot

**masculinidad** *nf* masculinity

**masculino, -a** *adj* (a) *Biol* male (b) (*varonil*) manly (c) *Gram* masculine

**mascullar** *vt* to mutter

**masía** *nf* = traditional Catalan or Aragonese farmhouse

**masificación** *nf* overcrowding (**de** in)

**masificar** [61] **1** *vt* to cause overcrowding in
**2 masificarse** *vpr* to become overcrowded

**masilla** *nf* putty

**masita** *nf CSur* shortcake biscuit

**masivo, -a** *adj* mass; **despido m.** mass sacking *o* redundancies

**masoca** *nmf Fam* masochist

**masón, -ona 1** *adj* masonic
**2** *nm,f* mason, freemason

**masonería** *nf* masonry, freemasonry

**masoquismo** *nm* masochism

**masoquista 1** *adj* masochistic
**2** *nmf* masochist

**mass media, mass-media** *nmpl* mass media

**mastectomía** *nf* mastectomy

**master** (*pl* masters) *nm* Master's (degree)

**masticar** [61] *vt* (a) (*mascar*) to chew (b) *Fig* (*pensar*) to chew over, to ponder

**mástil** *nm* (a) (*de barco*) mast; (*de bandera*) pole (b) (*de instrumento musical*) neck

**mastín** *nm* mastiff

**mastitis** *nf inv Med* mastitis

**mastodonte 1** *nm* mastodon
**2** *nmf Fam* giant

**mastodóntico, -a** *adj Fam* mammoth, ginormous

**mastuerzo** *nm Fam* idiot

**masturbación** *nf* masturbation

**masturbar 1** *vt* to masturbate
**2 masturbarse** *vpr* to masturbate

**mata** *nf* (a) (*arbusto*) bush, shrub; (*matojo*) tuft; **matas** scrub (b) (*de pelo*) mop (of hair)

**matadero** *nm* abattoir, slaughterhouse

**matador, -ora 1** *adj Fam* (a) (*cansado*) killing, exhausting (b) (*feo, de mal gusto*) awful, horrendous
**2** *nm Taurom* matador

**matambre** *nm CSur* cold cooked meat

**matamoscas** *nm inv* (*pala*) flyswat; (*espray*) flyspray

**matanza** *nf* (a) (*masacre*) slaughter (b) (*del cerdo*) pig-killing

**matar 1** *vt* (a) (*quitar la vida a*) to kill; **estar a m. (con alguien)** to be at daggers drawn (with sb); *Fam* **matarlas callando** to be up to something on the quiet (b) (*molestar*) to drive mad (c) (*apagar*) (*color*) to tone down; (*sed*) to slake, to quench; (*hambre*) to stave; (*fuego*) to put out (d) (*redondear, limar*) to round (off)
**2 matarse** *vpr* (a) (*morir*) to die; **se mató en un accidente de coche** he was killed in a car accident (b) (*suicidarse*) to kill oneself (c) *Fig* (*esforzarse*) **matarse a trabajar** to work oneself to death; **matarse por hacer algo** to kill oneself in order to do sth

**matarratas** *nm inv* (a) (*veneno*) rat poison (b) *Fig* (*bebida*) rotgut

**matasanos** *nmf inv Fam Pey* quack

**matasellos** *nm inv* postmark

**matasuegras** *nm inv* party blower

**match** [mat∫] *nm* match

**mate 1** *adj* matt
**2** *nm* (a) *Dep* (*en ajedrez*) mate, checkmate; (*en baloncesto*) dunk; (*en tenis*) smash (b) (*bebida*) maté; *Am* **yerba m.** bitter maté tea

**matemático, -a 1** *adj* mathematical
**2** *nm,f* (*científico*) mathematician
**3** *nfpl* **matemáticas** (*ciencia*) mathematics (*singular*)

**materia** *nf* (a) (*sustancia, asunto*) matter; **en m. de** on the subject of, concerning; **entrar en m.** to get down to business; **m. gris** grey matter (b) (*material*) material; **m. prima, primera m.** raw material (c) (*asignatura*) subject

**material 1** *adj* (a) (*físico*) physical; (*daños, consecuencias*) material (b) (*real*) real, actual
**2** *nm* (a) (*sustancia*) material; **m. de desecho** waste material (b) (*instrumentos*) equipment; **m. bélico** *o* **de guerra** war material

**materialismo** *nm* materialism; **m. dialéctico/histórico** dialectical/historical materialism

**materialista 1** *adj* materialistic
**2** *nmf* materialist

**materializar** [16] **1** *vt* (a) (*idea, proyecto*) to realize (b) (*hacer tangible*) to produce
**2 materializarse** *vpr* to materialize

**maternal** *adj* motherly, maternal

**maternidad** *nf* (a) *(cualidad)* motherhood (b) *(hospital)* maternity hospital

**materno, -a** *adj* maternal; **lengua materna** mother tongue

**matice** *etc ver* **matizar**

**matinal** *adj* morning; **sesión m.** *(de cine)* morning showing

**matinée** [mati'ne] *nf* matinée

**matiz** *nm* (a) *(de color, opinión)* shade; *(de sentido)* nuance, shade of meaning (b) *(atisbo)* trace, hint

**matizar** [16] *vt* (a) *(teñir)* to tinge (**de** with) (b) *Fig (distinguir) (rasgos, aspectos)* to distinguish; *(tema)* to explain in detail (c) *Fig (dar tono especial a)* to tinge, to colour (d) *Arte* to blend

**matojo** *nm (mata)* tuft; *(arbusto)* bush, shrub

**matón, -ona** *nm,f Fam* bully

**matorral** *nm* thicket

**matraca** *nf (instrumento)* rattle; *Fam* **dar la m.** to go on, to be a nuisance; *Fam* **ser una m.** to be a pain

**matraz** *nm* flask

**matriarcado** *nm* matriarchy

**matrícula** *nf* (a) *(inscripción)* registration (b) *(documento)* registration document (c) *Aut* number plate (d) *Educ* **m. de honor** top marks

**matriculación** *nf (inscripción)* registration

**matricular 1** *vt* to register

**2 matricularse** *vpr* to register

**matrimonial** *adj* marital; **vida m.** married life

**matrimonio** *nm* (a) *(boda)* marriage; **contraer m.** to get married; **m. civil** civil marriage (b) *(pareja)* married couple

**matriz 1** *nf* (a) *Anat* womb (b) *(de talonario)* (cheque) stub (c) *(molde)* mould (d) *Mat & Informát* matrix

**2** *adj (empresa)* parent; **casa m.** head office

**matrona** *nf* (a) *(madre)* matron (b) *(comadrona)* midwife

**matusalén** *nm Fam* very old person; **ser más viejo que M.** to be as old as Methuselah

**matute: de matute** *loc adv Fam (clandestinamente)* on the quiet

**matutino, -a** *adj* morning; **paseo m.** morning walk

**maullar** *vi* to miaow

**maullido** *nm* miaow, miaowing

**Mauricio** *n* Mauritius

**Mauritania** *n* Mauritania

**mauritano, -a** *adj & nm,f* Mauritanian

**máuser** *(pl* **máuseres** *o* **máusers**) *nm* Mauser

**mausoleo** *nm* mausoleum

**maxilar 1** *adj* maxillary, jaw; **hueso m.** jawbone, mandible

**2** *nm* jaw

**máxima** *nf* (a) *(sentencia, principio)* maxim (b) *(temperatura)* high, highest temperature

**maximalismo** *nm* maximalism

**maximalista** *adj & nmf* maximalist

**máxime** *adv* especially

**máximo, -a 1** *superlativo ver* **grande**

**2** *adj (capacidad, cantidad, temperatura)* maximum; *(honor, galardón)* highest; **la máxima puntuación** *(posible)* the maximum score; *(entre varias)* the highest score

**3** *nm* maximum; **al m.** to the utmost; **llegar al m.** to reach the limit; **como m.** *(a más tardar)* at the latest; *(como mucho)* at the most

**maxisingle** [maksi'singel] *(pl* **maxisingles**) *nm* twelve inch (single)

**maya 1** *adj* Mayan

**2** *nmf* Maya, Mayan

**3** *nm (lengua)* Maya

**mayestático, -a** *adj* majestic

**mayo** *nm* May; *ver también* **septiembre**

**mayonesa** *nf* mayonnaise

**mayor 1** *adj* (a) *(comparativo) (en tamaño)* bigger (**que** than); *(en importancia)* greater (**que** than); *(en edad)* older (**que** than); *(en número)* higher (**que** than)

(b) *(superlativo)* **el/la m....** *(en tamaño)* the biggest...; *(en importancia)* the greatest...; *(en edad)* the oldest...; *(en número)* the highest...

(c) *(adulto)* grown-up; **ser m. de edad** to be an adult

(d) *(anciano)* elderly; **ser muy m.** to be very old

(e) *Mús* **en do m.** in C major

(f) *Com* **al por m.** wholesale

**2** *nmf* **el/la m.** *(hijo, hermano)* the eldest; **mayores** *(adultos)* grown-ups; *(antepasados)* ancestors, forefathers

**3** *nm Mil* major

**mayoral** *nm* (a) *(capataz)* foreman, overseer (b) *(pastor)* chief herdsman

**mayorazgo** *nm Hist* (a) *(institución)* primogeniture (b) *(bienes)* entailed estate (c) *(persona)* heir to an entailed estate

**mayordomo** *nm* butler

**mayoreo** *nm Am* wholesale

**mayoría** *nf* (a) *(mayor parte)* majority; **la m. de** most of; **la m. de los españoles** most Spaniards; **en su m.** in the main; *Pol* **m. absoluta/relativa** absolute/relative majority; **m. silenciosa** silent majority (b) *(edad adulta)* **m. de edad** (age of) majority; **llegar a la m. de edad** to come of age

**mayorista 1** *adj* wholesale

**2** *nmf* wholesaler

**mayoritario, -a** *adj* majority; **decisión mayoritaria** majority decision

**mayúscula** *nf* capital letter; **en mayúsculas** in capitals *o* capital letters

**mayúsculo, -a** *adj* tremendous, enormous; **letra mayúscula** capital letter

**maza** *nf (arma)* mace; *(de bombo)* drumstick

**mazacote** *nm Fam* = dry, sticky food; **la paella era un auténtico m.** the paella was a gooey mess

**mazapán** *nm* marzipan

**mazazo** *nm también Fig* heavy blow

**mazmorra** *nf* dungeon

**mazo** *nm* **(a)** *(martillo)* mallet **(b)** *(de mortero)* pestle **(c)** *(conjunto) (de cartas, papeles)* bundle; *(de billetes)* wad; *(de naipes)* balance (of the deck)

**mazorca** *nf* cob; **m. de maíz** corncob

**mazurca** *nf Mús* mazurka

**MBA** *nm (abrev de* **Master of Business Administration***)* MBA

**MCCA** *(abrev de* **Mercado común Centroamericano***)* Central American Common Market

**me** *pron personal* **(a)** *(complemento directo)* me; **le gustaría verme** she'd like to see me **(b)** *(complemento indirecto)* (to) me; **me lo dio** he gave it to me; **me tiene miedo** he's afraid of me **(c)** *(reflexivo)* myself; **me visto** I get (myself) dressed

**meada** *nf Fam (acción, orina)* piss; *(mancha)* piss stain; **echar una m.** to have a pee *o* piss

**meadero** *nm muy Fam (váter) Br* bog

**meandro** *nm* meander

**meapilas** *nmf inv Fam Pey* holy Joe

**mear** *Fam* **1** *vi* to piss

**2 mearse** *vpr* to piss oneself; **mearse en la cama** to wet one's bed; *Fig* **mearse (de risa)** to piss oneself laughing

**MEC** [mek] *nm (abrev de* **Ministerio de Educación y Ciencia***)* = Spanish ministry of education and science

**meca** *nf* mecca; **La M.** Mecca

**mecachis** *interj Fam* **¡m.!** *Br* sugar!, *US* shoot!

**mecánica** *nf* **(a)** *(ciencia)* mechanics *(singular)* **(b)** *(funcionamiento)* mechanics

**mecanicismo** *nm* mechanism

**mecánico, -a 1** *adj* mechanical

**2** *nm,f (persona)* mechanic; **m. dentista** dental technician

**mecanismo** *nm* **(a)** *(estructura)* mechanism **(b)** *(funcionamiento)* way of working, modus operandi

**mecanización** *nf* mechanization

**mecanizado, -a** *adj* mechanized

**mecanizar** [16] *vt* to mechanize

**mecano®** *nm* Meccano

**mecanografía** *nf* typing; **m. al tacto** touch typing

**mecanografiar** [34] *vt* to type

**mecanógrafo, -a** *nm,f* typist

**mecapal** *nm CAm, Méx* porter's leather harness

**mecate** *nm Am* rope, cord

**mecedora** *nf* rocking chair

**mecenas** *nmf inv* patron

**mecenazgo** *nm* patronage

**mecer** [42] **1** *vt* to rock

**2 mecerse** *vpr (en silla)* to rock; *(en columpio, hamaca)* to swing; *(árbol, rama)* to sway

**mecha** *nf* **(a)** *(de vela)* wick; *(de explosivos)* fuse; *Fam* **a toda m.** flat out; *Fam* **aguantar m.** to grin and bear it **(b)** *(de pelo)* streak

**mechero** *nm* (cigarette) lighter

**mechón** *nm (de pelo)* lock; *(de lana)* tuft

**medalla** *nf* medal; **m. de oro/plata/bronce** gold/silver/bronze medal; *Fig* **ponerse medallas** to show off

**medallero** *nm* medals table

**medallista** *nmf (oficio)* maker of medals **(b)** *Dep* medallist

**medallón** *nm* **(a)** *(joya)* medallion **(b)** *Culin (rodaja)* médaillon; **m. de pescado** *(empanado)* fishcake

**médano** *nm* **(a)** *(duna)* (sand) dune **(b)** *(banco de arena)* sandbank

**media** *nf* **(a)** *(prenda)* **medias** tights, stockings; *Am* socks **(b)** *(promedio)* average; **m. aritmética/proporcional** arithmetic/proportional mean; **m. horaria** hourly average **(c)** *(hora)* **al dar la m.** on the half-hour

**mediación** *nf* mediation; **por m. de** through

**mediado, -a** *adj (a media capacidad)* half-full; **mediada la película** halfway through the film; **a mediados de abril/de año** in the middle of *o* halfway through April/the year

**mediador, -ora 1** *adj* mediating

**2** *nm,f* mediator

**mediana** *nf* **(a)** *Mat* median **(b)** *(de autopista) Br* central reservation

**medianamente** *adv* acceptably, tolerably; **habla francés m. bien** he can get by in French; **sólo entendí m. lo que dijo** I only half understood what he said

**medianía** *nf* average *o* mediocre person

**mediano, -a** *adj* **(a)** *(de tamaño)* medium; *(de calidad)* average **(b)** *(mediocre)* average, ordinary

**medianoche** *nf* **(a)** *(hora)* midnight; **a m.** at midnight **(b)** *(pl* **mediasnoches***) (bollo)* = sandwich made with a small bun

**mediante** *prep* by means of

**mediar** [15] *vi* (a) *(llegar a la mitad)* to be half-way through; **mediaba julio** it was mid-July (b) *(haber en medio)* **m. entre** to be between; **media un jardín/un kilómetro entre las dos casas** there is a garden/one kilometre between the two houses; **medió una semana** a week passed by (c) *(intervenir)* to mediate (**en/entre** in/between); *(interceder)* to intercede (**en favor de** *o* **por** on behalf of *o* for) (d) *(ocurrir)* to intervene, to happen; **media la circunstancia de que...** it so happens that...

**mediatizar** [16] *vt* to determine

**medicación** *nf* medication

**medicamento** *nm* medicine

**medicar** [61] **1** *vt* to give medicine to

**2 medicarse** *vpr* to take medicine

**medicina** *nf* medicine; **m. alternativa** alternative medicine; **m. interna** general medicine *o* practice; **m. preventiva/social** preventive/community medicine

**medicinal** *adj* medicinal

**medición** *nf* measurement

**médico, -a 1** *adj* medical

**2** *nm,f* doctor; **ir al m.** to go to the doctor; **m. de cabecera** *o* **familia** family doctor, general practitioner; **m. forense** specialist in forensic medicine; **m. de guardia** duty doctor; **m. interno** *Br* houseman, *US* intern

**medida** *nf* (a) *(dimensión)* measure; *(medición)* measurement; **a (la) m.** *(mueble)* custom-built; *(ropa)* made-to-measure; **medidas** *(del cuerpo)* measurements; **tomar las medidas a alguien** to take sb's measurements; **m. de capacidad** measure *(liquid or dry)*

(b) *(disposición)* measure, step; **tomar medidas** to take measures *o* steps

(c) *(moderación)* moderation; **sin m.** without moderation

(d) *(grado)* extent, degree; **en cierta/gran m.** to some/a large extent; **en la m. de lo posible** as far as possible; **a m. que entraban** as they were coming in

**medieval** *adj* medieval

**medievalismo** *nm* medievalism

**medievalista** *nmf* medievalist

**medievo** *nm* Middle Ages

**medio, -a 1** *adj* (a) *(mitad)* half; **a m. camino** *(en viaje)* halfway there; *(en trabajo)* halfway through; **media docena** half a dozen; **media hora** half an hour; **m. pueblo estaba allí** half the town was there; **a media luz** in the half-light; **un kilo y m.** one and a half kilos; **son las dos y media** it's half past two

(b) *(intermedio)* *(estatura, tamaño)* medium; *(posición, punto)* middle

(c) *(de promedio)* *(temperatura, velocidad)* average

(d) *(corriente)* ordinary, average

(e) **hacer algo a medias** to half-do sth; **pagar a medias** to go halves, to share the cost

**2** *adv* half; **m. borracho** half drunk; **a m. hacer** half done

**3** *nm* (a) *(mitad)* half

(b) *(centro)* middle, centre; **en m. (de)** in the middle (of); **estar por (en) m.** to be in the way; **equivocarse de m. a m.** to be completely wrong; **meterse** *o* **ponerse de por m.** to get in the way; *Fig* to interfere; **quitar de en m. a alguien** to get rid of sb, to get sb out of the way

(c) *(sistema, manera)* means *(singular)*, method; **por m. de** by means of, through; **por todos los medios** by all possible means; **los medios de comunicación** *o* **información** the media; **medios de producción/transporte** means of production/transport

(d) *(recursos)* **medios** means, resources

(e) *(elemento físico)* environment; **m. ambiente** environment

(f) *(ámbito)* **en medios bien informados** in well-informed circles

**medioambiental** *adj* environmental

**mediocampista** *nmf Dep* midfielder

**mediocre** *adj* mediocre, average

**mediocridad** *nf* mediocrity

**mediodía** *nm* (a) *(hora)* midday, noon; **al m.** at noon *o* midday (b) *(sur)* south

**medioevo** *nm* Middle Ages

**mediofondista** *nmf Dep* middle-distance runner

**mediopensionista** *nmf (en colegio)* = child who has lunch at school

**medique** *etc ver* **medicar**

**medir** [49] **1** *vt* (a) *(hacer mediciones)* to measure (b) *(sopesar)* to weigh up (c) *(palabras)* to weigh carefully (d) *(fuerzas)* to test out against each other

**2** *vi (tener de medida)* **¿cuánto mides?** how tall are you?; **mido 1,80** I'm 6 foot (tall); **mide diez metros** it's ten metres long

**3 medirse** *vpr* (a) *(tomarse medidas)* to measure oneself (b) *(moderarse)* to show restraint (c) *(enfrentarse)* **medirse con** to meet, to compete against

**meditabundo, -a** *adj* thoughtful, pensive

**meditación** *nf* meditation; **m. trascendental** transcendental meditation

**meditar 1** *vi* to meditate (**sobre** on)

**2** *vt* (a) *(considerar)* to meditate, to ponder (b) *(planear)* to plan, to think through

**meditativo, -a** *adj* pensive

**mediterráneo, -a 1** *adj* Mediterranean

**2** *nm* **el (mar) M.** the Mediterranean (Sea)

**médium** *nmf inv* medium

**medrar** vi (a) (prosperar) to prosper (b) (enriquecerse) to get rich (c) (crecer) to grow

**medro** nm **afán de m.** desire to get on in the world

**medroso, -a 1** adj (miedoso) fearful
**2** nm,f fearful person

**médula** nf (a) Anat (bone) marrow; **m. espinal** spinal cord (b) Fig (esencia) core

**medusa** nf jellyfish

**mefistotélico, -a** adj diabolical

**megabyte** [meɣaˈβait] (pl **megabytes**) nm Informát megabyte

**megafonía** nf public-address system

**megáfono** nm megaphone

**megahercio** nm megahertz

**megalito** nm megalith

**megalomanía** nf megalomania

**megalómano, -a** adj & nm,f megalomaniac

**megatón** nm megaton

**meiga** nf witch

**mejicanismo** nm Mexicanism

**mejicano, -a** adj & nm,f Mexican

**Méjico** n Mexico

**mejilla** nf cheek; Fig **ofrecer** o **poner la otra m.** to turn the other cheek

**mejillón** nm mussel

**mejor 1** adj (a) (comparativo) better (**que** than)
(b) (superlativo) **el/la m….** the best…; **lo m. fue que…** the best thing was that…; **a lo m.** maybe, perhaps
**2** nmf **el/la m. (de)** the best (in); **el m. de todos** the best of all
**3** adv (a) (comparativo) better (**que** than); **ahora veo m.** I can see better now; **es m. que no vengas** it would be better if you didn't come; **m. no se lo digas** it'd be better if you don't tell him; **estar m.** (no tan malo) to feel better; (recuperado) to be better; **m. dicho** (or) rather; **m. que m.** so much the better
(b) (superlativo) best; **el que la conoce m.** the one who knows her best

**mejora** nf (a) (progreso) improvement (b) (aumento) increase

**mejorable** adj improvable

**mejorana** nf sweet marjoram

**mejorar 1** vt (hacer mejor) to improve; (enfermo) to make better; **m. una oferta** to make a better offer
**2** vi to improve, to get better
**3 mejorarse** vpr to improve, to get better; **¡que te mejores!** get well soon!

**mejoría** nf improvement

**mejunje** nm Fam concoction

**melancolía** nf melancholy

**melancólico, -a 1** adj melancholic
**2** nm,f melancholic person

**melanina** nf melanin

**melaza** nf molasses

**melé** nf Dep scrum

**melena** nf (a) (de persona) long hair (b) (de león) mane; **melenas** mop of hair

**melenudo, -a 1** adj with a mop of hair
**2** nm,f person with a mop of hair

**melifluo, -a** adj honeyed, mellifluous

**Melilla** n Melilla

**melillense 1** adj of/from Melilla
**2** nmf person from Melilla

**melindre** nm (a) Culin = fried cake made from honey and sugar (b) **melindres** (afectación) affected scrupulousness

**melindroso, -a 1** adj affectedly scrupulous
**2** nm,f affectedly scrupulous person

**melisa** nf lemon balm

**mella** nf (a) (muesca, hendidura) nick; Fig **hacer m. en** (ahorros, moral) to make a dent in; Fig **hacer m. en alguien** to make an impression on sb (b) (en dentadura) gap

**mellado, -a** adj (a) (dañado) nicked (b) (sin dientes) gap-toothed

**mellar** vt (a) (hacer mellas) to nick, to chip (b) (menoscabar) to damage

**mellizo, -a** adj & nm,f twin

**melocotón** nm peach; **m. en almíbar** peaches in syrup

**melocotonero** nm peach tree

**melodía** nf melody, tune

**melódico, -a** adj melodic

**melodioso, -a** adj melodious

**melodrama** nm melodrama

**melodramático, -a** adj melodramatic

**melomanía** nf love of music

**melómano, -a** nm,f music lover

**melón** nm (a) (fruta) melon (b) Fam (idiota) lemon, idiot

**meloncillo** nm = European variety of mongoose

**melopea** nf Fam **agarrar** o **coger una m.** to get legless

**melosidad** nf (dulzura) sweetness; (empalago) sickliness

**meloso, -a** adj (como la miel) honey; Fig (dulce) sweet; (empalagoso) sickly

**membrana** nf membrane

**membranoso, -a** adj membranous

**membrete** nm letterhead

**membrillo** nm (a) (fruto) quince (b) (dulce) quince jelly

**memez** nf Fam (cualidad) stupidity; (acción, dicho) silly o stupid thing

**memo, -a 1** adj stupid
**2** nm,f idiot, fool

**memorable** adj memorable

**memorándum, memorando** (pl **memorandos**) nm (a) (cuaderno) notebook (b) (nota diplomática) memorandum

**memoria** nf (a) (capacidad de recordar) también Informát memory; **de m.** by heart; **hacer m.** to try to remember; **refrescar la m. (a alguien)** to refresh sb's memory; **traer a la m.** to call to mind; **ser flaco de m.** to be forgetful; **venir a la m.** to come to mind; Informát **m. de acceso aleatorio/de sólo lectura** random-access/read only memory; Informát **m. expandida/extendida/programable** expanded/extended/programmable memory; Informát **m. RAM/ROM** RAM/ROM
(b) (recuerdo) remembrance, remembering; **ser de feliz/ingrata m.** to be a happy/an unhappy memory; **memorias** (en literatura) memoirs
(c) (disertación) (academic) paper
(d) (informe) **m. (anual)** (annual) report
(e) (lista) list, record

**memorial** nm petition, request

**memorístico, -a** adj memory; **ejercicio m.** memory exercise

**memorización** nf memorizing

**memorizar** [16] vt to memorize

**ménage à trois** [me'naʃa'trwa] nm ménage à trois

**menaje** nm household goods and furnishings; **m. de cocina** kitchenware

**mención** nf mention; **hacer m. de** to mention

**mencionar** vt to mention

**menda** Fam **1** pron (el que habla) yours truly
**2** nmf (uno cualquiera) **vino un m. y...** this bloke came along and...

**mendacidad** nf Formal mendacity, untruthfulness

**mendaz** adj Formal mendacious, untruthful

**mendicidad** nf begging

**mendigar** [40] **1** vt to beg for
**2** vi to beg

**mendigo, -a** nm,f beggar

**mendrugo** nm (a) (de pan) crust (of bread) (b) Fam (idiota) fathead, idiot

**menear 1** vt (a) (mover) to move; (cabeza) to shake; (cola) to wag; (caderas) to wiggle (b) Fig (activar) to get moving
**2 menearse** vpr (a) (moverse) to move (about); (agitarse) to shake; (oscilar) to sway (b) (darse prisa, espabilarse) to get a move on (c) Fam **un susto de no te menees** a hell of a scare

**meneo** nm (movimiento) movement; (de cola) wagging; (de caderas) wiggle; Fam **dar un m. a algo** to knock sth; Fam **dar un m. a alguien** to give sb a hiding

**menester** nm necessity; **haber m. de algo** to be in need of sth; **ser m. que alguien haga algo** to be necessary for sb to do sth; **menesteres** (asuntos) business, matters

**menesteroso, -a** Formal **1** adj needy, poor
**2** nm,f needy o poor person

**menestra** nf vegetable stew

**mengano, -a** nm,f so-and-so

**mengua** nf (a) (reducción) reduction (b) (falta) lack (c) Fig (descrédito) discredit; **sin m. de** without detriment to

**menguado, -a** adj reduced, diminished

**menguante** adj (luna) waning; **en cuarto m.** on the wane

**menguar** [12] **1** vi (a) (disminuir) to decrease, to diminish; (luna) to wane (b) (en labor de punto) to decrease
**2** vt (a) (disminuir) to lessen, to diminish (b) (en labor de punto) to decrease

**menhir** nm menhir

**meninge** nf Anat meninx

**meningitis** nf inv Med meningitis

**menisco** nm Anat meniscus

**menopausia** nf menopause

**menor 1** adj (a) (comparativo) (en tamaño) smaller (**que** than); (en edad) younger (**que** than); (en importancia) less, lesser (**que** than); (en número) lower (**que** than)
(b) (superlativo) **el/la m....** (en tamaño) the smallest...; (en edad) the youngest...; (en importancia) the slightest...; (en número) the lowest...
(c) (en importancia) minor; **un problema m.** a minor problem
(d) **ser m. de edad** (para votar, conducir) to be under age; Der to be a minor
(e) Mús **en do m.** in C minor
(f) Com **al por m.** retail
**2** nmf (a) (superlativo) **el/la m.** (hijo, hermano) the youngest
(b) Der (niño) minor

**Menorca** n Minorca

**menorquín, -ina** adj & nm,f Minorcan

**menos 1** adj inv (a) (comparativo) (cantidad) less; (número) fewer; **m. aire** less air; **m. manzanas** fewer apples; **m.... que...** less/fewer... than...; **tiene m. experiencia que tú** she has less experience than you; **hace m. calor que ayer** it's not as hot as it was yesterday; **hay dos libros de m.** there are two books missing; **me han dado 100 ptas de m.** they've given me 100 pesetas too little
(b) (superlativo) (cantidad) the least; (número) the fewest; **el que compró m. acciones** the one

who bought the fewest shares; **lo que m. tiempo llevó** the thing that took the least time

**(c)** *Fam (peor)* **éste es m. coche que el mío** that car isn't as good as mine

**2** *adv* **(a)** *(comparativo)* less; **m. de/que** less than; **estás m. gordo** you're not as fat

**(b)** *(superlativo)* **el/la/lo m.** the least; **él es el m. indicado para criticar** he's the last person who should be criticizing; **ella es la m. adecuada para el cargo** she's the least suitable person for the job; **es lo m. que puedo hacer** it's the least I can do

**(c)** *(expresa resta)* minus; **tres m. dos igual a uno** three minus two is one

**(d)** *(con las horas)* to; **son las dos m. diez** it's ten to two

**(e)** *(expresiones)* **a m. que** unless; **no iré a m. que me acompañes** I won't go unless you come with me; **al m.** at least; **es lo de m.** that's the least of it, that's of no importance; **hacer de m. a alguien** to snub sb; **¡m. mal!** just as well!, thank God!; **nada m. (que)** no less (than); **ni mucho m.** nor anything like it; **no es para m.** not without (good) reason; **(por) lo m.** at least; **venir a m.** to go down in the world

**3** *nm inv Mat* minus (sign)

**4** *prep (excepto)* except (for); **todo m. eso** anything but that

**menoscabar** *vt (fama, honra)* to damage; *(derechos, intereses, salud)* to harm; *(belleza, perfección)* to diminish

**menoscabo** *nm (de fama, honra)* damage; *(de derechos, intereses, salud)* harm; *(de belleza, perfección)* diminishing; **(ir) en m. de** (to be) to the detriment of

**menospreciar** [15] *vt (despreciar)* to scorn, to despise; *(infravalorar)* to undervalue

**menosprecio** *nm* scorn, contempt

**mensáfono** *nm* pager

**mensaje** *nm también Informát* message

**mensajería** *nf* courier service

**mensajero, -a 1** *adj* message-carrying; *Fig* announcing, presaging

**2** *nm,f (portador)* messenger; *(de mensajería)* courier

**menstruación** *nf* menstruation

**menstrual** *adj* menstrual

**menstruar** [4] *vi* to menstruate, to have a period

**menstruo** *nm* menstruation

**mensual** *adj* monthly; **5.000 ptas mensuales** 5,000 pesetas a month

**mensualidad** *nf* **(a)** *(sueldo)* monthly salary **(b)** *(pago)* monthly payment *o* instalment

**menta** *nf* mint

**mentado, -a** *adj* **(a)** *(mencionado)* abovementioned, aforementioned **(b)** *(famoso)* famous

**mental** *adj* mental

**mentalidad** *nf* mentality

**mentalización** *nf* mental preparation

**mentalizar** [16] **1** *vt* to put into a frame of mind; **m. a alguien de algo** to make sb aware of sth

**2 mentalizarse** *vpr* to get into a frame of mind; **mentalizarse de que...** to get used to the idea that...

**mentar** [3] *vt* to mention

**mente** *nf* **(a)** *(pensamiento, intelecto)* mind; **tener en m. algo** to have sth in mind; **tener en m. hacer algo** to intend to do sth; **traer a la m.** to bring to mind **(b)** *(mentalidad)* mentality

**mentecato, -a** *nm,f* idiot

**mentir** [64] *vi* to lie; **miente más que habla** he's a born liar

**mentira** *nf* lie; **aunque parezca m.** strange as it may seem; **de m.** pretend, false; **parece m. (que...)** it hardly seems possible (that...), it's scarcely credible (that...); **es m.** it's a lie, it's not true; **una m. como una casa** a whopping great lie; **m. piadosa** white lie

**mentirijilla** *nf Fam* fib; **de mentirijillas** *(en broma)* as a joke, in fun; *(falso)* pretend, make-believe

**mentiroso, -a 1** *adj* lying; *(engañoso)* deceptive

**2** *nm,f* liar

**mentís** *nm inv* denial; **dar un m. (a)** to issue a denial (of)

**mentol** *nm* menthol

**mentolado, -a** *adj* menthol, mentholated

**mentón** *nm* chin

**mentor, -ora** *nm,f* mentor

**menú** *(pl menús) nm* **(a)** *(lista)* menu; *(comida)* food; **m. del día** set meal **(b)** *Informát* menu; **m. desplegable** pull-down menu

**menudear 1** *vi* to happen frequently

**2** *vt* to repeat, to do repeatedly

**menudencia** *nf* trifle, insignificant thing

**menudeo** *nm Andes, Méx* retailing

**menudillos** *nmpl* giblets

**menudo, -a** *adj* **(a)** *(pequeño)* small **(b)** *(insignificante)* trifling, insignificant **(c)** *(para enfatizar)* what!; **¡m. lío/gol!** what a mess/goal! **(d) a m.** often

**meñique** *nm* **(dedo) m.** little finger

**meódromo** *nm muy Fam* bog

**meollo** *nm* core, heart; **el m. de la cuestión** the nub of the question, the heart of the matter

**meón, -ona** *nm,f Fam* **es un m.** he has a weak bladder

**mequetrefe** *nmf Fam* good-for-nothing

**mercachifle** *nmf Pey* (a) *(comerciante)* pedlar (b) *(usurero)* money-grabber, shark

**mercader** *nmf* merchant, trader

**mercadería** *nf* merchandise, goods

**mercadillo** *nm* flea market

**mercado** *nm* market; *Com* **m. de abastos** wholesale food market; **m. alcista/bajista** bull/bear market; **m. bursátil** stock market; **m. de capitales/divisas/valores** capital/currency/securities market; **m. común** Common Market; **m. de futuros** futures market; **m. interbancario** interbank market; **m. libre/negro** free/black market; **m. de trabajo** labour *o* job market

**mercadotecnia** *nf* marketing

**mercancía 1** *nf* merchandise, goods

**2** *nm inv* **mercancías** *Ferroc* goods train, *US* freight train

**mercante 1** *adj* merchant

**2** *nm (barco)* merchantman, merchant ship

**mercantil** *adj* mercantile, commercial

**mercantilismo** *nm Econ* mercantilism; *Fig* commercialism

**mercantilizar** [16] *vt* to commercialize

**merced** *nf* favour; **m. a** thanks to; **a m. de algo/alguien** at the mercy of sth/sb

**mercenario, -a** *adj & nm,f* mercenary

**mercería** *nf* (a) *(género)* *Br* haberdashery, *US* notions (b) *(tienda)* *Br* haberdasher's (shop), *US* notions store

**MERCOSUR** *nm* = South American economic community consisting of Argentina, Brazil, Paraguay and Uruguay

**mercromina**® *nf (para heridas)* mercurochrome®

**Mercurio** *nm* Mercury

**mercurio** *nm* mercury

**mercurocromo** *nm* mercurochrome®

**merecedor, -ora** *adj* **m. de** worthy of

**merecer** [48] **1** *vt* to deserve, to be worthy of; **la isla merece una visita** the island is worth a visit; **no merece la pena** it's not worth it

**2** *vi* to be worthy; **en edad de m.** of marriageable age

**merecido** *nm* **darle a alguien su m.** to give sb his/her just deserts; **recibió su m.** he got his just deserts

**merendar** [3] **1** *vi* to have tea *(as a light afternoon meal)*

**2** *vt* to have for tea

**3 merendarse** *vpr Fam Fig* **merendarse a alguien** to thrash sb

**merendero** *nm* = open-air café or bar (in the country or on the beach)

**merendola** *nf Fam* slap-up tea

**merengue 1** *nm* (a) *Culin* meringue (b) *(baile)* merengue

**2** *adj Fam Dep* = relating to Real Madrid Football Club

**meretriz** *nf* prostitute

**merezca** *etc ver* **merecer**

**Mérida** *n* Merida

**meridiano, -a 1** *adj* (a) *(hora)* midday (b) *Fig (claro)* crystal-clear

**2** *nm* meridian

**meridional 1** *adj* southern

**2** *nmf* southerner

**merienda 1** *ver* **merendar**

**2** *nf* tea *(as a light afternoon meal)*; *(en el campo)* picnic; **fue una m. de negros** it was total chaos

**mérito** *nm* (a) *(cualidad)* merit; **hacer méritos para** to do everything possible to (b) *(valor)* value, worth; **tiene mucho m.** it's no mean achievement; **de m.** worthy, deserving

**meritorio, -a 1** *adj* worthy, deserving

**2** *nm,f* unpaid trainee *o* apprentice

**merluza** *nf* (a) *(pez, pescado)* hake (b) *Fam (borrachera)* **agarrar una m.** to get sozzled

**merluzo, -a** *nm,f Fam* idiot, fool

**merma** *nf* decrease, reduction

**mermar 1** *vi* to diminish, to lessen

**2** *vt* to reduce, to diminish

**mermelada** *nf* jam; **m. de naranja** marmalade

**mero, -a 1** *adj* (a) *(mere)*; **una mera excusa** just an excuse (b) *CAm, Méx* **aquí m.** right here; **el m. m.** the big shot; **ya m.** any minute now

**2** *nm* grouper

**merodeador, -ora** *nm,f* prowler, snooper

**merodear** *vi* to snoop, to prowl (**por** about)

**mes** *nm* (a) *(del año)* month (b) *(salario)* monthly salary (c) *Fam (menstruación)* period

**mesa** *nf* (a) *(mueble)* table; *(de oficina, despacho)* desk; **bendecir la m.** to say grace; **poner/quitar la m.** to set/clear the table; **m. camilla** small round table under which a heater is placed; **m. de mezclas** mixing desk; **m. (de) nido** nest of tables; **m. de operaciones** operating table; **m. plegable** folding table (b) *(comité)* board, committee; *(en un debate)* panel; **m. directiva** executive board *o* committee; **m. electoral** = group supervising the voting in each ballot box; **m. redonda** *(coloquio)* round table

**mesana** *nf* (a) *(mástil)* mizenmast (b) *(vela)* mizensail

**mescalina** *nf* mescalin

**mescolanza** *nf Fam* hotchpotch, mishmash

**mesero, -a** *nm,f Am* waiter, *f* waitress

**meseta** *nf* plateau, tableland

**mesianismo** *nm Rel* messianism; *Fig* blind faith in one person

**mesías** *nm inv también Fig* Messiah; **el M.** the Messiah

**mesilla** *nf* **m. (de noche)** bedside table

**mesnada** *nf* armed retinue

**mesocracia** *nf* = government by the middle classes

**mesón** *nm* (a) *Hist* inn (b) *(bar, restaurante)* = old, country-style restaurant and bar

**mesonero, -a** *nm,f* innkeeper

**Mesopotamia** *n* Mesopotamia

**mester** *nm Anticuado* trade, craft

**mestizaje** *nm (de razas)* racial mix, fusion of races; *Biol* cross-breeding; *Fig* mixing

**mestizo, -a** **1** *adj (persona)* of mixed race, half-caste; *(animal, planta)* cross-bred

**2** *nm,f* person of mixed race, half-caste

**mesura** *nf* (a) *(moderación)* moderation, restraint; **con m.** in moderation (b) *(cortesía)* courtesy, politeness (c) *(gravedad)* dignity, seriousness

**mesurado, -a** *adj* moderate, restrained

**mesurarse** *vpr* to restrain oneself

**meta** *nf* (a) *Dep (llegada)* finishing line; *(portería)* goal; **m. volante** *(en ciclismo)* hot spot sprint (b) *Fig (objetivo)* aim, goal; **fijarse una m.** to set oneself a target *o* goal

**metabólico, -a** *adj* metabolic

**metabolismo** *nm* metabolism

**metacrilato** *nm* methacrylate, = transparent resin used in furniture making

**metadona** *nf* methadone

**metafísica** *nf (disciplina)* metaphysics *(singular)*

**metafísico, -a 1** *adj* metaphysical

**2** *nm,f (filósofo)* metaphysicist

**metáfora** *nf* metaphor

**metafórico, -a** *adj* metaphorical

**metal** *nm* (a) *(material)* metal; **m. blanco** white metal; **metales preciosos** precious metals (b) *Mús* brass

**metalenguaje** *nm Informát & Ling* metalanguage

**metálico, -a 1** *adj (sonido, color)* metallic; *(objeto)* metal

**2** *nm* **pagar en m.** to pay (in) cash

**metalizado, -a** *adj (pintura)* metallic

**metalurgia** *nf* metallurgy

**metalúrgico, -a 1** *adj* metallurgical

**2** *nm,f* metallurgist

**metamórfico, -a** *adj* metamorphic

**metamorfismo** *nm* metamorphism

**metamorfosis** *nf inv también Fig* metamorphosis

**metano** *nm* methane

**metanol** *nm* methanol

**metástasis** *nf inv Med* metastasis

**metedura** *nf* **m. de pata** clanger

**meteórico, -a** *adj también Fig* meteoric

**meteorito** *nm* meteorite

**meteoro** *nm* meteor

**meteorología** *nf* meteorology

**meteorológico, -a** *adj* meteorological

**meteorólogo, -a** *nm,f* meteorologist; *Radio & TV* weatherman, *f* weatherwoman

**metepatas** *nmf inv Fam* **es un m.** he's always putting his foot in it

**meter 1** *vt* (a) *(introducir)* to put in; **m. algo/a alguien en algo** to put sth/sb in sth; **m. la llave en la cerradura** to put the key into the lock; **le metieron en la cárcel** they put him in prison; **m. dinero en el banco** to put money in the bank; **he metido mis ahorros en esa empresa** I've put all my savings into this venture; *Fam* **meterle ideas a alguien en la cabeza** to put ideas into sb's head; *Fam* **no consigo meterle en la cabeza (que...)** I can't get it into his head (that...)

(b) *(hacer participar)* **m. a alguien en algo** to get sb into sth

(c) *(obligar a)* **m. a alguien a hacer algo** to make sb start doing sth

(d) *(causar)* **m. prisa/miedo a alguien** to rush/scare sb; **m. ruido** to make a noise

(e) *Fam (asestar)* to give; **le metió un puñetazo** he gave him a punch

(f) *Fam (echar, soltar)* to give; **m. una bronca a alguien** to tell sb off; **me metió un rollo sobre la disciplina militar** he gave me this routine about military discipline

(g) *(prenda, ropa)* to take in; **m. el bajo de una falda** to take up a skirt

(h) **a todo m.** as quickly as possible

**2 meterse** *vpr* (a) *(entrar)* to get in; **meterse en** to get into; *Fam* **se le ha metido en la cabeza (que...)** he's got it into his head (that...)

(b) *(en frase interrogativa) (estar)* to get to; **¿dónde se ha metido ese chico?** where has that boy got to?

(c) *(dedicarse)* **meterse a** to become; **meterse a torero** to become a bullfighter

(d) *(involucrarse)* to get involved **(en** in)

(e) *(entrometerse)* to meddle, to interfere; **se mete en todo** he never minds his own business; **meterse por medio** to interfere

(f) *(empezar)* **meterse a hacer algo** to get started on doing sth

(g) **meterse con** *(incordiar)* to hassle; *(atacar)* to go for

(h) *Fam (comer)* to scoff

(i) *Fam (drogas)* **meterse coca/LSD** to do coke/LSD

**meterete, metete** *adj CSur Fam* meddling, meddlesome

**meticón, -ona** *adj Fam* busy-body, nosey-parker

**meticulosidad** *nf* meticulousness

**meticuloso, -a** *adj* meticulous

**metido, -a** *adj* (a) *(implicado)* **andar** *o* **estar m. en** to be involved in (b) *(abundante)* **m. en años** elderly; **m. en carnes** plump

**metódico, -a** *adj* methodical

**metodismo** *nm* Methodism

**metodista** *adj & nmf* Methodist

**método** *nm* (a) *(sistema)* method (b) *Educ* course

**metodología** *nf* methodology

**metodológico, -a** *adj* methodological

**metomentodo** *Fam* **1** *adj inv* meddlesome **2** *nmf* busybody

**metonimia** *nf* metonymy

**metraje** *nm* length, running time

**metralla** *nf* shrapnel

**metralleta** *nf* submachine gun

**métrica** *nf Lit* metrics

**métrico, -a** *adj* (a) *(del metro)* metric; **sistema m. decimal** metric system (b) *Lit* metrical

**metro** *nm* (a) *(unidad) & Lit* metre; **m. cuadrado/cúbico** square/cubic metre; **metros por segundo** metres per second (b) *(transporte) Br* underground, tube, *US* subway; **en m.** *Br* by underground *o* tube, *US* by *o* on the subway (c) *(cinta métrica)* tape measure

**metrópoli** *nf*, **metrópolis** *nf inv* (a) *(ciudad)* metropolis (b) *(nación)* home country

**metropolitano, -a 1** *adj* metropolitan **2** *nm (metro) Br* underground, tube, *US* subway

**mexicanismo** *nm* Mexicanism

**mexicano, -a** *adj & nm,f* Mexican

**México** ['meχiko] *n* Mexico

**mezcla** *nf* (a) *(unión, conjunto)* mixture; **una m. de tabacos** a blend of tobaccos (b) *(acción)* mixing (c) *Mús* mix

**mezclador, -ora 1** *nm,f (persona)* sound mixer **2** *nm (aparato)* mixer; **m. de imagen/sonido** vision/sound mixer

**mezclar 1** *vt* (a) *(combinar, unir)* to mix (b) *(confundir, desordenar)* to mix up (c) *Fig (implicar)* **m. a alguien en** to get sb mixed up in **2 mezclarse** *vpr* (a) *(juntarse)* to mix (con with) (b) *(difuminarse)* **mezclarse entre** to dis-

appear *o* blend into (c) *Fig (implicarse)* **mezclarse en** to get mixed up in

**mezclilla** *nf* = cloth woven from mixed fibres

**mezcolanza** *nf Fam* hotchpotch, mishmash

**mezquindad** *nf* (a) *(cualidad)* meanness (b) *(acción)* mean action

**mezquino, -a** *adj* mean

**mezquita** *nf* mosque

**mg** *(abrev de* **miligramo***)* mg

**MHz** *(abrev de* **megahercio***)* MHz

**mi**[1] *nm Mús* E; *(en solfeo)* mi

**mi**[2] *(pl* **mis***) adj posesivo* my; **mi casa** my house; **mis libros** my books

**mí** *pron personal (después de prep)* (a) *(en general)* me; **este trabajo no es para mí** this job isn't for me; **no se fía de mí** he doesn't trust me

(b) *(reflexivo)* myself; **debo pensar más en mí (mismo)** I should think more about myself

(c) *(expresiones)* **¡a mí qué!** so what?, why should I care?; **para mí** *(yo creo)* as far as I'm concerned, in my opinion; **por mí** as far as I'm concerned; **por mí, no hay inconveniente** it's fine by me

**mía** *adj & pron ver* **mío**

**miaja** *nf* crumb; *Fig* tiny bit

**mialgia** *nf Med* myalgia

**miasma** *nm* miasma

**miau** *nm* miaow

**mica** *nf* mica

**micción** *nf Med (acción)* urination

**micénico, -a** *adj* Mycenaean

**michelín** *nm Fam* spare tyre

**mico** *nm* (a) *(animal)* (long-tailed) monkey (b) *(expresiones)* **es un m.** *(pequeño)* he's tiny *o* a midget; *(feo)* he's an ugly devil; *Fig* **ser el último m.** to be the lowest of the low; **me volví m. para hacerlo** I had a devil of a job to do it

**micología** *nf* mycology

**micosis** *nf inv* mycosis

**micra** *nf* micron

**micro 1** *nm Fam (abrev de* **micrófono***)* mike **2** *nm o nf Andes, CSur (microbús)* minibus

**microbio** *nm* germ, microbe

**microbiología** *nf* microbiology

**microbús** *(pl* **microbuses***) nm* minibus

**microbusete** *nm Carib* minibus

**microcirugía** *nf* microsurgery

**microclima** *nm* microclimate

**microeconomía** *nf* microeconomics *(singular)*

**microelectrónica** *nf* microelectronics *(singular)*

**microficha** *nf* microfiche

**microfilm** *(pl* **microfilms***)*, **microfilme** *nm* microfilm

**micrófono** *nm* microphone

**microfotografía** *nf* microphotography

**microinformática** *nf Informát* microcomputing

**microonda** *nf* microwave

**microondas** *nm inv* microwave (oven)

**microordenador** *nm Informát* microcomputer

**microorganismo** *nm* microorganism

**microprocesador** *nm Informát* microprocessor

**microscópico, -a** *adj* microscopic

**microscopio** *nm* microscope; **m. electrónico** electron microscope

**microsurco** *nm* microgroove

**mida** *etc ver* **medir**

**midiera** *etc ver* **medir**

**miedica** *Fam* **1** *adj* yellow, chicken
  **2** *nmf* scaredy-cat, coward

**miedo** *nm* fear; **dar m.** to be frightening; **me da m. conducir** I'm afraid *o* frightened of driving; **meter m. a** to frighten; **temblar de m.** to tremble with fear; **tener m. a** *o* **de (hacer algo)** to be afraid of (doing sth); **tengo m. de que se estropee** I'm frightened it'll get damaged; *Fam* **Fig la película estuvo de m.** the film was brilliant; **lo pasamos de m.** we had a fantastic time; *muy Fam* **estar cagado de m.** to be shit-scared; **morirse de m.** to die of fright, to be terrified; **m. cerval** terrible fear, terror

**miedoso, -a** **1** *adj* fearful
  **2** *nm,f* fearful person

**miel** *nf* honey; **m. sobre hojuelas** all the better

**miembro** *nm* (a) *(integrante)* member (b) *(extremidad)* limb, member; **miembros superiores/inferiores** upper/lower limbs; **m. (viril)** penis

**mienta** (a) *ver* **mentar** (b) *ver* **mentir**

**mientes** *nfpl* mind; **parar m. (en algo)** to consider (sth); **traer a las m.** to bring to mind

**mientras** **1** *conj* (a) *(al tiempo que)* while; **leía m. comía** she was reading while she was eating (b) *(hasta que)* **m. no se pruebe lo contrario** until proved otherwise (c) *(por el contrario)* **m. (que)** whereas, whilst
  **2** *adv* **m. (tanto)** meanwhile, in the meantime

**miércoles** *nm inv* Wednesday; **M. de Ceniza** Ash Wednesday; *ver también* **sábado**

**mierda** *muy Fam* **1** *nf* (a) *(excremento)* shit (b) *(suciedad)* filth, shit (c) *(cosa sin valor)* **es una m.** it's (a load of) crap; **de m.** shitty, crappy (d) *(borrachera)* **agarrarse/tener una m.** to get/be shitfaced (e) *(expresiones)* **irse a la m.** *(proyecto)* to go down the tubes; **mandar a alguien a la m.** to tell sb to piss off; **¡vete a la m.!** go to hell!, piss off!
  **2** *nmf* shithead

**mies** **1** *nf (cereal)* ripe corn
  **2** *nfpl* **mieses** *(campo)* cornfields

**miga** *nf (de pan)* crumb; *Fam Fig* **tener m.** *(ser sustancioso)* to have a lot to it; *(ser complicado)* to have more to it than meets the eye; *Culin* **migas** fried breadcrumbs; *Fam* **hacer buenas/malas migas** to get on well/badly; *Fam* **hacerse migas** *(cosa)* to be smashed to bits; *Fam* **hacer migas a alguien** *(desmoralizar)* to shatter sb

**migaja** *nf* (a) *(trozo)* bit; *(de pan)* crumb (b) *Fig (pizca)* scrap; **migajas** *(restos)* leftovers

**migración** *nf* migration

**migraña** *nf* migraine

**migrar** *vi* to migrate

**migratorio, -a** *adj* migratory

**mijo** *nm* millet

**mil** *núm* thousand; **dos m.** two thousand; **m. pesetas** a thousand pesetas; *Fig* **m. y una/uno** a thousand and one; **miles (de)** *(gran cantidad)* thousands (of); *ver también* **seis**

**milagrero, -a** *Fam* **1** *adj* (a) *(crédulo)* = who believes in miracles (b) *(milagroso)* miraculous, miracle-working
  **2** *nm,f* = person who believes in miracles

**milagro** *nm* miracle; **de m.** miraculously, by a miracle; *Fig* **hacer milagros** to work wonders

**milagroso, -a** *adj* miraculous; *Fig* amazing

**milamores** *nf inv* valerian

**milanés, -esa** **1** *adj* of/from Milan
  **2** *nm,f* person from Milan

**milanesa** *nf Am* Wiener schnitzel, breaded veal escalope

**milano** *nm* kite

**milenario, -a** **1** *adj (antiguo)* ancient
  **2** *nm* millennium

**milenio** *nm (mil años)* millennium; *Fam (mucho tiempo)* (absolutely) ages

**milésimo, -a** **1** *núm* thousandth; **la milésima parte** a thousandth
  **2** *nf* **milésima** thousandth

**milhojas** *nm inv Culin* mille feuille

**mili** *nf Fam* military service; **hacer la m.** to do one's military service

**milicia** *nf* (a) *(profesión)* military (profession) (b) *(grupo armado)* militia; **milicias universitarias** = formerly in Spain, military service for students

**miliciano, -a** *nm,f* militiaman, *f* female soldier

**milico** *nm Andes, CSur Fam Pey (soldado)* soldier; **los milicos tomaron el poder** the military took power

**miligramo** *nm* milligram

**mililitro** *nm* millilitre

**milimetrado** *adj* **papel m.** graph paper

**milimétrico, -a** *adj* millimetric

**milímetro** *nm* millimetre; *Fig* **al m.** down to the last detail

**militancia** *nf* militancy

**militante** *adj & nmf* militant

**militar 1** *adj* military
 **2** *nmf* soldier; **los militares** the military
 **3** *vi* to be active **(en** in)

**militarismo** *nm* militarism

**militarista** *adj & nmf* militarist

**militarización** *nf* militarization

**militarizar** [16] *vt* to militarize

**militroncho** *nm Fam (soldado) Br* squaddie

**milla** *nf* mile; **m. (marina)** nautical mile

**millar** *nm* thousand; **un m. de personas** a thousand people

**millón** *núm* million; **dos millones** two million; **un m. de personas** a million people; **un m. de cosas que hacer** a million things to do; **un m. de gracias** thanks a million; **millones** *(dinero)* millions, a fortune

**millonada** *nf Fam* **una m.** a fortune, millions

**millonario, -a 1** *adj* **es m.** he's a millionaire
 **2** *nm,f* millionaire, *f* millionairess

**millonésima** *nf* millionth

**millonésimo, -a** *núm* millionth; **la millonésima parte** a millionth

**mimado, -a** *adj* spoilt

**mimar** *vt* to spoil, to pamper

**mimbre** *nm* wicker; **de m.** wickerwork

**mimético, -a** *adj* mimetic

**mimetismo** *nm (de animal, planta)* mimetism

**mimetizar** [16] *vt* to copy, to imitate

**mímica** *nf* (a) *(mimo)* mime (b) *(lenguaje)* sign language

**mímico, -a** *adj* mime; **lenguaje m.** sign language

**mimo** *nm* (a) *(zalamería)* mollycoddling (b) *(cariño)* show of affection; **hacerle mimos a alguien** to kiss and cuddle sb (c) *Teatro* mime; **hacer m.** to perform mime

**mimosa** *nf Bot* mimosa

**mimoso, -a** *adj* affectionate; *Fam* **el bebé está m.** the baby wants a cuddle

**min** *(abrev de* **minuto)** min

**mina** *nf* (a) *Geol & Mil* mine; **m. de carbón** coalmine (b) *Fig (chollo)* goldmine (c) *(de lápiz)* lead (d) *CSur Fam (chica) Br* bird, *US* babe

**minar** *vt* (a) *Mil* to mine (b) *Fig (aminorar)* to undermine

**minarete** *nm Arquit* minaret

**mineral 1** *adj* mineral
 **2** *nm* (a) *Geol* mineral (b) *Min* ore

**mineralizar** [16] **1** *vt* to mineralize
 **2 mineralizarse** *vpr* to become mineralized

**mineralogía** *nf* minerology

**minería** *nf* (a) *(técnica)* mining (b) *(sector)* mining industry

**minero, -a 1** *adj* mining; *(producción, riqueza)* mineral; **industria minera** mining industry
 **2** *nm,f* miner

**mineromedicinal** *adj* **agua m.** mineral water

**minestrone** *nf* minestrone

**mini** *nm Fam* **un m. de cerveza** a litre (glass) of beer

**miniatura** *nf* miniature; **el piso es una m.** the flat is tiny; **en m.** in miniature

**miniaturista** *nmf* miniaturist

**miniaturizar** [16] *vt* to miniaturize

**minicadena** *nf* midi system

**mini disk, mini disc** *nm inv* mini disc

**minifalda** *nf* mini skirt

**minifundio** *nm* small holding

**minigolf** *(pl* **minigolfs)** *nm* (a) *(lugar)* crazy golf course (b) *(juego)* crazy golf

**mínima** *nf* (a) *Meteo* low, lowest temperature (b) *(provocación)* **saltar a la m.** to blow up at the least thing

**minimalismo** *nm Mús* minimalism

**minimalista** *adj Mús* minimalist

**minimizar** [16] *vt* to play down

**mínimo, -a 1** *superlativo ver* **pequeño**
 **2** *adj* (a) *(lo más bajo posible o necesario)* minimum (b) *(lo más bajo temporalmente)* lowest (c) *(muy pequeño) (efecto, importancia)* minimal, very small; *(protesta, ruido)* slightest; **no tengo la más mínima idea** I haven't the slightest idea; **como m.** at the very least; **en lo más m.** in the slightest
 **3** *nm (límite)* minimum; **estar bajo mínimos** to have almost run out; **m. común múltiplo** lowest common multiple

**minino, -a** *nm,f Fam* pussy (cat)

**ministerial** *adj* ministerial

**ministerio** *nm* (a) *Pol (institución) Br* ministry, *US* department; *(periodo)* time as minister; **durante el m. de Sánchez** while Sánchez was minister; **M. de Asuntos Exteriores** *Br* Foreign Office, *US* State Department; **M. de Economía y Hacienda** *Br* Treasury, *US* Treasury Department; **M. del Interior** *Br* Home Office, *US* Department of the Interior (b) *Der* **m. público, m. fiscal** Department of Public Prosecution (c) *Rel* ministry

**ministro, -a** *nm,f* (a) *Pol Br* minister, *US* secretary; **m. sin cartera** minister without portfolio; **primer m.** prime minister (b) *Rel* minister; **m. de Dios** minister of God

**minoría** *nf* minority; **m. de edad** (legal) minority; **minorías étnicas** ethnic minorities

**minorista 1** *adj* retail
  **2** *nmf* retailer

**minoritario, -a** *adj* minority; **son un grupo m. dentro del partido** they are a minority within the party

**mintiera** *etc ver* **mentir**

**minucia** *nf* trifle, insignificant thing

**minuciosidad** *nf* meticulousness, attention to detail

**minucioso, -a** *adj* (a) *(meticuloso)* meticulous (b) *(detallado)* highly detailed

**minué** *nm* minuet

**minuendo** *nm Mat* figure from which another is to be subtracted, minuend

**minúscula** *nf* small letter; *Imprenta* lowercase letter

**minúsculo, -a 1** *adj* (a) *(tamaño)* tiny, minute (b) *(letra)* small; *Imprenta* lower-case

**minusvalía** *nf* (a) *Econ* depreciation (b) *(física)* handicap, disability

**minusválido, -a 1** *adj* disabled, handicapped
  **2** *nm,f* disabled o handicapped person

**minusvalorar** *vt* to underestimate

**minuta** *nf (factura)* fee

**minutero** *nm* minute hand

**minuto** *nm* minute; **al m.** *(al momento)* a moment later

**Miño** *nm* **el (río) M.** the River Miño

**mío, -a 1** *adj posesivo* mine; **este libro es m.** this book is mine; **un amigo m.** a friend of mine; **no es asunto m.** it's none of my business
  **2** *pron posesivo* **el m.** mine; **el m. es rojo** mine is red; *Fam* **esta es la mía** this is the chance I've been waiting for o my big chance; **lo m. es el teatro** *(lo que me va)* theatre is what I should be doing; *Fam* **los míos** *(mi familia)* my folks; *(mi bando)* my lot, my side

**miocardio** *nm Anat* myocardium

**miope 1** *adj* shortsighted, myopic; *Fig* **una política m.** a shortsighted policy
  **2** *nmf* shortsighted o myopic person

**miopía** *nf* shortsightedness, myopia

**MIR** [mir] *(abrev de* **médico interno residente***)* **1** *nm (examen)* = competitive national examination for placement in houseman's post
  **2** *nmf Br* houseman, *US* intern

**mira** *nf* (a) *(en instrumento, arma)* sight; **m. telescópica** telescopic sight (b) *Fig (intención, propósito)* intention; **con miras a** with a view to, with the intention of; **poner la m.** o **las miras en algo** to set one's sights on sth

**mirada** *nf (acción de mirar)* look; *(rápida)* glance; *(de cariño, placer, admiración)* gaze; **apartar la m.** to look away; **dirigir** o **lanzar la m.** a to glance at; **echar una m. (a algo)** to glance o to have a quick look (at sth); **fulminar con la m. a alguien** to look daggers at sb; **levantar la m.** to look up

**mirado, -a** *adj* (a) *(prudente)* careful (b) **ser bien m.** *(bien considerado)* to be well regarded; **es mal m.** *(mal considerado)* he's not well regarded o thought of

**mirador** *nm* (a) *(balcón)* enclosed balcony (b) *(para ver un paisaje)* viewpoint

**miramiento** *nm* consideration, circumspection; **andarse con miramientos** to stand on ceremony; **sin miramientos** just like that, without the least consideration

**miranda: de miranda** *loc adv Fam* **estar de m.** to be loafing about o around

**mirar 1** *vt* (a) *(dirigir la vista a)* to look at; *(observar)* to watch; *(fijamente)* to stare at; **m. algo de cerca/lejos** to look at sth closely/ from a distance; **m. algo por encima** to glance over sth, to have a quick look at sth; **m. a alguien bien/mal** to think highly/poorly of sb; **m. a alguien de arriba abajo** to look sb up and down; **m. a alguien por encima del hombro** to look down on sb; **de mírame y no me toques** very fragile
  (b) *(fijarse en)* to keep an eye on, to watch
  (c) *(examinar)* to check, to look through; **le miraron todas las maletas** they searched all her luggage
  (d) *(considerar)* to consider, to take a look at

**2** *vi* (a) *(dirigir la vista a)* to look; *(observar)* to watch; *(fijamente)* to stare; **¡mira!** look (at that!); **¡míralos!** look at them!; **mira, yo creo que…** look, I think (that)…; **mira que te avisé** I told you so; **mira por dónde…** guess what?, would you believe it?; **bien mirado…, mirándolo bien…** if you think about it…; **aunque bien m., podemos ir los dos** on second thoughts, we could both go; **¡mira que eres pesado/tonto!** you're being really tedious/silly!

(**b**) *(buscar)* to check, to look; **he mirado en todas partes** I've looked everywhere

(**c**) *(orientarse)* **m. a** to face

(**d**) *(cuidar)* **m. por alguien/algo** to look after sb/sth; **m. por los demás** to look out for other people

(**e**) *Fam (averiguar)* **m. a ver si** to see if *o* whether; **mira a ver si ha llegado la carta** (go and) see if the letter has arrived

**3 mirarse** *vpr (uno mismo)* to look at oneself; *(uno al otro)* to look at each other

**miríada** *nf* myriad

**mirilla** *nf* (**a**) *(en puerta)* spyhole (**b**) *(en arma)* sight

**mirlo** *nm* blackbird; *Fig* **ser un m. blanco** to be one in a million

**mirón, -ona** *Fam* **1** *adj (curioso)* nosey; *(con lascivia)* peeping

**2** *nm,f (espectador)* onlooker; *(curioso)* nosy parker; *(voyeur)* peeping Tom

**mirra** *nf* myrrh

**mirto** *nm* myrtle

**misa** *nf* mass; **cantar/decir/oír m.** to sing/say/hear mass; **ir a m.** to go or mass *o* church; *Fam Fig* to be gospel; *Fam Fig* **no saber de la m. la media** not to know half the story; **m. cantada/de campaña** sung/open-air mass; **m. de difuntos** requiem, mass for the dead; **m. del gallo** midnight mass *(on Christmas Eve)*

**misal** *nm* missal

**misantropía** *nf* misanthropy

**misántropo, -a** *nm,f* misanthrope, misanthropist

**miscelánea** *nf* miscellany

**miserable 1** *adj* (**a**) *(pobre)* poor; *(vivienda)* wretched, squalid (**b**) *(penoso, insuficiente)* miserable (**c**) *(vil)* contemptible, base (**d**) *(tacaño)* mean

**2** *nmf* (**a**) *(persona vil)* wretch, vile person (**b**) *(tacaño)* mean person, miser

**miseria** *nf* (**a**) *(pobreza)* poverty (**b**) *(desgracia)* misfortune (**c**) *(tacañería)* meanness (**d**) *(vileza)* baseness, wretchedness (**e**) *(poco dinero)* pittance; **le pagan una m.** they pay him next to nothing

**misericordia** *nf* compassion; **pedir m.** to beg for mercy; **para obras de m.** for charity

**misericordioso, -a 1** *adj* compassionate, merciful

**2** *nm,f Rel* **los misericordiosos** the merciful

**mísero, -a** *adj* (**a**) *(pobre, desdichado)* wretched, miserable; **ni un m....** not even a measly *o* miserable... (**b**) *(tacaño)* mean, stingy

**misil** *nm* missile; **m. de crucero** cruise missile

**misión** *nf* (**a**) *(delegación)* mission; *Rel* **misiones** (overseas) missions (**b**) *(cometido)* task, mission (**c**) *(expedición científica)* expedition

**misionero, -a** *adj & nm,f Rel* missionary

**misiva** *nf* missive

**Misisipí** *nm* **el M.** the Mississippi

**mismo, -a 1** *adj* (**a**) *(igual, no otro)* same; **del m. color/tipo que** the same colour/type as; **son del m. pueblo** they're from the same town/village (**b**) *(para enfatizar)* **yo m.** I myself; **en este m. sitio** in this very place; **delante de sus mismas narices** right in front of his nose; **por mí/ti m.** by myself/yourself; *Fam* **¡tú m.!** it's up to you!, suit yourself!

**2** *pron* **el m.** the same; **el m. que vi ayer** the same one I saw yesterday; **lo m.** the same (thing); **lo m. que the same as; **da** *o* **es lo m.** it doesn't matter, it doesn't make any difference; **me da lo m.** I don't care; *Fig* **estar en las mismas** to be no further forward

**3** *adv (para enfatizar)* **ahora/aquí m.** right now/here; **ayer m.** only yesterday; **por eso m.** precisely for that reason

**misoginia** *nf* misogyny

**misógino, -a 1** *adj* misogynistic

**2** *nm,f* misogynist

**miss** *(pl* **misses)** *nf* beauty queen

**Mississippi** [misi'sipi] *nm* **el M.** the Mississippi

**Missouri** [mi'suri] *nm* **el (río) M.** the (river) Missouri

**míster** *(pl* **místers)** *nm Dep* manager

**misterio** *nm* mystery

**misterioso, -a** *adj* mysterious

**mística** *nf (práctica)* mysticism

**misticismo** *nm* mysticism

**místico, -a 1** *adj* mystical

**2** *nm,f (persona)* mystic

**mistificación** *nf* mystification

**mistificar** [61] *vt* to mystify

**mitad** *nf* (**a**) *(parte)* half; **a m. de precio** at half price; **a m. de camino** halfway there; **a m. de película** halfway through the film; **la m. de** half (of); **la m. del tiempo no está** half the time she's not in; **m. y m.** half and half (**b**) *(centro)* middle; **en m. de** in the middle of; **(cortar algo) por la m.** (to cut sth) in half

**mítico, -a** *adj* mythical

**mitificar** [61] *vt* to mythologize

**mitigador, -ora** *adj* calming

**mitigar** [40] *vt (aplacar) (miseria, daño, efecto)* to alleviate, to reduce; *(ánimos)* to calm; *(sed)* to slake; *(hambre)* to take the edge off; *(choque, golpe)* to soften; *(dudas, sospechas)* to allay

**mitin** *(pl* **mítines)** *nm* rally, meeting

**mito** *nm* (a) *(ficción, leyenda)* myth (b) *(personaje)* mythical figure

**mitología** *nf* mythology

**mitológico, -a** *adj* mythological

**mitomanía** *nf* mythomania

**mitómano, -a** *adj & nm,f* mythomaniac

**mitón** *nm* (fingerless) mitten

**mitote** *nm Méx Fam (alboroto)* racket

**mitra** *nf* (a) *(tocado)* mitre (b) *(cargo)* office of archbishop/bishop

**mixtificar** [61] *vt* to mystify

**mixto, -a** *adj* mixed; **comisión mixta** joint committee

**mixtura** *nf* mixture

**mízcalo** *nm* = edible variety of milk cap mushroom

**ml** *(abrev de* **mililitro***)* ml

**mm** *(abrev de* **milímetro***)* mm

**MN** *(abrev de* **moneda nacional***)* national currency

**mnemónico, -a** *adj* mnemonic

**mnemotecnia** *nf* mnemonics *(singular)*

**moaré** *nm* moiré

**mobiliario** *nm* furniture; **m. urbano** street furniture

**moca** *nf* mocha

**mocasín** *nm* moccasin

**mocedad** *nf* youth

**mocetón, -ona** *nm,f Fam* strapping lad, *f* strapping lass

**mochales** *adj inv Fam* **estar m.** to have a screw loose, to be a bit touched

**moche: a troche y moche** *loc adv* haphazardly

**mochila** *nf* backpack

**mocho, -a 1** *adj (extremo, punta)* blunt; *(árbol)* lopped
**2** *nm (fregona)* mop

**mochuelo** *nm* little owl; *Fam* **cargar con el m.** to be landed with it

**moción** *nf* motion; *Pol* **m. de censura/confianza** motion of censure/confidence

**moco** *nm* (piece of) snot, bogey; *Med* mucus; **limpiarse los mocos** to wipe one's nose; **tener mocos** to have a runny nose; *Fam* **llorar a m. tendido** to cry one's eyes out; *Fam* **no ser m. de pavo** to be something not to be sneezed at, to be no mean feat

**mocoso, -a 1** *adj* runny-nosed
**2** *nm,f Fam* brat

**moda** *nf (uso, manera)* fashion; *(furor pasajero)* craze; **estar de m.** to be fashionable *o* in fashion; **estar pasado de m.** to be unfashionable *o* out of fashion; **ir a la última m.** to wear the latest fashion

**modal 1** *adj* modal
**2** *nmpl* **modales** manners; **tener buenos/malos modales** to have good/bad manners

**modalidad** *nf* form, type; *Dep* discipline; *Com* **m. de pago** method of payment

**modelado** *nm* modelling

**modelar** *vt* to model; *Fig* to form, to shape

**modelismo** *nm* modelling

**modelo 1** *adj* model
**2** *nmf (persona)* model
**3** *nm* (a) *(arquetipo, diseño, representación)* model; **m. económico/matemático** economic/mathematical model (b) *(prenda de vestir)* number

**módem** ['moðem] *(pl* **modems***) nm Informát* modem

**moderación** *nf* moderation

**moderado, -a** *adj & nm,f* moderate

**moderador, -ora 1** *adj* moderating
**2** *nm,f* chair, chairperson

**moderar 1** *vt* (a) *(templar, atenuar)* to moderate; *(velocidad)* to reduce (b) *(debate)* to chair
**2 moderarse** *vpr* to restrain oneself; **moderarse en algo** to moderate sth

**modernidad** *nf* modernity

**modernismo** *nm* (a) *Lit* modernism (b) *Arte* Art Nouveau

**modernista** *adj & nmf* (a) *Lit* modernist (b) *Arte* Art Nouveau

**modernización** *nf* modernization

**modernizar** [16] **1** *vt* to modernize
**2 modernizarse** *vpr* to modernize

**moderno, -a 1** *adj* modern
**2** *nm,f Fam* trendy (person)

**modestia** *nf* modesty; **falsa m.** false modesty

**modesto, -a 1** *adj* modest
**2** *nm,f* modest person

**módico, -a** *adj* modest

**modificación** *nf* alteration

**modificar** [61] *vt* (a) *(variar)* to alter (b) *Gram* to modify

**modismo** *nm* idiom

**modista** *nmf* (a) *(diseñador)* fashion designer (b) *(que cose)* tailor, *f* dressmaker

**modisto** *nm* (a) *(diseñador)* fashion designer (b) *(sastre)* tailor

**modo** *nm* (a) *(manera, forma)* way; **a m. de** as, by way of; **al m. de** in the style of; **de ese m.** in that way; **de ningún m.** in no way; **de todos modos** in any case, anyway; **de un m. u otro** one way or another; **en cierto m.** in some ways; **m. de empleo** instructions for use; **de m. que** *(de manera que)* in such a way that; *(así que)* so (b) **modos** *(modales)* manners; **buenos/malos modos** good/bad manners (**c**) *Gram* mood; **m. adverbial** adverbial phrase

**modorra** *nf Fam* drowsiness; **tener m.** to be o feel sleepy

**modoso, -a** *adj (recatado)* modest; *(formal)* well-behaved

**modulación** *nf* modulation; *Elec* **m. de frecuencia** frequency modulation

**modulador, -ora 1** *adj* modulating
**2** *nm* modulator

**modular 1** *adj* modular
**2** *vt* to modulate

**módulo** *nm* (**a**) *(pieza, unidad)* module (**b**) *(de muebles)* unit

**modus operandi** *nm inv* modus operandi

**modus vivendi** *nm inv* way of life

**mofa** *nf* mockery; **hacer m. de** to mock

**mofarse** *vpr* to scoff; **m. de** to mock

**mofeta** *nf* skunk

**moflete** *nm* chubby cheek

**mofletudo, -a** *adj* chubby-cheeked

**Mogadiscio** [moƔa'ðisƟio] *n* Mogadishu

**mogol, -a 1** *adj* Mongolian
**2** *nm,f (persona)* Mongol, Mongolian
**3** *nm (lengua)* Mongol, Mongolian

**mogollón 1** *nm Fam* (**a**) **m. de** *(muchos)* tons of, loads of (**b**) *(lío)* row, commotion; **entraron/salieron a m.** everyone rushed in/out at once
**2** *adv Fam* loads, heaps

**mogrebí** *adj & nmf* Maghrebi

**mohair** [mo'er] *nm* mohair

**mohín** *nm* grimace, face

**moho** *nm* (**a**) *(hongo)* mould (**b**) *(herrumbre)* rust

**mohoso, -a** *adj* (**a**) *(con hongo)* mouldy (**b**) *(oxidado)* rusty

**moisés** *nm inv* Moses basket

**mojado, -a** *adj (empapado)* wet; *(húmedo)* damp; *Fig* **llover sobre m.** to be just too much

**mojama** *nf* dried salted tuna

**mojar 1** *vt* to wet; *(humedecer)* to dampen; *(comida)* to dunk
**2** **mojarse** *vpr* (**a**) *(con agua)* to get wet (**b**) *Fam (comprometerse)* to come off the fence, to commit oneself

**mojigatería** *nf* (**a**) *(beatería)* prudery (**b**) *(falsa humildad)* sanctimoniousness

**mojigato, -a 1** *adj* (**a**) *(beato)* prudish (**b**) *(falsamente humilde)* sanctimonious
**2** *nm,f* (**a**) *(beato)* prude (**b**) *(falsamente humilde)* sanctimonious person

**mojón** *nm (piedra)* milestone; *(poste)* milepost

**moka** *nf* mocha

**molar¹ 1** *adj* **diente m.** molar
**2** *nm* molar

**molar²** *muy Fam* **1** *vt* ¡cómo me **mola esa moto/ese chico!** I think that motorbike/that guy is bloody gorgeous!
**2** *vi* to be bloody gorgeous

**molcajete** *nm Méx* mortar

**Moldavia** *n* Moldavia

**moldavo, -a** *adj & nm,f* Moldavian

**molde** *nm* mould

**moldeado** *nm* (**a**) *(del pelo)* soft perm, body-wave (**b**) *(de figura, cerámica)* moulding

**moldear** *vt* (**a**) *(dar forma)* to mould (**b**) *(sacar un molde)* to cast (**c**) *(cabello)* to give a soft perm to

**moldura** *nf* moulding

**mole 1** *nf* hulk
**2** *nm Méx* = sauce of chile and chocolate

**molécula** *nf* molecule

**molecular** *adj* molecular

**moler** [43] *vt* (**a**) *(pulverizar)* to grind; *(aceitunas)* to press; *(trigo)* to mill (**b**) *Fam Fig (cansar)* to wear out

**molestar 1** *vt* (**a**) *(perturbar)* to annoy; **¿le molesta que fume?** do you mind if I smoke?; **perdone que le moleste...** I'm sorry to bother you... (**b**) *(doler)* to hurt (**c**) *(ofender)* to offend
**2** **molestarse** *vpr* (**a**) *(incomodarse)* to bother; **no te molestes, yo lo haré** don't bother, I'll do it; **molestarse en hacer algo** to bother to do sth; **molestarse por alguien/algo** to put oneself out for sb/sth (**b**) *(ofenderse)* **molestarse (por algo)** to take offence (at sth)

**molestia** *nf* (**a**) *(incomodidad)* nuisance; **si no es demasiada m.** if it's not too much trouble; **tomarse la m. de hacer algo** to take the trouble to do sth (**b**) *(malestar)* discomfort

**molesto, -a** *adj* (**a**) *(incordiante)* annoying; *(visita)* inconvenient (**b**) *(irritado)* **m. (con)** annoyed (with) (**c**) *(con malestar)* in discomfort

**molido, -a** *adj* (**a**) *(pulverizado)* ground; *(trigo)* milled (**b**) *Fam Fig (cansado)* worn out; **estar m. de** to be worn out from

**molienda** *nf* *(acción de moler)* grinding; *(de trigo)* milling

**molinero, -a 1** *adj* milling
**2** *nm,f* miller

**molinete** *nm* (**a**) *(ventilador)* extractor fan (**b**) *(juguete)* toy windmill

**molinillo** *nm* grinder

**molino** *nm* mill; **m. de aceite** olive oil mill; **m. de viento** windmill

**molla** *nf* (**a**) *(parte blanda)* flesh (**b**) *(gordura)* flab

**molleja** *nf* gizzard

**mollera** *nf Fam (juicio)* brains; **ser duro de m.** *(estúpido)* to be thick in the head; *(testarudo)* to be pig-headed

**molusco** *nm* mollusc

**momentáneo, -a** *adj (de un momento)* momentary; *(pasajero)* temporary

**momento** *nm (instante)* moment; *(periodo)* time; **llegó un m. en que...** there came a time when...; **a cada m.** all the time; **al m.** straightaway; **de m., por el m.** for the time being o moment; **del m.** *(actual)* of the day; **de un m. a otro** any minute now; **desde el m. (en) que...** *(tiempo)* from the moment that...; *(causa)* seeing as...; **por momentos** by the minute

**momia** *nf* mummy

**momificar** [61] **1** *vt* to mummify
**2 momificarse** *vpr* to mummify

**momio, -a** *adj Chile Fam (carcamal)* square, untrendy

**mona** *nf Fam (borrachera)* **coger una m.** to get legless; **dormir la m.** to sleep it off

**monacal** *adj* monastic

**Mónaco** *n* Monaco

**monada** *nf Fam* (a) *(persona)* little beauty (b) *(cosa)* lovely thing (c) *(gracia)* antic

**monaguillo** *nm* altar boy

**monarca** *nm* monarch

**monarquía** *nf* monarchy; **m. absoluta/constitucional/parlamentaria** absolute/constitutional/parliamentary monarchy

**monárquico, -a 1** *adj* monarchic
**2** *nm,f* monarchist

**monasterio** *nm (de monjes)* monastery; *(de monjas)* convent

**monástico, -a** *adj* monastic

**Moncloa** *nf* **la M.** = residence of the Spanish premier which by extension refers to the Spanish government

**monda** *nf (piel)* peel; *Fam* **ser la m.** *(extraordinario)* to be amazing; *(gracioso)* to be a scream

**mondadientes** *nm inv* toothpick

**mondadura** *nf (piel)* peel

**mondar 1** *vt* to peel
**2 mondarse** *vpr Fam* **mondarse (de risa)** to laugh one's head off

**mondo, -a** *adj (pelado, limpio)* bare; *(huesos)* picked clean; *Fam* **dejaron el pollo m. y lirondo** they picked the chicken clean; **la verdad monda y lironda** the plain unvarnished truth

**mondongo** *nm Am* tripe

**moneda** *nf* (a) *(pieza)* coin; *Fig* **pagar a alguien con** o **en la misma m.** to pay sb back in kind; *Fig* **ser m. corriente** to be commonplace (b) *Fin (divisa)* currency; **m. corriente** legal tender; **m. débil/fuerte** weak/strong currency; **m. divisionaria** o **fraccionaria** minor unit of currency; **m. única** single currency

**monedero** *nm* purse; **m. electrónico** = smart card which is electronically credited with funds from the holder's account and which can be used for small purchases

**monegasco, -a** *adj & nm,f* Monacan, Monegasque

**monería** *nf Fam (gracia)* antic; *(bobada)* foolish act

**monetario, -a** *adj* monetary

**monetarismo** *nm Econ* monetarism

**monetarista** *adj Econ* monetarist

**mongol, -ola 1** *adj* Mongolian
**2** *nm,f (persona)* Mongol, Mongolian
**3** *nm (lengua)* Mongol, Mongolian

**Mongolia** *n* Mongolia

**mongólico, -a 1** *adj* Down's syndrome; **niño m.** child with Down's syndrome
**2** *nm,f* person with Down's syndrome

**mongolismo** *nm* Down's syndrome

**monigote** *nm* (a) *(muñeco)* rag o paper doll (b) *(dibujo)* doodle (c) *Fig (persona)* puppet

**monitor, -ora 1** *nm,f (persona)* instructor
**2** *nm Informát & Mec* monitor; **m. en color** colour monitor

**monitorio, -a** *adj Formal* admonitory

**monja** *nf* nun

**monje** *nm* monk

**monjil** *adj (de monje)* monk's; *(de monja)* nun's

**mono, -a 1** *adj Fam* lovely
**2** *nm,f (animal)* monkey; *Prov* **aunque la mona se vista de seda, mona se queda** you can't make a silk purse out of a sow's ear; *Fam* **ser el último m.** to be bottom of the heap
**3** *nm* (a) *(prenda) (con mangas)* overalls; *(con peto)* dungarees (b) *muy Fam (síndrome de abstinencia)* cold turkey

**monocarril** *adj & nm* monorail

**monocolor** *adj* monochrome

**monocorde** *adj* (a) *Fig (monótono)* monotonous (b) *Mús* single-stringed

**monóculo** *nm* monocle

**monoesquí** *(pl monoesquís) nm* monoski

**monofásico, -a** *adj Elec* single-phase

**monogamia** *nf* monogamy

**monógamo, -a 1** *adj* monogamous
**2** *nm,f* monogamous person

**monografía** *nf* monograph

**monográfico, -a** *adj* monographic

**monokini** *nm* monokini

**monolingüe** *adj* monolingual

**monolítico, -a** *adj* monolithic

**monolito** *nm* monolith

**monologar** [40] *vi* to give a monologue

**monólogo** *nm* monologue; *Teatro* soliloquy

**monomando 1** *adj* **grifo m.** mixer tap *(with single control)*
  **2** *nm* mixer tap *(with single control)*

**monomanía** *nf* obsession

**monomaniaco, -a, monomaníaco, -a** *adj & nm,f* obsessive

**monopatín** *nm* skateboard

**monoplano, -a 1** *adj* monoplane
  **2** *nm* monoplane

**monoplaza 1** *adj* single-seater; **avión m.** single-seater aeroplane
  **2** *nm* single-seater

**monopolio** *nm* monopoly

**monopolización** *nf* monopolization

**monopolizador, -ora 1** *adj* monopolistic
  **2** *nm,f* monopolist

**monopolizar** [16] *vt también Fig* to monopolize

**monorraíl** *adj & nm* monorail

**monosilábico, -a** *adj* monosyllabic

**monosílabo, -a 1** *adj* monosyllabic
  **2** *nm* monosyllable; **responder con monosílabos** to reply in monosyllables

**monoteísmo** *nm* monotheism

**monoteísta 1** *adj* monotheistic
  **2** *nmf* monotheist

**monotipo** *nm Imprenta* Monotype

**monotonía** *nf* (a) *(uniformidad)* monotony (b) *(entonación)* monotone

**monótono, -a** *adj* monotonous

**monovolumen** *nm Aut* people mover

**monóxido** *nm Quím* monoxide; **m. de carbono** carbon monoxide

**Monrovia** *n* Monrovia

**monseñor** *nm* Monsignor

**monserga** *nf Fam* drivel

**monstruo** *nm* (a) *(ser fantástico)* monster (b) *(prodigio)* giant, marvel

**monstruosidad** *nf* (a) *(anomalía)* freak (b) *(enormidad)* hugeness (c) *(crueldad)* monstrosity, atrocity (d) *(fealdad)* hideousness

**monstruoso, -a** *adj* (a) *(enorme)* huge, enormous (b) *(deforme)* terribly deformed (c) *(cruel)* monstrous (d) *(feo)* hideous

**monta** *nf* (a) *(suma)* total (b) *(importancia)* importance; **de poca/mucha m.** of little/great importance (c) *(en caballo)* ride, riding

**montacargas** *nm inv Br* goods lift, *US* freight elevator

**montado** *nm Culin* open sandwich

**montador, -ora** *nm,f* (a) *(obrero)* fitter (b) *Cine* editor

**montaje** *nm* (a) *(de máquina)* assembly (b) *Teatro* staging (c) *Fot* montage (d) *Cine* editing (e) *(farsa)* put-up job

**montante** *nm* (a) *Arquit (de armazón)* upright; *(de ventana)* mullion; *(de puerta)* jamb (b) *(ventanuco)* fanlight (c) *(importe)* total; *Com* **montantes compensatorios** compensating duties

**montaña** *nf* mountain; *Fam* **una m. de** *(un montón de)* heaps of; *Fig* **hacer una m. de algo** to make a big thing of sth; *Fig* **hacer una m. de un grano de arena** to make a mountain out of a molehill; **m. rusa** roller coaster

**Montañas Rocosas** *nfpl* **las M.** the Rocky Mountains

**montañero, -a 1** *adj* mountaineering
  **2** *nm,f* mountaineer

**montañés, -esa 1** *adj* (a) *(cántabro)* of/from Cantabria (b) *(de la montaña)* **pueblo m.** mountain village
  **2** *nm,f* (a) *(cántabro)* person from Cantabria (b) *(de la montaña)* **los montañeses** the people living in the mountains

**montañismo** *nm* mountaineering

**montañoso, -a** *adj* mountainous

**montar 1** *vt* (a) *(ensamblar)* *(máquina, estantería)* to assemble; *(tienda de campaña, tenderete)* to put up (b) *(encajar)* **m. algo en algo** to fit sth into sth (c) *(organizar)* *(negocio, piso)* to set up (d) *(cabalgar)* to ride (e) *(poner encima)* **m. a alguien en** to lift sb onto (f) *Culin (nata)* to whip; *(claras, yemas)* to beat (g) *Teatro* to stage (h) *Cine* to cut, to edit
  **2** *vi* (a) *(subir)* to get on; *(en vehículo)* to get in; **m. en** *(subir)* to get onto; *(coche)* to get into; *(animal)* to mount (b) *(ir montado)* to ride; **m. en bicicleta/a caballo** to ride a bicycle/a horse (c) *(sumar)* **m. a** to come to, to total; **tanto monta** it's all the same
  **3 montarse** *vpr* (a) *(subirse)* to get on; *(en vehículo)* to get in; **montarse en** *(subirse)* to get onto; *(vehículo)* to get into; *(caballo)* to mount (b) *Fam* **montárselo** to work it, to organize things

**Mont Blanc** *nm* **el M.** Mont Blanc

**monte** *nm* *(elevación)* mountain; *(terreno)* woodland; **echarse** *o* **tirarse al m.** to take to the hills; *Fig* to go to extremes; *Prov* **no todo el m. es orégano** life's not a bowl of cherries; **m. bajo** scrub; **m. de piedad** state pawnsbroker's; **m. de Venus** mons veneris

**montenegrino, -a** *adj & nm,f* Montenegran

**montepío** *nm* mutual aid society

**montera** *nf* bullfighter's hat

**montés** (*pl* **monteses**) *adj* wild

**Montevideo** *n* Montevideo

**montículo** *nm* hillock

**montilla** *nm* Montilla, = fortified sherry-type wine from Montilla near Córdoba

**monto** *nm* total

**montón** *nm* (a) (*pila*) heap, pile; **a** *o* **en m.** everything together *o* at once; *Fam* **del m.** ordinary, run-of-the-mill (b) *Fam* **un m. de** loads of; **a montones** by the bucketload

**Montreal** *n* Montreal

**montura** *nf* (a) (*cabalgadura*) mount (b) (*arreos*) harness; (*silla*) saddle (c) (*soporte*) (*de gafas*) frame; (*de joyas*) mounting

**monumental** *adj* (a) (*ciudad, lugar*) famous for its monuments (b) *Fig* (*fracaso, éxito*) monumental

**monumento** *nm* (*obra*) monument; *Fig* (*mujer atractiva*) stunner

**monzón** *nm* monsoon

**monzónico, -a** *adj* monsoon; **lluvias monzónicas** monsoon rains

**moña 1** *nf* (a) *Fam* (*borrachera*) **coger una m.** to get smashed (b) (*adorno*) ribbon

**2** *nm muy Fam* poof

**moño** *nm* bun (*of hair*); **agarrarse del m.** (*pegarse*) to pull each other's hair out; **estar hasta el m. (de)** to be sick to death (of)

**MOPU** ['mopu] *nm* (*abrev de* **Ministerio de Obras Públicas y Urbanismo**) *Antes* = Spanish ministry of public works and town planning

**moquear** *vi* to have a runny nose

**moqueta** *nf* fitted carpet

**moquillo** *nm* (*enfermedad de animal*) distemper

**mor**: **por mor de** *loc adv* on account of, for the sake of; **por m. de la verdad, debo decírselo** out of respect for the truth I have to tell him

**mora** *nf* (a) (*de la zarzamora*) blackberry (b) (*del moral*) mulberry

**morada** *nf* dwelling

**morado, -a 1** *adj* (a) (*color*) purple; *Fam Fig* **pasarlas moradas** to have a bad time of it; *Fam Fig* **ponerse m.** to stuff oneself (b) *muy Fam* **estar m.** (*de droga*) to be stoned; (*de alcohol*) *Br* to be pissed

**2** *nm* (a) (*color*) purple (b) (*moratón*) bruise (c) *muy Fam* **cogerse un m.** (*de droga*) to get stoned; (*de alcohol*) *Br* to get pissed

**morador, -ora** *nm,f* inhabitant

**moradura** *nf* bruise

**moral 1** *adj* moral

**2** *nf* (a) (*ética*) morality (b) (*ánimo*) morale; **estar bajo de m.** to be in poor spirits; **levantarle** *o* **subirle la m. a alguien** to lift sb's spirits, to cheer sb up

**3** *nm* (*árbol*) mulberry tree

**moraleja** *nf* moral

**moralidad** *nf* morality

**moralina** *nf* moralizing

**moralismo** *nm* moralism

**moralista** *nmf* moralist

**moralizar** [16] *vi* to moralize

**morapio** *nm Fam* cheap red wine, plonk

**morar** *vi* to dwell (**en** in)

**moratón** *nm* bruise

**mórbido, -a** *adj* (a) *también Med* morbid (b) (*delicado*) delicate

**morbilidad** *nf Med* morbidity

**morbo** *nm*, **morbosidad** *nf* morbid pleasure; *Fam* **tener m.** to hold a kinky *o* gruesome fascination; *Fam* **darle m. a alguien** to give sb a kinky thrill

**morboso, -a 1** *adj* (*persona, interés*) morbid, ghoulish; (*escena, descripción*) gruesome

**2** *nm,f* ghoul

**morcilla** *nf Culin Br* black pudding, *US* blood sausage; *Fam* **¡que te/os den m.!** you can stuff it, then!

**morcillo** *nm* foreknuckle

**morcón** *nm* cured pork sausage

**mordacidad** *nf* sharpness, mordacity

**mordaz** *adj* caustic, biting

**mordaza** *nf* gag

**mordedura** *nf* bite

**morder** [43] **1** *vt* (a) (*con los dientes*) to bite (b) (*gastar*) to eat into

**2** *vi* to bite; **está que muerde** he's hopping mad

**3 morderse** *vpr* **morderse la lengua/las uñas** to bite one's tongue/nails

**mordida** *nf Am Fam* (*soborno*) bribe

**mordisco** *nm* (a) (*con los dientes*) bite; **a mordiscos** by biting (b) *Fig* (*beneficio*) rake-off

**mordisquear** *vt* to nibble (at)

**morena** *nf* (*pez*) moray eel

**moreno, -a 1** *adj* (a) (*pelo, piel*) dark; (*por el sol*) tanned; **ponerse m.** to get a tan (b) (*pan, azúcar*) brown

**2** *nmf* (a) (*por el pelo*) dark-haired person; (*por la piel*) dark-skinned person (b) *Fam* (*negro*) coloured person, person of colour

**morera** *nf* white mulberry tree

**morería** *nf* Moorish quarter

**moretón** *nm* bruise

**morfema** *nm* morpheme

**morfina** *nf* morphine

**morfinómano, -a 1** *adj* addicted to morphine

**2** *nm,f* morphine addict

**morfología** *nf* morphology

**morganático, -a** *adj* morganatic

**morgue** *nf* morgue

**moribundo, -a 1** *adj* dying

**2** *nm,f* dying person

**morir** [29] **1** *vi* (a) *también Fig (fallecer)* to die (b) *(río, calle)* to come out (c) *(fuego)* to die down; *(luz)* to go out; *(día)* to come to a close

**2 morirse** *vpr* (a) *(fallecer)* to die (**de** of) (b) *Fig (sentir con fuerza)* **morirse de envidia/ira** to be burning with envy/rage; **morirse de risa** to die laughing; **me muero de ganas de ir a bailar** I'm dying to go dancing; **me muero de hambre/frío** I'm starving/freezing; **morirse por algo** to be dying for sth; **morirse por alguien** to be crazy about sb

**morisco, -a 1** *adj* = referring to Moors in Spain baptized after the Reconquista

**2** *nm,f* baptized Moor

**mormón, -ona** *adj & nm,f* Mormon

**moro, -a 1** *adj* (a) *Hist* Moorish (b) *muy Fam Fig (machista)* sexist

**2** *nm,f* (a) *Hist* Moor; **moros y cristianos** = traditional Spanish festival involving mock battle between Moors and Christians; *Fig* **no hay moros en la costa** the coast is clear (b) *Fam Pey (árabe)* Arab, = pejorative term referring to a North African or Arab person

**3** *nm muy Fam Fig (machista)* sexist (man).

**morocho, -a** *adj Andes, CSur (moreno)* dark-haired

**morosidad** *nf* (a) *Com* defaulting, failure to pay on time (b) *(lentitud)* slowness

**moroso, -a** *Com* **1** *adj* defaulting

**2** *nm,f* defaulter, bad debtor

**morral** *nm Mil* haversack; *(de cazador)* game-bag

**morralla** *nf* (a) *Pey (personas)* scum; *(cosas)* junk (b) *(pescado)* small fry (c) *Méx (suelto)* loose change

**morrear** *muy Fam* **1** *vi* to smooch

**2 morrearse** *vpr* to smooch

**morreo** *nm muy Fam* smooch

**morriña** *nf (por el país de uno)* homesickness; *(por el pasado)* nostalgia

**morro** *nm* (a) *(hocico)* snout (b) *(de coche, avión)* nose (c) *Fam (labios)* (thick) lips; **estar de morros** to be in a bad mood; **romperle los morros a alguien** to smash sb's face in (d) *Fam (caradura)* **¡qué m. tiene!** he's got a cheek!

**morrocotudo, -a** *adj Fam* tremendous

**morrón 1** *adj* **pimiento m.** red pepper

**2** *nm Fam* **darse un m.** to give oneself a real thump

**morsa** *nf* walrus

**morse** *nm* Morse (code)

**mortadela** *nf* mortadella

**mortaja** *nf* shroud

**mortal 1** *adj* mortal; *(caída, enfermedad)* fatal; *(aburrimiento, susto, enemigo)* deadly

**2** *nmf* mortal

**mortalidad** *nf* mortality

**mortandad** *nf* mortality

**mortecino, -a** *adj (luz, brillo)* faint; *(color, mirada)* dull

**mortero** *nm* mortar

**mortífero, -a** *adj* deadly

**mortificación** *nf* mortification

**mortificante** *adj* mortifying

**mortificar** [61] **1** *vt* to mortify

**2 mortificarse** *vpr (torturarse)* to torment oneself

**mortuorio, -a** *adj* death; **cámara mortuoria** funerary chamber

**moruno, -a** *adj* Moorish; *Culin* **pincho m.** = kebab of marinated pork

**mosaico** *nm* mosaic

**mosca** *nf* fly; **aflojar** *o* **soltar la m.** to cough up, to fork out; **cazar moscas** to twiddle one's thumbs; *Fam* **estar con** *o* **tener la m. detrás de la oreja** to be suspicious *o* distrustful; *Fam* **estar m.** *(con sospechas)* to smell a rat; *(enfadado)* to be in a mood; **no se oía ni una m.** you could have heard a pin drop; *Fam* **por si las moscas** just in case; *Fam Fig* **¿qué m. te ha picado?** what's up with you?; *Fam Fig* **m. muerta** slyboots, hypocrite; **m. tse-tsé** tsetse fly

**moscada** *adj* **nuez m.** nutmeg

**moscardón** *nm* (a) *Zool* blowfly (b) *Fam Fig (persona)* pest, creep

**moscatel** *nm* Muscatel, = dessert wine made from muscat grapes; **uvas de m.** muscat grapes

**moscón** *nm* (a) *Zool* meatfly, bluebottle (b) *Fam Fig (persona)* pest, creep

**moscovita** *adj & nmf* Muscovite

**Moscú** *n* Moscow

**mosqueado, -a** *adj Fam* (a) *(enfadado)* cross, in a mood; **estar m. con alguien** to be cross with sb (b) *(con sospechas)* suspicious

**mosquear** *Fam* **1** *vt* (a) *(enfadar)* to annoy, to irritate (b) *(hacer sospechar)* to make suspicious

**2 mosquearse** *vpr* (a) *(enfadarse)* to get cross (b) *(sospechar)* to smell a rat

**mosqueo** *nm Fam* (a) *(enfado)* annoyance, anger (b) *(sospechas)* **tener/cogerse un m.** to be/get suspicious

**mosquete** *nm* musket

**mosquetero** *nm* musketeer

**mosquetón** *nm* short carbine

**mosquitera** *nf,* **mosquitero** *nm* mosquito net

**mosquito** *nm* mosquito

**mosso d'esquadra** *nm* = member of the Catalan police force

**mostacho** *nm* moustache

**mostaza** *nf* mustard

**mosto** *nm (residuo)* must; *(zumo de uva)* grape juice

**mostrador** *nm (en tienda)* counter; *(en bar)* bar; *(en aeropuerto)* desk; **m. de información/ facturación** information/check-in desk

**mostrar** [65] **1** *vt* to show
 **2 mostrarse** *vpr* to appear, to show oneself; **se mostró muy interesado** he expressed great interest

**mostrenco, -a 1** *adj (sin dueño)* without an owner, unclaimed
 **2** *nm,f Fam (torpe)* thick *o* stupid person

**mota** *nf (de polvo)* speck; *(en una tela)* dot

**mote** *nm* nickname

**moteado, -a** *adj* speckled

**motejar** *vt (poner mote a)* to nickname; **m. a alguien de algo** to brand sb sth

**motel** *nm* motel

**motero, -a** *nm,f muy Fam* biker

**motín** *nm (del pueblo)* uprising, riot; *(de las tropas, en barco)* mutiny; *(en cárcel)* riot

**motivación** *nf* motive, motivation

**motivar** *vt* **(a)** *(causar)* to cause; *(impulsar)* to motivate **(b)** *(razonar)* to explain, to justify

**motivo** *nm* **(a)** *(causa)* reason, cause; *(de crimen)* motive; **con m. de** *(por causa de)* because of; *(para celebrar)* on the occasion of; *(con el fin de)* in order to; **dar m. a** to give reason to; **tener motivos para** to have reason to; **sin m.** for no reason **(b)** *Arte, Lit & Mús* motif

**moto** *nf Br* motorbike, motorcycle

**motocicleta** *nf* motorbike, motorcycle

**motociclismo** *nm* motorcycling

**motociclista** *nmf* motorcyclist

**motociclo** *nm* motorcycle

**motocross** *nm* motocross

**motonáutica** *nf* speedboat racing

**motonáutico, -a** *adj* speedboat; **competición motonáutica** speedboat race

**motor, -ora** *o* **-triz 1** *adj* motor
 **2** *nm* **(a)** *(aparato)* motor, engine; **m. de arranque** starter, starting motor; **m. de combustión interna** internal combustion engine; **m. diesel/de gasolina** diesel/fuel engine; **m. de dos/cuatro tiempos** two/four stroke engine; **m. eléctrico** electric motor; **m. de explosión** spark-ignition engine; **m. fuera borda** outboard motor; **m. de inyección/reacción** fuel-injection/jet engine

**(b)** *(fuerza)* dynamic force **(c)** *Fig (causa)* instigator, cause

**motora** *nf* motorboat

**motorismo** *nm* motorcycling

**motorista** *nmf* motorcyclist

**motorizado, -a** *adj* motorized; *Fam* **estar m.** *(tener coche)* to have wheels

**motorizar** [16] **1** *vt* to motorize
 **2 motorizarse** *vpr Fam* to get oneself some wheels

**motosierra** *nf* power saw

**motricidad** *nf* motivity

**motriz** *adj f ver* **motor**

**motu propio, motu proprio** *adv* **(de) m.** of one's own accord

**mousse** [mus] *nm inv Culin* mousse

**movedizo, -a** *adj* **(a)** *(movible)* movable, easily moved **(b)** *(inestable)* unsteady, unstable; **arenas movedizas** quicksand

**mover** [43] **1** *vt* **(a)** *(en general)* to move; *(mecánicamente)* to drive; *Informát* **m. un fichero** to move a file **(b)** *(cabeza) (afirmativamente)* to nod; *(negativamente)* to shake **(c)** *Fig (empujar)* **m. a alguien a hacer algo** to prompt sb to do sth; **m. a alguien a compasión** to excite sb's sympathy *o* pity **(d)** *(hacer trámites con)* to do something about
 **2 moverse** *vpr* **(a)** *(en general)* to move; *(en la cama)* to toss and turn **(b)** *(darse prisa)* to get a move on **(c)** *Fam (hacer gestiones)* to get things going *o* moving; **si te mueves puedes encontrar trabajo** if you make an effort you can get a job **(d)** *(relacionarse)* **moverse en/entre** to move in/among

**movible** *adj* movable

**movida** *nf Fam* **(a)** *(lío, problema)* problem; **mudarse es una m.** moving house is a real headache; **tener una m. con alguien** to have a spot of bother with sb **(b)** *(ambiente, actividad)* scene; **no me va esa m.** it's not my scene; **la m. madrileña** = the Madrid cultural scene of the late 1970s and early 80s

**movido, -a** *adj* **(a)** *(debate, torneo)* lively; *(jornada, viaje)* hectic **(b)** *Fot* blurred, fuzzy

**móvil 1** *adj* mobile, movable; **teléfono m.** mobile phone
 **2** *nm* **(a)** *(motivo)* motive **(b)** *(teléfono)* mobile **(c)** *(juguete)* mobile

**movilidad** *nf* mobility

**movilización** *nf* mobilization

**movilizar** [16] *vt* to mobilize

**movimiento** *nm* (a) *(desplazamiento, corriente)* movement; **m. obrero** working-class movement (b) *Fís & Mec* motion; **en m.** moving, in motion; **ponerse en m.** to start moving; **m. continuo/de rotación** perpetual/rotational motion; **m. sísmico** earth tremor (c) *(actividad)* activity; *(de vehículos)* traffic (d) *Com (de personal, mercancías)* turnover; *(de cuenta bancaria)* transaction; **m. de capital** cash flow (e) *Mús (parte de la obra)* movement; *(velocidad del compás)* tempo

**moviola** *nf* editing projector

**moza** *nf* (a) *(sirvienta)* girl, maid (b) *Am (camarera)* waitress

**mozalbete** *nm* young lad

**Mozambique** *n* Mozambique

**mozambiqueño, -a** *adj & nm,f* Mozambican

**mozárabe 1** *adj* Mozarabic, = Christian in the time of Moorish Spain

**2** *nmf (habitante)* Mozarab, = Christian of Moorish Spain

**3** *nm (lengua)* Mozarabic

**mozo, -a 1** *adj (joven)* young; *(soltero)* single, unmarried; **ser buen m.** to be a handsome young man

**2** *nm,f* (a) *(niño)* young boy, young lad; *(niña)* young girl, young lass (b) *(camarero)* waiter, *f* waitress

**3** *nm* (a) *(trabajador)* assistant (worker); **m. de cordel** *o* **de cuerda** porter; **m. de estación** (station) porter (b) *(recluta)* conscript

**mozzarella** [motsa'rela, moθa'rela] *nm* mozzarella

**mu** *nm (mugido)* moo; **no decir ni m.** not to say a word

**muaré** *nm* moiré

**mucamo, -a** *nm,f Andes, CSur* servant

**muchacha** *nf (sirvienta)* maid

**muchachada** *nf Am* group of youngsters

**muchacho, -a** *nm,f* boy, *f* girl

**muchedumbre** *nf (de gente)* crowd, throng; *(de cosas)* great number, masses

**mucho, -a 1** *adj* (a) *(gran cantidad de) (singular)* a lot of; *(plural)* many, a lot of; *(en frases interrogativas y negativas)* much, a lot of; **tengo m. sueño** I'm very sleepy; **no tengo m. tiempo** I haven't got much time

(b) *(singular) (demasiado)* **hay m. niño aquí** there are too many kids here

**2** *pron (singular)* a lot; *(plural)* many, a lot; **tengo m. que contarte** I have a lot to tell you; **¿queda dinero? – no m.** is there any money left? – not much *o* not a lot; **muchos piensan igual** a lot of *o* many people think the same

**3** *adv* (a) *(gran cantidad)* a lot; **habla m.** he talks a lot; **me canso m.** I get really *o* very tired;

**me gusta m.** I like it a lot *o* very much; **no me gusta m.** I don't like it much; **(no) m. más tarde** (not) much later

(b) *(largo tiempo)* **hace m. que no vienes** I haven't seen you for a long time; **¿dura m. la obra?** is the play long?; **m. antes/después** long before/after

(c) *(a menudo)* often; **¿vienes m. por aquí?** do you come here often?

(d) *(expresiones)* **como m.** at the most; **con m.** by far, easily; **ni m. menos** far from it, by no means; **no está ni m. menos decidido** it is by no means decided; **por m. que** no matter how much, however much; **por m. que insistas** no matter how much you insist, however much you insist

**mucosa** *nf* mucous membrane

**mucosidad** *nf* mucus

**mucoso, -a** *adj* mucous

**mucus** *nm inv* mucus

**muda** *nf* (a) *(de piel, plumas)* moulting (b) *(ropa interior)* change of underwear

**mudable** *adj (persona)* changeable; *(carácter)* fickle

**mudanza** *nf* (a) *(cambio)* change; *(de carácter)* changeability, fickleness; *(de plumas, piel)* moulting (b) *(de casa)* move; **estar de m.** to be moving

**mudar 1** *vt* (a) *(cambiar)* to change; *(casa)* to move; **cuando mude la voz** when his voice breaks (b) *(piel, plumas)* to moult

**2** *vi (cambiar)* **m. de** *(opinión, color)* to change; *(domicilio)* to move

**3 mudarse** *vpr* **mudarse (de casa)** to move (house); **mudarse (de ropa)** to change

**mudéjar** *adj & nmf* Mudejar

**mudez** *nf* muteness, inability to speak

**mudo, -a 1** *adj* (a) *(sin habla)* dumb (b) *(callado)* silent, mute; **se quedó m.** he was left speechless (c) *(sin sonido)* silent; **cine m.** silent cinema

**2** *nm,f* dumb person, mute

**mueble 1** *nm* piece of furniture; **los muebles** the furniture; **m. bar** cocktail cabinet

**2** *adj Der* **bienes muebles** moveables, goods and chattels

**mueca** *nf (gesto)* face, expression; *(de dolor)* grimace; **hacer una m.** to pull a face

**muela 1** *ver* **moler**

**2** *nf* (a) *(diente)* back tooth, molar; **m. del juicio** wisdom tooth (b) *(de molino)* millstone; *(para afilar)* grindstone

**muelle 1** *adj (vida)* easy, comfortable

**2** *nm* (a) *(resorte)* spring (b) *(en puerto)* dock, quay; *(en el río)* wharf; *(de carga y descarga)* loading bay

**muera** *etc ver* **morir**

**muerda** *etc ver* **morder**

**muérdago** *nm* mistletoe

**muerdo** *nm Fam* (a) *(mordisco)* bite (b) *muy Fam (beso)* French kiss

**muermo** *nm Fam* bore, drag; **ser un m.** to be boring *o* a bore

**muerte** *nf* (a) *(fin de la vida)* death; **a m.** *(lucha)* to the death; **un susto de m.** a terrible shock; **de mala m.** third-rate, lousy; **m. natural/violenta** natural/violent death; *Dep* **m. súbita** tie break (b) *(homicidio)* murder

**muerto, -a 1** *participio ver* **morir**

**2** *adj* (a) *(sin vida)* dead; **estar m. de miedo/frío** to be scared/freezing to death; **estar m. de hambre** to be starving; *Fig* **estar m. de risa** *(objeto)* to be lying around doing nothing (b) *(color)* dull

**3** *nm,f* dead person; *(cadáver)* corpse; **hubo dos muertos** two people died; **hacerse el m.** to pretend to be dead, to play dead; *Fig* **cargar con el m.** *(trabajo, tarea)* to be left holding the baby; *(culpa)* to get the blame; **hacer el m.** to float on one's back; **más m. que vivo de hambre/cansancio** half dead with hunger/exhaustion; **medio m.** *(cansado)* dead beat; **no tener donde caerse m.** not to have a penny to one's name

**muesca** *nf* (a) *(marca, concavidad)* notch, groove (b) *(corte)* nick

**muesli** *nm* muesli

**muestra 1** *ver* **mostrar**

**2** *nf* (a) *(cantidad representativa)* sample; **para m. (basta) un botón** one example is enough; **m. gratuita** free sample (b) *(señal)* sign, show; *(prueba)* proof; *(de cariño, aprecio)* token; **dar muestras de** to show signs of (c) *(modelo)* model, pattern (d) *(exposición)* show, exhibition

**muestrario** *nm* collection of samples

**muestreo** *nm* sampling

**mueva** *etc ver* **mover**

**mugido** *nm* (a) *(de vaca)* moo, mooing; **un m. a moo; el m. de las vacas** the mooing of the cows (b) *(de toro)* bellow, bellowing; **un m. a bellow; el m. de los toros** the bellowing of the bulls

**mugir** [26] *vi (vaca)* to moo; *(toro)* to bellow

**mugre** *nf* filth, muck

**mugriento, -a** *adj* filthy

**muguete** *nm* lily of the valley

**mujer** *nf* (a) *(en general)* woman; *(cónyuge)* wife; **m. de su casa** good housewife; **m. fatal** femme fatale; **m. de la limpieza** cleaning lady; **m. de negocios** businesswoman; **m. pública** prostitute

**mujeriego, -a 1** *adj* fond of the ladies

**2** *nm* womanizer, lady's man

**mujeril** *adj* female

**mujerzuela** *nf Pey* loose woman

**muladar** *nm Fig* tip, pigsty

**mulato, -a** *adj & nm,f* mulatto

**muleta** *nf* (a) *(para andar)* crutch; *Fig* prop, support (b) *Taurom* muleta, = red cape hanging from a stick used to tease the bull

**muletilla** *nf (frase)* pet phrase; *(palabra)* pet word

**Mulhacén** *nm* **el M.** Mulhacén

**mulillas** *nfpl Taurom* = team of mules which drag out the dead bull at the end of a fight

**mullido, -a** *adj* soft, springy

**mullir** *vt* to soften; *(lana, almohada)* to fluff up

**mulo, -a** *nm,f* (a) *(animal)* mule (b) *Fam Fig (persona)* brute, beast

**multa** *nf* fine; **poner una m. a alguien** to fine sb; **le pusieron mil pesetas de m.** he was fined a thousand pesetas

**multar** *vt* to fine

**multicolor** *adj* multicoloured

**multicopista** *nf* duplicator, duplicating machine

**multidisciplinario, -a, multidisciplinar** *adj* multidisciplinary

**multiforme** *adj* multiform, differently shaped

**multigrado** *adj* multigrade

**multilateral** *adj* multilateral

**multimedia** *adj inv Informát* multimedia

**multimillonario, -a 1** *adj* **un negocio m.** a multimillion pound *o* dollar business

**2** *nm,f* multimillionaire

**multinacional** *adj & nf* multinational

**múltiple** *adj (variado)* multiple; **múltiples** *(numerosos)* many, numerous

**multiplicable** *adj* multipliable

**multiplicación** *nf* multiplication

**multiplicador, -ora 1** *adj* multiplying

**2** *nm Mat* multiplier

**multiplicar** [61] **1** *vt (en general)* to multiply; *(efecto)* to magnify; *(riesgo, probabilidad)* to increase

**2** *vi* to multiply

**3 multiplicarse** *vpr* (a) *(reproducirse)* to multiply (b) *(esforzarse)* to do lots of things at the same time

**multiplicidad** *nf* multiplicity

**múltiplo** *nm* multiple

**multipropiedad** *nf* time-sharing

**multipuesto** *adj inv Informát* multiterminal; **red m.** multi-terminal network

**multisalas** *nm inv (cine)* multiplex cinema

**multitarea** *adj inv & nf Informát* multitasking

**multitud** *nf (de personas)* crowd; **m. de cosas** loads of *o* countless things

**multitudinario, -a** *adj* extremely crowded; **una manifestación multitudinaria** a massive demonstration

**multiuso** *adj inv* multipurpose

**mundanal** *adj* worldly

**mundano, -a** *adj* (a) *(del mundo)* worldly, of the world (b) *(de la vida social)* (high) society

**mundial 1** *adj (política, economía, guerra)* world; *(tratado, organización, fama)* worldwide
**2** *nm* World Championships; *(en fútbol)* World Cup

**mundialización** *nf* globalization

**mundillo** *nm* world, circles; **el m. literario** the literary world, literary circles

**mundo** *nm* (a) *(en general)* world; **el Nuevo M.** the New World; **el otro m.** the next world, the hereafter; **el Tercer M.** the Third World; **desde que el m. es m.** since the dawn of time; **el m. anda al revés** the world has been turned on its head; **el m. es un pañuelo** it's a small world; **medio m.** half the world, a lot of people; **no es cosa** o **nada del otro m.** it's nothing special; **ponerse el m. por montera** not to give a damn what people think; **por nada del m.** not for (all) the world; **se le cayó el m. encima** his world fell apart; **todo el m.** everyone, everybody; **traer al m.** to give birth to; **venir al m.** to come into the world, to be born
(b) *Fig (diferencia)* **hay un m. entre ellos** they're worlds apart
(c) *(experiencia)* **hombre/mujer de m.** man/woman of the world; **tener m.** to be worldlywise, to know the ways of the world; **ver** o **correr m.** to see life

**mundología** *nf* worldly wisdom, experience of life

**Munich** *n* Munich

**munición** *nf* ammunition; **municiones** ammunition

**municipal 1** *adj* town, municipal; *(elecciones)* local; *(instalaciones)* public; **las fiestas municipales** local/town festival
**2** *nmf (guardia)* (local) policeman, *f* policewoman

**municipalidad** *nf* (a) *(corporación)* local council (b) *(territorio)* town, municipality

**municipalizar** [16] *vt* to municipalize, to bring under municipal authority

**municipio** *nm* (a) *(corporación)* local council (b) *(edificio)* town hall (c) *(territorio)* town, municipality (d) *(habitantes)* **asistió todo el m.** the whole town was there

**munificencia** *nf* munificence

**muniqués, -esa 1** *adj* of/from Munich
**2** *nm,f* person from Munich

**muñeco, -a 1** *nm,f (juguete)* doll; *(marioneta)* puppet; *(peluche)* cuddly o soft toy
**2** *nm Fig* puppet; **m. de nieve** snowman
**3** *nf* **muñeca** (a) *Anat* wrist (b) *Fam Fig (mujer)* doll (c) *Andes, CSur Fam (enchufe)* **tener m.** to have friends in high places

**muñeira** *nf* = popular Galician dance and music

**muñequeo** *nm Am* fiddling

**muñequera** *nf* wristband

**muñón** *nm* stump

**mural 1** *adj (pintura)* mural; *(mapa)* wall
**2** *nm* mural

**muralla** *nf* wall

**Murcia** *n* Murcia

**murciano, -a** *adj & nm,f* Murcian

**murciélago** *nm* bat

**murga** *nf* (a) *(charanga)* band of street musicians (b) *Fam (pesadez)* drag, pain; **dar la m.** to be a pain

**muriera** *etc ver* **morir**

**murmullo** *nm (de agua, viento, voces)* murmur, murmuring; *(de hojas)* rustle, rustling

**murmuración** *nf* backbiting, gossip

**murmurador, -ora 1** *adj* backbiting, gossiping
**2** *nm,f* backbiter, gossip

**murmurar** *vi* (a) *(criticar)* to gossip, to backbite (**de** about) (b) *(susurrar) (persona)* to murmur, to whisper; *(agua, viento)* to murmur, to gurgle; *(hojas)* to rustle (c) *(rezongar, quejarse)* to grumble

**muro** *nm también Fig* wall; **m. de contención** retaining wall; **m. de las lamentaciones** Wailing Wall

**mus** *nm inv* = card game played in pairs with bidding and in which players communicate by signs

**musa** *nf* (a) *(inspiración)* muse (b) *Mitol* Muse

**musaraña** *nf Zool* shrew; *Fam* **mirar a las musarañas** to stare into space o thin air; *Fam* **pensar en las musarañas** to have one's head in the clouds

**musculación** *nf* body-building

**muscular** *adj* muscular

**musculatura** *nf* muscles

**músculo** *nm* muscle

**musculoso, -a** *adj* muscular

**museístico, -a** *adj* museum; **archivos museísticos** museum archives

**muselina** *nf* muslin

**museo** *nm* museum; **m. de arte** art gallery

**museología** *nf* museology

**musgo** *nm* moss

**música** *nf* music; *Fig* **irse con la m. a otra parte** to clear off; *Fig* **mandar a alguien con la m. a otra parte** to send sb packing; **m. ambiental** background music; *Fig* **m. celestial** hot air, empty words; **m. clásica/de cámara** classical/chamber music; **m. instrumental/vocal** instrumental/choral music; **m. ligera/pop** light/pop music

**musical** *adj & nm* musical

**musicalidad** *nf* musicality

**music-hall** ['musik'xɔl] (*pl* **music-halls**) *nm* music hall

**músico, -a 1** *adj* musical
 **2** *nm,f* (*persona*) musician

**musitar** *vt* to mutter, to mumble

**muslo** *nm* (*de persona*) thigh; (*de pollo, pavo*) (*entero*) leg; (*parte inferior*) drumstick

**mustela** *nf* (a) (*comadreja*) weasel (b) (*pez*) dogfish

**mustiar** [15] **1** *vt* to wither, to wilt
 **2 mustiarse** *vpr* to wither, to wilt

**mustio, -a** *adj* (a) (*flor, planta*) withered, wilted (b) (*persona*) down, gloomy

**musulmán, -ana** *adj & nm,f* Muslim, Moslem

**mutable** *adj* changeable, mutable

**mutación** *nf* (*cambio*) sudden change; *Biol* mutation

**mutante** *adj & nmf* mutant

**mutar** *vt* to mutate

**mutilación** *nf* mutilation

**mutilado, -a 1** *adj* mutilated
 **2** *nm,f* cripple; **m. de guerra** disabled war veteran

**mutilar** *vt* (*persona, texto*) to mutilate; (*estatua*) to vandalize

**mutis** *nm inv Teatro* exit; **hacer m.** (*marcharse*) to leave, to go away; *Teatro* to exit

**mutismo** *nm* (a) (*mudez*) muteness, dumbness (b) (*silencio*) silence

**mutua** *nf Br* friendly society, *US* mutual benefit society

**mutualidad** *nf* (a) (*asociación*) *Br* friendly society, *US* mutual benefit society (b) (*reciprocidad*) mutuality

**mutualista** *nmf* member of a *Br* friendly society *o US* mutual benefit society

**mutuo, -a** *adj* mutual

**muy** *adv* very; **m. bueno/cerca** very good/near; **m. de mañana** very early in the morning; **¡m. bien!** (*vale*) OK!, all right!; (*qué bien*) very good!, well done!; **eso es m. de ella** that's just like her; **eso es m. de los americanos** that's typically American; **¡el m. fresco!** the cheeky devil!; **¡la m. tonta!** the silly idiot!

**Myanmar** *n* (*Birmania*) Myanmar

# N

**N, n** ['ene] *nf (letra)* N, n; **el 20 N** 20th November, the date of Franco's death

**nabo** *nm* **(a)** *(planta)* turnip **(b)** *Vulg (pene)* prick

**nácar** *nm* mother-of-pearl

**nacarado, -a** *adj* mother-of-pearl; **piel nacarada** pearly skin

**nacatamal** *nm CAm* = steamed maize dumpling with savoury filling, wrapped in a banana leaf

**nacer** [44] *vi* **(a)** *(venir al mundo) (niño, animal)* to be born; *(planta)* to sprout, to begin to grow; *(pájaro)* to hatch (out); **n. de/en** to be born of/in; **n. de familia humilde** to be born into a poor family; **n. para algo** to be born for sth; **ha nacido cantante** she's a born singer; **volver a n.** to have a lucky escape **(b)** *(surgir) (pelo)* to grow; *(río)* to rise, to have its source; *(sol, luna)* to rise; *(costumbre, duda)* to have its roots

**nacido, -a 1** *adj* born
**2** *nm,f* **los nacidos hoy** those born today; **recién n.** new-born baby; **ser un mal n.** to be a wicked *o* vile person

**naciente** *adj* **(a)** *(día)* dawning; *(sol)* rising **(b)** *(Gobierno, Estado)* new, fledgling; *(interés)* budding, growing

**nacimiento** *nm* **(a)** *(de niño, animal)* birth; *(de planta)* sprouting; *(de ave, reptil)* hatching; **de n.** from birth **(b)** *(de río)* source **(c)** *(origen)* origin, beginning **(d)** *(belén)* Nativity scene

**nación** *nf (pueblo)* nation; *(territorio)* country; **Naciones Unidas** United Nations

**nacional** *adj* *(de la nación)* national; *(vuelo)* domestic, internal; *(mercado, noticias)* domestic, home; *Hist* **las fuerzas nacionales** *(en la guerra civil)* the Nationalist forces

**nacionalidad** *nf* nationality; **doble n.** dual nationality

**nacionalismo** *nm* nationalism

**nacionalista** *adj & nmf* nationalist

**nacionalización** *nf (de educación, bienes)* nationalization; *(de persona)* naturalization

**nacionalizar** [16] **1** *vt* **(a)** *(banca, bienes)* to nationalize **(b)** *(persona)* to naturalize
**2 nacionalizarse** *vpr* to become naturalized; **nacionalizarse español** to become a Spanish citizen, to acquire Spanish nationality

**nacionalsocialismo** *nm* National Socialism

**nada 1** *pron* **(a)** *(en general)* nothing; *(en negativas)* anything; **no he leído n. de Lorca** I haven't read anything by Lorca; **n. más** nothing else, nothing more; **no quiero n. más** I don't want anything else; **no dijo n. de n.** he didn't say anything at all; **no es n.** it's nothing serious; **te he traído un regalito de n.** I've brought you a little something; **cuesta cinco millones, ¡ahí es n.!** it costs five million, a real snip!; **casi n.** almost nothing; **como si n.** as if nothing was the matter, as if nothing had happened; **de n.** *(respuesta a 'gracias')* not at all, you're welcome; **dentro de n.** any second now; **esto no es n.** that's nothing; **¡n. de eso!** absolutely not!; **n. más salir de casa...** no sooner had I left the house than..., as soon as I left the house...
**(b)** *(en tenis)* love
**2** *adv* **(a)** *(en absoluto)* at all; **la película no me ha gustado n.** I didn't like the film at all **(b)** *(poco)* a little, a bit; **no hace n. que salió** he left just a minute ago; **n. menos que** *(cosa)* no less than; *(persona)* none other than
**3** *nf* **la n.** nothingness, the void

**nadador, -ora 1** *adj* swimming
**2** *nm,f* swimmer

**nadar** *vi* **(a)** *(avanzar en el agua)* to swim; *(flotar)* to float **(b)** *Fig* **n. en la abundancia** to be living in the lap of luxury

**nadería** *nf* trifle, little thing

**nadie 1** *pron* nobody, no one; **n. lo sabe** nobody knows; **no se lo dije a n.** I didn't tell anybody; **no ha llamado n.** nobody phoned
**2** *nm* **un don n.** a nobody

**nado: a nado** *loc adv* swimming

**nafta** *nf* **(a)** *Quím* naphtha **(b)** *CSur (gasolina)* *Br* petrol, *US* gasoline

**naftalina** *nf* naphthalene; **bolas de n.** mothballs

**naíf** (*pl* **naífs**) *adj Arte* naïve, primitivistic

**nailon** *nm* nylon

**naipe** *nm* (playing) card; **jugar a los naipes** to play cards

**Nairobi** *n* Nairobi

**nalga** *nf* buttock

**nana** *nf* (a) *(canción)* lullaby; *Fam* **más viejo que la n., del año de la n.** as old as the hills, ancient (b) *Fam (abuela)* grandma, nana

**nanay** *interj Fam* ¡n.! no way!, not likely!

**nao** *nf Literario* vessel

**napa** *nf* leather

**napalm** *nm* napalm

**napia** *nf Fam* snout, conk

**napoleónico, -a** *adj* Napoleonic

**naranja 1** *adj inv* orange
  **2** *nm (color)* orange
  **3** *nf (fruto)* orange; *Fam* ¡**naranjas de la china!** no way!; *Fam Fig* **media n.** other *o* better half

**naranjada** *nf* = orange juice drink

**naranjal** *nm* orange grove

**naranjo** *nm* (a) *(árbol)* orange tree (b) *(madera)* orange (wood)

**narcisismo** *nm* narcissism

**narcisista** *nmf* narcissist

**narciso** *nm* (a) *Bot* daffodil (b) *Fig (hombre)* narcissist

**narco** *nmf Fam (narcotraficante)* drug baron

**narcomanía** *nf* narcotism

**narcótico, -a 1** *adj* narcotic
  **2** *nm (somnífero)* narcotic; *(droga)* drug

**narcotizar** [16] *vt* to drug

**narcotraficante** *nmf* drug trafficker

**narcotráfico** *nm* drug trafficking

**nardo** *nm (flor)* nard, spikenard

**narices** *interj* ¡n.! no way!, not on your life!

**narigudo, -a 1** *adj* big-nosed
  **2** *nm,f* big-nosed person

**nariz** *nf* (a) *(órgano)* nose; **n. aguileña/chata/respingona** Roman/snub/turned-up nose (b) *(orificio)* nostril (c) *Fig (olfato)* sense of smell (d) *(expresiones)* **me da en la n. que...** I've got a feeling that...; **darse de narices con** *o* **contra algo/alguien** to bump into sth/sb; **de narices** *(estupendo)* great, brilliant; **delante de las narices** in front of one's nose; **estar hasta las narices (de algo)** to be fed up to the back teeth (with sth); **en sus propias narices** to his/her face; **me estás hinchando las narices** you're beginning to get up my nose; **meter las narices en algo** to poke *o* stick one's nose into sth; **tenemos que ir por narices** we have to go whether we like it or not; **restregar algo a alguien en las narices**

to rub sb's nose in sth; **romper las narices a alguien** to smash sb's face in; **romperse las narices** to fall flat on one's face; ¡**porque me sale de las narices!** because I damn well want to!

**narizotas** *nmf inv Fam* big-nose

**narración** *nf* (a) *(cuento, relato)* narrative, story (b) *(acción)* narration

**narrador, -ora** *nm,f* narrator

**narrar** *vt (contar)* to recount, to tell

**narrativa** *nf* narrative

**narrativo, -a** *adj* narrative

**NASA** ['nasa] *nf (abrev de* **National Aeronautics and Space Administration**) NASA

**nasal** *adj* nasal

**nasalizar** [16] *vt* to nasalize

**Nassau** *n* Nassau

**nata** *nf* (a) *(crema de leche)* cream; **n. batida** *o* **montada** whipped cream (b) *(en leche hervida)* skin

**natación** *nf* swimming

**natal** *adj (país, ciudad)* native; *(pueblo)* home

**natalicio** *nm (cumpleaños)* birthday

**natalidad** *nf (tasa* o *índice de)* **n.** birth rate

**natillas** *nfpl* custard

**natividad** *nf* nativity; **la N.** Christmas

**nativo, -a** *adj & nm,f* native

**nato, -a** *adj (de nacimiento)* born; **un criminal n.** a born criminal

**natura** *nf* nature; **contra n.** against nature, unnatural

**natural 1** *adj* (a) *(no artificial)* natural; *(flores, fruta, leche)* fresh; **al n.** *(en persona)* in the flesh; **ser n. en alguien** to be in sb's nature (b) *(lógico, normal)* natural, normal; **es n. que se enfade** it's natural that he should be angry (c) *(nativo)* native; **ser n. de** to come from (d) *(ilegítimo)* illegitimate; **hijo n.** illegitimate child
  **2** *nmf (nativo)* native
  **3** *nm (talante)* nature, disposition

**naturaleza** *nf* (a) *(en general)* nature; **por n.** by nature; **la madre n.** Mother Nature; **n. muerta** still life (b) *(complexión)* constitution

**naturalidad** *nf* naturalness; **con n.** naturally

**naturalismo** *nm Arte* naturalism

**naturalista** *nmf* naturalist

**naturalización** *nf* naturalization

**naturalizado, -a** *adj* naturalized

**naturalizar** [16] **1** *vt* to naturalize
  **2 naturalizarse** *vpr* to become naturalized; **naturalizarse español** to become a Spanish citizen, to acquire Spanish nationality

**naturalmente** *adv* (a) *(por naturaleza)* naturally (b) *(por supuesto)* of course

**naturismo** *nm (nudismo)* nudism

**naturista** *nmf (nudista)* nudist

**naturópata** *nmf* = practitioner of alternative medicine

**naufragar** [40] *vi* (a) *(barco)* to sink, to be wrecked; *(persona)* to be shipwrecked (b) *Fig (fracasar)* to fail, to collapse

**naufragio** *nm* (a) *(de barco)* shipwreck (b) *Fig (fracaso)* failure, collapse

**náufrago, -a 1** *adj* shipwrecked
 **2** *nm,f* shipwrecked person, castaway

**náusea** *nf* nausea, sickness; **me da náuseas** it makes me sick

**nauseabundo, -a** *adj* nauseating, sickening

**náutica** *nf* navigation, seamanship

**náutico, -a 1** *adj (de la navegación)* nautical; *Dep* **deportes náuticos** water sports; **club n.** yacht club
 **2** *nmpl* **náuticos** *(zapatos)* = lightweight lace-up shoes, made of coloured leather

**navaja** *nf* (a) *(cuchillo) (pequeño)* penknife; *(más grande)* jackknife; **n. de afeitar** razor (b) *(molusco)* razor-shell, razor clam

**navajazo** *nm* stab, slash

**navajero, -a** *nm,f* = thug who carries a knife

**naval** *adj* naval

**Navarra** *n* Navarre

**navarro, -a** *adj & nm,f* Navarrese

**nave** *nf* (a) *(barco)* ship; *Fig* **quemar las naves** to burn one's boats *o* bridges (b) *(vehículo)* craft; **n. espacial** spaceship, spacecraft (c) *(de fábrica)* shop, plant; *(almacén)* warehouse (d) *(de iglesia)* **n. central** nave; **n. de crucero** transepts; **n. lateral** side aisle

**navegable** *adj* navigable

**navegación** *nf* navigation; **n. aérea/fluvial/marítima** air/river/sea navigation; **n. de altura** ocean navigation

**navegador** *nm Informát* browser

**navegante 1** *adj (pueblo)* seafaring
 **2** *nmf* navigator

**navegar** [40] *vi (barco)* to sail; *(avión)* to fly; **n. por Internet** to surf the Net

**Navidad** *nf* (a) *(día)* Christmas (Day) (b) *(periodo)* Christmas (time); **felices Navidades** Merry Christmas

**navideño, -a** *adj* Christmas; **adornos navideños** Christmas decorations

**naviera** *nf (compañía)* shipping company

**naviero, -a 1** *adj* shipping
 **2** *nm (armador)* shipowner

**navío** *nm* large ship

**nazareno, -a 1** *adj & nm,f* Nazarene
 **2** *nm* = penitent in Holy Week processions; **el N.** Jesus of Nazareth

**nazca** *etc ver* **nacer**

**nazi** *adj & nmf* Nazi

**nazismo** *nm* Nazism

**NB** *(abrev de* **nota bene***)* NB

**neblina** *nf* mist

**neblinoso, -a** *adj* misty

**nebulosa** *nf Astron* nebula

**nebulosidad** *nf (de nubes)* cloudiness; *(de niebla)* fogginess

**nebuloso, -a** *adj* (a) *(con nubes)* cloudy; *(de niebla)* foggy (b) *Fig (poco claro)* vague

**necedad** *nf* (a) *(estupidez)* stupidity, foolishness (b) *(dicho, hecho)* stupid *o* foolish thing; **decir necedades** to talk nonsense

**necesario, -a** *adj* necessary; **es n. hacerlo** it needs to be done; **hacer n. algo** to make sth necessary; **no es n. que lo hagas** you don't need to do it; **si fuera n.** if need be

**neceser** *nm (bolsa)* toilet bag; *(maleta pequeña)* vanity case

**necesidad** *nf* (a) *(en general)* need; **de (primera) n.** essential; **no hay n. de algo** there's no need for sth; **no hay n. de hacer algo** there's no need to do sth; **obedecer a la n. (de)** to arise from the need (to); **tener n. de algo** to need sth; *Fam* **hacer (uno) sus necesidades** to answer a call of nature (b) *(obligación)* necessity; **por n.** out of necessity (c) *(hambre)* hunger

**necesitado, -a 1** *adj* needy; **n. de** in need of
 **2** *nm,f* needy *o* poor person; **los necesitados** the poor

**necesitar 1** *vt* to need; **necesito que me lo digas** I need you to tell me
 **2** *vi* to have need **(de** of**)**; **se necesita camarero** *(en letrero)* waiter wanted; **se necesita ser ignorante para no saber eso** you'd have to be an ignoramus not to know that

**necio, -a 1** *adj* stupid, foolish
 **2** *nm,f* idiot, fool

**nécora** *nf* small edible crab

**necrófago, -a** *adj* necrophagous

**necrofilia** *nf* necrophilia

**necrológica** *nm,f* obituary; **necrológicas** *(sección de periódico)* obituaries, obituary column

**necrológico, -a** *adj* **nota necrológica** obituary

**necrópolis** *nf inv* necropolis

**necrosis** *nf inv* necrosis

**néctar** *nm* nectar

**nectarina** *nf* nectarine

**neerlandés, -esa 1** *adj* Dutch
 **2** *nm,f* Dutchman, *f* Dutchwoman
 **3** *nm (idioma)* Dutch

**nefando, -a** *adj* abominable, odious

**nefasto, -a** *adj (funesto)* ill-fated; *(dañino)* bad, harmful; *(pésimo)* terrible, awful

**nefrítico, -a** *adj* renal, nephritic

**nefrología** *nf* nephrology

**negación** *nf* (a) *(desmentido)* denial (b) *(negativa)* refusal (c) *(lo contrario)* antithesis, negation (d) *Gram* negative

**negado, -a 1** *adj* useless, inept; **ser n. para algo** to be useless *o* no good at sth
**2** *nm,f* useless person, dead loss; **ser un n. para algo** to be useless *o* no good at sth

**negar** [45] **1** *vt* (a) *(rechazar)* to deny (b) *(denegar)* to refuse, to deny; **negarle algo a alguien** to refuse *o* deny sb sth
**2 negarse** *vpr* to refuse (a to); **negarse en redondo a hacer algo** to absolutely refuse to do sth

**negativa** *nf* (a) *(rechazo)* refusal (b) *(desmentido)* denial

**negativo, -a 1** *adj* (a) *(en general)* negative; **el análisis ha dado n.** the test results were negative (b) *Mat* minus, negative; **signo n.** minus sign
**2** *nm Fot* negative

**negligé** [negli'ʒe] *nm* negligée

**negligencia** *nf* negligence

**negligente** *adj* negligent

**negociable** *adj* negotiable

**negociación** *nf* negotiation; **n. colectiva** collective bargaining

**negociado** *nm* department, section

**negociador, -ora 1** *adj* negotiating
**2** *nm,f* negotiator

**negociante** *nmf (comerciante)* businessman, f businesswoman; *Fam Pey* sharp customer

**negociar** [15] **1** *vi* (a) *(comerciar)* to do business; **n. con** to deal *o* trade with (b) *(discutir)* to negotiate
**2** *vt* to negotiate

**negocio** *nm* (a) *(actividad, gestión)* business; **¿cómo va el n.?** how's business?; **el mundo de los negocios** the business world (b) *(transacción)* deal, (business) transaction; **n. sucio** shady deal, dirty business (c) *(operación ventajosa)* **(buen) n.** good deal, bargain; **hacer n.** to do well; **n. redondo** great bargain, excellent deal (d) *(comercio)* trade

**negra** *nf* (a) *Mús* crotchet (b) **tener la n.** to have bad luck; **se las va a ver negras para llegar a fin de mes** he'll have a hard job to get to the end of the month

**negrero, -a 1** *adj Fig (explotador)* tyrannical
**2** *nm,f* (a) *Hist* slave trader (b) *Fig (explotador)* slave driver

**negrita, negrilla** *adj* **(letra) n.** boldface; **en n.** in bold, in boldface

**negro, -a 1** *adj* (a) *(color)* black (b) *(bronceado, moreno)* tanned; **estar n.** to have a deep tan (c) *(pan)* brown (d) *(suerte)* awful, rotten; *(porvenir)* black, gloomy; **pasarlas negras** to have a hard time (e) *(furioso)* furious, fuming; **estar/ponerse n.** to be/get mad *o* angry (f) *(tabaco)* black, dark (g) *Cine* **cine n.** film noir
**2** *nm,f* black man, f black woman; *Fig* **trabajar como un n.** to work like a slave
**3** *nm* (a) *(color)* black (b) *(tabaco)* black *o* dark tobacco

**negroide** *adj* negroid

**negrura** *nf* blackness

**negruzco, -a** *adj* blackish

**negué** *etc ver* **negar**

**nemotecnia** *nf* mnemonics *(singular)*

**nemotécnico, -a** *adj* mnemonic

**nene, -a** *nm,f* (a) *Fam (niño)* baby (b) *(apelativo cariñoso)* dear, darling

**nenúfar** *nm* water lily

**neocapitalismo** *nm* neocapitalism

**neocelandés, -esa 1** *adj* New Zealand, of/from New Zealand; **un producto n.** a New Zealand product
**2** *nm,f* New Zealander

**neoclasicismo** *nm* neoclassicism

**neoclásico, -a 1** *adj* neoclassical
**2** *nm,f* neoclassicist

**neocolonialismo** *nm* neocolonialism

**neofascismo** *nm* neofascism

**neofascista** *adj & nmf* neofascist

**neófito, -a** *nm,f* (a) *Rel* neophyte (b) *(aprendiz)* novice

**neogótico, -a** *adj* Neo-Gothic

**neolatino, -a** *adj (lengua)* Romance

**neoliberalismo** *nm* neoliberalism

**neolítico, -a 1** *adj* Neolithic
**2** *nm* Neolithic (period)

**neologismo** *nm* neologism

**neón** *nm* (a) *Quím* neon (b) **(luz de) n.** neon light

**neonato, -a** *adj* newborn

**neonazi** *adj & nmf* neo-Nazi

**neoplasia** *nf* tumour

**neorrealismo** *nm* neorealism

**neoyorquino, -a 1** *adj* New York, of/from New York; **las calles neoyorquinas** the New York streets, the streets of New York
**2** *nm,f* New Yorker

**neozelandés, -esa 1** *adj* New Zealand, of/from New Zealand; **un producto n.** a New Zealand product
**2** *nm,f* New Zealander

**Nepal** *n* Nepal

**nepalés, -esa, nepalí** (*pl* **nepalíes**) **1** *adj & nm,f* Nepalese

**2** *nm* (*lengua*) Nepalese

**nepotismo** *nm* nepotism

**Neptuno** *n* Neptune

**nervio** *nm* (**a**) *Anat* nerve; **n. ciático/óptico** sciatic/optic nerve (**b**) **nervios** (*estado mental*) nerves; **me entraron los nervios** I got nervous; **perder los nervios** to lose one's cool *o* temper; **tener nervios** to be nervous; **tener nervios de acero** to have nerves of steel; **tener los nervios de punta** to be on edge; **poner los nervios de punta a alguien** to get on sb's nerves (**c**) (*en filete, carne*) sinew (**d**) *Bot* vein, rib (**e**) (*vigor*) energy, vigour (**f**) *Arquit* rib

**nerviosismo** *nm* nervousness, nerves

**nervioso, -a** *adj* (**a**) *Anat* (*sistema, enfermedad*) nervous; **centro/tejido n.** nerve centre/tissue (**b**) (*inquieto*) nervous; **ponerse n.** to get nervous (**c**) (*muy activo*) highly-strung (**d**) (*irritado*) worked-up, uptight; **poner n. a alguien** to get on sb's nerves; **ponerse n.** to get uptight *o* worked up

**nervudo, -a** *adj* sinewy

**neto, -a** *adj* (**a**) (*peso, sueldo*) net (**b**) (*claro*) clear, clean; (*verdad*) simple, plain

**neumático, -a 1** *adj* pneumatic

**2** *nm* tyre; **n. de repuesto** spare tyre

**neumonía** *nf* pneumonia

**neura** *Fam* **1** *adj* neurotic

**2** *nf* bug, mania; **le dio la n. de las maquetas** he caught the model-making bug

**neuralgia** *nf* neuralgia

**neurálgico, -a** *adj* (**a**) *Med* neuralgic (**b**) *Fig* (*importante*) critical

**neurastenia** *nf* nervous exhaustion

**neurasténico, -a** *Med* **1** *adj* neurasthenic

**2** *nm,f* neurasthenic person

**neuroanatomía** *nf* neuroanatomy

**neurobiología** *nf* neurobiology

**neurocirugía** *nf* neurosurgery

**neurocirujano, -a** *nm,f* neurosurgeon

**neurofisiología** *nf* neurophysiology

**neurología** *nf* neurology

**neurológico, -a** *adj* neurological

**neurólogo, -a** *nm,f* neurologist

**neurona** *nf* neuron, nerve cell

**neuropatía** *nf* neuropathy

**neuropsicología** *nf* neuropsychology

**neuropsiquiatría** *nf* neuropsychiatry

**neurosis** *nf inv* neurosis

**neurótico, -a** *adj & nm,f* neurotic

**neurotransmisor** *nm* neurotransmitter

**neutral** *adj & nmf* neutral

**neutralidad** *nf* neutrality

**neutralizable** *adj* (*efecto, consecuencia*) remediable

**neutralización** *nf* neutralization

**neutralizador, -ora** *adj* neutralizing

**neutralizar** [16] **1** *vt* to neutralize

**2 neutralizarse** *vpr* (*mutuamente*) to neutralize each other

**neutrino** *nm Fís* neutrino

**neutro, -a** *adj* (**a**) (*color, actitud, voz*) neutral (**b**) *Biol & Gram* neuter

**neutrón** *nm* neutron

**nevada** *nf* snowfall

**nevado, -a** *adj* snowy

**nevar** [3] *v impersonal* to snow

**nevera** *nf Br* fridge, *US* icebox

**nevisca** *nf* snow flurry

**neviscar** [61] *v impersonal* to snow lightly

**news** ['nius] *nfpl Informát* newsgroup

**newton** ['niuton] *nm Fís* newton

**nexo** *nm* link, connection

**ni 1** *conj* **ni... ni...** neither... nor...; **ni mañana ni pasado** neither tomorrow nor the day after; **no... ni...** neither... nor..., not... or... (either); **no es alto ni bajo** he's neither tall nor short, he's not tall or short (either); **no es rojo ni verde ni azul** it's neither red nor green nor blue; **ni un/una...** not a single...; **no me quedaré ni un minuto más** I'm not staying a minute longer; **ni uno/una** not a single one; **no he aprobado ni una** I haven't passed a single one; **ni que** as if; **¡ni que yo fuera tonto!** as if I were that stupid!

**2** *adv* not even; **ni siquiera** not even; **anda tan atareado que ni tiene tiempo para comer** he's so busy he doesn't even have time to eat

**Niágara** *nm* **las cataratas del N.** the Niagara Falls

**Niamey** *n* Niamey

**Nicaragua** *n* Nicaragua

**nicaragüense** *adj & nmf* Nicaraguan

**nicho** *nm* niche

**Nicosia** *n* Nicosia

**nicotina** *nf* nicotine

**nidada** *nf* (*pollitos*) brood; (*huevos*) clutch

**nidal** *nm* nest

**nidificar** [61] *vi* to (build a) nest

**nido** *nm* (**a**) (*refugio de animal*) nest; *Fig* **n. de víboras** nest of vipers (**b**) *Fig* (*escondrijo*) hiding-place (**c**) *Fig* (*origen*) breeding ground

**niebla** *nf* (**a**) (*densa*) fog; (*neblina*) mist; **hay n.** it's foggy/misty (**b**) *Fig* (*confusión*) fogginess, cloudiness

**niego** *etc ver* **negar**

**nieto, -a** *nm,f* grandson, *f* granddaughter

**nieva** *ver* **nevar**

**nieve** *nf* (a) *Meteo* snow; **nieves** *(nevada)* snows, snowfall; **n. carbónica** dry ice (b) *Fam (cocaína)* snow

**NIF** [nif] *nm (abrev de* **número de identificación fiscal)** *Br* ≃ National Insurance number, = identification number for tax purposes

**Níger** *nm* Niger

**Nigeria** *n* Nigeria

**nigeriano, -a** *adj & nm,f* Nigerian

**nigromancia** *nf* necromancy

**nigromante** *nmf* necromancer

**nihilismo** *nm* nihilism

**Nilo** *nm* **el N.** the (river) Nile

**nilón** *nm* nylon

**nimbo** *nm* (a) *(nube)* nimbus (b) *(de astro, santo)* halo, nimbus

**nimiedad** *nf* (a) *(cualidad)* insignificance, triviality (b) *(dicho, hecho)* trifle

**nimio, -a** *adj* insignificant, trivial

**ninfa** *nf* nymph

**ninfómana** *adj f & nf* nymphomaniac

**ninfomanía** *nf* nymphomania

**ninguno, -a**

> **Ningún** is used instead of **ninguno** before singular masculine nouns (e.g. **ningún hombre** no man).

**1** *adj* no; **no se dio ninguna respuesta** no answer was given; **no tengo ningún interés en hacerlo** I've no interest in doing it, I'm not at all interested in doing it; **no tengo ningún hijo/ninguna buena idea** I don't have any children/good ideas; **no tiene ninguna gracia** it's not funny; **en ningún momento** at no time

**2** *pron (cosa)* none, not any; *(persona)* nobody, no one; **n. funciona** none of them works; **no hay n.** there aren't any, there are none; **n. lo sabrá** no one *o* nobody will know; **n. de** none of; **n. de ellos** none of them; **n. de los dos** neither of them *o* the two

**niña** *nf* (a) *ver* **niño** (b) *(del ojo)* pupil; *Fig* **la n. de los ojos** the apple of one's eye

**niñato, -a** *nm,f Fam Pey* (a) *(inexperto)* amateur, novice (b) *(pijo)* spoiled brat

**niñera** *nf* nanny

**niñería** *nf* (a) *(cualidad)* childishness (b) *Fig (tontería)* silly *o* childish thing

**niñez** *nf (infancia)* childhood

**niño, -a1** *adj* young

**2** *nm,f* (a) *(crío) (varón)* child, boy; *(hembra)* child, girl; *(bebé)* baby; **los niños** the children; **estar como un n. con zapatos nuevos** to be as pleased as punch; **es culpa de la crisis – ¡qué crisis ni qué n. muerto!** it's the fault of the recession – don't talk to me about recession!; **ser el n. bonito de alguien** to be sb's pet *o* blue-eyed boy; *Pey* **n. bien** rich kid; **n. probeta** test-tube baby; **n. prodigio** child prodigy; **n. de teta** *o* **pecho** tiny baby

(b) *(joven)* young boy, f young girl

**nipón, -ona** *adj & nm,f* Japanese

**níquel** *nm* nickel

**niquelar** *vt* to nickel-plate

**niqui** *nm* T-shirt

**nirvana** *nm* nirvana

**níscalo** *nm* = edible variety of milk cap mushroom

**níspero** *nm* medlar

**nitidez** *nf (claridad)* clarity; *(de imagen, color)* sharpness

**nítido, -a** *adj (claro)* clear; *(imagen, color)* sharp

**nitrato** *nm* nitrate; **n. de Chile** sodium nitrate

**nítrico, -a** *adj* nitric

**nitrogenado, -a** *adj* nitrogenous

**nitrógeno** *nm* nitrogen

**nitroglicerina** *nf* nitroglycerine

**nitroso, -a** *adj* nitrous

**nivel** *nm* (a) *(altura)* level, height; **al n. de** level with; **al n. del mar** at sea level (b) *(grado)* level, standard; **al mismo n. (que)** on a level *o* par (with); **a n. europeo** at a European level; **n. mental** level of intelligence; **n. de vida** standard of living (c) *(instrumento)* spirit level

**nivelación** *nf* (a) *(allanamiento)* levelling (b) *(equilibrio)* levelling out, evening out

**niveladora** *nf* bulldozer

**nivelador, -ora** *adj* levelling

**nivelar** *vt* (a) *(allanar)* to level (b) *(equilibrar)* to even out; *Fin* to balance

**níveo, -a** *adj Formal* snow-white

**nixtamal** *nm CAm, Méx* maize dough

**no** *(pl* **noes)** **1** *adv* (a) *(negación)* not; *(en respuestas)* no; *(con sustantivos)* non-; **no sé** I don't know; **no veo nada** I can't see anything; **no es fácil** it's not easy, it isn't easy; **no tiene dinero** he has no money, he hasn't got any money; **todavía no vienen** they're not coming; **no ya...** are you coming? – no; **no fumadores** nonsmokers

(b) *(expresa duda, extrañeza)* **¿no irás a venir?** you're not coming, are you?; **estamos de acuerdo, ¿no?** we're agreed then, are we?; **es español, ¿no?** he's Spanish, isn't he?

(c) *(expresiones)* **no bien** as soon as; **no ya... sino que...** not only... but (also)...; **¡a que no lo haces!** I bet you don't do it!; **¿cómo no?**

of course; *Fam* **¡no es listo/guapo ni nada!** is he smart/good-looking or what?; **pues no** certainly not; **eso sí que no** certainly not; **¡que no!** I said no!

**2** *nm* no

**n°** *(abrev de* **número)** no

**Nobel** *nm (premio)* Nobel prize; *(galardonado)* Nobel prize winner

**nobiliario, -a** *adj* noble

**noble** *adj & nmf* noble; **los nobles** the nobility

**nobleza** *nf* nobility

**noche** *nf (en oposición a día)* night; *(atardecer)* evening; **ayer por la n.** last night; **esta n.** tonight; **hacer n. en** to stay the night in; **hacerse de n.** to get dark; **pasar la n. en claro** *o* **vela** to have a sleepless night; **por la n., de n.** at night; **buenas noches** *(saludo)* good evening; *(despedida)* good night; **de la n. a la mañana** overnight; **ser la n. y el día** to be as different as night and day

**Nochebuena** *nf* Christmas Eve

**Nochevieja** *nf* New Year's Eve

**noción** *nf (concepto)* notion; **tener n. (de)** to have an idea (of); **tener nociones de** *(conocimiento básico)* to have a smattering of

**nocividad** *nf (cualidad de dañino)* harmfulness; *(de gas)* noxiousness

**nocivo, -a** *adj (dañino)* harmful; *(gas)* noxious

**noctámbulo, -a 1** *adj* active at night; **animal n.** nocturnal animal

**2** *nm,f (persona)* night owl

**nocturnidad** *nf Der* **con n.** under cover of darkness

**nocturno, -a 1** *adj* **(a) tren/vuelo n.** night train/flight **(b)** *(animales, plantas)* nocturnal

**2** *nm Mús* nocturne

**nodo** *nm* node

**nodriza 1** *nf* wet nurse

**2** *adj* **buque/avión n.** refuelling ship/plane

**nódulo** *nm* nodule

**nogal** *nm* walnut

**nómada 1** *adj* nomadic

**2** *nmf* nomad

**nomadismo** *nm* nomadism

**nomás** *adv Am* just; **hasta allí n.** that far and no further

**nombrado, -a** *adj* **(a)** *(citado)* mentioned **(b)** *(famoso)* famous, well-known

**nombramiento** *nm* appointment

**nombrar** *vt* **(a)** *(citar)* to mention **(b)** *(designar)* to appoint

**nombre** *nm* **(a)** *(apelativo)* name; **a n. de** *(carta)* addressed to; *(cheque)* made out to; **de n. Juan** called Juan, Juan by name; **en n. de** on behalf of; **llamar a las cosas por su n.** to call a spade a spade; *Fam* **no tener n.** to be unspeakable; **n. y apellidos** full name; **n. artístico/comercial** stage/trade name; **n. de pila** first *o* Christian name; **n. de soltera** maiden name

**(b)** *(fama)* reputation; **tener mucho n.** to be renowned *o* famous

**(c)** *Gram* noun; **n. abstracto/colectivo** abstract/collective noun; **n. común/propio** common/proper noun

**nomenclatura** *nf* nomenclature

**nomeolvides** *nm inv* **(a)** *(flor)* forget-me-not **(b)** *(pulsera)* identity bracelet

**nómina** *nf* **(a)** *(lista de empleados)* payroll; **estar en n.** to be on the staff **(b)** *(pago)* wage packet, wages **(c)** *(hoja de salario)* payslip

**nominación** *nf* nomination

**nominado, -a** *adj* nominated

**nominal** *adj* nominal

**nominar** *vt* to nominate

**nominativo, -a 1** *adj Com* bearing a person's name, nominal

**2** *nm Gram* nominative

**non 1** *adj* odd, uneven

**2** *nm* odd number

**3** *adv Fam* **nones** *(no)* no way, absolutely not

**nonagenario, -a 1** *adj* ninety-year old

**2** *nm,f* person in his/her nineties

**nonagésimo, -a** *núm* ninetieth

**nono, -a** *núm Formal* ninth

**non plus ultra** *nm* **ser el n.** to be the best ever

**noquear** *vt Dep* to knock out

**nórdico, -a 1** *adj* **(a)** *(del norte)* northern, northerly **(b)** *(escandinavo)* Nordic

**2** *nm,f* Nordic person

**noreste, nordeste 1** *adj (posición, parte)* northeast, northeastern; *(dirección, viento)* northeasterly

**2** *nm* north-east

**noria** *nf* **(a)** *(para agua)* water wheel **(b)** *(de feria)* Br big wheel, US Ferris wheel

**norirlandés, -esa 1** *adj* Northern Irish

**2** *nm,f* person from Northern Ireland

**norma** *nf (patrón, modelo)* standard; *(regla)* rule; **es la n. hacerlo así** it's usual to do it this way; **por n.** as a rule; **n. de conducta** *(principios)* standards (of behaviour); *(pauta)* pattern of behaviour

**normal** *adj* normal

**normalidad** *nf* normality

**normalización** nf (a) (vuelta a la normalidad) normalization (b) (regularización) standardization

**normalizar** [16] **1** vt (a) (volver normal) to return to normal (b) (estandarizar) to standardize

**2 normalizarse** vpr to return to normal

**Normandía** n Normandy

**normando, -a 1** adj (a) (de Normandía) of/from Normandy **el paisaje n.** the Normandy countryside (b) Hist (nórdico) Norse; (de Normandía) Norman

**2** nm,f (a) (habitante de Normandía) person from Normandy (b) Hist (nórdico) Norseman, f Norsewoman; (de Normandía) Norman

**normativa** nf regulations

**normativo, -a** adj normative

**noroeste 1** adj (posición, parte) northwest, northwestern; (dirección, viento) northwesterly

**2** nm northwest

**norte 1** adj (posición, parte) north, northern; (dirección, viento) northerly

**2** nm (a) Geog north; **viento del n.** north wind; **ir hacia el n.** to go north(wards); **está al n. de Madrid** it's (to the) north of Madrid (b) Fig (objetivo) goal, objective; **perder el n.** to lose one's bearings o way

**norteafricano, -a** adj & nm,f North African

**norteamericano, -a** adj & nm,f North American, American

**norteño, -a 1** adj northern

**2** nm,f northerner

**Noruega** n Norway

**noruego, -a 1** adj & nm,f Norwegian

**2** nm (lengua) Norwegian

**nos** pron personal (a) (complemento directo) us; **le gustaría vernos** she'd like to see us

(b) (complemento indirecto) (to) us; **n. lo dio** he gave it to us; **n. tiene miedo** he's afraid of us

(c) (reflexivo) ourselves; **n. vestimos** we get (ourselves) dressed

(d) (recíproco) each other; **n. enamoramos** we fell in love (with each other)

**nosocomio** nm Am hospital

**nosotros, -as** pron personal (a) (sujeto) we (b) (predicado) **somos n.** it's us

(c) (después de prep & complemento) us; **lo arreglaremos entre n.** we'll sort it out among ourselves; **vente a comer con n.** come and eat with us; **entre n.** between you and me, just between the two of us

**nostalgia** nf (del pasado) nostalgia; (de país, amigos) homesickness

**nostálgico, -a 1** adj (del pasado) nostalgic; (de país, amigos) homesick

**2** nm,f nostalgic person

**nota** nf (a) también Mús note; **tomar n. de algo** (apuntar) to note sth down; (fijarse) to take note of sth; Fam **dar la n.** to make oneself conspicuous; **de mala n.** of ill repute; **forzar la n.** to go too far; **n. a pie de página** footnote; **n. bene** nota bene, N.B.; **n. dominante** prevailing mood; **notas de sociedad** society column

(b) Educ mark; **ir para n.** to go for top marks; **sacar** o **tener buenas notas** to get good marks; **n. de corte** = minimum marks for entry into university

(c) (cuenta) bill; **n. de gastos** expenses claim

**notable 1** adj remarkable, outstanding

**2** nm (a) Educ (pass with) credit (b) (persona) notable, distinguished person

**notar 1** vt (a) (advertir) to notice; **te noto cansado** you look tired to me; **hacer n. algo** to point sth out (b) (sentir) to feel

**2 notarse** vpr to be apparent; **se nota que le gusta** you can tell she likes it; Fam **¡pues no se nota!** you could have fooled me!

**notaría** nf (a) (profesión) profession of notary (b) (oficina) notary's office

**notariado** nm (profesión) profession of notary

**notarial** adj notarial

**notario, -a** nm,f notary (public)

**noticia** nf news (singular); **una n.** a piece of news; **tener noticias** to have news; **¿tienes noticias suyas?** have you heard from him?; **las noticias** the news; Fam **n. bomba** bombshell

**noticiario, noticiero** nm Cine newsreel; Radio & TV news bulletin

**notición** nm Fam bombshell

**notificación** nf notification

**notificar** [61] vt to notify, to inform

**notoriedad** nf (a) (fama) fame (b) (evidencia) obviousness

**notorio, -a** adj (a) (evidente) obvious (b) (conocido) widely-known

**novatada** nf (a) (broma) ragging (b) (error) beginner's mistake; **pagar la n.** to learn the hard way

**novato, -a 1** adj inexperienced

**2** nm,f novice, beginner

**novecientos, -as** núm nine hundred; ver también **seis**

**novedad** nf (a) (cualidad) (de nuevo) newness; (de novedoso) novelty; **novedades** (libros, discos) new releases; (moda) latest fashion (b) (cambio) change (c) (noticia) news (singular); **sin n.** without incident; Mil all quiet (d) (cosa nueva) new thing; (innovación) innovation

**novedoso, -a** adj novel, new

**novel** adj new, first-time

**novela** *nf* novel; **n. de caballerías** tale of chivalry; **n. por entregas** serial; **n. policíaca** detective story; **n. rosa** romance, romantic novel

**novelar** *vt* to fictionalize, to make into a novel

**novelero, -a 1** *adj* (a) *(fantasioso)* very imaginative (b) *(aficionado a las novelas)* fond of novels

**2** *nm,f* (a) *(fantasioso)* very imaginative person (b) *(aficionado a las novelas)* person fond of novels

**novelesco, -a** *adj* (a) *(de la novela)* fictional (b) *(fantástico)* fantastic, extraordinary

**novelista** *nmf* novelist

**novelón** *nm Fam* = hefty and badly written novel; *Fig* **¡menudo n.!** what a melodrama!

**novena** *nf Rel* novena

**noveno, -a** *núm* ninth; **la novena parte** a ninth

**noventa** *núm* ninety; **los (años) n.** the nineties; *ver también* **seis**

**noviazgo** *nm* engagement

**noviciado** *nm Rel* novitiate; *Fig (aprendizaje)* apprenticeship

**novicio, -a** *Rel & Fig nm,f* novice

**noviembre** *nm* November; *ver también* **septiembre**

**novillada** *nf Taurom* = bullfight with young bulls

**novillero, -a** *nm,f Taurom* apprentice bullfighter

**novillo, -a** *nm,f* young bull or cow; *Fam* **hacer novillos** *Br* to play truant, *US* to play hooky

**novio, -a** *nm,f* (a) *(compañero)* boyfriend, *f* girlfriend (b) *(prometido)* fiancé, *f* fiancée (c) *(recién casado)* bridegroom, *f* bride; **los novios** the newly-weds

**novocaína** *nf* Novocaine

**Ntra Sra** *(abrev de* **Nuestra Señora***)* Our Lady

**ntro.** *abrev de* **nuestro**

**nubarrón** *nm* storm cloud

**nube** *nf* (a) *(de lluvia, humo)* cloud; **como caído de las nubes** out of the blue; **estar en las nubes** to have one's head in the clouds; *Fam* **poner algo/a alguien por las nubes** to praise sth/sb to the skies; *Fam* **estar por las nubes** *(caro)* to be terribly expensive; *Fig* **n. de verano** short fit of anger (b) *(de personas, moscas)* swarm

**núbil** *adj Formal* nubile

**nublado, -a** *adj* (a) *(encapotado)* cloudy, overcast (b) *Fig (turbado)* clouded, darkened

**nublar 1** *vt también Fig* to cloud

**2 nublarse** *vpr* (a) *(cielo, vista)* to cloud over (b) *Fig (turbarse, oscurecerse)* to become clouded

**nubloso, -a** *adj* cloudy

**nubosidad** *nf* cloudiness, clouds

**nuboso, -a** *adj* cloudy

**nuca** *nf* nape, back of the neck

**nuclear** *adj* nuclear

**nuclearización** *nf* (a) *Ind* introduction of nuclear power (b) *Mil* acquisition of nuclear weapons

**nuclearizar [16]** *vt* (a) *Ind* to introduce nuclear power into (b) *Mil* to acquire nuclear weapons for

**núcleo** *nm* (a) *(centro)* nucleus; *Fig* centre; *Fís* **n. atómico** atomic nucleus; **n. de población** population centre (b) *(grupo)* core

**nudillo** *nm* knuckle; **llamar con los nudillos** *(a la puerta)* to knock (on *o* at the door)

**nudismo** *nm* nudism

**nudista** *adj & nmf* nudist

**nudo** *nm* (a) *(lazo)* knot; *Fig* **se le hizo un n. en la garganta** she got a lump in her throat; **n. corredizo** slipknot (b) *(cruce)* junction; **n. de comunicaciones** communications centre (c) *Fig (vínculo)* tie, bond (d) *Fig (punto principal)* crux, nub (e) *(en madera)* knot

**nudoso, -a** *adj* knotty, gnarled

**nuera** *nf* daughter-in-law

**nuestro, -a 1** *adj posesivo* our; **n. coche** our car; **este libro es n.** this book is ours, this is our book; **un amigo n.** a friend of ours; **no es asunto n.** it's none of our business

**2** *pron posesivo* **n.** ours; **el n. es rojo** ours is red; *Fam* **esta es la nuestra** this is the chance we've been waiting for *o* our big chance; **lo n. es el teatro** *(lo que nos va)* theatre is what we should be doing; *Fam* **los nuestros** *(nuestra familia)* our folks; *(nuestro bando)* our lot, our side

**nueva** *nf ver* **nuevo**

**Nueva Delhi** *n* New Delhi

**Nueva York** *n* New York

**Nueva Zelanda** *n* New Zealand

**nueve** *núm* nine; *ver también* **seis**

**nuevo, -a 1** *adj (reciente)* new; *(hortaliza)* new, fresh; *(vino)* young; **de n.** again; **ser n. en** to be new to; **estar/quedar como n.** to be as good as new

**2** *nm,f* newcomer

**3 nueva** *nf Literario* (piece of) news; **buena nueva** good news

**nuez** *nf* (a) *(de nogal)* walnut; **n. moscada** nutmeg (b) *Anat* Adam's apple

**nulidad** *nf* (a) *(no validez)* nullity (b) *(ineptitud)* incompetence (c) *Fam (persona)* nonentity; **ser una n.** to be useless

**nulo, -a** *adj* **(a)** *(sin validez)* null and void, invalid **(b)** *Fam (incapacitado)* useless **(para** at)

**núm.** *(abrev de* **número)** No

**numen** *nm Formal* inspiration, muse

**numeración** *nf* **(a)** *(acción)* numbering **(b)** *(sistema)* numerals, numbers; **n. arábiga** *o* **decimal** Arabic numerals; **n. binaria** binary numbers; **n. romana** Roman numerals

**numerador** *nm Mat* numerator

**numeral** *adj* numeral

**numerar 1** *vt* to number

**2 numerarse** *vpr (personas)* to number off

**numerario, -a** *adj (profesor, catedrático)* tenured, permanent; *(miembro)* full

**numérico, -a** *adj* numerical

**número** *nm* **(a)** *(signo)* number; **sin n.** *(muchos)* countless, innumerable; **en números rojos** in the red; **hacer números** to reckon up; **ser el n. uno** to be number one; *Quím* **n. atómico** atomic number **n. cardinal/ordinal** cardinal/ordinal number; **n. complejo/irracional** complex/irrational number; **n. complementario** *(en lotería)* bonus number; *Aut* **n. de matrícula** registration number; **n. dígito** digit; **n. entero** whole number, integer; **n. fraccionario** *o* **quebrado** fraction; **n. impar/par** odd/even number; **n. primo/redondo** prime/round number; **n. romano** Roman numeral

**(b)** *(tamaño, talla)* size

**(c)** *(de publicación)* issue, number; **n. atrasado** back number

**(d)** *(de lotería)* ticket

**(e)** *(de la Guardia Civil)* member

**(f)** *(de espectáculo)* turn, number; *Fam* **montar el n.** to make *o* cause a scene

**numeroso, -a** *adj* numerous; **un grupo n.** a large group

**numerus clausus** *nm inv Educ* = restriction on number of students in university course

**numismática** *nf (estudio)* numismatics *(singular)*

**numismático, -a 1** *adj* numismatic

**2** *nm,f (persona)* numismatist

**nunca** *adv (en frases afirmativas)* never; *(en frases negativas)* ever; **casi n.** viene he almost never comes, he hardly ever comes; **¿n. le has visto?** have you never seen her?, haven't you ever seen her?; **más que n.** more than ever; **n. jamás** *o* **más** never more *o* again

**nunciatura** *nf Rel* **(a)** *(cargo)* nunciature **(b)** *(edificio)* nuncio's residence **(c)** *(tribunal de la Rota)* = ecclesiastical court in Spain

**nuncio** *nm Rel* nuncio; **n. apostólico** papal nuncio

**nupcial** *adj* wedding; **ceremonia/lecho n.** marriage ceremony/bed

**nupcias** *nfpl* wedding, nuptials; **contraer segundas n.** to remarry

**nutria** *nf* otter

**nutrición** *nf* nutrition

**nutrido, -a** *adj* **(a)** *(alimentado)* nourished, fed; **mal n.** undernourished **(b)** *(numeroso)* large

**nutrir 1** *vt* **(a)** *(alimentar)* to nourish *o* feed **(con** *o* **de** with) **(b)** *Fig (fomentar)* to feed, to nurture **(c)** *Fig (suministrar)* to supply **(de** with)

**2 nutrirse** *vpr* **(a)** *(alimentarse)* **nutrirse de** *o* **con** to feed on **(b)** *Fig (proveerse)* **nutrirse de** *o* **con** to supply *o* provide oneself with

**nutritivo, -a** *adj* nutritious

**nylon** ['nailon] *(pl* **nylons)** *nm* nylon

**Ñ, ñ** ['ene] *nf (letra)* Ñ, ñ, = 15th letter of the Spanish alphabet
**ñato, -a** *adj Am* snub
**ñoñería, ñoñez** *nf* inanity

**ñoño, -a** *adj* (**a**) *(remilgado)* squeamish; *(quejica)* whining (**b**) *(soso)* dull, insipid
**ñoqui** *nm Culin* gnocchi
**ñu** *nm* gnu

# o

**O¹, o** [o] *nf (letra)* O, o

**o²**

---
**u** is used instead of **o** in front of words beginning with "o" or "ho" (e.g. **mujer u hombre** woman or man).

---

*conj* or; **o.... o.** either... or; **o sea (que)** in other words

**o/** *(abrev de* **orden***)*

**oasis** *nm inv también Fig* oasis

**obcecación** *nf* blindness, stubbornness

**obcecado, -a** *adj* **(a)** *(tozudo)* stubborn **(b)** *(obsesionado)* **o. por** *o* **con** blinded by

**obcecar** [61] **1** *vt* to blind

**2 obcecarse** *vpr* to become stubborn; **obcecarse en hacer algo** to stubbornly insist on doing sth

**obedecer** [48] **1** *vt* **o. a alguien** to obey sb

**2** *vi* **(a)** *(acatar)* to obey, to do as one is told **(b)** *(someterse)* **o. a** to respond to **(c)** *(estar motivado)* **o. a** to be due to

**obediencia** *nf* obedience

**obediente** *adj* obedient

**obelisco** *nm* obelisk

**obenque** *nm Náut* shroud

**obertura** *nf* overture

**obesidad** *nf* obesity

**obeso, -a 1** *adj* obese

**2** *nm,f* obese person

**óbice** *nm Formal* **no ser ó. para** not to be an obstacle to

**obispado** *nm* bishopric

**obispo** *nm* bishop

**óbito** *nm Formal* decease, demise

**obituario** *nm* obituary

**objeción** *nf* objection; **poner objeciones a** to raise objections to; **tener objeciones** to have objections; **o. de conciencia** conscientious objection

**objetar 1** *vt* to object to; **no tengo nada que o.** I have no objection

**2** *vi* to be a conscientious objector

**objetividad** *nf* objectivity

**objetivo, -a 1** *adj* objective

**2** *nm* **(a)** *(finalidad)* objective, aim **(b)** *Mil* target **(c)** *Fot* lens

**objeto** *nm* **(a)** *(asunto, cosa)* object; **ser o. de** to be the object of; **objetos perdidos** lost property; **objetos de valor** valuables **(b)** *(propósito)* purpose, object; **sin o.** *(inútilmente)* to no purpose, pointlessly; **al** *o* **con o. de hacer algo** in order to do sth, with the aim of doing sth

**objetor, -ora** *nm,f* objector; **o. de conciencia** conscientious objector

**oblación** *nf Rel* oblation

**oblea** *nf* wafer

**oblicuo, -a** *adj* **(a)** *(inclinado)* oblique, slanting; *(mirada)* sidelong **(b)** *Mat* oblique

**obligación** *nf* **(a)** *(deber, imposición)* obligation, duty; **por o.** out of a sense of duty **(b)** *Fin* bond, security; **o. convertible** convertible bond; **o. del Estado** Treasury bond

**obligacionista** *nmf Fin* bondholder

**obligado, -a** *adj* obligatory, compulsory

**obligar** [40] **1** *vt* **o. a alguien a hacer algo** to oblige *o* force sb to do sth

**2 obligarse** *vpr* **obligarse a hacer algo** to undertake to do sth

**obligatoriedad** *nf* obligatory *o* compulsory nature

**obligatorio, -a** *adj* obligatory, compulsory

**obligue** *etc ver* **obligar**

**obliterar** *vt Med* to obliterate

**oblongo, -a** *adj* oblong

**obnubilación** *nf* bewilderment

**obnubilar** *vt* to bewilder, to daze

**oboe 1** *nm (instrumento)* oboe

**2** *nmf (persona)* oboist

**óbolo** *nm* small contribution

**obra** *nf* **(a)** *(trabajo, acción)* work; **es o. suya** it's his doing; **poner en o.** to put into effect; **por o. (y gracia) de** thanks to; **o. de caridad** *(institución)* charity; **obras sociales** community work **(b)** *(de arte)* work (of art); *(de teatro)* play; *(de literatura)* book; *(de música)* opus; **obras completas** complete works; **o. maestra** masterpiece **(c)** *(construcción) (lugar)* building site; *(reforma)* alteration; **cerrado por obras** *(en letrero)* closed for alterations; **obras** *(en carretera)* roadworks; **obras públicas** public works

**obrador** *nm* workshop

**obrar 1** *vi* (**a**) *(actuar)* to act (**b**) *(causar efecto)* to work, to take effect (**c**) *(estar en poder)* **o. en manos de** to be in the possession of

**2** *vt* to work

**obrero, -a 1** *adj* **clase obrera** working class; **movimiento o.** labour movement

**2** *nm,f* *(en fábrica)* worker; *(en obra)* workman, labourer; **o. cualificado** skilled worker

**obscenidad** *nf* obscenity

**obsceno, -a** *adj* obscene

**obscurantismo** *nm* obscurantism

**obscurecer, obscuridad** *etc* = **oscurecer, oscuridad** *etc*

**obsequiar** [15] *vt* **o. a alguien con algo** to present sb with sth

**obsequio** *nm* gift, present; **o. de empresa** complimentary gift

**obsequiosidad** *nf* attentiveness, helpfulness

**obsequioso, -a** *adj* obliging, attentive

**observación** *nf* *(examen, contemplación)* observation; **hacer una o.** *(comentario)* to make a comment *o* observation

**observador, -ora 1** *adj* observant

**2** *nm,f* observer

**observancia** *nf* observance

**observar 1** *vt* (**a**) *(contemplar)* to observe, to watch (**b**) *(advertir)* to notice, to observe (**c**) *(acatar) (ley, normas)* to observe, to respect; *(conducta, costumbre)* to follow

**2 observarse** *vpr* to be noticed; **no se observan anomalías** no problems have been noted

**observatorio** *nm* observatory

**obsesión** *nf* obsession

**obsesionar 1** *vt* to obsess

**2 obsesionarse** *vpr* to be obsessed

**obsesivo, -a** *adj* obsessive

**obseso, -a 1** *adj* obsessed

**2** *nm,f* obsessed *o* obsessive person

**obsoleto, -a** *adj* obsolete

**obstaculizar** [16] *vt* to hinder, to hamper

**obstáculo** *nm* obstacle; **un o. para** an obstacle to; **poner obstáculos a algo/alguien** to hinder sth/sb

**obstante** *adv* **no o.** nevertheless, however

**obstar** *vi Formal* **eso no obsta para que vengas si quieres** that isn't to say that you can't come if you want to

**obstetricia** *nf* obstetrics *(singular)*

**obstinación** *nf* *(persistencia)* perseverance; *(terquedad)* obstinacy, stubbornness

**obstinado, -a** *adj* *(persistente)* persistent; *(terco)* obstinate, stubborn

**obstinarse** *vpr* to refuse to give way; **o. en** to persist in

**obstrucción** *nf también Fig* obstruction

**obstruccionismo** *nm* obstructionism, stonewalling

**obstruccionista** *adj & nmf* obstructionist

**obstruir** [36] **1** *vt* (**a**) *(bloquear)* to block, to obstruct (**b**) *(obstaculizar)* to obstruct, to impede

**2 obstruirse** *vpr* to get blocked (up)

**obtención** *nf* obtaining

**obtener** [67] *vt* *(beca, cargo, puntos)* to get; *(premio, victoria)* to win; *(ganancias)* to make; *(satisfacción)* to gain

**obturación** *nf* blockage, obstruction

**obturador** *nm Fot* shutter

**obturar** *vt* to block

**obtuso, -a 1** *adj* (**a**) *(sin punta)* blunt (**b**) *Fig (tonto)* obtuse, stupid

**2** *nm,f Fig* dimwit

**obtuviera** *etc ver* **obtener**

**obús** *(pl* **obuses)** *nm* (**a**) *(cañón)* howitzer (**b**) *(proyectil)* shell

**obviar** [15] *vt* to avoid, to get round

**obvio, -a** *adj* obvious

**oca** *nf* (**a**) *(animal)* goose (**b**) *(juego)* snakes and ladders

**ocarina** *nf* ocarina

**ocasión** *nf* (**a**) *(oportunidad)* opportunity, chance; **tener o. de hacer algo** to have the chance to do sth; *Fam* **la o. la pintan calva** this is my/your/etc big chance (**b**) *(momento)* moment, time; *(vez)* occasion; **en dos ocasiones** on two occasions; **en alguna o.** sometimes; **en cierta o.** once; **en otra o.** some other time (**c**) *(motivo)* **con o. de** on the occasion of; **dar o. para algo/hacer algo** to give cause for sth/to do sth (**d**) *(ganga)* bargain; **artículos de o.** bargains

**ocasional** *adj* (**a**) *(accidental)* accidental (**b**) *(irregular)* occasional

**ocasionar** *vt* to cause

**ocaso** *nm (puesta del sol)* sunset; *Fig (decadencia)* decline

**occidental 1** *adj* western

**2** *nmf* westerner

**occidentalismo** *nm* western nature

**occidentalizar** [16] **1** *vt* to westernize

**2 occidentalizarse** *vpr* to become westernized

**occidente** *nm* west; **el O.** *(bloque de países)* the West

**occipital** *adj* occipital

**OCDE** *nf (abrev de* **Organización para la Cooperación y el Desarrollo Económico)** OECD

**Oceanía** *n* Oceania *(including Australia and New Zealand)*

**oceánico, -a** adj (a) (de un océano) oceanic (b) (de Oceanía) Oceanian

**océano** nm ocean; Fig (inmensidad) sea, host

**oceanografía** nf oceanography

**oceanográfico, -a** adj oceanographical

**ochenta** núm eighty; **los (años) o.** the eighties; ver también **seis**

**ocho** núm eight; **de aquí en o. días** (en una semana) a week today; ver también **seis**

**ochocientos, -as** núm eight hundred; ver también **seis**

**ocio** nm (tiempo libre) leisure; (inactividad) idleness; **en sus ratos de o. se dedica a leer** he spends his spare time reading

**ociosidad** nf idleness

**ocioso, -a** adj (a) (inactivo) idle (b) (innecesario) unnecessary; (inútil) pointless

**oclusión** nf blockage

**oclusiva** nf Ling occlusive

**oclusivo, -a** adj occlusive

**ocre 1** nm ochre
**2** adj inv ochre

**octaedro** nm octahedron

**octagonal** adj octagonal

**octágono, -a 1** adj octagonal
**2** nm octagon

**octanaje** nm octane number o rating

**octano** nm octane

**octava** nf Mús octave

**octavilla** nf (a) (de propaganda) pamphlet, leaflet (b) (tamaño) octavo

**octavo, -a 1** núm eighth; **la octava parte** an eighth
**2** nm (a) (parte) eighth (b) Dep **octavos de final** round before the quarter final

**octeto** nm (a) Mús octet (b) Informát byte

**octogenario, -a** adj & nm,f octogenarian

**octogésimo, -a** núm eightieth

**octogonal** adj octagonal

**octógono** nm octagon

**octosílabo, -a 1** adj octosyllabic
**2** nm octosyllabic line

**octubre** nm October; ver también **septiembre**

**OCU** ['oku] nf (abrev de **Organización de Consumidores y Usuarios**) = Spanish consumer organization, Br ≃ CAB

**ocular** adj eye; **testigo o.** eyewitness

**oculista** nmf ophthalmologist

**ocultación** nf concealment, hiding; Der **o. de pruebas** concealment, non-disclosure

**ocultar 1** vt (a) (esconder) to hide; **o. algo a alguien** to hide sth from sb (b) Fig (delito) to cover up
**2 ocultarse** vpr to hide

**ocultismo** nm occultism

**ocultista** nmf occultist

**oculto, -a** adj (a) (escondido) hidden (b) (sobrenatural) **lo o.** the occult

**ocupa** nmf Fam squatter

**ocupación** nf (a) (de territorio) occupation; **o. ilegal de viviendas** squatting (b) (empleo) job, occupation

**ocupacional** adj occupational

**ocupado, -a** adj (a) (persona) busy; Fig **tengo las manos ocupadas** I've got my hands full (b) (teléfono, lavabo) engaged (c) (tiempo) **tengo toda la tarde ocupada** I'm busy all afternoon (d) (territorio) occupied; (plaza, asiento) taken; **casa ocupada** (ilegalmente) squat

**ocupante 1** adj occupying
**2** nmf occupant; **o. ilegal de viviendas** squatter

**ocupar 1** vt (a) (territorio, mente) to occupy; **han ocupado la casa** (ilegalmente) there are squatters in the house (b) (superficie, espacio) to take up; (habitación, piso) to live in; (mesa) to sit at; (sillón) to sit in; **los niños me ocupan mucho tiempo** the children take up a lot of my time (c) (cargo) to hold (d) (dar trabajo a) to find o provide work for
**2 ocuparse** vpr (encargarse) **ocúpate tú, yo no puedo** you do it, I can't; **ocuparse de** (tratar) to deal with; (cuidar de) to look after; **¡tú ocúpate de lo tuyo!** mind your own business!

**ocurrencia** nf (a) (idea) bright idea; **¡vaya o.!** the very idea!, what an idea! (b) (dicho gracioso) witty remark

**ocurrente** adj witty

**ocurrir 1** vi (a) (suceder) to happen; **lo que ocurre es que...** the thing is... (b) (pasar, preocupar) **¿qué le ocurre a Juan?** what's up with Juan?; **¿te ocurre algo?** is anything the matter?
**2 ocurrirse** vpr (venir a la cabeza) **no se me ocurre ninguna solución** I can't think of a solution; **¡ni se te ocurra!** don't even think about it!; **se me ocurre que...** it occurs to me that...

**oda** nf ode

**odalisca** nf odalisque

**odeón** nm odeon

**odiar** [15] vt & vi to hate; **o. a muerte** to loathe

**odio** nm hatred; **tener o. a algo/alguien** to hate sth/sb

**odioso, -a** adj hateful, horrible

**odisea** nf también Fig odyssey

**odontología** nf dentistry

**odontólogo, -a** nm,f dentist, dental surgeon

**odre** nm (de vino) wineskin

**OEA** nf (abrev de **Organización de Estados Americanos**) OAS

**oeste 1** adj (posición, parte) west, western; (dirección, viento) westerly

**2** nm west; **viento del o.** west wind; **ir hacia el o.** to go west(wards); **está al o. de Madrid** it's (to the) west of Madrid; **el lejano o.** the wild west

**ofender 1** vt (a) (injuriar) to insult; **tus palabras me ofenden** I feel insulted (b) (a la vista, al oído) to offend

**2** vi to cause offence

**3 ofenderse** vpr to take offence (**por** at)

**ofendido, -a 1** adj offended

**2** nm,f offended party

**ofensa** nf (a) (acción) offence; **una o. a la buena educación** an affront to good manners (b) (injuria) slight, insult

**ofensiva** nf offensive; **pasar a la o.** to go on the offensive

**ofensivo, -a** adj offensive

**ofensor, -ora** nm,f offender

**oferta** nf (a) (propuesta, ofrecimiento) offer; **ofertas de trabajo** o **empleo** situations vacant (b) Econ (suministro) supply; **la o. y la demanda** supply and demand; **o. monetaria** money supply (c) (rebaja) bargain, special offer; **de o.** bargain, on offer; **artículos de o.** sale goods, goods on offer; **estar de o.** to be on offer (d) Fin (proposición) bid, tender; Com **o. pública de adquisición** takeover bid

**ofertar** vt to offer

**ofertorio** nm Rel offertory

**office** ['ofis] nm inv scullery

**offset** nm Imprenta offset

**oficial¹ 1** adj official

**2** nm (a) Mil officer (b) (funcionario) clerk

**oficial², -ala** nm,f (obrero) time-served

**oficialidad** nf official nature

**oficialismo** nm Am (Gobierno) **el o.** the Government

**oficializar** [16] vt to make official

**oficiante** nmf Rel officiant

**oficiar** [15] **1** vt (misa) to celebrate; (ceremonia) to officiate at

**2** vi (a) (sacerdote) to officiate (b) **o. de** (actuar de) to act as

**oficina** nf office; **o. de correos** post office; **o. de empleo** job centre; Informát **o. inteligente** intelligent office; **o. de turismo** tourist office

**oficinista** nmf office worker

**oficio** nm (a) (profesión manual) trade; **de o.** by trade (b) (trabajo) job; **no tener o. ni beneficio** to have no trade (c) Der **de o.** (abogado) court-appointed, legal aid (d) (documento) official minute (e) (experiencia) **tener mucho o.** to be very experienced (f) Rel (ceremonia) service; **el Santo O.** the Holy Office, the Inquisition (g) (función) function, role

**oficioso, -a** adj unofficial

**ofidio** nm (serpiente) snake

**ofimática** nf office automation

**ofrecer** [48] **1** vt (a) (presentar, dar) to offer; **ofrecerle algo a alguien** to offer sb sth; **me ofrece la oportunidad de conocer la ciudad** it gives me the chance to get to know the city (b) (un aspecto) to present

**2 ofrecerse** vpr (a) (presentarse) to offer, to volunteer; **ofrecerse a** o **para hacer algo** to offer to do sth (b) **¿qué se le ofrece?** what can I do for you?

**ofrecimiento** nm offer

**ofrenda** nf Rel offering; Fig (por gratitud, amor) gift

**ofrendar** vt to offer up

**ofrezca** etc ver **ofrecer**

**oftalmología** nf ophthalmology

**oftalmólogo, -a** nm,f ophthalmologist

**ofuscación** nf blindness, confusion

**ofuscar** [61] **1** vt (a) (deslumbrar) to dazzle (b) (turbar) to blind

**2 ofuscarse** vpr to be blinded (**con** o **por** by)

**ogro** nm también Fig ogre

**oh** interj ¡oh! oh!

**ohmio** nm ohm

**oídas: de oídas** loc adv by hearsay

**oído** nm (a) (órgano) ear; **abrir los oídos** to pay close attention; **decir algo al o. a alguien** to whisper sth in sb's ear; **entrar por un o. y salir por el otro** to go in one ear and out the other; **hacer oídos sordos** to turn a deaf ear; Fig **lastimar los oídos** to offend one's ears; **si llega a oídos de ella...** if she gets to hear about this...; **me zumban los oídos** my ears are burning; **ser todo oídos** to be all ears (b) (sentido) (sense of) hearing; **ser duro de o.** to be hard of hearing; **tener o., tener buen o.** to have a good ear; **tocar de o.** to play by ear

**OIEA** nm (abrev de **Organismo Internacional para la Energía Atómica**) IAEA

**oigo** ver **oír**

**oír** [46] **1** *vt* (a) *(en general)* to hear; **como quien oye llover** without paying the least attention; **¡como lo oyes!** absolutely!, just like I'm telling you! (b) *(atender)* to listen to

**2** *vi* to hear; **¡oiga, por favor!** excuse me!; **¡oye!** hey!; *Fig* **o., ver y callar** hear no evil, see no evil, speak no evil

**OIT** *nf (abrev de* **Organización Internacional del Trabajo***)* ILO

**ojal** *nm* buttonhole

**ojalá** *interj* **¡o.!** I hope so!; **¡o. lo haga!** I hope she does it!; **¡o. fuera viernes!** I wish it was Friday!

**ojeada** *nf* glance, look; **echar una o. a algo/alguien** to take a quick glance at sth/sb, to take a quick look at sth/sb

**ojear** *vt* to have a look at

**ojeras** *nfpl* bags under the eyes

**ojeriza** *nf Fam* dislike; **tener o. a alguien** to have it in for sb

**ojeroso, -a** *adj* with bags under the eyes, haggard

**ojete** *nm* (a) *(bordado)* eyelet (b) *muy Fam* arsehole

**ojiva** *nf* (a) *Arquit* ogive (b) *Mil* warhead

**ojo 1** *nm* (a) *Anat* eye; *también Fig* **poner los ojos en blanco** to roll one's eyes; **o. a la funerala** *o* **a la virulé** black eye; *Fig* **ojos de carnero (degollado)** pleading eyes; **ojos rasgados** almond eyes; **ojos saltones** popping eyes

(b) *(agujero) (de aguja)* eye; *(de puente)* span; **o. de la cerradura** keyhole

(c) *(expresiones)* **a o. (de buen cubero)** roughly, approximately; **a ojos vistas** visibly; **abrir los ojos a alguien** to open sb's eyes; **andar con (mucho) o.** to be (very) careful; **cerrar los ojos ante algo** *(ignorar)* to close one's eyes to sth; *Fam* **¡dichosos los ojos que te ven!** how lovely to see you again!; **echar el o. a algo** to have one's eye on sth; **en un abrir y cerrar de ojos** in the twinkling of an eye; **estar o. alerta** *o* **avizor** to be on the lookout; **mirar algo con buenos/malos ojos** to look favourably/unfavourably on sth; **no pegar o.** not to get a wink of sleep; **no quitar los ojos de encima a alguien** not to take one's eyes off sb; **tener ojos de lince** to have eyes like a hawk; **poner los ojos en alguien** to set one's sights on sb; **ser todo ojos** to be all eyes; **tener (buen) o.** to have a good eye; **tener o. clínico para algo** to be a good judge of sth; **sólo tiene ojos para él** she only has eyes for him; **costar un o. de la cara** to cost an arm and a leg; *Prov* **o. por o., diente por diente** an eye for an eye, a tooth for a tooth; *Prov* **ojos que no ven, corazón que no siente** what the eye doesn't

see, the heart doesn't grieve over; **o. de buey** *(ventana)* porthole; **o. de gallo** *(callo)* corn; **o. de pez** *Fot* fish-eye lens

**2** *interj* **¡o.!** be careful!, watch out!

**ojotas** *nfpl Méx* sandals

**OK, okey** [o'kei] *interj* OK

**okapi** *nm* okapi

**okupa** *nmf Fam* squatter

**ola** *nf* wave; **o. de calor** heatwave; **o. de frío** cold spell; **la nueva o.** the New Wave; **hacer la o.** to do the Mexican wave

**ole, olé** *interj* **¡o.!** bravo!

**oleada** *nf* (a) *(del mar)* swell (b) *Fig (de protestas, atentados)* wave

**oleaginoso, -a** *adj* oleaginous

**oleaje** *nm* waves

**óleo** *nm* oil (painting); **al ó.** in oils

**oleoducto** *nm* oil pipeline

**oleoso, -a** *adj* oily

**oler** [47] **1** *vt* to smell

**2** *vi* (a) *(despedir olor)* to smell (a of); **o. a rayos** to stink (to high heaven) (b) *Fig (parecer)* **o. a** to smack of

**3 olerse** *vpr Fig* **olerse algo** to sense sth

**olfatear** *vt* (a) *(olisquear)* to sniff (b) *Fig (barruntar)* to smell, to sense; **o. en** *(indagar)* to pry into

**olfativo, -a** *adj* olfactory

**olfato** *nm* (a) *(sentido)* sense of smell (b) *Fig (sagacidad)* nose, instinct; **tener o. para algo** to be a good judge of sth

**oligarca** *nmf* oligarch

**oligarquía** *nf* oligarchy

**oligárquico, -a** *adj* oligarchic

**oligoelemento** *nm* trace element

**oligofrenia** *nf* mental handicap

**oligofrénico, -a 1** *adj* mentally handicapped

**2** *nm,f* mentally handicapped person

**oligopolio** *nm Econ* oligopoly

**olimpiada, olimpíada** *nf* Olympiad, Olympic Games; **las olimpiadas** the Olympics

**olímpicamente** *adv Fam* **paso o. de ayudarlos** I'm damned if I'm going to help them

**olímpico, -a** *adj Dep* Olympic

**olimpismo** *nm* Olympic movement

**olisquear** *vt* to sniff (at)

**oliva** *nf* olive

**oliváceo, -a** *adj* olive

**olivar** *nm* olive grove

**olivarero, -a 1** *adj* olive; **el sector o.** the olive growing industry

**2** *nm,f* olive-grower

**olivo** *nm* olive tree

**olla** *nf* (**a**) *(cacerola)* pot; **o. exprés** *o* **a presión** pressure cooker; *Fig* **o. de grillos** bedlam, madhouse; *Culin* **o. podrida** stew (**b**) *muy Fam (cabeza)* bonce, noggin

**olmeda** *nf* elm grove

**olmo** *nm* elm (tree)

**olor** *nm* smell (**a** of); **o. corporal** body odour; *Fam* **en o. de multitud** enjoying popular acclaim

**oloroso, -a 1** *adj* fragrant
**2** *nm* oloroso (sherry)

**OLP** *nf* (*abrev de* **Organización para la Liberación de Palestina**) PLO

**olvidadizo, -a** *adj* forgetful

**olvidar 1** *vt* (**a**) *(en general)* to forget (**b**) *(dejarse)* to leave; **olvidé las llaves en la oficina** I left my keys at the office
**2 olvidarse** *vpr* (**a**) *(en general)* to forget; **olvidarse de algo/hacer algo** to forget sth/ to do sth (**b**) *(dejarse)* to leave; **me he olvidado el paraguas en el tren** I've left my umbrella on the train

**olvido** *nm* (**a**) *(de un nombre, hecho)* forgetting; **caer en el o.** to fall into oblivion (**b**) *(descuido)* oversight

**Omán** *n* Oman

**ombligo** *nm* (**a**) *Anat* navel (**b**) *Fig (centro)* centre; **mirarse el propio o.** to contemplate one's navel; **se cree el o. del mundo** he thinks the world revolves around him

**ombudsman** *nm inv* ombudsman

**ominoso, -a** *adj* abominable

**omisión** *nf* omission

**omiso, -a** *adj* **hacer caso o. de algo** to ignore sth, to pay no attention to sth

**omitir** *vt* to omit

**ómnibus** *nm inv* (**a**) *Ferroc* local train (**b**) *CSur (autocar)* intercity bus

**omnipotencia** *nf* omnipotence

**omnipotente** *adj* omnipotent

**omnipresente** *adj* omnipresent

**omnívoro, -a 1** *adj* omnivorous
**2** *nm,f* omnivore

**omoplato, omóplato** *nm* shoulder-blade

**OMS** [oms] *nf* (*abrev de* **Organización Mundial de la Salud**) WHO

**onanismo** *nm* onanism

**ONCE** ['onθe] *nf* (*abrev de* **Organización Nacional de Ciegos Españoles**) = Spanish association for the blind, famous for its national lottery

**once 1** *núm* eleven; *ver también* **seis**
**2** *nm CSur* onces mid-morning snack

**onceavo, -a** *núm (fracción)* eleventh; **la onceava parte** an eleventh

**oncología** *nf* oncology

**oncólogo, -a** *nm,f* oncologist

**onda** *nf* wave; **o. corta/larga/media** short/ long/medium wave; **o. eléctrica** *o* **hertziana** Hertzian wave; **o. expansiva** shock wave; **o. luminosa/sonora** light/sound wave; *Fam* **estar en la o.** to be on the ball; *Fam* **me da mala o.** I've got bad vibes about him/her/it; *Fam* **tus primos tienen muy buena o.** your cousins are really cool

**ondeante** *adj* rippling

**ondear** *vi (bandera)* to flutter, to fly

**ondulación** *nf* (**a**) *(acción)* rippling (**b**) *(onda)* ripple; *(del pelo)* wave

**ondulado, -a** *adj* wavy

**ondulante** *adj* undulating

**ondular 1** *vi (agua)* to ripple; *(terreno)* to undulate
**2** *vt (pelo)* to wave

**ondulatorio, -a** *adj* wavelike

**oneroso, -a** *adj* (**a**) *(pesado)* burdensome, onerous (**b**) *(caro)* costly, expensive

**ONG** *nf inv* (*abrev de* **Organización no Gubernamental**) NGO

**ónice** *nm o nf* onyx

**onírico, -a** *adj* dreamlike; **experiencia onírica** dreamlike experience

**ónix** *nm o nf* onyx

**onomástica** *nf* name day

**onomástico, -a** *adj* onomastic

**onomatopeya** *nf* onomatopoeia

**onomatopéyico, -a** *adj* onomatopoeic

**Ontario** *nm* **el lago O.** Lake Ontario

**ontología** *nf* ontology

**ONU** ['onu] *nf* (*abrev de* **Organización de las Naciones Unidas**) UN

**onubense 1** *adj* of/from Huelva
**2** *nmf* person from Huelva

**ONUDI** [o'nuði] *nf* (*abrev de* **Organización de las Naciones Unidas para el Desarrollo Industrial**) UNIDO

**onza** *nf* (**a**) *(unidad de peso)* ounce (**b**) *(de chocolate)* square (**c**) *(guepardo)* cheetah

**op.** (*abrev de* **opus**) op.

**OPA** ['opa] *nf* (*abrev de* **oferta pública de adquisición**) takeover bid

**opacidad** *nf* también *Fig* opacity

**opaco, -a** *adj* opaque

**opalescente** *adj* opalescent

**opalina** *nf* opaline

**opalino, -a** *adj* opaline

**ópalo** *nm* opal

**opción** *nf* (**a**) *(elección)* option; **no hay o.** there is no alternative (**b**) *(derecho)* right; **dar o. a** to give the right to; **tener o. a** *(empleo, cargo)* to be eligible for

**opcional** *adj* optional

**open** *nm Dep* Open (tournament)

**OPEP** [o'pep] *nf* (*abrev de* **Organización de Países Exportadores de Petróleo**) OPEC

**ópera** *nf* opera; **ó. bufa** comic opera, opera buffa; **ó. prima** (*novela, película*) first work; **ó. rock** rock opera

**operación** *nf* (a) (*en general*) operation; **o. quirúrgica** (surgical) operation; **o. retorno/ salida** = police operation to assist traffic at the end/beginning of popular holiday periods (b) *Com* transaction

**operacional** *adj* operational

**operador, -ora 1** *nm,f* (a) *Informát & Telecom* operator (b) (*de la cámara*) cameraman; (*del proyector*) projectionist

**2** *nm* (a) **o. turístico** tour operator (b) *Mat* operator

**operar 1** *vt* (a) (*enfermo*) **o. a alguien (de algo)** (*enfermedad*) to operate on sb (for sth); **le operaron del hígado** they've operated on his liver (b) (*cambio*) to bring about, to produce

**2** *vi* to operate

**3 operarse** *vpr* (a) (*enfermo*) to be operated on, to have an operation; **operarse de algo** to be operated on for sth; **me voy a o. del hígado** I'm going to have an operation on my liver (b) (*cambio*) to occur, to come about

**operario, -a** *nm,f* worker

**operatividad** *nf* preparedness

**operativo, -a** *adj* operative

**opereta** *nf* operetta

**operístico, -a** *adj* operatic

**opiáceo, -a** *adj & nm* opiate

**opinar 1** *vt* to believe, to think

**2** *vi* to give one's opinion; **o. de algo/alguien, o. sobre algo/alguien** to think about sth/sb; **o. bien de alguien** to think highly of sb

**opinión** *nf* opinion; **expresar o dar una o.** to give an opinion; **reservarse la o.** to reserve judgment; **tener buena/mala o. de alguien** to have a high/low opinion of sb; **la o. pública** public opinion

**opio** *nm* opium

**opíparo, -a** *adj* sumptuous

**opondré** *etc ver* **oponer**

**oponente** *nmf* opponent

**oponer** [52] **1** *vt* (a) (*resistencia*) to put up (b) (*argumento, razón*) to put forward, to give

**2 oponerse** *vpr* (a) (*no estar de acuerdo*) to be opposed; **oponerse a algo** (*desaprobar*) to be opposed to sth, to oppose sth; (*contradecir*) to contradict sth; **me opongo a creerlo** I refuse to believe it (b) (*obstaculizar*) **oponerse a** to stand in the way of, to impede

**Oporto** *n* Oporto

**oporto** *nm* port (wine)

**oportunidad** *nf* (a) (*ocasión*) opportunity, chance; **aprovechar la o.** to seize the opportunity (b) (*conveniencia*) timeliness

**oportunismo** *nm* opportunism

**oportunista 1** *adj* opportunistic

**2** *nmf* opportunist

**oportuno, -a** *adj* (a) (*pertinente*) appropriate (b) (*propicio*) timely; **el momento o.** the right time

**oposición** *nf* (a) (*en general*) opposition; **los partidos de la o.** the opposition parties (b) (*resistencia*) resistance (c) (*examen*) = competitive public examination for employment in the civil service, education, legal system etc; **o. a profesor** = public examination to obtain a state teaching post; **preparar oposiciones** to be studying for a public examination

**opositar** *vi* = to sit a public entrance examination

**opositor, -ora** *nm,f* (a) (*a un cargo*) = candidate in a public entrance examination (b) (*oponente*) opponent

**opresión** *nf* (a) (*represión*) oppression (b) *Fig* (*molestia, ahogo*) **sentía una o. en el pecho** he felt a tightness in his chest

**opresivo, -a** *adj* oppressive

**opresor, -ora 1** *adj* oppressive

**2** *nm,f* oppressor

**oprimir** *vt* (a) (*apretar*) (*botón*) to press; (*garganta, brazo*) to squeeze; **la corbata le oprimía el cuello** his tie felt too tight (b) *Fig* (*reprimir*) to oppress (c) *Fig* (*angustiar*) to weigh down on, to burden

**oprobio** *nm* shame, disgrace

**optar** *vi* (a) (*escoger*) **o. (por algo)** to choose (sth); **o. por hacer algo** to choose to do sth; **o. entre** to choose between (b) (*aspirar*) **o. a** to aim for, to go for; **optan al puesto siete candidatos** there are seven candidates for the job

**optativa** *nf Educ* option, optional subject

**optativo, -a** *adj* optional

**óptica** *nf* (a) *Fís* optics (b) (*tienda*) optician's (shop) (c) *Fig* (*punto de vista*) point of view

**óptico, -a 1** *adj* optic

**2** *nm,f* (*persona*) optician

**optimismo** *nm* optimism

**optimista 1** *adj* optimistic

**2** *nmf* optimist

**optimización** *nf* optimization

**optimizar** *vt* to optimize

**óptimo, -a 1** *superlativo ver* **bueno**

**2** *adj* optimum

**opuesto, -a 1** *participio ver* **oponer**

**2** *adj* (**a**) *(contrario)* opposed, contrary (**a** to); **los dos hermanos son opuestos en todo** the two brothers are completely different; **opiniones opuestas** contrary *o* opposing opinions (**b**) *(del otro lado)* opposite

**opulencia** *nf (riqueza)* opulence; *(abundancia)* abundance; **vivir en la o.** to live in luxury; **nadar en la o.** to be filthy rich

**opulento, -a** *adj* (**a**) *(rico)* opulent (**b**) *(abundante)* abundant

**opus** *nm inv Mús* opus; **el O. Dei** the Opus Dei, = traditionalist religious organization, whose members include many professional people and public figures

**opúsculo** *nm* short work

**opusiera** *etc ver* **oponer**

**oquedad** *nf (cavidad)* hole; *(en pared)* recess

**ora** *conj* **o.... o....** now... now...

**oración** *nf* (**a**) *(rezo)* prayer; **o. fúnebre** memorial speech (**b**) *Gram* sentence; **o. principal/subordinada** main/subordinate clause

**oráculo** *nm* (**a**) *(mensaje, divinidad)* oracle (**b**) *Fig (persona)* fount of wisdom

**orador, -ora** *nm,f* speaker

**oral 1** *adj* oral

**2** *nm (examen)* oral exam

**órale** *interj Méx Fam* **¡ó.!** come on!

**orangután** *nm* orangutang

**orar** *vi* to pray

**oratoria** *nf* oratory

**oratorio, -a 1** *adj* oratorical

**2** *nm* (**a**) *(lugar)* oratory (**b**) *Mús* oratorio

**orbe** *nm* world, globe

**órbita** *nf* (**a**) *Astron* orbit; **entrar/poner en ó.** to go/put into orbit (**b**) *(de ojo)* eye socket (**c**) *Fig (ámbito)* sphere, realm

**orca** *nf* killer whale

**órdago** *nm* = all-or-nothing stake in the game of "mus"; *Fig* **de ó.** magnificent

**orden 1** *nm* (**a**) *(secuencia, categoría)* order; **en o.** *(bien colocado)* tidy, in its place; *(como debe ser)* in order; **llamar al o. a alguien** to call sb to order; **poner en o. algo** to tidy sth up; **por o.** in order; **sin o. ni concierto** in a haphazard way; **las fuerzas del o.** the forces of law and order; *Com* **o. de compra** purchase order; **o. del día** agenda; **o. público** law and order (**b**) *(tipo)* type, order; **problemas de o. económico** economic problems; **del o. de** around, approximately, of *o* in the order of; **en otro o. de cosas** on the other hand

**2** *nf* order; *Mil* **¡a la o.!, ¡a sus órdenes!** (yes) sir!; **dar órdenes** to give orders; **estar a la o. del día** to be the order of the day; **por o. de** by order of; **o. de busca y captura** warrant for search and arrest; **o. de caballería** order of knighthood; **o. de pago** payment order; **o. militar** military order

**ordenación** *nf* (**a**) *(organización)* ordering, arranging; *(disposición)* order, arrangement; *(de recursos, edificios)* planning; **o. territorial** administrative structure (**b**) *Rel* ordination

**ordenada** *nf Mat* ordinate

**ordenadamente** *adv (desfilar, salir)* in an orderly fashion *o* manner; *(colocar)* neatly

**ordenado, -a** *adj* (**a**) *(lugar, persona)* tidy (**b**) *(sacerdote)* ordained

**ordenador** *nm Informát* computer; **pasar algo a o.** to type sth up on a wordprocessor *o* computer; **o. central** mainframe computer; **o. personal** personal computer; **o. portátil** laptop computer

**ordenamiento** *nm* legislation, regulations

**ordenanza 1** *nm* (**a**) *(de oficina)* messenger (**b**) *Mil* orderly

**2** *nf* ordinance, law; **ordenanzas municipales** by-laws

**ordenar 1** *vt* (**a**) *(poner en orden) (alfabéticamente, numéricamente)* to arrange, to put in order; *(habitación, papeles)* to tidy (up) (**b**) *(mandar)* to order (**c**) *Rel* to ordain

**2 ordenarse** *vpr Rel* to be ordained

**ordeñadora** *nf* milking machine

**ordeñar** *vt* to milk

**ordeño** *nm* milking

**ordinal 1** *adj* ordinal

**2** *nm (número)* ordinal (number)

**ordinariez** *nf* commonness, coarseness; **decir/hacer una o.** to say/do something rude; **¡qué o.!** how vulgar!

**ordinario, -a 1** *adj* (**a**) *(común)* ordinary, usual; **de o.** usually (**b**) *(vulgar)* common, coarse (**c**) *(no selecto)* unexceptional (**d**) *(correo)* ≃ second class; *(tribunal)* of first instance

**2** *nm,f* common *o* coarse person

**orear 1** *vt* to air

**2 orearse** *vpr (ventilarse)* to air

**orégano** *nm* oregano

**oreja** *nf* (**a**) *Anat* ear; **calentarle a alguien las orejas** to box sb's ears; **con las orejas gachas** with one's tail between one's legs; **tirar a alguien de las orejas** to give sb a good telling-off; **verle las orejas al lobo** to see what's coming; **orejas de soplillo** stick-out ears (**b**) *(de sillón)* wing

**orejera** *nf (en gorra)* earflap; **orejeras** earmuffs

**orejón, -ona 1** *adj* big-eared

**2** *nm (dulce)* dried apricot/peach

**orejudo, -a** *adj* big-eared

**orensano, -a 1** *adj* of/from Orense

**2** *nm,f* person from Orense

**orfanato** *nm* orphanage

**orfandad** *nf* orphanhood; *Fig* abandonment, neglect

**orfebre** *nmf* *(de plata)* silversmith; *(de oro)* goldsmith

**orfebrería** *nf* (a) *(objetos) (de plata)* silver work; *(de oro)* gold work (b) *(oficio) (de plata)* silversmithing; *(de oro)* goldsmithing

**orfelinato** *nm* orphanage

**orfeón** *nm* choral group *o* society

**organdí** *(pl* organdíes*) nm* organdie

**orgánico, -a** *adj* organic

**organigrama** *nm también Informát* flowchart

**organillero, -a** *nm,f* organ-grinder

**organillo** *nm* barrel organ

**organismo** *nm* (a) *Biol* organism (b) *Anat* body (c) *Fig (entidad)* organization, body

**organista** *nmf* organist

**organización** *nf* organization

**organizador, -ora 1** *adj* organizing
**2** *nm,f* organizer

**organizar** [16] **1** *vt* to organize
**2 organizarse** *vpr* (a) *(persona)* to organize oneself (b) *(pelea, lío)* to break out, to happen suddenly

**organizativo, -a** *adj* organizing

**órgano** *nm* organ

**orgasmo** *nm* orgasm

**orgía** *nf* orgy

**orgiástico, -a** *adj* orgiastic

**orgullo** *nm* pride

**orgulloso, -a 1** *adj* proud
**2** *nm,f* proud person

**orientación** *nf* (a) *(dirección) (acción)* guiding; *(rumbo)* direction; **sentido de la o.** sense of direction (b) *(posicionamiento) (acción)* positioning; *(lugar)* position (c) *Fig (información)* guidance; **o. profesional** careers advice *o* guidance (d) *Fig (tendencia)* tendency, leaning; **o. sexual** sexual orientation

**oriental 1** *adj* (a) *(del este)* eastern; *(del Lejano Oriente)* oriental (b) *Arg (uruguayo)* Uruguayan
**2** *nmf* (a) *(del Lejano Oriente)* oriental (b) *Arg (uruguayo)* Uruguayan

**orientalismo** *nm* orientalism

**orientalista** *nmf* orientalist

**orientar 1** *vt* (a) *(dirigir)* to direct; **mi ventana está orientada hacia el sur** my window faces south *o* is south-facing (b) *Fig (aconsejar)* to give advice *o* guidance to (c) *Fig (medidas, fondos)* **o. hacia** to direct towards *o* at
**2 orientarse** *vpr* (a) *(dirigirse) (foco)* **orientarse a** to point towards *o* at (b) *(encontrar el camino)* to get one's bearings, to find one's way around (c) *Fig (encaminarse)* **orientarse hacia** to be aiming at

**oriente** *nm* east; **el O.** the East, the Orient; **O. Medio/Próximo** Middle/Near East; **Lejano** *o* **Extremo O.** Far East

**orificio** *nm* hole; *Mec* opening

**origen** *nm* (a) *(principio)* origin; *(ascendencia)* origins, birth; **de o. español** of Spanish origin (b) *(causa)* cause; **dar o. a** to give rise to

**original 1** *adj* (a) *(nuevo, primero)* original (b) *(raro)* eccentric, different
**2** *nm* original

**originalidad** *nf* (a) *(novedad)* originality (b) *(extravagancia)* eccentricity

**originar 1** *vt* to cause
**2 originarse** *vpr* *(acontecimiento)* to (first) start; *(costumbre, leyenda)* to originate

**originario, -a** *adj* (a) *(inicial, primitivo)* original (b) *(procedente)* **ser o. de** to come from (originally)

**orilla** *nf* (a) *(ribera) (de río)* bank; *(de mar)* shore; **a orillas de** *(río)* on the banks of; **a orillas del mar** by the sea (b) *(borde)* edge (c) *(acera)* pavement

**orillar** *vt* (a) *(dificultad, obstáculo)* to skirt around (b) *(tela)* to edge

**orín** *nm* *(herrumbre)* rust; **orines** *(orina)* urine

**orina** *nf* urine

**orinal** *nm* chamberpot

**orinar 1** *vi & vt* to urinate
**2 orinarse** *vpr* to wet oneself; **orinarse en la cama** to wet the bed

**Orinoco** *nm* **el O.** the Orinoco

**oriundo, -a 1** *adj* **o. de** native of
**2** *nm,f* *Dep* = non-Spanish footballer whose mother *o* father is Spanish

**orla** *nf* (a) *(adorno) (decorative)* trimming (b) *(fotografía)* graduation photograph

**orlar** *vt* to decorate with trimmings

**ornamentación** *nf* ornamentation

**ornamental** *adj* *(de adorno)* ornamental; *Fig (inútil)* merely decorative

**ornamentar** *vt* to decorate, to adorn

**ornamento** *nm* *(objeto)* ornament; *Rel* **ornamentos** vestments

**ornar** *vt* to decorate, to adorn

**ornato** *nm* decoration

**ornitología** *nf* ornithology

**ornitólogo, -a** *nm,f* ornithologist

**ornitorrinco** *nm* duck-billed platypus

**oro** *nm* gold; *Fig* money, riches; **de o.** gold; **guardar algo como o. en paño** to treasure sth; **hacerse de o.** to make one's fortune; **no es o. todo lo que reluce** all that glitters is not gold; **pedir el o. y el moro** to ask the earth; **oros** *(naipes)* = suit in Spanish deck of cards, with the symbol of a gold coin; **o. en barras** bullion; **o. negro** oil; **o. en polvo** gold dust

**orogénesis** *nf inv* orogenesis

**orografía** *nf* (a) *Geog* orography (b) *(relieve)* terrain

**orondo, -a** *adj Fam* (a) *(gordo)* plump (b) *(satisfecho)* self-satisfied, smug

**oropel** *nm Fig* glitter, glitz

**oropéndola** *nf* golden oriole

**orquesta** *nf* (a) *(músicos)* orchestra; **o. de cámara/sinfónica** chamber/symphony orchestra (b) *(lugar)* orchestra pit

**orquestación** *nf* orchestration

**orquestar** *vt también Fig* to orchestrate

**orquestina** *nf* dance band

**orquídea** *nf* orchid

**ortiga** *nf* (stinging) nettle

**ortodoncia** *nf* orthodontics *(singular);* **hacerse la o.** to have orthodontic work done

**ortodoxia** *nf* orthodoxy

**ortodoxo, -a 1** *adj* orthodox
  **2** *nm,f Rel* member of the Orthodox Church

**ortografía** *nf* spelling

**ortográfico, -a** *adj* spelling; **reglas ortográficas** spelling rules

**ortopedia** *nf* orthopaedics *(singular)*

**ortopédico, -a** *adj* (a) *(zapato, corsé)* orthopaedic; **pierna ortopédica** artificial leg (b) *Fam Fig (deforme)* misshapen

**ortopedista** *nmf* orthopaedist

**oruga** *nf* caterpillar

**orujo** *nm* = strong spirit made from grape pressings

**orzuelo** *nm* stye

**os** *pron personal* (a) *(complemento directo)* you; **me gustaría veros** I'd like to see you (b) *(complemento indirecto)* (to) you; **os lo dio** he gave it to you; **os tengo miedo** I'm afraid of you (c) *(reflexivo)* yourselves; **os vestís** you get (yourselves) dressed (d) *(recíproco)* each other; **os enamorasteis** you fell in love (with each other)

**osa** *nf ver* **oso**

**osadía** *nf* (a) *(valor)* boldness, daring (b) *(descaro)* audacity, cheek

**osado, -a** *adj* (a) *(valeroso)* daring, bold (b) *(descarado)* impudent, cheeky

**osamenta** *nf* skeleton

**osar** *vi* to dare

**osario** *nm* ossuary

**Óscar** *nm Cine* Oscar

**oscense 1** *adj* of/from Huesca
  **2** *nmf* person from Huesca

**oscilación** *nf* (a) *(movimiento)* swinging; *Fís* oscillation (b) *(espacio recorrido)* swing (c) *Fig (variación)* fluctuation

**oscilador** *nm* oscillator

**oscilar** *vi* (a) *(moverse)* to swing; *Fís* to oscillate (b) *Fig (variar)* to fluctuate; **el precio oscila entre las mil y las dos mil pesetas** the price can be anything between one and two thousand pesetas

**oscilatorio, -a** *adj* swinging; *Fís* oscillating

**ósculo** *nm Formal* kiss

**oscurantismo** *nm* obscurantism

**oscurecer** [48] **1** *vt* (a) *(privar de luz)* to darken (b) *Fig (mente)* to confuse, to cloud (c) *Fig (deslucir)* to overshadow
  **2** *v impersonal (anochecer)* to get dark
  **3 oscurecerse** *vpr* to grow dark

**oscurecimiento** *nm* darkening

**oscuridad** *nf* (a) *(falta de luz)* darkness (b) *(zona oscura)* **en la o.** in the dark (c) *Fig (falta de claridad)* obscurity

**oscuro, -a** *adj* (a) *(sin luz)* dark; **a oscuras** in the dark (b) *(nublado)* overcast (c) *Fig (infrecuente)* obscure (d) *Fig (incierto)* uncertain, unclear (e) *Fig (intenciones, asunto)* shady

**óseo, -a** *adj* bone; **médula ósea** bone marrow; **esqueleto ó.** bony skeleton

**osezno** *nm* bear cub

**osificarse** [61] *vpr* to ossify

**Oslo** *n* Oslo

**osmosis, ósmosis** *nf inv Fís & Fig* osmosis

**oso, -a** *nm,f* bear, **f** she-bear; **hacer el o.** to act the fool; *Fam* **¡anda la osa!** well I never!, upon my word!; **o. de felpa** *o* **peluche** teddy bear; **o. hormiguero** ant-eater; **Osa Mayor** Great Bear; **Osa Menor** Little Bear; **o. panda** panda; **o. polar** polar bear

**osobuco** *nm Culin* osso bucco

**ostensible** *adj* evident, clear

**ostentación** *nf* ostentation, show; **hacer o. de algo** to show sth off, to parade sth

**ostentador, -ora** *nm,f* show-off, ostentatious person

**ostentar** *vt* (a) *(poseer)* to hold, to have (b) *(exhibir)* to show off, to parade (c) *(cargo)* to hold, to occupy

**ostentoso, -a** *adj* ostentatious

**osteópata** *nmf* osteopath

**osteopatía** *nf (terapia)* osteopathy

**osteoplastia** *nf* osteoplasty

**osteoporosis** *nf inv* osteoporosis

**ostra 1** *nf* oyster; *Fam* **aburrirse como una o.** to be bored stiff
  **2** *interj Fam* **¡ostras!** blimey!

**ostracismo** *nm* ostracism; **o. político** political wilderness

**OTAN** ['otan] *nf (abrev de* **Organización del Tratado del Atlántico Norte)** NATO

**otear** *vt* to survey, to scan; *Fig* to study

**otero** *nm* hillock

**OTI** ['oti] *nf* (*abrev de* **Organización de Televisiones Iberoamericanas**) = association of all Spanish-speaking television networks; **el festival de la O.** = televised song competition across the Spanish-speaking world

**otitis** *nf inv* inflammation of the ear

**otomano, -a** *adj & nm,f* Ottoman

**otoñal** *adj Br* autumn, *Br* autumnal, *US* fall; **viento o.** autumn wind

**otoño** *nm también Fig Br* autumn, *US* fall

**otorgamiento** *nm* (*de favor, petición*) granting; (*de premio, beca*) award; *Der* (*de documento*) execution

**otorgar** [40] *vt* (*favor, petición*) to grant; (*honor, título*) to confer; (*premio, beca*) to award, to present; *Der* to execute

**otorrino, -a** *nm,f Fam* ear, nose and throat specialist

**otorrinolaringología** *nf* ear, nose and throat medicine

**otorrinolaringólogo, -a** *nm,f* ear, nose and throat specialist

**otro, -a 1** *adj* (a) (*distinto*) another; **otros/otras** other; **o. chico** another boy; **el o. chico** the other boy; **(los) otros chicos** (the) other boys; **no hacer otra cosa que llorar** to do nothing but cry; **el o. día** (*pasado*) the other day (b) (*nuevo*) another; **estamos ante o. Dalí** this is another Dalí; **otros tres goles** another three goals; **yo hubiera hecho o. tanto** I would have done just the same

**2** *pron* another (one); **otros/otras** others; **dame o.** give me another (one); **el o.** the other one; **(los) otros** (the) others; **yo no lo hice, fue o.** it wasn't me, it was somebody else; **o. habría abandonado, pero no él** anyone else would have given up, but not him; **¡o. que tal!** there's another one! **¡otra!** (*en conciertos*) encore!, more!; **¡hasta otra!** see you again!

**otrora** *adv Formal* formerly

**otrosí** *adv Formal* besides, moreover

**Ottawa** [o'tawa] *n* Ottawa

**OUA** *nf* (*abrev de* **Organización para la Unidad Africana**) OAU

**ouija** [u'iχa] *nf* (*mesa*) ouija board

**output** ['autput] (*pl* **outputs**) *nm Informát* output

**ovación** *nf* ovation

**ovacionar** *vt* to give an ovation to, to applaud

**oval** *adj* oval

**ovalado, -a** *adj* oval

**óvalo** *nm* oval

**ovárico** *adj* ovarian

**ovario** *nm* ovary

**oveja** *nf* sheep, ewe; **o. descarriada** lost sheep; **o. negra** black sheep

**overbooking** [oβer'βukin] (*pl* **overbookings**) *nm* overbooking

**ovetense 1** *adj* of/from Oviedo

**2** *nmf* person from Oviedo

**Oviedo** *n* Oviedo

**ovillar 1** *vt* to roll *o* wind into a ball

**2 ovillarse** *vpr* to curl up into a ball

**ovillo** *nm* ball (*of wool etc*); **hacerse un o.** to curl up into a ball

**ovino, -a** *adj* sheep; **productos ovinos** sheep products

**ovíparo, -a** *adj* oviparous

**ovni** *nm* (*abrev de* **objeto volador no identificado**) UFO

**ovoide** *adj* ovoid

**ovulación** *nf* ovulation

**ovular 1** *adj* ovular

**2** *vi* to ovulate

**óvulo** *nm* ovum

**oxidación** *nf* rusting

**oxidante 1** *adj* oxidizing

**2** *nm* oxidizing agent

**oxidar 1** *vt* to rust; *Quím* to oxidize

**2 oxidarse** *vpr también Fig* to get rusty

**óxido** *nm* (a) *Quím* oxide (b) (*herrumbre*) rust

**oxigenación** *nf* oxygenation

**oxigenado, -a** *adj* (a) *Quím* oxygenated (b) (*cabello*) peroxide; **una rubia oxigenada** a peroxide blonde

**oxigenar 1** *vt Quím* to oxygenate

**2 oxigenarse** *vpr* (a) (*airearse*) to get a breath of fresh air (b) (*cabello*) to bleach

**oxígeno** *nm* oxygen

**oye** *ver* **oír**

**oyente** *nmf* (a) *Radio* listener (b) (*alumno*) = student who attends a course but is not assessed

**oyera** *etc ver* **oír**

**ozono** *nm* ozone

**ozonosfera** *nf* ozonosphere

# P

**P, p** [pe] *nf (letra)* P, p

**p.** *(abrev de* **página)** p

**p.a. (a)** *(abrev de* **por ausencia) (b)** *(abrev de* **por autorización)** pp

**pabellón** *nm* **(a)** *(edificio)* pavilion **(b)** *(parte de un edificio)* block, section **(c)** *(en parques, jardines)* summerhouse **(d)** *(tienda de campaña)* bell tent **(e)** *(dosel)* canopy **(f)** *(bandera)* flag **(g) p. auditivo** outer ear

**pabilo, pábilo** *nm* wick

**pábulo: dar pábulo a** *loc verbal* to feed, to encourage

**PAC** [pak] *nf (abrev de* **política agrícola común)** CAP

**pacato, -a 1** *adj* **(a)** *(mojigato)* prudish **(b)** *(tímido)* shy

**2** *nm,f (mojigato)* prude

**pacense 1** *adj* of/from Badajoz

**2** *nmf* person from Badajoz

**paceño, -a 1** *adj* of/from La Paz

**2** *nm,f* person from La Paz

**pacer** [44] *vi* to graze

**pachá** *nm* pasha; *Fam* **vivir como un p.** to live like a lord

**pachanga** *nf Fam* rowdy celebration

**pachanguero, -a** *adj Fam (música)* catchy but mindless

**pacharán** *nm* = liqueur made from brandy and sloes

**pachorra** *nf Fam* calmness

**pachucho, -a** *adj Fam* off-colour

**pachulí** *(pl* **pachulíes)** *nm* patchouli

**paciencia** *nf* patience; **armarse de p.** to summon up one's patience; **perder la p.** to lose one's patience; **tener más p. que un santo** to have the patience of a saint; **tener p.** to be patient

**paciente** *adj & nmf* patient

**pacienzudo, -a** *adj* patient

**pacificación** *nf* pacification

**pacificar** [61] **1** *vt* **(a)** *(país)* to pacify **(b)** *(ánimos)* to calm

**2 pacificarse** *vpr (persona)* to calm down

**Pacífico 1** *nm* **el P.** the Pacific (Ocean)

**2** *adj* **el océano P.** the Pacific Ocean

**pacífico, -a** *adj (vida, relaciones)* peaceful; *(persona)* peaceable

**pacifismo** *nm* pacifism

**pacifista** *adj & nmf* pacifist

**pack** [pak] *(pl* **packs)** *nm* pack; **un p. de seis** a six-pack

**paco, -a** *nm,f Andes Fam* cop

**pacotilla: de pacotilla** *loc adj* trashy, third-rate

**pactar 1** *vt* to agree to; **p. un acuerdo** to reach an agreement

**2** *vi* to strike a deal **(con** with)

**pacto** *nm* agreement, pact; **hacer/romper un p.** to make/break an agreement; **p. electoral** electoral pact; **p. social** social contract

**padecer** [48] **1** *vt* to suffer, to endure; *(enfermedad)* to suffer from

**2** *vi* to suffer; *(enfermedad)* **p. del corazón/riñón** to suffer from a heart/kidney complaint

**padecimiento** *nm* suffering

**pádel** *nm Dep* = recently invented game similar to tennis, but where the ball can be bounced off the walls of the court

**padezca** *etc ver* **padecer**

**padrastro** *nm* **(a)** *(pariente)* stepfather **(b)** *(pellejo)* hangnail

**padrazo** *nm Fam* adoring father

**padre 1** *nm también Rel* father; **p. de familia** head of the family; **p. espiritual** confessor; *Rel* **Padres de la Iglesia** Fathers of the Christian Church; *Rel* **Santo P.** Holy Father, Pope; *Fam* **de p. y muy señor mío** incredible, tremendous

**2** *adj inv Fam* incredible, tremendous; *Méx* great; **fue el cachondeo p.** it was a great laugh

**3** *nmpl* **padres (a)** *(padre y madre)* parents **(b)** *(antepasados)* ancestors, forefathers

**padrenuestro** *nm* Lord's Prayer; **saberse algo como el p.** to know sth by heart, to have sth off pat

**padrino** *nm* **(a)** *(de bautismo)* godfather; *(de boda)* best man; **padrinos** *(padrino y madrina)* godparents **(b)** *(en duelos, torneos)* second **(c)** *Fig (protector)* patron

**padrísimo, -a** *adj Méx Fam* fantastic, great

**padrón** *nm (censo)* census; *(para votar)* electoral roll *o* register

**padrote** *nm Méx Fam* pimp

**paella** *nf* paella

**paellera** *nf* = large frying-pan for cooking paella

**paf** *interj* bang!, crash!

**pág.** *(abrev de* **página**) p

**paga** *nf (salario)* salary, wages; *(de niño)* pocket money; **p. extra** *o* **extraordinaria** = additional payment of a month's salary or wages made to Spanish workers in June and December

**pagadero, -a** *adj* payable; **p. a 90 días/a la entrega** payable within 90 days/on delivery

**pagado, -a** *adj* paid; **p. de sí mismo** pleased with oneself

**pagador, -ora 1** *adj* paying; **ser buen/mal p.** to be a reliable/unreliable payer

**2** *nm,f (de obreros)* paymaster

**paganismo** *nm* paganism

**pagano, -a** *adj & nm,f* pagan, heathen

**pagar** [40] **1** *vt (empleado, persona)* to pay; *(deuda)* to pay off, to settle; *(factura, gastos, delito)* to pay for; *(ayuda, favor)* to repay; **su padre le paga los estudios** his father is supporting him through college/university; **yo pago la cena** I'll pay for dinner; *Fam Fig* **me las pagarás** you'll pay for this; **el que la hace la paga** he/she/*etc* will pay for it in the end

**2** *vi* to pay

**pagaré** *(pl* pagarés) *nm Com* promissory note, IOU; **p. del Tesoro** Treasury note

**pagel** *nm* sea bream

**página** *nf* page; **las páginas amarillas** the Yellow Pages; *Informát* **p. web** Web page

**paginación** *nf* pagination

**paginar** *vt Informát* to paginate

**pago** *nm* (a) *(de dinero)* payment; *Fig* reward, payment; **en p. de** *o* **a** *(en recompensa por)* as a reward for; *(a cambio de)* in return for; **p. anticipado/inicial** advance/down payment (b) *(lugar)* **por estos pagos** around here (c) *Am (finca)* homestead

**pagoda** *nf* pagoda

**pague** *etc ver* **pagar**

**paila** *nf* (a) *Am (sartén)* frying pan (b) *Chile (huevos fritos)* fried eggs

**paipái** *(pl* paipáis), **paipay** *(pl* paipays) *nm* = rigid circular fan with handle

**país** *(pl* países) *nm* country; **los Países Bajos** the Netherlands; **los países bálticos** the Baltic States; **p. natal** native country, homeland; **p. satélite** satellite state; **países desarrollados/en vías de desarrollo/subdesarrollados** developed/developing/underdeveloped countries; **el P. Valenciano** the autonomous region of Valencia; **el P. Vasco** the Basque Country

**paisaje** *nm (pintura, terreno)* landscape; *(vista panorámica)* scenery, view

**paisajista 1** *adj* landscape; **pintor p.** landscape painter

**2** *nmf* landscape painter

**paisajístico, -a** *adj* landscape; **belleza paisajística** natural beauty

**paisanaje** *nm* civilians

**paisano, -a 1** *adj (del mismo país)* from the same country

**2** *nm,f* (a) *(del mismo país) (hombre)* compatriot, fellow countryman; *(mujer)* compatriot, fellow countrywoman (b) *(campesino)* country person, peasant

**3** *nm (civil)* civilian; **de p.** *(militar)* in civilian clothes; *(policía)* in plain clothes

**paja** *nf* (a) *(hierba, caña)* straw; *Fig (relleno)* waffle (b) *muy Fam (masturbación)* wank; **hacerse una p.** to have a wank

**pajar** *nm* straw loft

**pájara** *nf Fig* crafty *o* sly woman

**pajarera** *nf* aviary

**pajarería** *nf* pet shop

**pajarita** *nf* (a) *(corbata)* bow tie (b) *(de papel)* paper bird

**pájaro** *nm* (a) *(ave)* bird; **p. de mal agüero** bird of ill omen; *Fig* **matar dos pájaros de un tiro** to kill two birds with one stone; *Fig* **tener pájaros en la cabeza** to be scatterbrained *o* empty-headed; *Prov* **más vale p. en mano que ciento volando** a bird in the hand is worth two in the bush; **p. bobo** penguin; **p. carpintero** woodpecker (b) *Fig (persona)* crafty devil, sly old fox

**pajarraco** *nm Pey* (a) *(pájaro)* big ugly bird (b) *(persona)* nasty piece of work

**paje** *nm* page

**pajita, pajilla** *nf (drinking)* straw

**pajizo, -a** *adj (color, pelo)* straw-coloured

**pajolero, -a** *adj muy Fam* damn, blessed; **no tengo ni pajolera idea** I haven't the foggiest

**Pakistán** *n* Pakistan

**pakistaní** *(pl* pakistaníes) *adj & nmf* Pakistani

**pala** *nf* (a) *(herramienta)* spade; *(para recoger)* shovel; *Culin* slice; **p. mecánica** *o* **excavadora** excavator, digger (b) *(de frontón, ping-pong)* bat; **jugar a las palas** *(en la playa)* to play beach tennis (c) *(de remo, hélice)* blade (d) *(diente)* (upper) front tooth

**palabra** nf (a) *(en general)* word; **de p.** by word of mouth, verbally; **dejar a alguien con la p. en la boca** to cut sb off in mid-sentence; **en cuatro** o **dos palabras** in a few words; **en una p.** in a word; **estar bajo p.** to be on one's word of honour; **mantener uno su p.** to keep one's word; **medir las palabras** to weigh one's words (carefully); **no tiene p.** he's not a person of his word; **p. por p.** word for word; **ser palabras mayores** to be an important matter; **sin mediar p.** without a single word; **tomar la p. a alguien** to hold sb to their word; *Informát* **p. clave** keyword; **p. divina** o **de Dios** word of God; **p. de honor** word of honour (b) *(habla)* speech (c) *(derecho de hablar)* right to speak; **dar la p. a alguien** to give the floor to sb; **tomar la p.** to take the floor

**palabrería** nf *Fam* hot air

**palabrota** nf swearword, rude word; **decir palabrotas** to swear

**palacete** nm mansion, small palace

**palaciego, -a** adj palace, court; **lujo p.** palatial luxury; **intrigas palaciegas** court intrigues

**palacio** nm palace; **p. de congresos** conference centre; **P. de Justicia** Law Courts *(plural)*

**palada** nf (a) *(con pala)* spadeful, shovelful (b) *(con remo)* stroke

**paladar** nm *(en la boca)* palate; *Fig (gusto)* palate, taste

**paladear** vt to savour

**paladín** nm *Hist* paladin, heroic knight; *Fig (adalid)* champion, defender

**palanca** nf (a) *(barra, mando)* lever; *Aut* **p. de cambio** gear lever o stick, *US* gearshift; **p. de mando** joystick (b) *(trampolín)* diving board

**palangana** nf *(para fregar)* washing-up bowl; *(para lavarse)* washbowl

**palangre** nm fishing line with hooks

**palanqueta** nf jemmy, crowbar

**palatal** adj palatal

**palatino, -a** adj (a) *(de paladar)* palatine (b) *(de palacio)* palace, court; **oficio p.** position at court

**palco** nm box *(at theatre)*

**palentino, -a1** adj of/from Palencia
**2** nm,f person from Palencia

**paleocristiano, -a,** adj early Christian

**paleografía** nf paleography

**paleográfico, -a** adj paleographic

**paleógrafo, -a** nm,f paleographer

**paleolítico, -a1** adj paleolithic
**2** nm Paleolithic period

**paleontología** nf paleontology

**paleontólogo, -a** nm,f paleontologist

**Palermo** n Palermo

**Palestina** n Palestine

**palestino, -a** adj & nm,f Palestinian

**palestra** nf arena; *Fig* **salir** o **saltar a la p.** to enter the fray

**paleta** nf (a) *(pala pequeña)* small shovel, small spade; *(de albañil)* trowel; *(de pintor)* palette; *(en máquina)* blade, vane; *(de cocina)* slice

**paletada** nf *(con paleta)* shovelful, spadeful; *(de yeso)* trowelful

**paletilla** nf *Culin* shoulder blade

**paleto, -a** *Pey* **1** adj coarse, uncouth
**2** nm,f country bumpkin, yokel, *US* hick

**paliar** [15] vt (a) *(atenuar)* to ease, to relieve (b) *(disculpar)* to excuse, to justify

**paliativo, -a1** adj palliative
**2** nm (a) *(excusa)* excuse, mitigation; **sin paliativos** unmitigated (b) *Med* palliative

**palidecer** [48] vi *(ponerse pálido)* to go o turn pale; *Fig (perder importancia)* to pale, to fade

**palidez** nf paleness

**pálido, -a** adj pale; *Fig* dull; *Fig* **ser un p. reflejo** o **una pálida imagen de** to be a pale reflection of

**palier** nm *Aut* bearing

**palillero** nm toothpick holder

**palillo** nm (a) *(mondadientes)* toothpick (b) *(baqueta)* drumstick (c) *(para comida china)* chopstick (d) *Fig (persona delgada)* matchstick

**palio** nm canopy

**palique** nm *Fam* chat, natter; **estar de p.** to have a chat o a natter

**palisandro** nm rosewood

**palito** nm *Culin* **p. (de pescado)** fish finger

**paliza** nf (a) *(golpes, derrota)* beating (b) *(esfuerzo)* hard grind (c) *(rollo)* drag; **dar la p. (a alguien)** to go on and on (to sb)

**palma** nf (a) *(de mano)* palm; **conocer algo como la p. de la mano** to know sth like the back of one's hand (b) *(palmera)* palm (tree); *(hoja de palmera)* palm leaf; *Fig* **llevarse la p.** to be the best; *Irón* to take the biscuit (c) **palmas** *(aplausos)* clapping, applause; **batir** o **dar palmas** to clap (one's hands)

**palmada** nf (a) *(suave)* pat; *(más fuerte)* slap; **dar palmadas en la espalda a alguien** to pat someone on the back (b) *(aplauso)* clap; **palmadas** clapping

**palmar¹ 1** adj of the palm *(of the hand)*
**2** nm palm grove

**palmar²** *Fam* **1** vi to kick the bucket, to snuff it
**2** vt **palmarla** to kick the bucket, to snuff it

**palmarés** nm inv (a) *(historial)* record (b) *(lista)* list, roll

**palmear 1** vt (a) (aplaudir) to applaud (b) (espalda, hombro) to slap, to pat
2 vi to clap, to applaud

**palmeño, -a 1** adj of/from Las Palmas
2 nm,f person from Las Palmas

**palmera** nf (a) (árbol) palm (tree); (datilera) date palm (b) (pastel) = flat, heart-shaped pastry

**palmeral** nm palm grove

**palmesano, -a 1** adj of/from Palma (Mallorca)
2 nm,f person from Palma (Mallorca)

**palmípedo, -a 1** adj web-footed
2 nfpl **palmípedas** water fowl (plural)

**palmito** nm (a) (árbol) palmetto, fan palm (b) Culin palm heart (c) Fam (buena planta) good looks; **lucir el p.** to show off one's good looks

**palmo** nm handspan; Fig small amount; **p. a p.** bit by bit; Fam **dejar a alguien con un p. de narices** to bring sb down to earth with a bump

**palmotear** vi to clap

**palmoteo** nm clapping

**palo** nm (a) (trozo de madera) stick; Fam **a p. seco** (sin nada más) without anything else, on its own; (bebida) neat; Fig **dar palos de ciego** (criticar) to lash out (wildly); (no saber qué hacer) to grope around in the dark; Prov **de tal p. tal astilla** like father, like son
(b) (de golf) club
(c) (de portería) post
(d) (de escoba) handle
(e) (mástil) mast
(f) (golpe) blow (with a stick); Fig (mala crítica) bad review; Fam Fig (trauma) **¡qué p., me han suspendido!** this is the end! I've failed!; **se ha llevado muchos palos últimamente** he's had to put up with a lot recently; **moler a alguien a palos** to thrash sb
(g) (de baraja) suit
(h) (madera) **de p.** wooden
(i) Bot tree; **p. santo** lignum vitae
(j) Fam (pesadez) bind, drag
(k) Fam **me da p. hacerlo/decirlo** I hate having to do/say it

**paloma** nf dove, pigeon; **p. mensajera** carrier o homing pigeon; **p. torcaz** ringdove, wood pigeon

**palomar** nm (pequeño) dovecote; (grande) pigeon shed

**palometa** nf = type of cheap white fish

**palomilla** nf (a) (insecto) grain moth (b) (rosca) butterfly nut, wing nut (c) (soporte) bracket

**palomino** nm (ave) young dove o pigeon

**palomita** nf **palomitas (de maíz)** popcorn

**palomo** nm male dove o pigeon

**palote** nm (trazo) downstroke

**palpable** adj touchable, palpable; Fig obvious, clear

**palpación** nf palpation

**palpar 1** vt (a) (tocar) to feel, to touch; Med to palpate (b) Fig (percibir) to feel
2 vi to feel around

**palpitación** nf (de corazón) beating; (con fuerza) throbbing; **una p.** (de corazón) a beat; (con fuerza) a throb; Med **palpitaciones** palpitations

**palpitante** adj (a) (que palpita) beating; (con fuerza) throbbing (b) Fig (interesante) (discusión, competición) lively; (interés, deseo, cuestión) burning

**palpitar** vi (a) (latir) to beat; (con fuerza) to throb (b) Fig (sentimiento) to be evident

**pálpito** nm feeling, hunch

**palta** nf Andes, CSur avocado

**palúdico, -a** adj Med malarial

**paludismo** nm Med malaria

**palurdo, -a** Pey **1** adj coarse, uncouth
2 nm,f country bumpkin, yokel, US hick

**pamela** nf sun hat

**pampa** nf **la p.** the pampas (plural); CSur **pampas** open plains

**pampero, -a 1** adj of/from the pampas
2 nm,f inhabitant of the pampas

**pamplina** nf Fam trifle, unimportant thing; **¡no me vengas con pamplinas!** don't try that nonsense with me!

**Pamplona** n Pamplona

**pamplonés, -esa 1** adj of/from Pamplona
2 nm,f person from Pamplona

**pamplonica 1** adj of/from Pamplona
2 nmf person from Pamplona

**pan** nm (alimento) bread; (barra, hogaza) loaf; **a p. y agua** on bread and water; Fig on the breadline; **contigo, p. y cebolla** I'll go through thick and thin with you; **ganarse el p.** to earn a living; **llamar al p. p. y al vino vino** to call a spade a spade; Fam **ser p. comido** to be a piece of cake, to be as easy as pie; Fam **ser el p. nuestro de cada día** to be commonplace, to be part of the daily round; Fam **ser más bueno que el p.** to be kindness itself; Prov **a falta de p. buenas son tortas** you have to make the most of what you've got; **p. de molde** sliced bread; **p. francés** French bread; **p. integral** wholemeal bread; **p. moreno** o **negro** (integral) brown bread; (con centeno) black o rye bread; **p. rallado** breadcrumbs

**pana** nf corduroy; **pantalones/camisa de p.** corduroy trousers/shirt

**panacea** nf también Fig panacea

**panadería** nf bakery, baker's

**panadero, -a** nm,f baker

**panal** nm honeycomb

**Panamá** n Panama

**panamá** nm panama (hat)

**panameño, -a** adj & nm,f Panamanian

**panamericanismo** nm Pan-Americanism

**pancarta** nf placard, banner

**panceta** nf bacon

**panchitos** nmpl Fam salted peanuts

**pancho, -a** adj Fam calm, unruffled; **estar/quedarse tan p.** to be/remain perfectly calm

**páncreas** nm inv pancreas

**pancreático, -a** adj pancreatic

**panda 1** adj **oso p.** panda

  **2** nm panda

  **3** nf gang

**pandemónium** nm pandemonium

**pandereta** nf tambourine

**pandero** nm (a) (instrumento) tambourine (b) Fam (culo) bum

**pandilla** nf gang

**pandillero, -a** nm,f member of a gang

**panecillo** nm bread roll

**panegírico, -a 1** adj panegyrical, eulogistic

  **2** nm panegyric, eulogy

**panel** nm (a) (pared, biombo) screen (b) (tablero) board (c) (de personas) panel

**panera** nf (cesta) bread basket; (recipiente con tapa) bread bin

**panero** nm bread tray

**pánfilo, -a** Fam **1** adj simple, foolish

  **2** nm,f fool, simpleton

**panfletario, -a** adj propagandist

**panfleto** nm polemical pamphlet

**pánico** nm panic; **ser presa del p.** to be panic-stricken; **tenerle p. a** to be terrified of

**panificadora** nf (large) bakery

**panocha** nf ear, cob

**panoplia** nf (a) (armas) mounted display of weapons (b) Fig (conjunto, gama) range, gamut

**panorama** nm (a) (vista) panorama (b) Fig (situación) overall state; (perspectiva) outlook

**panorámica** nf panorama

**panorámico, -a** adj panoramic

**panqueque** nm Am cake

**pantagruélico, -a** adj gargantuan, enormous

**pantaletas** nfpl Méx, Ven knickers

**pantalla** nf (a) (de cine, televisión, ordenador) screen; **la pequeña p.** the small screen, television; **la p. grande** the big screen; **mostrar en p.** to show on the screen; **p. (acústica)** baffle; **p. de cristal líquido** liquid crystal display; **p. de radar** radar screen; **p. táctil** touch screen (b) (de lámpara) lampshade (c) (de chimenea) fireguard (d) Fig (encubridor) front

**pantalón** nm, **pantalones** nmpl trousers, US pants; Fam Fig **bajarse los pantalones** to climb down; Fam Fig **llevar los pantalones** to wear the trousers; **p. corto** short trousers, shorts; **p. largo** (long) trousers; **p. (de) pitillo** drainpipe trousers; **p. tejano** o **vaquero** jeans

**pantano** nm (a) (ciénaga) marsh; (laguna) swamp (b) (embalse) reservoir

**pantanoso, -a** adj (a) (cenagoso) marshy, boggy (b) Fig (difícil) tricky

**panteísta 1** adj pantheistic

  **2** nmf pantheist

**panteón** nm mausoleum, vault

**pantera** nf panther; **p. negra** black panther

**panti** nm tights

**pantimedias** nfpl Méx tights

**pantocrátor** nm Arte Christ Pantocrator

**pantomima** nf mime; Fig pantomime, acting

**pantorrilla** nf calf

**pantufla** nf slipper

**panty** (pl **pantis**) nm tights

**panza** nf belly

**panzada** nf (a) (en el agua) belly flop (b) Fam (hartura) bellyful; **darse una p. (de algo)** to stuff oneself (with sth)

**pañal** nm Br nappy, US diaper; Fam Fig **estar en pañales** (en sus inicios) to be in its infancy; (sin conocimientos) not to have a clue; Fam Fig **dejar a alguien en pañales** to leave sb standing o behind

**pañería** nf (producto) drapery; (tienda) draper's (shop), US dry-goods store

**paño** nm (a) (tela) cloth, material (b) (trapo) cloth; (para polvo) duster; (de cocina) tea towel (c) (lienzo) panel, length (d) (expresiones) **conocer el p.** to know the score; **ser el p. de lágrimas de alguien** to be a shoulder to cry on for sb; **en paños menores** in one's underthings; **paños calientes** half-measures

**pañol** nm Náut storeroom

**pañoleta** nf shawl, wrap

**pañuelo** nm (de nariz) handkerchief; (para el cuello) scarf; (para la cabeza) headscarf; **p. de papel** paper handkerchief, tissue; Fam **¡el mundo es un p.!** it's a small world!

**Papa** nm Pope

**papa** nf potato; Fam **no saber ni p.** not to have a clue

**papá** nm Fam dad, daddy, US pop; **P. Noel** Father Christmas

**papada** nf (de persona) double chin; (de animal) dewlap

**papado** nm papacy

**papagayo** nm parrot; **como un p.** parrot-fashion

**papal** *adj* papal

**papalote** *nm Méx (cometa)* kite

**papamoscas** *nm inv* flycatcher

**papanatas** *nmf inv Fam* sucker

**paparazzi** [papa'ratsi] *nmf inv* paparazzi

**paparruchas** *nfpl Fam* nonsense

**papaya** *nf (fruta)* papaya, pawpaw

**papear** *vi muy Fam* to scoff, to pig out

**papel** *nm* (a) *(material)* paper; *(hoja)* sheet of paper; *(trozo)* piece of paper; *Fam Fig* **ser p. mojado** to be worthless; *Fam Fig* **perder los papeles** to lose it; **p. biblia** bible paper; **p. carbón** carbon paper; **p. cebolla** onionskin; **p. celofán** Cellophane®; *Informát* **p. continuo** continuous paper; **p. de aluminio** *o* **estaño** *o* **plata** tin *o* aluminium foil; **p. de barba** bloom; **p. de embalar** *o* **de embalaje** wrapping paper; **p. de estraza** brown paper; **p. de fumar** cigarette paper; **p. de lija** sandpaper; **p. de regalo** wrapping paper, gift-wrapping; **p. higiénico** toilet paper; **p. milimetrado** graph paper; **p. pintado** wallpaper; **p. secante** blotting paper; **p. sellado** *o* **timbrado** stamp, stamped paper; **p. vegetal** tracing paper

(b) *(en película, teatro) & Fig* role, part; **desempeñar** *o* **hacer el p. de** to play the role *o* part of; **p. principal/secundario** main/minor part; **hacer buen/mal p.** to do well/badly

(c) *Fin* stocks and shares; **p. de pagos** = special stamps for making certain payments to the State; **p. del Estado** government bonds; **p. moneda** paper money, banknotes

**papela** *nf muy Fam (documentación)* I.D. card

**papeleo** *nm* paperwork, red tape

**papelera** *nf* (a) *(cesto)* wastepaper basket *o* bin; *(en la calle)* litter bin (b) *(fábrica)* paper mill

**papelería** *nf* stationer's (shop)

**papelero, -a** *adj* paper; **industria papelera** paper industry

**papeleta** *nf* (a) *(boleto)* ticket, slip (of paper); *(de votación)* ballot paper (b) *Educ* = slip of paper with university exam results (c) *Fig (problema)* **¡menuda p.!** that's a nasty one!

**papelina** *nf Fam* = sachet of paper containing drugs

**papelón** *nm Fam* spectacle; **hacer un p.** to make a fool of oneself, to be left looking ridiculous

**papeo** *nm muy Fam* grub

**paperas** *nfpl* mumps

**papi** *nm Fam* daddy, dad

**papila** *nf Anat* papilla

**papilla** *nf* (a) *(para niños)* baby food; *Fam* **echar** *o* **arrojar hasta la primera p.** to be as sick as a dog; *Fam* **hecho p.** *(cansado)* shattered, exhausted; *(roto)* smashed to bits, ruined (b) *Med* barium meal

**papiloma** *nm* papilloma

**papiro** *nm* papyrus

**papiroflexia** *nf* origami

**papirotazo** *nm* flick *(of finger)*

**papista** *nmf* papist; *Fam* **ser más p. que el Papa** to be more Catholic than the Pope

**papo** *nm Fam (moflete)* jowls; *Fig (descaro)* **tener mucho p.** to have a lot of cheek; *Fig* **¡tiene un p. que se lo pisa!** he's got some brass neck!

**páprika** *nf* paprika

**papú** (*pl* **papúes**) *adj & nmf* Papuan

**Papúa-Nueva Guinea** *n* Papua New Guinea

**paquebote** *nm* packet boat

**paquete** *nm* (a) *(de libros, regalos)* parcel; **p. bomba** parcel bomb; **p. postal** parcel (b) *(de cigarrillos, folios)* pack, packet; *(de azúcar, arroz)* bag (c) *(maleta, bulto)* bag (d) *Fig (conjunto)* package; **p. de acciones** share holding; **p. de medidas** package of measures; **p. turístico** package tour (e) *Informát* package (f) *Fam (cosa fastidiosa)* **me ha tocado el p. de hacer…** I've been lumbered with doing… (g) *muy Fam (genitales masculinos)* packet (h) *Fam* **meter un p. a alguien** *(castigar)* to come down on sb like a ton of bricks

**paquidermo** *nm* pachyderm

**Paquistán** *n* Pakistan

**paquistaní** (*pl* **paquistaníes**) *adj & nmf* Pakistani

**par 1** *adj* (a) *(número)* even (b) *(igual)* equal

**2** *nm* (a) *(de zapatos, pantalones)* pair (b) *(de personas, cosas)* couple (c) *(número indeterminado)* few, couple; **un p. de copas** a couple of *o* a few drinks; **un p. de veces** a couple of times, a few times; **sin p.** without equal, matchless; *(abierto)* **de p. en p.** *(puerta, ventana)* wide open (d) *(en golf)* par (e) *(noble)* peer

**3** *nf* **a la p.** (a) *(simultáneamente)* at the same time (b) *(a igual nivel)* at the same level (c) *Fin* at par

**para** *prep* (a) *(finalidad)* for; **es p. ti** it's for you; **una mesa p. el salón** a table for the living room; **esta agua no es buena p. beber** this water isn't fit for drinking *o* to drink; **te lo repetiré p. que te enteres** I'll repeat it so you understand; **¿p. qué?** what for?

(b) *(motivación)* (in order) to; **p. conseguir sus propósitos** in order to achieve his aims; **lo he hecho p. agradarte** I did it to please you

(c) *(dirección)* towards; **ir p. casa** to head (for) home; **salir p. el aeropuerto** to leave for the airport

(d) *(tiempo)* for; **tiene que estar acabado p. mañana** it has to be finished by *o* for tomorrow; *Am* **diez p. las once** ten to eleven

(e) *(comparación)* **está muy delgado p. lo que come** he's very thin considering how much he eats; **p. ser verano hace mucho frío** considering it's summer, it's very cold

(f) *(después de adj y antes de infin) (inminencia, propósito)* to; **la comida está lista p. servir** the meal is ready to be served; **el atleta está preparado p. ganar** the athlete is ready to win

(g) *(expresiones)* **p. con** towards; **es buena p. con los demás** she is kind towards other people; **p. mí/ti/***etc (en mi/tu opinión)* as far as I'm/you're/*etc* concerned; **p. mí que no van a venir** it looks to me like they're not coming

**parabién** (*pl* **parabienes**) *nm Formal* congratulations

**parábola** *nf* (a) *(alegoría)* parable (b) *Mat* parabola

**parabólica** *nf* satellite dish

**parabólico, -a** *adj* parabolic

**parabrisas** *nm inv* windscreen, *US* windshield

**paracas** *nmpl Fam Mil (paracaidistas)* Paras

**paracaídas** *nm inv* parachute

**paracaidismo** *nm* parachuting, parachute jumping

**paracaidista** *nmf* parachutist; *Mil* paratrooper

**parachispas** *nm inv* fireguard

**parachoques** *nm inv Aut* bumper, *US* fender; *Ferroc* buffer

**parada** *nf* (a) *(detención)* stop, stopping (b) *Dep* save (c) *(de autobús)* (bus) stop; *(de taxis)* taxi rank; *(de metro)* (underground) station; **p. discrecional** request stop (d) *Mil* parade

**paradero** *nm* (a) *(de persona)* whereabouts; **están en p. desconocido** their present whereabouts are unknown (b) *Am (parada de autobús)* bus stop

**paradigma** *nm* paradigm, example

**paradigmático, -a** *adj* paradigmatic

**paradisiaco, -a, paradisíaco, -a** *adj* heavenly

**parado, -a 1** *adj* (a) *(inmóvil) (vehículo)* stationary, standing; *(persona)* still, motionless; *(fábrica, proyecto)* at a standstill (b) *(pasivo)* lacking in initiative (c) *(sin empleo)* unemployed, out of work (d) **salir bien/mal p. de algo** to come off well/badly out of sth

**2** *nm,f (desempleado)* unemployed person; **los parados** the unemployed

**paradoja** *nf* paradox

**paradójico, -a** *adj* paradoxical, ironical

**parador** *nm* (a) *(mesón)* roadside inn (b) *(hotel)* **p. (nacional)** = state-owned luxury hotel, usually a building of historic or artistic importance

**parafernalia** *nf* paraphernalia

**parafina** *nf* paraffin

**parafrasear** *vt* to paraphrase

**paráfrasis** *nf inv* paraphrase

**paraguas** *nm inv* umbrella

**Paraguay** *nm* **(el)** P. Paraguay

**paraguayo, -a 1** *adj & nm,f* Paraguayan

**2** *nm (fruta)* = fruit similar to peach

**paragüero** *nm* umbrella stand

**paraíso** *nm* (a) *Rel* Paradise; *Fig* paradise; **p. fiscal** tax haven; **p. terrenal** earthly Paradise (b) *Teatro* **asientos de p.** seats in the gods

**paraje** *nm* spot, place

**paralela** *nf Mat* parallel (line); *Dep* **paralelas** parallel bars

**paralelismo** *nm* (a) *Mat* parallelism (b) *(semejanza)* similarity, parallels

**paralelo, -a 1** *adj* parallel (**a** to); *Dep* **barras paralelas** parallel bars

**2** *nm* (a) *Geog* parallel (b) *(comparación)* comparison; **trazar un p. con** to draw a comparison *o* parallel with (c) *Elec* **estar en p.** to be in parallel

**paralelogramo** *nm* parallelogram

**paralímpico, -a** *adj Dep* **juegos paralímpicos** Paralympic games, Paralympics

**parálisis** *nf inv* paralysis; **p. cerebral** cerebral palsy; **p. infantil** polio

**paralítico, -a** *adj & nm,f* paralytic

**paralización** *nf* paralysis; *Fig* halting

**paralizar [16] 1** *vt* to paralyse

**2** **paralizarse** *vpr Fig (producción, proyecto)* to come to a standstill

**Paramaribo** *n* Paramaribo

**paramento** *nm* (a) *(adorno)* adornment (b) *Constr* facing *(of a wall)*

**parámetro** *nm* parameter

**paramilitar** *adj* paramilitary

**páramo** *nm* moor; *Fig* wilderness; **los páramos** the moors, the moorland

**parangón** *nm* paragon; **sin p.** unparalleled; **tener p. con** to be comparable with

**paraninfo** *nm* assembly hall, auditorium

**paranoia** *nf* paranoia

**paranoico, -a** *adj & nm,f Med* paranoiac; *Fam* **estar p.** to be going up the wall

**paranormal** *adj* paranormal

**paraolímpico, -a** *adj Dep* **juegos paraolímpicos** Paralympic games, Paralympics

**parapente** *nm (desde montaña)* parapenting; *(a remolque de avión)* paragliding

**parapetarse** *vpr también Fig* to take refuge **(tras** behind)

**parapeto** *nm (antepecho)* parapet; *(barandilla)* bannister; *(barricada)* barricade

**paraplejía, paraplejia** *nf Med* paraplegia

**parapléjico, -a** *adj & nm,f Med* paraplegic

**parapsicología** *nf* parapsychology

**parapsicológico, -a** *adj* parapsychological

**parapsicólogo, -a** *nm,f* parapsychologist

**parar 1** *vi* (a) *(detenerse, interrumpirse)* to stop; **p. de hacer algo** to stop doing sth; **no para de molestarme** she keeps annoying me; *Fam* **no p.** to be always on the go; **sin p.** non-stop (b) *(alojarse)* to stay (c) *(recaer)* **p. en manos de alguien** to come into the possession of sb (d) *(acabar)* to end up; **¿en qué parará este lío?** where will it all end?; **ir a p. a** to end up in

**2** *vt* (a) *(detener, interrumpir)* to stop; *(golpe)* to parry (b) *Am (levantar)* to raise

**3** *pararse vpr* (a) *(detenerse)* to stop; **pararse a hacer algo** to stop to do sth (b) *Am (ponerse de pie)* to stand up

**pararrayos** *nm inv* lightning conductor

**parasitario, -a** *adj* parasitic

**parasitismo** *nm* parasitism

**parásito, -a 1** *adj Biol* parasitic

**2** *nm Biol & Fig* parasite; *Telecom* **parásitos** *(interferencias)* statics

**parasitología** *nf* parasitology

**parasol** *nm* parasol

**parcela** *nf* plot (of land)

**parcelación** *nf* parcelling out, division into plots

**parcelar** *vt* to parcel out, to divide into plots

**parcelario, -a** *adj* of *or* relating to plots of land

**parche** *nm* (a) *(de tela, goma)* patch (b) *(emplasto)* poultice (c) *(chapuza)* botch job; *(para salir del paso)* makeshift solution

**parchear** *vt Fig* to patch up

**parchís** *nm inv* ludo

**parcial 1** *adj* (a) *(no total)* partial (b) *(no ecuánime)* biased

**2** *nm (examen)* = end-of-term exam at university

**parcialidad** *nf* (a) *(tendenciosidad)* bias, partiality (b) *(bando)* faction

**parco, -a** *adj* (a) *(moderado)* sparing **(en** in) (b) *(escaso)* meagre; *(cena)* frugal; *(explicación)* brief, concise

**pardiez** *interj Anticuado o Hum* **¡p.!** good gracious!

**pardillo, -a 1** *adj Fam* (a) *(ingenuo)* naive (b) *(palurdo)* countrified

**2** *nm,f Fam* (a) *(ingenuo)* naive person (b) *(palurdo)* bumpkin

**3** *nm (pájaro)* linnet

**pardo, -a 1** *adj* greyish-brown, dull brown

**2** *nm* greyish-brown, dull brown

**parear** *vt* to pair

**parecer [48] 1** *nm* (a) *(opinión)* opinion; **cambiar de p.** to change one's mind (b) *(apariencia)* **de buen p.** good-looking

**2** *vi (semejar)* to look like; **parece un palacio** it looks like a palace

**3** *v copulativo* to look, to seem; **pareces cansado** you look *o* seem tired; **es alemán, pero no lo parece** he's German, but he doesn't look it

**4** *v impersonal* (a) *(expresa opinión)* **me parece que…** I think *o* it seems to me that…; **me parece que sí/no** I think/don't think so; **¿qué te parece?** what do you think (of it)? (b) *(tener aspecto de)* **parece que va a llover** it looks like it's going to rain; **parece que le gusta** it looks as if *o* it seems that she likes it; **eso parece** so it seems; **al p.** apparently

**5** *parecerse vpr* to be alike **(en** in); **parecerse a alguien** *(físicamente)* to look like sb; *(en carácter)* to be like sb

**parecido, -a 1** *adj* similar; **p. a** similar to, like; **bien p.** *(atractivo)* good-looking

**2** *nm* resemblance **(con/entre** to/between); **cualquier p. es pura coincidencia** any similarity is purely coincidental

**pared** *nf* (a) *(de construcción)* wall; **entre cuatro paredes** cooped-up at home; **las paredes oyen** walls have ears; **si las paredes hablasen…** if the walls could talk…; *Fig* **subirse por las paredes** to hit the roof, to go up the wall; **p. maestra** main wall (b) *(de montaña)* side (c) *Dep* one-two; **hacer la p.** to play a one-two

**paredón** *nm (muro)* (thick) wall; *(de fusilamiento)* (execution) wall

**pareja** *nf* (a) *(par)* pair; *(de novios)* couple; **por parejas** in pairs (b) *(miembro del par)* (persona) partner; *(guante, zapato)* other one; **la p. de este calcetín** the other sock of this pair

**parejo, -a** *adj* similar **(a** to)

**parentela** *nf* relations, family

**parentesco** *nm* relationship

**paréntesis** *nm inv* (a) *(signo)* bracket; **entre p.** in brackets, in parentheses (b) *(intercalación)* digression (c) *Fig (interrupción)* break; **hacer un p.** to have a break

**pareo** *nm* wraparound skirt

**parezca** *etc ver* **parecer**

**pargo** *nm* porgy

**paria** *nmf* pariah

**parida** *nf Fam* tripe, nonsense

**paridad** *nf* (a) *(semejanza)* similarity; *(igualdad)* evenness (b) *Fin & Informát* parity; **p. de cambio** parity of exchange

**parienta** *nf Fam (cónyuge)* missus

**pariente** *nm,f (familiar)* relation, relative

**parietal** *nm Anat* parietal

**parihuela** nf (camilla) stretcher

**paripé** nm Fam **hacer el p.** to put on an act, to pretend

**parir 1** vi to give birth; Fam **poner algo/a alguien a p.** to run sth/sb down, to badmouth sth/sb

**2** vt to give birth to

**París** n Paris

**parisiense** adj & nmf, **parisino, -a** adj & nm,f Parisian

**paritorio** nm delivery room

**parka** nf (abrigo) parka

**parking** ['parkin] (pl parkings) nm car park, US parking lot

**párkinson** nm Med Parkinson's disease

**parlamentar** vi to negotiate

**parlamentario, -a 1** adj parliamentary

**2** nm,f member of parliament

**parlamentarismo** nm parliamentary system

**parlamento** nm (a) Pol parliament (b) Teatro speech

**parlanchín, -ina 1** adj talkative

**2** nm,f chatterbox

**parlante** adj talking

**parlotear** vi Fam to chatter

**parloteo** nm Fam chatter

**parmesano, -a 1** adj queso p. Parmesan cheese

**2** nm (queso) Parmesan (cheese)

**parnaso** nm Formal parnassus

**parné** nm Fam dosh, loot

**paro** nm (a) (desempleo) unemployment; **estar en (el) p.** to be unemployed; **quedarse en p.** to be left unemployed; **p. cíclico/encubierto/estructural** cyclical/hidden/structural unemployment (b) (subsidio) unemployment benefit, dole money (c) (cesación) (acción) shutdown; (estado) stoppage; **p. cardiaco** cardiac arrest; **p. laboral** industrial action

**parodia** nf (de texto, estilo) parody; (de película) send-up, spoof; **hacer una p. de alguien** to do a send-up o take-off of sb

**parodiar** [15] vt (texto, estilo) to parody; (película) to send up, to spoof; (persona) to send up, to take off

**parón** nm sudden stoppage

**paroxismo** nm paroxysm

**paroxítono, -a** adj paroxytone, word where the penultimate syllable is stressed

**parpadeante** adj (luz) flickering

**parpadear** vi (ojos) to blink; Fig (luz) to flicker

**parpadeo** nm (de ojos) blinking; Fig (de luz) flickering

**párpado** nm eyelid

**parque** nm (a) (terreno) park; **p. acuático** waterpark; **p. de atracciones** amusement park; **p. nacional** national park; **p. natural** nature reserve; **p. tecnológico** science park; **(p.) zoológico** zoo (b) (vehículos) fleet; **p. de bomberos** fire station; **p. móvil** car pool (c) (para bebés) playpen

**parqué** nm (suelo) parquet (floor)

**parquear** vt Am to park

**parquedad** nf moderation; **con p.** sparingly

**parquet** [par'ke] nm (suelo) parquet (floor)

**parquímetro** nm parking meter

**parra** nf grapevine; Fam Fig **subirse a la p.** to get above oneself

**parrafada** nf earful, dull monologue; **soltar una p.** to go on (and on)

**párrafo** nm paragraph

**parral** nm (a) (emparrado) vine arbour (b) (terreno) vineyard

**parranda** nf Fam (juerga) **irse de p.** to go out on the town

**parrandear** vi Fam to go out on the town

**parricida** nmf parricide

**parricidio** nm parricide

**parrilla** nf (a) (utensilio) grill; **a la p.** grilled (b) (restaurante) grillroom, grill (c) Dep **p. (de salida)** (starting) grid (d) Am (baca) roof rack

**parrillada** nf mixed grill

**párroco** nm parish priest

**parroquia** nf (a) (iglesia) parish church (b) (jurisdicción) parish (c) (fieles) parishioners, parish (d) (clientela) clientele

**parroquial** adj parish; **iglesia p.** parish church

**parroquiano, -a** nm,f (a) (feligrés) parishioner (b) (cliente) customer, regular

**parsimonia** nf deliberation, calmness; **con p.** unhurriedly

**parsimonioso, -a** adj unhurried, deliberate

**parte 1** nm report; **dar p. (a alguien de algo)** to report (sth to sb); **p. facultativo** o **médico** medical report; **p. meteorológico** weather report

**2** nf (a) (porción, cantidad) part; **en p.** to a certain extent, partly; **la mayor p. de la gente** most people; **la tercera p. de** a third of; **por partes** bit by bit

(b) (lugar) part; **en alguna p.** somewhere; **no lo veo por ninguna p.** I can't find it anywhere; **¿de qué p. de España es?** what part of Spain is he from?, whereabouts in Spain is he from?; **en todas partes cuecen habas** it's the same the whole world over

(c) (bando, lado) side; Der party; **estar/ponerse de p. de alguien** to be on/to take sb's side; **por mi p.** for my part; **por p. de padre/madre** on one's father's/mother's side; **por una p.... por otra...** on the one hand... on the other (hand)...; **por otra p.** *(además)* what is more, besides; **tener a alguien de p. de uno** to have sb on one's side

(**d**) **partes** *(genitales)* private parts

(**e**) **formar p. de** to be part of; **tomar p. en algo** to take part in sth

(**f**) **de p. de** on behalf of, for; *Telecom* **¿de p. de (quién)?** who is calling, please?

**partenaire** [parte'ner] *nmf (pareja artística)* partner

**partera** *nf* midwife

**parterre** *nm* flowerbed

**partición** *nf (reparto)* sharing out; *(de territorio)* partitioning

**participación** *nf* (**a**) *(colaboración, intervención)* participation; **hubo mucha p.** *(en actividad)* many people took part; *(en elecciones)* there was a high turnout (**b**) *(de lotería)* = ticket representing a share in a lottery number (**c**) *(comunicación)* notice (**d**) *Econ* **p. en los beneficios** profit-sharing

**participante 1** *adj* participating
  **2** *nmf* participant

**participar 1** *vi* (**a**) *(colaborar, intervenir)* to take part *o* participate (**en** in); *Fin* to have a share (**en** in) (**b**) *(recibir)* to receive a share (**de** of) (**c**) *(compartir)* **p. de** to share
  **2** *vt* **p. algo a alguien** to notify sb of sth

**participativo, -a** *adj* **es muy p. en clase** he participates a lot in class

**partícipe 1** *adj* involved (**de** in); **hacer p. de algo a alguien** *(notificar)* to notify sb of sth; *(compartir)* to share sth with sb
  **2** *nmf* participant

**participio** *nm* participle

**partícula** *nf* particle

**particular 1** *adj* (**a**) *(especial)* particular; **tiene su sabor p.** it has its own particular taste; **en p.** in particular; **eso no tiene nada de p.** that's nothing special *o* unusual (**b**) *(privado)* private; **dar clases particulares** to teach private classes; **domicilio p.** home address; **la casa tiene jardín p.** the house has its own garden
  **2** *nmf (persona)* member of the public
  **3** *nm (asunto)* matter; **sin otro p.** without further ado

**particularidad** *nf* (**a**) *(rasgo)* distinctive characteristic, peculiarity (**b**) *(cualidad)* **la p. de su petición** the unusual nature of his request

**particularizar** [16] **1** *vt (caracterizar)* to characterize
  **2** *vi* (**a**) *(detallar)* to go into details (**b**) *(personalizar)* **p. en alguien** to single sb out
  **3** **particularizarse** *vpr (caracterizarse)* **particularizarse por** to be characterized by

**partida** *nf* (**a**) *(marcha)* departure (**b**) *(en juego)* game; **echar una p.** to have a game (**c**) *(documento)* certificate; **p. de defunción/matrimonio/nacimiento** death/marriage/birth certificate (**d**) *Com (mercancía)* consignment; *(entrada)* item, entry

**partidario, -a 1** *adj* **ser p. de** to be in favour of
  **2** *nm,f* supporter

**partidismo** *nm* partisanship, bias

**partidista** *adj* partisan, biased

**partido** *nm* (**a**) *Pol* party (**b**) *Dep* match; **p. amistoso** friendly (match) (**c**) *(futuro cónyuge)* match; **buen/mal p.** good/bad match (**d**) **sacar p. de, sacarle p. a** to make the most of; **tomar p. por** to side with

**partir 1** *vt* (**a**) *(dividir)* to divide, to split (**en** into) (**b**) *(repartir)* to share out (**c**) *(romper)* to break open; *(cascar)* to crack; *(tronco, loncha)* to cut; **párteme un pedazo de pan** break me off a piece of bread; **partirle la cara a alguien** to smash sb's face in (**d**) **a p. de** starting from; **a p. de aquí** from here on
  **2** *vi* (**a**) *(marchar)* to leave, to set off (**b**) *(empezar)* **p. de** to start from; **p. de cero** to start from scratch
  **3** **partirse** *vpr* (**a**) *(romperse)* to split; **partirse en dos** to split *o* break in two (**b**) *(rajarse)* to crack (**c**) *Fam (de risa)* **partirse (de risa)** to crack up (with laughter); **muy Fam partirse el culo** to piss oneself laughing; **¡yo me parto con su tío!** his uncle really kills me!

**partisano, -a** *adj & nm,f* partisan

**partitivo, -a 1** *adj* partitive
  **2** *nm* partitive

**partitura** *nf* score

**parto** *nm* birth; **estar de p.** to be in labour; **p. natural/prematuro** natural/premature birth

**parturienta** *nf* woman in labour

**parvulario** *nm* nursery school, kindergarten

**párvulo, -a** *nm,f* infant

**pasa** *nf (fruta)* raisin; **p. de Corinto** currant; **p. de Esmirna** sultana

**pasable** *adj* passable

**pasacalles** *nm inv* street procession *(during town festival)*

**pasada** *nf* (**a**) *(con el trapo)* wipe; **dar una segunda p. a** *(con la brocha)* to apply a second coat to; *Fig* **decir algo de p.** to say sth in passing (**b**) *(a texto)* **dar una p. a** to read through (**c**) *Fam* **es una p.** *(una barbaridad)* it's way over the top; **mala p.** dirty trick

**pasadizo** *nm* passage

**pasado, -a 1** *adj* (**a**) *(terminado)* past; **p. un año** a year later; **lo p., p. está** let bygones be bygones (**b**) *(último)* last; **el año p.** last year (**c**) *(podrido)* off, bad (**d**) *(muy hecho)* (*filete, carne*) well done

**2** *nm (tiempo)* past; *Gram* past (tense)

**pasador** *nm* (**a**) *(cerrojo)* bolt (**b**) *(para el pelo)* slide

**pasaje** *nm* (**a**) *(billete)* ticket, fare (**b**) *(pasajeros)* passengers (**c**) *(calle)* passage (**d**) *(fragmento)* passage

**pasajero, -a 1** *adj* passing; **es algo p.** it's sth temporary, it'll pass

**2** *nm,f* passenger

**pasamanería** *nm (adornos)* decorative fringe

**pasamanos** *nm inv (de escalera interior)* bannister; *(de escalera exterior)* handrail

**pasamontañas** *nm inv* balaclava (helmet)

**pasante** *nmf* articled clerk

**pasaporte** *nm* passport

**pasapuré** *nm*, **pasapurés** *nm inv* = hand-operated food mill

**pasar 1** *vt* (**a**) *(en general)* to pass; *(noticia, aviso)* to pass on; **¿me pasas la sal?** would you pass me the salt?; **p. algo por** *(filtrar)* to pass sth through

(**b**) *(cruzar)* to cross; **p. la calle** to cross the road; **pasé el río a nado** I swam across the river

(**c**) *(traspasar)* to pass through

(**d**) *(trasladar)* **p. algo a** to move sth to

(**e**) *(llevar adentro)* to show in; **el criado nos pasó al salón** the butler showed us into the living room

(**f**) *(contagiar)* **p. algo a alguien** to give sth to sb, to infect sb with sth; **me has pasado la tos** you've given me your cough

(**g**) *(consentir)* **p. algo a alguien** to let sb get away with sth

(**h**) *(rebasar)* *(en el espacio)* to go through; *(en el tiempo)* to have been through; **p. un semáforo en rojo** to go through a red light; **ya ha pasado lo peor** the worst is over now

(**i**) *(emplear)* *(tiempo)* to spend; **pasó dos años en Roma** he spent two years in Rome

(**j**) *(experimentar)* to go through, to experience; **pasarlo bien** to enjoy oneself, to have a good time; **pasarlo mal** to have a hard time of it; *Fam* **pasarlas canutas** to have a rough time

(**k**) *(sobrepasar)* **ya ha pasado los veinticinco** he's over twenty-five now; **mi hijo me pasa ya dos centímetros** my son is already two centimetres taller than me

(**l**) *(adelantar)* to overtake

(**m**) *Cine* to show

**2** *vi* (**a**) *(en general)* to pass, to go; **pasó por mi lado** he passed by my side; **el autobús pasa por mi casa** the bus goes past *o* passes in front of my house; **el Manzanares pasa por Madrid** the Manzanares goes *o* passes through Madrid; **he pasado por tu calle** I went down your street; **p. de... a...** to go *o* pass from... to...; **p. de largo** to go by

(**b**) *(entrar)* to go/come in; **¡pase!** come in!

(**c**) *(poder entrar)* to go (**por** through); **por ahí no pasa** it won't go through there

(**d**) *(ir un momento)* to pop in; **pasaré por mi oficina/por tu casa** I'll pop into my office/round to your place

(**e**) *(suceder)* to happen; **¿qué pasa aquí?** what's going on here?; **¿qué pasa?** what's the matter?; **¿qué le pasa?** what's wrong with him?, what's the matter with him?; **pase lo que pase** whatever happens, come what may

(**f**) *(terminarse)* to be over; **pasó la Navidad** Christmas is over

(**g**) *(transcurrir)* to go by; **pasaron tres meses** three months went by

(**h**) *(cambiar)* *(acción)* **p. a** to move on to; **pasemos a otra cosa** let's move on to something else

(**i**) *(conformarse)* **p. (con/sin algo)** to make do (with/without sth); **tendrá que p. sin coche** she'll have to make do without a car

(**j**) *(servir)* to be all right, to be usable; **puede p.** it'll do

(**k**) *Fam (prescindir)* **p. de algo/alguien** to want nothing to do with sth/sb; **paso de política** I'm not into politics; **paso olímpicamente de hacerlo** I'm damned if I'm going to do it

(**l**) *(tolerar)* **p. por algo** to put up with sth

**3 pasarse** *vpr* (**a**) *(acabarse)* to pass; **siéntate hasta que se te pase** sit down until you feel better

(**b**) *(emplear)* *(tiempo)* to spend, to pass; **se pasaron el día hablando** they spent all day talking

(**c**) *(desaprovecharse)* to slip by; **se me pasó la oportunidad** I missed my chance

(**d**) *(estropearse)* *(comida)* to go off; *(flores)* to fade

(**e**) *(cambiar de bando)* **pasarse a** to go over to

(**f**) *(omitir)* to miss out; **te has pasado una página** you've missed a page out

(**g**) *(olvidarse)* **pasársele a alguien** to slip sb's mind; **se me pasó decírtelo** I forgot to mention it to you

(**h**) *(no fijarse)* **pasársele a alguien** to escape sb's attention; **no se le pasa nada** he never misses a thing

(i) *(excederse)* **pasarse de generoso/bueno** to be far too generous/kind

(j) *Fam (propasarse)* to go too far, to go over the top; **te has pasado diciéndole eso** what you said went too far *o* was over the top

(k) *(divertirse)* **¿qué tal te lo estás pasando?** how are you enjoying yourself?; **pasárselo bien/mal** to have a good/bad time

(l) *(ir un momento)* to pop in; **me pasaré por mi oficina/por tu casa** I'll pop into my office/round to your place

**pasarela** *nf* (a) *(puente)* footbridge; *(para desembarcar)* gangway (b) *(en desfile de moda)* catwalk

**pasatiempo** *nm (hobby)* pastime, hobby; *Prensa* **pasatiempos** crossword and puzzles section

**pascua** *nf* (a) *(de los cristianos)* Easter; *Fam* **hacer la p. a alguien** *(ser pesado)* to pester sb; *(poner en apuros)* to land sb in it; **Pascuas** *(Navidad)* Christmas *(singular)*; **¡felices Pascuas!** Merry Christmas!; **de Pascuas a Ramos** once in a blue moon (b) *(de los judíos)* Passover

**pase** *nm* (a) *también Dep & Taurom* pass (b) *(proyección)* showing, screening (c) *(desfile)* parade; **p. de modelos** fashion parade (d) *Fam* **eso tiene un p.** that can be overlooked *o* forgiven

**paseante** *nmf* person out for a stroll

**pasear 1** *vi* to go for a walk

**2** *vt* to take for a walk; *(perro)* to walk; *Fig* to show off, to parade

**3 pasearse** *vpr* to go for a walk

**paseíllo** *nm Taurom* = parade of bullfighters when they come out into the ring before the bullfight starts

**paseo** *nm* (a) *(acción) (a pie)* walk; *(en coche)* drive; *(a caballo)* ride; *(en barca)* row; **dar un p.** *(a pie)* to go for a walk (b) *(lugar)* avenue; **p. marítimo** promenade (c) *Fam* **mandar** *o* **enviar a alguien a p.** to send sb packing

**pasillo** *nm* corridor; **p. deslizante** travelator; **hacer (el) p.** to form a corridor *(for people to walk down)*

**pasión** *nf* passion; **tener p. por algo/alguien** to adore sth/sb; *Rel* **la P.** the Passion

**pasional** *adj* passionate

**pasionaria** *nf* passion flower

**pasividad** *nf* passivity

**pasivo, -a 1** *adj* (a) *también Gram* passive (b) *(población)* inactive

**2** *nm Com* liabilities

**pasma** *nf muy Fam* **la p.** the fuzz *(plural)*, the cops

**pasmado, -a 1** *adj* (a) *(asombrado)* astonished, astounded (b) *(atontado)* stunned

**2** *nm,f* halfwit

**pasmar 1** *vt* to astound

**2 pasmarse** *vpr* to be astounded

**pasmarote** *nmf Fam* halfwit, dumbo

**pasmo** *nm* (a) *(asombro)* astonishment (b) *(de frío)* chill; **te va a dar un p.** you'll catch your death

**pasmoso, -a** *adj* astonishing

**paso** *nm* (a) *(con el pie)* step; *(huella)* footprint (b) *(acción)* passing; *(cruce)* crossing; *(camino de acceso)* way through, thoroughfare; **de p.** *(de pasada)* in passing; *(aprovechando)* while I'm/you're/*etc* at it; **el Ebro, a su p. por Zaragoza** the Ebro, as it flows through Zaragoza; *también Fig* **abrir p. a alguien** to make way for sb; **ceder el p. (a alguien)** to let sb past; *Aut* to give way (to sb); **ceda el p.** *(en letrero)* give way; **prohibido el p.** *(en letrero)* no entry; **su p. fugaz por la universidad** his brief spell at the university; **p. de cebra** zebra crossing; **p. del ecuador** = (celebration marking) halfway stage in a university course; **p. elevado** flyover; **p. a nivel** level crossing; **p. peatonal** *o* **de peatones** pedestrian crossing; **p. subterráneo** subway, *US* underpass

(c) *(forma de andar)* walk; *Fig (ritmo)* pace; *Fig* **a este p. no acabaremos nunca** at this rate we'll never finish; **a p. ligero** at a brisk pace; **marcar el p.** to keep time

(d) *Geog (en montaña)* pass; *(en el mar)* strait

(e) *(etapa, acontecimiento)* step; *(progreso)* step forward, advance; **dar los pasos necesarios** to take the necessary steps; **p. a p.** step by step

(f) *(mal momento)* **(mal) p.** difficult situation

(g) *(expresiones)* **a cada p.** every other minute; **está a dos** *o* **cuatro pasos** it's just down the road; **a pasos agigantados** with giant steps; **a p. de tortuga** at a snail's pace; **abrirse p. en la vida** to get on in life; **dar un p. en falso** to make a false move *o* a mistake; **estar de p.** to be passing through; **salirle al p. a alguien** to come up to sb; **salir del p.** to get out of trouble

**pasodoble** *nm* paso doble

**pasota** *Fam* **1** *adj* apathetic

**2** *nmf* dropout

**pasotismo** *nm Fam* couldn't-care-less attitude

**pasquín** *nm* lampoon

**pasta** *nf* (a) *(masa)* paste; *(de papel)* pulp; **p. dentífrica** toothpaste (b) *Culin (espaguetis, macarrones)* pasta; *(de pasteles)* pastry; **pastas alimenticias** pasta (c) *(pastelito)* shortcake biscuit (d) *Fam (dinero)* dough; **costar/ganar una p. gansa** to cost/earn a packet *o* fortune (e) *(encuadernación)* **de p. dura/blanda** hardback/paperback (f) *Fam* **ser de buena p.** to be good-natured

**pastar** *vi* to graze

**pastel** *nm* (**a**) *Culin (dulce)* cake; *(salado)* pie (**b**) *Arte* pastel; **colores p.** pastel colours (**c**) *(expresiones)* **descubrir el p.** to let the cat out of the bag; **repartirse el p.** to share things out

**pastelería** *nf* (**a**) *(establecimiento)* cake shop, patisserie (**b**) *(repostería)* pastries

**pastelero, -a 1** *adj* pastry; **crema pastelera** confectioner's custard; **la industria pastelera** the cake and biscuit manufacturing industry

**2** *nm,f (cocinero)* pastry cook; *(vendedor)* owner of a patisserie

**pasteurizado, -a, pasterizado, -a** *adj* pasteurized

**pasteurizar, pasterizar** [16] *vt* to pasteurize

**pastiche** *nm* pastiche

**pastilla** *nf* (**a**) *Med* pill, tablet (**b**) *(de jabón, chocolate)* bar (**c**) *Aut* shoe *(of brakes)* (**d**) *Elec* microchip (**e**) **a toda p.** at full pelt

**pastizal** *nm* pasture

**pasto** *nm* (**a**) *(hierba)* fodder (**b**) *(sitio)* pasture (**c**) *(expresiones)* **a todo p.** in abundance; **ser p. de las llamas** to go up in flames

**pastón** *nm Fam* **vale un p.** it costs a bomb

**pastor, -ora 1** *nm,f (de ganado)* shepherd, *f* shepherdess

**2** *nm* (**a**) *(sacerdote)* minister; **p. protestante** Protestant minister (**b**) *(perro)* **p. alemán** Alsatian, German shepherd

**pastoral** *adj* pastoral

**pastorear** *vt* to put out to pasture

**pastoreo** *nm* shepherding

**pastoso, -a** *adj* (**a**) *(blando)* pasty; *(arroz)* sticky (**b**) *(seco)* dry; **tener la boca pastosa** to have a furry tongue

**pata** *nf* (**a**) *(pierna)* (de mesa, animal) leg (**b**) *(pie)* foot; *(de perro, gato)* paw; *(de vaca, caballo)* hoof (**c**) *Fam (de persona)* leg; **a cuatro patas** on all fours; **a p.** on foot; **ir a la p. coja** to hop (**d**) *(de mueble)* leg; *(de gafas)* arm (**e**) *(ave)* duck (**f**) *(expresiones)* **estirar la p.** to kick the bucket; **meter la p.** to put one's foot in it; *también Fig* **poner algo patas arriba** to turn sth upside down; **tener mala p.** to be unlucky; *Am Fam* **patas** *(poca vergüenza)* cheek; **patas de gallo** *(arrugas)* crow's feet; **p. de gallo** *(tejido)* hound's-tooth check material; *Culin* **p. negra** = type of top-quality cured ham

**patada** *nf* kick; *(en el suelo)* stamp; **había turistas a patadas** there were loads of tourists; **dar una p. a** to kick; **me da cien patadas (que...)** it makes me mad (that...); **dar la p. a alguien** to kick sb out; *Fig* **en dos patadas** *(en seguida)* in two shakes; **sentar como una p. (en el estómago)** to be like a kick in the teeth; **tratar a alguien a patadas** to treat sb like dirt

**patagón, -ona** *adj & nm,f* Patagonian

**Patagonia** *n* **la P.** Patagonia

**patalear** *vi (en el aire)* to kick about; *(en el suelo)* to stamp one's feet

**pataleo** *nm (en el aire)* kicking, thrashing about; *(en el suelo)* stamping; *Fig* **derecho al p.** right to complain

**pataleta** *nf* tantrum

**patán 1** *adj m* uncivilized, uncouth

**2** *nm* bumpkin

**patata** *nf* potato; **patatas fritas** *(de sartén)* chips; *(de bolsa)* crisps; *Fig* **p. caliente** hot potato

**patatero, -a 1** *adj Fam* **un rollo p.** *(mentira)* a ridiculous spiel; **la película fue un rollo p.** the film was unbelievably boring

**2** *nm,f* potato farmer

**patatús** *(pl* patatuses*) nm Fam* funny turn

**paté** *nm* paté

**patear 1** *vt (dar un puntapié a)* to kick; *(pisotear)* to stamp on

**2** *vi* (**a**) *(patalear)* to stamp one's feet (**b**) *Fam Fig (andar)* to tramp

**3 patearse** *vpr Fam (recorrer)* to tramp

**patena** *nf* paten; **limpio** *o* **blanco como una p.** as clean as a new pin

**patentado, -a** *adj* patent, patented

**patentar** *vt* to patent

**patente 1** *adj* obvious; *(demostración, prueba)* clear

**2** *nf* (**a**) *(de invento)* patent (**b**) *(autorización)* licence (**c**) *Chile (matrícula)* number plate

**pateo** *nm Fam* stamping

**patera** *nf (embarcación)* small boat, dinghy

**paternal** *adj* fatherly, paternal; *Fig* paternal

**paternalismo** *nm* (**a**) *(actitud protectora)* paternalism (**b**) *(de padre)* fatherliness

**paternalista** *adj* paternalistic

**paternidad** *nf* fatherhood; *Der* paternity

**paterno, -a** *adj* paternal

**patético, -a** *adj* pathetic, moving

**patetismo** *nm* pathos

**patíbulo** *nm* scaffold, gallows

**patidifuso, -a** *adj Fam* stunned, floored

**patilla** *nf* (**a**) *(de pelo)* sideboard, sideburn (**b**) *(de gafas)* arm

**patín** *nm* (**a**) *(de hielo)* ice skate; *(de ruedas paralelas)* roller skate; *(en línea)* roller blade (**b**) *(patinete)* scooter (**c**) *(embarcación)* pedal boat

**pátina** *nf* patina

**patinador, -ora** *nm,f* skater

**patinaje** *nm* skating; **p. artístico** figure skating; **p. sobre hielo** ice skating; **p. sobre ruedas** roller skating; *(con patines en línea)* roller blading

**patinar** *vi* (**a**) *(sobre hielo)* to skate; *(sobre ruedas)* to roller-skate; *(con patines en línea)* to rollerblade (**b**) *(resbalar) (coche)* to skid; *(persona)* to slip; *Fam* **le patinan las neuronas** he's going a bit funny in the head (**c**) *Fam Fig (meter la pata)* to put one's foot in it

**patinazo** *nm* (**a**) *(de coche)* skid; *(de persona)* slip (**b**) *Fam Fig (equivocación)* blunder; **tener un p.** to make a blunder

**patinete** *nm* scooter

**patio** *nm (de casa)* courtyard; *(de escuela)* playground; *(de cuartel)* parade ground; *Fam* **¡cómo está el p.!** what a fine state of affairs!; **p. de butacas** stalls; **p. interior** *(en edificio)* lightshaft

**patita** *nf Fam Fig* **poner a alguien de patitas en la calle** to kick sb out

**patitieso, -a** *adj* (**a**) *(de frío)* frozen stiff (**b**) *(de sorpresa)* aghast, amazed

**patizambo, -a** *adj* knock-kneed

**pato, -a** *nm,f* duck; *Fig* **pagar el p.** to carry the can

**patochada** *nf Fam* piece of nonsense, idiocy; **la última p. del Gobierno** the government's latest cack-handed action

**patógeno, -a** *adj* infectious

**patología** *nf* pathology

**patológico, -a** *adj* pathological

**patoso, -a** *adj Fam* clumsy

**patraña** *nf* absurd story

**patria** *nf* native country, fatherland; **p. chica** home town; *Der* **p. potestad** parental authority

**patriarca** *nm* patriarch

**patriarcado** *nm* patriarchy

**patriarcal** *adj* patriarchal

**patricio, -a** *adj & nm,f* patrician

**patrimonial** *adj* hereditary

**patrimonio** *nm* (**a**) *(bienes) (heredados)* inheritance; *(propios)* wealth; *(económico)* national wealth (**b**) *(cultura)* heritage; **p. nacional** national heritage

**patrio, -a** *adj* native; **el suelo p.** one's native soil

**patriota 1** *adj* patriotic
**2** *nmf* patriot

**patriotero, -a** *adj Pey* jingoistic, chauvinistic

**patrioterismo** *nm Pey* jingoism, chauvinism

**patriótico, -a** *adj* patriotic

**patriotismo** *nm* patriotism

**patrocinador, -ora 1** *adj* sponsoring
**2** *nm,f* sponsor

**patrocinar** *vt* to sponsor

**patrocinio** *nm* sponsorship

**patrón, -ona 1** *nm,f* (**a**) *(de obreros)* boss; *(de criados)* master, *f* mistress (**b**) *(de pensión)* landlord, *f* landlady (**c**) *(santo)* patron saint
**2** *nm* (**a**) *(de barco)* skipper (**b**) *(medida)* standard; *Econ* **p. oro** gold standard (**c**) *(en costura)* pattern; *Fig* **estar cortados por el mismo p.** to be cast in the same mould

**patronal 1** *adj* (**a**) *(empresarial)* management; **organización p.** employers' organization (**b**) *Rel* **fiestas patronales** = celebrations for the feast day of a town's patron saint
**2** *nf (organización)* employers' organization

**patronato** *nm (dirección)* board of trustees; *(con fines benéficos)* trust

**patronímico, -a** *adj* patronymic

**patronista** *nmf* pattern cutter

**patrono, -a** *nm,f* (**a**) *(de empresa) (encargado)* boss; *(empresario)* employer (**b**) *(santo)* patron saint

**patrulla** *nf* patrol; **estar de p.** to be on patrol; **p. urbana** vigilante group

**patrullar** *vt & vi* to patrol

**patrullero, -a 1** *adj* patrol; **barco p.** patrol boat
**2** *nm,f (barco)* patrol boat

**patuco** *nm* bootee

**paulatino, -a** *adj* gradual

**pauperización** *nf* impoverishment

**paupérrimo, -a** *adj* very poor, impoverished

**pausa** *nf* pause, break; *Mús* rest; **con p.** unhurriedly; **hacer una p.** *(al hablar)* to pause; *(en actividad)* to take a break

**pausado, -a** *adj* deliberate, slow

**pauta** *nf* (**a**) *(modelo)* standard, model; **seguir una p.** to follow an example (**b**) *(en un papel)* guideline

**pautado, -a** *adj (papel)* lined, ruled

**pava** *nf* (**a**) *ver* **pavo** (**b**) *muy Fam (colilla)* dog end

**pavero, -a 1** *adj* boastful
**2** *nm,f* braggart

**pavimentación** *nf (de una carretera)* road surfacing; *(de la acera)* paving; *(de un suelo)* flooring

**pavimentar** *vt (carretera)* to surface; *(acera)* to pave; *(suelo)* to floor

**pavimento** *nm (de carretera)* road surface; *(de acera)* paving; *(de suelo)* flooring

**pavisoso, -a** *adj* dull, insipid

**pavo, -a 1** *adj Fam Pey* wet, drippy
**2** *nm,f* (**a**) *(ave)* turkey; **p. real** peacock, *f* peahen (**b**) *Fam Pey (persona)* drip (**c**) *Fam (cinco pesetas)* five pesetas; **cinco/cien pavos** twenty five/five hundred pesetas

**pavonearse** *vpr Pey* to boast, to brag (**de** about)

**pavoneo** *nm Pey* showing off, boasting

**pavor** *nm* terror

**pavoroso, -a** *adj* terrifying

**paya** *nf Arg, Chile* = improvised poem accompanied by guitar

**payasada** *nf* (**a**) *(graciosa)* piece of clowning; **hacer payasadas** to clown around (**b**) *(grotesca)* ludicrous thing to say/do

**payaso, -a 1** *adj* clownish
**2** *nm,f* clown

**payés, -esa** *nm,f* = peasant farmer from Catalonia or the Balearic Islands

**payo, -a** *adj & nm,f* non-gipsy

**paz** *nf* *(en general)* peace; *(tranquilidad)* peacefulness; **dejar a alguien en p.** to leave sb alone *o* in peace; **estar** *o* **quedar en p.** to be quits; **firmar la p.** to sign a peace treaty; **hacer las paces** to make (it) up; **que en p. descanse, que descanse en p.** may he/she rest in peace; **y en p.** and that's that

**pazguato, -a** *Fam* **1** *adj* *(simple)* simple; *(mojigato)* prudish
**2** *nm,f* *(simple)* simpleton; *(mojigato)* prude

**pazo** *nm* = Galician mansion, belonging to noble family

**PC** *nm* *(abrev de* **personal computer***)* PC

**PCE** *nm* *(abrev de* **Partido Comunista de España***)* Spanish communist party

**PCUS** [pe'kus] *nm* *(abrev de* **Partido Comunista de la Unión Soviética***)* Soviet communist party

**PD** *(abrev de* **posdata***)* PS

**pe** *nf Fam Fig* **de pe a pa** from beginning to end

**peaje** *nm* toll

**peana** *nf* pedestal

**peatón** *nm* pedestrian

**peatonal** *adj* pedestrian; **calle p.** pedestrian street

**peca** *nf* freckle

**pecado** *nm* sin; **p. mortal** mortal sin; **p. original** original sin; **pecados capitales** deadly sins; *también Fig* **ser un p.** to be a sin *o* crime

**pecador, -ora 1** *adj* sinful
**2** *nm,f* sinner

**pecaminoso, -a** *adj* sinful

**pecar** [61] *vi* (**a**) *Rel* to sin (**b**) *(pasarse)* **p. de confiado/generoso** to be overconfident/too generous

**pecera** *nf* *(acuario)* fish tank; *(redonda)* fish bowl

**pechera** *nf* *(de camisa)* shirt front; *(de blusa, vestido)* bust

**pecho** *nm* (**a**) *(tórax)* chest; *(de mujer)* bosom (**b**) *(mama)* breast; **dar el p.** a to breastfeed (**c**) *Fig (interior)* heart (**d**) *(expresiones)* **a lo hecho, p.** it's no use crying over spilt milk; **a p. descubierto** without protection *o* any form of defence; **tomarse algo a p.** to take sth to heart

**pechuga** *nf* (**a**) *(de ave)* breast *(meat)* (**b**) *Fam (de mujer)* bosom, bust

**pechugona** *adj Fam* busty, buxom

**pécora** *nf* **ser una mala p.** to be a bitch *o* harpy

**pecoso, -a** *adj* freckly

**pectoral 1** *adj* (**a**) *Anat* pectoral, chest; **músculos pectorales** pectorals (**b**) *Med* cough; **jarabe p.** cough syrup
**2** *nm* (**a**) *Anat* pectoral (**b**) *Med* cough mixture *o* medicine

**pecuario, -a** *adj* livestock; **actividad pecuaria** livestock raising

**peculiar** *adj* (**a**) *(característico)* typical, characteristic (**b**) *(raro, curioso)* peculiar

**peculiaridad** *nf* (**a**) *(cualidad)* uniqueness (**b**) *(detalle)* particular feature *o* characteristic

**pecuniario, -a** *adj* pecuniary

**pedagogía** *nf* education, pedagogy

**pedagógico, -a** *adj* educational

**pedagogo, -a** *nm,f* *(especialista)* educationist; *(profesor)* teacher, educator

**pedal** *nm* (**a**) *(de bicicleta, coche, piano)* pedal (**b**) *Fam (borrachera)* **agarrarse un p.** to get plastered

**pedalada** *nf* pedal, pedalling

**pedalear** *vi* to pedal

**pedante 1** *adj* pretentious
**2** *nmf* pretentious person

**pedantería** *nf* *(cualidad)* pretentiousness; *(dicho, hecho)* piece of pretentiousness

**pedazo** *nm* piece, bit; **hacer pedazos algo** to break sth to bits; *Fig* to destroy; **saltar en (mil) pedazos** to be smashed to pieces; **p. de alcornoque** *o* **de animal** *o* **de bruto** stupid oaf *o* brute; *Fig* **ser un p. de pan** to be an angel, to be a real sweetie

**pederasta** *nm* (**a**) *Der (contra menores)* child molester (**b**) *(homosexual)* (active) homosexual

**pederastia** *nf* (**a**) *Der (contra menores)* child molesting (**b**) *(sodomía)* sodomy

**pedernal** *nm* flint

**pedestal** *nm* pedestal, stand; **poner/tener a alguien en un p.** to put sb on a pedestal

**pedestre** *adj* (**a**) *(a pie)* on foot (**b**) *(corriente)* pedestrian, prosaic

**pediatra** *nmf* paediatrician

**pediatría** *nf* paediatrics *(singular)*

**pediculo, -a** *nm,f Br* chiropodist, *US* podiatrist

**pedido** *nm Com* order; **hacer un p.** to place an order

**pedigrí** (*pl* **pedigríes**) *nm* pedigree

**pedigüeño, -a 1** *adj* demanding, clamouring

**2** *nm,f* (*que pide*) demanding person; (*mendigo*) beggar

**pedir** [49] **1** *vt* (a) (*en general*) to ask for; (*en comercios, restaurantes*) to order; **p. a alguien que haga algo** to ask sb to do sth; **p. a alguien (en matrimonio)** to ask for sb's hand (in marriage); **p. prestado algo a alguien** to borrow sth from sb; **pide un millón por la moto** he's asking a million for the motorbike (b) (*exigir*) to demand (c) (*requerir*) to call for, to need

**2** *vi* (*mendigar*) to beg

**pedo 1** *nm* (a) (*ventosidad*) fart; **tirarse un p.** to fart (b) *Fam* (*borrachera*) **agarrarse un p.** to get pissed

**2** *adj Fam* **estar p.** to be pissed

**pedofilia** *nf* paedophilia

**pedorrear** *vi Fam* to fart a lot

**pedorreta** *nf Fam* raspberry (*sound*)

**pedorro, -a** *nm,f Fam* (a) (*que se tira pedos*) person who farts a lot (b) (*tonto, pesado*) pain, bore

**pedrada** *nf* (a) (*acción*) throw of a stone (b) (*golpe*) blow *o* hit with a stone; **a pedradas** by stoning

**pedrea** *nf* (a) (*en lotería*) = group of smaller prizes in the Spanish national lottery (b) (*lucha*) stone fight

**pedregal** *nm* stony ground

**pedregoso, -a** *adj* stony

**pedrera** *nf* stone quarry

**pedrería** *nf* precious stones

**pedrisco** *nm* hail

**pedrusco** *nm* rough stone

**peeling** ['pilin] (*pl* **peelings**) *nm* face mask *o* pack

**pega** *nf* (a) (*pegamento*) glue (b) (*obstáculo*) difficulty, hitch; **poner pegas (a)** to find problems (with) (c) **de p.** false, fake

**pegadizo, -a** *adj* (a) (*música*) catchy (b) *Fig* (*contagioso*) catching

**pegado** *nm* (*parche*) plaster

**pegajoso, -a** *adj* sticky; *Fig* clinging

**pegamento** *nm* glue

**pegar** [40] **1** *vt* (a) (*adherir*) to stick; (*con pegamento*) to glue; (*póster, cartel*) to fix, to put up; (*botón*) to sew on

(b) (*arrimar*) **p. algo a** to put *o* place sth against

(c) (*golpear*) to hit

(d) (*propinar*) (*bofetada, paliza*) to give; (*golpe*) to deal

(e) (*contagiar*) **p. algo a alguien** to give sb sth, to pass sth on to sb

(f) (*corresponder a, ir bien a*) to suit, to go with; **no le pega ese novio/vestido** that boyfriend/dress doesn't suit her

(g) *Informát* to paste

**2** *vi* (a) (*adherir*) to stick

(b) (*golpear*) to hit

(c) (*armonizar*) to go together, to match; **p. con** to go with

(d) (*sol*) to beat down

**3 pegarse** *vpr* (a) (*adherirse*) to stick

(b) (*agredirse*) to fight, to hit one another

(c) (*golpearse*) **pegarse (un golpe) con algo** to hit oneself against sth

(d) *Fig* (*contagiarse*) (*enfermedad*) to be transmitted, to be passed on; (*canción*) to be catchy; **se me pegó su acento** I picked up his accent

(e) *Fig* (*engancharse*) **pegarse a alguien** to stick to sb

(f) *Fam Fig* **pegársela a alguien** to have sb on, to deceive sb; (*cónyuge*) to cheat on sb; **se la pega a su marido con el vecino** she's cheating on her husband with the man next door

**pegatina** *nf* sticker

**pego** *nm Fam Fig* **dar el p.** to look like the real thing

**pegote** *nm Fam* (a) (*masa pegajosa*) sticky mess (b) (*chapucería*) botch

**pegue** *etc ver* **pegar**

**peinado** *nm* (*estilo, tipo*) hairstyle; (*más elaborado*) hairdo

**peinador** *nm* dressing gown

**peinar 1** *vt también Fig* to comb

**2 peinarse** *vpr* to comb one's hair

**peine** *nm* comb; *Fam Fig* **enterarse de** *o* **saber lo que vale un p.** to find out what's what *o* a thing or two

**peineta** *nf* decorative comb worn in hair

**p.ej.** (*abrev de* **por ejemplo**) e.g

**pejiguera** *nf Fam* drag, pain

**Pekín** *n* Peking, Beijing

**pela** *nf Fam* peseta; **no tengo pelas** I'm skint

**peladilla** *nf* sugared almond

**pelado, -a** *adj* (a) (*cabeza*) shorn (b) (*piel, cara*) peeling; (*fruta*) peeled (c) (*habitación, monte, árbol*) bare (d) (*número*) exact, round; **saqué un aprobado p.** I passed, but only just (e) *Fam* (*sin dinero*) broke, skint

**peladura** *nf* peeling

**pelagatos** *nmf inv Fam Pey* nobody

**pelaje** *nm (de gato, oso, conejo)* fur; *(de perro, caballo)* coat

**pelambre** *nm* mane *o* mop of hair

**pelambrera** *nf* long thick hair

**pelandusca** *nf Fam Pey* tart, slut

**pelar 1** *vt* (a) *(persona)* to cut the hair of (b) *(fruta, patatas)* to peel; *(guisantes, marisco)* to shell (c) *(aves)* to pluck; *(conejos)* to skin; **p. la pava** *(novios)* to flirt, to have a lovey-dovey conversation (d) *Fam Fig (dejar sin dinero)* to fleece (e) *Fam* **hace un frío que pela** it's freezing cold

**2 pelarse** *vpr* (a) *(cortarse el pelo)* to have one's hair cut (b) *(piel, espalda)* to peel (c) **pelarse de frío** to be frozen stiff, to be freezing cold

**peldaño** *nm (escalón)* step; *(de escalera de mano)* rung

**pelea** *nf* (a) *(a golpes)* fight (b) *(riña)* row, quarrel

**pelear 1** *vi* (a) *(a golpes)* to fight (b) *(a gritos)* to have a row *o* quarrel (c) *(esforzarse)* to struggle

**2 pelearse** *vpr* (a) *(a golpes)* to fight (b) *(a gritos)* to have a row *o* quarrel (c) *(enfadarse)* to fall out; **se ha peleado con su hermano** he's fallen out with his brother

**pelele** *nm* (a) *Fam Pey (persona)* puppet (b) *(muñeco)* guy, straw doll (c) *(prenda de bebé)* rompers

**peleón, -ona** *adj* (a) *(persona)* aggressive (b) *(vino)* rough

**peletería** *nf* (a) *(tienda)* fur shop, furrier's (b) *(oficio)* furriery (c) *(pieles)* furs; **artículos de p.** furs

**peletero, -a** *nm,f* furrier

**peliagudo, -a** *adj* tricky

**pelícano, pelicano** *nm* pelican

**película** *nf* (a) *(de cine)* film; **echar** *o* **poner una p.** to show a film; **de p.** amazing; **casa/vacaciones de p.** dream house/holiday; **p. muda/de terror** silent/horror film; **p. del Oeste** western (b) *Fot* **p. virgen** blank film (c) *(capa)* film (d) *Fam (historia increíble)* (tall) story; **montarse una p.** to dream up an incredible story

**peliculero, -a** *nm,f Fam* teller of tall stories

**peliculón** *nm Fam (película buena)* fantastic *o* great film

**peligrar** *vi* to be in danger

**peligro** *nm* danger; **correr p. (de)** to be in danger (of); **estar/poner en p.** to be/put at risk; **fuera de p.** out of danger; **¡p. de muerte!** *(en letrero)* danger!; **ser un p.** to be dangerous *o* a menace

**peligrosidad** *nf* danger

**peligroso, -a** *adj* dangerous

**pelillo** *nm* **¡pelillos a la mar!** let bygones be bygones

**pelín** *nm Fam* mite, tiny bit

**pelirrojo, -a 1** *adj* ginger, red-headed

**2** *nm,f* redhead

**pella** *nf Fam* **hacer pellas** *Br* to skive off (school)

**pellejo** *nm* (a) *(piel, vida)* skin; **estar/ponerse en el p. de otro** to be/put oneself in someone else's shoes; **salvar el p.** to save one's skin (b) *(padrastro)* hangnail

**pelliza** *nf* fur jacket

**pellizcar** [61] *vt* (a) *(persona)* to pinch (b) *(pan)* to pick at

**pellizco** *nm* pinch; *Fig* **un buen p.** *(de dinero)* a tidy sum

**pelma, pelmazo, -a** *Fam* **1** *adj* annoying, tiresome

**2** *nm,f* bore, pain

**pelo** *nm* (a) *(cabello)* hair

(b) *(de oso, conejo, gato)* fur; *(de perro, caballo)* coat

(c) *(de melocotón)* down

(d) *(de una tela)* nap

(e) *(expresiones)* **se le va a caer el p.** he'll be in big trouble; **con pelos y señales** with all the details; **de medio p.** second-rate; **le luce el p.** he's as fit as a fiddle; **montar a caballo a p.** to ride bareback; **presentarse a un examen a p.** to enter an exam unprepared; **no tener un p. de tonto** to be nobody's fool; **no tener pelos en la lengua** not to mince one's words; **no verle el p. a alguien** not to see hide nor hair of sb; **poner a alguien los pelos de punta** to make sb's hair stand on end; **por los pelos, por un p.** by the skin of one's teeth, only just; **ser un hombre de p. en pecho** to be a real man; **soltarse el p.** to let one's hair down; **tomar el p. a alguien** to pull sb's leg; **venir al p. a alguien** to be just right for sb; *también Fig* **a contra p.** against the grain

**pelón, -ona** *adj Fam (sin pelo)* bald

**pelota1** *nf* (a) *también Dep* ball; **jugar a la p.** to play ball; **devolver la p. a alguien** to put the ball back into sb's court; *Fam* **hacer la p. (a alguien)** to suck up (to sb); **p. base** baseball; **p. vasca** pelota (b) *Fam (cabeza)* nut (c) *Vulg (testículo)* **pelotas** balls; *muy Fam* **en pelotas** starkers, in the nude

**2** *nmf Fam Pey (persona) (en colegio)* apple-polisher; *(en oficina)* yes-man, sycophant

**pelotari** *nmf* pelota player

**pelotazo** *nm* (a) *(con pelota)* kick *o* throw of a ball (b) *Fig* **la cultura del p.** = ruthless obsession with money and power

**pelotear** *vi (en tenis)* to knock up

**peloteo** nm (a) (en tenis) knock-up (b) Fam (adulación) fawning (con on)

**pelotera** nf Fam scrap, fight

**pelotero, -a** Fam Pey 1 adj fawning

2 nm,f (en colegio) apple-polisher; (en oficina) yes-man, sycophant

**pelotilla** nf Fam (a) **hacer la p. a alguien** to suck up to sb (b) (de suciedad) = ball of grime rubbed from skin

**pelotón** nm (de soldados) squad; (de gente) crowd; Dep pack; **p. de ejecución** firing squad

**pelotudo, -a** adj CSur Fam stupid

**peluca** nf wig

**peluche** nm (a) (material) plush (b) (muñeco) cuddly toy; **osito de p.** teddy bear

**peludo, -a** adj hairy

**peluquería** nf (a) (establecimiento) hairdresser's (shop) (b) (oficio) hairdressing

**peluquero, -a** nm,f hairdresser

**peluquín** nm toupee

**pelusa** nf (a) (de tela) fluff (b) (vello) down (c) (de polvo) ball of fluff (d) (celos) **tener p. de** to be jealous of

**pélvico, -a** adj pelvic

**pelvis** nf inv pelvis

**pena** nf (a) (lástima) shame, pity; **¡qué p.!** what a shame o pity!; **dar p.** to inspire pity; **el pobre me da p.** I feel sorry for the poor chap (b) (tristeza) sadness, sorrow (c) (desgracia) problem, trouble (d) (dificultad) struggle; **a duras penas** with great difficulty (e) (castigo) punishment; **so** o **bajo p. de** under penalty of; **p. capital** o **de muerte** death penalty (f) Am (vergüenza) shame, embarrassment; **me da p.** I'm ashamed of it (g) Am **me da mucha p.** I'm very sorry (h) (expresiones) **de p.** (muy malo) atrocious, appalling; **dibuja/cocina de p.** he can't draw/cook to save his life; **hecho una p.** in a real mess, in a terrible state; **(no) valer** o **merecer la p.** (not) to be worthwhile o worth it; **una película que merece la p.** a film that's worth seeing; **sin p. ni gloria** without distinction

**penacho** nm (a) (de pájaro) crest (b) (adorno) plume

**penado, -a** nm,f convict

**penal 1** adj criminal

2 nm prison

**penalidad** nf suffering, hardship

**penalista** nmf (abogado) criminal lawyer

**penalización** nf (a) (acción) penalization (b) (sanción) penalty

**penalizar** [16] vt también Dep to penalize

**penalti** nm Dep penalty; **parar un p.** to save a penalty (shot); Fam **casarse de p.** to have a shotgun wedding

**penar 1** vt (castigar) to punish

2 vi (sufrir) to suffer

**pendejada** nf Am (tontería) stupid thing to do/say

**pendejo** nm Fam (a) (cobarde) coward (b) (tonto) prat, idiot

**pendenciero, -a 1** adj who always gets into a fight

2 nm,f = person who is always getting into fights

**pender** vi (a) (colgar) to hang (de from); Fig **p. de un hilo** to be hanging by a thread (b) Fig (amenaza) **p. sobre** to hang over (c) Fig (sentencia) to be pending

**pendiente 1** adj (a) (por resolver) pending; (deuda) outstanding; **estar p. de** (atento a) to keep an eye on; (a la espera de) to be waiting for; Fig **estar p. de un hilo** to be hanging by a thread (b) (asignatura) failed

2 nm earring

3 nf slope; **el terreno está en p.** the ground slopes o is on a slope

**pendón¹** nm (estandarte) banner

**pendón², -ona** nm,f Fam libertine

**pendonear** vi Fam to hang out

**pendular** adj (movimiento) swinging, swaying

**péndulo** nm pendulum

**pene** nm penis

**penene** nmf = untenured teacher or lecturer

**penetración** nf (a) (introducción) penetration; Econ **p. de mercado** market penetration (b) (sagacidad) astuteness, sharpness

**penetrante** adj (a) (intenso) (dolor) acute; (olor) sharp; (frío) biting; (mirada) penetrating; (voz, sonido) piercing (b) (sagaz) sharp, penetrating

**penetrar 1** vi **penetrar en** (internarse en) to enter; (filtrarse por) to get into, to penetrate; (perforar) to pierce; (llegar a conocer) to get to the bottom of

2 vt (a) (introducirse en) (sujeto: arma, sonido) to pierce, to penetrate; (sujeto: humedad, líquido) to permeate; (sujeto: emoción, sentimiento) to pierce (b) (secreto, misterio) to get to the bottom of (c) (sexualmente) to penetrate

**peneuvista 1** adj of/relating to the Basque nationalist party PNV

2 nmf member/supporter of the Basque nationalist party PNV

**penicilina** nf penicillin

**península** nf peninsula

**peninsular 1** adj peninsular

2 nmf peninsular Spaniard

**penique** nm penny; **peniques** pence

**penitencia** *nf* penance; **hacer p.** to do penance

**penitenciaría** *nf* prison

**penitenciario, -a** *adj* prison; **régimen p.** prison regime

**penitente** *nmf* penitent

**penoso, -a** *adj* (a) *(trabajoso)* laborious (b) *(lamentable)* distressing; *(aspecto, espectáculo)* sorry

**pensado, -a** *adj* **mal p.** twisted, evil-minded; **en el día/momento menos p.** when you least expect it; **un mal p.** a twisted person; **bien p.** on reflection

**pensador, -ora** *nm,f* thinker

**pensamiento** *nm* (a) *(facultad)* thought; *(mente)* mind; *(idea)* idea, thought; **leer el p. a alguien** to read sb's mind *o* thoughts (b) *Bot* pansy

**pensar** [3] **1** *vi* to think; **p. en algo/en alguien/en hacer algo** to think about sth/about sb/about doing sth; **piensa en un número/buen regalo** think of a number/good present; **dar que p. a alguien** to give sb food for thought

**2** *vt* (a) *(reflexionar sobre)* to think about *o* over (b) *(opinar, creer)* to think; **p. algo de alguien/algo** to think sth of sb/sth; **pienso que no vendrá** I don't think she'll come (c) *(idear)* to think up (d) *(tener la intención de)* **p. hacer algo** to intend to do sth; **¡ni pensarlo!** no way!, not a chance!; **no pienso decírtelo** I have no intention of telling you; **¿qué piensas hacer?** what are you going to do?, what are you thinking of doing?

**3 pensarse** *vpr* **pensarse algo** to think about sth, to think sth over

**pensativo, -a** *adj* pensive, thoughtful

**pensión** *nf* (a) *(dinero)* pension; **p. alimenticia** *o* **alimentaria** maintenance; **p. de jubilación/de viudedad** retirement/widow's pension (b) *(de huéspedes)* guest house; **media p.** *(en hotel)* half board; **estar a media p.** *(en colegio)* to have school dinners; **p. completa** full board

**pensionado** *nm* boarding school

**pensionista** *nmf* (a) *(jubilado)* pensioner (b) *(en una pensión)* guest, lodger (c) *(en un colegio)* boarder

**pentaedro** *nm* pentahedron

**pentagonal** *adj* pentagonal

**pentágono** *nm* pentagon

**pentagrama** *nm Mús* stave

**pentatlón** *nm* pentathlon

**Pentecostés** *nm* (a) *(cristiano)* Whitsun, Pentecost (b) *(judío)* Pentecost

**pentotal** *nm* Pentothal

**penúltimo, -a** *adj & nm,f* penultimate, last but one

**penumbra** *nf* semi-darkness, half-light; **en p.** in semi-darkness

**penuria** *nf* (a) *(pobreza)* penury, poverty (b) *(escasez)* paucity, dearth

**peña** *nf* (a) *(roca)* crag, rock; *(monte)* cliff (b) *(grupo de amigos)* circle, group; *(club)* club; *(quinielística)* pool

**peñasco** *nm* large crag *o* rock

**peñón** *nm* rock; **el P. (de Gibraltar)** the Rock (of Gibraltar)

**peón** *nm* (a) *(obrero)* unskilled labourer; **p. caminero** navvy (b) *(en ajedrez)* pawn (c) *(peonza)* (spinning) top

**peonada** *nf* (a) *(día de trabajo)* day's work (b) *(sueldo)* day's wages (c) *Am (obreros)* group of workers

**peonza** *nf* (spinning) top

**peor 1** *adj* (a) *(comparativo)* worse **(que** than) (b) *(superlativo)* **el/la p....** the worst...; **lo p. fue que...** the worst thing was that...

**2** *pron* **el/la p. (de)** the worst (in); **el p. de todos** the worst of all

**3** *adv* (a) *(comparativo)* worse **(que** than); **ahora veo p.** I see worse now; **estar p.** *(enfermo)* to get worse; **estoy p. (de salud)** I feel worse; **p. que p.** so much the worse (b) *(superlativo)* worst; **el que lo hizo p.** the one who did it (the) worst

**pepinillo** *nm* gherkin

**pepino** *nm* cucumber; *Fam* **me importa un p.** I couldn't care less, I don't give a damn

**pepita** *nf* (a) *(de fruta)* pip (b) *(de oro)* nugget

**pepito** *nm* (a) *(de carne)* grilled meat sandwich (b) *(dulce)* = long, cream-filled cake made of dough similar to doughnut

**pepona** *nf* large cardboard doll

**peque¹** *nmf* *(diminutivo de* **pequeño)** *Fam (niño)* kid

**peque²** *etc ver* **pecar**

**pequeñez** *nf* *(cualidad)* smallness; *Fig (cosa insignificante)* trifle

**pequeño, -a 1** *adj* small, little; *(hermano)* little; *(posibilidad)* slight; *(ingresos, cifras)* low

**2** *nm,f (niño)* little one; **de p.** as a child; **el p., la pequeña** *(benjamín)* the youngest, the baby

**pequeñoburgués, -esa 1** *adj* petit bourgeois

**2** *nm,f* petit bourgeois, *f* petite bourgeoise

**pequinés, -esa 1** *adj & nm,f* Pekinese

**2** *nm (perro)* Pekinese

**PER** *nm (abrev de* **Plan de Empleo Rural)** = Spanish government project to support rural employment

**pera 1** *nf* (a) *(fruta)* pear (b) *(de goma)* (rubber) bulb (c) *(interruptor)* = light switch on cord (d) *(expresiones)* **partir peras** to fall out; **pedir peras al olmo** to ask (for) the impossible; *Fam* **ser la p.** to be the limit

**2** *adj inv Fam* posh; **niño p.** spoilt *o* posh brat

**peral** *nm* pear-tree

**peralte** *nm* (de carretera) banking

**perborato** *nm* perborate

**perca** *nf* perch

**percal** *nm* percale; **conocer el p.** to know the score *o* what's what

**percance** *nm* mishap

**per cápita** *adj & adv* per capita

**percatarse** *vpr* **p. (de algo)** to notice (sth)

**percebe** *nm* (a) *(marisco)* goose barnacle (b) *Fam (persona)* twit

**percepción** *nf* (a) *(por los sentidos, la inteligencia)* perception; **p. extrasensorial** extrasensory perception (b) *(cobro)* receipt, collection

**perceptible** *adj* (a) *(por los sentidos)* noticeable, perceptible (b) *(que se puede cobrar)* receivable, payable

**perceptivo, -a** *adj* sensory

**percha** *nf* (a) *(de armario)* (coat) hanger (b) *(de pared)* coat rack (c) *(de pie)* coat stand, hat stand (d) *(para pájaros)* perch (e) *Fam* **ser una buena p.** to have a good figure

**perchero** *nm* (de pared) coat rack; (de pie) coat stand, hat stand

**percibir** *vt* (a) *(con los sentidos)* to perceive, to notice; *(por los oídos)* to hear (b) *(cobrar)* to receive, to get

**percusión** *nf* percussion

**percusionista** *nmf* percussionist

**percusor, percutor** *nm* hammer, firing pin

**perdedor, -ora 1** *adj* losing

**2** *nm,f* loser

**perder** [66] **1** *vt* (a) *(dinero, objeto, amigo)* to lose (b) *(desperdiciar)* to waste (c) *(tren, oportunidad)* to miss (d) *(perjudicar)* to be the ruin of; **le pierde su pasión por el juego** his passion for gambling is ruining him

**2** *vi* (a) *(salir derrotado)* to lose (b) *(empeorar)* to go downhill (c) *(dejar escapar aire)* to deflate, to go down (d) **echar algo a p.** to spoil sth; **echarse a p.** *(alimento)* to go off, to spoil

**3 perderse** *vpr* (a) *(extraviarse)* to get lost; **me he perdido** I'm lost (b) *(desaparecer)* to disappear; *Fam* **¡piérdete!** get lost! (c) *(desperdiciarse)* to be wasted (d) *(desaprovechar)* **perderse algo** to miss out on sth; **¡no te lo pierdas!** don't miss it! (e) *Fig (por los vicios)* to be beyond salvation (f) *Fig* **perderse por** *(anhelar)* to be mad about

**perdición** *nf* ruin, undoing

**pérdida** *nf* (a) *(en general)* loss; **no tiene p.** you can't miss it (b) *(de tiempo, dinero)* waste (c) *(escape)* leak (d) *Fin & Mil* **pérdidas** losses (e) **pérdidas** *(daños)* damage

**perdidamente** *adv* hopelessly

**perdido, -a 1** *adj* (a) *(extraviado)* lost; *(animal, bala)* stray (b) *(sucio)* filthy; **ponerse p. de pintura/barro** to get (oneself) covered in paint/mud; *Fig* **¡estamos perdidos!** we're done for!, we're lost! (c) *(tiempo)* wasted; *(ocasión)* missed (d) *Fam (de remate)* complete, utter; **es idiota p.** he's a complete idiot

**2** *nm,f* reprobate

**perdigón** *nm* pellet

**perdigonada** *nf* (a) *(tiro)* shot (b) *(herida)* gunshot wound

**perdiguero** *nm* English setter

**perdiz** *nf* partridge; **fueron felices y comieron perdices** they all lived happily ever after

**perdón** *nm* pardon, forgiveness; **con p.** if you'll forgive the expression; **no tener p.** to be unforgivable; **pedir p.** to apologize; **¡p.!** *(lo siento)* sorry!; **perdón, ¿me deja pasar?** excuse me – can I get past?

**perdonar** *vt* (a) *(ofensa, falta)* to forgive; **perdonarle algo a alguien** to forgive sb for sth; **perdone que le moleste** sorry to bother you; **perdone, ¿me deja salir?** excuse me – can I get past? (b) *(eximir de) (deuda, condena)* **p. algo a alguien** to let sb off sth; **perdonarle la vida a alguien** to spare sb their life (c) *(desperdiciar)* **no p. algo** not to miss sth

**perdonavidas** *nmf inv Fam* bully

**perdurable** *adj* (a) *(que dura siempre)* eternal (b) *(que dura mucho)* long-lasting

**perdurar** *vi* (a) *(durar mucho)* to endure, to last (b) *(persistir)* to persist

**perecedero, -a** *adj* (a) *(productos)* perishable (b) *(naturaleza)* transitory

**perecer** [48] *vi* to perish, to die

**peregrina** *nf* (a) *ver* **peregrino** (b) *(vieira)* scallop

**peregrinación** *nf*, **peregrinaje** *nm Rel* pilgrimage; *Fig (a un lugar)* trek

**peregrinar** *vi Rel* to make a pilgrimage; *Fig (a un lugar)* to trail, to trek

**peregrino, -a 1** *adj* (a) *(ave)* migratory (b) *Fig (extraño)* strange, bizarre

**2** *nm,f (persona)* pilgrim

**perejil** *nm* parsley

**perenne** *adj* (a) *Bot* perennial (b) *(recuerdo)* enduring (c) *(continuo)* constant

**perentorio, -a** *adj* urgent, pressing; *(gesto, tono)* peremptory; **plazo p.** fixed time limit

**perestroika** *nf* perestroika

**pereza** *nf* idleness; **me da p. ir a pie** I can't be bothered walking; **sacudirse la p.** to wake oneself up

**perezoso, -a 1** *adj* (a) *(vago)* lazy (b) *(lento)* slow, sluggish

  **2** *nm,f (vago)* lazy person, idler

  **3** *nm (animal)* sloth

**perfección** *nf* perfection; **es de una gran p.** it's exceptionally good; **a la p.** perfectly

**perfeccionamiento** *nm* (a) *(acabado)* perfecting (b) *(mejoramiento)* improvement

**perfeccionar** *vt* (a) *(redondear)* to perfect (b) *(mejorar)* to improve

**perfeccionismo** *nm* perfectionism

**perfeccionista** *adj & nmf* perfectionist

**perfectamente** *adv* (a) *(sobradamente)* perfectly (b) *(muy bien)* fine; **¿cómo estás? – estoy p.** how are you? – I'm fine (c) *(de acuerdo)* **¡p.!** fine!, great!

**perfectivo, -a** *adj* perfective

**perfecto, -a** *adj* perfect; **¡p.!** *(de acuerdo)* fine!, great!

**perfidia** *nf* perfidy, treachery

**pérfido, -a 1** *adj* perfidious, treacherous

  **2** *nm,f* treacherous person

**perfil** *nm* (a) *(contorno)* outline, shape (b) *(de cara, cuerpo)* profile; **de p.** in profile (c) *Fig (característica)* characteristic (d) *Fig (retrato moral)* profile

**perfilar** *vt* **1** to outline

  **2 perfilarse** *vpr* (a) *(destacarse)* to be outlined (b) *(concretarse)* to shape up

**perforación** *nf* (a) *también Med* perforation (b) *(taladro)* bore-hole

**perforador, -ora** *adj* drilling

**perforadora** *nf* (a) *(herramienta)* drill (b) *(para papel)* paper punch

**perforar 1** *vt (agujerear)* to cut a hole/holes in; *(con taladro)* to drill a hole/holes in; **la bala le perforó el pulmón** the bullet pierced his lung

  **2 perforarse** *vpr* **p. las orejas** to have o get one's ears pierced

**perfumar 1** *vt* to perfume

  **2 perfumarse** *vpr* to put perfume on

**perfume** *nm* perfume

**perfumería** *nf* (a) *(tienda, arte)* perfumery (b) *(productos)* perfumes

**pergamino** *nm* parchment

**pergeñar** *vt (plan, idea)* to rough out; *(comida)* to whip up

**pérgola** *nf* pergola

**pericia** *nf* skill

**pericial** *adj* expert

**perico** *nm* (a) *Fam (pájaro)* parakeet (b) *muy Fam (cocaína)* snow (c) *Col (café con leche)* white coffee

**periferia** *nf (contorno)* periphery; *(alrededores)* outskirts

**periférico, -a 1** *adj* peripheral; **barrio p.** outlying district

  **2** *nm Informát* peripheral

**perifollos** *nmpl Fam* frills (and fripperies)

**perífrasis** *nf inv* wordy explanation; *Gram* **p. verbal** compound verb

**perifrástico, -a** *adj* long-winded

**perilla** *nf* goatee; **venir de p.** *o* **perillas** to be just the right thing

**perímetro** *nm* perimeter

**periodicidad** *nf (regularidad, frecuencia)* frequency; *Mec* periodicity

**periódico, -a 1** *adj* (a) *(regular)* regular, periodic (b) *Mat* recurrent

  **2** *nm* newspaper

**periodismo** *nm* journalism

**periodista** *nmf* journalist

**periodístico, -a** *adj* journalistic

**período, periodo** *nm* period; *Dep* half; **p. de prácticas** trial period

**peripatético, -a 1** *adj* (a) *Filosofía* Peripatetic (b) *Fam (ridículo)* ludicrous

  **2** *nm,f* Peripatetic

**peripecia** *nf* incident, adventure; **sus peripecias en la selva** his adventures in the jungle

**periplo** *nm* journey, voyage

**peripuesto, -a** *adj Fam* dolled-up, tarted-up

**periquete** *nm* **en un p.** in a jiffy

**periquito 1** *nm* parakeet

  **2** *adj Fam Dep* = of/relating to the Español Football Club

**periscopio** *nm* periscope

**perista** *nmf Fam* fence, = receiver of stolen goods

**peritaje** *nm* (a) *(trabajo)* expert work; *(informe)* expert's report (b) *(estudios)* professional training

**peritar** *vt (casa)* to value; *(coche)* to assess the value of, to assess the damage to

**perito** *nm* (a) *(experto)* expert; **p. agrónomo** agronomist (b) *(ingeniero técnico)* technician

**perjudicado, -a 1** *adj* affected; *Der* **la parte perjudicada** the injured party

  **2** *nm,f* **los perjudicados por la inundación** those affected by the flood; *Der* **el p.** the injured party

**perjudicar [61]** *vt* to damage, to harm

**perjudicial** *adj* harmful **(para** to)

**perjuicio** *nm* harm, damage; **causar perjuicios** (a) to do harm *o* damage (to); **ir en p. de** to be detrimental to; **sin p. de** despite

**perjurar** *vi* (a) *(jurar mucho)* **juró y perjuró que no había sido él** he swore blind that he hadn't done it (b) *(jurar en falso)* to commit perjury

**perjurio** *nm* perjury

**perjuro, -a 1** *adj* perjured

**2** *nm,f* perjurer

**perla** *nf* pearl; *Fig (maravilla)* gem, treasure; **de perlas** great, fine; **me viene de perlas** it's just the right thing

**perlado, -a** *adj (de gotas)* beaded

**permanecer** [48] *vi* (a) *(en un lugar)* to stay (b) *(en un estado)* to remain, to stay

**permanencia** *nf* (a) *(en un lugar)* staying, continued stay (b) *(en un estado)* continuation

**permanente 1** *adj* permanent; *(comisión)* standing

**2** *nf* perm; **hacerse la p.** to have a perm

**permeabilidad** *nf* permeability

**permeable** *adj* permeable

**permisible** *adj* permissible, acceptable

**permisividad** *nf* permissiveness

**permisivo, -a** *adj* permissive

**permiso** *nm* (a) *(autorización)* permission; **con p.** if I may, if you'll excuse me; **pedir p. para hacer algo** to ask permission to do sth (b) *(documento)* licence, permit; **p. de armas** gun licence; **p. de conducir** *Br* driving licence, *US* driver's license; **p. de residencia** residence permit; **p. de trabajo** work permit (c) *(vacaciones)* leave; **estar de p.** to be on leave

**permitido, -a** *adj* permitted, allowed

**permitir 1** *vt* to allow; **p. a alguien hacer algo** to allow sb to do sth; **¿me permite?** may I?

**2 permitirse** *vpr* to allow oneself (the luxury of); **no puedo permitírmelo** I can't afford it

**permuta** *nf* exchange

**permutable** *adj* exchangeable

**permutación** *nf* (a) *(permuta)* exchange (b) *Mat* permutation

**permutar** *vt* to exchange, to swap

**pernera** *nf* trouser leg

**pernicioso, -a** *adj* damaging, harmful

**pernil** *nm* leg of ham

**perno** *nm* bolt

**pernoctar** *vi* to stay overnight

**pero 1** *conj* but; **el reloj es viejo, p. funciona bien** the watch is old but it keeps good time; **p. ¿qué es todo este ruido?** what on earth is all this noise about?

**2** *nm* snag, fault; **poner peros a todo** to find fault with everything

**perogrullada** *nf Fam* truism

**Perogrullo** *nm* **una verdad de P.** a truism

**perol** *nm* casserole (dish)

**peroné** *nm* fibula

**peronismo** *nm Pol* Peronism

**peronista** *adj & nmf Pol* Peronist

**perorar** *vi Fam Pey* to speechify

**perorata** *nf* long-winded speech

**peróxido** *nm* peroxide

**perpendicular 1** *adj* perpendicular; **ser p. a algo** to be at right angles to sth'

**2** *nf* perpendicular (line)

**perpetrar** *vt* to perpetrate, to commit

**perpetuar** [4] **1** *vt* to perpetuate

**2 perpetuarse** *vpr* to last, to endure

**perpetuidad** *nf* perpetuity; **a p.** in perpetuity; **presidente a p.** president for life; **condenado a p.** condemned to life imprisonment

**perpetuo, -a** *adj* (a) *(para siempre)* perpetual (b) *(vitalicio)* lifelong; *Der* **cadena perpetua** life imprisonment

**perplejidad** *nf* perplexity, bewilderment

**perplejo, -a** *adj* perplexed, bewildered

**perra** *nf* (a) *(animal)* bitch (b) *Fam (rabieta)* tantrum; **coger una p.** to throw a tantrum (c) *Fam (dinero)* penny; **estoy sin una p.** I'm flat broke; **no tiene una p. gorda** *o* **chica** he hasn't got a bean; **no vale una p. gorda** *o* **chica** it isn't worth a bean

**perrera** *nf* (a) *(lugar)* kennels (b) *(vehículo)* dogcatcher's van

**perrería** *nf Fam* **hacer perrerías a alguien** to play dirty tricks on sb

**perrero, -a** *nm,f (persona)* dogcatcher

**perrito** *nm* **p. (caliente)** hot dog

**perro, -a 1** *adj Fam* wretched, lousy; **¡que vida más perra!** life's a bitch!

**2** *nm* (a) *(animal)* dog; **andar como el p. y el gato** to fight like cat and dog; **de perros** *(tiempo)* wretched, lousy; **ser p. viejo** to be an old hand; **allí no atan los perros con longaniza** money doesn't grow on trees there; *Prov* **p. ladrador poco mordedor** his/her bark is worse than his/her bite; *Prov* **muerto el p., se acabó la rabia** deal with a problem at its source; **p. callejero/de caza** stray/hunting dog; **p. faldero** lapdog; *Fig* lackey; **p. lazarillo/policía** guide/police dog; **p. lobo** alsatian; **p. pastor** sheepdog; **p. salchicha** sausage dog, dachshund (b) *Fam (persona)* swine, dog

**perruno, -a** *adj* canine

**persa 1** *adj & nmf* Persian

**2** *nm (idioma)* Persian, Farsi

**persecución** *nf* (a) *(seguimiento)* pursuit (b) *(acoso)* persecution

**per sécula seculorum** *adv* for ever and ever

**persecutorio, -a** *adj* **complejo p.** persecution complex

**perseguir** [63] *vt* (a) *(seguir, tratar de obtener)* to pursue (b) *(acosar)* to persecute; *Fig* **le persigue la mala suerte** she's dogged by bad luck

**perseverancia** *nf* perseverance

**perseverante** *adj* persistent

**perseverar** *vi* to persevere (**en** with), to persist (**en** in)

**Persia** *n* Persia

**persiana** *nf* blind

**persignarse** *vpr Rel* to cross oneself

**persigo** *etc ver* **perseguir**

**persiguiera** *etc ver* **perseguir**

**persistencia** *nf* persistence

**persistente** *adj* persistent

**persistir** *vi* to persist (**en** in)

**persona** *nf* (a) *(individuo)* person; **cien personas** a hundred people; **en p.** in person; **por p.** per head; **ser buena p.** to be nice; **p. mayor** adult, grown-up; **p. non grata** persona non grata (b) *Der* party; **p. física** private individual; **p. jurídica** legal entity *o* person (c) *Gram* person

**personaje** *nm* (a) *(persona importante)* important person, celebrity; **¡menudo p.!** *(persona despreciable)* what an unpleasant individual! (b) *(en novela, teatro)* character

**personal 1** *adj* *(privado, íntimo)* personal; **una opinión/pregunta p.** a personal opinion/question; **p. e intransferible** non-transferable
**2** *nm* (a) *(trabajadores)* staff, personnel (b) *Fam (gente)* people *(plural)*
**3** *nf* *(en baloncesto)* personal foul

**personalidad** *nf* (a) *(características)* personality (b) *(identidad)* identity (c) *(persona importante)* important person, celebrity (d) *Der* legal personality *o* status

**personalismo** *nm* (a) *(parcialidad)* favouritism (b) *(egocentrismo)* self-centredness

**personalizar** [16] *vi* (a) *(nombrar)* to name names (b) *(aludir)* to get personal

**personalmente** *adv* personally; **me encargaré yo p.** I'll deal with it myself *o* personally; **a mí, p., no me importa** it doesn't matter to me personally; **les afecta p.** it affects them personally

**personarse** *vpr* to turn up

**personero, -a** *nm,f Am* government representative

**personificación** *nf* personification

**personificar** *vt* to personify

**perspectiva** *nf* (a) *(punto de vista)* perspective; **en p.** *(dibujo)* in perspective (b) *(paisaje)* view (c) *(futuro)* prospect; **en p.** in prospect

**perspicacia** *nf* insight, perceptiveness

**perspicaz** *adj* sharp, perceptive

**persuadir 1** *vt* to persuade; **p. a alguien para que haga algo** to persuade sb to do sth
**2 persuadirse** *vpr* to convince oneself; **persuadirse de algo** to become convinced of sth

**persuasión** *nf* persuasion

**persuasiva** *nf* persuasive power

**persuasivo, -a** *adj* persuasive

**pertenecer** [48] *vi* **p. a** *(ser propiedad de)* to belong to; *(corresponder a)* to be up to, to be a matter for

**perteneciente** *adj* **p. a** belonging to

**pertenencia** *nf* (a) *(propiedad)* ownership (b) *(afiliación)* membership; **pertenencias** *(efectos personales)* belongings

**pértiga** *nf* (a) *(vara)* pole (b) *Dep* **(salto con) p.** pole-vault

**pertinaz** *adj* (a) *(terco)* stubborn (b) *(persistente)* persistent

**pertinencia** *nf* (a) *(adecuación)* appropriateness (b) *(relevancia)* relevance

**pertinente** *adj* (a) *(adecuado)* appropriate (b) *(relativo)* relevant, pertinent

**pertrechar 1** *vt Mil* to supply with food and ammunition; *(equipar)* to equip
**2 pertrecharse** *vpr* **pertrecharse de** to equip oneself with

**pertrechos** *nmpl* (a) *Mil* supplies and ammunition (b) *(utensilios)* gear

**perturbación** *nf* (a) *(desconcierto)* disquiet, unease (b) *(disturbio)* disturbance; **p. del orden público** breach of the peace (c) *Med* mental imbalance (d) *Meteo* **p. atmosférica** atmospheric disturbance

**perturbado, -a 1** *adj* (a) *Med* disturbed, mentally unbalanced (b) *(desconcertado)* perturbed
**2** *nm,f Med* mentally unbalanced person

**perturbador, -ora 1** *adj* unsettling
**2** *nm,f* troublemaker

**perturbar** *vt* (a) *(trastornar)* to disrupt (b) *(inquietar)* to disturb, to unsettle (c) *(enloquecer)* to perturb

**Perú** *nm* **(el)** P. Peru

**peruano, -a** *adj & nm,f* Peruvian

**perversidad** *nf* wickedness

**perversión** *nf* perversion

**perverso, -a** *adj* depraved

**pervertido, -a** *nm,f* pervert

**pervertidor, -ora 1** *adj* pernicious, corrupting
**2** *nm,f* reprobate, corrupter

**pervertir** [64] **1** *vt* to corrupt
**2 pervertirse** *vpr* to become corrupt, to be corrupted

**pervivir** *vi* to survive

**pesa** nf (**a**) (balanza, contrapeso) weight (**b**) Dep **pesas** weights; Fam **hacer pesas** to do weight training; **levantamiento de pesas** weightlifting

**pesabebés** nm inv baby-weighing scales

**pesacartas** nm inv letter-weighing scales

**pesadez** nf (**a**) (peso) weight (**b**) (sensación) heaviness (**c**) (molestia, fastidio) drag, pain (**d**) (aburrimiento) ponderousness

**pesadilla** nf también Fig nightmare

**pesado, -a 1** adj (**a**) (que pesa) heavy (**b**) (calor) oppressive (**c**) (sueño) deep (**d**) (lento) ponderous, sluggish (**e**) (tarea, trabajo) difficult, tough (**f**) (aburrido) boring (**g**) (molesto) annoying, tiresome; **¡qué pesada eres!** you're so annoying!; **ponerse p.** to be a pain
**2** nm,f bore, pain

**pesadumbre** nf grief, sorrow

**pésame** nm sympathy, condolences; **dar el p.** to offer one's condolences

**pesar 1** nm (**a**) (tristeza) grief (**b**) (arrepentimiento) remorse (**c**) (expresiones) **a p. de** despite; Fam **a p. de los pesares** in spite of everything; **a p. mío** against my will; **a p. de que** in spite of the fact that
**2** vt (**a**) (en balanza) to weigh (**b**) (examinar) to weigh up
**3** vi (**a**) (tener peso) to weigh (**b**) (ser pesado) to be heavy (**c**) (importar) to play an important part (**d**) (molestar) **me pesa tener que hacerlo** it grieves me to have to do it; **pese a** in spite of; **pese a quien pese** in spite of everything (**e**) (entristecer) **me pesa tener que decirte esto** I'm sorry to have to tell you this
**4 pesarse** vpr to weigh oneself

**pesaroso, -a** adj (**a**) (arrepentido) remorseful (**b**) (afligido) sad

**pesca** nf (**a**) (acción) fishing; **ir de p.** to go fishing; **p. de altura/bajura** deep-sea/coastal fishing; **p. submarina** underwater fishing (**b**) (captura) catch (**c**) Fam **... y toda la p. ...** the (whole) works

**pescadería** nf fishmonger's (shop)

**pescadero, -a** nm,f fishmonger

**pescadilla** nf whiting; Fam Fig **ser como la p. que se muerde la cola** to be a vicious circle

**pescado** nm fish; **p. azul/blanco** blue/white fish

**pescador, -ora** nm,f fisherman, f fisherwoman

**pescante** nm (**a**) (de carruaje) driver's seat (**b**) Náut davit

**pescar [61] 1** vt (**a**) (peces) to catch (**b**) Fam (pillar) to catch (**c**) Fam (conseguir) to get oneself, to land (**d**) Fam (entender) to pick up, to understand
**2** vi to fish, to go fishing

**pescuezo** nm neck; Fam **retorcer el p. a alguien** to wring sb's neck

**pese 1** etc ver **pesar**
**2: pese a** loc adv despite

**pesebre** nm (**a**) (para los animales) manger (**b**) (belén) crib, Nativity scene

**pesero** nm CAm, Méx fixed-rate taxi service

**peseta** nf (unidad) peseta; **pesetas** (dinero) money; Fam Fig **mirar la p.** to watch one's money

**pesetero, -a** Fam Pey **1** adj money-grubbing
**2** nm,f moneygrubber

**pesimismo** nm pessimism

**pesimista 1** adj pessimistic
**2** nmf pessimist

**pésimo, -a 1** superlativo ver **malo**
**2** adj terrible, awful

**peso** nm (**a**) (en general) weight; **tiene un kilo de p.** it weighs a kilo; **de p.** (razones) weighty, sound; (persona) influential; **caer por su propio p.** to be self-evident; **pagar algo a p. de oro** to pay a fortune for sth; **quitarse un p. de encima** to take a weight off one's mind; **p. atómico/molecular** atomic/molecular weight; **p. bruto/neto** gross/net weight; **p. ligero** lightweight; **p. medio** middleweight; **p. mosca** flyweight; **p. muerto** dead weight; **p. pesado** heavyweight (**b**) (balanza) scales (**c**) Dep shot; **lanzamiento de p.** shot-put, shot-putting (**d**) (moneda) peso

**pespunte** nm backstitch

**pespuntear** vt to backstitch

**pesque** etc ver **pescar**

**pesquería** nf (sitio) fishery, fishing ground

**pesquero, -a 1** adj fishing
**2** nm fishing boat

**pesquisa** nf investigation, inquiry

**pestaña** nf (**a**) (de párpado) eyelash; Fam Fig **quemarse las pestañas** to burn the midnight oil (**b**) (de recortable) flap (**c**) Mec flange

**pestañear** vi to blink; **sin p.** (con serenidad) without batting an eyelid; (con atención) without losing concentration once

**peste** nf (**a**) (enfermedad) plague; **p. bubónica** bubonic plague (**b**) Fam (mal olor) stink, stench (**c**) Fam (molestia) pest (**d**) (expresiones) **decir pestes de alguien** to heap abuse on sb; **echar pestes** to curse, to swear

**pesticida 1** adj pesticidal
**2** nm pesticide

**pestilencia** nf stench

**pestilente** adj foul-smelling

**pestillo** nm (cerrojo) bolt; (mecanismo, en verjas) latch; **correr o echar el p.** to shoot the bolt

**petaca** *nf* (a) *(para cigarrillos)* cigarette case; *(para tabaco)* tobacco pouch (b) *(para bebidas)* flask (c) *Am (maleta)* suitcase (d) *Fam* **hacer la p.** *(como broma)* to make an apple-pie bed

**petalo** *nm Fam* pin-ball machine

**pétalo** *nm* = petal

**petanca** *nf* = game similar to bowls played in parks, on beach etc

**petardo 1** *nm* (a) *(cohete)* banger, firecracker (b) *Fam (aburrimiento)* bore; **¡qué p. de película!** what a boring film! (c) *muy Fam (porro)* joint
2 *nmf Fam (persona fea)* horror, ugly person

**petate** *nm* kit bag; *Fam* **liar el p.** *(marcharse)* to pack one's bags and go; *(morir)* to kick the bucket

**petenera** *nf* = Andalusian popular song; *Fam* **salir por peteneras** to go off at a tangent

**petición** *nf* (a) *(acción)* request; **a p. de** at the request of; **p. de mano** proposal (of marriage) (b) *Der (escrito)* petition

**petimetre** *nm* fop, dandy

**petirrojo** *nm* robin

**petiso, -a** *adj Am Fam* short

**peto** *nm* (a) *(de prenda)* bib (b) *(de armadura)* breastplate (c) *Dep* breastguard

**pétreo, -a** *adj (de piedra)* stone; *(como piedra)* stony

**petrificar** [61] *vt también Fig* to petrify

**petrodólar** *nm* petrodollar

**petróleo** *nm* oil, petroleum; **p. crudo** crude oil

**petrolero, -a 1** *adj* oil; **compañía petrolera** oil company
2 *nm* oil tanker

**petrolífero, -a** *adj* oil; **pozo p.** oil well

**petroquímico, -a 1** *adj* petrochemical
2 *nf* **petroquímica** petrochemistry

**petulancia** *nf* arrogance

**petulante 1** *adj* opinionated, arrogant
2 *nmf* opinionated person

**petunia** *nf* petunia

**peúco** *nm* bootee

**peyorativo, -a** *adj* pejorative

**pez 1** *nm (animal)* fish; *Fig* **estar como p. en el agua** to be in one's element; *Fam* **estar p. (en algo)** to have no idea (about sth); **p. espada** swordfish; *Fam* **p. gordo** big shot; **p. martillo** hammerhead shark; **p. de río** freshwater fish; **p. volador** flying fish
2 *nf (sustancia)* pitch, tar

**pezón** *nm* (a) *(de teta)* nipple (b) *(de planta)* stalk

**pezuña** *nf* (a) *(de animal)* hoof (b) *Fam (mano)* paw

**Phnom Penh** [nom'pen] *n* Phnom Penh

**pi** *nf Mat* pi

**piadoso, -a** *adj* (a) *(compasivo)* kind-hearted (b) *(religioso)* pious

**Piamonte** *nm* **(el)** P. Piedmont

**pianista** *nmf* pianist

**piano 1** *nm* piano; **p. bar** piano bar; **p. de cola** grand piano; **p. de media cola** baby grand
2 *adv Mús* piano

**pianola** *nf* pianola

**piar** [34] *vi* to cheep, to tweet

**piara** *nf* herd

**piastra** *nf* piastre, piaster

**PIB** *nm (abrev de* **producto interior bruto***)* GDP

**pibe, -a** *nm,f CSur Fam (niño)* kid, boy; *(niña)* kid, girl

**PIC** [pik] *nm (abrev de* **punto de información cultural***)* = computer terminal for accessing cultural information

**pica** *nf* (a) *(lanza)* pike; *Fig* **poner una p. en Flandes** to do the impossible (b) *Taurom* goad, picador's spear (c) *Fam (revisor de tren)* ticket inspector (d) **picas** *(palo de baraja)* spades

**picada** *nf (de mosquito, serpiente)* bite; *(de avispa, escorpión, ortiga)* sting

**picadero** *nm* (a) *(de caballos)* riding school (b) *Fam (de soltero)* bachelor pad

**picadillo** *nm (de carne)* mince; *(de verdura)* chopped vegetables; *Fam* **hacer p. a alguien** to beat sb to a pulp

**picado, -a** *adj* (a) *(marcado) (piel)* pockmarked; *(fruta)* bruised (b) *(agujereado)* perforated; **p. de polilla** moth-eaten (c) *(triturado) (alimento)* chopped; *(carne)* minced; *(tabaco)* cut (d) *(vino)* sour (e) *(diente)* decayed (f) *(mar)* choppy (g) *Fam (enfadado)* annoyed (h) *Av* **hacer un p.** to dive; *Fig* **caer en p.** to plummet

**picador, -ora** *nm,f* (a) *Taurom* picador (b) *(domador)* (horse) trainer (c) *(minero)* face worker

**picadora** *nf* mincer

**picadura** *nf* (a) *(de mosquito, serpiente)* bite; *(de avispa, ortiga, escorpión)* sting (b) *(de viruela)* pockmark (c) *(de diente)* decay (d) *(tabaco) (cut)* tobacco

**picajoso, -a** *adj Fam* touchy

**picante 1** *adj* (a) *(comida)* spicy, hot (b) *Fig (chiste, comedia)* saucy
2 *nm (comida)* spicy food; *(sabor)* spiciness

**picantería** *nf Andes* cheap restaurant

**picapica** *nm* **(polvos de) p.** = powder which causes sneezing and itching

**picapleitos** *nmf inv Pey* bad lawyer

**picaporte** *nm* (a) *(mecanismo)* latch (b) *(aldaba)* doorknocker

**picar** [61] **1** vt (a) (*sujeto: mosquito, serpiente*) to bite; (*sujeto: avispa, escorpión, ortiga*) to sting
(**b**) (*sujeto: ave*) to peck
(**c**) (*escocer*) to itch; **me pican los ojos** my eyes are stinging
(**d**) (*triturar*) (*verdura*) to chop; (*carne*) to mince
(**e**) (*piedra, hielo*) to break up
(**f**) (*pared*) to chip the plaster off
(**g**) (*aperitivo*) to pick at
(**h**) *Fam* (*enojar*) to irritate
(**i**) *Fig* (*estimular*) (*persona, caballo*) to spur on; (*curiosidad*) to prick
(**j**) (*perforar*) (*billete, ficha*) to punch
(**k**) *Taurom* to goad
**2** vi (a) (*alimento*) to be spicy o hot
(**b**) (*pez*) to bite; *Fig* (*dejarse engañar*) to take the bait
(**c**) (*escocer*) to itch
(**d**) (*ave*) to peck
(**e**) (*tomar un aperitivo*) to nibble
(**f**) (*sol*) to burn
(**g**) **p. (muy) alto** to have great ambitions
**3** **picarse** vpr (a) (*vino*) to turn sour
(**b**) (*ropa*) to become moth-eaten
(**c**) (*mar*) to get choppy
(**d**) (*diente*) to get a cavity
(**e**) (*oxidarse*) to go rusty
(**f**) *Fam* (*enfadarse*) to get annoyed o cross
(**g**) *muy Fam* (*inyectarse droga*) to shoot up

**picardía** nf (a) (*astucia*) sharpness, craftiness (**b**) (*travesura*) naughty trick, mischief (**c**) (*atrevimiento*) brazenness (**d**) (*prenda femenina*) negligee

**picaresca** nf (a) *Lit* picaresque literature (**b**) (*modo de vida*) roguery

**picaresco, -a** adj mischievous, roguish

**pícaro, -a** nm,f (a) (*astuto*) sly person, rogue (**b**) (*travieso*) rascal (**c**) (*atrevido*) brazen person

**picatoste** nm crouton

**picazón** nf (a) (*en el cuerpo*) itch (**b**) *Fam* (*inquietud*) uneasiness

**picha** nf *muy Fam* dick, knob; **hacerse la p. un lío** to get oneself in a right mess

**pichi** nm pinafore (dress)

**pichichi** nm *Dep* top scorer

**pichincha** nf *CSur Fam* snip, bargain

**pichón** nm (a) (*ave*) young pigeon (**b**) *Fam* (*apelativo cariñoso*) darling, sweetheart

**pichula** nf *Am Vulg* dick, cock

**picnic** (*pl* picnics) nm picnic

**pico** nm (a) (*de ave*) beak (**b**) *Fam* (*boca*) gob, mouth; **cerrar el p.** (*callar*) to shut up; **darle al p.** to talk a lot, to rabbit on; **ser** o **tener un p. de oro** to be a smooth talker, to have the gift of the gab (**c**) (*punta, saliente*) corner (**d**) (*herramienta*) pick, pickaxe (**e**) (*cumbre*) peak (**f**) (*cantidad indeterminada*) **cincuenta y p.** fifty-odd, fifty-

something; **llegó a las cinco y p.** he got there just after five; **le costó un p.** (*cantidad elevada*) it cost her a fortune (**g**) *Fam* **andar/irse de picos pardos** to be/go out on the town (**h**) *muy Fam* (*inyección de heroína*) fix; **meterse un p.** to give oneself a fix

**picor** nm itch

**picoso, -a** adj *Méx* spicy, hot

**picota** nf (a) (*de ajusticiados*) pillory; *Fig* **poner a alguien en la p.** to pillory sb (**b**) (*cereza*) cherry

**picotazo** nm peck

**picotear** vt (a) (*ave*) to peck (**b**) *Fig* (*comer*) to pick at

**pictórico, -a** adj pictorial

**pida** etc ver **pedir**

**pidiera** etc ver **pedir**

**pie** nm (a) (*de persona*) foot; **a p.** on foot; **estar de** o **en p.** to be on one's feet o standing; **ponerse de** o **en p.** to stand up; *Fig* **de pies a cabeza** from head to toe; **perder/no hacer p.** to go/to be out of one's depth; **p. de atleta** athlete's foot; **pies de cerdo** (pig's) trotters; **pies planos** flat feet
(**b**) (*de lámpara, micrófono*) stand; (*de copa*) stem; (*de montaña, árbol*) foot; **p. de foto** caption
(**c**) *Teatro* cue
(**d**) (*expresiones*) **al p. de la letra** to the letter, word for word; **al p. del cañón** ready for action; **andar con pies de plomo** to tread carefully; **a pies juntillas** unquestioningly; **a sus pies** at your service; **buscarle (los) tres pies al gato** to split hairs; **cojear del mismo p.** to fall at the same fence; **con buen p.** on the right footing; **dar p. a alguien para que haga algo** to give sb cause to do sth; **el ciudadano de a p.** the man in the street; **en p. de igualdad** on an equal footing; **en p. de guerra** at war; **levantarse con el p. izquierdo** to get out of bed on the wrong side; **no dar p. con bola** to get everything wrong; **no tener ni pies ni cabeza** to make no sense at all; **no tenerse de** o **en p.** (*por cansancio*) not to be able to stand up a minute longer; *Fig* (*por ser absurdo*) not to stand up; **pararle los pies a alguien** to put sb in their place; **poner pies en polvorosa** to make a run for it; **saber de qué p. cojea alguien** to know sb's weaknesses; *Fig* **seguir en p.** (*propuesta*) to be still valid; **tener un p. en la tumba** to have one foot in the grave

**piedad** nf (a) (*compasión*) pity; **tener p. de** to take pity on (**b**) (*religiosidad*) piety (**c**) *Arte* Pietà

**piedra** nf (a) (*material, roca*) stone; **poner la primera p.** (*inaugurar*) to lay the foundation stone; *Fig* to lay the foundations; **no dejar p. sobre p.** to leave no stone standing; **quedarse de p.** to be thunderstruck; *Fig* **tirar la p. y**

**esconder la mano** to play the innocent; *también Fig* **p. angular** cornerstone; **p. pómez/ preciosa** pumice/precious stone (**b**) *(de mechero)* flint

**piel** *nf* (**a**) *(epidermis)* skin; **dejar** *o* **jugarse la p.** to risk one's neck; **ser de la p. del diablo** to be a little devil; **p. roja** redskin (**b**) *(cuero)* leather; **cazadora/guantes de p.** leather jacket/gloves (**c**) *(pelo)* fur; **abrigo de p.** fur coat (**d**) *(cáscara)* skin, peel

**pienso 1** *ver* **pensar**
  **2** *nm* fodder

**pierda** *etc ver* **perder**

**pierna** *nf* leg; **dormir a p. suelta** to sleep like a log; **estirar las piernas** to stretch one's legs; *Fam* **salir por piernas** to go haring off, to take to one's heels

**pieza** *nf* (**a**) *(pedazo, parte)* piece; *(de mecanismo)* part; **dejar/quedarse de una p.** to leave/ be thunderstruck; **un dos piezas** a two-piece suit; **p. de recambio** *o* **repuesto** spare part, *US* extra (**b**) *(de pesca)* catch, *(de caza)* kill (**c**) *Irón (persona)* **ser una buena p.** to be a fine one *o* a right one (**d**) *(parche)* patch (**e**) *(obra dramática)* play (**f**) *(habitación)* room

**pifia** *nf Fam* blunder

**pifiar** [15] *vt Fam* **pifiarla** to put one's foot in it

**pigmentación** *nf* pigmentation

**pigmento** *nm* pigment

**pigmeo, -a** *nm,f* pygmy

**pijada** *nf Fam (dicho)* trivial remark; *(hecho)* trifle

**pijama** *nm* pyjamas

**pijería** *nf Fam (dicho)* trivial remark; *(hecho)* trifle

**pijo, -a 1** *adj Fam* posh
  **2** *nm,f Fam (persona)* spoilt rich brat
  **3** *nm muy Fam (pene)* prick, cock

**pila** *nf* (**a**) *(generador)* battery; **p. atómica** atomic pile; **p. solar** solar cell (**b**) *(montón)* pile; **tiene una p. de deudas** he's up to his neck in debt (**c**) *(fregadero)* sink; **p. bautismal** (baptismal) font (**d**) *Arquit* pile

**pilar** *nm también Fig* pillar

**pilastra** *nf* pilaster

**píldora** *nf (pastilla)* pill; **la p.** *(anticonceptivo)* the pill; *Fam* **dorar la p.** to sugar the pill

**pileta** *nf CSur* swimming pool

**pilila** *nf Fam* willie

**pillaje** *nm* pillage

**pillar 1** *vt* (**a**) *(coger, tomar, atrapar)* to catch; *Fam* **p. una pulmonía/un taxi** to catch pneumonia/a taxi (**b**) *(atropellar)* to knock down (**c**) *Fam (chiste, explicación)* to get; **no lo pillo** I don't get it
  **2** *vi (hallarse, coger)* **me pilla lejos** it's out of the way for me; **me pilla de camino** it's on my way
  **3 pillarse** *vpr* **pillarse los dedos** to catch one's fingers; *Fig* to get burned

**pillastre** *nmf Fam* rogue, crafty person

**pillo, -a 1** *adj* (**a**) *(travieso)* mischievous (**b**) *(astuto)* crafty
  **2** *nm,f* (**a**) *(pícaro)* rascal (**b**) *(astuto)* crafty person

**pilón** *nm* (**a**) *(pila) (para lavar)* basin; *(para animales)* trough (**b**) *(torre eléctrica)* pylon (**c**) *(pilar grande)* post

**pilotar** *vt (avión)* to fly, to pilot; *(coche)* to drive; *(barco)* to steer

**piloto 1** *nmf (de avión, barco)* pilot; *(de coche)* driver; **p. automático** automatic pilot; **p. de pruebas** test pilot
  **2** *nm (luz) (de coche)* tail light; *(de aparato)* pilot lamp
  **3** *adj inv* pilot; **piso p.** show flat; **proyecto p.** pilot project

**piltra** *nf muy Fam* pit, bed

**piltrafa** *nf (de comida)* scrap; *Fam (persona débil)* wreck; *Fam (cosa inservible)* piece of junk; **estar hecho una p.** *(persona, coche)* to be a wreck; *(chaqueta, zapatos)* to be worn out

**pimentón** *nm* paprika

**pimienta** *nf* pepper; **p. blanca/negra** white/black pepper

**pimiento** *nm (fruto)* pepper, capsicum; *(planta)* pimiento, pepper plant; **p. morrón** sweet pepper

**pimpante** *adj Fam* (**a**) *(satisfecho)* well-pleased (**b**) *(garboso)* swish, smart

**pimpinela** *nf* pimpernel

**pimplar** *Fam* **1** *vi* to booze
  **2 pimplarse** *vpr* **se pimpló dos botellas él solo** he downed two bottles on his own

**pimpollo** *nm* (**a**) *(de rama, planta)* shoot; *(de flor)* bud (**b**) *Fam Fig (persona atractiva)* gorgeous person

**PIN** *nm (abrev de* **producto interior neto**) NDP

**pin** *nm Fam* = small metal decorative badge

**pinacoteca** *nf* art gallery

**pináculo** *nm* (**a**) *(de edificio)* pinnacle (**b**) *(juego de naipes)* pinochle

**pinar** *nm* pine wood *o* grove

**pinaza** *nf* pine needles

**pincel** *nm* (**a**) *(para pintar)* paintbrush; *(para maquillar)* brush (**b**) *Fig (estilo)* style

**pincelada** *nf* brushstroke; *Fig* **a grandes pinceladas** in broad terms

**pinchadiscos** *nmf inv* disc jockey

**pinchar 1** *vt* (a) *(punzar)* to prick; *(rueda)* to puncture; *(globo, balón)* to burst (b) *(penetrar)* to pierce (c) *(con chinchetas, alfileres)* **p. algo en la pared** to pin sth to the wall (d) *Fam (teléfono)* to tap (e) *Fam (irritar)* to torment (f) *Fig (incitar)* **p. a alguien para que haga algo** to urge sb to do sth

**2** *vi* (a) *(rueda)* to get a puncture (b) *(barba)* to be prickly (c) *(expresiones)* **ella ni pincha ni corta** she cuts no ice; **p. en hueso** to go wide of the mark, to misfire

**3 pincharse** *vpr* (a) *(punzarse) (persona)* to prick oneself; *(rueda)* to get a puncture (b) *Fig (irritarse)* to get annoyed (c) *(inyectarse)* **pincharse (algo)** *(medicamento)* to inject oneself (with sth); *Fam (droga)* to shoot up (with sth)

**pinchazo** *nm* (a) *(punzada)* prick (b) *(marca)* needle mark (c) *(de neumático, balón)* puncture, *US* flat

**pinche 1** *nmf* kitchen boy, *f* maid
**2** *adj Méx muy Fam* bloody, lousy

**pinchito** *nm (tapa)* aperitif on a stick

**pincho** *nm* (a) *(punta)* (sharp) point (b) *(espina) (de planta)* prickle, thorn (c) *(varilla)* pointed stick (d) *(tapa)* aperitif on a stick; **p. moruno** shish kebab

**pindonguear** *vi Fam* to loaf about

**pinga** *nf Andes, Méx Vulg* prick, cock

**pingajo** *nm Fam* rag

**pingo** *nm* (a) *Fam (pingajo)* rag (b) *(mamarracho)* **ir hecho un p.** to look a state, to be dressed in rags (c) *Fam (persona despreciable)* rotter, dog

**pingonear** *vi Fam* to loaf about

**ping-pong** [pim'pon] *nm* ping-pong, table-tennis

**pingüe** *adj* plentiful; **pingües beneficios** fat profit

**pingüino** *nm* penguin

**pinitos** *nmpl Fam* **hacer p.** to take one's first steps

**pino** *nm* pine; *Fam* **en el quinto p.** in the back of beyond; **hacer el p.** to do a handstand

**pinsapo** *nm* Spanish fir

**pinta** *nf* (a) *(lunar)* spot (b) *Fig (aspecto)* appearance; **tener p. de algo** to look o seem sth; **tiene buena p.** it looks good (c) *(unidad de medida)* pint (d) *Méx (pintada)* graffiti

**pintada** *nf* (a) *(en pared)* graffiti (b) *(ave)* guinea fowl

**pintado, -a** *adj* (a) *(coloreado)* coloured; **recién p.** *(en letrero)* wet paint (b) *(maquillado)* made-up (c) *(moteado)* speckled (d) *(expresiones)* **el más p.** the best person around; **venir que ni p.** to be just the thing

**pintalabios** *nm inv* lipstick

**pintamonas** *nmf inv Fam Pey* hack painter, dauber

**pintar 1** *vt* to paint; **p. algo de verde/azul** to paint sth green/blue

**2** *vi* (a) *(con pintura)* to paint (b) *Fam (significar, importar)* to count; **aquí no pinto nada** there's no place for me here; **¿qué pinto yo en este asunto?** where do I come in?

**3 pintarse** *vpr* (a) *(maquillarse)* to make oneself up (b) *(manifestarse)* to show, to be evident (c) **pintárselas uno solo para algo** to be a past master at sth

**pintarrajear** *vt Fam* to daub

**pinto, -a** *adj* speckled, spotted

**pintor, -ora** *nm,f* painter; **p. de brocha gorda** painter and decorator; *Pey* dauber

**pintoresco, -a** *adj (bonito)* picturesque; *Fig (extravagante)* colourful

**pintura** *nf* (a) *Arte* painting; *Fig* **no poder ver a alguien ni en p.** not to be able to stand the sight of sb; **p. a la acuarela** watercolour; **p. al óleo** oil painting; **la p. renacentista** Renaissance painting; **p. rupestre** cave painting (b) *(materia)* paint (c) *Fig (descripción)* description, portrayal

**pinza** *nf* (a) *(instrumento)* tweezers; *(de tender ropa)* peg, *US* clothespin; *Fam Fig* **coger algo con pinzas** to handle sth with great care (b) *(de animal)* pincer, claw (c) *(pliegue)* fold

**piña** *nf* (a) *(del pino)* pine cone (b) *(fruta tropical)* pineapple; **p. colada** piña colada (c) *Fig (conjunto de gente)* close-knit group (d) *Fam (golpe)* knock, bash

**piñata** *nf* = pot full of sweets

**piñón** *nm* (a) *(fruto)* pine nut o kernel; **estar a partir un p. con alguien** to be hand in glove with sb (b) *(rueda dentada)* pinion; **ser de p. fijo** to be fixed o rigid

**pío¹** *onomatopeya* cheep; **¡p., p.!** cheep, cheep!; *Fig* **no decir ni p.** not to make a peep

**pío², -a** *adj* pious

**piojo** *nm* louse

**piojoso, -a 1** *adj* lousy, covered in lice; *Fig (sucio)* flea-bitten, filthy
**2** *nm,f (con piojos)* louse-ridden person; *Fig (sucio)* filthy person

**piola** *adj Arg Fam* (a) *(astuto)* shrewd (b) *(estupendo)* fabulous

**piolet** *nm* ice axe

**pionero, -a** *nm,f* pioneer

**piorrea** *nf* pyorrhoea

**pipa** nf (a) *(para fumar)* pipe; **fumar en p.** to smoke a pipe (b) *(pepita)* seed, pip; **pipas (de girasol)** = unshelled sunflower seeds sold as a snack (c) *(tonel)* barrel (d) **pasarlo** o **pasárselo p.** to have a whale of a time

**pipermín** nm peppermint liqueur

**pipeta** nf pipette

**pipí** nm Fam wee-wee; **hacer p.** to have a wee-wee

**pique**1 ver **picar**

**2** nm (a) *(enfado)* grudge; **tener un p. con alguien** to have a grudge against sb (b) *(rivalidad)* rivalry (c) **irse a p.** *(barco)* to sink; *(negocio)* to go under; *(plan)* to fail

**piqué** *(pl piqués)* nm piqué

**piquera** nf Méx *(antro)* dive, seedy bar

**piqueta** nf *(herramienta)* pickaxe; *(en tienda de campaña)* metal tent-peg

**piquete** nm (a) *(herramienta)* peg, stake (b) *(grupo)* **p. de ejecución** firing squad; **p. (de huelga)** picket

**pira** nf pyre

**pirado, -a** Fam1 adj crazy

**2** nm,f nutter, loony

**piragua** nf canoe

**piragüismo** nm canoeing

**piramidal** adj pyramid-shaped, pyramidal

**pirámide** nf pyramid

**piraña** nf piranha

**pirarse** vpr Fam to clear off; **¡nos piramos!** that's us off; **¿ya os piráis?** is that you off, then?

**pirata**1 adj (a) *(barco, ataque)* pirate (b) *(radio, edición, vídeo)* pirate; *(casete, grabación)* bootleg

**2** nmf también Fig pirate; **p. del aire** hijacker; **p. informático** hacker

**piratear** vi (a) *(asaltar barcos)* to be involved in piracy (b) Informát to hack

**2** vt (a) *(propiedad intelectual)* to pirate (b) Informát to hack into

**pirateo** nm Fam *(de programa informático, de vídeos)* = illegal reproduction and sale

**piratería** nf también Fig piracy; **p. aérea** hijacking; **p. informática** *(copias ilegales)* software piracy; *(acceso no autorizado)* hacking

**pirenaico, -a** adj Pyrenean

**pírex** nm Pyrex

**pirindolo** nm Fam decorative knob

**Pirineos** nmpl **los P.** the Pyrenees

**piripi** adj Fam tipsy

**pirita** nf pyrite

**piro** nm muy Fam **darse el p.** to scarper, to clear off

**pirograbado** nm *(técnica)* pokerwork

**piromanía** nf pyromania

**pirómano, -a**1 adj pyromaniacal

**2** nm,f pyromaniac

**piropear** vt Fam = to make flirtatious comments to, to wolf-whistle at

**piropo** nm Fam flirtatious remark

**pirotecnia** nf pyrotechnics *(singular)*

**pirotécnico, -a** 1 adj firework; **un montaje p.** a firework display

**2** nm,f firework specialist

**pirrar** Fam1 vt **me pirran las albóndigas** I just adore o love meatballs

**2** pirrarse vpr **p. por algo/alguien** to be dead keen on sth/sb

**pírrico, -a** adj Pyrrhic

**pirueta** nf pirouette; Fig **hacer piruetas** *(esfuerzo)* to perform miracles

**piruleta** nf lollipop

**pirulí** *(pl pirulís)* nm lollipop

**pis** *(pl pises)* nm Fam pee; **hacer p.** to have a pee; **hacerse p.** *(tener ganas)* to be dying o bursting for a pee

**Pisa** n Pisa

**pisada** nf (a) *(acción)* footstep; **seguir las pisadas de alguien** to follow in sb's footsteps (b) *(huella)* footprint

**pisadura** nf footprint

**pisapapeles** nm inv paperweight

**pisar** vt (a) *(con el pie)* to tread on; Fig **venir pisando fuerte** to be on the road to success (b) *(uvas)* to tread (c) Fig *(llegar a)* to set foot in (d) Fig *(despreciar)* to trample on (e) Fig *(anticiparse)* **p. un contrato a alguien** to beat sb to a contract; **p. una idea a alguien** to think of something before sb

**piscicultura** nf fish farming

**piscifactoría** nf fish farm

**piscina** nf swimming pool

**piscis** 1 nm *(zodíaco)* Pisces; **ser p.** to be (a) Pisces

**2** nmf inv *(persona)* Pisces

**piscolabis** nm inv Fam snack

**piso** nm (a) *(vivienda)* flat; **p. franco** safe house (b) *(planta)* floor (c) *(suelo)* *(de carretera)* surface; *(de habitación)* floor (d) *(capa)* layer; **un sandwich de dos pisos** a double-decker sandwich

**pisotear** vt (a) *(con el pie)* to trample on (b) *(humillar)* to scorn (c) *(desobedecer)* to trample over

**pisotón** nm stamp *(of the foot)*; **darle un p. a alguien** to stamp on sb's foot

**pista** *nf* (a) *(carretera)* unsurfaced road; **p. de aterrizaje** runway; **p. forestal** = minor road through forest or mountain area (b) *(superficie, terreno)* **p. de baile** dance floor; **p. de esquí** ski slope; **p. de hielo** ice rink; **p. de tenis** tennis court (c) *Fig (indicio)* clue; **seguir la p. a alguien** to be on sb's trail

**pistacho** *nm* pistachio

**pistilo** *nm* pistil

**pisto** *nm* ratatouille; *Fam* **darse p.** to be big-headed

**pistola** *nf* (a) *(arma) (con cilindro)* gun; *(sin cilindro)* pistol; **p. de agua** water pistol (b) *(pulverizador)* spraygun; **pintar a p.** to spray-paint (c) *(herramienta)* gun (d) *(de pan)* French loaf

**pistolera** *nf* (a) *(funda)* holster (b) *Fam* **pistoleras** *(celulitis)* saddlebags

**pistolero, -a** *nm,f (persona)* gunman

**pistoletazo** *nm* pistol shot; **p. de salida** shot from the starter's gun

**pistón** *nm* (a) *Mec* piston (b) *Mús (corneta)* cornet; *(llave)* key (c) *(de arma)* percussion cap

**pita** *nf* agave

**pitada** *nf Am Fam (calada)* drag, puff

**pitanza** *nf* (a) *(ración de comida)* daily rations (b) *Fam (alimento)* grub

**pitar 1** *vt* (a) *(arbitrar) (partido)* to referee; *(falta)* to blow for (b) *(abuchear)* **p. a alguien** to whistle at sb in disapproval (c) *Am Fam (dar una calada a)* to puff (on)

**2** *vi* (a) *(tocar el pito)* to blow a whistle; *(del coche)* to toot one's horn (b) *(funcionar) (cosa)* to work; *(persona)* to get on (c) **salir/irse pitando** to rush out/off; **venir pitando** to come rushing

**pitido** *nm (con pito)* whistle; *(de aparato electrónico)* beep, bleep; **los pitidos de los coches** the honking of car horns

**pitillera** *nf* cigarette case

**pitillo** *nm* (a) *(cigarrillo)* cigarette (b) *Col (paja)* drinking straw

**pito** *nm* (a) *(silbato)* whistle (b) *(claxon)* horn (c) *Fam (cigarrillo)* fag (d) *Fam (pene)* willie (e) *(expresiones)* **entre pitos y flautas** what with one thing and another; **(no) me importa un p.** I couldn't give a damn; **por pitos o por flautas** for one reason or another; **tomar a alguien por el p. del sereno** not to take sb seriously

**pitón 1** *nm* (a) *(cuerno)* horn (b) *(pitorro)* spout

**2** *nf (serpiente)* python

**pitonisa** *nf* fortune-teller

**pitorrearse** *vpr Fam* to take the mickey (**de** out of)

**pitorreo** *nm* making fun, joking; **tomarse algo a p.** to treat sth as a joke

**pitorro** *nm* spout

**pitote** *nm (jaleo)* row, fuss; **armar un p.** to kick up a row o fuss

**pituitaria** *nf* pituitary gland

**pívot** ( *pl* **pivots**) *nmf (en baloncesto)* pivot

**pivotar** *vi Dep* to pivot

**pivote** *nmf* (a) *(eje)* pivot (b) *Dep* pivot

**píxel** *nm* pixel

**pizarra** *nf* (a) *(roca, material)* slate (b) *(encerado)* blackboard

**pizca** *nf Fam (poco)* tiny bit; *(de sal)* pinch; **ni p.** not one bit

**pizpireta** *adj Fam (niña, mujer)* spirited, zippy

**pizza** ['pitsa] *nf* pizza

**pizzería** [pitse'ria] *nf* pizzeria, pizza parlour

**placa** *nf* (a) *(lámina)* plate; *(de madera)* sheet; **p. solar** solar panel (b) *(inscripción)* plaque; *(de policía)* badge (c) *(de cocina)* ring; **p. de vitrocerámica** ceramic hob (d) *Aut* **p. (de matrícula)** number plate (e) *Geol* plate (f) *Elec* board; *Informát* **p. madre** motherboard (g) *Med* **p. dental** dental plaque

**placaje** *nm Dep* tackle

**placar** [61] *vt Dep* to tackle

**placebo** *nm* placebo

**placenta** *nf* placenta

**placentero, -a** *adj* pleasant

**placer 1** *nm* pleasure; **ha sido un p. (conocerle)** it has been a pleasure meeting you

**2** *vt* to please; **si me place** if I want to, if I feel like it

**plácet** *nm Formal (aprobación)* approval; **dar el p. a un embajador** to accept an ambassador's credentials

**placidez** *nf (de persona)* placidness; *(de día, vida, conversación)* peacefulness

**plácido, -a** *adj (persona)* placid; *(día, vida, conversación)* peaceful

**plafón** *nm Arquit* soffit

**plaga** *nf* (a) *(abundancia de algo malo)* plague; **p. de langosta** plague of locusts (b) *Fig (de gente)* swarm (c) *(epidemia)* epidemic

**plagado, -a** *adj (de insectos)* infested (**de** with); **p. de dificultades** beset o plagued with difficulties; *Fig* **la ciudad está plagada de turistas** the city is overrun with tourists

**plagar** [40] *vt* **p. de** *(propaganda)* to swamp with; *(moscas)* to infest with

**plagiar** [15] *vt* (a) *(copiar)* to plagiarize (b) *Am (secuestrar)* to kidnap

**plagiario, -a** *nm,f Am* kidnapper

**plagio** *nm* (a) *(copia)* plagiarism (b) *Am (secuestro)* kidnapping

**plaguicida 1** *adj* pesticidal

**2** *nm* pesticide

**plan** *nm* (a) *(proyecto, programa)* plan; **p. de estudios** syllabus; **p. de pensiones** pension plan (b) *Fam (ligue)* date (c) *Fam (modo, forma)* **a todo p.** in the greatest luxury, with no expense spared; **lo dijo en p. serio** he was serious about it; **¡vaya p. de vida!** what a life!; **si te pones en ese p....** if you're going to be like that about it...; **no es p.** it's just not on

**plana** *nf* (a) *(página)* page; **en primera p.** on the front page (b) *(llanura)* plain (c) *Mil* **p. mayor** staff

**plancha** *nf* (a) *(para planchar)* iron (b) *(para cocinar)* grill; **a la p.** grilled (c) *(placa)* plate; *(de madera)* sheet (d) *Fam (metedura de pata)* boob, blunder (e) *(en fútbol)* diving header (f) *Imprenta* plate

**planchado** *nm* ironing

**planchar** *vt* to iron

**planchazo** *nm Fam* boob, blunder

**plancton** *nm* plankton

**planeador** *nm* glider

**planeadora** *nf (lancha)* speedboat

**planear 1** *vt* to plan
**2** *vi* (a) *(hacer planes)* to plan (b) *(en el aire)* to glide

**planeta** *nm* planet

**planetario, -a 1** *adj* (a) *(de un planeta)* planetary (b) *(mundial)* world; **a nivel p.** on a global scale
**2** *nm* planetarium

**planicie** *nf* plain

**planificación** *nf* planning; **p. familiar** family planning

**planificar** [61] *vt* to plan

**planilla** *nf Am (formulario)* form

**planisferio** *nm* planisphere

**planning** ['planin] (*pl* **plannings**) *nm* scheduling

**plano, -a 1** *adj* flat
**2** *nm* (a) *(diseño, mapa)* plan (b) *(nivel, aspecto)* level (c) *Cine* shot; **primer p.** close-up; *Fig* **en segundo p.** in the background (d) *Mat* plane (e) *(expresiones)* **de p.** *(golpear)* right, directly; *(negar)* flatly; **cantar de p.** to make a full confession

**planta** *nf* (a) *Bot & Ind* plant; **p. depuradora** purification plant; **p. de envase** *o* **envasadora** packaging plant (b) *(piso)* floor; **p. baja** ground floor (c) *(del pie)* sole (d) *(expresiones)* **de nueva p.** brand new; **tener buena p.** to be good-looking

**plantación** *nf* (a) *(terreno)* plantation (b) *(acción)* planting

**plantado, -a** *adj* (a) *(planta, árbol)* planted; **un terreno p. de trigo** a field planted with wheat (b) *(expresiones) Fam* **dejar p. a alguien** *(no acudir)* to stand sb up; **ser bien p.** to be good-looking

**plantar 1** *vt* (a) *(sembrar)* to plant (**de** with) (b) *(fijar) (tienda de campaña)* to pitch; *(poste)* to put in (c) *Fam (bofetada)* to deal, to land; *(beso)* to plant (d) *Fam (decir con brusquedad)* **le plantó cuatro frescas** she gave him a piece of her mind (e) *Fam (dejar plantado)* **p. a alguien** to stand sb up (f) *Fam (construcción, mueble, objeto)* to plonk; **plantó los pies en el sofá** she plonked her feet on the sofa
**2 plantarse** *vpr* (a) *(ponerse, colocarse)* to plant oneself (b) *(en un sitio con rapidez)* **plantarse en** to get to, to make it to (c) *(en una actitud)* **plantarse en algo** to stick to sth, to insist on sth (d) *(en naipes)* to stick

**plante** *nm* (a) *(para protestar)* protest (b) *(plantón)* **dar** *o* **hacer un p. a alguien** to stand sb up

**planteamiento** *nm* (a) *(exposición)* raising, posing (b) *(enfoque)* approach

**plantear 1** *vt* (a) *(exponer) (problema)* to pose; *(posibilidad, dificultad, duda)* to raise (b) *(enfocar)* to approach
**2 plantearse** *vpr* **plantearse algo** to consider sth, to think about sth

**plantel** *nm* (a) *(criadero)* nursery bed (b) *Fig (conjunto)* group

**plantilla** *nf* (a) *(de empresa)* staff; **estar en p.** to be on the staff (b) *(para zapatos)* insole (c) *(patrón)* pattern, template

**plantío** *nm* plot (of land)

**plantón** *nm Fam* **dar un p. a alguien** to stand sb up

**plañidero, -a** *adj* plaintive, whining

**plañido** *nm* moan

**plañir 1** *vt* to bewail
**2** *vi* to moan, to wail

**plaqueta** *nf Biol* platelet

**plasma** *nm* plasma

**plasmar 1** *vt* (a) *(reflejar) (sentimientos)* to give expression to; *(realidad)* to reflect (b) *(modelar)* to shape, to mould
**2 plasmarse** *vpr* to emerge, to take shape

**plasta 1** *adj Fam* **ser p.** to be a pain; **un tío p.** a real bore, a pain in the neck
**2** *nmf Fam (pesado)* pain, drag
**3** *nf* (a) *(cosa blanda)* mess (b) *Fam Fig (cosa mal hecha)* botchup

**plastelina®** *nf* Plasticine®

**plástica** *nf* plastic art

**plasticidad** *nf* (a) *(moldeabilidad)* plasticity (b) *(expresividad)* expressiveness

**plástico, -a 1** adj (a) (moldeable) plastic (b) (expresivo) expressive

**2** nm (a) (material) plastic (b) Fam (tarjetas de crédito) plastic (money)

**plastificar** [61] vt (carné, tarjeta) to cover in plastic

**plastilina**® nf Plasticine®

**plata** nf (a) (metal) silver; Fam **hablar en p.** to speak bluntly; **p. de ley** sterling silver (b) (objetos de plata) silverware (c) Am (dinero) money

**plataforma** nf (a) (superficie elevada, estrado) platform (b) **p. petrolífera** oil rig (c) Fig (punto de partida) launching pad (d) Geol shelf; **p. continental** continental shelf

**platanal, platanar** nm banana plantation

**platanera** nf, **platanero** nm banana tree

**plátano** nm (a) (fruta) banana (b) (árbol de sombra) plane tree

**platea** nf stalls

**plateado, -a** adj (a) (con plata) silver-plated (b) Fig (color) silvery

**plateresco, -a** adj plateresque

**platería** nf (a) (arte, oficio) silversmithing (b) (tienda) jeweller's (shop)

**platero, -a** nm,f silversmith

**plática** nf (a) Am (charla) talk, chat (b) Rel sermon

**platicar** [61] vi Am to talk, to chat

**platillo** nm (a) (plato pequeño) small plate; (de taza) saucer; **p. volante** flying saucer (b) (de una balanza) pan (c) Mús **platillos** cymbals

**platina** nf (a) (de casete) cassette deck (b) (de microscopio) slide

**platino** nm (metal) platinum; Aut & Mec **platinos** contact points

**plato** nm (a) (recipiente) plate, dish; **lavar los platos** to do the washing-up; Fig **comer en el mismo p.** to be great friends; Fig **pagar los platos rotos** to carry the can; Fig **parece que no ha roto un p. en su vida** he looks as if butter wouldn't melt in his mouth; **estaba el mar como un p.** the sea was like a millpond; **p. hondo** o **sopero** soup dish o plate; **p. llano** plate; **p. de postre** dessert plate

(b) (parte de una comida) course; **primer p.** first course, starter; **de primer p.** for starters; **segundo p.** second course, main course; **p. fuerte** (en una comida) main course; Fig main part; **p. principal** main course

(c) (comida) dish; **p. combinado** = single-course meal which usually consists of meat or fish accompanied by chips and vegetables; **p. preparado** ready-prepared meal

(d) (de tocadiscos, microondas) turntable

(e) (de bicicleta) chain wheel

(f) Dep clay-pigeon

**plató** nm set

**platónico, -a** adj platonic

**platudo, -a** adj Am Fam loaded, rolling in it

**plausibilidad** nf (a) (admisibilidad) acceptability (b) (posibilidad) plausibility

**plausible** adj (a) (admisible) acceptable (b) (posible) plausible

**playa** nf (a) (en el mar) beach; **ir a la p. de vacaciones** to go on holiday to the seaside (b) Am (aparcamiento) **p. de estacionamiento** car park

**play-back** ['pleiβak] (pl play-backs) nm **hacer p.** to mime (the lyrics)

**play-boy** [plei'βoi] (pl play-boys) nm play-boy

**playero, -a 1** adj beach; **toalla playera** beach towel

**2** nfpl **playeras** (a) (de deporte) tennis shoes (b) (para la playa) canvas shoes

**plaza** nf (a) (en una población) square; **la p. del pueblo** the village o town square (b) (sitio) place; **tenemos plazas limitadas** there are a limited number of places available (c) (asiento) seat; **un vehículo de dos plazas** a two-seater vehicle (d) (puesto de trabajo) position, job; **p. vacante** vacancy (e) (mercado) market, marketplace (f) Taurom **p. (de toros)** bull-ring (g) Com (zona) area (h) (fortificación) **p. fuerte** stronghold

**plazo** nm (a) (de tiempo) period (of time); **en el p. de un mes** within a month; **mañana termina el p. de inscripción** the deadline for registration is tomorrow; **a corto/largo p.** in the short/long term o run; Econ short/long term; Com **p. de entrega** delivery time (b) (de dinero) instalment; **a plazos** in instalments, on hire purchase

**plazoleta, plazuela** nf small square

**pleamar** nf high tide

**plebe** nf también Fig **la p.** the plebs

**plebeyo, -a** adj (a) Hist plebeian (b) (vulgar) common

**plebiscito** nm plebiscite

**plegable** adj collapsible, foldaway; (silla) folding

**plegar** [45] **1** vt (papel) to fold; (mesita, hamaca) to fold away

**2 plegarse** vpr **plegarse a algo** to give in o yield to sth

**plegaria** nf prayer

**pleitear** vi Der to litigate, to conduct a lawsuit

**pleitesía** nf homage; **rendir p. a alguien** to pay homage to sb

**pleito** nm Der (litigio) legal action, lawsuit; (disputa) dispute; **poner un p. (a alguien)** to take legal action (against sb)

**plenario, -a** adj plenary

**plenilunio** nm full moon

**plenipotenciario, -a 1** *adj* plenipotentiary

**2** *nm,f* envoy

**plenitud** *nf* (**a**) *(apogeo)* completeness, fullness; **en la p. de** at the height of (**b**) *(abundancia)* abundance

**pleno, -a 1** *adj* full, complete; **en p. día** in broad daylight; **en plena guerra** in the middle of the war; **le dio en plena cara** she hit him right in the face; **en plena forma** on top form; **en plena naturaleza** in the middle of the country(side); **en p. uso de sus facultades** in full command of his faculties; **la reunión en p.** the meeting as a whole, everyone at the meeting; **miembro de p. derecho** full member

**2** *nm* (**a**) *(reunión)* plenary meeting (**b**) *(en las quinielas)* full claim *(14 correct predictions)*; **p. al quince** full claim *(14 correct predictions plus bonus)*

**pletina** *nf* cassette deck

**pletórico, -a** *adj* **p. de** full of

**pleura** *nf* pleural membrane

**pleuresía** *nf Med* pleurisy

**plexiglás®** *nm inv* Perspex®

**pléyade** *nf (conjunto)* cluster

**pliego 1** *ver* **plegar**

**2** *nm* (**a**) *(de papel, de cartulina)* sheet (**b**) *(carta, documento)* sealed document *o* letter; **p. de condiciones** specifications; **p. de descargos** list of rebuttals (**c**) *Imprenta* signature

**pliegue** *nm* (**a**) *también Geol* fold (**b**) *(en un plisado)* pleat

**plinto** *nm Dep* vaulting box

**plisado** *nm* pleating

**plisar** *vt* to pleat

**plomada** *nf* plumb line

**plomería** *nf Am* plumber's

**plomero** *nm Am* plumber

**plomizo, -a** *adj (color, cielo)* leaden

**plomo** *nm* (**a**) *(metal)* lead; **sin p.** *(gasolina)* unleaded; *Fig* **caer a p.** to fall *o* drop like a stone (**b**) *(pieza de metal)* lead weight (**c**) *(fusible)* fuse (**d**) *Fam Fig (pelmazo)* bore, drag

**plóter, plotter** *(pl* **plotters)** *nm Informát* plotter

**pluma 1** *nf* (**a**) *(de ave)* feather (**b**) *(para escribir)* (fountain) pen; *(de ave)* quill (pen); **p. estilográfica** fountain pen (**c**) *Fig (estilo de escribir)* style (**d**) *Fig (escritor)* writer (**e**) **tener mucha p.** to be camp

**2** *adj inv Dep* featherweight; **peso p.** featherweight

**plumaje** *nm* (**a**) *(de ave)* plumage (**b**) *(adorno)* plume

**plumazo** *nm* stroke of the pen; **de un p.** *(al tachar)* with a stroke of one's pen; *Fig (al hacer algo)* in one fell swoop, at a stroke

**plúmbeo, -a** *adj Fig* tedious, heavy

**plum-cake** [pluŋ'keik] *(pl* **plum-cakes)** *nm* fruit cake

**plumero** *nm* feather duster; *Fam Fig* **se le ve el p.** you can see through him

**plumier** *(pl* **plumiers)** *nm* pencil box

**plumífero** *nm (anorak)* feather-lined anorak

**plumilla** *nf* nib

**plumín** *nm* nib

**plumón** *nm (de ave)* down

**plural 1** *adj* (**a**) *(múltiple)* pluralistic (**b**) *Gram* plural

**2** *nm Gram* plural

**pluralidad** *nf* diversity

**pluralismo** *nm* pluralism

**pluralizar** [16] *vi* to generalize

**pluricelular** *adj* multicellular

**pluriempleado, -a 1** *adj* **estar p.** to have more than one job

**2** *nm,f* = person with more than one job

**pluriempleo** *nm* **hacer p.** to have more than one job

**pluripartidismo** *nm* multi-party system

**plurivalente** *adj* polyvalent

**plus** *(pl* **pluses)** *nm* bonus; **p. familiar** family allowance; **p. de peligrosidad** danger money

**pluscuamperfecto** *adj & nm* pluperfect

**plusmarca** *nf* record

**plusmarquista** *nmf* record-holder

**plusvalía** *nf Econ* appreciation, added value

**plutocracia** *nf* plutocracy

**Plutón** *n* Pluto

**plutonio** *nm* plutonium

**pluvial** *adj* rain; **régimen p.** annual rainfall pattern

**pluviómetro** *nm* rain gauge

**pluviosidad** *nf* rainfall

**pluvioso, -a** *adj Formal* rainy

**PM** *nf (abrev de* **policía militar)** MP

**p.m.** *(abrev de* **post meridiem)** p.m

**PNB** *nm (abrev de* **producto nacional bruto)** GNP

**PNN** *nmf (abrev de* **profesor no numerario)** *Antes* = university lecturer who does not have tenure

**PNV** *nm (abrev de* **Partido Nacionalista Vasco)** = Basque nationalist party to the right of the political spectrum

**Po** *nm* **el P.** the (River) Po

**p.o., p/o** *(abrev de* **por orden)** pp

**población** nf (a) (ciudad) town, city; (pueblo) village (b) (personas, animales) population; **p. activa/flotante** working/floating population (c) (acción de poblar) settlement, populating

**poblado, -a 1** adj (a) (habitado) inhabited; **una zona muy poblada** a densely populated area (b) Fig (lleno) full; (barba, cejas) bushy

**2** nm settlement

**poblador, -ora** nm,f (habitante) inhabitant; (colono) settler

**poblano, -a 1** adj of/from Puebla

**2** nm,f person from Puebla

**poblar** [65] **1** vt (a) (establecerse en) to settle, to colonize (b) (habitar) to inhabit (c) Fig (llenar) **p. (de)** (plantas, árboles) to plant (with); (peces) to stock (with)

**2 poblarse** vpr to fill up (**de** with)

**pobre 1** adj poor; **¡p. hombre!** poor man!; **p. en** lacking in; **¡p. de mí!** poor me!

**2** nmf (a) (sin dinero, infeliz) poor person; **los pobres** the poor, poor people; **¡el p.!** poor thing! (b) (mendigo) beggar

**pobreza** nf poverty; **p. de** lack o scarcity of; **p. de espíritu** weakness of character

**pocha** nf (judía) haricot bean

**pocho, -a** adj (a) (persona) off-colour (b) (fruta) over-ripe (c) Méx Fam (americanizado) Americanized

**pocholada** nf Fam **una p. de niño/vestido** a cute little child/dress

**pocholo, -a** adj Fam cute

**pocilga** nf también Fig pigsty

**pocillo** nm Am small cup

**pócima** nf (a) (poción) potion (b) (bebida de mal sabor) concoction

**poción** nf potion

**poco, -a 1** adj (singular) little, not much; (plural) few, not many; **poca agua** not much water; **de poca importancia** of little importance; **hay pocos árboles** there aren't many trees; **pocas personas lo saben** few o not many people know it; **tenemos p. tiempo** we don't have much time; **hace p. tiempo** not long ago; **dame unos pocos días** give me a few days

**2** pron (singular) little, not much; (plural) few, not many; **queda p.** there's not much left; **tengo muy pocos** I don't have very many, I have very few; **pocos hay que sepan tanto** not many people know so much; **un p.** a bit; **¿me das un p.?** can I have a bit?; **un p. de** a bit of; **un p. de sentido común** a bit of common sense; **unos pocos** a few

**3** adv (a) (escasamente) not much; **este niño come p.** this boy doesn't eat much; **es p. común** it's not very common; **es un p. triste** it's rather sad

(b) (brevemente) **tardaré muy p.** I won't be long; **al p. de...** shortly after...; **dentro de p.** soon, in a short time; **hace p.** a little while ago, not long ago

(c) (no a menudo) not often; **voy p. por allí** I don't go there very often; **voy muy p. por allí** I seldom go there

(d) (expresiones) **p. a p.** (progresivamente) little by little, bit by bit; **¡p. a p.!** (despacio) steady on!, slow down!; **p. más o menos** more or less; **por p.** almost, nearly; **tener en p. a alguien** not to think much of sb

**poda** nf (a) (acción) pruning (b) (tiempo) pruning time

**podadera** nf garden shears

**podar** vt to prune

**podenco** nm hound

**poder** [51] **1** nm (a) (mando, competencia) power; **estar en/hacerse con el p.** to be in/to seize power; **tener poderes** (paranormales) to be psychic, to have psychic powers; **p. adquisitivo** purchasing power; **p. calorífico** calorific value; **p. de convicción** persuasive powers; **tener p. de convocatoria** to be a crowd-puller; **p. ejecutivo/legislativo/judicial** executive/legislature/judiciary power; **poderes fácticos** the church, military and press; **poderes públicos** public authorities

(b) (posesión) **estar en p. de alguien** to be in sb's hands

(c) (autorización) power, authorization; **dar poderes a alguien para que haga algo** to authorize sb to do sth; **por poderes** by proxy

**2** vi (a) (tener facultad) can, to be able to; **no puedo decírtelo** I can't tell you, I'm unable to tell you

(b) (tener permiso) can, may; **no puedo salir por la noche** I'm not allowed o I can't go out at night; **¿puedo fumar aquí?** may I smoke here?

(c) (ser capaz moralmente) can; **no podemos portarnos así con él** we can't treat him like that

(d) (tener posibilidad, ser posible) may, can; **podías haber cogido el tren** you could have caught the train; **puede estallar la guerra** war could o may break out; **¡hubiera podido invitarnos!** (expresa enfado) she could o might have invited us!

(e) (expresiones) **a** o **hasta más no p.** as much as can be; **es avaro a más no p.** he's as miserly as can be; **no p. más** (estar cansado) to be too tired to carry on; (estar harto de comer) to be full (up); (estar enfadado) to have had enough; **¿se puede?** may I come in?; **p. con** (enfermedad, rival) to be able to overcome; (tarea, problema) to be able to cope with; **no p. con algo/alguien** (no soportar) not to be able to stand sth/sb; **no**

**puedo con la hipocresía** I can't stand hypocrisy

**3** *v impersonal (ser posible)* may; **puede que llueva** it may *o* might rain; **¿vendrás mañana? – puede** will you come tomorrow? – I may do; **puede ser** perhaps, maybe

**4** *vt (ser más fuerte que)* to be stronger than; **tú eres más alto, pero yo te puedo** you may be taller than me, but I could still beat you up

**poderío** *nm* **(a)** *(poder, fuerza)* power **(b)** *(riqueza)* riches

**poderoso, -a 1** *adj* powerful

**2** *nm,f* powerful person; **los poderosos** the powerful

**podio, pódium** *nm* podium

**podología** *nf* chiropody

**podólogo, -a** *nm,f* chiropodist

**podré** *etc ver* **poder**

**podredumbre** *nf (putrefacción)* putrefaction; *Fig (inmoralidad)* corruption

**podría** *etc ver* **poder**

**podrido, -a 1** *participio ver* **pudrir**

**2** *adj* rotten

**poema** *nm* poem; **ser todo un p.** to be pathetic

**poesía** *nf* **(a)** *(género literario)* poetry **(b)** *(poema)* poem

**poeta** *nmf* poet

**poética** *nf* poetics *(singular)*

**poético, -a** *adj* poetic

**poetisa** *nf* female poet

**póker** *nm* **(a)** *(juego)* poker **(b)** *(jugada)* four of a kind

**polaco, -a 1** *adj & nm,f* **(a)** Polish **(b)** *Fam Pey (catalán)* = pejorative term for a Catalan

**2** *nm (lengua)* Polish

**polaina** *nf* leggings

**polar** *adj* polar

**polaridad** *nf* polarity

**polarizar** [16] **1** *vt* **(a)** *Fig (miradas, atención, esfuerzo)* to concentrate **(b)** *Fís* to polarize

**2 polarizarse** *vpr (vida política, opinión pública)* to become polarized

**polaroid**® *nf inv* Polaroid®

**polca** *nf* polka

**polea** *nf* pulley

**polémica** *nf* controversy

**polémico, -a** *adj* controversial

**polemizar** [16] *vi* to argue, to debate

**polen** *nm* pollen

**polenta** *nf* polenta

**poleo** *nm (planta)* pennyroyal; *(infusión)* = herbal tea similar to mint

**poli** *Fam* **1** *nmf* cop

**2** *nf* cops

**poliamida** *nf* polyamide

**polichinela** *nm* **(a)** *(personaje)* Punchinello **(b)** *(títere)* puppet, marionette

**policía 1** *nmf* policeman, *f* policewoman

**2** *nf* **la p.** the police; **viene la p.** the police are coming; **p. antidisturbios** riot police; **p. militar/secreta** military/secret police; **p. de tráfico** traffic police

**policiaco, -a, policíaco, -a** *adj* **película/novela policiaca** detective film/novel

**policial** *adj* police; **investigación p.** police investigation *o* enquiry

**policlínica** *nf* private hospital

**policromado, -a** *adj Arte* polychrome

**policromía** *nf Arte* polychromy

**policromo, -a, polícromo, -a** *adj* polychromatic

**polideportivo, -a 1** *adj* multi-sport; *(gimnasio)* multi-use

**2** *nm* sports centre

**poliedro** *nm* polyhedron

**poliéster** *nm inv* polyester

**polietileno** *nm Br* polythene, *US* polyethylene

**polifacético, -a** *adj (persona)* multifaceted; *(actor)* versatile

**polifónico, -a** *adj* polyphonic

**poligamia** *nf* polygamy

**polígamo, -a 1** *adj* polygamous

**2** *nm,f* polygamist

**políglota** *adj & nmf* polyglot

**poligonal** *adj* polygonal

**polígono** *nm* **(a)** *Mat* polygon **(b)** *(terreno)* **p. industrial/residencial** industrial/housing estate; **p. de tiro** firing range

**polilla** *nf* moth

**polímero** *nm* polymer

**Polinesia** *n* Polynesia

**polinesio, -a** *adj & nm,f* Polynesian

**polinización** *nf* pollination

**polinomio** *nm* polynomial

**polio, poliomielitis** *nf inv* polio

**polipiel** *nf* artificial skin

**pólipo** *nm* polyp

**Polisario** *nm* **el (Frente) P.** Polisario, = Western Sahara liberation front

**polisemia** *nf* polysemy

**polisílabo, -a 1** *adj* polysyllabic

**2** *nm* polysyllable

**politburó** *nm* politburo

**politécnico, -a** *adj* polytechnic; **universidad politécnica** technical university

**politeísta** *adj* polytheistic

**política** *nf* **(a)** *(arte de gobernar)* politics *(singular)*; **hablar de p.** to discuss politics, to talk (about) politics **(b)** *(modo de gobernar, táctica)* policy; **p. monetaria** monetary policy

**politicastro** *nm Pey* bad politician

**político, -a 1** *adj* (a) *(de gobierno)* political (b) *Fig (prudente)* tactful (c) *(pariente)* **hermano p.** brother-in-law; **familia política** in-laws
**2** *nm* politician

**politiqueo** *nm* politicking

**politización** *nf* politicization

**politizar** [16] **1** *vt* to politicize
**2 politizarse** *vpr* to become politicized

**poliuretano** *nm* polyurethane

**polivalencia** *nf* polyvalency

**polivalente** *adj (vacuna, suero)* polyvalent

**póliza** *nf* (a) *(de seguro)* (insurance) policy (b) *(sello)* = stamp on a document showing that a certain tax has been paid

**polizón** *nm* stowaway

**polizonte** *nm Fam* cop

**polla** *nf Vulg* cock, prick; **¡una p.!** *(no)* not bloody likely!, no fucking way!

**pollera** *nf Andes, CSur* skirt

**pollería** *nf* poultry shop

**pollino** *nm* donkey

**pollito** *nm* chick

**pollo, -a 1** *nm,f (animal)* chick; **polla de agua** *(ave)* moorhen
**2** *nm* (a) *Culin* chicken (b) *Anticuado o Hum (joven)* young shaver

**polluelo** *nm* chick

**polo** *nm* (a) *(de la tierra)* pole; *Fig* **ser polos opuestos** to be poles apart; *Fig* **p. de atracción** *o* **atención** centre of attraction; **p. magnético** magnetic pole; **p. Norte/Sur** North/South Pole (b) *Elec* terminal; **p. negativo/positivo** negative/positive terminal (c) *(helado)* ice lolly (d) *(jersey)* polo shirt (e) *Dep* polo

**pololear** *vi Andes, CSur Fam* to go out (together)

**pololeo** *nm Andes Fam* small job

**pololo, -a** *nm,f Andes Fam* boyfriend, f girlfriend

**Polonia** *n* Poland

**poltrona** *nf* easy chair

**poltrón, -ona** *adj* lazy

**polución** *nf* (a) *(contaminación)* pollution (b) *(eyaculación)* **p. nocturna** wet dream

**polucionar** *vt* to pollute

**polvareda** *nf* dust cloud; *Fig* **levantar una gran p.** to cause a commotion

**polvera** *nf* powder compact

**polvo** *nm* (a) *(en el aire)* dust; **limpiar** *o* **quitar el p.** to do the dusting (b) *(de un producto)* powder; **en p.** powdered; *Fam* **estar hecho p.** to be knackered; **hacer p. algo** to smash sth; **morder el p.** to be humiliated; **polvos** *(maquillaje)* powder; **polvos de talco** talcum powder (c) *Vulg (coito)* fuck, screw; **echar un p.** to have a screw

**pólvora** *nf (sustancia explosiva)* gunpowder; **correr como la p.** to spread like wildfire; *Fam* **no ha inventado la p.** he's not the most intelligent person in the world

**polvoriento, -a** *adj (superficie)* dusty; *(sustancia)* powdery

**polvorín** *nm* munitions dump; *Fig* powder keg

**polvorón** *nm* = very crumbly shortbread biscuit

**pomada** *nf* ointment

**pomelo** *nm* (a) *(fruto)* grapefruit (b) *(árbol)* grapefruit tree

**pómez** *adj* **piedra p.** pumice stone

**pomo** *nm* knob

**pompa** *nf* (a) *(suntuosidad)* pomp (b) *(ostentación)* show, ostentation (c) **p. (de jabón)** (soap) bubble (d) **pompas fúnebres** *(servicio)* undertaker's; *(ceremonia)* funeral

**Pompeya** *n* Pompeii

**pompis** *nm inv Fam* behind, bottom

**pompón** *nm* pompom

**pomposidad** *nf* (a) *(suntuosidad)* splendour, pomp; *(ostentación)* showiness (b) *(en el lenguaje)* pomposity

**pomposo, -a** *adj* (a) *(suntuoso)* sumptuous, magnificent; *(ostentoso)* showy (b) *(lenguaje)* pompous

**pómulo** *nm* (a) *(hueso)* cheekbone (b) *(mejilla)* cheek

**pon** *ver* **poner**

**ponchadura** *nf Am* puncture, *US* blowout

**ponchar** *Guat, Méx* **1** *vt* to puncture
**2 poncharse** *vpr* to get a puncture

**ponche** *nm* (a) *(en fiesta)* punch (b) *(con leche y huevo)* eggnog

**ponchera** *nf* punch bowl

**poncho** *nm* poncho, blanket *(for wearing)*

**ponderación** *nf* (a) *(alabanza)* praise (b) *(moderación)* deliberation, considered nature (c) *(en estadística)* weighting

**ponderado, -a** *adj* (a) *(moderado)* considered (b) *(en estadística)* weighted

**ponderar** *vt* (a) *(alabar)* to praise (b) *(considerar)* to consider, to weigh up (c) *(en estadística)* to weight

**pondré** *etc ver* **poner**

**ponedero** *nm* nesting box

**ponedor, -ora 1** *adj* egg-laying

**2** *nm (ponedor)* nesting box

**ponencia** *nf (conferencia)* lecture, paper; *(informe)* report

**ponente** *nmf (en congreso)* speaker; *(relator)* reporter, rapporteur

**poner** [52] **1** *vt* **(a)** *(en general)* to put; *(colocar)* to place, to put

**(b)** *(vestir)* **p. algo a alguien** to put sth on sb

**(c)** *(contribuir, invertir)* to put in; **p. dinero en el negocio** to put money into the business; **p. algo de mi/tu/etc parte** to do my/your/etc bit; **p. mucho empeño en (hacer) algo** to put a lot of effort into (doing) sth

**(d)** *(hacer estar de cierta manera)* **p. a alguien en un aprieto/de mal humor** to put sb in a difficult position/in a bad mood; **le has puesto colorado/nervioso** you've made him blush/feel nervous; **poner cara de tonto/ inocente** to put on a stupid/an innocent face

**(e)** *(calificar)* **p. a alguien de algo** to call sb sth; **p. bien algo/a alguien** to praise sth/sb; **p. mal algo/a alguien** to criticize sth/sb.

**(f)** *(oponer)* **p. obstáculos a algo** to hinder sth; **p. pegas a algo** to raise objections to sth

**(g)** *(asignar)* *(precio, medida)* to fix, to settle; *(multa, tarea)* to give; **le pusieron Mario** they called him Mario; **le pusieron un cinco en el examen** he got five out of ten in the exam

**(h)** *Telecom (telegrama, fax)* to send; *(conferencia)* to make; **¿me pones con él?** can you put me through to him?

**(i)** *(conectar)* *(televisión, radio)* to switch *o* put on; *(despertador)* to set; *(instalación, gas)* to put in

**(j)** *Cine Teatro & TV* to show; **¿qué ponen en la tele?** what's on the telly?

**(k)** *(montar)* to set up; **ha puesto una tienda** she has opened a shop; **p. la mesa** to lay the table

**(l)** *(decorar)* to do up; **han puesto su casa con mucho lujo** they've done up their house in real style

**(m)** *(suponer)* to suppose; **pongamos que sucedió así** (let's) suppose that's what happened; **pon que necesitemos cinco días** suppose we need five days; **poniendo que todo salga bien** assuming everything goes according to plan

**(n)** *(decir)* to say; **¿qué pone ahí?** what does it say?

**(o)** *(huevo)* to lay

**2** *vi (ave)* to lay (eggs)

**3** *v impersonal Am Fam (parecer)* **se me pone que…** it seems to me that…

**4 ponerse** *vpr* **(a)** *(colocarse)* to put oneself; **ponerse de pie** to stand up; **ponte en la ventana** stand by the window

**(b)** *(ropa, gafas, maquillaje)* to put on

**(c)** *(volverse de cierta manera)* to go, to become; **se puso rojo de ira** he went red with anger; **se puso colorado** he blushed; **se puso muy guapa** she made herself look attractive; **¡cómo te pones por una nadería!** there's no need to react like that!; **¡no te pongas así!** *(no te enfades)* don't be like that!; *(no te pongas triste)* don't get upset!, don't be sad!

**(d)** *(iniciar)* **ponerse a hacer algo** to start doing sth

**(e)** *(de salud)* **ponerse malo** *o* **enfermo** to fall ill; **ponerse bien** to get better

**(f)** *(llenarse)* **ponerse de algo** to get covered in sth; **se puso de barro hasta las rodillas** he got covered in mud up to the knees

**(g)** *(sol, luna)* to set

**(h)** *(llegar)* **ponerse en** to get to

**poney** ['poni] *nm* pony

**pongo** *ver* **poner**

**poni** *nm* pony

**poniente** *nm (occidente)* West; *(viento)* west wind

**pontevedrés, -esa 1** *adj* of/from Pontevedra

**2** *nm,f* person from Pontevedra

**pontificado** *nm* papacy

**pontifical** *adj* papal

**pontifice** *nm (obispo)* bishop; *(Papa)* Pope; **el Sumo P.** the Supreme Pontiff, the Pope

**pontificio, -a** *adj (de los obispos)* episcopal; *(del Papa)* papal

**pontón** *nm* pontoon

**ponzoña** *nf (veneno)* venom, poison; *Fig* venom

**ponzoñoso, -a** *adj (venenoso)* venomous, poisonous; *Fig* venomous

**pop 1** *adj* pop

**2** *nm (música)* pop (music)

**popa** *nf* stern

**pope** *nm* **(a)** *Rel* = priest of the Orthodox church **(b)** *Fam Fig (pez gordo)* big shot

**popelín** *nm*, **popelina** *nf* poplin

**popote** *nm Méx* drinking straw

**populachero, -a** *adj Pey* **(a)** *(fiesta)* common, popular **(b)** *(discurso)* populist

**populacho** *nm Pey* mob, masses

**popular** *adj* **(a)** *(del pueblo)* of the people; *(arte, música)* folk **(b)** *(famoso)* popular

**popularidad** *nf* popularity

**popularizar** [16] **1** *vt* to popularize

**2 popularizarse** *vpr* to become popular

**popularmente** *adv* **p. conocido como…** more commonly known as…

**populismo** *nm* populism

**populista** *adj & nmf* populist

**populoso, -a** *adj* populous, crowded

**popurrí** nm potpourri

**póquer** nm (a) (juego) poker (b) (jugada) four of a kind

**poquito** nm un **p.** a little bit

**por** prep (a) (causa) because of; **se enfadó p. tu comportamiento** she got angry because of your behaviour; **¿p. qué?** why?; **¿p. qué lo dijo?** why did she say it?; **¿p. qué no vienes?** why don't you come?; Fam **¿p.?** why?

(b) (finalidad) (antes de infinitivo) (in order) to; (antes de sustantivo o pronombre) for; **lo hizo p. complacerte** he did it to please you; **lo hice p. ella** I did it for her

(c) (medio, modo, agente) by; **p. mensajero/fax/teléfono** by courier/fax/telephone; **p. escrito** in writing; **lo cogieron p. el brazo** they took him by the arm; **el récord fue batido p. el atleta** the record was broken by the athlete

(d) (tiempo aproximado) **creo que la boda será p. abril** I think the wedding will be some time in April

(e) (tiempo concreto) **p. la mañana/tarde** in the morning/afternoon; **p. la noche** at night; **ayer salimos p. la noche** we went out last night; **p. unos días** for a few days

(f) (lugar) **¿p. dónde vive?** whereabouts does he live?; **vive p. las afueras** he lives somewhere on the outskirts; **había papeles p. el suelo** there were papers all over the floor; **p. delante parece muy bonita** it looks very nice from the front; **está escrito p. detrás** there's writing on the back; **sólo quedaba sitio p. detrás** there was only room at the back

(g) (a través de) through; **vamos p. aquí/allí** let's go this/that way; **iba paseando p. el bosque/la calle** she was walking through the forest/along the street; **pasar p. la aduana** to go through customs

(h) (a cambio de, en lugar de) for; **lo ha comprado p. poco dinero** she bought it for very little; **cambió el coche p. la moto** he exchanged his car for a motorbike; **él lo hará p. mí** he'll do it for me

(i) (distribución) per; **cien pesetas p. unidad** a hundred pesetas each; **mil unidades p. semana** a thousand units a o per week; **uno p. uno** one by one; **20 kms p. hora** 20 km an o per hour

(j) Mat **dos p. dos igual a cuatro** two times two is four

(k) (en busca de) for; **baja p. tabaco** go down to the shops for some cigarettes, go down to get some cigarettes; **a p.** for; **vino a p. las entradas** she came for the tickets

(l) (concesión) **p. más** o **mucho que lo intentes no lo conseguirás** however hard you try o try as you might, you'll never manage it;

**no me cae bien, p. (muy) simpático que te parezca** you may think he's nice, but I don't like him

(m) **p. mí/nosotros** as far as I'm/we're concerned

**porcelana** nf (a) (material) porcelain, china (b) (objeto) piece of porcelain o china

**porcentaje** nm percentage

**porcentual** adj percentage; **seis puntos porcentuales** six percentage points

**porche** nm (entrada) porch; (soportal) arcade

**porcino, -a** adj pig; **ganado p.** pigs

**porción** nf portion, piece

**pordiosero, -a 1** adj begging

**2** nm,f beggar

**porfía** nf (a) (disputa) dispute; **a p.** determinedly (b) (insistencia) persistence; (tozudez) stubbornness

**porfiado, -a** adj (insistente) persistent; (tozudo) stubborn

**porfiar** [34] vi (a) (disputar) to argue obstinately (b) (empeñarse) **p. en** to be insistent on

**pormenor** nm detail

**pormenorizar** [16] **1** vt to describe in detail

**2** vi to go into detail

**porno** adj Fam porn, porno

**pornografía** nf pornography

**pornográfico, -a** adj pornographic

**poro** nm pore

**poroso, -a** adj porous

**poroto** nm Andes, CSur kidney bean; **p. verde** green bean

**porque** conj (a) (debido a que) because; **¡p. sí/no!** just because!; **no voy a hacerlo p. sí** I'm not going to do it just because I'm told to (b) (para que) so that, in order that

**porqué** nm reason; **el p. de** the reason for

**porquería** nf (a) (suciedad) filth (b) (cosa de mala calidad) rubbish; **es una p. de libro** the book stinks (c) **porquerías** (comida) junk food, rubbish

**porqueriza** nf pigsty

**porquero, -a** nm,f swineherd

**porra 1** nf (a) (palo) club; (de policía) truncheon (b) Culin = deep-fried pastry sticks (c) Fam **mandar a alguien a la p.** to tell sb to go to hell (d) Fam **¿por qué/dónde porras...?** why/where the blazes...?; **¡una p.!** no way! not bloody likely!

**2** interj Fam **¡porras!** hell!, damn it!

**porrada** nf Fam **una p. (de)** heaps o tons (of)

**porrazo** nm (golpe) bang, blow; (caída) bump

**porreta 1** nmf muy Fam (fumador de porros) pothead

**2** nf Fam (a) (nariz) hooter (b) **en p.** (desnudo) in the altogether

**porrillo: a porrillo** *loc adv Fam* by the bucket

**porro** *nm Fam (de droga)* joint

**porrón** *nm* (a) *(vasija)* = glass wine jar used for drinking wine from its long spout (b) *Fam* **un p. de** loads of

**portaaviones** *nm inv* aircraft carrier

**portada** *nf* (a) *(de libro)* title page; *(de revista)* (front) cover; *(de periódico)* front page (b) *(de disco)* sleeve (c) *Arquit* façade

**portador, -ora 1** *adj* carrying, bearing
  **2** *nm,f* carrier, bearer; *Com* **al p.** to the bearer

**portaequipajes** *nm inv (maletero) Br* boot, *US* trunk; *(baca)* roof *o* luggage rack

**portaestandarte** *nm* standard-bearer

**portafolio** *nm*; **portafolios** *nm inv (carpeta)* file; *(maletín)* attaché case

**portal** *nm* (a) *(entrada)* entrance hall; *(puerta)* main door; **viven en aquel p.** they live at that number (b) *(belén)* crib, Nativity scene

**portalámparas** *nm inv* socket

**portaligas** *nm inv Am* suspender belt

**portalón** *nm* = large doors or gate giving access to interior courtyard from street

**portamaletas** *nm inv Am Br* boot, *US* trunk

**portamonedas** *nm inv* purse

**portapapeles** *nm inv Informát* clipboard

**portar 1** *vt* to carry
  **2 portarse** *vpr* to behave; **se ha portado bien conmigo** she has treated me well; **portarse mal** to misbehave

**portátil 1** *adj* portable
  **2** *nm (ordenador)* lap-top

**portaviones** *nm inv* aircraft carrier

**portavoz 1** *nmf (persona)* spokesman, *f* spokeswoman
  **2** *nm (periódico)* voice

**portazo** *nm* **dar un p.** to slam the door; **la puerta se cerró de un p.** the door slammed shut

**porte** *nm* (a) *(gasto de transporte)* carriage, transport costs; *Com* **p. debido/pagado** carriage due/paid (b) *(transporte)* carriage, transport; **una empresa de portes y mudanzas** a removal firm (c) *(aspecto)* bearing, demeanour

**porteador, -ora 1** *adj* bearing, carrying
  **2** *nm,f* porter

**portento** *nm* wonder, marvel

**portentoso, -a** *adj* wonderful, amazing

**porteño, -a 1** *adj (bonaerense)* of/from Buenos Aires
  **2** *nm,f (bonaerense)* person from Buenos Aires

**portería** *nf* (a) *(de casa, colegio)* caretaker's office *o* lodge; *(de hotel, ministerio)* porter's office *o* lodge (b) *Dep* goal, goalmouth

**portero, -a** *nm,f* (a) *(de casa, colegio)* caretaker; *(de hotel, ministerio)* porter; **p. automático** *o* **eléctrico** entry-phone (b) *Dep* goalkeeper

**portezuela** *nf (de coche)* door

**pórtico** *nm* (a) *(fachada)* portico (b) *(arcada)* arcade

**portilla** *nf Náut* porthole

**portillo** *nm* (a) *(abertura)* opening, gap (b) *(puerta pequeña)* wicket gate

**portón** *nm* large door *o* entrance

**portorriqueño, -a** *adj & nm,f* Puerto Rican

**portuario, -a** *adj* (a) *(del puerto)* port; **ciudad portuaria** port (b) *(de los muelles)* dock; **trabajador p.** docker; **la zona portuaria** the docks (area)

**Portugal** *n* Portugal

**portugués, -esa 1** *adj & nm,f* Portuguese
  **2** *nm (lengua)* Portuguese

**porvenir** *nm* future

**pos: en pos de** *loc prep (detrás de)* behind; *(en busca de)* after

**posada** *nf* (a) *(fonda)* inn, guest house (b) *(hospedaje)* lodging, accommodation

**posaderas** *nfpl Fam* backside, bottom

**posadero, -a** *nm,f* innkeeper

**posar 1** *vt (dejar, poner) (objeto)* to put *o* lay down; *(mano, mirada)* to rest
  **2** *vi* to pose
  **3 posarse** *vpr* (a) *(insecto, polvo)* to settle (b) *(pájaro)* to perch; *(nave, helicóptero)* to come down

**posavasos** *nm inv* coaster

**posdata** *nf* postscript

**pose** *nf* pose

**poseedor, -ora 1** *adj (propietario)* owning, possessing; *(de cargo, acciones, récord)* holding
  **2** *nm,f (propietario)* owner; *(de cargo, acciones, récord)* holder

**poseer** [39] *vt* (a) *(ser dueño de)* to own; *(estar en poder de)* to have, to possess (b) *(sexualmente)* to have

**poseído, -a 1** *adj* **p. por** possessed by
  **2** *nm,f* possessed person

**posesión** *nf* possession; **tomar p. de un cargo** to take up a position *o* post

**posesivo, -a 1** *adj* possessive
  **2** *nm Gram* possessive

**poseso, -a 1** *adj* possessed
  **2** *nm,f* possessed person; **gritar como un p.** to scream like one possessed

**poseyera** *etc ver* **poseer**

**posgraduado, -a** *adj & nm,f* postgraduate

**posguerra** *nf* post-war period

**posibilidad** *nf* possibility, chance; **cabe la p. de que…** there is a chance that…; **posibilidades económicas** financial means *o* resources

**posibilitar** *vt* to make possible

**posible 1** *adj* possible; **es p. que llueva** it could rain; **dentro de lo p.** as far as possible; **de ser p.** if possible; **hacer (todo) lo p.** to do everything possible; **lo antes p.** as soon as possible

  **2** *nmpl* **posibles** (financial) means

**posición** *nf* (a) *(lugar, postura)* position (b) *(categoría) (social)* status; *(económica)* situation

**posicionamiento** *nm* position; **su p. con respecto a algo** his position on sth

**posicionarse** *vpr* to take a position *o* stance

**positivar** *vt* Fot *(negativos)* to print

**positivismo** *nm* (a) *(realismo)* pragmatism (b) *Filosofía* positivism

**positivista** *adj & nmf* Filosofía positivist

**positivo, -a 1** *adj también Elec* positive

  **2** *nm* Fot print

**posmodernidad** *nf* post-modernism

**posmoderno, -a** *adj & nm,f* postmodernist

**poso** *nm* sediment; *Fig* trace

**posología** *nf* dosage

**posponer** [52] *vt* (a) *(relegar)* to put behind, to relegate (b) *(aplazar)* to postpone

**pospuesto, -a** *participio ver* **posponer**

**pospusiera** *etc ver* **posponer**

**posta: a posta** *loc adv* on purpose

**postal 1** *adj* postal

  **2** *nf* postcard

**postdata** *nf* postscript

**poste** *nm* post, pole; *Dep* post

**póster** *(pl* posters*)* *nm* poster

**postergación** *nf* *(aplazamiento)* postponement

**postergar** [40] *vt* (a) *(aplazar)* to postpone (b) *(relegar)* to put behind, to relegate

**posteridad** *nf* (a) *(generación futura)* posterity; **quedar para la p.** to be left to posterity (b) *(futuro)* future

**posterior** *adj* (a) *(en el espacio)* rear, back; **p. a** behind (b) *(en el tiempo)* subsequent, later; **p. a** subsequent to, after

**posteriori: a posteriori** *loc adv* with hindsight; **habrá que juzgarlo a p.** we'll have to judge it after the event

**posterioridad** *nf* **con p.** later, subsequently

**postgraduado, -a** *adj & nm,f* postgraduate

**postguerra** *nf* post-war period

**postigo** *nm* (a) *(contraventana)* shutter (b) *(puerta)* wicket gate

**postilla** *nf* scab

**postín** *nm* showiness, boastfulness; **darse p.** to show off; **de p.** posh

**post-it®** *nm inv* Post-it®

**postizo, -a 1** *adj* (a) *(falso)* false (b) *(añadido)* detachable

  **2** *nm* hairpiece

**postoperatorio, -a 1** *adj* post-operative

  **2** *nm* *(período)* post-operative period

**postor, -ora** *nm,f* bidder; **mejor p.** highest bidder

**postración** *nf* prostration

**postrado, -a** *adj* prostrate

**postrar 1** *vt* to weaken, to (make) prostrate

  **2 postrarse** *vpr* to prostrate oneself

**postre** *nm* dessert, pudding; **de p.** for dessert; *Fig* **a la p.** in the end; *Fig* **para p.** to cap it all

**postrero, -a**

> **Postrer** is used instead of **postrero** before singular masculine nouns (e.g. **el postrer día** the last day).

*adj* last, final

**postrimerías** *nfpl* final stages; **en las p. del siglo XIX** at the end *o* close of the 19th century

**postulado** *nm* postulate

**postulante, -a** *nm,f* *(en colecta)* collector; *Rel* postulant

**postular 1** *vt* *(exigir)* to call for

  **2** *vi* *(en colecta)* to collect

**póstumo, -a** *adj* posthumous

**postura** *nf* (a) *(posición)* position, posture (b) *(actitud)* attitude, stance (c) *(en subasta)* bid

**posventa, postventa** *adj inv Com* after-sales; **servicio p.** after-sales service

**pota** *nf* muy Fam *(vómito)* puke; **echar la p.** to puke (up)

**potable** *adj* (a) *(bebible)* drinkable; **agua p.** drinking water (b) *Fam (aceptable)* acceptable, passable

**potaje** *nm* *(guiso)* vegetable stew; *(caldo)* vegetable stock; *Fam (brebaje)* potion, brew

**potar** *vi* muy Fam to puke (up)

**potasa** *nf* potash

**potásico, -a** *adj* Quím **cloruro p.** potassium chloride

**potasio** *nm* potassium

**pote** *nm* pot

**potencia** *nf* (a) *(capacidad, fuerza, poder)* power; **tiene mucha p.** it's very powerful; **las grandes potencias** the major (world) powers (b) *(posibilidad)* **en p.** potentially; **una campeona en p.** a potential champion (c) *Mat* **a la tercera/cuarta p.** to the third/fourth power

**potencial 1** *adj* potential

**2** *nm* (a) *(fuerza)* power (b) *(posibilidades)* potential (c) *Gram* conditional (d) *Elec* (electric) potential

**potenciar** [15] *vt* (a) *(fomentar)* to encourage, to promote (b) *(reforzar)* to boost, to strengthen

**potentado, -a** *nm,f* potentate

**potente** *adj* powerful

**potestad** *nf* authority, power

**potingue** *nm Fam (cosmético)* potion

**potra** *nf* (a) *(yegua joven)* filly (b) *Fam (suerte)* luck; **tener p.** to be jammy

**potranco, -a** *nm,f* = horse under three years of age

**potrero** *nm Am* field, pasture

**potro** *nm* (a) *(caballo joven)* colt (b) *Dep* vaulting horse (c) *(aparato de tormento)* rack

**poza** *nf (de río)* pool, deep section of small river

**pozo** *nm (de agua)* well; *(de mina)* shaft; **p. negro** cesspool; **p. de petróleo** oil well; *Fig* **ser un p. de algo** to be a fountain of sth

**p.p.** (a) *(abrev de* **por poder***)* pp (b) *(abrev de* **porte pagado***)* c/p

**PP** *nm (abrev de* **Partido Popular***)* = Spanish political party to the right of the political spectrum

**práctica** *nf* (a) *(ejercicio, destreza)* practice; *(de un deporte)* playing; **llevar algo a la p., poner algo en p.** to put sth into practice; **en la p.** in practice (b) *(clase no teórica)* practical

**practicable** *adj* (a) *(realizable)* practicable (b) *(transitable)* passable

**prácticamente** *adv (casi)* practically

**practicante 1** *adj* practising

**2** *nmf* (a) *(de deporte)* practitioner; *(de religión)* practising member of a Church (b) *Med* medical assistant

**practicar** [61] **1** *vt* (a) *(ejercitar )* to practise; *(deporte)* to play (b) *(realizar)* to carry out, to perform

**2** *vi* to practise

**práctico, -a 1** *adj* practical

**2** *nm Náut* pilot

**pradera** *nf* large meadow, prairie

**prado** *nm* meadow; **el (Museo del) P.** the Prado (Museum)

**Praga** *n* Prague

**pragmática** *nf* (a) *Hist (edicto)* royal edict (b) *Ling* pragmatics *(singular)*

**pragmático, -a 1** *adj* pragmatic

**2** *nm,f (persona)* pragmatist

**pragmatismo** *nm* pragmatism

**praguense 1** *adj* of/from Prague

**2** *nmf* person from Prague

**praliné** *nm* praline

**praxis** *nf inv* practice; *Filosofía* praxis

**preacuerdo** *nm* draft agreement

**preámbulo** *nm* (a) *(introducción)* (de libro) foreword, preface; *(de congreso, conferencia)* introduction, preamble (b) *(rodeo)* digression

**preaviso** *nm* prior notice

**prebenda** *nf* (a) *Rel* prebend (b) *Fig (privilegio)* sinecure

**preboste** *nm* provost

**precalentamiento** *nm Dep* warm-up

**precalentar** [3] *vt* (a) *Culin* to pre-heat (b) *Dep* to warm up

**precampaña** *nf Pol* run-up to election

**precariedad** *nf* precariousness

**precario, -a** *adj* precarious

**precaución** *nf* (a) *(prudencia)* caution, care (b) *(medida)* precaution; **tomar precauciones** to take precautions

**precaver 1** *vt* to guard against

**2 precaverse** *vpr* to take precautions; **precaverse de** *o* **contra** to guard (oneself) against

**precavido, -a** *adj* (a) *(prevenido)* prudent; **es muy p.** he always comes prepared (b) *(cauteloso)* wary

**precedente 1** *adj* previous, preceding

**2** *nm* precedent; **sentar p.** to set a precedent; **sin precedentes** unprecedented

**preceder** *vt* to go before, to precede

**preceptiva** *nf* rules

**preceptivo, -a** *adj* obligatory, compulsory

**precepto** *nm* precept; *Rel* **fiestas de p.** days of obligation

**preceptor, -ora** *nm,f* (private) tutor

**preces** *nfpl Formal* prayers

**preciado, -a** *adj* valuable, prized

**preciar** [15] **1** *vt* to appreciate

**2 preciarse** *vpr* to have self-respect; **preciarse de** to pride oneself on

**precintado** *nm* sealing

**precintadora** *nf* sealing machine

**precintar** *vt* to seal

**precinto** *nm* seal

**precio** *nm* price; **a cualquier p.** at any price; *Fig* **al p. de** at the cost of; **p. de fábrica/de coste** factory/cost price; **p. de compra** purchase price; *Econ* **p. indicativo** guide price; **p. de mercado** market price; **p. prohibitivo** prohibitively high price; **p. de salida** starting price; **p. de venta (al público)** retail price; *Fig* **no tener p.** to be priceless

**preciosidad** *nf* (a) *(cosa, persona)* **¡es una p.!** it's lovely *o* beautiful! (b) *(valor)* value

**precioso, -a** *adj* (a) *(valioso)* precious (b) *(bonito)* lovely, beautiful

**precipicio** *nm* precipice

**precipitación** nf (a) *(apresuramiento)* haste (b) *Meteo* **precipitaciones** *(lluvia)* rain; **precipitaciones en forma de nieve** snow (c) *Quím* precipitation

**precipitado, -a 1** adj hasty
**2** nm *Quím* precipitate

**precipitar 1** vt (a) *(arrojar)* to throw o hurl down (b) *(acelerar)* to hasten, to speed up (c) *Quím* to precipitate

**2 precipitarse** vpr (a) *(caer)* to plunge (down) (b) *(acelerarse) (acontecimientos)* to speed up (c) *(apresurarse)* to rush (**hacia** towards) (d) *(obrar irreflexivamente)* to act rashly

**precisamente** adv *(con precisión)* precisely (b) *(justamente)* ¡p.! exactly!, precisely!; **p. por eso** for that very reason; **p. tú lo sugeriste** in fact it was you who suggested it

**precisar** vt (a) *(determinar)* to fix, to set; *(aclarar)* to specify exactly (b) *(necesitar)* to need, to require

**precisión** nf accuracy, precision; **instrumento de p.** precision instrument

**preciso, -a** adj (a) *(determinado, conciso)* precise (b) *(necesario)* **ser p. para (algo/hacer algo)** to be necessary (for sth/to do sth); **es p. que vengas** you must come

**precocidad** nf precociousness

**precocinado, -a** adj pre-cooked

**precolombino, -a** adj pre-Columbian

**preconcebido, -a** adj *(idea)* preconceived; *(plan)* drawn up in advance

**preconcebir** [49] vt to draw up in advance

**preconizar** [16] vt to recommend, to advise

**precoz** adj (a) *(persona)* precocious (b) *(lluvias, frutos)* early

**precursor, -ora** nm,f precursor

**predador, -ora 1** adj predatory
**2** nm predator

**predatorio, -a** adj *(animal, instinto)* predatory

**predecesor, -ora** nm,f predecessor

**predecible** adj predictable

**predecir** [53] vt to predict

**predestinado, -a** adj predestined (**a** to)

**predestinar** vt to predestine

**predeterminación** nf predetermination

**predeterminar** vt to predetermine

**prédica** nf sermon

**predicado** nm *Gram* predicate

**predicador, -ora** nm,f preacher

**predicar** [61] vt & vi to preach; **es como p. en el desierto** it's like talking to a brick wall

**predicción** nf prediction

**predice** ver **predecir**

**predicho, -a** participio ver **predecir**

**predigo** ver **predecir**

**predijera** etc ver **predecir**

**predilección** nf preference (**por** for)

**predilecto, -a** adj favourite

**predio** nm (a) *(finca)* estate, property (b) *Am (edificio)* building

**predisponer** [52] vt to predispose (**a** to)

**predisposición** nf (a) *(aptitud)* **p. para** aptitude for (b) *(tendencia)* **p. a** a predisposition to

**predispuesto, -a 1** participio ver **predisponer**
**2** adj predisposed (**a** to)

**predominancia** nf predominance

**predominante** adj *(que prevalece)* predominant; *(viento, actitudes)* prevailing

**predominar** vi to predominate, to prevail (**sobre** over)

**predominio** nm preponderance, predominance

**preeminencia** nf preeminence

**preeminente** adj preeminent

**preescolar 1** adj preschool, nursery; **educación p.** nursery education
**2** nm nursery school, kindergarten

**preestreno** nm preview

**preexistente** adj pre-existing

**prefabricado, -a** adj prefabricated

**prefabricar** [61] vt to prefabricate

**prefacio** nm preface

**prefecto** nm prefect

**prefectura** nf prefecture; **p. de tráfico** traffic division

**preferencia** nf preference; **con** o **de p.** preferably; *Aut* **tener p.** to have right of way; **tener p. por** to have a preference for

**preferente** adj preferential

**preferentemente** adv preferably

**preferible** adj preferable (**a** to)

**preferido, -a** adj favourite

**preferir** [64] vt **p. algo (a algo)** to prefer sth (**to** sth)

**prefigurar** vt to prefigure

**prefijar** vt to fix in advance

**prefijo** nm (a) *Gram* prefix (b) *Telecom* (telephone) dialling code

**prefiriera** etc ver **preferir**

**pregón** nm (a) *(bando)* proclamation, announcement (b) *(discurso)* speech

**pregonar** vt (a) *(bando)* to proclaim, to announce (b) *(secreto)* to spread about

**pregonero, -a** nm,f (a) *(de pueblo)* town crier; *Fig (bocazas)* blabbermouth

**pregunta** nf question; **hacer una p.** to ask a question; **p. capciosa** catch question; **andar a la cuarta** o **última p.** to be broke

**preguntar 1** *vt* to ask; **p. algo a alguien** to ask sb sth

**2** *vi* **p. por** to ask about *o* after

**3 preguntarse** *vpr* to wonder (**si** whether)

**prehistoria** *nf* prehistory

**prehistórico, -a** *adj* prehistoric

**prejuicio** *nm* prejudice

**prejuzgar** [40] *vt & vi* to prejudge

**prelado** *nm Rel* prelate

**preliminar 1** *adj* preliminary

**2** *nm* preliminary

**preludio** *nm también Mús* prelude

**premamá** *adj inv (ropa)* maternity

**prematrimonial** *adj* premarital; **relaciones prematrimoniales** premarital sex

**prematuro, -a 1** *adj* premature

**2** *nm,f* premature baby

**premeditación** *nf* premeditation; *Der & Fig* **con p. y alevosía** with malice aforethought

**premeditado, -a** *adj* premeditated

**premeditar** *vt* to think out in advance

**premiar** [15] *vt* (a) *(recompensar)* to reward (b) *(dar un premio a)* to give a prize to

**premier** *nm* British prime minister

**premio** *nm* (a) *(en competición)* prize; *(recompensa)* reward; **p. de consolación** consolation prize; **p. gordo** first prize (b) *(ganador)* prizewinner

**premisa** *nf* premise

**premolar** *adj & nm* premolar

**premonición** *nf* premonition

**premonitorio, -a** *adj* warning

**premura** *nf* (a) *(urgencia)* urgency (b) *(escasez)* lack, shortage

**prenatal** *adj* prenatal, antenatal

**prenda** *nf* (a) *(vestido)* garment, article of clothing (b) *(garantía)* pledge; **dejar algo en p.** to leave sth as a pledge (c) *(en juego)* forfeit (d) *(virtud)* talent, gift (e) *(apelativo cariñoso)* darling, treasure (f) *Fam* **no soltar p.** not to say a word

**prendar 1** *vt* to enchant

**2 prendarse** *vpr* **prendarse de** to fall in love with

**prendedor** *nm* brooch

**prender 1** *vt* (a) *(arrestar)* to arrest, to apprehend (b) *(sujetar)* to fasten (c) *(encender)* to light (d) *(agarrar)* to grip

**2** *vi* (a) *(arder)* to catch (fire) (b) *(planta)* to take root (c) *Fig (propagarse)* to spread, to take root

**3 prenderse** *vpr (arder)* to catch fire

**prendido, -a** *adj* caught; *Fig* **quedar p. de** to be captivated by

**prensa** *nf* (a) *(periódicos, periodistas)* press; **la p. amarilla** the gutter press, the tabloids; **p. del corazón** romantic magazines; *Fig* **tener buena/mala p.** to have a good/bad press (b) *(imprenta)* printing press (c) *(máquina)* press

**prensar** *vt* to press

**prenupcial** *adj* premarital

**preñado, -a 1** *adj* (a) *(hembra)* pregnant (b) *Fig (lleno)* **p. de** full of

**2** *nf* **preñada** pregnant woman

**preñar** *vt* (a) *(hembra)* to make pregnant (b) *Fig (llenar)* **p. de** to fill with

**preñez** *nf* pregnancy

**preocupación** *nf* concern, worry

**preocupado, -a** *adj* worried, concerned (**por** about)

**preocupante** *adj* worrying

**preocupar 1** *vt* (a) *(inquietar)* to worry (b) *(importar)* to bother

**2 preocuparse** *vpr* (a) *(inquietarse)* to worry (**por** about), to be worried (**por** about) (b) *(encargarse)* **preocuparse de algo** to take care of sth; **preocuparse de hacer algo** to see to it that sth is done; **preocuparse de que...** to make sure that...

**preolímpico, -a** *adj Dep* in the run-up to the Olympics; **torneo p.** Olympic qualifying competition

**preparación** *nf* (a) *(disposición, elaboración)* preparation (b) *(conocimientos)* training (c) *(para microscopio)* specimen

**preparado, -a 1** *adj* (a) *(dispuesto)* ready; *(de antemano)* prepared; **preparados, listos, ¡ya!** ready, steady, go! (b) *(capacitado)* competent, talented (**para** in)

**2** *nm (medicamento)* preparation

**preparador, -ora** *nm,f Dep (entrenador)* coach

**preparar 1** *vt* (a) *(disponer, elaborar)* to prepare; *(trampa)* to set, to lay; *(maletas)* to pack (b) *(examen)* to prepare for (c) *Dep* to train

**2 prepararse** *vpr* to prepare oneself, to get ready (**para algo** for sth); **prepararse para hacer algo** to prepare *o* get ready to do sth

**preparativo, -a 1** *adj* preparatory, preliminary

**2** *nmpl* **preparativos** preparations

**preparatorio, -a** *adj* preparatory

**preponderancia** *nf* preponderance; **tener p. (sobre)** to predominate (over)

**preponderante** *adj* prevailing

**preponderar** *vi* to prevail

**preposición** *nf* preposition

**preposicional** *adj* prepositional

**prepotencia** *nf* (a) *(arrogancia)* arrogance (b) *(poder)* dominance, power

**prepotente** *adj* (a) *(arrogante)* domineering, overbearing (b) *(poderoso)* very powerful

**prepucio** *nm* foreskin

**prerrogativa** *nf* prerogative

**presa** *nf* (a) *(captura) (de cazador)* catch; *(de animal)* prey; **hacer p. en alguien** to seize o grip sb; **ser p. de** to be prey to; **ser p. del pánico** to be panic-stricken (b) *(dique)* dam

**presagiar** [15] *vt* *(prever)* to foretell, to foresee; *(tormenta, problemas)* to warn of

**presagio** *nm* (a) *(premonición)* premonition (b) *(señal)* omen

**presbiterianismo** *nm* Presbyterianism

**presbiteriano, -a** *adj & nm,f* Presbyterian

**presbiterio** *nm* presbytery

**presbítero** *nm* Rel priest

**prescindir** *vi* **p. de** *(renunciar a)* to do without; *(omitir)* to dispense with

**prescribir 1** *vt* to prescribe

**2** *vi* (a) *(ordenar)* to prescribe (b) Der *(plazo, deuda)* to expire, to lapse

**prescripción** *nf* prescription; **por p. facultativa** on medical advice, on doctor's orders

**prescrito, -a** *participio ver* **prescribir**

**preselección** *nf* short list, shortlisting

**preseleccionar** *vt* to shortlist; Dep to name in the squad

**presencia** *nf* *(asistencia, aspecto)* presence; **en p. de** in the presence of; **buena p.** good looks; **mucha/poca p.** great/little presence; **p. de ánimo** presence of mind

**presencial** *adj* **testigo p.** eyewitness

**presenciar** [15] *vt* *(asistir)* to be present at; *(ser testigo de)* to witness

**presentable** *adj* presentable

**presentación** *nf* (a) *(en general)* presentation (b) *(entre personas)* introduction

**presentador, -ora** *nm,f* presenter

**presentar 1** *vt* (a) *(en general)* to present; *(dimisión)* to tender; *(tesis, pruebas, propuesta)* to hand in, to submit; *(solicitud, recurso, denuncia)* to lodge; *(moción)* to propose (b) *(ofrecer) (disculpas, excusas)* to make; *(respetos)* to pay (c) *(persona)* to introduce; **me presentó a sus amigos** she introduced me to her friends (d) *(tener) (aspecto)* to have, to show; **presenta difícil solución** it's going to be difficult to solve (e) *(proponer)* **p. a alguien para** to propose sb for, to put sb forward for

**2 presentarse** *vpr* (a) *(personarse)* to turn up, to appear (b) *(en juzgado, comisaría)* to report (**en** to); **presentarse a un examen** to sit an exam (c) *(darse a conocer)* to introduce oneself (d) *(para un cargo)* to stand, to run (**a** for) (e) *(futuro)* to appear, to look (f) *(problema, situación)* to arise, to come up

**presente 1** *adj* (a) *(asistente, que está delante)* present; **aquí p.** here present; **hacer p. algo a alguien** to notify sb of sth; **tener p.** *(recordar)* to remember; *(tener en cuenta)* to bear in mind; **¡p.!** present! (b) *(en curso)* current; **del p. mes** of this month

**2** *nmf* (a) *(en un lugar)* **los (aquí) presentes** all those present (b) *(escrito)* **por la p. le informo...** I hereby inform you...

**3** *nm* (a) *también* Gram present; **p. histórico** historical present (b) *(regalo)* gift, present (c) *(corriente)* **el p.** *(mes)* the current month; *(año)* the current year (d) **mejorando lo p.** present company excepted

**presentimiento** *nm* presentiment, feeling

**presentir** [64] *vt* to foresee; **p. que algo va a pasar** to have a feeling that sth is going to happen; **p. lo peor** to fear the worst

**preservación** *nf* preservation

**preservar 1** *vt* to protect

**2 preservarse** *vpr* **preservarse de** to protect oneself o shelter from

**preservativo, -a 1** *adj* protective

**2** *nm* condom; **p. femenino** female condom

**presidencia** *nf* *(de nación)* presidency; *(de asamblea, empresa)* chairmanship

**presidencialismo** *nm* Pol presidential system

**presidencialista 1** *adj* Pol presidential

**2** *nmf* supporter of the presidential system

**presidente, -a** *nm,f* *(de nación)* president; *(de asamblea, empresa)* chairman, f chairwoman; **p. (del Gobierno)** prime minister

**presidiario, -a** *nm,f* convict

**presidio** *nm* prison

**presidir** *vt* (a) *(ser presidente de)* to preside over; *(reunión)* to chair (b) *(predominar sobre)* to dominate

**presienta** *etc ver* **presentir**

**presintiera** *etc ver* **presentir**

**presintonía** *nf* *(de radio)* pre-set station selector

**presión** *nf* pressure; **a p.** under pressure; **p. atmosférica** atmospheric pressure; **p. arterial** o **sanguínea** blood pressure; Econ **p. fiscal** tax burden

**presionar** *vt* (a) *(apretar)* to press (b) Fig *(coaccionar)* to pressurize, to put pressure on

**preso, -a 1** *adj* imprisoned

**2** *nm,f* prisoner

**prestación** *nf* (a) *(de servicio) (acción)* provision; *(resultado)* service; **p. social** social security benefit; **p. social sustitutoria** = community service done as alternative to military service (b) *(de dinero)* lending (c) **prestaciones** *(de coche)* performance features

**prestado, -a** *adj* on loan; **dar p.** algo to lend sth; **pedir/tomar p.** algo to borrow sth; **de p.** *(con cosas prestadas)* with borrowed things; *(de modo precario)* on borrowed time

**prestamista** *nmf* moneylender

**préstamo** *nm* (a) *(acción) (de prestar)* lending; *(de pedir prestado)* borrowing (b) *(cantidad)* loan

**prestancia** *nf* excellence, distinction

**prestar** *vt* (a) *(dejar) (dinero, cosa)* to lend, to loan (b) *(dar) (ayuda)* to give, to offer; *(servicio)* to offer, to provide; *(atención)* to pay; *(declaración, juramento)* to make

  **2 prestarse** *vpr* **prestarse a** *(ofrecerse a)* to offer to; *(acceder a)* to consent to; *(dar motivo a)* to be open to

**presteza** *nf* promptness, speed

**prestidigitación** *nf* conjuring

**prestidigitador, -ora** *nm,f* conjuror

**prestigio** *nm* prestige

**prestigioso, -a** *adj* prestigious

**presto, -a** *adj* **1** (a) *(dispuesto)* ready (a to) (b) *(rápido)* prompt
  **2** *adv Mús* presto

**presumible** *adj* probable, likely

**presumido, -a1** *adj* conceited, vain
  **2** *nm,f* conceited *o* vain person

**presumir** **1** *vt* *(suponer)* to presume, to assume
  **2** *vi* (a) *(jactarse)* to show off; **presume de guapa** she thinks she's pretty (b) *(ser vanidoso)* to be conceited *o* vain

**presunción** *nf* (a) *(suposición)* presumption (b) *(vanidad)* conceit, vanity

**presunto, -a** *adj* *(supuesto)* presumed, supposed; *(criminal)* alleged, suspected

**presuntuoso, -a** **1** *adj* *(vanidoso)* conceited; *(pretencioso)* pretentious
  **2** *nm,f* conceited person

**presuponer** [52] *vt* to presuppose

**presuposición** *nf* assumption

**presupuestar** *vt* *(hacer un presupuesto para)* to give an estimate for; *Fin* to budget for

**presupuestario, -a** *adj* budgetary

**presupuesto, -a** **1** *participio ver* **presuponer**
  **2** *nm* (a) *(dinero disponible)* budget; *(cálculo de costes)* estimate; *Econ* **Presupuestos Generales del Estado** Spanish national budget (b) *(suposición)* assumption

**presuroso, -a** *adj* in a hurry

**prêt-à-porter** [pretapor'te] **1** *adj* *(ropa, moda)* off-the-peg, ready-to-wear
  **2** *nm* off-the-peg clothing

**pretencioso, -a** **1** *adj* *(persona)* pretentious; *(cosa)* showy
  **2** *nm,f* pretentious person

**pretender** *vt* (a) *(intentar)* **p. hacer** algo to try to do sth (b) *(aspirar a)* **p. hacer** algo to aspire *o* want to do sth; **p. que alguien haga algo** to want sb to do sth; **¿qué pretendes decir?** what do you mean? (c) *(afirmar)* to claim (d) *(solicitar)* to apply for (e) *(cortejar)* to court

**pretendido, -a** *adj* supposed

**pretendiente** **1** *nmf* (a) *(aspirante)* candidate (a for) (b) *(a un trono)* pretender (a to)
  **2** *nm* *(a noviazgo, matrimonio)* suitor

**pretensión** *nf* (a) *(intención)* aim, intention (b) *(aspiración)* aspiration (c) *(supuesto derecho)* claim (a *o* **sobre** to) (e) *(afirmación)* claim (e) **pretensiones** *(exigencias)* demands

**pretérito, -a1** *adj* past
  **2** *nm Gram* preterite, past; **p. imperfecto** imperfect; **p. indefinido** simple past; **p. perfecto** (present) perfect; **p. pluscuamperfecto** pluperfect

**pretextar** *vt* to use as a pretext, to claim

**pretexto** *nm* pretext, excuse

**pretil** *nm* parapet

**Pretoria** *n* Pretoria

**preuniversitario, -a1** *adj* pre-university
  **2** *nm Antes* = in Spain, former one-year course of study, successful completion of which allowed pupils to go to university

**prevalecer** [48] *vi* to prevail (**sobre** over)

**prevaler** [70] **1** *vi* to prevail (**sobre** over)
  **2 prevalerse** *vpr* to take advantage (**de** of)

**prevaricación** *nf Der* breach of trust

**prevaricar** [61] *vi Der* to betray one's trust

**prevención** *nf* (a) *(acción)* prevention; *(medida)* precaution; **en p. de** as a precaution against (b) *(prejuicio)* prejudice

**prevengo** *ver* **prevenir**

**prevenido, -a** *adj* (a) *(previsor)* **ser p.** to be cautious (b) *(avisado, dispuesto)* **estar p.** to be prepared

**prevenir** [71] *vt* (a) *(evitar)* to prevent; *Prov* **más vale p. que curar** prevention is better than cure (b) *(avisar)* to warn (c) *(prever)* to foresee, to anticipate (d) *(predisponer)* **p. a alguien contra algo/alguien** to prejudice sb against sth/sb

**preventivo, -a** *adj* *(medicina, prisión)* preventive; *(medida)* precautionary

**prever** [72] *vt* (a) *(conjeturar)* to foresee, to anticipate (b) *(planear)* to plan (c) *(predecir)* to forecast

**previera** *etc ver* **prever**

**previniera** *etc ver* **prevenir**

**previo, -a1** *adj* prior; **p. pago de multa** on payment of a fine
  **2** *nm Cine* prescoring, playback

**previó** ver **prever**

**previsible** adj foreseeable

**previsión** nf (a) (predicción) forecast (b) (visión de futuro) foresight (c) (precaución) **en p. de** as a precaution against

**previsor, -ora** adj prudent, farsighted

**previsto, -a 1** participio ver **prever**

**2** adj (conjeturado) predicted; (planeado) forecast, expected, planned

**PRI** [pri] nm (abrev de **Partido Revolucionario Institucional**) = Mexican political party, the governing party since 1929

**prieto, -a** adj (a) (ceñido) tight; **íbamos muy prietos en el coche** we were really squashed together in the car (b) Méx Fam (moreno) dark-skinned

**prima** nf (a) (paga extra) bonus (b) (de seguro) premium; **p. de riesgo** risk premium (c) (subvención) subsidy

**primacía** nf primacy

**primado** nm Rel primate

**primar 1** vi to have priority (**sobre** over)

**2** vt to give a bonus to

**primario, -a** adj primary; Fig primitive

**primate** nm (simio) primate

**primavera** nf (a) (estación) spring (b) Fig (juventud) springtime (c) Fig (año) **tiene diez primaveras** she is ten years old, she has seen ten summers

**primaveral** adj spring; **día p.** spring day

**primer** núm adj ver **primero**

**primera** nf (a) Aut first (gear); **meter (la) p.** to go into first (gear) (b) Av & Ferroc first class; **viajar en p.** to travel first class (c) Dep first division; **subir a p.** to go up into the first division (d) (expresiones) **de p.** first-class, excellent

**primeriza** nf (madre) first-time mother

**primerizo, -a 1** adj (a) (principiante) novice (b) (embarazada) first-time

**2** nm,f (principiante) beginner

**primero, -a**

> Primer is used instead of primero before singular masculine nouns (e.g. **el primer hombre** the first man).

**1** núm adj (a) (en orden) first (b) (en importancia) main, basic; **lo p.** the most important o main thing; **lo p. es lo p.** first things first

**2** núm nm,f (a) (en orden) **el p.** the first one; **llegó el p.** he came first; **es el p. de la clase** he's top of the class (b) (mencionado antes) **vinieron Pedro y Juan, el p. con...** Pedro and Juan arrived, the former with...

**3** adv (a) (en primer lugar) first (b) (antes) **p.... que... rather... than...; p. morir que traicionarle** I'd rather die than betray him

**4** nm (a) (piso) first floor (b) (curso) first year

(c) **a primeros** (de mes, año) at the beginning; **a primeros de junio** at the beginning of June, in early June

**primicia** nf scoop, exclusive

**primitiva** nf (lotería) ≃ national lottery

**primitivo, -a** adj (a) (arcaico, rudimentario) primitive (b) (original) original (c) **lotería primitiva** ≃ national lottery

**primo, -a 1** adj Mat (número) prime

**2** nm,f (a) (pariente) cousin; **p. carnal** o **hermano** first cousin; **p. segundo** second cousin (b) Fam (tonto) sucker; **hacer el p.** to be taken for a ride

**primogénito, -a** adj & nm,f first-born

**primor** nm (a) (persona) treasure, marvel; (cosa, trabajo) fine thing; **hecho un p.** spick and span (b) (esmero) **con p.** with skill

**primordial** adj fundamental

**primoroso, -a** adj (a) (delicado) exquisite, fine (b) (hábil) skilful

**princesa** nf princess

**principado** nm principality

**principal 1** adj main, principal; **puerta p.** front door

**2** nm (a) (piso) first floor (b) (jefe) chief, boss

**príncipe** nm prince; Fig **p. azul** Prince Charming; **p. consorte** prince consort; **p. heredero** crown prince

**principesco, -a** adj princely

**principiante, -a 1** adj novice, inexperienced

**2** nm,f novice, beginner

**principio** nm (a) (comienzo) beginning, start; **a principios de** at the beginning of; **en un p.** at first (b) (fundamento, ley) principle; **en p.** in principle; **por p.** on principle (c) (origen) origin, source (d) (elemento) element; **p. activo** active ingredient; **principios** (reglas de conducta) principles; (nociones) rudiments, first principles

**pringado, -a** nm,f Fam (desgraciado) mug, sucker

**pringar [40] 1** vt (a) (ensuciar) to make greasy (b) (mojar) to dip (c) Fam (comprometer) to involve

**2** vi Fam Fig to get stuck in

**2 pringarse** vpr (a) (ensuciarse) to get covered in grease (b) Fam (en asunto sucio) to get one's hands dirty

**pringoso, -a** adj (grasiento) greasy; (pegajoso) sticky

**pringue 1** ver **pringar**

**2** nm (suciedad) muck, dirt; (grasa) grease

**prior** nm Rel prior

**priora** nf Rel prioress

**priorato** nm (a) Rel priorate (b) (vino) = wine from El Priorato in Tarragona

**priori: a priori** *loc adv* in advance, a priori

**prioridad** *nf* priority; *Aut* right of way

**prioritario, -a** *adj* priority; **objetivo p.** key objective *o* aim; **ser p.** to be a priority

**prisa** *nf* haste, hurry; **de p.** quickly; **a toda p.** very quickly; **correr p.** to be urgent; **darse p.** to hurry (up); **meter p. a alguien** to hurry *o* rush sb; **tener p.** to be in a hurry; **de p. y corriendo** in a slapdash way

**prisión** *nf* (**a**) *(cárcel)* prison (**b**) *(encarcelamiento)* imprisonment

**prisionero, -a** *nm,f* prisoner; **hacer p. a alguien** to take sb prisoner

**prisma** *nm* (**a**) *Fís & Geom* prism (**b**) *Fig (perspectiva)* viewpoint, perspective

**prismático, -a1** *adj* prismatic

2 *nmpl* **prismáticos** binoculars

**priva** *nf muy Fam (bebida)* booze

**privación** *nf* deprivation; **p. de libertad** loss of freedom; **pasar privaciones** to suffer hardship

**privado, -a** *adj* private; **en p.** in private

**privar 1** *vt* (**a**) **p. a alguien/algo de** *(dejar sin)* to deprive sb/sth of (**b**) **p. a alguien de hacer algo** *(prohibir)* to forbid sb to do sth

2 *vi* (**a**) *(gustar)* **le privan los pasteles** he adores cakes (**b**) *(estar de moda)* to be in (fashion) (**c**) *muy Fam (beber)* to booze

3 **privarse** *vpr* **privarse de** to go without

**privativo, -a** *adj* exclusive

**privatización** *nf* privatization

**privatizar** [16] *vt* to privatize

**privilegiado, -a1** *adj* (**a**) *(favorecido)* privileged (**b**) *(excepcional)* exceptional

2 *nm,f* (**a**) *(afortunado)* privileged person (**b**) *(muy dotado)* very gifted person

**privilegiar** [15] *vt (persona)* to favour; *(intereses)* to put first

**privilegio** *nm* privilege

**pro1** *prep* for, supporting; **una asociación p. derechos humanos** a human rights organization

2 *nm* advantage; **los pros y los contras** the pros and cons; **en p. de** for, in support of

**proa** *nf Náut* prow, bows; *Av* nose

**probabilidad** *nf también Mat* probability; *(oportunidad)* likelihood, chance

**probable** *adj* probable, likely; **es p. que llueva** it'll probably rain; **es p. que no diga nada** he probably won't say anything

**probador** *nm* fitting room

**probar** [65] **1** *vt* (**a**) *(demostrar, indicar)* to prove (**b**) *(comprobar)* to test, to check (**c**) *(experimentar)* to try (**d**) *(degustar)* to taste, to try

2 *vi* **p. a hacer algo** to try to do sth

3 **probarse** *vpr (ropa)* to try on

**probeta1** *adj* bebé *o* **niño p.** test-tube baby

2 *nf* test tube

**probidad** *nf Formal* integrity

**problema** *nm* problem

**problemática** *nf* problems

**problemático, -a** *adj* problematic

**probo, -a** *adj Formal* honest

**procacidad** *nf (desvergüenza)* obscenity; *(acto)* indecent act

**procaz** *adj* indecent, obscene

**procedencia** *nf* (**a**) *(origen)* origin (**b**) *(punto de partida)* point of departure; **con p. de** *(arriving)* from (**c**) *(pertinencia)* properness, appropriateness

**procedente** *adj* (**a**) *(originario)* **p. de** *(proveniente de)* originating in; *(avión, tren)* (arriving) from (**b**) *(oportuno)* appropriate; *Der* fitting, right and proper

**proceder 1** *nm* conduct, behaviour

2 *vi* (**a**) *(originarse)* **p. de** to come from (**b**) *(actuar)* to act (**con** with) (**c**) *(empezar)* to proceed (**a** with) (**d**) *(ser oportuno)* to be appropriate

**procedimiento** *nm* (**a**) *(método)* procedure, method (**b**) *Der* proceedings

**prócer** *nm Formal* great person

**procesado, -a** *nm,f* accused, defendant

**procesador** *nm Informát* processor; **p. de textos** word processor

**procesamiento** *nm* (**a**) *Der* prosecution (**b**) *Informát* processing; **p. de textos** word processing

**procesar** *vt* (**a**) *Der* to prosecute (**b**) *Informát* to process

**procesión** *nf* (**a**) *Rel & Fig* procession; **la p. va por dentro** he/she is putting on a brave face (**b**) *(transcurso)* succession

**procesionaria** *nf* processionary moth

**proceso** *nm* (**a**) *(fenómeno, operación)* process (**b**) *(transcurso, intervalo)* course (**c**) *Der (juicio)* trial; *(causa)* lawsuit; **abrir un p. contra** to bring an action against

**proclama** *nf* proclamation

**proclamación** *nf* (**a**) *(anuncio)* notification (**b**) *(acto, ceremonia)* proclamation

**proclamar 1** *vt* (**a**) *(nombrar)* to proclaim (**b**) *Fig (aclamar)* to acclaim (**c**) *(anunciar)* to declare

2 **proclamarse** *vpr* (**a**) *(nombrarse)* to proclaim oneself (**b**) *(conseguir un título)* **proclamarse campeón** to become champion

**proclive** *adj* **p. a** prone to

**procreación** *nf* procreation

**procrear 1** *vi* to procreate

2 *vt* to generate, to bear

**procurador, -ora** *nm,f Der* attorney; *Hist* **p. en Cortes** Member of Spanish Parliament *(in 19th century or under Franco)*

**procurar 1** *vt* (a) *(intentar)* **p. hacer algo** to try to do sth; **p. que...** to make sure that... (b) *(proporcionar)* to get, to secure

**2 procurarse** *vpr* to get, to obtain (for oneself)

**prodigalidad** *nf* (a) *(derroche)* prodigality (b) *(abundancia)* profusion

**prodigar** [40] **1** *vt* **p. algo a alguien** to lavish sth on sb

**2 prodigarse** *vpr* (a) *(exhibirse)* to appear a lot in public (b) *(excederse)* **prodigarse en** to be lavish with

**prodigio 1** *adj* **niño p.** child prodigy

**2** *nm (suceso)* miracle; *(persona)* wonder, prodigy

**prodigioso, -a** *adj* (a) *(sobrenatural)* miraculous (b) *(extraordinario)* wonderful, marvellous

**pródigo, -a 1** *adj* (a) *(derrochador)* extravagant; **el hijo p.** *(en la Biblia)* the prodigal son (b) *(generoso)* generous, lavish

**2** *nm,f* spendthrift

**producción** *nf* (a) *también Cine* production; *Ind* **p. en serie** mass production (b) *(productos)* products

**producir** [20] **1** *vt* (a) *(hacer) & Cine* to produce (b) *(ocasionar)* to cause, to give rise to (c) *(interés, fruto)* to yield, to bear

**2 producirse** *vpr (ocurrir)* to take place, to come about

**productividad** *nf* productivity

**productivo, -a** *adj (trabajador, método)* productive; *(inversión, negocio)* profitable

**producto** *nm* (a) *(bien, objeto) & Mat* product; **productos** *(agrícolas)* produce; **p. acabado/manufacturado** finished/manufactured product; *Econ* **p. interior/nacional bruto** gross domestic/national product; **p. químico** chemical (b) *(ganancia)* profit (c) *Fig (resultado)* result

**productor, -ora 1** *adj* producing; **país p. de petróleo** oil-producing country

**2** *nm,f Cine (persona)* producer

**productora** *nf (de cine, televisión)* production company

**proeza** *nf* exploit, deed

**prof.** *(abrev de* **profesor)** Prof

**profanación** *nf* desecration

**profanar** *vt* to desecrate

**profano, -a 1** *adj* (a) *(no sagrado)* profane, secular (b) *(ignorante)* ignorant, uninitiated

**2** *nm,f (hombre)* layman, lay person; *(mujer)* laywoman, lay person

**profecía** *nf (predicción)* prophecy

**proferir** [6] *vt (palabras, sonidos)* to utter; *(insultos)* to hurl

**profesar 1** *vt* (a) *(religión)* to follow; *(arte, oficio)* to practise (b) *(admiración, amistad)* to profess

**2** *vi Rel* to take one's vows

**profesión** *nf* profession; **de p.** by profession; **p. liberal** liberal profession

**profesional** *adj & nmf* professional

**profesionalidad** *nf,* **profesionalismo** *nm* professionalism

**profesionalización** *nf* professionalization

**profesionalizar** [16] *vt* to professionalize

**profesionista** *nmf Am* professional

**profeso, -a 1** *adj* professed

**2** *nm,f* professed monk, *f* professed nun

**profesor, -ora** *nm,f (maestro)* teacher; *(de universidad)* lecturer; *(de autoescuela, esquí)* instructor; **p. agregado** lecturer; **p. asociado** associate lecturer; **p. ayudante** assistant lecturer; **p. particular** (private) tutor; **p. titular** (full) lecturer

**profesorado** *nm* (a) *(plantilla)* teaching staff, *US* faculty; *(profesión)* teachers, teaching profession (b) *(cargo)* post of teacher; *(en universidad)* lectureship

**profeta** *nm* prophet

**profético, -a** *adj* prophetic

**profetisa** *nf* prophetess

**profetizar** [16] *vt* to prophesy

**profiláctico, -a 1** *adj* prophylactic

**2** *nm* prophylactic, condom

**profilaxis** *nf inv* prophylaxis

**prófugo, -a 1** *adj & nm,f* fugitive; **p. de la justicia** fugitive from justice

**2** *nm Mil* = person evading military service

**profundidad** *nf también Fig* depth; **tiene dos metros de p.** it's two metres deep

**profundizar** [16] **1** *vt (hoyo, conocimientos)* to deepen

**2** *vi (en excavación)* to dig deeper; *Fig (en estudio, conocimientos)* to go into depth; **p. en** *(tema)* to study in depth

**profundo, -a** *adj* (a) *(hoyo, río, raíces, herida)* deep (b) *Fig (libro, sentimiento)* profound, deep; *(sueño)* deep; *(dolor, alegría)* intense

**profusión** *nf* profusion

**profuso, -a** *adj* profuse

**progenie** *nf Formal* (a) *(familia)* lineage (b) *(descendencia)* offspring

**progenitor, -ora** *nm,f* father, *f* mother; **progenitores** parents

**progesterona** *nf* progesterone

**programa** *nm* (a) *(de actividades, proyecto, espectáculo)* programme; **p. espacial** space programme; **p. de intercambio** exchange (programme) (b) *(de actividades)* schedule, programme; *(de curso, asignatura)* syllabus (c) *Informát* program

**programación** *nf* (a) *Informát* programming (b) *TV* scheduling; **la p. del lunes** Monday's programmes

**programador, -ora 1** *nm,f (persona)* programmer

 **2** *nm (aparato)* programmer

**programar** *vt* (a) *(actividades, proyecto)* to plan (b) *TV* to schedule; *Cine* to put on (c) *Mec* to programme; *Informát* to program

**progre** *Fam* **1** *adj* liberal, permissive

 **2** *nmf* progressive

**progresar** *vi* to progress, to make progress; **p. en** to make progress in

**progresión** *nf* progression, advance; **p. aritmética/geométrica** arithmetic/geometric progression

**progresismo** *nm* progressivism

**progresista** *adj & nmf* progressive

**progresivo, -a** *adj* progressive

**progreso** *nm* progress; **hacer progresos** to make progress

**prohibición** *nf* ban, banning

**prohibido, -a** *adj* prohibited, banned; **p. aparcar/fumar** *(en letrero)* no parking/smoking, parking/smoking prohibited; **prohibida la entrada** *(en letrero)* no entry

**prohibir** *vt* (a) *(impedir, proscribir)* to forbid; **p. a alguien hacer algo** to forbid sb to do sth; **se prohíbe el paso** *(en letrero)* no entry (b) *(por ley) (de antemano)* to prohibit; *(a posteriori)* to ban

**prohibitivo, -a** *adj* prohibitive

**prohijar** *vt* to adopt

**prohombre** *nm Formal* great man

**prójimo** *nm* fellow human being, neighbour

**prole** *nf* offspring

**prolegómenos** *nmpl (de una obra)* preface

**proletariado** *nm* proletariat

**proletario, -a** *adj & nm,f* proletarian

**proliferación** *nf* proliferation; **p. nuclear** proliferation (of nuclear arms)

**proliferar** *vi* to proliferate

**prolífico, -a** *adj* prolific

**prolijo, -a** *adj* (a) *(extenso)* long-winded (b) *(esmerado)* meticulous; *(detallado)* exhaustive

**prologar** *vt* to preface

**prólogo** *nm (de libro)* preface, foreword; *(de obra de teatro)* prologue; *Fig* prelude

**prolongación** *nf* extension

**prolongado, -a** *adj (alargado)* long; *Fig (dilatado)* lengthy

**prolongar** [40] *vt (alargar)* to extend; *(espera, visita, conversación)* to prolong; *(cuerda, tubo)* to lengthen

**promedio** *nm* average

**promesa** *nf* (a) *(compromiso)* promise (b) *Fig (persona)* promising talent

**prometedor, -ora** *adj* promising

**prometer 1** *vt* to promise

 **2** *vi (tener futuro)* to show promise

 **3 prometerse** *vpr* (a) *(novios)* to get engaged (b) *Fam (esperar)* **se las promete muy felices** he thinks he's got it made

**prometido, -a 1** *nm,f* fiancé, *f* fiancée

 **2** *adj* (a) *(para casarse)* engaged (b) *(asegurado)* **lo p.** what has been promised, promise; **cumplir lo p.** to keep one's promise; **lo p. es deuda** a promise is a promise

**prominencia** *nf* (a) *(abultamiento)* protuberance (b) *(elevación)* rise (c) *(importancia)* prominence

**prominente** *adj* (a) *(abultado)* protruding (b) *(elevado, ilustre)* prominent

**promiscuidad** *nf* promiscuity

**promiscuo, -a** *adj* promiscuous

**promoción** *nf* (a) *(ascenso)* & *Dep* promotion; *Com* **p. de ventas** sales promotion (b) *(curso)* class, year

**promocional** *adj* promotional

**promocionar 1** *vt* to promote

 **2 promocionarse** *vpr* to put oneself forward, to promote oneself

**promontorio** *nm* promontory

**promotor, -ora 1** *adj* promoting

 **2** *nm,f (organizador)* organizer; *Com* **p. inmobiliario** real estate developer

**promover** [43] *vt* (a) *(iniciar)* to initiate, to bring about; *(impulsar)* to promote (b) *(ocasionar)* to cause (c) *(ascender)* **p. a alguien a** to promote sb to

**promulgación** *nf (de ley)* passing

**promulgar** [40] *vt (ley)* to pass

**pronombre** *nm Gram* pronoun; **p. demostrativo** demonstrative pronoun; **p. indefinido** indefinite pronoun; **p. interrogativo** interrogative pronoun; **p. personal** personal pronoun; **p. posesivo** possessive pronoun; **p. relativo** relative pronoun

**pronominal** *Gram* **1** *adj* pronominal

 **2** *nm* pronominal verb

**pronosticar** [61] *vt* to predict, to forecast

**pronóstico** *nm* (a) *(predicción)* forecast (b) *Med* prognosis; **de p. leve** suffering from a mild condition; **de p. grave** in a serious condition; **de p. reservado** under observation

**prontitud** *nf* promptness

**pronto, -a 1** adj (rápido) quick, fast; (respuesta) prompt, early; (curación, tramitación) speedy

**2** adv (a) (rápidamente) quickly; **tan p. como** as soon as (b) (temprano) early; **salimos p.** we left early (c) (dentro de poco) soon; **¡hasta p.!** see you soon!

**3** nm Fam sudden impulse; **le dio un p. y se fue** something got into him and he left; **al p.** at first; **de p.** suddenly; **por lo p.** (de momento) for the time being; (para empezar) to start with

**pronunciación** nf pronunciation

**pronunciado, -a** adj (facciones) pronounced; (curva) sharp; (pendiente, cuesta) steep

**pronunciamiento** nm (a) (golpe) (military) coup (b) Der pronouncement

**pronunciar** [15] **1** vt (a) (palabra) to pronounce; (discurso) to deliver, to make (b) (acentuar, realzar) to accentuate (c) Der to pronounce, to pass

**2 pronunciarse** vpr (a) (definirse) to state an opinion (**sobre** on) (b) (sublevarse) to stage a coup

**propagación** nf (a) (extensión, divulgación) spreading (b) (de especies, ondas) propagation

**propaganda** nf (a) (publicidad) advertising (b) (prospectos) publicity leaflets; (por correo) junk mail; **repartir p.** to distribute advertising leaflets; (en la calle) to hand out advertising leaflets; **p. electoral** (folletos) election literature; (anuncios, emisiones) election campaign advertising (c) (política, religiosa) propaganda

**propagandístico, -a** adj (a) (publicitario) advertising; **campaña propagandística** advertising campaign (b) Pol propaganda; **actividad propagandística** propaganda activity

**propagar** [40] **1** vt (extender) to spread; (especies) to propagate

**2 propagarse** vpr (a) (extenderse) to spread (b) (especies, ondas) to propagate

**propalar** vt to divulge

**propano** nm propane

**propasarse** vpr to go too far (**con** with); **p. con alguien** (sexualmente) to take liberties with sb

**propensión** nf propensity, tendency

**propenso, -a** adj **p. a algo/a hacer algo** prone to sth/to doing sth

**propiamente** adv (adecuadamente) properly; (verdaderamente) really, strictly; **p. dicho** strictly speaking

**propiciar** [15] vt (favorecer) to be conducive to

**propiciatorio, -a** adj propitiatory

**propicio, -a** adj (a) (favorable) propitious, favourable (b) (adecuado) suitable, appropriate

**propiedad** nf (a) (derecho) ownership; (bienes) property; **tener algo en p.** to own sth; **p. horizontal** joint-ownership (in a block of flats); **p. industrial** patent rights; **p. intelectual** copyright; **p. privada** private property; **p. pública** public ownership (b) (facultad) property (c) (exactitud) accuracy; **expresarse/hablar con p.** to express oneself precisely, to use words properly

**propietario, -a** nm,f (de bienes) owner; (de cargo) holder

**propina** nf tip; Fig **de p.** (por añadidura) on top of that

**propinar** vt (paliza) to give; (golpe) to deal

**propio, -a** adj (a) (en propiedad) own; **tiene coche p.** she has a car of her own, she has her own car; **por tu p. bien** for your own good (b) (peculiar) **p. de** typical o characteristic of; **no es p. de él** it's not like him (c) (adecuado) suitable, right (**para** for) (d) (correcto) proper, true (**en persona**) himself, f herself; **el p. compositor** the composer himself (f) (semejante) true to life

**proponer** [52] **1** vt (sugerir) to propose, to suggest; (candidato) to put forward

**2 proponerse** vpr **proponerse hacer algo** to plan o intend to do sth

**proporción** nf (a) (también Mat proportion; **guardar p.** (**con**) to be in proportion (to) (b) **proporciones** (tamaño) size; Fig (importancia) extent, scale

**proporcionado, -a** adj (tamaño, sueldo) commensurate (**a** with); (medidas) proportionate (**a** to); **bien p.** well-proportioned

**proporcional** adj proportional

**proporcionar** vt (a) (ajustar) **p. algo a algo** to adapt sth to sth (b) (facilitar) **p. algo a alguien** to provide sb with sth (c) Fig (conferir) to lend, to add

**proposición** nf (a) (propuesta) proposal; **hacer proposiciones a alguien** to proposition sb; **proposiciones deshonestas** improper suggestions (b) Gram clause

**propósito** nm (a) (intención) intention (b) (objetivo) purpose; **a p.** (adecuado) suitable; **hacer algo a p.** (adrede) to do sth on purpose; **a p. de** with regard to, concerning

**propuesta** nf proposal

**propuesto, -a** participio ver **proponer**

**propugnar** vt to advocate, to support

**propulsar** vt (a) (impulsar) to propel (b) Fig (promover) to promote

**propulsión** nf propulsion; **p. a chorro** jet propulsion

**propulsor, -ora 1** adj propulsive

**2** nm (a) (dispositivo) engine (b) (combustible) propellent

**propusiera** *etc ver* **proponer**

**prorrata** *nf* quota, share; **a p.** pro rata

**prórroga** *nf* (**a**) *(de plazo, tiempo)* extension; *(de estudios, servicio militar)* deferment (**b**) *Dep* extra time

**prorrogable** *adj* *(plazo)* which can be extended

**prorrogar** [40] *vt* *(alargar)* to extend; *(aplazar)* to defer, to postpone

**prorrumpir** *vi* **p. en** to burst into

**prosa** *nf* prose; **en p.** in prose

**prosaico, -a** *adj* *(trivial)* mundane, prosaic; *(materialista)* materialistic

**prosapia** *nf* lineage, ancestry

**proscribir** *vt* (**a**) *(prohibir)* to ban (**b**) *(desterrar)* to banish

**proscrito, -a** [1] *participio ver* **proscribir**
  **2** *adj* (**a**) *(prohibido)* banned (**b**) *(desterrado)* banished
  **3** *nm,f* (**a**) *(desterrado)* exile (**b**) *(fuera de la ley)* outlaw

**prosecución** *nf* *Formal* continuation

**proseguir** [63] **1** *vt* to continue
  **2** *vi* to go on, to continue

**proselitismo** *nm* proselytism; **hacer p.** to proselytize

**prosélito, -a** *nm,f* proselyte

**prosiga** *etc ver* **proseguir**

**prosiguiera** *etc ver* **proseguir**

**prosista** *nmf* prose writer

**prosodia** *nf* prosody

**prospección** *nf* *(petrolífera, minera)* prospecting; **p. de mercados** market research

**prospectivo, -a** *adj* exploratory

**prospecto** *nm* *(folleto)* leaflet; *(de medicamento)* = leaflet giving directions for use

**prosperar** *vi* (**a**) *(mejorar)* to prosper, to thrive (**b**) *(triunfar)* to be successful

**prosperidad** *nf* (**a**) *(mejora)* prosperity (**b**) *(éxito)* success

**próspero, -a** *adj* prosperous, flourishing

**próstata** *nf* prostate

**prosternarse** *vpr* to prostrate oneself

**prostíbulo** *nm* brothel

**prostitución** *nf* (**a**) *(actividad)* prostitution (**b**) *Fig (corrupción)* corruption

**prostituir** [36] *también Fig* **1** *vt* to prostitute
  **2 prostituirse** *vpr* to prostitute oneself

**prostituta** *nf* prostitute

**protagonismo** *nm* leading role

**protagonista** *nmf* (**a**) *(de libro, película)* main character, hero, f heroine; *Teatro* lead, leading role (**b**) *Fig* **ser p. de** *(acontecimiento histórico)* to play a leading part in; *(accidente)* to be one of the main people involved in; *(entrevista, estudio)* to be the subject of

**protagonizar** [16] *vt* (**a**) *(obra, película)* to play the lead in, to star in (**b**) *Fig (acontecimiento histórico)* to play a leading part in; *(accidente)* to be one of the main people involved in; *(entrevista, estudio)* to be the subject of

**protección** *nf* protection; **p. civil** civil defence

**proteccionismo** *nm Econ* protectionism

**protector, -ora 1** *adj* protective
  **2** *nm,f* *(persona)* protector
  **3** *nm* (**a**) *Informát* **p. de pantalla** *(salvapantallas)* screensaver (**b**) *(en boxeo)* gumshield (**c**) **p. labial** lip salve

**protectorado** *nm* protectorate

**proteger** [54] **1** *vt* to protect; **p. algo de algo** to protect sth from sth
  **2 protegerse** *vpr* to take cover *o* refuge (**de** *o* **contra** from)

**protege-slips** *nm inv* panty liner

**protegido, -a 1** *adj* protected
  **2** *nm,f* protégé, f protégée

**proteico, -a** *adj* protean

**proteína** *nf* protein

**protésico, -a 1** *adj* prosthetic
  **2** *nm,f* prosthetist; **p. dental** dental technician

**prótesis** *nf inv* (**a**) *Med* prosthesis; *(miembro)* artificial limb (**b**) *Gram* prothesis

**protesta** *nf* protest; *Der* objection

**protestante** *adj & nmf* Protestant

**protestantismo** *nm* Protestantism

**protestar** *vi* (**a**) *(quejarse)* to protest (**por/ contra** about/against); *Der* **¡protesto!** objection! (**b**) *(refunfuñar)* to grumble

**protesto** *nm Com* **p. de letra** noting bill of exchange

**protestón, -ona** *Fam* **1** *adj* **es muy p.** *(que se queja)* he's always complaining; *(que refunfuña)* he's always moaning
  **2** *nm,f* *(que se queja)* complainer, awkward customer; *(que refunfuña)* grumbler, moaner

**protocolario, -a** *adj* formal

**protocolo** *nm* (**a**) *(ceremonial)* etiquette (**b**) *Der* documents handled by a solicitor (**c**) *Informát* protocol; **p. de comunicación** communications protocol

**protohistoria** *nf* protohistory

**protón** *nm* proton

**prototipo** *nm* (**a**) *(modelo)* archetype (**b**) *(primer ejemplar)* prototype

**protozoo** *nm* protozoan, protozoon

**protuberancia** *nf* protuberance, bulge

**protuberante** *adj* protuberant; **nariz p.** big nose

**provecho** *nm* benefit; **de p.** *(persona)* worthy; **sacar p. de** to make the most of, to take advantage of; **hacer p. a alguien** to do sb good; **en p. propio** in one's own interest, for one's own benefit; **¡buen p.!** enjoy your meal!

**provechoso, -a** *adj* (a) *(ventajoso)* beneficial, advantageous (b) *(lucrativo)* profitable

**proveedor, -ora** *nm,f* supplier

**proveer** [39] 1 *vt* (a) *(abastecer)* to supply, to provide; **p. a alguien de algo** to provide *o* supply sb with sth (b) *(puesto, cargo)* to fill
  2 **proveerse** *vpr* **proveerse de** *(ropa, víveres)* to stock up on; *(medios, recursos)* to arm oneself with

**provengo** *ver* **provenir**

**proveniente** *adj* **p. de** (coming) from

**provenir** [71] *vi* **p. de** to come from

**Provenza** *n* Provence

**provenzal 1** *adj & nmf* Provençal
  2 *nm (lengua)* Provençal

**proverbial** *adj* proverbial

**proverbio** *nm* proverb

**providencia** *nf* (a) *(medida)* measure, step (b) *Der* ruling (c) **la (Divina) P.** (Divine) Providence

**providencial** *adj también Fig* providential

**provincia** *nf (división administrativa)* province; **provincias** *(no la capital)* the provinces

**provincial** *adj & nm* provincial

**provincianismo** *nm* provincialism

**provinciano, -a** *adj & nm,f* provincial

**proviniera** *etc ver* **provenir**

**provisión** *nf* (a) *(suministro)* supply, provision; *(de una plaza)* filling; **provisiones** *(alimentos)* provisions; **p. de fondos** financial reserves (b) *(disposición)* measure

**provisional** *adj* provisional

**provisto, -a** *participio ver* **proveer**

**provocación** *nf* (a) *(irritación, estimulación, hostigamiento)* provocation (b) *(de incendio)* starting; *(de incidente)* causing; *(de revuelta)* instigation

**provocador, -ora 1** *adj* provocative
  2 *nm,f* agitator

**provocar** [61] *vt* (a) *(incitar)* to provoke (b) *(causar)* *(accidente, muerte)* to cause, to bring about; *(incendio, rebelión)* to start; *(sonrisa, burla)* to elicit; **p. las iras de alguien** to anger sb (c) *(excitar sexualmente)* to lead on (d) *Andes Fig (apetecer a)* **¿te provoca hacerlo?** do you feel like doing it?

**provocativo, -a** *adj* provocative

**proxeneta** *nmf* pimp, *f* procuress

**proxenetismo** *nm* pimping, procuring

**próximamente** *adv* soon, shortly; *Cine* coming soon

**proximidad** *nf (cercanía)* closeness, proximity; **proximidades** *(de ciudad)* surrounding area; *(de lugar)* vicinity

**próximo, -a** *adj* (a) *(cercano)* near, close; **en fecha próxima** shortly (b) *(parecido)* similar, close (c) *(siguiente)* next; **el p. año** next year

**proyección** *nf* (a) *(de mapa)* *& Mat* projection (b) *Cine* screening, showing (c) *(lanzamiento)* throwing forwards (d) *Fig (trascendencia)* importance; **con p. de futuro** with a promising future

**proyeccionista** *nmf Cine* projectionist

**proyectar** *vt* (a) *(luz)* to shine, to direct; *(sombra)* to cast (b) *(mostrar)* *(película)* to project, to screen; *(diapositivas)* to show (c) *(planear)* *(viaje, operación, edificio)* to plan; *(puente, obra)* to design (d) *(arrojar)* to throw forwards (e) *Mat* to project

**proyectil** *nm* projectile, missile

**proyectista** *nmf* designer

**proyecto** *nm* (a) *(intención)* project (b) *(plan)* plan; **tener en p. hacer algo** to be planning to do sth (c) *(diseño)* *Arquit* design; *Ind & Mec* plan (d) *(borrador)* draft; **p. de ley** bill (e) *Educ* **p. fin de carrera** final-year project; **p. de investigación** *(de un grupo)* research project; *(de una persona)* dissertation

**proyector, -ora 1** *adj* projecting
  2 *nm* (a) *(de cine, diapositivas)* projector (b) *(foco)* searchlight; *(en el teatro)* spotlight

**prudencia** *nf (cuidado, cautela)* caution, care; *(previsión, sensatez)* prudence; **con p.** carefully, cautiously (b) *(moderación)* moderation; **con p.** in moderation

**prudencial** *adj (sensato)* sensible; *(moderado)* moderate

**prudente** *adj (cuidadoso)* careful, cautious; *(previsor, sensato)* sensible (b) *(razonable)* reasonable

**prueba 1** *ver* **probar**
  2 *nf* (a) *(demostración)* proof; *Der* evidence, proof; **no tengo pruebas** I have no proof (b) *(manifestación, señal)* sign, token; **en** *o* **como p. de** *o* as proof of (c) *(trance)* ordeal, trial (d) *(examen)* test; **p. de acceso** entrance examination (e) *(comprobación)* test; **a** *o* **de p.** *(trabajador)* on trial; *(producto comprado)* on approval; **a p. de balas** bulletproof; **fe a toda p.** *o* **a p. de bombas** unshakeable faith; **poner a p.** to (put to the) test; **la p. de fuego** the acid test (f) *Dep* event (g) *Imprenta* proof

**prurito** *nm Med* itch, itching; *Fig* urge

**Prusia** *n Hist* Prussia

**prusiano, -a** *adj & nm,f Hist* Prussian

**PS** *(abrev de* **post scriptum***)* PS

**pseudo** *adj* pseudo

**pseudónimo** *nm* pseudonym

**psicoanálisis** *nm inv* psychoanalysis

**psicoanalista** *nmf* psychoanalyst

**psicoanalítico, -a** *adj* psychoanalytic(al)

**psicoanalizar** [16] *vt* to psychoanalyze

**psicodélico, -a** *adj* psychedelic

**psicodrama** *nm* psychodrama

**psicofármaco** *nm* psychotropic *o* psycho-active drug

**psicología** *nf también Fig* psychology

**psicológico, -a** *adj* psychological

**psicólogo, -a** *nm,f* psychologist

**psicometría** *nf* psychometrics *(singular)*

**psicomotor, -ora** *adj* psychomotor

**psicomotricidad** *nf* psychomotricity

**psicópata** *nmf* psychopath

**psicopatía** *nf* psychopathy, psychopathic personality

**psicosis** *nf inv* psychosis; **p. maniaco-depresiva** manic-depressive psychosis

**psicosomático, -a** *adj* psychosomatic

**psicotécnico, -a** 1 *adj* psychotechnical
  2 *nm,f* psychotechnician
  3 *nm (prueba)* psychotechnical test

**psicoterapia** *nf* psychotherapy

**psicotrópico, -a** *adj* psychotropic, psychoactive

**psique** *nf* psyche

**psiquiatra** *nmf* psychiatrist

**psiquiatría** *nf* psychiatry

**psiquiátrico, -a** 1 *adj* psychiatric
  2 *nm* psychiatric *o* mental hospital

**psíquico, -a** *adj* psychic

**psiquis** *nf inv* psyche

**PSOE** [pe'soe, soe] *nm (abrev de **Partido Socialista Obrero Español**)* = Spanish political party to the centre-left of the political spectrum

**PSS** *nf (abrev de **Prestación Social Sustitutoria**)* = community service done as alternative to military service

**pta.** *(pl ptas.) (abrev de **peseta**)* pta

**púa** *nf* (a) *(de planta)* thorn; *(de erizo)* barb, quill; *(de peine)* spine, tooth; *(de tenedor)* prong (b) *Mús* plectrum

**pub** [paβ, paf] *(pl pubs)* *nm* bar *(open late, usually with music)*

**púber** *adj Formal* adolescent

**púbero, -a** *nm,f Formal* adolescent

**pubertad** *nf* puberty

**púbico, -a, pubiano, -a** *adj* pubic

**pubis** *nm inv* pubes

**publicación** *nf* publication

**publicar** [61] *vt* (a) *(libro, revista)* to publish (b) *(difundir)* to publicize; *(noticia)* to make known, to make public; *(aviso)* to issue; *(ley) =* to bring a law into effect by publishing it in the official government gazette

**publicidad** *nf* (a) *(difusión)* publicity; **dar p. a algo** to publicize sth (b) *Com* advertising; *TV* adverts, commercials; **p. directa** direct mailing; **p. subliminal** subliminal advertising (c) *(folletos)* advertising material

**publicista** *nmf* advertising agent

**publicitario, -a** 1 *adj* advertising; **pausa publicitaria** commercial break
  2 *nm,f* advertising agent

**público, -a** 1 *adj* public; **ser p.** *(conocido)* to be common knowledge; **en p.** in public; **hacer algo p.** to make sth public; **personaje p.** public figure
  2 *nm* (a) *Cine, Teatro & TV* audience; *Dep* crowd; **para todos los públicos** *(suitable)* for all ages (b) *(comunidad)* public; **el gran p.** the (general) public

**publirreportaje** *nm (anuncio de televisión)* promotional film; *(en revista)* advertising spread

**pucha** *interj Andes, CSur* good heavens!

**pucherazo** *nm Fig* electoral fraud

**puchero** *nm* (a) *(perola)* cooking pot (b) *(comida)* stew (c) *(gesto)* pout; **hacer pucheros** to pout

**pucho** *nm CSur (colilla)* cigarette butt

**pudding** ['puðin] *(pl puddings)* *nm* (plum) pudding

**pudendo, -a** *adj* **partes pudendas** private parts

**pudibundez** *nf* prudishness

**pudibundo, -a** *adj* prudish

**púdico, -a** *adj* modest, demure

**pudiente** 1 *adj* wealthy, well-off
  2 *nmf* wealthy person

**pudiera** *etc ver* **poder**

**pudin** *(pl púdines)*, **pudín** *(pl pudines)* *nm* (plum) pudding

**pudor** *nm* (a) *(recato)* shyness; *(vergüenza)* (sense of) shame (b) *(modestia)* modesty

**pudoroso, -a** *adj* (a) *(recatado)* modest, demure (b) *(modesto)* modest, shy

**pudridero** *nm* rubbish dump

**pudrir** 1 *vt* to rot
  2 **pudrirse** *vpr* to rot

**pueblerino, -a** 1 *adj Pey* rustic, provincial
  2 *nm,f* villager; *Pey* yokel

**pueblo** 1 *ver* **poblar**
  2 *nm* (a) *(población) (pequeña)* village; *(grande)* town; *Fig Pey* **ser de p.** to be a yokel *o* country bumpkin; *Am* **p. nuevo** *o* **joven** shanty town

**(b)** *(nación, ciudadanos)* people; **el p. español** the Spanish people **(c)** *(proletariado)* **el p.** the (common) people

**puedo** *etc ver* **poder**

**puente** *nm* **(a)** *(construcción)* bridge; **p. colgante** suspension bridge; **p. levadizo** drawbridge **(b)** *(días festivos)* ≃ long weekend *(consisting of a public holiday, the weekend and the day in between);* **hacer p.** = to take an extra day off to join a public holiday with the weekend **(c) p. aéreo** *(civil)* air shuttle; *(militar)* airlift **(d)** *Fam* **hacer un p.** *(para arrancar un coche)* to hotwire a car **(e)** *(dientes)* bridge

**puentear** *vt Elec (circuito)* to bridge; *(para arrancar un coche)* to hot-wire

**puenting** *nm* bungee-jumping; **hacer p.** to go bungee-jumping

**puerco, -a1** *adj* dirty, filthy

 **2** *nm,f* **(a)** *(animal)* pig, *f* sow **(b)** *Fam Fig (persona)* pig, swine

**puercoespín** *nm* porcupine

**puericultor, -ora** *nm,f* nursery nurse

**puericultura** *nf* childcare

**pueril** *adj* childish

**puerilidad** *nf* childishness

**puerperio** *nm* puerperium

**puerro** *nm* leek

**puerta** *nf* **(a)** *(de casa)* door; *(de jardín, ciudad)* gate; **de p. en p.** from door to door; **p. principal/trasera** front/back door; **p. corrediza/giratoria** sliding/revolving door; **p. blindada/vidriera** reinforced/glass door **(b)** *Fig (posibilidad)* gateway, opening **(c)** *Dep* goal, goalmouth **(d)** *(expresiones)* **a las puertas de** on the verge of; **a p. cerrada** *(reunión)* behind closed doors; *(juicio)* in camera; **coger la p. y marcharse** to up and go; **dar a alguien con la p. en las narices** to slam the door in sb's face; *Fam* **dar p. a alguien** to give sb the boot, to send sb packing; **estar en puertas** to be knocking on the door, to be imminent

**puerto** *nm* **(a)** *(de mar)* port; **llegar a p.** to come into port; *Fig* to make it in the end; **p. deportivo** marina; **p. franco** *o* **libre** free port **(b)** *(de montaña)* pass; **subir/bajar un p.** to go up/down a mountain pass **(c)** *Informát* port; **p. paralelo/serie** parallel/serial port **(d)** *Fig (refugio)* haven

**Puerto España** *n* Port of Spain

**Puerto Príncipe** *n* Port-au-Prince

**Puerto Rico** *n* Puerto Rico

**puertorriqueño, -a** *adj & nm,f* Puerto Rican

**pues** *conj* **(a)** *(dado que)* since, as **(b)** *(por lo tanto)* therefore, so; **creo, p., que…** so, I think that… **(c)** *(así que)* so; **querías verlo, p. ahí está** you wanted to see it, so here it is **(d)** *(enfático)* **¡p. ya está!** well, that's it!; **¡p. claro!** but of course!; **¡p. vaya amigo que tienes!** some friend he is!

**puesta** *nf* **(a)** *(acción) (de un motor)* tuning; **p. al día** updating; **p. en escena** staging, production; **p. de largo** debut (in society); **p. en marcha** *(de máquina)* starting, start-up; *(de acuerdo, proyecto)* implementation; **p. en órbita** putting into orbit; **p. a punto** *(de una técnica)* perfecting **(b)** *(de ave)* laying **(c) p. de sol** sunset

**puesto, -a1** *participio ver* **poner**

 **2** *adj* **ir muy p.** to be all dressed up; **iba sólo con lo p.** all she had with her were the clothes on her back; *Fam* **estar muy p. en algo** to be well up on sth

 **3** *nm* **(a)** *(empleo)* post, position; **escalar puestos** to work one's way up **(b)** *(en fila, clasificación)* place **(c)** *(tenderete)* stall, stand **(d)** *Mil* post; **p. de mando/vigilancia** command/sentry post; **p. de policía** police station; **p. de socorro** first-aid post

 **4** *conj* **p. que** since, as

**puf** *(pl* **pufs***) nm* pouf, pouffe

**pufo** *nm Fam* swindle, swizz

**púgil** *nm* boxer

**pugilato** *nm Fig* ding-dong battle

**pugilístico, -a** *adj* boxing; **combate p.** boxing match

**pugna** *nf* fight, battle

**pugnar** *vi* **(a)** *(luchar)* to fight **(b)** *Fig (esforzarse)* to struggle **(por** for), to fight **(por** for)

**puja** *nf* **(a)** *(en subasta) (acción)* bidding; *(cantidad)* bid **(b)** *(lucha)* struggle

**pujante** *adj* vigorous

**pujanza** *nf* vigour, strength

**pujar1** *vi* **(a)** *(en subasta)* to bid higher **(b)** *Fig (luchar)* to struggle

 **2** *vt* to bid

**pulcritud** *nf* neatness, tidiness

**pulcro, -a** *adj* neat, tidy

**pulga** *nf* **(a)** *(insecto)* flea; *Fig* **tener malas pulgas** to be bad-tempered **(b)** *(bocadillo)* small filled roll

**pulgada** *nf* inch

**pulgar** *nm (dedo)* thumb

**pulgón** *nm* plant louse, aphid

**pulgoso, -a** *adj* flea-ridden

**pulido, -a1** *adj* polished, clean

 **2** *nm* **durante el p. del suelo** while polishing the floor

**pulidor, -ora** *adj* polishing

**pulidora** *nf* polisher

**pulimentar** *vt* to polish

**pulimento** *nm* polish, polishing

**pulir 1** *vt* to polish

**2 pulirse** *vpr Fam (gastarse)* to blow, to throw away

**pulla** *nf* gibe

**pulmón** *nm* lung; **a pleno p.** *(gritar)* at the top of one's voice; *(respirar)* deeply; **tener buenos pulmones** *(vozarrón)* to have a powerful voice; *Fig* **el p. de la ciudad** *(parque)* the lungs of the city; **p. de acero** *o* **artificial** iron lung

**pulmonar** *adj* pulmonary, lung; **enfermedad p.** lung disease

**pulmonía** *nf* pneumonia

**pulóver** *nm* pullover

**pulpa** *nf (de fruta)* flesh; *(de papel)* pulp

**púlpito** *nm* pulpit

**pulpo** *nm* (a) *(animal)* octopus (b) *Fam Pey (hombre)* **es un p.** he can't keep his hands off women (c) *(correa elástica)* spider strap

**pulque** *nm Méx* = fermented maguey juice

**pulsación** *nf* (a) *(del corazón)* beat, beating (b) *(en máquina de escribir)* keystroke, tap; *(en piano)* touch; **pulsaciones por minuto** keystrokes per minute

**pulsador** *nm* button, push button

**pulsar** *vt* (a) *(botón, timbre)* to press; *(teclas de ordenador)* to press, to strike; *(teclas de piano)* to play; *(cuerdas de guitarra)* to pluck (b) *Fig (opinión pública)* to sound out

**púlsar** *nm Astron* pulsar

**pulsera** *nf* bracelet

**pulso** *nm* (a) *(latido)* pulse; **tomar el p. a alguien** to take sb's pulse; *Fig* **tomar el p. a algo/alguien** to sound sth/sb out (b) *(firmeza)* **tener buen p.** to have a steady hand; **a p.** unaided (c) *(lucha)* **echar un p. (con alguien)** to arm-wrestle (with sb); *Fig* **mantener un p. con alguien** to be locked in struggle with sb (d) *Fig (cuidado)* tact

**pulular** *vi* to swarm

**pulverización** *nf (de sólido)* pulverization; *(de líquido)* spraying

**pulverizador** *nm* spray

**pulverizar** [16] *vt* (a) *(líquido)* to spray (b) *(sólido)* to reduce to dust; *Mec* to pulverize (c) *Fig (aniquilar)* to pulverize

**pum** *interj* **¡p.!** bang!

**puma** *nm* puma

**pumba** *interj* **¡p.!** wham!, bang!

**puna** *nf Andes* (a) *Geog* Andean plateau (b) *(mal de altura)* altitude sickness

**punción** *nf* puncture

**pundonor** *nm* pride

**punible** *adj* punishable

**punición** *nf* punishment

**punitivo, -a** *adj* punitive

**punk** [paŋk] *(pl* **punks), punki** *adj & nmf* punk

**punta** *nf* (a) *(extremo)* *(de cuchillo, lápiz, aguja)* point; *(de pan, pelo)* end; *(de dedo, cuerno)* tip; **a p. de pistola** at gunpoint; **a p. (de) pala** by the dozen *o* bucket; **estar de p. con alguien** to be on edge with sb; **ir de p. en blanco** to be dressed up to the nines; **sacar p. a un lápiz** to sharpen a pencil; *Fam Fig* **sacarle p. a algo** to read too much into sth; *Fig* **la p. del iceberg** the tip of the iceberg; *Fig* **tener algo en la p. de la lengua** to have sth on the tip of one's tongue (b) *(pizca)* touch, bit; *(de sal)* pinch (c) *(clavo)* small nail (d) *Geog* point, headland

**puntada** *nf (pespunte)* stitch

**puntal** *nm (madero)* prop; *Fig (apoyo)* mainstay

**puntapié** *nm* kick; **echar a alguien a puntapiés** to kick sb out; *Fig* **tratar a alguien a puntapiés** to be nasty to sb

**punteado, -a 1** *adj (línea)* dotted

**2** *nm Mús* plucking

**puntear** *vt Mús* to pluck

**punteo** *nm* guitar solo

**puntera** *nf (de zapato)* toecap; *(de calcetín)* toe

**puntería** *nf* (a) *(destreza)* marksmanship; **tener p.** to be a good shot (b) *(orientación para apuntar)* aim

**puntero, -a 1** *adj* leading

**2** *nm,f (líder)* leader

**3** *nm (para señalar)* pointer

**puntiagudo, -a** *adj* pointed

**puntilla** *nf* (a) *(encaje)* point lace (b) *Fig* **dar la p.** to give the coup de grâce (c) **de puntillas** on tiptoe

**puntillismo** *nm Arte* pointillism

**puntillo** *nm* pride

**puntilloso, -a** *adj* (a) *(susceptible)* touchy (b) *(meticuloso)* punctilious

**punto** *nm* (a) *(marca)* spot, dot; *(en geometría)* point

(b) *(signo ortográfico)* dot; **p. y aparte** full stop, new paragraph; **p. y coma** semi-colon; **p. y seguido** full stop; **puntos suspensivos** dots, suspension points; **dos puntos** colon; *Fig* **poner los puntos sobre las íes** to dot the i's and cross the t's; *Fig* **poner p. final a algo** to bring sth to a close; *Fam* **y p.** and that's that

(c) *(unidad)* point; **ganar/perder por seis puntos** to win/lose by six points

(d) *(asunto)* point; **p. débil/fuerte** weak/strong point; **puntos a tratar** matters to be discussed; **p. de vista** point of view, viewpoint

(e) *(lugar)* spot, place; **p. de apoyo** fulcrum; *Fig* backup, support; **p. cardinal** cardinal point; **p. negro** *(grano)* blackhead; *(en carretera)* accident blackspot; *Com* **p. de venta** point of sale

**(f)** *(momento)* point, moment; **al p.** at once, there and then; **en p.** exactly, on the dot; **a las seis en p.** on the stroke of six; **estar a p.** to be ready; **estar a p. de hacer algo** to be on the point of doing sth; **llegar a p. (para hacer algo)** to arrive just in time (to do sth)

**(g)** *(estado, fase)* state; **estando las cosas en este p.** things being as they are; **llegar a un p. en que...** to reach the stage where...; **estar a p. de caramelo para** to be ripe for; **estar en su p.** to be just right; **poner a p.** *(motor)* to tune; *Fig* to fine-tune; **p. culminante** high point; **p. de ebullición/fusión** boiling/melting point; **batir a p. de nieve** to beat until stiff; **p. de partida** starting point; **p. de referencia** point of reference

**(h)** *(grado)* degree; **de todo p.** *(completamente)* absolutely; **hasta tal p. que** to such an extent that; **hasta cierto p.** to some extent, up to a point

**(i)** *(cláusula)* clause

**(j)** *Aut* **p. muerto** neutral; *Fig* deadlock; **estar en un p. muerto** to be deadlocked

**(k)** *(puntada)* stitch; **p. de cruz** cross-stitch

**(l)** *(estilo de tejer)* knitting; **hacer p.** to knit; **un jersey de p.** a knitted jumper; **p. de ganchillo** crochet

**(m)** *(pizca, toque)* touch

**(n)** *muy Fam (borrachera ligera)* **cogerse/tener un p.** to get/be merry

**(o)** *muy Fam (reacción, estado de ánimo)* **le dan unos puntos muy raros** he can be really weird sometimes; **le dio el p. generoso** he had a fit of generosity

**(p)** *Fam* **¡qué p.!** that's great o fantastic!

**puntuable** *adj* **p. para** that counts towards

**puntuación** *nf* **(a)** *(calificación)* mark; *(en concursos, competiciones)* score **(b)** *(ortográfica)* punctuation

**puntual** *adj* **(a)** *(en el tiempo)* punctual **(b)** *(exacto, detallado)* detailed **(c)** *(aislado)* isolated, one-off

**puntualidad** *nf* **(a)** *(en el tiempo)* punctuality **(b)** *(exactitud)* exactness

**puntualización** *nf* clarification

**puntualizar** [16] *vt (aclarar)* to specify, to clarify

**puntuar** [4] **1** *vt* **(a)** *(calificar)* to mark; *Dep* to award marks to **(b)** *(escrito)* to punctuate

**2** *vi* **(a)** *(calificar)* to mark **(b)** *(entrar en el cómputo)* to count **(para** towards**)**

**punzada** *nf* **(a)** *(pinchazo)* prick **(b)** *(dolor intenso)* stabbing pain; *Fig* pang, twinge

**punzante** *adj* **(a)** *(que pincha)* sharp **(b)** *(intenso)* sharp, stabbing **(c)** *(mordaz)* caustic

**punzar** [16] *vt* **(a)** *(pinchar)* to prick **(b)** *(sujeto: dolor)* to stab; *Fig (sujeto: actitud)* to wound

**punzón** *nm (herramienta)* punch

**puñado** *nm* handful; *Fig* **a puñados** hand over fist

**puñal** *nm* dagger

**puñalada** *nf (acción)* stab; *(herida)* stab wound; *Fig* **coser a puñaladas** to stab repeatedly; *Fig* **p. trapera** stab in the back

**puñeta 1** *nf* **(a)** *Fam (tontería)* **hacer la p.** to be a pain; **mandar a alguien a hacer puñetas** to tell sb to get lost **(b)** *(bocamanga)* border

**2** *interj Fam* **¡p.!, ¡puñetas!** damn it!

**puñetazo** *nm* punch; **darle un p. a alguien** to punch sb; **dio un p. en la mesa** he thumped his fist on the table

**puñetería** *nf* *Fam* **(a)** *(molestia)* bloody-mindedness **(b)** *(menudencia)* trifle, unimportant thing

**puñetero, -a** *nf Fam* **1** *adj* **(a)** *(persona)* damn **(b)** *(cosa)* tricky, awkward

**2** *nm,f* pain

**puño** *nm* **(a)** *(mano cerrada)* fist; **son verdades como puños** it's as clear as daylight; **de su p. y letra** in his/her own handwriting; **meter** *o* **tener a alguien en un p.** to have sb under one's thumb **(b)** *(de manga)* cuff **(c)** *(empuñadura) (de espada)* hilt; *(de paraguas)* handle

**pupa** *nf* **(a)** *(erupción)* blister **(b)** *Fam (daño)* pain; **hacerse p.** to hurt oneself **(c)** *(crisálida)* pupa

**pupila** *nf* pupil

**pupilo, -a** *nm,f* **(a)** *(discípulo)* pupil **(b)** *(huérfano)* ward

**pupitre** *nm* desk

**pupusa** *nf CAm* maize dumpling

**purasangre** *nm inv* thoroughbred

**puré** *nm Culin* thick soup; **p. de patatas** mashed potatoes; *Fam* **estar hecho p.** to be knackered

**pureta** *muy Fam* **1** *adj* fogeyish

**2** *nmf* old fogey

**pureza** *nf* purity

**purga** *nf* **(a)** *Med* purgative **(b)** *Fig (depuración)* purge

**purgaciones** *nfpl Med* gonorrhoea

**purgante** *adj & nm* purgative

**purgar** [40] **1** *vt también Fig* to purge

**2 purgarse** *vpr* to take a purge

**purgatorio** *nm* purgatory

**purgue** *etc ver* **purgar**

**purificación** *nf* purification

**purificar** [61] *vt (agua, sangre, aire)* to purify; *(mineral, metal)* to refine

**purista 1** *adj* purist; **una corriente p. a** purist tendency
**2** *nmf* purist
**puritanismo** *nm* puritanism
**puritano, -a** *adj & nm,f* puritan
**puro, -a 1** *adj* (**a**) *(limpio, sin mezcla)* pure; *(oro)* solid (**b**) *(cielo, atmósfera)* clear (**c**) *(conducta, persona)* decent, honourable (**d**) *(mero)* sheer; *(verdad)* plain; **por pura casualidad** by pure chance
**2** *nm* (**a**) *(cigarro)* cigar (**b**) *Fam* **meterle un p. a alguien** *(regañina)* to give sb a row *o* rocket; *(castigo)* to throw the book at sb
**púrpura 1** *adj inv* purple
**2** *nm (color)* purple
**purpúreo, -a** *adj* purple
**purpurina** *nf* purpurin
**purulencia** *nf* purulence
**purulento, -a** *adj* purulent
**pus** *nm* pus
**puse** *ver* **poner**
**pusiera** *etc ver* **poner**
**pusilánime** *adj* cowardly
**pústula** *nf* pustule
**puta 1** *adj Vulg ver* **puto**
**2** *nf* whore; *Vulg* **de p. madre** *(estupendo)* bloody brilliant; *Vulg* **nos lo pasamos de p. madre** we had a bloody marvellous time
**putada** *nf Vulg* **hacerle una p. a alguien** to be a mean bastard to sb; **¡qué p.!** what a bummer!
**putativo, -a** *adj* putative

**puteado, -a** *adj Vulg* **tengo la espalda puteada** my back is knackered *o* fucked; **está p. en el trabajo** he's being messed around at work; **está p. porque no tiene dinero** he's screwed because he's short of money
**putear 1** *vt Vulg (fastidiar)* **p. a alguien** to mess sb around; **me está puteando el dolor de espalda** my back is bloody killing me
**2** *vi Fam (salir con prostitutas)* to go whoring
**puteo** *nm* (**a**) *Vulg (fastidio)* **es un p.** it's a pain in the arse (**b**) *Fam (con prostitutas)* **ir de p.** to go whoring
**putero, -a** *adj Fam* whoremonger
**puticlub** *nm Fam* brothel, knocking shop
**puto, -a 1** *adj Vulg* (**a**) *(maldito)* bloody (**b**) *(difícil)* bloody difficult
**2** *nm Fam* male prostitute
**putrefacción** *nf* rotting, putrefaction
**putrefacto, -a** *adj* rotting
**pútrido, -a** *adj* putrid
**puya** *nf* (**a**) *(punta de vara)* goad (**b**) *Fam Fig (palabras)* taunt
**puyazo** *nm* (**a**) *(golpe)* jab *(with goad)* (**b**) *Fam Fig (palabras)* taunt
**puzzle** ['puθle], **puzle** *nm* jigsaw puzzle
**PVC** *nm (abrev de* **cloruro de polivinilo**) PVC
**PVP** *nm (abrev de* **precio de venta al público**) RRP
**PYME** ['pime] *nf (abrev de* **Pequeña y Mediana Empresa**) SME
**pyrex®** *nm* Pyrex®
**pza.** *(abrev de* **plaza**) Sq

# Q

**Q, q** [ku] *nf (letra)* Q, q

**Qatar** *n* Qatar

**q.e.p.d.** *(abrev de* **que en paz descanse)** RIP

**quark** *nm Fís* quark

**quásar** *nm Astron* quasar

**que 1** *pron relat* (**a**) *(sujeto) (persona)* who, that; *(cosa)* that, which; **la mujer q. me saluda** the woman (who *o* that is) waving to me; **el q. me lo compró** the one who bought it from me; **la moto q. me gusta** the motorbike (that) I like; **el q. más y el q. menos** every last one of us, all of us without exception

(**b**) *(complemento directo) (se puede omitir en inglés) (persona)* who, whom; *(cosa)* that, which; **el hombre q. conociste ayer** the man (who *o* whom) you met yesterday; **ese coche es el q. me quiero comprar** that car is the one (that *o* which) I want to buy

(**c**) *(complemento indirecto) (se puede omitir en inglés)* **al q., a la q., a los/las q.** (to) who, (to) whom; **ese es el chico al q. presté dinero** that's the boy I lent some money to

(**d**) *(complemento circunstancial)* **la playa a la q. fui** the beach where I went; the beach I went to; **la mujer con la q. hablas** the woman (who) you are talking to; **la mesa en la que escribes** the table on which you are writing, the table you are writing on

(**e**) *(complemento de tiempo)* **(en) q.** when; **el día (en) q. me fui** the day (when) I left

**2** *conj* (**a**) *(con oraciones de sujeto)* that; **es importante q. me escuches** it's important that you listen to me

(**b**) *(con oraciones de complemento directo)* that; **me ha confesado q. me quiere** he has told me that he loves me

(**c**) *(comparativo)* than; **es más rápido q. tú** he's quicker than you; **antes morir q. vivir la guerra** I'd rather die than live through a war

(**d**) *(expresa causa)* **hemos de esperar, q. todavía no es la hora** we'll have to wait, as it isn't time yet

(**e**) *(expresa consecuencia)* that; **tanto me lo pidió q. se lo di** he asked me for it so insistently that I gave it to him

(**f**) *(expresa finalidad)* so (that); **ven aquí q. te vea** come over here so (that) I can see you

(**g**) *(expresa deseo)* that; **quiero q. lo hagas** I want you to do it; **espero q. te diviertas** I hope (that) you have fun

(**h**) *(en oraciones exclamativas)* **¡q. te diviertas!** have fun!; **¡q. te doy un bofetón!** do that again and I'll slap you!; **¿no vas a venir? – ¡q. sí!** aren't you coming? – of course I am!; **¿pero de verdad no quieres venir? – ¡q. no!** but do you really not want to come? – definitely not!; **¡q. me dejes!** just leave me alone!

(**i**) *(en oraciones interrogativas)* **¿q. quiere venir? pues que venga** so she wants to come? then let her

(**j**) *(para explicar)* **es que…** the thing is that…, it's just that…

(**k**) *(expresa hipótesis)* if; **q. no quieres hacerlo, pues no pasa nada** it doesn't matter if you don't want to do it

(**l**) *(expresa disyunción)* or; **quieras q. no, harás lo que yo mando** you'll do what I tell you, whether you like it or not

(**m**) *(expresa reiteración)* **estuvieron charla q. te charla toda la mañana** they were nattering away all morning

**qué 1** *adj (interrogativo) (en general)* what; *(al elegir, al concretar)* which; **¿q. hora es?** what's the time?; **¿q. coche prefieres?** which car do you prefer?; **¿a q. distancia?** how far away?

**2** *pron (interrogativo)* what; **¿q. te dijo?** what did he tell you?; **no sé q. hacer** I don't know what to do; **¿q.?** *(¿cómo dices?)* sorry? pardon?; **¿y q.?** so what?

**3** *adv* (**a**) *(exclamativo)* how; **¡q. horror!** how awful!; **¡q. tonto eres!** how stupid you are!, you're so stupid!; **¡q. casa más bonita!** what a lovely house!

(**b**) *(expresa gran cantidad)* **¡q. de…!** what a lot of…!; **¡q. de gente hay aquí!** what a lot of people there are here!, there are so many people here!

(**c**) *(expresiones)* **¿q. tal?** how are things?, how are you doing?; **¿q. tal la fiesta/película?** how was the party/film?; **¿por q.?** why?

**Quebec** *nm* **(el) Q.** Quebec

**quebequés, -esa 1** *adj* Quebecois

  **2** *nm,f* Quebecois, Quebecker

**quebrada 1** *adj ver* **quebrado**

  **2** *nf* *(desfiladero)* gorge

**quebradero** *nm* **q. de cabeza** headache, problem

**quebradizo, -a** *adj* (a) *(frágil)* fragile, brittle (b) *(débil)* frail (c) *(voz)* wavering, faltering

**quebrado, -a 1** *adj* (a) *(terreno)* rough, uneven; *(perfil)* rugged (b) *(fraccionario)* **número q.** fraction (c) *Lit* broken

  **2** *nm (fracción)* fraction

**quebradura** *nf* (a) *(grieta)* crack, fissure (b) *Med* rupture

**quebrantado, -a** *adj* frail

**quebrantahuesos** *nm inv* bearded vulture, lammergeier

**quebrantamiento** *nm* (a) *(incumplimiento)* breaking (b) *(rotura)* cracking; *Fig (de moral, resistencia)* breaking (c) *(debilitamiento)* weakening

**quebrantar 1** *vt* (a) *(incumplir) (promesa, ley)* to break; *(obligación)* to fail in (b) *(romper)* to crack; *Fig (moral, resistencia)* to break (c) *(debilitar)* to weaken

  **2 quebrantarse** *vpr* (a) *(romperse)* to crack (b) *(debilitarse)* to decline, to deteriorate

**quebranto** *nm* (a) *(pérdida)* loss (b) *(debilitamiento)* weakening, debilitation (c) *(pena)* grief

**quebrar [3] 1** *vt* (a) *(romper)* to break; *Fig (esperanzas, ilusiones)* to destroy, to shatter (b) *(debilitar)* to weaken

  **2** *vi* *Fin* to go bankrupt

  **3 quebrarse** *vpr* (a) *(romperse)* to break; *Fam Fig* **quebrarse la cabeza** to give oneself a headache (b) *(voz)* to break, to falter

**quechua 1** *adj* Quechuan

  **2** *nmf (persona)* Quechua

  **3** *nm (idioma)* Quechua

**queda** *nf* **toque de q.** curfew

**quedar 1** *vi* (a) *(permanecer)* to remain, to stay; **el viaje quedó en proyecto** the trip never got beyond the planning stage

  (b) *(haber aún, faltar)* to be left, to remain; **¿queda azúcar?** is there any sugar left?; **nos quedan 100 pesetas** we have 100 pesetas left; **¿cuánto queda para León?** how much further is it to León?; **q. por hacer** to remain to be done; **queda por fregar el suelo** the floor has still to be cleaned

  (c) *(mostrarse)* **q. bien/mal (con alguien)** to make a good/bad impression (on sb); **q. como un idiota** to look stupid, to end up looking stupid; **le gusta q. bien con todo el mundo** he likes to keep everyone happy

  (d) *(llegar a ser, resultar)* **el trabajo ha quedado perfecto** the job turned out perfectly; **el**

**cuadro queda muy bien ahí** the picture looks great there

  (e) *(llegar)* **q. en** to end in; **q. en quinto lugar, q. el quinto** to come fifth; **q. en nada** to come to nothing

  (f) *(sentar)* to look; **te queda un poco corto el traje** your suit is a bit too short; **q. bien/ mal a alguien** to look good/bad on sb; **q. bien/mal con algo** to go well/badly with sth

  (g) *(citarse)* **q. (con alguien)** to arrange to meet (sb); **hemos quedado el lunes** we've arranged to meet on Monday; **he quedado con Juan esta noche** I've arranged to meet Juan this evening

  (h) *(acordar)* **quedar en algo/en hacer algo** to agree on sth/to do sth; **quedar en que...** to agree that...; **¿en qué quedamos?** what's it to be, then?

  (i) *Fam (estar situado)* to be; **queda por las afueras** it's somewhere on the outskirts; **¿por dónde queda?** whereabouts is it?

  **2** *v impersonal* **por mí que no quede** don't let me be the one to stop you; **que no quede por falta de dinero** we don't want it to fall through for lack of money

  **3 quedarse** *vpr* (a) *(permanecer)* to stay, to remain

  (b) *(terminar en un estado)* **quedarse ciego/ sordo** to go blind/deaf; **quedarse triste** to be *o* feel sad; **quedarse sin dinero** to be left penniless; **la pared se ha quedado limpia** the wall is clean now

  (c) *(comprar, elegir)* to take; **me quedo éste** I'll take this one

  (d) **quedarse con** *(retener, guardarse)* to keep

  (e) **quedarse con** *(preferir)* to go for, to prefer

  (f) *Fam (morir)* to kick the bucket

  (g) *Fam* **quedarse con alguien** *(burlarse de)* to wind sb up

**quedo, -a 1** *adj* quiet, soft

  **2** *adv* quietly, softly

**quehacer** *nm* task; **quehaceres domésticos** housework

**queimada** *nf* = punch made from spirits and sugar, which is set alight to burn off some of the alcohol before being drunk

**queja** *nf* (a) *(lamento)* moan, groan (b) *(protesta)* complaint; **presentar una q.** *(formalmente)* to make *o* lodge a complaint; **tener q. de algo/alguien** to have a complaint about sth/ sb

**quejarse** *vpr* (a) *(expresar dolor, pena)* to groan, to moan (b) *(protestar)* to complain **(de** about); *(refunfuñar)* to moan **(de** about); *Fam* **q. de vicio** to complain about nothing

**quejica, quejicoso, -a** *Fam Pey* **1** *adj* whining, whingeing

**2** *nmf* whinger

**quejido** *nm* cry, moan

**quejoso, -a** *adj* **estar q. de** *o* **por** to be unhappy *o* dissatisfied with

**quejumbroso, -a** *adj* whining

**quema** *nf* burning

**quemado, -a** *adj* **(a)** *(por fuego)* burnt; *(por agua hirviendo)* scalded; *(por electricidad)* burntout **(b)** *(por sol)* sunburnt **(c)** *Fam* **estar q.** *(agotado)* to be burnt-out; *(harto)* to be fed up

**quemador** *nm Br* gas ring, *US* burner

**quemadura** *nf (por fuego)* burn; *(por agua hirviendo)* scald; **hacerse una q.** to burn/scald oneself

**quemar 1** *vt* **(a)** *(con fuego, calor, sol)* to burn; *(con líquido hirviendo)* to scald **(b)** *(plantas)* **la helada quemó las plantas** frost killed the plants; **el sol quemó las plantas** the plants withered in the sun **(c)** *Fig (malgastar)* to go through, to fritter away **(d)** *Fig (desgastar)* to burn out **(e)** *Fig (hartar)* to make fed up

**2** *vi* **(a)** *(estar caliente)* to be (scalding) hot **(b)** *Fam Fig (desgastar)* **la política quema** politics burns you out

**3 quemarse** *vpr* **(a)** *(por fuego)* to burn down; *(por agua hirviendo)* to get scalded; *(por calor)* to burn; *(por electricidad)* to burn out **(b)** *(por el sol)* to get (sun)burnt **(c)** *Fam Fig (desgastarse)* to burn out; *(hartarse)* to get fed up

**quemarropa: a quemarropa** *loc adv* point-blank

**quemazón** *nf (ardor)* burning (sensation); *(picor)* itch

**quena** *nf* Andean flute

**quepa** *etc ver* **caber**

**quepis** *nm inv* kepi

**quepo** *ver* **caber**

**queratina** *nf* keratin

**querella** *nf* **(a)** *Der (acusación)* charge **(b)** *(discordia)* dispute

**querellante** *adj & nmf Der* plaintiff

**querellarse** *vpr Der* to bring an action **(contra** against)

**querencia** *nf* homing instinct

**querer [55] 1** *vt* **(a)** *(desear)* to want; **quiero una bicicleta** I want a bicycle; **¿quieren ustedes algo más?** would you like anything else?; **q. que alguien haga algo** to want sb to do sth; **quiero que lo hagas tú** I want you to do it; **q. que pase algo** to want sth to happen; **queremos que las cosas te vayan bien** we want things to go well for you; **quisiera hacerlo, pero…** I'd like to do it, but… **(b)** *(amar)* to love **(c)** *(en preguntas) (con amabilidad)* **¿quiere**

**decirle a su amigo que pase?** could you tell your friend to come in, please?

**(d)** *(pedir)* **q. algo (por)** to want sth (for); **¿cuánto quieres por el coche?** how much do you want for the car?

**(e)** *Fig (dar motivos para)* **tú lo que quieres es que te pegue** you're asking for a smack

**(f)** *(expresiones)* **como quien no quiere la cosa** as if it were nothing; *Prov* **quien bien te quiere te hará llorar** you have to be cruel to be kind

**2** *vi* to want; **ven cuando quieras** come whenever you like *o* want; **no me voy porque no quiero** I'm not going because I don't want to; **queriendo** on purpose; **sin q.** accidentally; **q. decir** to mean; **¿qué quieres decir con eso?** what do you mean by that?; **q. es poder** where there's a will there's a way

**3** *v impersonal (haber atisbos)* **parece que quiere llover** it looks like rain

**4 quererse** *vpr* to love each other

**5** *nm (amor)* love

**querido, -a 1** *adj* dear

**2** *nm,f (amante)* lover; *(apelativo afectuoso)* darling

**queroseno** *nm* kerosene

**querré** *etc ver* **querer**

**querubín** *nm* cherub

**quesadilla** *nf Am* = filled fried tortilla

**quesera** *nf* cheese dish

**quesería** *nf* cheese shop

**quesero, -a 1** *adj* cheese; **la industria quesera** the cheese-making industry

**2** *nm,f (persona)* cheese maker

**quesito** *nm* cheese portion *o* triangle

**queso** *nm* cheese; **q. gruyère/parmesano/roquefort** Gruyère/Parmesan/Roquefort (cheese); **q. de bola** Dutch cheese; **q. manchego** = hard yellow cheese made in La Mancha; **q. en porciones** cheese portions *o* triangles; **q. rallado** grated cheese

**quetzal** [ket'sal] *nm* quetzal

**quevedos** *nmpl* pince-nez

**quia** *interj Fam* **¡q.!** huh!, ha!

**quicio** *nm (de puerta)* (door)jamb *(on hinge side)*; *Fig* **estar fuera de q.** to be out of kilter; *Fig* **sacar de q. a alguien** to drive sb mad; *Fig* **sacar las cosas de q.** to blow things (up) out of all proportion

**quiche** *nf* quiche

**quid** *(pl* **quids)** *nm* crux; **el q. de la cuestión** the crux of the matter

**quiebra 1** *ver* **quebrar**

**2** *nf* **(a)** *(ruina)* bankruptcy; *(en Bolsa)* crash; *Der* **q. fraudulenta** fraudulent bankruptcy; **ir a la q.** to go bankrupt **(b)** *Fig (pérdida)* collapse; **q. moral** moral bankruptcy

**quiebro** *nm* (a) *(ademán)* swerve (b) *Mús* trill

**quien** *pron* (a) *(relativo) (sujeto)* who; *(complemento)* whom; **fue mi hermano q. me lo explicó** it was my brother who explained it to me; **era Pepe a q. vi/de q. no me fiaba** it was Pepe (whom) I saw/didn't trust

(b) *(indefinido)* **quienes quieran verlo que se acerquen** whoever wants to see it will have to come closer; **hay q. lo niega** there are those who deny it; **q. más q. menos** everyone

**quién** *pron* (a) *(interrogativo) (sujeto)* who; *(complemento)* who, whom; **¿q. es ese hombre?** who's that man?; **no sé q. viene** I don't know who is coming; **¿a quiénes has invitado?** who *o* whom have you invited?; **¿de q. es?** whose is it?; **¿q. es?** *(en la puerta)* who is it?; *(al teléfono)* who's calling?

(b) *(exclamativo)* **¡q. pudiera verlo!** if only I could see!

**quienquiera** *(pl* **quienesquiera***) pron* whoever; **q. que venga** whoever comes

**quiera** *etc ver* **querer**

**quieto, -a** *adj* (a) *(parado)* still; **¡estate q.!** keep still!; **¡q. ahí!** don't move! (b) *Fig (tranquilo)* quiet

**quietud** *nf* (a) *(inmovilidad)* stillness (b) *(tranquilidad)* quietness

**quif** *nm* hashish

**quijada** *nf* jaw

**quijotada** *nf* quixotic deed

**quijote** *nm* do-gooder

**quijotesco, -a** *adj* quixotic

**quijotismo** *nm* quixotism

**quilate** *nm* carat

**quilla** *nf* (a) *Náut* keel (b) *(de ave)* breastbone

**quilo** *etc ver* **kilo** *etc*

**quimbambas** *nfpl Fam* **en las q.** in the back of beyond

**quimera** *nf* fantasy

**quimérico, -a** *adj* fanciful, unrealistic

**química** *nf* chemistry

**químico, -a 1** *adj* chemical

**2** *nm,f (científico)* chemist

**quimioterapia** *nf* chemotherapy

**quimono** *nm* kimono

**quina** *nf (extracto)* quinine; **árbol de la q.** cinchona; **ser más malo que la q.** to be truly horrible; **tragar q.** to grin and bear it

**quincalla** *nf* trinket

**quincallería** *nf (chatarra)* trinkets

**quince** *núm* fifteen; **q. días** a fortnight; *ver también* **seis**

**quinceañero, -a 1** *adj* teenage

**2** *nm,f* teenager

**quinceavo, -a** *núm (fracción)* fifteenth; **la quinceava parte** a fifteenth

**quincena** *nf* fortnight

**quincenal** *adj* fortnightly

**quincuagésimo, -a** *núm* fiftieth

**quiniela** *nf (boleto)* pools coupon; **hacer/ echar una q.** to do the pools; **quinielas** *(apuestas)* (football) pools; **q. hípica** sweepstake

**quinielista** *nmf* = person who does the football pools

**quinielístico, -a** *adj* **peña quinielística** football pools syndicate

**quinientos, -as** *núm* five hundred; *ver también* **seis**

**quinina** *nf* quinine

**quino** *nm (árbol)* cinchona

**quinqué** *nm* oil lamp

**quinquenal** *adj* five-year; **plan q.** five-year plan

**quinquenio** *nm* (a) *(periodo)* five-year period (b) *(paga)* = five-yearly increment of salary

**quinqui** *nmf muy Fam (macarra)* lout, *Br* yob

**quinta** *nf* (a) *(finca)* country house (b) *Mil* call-up year; **entrar en quintas** to be called up; *Fig* **Juan es de mi q.** *(tiene mi edad)* Juan is my age

**quintacolumnista** *nmf* fifth columnist

**quintaesencia** *nf inv* quintessence

**quintal** *nm* = weight measure equivalent to 46 kilos; **q. métrico** 100 kilos; *Fig* **pesar un q.** to weigh a ton

**quinteto** *nm* quintet

**quintillizo, -a** *adj & nm,f* quintuplet

**quinto, -a 1** *núm* fifth; **la quinta parte** a fifth

**2** *nm* (a) *(parte)* fifth (b) *Mil* recruit, conscript (c) *(de cerveza)* small bottle of beer *(0.2 litre)*

**quintuplicar** [61] **1** *vt* to increase fivefold

**2 quintuplicarse** *vpr* to increase fivefold

**quíntuplo, -a, quíntuple 1** *adj* quintuple

**2** *nm* quintuple

**quiosco** *nm (tenderete)* kiosk; *(de periódicos)* newspaper stand; **q. de música** bandstand

**quiosquero, -a** *nm,f* = person selling newspapers, drinks etc from a kiosk

**quiquiriquí** *(pl* **quiquiriquíes***)* **1** *nm* crowing

**2** *interj* cock-a-doodle-do

**quirófano** *nm* operating theatre, *US* operating room

**quiromancia** *nf* palmistry, chiromancy

**quiromántico, -a 1** *adj* chiromantic

**2** *nm,f* palmist

**quiromasaje** *nm* (manual) massage

**quiropráctico, -a 1** *adj* chiropractic

**2** *nm,f* chiropractor

**quirúrgico, -a** *adj* surgical

**quisiera** *etc ver* **querer**

**quisque, quisqui** *nm* cada·o todo q. every man Jack, everyone

**quisquilla** *nf* shrimp

**quisquilloso, -a 1** *adj* (**a**) *(detallista)* pernickety (**b**) *(susceptible)* touchy, over-sensitive

**2** *nm,f* (**a**) *(detallista)* nit picker (**b**) *(susceptible)* touchy person

**quiste** *nm* cyst; **q. ovárico** ovarian cyst

**quitaesmalte** *nm* nail-polish remover

**quitamanchas** *nm inv* stain remover

**quitamiedos** *nm inv* *(en carretera)* crash barrier; *(para evitar caída)* railing

**quitanieves** *nm inv* snow plough

**quitapenas** *nm inv* Fam *(licor)* pick-me-up

**quitar 1** *vt* (**a**) *(en general)* to remove; *(ropa, zapatos)* to take off; **quitarle algo a alguien** to take sth away from sb; **de quita y pon** removable; *(capucha)* detachable

(**b**) *(dolor, ansiedad)* to take away, to relieve; *(sed)* to quench; **el aperitivo me ha quitado el hambre** the snack has taken away my appetite

(**c**) *(tiempo)* to take up

(**d**) *(robar)* to take, to steal

(**e**) *(impedir)* **esto no quita que sea un vago** that doesn't change the fact that he's a lay-about

(**f**) *(exceptuar)* **quitando el queso, me gusta todo** apart from cheese, I like everything

(**g**) *(desconectar)* to switch off

**2 quitarse** *vpr* (**a**) *(apartarse)* to get out of the way; **¡quítate de en medio!** get out of the way!

(**b**) *(ropa)* to take off

(**c**) *(sujeto: mancha)* to come out

(**d**) *(expresiones)* **quitarse la vida** to take one's own life; **quitarse a alguien de encima** *o* **de en medio** to get rid of sb

**quitasol** *nm* Br sunshade, parasol

**quite** *nm* Dep parry; **estar al q.** to be on hand to help; Fam *(alerta)* to keep one's ears/eyes open

**quiteño, -a** *adj* of/from Quito

**Quito** *n* Quito

**quizá, quizás** *adv* perhaps; **q. llueva mañana** it might rain tomorrow; **q. no lo creas** you may not believe it; **q. sí** maybe; **q. no** maybe not

**quórum** *nm* quorum; **hay q.** we have a quorum, we are quorate; **no hay q.** we are inquorate

# R

**R, r** ['erre] *nf (letra)* R, r

**rabadilla** *nf* coccyx

**rábano** *nm* radish; *Fam* **me importa un r.** I couldn't care less, I don't give a damn

**Rabat** *n* Rabat

**rabel** *nm* rebec

**rabia** *nf* (a) *(enfado)* rage; **me da r.** it makes me mad; *Fig* **tenerle r. a alguien** not to be able to stand sb (b) *(enfermedad)* rabies

**rabiar** [15] *vi* (a) *(sufrir)* to writhe in pain (b) *(enfadarse)* to be furious; **estar a r. (con alguien)** to be furious (with sb); **hacer r. a alguien** to make sb furious (c) *(desear)* **r. por algo/hacer algo** to be dying for sth/to do sth; **me gusta a r.** I'm crazy about it (d) *Fam* **pica que rabia** *(comida)* it's incredibly hot

**rabicorto, -a** *adj* short-tailed

**rabieta** *nf Fam* tantrum

**rabilargo, -a** *adj* long-tailed

**rabillo** *nm* (a) *(de fruta, hoja)* stalk (b) *(del ojo)* corner; **mirar algo con el r. del ojo** to look at sth out of the corner of one's eye

**rabino** *nm* rabbi

**rabiosamente** *adv* (a) *(mucho)* terribly (b) *(con enfado)* furiously, in a rage

**rabioso, -a** *adj* (a) *(furioso)* furious (b) *(excesivo)* terrible; *Fig* **de rabiosa actualidad** *(libro, emisión)* extremely topical (c) *(enfermo de rabia)* rabid (d) *(chillón)* loud, gaudy

**rabo** *nm* (a) *(de animal)* tail; **r. de buey** oxtail; **irse** *o* **salir con el r. entre las piernas** to go off with one's tail between one's legs (b) *(de hoja, fruto)* stem (c) *Vulg (pene)* prick, cock

**rabona** *nf* **hacer r.** to play truant

**racanear** *Fam* **1** *vt* to be stingy with
**2** *vi* (a) *(ser tacaño)* to be stingy (b) *(holgazanear)* to loaf about

**racaneo** *nm,* **racanería** *nf Fam* stinginess

**rácano, -a** *Fam* **1** *adj* (a) *(tacaño)* mean, stingy (b) *(gandul)* idle, lazy
**2** *nm,f* (a) *(tacaño)* mean devil (b) *(gandul)* lazybones

**RACE** ['rraθe] *nm (abrev de* **Real Automóvil Club de España**) *Br* ≃ AA, RAC, ≃ *US* AAA, = Spanish automobile association

**racha** *nf* (a) *(época)* spell; *(serie)* string; **buena/mala r.** good/bad patch; **a rachas** in fits and starts (b) *(ráfaga)* gust (of wind)

**racheado, -a** *adj* gusty, squally

**racial** *adj* racial

**racimo** *nm (de uvas)* bunch

**raciocinio** *nm* (a) *(razón)* (power of) reason (b) *(razonamiento)* reasoning

**ración** *nf* (a) *(porción)* portion (b) *(en bar, restaurante)* = portion of a dish served as a substantial snack

**racionado, -a** *adj* rationed

**racional** *adj* rational

**racionalidad** *nf* rationality

**racionalismo** *nm* rationalism

**racionalización** *nf* rationalization

**racionalizar** [16] *vt* to rationalize

**racionamiento** *nm* rationing

**racionar** *vt* to ration

**racismo** *nm* racism

**racista** *adj & nmf* racist

**rada** *nf* roadstead, inlet

**radar** *(pl* **radares**) *nm* radar

**radiación** *nf* radiation; **r. solar** solar radiation

**radiactividad** *nf* radioactivity

**radiactivo, -a** *adj* radioactive

**radiado, -a** *adj* (a) *(mensaje)* radioed; **programa r.** radio programme (b) *(radial)* radiate

**radiador** *nm* radiator

**radial** *adj (del radio)* radial; **longitud r.** length of the radius

**radiante** *adj también Fig* radiant; **estar r. de felicidad** to be beaming with joy

**radiar** [34] *vt* (a) *(irradiar)* to radiate (b) *Fís* to irradiate; *Med* to give X-ray treatment to (c) *(por radio)* to broadcast

**radicación** *nf (establecimiento)* settling

**radical 1** *adj & nmf* radical
**2** *nm* (a) *Gram & Mat* root (b) *Quím* radical

**radicalismo** *nm* (a) *(intransigencia)* inflexibility, unwillingness to compromise (b) *Pol* radicalism

**radicalización** *nf* radicalization

**radicalizar** [16] **1** *vt* to harden, to make more radical

**2 radicalizarse** *vpr* to become more radical o extreme

**radicar** [61] **1** *vi* (a) *(consistir)* **r. en** to lie in (b) *(estar situado)* to be (situated) (**en** in)

**2 radicarse** *vpr (establecerse)* to settle (**en** in)

**radio 1** *nm* (a) *(Anat & Geom* radius; **en un r. de** within a radius of; **r. de acción** *Mec* range; *Fig* sphere of influence (b) *(de rueda)* spoke (c) *Quím* radium (d) *Andes* radio

**2** *nf* radio; **oír algo por la r.** to hear sth on the radio

**radioactividad** *nf* radioactivity

**radioactivo, -a** *adj* radioactive

**radioaficionado, -a** *nm,f* radio ham

**radiocasete** *nm* radio cassette (player)

**radiocontrol** *nm* remote control

**radiodespertador** *nm* clock radio

**radiodifusión** *nf* broadcasting

**radioemisor, -ora** *adj* radio broadcasting

**radioemisora** *nf* radio station, radio transmitter

**radioenlace** *nm* radio link

**radioescucha** *nmf inv* listener

**radiofonía** *nf* radio *(technology)*

**radiofónico, -a** *adj* radio; **programa r.** radio programme

**radiofrecuencia** *nf* radio frequency

**radiografía** *nf (fotografía)* X-ray

**radiografiar** [34] *vt* to X-ray

**radiología** *nf* radiology

**radiológico, -a** *adj* X-ray, radiological; **examen r.** X-ray examination

**radiólogo, -a** *nm,f* radiologist

**radionovela** *nf* radio soap opera

**radiooperador, -ora** *nm,f* radio operator

**radiorreceptor** *nm* radio (receiver)

**radiorreloj** *nm* clock radio

**radiotaxi** *nm (aparato de radio)* = taxi-driver's two-way radio; *(taxi)* minicab

**radioteléfono** *nm* radiotelephone

**radiotelegrafía** *nf* radiotelegraphy

**radiotelegrafista** *nmf* wireless operator

**radiotelescopio** *nm* radio telescope

**radiotelevisión** *nf* **empresa de r.** broadcasting company

**radioterapia** *nf* radiotherapy

**radiotransmisión** *nf* broadcasting

**radiotransmisor** *nm* radio transmitter

**radioyente** *nmf* listener

**radique** *etc ver* **radicar**

**RAE** ['rrae] *nf (abrev de* **Real Academia Española**) = institution that sets lexical and syntactical standards for Spanish

**raer** [56] *vt* to scrape (off)

**ráfaga** *nf (de aire, viento)* gust; *(de disparos)* burst; *(de luces)* flash

**rafia** *nf* raffia

**rafting** *nm Dep* rafting

**raglán** *adj* **manga r.** raglan sleeve

**ragout** [rra'ɣu] *(pl* **ragouts)** *nm* ragout

**ragú** *nm* ragout

**raido, -a** *adj (desgastado)* threadbare; *(por los bordes)* frayed

**raigambre** *nf* (a) *(tradición)* tradition; **de r.** traditional (b) *(origen)* roots

**raíl, rail** *nm* rail

**raíz** *(pl* **raíces)** *nf también Mat* root; *Fig (causa)* root cause, origin; **a r. de** as a result of, following; **arrancar algo de r.** to root sth out completely; **cortar algo de r.** to nip sth in the bud; **echar raíces** to put down roots; **r. cuadrada/cúbica** square/cube root

**raja** *nf* (a) *(porción)* slice (b) *(grieta)* crack

**rajá** *(pl* **rajaes)** *nm* rajah

**rajado, -a** *nm,f Fam* (a) *(cobarde)* chicken (b) **¡eres un r.!** *(siempre te echas atrás)* you're always pulling out at the last minute!; *(nunca te unes)* you never join in anything!

**rajar 1** *vt* (a) *(partir)* to crack; *(melón)* to slice (b) *Fam (apuñalar)* to slash, to cut up

**2** *vi muy Fam (hablar)* to natter on, to witter on

**3 rajarse** *vpr* (a) *(partirse)* to crack (b) *Fam (echarse atrás)* to back o pull out

**rajatabla: a rajatabla** *loc adv* to the letter, strictly

**ralea** *nf Pey* breed, ilk

**ralentí** *nm* neutral; **al r.** *Aut* ticking over; *Cine* in slow motion

**ralentización** *nf* slowing down

**ralentizar 1** *vt* to slow down

**2 ralentizarse** *vpr* to slow down

**rallado, -a 1** *adj* grated; **pan r.** breadcrumbs

**2** *nm* grating

**rallador** *nm* grater

**ralladura** *nf* grating; **r. de limón** grated lemon rind

**rallar** *vt* to grate

**rally** ['rrali] *(pl* **rallys)** *nm* rally

**ralo, -a** *adj (pelo, barba)* sparse, thin; *(dientes)* with gaps between them

**RAM** [rram] *nf (abrev de* **random access memory)** RAM

**rama** *nf* branch; **en r.** raw; *Fam Fig* **andarse por las ramas** to beat about the bush

**ramadán** *nm* Ramadan

**ramaje** *nm* branches

**ramal** *nm (de carretera, ferrocarril)* branch

**ramalazo** *nm* (a) *Fam (hecho que delata)* give-away sign; **tener r.** *(ser afeminado)* to be limp-wristed (b) *(ataque)* fit

**rambla** *nf* (a) *(avenida)* avenue, boulevard (b) *(río)* watercourse

**ramera** *nf* whore, *US* hooker

**ramificación** *nf* (a) *(acción de dividirse)* branching (b) *(rama)* branch (c) *(consecuencia)* ramification

**ramificarse** [61] *vpr* to branch out

**ramillete** *nm* bunch, bouquet; *Fig* handful

**ramo** *nm* (a) *(de flores)* bunch, bouquet (b) *(rama)* branch; **el r. de la construcción** the building industry

**rampa** *nf* (a) *(para subir y bajar)* ramp; **r. de lanzamiento** launch pad (b) *(cuesta)* steep incline (c) *(calambre)* cramp

**ramplón, -ona** *adj* vulgar, coarse

**rana** *nf* frog; **te devolverá el libro cuando las ranas críen pelo** you'll be waiting till the cows come home for him to give you that book back; *Fam* **salir r.** to turn out sadly, to be a disappointment

**ranchera** *nf* (a) *Mús* popular Mexican song (b) *Aut* estate car

**ranchero, -a** *nm,f* rancher

**rancho** *nm* (a) *(comida)* mess (b) *(granja)* ranch (c) *Am* **ranchos** slums, shanty town

**rancio, -a** *adj* (a) *(pasado)* *(butter, oil)* rancid; *(bread)* stale (b) *(antiguo)* ancient (c) *(añejo)* **vino r.** mellow wine (d) *(persona)* sour, unpleasant

**ranglan** *adj* **manga r.** raglan sleeve

**rango** *nm* (a) *(social)* standing (b) *(jerárquico)* rank; **de alto r.** high-ranking

**Rangún** *n* Rangoon

**ranking** ['rraŋkin] *(pl* **rankings)** *nm* ranking

**ranúnculo** *nm* buttercup

**ranura** *nf* *(para monedas)* slot; *(debajo de la puerta, ventana)* gap; *(surco)* groove

**rap** *nm Mús* rap

**rapacidad** *nf* rapacity, greed

**rapado, -a** *adj* shaven

**rapapolvo** *nm Fam* ticking-off; **dar** *o* **echar un r. a alguien** to tick sb off

**rapar 1** *vt (barba, bigote)* to shave off; *(cabeza)* to shave; *(persona)* to shave the hair of

**2 raparse** *vpr* to shave one's head

**rapaz¹ 1** *adj* (a) *(que roba)* rapacious, greedy (b) *Zool* **ave r.** bird of prey

**2** *nf Zool* bird of prey

**rapaz², -aza** *nm,f Fam (muchacho)* lad, *f* lass

**rape** *nm* (a) *(pez)* monkfish (b) **cortar el pelo al r. a alguien** to crop sb's hair

**rapé** *nm* snuff

**rápidamente** *adv* quickly

**rapidez** *nf* speed; **con r.** quickly

**rápido, -a 1** *adj (veloz)* quick, fast; *(coche)* fast; *(beneficio, decisión)* quick

**2** *adv* quickly; **más r.** quicker; **¡ven, r.!** come, quick!

**3** *nm* (a) *(tren)* express train (b) *(de río)* **rápidos** rapids

**rapiña** *nf* (a) *(robo)* robbery with violence (b) **ave de r.** bird of prey

**rapiñar** *vt* to steal

**raposo, -a** *nm,f* fox, *f* vixen

**rappel** ['rrapel] *(pl* **rappels)** *nm Dep* abseiling; **hacer r.** to abseil

**rapsodia** *nf* rhapsody

**raptar** *vt* to abduct, to kidnap

**rapto** *nm* (a) *(secuestro)* abduction, kidnapping (b) *(ataque)* fit

**raptor, -ora** *nm,f* abductor, kidnapper

**raqueta** *nf* (a) *(para jugar)* *(al tenis)* racquet; *(al ping pong)* bat (b) *(para la nieve)* snowshoe

**raquianestesia** *nf Med* epidural (anaesthetic)

**raquídeo, -a** *adj Anat* **bulbo r.** medulla oblongata

**raquis** *nm inv* vertebral column

**raquítico, -a 1** *adj* (a) *Fig (canijo)* scrawny (b) *(escaso)* miserable (c) *Med* rachitic

**2** *nm,f Med* rickets sufferer

**raquitismo** *nm Med* rickets

**rareza** *nf* (a) *(de persona, cosa)* rarity (b) *(de visita)* infrequency (c) *(extravagancia)* idiosyncrasy, eccentricity

**raro, -a** *adj* (a) *(extraño)* strange; **¡qué r.!** how odd *o* strange!; **rara avis** oddity (b) *(excepcional)* unusual, rare; *(visita)* infrequent; **rara vez** rarely (c) *(extravagante)* odd, eccentric (d) *(escaso)* rare

**ras** *nm* **a r. de** level with; **a r. de tierra** at ground level; **volar a r. de tierra** to fly low

**rasante 1** *adj (vuelo)* low-level; *(tiro)* grazing

**2** *nf (de carretera)* **cambio de r.** brow of a hill; *(en letrero)* blind hill

**rasar** *vt* to skim, to graze

**rasca** *nf muy Fam (frío)* freezing cold; **hace r.** it's bloody freezing

**rascacielos** *nm inv* skyscraper

**rascador** *nm* (a) *(herramienta)* scraper (b) *(para las cerillas)* striking surface

**rascar** [61] **1** *vt* (a) *(con uñas, clavo)* to scratch (b) *(con espátula)* to scrape (off); *(con cepillo)* to scrub (c) *(instrumento)* to scrape away at

**2** *vi* to be rough

**3 rascarse** *vpr* to scratch oneself

**RASD** [rrasð] *nf (abrev de* **República Árabe Saharaui Democrática)** Democratic Arab Republic of the Western Sahara

**rasera** *nf* fish slice

**rasero** *nm* strickle; **medir por el mismo r.** to treat alike

**rasgado, -a** *adj* **ojos rasgados** almond (-shaped) eyes

**rasgar [40] 1** *vt* to tear; **r. un sobre** to tear open an envelope

**2 rasgarse** *vpr* to tear; *Fig* **rasgarse las vestiduras** to kick up a fuss

**rasgo** *nm* (a) *(característica)* trait, characteristic; *(del rostro)* feature (b) *(acto elogiable)* act (c) *(trazo)* flourish, stroke (d) *(expresiones)* **a grandes rasgos** in general terms; **explicar algo a grandes rasgos** to outline sth

**rasgón** *nm* tear

**rasgue** *etc ver* **rasgar**

**rasguear** *vt (guitarra)* to strum

**rasguñar 1** *vt* to scratch

**2 rasguñarse** *vpr* to scratch; **se rasguñó la rodilla** she scraped *o* grazed her knee

**rasguño** *nm* scratch; **sin un r.** without a scratch

**rasilla** *nf (ladrillo)* = type of thin, hollow brick

**raso, -a 1** *adj* (a) *(terreno)* flat (b) *(cucharada)* level (c) *(cielo)* clear (d) *(a poca altura)* low (e) *Mil* **soldado r.** private

**2** *nm* (a) *(tela)* satin (b) **al r.** in the open air

**raspa** *nf* backbone (of fish)

**raspado** *nm* (a) *Med* scrape (b) *(de pieles)* scraping (c) *Am (refresco)* slush, = flavoured crushed ice

**raspador** *nm* scraper

**raspadura** *nf (señal)* scratch

**raspar 1** *vt* (a) *(rascar)* to scrape (off) (b) *(rasguñar)* to graze, to scrape; **se raspó el codo** she grazed *o* scraped her elbow

**2** *vi* to be rough

**raspón, rasponazo** *nm* graze, scrape

**rasposo, -a** *adj* rough

**rasque** *etc ver* **rascar**

**rasta** *adj Fam (rastafari)* Rasta; **pelo** *o* **peinado r.** dreadlocks

**rastafari** *adj & nmf* Rastafarian

**rastras: a rastras** *loc adv también Fig* **llevar algo/a alguien a r.** to drag sth/sb along

**rastreador, -ora 1** *adj* tracker; **perro r.** tracker dog

**2** *nm,f* tracker

**rastrear 1** *vt* (a) *(persona, información)* to track (b) *(bosque, zona)* to search, to comb

**2** *vi Fig (indagar)* to make enquiries

**rastreo** *nm (de una zona)* searching, combing

**rastrero, -a** *adj (despreciable)* despicable

**rastrillar** *vt* to rake (over)

**rastrillo** *nm* (a) *(instrumento)* rake (b) *(mercado)* flea market; *(benéfico)* jumble sale

**rastro** *nm* (a) *(pista)* trail; **perder el r. de alguien** to lose track of sb (b) *(vestigio)* trace; **sin dejar r.** without trace; **no hay** *o* **queda ni r. de él** there's no sign of him (c) *(mercado)* flea market

**rastrojo** *nm* stubble

**rasurar 1** *vt* to shave

**2 rasurarse** *vpr* to shave

**rata 1** *adj Fam* stingy, mean

**2** *nmf Fam* stingy person

**3** *nf* rat; *Fam* **r. de sacristía** fanatical churchgoer; *Fam* **más pobre que las ratas** as poor as a church mouse

**rataplán** *nm* ratatat

**ratear** *vi* to pilfer, to steal

**ratería** *nf* pilfering, stealing

**ratero, -a** *nm,f* petty thief

**raticida** *nm* rat poison

**ratificación** *nf* ratification

**ratificar [61] 1** *vt* to ratify

**2 ratificarse en** *vpr* to stand by, to stick to

**rato** *nm* while; **estuvimos hablando mucho r.** we were talking for quite a while; **al poco r. (de)** shortly after; **con esto hay para r.** that should keep us going for a while; **pasar el r.** to kill time, to pass the time; **pasar un mal r.** to have a hard time of it; **ratos libres** spare time; **a ratos** at times; **a ratos perdidos** at odd moments; *Fig* **un r. (largo)** really, terribly; **va para r.** it will take some (considerable) time

**ratón** *nm también Informát* mouse; **r. de biblioteca** bookworm

**ratonera** *nf* (a) *(para ratas)* mousetrap (b) *Fig (trampa)* trap

**raudal** *nm* (a) *(de agua)* torrent (b) *Fig (montón)* abundance; *(de lágrimas)* flood; *(de desgracias)* string; **a raudales** in abundance, by the bucket

**raudo, -a** *adj* fleet, swift

**ravioli** *nm* (piece of) ravioli; **raviolis** ravioli

**raya 1** *ver* **raer**

**2** *nf* (a) *(línea)* line; *(en tejido)* stripe; **a rayas** striped (b) *(del pelo)* parting; **hacerse la r.** to part one's hair (c) *(de pantalón)* crease (d) *Fig (límite)* limit; **pasarse de la r.** to overstep the mark; **mantener** *o* **tener a r. a alguien** to keep sb in line (e) *(señal) (en disco, pintura)* scratch (f) *(pez)* ray (g) *(guión)* dash

**rayado, -a 1** *adj* (a) *(a rayas) (tela)* striped; *(papel)* ruled (b) *(disco, superficie)* scratched (c) *muy Fam (loco)* **estar r.** to be a headcase *o* *Br* nutter

**2** *nm (rayas)* stripes

**rayano, -a** *adj Fig* **r. en** bordering on

**rayar 1** vt **(a)** *(disco, superficie)* to scratch **(b)** *(papel)* to rule lines on

**2** vi **(a)** *(aproximarse)* **r. en algo** to border on sth; **raya en los cuarenta** he's pushing forty **(b)** *(alba)* to break

**3 rayarse** vpr **(a)** *(disco, superficie)* to get scratched; *Fig* **parece que te has rayado** you're like a broken record **(b)** muy Fam *(volverse loco)* to go crazy o Br off one's head

**rayo 1** ver **raer**

**2** nm **(a)** *(de luz)* ray; **r. solar** sunbeam **(b)** *Fís* beam, ray; **r. láser** laser beam; **rayos infrarrojos/ultravioleta/uva** infrared/ultravioleta/UVA rays; **rayos X** X-rays **(c)** *Meteo* bolt of lightning; *Fig* **caer como un r.** to be a bombshell; *Fam* **¡que le parta un r.!** he can go to hell!, to hell with him!; **rayos** lightning **(d)** *(persona)* **ser un r.** to be like greased lightning; **pasar como un r.** to flash by

**rayón** nm rayon

**rayuela** nf *(juego)* hopscotch

**raza** nf **(a)** *(humana)* race; **r. humana** human race **(b)** *(animal)* breed; **de r.** *(caballo)* thoroughbred; *(perro)* pedigree

**razón** nf **(a)** *(en general )* reason; **atender a razones** to listen to reason; **a r. de** at a rate of; **¡con r. no quería venir!** no wonder he didn't want to come!; **dar la r. a alguien** to say that sb is right; **en r. de** o **a** in view of; **entrar en r.** to see reason; **perder la r.** to lose one's reason o mind; **tener r. (en** o **al hacer algo)** to be right (to do sth); **no tener r.** to be wrong; **y con r.** and quite rightly so; **r. de ser** raison d'être; *Pol* **r. de Estado** reasons of state; *Com* **r. social** trade name *(of company)*

**(b)** *(información)* **se vende piso: r. aquí** flat for sale: enquire within; **dar r. de** to give an account of

**(c)** *Mat* ratio

**razonable** adj reasonable

**razonado, -a** adj reasoned

**razonamiento** nm reasoning

**razonar 1** vt *(argumentar)* to reason out

**2** vi *(pensar)* to reason

**RDA** nf *(abrev de* **República Democrática Alemana**) *Antes* GDR

**RDSI** nf *Informát & Telecom (abrev de* **Red Digital de Servicios Integrados**) ISDN

**re** nm *Mús* D; *(en solfeo)* re

**reabrir 1** vt to reopen

**2 reabrirse** vpr to reopen

**reabsorber 1** vt to reabsorb

**2 reabsorberse** vpr to be reabsorbed

**reacción** nf reaction; **r. en cadena** chain reaction; **avión/motor a r.** jet plane/engine

**reaccionar** vi to react

**reaccionario, -a** adj & nm,f reactionary

**reacio, -a** adj stubborn; **r. a algo** resistant to sth; **ser r. a hacer algo** to be reluctant to do sth

**reactivación** nf recovery

**reactivar** vt to revive; **r. la economía** to kick-start the economy

**reactivo, -a 1** adj reactive

**2** nm *Quím* reagent

**reactor** nm **(a)** *(propulsor)* reactor **(b)** *(avión)* jet (plane) **(c)** *(nuclear)* reactor

**readaptación** nf readjustment

**readaptar 1** vt to adapt

**2 readaptarse** vpr to readjust

**readmitir** vt to accept o take back

**reafirmar 1** vt to confirm; **r. a alguien en algo** to confirm sb in sth

**2 reafirmarse** vpr to assert oneself; **reafirmarse en algo** to become confirmed in sth

**reagrupar** vt *(reunir)* to regroup; *(reorganizar)* to reorganize

**reajustar** vt **(a)** *(corregir)* to rearrange **(b)** *(precios, impuestos)* to make changes to, to adjust; *(sector)* to streamline

**reajuste** nm **(a)** *(cambio)* readjustment; **r. ministerial** cabinet reshuffle **(b)** *Econ (de precios, impuestos)* increase; *(de sector)* streamlining; *(de salarios)* reduction; **r. de plantilla** staff redeployment

**real 1** adj **(a)** *(verdadero)* real **(b)** *(de la realeza)* royal

**2** nm *Anticuado* = old Spanish coin worth one quarter of a peseta; **no valer un r.** to be worthless

**realce 1** ver **realzar**

**2** nm **(a)** *(esplendor)* glamour; **dar r. a algo/ alguien** to enhance sth/sb **(b)** *(en arquitectura, escultura)* relief

**realeza** nf **(a)** *(monarcas)* royalty **(b)** *(grandeza)* magnificence

**realidad** nf **(a)** *(mundo real)* reality; **r. virtual** virtual reality **(b)** *(verdad)* truth; **en r.** actually, in fact; **hacerse r.** to come true

**realismo** nm realism; *Lit* **r. mágico** magic(al) realism

**realista 1** adj realistic

**2** nmf *Arte* realist

**realizable** adj **(a)** *(factible)* feasible **(b)** *Fin* realizable

**realización** nf **(a)** *(ejecución)* carrying-out; *(de proyecto, medidas)* implementation; *(de sueños, deseos)* fulfilment; **r. de beneficios** profit-taking **(b)** *(obra)* achievement **(c)** *Cine (película)* production; *(actividad)* direction

**realizado, -a** adj **(a)** *(hecho)* carried out, performed **(b)** *(satisfecho)* fulfilled; **sentirse r.** to feel fulfilled

**realizador, -ora** nm,f *Cine & TV* director

**realizar** [16] **1** *vt* (a) *(ejecutar) (esfuerzo, viaje, inversión)* to make; *(operación, experimento, trabajo)* to perform; *(encargo)* to carry out; *(plan, reformas)* to implement; *(desfile)* to go on (b) *(hacer real)* to fulfil, to realize (c) *Cine* to direct

**2 realizarse** *vpr* (a) *(en un trabajo, actividad)* to find fulfilment (b) *(hacerse real) (sueño, predicción, deseo)* to come true; *(esperanza, ambición)* to be fulfilled (c) *(ejecutarse)* to be carried out

**realmente** *adv* (a) *(en verdad)* in fact, actually (b) *(muy)* really, very

**realquilado, -a 1** *adj* sub-let
**2** *nm,f* sub-tenant

**realquilar** *vt* to sublet

**realzar** [16] *vt* *(destacar)* to enhance

**reanimación** *nf* (a) *(física, moral)* recovery (b) *Med* resuscitation

**reanimar 1** *vt* (a) *(físicamente)* to revive (b) *(moralmente)* to cheer up (c) *Med* to resuscitate
**2 reanimarse** *vpr* to revive

**reanudación** *nf* *(de conversación, actividad)* resumption; *(de amistad)* renewal

**reanudar 1** *vt* *(conversación, actividad)* to resume; *(amistad)* to renew
**2 reanudarse** *vpr* *(conversación, actividad)* to resume; *(amistad)* to be renewed

**reaparecer** [48] *vi* to reappear

**reaparición** *nf* *(de enfermedad, persona)* reappearance; *(de artista)* comeback

**reapertura** *nf* reopening

**rearmar** *vt* to rearm

**rearme** *nm* rearmament

**reaseguro** *nm* reinsurance

**reavivar** *vt* to revive

**rebaja** *nf* (a) *(acción)* reduction (b) *(descuento)* discount; **hacer una r. a alguien** to give sb a discount; **estar de rebajas** to have a sale on; **grandes rebajas** *(en letrero)* massive reductions; **las rebajas** the sales

**rebajado, -a** *adj* (a) *(precio)* reduced (b) *(humillado)* humiliated (c) *(diluido)* diluted *(con* with)

**rebajar 1** *vt* (a) *(precio)* to reduce; **te rebajo 100 pesetas** I'll knock 100 pesetas off for you (b) *(persona)* to humiliate (c) *(intensidad)* to tone down (d) *(altura)* to lower (e) *(diluir)* to dilute
**2 rebajarse** *vpr* *(persona)* to humble oneself; **rebajarse a hacer algo** to lower oneself *o* stoop to do sth

**rebanada** *nf* slice

**rebanar** *vt* *(pan)* to slice; *(dedo, cabeza)* to cut off

**rebañar** *vt* to scrape clean

**rebaño** *nm* *(de ovejas)* flock; *(de vacas)* herd

**rebasar** *vt* *(sobrepasar)* to exceed, to surpass; *(corredor, coche)* to pass, to overtake; **el agua rebasó el borde de la bañera** the bath overflowed
**2** *vi Méx (adelantar)* to overtake

**rebatible** *adj* refutable

**rebatir** *vt* to refute

**rebato** *nm* alarm; **tocar a r.** to sound the alarm

**rebeca** *nf* cardigan

**rebeco** *nm* chamois

**rebelarse** *vpr* to rebel

**rebelde 1** *adj* (a) *(sublevado)* rebel; **ejército r.** rebel army (b) *(desobediente)* rebellious; **ese niño es muy r.** that child is very disobedient (c) *(difícil de dominar) (pelo)* unmanageable; *(tos)* persistent; *(pasiones)* unruly (d) *Der* defaulting
**2** *nmf* (a) *(sublevado, desobediente)* rebel (b) *Der* defaulter

**rebeldía** *nf* (a) *(cualidad)* rebelliousness (b) *(acción)* (act of) rebellion (c) *Der* default; **declarar a alguien en r.** to declare sb in default

**rebelión** *nf* rebellion

**rebenque** *nm CSur (látigo)* whip

**reblandecer** [48] **1** *vt* to soften
**2 reblandecerse** *vpr* to get soft

**reblandecimiento** *nm* softening

**rebobinado** *nm* rewinding

**rebobinar** *vt* to rewind

**reboce** *etc ver* **rebozar**

**reborde** *nm* edge

**rebosante** *adj* brimming *o* overflowing *(de* with); *Fig (persona)* brimming *(de* with)

**rebosar 1** *vt* to overflow with, to brim with
**2** *vi* to overflow; **estar (lleno) a r.** to be full to overflowing; **r. de** to be overflowing with; *Fig (persona)* to brim with

**rebotado, -a** *adj* (a) *(cura)* who has given up the cloth *o* left the priesthood (b) *Fam (enfadado)* Br cheesed off, US pissed

**rebotar 1** *vi* to bounce *(en* off), to rebound *(en* off)
**2 rebotarse** *vpr Fam (irritarse)* to get Br cheesed *o* US pissed

**rebote** *nm* (a) *(bote)* bounce, bouncing; *Fig* **de r.** by chance, indirectly (b) *Dep* rebound; **de r.** on the rebound (c) *Fam (enfado)* **pillarse un r.** to get Br cheesed *o* US pissed

**rebozado, -a** *adj Culin* coated in batter *o* breadcrumbs; *Fig* **r. de** *o* **en** *(barro)* covered in

**rebozar** [16] *vt Culin* to coat in batter *o* breadcrumbs; *Fig* **r. de** *o* **en** *(barro)* to cover in

**rebozo** *nm Am* wrap, shawl; *Fig* **sin r.** *(con franqueza)* frankly

**rebrotar** *vi Bot* to sprout; *(fenómeno)* to reappear

**rebufo** *nm (de vehículo)* slipstream; **ir a r. de algo/alguien** to travel along in the wake of sth/sb

**rebuscado, -a** *adj (lenguaje)* obscure, recherché; **una explicación rebuscada** a roundabout explanation

**rebuscamiento** *nm (de lenguaje)* obscurity; *(de explicación)* roundabout nature

**rebuscar** [61] *vt* to search (around in)

**rebuznar** *vi* to bray

**rebuzno** *nm* bray, braying

**recabar** *vt (pedir)* to ask for; *(conseguir)* to manage to get

**recadero, -a** *nm,f (de mensajes)* messenger; *(de encargos)* errand boy, *f* errand girl

**recado** *nm* (a) *(mensaje)* message (b) *(encargo)* errand; **hacer recados** to run errands

**recaer** [14] *vi* (a) *(enfermo)* to have a relapse (b) *(ir a parar)* **r. sobre** to fall on (c) *(reincidir)* **r. en** to relapse into

**recaída** *nf* relapse

**recaiga** *etc ver* **recaer**

**recalar** *vi Náut* to put in (**en** at); *Fam (aparecer, pasar por)* to drop *o* look in (**en** *o* **por** at)

**recalcar** [61] *vt* to stress, to emphasize

**recalcitrante** *adj (persona, mancha, actitud)* stubborn

**recalentar** [3] **1** *vt* (a) *(volver a calentar)* to warm up (b) *(calentar demasiado)* to overheat
**2 recalentarse** *vpr* to overheat

**recámara** *nf* (a) *(habitación)* dressing room (b) *(de arma de fuego)* chamber (c) *CAm, Méx (dormitorio)* bedroom

**recamarera** *nf CAm, Méx* maid

**recambiar** [15] *vt* to replace

**recambio** *nm (repuesto)* spare; *(para pluma, cuaderno)* refill; **de r.** spare

**recapacitar** *vi* to reflect, to think

**recapitalización** *nf* recapitalization

**recapitulación** *nf* recap, recapitulation

**recapitular** *vt* to recapitulate, to summarize

**recargable** *adj (batería, pila)* rechargeable; *(encendedor)* refillable

**recargado, -a** *adj (estilo)* over-elaborate, affected

**recargar** [40] *vt* (a) *(volver a cargar) (encendedor, recipiente)* to refill; *(batería, pila)* to recharge; *(fusil, camión)* to reload (b) *(cargar demasiado)* to overload (c) *(adornar en exceso)* to overelaborate (d) *(cantidad)* **r. 1.000 pesetas a alguien** to charge sb 1,000 pesetas extra (e) *(poner en exceso)* **r. algo de algo** to put too much of sth in sth

**recargo** *nm* extra charge, surcharge

**recatado, -a** *adj (pudoroso)* modest, demure

**recatarse** *vpr* **r. de hacer algo** to shy away from doing sth; **sin r.** openly

**recato** *nm* (a) *(pudor)* modesty, demureness (b) *(reserva)* **sin r.** openly, without reserve (c) *(cautela)* prudence, caution

**recauchutado** *nm* retread

**recauchutar** *vt* to retread

**recaudación** *nf* (a) *(acción)* collection, collecting; **r. de impuestos** tax collection (b) *(cantidad)* takings; *Dep* gate; *Teatro* box office takings

**recaudador, -ora** *nm,f* **r. (de impuestos)** tax collector

**recaudar** *vt* to collect

**recaudo** *nm* **a buen r.** in safe-keeping; **poner a buen r.** to put in a safe place

**recayera** *etc ver* **recaer**

**rece** *etc ver* **rezar**

**recelar 1** *vt* (a) *(sospechar)* to suspect (b) *(temer)* to fear
**2** *vi* to be mistrustful; **r. de** to mistrust

**recelo** *nm* mistrust, suspicion

**receloso, -a** *adj* mistrustful, suspicious

**recensión** *nf* review, write-up

**recepción** *nf* (a) *(de hotel, sonido)* reception (b) *(de carta, paquete)* receipt

**recepcionista** *nmf* receptionist

**receptáculo** *nm* receptacle

**receptividad** *nf* receptiveness

**receptivo, -a** *adj* receptive

**receptor, -ora 1** *adj* receiving
**2** *nm,f (persona)* recipient; **r. de órgano** organ recipient
**3** *nm (aparato)* receiver

**recesión** *nf* recession

**recesivo, -a** *adj* (a) *Econ* recessionary (b) *Biol* recessive

**receta** *nf* (a) *Culin & Fig* recipe (b) *Med* prescription

**recetar** *vt* to prescribe

**recetario** *nm* (a) *Med* prescription pad (b) *Culin* recipe book

**rechazar** [16] *vt* (a) *también Med* to reject; *(oferta)* to turn down (b) *(repeler) (a una persona)* to push away; *Mil* to drive back, to repel

**rechazo** *nm* (a) *también Med* rejection; *(hacia una ley, un político)* disapproval; **mostró su r.** he made his disapproval clear; **r. a hacer algo** refusal to do sth (b) *(negación)* denial

**rechinar** *vi* (a) *(puerta)* to creak; *(dientes)* to grind; *(frenos, ruedas)* to screech; *(metal)* to clank (b) *(dando dentera)* to grate

**rechistar** *vi* to answer back; **sin r.** without a word of protest

**rechoncho, -a** *adj Fam* tubby, chubby

**rechupete** *nm Fam* **de r.** *(comida)* delicious, scrumptious; *Fig* brilliant, great

**recibí** *nm (en documentos)* received

**recibidor** nm entrance hall

**recibimiento** nm reception, welcome

**recibir 1** vt (a) (tomar, aceptar) to receive; (clase, instrucción) to have (b) (dar la bienvenida a) to welcome (c) (ir a buscar) to meet

**2** vi (atender pacientes) to hold surgery

**recibo** nm (de compra) receipt; Fam (del gas, de la luz) bill; **acusar r. de** to acknowledge receipt of; Fam **no ser de r.** not to be up to scratch

**reciclado, -a** adj recycled

**reciclaje** nm (a) (de residuos) recycling (b) (de personas) retraining

**reciclar** vt (a) (residuos) to recycle (b) (personas) to retrain

**reciedumbre** nf strength

**recién** adv (a) (hace poco) recently, newly; **los r. casados** the newly-weds; **los r. llegados** the newcomers; **el r. nacido** the newborn baby (b) Am (hace poco) just now, recently; **regresó recién ayer** she just got back yesterday

**reciente** adj (a) (acontecimiento) recent (b) (pintura, pan) fresh

**recientemente** adv (a) (hace poco) recently (b) (en los últimos tiempos) recently, of late

**recinto** nm (zona cercada) enclosure; (área) place, area; (alrededor de edificios) grounds; **r. ferial** fairground (of trade fair)

**recio, -a** adj (a) (persona) robust (b) (voz) gravelly (c) (objeto) solid (d) (material, tela) tough, strong (e) (lluvia, viento) harsh

**recipiente** nm container, receptacle

**reciprocidad** nf reciprocity; **en r. a** in return for

**recíproco, -a** adj mutual, reciprocal

**recital** nm (a) (de música clásica) recital; (de rock) concert (b) (de lectura) reading

**recitar** vt to recite

**reclamación** nf (a) (petición) claim, demand (b) (queja) complaint

**reclamar 1** vt (a) (pedir, exigir) to demand, to ask for (b) (necesitar) to demand, to need

**2** vi (protestar) to protest (**contra** against); (quejarse) to complain (**contra** about)

**reclamo** nm (para atraer) inducement; **r. publicitario** advertising gimmick (b) (para cazar) decoy, lure (c) (de ave) call

**reclinable** adj reclining

**reclinar 1** vt to lean (**sobre** on)

**2 reclinarse** vpr to lean back (**sobre** against)

**reclinatorio** nm prie-dieu, prayer stool

**recluir** [36] **1** vt to shut o lock away, to imprison

**2 recluirse** vpr to shut oneself away

**reclusión** nf (a) (encarcelamiento) imprisonment (b) Fig (encierro) seclusion

**recluso, -a** nm,f (preso) prisoner

**recluta** nm (obligatorio) conscript; (voluntario) recruit

**reclutamiento** nm (a) (de soldados) (obligatorio) conscription; (voluntario) recruitment (b) (de trabajadores) recruitment

**reclutar** vt (a) (soldados) (obligatoriamente) to conscript; (voluntariamente) to recruit (b) (trabajadores) to recruit

**recobrar 1** vt (recuperar) to recover; (conocimiento) to regain; (tiempo perdido) to make up for

**2 recobrarse** vpr to recover (**de** from)

**recochinearse** vpr Fam **r. de alguien** to take the mickey out of sb

**recochineo** nm Fam crowing, gloating; **decir algo con r.** to say sth to really rub it in

**recodo** nm bend

**recogedor** nm dustpan

**recogemigas** nm inv crumb scoop

**recogepelotas** nmf inv ball boy, f ball girl

**recoger** [54] **1** vt (a) (coger) to pick up (b) (reunir) to collect, to gather (c) (ordenar, limpiar) (mesa) to clear; (habitación, cosas) to tidy o clear up (d) (ir a buscar) to pick up, to fetch (e) (albergar) to take in (f) (cosechar) to gather, to harvest; (fruta) to pick (g) (acortar) (prenda) to take up, to shorten

**2 recogerse** vpr (a) (a dormir, meditar) to retire (b) **recogerse el pelo** to put one's hair up

**recogida** nf (a) (acción) collection; **hacer una r. de firmas** to collect signatures (b) (cosecha) harvest, gathering; (de fruta) picking

**recogido, -a** adj (a) (vida) quiet, withdrawn; (lugar) secluded (b) (cabello) tied back

**recogimiento** nm (a) (concentración) concentration, absorption (b) (retiro) withdrawal, seclusion

**recoja** etc ver **recoger**

**recolección** nf (a) (cosecha) harvest, gathering (b) (recogida) collection

**recolectar** vt (a) (cosechar) to harvest, to gather; (fruta) to pick (b) (reunir) to collect

**recolector, -ora 1** adj harvesting

**2** nm,f (de cosecha) harvester; (de fruta) picker

**recoleto, -a** adj quiet, secluded

**recombinante** adj Biol recombinant

**recomendable** adj recommendable; **no es r.** it's not a good idea; **esa zona no es r.** it's not a very nice area; **va con gente poco r.** he keeps bad company

**recomendación** nf (a) (consejo) recommendation; **por r. de alguien** on sb's advice o recommendation (b) (referencia) (**carta de**) **r.** letter of recommendation

**recomendado, -a** nm,f Pey = person who gets a job, passes an exam etc through influence or connections; **es un r. del jefe** the boss got him the job

**recomendar** [3] *vt* to recommend; **r. a alguien que haga algo** to recommend that sb do sth, to advise sb to do sth

**recomenzar** [19] *vt* to begin *o* start again, to recommence

**recompensa** *nf* reward; **en r. por** in return for

**recompensar** *vt* (a) *(premiar)* to reward (b) *(compensar)* **r. a alguien algo** to compensate *o* reward sb for sth

**recomponer** [52] *vt* to repair, to mend

**recompuesto, -a** *participio ver* **recomponer**

**reconcentrar 1** *vt* (a) *(reunir)* to bring together (b) *(concentrar)* **r. algo en** to centre *o* concentrate sth on (c) *(hacer denso)* to thicken
**2 reconcentrarse** *vpr* to concentrate (**en** on), to be absorbed (**en** in)

**reconciliación** *nf* reconciliation

**reconciliar** [15] *vt* to reconcile
**2 reconciliarse** *vpr* to be reconciled

**reconcomerse** *vpr* to get worked up

**reconcomio** *nm* grudge, resentment

**recóndito, -a** *adj* hidden, secret; **en lo más r. de mi corazón** in the depths of my heart

**reconducir** [20] *vt* *(desviar)* to redirect; *(devolver)* to return

**reconfortante** *adj* (a) *(anímicamente)* comforting (b) *(físicamente)* revitalizing

**reconfortar** *vt* (a) *(anímicamente)* to comfort (b) *(físicamente)* to revitalize

**reconocer** [21] **1** *vt* (a) *(identificar, admitir)* to recognize (b) *Med* to examine (c) *(terreno)* to survey
**2 reconocerse** *vpr* (a) *(identificarse)* to recognize each other (b) *(confesarse)* **reconocerse culpable** to admit one's guilt

**reconocible** *adj* recognizable

**reconocido, -a** *adj* (a) *(admitido)* recognized, acknowledged (b) *(agradecido)* grateful

**reconocimiento** *nm* (a) *(identificación, admisión)* recognition; *Informát & Ling* **r. del habla** speech recognition; *Informát* **r. óptico de caracteres** optical character recognition (b) *(agradecimiento)* gratitude (c) *Med* examination (d) *Mil* reconnaissance

**reconquista** *nf* reconquest, recapture; *Hist* **la R.** = the Reconquest of Spain, when the Christian Kings retook the country from the Muslims

**reconquistar** *vt* to recapture, to reconquer; *Fig* to regain, to win back

**reconsiderar** *vt* to reconsider

**reconstituir** [36] **1** *vt* (a) *(rehacer)* to reconstitute (b) *(reproducir)* to reconstruct
**2 reconstituirse** *vpr* *(país, organización)* to rebuild itself

**reconstituyente** *adj & nm* tonic

**reconstrucción** *nf* (a) *(de edificios, país)* rebuilding (b) *(de sucesos)* reconstruction

**reconstruir** [36] *vt* (a) *(edificio, país)* to rebuild (b) *(suceso)* to reconstruct

**reconvención** *nf* reprimand, reproach

**reconvenir** [71] *vt* to reprimand, to reproach

**reconversión** *nf* restructuring; **r. industrial** rationalization of industry

**reconvertir** [64] *vt* *(reestructurar)* to restructure; *(industria)* to rationalize

**recopa** *nf* Cup-Winners' Cup

**recopilación** *nf* (a) *(acción)* collecting, gathering (b) *(libro)* collection, anthology; *(disco)* compilation; *(de leyes)* code

**recopilar** *vt* (a) *(recoger)* to collect, to gather (b) *(escritos, leyes)* to compile

**récord** (*pl* **récords**) *nm* record; **batir un r.** to break a record; **establecer un r.** to set a new record; **tener el r.** to hold the record; **en un tiempo r.** in record time

**recordar** [65] **1** *vt* (a) *(acordarse de)* to remember (b) *(traer a la memoria)* to remind; **me recuerda a un amigo mío** he reminds me of a friend of mine
**2** *vi* to remember; **si mal no recuerdo** as far as I can remember

**recordatorio** *nm* (a) *(aviso)* reminder (b) *(estampa)* = card given to commemorate sb's first communion, a death etc

**recorrer** *vt* (a) *(atravesar)* *(lugar, país)* to travel through *o* across, to cross; *(ciudad)* to go round (b) *(distancia)* to cover (c) *Fig* *(con la mirada)* to look over

**recorrida** *nf Am* trip

**recorrido** *nm* (a) *(trayecto)* route, path; *Fig* **hacer un r. (mental) por algo** *(narración)* to run over sth (in one's head) (b) *(viaje)* journey

**recortable 1** *adj* cutout
**2** *nm* cutout (figure)

**recortado, -a** *adj* (a) *(cortado)* cut (b) *(borde)* jagged

**recortar 1** *vt* (a) *(cortar)* *(lo que sobra)* to cut off *o* away; *(figuras)* to cut out (b) *(pelo, flequillo)* to trim (c) *Fig* *(reducir)* to cut
**2 recortarse** *vpr* *(perfil)* to stand out (**en** against), to be outlined (**en** against)

**recorte** *nm* (a) *(pieza cortada)* cut, trimming; *(de periódico, revista)* cutting, clipping (b) *(reducción)* cut, cutback; **r. presupuestario/salarial** budget/salary cut (c) *(cartulina)* cutout (d) *Dep* swerve, sidestep

**recostar** [65] **1** vt to lean (back)
**2 recostarse** vpr (tumbarse) to lie down;
**recostarse en** (apoyarse) to lean on o against

**recoveco** nm (a) (rincón) nook, hidden corner (b) Fig (complicación) **sin recovecos** uncomplicated (c) Fig (lo más oculto) **los recovecos del alma** the innermost recesses of the soul

**recreación** nf re-creation

**recrear 1** vt (a) (volver a crear) to recreate (b) (entretener) to amuse, to entertain
**2 recrearse** vpr (a) (entretenerse) to amuse oneself, to entertain oneself (b) (regodearse) to take delight o pleasure

**recreativo, -a** adj recreational

**recreo** nm (a) (entretenimiento) recreation, amusement (b) Educ (en primaria) playtime; (en secundaria) break

**recriminación** nf reproach, recrimination

**recriminar 1** vt to reproach
**2 recriminarse** vpr (mutuamente) to reproach each other

**recriminatorio, -a** adj reproachful

**recrudecer** [48] **1** vi to get worse
**2 recrudecerse** vpr to get worse

**recrudecimiento** nm (de crisis) worsening; (de criminalidad) upsurge (**de** in)

**recta** nf straight line; también Fig **la r. final** the home straight

**rectal** adj rectal

**rectangular** adj (a) (de forma) rectangular (b) Mat right-angled

**rectángulo** nm rectangle

**rectificable** adj rectifiable

**rectificación** nf (de error) rectification; (en periódico) correction

**rectificar** [61] vt (a) (error) to rectify, to correct (b) (conducta, actitud) to improve (c) (ajustar) to put right

**rectilíneo, -a** adj Mat rectilinear; **una carretera rectilínea** a straight road

**rectitud** nf straightness; Fig rectitude, uprightness

**recto, -a 1** adj (a) (sin curvas, vertical) straight (b) Fig (íntegro) upright, honourable (c) Fig (justo, verdadero) true, correct (d) Fig (literal) literal, true
**2** nm Anat rectum
**3** adv straight on o ahead; **todo r.** straight on o ahead

**rector, -ora 1** adj governing, guiding
**2** nm,f (a) (de universidad) Br vice-chancellor, US president (b) (dirigente) leader, head
**3** nm Rel rector

**rectorado** nm (a) (cargo) Br vice-chancellorship, US presidency (b) (lugar) vice-chancellor's office, rector's office

**rectoría** nf (a) (cargo) rectorate, rectorship (b) (casa) rectory

**recuadro** nm box

**recubierto, -a** participio ver **recubrir**

**recubrimiento** nm covering, coating

**recubrir** vt (cubrir) to cover; (con pintura, barniz) to coat

**recuento** nm (por primera vez) count; (otra vez) recount

**recuerdo 1** ver **recordar**
**2** nm (a) (rememoración) memory; **quedar en el r. (de)** to be remembered (by); **traer recuerdos a alguien de algo** to bring back memories of sth to sb; **tengo muy buen/mal r. de ese viaje** I have very fond/bad memories of that trip (b) (objeto) (de viaje) souvenir; (de persona) keepsake (c) **recuerdos** (saludos) regards; **dar recuerdos a alguien (de parte de alguien)** to give one's regards to sb (on sb's behalf); **dale recuerdos de mi parte** give her my regards

**recuesto** etc ver **recostar**

**recular** vi (a) (retroceder) to go o move back (b) Fig (ceder) to back down

**recuperable** adj (información, objeto) recoverable, retrievable; **esta clase es r.** you can catch o make this class up later

**recuperación** nf (a) (de lo perdido, la salud, la economía) recovery; (de espacios naturales) reclamation (b) (fisioterapia) physiotherapy (c) Educ (examen) resit; (clase de) **r.** = extra class for pupils or students who have to resit their exams

**recuperar 1** vt (lo perdido, la salud) to recover; (espacios naturales) to reclaim; (horas de trabajo) to make up; (conocimiento) to regain; (examen) to resit
**2 recuperarse** vpr (a) (enfermo) to recuperate, to recover (b) (de una crisis) to recover; (negocio) to pick up; **recuperarse de algo** to get over sth

**recurrente 1** adj (a) Der appellant (b) (repetido) recurrent
**2** nmf Der appellant

**recurrir** vi (a) (buscar ayuda) **r. a alguien** to turn to sb; **r. a algo** to resort to sth (b) Der to appeal

**recurso** nm (a) (medio) resort; **como último r.** as a last resort (b) Der appeal; **r. de alzada** appeal (against an official decision); **r. de apelación** appeal; **r. de casación** High Court appeal (c) (bien, riqueza) resource; **recursos**

**humanos** human resources; **recursos naturales** natural resources; *Econ* **recursos propios** equities

**recusar** *vt* (a) *Der* to challenge (b) *(rechazar)* to reject, to refuse

**red** *nf* (a) *(malla)* net; *(para cabello)* hairnet; *Fig* **caer en las redes de alguien** to fall into sb's trap (b) *(sistema)* network, system; *(de electricidad, agua)* mains *(singular)*; **conectar algo a la r.** to connect sth to the mains; **r. viaria** road network *o* system (c) *(organización) (de espionaje)* ring; *(de tiendas)* chain (d) *Informát* network; **r. local/neuronal** local (area)/neural network; **la r. (de redes)** *(Internet)* the Net, the Internet

**redacción** *nf* (a) *(acción)* writing; *(de periódico)* editing (b) *(estilo)* wording (c) *(equipo de redactores)* editorial team *o* staff (d) *(oficina)* editorial office (e) *Educ* essay

**redactar** *vt* to write; **r. un contrato/un tratado** to draw up a contract/a treaty

**redactor, -ora** *nm,f Prensa (escritor)* writer; *(editor)* editor; **r. jefe** editor-in-chief

**redada** *nf Fig (de policía) (en un solo lugar)* raid; *(en varios lugares)* round-up

**redaños** *nmpl (valor)* spirit; **no tener r. para hacer algo** not to have the courage to do sth

**redecilla** *nf (de pelo)* hairnet

**rededor: en rededor** *loc adv* around

**redención** *nf* redemption

**redentor, -ora** *nm,f (persona)* redeemer; *Rel* **el R.** the Redeemer

**redicho, -a** *adj Fam* affected, pretentious

**rediez** *interj Fam* ¡r.! good grief!, my goodness!

**redil** *nm* fold, pen; *Fig* **volver al r.** to return to the fold

**redimir** **1** *vt Rel & Fin* to redeem (**de** from)
**2 redimirse** *vpr* to redeem oneself

**redistribución** *nf* redistribution

**redistribuir** [36] *vt* to redistribute

**rédito** *nm* interest, yield

**redoblar 1** *vt (aumentar)* to redouble
**2** *vi (tambor)* to roll

**redoble** *nm* roll, drumroll

**redomado, -a** *adj* out-and-out

**redonda** *nf Mús Br* semibreve, *US* whole note

**redondeado, -a** *adj* rounded

**redondear** *vt* (a) *(hacer redondo)* to round, to make round (b) *(negocio, acuerdo)* to round off (c) *(cifra, precio)* to round up/down

**redondel** *nm* (a) *(círculo)* circle, ring (b) *Taurom* bullring

**redondo, -a 1** *adj* (a) *(circular, esférico)* round; **a la redonda** around; **en quince kilómetros a la redonda** within a fifteen kilometre radius; *Fig* **caerse r.** to collapse in a heap (b) *(perfecto)* excellent; **salir r.** to go like a dream, to turn out perfectly (c) *(rotundo)* categorical (d) *(cantidad)* round; **mil pesetas redondas** a round thousand pesetas
**2** *nm Culin* topside

**reducción** *nf* (a) *(disminución)* reduction; **r. al absurdo** reductio ad absurdum (b) *(sometimiento) (de rebelión)* suppression; *(de ejército)* defeat

**reducido, -a** *adj* (a) *(pequeño)* small (b) *(limitado)* limited (c) *(estrecho)* narrow

**reducir** [20] **1** *vt* (a) *(disminuir)* to reduce; **r. algo a algo** to reduce sth to sth; **r. algo al absurdo** to make a nonsense of sth (b) *(someter) (país, ciudad)* to suppress, to subdue; *(sublevados, atracadores)* to bring under control (c) *Mat (convertir)* to convert (d) *Med* to set
**2** *vi Aut* to change down
**3 reducirse a** *vpr* (a) *(limitarse a)* to be reduced to (b) *(equivaler a)* to boil *o* come down to

**reducto** *nm* (a) *(fortificación)* redoubt (b) *Fig (refugio)* stronghold, bastion

**redujera** *etc ver* **reducir**

**redundancia** *nf* redundancy, superfluousness

**redundante** *adj* redundant, superfluous

**redundar** *vi* **r. en algo** to have an effect on sth; **redunda en beneficio nuestro** it is to our advantage

**reduplicar** [61] *vt* to redouble

**reduzco** *ver* **reducir**

**reedición** *nf (nueva edición)* new edition; *(reimpresión)* reprint

**reedificación** *nf* rebuilding

**reedificar** *vt* to rebuild

**reeditar** *vt (publicar nueva edición de)* to bring out a new edition of; *(reimprimir)* to reprint

**reelección** *nf* re-election

**reelegir** [57] *vt* to re-elect

**reembolsable** *adj (gastos)* reimbursable; *(fianza)* refundable; *(deuda)* repayable

**reembolsar 1** *vt (gastos)* to reimburse; *(fianza)* to refund; *(deuda)* to repay
**2 reembolsarse** *vpr* to be reimbursed

**reembolso** *nm (de gastos)* reimbursement; *(de fianza, dinero)* refund; *(de deuda)* repayment; **contra r.** cash on delivery

**reemplazar** [16] *vt también Informát* to replace

**reemplazo** *nm* (a) *también Informát* replacement (b) *Mil* call-up, draft; **soldados de r.** conscripts

**reemprender** *vt* to start again

**reencarnación** *nf* reincarnation

**reencarnar 1** *vt* to reincarnate

**2 reencarnarse** *vpr* to be reincarnated (**en** as)

**reencontrar** [65] **1** *vt* to find again

**2 reencontrarse** *vpr (varias personas)* to meet again

**reencuentro** *nm* reunion

**reengancharse** *vpr Mil* to re-enlist

**reestrenar** *vt Cine* to re-run; *Teatro* to revive

**reestreno** *nm* (a) *Cine* rerun, re-release; **cine de r.** second-run cinema; **reestrenos, películas de r.** *(en cartelera)* re-releases (b) *Teatro* revival

**reestructuración** *nf* restructuring

**reestructurar** *vt* to restructure

**reexpedir** [49] *vt* to forward, to send on

**reexportación** *nf* re-exportation

**reexportar** *vt* to re-export

**refacción** *nf* (a) *Am (reparaciones)* repairs (b) *Chile, Méx (recambios)* spare parts

**refaccionar** *vt Am* to repair, to fix

**refectorio** *nm* refectory

**referencia** *nf* reference; **con r.** a with reference to; **hacer r.** a to make reference to, to refer to; **referencias** *(información)* information; *(para puesto de trabajo)* references

**referéndum** *(pl referendos) nm* referendum

**referente** *adj* **r.** a concerning, relating to

**referir** [64] **1** *vt* (a) *(narrar)* to tell, to recount (b) *(remitir)* **r.** a alguien a to refer sb to (c) *(relacionar)* **r.** algo a to relate sth to (d) *Com (convertir)* **r.** algo a to convert sth into

**2 referirse** *vpr* to refer to; **¿a qué te refieres?** what do you mean?; **por o en lo que se refiere a…** as far as… is concerned

**refilón: de refilón** *loc adv (de lado)* sideways; *(de pasada)* briefly; **mirar algo de r.** to look at sth out of the corner of one's eye

**refinado, -a 1** *adj* refined

**2** *nm* refining

**refinamiento** *nm* refinement

**refinanciación** *nf* refinancing

**refinanciar** [15] *vt* to refinance

**refinar** *vt* to refine

**refinería** *nf* refinery

**refiriera** *etc ver* **referir**

**reflectar** *vt* to reflect

**reflector** *nm* (a) *Elec* spotlight; *Mil* searchlight (b) *(telescopio)* reflector

**reflejar 1** *vt también Fig* to reflect

**2 reflejarse** *vpr también Fig* to be reflected (**en** in)

**reflejo, -a 1** *adj* (a) *(onda, rayo)* reflected (b) *(movimiento, dolor)* reflex; **acto r.** reflex action

**2** *nm* (a) *(imagen, manifestación)* reflection (b) *(destello)* glint, gleam (c) *Anat* reflex; *también Fig* **tener buenos reflejos** to have good o quick reflexes; **r. condicional** o **condicionado** conditioned reflex o response (d) *(de peluquería)* **reflejos** highlights; **hacerse** o **darse reflejos** to have highlights put in one's hair

**réflex** *Fot* **1** *adj inv* reflex, SLR

**2** *nf inv (cámara)* reflex o SLR camera

**reflexión** *nf* reflection; **sin previa r.** without thinking

**reflexionar** *vi* to reflect (**sobre** on), to think (**sobre** about)

**reflexivo, -a** *adj* (a) *(que piensa)* reflective, thoughtful (b) *Gram* reflexive

**reflorecimiento** *nm* resurgence, rebirth; **r. de la economía** economic recovery

**refluir** [36] *vi* to flow back o out

**reflujo** *nm* ebb (tide)

**refocilarse** *vpr* **r. haciendo algo** to take delight in doing sth; **r. en la desgracia ajena** to gloat over others' misfortune

**reforestación** *nf* reforestation

**reforestar** *vt* to reforest

**reforma** *nf* (a) *(modificación)* reform; **r. agraria** agrarian reform (b) *(en local, casa)* alterations (c) *Rel* **la R.** the Reformation

**reformar 1** *vt* (a) *también Rel* to reform (b) *(local, casa)* to renovate, to do up

**2 reformarse** *vpr* to mend one's ways

**reformatorio** *nm (de menores) Br* youth custody centre, *US* reformatory; *(de menores de 15 años)* remand home

**reformismo** *nm* reformism

**reformista** *adj & nmf* reformist

**reformular** *vt* to reformulate, to put another way

**reforzado, -a** *adj* reinforced

**reforzar** [33] *vt* to reinforce

**refracción** *nf* refraction

**refractar** *vt* to refract

**refractario, -a** *adj* (a) *(material)* refractory, heat-resistant (b) *(opuesto)* **r.** a averse to (c) *(inmune)* **r.** a immune to

**refrán** *nm* proverb, saying

**refranero** *nm* collection of proverbs o sayings

**refregar** [45] *vt* (a) *(frotar)* to scrub (b) *Fig (restregar)* **r. algo a alguien** to rub sb's nose in sth

**refreír** [58] *vt* (a) *(volver a freír)* to re-fry (b) *(freír en exceso)* to over-fry

**refrenar 1** *vt* to curb, to restrain

**2 refrenarse** *vpr* to hold back, to restrain oneself

**refrendar** vt (a) (confirmar) to confirm; (aprobar) to approve (b) (legalizar) to endorse, to countersign

**refrescante** adj refreshing

**refrescar** [61] **1** vt (a) (enfriar) to refresh; (bebidas) to chill (b) Fig (conocimientos) to brush up; **r. la memoria a alguien** to refresh sb's memory

**2** vi (bebida) to be refreshing

**3** v impersonal to cool down

**4 refrescarse** vpr (a) (tomar aire fresco) to get a breath of fresh air (b) (mojarse con agua fría) to splash oneself down

**refresco** nm (a) (bebida) soft drink; **refrescos** refreshments (b) Mil **de r.** new, fresh

**refría** etc ver **refreír**

**refriega** **1** ver **refregar**

**2** nf scuffle; Mil fracas, skirmish

**refriera** etc ver **refreír**

**refrigeración** nf (a) (aire acondicionado) air-conditioning (b) (de alimentos) refrigeration (c) (de máquinas, motores) cooling; **(sistema de) r.** cooling system

**refrigerado, -a** adj (a) (local) air-conditioned (b) (alimentos) refrigerated (c) (líquido, gas) cooled

**refrigerador** nm (a) (frigorífico) refrigerator, Br fridge, US icebox (b) (de máquinas, motores) cooling system

**refrigerante** adj (a) (para alimentos) refrigerating (b) (para motores) cooling

**refrigerar** vt (a) (local) to air-condition (b) (alimentos) to refrigerate (c) (máquina, motor) to cool

**refrigerio** nm refreshments

**refrito, -a 1** participio ver **refreír**

**2** adj (demasiado frito) over-fried; (frito de nuevo) re-fried

**3** nm (a) Culin = sauce made from fried tomato and onion (b) Fig (cosa rehecha) rehash

**refuerce** etc ver **reforzar**

**refuerzo** nm reinforcement; Mil **refuerzos** reinforcements

**refugiado, -a 1** adj refugee

**2** nm,f refugee

**refugiar** [15] **1** vt to give refuge to

**2 refugiarse** vpr to take refuge; **refugiarse de algo** to shelter from sth

**refugio** nm (a) (lugar) shelter, refuge; **r. antiaéreo** air-raid shelter; **r. atómico** nuclear bunker; **r. de montaña** (muy básico) mountain shelter; (albergue) mountain refuge; **r. subterráneo** bunker, underground shelter (b) Fig (amparo, consuelo) refuge, comfort (c) Aut traffic island

**refulgencia** nf brilliance

**refulgente** adj brilliant

**refulgir** [26] vi to shine brightly

**refundir** vt (a) (material) to re-cast (b) Lit to adapt (c) Fig (unir) to bring together

**refunfuñar** vi to grumble

**refunfuñón, -ona 1** adj grumpy

**2** nm,f grumbler

**refutable** adj refutable

**refutación** nf refutation

**refutar** vt to refute

**regadera** nf (para regar) watering can; Fig **estar como una r.** to be as mad as a hatter

**regadío** nm irrigated land; **de r.** irrigated, irrigable

**regalado, -a** adj (a) (muy barato) dirt cheap; Fig **te lo doy r.** I'm giving it away to you (b) (agradable) comfortable, easy

**regalar 1** vt (a) (dar) (de regalo) to give (as a present); (gratis) to give away (b) (agasajar) **r. a alguien con algo** to shower sb with sth

**2 regalarse con** vpr to treat oneself to

**regalía** nf royal prerogative

**regaliz** nm liquorice

**regalo** nm (a) (obsequio) present, gift (b) (placer) joy, delight (c) (en rifa) prize

**regalón, -ona** adj CSur, Chile Fam spoilt

**regalonear** vt CSur, Chile Fam to spoil

**regañadientes: a regañadientes** loc adv Fam unwillingly, reluctantly

**regañar 1** vt (reprender) to tell off

**2** vi (pelearse) to fall out, to argue

**regañina** nf (a) (reprimenda) ticking off (b) (enfado) argument, row

**regaño** nm telling off

**regañón, -ona 1** adj **es muy r.** he's always telling people off for nothing

**2** nm,f **es un r.** he's always telling people off for nothing

**regar** [45] vt (a) (con agua) (planta, campo) to water; (calle) to hose down (b) (sujeto: río) to flow through (c) (sujeto: vasos sanguíneos) to supply with blood (d) Fig (desparramar) to sprinkle, to scatter

**regata** nf (a) Náut regatta, boat race (b) (reguera) irrigation channel

**regate** nm (a) Dep swerve, sidestep (b) Fig (evasiva) dodge

**regatear 1** vt (a) (escatimar) to be sparing with; **no ha regateado esfuerzos** he has spared no effort (b) Dep to beat, to dribble past (c) (precio) to haggle over

**2** vi (a) (negociar el precio) to barter, to haggle (b) Náut to race

**regateo** nm bartering, haggling

**regato** nm brook, rivulet

**regazo** nm lap

**regencia** *nf* (a) *(reinado)* regency (b) *(administración)* running, management

**regeneración** *nf (recuperación, restablecimiento)* regeneration; *(de delincuente, degenerado)* reform

**regeneracionismo** *nm* political reform movement

**regenerar 1** *vt (recuperar, restablecer)* to regenerate; *(delincuente, degenerado)* to reform

**2 regenerarse** *(recuperarse, restablecerse)* to regenerate; *(delincuente, degenerado)* to reform

**regenta** *nf* wife of the regent

**regentar** *vt (país)* to run, to govern; *(negocio)* to run, to manage; *(puesto)* to hold *(temporarily)*

**regente 1** *adj* regent

**2** *nmf* (a) *(de un país)* regent (b) *(administrador)* *(de tienda)* manager; *(de colegio)* governor (c) *Méx (alcalde)* mayor, *f* mayoress

**reggae** ['rrivi, 'rrevi] *nm* reggae

**regicida** *nmf* regicide

**regicidio** *nm* regicide

**regidor, -ora** *nm,f* (a) *Teatro* stage manager; *Cine & TV* assistant director (b) *(concejal)* councillor

**régimen** (*pl* **regímenes**) *nm* (a) *(sistema político)* regime; **r. parlamentario** parliamentary system (b) *(normativa)* rules (c) *(dieta)* diet; **estar/ponerse a r.** to be/go on a diet (d) *(rutina)* pattern; **r. de lluvias** pattern of rainfall; **r. de vida** lifestyle (e) *Ling* government

**regimiento** *nm Mil & Fig* regiment

**regio, -a** *adj* (a) *(real)* royal (b) *Am* great, fabulous

**regiomontano, -a 1** *adj* of/from Monterrey

**2** *nm,f* person from Monterrey

**región** *nf* region; *Mil* district

**regional** *adj* regional

**regionalismo** *nm* regionalism

**regionalista** *adj & nmf* regionalist

**regionalizar** [16] *vt* to regionalize

**regir** [57] **1** *vt* (a) *(gobernar)* to rule, to govern (b) *(administrar)* to run, to manage (c) *Ling* to govern (d) *Fig (determinar)* to govern, to determine

**2** *vi* (a) *(ley)* to be in force, to apply (b) *Fig (persona)* to be of sound mind

**3 regirse por** *vpr* to trust in, to be guided by

**registrado, -a** *adj* (a) *(grabado, anotado)* recorded (b) *(patentado, inscrito)* registered

**registrador, -ora 1** *adj* registering

**2** *nm,f* registrar

**registrar 1** *vt* (a) *(zona, piso, persona)* to search (b) *(datos, hechos)* to register, to record (c) *(grabar)* to record

**2 registrarse** *v impersonal* (a) *(suceder)* to occur, to happen (b) *(observarse)* to be recorded

**registro** *nm* (a) *(oficina)* registry (office); **r. civil** registry (office); **r. mercantil** *o* **de comercio** business registry office; **r. de la propiedad** land registry office (b) *(inscripción)* registration; **llevar el r. de algo** to keep a record of sth (c) *(libro)* register (d) *(inspección)* search, searching (e) *(de libro)* bookmark (f) *Informát* record (g) *Ling & Mús* register

**regla** *nf* (a) *(para medir)* ruler, rule; **r. de cálculo** slide rule (b) *(norma)* rule; **en r.** in order; **por r. general** as a rule, generally; **salirse de la r.** to overstep the mark *o* line (c) *Mat* operation; **r. de tres** rule of three (d) *Fam (menstruación)* period; **tener la r.** to have one's period (e) *(modelo)* example, model

**reglaje** *nm (de motor)* tuning

**reglamentación** *nf (acción)* regulation; *(reglas)* rules, regulations

**reglamentar** *vt* to regulate

**reglamentario, -a** *adj (legal)* lawful; *Der* statutory; **arma reglamentaria** regulation weapon

**reglamento** *nm (normas)* regulations, rules; **balón de r.** regulation football

**reglar** *vt* to regulate

**regocijar 1** *vt* to delight

**2 regocijarse** *vpr* to rejoice **(de** *o* **con** in)

**regocijo** *nm* joy, delight

**regodearse** *vpr* to take pleasure *o* delight **(en** *o* **con** in)

**regodeo** *nm (deleite)* delight, pleasure; *(malicioso)* (cruel) delight *o* pleasure

**regordete** *adj* chubby, tubby

**regresar 1** *vi (yendo)* to go back, to return; *(viniendo)* to come back, to return

**2** *vt Am (devolver)* to give back

**3 regresarse** *vpr Am (volver)* to come back

**regresión** *nf* (a) *(de economía, exportaciones)* drop, decline (b) *(de epidemia)* regression

**regresivo, -a** *adj* regressive

**regreso** *nm* return; **estar de r.** to be back

**regué** *etc ver* **regar**

**regüeldo** *nm* belch

**reguero** *nm* (a) *(rastro)* *(de sangre, agua)* trickle; *(de harina, arena)* trail; **correr como un r. de pólvora** to spread like wildfire (b) *(canal)* irrigation ditch

**regulable** *adj* adjustable, variable

**regulación** nf *(de actividad, economía)* regulation; *(de nacimientos, tráfico)* control; *(de mecanismo)* adjustment; **r. de empleo** streamlining, redundancies

**regulador, -ora** adj regulating, regulatory

**regular 1** adj **(a)** *(uniforme)* regular; **de un modo r.** regularly **(b)** *(mediocre)* average, fair **(c)** *(normal)* normal, usual; *(de tamaño)* medium; **por lo r.** as a rule, generally

**2** nm Mil regular

**3** adv *(no muy bien)* so-so

**4** vt *(actividad, economía, tráfico)* to control, to regulate; *(mecanismo)* to adjust

**regularidad** nf regularity; **con r.** regularly

**regularización** nf regularization

**regularizar** [16] **1** vt **(a)** *(devolver a la normalidad)* to get back to normal **(b)** *(legalizar)* to regularize

**2 regularizarse** vpr **(a)** *(volver a la normalidad)* to return to normal **(b)** *(legalizarse)* to become legitimate

**regurgitar** vt & vi to regurgitate

**regusto** nm *(sabor)* aftertaste; *(semejanza, aire)* flavour, hint

**rehabilitación** nf **(a)** *(de enfermo, de delincuente)* rehabilitation; *(en un puesto)* reinstatement **(b)** *(de local, edificio)* refurbishment

**rehabilitar** vt **(a)** *(enfermo, delincuente)* to rehabilitate; *(en un puesto)* to reinstate **(b)** *(local, edificio)* to refurbish

**rehacer** [35] **1** vt **(a)** *(volver a hacer)* to redo, to do again **(b)** *(reconstruir)* to rebuild

**2 rehacerse** vpr *(recuperarse)* to recuperate, to recover

**rehecho, -a** participio ver **rehacer**

**rehén** *(pl* rehenes*)* nm hostage

**rehíce** etc ver **rehacer**

**rehiciera** etc ver **rehacer**

**rehogar** [40] vt = to fry over a low heat

**rehuir** [36] vt to avoid

**rehusar** vt & vi to refuse

**rehuya** etc ver **rehuir**

**rehuyera** etc ver **rehuir**

**Reikiavik** n Reykjavik

**reimplantar** vt **(a)** *(reintroducir)* to reintroduce **(b)** Med to implant again

**reimportación** nf reimporting

**reimpresión** nf *(tirada)* reprint; *(acción)* reprinting

**reimprimir** vt to reprint

**reina** nf *(en general)* queen; *(apelativo)* love, darling; **ven aquí, mi r.** come here, princess

**reinado** nm también Fig reign

**reinante** adj **(a)** *(monarquía, persona)* reigning, ruling **(b)** *(viento, ambiente)* prevailing

**reinar** vi también Fig to reign

**reincidencia** nf *(en un vicio)* relapse; *(en un delito)* recidivism

**reincidente** adj & nmf recidivist

**reincidir** vi **r. en** *(falta, error)* to relapse into, to fall back into; *(delito)* to repeat

**reincorporación** nf return (**a** to)

**reincorporar 1** vt to reincorporate

**2 reincorporarse a** vpr to rejoin, to go back to

**reineta** nf **(manzana) r.** = type of apple with tart flavour, used for cooking and eating

**reingresar** vi to return (**en** to)

**reinicializar** [16] vt Informát *(ordenador)* to reboot; *(impresora)* to reset

**reino** nm Biol & Pol kingdom; Fig realm; **el r. de los cielos** the kingdom of Heaven

**Reino Unido** nm **el R.** the United Kingdom

**reinserción** nf **r. (social)** rehabilitation o reintegration (into society); **la r. (laboral) de los desempleados de larga duración** getting the long-term unemployed back to work

**reinsertar** vt **(a)** *(en sociedad)* to reintegrate, to rehabilitate **(b)** *(en ranura)* to reinsert

**reinstaurar** vt to reestablish

**reintegración** nf **(a)** *(a puesto)* reinstatement **(b)** *(de dinero)* repayment, reimbursement

**reintegrar 1** vt **(a)** *(a un puesto)* to reinstate **(b)** *(dinero)* to repay, to reimburse

**2 reintegrarse** vpr to return (**a** to)

**reintegro** nm **(a)** *(de dinero)* repayment, reimbursement; Com withdrawal **(b)** *(en lotería)* = refund of one's stake as prize

**reinversión** nf reinvestment

**reinvertir** [64] vt to reinvest

**reír** [58] **1** vi to laugh

**2** vt to laugh at

**3 reírse** vpr to laugh (**de** at)

**reiteración** nf reiteration, repetition

**reiterar 1** vt to reiterate, to repeat

**2 reiterarse en** vpr to reaffirm

**reiterativo, -a** adj repetitive, repetitious

**reivindicación** nf claim, demand; **r. salarial** pay claim; **estamos a la espera de la r. del atentado** no-one has yet claimed responsibility for the attack

**reivindicar** [61] vt **(a)** *(derechos, salario)* to claim, to demand **(b)** *(atentado)* to claim responsibility for **(c)** *(herencia, territorio)* to lay claim to

**reivindicativo, -a** adj **jornada reivindicativa** day of protest; **plataforma reivindicativa** pressure group

**reja** nf *(barrotes)* bars; *(en el suelo)* grating; *(en ventana)* grille; **poner una r. en la ventana** to put bars on the window; **estar entre rejas** to be behind bars

**rejilla** *nf* (a) *(enrejado)* grid, grating; *(de ventana)* grille; *(de cocina)* grill *(on stove)*; *(de horno)* gridiron (b) *(en sillas, muebles)* wickerwork; **silla de r.** chair with a wickerwork seat (c) *(para equipaje)* luggage rack

**rejón** *nm Taurom* = type of "banderilla" used by mounted bullfighter

**rejoneador, -ora** *nm,f Taurom* = bullfighter on horseback who uses the "rejón"

**rejuntarse** *vpr muy Fam (pareja)* to shack up together; **r. con alguien** to move in with sb

**rejuvenecer** [48] **1** *vt & vi* to rejuvenate
**2 rejuvenecerse** *vpr* to be rejuvenated

**rejuvenecimiento** *nm* rejuvenation

**relación** *nf* (a) *(nexo)* relation, connection; **con r. a, en r. con** in relation to, with regard to; **r. precio-calidad** value for money
(b) *(comunicación, trato)* relations, relationship; **relaciones amorosas** (love) affair; **relaciones comerciales** *(vínculos)* business links; *(comercio)* trade; **relaciones diplomáticas** diplomatic relations; **relaciones laborales** industrial relations; **relaciones públicas** public relations, PR
(c) *(lista)* list
(d) *(descripción)* account
(e) *(informe)* report
(f) **relaciones** *(noviazgo)* relationship; **llevan cinco años de relaciones** they've been going out together for five years; **relaciones prematrimoniales** premarital sex
(g) **relaciones** *(contactos)* contacts, connections
(h) *Mat* ratio; **una r. 5:1** a ratio of 5 to 1

**relacionar** **1** *vt* (a) *(vincular)* to relate, to connect; **estar bien relacionado** to be well-connected (b) *(enumerar)* to list, to enumerate
**2 relacionarse** *vpr (alternar)* to mix (**con** with)

**relajación** *nf*, **relajamiento** *nm* relaxation; **r. de la moral** lowering of moral standards

**relajante 1** *adj* relaxing
**2** *nm* relaxant

**relajar 1** *vt* to relax
**2 relajarse** *vpr* to relax

**relajo** *nm Am Fam (alboroto)* racket, din

**relamer 1** *vt* to lick repeatedly
**2 relamerse** *vpr* (a) *(persona)* to lick one's lips; **relamerse de gusto** to smack one's lips; *Fig* **se relamía de gusto al pensar en...** he savoured the thought of... (b) *(animal)* to lick its chops

**relamido, -a** *adj* prim and proper

**relámpago** *nm (descarga)* flash of lightning; *(destello)* flash; **hubo muchos relámpagos** there was a lot of lightning; *Fig* **pasar como un r.** to pass by as quick as lightning, to flash past

**relampaguear 1** *v impersonal* **relampagueó** lightning flashed
**2** *vi Fig* to flash

**relampagueo** *nm Meteo* lightning; *(destello)* flashing

**relanzamiento** *nm* relaunch

**relanzar** [16] *vt* to relaunch

**relatar** *vt (suceso)* to relate, to recount; *(historia)* to tell

**relatividad** *nf* relativity

**relativismo** *nm* relativism

**relativizar** [16] *vt* to play down

**relativo, -a** *adj* (a) *(no absoluto)* relative (b) *(relacionado, tocante)* relating; **en lo r. a...** regarding... (c) *(escaso)* limited

**relato** *nm (exposición)* account, report; *(cuento)* tale, story

**relax** *nm inv* (a) *(relajación)* relaxation (b) *(sección de periódico)* personal column

**relé** *nm Elec* relay

**releer** [39] *vt* to re-read

**relegar** [40] *vt* to relegate (**a** to); **r. algo al olvido** to banish sth from one's mind

**relente** *nm (night)* dew

**relevancia** *nf* importance

**relevante** *adj* outstanding, important

**relevar** *vt* (a) *(sustituir)* to relieve, to take over from (b) *(destituir)* to dismiss (**de** from), to relieve (**de** of) (c) *(eximir)* to free (**de** from) (d) *Dep (en partidos)* to substitute; *(en relevos)* to take over from

**relevo** *nm* (a) *(sustitución, cambio)* change; **tomar el r.** to take over; **el r. de la guardia** the changing of the guard (b) *(sustituto, grupo)* relief (c) *Dep (acción)* relay; *(carrera)* **relevos** relay (race)

**releyera** *etc ver* **releer**

**relicario** *nm Rel* reliquary; *(estuche)* locket

**relieve** *nm* (a) *también Arte & Geog* relief; **alto r.** high relief; **bajo r.** bas-relief; **en r.** in relief (b) *(importancia)* importance; **de r.** important; **poner de r.** to underline (the importance of), to highlight

**religión** *nf* religion

**religiosamente** *adv también Fig* religiously

**religiosidad** *nf también Fig* religiousness

**religioso, -a 1** *adj* religious
**2** *nm,f (monje)* monk; *(monja)* nun; *(cura)* priest *(of a religious order)*

**relinchar** *vi* to neigh, to whinny

**relincho** *nm* neigh, neighing

**reliquia** nf (restos) relic; (familiar) heirloom; Fig **este ordenador es una r.** this computer is an antique

**rellano** nm (a) (de escalera) landing (b) (de terreno) shelf

**rellenar** vt (a) (volver a llenar) to refill (b) (documento, formulario) to fill in o out (c) (pollo, cojín) to stuff; (tarta, pastel) to fill

**relleno, -a 1** adj (a) (lleno) stuffed; (tarta, pastel) filled (b) (gordo) plump
**2** nm (de pollo, almohadón) stuffing; (de pastel) filling; Fig **páginas de r.** padding

**reloj** nm (de pared, en torre) clock; (de pulsera) watch; Dep **(carrera) contra r.** time trial; Fig **hacer algo contra r.** to do sth against the clock; Fig **funcionar como un r.** to go like clockwork; **r. analógico/digital** analogue/ digital watch; **r. de arena** hourglass; **r. de bolsillo** pocket watch; **r. de cuco** cuckoo clock; **r. despertador** alarm clock; Informát **r. interno** internal clock; **r. de pulsera** watch, wristwatch; **r. de sol** sun dial

**relojería** nf (a) (tienda) watchmaker's (shop) (b) (arte) watchmaking

**relojero, -a** nm,f watchmaker

**reluciente** adj shining, gleaming

**relucir** [41] vi también Fig to shine; **sacar algo a r.** to bring sth up, to mention sth

**relumbrar** vi to shine brightly

**reluzca** etc ver **relucir**

**remachar** vt (a) (machacar) to rivet (b) Fig (recalcar) to drive home, to stress

**remache** nm (a) (acción) riveting (b) (clavo) rivet

**remake** [rri'meik] (pl remakes) nm remake

**remanente** nm (a) (de géneros) surplus stock; (de productos agrícolas) surplus (b) (en cuenta bancaria) balance (c) (de beneficios) net profit

**remangar** [40] **1** vt to roll up
**2 remangarse** vpr (mangas, camisa) to roll up one's sleeves; **remangarse los pantalones** to roll up one's trouser legs

**remanguillé** nf Fam **a la r.** any old how; **la casa estaba a la r.** the house was in an awful mess

**remanso** nm still pool; **r. de paz** oasis of peace

**remar** vi to row

**remarcar** [61] vt (recalcar) to underline, to stress

**rematadamente** adv absolutely, utterly

**rematado, -a** adj utter, complete

**rematar 1** vt (a) (acabar) to finish (b) (matar) to finish off; Fig **para r.** (para colmo) to cap o crown it all (c) Dep to shoot (d) (liquidar, vender) to sell off cheaply (e) (costura) to finish off (f) (adjudicar en subasta) to knock down
**2** vi Dep to shoot; **r. de cabeza** to head at goal

**remate** nm (a) (fin, colofón) end; **de r.** totally, completely; **para r.** (colmo) to cap it all (b) (costura) overstitch (c) Arquit top (d) Dep shot; **r. de cabeza** header (at goal)

**remedar** vt (imitar) to imitate; (por burla) to ape, to mimic

**remediar** [15] vt (daño) to remedy, to put right; (problema) to solve; (peligro) to avoid, to prevent; **no lo puedo r.** I can't help it

**remedio** nm (a) (solución) solution, remedy; **como último r.** as a last resort; **no hay o queda más r. que...** there's nothing for it but...; **no tener más r. (que)** to have no alternative o choice (but); **no tiene r.** (persona) he's a hopeless case; (problema) nothing can be done about it; **poner r. a algo** to do sth about sth; **¡qué r.!** there's no alternative!, what else can I/we etc do?; **sin r.** (sin cura, solución) hopeless; (ineludiblemente) inevitably
(b) (consuelo) comfort, consolation
(c) (medicamento) remedy, cure; **r. casero** home remedy

**remedo** nm (imitación) imitation; (por burla) parody

**rememorar** vt to remember, to recall

**remendado, -a** adj (con parches) patched; (zurcido) darned, mended

**remendar** [3] vt (con parches) to patch, to mend; (zurcir) to darn, to mend

**remendón, -ona** adj **zapatero r.** cobbler

**remera** nf CSur (prenda) T-shirt

**remero, -a** nm,f (persona) rower

**remesa** nf (de productos) consignment; (de dinero) shipment, remittance

**remeter** vt to tuck in

**remiendo 1** ver **remendar**
**2** nm (a) (parche) mend, darn (b) Fam (apaño) patching up, makeshift mending

**remilgado, -a** adj (a) (afectado) affected (b) (escrupuloso) squeamish; (con comida) fussy, finicky

**remilgo** nm (a) (afectación) affectation (b) (escrúpulos) squeamishness; (con comida) fussiness; **hacerle remilgos a algo** to turn one's nose up at sth

**reminiscencia** nf reminiscence; **tener reminiscencias de** to be reminiscent of

**remisión** nf (a) (envío) sending (b) (en texto) cross-reference, reference (c) (perdón) remission, forgiveness; **sin r.** without hope of a reprieve

**remiso, -a** *adj (reacio)* reluctant; **ser r. a hacer algo** to be reluctant to do sth

**remite** *nm* = sender's name and address

**remitente** *nmf* sender

**remitir 1** *vt* **(a)** *(enviar)* to send; **r. algo a** to refer sth to **(b)** *(perdonar)* to forgive, to remit

**2** *vi* **(a)** *(en texto)* to refer **(a to) (b)** *(disminuir) (tormenta, viento)* to subside; *(fiebre, temperatura)* to go down; *(enfermedad)* to go into remission; *(lluvia, calor)* to ease off

**3 remitirse** *vpr* **(a)** *(atenerse a)* to comply with, to abide by **(b)** *(referirse a)* to refer to

**remo** *nm* **(a)** *(pala)* oar **(b)** *(deporte)* rowing

**remodelación** *nf (modificación)* redesign; *(conversión)* conversion; *(de Gobierno)* reshuffle

**remodelar** *vt (modificar)* to redesign; *(gobierno)* to reshuffle; **r. algo para convertirlo en** to convert sth into

**remojar** *vt* **(a)** *(mojar)* to soak **(b)** *Fam (celebrar bebiendo)* to celebrate with a drink

**remojo** *nm* **poner en** *o* **a r.** to leave to soak; **estar en r.** to be soaking

**remojón** *nm (en la piscina, el mar)* dip; *(bajo la lluvia)* soaking, drenching; **darse un r.** to go for a dip

**remolacha** *nf Br* beetroot, *US* beet; **r. azucarera** (sugar) beet

**remolcador, -ora 1** *adj (vehículo)* **camión r.** tow truck; *(barco)* **lancha remolcadora** tug, tugboat

**2** *nm (camión)* tow truck; *(barco)* tug, tugboat

**remolcar** [61] *vt (coche)* to tow; *(barco)* to tug

**remolino** *nm* **(a)** *(de agua)* eddy, whirlpool; *(de viento)* whirlwind; *(de humo)* cloud, swirl **(b)** *(de gente)* throng, mass **(c)** *(de ideas)* confusion **(d)** *(de pelo)* cowlick

**remolón, -ona 1** *adj* lazy

**2** *nm,f* **hacerse el r.** to shirk, to be lazy

**remolonear** *vi Fam (perder el tiempo)* to shirk, to be lazy; *(en la cama)* to laze about in bed

**remolque** *nm* **(a)** *(acción)* towing; **ir a r. de** to be towed along by; *Fig* to follow along behind, to be led by **(b)** *(vehículo)* trailer

**remontar 1** *vt (pendiente, río)* to go up; *(obstáculo)* to get over, to overcome; *(puestos)* to pull back, to catch up; **r. el vuelo** to soar

**2 remontarse** *vpr* **(a)** *(ave, avión)* to soar, to climb high **(b)** *(gastos)* **remontarse a** to amount *o* come to **(c)** *Fig (datar)* **remontarse a** to go *o* date back to

**remonte** *nm* ski lift

**rémora** *nf* **(a)** *(pez)* remora **(b)** *Fam Fig (impedimento)* hindrance

**remorder** [43] *vt* **me remuerde (la conciencia) haberle mentido** I feel guilty *o* bad about lying to him

**remordimiento** *nm* remorse; **tener remordimientos (por)** to feel remorse (about)

**remoto, -a** *adj también Informát* remote; **no tengo ni la más remota idea** I haven't got the faintest idea

**remover** [43] **1** *vt* **(a)** *(agitar) (sopa, café)* to stir; *(ensalada)* to toss; *(tierra)* to turn over, to dig up **(b)** *(recuerdos, pasado)* to stir up, to rake up **(c)** *Am (despedir)* to dismiss, to sack

**2 removerse** *vpr (moverse)* to fidget; *(en la cama)* to toss and turn

**remozar** *vt (edificio, fachada)* to renovate; *Fig (equipo)* to give a new look to

**remplazar** [16] *vt también Informát* to replace

**remplazo** *nm* **(a)** *también Informát* replacement **(b)** *Mil* call-up, draft; **soldados de r.** conscripts

**remuerda** *etc ver* **remorder**

**remuevo** *etc ver* **remover**

**remuneración** *nf* remuneration

**remunerado, -a** *adj* paid; **bien r.** well-paid; **mal r.** badly-paid; **no r.** unpaid

**remunerar** *vt* **(a)** *(pagar)* to remunerate **(b)** *(recompensar)* to reward

**renacentista 1** *adj* Renaissance; **pintor r.** Renaissance painter

**2** *nmf (artista)* Renaissance artist

**renacer** [44] *vi* **(a)** *(flores, hojas)* to grow again **(b)** *(sentimiento, interés)* to return, to revive; **sentirse r.** to feel reborn, to feel one has a new lease of life

**Renacimiento** *nm* **el R.** the Renaissance

**renacimiento** *nm* **(a)** *(de flores, hojas)* budding **(b)** *(de sentimiento, interés)* revival, return; **r. espiritual** spiritual rebirth

**renacuajo** *nm* tadpole; *Fam Fig* tiddler

**renal** *adj* renal, kidney; **infección r.** kidney infection

**renazca** *etc ver* **renacer**

**rencilla** *nf* (long-standing) quarrel, feud

**rencor** *nm* resentment, bitterness; **guardar r. a alguien** to have *o* bear a grudge against sb

**rencoroso, -a 1** *adj* resentful, bitter

**2** *nm,f* resentful *o* bitter person

**rendición** *nf* surrender; **r. incondicional** unconditional surrender

**rendido, -a** *adj* **(a)** *(agotado)* exhausted, worn-out **(b)** *(sumiso)* submissive; *(admirador)* servile, devoted

**rendija** *nf* crack, gap

**rendimiento** *nm* **(a)** *(de inversión, negocio)* yield, return; *(de trabajador, fábrica)* productivity; *(de tierra, cosecha)* performance, yield **(b)** *(de motor)* performance

**rendir** [49] **1** vt (**a**) (cansar) to wear out, to tire out (**b**) (rentar) to yield (**c**) (vencer) to defeat, to subdue (**d**) (ofrecer) to give, to present; (pleitesía) to pay; **r. culto a** to worship

**2** vi (**a**) (máquina) to perform well; (negocio) to be profitable; (fábrica, trabajador) to be productive (**b**) (dar de sí) **esta pintura rinde mucho** a little of this paint goes a long way; **me rinde mucho el tiempo** I get a lot done (in the time)

**3 rendirse** vpr (**a**) (entregarse) to give oneself up, to surrender (**b**) (ceder, abandonar) to submit, to give in; **rendirse a la evidencia** to bow to the evidence; **¡me rindo!** (en adivinanza) I give in o up!

**renegado, -a** adj & nm,f renegade

**renegar** [45] vi (**a**) (repudiar) **r. de** Rel to renounce; (familia) to disown (**b**) Fam (gruñir) to grumble

**renegociar** [15] vt to renegotiate

**renegrido, -a** adj grimy, blackened

**renegué** ver **renegar**

**Renfe** nf (abrev de **Red Nacional de los Ferrocarriles Españoles**) = Spanish state railway company

**renglón** nm line; Fig **a r. seguido** in the same breath, straight after; **escribir a alguien unos renglones** to drop sb a line

**reniego** etc ver **renegar**

**reno** nm reindeer

**renombrado, -a** adj renowned, famous

**renombrar** vt Informát to rename

**renombre** nm renown, fame; **de r.** famous

**renovable** adj renewable

**renovación** nf (de carné, contrato) renewal; (de mobiliario, local) renovation

**renovado, -a** adj (carné, contrato) renewed; **con renovados bríos** with renewed energy

**renovador, -ora** **1** adj innovative; Pol reformist

**2** nm,f innovator; Pol reformer

**renovar** [43] vt (**a**) (cambiar) (mobiliario, local) to renovate; (personal, plantilla) to make changes to, to shake out; **r. el vestuario** to buy new clothes, to update one's wardrobe (**b**) (rehacer) (carné, contrato, ataques) to renew (**c**) (restaurar) to restore (**d**) (transformar) to revitalize; Pol to reform

**renqueante** adj limping, hobbling; Fig struggling

**renquear** vi to limp, to hobble; Fig to struggle along

**renta** nf (**a**) (ingresos) income; **vivir de las rentas** to live off one's (private) income; **r. fija** fixed income; **r. per cápita** o **por habitante** per capita income; **r. variable/vitalicia** variable/life annuity; **r. del trabajo** wage income; **r. del capital** capital yield (**b**) (alquiler) rent (**c**) (beneficios) return (**d**) (intereses) interest (**e**) (deuda pública) national o public debt

**rentabilidad** nf profitability

**rentabilizar** [16] vt to make profitable

**rentable** adj profitable

**rentar** **1** vt (**a**) (rendir) to produce, to yield (**b**) Am (alquilar) to rent; **se renta** (en letrero) for rent
**2** vi to be profitable

**rentista** nmf = person of independent means

**renuencia** nf reluctance, unwillingness

**renuente** adj reluctant (**a** to), unwilling (**a** to)

**renuevo** etc ver **renovar**

**renuncia** nf (**a**) (abandono) giving up (**b**) (dimisión) resignation; **presentó su r.** he handed in his (letter of) resignation

**renunciar** [15] vi (**a**) **r. a algo** (abandonar, prescindir de) to give sth up; **r. a un proyecto** to abandon a project; **r. al tabaco** to give up o stop smoking (**b**) (dimitir) to resign (**c**) (rechazar) **r. a hacer algo** to refuse to do sth; **r. a algo** (premio, oferta) to turn sth down

**reñido, -a** adj (**a**) (enfadado) on bad terms o at odds (**con** with); **están reñidos** they've fallen out (**b**) (disputado) fierce, hard-fought (**c**) (incompatible) **estar r. con** to be at odds with, to be incompatible with

**reñir** [49] **1** vt (regañar) to tell off
**2** vi (enfadarse) to argue, to squabble; **r. con** to fall out with

**reo** nmf (culpado) offender, culprit; (acusado) accused, defendant

**reoca** nf Fam **ser la r.** (gracioso) to be a scream; (el colmo) to be the limit

**reojo: de reojo** loc adv **mirar algo/a alguien de r.** to look at sth/sb out of the corner of one's eye

**reordenación** nf restructuring, reorganization

**reorganización** nf (reestructuración) reorganization; (del gobierno) reshuffle

**reorganizar** [16] vt (reestructurar) to reorganize; (gobierno) to reshuffle

**reorientar** **1** vt (carrera, empresa, vida) to give a new direction to; (energías, interés) to re-focus (**hacia** on), to redirect (**hacia** towards)
**2 reorientarse** (carrera, empresa, vida) to take a new direction; (energías, interés) to re-focus (**hacia** on), to be redirected (**hacia** towards)

**repanchigarse, repanchingarse** [40] vpr Fam to sprawl out

**repanocha** nf Fam **ser la r.** (gracioso) to be a scream; (el colmo) to be the limit

**repantigarse, repantingarse [40]** vpr Fam to sprawl out

**reparación** nf (a) (arreglo) repair; **necesita varias reparaciones** it needs several things repairing; **en r.** under repair (b) (compensación) reparation, redress

**reparador, -ora** adj (descanso, sueño) refreshing

**reparar 1** vt (coche, aparato) to repair, to fix; (error, daño) to make amends for; (fuerzas) to make up for, to restore

**2** vi (advertir) **r. en algo** to notice sth; **no r. en gastos** to spare no expense

**reparo** nm (a) (objeción) objection; **poner reparos a algo** to raise objections to sth (b) (apuro) **con reparos** with hesitation o reservations; **me da r.** I feel awkward about it; **no tener reparos en hacer algo** to have no qualms o scruples about doing sth; **sin reparos** without reservation, with no holds barred

**repartición** nf (reparto) sharing out

**repartidor, -ora 1** adj delivery; **camión r.** delivery lorry

**2** nm,f (de butano, carbón) deliveryman, f deliverywoman; (de leche) milkman, f milklady; (de periódicos) paperboy, f papergirl; **es r. de publicidad** (en la calle) he hands out advertising leaflets; (en buzones) he distributes advertising leaflets

**repartir 1** vt (a) (dividir) to share out, to divide (b) (distribuir) (leche, periódicos, correo) to deliver; (naipes) to deal (out) (c) (esparcir) (pintura, mantequilla) to spread (d) (asignar) (trabajo, órdenes) to give out, to allocate; (papeles) to assign (e) Fig (administrar) to administer, to dish out

**2 repartirse** vpr (a) (dividirse) to divide up, to share out; **se repartieron el botín** they divided up o shared out the loot (b) (distribuirse) to spread out

**reparto** nm (a) (división) division, distribution; **hacer el r.** to divide sth up o share sth out; Econ **r. de beneficios** profit sharing (b) (distribución) (de leche, periódicos, correo) delivery; (de naipes) dealing (c) (asignación) giving out, allocation; **r. de premios** prizegiving (d) Cine & Teatro cast

**repasar** vt (a) (revisar) to go over, to check (b) (estudiar) to revise (c) (zurcir) to darn, to mend

**repaso** nm (a) (revisión) check (b) (estudio) revision; **dar un r. a** to revise (c) (de ropa) darning, mending (d) Fam **dar un r. a alguien** (regañar) to give sb a telling off o a ticking off; (apabullar) to cut sb down to size

**repatear** vt Fam **me repatea que…** it really annoys me that…; **ese tipo me repatea** I can't stand that guy

**repatriación** nf repatriation

**repatriar [34] 1** vt to repatriate

**2 repatriarse** vpr to return home

**repecho** nm steep slope

**repeinado, -a** adj dolled up

**repelencia** nf repulsion

**repelente 1** adj (a) (desagradable, repugnante) repulsive (b) (de insectos) repellent

**2** nm insect repellent

**repeler** vt (a) (rechazar) to repel (b) (repugnar) to repulse, to disgust

**repelús** nm **me da r.** it gives me the shivers

**repeluzno** nm shiver

**repente** nm (arrebato) fit; **de r.** suddenly

**repentinamente** adv suddenly

**repentino, -a** adj sudden

**repera** nf Fam **ser la r.** to be the limit

**repercusión** nf (a) Fig (consecuencia) repercussion (b) (resonancia) echoes

**repercutir** vi (a) Fig (afectar) to have repercussions (**en** on) (b) (resonar) to resound, to echo

**repertorio** nm (a) (obras) repertoire (b) Fig (serie) selection

**repesca** nf (a) Educ resit (b) Dep repêchage

**repescar [61]** vt (a) Educ to allow a resit (b) Dep to allow into the repêchage

**repetición** nf (de acción, dicho) repetition; (de una jugada) action replay

**repetido, -a** adj (a) (reiterado) repeated; **repetidas veces** time and time again (b) (duplicado) **tengo este libro r.** I've got two copies of this book

**repetidor, -ora 1** adj repeating the year

**2** nm,f Educ = student repeating a year

**3** nm (de radio, televisión) repeater

**repetir [49] 1** vt (hacer, decir de nuevo) to repeat; (ataque) to renew; (en comida) to have seconds of

**2** vi (a) (alumno) to repeat a year (b) (sabor, alimento) **r. (a alguien)** to repeat (on sb) (c) (comensal) to have seconds

**3 repetirse** vpr (a) (fenómeno) to recur (b) (persona) to repeat oneself

**repetitivo, -a** adj repetitive

**repicar [61] 1** vt (campanas) to ring; (tambor) to beat

**2** vi (campanas) to ring; (tambor) to sound

**repipi 1** adj (irritatingly) precocious

**2** nmf precocious brat

**repique 1** ver **repicar**

**2** nm peal, ringing

**repiquetear** vi *(campanas)* to ring out; *(tambor)* to beat; *(timbre)* to ring; *(lluvia, dedos)* to drum

**repiqueteo** nm *(de campanas)* pealing; *(de tambor)* beating; *(de timbre)* ringing; *(de lluvia, dedos)* drumming

**repisa** nf (a) *(estante)* shelf; *(sobre chimenea)* mantelpiece (b) *Arquit* bracket

**repitiera** etc ver **repetir**

**repito** etc ver **repetir**

**replantar** vt to replant

**replanteamiento** nm restatement, reconsideration

**replantear 1** vt (a) *(situación, problema)* to restate (b) *(cuestión) (de nuevo)* to raise again; *(parafrasear)* to rephrase
**2 replantearse** vpr to reconsider

**replegar** [45] **1** vt *(ocultar)* to retract
**2 replegarse** vpr *(retirarse)* to withdraw, to retreat

**repleto, -a** adj *(habitación, autobús)* packed (**de** with); **estoy r.** *(de comida)* I'm full (up)

**réplica** nf (a) *(respuesta)* reply (b) *(copia)* replica

**replicación** nf *Biol* replication

**replicar** [61] **1** vt *(responder)* to answer; *(objetar)* to answer back, to retort
**2** vi *(objetar)* to answer back

**repliego** etc ver **replegar**

**repliegue** nm (a) *(retirada)* withdrawal, retreat (b) *(pliegue)* fold

**repoblación** nf *(con gente)* repopulation; *(con peces)* restocking; **r. forestal** reafforestation

**repoblar** [65] **1** vt *(con gente)* to repopulate; *(con peces)* to restock; *(con árboles)* to replant, to reafforest
**2 repoblarse** vpr *(gente)* to be repopulated (**de** with); *(peces)* to be restocked (**de** with); *(árboles)* to be replanted o reafforested (**de** with)

**repollo** nm cabbage

**reponer** [52] **1** vt (a) *(existencias, trabajador)* to replace (b) *Cine & Teatro* to re-run; *TV* to repeat (c) *(replicar)* **r. que** to reply that
**2 reponerse** vpr to recover (**de** from)

**reportaje** nm *Rad & TV* report; *Prensa* article; **r. gráfico** illustrated feature

**reportar 1** vt (a) *(traer)* to bring; **no le ha reportado más que problemas** it has caused him nothing but problems (b) *Méx (informar)* to report
**2 reportarse** vpr *(reprimirse)* to control oneself

**reporte** nm *Méx* report

**reportero, -a** nm,f reporter; **r. gráfico** press photographer

**reposacabezas** nm inv headrest

**reposado, -a** adj relaxed, calm

**reposapiés** nm inv footrest

**reposar** vi (a) *(descansar)* to (have a) rest (b) *(sedimentarse)* to stand (c) *Fig (yacer)* to lie

**reposera** nf *CSur* easy chair

**reposición** nf (a) *Cine* rerun; *Teatro* revival; *TV* repeat (b) *(de existencias, pieza)* replacement

**reposo** nm *(descanso)* rest; **en r.** *(cuerpo, persona)* at rest; *(máquina)* not in use; *Culin* standing

**repostar 1** vi *(coche)* to fill up; *(avión)* to refuel
**2** vt (a) *(gasolina)* to fill up with (b) *(provisiones)* to stock up on

**repostería** nf (a) *(establecimiento)* confectioner's (shop) (b) *(oficio, productos)* confectionery

**repostero, -a 1** nm,f *(persona)* confectioner
**2** nm *Andes (armario)* larder, pantry

**reprender** vt *(a niños)* to tell off; *(a empleados)* to reprimand

**reprensible** adj reprehensible

**reprensión** nf *(a niños)* telling-off; *(a empleados)* reprimand

**represa** nf dam

**represalia** nf reprisal; **tomar represalias** to retaliate, to take reprisals

**representación** nf (a) *también Com* representation; **en r. de** on behalf of; *Com* **tener la r. de** to act as a representative for (b) *Teatro* performance

**representante 1** adj representative
**2** nmf (a) *también Com* representative (b) *(de artista)* agent

**representar** vt (a) *también Com* to represent (b) *(aparentar)* to look; **representa unos 40 años** she looks about 40 (c) *(significar)* to mean; **representa el 50% del consumo interno** it accounts for 50% of domestic consumption (d) *Teatro (función)* to perform; *(papel)* to play

**representatividad** nf representativeness

**representativo, -a** adj representative

**represión** nf repression

**represivo, -a** adj repressive

**represor, -ora 1** adj repressive
**2** nm,f oppressor

**reprimenda** nf reprimand

**reprimido, -a 1** adj repressed
**2** nm,f repressed person

**reprimir 1** vt (a) *(llanto, risa)* to suppress (b) *(minorías, disidentes)* to repress
**2 reprimirse** vpr **reprimirse (de hacer algo)** to restrain oneself (from doing sth)

**reprís, reprise** *(pl reprises)* nm acceleration

**reprobable** adj reprehensible

**reprobación** nf reproof, censure

**reprobar** [65] vt to censure, to condemn

**reprobatorio, -a** *adj* reproving

**réprobo, -a 1** *adj* damned

**2** *nm,f* lost soul

**reprochar 1** *vt* r. algo a alguien to reproach sb for sth

**2 reprocharse** *vpr* reprocharse algo (uno mismo) to reproach oneself for sth

**reproche** *nm* reproach; hacer un r. a alguien to reproach sb

**reproducción** *nf* reproduction; tratamiento de r. asistida fertility treatment

**reproducir** [20] **1** *vt también Arte* to reproduce; (gestos) to copy, to imitate

**2 reproducirse** *vpr* (a) (volver a suceder) to recur (b) (procrear) to reproduce

**reproductor, -ora** *adj* reproductive

**reprografía** *nf* reprographics; (servicio de) r. copying service

**repruebo** *etc ver* **reprobar**

**reptar** *vi* to crawl

**reptil** *nm* reptile

**república** *nf* republic

**República Centroafricana** *nf* Central African Republic

**República Checa** *nf* Czech Republic

**República Dominicana** *nf* Dominican Republic

**republicanismo** *nm* republicanism

**republicano, -a** *adj & nm,f* republican

**repudiar** [15] *vt* (a) (condenar) to condemn (b) (rechazar) to disown

**repudio** *nm* (a) (condena) condemnation (b) (rechazo) disowning

**repueblo** *etc ver* **repoblar**

**repuesto, -a 1** *participio ver* **reponer**

**2** *adj* recovered (de from)

**3** *nm* (provisión extra) reserve; Aut spare part; de r. spare, in reserve; la rueda de r. the spare wheel

**repugnancia** *nf* disgust

**repugnante** *adj* disgusting

**repugnar 1** *vt* me repugna ese olor/su actitud I find that smell/her attitude disgusting; me repugna hacerlo I'm loath to do it

**2** *vi* to be disgusting

**repujado, -a 1** *adj* embossed

**2** *nm* embossed work

**repujar** *vt* to emboss

**repulsa** *nf* (censura) condemnation

**repulsión** *nf* repulsion

**repulsivo, -a** *adj* repulsive

**repusiera** *etc ver* **reponer**

**reputación** *nf* reputation; tener mucha r. to be very famous

**reputado, -a** *adj* highly reputed

**reputar** *vt* to consider

**requemado, -a** *adj* burnt

**requemar 1** *vt* (quemar) to burn; (planta, tierra) to scorch

**2 requemarse** *vpr* to get burnt, to burn

**requerimiento** *nm* (a) (demanda) entreaty; a r. de on the request of (b) Der (intimación) writ, injunction; (aviso) summons (singular)

**requerir** [64] **1** *vt* (a) (necesitar) to require (b) (ordenar) to demand (c) (pedir) r. a alguien (para) que haga algo to ask sb to do sth (d) Der to order

**2 requerirse** *vpr* (ser necesario) to be required o necessary

**requesón** *nm* = ricotta-type cheese

**requiebro** *nm* flirtatious remark

**réquiem** (pl requiems) *nm* requiem

**requiero** *etc ver* **requerir**

**requiriera** *etc ver* **requerir**

**requisa** *nf* (a) (requisición) Mil requisition; (en aduana) seizure (b) (inspección) inspection

**requisar** *vt* Mil to requisition; (en aduana) to seize

**requisito** *nm* requirement; cumplir los requisitos to fulfil all the requirements; r. previo prerequisite

**res** (pl reses) *nf* (a) (animal) beast, animal (b) Am reses (ganado vacuno) cattle

**resabiado, -a** *adj* estar r. to be hardened; un caballo r. a vicious horse

**resabio** *nm* (a) (sabor) nasty aftertaste (b) (vicio) persistent bad habit

**resaca** *nf* (a) (de borrachera) hangover (b) (de las olas) undertow

**resalado, -a** *adj* Fam charming

**resaltar 1** *vi* (a) (destacar) to stand out (b) (en edificios) (balcón) to stick out; (decoración) to stand out

**2** *vt* (destacar) to highlight

**resarcir** [74] **1** *vt* r. a alguien (de) to compensate sb (for)

**2 resarcirse** *vpr* (daño, pérdida) to be compensated (de for); se resarció de la derrota del mes pasado he gained revenge for his defeat the previous month

**resbalada** *nf* Am Fam slip

**resbaladizo, -a** *adj también Fig* slippery

**resbalar 1** *vi* (a) (caer) to slip (con o en on) (b) (deslizarse) to slide (c) (estar resbaladizo) to be slippery

**2** *vt* Fam Fig resbalarle a alguien to leave sb cold

**3 resbalarse** *vpr* to slip (over)

**resbalón** *nm también Fig* slip; dar o pegar un r. to slip

**resbaloso, -a** *adj* slippery

**rescatar** vt (a) *(liberar, salvar)* to rescue; *(pagando rescate)* to ransom (b) *(recuperar) (herencia)* to recover

**rescate** nm (a) *(liberación, salvación)* rescue (b) *(dinero)* ransom (c) *(recuperación)* recovery

**rescindir** vt to rescind

**rescisión** nf cancellation

**rescoldo** nm ember; *Fig* lingering feeling, flicker

**resecar** [61] **1** vt (a) *(piel)* to dry out (b) *(tierra)* to parch

**2 resecarse** vpr (a) *(piel)* to dry out (b) *(tierra)* to become parched

**reseco, -a** adj (a) *(piel, garganta, pan)* very dry (b) *(tierra)* parched (c) *(flaco)* emaciated

**resentido, -a 1** adj bitter, resentful; **estar r. con alguien** to be really upset with sb

**2** nm,f bitter o resentful person

**resentimiento** nm resentment, bitterness

**resentirse** [64] vpr (a) *(debilitarse)* to be weakened; *(salud)* to deteriorate (b) *(sentir molestias)* **r. de** to be suffering from (c) *(ofenderse)* to be offended

**reseña** nf *(de libro, concierto)* review; *(de partido, conferencia)* report

**reseñar** vt (a) *(criticar) (libro, concierto)* to review; *(partido, conferencia)* to report on (b) *(describir)* to describe

**reseque** etc ver **resecar**

**reserva 1** nf (a) *(de hotel, avión)* reservation (b) *(provisión)* reserves; **tener algo de r.** to keep sth in reserve; **reservas** *(energía acumulada)* energy reserves; *(recursos)* resources; *Econ* **reservas de divisas** foreign currency; **reservas monetarias** monetary reserves

(c) *(objeción, cautela)* reservation; **sin reservas** without reservations

(d) *(discreción)* discretion

(e) *(de indígenas)* reservation

(f) *(de animales)* reserve; **r. natural** nature reserve

(g) *Mil* reserve; **pasar a la r.** to become a reservist

**2** nmf *Dep* reserve, substitute

**3** nm *(vino)* vintage (wine)

**reservado, -a 1** adj (a) *(mesa)* reserved (b) *(tema, asunto)* confidential (c) *(persona)* reserved

**2** nm *(en restaurante)* private room; *Ferroc* reserved compartment

**reservar 1** vt (a) *(billete, habitación)* to book, to reserve (b) *(guardar, apartar)* to set aside; **reservan la primera fila para los críticos** the front row is reserved for the critics (c) *(callar) (opinión, comentarios)* to reserve

**2 reservarse** vpr (a) *(esperar)* **reservarse para** to save oneself for (b) *(guardar para sí)*

*(secreto)* to keep to oneself; *(dinero, derecho)* to retain (for oneself)

**reservista** *Mil* **1** adj reserve; **militar r.** officer in the reserve

**2** nmf reservist

**resfriado, -a 1** adj **estar r.** to have a cold

**2** nm cold

**resfriarse** [34] vpr *(constiparse)* to catch a cold

**resfrío** nm *Am* cold

**resguardar 1** vt & vi **r. de** to protect against

**2 resguardarse** vpr *(en un portal)* to shelter (**de** from); *(con abrigo, paraguas)* to protect oneself (**de** against)

**resguardo** nm (a) *(documento)* receipt (b) *(protección)* protection; **al r. de** safe from

**residencia** nf (a) *(establecimiento) (de estudiantes)* hall of residence; *(de ancianos)* old people's home; *(de oficiales)* residence (b) *(hotel)* boarding house (c) *(hospital)* hospital (d) *(permiso para extranjeros)* residence permit (e) *(periodo de formación)* residency (f) *(estancia)* stay (g) *(localidad, domicilio)* residence

**residencial** adj residential; **barrio r.** *(lujoso)* residential area

**residente** adj & nmf resident

**residir** vi (a) *(vivir)* to reside (b) *(radicar)* to lie (**en** in), to reside (**en** in)

**residual** adj residual; **aguas residuales** sewage

**residuo** nm (a) *(material inservible)* waste; *Quím* residue; **residuos nucleares** nuclear waste (b) *(restos)* leftovers

**resiento** etc ver **resentirse**

**resignación** nf resignation

**resignarse** vpr **r. (a hacer algo)** to resign oneself (to doing sth)

**resina** nf resin

**resinoso, -a** adj resinous

**resintiera** etc ver **resentirse**

**resistencia** nf (a) *también Elec & Pol* resistance; **ofrecer r.** to put up resistance; **r. pasiva** passive resistance (b) *(de puente, cimientos)* strength (c) *(para correr, hacer deporte)* stamina

**resistente** adj *(fuerte)* tough, strong; **r. al calor** heat-resistant

**resistir 1** vt (a) *(dolor, peso, críticas)* to withstand (b) *(tentación, impulso, deseo)* to resist (c) *(tolerar)* to tolerate, to stand; **no lo resisto más, me voy** I can't stand it any longer, I'm off

**2** vi (a) *(ejército, ciudad)* **r. (a algo/a alguien)** to resist (sth/sb) (b) *(persona)* to keep going; **ese corredor resiste mucho** that runner has a lot of stamina; **r. a algo** to stand up to sth, to withstand sth (c) *(mesa, dique)* to take the strain; **r. a algo** to withstand sth (d) *(mostrarse firme)* *(ante tentaciones)* to resist (it); **r. a algo** to resist sth

**3 resistirse** *vpr* **resistirse (a algo)** to resist (sth); **resistirse a hacer algo** to refuse to do sth; **me resisto a creerlo** I refuse to believe it; **no hay hombre que se le resista** no man can resist her; **se le resisten las matemáticas** she just can't get the hang of maths

**resma** *nf* ream

**resol** *nm* (sun's) glare; **hace r.** it's cloudy but very bright

**resollar** [65] *vi (jadear)* to pant; *(respirar)* to breathe

**resolución** *nf* (a) *(solución) (de una crisis)* resolution; *(de un crimen)* solution (b) *(firmeza)* determination (c) *(decisión)* decision; *Der* ruling; **tomar una r.** to take a decision (d) *(de Naciones Unidas)* resolution

**resoluto, -a** *adj* resolute

**resolver** [43] **1** *vt* (a) *(solucionar) (duda, crisis)* to resolve; *(problema, caso)* to solve (b) *(decidir)* **r. hacer algo** to decide to do sth (c) *(partido, disputa, conflicto)* to settle

**2 resolverse** *vpr* (a) *(solucionarse) (duda, crisis)* to be resolved; *(problema, caso)* to be solved (b) *(decidirse)* **resolverse a hacer algo** to decide to do sth (c) *(en disputa, conflicto)* **resolverse en** to come to nothing more than

**resonancia** *nf* (a) *también Fís* resonance; *Med* **r. magnética** magnetic resonance (b) *Fig (importancia)* repercussions

**resonante** *adj (que suena, retumba)* resounding; *Fís* resonant; *Fig* important

**resonar** [65] *vi* to resound, to echo

**resoplar** *vi (de cansancio)* to pant; *(de enfado)* to snort

**resoplido** *nm (por cansancio)* pant; *(por enfado)* snort

**resorte** *nm* spring; *Fig* means; **tocar todos los resortes** to pull out all the stops

**respaldar 1** *vt* to back, to support

**2 respaldarse** *vpr Fig (apoyarse)* **respaldarse en** to fall back on

**respaldo** *nm* (a) *(de asiento)* back (b) *Fig (apoyo)* backing, support

**respectar** *v impersonal* **por** *o* **en lo que respecta a alguien/a algo** as far as sb/sth is concerned

**respectivo, -a** *adj* respective; **en lo r. a** with regard to

**respecto** *nm* **al r., a este r.** in this respect; **no sé nada al r.** I don't know anything about it; **(con) r. a, r. de** regarding

**respetabilidad** *nf* respectability

**respetable 1** *adj (venerable)* respectable

**2** *nm Fam (público)* **el r.** the audience

**respetar** *vt* (a) *(persona, costumbre)* to respect; *(la palabra)* to honour; **hacerse r.** to make oneself respected (b) *(no destruir)* to spare; **respetad las plantas** *(en letrero)* keep off the flowerbeds

**respeto** *nm* respect (**a** *o* **por** for); **es una falta de r.** it shows a lack of respect; **faltar al r. a alguien** to be disrespectful to sb; **por r. a** out of consideration for; **presentar uno sus respetos a alguien** to pay one's respects to sb

**respetuoso, -a** *adj* respectful (**con** of)

**respingar** [40] *vi (protestar)* to make a fuss, to complain

**respingo** *nm* (a) *(movimiento)* start, jump; **dar un r.** to start (b) *(contestación)* shrug (of annoyance)

**respingón, -ona** *adj (nariz)* snub; *(trasero)* pert

**respiración** *nf* breathing; *Med* respiration; **r. artificial** *o* **asistida** artificial respiration; **r. boca a boca** mouth-to-mouth resuscitation, the kiss of life; *Fig* **quedarse sin r.** *(asombrado)* to be stunned

**respiradero** *nm (hueco)* vent; *(conducto)* ventilation shaft

**respirar 1** *vt* (a) *(aire)* to breathe (b) *Fig (bondad)* to exude

**2** *vi* to breathe; *Fig (sentir alivio)* to breathe again; *Fig* **no dejar r. a alguien** not to allow sb a moment's peace; **sin r.** *(sin descanso)* without a break; *(atentamente)* with great attention

**respiratorio, -a** *adj* respiratory

**respiro** *nm* (a) *(descanso)* rest (b) *(alivio)* relief, respite

**resplandecer** [48] *vi* (a) *(brillar)* to shine (b) *Fig (destacar)* to shine, to stand out; **r. de algo** to shine with sth

**resplandeciente** *adj (brillante)* shining; *(sonrisa)* beaming; *(época)* glittering; *(vestimenta, color)* resplendent

**resplandor** *nm* (a) *(luz)* brightness; *(de fuego)* glow (b) *(brillo)* gleam

**responder 1** *vt (contestar)* to answer; *(con insolencia)* to answer back

**2** *vi* (a) *(contestar)* **r. (a algo)** to answer (sth); **responde al nombre de Toby** he answers to the name of Toby (b) *(reaccionar)* to respond (a to) (c) *(responsabilizarse)* **r. de algo/por alguien** to answer for sth/for sb; **¡no respondo de mis actos!** I can't be responsible for what I might do! (d) *(replicar)* to answer back (e) *(corresponder)* **r. a** to correspond to; **las medidas responden a la crisis** the measures are in keeping with the nature of the crisis

**respondón, -ona 1** *adj* insolent

**2** *nm,f* insolent person

**responsabilidad** *nf* responsibility; *Der* liability; **puesto de r.** responsible position; **tener la r. de algo** to be responsible for sth; *Der* **r. civil/penal** civil/criminal liability; **r. limitada** limited liability

**responsabilizar** [16] **1** *vt* **r. a alguien (de algo)** to hold sb responsible (for sth)

**2 responsabilizarse** *vpr* to accept responsibility (**de** for)

**responsable 1** *adj* responsible; **r. de** responsible for; **hacerse r. de** *(responsabilizarse de)* to take responsibility for; *(atentado, secuestro)* to claim responsibility for

**2** *nmf* (a) *(culpable, autor)* person responsible (b) *(encargado)* person in charge

**responso** *nm* prayer for the dead

**respuesta** *nf* (a) *(contestación)* answer, reply; *(en exámenes)* answer; **en r. a** in reply to (b) *Fig (reacción)* response

**resquebrajadura** *nf* crack

**resquebrajamiento** *nm* (a) *(grieta)* crack (b) *(cuarteamiento)* cracking; *Fig* crumbling

**resquebrajar 1** *vt* to crack

**2 resquebrajarse** *vpr (piedra, loza, plástico)* to crack; *(madera)* to split; *Fig* **se está resquebrajando la sociedad** society is beginning to fall apart

**resquemor** *nm* resentment, bitterness

**resquicio** *nm* (a) *(abertura)* chink; *(grieta)* crack (b) *Fig (pizca)* glimmer

**resta** *nf* *Mat* subtraction

**restablecer** [48] **1** *vt* to reestablish, to restore

**2 restablecerse** *vpr* (a) *(curarse)* to recover (**de** from) (b) *(reinstaurarse)* to be reestablished

**restablecimiento** *nm* (a) *(reinstauración)* restoration, reestablishment (b) *(cura)* recovery

**restallar** *vt & vi (látigo)* to crack; *(lengua)* to click

**restante** *adj* remaining; **lo r.** the rest

**restar 1** *vt* (a) *Mat* to subtract; **r. una cantidad de otra** to subtract one figure from another (b) *(disminuir)* **r. importancia a algo/méritos a alguien** to play down the importance of sth/sb's qualities

**2** *vi (faltar)* to be left

**restauración** *nf* restoration

**restaurador, -ora** *nm,f* restorer

**restaurante** *nm* restaurant

**restaurar** *vt* to restore

**restitución** *nf* return

**restituir** [36] **1** *vt* (a) *(devolver) (objeto)* to return; *(salud)* to restore (b) *(restaurar)* to restore

**2 restituirse** *vpr (regresar)* **restituirse a** to return to

**resto** *nm* (a) **el r.** the rest; *Mat* the remainder; *Fig* **echar el r.** to do one's utmost; **restos** *(sobras)* leftovers; *(cadáver)* remains; *(ruinas)* ruins; **restos mortales** mortal remains (b) *(en tenis)* return

**restregar** [45] **1** *vt (frotar)* to rub hard; *(para limpiar)* to scrub

**2 restregarse** *vpr (frotarse)* to rub

**restregón** *nm* scrub; **dar un r. a alguien** to give sb a scrub

**restricción** *nf* restriction; **restricciones de agua** water rationing; **restricciones eléctricas** power cuts

**restrictivo, -a** *adj* restrictive

**restringir** [26] *vt* to limit, to restrict

**resucitar 1** *vt (persona)* to bring back to life; *(costumbre)* to resurrect, to revive

**2** *vi (persona)* to rise from the dead

**resuello 1** *ver* **resollar**

**2** *nm (jadeo)* pant, panting; **quedarse sin r.** to be out of breath

**resuelto, -a 1** *participio ver* **resolver**

**2** *adj* (a) *(solucionado)* solved (b) *(decidido)* determined; **estar r. a hacer algo** to be determined to do sth

**resuelvo** *etc ver* **resolver**

**resueno** *etc ver* **resonar**

**resultado** *nm* result; **dar r.** to work (out), to have the desired effect; **dar buenos resultados** to work well

**resultante** *adj & nf* resultant

**resultar 1** *vi* (a) *(salir)* to turn out to) be; **¿cómo resultó?** how did it turn out?; **resultó un éxito** it was a success; **resultó ileso** he was uninjured; **nuestro equipo resultó vencedor** our team came out on top (b) *(originarse)* **r. de** to come of, to result from (c) *(ser)* to be; **resulta sorprendente** it's surprising; **me resultó imposible terminar antes** I was unable to finish earlier; **r. útil** to be useful

**2** *v impersonal (suceder)* **r. que** to turn out that; **ahora resulta que no quiere alquilarlo** now it seems that she doesn't want to rent it

**resultas** *nfpl* **de r. de** as a result of

**resultón, -ona** *adj Fam* attractive

**resumen** *nm* summary; **en r.** in short

**resumir 1** *vt (abreviar)* to summarize; *(discurso)* to sum up

**2 resumirse** *vpr* **se resume en pocas palabras** it can be summed up in a few words

**resurgimiento** *nm* resurgence

**resurgir** [26] *vi* to undergo a resurgence, to be revived

**resurrección** *nf* resurrection

**retablo** *nm* altarpiece

**retaco** *nm Fam* shorty, midget

**retaguardia** *nf (tropa)* rearguard; *(territorio)* rear

**retahíla** *nf* string, series

**retal** *nm* remnant

**retama** *nf* broom

**retar** *vt* to challenge (**a** to)

**retardado, -a** *adj* delayed

**retardar** *vt (retrasar)* to delay; *(frenar)* to hold up, to slow down

**retazo** *nm* remnant; *Fig* fragment

**rete-** *prefijo Am Fam* very

**retén** *nm* reserve

**retención** *nf* (**a**) *(en comisaría)* detention (**b**) *(en el sueldo)* deduction; **r. fiscal** tax (**c**) *(de tráfico)* hold-up, delay (**d**) *Med* retention

**retener** [67] *vt* (**a**) *(detener)* to hold back; *(en comisaría)* to detain (**b**) *(contener) (impulso, ira)* to hold back, to restrain; *(aliento)* to hold (**c**) *(conservar)* to retain (**d**) *(quedarse con)* to hold on to, to keep (**e**) *(memorizar)* to remember (**f**) *(deducir del sueldo)* to deduct

**retengo** *ver* **retener**

**reticencia** *nf* (**a**) *(resistencia)* unwillingness (**b**) *(insinuación)* insinuation, innuendo

**reticente** *adj* (**a**) *(reacio}* unwilling, reluctant (**b**) *(con insinuaciones)* full of insinuation

**retícula** *nf* reticle

**reticular** *adj Anat* reticular

**retículo** *nm* reticle

**retiene** *ver* **retener**

**retina** *nf* retina

**retintín** *nm* (**a**) *(ironía)* sarcastic tone; **con r.** sarcastically (**b**) *(tintineo)* ringing

**retirada** *nf* (**a**) *Mil* retreat; **batirse en r.** to beat a retreat; **cubrir la r.** *Mil* to cover the retreat; *Fig (tomar precauciones)* not to burn one's bridges, to cover oneself (**b**) *(de fondos, moneda, carné)* withdrawal (**c**) *(de competición, actividad)* withdrawal

**retirado, -a 1** *adj* (**a**) *(jubilado)* retired (**b**) *(solitario, alejado)* isolated, secluded
**2** *nm,f (jubilado)* retired person

**retirar 1** *vt* (**a**) *(quitar, sacar)* to remove; *(dinero, moneda, carné)* to withdraw; *(nieve)* to clear; *(mano)* to withdraw (**b**) *(jubilar) (a deportista)* to force to retire; *(a empleado)* to retire (**c**) *(retractarse de)* to take back
**2 retirarse** *vpr* (**a**) *(jubilarse)* to retire (**b**) *(de competición, elecciones)* to withdraw; *(de reunión)* to leave; *(irse a dormir)* to retire (for the evening) (**c**) *(de campo de batalla)* to retreat (**d**) *(apartarse)* to move away

**retiro** *nm* (**a**) *(jubilación)* retirement; *(pensión)* pension (**b**) *(refugio, ejercicio)* retreat

**reto** *nm* challenge

**retocar** [61] *vt (prenda de vestir)* to alter; **r. la pintura** to touch up the painting

**retoce** *etc ver* **retozar**

**retomar** *vt* to take up again

**retoño** *nm* (**a**) *Bot* sprout, shoot (**b**) *(hijo)* **mis retoños** my offspring

**retoque 1** *ver* **retocar**
**2** *nm (toque)* touching-up; *(de prenda de vestir)* alteration; **dar los últimos retoques a algo** to put the finishing touches to sth

**retorcer** [17] **1** *vt* (**a**) *(torcer) (brazo, alambre)* to twist; *(ropa, cuello)* to wring (**b**) *Fig (tergiversar)* to twist
**2 retorcerse** *vpr (de risa)* to double up (**de** with); *(de dolor)* to writhe about (**de** in)

**retorcido, -a** *adj* (**a**) *(torcido) (brazo, alambre)* twisted; *(ropa)* wrung out (**b**) *Fig (rebuscado)* complicated, involved (**c**) *Fig (malintencionado)* twisted, warped

**retórica** *nf Lit & Fig* rhetoric

**retórico, -a 1** *adj* rhetorical
**2** *nm,f (persona)* rhetorician

**retornable** *adj* returnable; **no r.** non-returnable

**retornar** *vt & vi* to return

**retorno** *nm también Informát* return; **r. de carro** carriage return

**retortijón** *nm* stomach cramp

**retozar** [16] *vi (niños, cachorros)* to gambol, to frolic; *(amantes)* to romp about

**retozón, -ona** *adj* playful

**retractación** *nf* retraction

**retractarse** *vpr (de una promesa)* to go back on one's word; *(de una opinión)* to take back what one has said; **r. de** *(lo dicho)* to retract, to take back

**retráctil** *adj (antena, brazo mecánico)* retractable; *(uña)* retractile

**retraer** [68] **1** *vt* (**a**) *(encoger)* to retract (**b**) *(disuadir)* **r. a alguien de hacer algo** to persuade sb not to do sth
**2 retraerse** *vpr* (**a**) *(encogerse)* to retract (**b**) *(aislarse, retroceder)* to withdraw, to retreat; **se retrae cuando hay extraños** he becomes very withdrawn in the company of strangers

**retraído, -a** *adj* withdrawn, retiring

**retraimiento** *nm* shyness, reserve

**retransmisión** *nf* broadcast; **r. en directo/diferido** live/recorded broadcast

**retransmitir** *vt* to broadcast

**retrasado, -a 1** *adj* **(a)** *(país, industria)* backward; *(reloj)* slow; *(tren)* late, delayed; **número r.** *(de periódico, revista)* back number *o* issue **(b)** *(en el pago, los estudios)* behind **(c)** *Med* retarded, backward

**2** *nm,f* **r. (mental)** mentally retarded person; *Fig (tonto)* retard

**retrasar 1** *vt* **(a)** *(aplazar)* to postpone **(b)** *(demorar)* to delay, to hold up **(c)** *(hacer más lento)* to slow down, to hold up **(d)** *(en el pago, los estudios)* to set back **(e)** *(reloj)* to put back **(f)** *Dep (balón)* to pass back

**2** *vi (reloj)* to be slow

**3 retrasarse** *vpr* **(a)** *(llegar tarde)* to be late **(b)** *(quedarse atrás)* to fall behind **(c)** *(aplazarse)* to be put off **(d)** *(reloj)* to lose time

**retraso** *nm* **(a)** *(demora)* delay; **llegar con (15 minutos de) r.** to be (15 minutes) late; **los trenes circulan hoy con (una hora de) r.** trains are running (an hour) late today **(b)** *(por sobrepasar un límite)* **el proyecto lleva dos semanas de r.** the project is two weeks behind schedule; **llevo en mi trabajo un r. de 20 páginas** I'm 20 pages behind with my work **(c)** *(subdesarrollo)* backwardness; **llevar (siglos de) r.** to be (centuries) behind; *Med* **r. mental** mental deficiency

**retratar 1** *vt* **(a)** *(fotografiar)* to photograph **(b)** *(dibujar)* to do a portrait of **(c)** *Fig (describir)* to portray

**2 retratarse** *vpr* **(a)** *Fig (describirse)* to describe oneself **(b)** *Fam (pagar)* to cough up

**retratista** *nmf Arte* portraitist; *Fot* (portrait) photographer

**retrato** *nm* **(a)** *(dibujo)* portrait; *(fotografía)* photograph; **ser el vivo r. de alguien** to be the spitting image of sb; **r. robot** photofit picture **(b)** *Fig (descripción)* portrayal

**retreta** *nf Mil* retreat

**retrete** *nm* toilet

**retribución** *nf (pago)* payment; *(recompensa)* reward

**retribuir** [36] *vt (pagar)* to pay; *(recompensar)* to reward

**retro** *adj* **(a)** *(estilo, moda)* retro **(b)** *Pol* reactionary

**retroactividad** *nf (de ley)* retroactivity; *(del pago)* backdating

**retroactivo, -a** *adj (ley)* retrospective, retroactive; *(pago)* backdated; **con efecto** *o* **con carácter r.** retroactively

**retroceder** *vi* to go back; *Fig* to back down; **no retrocederé ante nada** there's no stopping me now

**retroceso** *nm* **(a)** *(movimiento hacia atrás, regresión)* backward movement; *(de fusil, cañón)* recoil; *(en negociaciones)* setback; *(en la economía)* recession **(b)** *(en enfermedad)* deterioration

**retrógrado, -a** *adj Pey* backward-looking, hidebound; *Pol* reactionary

**retropropulsión** *nf* jet propulsion

**retroproyector** *nm* overhead projector

**retrospección** *nf* retrospection

**retrospectiva** *nf* retrospective

**retrospectivo, -a** *adj* retrospective; **echar una mirada retrospectiva a** to look back over

**retrotraer** [68] **1** *vt (relato)* to set in the past

**2 retrotraerse** *vpr (al pasado)* to cast one's mind back, to go back

**retrovisor** *nm* rear-view mirror

**retuerzo** *ver* **retorcer**

**retumbante** *adj* resounding

**retumbar** *vi (resonar)* to resound; *(hacer ruido)* to thunder, to boom; *Fam* **me retumban los oídos** my ears are ringing

**retuviera** *etc ver* **retener**

**reuma, reúma** *nm o nf* rheumatism

**reumático, -a** *adj & nm,f* rheumatic

**reumatismo** *nm* rheumatism

**reumatología** *nf* rheumatology

**reumatólogo, -a** *nm,f* rheumatologist

**reunificación** *nf* reunification

**reunificar** [61] **1** *vt* to reunify

**2 reunificarse** *vpr* to reunify

**reunión** *nf* **(a)** *(encuentro, asistentes)* meeting **(b)** *(recogida)* gathering, collection

**reunir 1** *vt* **(a)** *(público, tendencias)* to bring together **(b)** *(objetos, información)* to collect, to bring together; *(fondos)* to raise **(c)** *(requisitos, condiciones)* to meet, to fulfil; *(cualidades)* to possess, to combine **(d)** *(volver a unir)* to put back together

**2 reunirse** *vpr (congregarse, juntarse)* to meet; **reunirse con alguien** to meet sb

**reutilizable** *adj* reusable

**reutilizar** [16] *vt* to reuse

**reválida** *nf* **(a)** *Antes* = qualifying exam for higher stages of secondary education (taken at 14 and 16) **(b)** *Fig (confirmación)* **pasó la r. del título** he successfully defended the title

**revalidar** *vt* to confirm

**revalorización** *nf* **(a)** *(aumento del valor)* appreciation; *(de moneda)* revaluation **(b)** *(restitución del valor)* favourable reassessment

**revalorizar** [16] **1** vt (a) *(aumentar el valor de)* to increase the value of; *(moneda)* to revalue (b) *(restituir el valor de)* to reassess in a favourable light

**2 revalorizarse** vpr (a) *(aumentar de valor)* to appreciate; *(moneda)* to be revalued (b) *(recuperar valor)* to be reassessed favourably

**revancha** nf *(venganza)* revenge; **tomarse la r.** to take revenge

**revanchismo** nm vengefulness

**revelación** nf revelation

**revelado** nm Fot developing

**revelador, -ora 1** adj *(aclarador)* revealing
**2** nm Fot developer

**revelar 1** vt (a) *(descubrir)* to reveal (b) *(manifestar)* to show (c) Fot to develop
**2 revelarse** vpr **revelarse como** to show oneself to be

**revendedor, -ora** nm,f ticket tout

**revender** vt *(productos, bienes)* to resell; *(entradas)* to tout

**reventa** nf *(de productos, bienes)* resale; *(de entradas)* touting

**reventado, -a** adj Fam *(cansado)* shattered, whacked

**reventador** nm *(boicoteador)* heckler

**reventar** [3] **1** vt (a) *(explotar)* to burst (b) *(echar abajo)* to break down; *(con explosivos)* to blow up (c) *(hacer fracasar)* to ruin, to spoil; *(boicotear)* to disrupt (d) Fam *(cansar mucho)* to shatter (e) Fam *(fastidiar)* to annoy
**2** vi (a) *(explotar)* to burst (b) *(estar lleno)* **r. de** to be bursting with (c) *(desear mucho)* **r. por hacer algo** to be bursting to do sth (d) Fam Fig *(perder los nervios)* to explode (de with)
**3 reventarse** vpr (a) *(explotar)* to explode; *(rueda, tuberías)* to burst (b) Fam *(cansarse)* to get whacked, to tire oneself to death

**reventón** nm (a) *(pinchazo)* blowout, US flat, Br puncture (b) *(estallido)* burst

**reverberación** nf *(de sonido)* reverberation; *(de luz, calor)* reflection

**reverberar** vi *(sonido)* to reverberate; *(luz, calor)* to reflect

**reverdecer** [48] vi (a) *(campos)* to become green again (b) Fig *(interés, sentimientos)* to revive

**reverencia** nf (a) *(respeto)* reverence (b) *(saludo) (inclinación)* bow; *(flexión de piernas)* curtsy (c) *(tratamiento)* **su r.** Your/His Reverence

**reverenciar** [15] vt to revere

**reverendo, -a** adj & nm reverend

**reverente** adj reverent

**reversibilidad** nf reversibility

**reversible** adj reversible

**reverso** nm *(parte de atrás)* back, other side; *(de moneda, medalla)* reverse; **ser el r. de la medalla** to be the other side of the coin

**revertir** [64] vi (a) *(resultar)* **r. en** to result in; **r. en beneficio/perjuicio de** to be to the advantage/detriment of (b) *(volver)* **r. a** to revert to

**revés** *(pl reveses)* nm (a) *(parte opuesta) (de papel, mano)* back; *(de tela)* other side, wrong side; **al r.** *(en sentido contrario)* the wrong way round; *(en forma opuesta)* the other way round; **del r.** *(lo de detrás, delante)* the wrong way round, back to front; *(lo de dentro, fuera)* inside out; *(lo de arriba, abajo)* upside down (b) *(contratiempo)* setback, blow (c) *(bofetada)* slap (d) Dep backhand

**revestimiento** nm *(por fuera)* covering; *(por dentro)* lining

**revestir** [49] **1** vt (a) *(recubrir)* to cover; *(con pintura)* to coat; *(con forro)* to line (b) *(poseer) (solemnidad, gravedad)* to take on, to have (c) Fig *(adornar)* to dress up (de in), to adorn (de with) (d) Fig *(disfrazar)* to disguise, to cover up
**2 revestirse** vpr **revestirse de** *(actitud)* to arm oneself with

**reviento** etc ver **reventar**

**revierta** etc ver **revertir**

**revirtiera** etc ver **revertir**

**revisar** vt (a) *(repasar)* to go over again (b) *(inspeccionar)* to inspect; *(cuentas)* to audit (c) *(modificar)* to revise

**revisión** nf (a) *(repaso)* revision (b) *(inspección)* inspection; Aut service; **r. de cuentas** audit; **r. médica** check-up (c) *(modificación)* amendment

**revisionismo** nm revisionism

**revisionista** nmf revisionist

**revisor, -ora** nm,f *(en tren, autobús)* ticket inspector

**revista 1** ver **revestir**
**2** nf (a) *(publicación)* magazine; *(académica)* journal; **r. del corazón** gossip magazine (b) *(espectáculo teatral)* revue (c) *(inspección)* **pasar r. a** Mil to inspect, to review; *(examinar)* to examine

**revistero** nm *(mueble)* magazine rack

**revistiera** etc ver **revestir**

**revitalizar** [16] vt to revitalize

**revival** [rri'βaiβal] nm inv revival

**revivificar** [61] vt to revive

**revivir 1** vi también Fig to revive
**2** vt Fig *(recordar)* to revive memories of; *(resucitar)* to revive, to rekindle

**revocable** adj revocable

**revocación** nf revocation

**revocar** [61] *vt* (a) *(orden, decisión)* to revoke (b) *Constr* to plaster

**revolcar** [69] **1** *vt* to throw to the ground, to upend

**2 revolcarse** *vpr* (a) *(por el suelo)* to roll about (b) *Fam (amantes)* to roll around *(kissing and canoodling)*

**revolcón** *nm* (a) *(caída)* tumble, fall (b) *Fam (juegos amorosos)* **darse un r.** to roll around *(kissing and canoodling)*

**revolotear** *vi* (a) *(pájaro, mariposa)* to flutter (about) (b) *Fig (persona)* to flit about

**revoloteo** *nm* (a) *(de pájaro, mariposa)* fluttering (about) (b) *Fig (de persona)* flitting about

**revoltijo, revoltillo** *nm* jumble

**revoltoso, -a 1** *adj (rebelde)* rebellious; *(travieso)* naughty

**2** *nm,f (alborotador)* troublemaker; *(sedicioso)* rebel; *(travieso)* rascal

**revolución** *nf* revolution

**revolucionar** *vt* (a) *(agitar) (crear conflicto en)* to cause uproar in; *(crear excitación en)* to cause a stir in; **¡no revoluciones a los niños!** don't get the children all excited! (b) *(transformar)* to revolutionize

**revolucionario, -a** *adj & nm,f* revolutionary

**revolver** [43] **1** *vt* (a) *(mezclar) (líquido)* to stir; *(ensalada)* to toss; *(objetos)* to mix (b) *(desorganizar)* to turn upside down, to mess up; *(cajones)* to turn out (c) *(irritar)* to upset; **me revuelve el estómago** *o* **las tripas** it makes my stomach turn

**2** *vi* **r. en** *(armario, pasado)* to rummage around in

**3 revolverse** *vpr* (a) *(moverse) (en un sillón)* to shift about; *(en la cama)* to toss and turn; **revolverse contra alguien** to turn on sb (b) *(el mar)* to become rough; *(el tiempo)* to turn stormy

**revólver** ( *pl* **revólveres**) *nm* revolver

**revoque** *etc ver* **revocar**

**revuelco** *etc ver* **revolcar**

**revuelo** *nm (agitación)* commotion; **armar** *o* **causar un gran r.** to cause a stir

**revuelque** *etc ver* **revolcar**

**revuelta** *nf* (a) *(disturbio)* riot, revolt (b) *(curva)* bend

**revuelto, -a 1** *participio ver* **revolver**

**2** *adj* (a) *(desordenado) (habitación)* upside down, in a mess; *(época)* troubled, turbulent; *(pelo)* dishevelled (b) *(mezclado)* mixed up; **viven todos revueltos** they live on top of one another; **huevos revueltos** scrambled eggs (c) *(clima)* unsettled; *(aguas)* choppy, rough

**3** *nm Culin* scrambled eggs; **r. de espárragos** = scrambled egg with asparagus

**revuelvo** *etc ver* **revolver**

**revulsión** *nf* revulsion

**revulsivo, -a 1** *adj Fig* stimulating, revitalizing

**2** *nm Fig* kick-start, stimulus

**rey** *nm* king; **hablando del r. de Roma** talk *o* speak of the devil; **los Reyes** the King and Queen; **(Día de) Reyes** Twelfth Night; **los Reyes Católicos** the Spanish Catholic monarchs Ferdinand V and Isabella; **los Reyes Magos** the Three Kings, the Three Wise Men

**reyerta** *nf* fight, brawl

**rezagado, -a 1** *adj* **ir r.** to lag behind

**2** *nm,f* straggler

**rezagarse** [40] *vpr* to lag *o* fall behind

**rezar** [16] **1** *vt (oración)* to say

**2** *vi* (a) *(orar)* to pray (a to); **r. por alguien/algo** to pray for sb/sth (b) *(decir)* to read, to say (c) *Fam (tener que ver)* **esto no reza conmigo** that has nothing to do with me

**rezo** *nm* (a) *(acción)* praying (b) *(oración)* prayer

**rezongar** [40] *vi* to grumble, to moan

**rezumar 1** *vt* (a) *(transpirar)* to ooze (b) *Fig (manifestar)* to be overflowing with

**2** *vi* to ooze *o* seep out

**RFA** *nf (abrev de* **República Federal de Alemania***)* FRG

**Rhin** *nm* = **Rin**

**ría 1** *ver* **reír**

**2** *nf* ria, = long narrow sea inlet, especially those found in Galicia

**riachuelo** *nm* brook, stream

**Riad** *n* Riyadh

**riada** *nf también Fig* flood

**ribazo** *nm (terreno inclinado)* slope; *(del río)* sloping bank

**ribeiro** *nm* = wine from the province of Orense, Spain

**ribera** *nf (del río)* bank; *(del mar)* shore; **la r. del Ebro** the banks of the Ebro

**ribereño, -a 1** *adj (de río)* riverside; *(de mar)* coastal

**2** *nm,f* = person who lives by a river

**ribete** *nm* edging, trimming; *Fig* **ribetes** touches, nuances; **tener ribetes de poeta/orador** to be something of a poet/an orator

**ribeteado, -a** *adj* edged, trimmed

**ribetear** *vt* to edge, to trim

**ribonucleico** *adj Biol* **ácido r.** ribonucleic acid

**ricachón, -ona** *nm,f Pey* filthy *o* stinking rich person

**ricamente** *adv* **tan r.** quite happily

**rice** *etc ver* **rizar**

**ricino** *nm (planta)* castor oil plant

**rico, -a 1** *adj* **(a)** *(adinerado)* rich **(b)** *(abundante)* rich **(en** in**) (c)** *(fértil)* fertile, rich **(d)** *(sabroso)* delicious **(e)** *(simpático)* cute **(f)** *Fam (apelativo)* **¡oye r.!** hey, sunshine!

**2** *nm,f* rich person; **los ricos** the rich; **los nuevos ricos** the nouveaux riches

**rictus** *nm inv (de dolor)* wince; *(de ironía)* smirk; *(de desprecio)* sneer; **un r. de amargura** a bitter expression

**ricura** *nf Fam* **(a)** *(persona)* delight, lovely person; **¡qué r. de niño!** what a lovely *o* charming child! **(b)** *(guiso)* **¡qué r. de sopa!** what delicious soup!

**ridiculez** *nf* **(a)** *(payasada)* silly thing, nonsense **(b)** *(nimiedad)* trifle; **cuesta una r.** it costs next to nothing

**ridiculizar** [16] *vt* to ridicule

**ridículo, -a 1** *adj (irrisorio)* ridiculous; *(precio, suma)* laughable, derisory

**2** *nm* ridicule; **hacer el r.** to make a fool of oneself; **poner** *o* **dejar en r. a alguien** to make sb look stupid; **quedar en r.** to look like a fool

**ríe** *ver* **reír**

**riego 1** *ver* **regar**

**2** *nm (de campo)* irrigation; *(de jardín)* watering; **r. sanguíneo** (blood) circulation

**riegue** *etc ver* **regar**

**riel** *nm* **(a)** *(de vía)* rail **(b)** *(de cortina)* (curtain) rail

**rienda** *nf* **(a)** *(de caballería)* rein; *Fig* **comer a r. suelta** to eat one's fill; *Fig* **dar r. suelta a** to give free rein to **(b)** *Fig (dirección)* **aflojar las riendas** to ease up; **llevar** *o* **tener las riendas** to hold the reins, to be in control **(c)** *(moderación)* restraint

**riera** *etc ver* **reír**

**riesgo** *nm* risk; **a todo r.** *(seguro, póliza)* comprehensive; **correr (el) r. de** to run the risk of; **a r. de** at the risk of

**rifa** *nf* raffle

**rifar 1** *vt* to raffle

**2 rifarse** *vpr Fig* to fight over, to contest

**rifirrafe** *nm Fam* skirmish, flare-up

**rifle** *nm* rifle

**Riga** *n* Riga

**rige** *ver* **regir**

**rigidez** *nf* **(a)** *(de objeto, material)* rigidity **(b)** *(de pierna, brazo)* stiffness **(c)** *(del rostro)* stoniness **(d)** *Fig (severidad)* strictness, harshness

**rígido, -a** *adj* **(a)** *(objeto, material)* rigid **(b)** *(pierna, brazo)* stiff **(c)** *(rostro)* stony **(d)** *(severo) (normas)* harsh; *(carácter)* inflexible

**rigiera** *etc ver* **regir**

**rigor** *nm* **(a)** *(severidad)* strictness **(b)** *(exactitud)* accuracy, rigour; **en r.** strictly (speaking); **de r.** essential **(c)** *(inclemencia)* harshness **(d)** *(rigidez)* **r. mortis** rigor mortis

**rigurosidad** *nf* **(a)** *(severidad)* strictness **(b)** *(exactitud)* accuracy, rigour **(c)** *(inclemencia)* harshness

**riguroso, -a** *adj* **(a)** *(severo)* strict **(b)** *(exacto)* rigorous, disciplined **(c)** *(inclemente)* harsh

**rijo** *etc ver* **regir**

**rijoso, -a** *adj* **(a)** *(pendenciero)* always getting into fights **(b)** *(lujurioso)* lustful

**rima** *nf* rhyme

**rimar** *vt & vi* to rhyme

**rimbombancia** *nf* **(a)** *(de estilo, frases)* pomposity **(b)** *(de desfile, fiesta)* razzmatazz

**rimbombante** *adj* **(a)** *(estilo, frases)* pompous **(b)** *(desfile, fiesta)* spectacular

**rímel** *nm* mascara

**Rin, Rhin** *nm* **el R.** the Rhine

**rincón** *nm* corner *(inside)*

**rinconera** *nf* corner piece

**rindiera** *etc ver* **rendir**

**rindo** *etc ver* **rendir**

**ring** [rrin] *(pl* **rings**) *nm* (boxing) ring

**rinitis** *nf inv Med* rhinitis

**rinoceronte** *nm* rhinoceros, rhino

**riña 1** *ver* **reñir**

**2** *nf (disputa)* quarrel; *(pelea)* fight

**riñera** *etc ver* **reñir**

**riñón** *nm* kidney; **r. artificial** kidney machine; *Fig* **costar** *o* **valer un r.** to cost/be worth a fortune; *Fam Fig* **tener el r. bien cubierto** to be well-heeled; **riñones** *(región lumbar)* lower back

**riñonada** *nf (región lumbar)* lower back

**riñonera** *nf (pequeño bolso) Br* bum bag, *US* fanny pack

**río 1** *ver* **reír**

**2** *nm también Fig* river; **ir r. arriba/abajo** to go upstream/downstream; **¡de perdidos, al r.!** what the hell!; *Prov* **a r. revuelto, ganancia de pescadores** it's an ill wind that blows nobody any good; *Prov* **cuando el r. suena, agua lleva** there's no smoke without fire

**Río de Janeiro** *nm* Rio de Janeiro

**Río de la Plata** *nm* River Plate

**rioja** *nm* Rioja (wine)

**riojano, -a** *adj & nm,f* Riojan

**rioplatense** *adj* of/from the River Plate region

**RIP** [rrip] *(abrev de* **requiescat in pace**) RIP

**ripio** *nm* **(a)** *Lit* = word or phrase included to complete a rhyme; *Fig (relleno)* padding; **no perder r.** to be all ears **(b)** *(cascote)* rubble

**riqueza** nf (a) (fortuna) wealth (b) (abundancia) richness

**risa** nf laughter; **me da r.** I find it funny; **¡qué r.!** how funny!; Fam Fig **caerse** o **morirse** o **partirse de r.** to die laughing, to split one's sides (laughing); **se me escapó la r.** I burst out laughing; **se oían risas** laughter could be heard; **tiene una r. muy contagiosa** she has a very infectious laugh; **tomar algo a r.** to take sth as a joke

**risco** nm cliff, crag

**risible** adj laughable

**risotada** nf guffaw; **soltar una r.** to let out a guffaw, to guffaw

**ristra** nf también Fig string; **r. de ajos** string of garlic

**ristre** nm **en r.** at the ready

**risueño, -a** adj (a) (alegre) smiling (b) (próspero) sunny, promising

**rítmico, -a** adj rhythmic

**ritmo** nm (a) (compás, repetición) rhythm, beat; (cardíaco) beat (b) (velocidad) pace

**rito** nm (a) Rel rite (b) (costumbre) ritual

**ritual** adj & nm ritual

**rival** adj & nmf rival

**rivalidad** nf rivalry

**rivalizar** [16] vi to compete (**con/por** with/for)

**rivera** nf brook, stream

**rizado, -a** 1 adj (a) (pelo) curly (b) (mar) choppy

2 nm (en peluquería) **hacerse un r.** to have one's hair curled

**rizar** [16] 1 vt (a) (pelo) to curl (b) (mar) to ripple

2 **rizarse** vpr (a) (pelo) to curl (b) (mar) to get choppy

**rizo, -a** 1 adj (a) (pelo) curly (b) (mar) choppy

2 nm (a) (de pelo) curl (b) (del agua) ripple (c) (de avión) loop; **rizar el r.** to loop the loop; Fig (complicar) to overcomplicate (things); Fig **para rizar el r. hizo un doble salto mortal** as if all that wasn't impressive enough, he performed a double somersault (d) (tela) towelling, terry

**RNE** nf (abrev de **Radio Nacional de España**) = Spanish national radio station

**roast-beef** [rros'βif] (pl **roast-beefs**) nm roast beef

**róbalo, robalo** nm sea bass

**robar** vt (a) (sustraer) to steal; (casa) to burgle; **r. a alguien** to rob sb; Fig **r. el corazón a alguien** to steal sb's heart (b) (en naipes) to draw (c) (cobrar caro) to rob

**roble** nm (a) (árbol, madera) oak (b) Fig (persona) strong person

**robledal, robledo** nm oak wood o grove

**robo** nm (a) (atraco, hurto) robbery, theft; (en casa) burglary; **r. a mano armada** armed robbery; **ser un r.** (precios) to be daylight robbery (b) (cosa robada) stolen goods

**robot** (pl **robots**) nm también Informát robot; **r. de cocina** food processor; **actuar como un r.** to behave like a machine o robot

**robótica** nf robotics (singular)

**robotización** nf automation

**robotizar** [16] vt to automate

**robustecer** [48] 1 vt to strengthen

2 **robustecerse** vpr to get stronger

**robustez** nf robustness

**robusto, -a** adj robust

**roca** nf rock

**rocalla** nf rubble

**rocambolesco, -a** adj fantastic, incredible; **nos sucedió una aventura rocambolesca** the most incredible series of things happened to us

**roce** 1 ver **rozar**

2 nm (a) (contacto) rubbing; Fís friction; **el r. de la seda contra su piel** the feel of the silk against her skin; **el r. de su mano en la mejilla** the touch of his hand on her cheek

(b) (desgaste) **el r. de la silla con la pared ha desgastado la pintura** the back of the chair has worn away some of the paint on the wall; **el r. del viento en la piedra** the weathering effect of the wind on the stone

(c) (rasguño) (en piel) graze; (en madera, zapato) scuffmark; (en metal) scratch

(d) (trato) close contact

(e) (desavenencia) brush, quarrel; **tener un r. con alguien** to have a brush with sb

**rociada** nf (a) (rocío) dew (b) (aspersión) sprinkling (c) (de insultos, perdigones) shower

**rociar** [34] 1 vt (a) (arrojar gotas) to sprinkle; (con espray) to spray (b) (arrojar cosas) **r. algo/alguien (de)** to shower sth/sb (with)

2 v impersonal (caer rocío) **roció anoche** a dew fell last night

**rocín** nm nag

**rocío** nm dew

**rock** nm inv rock; **r. duro** hard rock

**rock and roll** nm inv rock and roll

**rocker** nm Fam rocker

**rockero, -a** 1 adj rock; **grupo r.** rock band

2 nm,f (a) (músico) rock musician (b) (fan) rock fan

**rococó** adj inv & nm rococo

**rocoso, -a** adj rocky

**roda** nf Náut stem

**rodaballo** nm turbot

**rodada** nf tyre track

**rodado, -a** adj (a) (por carretera) road; **tráfico r.** road traffic (b) (piedra) rounded (c) (expresiones) **estar muy r.** (persona) to be very experienced; **venir r. para** to be the perfect opportunity to

**rodaja** nf slice; **en rodajas** sliced

**rodaje** nm (a) (filmación) shooting (b) (de motor) running-in (c) (experiencia) experience

**rodamiento** nm bearing

**Ródano** nm **el R.** the (River) Rhone

**rodapié** nm skirting board

**rodar** [65] **1** vi (a) (deslizar) to roll (b) (circular) to travel, to go (c) (girar) to turn (d) (caer) to tumble (**por** down) (e) (ir de un lado a otro) to go around (f) Cine to shoot

**2** vt (a) Cine to shoot (b) (automóvil) to run in

**Rodas** n Rhodes

**rodear 1** vt (a) (poner o ponerse alrededor) to surround; **le rodeó el cuello con los brazos** she put her arms around his neck (b) (dar la vuelta a) to go around (c) (eludir) to skirt around

**2 rodearse de** vpr to surround oneself with

**rodeo** nm (a) (camino largo) detour; **dar un r.** to make a detour (b) (evasiva) **rodeos** evasiveness; **andar** o **ir con rodeos** to beat about the bush; **hablar sin rodeos** to come straight to the point (c) (espectáculo) rodeo (d) (reunión de ganado) rounding up

**rodete** nm round pad

**rodilla** nf knee; **de rodillas** on one's knees; **doblar** o **hincar la r.** (arrodillarse) to go down on one knee; Fig to bow (down), to humble oneself; **hincarse de rodillas** to kneel (down)

**rodillera** nf (a) (protección) knee pad (b) (remiendo) knee patch

**rodillo** nm (a) (para amasar) rolling pin (b) (en máquina) roller (c) (para pintar) (paint) roller

**rododendro** nm rhododendron

**rodrigón** nm stake, prop

**rodríguez** nm inv Fam grass widower; **estar** o **quedarse de r.** to be a grass widower

**roedor, -ora 1** adj Zool rodent; **animal r.** rodent

**2** nm rodent

**roedura** nf (a) (acción) gnawing (b) (señal) gnaw mark

**roer** [59] vt (a) (con dientes) to gnaw (at) (b) Fig (gastar) to eat away (at) (c) Fig (atormentar) to nag o gnaw (at) (d) **ser duro de r.** to be a tough nut to crack

**rogar** [18] vt (implorar) to beg; (pedir) to ask; **r. a alguien que haga algo** to ask o beg sb to do sth; **le ruego (que) me perdone** I beg your pardon; **hacerse (de) r.** to play hard to get; **se ruega silencio** (en letrero) silence, please

**rogativa** nf rogation

**rogué** etc ver **rogar**

**rojez** nf (a) (cualidad) redness (b) (en la piel) (red) blotch

**rojizo, -a** adj reddish

**rojo, -a 1** adj red; **ponerse r.** (semáforo) to turn red; (ruborizarse) to blush

**2** nm,f Pol red

**3** nm (color) red; **al r. vivo** (incandescente) red hot; Fig heated

**rol** (pl **roles**) nm (a) (papel) role; **juegos de r.** (técnica terapéutica, de enseñanza) role-play; (juegos de fantasía) fantasy roleplaying games (b) Náut muster

**rollizo, -a** adj chubby, plump

**rollo** nm (a) (cilindro) roll; Culin r. de primavera spring roll

(b) Cine reel

(c) Fam (pesadez, aburrimiento) drag, bore; **¡qué r.!** what a bore o drag!; **un r. de discurso/tío** an incredibly boring speech/guy; **el r. de costumbre** the same old story; **soltar el r.** to go on and on; **tener mucho r.** to witter on

(d) (embuste) tall story; **meter un r. a alguien** (engañar) to put one over on sb; **r. patatero** (mentira) ridiculous spiel

(e) Fam (tema, historia) stuff; (ambiente, tipo de vida) scene; **¿de qué va el r.?** what's it all about?; **no me va ese r.** it's not my scene, I'm not into all that; **¡vamos, suelta el r.!** come on, out with it!

(f) Fam (relación) relationship; **tener un r. (con)** to have a fling (with); **tener buen/mal r. (con alguien)** to get on/not to get on (with sb)

**ROM** [rrom] nf (abrev de **read-only memory**) ROM

**Roma** n Rome; Prov **todos los caminos llevan a R.** all roads lead to Rome

**romance 1** adj Romance

**2** nm (a) Ling Romance language (b) Lit romance (c) (idilio) romance

**romancero** nm Lit collection of romances

**románico, -a 1** adj (a) Arquit & Arte Romanesque (b) Ling Romance

**2** nm **el (estilo) r.** the Romanesque (style)

**romanización** nf Romanization

**romanizar** [16] vt to Romanize

**romano, -a 1** adj Roman; Rel Roman Catholic

**2** nm,f Roman

**romanticismo** nm (a) Arte, Hist & Lit Romanticism (b) (sentimentalismo) romanticism

**romántico, -a** adj & nm,f (a) Arte & Lit Romantic (b) (sentimental) romantic

**romanza** nf Mús ballad

**rombo** nm (figura) rhombus; Imprenta lozenge

**romeo** nm Fig = person very much in love

**romería** *nf* (a) *(peregrinación)* pilgrimage (b) *(fiesta)* = open-air festivities to celebrate a religious event (c) *Fig (mucha gente)* throng, crowd

**romero, -a 1** *nm,f (peregrino)* pilgrim
**2** *nm (arbusto, condimento)* rosemary

**romo, -a** *adj* (a) *(sin filo)* blunt (b) *(de nariz)* snub-nosed

**rompecabezas** *nm inv* (a) *(juego)* jigsaw (b) *Fam (problema)* puzzle

**rompehielos** *nm inv* ice-breaker

**rompeolas** *nm inv* breakwater

**romper 1** *vt* (a) *(partir, fragmentar)* to break; *(hacer añicos)* to smash; *(rasgar)* to tear (b) *(estropear)* to break (c) *(desgastar)* to wear out (d) *(interrumpir) (monotonía, silencio, hábito)* to break; *(hilo del discurso)* to break off; *(tradición)* to put an end to, to stop (e) *(terminar)* to break off
**2** *vi* (a) *(terminar una relación)* **r. (con alguien)** to break up *o* split up (with sb); **r. con la tradición** she broke with tradition; **rompió con el partido** she broke with the party (b) *(empezar) (día)* to break; *(hostilidades)* to break out; **al r. el alba** *o* **día** at daybreak; **r. a hacer algo** to suddenly start doing sth; **r. a llorar** to burst into tears; **r. a reír** to burst out laughing (c) *(olas)* to break (d) *Fam* **es una mujer de rompe y rasga** she's a woman who knows what she wants *o* knows her own mind
**3 romperse** *vpr* (a) *(partirse)* to break; *(rasgarse)* to tear; **se ha roto una pierna** he has broken a leg (b) *(estropearse)* to break; **se ha roto la tele** the TV is broken (c) *(desgastarse)* to wear out

**rompiente** *nm* reef, shoal

**rompimiento** *nm (rotura)* breaking; *(de relaciones)* breaking-off

**ron** *nm* rum

**roncar** [61] *vi* to snore

**roncha** *nf* lump *(on skin)*

**ronco, -a** *adj (persona, voz)* hoarse; *(sonido)* harsh

**ronda** *nf* (a) *(de vigilancia)* patrol; **salir de r.** to go out on patrol (b) *(de visitas)* **hacer la r.** to do one's rounds; **salir de r.** *(músico)* to go (out) serenading (c) *(de conversaciones, en el juego)* round; *Fam* **pagar una r.** *(de bebidas)* to buy a round (d) *(avenida)* avenue; **r. de circunvalación** ring road (e) *Dep (carrera ciclista)* tour; **la r. francesa** the Tour de France

**rondalla** *nf* group of minstrels

**rondar 1** *vt* (a) *(vigilar)* to patrol (b) *(parecer próximo)* **me está rondando un resfriado** I've got a cold coming on; **le ronda el sueño** he's about to drop off (c) *(cortejar)* to court (d) *(edad, cifra)* to be around; **ronda los cuarenta años** he's about forty

**2** *vi (merodear)* to wander (**por** around); **me ronda una idea por la cabeza** I've been turning over an idea in my head

**rondón** *nm Fam* **entrar de r.** to barge in

**rondín** *nm Andes* (a) *(vigilante)* watchman, guard (b) *(armónica)* mouth organ

**ronque** *etc ver* **roncar**

**ronquear** *vi* to be hoarse

**ronquera** *nf* hoarseness

**ronquido** *nm* snore, snoring

**ronroneante** *adj* purring

**ronronear** *vi* to purr

**ronroneo** *nm* purr, purring

**roña 1** *adj Fam (tacaño)* stingy, tight
**2** *nmf Fam (tacaño)* stingy person
**3** *nf* (a) *(suciedad)* filth, dirt (b) *Fam (tacañería)* stinginess (c) *(enfermedad de animal)* mange

**roñería** *nf Fam* stinginess

**roñica** *Fam* **1** *adj* stingy, tight
**2** *nmf* stingy person

**roñoso, -a 1** *adj* (a) *(sucio)* dirty (b) *Fam (tacaño)* mean, tight-fisted
**2** *nm,f Fam* mean person, skinflint

**ropa** *nf* clothes; **ligero de r.** scantily clad; *Fig* **lavar la r. sucia en público** to wash one's dirty linen in public; *Fig* **nadar y guardar la r.** to cover one's back; **r. de abrigo** warm clothes; **r. blanca** linen; **r. de cama** bed linen; **r. deportiva** sportswear; **r. hecha** ready-to-wear clothes; **r. interior** underwear; **r. usada** second-hand *o* old clothes

**ropaje** *nm* robes

**ropero** *nm* (a) *(armario)* wardrobe; *(habitación)* walk-in wardrobe (b) *(guardarropa)* cloakroom

**roque 1** *adj Fam* **estar r.** to be out for the count; **quedarse r.** to drop *o* nod off
**2** *nm (en ajedrez)* castle

**roquefort** [roke'for] *nm* Roquefort (cheese)

**roquero, -a 1** *adj* rock; **grupo r.** rock band
**2** *nm,f* (a) *(músico)* rock musician (b) *(fan)* rock fan

**rorro** *nm Fam* baby

**rosa 1** *adj (color)* pink; *Fig* **verlo todo de color (de) r.** to see everything through rose-tinted spectacles
**2** *nm (color)* pink
**3** *nf (flor)* rose; **estar (fresco) como una r.** to be as fresh as a daisy; **r. de los vientos** compass rose

**rosáceo, -a** *adj* pinkish

**rosado, -a 1** *adj* pink
**2** *nm (vino)* rosé

**rosal** *nm (arbusto)* rose bush

**rosaleda** *nf* rose garden

**rosario** nm (a) *Rel* rosary; **rezar el r.** to say one's rosary (b) *Fig (serie)* string; **un r. de desgracias** a string of disasters (c) *Fam* **acabar como el r. de la aurora** to finish up badly

**rosbif** (*pl* **rosbifs**) nm roast beef

**rosca** nf (a) *(de tornillo)* thread (b) *(forma) (de anillo)* ring; *(espiral)* coil (c) *Culin* = ring-shaped bread roll; *Méx* sponge cake (d) *(expresiones)* **nunca se come una r.** he never gets off with anyone; **hacerle la r. a alguien** to suck up to sb; **pasarse de r.** *(persona)* to go over the top

**rosco** nm = ring-shaped bread roll; *Fam Fig* **nunca se come un r.** he never gets off with anyone

**roscón** nm = ring-shaped bread roll; **r. de Reyes** = ring-shaped pastry eaten on 6th January

**roseta** nf (a) *(rubor)* flush (b) *(de regadera)* nozzle (c) **rosetas** *(palomitas)* popcorn

**rosetón** nm (a) *Arquit (ventana)* rose window (b) *(adorno)* ceiling rose

**rosquete** adj *Perú Fam Pey* queer

**rosquilla** nf ring doughnut; *Fam* **venderse como rosquillas** to sell like hot cakes

**rostro** nm face; *Fam Fig* **tener (mucho) r.** to have a (lot of) nerve

**rotación** nf (a) *(giro)* rotation (b) *(alternancia)* rota; **r. de cultivos** crop rotation; **por r.** in turn

**rotar** vi (a) *(girar)* to rotate, to turn (b) *(alternar)* to rotate

**rotativa** nf rotary press

**rotativo, -a 1** adj rotary, revolving
  **2** nm newspaper

**rotatorio, -a** adj rotary, revolving

**roto, -a 1** *participio ver* **romper**
  **2** adj (a) *(partido, rasgado)* broken; *(tela, papel)* torn (b) *(estropeado)* broken (c) *Fig (deshecho) (vida)* destroyed; *(corazón)* broken (d) *Fam Fig (exhausto)* shattered
  **3** nm,f *Chile (trabajador)* worker
  **4** nm *(en tela)* tear, rip

**rotonda** nf (a) *Aut* roundabout (b) *(plaza)* circus (c) *(edificio)* rotunda

**rotoso, -a** adj *Andes, CSur* ragged, in tatters

**Rotterdam** n Rotterdam

**rótula** nf kneecap

**rotulador** nm felt-tip pen; **r. fluorescente** highlighter (pen)

**rotular** vt (a) *(con rotulador)* to highlight (b) *(carta, artículo)* to head with fancy lettering (c) *(mapa, gráfico)* to label

**rótulo** nm (a) *(letrero)* sign (b) *(encabezamiento)* headline, title

**rotundidad** nf firmness, categorical nature; **con r.** categorically

**rotundo, -a** adj (a) *(negativa, persona)* categorical (b) *(lenguaje, estilo)* emphatic, forceful (c) *(completo)* total; **r. fracaso** total o complete failure

**rotura** nf *(en general)* break; *(de hueso)* fracture; *(en tela)* rip, hole

**roturar** vt to plough

**roulotte** [rru'lod] nf *Br* caravan, *US* trailer

**royalty** [rro'jalti] (*pl* **royalties**) nm royalty

**royera** *etc ver* **roer**

**rozadura** nf (a) *(señal)* scratch, scrape (b) *(herida)* graze

**rozamiento** nm *(fricción)* rubbing; *Fís* friction

**rozar** [16] **1** vt (a) *(tocar, frotar)* to rub; *(suavemente)* to brush; **me roza el zapato** my shoe is rubbing my heel (b) *(pasar cerca de)* to skim, to shave (c) *Fig (estar cerca de)* to border on; **roza los cuarenta** he's almost forty
  **2** vi **r. con** *(tocar)* to brush against; *Fig (relacionarse con)* to touch on
  **3** **rozarse** vpr (a) *(tocarse)* to touch (b) *(pasar cerca)* to brush past each other (c) *(rasguñarse)* to graze (d) *Fig (tener trato)* **rozarse con** to rub shoulders with

**Rte.** *(abrev de* **remitente***)* sender

**RTVE** nf *(abrev de* **Radiotelevisión Española***)* = Spanish state broadcasting company

**rúa** nf street

**ruana** nf *Andes* poncho

**Ruanda** n Rwanda

**ruandés, -esa** adj & nm,f Rwandan

**rubeola, rubéola** nf German measles

**rubí** (*pl* **rubíes** o **rubís**) nm ruby

**rubia** nf (a) *ver* **rubio** (b) *Fam Anticuado (moneda)* peseta

**rubiales** *Fam* **1** adj inv blond(e), fair-haired
  **2** nmf inv blonde

**rubicundo, -a** adj ruddy

**rubio, -a 1** adj (a) *(pelo, persona)* blond(e), fair; **r. platino** platinum blonde (b) *(tabaco)* **tabaco r.** Virginia tobacco *(as opposed to black tobacco)* (c) *(cerveza)* **cerveza rubia** lager
  **2** nm,f *(persona)* blond(e), fair-haired person; **rubia platino** platinum blonde
  **3** nm *(tabaco)* Virginia tobacco *(as opposed to black tobacco)*

**rublo** nm rouble

**rubor** nm (a) *(vergüenza)* embarrassment; **causar r.** to embarrass (b) *(sonrojo)* blush

**ruborizado, -a** adj flushed

**ruborizar** [16] **1** vt to make blush; *Fig* to embarrass
  **2** **ruborizarse** vpr to blush

**ruboroso, -a** adj blushing

**rúbrica** *nf* (**a**) *(de firma)* flourish (**b**) *(título)* title (**c**) *Fig (conclusión)* final flourish; **poner r. a algo** to complete sth

**rubricar** [61] *vt* (**a**) *(firmar)* to sign with a flourish (**b**) *Fig (confirmar)* to confirm (**c**) *Fig (concluir)* to complete

**rucio, -a 1** *adj* (**a**) *(gris)* grey (**b**) *Am Fam* blond(e)

  **2** *nm* ass, donkey

**rudeza** *nf* (**a**) *(tosquedad)* roughness (**b**) *(grosería, descortesía)* coarseness (**c**) *(dureza, rigurosidad)* harshness

**rudimentario, -a** *adj* rudimentary

**rudimentos** *nmpl* rudiments

**rudo, -a** *adj* (**a**) *(tosco, basto)* rough (**b**) *(brusco)* sharp, brusque; *(grosero)* rude, coarse (**c**) *(riguroso, duro)* harsh

**rueca** *nf* distaff

**rueda** *nf* (**a**) *(pieza)* wheel; *Fig Dep* **chupar r.** to tag on behind another cyclist; to slipstream; *Fig* **comulgar con ruedas de molino** to be very gullible; *Fig* **ir sobre ruedas** to go smoothly; **r. delantera/trasera** front/rear wheel; **r. dentada** cogwheel; *Fig* **la r. de la fortuna** *o* **del destino** the wheel of fortune; **r. de repuesto** *o* **recambio** spare wheel (**b**) *(corro)* circle; **r. de prensa** press conference; **r. de reconocimiento** identification parade (**c**) *(rodaja)* slice

**ruedo 1** *ver* **rodar**

  **2** *nm* (**a**) *Taurom* bullring (**b**) *Fig (mundo)* sphere, world; **echarse al r.** to enter the fray

**ruego 1** *ver* **rogar**

  **2** *nm* request; **ruegos y preguntas** any other business

**rufián** *nm* villain

**rufianesco, -a 1** *adj* villainous

  **2** *nf* **la rufianesca** the underworld

**rugby** *nm* rugby

**rugido** *nm* *(de animales, mar, viento)* roar; *(de persona)* bellow; *(de tripas)* rumble

**rugir** [26] *vi* *(animal, mar, viento)* to roar; *(persona)* to bellow; *(tripas)* to rumble

**rugosidad** *nf* (**a**) *(cualidad)* roughness (**b**) *(arruga, de piel)* wrinkle; *(de tejido)* crinkle

**rugoso, -a** *adj* (**a**) *(áspero)* rough (**b**) *(con arrugas) (piel)* wrinkled; *(tejido)* crinkled

**Ruhr** *nm* **el R.** the (River) Ruhr

**ruibarbo** *nm* rhubarb

**ruido** *nm* (**a**) *(sonido)* noise; **r. de fondo** background noise; **mucho r. y pocas nueces** much ado about nothing (**b**) *Fig (alboroto)* row; **hacer** *o* **meter r.** to cause a stir

**ruidoso, -a** *adj* (**a**) *(que hace ruido)* noisy (**b**) *Fig (escandaloso)* controversial, sensational

**ruin** *adj* (**a**) *(vil)* low, contemptible (**b**) *(avaro)* mean

**ruina** *nf* (**a**) *(quiebra)* ruin; **dejar en** *o* **llevar a la r. a alguien** to ruin sb; **estar en la r.** to be ruined; **su negocio es una r.** his business is swallowing up his money (**b**) *(destrucción)* destruction; **amenazar r.** *(edificio)* to be about to collapse; **el alcohol será su r.** drink will be the ruin *o* ruination of him (**c**) **ruinas** *(de una construcción)* ruins (**d**) *(persona)* wreck; **estar hecho una r.** to be a wreck

**ruindad** *nf* (**a**) *(cualidad)* meanness, baseness (**b**) *(acto)* vile deed

**ruinoso, -a** *adj* (**a**) *(poco rentable)* ruinous (**b**) *(edificio)* ramshackle

**ruiseñor** *nm* nightingale

**ruja** *etc ver* **rugir**

**rular** *vi muy Fam* to go, to work; **esta tele no rula** this telly is bust

**ruleta** *nf* roulette; **r. rusa** Russian roulette

**ruletear** *vi Méx* to drive a taxi

**ruletero** *nm Méx (de taxi)* taxi driver; *(de camión)* truck driver

**rulo** *nm* (**a**) *(para el pelo)* roller, curler (**b**) *(rizo)* curl

**rulot** *nf Br* caravan, *US* trailer

**Rumanía, Rumania** *n* Romania

**rumano, -a 1** *adj & nm,f* Romanian

  **2** *nm (lengua)* Romanian

**rumba** *nf* rumba

**rumbo** *nm (dirección)* direction, course; *Fig* path, direction; **ir con r. a** to be heading for; **corregir el r.** to correct one's course; *Fig* **habrá que corregir el r. de la empresa** we will have to change the company's direction; **mantener el r.** to maintain one's course; **poner r. a** to set course for; **perder el r.** *(barco)* to go off course; *Fig (persona)* to lose one's way; **el r. de los acontecimientos** the course of events

**rumboso, -a** *adj Fam* generous

**rumiante** *adj & nm* ruminant

**rumiar** [15] **1** *vt (masticar)* to chew; *Fig* to ruminate, to chew over

  **2** *vi (masticar)* to ruminate, to chew the cud

**rumor** *nm* (**a**) *(ruido sordo)* murmur; **un r. de voces** the sound of voices (**b**) *(chisme)* rumour; **corre un r.** there's a rumour going round

**rumorearse** *v impersonal* **se rumorea que…** it is rumoured that…

**runrún** *nm* (**a**) *(ruido)* hum, humming (**b**) *(chisme)* rumour

**runrunearse** *v impersonal* **se runrunea que…** it is rumoured that…

**runruneo** *nm (ruido)* hum, humming

**rupestre** *adj* cave; **arte r.** cave paintings

**rupia** *nf* rupee

**ruptura** *nf (rotura)* break; *(de relaciones, conversaciones)* breaking-off; *(de pareja)* break-up; *(de contrato)* breach

**rural** *adj* rural

**Rusia** *n* Russia

**ruso, -a 1** *adj & nm,f* Russian
**2** *nm (lengua)* Russian

**rústica** *nf* **en r.** *(encuadernación)* paperback

**rústico, -a** *adj* **(a)** *(del campo)* country; **casa rústica** country cottage **(b)** *(tosco)* rough, coarse

**ruta** *nf* route; *Fig* way, course; **en r. (hacia)** en route (to); **en r.** *(en carretera)* on the road; **la seguridad en r.** safety on the roads, road safety

**rutilante** *adj* shining

**rutilar** *vi* to shine brightly

**rutina** *nf también Informát* routine; **de r.** routine; **por r.** as a matter of course

**rutinario, -a** *adj* routine

**Rvda.** *(abrev de **Reverenda**)* Rev. *(Mother etc)*

**Rvdo.** *(abrev de **Reverendo**)* Rev. *(Father etc)*

# S

**S, s** ['ese] *nf (letra)* S, s

**S.** (a) *(abrev de* **San**) St (b) *(abrev de* **Sur**) S

**s.**[1] (a) *(abrev de* **san**) St (b) *(abrev de* **siglo**) C (c) *(abrev de* **segundo**) s

**s.**[2], **sig.** *(abrev de* **siguiente**) following

**S.A.** *nf (abrev de* **sociedad anónima**) Ltd, PLC

**sábado** *nm* Saturday; **¿qué día es hoy? – (es) s.** what day is it (today)? – (it's) Saturday; **cada s., todos los sábados** every Saturday; **cada dos sábados, un s. sí y otro no** every other Saturday; **caer en s.** to be on a Saturday; **te llamo el s.** I'll call you on Saturday; **el próximo s., el s. que viene** next Saturday; **el s. pasado** last Saturday; **el s. por la mañana/tarde/noche** Saturday morning/afternoon/night; **en s.** on Saturdays; **nací en s.** I was born on a Saturday; **este s.** *(pasado)* last Saturday; *(próximo)* this (coming) Saturday; **¿trabajas los sábados?** do you work (on) Saturdays?; **trabajar un s.** to work on a Saturday; **un s. cualquiera** on any Saturday

**sabana** *nf* savannah

**sábana** *nf* sheet; **s. bajera/encimera** bottom/top sheet; *Fig* **se le pegan las sábanas** she's not good at getting up; *Fig* **se me han pegado las sábanas** I slept in, I overslept

**sabandija** *nf* (a) *(animal)* creepy-crawly, bug (b) *Fig (persona)* worm

**sabañón** *nm* chilblain

**sabático, -a** *adj (de descanso)* sabbatical; **año s.** sabbatical year

**sabedor, -ora** *adj* **ser s. de** to be aware of

**sabelotodo** *nmf inv Fam* know-all

**saber** [60] **1** *nm* knowledge; *Prov* **el s. no ocupa lugar** you can never know too much

**2** *vt* (a) *(conocer)* to know; **ya lo sé** I know; **hacer s. algo a alguien** to inform sb of sth, to tell sb sth

(b) *(ser capaz de)* **s. hacer algo** to know how to do sth, to be able to do sth; **sabe hablar inglés/montar en bici** she can speak English/ride a bike

(c) *(enterarse de)* to learn, to find out; **lo supe ayer** I found out yesterday

(d) *(entender de)* to know about; **sabe mucha física** he knows a lot about physics

(e) *(expresiones)* **no s. dónde meterse** not to know where to put oneself; **no sabe lo que se hace** she doesn't know what she's doing; **no sabe lo que tiene** he doesn't realize just how lucky he is; **no sé qué decir** I don't know what to say; **¡qué sé yo!** how should I know!

**3** *vi* (a) *(tener sabor)* to taste (a of); **s. bien/mal** to taste good/bad; *Fam Fig* **s. a cuernos** *o* **rayos** to taste disgusting *o* revolting; *Fam Fig* **sus comentarios le supieron a cuernos** *o* **rayos** her comments infuriated *o* incensed him; *Fig* **le supo mal** *(le enfadó)* it upset *o* annoyed him; *Fig* **me sabe mal mentirle** I feel bad about lying to him

(b) *(entender)* **s. de algo** to know about sth; **ése sí que sabe** he's a canny one

(c) *(tener noticia)* **s. de alguien** to hear from sb; **s. de algo** to learn of sth

(d) *(parecer)* **eso me sabe a disculpa** that sounds like an excuse to me

(e) *(expresiones)* **a s.** *(es decir)* namely; **no s. uno por dónde se anda** not to have a clue; **que yo sepa** as far as I know; **¡quién sabe!, ¡vete a s.!** who knows!

**4 saberse** *vpr* **saberse algo** to know sth; **saberse algo al dedillo** to know sth inside out; *Fig* **sabérselas todas** to know all the tricks; **llegar a saberse** to come to light

**sabido, -a** *adj* **como es (bien) s.** as everyone knows

**sabiduría** *nf* (a) *(conocimientos)* knowledge, learning (b) *(prudencia)* wisdom

**sabiendas: a sabiendas** *loc adv* knowingly; **a s. de que...** knowing that..., quite aware of the fact that...

**sabihondo, -a, sabiondo, -a** *nm,f Fam* know-all

**sabina** *nf (arbusto)* savin

**sabio, -a 1** *adj* (a) *(sensato, inteligente)* wise (b) *(docto)* learned (c) *(amaestrado)* trained

**2** *nm,f* (a) *(sensato, inteligente)* wise person (b) *(docto)* learned person

**sablazo** *nm* (a) *Fam Fig (de dinero)* scrounging; **dar** *o* **pegar un s. a alguien** to scrounge money off sb (**b**) *(golpe)* blow with a sabre (**c**) *(herida)* sabre wound

**sable** *nm* sabre

**sableador, -ora** *nm,f Fam* scrounger

**sablear** *vi Fam* to scrounge money

**sablista** *nmf Fam* scrounger

**sabor** *nm* (**a**) *(gusto)* taste, flavour; **tener s. a algo** to taste of sth; *Fig* **dejar mal/buen s. (de boca)** to leave a nasty taste in one's mouth/a warm feeling (**b**) *Fig (estilo)* flavour

**saborear** *vt también Fig* to savour

**sabotaje** *nm* sabotage

**saboteador, -ora** *nm,f* saboteur

**sabotear** *vt* to sabotage

**sabré** *etc ver* **saber**

**sabroso, -a** *adj* (**a**) *(gustoso)* tasty (**b**) *Fig (substancioso)* tidy, considerable (**c**) *Fig (gracioso)* juicy, tasty; *(malicioso)* mischievous

**sabueso** *nm* (**a**) *(perro)* bloodhound (**b**) *Fig (detective)* sleuth, detective

**saca** *nf* sack

**sacacorchos** *nm inv* corkscrew

**sacamuelas** *nm inv Fam* dentist

**sacapuntas** *nm inv* pencil sharpener

**sacar** [61] **1** *vt* (**a**) *(poner fuera, hacer salir)* to take out; *(lengua)* to stick out; **s. algo de** to take sth out of; **nos sacaron algo de comer** they gave us something to eat

(**b**) *(quitar)* to remove (**de** from)

(**c**) *(librar, salvar)* **s. a alguien de algo** to get sb out of sth

(**d**) *(obtener) (carné, buenas notas)* to get, to obtain; *(premio)* to win; *(dinero del banco)* to withdraw; **la sidra se saca de las manzanas** cider is made from apples

(**e**) *(foto)* to take; *(fotocopia)* to make

(**f**) *(sonsacar)* **s. algo a alguien** to get sth out of sb

(**g**) *(fabricar)* to produce; *(modelo, disco)* to bring out

(**h**) *(manifestar)* **s. a relucir algo** to bring sth up; **sacó su mal humor a relucir** he let his bad temper show

(**i**) *(resolver, encontrar)* to work out; **s. una conclusión** to come to a conclusion; **s. la cuenta/la solución** to work out the total/the answer; **s. la respuesta correcta** to get the right answer

(**j**) *(deducir)* to gather, to understand; **lo leí tres veces, pero no saqué nada en claro** *o* **limpio** I read it three times, but I couldn't make much sense of it

(**k**) *(entradas, billetes)* to get, to buy

(**l**) *(prenda) (de ancho)* to let out; *(de largo)* to let down

(**m**) *(aventajar en)* **sacó tres minutos a su rival** he was three minutes ahead of his rival

(**n**) **s. adelante** *(hijos)* to bring up; *(negocio)* to make a go of

(**o**) *Dep (con la mano)* to throw in; *(con la raqueta)* to serve

**2** *vi Dep* to put the ball into play; *(con la raqueta)* to serve

**3 sacarse** *vpr* (**a**) *(poner fuera)* **sacarse algo (de)** to take sth out (of); *Fam Fig* **sacarse algo de la manga** to make sth up (on the spur of the moment)

(**b**) *(carné, título)* to get

**sacárido** *nm Quím* saccharide

**sacarina** *nf* saccharine

**sacarosa** *nf* sucrose

**sacerdocio** *nm* priesthood; *Fig* vocation

**sacerdotal** *adj* priestly

**sacerdote, -isa** **1** *nm,f (pagano)* priest, *f* priestess

**2** *nm (cristiano)* priest; **mujer s.** woman priest

**saciar** [15] **1** *vt (satisfacer) (sed)* to quench; *(hambre)* to satisfy, to sate; *Fig (curiosidad)* to satisfy; *(ambición)* to fulfil

**2 saciarse** *vpr* to have had one's fill; *Fig* to be satisfied

**saciedad** *nf* **comió hasta la s.** she ate until she couldn't eat any more; *Fig* **repetir algo hasta la s.** to repeat sth over and over

**saco** *nm* (**a**) *(bolsa)* sack, bag; **s. de dormir** sleeping bag (**b**) *Fig (persona)* **ser un s. de mentiras** to be full of lies (**c**) *Am* jacket (*expresiones*) **entrar a s. en** to sack, to pillage; **no echar algo en s. roto** to take good note of sth; **ser (como) un s. sin fondo** to be (like) a bottomless pit

**sacralizar** [16] *vt* to consecrate

**sacramental** *adj* sacramental

**sacramentar** *vt* to administer the last rites to

**sacramento** *nm* sacrament

**sacrificar** [61] **1** *vt* (**a**) *(renunciar a)* to sacrifice, to give up (**b**) *(matar) (para consumo)* to slaughter; *(por enfermedad)* to put down; *(a los dioses)* to sacrifice (**a** to)

**2 sacrificarse** *vpr* **sacrificarse (para hacer algo)** to make sacrifices (in order to do sth); **sacrificarse por alguien** to make sacrifices for sb

**sacrificio** *nm también Fig* sacrifice

**sacrilegio** *nm también Fig* sacrilege

**sacrílego, -a 1** *adj* sacrilegious

**2** *nm,f* sacrilegious person

**sacristán, -ana** *nm,f* sacristan, sexton

**sacristía** *nf* sacristy

**sacro, -a 1** *adj* (**a**) *(sagrado)* holy, sacred (**b**) *Anat* sacral

**2** *nm Anat* sacrum

**sacrosanto, -a** *adj* sacrosanct

**sacudida** *nf* (a) *(movimiento)* shake; *(de la cabeza)* toss; *(de tren, coche)* jolt (b) *(terremoto)* tremor (c) *Fig (conmoción)* shock; **s. eléctrica** electric shock

**sacudidor** *nm* carpet beater

**sacudir 1** *vt* (a) *(agitar)* to shake (b) *(golpear)* *(alfombra)* to beat; *Fam (persona)* to smack, to give a hiding to (c) *Fig (conmover)* to shake, to shock
**2 sacudirse** *vpr (persona)* to get rid of; *(responsabilidad, tarea)* to get out of

**sádico, -a 1** *adj* sadistic
**2** *nm,f* sadist

**sadismo** *nm* sadism

**sadomasoquismo** *nm* sadomasochism

**sadomasoquista 1** *adj* sadomasochistic
**2** *nmf* sadomasochist

**saeta** *nf* (a) *(flecha)* arrow (b) *(de reloj)* hand; *(de brújula)* needle (c) *Mús* = flamenco-style song sung on religious occasions

**safari** *nm* (a) *(expedición)* safari; **ir de s.** to go on safari; **s. fotográfico** = holiday/trip photographing African wildlife (b) *(zoológico)* safari park

**saga** *nf* saga

**sagacidad** *nf* astuteness

**sagaz** *adj* astute, shrewd

**sagitario 1** *nm (zodiaco)* Sagittarius; **ser s.** to be (a) Sagittarius
**2** *nmf (persona)* Sagittarian

**sagrado, -a** *adj* holy, sacred; *Fig* sacred

**sagrario** *nm* (a) *(parte del templo)* shrine (b) *(tabernáculo)* tabernacle

**Sáhara** *nm* **el (desierto del) S.** the Sahara (Desert)

**saharaui** *adj & nmf* Saharan

**sahariana** *nf (prenda)* safari jacket

**sahariano, -a** *adj & nm,f* Saharan

**SAI** ['sai] *nm Informát (abrev de* **sistema de alimentación ininterrumpida)** uninterrupted power supply, UPS

**sainete** *nm Teatro* = short, popular comic play

**sajar** *vt* to cut open

**sajón, -ona** *adj & nm,f* Saxon

**Sajonia** *nf* Saxony

**sal 1** *nf* (a) *Culin & Quím* salt; **s. común** *o* **de cocina** cooking salt; **s. gorda** coarse salt; **s. marina** sea salt; (b) *Fig (gracia)* wit; **es la s. de la vida** it's one of the little things that makes life worth living (c) *Fig (garbo)* charm
**2** *nfpl* **sales** (a) *(para reanimar)* smelling salts (b) *(para baño)* bath salts

**sala** *nf* (a) *(habitación)* room; *(de una casa)* lounge, living room; *(de hospital)* ward; **s. de espera** waiting room; **s. de estar** lounge, living room; **s. de juntas** boardroom; **s. de lectura** reading room; **s. de máquinas** machine room; **s. de operaciones** operating theatre; **s. de partos** delivery room
(b) *(local) (de conferencias, conciertos)* hall; *(de cine, teatro)* auditorium; **un cine de 8 salas** an 8-screen cinema *o* multiplex; **s. de fiestas** discotheque; **s. X** = cinema showing pornographic films
(c) *Der (lugar)* court(room); *(magistrados)* bench

**saladero** *nm* salting room

**saladillo, -a** *adj* salted

**salado, -a** *adj* (a) *(con sal)* salted; *(con demasiada sal)* salty; **estar s.** to be (too) salty; **agua s.** salt water (b) *(opuesto a lo dulce)* savoury (c) *Fig (gracioso)* witty

**salamandra** *nf (animal)* salamander

**salami** *nm* salami

**salar** *vt* (a) *(para conservar)* to salt (b) *(para cocinar)* to add salt to

**salarial** *adj* wage; **congelación s.** pay freeze; **incremento s.** pay rise

**salario** *nm* salary, wages; *(semanal)* wage; **s. base** *o* **básico** basic wage; **s. bruto/neto** gross/net wage; **s. mínimo (interprofesional)** minimum wage; **s. social** = benefit paid by local authorities to low-income families

**salaz** *adj* salacious

**salazón 1** *nf (acción)* salting
**2** *nfpl* **salazones** *(carne)* salted meat; *(pescado)* salted fish

**salchicha** *nf* sausage

**salchichón** *nm* = cured pork sausage similar to salami

**saldar 1** *vt* (a) *(pagar) (cuenta)* to close; *(deuda)* to settle; *Fig (asunto)* to settle (b) *Com* to sell off
**2 saldarse** *vpr (acabar)* **saldarse con** to produce; **la pelea se saldó con 11 heridos** 11 people were injured in the brawl

**saldo** *nm* (a) *(de cuenta)* balance; **s. acreedor/deudor** credit/debit balance; **s. medio** average (bank) balance; **s. negativo** overdraft; *Fig* **la iniciativa tuvo un s. positivo** on balance, the outcome of the initiative was positive (b) *(de deudas)* settlement (c) *(restos de mercancías)* remnant; **saldos** *(rebajas)* sale; **de s.** bargain

**saldré** *etc ver* **salir**

**saledizo** *nm Arquit* overhang

**salero** *nm* (a) *(recipiente)* salt cellar (b) *Fam (gracia, donaire)* **baila con s.** she dances with great verve; **tiene mucho s. al hablar** she's a lively and entertaining conversationalist; **cuenta chistes con s.** she's good at telling jokes

**saleroso, -a** *adj Fam (gracioso)* witty, funny; *(garboso)* charming

**salesiano, -a** *adj & nm,f Rel* Salesian

**salga** *etc ver* **salir**

**sálico, -a** *adj Hist* **ley sálica** Salic law

**salida** *nf* (a) *(partida)* departure

(b) *Dep* start; **s. nula** false start

(c) *(lugar)* exit, way out; **s. de emergencia/incendios** emergency/fire exit; **s. de humos** air vent

(d) *(viaje)* trip

(e) *(aparición) (de sol, luna)* rise; *(de revista, nuevo modelo)* appearance; **esta llave regula la s. del agua** this tap controls the flow of water

(f) *(momento)* **quedamos a la s. del trabajo** we agreed to meet after work

(g) *Com (producción)* output; *(posibilidades)* market; **este producto no tiene s.** there's no market for this product

(h) *Informát* output

(i) *Fig (solución)* way out; **si no hay otra s.** if there's no alternative

(j) *(ocurrencia)* witty remark; *(pretexto)* excuse; **tener salidas** to be witty; **s. de tono** out-of-place remark; **salidas** *Fig (posibilidades laborales)* opening, opportunity; **carreras con salidas** university courses with good job prospects

**salido, -a 1** *adj* (a) *(saliente)* projecting, sticking out; *(ojos)* bulging; **dientes salidos** buck teeth (b) *(animal)* on heat (c) *muy Fam (persona)* horny

**2** *nm,f muy Fam (persona)* horny bugger

**saliente 1** *adj* (a) *(destacable)* salient, important (b) *(presidente, ministro)* outgoing

**2** *nm* projection

**salina** *nf* (a) *Min* salt mine (b) *(en el mar)* **salinas** saltworks *(singular)*

**salinidad** *nf* salinity

**salino, -a** *adj* saline

**salir** [62] **1** *vi* (a) *(ir fuera)* to go out; *(venir fuera)* to come out; **s. de** to go/come out of; **¿salimos al jardín?** shall we go out into the garden?; **¡sal aquí fuera!** come out here!

(b) *(ser novios)* to go out (**con** with); **están saliendo** they are going out (together)

(c) *(marcharse)* **s. (de/para)** to leave (from/for); **s. de viaje** to go away (on a trip)

(d) *(desembocar) (calle)* **s. a** to open onto

(e) *(separarse) (tapón, anillo)* **s. (de algo)** to come off (sth)

(f) *(resultar)* to turn out; **ha salido muy estudioso** he has turned out to be very studious; **¿qué salió en la votación?** what was the result of the vote?; **s. elegida actriz del año** to be voted actress of the year; **s. premiado** to be awarded a prize; **s. bien/mal** to turn out

well/badly; **s. ganando/perdiendo** to come off well/badly

(g) *(dar resultado)* to turn out; **me ha salido mal** *(examen, entrevista)* it didn't go very well; *(plato, dibujo)* it didn't turn out very well; *(cuenta)* I got the wrong result; **¿qué tal te ha salido?** how did it go?

(h) *(proceder)* **s. de** to come from; **el vino sale de la uva** wine comes from grapes

(i) *(a divertirse)* to go out; **salen mucho a cenar** they eat out a lot

(j) *(surgir) (luna, estrellas, planta)* to come out; *(sol)* to rise; *(dientes)* to come through; **le ha salido un sarpullido en la espalda** her back has come out in a rash

(k) *(aparecer) (publicación, producto, traumas)* to come out; *(moda, ley)* to come in; *(en imagen, prensa, televisión)* to appear; **¡qué bien sales en la foto!** you look great in the photo!; **ha salido en los periódicos/en la tele** it's been in the papers/on TV; *Cine & Teatro* **s. de** to appear as

(l) *(en sorteo)* to come up

(m) *(presentarse) (ocasión, oportunidad)* to turn up, to come along; *(problema, contratiempo)* to arise; *Fig* **a lo que salga, salga lo que salga** whatever happens

(n) *(costar)* to work out (**a** *o* **por** at); **s. caro** *(de dinero)* to be expensive; *(por las consecuencias)* to be costly

(o) *(decir u obrar inesperadamente)* **nunca se sabe por dónde va a s.** you never know what she's going to do/come out with next

(p) *(parecerse)* **s. a alguien** to turn out like sb, to take after sb

(q) *(en juegos)* to lead; **te toca s. a ti** it's your lead

(r) *(desaparecer)* to come out; **la mancha de vino no sale** the wine stain won't come out

(s) *(librarse)* **s. de un apuro** to get out of a tight spot; **no sé si podremos s. de esta** I don't know how we're going to get out of this one

(t) *Informát* **s. (de)** to quit, to exit

(u) *Fam* **porque (no) me sale de las narices** because I can't be bloody well bothered

(v) **s. adelante** *(persona, empresa)* to get by; *(proyecto, propuesta, ley)* to be successful

**2 salirse** *vpr* (a) *(marcharse)* **salirse (de)** to leave; **me salí del agua porque tenía frío** I came out of the water because I was cold

(b) *(filtrarse) (líquido, gas)* to leak, to escape (**por** through); *(humo, aroma)* to come out (**por** through)

(c) *(rebosar)* to overflow; *(leche)* to boil over; **el río se salió del cauce** the river broke its banks

(d) *(desviarse)* **salirse (de)** to come off; **el**

**coche se salió de la carretera** the car came off o left the road

(e) *Fig (escaparse)* **salirse de** *(límites)* to go beyond; **salirse del tema** to digress

(f) **salirse con la suya** to get one's own way

**salitre** *nm* saltpetre

**salitroso, -a** *adj* containing saltpetre

**saliva** *nf* saliva; *Fam Fig* **gastar s. (en balde)** to waste one's breath; *Fig* **tragar s.** to bite one's tongue

**salivación** *nf* salivation

**salival, salivar**[1] *adj* salivary

**salivar**[2] *vi* to salivate

**salivazo** *nm* spit; **echar un s.** to spit

**salmantino, -a**[1] *adj* of/from Salamanca

2 *nm,f* person from Salamanca

**salmo** *nm* psalm

**salmodia** *nf* singing of psalms; *Fig* drone

**salmodiar** [15] *vt* to sing in a monotone

**salmón 1** *adj & nm inv (color)* salmon (pink)

2 *nm (pez)* salmon

**salmonella** *nf* salmonella *(bacterium)*

**salmonelosis** *nf inv* salmonella *(illness)*

**salmonete** *nm* red mullet

**salmuera** *nf* brine

**salobre** *adj* salty

**salobridad** *nf* saltiness

**salomón** *nm Fig* sage, wise person

**salomónico, -a** *adj* equitable, even-handed

**salón** *nm* (a) *(en vivienda)* lounge, sitting room (b) *(para reuniones, ceremonias)* hall; **s. de actos** assembly hall; **s. de sesiones** meeting room (c) *(mobiliario)* lounge suite (d) *(feria)* show, exhibition (e) *(establecimiento)* shop; **s. de belleza/masaje** beauty/massage parlour; **s. recreativo** amusement arcade; **s. de té** tearoom; *Fig* **revolucionario de s.** armchair revolutionary; **intelectual de s.** pseudo-intellectual

**salpicadera** *nf Méx Br* mudguard, *US* fender

**salpicadero** *nm* dashboard

**salpicadura** *nf (acción)* splashing, spattering; *(mancha)* spot, spatter

**salpicar** [61] *vt* (a) *(con líquido)* to splash, to spatter; *Fig (en reputación)* **el escándalo salpicó al presidente** the president was tainted by the scandal (b) *Fig (diseminar)* to pepper **(de** with)

**salpicón** *nm Culin* = cold dish of chopped fish or meat, seasoned with pepper, salt, vinegar and onion

**salpimentar** [3] *vt Culin* to season (with salt and pepper)

**salsa** *nf* (a) *Culin* sauce; *(de carne)* gravy; *Fig* **en su (propia) s.** in one's element; **s. agridulce** sweet-and-sour sauce; **s. bearnesa** bearnaise sauce; **s. bechamel** o **besamel** bechamel o white sauce; **s. mahonesa** o **mayonesa** mayonnaise; **s. rosa** thousand island dressing; **s. tártara** tartare sauce; **s. de tomate** tomato sauce (b) *Fig (interés)* spice; **ser la s. de la vida** to make life worth living (c) *Mús* salsa

**salsera** *nf* gravy boat

**saltador, -ora**[1] *adj* jumping

2 *nm,f Dep* jumper; **s. de altura** high-jumper; **s. de longitud** long-jumper

**saltamontes** *nm inv* grasshopper

**saltar 1** *vt* (a) *(obstáculo)* to jump (over)

(b) *(omitir)* to skip, to miss out

2 *vi* (a) *(en general)* to jump; *(al agua)* to dive; **s. sobre alguien** *(abalanzarse)* to set upon sb; **s. a la comba** to skip; **s. de un tema a otro** to jump (around) from one subject to another; **los jugadores saltan al campo** the players are coming out onto the field

(b) *(levantarse)* to jump up; **s. de la silla** to jump out of one's seat

(c) *(salir disparado) (objeto)* to jump, to shoot; *(aceite)* to spurt; *(corcho, válvula)* to pop out; *(chispas)* to fly

(d) *(explotar)* to explode, to blow up; **han saltado los plomos** the fuses have blown

(e) *(romperse)* to break

(f) *(sorprender, intervenir)* **s. con** to suddenly come out with

(g) *Fig (reaccionar bruscamente)* to explode; **s. a la mínima** to be quick to lose one's temper

(h) *(agua, cascada)* **s. por** to gush down, to pour down

(i) *(alarma)* to go off; **hacer s.** to set off

(j) *(expresiones)* **salta a la vista que...** it's patently obvious that...; **estar a la que salta** to be always on the lookout

3 **saltarse** *vpr* (a) *(omitir)* to skip, to miss out

(b) *(salir despedido)* to pop off

(c) *(no respetar) (cola, semáforo)* to jump; *(ley, normas)* to break

**saltarín, -ina**[1] *adj* fidgety

2 *nm,f* fidget

**salteado, -a** *adj* (a) *Culin* sautéed (b) *(espaciado)* unevenly spaced; **en días salteados** every other day; **se sentaron en pupitres salteados** they sat at alternate desks

**salteador, -ora** *nm,f* **s. de caminos** highway robber

**saltear** *vt* (a) *(asaltar)* to assault (b) *Culin* to sauté

**saltimbanqui** *nmf* acrobat

**salto** *nm* (a) *también Dep* jump; *(grande)* leap; *(al agua)* dive; **dar** *o* **pegar un s.** to jump; *(grande)* to leap; **s. de altura/longitud** high/long jump; **s. mortal** somersault; **s. con pértiga** pole vault; **triple s.** triple jump

(b) *Fig (diferencia, omisión)* gap

(c) *Fig (progreso)* leap forward; **un s. hacia atrás** a major step backwards

(d) *(despeñadero)* precipice; **s. de agua** waterfall

(e) **s. de cama** *(prenda)* negligée

(f) *(expresiones)* **vivir a s. de mata** to live from one day to the next; **dar saltos de alegría** *o* **contento** to jump with joy

**saltón, -ona** *adj (ojos)* bulging; *(dientes)* sticking out

**salubre** *adj* healthy

**salubridad** *nf* healthiness

**salud 1** *nf también Fig* health; **estar bien/mal de s.** to be well/unwell; **beber** *o* **brindar a la s. de alguien** to drink to sb's health; **curarse en s.** to cover one's back; **rebosar de s.** to glow with health; **s. pública** public health

**2** *interj* **¡s.!** *(para brindar)* cheers!; *(después de estornudar)* bless you!; *(para saludar)* hello!

**saludable** *adj* (a) *(sano)* healthy (b) *Fig (provechoso)* beneficial

**saludar 1** *vt* to greet; *Mil* to salute; **me saludó con la mano** he waved to me (in greeting); **saluda a Ana de mi parte** give my regards to Ana; **le saluda atentamente** yours faithfully

**2 saludarse** *vpr* to greet one another

**saludo** *nm* greeting; *Mil* salute; **Ana te manda saludos** *(en carta)* Ana sends you her regards; *(al teléfono)* Ana says hello; **dale saludos de mi parte** give her my regards; **un s. afectuoso** *(en cartas)* yours sincerely

**salva** *nf Mil* salvo; *Fig* **una s. de aplausos** a round of applause

**salvación** *nf* (a) *(remedio, solución)* **no tener s.** to be beyond hope; **las lluvias fueron la s. de los agricultores** the rains were the farmers' salvation (b) *(rescate)* rescue (c) *Rel* salvation

**salvado** *nm* bran

**Salvador** *nm* (a) *Rel* **el S.** the Saviour (b) *Geog* **El S.** El Salvador

**salvador, -ora 1** *adj* saving

**2** *nm,f (persona)* saviour

**salvadoreño, -a** *adj & nm,f* Salvadoran

**salvaguardar** *vt* to safeguard

**salvaguardia, salvaguarda** *nf* (a) *(defensa)* safeguard (b) *(salvoconducto)* safeconduct, pass

**salvajada** *nf* atrocity

**salvaje 1** *adj* (a) *(animal, terreno)* wild (b) *(pueblo, tribu)* savage (c) *(cruel, brutal)* brutal, savage (d) *(incontrolado)* **acampada s.** unauthorized camping

**2** *nmf* (a) *(primitivo)* savage (b) *(bruto)* maniac

**salvajismo** *nm* savagery

**salvamanteles** *nm inv (plano)* table mat; *(con pies)* trivet

**salvamento** *nm* rescue, saving; **equipo de s.** rescue team

**salvapantallas** *nm inv Informát* screensaver

**salvar 1** *vt* (a) *(librar de peligro)* to save (b) *(rescatar)* to rescue (c) *(superar) (dificultad)* to overcome; *(obstáculo)* to go over *o* around (d) *(recorrer)* to cover (e) *(exceptuar)* **salvando algunos detalles** except for a few details; **salvando las distancias** allowing for the obvious differences

**2 salvarse** *vpr* (a) *(librarse)* to escape; **sálvese quien pueda** every man for himself (b) *Rel* to be saved

**salvavidas 1** *adj inv* **bote s.** lifeboat; **chaleco s.** lifejacket

**2** *nm (chaleco)* lifejacket; *(flotador)* lifebelt

**salve¹** *interj* hail!

**salve²** *nf* = prayer or hymn to the Virgin Mary

**salvedad** *nf* exception; **con la s. de** with the exception of

**salvia** *nf* sage

**salvo, -a 1** *adj* **sano y s.** safe and sound

**2** *prep* except; **s. que** unless; **s. error u omisión** errors and omissions excepted

**3** *nm* **estar a s.** to be safe; **poner algo a s.** to put sth in a safe place

**salvoconducto** *nm* safe-conduct, pass

**Salzburgo** [sals'βurɣo] *n* Salzburg

**samaritano, -a** *adj & nm,f* Samaritan

**samba** *nf* samba

**sambenito** *nm Fig (descrédito)* disgrace; **poner** *o* **colgar a alguien el s. de borracho** to brand sb a drunk

**Samoa Occidental** *n* Western Samoa

**samovar** *nm* samovar

**sámpler** *nm Mús* sampler

**samurái** *(pl* **samuráis)**, **samuray** *nm* samurai

**san** *adj* Saint; **s. José** Saint Joseph

**Saná** *n* Sanaa

**sanar 1** *vt (persona)* to cure; *(herida)* to heal

**2** *vi (persona)* to get better; *(herida)* to heal

**sanatorio** *nm* sanatorium

**sanción** *nf* (a) *(castigo, multa)* punishment; *Econ* sanction (b) *(aprobación)* approval

**sancionar** vt (a) *(castigar, multar)* to punish; *Econ* to impose sanctions on (b) *(aprobar)* to approve, to sanction

**sancocho** nm *Carib* stew of meat and vegetables

**sanctasanctórum** nm inv *también Fig* sanctum

**sandalia** nf sandal

**sándalo** nm sandalwood

**sandez** nf silly thing; **decir sandeces** to talk nonsense

**sandía** nf watermelon

**sandinismo** nm Sandinista movement

**sandinista** adj & nmf Sandinista

**sandunguero, -a** adj witty, charming

**sándwich** ['sanwitʃ, 'saŋwis] (pl **sándwiches**) nm *(sin tostar)* sandwich; *(tostado)* toasted sandwich

**sandwichera** [saŋwi'tʃera] nf toasted sandwich maker

**saneado, -a** adj *Fin (bienes)* written off, written down; *(economía)* sound, healthy; *(cuenta)* regularized

**saneamiento** nm (a) *(limpieza)* disinfection; *(fontanería)* plumbing; *(de río)* clean-up; **artículos de s.** bathroom furniture (b) *Fin (de bienes)* write-off, write-down; *(de moneda)* stabilization; *(de economía)* putting back on a sound footing

**sanear** vt (a) *(higienizar) (tierras)* to drain; *(edificio)* to disinfect (b) *Fin (bienes)* to write off o down; *(moneda)* to stabilize; *(economía)* to put back on a sound footing

**sanfermines** nmpl = festival held in Pamplona in July during which bulls are run through the streets of the town

**sangrante** adj *(herida)* bleeding; *Fig (situación, injusticia)* shameful, outrageous

**sangrar 1** vi to bleed
**2** vt (a) *(sacar sangre a)* to bleed (b) *(árbol)* to tap (c) *Fam (robar)* to bleed dry (d) *Imprenta* to indent

**sangre** nf blood; *Zool* **de s. caliente** warmblooded; *Zool* **de s. fría** cold-blooded; **s. azul** blue blood; *Fam Fig* **chuparle a alguien la s.** to bleed sb dry; *Fam Fig* **encender** o **quemar la s. a alguien** to make sb's blood boil; **llevar algo en la s.** to have sth in one's blood; *Fig* **no llegó la s. al río** it didn't get too nasty; *Fig* **no tiene s. en las venas** he's got no life in him; *Fam* **se le subió la s. a la cabeza** he saw red; *Fig* **sudar s.** to sweat blood; *Fam* **hacerse mala s.** to get worked up; **tener mala s.** to be malicious; *Fig* **tener s. de horchata** to be as cool as a cucumber; **un baño de s.** a bloodbath; **evitar un derramamiento de s.** to

avoid bloodshed; **s. fría** sangfroid; **a s. fría** in cold blood

**sangría** nf (a) *(bebida)* sangria (b) *Fig (matanza)* bloodbath (c) *Fig (ruina)* drain (d) *Med* bloodletting

**sangriento, -a** adj (a) *(ensangrentado, cruento)* bloody (b) *(despiadado, hiriente)* cruel

**sanguijuela** nf *también Fig* leech

**sanguinario, -a** adj bloodthirsty

**sanguíneo, -a** adj blood; **presión sanguínea** blood pressure

**sanguinolento, -a** adj *(que echa sangre)* bleeding; *(bañado en sangre)* bloody; *(manchado de sangre)* bloodstained; *(ojos)* bloodshot

**sanidad** nf (a) *(salubridad)* health, healthiness (b) *(ministerio)* health department; **s. (pública)** public health service; **s. privada** private healthcare

**sanitario, -a 1** adj health; **personal s.** healthcare workers
**2** nm,f *(persona)* health officer
**3** nm *(retrete)* toilet; **sanitarios** *(bañera, lavabo, retrete)* bathroom furniture

**sanjacobo** nm *Culin* = two slices of steak or ham with a slice of cheese in between, fried in breadcrumbs

**San José** n San José

**San Marino** n San Marino

**sano, -a** adj (a) *(saludable)* healthy; **s. y salvo** safe and sound (b) *(positivo) (principios, persona)* sound; *(ambiente, educación)* wholesome (c) *(entero)* intact, undamaged (d) **cortar por lo s.** to make a clean break

**San Salvador** n San Salvador

**sánscrito, -a** adj & nm Sanskrit

**sanseacabó** interj *Fam* ¡s.! that's an end to it!

**sansón** nm very strong man

**Santander** n Santander

**santaderino, -a 1** adj of/from Santander
**2** nm,f person from Santander

**santero, -a** adj pious

**Santiago (de Chile)** n Santiago

**Santiago de Compostela** n Santiago de Compostela

**Santiago de Cuba** n Santiago de Cuba

**santiagués, -esa 1** adj of/from Santiago de Compostela
**2** nm,f person from Santiago de Compostela

**santiaguero, -a 1** adj of/from Santiago de Cuba
**2** nm,f person from Santiago de Cuba

**santiaguino, -a 1** adj of/from Santiago (de Chile)
**2** nm,f person from Santiago (de Chile)

**santiamén** nm *Fam* **en un s.** in a flash

**santidad** *nf* (a) *(cualidad)* saintliness, holiness (b) **Su S.** His Holiness

**santificación** *nf* sanctification

**santificar** [61] *vt Rel* (a) *(consagrar)* to sanctify (b) *(respetar) (días festivos)* to keep holy; *(padres)* to honour

**santiguar** [12] **1** *vt* to make the sign of the cross over
**2 santiguarse** *vpr* to cross oneself

**santo, -a 1** *adj* (a) *(sagrado)* holy (b) *(virtuoso)* saintly (c) *Fam Fig (beneficioso)* miraculous (d) *Fam Fig (dichoso)* damn; **todo el s. día** all day long
**2** *nm,f Rel & Fig* saint
**3** *nm* (a) *(onomástica)* saint's day; **el día de todos los santos** All Saints' Day (b) *(ilustración)* illustration (c) *(contraseña)* **s. y seña** password (d) *(expresiones)* **¿a s. de qué?** why on earth?, for what earthly reason?; **se le fue el s. al cielo** he/she completely forgot; **llegar y besar el s.** to get it at the first attempt; **no es s. de mi devoción** he's not my cup of tea; **quedarse para vestir santos** to be left on the shelf; **desnudar a un s. para vestir a otro** to rob Peter to pay Paul

**Santo Domingo** *n* Santo Domingo

**santón** *nm* (a) *Rel* holy man (b) *Fig (persona influyente)* guru

**santoral** *nm* (a) *(libro)* = book containing lives of saints (b) *(onomásticas)* = list of saints' days

**Santo Tomé** *n* São Tomé

**Santo Tomé y Príncipe** *n* Sao Tomé and Príncipe

**santuario** *nm* shrine; *Fig* sanctuary

**santurrón, -ona 1** *adj* excessively pious
**2** *nm,f* excessively pious person

**santurronería** *nf* sanctimoniousness

**saña** *nf* viciousness, malice; **con s.** viciously, maliciously

**sañudo, -a** *adj* vicious, malicious

**Sao Paulo** *n* São Paulo

**sapiencia** *nf Formal* knowledge

**sapo** *nm* toad; *Fig* **echar sapos y culebras** to rant and rave

**saque 1** *ver* **sacar**
**2** *nm* (a) *(en fútbol)* **s. de banda** throw-in; **s. inicial** *o* **de centro** kick-off; **s. de esquina** corner kick; **s. de puerta** *o* **meta** goal kick; **s. de honor** = ceremonial kick-off by celebrity (b) *(en rugby)* **s. de banda** line-out (c) *(en tenis, voleibol)* serve; **tener buen s.** to have a good serve (d) *Fig (apetito)* **tener buen s.** to have a hearty appetite

**saqueador, -ora 1** *adj* looting, plundering
**2** *nm,f* looter

**saquear** *vt* (a) *(ciudad, población)* to sack (b) *(tienda)* to loot; *Fam (nevera, armario)* to raid

**saqueo** *nm (de ciudad)* sacking; *(de tienda)* looting

**S.A.R.** *(abrev de* **Su Alteza Real**) HRH

**Sarajevo** *n* Sarajevo

**sarampión** *nm* measles

**sarao** *nm* (a) *(fiesta)* party (b) *Fam (jaleo)* row, rumpus

**sarasa** *nm Fam Pey* poof, queer

**sarcasmo** *nm* sarcasm

**sarcástico, -a 1** *adj* sarcastic
**2** *nm,f* sarcastic person

**sarcófago** *nm* sarcophagus

**sarcoma** *nm* sarcoma

**sardana** *nf* = traditional Catalan dance and music

**sardina** *nf* sardine; **como sardinas en lata** like sardines

**sardinero, -a** *adj* sardine; **barco s.** sardine fishing boat

**sardo, -a 1** *adj & nm,f* Sardinian
**2** *nm (lengua)* Sardinian

**sardónico, -a** *adj* sardonic

**Sargazos** *nmpl* **el mar de los S.** the Sargasso Sea

**sargento 1** *nmf* (a) *Mil* sergeant (b) *Fam Pey (mandón)* dictator, little Hitler
**2** *nm (herramienta)* small clamp

**sari** *nm* sari

**sarmiento** *nm* vine shoot

**sarna** *nf Med* scabies; *(en animales)* mange; *Prov* **s. con gusto no pica** I'm/he's *etc* more than happy to put up with it

**sarnoso, -a 1** *adj (perro)* mangy
**2** *nm,f (persona)* scabies sufferer

**sarpullido** *nm* rash

**sarraceno, -a** *adj & nm,f* Saracen

**sarrio** *nm* chamois

**sarro** *nm* (a) *(de dientes)* tartar (b) *(poso)* sediment

**sarta** *nf también Fig* string; **una s. de insultos/mentiras** a string of insults/lies

**sartén** *nf* frying pan; *Fam Fig* **tener la s. por el mango** to call the shots

**sastre, -tra** *nm,f* tailor

**sastrería** *nf (oficio)* tailoring; *(taller)* tailor's (shop); *Cine & Teatro* wardrobe (department)

**Satanás** *nm* Satan

**satánico, -a** *adj* satanic

**satanismo** *nm* Satanism

**satélite 1** *adj inv Fig* satellite; **las ciudades s. de Madrid** the towns around Madrid; **estado s.** satellite (state)
**2** *nm* satellite; **s. artificial** satellite; **s. espía/meteorológico** spy/weather satellite

**satén** *nm (de seda)* satin; *(de algodón)* sateen

**satinado, -a 1** *adj (papel)* glossy; *(tela)* shiny, satiny; *(pintura)* satin

**2** *nm (de papel)* glossy finish; *(de tela)* shiny o satiny finish; *(de pintura)* satin finish

**satinar** *vt* to make glossy

**sátira** *nf* satire

**satírico, -a 1** *adj* satirical

**2** *nm,f* satirist

**satirizar** [16] *vt* to satirize

**sátiro** *nm* (a) *Mitol* satyr (b) *Fig (lujurioso)* lecher

**satisfacción** *nf* satisfaction; **sentir una gran s. personal** to feel a sense of fulfilment o satisfaction

**satisfacer** [35] **1** *vt* (a) *(saciar)* to satisfy; **s. el hambre/la curiosidad** to satisfy one's hunger/curiosity; **s. la sed** to quench one's thirst (b) *(gustar, agradar)* to please (c) *(deuda, pago)* to pay, to settle (d) *(ofensa, daño)* to redress (e) *(duda, pregunta)* to answer (f) *(cumplir) (requisitos, exigencias)* to meet

**2 satisfacerse** *vpr* to be satisfied; **no se satisfacen con nada** nothing seems to satisfy them

**satisfactorio, -a** *adj (suficientemente bueno)* satisfactory; *(gratificante)* rewarding, satisfying

**satisfecho, -a 1** *participio ver* **satisfacer**

**2** *adj* satisfied; **s. de sí mismo** self-satisfied; **darse por s.** to be satisfied; **dejar s. a alguien** to satisfy sb

**saturación** *nf* saturation; *Fig* **hasta la s.** ad nauseam

**saturado, -a** *adj* saturated (**de** with); *Fig* **estar s. de trabajo** to have all the work one can manage

**saturar 1** *vt* to saturate

**2 saturarse** *vpr* to become saturated (**de** with)

**saturnismo** *nm Med* lead poisoning

**Saturno** *nm* Saturn

**sauce** *nm* willow; **s. llorón** weeping willow

**saúco** *nm* elder

**saudí** ( *pl* **saudíes**), **saudita** *adj & nmf* Saudi

**sauna** *nf* sauna

**saurio** *nm* lizard, saurian

**savia** *nf* sap; *Fig* vitality; *Fig* **s. nueva** new blood

**saxo 1** *nm (instrumento)* sax

**2** *nmf (persona)* sax player

**saxofón, saxófono 1** *nm (instrumento)* saxophone

**2** *nmf (persona)* saxophonist

**saxofonista** *nmf* saxophonist

**saya** *nf Anticuado* petticoat

**sayal** *nm Anticuado* sackcloth

**sayo** *nm Anticuado* smock

**sazón** *nf* (a) *(madurez)* ripeness; **en s.** ripe (b) *(sabor)* seasoning, flavouring (c) **a la s.** then, at that time

**sazonado, -a** *adj* seasoned

**sazonar** *vt* to season

**scooter** [es'kuter] ( *pl* **scooters**) *nm (motor)* scooter

**scout** [es'kaut] ( *pl* **scouts**) **1** *adj* **un grupo s.** a Scout troop

**2** *nmf (boy)* scout, f girl guide

**script** [es'kript] ( *pl* **scripts**) **1** *nm* script

**2** *nf* script girl

**SE** *(abrev de* **Su Excelencia***)* HE

**se** *pron personal* (a) *(reflexivo) (de personas) (singular)* himself, f herself; *(plural)* themselves; *(usted mismo)* yourself; *(ustedes mismos)* yourselves; *(de cosas, animales) (singular)* itself; *(plural)* themselves; **se está lavando, está lavándose** she is washing (herself); **se lavó los dientes** she cleaned her teeth; **espero que se diviertan** I hope you enjoy yourselves; **el perro se lame** the dog is licking itself; **se lame la herida** it's licking its wound; **se levantaron y se fueron** they got up and left

(b) *(reflexivo impersonal)* oneself; **hay que afeitarse todos los días** one has to shave every day, you have to shave every day

(c) *(recíproco)* each other, one another; **se aman** they love each other; **se escriben cartas** they write to each other

(d) *(impersonal)* **en esta sociedad ya no se respeta a los ancianos** in our society old people are no longer respected; **se ha suspendido la reunión** the meeting has been cancelled; **se dice que...** it is said that..., people say that...; **se prohíbe fumar** *(en cartel)* no smoking; **se habla español** *(en cartel)* Spanish spoken

(e) *(como complemento indirecto) (de personas) (singular)* (to) him, f (to) her; *(plural)* (to) them; *(de cosas, animales) (singular)* (to) it; *(plural)* (to) them; *(usted, ustedes)* (to) you; **se lo dio** he gave it to him/her/etc; **se lo dije, pero no me hizo caso** I told her, but she didn't listen; **si usted quiere, yo se lo arreglo en un minuto** if you like, I'll sort it out for you in a minute

**sé** (a) *ver* **saber** (b) *ver* **ser**

**sebáceo, -a** *adj* sebaceous

**sebo** *nm (grasa sólida)* fat; *(para jabón, velas)* tallow

**seborrea** *nf* seborrhoea

**seboso, -a** *adj* fatty

**secadero** *nm* drying room

**secado** *nm* drying

**secador** *nm* dryer; **s. (de pelo)** hair-dryer

**secadora** nf clothes o tumble dryer

**secano** nm unirrigated o dry land; **cultivos de s.** = crops suitable for unirrigated land

**secante 1** adj (a) (secador) drying (b) **papel s.** blotting paper (c) Mat secant; **línea s.** secant

  **2** nf Mat secant

**secar** [61] **1** vt (a) (quitar humedad a) to dry (b) (enjugar) to wipe away; (con fregona) to mop up

  **2 secarse** vpr (planta, pozo) to dry up; (vajilla, suelo, ropa) to dry

**sección** nf (a) también Mat section (b) (departamento) department

**seccionar** vt (a) (cortar) to cut; Mec to section (b) (dividir) to divide (up)

**secesión** nf secession

**secesionismo** nm secessionism

**secesionista** adj secessionist

**seco, -a** adj (a) (en general) dry; (plantas, flores) withered; (higos, pasas) dried (b) (persona, actitud) brusque (c) (flaco) thin, lean (d) (ruido) dull; (tos) dry; (voz) sharp; **un golpe s.** a rap (e) Fam (sediento) thirsty; **estar s.** to be thirsty (f) (expresiones) **dejar a alguien s.** (matar) to kill sb stone dead; (pasmar) to stun sb; **parar en s.** to stop dead; **a secas** simply, just; **llámame Juan a secas** just call me Juan

**secoya** nf sequoia

**secreción** nf secretion

**secretar** vt to secrete

**secretaría** nf (a) (cargo) post of secretary (b) (oficina, lugar) secretary's office (c) (organismo) secretariat; **S. de Estado** = subdivision of government ministry

**secretariado** nm (a) Educ secretarial skills; **estudia s.** she's doing a secretarial course (b) (cargo) post of secretary (c) (oficina, lugar) secretary's office (d) (organismo) secretariat

**secretario, -a** nm,f secretary; **s. de dirección** secretary to the director; **s. de Estado** Secretary of State; **s. general** General Secretary

**secretear** vi Fam to whisper, to talk secretively

**secreter** nm bureau, writing desk

**secretismo** nm (excessive) secrecy

**secreto, -a 1** adj (reservado) secret; (confidencial) confidential

  **2** nm (a) (en general) secret; **s. a voces** open secret; **s. bancario** banking confidentiality; **s. de confesión** secrecy of the confessional; **s. de Estado** State o official secret; **s. profesional** professional secret; **decretar el s. sumarial** = to deny public access to information relating to a judicial investigation (b) (sigilo) secrecy; **en s.** in secret

**secta** nf sect

**sectario, -a 1** adj sectarian

  **2** nm,f (a) (miembro de secta) sect member (b) (fanático) fanatic

**sectarismo** nm sectarianism

**sector** nm (a) (división) section; Econ sector; **s. cuaternario** leisure industries o sector; **s. primario/secundario** primary/secondary sector; **s. privado/público** private/public sector; **s. servicios** o **terciario** service industries o sector (b) (zona) sector, area

**sectorial** adj sectorial

**secuaz** nmf Pey minion

**secuela** nf consequence; **dejar secuelas a alguien** to leave sb suffering from the after-effects

**secuencia** nf sequence

**secuenciador** nm Mús & Informát sequencer

**secuencial** adj sequential

**secuestrador, -ora** nm,f kidnapper

**secuestrar** vt (a) (raptar) to kidnap (b) (avión, barco) to hijack (c) (embargar) to seize

**secuestro** nm (a) (rapto) kidnapping (b) (de avión, barco) hijack (c) (de bienes) seizure, confiscation

**secular** adj (a) (seglar) secular, lay; **clero s.** secular clergy (b) (centenario) centuries-old, age-old

**secularización** nf secularization

**secularizar** [16] vt to secularize

**secundar** vt to support, to back (up); **s. una propuesta** to second a proposal

**secundario, -a** adj secondary; **actor s.** supporting actor

**secuoya** nf sequoia

**sed 1** ver **ser**

  **2** nf thirst; **tener s.** to be thirsty; Fig **s. de** thirst for

**seda** nf silk; **ir como una** o **la s.** to go smoothly; **s. artificial** rayon, artificial silk; **s. cruda** raw silk; **s. dental** dental floss; **s. natural** pure silk

**sedal** nm fishing line

**sedán** nm saloon

**sedante 1** adj Med sedative; (música) soothing

  **2** nm sedative

**sedar** vt Med to sedate; (sujeto: música) to soothe, to calm

**sede** nf (a) (de organización, empresa) headquarters; (de Gobierno) seat; (de acontecimiento) venue (de for); **s. social** head office (b) Rel see; **la Santa S.** the Holy See

**sedentario, -a** adj sedentary

**sedentarismo** nm **el s. avanza** people are adopting an increasingly sedentary lifestyle

**sedente** *adj* seated

**sedición** *nf* sedition

**sedicioso, -a 1** *adj* seditious
 **2** *nm,f* rebel

**sediento, -a** *adj* (*de agua*) thirsty; *Fig* **s. de** (*deseoso*) hungry for

**sedimentación** *nf* sedimentation

**sedimentar 1** *vt* to deposit
 **2 sedimentarse** *vpr* to settle

**sedimentario, -a** *adj* sedimentary

**sedimento** *nm* (a) (*poso*) sediment (b) *Fig* (*huella*) residue

**sedoso, -a** *adj* silky

**seducción** *nf* (a) (*cualidad*) seductiveness (b) (*atracción*) attraction, charm; (*sexual*) seduction

**seducir** [20] *vt* (a) (*atraer*) to attract, to charm; (*sexualmente*) to seduce (b) (*persuadir*) **s. a alguien para que haga algo** to charm sb into doing sth

**seductor, -ora 1** *adj* (a) (*atractivo*) attractive, charming; (*sexualmente*) seductive (b) (*persuasivo*) persuasive, charming
 **2** *nm,f* seducer

**sedujera** *etc ver* **seducir**

**seduzca** *etc ver* **seducir**

**sefardí** (*pl* sefardíes), **sefardita 1** *adj* Sephardic
 **2** *nmf* (*persona*) Sephardi
 **3** *nm* (*lengua*) Sephardi

**segador, -ora** *nm,f* (*agricultor*) reaper

**segadora** *nf* (*máquina*) reaping machine

**segar** [45] *vt* (a) *Agr* to reap (b) (*cortar*) to cut off (c) *Fig* (*truncar*) **la epidemia segó la vida de cientos de personas** the epidemic claimed the lives of hundreds of people

**seglar 1** *adj* secular, lay
 **2** *nm* lay person

**segmentación** *nf* division

**segmentar** *vt* to cut *o* divide into pieces

**segmento** *nm* (a) *Mat & Zool* segment (b) (*trozo*) piece

**segoviano, -a 1** *adj* of/from Segovia
 **2** *nm,f* person from Segovia

**segregación** *nf* (a) (*separación, discriminación*) segregation; **s. racial** racial segregation (b) (*secreción*) secretion

**segregacionismo** *nm* policy of racial segregation

**segregacionista** *adj* segregationist; **política s.** policy of racial segregation

**segregar** [40] *vt* (a) (*separar, discriminar*) to segregate (b) (*secretar*) to secrete

**segué** *etc ver* **segar**

**segueta** *nf* fretsaw

**seguidamente** *adv* next, immediately afterwards

**seguidilla** *nf* (a) *Lit* = poem containing four or seven verses used in popular songs (b) (*cante flamenco*) = mournful flamenco song

**seguido, -a 1** *adj* (a) (*consecutivo*) consecutive; **diez años seguidos** ten years in a row; **llamó a la puerta cinco veces seguidas** she knocked at the door five times (b) (*sin interrupción*) continuous; **llevan reunidos cuatro horas seguidas** they've been in the meeting for four hours without a break; **ha nevado durante dos semanas seguidas** it's been snowing for two weeks solid (c) (*inmediatamente después*) **s. de** followed by; **sopa, seguida de carne o pescado** soup, followed by meat or fish (d) (*expresiones*) **en seguida** straight away, at once; **en seguida nos vamos** we're going right away
 **2** *adv* (a) (*sin interrupción*) continuously (b) (*en línea recta*) straight on; **todo s.** straight on *o* ahead

**seguidor, -ora** *nm,f* follower

**seguimiento** *nm* (*de noticia*) following; (*de clientes*) follow-up; **efectuar un s. de una epidemia** to monitor the course of an epidemic

**seguir** [63] **1** *vt* (a) (*en general*) to follow (b) (*perseguir*) to chase (c) (*reanudar*) to continue, to resume (d) (*cursar*) **sigue un curso de italiano** he's doing an Italian course
 **2** *vi* (a) (*sucederse*) **s. a algo** to follow sth; **la lluvia siguió a los truenos** the thunder was followed by rain (b) (*continuar*) to continue, to go on; **¡sigue, no te pares!** go *o* carry on, don't stop!; **sigo trabajando en la fábrica** I'm still working at the factory; **debes s. haciéndolo** you should keep on *o* carry on doing it; **sigo pensando que está mal** I still think it's wrong; **sigue enferma/en el hospital** she's still ill/in hospital
 **3 seguirse** *v impersonal* to follow; **seguirse de algo** to follow *o* be deduced from sth; **de esto se sigue que estás equivocado** it therefore follows that you are wrong

**según 1** *prep* (a) (*de acuerdo con*) according to; **s. su opinión, ha sido un éxito** in her opinion *o* according to her, it was a success; **s. yo/tú/***etc* in my/your/*etc* opinion
 (b) (*dependiendo de*) depending on; **s. la hora que sea** depending on the time
 **2** *adv* (a) (*como*) (just) as; **todo permanecía s. lo recordaba** everything was just as she remembered it; **actuó s. se le recomendó** he did as he had been advised
 (b) (*a medida que*) as; **entrarás en forma s. vayas entrenando** you'll get fit as you train
 (c) (*dependiendo*) **¿te gusta la música? – s.** do

you like music? – it depends; **lo intentaré s. esté de tiempo** I'll try to do it, depending on how much time I have; **s. que** depending on whether; **s. qué** certain; **s. qué días la clase es muy aburrida** some days the class is really boring

**segunda** *nf* (a) *Aut* second (gear); **meter (la) s.** to go into second (gear) (b) *Av & Ferroc* second class; **viajar en s.** to travel second class (c) *Dep* second division; **bajar a s.** to be relegated to the second division (d) *(expresiones)* **con segundas (intenciones)** with ulterior motives; **¿me lo dices con segundas?** are you telling me this for any particular reason?

**segundero** *nm* second hand

**segundo, -a 1** *núm adj* second

**2** *núm nm,f* (a) *(en orden)* **el s.** the second one; **llegó el s.** he came second (b) *(mencionado antes)* **vinieron Pedro y Juan, el s. con...** Pedro and Juan arrived, the latter with... (c) *(ayudante)* number two; *Náut* **s. de abordo** first mate

**3** *nm (en general)* second; *(piso)* second floor

**segundón, -ona** *nm,f* second son; *Fig Pey* **ser el eterno s.** to be one of life's eternal bridesmaids

**seguramente** *adv* probably; **s. iré, pero aún no lo sé** the chances are I'll go, but I'm not sure yet

**seguridad** *nf* (a) *(ausencia de peligro)* safety; **de s.** *(cinturón, cierre)* safety; **s. vial** road safety (b) *(protección)* security; *(puerta, guardia)* security; **s. ciudadana** public safety; **S. Social** Social Security (c) *(estabilidad, firmeza)* security; **una inversión que ofrece s.** a safe *o* secure investment (d) *(certidumbre)* certainty; **con s.** for sure, definitely; **con toda s.** with absolute certainty *(en confianza)* confidence; **s. en sí mismo** self-confidence; **mostrar una falsa s.** to put on a show of confidence

**seguro, -a 1** *adj* (a) *(sin peligro)* safe; **sobre s.** safely, without risk; **es una inversión segura** it's a safe investment

(b) *(protegido, estable)* secure

(c) *(fiable)* reliable

(d) *(indudable, cierto)* definite, certain; **su nombramiento es s.** he's certain to be given the post; **ya sabemos la fecha segura de su llegada** we've now got a definite date for his arrival

(e) *(confiado)* sure; **estar s. de algo** to be sure about sth; **tener por s. que** to be sure that

**2** *nm* (a) *(contrato)* insurance; **s. de cambio** exchange rate hedge; **s. del coche/de la vivienda** car/house insurance; **s. de incendios** fire insurance; **s. de invalidez** *o* **incapacidad** disability insurance; **s. mutuo** joint insurance;

**s. de paro** *o* **de desempleo** unemployment benefit; **s. a todo riesgo/a terceros** comprehensive/third party insurance; **s. de vida** life insurance

(b) *Fam (seguridad social)* **ir al s.** to go to the hospital/health centre; **ese tratamiento no lo cubre el s.** you can't get that treatment on the National Health

(c) *(dispositivo)* safety device; *(de armas)* safety catch (d) *Méx (imperdible)* safety pin

**3** *adv* for sure, definitely; **s. que vendrá** she's bound to come

**seis 1** *núm adj inv* (a) *(para contar)* six; **tiene s. años** she's six (years old)

(b) *(para ordenar)* (number) six; **la página s.** page six

**2** *núm nm* (a) *(número)* six; **el s.** number six; **doscientos s.** two hundred and six; **treinta y s.** thirty-six

(b) *(en fechas)* sixth; **el s. de agosto** the sixth of August

(c) *(en direcciones)* **calle Mayor (número) s.** number six calle Mayor

(d) *(en naipes)* six; **el s. de diamantes** the six of diamonds; **echar** *o* **tirar un s.** to play a six

**3** *núm mpl* (a) *(referido a grupos)* **invité a diez y sólo vinieron s.** I invited ten and only six came along; **somos s.** there are six of us; **de s. en s.** in sixes; **los s.** the six of them

(b) *(en temperaturas)* **estamos a s. bajo cero** the temperature is six below zero

(c) *(en puntuaciones)* **empatar a s.** to draw six all; **s. a cero** six-nil

**4** *núm fpl (hora)* **las s.** six o'clock; **son las s.** it's six o'clock

**seiscientos, -as** *núm* six hundred; *ver también* **seis**

**seísmo** *nm* earthquake

**selección** *nf* (a) *(en general)* selection; *(de personal)* recruitment; **test de s. múltiple** multiple choice test; **s. natural** natural selection (b) *(equipo)* team; **s. nacional** national team

**seleccionador, -ora 1** *adj* (a) *Dep* selecting (b) *(de personal)* recruiting

**2** *nm,f* (a) *Dep* selector, manager (b) *(de personal)* recruiter

**seleccionar** *vt* to pick, to select

**selectividad** *nf* (a) *(selección)* selectivity (b) *(examen)* university entrance examination

**selectivo, -a** *adj* selective

**selecto, -a** *adj* select

**selector, -ora 1** *adj* selecting

**2** *nm* selector (button)

**selenio** *nm* selenium

**selenita 1** *nf* selenite

**2** *nmf (habitante)* moon dweller

**self-service** [selfˈserβis] *nm inv* self-service restaurant

**sellado, -a 1** *adj (documento)* sealed; *(pasaporte, carta)* stamped

**2** *nm (de documento)* sealing; *(de pasaporte, carta)* stamping

**sellar** *vt* **(a)** *(timbrar)* to stamp **(b)** *(lacrar)* to seal **(c)** *Fig (pacto, labios)* to seal

**sello** *nm* **(a)** *(timbre)* stamp **(b)** *(tampón)* rubber stamp; *(marca)* stamp **(c)** *(lacre)* seal **(d)** *(sortija)* signet ring **(e)** *Fig (carácter)* hallmark; **ese libro lleva el s. de su autor** this book is unmistakably the author's work **(f) s. discográfico** record label

**selva** *nf (jungla)* jungle; *(bosque)* forest; *Fig* **una s. de libros** mountains of books; **s. tropical** tropical rainforest; **s. virgen** virgin forest

**Selva Negra** *nf* **la S.** the Black Forest

**selvático, -a** *adj* woodland; **zona selvática** woodland area

**semáforo** *nm* traffic lights; **s. sonoro** pelican crossing *(with audible signal)*

**semana** *nf* week; **entre s.** during the week; **s. laboral** working week; **dos veces por s.** twice a week, twice weekly; **S. Santa** Easter; *Rel* Holy Week

**semanal** *adj* weekly

**semanalmente** *adv* every week, once a week; **se publica s.** it's published weekly

**semanario, -a 1** *adj* weekly

**2** *nm (publicación semanal)* weekly

**semántica** *nf* semantics *(singular)*

**semántico, -a** *adj* semantic

**semblante** *nm* countenance, face

**semblanza** *nf* portrait, profile

**sembrado, -a 1** *adj* **(a)** *(plantado)* sown **(b)** *Fig (lleno)* **s. de** scattered *o* plagued with

**2** *nm* sown field

**sembrador, -ora 1** *adj* sowing

**2** *nm,f (persona)* sower

**sembradora** *nf (máquina)* seed drill

**sembrar** [3] *vt* **(a)** *(plantar)* to sow **(b)** *Fig (llenar)* to scatter, to strew **(c)** *Fig (confusión, pánico)* to sow

**semejante 1** *adj* **(a)** *(parecido)* similar **(a** to**) (b)** *(tal)* such; **jamás aceptaría s. invitación** I would never accept such an invitation; **una propuesta de s. talante** a proposal of this nature, such a proposal

**2** *nm* fellow (human) being

**semejanza** *nf* similarity

**semejar 1** *vt* to resemble

**2 semejarse** *vpr* to be alike, to resemble each other; **semejarse a alguien/algo** to resemble sb/sth

**semen** *nm* semen

**semental 1** *adj* stud; **toro s.** stud bull

**2** *nm* stud; *(caballo)* stallion

**sementera** *nf (tierra)* sown land

**semestral** *adj* half-yearly, six-monthly

**semestre** *nm* period of six months, *US* semester; **cada s.** every six months

**semiautomático, -a** *adj* semiautomatic

**semicircular** *adj* semicircular

**semicírculo** *nm* semicircle

**semiconductor** *nm* semiconductor

**semiconsciente** *adj* semiconscious

**semiconsonante** *nf* semiconsonant

**semicorchea** *nf Mús Br* semiquaver, *US* sixteenth note

**semiderruido, -a** *adj* crumbling

**semidesconocido, -a 1** *adj* almost unknown

**2** *nm,f* **es un s.** he is almost unknown

**semidesierto, -a 1** *adj (calle, playa)* almost deserted; *(sala, oficina)* almost empty

**2** *nm Geog* semidesert

**semidesnatado, -a** *adj* semi-skimmed

**semidesnudo, -a** *adj* half-naked

**semidiós, -osa** *nm,f* demigod, *f* demigoddess

**semidirecto, -a 1** *adj* express

**2** *nm (tren)* = through train, a section of which becomes a stopping train

**semiesférico, -a** *adj* semispherical

**semifinal** *nf* semifinal

**semifinalista 1** *adj* semifinalist; **equipo s.** semifinalist

**2** *nmf* semifinalist

**semifusa** *nf Mús Br* hemidemisemiquaver, *US* sixty-fourth note

**semilla** *nf también Fig* seed

**semillero** *nm* **(a)** *(para plantar)* seedbed **(b)** *(para guardar)* seed box

**seminario** *nm* **(a)** *(escuela para sacerdotes)* seminary **(b)** *Educ (curso, conferencia)* seminar; *(departamento)* department, school

**seminarista** *nm* seminarist

**seminuevo, -a** *adj* almost new

**semioculto, -a** *adj* partially hidden

**semiología** *nf Ling & Med* semiology

**semiólogo, -a** *nm,f Ling & Med* semiologist

**semiótica** *nf Ling & Med* semiotics *(singular)*

**semipesado, -a** *Dep* **1** *adj* light heavyweight; **peso s.** light heavyweight

**2** *nm* light heavyweight

**semiprecioso, -a** *adj* semiprecious

**semiseco, -a** *adj* medium-dry

**semita 1** *adj* Semitic

**2** *nmf* Semite

**semítico, -a** *adj* Semitic

**semitismo** *nm* Semitism

**semitono** *nm Mús* semitone

**semitransparente** *adj* translucent

**semivocal** *nf Ling* semivowel

**sémola** *nf* semolina

**sempiterno, -a** *adj Formal* eternal

**Sena** *nm* el S. the (river) Seine

**senado** *nm* senate

**senador, -ora** *nm,f* senator

**senatorial** *adj* (a) *(del senado)* senate; **comité s.** senate committee (b) *(de senador)* senatorial

**sencillamente** *adv* simply

**sencillez** *nf* (a) *(facilidad)* simplicity (b) *(modestia)* unaffectedness, naturalness (c) *(discreción)* plainness

**sencillo, -a 1** *adj* (a) *(fácil, sin lujo, llano)* simple (b) *(campechano)* natural, unaffected (c) *(billete) Br* single, *US* one-way (d) *(no múltiple)* single; **habitación sencilla** single room

**2** *nm* (a) *(disco)* single (b) *Am Fam (cambio)* loose change

**senda** *nf*, **sendero** *nm* path

**senderismo** *nm* hill walking, hiking

**sendos, -as** *adj pl* **llegaron con s. paquetes** they each arrived with a parcel

**senectud** *nf* old age

**Senegal** *nm* (el) S. Senegal

**senegalés, -esa** *adj & nm,f* Senegalese

**senil** *adj* senile

**senilidad** *nf* senility

**sénior** (*pl* **séniors**) *adj & nm* senior

**seno** *nm* (a) *(pecho)* breast; **senos** breasts, bosom (b) *Fig (amparo, cobijo)* refuge, shelter; **acogieron en su s. a los refugiados** they gave shelter to *o* took in the refugees (c) *(útero)* **s.** *(materno)* womb (d) *Fig (de una organización)* heart; **en el s. de** within (e) *(concavidad)* hollow (f) *Mat* sine (g) *Anat (de la nariz)* sinus

**sensación** *nf* (a) *(percepción)* feeling, sensation; **una s. de dolor** a painful sensation; **tengo la s. de que estoy perdiendo el tiempo** I get the feeling I'm wasting my time (b) *(efecto)* sensation; **causar s.** to cause a sensation; **causar una gran s. a alguien** to make a great impression on sb (c) *(premonición)* feeling; **tener la s. de que** to have a feeling that

**sensacional** *adj* sensational

**sensacionalismo** *nm* sensationalism

**sensacionalista** *adj* sensationalist

**sensatez** *nf* wisdom, common sense

**sensato, -a** *adj* sensible

**sensibilidad** *nf* (a) *(percepción)* feeling; **no tiene s. en los brazos** she has no feeling in her arms (b) *(emotividad)* sensitivity; **tener la s. a flor de piel** to be easily hurt, to be very sensitive (c) *(inclinación)* feeling; **s. artística/ musical** feeling for art/music (d) *(de instrumento, película)* sensitivity; **un termómetro de gran s.** a very sensitive thermometer

**sensibilización** *nf* (a) *(concienciación)* increased awareness (b) *Fot* sensitization

**sensibilizar** [16] *vt* (a) *(concienciar)* to raise the awareness of (b) *Fot* to sensitize

**sensible** *adj* (a) *(en general)* sensitive (b) *(evidente)* perceptible; *(importante)* significant; **pérdidas sensibles** significant losses; **mostrar una s. mejoría** to show a perceptible improvement

**sensiblería** *nf Pey* mushiness

**sensiblero, -a** *adj Pey* mushy, sloppy

**sensitivo, -a** *adj* (a) *(de los sentidos)* sensory (b) *(receptible)* sensitive

**sensor** *nm* sensor

**sensorial** *adj* sensory

**sensual** *adj* sensual

**sensualidad** *nf* sensuality

**sentada** *nf* (a) *(protesta)* sit-in (b) *Fam* **hacer algo de una s.** to do sth at one sitting *o* in one go

**sentado, -a** *adj* (a) *(en asiento)* seated; **estar s.** to be sitting down (b) *(establecido)* **dar algo por s.** to take sth for granted; **dejar s. que…** to make it clear that…

**sentar** [3] **1** *vt* (a) *(en asiento)* to seat, to sit (b) *(establecer)* to establish

**2** *vi* (a) *(ropa, color)* to suit; **no le sienta bien** it doesn't suit her (b) *(comida)* **s. bien/mal a alguien** to agree/disagree with sb (c) *(vacaciones, medicamento)* **s. bien a alguien** to do sb good (d) *(comentario, consejo)* **le sentó mal** it upset her; **le sentó bien** she appreciated it

**3 sentarse** *vpr* to sit down; **sentarse a hacer algo** to sit down and do sth

**sentencia** *nf* (a) *Der* sentence; **visto para s.** ready for judgment (b) *(proverbio, máxima)* maxim

**sentenciar** [15] *vt* (a) *Der* to sentence (a **alguien a algo** sb to sth) (b) *Fig (condenar, juzgar)* to condemn

**sentencioso, -a** *adj* sententious

**sentido, -a 1** *adj* (a) *(profundo)* heartfelt (b) *(sensible)* **ser muy s.** to be very sensitive

**2** *nm* (a) *(en general)* sense; **s. común** common sense; **s. del humor** sense of humour; **s. de la orientación** sense of direction; **s. del ridículo** sense of the ridiculous; **sexto s.** sixth sense (b) *(conocimiento)* consciousness; **perder/recobrar el s.** to lose/regain consciousness; **sin s.**

unconscious (**c**) *(significado)* meaning, sense; **tener s.** to make sense; **sin s.** *(ilógico)* meaningless; *(inútil, irrelevante)* pointless; **doble s.** double meaning; **un sin s.** nonsense (**d**) *(dirección)* direction; **de s. único** one-way

**sentimental 1** *adj* sentimental
**2** *nmf* **es un s.** he's very sentimental

**sentimentalismo** *nm* sentimentality

**sentimentaloide** *adj* mushy, sloppy

**sentimiento** *nm* (**a**) *(en general)* feeling; **s. de culpabilidad/pena** feeling of guilt/sorrow; **le acompaño en el s.** my deepest sympathy (**b**) **sentimientos** feelings; **dejarse llevar por los sentimientos** to get carried away; **¡no tienes sentimientos!** you have no feelings!

**sentir** [64] **1** *vt* (**a**) *(en general)* to feel (**b**) *(lamentar)* to regret, to be sorry about; **siento que no puedas venir** I'm sorry you can't come; **lo siento (mucho)** I'm (really) sorry (**c**) *(oír)* to hear
**2** *vi* to feel; *Fig* **sin s.** without noticing
**3** *nm* feelings, sentiments
**4 sentirse** *vpr* to feel; **me siento mareada** I feel sick; **se siente superior** she considers herself superior

**senyera** *nf* Catalan national flag

**seña 1** *nf* *(gesto, indicio, contraseña)* sign, signal
**2** *nfpl* **señas** (**a**) *(dirección)* address; **señas personales** *(personal)* description (**b**) *(gesto, indicio)* signs; **dar señas de algo** to show signs of sth; **hablar por señas** to talk in sign language; **hacer señas (a alguien)** to signal (to sb) (**c**) *(detalle)* details; **para** *o* **por más señas** to be precise

**señal** *nf* (**a**) *también Telecom* signal; *(de teléfono)* tone; **s. de alarma/salida** alarm/starting signal (**b**) *(indicio, símbolo)* sign; **dar señales de vida** to show signs of life; **s. de la cruz** sign of the Cross; **s. de tráfico** road sign; **en s. de** as a mark *o* sign of (**c**) *(marca, huella)* mark; **no quedó ni s. de él** there was no sign of him left; **no dejó ni s.** she didn't leave a trace (**d**) *(cicatriz)* scar, mark (**e**) *(fianza)* deposit

**señalado, -a** *adj* (**a**) *(importante) (fecha)* special; *(personaje)* distinguished (**b**) *(con cicatrices)* scarred, marked

**señalar 1** *vt* (**a**) *(marcar, denotar)* to mark; *(hora, temperatura)* to indicate, to say (**b**) *(indicar)* to point out; **nos señaló con el dedo** he pointed at us; **no quiero s. a nadie, pero...** I don't want to point the finger at anyone, but... (**c**) *(fijar)* to set, to fix; **señaló su valor en 1.000 dólares** he set *o* fixed its value at $1,000
**2 señalarse** *vpr (destacar)* to stand out

**señalización** *nf* (**a**) *(conjunto de señales)* signs (**b**) *(colocación de señales)* signposting

**señalizar** [16] *vt* to signpost

**señera** *nf* Catalan flag

**señor, -ora 1** *adj* (**a**) *(refinado)* noble, refined (**b**) *Fam (gran)* real; *(excelente)* wonderful, splendid; **tienen una señora casa/un s. problema** that's some house/problem they've got
**2** *nm* (**a**) *(tratamiento) (antes de nombre, cargo)* Mr; *(al dirigir la palabra)* Sir; **el s. López** Mr López; **los señores Ruiz** Mr and Mrs Ruiz; **¡s. presidente!** Mr President!; **¿qué desea el s.?** what would you like, Sir?; **Muy s. mío** *(en cartas)* Dear Sir
(**b**) *(hombre)* man
(**c**) *(caballero)* gentleman
(**d**) *(dueño)* owner
(**e**) *(amo)* master
(**f**) *Rel* **el S.** the Lord

**señora** *nf* (**a**) *(tratamiento) (antes de nombre, cargo)* Mrs; *(al dirigir la palabra)* Madam; **la s. López** Mrs López; **¡s. presidenta!** Madam President!; **¿qué desea la s.?** what would you like, Madam?; **¡señoras y señores!** Ladies and Gentlemen!; **Estimada s.** *(en cartas)* Dear Madam; **¿es usted s. o señorita?** are you a Mrs or a Miss?
(**b**) *(mujer)* lady; **s. de compañía** female companion
(**c**) *(dama)* lady
(**d**) *(dueña)* owner
(**e**) *(ama)* mistress
(**f**) *(esposa)* wife; **el señor Ruiz y s.** Mr and Mrs Ruiz; **mi s. esposa** my (good) wife
(**g**) *Rel* **Nuestra S.** Our Lady

**señorear** *vt (dominar)* to control, to rule

**señoría** *nf* lordship, *f* ladyship; **su s.** *(en general)* his lordship; *(a un noble)* Your Lordship; *(a un parlamentario)* the Right Honourable gentleman/lady; *(a un juez)* your Honour

**señorial** *adj* (**a**) *(majestuoso)* stately (**b**) *(del señorío)* lordly

**señorío** *nm* (**a**) *(dominio)* dominion, rule (**b**) *(distinción)* nobility

**señorita** *nf* (**a**) *(soltera, tratamiento)* Miss (**b**) *(joven)* young lady (**c**) *(maestra)* **la s.** miss, the teacher (**d**) *Anticuado (hija del amo)* mistress

**señorito, -a 1** *adj Fam Pey (refinado)* lordly
**2** *nm* (**a**) *Anticuado (hijo del amo)* master (**b**) *Fam Pey (niñato)* rich kid

**señuelo** *nm* (**a**) *(reclamo)* decoy (**b**) *Fig (trampa)* bait, lure

**seo** *nf (catedral)* cathedral

**sepa** *etc ver* **saber**

**sépalo** *nm Bot* sepal

**separación** *nf* (a) *(en general)* separation (b) *(espacio)* space, distance (c) *Der* **s. de bienes** separate estates (in matrimony)

**separado, -a 1** *adj* (a) *(en general)* separate; **está muy s. de la pared** it's too far away from the wall; **por s.** separately (b) *(del cónyuge)* separated
  **2** *nm,f* separated person

**separar 1** *vt* (a) *(en general)* to separate (**de** from) (b) *(desunir)* to take off, to remove (c) *(apartar)* to move away (**de** from) (d) *(reservar)* to put aside (e) *(destituir)* **s. de** to remove *o* dismiss from
  **2 separarse** *vpr* (a) *(apartarse)* to move apart; **separarse de** to move away from (b) *(ir por distinto lugar)* to separate, to part company (c) *(matrimonio)* to separate (**de alguien** from sb) (d) *(desprenderse)* to come away *o* off

**separata** *nf* pull-out supplement

**separatismo** *nm* separatism

**separatista** *adj & nmf* separatist

**separo** *nm Méx* cell

**sepelio** *nm* burial

**sepia 1** *adj & nm inv (color)* sepia
  **2** *nf (molusco)* cuttlefish

**septentrional 1** *adj* northern
  **2** *nmf* northerner

**septicemia** *nf Med* septicaemia

**séptico, -a** *adj* septic

**septiembre, setiembre** *nm* September; **el 1 de s.** the 1st of September; **uno de los septiembres más lluviosos de la última década** one of the rainiest Septembers in the last decade; **a principios/mediados/finales de s.** at the beginning/in the middle/at the end of September; **el pasado/próximo (mes de) s.** last/next September; **en s.** in September; **en pleno s.** in mid-September; **este (mes de) s.** *(pasado)* (this) last September; *(próximo)* next September, this coming September; **para s.** by September

**séptimo, -a** *núm* seventh; **la séptima parte** a seventh

**septuagésimo, -a** *núm* seventieth

**septuplicar [61] 1** *vt* to multiply by seven
  **2 septuplicarse** *vpr* to increase sevenfold

**sepulcral** *adj* (a) *(del sepulcro)* **arte s.** funerary art (b) *Fig (profundo) (voz, silencio)* lugubrious, gloomy; *(frío)* deathly

**sepulcro** *nm* tomb

**sepultar** *vt* to bury

**sepultura** *nf* (a) *(enterramiento)* burial (b) *(fosa)* grave

**sepulturero, -a** *nm,f* gravedigger

**seque** *etc ver* **secar**

**sequedad** *nf* (a) *(falta de humedad)* dryness (b) *Fig (antipatía)* abruptness, brusqueness

**sequía** *nf* drought

**séquito** *nm (comitiva)* retinue, entourage

**ser [2]**

> The auxiliary verb **ser** is used with the past participle of a verb to form the passive (e.g. **la película fue criticada** the film was criticized).

**1** *v aux (para formar la voz pasiva)* to be; **fue visto por un testigo** he was seen by a witness

**2** *v copulativo* (a) *(en general)* to be; **es alto/gracioso** he is tall/funny; **es azul/difícil** it's blue/difficult; **es un amigo/el dueño** he is a friend/the owner

(b) *(empleo, dedicación)* to be; **soy abogado/actriz** I'm a lawyer/an actress; **son estudiantes** they're students

**3** *vi* (a) *(en general)* to be; **fue aquí** it was here; **lo importante es decidirse** the important thing is to reach a decision; **s. de** *(estar hecho de)* to be made of; *(provenir de)* to be from; *(ser propiedad de)* to belong to; *(formar parte de)* to be a member of; **¿de dónde eres?** where are you from?; **los juguetes son de mi hijo** the toys are my son's

(b) *(con precios, horas, números)* to be; **¿cuánto es?** how much is it?; **son 300 pesetas** that'll be 300 pesetas; **¿qué (día) es hoy?** what day is it today?, what's today?; **mañana será 15 de julio** tomorrow (it) will be the 15th of July; **¿qué hora es?** what time is it?, what's the time?; **son las tres (de la tarde)** it's three o'clock (in the afternoon), it's three (pm)

(c) *(servir, ser adecuado)* **s. para** to be for; **este trapo es para (limpiar) las ventanas** this cloth is for (cleaning) the windows; **este libro es para niños** this book is (meant) for children

(d) *(uso partitivo)* **s. de los que...** to be one of those (people) who...; **ése de los que están en huelga** he is one of those on strike

**4** *v impersonal* (a) *(expresa tiempo)* to be; **es muy tarde** it's rather late; **era de noche/de día** it was night/day

(b) *(expresa necesidad, posibilidad)* **es de desear que...** it is to be hoped that...; **es de suponer que aparecerá** presumably, he'll turn up

(c) *(expresa motivo)* **es que no vine porque estaba enfermo** the reason I didn't come is that I was ill

(d) *(expresiones)* **a no s. que** unless; **como sea** one way or another, somehow or other; **de no s. por** had it not been for; **érase una vez, érase que se era** once upon a time; **no es para menos** not without reason; **o sea** that is (to say), I mean; **por si fuera poco** as if that wasn't enough

**5** *nm (ente)* being; **s. humano** human being; **los seres vivos** living things

**serafín** *nm* seraph

**Serbia** *n* Serbia

**serbio, -a** *adj & nm,f* Serbian

**serbocroata 1** *adj & nmf* Serbo-Croat

**2** *nm (idioma)* Serbo-Croat

**serenar 1** *vt (calmar)* to calm

**2 serenarse** *vpr (calmarse)* to calm down; *(tiempo)* to clear up; *(viento)* to die down; *(aguas)* to grow calm

**serenata** *nf Mús* serenade

**serenidad** *nf* (a) *(tranquilidad)* calm (b) *(quietud)* tranquility

**sereno, -a 1** *adj* (a) *(sobrio)* sober (b) *(tranquilo)* calm

**2** *nm* (a) *Antes (vigilante)* night watchman (b) *(humedad)* night dew

**serial** *nm* serial

**serie** *nf* (a) *también TV* series *(singular)*; *(de hechos, sucesos)* chain; *(de mentiras)* string (b) *(de sellos, monedas)* set (c) *(producción)* **fabricación en s.** mass-production; **con ABS de s.** with ABS as standard; *Fig* **ser un fuera de s.** to be unique, to be one of a kind (d) *Elec* **en s.** in series

**seriedad** *nf* (a) *(gravedad, importancia)* seriousness; **viste con demasiada s.** he dresses too formally (b) *(responsabilidad)* sense of responsibility; *(formalidad)* reliability; **¡qué falta de s.!** what an irresponsible way to behave!

**serigrafía** *nf* silkscreen printing

**serio, -a** *adj* (a) *(grave, importante)* serious; **estar s.** to look serious; **¿vas en s.?** are you (being) serious? (b) *(responsable)* responsible; *(cumplidor, formal)* reliable; **no son gente seria** they are very unreliable; **¡esto no es s.!** this is ridiculous! (c) *(expresiones)* **en s.** seriously; **lo digo en s.** I'm serious; **tomarse algo/a alguien en s.** to take sth/sb seriously

**sermón** *nm también Fig* sermon

**sermoneador, -ora** *adj* sermonizing

**sermonear** *vt* to give a lecture *o* ticking-off to

**seropositivo, -a** *Med* **1** *adj* HIV-positive

**2** *nm,f* HIV-positive person

**serpentear** *vi* (a) *(río, camino)* to wind, to snake (b) *(culebra)* to wriggle

**serpentina** *nf* streamer

**serpiente** *nf (culebra)* snake; *Lit* serpent; **s. de cascabel** rattlesnake; **s. pitón** python

**serrallo** *nm* seraglio

**serranía** *nf* mountainous region

**serrano, -a 1** *adj* (a) *(de la sierra)* mountain, highland; **aire/pueblo s.** mountain air/village (b) *(jamón)* cured (c) *Fam (expresiones)* **¡vaya cuerpo s.!** what a great bod!; **¡vaya cuerpo s. tengo!** I feel like death warmed up!

**2** *nm,f Am* person from the mountains

**serrar** [3] *vt* to saw (up)

**serrería** *nf* sawmill

**serrín** *nm* sawdust

**serrucho** *nm* handsaw

**servicial** *adj* attentive, helpful

**servicio** *nm* (a) *(en general)* service; **s. de inteligencia** *o* **secreto** intelligence *o* secret service; **s. discrecional** private service; **s. a domicilio** home delivery service; **s. de mesa** dinner service; **s. militar** military service; **servicios mínimos** skeleton service; **s. de paquetería** parcel service; **s. posventa** after-sales service; **s. de prensa** press department; **s. público** public service; **s. de té** tea set; **s. de urgencias** casualty department

(b) *(servidumbre)* servants; **s. doméstico** domestic help

(c) *(turno)* duty; **estar de s.** to be on duty

(d) *(WC)* toilet, lavatory; **¿dónde están los servicios?** where are the toilets?

(e) *Dep* serve, service

(f) *(cubierto)* place setting

**servidor, -ora 1** *nm,f* (a) *(criado)* servant (b) *(en cartas)* **su seguro s.** yours faithfully (c) *(yo)* yours truly, me; **¿quién es el último? – s.** who's last? – I am

**2** *nm Informát* server

**servidumbre** *nf* (a) *(criados)* servants (b) *(dependencia)* servitude

**servil** *adj* servile

**servilismo** *nm* subservience

**servilleta** *nf* serviette, napkin

**servilletero** *nm* serviette *o* napkin ring

**servir** [49] **1** *vt* to serve; **sírvanos dos cervezas** bring us two beers; **¿te sirvo más patatas?** would you like some more potatoes?; **¿en qué puedo servirle?** what can I do for you?

**2** *vi* (a) *(en general)* to serve; **s. en el Ejército** to serve in the Army (b) *(valer, ser útil)* to serve, to be useful; **no sirve para estudiar** he's no good at studying; **de nada sirve que se lo digas** it's no use telling him; **s. de algo** to serve as sth (c) *(como criado)* to be in service

**3 servirse** *vpr* (a) *(aprovecharse)* **servirse de** to make use of; **sírvase llamar cuando quiera** please call whenever you want (b) *(comida, bebida)* to help oneself; **que cada uno se sirva lo que prefiera** help yourselves to whatever you like

**servoasistido, -a** *adj Aut* servo; **dirección servoasistida** power steering

**servodirección** *nf* power steering

**servofreno** *nm* servo brake

**sésamo** *nm* sesame

**sesear** *vi Gram* = to pronounce "c" and "z" as "s", as in Andalusian and Latin American dialects

**sesenta** *núm* sixty; **los (años) s.** the sixties; *ver también* **seis**

**sesentón, -a** *nm,f Fam* person in their sixties

**seseo** *nm Gram* = pronunciation of "c" and "z" as an "s"

**sesera** *nf Fam* (a) *(cabeza)* skull, nut (b) *Fig (inteligencia)* brains

**sesgado, -a** *adj* biased, partial; **información sesgada** biased information

**sesgar** [40] *vt* to cut on the bias

**sesgo** *nm* (a) *(oblicuidad)* slant; **al s.** *(en general)* on a slant; *(costura)* on the bias (b) *Fig (rumbo)* course, path

**sesgue** *etc ver* **sesgar**

**sesión** *nf* (a) *(reunión)* meeting, session; *Der* sitting, session; **abrir la s.** to open the meeting; **s. plenaria** *(de congreso)* plenary (session); *(de organización)* plenary assembly (b) *(proyección, representación)* show, performance; **s. continua** continuous showing; **s. doble** double bill; **s. matinal** matinée; **s. de noche** evening showing; **s. de tarde** afternoon matinée (c) *(periodo)* session

**seso** *nm* (a) *(cerebro)* brain; *Culin* **sesos** brains (b) *(sensatez)* brains, sense (c) *(expresiones)* **calentarse** *o* **devanarse los sesos** to rack one's brains; **sorber el s.** *o* **los sesos a alguien** to brainwash sb; *Fam* **tener poco s.** not to be very bright

**sestear** *vi* to have a nap

**sesudo, -a** *adj* (a) *(inteligente)* brainy (b) *(sensato)* wise, sensible

**set** *(pl* sets*) nm también Dep* set

**seta** *nf* mushroom; **s. venenosa** poisonous mushroom

**setecientos, -as** *núm* seven hundred; *ver también* **seis**

**setenta** *núm* seventy; **los (años) s.** the seventies; *ver también* **seis**

**setiembre** *nm* = **septiembre**

**sétimo, -a** *núm* seventh; **la sétima parte** a seventh

**seto** *nm* fence; **s. vivo** hedge

**setter** ['seter] *(pl* setters*) nm* setter

**seudo** *adj* pseudo

**seudónimo** *nm* pseudonym

**Seúl** *n* Seoul

**s.e.u.o.** *(abrev de* **salvo error u omisión**) E. & O.E.

**severidad** *nf* (a) *(de castigo, clima)* severity, harshness; *(de enfermedad)* severity, seriousness (b) *(de persona)* strictness

**severo, -a** *adj* (a) *(castigo, clima)* severe, harsh; *(enfermedad)* serious (b) *(persona)* strict

**Sevilla** *n* Seville

**sevillana** *nf* = Andalusian dance and song

**sevillano, -a** *adj & nm,f* Sevillian

**sexagenario, -a** *adj & nm,f* sexagenarian

**sexagésimo, -a** *núm* sixtieth; **s. primero** sixty-first

**sex-appeal** [seksa'pil] *nm inv* sex appeal

**sexi** *adj Fam* sexy

**sexismo** *nm* sexism

**sexista** *adj & nmf* sexist

**sexo** *nm* (a) *(en general)* sex; **bello s., s. débil** fair sex (b) *(genitales)* genitals

**sexología** *nf* sexology

**sexólogo, -a** *nm,f* sexologist

**sex-shop** [sek'ʃop] *(pl* sex-shops*) nm* sex shop

**sex-symbol** *nm* sex symbol

**sextante** *nm* sextant

**sexteto** *nm* (a) *Mús* sextet (b) *Lit* sestina

**sexto, -a** *núm* sixth; **la sexta parte** a sixth; **s. sentido** sixth sense

**sextuplicar** [61] **1** *vt* to multiply by six **2 sextuplicarse** *vpr* to increase sixfold

**séxtuplo, -a 1** *adj* sixfold **2** *nm* sextuple

**sexuado, -a** *adj* sexed

**sexual** *adj* sexual; **educación/vida s.** sex education/life

**sexualidad** *nf* sexuality

**sexy** *adj Fam* sexy

**Seychelles** [sei'ʃels] *nfpl* **las (islas) S.** the Seychelles

**SGAE** *nf (abrev de* **Sociedad General de Autores de España**) = society that safeguards the interests of Spanish authors, musicians etc

**SGBD** *nm (abrev de* **Sistema de Gestión de Bases de Datos**) database management system

**sha** [sa, ʃa] *nm* shah

**shakesperiano, -a** [ʃespi'rjano] *adj* Shakespearian

**Shanghai** [ʃaŋ'gai] *n* Shanghai

**sheriff** ['ʃerif] *(pl* sheriffs*) nm* sheriff

**sherpa** ['serpa, 'ʃerpa] *nm* sherpa

**shiatsu** ['ʃiatsu] *nm* shiatsu

**shock** [ʃok] *(pl* shocks*) nm* shock

**shorts** [ʃorts] *nmpl* shorts

**show** [ʃou, tʃou] *(pl* shows*) nm* show; *Fig* **montar un s.** to cause a scene

**si¹** (*pl* sis) *nm Mús* B; (*en solfeo*) ti

**si²** *conj* (**a**) (*condicional*) if; **si no te das prisa perderás el tren** if you don't hurry up you'll miss the train; **si viene él yo me voy** if he comes, then I'm going; **si hubieses venido te habrías divertido** if you had come, you would have enjoyed yourself; **si no** if not, otherwise

(**b**) (*en oraciones interrogativas indirectas*) if, whether; **ignoro si lo sabe** I don't know if *o* whether she knows

(**c**) (*expresa protesta*) but; **¡si te dije que no lo hicieras!** but I told you not to do it!

**sí** (*pl* síes) **1** *adv* (**a**) (*afirmación*) yes; **¿vendrás? – sí** will you come? - yes, I will; **claro que sí** of course; **creo que sí** I think so; **¿están de acuerdo? – algunos sí** do they agree? - some do; **un día sí y uno no** every other day

(**b**) (*uso enfático*) **sí que** really, certainly; **sí que me gusta** I certainly do *o* really like it; **éste sí que me gusta** this one I DO like

(**c**) (*expresiones*) **no creo que puedas hacerlo – ¡a que sí!** I don't think you can do it - I bet I can!; **van a subir la gasolina – ¡pues sí que...!** petrol prices are going up - what a pain!; **¿sí?** (*incredulidad*) really?; (*¿de acuerdo?*) all right?

**2** *pron personal* (**a**) (*reflexivo*) (*de personas*) (*singular*) himself, *f* herself, (*plural*) themselves; (*usted*) yourself, *pl* yourselves; (*de cosas, animales*) itself, *pl* themselves; **lo quiere todo para sí (misma)** she wants everything for herself; **se acercó la silla hacia sí** he drew the chair nearer (himself); **de (por) sí** (*cosa*) in itself

(**b**) (*reflexivo impersonal*) oneself; **cuando uno piensa en sí mismo** when one thinks about oneself, when you think about yourself

**3** *nm* consent; **dar el sí** to give one's consent

**Siam** *n* Siam

**siamés, -esa 1** *adj* Siamese; **hermanos siameses** Siamese twins

**2** *nm,f* (**a**) (*de Siam*) Siamese person, Thai (**b**) (*gemelo*) Siamese twin

**3** *nm* (*gato*) Siamese

**sibarita 1** *adj* sybaritic

**2** *nmf* sybarite, epicure

**sibaritismo** *nm* sybaritism, epicureanism

**Siberia** *n* Siberia

**siberiano, -a** *adj & nm,f* Siberian

**sibila** *nf Mitol* sibyl

**sibilante** *adj* sibilant

**sibilino, -a** *adj* (*incomprensible*) mysterious, cryptic

**sicario** *nm* hired assassin

**Sicilia** *n* Sicily

**siciliano, -a** *adj & nm,f* Sicilian

**sicoanálisis** *nm inv* psychoanalysis

**sicoanalista** *nmf* psychoanalyst

**sicoanalítico, -a** *adj* psychoanalytic(al)

**sicoanalizar** [16] *vt* to psychoanalyze

**sicodélico, -a** *adj* psychedelic

**sicodrama** *nm* psychodrama

**sicofármaco** *nm* psychotropic *o* psychoactive drug

**sicología** *nf también Fig* psychology

**sicológico, -a** *adj* psychological

**sicólogo, -a** *nm,f* psychologist

**sicometría** *nf* psychometrics (*singular*)

**sicomoro, sicómoro** *nm* (*planta*) sycamore

**sicomotricidad** *nf* psychomotricity

**sicópata** *nmf* psychopath

**sicopatía** *nf* psychopathy, psychopathic personality

**sicosis** *nf inv* psychosis

**sicosomático, -a** *adj* psychosomatic

**sicotécnico, -a 1** *adj* psychotechnical

**2** *nm,f* psychotechnician

**3** *nm* (*prueba*) psychotechnical test

**sicoterapia** *nf* psychotherapy

**sicotrópico, -a** *adj* psychotropic, psychoactive

**sida** *nm* (*abrev de* **síndrome de inmunodeficiencia adquirida**) AIDS

**sidecar** [siðe'kar] (*pl* sidecares) *nm* sidecar

**sideral** *adj* sidereal

**siderurgia** *nf* iron and steel industry

**siderúrgico, -a** *adj Ind* iron and steel; **el sector s.** the iron and steel industry

**sidoso, -a** *Fam Pey* **1** *adj* suffering from AIDS

**2** *nm,f* AIDS sufferer

**sidra** *nf* cider

**siega 1** *ver* **segar**

**2** *nf* (**a**) (*acción*) reaping, harvesting (**b**) (*época*) harvest (time)

**siembra 1** *ver* **sembrar**

**2** *nf* (**a**) (*acción*) sowing (**b**) (*época*) sowing time

**siempre** *adv* (**a**) (*en general*) always; **como s.** as usual; **de s.** usual; **lo de s.** the usual; **somos amigos de s.** we've always been friends; **es así desde s.** it has always been that way; **para s., para s. jamás** for ever and ever; **s. que** (*cada vez que*) whenever; **s. y cuando, s. que** provided that, as long as (**b**) (*sin duda*) **s. es mejor estar preparado** it's always better to be prepared (**c**) *Am* (*sin duda*) really (**d**) *Am* (*a pesar de todo*) despite everything (**e**) *Am* (*todavía*) still

**siempreviva** *nf* everlasting flower

**sien** *nf* temple

**siento** *etc* (**a**) *ver* **sentar** (**b**) *ver* **sentir**

**sierpe** nf Anticuado serpent

**sierra1** ver **serrar**

**2** nf (a) (herramienta) saw; **s. eléctrica** power saw (b) (cordillera) mountain range (c) (región montañosa) mountains; **se van a la s. los fines de semana** they go to the mountains at the weekend

**Sierra Leona** n Sierra Leone

**siervo, -a** nm,f (a) (esclavo) serf (b) Rel servant

**siesta** nf siesta, nap; **dormir** o **echarse la s.** to have an afternoon nap

**siete 1** núm seven; **las s. y media** = card game in which players aim to get 7 points, court cards counting for point; ver también **seis**

**2** nm (roto) tear (right-angled in shape)

**3** nf CSur Fam **de la gran s.** amazing, incredible; **¡la gran s.!** good heavens!

**sietemesino, -a 1** adj premature (by two months)

**2** nm,f premature baby (by two months)

**sífilis** nf inv syphilis

**sifilítico, -a** adj & nm,f Med syphilitic

**sifón** nm (a) (agua carbónica) soda (water) (b) (de WC) trap, U-bend (c) (tubo) siphon

**SIG** [siɣ] nm Informát (abrev de **sistema de información geográfica**) GIS

**sigilo** nm (secreto) secrecy; (al robar, escapar) stealth

**sigiloso, -a** adj (discreto) secretive; (al robar, escapar) stealthy

**sigla** nf letter (in an acronym); **siglas (de)** (acrónimo) acronym (for)

**siglo** nm (a) (cien años) century; **el s. XX** the 20th century; **el s. de las Luces** the Age of Enlightenment (b) Fig (mucho tiempo) **hace siglos que no la veo** I haven't seen her for ages; **por los siglos de los siglos** for ever and ever

**signatario, -a** adj & nm,f signatory

**signatura** nf (a) (en biblioteca) catalogue number (b) (firma) signature

**significación** nf (a) (importancia) significance (b) (significado) meaning

**significado, -a1** adj important

**2** nm (a) (sentido) meaning (b) Ling signifier

**significante** nm Ling signifiant

**significar [61] 1** vt (a) (querer decir) to mean (b) (expresar) to express

**2** vi (tener importancia) **no significa nada para mí** it means nothing to me

**3 significarse** vpr **significarse por** to become known for

**significativo, -a** adj significant

**signo** nm (a) (en general) sign; **s. de multiplicar/dividir** multiplication/division sign; **s. del zodiaco** sign of the zodiac (b) (en la escritura) mark; **s. de admiración/interrogación** exclamation/question mark (c) (símbolo) symbol

**sigo** etc ver **seguir**

**siguiente 1** adj (a) (en el tiempo, espacio) next (b) (a continuación) following; **el día s. a la catástrofe** the day after the disaster

**2** nmf (a) (el que sigue) **el s.** the next one; **¡el s.!** next, please! (b) (lo que sigue) **lo s.** the following

**siguiera** etc ver **seguir**

**sij** (pl sijs) adj & nmf Sikh

**sílaba** nf syllable

**silabear 1** vt to spell out syllable by syllable

**2** vi to read syllable by syllable

**silábico, -a** adj syllabic

**silbante** adj (respiración) whistling

**silbar 1** vt (a) (en general) to whistle (b) (abuchear) to hiss, to catcall

**2** vi (a) (en general) to whistle (b) (abuchear) to hiss, to catcall (c) Fig (oídos) to ring

**silbato** nm whistle

**silbido** nm (a) (sonido) whistle (b) (para abuchear, de serpiente) hiss, hissing

**silenciador** nm silencer

**silenciar [15]** vt to hush up, to keep quiet

**silencio** nm (a) (en general) silence; **en s.** in silence; **guardar s. (sobre algo)** to keep silent (about sth); **guardaron un minuto de s.** they held a minute's silence; **imponer s. a alguien** to make sb be silent; **romper el s.** to break the silence; **s. administrativo** = lack of official response to a request, claim, etc. within a given period, signifying refusal or tacit assent, depending on circumstances (b) Mús rest

**silencioso, -a** adj silent, quiet

**sílex** nm inv flint

**sílfide** nf sylph; **está hecha una s.** she's really slim

**silicato** nm silicate

**sílice** nf silica

**silicio** nm silicon

**silicona** nf silicone

**silicosis** nf inv silicosis

**silla** nf chair; **s. eléctrica** electric chair; **s. (de montar)** saddle; **s. de la reina** = seat made by two people joining hands; **s. de ruedas** wheelchair

**sillería** nf (sillas) set of chairs; **la s. del coro** the choir stalls

**sillín** nm saddle, seat

**sillón** nm armchair

**silo** nm silo

**silogismo** nm syllogism

**silueta** nf (a) (cuerpo) figure (b) (contorno) outline (c) (dibujo) silhouette

**silvestre** adj wild

**silvicultura** nf forestry

**sima** nf chasm

**simbiosis** nf inv symbiosis

**simbólico, -a** adj symbolic

**simbolismo** nm symbolism

**simbolizar** [16] vt to symbolize

**símbolo** nm symbol

**simbología** nf system of symbols

**simetría** nf symmetry

**simétrico, -a** adj symmetrical

**simiente** nf seed

**simiesco, -a** adj simian, apelike

**símil** nm (a) (paralelismo) similarity, resemblance (b) Lit simile

**similar** adj similar (a to)

**similitud** nf similarity

**simio, -a** nm,f simian, ape

**simpatía** nf (a) (cordialidad) friendliness (b) (cariño) affection; **coger s. a alguien** to take a liking to sb; **tener s. a, sentir s. por** to like (c) Med sympathy

**simpático, -a** adj (a) (agradable) (persona) nice, likeable; (ocasión) agreeable, pleasant (b) (abierto, cordial) friendly; **estuvo muy s. conmigo** he was very friendly to me; **hacerse el s.** to come over all friendly (c) (anécdota, comedia) amusing, entertaining (d) Anat sympathetic

**simpatizante 1** adj sympathizing
  **2** nmf sympathizer

**simpatizar** [16] vi (persona) to hit it off (con with), to get on (con with); (cosa) to sympathize (con with); **simpatiza con la ideología comunista** she has communist sympathies

**simple 1** adj (a) (sencillo, tonto) simple (b) (fácil) easy, simple (c) (único, sin componentes) single; **dame una s. razón** give me one single reason (d) (mero) mere; **por s. estupidez** through sheer stupidity (e) Mat prime
  **2** nmf (persona) simpleton

**simplemente** adv simply; **simple y llanamente** purely and simply

**simpleza** nf (a) (de persona) simplemindedness (b) (tontería) trifle

**simplicidad** nf simplicity

**simplificación** nf simplification

**simplificar** [61] **1** vt to simplify
  **2 simplificarse** vpr to be simplified

**simplismo** nm oversimplification

**simplista 1** adj simplistic
  **2** nmf naïve person

**simplón, -ona 1** adj simple, simpleminded
  **2** nm,f simpleminded person

**simposio, simposium** nm symposium

**simulación** nf pretence, simulation

**simulacro** nm simulation; **s. de combate** mock battle; **s. de incendio** fire drill

**simulado, -a** adj (a) (fingido) feigned; **su tristeza era simulada** he was only pretending to be sad (b) (de prueba) simulated

**simulador** nm simulator; **s. de vuelo** flight simulator

**simular** vt (a) (aparentar) to feign; **s. una enfermedad** to pretend to have an illness; **simuló que no me había visto** he pretended not to have seen me (b) (copiar, emular) to simulate

**simultanear** vt to do at the same time (con as)

**simultaneidad** nf simultaneousness

**simultáneo, -a** adj simultaneous

**sin** prep without; **s. alcohol** alcohol-free; **estoy s. una peseta** I'm penniless; **ha escrito cinco libros s. (contar) las novelas** he has written five books, not counting his novels; **está s. hacer** it hasn't been done yet; **estamos s. vino** we're out of wine; **lleva tres noches s. dormir** she hasn't slept for three nights; **s. que** without; **s. que nadie se enterara** without anyone noticing; **s. embargo** however

**sinagoga** nf synagogue

**Sinaí** nm **el monte S.** Mount Sinai; **el S., la península del S.** the Sinai Peninsula

**sincerarse** vpr to open one's heart (con alguien to sb)

**sinceridad** nf sincerity; **con toda s.** in all honesty o sincerity

**sincero, -a** adj sincere; **para serte s.,...** to be honest o frank,...

**síncopa** nf (a) (en palabra) syncope (b) Mús syncopation

**sincopado, -a** adj syncopated

**sincopar** vt to syncopate

**síncope** nm blackout; Fam Fig **le dio un s.** he had a fit

**sincretismo** nm syncretism

**sincronía** nf (a) (simultaneidad) simultaneity (b) Ling synchrony

**sincrónico, -a** adj (a) (simultáneo) simultaneous (b) (coordinado) synchronous (c) Ling synchronic

**sincronismo** nm (a) (simultaneidad) simultaneity (b) Fís tuning

**sincronización** nf synchronization

**sincronizar** [16] vt (a) (coordinar) to synchronize; **sincronizaron los relojes** they synchronized their watches (b) Fís to tune

**síncrono, -a** adj Informát synchronous

**sindicación** *nf* trade union membership

**sindicado, -a** *adj* belonging to a trade union

**sindical** *adj* (trade) union; **organización s.** trade-union organization

**sindicalismo** *nm* trade unionism

**sindicalista** *nmf* trade unionist

**sindicar [61] 1** *vt* to unionize

**2 sindicarse** *vpr* to join a union

**sindicato** *nm* trade union, *US* labor union; **s. amarillo** yellow union, = conservative trade union that leans towards the employers' interests; **s. vertical** = workers' and employers' union during the Franco period

**síndico** *nm* (a) *(representante)* community representative (b) *(administrador)* (official) receiver (c) *Econ* trustee; **s. de la Bolsa** = Chairman of the Spanish Stock Exchange Commission

**síndrome** *nm* syndrome; **s. de abstinencia** withdrawal symptoms; **s. de Down** Down's syndrome; **s. de Estocolmo** Stockholm syndrome; **s. de inmunodeficiencia adquirida** acquired immune deficiency syndrome; **s. tóxico** = toxic syndrome caused by ingestion of adulterated rapeseed oil in late 1970s

**sinecura** *nf* sinecure

**sine die 1** *adj* **un aplazamiento s.** an indefinite postponement

**2** *adv* indefinitely

**sinergia** *nf* synergy

**sinestesia** *nf* synaesthesia

**sinfín** *nm* vast number; **un s. de problemas** no end of problems

**sinfonía** *nf* symphony

**sinfónico, -a** *adj* symphonic

**Singapur** *n* Singapore

**singladura** *nf* *Naút (distancia)* day's run; *Fig (dirección)* course

**single** ['singel] *nm* single

**singular 1** *adj* (a) *(raro)* peculiar, odd (b) *(único)* unique; **s. batalla** single combat (c) *Gram* singular

**2** *nm* *Gram* singular; **en s.** in the singular

**singularidad** *nf* (a) *(rareza, peculiaridad)* peculiarity; **una de las singularidades de esta especie** one of the special characteristics of this species (b) *(exclusividad)* uniqueness

**singularizar [16] 1** *vt* to distinguish, to single out

**2 singularizarse** *vpr* to stand out, to be conspicuous

**siniestrado, -a 1** *adj (coche, avión)* crashed, smashed up; *(edificio)* ruined, destroyed

**2** *nm,f* victim

**siniestralidad** *nf* accident rate

**siniestra** *nf* *Anticuado* left hand

**siniestro, -a 1** *adj* (a) *(malo)* sinister (b) *(desgraciado)* disastrous

**2** *nm* *(daño, catástrofe)* disaster; *(accidente de coche)* accident, crash; *(incendio)* fire; *(atentado)* terrorist attack; **s. total** write-off

**sinnúmero** *nm* **un s. de** countless

**sino¹** *nm* fate, destiny

**sino²** *conj* (a) *(para contraponer)* but; **no lo hizo él, s. ella** he didn't do it, she did; **no sólo es listo, s. también trabajador** he's not only clever but also hardworking (b) *(para exceptuar)* except, but; **¿quién s. tú lo haría?** who else but you would do it?; **no quiero s. que se haga justicia** I only want justice to be done

**sínodo** *nm* synod

**sinonimia** *nf* synonymy

**sinónimo, -a 1** *adj* synonymous

**2** *nm* synonym

**sinopsis** *nf inv* synopsis

**sinóptico, -a** *adj* synoptic; **cuadro s.** tree diagram

**sinovial** *adj* synovial

**sinrazón** *nf* injustice

**sinsabores** *nmpl* trouble, upsetting experiences; **ese trabajo me causó muchos s.** the job gave me a lot of headaches

**sinsentido** *nm* **decir un s.** to say something stupid

**sintáctico, -a** *adj* syntactic

**sintagma** *nm* **s. nominal/verbal** noun/verb phrase

**sintaxis** *nf inv* syntax

**síntesis** *nf inv* synthesis; **en s.** in short; **esta obra hace una s. de sus ideas sobre el tema** this work draws together his ideas on the subject; *Informát & Ling* **s. del habla** speech synthesis

**sintético, -a** *adj* (a) *(artificial)* synthetic (b) *(conciso)* concise

**sintetizador, -ora 1** *adj* synthesizing

**2** *nm* synthesizer

**sintetizar [16]** *vt* (a) *(resumir)* to summarize; *(reunir)* to draw together (b) *(fabricar artificialmente)* to synthesize

**sintiera** *etc ver* **sentir**

**sintoísmo** *nm* Shintoism

**síntoma** *nm* symptom

**sintomático, -a** *adj* symptomatic

**sintomatología** *nf* symptoms

**sintonía** *nf* (a) *(música)* signature tune (b) *(conexión)* tuning (c) *Fig (compenetración)* harmony

**sintonización** *nf* (a) *(conexión)* tuning (b) *Fig (compenetración)* harmonization

**sintonizador** *nm* tuner, tuning dial

**sintonizar** [16] **1** *vt (conectar)* to tune in to

**2** *vi* **(a)** *(conectar)* to tune in **(con** to) **(b)** *Fig (compenetrarse)* **s. en algo (con alguien)** to be on the same wavelength (as sb) about sth

**sinuosidad** *nf* bend, wind

**sinuoso, -a** *adj* **(a)** *(camino)* winding **(b)** *(movimiento)* sinuous **(c)** *Fig (disimulado)* devious

**sinusitis** *nf inv* sinusitis

**sinvergüenza 1** *adj* **(a)** *(canalla)* shameless **(b)** *(fresco, descarado)* cheeky

**2** *nmf* **(a)** *(canalla)* rogue **(b)** *(fresco, descarado)* cheeky person

**sionismo** *nm* Zionism

**sionista** *adj & nmf* Zionist

**sioux** ['siuks] *adj inv & nmf inv* Sioux

**siquiatra** *nmf* psychiatrist

**siquiatría** *nf* psychiatry

**siquiátrico, -a 1** *adj* psychiatric

**2** *nm* psychiatric *o* mental hospital

**síquico, -a** *adj* psychic

**siquiera 1** *conj (aunque)* even if; **ven s. por pocos días** do come, even if it's only for a few days

**2** *adv (por lo menos)* at least; **dime s. tu nombre** (you could) at least tell me your name; **ni (tan) s.** not even; **ni (tan) s. me hablaron** they didn't even speak to me

**sirena** *nf* **(a)** *Mitol* mermaid, siren **(b)** *(señal)* siren

**Siria** *n* Syria

**sirimiri** *nm* drizzle

**sirio, -a** *adj & nm,f* Syrian

**sirlero, -a** *nm,f muy Fam* = thug who carries a knife

**siroco** *nm* sirocco; *Fam* **le ha dado el s.** she's had a brainstorm

**sirope** *nm* golden syrup; **s. de fresa/chocolate** *(para helado)* strawberry/chocolate sauce

**sirviente, -a** *nm,f* servant

**sirviera** *etc ver* **servir**

**sirvo** *etc ver* **servir**

**sisa** *nf* **(a)** *(de manga)* armhole **(b)** *(de dinero)* pilfering

**sisar** *vt & vi* to pilfer

**sisear** *vt & vi* to hiss

**siseo** *nm* hiss, hissing

**sísmico, -a** *adj* seismic; **zona sísmica** earthquake zone

**sismo** *nm* earthquake

**sismógrafo** *nm* seismograph

**sisón, -ona 1** *adj* pilfering

**2** *nm,f (ladrón)* pilferer, petty thief

**3** *nm (ave)* little bustard

**sistema** *nm* **(a)** *también Informát* system; **por s.** systematically; *Aut* **s. ABS** ABS (brake) system; **s. circulatorio/nervioso** circulatory/nervous system; *TV* **s. dual** = system enabling dubbed TV programmes to be heard in the original language; *Informát* **s. experto/operativo** expert/operating system; **s. fiscal** *o* **impositivo** tax system; *Informát* **s. de gestión de bases de datos** database management system; **s. internacional de unidades** SI system; **s. métrico (decimal)** metric (decimal) system; **s. monetario europeo** European Monetary System; **s. montañoso** mountain chain *o* range; **s. periódico de los elementos** periodic table of elements; **s. solar** solar system

**(b)** *(método, orden)* method

**Sistema Ibérico** *nm* **el S.** the Iberian mountain chain

**sistemático, -a** *adj* systematic

**sistematización** *nf* systematization

**sistematizar** [16] *vt* to systematize

**sístole** *nf* systole

**sitiado, -a** *adj* besieged

**sitiador, -a 1** *adj* besieging

**2** *nm,f* besieger

**sitial** *nm Formal* seat of honour

**sitiar** [15] *vt* **(a)** *(cercar)* to besiege **(b)** *Fig (acorralar)* to surround

**sitio** *nm* **(a)** *(lugar)* place; **cambiar de s. (con alguien)** to change places (with sb); **en cualquier s.** anywhere; **en otro s.** elsewhere; **en todos los sitios** everywhere; *Fig* **poner a alguien en su s.** to put sb in their place **(b)** *(espacio)* room, space; **hacer s. a alguien** to make room for sb; **no queda más s.** there's no more room **(c)** *(cerco)* siege

**sito, -a** *adj* located

**situación** *nf* **(a)** *(circunstancias)* situation; *(legal, social)* status; **s. económica** economic situation; **s. límite** extreme *o* critical situation **(b)** *(estado, condición)* state, condition; **estar en s. de hacer algo** *(en general)* to be in a position to do sth; *(sujeto: enfermo, borracho)* to be in a fit state to do sth **(c)** *(ubicación)* location

**situado, -a** *adj* **(a)** *(ubicado)* located; **estar bien s.** *(casa)* to be conveniently located; *Fig* to be well-placed **(b)** *(acomodado)* comfortably off

**situar** [4] **1** *vt* **(a)** *(colocar)* to place, to put; *(edificio, ciudad)* to site, to locate; *Fig* **me suena pero no lo sitúo** he sounds familiar, but I can't place him **(b)** *(en clasificación)* to place, to rank

**2 situarse** *vpr* **(a)** *(colocarse)* to take up position **(b)** *(ubicarse)* to be located **(c)** *(desarrollarse) (acción)* to be set **(d)** *(acomodarse, establecerse)* to get oneself established (**e**) *(en clasificación)* to be placed; **se sitúa entre los mejores** he's (ranked) amongst the best

**siútico, -a** *adj Chile Fam* stuck-up

**skay** [es'kai] *nm* Leatherette®

**skateboard** [es'keidβor] *(pl skateboards) nm* (**a**) *(tabla)* skateboard (**b**) *(deporte)* skateboarding

**sketch** [es'ketʃ] *(pl sketches) nm Cine & Teatro* sketch

**skin head** [es'kinχeð] *(pl skin heads) nmf* skinhead

**S.L.** *nf (abrev de sociedad limitada)* Ltd

**slalom** [es'lalom] *(pl slaloms) nm Dep* slalom; **s. gigante** giant slalom

**slip** [es'lip] *(pl slips) nm* briefs

**SM** *(abrev de Su Majestad)* HM

**smash** [es'maʃ] *(pl smashes) nm Dep* smash

**SME** *nm (abrev de Sistema Monetario Europeo)* EMS

**SMI** *nm (abrev de sistema monetario internacional)* IMS

**s/n** *(abrev de sin número)* = abbreviation used in addresses after the street name, where the building has no number

**snob 1** *adj* trying to be trendy
**2** *nmf* person who wants to be trendy

**snobismo** *nm* desire to be trendy

**snowboard** [es'nouβor] *(pl snowboards) nm* (**a**) *(tabla)* snowboard (**b**) *(deporte)* snowboarding

**so** *prep* under; **s. pretexto de** under the pretext of
**2** *adv* ¡s. tonto! you idiot!
**3** *interj* ¡s., caballo! whoa!

**soba** *nf Fam Fig (paliza)* hiding; **dar una s. a alguien** to give sb a good hiding

**sobaco** *nm* armpit

**sobado, -a** *adj* (**a**) *(cuello, puños)* worn, shabby; *(libro)* dog-eared (**b**) *Fig (argumento, tema)* well-worn, hackneyed

**sobao** *nm Culin* = small, flat, square sponge cake

**sobaquera** *nf* armhole

**sobaquina** *nf Fam* body odour, BO

**sobar 1** *vt* (**a**) *(tocar)* to finger, to paw; *Fam (persona)* to touch up, to fondle (**b**) *(ablandar)* to soften
**2** *vi muy Fam* to kip

**soberanamente** *adv* (**a**) *(independientemente)* independently, free from outside interference (**b**) *(enormemente)* incredibly, unbelievably

**soberanía** *nf* sovereignty

**soberano, -a 1** *adj* (**a**) *(independiente)* sovereign (**b**) *Fig (grande)* massive; *(paliza)* thorough; *(belleza, calidad)* supreme, unrivalled; **decir/hacer una s. tontería** to say/do something unbelievably stupid
**2** *nm,f* sovereign

**soberbia** *nf* (**a**) *(arrogancia)* pride, arrogance (**b**) *(magnificencia)* grandeur, splendour

**soberbio, -a 1** *adj* (**a**) *(arrogante)* proud, arrogant (**b**) *(magnífico)* superb, magnificent
**2** *nm,f (persona)* arrogant *o* proud person

**sobón, -ona** *adj & nm,f Fam* groper

**sobornable** *adj* bribable

**sobornar** *vt* to bribe

**soborno** *nm* (**a**) *(acción)* bribery (**b**) *(dinero, regalo)* bribe

**sobra 1** *nf* excess, surplus; **de s.** *(en exceso)* more than enough; *(de más)* superfluous; **aquí estoy de s., me voy** I'm off, it's obvious I'm not wanted here; **lo sabemos de s.** we know it only too well
**2** *nfpl* **sobras** (**a**) *(de comida)* leftovers (**b**) *(de tela)* remnants

**sobradamente** *adv* **s. conocido** extremely well-known; **como es s. conocido...** as I/we *etc* know all too well...

**sobrado, -a** *adj* (**a**) *(de sobra)* more than enough, plenty of (**b**) *(de dinero)* well-off; **estar s. de dinero** to have more than enough money

**sobrante 1** *adj* remaining
**2** *nm* surplus

**sobrar** *vi* (**a**) *(quedar, restar)* to be left over, to be spare; **nos sobró comida** we had some food left over (**b**) *(haber de más)* to be more than enough; **parece que van a s. bocadillos** it looks like there are going to be too many sandwiches (**c**) *(estar de más)* to be superfluous; **lo que dices sobra** that goes without saying; *Fig* **aquí sobra alguien** someone here is not welcome

**sobrasada** *nf* = Mallorcan spicy pork sausage that can be spread

**sobre¹** *nm* (**a**) *(para cartas)* envelope (**b**) *(para alimentos, medicamentos)* sachet, packet (**c**) *muy Fam (cama)* sack; **irse al s.** to hit the sack

**sobre²** *prep* (**a**) *(encima de)* on (top of); **el libro está s. la mesa** the book is on (top of) the table
(**b**) *(por encima de)* over, above; **el pato vuela s. el lago** the duck is flying over the lake
(**c**) *(superioridad)* above; **su opinión está s. las de los demás** his opinion is more important than that of the others; **tiene muchas ventajas s. el antiguo modelo** it has a lot of advantages over the old model
(**d**) *(acerca de)* about, on; **un libro s. el amor** a book about *o* on love; **una conferencia s. el**

**desarme** a conference on disarmament

(e) *(aproximadamente)* about; **llegarán s. las diez** they'll arrive at about ten o'clock

(f) *(acumulación)* upon; **nos contó mentira s. mentira** he told us lie upon lie o one lie after another

(g) *(cerca de)* upon; **la desgracia estaba ya s. nosotros** the disaster was already upon us

**sobreabundancia** *nf* excess

**sobreabundante** *adj* excessive

**sobreabundar** *vi* to abound

**sobreactuar** *vi* to overact

**sobrealimentación** *nf* overfeeding

**sobrealimentar** *vt* to overfeed

**sobreañadido** *nm* unnecessary addition

**sobreañadir** *vt* to add on top of

**sobrecalentamiento** *nm* overheating

**sobrecalentar** [3] *vt* to overheat

**sobrecarga** *nf* (a) *(exceso de carga)* excess weight (b) *(saturación)* overload

**sobrecargado, -a** *adj* overloaded

**sobrecargar** [40] *vt* (con peso, trabajo) to overload; *(decoración)* to overdo

**sobrecargo** *nm* (a) *Náut* supercargo; *Av* flight attendant (b) *Com* surcharge

**sobrecogedor, -ora** *adj* frightening, startling

**sobrecoger** [54] 1 *vt* to frighten, to startle

**2 sobrecogerse** *vpr* to be frightened, to be startled

**sobrecoste, sobrecosto** *nm* extra costs

**sobrecubierta** *nf* (a) *(de libro)* (dust) jacket (b) *(de barco)* upper deck

**sobredosis** *nf inv* overdose

**sobreentender** [66] 1 *vt* to understand, to deduce

**2 sobreentenderse** *vpr* to be inferred o implied

**sobreentendido, -a** *adj* implied, implicit

**sobreesdrújula** *nf* = word stressed on the fourth-last syllable

**sobreesdrújulo, -a** *adj* = stressed on the fourth-last syllable

**sobreexcitar** 1 *vt* to overexcite

**2 sobreexcitarse** *vpr* to get overexcited

**sobreexponer** [52] *vt* to overexpose

**sobreexposición** *nf* overexposure

**sobrefusión** *nf* supercooling

**sobregiro** *nm Com* overdraft

**sobrehilar** *vt* to whipstitch

**sobrehumano, -a** *adj* superhuman

**sobreimpresión** *nf* superimposing

**sobreimprimir** *vt* to superimpose

**sobrellevar** *vt* to bear, to endure

**sobremanera** *adv* exceedingly

**sobremesa** *nf* quedarse de s. to stay at the table *(talking, playing cards etc)*; **la programación de s.** afternoon TV (programmes)

**sobrenadar** *vi* to float

**sobrenatural** *adj* supernatural; **poderes sobrenaturales** supernatural powers

**sobrenombre** *nm* nickname

**sobrentender** [66] 1 *vt* to understand, to deduce

**2 sobrentenderse** *vpr* to be inferred o implied

**sobrentendido, -a** *adj* implied, implicit

**sobrepasar** *vt* (a) *(exceder)* to exceed (b) *(aventajar)* **s. a alguien** to overtake sb

**sobrepelliz** *nf* surplice

**sobrepeso** *nm* excess weight

**sobreponer** [52] 1 *vt* (a) *(poner encima)* to put on top (b) *Fig (anteponer)* **s. algo a algo** to put sth before sth

**2 sobreponerse** *vpr* **sobreponerse a algo** to overcome sth

**sobreposición** *nf* superimposing

**sobreproducción** *nf Econ* overproduction

**sobreproteger** [54] *vt* to overprotect

**sobrepuesto, -a 1** *participio ver* **sobreponer**

**2** *adj* superimposed

**sobrepujar** *vt* to outdo, to surpass

**sobresaliente 1** *adj (destacado)* outstanding

**2** *nm (nota)* excellent, $\simeq$ A

**sobresalir** [62] *vi* (a) *(en tamaño)* to jut out (b) *(en importancia)* to stand out

**sobresaltar 1** *vt* to startle

**2 sobresaltarse** *vpr* to be startled, to start

**sobresalto** *nm* start, fright; **dar un s. a alguien** to make sb start, to give sb a fright

**sobresaturar** *vt* to supersaturate

**sobrescribir** *vt* to overwrite

**sobrescrito, -a** *participio ver* **sobrescribir**

**sobresdrújula** *nf* = word stressed on the fourth-last syllable

**sobresdrújulo, -a** *adj* = stressed on the fourth-last syllable

**sobreseer** [39] *vt Der* to discontinue, to stay

**sobreseimiento** *nm Der* stay

**sobrestimar** *vt* to overestimate

**sobresueldo** *nm* extra money on the side

**sobretasa** *nf* surcharge

**sobretodo** *nm* overcoat

**sobrevalorado, -a** *adj (artista, obra)* overrated; *(casa, acciones)* overvalued

**sobrevalorar 1** *vt (artista, obra)* to overrate; *(casa, acciones)* to overvalue

**2 sobrevalorarse** *vpr* to have too high an opinion of oneself

**sobrevenir** [71] *vi* to happen, to ensue; **sobrevino la guerra** the war intervened

**sobreviviente 1** *adj* surviving

**2** *nmf* survivor

**sobrevivir** *vi* to survive; **s. a alguien** to outlive sb

**sobrevolar** [65] *vt* to fly over

**sobrexcitar 1** *vt* to overexcite

**2 sobrexcitarse** *vpr* to get overexcited

**sobrexponer** [52] *vt* to overexpose

**sobrexposición** *nf* overexposure

**sobriedad** *nf* (a) *(moderación)* restraint, moderation; *(sencillez)* simplicity, sobriety (b) *(no embriaguez)* soberness

**sobrino, -a** *nm,f* nephew, *f* niece

**sobrio, -a** *adj* (a) *(moderado)* restrained; *(no excesivo)* simple; **s. en** moderate in (b) *(austero, no borracho)* sober

**SOC** *nm* (*abrev de* **Sindicato de Obreros del Campo**) Spanish farm-workers' union

**socaire** *nm Náut* lee; *Fig* **al s. de** under the protection of

**socarrado, -a** *adj* burnt, scorched

**socarrar 1** *vt* *(quemar)* to burn, to scorch

**2 socarrarse** *vpr* to burn

**socarrón, -ona** *adj* ironic

**socarronería** *nf* irony, ironic humour

**socavar** *vt* *(excavar por debajo)* to dig under; *Fig* *(debilitar)* to undermine

**socavón** *nm* (a) *(hoyo)* hollow; *(en la carretera)* pothole (b) *Min* gallery

**sociabilidad** *nf* sociability

**sociable** *adj* sociable

**social** *adj* (a) *(en general)* social (b) *Com* company; **capital s.** share capital

**socialdemocracia** *nf* social democracy

**socialdemócrata 1** *adj* social democratic

**2** *nmf* social democrat

**socialismo** *nm* socialism

**socialista** *adj & nmf* socialist

**socialización** *nf Econ* nationalization

**socializar** [16] *vt Econ* to nationalize

**sociedad** *nf* (a) *(en general)* society; **entrar** *o* **presentarse en s.** to come out, to make one's debut; **alta s.** high society; **notas de s.** society column; **s. de consumo/del ocio** consumer/leisure society; **s. deportiva** sports club; **s. gastronómica** dining club, gourmet club; **s. literaria** literary society; *Hist* **S. de Naciones** League of Nations

(b) *Com (empresa)* company; **s. anónima** *Br* public (limited) company, *US* incorporated company; **s. de cartera** portfolio company; **s. civil** non-profit making company; **s. colectiva** general partnership; **s. comanditaria** *o* **en comandita** general and limited partnership; **s.**

**cooperativa** cooperative; **s. industrial** industrial society; **s. mercantil** trading company; **s. (de responsabilidad) limitada** private limited company

**socio, -a** *nm,f* (a) *Com* partner; **s. capitalista** *o* **comanditario** *Br* sleeping partner, *US* silent partner; **s. fundador** founding partner; **s. mayoritario** majority shareholder (b) *(miembro)* member; **s. honorario** *o* **de honor** honorary member; **s. vitalicio** life member (c) *Fam (amigo)* mate

**sociocultural** *adj* sociocultural

**socioeconomía** *nf* socioeconomics *(singular)*

**socioeconómico, -a** *adj* socioeconomic

**sociolingüística** *nf* sociolinguistics *(singular)*

**sociolingüístico, -a** *adj* sociolinguistic

**sociología** *nf* sociology

**sociológico, -a** *adj* sociological

**sociólogo, -a** *nm,f* sociologist

**sociopolítico, -a** *adj* sociopolitical

**socorrer** *vt* to help

**socorrido, -a** *adj (útil)* useful, handy

**socorrismo** *nm* first aid; *(en la playa)* lifesaving

**socorrista** *nmf* first aid worker; *(en la playa)* lifeguard

**socorro 1** *nm* help, aid

**2** *interj* ¡s.! help!

**soda** *nf (bebida)* soda water

**sódico, -a** *adj* sodium; **cloruro s.** sodium chloride

**sodio** *nm* sodium

**sodomía** *nf* sodomy

**sodomita** *adj & nmf* sodomite

**sodomizar** [16] *vt* to sodomize

**soez** *adj* vulgar, dirty

**sofá** (*pl* **sofás**) *nm* sofa; **s. cama** *o* **nido** sofa bed

**Sofía** *n* Sofia

**sofisma** *nm* sophism

**sofisticación** *nf* sophistication

**sofisticado, -a** *adj* sophisticated

**sofocado, -a** *adj* (a) *(por cansancio)* gasping for breath; *(por calor)* suffocating (b) *(por vergüenza)* mortified (c) *(por irritación)* hot under the collar

**sofocante** *adj* suffocating, stifling

**sofocar** [61] **1** *vt* (a) *(ahogar)* to suffocate, to stifle (b) *(incendio)* to put out, to smother (c) *Fig (rebelión)* to suppress, to quell (d) *Fig (avergonzar)* to mortify

**2 sofocarse** *vpr* (a) *(ahogarse)* to suffocate (b) *Fig (avergonzarse)* to go red as a beetroot

**(c)** *Fig (irritarse)* to get hot under the collar (**por about**)

**sofoco** *nm* **(a)** *(ahogo)* breathlessness; *(sonrojo, bochorno)* hot flush **(b)** *Fig (vergüenza)* mortification **(c)** *Fig (disgusto)* **llevarse un s.** to have a fit

**sofocón** *nm Fam* **llevarse un s.** to get hot under the collar

**sofoque** *etc ver* **sofocar**

**sofreír** [58] *vt* to fry lightly over a low heat

**sofría, sofriera** *etc ver* **sofreír**

**sofrito, -a 1** *participio ver* **sofreír**

**2** *nm* = lightly fried onions and garlic, used as a base for sauces, stews etc

**sofrología** *nf* relaxation therapy

**software** ['sofwer] *nm Informát* software; **paquete de s.** software package; **s. integrado** integrated software; **s. de dominio público** public domain software

**soga** *nf* rope; *(para ahorcar)* noose; *Fig* **estar con la s. al cuello** to be in dire straits; *Fig* **mentar la s. en casa del ahorcado** to really put one's foot in it *(by mentioning a sensitive subject)*

**sois** *ver* **ser**

**soja** *nf* soya

**sojuzgar** [40] *vt* to subjugate

**sol** *nm* **(a)** *(astro)* sun; **hace s.** it's sunny; **de s. a s.** from dawn to dusk; *Fam* **no dejar a alguien ni a s. ni a sombra** to follow sb around wherever they go; **s. naciente/poniente** rising/setting sun

**(b)** *(rayos, luz)* sunshine, sun; **tomar el s.** to sunbathe; **hace un s. de justicia** it's blazing hot; **siempre se arrima al s. que más calienta** he sides with whoever is most beneficial for him at the time

**(c)** *Fig (ángel, ricura)* darling, angel

**(d)** *Mús* G; *(en solfeo)* so

**(e)** *(moneda)* sol

**(f)** *Taurom* = seats in the sun, the cheapest in the bullring

**(g) s. y sombra** *(bebida)* mixture of brandy and anisette

**solamente** *adv* only, just; **vino s. él** only he came

**solana** *nf* **(a)** *(lugar)* sunny spot **(b)** *(galería)* sun lounge

**solano** *nm* east wind

**solapa** *nf* **(a)** *(de prenda)* lapel **(b)** *(de libro, sobre)* flap

**solapado, -a** *adj* underhand, devious

**solapar** *vt* to cover up

**solar 1** *adj* solar

**2** *nm* undeveloped plot (of land)

**solariego, -a** *adj* ancestral

**solario, solárium** *(pl* solariums) *nm* solarium

**solaz** *nm* **(a)** *(entretenimiento)* amusement, entertainment **(b)** *(descanso)* rest

**solazar** [16] **1** *vt* to amuse, to entertain

**2 solazarse** *vpr* to enjoy oneself

**soldada** *nf* pay

**soldado** *nm* soldier; **s. de primera** lance corporal; **s. raso** private

**soldador, -ora 1** *nm,f (persona)* welder

**2** *nm (aparato)* soldering iron

**soldadura** *nf* **(a)** *(acción)* soldering, welding **(b)** *(juntura)* weld, soldered joint

**soldar** [65] *vt* to solder, to weld

**soleá** *(pl* soleares) *nf* = type of flamenco song and dance

**soleado, -a** *adj* sunny

**solear** *vt* to put in the sun

**solecismo** *nm* solecism

**soledad** *nf* loneliness; **vive en completa s.** he lives in complete solitude

**solemne** *adj* **(a)** *(con pompa, importante)* formal, solemn; *(serio)* solemn; **una promesa s.** a solemn promise **(b)** *Fig (enorme)* utter, complete; **hacer/decir una s. tontería** to do/say something incredibly stupid

**solemnidad** *nf* **(a)** *(suntuosidad)* pomp, solemnity **(b)** *(acto)* ceremony

**solemnizar** [16] *vt* to celebrate, to commemorate

**soler** *vi* **s. hacer algo** to do sth usually; **aquí suele llover mucho** it usually rains a lot here; **solíamos ir a la playa cada día** we used to go to the beach every day; **como se suele hacer en estos casos** as is customary in such cases

**solera** *nf* **(a)** *(tradición)* tradition **(b) vino de s.** *(añejo)* vintage wine

**solfa** *nf* **(a)** *Mús (tonic)* sol-fa **(b)** *Fam (paliza)* thrashing **(c)** *Fam* **poner algo en s.** to make fun of sth

**solfeo** *nm Mús* solfeggio; **estudiar s.** to learn to read music; **saber s.** to be able to read music

**solicitante 1** *adj* applying

**2** *nmf* applicant

**solicitar** *vt* **(a)** *(pedir)* to request; *(empleo)* to apply for; **s. algo a o de alguien** to request sth of sb **(b)** *(persona)* to ask for; **le solicita el director de ventas** the sales manager wants to see you; **estar muy solicitado** to be very popular, to be much sought after

**solícito, -a** *adj* solicitous, obliging

**solicitud** *nf* **(a)** *(petición)* request **(b)** *(documento)* application **(c)** *(atención)* care

**solidaridad** *nf* solidarity

**solidario, -a** *adj* **(a)** *(adherido)* sympathetic (**con** to), supporting (**con** of); **un gesto s.** a gesture of solidarity **(b)** *(obligación, compromiso)* mutually binding

**solidarizarse** [16] *vpr* to make common cause, to show one's solidarity

**solidez** *nf (física)* solidity; *(moral)* firmness

**solidificación** *nf* solidification

**solidificar** [61] **1** *vt* to solidify
**2 solidificarse** *vpr* to solidify

**sólido, -a 1** *adj* **(a)** *(en general)* solid; *(cimientos, fundamento)* firm **(b)** *(argumento, conocimiento, idea)* sound **(c)** *(color)* fast
**2** *nm* solid

**soliloquio** *nm* soliloquy

**solista 1** *adj* solo
**2** *nmf* soloist

**solitaria** *nf (tenia)* tapeworm

**solitario, -a 1** *adj* **(a)** *(persona, vida)* solitary **(b)** *(lugar)* lonely, deserted
**2** *nm,f (persona)* loner
**3** *nm* **(a)** *(diamante)* solitaire **(b)** *(juego)* patience, *US* solitaire

**soliviantar 1** *vt* **(a)** *(excitar, incitar)* to stir up **(b)** *(indignar)* to exasperate
**2 soliviantarse** *vpr* to be infuriated

**solla** *nf* plaice

**sollozar** [16] *vi* to sob

**sollozo** *nm* sob

**solo, -a 1** *adj* **(a)** *(sin nadie)* alone; **se quedó s. a temprana edad** he was on his own from an early age; *Fig* **estar más s. que la una** to be all on one's own; **a solas** alone, by oneself **(b)** *(sin nada)* on its own; *(café)* black; *(whisky)* neat **(c)** *(único)* single, sole; **ni una sola gota** not a (single) drop; **dame una sola cosa** give me just one thing **(d)** *(solitario)* lonely
**2** *nm Mús* solo

**sólo** *adv* only, just; **no s.... sino (también)...** not only... but (also)...; **con s., s. con** just by; **s. que...** only...

**solomillo** *nm* sirloin

**solsticio** *nm* solstice

**soltar** [65] **1** *vt* **(a)** *(desasir)* to let go of **(b)** *(desatar)* to unfasten; *(nudo)* to untie; *(hebilla, cordones)* to undo **(c)** *(dejar ir)* *(preso, animales, freno)* to release; **no suelta ni un duro** you can't get a penny out of her **(d)** *(desenrollar)* *(cable, cuerda)* to let o lay out **(e)** *(patada, grito, suspiro)* to give **(f)** *(decir bruscamente)* to come out with **(g)** *(desprender)* **s. mucha grasa** to give out a lot of fat **(h)** *(laxar)* **s. el vientre** to loosen one's bowels
**2 soltarse** *vpr* **(a)** *(desasirse)* to break free **(b)** *(desatarse)* to come undone **(c)** *(desprenderse)* to come off **(d)** *Fam (perder timidez)* to let go; **soltarse en algo** *(adquirir habilidad)* to get the hang of sth

**soltería** *nf (de hombre)* bachelorhood; *(de mujer)* spinsterhood

**soltero, -a 1** *adj* single, unmarried
**2** *nm,f* bachelor, *f* single woman

**solterón, -ona 1** *adj* unmarried
**2** *nm,f* old bachelor, *f* spinster, *f* old maid

**soltura** *nf* **(a)** *(fluidez)* fluency **(b)** *(facilidad, desenvoltura)* assurance; **con s.** fluently

**soluble** *adj* **(a)** *(que se disuelve)* soluble **(b)** *(que se soluciona)* solvable

**solución** *nf* solution; **s. de continuidad** interruption; **sin s. de continuidad** uninterrupted

**solucionar** *vt (problema)* to solve; *(disputa)* to resolve

**solvencia** *nf* **(a)** *(económica)* solvency **(b)** *(capacidad)* reliability

**solventar** *vt* **(a)** *(pagar)* to settle **(b)** *(resolver)* to resolve

**solvente** *adj* **(a)** *(económicamente)* solvent **(b)** *Fig (fuentes)* reliable

**somalí** *(pl* **somalíes) 1** *adj & nmf* Somali
**2** *nm (lengua)* Somali

**Somalia** *n* Somalia

**somanta** *nf Fam (paliza)* hiding; **s. de palos** beating, thrashing

**somático, -a** *adj* somatic

**somatizar** [16] *vt Med* to convert into physical symptoms

**sombra** *nf* **(a)** *(proyección)* *(fenómeno)* shadow; *(zona)* shade; **a la s.** in the shade; *Fam (en la cárcel)* in the slammer; **dar s. a** to cast a shadow over; *Fig* **hacer s. a alguien** to overshadow sb; *Fam Fig* **no se fía ni de su propia s.** he wouldn't trust his own mother; **reírse de su propia s.** to make a joke of everything, to laugh at everything; *Fig* **ser la s. de alguien** to be sb's shadow; *Fam Fig* **tener mala s.** to be nasty o a swine; **sombras chinescas** *(marionetas)* shadow puppets; **hacer sombras chinescas** *(con las manos)* to make shadow pictures; **s. de ojos** eyeshadow
**(b)** *(en pintura)* shade
**(c)** *Fig (anonimato)* background; **permanecer en la s.** to stay out of the limelight
**(d)** *Fig (imperfección)* stain, blemish
**(e)** *Fig (atisbo, apariencia)* trace, touch; **no tener ni s. de** not to have the slightest bit of
**(f)** *(suerte)* **buena/mala s.** good/bad luck
**(g)** *Taurom =* most expensive seats in bullring, located in the shade
**(h)** *(oscuridad, inquietud)* darkness
**(i)** *(ignorancia)* gaps in one's knowledge

**sombreado** *nm* shading

**sombrear** *vt (dibujo)* to shade

**sombrerería** *nf* **(a)** *(fábrica)* hat factory **(b)** *(tienda)* hat shop

**sombrero** nm (a) (prenda) hat; Fig **pasar el s.** to pass round the hat; Fig **quitarse el s. (ante)** to take one's hat off (to); **s. de copa** top hat; **s. hongo** bowler hat, US derby (b) (de setas) cap

**sombrilla** nf sunshade, parasol

**sombrío, -a** adj (a) (oscuro) gloomy, dark (b) Fig (triste, lúgubre) sombre, gloomy

**somero, -a** adj superficial

**someter 1** vt (a) (dominar, subyugar) to subdue (b) (presentar) **s. algo a la aprobación de alguien** to submit sth for sb's approval; **s. algo a votación** to put sth to the vote (c) (subordinar) to subordinate (d) (a interrogatorio, presiones) **s. a alguien a algo** to subject sb to sth; **s. a alguien a una operación** to operate on sb

**2 someterse** vpr (a) (rendirse) to surrender (b) (conformarse) **someterse a algo** to yield o bow to sth (c) (a interrogatorio, pruebas) to undergo; **someterse a una operación** to have an operation

**sometimiento** nm (a) (en general) submission; **evitar el s. a los rayos del sol** (en frasco, envoltorio) keep out of direct sunlight (b) (dominio) subjugation

**somier** (pl **somieres**) nm (de muelles) bed springs; (de tablas) slats (of bed)

**somnífero, -a 1** adj somniferous
**2** nm sleeping pill

**somnolencia** nf sleepiness, drowsiness

**somnoliento, -a** adj drowsy, sleepy

**somos** ver **ser**

**son 1** ver **ser**
**2** nm (a) (sonido) sound; Fig **bailar al s. que le tocan** to toe the line (b) (estilo) way; **en s. de in** the manner of); **en s. de paz** in peace

**sonado, -a** adj (a) (renombrado) famous (b) Fam (loco) crazy (c) (boxeador) punch drunk

**sonajero** nm rattle

**sonambulismo** nm sleepwalking

**sonámbulo, -a 1** adj sleepwalking; **es s. he** walks in his sleep
**2** nm,f sleepwalker

**sonante** adj **dinero contante y s.** hard cash

**sonar¹** nm Náut sonar

**sonar² [65] 1** vi (a) (producir sonido) to sound; (timbre) to ring; **sonaron las doce** the clock struck twelve; **suena a falso/chiste** it sounds false/like a joke; **(así o tal) como suena** literally, in so many words (b) (ser conocido, familiar) to be familiar; **me suena** it rings a bell; **no me suena su nombre** I don't remember hearing her name before (c) (pronunciarse) to be pronounced; **la letra 'h' no suena** the 'h' is silent (d) (mencionarse, citarse) to be mentioned; **su nombre suena como futuro ministro** his

name is being mentioned as a future minister
**2 sonarse** vpr to blow one's nose

**sonata** nf sonata

**sonda** nf (a) Med & Mec probe; **s. espacial** space probe (b) Náut sounding line (c) Min drill, bore

**sondar** vt (a) Med to sound, to probe (b) Náut to sound (c) Min (terreno) to test; (roca) to drill

**sondear** vt (a) (indagar) to sound out (b) Min (terreno) to test; (roca) to drill

**sondeo** nm (a) (encuesta) (opinion) poll (b) Min drilling, boring (c) Náut sounding

**soneto** nm sonnet

**sonido** nm sound

**soniquete** nm (sonido) monotonous noise; Fam **el s. de siempre** the same old story

**sonora** nf Gram voiced consonant

**sonoridad** nf (a) (armonía) sonority (b) (acústica) acoustics (c) (resonancia) resonance

**sonorización** nf soundtrack recording

**sonorizar [16]** vt (a) (con amplificadores) to fit with a public address system (b) Cine (poner sonido a) to record the soundtrack for (c) Gram to voice

**sonoro, -a** adj (a) (del sonido) sound; (película) talking; **ondas sonoras** sound waves (b) (ruidoso, resonante, vibrante) resonant (c) Gram voiced

**sonotone®** nm hearing aid

**sonreír [58] 1** vi (a) (reír levemente) to smile (b) Fig (ser favorable) to smile on
**2 sonreírse** vpr to smile

**sonriente** adj smiling; **estás muy s. hoy** you're looking very cheerful today

**sonriera** etc ver **sonreír**

**sonrisa** nf smile

**sonrojar 1** vt to cause to blush
**2 sonrojarse** vpr to blush

**sonrojo** nm blush, blushing

**sonrosado, -a** adj rosy

**sonrosar** vt to colour pink

**sonsacar [61]** vt **s. algo a alguien** to extract sth from sb

**sonso, -a** adj Am Fam silly

**sonsonete** nm (a) (ruido) tapping (b) Fig (entonación) monotonous intonation (c) Fig (cantinela) old tune (d) Fig (sarcasmo) hint of sarcasm

**soñador, -ora 1** adj dreamy
**2** nm,f dreamer

**soñar [65] 1** vt también Fig to dream; **¡ni soñarlo!, ¡ni lo sueñes!** not on your life!
**2** vi también Fig to dream (**con** o about); **s. con los angelitos** to have sweet dreams; **s. despierto** to daydream

**soñarrera** *nf Fam* **tener una s.** to feel drowsy

**soñoliento, -a** *adj* sleepy, drowsy

**sopa** *nf* (a) *(guiso)* soup; **s. de ajo** garlic soup; *Am* **s. inglesa** trifle; **s. juliana** *o* **de verduras** vegetable soup (b) *(de pan)* sop, piece of soaked bread; **hacer sopas (en)** to dip bread (into) (c) *(expresiones)* **andar a la s. boba** to scrounge; **dar s. con hondas a alguien** to knock the spots off sb; **encontrarse a alguien hasta en la s.** not to be able to get away from sb; **estar como una s.** to be sopping wet

**sopapo** *nm* slap

**sopera** *nf (recipiente)* soup tureen

**sopero, -a** *adj* soup; **plato s.** soup plate

**sopesar** *vt* to try the weight of; *Fig* to weigh up

**sopetón: de sopetón** *loc adv* suddenly, abruptly

**soplado** *nm (del vidrio)* glassblowing

**soplagaitas** *nmf inv Fam (estúpido, pesado)* Br prat, *US* jerk

**soplamocos** *nm inv Fam* box on the ears

**soplar 1** *vt* (a) *(vela, fuego)* to blow out (b) *(ceniza, polvo)* to blow off (c) *(globo)* to blow up (d) *(vidrio)* to blow (e) *Fig (en examen)* to prompt; **me sopló las respuestas** he whispered the answers to me (f) *Fig (denunciar)* to squeal (g) *Fig (hurtar)* to pinch, to nick

**2** *vi* (a) *(echar aire)* to blow (b) *Fam (beber)* to booze

**3 soplarse** *vpr Fam (comer)* to gobble up; *(beber)* to knock back

**soplete** *nm* blowlamp

**soplido** *nm* blow, puff

**soplo** *nm* (a) *(soplido)* blow, puff (b) *Fig (instante)* breath, moment (c) *Med* murmur (d) *Fam (chivatazo)* tip-off; **dar el s.** to squeal, to grass

**soplón, -ona** *nm,f Fam* grass

**soponcio** *nm Fam* fainting fit; **le dio un s.** she passed out

**sopor** *nm* drowsiness

**soporífero, -a** *adj también Fig* soporific

**soportable** *adj* bearable, endurable

**soportal** *nm (pórtico)* porch; **soportales** arcade

**soportar 1** *vt* (a) *(sostener)* to support (b) *(resistir, tolerar)* to stand; **¡no lo soporto!** I can't stand him/it! (c) *(sobrellevar)* to endure, to bear

**2 soportarse** *vpr (mutuamente)* to stand one another

**soporte** *nm* (a) *(apoyo)* support; **s. publicitario** publicity medium (b) *Informát* medium; **s. físico/lógico** hardware/software

**soprano** *nmf* soprano

**sor** *nf Rel* sister

**sorber** *vt* (a) *(beber)* to sip; *(haciendo ruido)* to slurp (b) *(absorber)* to soak up, to absorb (c) *(atraer)* to draw *o* suck in (d) *Fig (escuchar atentamente)* to drink in

**sorbete** *nm* sorbet; *CAm (helado)* ice cream

**sorbetería** *nf CAm* ice cream shop

**sorbo** *nm* (a) *(acción)* gulp, swallow; *(pequeño)* sip; **beber a sorbos** to sip (b) *(trago)* mouthful; *(pequeño)* sip (c) *(cantidad pequeña)* drop

**sorda** *nf Gram* voiceless consonant

**sordera** *nf* deafness

**sordidez** *nf* (a) *(miseria)* squalor (b) *(obscenidad, perversión)* sordidness

**sórdido, -a** *adj* (a) *(miserable)* squalid (b) *(obsceno, perverso)* sordid

**sordina** *nf* (a) *Mús (en instrumentos de viento, cuerda)* mute; *(en pianos)* damper; *Fig* **con s.** *(hablar)* under one's breath (b) *(de reloj)* muffle

**sordo, -a 1** *adj* (a) *(que no oye)* deaf; *Fig* **permanecer s. a** *o* **ante algo** to be deaf to sth; **estar más s. que una tapia** to be stone deaf (b) *(pasos)* quiet, muffled (c) *(ruido, dolor)* dull (d) *Gram* voiceless, unvoiced

**2** *nm,f (persona)* deaf person; **los sordos** the deaf; **hacerse el s.** to turn a deaf ear

**sordomudo, -a 1** *adj* deaf and dumb

**2** *nm,f* deaf-mute

**sorgo** *nm* sorghum

**soriano, -a 1** *adj* of/from Soria

**2** *nm,f* person from Soria

**soriasis** *nf inv* psoriasis

**sorna** *nf* **con s.** ironically, mockingly

**soroche** *nm Am* altitude sickness

**sorprendente** *adj* surprising

**sorprender 1** *vt* (a) *(asombrar)* to surprise (b) *(atrapar, pillar)* **s. a alguien (haciendo algo)** to catch sb (doing sth) (c) *(coger desprevenido)* to catch unawares (d) *(descubrir)* to discover

**2 sorprenderse** *vpr* to be surprised (**de** by *o* at)

**sorprendido, -a** *adj* surprised

**sorpresa** *nf* surprise; **dar una s. a alguien** to surprise sb; **llevarse una s.** to get a surprise; **de** *o* **por s.** unexpectedly; **pillar a alguien por s.** to catch sb by surprise

**sorpresivo, -a** *adj* unexpected

**sortear 1** *vt* (a) *(rifar)* to raffle (b) *(echar a suertes)* to draw lots for (c) *Fig (superar)* to get round (d) *Fig (esquivar)* to dodge

**2 sortearse** *vpr* **sortearse algo** to draw lots for sth

**sorteo** *nm (lotería)* draw; *(rifa)* raffle; **haremos un s. con los premios** we'll raffle the prizes

**sortija** *nf* ring

**sortilegio** *nm* (a) *(hechizo)* spell (b) *Fig (atractivo)* charm, magic

**SOS** *nm* SOS

**sosa** *nf* soda; **s. cáustica** caustic soda

**sosaina 1** *adj (sin gracia)* dull, insipid
  **2** *nmf* dull person, bore

**sosegado, -a** *adj* calm

**sosegar** [45] **1** *vt* to calm
  **2 sosegarse** *vpr* to calm down

**soseras** *nmf inv Fam* dull person, bore

**sosería** *nf* lack of sparkle

**sosia** *nm inv* double, lookalike

**sosiego 1** *ver* **sosegar**
  **2** *nm* calm

**soslayar** *vt* to avoid

**soslayo: de soslayo** *loc adv (oblicuamente)* sideways, obliquely; **mirar a alguien de s.** to look at sb out of the corner of one's eye

**soso, -a 1** *adj* (a) *(sin sal)* bland, tasteless (b) *(sin gracia)* dull, insipid
  **2** *nm,f* dull person, bore

**sospecha** *nf* suspicion; **despertar sospechas** to arouse suspicion

**sospechar 1** *vt (creer, suponer)* to suspect; **sospecho que no lo terminará** I doubt whether she'll finish it
  **2** *vi* **s. de** to suspect

**sospechoso, -a 1** *adj* suspicious
  **2** *nm,f* suspect

**sostén** *nm* (a) *(apoyo)* support (b) *(sustento)* main support; *(alimento)* sustenance (c) *(sujetador)* bra, brassiere

**sostener** [67] **1** *vt* (a) *(sujetar)* to support, to hold up (b) *(defender) (idea, opinión, tesis)* to defend; *(promesa, palabra)* to stand by, to keep; **s. que...** to maintain that... (c) *(mantener, costear)* to support (d) *(tener) (conversación)* to hold, to have; *(correspondencia)* to keep up
  **2 sostenerse** *vpr (en pie)* to stay on one's feet; *(suspendido)* to hang; **con ese clavito no se va a s.** it'll never stay up on that little nail

**sostenido, -a 1** *adj* (a) *(persistente)* sustained (b) *Mús* sharp
  **2** *nm Mús* sharp

**sostiene, sostuviera** *etc ver* **sostener**

**sota** *nf* jack

**sotabanco** *nm (ático)* attic

**sotabarba** *nf* double chin

**sotana** *nf* cassock

**sótano** *nm* basement, cellar

**sotavento** *nm* leeward

**soterrado, -a** *adj (enterrado)* buried; *Fig* hidden

**soterrar** [3] *vt (enterrar)* to bury; *Fig* to hide

**sotobosque** *nm* undergrowth

**sotto voce** [soto'βotʃe] *adv* sotto voce

**soufflé** [su'fle] *(pl soufflés)* *nm* soufflé

**soul** *nm Mús* soul (music)

**souvenir** [suβe'nir] *(pl souvenirs)* *nm* souvenir

**soviet** *(pl soviets)* *nm* soviet; *Antes* **el s. supremo** the Supreme Soviet

**soviético, -a 1** *adj (de la URSS)* Soviet
  **2** *nm,f* Soviet

**soy** *ver* **ser**

**SP** *(abrev de* **servicio público***)* = sign indicating public transport vehicle

**spaghetti** [espa'veti] *nm* = **espagueti**

**spaniel** [es'paniel] *(pl spaniels)* *nm* spaniel

**sparring** [es'parrin] *(pl sparrings)* *nm Dep* sparring partner

**speed** [es'piθ] *nm (droga)* speed

**sport** [es'por]: **de sport** *loc adj* **chaqueta de s.** sports jacket; **ropa de s.** casual clothes

**spot** [es'pot] *(pl spots)* *nm* (TV) advert; **un s. publicitario** a (television) commercial

**spray** [es'prai] *(pl sprays)* *nm* spray

**sprint** [es'prin] *(pl sprints)* *nm* sprint

**sprinter** [es'printer] *(pl sprinters)* *nmf* sprinter

**squash** [es'kwas] *nm inv Dep* squash

**Sr.** *(abrev de* **señor***)* Mr

**Sra.** *(abrev de* **señora***)* Mrs

**Sres.** *(abrev de* **señores***)* Messrs

**Sri Lanka** *n* Sri Lanka

**Srta.** *(abrev de* **señorita***)* Miss

**SS** *(abrev de* **Su Santidad***)* HH

**Sta.** *(abrev de* **santa***)* St

**stand** [es'tan] *(pl stands)* *nm* stall, stand

**standing** [es'tandin] *nm* standing, social status; **un apartamento de alto s.** a luxury flat; **una compañía de alto s.** a top company

**starter** [es'tarter] *(pl starters)* *nm* = **estárter**

**statu quo** [es'tatu'kwo] *nm inv* status quo

**stick** [es'tik] *(pl sticks)* *nm Dep* hockey stick

**Sto.** *(abrev de* **santo***)* St

**stock** [es'tok] *(pl stocks)* *nm Com* stock

**stop** [es'top] *(pl stops)* *nm* (a) *Aut* stop sign (b) *(en telegrama)* stop

**strip-tease** [es'tribtis] *nm inv* striptease

**su** *(pl sus)* *adj posesivo (de él)* his; *(de ella)* her; *(de cosa, animal)* its; *(de uno)* one's; *(de ellos, ellas)* their; *(de usted, ustedes)* your; **su libro** his/her/your/their book; **sus libros** his/her/your/their books; **su hocico** its snout

**suahili** [swa'xili], **suajili** *nm (lengua)* Swahili

**suave** *adj* (**a**) *(al tacto)* soft (**b**) *(liso, no brusco)* smooth; **este coche tiene la dirección muy s.** this car has very smooth steering (**c**) *(sabor, olor, color)* delicate (**d**) *(apacible) (persona, carácter)* gentle; *(clima)* mild (**e**) *(fácil, lento) (cuesta, tarea, ritmo)* gentle

**suavidad** *nf* (**a**) *(de tacto)* softness (**b**) *(lisura, falta de brusquedad)* smoothness (**c**) *(de sabor, olor, color)* delicacy (**d**) *(de carácter)* gentleness (**e**) *(de clima)* mildness (**f**) *(de cuesta, tarea, ritmo)* gentleness

**suavizante** **1** *adj (para ropa, cabello)* conditioning; *(para piel)* moisturizing

  **2** *nm* conditioner; **s. para la ropa** fabric conditioner *o* softener

**suavizar** [16] *vt* (**a**) *(poner blando)* to soften; *(hacer liso)* to smooth; *(ropa, cabello)* to condition (**b**) *(hacer dócil)* to temper (**c**) *Fig (dificultad, tarea)* to ease; *(conducción)* to make smoother; *(clima)* to make milder (**d**) *(sabor, olor, color)* to tone down

**Suazilandia** *n* Swaziland

**subacuático, -a** *adj* subaquatic

**subafluente** *nm* minor tributary

**subalimentación** *nf* undernourishment

**subalimentar** *vt* to undernourish

**subalquilar** *vt* to sublet

**subalterno, -a** **1** *adj (subordinado)* auxiliary

  **2** *nm,f (empleado)* subordinate

  **3** *nm Taurom* assistant to bullfighter

**subarrendar** [3] *vt* to sublet

**subarrendatario, -a** *nm,f* subtenant

**subarriendo** *nm* (**a**) *(acción)* subtenancy (**b**) *(contrato)* sublease (agreement)

**subasta** *nf* (**a**) *(venta pública)* auction; **sacar algo a s.** to put sth up for auction (**b**) *(contrata pública)* tender; **sacar algo a s.** to put sth out to tender

**subastador, -ora** *nm,f* auctioneer

**subastar** *vt* to auction

**subcampeón, -ona** *nm,f* runner-up

**subcampeonato** *nm* second place, runner-up's position

**subclase** *nf* subclass

**subcomisión** *nf* subcommittee

**subconjunto** *nm Mat* subset

**subconsciencia** *nf* subconscious

**subconsciente** *adj & nm* subconscious

**subcontratar** *vt* to subcontract

**subcontrato** *nm* subcontract

**subcutáneo, -a** *adj* subcutaneous

**subdelegación** *nf* subdelegation

**subdelegado, -a** *nm,f* subdelegate

**subdesarrollado, -a** *adj* underdeveloped

**subdesarrollo** *nm* underdevelopment

**subdirección** *nf (puesto)* post of assistant manager

**subdirector, -ora** *nm,f* assistant manager

**subdirectorio** *nm Informát* subdirectory

**súbdito, -a** *nm,f* (**a**) *(de monarca)* subject (**b**) *(ciudadano)* citizen, national

**subdividir** *vt* to subdivide

  **2 subdividirse** *vpr* to be subdivided (**en** into)

**subdivisión** *nf* subdivision

**subemplear** *vt* to underemploy

**subempleo** *nm* underemployment

**subespecie** *nf* subspecies

**subestimar** **1** *vt* to underestimate; *(infravalorar)* to underrate

  **2 subestimarse** *vpr* to underrate oneself

**subgénero** *nm* subgenus

**subgrupo** *nm* subgroup

**subida** *nf* (**a**) *(cuesta)* hill (**b**) *(ascensión)* ascent, climb (**c**) *(aumento)* increase, rise

**subido, -a** *adj* (**a**) *(intenso)* strong, intense (**b**) *Fam (en cantidad)* **tiene el guapo s.** he really fancies himself; **está de un imbécil s.** he has been acting like an idiot recently (**c**) *Fam (atrevido)* risqué; **s. de tono** *(impertinente)* impertinent

**subíndice** *nm* subscript

**subinspector, -ora** *nm,f* deputy inspector

**subir** **1** *vi* (**a**) *(a piso, azotea)* to go/come up; *(a montaña, cima)* to climb

  (**b**) *(aumentar) (precio, temperatura)* to go up, to rise; *(cauce, marea)* to rise; **s. de categoría** *(mejorar)* to improve; *(ser ascendido)* to be promoted

  (**c**) *(montar) (en avión, barco)* to get on; *(en coche)* to get in; **sube al coche** get into the car

  (**d**) *(cuenta, importe)* **s. a** to come *o* amount to

  (**e**) *Culin (crecer)* to rise

  **2** *vt* (**a**) *(ascender) (calle, escaleras)* to go/come up; *(pendiente, montaña)* to climb

  (**b**) *(poner arriba)* to lift up; *(llevar arriba)* to take/bring up

  (**c**) *(aumentar) (precio, peso)* to put up, to increase; *(volumen)* to turn up; *(voz)* to raise

  (**d**) *(montar)* **s. algo/a alguien a** to lift sth/sb onto

  (**e**) *(alzar) (mano, bandera, voz)* to raise; *(persiana)* to roll up; *(ventanilla)* to wind up

  (**f**) *Mús* to raise the pitch of

  **3 subirse** *vpr* (**a**) *(ascender)* **subirse a** *(árbol)* to climb up; *(mesa)* to climb onto; *(piso)* to go/come up to; *Fig* **subirse por las paredes** to hit the roof

  (**b**) *(montarse)* **subirse a** *(tren, avión)* to get on, to board; *(caballo, bicicleta)* to mount, to get on; *(coche)* to get into; **el taxi paró y me subí** the taxi stopped and I got in

  (**c**) *(alzarse) (pernera, mangas)* to roll up;

*(cremallera)* to do up; *(pantalones, calcetines)* to pull up

(**d**) **subirse (a la cabeza)** *(alcohol, éxito)* to go to one's head

**súbito, -a** *adj* sudden; **de s.** suddenly

**subjefe, -a** *nm,f* deputy manager

**subjetividad** *nf* subjectivity

**subjetivismo** *nm* subjectivism

**subjetivo, -a** *adj* subjective

**sub júdice** [suβ'juðiθe] *adj Der* sub judice

**subjuntivo, -a** *adj & nm* subjunctive

**sublevación** *nf*, **sublevamiento** *nm* uprising

**sublevar 1** *vt* (**a**) *(amotinar)* to stir up (**b**) *(indignar)* to infuriate

**2 sublevarse** *vpr (amotinarse)* to rise up, to rebel

**sublimación** *nf* (**a**) *(exaltación)* exaltation (**b**) *Psi & Quím* sublimation

**sublimar** *vt* (**a**) *(exaltar)* to exalt (**b**) *Psi & Quím* to sublimate

**sublime** *adj* sublime

**sublimidad** *nf* sublimity

**subliminal** *adj* subliminal

**submarinismo** *nm* scuba diving

**submarinista** *nmf* scuba diver

**submarino, -a 1** *adj* underwater; **fotografía submarina** underwater photography

**2** *nm* submarine

**submúltiplo, -a** *adj & nm* submultiple

**subnormal 1** *adj* (**a**) *(retrasado)* mentally retarded (**b**) *Fig Pey (imbécil)* moronic

**2** *nmf* (**a**) *(retrasado)* mentally retarded person (**b**) *Fig Pey (imbécil)* moron, cretin

**subnormalidad** *nf* **una campaña de prevención de la s.** a campaign aimed at preventing children from being born with a mental handicap; **la actitud de la sociedad ante la s.** society's attitude to the mentally retarded

**suboficial** *nmf Mil* non-commissioned officer

**suborden** *nm Biol* suborder

**subordinación** *nf también Gram* subordination

**subordinado, -a** *adj & nm,f* subordinate

**subordinante** *adj Gram* subordinating

**subordinar 1** *vt también Gram* to subordinate

**2 subordinarse** *vpr* to be subordinate (**a** to)

**subproducto** *nm* by-product

**subrayado, -a 1** *adj* underlined

**2** *nm* underlining

**subrayar** *vt también Fig* to underline

**subrepticio, -a** *adj* surreptitious

**subrogación** *nf* subrogation

**subrogar** [40] *vt* to subrogate

**subsahariano, -a** *adj* sub-Saharan

**subsanable** *adj* (**a**) *(solucionable)* solvable (**b**) *(corregible)* rectifiable

**subsanación** *nf (de errores)* correction

**subsanar** *vt* (**a**) *(solucionar)* to resolve (**b**) *(corregir)* to correct (**c**) *(disculpar)* to excuse

**subscribir** *vt*, **subscripción** *nf etc* = **suscribir, suscripción** *etc*

**subsecretaría** *nf* (**a**) *(oficina)* undersecretary's office (**b**) *(cargo)* undersecretaryship

**subsecretario, -a** *nm,f* (**a**) *(de secretario)* assistant secretary (**b**) *(de ministro)* undersecretary

**subsidiar** [15] *vt* to subsidize

**subsidiario, -a** *adj* (**a**) *(empresa, compañía)* subsidiary (**b**) *Der* ancillary (**c**) *(de subvención)* paid for by the State

**subsidio** *nm* benefit, allowance; **s. de desempleo** unemployment benefit; **s. de invalidez** disability allowance

**subsiguiente** *adj* subsequent

**subsistencia** *nf* (**a**) *(vida)* subsistence (**b**) *(conservación)* continued existence (**c**) **subsistencias** *(provisiones)* provisions

**subsistente** *adj* surviving

**subsistir** *vi* (**a**) *(vivir)* to live, to exist (**b**) *(sobrevivir)* to survive

**substancia** *nf*, **substancial** *adj etc* = **sustancia, sustancial** *etc*

**substantivar** *vt*, **substantivo, -a** *adj & nm etc* = **sustantivar, sustantivo** *etc*

**substitución** *nf*, **substituir** [36] *vt etc* = **sustitución, sustituir** *etc*

**substracción** *nf* = **sustracción**

**substraer** [68] *vt* = **sustraer**

**substrato** *nm* = **sustrato**

**subsuelo** *nm* subsoil

**subte** *nm Arg* metro, *Br* underground, *US* subway

**subteniente** *nm* sub-lieutenant

**subterfugio** *nm* subterfuge; **sin subterfugios** without subterfuge

**subterráneo, -a 1** *adj* subterranean, underground

**2** *nm* underground tunnel

**subtipo** *nm Biol* subtype

**subtitular** *vt también Cine* to subtitle

**subtítulo** *nm también Cine* subtitle

**subtropical** *adj* subtropical

**suburbano, -a 1** *adj* suburban

**2** *nm (tren)* suburban train

**suburbial** *adj* **barrio s.** poor suburb

**suburbio** *nm* poor suburb

**subvalorar** *vt* to undervalue, to underrate

**subvención** nf (para un proyecto) grant; (para proteger precios, una industria) subsidy; **la orquesta recibe una s. del ayuntamiento** the orchestra receives financial support from the town council

**subvencionar** vt (precios, industria) to subsidize; (proyecto, actividad cultural, estudios) to provide financial support for

**subversión** nf subversion

**subversivo, -a** adj subversive

**subvertir** [64] vt to subvert

**subyacente** adj underlying

**subyacer** vi (ocultarse) **s. bajo algo** to underlie sth

**subyugador, -ora, subyugante** adj (a) (dominador) conquering (b) (atrayente) captivating

**subyugar** [40] vt (a) (someter) to subjugate; Fig to quell, to master (b) Fig (atraer) to captivate

**succión** nf suction

**succionar** vt (sujeto: raíces) to suck up; (sujeto: bebé) to absorb, to suck

**sucedáneo, -a 1** adj ersatz, substitute
**2** nm (sustituto) substitute; Fig **ser un s. de** (mala copia) to be an apology for

**suceder 1** v impersonal (ocurrir) to happen; **suceda lo que suceda** whatever happens
**2** vt (sustituir) to succeed (**en** in)
**3** vi (venir después) **s.** a to come after, to follow; **a la guerra sucedieron años muy tristes** the war was followed by years of misery

**sucesión** nf (a) (serie) succession (b) (cambio) (de monarca) succession; (de cargo importante) changeover (c) (descendencia) **morir sin s.** to die without issue

**sucesivamente** adv successively; **y así s.** and so on

**sucesivo, -a** adj (a) (consecutivo) successive, consecutive (b) (siguiente) **en días sucesivos les informaremos** we'll let you know over the next few days; **en lo s.** in future

**suceso** nm (a) (acontecimiento) event (b) (hecho delictivo) crime; (incidente) incident; **sección de sucesos** (en prensa) = section of newspaper dealing with accidents, crimes, disasters etc

**sucesor, -ora 1** adj succeeding
**2** nm,f successor

**suciedad** nf (a) (cualidad) dirtiness (b) (porquería) dirt, filth

**sucinto, -a** adj (a) (conciso) succinct (b) (pequeño, corto) skimpy

**sucio, -a 1** adj (a) (sin limpieza) dirty; (al comer, trabajar) messy; **el blanco es un color muy s.** white is a colour that gets dirty easily; **en s.** in rough (b) (conciencia) bad, guilty
**2** adv **jugar s.** to play dirty

**sucre** nm (moneda) sucre

**suculento, -a** adj tasty

**sucumbir** vi (a) (rendirse, ceder) to succumb (**a** to) (b) (fallecer) to die

**sucursal** nf branch

**sudaca** adj & nmf Fam = term used to refer to Latin American people, which can sometimes be pejorative

**sudadera** nf (a) (prenda) sweatshirt (b) (sudor) sweat

**Sudáfrica** n South Africa

**sudafricano, -a** adj & nm,f South African

**Sudamérica** n South America

**sudamericano, -a** adj & nm,f South American

**Sudán** n Sudan

**sudanés, -esa** adj & nm,f Sudanese

**sudar 1** vi (transpirar) to sweat; (pared) to run with condensation; Fam **sudaban a chorros** they were running with sweat; Fam **s. la gota gorda** to sweat buckets; Fig (trabajar duro) to sweat blood
**2** vt (a) (empapar) to make sweaty (b) Fam Fig (trabajar duro por) to work hard for

**sudario** nm shroud

**sudeste 1** adj (posición, parte) southeast, southeastern; (dirección, viento) southeasterly
**2** nm southeast

**sudista** Hist **1** adj Southern (in US Civil War)
**2** nmf Southerner (in US Civil War)

**sudoeste 1** adj (posición, parte) southwest, southwestern; (dirección, viento) southwesterly
**2** nm southwest

**sudor** nm (transpiración) sweat; (de pared) condensation; **con el s. de mi frente** by the sweat of my brow

**sudoración** nf sweating, perspiration

**sudoriento, -a** adj sweaty

**sudoríparo, -a** adj sweat; **glándula sudorípara** sweat gland

**sudoroso, -a** adj sweaty

**Suecia** n Sweden

**sueco, -a 1** adj Swedish
**2** nm,f (persona) Swede; Fig **hacerse el s.** to play dumb, to pretend not to understand
**3** nm (lengua) Swedish

**suegro, -a** nm,f father-in-law, f mother-in-law

**suela** nf sole; Fig **no llegarle a alguien a la s. del zapato** not to hold a candle to sb

**sueldo 1** ver **soldar**
**2** nm salary, wages; (semanal) wage; **a s.** (empleado) salaried; (asesino) hired; **s. base** basic salary; (semanal) basic wage

**suelo 1** *ver* **soler**

**2** *nm* **(a)** *(pavimento) (en interiores)* floor; *(en el exterior)* ground **(b)** *(terreno, territorio)* soil; *(para edificar)* land **(c)** *(expresiones)* **arrastrarse por el s.** to grovel, to humble oneself; **besar el s.** to fall flat on one's face; **echar por el s. un plan** to ruin a project; **estar por los suelos** *(persona, precio)* to be at rock bottom; *(productos)* to be dirt cheap; **poner** *o* **tirar por los suelos** to run down, to criticize

**suelta** *nf (liberación)* release

**suelto, -a 1** *ver* **soltar**

**2** *adj* **(a)** *(en general)* loose; *(cordones)* undone; **¿tienes cinco duros sueltos?** have you got 25 pesetas in loose change?; **andar s.** *(en libertad)* to be free; *(en fuga)* to be at large; *(con diarrea)* to have diarrhoea **(b)** *(separado)* separate; *(desparejado)* odd; **no los vendemos sueltos** we don't sell them separately **(c)** *(arroz)* fluffy **(d)** *(lenguaje, estilo)* fluent, fluid **(e)** *(desenvuelto)* comfortable, at ease

**3** *nm (calderilla)* loose change

**sueno** *etc ver* **sonar**

**sueño 1** *ver* **soñar**

**2** *nm* **(a)** *(ganas de dormir)* sleepiness; *(por medicamento)* drowsiness; **¡qué s.!** I'm really sleepy!; **tener s.** to be sleepy

**(b)** *(estado)* sleep; **coger el s.** to get to sleep; **conciliar el s.** to get to sleep; **descabezar un s.** to have a nap; *Fam* **no me quita el s.** I'm not losing any sleep over it; *Fig* **s. eterno** eternal rest; **s. pesado/ligero** heavy/light sleep

**(c)** *(imagen mental, objetivo, quimera)* dream; *Fam* **esta casa es un s.** this house is a dream; **en sueños** in a dream; *Fig* **ni en sueños** no way, under no circumstances

**suero** *nm* **(a)** *Med* serum; **s. artificial** saline solution **(b)** *(de la leche)* whey

**suerte** *nf* **(a)** *(azar)* chance; **echar** *o* **tirar algo a suertes** to draw lots for sth; **la s. está echada** the die is cast **(b)** *(fortuna)* luck; *(destino)* fate; **por s.** luckily; **probar s.** to try one's luck; **¡qué s.!** that was lucky!; **tener s.** to be lucky; **tener buena/mala s.** to be lucky/unlucky; **tener la s. de espaldas** to be having a run of bad luck; **tentar a la s.** to tempt fate; **tocar** *o* **caer en s. a alguien** to fall to sb's lot **(c)** *(situación)* situation, lot **(d)** *(clase)* **toda s. de** all manner of; **ser una s. de** to be a kind *o* sort of **(e)** *(manera)* manner, fashion; **de s. que** in such a way that

**suertudo, -a** *nm,f Fam* lucky devil

**suéter** ( *pl* **suéteres**) *nm* sweater

**Suez** *n* Suez

**suficiencia** *nf* **(a)** *(capacidad)* proficiency **(b)** *(idoneidad)* suitability; *(de medidas, esfuerzos)* adequacy **(c)** *(presunción)* smugness, self-importance **(d)** *Educ (examen)* = resit of secondary school end-of-year examination at end of June

**suficiente 1** *adj* **(a)** *(bastante)* enough; *(medidas, esfuerzos)* adequate; **no llevo (dinero) s.** I don't have enough (money) on me; **no tienes la estatura s.** you're not tall enough **(b)** *(presuntuoso)* smug, full of oneself

**2** *nm (nota)* pass

**suficientemente** *adv* enough, sufficiently

**sufijo** *nm* suffix

**suflé** *nm Culin* soufflé

**sufragar** [40] *vt* to defray

**sufragio** *nm* suffrage; **s. directo/indirecto** direct/indirect suffrage; **s. restringido/universal** restricted/universal suffrage

**sufragismo** *nm Hist* suffragette movement

**sufragista** *Hist* **1** *adj* suffragette; **movimiento s.** suffragette movement

**2** *nmf* suffragette

**sufrido, -a** *adj* **(a)** *(resignado)* patient, uncomplaining; *(durante mucho tiempo)* long-suffering **(b)** *(resistente) (tela)* hardwearing; *(color)* that does not show the dirt

**sufridor, -ora** *adj* easily worried

**sufrimiento** *nm* suffering

**sufrir 1** *vt* **(a)** *(padecer)* to suffer; *(accidente)* to have **(b)** *(soportar)* to bear, to stand; **tengo que s. sus manías** I have to put up with his idiosyncrasies **(c)** *(experimentar)* to undergo, to experience

**2** *vi* **(a)** *(padecer)* to suffer; **s. de** *(enfermedad)* to suffer from; **s. del estómago** to have a stomach complaint

**sugerencia** *nf* suggestion

**sugerente** *adj* evocative

**sugerir** [64] *vt* **(a)** *(proponer)* to suggest **(b)** *(evocar)* to evoke

**sugestión** *nf* suggestion

**sugestionable** *adj* impressionable

**sugestionar 1** *vt* to influence

**2 sugestionarse** *vpr* **(a)** *(obsesionarse)* to become obsessed **(b)** *Psi* to use autosuggestion

**sugestivo, -a** *adj* attractive

**sugiero** *etc ver* **sugerir**

**sugiriera** *etc ver* **sugerir**

**suich** *nm Méx* switch

**suicida 1** *adj* suicidal

**2** *nmf (por naturaleza)* suicidal person; *(suicidado)* person who has committed suicide

**suicidarse** *vpr* to commit suicide

**suicidio** *nm* suicide

**sui géneris** *adj inv* unusual, individual

**suite** [suit] *nf también Mús* suite

**Suiza** *n* Switzerland

**suizo, -a 1** *adj & nm,f* Swiss

　**2** *nm Culin* = type of sugared bun

**sujeción** *nf* (a) *(atadura)* fastening (b) *(sometimiento)* subjection

**sujetador** *nm* bra, brassiere

**sujetalibros** *nm inv* bookend

**sujetapapeles** *nm inv* paper clip

**sujetar 1** *vt* (a) *(agarrar) (para mantener en su sitio)* to hold in place; *(sobre una superficie, con un peso)* to hold down; *(para que no se caiga)* to hold up; **s. con clavos/cola** to fasten with nails/glue; **sujeta los papeles con un clip** fasten the papers together with a paper clip; **intentó escapar, pero la sujetaron firmemente** she tried to escape, but they kept a firm grip on her (b) *(sostener)* to hold

　**2 sujetarse** *vpr* (a) *(agarrarse)* **sujetarse a** to hold on to, to cling to (b) *(aguantarse)* to keep in place (c) *(someterse)* **sujetarse a** to keep o stick to

**sujeto, -a 1** *adj* (a) *(agarrado)* fastened (b) *(expuesto)* subject (a to)

　**2** *nm* (a) *(de acción, frase)* subject (b) *(individuo)* individual; **un s. sospechoso** a suspicious individual; *Econ* **s. pasivo** taxpayer

**sulfamida** *nf Med* sulphonamide

**sulfatarse** *vpr (pilas)* to leak

**sulfato** *nm* sulphate

**sulfurar 1** *vt* (a) *(encolerizar)* to infuriate (b) *Quím* to sulphurate

　**2 sulfurarse** *vpr (encolerizarse)* to get mad

**sulfúrico, -a** *adj* sulphuric

**sulfuro** *nm* sulphide

**sulfuroso, -a** *adj Quím* sulphurous

**sultán, -ana** *nm,f* sultan, *f* sultana

**suma** *nf* (a) *Mat (acción)* addition; *(resultado)* total (b) *(conjunto) (de conocimientos, datos)* total, sum; *(de dinero)* sum (c) *(resumen)* **en s.** in short

**sumamente** *adv* extremely

**sumando** *nm Mat* = amount to be added, addend

**sumar 1** *vt* (a) *Mat* to add together; **tres y cinco suman ocho** three and five are o make eight; *Fam Fig* **¡suma y sigue!** here we go again! (b) *(costar)* to come to

　**2 sumarse** *vpr* to join (a in)

**sumarial** *adj* pertaining to an indictment

**sumario, -a 1** *adj* (a) *(conciso)* brief (b) *Der* summary

　**2** *nm* (a) *Der* indictment (b) *(resumen)* summary

**sumarísimo, -a** *adj Der* swift, expeditious

**Sumatra** *n* Sumatra

**sumergible 1** *adj* waterproof

　**2** *nm* submarine

**sumergir** [26] **1** *vt (hundir)* to submerge; *(con fuerza)* to plunge; *(bañar)* to dip; *Fig* **s. en el caos** to plunge into chaos; *Fig* **el libro sumerge al lector en otra época** the book immerses the reader in another age

　**2 sumergirse** *vpr* (a) *(hundirse)* to submerge; *(con fuerza)* to plunge (b) *(abstraerse)* to immerse oneself (**en** in)

**sumidero** *nm* drain

**sumiller** *(pl* **sumillers***) nm* sommelier, wine waiter

**suministrador, -ora** *nm,f* supplier

**suministrar** *vt* to supply; **s. algo a alguien** to supply sb with sth

**suministro** *nm (productos)* supply; *(acción)* supplying

**sumir 1** *vt* **s. a alguien en** to plunge sb into

　**2 sumirse en** *vpr* (a) *(depresión, sueño)* to sink into (b) *(estudio, tema)* to immerse oneself in

**sumisión** *nf* (a) *(obediencia) (acción)* submission; *(cualidad)* submissiveness (b) *(rendición)* surrender

**sumiso, -a** *adj* submissive

**súmmum** *nm* **el s. de** the height of; **esto es el s.** this is wonderful o magnificent

**sumo, -a** *adj* **1** (a) *(supremo)* highest, supreme (b) *(gran)* extreme, great; **a lo s.** at most

　**2** *nm (lucha japonesa)* sumo (wrestling)

**sunnita 1** *adj* Sunni

　**2** *nmf* Sunnite, Sunni Moslem

**suntuosidad** *nf* sumptuousness, magnificence

**suntuoso, -a** *adj* sumptuous, magnificent

**supe** *ver* **saber**

**supeditación** *nf* subordination

**supeditar 1** *vt* to subordinate (a to); **estar supeditado a** to be dependent on

　**2 supeditarse** *vpr* **supeditarse a** to submit to

**súper 1** *adj Fam* great, super

　**2** *adv Fam* **pasarlo s.** to have a great time

　**3** *nm Fam* supermarket

　**4** *nf (gasolina)* **s.** four-star (petrol)

**super-** *prefijo Fam (muy)* really; **es supermajo** he's lovely o really nice; **superfácil** really o incredibly easy

**superable** *adj* surmountable

**superabundancia** *nf* excess

**superabundante** *adj* excessive

**superabundar** *vi* to abound

**superación** *nf* overcoming; **afán de s.** drive to improve

**superar 1** vt (a) (vencer) to beat; (récord) to break; **s. algo/a alguien en algo** to beat sth/sb for sth; **me supera en altura/inteligencia** he's taller/cleverer than me (b) (adelantar) to overtake, to pass (c) (época, técnica) **estar superado** to have been superseded (d) (resolver) to overcome; **s. un examen** to get through an exam

**2 superarse** vpr (a) (mejorar) to better oneself; **se supera día a día** he goes from strength to strength (b) (lucirse) to excel oneself

**superávit** nm inv surplus

**supercarburante** nm high-grade fuel

**superchería** nf (a) (engaño) fraud, hoax (b) (superstición) superstition

**superconductor** nm superconductor

**supercopa** nf = cup contested by the league champions and the winner of the league cup at the end of the season

**superdotado, -a 1** adj extremely gifted

**2** nm,f extremely gifted person

**superego** nm Psi superego

**superestructura** nf superstructure

**superficial** adj también Fig superficial

**superficialidad** nf superficiality

**superficie** nf (a) (parte exterior) surface (b) (área) area

**superfino, -a** adj superfine

**superfluo, -a** adj superfluous; (gasto) unnecessary

**superhombre** nm superman

**superíndice** nm superscript

**superintendente** nmf superintendent

**superior¹ 1** adj (a) (de arriba) top (b) (mayor) higher (a than) (c) (mejor) superior (a to) (d) (excelente) excellent (e) Anat & Geog upper (f) Educ higher

**2** nm (jefe) superior

**superior², -ora** Rel **1** adj superior

**2** nm,f superior, f mother superior

**superioridad** nf también Fig superiority

**superlativo, -a 1** adj (a) (belleza, inteligencia) exceptional (b) Gram superlative

**2** nm Gram superlative

**supermán** nm superman

**supermercado** nm supermarket

**superministro, -a** nm,f = powerful government minister in charge of more than one department

**supernova** nf supernova

**superpetrolero** nm supertanker

**superpoblación** nf overpopulation

**superpoblado, -a** adj overpopulated

**superponer** [52] vt (poner encima) to put on top (a of)

**superposición** nf superimposing

**superpotencia** nf superpower

**superproducción** nf (a) Econ overproduction (b) Cine blockbuster

**superpuesto, -a 1** participio ver **superponer**

**2** adj superimposed

**supersónico, -a** adj supersonic

**superstición** nf superstition

**supersticioso, -a** adj superstitious

**supervalorar** vt (artista, obra) to overrate; (casa, acciones) to overvalue

**supervisar** vt to supervise

**supervisión** nf supervision

**supervisor, -ora 1** adj supervisory

**2** nm,f supervisor

**supervivencia** nf survival

**superviviente 1** adj surviving

**2** nmf survivor

**supiera** etc ver **saber**

**supino, -a** adj **1** (a) (tendido) supine (b) Fig (excesivo) utter

**2** nm Gram supine

**suplantación** nf **s. (de personalidad)** impersonation

**suplantador, -ora** nm,f impostor

**suplantar** vt to take the place of

**suplementario, -a** adj supplementary, extra

**suplemento** nm (a) (añadido) & Prensa supplement; **s. dominical** Sunday supplement (b) (complemento) attachment

**suplencia** nf hacer una **s.** (profesor) to do Br supply teaching o US substitute teaching; (médico) to do a locum

**suplente 1** adj stand-in; **profesor s.** Br supply teacher, US substitute teacher

**2** nmf (sustituto) stand-in; Teatro understudy; Dep substitute

**supletorio, -a 1** adj additional, extra

**2** nm Telecom extension

**súplica** nf (a) (ruego) plea, entreaty (b) Der petition

**suplicar** [61] vt (a) (rogar) **s. algo (a alguien)** to plead for sth (with sb); **s. a alguien que haga algo** to beg sb to do sth (b) Der to appeal to

**suplicatorio** nm Der (a tribunal superior) = request by lower court for assistance from a higher court; (a órgano legislativo) = request by court for the parliamentary immunity of the accused to be waived

**suplicio** nm también Fig torture; **es un s.** it's torture; **¡qué s.!** what a life!

**suplique** etc ver **suplicar**

**suplir** vt (**a**) (sustituir) to replace (**con** with) (**b**) (compensar) **s. algo (con)** to compensate for sth (with)

**supo** ver **saber**

**suponer** [52] 1 vt (**a**) (creer, presuponer) to suppose (**b**) (implicar) to involve, to entail (**c**) (significar) to mean (**d**) (conjeturar) to imagine; **lo suponía** I guessed as much; **te suponía mayor** I thought you were older

2 vi to be important

3 nm **ser un s.** to be conjecture

4 **suponerse** vpr to suppose

**suposición** nf assumption

**supositorio** nm suppository

**supranacional** adj supranational

**suprarrenal** adj suprarenal

**supremacía** nf supremacy

**supremo, -a** 1 adj también Fig supreme

2 nm Der **el (Tribunal) S.** Br ≃ the High Court, US ≃ the Supreme Court

**supresión** nf (**a**) (de ley, impuesto, derecho) abolition; (de sanciones, restricciones) lifting (**b**) (de palabras, texto) deletion (**c**) (de puestos de trabajo, proyectos) axing

**suprimir** vt (**a**) (ley, impuesto, derecho) to abolish; (sanciones, restricciones) to lift (**b**) (palabras, texto) to delete (**c**) (puestos de trabajo, proyectos) to axe

**supuesto, -a** 1 participio ver **suponer**

2 adj supposed; (culpable, asesino) alleged; (nombre) false; **dar algo por s.** to take sth for granted; **por s.** of course

3 nm assumption; **en el s. de que...** assuming...

**supuración** nf suppuration

**supurar** vi to suppurate, to fester

**supusiera** etc ver **suponer**

**sur** 1 adj (posición, parte) south, southern; (dirección, viento) southerly

2 nm south; **viento del s.** south wind; **ir hacia el s.** to go south(wards); **está al s. de Madrid** it's (to the) south of Madrid

**Suramérica** n South America

**suramericano, -a** adj & nm,f South American

**surcar** [61] vt (tierra) to plough; (aire, agua) to cut o slice through

**surco** nm (**a**) (zanja) furrow (**b**) (señal) (de disco) groove; (de rueda) rut (**c**) (arruga) line, wrinkle

**sureño, -a** 1 adj southern; (viento) southerly

2 nm,f southerner

**sureste** 1 adj (posición, parte) southeast, southeastern; (dirección, viento) southeasterly

2 nm southeast

**surf, surfing** nm surfing

**surfista** nmf surfer

**surgir** [26] vi (**a**) (brotar) to spring forth (**b**) (aparecer) to appear (**c**) Fig (producirse) to arise

**Surinam** n Surinam

**suroeste** 1 adj (posición, parte) southwest, southwestern; (dirección, viento) southwesterly

2 nm southwest

**surque** etc ver **surcar**

**surrealismo** nm surrealism

**surrealista** adj & nmf surrealist

**surtido, -a** 1 adj (**a**) (bien aprovisionado) well-stocked (**b**) (variado) assorted

2 nm (**a**) (gama) range (**b**) (caja surtida) assortment

**surtidor** nm (de gasolina) pump; (de un chorro) spout

**surtir** 1 vt (proveer) to supply (**de** with)

2 vi (brotar) to spout, to spurt (**de** from)

3 **surtirse** vpr (proveerse) **surtirse de** to stock up on

**susceptibilidad** nf oversensitivity

**susceptible** adj (**a**) (sensible) oversensitive (**b**) (posible) **s. de** liable to

**suscitar** vt (discusión) to give rise to; (dificultades) to cause, to create; (interés, simpatía, sospechas) to arouse; (dudas) to raise

**suscribir** 1 vt (**a**) (firmar) to sign (**b**) (ratificar) to endorse (**c**) Com (acciones) to subscribe for

2 **suscribirse** vpr (**a**) Prensa to subscribe (**a** to) (**b**) Com **suscribirse a** to take out an option on

**suscripción** nf subscription

**suscriptor, -ora** nm,f subscriber

**suscrito, -a** 1 participio ver **suscribir**

2 adj **estar s. a** to subscribe to

**susodicho, -a** adj above-mentioned

**suspender** vt (**a**) (colgar) to hang (up) (**b**) Educ to fail (**c**) (interrumpir) to suspend (**d**) (aplazar) to postpone; (reunión, sesión) to adjourn (**e**) (de un cargo) to suspend; **s. de empleo y sueldo** to suspend without pay

**suspense** nm suspense

**suspensión** nf (**a**) también Aut suspension; **en s.** in suspension; **s. de empleo** suspension on full pay; **s. de pagos** suspension of payments (**b**) (aplazamiento) postponement; (de reunión, sesión) adjournment

**suspenso, -a** adj 1 (**a**) (colgado) **s. de** hanging from (**b**) (no aprobado) **estar s.** to have failed (**c**) Fig (interrumpido) **en s.** pending

2 nm (nota) **sacar un s.** to fail

**suspensorio** nm jockstrap

**suspicacia** nf suspicion

**suspicaz** adj suspicious

**suspirar** vi (**a**) (dar suspiros) to sigh; **s. de** to sigh with (**b**) Fig (desear) **s. por algo/por hacer algo** to long for sth/to do sth

**suspiro** nm (**a**) (aspiración) sigh; **dar un s.** to heave a sigh (**b**) (instante) **en un s.** in no time at all

**sustancia** *nf* (a) *(materia)* substance; **sin s.**
lacking in substance; **s. gris** grey matter (b)
*(esencia)* essence (c) *(de alimento)* nutritional
value

**sustancial** *adj* substantial, significant

**sustanciar** [15] *vt* (a) *(resumir)* to
summarize (b) *Der* to substantiate

**sustancioso, -a** *adj* substantial

**sustantivación** *nf* *Gram* nominalization,
use as a noun

**sustantivar** *vt* *Gram* to nominalize, to use as
a noun

**sustantivo, -a 1** *adj* *Formal (fundamental)*
substantial, significant
  **2** *nm* *Gram* noun

**sustentación** *nf* support

**sustentar** *vt* (a) *(sostener)* to support (b) *Fig
(mantener) (la moral)* to keep up; *(argumento,
teoría)* to defend

**sustento** *nm* (a) *(alimento)* sustenance;
*(mantenimiento)* livelihood; **ganarse el s.** to
earn one's living (b) *(apoyo)* support

**sustitución** *nf* (a) *(cambio)* replacement (b)
*Der* subrogation

**sustituible** *adj* replaceable

**sustituir** [36] *vt* to replace (**por** with)

**sustitutivo, -a** *adj & nm* substitute (**de** for)

**sustituto, -a** *nm,f* substitute, replacement

**susto** *nm* fright; **dar** *o* **pegar un s. a alguien**
to give sb a fright; **darse** *o* **pegarse un s.** to get
a fright; *Fam Fig* **darse un s. mortal** *o* **de
muerte** to be scared to death; **no ganar para
sustos** to have no end of troubles

**sustracción** *nf* (a) *(robo)* theft (b) *Mat*
subtraction

**sustraendo** *nm* *Mat* = amount to be
subtracted, subtrahend

**sustraer** [68] **1** *vt* (a) *(robar)* to steal (b) *Mat*
to subtract
  **2 sustraerse** *vpr* **sustraerse a** *o* **de**
*(obligación, problema)* to avoid

**sustrato** *nm* substratum

**susurrador, -ora, susurrante** *adj*
whispering

**susurrar** *vt & vi* to whisper

**susurro** *nm* whisper; *Fig* murmur

**sutil** *adj* *(en general)* subtle; *(velo, tejido)* delicate,
thin; *(brisa)* gentle; *(hilo, línea)* fine

**sutileza** *nf* *(en general)* subtlety; *(de velo, tejido)*
delicacy, thinness; *(de brisa)* gentleness; *(de hilo,
línea)* fineness

**sutura** *nf* suture

**suturar** *vt* to stitch

**Suva** *n* Suva

**suyo, -a 1** *adj posesivo (de él)* his; *(de ella)* hers;
*(de uno)* one's (own); *(de ellos, ellas)* theirs; *(de
usted, ustedes)* yours; **este libro es s.** this book
is his/hers/etc; **un amigo s.** a friend of his/
hers/etc; **no es asunto s.** it's none of his/her/
*etc* business; *Fam Fig* **es muy s.** he's a law unto
himself
  **2** *pron posesivo* (a) **el s.** *(de él)* his; *(de ella)* hers;
*(de cosa, animal)* its (own); *(de uno)* one's own;
*(de ellos, ellas)* theirs; *(de usted, ustedes)* yours
  (b) *(expresiones)* **de s.** in itself; **hacer de las
suyas** to be up to his/her/etc usual tricks;
**hacer s.** to make one's own; *Fam* **esta es la
suya** this is the chance he's been waiting for *o*
his big chance; **lo s. es el teatro** he/she/etc
should be on the stage; **lo s. sería volver** the
proper thing to do would be to go back; *Fam*
**los suyos** *(su familia)* his/her/etc folks; *(su
bando)* his/her/etc lot *o* side

**svástica** [es'βastika] *nf* swastika

**SWAPO** ['swapo] *nm (abrev de* **South
West African People's Organization)** SWAPO

**swing** [swin] *nm* *Mús* swing

**Sydney** *n* Sydney

# T

**T¹, t** [te] *nf (letra)* T, t

**t²** (a) *(abrev de* **tonelada)** t (b) *(abrev de* **tomo)** vol

**taba** *nf* **jugar a las tabas** to play at fivestones

**Tabacalera** *nf* = state tobacco monopoly in Spain

**tabacalero, -a** *adj* tobacco; **la industria tabacalera** the tobacco industry

**tabaco 1** *nm* (a) *(planta)* tobacco plant (b) *(picadura)* tobacco; **t. de liar** rolling tobacco; **t. negro/rubio** dark/Virginia tobacco; **t. de pipa** pipe tobacco (c) *(cigarrillos)* cigarettes
**2** *adj inv (color)* light brown

**tábano** *nm* horsefly

**tabaquería** *nf Br* tobacconist's (shop), *US* cigar store

**tabaquismo** *nm* = addiction to tobacco, and its damaging effects on one's health

**tabarra** *nf Fam* **dar la t.** to be a pest, to play up; **dar la t. con algo** to go on and on about sth

**tabasco** *nm* Tabasco® (sauce)

**taberna** *nf (bar)* bar *(old-fashioned in style)*; *(antiguo)* tavern, inn

**tabernáculo** *nm* tabernacle

**tabernario, -a** *adj* coarse

**tabernero, -a** *nm,f (propietario)* landlord, *f* landlady; *(encargado)* bartender, barman, *f* barmaid

**tabicar** [61] *vt* to wall up

**tabique** *nm* (a) *(pared)* partition (wall) (b) *Anat* **t. nasal** nasal septum

**tabla 1** *nf* (a) *(de madera)* plank; **t. de planchar** ironing board (b) *(pliegue)* pleat (c) *(lista, gráfico)* table; **t. de multiplicación** multiplication table (d) *Culin* **t. de cocina** chopping board; **t. de quesos** cheeseboard; **t. de patés** selection of pâtés (e) *(de surf, vela)* board (f) *Arte* panel (g) *(expresiones)* **ser una t. de salvación** to be a last resort *o* hope; **hacer t. rasa** to wipe the slate clean
**2** *nfpl* **tablas** (a) *(en ajedrez)* **quedar en** *o* **hacer tablas** to end in stalemate (b) *Teatro* stage, boards; *Teatro* **tener (muchas) tablas** to be an experienced actor; *Fig* to be an old hand (c) *Taurom* fence surrounding bullring

**tablado** *nm (de teatro)* stage; *(de baile)* dancefloor; *(plataforma)* platform

**tablao** *nm (local)* = club where flamenco dancing and singing is performed

**tableado, -a** *adj (falda)* pleated

**tablero** *nm* (a) *(tabla)* board; **t. de ajedrez** chessboard (b) *(en baloncesto)* backboard (c) **t. (de mandos)** *(de avión)* instrument panel; *(de coche)* dashboard

**tableta** *nf* (a) *Med* tablet (b) *(de chocolate)* bar

**tablilla** *nf Med (para entablillar)* splint

**tablón** *nm (tabla)* plank; *(viga)* beam; **t. de anuncios** notice board

**tabú** (*pl* **tabúes** *o* **tabús**) *adj & nm* taboo

**tabulación** *nf* tab-settings

**tabulador** *nm (tecla)* tabulator, tab (key)

**tabular** *vt & vi* to tabulate

**taburete** *nm* stool

**tacañería** *nf* meanness, miserliness

**tacaño, -a 1** *adj* mean, miserly
**2** *nm,f* mean *o* miserly person

**tacataca, tacatá** *nm* babywalker

**tacha** *nf* (a) *(defecto)* flaw, fault; **sin t.** faultless (b) *(clavo)* tack

**tachadura** *nf* crossing out

**tachar** *vt* (a) *(lo escrito)* to cross out (b) *Fig (acusar)* **t. a alguien de mentiroso/cobarde** to accuse sb of being a liar/coward

**tacho** *nm CSur* bucket

**tachón** *nm* (a) *(tachadura)* crossing out (b) *(clavo)* stud

**tachonado, -a** *adj (salpicado)* studded **(de** with)

**tachonar** *vt* (a) *(poner clavos)* to decorate with studs (b) *Fig (salpicar)* to stud

**tachuela** *nf* tack

**tácito, -a** *adj (acuerdo)* tacit; *(norma, regla)* unwritten

**taciturno, -a** *adj* taciturn

**taco** *nm* (a) *(tarugo)* plug; *(para tornillo)* Rawlplug® (b) *(cuña)* wedge (c) *Fam Fig (palabrota)* swearword; **decir tacos** to swear (d) *Fam Fig (confusión)* mess, muddle; **armarse un t. (con algo)** to get into a muddle (over sth) (e) *(de billar)* cue (f) *(de billetes de banco)* wad; *(de billetes* *de autobús, metro)* book; *(de hojas)* pile, stack **(g)** *(de jamón, queso)* cube **(h)** *Fam* **tacos** *(años)* years (of age) **(i)** *CAm, Méx Culin* taco, = filled tortilla **(j)** *Am (tacón)* heel

**tacógrafo** *nm* tachograph

**tacón** *nm* heel; **de t. (alto)** high-heeled; **t. de aguja** stiletto heel

**taconazo** *nm* stamp (of the heel); **dar un t.** to stamp one's foot

**taconear** *vi* **(a)** *(bailarín)* to stamp one's feet **(b)** *Mil* to click one's heels

**taconeo** *nm (de bailarín)* foot-stamping

**táctica** *nf también Fig* tactics

**táctico, -a** *adj* tactical

**táctil** *adj* tactile

**tacto** *nm* **(a)** *(sentido)* sense of touch **(b)** *(textura)* feel; **áspero/suave al t.** rough/soft to the touch **(c)** *Fig (delicadeza)* tact; **con t.** tactfully; **tener t.** to be tactful **(d)** *Med* manual examination

**TAE** ['tae] *nf (abrev de* **tasa anual equivalente)** Annual Percentage Rate, APR

**taekwondo** ['tae'kwondo] *nm* tae kwon do

**tafetán** *nm* taffeta

**tafilete** *nm* morocco leather

**tagalo, -a 1** *adj & nm,f* Tagalog
**2** *nm (lengua)* Tagalog

**tahona** *nf* bakery

**tahúr, -ura** *nm,f* cardsharp

**taifa** *nf Hist* = independent Muslim kingdom in Iberian peninsula

**taiga** *nf* taiga

**tailandés, -esa 1** *adj & nm,f* Thai
**2** *nm (lengua)* Thai

**Tailandia** *n* Thailand

**taimado, -a 1** *adj* crafty
**2** *nm,f* crafty person

**Taipei** *n* Taipei

**Taiwán** [tai'wan] *n* Taiwan

**taiwanés, -esa** *adj & nm,f* Taiwanese

**tajada** *nf* **(a)** *(rodaja)* slice **(b)** *Fig (parte)* share; **sacar t. de algo** to get something out of sth **(c)** *Fam Fig (borrachera)* **agarrarse una t. (como un piano)** to get plastered *o* legless

**tajante** *adj (respuesta, rechazo)* categorical; *(tono)* emphatic

**tajar** *vt (cortar)* to cut *o* slice up; *(en dos)* to slice in two

**Tajo** *nm* **el (río) T.** the (River) Tagus

**tajo** *nm* **(a)** *(corte)* deep cut **(b)** *(trabajo)* workplace, work **(c)** *(de carnicero)* chopping block **(d)** *(acantilado)* precipice

**tal 1** *adj* **(a)** *(semejante, tan grande)* such; **¡jamás se vio cosa t.!** you've never seen such a thing!; **lo dijo con t. seguridad que...** he said it with such conviction that...; **dijo cosas tales como...** he said such things as... **(b)** *(sin especificar)* such and such; **a t. hora** at such and such a time **(c)** *(desconocido)* **un t. Pérez** a (certain) Mr Pérez

**2** *pron* **(a)** *(alguna cosa)* such a thing **(b)** *(expresiones)* **que si t. que si cual** this, that and the other; **ser t. para cual** to be two of a kind; **t. y cual, t. y t.** this and that; **y t.** *(etcétera)* and so on

**3** *adv* **¿qué t...?** how...?; **¿qué t. (estás)?** how's it going?, how are you doing?; **¿qué t. el viaje?** how was the journey?; **déjalo t. cual** leave it just as it is; **con t. de** as long as, provided; **con t. de volver pronto...** as long as we're back early...; **con t. (de) que** as long as, provided; **t. (y) como** just as *o* like; *Fam* **t. que** *(como por ejemplo)* like

**tala** *nf* felling

**taladrador, -ora 1** *adj* drilling
**2** *nm,f (para pared, madera)* drill; *(para papel)* paper punch

**taladrar** *vt* to drill; *Fig* **este ruido te taladra los tímpanos** the noise is ear-piercing

**taladro** *nm* **(a)** *(taladradora)* drill **(b)** *(agujero)* drill hole

**tálamo** *nm* **(a)** *Formal (cama)* marriage bed **(b)** *Anat & Bot* thalamus

**talante** *nm* **(a)** *(humor)* mood; **estar de buen t.** to be in good humour **(b)** *(carácter)* character, disposition

**talar** *vt* to fell

**talco** *nm* talc; **polvos de t.** talcum powder

**talega** *nf* sack

**talento** *nm* **(a)** *(don natural)* talent **(b)** *(inteligencia)* intelligence

**talentoso, -a, talentudo, -a** *adj* talented

**talgo** *nm (abrev de* **tren articulado ligero de Goicoechea Oriol)** = Spanish intercity high-speed train

**talidomida** *nf* thalidomide

**talión** *nm* **la ley del t.** an eye for an eye and a tooth for a tooth

**talismán** *nm* talisman

**talla** *nf* **(a)** *(medida)* size; **¿qué t. usas?** what size are you? **(b)** *(estatura)* height **(c)** *Fig (capacidad)* stature; **dar la t.** to be up to it **(d)** *Arte (en madera)* carving; *(en piedra)* sculpture **(e)** *(de piedras preciosas)* cutting

**tallado, -a 1** *adj (madera)* carved; *(piedras preciosas)* cut
**2** *nm (de madera, piedra)* carving; *(de piedras preciosas)* cutting

**tallar** vt **(a)** *(esculpir) (madera, piedra)* to carve; *(piedra preciosa)* to cut **(b)** *(medir)* to measure (the height of)

**tallarines** nmpl *(chinos)* noodles; *(italianos)* tagliatelle

**talle** nm **(a)** *(cintura)* waist **(b)** *(figura, cuerpo)* figure **(c)** *(medida)* measurement

**taller** nm **(a)** *(lugar de trabajo)* workshop; *(de artista)* studio **(b)** *Aut* garage **(c)** *(cursillo, seminario)* workshop

**Tallin** n Tallin

**tallista** nmf *(de madera)* wood carver; *(de piedra)* stone carver

**tallo** nm *(de planta, flor)* stem; *(brote)* sprout, shoot

**talludito, -a** adj estar o ser t. to be getting on (a bit)

**talludo, -a** adj **(a)** *(planta)* thick-stemmed **(b)** *Fig (persona) (alta)* tall

**Talmud** nm el T. the Talmud

**talón** nm **(a)** *(de pie)* heel; *Fig* t. de Aquiles Achilles' heel; **pisarle a alguien los talones** to be hot on sb's heels **(b)** *(cheque)* cheque; *(matriz)* stub; **t. cruzado/devuelto/en blanco** crossed/bounced/blank cheque; **t. bancario** *Br* cashier's cheque, *US* cashier's check; **t. sin fondos** bad cheque

**talonario** nm *(de cheques)* chequebook; *(de recibos)* receipt book

**talonera** nf heelpiece

**talud** nm bank, slope; **t. continental** continental slope

**tamal** nm *CAm, Méx* tamale, = steamed maize dumpling with savoury or sweet filling, wrapped in maize husks or a banana leaf

**tamaño, -a 1** adj such; **¡cómo pudo decir tamaña estupidez!** how could he say such a stupid thing!
**2** nm size; **de gran t.** large; **de t. natural** life-size

**tamarindo** nm tamarind

**tambaleante** adj **(a)** *(inestable) (mesa)* wobbly, unsteady; *(persona)* staggering **(b)** *Fig (Gobierno, economía)* unstable, shaky

**tambalearse** vpr **(a)** *(bambolearse) (persona)* to stagger, to totter; *(mueble)* to wobble, to be unsteady; *(tren)* to sway **(b)** *Fig (gobierno, sistema)* to totter

**tambaleo** nm *(de tren)* rocking motion; *(de mueble)* wobble; *(de persona)* staggering

**también** adv also, too; **yo t.** me too; **t. a mí me gusta** I like it too, I also like it

**tambor 1** nm **(a)** *Mús & Mec* drum; *(de pistola)* cylinder **(b)** *Anat* eardrum
**2** nmf *(tamborilero)* drummer

**tamboril** nm small drum

**tamborilear** vi *Mús & Fig* to drum

**tamborileo** nm drumming

**tamborilero, -a** nm,f drummer

**Támesis** nm el **(río)** T. the (River) Thames

**tamice** etc ver **tamizar**

**tamil 1** adj & nmf Tamil
**2** nm *(lengua)* Tamil

**tamiz** nm **(a)** *(cedazo)* sieve **(b)** *Fig (selección)* **la prueba es un t. para eliminar a los peores** the test is designed to weed out the weaker candidates

**tamizar** [16] vt **(a)** *(cribar)* to sieve **(b)** *Fig (seleccionar)* to screen

**tampoco** adv neither, not… either; **ella no va y tú t.** she's not going and neither are you o and you aren't either; **yo no voy – yo t.** I'm not going – neither am I o me neither; **yo t. lo veo** I can't see it either; **¡t. nos íbamos a presentar sin un regalo!** we were hardly going to turn up without a present!

**tampón** nm **(a)** *(sello)* stamp; *(almohadilla)* inkpad **(b)** *(para la menstruación)* tampon; **t. contraceptivo** contraceptive sponge

**tam-tam** nm tom tom

**tan** adv **(a)** *(mucho)* so; **t. grande/deprisa (que…)** so big/quickly (that…); **¡qué película t. larga!** what a long film!; **t. es así que…** so much so that…; **de t. amable que es, se hace inaguantable** she's so kind it can get unbearable **(b)** *(en comparaciones)* **t.… como…** as… as… **(c)** **t. sólo** only

**tanatorio** nm = building where relatives and friends of a dead person can stand vigil over the deceased in a private room on the night before the burial

**tanda** nf **(a)** *(grupo, lote)* group, batch **(b)** *(serie)* series

**tándem** *(pl tándemes)* nm **(a)** *(bicicleta)* tandem **(b)** *(pareja)* duo, pair

**tanga** nm tanga

**Tanganica** nm el lago T. Lake Tanganyika

**tangencial** adj tangential

**tangente 1** adj tangential
**2** nf tangent; **irse** o **salirse por la t.** to go off at a tangent

**Tánger** n Tangiers

**tangible** adj tangible

**tango** nm tango

**tanino** nm tannin

**tanque** nm **(a)** *Mil* tank **(b)** *(vehículo cisterna)* tanker **(c)** *(depósito)* tank **(d)** *(de cerveza)* beer mug

**tanqueta** nf armoured car

**tanteador** nm *(marcador)* scoreboard

**tantear 1** vt (**a**) *(probar, sondear)* to test (out); *(toro, contrincante)* to size up; *Fig* **t. el terreno** to see how the land lies, to test the waters (**b**) *(sopesar)* *(peso, precio, cantidad)* to try to guess; *(problema, posibilidades, ventajas)* to weigh up

**2** vi *(andar a tientas)* to feel one's way

**tanteo** nm (**a**) *(prueba, sondeo)* testing out; *(de posibilidades, ventajas)* weighing up; *(de contrincante, puntos débiles)* sizing up (**b**) *(cálculo aproximado)* rough calculation, estimate; **a t.** roughly (**c**) *(puntuación)* score (**d**) *Der* first option *(on a purchase)*

**tanto, -a 1** adj (**a**) *(gran cantidad)* so much; **tantos** so many; **t. dinero** so much money, such a lot of money; **tanta gente** so many people; **tiene t. entusiasmo/tantos amigos que...** she has so much enthusiasm/so many friends that...

(**b**) *(cantidad indeterminada)* so much; **tantos** so many; **nos daban tantas pesetas al día** they used to give us so many pesetas per day; **cuarenta y tantos** forty-something, forty-odd; **nos conocimos en el sesenta y tantos** we met sometime in the Sixties

(**c**) *(en comparaciones)* **t.... como** as much... as; **tantos... como** as many... as.

**2** pron (**a**) *(gran cantidad)* so much; **tantos** so many; **¿cómo puedes tener tantos?** how can you have so many?

(**b**) *(cantidad indeterminada)* so much; **tantos** so many; **a tantos de agosto** on such and such a date in August

(**c**) *(igual cantidad)* as much; **tantos** as many; **había mucha gente aquí, pero allí no había tanta** there were a lot of people here, but there weren't as many there; **otro t.** as much again, the same again; **otro t. le ocurrió a los demás** the same thing happened to the rest of them

(**d**) *(expresiones)* **en t. (que)** while; **entre t.** meanwhile; **por (lo) t.** therefore, so; **ser uno de tantos** to be nothing special; **un t.** *(un poco)* a bit, rather; **¡y t.!** most certainly!, you bet!

**3** nm (**a**) *(punto)* point; *(gol)* goal; **marcar un t.** to score

(**b**) *Fig (ventaja)* point; **apuntarse un t. a favor** to earn oneself a point in one's favour

(**c**) *(cantidad indeterminada)* **un t.** so much, a certain amount; **t. por ciento** percentage

(**d**) **estar al t. (de)** to be on the ball *(about)*

**4** adv (**a**) *(mucho)* **t. (que...)** *(cantidad)* so much (that...); *(tiempo)* so long (that...); **no bebas t.** don't drink so much; **de eso hace t. que ya no me acordaba** it's been so long since that happened that I don't even remember; **t. (es así) que** so much so that; **t. mejor/peor** so much the better/worse

(**b**) *(en comparaciones)* **t. como** as much as; **t.**

**hombres como mujeres** both men and women; **t. si estoy como si no** whether I'm there or not

**5** nfpl **tantas** *Fam* **eran las tantas** it was very late

**Tanzania** n Tanzanía

**tanzano, -a** adj & nm,f Tanzanian

**tañer** vt *(instrumento)* to play; *(campana)* to ring

**tañido** nm *(de instrumento)* sound; *(de campana)* ringing

**taoísmo** nm Taoism

**tapa** nf (**a**) *(para cerrar)* lid; *Fam* **levantarse la t. de los sesos** to blow one's brains out (**b**) *Culin* snack, tapa (**c**) *(portada)* *(de libro)* cover; *(de disco)* sleeve (**d**) *(de zapato)* heel plate (**e**) *(trozo de carne)* topside (**f**) *Am (de botella)* top; *(de frasco)* stopper

**tapabarro** nm *Andes* mudguard

**tapacubos** nm inv hubcap

**tapadera** nf (**a**) *(tapa)* lid (**b**) *(para encubrir)* front

**tapadillo: de tapadillo** loc adv on the sly

**tapado** nm *CSur (abrigo)* overcoat

**tapar 1** vt (**a**) *(cerrar)* *(ataúd, cofre)* to close (the lid of); *(olla, caja)* to put the lid on; *(botella)* to put the top on (**b**) *(ocultar, cubrir)* to cover; *(no dejar ver)* to block out; **quítate, que me tapas la tele** could you move out of the way? – I can't see the TV with you in the way (**c**) *(abrigar)* to cover up; *(en la cama)* to tuck in (**d**) *Fig (encubrir)* to cover up

**2** taparse vpr (**a**) *(cubrirse)* to cover (up) (**b**) *(abrigarse)* *(con ropa)* to wrap up; *(en la cama)* to tuck oneself in

**taparrabos** nm inv (**a**) *(de hombre primitivo)* loincloth (**b**) *(tanga)* tanga briefs

**tapete** nm *(paño)* runner; *(en mesa de billar, para cartas)* baize; *Am (moqueta)* carpet; *Fig* **estar sobre el t.** to be up for discussion; **poner algo sobre el t.** to put sth up for discussion; **t. verde** *(mesa de juego)* card table

**tapia** nf *(stone)* wall; *Fam* **estar sordo como una t.** to be (as) deaf as a post

**tapiar** [15] vt (**a**) *(obstruir)* to brick up (**b**) *(cercar)* to wall in

**tapice** etc ver **tapizar**

**tapicería** nf (**a**) *(tela)* upholstery (**b**) *(tienda)* *(para muebles)* upholsterer's; *(para cortinas)* draper's (**c**) *(tapices)* tapestries (**d**) *(oficio)* *(de muebles)* upholstery; *(de tapices)* tapestry making

**tapicero, -a** nm,f (**a**) *(de muebles)* upholsterer (**b**) *(de tapices)* tapestry maker

**tapioca** nf tapioca

**tapir** nm tapir

**tapiz** nm *(para la pared)* tapestry

**tapizado 1** *adj (sillón)* upholstered (**en** *o* **con** with); *(pared)* lined (**en** *o* **con** with)

**2** *nm* (**a**) *(de mueble)* upholstery (**b**) *(de pared)* tapestries

**tapizar** [16] *vt (mueble)* to upholster

**tapón** *nm* (**a**) *(para tapar) (botellas, frascos)* stopper; *(de corcho)* cork; *(de metal, plástico)* cap, top; *(de bañera, lavabo)* plug; **t. de rosca** screwtop (**b**) *(atasco)* traffic jam (**c**) *(en el oído) (de cerumen)* wax in the ear; *(de algodón, goma)* earplug (**d**) *Fam (persona baja)* shorty (**e**) *(en baloncesto)* block; **poner un t.** to block a shot

**taponamiento** *nm* (**a**) *Med* tamponage (**b**) *Mec* plugging

**taponar 1** *vt* (**a**) *(cerrar) (botella)* to put the top on; *(lavadero)* to put the plug in; *(salida)* to block; *(tubería)* to stop up (**b**) *Med* to tampon

**2 taponarse** *vpr* to get blocked

**tapujo** *nm* subterfuge; **hacer algo con/sin tapujos** to do sth deceitfully/openly

**taquicardia** *nf* tachycardia

**taquigrafía** *nf* shorthand, stenography

**taquigrafiar** [34] *vt* to write (down) in shorthand

**taquígrafo, -a** *nm,f* shorthand writer, stenographer

**taquilla** *nf* (**a**) *(ventanilla)* ticket office, booking office; *(de cine, teatro)* box office (**b**) *(armario)* locker (**c**) *(recaudación)* takings (**d**) *(casillero)* set of pigeonholes

**taquillero, -a 1** *adj* **es un espectáculo t.** the show is a box-office hit

**2** *nm,f* ticket clerk

**taquimecanografía** *nf* shorthand and typing

**taquimecanógrafo, -a** *nm,f* shorthand typist

**taquímetro** *nm (en topografía)* tacheometer

**tara** *nf* (**a**) *(defecto)* defect; **artículos con t.** seconds (**b**) *(peso)* tare

**taracea** *nf* inlay

**tarado, -a 1** *adj* (**a**) *(defectuoso)* defective (**b**) *(tonto)* thick

**2** *nm,f* idiot

**tarambana** *nmf Fam* ne'er-do-well

**tarántula** *nf* tarantula

**tarar** *vt* to tare

**tararear** *vt* to hum, to sing

**tarareo** *nm* humming, singing

**tardanza** *nf* lateness

**tardar** *vi* (**a**) *(llevar tiempo)* to take; **tardó un año en hacerlo** she took a year to do it; **¿cuánto tardarás (en hacerlo)?** how long will you be (doing it)?, how long will it take you (to do it)? (**b**) *(retrasarse)* to be late; *(ser lento)* to be slow; **t. en hacer algo** to take a long time to do sth; **no tardará en llegar** he won't be long (in coming); **no tardaron en hacerlo** they were quick to do it; **a más t.** at the latest; **sin t.** promptly

**tarde 1** *nf (hasta las cinco)* afternoon; *(después de las cinco)* evening; **por la t.** *(hasta las cinco)* in the afternoon; *(después de las cinco)* in the evening; **buenas tardes** *(hasta las cinco)* good afternoon; *(después de las cinco)* good evening; **de t. en t.** from time to time

**2** *adv* late; *(demasiado)* **t.** too late; **ya es t. para eso** it's too late for that now; **llegar t.** to be late; **se está haciendo t.** it's getting late; **t. o temprano** sooner or later; **más vale t. que nunca** better late than never

**tardíamente** *adv* belatedly

**tardío, -a** *adj (que ocurre tarde)* late; *(que ocurre demasiado tarde)* belated

**tardo, -a** *adj* (**a**) *(lento)* slow (**b**) *(torpe)* dull; **t. de oído** hard of hearing

**tardón, -ona** *nm,f* (**a**) *(impuntual)* person who is always late (**b**) *(lento)* slowcoach

**tarea** *nf (trabajo)* task; *Educ* homework; **tareas domésticas** household chores, housework

**tarifa** *nf* (**a**) *(precio)* charge; *(en transportes)* fare; *(de médico, abogado)* fee; *Com* tariff; *Informát* **t. plana** flat-rate (**b**) *(lista)* price list

**tarifar 1** *vt* to price

**2** *vi Fam (pelear)* to have a row

**tarima** *nf* platform

**tarjeta** *nf también Informát* card; *Dep* **t. amarilla/roja** yellow/red card; **t. de compra** store card, charge card; **t. de crédito** credit card; **t. de embarque** boarding pass; **t. inteligente** smart card; **t. multiviaje** travel pass; **t. postal** postcard; **t. sanitaria** = card bearing national insurance number and doctor's address; *Informát* **t. de sonido** sound card; **t. de visita** visiting *o* calling card

**tarjetero** *nm* credit-card wallet

**tarot** *nm* tarot

**tarraconense 1** *adj* of/from Tarragona

**2** *nmf* person from Tarragona

**tarrina** *nf (envase)* tub; *Culin* terrine

**tarro** *nm* (**a**) *(recipiente)* jar (**b**) *muy Fam (cabeza)* nut, bonce

**tarso** *nm* tarsus

**tarta** *nf (pastel)* cake; *(plana, con base de pasta dura)* tart; *(plana, con base de bizcocho)* flan; **t. de cumpleaños** birthday cake

**tartaja** *Fam* **1** *adj* **ser t.** to have a stammer *o* stutter

**2** *nmf* **ser un t.** to have a stammer *o* stutter

**tartajear** *vi Fam* to stammer, to stutter

**tartajeo** *nm Fam* stammer, stutter

**tartaleta** *nf* tartlet

**tartamudear** *vi* to stammer, to stutter

**tartamudeo** *nm* stammer, stutter

**tartamudez** *nf* stammer, stutter

**tartamudo, -a** **1** *adj* stammering, stuttering

**2** *nm,f* stammerer, stutterer

**tartán** *nm inv* tartan

**tartana** *nf* (a) *(carruaje)* trap (b) *Fam (coche viejo)* banger

**tártaro, -a** **1** *adj* (a) *(pueblo)* Tartar (b) *Culin* **salsa tártara** tartar sauce

**2** *nm,f* Tartar

**tartera** *nf (fiambrera)* lunch box

**tarugo** *nm* (a) *Fam (necio)* blockhead (b) *(de madera)* block of wood (c) *(de pan)* chunk (of stale bread)

**tarumba** *adj Fam* crazy

**tasa** *nf* (a) *(índice)* rate; **t. de mortalidad/natalidad** death/birth rate; **t. de paro** *o* **desempleo** (level of) unemployment; **t. de crecimiento** growth rate (b) *(impuesto)* tax (c) *Educ* fee (d) *(tasación)* valuation

**tasación** *nf* valuation

**tasador, -ora** **1** *adj* evaluating

**2** *nm,f* valuer

**tasar** *vt* (a) *(valorar)* to value (b) *(fijar precio)* to fix a price for

**tasca** *nf* cheap bar; **ir de tascas** to go on a pub crawl

**Tasmania** *n* Tasmania

**tasquear** *vi* to go on a pub crawl

**tasqueo** *nm* pubcrawling

**tata** *nf (niñera)* nanny

**tatarabuelo, -a** *nm,f* great-great-grandfather, *f* great-great-grandmother

**tataranieto, -a** *nm,f* great-great-grandson, *f* great-great-granddaughter

**tate** *interj* ¡t.! *(¡cuidado!)* watch out!; *(¡ya comprendo!)* I see!

**tato, -a** *Fam nm,f (hermano)* big brother, *f* big sister

**tatuaje** *nm* (a) *(dibujo)* tattoo (b) *(acción)* tattooing

**tatuar** [4] **1** *vt* to tattoo

**2** *vi* to make a tattoo

**3** **tatuarse** *vpr* to have a tattoo done

**taumaturgia** *nf* miracle-working

**taumaturgo, -a** *nm,f* miracle-worker

**taurino, -a** *adj* bullfighting; **temporada taurina** bullfighting season

**tauro** **1** *nm (zodiaco)* Taurus; **ser t.** to be (a) Taurus

**2** *nmf (persona)* Taurean

**tauromaquia** *nf* bullfighting

**tautología** *nf* tautology

**tautológico, -a** *adj* tautological

**taxativo, -a** *adj (órdenes)* strict

**taxi** *nm* taxi, cab

**taxidermia** *nf* taxidermy

**taxidermista** *nmf* taxidermist

**taxímetro** *nm* taximeter

**taxista** *nmf* taxi driver

**taxonomía** *nf* taxonomy

**taxonómico, -a** *adj* taxonomic

**taxonomista** *nmf* taxonomist

**Tayikistán** *n* Tadzhikistan

**taza** *nf* (a) *(para beber)* cup (b) *(de retrete)* bowl

**tazón** *nm* bowl

**TC** *nm (abrev de* **Tribunal Constitucional)** constitutional court

**te** *pron personal* (a) *(complemento directo)* you; **le gustaría verte** she'd like to see you (b) *(complemento indirecto)* (to) you; **te lo dio** he gave it to you, he gave you it; **te tiene miedo** he's afraid of you (c) *(reflexivo)* yourself; **¡vístete!** get (yourself) dressed! (d) *(valor impersonal)* **si te dejas pisar, estás perdido** if you let people walk all over you, you've had it

**té** *(pl* **tés)** *nm* tea

**tea** *nf (antorcha)* torch

**teatral** *adj* (a) *(de teatro)* theatre; **grupo t.** drama group; **temporada t.** theatre season (b) *(exagerado)* theatrical

**teatralidad** *nf también Fig* theatricality

**teatralizar** [16] *vt* to exaggerate

**teatrero, -a** *adj Fam (persona)* **¡no seas tan t.!** don't be such a drama queen!

**teatro** *nm* (a) *(espectáculo, edificio)* theatre; **t. de variedades** *Br* music hall, *US* variety, vaudeville; **t. lírico** opera and light opera (b) *Fig (fingimiento)* play-acting; **hacer t.** to playact (c) *Fig (escenario)* scene

**tebeo** *nm (children's)* comic; **estar más visto que el t.** to be old hat

**teca** *nf* teak

**techado** *nm* roof; **bajo t.** under cover

**techar** *vt* to roof

**techo** *nm* (a) *(tejado)* roof; *(dentro de casa)* ceiling; **t. solar** *(en coche)* sun roof; **bajo t.** under cover (b) *Fig (límite)* ceiling; **tocar t.** *(inflación, precios)* to level off and start to drop; **la crisis ha tocado techo** the worst of the recession is behind us

**techumbre** *nf* roof

**tecla** *nf Informát & Mús* key; *(botón)* button; **t. de borrado/control/función/retorno** erase/control/function/return key; **pulsar** *o* **tocar una t.** to press *o* strike a key; **tocar muchas teclas** *(contactar)* to pull lots of strings; *(abarcar mucho)* to have too many things on the go at once

**teclado** *nm también Informát & Mús* keyboard; **t. expandido** expanded *o* enhanced keyboard; **t. numérico** (numeric) keypad

**teclear 1** *vt (en ordenador)* to type; *(en piano)* to play; **teclee su número secreto** enter your PIN number

**2** *vi (en ordenador)* to type; *(en piano)* to play

**tecleo** *nm (en piano)* playing; *(en máquina de escribir)* clattering

**teclista** *nmf* keyboard player

**técnica** *nf* (a) *(procedimiento)* technique (b) *(tecnología)* technology

**tecnicismo** *nm* (a) *(cualidad)* technical nature (b) *(término)* technical term

**técnico, -a 1** *adj* technical

**2** *nm,f* (a) *(mecánico)* technician (b) *(experto)* expert

**tecnicolor** *nm* Technicolor

**tecnificación** *nf* application of technology

**tecnificar** [61] *vt* to apply technology to

**tecno** *nm inv* techno *(music)*

**tecnocracia** *nf* technocracy

**tecnócrata 1** *adj* technocratic

**2** *nmf* technocrat

**tecnología** *nf* technology; **t. punta** state-of-the-art technology

**tecnológico, -a** *adj* technological

**tecnólogo, -a** *nm,f* technologist

**tecolote** *nm CAm, Méx* owl

**tectónica** *nf* tectonics *(singular)*

**tectónico, -a** *adj* tectonic

**tedéum** *nm inv* Te Deum

**tedio** *nm* boredom, tedium

**tedioso, -a** *adj* tedious

**teflón** *nm* Teflon

**Tegucigalpa** *n* Tegucigalpa

**tegumento** *nm Biol* integument

**Teherán** *n* Teheran

**Teide** *nm* **el T.** (Mount) Teide

**teína** *nf* caffeine *(contained in tea)*

**teísmo** *nm* theism

**teja** *nf (de tejado)* tile; **color t.** brick red

**tejado** *nm* roof

**tejano, -a 1** *adj* (a) *(de Texas)* Texan (b) *(tela)* denim

**2** *nm,f (persona)* Texan

**tejanos** *nmpl (pantalones)* jeans

**tejar 1** *nm* brickworks *(singular)*

**2** *vt & vi* to tile

**tejedor, -ora 1** *adj* weaving

**2** *nm,f* weaver

**tejeduría** *nf* (a) *(arte)* weaving (b) *(taller)* weaver's shop

**tejemaneje** *nm Fam* (a) *(maquinación)* intrigue (b) *(ajetreo)* to-do, fuss

**tejer 1** *vt* (a) *(hilos, mimbre)* to weave (b) *(labor de punto)* to knit (c) *(telaraña)* to spin (d) *Fig (labrar) (porvenir)* to carve out; *(ruina)* to bring about (e) *Fig (tramar)* to plot; **t. un plan** to forge a plot

**2** *vi (hacer punto)* to knit; *Fig* **t. y destejer** to chop and change

**tejido** *nm* (a) *(tela)* fabric, material; *Ind* textile (b) *Anat* tissue

**tejo** *nm* (a) *(juego)* hopscotch (b) *Bot* yew (c) *Fam Fig* **creo que te está tirando los tejos** I think he's rather keen on you

**tejón** *nm* badger

**tel.** *(abrev de* **teléfono***)* tel.

**tela** *nf* (a) *(tejido)* fabric, material; *(retal)* piece of material; **t. de araña** cobweb; **t. asfáltica** asphalt roofing/flooring; **t. metálica** wire netting

(b) *Arte (lienzo)* canvas

(c) *Fam (dinero)* dough

(d) *Fam (cosa complicada)* **el examen era t.** the exam was really tricky; **tener (mucha) t.** *(ser difícil)* to be (very) tricky; **hay t. (para rato)** *(trabajo)* there's no shortage of things to do; **¡t. marinera!** that's too much!

(e) **poner en t. de juicio** to call into question

**telar** *nm* (a) *(máquina)* loom (b) *Teatro* gridiron (c) **telares** *(fábrica)* textiles mill

**telaraña** *nf* spider's web, cobweb

**tele** *nf Fam* telly

**teleadicto, -a** *nm,f* telly-addict

**telearrastre** *nm* ski-tow

**telecabina** *nf* cable-car

**telecomedia** *nf* television comedy programme

**telecompra** *nf* teleshopping, home shopping

**telecomunicación** *nf (medio)* telecommunication; **telecomunicaciones** telecommunications

**telecontrol** *nm* remote control

**telediario** *nm* television news

**teledirigido, -a** *adj* remote-controlled

**teledirigir** [26] *vt* to operate by remote control

**teléf.** *(abrev de* **teléfono***)* tel.

**telefax** *nm inv* fax

**teleférico** *nm* cable car

**telefilme, telefilm** *(pl* **telefilmes, telefilms***) nm* TV film

**telefonazo** nm Fam ring, buzz; Fig **dar un t. a alguien** to give sb a ring o buzz

**telefonear** vi to phone

**telefonía** nf telephony; **sistema de t. móvil** mobile phone system

**Telefónica** nf = main Spanish telephone company, formerly a state-owned monopoly

**telefónico, -a** adj telephone; **llamada telefónica** telephone call

**telefonista** nmf telephonist

**telefonillo** nm (portero automático) entry-phone

**teléfono** nm (a) (aparato, sistema) telephone, phone; **coger el t.** to answer o pick up the phone; **hablar por t.** to be on the phone; **t. inalámbrico** cordless phone; **t. modular** o **inteligente** cellphone; **t. móvil** mobile phone; **t. público** public phone; **t. rojo** hot line; **t. sin manos** phone with hands-free facility (b) (número) telephone number

**telefotografía** nf telephotography

**telegrafía** nf telegraphy

**telegrafiar** [34] vt & vi to telegraph

**telegráfico, -a** adj también Fig telegraphic

**telegrafista** nmf telegraphist

**telégrafo** nm (medio, aparato) telegraph; **telégrafos** (oficina) telegraph office

**telegrama** nm telegram

**telejuego** nm television game show

**telele** nm Fam **le dio un t.** (desmayo) he passed out, he fainted; (enfado, susto) he had a fit

**telemando** nm remote control

**telemática** nf electronic communications technology

**telémetro** nm telemeter

**telenovela** nf television soap opera

**teleobjetivo** nm telephoto lens

**telepatía** nf telepathy

**telepático, -a** adj telepathic

**telequinesia** nf telekinesis

**telerruta** nf = telephone service giving traffic information

**telescópico, -a** adj telescopic

**telescopio** nm telescope

**telesilla** nm chair lift

**telespectador, -ora** nm,f viewer

**telesquí** nm ski lift

**teletexto** nm Teletext®

**teletienda** nf home shopping programme

**teletipo** nm (a) (aparato) teleprinter (b) (texto) Teletype®

**teletrabajo** nm teleworking

**televendedor, -ora** nm,f telesales assistant

**televenta** nf (a) (por teléfono) telesales (b) (por televisión) teleshopping, home shopping

**televidente** nmf viewer

**televisado, -a** adj televised

**televisar** vt to televise

**televisión** nf television; **t. en blanco y negro/en color** black and white/colour television; **t. por cable/satélite** cable/satellite television; **t. digital** digital television; **t. privada/pública** privately owned/public television

**televisivo, -a** adj television; **concurso t.** television game show

**televisor** nm television (set)

**télex** nm inv telex; **mandar por t.** to telex

**telón** nm (de escenario) (delante) curtain; (detrás) backcloth; Fig **t. de acero** Iron Curtain; Fig **t. de fondo** backdrop

**telonero, -a 1** adj grupo t. support (band) **2** nm,f (cantante) supporting artist; (grupo) support (band)

**telúrico, -a** adj telluric

**tema** nm (a) (asunto) subject; **cambiar de t.** to change the subject; **temas de actualidad** current affairs (b) Educ (lección) topic (c) Mús theme; (canción) track, song

**temario** nm (a) (de una asignatura) syllabus; (de oposiciones) = list of topics for public examination (b) (de reunión, congreso) agenda

**temática** nf subject matter

**temático, -a** adj thematic; **parque t.** theme park

**tembladera** nf trembling fit

**temblar** [3] vi (a) (persona) (de miedo) to tremble (de with); (de frío) to shiver (de with); Fig **tiemblo por lo que pueda pasarle** I shudder to think what could happen to him (b) (suelo, máquina) to shudder, to shake

**tembleque** nm trembling fit; **le dio** o **entró un t.** he got the shakes

**temblequear** vi (a) (persona) to tremble; (de frío) to shiver (b) (suelo, máquina) to shudder, to shake

**temblón, -ona** adj shaky, trembling

**temblor** nm shaking, trembling; **t. de tierra** earthquake

**tembloroso, -a** adj trembling, shaky

**temer 1** vt (a) (tener miedo de) to fear, to be afraid of (b) (sospechar) to fear **2** vi to be afraid; **no temas** don't worry; **t. por** to fear for

**3 temerse** vpr **temerse que** to be afraid that, to fear that; **me temo que no vendrá** I'm afraid she won't come; **temerse lo peor** to fear the worst

**temerario, -a** adj rash, reckless; **conducción temeraria** reckless driving

**temeridad** nf (a) (cualidad) recklessness (b) (acción) folly, reckless act

**temeroso, -a** *adj (receloso)* fearful

**temible** *adj* fearsome

**temor** *nm* fear (**a** *o* **de** of); **por t. a** *o* **de** for fear of

**témpano** *nm* t. **(de hielo)** ice floe

**témpera** *nf Arte* tempera

**temperado, -a** *adj* temperate

**temperamental** *adj* (a) *(cambiante)* temperamental (b) *(impulsivo)* impulsive

**temperamento** *nm* temperament

**temperancia** *nf* temperance

**temperar** *vt (moderar)* to temper

**temperatura** *nf* temperature; **tomar la t. a alguien** to take sb's temperature; **t. máxima/mínima** highest/lowest temperature; **t. ambiental** room temperature

**tempestad** *nf* storm

**tempestuoso, -a** *adj también Fig* stormy

**templado, -a** *adj* (a) *(agua, comida)* lukewarm (b) *Geog (clima, zona)* temperate (c) *(nervios)* steady (d) *(persona, carácter)* calm, composed

**templanza** *nf* (a) *(serenidad)* composure (b) *(moderación)* moderation (c) *(benignidad) (del clima)* mildness

**templar 1** *vt* (a) *(entibiar) (lo frío)* to warm (up); *(lo caliente)* to cool down (b) *(calmar) (nervios, ánimos)* to calm; *(ira, pasiones)* to restrain; *(voz)* to soften (c) *Mec (metal)* to temper (d) *Mús* to tune (e) *(tensar)* to tighten (up)

**2** *vi (entibiarse)* to get milder

**3 templarse** *vpr* (a) *(calentarse)* to warm up (b) *Am (enamorarse)* to fall in love

**templario** *nm* Templar

**temple** *nm* (a) *(serenidad)* composure; **estar de buen/mal t.** to be in a good/bad mood (b) *Mec* tempering (c) *(pintura) (témpera)* tempera; *(para paredes)* distemper

**templete** *nm* pavilion

**templo** *nm* (a) *(edificio) (no cristiano)* temple; *(católico, protestante)* church; *(judío)* synagogue; *(musulmán)* mosque (b) *Fig (lugar mitificado)* temple

**tempo** *nm* tempo

**temporada** *nf* (a) *(periodo concreto)* season; *(de exámenes)* period; **de t.** *(fruta, trabajo)* seasonal; **t. alta/baja** high/low season; **t. media** mid-season (b) *(periodo indefinido)* (period of) time; **pasé una t. en el extranjero** I spent some time abroad

**temporal 1** *adj* (a) *(no permanente)* temporary (b) *(del tiempo)* time; **el factor t.** the time factor (c) *Anat & Rel* temporal

**2** *nm* (a) *(tormenta)* storm (b) *Anat* temporal bone

**temporalidad** *nf (transitoriedad)* temporary nature

**témporas** *nfpl Rel* Ember days

**temporero, -a 1** *adj* temporary

**2** *nm,f* casual labourer

**temporizador** *nm* timer

**tempranero, -a** *adj (persona)* early-rising

**temprano, -a** *adj & adv* early

**ten 1** *ver* **tener**

**2** *nm* tener t. **con t.** to be tactful

**tenacidad** *nf* tenacity

**tenacillas** *nfpl (para rizar el pelo)* curling tongs

**tenaz** *adj* (a) *(perseverante)* tenacious (b) *(persistente)* stubborn

**tenaza** *nf*, **tenazas** *nfpl* (a) *(herramienta)* pliers (b) *(pinzas)* tongs (c) *Zool* pincer

**tendal** *nm* awning

**tendedero** *nm* (a) *(armazón)* clothes horse; *(cuerda)* clothes line (b) *(lugar)* drying place

**tendencia** *nf* (a) *(inclinación)* tendency; **tener t. a hacer algo** to have a tendency to do sth; **t. a la depresión** tendency to get depressed (b) *(corriente)* trend; **las últimas tendencias de la moda** the latest fashion trends

**tendenciosidad** *nf* tendentiousness

**tendencioso, -a** *adj* tendentious

**tendente** *adj* t. **a** intended *o* designed to; **medidas tendentes a mejorar la economía** measures (intended *o* designed) to improve the economy

**tender** [66] **1** *vt* (a) *(ropa)* to hang out (b) *(tumbar)* to lay (out) (c) *(extender)* to stretch (out); *(mantel)* to spread (d) *(dar) (cosa)* to hand; *(mano)* to hold out, to offer (e) *(entre dos puntos) (cable, vía)* to lay; *(puente)* to build; *(cuerda)* to stretch (f) *Fig (trampa, emboscada)* to lay

**2** *vi* t. **a hacer algo** to tend to do something; **t. a la depresión** to have a tendency to get depressed; *Mat* **cuando x tiende a 1** as x approaches 1

**3 tenderse** *vpr* to stretch out, to lie down

**tenderete** *nm (puesto)* stall

**tendero, -a** *nm,f* shopkeeper

**tendido, -a 1** *adj* (a) *(extendido, tumbado)* stretched out (b) *(colgado) (ropa)* hung out, on the line

**2** *nm* (a) *(instalación) (de puente)* construction; *(de cable)* laying; **t. eléctrico** power lines (b) *Taurom* front rows; *Fig* **saludar al t.** *(monarca, personaje público)* to wave to the crowd

**tendón** *nm* tendon

**tendré** *etc ver* **tener**

**tenebrismo** *nm* tenebrism

**tenebroso, -a** *adj* dark, gloomy; *Fig* shady, sinister

**tenedor[1]** *nm (utensilio)* fork

**tenedor²**, **-ora** *nm,f (poseedor)* holder; **t. de acciones** shareholder; **t. de libros** bookkeeper

**teneduría** *nf Com* **t. (de libros)** bookkeeping

**tenencia** *nf* possession; **t. ilícita de armas** illegal possession of arms

**tener** [67] **1** *v aux* **(a)** *(antes de participio) (haber)* **teníamos pensado ir al teatro** we had thought of going to the theatre

  **(b)** *(antes de adj) (hacer estar)* **me tuvo despierto** it kept me awake; **eso la tiene despistada** that has confused her

  **(c)** *(expresa obligación)* **t. que hacer algo** to have to do sth; **tiene que ser así** it has to be this way

  **(d)** *(expresa propósito)* **tenemos que ir a cenar un día** we ought to *o* should go for dinner some time

**2** *vt* **(a)** *(en general)* to have; **tengo un hermano** I have *o* I've got a brother; **t. fiebre** to have a temperature; **tuvieron una pelea** they had a fight; **t. un niño** to have a baby; **¡que tengan buen viaje!** have a good journey!; **tengo las vacaciones en agosto** my holidays are in August

  **(b)** *(medida, años, sensación, cualidad)* to be; **tiene 3 metros de ancho** it's 3 metres wide; **¿cuántos años tienes?** how old are you?; **tiene diez años** she's ten (years old); *Am* **tengo tres años aquí** I've been here for three years; **t. hambre/miedo** to be hungry/afraid; **t. mal humor** to be bad-tempered; **le tiene lástima** he feels sorry for her

  **(c)** *(sujetar)* to hold; **tenlo por el asa** hold it by the handle

  **(d)** *(tomar)* **ten el libro que me pediste** here's the book you asked me for; **¡aquí tienes!, ¡ten!** here you are!

  **(e)** *(recibir)* to get; **tuve un verdadero desengaño** I was really disappointed; **tendrá una sorpresa** he'll get a surprise

  **(f)** *(valorar)* **me tienen por tonto** they think I'm stupid; **t. a alguien en mucho** to think the world of sb

  **(g)** *(guardar, contener)* to keep

  **(h)** *(expresiones)* **no las tiene todas consigo** he is not too sure about it; **t. a bien hacer algo** to be kind enough to do sth; **t. que ver con algo/alguien** *(existir relación)* to have something to do with sth/sb; *(existir semejanza)* to be in the same league as sth/sb

**3 tenerse** *vpr* **(a)** *(sostenerse)* **tenerse de pie** to stand upright

  **(b)** *(considerarse)* **se tiene por listo** he thinks he's clever

**tengo** *ver* **tener**

**tenia** *nf* tapeworm

**teniente 1** *nm* **(a)** *Mil* lieutenant; **t. coronel/general** lieutenant colonel/general **(b)** *(sustituto)* deputy; **t. (de) alcalde** deputy mayor

**2** *adj Fam (sordo)* **estar t.** to be a bit deaf

**tenis** *nm inv* tennis; **t. de mesa** table tennis

**tenista** *nmf* tennis player

**tenístico, -a** *adj* tennis; **campeonato t.** tennis championship

**Tenochtitlán** *n* Tenochtitlan *(Aztec capital)*

**tenor** *nm* **(a)** *Mús* tenor **(b)** *(estilo)* tone; **a este t.** *(de la misma manera)* in the same vein; **a t. de** in view of

**tenorio** *nm* ladies' man, Casanova

**tensado** *nm* tightening

**tensar** *vt (cable, cuerda)* to tauten; *(arco)* to draw

**tensión** *nf* **(a)** *(estado emocional)* tension; **estar en t.** to be tense; **t. nerviosa** nervous tension **(b)** *Mec (tirantez)* stress; **en t.** tensed **(c)** *Med* **t. (arterial)** blood pressure; **tener la t. alta/baja** to have high/low blood pressure **(d)** *Elec* voltage; **alta t.** high voltage

**tenso, -a** *adj* taut; *Fig* tense

**tensor, -ora 1** *adj* tightening

**2** *nm* **(a)** *(dispositivo)* turnbuckle **(b)** *Anat* tensor

**tentación** *nf* temptation; **caer en la t.** to give in to temptation; **tener la t. de** to be tempted to

**tentáculo** *nm* tentacle

**tentador, -ora** *adj* tempting

**tentar** [3] *vt* **(a)** *(palpar)* to feel **(b)** *(atraer, incitar)* to tempt

**tentativa** *nf* attempt; **t. de asesinato** attempted murder; **t. de suicidio** suicide attempt

**tentempié** *(pl* tentempiés*)* *nm* snack

**tentetieso** *nm* = wobbly toy which always returns to an upright position

**tenue** *adj* **(a)** *(tela, hilo, lluvia)* fine **(b)** *(luz, sonido, dolor)* faint **(c)** *(relación)* tenuous

**teñido, -a 1** *adj (pelo, tela)* dyed

**2** *nm* dyeing

**teñir** [49] **1** *vt* **(a)** *(ropa, pelo)* **t. algo (de rojo/verde)** to dye sth (red/green) **(b)** *Fig (matizar)* to tinge sth **(de** with)

**2 teñirse** *vpr* **teñirse (el pelo)** to dye one's hair

**teocracia** *nf* theocracy

**teodolito** *nm* theodolite

**teologal** *adj* theological

**teología** *nf* theology; **t. de la liberación** liberation theology

**teológico, -a** *adj* theological

**teólogo, -a** *nm,f* theologian

**teorema** *nm* theorem

**teoría** *nf* theory; **en t.** in theory; **t. del conocimiento** epistemology; **t. de la información** information theory; **t. monetaria** monetary theory

**teóricamente** *adv* theoretically

**teórico, -a 1** *adj* theoretical
**2** *nm,f (persona)* theorist

**teorizador, -ora** *adj* theorizing

**teorizar** [16] *vi* to theorize

**tequila** *nmf* tequila

**terapeuta** *nmf (médico)* doctor; *(fisioterapeuta)* physiotherapist

**terapéutica** *nf* therapeutics *(singular)*

**terapéutico, -a** *adj* therapeutic

**terapia** *nf* therapy; **t. ocupacional/de grupo** occupational/group therapy; **t. genética** gene therapy

**tercer** *adj ver* **tercero**

**tercera** *nf Aut* third (gear)

**tercermundismo** *nm* underdevelopment; *Fig* backwardness

**tercermundista** *adj* third-world; **un país t.** a third-world country; *Fig* **¡este servicio es t.!** this service is appalling *o* a disgrace!

**tercero, -a**

> **tercer** is used instead of **tercero** before masculine singular nouns (e.g. **el tercer piso** the third floor).

**1** *núm* third; **a la tercera va la vencida** third time lucky; **la tercera edad** senior citizens; **durante la tercera edad** in old age
**2** *nm* (a) *(piso)* third floor (b) *(curso)* third year (c) *(mediador, parte interesada)* third party; **el t. en discordia** the third party

**terceto** *nm* (a) *(estrofa)* tercet (b) *Mús* trio

**terciado, -a** *adj (mediano)* medium-sized

**terciar** [15] **1** *vt* (a) *(poner en diagonal)* to place diagonally; *(sombrero)* to tilt (b) *(dividir)* to divide into three
**2** *vi* (a) *(mediar)* to mediate (**en** in) (b) *(participar)* to intervene, to take part
**3 terciarse** *vpr* to arise; **si se tercia** if the opportunity arises

**terciario, -a 1** *adj* tertiary
**2** *nm Geol* **el t.** the Tertiary (era)

**tercio** *nm* (a) *(tercera parte)* third (b) *Mil* regiment; **t. de la guardia civil** Civil Guard division (c) *Taurom* stage (of bullfight) (d) *(de cerveza)* bottle of beer (0.33 litre)

**terciopelo** *nm* velvet

**terco, -a 1** *adj* stubborn; **t. como una mula** as stubborn as a mule
**2** *nm,f* stubborn person; **ser un t.** to be stubborn

**tergal**® *nm* = type of synthetic fibre containing polyester

**tergiversación** *nf* distortion

**tergiversador, -ora 1** *adj* distorting
**2** *nm,f* person who distorts the facts

**tergiversar** *vt* to distort, to twist

**termal** *adj* thermal; **fuente de aguas termales** hot spring

**termas** *nfpl (baños)* hot baths, spa

**termes** *nm inv* = **termita**

**térmico, -a** *adj* (a) *(de la temperatura)* temperature; **descenso t.** drop in temperature (b) *(aislante)* thermal

**terminación** *nf* (a) *(finalización)* completion (b) *(parte final)* end (c) *Gram* ending

**terminal 1** *adj* (a) *(del fin)* final; *(del extremo)* end (b) *(enfermedad)* terminal; **es un enfermo t.** he's terminally ill
**2** *nm Elec & Informát* terminal; **t. videotexto** videotext terminal
**3** *nf (de aeropuerto)* terminal; *(de autobuses)* terminus

**terminante** *adj (categórico)* categorical; *(prueba)* conclusive

**terminar 1** *vt* to finish
**2** *vi* (a) *(acabar)* to end; *(tren)* to stop, to terminate; **t. en** *(objeto)* to end in; **terminamos de desayunar a las nueve** we finished having breakfast at nine (b) *(reñir)* to finish, to split up (c) *(ir a parar)* **terminó de camarero/en la cárcel** he ended up as a waiter/in jail; **t. por hacer algo** to end up doing sth
**3 terminarse** *vpr* (a) *(finalizar)* to finish (b) *(agotarse)* to run out

**término** *nm* (a) *(fin, extremo)* end; **dar t. a algo** to bring sth to a close; **llegó a su t.** it came to an end; **poner t. a algo** to put a stop to sth
(b) *(territorio)* **t. municipal** = area under the jurisdiction of a town council
(c) *(plazo)* period; **en el t. de un mes** within (the space of) a month
(d) *(lugar, posición)* place; *Arte & Fot* **en primer t.** in the foreground; **en último t.** in the background; *Fig (si es necesario)* as a last resort; *(en resumidas cuentas)* in the final analysis
(e) *(elemento)* point; **t. medio** *(media)* average; *(compromiso)* compromise, happy medium; **por t. medio** on average
(f) *(palabra)* term; **en términos generales** generally speaking; **los términos del contrato** the terms of the contract
(g) *(de transportes)* terminus
(h) *(relaciones)* **estar en buenos/malos términos (con)** to be on good/bad terms (with)

**terminología** *nf* terminology

**terminológico, -a** *adj* terminological

**termita** *nf* termite

**termitero** *nm* termite mound *o* nest

**termo** *nm* Thermos®

**termoaislante** *adj* heat insulating

**termodinámica** *nf* thermodynamics *(singular)*

**termodinámico, -a** *adj* thermodynamic

**termometría** *nf* thermometry

**termométrico, -a** *adj* thermometric

**termómetro** *nm* thermometer; **t. centigrado/clínico** centigrade/clinical thermometer; **poner el t. a alguien** to take sb's temperature

**termonuclear** *adj* thermonuclear

**termorregulador** *nm* thermostat

**termostato** *nm* thermostat

**terna** *nf Pol* = shortlist of three candidates

**ternario, -a** *adj* ternary

**ternasco** *nm* suckling lamb

**ternera** *nf (carne)* veal

**ternero, -a** *nm,f (animal)* calf

**ternilla** *nf* (a) *Culin* gristle (b) *Anat* cartilage

**terno** *nm* (a) *(trío)* trio (b) *(traje)* three-piece suit

**ternura** *nf* tenderness

**terquedad** *nf* stubbornness

**terracota** *nf* terracotta

**terrado** *nm* terrace roof

**terral** *nm Am* dust cloud

**Terranova** *n* Newfoundland

**terraplén** *nm* steep embankment

**terráqueo, -a** *adj* Earth; **globo t.** *(Tierra)* Earth; *(representación)* globe

**terrario, terrarium** *nm* terrarium

**terrateniente** *nmf* landowner

**terraza** *nf* (a) *(balcón)* balcony (b) *(de café)* terrace, patio (c) *(azotea)* terrace roof (d) *(bancal)* terrace

**terrazo** *nm* terrazzo, = polished composite floor covering made from stone chips

**terremoto** *nm* earthquake; *Fig* **es un t.** *(destructivo)* he leaves a trail of destruction wherever he goes

**terrenal** *adj* earthly

**terreno, -a 1** *adj* earthly

**2** *nm* (a) *(suelo)* land; *Geol* terrain; *Agr* soil; **t. irregular** uneven ground

(b) *(solar)* plot (of land); **t. edificable** building land

(c) *Dep* **t. (de juego)** field, pitch

(d) *Fig (ámbito)* field

(e) *(expresiones)* **estar** *o* **encontrarse en su propio t.** to be on home ground; **ganar t.** *(imponerse)* to gain ground; **le está ganando t. a su rival** he's gaining ground on his rival; **perder t.** to lose ground; **preparar** *o* **trabajar**

**el t. (para)** to pave the way (for); **reconocer** *o* **tantear el t.** to see how the land lies; **saber uno el t. que pisa** to know what one is about; **ser t. abonado (para algo)** to be fertile ground (for sth); **sobre el t.** on the spot

**térreo, -a** *adj* earthy

**terrestre 1** *adj* (a) *(del planeta)* terrestrial (b) *(de la tierra)* land; **animales terrestres** land animals

**2** *nmf* terrestrial, Earth-dweller

**terrible** *adj* (a) *(tremendo)* terrible (b) *(aterrador)* terrifying

**terrícola** *nmf* earthling

**terrier** *nm* terrier

**territorial** *adj* territorial

**territorialidad** *nf Der* territoriality

**territorio** *nm* territory; **por todo el t. nacional** across the country, nationwide

**terrón** *nm (de tierra)* clod of earth; **t. de azúcar** sugar lump

**terror** *nm* terror; **de t.** *(cine)* horror; **dar t.** to terrify

**terrorífico, -a** *adj* terrifying

**terrorismo** *nm* terrorism

**terrorista** *adj & nmf* terrorist

**terroso, -a** *adj* (a) *(parecido a la tierra)* earthy (b) *(con tierra)* muddy

**terruño** *nm* (a) *(terreno)* plot of land (b) *(patria)* homeland

**tersar** *vt* to make smooth

**terso, -a** *adj* (a) *(piel, superficie)* smooth (b) *(aguas, mar)* clear (c) *(estilo, lenguaje)* polished

**tersura** *nf* (a) *(de piel, superficie)* smoothness (b) *(de aguas, mar)* clarity (c) *(de estilo, lenguaje)* polish

**tertulia** *nf* = regular informal social gathering where issues of common interest are discussed; *Fam* **estar de t.** to sit (there) chatting; **t. literaria** literary circle

**Tesalónica** *n* Thessalonica

**tesina** *nf* (undergraduate) dissertation

**tesis** *nf inv* thesis

**tesitura** *nf* (a) *(situación)* circumstances, situation (b) *Mús* tessitura, pitch

**tesón** *nm* (a) *(tenacidad)* tenacity, perseverance (b) *(firmeza)* firmness

**tesorería** *nf* (a) *(cargo)* treasurership (b) *(oficina)* treasurer's office (c) *Com* liquid capital

**tesorero, -a** *nm,f* treasurer

**tesoro** *nm* (a) *(botín)* treasure; **el cofre del t.** the treasure chest (b) *(hacienda pública)* treasury, exchequer; *Econ* **el T.** the Treasury (c) *Fig (persona valiosa)* gem, treasure (d) *Fig (apelativo)* my treasure

**test** [tesd] (*pl* tests) *nm* test; **hacer un t.** to do *o* take a test; **hacer un t. a alguien** to give sb a test; **tipo t.** *(examen, pregunta)* multiple choice; **t. de embarazo** pregnancy test

**testa** *nf* head

**testado, -a** *adj (persona)* testate; *(herencia)* testamentary

**testaferro** *nm* front man

**testamentaría** *nf* **(a)** *(documentos)* documentation *(of a will)* **(b)** *(bienes)* estate, inheritance

**testamentario, -a1** *adj* testamentary

**2** *nm,f* executor

**testamento** *nm* will; **hacer t.** to write one's will; **Antiguo/Nuevo T.** Old/New Testament

**testar** *vi* to make a will

**testarudez** *nf* stubbornness

**testarudo, -a1** *adj* stubborn

**2** *nm,f* stubborn person

**testículo** *nm* testicle

**testificación** *nf* testimony; **es la t. de su talento** it is proof of her talent

**testificar** [61] **1** *vt* to testify; *Fig* to testify to

**2** *vi* to testify, to give evidence

**testigo 1** *nmf (persona)* witness; **poner por t. a alguien** to cite sb as a witness; **t. de cargo/descargo** witness for the prosecution/defence; **t. ocular** *o* **presencial** eyewitness; **t. de Jehová** Jehovah's Witness

**2** *nm* **(a)** *Fig (prueba)* **t. de** proof of **(b)** *Dep* baton

**testimonial** *adj* **(a)** *(documento, prueba)* testimonial **(b)** *Fig (simbólico)* token, symbolic

**testimoniar** [15] **1** *vt* to testify; *Fig* to testify to, to bear witness to

**2** *vi* to testify, to give evidence

**testimonio** *nm* **(a)** *Der* testimony; **falso t.** perjury, false evidence **(b)** *(prueba)* proof; **como t. de** as proof of; **dar t. de** to prove

**testosterona** *nf* testosterone

**testuz** *nm o nf* **(a)** *(frente)* brow **(b)** *(nuca)* nape

**teta** *nf* **(a)** *Fam (de mujer)* tit; **dar la t.** to breast-feed; **de t.** nursing **(b)** *(de animal)* teat

**tétanos** *nm inv* tetanus

**tetera** *nf* teapot

**tetilla** *nf* **(a)** *(de hombre, animal)* nipple **(b)** *(de biberón)* teat

**tetina** *nf* teat

**tetona** *adj f Fam* busty, top-heavy; **es muy t.** she has big boobs

**tetrabrik**® (*pl* tetrabriks) *nm* tetrabrick

**tetraedro** *nm* tetrahedron

**tetralogía** *nf Lit* tetralogy

**tetraplejía** *nf* quadriplegia

**tetrapléjico, -a** *adj & nm,f* quadriplegic

**tétrico, -a** *adj* gloomy

**teutón, -ona1** *adj Hist* Teutonic

**2** *nm,f* Teuton

**teutónico, -a** *adj Hist* Teutonic

**Texas** ['teχas] *n* Texas

**textil** *adj & nm* textile

**texto** *nm* **(a)** *(palabras, libro)* text **(b)** *(pasaje)* passage

**textual** *adj* **(a)** *(del texto)* textual **(b)** *(exacto)* exact; **dijo, palabras textuales, que era horroroso** her exact words were "it was terrible"

**textualmente** *adv* literally, word for word

**textura** *nf* **(a)** *(de superficie, tela)* texture **(b)** *Fig (estructura)* structure

**tez** *nf* complexion

**thriller** ['triler, 'θriler] (*pl* thrillers) *nm* thriller

**ti** *pron personal (después de prep)* **(a)** *(en general)* you; **siempre pienso en ti** I'm always thinking about you; **me acordaré de ti** I'll remember you **(b)** *(reflexivo)* yourself; **sólo piensas en ti (mismo)** you only think about yourself

**tía** *nf ver* **tío**

**tianguis** *nm inv Méx* open-air market

**tiara** *nf* tiara

**Tibet** *nm* **el T.** Tibet

**tibetano, -a** *adj & nm,f* Tibetan

**tibia** *nf* shinbone, tibia

**tibieza** *nf* **(a)** *(calidez)* warmth; *(falta de calor)* lukewarmness **(b)** *Fig (frialdad)* lack of enthusiasm

**tibio, -a** *adj* **(a)** *(cálido)* warm; *(falto de calor)* tepid, lukewarm **(b)** *Fig (frío)* lukewarm **(c)** *(expresiones)* **poner t. a alguien** to speak ill of sb; *Fam* **ponerse t. de algo** to stuff one's face with sth

**tiburón** *nm* **(a)** *(pez)* shark **(b)** *Fin* raider

**tic** *nm* tic

**ticket** ['tike] (*pl* tickets) *nm* **(a)** *(billete)* ticket **(b)** *(recibo)* **t. (de compra)** receipt

**tictac** *nm* tick tock

**tiemblo** *etc ver* **temblar**

**tiempo** *nm* **(a)** *(en general)* time; **al poco t.** soon afterwards; **a t. (de hacer algo)** in time (to do sth); **a un t., al mismo t.** at the same time; **cada cierto t.** every so often; **con el t.** in time; **con t.** with plenty of time to spare, in good time; **dar t. al t.** to give things time; **del t.** *(fruta)* of the season; *(bebida)* at room temperature; **de un t. a esta parte** recently, for a while now; **en mis tiempos** in my day *o* time; **estar a** *o* **tener t. de** to have time to; **fuera de t.** at the wrong moment; **ganar t.** to save time; **hace mucho t. que no lo veo** I haven't seen him for ages; **hacer t.** to pass the time; **matar** *o*

**engañar el t.** to kill time; **perder el t.** to waste time; **en tiempos de Maricastaña** donkey's years ago; **t. libre** *o* **de ocio** spare time; **a t. completo** full-time; **a t. parcial** part-time; *Informát* **t. de acceso** access time; *Dep* **t. muerto** time out; *Informát* **t. real** real time

**(b)** *(período largo)* long time; **hace t. que** it is a long time since; **hace t. que no vive aquí** he hasn't lived here for some time; **tomarse uno su t.** to take one's time

**(c)** *(edad)* age; **¿qué t. tiene?** how old is he?

**(d)** *(movimiento)* movement; **motor de cuatro tiempos** four-stroke engine

**(e)** *(clima)* weather; **hizo buen/mal t.** the weather was good/bad; **si el t. lo permite** *o* **no lo impide** weather permitting; **hace un t. de perros** it's a foul day; **poner a** *o* **al mal t. buena cara** to put a brave face on things

**(f)** *Dep* half

**(g)** *Gram* tense; **t. simple/compuesto** simple/composite tense

**(h)** *Mús (compás)* time; *(ritmo)* tempo

**tienda** *nf* **(a)** *(establecimiento)* shop; **ir de tiendas** to go shopping; **t. libre de impuestos** duty-free shop **(b)** *(para acampar)* **t. (de campaña)** tent

**tiendo** *ver* **tender**

**tiene** *ver* **tener**

**tienta** *nf* **(a)** *Taurom* trial *(of the bulls)* **(b) a tientas** blindly; **buscar algo a tientas** to grope about *o* around for sth; **andar a tientas** to grope along

**tiento 1** *ver* **tentar**

**2** *nm* **(a)** *(cuidado)* care; *(tacto)* tact **(b) dar un t. a algo** *(probar)* to try sth **(c)** *(de ciego)* white stick **(d)** *(de equilibrista)* balancing pole

**tierno, -a 1** *adj* **(a)** *(blando, cariñoso)* tender **(b)** *(del día)* fresh

**2** *nm Am* baby

**tierra** *nf* **(a)** *(terrenos, continentes)* land; **t. adentro** inland; **t. firme** terra firma, dry land; **t. de nadie** no-man's-land; **t. prometida** Promised Land; **t. virgen** virgin land; **la T. the** Earth; **T. del Fuego** Tierra del Fuego; **T. Santa** the Holy Land

**(b)** *(materia inorgánica)* earth, soil; **dar t. a alguien** to bury sb; **un camino de t.** a dirt track

**(c)** *(suelo)* ground; *Fig* **besar la t.** to fall flat on one's face; **caer a t.** to fall to the ground; **tomar t.** to touch down; **Ejército de T.** army

**(d)** *(patria)* homeland, native land; **vino/queso de la t.** local wine/cheese

**(e)** *Elec Br* earth, *US* ground

**(f)** *(expresiones)* **echar por t. algo** to ruin sth; **echar t. a un asunto** to hush up an affair; **poner t. por medio** to make oneself scarce; **quedarse en t.** to miss the boat/train/plane/

*etc; Fam* **¡t., trágame!** I wish the earth would swallow me up!; **venir** *o* **venirse a t.** to come to nothing

**tierral** *nm Am* dust cloud

**tieso, -a** *adj* **(a)** *(rígido)* stiff; *Fig* **dejar t. a alguien** to kill sb; **quedarse t.** *(de frío)* to freeze **(b)** *(erguido)* erect **(c)** *Fig (engreído)* haughty **(d)** *Fig (distante)* distant

**tiesto** *nm* flowerpot

**tifoideo, -a** *adj* typhoid; **fiebres tifoideas** typhoid fever

**tifón** *nm* typhoon

**tifus** *nm inv* typhus

**tigre** *nm* **(a)** *(animal)* tiger; *Fig* **los tigres económicos del sudeste asiático** the tiger economies of South-East Asia; *Fam Fig* **oler a t.** to stink **(b)** *muy Fam (WC) Br* bog, *US* john

**tigresa** *nf* tigress

**Tigris** *nm* **el T.** the (River) Tigris

**TIJ** [tix] *nm (abrev* **Tribunal Internacional de Justicia)** ICJ, International Court of Justice

**tijera** *nf (en general)* scissors; *(de jardinero, esquilador)* shears; **unas tijeras** (a pair of) scissors/ shears; **de t.** *(escalera, silla)* folding; **tijeras de podar** secateurs

**tijereta** *nf* **(a)** *(insecto)* earwig **(b)** *Dep* scissors

**tijeretazo** *nm* snip

**tijeretear** *vt* to snip

**tila** *nf* **(a)** *(flor)* lime blossom **(b)** *(infusión)* lime blossom tea

**tildar** *vt* **t. a alguien de algo** to brand *o* call sb sth

**tilde** *nf (acento gráfico)* accent

**tilín** *nm* tinkle, tinkling; *Fam* **me hace t.** I like the look of him/her/it; *Fam* **no me hizo mucho t.** he/she/it didn't do much for me

**tilo** *nm* **(a)** *(árbol)* linden *o* lime tree **(b)** *(madera)* lime

**timador, -ora** *nm,f* confidence trickster, swindler

**timar** *vt* **(a)** *(estafar)* **t. a alguien** to swindle sb; **t. algo a alguien** to swindle sb out of sth **(b)** *Fig (engañar)* to cheat, to con

**timba** *nf* card game *(in gambling den)*

**timbal** *nm Mús (de orquesta)* kettledrum, timbal; *(tamboril)* small drum

**timbrado, -a** *adj* **(a)** *(sellado)* stamped **(b)** *(sonido)* clear

**timbrar** *vt* to stamp

**timbrazo** *nm* loud ring

**timbre** *nm* **(a)** *(aparato)* bell; **tocar el t.** to ring the bell; **t. de alarma** alarm (bell) **(b)** *(de voz, sonido)* timbre; **el t. de su voz** the sound of her voice **(c)** *(sello) (de documentos)* (official) stamp; *(de impuestos)* seal

**timidez** *nf* shyness

**tímido, -a 1** *adj* shy

**2** *nm,f* shy person

**timo** *nm* (a) *(estafa)* swindle; *Fam Fig* ¡eso es el t. de la estampita! it's a complete rip-off! (b) *Fam (engaño)* trick (c) *Anat* thymus

**timón** *nm* (a) *Av & Náut* rudder (b) *Fig (gobierno)* helm; **llevar el t. de** to be at the helm of (c) *Andes (volante)* steering wheel

**timonear** *vi* to steer

**timonel, timonero** *nm Náut* helmsman

**timorato, -a** *adj* (a) *(mojigato)* prudish (b) *(tímido)* fearful

**tímpano** *nm* (a) *Anat* eardrum (b) *Mús (tamboril)* small drum; *(de cuerda)* hammer dulcimer (c) *Arquit* tympanum

**tina** *nf* (a) *(tinaja)* pitcher (b) *(gran cuba)* vat (c) *(bañera)* bathtub

**tinaja** *nf* (large) pitcher

**tinción** *nf* dyeing

**tinerfeño, -a 1** *adj* of/from Tenerife

**2** *nm,f* person from Tenerife

**tinglado** *nm* (a) *(cobertizo)* shed (b) *(armazón)* platform (c) *Fig (lío)* fuss; *(maquinación)* plot

**tinieblas** *nfpl* darkness; *Fig* confusion, uncertainty; **estar en t. sobre algo** to be in the dark about sth

**tino** *nm* (a) *(puntería)* good aim (b) *Fig (habilidad)* skill (c) *Fig (juicio)* sense, good judgment (d) *Fig (prudencia)* moderation

**tinta** *nf* ink; **andarse con medias tintas** to be wishy-washy; **cargar** *o* **recargar las tintas** to exaggerate; **se han escrito ríos de t. sobre el tema** people have written reams on the subject; **saberlo de buena t.** to have it on good authority; **sudar t.** to sweat blood; **t. china** Indian ink; **t. simpática** invisible ink

**tintar** *vt* to dye

**tinte** *nm* (a) *(sustancia)* dye (b) *(operación)* dyeing (c) *(tintorería)* dry cleaner's (d) *Fig (tono)* shade, tinge (e) *Fig (apariencia)* suggestion, semblance

**tintero** *nm (frasco)* ink pot; *(en la mesa)* inkwell; **dejarse algo en el t.** to leave sth unsaid

**tintinear** *vi* to jingle, to tinkle

**tintineo** *nm* tinkle, tinkling

**tinto, -a 1** *adj* (a) *(vino)* red (b) *(teñido)* dyed (c) *(manchado)* stained

**2** *nm (vino)* red wine

**tintorera** *nf* blue shark

**tintorería** *nf* dry cleaner's

**tintorero, -a** *nm,f* dry cleaner

**tintorro** *nm Fam* red plonk

**tintura** *nf* (a) *Quím* tincture; **t. de yodo** (tincture of) iodine (b) *(tinte)* dye; *(proceso)* dyeing

**tiña** *nf Med* ringworm

**tiñera** *etc ver* **teñir**

**tiño** *ver* **teñir**

**tiñoso, -a** *adj* (a) *Med* suffering from ringworm (b) *Fam (miserable)* grotty

**tío, -a** *nm,f* (a) *(familiar)* uncle, *f* aunt; **t. abuelo** great uncle, *f* great aunt; **t. carnal** uncle, *f* aunt *(blood relative)*; *Fig* **el t. Sam** Uncle Sam

(b) *Fam (hombre)* guy, *Br* bloke; *(mujer)* woman; *(mujer joven)* girl

(c) *Fam (apelativo) (hombre)* pal, *Br* mate; *(mujer)* ¡tía, déjame en paz! leave me alone, will you?; ¡tía, qué guapa estás! wow, you look fantastic!

(d) *Fam* **no hay tu tía, no puedo abrir el cajón** this drawer just refuses to open; **por más que se lo pido, no hay tu tía** I've asked him and asked him, but he's not having any of it

**tiovivo** *nm* merry-go-round

**tipazo** *nm Fam (de mujer)* great figure; *(de hombre)* good build

**tipejo, -a** *nm,f Fam Pey* individual, character

**típico, -a** *adj (característico)* typical (**de** of); *(traje, restaurante)* traditional

**tipificación** *nf* (a) *también Der* classification (b) *(normalización)* standardization (c) *(paradigma, representación)* epitome

**tipificar** [61] *vt* (a) *también Der* to classify (b) *(normalizar)* to standardize (c) *(representar)* to epitomize, to typify

**tipismo** *nm* local colour

**tiple 1** *nmf (cantante)* soprano

**2** *nm* (a) *(voz)* soprano (b) *(guitarra)* treble guitar

**tipo, -a 1** *nm,f Fam (hombre)* guy, *Br* bloke; *(mujer)* woman; *(mujer joven)* girl

**2** *nm* (a) *(clase)* type, sort; **no es mi t.** he's not my type; **todo t. de** all sorts of (b) *(cuerpo) (de mujer)* figure; *(de hombre)* build (c) *Econ* rate; **t. de descuento** base rate; **t. de interés/cambio** interest/exchange rate; **t. impositivo** tax band (d) *Imprenta* type (e) *(expresiones)* **jugarse el t.** to risk one's neck; **aguantar** *o* **mantener el t.** to keep one's cool, not to lose one's head

**tipografía** *nf* (a) *(procedimiento)* printing (b) *(taller)* printing works *(singular)*

**tipográfico, -a** *adj* typographical, printing; **industria tipográfica** printing industry

**tipógrafo, -a** *nm,f* printer

**tipología** *nf* typology

**tíquet** ( *pl* **tíquets**) *nm* (a) *(billete)* ticket (b) *(recibo)* **t. (de compra)** receipt

**tiquismiquis 1** *adj inv (maniático)* pernickety

**2** *nmf inv (maniático)* fusspot

**3** *nmpl* (a) *(riñas)* squabbles (b) *(bagatelas)* trifles

**tira** *nf* (a) *(banda cortada)* strip (b) *(tirante)* strap (c) *(de viñetas)* comic strip (d) *Fam* **la t. de** loads of

**tirabeque** *nm* mangetout

**tirabuzón** *nm* (a) *(rizo)* curl (b) *(sacacorchos)* corkscrew

**tirachinas** *nm inv* catapult

**tirada** *nf* (a) *(lanzamiento)* throw (b) *Imprenta (número de ejemplares)* print run; *(reimpresión)* reprint (c) *(sucesión)* series (d) *Fam (distancia)* **hay una buena t. hasta allí** it's a fair way *o* quite a stretch; **de** *o* **en una t.** in one go

**tiradero** *nm Méx* rubbish dump

**tirado, -a** *Fam* **1** *adj* (a) *(barato)* dirt cheap (b) *(fácil)* simple, dead easy; **estar t.** to be a cinch (c) *(débil, cansado)* worn-out (d) *(miserable)* seedy (e) *(abandonado, plantado)* **dejar t. a alguien** to leave sb in the lurch

**2** *nm,f (persona)* wretch

**tirador, -ora 1** *nm,f (persona)* marksman, *f* markswoman

**2** *nm* (a) *(mango)* handle (b) *(de campanilla)* bell rope

**tiragomas** *nm inv* catapult

**tiralíneas** *nm inv* ruling pen, = pen used with bottled ink for drawing geometrical figures, plans etc

**Tirana** *n* Tirana

**tiranía** *nf* tyranny

**tiránico, -a** *adj* tyrannical

**tiranizar** [16] *vt* to tyrannize

**tirano, -a 1** *adj* tyrannical

**2** *nm,f* tyrant

**tirante 1** *adj* (a) *(estirado)* taut (b) *Fig (violento, tenso)* tense; **estoy t. con él** there's tension between us

**2** *nm* (a) *(de tela)* strap; **tirantes** *(para pantalones) Br* braces, *US* suspenders (b) *Arquit* brace

**tirantez** *nf también Fig* tension

**tirar 1** *vt* (a) *(lanzar)* to throw; **t. algo a alguien/algo** *(para hacer daño)* to throw sth at sb/sth; **tírame una manzana** throw me an apple

(b) *(dejar caer)* to drop; *(derramar)* to spill; *(volcar)* to knock over

(c) *(desechar, malgastar)* to throw away; **t. algo a la basura** to throw sth away

(d) *(disparar)* to fire; *(bomba)* to drop; *(petardo, cohete)* to let off; **t. una foto** to take a picture

(e) *(derribar)* to knock down

(f) *(jugar) (carta)* to play; *(dado)* to throw

(g) *Dep (falta, penalti)* to take; *(balón)* to pass; **t. a gol** to shoot, to have a shot at goal

(h) *(imprimir)* to print

(i) *Fam (suspender)* to fail

**2** *vi* (a) *(estirar, arrastrar)* **t. (de algo)** to pull (sth); **tira y afloja** give and take

(b) *(disparar)* to shoot; **t. a matar** to shoot to kill

(c) *Fam (atraer)* to have a pull; **me tira la vida del campo** I feel drawn towards life in the country; **t. de algo** to attract sth

(d) *(cigarrillo, chimenea)* to draw

(e) *Fam (funcionar)* to go, to work

(f) *(dirigirse)* to go, to head; **tira por esa calle** go up *o* take that street

(g) *Fam* **ir tirando** *(apañárselas)* to get by; **voy tirando** I'm O.K., I've been worse

(h) *(durar)* to last

(i) *(parecerse)* **tira a gris** it's greyish; **tira a su abuela** she takes after her grandmother; **tirando a** approaching, not far from

(j) *(tender)* **t. para algo** *(persona)* to have the makings of sth; **este programa tira a (ser) hortera** this programme is a bit on the tacky side; **el tiempo tira a mejorar** the weather looks as if it's getting better

(k) *(jugar)* to (have one's) go

(l) *Dep (con el pie)* to kick; *(con la mano)* to throw; *(a meta, canasta)* to shoot

**3 tirarse** *vpr* (a) *(lanzarse) (al agua)* to dive (a into); *(al aire)* to jump (a into); **tirarse sobre alguien** to jump on top of sb; **tirarse de** to jump from; *(para bajar)* to jump down from; *(para matarse)* to throw oneself from

(b) *(tumbarse)* to stretch out

(c) *Fam (tiempo)* to spend

(d) *muy Fam* **tirarse a alguien** to lay *o Br* bonk sb

**tirita** *nf Br* (sticking) plaster, *US* Bandaid®

**tiritar** *vi* to shiver (de with)

**tiritona, tiritera** *nf* **le dio una t.** he had a fit of shivering

**tiro** *nm* (a) *(disparo)* shot; **pegar un t. a alguien** to shoot sb; **pegarse un t.** to shoot oneself; **t. de gracia** coup de grâce; *Dep* **t. libre** *(en fútbol)* free kick; *(en baloncesto)* free throw; **este cajón no se abre ni a tiros** this drawer just refuses to open; **esta cuenta no me sale ni a tiros** however hard I try I don't seem to be able to get this sum right; **me salió el t. por la culata** it backfired on me; **no van por ahí los tiros** you're a bit wide of the mark there; *Fam* **sentar como un t. (a alguien)** to go down badly (with sb)

(b) *(acción)* shooting; **t. al blanco** *(deporte)* target shooting; *(lugar)* shooting range; **t. al plato** clay-pigeon shooting; **t. con arco** archery

(c) *(huella, marca)* bullet mark; *(herida)* gunshot wound

(d) *(alcance)* range; **a t. de** within the range of;

**a t. de piedra** a stone's throw away; **ponerse/estar a t.** *(de arma)* to come/be within range; *Fig (de persona)* to come/be within one's reach

(e) *(de chimenea, horno)* draw

(f) *(de pantalón)* = distance between crotch and waist; **vestirse** *o* **ponerse de tiros largos** to dress oneself up to the nines

(g) *(de caballos)* team

**tiroideo, -a** *adj* thyroid; **glándula tiroidea** thyroid (gland)

**tiroides** *nm inv* thyroid (gland)

**tirolés, -esa 1** *adj* Tyrolean; **sombrero t.** Tyrolean hat

**2** *nm,f* Tyrolean

**tirón** *nm* (a) *(estirón)* pull; **de un t.** in one go (b) *(robo)* bagsnatching

**tironear** *vt* to tug (at)

**tirotear 1** *vt* to fire at

**2** *vi* to shoot

**3 tirotearse** *vpr* to fire at each other

**tiroteo** *nm (tiros)* shooting; *(intercambio de disparos)* shootout

**Tirreno** *nm* **el (mar) T.** the Tyrrhenian Sea

**tirria** *nf Fam* dislike; **tenerle t. a alguien** to have a grudge against sb

**tisana** *nf* herbal tea

**tísico, -a** *adj & nm,f Med* consumptive

**tisis** *nf inv Med* (pulmonary) tuberculosis

**tisú** *(pl* tisús) *nm (tela)* lamé

**titán** *nm Fig* giant

**titánico, -a** *adj* titanic

**titanio** *nm* titanium

**títere** *nm también Fig* puppet; **no dejar t. con cabeza** *(destrozar)* to destroy everything in sight; *(criticar)* to spare nobody; **títeres** *(guiñol)* puppet show

**titi** *nf muy Fam (chica) Br* bird, *US* broad

**tití** *nm (mono)* titi, = small monkey common in Central and South America

**Titicaca** *nm* **el lago T.** Lake Titicaca

**titilar** *vi* (a) *(temblar)* to tremble (b) *(estrella, luz)* to flicker

**titiritar** *vi* to shiver **(de** with)

**titiritero, -a** *nm,f* (a) *(de títeres)* puppeteer (b) *(acróbata)* acrobat

**titubeante** *adj (actitud)* hesitant; *(voz)* hesitant, faltering

**titubear** *vi (dudar)* to hesitate; *(al hablar)* to falter, to hesitate

**titubeo** *nm (duda, al hablar)* hesitation, hesitancy; **tras muchos titubeos** after much hesitation

**titulación** *nf (académica)* qualifications

**titulado, -a 1** *adj (diplomado)* qualified; *(licenciado)* graduate; **abogado t.** law graduate; **t. en** with a qualification/degree in

**2** *nm,f (diplomado)* holder of a qualification; *(licenciado)* graduate

**titular 1** *adj (profesor)* tenured

**2** *nmf (poseedor)* holder; *(profesor)* tenured lecturer

**3** *nm Prensa* headline; **con grandes titulares** splashed across the front page

**4** *vt (libro, cuadro)* to call, to title

**5 titularse** *vpr* (a) *(llamarse)* to be titled *o* called (b) *(licenciarse)* to graduate **(en** in) (c) *(diplomarse)* to obtain a qualification **(en** in)

**título** *nm* (a) *(en general)* title; **t. de propiedad** title deed (b) *(licenciatura)* degree; *(diploma)* diploma; **tiene muchos títulos** she has a lot of qualifications (c) *Fig (derecho)* right (d) *Econ* bond, security (e) **a t. de** as

**tiza** *nf* chalk; **una t.** a piece of chalk

**tiznadura** *nf* (a) *(acción)* blackening, dirtying (b) *(mancha)* black mark

**tiznar 1** *vt* to blacken

**2 tiznarse** *vpr* to be blackened

**tizne** *nm o nf* soot

**tizón** *nm* burning stick *o* log

**tizona** *nf* sword

**tlapalería** *nf Méx* ironmonger's (shop)

**TLC** *nm (abrev de* **Tratado de Libre Comercio)** *nm* NAFTA, North American Free Trade Agreement

**TNT** *nm (abrev de* **trinitrotolueno)** TNT

**toalla** *nf* (a) *(para secarse)* towel; **t. de ducha/manos** bath/hand towel; *Fig* **arrojar** *o* **tirar la t.** to throw in the towel (b) *(tejido)* towelling

**toallero** *nm* towel rail

**toba** *nf Fam (papirotazo)* flick

**tobera** *nf (de horno)* air inlet; *(de propulsor)* nozzle

**tobillera** *nf* ankle support

**tobillo** *nm* ankle

**tobogán** *nm* (a) *(rampa)* slide; *(en parque de atracciones)* helter-skelter; *(en piscina)* chute, flume (b) *(trineo)* toboggan; *(pista)* toboggan run

**toca** *nf* wimple

**tocadiscos** *nm inv* record player

**tocado, -a 1** *adj* (a) *Fam (loco)* **t. (del ala)** soft in the head (b) *(fruta)* bad, rotten

**2** *nm* (a) *(prenda)* headgear (b) *(peinado)* hairdo

**tocador** *nm* (a) *(mueble)* dressing table (b) *(habitación) (en lugar público)* powder room; *(en casa)* boudoir

**tocante** *adj* **(en lo) t.** a regarding

**tocar** [61] **1** vt (a) (en general) to touch; (palpar) to feel

(b) (instrumento, canción) to play; (bombo) to bang; (sirena, alarma) to sound; (campana, timbre) to ring; **el reloj tocó las doce** the clock struck twelve

(c) (tema) to touch on

(d) Fig (conmover) to touch; (herir) to wound

(e) Fig (concernir) **por lo que a mí me toca/a eso le toca** as far as I'm/that's concerned; **t. a alguien de cerca** to concern sb closely

**2** vi (a) (entrar en contacto) to touch

(b) (estar próximo) **t. con** to be touching; (país, jardín) to border (on)

(c) (a la puerta, ventana) to knock

(d) (en un reparto) **t. a alguien** to be due to sb; **le tocó la mitad** he got half of it; **tocamos a dos trozos cada uno** there's enough for two slices each; **tocamos a mil cada uno** (nos deben) we're due a thousand each; (debemos) it's a thousand each; **te toca a ti hacerlo** (turno) it's your turn to do it; (responsabilidad) it's up to you to do it

(e) (caer en suerte) **me ha tocado la lotería** I've won the lottery; **le ha tocado sufrir mucho** he has had to suffer a lot

(f) (llegar el momento) **hoy toca limpiar** it's cleaning day today

**3 tocarse** vpr (a) (estar en contacto) to touch

(b) (mutuamente) to touch each other

**tocata 1** nm Fam (tocadiscos) record player

**2** nf Mús toccata

**tocateja: a tocateja** loc adv in cash

**tocayo, -a** nm,f namesake; **somos tocayos** we have the same (first) name

**tocho 1** adj Fam (grande) huge

**2** nm (a) Fam (cosa grande) massive o huge great thing; (libro) massive tome (b) (hierro) iron ingot

**tocinería** nf pork butcher's (shop)

**tocinero, -a** nm,f pork butcher

**tocino** nm (para cocinar) lard; (para comer) fat (of bacon); **t. entreverado** streaky bacon; **t. de cielo** = dessert made of syrup and eggs

**tocología** nf obstetrics

**tocólogo, -a** nm,f obstetrician

**tocomocho** nm = confidence trick involving the sale of a lottery ticket, claimed to be a certain winner, for a large amount of money

**tocón** nm stump

**todavía** adv (a) (aún) still; (con negativo) yet, still; **t. no** not yet; **t. no lo he recibido** I still haven't got it, I haven't got it yet; **están t. aquí** they are still here (b) (sin embargo) still (c) (incluso) even; **t. más** even more

**todo, -a 1** adj (a) (en general) all; **t. el mundo** everybody; **t. el libro** the whole book, all (of) the book; **t. el día** all day

(b) (cada, cualquier) **todos los días/lunes** every day/Monday; **t. español** every Spaniard, all Spaniards

(c) (para enfatizar) **es t. un hombre** he's every inch a man; **ya es toda una mujer** she's a grown woman now; **fue t. un éxito** it was a great success

**2** pron (a) (todas las cosas) (singular) everything; (plural) all of them; **lo vendió t.** he sold everything, he sold it all; **todos están rotos** they're all broken, all of them are broken; **de t.** everything (you can think of)

(b) **todos** (todas las personas) everybody; **todos vinieron** everybody o they all came

(c) (expresiones) **del t.** completely; **no estoy del t. contento** I'm not entirely happy; **no lo hace mal del t.** she doesn't do it at all badly; **en t. y por t.** entirely; **ante t.** (sobre todo) above all; (en primer lugar) first of all; **con t.** despite everything; **después de t.** after all; **de todas todas** without a shadow of a doubt; **sobre t.** above all; **t. lo más** at the most; **está en t.** he thinks of everything; **me invitó a cenar y t.** she even asked me to dinner

**3** nm whole; **jugarse el t. por el t.** to stake everything

**todopoderoso, -a** adj almighty; **el T.** the Almighty

**todoterreno** nm (a) (vehículo) all-terrain vehicle (b) Fig (persona) all-rounder

**toffee** ['tofe] (pl **toffees**) nm coffee-flavoured toffee

**tofu** nm tofu

**toga** nf (a) (romana) toga (b) (de académico) gown; (de magistrado) robes (c) (en el pelo) **hacerse la t.** = to wrap one's wet hair round one's head and cover it with a towel to dry, in order to straighten out curls

**togado, -a** adj robed

**Togo** n Togo

**toilette** [twa'let] (pl **toilettes**) nf Anticuado **hacer la t.** to perform one's toilet(te)

**toisón** nm **t. de oro** (insignia) golden fleece

**tojo** nm gorse

**Tokio** n Tokyo

**toldo** nm (de tienda) awning; (de playa) sunshade

**toledano, -a 1** adj of/from Toledo

**2** nm,f person from Toledo

**Toledo** n Toledo

**tolerable** adj (a) (aguantable) tolerable (b) (perdonable) acceptable

**tolerado, -a** adj (película) suitable for all ages, Br ≃ U

**tolerancia** *nf* tolerance

**tolerante 1** *adj* tolerant

 **2** *nmf* tolerant person

**tolerar** *vt* (a) *(consentir aceptar)* to tolerate; **t. que alguien haga algo** to tolerate sb doing sth (b) *(aguantar)* to stand

**tolva** *nf* hopper

**toma** *nf* (a) *(de biberón, papilla)* feed (b) *(de medicamento)* dose (c) *(de ciudad)* capture (d) *(de agua, aire)* inlet; *Elec* **t. de corriente** socket; *Elec* **t. de tierra** earth (e) *Cine (plano)* take (f) *(expresiones)* **ser un t. y daca** to be give and take; **la t. de conciencia tardó mucho tiempo** it took some time for people to become aware of the true situation; **t. de posesión** *(de gobierno, presidente)* investiture; *(de cargo)* undertaking

**tomadura** *nf* **t. de pelo** hoax

**tomahawk** [toma'xauk] *(pl* **tomahawks***) nm* tomahawk

**tomar 1** *vt* (a) *(en general)* to take; *(actitud, costumbre)* to adopt; **tomarle manía/cariño a algo/alguien** to take a dislike/a liking to sth/sb

 (b) *(datos, información)* to take down

 (c) *(comida, bebida)* to have; *Am (beber alcohol)* to drink (alcohol); **¿qué quieres t.?** what would you like (to drink/eat)?

 (d) *(autobús, tren)* to catch; *(taxi)* to take

 (e) *(contratar)* to take on

 (f) *(considerar, confundir)* **t. a alguien por algo/alguien** to take sb for sth/sb

 (g) **t. el sol** to sunbathe; **t. el aire** *o* **el fresco** to go out for a breath of fresh air

 (h) *Fam* **tomarla con alguien** to have it in for sb; **¡toma!** *(al dar algo)* here you are!; *(expresa sorpresa)* well I never!; *Fam* **¡toma (ésa)!** *(expresa venganza)* take that!

 **2** *vi (encaminarse)* to go, to head

 **3 tomarse** *vpr* (a) *(comida, bebida)* to have; *(medicina, drogas)* to take

 (b) *(interpretar)* to take; **tomarse algo bien/a mal/en serio** to take sth well/badly/seriously

**tomate** *nm* (a) *(fruto)* tomato; **t. frito** = unconcentrated purée made by frying peeled tomatoes; **ponerse como un t.** to go as red as a beetroot

 (b) *Fam (de calcetín)* hole

 (c) *Fam (jaleo)* uproar, commotion

**tomatera** *nf* tomato plant

**tomavistas** *nm inv* cine camera

**tómbola** *nf* tombola

**tomillo** *nm* thyme

**tomo** *nm* (a) *(volumen)* volume (b) *(libro)* tome

**tomografía** *nf* tomography

**ton:** **sin ton ni son** *loc adv* for no apparent reason

**tonada** *nf* tune

**tonadilla** *nf* ditty

**tonadillero, -a** *nm,f* ditty singer/writer

**tonal** *adj* tonal

**tonalidad** *nf* (a) *Mús* key (b) *(de color)* tone

**tonel** *nm* *(recipiente)* barrel; **estar/ponerse como un t.** to be/become (like) an elephant *o* a whale

**tonelada** *nf* tonne; **t. métrica** metric ton, tonne; **pesar una t.** to weigh a ton

**tonelaje** *nm* tonnage

**tóner** *nm* toner

**Tonga** *n* Tonga

**tongada** *nf* layer

**tongo** *nm (engaño)* **en la pelea hubo t.** the fight was fixed

**tónico, -a 1** *adj* (a) *(reconstituyente)* revitalizing (b) *Gram & Mús* tonic

 **2** *nm* (a) *(reconstituyente)* tonic (b) *(cosmético)* skin toner

 **3** *nf* (a) *(tendencia)* trend (b) *Mús* tonic (c) *(bebida)* tonic water

**tonificación** *nf* invigoration

**tonificante, tonificador, -ora** *adj* invigorating

**tonificar** [61] *vt* to invigorate

**tonillo** *nm Pey (retintín)* sarcastic tone of voice

**tono** *nm* (a) *(en general)* tone; **estar a t. (con)** to be appropriate (for); **fuera de t.** out of place (b) *Mús (tonalidad)* key; *(altura)* pitch (c) *(de color)* shade; **t. de piel** complexion (d) *(expresiones)* **darse t.** to give oneself airs; **ponerse a t. con algo** *(emborracharse)* to get drunk on sth; *(ponerse al día)* to get to grips with sth; **subir el t., subirse de t.** to get angrier and angrier

**tonsura** *nf* tonsure

**tonsurado** *nm (sacerdote)* priest

**tontaina** *Fam* **1** *adj* daft

 **2** *nmf* daft idiot

**tontear** *vi* (a) *(hacer el tonto)* to fool about (b) *(coquetear)* **t. (con alguien)** to flirt (with sb)

**tontería** *nf* (a) *(estupidez)* stupid thing; **decir una t.** to say something stupid, to talk nonsense; **hacer una t.** to do sth foolish (b) *(cosa sin importancia o valor)* trifle

**tonto, -a 1** *adj* (a) *(estúpido)* stupid; *(simple)* silly; **a lo t.** *(sin notarlo)* without realizing it; **ponerse t.** *(persona)* to be difficult; **t. de capirote** *o* **remate** daft as a brush (b) *(retrasado)* retarded, mentally handicapped

 **2** *nm,f* idiot; **hacer el t.** to play the fool; **hacerse el t.** to act innocent; **a tontas y a locas** without thinking

**tontorrón, -ona 1** *adj* daft

 **2** *nmf* daft idiot

**toña** *nf muy Fam (borrachera)* **cogerse una t.** to get pissed

**top** (*pl* **tops**) *nm* (*prenda*) cropped top

**topacio** *nm* topaz

**topadora** *nf CSur* bulldozer

**topar 1** *vi* (**a**) (*chocar*) to bump into each other (**b**) (*encontrarse*) **t. con alguien** to bump into sb; **t. con algo** to come across sth

**2 toparse** *vpr* **toparse con** (*persona*) to bump into; (*cosa*) to come across

**tope 1** *adj inv* (**a**) (*máximo*) top, maximum; **fecha t.** deadline (**b**) *muy Fam* (*genial*) fab, *Br* brill

**2** *adv muy Fam* (*muy*) mega, really

**3** *nm* (**a**) (*pieza*) block; (*para puerta*) doorstop (**b**) *Ferroc* buffer (**c**) (*límite máximo*) limit; (*de plazo*) deadline (**d**) (*freno*) **poner t. a** to rein in, to curtail (**e**) (*expresiones*) **a t.** (*de velocidad, intensidad*) flat out; (*lleno*) packed; **abrir el grifo a t.** to turn the tap on full; **estar hasta los topes** to be bursting at the seams

**topera** *nf* molehill

**topetazo** *nm* bump; **darse un t.** (*en la cabeza*) to bump oneself on the head

**topetear** *vi* to butt

**tópico, -a 1** *adj* (**a**) *Med* topical (**b**) (*manido*) clichéd

**2** *nm* cliché

**topless** ['tobles] *nm inv* topless sunbathing; **en t.** topless; **hacer t.** to go topless

**topo** *nm* (**a**) *Zool & Fig* mole (**b**) (*lunar en tela*) polka dot; **una falda de topos** a polka-dot skirt

**topografía** *nf* topography

**topográfico, -a** *adj* topographical

**topógrafo, -a** *nm,f* topographer

**topología** *nf* topology

**toponimia** *nf* (**a**) (*nombres*) place names (**b**) (*ciencia*) toponymy

**topónimo** *nm* place name

**toque 1** *ver* **tocar**

**2** *nm* (**a**) (*golpe*) knock; **dio unos toques en la puerta** she knocked on the door

(**b**) (*detalle*) touch; **dar los últimos toques a algo** to put the finishing touches to sth

(**c**) (*aviso*) warning; **dar un t. a alguien** (*llamar*) to call sb; (*llamar la atención*) to prod sb, to warn sb; **t. de atención** warning

(**d**) (*sonido*) (*de campana*) chime; (*de tambor*) beat; (*de sirena*) blast; **t. de diana** reveille; **t. de difuntos** death knell; **t. de queda** curfew

**toquetear 1** *vt* (*manosear*) (*cosa*) to fiddle with; (*persona*) to fondle

**2** *vi Fam* (*sobar*) to fiddle about

**toqueteo** *nm* (*de cosa*) fiddling; (*a persona*) fondling

**toquilla** *nf* shawl

**tora** *nf* (*libro*) Torah

**torácico, -a** *adj* thoracic

**tórax** *nm inv* thorax

**torbellino** *nm* (**a**) (*remolino*) (*de aire*) whirlwind; (*de agua*) whirlpool; (*de polvo*) dustcloud (**b**) *Fig* (*mezcla confusa*) spate (**c**) *Fig* (*persona inquieta*) whirlwind

**torcaz** *adj* **paloma t.** ringdove, wood pigeon

**torcedura** *nf* (**a**) (*torsión*) twist (**b**) (*esguince*) sprain

**torcer** [17] **1** *vt* (**a**) (*retorcer*) to twist; (*doblar*) to bend (**b**) (*girar*) to turn (**c**) (*desviar*) to deflect; *Fig* (*persona*) to corrupt; **t. el gesto** to pull a face

**2** *vi* (*girar*) to turn

**3 torcerse** *vpr* (**a**) (*retorcerse*) to twist; (*doblarse*) to bend; **me tuerzo al andar/escribir** I can't walk/write in a straight line (**b**) (*lastimarse*) **torcerse el tobillo** to twist one's ankle (**c**) (*ir mal*) (*esperanzas, negocios, día*) to go wrong; (*persona*) to go astray

**torcido, -a** *adj* (*enroscado*) twisted; (*doblado*) bent; (*cuadro, corbata*) crooked

**tordo, -a 1** *adj* dappled

**2** *nm,f* (*caballo*) dapple (horse)

**3** *nm* (*pájaro*) thrush

**toreador, -ora** *nm,f* bullfighter

**torear 1** *vt* (**a**) (*lidiar*) to fight (*bulls*) (**b**) *Fig* (*eludir*) to dodge (**c**) *Fig* (*burlarse de*) **t. a alguien** to mess sb about

**2** *vi* (*lidiar*) to fight bulls

**toreo** *nm* bullfighting

**torera** *nf* (**a**) (*prenda*) bolero (jacket) (**b**) *Fig* **saltarse algo a la t.** to flout sth

**torero, -a** *nm,f* (*persona*) bullfighter

**toril** *nm* bullpen (*in bullring*)

**tormenta** *nf también Fig* storm; **t. eléctrica** electric storm; *Fig* **esperar a que pase la t.** to wait until things have calmed down

**tormento** *nm* torment; **ser un t.** (*persona*) to be a torment; (*cosa*) to be torture

**tormentoso, -a** *adj* (*cielo, día, relación*) stormy; *Fig* (*época*) troubled, turbulent

**tornadizo, -a** *adj* fickle

**tornado** *nm* tornado

**tornar 1** *vt* (**a**) (*convertir*) **t. algo en algo** to turn sth into sth (**b**) (*devolver*) to return

**2** *vi* (**a**) (*regresar*) to return (**b**) (*volver a hacer*) **t. a hacer algo** to do sth again

**3 tornarse** *vpr* (**a**) (*volverse*) to become (**b**) (*convertirse*) **tornarse en** to turn into

**tornas** *nfpl* **volver las t.** to turn the tables; **las t. han cambiado** the boot is on the other foot

**tornasol** *nm* (**a**) (*girasol*) sunflower (**b**) (*reflejo*) sheen (**c**) *Quím* **papel de t.** litmus paper

**tornasolado, -a** *adj* iridescent

**torneado, -a 1** *adj* (**a**) *(madera)* turned (**b**) *(brazos, piernas)* shapely
 **2** *nm (de madera)* turning

**tornear** *vt* to turn

**torneo** *nm* tournament

**tornero, -a** *nm,f (con madera)* lathe operator

**tornillo** *nm* (**a**) *(con punta)* screw; *(con tuerca)* bolt (**b**) *(expresiones)* **apretar los tornillos a alguien** to put the screws on sb; *Fam* **le falta un t.** he has a screw loose

**torniquete** *nm* (**a**) *Med* tourniquet (**b**) *(en entrada)* turnstile

**torno** *nm* (**a**) *(de dentista)* drill (**b**) *(de alfarero)* (potter's) wheel (**c**) *(de carpintero)* lathe (**d**) *(para pesos)* winch (**e**) **en t. a** *(alrededor de)* around; *(acerca de)* about; **girar en t. a** to be about

**toro** *nm* bull; **t. de lidia** fighting bull; *Fig* **agarrar** *o* **coger el t. por los cuernos** to take the bull by the horns; *Fig* **ver los toros desde la barrera** to watch from the wings; **toros** *(lidia)* bullfighting; **ir a los toros** to go to a bullfight; *Fig* **nos va a pillar el t.** we're going to be late

**toronja** *nf* grapefruit

**Toronto** *n* Toronto

**torpe** *adj* (**a**) *(desmañado, inconveniente)* clumsy; **es muy t. conduciendo** he's a terrible driver (**b**) *(necio)* slow, dim-witted

**torpedear** *vt* to torpedo

**torpedero** *nm* torpedo boat

**torpedo** *nm* (**a**) *(proyectil)* torpedo (**b**) *(pez)* electric ray

**torpeza** *nf* (**a**) *(desmaña, inconveniencia)* clumsiness; **fue una t. hacerlo/decirlo** it was a clumsy thing to do/say (**b**) *(falta de inteligencia)* slowness

**torrar 1** *vt* to toast
 **2 torrarse** *vpr Fam* to be roasting

**torre** *nf* (**a**) *(construcción)* tower; **t. (de apartamentos)** tower block; **t. de control** control tower; **t. del homenaje** keep; *Fig* **t. de marfil** ivory tower; **t. de perforación** oil derrick (**b**) *(en ajedrez)* rook, castle (**c**) *Mil* turret (**d**) *Elec* pylon

**torrefacto, -a** *adj* high-roast; **café t.** high-roast coffee

**torrencial** *adj* torrential

**torrente** *nm* torrent; *Fig* **un t. de** *(gente, palabras)* a stream *o* flood of; *(dinero, energía)* masses of

**torrentera** *nf* channel *(made by flowing water)*

**torreón** *nm* large fortified tower

**torreta** *nf* (**a**) *Mil* turret (**b**) *Elec* pylon

**torrezno** *nm* = chunk of fried bacon

**tórrido, -a** *adj* torrid

**torrija** *nf* = French toast topped with cinnamon and sugar or golden syrup, typically eaten at Easter

**torsión** *nf* (**a**) *(del cuerpo, brazo)* twist, twisting (**b**) *Mec* torsion

**torso** *nm* torso

**torta** *nf* (**a**) *Culin* cake; *Méx* filled roll; **nos costó la t. un pan** it cost us an arm and a leg (**b**) *Fam (bofetada)* slap (in the face); **dar** *o* **pegar una t. a alguien** to slap sb (in the face) (**c**) *Fam (golpe, accidente)* thump; **darse** *o* **pegarse una t.** *(al caer)* to bang oneself; *(con el coche)* to have a smash (**d**) *Fam* **ni t.** not a thing

**tortazo** *nm Fam* (**a**) *(bofetón)* slap (in the face); **dar** *o* **pegar un t. a alguien** to slap sb (in the face); **liarse a tortazos** to come to blows (**b**) *(golpe, accidente)* thump, wallop; **darse** *o* **pegarse un t.** to give oneself a real thump *o* wallop; *(con el coche)* to have a crash

**tortícolis** *nf inv* = crick in the neck

**tortilla** *nf* (**a**) *(de huevo)* omelette; **t. (a la) española** Spanish *o* potato omelette; **t. (a la) francesa** French *o* plain omelette; **se ha dado la vuelta a la t.** the boot is on the other foot (**b**) *(de maíz)* tortilla, = thin maize pancake

**tortillera** *nf muy Fam* dyke, lesbian

**tortillería** *nf Am* = shop selling (corn) tortillas

**tortita** *nf* small pancake

**tórtola** *nf* turtledove

**tortolito, -a** *nm,f* (**a**) *(inexperto)* novice (**b**) *Fam (enamorado)* lovebird

**tortuga** *nf (terrestre)* tortoise; *(marina)* turtle; *(fluvial)* terrapin; *Fig* **ser una t.** *(ser lento)* to be a snail

**tortuosidad** *nf* (**a**) *(sinuosidad)* tortuousness (**b**) *Fig (perversidad)* deviousness

**tortuoso, -a** *adj* (**a**) *(sinuoso)* tortuous, winding (**b**) *Fig (perverso)* devious

**tortura** *nf* torture

**torturador, -ora 1** *adj* torturing
 **2** *nm,f* torturer

**torturar 1** *vt* to torture
 **2 torturarse** *vpr* to torture oneself

**torunda** *nf (de algodón)* swab

**torvo, -a** *adj* fierce

**torzamos** *ver* **torcer**

**tos** *(pl* **toses***) nf* cough; **t. ferina** whooping cough

**Toscana** *nf* **(la) T.** Tuscany

**toscano, -a** *adj & nm,f* Tuscan

**tosco, -a** *adj* (**a**) *(primitivo)* crude (**b**) *Fig (persona, modales)* rough

**toser** *vi* to cough

**tosferina** *nf* whooping cough

**tosquedad** nf (a) (de objeto) crudeness (b) Fig (de persona, modales) roughness

**tostada** nf piece of toast; **tostadas** toast

**tostadero** nm (de café) roaster

**tostado, -a** adj (a) (pan) toasted; (almendras, café) roasted (b) (color) brownish (c) (piel) tanned

**tostador** nm toaster

**tostar** [65] 1 vt (a) (dorar, calentar) (pan) to toast; (café, almendras) to roast; (carne) to brown (b) (broncear) to tan

2 **tostarse** vpr to get brown; **tostarse al sol** to sunbathe

**tostón** nm (a) Fam Fig (rollo, aburrimiento) bore, drag; **dar el t. a alguien** to pester sb, to go on and on at sb (b) Fam Fig (persona molesta) pain (c) Culin crouton

**total 1** adj (completo) total; muy Fam (fantástico) fab, Br brill

2 nm (a) (suma) total (b) (totalidad, conjunto) whole; **el t. del grupo** the whole group; **en t.** in all

3 adv anyway; **t. que me marché** so anyway, I left

**totalidad** nf whole; **en su t.** as a whole

**totalitario, -a** adj & nm,f totalitarian

**totalitarismo** nm totalitarianism

**totalizar** [16] vt to add up to, to amount to

**tótem** (pl tótems o tótemes) nm totem

**totémico, -a** adj totemic

**toûr** [tur] (pl tours) nm tour; **t. de force** tour de force; **t. operador** tour operator

**tournedos** [turne'ðo] nm inv tournedos

**tournée** [tur'ne] (pl tournées) nf tour; **estar de t.** to be on tour

**toxicidad** nf toxicity

**tóxico, -a1** adj toxic, poisonous

2 nm poison

**toxicología** nf toxicology

**toxicológico, -a** adj toxicological

**toxicomanía** nf drug addiction

**toxicómano, -a1** adj addicted to drugs

2 nm,f drug addict

**toxina** nf toxin

**tozudez** nf stubbornness, obstinacy

**tozudo, -a1** adj stubborn

2 nm,f stubborn person

**traba** nf (a) (obstáculo) obstacle; **poner trabas (a alguien)** (b) (para coche) chock (c) (de mesa) cross-piece to put obstacles in the way (of sb)

**trabado, -a** adj (a) (unido) (salsa) smooth; (discurso) coherent (b) (atascado) jammed (c) Gram ending in a consonant

**trabajado, -a** adj (a) (obra) carefully worked (b) (músculo) developed

**trabajador, -ora1** adj hard-working

2 nm,f worker; **t. por cuenta propia** self-employed person

**trabajar 1** vi (a) (en general) to work; **t. de/en** to work as/in; **t. en una empresa** to work for a firm (b) Cine & Teatro to act

2 vt (a) (hierro, barro, tierra) to work; (masa) to knead (b) (mejorar) to work on o at (c) Fig (engatusar, convencer) **t. a alguien (para que haga algo)** to work on sb (so that they do sth)

**trabajo** nm (a) (en general) work; **hacer un buen t.** to do a good job; **t. en o de equipo** teamwork; **t. intelectual/físico** mental/physical effort; **t. manual** manual labour; **trabajos forzados o forzosos** hard labour; **trabajos manuales** (en el colegio) arts and crafts; **ser un t. de chinos** to be a finicky job (b) (empleo) job; **no tener t.** to be out of work (c) (estudio escrito) piece of work, essay (d) Pol labour (e) Fig (esfuerzo) effort; **costar mucho t.** to take a lot of effort

**trabajoso, -a** adj (a) (difícil) hard, difficult (b) (molesto) tiresome

**trabalenguas** nm inv tongue-twister

**trabar 1** vt (a) (sujetar) to fasten; (a preso) to shackle (b) (unir) to join (c) (iniciar) (conversación, amistad) to strike up (d) (obstaculizar) to obstruct, to hinder (e) (espesar) to thicken

2 **trabarse** vpr (a) (enredarse) to get tangled (b) (espesarse) to thicken (c) (al hablar) to get one's tongue tied in knots; **se le trabó la lengua** he tripped over his tongue

**trabazón** nf (a) (unión) assembly (b) Fig (conexión) link, connection

**trabilla** nf (de pantalón) belt loop

**trabucar 1** vt to mix up

2 **trabucarse** vpr (liarse) to get things mixed up; (al hablar) to get one's tongue tied in knots

**trabuco** nm (arma de fuego) blunderbuss

**traca** nf string of firecrackers

**tracción** nf traction; **vehículo de t. animal** vehicle drawn by an animal; **t. delantera/trasera** front-wheel/rear-wheel drive; **t. a las cuatro ruedas** four-wheel drive

**trace** etc ver **trazar**

**tracoma** nm trachoma

**tracto** nm tract; **t. digestivo** digestive tract

**tractor** nm tractor

**tractorista** nmf tractor driver

**tradición** nf tradition

**tradicional** adj traditional

**tradicionalismo** nm traditionalism; Pol conservatism

**tradicionalista** adj & nmf traditionalist

**traducción** *nf* translation; **t. automática/ simultánea** machine/simultaneous translation; **t. directa/inversa** translation into/out of one's own language

**traducir** [20] **1** *vt* (a) *(a otro idioma)* to translate (b) *Fig (expresar)* to express
**2** *vi* to translate **(de/a** from/into)
**3 traducirse** *vpr* (a) *(a otro idioma)* traducirse **(por)** to be translated (by *o* as) (b) *Fig* **traducirse en** *(ocasionar)* to lead to

**traductor, -ora 1** *adj* translating
**2** *nm,f* translator; **t. jurado** = translator qualified to work in court

**traer** [68] **1** *vt* (a) *(trasladar, provocar)* to bring; *(consecuencias)* to carry, to have; **t. consigo** *(implicar)* to mean, to lead to (b) *(llevar)* to carry; **¿qué traes ahí?** what have you got there? (c) *(llevar adjunto, dentro)* to have; **trae un artículo interesante** it has an interesting article in it (d) *(llevar puesto)* to wear (e) *Fam Fig (persona)* **t. a alguien loco** *o* **de cabeza** to be driving sb mad
**2 traerse** *vpr Fam Fig* **traérselas** to be a real handful

**tráfago** *nm* drudgery

**traficante** *nmf (de drogas, armas)* trafficker

**traficar** [61] *vi* to traffic **(en/con** in)

**tráfico** *nm* traffic; **t. de drogas/armas** drug/arms trafficking; **t. de influencias** political corruption; **t. rodado** road traffic

**tragaderas** *nfpl Fam* **tener (buenas) t.** *(ser crédulo)* to fall for anything; *(ser tolerante)* to be able to stomach anything

**tragaldabas** *nmf inv Fam* greedy-guts, human dustbin

**tragaluz** *nm* skylight

**tragaperras** *nf inv* slot machine

**tragar** [40] **1** *vt* (a) *(ingerir, creer)* to swallow (b) *(absorber)* to swallow up (c) *Fig (soportar)* to put up with; **no (poder) t. a alguien** not to be able to stand sb (d) *Fam (consumir mucho)* to devour, to guzzle
**2** *vi* (a) *(ingerir, creerse)* to swallow (b) *Fam (acceder)* to give in
**3 tragarse** *vpr* (a) *(ingerir, creerse)* to swallow (b) *Fig (disimular)* to contain, to keep to oneself; *(lágrimas)* to choke back (c) *Fig (soportarse)* **no se tragan** they can't stand each other

**tragedia** *nf* tragedy

**trágico, -a 1** *adj* tragic
**2** *nm,f* tragedian

**tragicomedia** *nf* tragicomedy

**tragicómico, -a** *adj* tragicomic

**trago** *nm* (a) *(de líquido)* mouthful; **de un t.** in one gulp (b) *Fam (copa)* drink; **echar** *o* **tomar un t.** to have a quick drink (c) *Fam Fig (disgusto)* **ser un t. para alguien** to be tough on sb; **pasar un mal t.** to have a tough time of it

**tragón, -ona** *Fam* **1** *adj* greedy
**2** *nm,f* **ser un t.** to have a healthy appetite

**trague** *etc ver* **tragar**

**traición** *nf* (a) *(infidelidad)* betrayal; **a t.** treacherously (b) *Der* treason; **alta t.** high treason

**traicionar** *vt* (a) *(ser infiel a)* to betray; *Fig* **su accento lo traicionó** his accent gave him away

**traicionero, -a 1** *adj* (a) *(desleal)* treacherous; *Der* treasonous (b) *(peligroso, dañino)* treacherous, dangerous
**2** *nm,f* traitor

**traído, -a** *adj* worn-out; **t. y llevado** wellworn, hackneyed

**traidor, -ora 1** *adj* (a) *(desleal)* treacherous; *Der* treasonous (b) *(peligroso, dañino)* treacherous, dangerous
**2** *nm,f* traitor

**traigo** *etc ver* **traer**

**tráiler** ['trailer] *(pl* **tráilers)** *nm* (a) *Cine* trailer (b) *(remolque)* trailer; *(camión)* articulated lorry

**trainera** *nf* = small boat, for fishing or rowing in races

**traje 1** *ver* **traer**
**2** *nm* (a) *(con chaqueta)* suit; *(de una pieza)* dress; **t. de baño** swimsuit; **t. de bucear** wet suit; **llevar t. de ceremonia** *o* **de gala** to wear formal dress; **t. de chaqueta** woman's twopiece suit; **t. de etiqueta** evening dress; **t. de noche** evening dress; **t. pantalón** trouser suit (b) *(regional, disfraz)* costume; **t. de luces** matador's outfit (c) *(ropa)* clothes; **t. de diario** everyday clothes; **t. de paisano** *(de militar)* civilian clothes; *(de policía)* plain clothes

**trajeado, -a** *adj* (a) *(con chaqueta)* wearing a jacket (b) *Fam (arreglado)* spruced up

**trajear 1** *vt* to dress in a suit
**2 trajearse** *vpr* to wear a suit

**trajera** *etc ver* **traer**

**trajín** *nm* (a) *Fam Fig (ajetreo)* bustle (b) *(transporte)* haulage, transport

**trajinar 1** *vi Fam Fig* to bustle about
**2** *vt* to transport
**3 trajinarse a** *vpr muy Fam (ligarse a)* to get off with

**tralla** *nf* (a) *(látigo)* whip (b) *Fam* **dar t. a** *(criticar)* to slate

**trama** *nf* (a) *(historia)* plot (b) *Fig (confabulación)* plot, intrigue (c) *(de hilos)* weft

**tramar** vt (a) (hilo) to weave (b) Fig (planear) to plot; (complot) to hatch; **estar tramando algo** to be up to something

**tramitación** nf (acción) processing; **está en t.** it is being processed

**tramitar** vt (sujeto: autoridades) (pasaporte, solicitud) to process; (sujeto: solicitante) to be in the process of applying for; **me están tramitando la renovación de la licencia** my application for a new licence is being processed

**trámite** nm (gestión) formal step; **de t.** routine, formal; **trámites** (proceso) procedure; (papeleo) paperwork

**tramo** nm (a) (espacio) section, stretch (b) (de escalera) flight (of stairs)

**tramontana** nf north wind

**tramoya** nf (a) Teatro stage machinery (b) Fig (enredo) intrigue

**tramoyista** nmf (a) Teatro stagehand (b) Fig (tramposo) schemer

**trampa** nf (a) (para cazar) trap (b) (trampilla) trapdoor (c) Fig (engaño) trick; **caer en la t.** to fall into the trap; **tender una t. (a alguien)** to set o lay a trap (for sb); **hacer trampas** to cheat (d) Fig (deuda) debt

**trampear** vi Fam (a) (estafar) to swindle money (b) (ir tirando) to struggle along

**trampero, -a** nm,f trapper

**trampilla** nf (puerta) trapdoor

**trampolín** nm (a) (de piscina) diving board; (de esquí) ski jump; (en gimnasia) springboard (b) Fig (medio, impulso) springboard

**tramposo, -a 1** adj cheating
**2** nm,f cheat

**tranca** nf (a) (de puerta) bar; **poner una t. en la puerta** to bar the door (b) (arma) cudgel, stick (c) Fam (borrachera) **coger una t.** to get plastered (d) Fam **a trancas y barrancas** with great difficulty

**trancazo** nm (a) (golpe) blow (with a stick) (b) Fam Fig (gripe) bout of the flu

**trance** nm (a) (situación crítica) difficult situation; **pasar por un mal t.** to go through a bad patch; **a todo t.** at all costs (b) (estado hipnótico) trance; **estar en t.** to be in a trance

**tranco** nm stride

**tranquilidad** nf peacefulness, calmness; **para mayor t.** to be on the safe side; **para tu t.** to put your mind at rest

**tranquilizador, -ora** adj calming

**tranquilizante 1** adj (a) (música, color) soothing (b) Med tranquilizing
**2** nm Med tranquilizer

**tranquilizar [16] 1** vt (a) (calmar) to calm (down) (b) (dar confianza a) to reassure
**2 tranquilizarse** vpr (a) (calmarse) to calm down (b) (ganar confianza) to feel reassured

**tranquillo** nm Fam **cogerle el t. a algo** to get the knack of sth

**tranquilo, -a** adj (a) (sosegado) (lugar, música) peaceful; (persona, tono de voz, mar) calm; (viento) gentle; Fam **¡(tú) t.!** don't you worry! (b) (velada, charla, negocio) quiet (c) (mente) untroubled; (conciencia) clear (d) (despreocupado) casual, laid-back; **quedarse tan t.** not to bat an eyelid

**transacción** nf Com transaction

**transalpino, -a, trasalpino, -a** adj transalpine

**transandino, -a, trasandino, -a** adj trans-Andean

**transar** vi Am to compromise, to give in

**transatlántico, -a, trasatlántico, -a**
**1** adj transatlantic
**2** nm Náut (ocean) liner

**transbordador, trasbordador** nm (a) Náut ferry (b) Av **t. (espacial)** space shuttle

**transbordar, trasbordar** vi to change (trains)

**transbordo, trasbordo** nm **hacer t.** to change (trains)

**transcendencia** nf, **transcendental** adj etc = **trascendencia, trascendental** etc

**transcontinental** adj transcontinental

**transcribir, trascribir** vt (a) (escribir) to transcribe (b) Fig (expresar) to express in writing

**transcripción, trascripción** nf transcription

**transcriptor, -ora, trascriptor, -ora**
**1** nm,f (persona) transcriber
**2** nm (aparato) transcriber

**transcrito, -a, trascrito, -a** adj transcribed

**transcurrir, trascurrir** vi (a) (tiempo) to pass, to go by (b) (ocurrir) to take place, to happen; **t. sin incidentes** to go off without incident

**transcurso, trascurso** nm (a) (paso de tiempo) passing (b) (periodo de tiempo) **en el t. de** in the course of

**transeúnte 1** adj passing
**2** nmf (a) (paseante) passer-by (b) (residente temporal) temporary resident

**transexual** adj & nmf transsexual

**transferencia, trasferencia** nf transfer; **t. electrónica de fondos** electronic transfer of funds

**transferir, trasferir [64]** vt to transfer

**transfiguración, trasfiguración** nf transfiguration

**transfigurar, trasfigurar 1** *vt* to transfigure

**2 transfigurarse** *vpr* to become transfigured

**transformación, trasformación** *nf* transformation

**transformador, -ora, trasformador, -ora 1** *adj* transforming

**2** *nm Electr* transformer

**transformar, trasformar 1** *vt* (a) *(cambiar radicalmente)* **t. algo/a alguien (en)** to transform sth/sb (into) (b) *(convertir)* **t. algo (en)** to convert sth (into) (c) *(en rugby)* to convert

**2 transformarse** *vpr* (a) *(cambiar radicalmente)* to be transformed (b) *(convertirse)* **transformarse en algo** to be converted into sth

**transformismo, trasformismo** *nm* evolution

**transformista, trasformista 1** *adj* evolutionary

**2** *nmf* (a) *(seguidor)* evolutionist (b) *(artista) (que cambia de trajes)* quick-change artist

**3** *nm (travestido)* drag artist

**transfronterizo, -a** *adj* cross-border

**tránsfuga, trásfuga** *nmf Pol* defector

**transfuguismo, trasfuguismo** *nm Pol* defection *(to another party)*

**transfusión, trasfusión** *nf* transfusion

**transfusor, -ora, trasfusor, -ora** *nm (aparato)* transfuser

**transgénico, -a** *adj* transgenic

**transgredir, trasgredir** *vt* to transgress

**transgresión, trasgresión** *nf* transgression

**transgresor, -ora, trasgresor, -ora** *nm,f* transgressor

**transiberiano** *nm* Trans-Siberian railway

**transición** *nf* transition; **periodo de t.** transition period; **t. democrática** transition to democracy

**transido, -a** *adj* stricken (**de** with); **t. de pena** grief-stricken

**transigencia** *nf* (a) *(espíritu negociador)* willingness to compromise (b) *(tolerancia)* tolerance

**transigente** *adj* (a) *(que cede)* willing to compromise (b) *(tolerante)* tolerant

**transigir** [26] *vi* (a) *(ceder)* to compromise (**en** on) (b) *(ser tolerante)* to be tolerant

**transistor** *nm* transistor

**transitable** *adj (franqueable)* passable; *(no cerrado al tráfico)* open to traffic

**transitar** *vi* to go (along)

**transitivo, -a** *adj* transitive

**tránsito** *nm* (a) *(circulación)* movement; *(de coches)* traffic; **t. rodado** road traffic; **pasajeros en t. hacia Roma** *(en aeropuerto)* passengers with connecting flights to Rome (b) *(transporte)* transit

**transitoriedad** *nf* temporary nature; **la t. de la vida** the transience of life

**transitorio, -a** *adj (temporal)* transitory; *(residencia)* temporary; *(régimen, medida)* transitional, interim

**translación** *nf* = **traslación**

**translúcido, -a, traslúcido, -a** *adj* translucent

**traslucirse** [41] *vpr* = **traslucirse**

**transmediterráneo, -a, trasmediterráneo, -a** *adj* transmediterranean

**transmisible, trasmisible** *adj (enfermedad)* transmittable (b) *(título, posesiones)* transferrable

**transmisión, trasmisión** *nf* (a) *también Aut* transmission; *(de saludos, noticias)* passing on; **t. del pensamiento** telepathy (b) *Rad & TV (programa)* broadcast; *(servicio)* broadcasting (c) *(de herencia, poderes)* transference

**transmisor, -ora, trasmisor, -ora 1** *adj* transmitting

**2** *nm* transmitter

**transmitir, trasmitir 1** *vt* (a) *(sonido, onda)* to transmit; *(saludos, noticias)* to pass on (b) *Rad & TV* to broadcast (c) *(ceder)* to transfer

**2 transmitirse** *vpr* to be transmitted

**transmutación, trasmutación** *nf* transmutation

**transmutar, trasmutar** *vt* to transmute

**transnacional, trasnacional** *adj* transnational

**transoceánico, -a** *adj* transoceanic

**transparencia, trasparencia** *nf* transparency

**transparentarse, trasparentarse** *vpr* (a) *(ser transparente) (tela)* to be see-through; *(cristal, líquido)* to be transparent (b) *(verse)* to show through; *Fig* **se transparentan sus intenciones/sentimientos** her intentions/feelings are obvious

**transparente, trasparente** *adj (cristal, líquido)* transparent; *(tela)* see-through

**transpiración, traspiración** *nf* perspiration; *Bot* transpiration

**transpirar, traspirar** *vi* (a) *(sudar)* to perspire; *Bot* to transpire (b) *Fig (exudar)* to exude

**transpirenaico, -a, traspirenáico, -a** *adj* trans-Pyrenean

**transplantar** *vt* = **trasplantar**

**transplante** *nm* = **trasplante**

**transponer, trasponer** [52] **1** *vt* (a) *(cambiar)* to switch (b) *(desaparecer detrás de)* to disappear behind

**2 transponerse** *vpr* (a) *(adormecerse)* to doze off (b) *(ocultarse)* to disappear; *(sol)* to set

**transportable** *adj* portable

**transportador** *nm* (a) *(para transportar)* **t. aéreo** cableway; **t. de cinta** conveyor belt (b) *(para medir ángulos)* protractor

**transportar 1** *vt* (a) *(trasladar)* to transport (b) *(embelesar)* to captivate

**2 transportarse** *vpr (embelesarse)* to go into raptures

**transporte** *nm* transport; **t. público** *o* **colectivo** public transport

**transportista** *nmf Com* carrier

**transposición, trasposición** *nf* transposition

**transpuesto, -a, traspuesto, -a** *adj (dormido)* dozing; **quedarse t.** to doze off

**transubstanciación** *nf Rel* transubstantiation

**transvasar, trasvasar** *vt* (a) *(líquido)* to decant (b) *(agua de río)* to transfer

**transvase, trasvase** *nm* (a) *(de líquido)* decanting (b) *(entre ríos)* transfer

**transversal, trasversal 1** *adj* transverse

**2** *nf Mat* transversal

**tranvía** *nm* tram, *US* streetcar

**trapecio** *nm* (a) *Mat* trapezium (b) *(de gimnasia)* trapeze (c) *Anat (músculo)* trapezius

**trapecista** *nmf* trapeze artist

**trapense** *adj & nmf* Trappist

**trapero, -a** *nm,f* rag-and-bone man

**trapezoide** *nm Anat & Geom* trapezoid

**trapichear** *vi Fam* to be on the fiddle

**trapicheo** *nm Fam* (a) *(negocio sucio)* fiddle (b) *(tejemaneje)* scheme; **estoy harto de sus trapicheos** I'm sick of his scheming

**trapillo: de trapillo** *loc adv Fam* **vestir de t.** to wear any old thing

**trapío** *nm Formal* (a) *(garbo)* elegance (b) *Taurom* good bearing

**trapisonda** *nf Fam* (a) *(riña)* row, commotion (b) *(enredo)* scheme

**trapisondear** *vi Fam* (a) *(reñir)* to kick up a row (b) *(liar, enredar)* to scheme

**trapisondista** *nmf Fam* (a) *(camorrista)* troublemaker (b) *(liante)* schemer

**trapo 1** *nm* (a) *(trozo de tela)* rag (b) *(gamuza, bayeta)* cloth; *Fam Fig* **sacar los trapos sucios (a relucir)** to wash one's dirty linen in public; *Fam* **poner a alguien como un t.** to tear sb to pieces; **t. del polvo** duster; **t. de secar (los platos)** dishcloth (c) *Taurom* cape (d) *Fam* a

**todo t.** at full pelt

**2** *nmpl Fam (ropa)* clothes

**tráquea** *nf* windpipe, trachea

**traqueotomía** *nf Med* tracheotomy

**traquetear 1** *vt* to shake

**2** *vi (hacer ruido)* to rattle

**traqueteo** *nm (ruido)* rattling

**tras** *prep* (a) *(detrás de)* behind (b) *(después de, en pos de)* after; **uno t. otro** one after the other; **andar t. algo** to be after sth

**trasalpino, -a** *adj* = **transalpino**

**trasandino, -a** *adj* = **transandino**

**trasatlántico, -a** *adj* = **transatlántico**

**trasbordador** *nm* = **transbordador**

**trasbordar** *vt & vi* = **transbordar**

**trasbordo** *nm* = **transbordo**

**trascendencia, transcendencia** *nf* importance, significance; **esta decisión tendrá una gran t.** this decision will be of major significance

**trascendental, transcendental** *adj* (a) *(importante)* momentous (b) *(filosófico, elevado)* transcendental; *Fam* **ponerse t.** to wax philosophical

**trascendente, transcendente** *adj* momentous

**trascender, transcender** [66] *vi* (a) *(extenderse)* to spread (a across) (b) *(filtrarse)* to be leaked (c) *(sobrepasar)* **t. de** to transcend, to go beyond

**trascribir** *vt*, **trascripción** *nf etc* = **transcribir, transcripción** *etc*

**trascurrir** *vi* = **transcurrir**

**trascurso** *nm* = **transcurso**

**trasegar** [45] *vt* (a) *(desordenar)* to rummage about amongst (b) *(transvasar)* to decant

**trasera** *nf* rear

**trasero, -a 1** *adj* back, rear

**2** *nm* backside

**transferencia** *nf* = **transferencia**

**trasferir** [64] *vt* = **transferir**

**trasfiguración** *nf* = **transfiguración**

**trasfigurar** *vt* = **transfigurar**

**trasfondo** *nm (contexto)* background; *(de palabras, intenciones)* undertone

**trasformar** *vt*, **trasformación** *nf etc* = **transformar, transformación** *etc*

**trásfuga** *nmf* = **tránsfuga**

**trasfuguismo** *nm* = **transfuguismo**

**trasfusión** *nf* = **transfusión**

**trasfusor, -ora** *adj & nm* = **transfusor**

**trasgredir** *vt*, **trasgresión** *nf etc* = **transgredir, transgresión** *etc*

**trashumancia** *nf* seasonal migration *(of livestock)*

**trashumante** *adj* seasonally migratory

**trashumar** *vi* to migrate seasonally

**trasiego 1** *ver* **trasegar**

**2** *nm* (a) *(movimiento)* comings and goings (b) *(transvase)* decanting

**trasiegue** *etc ver* **trasegar**

**traslación, translación** *nf* Astron passage

**trasladar 1** *vt* (a) *(desplazar)* to move (b) *(a empleado, funcionario)* to transfer (c) *(reunión, fecha)* to postpone, to move back (d) *(traducir)* to translate (e) *Fig (expresar)* **t. algo al papel** to transfer sth onto paper

**2 trasladarse** *vpr* (a) *(desplazarse)* to go (b) *(mudarse)* to move; **me traslado de piso** I'm moving flats

**traslado** *nm* (a) *(de casa, empresa)* move; **el t. de los muebles** the moving of the furniture (b) *(de trabajo)* transfer (c) *(de personas)* movement

**traslúcido, -a** *adj* = **translúcido**

**traslucirse, translucirse** [41] *vpr* Fig to show through, to be obvious

**trasluz** *nm* reflected light; **al t.** against the light

**trasmano: a trasmano** *loc adv (fuera de alcance)* out of reach; *(lejos)* out of the way

**trasmediterráneo, -a** *adj* = **transmediterráneo**

**trasmisible** *adj*, **trasmisión** *nf etc* = **transmisible, transmisión** *etc*

**trasmutación** *nf* = **transmutación**

**trasmutar** *vt* = **transmutar**

**trasnacional** *adj* = **transnacional**

**trasnochado, -a** *adj Fam* estar **t.** to be old-hat

**trasnochador, -ora 1** *adj* given to staying up late

**2** *nm,f* night owl

**trasnochar** *vi* to stay up late, to go to bed late

**traspapelar 1** *vt (papeles, documentos)* to mislay, to misplace

**2 traspapelarse** *vpr* to get mislaid *o* misplaced

**trasparencia** *nf*, **trasparentarse** *vpr etc* = **transparencia, transparentarse** *etc*

**traspasable** *adj (camino)* passable; *(río)* crossable

**traspasar** *vt* (a) *(atravesar)* to go through, to pierce; **t. la puerta** to go through the doorway; **t. una valla saltando** to jump over a fence; **la tinta traspasó el papel** the ink soaked through the paper (b) *(transferir) (jugador)* to transfer; *(negocio)* to sell (as a going concern); **se traspasa (negocio)** *(en cartel)* (business) for sale (c) *(desplazar)* to move (d) *Fig (exceder)* to go beyond

**traspaso** *nm* (a) *(venta) (de jugador)* transfer; *(de negocio)* sale (as a going concern) (b) *(precio) (de jugador)* transfer fee; *(de negocio)* takeover fee

**traspié** (*pl* **traspiés**) *nm* (a) *(resbalón)* trip, stumble; **dar un t.** to trip up (b) *Fig (error)* blunder, slip; **dar un t.** to slip up, to make a mistake

**traspiración** *nf* = **transpiración**

**traspirar** *vi* = **transpirar**

**traspirenaico, -a** *adj* = **transpirenaico**

**trasplantar, transplantar** *vt* to transplant

**trasplante, transplante** *nm* transplant, transplanting

**trasponer** [52] *vt*, **trasposición** *nf etc* = **transponer, transposición** *etc*

**trasportín** *nm (rejilla)* rear rack *(on bike)*; *(caja)* = container carried on rear rack

**trasquilado, -a** *adj* Fig **salir t.** to come off badly

**trasquilar** *vt* (a) *(esquilar)* to shear (b) *Fam* **me trasquilaron (el pelo)** they gave me a terrible haircut

**trasquilón** *nm Fam* **hacerle un t. a alguien** *(cortar el pelo)* to give sb a terrible haircut

**trastabillar** *vi* to stagger; *Am (caerse)* to fall over

**trastada** *nf Fam (travesura)* prank

**trastazo** *nm* bump, bang; **darse** *o* **pegarse un t.** to bang *o* bump oneself

**traste** *nm* (a) *Mús* fret (b) **dar al t. con algo** to ruin sth; **irse al t.** to fall through

**trastero 1** *adj* **cuarto t.** lumber room

**2** *nm* lumber room

**trastienda** *nf* backroom

**trasto** *nm* (a) *(utensilio inútil)* piece of junk; **trastos** junk (b) *Fam Fig (persona traviesa)* menace, nuisance (c) *Fam Fig (persona inútil)* **t. (viejo)** dead loss (d) *Fam* **trastos** *(pertenencias, equipo)* things, stuff; **tirarse los trastos a la cabeza** to have a flaming row

**trastocar** [69] **1** *vt* (a) *(cambiar)* to turn upside down (b) *(enloquecer)* **t. a alguien** to drive sb mad, to unbalance sb's mind

**2 trastocarse** *vpr (enloquecer)* to go mad

**trastornable** *adj* oversensitive

**trastornado, -a** *adj* disturbed, unbalanced

**trastornar 1** *vt* (a) *(volver loco)* to drive mad (b) *(inquietar)* to worry, to trouble (c) *(alterar)* to turn upside down; *(planes)* to disrupt, to upset (d) *(estómago)* to upset

**2 trastornarse** *vpr (volverse loco)* to go mad

**trastorno** *nm* (a) *(mental)* disorder; *(digestivo)* upset (b) *(alteración)* **causar trastornos** *o* **un t.** *(huelga, nevada)* to cause trouble *o* disruption; *(guerra)* to cause upheaval

**trasvasar** *vt* = **transvasar**

**trasvase** *nm* = **transvase**

**trasversal** *adj* = **transversal**

**trata** *nf* slave trade; **t. de blancas** white slave trade

**tratable** *adj* easy-going, friendly

**tratadista** *nmf* treatise writer, essayist

**tratado** *nm* (a) *(convenio)* treaty; **T. de Libre Comercio** *(entre EE.UU., Canadá y México)* NAFTA Treaty (b) *(escrito)* treatise

**tratamiento** *nm* (a) *también Med* treatment (b) *(título)* title, form of address; **apear el t. a alguien** to address sb more informally (c) *Informát* processing; **t. de datos/textos** data/word processing; **t. por lotes** batch processing

**tratante** *nmf* dealer; **t. de vinos** wine merchant

**tratar 1** *vt* (a) *también Med* to treat (b) *(discutir)* to discuss (c) *Informát* to process (d) *(dirigirse a)* **t. a alguien de usted/tú** to address sb formally/informally (e) *(llamar)* **t. a alguien de cretino/tonto** to call sb a cretin/an idiot

**2** *vi* (a) *(versar)* **t. de** *o* **sobre** to be about (b) *(tener relación)* **t. con alguien** to mix with sb, to have dealings with sb (c) *(intentar)* **t. de hacer algo** to try to do sth (d) *(comerciar)* to deal (en in)

**3 tratarse** *vpr* (a) *(relacionarse)* **tratarse con** to mix with, to have dealings with (b) *(versar)* **tratarse de** to be about; **¿de qué se trata?** what's it about?

**trato** *nm* (a) *(comportamiento, conducta)* treatment; **de t. agradable** pleasant; **malos tratos** battering *(of child, wife)* (b) *(relación)* dealings; **tener t. con** to associate with, to be friendly with (c) *(acuerdo)* deal; **cerrar** *o* **hacer un t.** to do *o* make a deal; **no querer tratos con alguien** to want (to have) nothing to do with sb; **¡t. hecho!** it's a deal! (d) *(tratamiento)* title, term of address

**trauma** *nm* trauma

**traumático, -a** *adj* traumatic

**traumatismo** *nm* traumatism

**traumatizante** *adj* traumatic

**traumatizar** [16] **1** *vt* to traumatize

**2 traumatizarse** *vpr* to be devastated

**traumatología** *nf* traumatology

**traumatólogo, -a** *nm,f* traumatologist

**travellers** ['traβelers] *nmpl* travellers' cheques

**travelling** ['traβelin] *(pl* **travellings)** *nm* *Cine* travelling shot

**través** *nm* (a) **a t. de** *(de un lado a otro de)* across, over; *(por, por medio de)* through (b) **de t.** *(transversalmente)* crossways; *(de lado)* crosswise, sideways; *Fig* **mirar de t.** to give a sidelong glance

**travesaño** *nm* (a) *Arquit* crosspiece (b) *Dep* crossbar

**travesero, -a** *adj* **flauta travesera** flute

**travesía** *nf* (a) *(viaje)* *(por mar)* voyage, crossing; *(por aire)* flight (b) *(calle)* *(entre otras dos)* cross-street, connecting street; *(en pueblo)* = main road through a town

**travestí** *(pl* **travestís)** *nmf,* **travestido, -a** *nm,f* transvestite

**travestirse** [49] *vpr* to cross-dress

**travestismo** *nm* transvestism

**travesura** *nf* prank, mischief

**traviesa** *nf* (a) *Ferroc* sleeper *(on track)* (b) *Constr* crossbeam, tie beam

**travieso, -a** *adj* mischievous

**trayecto** *nm* (a) *(distancia)* distance; *(ruta)* route; **final de t.** end of the line (b) *(viaje)* journey, trip

**trayectoria** *nf* (a) *(recorrido)* trajectory (b) *Fig (evolución)* path, development

**traza** *nf* (a) *(aspecto)* appearance, looks (b) *(boceto, plano)* plan, design (c) *(habilidad)* **tener buena/mala t. (para algo)** to be good/no good (at sth)

**trazado 1** *adj* designed, laid out

**2** *nm* (a) *(trazo)* outline, sketching (b) *(diseño)* plan, design (c) *(recorrido)* route

**trazar** [16] *vt* (a) *(dibujar)* to draw, to trace; *(ruta)* to plot (b) *(indicar, describir)* to outline (c) *(idear)* to draw up

**trazo** *nm* (a) *(de dibujo, rostro)* line (b) *(de letra)* stroke

**trébol** *nm* (a) *(planta)* clover (b) **tréboles** *(naipes)* clubs

**trece** *núm* thirteen; **mantenerse** *o* **seguir en sus t.** to stick to one's guns; *ver también* **seis**

**treceavo, -a** *núm (fracción)* thirteenth; **la treceava parte** a thirteenth

**trecho** *nm* *(espacio)* distance; *(tiempo)* time, while; **de t. en t.** every so often

**tregua** *nf* truce; *Fig* respite

**treinta** *núm* thirty; **los (años) t.** the Thirties; *ver también* **seis**

**treintañero, -a** *adj & nm,f* *Fam* thirtysomething

**treintavo, -a** *núm (fracción)* thirtieth; **la treintava parte** a thirtieth

**treintena** *nf* thirty; **andará por la t.** he must be about thirty; **una t. de...** *(unos treinta)* about thirty...; *(treinta)* thirty...

**trekking** *nm* hiking

**tremebundo, -a** *adj* terrifying

**tremenda** *nf* **tomar** *o* **tomarse algo a la t.** to take sth hard

**tremendismo** *nm* (a) (*exageración*) alarmism (b) *Lit* = gloomy Spanish post-war realism

**tremendista** *adj & nmf* (*exagerado*) alarmist

**tremendo, -a** *adj* (a) (*enorme*) tremendous, enormous (b) (*enfadado*) **ponerse t.** to get very angry

**trementina** *nf* turpentine

**tremolar** *vi Formal* to wave, to flutter

**tremolina** *nf* row, uproar

**trémolo** *nm Mús* tremolo

**trémulo, -a** *adj* (*voz*) trembling; (*luz*) flickering

**tren** *nm* (a) (*ferrocarril*) train; **t. de alta velocidad/largo recorrido** high-speed/long-distance train; **t. de carga** *o* **mercancías** freight *o* goods train; **t. de cercanías** local train, suburban train; **t. correo** mail train; **t. de cremallera** rack *o* cog railway train; **t. directo** through train; **t. mixto** passenger and goods train; **t. semidirecto** = through train, a section of which becomes a stopping train

(b) *Mec* line; **t. de aterrizaje** undercarriage, landing gear; **t. de lavado** car wash

(c) *Fig* (*estilo*) **vivir a todo t.** to live in style; **t. de vida** lifestyle

(d) (*expresiones*) *Fam* **estar como (para parar) un t.** to be really gorgeous; *Fam* **nos dieron comida como para parar un t.** (*en grandes cantidades*) they gave us enough food to feed an army; **ir a buen t.** to be going well; *Fig* **perder el t.** to miss the boat; *Fig* **subirse al t.** to climb on the bandwagon

**trena** *nf muy Fam* nick, slammer

**trenca** *nf* duffle coat

**trence** *etc ver* **trenzar**

**trencilla** *nm Dep Fam* ref

**trenza** *nf* (a) (*de pelo*) plait; (*de fibras*) braid (b) *Culin* = sweet bun made of plaited dough

**trenzado, -a 1** *adj* plaited

**2** *nm* (a) (*peinado*) plait (b) (*en danza*) entrechat

**trenzar** [16] *vt* (a) (*pelo*) to plait (b) (*fibras*) to braid

**trepa** *nmf Fam Pey* social climber

**trepador, -ora 1** *adj* **planta trepadora** climbing plant

**2** *nm,f Fam* social climber

**trepanación** *nf* trepanation

**trepanar** *vt* to trepan

**trepar 1** *vt* to climb

**2** *vi* (a) (*subir*) to climb (b) *Fam Fig* (*medrar*) to be a social climber

**trepidación** *nf* shaking, vibration

**trepidante** *adj* (a) (*rápido, vivo*) frenetic (b) (*que tiembla*) shaking, vibrating

**trepidar** *vi* to shake, to vibrate

**tres 1** *núm* three; *Fam* **de t. al cuarto** cheap, third-rate; *Fam* **no ver t. en un burro** to be as blind as a bat; **t. cuartos de lo mismo** same thing; *Fam* **no le convencimos ni a la de t.** there was no way we could convince him; *ver también* **seis**

**2** *nm inv* **t. cuartos** (*abrigo*) three-quarter-length coat

**3** *nm* **t. en raya** *Br* noughts and crosses, *US* tick-tack-toe

**trescientos, -as** *núm* three hundred; *ver también* **seis**

**tresillo** *nm* (a) (*sofá*) three-piece suite (b) (*juego de naipes*) ombre, = card game (c) *Mús* triplet

**treta** *nf* (*engaño*) trick

**tri-** *prefijo* tri-

**tríada** *nf* triad

**trial** *nm Dep* trial; **t. indoor** indoor trial

**triangular** *adj* triangular

**triángulo** *nm* (a) *Mat & Mús* triangle; **triángulo equilátero/rectángulo** equilateral/right-angled triangle; **triángulo escaleno/isósceles** scalene/isosceles triangle (b) *Fam* **t. amoroso** love triangle

**triatlón** *nm Dep* triathlon

**tribal** *adj* tribal

**tribalismo** *nm* tribalism

**tribu** *nf* tribe; **t. urbana** = identifiable social group, such as punks or yuppies, made up of young people living in urban areas

**tribulación** *nf* tribulation

**tribuna** *nf* (a) (*estrado*) rostrum, platform; (*del jurado*) jury box (b) *Dep* (*localidad*) stand; (*graderío*) grandstand; **t. de prensa** press box (c) *Prensa* **t. libre** open forum

**tribunal** *nm* (a) (*de justicia*) court; **llevar a alguien/acudir a los tribunales** to take sb/go to court; **T. Constitucional** Constitutional Court; **T. de Cuentas** (*español*) ≃ National Audit Office; (*europeo*) Court of Audit; **T. Supremo** = Spanish Supreme Court; **T. Tutelar de Menores** Juvenile Court (b) (*de examen*) board of examiners; (*de concurso*) panel

**tributable** *adj* taxable

**tributación** *nf* (a) (*impuesto*) tax (b) (*sistema*) taxation

**tributar 1** *vt* (*homenaje*) to pay; **t. respeto** *o* **admiración a** to have respect *o* admiration for

**2** *vi* (*pagar impuestos*) to pay taxes

**tributario, -a 1** *adj* tax; **sistema t.** tax system; **derecho t.** tax law

**2** *nm,f* taxpayer

**tributo** nm (a) (impuesto) tax (b) Fig (precio) price (c) (homenaje) tribute

**tricéfalo, -a** adj three-headed

**tricentenario** nm tricentenary

**tríceps** nm inv triceps

**triciclo** nm tricycle

**tricolor 1** adj tricolour, three-coloured
**2** nf tricolour

**tricornio** nm three-cornered hat

**tricot** nm inv knitting

**tricotar** vt & vi to knit

**tricotosa** nf knitting machine

**tridente** nm trident

**tridimensional** adj three-dimensional

**trienal** adj triennial, three-yearly

**trienio** nm (a) (tres años) three years (b) (paga) three-yearly salary increase

**trifásico, -a** adj (a) Elec three-phase (b) (de tres fases) three-part

**trifulca** nf Fam row, squabble

**trigal** nm wheat field

**trigésimo, -a** núm thirtieth

**trigo** nm wheat

**trigonometría** nf trigonometry

**trigueño, -a** adj (tez) olive; (cabello) corn-coloured

**triguero, -a** adj (del trigo) wheat; **espárrago t.** wild asparagus

**trilateral** adj trilateral

**trilero, -a** nm,f Fam = person who runs a game such as find-the-lady, the shell game etc, where people bet on which is the correct card, shell etc out of three

**trilingüe** adj trilingual

**trilita** nf trinitrotoluene, TNT

**trilla** nf (a) (acción) threshing (b) (tiempo) threshing time o season

**trillado, -a** adj Fig well-worn, trite

**trillador, -ora 1** adj threshing
**2** nm,f (persona) thresher

**trilladora** nf (máquina) threshing machine

**trillar** vt to thresh

**trillizo, -a** nm,f triplet

**trilogía** nf trilogy

**trimestral** adj three-monthly, quarterly; **exámenes/notas trimestrales** end-of-term exams/marks

**trimestre** nm three months, quarter; Educ term

**trimotor 1** adj three-engined
**2** nm three-engined aeroplane

**trinar** vi to chirp, to warble; Fam Fig **está que trina** she's fuming

**trinca** nf trio

**trincar** [61] vt Fam to grab; **han trincado al ladrón** they've caught the thief

**trincha** nf strap

**trinchante** nm (a) (cuchillo) carving knife (b) (tenedor) meat fork

**trinchar** vt to carve

**trinchera** nf Mil trench

**trineo** nm (pequeño) sledge; (grande) sleigh

**Trinidad** nf la **(Santísima) T.** the (Holy) Trinity

**Trinidad y Tobago** n Trinidad and Tobago

**trinitario, -a** adj & nm,f Rel Trinitarian

**trinitrotolueno** nm trinitrotoluene

**trino** nm (de pájaros) chirp; Mús trill

**trinque** etc ver **trincar**

**trinquete** nm Náut foremast

**trío** nm (en general) trio; (de naipes) three of a kind

**tripa** nf (a) (intestino) gut, intestine; Fam Fig **echar las tripas** to throw up, to puke; Fam Fig **hacer de tripas corazón** to pluck up one's courage; Fam Fig **¿qué t. se te ha roto?** what's up with you, then?, what's bugging you?; Fam Fig **revolverle las tripas a alguien** to turn sb's stomach (b) Fam (barriga) gut, belly; **está echando t.** he's getting a pot belly o a bit of a gut (c) Fam Fig **tripas** (interior) insides

**tripartito, -a** adj tripartite

**tripi** nm muy Fam (de LSD) tab

**triple 1** adj triple
**2** nm (a) **el t.** three times as much; **el t. de gente** three times as many people (b) Elec three-way adapter

**triplicado** nm second copy, triplicate; **por t.** in triplicate

**triplicar** [61] **1** vt to triple, to treble
**2 triplicarse** vpr to triple, to treble

**trípode** nm tripod

**Trípoli** n Tripoli

**tripón, -ona** nm,f Fam paunchy o pot-bellied person

**tríptico** nm (a) Arte triptych (b) (folleto) leaflet (folded twice to form three parts)

**triptongo** nm Gram triphthong

**tripudo, -a** nm,f Fam paunchy o pot-bellied person

**tripulación** nf crew

**tripulante** nmf crew member

**tripular** vt to man

**triquina** nf trichina

**triquinosis** nf inv trichinosis

**triquiñuela** nf Fam (truco) trick

**triquitraque** nm (apagado) creaking; (fuerte) rattling

**tris: en un tris** loc adv Fig **estar en un t. de** to be within a whisker of

**trisílabo, -a** *Gram***1** *adj* trisyllabic
  **2** *nm,f* three-syllable word

**triste** *adj* **(a)** *(en general)* sad; *Fig (día, tiempo, paisaje)* gloomy, dreary; *(color, vestido, luz)* pale, faded; **es t. que...** it's a shame *o* pity that... **(b)** *(humilde)* poor; **un t. viejo** a poor old man; **un t. sueldo** a miserable salary **(c) ni un t....** not a single...

**tristeza** *nf (en general)* sadness; *(de paisaje, día)* gloominess, dreariness; *(de color, vestido, luz)* paleness

**tristón, -ona** *adj* rather sad *o* miserable

**tritón** *nm* newt

**trituración** *nf* grinding, crushing

**triturador** *nm (de basura)* waste-disposal unit; *(de papeles)* shredder; *(de ajos)* garlic press

**trituradora** *nf* crushing machine, grinder

**triturar** *vt* **(a)** *(moler, desmenuzar)* to crush, to grind; *(papel)* to shred **(b)** *(mascar)* to chew

**triunfador, -ora 1** *adj* winning, victorious
  **2** *nm,f* winner

**triunfal** *adj* triumphant

**triunfalismo** *nm* triumphalism

**triunfalista** *adj* triumphalist

**triunfante** *adj* victorious; **salir t.** to win, to emerge triumphant *o* victorious

**triunfar** *vi* **(a)** *(vencer)* to win, to triumph **(b)** *(tener éxito)* to succeed, to be successful

**triunfo** *nm* **(a)** *(victoria)* triumph; *(en encuentro, elecciones)* victory, win; *Fam* **le costó un t. hacerlo** it was a great effort for him to do it **(b)** *(en juegos de naipes)* trump; **sin t.** no trump

**triunvirato** *nm* triumvirate

**trivial** *adj* trivial

**trivialidad** *nf* triviality

**trivializar** [16] *vt* to trivialize

**trizas** *nfpl* **hacer t. algo** *(hacer añicos)* to smash sth to pieces; *(desgarrar)* to tear sth to shreds; *Fig* **hacer t. a alguien** to tear *o* pull sb to pieces; *Fig* **estar hecho t.** *(persona)* to be shattered

**trocar** [69] **1** *vt* **(a)** *(transformar)* **t. algo (en algo)** to change sth (into sth) **(b)** *(intercambiar)* to swap, to exchange **(c)** *(malinterpretar)* to mix up
  **2 trocarse** *vpr (transformarse)* **trocarse (en)** to change (into)

**trocear** *vt* to cut up (into pieces)

**trocha** *nf Am* path

**troche: a troche y moche** *loc adv* haphazardly

**trofeo** *nm* trophy

**troglodita 1** *adj* **(a)** *(cavernícola)* cave dwelling **(b)** *Fam (bárbaro, tosco)* rough, brutish
  **2** *nmf* **(a)** *(cavernícola)* cave dweller **(b)** *Fam (bárbaro, tosco)* brute

**troika** *nf* troika

**trola** *nf Fam* fib, lie

**trolebús** *( pl* **trolebuses***)* *nm* trolleybus

**trolero, -a** *Fam***1** *adj* fibbing, lying
  **2** *nm,f* fibber, liar

**tromba** *nf* waterspout; *Fig* **entrar en t.** to burst in; **t. de agua** heavy downpour

**trombo** *nm* thrombus

**trombón** *nm Mús (instrumento)* trombone; *(músico)* trombonist; **t. de pistones** *o* **de llaves** valve trombone; **t. de varas** slide trombone

**trombosis** *nf inv* thrombosis

**trompa 1** *nf* **(a)** *Mús* horn **(b)** *(de elefante)* trunk; *(de oso hormiguero)* snout; *(de insecto)* proboscis **(c)** *Anat* tube; **t. de Eustaquio/de Falopio** Eustachian/Fallopian tube **(d)** *(músico)* horn player **(e)** *Fam (borrachera)* **coger** *o* **pillar una t.** to get plastered
  **2** *adj Fam (borracho)* plastered

**trompazo** *nm* bang; **darse** *o* **pegarse un t. con** to bang into

**trompeta 1** *nf* trumpet
  **2** *nmf* trumpeter

**trompetilla** *nf* ear trumpet

**trompetista** *nmf* trumpeter

**trompicar** *vi* to stumble

**trompicón** *nm (tropezón)* stumble; **a trompicones** in fits and starts

**trompo** *nm* **(a)** *(peonza )* spinning top **(b)** *(giro)* spin

**tronada** *nf* thunderstorm

**tronado, -a** *adj Fam (loco)* crazy

**tronar** [65] **1** *v impersonal* to thunder
  **2** *vi Méx* to fail
  **3 tronarse** *vpr Am Fam* to shoot oneself

**troncal** *adj* **carretera t.** trunk road; **asignatura t.** compulsory *o* core subject

**tronchante** *adj Fam* hilarious

**tronchar 1** *vt (partir)* to snap
  **2 troncharse** *vpr Fam* **troncharse (de risa)** to split one's sides laughing

**troncho** *nm (de lechuga)* heart

**tronco** *nm* **(a)** *Anat & Bot* trunk; *(talado y sin ramas)* log; *Fam* **dormir como un t.** to sleep like a log **(b)** *Culin* **t. (de Navidad)** yule log **(c)** *Univ* **t. común** compulsory subjects **(d)** *Fam (compañero)* pal, *Br* mate; **¿qué pasa, t.?** how's it going, mate?

**tronera** *nf* **(a)** *Arquit & Hist* embrasure **(b)** *(en billar)* pocket

**trono** *nm* throne

**tropa** *nf* **(a)** *Mil (no oficiales)* rank and file; *(ejército)* troops; **tropas de asalto** assault troops **(b)** *Fam (multitud)* troop, flock

**tropecientos, -as** *adj inv Fam* hundreds (and hundreds) of, umpteen

**tropel** *nm* (a) *(de personas)* mob, crowd; **en t.** in a mad rush, en masse (b) *(de cosas)* mass, heap

**tropelía** *nf* outrage

**tropezar** [19] 1 *vi (trompicar)* to trip o stumble (**con** on); **t. con** *(problema, persona)* to run into, to come across

2 **tropezarse** *vpr Fam (encontrarse)* to bump into each other, to come across one another; **tropezarse con alguien** to bump into sb

**tropezón** *nm* (a) *(tropiezo)* trip, stumble; **dar un t.** to trip up, to stumble; **a tropezones** *(hablar)* haltingly; *(moverse)* in fits and starts (b) *Fig (desacierto)* slip-up, blunder (c) *Culin* **tropezones** = finely chopped ham, boiled egg etc added as a garnish to soups or other dishes

**tropical** *adj* tropical

**trópico** *nm* tropic

**tropiece** *etc ver* **tropezar**

**tropiezo** *nm* (a) *(tropezón)* trip, stumble; **dar un t.** to trip up, to stumble (b) *Fig (impedimento)* obstacle, stumbling block; *(revés)* setback (c) *Fig (equivocación)* blunder, slip-up; *(desliz sexual)* indiscretion; **tener un t.** to commit an indiscretion

**tropismo** *nm* tropism

**tropo** *nm* figure of speech, trope

**troposfera** *nf* troposphere

**troqué** *ver* **trocar**

**troquel** *nm* (a) *(molde)* mould, die (b) *(cuchilla)* cutter

**troquelado** *nm (acuñado) (de moneda)* minting, mintage; *(de medallas)* die-casting

**troquelar** *vt (acuñar) (monedas)* to mint; *(medallas)* to cast (b) *(recortar)* to cut

**troquemos** *ver* **trocar**

**trotamundos** *nmf inv* globe-trotter

**trotar** *vi* to trot; *Fam Fig (andar mucho)* to dash o run around

**trote** *nm* (a) *(de caballo)* trot; **al t.** at a trot (b) *Fam (actividad)* **no estar para (estos) trotes** not to be up to it o to that kind of thing; **le he dado un buen t. a esta chaqueta** I've got good wear out of this jacket

**trotskismo** [tros'kismo] *nm* Trotskyism

**trotskista** [tros'kista] *adj & nmf* Trotskyite

**troupe** [trup, 'trupe] *( pl* **troupes** *) nf* troupe

**trova** *nf Lit* lyric

**trovador** *nm* troubadour

**troyano, -a** *adj & nm,f* Trojan

**trozo** *nm (pedazo)* piece; *(de obra)* extract; *(de película)* snippet; **hacer algo a trozos** to do sth bit by bit; **cortar algo en trozos** to cut sth into pieces

**trucaje** *nm* trick effect; **t. fotográfico** trick photography

**trucar** [61] *vt* to doctor; **t. el motor** to soup up the engine; **esta foto está trucada** this is a trick photograph

**trucha** *nf (pez)* trout; **t. arcoiris** rainbow trout; *Culin* **t. a la navarra** = fried trout stuffed with ham

**truchero, -a** *adj* **río t.** trout river

**truco** *nm* (a) *(trampa, engaño)* trick (b) *(habilidad, técnica)* knack; **pillarle el t. (a algo)** to get the knack (of sth); **tiene t.** there's a knack to it; **t. publicitario** advertising gimmick

**truculencia** *nf* horror, terror

**truculento, -a** *adj* horrifying, terrifying

**truena** *ver* **tronar**

**trueno** *nm* (a) *Meteo* clap of thunder; **truenos** thunder (b) *Fig (ruido)* thunder, boom

**trueque 1** *ver* **trocar**

2 *nm (intercambio)* exchange, swap; *Com & Hist* barter

**trufa** *nf (hongo, bombón)* truffle

**trufar** *vt Culin* to stuff with truffles

**truhán, -ana 1** *adj* crooked

2 *nm,f* rogue, crook

**trullo** *nm muy Fam* slammer, nick

**truncado, -a** *adj* (a) *(frustrado) (vida, carrera)* cut short; *(planes, ilusiones)* ruined (b) *Mat* truncated

**truncar** [61] *vt (frustrar) (vida, carrera)* to cut short; *(planes, ilusiones)* to spoil, to ruin

**truque** *etc ver* **trucar**

**trust** [trusd] *( pl* **trusts** *) nm* trust, cartel

**TS** *nm (abrev de* **Tribunal Supremo** *)* = Spanish Supreme Court

**tsé-tsé** *adj inv* **mosca t.** tsetse fly

**tu** *( pl* **tus** *) adj poses* your; **tu casa** your house; **tus libros** your books

**tú**

> Usually omitted in Spanish except for emphasis or contrast.

*pron personal* you; **tú te llamas Sara** your name is Sara; **es más alta que tú** she's taller than you; **hablar** *o* **tratar de tú a alguien** = to address sb as "tú", i.e. informally

**tuareg** *adj inv & mf inv* Tuareg

**tuba** *nf* tuba

**tuberculina** *nf* tuberculin

**tubérculo** *nm* tuber, root vegetable

**tuberculosis** *nf inv* tuberculosis

**tuberculoso, -a 1** *adj* (a) *Med* tuberculous (b) *Bot* tuberous

2 *nm,f* tuberculosis sufferer

**tubería** *nf* (a) *(cañerías)* pipes, pipework (b) *(tubo)* pipe

**tubo** nm (a) *(tubería)* pipe; **t. del desagüe** drainpipe; *Aut* **t. de escape** exhaust (pipe) (b) *(recipiente)* tube; **t. de ensayo** test tube; **t. fluorescente** fluorescent light strip (c) *Anat* tract; **t. digestivo** digestive tract, alimentary canal (d) *Fam* **por un t.** a hell of a lot (e) *Fam (de cerveza)* = tall glass of beer

**tubular 1** *adj* tubular
 **2** nm bicycle tyre

**tucán** nm toucan

**tuerca** nf nut; **apretar las tuercas a alguien** to tighten the screws on sb

**tuerce** *ver* **torcer**

**tuerto, -a 1** *adj (sin un ojo)* one-eyed; *(ciego de un ojo)* blind in one eye
 **2** nm,f *(sin un ojo)* one-eyed person; *(ciego de un ojo)* person who is blind in one eye

**tuerzo** *ver* **torcer**

**tueste** nm **t. natural** medium roast; **t. torrefacto** high roast

**tuesto** *etc ver* **tostar**

**tuétano** nm (a) *Anat (bone)* marrow (b) *Fig (meollo)* crux, heart; **hasta el t.** o **los tuétanos** to the core; **mojado hasta los tuétanos** soaked through o to the skin

**tufarada** nf waft

**tufillo** nm whiff

**tufo** nm (a) *Fam (mal olor)* stench, foul smell (b) *(emanación)* vapour

**tugurio** nm hovel

**tul** nm tulle

**tulipa** nf (a) *(tulipán)* tulip (b) *(de lámpara)* tulip-shaped lampshade

**tulipán** nm tulip

**tullido, -a 1** *adj* paralyzed, crippled
 **2** nm,f cripple, disabled person

**tullir** vt to paralyze, to cripple

**tumba** nf (a) *(derribar)* grave, tomb; *Fam* **a t. abierta** at breakneck speed; *Fam* **ser (como) una t.** to be as silent as the grave

**tumbar 1** vt (a) *(derribar)* to knock over o down; *Fam Fig* **tiene un olor que tumba** it stinks to high heaven (b) *(reclinar)* **t. al paciente** lie the patient down (c) *Fam Fig (suspender)* to fail
 **2 tumbarse** vpr (a) *(acostarse)* to lie down (b) *(repantigarse)* to lounge, to stretch out

**tumbo** nm jolt, jerk; **dar tumbos** o **un t.** *(coche)* to jolt, to jerk; *Fig* **ir dando tumbos** *(persona)* to have a lot of ups and downs

**tumbona** nf *(en la playa)* deck chair; *(en el jardín)* (sun) lounger

**tumefacción** nf swelling

**tumefacto, -a** *adj* swollen

**tumor** nm tumour

**tumoración** nf lump, swelling

**túmulo** nm (a) *(sepulcro)* tomb (b) *(montecillo)* burial mound (c) *(catafalco)* catafalque

**tumulto** nm (a) *(disturbio)* riot, disturbance (b) *(alboroto)* uproar, tumult

**tumultuoso, -a** *adj* (a) *(conflictivo)* tumultuous, riotous (b) *(turbulento)* rough, stormy

**tuna** nf (a) *(agrupación musical)* = group of student minstrels (b) *Am* prickly pear

**tunante, -a** nm,f crook, scoundrel

**tunco** nm *Am* pig

**tunda** nf *Fam* (a) *(paliza)* beating, thrashing (b) *(esfuerzo)* drag, exhausting job

**tundra** nf tundra

**tunecino, -a** *adj & nm,f* Tunisian

**túnel** nm tunnel; *Fig* **salir del t.** to turn the corner; *Dep* **hacerle el t. a alguien** to nutmeg sb; **T. del Canal de la Mancha** Channel Tunnel; *Aut* **t. de lavado** car wash

**Túnez** n (a) *(capital)* Tunis (b) *(país)* Tunisia

**tungsteno** nm tungsten

**túnica** nf tunic

**Tunicia** n Tunisia

**tuno, -a** nm,f (a) *(tunante)* rogue, scoundrel (b) *(músico)* student minstrel

**tuntún** nm **al (buen) t.** without thinking

**tupamaro, -a** nm,f *Pol* = member of a Uruguayan Marxist urban guerrilla group of the 1960s and 70s, Tupamaro

**tupé** nm (a) *(cabello)* quiff (b) *Fam Fig (atrevimiento)* cheek, nerve

**tupido, -a** *adj* thick, dense

**tupir** vt to pack tightly

**tupperware®** [taper'wer] nm Tupperware®

**turba** nf (a) *(combustible)* peat, turf (b) *(muchedumbre)* mob

**turbación** nf (a) *(desconcierto)* upset, disturbance (b) *(vergüenza)* embarrassment

**turbador, -ora** *adj* (a) *(desconcertante)* disconcerting, troubling (b) *(emocionante)* upsetting, disturbing

**turbante** nm turban

**turbar 1** vt (a) *(alterar)* to disturb (b) *(emocionar)* to upset (c) *(desconcertar)* to trouble, to disconcert
 **2 turbarse** vpr *(emocionarse)* to get upset

**turbera** nf peat bog

**turbiedad** nf (a) *(de líquido)* cloudiness (b) *Fig (de negocios)* shadiness

**turbina** nf turbine

**turbio, -a** *adj* (a) *(líquido)* cloudy (b) *(vista)* blurred (c) *Fig (negocio)* shady (d) *Fig (época, periodo)* turbulent, troubled

**turbión** nm downpour

**turbo** nm turbocharger; **poner el t.** to put one's foot down (on the accelerator)

**turbodiesel** *adj* **motor t.** turbocharged diesel engine

**turbopropulsor** *nm* turboprop

**turborreactor** *nm* turbojet (engine)

**turbulencia** *nf* (a) *(de fluido)* turbulence (b) *(alboroto)* uproar, clamour

**turbulento, -a** *adj* (a) *(situación, aguas)* turbulent (b) *(persona)* unruly, rebellious

**turco, -a 1** *adj* Turkish
**2** *nm,f (persona)* Turk
**3** *nm (lengua)* Turkish

**turcochipriota 1** *adj* Turkish-Cypriot
**2** *nmf* Turkish Cypriot

**turgente** *adj (formas, muslos)* well-rounded

**turismo** *nm* (a) *(actividad)* tourism; **hacer t. (por)** to go touring (round) (b) *Aut* private car

**turista** *nmf* tourist

**turístico, -a** *adj* tourist; **atracción turística** tourist attraction

**Turkmenistán** *n* Turkmenistan

**turmalina** *nf* tourmaline

**túrmix**® *nf inv* blender, liquidizer

**turnarse** *vpr* to take turns (**con** with)

**turnedó** *(pl* **turnedós)** *nm* tournedos

**turno** *nm* (a) *(tanda)* turn, go (b) *(de trabajo)* shift; **t. de día/noche** day/night shift; **de t.** on duty; **el médico de t.** the doctor on duty; **el gracioso de t.** the inevitable smart alec

**turolense 1** *adj* of/from Teruel
**2** *nmf* person from Teruel

**turón** *nm* polecat

**turquesa 1** *nf (mineral)* turquoise
**2** *adj inv (color)* turquoise
**3** *nm (color)* turquoise

**Turquía** *n* Turkey

**turrón** *nm* = Christmas sweet similar to marzipan or nougat, made with almonds and honey

**turulato, -a** *adj Fam* flabbergasted, dumbfounded

**tururú** *interj Fam* ¡t.! get away!, you must be joking!

**tute** *nm* (a) *(juego)* = card game similar to whist (b) *Fam Fig (trabajo intenso)* hard slog; **darse** *o* **pegarse un (buen) t.** *(trabajar)* to slog away

**tutear 1** *vt* = to address as "tú", i.e. informally
**2 tutearse** *vpr* = to address each other as "tú", i.e. informally

**tutela** *nf* (a) *Der* guardianship (b) *(cargo)* responsibility (**de** for); **bajo la t. de** under the protection of

**tutelaje** *nm Der* guardianship

**tutelar 1** *adj* (a) *Der* tutelary (b) *(protector)* protecting
**2** *vt* to act as guardian to

**tuteo** *nm* = use of "tú", familiar form of address

**tutiplén: a tutiplén** *loc adv* to excess, in abundance

**tutor, -ora** *nm,f* (a) *Der* guardian (b) *(profesor) (privado)* tutor; *(de un curso)* form teacher

**tutoría** *nf* (a) *Der* guardianship (b) *(clase)* ≃ form class

**tutti frutti, tuttifrutti** *nm* tutti frutti

**tutú** *(pl* **tutús)** *nm* tutu

**tutuma** *nf Am Fam* = variety of nut

**tuviera** *etc ver* **tener**

**tuyo, -a 1** *adj poses* yours; **este libro es t.** this book is yours; **un amigo t.** a friend of yours; **no es asunto t.** it's none of your business
**2** *pron poses* **el t.** yours; **el tuyo es rojo** yours is red; *Fam* **esta es la tuya** this is the chance you've been waiting for *o* your big chance; **lo tuyo es el teatro** *(lo que haces bien)* you should be on the stage; *Fam* **los tuyos** *(tu familia)* your folks; *(tu bando)* your lot, your side

**TV** *nf (abrev de* **televisión)** TV

**TV3** [teβe'tres] *nf (abrev de* **Televisión de Cataluña)** = Catalan television channel

**TVE** *nf (abrev de* **Televisión Española)** = Spanish state television network

**TVG** *nf (abrev de* **Televisión de Galicia)** = Galician television channel

**TWA** ['tua] *nf (abrev de* **Trans World Airlines)** TWA

**twist** [twist] *nm inv* twist *(dance)*

# U

**U, u**[1] [u] *nf (letra)* U, u

**u**[2] *conj* or; *ver también* **o**

**ubérrimo, -a** *adj Formal (tierra)* extremely fertile; *(vegetación)* luxuriant, abundant

**ubicación** *nf* position, location

**ubicado, -a** *adj (edificio)* located, situated

**ubicar** [61] **1** *vt (en general)* to place, to position; *(edificio)* to locate

**2 ubicarse** *vpr (edificio)* to be situated, to be located

**ubicuidad** *nf* ubiquity; *Fig* **tiene el don de la u.** he seems to be everywhere at once

**ubicuo, -a** *adj* ubiquitous

**ubique** *etc ver* **ubicar**

**ubre** *nf* udder

**UCD** *nf (abrev de* **Unión de Centro Democrático**) = former Spanish political party at the centre of the political spectrum

**UCI** ['uθi] *nf (abrev de* **unidad de cuidados intensivos**) ICU, intensive care unit

**Ucrania** *n* the Ukraine

**ucraniano, -a** *adj & nm,f* Ukrainian

**Ud.** *abrev de* **usted**

**UDC** *nf (abrev de* **universal decimal classification**) UDC

**Uds.** *abrev de* **ustedes**

**UE** *nf (abrev de* **Unión Europea**) EU

**UEFA** ['uefa] *nf (abrev de* **Union of European Football Associations**) UEFA

**UEM** [uem] *nf (abrev de* **unión económica y monetaria**) EMU

**UEO** *nf (abrev de* **Unión Europea Occidental**) WEU

**uf** *interj* ¡uf! *(expresa cansancio, calor)* phew!; *(expresa fastidio)* tut!; *(expresa repugnancia)* ugh!

**ufanarse** *vpr* **u. de** to boast about

**ufano, -a** *adj* **(a)** *(satisfecho)* proud, pleased **(b)** *(engreído)* boastful, conceited **(c)** *(lozano)* luxuriant, lush

**ufología** *nf* ufology

**ufólogo, -a** *nm,f* ufologist

**Uganda** *n* Uganda

**ugandés, -esa** *adj & nm,f* Ugandan

**ugetista 1** *adj* = of or belonging to the "UGT"

**2** *nmf* = member of the "UGT"

**UGT** *nf (abrev de* **Unión General de los Trabajadores**) = major socialist Spanish trade union

**UHF** *nf (abrev de* **ultra high frequency**) UHF

**UHT** *adj (abrev de* **ultra heat treated**) UHT

**ujier** *(pl* ujieres) *nm* usher

**ukelele** *nm* ukelele

**Ulan-Bator** *n* Ulan-Bator

**úlcera** *nf Med* ulcer; **ú. de estómago** stomach ulcer

**ulceración** *nf* ulceration

**ulcerar 1** *vt* to ulcerate

**2 ulcerarse** *vpr Med* to ulcerate

**ulceroso, -a** *adj* ulcerous

**Ulster** *nm* **(el)** U. Ulster

**ulterior** *adj* **(a)** *(en el tiempo)* subsequent, ulterior **(b)** *(en el espacio)* further

**ulteriormente** *adv* subsequently

**ultimación** *nf* conclusion, completion

**últimamente** *adv* recently, of late

**ultimar** *vt* **(a)** *(terminar)* to conclude, to complete **(b)** *Am (matar)* to kill

**ultimátum** *(pl* ultimátums *o* ultimatos) *nm* ultimatum

**último, -a 1** *adj* **(a)** *(en general)* last; **por ú.** lastly, finally; **ser lo ú.** *(lo final)* to come last; *(el último recurso)* to be a last resort; *(el colmo)* to be the last straw **(b)** *(más reciente)* latest, most recent; *Fam* **ser lo ú. en...** to be the latest thing in... **(c)** *(más remoto)* furthest, most remote **(d)** *(más bajo)* bottom **(e)** *(más alto)* top **(f)** *(de más atrás)* back

**2** *nm,f* **(a)** *(en fila, carrera)* **el ú.** the last (one); **llegar el ú.** to come last **(b)** *(en comparaciones, enumeraciones)* **este ú....** the latter... **(c)** *(expresiones)* **a últimos de mes** at the end of the month; **estar en las últimas** *(muriéndose)* to be on one's deathbed; *(sin dinero)* to be down to one's last penny; *(sin provisiones)* to be down to one's last provisions; *Fam* **ir a la última** to wear the latest fashion

**ultra** *adj & nmf Pol* extremist

**ultracongelado, -a** *adj* deep-frozen; **ultracongelados** deep-frozen food

**ultraconservador, -ora** *adj & nmf* ultraconservative

**ultraderecha** *nf* far right

**ultraderechista 1** *adj* far right
 **2** *nmf* extreme right-winger

**ultraizquierda** *nf* far left

**ultraizquierdista 1** *adj* far left
 **2** *nmf* extreme left-winger

**ultrajante** *adj* insulting, offensive

**ultrajar** *vt* to insult, to offend

**ultraje** *nm* insult

**ultraligero** *nm* microlight

**ultramar** *nm* overseas; **territorios de u.** overseas territories

**ultramarino, -a** *adj* overseas; **posesiones ultramarinas** overseas territories

**ultramarinos** *nmpl* (a) *(comestibles)* groceries (b) *(tienda)* grocer's (shop)

**ultramicroscopio** *nm* ultramicroscope

**ultramoderno, -a** *adj* ultramodern

**ultramontano, -a 1** *adj* (a) *Rel* ultramontane (b) *Fig (reaccionario)* reactionary
 **2** *nm,f* (a) *Rel* ultramontane (b) *Fig (reaccionario)* reactionary

**ultranza** *nf* a u. *(con decisión)* to the death; *(acérrimamente)* out-and-out

**ultrasecreto, -a** *adj* top-secret

**ultrasonido** *nm* ultrasound

**ultratumba** *nf* de u. from beyond the grave

**ultravioleta** *adj inv* ultraviolet

**ulular** *vi* (a) *(viento, lobo)* to howl (b) *(búho)* to hoot

**umbilical** *adj* **cordón u.** umbilical cord

**umbral** *nm* (a) *(de puerta, periodo)* threshold (b) *Fig (límite)* bounds, realms; **el u. de la pobreza** the poverty line

**umbrío, -a** *adj* shady

**un, una**

> **un** is used instead of **una** before feminine nouns which begin with a stressed "a" or "ha" (e.g. **un águila** an eagle; **un hacha** an axe).

**1** *artículo* a; *(ante sonido vocálico)* an; **un hombre/coche** a man/car; **una mujer/mesa** a woman/table; **una hora** an hour
 **2** *adj ver* **uno**

**unánime** *adj* unanimous

**unanimidad** *nf* unanimity; **por u.** unanimously

**unción** *nf* unction

**uncir** [74] *vt* to yoke

**UNCTAD** [uŋg'tad] *nf (abrev de* **United Nations Conference on Trade and Development)** UNCTAD

**undécimo, -a** *núm* eleventh

**underground** [ander'vraun] *adj inv* underground

**UNED** [u'neð] *nf (abrev de* **Universidad Nacional de Educación a Distancia)** = Spanish open university

**Unesco** [u'nesko] *nf (abrev de* **United Nations Educational, Scientific and Cultural Organization)** UNESCO

**ungimiento** *nm* unction

**ungir** [26] *vt* to put ointment on; *Rel* to anoint

**ungüento** *nm* ointment

**únicamente** *adv* only, solely

**unicameral** *adj* single-chamber

**Unicef** [uni'θef] *nm (abrev de* **United Nations Children's Fund)** UNICEF

**unicelular** *adj* single-cell, unicellular

**unicidad** *nf* uniqueness

**único, -a** *adj* (a) *(solo)* only; **es lo ú. que quiero** it's all I want; **lo ú. es que...** the (only) thing is..., it's just that...; **única y exclusivamente** only, exclusively (b) *(excepcional)* unique (c) *(precio, función, razón)* single

**unicornio** *nm* unicorn; **u. marino** narwhal

**unidad** *nf* (a) *(elemento)*, *Mat & Mil* unit; **25 pesetas la u.** 25 pesetas each; *Informát* **u. central de proceso** central processing unit; **u. de combate** combat unit; **u. de cuidados intensivos** *o* **vigilancia intensiva** intensive care (unit); *Informát* **u. de disco/CD-ROM** disk/CD-ROM drive; *TV* **u. móvil** mobile unit (b) *(cohesión, acuerdo)* unity

**unidireccional** *adj* unidirectional, one-way

**unido, -a** *adj (junto, reunido)* united; *(familia, amigos)* close

**unifamiliar** *adj* **vivienda u.** house *(detached, semi-detached or terraced)*

**unificación** *nf* (a) *(unión)* unification (b) *(uniformización)* standardization

**unificador, -ora** *adj* (a) *(que une)* unifying (b) *(que uniformiza)* standardizing

**unificar** [61] *vt* (a) *(unir)* to unite, to join; *(países)* to unify (b) *(uniformar)* to standardize

**uniformado, -a** *adj* (a) *(igual, normalizado)* standardized (b) *(policía, soldado)* uniformed

**uniformar** *vt* (a) *(igualar, normalizar)* to standardize (b) *(poner uniforme a)* to put into uniform

**uniforme 1** *adj (igual, normalizado)* uniform; *(superficie)* even
 **2** *nm* uniform; **de u.** in uniform

**uniformidad** *nf (igualdad, homogeneidad)* uniformity; *(de superficie)* evenness

**uniformización** *nf (normalización)* standardization

**uniformizar** [16] *vt (normalizar)* to standardize

**unilateral** *adj* unilateral

**unión** *nf* (a) *(asociación)* union; **en u. con** together with; **u. aduanera** customs union; **la U. Europea** the European Union; *Antes* **U. Soviética** Soviet Union (b) *(suma, adherimiento)* joining together (c) *Mec* join, joint

**unionismo** *nm Pol* unionism

**unionista** *Pol adj & nmf* unionist

**unipersonal** *adj* = designed for one person; **verbo u.** impersonal verb

**unir 1** *vt* (a) *(juntar) (pedazos, habitaciones)* to join; *(empresas, estados, facciones)* to unite (b) *(comunicar, conectar)* to connect, to link; **les une su pasión por la música** they share a passion for music; **u. a dos personas en matrimonio** to join two people in matrimony (c) *(combinar)* to combine (d) *(añadir)* **u. algo a algo** to add sth to sth; **u. la mantequilla con el azúcar** cream together the butter and the sugar

**2 unirse** *vpr* (a) *(juntarse)* to join together; **unirse a algo** to join sth (b) *(casarse)* **unirse en matrimonio** to join in wedlock *o* matrimony

**unisex** *adj inv* unisex

**unisexual** *adj* unisexual

**unísono** *nm* **al u.** in unison

**UNITA** [u'nita] *nf (abrev de* **Unión Nacional para la Independencia Total de Angola)** UNITA

**unitario, -a** *adj (unido, único)* single; *(de una unidad)* unitary; **precio u.** unit price

**unitarismo** *nm Rel* Unitarianism

**universal** *adj* (a) *(total)* universal (b) *(mundial)* world; **historia u.** world history; *Filosofía* **universales** universals

**universalidad** *nf* universality

**universalismo** *nm* universalism

**universalizar** [16] **1** *vt* to make widespread
**2 universalizarse** *vpr (costumbre, uso)* to become widespread

**universidad** *nf* university; **u. a distancia** *Br ≃* Open University

**universitario, -a 1** *adj* university; **estudiante u.** university student

**2** *nm,f* (a) *(estudiante)* university student (b) *(profesor)* university lecturer (c) *(licenciado)* university graduate

**universo** *nm* (a) *Astron* universe (b) *Fig (mundo)* world

**unívoco, -a** *adj* univocal, unambiguous

**UNIX** *nm Informát* UNIX

**unjo** *etc ver* **ungir**

**uno, -a**

**un** is used instead of **uno** before singular masculine nouns (e.g. **un perro** a dog; **un coche** a car).

**1** *artículo* (a) *(indefinido)* one; **un día volveré** one *o* some day I'll return; **había unos coches mal aparcados** there were some badly parked cars; **había unos 12 muchachos** there were about *o* some 12 boys there

(b) *(numeral)* one; **un hombre, un voto** one man, one vote

**2** *pron* (a) *(indefinido)* one; **coge u.** take one; **u. de vosotros** one of you; **unos... otros...** some... others...; **u. a otro, unos a otros** each other, one another; **u. y otro** both; **unos y otros** all of them

(b) *(cierta persona)* someone, somebody; **hablé con u. que te conoce** I spoke to someone who knows you; **me lo han contado unos** certain people told me so

(c) *(yo)* one; **u. ya no está para estos trotes** one isn't really up to this sort of thing any more

(d) *(expresiones)* **a una** together; **todos a una** *(a la vez)* everyone at once; **de u. en u., u. a u., u. por u.** one by one; **juntar varias cosas en una** to combine several things into one; **lo u. por lo otro** it all evens out in the end; **más de u.** many people; *(unánimemente)* as one; **una de dos** it's either one thing or the other; **una de las suyas** one of his/her/their tricks *o* pranks; **unos cuantos** a few; **u. de tantos** of many; **una y no más** once was enough, once bitten, twice shy

**3** *nm (número)* (number) one; **el u.** number one; **la fila u.** row one; **la una** *(hora)* one o'clock; *ver también* **seis**

**untar 1** *vt* (a) *(piel, cara)* to smear **(con** *o* **de** with); **u. el paté en el pan** to spread the pâté on the bread (b) *Fam Fig (sobornar)* to grease the palm of, to bribe

**2 untarse** *vpr* (a) *(embadurnarse)* **untarse la piel/cara (con** *o* **de)** to smear one's skin/face (with) (b) *Fam (enriquecerse)* to line one's pockets

**unto** *nm (grasa)* grease

**untuosidad** *nf* greasiness, oiliness

**untuoso, -a** *adj* greasy, oily

**untura** *nf* (a) *(ungüento)* ointment (b) *(grasa)* grease

**uña** *nf* (a) *(de mano)* fingernail, nail; **hacerse las uñas** to do one's nails; *también Fig* **comerse** *o* **morderse las uñas** to bite one's nails; *Fig* **con uñas y dientes** *(agarrarse)* doggedly; *(defender)* fiercely; *Fig* **ser u. y carne** to be as thick as thieves (b) *(de pie)* toenail (c) *(garra)* claw; **enseñar** *o* **sacar las uñas** to get one's claws out (d) *(casco)* hoof

**uñero** *nm* (a) *(inflamación)* whitlow (b) *(uña encarnada)* ingrowing nail

**uperisación, uperización** *nf* U.H.T. treatment

**uperisar, uperizar** [16] *vt* to give U.H.T. treatment

**Ural** *nm* **el U.** the River Ural

**Urales** *nmpl* **los U.** the Urals

**uralita®** *nf Constr* = material made of asbestos and cement, usually corrugated and used mainly for roofing

**uranio** *nm* uranium

**Urano** *nm* Uranus

**urbanidad** *nf* politeness, courtesy

**urbanismo** *nm* town planning

**urbanista** *nmf* town planner

**urbanístico, -a** *adj* town-planning; **plan u.** urban development plan

**urbanización** *nf* (a) *(zona residencial)* (private) housing development (b) *(acción)* urbanization

**urbanizador, -ora 1** *adj* developing

  **2** *nm,f* developer

**urbanizar** [16] *vt* to develop, to urbanize

**urbano, -a** *adj* urban, city; **autobús u.** city bus; **guardia u.** local policeman, *f* local policewoman

**urbe** *nf* large city

**urdimbre** *nf* (a) *(de hilos)* warp (b) *(plan)* plot

**urdir** *vt* (a) *(plan)* to plot, to forge (b) *(hilos)* to warp

**urea** *nf* urea

**uremia** *nf* uraemia

**uréter** *nm* ureter

**uretra** *nf* urethra

**urgencia** *nf* (a) *(cualidad)* urgency (b) *(necesidad)* urgent need; **en caso de u.** in case of emergency; **urgencias** casualty (department)

**urgente** *adj* (a) *(apremiante)* urgent (b) *(correo)* express

**urgir** [26] *v impersonal* to be urgently necessary; **me urge hacerlo** I urgently need to do it

**úrico, -a** *adj* uric

**urinario, -a 1** *adj* urinary

  **2** *nm* urinal, *US* comfort station

**URL** *nm Informát (abrev de* **uniform resource location)** URL

**urna** *nf* (a) *(caja de cristal)* glass case; *(para votar)* ballot box; **acudir a la urnas** to go to the polls (b) *(vasija)* urn; **u. cineraria** urn *(for somebody's ashes)*

**uro** *nm* aurochs, urus

**urogallo** *nm* capercaillie

**urogenital** *adj* urogenital

**urología** *nf* urology

**urólogo, -a** *nm,f* urologist

**urraca** *nf* magpie

**URSS** [urs] *nf (abrev de* **Unión de Repúblicas Socialistas Soviéticas)** *Antes* USSR

**ursulina** *nf* (a) *Rel* Ursuline (nun) (b) *Fig (mujer recatada)* prudish woman

**urticaria** *nf* nettle rash, urticaria

**Uruguay** *nm* **(el) U.** Uruguay

**uruguayo, -a** *adj & nm,f* Uruguayan

**usado, -a** *adj* (a) *(utilizado)* used; **muy u.** widely-used (b) *(gastado)* worn-out, worn (c) *(de segunda mano)* second-hand

**usanza** *nf* custom, usage; **a la vieja** *o* **antigua u.** in the old way *o* style

**usar 1** *vt* (a) *(utilizar)* to use (b) *(llevar puesto)* to wear

  **2** *vi* **u. de** to use, to make use of

  **3 usarse** *vpr* (a) *(utilizarse)* to be used (b) *(llevarse puesto)* to be worn (c) *(estar de moda)* **ya casi no se usan las máquinas de escribir** people hardly use typewriters any more

**usía** *nmf Anticuado* Your Lordship, *f* Your Ladyship

**uso** *nm* (a) *(utilización)* use; **hacer u. de** *(utilizar)* to make use of, to use; *(de prerrogativa, derecho)* to exercise; **de u. externo** *(medicamento)* for external use only; **fuera de u.** out of use, obsolete; **tener el u. de la palabra** to have the floor; **u. de razón** age of reason (b) *(costumbre)* custom; **al u.** fashionable; **al u. andaluz** in the Andalusian style (c) *Ling* usage (d) *(desgaste)* wear and tear

**usted** *pron personal (tratamiento de respeto)* you; **ustedes** you *(plural)*; **contesten ustedes a las preguntas** please answer the questions; **de u./ustedes** yours; **me gustaría hablar con u.** I'd like to talk to you; **hablar** *o* **tratar de u. a alguien** = to address sb as "usted", i.e. formally

**usual** *adj* usual; **lo u. es hacerlo así** people usually do it this way; **no es u. verlo por aquí** it's unusual to see him here

**usuario, -a** *nm,f* user

**usufructo** *nm Der* usufruct, use

**usufructuar** [4] *vt Der* to have the usufruct *o* use of

**usufructuario, -a** *adj & nm,f Der* usufructuary

**usura** *nf* usury

**usurero, -a** *nm,f* usurer

**usurpación** *nf* usurpation

**usurpador, -ora 1** *adj* usurping

  **2** *nm,f* usurper

**usurpar** *vt* to usurp

**utensilio** *nm (instrumento)* tool, implement; *Culin* utensil; **utensilios de pesca** fishing tackle

**uterino, -a** *adj* uterine

**útero** *nm* womb, uterus

**útil 1** *adj* (**a**) *(beneficioso, aprovechable)* useful (**b**) *(eficiente)* helpful

  **2** *nm (herramienta)* tool; *Agr* implement

**utilería** *nf (útiles)* equipment; *Cine & Teatro* props

**utilidad** *nf* (**a**) *(cualidad)* usefulness (**b**) *(beneficio)* profit

**utilitario, -a1** *adj* (**a**) *(persona)* utilitarian (**b**) *Aut* run-around, utility

  **2** *nm Aut* run-around car, utility car

**utilitarismo** *nm* utilitarianism

**utilización** *nf* use

**utilizar** [16] *vt (usar)* to use

**utillaje** *nm* tools

**utopía** *nf* utopia

**utópico, -a** *adj* utopian

**uva** *nf* grape; **de uvas a peras** once in a blue moon; **estar de mala u.** to be in a bad mood; **tener mala u.** to be a bad sort, to be a nasty piece of work; **uvas de la suerte** = grapes eaten for good luck as midnight chimes on New Year's Eve; **nos van a dar las uvas** we're going to be here for ever!, this is taking for ever!

**UVI** ['uβi] *nf (abrev de **unidad de vigilancia intensiva**)* ICU, intensive care unit

**úvula** *nf* uvula

**Uzbekistán** *n* Uzbekistan

# V

**V, v** ['uβe] *nf (letra)* V, v; **v doble** W

**v.** *(abrev de* **véase)** v., vide

**va** *ver* **ir**

**vaca** *nf* (a) *(animal)* cow; *Fam* **estar como una v.** *(gordo)* to be as fat as an elephant; **v. lechera/sagrada** dairy/sacred cow; **v. marina** manatee; *Fam* **vacas flacas** lean years; *Fam* **vacas gordas** years of plenty (b) *(carne)* beef

**vacaciones** *nfpl* holiday, *Br* holidays, *US* vacation; **coger** *o* **tomar (las) v.** to take one's holidays; **estar/irse de v.** to be/go on holiday; **diez días de v.** ten days' holiday

**vacacional** *adj* holiday; **período v.** holiday period

**vacante 1** *adj* vacant
**2** *nf* vacancy

**vaciado** *nm* (a) *(de recipiente)* emptying (b) *(de escultura)* casting, moulding

**vaciar** [34] *vt* (a) *(recipiente)* to empty (**de** of); *(líquido)* to pour; **v. el agua de la botella** to pour the water out of the bottle (b) *(dejar hueco)* to hollow (out) (c) *Arte* to cast, to mould (d) *(texto)* to copy out

**vaciedad** *nf (tontería)* trifle

**vacilación** *nf* (a) *(duda)* hesitation; *(al elegir)* indecision (b) *(oscilación)* swaying; *(de la luz)* flickering

**vacilante** *adj* (a) *(dudoso, indeciso)* hesitant; *(al elegir)* indecisive (b) *(luz)* flickering; *(pulso)* irregular; *(paso)* swaying, unsteady

**vacilar 1** *vi* (a) *(dudar)* to hesitate; *(al elegir)* to be indecisive (b) *(voz, principios, régimen)* to falter (c) *(fluctuar) (luz)* to flicker; *(pulso)* to be irregular (d) *(tambalearse)* to wobble, to sway (e) *Fam (chulear)* to swank, to show off (f) *Fam (bromear)* to take the mickey
**2** *vt Fam* **v. a alguien** *(tomar el pelo)* to take the mickey out of sb

**vacile** *nm Fam (tomadura de pelo)* joke, *Br* wind-up; **estar de v.** *(de broma)* to be kidding *o* joking

**vacilón, -ona** *Fam* **1** *adj* (a) *(chulo)* swanky (b) *(bromista)* jokey, teasing
**2** *nm,f* (a) *(chulo)* show-off (b) *(bromista)* tease
**3** *nm Am (fiesta)* party

**vacío, -a 1** *adj* empty; **v. de** *(contenido)* devoid of
**2** *nm* (a) *Fís* vacuum; **envasar al v.** to vacuum-pack (b) *(abismo, carencia)* void; **v. legal** legal vacuum; *Pol* **v. de poder** power vacuum (c) *(hueco)* space, gap (d) *(expresiones)* **caer en el v.** *(palabras)* to fall on deaf ears; **hacer el v. a alguien** to send sb to Coventry; **tener un v. en el estómago** to feel hungry

**vacuidad** *nf (trivialidad)* shallowness, vacuity

**vacuna** *nf* vaccine

**vacunación** *nf* vaccination

**vacunar 1** *vt* to vaccinate
**2 vacunarse** *vpr* to get vaccinated

**vacuno, -a 1** *adj* bovine
**2** *nm* cattle; **carne de v.** beef

**vacuo, -a** *adj (trivial)* shallow, vacuous

**vadeable** *adj* fordable

**vadear** *vt* to ford; *Fig* to overcome

**vademécum** *(pl* **vademecums)** *nm* vademecum, handbook

**vade retro** *interj Hum & Formal (márchate)* get thee gone!

**vado** *nm* (a) *(en acera)* lowered kerb; **v. permanente** *(en letrero)* keep clear at all times (b) *(de río)* ford

**Vaduz** *n* Vaduz

**vagabundear** *vi* (a) *(ser un vagabundo)* to lead a vagrant's life (b) *(vagar)* **v. (por)** to wander, to roam

**vagabundeo** *nm* vagrant's life

**vagabundo, -a 1** *adj (persona)* vagrant; *(perro)* stray
**2** *nm,f* tramp, vagrant, *US* bum

**vagamente** *adv* vaguely

**vagancia** *nf* (a) *(holgazanería)* laziness, idleness (b) *(vagabundeo)* vagrancy

**vagar** [40] *vi* **v. (por)** to wander, to roam

**vagido** *nm* = cry of a newborn baby

**vagina** *nf* vagina

**vaginal** *adj* vaginal

**vago, -a 1** *adj* (a) *(perezoso)* lazy, idle (b) *(impreciso)* vague
**2** *nm,f* lazy person, idler

**vagón** *nm (de pasajeros)* carriage; *(de mercancías)* wagon; **v. cisterna** tanker, tank wagon; **v. de mercancías** goods wagon *o* van; **v. de primera/segunda** first-class/second-class carriage; **v. restaurante** dining car, restaurant car

**vagoneta** *nf* wagon

**vaguada** *nf* valley floor

**vague** *etc ver* **vagar**

**vaguear** *vi* to laze around

**vaguedad** *nf* **(a)** *(cualidad)* vagueness **(b)** *(dicho)* vague remark

**vaguería** *nf Fam (holgazanería)* laziness, idleness

**vaharada** *nf (de olor)* whiff

**vahído** *nm* blackout, fainting fit; **me dio un v.** I fainted

**vaho** *nm* **(a)** *(vapor)* steam; *Med* **hacer vahos** to inhale (medicinal vapours) **(b)** *(aliento)* breath

**vaina** *nf* **(a)** *(en planta)* pod **(b)** *(de espada)* scabbard **(c)** *Am Fam (asunto, tontería)* bloody thing; **¡qué v.!** what a business!

**vainica** *nf* hemstitch

**vainilla** *nf* vanilla

**vainitas** *nfpl Am* green beans

**vaivén** *nm* **(a)** *(balanceo) (de barco)* swaying, rocking; *(de péndulo, columpio)* swinging **(b)** *(altibajo)* ups-and-downs

**vajilla** *nf* crockery; **una v.** a dinner service

**valdepeñas** *nm inv* Valdepeñas, = Spanish wine from the La Mancha region, usually red

**valdrá** *etc ver* **valer**

**vale 1** *nm* **(a)** *(bono)* coupon, voucher **(b)** *(entrada gratuita)* free ticket **(c)** *(comprobante)* receipt **(d)** *(pagaré)* IOU **(e)** *Col, Méx, Ven Fam (compañero)* mate

**2** *interj* **¡v.!** okay!, all right!; **¿v.?** okay?, all right?; **¡v. (ya)!** that's enough!

**valedero, -a** *adj* valid

**valedor, -ora** *nm,f* protector

**Valencia** *n* Valencia

**valencia** *nf Quím* valency

**valenciano, -a 1** *adj & nm,f* Valencian

**2** *nm (idioma)* Valencian

**valentía** *nf* **(a)** *(valor)* bravery **(b)** *(hazaña)* act of bravery

**valentón, -ona** *nm,f* **hacer el v.** to boast of one's bravery

**valer [70] 1** *vt* **(a)** *(costar) (precio)* to cost; *(tener un valor de)* to be worth; **¿cuánto vale?** how much does it cost?, how much is it?

**(b)** *(suponer)* to earn

**(c)** *(merecer)* to deserve, to be worth

**(d)** *(equivaler)* to be equivalent *o* equal to

**(e)** *(amparar)* **¡válgame Dios!** good God *o* heavens!

**2** *vi* **(a)** *(merecer aprecio)* to be worthy; **hacerse v.** to show one's worth

**(b)** *(servir)* **v. para algo** to be for sth; **eso aún vale** you can still use that; **¿para qué vale?** what's it for?

**(c)** *(ser válido)* to be valid; *(en juegos)* to be allowed

**(d)** *(ayudar)* to help, to be of use

**(e)** *(tener calidad)* to be of worth; **no v. nada** to be worthless *o* useless

**(f)** *(equivaler)* **v. por** to be worth

**(g)** *(expresiones)* **más vale tarde que nunca** better late than never; **más vale que te calles/vayas** it would be better if you shut up/left

**3** *nm* worth, value

**4** **valerse** *vpr* **(a)** *(servirse)* **valerse de algo/alguien** to use sth/sb

**(b)** *(desenvolverse)* **valerse (por sí mismo)** to manage on one's own

**valeriana** *nf* valerian, allheal

**valeroso, -a** *adj* brave, courageous

**valgo** *ver* **valer**

**valía** *nf* value, worth

**validación** *nf (de documento, billete)* validation

**validar** *vt (documento, billete)* to validate; *(resultado)* to (officially) confirm

**validez** *nf* validity; **dar v. a** to validate

**válido, -a** *adj* valid

**valido, -a** *nm,f Hist* royal adviser, éminence grise

**valiente 1** *adj* **(a)** *(valeroso)* brave **(b)** *Irón (menudo)* **¡en v. lío te has metido!** you've got yourself into some mess *o* into a fine mess!

**2** *nmf (valeroso)* brave person

**valija** *nf* **(a)** *(maleta)* case, suitcase; **v. diplomática** diplomatic bag **(b)** *(de correos)* mailbag

**valioso, -a** *adj* **(a)** *(de valor)* valuable **(b)** *(intento, esfuerzo)* worthy

**valla** *nf* **(a)** *(cerca)* fence; **v. publicitaria** billboard, hoarding **(b)** *Dep* hurdle

**vallado** *nm* fence

**Valladolid** *n* Valladolid

**vallar** *vt* to put a fence round

**valle** *nm* valley

**vallisoletano, -a** *adj* of/from Valladolid

**valón, -ona** *adj & nm,f* Walloon

**valor** *nm* **(a)** *también Mat & Mús* value; **de v.** valuable; **joyas por v. de...** jewels worth...; **sin v.** worthless; **tener v.** *(ser valioso)* to be valuable; *(ser válido)* to be valid; **v. adquisitivo** purchasing power; *Econ* **v. añadido** added value; **v. nominal** face *o* nominal value; **v. nutritivo** nutritional value

**(b)** *(importancia)* importance; **dar v. a** to give *o* attach importance to; **quitar v. a algo** to take away from sth, to diminish the importance of sth

(c) *(valentía)* bravery; **armarse de v.** to pluck up one's courage

(d) *(desvergüenza)* cheek, nerve

(e) *Fam (personaje)* **un joven v.** a young prospect

(f) **valores** *(principios)* values

(g) *Fin* **valores** securities, bonds; **valores en cartera** investments

**valoración** *nf* (a) *(de precio, pérdidas)* valuation (b) *(de mérito, cualidad, ventajas)* evaluation, assessment (c) *(revalorización)* appreciation, increase in value

**valorar** 1 *vt* (a) *(tasar, apreciar)* to value (b) *(evaluar)* to evaluate, to assess (c) *(revalorizar)* to (cause to) increase in value

2 **valorarse** *vpr* (a) *(tasarse, apreciarse)* to be valued (**en** at) (b) *(revalorizarse)* to appreciate, to increase in value

**valorización** *nf (revalorización)* appreciation, increase in value

**valorizar** [16] 1 *vt* to increase the value of

2 **valorizarse** *vpr* to increase in value

**valquiria** *nf* Valkyrie

**vals** *(pl* **valses)** *nm* waltz

**valuar** [4] *vt* to value

**valva** *nf Bot & Zool* valve

**válvula** *nf* valve; *Fig* **v. de escape** means of letting off steam; **v. de seguridad** safety valve

**vamos** *ver* **ir**

**vampiresa** *nf Fam* vamp, femme fatale

**vampirismo** *nm* vampirism

**vampiro** *nm* (a) *(personaje)* vampire (b) *(murciélago)* vampire bat

**vanagloriarse** [15] *vpr* to boast (**de** about), to show off (**de** about)

**Vancouver** *n* Vancouver

**vandálico, -a** *adj (salvaje)* vandalistic; **un acto v.** an act of vandalism

**vandalismo** *nm* vandalism

**vándalo, -a** 1 *nm,f Hist* Vandal

2 *nm Fig (salvaje)* vandal

**vanguardia** *nf* (a) *Mil* vanguard; *Fig* **ir a la v. de** to be at the forefront of (b) *(cultural)* avant-garde, vanguard

**vanguardismo** *nm* avant-garde

**vanguardista** 1 *adj* avant-garde

2 *nmf* member of the avant-garde

**vanidad** *nf* (a) *(orgullo)* vanity (b) *(inutilidad)* futility

**vanidoso, -a** 1 *adj* vain, conceited

2 *nm,f* vain person

**vano, -a** 1 *adj* (a) *(inútil, infundado)* vain; **en v.** in vain (b) *(vacío, superficial) (palabras)* shallow, superficial; *(persona)* vain, conceited

2 *nm Arquit (de puerta)* doorway

**Vanuatú** *n* Vanuatu

**vapor** *nm (emanación)* vapour; *(de agua)* steam; *Culin* **al v.** steamed; **barco de v.** steamer, steamship; **máquina de v.** steam engine; *Fís & Quím* **v. de agua** water vapour

**vaporización** *nf* (a) *(pulverización)* spraying (b) *Fís* vaporization

**vaporizador** *nm* (a) *(pulverizador)* spray (b) *(para evaporar)* vaporizer

**vaporizar** [16] 1 *vt* (a) *Fís* to vaporize (b) *(pulverizar)* to spray

2 **vaporizarse** *vpr Fís* to evaporate, to vaporize

**vaporoso, -a** *adj* (a) *(tela, vestido)* diaphanous, sheer (b) *(con vapor) (ducha, baño)* steamy; *(cielo)* hazy, misty

**vapulear** *vt* (a) *(golpear)* to beat, to thrash; *(zarandear)* to shake about (b) *Fig (criticar)* to slate; **v. los derechos de alguien** to trample on sb's rights

**vapuleo** *nm* (a) *(golpes)* beating; *(zarandeo)* shaking about (b) *Fig (crítica)* slating; *(falta de respeto)* contemptuous treatment, abuse

**vaquería** *nf* dairy

**vaquero, -a** 1 *adj (tela)* denim; **tela vaquera** denim; **pantalón v.** jeans, denims

2 *nm,f (persona)* cowboy, *f* cowgirl; **una película de vaqueros** a western, a cowboy film

3 *nm (pantalón)* jeans; **unos vaqueros** (a pair of) jeans

**vaquilla** *nf (vaca)* heifer; *(toro)* young bull

**vara** *nf* (a) *(rama, palo)* stick (b) *(pértiga)* pole (c) *(fabricada)* rod (d) *(tallo)* stem, stalk (e) *(de trombón)* slide (f) *(insignia)* staff

**varadero** *nm* dry dock

**varado, -a** *adj Náut (encallado)* aground, stranded; *(en el dique seco)* in dry dock

**varapalo** *nm (paliza)* hiding

**varar** *vi Náut* to run aground

**varear** *vt (golpear)* to beat (with a pole); **v. las aceitunas** = to knock the branches of olive trees with a pole to bring down the ripe olives

**variabilidad** *nf* changeability, variability

**variable** 1 *adj* changeable, variable

2 *nf Mat* variable

**variación** *nf (cambio)* variation; *(del tiempo)* change; **v. magnética** magnetic declination

**variado, -a** *adj (diverso)* varied; *(galletas, bombones)* assorted

**variante** 1 *adj* variant

2 *nf* (a) *(variación)* variation; *(versión)* version (b) *Aut* by-pass (c) *(en quiniela)* draw or away win (d) **variantes** mixed pickles

**variar** [34] 1 *vt* (a) *(modificar)* to alter, to change (b) *(dar variedad)* to vary

2 *vi* (a) *(cambiar)* **v.** (**de**) to change; *también Irón* **para v.** (just) for a change (b) *(ser diferente)* to vary, to differ (**de** from)

**varicela** *nf* chickenpox

**varicoso, -a** *adj* varicose

**variedad** *nf* (**a**) *(diversidad)* variety (**b**) *Teatro* **variedades** variety, music hall

**varilla** *nf* *(barra delgada)* rod; *(de abanico, paraguas)* spoke, rib; *(de gafas)* arm

**varillaje** *nm* *(de abanico, paraguas)* spokes, ribbing; *(de gafas)* arms

**vario, -a 1** *adj* *(variado)* *(singular)* varied, different; *(plural)* various, several

  **2** *pron pl* **varios, -as** several

**variopinto, -a** *adj* diverse

**varita** *nf* wand; **v. mágica** magic wand

**variz** *nf* varicose vein

**varón** *nm* *(hombre)* male, man; *(chico)* boy

**varonil** *adj* *(masculino)* masculine, male; *(viril)* manly, virile

**Varsovia** *n* Warsaw

**varsoviano, -a 1** *adj* of/from Warsaw

  **2** *nm,f* person from Warsaw

**vasallo, -a** *nm,f* (**a**) *(siervo)* vassal (**b**) *(súbdito)* subject

**vasco, -a 1** *adj & nm,f* Basque

  **2** *nm (lengua)* Basque

**vascofrancés, -esa 1** *adj* of/from the French Basque provinces

  **2** *nm* French Basque

**Vascongadas** *nfpl* **las V.** the Basque provinces of Spain

**vascuence** *nm (lengua)* Basque

**vascular** *adj* vascular

**vasectomía** *nf* vasectomy

**vaselina** *nf* Vaseline®

**vasija** *nf* *(de barro)* earthenware vessel

**vaso** *nm* (**a**) *(recipiente, contenido)* glass; **un v. de plástico** a plastic cup; **ahogarse en un v. de agua** to make a mountain out of a molehill (**b**) *Anat* vessel; **vasos capilares** capillaries; **vasos sanguíneos** blood vessels (**c**) *Bot* vein

**vástago** *nm* (**a**) *(descendiente)* offspring (**b**) *(brote)* shoot (**c**) *(varilla)* rod

**vastedad** *nf* vastness

**vasto, -a** *adj* vast

**vate** *nm* *Formal* bard

**váter** (*pl* **váteres**) *nm* toilet

**Vaticano** *n* **el V.** the Vatican

**vaticinar** *vt* to prophesy, to predict

**vaticinio** *nm* prophecy, prediction

**vatio** *nm* watt

**vaya 1** *ver* **ir**

  **2** *interj* (**a**) *(sorpresa)* ¡v.! well! (**b**) *(énfasis)* ¡**v. moto!** what a motorbike! (**c**) *(contrariedad, disgusto)* ¡v.! oh no!, blast!

**VB** *(abrev de* **visto bueno***)* *(en ejercicios escolares)* = abbreviation equivalent to a tick on a piece of schoolwork

**Vd.** *abrev de* **usted**

**Vda.** *(abrev de* **viuda***)* widow

**Vds.** *abrev de* **ustedes**

**ve** *ver* **ir**

**véase** *ver* **ver**

**vecinal** *adj* (**a**) *(relaciones, trato)* neighbourly (**b**) *(camino, impuestos)* local

**vecindad** *nf* (**a**) *(vecindario)* neighbourhood (**b**) *(cualidad)* neighbourliness (**c**) *(alrededores)* vicinity (**d**) *Méx* urban slum

**vecindario** *nm (de barrio)* neighbourhood; *(de población)* community, inhabitants

**vecino, -a 1** *adj* *(cercano)* neighbouring; **v.** a next to

  **2** *nm,f* (**a**) *(de la misma casa, calle)* neighbour; *(de un barrio)* resident (**b**) *(de una localidad)* inhabitant

**vector** *nm* vector

**vectorial** *adj* vectorial

**veda** *nf* (**a**) *(prohibición)* ban *(on hunting and fishing);* **levantar la v.** to open the season (**b**) *(periodo)* close season

**vedado, -a 1** *adj* prohibited

  **2** *nm* reserve

**vedar** *vt* to prohibit

**vedette** [be'ðet] (*pl* **vedettes**) *nf* star

**vedismo** *nm* Vedaism

**vega** *nf* fertile plain

**vegetación 1** *nf* vegetation

  **2** *nfpl* **vegetaciones** *Med* adenoids

**vegetal 1** *adj* (**a**) *Biol* vegetable, plant; **aceite v.** vegetable oil; **el mundo v.** the plant kingdom (**b**) *Culin* salad; **sandwich v.** salad sandwich

  **2** *nm* vegetable

**vegetar** *vi* (**a**) *(planta)* to grow (**b**) *Fam (holgazanear)* to vegetate

**vegetarianismo** *nm* vegetarianism

**vegetariano, -a** *adj & nm,f* vegetarian

**vegetativo, -a** *adj* vegetative

**vehemencia** *nf* (**a**) *(pasión, entusiasmo)* vehemence (**b**) *(irreflexión)* impulsiveness, impetuosity

**vehemente** *adj* (**a**) *(apasionado, entusiasta)* vehement (**b**) *(irreflexivo)* impulsive, impetuous

**vehículo** *nm* (**a**) *(medio de transporte)* vehicle (**b**) *(medio de propagación)* *(de enfermedad)* carrier; *(de ideas)* vehicle

**veinte** *núm* twenty; **los (años) v.** the twenties; *ver también* **seis**

**veinteañero, -a 1** *adj* = in one's (early) twenties

  **2** *nm,f* = person in their (early) twenties

**veinteavo, -a** *núm (fracción)* twentieth; **la veinteava parte** a twentieth

**veintena** *nf* twenty; **andará por la v.** he must be about twenty; **una v. de...** *(unos veinte)* about twenty...; *(veinte)* twenty...

**veintitantos, -as** *núm Fam* twenty-odd

**vejación** *nf,* **vejamen** *nm* humiliation

**vejar** *vt* to humiliate

**vejatorio, -a** *adj* humiliating

**vejestorio** *nm Fam Pey* old codger *o Br* crock

**vejete** *nm Fam* old guy *o Br* bloke

**vejez** *nf* old age; **¡a la v. viruelas!** fancy that at his/her age!

**vejiga** *nf* bladder; **v. de la bilis** gall bladder

**vela 1** *nf* (a) *(para dar luz)* candle; **estar a dos velas** not to have two halfpennies to rub together; *Fam Fig* **quedarse a dos velas** to be left none the wiser; *Fam Fig* **¿quién te ha dado v. en este entierro?** *Br* who asked you to stick your oar in?, *Am* who asked you to butt in?

(b) *(de barco)* sail; **a toda v.** under full sail; **v. mayor** mainsail

(c) *Dep* sailing

(d) *(vigilia)* vigil; **pasar la noche en v.** *(adrede)* to stay awake all night; *(desvelado)* to have a sleepless night

**2** *nfpl* **velas** *Fam (mocos)* bogies, snot

**velada** *nf* evening

**veladamente** *adv* covertly; **le acusó v. de ser el culpable** she hinted he was the guilty one

**velado, -a** *adj* (a) *(oculto)* veiled, hidden (b) *Fot* damaged by exposure to sunlight

**velador** *nm (mesa)* pedestal table

**velamen** *nm* sails

**velar**[1] *adj Anat & Ling* velar

**velar**[2] **1** *vi* (a) *(cuidar)* **v. por** to look after, to watch over (b) *(no dormir)* to stay awake

**2** *vt* (a) *(de noche) (muerto)* to keep a vigil over; *(enfermo)* to sit up with (b) *(ocultar)* to mask, to veil (c) *Fot* to damage by exposure to sunlight

**3 velarse** *vpr Fot* to be damaged by exposure to sunlight

**velatorio** *nm* (a) *(acto)* wake, vigil (b) *(lugar)* = room where vigil is held over a dead person's remains on the night before burial

**velcro®** *nm* Velcro®

**veleidad** *nf* (a) *(inconstancia)* fickleness, capriciousness (b) *(antojo, capricho)* whim, caprice

**veleidoso, -a** *adj* (a) *(inconstante)* fickle (b) *(caprichoso)* capricious

**velero** *nm* sailing boat *o* ship

**veleta 1** *nf* weather vane

**2** *nmf Fig* capricious person

**velista** *nmf* yachtsman, *f* yachtswoman

**vello** *nm* (a) *(pelusilla)* down (b) *(pelo)* hair

**vellocino** *nm* fleece

**vellón** *nm (lana)* fleece

**vellosidad** *nf (presencia de pelo)* hairiness; *(más fino)* downiness

**velloso, -a** *adj (con pelo)* hairy; *(más fino)* downy

**velludo, -a** *adj* hairy

**velo** *nm* (a) *también Fig* veil; *Fam* **correr** *o* **echar un (tupido) v. sobre algo** to draw a veil over sth (b) **v. del paladar** soft palate

**velocidad** *nf* (a) *(rapidez)* speed; *Mec* velocity; **a toda v.** at full speed; **de alta v.** high-speed; **con la v. de un rayo** as quick as lightning; **v. de crucero** cruising speed; **v. punta** *o* **máxima** top speed (b) *Aut (marcha)* gear; **cambiar de v.** to change gear

**velocímetro** *nm* speedometer

**velocípedo** *nm* velocipede

**velocista** *nmf* sprinter

**velódromo** *nm* cycle track, velodrome

**velomotor** *nm* moped

**velorio** *nm* wake

**veloz** *adj* fast, quick

**velozmente** *adv* quickly, rapidly

**ven** *ver* **venir**

**vena** *nf* (a) *también Anat & Min* vein (b) *(inspiración)* inspiration; *Fam* **estar en v., tener la v.** to be on form; *Fam* **le dio la v. de hacerlo** she took it into her head to do it (c) *(don)* vein, streak; **tener v. de pintor** to have a gift for painting

**venado** *nm Zool* deer; *Culin* venison

**venal** *adj* (a) *(sobornable)* venal, corrupt (b) *(vendible)* for sale, saleable

**vencedor, -ora 1** *adj* winning, victorious

**2** *nm,f* winner

**vencejo** *nm (pájaro)* swift

**vencer** [42] **1** *vt* (a) *(ganar, derrotar)* to beat, to defeat; **venció al cansancio/sueño** she overcame her exhaustion/sleepiness (b) *(aventajar)* **v. a alguien** *a o* **en algo** to outdo sb at sth (c) *(superar) (miedo, obstáculos)* to overcome; *(tentación)* to resist

**2** *vi* (a) *(ganar)* to win, to be victorious (b) *(caducar) (garantía, contrato, plazo)* to expire; *(deuda, pago)* to fall due, to be payable; *(bono)* to mature (c) *(prevalecer)* to prevail

**3 vencerse** *vpr (estante)* to give way, to collapse

**vencido, -a 1** *adj* (a) *(derrotado)* defeated; **darse por v.** to give up (b) *(caducado) (garantía, contrato, plazo)* expired; *(pago, deuda)* due, payable; *(bono)* mature

**2** *nm,f* (en guerra) conquered *o* defeated person; *(en deportes, concursos)* loser

**vencimiento** *nm* (a) *(término) (de garantía, contrato, plazo)* expiry; *(de pago, deuda)* falling due; *(de bono)* maturing (b) *(inclinación)* giving way, collapse

**venda** nf bandage; Fig **tener una v. en o delante de los ojos** to be blind

**vendaje** nm bandaging

**vendar** vt to bandage; **v. los ojos a alguien** to blindfold sb

**vendaval** nm gale

**vendedor, -ora 1** adj selling

**2** nm,f (en general) seller; (en tienda) shop o sales assistant; (de coches, seguros) salesman, f saleswoman; **v. ambulante** pedlar, hawker

**vender 1** vt también Fig to sell; **v. algo a o por** to sell sth for

**2 venderse** vpr (a) (ser vendido) to be sold o on sale; **se vende** (en letrero) for sale (b) (dejarse sobornar) to sell oneself, to be bribed

**vendetta** nf vendetta

**vendido, -a** adj sold; Fig **estar o ir v.** not to stand a chance

**vendimia** nf grape harvest

**vendimiador, -ora** nm,f grape picker

**vendimiar** [15] **1** vt to harvest (grapes)

**2** vi to pick grapes

**vendré** etc ver **venir**

**Venecia** n Venice

**veneciano, -a** adj & nm,f Venetian

**veneno** nm (a) (sustancia tóxica) poison; (de serpiente, insecto) venom (b) Fig (mala intención) venom

**venenoso, -a** adj (a) (tóxico) poisonous (b) Fig (malintencionado) venomous

**venerable** adj venerable

**veneración** nf veneration, worship

**venerador, -ora 1** adj venerational

**2** nm,f venerator

**venerar** vt to venerate, to worship

**venéreo, -a** adj venereal

**venezolano, -a** adj & nm,f Venezuelan

**Venezuela** n Venezuela

**venga** interj Fam **¡v.!** come on!

**vengador, -ora 1** adj avenging

**2** nm,f avenger

**venganza** nf vengeance, revenge

**vengar** [40] **1** vt to avenge

**2 vengarse** vpr to take revenge (**de** on), to avenge oneself (**de** on)

**vengativo, -a** adj vengeful, vindictive

**vengo** ver **venir**

**vengue** etc ver **vengar**

**venia** nf (a) (permiso) permission; **con la v.** (tomando la palabra) by your leave (b) (perdón) pardon

**venial** adj petty, venial

**venialidad** nf veniality, pettiness

**venida** nf (a) (llegada) arrival (b) (regreso) return

**venidero, -a** adj coming, future

**venir** [71] **1** vi (a) (en general) to come; **v. a/de hacer algo** to come to do sth/from doing sth; **v. de algo** (proceder, derivarse) to come from sth; **v. a alguien con algo** to come to sb with sth; **no me vengas con exigencias** don't come to me making demands; **el año que viene** next year

(b) (llegar) to arrive; **vino a las doce** he arrived at twelve o'clock

(c) (hallarse) to be; **su foto viene en primera página** his photo is o appears on the front page; **el texto viene en inglés** the text is in English; **vienen en todos los tamaños** they come in every size; **las anchoas vienen en lata** anchovies come in tins

(d) (acometer, sobrevenir) **me viene sueño** I'm getting sleepy; **le vinieron ganas de reír** he was seized by a desire to laugh; **le vino una tremenda desgracia** he suffered a great misfortune

(e) (ropa, calzado) **v. a alguien** to fit sb; **¿qué tal te viene?** does it fit all right?; **el abrigo le viene pequeño** the coat is too small for her

(f) (convenir) **v. bien/mal a alguien** to suit/not to suit sb

(g) (aproximarse) **viene a costar un millón** it costs almost a million

(h) (indica resultado) **esto viene a significar...** this means...; **v. a parar en** to end in; **v. a ser** to amount to

(i) (expresiones) **¿a qué viene esto?** what do you mean by that?, what's that in aid of?; **v. a menos** (negocio) to go downhill; (persona) to go down in the world

**2** v aux (a) (antes de gerundio) (haber estado) **v. haciendo algo** to have been doing sth; **las peleas vienen sucediéndose desde hace tiempo** fighting has been going on for some time

(b) (antes de participio) (estar) **los cambios vienen motivados por la presión de la oposición** the changes have resulted from pressure on the part of the opposition

**3 venirse** vpr (a) (venir) to come; **venirse (de)** (volver) to come back o return (from); **¿te vienes?** are you coming?

(b) **venirse abajo** (techo, estante) to collapse; (ilusiones) to be dashed

**venoso, -a** adj venous

**venta** nf (a) (acción) sale, selling; **de v. en...** on sale at...; **estar en v.** to be for sale; **poner a la v.** (casa) to put up for sale; (producto) to put on sale; **v. por correo o por correspondencia** mail-order sale; **v. por catálogo** mail-order selling; **v. automatizada** vending-machine sale; **v. al contado** cash sale; **v. a crédito** credit sale; **v. a domicilio** door-to-door selling; **v. a plazos** sale by instalments; **v. pública**

public auction; **v. sobre plano** sale of customized goods **(b)** *(cantidad)* sales **(c)** *(posada)* country inn

**ventaja** *nf* **(a)** *(hecho favorable)* advantage **(b)** *(en competición)* lead; **dar v.** to give a start; **llevar v. a alguien** to have a lead over sb

**ventajista** *adj & nmf* opportunist

**ventajoso, -a** *adj* advantageous

**ventana** *nf* **(a)** *también Informát* window; *Fig* **echar** *o* **tirar algo por la v.** to let sth go to waste; **v. de guillotina** sash window; **v. de socorro** emergency exit (window) **(b)** *(de nariz)* nostril

**ventanal** *nm* large window

**ventanilla** *nf* **(a)** *(de vehículo, sobre)* window **(b)** *(taquilla)* counter

**ventarrón** *nm Fam* strong *o* blustery wind

**ventear 1** *v impersonal* to be very windy

**2** *vi* to sniff the air

**ventero, -a** *nm,f* innkeeper

**ventilación** *nf* ventilation

**ventilador** *nm* ventilator, fan

**ventilar 1** *vt* **(a)** *(airear)* to air **(b)** *(resolver)* to clear up **(c)** *(discutir)* to air **(d)** *(difundir)* to spread, to make public

**2 ventilarse** *vpr* **(a)** *(airearse)* to air **(b)** *Fam (terminarse)* to knock *o* finish off **(c)** *Fam (asesinar)* to rub out

**ventisca** *nf* blizzard

**ventiscar [61]**, **ventisquear** *v impersonal* to blow a blizzard

**ventisquero** *nm (nieve amontonada)* snowdrift

**ventolera** *nf* **(a)** *(viento)* gust of wind **(b)** *Fam (idea extravagante)* wild idea; **le ha dado la v. de hacerlo** she has taken it into her head to do it

**ventosa** *nf también Zool* sucker

**ventosear** *vi* to break wind

**ventosidad** *nf* wind, flatulence

**ventoso, -a** *adj* windy

**ventricular** *adj* ventricular

**ventrículo** *nm* ventricle

**ventrílocuo, -a** *nm,f* ventriloquist

**ventriloquía** *nf* ventriloquism

**ventura** *nf* **(a)** *(felicidad)* happiness, contentment **(b)** *(suerte)* luck; **por v.** luckily; **a la (buena) v.** *(al azar)* at random, haphazardly; *(sin nada previsto)* without planning *o* a fixed plan

**venturoso, -a** *adj* happy, fortunate

**Venus** *nm* Venus

**venza** *etc ver* **vencer**

**veo-veo** *nm* I-spy

**ver** **[72] 1** *vt* **(a)** *(en general)* to see; *(mirar)* to look at; *(televisión, partido de fútbol)* to watch; **¿ves algo?** can you see anything?; **he estado viendo tu trabajo** I've been looking at your work; **ya veo que estás de mal humor** I can see you're in a bad mood; **¿ves lo que quiero decir?** do you see what I mean?; **ir a v. lo que pasa** to go and see what's going on; **es una manera de v. las cosas** that's one way of looking at it; **yo no lo veo tan mal** I don't think it's that bad

**(b)** *(expresiones)* **eso habrá que verlo** that remains to be seen; **¡hay que v. qué lista es!** you wouldn't believe how clever she is!; *Fam* **no puedo verlo (ni en pintura)** I can't stand him; **si no lo veo, no lo creo** I would never have believed this was possible; **pero ahora, si te he visto, no me acuerdo** but now he/she etc doesn't want anything to do with me; **v. venir a alguien** to see what sb is up to

**2** *vi* **(a)** *(en general)* to see

**(b)** *(expresiones)* **a v.** *(veamos)* let's see; **¿a v.?** *(mirando con interés)* let me see, let's have a look; **¡a v.!** *(¡pues claro!)* what do you expect?; *(al empezar algo)* right!; **dejarse v. (por un sitio)** to show one's face (somewhere); **eso está por v.** that remains to be seen; **ni visto ni oído** in the twinkling of an eye; **ya veremos** we'll see

**3** *nm* **estar de buen v.** to be good-looking

**4 verse** *vpr* **(a)** *(mirarse, imaginarse)* to see oneself; **verse en el espejo** to see oneself in the mirror; **ya me veo cargando el camión yo solo** I can see myself having to load the lorry on my own

**(b)** *(percibirse)* **desde aquí se ve el mar** you can see the sea from here

**(c)** *(encontrarse)* to meet, to see each other; **hace mucho que no nos vemos** we haven't seen each other for a long time

**(d)** *(darse, suceder)* to be seen

**(e)** *(expresiones)* **vérselas y deseárselas para hacer algo** to have a real struggle doing sth; **por lo visto, por lo que se ve** apparently; **véase** *(en textos)* see

**vera** *nf* **(a)** *(orilla) (de río, lago)* bank; *(de camino)* edge, side **(b)** *Fig (lado)* side; **a la v. de** next to

**veracidad** *nf* truthfulness

**veraneante 1** *adj* holiday-making

**2** *nmf* holidaymaker, *US* (summer) vacationer

**veranear** *vi* **v. en** to spend one's summer holidays in

**veraneo** *nm* summer holidays; **irse de v.** to go on (one's summer) holiday

**veraniego, -a** *adj* summer; **ropa veraniega** summer clothing

**veranillo** *nm* Indian summer

**verano** *nm* summer; *Am (estación seca)* dry season

**veras** *nfpl* truth; **de v.** *(verdaderamente)* really; *(en serio)* seriously

**veraz** *adj* truthful

**verbal** *adj* verbal

**verbalizar** [16] *vt* to verbalize

**verbena** *nf* (a) *(fiesta)* street party (b) *(planta)* verbena

**verbenero, -a** *adj* street-party; **ambiente v.** festive atmosphere

**verbigracia** *adv Formal* for example, for instance

**verbo** *nm* (a) *Gram* verb (b) *(lenguaje)* language

**verborrea** *nf* verbal diarrhoea, verbosity

**verbosidad** *nf* verbosity

**verboso, -a** *adj* verbose

**verdad 1** *nf* (a) *(en general)* truth; **¿es v.?** is that true *o* right?; **a decir v.** to tell the truth; **en v.** truly, honestly; *Fam* **una v. como un puño** an undeniable fact; **no te gusta, ¿v.?** you don't like it, do you?; **está bueno, ¿v.?** it's good, isn't it? (b) *(principio aceptado)* fact (c) **de v.** *(en serio)* seriously; *(realmente)* really; *(auténtico)* real

2 *nfpl* **verdades** *(opinión sincera)* true thoughts; *Fig* **cantar las verdades** to speak one's mind; *Fig* **cantarle** *o* **decirle a alguien cuatro verdades** to tell sb a few home truths

**verdadero, -a** *adj* (a) *(cierto, real)* true, real (b) *(sin falsificar)* real (c) *(enfático)* real; **fue un v. lío** it was a real mess

**verde 1** *adj* (a) *(en general)* green; **v. botella** bottle green; **v. oliva** olive (green); *Fam* **poner v. a alguien** to run sb down (b) *(poco maduro)* *(fruta)* unripe, green; *Fam Fig (persona)* green, wet behind the ears; *(proyecto, plan)* in its early stages (c) *(ecologista)* Green, green (d) *Fig (obsceno)* blue, dirty (e) *Fam (billete)* = 1,000 peseta note

2 *nm (color)* green

3 *nmpl* **los Verdes** *(partido)* the Greens

**verdear** *vi* (a) *(parecer verde)* to look green (b) *(plantas)* to turn *o* go green

**verdecer** [48] *vi* to turn *o* go green

**verdinegro, -a** *adj* very dark green

**verdor** *nm* (a) *(color)* greenness (b) *(madurez)* lushness

**verdoso, -a** *adj* greenish

**verdugo** *nm* (a) *(de preso)* executioner; *(que ahorca)* hangman (b) *Fig (tirano)* tyrant (c) *(pasamontañas)* balaclava helmet

**verdulera** *nf Fam Fig (ordinaria)* fishwife

**verdulería** *nf* greengrocer's *(shop)*

**verdulero, -a** *nm,f (tendero)* greengrocer

**verdura** *nf* (a) *(comestible)* vegetables, greens (b) *(color verde)* greenness

**verdusco, -a** *adj* dirty green

**vereda** *nf* (a) *(senda)* path; *Fam* **hacer entrar** *o* **meter a alguien en v.** to bring sb into line (b) *Am (acera) Br* pavement, *US* sidewalk

**veredicto** *nm* verdict

**verga** *nf* (a) *Anat* penis (b) *Náut* yard

**vergel** *nm* lush, fertile place

**vergonzante** *adj* shameful

**vergonzoso, -a 1** *adj* (a) *(deshonroso)* shameful (b) *(tímido)* bashful

2 *nm,f* bashful person

**vergüenza 1** *nf* (a) *(en general)* shame; **sentir v.** to feel ashamed (b) *(bochorno)* embarrassment; **dar v.** to embarrass; **¡qué v.!** how embarrassing!; **sentir v.** to feel embarrassed; **sentir v. ajena** to feel embarrassed for sb; **¿quién quiere el de la v.?** who wants the last one? (c) *(timidez)* bashfulness; **perder la v.** to lose one's inhibitions; *Fig* **tener poca v.** to be shameless (d) *(deshonra, escándalo)* disgrace; **¡es una v.!** it's disgraceful!

2 *nfpl* **vergüenzas** *(genitales)* private parts, privates

**vericueto** *nm (camino difícil)* rough track; *Fig* **vericuetos** ins and outs

**verídico, -a** *adj* (a) *(cierto)* true, truthful (b) *Fig (verosímil)* true-to-life, real

**verificable** *adj* verifiable

**verificación** *nf* check, checking

**verificador, -ora 1** *adj (confirmador)* checking; *(examinador)* testing, inspecting

2 *nm,f* tester, inspector

**verificar** [61] **1** *vt* (a) *(verdad, autenticidad)* to check, to verify (b) *(funcionamiento, buen estado)* to check, to test (c) *(fecha, cita)* to confirm (d) *(llevar a cabo)* to carry out

2 **verificarse** *vpr* (a) *(tener lugar)* to take place (b) *(resultar cierto) (predicción)* to come true; *(comprobarse)* to be verified

**verja** *nf* (a) *(puerta)* iron gate (b) *(valla)* railings (c) *(enrejado)* grille

**vermú** *(pl* vermús*)*, **vermut** *(pl* vermuts*)* *nm (bebida)* vermouth

**vernáculo, -a** *adj* vernacular

**verónica** *nf* (a) *Taurom* = pass in which the matador swings his cape away from the bull (b) *(planta)* veronica

**verosímil** *adj* (a) *(creíble)* believable, credible (b) *(probable)* likely, probable

**verosimilitud** *nf* (a) *(credibilidad)* credibility (b) *(probabilidad)* likeliness

**verraco** *nm* boar

**verruga** *nf* wart

**verrugoso, -a** *adj* warty

**versado, -a** *adj* versed *(en* in*)*

**versal** *nf* capital (letter)

**versalita** *nf* small capital

**Versalles** *n* Versailles

**versallesco, -a** adj Fam (cortés) gallant, chivalrous

**versar** vi **v. sobre** to be about, to deal with

**versátil** adj (a) (voluble) changeable, fickle (b) (polifacético) versatile

**versatilidad** nf (a) (volubilidad) changeability, fickleness (b) (adaptabilidad) versatility

**versículo** nm verse

**versificación** nf versification

**versificar** [61] **1** vi to write (in) verse
**2** vt to put into verse

**versión** nf (a) (en general) version; (en música pop) cover version; Cine **v. original** original (version) (b) (traducción) translation, version

**versionar** vt Fam (en música pop) to cover

**verso** nm (a) (género) verse; **en v.** in verse; **v. blanco/libre** blank/free verse (b) (unidad rítmica) line (of poetry)

**vértebra** nf vertebra

**vertebrado, -a 1** adj vertebrate
**2** nmpl Zool **vertebrados** vertebrates

**vertebral** adj vertebral

**vertebrar** vt Fig to form the backbone of

**vertedero** nm (a) (de basuras) rubbish tip o dump (b) (de pantano) drain, spillway

**verter** [66] **1** vt (a) (derramar) to spill (b) (vaciar) (líquido) to pour (out); (recipiente) to empty; (basura, residuos) to dump (c) (traducir) to translate (a into) (d) Fig (decir) to tell
**2** vi **v. a** o **en** to flow into
**3** verterse vpr (derramarse) to spill

**vertical 1** adj Mat vertical; (derecho) upright
**2** nm Astron vertical circle
**3** nf Mat vertical

**verticalidad** nf verticality, vertical position

**verticalmente** adv vertically

**vértice** nm (en general) vertex; (de cono) apex; **v. geodésico** triangulation pillar

**vertido** nm (a) (residuo) waste; **vertidos radiactivos** radioactive waste (b) (acción) dumping; **v. de residuos** waste dumping

**vertiente** nf (a) (pendiente) slope (b) Fig (aspecto) side, aspect

**vertiginosamente** adv with dizzying speed

**vertiginosidad** nf dizziness

**vertiginoso, -a** adj (a) (mareante) dizzy (b) Fig (raudo) giddy

**vértigo** nm (a) (enfermedad) vertigo; (mareo) dizziness; **trepar me da v.** climbing makes me dizzy; **Fig sólo de pensarlo me da v.** just thinking about it makes me feel dizzy; **Fig de v.** (velocidad, altura) giddy; (cifras) mind-boggling (b) Fig (apresuramiento) mad rush, hectic pace

**vesícula** nf (ampolla) blister; **v. biliar** gall bladder

**vesicular** adj vesicular

**vespa®** nf Vespa®, motor scooter

**vespertino, -a 1** adj evening; **diario v.** evening (news)paper
**2** nm (periódico) evening (news)paper

**vespino®** nm = small motor scooter

**vestal** nf vestal (virgin)

**vestíbulo** nm (de casa) (entrance) hall; (de hotel, oficina) lobby, foyer

**vestido, -a 1** adj dressed
**2** nm (a) (indumentaria) clothes (b) (prenda femenina) dress

**vestidor** nm dressing room (in house)

**vestiduras** nfpl clothes; Rel vestments

**vestigio** nm vestige; Fig sign, trace

**vestimenta** nf clothes, wardrobe

**vestir** [49] **1** vt (a) (en general) to dress; Prov **vísteme despacio que tengo prisa** more haste, less speed (b) (llevar puesto) to wear (c) (cubrir) to cover (d) Fig (encubrir) **v. algo de** to invest sth with
**2** vi (a) (ser elegante) to be dressy; **de (mucho) v.** (very) dressy (b) (llevar ropa) to dress (c) Fig (estar bien visto) to be the done thing (d) (expresiones) **¿de verdad que estuvo el rey? – el mismo que viste y calza** was the king really there? – he certainly was
**3** vestirse vpr (a) (ponerse ropa) to get dressed, to dress (b) (adquirir ropa) **vestirse en** to buy one's clothes at (c) Fig (cubrirse) **vestirse de** to be covered in

**vestuario** nm (a) (vestimenta) clothes, wardrobe; Teatro costumes (b) (guardarropa) cloakroom (c) (para cambiarse) changing room; (de actores) dressing room

**veta** nf (a) (de mineral) seam (b) (en madera) knot; (en mármol) vein

**vetar** vt to veto

**veteado, -a** adj grained

**vetear** vt to grain

**veteranía** nf seniority, age

**veterano, -a** adj & nm,f veteran

**veterinaria** nf (ciencia) veterinary science

**veterinario, -a 1** adj veterinary
**2** nm,f (persona) vet, veterinary surgeon

**veto** nm veto; **poner v. a algo** to veto sth

**vetusto, -a** adj Formal ancient, very old

**vez** nf (a) (en general) time; **una v.** once; **dos veces** twice; **tres veces** three times; **¿has estado allí alguna v.?** have you ever been there?; **a mi/tu/etc v.** in my/your/etc turn; **a la v. (que)** at the same time (as); **alguna que otra v.** occasionally; **a veces, algunas veces** sometimes, at times; **cada v. (que)** every time; **cada v. más** more and more; **cada v. menos** less and less; **cada v. la veo más feliz** she seems happier and happier; **de una v.** in one go; **de una v. para siempre** o **por todas** once and for all; **de v. en cuando** from time to time, now and again; **cállate de una v.** why don't you just shut up!; **vete de una v.** just go, for heaven's sake; **en v. de** instead of; **érase una v.** once upon a time; **hacer las veces de** to act as; **muchas veces** often, a lot; **otra v.** again; **pocas veces, rara v.** rarely, seldom; **por última/enésima v.** for the last/umpteenth time; **tal v.** perhaps, maybe; **una v. más** once again; **una v. que** once, after; **una y otra v.** time and again **(b)** *(turno)* turn; **¿quién lleva** *o* **da la v.?** who's the last in the *Br* queue *o Am* line?

**v.g., v.gr.** *(abrev de* **verbigracia***)* e.g.

**VHF** *nf (abrev de* **very high frequency***)* VHF

**VHS** *nm (abrev de* **video home system***)* VHS

**vía 1** *nf* **(a)** *(medio de transporte)* route; **por v. aérea** *(en general)* by air; *(correo)* (by) airmail; **por v. marítima** by sea; **por v. terrestre** overland, by land; **v. de comunicación** communication route; **v. fluvial** waterway
**(b)** *(calzada, calle)* road; **v. pública** public thoroughfare; **V. Láctea** Milky Way
**(c)** *Ferroc (raíl)* rails, track; *(andén)* platform; **v. estrecha** narrow gauge; **v. férrea** *(ruta)* railway line; **v. muerta** siding
**(d)** *(proceso)* **estar en vías de** to be in the process of; **país en vías de desarrollo** developing country; **una especie en vías de extinción** an endangered species
**(e)** *Anat* tract; **por v. oral** orally
**(f)** *(opción)* channel, path; **por v. oficial/judicial** through official channels/the courts
**(g)** *(camino)* way; **dar v. libre** *(dejar paso)* to give way; *(dar libertad de acción)* to give a free rein
**(h)** *(en barco)* **v. de agua** leakage, hole (below the water line)
**(i)** *Der* procedure
**2** *prep* via

**viabilidad** *nf* viability

**viabilizar** *vt* to make viable

**viable** *adj Fig (posible)* viable

**vía crucis** *nm inv Rel* Stations of the Cross, Way of the Cross

**viaducto** *nm* viaduct

**viajante** *nmf* travelling salesperson

**viajar** *vi* **(a)** *(trasladarse, irse)* to travel **(en** by**)** **(b)** *(circular)* to run

**viaje** *nm* **(a)** *(en general)* journey, trip; *(en barco)* voyage; **¡buen v.!** have a good journey *o* trip!; **estar/ir de v.** to be/go away (on a trip); **hay 11 días de v.** it's an 11-day journey; **los viajes de Colón** the voyages of Columbus; **v. de Estado/oficial** state/official visit; **v. de ida/de**

**vuelta** outward/return journey; **v. de ida y vuelta** return journey *o* trip; **v. de novios** honeymoon; **v. relámpago** lightning trip *o* visit **(b)** *Fig (recorrido)* trip; **di varios viajes para trasladar los muebles** it took me a good few trips to move all the furniture **(c)** *Fam Fig (alucinación)* trip **(d)** *Fam Fig (golpe)* bang, bump

**viajero, -a 1** *adj (persona)* travelling; *(ave)* migratory
**2** *nm,f* **(en general)** traveller; *(en transporte público)* passenger

**vial 1** *adj* road; **seguridad v.** road safety
**2** *nm (frasco)* phial

**vialidad** *nf* **departamento de v.** roads and highways department

**vianda** *nf* food

**viandante** *nmf* **(a)** *(peatón)* pedestrian **(b)** *(transeúnte)* passer-by

**viario, -a** *adj* road; **red viaria** road network

**viático** *nm* **(a)** *(dieta)* expenses allowance **(b)** *Rel* last rites, viaticum

**víbora** *nf* adder, viper; *Fig* viper

**vibración** *nf* vibration

**vibrador, -ora 1** *adj* vibrating
**2** *nm* vibrator

**vibráfono** *nm* vibraphone

**vibrante** *adj* **(a)** *(oscilante)* vibrating **(b)** *Fig (emocionante)* vibrant **(c)** *Ling* rolled, trilled

**vibrar** *vi* **(a)** *(oscilar)* to vibrate **(b)** *Fig (voz, rodillas)* to shake **(c)** *Fig (público)* to get excited

**vibrátil** *adj* vibratile

**vibratorio, -a** *adj* vibratory

**vicaría** *nf* **(a)** *(cargo)* vicarship, vicariate **(b)** *(residencia)* vicarage **(c)** *Fam* **pasar por la v.** *(casarse)* to tie the knot

**vicario** *nm* vicar

**vicealmirante** *nm* vice-admiral

**vicecónsul** *nm* vice-consul

**vicepresidencia** *nf (de país, asociación)* vice-presidency; *(de comité, empresa)* vice-chairmanship

**vicepresidente, -a** *nm,f (de país, asociación)* vice-president; *(de comité, empresa)* vice-chairman

**vicerrector, -ora** *nm,f* = deputy to the vice-chancellor of a university

**vicesecretario, -a** *nm,f* assistant secretary

**viceversa** *adv* vice versa

**vichy** [bi't∫i] *(pl* **vichys***) nm (tejido)* gingham

**vichyssoise** [bit∫i'swas] *(pl* **vichyssoises***) nf Culin* vichyssoise

**viciado, -a** *adj (aire) (maloliente)* stuffy; *(contaminado)* polluted

**viciar** [15] **1** *vt* (**a**) *(enviciar)* **v. a alguien** to get sb into a bad habit; *(pervertir)* to corrupt sb (**b**) *Fig (falsear)* to falsify; *(tergiversar)* to distort, to twist

**2 viciarse** *vpr* (**a**) *(enviciarse)* to get into a bad habit; *(pervertirse)* to become *o* get corrupted; **es muy fácil viciarse con estos bombones** it's very easy to get addicted to these chocolates (**b**) *(aire)* to get stuffy (**c**) *(deformarse)* to warp

**vicio** *nm* (**a**) *(libertinaje)* vice (**b**) *(mala costumbre)* bad habit, vice; **quejarse** *o* **llorar de v.** to complain for no (good) reason; *Fam Fig* **para mí, viajar es un v.** I'm addicted to travelling; *Fam* **de v.** *(fenomenal)* brilliant (**c**) *(defecto, error)* defect; *(de dicción)* speech defect; **tiene un v. al andar** he walks in a strange way

**vicioso, -a 1** *adj* (**a**) *(depravado)* depraved (**b**) *(enviciado)* **es un jugador muy v.** he's heavily addicted to gambling

**2** *nm,f* (**a**) *(depravado)* depraved person (**b**) *(enviciado)* addict; *Fam Fig* **es un v. de las novelas policíacas** he's addicted to detective novels

**vicisitudes** *nfpl* vicissitudes, ups and downs

**víctima** *nf (por mala suerte o negligencia)* victim; *(en accidente, guerra)* casualty; **v. propiciatoria** scapegoat

**Victoria** *n* **el lago V.** Lake Victoria

**victoria** *nf* victory; **adjudicarse la v.** to win a victory; **cantar v.** to claim victory

**victoriano, -a** *adj* Victorian

**victorioso, -a** *adj* victorious

**vicuña** *nf* vicuña

**vid** *nf* vine

**vid.** *(abrev de* **véase***)* v., vide

**vida** *nf* life; **amargarse la v.** to make one's life a misery; **buscarse la v.** to try to earn one's own living; *Fig* **dar la v. por** to give one's life for; **de toda la v.** *(amigo)* lifelong; **le conozco de toda la v.** I've known him all my life; **de por v.** for life; **una mujer de v. alegre** a loose woman; **en v. de** during the life *o* lifetime of; **en mi/tu/***etc* **v.** never (in my/your/*etc* life); **estar con v.** to be alive; **estar entre la v. y la muerte** to be at death's door; **ganarse la v.** to earn a living; **pasar a mejor v.** to pass away; **pasarse la v. haciendo algo** to spend one's life doing sth; **se pasa la v. quejándose** he does nothing but complain all the time; **perder la v.** to lose one's life; **quitar la v. a alguien** to kill sb; **su v. es el teatro** the theatre is her life; **v. privada/sentimental** private/love life; **v. eterna** eternal life; **la otra v.** the next life; **¡así es la v.!** that's life!, such is life!; **darse** *o* **pegarse la gran v., darse** *o* **pegarse la v. padre** to live the life of Riley; **enterrarse en v.** to forsake the world; **la v. y milagros de alguien**

sb's life story; **llevar una v. de perros** to lead a dog's life; **¡mi v.!, ¡v. mía!** my darling!; **¿qué es de tu v.?** how's life?; **tener la v. pendiente de un hilo** to have one's life hanging by a thread; **tener siete vidas (como los gatos)** to have nine lives

**vidente** *nmf* clairvoyant

**vídeo** *nm (aparato, sistema)* video; *(cinta)* video(tape); *(videoclip)* (pop) video; **en v.** on video; **grabar en v.** to videotape, to record on video; **cámara de v.** *(profesional)* video camera; *(de aficionado)* camcorder; **v. comunitario** = system enabling one video to be shown simultaneously on different television sets in one block of flats; **v. doméstico** home video; **v. interactivo** interactive video

**videocámara** *nf* camcorder

**videocasete** *nm* video, videocassette

**videocinta** *nf* video, videotape

**videoclip** *nm* (pop) video

**videoclub** *(pl* **videoclubes***) nm* video (rental) shop

**videoconferencia** *nf* videoconference

**videodisco** *nm* videodisc

**videoedición** *nf* video editing

**videojuego** *nm* video game

**videoteca** *nf* video library

**videoteléfono** *nm* videophone

**videoterminal** *nm* video terminal

**videotexto** *nm*, **videotex** *nm inv (por señal de televisión)* teletext; *(por línea telefónica)* videotext, viewdata

**vidorra** *nf Fam* **pegarse una gran v.** to live the life of Riley

**vidriado, -a 1** *adj* glazed

**2** *nm* (**a**) *(técnica)* glazing (**b**) *(material)* glaze

**vidriera** *nf (puerta)* glass door; *(ventana)* glass window; *(en catedrales)* stained glass window

**vidriero, -a** *nm,f* (**a**) *(que fabrica cristales)* glass merchant *o* manufacturer (**b**) *(que coloca cristales)* glazier

**vidrio** *nm* (**a**) *(material)* glass (**b**) *(de ventana)* window (pane); **pagar los vidrios rotos** to carry the can

**vidrioso, -a** *adj* (**a**) *(quebradizo)* brittle (**b**) *Fig (tema, asunto)* thorny, delicate (**c**) *Fig (ojos)* glazed

**vieira** *nf* scallop

**viejo, -a 1** *adj* old; **hacerse v.** to get *o* grow old

**2** *nm,f* (**a**) *(anciano)* old man, *f* old lady; **los viejos** the elderly; **v. verde** dirty old man (**b**) *Fam (padre, madre)* old man, *f* old girl; **mis viejos** my folks (**c**) *Am Fam (amigo)* pal, mate (**d**) *Am* **V. de Pascua** Father Christmas

**Viena** *n* Vienna

**viene** *ver* **venir**

**vienés, -esa** adj & nm,f Viennese

**viento** nm (a) (aire) wind; **v. de costado** o **de lado** crosswind (b) (cuerda) guy (rope) (c) Náut (rumbo) course, bearing (d) (expresiones) **a los cuatro vientos; beber los vientos por alguien** to be head over heels in love with sb; **contra v. y marea** in spite of everything; **despedir** o **echar a alguien con v. fresco** to send sb packing; **mis esperanzas se las llevó el v.** my hopes flew out of the window; **v. en popa** splendidly, very nicely

**vientre** nm (a) (de persona) stomach, belly; **hacer de v.** to have a bowel movement; **bajo v.** lower abdomen (b) (de vasija) belly, rounded part

**viera** etc ver **ver**

**viernes** nm inv Friday; **V. Santo** Good Friday; ver también **sábado**

**vierto** etc ver **verter**

**viese** etc ver **ver**

**Vietnam** n Vietnam

**vietnamita** adj & nmf Vietnamese

**viga** nf (de madera) beam, rafter; (de metal) girder; **v. maestra** main beam

**vigencia** nf (de ley) validity; (de costumbre) use

**vigente** adj (ley) in force; (costumbre) in use

**vigésimo, -a** núm twentieth

**vigía 1** nmf lookout
  **2** nf (atalaya) watchtower

**vigilancia** nf (a) (cuidado) vigilance (b) (seguridad) security; **tras la fuga aumentaron la v.** after the escape security was increased

**vigilante 1** adj vigilant
  **2** nmf guard; **v. nocturno** night watchman

**vigilar 1** vt (enfermo) to watch over; (presos, banco) to guard; (niños, bolso) to keep an eye on; (proceso) to oversee; **vigila que nadie toque esto** make sure no-one touches this
  **2** vi to keep watch

**vigilia** nf (a) (vela) wakefulness; (periodo) period of wakefulness (b) (insomnio) sleeplessness (c) (víspera) vigil

**vigor** nm (a) (fuerza) vigour (b) (vigencia) **en v.** in force; **entrar en v.** to come into force, to take effect

**vigorizador, -ora, vigorizante** adj (medicamento) fortifying; (actividad) invigorating

**vigorizar** [16] vt (a) (fortalecer) to fortify (b) Fig (animar) to animate, to encourage

**vigoroso, -a** adj (robusto) vigorous; (colorido) strong

**vigués, -esa 1** adj of/from Vigo
  **2** nm,f person from Vigo

**vikingo, -a** adj & nm,f Viking

**vil** adj vile, despicable; Hum **el v. metal** filthy lucre

**vileza** nf (a) (acción) vile o despicable act (b) (cualidad) vileness

**vilipendiar** [15] vt (a) (ofender) to vilify, to revile (b) (despreciar) to despise; (humillar) to humiliate

**vilipendio** nm (a) (ofensa) vilification (b) (desprecio) scorn, contempt; (humillación) humiliation

**vilipendioso, -a** adj (a) (ofensivo) vilifying (b) (despreciativo) scornful, contemptuous; (humillante) humiliating

**villa** nf (a) (población) small town, **v. olímpica** Olympic village (b) (casa) villa, country house (c) Am **v. miseria** shanty town

**Villadiego** nm Fig **coger** o **tomar las de V.** to take to one's heels

**villancico** nm (navideño) Christmas carol

**villanía** nf vile o despicable act, villainy

**villano, -a 1** adj villainous
  **2** nm,f villain

**villorrio** nm Pey one-horse town, backwater

**Vilna** n Vilnius

**vilo** nm **v.** (suspendido) in the air, suspended; (inquieto) on tenterhooks; **tener a alguien en v.** to keep sb in suspense

**vinagre** nm vinegar

**vinagrera** nf (vasija) vinegar bottle; **vinagreras** (para aceite y vinagre) cruet set

**vinagreta** nf vinaigrette, French dressing

**vinatero, -a** nm,f vintner, wine merchant

**vinculación** nf link, connection

**vinculante** adj Der binding

**vincular 1** vt (a) (enlazar) to link; (por obligación) to tie, to bind (b) Der to entail
  **2 vincularse** vpr (enlazarse) **vincularse con** o **a** to form links with

**vínculo** nm (a) (lazo) (entre hechos, países) link; (personal, familiar) tie, bond (b) Der entail

**vindicación** nf (a) (venganza) vengeance, revenge (b) (defensa, rehabilitación) vindication

**vindicar** [61] vt (a) (vengar) to avenge, to revenge (b) (defender, rehabilitar) to vindicate (c) (reivindicar) to claim

**vindicatorio, -a, vindicativo, -a** adj (reivindicativo) in defence (**de** of)

**vinícola** adj (país, región) wine-producing; **industria v.** wine industry

**vinicultor, -ora** nm,f wine producer

**vinicultura** nf wine producing

**viniera** etc ver **venir**

**vinilo** nm vinyl

**vino 1** *ver* **venir**

  **2** *nm* wine; **v. blanco/tinto** white/red wine; **v. clarete** light red wine; **v. dulce/seco** sweet/dry wine; **v. espumoso** sparkling wine; **v. generoso** full-bodied wine; **v. de mesa** table wine; **v. peleón** plonk, cheap wine; **v. rosado** rosé

**viña** *nf* vineyard

**viñedo** *nm* (large) vineyard

**viñeta** *nf* (a) *(de tebeo)* (individual) cartoon (b) *(de libro)* vignette

**vio** *ver* **ver**

**viola 1** *nf* viola

  **2** *nmf* viola player

**violáceo, -a** *adj & nm* violet

**violación** *nf* (a) *(de ley, derechos)* violation, infringement (b) *(de persona)* rape (c) **v. de domicilio** unlawful entry

**violador, -ora** *adj & nm,f* rapist

**violar** *vt* (a) *(ley, derechos, domicilio)* to violate, to infringe (b) *(persona)* to rape

**violencia** *nf* (a) *(agresividad)* violence (b) *(de viento, pasiones)* force (c) *(incomodidad)* awkwardness

**violentar 1** *vt* (a) *(incomodar)* **v. a alguien** to make sb feel awkward (b) *(forzar) (cerradura)* to force; *(domicilio)* to break into

  **2 violentarse** *vpr (incomodarse)* to feel awkward

**violento, -a** *adj* (a) *(agresivo)* violent; *(intenso)* intense; *(viento)* fierce (b) *(incómodo)* awkward

**violeta 1** *nf (flor)* violet

  **2** *adj inv & nm (color)* violet

**violetera** *nf* violet seller

**violín 1** *nm* violin

  **2** *nmf* violinist

**violinista** *nmf* violinist

**violón 1** *nm* double bass

  **2** *nmf* double bass player

**violonchelista, violoncelista** *nmf* cellist

**violonchelo, violoncelo 1** *nm* cello

  **2** *nmf* cellist

**VIP** [bib] *nmf (abrev de* **very important person***)* VIP

**viperino, -a** *adj Fig* venomous

**viraje** *nm* (a) *(giro)* Aut turn; Náut tack (b) *(curva)* bend, curve (c) Fot toning (d) Fig *(cambio)* change of direction

**viral** *adj* viral

**virar 1** *vt* (a) *(girar)* to turn (round); Náut to tack, to put about (b) Fot to tone

  **2** *vi (girar)* to turn (round); **v. en redondo** to turn round; Fig *(persona)* to do a volte-face o U-turn; Fig *(ideas, política)* to change radically

**virgen 1** *adj (en general)* virgin; *(cinta)* blank; *(película)* unused

  **2** *nmf (persona)* virgin

  **3** *nf* Arte Madonna; Rel **la V.** the Virgin (Mary)

**virginal** *adj (puro)* virginal

**virginidad** *nf* virginity

**virgo 1** *nmf (persona)* Virgo

  **2** *nm* (a) *(virginidad)* virginity; *(himen)* hymen (b) *(zodiaco)* Virgo; **ser V.** to be (a) Virgo

**virguería** *nf Fam* gem; **hacer virguerías** to do wonders

**vírico, -a** *adj* viral

**viril** *adj* virile, manly

**virilidad** *nf* virility

**virola** *nf (de bastón, paraguas)* ferrule

**virolento, -a** *adj* pockmarked

**virología** *nf* virology

**virreina** *nf* vicereine

**virreinato, virreino** *nm* viceroyalty

**virrey** *nm* viceroy

**virtual** *adj* (a) *(posible)* possible, potential (b) *(casi real)* virtual

**virtualidad** *nf* potential

**virtud** *nf* (a) *(cualidad)* virtue; **v. cardinal/ teologal** cardinal/theological virtue (b) *(poder, facultad)* power; **tener la v. de** to have the power o ability to; **en v. de** by virtue of

**virtuosismo** *nm* virtuosity

**virtuoso, -a 1** *adj (honrado)* virtuous

  **2** *nm,f (genio)* virtuoso

**viruela** *nf* (a) *(enfermedad)* smallpox (b) *(pústula)* pockmark; **picado de viruelas** pockmarked

**virulé** *nf* **a la v.** *(torcido)* crooked; **un ojo a la v.** a black eye

**virulencia** *nf también Fig* virulence

**virulento, -a** *adj también Fig* virulent

**virus** *nm inv también Informát* virus

**viruta** *nf* shaving

**vis** *nf* (a) **v. a v.** face-to-face meeting (b) **v. cómica** sense of humour

**visado** *nm* visa

**visar** *vt (pasaporte)* to put a visa in

**víscera** *nf* internal organ; **vísceras** entrails

**visceral** *adj también Fig* visceral; **un sentimiento/una reacción v.** a gut feeling/reaction

**viscosa** *nf (tejido)* viscose

**viscosidad** *nf* (a) *(cualidad)* viscosity (b) *(substancia)* slime

**viscoso, -a** *adj (denso)* viscous; *(baboso)* slimy

**visera** *nf* (a) *(de gorra)* peak (b) *(de casco, suelta)* visor (c) *(de automóvil)* sun visor

**visibilidad** *nf* visibility

**visible** *adj* visible; **estar v.** *(presentable)* to be decent *o* presentable

**visigodo, -a 1** *adj* Visigothic
**2** *nm,f* Visigoth

**visillo** *nm* net curtain, lace curtain

**visión** *nf* **(a)** *(sentido, lo que se ve)* sight **(b)** *(alucinación, lucidez)* vision; **ver visiones** to be seeing things; **tener v. de futuro** to be forward-looking **(c)** *(punto de vista)* (point of) view; **una v. clara de la situación** a clear view *o* appreciation of the situation

**visionar** *vt* Cine to view *(during production or before release)*

**visionario, -a** *adj & nm,f* visionary

**visir** ( *pl* **visires**) *nm* vizier

**visita** *nf* **(a)** *(en general)* visit; *(breve)* call; **estar de v.** to be visiting *o* on a visit; **hacer una v. a alguien** to visit sb, to pay sb a visit; **ir de v.** to go visiting; *Med* **pasar v.** to see one's patients; **visitas médicas** doctor's rounds; **v. de cumplido** courtesy visit *o* call; **v. relámpago** flying visit **(b)** *(visitante)* visitor; **tener v.** *o* **visitas** to have visitors

**visitador, -ora 1** *adj* fond of visiting
**2** *nm,f* **(a)** *(de laboratorio)* medical sales representative **(b)** *(visitante)* visitor

**visitante 1** *adj* Dep visiting, away
**2** *nmf* visitor

**visitar** *vt* *(en general)* to visit; **el médico visitó al paciente** the doctor called on *o* visited the patient

**vislumbrar 1** *vt* **(a)** *(entrever)* to make out, to discern **(b)** *(adivinar)* to have an inkling of
**2 vislumbrarse** *vpr* **(a)** *(entreverse)* to be barely visible **(b)** *(adivinarse)* to become a little clearer

**vislumbre** *nf también Fig* glimmer

**viso** *nm* **(a)** *(aspecto)* **tener visos de** to seem; **tiene visos de verdad** it seems pretty true; **tiene visos de hacerse realidad** it could become a reality **(b)** *(reflejo)* *(de tejido)* sheen; *(de metal)* glint **(c)** *(de prenda)* lining

**visón** *nm* mink

**visor** *nm* **(a)** *Fot* viewfinder **(b)** *(de arma)* sight **(c)** *(en fichero)* file tab

**víspera** *nf* **(a)** *(día antes)* day before, eve; **en vísperas de** on the eve of **(b)** *Rel* **vísperas** evensong, vespers

**vista 1** *adj ver* **visto**
**2** *nf* **(a)** *(sentido)* sight, eyesight; *(ojos)* eyes; **perder la v.** to lose one's sight, to go blind; **corto de v.** short-sighted; **v. cansada** eye-strain
**(b)** *(observación)* watching
**(c)** *(mirada)* gaze; **fijar la v. en** to fix one's eyes on, to stare at; **a la v. (de)** in full view (of); **a primera** *o* **simple v.** *(aparentemente)* at

first sight, on the face of it; **estar a la v.** *(visible)* to be visible; *(muy cerca)* to be staring one in the face
**(d)** *(panorama)* view; **vistas** view; **con vistas al mar** with a sea view
**(e)** *Der* hearing
**(f)** *Com* **a la v.** at sight
**(g)** *(expresiones)* **a v. de pájaro** seen from above; **conocer a alguien de v.** to know sb by sight; **en v. de** in view of, considering; **en v. de que** since, seeing as; **con vistas a** *(con la intención de)* with a view to; **hacer la v. gorda** to turn a blind eye; **¡hasta la v.!** see you!; **no perder de v. a alguien/algo** *(vigilar)* not to let sb/sth out of one's sight; *(tener en cuenta)* not to lose sight of sb/sth, not to forget about sb/sth; **perder de v.** *(dejar de ver)* to lose sight of; *(perder contacto)* to lose touch with; **saltar a la v.** to be blindingly obvious; **tener v.** to have vision *o* foresight; **volver la v. atrás** to look back

**vistazo** *nm* glance, quick look; **echar** *o* **dar un v. a** to have a quick look at

**viste** *ver* **ver**

**vistiera** *etc ver* **vestir**

**visto, -a 1** *participio ver* **ver**
**2** *ver* **vestir**
**3** *adj* **estar muy v.** to be old-fashioned; **estar bien/mal v.** to be considered good/frowned upon; **es lo nunca v.** you've never seen anything like it; **fue v. y no v.** it happened just like that, it was over in a flash
**4** *nm* **(a)** **por lo v.** apparently; **v. que** seeing *o* given that **(b)** **el v. bueno** the go-ahead; **dar el v. bueno (a algo)** to give the go-ahead (to sth); **v. bueno** *(en documento)* approved

**vistoso, -a** *adj* eye-catching

**Vístula** *nm* **el V.** the Vistula

**visual 1** *adj* visual
**2** *nf* line of sight

**visualización** *nf* **(a)** *(en general)* visualization **(b)** *Informát* display

**visualizar** [16] *vt* **(a)** *(en general)* to visualize **(b)** *Informát* to display

**vital** *adj* **(a)** *(de la vida, esencial)* vital; **ciclo v.** life cycle **(b)** *(persona)* full of life, vivacious

**vitalicio, -a 1** *adj* for life, life; **renta vitalicia** life annuity
**2** *nm* **(a)** *(pensión)* life annuity **(b)** *(seguro)* life insurance policy

**vitalidad** *nf* vitality

**vitalizar** [16] *vt* to vitalize

**vitamina** *nf* vitamin

**vitaminado, -a** *adj* with added vitamins, vitamin-enriched

**vitamínico, -a** *adj* vitamin; **complejo v.** vitamin complex

**vitícola** *adj* *(región, industria)* grape-producing

**viticultor, -ora** *nm,f* grape grower, viticulturist

**viticultura** *nf* grape growing, viticulture

**vítor** *nm* cheer; **los vítores de la multitud** the cheers *or* cheering of the crowd

**vitorear** *vt* to cheer

**Vitoria** *n* Vitoria

**vitoriano, -a** *adj* of/from Vitoria

**vitral** *nm* stained-glass window

**vítreo, -a** *adj* vitreous

**vitrificar** [61] *vt* to vitrify

**vitrina** *nf* *(en casa)* display cabinet; *(en tienda)* showcase, glass case

**vitriolo** *nm* vitriol

**vitrocerámica** *nf* **cocina (de) v.** ceramic hob

**vituallas** *nfpl* provisions

**vituperar** *vt* to criticize harshly, to condemn

**vituperio** *nm* harsh criticism, condemnation

**viudedad** *nf* **(a)** *(viudez) (de mujer)* widowhood; *(de hombre)* widowerhood **(b)** **(pensión de) v.** widow's/widower's pension

**viudo, -a 1** *adj* widowed

**2** *nm,f* widower, *f* widow

**viva 1** *nm* cheer

**2** *interj* ¡v.! hurrah!; ¡v. el rey! long live the King!

**vivac** *nm* bivouac; **hacer v.** to bivouac

**vivacidad** *nf* liveliness

**vivalavirgen** *nmf inv* = person with a devil-may-care attitude

**vivales** *nmf inv* crafty person

**vivamente** *adv* **(a)** *(relatar, describir)* vividly **(b)** *(afectar, emocionar)* deeply

**vivaque** *nm* bivouac

**vivaquear** *vi* to bivouac

**vivaracho, -a** *adj* lively, vivacious

**vivaz** *adj* **(a)** *(despierto)* alert, sharp **(b)** *Bot* perennial

**vivencia** *nf* experience

**víveres** *nmpl* provisions, food (supplies)

**vivero** *nm* **(a)** *(de plantas)* nursery **(b)** *(de peces)* fish farm; *(de moluscos)* bed

**viveza** *nf* **(a)** *(de colorido, descripción)* vividness **(b)** *(de persona, discusión, ojos)* liveliness; *(de ingenio, inteligencia)* sharpness

**vívido, -a** *adj* real-life, true

**vívido, -a** *adj* vivid

**vividor, -ora** *nm,f* parasite, scrounger

**vivienda** *nf* **(a)** *(morada)* dwelling; **v. de protección oficial** council house; **v. de renta limitada** council house with fixed maximum rent *o* price **(b)** *(alojamiento)* housing; **plan de v.** housing plan

**viviente** *adj* living

**vivificante** *adj* *(que da vida)* life-giving; *(que reanima)* revitalizing

**vivificar** [61] *vt* *(dar vida)* to give life to; *(reanimar)* to revitalize

**vivíparo, -a** *adj* viviparous

**vivir 1** *vt* *(experimentar)* to experience, to live through; **vivió la guerra** he lived through the war

**2** *vi* to live; *(estar vivo)* to be alive; **vivió noventa años** she lived for ninety years; **v. de** to live on *o* off; **v. para algo/alguien** to live for sth/sb; **v. bien** *(económicamente)* to be well-off; *(en armonía)* to be happy; **no dejar v. a alguien** not to give sb any peace; **¿quién vive?** who goes there?; **v. para ver** who'd have thought it?

**vivisección** *nf* vivisection

**vivito, -a** *adj Fam* **v. y coleando** alive and kicking

**vivo, -a 1** *adj* **(a)** *(ser, lengua)* living; **estar v.** *(persona, costumbre, recuerdo)* to be alive **(b)** *(dolor, deseo, olor)* intense; *(luz, color, tono)* bright; **un v. interés por algo** a lively interest in sth **(c)** *(gestos, ojos, descripción)* lively, vivid; **es el v. retrato de su padre** he's the spitting image of his father **(d)** *(ingenio, niño)* quick, sharp; *(ciudad)* lively **(e)** *(genio)* quick, hot

**2** *nm,f* **los vivos** the living

**3** *nm* **en v.** *(en directo)* live; *(sin anestesia)* without anaesthetic

**vizcaíno, -a** *adj & nm,f* Biscayan

**Vizcaya** *n* Vizcaya; **Golfo de V.** Bay of Biscay

**vizconde, -esa** *nm,f* viscount, *f* viscountess

**V.O.** *nf* *(abrev de* **versión original***)* original language version; **V.O. subtitulada** subtitled version

**vocablo** *nm* word, term

**vocabulario** *nm* **(a)** *(riqueza léxica)* vocabulary **(b)** *(diccionario)* dictionary

**vocación** *nf* vocation, calling

**vocacional** *adj* vocational

**vocal 1** *adj* vocal

**2** *nmf* member

**3** *nf* vowel

**vocálico, -a** *adj* **sonido v.** vowel sound

**vocalista** *nmf* vocalist

**vocalización** *nf* vocalization

**vocalizar** [16] *vi* to enunciate clearly

**vocativo** *nm* vocative

**vocear 1** *vt* **(a)** *(gritar)* to shout out, to call out **(b)** *(llamar)* to shout to, to call to **(c)** *(vitorear)* to cheer **(d)** *(pregonar) (mercancía)* to hawk; *(secreto)* to publicize

**2** *vi* *(gritar)* to shout

**vocerío** *nm* shouting

**vocero, -a** *nm,f* *(portavoz)* spokesperson

**vociferante** *adj* shouting

**vociferar** *vi* to shout

**vodevil** *nm* vaudeville

**vodka** ['boðka] *nm o nf* vodka

**vol.** (*abrev de* **volumen**) vol

**voladizo** *nm* ledge

**volado, -a** *adj Fam (ido)* **estar v.** to be away with the fairies

**volador, -ora 1** *adj* flying

**2** *nm* **(a)** *(pez)* flying fish **(b)** *(calamar)* = type of squid **(c)** *(cohete)* rocket

**voladura** *nf (en guerras, atentados)* blowing-up; *(de edificio en ruinas)* demolition *(with explosives)*; *Min* blasting

**volandas** *nfpl* **levantar a alguien en v.** to lift sb off the ground; **la multitud le llevó en v.** the crowd carried him on their shoulders

**volantazo** *nm* **dar un v.** to slew one's car round, to swerve

**volante 1** *adj* flying

**2** *nm* **(a)** *(para conducir)* (steering) wheel; **estar o ir al v.** to be at the wheel **(b)** *(automovilismo)* motor racing **(c)** *(de tela)* frill, flounce **(d)** *(del médico)* (referral) note **(e)** *(en bádminton)* shuttlecock

**volantín** *nm Chile* kite

**volapié** *nm Taurom* = method of killing the bull

**volar [65] 1** *vt (en guerras, atentados)* to blow up; *(caja fuerte, puerta)* to blow open; *(edificio en ruinas)* to demolish *(with explosives)*; *Min* to blast

**2** *vi* **(a)** *(en el aire)* to fly; *(papeles)* to blow away; **v. a** *(una altura)* to fly at; *(un lugar)* to fly to; **echar(se) a v.** to fly away *o* off **(b)** *Fam (desaparecer)* to disappear, to vanish **(c)** *Fig (correr)* to fly (off), to rush (off); **v. a hacer algo** to rush off to do sth; **hacer algo volando** to do sth at top speed; **me voy volando** I must fly *o* dash **(d)** *Fig (días, años)* to fly by

**3 volarse** *vpr (papeles)* to be blown away

**volatería** *nf* birds, fowl

**volátil** *adj Quím & Fig* volatile

**volatilización** *nf* volatilization

**volatilizar [16] 1** *vt* to volatilize

**2 volatilizarse** *vpr* **(a)** *Fís* to volatilize, to evaporate **(b)** *Fam Fig (desaparecer)* to vanish into thin air

**volatinero, -a** *nm,f* acrobat

**volcado** *nm Informát* **v. de pantalla** screen dump; **v. de pantalla en impresora** hard copy

**volcán** *nm* volcano

**volcánico, -a** *adj* volcanic

**volcar [69] 1** *vt* **(a)** *(tirar)* to knock over; *(carretilla)* to tip up **(b)** *(vaciar)* to empty out

**2** *vi (coche, camión)* to overturn; *(barco)* to capsize

**3 volcarse** *vpr* **(a)** *(caerse)* to fall over **(b)** *(esforzarse)* to bend over backwards **(con/en** for/in)

**volea** *nf* volley

**voleibol** *nm* volleyball

**voleo** *nm* volley; **a o al v.** randomly, any old how; **sembrar a v.** to sow seed by hand

**Volga** *nm* **el V.** the (River) Volga

**volitivo, -a** *adj* voluntary

**volován** *nm* vol-au-vent

**volqué** *etc ver* **volcar**

**volquete** *nm* dumper truck, *US* dump truck

**voltaico, -a** *adj* voltaic

**voltaje** *nm* voltage

**volteador, -ora** *nm,f* acrobat

**voltear 1** *vt* **(a)** *(heno, crepe, torero)* to toss; *(tortilla)* to turn over; *(mesa, silla)* to turn upside-down **(b)** *Am (derribar)* to knock over **(c)** *Am (dar la vuelta)* to turn over

**2 voltearse** *vpr Am* **(a)** *(volverse)* to turn around **(b)** *(volcarse)* to overturn

**voltereta** *nf (en el suelo)* handspring; *(en el aire)* somersault; **dar una v.** to do a somersault; **v. lateral** cartwheel

**voltímetro** *nm* voltmeter

**voltio** *nm* **(a)** *(electricidad)* volt **(b)** *Fam (paseo)* walk, stroll; **dar un v.** to go for a walk

**volubilidad** *nf* changeability, fickleness

**voluble** *adj* **(a)** *(persona)* changeable, fickle **(b)** *Bot* climbing

**volumen** *nm* **(a)** *también Com* volume; **subir/bajar el v.** *(de aparato)* to turn up/down the volume; **sube el v. que no te oímos** speak up, please, we can't hear you; **a todo v.** at full volume; *Econ* **v. de contratación** trading volume; **v. de negocio o ventas** turnover **(b)** *(espacio ocupado)* size, bulk

**voluminoso, -a** *adj* bulky

**voluntad** *nf* **(a)** *(determinación)* will, willpower; **v. de hierro** iron will **(b)** *(intención)* intention; **buena v.** goodwill; **mala v.** ill will **(c)** *(deseo)* wishes, will; **contra la v. de alguien** against sb's will **(d)** *(albedrío)* free will; **a v.** *(cuanto se quiere)* as much as one likes; **¿qué le debo? – la v.** what do I owe you? – whatever you think fit; **por v. propia** of one's own free will

**voluntariado** *nm* volunteers; **la ley del v.** = law governing voluntary work

**voluntariedad** *nf* **(a)** *(intencionalidad)* volition **(b)** *(no obligatoriedad)* voluntary nature

**voluntario, -a 1** *adj* voluntary

**2** *nm,f* volunteer

**voluntarioso, -a** *adj* willing

**voluptuosidad** *nf* voluptuousness

**voluptuoso, -a** *adj* voluptuous

**voluta** *nf* spiral

**volver** [43] 1 *vt* (a) *(dar la vuelta a)* to turn round; *(lo de arriba abajo)* to turn over (b) *(poner del revés) (boca abajo)* to turn upside down; *(lo de dentro fuera)* to turn inside out; *(lo de detrás delante)* to turn back to front (c) *(cabeza, ojos)* to turn (d) *(convertir en)* **eso le volvió un delincuente** that made him a criminal, that turned him into a criminal; **la lejía volvió blanca la camisa** the bleach turned the shirt white

2 *vi* (a) *(ir de vuelta)* to go back, to return; *(venir de vuelta)* to come back, to return; **yo allí no vuelvo** I'm not going back there; **vuelve, no te vayas** come back, don't go; **v. en sí** to come to, to regain consciousness (b) *(reanudar)* **v. a la tarea** to return to one's work; *(hacer otra vez)* **v. a hacer algo** to do sth again; *Fig* **v. a nacer** to be reborn

3 **volverse** *vpr* (a) *(darse la vuelta, girar la cabeza)* to turn round (b) *(ir de vuelta)* to go back, to return; *(venir de vuelta)* to come back, to return (c) *(convertirse en)* to become; **volverse loco/pálido** to go mad/pale (d) *(de una afirmación, promesa)* to go back on one's word; *(de una decisión)* to change one's mind, to back out; **volverse (en) contra (de)** alguien to turn against sb

**vomitar 1** *vt* to vomit, to bring up

2 *vi* to vomit, to be sick; *Fig* **me dan** *o* **entran ganas de v.** it makes me want to throw up

**vomitera** *nf* acute vomiting

**vomitivo, -a 1** *adj* (a) *Med* emetic (b) *Fam Fig (asqueroso)* sick-making

2 *nm* emetic

**vómito** *nm* (a) *(acción)* vomiting (b) *(substancia)* vomit

**vomitona** *nf Fam* **me dio una v.** I threw up

**voracidad** *nf* voraciousness

**vorágine** *nf Fig* confusion, whirl

**voraz** *adj* (a) *(persona, apetito)* voracious (b) *Fig (fuego, enfermedad)* raging

**vórtice** *nm* (a) *(de agua)* whirlpool, vortex (b) *(de aire)* whirlwind

**vos** *pron personal CAm, CSur (tú)* you

**V.O.S.E.** *nf* (*abrev de* **versión original subtitulada en español**) = original language version subtitled in Spanish

**voseo** *nm* = practice of using the "vos" pronoun with its corresponding verb form instead of the second person singular when addressing friends, typical of Argentina and Uruguay

**vosotros, -as** *pron personal* you *(plural)*; **v. bailáis muy bien** you dance very well; **son más fuertes que v.** they're stronger than you

**votación** *nf* vote, voting; **decidir algo por v.** to put sth to the vote; **v. a mano alzada** show of hands

**votante** *nmf* voter

**votar 1** *vt* (a) *(partido, candidato)* to vote for; *(ley)* to vote on (b) *(aprobar)* to pass, to approve *(by vote)*

2 *vi* to vote; **v. por** *(emitir un voto por)* to vote for; *Fig (estar a favor de)* to be in favour of; **v. por que…** to vote (that)…; **v. en blanco** to return a blank ballot paper

**voto** *nm* (a) *(en general)* vote; **v. afirmativo** *o* a favor vote in favour; **v. de calidad** casting vote; **v. de castigo** vote against one's own party; **v. de confianza/censura** vote of confidence/no confidence; **v. en blanco** unmarked ballot; **v. por correspondencia** *o* **correo** postal vote; **v. nulo** spoilt ballot; **v. secreto** secret ballot

(b) *Rel* vow; **hacer v. de** to vow to; **v. de castidad/pobreza/silencio** vow of chastity/poverty/silence

(c) *(ruego)* prayer, plea; **hacer votos por** to pray for; **votos de felicidad** best wishes

**vox populi** *nf* **ser v. que…** to be common knowledge that…

**voy** *ver* **ir**

**voyeur** [bwa'jer] (*pl* **voyeurs**) *nmf* voyeur

**voyeurismo** [bwaje'rismo] *nm* voyeurism

**voyeurístico, -a** [bwaje'ristiko] *adj* voyeuristic

**voz** *nf* (a) *también Gram* voice; **a media v.** in a low voice, under one's breath; **a v. en cuello** *o* **grito** at the top of one's voice; **aclarar** *o* **aclararse la v.** to clear one's throat; **alzar** *o* **levantar la v. a alguien** to raise one's voice to sb; **de viva v.** by word of mouth; **en v. alta** aloud; **en v. baja** softly, in a low voice; **mudó la v.** his voice broke; **tener la v. tomada** to be hoarse; *Gram* **v. activa/pasiva** active/passive voice; **la v. de la conciencia** the voice of conscience; **v. en off** *Cine* voice-over; *Teatro* voice offstage

(b) *(grito)* shout; **a voces** shouting; **dar voces** to shout

(c) *(vocablo)* word; **dar la v. de alerta** to raise the alarm; **v. de mando** order, command

(d) *(derecho a expresarse)* say, voice; **no tener ni v. ni voto** to have no say in the matter

(e) *(rumor)* rumour; **corre la v. de que va a dimitir** people are saying that she's going to resign

(f) *(expresiones)* **correr la v.** to spread the word; **estar pidiendo algo a voces** to be crying out for sth; **llevar la v. cantante** to be the boss

**vozarrón** *nm* loud voice

**VPO** nf (abrev de **viviendas de protec-ción oficial**) = low-cost housing subsidized by the government

**VTR** nf (abrev de **videotape recording**) VTR

**vudú** nm voodoo

**vuelco 1** ver **volcar**

**2** nm upset; **dar un v.** (coche) to overturn; (relaciones, vida) to change completely; (empresa) to go to ruin; **me dio un v. el corazón** my heart missed o skipped a beat

**vuelo 1** ver **volar**

**2** nm (a) también Av flight; **alzar** o **empren-der** o **levantar el v.** (despegar) to take flight, to fly off; Fig (irse de casa) to fly the nest; **coger algo al v.** (en el aire) to catch sth in flight; Fig (rápido) to catch on to sth very quickly; **remontar el v.** to soar; **de altos vuelos, de mucho v.** of great importance; **no se oía el v. de una mosca** you could have heard a pin drop; **v. chárter/regular** charter/scheduled flight; **v. espacial** space flight; **v. libre** hang-gliding; **v. sin escalas** direct flight; **v. sin motor** gliding; **vuelos nacionales** domestic flights (b) (de vestido) fullness; **una falda de v.** a full skirt (c) Arquit projection

**vuelque** etc ver **volcar**

**vuelta** nf (a) (en general) turn; (acción) turning; **dar una v. (a algo)** (recorriéndolo) to go round (sth); **darse la v.** to turn round; **dar vueltas (a algo)** (girándolo) to turn (sth) round; Mil **me-dia v.** about-turn; Aut U-turn; Taurom **v. al ruedo** bullfighter's lap of honour

(b) Dep lap; **v. (ciclista)** tour; **v. de honor** lap of honour

(c) (regreso, devolución) return; **a la v.** (volviendo) on the way back; (al llegar) on one's return; **estar de v.** to be back

(d) (paseo) **dar una v.** (a pie) to go for a walk; (en coche) to go for a drive o spin; **dar vueltas** (en coche) to drive round and round

(e) (dinero sobrante) change

(f) (ronda, turno) **dar la primera/se-gunda v.** the first/second round

(g) (parte opuesta) back, other side; también Fig **a la v. de la esquina** round the corner; **a la v. de la página** over the page

(h) (cambio, avatar) change; Fig **dar la** o **una v.** to turn around completely

(i) (de pantalón) Br turn-up, US cuff; (de manga) cuff

(j) (en labor de punto) row

(k) (expresiones) **a la v. de** (tras) at the end of;

**a v. de correo** by return of post; Fam **dar la v. a la tortilla** to turn the tables; Fam **darle cien vueltas a alguien** to knock spots off sb; **dar una v./dos/**etc **vueltas de campana** (coche) to turn over once/twice/etc; **darle vueltas a algo** to turn sth over in one's mind; **estar de v. de algo** to be blasé about sth; **estar de v. de todo** to have seen it all before; **la cabeza me da vueltas** my head's spinning; **no tiene v. de hoja** there are no two ways about it; Fam **poner a alguien de v. y media** (criticar) to call sb all the names under the sun; (regañar) to give sb a good telling-off; **sin v. de hoja** irrevocable

**vuelto, -a 1** participio ver **volver**

**2** adj turned

**3** nm Am change

**vuelvo** etc ver **volver**

**vuestro, -a 1** adj posesivo your; **v. libro/ amigo** your book/friend; **este libro es v.** this book is yours; **un amigo v.** a friend of yours; **no es asunto v.** it's none of your business

**2** pron poses **el v.** yours; **los vuestros están en la mesa** yours are on the table; Fam **ésta es la vuestra** this is the chance you've been wait-ing for o your big chance; **lo v. es el teatro** (lo que hacéis bien) you should be on the stage; Fam **los vuestros** (vuestra familia) your folks; (vuestro bando) your lot, your side

**vulcanología** nf vulcanology

**vulcanólogo, -a** nm,f vulcanologist

**vulgar** adj (a) (no refinado) vulgar (b) (corriente, común) ordinary, common (c) (no técnico) non-technical, lay

**vulgaridad** nf (a) (grosería) vulgarity; **ha-cer/decir una v.** to do/say something vulgar (b) (banalidad) banality

**vulgarismo** nm Gram vulgarism

**vulgarización** nf popularization

**vulgarizar** [16] **1** vt to popularize

**2 vulgarizarse** vpr to become popular o common

**vulgo** nm **el v.** (plebe) the masses, the common people; (no expertos) the lay public

**vulnerabilidad** nf vulnerability

**vulnerable** adj vulnerable

**vulneración** nf (a) (de prestigio, reputación) harming, damaging; (de intimidad) invasion (b) (de ley, pacto) violation, infringement

**vulnerar** vt (a) (prestigio, reputación) to harm, to damage; (intimidad) to invade (b) (ley, pacto) to violate, to break

**vulva** nf vulva

# W

**W, w** [uβe'ðoβle] *nf (letra)* W, w

**walkie-talkie** ['walki'talki] *(pl* **walkie-talkies)** *nm* walkie-talkie

**walkman**® ['walman] *(pl* **walkmans)** *nm* Walkman®

**Washington** ['wasinton] *n* Washington

**wáter** ['bater] *(pl* **wáteres)** *nm* toilet

**waterpolista** [waterpo'lista] *nmf* water polo player

**waterpolo** [water'polo] *nm* water polo

**watio** ['batio] *nm* watt

**WC** *nm (abrev de* **water closet)** WC

**Web, web** [web] *Informát* **1** *nf (World Wide Web)* la W. the Web
**2** *nm o nf (página Web)* web site

**Wellington** ['welinton] *n* Wellington

**western** ['wester] *(pl* **westerns)** *nm Cine* western

**whiskería** [wiske'ria] *nf* = bar where hostesses chat with clients

**whisky** ['wiski] *nm* whisky

**windsurf** ['winsurf], **windsurfing** ['winsurfin] *nm* windsurfing

**windsurfista** [winsur'fista] *nmf* windsurfer

**WWW** *nf (abrev de* **World Wide Web)** WWW

# X

**X, x** ['ekis] **1** *nf (letra)* X, x
**2** *nmf* la señora X Mrs X

**xenofobia** *nf* xenophobia

**xenófobo, -a 1** *adj* xenophobic
**2** *nm,f* xenophobe

**xerografía** *nf* photocopying

**xerografiar** *vt* to photocopy

**xilofón, xilófono** *nm* xylophone

**xilofonista** *nmf* xylophone player

**xilografía** *nf* **(a)** *(técnica)* woodcut printing **(b)** *(impresión)* woodcut

**Xunta** ['ʃunta] *nf* = autonomous government of the region of Galicia

# Y

**Y, y[1]** [i'grjeɣa] *nf (letra)* Y, y

**y[2]**

> **e** is used instead of **y** before words beginning with "i" or "hi" (e.g. *Pérez e hijos* Perez and Sons).

*conj* **(a)** *(en general)* and; **un ordenador y una impresora** a computer and a printer; **horas y horas de espera** hours and hours of waiting

**(b)** *(en preguntas)* what about; **¿y tu mujer?** what about your wife?

**ya 1** *adv* **(a)** *(en el pasado)* already; **ya me lo habías contado** you had already told me; **ya en 1926** as long ago as 1926

**(b)** *(ahora)* now; *(inmediatamente)* at once; **hay que hacer algo ya** something has to be done now/at once; **bueno, yo ya me voy** right, I'm off now; **ya no es así** it's no longer like that; **¡ya voy!** I'm coming!

**(c)** *(en el futuro)* **ya te llamaré** I'll give you a ring some time; **ya hablaremos** we'll talk later; **ya nos habremos ido** we'll already have gone; **ya verás** you'll (soon) see

**(d)** *(refuerza al verbo)* **ya entiendo/lo sé** I understand/know

**2** *conj* **(a)** *(distributiva)* **ya (sea) por... ya (sea) por...** whether for... or...

**(b)** *(adversativa)* **ya no... sino, no ya ... sino** not only... but

**(c)** *(consecutiva)* **ya que** since; **ya que has venido, ayúdame con esto** since you're here, give me a hand with this

**3** *interj* **¡ya!** *(expresa asentimiento)* right!; *(expresa comprensión)* yes!; *Irón* **¡ya, ya!** sure!, yes, of course!

**yac, yak** *nm*

**yacaré** *nm* cayman

**yacente, yaciente** *adj (tumbado)* lying; *Arte* recumbent, reclining

**yacer** [73] *vi* **(a)** *(estar tumbado, enterrrado)* to lie; **aquí yace...** here lies... **(b)** *(tener relaciones sexuales)* to lie together

**yacimiento** *nm (minero)* bed, deposit; *(arqueológico)* site; **y. de petróleo** oilfield

**yago** *ver* **yacer**

**Yakarta** *n* Jakarta

**yanqui 1** *adj* **(a)** *Hist* Yankee **(b)** *Fam (estadounidense)* American; **un político y.** an American politician

**2** *nmf* **(a)** *Hist* Yankee **(b)** *Fam (estadounidense)* Yank

**yantar** *Anticuado* **1** *nm* fare, food

**2** *vt* to eat

**Yaoundé** [jaun'de] *n* Yaoundé

**yarda** *nf* yard

**yate** *nm* yacht

**yayo, -a** *nm,f Fam* grandad, *f* grandma

**yazco** *ver* **yacer**

**yazgo** *ver* **yacer**

**yegua** *nf* mare

**yeguada** *nf* herd of horses; **tiene una gran y.** he's got a lot of horses

**yeísmo** *nm* = pronunciation of Spanish "ll" as "y", widespread in practice, though regarded as incorrect by purists

**yeísta** *nmf* = person who pronounces Spanish "ll" as "y"

**yelmo** *nm* helmet

**yema** *nf* **(a)** *(de huevo)* yolk **(b)** *(de planta)* bud, shoot **(c)** *(de dedo)* fingertip **(d)** *Culin* = sweet made from sugar and egg yolk

**Yemen** *nm* **(el) Y.** Yemen

**yemení** *(pl* yemeníes*)*, **yemenita** *adj & nmf* Yemeni

**yen** *(pl* yenes*) nm* yen

**yerba** *nf* = **hierba**

**yerbatero** *nm Am* healer

**Yereván** *n* Yerevan

**yergo** *etc ver* **erguir**

**yermar** *vt* to leave unsown *o* fallow

**yermo, -a 1** *adj* **(a)** *(estéril)* barren **(b)** *(despoblado)* uninhabited

**2** *nm* wasteland

**yerno** *nm* son-in-law

**yerro 1** *ver* **errar**

**2** *nm* mistake, error

**yerto, -a** *adj* rigid, stiff

**yesca** *nf* tinder

**yesería** *nf (fábrica)* gypsum kiln

**yesero, -a 1** *adj* plaster; **producción ye-sera** plaster production

  **2** *nm,f* **(a)** *(fabricante)* plaster manufacturer **(b)** *(obrero)* plasterer

**yeso** *nm* **(a)** *Geol* gypsum **(b)** *Constr* plaster **(c)** *Arte* gesso

**yeti** *nm* yeti

**yeyé** *adj inv Fam* **música/ropa y.** sixties music/clothes

**Yibuti** *n* Djibouti

**yiddish** *nm* Yiddish

**yihad** *nf* jihad

**yiu-yitsu** *nm* jujitsu

**yo**

> Usually omitted as a personal pronoun in Spanish except for emphasis or contrast.

  **1** *pron personal* **(a)** *(sujeto)* I; **yo me llamo Luis** I'm called Luis

  **(b)** *(predicado)* **soy yo** it's me

  **(c)** **yo de ti/él/***etc* if I were you/him/*etc; Fam* **yo que tú/ él/***etc* if I were you/him/*etc*

  **2** *nm Psi* **el yo** the ego

**yodado, -a** *adj* iodized

**yodo** *nm* iodine

**yoga** *nm* yoga

**yogui** *nmf* yogi

**yogur** (*pl* **yogures**), **yogurt** (*pl* **yogurts**) *nm* yoghurt

**yogurtera** *nf* yoghurt maker

**yonqui** *nmf Fam* junkie

**yóquey** (*pl* **yóqueys**) *nm* jockey

**yoyó** *nm* yoyo

**yuca** *nf* **(a)** *Bot* yucca **(b)** *Culin* cassava, manioc

**yudo** *nm* judo

**yudoka** *nmf* judo player, judoka

**yugo** *nm también Fig* yoke

**Yugoslavia** *n* Yugoslavia

**yugoslavo, -a 1** *adj* Yugoslavian

  **2** *nm,f* Yugoslav

**yugular** *adj & nf* jugular

**yunque** *nm* anvil

**yunta** *nf* *(de bueyes, vacas)* yoke, team

**yupi** *interj Fam* **¡y.!** yippee!

**yuppie** ['jupi] (*pl* **yuppies**), **yuppi** *nmf* yuppie

**yute** *nm* jute

**yuxtaponer** [52] **1** *vt* to juxtapose

  **2 yuxtaponerse** *vpr* to be juxtaposed (**a** with)

**yuxtaposición** *nf* juxtaposition

**yuxtapuesto, -a** *participio ver* **yuxtaponer**

# Z

**Z, z** ['θeta] *nf (letra)* Z, z

**zafarrancho** *nm* **(a)** *Náut* clearing of the decks; *Mil* **z. de combate** call to action stations **(b)** *Fig (destrozo)* mess **(c)** *Fig (riña)* row, fracas

**zafarse** *vpr* to get out of it, to escape; **z. de** *(persona)* to get rid of; *(obligación)* to get out of

**zafiedad** *nf* roughness, uncouthness

**zafio, -a** *adj* rough, uncouth

**zafiro** *nm* sapphire

**zaga** *nf Dep* defence; **a la z.** behind, at the back; *Fam* **no irle a la z. a alguien** to be every bit *o* just as good as sb

**zagal, -ala** *nm,f* **(a)** *(muchacho)* adolescent, teenager **(b)** *(pastor)* shepherd, *f* shepherdess

**zaguán** *nm* (entrance) hall

**zaguero, -a** *nm,f Dep* defender; *(en rugby)* fullback

**zaherir** *vt* **(a)** *(herir)* to hurt **(b)** *(burlarse de)* to mock **(c)** *(criticar)* to pillory

**zahorí** (*pl* **zahoríes**) *nmf* **(a)** *(de agua)* water diviner **(b)** *Fig (clarividente)* mind reader

**zaino, -a** *adj* **(a)** *(caballo)* chestnut **(b)** *(res)* black

**Zaire** *n Antes* Zaire

**zaireño, -a** *adj & nm,f* Zairean

**zalamería** *nf* flattery, fawning

**zalamero, -a 1** *adj* flattering, fawning

  **2** *nm,f* flatterer

**zamarra** *nf* sheepskin jacket

**Zambia** *n* Zambia

**zambo, -a 1** *adj* knock-kneed

  **2** *nm,f* knock-kneed person

**zambomba 1** *nf Mús* type of rustic drum
**2** *interj Fam* ¡z.! wow!
**zambombazo** *nm* (a) *(ruido)* bang (b) *Dep* cracker of a shot, rocket
**zambullida** *nf* dive; **darse una z.** *(baño)* to go for a dip
**zambullir 1** *vt* to dip, to submerge
**2 zambullirse** *vpr (agua)* to dive (**en** into); *(actividad)* to immerse oneself (**en** in)
**zamorano, -a 1** *adj* of/from Zamora
**2** *nm,f* person from Zamora
**zampabollos** *nmf inv Fam* human dustbin
**zampar** *Fam* **1** *vi* to gobble
**2 zamparse** *vpr* to scoff, to wolf down
**zampoña** *nf* pan pipes
**zanahoria** *nf* carrot
**zanca** *nf (de ave)* leg, shank
**zancada** *nf* stride
**zancadilla** *nf* trip; **poner una** *o* **la z. a alguien** *(hacer tropezar)* to trip sb up; *Fig* to put a spoke in sb's wheel
**zancadillear** *vt* **z. alguien** to trip sb up; *Fig* to put a spoke in sb's wheel
**zanco** *nm* stilt
**zancuda** *nf* wader
**zancudo, -a 1** *adj* long-legged
**2** *nm Am* mosquito
**zanganear** *vi Fam* to laze about
**zángano, -a 1** *nm,f Fam (persona)* lazy oaf, idler
**2** *nm (abeja)* drone
**zanja** *nf* ditch
**zanjar** *vt (poner fin a)* to put an end to; *(resolver)* to settle, to resolve
**zapa** *nf Fig* **les acusó de hacer labor de z.** she accused them of undermining her
**zapador** *nm Mil* sapper
**zapallo** *nm Am* sweet pumpkin
**zapapico** *nm* pickaxe
**zapata** *nf* (a) *(cuña)* wedge (b) *(de freno)* shoe
**zapatazo** *nm* stamp (of the foot)
**zapateado** *nm* = type of flamenco music and dance
**zapatear** *vi* to stamp one's feet
**zapatería** *nf* (a) *(oficio)* shoemaking (b) *(taller)* shoemaker's (c) *(tienda)* shoe shop
**zapatero, -a 1** *adj* **industria zapatera** shoe-making industry
**2** *nm,f* (a) *(fabricante)* shoemaker (b) *(reparador)* z. **de viejo** *o* **remendón** cobbler; *Fig* ¡z. **a tus zapatos!** mind your own business! (c) *(vendedor)* shoe seller (d) *(insecto)* pondskater
**zapatilla** *nf* (a) *(de baile)* shoe, pump; *(de estar en casa)* slipper; *(de deporte)* sports shoe, trainer, *US* sneaker (b) *(de grifo)* washer
**zapatillazo** *nm* whack *(with a slipper)*

**zapatista** *adj & nmf Pol* = member of the Zapatista Front, a mainly indigenous insurrectionist group in the Southern Mexican state of Chiapas; *Hist* = follower or supporter of the Mexican revolutionary Emiliano Zapata (1879–1919)
**zapato** *nm* shoe; *Fig* **saber alguien dónde le aprieta el z.** to know which side one's bread is buttered
**zape** *interj Fam (sorpresa)* ¡z.! wow!
**zapear** *vi Fam* to channel-hop
**zapeo** *nm Fam* channel-hopping
**zapping** ['θapin] *nm inv Fam* channel-hopping; **hacer z.** to channel-hop
**zar** *nm* tsar, czar
**zarabanda** *nf* (a) *(danza)* saraband (b) *Fig (jaleo)* commotion, uproar
**Zaragoza** *n* Saragossa
**zaragozano, -a** *adj* of/from Saragossa
**zarajo** *nm* = lamb intestines, rolled round two crossed sticks and fried
**zarandajas** *nfpl Fam* nonsense, trifles
**zarandeado, -a** *adj* eventful, turbulent
**zarandear** *vt (cosa)* to shake; *(persona)* to jostle, to knock about
**zarandeo** *nm* (a) *(sacudida)* shake, shaking (b) *(empujón)* pushing *o* knocking about
**zarcillo** *nm* earring
**zarco, -a** *adj* light blue
**zarina** *nf* tsarina, czarina
**zarismo** *nm* **el fin del z.** the end of the Tsars *o* Czars
**zarista** *adj & nmf* Tsarist, Czarist
**zarpa** *nf* (a) *(de animal) (uña)* claw; *(mano)* paw (b) *Fam (de persona)* paw, hand
**zarpar** *vi* to weigh anchor, to set sail
**zarpazo** *nm* clawing
**zarrapastroso, -a** *Fam* **1** *adj* scruffy, shabby
**2** *nm,f* scruff
**zarza** *nf* bramble, blackberry bush
**zarzal** *nm* bramble patch
**zarzamora** *nf* blackberry
**zarzaparrilla** *nf* sarsaparilla
**zarzuela** *nf* (a) *Mús* zarzuela, = Spanish light opera (b) *Culin* = fish and/or seafood stew
**zas** *interj* ¡z.! wham!, bang!
**zascandil** *nm Fam* fidget, restless person
**zascandilear** *vi Fam* to faff about *o* around
**zen** *adj inv & nm* Zen
**zenit** *nm también Fig* zenith
**zepelín** *(pl zepelines) nm* zeppelin
**zeta** *nf Fam (coche)* z. *(de policía)* police patrol car
**zigoto** *nm* zygote

**zigzag** (*pl* **zigzags** *o* **zigzagues**) *nm* zigzag

**zigzagueante** *adj* **una carretera z.** a winding road

**zigzaguear** *vi* to zigzag

**zigzagueo** *nm* (*de carretera, sendero*) twisting and turning

**Zimbabue** *n* Zimbabwe

**zinc** *nm* zinc

**zíngaro, -a** *adj & nm,f* Gypsy

**zíper** *nm Méx* zip, *US* zipper

**zipizape** *nm Fam* squabble, set-to

**zócalo** *nm* (**a**) (*de pared*) skirting board (**b**) (*de edificio, pedestal*) plinth (**c**) (*pedestal*) pedestal (**d**) *Méx* main square

**zoco** *nm* souk, Arabian market

**zodiac**® *nf* = rubber dinghy with outboard motor

**zodiacal** *adj* zodiacal

**zodiaco, zódiaco** *nm* zodiac

**zombi, zombie 1** *adj Fam* (*atontado*) zonked
  **2** *nmf también Fig* zombie

**zona** *nf* (*espacio*) zone, area; (*en baloncesto*) key; *Aut* **z. azul** restricted parking zone; **z. catastrófica** disaster area; **z. comercial** shopping area; *Com* **z. franca** free-trade zone; **z. de guerra** war zone; **z. peatonal** pedestrian precinct; **z. de urgente reindustrialización** *Br* ≃ enterprise zone, = region given priority status for industrial investment; **z. verde** (*grande*) park; (*pequeño*) lawn

**zoo** *nm* zoo

**zoofilia** *nf* bestiality

**zoología** *nf* zoology

**zoológico, -a 1** *adj* zoological
  **2** *nm* zoo

**zoólogo, -a** *nm,f* zoologist

**zoom** [θum] (*pl* **zooms**) *nm Fot* zoom

**zopenco, -a** *Fam* **1** *adj* idiotic, daft
  **2** *nm,f* idiot, nitwit

**zopilote** *nm Am* vulture

**zoquete 1** *adj Fam* thick, dense
  **2** *nm* (*calcetín*) *CSur* ankle sock
  **3** *nmf Fam* (*tonto*) blockhead, idiot

**zorra** *nf Fam Pey* (*ramera*) whore, tart, *US* hooker

**zorro, -a 1** *adj* foxy, crafty; *Vulg* **no tengo ni zorra** (**idea**) I haven't got a bloody clue
  **2** *nm,f también Fig* fox; **z. azul/ártico** blue/arctic fox
  **3** *nm* (*piel*) fox (fur)
  **4** *nmpl* **zorros** (*utensilio*) feather duster; *Fam* **estar hecho unos zorros** (*cansado, maltrecho*) to be whacked, to be done in; (*enfurecido*) to be fuming

**zozobra** *nf* (**a**) (*inquietud*) anxiety, worry (**b**) (*naufragio*) sinking; *Fig* (*de empresa, planes*) ruin, end

**zozobrar** *vi* (**a**) (*naufragar*) to be shipwrecked (**b**) *Fig* (*fracasar*) to fall through

**zueco** *nm* clog

**zulo** *nm* hiding place

**zulú** (*pl* **zulúes**) *adj & nmf* Zulu

**zumbado, -a** *Fam* **1** *adj* halfwitted, crazy
  **2** *nm,f* halfwit, nut

**zumbador** *nm* buzzer

**zumbar 1** *vi* (*producir ruido*) to buzz; (*máquinas*) to whirr, to hum; **me zumban los oídos** my ears are buzzing; *Fig* **venir zumbando** to come running
  **2** *vt Fam* (*golpear*) to beat, to thump

**zumbido** *nm* (*ruido*) buzz, buzzing; (*de máquinas*) whirr, whirring

**zumbón, -ona** *Fam* **1** *adj* funny, joking
  **2** *nm,f* joker, tease

**zumo** *nm* juice

**zurcido** *nm* (**a**) (*acción*) darning (**b**) (*remiendo*) darn

**zurcidor, -ora** *nm,f* darner, mender

**zurcir** [74] *vt* to darn; *Fam* **¡anda y que te zurzan!** on your bike!, get lost!

**zurda** *nf* (**a**) (*mano*) left hand (**b**) (*pierna*) left foot

**zurdazo** *nm* left-footed kick

**zurdo, -a 1** *adj* (*mano, pierna*) left; (*persona*) left-handed
  **2** *nm,f* (*persona*) left-handed person

**Zurich** ['θurik] *n* Zurich

**zurra** *nf Fam* beating, hiding

**zurrar** *vt Fam* (*pegar*) to beat, to thrash

**zurrón** *nm* shepherd's shoulder bag

**zurzo** *ver* **zurcir**

**zutano, -a** *nm,f* (*hombre*) so-and-so, what's-his-name; (*mujer*) so-and-so, what's-her-name

# Supplement
# Suplemento

# Verbos Irregulares Ingleses

| Infinitivo | Pretérito | Participio |
|---|---|---|
| arise | arose | arisen |
| awake | awoke | awoken |
| awaken | awoke, awakened | awakened, awoken |
| be | were/was | been |
| bear | bore | borne |
| beat | beat | beaten |
| become | became | become |
| begin | began | begun |
| bend | bent | bent |
| beseech | besought, beseeched | besought, beseeched |
| bet | bet, betted | bet, betted |
| bid | bade, bid | bidden, bid |
| bind | bound | bound |
| bite | bit | bitten |
| bleed | bled | bled |
| blow | blew | blown |
| break | broke | broken |
| breed | bred | bred |
| bring | brought | brought |
| build | built | built |
| burn | burnt, burned | burnt, burned |
| burst | burst | burst |
| bust | bust, busted | bust, busted |
| buy | bought | bought |
| cast | cast | cast |
| catch | caught | caught |
| chide | chided, chid | chided, chidden |
| choose | chose | chosen |
| cleave | cleaved, cleft, clove | cleaved, cleft, cloven |
| cling | clung | clung |
| clothe | clad, clothed | clad, clothed |
| come | came | come |
| cost | cost | cost |
| creep | crept | crept |
| crow | crowed, crew | crowed |
| cut | cut | cut |
| deal | dealt | dealt |
| dig | dug | dug |
| dive | dived, *US* dove | dived |
| do | did | done |
| draw | drew | drawn |
| dream | dreamt, dreamed | dreamt, dreamed |
| drink | drank | drunk |

| Infinitivo | Pretérito | Participio |
|---|---|---|
| drive | drove | driven |
| dwell | dwelt | dwelt |
| eat | ate | eaten |
| fall | fell | fallen |
| feed | fed | fed |
| feel | felt | felt |
| fight | fought | fought |
| find | found | found |
| flee | fled | fled |
| fling | flung | flung |
| fly | flew | flown |
| forget | forgot | forgotten |
| forgive | forgave | forgiven |
| forsake | forsook | forsaken |
| freeze | froze | frozen |
| get | got | got, US gotten |
| gild | gilded, gilt | gilded, gilt |
| gird | girded, girt | girded, girt |
| give | gave | given |
| go | went | gone |
| grind | ground | ground |
| grow | grew | grown |
| hang | hung/hanged | hung/hanged |
| have | had | had |
| hear | heard | heard |
| hew | hewed | hewn, hewed |
| hide | hid | hidden |
| hit | hit | hit |
| hold | held | held |
| hurt | hurt | hurt |
| keep | kept | kept |
| kneel | knelt | knelt |
| knit | knitted, knit | knitted, knit |
| know | knew | known |
| lay | laid | laid |
| lead | led | led |
| lean | leant, leaned | leant, leaned |
| leap | leapt, leaped | leapt, leaped |
| learn | learnt, learned | learnt, learned |
| leave | left | left |
| lend | lent | lent |
| let | let | let |
| lie | lay | lain |
| light | lit | lit |

| Infinitivo | Pretérito | Participio |
|---|---|---|
| lose | lost | lost |
| make | made | made |
| mean | meant | meant |
| meet | met | met |
| mow | mowed | mown |
| pay | paid | paid |
| plead | pleaded, *US* pled | pleaded, *US* pled |
| prove | proved | proved, proven |
| put | put | put |
| quit | quit, quitted | quit, quitted |
| read | read [red] | read [red] |
| rend | rent | rent |
| rid | rid | rid |
| ride | rode | ridden |
| ring | rang | rung |
| rise | rose | risen |
| run | ran | run |
| saw | sawed | sawn, sawed |
| say | said | said |
| see | saw | seen |
| seek | sought | sought |
| sell | sold | sold |
| send | sent | sent |
| set | set | set |
| sew | sewed | sewn |
| shake | shook | shaken |
| shear | sheared | shorn, sheared |
| shed | shed | shed |
| shine | shone | shone |
| shit | shitted, shat | shitted, shat |
| shoe | shod | shod |
| shoot | shot | shot |
| show | showed | shown |
| shrink | shrank | shrunk |
| shut | shut | shut |
| sing | sang | sung |
| sink | sank | sunk |
| sit | sat | sat |
| slay | slew | slain |
| sleep | slept | slept |
| slide | slid | slid |
| sling | slung | slung |
| slink | slunk | slunk |
| slit | slit | slit |
| smell | smelled, smelt | smelled, smelt |
| smite | smote | smitten |
| sneak | sneaked, *US* snuck | sneaked, *US* snuck |

(iv)

| Infinitivo | Pretérito | Participio |
|---|---|---|
| sow | sowed | sown, sowed |
| speak | spoke | spoken |
| speed | sped, speeded | sped, speeded |
| spell | spelt, spelled | spelt, spelled |
| spend | spent | spent |
| spill | spilt, spilled | spilt, spilled |
| spin | span | spun |
| spit | spat, *US* spit | spat, *US* spit |
| split | split | split |
| spoil | spoilt, spoiled | spoilt, spoiled |
| spread | spread | spread |
| spring | sprang | sprung |
| stand | stood | stood |
| stave in | staved in, stove in | staved in, stove in |
| steal | stole | stolen |
| stick | stuck | stuck |
| sting | stung | stung |
| stink | stank, stunk | stunk |
| strew | strewed | strewed, strewn |
| stride | strode | stridden |
| strike | struck | struck |
| string | strung | strung |
| strive | strove | striven |
| swear | swore | sworn |
| sweep | swept | swept |
| swell | swelled | swollen, swelled |
| swim | swam | swum |
| swing | swung | swung |
| take | took | taken |
| teach | taught | taught |
| tear | tore | torn |
| tell | told | told |
| think | thought | thought |
| thrive | thrived, throve | thrived |
| throw | threw | thrown |
| thrust | thrust | thrust |
| tread | trod | trodden |
| wake | woke | woken |
| wear | wore | worn |
| weave | wove, weaved | woven, weaved |
| weep | wept | wept |
| wet | wet, wetted | wet, wetted |
| win | won | won |
| wind | wound | wound |
| wring | wrung | wrung |
| write | wrote | written |

# Spanish Verbs

This guide to Spanish verbs opens with the three regular conjugations (verbs ending in "-ar", "-er" and "-ir"), followed by the two most common auxiliary verbs: **haber**, which is used to form the perfect tenses and **ser**, which is used to form the passive. These five verbs are given in full.

These are followed by a list of Spanish irregular verbs, numbered 3-74. A number refers you to these tables after irregular verbs in the main part of the dictionary.

The first person of each tense is always shown, even if it is regular. Of the other forms, only those which are irregular

| INDICATIVE | | | | |
| Present | Imperfect | Preterite | Present Perfect | Future |
|---|---|---|---|---|
| **Regular "-ar"** | **amar** | | | |
| yo amo | yo amaba | yo amé | yo he amado | yo amaré |
| tú amas | tú amabas | tú amaste | tú has amado | tú amarás |
| él ama | él amaba | él amó | él ha amado | él amará |
| nosotros amamos | nosotros amábamos | nosotros amamos | nosotros hemos amado | nosotros amaremos |
| vosotros amáis | vosotros amabais | vosotros amasteis | vosotros habéis amado | vosotros amaréis |
| ellos aman | ellos amaban | ellos amaron | ellos han amado | ellos amarán |
| **Regular "-er"** | **temer** | | | |
| yo temo | yo temía | yo temí | yo he temido | yo temeré |
| tú temes | tú temías | tú temiste | tú has temido | tú temerás |
| él teme | él temía | él temió | él ha temido | él temerá |
| nosotros tememos | nosotros temíamos | nosotros temimos | nosotros hemos temido | nosotros temeremos |
| vosotros teméis | vosotros temíais | vosotros temisteis | vosotros habéis temido | vosotros temeréis |
| ellos temen | ellos temían | ellos temieron | ellos han temido | ellos temerán |
| **Regular "-ir"** | **partir** | | | |
| yo parto | yo partía | yo partí | yo he partido | yo partiré |
| tú partes | tú partías | tú partiste | tú has partido | tú partirás |
| él parte | él partía | él partió | él ha partido | él partirá |
| nosotros partimos | nosotros partíamos | nosotros partimos | nosotros hemos partido | nosotros partiremos |
| vosotros partís | vosotros partíais | vosotros partisteis | vosotros habéis partido | vosotros partiréis |
| ellos parten | ellos partían | ellos partieron | ellos han partido | ellos partirán |
| **1 haber** | | | | |
| yo he | yo había | yo hube | yo he habido | yo habré |
| tú has | tú habías | tú hubiste | tú has habido | tú habrás |
| él ha | él había | él hubo | él ha habido | él habrá |
| nosotros hemos | nosotros habíamos | nosotros hubimos | nosotros hemos habido | nosotros habremos |
| vosotros habéis | vosotros habíais | vosotros hubisteis | vosotros habéis habido | vosotros habréis |
| ellos han | ellos habían | ellos hubieron | ellos han habido | ellos habrán |

are given. An *etc* after a form indicates that the other forms of that tense use the same irregular stem, e.g. the future of **decir** is **yo diré** *etc*, i.e.: **yo diré, tú dirás, él dirá, nosotros diremos, vosotros diréis, ellos dirán.**

When the first person of a tense is the only irregular form, then it is not followed by *etc*, e.g. the present indicative of **placer** is **yo plazco** (irregular), but the other forms (**tú places, él place, nosotros placemos, vosotros placéis, ellos placen**) are regular and are thus not shown.

| CONDITIONAL | SUBJUNCTIVE | | IMPERATIVE | PARTICIPLE | |
|-------------|-------------|-----------|------------|------------|------|
| Present | Present | Imperfect | | Present | Past |
| yo amaría | yo ame | yo amara *o* amase | | amando | amado |
| tú amarías | tú ames | tú amaras *o* amases | ama (tú) | | |
| él amaría | él ame | él amara *o* amase | ame (él, ella) | | |
| nosotros amaríamos | nosotros amemos | nosotros amáramos *o* amásemos | amemos (nosotros) | | |
| vosotros amaríais | vosotros améis | vosotros amarais *o* amaseis | amad (vosotros) | | |
| ellos amarían | ellos amen | ellos amaran *o* amasen | amen (ellos, ellas) | | |
| yo temería | yo tema | yo temiera *o* temiese | | temiendo | temido |
| tú temerías | tú temas | tú temieras *o* temieses | teme (tú) | | |
| él temería | él tema | él temiera *o* temiese | tema (él, ella) | | |
| nosotros temeríamos | nosotros temamos | nosotros temiéramos *o* temiésemos | temamos (nosotros) | | |
| vosotros temeríais | vosotros temáis | vosotros temierais *o* temieseis | temed (vosotros) | | |
| ellos temerían | ellos teman | ellos temieran *o* temiesen | teman (ellos, ellas) | | |
| yo partiría | yo parta | yo partiera *o* partiese | | partiendo | partido |
| tú partirías | tú partas | tú partieras *o* partieses | parte (tú) | | |
| él partiría | él parta | él partiera *o* partiese | parta (él, ella) | | |
| nosotros partiríamos | nosotros partamos | nosotros partiéramos *o* partiésemos | partamos (nosotros) | | |
| vosotros partiríais | vosotros partáis | vosotros partierais *o* partieseis | partid (vosotros) | | |
| ellos partirían | ellos partan | ellos partieran *o* partiesen | partan (ellos, ellas) | | |
| yo habría | yo haya | yo hubiera *o* hubiese | | habiendo | habido |
| tú habrías | tú hayas | tú hubieras *o* hubieses | he (tú) | | |
| él habría | él haya | él hubiera *o* hubiese | haya (él, ella) | | |
| nosotros habríamos | nosotros hayamos | nosotros hubiéramos *o* hubiésemos | hayamos (nosotros) | | |
| vosotros habríais | vosotros hayáis | vosotros hubierais *o* hubieseis | habed (vosotros) | | |
| ellos habrían | ellos hayan | ellos hubieran *o* hubiesen | hayan (ellos, ellas) | | |

| | Present | Imperfect | Preterite | Present Perfect | Future |
|---|---|---|---|---|---|
| **2** | **ser** | | | | |
| | yo soy | yo era | yo fui | yo he sido | yo seré |
| | tú eres | tú eras | tú fuiste | tú has sido | tú serás |
| | él es | él era | él fue | él ha sido | él será |
| | nosotros somos | nosotros éramos | nosotros fuimos | nosotros hemos sido | nosotros seremos |
| | vosotros sois | vosotros erais | vosotros fuisteis | vosotros habéis sido | vosotros seréis |
| | ellos son | ellos eran | ellos fueron | ellos han sido | ellos serán |
| **3** | **acertar** | | | | |
| | yo acierto | yo acertaba | yo acerté | yo he acertado | yo acertaré |
| | tú aciertas | | | | |
| | él acierta | | | | |
| | ellos aciertan | | | | |
| **4** | **actuar** | | | | |
| | yo actúo | yo actuaba | yo actué | yo he actuado | yo actuaré |
| | tú actúas | | | | |
| | él actúa | | | | |
| | ellos actúan | | | | |
| **5** | **adecuar** | | | | |
| | yo adecuo | yo adecuaba | yo adecué | yo he adecuado | yo adecuaré |
| **6** | **adquirir** | | | | |
| | yo adquiero | yo adquiría | yo adquirí | yo he adquirido | yo adquiriré |
| | tú adquieres | | | | |
| | él adquiere | | | | |
| | ellos adquieren | | | | |
| **7** | **agorar** | | | | |
| | yo agüero | yo agoraba | yo agoré | yo he agorado | yo agoraré |
| | tú agüeras | | | | |
| | él agüera | | | | |
| | ellos agüeran | | | | |
| **8** | **andar** | | | | |
| | yo ando | yo andaba | yo anduve | yo he andado | yo andaré |
| | | | tú anduviste | | |
| | | | él anduvo | | |
| | | | nosotros anduvimos | | |
| | | | vosotros anduvisteis | | |
| | | | ellos anduvieron | | |
| **9** | **argüir** | | | | |
| | yo arguyo | yo argüía | yo argüí | yo he argüido | yo argüiré |
| | tú arguyes | | | | |
| | él arguye | | él arguyó | | |
| | ellos arguyen | | ellos arguyeron | | |
| **10** | **asir** | | | | |
| | yo asgo | yo asía | yo así | yo he asido | yo asiré |
| **11** | **avergonzar** | | | | |
| | yo avergüenzo | yo avergonzaba | yo avergoncé | yo he avergonzado | yo avergonzaré |
| | tú avergüenzas | | | | |
| | él avergüenza | | | | |
| | ellos avergüenzan | | | | |

| CONDITIONAL | SUBJUNCTIVE | | IMPERATIVE | PARTICIPLE | |
|---|---|---|---|---|---|
| Present | Present | Imperfect | | Present | Past |
| yo sería | yo sea | yo fuera *o* fuese | | siendo | sido |
| tú serías | tú seas | tú fueras *o* fueses | sé (tú) | | |
| él sería | él sea | él fuera *o* fuese | sea (él, ella) | | |
| nosotros seríamos | nosotros seamos | nosotros fuéramos *o* fuésemos | seamos (nosotros) | | |
| vosotros seríais | vosotros seáis | vosotros fuerais *o* fueseis | sed (vosotros) | | |
| ellos serían | ellos sean | ellos fueran *o* fuesen | sean (ellos, ellas) | | |
| yo acertaría | yo acierte | yo acertara *o* acertase | acierta (tú) | acertando | acertado |
| | tú aciertes | | | | |
| | él acierte | | | | |
| | ellos acierten | | | | |
| yo actuaría | yo actúe | yo actuara *o* actuase | actúa (tú) | actuando | actuado |
| yo adecuaría | yo adecue | yo adecuara *o* adecuase | adecua (tú) | adecuando | adecuado |
| yo adquiriría | yo adquiera | yo adquiriera *o* adquiriese | adquiere (tú) | adquiriendo | adquirido |
| | tú adquieras | | | | |
| | él adquiera | | | | |
| | ellos adquieran | | | | |
| yo agoraría | yo agüere | yo agorara *o* agorase | agüera (tú) | agorando | agorado |
| | tú agüeres | | | | |
| | él agüere | | | | |
| | ellos agüeren | | | | |
| yo andaría | yo ande | yo anduviera *o* anduviese *etc* | anda (tú) | andando | andado |
| yo argüiría | yo arguya *etc* | yo arguyera *o* arguyese *etc* | arguye (tú) | arguyendo | argüido |
| yo asiría | yo asga *etc* | yo asiera *o* asiese | ase (tú) | asiendo | asido |
| yo avergonzaría | yo avergüence | yo avergonzara *o* avergonzase | avergüenza (tú) | avergon- zando | avergon- zado |
| | tú avergüences | | | | |
| | él avergüence | | | | |
| | nosotros avergoncemos | | | | |
| | vosotros avergoncéis | | | | |
| | ellos avergüencen | | | | |

| INDICATIVE Present | Imperfect | Preterite | Present Perfect | Future |
|---|---|---|---|---|
| **12 averiguar** | | | | |
| yo averiguo | yo averiguaba | yo averigüé | yo he averiguado | yo averiguaré |
| **13 caber** | | | | |
| yo quepo | yo cabía | yo cupe | yo he cabido | yo cabré *etc* |
| | | tú cupiste | | |
| | | él cupo | | |
| | | nosotros cupimos | | |
| | | vosotros cupisteis | | |
| | | ellos cupieron | | |
| **14 caer** | | | | |
| yo caigo | yo caía | yo caí | yo he caído | yo caeré |
| | | tú caíste | | |
| | | él cayó | | |
| | | nosotros caímos | | |
| | | vosotros caísteis | | |
| | | ellos cayeron | | |
| **15 cambiar** | | | | |
| yo cambio | yo cambiaba | yo cambié | yo he cambiado | yo cambiaré |
| **16 cazar** | | | | |
| yo cazo | yo cazaba | yo cacé | yo he cazado | yo cazaré |
| **17 cocer** | | | | |
| yo cuezo | yo cocía | yo cocí | yo he cocido | yo coceré |
| tú cueces | | | | |
| él cuece | | | | |
| | | | | |
| ellos cuecen | | | | |
| **18 colgar** | | | | |
| yo cuelgo | yo colgaba | yo colgué | yo he colgado | yo colgaré |
| tú cuelgas | | | | |
| él cuelga | | | | |
| | | | | |
| ellos cuelgan | | | | |
| **19 comenzar** | | | | |
| yo comienzo | yo comenzaba | yo comencé | yo he comenzado | yo comenzaré |
| | | | | |
| tú comienzas | | | | |
| él comienza | | | | |
| | | | | |
| | | | | |
| ellos comienzan | | | | |
| **20 conducir** | | | | |
| yo conduzco | yo conducía | yo conduje | yo he conducido | yo conduciré |
| | | tú condujiste | | |
| | | él condujo | | |
| | | nosotros condujimos | | |
| | | vosotros condujisteis | | |
| | | ellos condujeron | | |
| **21 conocer** | | | | |
| yo conozco | yo conocía | yo conocí | yo he conocido | yo conoceré |

| CONDITIONAL | SUBJUNCTIVE | | IMPERATIVE | PARTICIPLE | |
|---|---|---|---|---|---|
| Present | Present | Imperfect | | Present | Past |
| yo averiguaría | yo averigüe *etc* | yo averiguara *o* averiguase | averigua (tú) | averiguando | averiguado |
| yo cabría *etc* | yo quepa *etc* | yo cupiera *o* cupiese *etc* | cabe (tú) | cabiendo | cabido |
| yo caería | yo caiga *etc* | yo cayera *o* cayese *etc* | cae (tú) | cayendo | caído |
| yo cambiaría | yo cambie | yo cambiara *o* cambiase | cambia (tú) | cambiando | cambiado |
| yo cazaría | yo cace *etc* | yo cazara *o* cazase | caza (tú) | cazando | cazado |
| yo cocería | yo cueza<br>tú cuezas<br>él cueza<br>nosotros cozamos<br>vosotros cozáis<br>ellos cuezan | yo cociera *o* cociese | cuece (tú) | cociendo | cocido |
| yo colgaría | yo cuelgue<br>tú cuelgues<br>él cuelgue<br>nosotros colguemos<br>vosotros colguéis<br>ellos cuelguen | yo colgara *o* colgase | cuelga (tú) | colgando | colgado |
| yo comenzaría | yo comience<br><br>tú comiences<br>él comience<br>nosotros comencemos<br>vosotros comencéis<br>ellos comiencen | yo comenzara *o* comenzase | comienza (tú) | comenzando | comenzado |
| yo conduciría | yo conduzca *etc* | yo condujera *o* condujese *etc* | conduce (tú) | conduciendo | conducido |
| yo conocería | yo conozca *etc* | yo conociera *o* conociese | conoce (tú) | conociendo | conocido |

| INDICATIVE | | | | |
| Present | Imperfect | Preterite | Present Perfect | Future |
| --- | --- | --- | --- | --- |
| **22 dar** | | | | |
| yo doy | yo daba | yo di<br>tú diste<br>él dio<br>nosotros dimos<br>vosotros disteis<br>ellos dieron | yo he dado | yo daré |
| **23 decir** | | | | |
| yo digo<br>tú dices<br>él dice<br><br>ellos dicen | yo decía | yo dije<br>tú dijiste<br>él dijo<br>nosotros dijimos<br>vosotros dijisteis<br>ellos dijeron | yo he dicho | yo diré *etc* |
| **24 delinquir** | | | | |
| yo delinco | yo delinquía | yo delinquí | yo he delinquido | yo delinquiré |
| **25 desosar** | | | | |
| yo deshueso<br>tú deshuesas<br>él deshuesa<br>ellos deshuesan | yo deshuesaba *etc* | yo desosé | yo he desosado | yo desosaré |
| **26 dirigir** | | | | |
| yo dirijo | yo dirigía | yo dirigí | yo he dirigido | yo dirigiré |
| **27 discernir** | | | | |
| yo discierno<br><br>tú disciernes<br>él discierne<br>ellos disciernen | yo discernía | yo discerní | yo he discernido | yo discerniré |
| **28 distinguir** | | | | |
| yo distingo | yo distinguía | yo distinguí | yo he distinguido | yo distinguiré |
| **29 dormir** | | | | |
| yo duermo<br><br>tú duermes<br>él duerme<br><br>ellos duermen | yo dormía | yo dormí<br><br>él durmió<br><br>ellos durmieron | yo he dormido | yo dormiré |
| **30 erguir** | | | | |
| yo irgo *o* yergo<br>tú irgues *o* yergues<br>él irgue *o* yergue<br>nosotros erguimos<br>vosotros erguís<br>ellos irguen o<br>yerguen | yo erguía | yo erguí<br><br>él irguió<br><br>ellos irguieron | yo he erguido | yo erguiré |
| **31 errar** | | | | |
| yo yerro<br>tú yerras<br>él yerra<br>ellos yerran | yo erraba | yo erré | yo he errado | yo erraré |

| CONDITIONAL Present | SUBJUNCTIVE Present | Imperfect | IMPERATIVE | PARTICIPLE Present | Past |
|---|---|---|---|---|---|
| yo daría | yo dé | yo diera o diese etc | da (tú) | dando | dado |
| yo diría etc | yo diga etc | yo dijera o dijese etc | di (tú) | diciendo | dicho |
| yo delinquiría | yo delinca etc | yo delinquiera o delinquiese | delinque (tú) | delinquiendo | delinquido |
| yo desosaría | yo deshuese tú deshueses él deshuese ellos deshuesen | yo desosara o desosase | deshuesa (tú) | desosando | desosado |
| yo dirigiría | yo dirija etc | yo dirigiera o dirigiese | dirige (tú) | dirigiendo | dirigido |
| yo discerniría | yo discierna tú disciernas él discierna ellos disciernan | yo discerniera o discerniese | discierne (tú) | discerniendo | discernido |
| yo distinguiría | yo distinga etc | yo distinguiera o distinguiese | distingue (tú) | distinguiendo | distinguido |
| yo dormiría | yo duerma nosotros durmamos vosotros durmáis | yo durmiera o durmiese etc | duerme (tú) | durmiendo | dormido |
| yo erguiría | yo irga o yerga tú irgas o yergas él irga o yerga nosotros irgamos vosotros irgáis ellos irgan o yergan | yo irguiera o irguiese | irgue o yergue (tú) | irguiendo | erguido |
| yo erraría | yo yerre tú yerres él yerre ellos yerren | yo errara o errase | yerra (tú) | errando | errado |

| INDICATIVE | | | | |
|---|---|---|---|---|
| **Present** | **Imperfect** | **Preterite** | **Present Perfect** | **Future** |
| **32 estar** | | | | |
| yo estoy | yo estaba | yo estuve | yo he estado | yo estaré |
| tú estás | | tú estuviste | | |
| él está | | él estuvo | | |
| nosotros estamos | | nosotros estuvimos | | |
| vosotros estáis | | vosotros estuvisteis | | |
| ellos están | | ellos estuvieron | | |
| **33 forzar** | | | | |
| yo fuerzo | yo forzaba | yo forcé | yo he forzado | yo forzaré |
| tú fuerzas | | | | |
| él fuerza | | | | |
| ellos fuerzan | | | | |
| **34 guiar** | | | | |
| yo guío | yo guiaba | yo guié | yo he guiado | yo guiaré |
| tú guías | | | | |
| él guía | | | | |
| ellos guían | | | | |
| **35 hacer** | | | | |
| yo hago | yo hacía | yo hice | yo he hecho | yo haré *etc* |
| | | tú hiciste | | |
| | | él hizo | | |
| | | nosotros hicimos | | |
| | | vosotros hicisteis | | |
| | | ellos hicieron | | |
| **36 huir** | | | | |
| yo huyo | yo huía | yo huí | yo he huido | yo huiré |
| tú huyes | | | | |
| él huye | | él huyó | | |
| ellos huyen | | ellos huyeron | | |
| **37 ir** | | | | |
| yo voy | yo iba | yo fui | yo he ido | yo iré |
| tú vas | | tú fuiste | | |
| él va | | él fue | | |
| nosotros vamos | | nosotros fuimos | | |
| vosotros vais | | vosotros fuisteis | | |
| ellos van | | ellos fueron | | |
| **38 jugar** | | | | |
| yo juego | yo jugaba | yo jugué | yo he jugado | yo jugaré |
| tú juegas | | | | |
| él juega | | | | |
| ellos juegan | | | | |
| **39 leer** | | | | |
| yo leo | yo leía | yo leí | yo he leído | yo leeré |
| | | tú leíste | | |
| | | él leyó | | |
| | | nosotros leímos | | |
| | | vosotros leísteis | | |
| | | ellos leyeron | | |
| **40 llegar** | | | | |
| yo llego | yo llegaba | yo llegué | yo he llegado | yo llegaré |
| **41 lucir** | | | | |
| yo luzco | yo lucía | yo lucí | yo he lucido | yo luciré |
| **42 mecer** | | | | |
| yo mezo | yo mecía | yo mecí | yo he mecido | yo meceré |

| CONDITIONAL | SUBJUNCTIVE | | IMPERATIVE | PARTICIPLE | |
|---|---|---|---|---|---|
| Present | Present | Imperfect | | Present | Past |
| yo estaría | yo esté *etc* | yo estuviera *o* estuviese *etc* | está (tú) | estando | estado |
| yo forzaría | yo fuerce<br>tú fuerces<br>él fuerce<br>nosotros forcemos<br>vosotros forcéis<br>ellos fuercen | yo forzara *o* forzase | fuerza (tú) | forzando | forzado |
| yo guiaría | yo guíe<br>tú guíes<br>él guíe<br>ellos guíen | yo guiara *o* guiase | guía (tú) | guiando | guiado |
| yo haría *etc* | yo haga *etc* | yo hiciera *o* hiciese *etc* | haz (tú) | haciendo | hecho |
| yo huiría | yo huya *etc* | yo huyera *o* huyese *etc* | huye (tú) | huyendo | huido |
| yo iría | yo vaya *etc* | yo fuera *o* fuese *etc* | ve (tú) | yendo | ido |
| yo jugaría | yo juegue<br>tú juegues<br>él juegue<br>nosotros juguemos<br>vosotros juguéis<br>ellos jueguen | yo jugara *o* jugase | juega (tú) | jugando | jugado |
| yo leería | yo lea | yo leyera *o* leyese *etc* | lee (tú) | leyendo | leído |
| yo llegaría | yo llegue *etc* | yo llegara *o* llegase | llega (tú) | llegando | llegado |
| yo luciría | yo luzca *etc* | yo luciera *o* luciese | luce (tú) | luciendo | lucido |
| yo mecería | yo meza *etc* | yo meciera *o* meciese | mece (tú) | meciendo | mecido |

| INDICATIVE | | | | |
| Present | Imperfect | Preterite | Present Perfect | Future |
|---|---|---|---|---|
| **43 mover** | | | | |
| yo muevo | yo movía | yo moví | yo he movido | yo moveré |
| tú mueves | | | | |
| él mueve | | | | |
| ellos mueven | | | | |
| **44 nacer** | | | | |
| yo nazco | yo nacía | yo nací | yo he nacido | yo naceré |
| **45 negar** | | | | |
| yo niego | yo negaba | yo negué | yo he negado | yo negaré |
| tú niegas | | | | |
| él niega | | | | |
| ellos niegan | | | | |
| **46 oír** | | | | |
| yo oigo | yo oía | yo oí | yo he oído | yo oiré |
| tú oyes | | | | |
| él oye | | él oyó | | |
| ellos oyeron | | ellos oyeron | | |
| **47 oler** | | | | |
| yo huelo | yo olía | yo olí | yo he olido | yo oleré |
| tú hueles | | | | |
| él huele | | | | |
| ellos huelen | | | | |
| **48 parecer** | | | | |
| yo parezco | yo parecía | yo parecí | yo he parecido | yo pareceré |
| **49 pedir** | | | | |
| yo pido | yo pedía | yo pedí | yo he pedido | yo pediré |
| tú pides | | | | |
| él pide | | él pidió | | |
| ellos piden | | ellos pidieron | | |
| **50 placer** | | | | |
| yo plazco | yo placía | yo plací | yo he placido | yo placeré |
| | | él plació *o* plugo | | |
| | | ellos placieron *o* plugieron | | |
| **51 poder** | | | | |
| yo puedo | yo podía | yo pude | yo he podido | yo podré *etc* |
| tú puedes | | tú pudiste | | |
| él puede | | él pudo | | |
| | | nosotros pudimos | | |
| | | vosotros pudisteis | | |
| ellos pueden | | ellos pudieron | | |
| **52 poner** | | | | |
| yo pongo | yo ponía | yo puse | yo he puesto | yo pondré *etc* |
| | | tú pusiste | | |
| | | él puso | | |
| | | nosotros pusimos | | |
| | | vosotros pusisteis | | |
| | | ellos pusieron | | |

| CONDITIONAL | SUBJUNCTIVE | | IMPERATIVE | PARTICIPLE | |
|---|---|---|---|---|---|
| Present | Present | Imperfect | | Present | Past |
| yo movería | yo mueva<br>tú muevas<br>él mueva<br>ellos muevan | yo moviera o moviese | mueve (tú) | moviendo | movido |
| yo nacería | yo nazca *etc* | yo naciera o naciese | nace (tú) | naciendo | nacido |
| yo negaría | yo niegue<br>tú niegues<br>él niegue<br>nosotros neguemos<br>vosotros neguéis<br>ellos nieguen | yo negara o negase | niega (tú) | negando | negado |
| yo oiría | yo oiga *etc* | yo oyera u oyese *etc* | oye (tú) | oyendo | oído |
| yo olería | yo huela<br>tú huelas<br>él huela<br>ellos huelan | yo oliera u oliese | huele (tú) | oliendo | olido |
| yo parecería | yo parezca *etc* | yo pareciera o pareciese | parece (tú) | pareciendo | parecido |
| yo pediría | yo pida *etc* | yo pidiera o pidiese *etc* | pide (tú) | pidiendo | pedido |
| yo placería | yo plazca<br>tú plazcas<br>él plazca o plegue<br>nosotros plazcamos<br>vosotros plazcáis<br>ellos plazcan | yo placiera o placiese<br>tú placieras o placieses<br>él placiera, placiese,<br>pluguiera o pluguiese<br>nosotros placiéramos o<br>placiésemos<br>vosotros placierais o<br>placieseis<br>ellos placieran, placiesen,<br>puguieran o pluguiesen | place (tú) | placiendo | placido |
| yo podría *etc* | yo pueda<br>tú puedas<br>él pueda<br>ellos puedan | yo pudiera o<br>pudiese *etc* | puede (tú) | pudiendo | podido |
| yo pondría *etc* | yo ponga *etc* | yo pusiera o<br>pusiese *etc* | pon (tú) | poniendo | puesto |

| | Present | Imperfect | Preterite | Present Perfect | Future |
|---|---|---|---|---|---|
| **53** | **predecir** | | | | |
| | yo predigo | yo predecía | yo predije | yo he predicho | yo prediciré |
| | | | tú predijiste | | |
| | | | él predijo | | |
| | | | nosotros predijimos | | |
| | | | vosotros predijisteis | | |
| | | | ellos predijeron | | |
| **54** | **proteger** | | | | |
| | yo protejo | yo protegía | yo protegí | yo he protegido | yo protegeré |
| **55** | **querer** | | | | |
| | yo quiero | yo quería | yo quise | yo he querido | yo querré *etc* |
| | tú quieres | | tú quisiste | | |
| | él quiere | | él quiso | | |
| | | | nosotros quisimos | | |
| | | | vosotros quisisteis | | |
| | ellos quieren | | ellos quisieron | | |
| **56** | **raer** | | | | |
| | yo rao, raigo *o* rayo | yo raía | yo raí | yo he raído | yo raeré |
| | | | tú raíste | | |
| | | | él rayó | | |
| | | | nosotros raímos | | |
| | | | vosotros raísteis | | |
| | | | ellos rayeron | | |
| **57** | **regir** | | | | |
| | yo rijo | yo regía | yo regí | yo he regido | yo regiré |
| | tú riges | | | | |
| | él rige | | él rigió | | |
| | ellos rigen | | ellos rigieron | | |
| **58** | **reír** | | | | |
| | yo río | yo reía | yo reí | yo he reído | yo reiré |
| | tú ríes | | | | |
| | él ríe | | él rió | | |
| | | | | | |
| | | | ellos rieron | | |
| **59** | **roer** | | | | |
| | yo roo, roigo *o* royo | yo roía | yo roí | yo he roído | yo roeré |
| | | | él royó | | |
| | | | ellos royeron | | |
| **60** | **saber** | | | | |
| | yo sé | yo sabía | yo supe | yo he sabido | yo sabré *etc* |
| | | | tú supiste | | |
| | | | él supo | | |
| | | | nosotros supimos | | |
| | | | vosotros supisteis | | |
| | | | ellos supieron | | |
| **61** | **sacar** | | | | |
| | yo saco | yo sacaba | yo saqué | yo he sacado | yo sacaré |
| **62** | **salir** | | | | |
| | yo salgo | yo salía | yo salí | yo he salido | yo saldré *etc* |
| **63** | **seguir** | | | | |
| | yo sigo | yo seguía | yo seguí | yo he seguido | yo seguiré |
| | tú sigues | | | | |
| | él sigue | | él siguió | | |
| | ellos siguen | | ellos siguieron | | |

| CONDITIONAL | SUBJUNCTIVE | | IMPERATIVE | PARTICIPLE | |
|---|---|---|---|---|---|
| Present | Present | Imperfect | | Present | Past |
| yo predeciría | yo prediga *etc* | yo predijera *o* predijese *etc* | predice (tú) | prediciendo | predicho |
| yo protegería | yo proteja *etc* | yo protegiera *o* protegiese | protege (tú) | protegiendo | protegido |
| yo querría *etc* | yo quiera<br>tú quieras<br>él quiera<br><br>ellos quieran | yo quisiera *o* quisiese *etc* | quiere (tú) | queriendo | querido |
| yo raería | yo raiga *o* raya *etc* | yo rayera *o* rayese *etc* | rae (tú) | rayendo | raído |
| yo regiría | yo rija *etc* | yo rigiera *o* rigiese *etc* | rige (tú) | rigiendo | regido |
| yo reiría | yo ría<br>tú rías<br>él ría<br>nosotros riamos<br>vosotros riáis<br>ellos rían | yo riera *o* riese *etc* | ríe (tú) | riendo | reído |
| yo roería | yo roa, roiga *o* roya *etc* | yo royera *o* royese *etc* | roe (tú) | royendo | roído |
| yo sabría *etc* | yo sepa *etc* | yo supiera *o* supiese *etc* | sabe (tú) | sabiendo | sabido |
| yo sacaría | yo saque *etc* | yo sacara *o* sacase *etc* | saca (tú) | sacando | sacado |
| yo saldría *etc* | yo salga *etc* | yo saliera *o* saliese | sal (tú) | saliendo | salido |
| yo seguiría | yo siga *etc* | yo siguiera *o* siguiese *etc* | sigue (tú) | siguiendo | seguido |

| INDICATIVE | | | | |
|---|---|---|---|---|
| Present | Imperfect | Preterite | Present Perfect | Future |
| **64 sentir** | | | | |
| yo siento | yo sentía | yo sentí | yo he sentido | yo sentiré |
| tú sientes | | | | |
| él siente | | él sintió | | |
| ellos sienten | | ellos sintieron | | |
| **65 sonar** | | | | |
| yo sueno | yo sonaba | yo soné | yo he sonado | yo sonaré |
| tú suenas | | | | |
| él suena | | | | |
| ellos suenan | | | | |
| **66 tender** | | | | |
| yo tiendo | yo tendía | yo tendí | yo he tendido | yo tenderé |
| tú tiendes | | | | |
| él tiende | | | | |
| ellos tienden | | | | |
| **67 tener** | | | | |
| yo tengo | yo tenía | yo tuve | yo he tenido | yo tendré *etc* |
| tú tienes | | tú tuviste | | |
| él tiene | | él tuvo | | |
| | | nosotros tuvimos | | |
| | | vosotros tuvisteis | | |
| ellos tienen | | ellos tuvieron | | |
| **68 traer** | | | | |
| yo traigo | yo traía | yo traje | yo he traído | yo traeré |
| | | tú trajiste | | |
| | | él trajo | | |
| | | nosotros trajimos | | |
| | | vosotros trajisteis | | |
| | | ellos trajeron | | |
| **69 trocar** | | | | |
| yo trueco | yo trocaba | yo troqué | yo he trocado | yo trocaré |
| tú truecas | | | | |
| él trueca | | | | |
| ellos truecan | | | | |
| **70 valer** | | | | |
| yo valgo | yo valía | yo valí | yo he valido | yo valdré *etc* |
| **71 venir** | | | | |
| yo vengo | yo venía | yo vine | yo he venido | yo vendré *etc* |
| tú vienes | | tú viniste | | |
| él viene | | él vino | | |
| | | nosotros vinimos | | |
| | | vosotros vinisteis | | |
| ellos vienen | | ellos vinieron | | |
| **72 ver** | | | | |
| yo veo | yo veía *etc* | yo vi | yo he visto | yo veré |
| **73 yacer** | | | | |
| yo yazco, yazgo *o* yago | yo yacía | yo yací | yo he yacido | yo yaceré |
| **74 zurcir** | | | | |
| yo zurzo | yo zurcía | yo zurcí | yo he zurcido | yo zurciré |

| CONDITIONAL Present | SUBJUNCTIVE Present | Imperfect | IMPERATIVE | PARTICIPLE Present | Past |
|---|---|---|---|---|---|
| yo sentiría | yo sienta<br><br>tú sientas<br>él sienta<br>nosotros sintamos<br>vosotros sintáis<br>ellos sientan | yo sintiera o<br>sintiese *etc* | siente (tú) | sintiendo | sentido |
| yo sonaría | yo suene<br>tú suenes<br>él suene<br>ellos suenen | yo sonara o sonase | suena (tú) | sonando | sonado |
| yo tendería | yo tienda<br>tú tiendas<br>él tienda<br>ellos tiendan | yo tendiera o tendiese | tiende (tú) | tendiendo | tendido |
| yo tendría *etc* | yo tenga *etc* | yo tuviera o<br>tuviese *etc* | ten (tú) | teniendo | tenido |
| yo traería | yo traiga *etc* | yo trajera o trajese *etc* | trae (tú) | trayendo | traído |
| yo trocaría | yo trueque<br>tú trueques<br>él trueque<br>ellos truequen | yo trocara o trocase | troca (tú) | trocando | trocado |
| yo valdría *etc* | yo valga *etc* | yo valiera o valiese | vale (tú) | valiendo | valido |
| yo vendría *etc* | yo venga *etc* | yo viniera o viniese *etc* | ven (tú) | viniendo | venido |
| yo vería | yo vea *etc* | yo viera o viese | ve (tú) | viendo | visto |
| yo yacería | yo yazca, yazga o<br>yaga *etc* | yo yaciera o yaciese | yace o yaz (tú) | yaciendo | yacido |
| yo zurciría | yo zurza *etc* | yo zurciera o zurciese | zurce (tú) | zurciendo | zurcido |

# English-Spanish

---

# Inglés-Español

# A

**A, a¹** [eɪ] *n* (**a**) *(letter)* A, a *f*; **to get from A to B** ir de un lugar a otro; **from A–Z** de principio a fin; **A bomb** bomba *f* atómica; *Br Sch* **A level** = examen final o diploma en una asignatura de los estudios preuniversitarios; **A road** ≃ carretera *f* nacional *or* general; **A side** *(of record)* cara *f* A, primera cara *f*; **A–Z** *(street guide)* callejero *m*; **an A–Z of gardening** una guía completa de jardinería (**b**) *Sch (grade)* sobresaliente *m*; **to get an A** *(in exam, essay)* sacar un sobresaliente (**c**) *Mus* la *m*

**a²** [ə, *stressed* eɪ]

> Antes de vocal o ''h'' muda se usa **an** [ən, *stressed* æn].

*indefinite article* (**a**) *(in general)* un, una; **a man** un hombre; **a woman** una mujer; **an hour** una hora; **he has a red nose** tiene la nariz roja; **I haven't got a car** no tengo coche; **he is an Englishman/a father/a barrister** es inglés/padre/abogado
(**b**) *(expressing prices, rates)* **30 pence a kilo** 30 peniques el kilo; **three times a week/a year** tres veces a la semana/al año; **50 kilometres an hour** 50 kilómetros por hora
(**c**) *(a certain)* **a Mr Watkins phoned** llamó un tal Sr. Watkins

**AA** [eɪ'eɪ] *n* (**a**) *Br (abbr* **Automobile Association**) = asociación automovilística británica (**b**) *(abbr* **Alcoholics Anonymous**) AA, alcohólicos *mpl* anónimos

**AAA** *n* (**a**) ['θriː'eɪz] *Br Formerly (abbr* **Amateur Athletics Association**) = federación británica de atletismo aficionado (**b**) [eɪeɪ'eɪ] *US (abbr* **American Automobile Association**) = asociación automovilística estadounidense

**AB** [eɪ'biː] *n US Univ (abbr* **artium baccalaureus**) *(qualification)* = licenciatura en letras; *(person)* = licenciado en letras

**aback** [ə'bæk] *adv* **to be taken a. (by)** quedarse desconcertado(a) (por)

**abacus** ['æbəkəs] *(pl* **abaci** [æbəsaɪ] *or* **abacuses** [æbəkəsɪz]) *n* ábaco *m*

**abandon** [ə'bændən] **1** *n* **with reckless a.** como loco(a)
**2** *vt (give up, leave)* abandonar; *(match)* suspender; **to a. ship** abandonar el barco

**abase** [ə'beɪs] *vt* **to a. oneself** humillarse, degradarse

**abashed** [ə'bæʃt] *adj* **to be a.** estar avergonzado(a) *or* abochornado(a)

**abate** [ə'beɪt] *vi (of storm, wind)* amainar; *(of pain)* remitir; *(of noise)* disminuir

**abattoir** ['æbətwɑː(r)] *n* matadero *m*

**abbess** ['æbes] *n* abadesa *f*

**abbey** ['æbɪ] *(pl* **abbeys**) *n* abadía *f*

**abbot** ['æbət] *n* abad *m*

**abbreviate** [ə'briːvɪeɪt] *vt* abreviar

**abbreviation** [əbriːvɪ'eɪʃən] *n* abreviatura *f*

**ABC** [eɪbiː'siː] *n* (**a**) *(alphabet)* abecedario *m*; **an A. of gardening** una guía básica de jardinería (**b**) *(abbr* **American Broadcasting Corporation**) cadena *f* ABC *(de radio y televisión estadounidense)* (**c**) *(abbr* **Australian Broadcasting Corporation**) = radiotelevisión pública australiana

**abdicate** ['æbdɪkeɪt] **1** *vt (throne)* abdicar; *(responsibility)* desatender, abandonar
**2** *vi (of monarch)* abdicar

**abdication** [æbdɪ'keɪʃən] *n (of throne)* abdicación *f*; *(of responsibilities)* descuido *m*, abandono *m*

**abdomen** ['æbdəmən] *n Anat & Zool* abdomen *m*

**abdominal** [əb'dɒmɪnəl] *adj Anat* abdominal

**abduct** [əb'dʌkt] *vt* raptar, secuestrar

**abduction** [əb'dʌkʃən] *n* rapto *m*, secuestro *m*

**aberration** [æbə'reɪʃən] *n* anomalía *f*, aberración *f*; **mental a.** desvarío *m*, despiste *m*

**abet** [ə'bet] *(pt & pp* **abetted**) *vt Law* **to aid and a. sb** ser cómplice de alguien

**abetting** [ə'betɪŋ] *n Law* **to be accused of aiding and a.** ser acusado(a) de complicidad

**abeyance** [ə'beɪəns] *n* **to fall into a.** *(of law, custom)* caer en desuso

**abhor** [əb'hɔː(r)] *(pt & pp* **abhorred**) *vt* aborrecer

**abhorrence** [əb'hɒrəns] *n* aversión *f* **(of** hacia *or* por), aborrecimiento *m* **(of** hacia *or* por)

**abhorrent** [əb'hɒrənt] *adj* aborrecible, repugnante; **it is a. to me** me resulta repugnante

**abide** [ə'baɪd] vt (tolerate) soportar; **I can't a. him** no lo soporto

▸**abide by** vt insep (promise) cumplir; (rule, decision) acatar, atenerse a

**abiding** [ə'baɪdɪŋ] adj (interest, impression) duradero(a); **my a. memory of Spain is...** mi recuerdo más destacado de España es...

**ability** [ə'bɪlɪtɪ] n (a) (talent, skill) aptitud f, habilidad f; **he did it to the best of his a.** lo hizo lo mejor que supo (b) (capability) capacidad f; **we now have the a. to record all calls** ahora podemos grabar todas las llamadas

**abject** ['æbdʒekt] adj (very bad) deplorable; **to look a.** (unhappy) tener un aspecto lamentable; **an a. apology** una disculpa degradante; **a. poverty** pobreza f extrema

**ablaze** [ə'bleɪz] adj **to be a.** estar ardiendo or en llamas; **to set sth a.** prender fuego a algo; Fig **her eyes were a. with passion** sus ojos ardían de pasión

**able** ['eɪbəl] adj (a) **to be a. to do sth** (have the capability) ser capaz de hacer algo, poder hacer algo; (manage) conseguir or poder hacer algo; **I was a. to speak to him myself** conseguí or pude hablar con él; **she was a. to see exactly what was happening** pudo ver exactamente lo que estaba sucediendo (b) (competent) (person) capaz; (piece of work, performance) logrado(a), conseguido(a)

**able-bodied** ['eɪbəl'bɒdɪd] adj sano(a); Naut **a. seaman** marinero m de primera

**abnormal** [æb'nɔːməl] adj anormal, anómalo(a)

**abnormality** [æbnɔː'mælɪtɪ] n anormalidad f, anomalía f

**aboard** [ə'bɔːd] **1** adv a bordo; **to go a.** subir a bordo

**2** prep (ship, aeroplane) a bordo de; (bus, train) en; **a. ship** a bordo (del barco)

**abode** [ə'bəʊd] n Literary morada f; Law **of no fixed a.** sin domicilio fijo; Law **right of a.** derecho m de residencia

**abolish** [ə'bɒlɪʃ] vt (law, custom) abolir

**abolition** [æbə'lɪʃən] n (of law, custom) abolición f

**abominable** [ə'bɒmɪnəbəl] adj espantoso(a), abominable; **the a. snowman** el abominable hombre de las nieves

**abomination** [əbɒmɪ'neɪʃən] n (thing, action) abominación f, horror m; (disgust) repugnancia f, aversión f

**aborigine** [æbə'rɪdʒɪnɪ] n aborigen mf (de Australia)

**abort** [ə'bɔːt] **1** vt (a) Med **the foetus was aborted in the 14th week of pregnancy** se provocó un aborto en la 14 semana de embarazo (b) (project) interrumpir, suspender;

Comptr cancelar

**2** vi abortar

**abortion** [ə'bɔːʃən] n aborto m (provocado); **to have an a.** abortar, tener un aborto

**abortive** [ə'bɔːtɪv] adj (attempt, plan) fallido(a), malogrado(a)

**abound** [ə'baʊnd] vi abundar (**in** or **with** en)

**about** [ə'baʊt] **1** prep (a) (regarding) sobre, acerca de; **a book a. France** un libro sobre Francia; **the good/bad thing a....** lo bueno/malo de...; **to talk/argue a. sth** hablar/discutir de or sobre algo; **we must do something a. this problem** tenemos que hacer algo con este problema or para solucionar este problema (b) (in various parts of) por; **to walk a. the town** caminar por la ciudad

**2** adv (a) (in different directions, places) **to run a.** correr de aquí para allá; **to walk a.** caminar or pasear por ahí; **there were books lying all a.** había libros por todas partes

(b) (in the general area) **is Jack a.?** ¿está Jack por ahí?; **there was nobody a.** no había nadie (por allí)

(c) (approximately) más o menos; **a. thirty** unos treinta; **at a. one o'clock** alrededor de la una, a eso de la una; **a. a week** una semana más o menos; **she's a. as tall as you** es más o menos como tú de alta; **I've just a. finished** estoy a punto de acabar; **that's a. enough** con eso basta; **a. time!** ¡ya era hora!

(d) (on the point of) **to be a. to do sth** estar a punto de hacer algo; **I'm not a. to...** (have no intention of) no tengo la más mínima intención de...

**about-face** [ə'baʊt'feɪs], **about-turn** [ə'baʊt'tɜːn] n (radical change) giro m radical or de 180 grados

**above** [ə'bʌv] **1** prep (a) (physically) por encima de; **a. sea level** sobre el nivel del mar; **the Ebro a. Zaragoza** el Ebro, antes de llegar a Zaragoza

(b) (with numbers) **a. twenty** por encima de veinte; **a. $100** más de 100 dólares; **the temperature didn't rise a. 10°C** la temperatura no pasó de or superó los 10 grados

(c) (in importance, rank) **a. all** por encima de todo, sobre todo; **he is a. me** está por encima de mí

(d) (not subject to) **to be a. suspicion** estar libre de sospecha; **she thinks she's a. criticism** cree que está por encima de las críticas

(e) (superior to) **he thinks he's a. all that** cree que hacer eso sería humillarse; **he's not a. telling the occasional lie** incluso él miente de vez en cuando; **to get a. oneself** darse muchos humos

**2** adv (a) (in general) **the tenants (of the flat) a.** los inquilinos de arriba; **to have a view from a.** ver desde arriba; **imposed from a.**

impuesto(a) desde arriba

(**b**) *(in book, document)* **the paragraph a.** el párrafo anterior; **as noted a.,...** como se dice más arriba,...

(**c**) *(with numbers)* **women aged 18 and a.** las mujeres a partir de los 18 años

**above-board** [ə'bʌvbɔːd] *adj (honest)* honrado(a), sincero(a)

**above-mentioned** [əbʌv'menʃənd], **above-named** [əbʌv'neɪmd] *adj* arriba mencionado(a), susodicho(a)

**abrasion** [ə'breɪʒən] *n (on skin)* abrasión *f*

**abrasive** [ə'breɪsɪv] **1** *n (substance)* abrasivo *m*
**2** *adj (surface, substance)* abrasivo(a); *(person, manner)* acre, corrosivo(a)

**abreast** [ə'brest] *adv* three/four a. en fila de a tres/cuatro, de tres/cuatro en fondo; **to come a. of** situarse a la altura de; **to keep a. of sth** mantenerse al tanto de algo

**abridged** [ə'brɪdʒd] *adj* abreviado(a)

**abroad** [ə'brɔːd] *adv* en el extranjero, fuera del país; **to be/live a.** estar/vivir en el extranjero; **to go a.** ir al extranjero; **to get a.** *(of news)* difundirse

**abrupt** [ə'brʌpt] *adj* (**a**) *(sudden)* brusco(a), repentino(a); **the evening came to an a. end** la velada terminó bruscamente (**b**) *(curt)* brusco(a), abrupto(a)

**abruptly** [ə'brʌptlɪ] *adv* (**a**) *(suddenly)* bruscamente, repentinamente (**b**) *(curtly)* bruscamente

**ABS** [eɪbiː'es] *n Aut (abbr* **antilock braking system**) ABS *m*

**abscess** ['æbses] *n* absceso *m*; *(in mouth)* flemón *m*

**abscond** [əb'skɒnd] *vi Formal* darse a la fuga, huir

**abseil** [æb'seɪl] *vi* hacer rappel; **to a. down sth** bajar algo haciendo rappel

**abseiling** ['æbseɪlɪŋ] *n* rappel *m*; **to go a.** ir a hacer rappel

**absence** ['æbsəns] *n (of person, thing)* ausencia *f*; *(of evidence, information)* ausencia *f*, falta *f* (**of** de); **in the a. of...** a falta de...; *Law* **sentenced in one's a.** juzgado(a) en rebeldía; *Prov* **a. makes the heart grow fonder** la ausencia aviva el cariño

**absent 1** *adj* ['æbsənt] *(pupil, expression)* ausente; *Mil* **a. without leave** ausente sin permiso
**2** *vt* [æb'sent] **to a. oneself (from)** ausentarse (de)

**absentee** [æbsən'tiː] *n* ausente *mf*; **a. landlord** (propietario(a) *m,f*) absentista *mf*

**absenteeism** [æbsən'tiːɪzəm] *n* absentismo *m*

**absent-minded** [æbsənt'maɪndɪd] *adj* distraído(a), despistado(a)

**absinthe** ['æbsɪnθ] *n* absenta *f*, ajenjo *m*

**absolute** ['æbsəluːt] *adj* (**a**) *(in general)* absoluto(a); **a. majority** mayoría *f* absoluta (**b**) *(emphatic)* absoluto(a), auténtico(a); **he's an a. fool!** ¡es un completo idiota!; **a. rubbish!** ¡no son más que tonterías!; **it's an a. disgrace!** ¡es una auténtica vergüenza!

**absolutely** [æbsə'luːtlɪ] *adv* absolutamente, completamente; **you're a. right** tienes toda la razón; **do you support him? – a.** ¿lo apoyas? – completamente; **a. not!** ¡en absoluto!; **it is a. forbidden** está terminantemente prohibido

**absolution** [æbsə'luːʃən] *n Rel* absolución *f*

**absolutism** [æbsə'luːtɪzəm] *n Hist* absolutismo *m*

**absolve** [əb'zɒlv] *vt (person)* absolver (**from** or **of** de)

**absorb** [əb'zɔːb] *vt (liquid)* absorber; *Fig (information, ideas)* asimilar; **paperwork absorbs too much of my time** paso demasiado tiempo ocupado en papeleos; **to be absorbed in sth** estar absorto en algo

**absorbent** [əb'zɔːbənt] *adj* absorbente

**absorbing** [əb'zɔːbɪŋ] *adj (book, work)* absorbente

**abstain** [əb'steɪn] *vi* abstenerse (**from** de)

**abstemious** [əb'stiːmɪəs] *adj* frugal, mesurado(a)

**abstention** [əb'stenʃən] *n* abstención *f*

**abstinence** ['æbstɪnəns] *n* abstinencia *f*

**abstract 1** *n* ['æbstrækt] (**a**) **in the a.** en abstracto (**b**) *(of article)* resumen *m*
**2** *adj* ['æbstrækt] abstracto(a)
**3** *vt* [æb'strækt] *Formal (remove)* extraer (**from** de); *(steal)* sustraer (**from** de)

**abstraction** [æb'strækʃən] *n* abstracción *f*

**abstruse** [əb'struːs] *adj* abstruso(a), impenetrable

**absurd** [əb'sɜːd] *adj* absurdo(a)

**absurdity** [əb'sɜːdɪtɪ] *n* irracionalidad *f*

**ABTA** ['æbtə] *n Br (abbr* **Association of British Travel Agents**) = asociación británica de agencias de viajes

**abundance** [ə'bʌndəns] *n* abundancia *f*; **in a.** en abundancia

**abundant** [ə'bʌndənt] *adj* abundante (**in** en)

**abundantly** [ə'bʌndəntlɪ] *adv* en abundancia; **it is a. clear that...** está clarísimo que...

**abuse 1** *n* [ə'bjuːs] (**a**) *(of power)* abuso *m*, mal uso *m* (**b**) *(insults)* insultos *mpl*, improperios *mpl*; **term of a.** insulto *m*, término *m* ofensivo; **to shower a. on sb** despotricar contra alguien (**c**) *(cruelty)* malos tratos *mpl*; **(sexual) a.** abuso *m* (sexual)
**2** *vt* [ə'bjuːz] (**a**) *(misuse)* abusar de (**b**) *(insult)* insultar (**c**) *(ill-treat) (physically)* maltratar; *(sexually)* abusar de

**abusive** [əˈbjuːsɪv] *adj* *(person)* grosero(a); *(language)* injurioso(a)

**ABV** *(abbr* **alcohol by volume)** A. 3.8% 3,8% Vol.

**abysmal** [əˈbɪzməl] *adj* *(stupidity, ignorance)* profundo(a); *(performance, quality)* pésimo(a)

**abyss** [əˈbɪs] *n also Fig* abismo *m*

**AC** [ˈeɪsiː] *n Elec (abbr* **alternating current)** corriente *f* alterna

**a/c** *(abbr* **account)** cuenta *f*

**academic** [ækəˈdemɪk] **1** *n (university teacher)* profesor(ora) *m,f* de universidad; *(intellectual)* erudito(a) *m,f*
**2** *adj* **(a)** *(of school, university)* académico(a) **(b)** *(intellectual)* académico(a), intelectual **(c)** **it's entirely a. now** ya carece por completo de relevancia

**academy** [əˈkædəmɪ] *n* academia *f;* **a. of music** conservatorio *m*

**ACAS** [ˈeɪkæs] *n Br (abbr* **Advisory, Conciliation and Arbitration Service)** = organismo independiente de arbitraje para conflictos laborales, ≃ IMAC *m*

**accede** [ækˈsiːd] *vi Formal* **(a)** *(agree)* **to a. to** acceder a **(b)** *(of monarch)* **to a. to the throne** acceder al trono

**accelerate** [əkˈseləreɪt] **1** *vt (rate, progress)* acelerar
**2** *vi (of car, driver)* acelerar; *(rate, growth)* acelerarse

**acceleration** [əkseləˈreɪʃən] *n* aceleración *f*

**accelerator** [əkˈseləreɪtə(r)] *n also Comptr* acelerador *m*

**accent** [ˈæksənt] *n (when speaking)* acento *m;* *(in writing)* acento *m,* tilde *f;* **to put the a. on sth** *(emphasize)* hacer hincapié en algo

**accentuate** [ækˈsentʃueɪt] *vt* acentuar

**accept** [əkˈsept] *vt* **(a)** *(invitation, apology, defeat)* aceptar; *(reasons)* aceptar, admitir; *(blame)* admitir; **the machine won't a. foreign coins** la máquina no funciona con *or* no admite monedas extranjeras; **to a. responsibility for sth** asumir la responsabilidad de algo; **it is generally accepted that...** en general, se acepta *or* se admite que... **(b)** *(into university)* admitir

**acceptable** [əkˈseptəbəl] *adj* aceptable, admisible; **to be a. to sb** *(suit)* venirle bien a alguien

**acceptance** [əkˈseptəns] *n (of invitation, apology, defeat)* aceptación *f;* **to find a.** tener aceptación; **a. speech** discurso *m* de agradecimiento *(al recibir un premio)*

**access** [ˈækses] **1** *n* acceso *m;* **to gain a. to sth** acceder a algo; **a. road** (vía *f* de) acceso *m; Comptr* **a. code** código *m* de acceso; *Comptr* **a. time** tiempo *m* de acceso
**2** *vt Comptr (data)* acceder a

**accessible** [əkˈsesəbəl] *adj (place, person, explanation)* accesible; **the beach is easily a. by car** se puede acceder fácilmente a la playa en coche

**accession** [əkˈseʃən] *n (to power, throne)* acceso *m; (library book)* adquisición *f*

**accessory** [əkˈsesərɪ] *n* **(a)** *(for car, camera)* accesorio *m;* **accessories** *(handbag, gloves etc)* complementos *mpl* **(b)** *Law* **a. (to a crime)** cómplice *mf* (de un delito)

**accident** [ˈæksɪdənt] *n* accidente *m;* **by a.** *(by chance)* por casualidad; *(unintentionally)* sin querer; **to have an a.** tener *or* sufrir un accidente; **that was no a.** eso no fue casualidad; **car** *or* **road a.** accidente de coche or de tráfico; **a. insurance** seguro *m* de accidentes

**accidental** [æksɪˈdentəl] *adj* accidental, casual; *Law* **a. death** muerte *f* accidental

**accidentally** [æksɪˈdentəlɪ] *adv (unintentionally)* sin querer, accidentalmente; *(by chance)* por casualidad

**accident-prone** [ˈæksɪdəntprəʊn] *adj* propenso(a) a tener accidentes

**acclaim** [əˈkleɪm] **1** *n* alabanza *f,* elogios *mpl*
**2** *vt* alabar, elogiar

**acclamation** [ækləˈmeɪʃən] *n* aclamación *f*

**acclimatize** [əˈklaɪmətaɪz] *vi* aclimatarse **(to** a)

**accolade** [ˈækəleɪd] *n (praise)* elogio *m; (prize)* galardón *m*

**accommodate** [əˈkɒmədeɪt] *vt* **(a)** *(provide room for)* alojar, acomodar; **the hotel can a. 300 people** el hotel puede albergar *or* alojar a 300 personas **(b)** *(satisfy)* complacer; *(point of view)* tener en cuenta

**accommodating** [əˈkɒmədeɪtɪŋ] *adj (helpful)* servicial; *(easy to please)* flexible

**accommodation** [əkɒməˈdeɪʃən] *n* **(a)** *(lodging)* alojamiento *m;* **there is a. in this hotel for fifty people** este hotel alberga a cincuenta personas **(b)** *Formal (agreement)* **to come to an a.** llegar a un acuerdo satisfactorio

**accompaniment** [əˈkʌmpənɪmənt] *n* acompañamiento *m*

**accompany** [əˈkʌmpənɪ] *vt* acompañar

**accomplice** [əˈkʌmplɪs] *n* cómplice *mf*

**accomplish** [əˈkʌmplɪʃ] *vt (task)* realizar; *(aim)* cumplir, alcanzar; **we didn't a. much** no logramos *or* conseguimos gran cosa

**accomplished** [əˈkʌmplɪʃt] *adj (performer)* hábil; *(performance)* logrado(a), conseguido(a)

**accord** [əˈkɔːd] **1** *n (agreement, pact)* acuerdo *m;* **in a. with** de acuerdo con, acorde con; **with one a.** unánimemente, al unísono; **of one's own a.** de motu propio
**2** *vt* conceder **(to** a)
▸**accord with** *vt insep* ser acorde con, estar de acuerdo con

**accordance** [ə'kɔ:dəns] *n* **in a. with** de acuerdo con

**accordingly** [ə'kɔ:dıŋlı] *adv* (**a**) *(appropriately)* como corresponde; **to act a.** actuar en consecuencia (**b**) *(therefore)* así pues, por consiguiente

**according to** [ə'kɔ:dıŋtu:] *prep* (**a**) *(depending on)* **a. whether one is rich or poor** dependiendo de si se es rico o pobre, según se sea rico o pobre (**b**) *(in conformity with)* **a. instructions** según las instrucciones; **everything went a. plan** todo fue de acuerdo con lo planeado (**c**) *(citing a source)* según

**accordion** [ə'kɔ:dıən] *n* acordeón *m*

**accost** [ə'kɒst] *vt (person)* abordar

**account** [ə'kaʊnt] *n* (**a**) *(at bank)* cuenta *f*; **to open an a.** abrir una cuenta; *Com* **accounts department** departamento *m* de contabilidad (**b**) *(reckoning)* **to keep (an) a. of sth** llevar la cuenta de algo; **to take sth into a., to take a. of sth** tener *or* tomar algo en cuenta; **to call sb to a.** pedir cuentas a alguien; **the terrorists will be brought to a.** los terroristas tendrán que responder de sus acciones (**c**) *(importance)* **of no a.** sin importancia (**d**) **on a. of** *(because of)* a causa de; **on no a., not on any a.** bajo ningún concepto; **on one's own a.** por cuenta propia; **don't do it on my a.!** ¡no lo hagas por mí! (**e**) *(report)* relato *m*, descripción *f*; *Fig* **to give a good a. of oneself** *(in fight, contest)* salir airoso(a), lucirse; **by all accounts** a decir de todos

▸**account for** *vt insep* (**a**) *(explain, justify)* explicar; **I can't a. for it** no puedo dar cuenta de ello; **five people have still not been accounted for** todavía no se conoce la suerte de cinco personas; **there's no accounting for taste** sobre gustos no hay nada escrito (**b**) *(constitute)* constituir

**accountability** [ə'kaʊntəbılıtı] *n* responsabilidad *f*

**accountable** [ə'kaʊntəbəl] *adj* **to be a. (to sb/for sth)** ser responsable (ante alguien/de algo); **to hold sb a.** considerar a alguien responsable

**accountancy** [ə'kaʊntənsı] *n* contabilidad *f*

**accountant** [ə'kaʊntənt] *n* contable *mf*

**accounting** [ə'kaʊntıŋ] *n* contabilidad *f*; **a. period** período *m* contable

**accrue** [ə'kru:] *vi Fin (of interest)* acumularse; **to a. to sb** *(of interest, benefits)* ir a parar a alguien

**accumulate** [ə'kju:mjʊleıt] **1** *vt* acumular
**2** *vi* acumularse

**accumulation** [əkju:mjʊ'leıʃən] *n* acumulación *f*

**accuracy** ['ækjʊrəsı] *n (of calculation, report, measurement)* exactitud *f*, precisión *f*; *(of translation, portrayal)* fidelidad *f*; *(of firearm, shot)* precisión *f*

**accurate** ['ækjʊrət] *adj (calculation, report, measurement)* exacto(a), preciso(a); *(translation, portrayal)* fiel; *(firearm, shot)* certero(a)

**accurately** ['ækjʊrətlı] *adv (calculate)* exactamente; *(measure, aim, report)* con exactitud, con precisión; *(translate, portray)* fielmente

**accusation** [ækjʊ'zeıʃən] *n* acusación *f*

**accusative** [ə'kju:zətıv] *n & adj* acusativo *m*

**accuse** [ə'kju:z] *vt* acusar; **to a. sb of sth/of doing sth** acusar a alguien de algo/de hacer algo

**accused** [ə'kju:zd] *n Law* **the a.** el/la acusado(a)

**accuser** [ə'kju:zə(r)] *n* acusador(ora) *m,f*

**accusing** [ə'kju:zıŋ] *adj (look, stare)* acusador(ora)

**accustom** [ə'kʌstəm] *vt* acostumbrar; **to be accustomed to sth/to doing sth** estar acostumbrado(a) a algo/a hacer algo; **to get** *or* **grow accustomed to sth/to doing sth** acostumbrarse a algo/a hacer algo

**AC/DC** ['eısı'di:si:] *n Elec (abbr* **alternating current/direct current)** corriente *f* alterna/continua

**ace** [eıs] **1** *n* (**a**) *(in cards)* as *m*; **a. of spades** as de picas; *Fig* **to have an a. up one's sleeve** tener un as en la manga; **she came within an a. of winning** *(very near to)* estuvo a punto *or* en un tris de ganar (**b**) *(tennis)* ace *m* (**c**) *Fam (expert)* as *m*; **a flying a.** un as del vuelo
**2** *adj Fam (very good)* de buten, guay

**acerbic** [ə'sɜ:bık] *adj (wit, remark)* acre, mordaz

**acetate** ['æsıteıt] *n Chem* acetato *m*

**acetic acid** [æ'si:tık'æsıd] *n* ácido *m* acético

**ache** [eık] **1** *n* dolor *m*; **aches and pains** achaques *mpl*
**2** *vi* doler; **my head aches** me duele la cabeza; **I a. all over** me duele todo; *Fig* **to be aching to do sth** estar deseando hacer algo

**achieve** [ə'tʃi:v] *vt* conseguir, lograr

**achievement** [ə'tʃi:vmənt] *n (action)* realización *f*, consecución *f*; *(thing achieved)* logro *m*

**acid** ['æsıd] **1** *n* (**a**) *(chemical)* ácido *m* (**b**) *Fam (LSD)* ácido *m*, **a. house** *(music)* acid house *m*
**2** *adj* (**a**) *(chemical, taste)* ácido(a); **a. rain** lluvia *f* ácida; *Fig* **a. test** prueba *f* de fuego (**b**) *(tone, remark)* sarcástico(a)

**acidic** [ə'sıdık] *adj* ácido(a)

**acidity** [ə'sıdıtı] *n (of chemical, taste)* acidez *f*; *(of tone, remark)* sarcasmo *m*

**acknowledge** [ək'nɒlıdʒ] *vt (mistake, debt, truth)* reconocer, admitir; **to a. (receipt of) a letter** acusar recibo de una carta; **to a. defeat** admitir una derrota; **she didn't a. me** *or* **my presence** no me saludó

**acknowledg(e)ment** [ək'nɒlɪdʒmənt] *n* *(of mistake, debt, truth)* reconocimiento *m*; *(of letter)* acuse *m* de recibo; **in a. of** en reconocimiento a; **acknowledgements** *(in book)* menciones *fpl*, agradecimientos *mpl*

**ACLU** ['eɪsi:elju:] *n* *US* (*abbr* **American Civil Liberties Union**) = organización americana para la defensa de las libertades civiles

**acne** ['ækni] *n* acné *m*

**acolyte** ['ækəlaɪt] *n* acólito *m*

**acorn** ['eɪkɔ:n] *n* bellota *f*

**acoustic** [ə'ku:stɪk] *adj* acústico(a); **a. guitar** guitarra *f* acústica

**acoustics** [ə'ku:stɪks] *npl* acústica *f*

**acquaint** [ə'kweɪnt] *vt* (a) *(with person)* **to be acquainted with sb** conocer a alguien; **to become** *or* **get acquainted** entablar relación (b) *(with facts, situation)* **to be acquainted with sth** conocer algo, estar al corriente de algo; **to a. sb with sth** poner al corriente de algo a alguien; **to a. oneself with sth** familiarizarse con algo

**acquaintance** [ə'kweɪntəns] *n* (a) *(person)* conocido(a) *m,f* (b) *(familiarity)* *(with person)* relación *f*; *(with facts)* conocimiento *m* (**with** de); **to make sb's a.** conocer a alguien

**acquiesce** [ækwɪ'es] *vi* acceder (**in** a)

**acquiescence** [ækwɪ'esəns] *n* aquiescencia *f*, consentimiento *m*

**acquiescent** [ækwɪ'esənt] *adj* aquiescente

**acquire** [ə'kwaɪə(r)] *vt* adquirir; **to a. a taste for sth** aprender a disfrutar de algo; **it's an acquired taste** es un placer adquirido con el tiempo

**acquisition** [ækwɪ'zɪʃən] *n* adquisición *f*

**acquisitive** [ə'kwɪzɪtɪv] *adj* *(person)* consumista

**acquit** [ə'kwɪt] (*pt & pp* **acquitted**) *vt* (a) *Law* absolver, declarar inocente (b) **to a. oneself well/badly** salir bien/mal parado(a)

**acquittal** [ə'kwɪtəl] *n* *Law* absolución *f*

**acre** ['eɪkə(r)] *n* acre *m*, = 4047 m²; *Fam* **acres of space** *(lots)* la mar de espacio

**acrid** ['ækrɪd] *adj* acre

**acrimonious** [ækrɪ'məʊnɪəs] *adj* *(discussion, debate)* agrio(a); *(words, remark)* mordaz, acre

**acrimony** ['ækrɪmənɪ] *n* acritud *f*, acrimonia *f*

**acrobat** ['ækrəbæt] *n* acróbata *mf*

**acrobatic** [ækrə'bætɪk] *adj* acrobático(a)

**acrobatics** [ækrə'bætɪks] **1** *n* acrobacias *fpl*
  **2** *npl Fig* **mental a.** gimnasia *f* mental

**acronym** ['ækrənɪm] *n* siglas *fpl*, acrónimo *m*

**across** [ə'krɒs] *prep* **1** (a) *(from one side to the other of)* a través de; **to go a. sth** cruzar algo; **he ran a. the road** cruzó corriendo la calle; **to run a. the road** cruzar la calle corriendo; **we drove a. the desert** cruzamos el desierto en coche; **she swam a. the river** cruzó el río a nado; **the bridge a. the river** el puente que cruza el río; **she threw it a. the room** lo tiró al otro lado de la habitación
  (b) *(on the other side of)* al otro lado de; **a. the street/border** al otro lado de la calle/frontera; **I saw him a. the room** lo vi en el otro extremo de la sala
  (c) *(throughout)* **a. the country** por todo el país; **changes have been introduced a. the syllabus** se han introducido cambios en todo el programa
  **2** *adv* (a) *(from one side to the other)* de un lado a otro **to run/swim a.** cruzar corriendo/a nado
  (b) *(with distance)* **it's 10 cm/2 km a.** tiene 10 cms/2 kms de ancho
  (c) **a. from me/my house** enfrente
  (d) *(in crosswords)* **8 a.** 8 horizontal

**across-the-board** [ə'krɒsðə'bɔ:d] *adj* generalizado(a); **an a. increase** *(in salary)* un aumento lineal

**acrylic** [ə'krɪlɪk] **1** *n* acrílico *m*
  **2** *adj* acrílico(a)

**act** [ækt] **1** *n* (a) *(thing done)* acto *m*; **to catch sb in the a.** pillar *or* atrapar a alguien in fraganti; **to catch sb in the a. of doing sth** pillar a alguien haciendo algo; **to be in the a. of doing sth** estar haciendo algo (precisamente); *Fam* **to get in on the a.** *(get involved)* apuntarse; **an a. of war** una acción de guerra; *Law* **a. of God** caso *m* de fuerza mayor
  (b) *(in play)* acto *m*; *(in cabaret, circus)* número *m*; *Fig* **to put on an a.** hacer teatro; *Fig* **it's all an a.** es puro teatro *or* pura farsa; *Fig* **to get one's a. together** organizarse, ponerse las pilas
  (c) *Law* **a. (of parliament)** ley *f*

  **2** *vt* (a) *(of actor)* interpretar; *Fig* **he was acting the part of the caring husband** estaba interpretando *or* haciendo el papel del marido solícito
  (b) *(behave like)* **to a. the fool** *or* **the goat** hacer el tonto; *Fam* **a. your age!** ¡no seas infantil!

  **3** *vi* (a) *(take action)* actuar; **to a. for sb** *(of lawyer)* representar a alguien; **to a. as secretary/chairperson** actuar *or* hacer de secretario(a)/presidente(a); **to a. as a warning/an incentive** servir de advertencia/incentivo
  (b) *(behave)* actuar, comportarse; **to a. stupid** hacerse el tonto
  (c) *(of actor)* actuar

▸**act out** *vt sep (fantasy)* realizar; *(scene)* representar

▸**act up** *vi (of child, car, injury)* dar guerra

**acting** ['æktɪŋ] **1** *n* *(performance)* interpretación *f*, actuación *f*; *(profession)* interpretación *f*, profesión f de actor/actriz

**2** adj (temporary) en funciones

**action** ['ækʃən] n (**a**) (individual act) acto m, acción f; **to be responsible for one's actions** ser responsable de los propios actos; Prov **actions speak louder than words** hechos son amores y no buenas razones

(**b**) (activity) acción f; **to take a.** actuar; **in a.** en acción; **to go into a.** ponerse en acción; **to be out of a.** (machine) no funcionar; (person) estar fuera de combate; **to put a plan into a.** poner en marcha un plan; Fam **they were looking for some a.** (excitement) estaban buscando acción; Com **a. plan** plan m de acción

(**c**) Mil (acción f de) combate m; **to see a.** entrar en combate; **missing in a.** desaparecido(a) en combate

(**d**) (of film, novel) acción f; TV **a. replay** repetición f

(**e**) Law demanda f; **to bring an a. against sb** poner una demanda a alguien, demandar a alguien

**activate** ['æktɪveɪt] vt (alarm, mechanism) activar

**active** ['æktɪv] adj (**a**) (person, imagination, life) activo(a); (interest, dislike) profundo(a); (volcano) activo(a); **to take an a. part in sth** participar activamente en algo; Mil **on a. service** en servicio activo (**b**) Gram activo(a)

**actively** ['æktɪvlɪ] adv activamente; **I a. dislike him** me desagrada profundamente

**activist** ['æktɪvɪst] n Pol activista mf

**activity** [æk'tɪvɪtɪ] n actividad f

**actor** ['æktə(r)] n actor m

**actress** ['æktrɪs] n actriz f

**actual** ['æktʃʊəl] adj (real) verdadero(a), real; **her a. words were...** lo que dijo exactamente fue...; **an a. example** un ejemplo real; **in a. fact** de hecho, en realidad; **although the garden is big, the a. house is small** aunque el jardín es grande, la casa en sí es pequeña

**actually** ['æktʃʊəlɪ] adv (**a**) (really) en realidad; **what a. happened?** ¿qué ocurrió en realidad?; **what she a. means is...** lo que quiere decir en realidad es...; **he a. believed me!** ¡me creyó y todo! (**b**) (in fact) **a., I rather like it** la verdad es que me gusta; **a., it WAS the right number** de hecho, sí que era el número correcto; **I'm not sure, a.** pues... no estoy seguro

**actuary** ['æktʃʊərɪ] n actuario(a) m,f de seguros

**acumen** ['ækjʊmən] n perspicacia f, sagacidad f; **business a.** perspicacia para los negocios

**acupuncture** ['ækjʊpʌŋktʃə(r)] n acupuntura f

**acute** [ə'kjuːt] adj (pain, mind, eyesight) Gram & Math agudo(a); (hearing, sense of smell) muy fino(a); (problem, shortage) acuciante; (remorse, embarrassment) intenso(a)

**acutely** [ə'kjuːtlɪ] adv (painful, embarrassing) extremadamente; **to be a. aware of sth** ser plenamente consciente de algo

**AD** [eɪ'diː] adv (abbr **Anno Domini**) d. J.C., d.C.

**ad** [æd] n Fam (advertisement) anuncio m

**Adam** ['ædəm] n Fam **I wouldn't know him from A.** no lo conozco de nada; **A.'s apple** nuez f, bocado m de Adán

**adamant** ['ædəmənt] adj inflexible; **she is a. that she saw him** insiste en que lo vio

**adapt** [ə'dæpt] **1** vt adaptar (**for** a); **to a. oneself to sth** adaptarse a algo

**2** vi adaptarse

**adaptable** [ə'dæptəbəl] adj (instrument, person) adaptable; **she's very a.** se adapta a todo

**adaptation** [ædæp'teɪʃən] n adaptación f

**adaptor, adapter** [ə'dæptə(r)] n (for several plugs) ladrón m; (for different socket) adaptador m

**ADC** [eɪdiː'siː] n Mil (abbr **aide-de-camp**) ayudante m de campo, edecán f

**add** [æd] vt añadir (**to** a); Math sumar

**▸add up 1** vt sep (figures) sumar

**2** vi (give correct total) cuadrar; (make sense) encajar

**▸add up to** (amount to) **it adds up to £126** suma un total de 126 libras; **it all adds up to an enjoyable day out** todo esto da como resultado una agradable excursión; **it doesn't a. up to much** no viene a ser gran cosa

**adder** ['ædə(r)] n víbora f

**addict** ['ædɪkt] n adicto(a) m,f; (drug) a. drogadicto(a) m,f, toxicómano(a) m,f; **heroin a.** heroinómano(a) m,f; TV **a.** teleadicto(a) m,f

**addicted** [ə'dɪktɪd] adj **to be a. to sth** ser adicto(a) a algo; **to become** or **get a. to sth** hacerse or volverse adicto(a) a algo

**addiction** [ə'dɪkʃən] n adicción f

**addictive** [ə'dɪktɪv] adj also Fig adictivo(a)

**Addis Ababa** ['ædɪs'æbəbə] n Addis Abeba

**addition** [ə'dɪʃən] n (**a**) Math suma f (**b**) (action) incorporación f, adición f; (thing added) incorporación f, añadido m; **in a. (to)** además (de); **an a. to the family** un nuevo miembro en la familia

**additional** [ə'dɪʃənəl] adj adicional

**additive** ['ædɪtɪv] n aditivo m

**addled** ['ædəld] adj (mind) embarullado(a), abotargado(a)

**add-on** ['ædɒn] n Comptr extra m

**address** [ə'dres] **1** n (**a**) (of person, letter) dirección f, domicilio m; **a. book** agenda f de direcciones (**b**) (speech) alocución f, discurso m; **form of a.** (when speaking to sb) tratamiento m

**2** *vt* (**a**) *(letter, remarks, criticism)* dirigir (**to** a) (**b**) *(speak to)* (*person, crowd*) dirigirse a; **he addressed her as 'Your Majesty'** le dio el tratamiento de "Su Majestad" (**c**) *(question, problem)* abordar; **to a. oneself to sth** abordar algo

**addressee** [ædre'si:] *n* destinatario(a) *m,f*

**adenoids** ['ædɪnɔɪdz] *npl Anat* vegetaciones *fpl* (adenoideas)

**adept** [ə'dept] *adj* **she is a. at getting her own way** siempre consigue lo que quiere; **he had always been a. at persuading people to support him** siempre se le había dado muy bien conseguir el apoyo de la gente

**adequate** ['ædɪkwət] *adj* (*enough*) suficiente; (*satisfactory*) adecuado(a), apropiado(a)

**adhere** [əd'hɪə(r)] *vi* (**a**) (*stick*) adherirse (**to** a) (**b**) **to a. to** *(rule)* cumplir, observar; (*belief, plan*) atenerse a

**adherence** [əd'hɪərəns] *n* (*to rule*) cumplimiento *m*, observancia *f* (**to** de); (*to belief, plan*) adhesión *f*, apoyo *m* (**to** a)

**adherent** [əd'hɪərənt] *n* adepto(a) *m,f*

**adhesion** [əd'hi:ʒən] *n* (**a**) (*stickiness*) adherencia *f* (**b**) (*to belief, plan*) adhesión *f* (**to** a), apoyo *m* (**to** a)

**adhesive** [əd'hi:sɪv] **1** *n* adhesivo *m*
**2** *adj* adhesivo(a), adherente; **a. tape** cinta *f* adhesiva

**ad hoc** ['æd'hɒk] *adj* improvisado(a); **on an a. basis** improvisadamente; **a. committee** comisión *f* especial

**ad infinitum** ['ædɪnfɪ'naɪtəm] *adv* hasta el infinito

**adjacent** [ə'dʒeɪsənt] *adj* adyacente, contiguo(a); **to be a. to** estar al lado de

**adjectival** [ædʒek'taɪvəl] *adj* adjetival; **an a. use** un uso adjetival

**adjective** ['ædʒɪktɪv] *n* adjetivo *m*

**adjoin** [ə'dʒɔɪn] *vt* (*of building, land*) lindar con

**adjoining** [ə'dʒɔɪnɪŋ] *adj* (*building, room*) contiguo(a)

**adjourn** [ə'dʒɜ:n] **1** *vt* (*meeting, trial*) aplazar, posponer
**2** *vi* **the trial/meeting adjourned** se levantó la sesión (*tras juicio/reunión*); **to a. to another room** pasar a otra habitación

**adjournment** [ə'dʒɜ:nmənt] *n* (*of meeting, trial*) aplazamiento *m*

**adjudge** [ə'dʒʌdʒ] *vt* **to a. sb guilty** declarar a alguien culpable; **to a. sb the winner** proclamar a alguien ganador

**adjudicate** [ə'dʒu:dɪkeɪt] *vt* juzgar

**adjudication** [ədʒu:dɪ'keɪʃən] *n* fallo *m*

**adjudicator** [ə'dʒu:dɪkeɪtə(r)] *n* (*of dispute*) árbitro *m*; (*of contest*) juez *mf*

**adjunct** ['ædʒʌŋkt] *n* apéndice *m*

**adjust** [ə'dʒʌst] **1** *vt* (*machine, mechanism*) ajustar, regular; (*method*) ajustar, adaptar; **to a. one's tie** ajustarse la corbata; **to a. oneself to sth** adaptarse a algo
**2** *vi* (*of person*) adaptarse (**to** a)

**adjustable** [ə'dʒʌstəbəl] *adj* ajustable, regulable; **a. spanner** llave *f* inglesa

**adjustment** [ə'dʒʌstmənt] *n* ajuste *m*; **to make an a. to sth** hacer un ajuste a algo, ajustar algo

**ad-lib** ['æd'lɪb] **1** *adv* improvisadamente
**2** *vi* (*pt & pp* **ad-libbed**) improvisar

**adman** ['ædmæn] *n Fam* publicista *m*, publicitario *m*

**admin** ['ædmɪn] *n Fam* (*work*) papeleo *m*

**administer** [əd'mɪnɪstə(r)] *vt* (**a**) (*estate, funds*) administrar (**b**) (*give*) (*punishment*) aplicar; (*blow*) propinar; (*medication*) administrar

**administration** [ədmɪnɪ'streɪʃən] *n* (**a**) (*act, activity*) administración *f* (**b**) (*government*) gobierno *m*, administración *f*

**administrative** [əd'mɪnɪstrətɪv] *adj* administrativo(a)

**administrator** [əd'mɪnɪstreɪtə(r)] *n* administrador(ora) *m,f*

**admirable** ['ædmərəbəl] *adj* admirable

**admiral** ['ædmərəl] *n* almirante *m*

**Admiralty** ['ædmərəltɪ] *n* Ministerio *m* de Marina, Almirantazgo *m*

**admiration** [ædmə'reɪʃən] *n* admiración *f*

**admire** [əd'maɪə(r)] *vt* admirar

**admirer** [əd'maɪərə(r)] *n* admirador(ora) *m,f*

**admiring** [əd'maɪrɪŋ] *adj* (*look, glance*) de admiración

**admissible** [əd'mɪsɪbəl] *adj* admisible

**admission** [əd'mɪʃən] *n* (**a**) (*entry*) (*to school, hospital*) ingreso *m* (**to** en); (*to museum, exhibition*) visita *f* (**to** a), entrada *f* (**to** a); (*price*) entrada *f*; **a. free** entrada gratuita; **no a. to unaccompanied children** (*sign*) prohibida la entrada a menores no acompañados (**b**) (*acknowledgement*) (*of guilt, mistake*) confesión *f*; **by his own a.** según él mismo admite

**admit** [əd'mɪt] (*pt & pp* **admitted**, *continuous* **admitting**) **1** *vt* (**a**) (*allow to enter*) admitir, dejar pasar; **he was admitted to hospital** ingresó en un hospital; **children not admitted** (*sign*) prohibida la entrada a niños; **admits one** (*on ticket*) individual (**b**) (*acknowledge*) (*fact, mistake*) admitir; (*crime, guilt*) confesar; **I must a. that…** tengo que reconocer o debo confesar que…; **to a. defeat** darse por vencido(a)
**2** *vi* **to a. to** (*mistake*) admitir; (*crime*) confesar; **to a. to doing sth** admitir haber hecho algo

**admittance** [əd'mɪtəns] *n* (*entry*) acceso *m*, admisión *f*; **to gain a.** ser admitido(a); **to refuse sb a.** no dejar entrar a alguien; **no a.** (*sign*) prohibido el paso

**admittedly** [əd'mɪtɪdlɪ] *adv* es cierto que; **a., it was dark when I saw him** es cierto que estaba oscuro cuando lo vi; **an a. serious case** un caso sin duda serio

**admonish** [əd'mɒnɪʃ] *vt (reprimand)* reprender **(for** por)

**ad nauseam** [æd'nɔ:sɪæm] *adv* hasta la saciedad

**ado** [ə'du:] *n* **without further a.** sin más dilación; *Prov* **much a. about nothing** mucho ruido y pocas nueces

**adobe** [ə'dəʊbɪ] *n (clay)* adobe *m*

**adolescence** [ædə'lesəns] *n* adolescencia *f*

**adolescent** [ædə'lesənt] *n* adolescente *mf*

**adopt** [ə'dɒpt] *vt (child, approach, measure)* adoptar; *(candidate)* nombrar

**adopted** [ə'dɒptɪd] *adj (country)* adoptivo(a), de adopción; **a. daughter** hija *f* adoptiva; **a. son** hijo *m* adoptivo

**adoption** [ə'dɒpʃən] *n* adopción *f*

**adorable** [ə'dɔ:rəbəl] *adj* encantador(ora)

**adoration** [ædə'reɪʃən] *n* adoración *f*

**adore** [ə'dɔ:(r)] *vt (person)* adorar; **I adored her last film** me encantó su última película

**adorn** [ə'dɔ:n] *vt* adornar

**adornment** [ə'dɔ:nmənt] *n* adorno *m*, ornamento *m*

**ADP** [eɪdɪ:'pi:] *n Comptr (abbr* **automatic data processing)** proceso *m or* procesamiento *m* automático de datos

**adrenalin(e)** [ə'drenəlɪn] *n* adrenalina *f*

**Adriatic** [eɪdrɪ'ætɪk] *n* **the A. (Sea)** el (mar) Adriático

**adrift** [ə'drɪft] *adv* **to be a.** *(of boat)* ir a la deriva; *Fig* **to go a.** *(of plan)* irse a pique *or* al garete

**adroit** [ə'drɔɪt] *adj* diestro(a), hábil

**adulation** [ædjʊ'leɪʃən] *n* adulación *f*

**adult** ['ædʌlt, ə'dʌlt] **1** *n* adulto(a) *m,f*

**2** *adj (person, animal)* adulto(a); *(attitude)* adulto(a), maduro(a); *(film)* para adultos; **a. education** educación *f* de *or* para adultos

**adulterate** [ə'dʌltəreɪt] *vt* adulterar

**adulteration** [ədʌltə'reɪʃən] *n* adulteración *f*

**adulterer** [ə'dʌltərə(r)] *n* adúltero(a) *m,f*

**adulteress** [ə'dʌltərəs] *n* adúltera *f*

**adulterous** [ə'dʌltərəs] *adj* adúltero(a)

**adultery** [ə'dʌltərɪ] *n* adulterio *m*; **to commit a.** cometer adulterio

**adulthood** ['ædʌlthʊd] *n* edad *f* adulta

**advance** [əd'vɑ:ns] **1** *n* **(a)** *(forward movement)* avance *m*; *(progress)* avance *m*, progreso *m*; **to make advances to sb** *(sexual)* insinuarse a alguien; *(in business)* hacer una propuesta inicial a alguien; **in a.** *(pay)* por adelantado; *(give notice)* con antelación; **six weeks in a.** con seis semanas de antelación; **a. booking** reserva *f* (anticipada); **a. notice** aviso *m* previo; **a. warning** advertencia *f* previa **(b)** *(loan)* anticipo *m*, adelanto *m*

**2** *vt* **(a)** *(move forward) (chesspiece, troops)* avanzar, adelantar; *(science, knowledge)* hacer avanzar, adelantar **(b)** *(idea, opinion)* presentar **(c)** *(loan)* anticipar, adelantar

**3** *vi (move forward, make progress)* avanzar; **the troops advanced on the city** las tropas avanzaron hacia la ciudad

**advanced** [əd'vɑ:nst] *adj (child, student)* avanzado(a), aventajado(a); *(country)* avanzado(a); **she's very a. for her age** está muy adelantada para su edad

**advantage** [əd'vɑ:ntɪdʒ] *n* ventaja *f*; **to have an a. over** tener ventaja sobre; **to take a. of** aprovecharse de; **to turn sth to one's a.** sacar provecho de algo; **it would be to your a.** te conviene; **a. Sampras** *(in tennis)* ventaja de *or* para Sampras

**advantageous** [ædvən'teɪdʒəs] *adj* ventajoso(a)

**advent** ['ædvənt] *n (arrival)* llegada *f*, advenimiento *m*; *Rel* **A.** Adviento *m*

**adventure** [əd'ventʃə(r)] *n* aventura *f*; **a. playground** parque *m* infantil; **a. story** historia *f* de aventuras

**adventurer** [əd'ventʃərə(r)] *n* **(a)** *(person fond of adventure)* aventurero(a) *m,f* **(b)** *(dishonest person)* sinvergüenza *mf*

**adventurous** [əd'ventʃərəs] *adj (plan, choice)* aventurado(a), arriesgado(a); *(person)* aventurero(a)

**adverb** ['ædvɜ:b] *n* adverbio *m*

**adverbial** [əd'vɜ:bɪəl] *adj* adverbial; **an a. use** un uso adverbial

**adversary** ['ædvəsərɪ] *n* adversario(a) *m,f*

**adverse** ['ædvɜ:s] *adj* adverso(a), desfavorable

**adversely** ['ædvɜ:slɪ] *adv* desfavorablemente, negativamente; **to be a. affected by sth** resultar perjudicado(a) por algo

**adversity** [əd'vɜ:sɪtɪ] *n* adversidad *f*; **in a.** en la adversidad

**advert** ['ædvɜ:t] *n* anuncio *m*

**advertise** ['ædvətaɪz] **1** *vt* **(a)** *(product, job)* anunciar **(b)** *(call attention to)* **he didn't want to a. his presence** no quería llamar la atención

**2** *vi* poner un anuncio; **to a. for sth/sb** poner un anuncio pidiendo algo/a alguien

**advertisement** [əd'vɜ:tɪsmənt] *n (on TV, in newspaper)* anuncio *m*; *Fig* **you're not a good a. for your school** no le haces buena publicidad a tu colegio

**advertiser** ['ædvətaɪzə(r)] *n* anunciante *mf*

**advertising** [ˈædvətaɪzɪŋ] *n* publicidad *f*; **a. agency** agencia *f* de publicidad; **a. campaign** campaña *f* publicitaria

**advice** [ədˈvaɪs] *n* consejo *m*; **a piece of a.** un consejo; **that's good a.** es un buen consejo; **to give sb a.** aconsejar a alguien; **to ask sb's a.** pedir consejo a alguien; **to take sb's a.** seguir el consejo de alguien

**advisable** [ədˈvaɪzəbəl] *adj* aconsejable, recomendable

**advise** [ədˈvaɪz] *vt* (**a**) *(give advice to)* aconsejar; **to a. sb to do sth** aconsejar a alguien hacer *or* que haga algo; **to a. sb against doing sth** aconsejar a alguien que no haga algo; **you'd be well advised to take an umbrella** más vale que lleves un paraguas (**b**) *(inform)* **to a. sb that…** informar a alguien de que…; **to a. sb of sth** informar a alguien de algo (**c**) *(give professional guidance)* asesorar (**on** sobre)

**adviser, advisor** [ədˈvaɪzə(r)] *n* consejero(a) *m,f*; *(professional)* asesor(ora) *m,f*

**advisory** [ədˈvaɪzərɪ] *adj* asesor(ora); **in an a. capacity** en calidad de asesor(ora)

**advocate 1** *n* [ˈædvəkət] (**a**) *Scot Law* abogado(a) *m,f*; **the Lord A.** el fiscal general (**b**) *(of cause, doctrine)* defensor(ora) *m,f*
**2** *vt* [ˈædvəkeɪt] *(policy, plan)* abogar por, defender

**A & E** [eɪənˈdiː] *n* (*abbr* **Accident and Emergency**) = urgencias

**AEA** [eiːˈeɪ] *n Br* (*abbr* **Atomic Energy Authority**) = agencia británica para la energía nuclear

**AEC** [eiːˈsiː] *n US* (*abbr* **Atomic Energy Commission**) = comisión americana para la energía nuclear

**Aegean** [ɪˈdʒiːən] *n* **the A. (Sea)** el (mar) Egeo

**aegis, US egis** [ˈiːdʒɪs] *n* **under the a. of…** bajo los auspicios de…

**aeon, US eon** [ˈiːən] *n* eón; *Fam* **aeons ago** hace siglos

**aerate** [ˈeəreɪt] *vt (blood)* oxigenar

**aerial** [ˈeərɪəl] **1** *n (of radio, TV)* antena *f*
**2** *adj* aéreo(a); **a. photography** fotografía *f* aérea

**aerobics** [eəˈrəʊbɪks] *n* aerobic *m*, aeróbic *m*

**aerodrome** [ˈeərədrəʊm] *n* aeródromo *m*

**aerodynamic** [eərəʊdəˈnæmɪk] *adj* aerodinámico(a)

**aerogram(me)** [ˈeərəgræm] *n* aerograma *m*

**aeronautic(al)** [eərəˈnɔːtɪk(əl)] *adj* aeronáutico(a)

**aeroplane** [ˈeərəpleɪn], *US* **airplane** [ˈeəpleɪn] *n* avión *m*

**aerosol** [ˈeərəsɒl] *n* aerosol *m*; **a. spray** aerosol *m*

**aesthetic** [ɪsˈθetɪk] *adj* estético(a)

**afar** [əˈfɑː(r)] *adv Literary* **from a.** desde lejos

**affable** [ˈæfəbəl] *adj* afable, amable

**affair** [əˈfeə(r)] *n (a) (matter, concern)* asunto *m*; **that's my a.** eso es asunto mío; **she put her affairs in order** puso sus asuntos en orden; **in the present state of affairs** tal y como están las cosas; **foreign affairs** asuntos exteriores; **current affairs** (temas *mpl* de) actualidad *f*; **affairs of state** asuntos de Estado (**b**) *(sexual)* aventura *f*, lío *m*; **to have an a. with sb** tener una aventura con alguien (**c**) *(event)* acontecimiento *m*; **the wedding was a quiet a.** fue una boda discreta

**affect¹** [əˈfekt] *vt* (**a**) *(have effect on) (person, organ, health)* afectar; *(decision)* afectar a, influir en (**b**) *(move emotionally)* afectar; **to be deeply affected by sth** estar muy afectado(a) por algo

**affect²** *vt (indifference, interest)* afectar, fingir; **to a. an accent** poner un acento

**affectation** [æfekˈteɪʃən] *n* afectación *f*, amaneramiento *m*

**affected** [əˈfektɪd] *adj (unnatural, pretended)* afectado(a), artificial

**affection** [əˈfekʃən] *n* afecto *m*, cariño *m*

**affectionate** [əˈfekʃənət] *adj* afectuoso(a), cariñoso(a)

**affidavit** [æfɪˈdeɪvɪt] *n Law* declaración *f* jurada

**affiliate 1** *n* [əˈfɪlɪət] filial *f*
**2** *vt* [əˈfɪlɪeɪt] afiliar (**to** *or* **with** a); **affiliated company** (empresa *f*) filial *f*

**affiliation** [əfɪlɪˈeɪʃən] *n (link, connection)* conexión *f*; *(political, religious)* filiación *f*

**affinity** [əˈfɪnɪtɪ] *n* (**a**) *(liking, attraction)* afinidad *f* (**with/between** con/entre); **she felt an a. for such places** sentía atracción por ese tipo de lugares (**b**) *(relationship, connection)* afinidad *f* (**between/with** entre/con)

**affirm** [əˈfɜːm] *vt* afirmar

**affirmation** [æfəˈmeɪʃən] *n* afirmación *f*

**affirmative** [əˈfɜːmətɪv] **1** *n* **to answer in the a.** responder afirmativamente
**2** *adj (answer)* afirmativo(a); **a. action** discriminación *f* positiva

**affix 1** *n* [ˈæfɪks] *Ling* afijo *m*
**2** *vt* [əˈfɪks] *(notice, poster)* pegar (**to** a)

**afflict** [əˈflɪkt] *vt* afligir; **to be afflicted with sth** padecer algo

**affliction** [əˈflɪkʃən] *n (suffering)* padecimiento *m*; *(misfortune)* desgracia *f*

**affluent** [ˈæfluənt] *adj* opulento(a), acomodado(a); **the a. society** la sociedad opulenta

**afford** [əˈfɔːd] *vt* (**a**) *(financially)* permitirse; **to be able to a. sth** poder permitirse algo; **I can't a. it** no me lo puedo permitir (**b**) *(non-financial use)* **I can a. to wait** puedo esperar; **can you a. the time?** ¿tienes tiempo?; **I can't**

**a. not to** no puedo permitirme no hacerlo; **we can't a. another mistake** no podemos permitirnos cometer otro error (**c**) Formal (give) proporcionar

**affordable** [ə'fɔ:dəbəl] adj (price, purchase) asequible

**affray** [ə'freɪ] (pl **affrays**) n altercado m, reyerta f

**affront** [ə'frʌnt] **1** n afrenta f, ofensa f
**2** vt afrentar, ofender; **to be/feel affronted** estar/sentirse ofendido(a)

**Afghan** ['æfɡæn] **1** n (**a**) (person) afgano m,f (**b**) (dog) (galgo m) afgano m
**2** adj afgano(a); **A. hound** galgo m afgano

**Afghanistan** [æf'ɡænɪstɑ:n] n Afganistán

**afield** [ə'fi:ld] adv **to go further a.** ir más allá; **to look further a.** buscar más

**AFL/CIO** [eɪef'elsiː'aɪ'əʊ] n (abbr **American Federation of Labor and Congress of Industrial Organizations**) = federación estadounidense de sindicatos

**afloat** [ə'fləʊt] adv a flote; **to stay a.** (of boat, company) mantenerse a flote

**afoot** [ə'fʊt] adv **there's something a.** se está tramando algo

**aforementioned** [ə'fɔ:menʃənd] adj susodicho(a), mencionado(a)

**aforesaid** [ə'fɔ:sed] adj mencionado(a), citado(a)

**afraid** [ə'freɪd] adj (**a**) (scared) **to be a.** tener miedo; **I'm a. of him** me da miedo; **I'm a. of dogs** tengo miedo a los perros; **I'm a. of making a mistake** tengo miedo de equivocarme; **that's exactly what I was a. of!** ¡eso es precisamente lo que me temía!; **I was a. there would be an accident** temía que ocurriera un accidente
(**b**) (sorry) **I'm a. so/not** me temo que sí/no; **I'm a. she's out** me temo que ha salido; **I'm a. I can't help you** lo siento, no puedo ayudarle

**afresh** [ə'freʃ] adv de nuevo, otra vez; **to start a.** empezar de nuevo

**Africa** ['æfrɪkə] n África

**African** ['æfrɪkən] **1** n africano(a) m,f
**2** adj africano(a); **A. American** afroamericano(a) m,f

**Afrikaans** [æfrɪ'kɑ:nz] n afrikaans m

**aft** [ɑ:ft] adv Naut a popa

**after** ['ɑ:ftə(r)] **1** prep (**a**) (with time) después de; **a. today** a partir de hoy; **a. dinner** después de cenar; **the day a. tomorrow** pasado mañana; **it's a. five** son más de las cinco; US **it's twenty a. six** son las seis y veinte; **a. all** (all things considered) después de todo; (despite everything) a pesar de todo
(**b**) (with motion) **to run a. sb** correr tras (de) alguien; **close the door a. you** cierra la puerta

al salir
(**c**) (looking for) **to be a. sb** buscar a alguien, andar detrás de alguien; **the police are a. him** la policía lo busca; **I think she's a. a pay-rise** me parece que anda detrás de or va buscando un aumento de sueldo
(**d**) (expressing order) **a. you!** (you first) ¡después de usted!; **am I a. you (in the queue)?** ¿voy detrás de usted (en la cola)?; **the first crossing a. the traffic lights** el primer cruce después del semáforo; **a. her, he is the best** después de ella, el mejor es él
(**e**) (expressing repetition) **day a. day** un día tras otro; **time a. time** una y otra vez; **year a. year** año tras año; **one a. the other** uno tras otro; **page a. page of statistics** páginas y más páginas de estadísticas
(**f**) Br (in honour of) **to name sb/sth a. sb** ponerle a alguien/algo el nombre de alguien
**2** adv después; **soon/long a.** poco/mucho después; **the day/the week a.** el día/la semana siguiente
**3** conj después de que; **I came a. he left** llegué cuando él ya se había ido; **a. doing sth** después de hacer algo

**afterbirth** ['ɑ:ftəbɜ:θ] n placenta f, secundinas fpl

**aftercare** ['ɑ:ftəkeə(r)] n (after operation) atención f posoperatoria; (of convalescent, delinquent) seguimiento m

**aftereffects** ['ɑ:ftərɪfekts] npl (of accident, crisis) secuelas fpl; (of drug) efectos mpl secundarios

**afterlife** ['ɑ:ftəlaɪf] n otra vida f, vida f de ultratumba

**aftermath** ['ɑ:ftəmæθ] n (period) periodo m posterior; (result) secuelas fpl, consecuencias fpl

**afternoon** [ɑ:ftə'nu:n] n tarde f; **in the a.** por la tarde; **at 2 o'clock in the a.** a las dos de la tarde; **good a.!** ¡buenas tardes!

**after-sales service** ['ɑ:ftə'seɪlz'sɜ:vɪs] n Com servicio m posventa

**aftershave** ['ɑ:ftəʃeɪv] n (as perfume) colonia f; **a. balm** or **lotion** (to protect skin) loción f para después del afeitado

**aftertaste** ['ɑ:ftəteɪst] n also Fig regusto m; **it leaves an unpleasant a.** deja mal sabor de boca

**afterthought** ['ɑ:ftəθɔ:t] n idea f tardía; **it was an a.** se me ocurrió después

**afterwards** ['ɑ:ftəwədz] adv después

**again** [ə'ɡen] adv (**a**) (in general) de nuevo, otra vez; **to begin a.** volver a empezar; **he never came back a.** no volvió nunca más; **once a.** una vez más; **don't do it a.!** ¡no lo vuelvas a hacer!; **not you a.!** ¡otra vez tú!; **a. and a.** una y otra vez; **now and a.** de vez en cuando; **half as much a.** la mitad más; **what**

**did you say a.?** ¿qué?, ¿cómo has dicho?
**(b)** *(besides)* además; **(then) a.** *(on the other hand)* por otra parte; **a., I may have imagined it** en fin, puede que me lo haya imaginado

**against** [ə'genst] *prep* **(a)** *(in opposition to)* contra, en contra de; **to be a. sb/sth** estar en contra de alguien/algo; **to have something a. sb/sth** tener algo en contra de alguien/algo; **to have nothing a. sb/sth** no tener nada en contra de alguien/algo; **it was a. my principles** iba (en) contra (de) mis principios; **a. the law** ilegal; **a. my will** en contra de mi voluntad
**(b)** *(as protection from)* contra; **to warn sb a. sb/sth** poner a alguien en guardia contra alguien/algo
**(c)** *(in contact with)* contra; **to lean a. sth** apoyarse en algo; **she put the ladder a. the wall** apoyó la escalera contra la pared
**(d)** *(in comparison with)* frente a; **the pound rose/fell a. the dollar** la libra subió/bajó frente al dólar; **inflation was 4.1%, as a. 3.2% last year** hubo una inflación del 4,1% frente a un 3,2% del año pasado; **a. the light** a contraluz

**age** [eɪdʒ] *(continuous* **aging** *or* **ageing**) **1** *n*
**(a)** *(of person)* edad *f*; **to be twenty years of a.** tener veinte años; **what a. is she?, what's her a.?** ¿qué edad tiene?, ¿cuántos años tiene?; **he doesn't look his a.** no aparenta la edad que tiene; **at the a. of twenty** a los veinte años; **people of all ages** gente de todas las edades; **the fifteen-to-twenty a. group** la franja de edad comprendida entre los quince y los veinte años; **a. of consent** edad *f* núbil; **a. limit** límite *m* de edad
**(b)** *(old)* **a.** vejez *f*
**(c)** *(adulthood)* **to come of a.** alcanzar la mayoría de edad; **to be under a.** ser menor *(para beber, tener relaciones sexuales etc)*
**(d)** *(era)* época *f*, edad *f*; **through the ages** a lo largo del tiempo
**(e)** *Fam (long time)* **it's ages since I saw him** hace siglos que no lo veo; **I've been waiting (for) ages** llevo esperando una eternidad
**2** *vt & vi* envejecer

**aged** *adj* **(a)** [eɪdʒd] *(of the age of)* **a. twenty** de veinte años (de edad) **(b)** ['eɪdʒɪd] *(old)* anciano(a)

**ageing** ['eɪdʒɪŋ] **1** *n (of person, wine)* envejecimiento *m*; **a. process** proceso *m* de envejecimiento
**2** *adj (old)* viejo(a); **the problem of Britain's a. population** el problema del envejecimiento de la población británica

**ageism** ['eɪdʒɪzəm] *n* discriminación *f* por motivos de edad

**agency** ['eɪdʒənsɪ] *n* **(a)** *Com* agencia *f*; **advertising/travel a.** agencia de publicidad/viajes **(b) through the a. of** mediante la intervención de

**agenda** [ə'dʒendə] *n (of meeting)* orden *m* del día, programa *m*; *Fig* **to be on top of the a.** ser un asunto prioritario; *Fig* **what is his real a.?** ¿cuáles son sus verdaderas intenciones?

**agent** ['eɪdʒənt] *n* **(a)** *(representative)* agente *mf*, representante *mf* **(b) (secret) a.** agente *mf* secreto(a) **(c)** *(instrument)* **to be the a. of** ser la causa de

**age-old** ['eɪdʒəʊld] *adj (custom, problem)* antiguo(a)

**aggravate** ['ægrəveɪt] *vt* **(a)** *(worsen)* agravar **(b)** *Fam (annoy)* fastidiar, molestar

**aggravating** ['ægrəveɪtɪŋ] *adj* **(a)** *Law* agravante **(b)** *Fam (annoying)* molesto(a); **it's very a.** fastidia un montón

**aggravation** [ægrə'veɪʃən] *n* **(a)** *(worsening)* agravamiento *m*, empeoramiento *m* **(b)** *Fam (annoyance)* fastidio *m*, molestia *f*

**aggregate** ['ægrɪgət] **1** *n* conglomerado *m*; *Sport* **on a.** en el total de la eliminatoria
**2** *adj* total, conjunto(a); **a. score** puntuación *f* total

**aggression** [ə'greʃən] *n (violence)* agresividad *f*; **an act of a.** una agresión

**aggressive** [ə'gresɪv] *adj (violent)* agresivo(a); *(vigorous, dynamic)* enérgico(a), agresivo(a),

**aggressively** [ə'gresɪvlɪ] *adv (violently)* agresivamente; *(vigorously)* enérgicamente, agresivamente

**aggressor** [ə'gresə(r)] *n* agresor(ora) *m,f*

**aggrieved** [ə'griːvd] *adj* agraviado(a), ofendido(a); **to be a.** estar ofendido(a)

**aggro** ['ægrəʊ] *n Fam (violence)* camorra *f*, pelea *f*; *(trouble)* follones *mpl*, líos *mpl*

**aghast** [ə'gɑːst] *adj* horrorizado(a), espantado(a)

**agile** ['ædʒaɪl] *adj* ágil

**agility** [ə'dʒɪlɪtɪ] *n* agilidad *f*

**agitate** ['ædʒɪteɪt] **1** *vt (liquid)* revolver, agitar; *(person)* inquietar, agitar
**2** *vi* **to a. for/against sth** hacer campaña a favor de/en contra de algo

**agitated** [ædʒɪteɪtɪd] *adj* inquieto(a), agitado(a); **to be a.** estar inquieto(a) or agitado(a)

**agitation** [ædʒɪ'teɪʃən] *n* **(a)** *(of person)* inquietud *f*, agitación *f* **(b)** *(campaign)* campaña *f*

**agitator** ['ædʒɪteɪtə(r)] *n Pol* agitador(ora) *m,f*, activista *mf*

**aglow** [ə'gləʊ] *adj* **to be a. with** *(with colour)* estar encendido(a) de; *(with pleasure, excitement)* estar rebosante de

**AGM** [eɪdʒiː'em] n Com (abbr **annual general meeting**) asamblea f or junta f general anual

**agnostic** [æg'nɒstɪk] n & adj agnóstico(a) m,f

**ago** [ə'gəʊ] adv **ten years a.** hace diez años; **a little while a., a short time a.** hace un rato; **long a.** hace mucho (tiempo); **not long a.** no hace mucho (tiempo); **as long a. as 1840** ya en 1840; **how long a. was that?** ¿hace cuánto tiempo fue (eso)?

**agog** [ə'gɒg] adj **to be a. at sth** estar entusiasmado(a) or emocionado(a) con algo

**agonize** ['ægənaɪz] vi angustiarse, agobiarse (**over** por or con)

**agonizing** ['ægənaɪzɪŋ] adj (pain, death) atroz; (silence, wait) angustioso(a); (decision, dilemma) peliagudo(a)

**agony** ['ægənɪ] n (physical pain) dolor m intenso; (anguish) angustia f, agonía f; **to be in a.** morirse de dolor; **it's a. walking in these shoes** andar con estos zapatos es un martirio; **a. aunt** (in newspaper) consultor(ora) m,f sentimental; **a. column** (in newspaper) consultorio m sentimental

**agoraphobia** [ægərə'fəʊbɪə] n agorafobia f

**agrarian** [ə'greərɪən] adj agrario(a)

**agree** [ə'griː] **1** vt (a) (reach agreement on) (price, conditions) acordar, pactar; **(are we) agreed?** ¿(estamos) de acuerdo?
(b) (concur) **to a. (that)...** estar de acuerdo en que...
(c) (consent) **to a. to do sth** acordar hacer algo; **we agreed to meet at six** quedamos a las seis; **he agreed to pay** estuvo de acuerdo en pagar él; **we'll have to a. to differ on that** tendremos que aceptar las discrepancias en cuanto a eso; **it is generally agreed that...** se suele admitir que...
**2** vi (a) (be of same opinion, concur) estar de acuerdo (**about/with** en cuanto a/con); **I quite** or **entirely a.** estoy completamente de acuerdo; **I'm afraid I can't a.** lo siento, pero no puedo estar conforme; **I couldn't a. more!** ¡estoy completamente de acuerdo!; **at least we a. about that** al menos estamos de acuerdo en eso; **I don't a. with all this violence on television** no me parece bien toda esa violencia que aparece en televisión
(b) (match) (of statements, facts, opinions) coincidir, concordar (**with** con); Gram concordar
(c) (accept) acceder, consentir

▸**agree on** vt insep (be in agreement) estar de acuerdo en; (reach agreement) ponerse de acuerdo en

▸**agree to** vt insep acceder a, aceptar; **he'll never a. to that** nunca accederá a eso; **to a. to** a condition/a proposal aceptar una condición/una propuesta

▸**agree with** vt insep (of food, climate) sentar bien a

**agreeable** [ə'griːəbəl] adj (a) (pleasant) agradable; (person) simpático(a) (b) (acceptable) **if that is a. to you** si te parece bien

**agreed** [ə'griːd] adj (price, time) fijado(a)

**agreement** [ə'griːmənt] n (a) (contract, assent) acuerdo m; **to come to an a.** llegar a un acuerdo; **by mutual a.** de mutuo acuerdo; **the proposal met with unanimous a.** la propuesta recibió un apoyo unánime; **to be in a. with sb/sth** estar de acuerdo con alguien/algo (b) (of facts, account) **to be in a. (with)** concordar, coincidir (con) (c) Gram concordancia f

**agricultural** [ægrɪ'kʌltʃərəl] adj agrícola; **a. college** escuela f de agricultura; **a. labourer** trabajador(ora) m,f agrícola

**agriculture** ['ægrɪkʌltʃə(r)] n agricultura f

**agronomy** [ə'grɒnəmɪ] n agronomía f

**aground** [ə'graʊnd] adv Naut **to run a.** (of ship) varar, encallar; (of project, government) encallar

**ahead** [ə'hed] adv (a) (forwards) adelante, (in front) delante; **to go on a.** adelantarse; **to send sb (on) a.** enviar a alguien por delante; **a. of** delante de; **the road a. was clear** no había nadie en la carretera delante de nosotros
(b) (winning) **to be a. (of)** (in race, opinion poll) ir por delante (de); (in match) ir ganando (a); **Liverpool are two goals a.** el Liverpool gana por dos goles; **to get a.** (in career) triunfar; **to get a. of sb** adelantar a alguien
(c) (in time) **to plan a.** hacer planes con antelación or por adelantado; **in the years a.** en los años venideros; **a. of time** antes de tiempo; **he was a. of his time** se adelantó a su tiempo; **how far a. should one book?** ¿con cuánta antelación hace falta reservar?; **the project is a. of schedule** el proyecto va por delante del calendario previsto

**ahoy** [ə'hɔɪ] exclam **a. there!** ¡ha del barco!; **ship a.!** ¡barco a la vista!

**AI** ['eɪaɪ] n (a) Comptr (abbr **artificial intelligence**) inteligencia f artificial (b) Biol (abbr **artificial insemination**) inseminación f artificial (c) Pol (abbr **Amnesty International**) AI, Amnistía f Internacional

**aid** [eɪd] **1** n (a) (help, for disaster relief) ayuda f; **with the a. of** con la ayuda de; **to go to sb's a.** acudir en ayuda de alguien; **in a. of** (fundraising event) a beneficio de; Fam **what's (all) this in a. of?** ¿a qué se debe (todo) esto? (b) (device) ayuda f; **teaching aids** material m didáctico or docente
**2** vt (growth, development) ayudar a, contribuir a;

*(person)* ayudar; *Law* **to a. and abet sb** ser cómplice de alguien

**aide** [eɪd] *n* asistente *mf*

**aide-de-camp** ['eɪd'dɒkɒŋ] *(pl* **aides-de-camp***) n Mil* ayudante *mf* de campo, edecán *m*

**AIDS** [eɪdz] *n (abbr* **Acquired Immuno-deficiency Syndrome)** SIDA *m*; **A. sufferer** enfermo(a) *m,f* de SIDA; **A. clinic** clínica *f* para enfermos de SIDA; **A. virus** virus *m* del SIDA

**ailing** ['eɪlɪŋ] *adj (person)* enfermo(a); *(company, economy)* enfermizo(a), débil

**ailment** ['eɪlmənt] *n* achaque *m*

**aim** [eɪm] **1** *n* **(a)** *(at target)* puntería *f*; **to take a. at** apuntar a; **her a. was good** tenía buena puntería **(b)** *(goal)* objetivo *m*, propósito *m*; **with the a. of doing sth** con el propósito de hacer algo
**2** *vt (blow, remark, TV programme)* dirigir (**at** a); *(gun, camera)* apuntar (**at** hacia *or* a); **to be aimed at sb** *(of remarks, TV programme)* estar dirigido(a) a alguien
**3** *vi* **to a. at sth/sb** *(with gun)* apuntar a *or* hacia algo/alguien; **to a. to do sth** *(intend)* tener la intención de hacer algo

**aimless** ['eɪmlɪs] *adj (existence)* sin objetivos; *(remark)* vago(a)

**ain't** [eɪnt] *very Fam* **(a)** = **is not, am not, are not (b)** = **has not, have not**

**air** [eər] **1** *n* **(a)** *(in general)* aire *m*; **by a.** en avión; **to be on the a.** *(of person, programme)* estar en el aire; **to throw sth (up) in the a.** lanzar algo al aire; **our plans are up in the a.** *(undecided)* nuestros planes están en el aire; **there's a feeling of hope in the a.** hay (un) ambiente de esperanza; *Aut* **a. bag** airbag *m*; **a. bed** colchón *m* hinchable; **a. filter** filtro *m* del aire; **the A. Force** las Fuerzas Aéreas; **a. freight** transporte *m* aéreo; **a. freshener** ambientador *m*; **a. hostess** azafata *f* de vuelo; **a. raid** ataque *m* aéreo; **a. rifle** escopeta *f* de aire comprimido; **a. show** demostración *f or* exhibición *f* aérea; **a. steward** auxiliar *m* de vuelo; **a. stewardess** auxiliar *f* de vuelo; **a. terminal** terminal *f* de vuelo; **a. traffic control** control *m* (del tráfico) aéreo; **a. traffic controller** controlador(ora) *m,f* (del tráfico) aéreo(a)
**(b)** *(melody)* melodía *f*, aire *m*
**(c)** *(look)* aire *m*; **he has the a. of somebody who has travelled** tiene aire de haber viajado mucho; **to give oneself airs, to put on airs** darse aires, darse tono
**2** *vt (room, opinions, grievances)* ventilar, airear; *(clothing, bedding)* airear, orear

**airborne** ['eəbɔːn] *adj (aircraft)* en vuelo; *(seeds, particles)* transportado(a) por el viento; *(troops)* aerotransportado(a); **to be a.** *(of aircraft)* estar volando

**air-conditioned** ['eəkən'dɪʃənd] *adj* climatizado(a), con aire acondicionado; **to be a.** *(of room)* tener aire acondicionado

**air-conditioning** ['eəkən'dɪʃənɪŋ] *n* aire acondicionado

**air-cooled** ['eəkuːld] *adj* con refrigeración de aire

**aircraft** ['eəkrɑːft] *(pl* **aircraft)** *n (aeroplane)* avión *m*; *(any flying vehicle)* aeronave *f*; **a. carrier** portaaviones *m inv*

**aircrew** ['eəkruː] *n Av* tripulación *f*

**airfield** ['eəfiːld] *n* campo *m* de aviación

**airhead** ['eəhed] *n Fam* cabeza de chorlito, simple

**airing** ['eərɪŋ] *n* **to give sth an a.** *(room, opinions, grievances)* ventilar *or* airear algo; *(clothing)* airear *or* orear algo; **a. cupboard** = ropero en el que se encuentra la caldera del agua caliente, y que se utiliza para orear la ropa, sábanas, etc

**airless** ['eəlɪs] *adj (evening, atmosphere)* cargado(a); **an a. room** una habitación en la que falta el aire

**airlift** ['eəlɪft] **1** *n* puente *m* aéreo
**2** *vt (supplies, troops)* transportar mediante un puente aéreo

**airline** ['eəlaɪn] *n* línea *f* aérea; **a. pilot** piloto *mf* comercial

**airlock** ['eəlɒk] *n* **(a)** *(in submarine, spacecraft)* compartimento *m* estanco, esclusa *f* de aire **(b)** *(in pipe)* burbuja *f* de aire

**airmail** ['eəmeɪl] **1** *n* correo *m* aéreo; **a. letter** carta *f* por vía aérea
**2** *adv* **to send sth a.** enviar algo por vía aérea
**3** *vt (letter)* mandar por vía aérea

**airplane** ['eəpleɪn] *n US* avión *m*

**airport** ['eəpɔːt] *n* aeropuerto *m*

**air-sea rescue** ['eəsiː'reskjuː] *n* rescate *m* marítimo desde el aire

**airship** ['eəʃɪp] *n* dirigible *m*

**airsick** ['eəsɪk] *adj* **to be a.** marearse *(en un avión)*

**airspace** ['eəspeɪs] *n* espacio *m* aéreo

**airstrip** ['eəstrɪp] *n* pista *f* de aterrizaje

**airtight** ['eətaɪt] *adj* hermético(a)

**airtime** ['eətaɪm] *n Rad TV* tiempo *m* de emisión

**airwaves** ['eəweɪvz] *npl* **his voice came over the a.** su voz llegó a través de las ondas

**airworthy** ['eəwɜːðɪ] *adj Av* **to be a.** estar en condiciones de volar

**airy** ['eərɪ] *adj* **(a)** *(room, house)* aireado(a) y espacioso(a) **(b)** *(person, attitude)* ligero(a), despreocupado(a)

**airy-fairy** ['eərɪ'feərɪ] *adj Fam (idea, scheme)* fantasioso(a), poco realista

**aisle** [aɪl] *n (in church)* nave *f* lateral; *(in plane, bus, cinema)* pasillo *m*; *Fam* **to have them rolling in the aisles** *(of comedian)* hacer que se caigan por los suelos de risa; **a. seat** *(in plane)* asiento *m* de pasillo

**ajar** [ə'dʒɑː(r)] *adj & adv* entornado(a)

**aka** [eɪkeɪ'eɪ] *adv (abbr* **also known as)** alias

**akin** [ə'kɪn] *adj & adv* **a. to** parecido(a) a

**alabaster** ['æləbæstə(r)] *n* alabastro *m*

**alacrity** [ə'lækrɪtɪ] *n* presteza *f*

**alarm** [ə'lɑːm] **1** *n* alarma *f*; **to raise** *or* **give the a.** dar la alarma; **there's no cause for a.** no hay motivo de alarma; **a. clock** (reloj *m*) despertador *m*; **a. signal** señal *f* de alarma
   **2** *vt* alarmar; **to be alarmed at sth** estar alarmado(a) por algo

**alarming** [ə'lɑːmɪŋ] *adj* alarmante

**alarmist** [ə'lɑːmɪst] *n & adj* alarmista *mf*

**alas** [ə'læs] **1** *exclam* ¡ay de mí!
   **2** *adv* desgraciadamente

**Albania** [æl'beɪnɪə] *n* Albania

**Albanian** [æl'beɪnɪən] **1** *n* **(a)** *(person)* albanés(esa) *m,f* **(b)** *(language)* albanés *m*
   **2** *adj* albanés(esa)

**albatross** ['ælbətrɒs] *n* albatros *m inv*

**albeit** [ɔːl'biːɪt] *conj* aunque; **a brilliant, a. uneven, novel** una novela brillante, aunque desigual

**albino** [æl'biːnəʊ] *( pl* **albinos**) *n* albino(a) *m,f*

**album** ['ælbəm] *n (for photos, stamps, record)* álbum *m*

**albumen** ['ælbjʊmɪn] *n* **(a)** *(in egg)* albumen *m* **(b)** *(in blood)* albúmina *f*

**alchemy** ['ælkəmɪ] *n* alquimia *f*

**alcohol** ['ælkəhɒl] *n* alcohol *m*

**alcoholic** [ælkə'hɒlɪk] **1** *n (person)* alcohólico(a) *m,f*
   **2** *adj* alcohólico(a)

**alcoholism** ['ælkəhɒlɪzəm] *n* alcoholismo *m*

**alcove** ['ælkəʊv] *n* hueco *m*

**alder** ['ɔːldə(r)] *n (tree)* aliso *m*

**ale** [eɪl] *n* = cerveza inglesa de malta

**alert** [ə'lɜːt] **1** *n* alerta *f*; **to be on the a.** estar alerta
   **2** *adj (mind)* lúcido(a); **to be a.** *(watchful)* estar alerta *or* vigilante; *(lively)* ser despierto(a) *or* espabilado(a); **to be a. to sth** *(aware of)* ser consciente de algo
   **3** *vt* alertar; **he alerted them to the danger** los alertó del peligro

**Aleutian Islands** [æl'uːʃən'aɪləndz] *npl* the A. las (Islas) Aleutianas

**Alexandria** [ælɪg'zɑːndrɪə] *n* Alejandría

**alfalfa** [æl'fælfə] *n* alfalfa *f*

**alfresco** [æl'freskəʊ] *adj & adv* al aire libre

**algae** ['ældʒiː] *npl* algas *fpl*

**algebra** ['ældʒɪbrə] *n* álgebra *f*

**Algeria** [æl'dʒɪərɪə] *n* Argelia

**Algerian** [æl'dʒɪərɪən] *n & adj* argelino(a) *m,f*

**Algiers** [æl'dʒɪəz] *n* Argel

**algorithm** ['ælgərɪðəm] *n* *Comptr* algoritmo *m*

**alias** ['eɪlɪəs] **1** *n* alias *m inv*
   **2** *adv* alias

**alibi** ['ælɪbaɪ] *n* *Law* coartada *f*

**alien** ['eɪlɪən] **1** *n* **(a)** *Formal (foreigner)* extranjero(a) *m,f* **(b)** *(from outer space)* extraterrestre *mf*, alienígena *mf*
   **2** *adj* **(a)** *(strange)* extraño(a); **it was a. to her nature** era ajeno a su carácter **(b)** *(from outer space)* extraterrestre, alienígena

**alienate** ['eɪlɪəneɪt] *vt (supporters, readers)* alejar, provocar el distanciamiento de; **they feel alienated from society** se sienten marginados de la sociedad

**alight¹** [ə'laɪt] *adj (burning)* **to be a.** estar ardiendo *or* en llamas; **to set sth a.** prender fuego a algo

**alight²** [ *pt & pp* **alighted** *or* **alit**) *vi* **(a)** *Formal (from train, car)* apearse **(at en) (b)** *(of bird, glance)* posarse **(on** sobre *or* en)

**align** [ə'laɪn] *vt* alinear; **to a. oneself with/against sb** alinearse con/contra alguien

**alignment** [ə'laɪnmənt] *n* alineamiento *m*, alineación *f*; **out of a.** desalineado(a), no alineado(a); **in a.** alineado

**alike** [ə'laɪk] **1** *adj* igual; **to look a.** parecerse; **you are all a.!** ¡todos sois iguales!
   **2** *adv (treat, dress, think)* igual; **old and young a.** jovenes y viejos por igual

**alimentary canal** [ælɪ'mentərɪkə'næl] *n* *Anat* tracto *m* alimentario, tubo *m* digestivo

**alimony** ['ælɪmənɪ] *n* *Law* pensión *f* (matrimonial) compensatoria

**alit** *pt & pp of* **alight**

**alive** [ə'laɪv] *adj* **(a)** *(living)* vivo(a); **to be a.** estar vivo(a); **to keep sb a.** mantener vivo(a) a alguien; **to keep a memory a.** mantener un recuerdo vivo; **to stay a.** sobrevivir; **to be burnt/buried a.** ser quemado(a)/enterrado(a) vivo(a); **to be a. and well** *(still living)* estar a salvo; **the oldest man a.** el hombre más viejo del mundo
   **(b)** *(aware)* **to be a. to sth** ser consciente de algo, darse cuenta de algo
   **(c)** *(full of vitality)* **I've never felt so a.** nunca me he sentido tan lleno de vida; **he came a. when someone mentioned food** revivió cuando alguien nombró la comida
   **(d)** *(teeming)* **to be a. with sth** ser un hervidero de algo

**alkali** ['ælkəlaɪ] *n* álcali *m*, base *f*

**alkaline** ['ælkəlaɪn] *adj* alcalino(a)

**all** [ɔ:l] **1** adj (**a**) *(every one of)* todos(as); **a. men** todos los hombres; **a. the others** todos los demás; **a. four of them** los cuatro; **a. the books** todos los libros; **they are a. smokers** todos fuman, todos son fumadores; **at a. hours** a todas horas, continuamente

(**b**) *(the whole of)* todo(a); **a. the wine** todo el vino; **a. day** todo el día; **a. week** toda la semana; **she has lived here a. her life** ha vivido aquí toda la *or* su vida; **a. the time** todo el tiempo; **he leaves the door open a. the time** siempre se deja la puerta abierta; **is that a. the money you're taking?** ¿no te llevas más que ese dinero?

(**c**) *(for emphasis)* **she helped me in a. sorts of ways** me ayudó de mil maneras; **what's a. that noise?** ¿qué es ese escándalo?; **in a. honesty** para ser francos; *Fam* **and a. that** y todo eso; **it's not a. that easy** no es tan fácil; **for a. her apparent calm, she was actually very nervous** a pesar de su aparente tranquilidad, estaba realmente muy nerviosa; **you, of a. people, should understand** tú deberías comprenderlo mejor que nadie; **of a. the times to phone!** ¡vaya un momento para llamar!

**2** pron (**a**) *(everyone)* todos(as) *m,fpl*; **a. of them say that..., they a. say that...** todos dicen que....; **a. of us** todos (nosotros); **we a. love him** todos lo queremos; **a. together** todos juntos

(**b**) *(everything)* *(replacing uncountable noun)* todo(a) *m,f*; *(replacing plural noun)* todos(as) *m,fpl*; **I want a. of it** lo quiero todo; **a. of them are blue, they are a. blue** todos son azules; **I did a. I could** hice todo lo que pude; **it was a. I could do not to laugh** apenas pude aguantar la risa; **best/worst of a.,...** y lo que es mejor/peor,...; **I like this one best of a.** este es el que más me gusta; **most of a.** ante todo; **when I was busiest of a.** cuando estaba más ocupado; **that's a.** eso es todo; **is that a.?** ¿nada más?, ¿es eso todo?; **a. I said was "good morning"** sólo dije "buenos días"; **when a.'s said and done** a fin de cuentas; **for a. I know** por lo que yo sé; **it's a. the same to me** me da lo mismo; **thirty men in a.** treinta hombres en total; **a. in a.** en resumen, en suma; **it cost £260, a. in** costó 260 libras con todo incluido; *Ironic* **it cost a. of £2** costó la increíble suma de 2 libras

**3** adv (**a**) *(entirely)* totalmente, completamente; **he was left a. alone** lo dejaron (completamente) solo(a); **he did it a. on his own** lo hizo él solo; **to be (dressed) a. in black** ir (vestido) todo de negro; **to be a. for sth** ser partidario(a) de algo; **to be a. ears** ser todo oídos; **he's not a. bad** no es del todo malo; **a. around the room** por toda la habitación; **a.

over (the place)** por todas partes; **a. too soon** demasiado pronto; **a. at once** *(suddenly)* de repente; *(at the same time)* a la vez; **a. along** desde el principio; **a. but** *(almost)* casi; **it's a. yours** es todo tuyo; *Fam* **a. in** *(exhausted)* hecho(a) polvo

(**b**) **do you know him at a.?** ¿lo conoces de algo?; **if at a. possible** a ser posible; **not at a.** *(not in the slightest)* en absoluto; *(when thanked)* de nada; **I'm not at a. astonished** no estoy en absoluto sorprendido

(**c**) *(with comparatives)* **a. the better/worse** tanto mejor/peor; **the noise made it a. the harder to hear them** con el ruido era aún más difícil oírlos

(**d**) *(in games)* **two a.** *(in football)* empate *m* a dos; **four (games) a.** *(in tennis)* empate a cuatro juegos; **fifteen a.** *(in tennis)* quince iguales

**4** *n* **to give one's a.** darlo todo

**Allah** ['ælə] *n* Alá *m*

**allay** [ə'leɪ] *vt (doubts, suspicions)* despejar; *(fear, pain)* apaciguar, aplacar

**all-clear** ['ɔ:l'klɪə(r)] *n (after air-raid)* señal *f* de que pasó el peligro; *Fig (for project)* luz *f* verde

**allegation** [ælɪ'geɪʃən] *n* acusación *f*

**allege** [ə'ledʒ] *vt* alegar; **it is alleged that...** se dice que...

**alleged** [ə'ledʒd] *adj* presunto(a)

**allegedly** [ə'ledʒɪdlɪ] *adv* presuntamente

**allegiance** [ə'li:dʒəns] *n* lealtad *f*

**allegory** ['ælɪgərɪ] *n* alegoría *f*

**all-embracing** [ɔ:lɪm'breɪsɪŋ] *adj* general, global

**allergic** [ə'lɜ:dʒɪk] *adj* alérgico(a) (**to** a)

**allergy** ['ælədʒɪ] *n* alergia *f*; **to have an a. to sth** tener alergia a algo

**alleviate** [ə'li:vɪeɪt] *vt (pain, symptoms)* aliviar

**alley** ['ælɪ] (*pl* **alleys**) *n* callejón *m*, callejuela *f*; **a. cat** gato *m* callejero

**alleyway** ['ælɪweɪ] *n* callejón *m*, callejuela *f*

**alliance** [ə'laɪəns] *n* alianza *f*; **to enter into an a. (with)** formar una alianza (con), aliarse (con)

**allied** ['ælaɪd] *adj (countries)* aliado(a); *(issues, phenomena)* afín, asociado(a)

**alligator** ['ælɪgeɪtə(r)] *n* caimán *m*; **a. shoes/handbag** zapatos *mpl*/bolso *m* de cocodrilo

**all-important** ['ɔ:lɪm'pɔ:tənt] *adj* fundamental, esencial

**all-in** ['ɔ:lɪn] *adj (price)* con todo incluido; **a. wrestling** lucha *f* libre

**alliteration** [əlɪtə'reɪʃən] *n* aliteración *f*

**all-night** ['ɔ:lnaɪt] *adj (party, session)* de toda la noche

**allocate** ['æləkeɪt] *vt* asignar (**to** a)

**allocation** [ælə'keɪʃən] *n* asignación *f*

**allot** [ə'lɒt] (*pt & pp* **allotted**) *vt* asignar; **in the allotted time** en el tiempo asignado

**allotment** [ə'lɒtmənt] *n* (**a**) *(plot of land)* huerto *m* de ocio, parcela *f* *(arrendada por el ayuntamiento para cultivo)* (**b**) *(of time, money)* asignación *f*

**all-out** [ɔ:'laʊt] *adj (effort)* supremo(a); *(opposition, resistance)* total; *(war)* sin cuartel; *(attack)* frontal; **an a. strike** una huelga general

**allow** [ə'laʊ] *vt* (**a**) *(permit)* permitir; **to a. sb to do sth** permitir a alguien hacer *or* que haga algo, dejar a alguien hacer algo; **smoking is not allowed** se prohíbe *or* no se permite fumar; **they'll never a. you to do it** nunca te dejarán hacerlo; **a. me!** *(offering help)* ¡permítame!; **I am allowed to do it** tengo permiso para hacerlo; **to a. oneself to be deceived/persuaded** dejarse engañar/convencer (**b**) *(allocate, grant)* dar, conceder; **a. an hour to get to the airport** deja una hora para llegar al aeropuerto

▸**allow for** *vt insep* tener en cuenta; **add another hour to a. for delays** añade una hora más *por* si hay retraso

**allowable** [ə'laʊəbəl] *adj (error, delay)* permisible

**allowance** [ə'laʊəns] *n* (**a**) *(money given)* asignación *f*, gastos *mpl* de viaje, dietas *fpl* (**b**) **to make a. for sth** *(take into account)* tener algo en cuenta; **I'm tired of making allowances for his inexperience** estoy harto de hacer concesiones *or* de disculparle por su falta de experiencia

**alloy** ['ælɔɪ] *n* aleación *f*

**all-powerful** [ɔ:'paʊəfʊl] *adj* todopoderoso(a)

**all-purpose** [ɔ:'pɜ:pəs] *adj* multiuso; **a. cleaner/adhesive** limpiador *m*/adhesivo *m* multiuso

**all right** [ɔ:l'raɪt] **1** *adj (well)* **to be a.** estar bien; **are you a.?** ¿estás bien?; **he was in a car crash but he's a.** tuvo un accidente, pero no le pasó nada; **it's a.** *(acceptable)* no está mal; *(not a problem)* está bien; **to be a. for money** tener dinero suficiente; **she's a. at dancing/at French** no se le da mal el baile/el francés; *Fam* **she's a bit of a.!** ¡está buenísima!

**2** *adv (yes)* vale; **is it a. if I smoke?** ¿puedo fumar?; **a., let's get started** venga, vamos a empezar

**all-round** [ɔ:l'raʊnd] *adj (education, improvement)* general; **an a. athlete** un/una atleta completo(a)

**all-rounder** [ɔ:l'raʊndə(r)] *n* **he's an a.** todo se le da bien

**allspice** ['ɔ:lspaɪs] *n* pimienta *f* inglesa

**all-star** [ɔ:l'stɑ:(r)] *adj* **an a. cast** un reparto de primeras figuras, un reparto estelar

**all-time** [ɔ:l'taɪm] *adj (record)* sin precedentes; *(favourite)* de todos los tiempos; **a. high/low** máximo *m*/mínimo *m* histórico

**allude** [ə'lu:d] *vi* aludir (**to** a)

**allure** [ə'lʊə(r)] *n* atractivo *m*, encanto *m*

**allusion** [ə'lu:ʒən] *n* alusión *f*; **to make an a. (to)** hacer (una) alusión (a)

**ally 1** *n* ['ælaɪ] aliado(a) *m,f*

**2** *vt* [ə'laɪ] **to a. oneself with...** aliarse con...

**almanac** ['ælmənæk] *n (calendar)* almanaque *m*

**almighty** [ɔ:l'maɪtɪ] **1** *n* **the A.** el Todopoderoso

**2** *adj Fam (fuss, row)* de mil demonios

**almond** ['ɑ:mənd] *n* almendra *f*; **a. tree** almendro *m*

**almost** ['ɔ:lməʊst] *adv* casi; **it's a. six o'clock** son casi las seis; **we're a. there** *(in journey)* casi hemos llegado; *(in task)* casi hemos acabado

**alms** [ɑ:mz] *npl* limosna *f*

**aloft** [ə'lɒft] *adv* por el aire, en vilo; **to hold sth a.** levantar a algo en el aire

**alone** [ə'ləʊn] *adj & adv* solo(a); **to be a.** estar solo(a); **to leave sth/sb a.** dejar algo/a alguien en paz; **I did it a.** lo hice yo solo; **to go it a.** ir por libre; **we are not a. in thinking that...** no somos los únicos que pensamos que...; **you a. can help me** tú eres el/la único(a) que me puede ayudar; **my salary a. isn't enough** con mi sueldo sólo no es suficiente; **let a....** mucho menos...; **I can't afford a bicycle, let a. a car!** no puedo comprarme una bicicleta, mucho menos un coche

**along** [ə'lɒŋ] **1** *prep* a lo largo de; **to walk a. the shore/a street** caminar por la costa/una calle; **somewhere a. the way** en algún punto (del camino)

**2** *adv* **to move a.** avanzar; **he'll be a. in ten minutes** vendrá en diez minutos; **to bring sth/sb a.** traerse algo/a alguien (consigo); **he knew all a.** lo sabía todo el tiempo, lo sabía desde el principio; **a. with** *(as well as)* además de, junto con

**alongside** [ə'lɒŋ'saɪd] *prep (next to)* junto a; *(together with)* junto con; *Naut* **to come a. the quay** arrimarse de costado al muelle

**aloof** [ə'lu:f] **1** *adj (person, manner)* distante

**2** *adv* al margen; **to remain a. (from)** mantenerse al margen (de)

**aloud** [ə'laʊd] *adv* en alto, en voz alta; **I was thinking a.** estaba pensando en voz alta

**alpha** ['ælfə] *n* alfa *f*; *Phys* **a. rays** radiación *f* *or* rayos *mpl* alfa

**alphabet** ['ælfəbet] *n* alfabeto *m*

**alphabetical** [ælfə'betɪkl] *adj* alfabético(a); **in a. order** en orden alfabético

**alphabetically** [ælfə'betɪklɪ] *adv* alfabéticamente

**alpine** ['ælpaɪn] *adj* alpino(a)

**Alps** [ælps] *npl* the A. los Alpes

**already** [ɔːl'redɪ] *adv* ya

**alright** = **all right**

**Alsatian** [æl'seɪʃən] **1** *n (dog)* pastor *m* alemán; *(person from Alsace)* alsaciano(a) *m,f*
**2** *adj (from Alsace)* alsaciano(a)

**also** ['ɔːlsəʊ] *adv* también, además; **not only... but a....** no sólo..., sino también...

**also-ran** ['ɔːlsəʊræn] *n (in horse race)* = caballo no clasificado entre los tres primeros; *Fig (person)* **he is just an a.** sólo es uno más o uno del montón

**altar** ['ɔːltə(r)] *n* altar *m*; **a. boy** monaguillo *m*

**alter** ['ɔːltə(r)] **1** *vt (person, design, plan)* cambiar, alterar; *(garment)* arreglar; **he altered his opinion** cambió de opinión; **that doesn't a. the fact that...** eso no cambia el hecho de que...
**2** *vi* cambiar, alterarse

**alteration** [ɔːltə'reɪʃən] *n (to design, plan)* cambio *m*, alteración *f*; *(to timetable)* alteración *f*; *(to garment)* arreglo *m*

**altercation** [ɔːltə'keɪʃən] *n* altercado *m*

**alter ego** ['æltə'riːgəʊ] *(pl* **alter egos)** *n* álter ego *m*

**alternate 1** *adj* [ɔːl'tɜːnət] alterno(a); **on a. days** en días alternos, cada dos días
**2** *vt* ['ɔːltəneɪt] alternar
**3** *vi* alternar (**with** con)

**alternately** [ɔːl'tɜːnətlɪ] *adv* alternativamente

**alternating** ['ɔːltəneɪtɪŋ] *adj* alterno(a); *Elec* **a. current** corriente *f* alterna

**alternative** [ɔːl'tɜːnətɪv] **1** *n (choice)* alternativa *f*; **there is no a.** no hay alternativa; **she had no a. but to obey** no tenía más remedio que obedecer
**2** *adj (plan, route, music, comedy)* alternativo(a); **an a. proposal** una alternativa; **a. energy** energía *f* alternativa; **a. medicine** medicina *f* alternativa

**alternatively** [ɔːl'tɜːnətɪvlɪ] *adv (on the other hand)* si no; **a., we could go to the beach** si no, podríamos ir a la playa

**alternator** ['ɔːltəneɪtə(r)] *n Elec* alternador *m*

**although** [ɔːl'ðəʊ] *conj* aunque

**altitude** ['æltɪtjuːd] *n* altitud *f*; **a. sickness** mal *m* de altura, *Andes* soroche *m*

**alto** ['æltəʊ] *Mus* **1** *n (pl* **altos)** contralto *m,f*
**2** *adj* contralto; **a. saxophone** saxo *m* alto

**altogether** [ɔːltə'geðə(r)] **1** *adv* **(a)** *(entirely)* completamente, enteramente; **I was not a. pleased** no estaba del todo contento **(b)** *(in total)* en total **(c)** *(on the whole)* en general

**2** *n Fam* **in the a.** *(naked)* como Dios lo trajo al mundo, en cueros

**altruism** ['æltrʊɪzm] *n* altruismo *m*

**altruistic** [æltrʊ'ɪstɪk] *adj* altruista

**aluminium** [ælju'mɪnɪəm], *US* **aluminum** [ə'luːmɪnəm] *n* aluminio *m*; **a. foil** papel *m* de aluminio

**always** ['ɔːlweɪz] *adv* siempre; **I can a. try** siempre puedo intentarlo

**AM** ['eɪ'em] *n Rad (abbr* **amplitude modulation)** AM, onda *f* media

**am** [æm] *1st person singular of* **be**

**a.m.** ['eɪ'em] *adv (abbr* **ante meridiem)** a.m., de la mañana; **5 a.m.** las 5 de la mañana

**amalgam** [ə'mælgəm] *n* amalgama *f*

**amalgamate** [ə'mælgəmeɪt] **1** *vt (metals, ideas)* amalgamar; *(companies)* fusionar
**2** *vi (of companies)* unirse, fusionarse

**amass** [ə'mæs] *vt (wealth)* amasar; *(objects, information, evidence)* acumular, reunir

**amateur** ['æmətə(r)] **1** *n (non-professional)* aficionado(a) *m,f*
**2** *adj (painter, musician)* aficionado(a); *(work, performance)* de aficionado; **it was a rather a. job** fue un trabajo chapucero *or* de aficionados

**amateurish** [æmə'tɜːrɪʃ] *adj Pej* chapucero(a)

**amaze** [ə'meɪz] *vt* asombrar, pasmar; **to be amazed at** *or* **by sth** quedarse atónito(a) *or* pasmado(a) ante algo

**amazement** [ə'meɪzmənt] *n* asombro *m*, estupefacción *f*; **she watched in a.** miró asombrada

**amazing** [ə'meɪzɪŋ] *adj* **(a)** *(surprising)* asombroso(a), extraordinario(a); **it's a. that no one was hurt** es increíble que nadie resultara herido **(b)** *(excellent)* genial, extraordinario(a)

**Amazon** ['æməzən] *n* **(a)** the A. *(river)* el Amazonas; *(region)* la Amazonia **(b)** *(female warrior)* amazona *f*

**ambassador** [æm'bæsədə(r)] *n* embajador(ora) *m,f*

**amber** ['æmbə(r)] **1** *n* ámbar *m*
**2** *adj* ambarino(a)

**ambidextrous** [æmbɪ'dekstrəs] *adj* ambidextro(a), ambidiestro(a)

**ambience, ambiance** ['æmbɪəns] *n* ambiente *m*

**ambiguity** [æmbɪ'gjuːɪtɪ] *n* ambigüedad *f*

**ambiguous** [æm'bɪgjʊəs] *adj* ambiguo(a)

**ambition** [æm'bɪʃən] *n* ambición *f*

**ambitious** [æm'bɪʃəs] *adj* ambicioso(a)

**ambivalent** [æm'bɪvələnt] *adj* ambivalente

**amble** ['æmbəl] *vi (of person)* deambular

**ambulance** ['æmbjʊləns] *n* ambulancia *f*; **a. man/woman** hombre *m*/mujer *f* de la ambulancia

**ambush** ['æmbʊʃ] **1** *n also Fig* emboscada *f*
**2** *vt also Fig* tender una emboscada a

**ameba** *US* = **amoeba**

**amen** ['ɑː'men] *exclam Rel* amén

**amenable** [ə'miːnəbəl] *adj* receptivo(a); **to be a. to reason** atender a razones; **to prove a. to a suggestion** acoger bien una sugerencia

**amend** [ə'mend] *vt (text, law)* enmendar, modificar; *(plans, schedule)* modificar; *(error)* corregir

**amendment** [ə'mendmənt] *n (to text, law)* enmienda *f* (**to** a), modificación *f* (**to** de); *(to plans, schedule)* modificación *f*; *(of error)* corrección *f*

**amends** [ə'mendz] *npl* **to make a. (for sth)** compensar (algo); **to make a. to sb for sth** resarcir a alguien por *or* de algo

**amenities** [ə'miːnɪtɪz] *npl* comodidades *fpl*, servicios *mpl*

**America** [ə'merɪkə] *n (United States)* Estados Unidos, América; *(continent)* América

**American** [ə'merɪkən] **1** *n (from USA)* estadounidense *mf*, americano(a) *m,f*
**2** *adj (of USA)* estadounidense, americano(a); *(of continent)* americano(a); **the A. Civil War** la guerra civil *or* de secesión americana; **A. football** fútbol *m* americano; **A. Indian** amerindio(a) *m,f*

**amethyst** ['æmɪθɪst] *n* amatista *f*

**amiable** ['eɪmɪəbəl] *adj* afable, amable

**amicable** ['æmɪkəbəl] *adj (relationship, agreement)* amistoso(a), amigable

**amid** [ə'mɪd], **amidst** [ə'mɪdst] *prep* entre, en medio de

**amino acid** [ə'miːnəʊ'æsɪd] *n* aminoácido *m*

**amiss** [ə'mɪs] *adj & adv* **there's something a.** algo va mal; **to take sth a.** tomarse algo a mal; **a cup of coffee wouldn't go a.** no vendría mal un café

**ammeter** ['æmɪtə(r)] *n Elec* amperímetro *m*

**ammonia** [ə'məʊnɪə] *n* amoniaco *m*

**ammunition** [æmjʊ'nɪʃən] *n (for guns)* munición *f; Fig (in debate, argument)* argumentos *mpl*

**amnesia** [æm'niːzɪə] *n Med* amnesia *f*

**amnesty** ['æmnɪstɪ] *n* amnistía *f*

**amniotic** [æmnɪ'ɒtɪk] *adj* amniótico(a); **a. fluid** líquido *m* amniótico

**amoeba**, *US* **ameba** [ə'miːbə] *n* ameba *f*

**amok** [ə'mʌk] *adv* **the demonstrators ran a. through the town** los manifestantes se descontrolaron y recorrieron la ciudad destrozando todo a su paso; **a gunman ran a.** un hombre perturbado disparó indiscriminadamente contra la multitud

**among** [ə'mʌŋ], **amongst** [ə'mʌŋst] *prep* entre; **we are a. friends** estamos entre amigos; **a. the best** entre los mejores; **a. other**

**things** entre otras cosas; **they quarrel a. themselves** se pelean entre ellos; **the money was divided a. them** se repartió el dinero entre ellos

**amoral** [eɪ'mɒrəl] *adj* amoral

**amorphous** [ə'mɔːfəs] *adj* amorfo(a)

**amount** [ə'maʊnt] *n* cantidad *f*; **a certain a. of discomfort** una cierta incomodidad; **no a. of money could persuade her to do it** no lo haría ni por todo el oro del mundo

▶**amount to** *vt insep* **(a)** *(add up to)* ascender a; **her debts a. to £700** sus deudas ascienden a 700 libras **(b)** *(mean)* **it amounts to the same thing** viene a ser lo mismo, equivale a lo mismo; **he'll never a. to much** nunca llegará a nada

**amp** [æmp] *n* **(a)** *Elec (unit)* amperio *m*; **a 13-a. plug** un enchufe (con fusible) de 13 amperios **(b)** *(amplifier)* amplificador *m*

**ampere** ['æmpeə(r)] *n Elec* amperio *m*

**ampersand** ['æmpəsænd] *n Typ* = signo '&'

**amphetamine** [æm'fetəmɪn] *n* anfetamina *f*

**amphibian** [æm'fɪbɪən] *n & adj* anfibio *m*

**amphibious** [æm'fɪbɪəs] *adj (animal, vehicle)* anfibio(a)

**amphitheatre,** *US* **amphitheater** ['æmfɪθɪətə(r)] *n* anfiteatro *m*

**ample** ['æmpəl] *adj (large) (garment)* amplio(a); *(bosom, proportions)* abundante; *(plentiful)* sobrado(a), abundante; **this will be a.** esto será más que suficiente; **to have a. time/ opportunity to do sth** tener tiempo/ocasiones de sobra para hacer algo

**amplification** [æmplɪfɪ'keɪʃən] *n (of sound)* amplificación *f*; *(of remark)* ampliación *f*

**amplifier** ['æmplɪfaɪə(r)] *n* amplificador *m*

**amplify** ['æmplɪfaɪ] *vt (essay, remarks)* ampliar; *(current, volume)* amplificar

**amputate** ['æmpjʊteɪt] *vt* amputar

**amputation** [æmpjʊ'teɪʃən] *n* amputación *f*

**Amsterdam** [æmstə'dæm] *n* Amsterdam

**amuck** [ə'mʌk] = **amok**

**amulet** ['æmjʊlet] *n* amuleto *m*

**amuse** [ə'mjuːz] *vt* **(a)** *(make laugh)* divertir **(b)** *(occupy)* distraer; **to a. oneself by doing sth** divertirse haciendo algo; **to keep sb amused** entretener a *or* distraer a alguien

**amusement** [ə'mjuːzmənt] *n* **(a)** *(enjoyment)* diversión *f*; **much to everyone's a.** para regocijo *or* diversión de todos **(b)** *(pastime)* distracción *f*, entretenimiento *m*; **a. arcade** salón *m* de juegos (recreativos); **a. park** parque *m* de atracciones

**amusing** [ə'mjuːzɪŋ] *adj* divertido(a)

**an** [æn] *see* **a²**

**anabolic steroid** [æn'bɒlɪk'stɪərɔɪd] *n* (esteroide *m*) anabolizante *m*

**anachronism** [ə'nækrənɪzəm] *n* anacronismo *m*

**anaconda** [ænə'kɒndə] *n* anaconda *f*

**anaemia,** US **anemia** [ə'ni:mɪə] *n* anemia *f*

**anaemic,** US **anemic** [ə'ni:mɪk] *adj Med* anémico(a); *Fig (weak)* pobre

**anaesthetic,** US **anesthetic** [ænəs-'θetɪk] *n* anestesia *f*, anestésico *m*; **under a.** bajo (los efectos de la) anestesia; **local/general a.** anestesia local/general

**anaesthetist,** US **anesthetist** [ə'ni:sθətɪst] *n* anestesista *mf*

**anaesthetize,** US **anesthetize** [ə'ni:sθətaɪz] *vt Med* anestesiar

**anagram** ['ænəgræm] *n* anagrama *m*

**anal** ['eɪnəl] *adj Anat* anal

**analgesic** [ænəl'dʒi:zɪk] **1** *n* analgésico *m*
**2** *adj* analgésico(a)

**analog** US = **analogue**

**analogous** [ə'næləgəs] *adj* análogo(a) (**to** a)

**analogue,** US **analog** ['ænəlɒg] **1** *n* equivalente *m*
**2** *adj* analógico(a); **a. clock** reloj *m* analógico

**analogy** [ə'nælədʒɪ] *n* analogía *f*; **to draw an a. between two things** establecer una analogía entre dos cosas

**analyse,** US **analyze** ['ænəlaɪz] *vt* analizar; *Psy* psicoanalizar

**analysis** [ə'næləsɪs] (*pl* **analyses** [ə'næləsi:z]) *n* análisis *m inv*; *Psy* psicoanálisis *m inv*; **in the final a.** a fin de cuentas

**analyst** ['ænəlɪst] *n* analista *mf*; *Psy* psicoanalista *mf*

**analytic(al)** [ænə'lɪtɪk(əl)] *adj* analítico(a)

**analyze** US = **analyse**

**anarchic** [ə'nɑ:kɪk] *adj* anárquico(a)

**anarchist** ['ænəkɪst] *n* anarquista *mf*

**anarchy** ['ænəkɪ] *n* anarquía *f*

**anathema** [ə'næθəmə] *n* (**a**) *Rel* anatema *m* (**b**) *(repellent)* **the very idea was a. to her** la sola idea le resultaba repugnante

**anatomical** [ænə'tɒmɪkəl] *adj* anatómico(a)

**anatomy** [ə'nætəmɪ] *n* anatomía *f*

**ANC** [eɪen'si:] *n* (*abbr* **African National Congress**) ANC *m*, Congreso *m* Nacional Africano

**ancestor** ['ænsestə(r)] *n* ancestro *m*, antepasado(a) *m,f*

**ancestral** [æn'sestrəl] *adj* de los antepasados; **a. home** casa *f* solariega

**ancestry** ['ænsestrɪ] *n* (*descent)* linaje *m*, abolengo *m*

**anchor** ['æŋkə(r)] **1** *n Naut* ancla *f*; *Fig (of team)* eje *m*; **at a.** fondeado(a), anclado(a); **to**

**drop a.** echar el ancla, fondear; **to weigh a.** levar anclas
**2** *vt* (**a**) *Naut* fondear, anclar (**b**) *(fix securely)* sujetar, anclar (**to** a) (**c**) *(radio, TV programme)* presentar
**3** *vi Naut* fondear, anclar

**anchorman** ['æŋkəmən] *n* (*in radio, TV programme)* presentador *m*, locutor *m*

**anchorwoman** ['æŋkəwʊmən] *n* (*in radio, TV programme)* presentadora *f*, locutora *f*

**anchovy** ['æntʃəvɪ] *n* anchoa *f*

**ancient** ['eɪnʃənt] **1** *n* **the ancients** los antiguos
**2** *adj* antiguo(a); *Fam (car, clothes)* vetusto(a); **you're 40? – that's a.!** ¿40 años? – ¡estás hecho un carroza!; **a. history** historia *f* antigua; **A. Rome** la antigua Roma

**ancillary** [æn'sɪlərɪ] *adj (staff, workers)* auxiliar

**and** [ænd, *unstressed* ənd, ən] *conj* (**a**) *(in general)* y; *(before* i, hi) e; **she can read a. write** sabe leer y escribir; **father a. son** padre e hijo; **my father a. brother** mi padre y mi hermano; **chicken a. chips** pollo con patatas fritas; **go a. look for it** ve a buscarlo; **come a. see me** ven a verme; **try a. help me** intenta ayudarme; **wait a. see** espera a ver; **nice a. warm** bien calentito(a); **do that again a. I'll hit you!** como lo vuelvas a hacer, te pego (**b**) *(in numbers)* **two hundred a. two** doscientos dos; **four a. a half** cuatro y medio; **an hour a. twenty minutes** una hora y veinte minutos; **four a. five make nine** cuatro y cinco, nueve (**c**) *(expressing repetition)* **hours a. hours** horas y horas; **better a. better** cada vez mejor; **she talked a. talked** no paraba de hablar (**d**) **a. so on a. so forth** etcétera, etcétera

**Andalusia** [ændə'lu:sɪə] *n* Andalucía

**Andalusian** [ændə'lu:sɪən] *n & adj* andaluz(uza) *m,f*

**Andean** ['ændɪən] *adj* andino(a)

**Andes** ['ændi:z] *npl* **the A.** los Andes

**Andorra** [æn'dɔ:rə] *n* Andorra

**Andorran** [æn'dɔ:rən] *n & adj* andorrano(a) *m,f*

**anecdotal** [ænɪk'dəʊtəl] *adj* anecdótico(a)

**anecdote** ['ænɪkdəʊt] *n* anécdota *f*

**anemia, anemic** US = **anaemia, anaemic**

**anemone** [ə'nemənɪ] *n (flower)* anémona *f*; **sea a.** anémona *f* de mar

**anesthetic, anesthetist** *etc* US = **anaesthetic, anaesthetist** *etc*

**anew** [ə'nju:] *adv* de nuevo

**angel** ['eɪndʒəl] *n* ángel *m*; *Fam* **you're an a.!** ¡eres un ángel *or* un sol!

**Angeleno** [ændʒə'li:nəʊ] (*pl* **Angelenos**) *n* = habitante o nativo de Los Angeles

**angelic** [æn'dʒelɪk] *adj* angelical

**anger** ['æŋgə(r)] **1** *n* ira *f*, enfado *m*; **a fit of a.** un ataque de ira; **to speak in a.** hablar con ira
**2** *vt* enojar, enfadar
**3** *vi* **to be slow to a.** tardar en enfadarse; **to be quick to a.** enfadarse con facilidad

**angina** [æn'dʒaɪnə] *n Med* angina *f* (de pecho)

**angle** ['æŋgəl] **1** *n* **(a)** *Math* ángulo *m* **(b)** *(viewpoint)* ángulo *m*, punto *m* de vista; **seen from this a.** visto(a) desde este ángulo
**2** *vi* **(a)** *(fish)* pescar con caña **(b)** *Fam* **to a. for an invitation** andar a la caza de una invitación

**angler** ['æŋglə(r)] *n (person)* pescador(ora) *m,f (con caña)*; **a. fish** rape *m*

**Anglican** ['æŋglɪkən] *n & adj Rel* anglicano(a) *m,f*

**angling** ['æŋglɪŋ] *n* pesca *f* con caña

**Anglo-American** ['æŋgləʊə'merɪkən] *adj* angloamericano(a)

**Anglo-Saxon** ['æŋgləʊ'sæksən] *n & adj* anglosajón(ona) *m,f*

**Angola** [æŋ'gəʊlə] *n* Angola

**Angolan** [æŋ'gəʊlən] *n & adj* angoleño(a) *m,f*

**angora** [æŋ'gɔːrə] *n (textile)* angora *f*; **a. goat** cabra *f* de angora; **a. jumper** jersey *m* de angora; **a. rabbit** conejo *m* de angora; **a. wool** lana *f* de angora

**angrily** ['æŋgrɪlɪ] *adv* airadamente, con enfado

**angry** ['æŋgrɪ] *adj (person)* enfadado(a), enojado(a); *(voice, letter)* airado(a); **to be a.** estar enfadado(a) or enojado(a); **to get a.** enfadarse, enojarse; **to make sb a.** (hacer) enfadar a alguien, hacer que alguien se enfade

**anguish** ['æŋgwɪʃ] *n* angustia *f*

**anguished** ['æŋgwɪʃt] *adj (look, cry)* angustiado(a)

**angular** ['æŋgjʊlə(r)] *adj (face, shape)* anguloso(a)

**animal** ['ænɪməl] *n (creature)* animal *m*; **the a. kingdom** el reino animal; **a. rights** derechos *mpl* de los animales; **he's an a.** *(uncivilized person)* es un animal, es una bestia

**animate 1** *adj* ['ænɪmɪt] animado(a)
**2** *vt* ['ænɪmeɪt] animar

**animated** ['ænɪmeɪtɪd] *adj (expression, discussion)* animado(a); **to be a.** estar animado(a); **to become a.** animarse; **a. cartoon** dibujos *mpl* animados

**animation** [ænɪ'meɪʃən] *n* animación *f*

**animator** ['ænɪmeɪtə(r)] *n Cin* animador(ora) *m,f*

**animism** ['ænɪmɪzəm] *n Rel* animismo *m*

**animosity** [ænɪ'mɒsɪtɪ] *n* animosidad *f*

**aniseed** ['ænɪsiːd] *n* anís *m*

**Ankara** ['æŋkərə] *n* Ankara

**ankle** ['æŋkəl] *n* tobillo *m*; **a. boots** botines *mpl*; **a. socks** calcetines *mpl* cortos

**anklet** ['æŋklət] *n (ankle bracelet)* pulsera *f* para el tobillo

**annals** ['ænəlz] *npl* anales *mpl*

**annex 1** *vt* [ə'neks] *(territory)* anexionar, anexar
**2** *n* ['æneks] *US* = **annexe**

**annexation** [ænek'seɪʃən] *n* anexión *f*

**annexe,** *US* **annex** ['æneks] *n (of building)* edificio *m* anejo; *(of document)* anexo *m*

**annihilate** [ə'naɪəleɪt] *vt* aniquilar

**annihilation** [ənaɪə'leɪʃən] *n* aniquilación *f*

**anniversary** [ænɪ'vɜːsərɪ] *n* aniversario *m*; **wedding a.** aniversario de boda

**anno Domini** ['ænəʊ'dɒmɪnaɪ] *adv* después de Cristo

**annotate** ['ænəteɪt] *vt* anotar

**announce** [ə'naʊns] *vt* anunciar; **"I think you're all wrong,"** she announced "creo que estáis todos equivocados", declaró or anunció

**announcement** [ə'naʊnsmənt] *n (of news)* anuncio *m*; *(formal statement)* declaración *f*, anuncio *m*

**announcer** [ə'naʊnsə(r)] *n (on radio, TV programme)* presentador(ora) *m,f*

**annoy** [ə'nɔɪ] *vt* fastidiar, enfadar; **to get annoyed** molestarse, enfadarse; **to be annoyed with sb** estar molesto(a) or enfadado(a) con alguien

**annoyance** [ə'nɔɪəns] *n (feeling)* enfado *m*; *(annoying thing)* molestia *f*, fastidio *m*

**annoying** [ə'nɔɪŋ] *adj* molesto(a), irritante; **he has an a. habit of interrupting me** tiene la mala or molesta costumbre de interrumpirme; **how a.!** ¡qué fastidio!

**annual** ['ænjʊəl] **1** *n* **(a)** *(plant)* planta *f* anual **(b)** *(book)* anuario *m*; *(for children)* = recopilación de historietas de tebeo en un libro grueso
**2** *adj* anual; **a. general meeting** asamblea *f* or junta *f* general anual

**annually** ['ænjʊəlɪ] *adv* anualmente

**annuity** [ə'njuːɪtɪ] *n* anualidad *f*

**annul** [ə'nʌl] *(pt & pp* annulled) *vt Law (contract, marriage)* anular

**annulment** [ə'nʌlmənt] *n* anulación *f*

**anode** ['ænəʊd] *n Elec* ánodo *m*

**anodyne** ['ænəʊdaɪn] *adj (bland)* anodino(a), insulso(a)

**anoint** [ə'nɔɪnt] *vt* ungir (**with** con)

**anomalous** [ə'nɒmələs] *adj* anómalo(a)

**anomaly** [ə'nɒməlɪ] *n* anomalía *f*

**anon¹** [ə'nɒn] *adv Literary (soon)* pronto

**anon²** *n (abbr* **anonymous**) anón., anónimo(a)

**anonymity** [ænə'nɪmɪtɪ] *n* anonimato *m*

**anonymous** [əˈnɒnɪməs] *adj (gift, donor)* anónimo(a); **to remain a.** permanecer en el anonimato; **a. letter** carta *f* anónima, anónimo *m*

**anorak** [ˈænəræk] *n* anorak *m*

**anorexia** [ænəˈreksɪə] *n Med* anorexia *f*; **a. nervosa** anorexia nerviosa

**anorexic** [ænəˈreksɪk] *adj Med* anoréxico(a)

**another** [əˈnʌðə(r)] **1** *adj* otro(a); **a. cup of tea** otra taza de té; **it lasted for a. fifty years** duró otros cincuenta años *or* cincuenta años más; **don't say a. word** ni una palabra más; **that's quite a. matter** eso es algo (totalmente) distinto; **a. time, perhaps** *(declining invitation)* quizá en otra ocasión; **let's do it a. way** vamos a hacerlo de otra manera

**2** *pron* **(a)** *(in general)* otro(a) *m,f*; **give me a. dame** otro; **what with one thing and a., I forgot** entre unas cosas y otras, se me olvidó **(b)** *(reciprocal)* **they saw one a.** se vieron; **we always help one a.** siempre nos ayudamos el uno al otro

**answer** [ˈɑːnsə(r)] **1** *n (to question, letter)* respuesta *f*, contestación *f*; *(to problem)* solución *f*; **I knocked but there was no a.** llamé a la puerta, pero no hubo respuesta; **there's no a.** *(on telephone)* no contestan; **he has an a. to everything** tiene respuesta para todo; **Forin a. to your letter** en respuesta a su carta

**2** *vt (person, question, letter)* responder, contestar; **to a. the telephone** coger *or* contestar el teléfono; **to a. the door** abrir la puerta; **to a. a description/need** responder a una descripción/una necesidad

**3** *vi (of person)* responder, contestar

▸**answer back** *vi (be impertinent)* replicar, contestar; **don't a. back!** ¡no me repliques!

▸**answer for** *vt insep* responder de, ser responsable de; **he has a lot to a. for** tiene mucho que explicar

▸**answer to** *vt insep* **(a)** *(be accountable to)* **to a. to sb (for sth)** ser responsable ante alguien (de algo), responder ante alguien (de algo) **(b)** *(correspond to)* *(description)* responder a **(c)** **the dog answers to the name of Rover** el perro responde al nombre de Rover

**answerable** [ˈɑːnsərəbəl] *adj* **to be a. to sb** ser responsable ante alguien, responder ante alguien

**answering machine** [ˈɑːnsərɪŋˈməʃiːn], **answerphone** [ˈɑːnsəfəʊn] *n* contestador *m* (automático)

**ant** [ænt] *n* hormiga *f*; **a. hill** hormiguero *m*

**antagonism** [ænˈtæɡənɪzəm] *n* antagonismo *m*

**antagonist** [ænˈtæɡənɪst] *n* antagonista *mf*

**antagonize** [ænˈtæɡənaɪz] *vt* enfurecer, enfadar

**Antarctica** [ænˈtɑːktɪkə] *n* la Antártida

**ante** [ˈæntɪ] *n* **to up the a.** *Fam (in gambling, conflict)* elevar la apuesta

**anteater** [ˈæntiːtə(r)] *n* oso *m* hormiguero

**antecedents** [æntɪˈsiːdənts] *npl* antecedentes *mpl*

**antelope** [ˈæntɪləʊp] *(pl* **antelopes** *or* **antelope)** *n* antílope *m*

**antenatal** [æntɪˈneɪtəl] *adj* prenatal; **a. clinic** clínica *f* de obstetricia *or* de preparación para el parto

**antenna** [ænˈtenə] *n* **(a)** *(pl* **antennae** [ænˈteniː]) *(of insect, snail)* antena *f* **(b)** *(pl* **antennas)** *(of radio, TV)* antena *f*

**anteroom** [ˈæntruːm] *n* antesala *f*

**anthem** [ˈænθəm] *n* himno *m*; **national a.** himno nacional

**anthology** [ænˈθɒlədʒɪ] *n* antología *f*

**anthracite** [ˈænθrəsaɪt] *n* antracita *f*

**anthrax** [ˈænθræks] *n Med* carbunco *m*, ántrax *m inv*

**anthropologist** [ænθrəˈpɒlədʒɪst] *n* antropólogo(a) *m,f*

**anthropology** [ænθrəˈpɒlədʒɪ] *n* antropología *f*

**anti-** [ˈæntɪ] *pref* anti-; **a.-American** antiamericano(a)

**anti-aircraft** [ˈæntɪˈeəkrɑːft] *adj (gun, defences)* antiaéreo(a)

**antibiotic** [æntɪbaɪˈɒtɪk] *n* antibiótico *m*

**antibody** [ˈæntɪbɒdɪ] *n Med* anticuerpo *m*

**Antichrist** [ˈæntɪkraɪst] *n* Anticristo *m*

**anticipate** [ænˈtɪsɪpeɪt] *vt* **(a)** *(expect)* esperar; *(foresee)* prever; **as anticipated, there was trouble** como se preveía, hubo problemas **(b)** *(foreshadow)* anticipar, anunciar **(c)** *(do or say before)* adelantarse a

**anticipation** [æntɪsɪˈpeɪʃən] *n* **(a)** *(foresight)* previsión *f*; **in a. of trouble** en previsión de posibles problemas; **thanking you in a.** *(in letter)* le doy las gracias de antemano; **to show great a.** *(of tennis player, footballer)* tener mucha visión de juego **(b)** *(eagerness)* ilusión *f*, expectación *f*

**anticlimax** [æntɪˈklaɪmæks] *n* gran decepción *f*

**anti-clockwise** [æntɪˈklɒkwaɪz], *US* **counter-clockwise** [ˈkaʊntəˈklɒkwaɪz] **1** *adj* **in an a. direction** en sentido contrario al de las agujas del reloj

**2** *adv* en sentido contrario al de las agujas del reloj

**antics** [ˈæntɪks] *npl* payasadas *fpl*; **he's been up to his usual a.** ha estado haciendo las payasadas de costumbre

**anticyclone** [æntɪˈsaɪkləʊn] *n Met* anticiclón *m*

**antidepressant** [æntɪdɪ'presənt] *n & adj* antidepresivo *m*

**antidote** ['æntɪdəʊt] *n also Fig* antídoto *m* (**to** contra)

**antifreeze** ['æntɪfriːz] *n* anticongelante *m*

**Antigua and Barbuda** [æn'tiːgənbɑː 'bjuːdə] *n* Antigua y Barbuda

**antihistamine** [æntɪ'hɪstəmiːn] **1** *n* antihistamina *f*

  **2** *adj* antihistamínico(a); **a. drug** antihistamínico *m*

**anti-inflammatory** [æntɪm'flæmətərɪ] **1** *n* antiinflamatorio *m*

  **2** *adj* antiinflamatorio(a); **a. drug** antiinflamatorio *m*

**antipathy** [æn'tɪpəθɪ] *n* antipatía *f*

**antiperspirant** [æntɪ'pɜːspɪrənt] *n* antitranspirante *m*

**Antipodes** [æn'tɪpədiːz] *npl* **the A.** las antípodas (*Australia y Nueva Zelanda*)

**antiquarian** [æntɪ'kweərɪən] **1** *n* (*dealer*) anticuario(a) *m,f*; (*collector*) coleccionista *mf* de antigüedades

  **2** *adj* (*book*) antiguo(a); **a. bookshop** = librería especializada en libros antiguos

**antiquated** ['æntɪkweɪtɪd] *adj* anticuado(a)

**antique** [æn'tiːk] **1** *n* antigüedad *f*; **a. dealer** anticuario(a) *m,f*; **a. shop** tienda *f* de antigüedades

  **2** *adj* antiguo(a); **a. furniture** muebles *mpl* antiguos

**antiquity** [æn'tɪkwɪtɪ] *n* antigüedad *f*

**antiracist** [æntɪ'reɪsɪst] *adj* antirracista

**anti-Semitic** [æntɪsɪ'mɪtɪk] *adj* (*person*) antisemita; (*beliefs, remarks*) antisemítico(a)

**antiseptic** [æntɪ'septɪk] **1** *n Med* antiséptico *m*

  **2** *adj* **(a)** (*anti-bacterial*) antiséptico(a) **(b)** *Fig* (*lacking character or warmth*) aséptico(a)

**antisocial** [æntɪ'səʊʃəl] *adj* **(a)** (*disruptive*) incívico(a), antisocial **(b)** (*unsociable*) insociable

**antithesis** [æn'tɪθɪsɪs] (*pl* **antitheses** [æn'tɪθɪsiːz]) *n* antítesis *f inv*

**antler** ['æntlə(r)] *n* cuerno *m*; **antlers** cornamenta *f*

**antonym** ['æntənɪm] *n* antónimo *m*

**Antwerp** ['æntwɜːp] *n* Amberes

**anus** ['eɪnəs] *n* ano *m*

**anvil** ['ænvɪl] *n* yunque *m*

**anxiety** [æŋ'zaɪətɪ] *n* **(a)** (*worry, concern*) preocupación *f*; (*anguish, impatience*) ansiedad *f*; **her behaviour has been the cause of great a.** su comportamiento ha causado gran preocupación **(b)** (*eagerness*) ansia *f*, afán *m*; **in her a. not to offend...** en su afán por no ofender...

**anxious** ['æŋkʃəs] *adj* **(a)** (*worried*) preocupado(a); (*anguished, impatient*) ansioso(a); **to be a.**

**(for)** estar preocupado(a) (por); **I am a. about his health** me preocupa su salud; **he was a. that all his work might come to nothing** temía que todo su trabajo quedara en nada **(b)** (*worrying*) **an a. moment** un momento de preocupación; **it was an a. time for us** en esos momentos estábamos muy preocupados **(c)** (*eager*) **to be a. to do sth** estar ansioso(a) por hacer algo

**anxiously** ['æŋkʃəslɪ] *adv* **(a)** (*worriedly*) con preocupación **(b)** (*with anguish, impatience*) ansiosamente

**any** ['enɪ] **1** *pron* **(a)** (*some*) **have you got a.?** (*with plural nouns*) ¿tienes alguno(a)?; (*with uncountable nouns*) ¿tienes algo?; **I fancy some biscuits – have you got a.?** me apetecen unas galletas, ¿tienes?; **are there a. left?** ¿queda alguno(a)?; **is there a. left?** ¿queda algo?; **is there a. more?** ¿hay más?; **can a. of them speak English?** ¿alguno (de ellos) habla inglés?

  **(b)** (*in negatives*) ninguno(a) *m,f*; **I haven't got a.** no tengo; **there was nothing in a. of the boxes** no había nada en ninguna de las cajas; **few, if a., can read** pocos, o ninguno, saben leer

  **(c)** (*no particular one*) cualquiera; (*before noun*) cualquier; **a. of us** cualquiera de nosotros; **take a. of the bottles** coge cualquier botella *or* una botella cualquiera

  **(d)** (*every one*) **keep a. you find** quédate con todos los que encuentres

  **2** *adj* **(a)** (*some*) **have you a. milk/sugar?** ¿tienes leche/azúcar?; **have you a. apples/cigarettes?** ¿tienes manzanas/cigarrillos?; **is there a. hope?** ¿hay alguna esperanza?

  **(b)** (*in negatives*) ninguno(a); (*before masculine singular noun*) ningún; **he hasn't got a. money** no tiene dinero; **I didn't get a. of your letters** no recibí ninguna de tus cartas; **without a. help** sin ninguna ayuda

  **(c)** (*no particular*) (*before noun*) cualquier; (*after noun*) cualquiera; **come a. day** ven cualquier día, ven un día cualquiera; **a. doctor will tell you the same** cualquier médico te diría lo mismo; **a. minute now** de un momento a otro; **I don't want just a. (old) wine** no quiero un vino cualquiera

  **(d)** (*every*) **a. pupil who forgets his books will be punished** los alumnos que olviden sus libros serán castigados; **I'll take a. books you don't want** me quedaré con todos los libros que no quieras; **at a. rate, in a. case** en cualquier caso

  **3** *adv* **(a)** (*with comparative*) **I'm not a. better** no me encuentro mejor; **the weather couldn't be a. worse** el tiempo no podía ser peor; **have you a. more milk?** ¿tienes más leche?; **we don't see them a. longer** *or* **more**

ya no los vemos; **I don't like her a. more than you do** a mí no me gusta más que a ti; **is that a. easier?** ¿es así más fácil?

**(b)** *Fam* **a. old how** de cualquier manera, a la buena de Dios; **that didn't help us a.** eso no nos ayudó para nada

**anybody** ['enɪbɒdɪ] *pron* **(a)** *(indeterminate)* alguien; **would a. like some more cake?** ¿quiere alguien más pastel?; **does a. mind if I close the window?** ¿les importa que cierre la ventana?; **she'll know if a. does** si alguien lo sabe es ella

**(b)** *(in negatives)* nadie; **there isn't a. here** aquí no hay nadie; **there was hardly a.** no había apenas nadie, apenas había nadie

**(c)** *(no matter who)* cualquiera; **a. will tell you so** cualquiera te lo dirá; **bring along a. you like** trae a quien quieras; **a. but her would have refused** cualquiera menos ella se habría negado; **I don't want just a.!** ¡no quiero a cualquiera!

**(d)** *(person with status)* **he'll never be a.** nunca será nadie

**anyhow** ['enɪhaʊ] *adv* **(a)** *(however)* de todas maneras *or* formas, de todos modos; **a., let's get back to what we were saying** bueno, volvamos a lo que estábamos diciendo **(b)** *Fam (carelessly)* a la buena de Dios, de cualquier manera; **I don't want it done just a.** no quiero que se haga de cualquier manera

**anyone** ['enɪwʌn] = **anybody**

**anyplace** ['enɪpleɪs] *US* = **anywhere**

**anything** ['enɪθɪŋ] **1** *pron* **(a)** *(indeterminate)* algo; **is there a. I can do (to help)?** ¿puedo ayudarte en algo?; **have you a. to write with?** ¿tienes con qué escribir?; **will there be a. else?** *(in shop)* ¿algo más?; **have you a. smaller?** ¿tendría algo más pequeño?; **if a. should happen to me** si me ocurriera algo; **do you notice a. strange about him?** ¿le notas algo raro?; **is (there) a. the matter?** ¿ocurre algo?

**(b)** *(in negatives)* nada; **he doesn't do a.** no hace nada; **hardly a.** apenas nada

**(c)** *(no matter what)* cualquier cosa; **he eats a.** come cualquier cosa; **a. you want** lo que quieras; **I love a. French** me gusta todo lo francés; **he would do a. for me** haría cualquier cosa por mí; **he was a. but friendly** fue todo menos amable; **are you angry? – a. but** ¿estás enfadado? – ni mucho menos

**2** *adv* **is it a. like the last one?** ¿se parece en algo al anterior?; **it didn't cost a. like £500** no costó 500 libras, ni muchísimo menos; **the food wasn't a. like as bad as they said it** la comida no fue en absoluto tan mala como decían; *Fam* **as funny as a.** divertidísimo(a); *Fam* **to work like a.** trabajar como loco(a); *Fam*

**it's not that you were wrong or a.** no es que estuvieras equivocado ni nada parecido

**anyway** ['enɪweɪ] *adv (however)* de todas maneras *or* formas, de todos modos; **a., let's get back to what we were saying** bueno, volvamos a lo que estábamos diciendo

**anywhere** ['enɪweə(r)], *US* **anyplace** ['enɪpleɪs] *adv* **(a)** *(in questions)* **can you see it a.?** ¿lo ves por alguna parte?; **have you found a. to live?** ¿has encontrado un lugar *or* algún sitio para vivir?; **did you go a. yesterday?** ¿fuiste a alguna parte ayer?

**(b)** *(in negatives)* **I can't find it a.** no lo encuentro por ningún sitio; **we never go a. interesting** nunca vamos a ningún sitio interesante; **we're not getting a.** no estamos consiguiendo nada; **he isn't a. near as clever as her** no es ni mucho menos tan listo como ella

**(c)** *(no matter where)* en cualquier lugar, en cualquier sitio; **put it a.** ponlo en cualquier sitio; **I'd know him a.** lo reconocería en cualquier parte; **it's miles from a.** está en un lugar muy aislado; **a. else** en cualquier otro lugar

**AO(C)B** [eɪəʊ(siː)'biː] *Com (abbr* **any other (competent) business)** ruegos *mpl* y preguntas

**aorta** [eɪ'ɔːtə] *n Anat* aorta *f*

**apart** [ə'pɑːt] *adv* **(a)** *(at a distance)* alejado(a), separado(a); **to stand a.** estar separado(a)

**(b)** *(separated)* **the two towns are 10 kilometres a.** las dos ciudades están a 10 kilómetros una de la otra; **boys and girls were kept a.** los chicos y las chicas estaban separados; **they're never a.** no se separan nunca; **with one's legs a.** con las piernas abiertas *or* separadas; **they were born two years a.** nacieron con dos años de diferencia; **they've lived a. since 1987** viven separados desde 1987; **it is difficult to tell them a.** es difícil distinguirlos

**(c)** *(to pieces)* **to take sth a.** desmontar algo; **to come a.** destrozarse

**(d) a. from** *(excepting)* aparte de; **quite a. from the fact that...** independientemente del hecho de que...; **joking a.** bromas aparte

**apartheid** [ə'pɑːtaɪt] *n* apartheid *m*

**apartment** [ə'pɑːmənt] *n US* piso *m*, *Am* departamento *m*; **a. building** bloque *m* de pisos

**apathetic** [æpə'θetɪk] *adj* apático(a) (**about** respecto a)

**apathy** ['æpəθɪ] *n* apatía *f*

**ape** [eɪp] **1** *n (animal)* simio *m*; *US Fam* **to go a.** ponerse hecho(a) una furia

**2** *vt (imitate)* imitar, remedar

**aperitif** [əperɪ'tiːf] *n* aperitivo *m (bebida)*

**aperture** ['æpətjʊə(r)] *n (opening)* abertura *f*; *(of camera)* (apertura *f* del) diafragma *m*

**APEX** ['eɪpeks] *adj* **A. ticket** billete *m* (con tarifa) APEX

**apex** ['eɪpeks] *n (of triangle)* vértice *m*; *(of career)* cima *f*, cumbre *f*

**aphasia** [ə'feɪzɪə] *n Med* afasia *f*

**aphid** ['eɪfɪd] *n* pulgón *m*

**aphorism** ['æfərɪzəm] *n* aforismo *m*

**aphrodisiac** [æfrəʊ'dɪzɪæk] **1** *n* afrodisíaco *m*
**2** *adj* afrodisíaco(a)

**apiece** [ə'piːs] *adv* cada uno(a); **they cost £3 a.** cuestan 3 libras cada uno, están a 3 libras

**aplenty** [ə'plentɪ] *adv* en abundancia; **there was wine a.** corría el vino a raudales

**aplomb** [ə'plɒm] *n* aplomo *m*

**apocalypse** [ə'pɒkəlɪps] *n* apocalipsis *m inv*

**apocalyptic** [əpɒkə'lɪptɪk] *adj* apocalíptico(a)

**apolitical** [eɪpə'lɪtɪkəl] *adj* apolítico(a)

**apologetic** [əpɒlə'dʒetɪk] *adj (tone, smile)* de disculpa; **she was quite a. about it** lo sentía mucho

**apologize** [ə'pɒlədʒaɪz] *vi* disculparse **(to sb/for sth** ante alguien/por algo); **I had to a. for you** tuve que pedir disculpas por ti; **there's no need to a.** no hay por qué disculparse

**apology** [ə'pɒlədʒɪ] *n* disculpa *f*; **to make/offer an a.** disculparse; **I owe you an a.** te debo una disculpa; **please accept my apologies** le ruego (que) acepte mis disculpas; *Pej* **an a. for a dinner** una birria de cena

**apoplectic** [æpə'plektɪk] *adj* **(a)** *(angry)* **to be a. (with rage)** estar hecho(a) una furia **(b)** *Med* **to be a.** tener apoplejía

**apoplexy** ['æpəpleksɪ] *n Med* apoplejía *f*; *Fig (anger)* furia *f*

**apostle** [ə'pɒsəl] *n* apóstol *m*

**apostolic(al)** [æpɒs'tɒlɪk(əl)] *adj* apostólico(a)

**apostrophe** [ə'pɒstrəfɪ] *n* apóstrofo *m*

**appal** [ə'pɔːl] *(pt & pp* **appalled***) vt* horrorizar, espantar; **to be appalled at** *or* **by sth** horrorizarse por algo

**appall** *US* = **appal**

**appalling** [ə'pɔːlɪŋ] *adj* espantoso(a), horroroso(a)

**apparatus** [æpə'reɪtəs] *n (in laboratory, gym)* aparatos *mpl*; **a piece of a.** un aparato

**apparel** [ə'pærəl] *n* atuendo *m*, atavío *m*

**apparent** [ə'pærənt] *adj* **(a)** *(obvious)* evidente; **to become a.** hacerse patente *or* evidente **(b)** *(seeming)* aparente

**apparently** [ə'pærəntlɪ] *adv* al parecer; **a. easy/innocent** aparentemente fácil/inocente; **a. not** parece que no

**apparition** [æpə'rɪʃən] *n* aparición *f*

**appeal** [ə'piːl] **1** *n* **(a)** *(call)* llamamiento *m*; **to make an a. for sth** hacer un llamamiento para solicitar algo; **an a. for calm** un llamamiento a la calma; **charity a.** = campaña de recaudación de fondos para fines benéficos
**(b)** *Law* apelación *f*; **to lodge an a.** presentar una apelación; **A. Court, Court of A.** tribunal *m* de apelación
**(c)** *(attraction)* atractivo *m*; **to have** *or* **hold little a. for sb** no atraer mucho a alguien; **to have great a.** ser muy atractivo(a); **their music has a wide a.** su música gusta a gente muy diversa
**2** *vt US Law* **to a. a decision** entablar recurso de apelación contra una decisión
**3** *vi* **(a)** *(make a plea)* **to a. (to sb) for help/money** solicitar ayuda/dinero (a alguien); **to a. to sb's generosity** apelar a la generosidad de alguien
**(b)** *(attract)* **to a. to sb** atraer a alguien; **it doesn't a. to me** no me atrae
**(c)** *Law* apelar, recurrir; **to a. against a decision** entablar recurso de apelación contra una decisión

**appealing** [ə'piːlɪŋ] *adj* atractivo(a), atrayente

**appear** [ə'pɪə(r)] *vi* **(a)** *(come into view)* aparecer; *(of publication, film)* salir, aparecer; **where did you a. from?** ¿de dónde has salido?; **to a. from nowhere** aparecer de repente; **to a. on TV** salir en televisión
**(b)** *Law* **to a. before a court** comparecer ante un tribunal; **to a. for sb** *(of counsel)* representar a alguien
**(c)** *(look, seem)* parecer; **to a. to be lost** parecer perdido(a); **there appears to be a mistake** parece que hay un error; **so it would a.** eso parece

**appearance** [ə'pɪərəns] *n* **(a)** *(arrival)* aparición *f*; **to put in an a.** hacer acto de presencia **(b)** *(of actor)* aparición *f* **(c)** *(of publication)* publicación *f* **(d)** *Law (in court)* comparecencia *f* **(e)** *(looks, demeanour)* apariencia *f*, aspecto *m*; **you should not judge by appearances** no se debe juzgar por las apariencias; **it has all the appearances of a conspiracy** tiene todo el aspecto de ser una conspiración; **appearances can be deceptive** las apariencias engañan; **to keep up appearances** guardar las apariencias

**appease** [ə'piːz] *vt (anger)* aplacar, apaciguar; *(person)* calmar, apaciguar; *Pol* contemporizar con

**appeasement** [ə'piːzmənt] *n (of person, anger)* apaciguamiento *m*; *Pol* contemporización *f*

**append** [ə'pend] *vt (list, document)* adjuntar; *(one's signature)* añadir

**appendage** [ə'pendɪdʒ] *n* apéndice *m*; **she was tired of being treated as his a.** estaba harta de que se la tratara como si fuera un mero apéndice de él

**appendicitis** [əpendɪ'saɪtɪs] *n* apendicitis *f inv*

**appendix** [ə'pendɪks] (*pl* **appendices** [ə'pendɪsi:z]) *n* (**a**) *Anat* apéndice *m*; **to have one's a. (taken) out** operarse de apendicitis (**b**) (*of book*) apéndice *m*

**appetite** ['æpɪtaɪt] *n* (**a**) (*for food*) apetito *m*; **to have a good a.** tener buen apetito; **to spoil sb's a.** quitarle el apetito a alguien; **to give sb an a.** abrirle el apetito a alguien (**b**) (*for knowledge, sex*) afán *m*, apetito *m* (**for** de)

**appetizer** ['æpɪtaɪzə(r)] *n also Fig* aperitivo *m*

**appetizing** ['æpɪtaɪzɪŋ] *adj* apetitoso(a)

**applaud** [ə'plɔ:d] *vt & vi* aplaudir

**applause** [ə'plɔ:z] *n* (*clapping*) aplauso *m*, ovación *f*; (*approval*) aplauso *m*, aprobación *f*

**apple** ['æpəl] *n* manzana *f*; **she was the a. of his eye** (*his favourite*) era la niña de sus ojos; **a. core** corazón *m* de una manzana; **a. juice** zumo *m* de manzana; **a. pie** pastel *m* de manzana; **as American as a. pie** típicamente americano(a); **a. tart** tarta *f* de manzana; **a. tree** manzano *m*

**applecart** ['æpɪkɑ:t] *n* **to upset the a.** (*spoil plan*) estropearlo todo

**apple-pie** ['æpəlpaɪ] *adj* **in a. order** en perfecto orden

**appliance** [ə'plaɪəns] *n* (**electrical** *or* **domestic**) **a.** electrodoméstico *m*

**applicable** [ə'plɪkəbəl] *adj* válido(a) (**to** para), aplicable (**to** a); **delete where not a.** (*on form*) táchese lo que no proceda

**applicant** ['æplɪkənt] *n* (*for job*) solicitante *mf*

**application** [æplɪ'keɪʃən] *n* (**a**) (*for job, patent*) solicitud *f*; **to make an a. for sth** solicitar algo; **a. form** (*for job*) impreso *m* de solicitud (**b**) (*of law, rule*) aplicación *f* (**c**) (*effort*) aplicación *f*, entrega *f* (**d**) *Comptr* aplicación *f*

**applied** [ə'plaɪd] *adj* (*maths, physics*) aplicado(a)

**apply** [ə'plaɪ] **1** *vt* (**a**) (*put on*) aplicar; **to a. pressure to** ejercer presión sobre, presionar (**b**) (*use*) (*system, theory*) aplicar; **to a. one's mind to sth** concentrarse en algo; **to a. oneself to one's work** aplicarse en el trabajo

**2** *vi* (**a**) (*for job, grant*) **to a. (to sb) for sth** solicitar algo (a alguien) (**b**) (*of law, rule*) **rule 26b applies in all other cases** la norma 26b se aplicará en todos los demás casos; **this clause no longer applies** esta cláusula ya no está en vigor; **that applies to all of you!** ¡esto es válido *or* vale para todos vosotros!

**appoint** [ə'pɔɪnt] *vt* (*person, committee*) nombrar, designar; **to a. sb to a post** designar a alguien para un cargo

**appointed** [ə'pɔɪntɪd] *adj Formal* (*agreed*) (*place, hour*) fijado(a)

**appointment** [ə'pɔɪntmənt] *n* (**a**) (*meeting*) cita *f*; **to make an a. with sb** concertar una cita con alguien; **she didn't keep the a.** faltó a la cita; **I've made/got an a. with the doctor** he pedido/tengo hora con el médico; **by a. only** con cita previa (**b**) (*to job, of committee*) nombramiento *m*, designación *f*; **to make an a.** hacer un nombramiento; *Com* **by a. to His/Her Majesty** proveedores de la Casa Real; **appointments** (*in newspaper*) ofertas *fpl* de empleo

**apportion** [ə'pɔ:ʃən] *vt* (*food, praise*) distribuir, repartir; **to a. blame** repartir la culpa

**appraisal** [ə'preɪzəl] *n* (*of standards, personnel*) evaluación *f*, valoración *f*

**appraise** [ə'preɪz] *vt* (*performance, situation*) evaluar, valorar; **to a. the value of sth** tasar algo

**appreciable** [ə'pri:ʃəbəl] *adj* (*change, difference*) apreciable

**appreciate** [ə'pri:ʃɪeɪt] **1** *vt* (**a**) (*be grateful for*) agradecer; **I a. your helping me** te agradezco tu ayuda; **I would a. it if you didn't shout** te agradecería que no gritaras (**b**) (*grasp, understand*) darse cuenta de; **I fully a. (the fact) that…** me doy perfecta cuenta de que…; **we a. the risks** somos conscientes de los riesgos (**c**) (*value*) apreciar

**2** *vi* (*of goods, investment*) revalorizarse, aumentar de valor

**appreciation** [pri:ʃɪ'eɪʃən] *n* (**a**) (*gratitude*) gratitud *f*, agradecimiento *m*; **in a. of** en agradecimiento por

(**b**) (*understanding*) apreciación *f*, percepción *f*; **she has no a. of what is involved** no se da cuenta de lo que implica

(**c**) (*review, assessment*) (*of film, author's work*) reseña *f*, crítica *f*; **a musical/wine a. society** una asociación de amigos de la música/del vino (**d**) (*valuing*) (*of music, art*) valorización *f*

(**e**) *Fin* **a. of assets** revalorización *f* de activos

**appreciative** [ə'pri:ʃɪətɪv] *adj* (*person, response, audience*) agradecido(a); (*review*) elogioso(a); **to be a. of sb's help/efforts** sentirse muy agradecido(a) por la ayuda/los esfuerzos de alguien

**apprehend** [æprɪ'hend] *vt* (**a**) (*arrest*) detener, aprehender (**b**) *Formal* (*understand*) aprehender, comprender

**apprehension** [æprɪ'henʃən] *n* (**a**) (*fear*) aprensión *f* (**b**) *Law* (*arrest*) detención *f*, aprehensión *f*

**apprehensive** [æprɪ'hensɪv] *adj* (*look, smile*) temeroso(a), receloso(a); **to be a. about (doing) sth** tener miedo de (hacer) algo

**apprentice** [ə'prentıs] **1** n aprendiz(iza) m,f
**2** vt he was apprenticed to a tailor estaba de aprendiz con un sastre

**apprenticeship** [ə'prentıʃıp] n also Fig aprendizaje m; **to serve one's a.** hacer el aprendizaje

**approach** [ə'prəutʃ] **1** n (a) (coming) (of person, season) llegada f; (of night) caída f; **to make an a. to sb** (proposal) hacer una propuesta inicial a alguien (b) (method) enfoque m, planteamiento m (c) (route of access) acceso m; **the approaches to a town** los accesos a una ciudad; Aut **a. road** (vía f de) acceso m
**2** vt (a) (get nearer to) acercarse a, aproximarse a; **I'm approaching forty-five** tengo casi cuarenta y cinco años (b) (go up to) acercarse a, aproximarse a; **she approached several organizations** acudió or se dirigió a varias organizaciones; **to be easy/difficult to a.** ser/no ser accesible (c) (tackle) abordar, enfocar
**3** vi acercarse, aproximarse

**approachable** [ə'prəutʃəbəl] adj (person) accesible

**approaching** [ə'prəutʃıŋ] adj (holiday, season) próximo(a); **the a. car** el coche que viene de frente

**appropriate¹** [ə'prəupriət] adj (suitable) apropiado(a), adecuado(a); (moment) oportuno(a), adecuado(a)

**appropriate²** [ə'prəuprieıt] vt (a) (take, steal) apropiarse de (b) (set aside) (money, funds) destinar, asignar

**appropriately** [ə'prəupriətlı] adv (suitably) apropiadamente, adecuadamente; (properly) con propiedad

**appropriation** [əprəuprı'eıʃən] n (of funds) apropiación f

**approval** [ə'pru:vəl] n aprobación f; **he gave/withheld his a.** dio/no dio su aprobación; Com **on a.** a prueba

**approve** [ə'pru:v] vt aprobar
▸**approve of** vt insep aprobar; **she doesn't a. of them smoking** no aprueba que fumen; **I don't a. of your friends** no me gustan tus amigos

**approved school** [ə'pru:vd'sku:l] n Br Formerly reformatorio m, correccional m

**approving** [ə'pru:vıŋ] adj de aprobación

**approx** [ə'prɒks] (abbr **approximately**) aprox., aproximadamente

**approximate 1** adj [ə'prɒksımıt] aproximado(a)
**2** vi [ə'prɒksımeıt] **to a. to** aproximarse a

**approximately** [ə'prɒksımətlı] adv aproximadamente

**approximation** [əprɒksı'meıʃən] n aproximación f

**APR** [eıpi:'ɑ:] n Fin (abbr **annual percentage rate**) TAE m o f

**Apr** (abbr **April**) abril m

**apricot** ['eıprıkɒt] n (fruit) albaricoque m, Am damasco m, Méx chabacano m; **a. tree** albaricoquero m

**April** ['eıprıl] n abril m; **A. showers** lluvias fpl de abril; **A. Fool's Day** ≃ día m de los (Santos) Inocentes (uno de abril); see also **May**

**apron** ['eıprən] n (a) (clothing) delantal m; Fam **he's still tied to his mother's a. strings** (dependent on her) sigue pegado a las faldas de su madre (b) Av área f de estacionamiento

**apt** [æpt] adj (a) (word, description) apropiado(a), acertado(a) (b) (likely) **to be a. to do sth** ser propenso(a) a hacer algo

**aptitude** ['æptıtju:d] n aptitud f; **to have an a. for** tener aptitudes para; **a. test** prueba f de aptitud

**aptly** ['æptlı] adv acertadamente

**aquamarine** [ækwəmə'ri:n] **1** n (gem) aguamarina f
**2** adj (colour) azul verdoso(a)

**aquarium** [ə'kweərıəm] n acuario m

**Aquarius** [ə'kweərıəs] n (sign of zodiac) acuario m; **to be (an) A.** ser acuario

**aquatic** [ə'kwætık] adj acuático(a)

**aqueduct** ['ækwıdʌkt] n acueducto m

**aquiline** ['ækwılaın] adj aguileño(a), aquilino(a)

**Arab** ['ærəb] n & adj árabe mf

**Arabia** [ə'reıbıə] n Arabia

**Arabian** [ə'reıbıən] adj árabe; **the A. Sea** el Mar de Arabia or de Omán

**Arabic** ['ærəbık] **1** n (language) árabe m
**2** adj árabe; **A. numerals** números mpl arábigos

**arable** ['ærəbəl] adj cultivable, arable

**arachnid** [ə'ræknıd] n Zool arácnido m

**Aragon** ['ærəgən] n Aragón

**Aragonese** [ærəgə'ni:z] n & adj aragonés(esa) m,f

**arbiter** ['ɑ:bıtə(r)] n (of taste, fashion) árbitro m

**arbitrary** ['ɑ:bıtrərı] adj arbitrario(a)

**arbitrate** ['ɑ:bıtreıt] **1** vt arbitrar
**2** vi arbitrar (between entre)

**arbitration** [ɑ:bı'treıʃən] n arbitraje m; **the dispute went to a.** el conflicto se llevó ante un árbitro

**arbitrator** ['ɑ:bıtreıtə(r)] n (in dispute) árbitro m

**arc** [ɑ:k] n arco m; **a. lamp** lámpara f de arco (voltaico)

**arcade** [ɑ:'keıd] n (a) (for shopping) galería f comercial (b) Archit galería f

**arch¹** [ɑ:tʃ] **1** n (a) Archit arco m (b) (of foot) puente m; **to have fallen arches** tener los pies planos

**2** *vt* **to a. one's back** arquear la espalda

**arch²** *adj* **a. enemy** mayor enemigo(a) *m,f;* **a. traitor** gran traidor(ora) *m,f*

**arch³** *adj (mischievous)* pícaro(a)

**archaeological,** *US* **archeological** [ɑ:kɪə'lɒdʒɪkəl] *adj* arqueológico(a)

**archaeologist,** *US* **archeologist** [ɑ:kɪ'ɒlədʒɪst] *n* arqueólogo(a) *m,f*

**archaeology,** *US* **archeology** [ɑ:kɪ'ɒlədʒɪ] *adj* arqueología *f*

**archaic** [ɑ:'keɪɪk] *adj* arcaico(a)

**archangel** ['ɑ:keɪndʒəl] *n* arcángel *m*

**archbishop** [ɑ:tʃ'bɪʃəp] *n* arzobispo *m*

**archduke** [ɑ:tʃ'dju:k] *n* archiduque *m*

**archeological, archeologist** *etc US* = **archaeological, archaeologist** *etc*

**archer** ['ɑ:tʃə(r)] *n* arquero *m*

**archery** ['ɑ:tʃərɪ] *n* tiro *m* con arco

**archetypal** [ɑ:kɪ'taɪpəl] *adj* arquetípico(a), típico(a)

**archetype** ['ɑ:kɪtaɪp] *n* arquetipo *m*, modelo *m*

**archipelago** [ɑ:kɪ'pelɪgəʊ] *n* archipiélago *m*

**architect** ['ɑ:kɪtekt] *n (of building)* arquitecto(a) *m,f; Fig (of scheme)* artífice *mf*

**architecture** ['ɑ:kɪtektʃə(r)] *n* arquitectura *f*

**archives** ['ɑ:kaɪvz] *npl* archivos *mpl*

**archway** ['ɑ:tʃweɪ] *n (passage)* arcada *f; (entrance)* arco *m*

**arctic** ['ɑ:ktɪk] **1** *n* the A. el Ártico

**2** *adj* **(a)** *(climate)* ártico(a); **the A. Circle** el Círculo Polar Ártico; **the A. Ocean** el Océano Glacial Ártico **(b)** *Fam (very cold)* gélido(a), glacial

**ardent** ['ɑ:dənt] *adj (desire, love)* ardiente; *(admirer, believer)* ferviente

**ardour** ['ɑ:də(r)] *n* ardor *m*, fervor *m*

**arduous** ['ɑ:djʊəs] *adj* arduo(a)

**are** [ɑ:(r)] *plural and 2nd person singular of* **be**

**area** ['eərɪə] *n* **(a)** *(surface)* área *f* **(b)** *(region)* área *f*, zona *f; (of town, city)* zona *f*, barrio *m; (of knowledge)* área *f*, ámbito *m;* **the London a.** la región londinense; **an a. of agreement** un área de acuerdo; *US Tel* **a. code** prefijo *m; Com* **a. manager** jefe *m* de zona

**arena** [ə'ri:nə] *n* **(a)** *(stadium)* estadio *m* **(b)** *(area of activity) (economic, international)* ruedo *m;* **to enter the a.** salir al ruedo, saltar a la palestra

**aren't** [ɑ:nt] **(a)** = **are not (b)** a. I? = **am I not?**

**Argentina** [ɑ:dʒən'ti:nə] *n* Argentina

**Argentine** ['ɑ:dʒəntaɪn] **1** *n (person)* argentino(a) *m,f; Old-fashioned* **the A.** *(country)* (la) Argentina

**2** *adj* argentino(a)

**Argentinian** [ɑ:dʒən'tɪnɪən] *n & adj* argentino(a) *m,f*

**argon** ['ɑ:gən] *n Chem* argón *m*

**arguable** ['ɑ:gjʊəbəl] *adj* **(a)** *(questionable)* discutible; **it is a. whether it would have made any difference** cabe dudar que las cosas hubiesen sido distintas **(b)** *(conceivable)* **it is a. that…** se podría afirmar que…

**arguably** ['ɑ:gjʊəblɪ] *adv* **it's a. the city's best restaurant** es, probablemente, el mejor restaurante de la ciudad

**argue** ['ɑ:gju:] **1** *vt (case, position)* argumentar; **to a. that…** aducir *or* argumentar que…

**2** *vi (quarrel)* discutir; **to a. about sth** discutir sobre algo; **to a. for** *(defend)* abogar por; **to a. against** *(oppose)* oponerse a

**argument** ['ɑ:gjʊmənt] *n* **(a)** *(quarrel)* discusión *f*, pelea *f;* **to have an a. (about sth)** discutir (por algo); **to get into an a.** meterse en una discusión; **and I don't want any arguments!** ¡y punto! **(b)** *(reason)* argumento *m;* **an a. for/against doing sth** un argumento a favor de/en contra de hacer algo; **suppose for a.'s sake that…** pongamos por caso que…

**argumentative** [ɑ:gjʊ'mentətɪv] *adj* discutidor(ora), peleón(ona)

**aria** ['ɑ:rɪə] *n Mus* aria *f*

**arid** ['ærɪd] *adj* árido(a)

**Aries** ['eərɪ:z] *n (sign of zodiac)* aries *m;* **to be (an) A.** ser aries

**arise** [ə'raɪz] *(pt* **arose** [ə'rəʊz], *pp* **arisen** [ə'rɪzən]) *vi (of problem, situation)* surgir; **the question has not yet arisen** todavía no se ha presentado la cuestión; **should the need a.** si surgiera la necesidad; **a storm arose** se formó una tormenta

**aristocracy** [ærɪs'tɒkrəsɪ] *n* aristocracia *f*

**aristocrat** ['ærɪstəkræt] *n* aristócrata *mf*

**aristocratic** [ærɪstə'krætɪk] *adj* aristocrático(a)

**arithmetic** [ə'rɪθmətɪk] *n (calculations)* cálculos *mpl*, aritmética *f; (subject)* aritmética *f*

**arithmetical** [ærɪθ'metɪkəl] *adj* aritmético(a)

**ark** [ɑ:k] *n* arca *f*

**arm** [ɑ:m] **1** *n* **(a)** *(of person, chair)* brazo *m; (of garment)* manga *f;* **to carry sth/sb in one's arms** llevar algo/a a alguien en brazos; **he took my a.** me tomó *or* cogió del brazo; **to walk a. in a.** caminar *or* ir del brazo; **to receive sb with open arms** *(warmly welcome)* recibir a alguien con los brazos abiertos; *Fig* **to keep sb at a.'s length** mantenerse a una distancia prudencial de alguien **(b)** **arms** *(weapons)* armas *fpl;* **arms race** carrera *f* armamentística **(c)** *(in heraldry)* **(coat of) arms** escudo *m* de armas

**2** *vt* (*person, country*) armar; **to a. oneself with the facts** armarse de datos

**armadillo** [ɑːməˈdɪləʊ] (*pl* **armadillos**) *n* armadillo *m*

**Armageddon** [ɑːməˈgedən] *n* apocalipsis *m inv*

**armaments** [ˈɑːməmənts] *npl* armamento *m*

**armband** [ˈɑːmbænd] *n* (*at funeral, for swimming*) brazalete *m*

**armchair** [ˈɑːmtʃeə(r)] *n* sillón *m*; **an a. strategist** un estratega de salón

**armed** [ɑːmd] *adj* armado(a); **to be a.** estar armado(a); **a. forces** fuerzas *fpl* armadas; **a. robbery** atraco *m* a mano armada

**Armenia** [ɑːˈmiːnɪə] *n* Armenia

**Armenian** [ɑːˈmiːnɪən] *n & adj* armenio(a) *m,f*

**armhole** [ˈɑːmhəʊl] *n* sisa *f*

**armistice** [ˈɑːmɪstɪs] *n* armisticio *m*; **A. Day** = día en que se conmemora el final de la primera Guerra Mundial

**armour** [ˈɑːmə(r)] *n* (**a**) (*of knight*) armadura *f*; **suit of a.** armadura *f* (**b**) *Mil* (*of tank*) blindaje *m*; (*tanks*) división *f* acorazada

**armoured car** [ˈɑːməd] *n* carro *m* de combate

**armoury** [ˈɑːmərɪ] *n* arsenal *m*

**armpit** [ˈɑːmpɪt] *n* axila *f*, sobaco *m*

**armrest** [ˈɑːmrest] *n* reposabrazos *m inv*

**army** [ˈɑːmɪ] *n* ejército *m*; **to be in the a.** ser militar; *Fig* **an a. of workers/assistants** un ejército de obreros/ayudantes

**aroma** [əˈrəʊmə] *n* aroma *m*

**aromatic** [ærəʊˈmætɪk] *adj* aromático(a)

**arose** [əˈrəʊz] *pt of* **arise**

**around** [əˈraʊnd] **1** *prep* (**a**) (*indicating position*) alrededor de; **a. the table** en torno a la mesa; **there were hills all a. the town** la ciudad estaba rodeada de colinas; **a. here** por aquí (*cerca*)

(**b**) (*indicating motion*) **to look a. the room** mirar por toda la habitación; **to travel a. the world** viajar por todo el mundo; **to walk a. the town/the streets** caminar por la ciudad/las calles

**2** *adv* (**a**) (*surrounding*) alrededor; **a garden with a fence a.** un jardín rodeado por una valla; **there were open fields all a.** estábamos rodeados de campo por todas partes; **for miles a.** en millas a la redonda

(**b**) (*in different directions*) **to walk a.** pasear (por ahí); **there were books lying all a.** había libros por todas partes

(**c**) (*in the general area*) **is Jack a.?** (*there*) ¿está Jack por ahí?; (*here*) ¿está Jack por aquí?; **there was nobody a.** no había nadie; **there's never a policeman a. when you need one**

nunca hay un policía a mano cuando lo necesitas

(**d**) (*approximately*) **a. thirty** unos treinta; **a. ten years** unos diez años; **at a. one o'clock** alrededor de la una

**arousal** [əˈraʊzəl] *n* excitación *f*

**arouse** [əˈraʊz] *vt* (*sleeping person*) despertar; (*emotion, desire*) despertar, provocar; (*suspicion*) levantar, despertar; (*sexually*) excitar

**arr** *Rail* (*abbr* **arrival**) llegada *f*

**arraign** [əˈreɪn] *vt Law* hacer comparecer, citar

**arraignment** [əˈreɪnmənt] *n Law* acusación *f*

**arrange** [əˈreɪndʒ] **1** *vt* (**a**) (*put in order*) (*books, furniture*) ordenar, colocar; (*hair, flowers*) arreglar (**b**) (*organize*) (*wedding, meeting*) organizar; (*time, date*) fijar; (*accommodation*) buscar; **to a. to do sth** quedar en hacer algo; **to a. to meet** quedar; **to a. what to do** planear qué hacer; **it was arranged that...** se quedó en que...; **an arranged marriage** un matrimonio concertado

**2** *vi* **to a. for sth to be done** disponer que se haga algo

**arrangement** [əˈreɪndʒmənt] *n* (**a**) (*order, placing*) disposición *f* (**b**) (*plan, preparations*) **to make arrangements** hacer los preparativos (**c**) (*agreement*) acuerdo *m*; **to come to an a.** (**with sb**) llegar a un acuerdo (con alguien); **by a.** con cita previa (**d**) *Mus* arreglo *m*

**array** [əˈreɪ] *n* (*collection*) muestrario *m*

**arrears** [əˈrɪəz] *npl* atrasos *mpl*; **to be in a. with the rent/with one's work** ir atrasado(a) en el pago del alquiler/en el trabajo; **I am paid monthly in a.** me pagan al final de cada mes

**arrest** [əˈrest] **1** *n* detención *f*, arresto *m*; **to be under a.** estar detenido(a); **to make an a.** realizar o practicar una detención

**2** *vt* (*person, development*) detener; **my attention was arrested by...** me llamó poderosamente la atención...

**arresting** [əˈrestɪŋ] *adj* (*expression, look*) llamativo(a)

**arrival** [əˈraɪvəl] *n* llegada *f*; **on a.** al llegar; **a new a.** (*at work, in club*) un/una recién llegado(a); (*baby*) un/una recién nacido(a)

**arrive** [əˈraɪv] *vi* (**a**) (*at place*) llegar; **to a. at a decision/solution** llegar a una decisión/solución (**b**) *Fam* (*attain success*) triunfar

**arrogance** [ˈærəgəns] *n* arrogancia *f*

**arrogant** [ˈærəgənt] *adj* arrogante

**arrow** [ˈærəʊ] *n* flecha *f*

**arrowhead** [ˈærəʊhed] *n* punta *f* de flecha

**arrowroot** [ˈærəʊruːt] *n Culin* arrurruz *m*

**arse** [ɑːs] *n Br Vulg* (**a**) (*buttocks*) culo *m* (**b**) (*stupid person*) gilipollas *mf inv*; **to make an a. of oneself** hacer el gilipollas

▶**arse about, arse around** vi Vulg hacer el gilipollas

**arsehole** ['ɑːshəʊl] n Vulg **(a)** (anus) ojete m **(b)** (unpleasant person) gilipollas mf inv

**arsenal** ['ɑːsənəl] n arsenal m

**arsenic** ['ɑːsənɪk] n Chem arsénico m

**arson** ['ɑːsən] n incendio m provocado

**arsonist** ['ɑːsənɪst] n incendiario(a) m,f, pirómano(a) m,f

**art** [ɑːt] n **(a)** (in general) arte m; **the arts** las artes; **arts and crafts** artes fpl y oficios; **a. exhibition** exposición f (artística); **a. form** manifestación f artística; **a. gallery** (for sale) galería f de arte; (for exhibition) museo m; **a. school** escuela f de bellas artes **(b)** Univ **arts** letras fpl **(c)** (technique) arte m; **there's an a. to making omelettes** hacer tortillas tiene su arte; **the a. of war/conversation** el arte de la guerra/la conversación

**artefact** ['ɑːtɪfækt] n utensilio m

**arteriosclerosis** [ɑː'tɪərɪəʊsklə'rəʊsɪs] n Med arteriosclerosis f inv

**artery** ['ɑːtərɪ] n arteria f

**artful** ['ɑːtfʊl] adj (person) astuto(a), artero(a); (solution) astuto(a), hábil

**arthritic** [ɑː'θrɪtɪk] adj artrítico(a)

**arthritis** [ɑː'θraɪtɪs] n artritis f inv

**arthropod** ['ɑːθrəpɒd] n Zool artrópodo m

**arthrosis** [ɑː'θrəʊsɪs] n Med artrosis f inv

**artichoke** ['ɑːtɪtʃəʊk] n **(globe) a.** alcachofa f

**article** ['ɑːtɪkəl] **1** n artículo m; **a. of clothing** prenda f de vestir; Gram **definite/indefinite a.** artículo m determinado/indeterminado
**2** vt Law **to be articled to a firm of solicitors** trabajar en prácticas or hacer una pasantía en un bufete de abogados

**articled** ['ɑːtɪkəld] adj **a. clerk** abogado(a) m,f en prácticas

**articulate**¹ [ɑː'tɪkjʊlət] adj (person) elocuente; (description, account) claro(a), comprensible

**articulate**² [ɑː'tɪkjʊleɪt] vt (word) articular; (idea, feeling) formular, expresar

**articulated lorry** [ɑː'tɪkjʊleɪtɪd'lɒrɪ] n camión m articulado

**articulation** [ɑːtɪkjʊ'leɪʃən] n (of words) articulación f; (of ideas, feelings) formulación f

**artifice** ['ɑːtɪfɪs] n artificio m

**artificial** [ɑːtɪ'fɪʃəl] adj (conditions, light, distinction) artificial; (limb, hair) postizo(a), artificial; (smile) afectado(a), artificial; **a. insemination** inseminación f artificial; Comptr **a. intelligence** inteligencia f artificial; **a. respiration** respiración f artificial

**artificially** [ɑːtɪ'fɪʃəlɪ] adv artificialmente

**artillery** [ɑː'tɪlərɪ] n artillería f

**artisan** [ɑːtɪ'zæn] n artesano(a) m,f

**artist** ['ɑːtɪst] n artista mf

**artistic** [ɑː'tɪstɪk] adj artístico(a); **she is very a.** tiene mucha sensibilidad artística

**artistry** ['ɑːtɪstrɪ] n arte m, destreza f

**artless** ['ɑːtlɪs] adj (simple) inocente, ingenuo(a); (clumsy) torpe

**artwork** ['ɑːtwɜːk] n (in book, magazine) ilustraciones fpl

**arty** ['ɑːtɪ] adj Fam (person) = que se interesa por las artes

**Aryan** ['eərɪən] n & adj ario(a) m,f

**as** [əz] stressed [æz] **1** prep como; **to work as a team** trabajar en equipo; **to regard sb as a friend** considerar a alguien un amigo; **to treat sb as a stranger** tratar a alguien como a un extraño; **to act/serve as a protection against sth** actuar/servir de protección contra algo; **she used it as a bandage** lo utilizó a modo de venda; **as a woman, I think that...** como mujer, creo que...
**2** adv **(a)** (with manner) (tal y) como; **we arrived at eight o'clock, as requested** llegamos a las ocho, tal y como se nos había pedido; **we did exactly as we had been told** hicimos exactamente lo que nos habían dicho; **B as in Birmingham** B de Birmingham
**(b)** (in comparisons) **as... as...** tan... como...; **not as** or **so... as...** no tan... como...; **as tall as me** tan alto como yo; **as white as a sheet** blanco(a) como la nieve; **twice as big** el doble de grande; **I pushed/tried as hard as I could** empujé/lo intenté con todas mis fuerzas; **as many as you want** todos los que quieras; **as much as you want** todo lo que quieras; **as recently as last week** hace tan sólo una semana; **as soon as possible** cuanto antes
**(c)** (phrases) como si; **she looked as if** or **though she was upset** parecía (como si estuviera) disgustada; **it isn't as if** or **though I haven't tried** no será porque no lo he intentado, no es que no lo haya intentado; **it looks as if...** parece que..., a lo que parece...; **as for the cost/the food,...** en or por lo que se refiere al coste/a la comida,...; **as well** también
**3** conj **(a)** (with time) (when) cuando; (whilst) mientras; **he went out as I came in** salió cuando yo entraba; **she talked to me as I worked** me hablaba mientras trabajaba; **as you get older...** a medida que te haces mayor...; **as necessary** según sea necesario; **as always** como siempre
**(b)** (because) como; **as he has now left,...** como se ha ido..., ahora que se ha ido...
**(c)** (concessive) **late as it was,...** aunque era tarde...; **try as she might,...** por mucho que lo intentara...; **unlikely as it might**

**seem,...** por improbable que parezca,...; **stupid as he is, even if he saw the mistake** hasta él, que es tan estúpido, se dio cuenta del error

**(d)** *(with manner)* como; **as I was saying,...** como iba diciendo,...; **do as you like** haz lo que quieras; **as often happens,...** como suele suceder,...; **it's hard enough as it is without this happening!** ¡ya es lo bastante duro como para que ahora pase esto!; **it's far enough as it is!** ¡ya está suficientemente lejos así!

**(e)** *(in addition)* **I'm well, as are the children** estoy bien y los niños también

**asap** [eɪeser'piː] *adv (abbr* **as soon as possible)** cuanto antes, lo antes posible

**asbestos** [æs'bestəs] *n* amianto *m*, asbesto *m*

**asbestosis** [æsbes'təʊsɪs] *n Med* asbestosis *f inv*

**ascend** [ə'send] **1** *vt (mountain)* ascender, subir; *(throne)* ascender a, subir a

**2** *vi* ascender

**ascendancy, ascendency** [ə'sendənsɪ] *n* dominio *m*, ascendiente *m*

**ascendant, ascendent** [ə'sendənt] *n* **to be in the a.** ir en ascenso

**Ascension** [ə'senʃən] *n Rel* Ascensión *f*; **A. Island** Ascensión

**ascent** [ə'sent] *n (of mountain)* ascenso *m*, subida *f*; **her a. to power** su ascenso al poder

**ascertain** [æsə'teɪn] *vt (establish)* precisar, determinar; *(find out)* averiguar

**ascetic** [ə'setɪk] **1** *n* asceta *mf*

**2** *adj* ascético(a)

**ASCII** ['æskɪ] *n Comptr (abbr* **American Standard Code for Information Interchange)** ASCII *m*

**ascribe** [ə'skraɪb] *vt* atribuir

**ASEAN** ['æzɪæn] *n (abbr* **Association of South-East Asian Nations)** ASEAN *f*

**aseptic** [eɪ'septɪk] *adj* aséptico(a)

**asexual** [eɪ'seksjʊəl] *adj* asexual

**ash¹** [æʃ] *n (tree)* fresno *m*

**ash²** *n (from fire, cigarette)* ceniza *f*; *Rel* **A. Wednesday** Miércoles *m inv* de Ceniza

**ashamed** [ə'ʃeɪmd] *adj* avergonzado(a); **to be a. (of)** estar avergonzado(a) (de); **to feel a.** sentir vergüenza; **I'm a. of you!** ¡me das vergüenza!; **I am a. to say that...** me avergüenza decir que...; **there is nothing to be a. of** no hay de qué avergonzarse; **you ought to be a. of yourself!** ¡debería darte vergüenza!

**ashen** ['æʃən] *adj* pálido(a)

**ashore** [ə'ʃɔː(r)] *adv* en tierra; **to go a.** desembarcar

**ashtray** ['æʃtreɪ] *n* cenicero *m*

**Asia** ['eɪʒə] *n* Asia; **A. Minor** Asia Menor

**Asian** ['eɪʒən] **1** *n* asiático(a) *m,f*; *Br (person from Indian sub-continent)* = persona de la India,

Paquistán o Bangladesh

**2** *adj* asiático(a); *Br (from Indian sub-continent)* de la India, Paquistán o Bangladesh; *US* **A. American** = americano(a) de origen asiático

**Asiatic** [eɪsɪ'ætɪk] *n & adj* asiático(a) *m,f*

**aside** [ə'saɪd] **1** *adv* aparte, a un lado; **a. from** aparte de; **to put** *or* **set sth a.** apartar *or* reservar algo; **stand a. please!** ¡apártense, por favor!; **to take sb a.** llevarse a alguien aparte; **politics a.,...** dejando a un lado la política,...

**2** *n Th* aparte *m*

**asinine** ['æsɪnaɪn] *adj* cretino(a), majadero(a)

**ask** [ɑːsk] **1** *vt* **(a)** *(enquire about)* preguntar; **to a. sb sth** preguntar algo a alguien; **to a. (sb) a question** hacer una pregunta (a alguien); **to a. sb the time** preguntar la hora a alguien; **to a. sb the way** preguntar a alguien el camino; **don't a. me!** ¿a mí me lo vas a preguntar?

**(b)** *(request)* pedir; **to a. sb for sth** pedir algo a alguien; **to a. to do sth** pedir hacer algo; **to a. sb to do sth** pedir a alguien que haga algo; **to a. a favour of sb, to a. sb a favour** pedir un favor a alguien; **if it isn't asking too much** si no es mucho pedir; **to a. sb's permission to do sth** pedir permiso a alguien para hacer algo

**(c)** *(invite)* invitar, convidar; **to a. sb to lunch** invitar a alguien a comer

**2** *vi* **(a)** *(enquire)* preguntar **(about** por)

**(b)** *(request)* **to a. for sth** pedir algo; **you only have to a.!** ¡no tienes más que pedirlo!; *Fam* **he was asking for it!** *(deserved it)* ¡se lo estaba buscando!

▸**ask after** *vt insep* preguntar por

**askance** [ə'skæns] *adv* **to look a. at sb** mirar a alguien con recelo

**askew** [ə'skjuː] *adv* **her dress was a.** llevaba el vestido torcido

**asking** ['ɑːskɪŋ] *n* **it's yours for the a.** si lo pides, es tuyo; **a. price** precio *m* de salida

**ASL** [eɪes'el] *n US (abbr* **American Sign Language)** = lenguaje de signos para sordos

**asleep** [ə'sliːp] *adj* **to be a.** estar dormido(a) *or* durmiendo; **to be fast** *or* **sound a.** estar profundamente dormido(a); **to fall a.** quedarse dormido(a), dormirse

**asocial** [eɪ'səʊʃəl] *adj* asocial

**asparagus** [ə'spærəgəs] *n (plant)* esparraguera *f*; *(vegetable)* espárragos *mpl*

**aspect** ['æspekt] *n* **(a)** *(of problem, subject)* aspecto *m* **(b)** *(of building)* orientación *f*

**asperity** [æ'sperɪtɪ] *n* aspereza *f*

**aspersions** [əs'pɜːʃənz] *npl* **to cast a. on sth** poner en duda algo

**asphalt** ['æsfælt] *n* asfalto *m*

**asphyxiate** [æs'fɪksɪeɪt] **1** *vt* asfixiar

**2** *vi* asfixiarse

**asphyxiation** [æsfɪksɪ'eɪʃən] *n* asfixia *f*

**aspic** ['æspɪk] *n Culin* gelatina *f; Fig* it was as if the house had been preserved in a. parecía que hubieran conservado la casa en alcanfor

**aspirate** ['æspərət] *adj Ling* aspirado(a)

**aspirant** ['æspɪrənt] *n* aspirante *mf*

**aspiration** [æspɪ'reɪʃən] *n (ambition)* aspiración *f*

**aspire** [ə'spaɪə(r)] *vi* to a. to do sth aspirar a hacer algo

**aspirin** ['æsprɪn] *n* aspirina® *f*

**aspiring** [ə'spaɪrɪŋ] *adj* to be an a. actor aspirar a ser actor

**ass¹** [æs] *n* (a) *(animal)* burro *m*, asno *m* (b) *Fam (idiot)* burro(a) *m,f*, tonto(a) *m,f*; to make an a. of oneself quedar como un tonto

**ass²** *n US very Fam* culo *m*

**assail** [ə'seɪl] *vt (attack)* asaltar, agredir (with con); to a. sb with questions asediar a alguien a preguntas; assailed by doubt asaltado por la duda

**assailant** [ə'seɪlənt] *n* asaltante *mf*, agresor(ora) *m,f*

**assassin** [ə'sæsɪn] *n* asesino(a) *m,f*

**assassinate** [ə'sæsɪneɪt] *vt* asesinar

**assassination** [əsæsɪ'neɪʃən] *n* asesinato *m*

**assault** [ə'sɔːlt] 1 *n* ataque *m* (on a), asalto *m* (on a); *Law* agresión *f; Mil* a. course pista *f* de entrenamiento
2 *vt* atacar, asaltar; *Law* agredir; to be sexually assaulted ser objeto de una agresión sexual

**assemble** [ə'sembəl] 1 *vt (people)* reunir, congregar; *(facts, objects)* reunir, juntar; *(machine, furniture)* montar, ensamblar
2 *vi (of people)* reunirse, congregarse

**assembly** [ə'semblɪ] *n* (a) *(gathering)* reunión *f; Br Sch* = reunión de todos los profesores y los alumnos al principio de la jornada escolar; a. hall *(in school)* salón *m* de actos (b) *(of machine, furniture)* montaje *m*, ensamblaje *m*; a. instructions instrucciones *fpl* de montaje; *Ind* a. line cadena *f* de montaje

**assent** [ə'sent] 1 *n* asentimiento *m*, consentimiento *m*; she gave/withheld her a. dio/no dio su consentimiento
2 *vi* dar el consentimiento (to a)

**assert** [ə'sɜːt] *vt (one's rights, point of view, authority)* afirmar, hacer valer; to a. oneself mostrarse firme, imponerse; to a. that... afirmar que...

**assertion** [ə'sɜːʃən] *n (of right)* afirmación *f; (statement)* afirmación *f*, aseveración *f*

**assertive** [ə'sɜːtɪv] *adj* a course aimed at teaching women to be more a. un curso para potenciar la afirmación personal de las mujeres

**assertiveness** [ə'sɜːtɪvnəs] *n* afirmación *f* personal, autoafirmación *f*; a. training cursos *mpl* de afirmación personal

**assess** [ə'ses] *vt* (a) *(estimate) (value)* tasar, valorar; *(damage)* evaluar, valorar; to a. sb's income *(for tax purposes)* evaluar la renta de alguien (b) *(analyse)* evaluar

**assessment** [ə'sesmənt] *n* (a) *(estimate) (of value)* tasación *f*, valoración *f*; *(of damage)* evaluación *f*, valoración *f*; *(for insurance or tax purposes)* tasación *f* (b) *(analysis)* evaluación *f*

**assessor** [ə'sesə(r)] *n Fin* tasador(ora) *m,f*

**asset** ['æset] *n* ventaja *f*, beneficio *m*; she is a great a. to the firm es una valiosa aportación a la empresa; *Fin* assets activos *mpl; Fin* a. stripper liquidador(ora) *m,f* de activos; *Fin* a. stripping liquidación *f* (especulativa) de activos

**assiduous** [ə'sɪdjʊəs] *adj* perseverante

**assign** [ə'saɪn] *vt (task, funds)* asignar (to a); *(importance)* atribuir; to a. sb to do sth asignar a alguien la tarea de hacer algo

**assignation** [æsɪg'neɪʃən] *n Formal (meeting)* cita *f*

**assignment** [ə'saɪnmənt] *n* (a) *(allocation)* asignación *f* (b) *(task) Sch* tarea *f*, trabajo *m; Journ* encargo *m*, trabajo *m; Mil* misión *f*

**assimilate** [ə'sɪmɪleɪt] 1 *vt (food, ideas)* asimilar
2 *vi (of immigrants)* integrarse

**assimilation** [əsɪmɪ'leɪʃən] *n (of food, ideas)* asimilación *f; (of immigrants)* integración *f*

**assist** [ə'sɪst] 1 *vt (person)* ayudar; *(process, development)* colaborar en, contribuir a; to a. sb in doing *or* to do sth ayudar a alguien a hacer algo
2 *vi* prestar ayuda; to a. in sth colaborar en algo

**assistance** [ə'sɪstəns] *n* ayuda *f*, asistencia *f*; to come to sb's a. acudir en ayuda de alguien; can I be of any a.? ¿puedo ayudar en algo?

**assistant** [ə'sɪstənt] *n* ayudante *mf*; (shop) a. dependiente(a) *m,f*; a. manager subdirector(ora) *m,f*

**assizes** [ə'saɪzɪz] *npl Law* ≃ audiencia *f* provincial

**associate** 1 *n* [ə'səʊsɪət] *(in business)* socio(a) *m,f*; *(in crime)* cómplice *mf*
2 *adj (company)* asociado(a)
3 *vt* [ə'səʊsɪeɪt] (a) *(mentally)* asociar (b) to be associated with estar asociado(a) *or* relacionado(a) con
4 *vi* to a. with sb frecuentar *or* tratar con alguien

**associated** [ə'səʊsɪeɪtɪd] *adj* asociado(a); a. company empresa *f* asociada

**association** [əsəʊsɪ'eɪʃən] *n* asociación *f*; the name has unfortunate associations

**for her** ese nombre le trae malos recuerdos, ese nombre tiene connotaciones desagradables para ella; **in a. with...** conjuntamente con...; **to form an a.** crear una asociación

**assonance** ['æsənəns] *n* asonancia *f*

**assorted** [ə'sɔːtɪd] *adj (colours, flavours)* diverso(a); *(biscuits, sweets)* surtido(a)

**assortment** [ə'sɔːtmənt] *n (of colours, reasons)* diversidad *f*; *(of biscuits, sweets)* surtido *m*

**assuage** [ə'sweɪdʒ] *vt Formal (anger, person)* apaciguar; *(hunger, thirst)* aplacar

**assume** [ə'sjuːm] *vt* **(a)** *(suppose)* suponer; **I a. so/not** supongo que sí/no; **he was assumed to be rich** se suponía que era rico; **let us a. that...** supongamos que... **(b)** *(take over) (duty, power)* asumir; *(name)* adoptar; **to a. responsibility for sth** asumir la responsabilidad de algo; **an assumed name** un nombre falso **(c)** *(take on) (appearance, shape)* adquirir, adoptar

**assumption** [ə'sʌmpʃən] *n* **(a)** *(supposition)* suposición *f*; **to work on the a. that...** trabajar sobre la base de que... **(b)** *(of power, responsibility)* asunción *f* **(c)** *Rel* **the A.** la Asunción

**assurance** [ə'ʃuərəns] *n* **(a)** *(guarantee)* garantía *f*; **to give sb one's a.** dar garantías a alguien **(b)** *(confidence)* seguridad *f*; **to answer with a.** responder con seguridad **(c)** *Br (insurance)* seguro *m*; **life a.** seguro de vida

**assure** [ə'ʃuə(r)] *vt* asegurar; **to a. sb of sth** asegurar algo a alguien

**assured** [ə'ʃuəd] *adj (certain, confident)* seguro(a); **to be a. of sth** tener algo asegurado(a); **he gave a very a. performance** se mostró muy seguro en su actuación

**assuredly** [ə'ʃuərɪdlɪ] *adv (undoubtedly)* sin duda

**asterisk** ['æstərɪsk] *n* asterisco *m*

**asteroid** ['æstərɔɪd] *n* asteroide *m*

**asthma** ['æsmə] *n* asma *f*

**asthmatic** [æs'mætɪk] *n & adj* asmático(a) *m,f*

**astonish** [ə'stɒnɪʃ] *vt* asombrar; **to be astonished at** *or* **by** quedarse asombrado(a) por; **I am astonished that...** me asombra que...

**astonishing** [ə'stɒnɪʃɪŋ] *adj* asombroso(a); **I find it a. that...** me parece asombroso que...

**astonishment** [ə'stɒnɪʃmənt] *n* asombro *m*; **to my a.** para mi asombro

**astound** [ə'staʊnd] *vt* dejar atónito(a), pasmar; **I was astounded** me quedé atónito(a)

**astounding** [ə'staʊndɪŋ] *adj* pasmoso(a), asombroso(a)

**astral** ['æstrəl] *adj* astral

**astray** [ə'streɪ] *adv* **to go a.** *(become lost)* perderse, extraviarse; **to lead sb a.** descarriar a alguien

**astride** [ə'straɪd] *prep* **to sit a. sth** sentarse a horcajadas sobre algo

**astringent** [ə'strɪndʒənt] *n & adj* astringente *m*

**astrologer** [ə'strɒlədʒə(r)] *n* astrólogo(a) *m,f*

**astrological** [æstrə'lɒdʒɪkəl] *adj* astrológico(a); **a. chart** carta *f* astral

**astrology** [ə'strɒlədʒɪ] *n* astrología *f*

**astronaut** ['æstrənɔːt] *n* astronauta *mf*

**astronomer** [ə'strɒnəmə(r)] *n* astrónomo(a) *m,f*

**astronomic(al)** [æstrə'nɒmɪk(əl)] *adj* astronómico(a)

**astronomy** [ə'strɒnəmɪ] *n* astronomía *f*

**astrophysics** [æstrəʊ'fɪzɪks] *npl* astrofísica *f*

**Astroturf®** ['æstrəʊtɜːf] *n Sport (césped m de)* hierba *f* artificial

**Asturian** [æ'stʊərɪən] *n & adj* asturiano(a) *m,f*

**Asturias** [æ'stʊərɪəs] *n* Asturias

**astute** [ə'stjuːt] *adj* astuto(a), sagaz

**astutely** [ə'stjuːtlɪ] *adv* astutamente, con sagacidad

**asunder** [ə'sʌndə(r)] *adv Literary* **to tear sth a.** hacer pedazos algo

**asylum** [ə'saɪləm] *n* asilo *m*; **to seek a.** buscar asilo; **(mental) a.** manicomio *m*; **political a.** asilo político

**asymmetric(al)** [eɪsɪ'metrɪk(əl)] *adj* asimétrico(a)

**asymmetry** [eɪ'sɪmɪtrɪ] *n* asimetría *f*

**at** [æt, *unstressed* ət] *prep* **(a)** *(with place)* en; **at the top/bottom** (en la parte de) arriba/abajo; **at university/the station** en la universidad/ la estación; **at the side** al lado; **at John's (house)** en casa de John; **at home** en casa

**(b)** *(with time)* **at six o'clock** a las seis; **at night** por la noche; **at Christmas** en Navidad; **at a good time** en un momento oportuno; **at the beginning/end** al principio/final; **at (the age of) twenty** a los veinte años

**(c)** *(with price, speed)* a; **at 60 km/h** a 60 km/h; **at 50p a kilo** a 50 peniques el kilo

**(d)** *(with direction)* a; **to throw a stone at sb** tirarle una piedra a alguien; **to look at sth/sb** mirar algo/a alguien

**(e)** *(with cause)* **to be angry at sb** estar enfadado con alguien; **to be surprised at sth** sorprenderse de algo

**(f)** *(with activity)* **to be at work/play** estar trabajando/jugando; **she's been at it all weekend** *(working)* ha pasado todo el fin de semana trabajando; **while you're at it, could**

**you buy some sugar?** ya que vas, ¿podrías comprar azúcar?; **I am good at languages** los idiomas se me dan bien; **he's bad at sport** se le dan mal los deportes

(**g**) **do you know him at all?** ¿lo conoces de algo?; **anything at all** cualquier cosa; **nothing at all** nada en absoluto; **not at all** *(not in the slightest)* en absoluto; *(when thanked)* de nada

**atavistic** [ætə'vɪstɪk] *adj* atávico(a)

**ate** [eɪt] *pt of* **eat**

**atheism** ['eɪθɪɪzəm] *n* ateísmo *m*

**atheist** ['eɪθɪɪst] *n* ateo(a) *m,f*

**Athenian** [ə'θi:nɪən] *n & adj* ateniense *mf*

**Athens** ['æθənz] *n* Atenas

**athlete** ['æθli:t] *n* atleta *mf*; *Med* **a.'s foot** pie *m* de atleta

**athletic** [æθ'letɪk] *adj* atlético(a)

**athletics** [æθ'letɪks] *npl* atletismo *m*

**Atlantic** [ət'læntɪk] **1** *n* **the A.** el (océano) Atlántico

**2** *adj* atlántico(a); **the A. Ocean** el océano Atlántico

**atlas** ['ætləs] *n* atlas *m inv*

**ATM** [eɪti:'em] *n Fin (abbr* **automated teller machine)** cajero *m* automático

**atmosphere** ['ætməsfɪə(r)] *n* atmósfera *f*; *Fig* ambiente *m*

**atmospheric** [ætməs'ferɪk] *adj (pressure)* atmosférico(a); *Fig* **the music was very a.** la música te ponía la carne de gallina

**atoll** ['ætɒl] *n Geog* atolón *m*

**atom** ['ætəm] *n* átomo *m*; **a. bomb** bomba *f* atómica

**atomic** [ə'tɒmɪk] *adj* atómico(a); **a. bomb** bomba *f* atómica; **a. energy** energía *f* atómica *or* nuclear; **a. warfare** guerra *f* nuclear

**atomizer** ['ætəmaɪzə(r)] *n* atomizador *m*

▸**atone for** [ə'təʊn] *vt insep (sin, crime)* expiar; *(mistake)* subsanar

**atonement** [ə'təʊnmənt] *n (for sin, crime)* expiación *f*; *(for mistake, behaviour)* subsanación *f*

**atrocious** [ə'trəʊʃəs] *adj (crime, behaviour)* atroz, cruel; *(mistake, decision, weather, meal)* atroz, terrible

**atrocity** [ə'trɒsɪtɪ] *n* atrocidad *f*

**atrophy** ['ætrəfɪ] *vi* atrofiarse

**attach** [ə'tætʃ] *vt (label, cheque)* sujetar, fijar **(to** a); *(document)* adjuntar **(to** a); *(blame, responsibility, importance)* atribuir **(to** a); **to a. oneself to sb** pegarse a alguien; **to be very attached to sb/sth** tenerle mucho cariño a alguien/algo

**attaché** [ə'tæʃeɪ] *n* agregado(a) *m,f*; **military a.** agregado(a) militar; **a. case** maletín *m*

**attachment** [ə'tætʃmənt] *n* (**a**) *(device)* accesorio *m* (**b**) *(secondment)* **to be on a. to a department** estar destinado(a) a un departa-

mento (**c**) *(fondness)* cariño *m*; **to form an a. to sb** tomar cariño a alguien

**attack** [ə'tæk] **1** *n* ataque *m*; **to be under a.** estar siendo atacado(a); **to come under a.** ser atacado(a); **to launch an a. on sb** lanzar un ataque contra alguien; **an a. of nerves** un ataque de nervios; **I had an a. of doubt** me asaltaron las dudas; **an a. of fever** un acceso de fiebre

**2** *vt* atacar; *(problem)* acometer, abordar; **he was attacked in the street** lo asaltaron en la calle

**attacker** [ə'tækə(r)] *n (assailant, sportsperson)* atacante *mf*

**attain** [ə'teɪn] *vt (ambition, age)* alcanzar; *(rank)* llegar a

**attainable** [ə'teɪnəbəl] *adj (goal, ambition)* alcanzable

**attainment** [ə'teɪnmənt] *n (of goal, ambition)* consecución *f*, logro *m*

**attempt** [ə'tempt] **1** *n (effort)* intento *m*, tentativa *f*; **to make an a. at doing sth** *or* **to do sth** intentar hacer algo; **they made no a. to help** no trataron de ayudar; **to make an a. on sb's life** atentar contra la vida de alguien; **at the first a.** al primer intento

**2** *vt (task)* intentar; **to a. to do sth** tratar de *or* intentar hacer algo; **to a. a smile** intentar sonreír; *Law* **attempted murder/robbery** intento *m* de asesinato/robo

**attend** [ə'tend] **1** *vt* (**a**) *(meeting, school)* asistir a, acudir a (**b**) *(patient)* atender; **we were attended by three waiters** nos atendieron tres camareros

**2** *vi (be present)* asistir

▸**attend to** *vt insep (matter, problem)* ocuparse de; *(patient)* atender, asistir; *(customer)* atender

**attendance** [ə'tendəns] *n (presence, people present)* asistencia *f*; **there was a good/poor a.** acudió mucha/poca gente; **a. register** lista *f* de asistencia

**attendant** [ə'tendənt] *n (in museum)* vigilante *mf*; *(in car park, cloakroom)* encargado(a) *m,f*

**attention** [ə'tenʃən] *n* (**a**) *(in general)* atención *f*; **to pay a. to sth** prestar atención a alguien/algo; **to pay a. to detail** fijarse en los detalles; **to give sth/sb one's full a.** atender bien algo/a alguien; **to attract** *or* **catch sb's a.** llamar la atención de alguien; **to draw a. to oneself** llamar la atención; **your a. please, ladies and gentlemen** atención, señoras y señores; **for the a. of** a la atención de

(**b**) *(repairs)* **the engine needs some a.** hay que revisar el motor

(**c**) *Mil* **a.!** ¡firmes!; **to stand at** *or* **to a.** ponerse firme, cuadrarse

**attentive** [ə'tentɪv] adj (paying attention, considerate) atento(a); **to be a. to sb** estar pendiente de alguien

**attentively** [ə'tentɪvlɪ] adv atentamente

**attest** [ə'test] **1** vt (affirm, prove) atestiguar
**2** vi **to a. to** dar testimonio de

**attic** ['ætɪk] n (storage space) desván m; (room) ático m

**attire** [ə'taɪə(r)] n atuendo m, atavío m

**attitude** ['ætɪtjuːd] n **(a)** (opinion, behaviour) actitud f; **what's your a. to abortion?** ¿cuál es tu actitud or postura ante el aborto?; **to take the a. that...** adoptar la actitud de que...; **I don't like your a.** no me gusta tu actitud; Com **a. survey** = estudio de la actitud del personal en materia laboral **(b)** (pose) postura f; **to strike an a.** adoptar una pose

**attn** Com (abbr **for the attention of**) a la atención de

**attorney** [ə'tɜːnɪ] (pl attorneys) n US Law abogado(a) m,f

**attract** [ə'trækt] vt atraer; **to a. sb's attention** llamar la atención de alguien; **to be attracted to sb/sth** sentirse atraído(a) por alguien/algo

**attraction** [ə'trækʃən] n **(a)** (power) atracción f; **the prospect holds little a. for me** la perspectiva no me atrae mucho **(b)** (attractive aspect) atractivo m

**attractive** [ə'træktɪv] adj (person, offer, prospect) atractivo(a)

**attributable** [ə'trɪbjʊtəbəl] adj atribuible

**attribute 1** n ['ætrɪbjuːt] atributo m
**2** vt [ə'trɪbjuːt] atribuir (**to** a)

**attributive** [ə'trɪbjʊtɪv] adj atributivo(a); **an a. use** un uso atributivo

**attrition** [ə'trɪʃən] n desgaste m; **war of a.** guerra f de desgaste

**attuned** [ə'tjuːnd] adj **he's a. to their way of thinking** sintoniza muy bien con su manera de pensar

**atypical** [eɪ'tɪpɪkəl] adj atípico(a)

**aubergine** ['əʊbəʒiːn] n Br berenjena f

**auburn** ['ɔːbən] adj (hair) (color) caoba

**auction** ['ɔːkʃən] **1** n subasta f; **to put sth up for a.** sacar algo a subasta; **a. room** sala f de subastas
**2** vt subastar

▶**auction off** vt sep liquidar mediante subasta, subastar

**auctioneer** [ɔːkʃə'nɪə(r)] n subastador(ora) m,f

**audacious** [ɔː'deɪʃəs] adj audaz

**audacity** [ɔː'dæsɪtɪ] n audacia f

**audible** ['ɔːdɪbəl] adj audible

**audience** ['ɔːdɪəns] n **(a)** (spectators) público m; TV & Radio audiencia f; **a. participation**

participación f del público **(b)** (meeting with monarch, Pope) audiencia f; **to grant sb an a.** conceder una audiencia a alguien

**audio** ['ɔːdɪəʊ] adj **a. cassette** cinta f de audio; **a. equipment** equipo m de sonido

**audiotypist** ['ɔːdɪəʊ'taɪpɪst] n mecanógrafo(a) m,f con dictáfono

**audiovisual** [ɔːdɪəʊ'vɪzjʊəl] adj audiovisual

**audit** ['ɔːdɪt] Fin **1** n auditoría f
**2** vt auditar

**audition** [ɔː'dɪʃən] Th **1** n prueba f, audición f; **to hold auditions for a play** realizar pruebas a actores para una obra de teatro
**2** vt (of director) hacer una prueba a
**3** vi (of actor) hacer una prueba

**auditor** ['ɔːdɪtə(r)] n Fin auditor(ora) m,f

**auditorium** [ɔːdɪ'tɔːrɪəm] n auditorio m

**auditory** ['ɔːdɪtrɪ] adj auditivo(a)

**Aug** (abbr **August**) agosto m

**augment** [ɔːg'ment] vt incrementar, aumentar

**augur** ['ɔːgə(r)] vi **to a. well/badly** ser un buen/mal augurio

**August** ['ɔːgəst] n agosto m; see also **May**

**august** [ɔː'gʌst] adj Literary (distinguished) augusto(a)

**aunt** [ɑːnt] n tía f

**auntie, aunty** ['ɑːntɪ] n Fam tita f

**au pair** [əʊ'peə(r)] n au pair f

**aura** ['ɔːrə] n aura f

**aural** ['ɔːrəl] adj auditivo(a)

**auspices** ['ɔːspɪsɪz] npl **under the a. of** bajo los auspicios de

**auspicious** [ɔː'spɪʃəs] adj prometedor(a), halagüeño(a)

**Aussie** ['ɒzɪ] n & adj Fam australiano(a) m,f

**austere** [ɒ'stɪə(r)] adj austero(a)

**austerity** [ɒ'sterɪtɪ] n austeridad f

**Australasia** [ɒstrə'leɪʒə] n Australasia

**Australasian** [ɒstrə'leɪʒən] adj de Australasia

**Australia** [ɒ'streɪlɪə] n Australia

**Australian** [ɒ'streɪlɪən] n & adj australiano(a) m,f

**Austria** ['ɒstrɪə] n Austria

**Austrian** ['ɒstrɪən] n & adj austriaco(a) m,f

**autarchy** ['ɔːtɑːkɪ] n autarquía f

**authentic** [ɔː'θentɪk] adj auténtico(a)

**authenticate** [ɔː'θentɪkeɪt] vt autentificar, autenticar

**authenticity** [ɔːθen'tɪsɪtɪ] n autenticidad f

**author** ['ɔːθə(r)] n (by profession) escritor(ora) m,f; (of a book) autor(a) m,f

**authoritarian** [ɔːθɒrɪ'teərɪən] n & adj autoritario(a) m,f

**authoritative** [ɔːˈθɒrɪtətɪv] *adj* (a) *(manner, voice, person)* autoritario(a) (b) *(study, source)* autorizado(a)

**authority** [ɔːˈθɒrɪtɪ] *n* (a) *(power)* autoridad *f*; **the authorities** las autoridades; **I'd like to speak to someone in a.** quisiera hablar con el responsable; **to have an air of a.** mostrar seguridad *or* aplomo

(b) *(authorization)* autorización *f*; **to give sb a. to do sth** autorizar a alguien a hacer algo; **he did it on his own a.** lo hizo bajo su responsabilidad

(c) *(expert)* autoridad *f*; **to be an a. on sth** ser una autoridad en algo; **to have it on good a.** saberlo de buena tinta

**authorization** [ɔːθəraɪˈzeɪʃən] *n* autorización *f*

**authorize** [ˈɔːθəraɪz] *vt* autorizar; **to a. sb to do sth** autorizar a alguien a hacer algo

**autism** [ˈɔːtɪzəm] *n* autismo *m*

**autistic** [ɔːˈtɪstɪk] *adj* autista

**auto** [ˈɔːtəʊ] *(pl* **autos***)* *n US* coche *m*, automóvil *m*

**auto-** [ˈɔːtəʊ] *pref* auto-

**autobiographical** [ɔːtəʊbaɪəˈɡræfɪkəl] *adj* autobiográfico(a)

**autobiography** [ɔːtəʊbaɪˈɒɡrəfɪ] *n* autobiografía *f*

**autocrat** [ˈɔːtəkræt] *n* autócrata *mf*

**autocratic** [ɔːtəˈkrætɪk] *adj* autocrático(a)

**Autocue**® [ˈɔːtəkjuː] *n TV* teleapuntador *m*

**autograph** [ˈɔːtəɡrɑːf] **1** *n* autógrafo *m*; **a. album** álbum *m* de autógrafos

**2** *vt* autografiar, firmar

**automat** [ˈɔːtəmæt] *n US* = restaurante en el que la comida se obtiene de máquinas expendedoras

**automate** [ˈɔːtəmeɪt] *vt* automatizar

**automatic** [ɔːtəˈmætɪk] **1** *n (car)* coche *m* (con cambio) automático; *(pistol)* pistola *f* automática; *(washing machine)* lavadora *f* (automática)

**2** *adj* automático(a); *Comptr* **a. data processing** proceso *m or* procesamiento *m* automático de datos; *Av* **a. pilot** piloto *m* automático; *Fig* **to be on a. pilot** tener puesto el piloto automático

**automatically** [ɔːtəˈmætɪklɪ] *adv* automáticamente

**automation** [ɔːtəˈmeɪʃən] *n* automatización *f*

**automaton** [ɔːˈtɒmətən] *n* autómata *m*

**automobile** [ˈɔːtəməʊbiːl] *n US* coche *m*, automóvil *m*

**autonomous** [ɔːˈtɒnəməs] *adj* autónomo(a)

**autonomy** [ɔːˈtɒnəmɪ] *n* autonomía *f*

**autopsy** [ˈɔːtɒpsɪ] *n* autopsia *f*

**autumn** [ˈɔːtəm] *n* otoño *m*; **in (the) a.** en otoño

**autumnal** [ɔːˈtʌmnəl] *adj* otoñal

**auxiliary** [ɔːɡˈzɪlɪ(ə)rɪ] **1** *n* (a) *(person)* auxiliar *mf* (b) **a. (verb)** (verbo *m*) auxiliar *m*

**2** *adj* auxiliar

**avail** [əˈveɪl] **1** *n* **of no a.** *(not useful)* inútil; **to no a.** *(in vain)* en vano

**2** *vt* **to a. oneself of sth** aprovechar algo

**availability** [əveɪləˈbɪlɪtɪ] *n* disponibilidad *f*

**available** [əˈveɪləbəl] *adj (information, services, products)* disponible; *(person)* disponible, libre; **to be a.** *(of person)* estar disponible *or* libre; **tickets are still a.** todavía quedan entradas; **money is a. for…** hay dinero para…

**avalanche** [ˈævəlɑːntʃ] *n also Fig* avalancha *f*

**avant-garde** [ævɒ̃ˈɡɑːd] *adj* vanguardista

**avarice** [ˈævərɪs] *n* avaricia *f*

**Ave** *(abbr* **Avenue***)* Avda., avenida *f*

**avenge** [əˈvendʒ] *vt (person, crime)* vengar; **to a. oneself on sb** vengarse de alguien

**avenue** [ˈævɪnjuː] *n* avenida *f*; *Fig* **an a. to success/fame** un camino hacia el éxito/la fama

**aver** [əˈvɜː(r)] *(pt & pp* **averred***)* *vt Formal* aseverar

**average** [ˈævərɪdʒ] **1** *n* promedio *m*, media *f*; **on a.** de media, como promedio; **above/below a.** por encima/debajo del promedio *or* de la media

**2** *adj* (a) *(mean, typical)* medio(a); **the a. Englishman** el inglés medio (b) *(unexceptional)* regular

**3** *vt* alcanzar una media *or* un promedio de; **to a. eight hours work a day** trabajar un promedio de ocho horas diarias

▸**average out** *vi* **my expenses a. out at £400 per month** tengo una media de gastos de 400 libras al mes

**averse** [əˈvɜːs] *adj* reacio(a) *(to* a); **to be a. to sth** ser reacio a algo; **he is not a. to the occasional glass of wine** no le hace ascos a un vino de vez en cuando

**aversion** [əˈvɜːʃən] *n (feeling)* aversión *f*; **to have an a. to sb/sth** sentir aversión por alguien/algo

**avert** [əˈvɜːt] *vt* (a) *(turn away) (eyes, thoughts)* apartar, desviar (b) *(prevent) (misfortune, accident)* evitar, impedir

**aviary** [ˈeɪvɪərɪ] *n* pajarera *f*

**aviation** [eɪvɪˈeɪʃən] *n* aviación *f*

**avid** [ˈævɪd] *adj* ávido(a) **(for** de)

**avidly** [ˈævɪdlɪ] *adv* ávidamente

**avocado** [ævəˈkɑːdəʊ] *(pl* **avocados***)* *n* **a. (pear)** aguacate *m*, *Andes, CSur* palta *f*

**avoid** [əˈvɔɪd] *vt (person, thing)* evitar; *(punishment, danger, question)* evitar, eludir; **to a. doing**

**sth** evitar hacer algo; **to a. sb/sth like the plague** huir de alguien/algo como de la peste

**avoidable** [ə'vɔɪdəbəl] *adj* evitable

**avowed** [ə'vaʊd] *adj* declarado(a)

**AWACS** ['eɪwæks] *n Mil (abbr* **Airborne Warning and Control System)** AWACS *m*, = sistema de control y alarma aéreo

**await** [ə'weɪt] *vt* aguardar, esperar; **a nasty surprise awaited her** le esperaba una desagradable sorpresa; *Law* **to be awaiting trial** estar en espera de juicio

**awake** [ə'weɪk] **1** *adj* **to be a.** estar despierto(a); **he lay a. for hours** permaneció despierto en la cama durante horas; **the coffee kept her a.** el café la mantuvo despierta; *Fig* **he was a. to the danger** era consciente del peligro

**2** *vt (pt* **awoke** [ə'wəʊk], *pp* **awoken** [ə'wəʊkən])** despertar

**3** *vi* despertarse; *Fig* **to a. to a danger** tomar conciencia de un peligro

**awaken** [ə'weɪkən] (*pt* **awakened** *or* **awoke** [ə'wəʊk], *pp* **awakened** *or* **awoken** [ə'wəʊkən]) **1** *vt* despertar

**2** *vi* despertarse

**awakening** [ə'weɪkənɪŋ] *n* despertar *m*

**award** [ə'wɔːd] **1** *n (prize)* premio *m*; *Law* indemnización *f*

**2** *vt (prize, contract, damages)* otorgar, conceder; **to a. sb for sth** premiar a alguien por algo

**award-winning** [ə'wɔːdwɪnɪŋ] *adj* premiado(a)

**aware** [ə'weə(r)] *adj* **to be a. of** ser consciente de; **to be a. that...** ser consciente de que...; **not that I am a. of** no, que yo sepa; **as far as I'm a.** por lo que yo sé; **to become a. of** darse cuenta de; **environmentally a.** preocupado(a) por los temas del medio ambiente

**awareness** [ə'weənɪs] *n* conciencia *f* (**of** de)

**awash** [ə'wɒʃ] *adj* **to be a. (with)** estar inundado(a)

**away** [ə'weɪ] *adv* (**a**) *(with distance)* **a long way a., far a.** muy lejos; **it's 10 kilometres a.** está a 10 kilómetros; **to keep a. from sb/sth** mantenerse alejado(a) de alguien/algo; **to go a.** marcharse, irse; **go a.!** ¡vete!; **to put sth a.** recoger *or* guardar algo; **to take sth a. from sb** quitarle algo a alguien; **to stand a. from sth** mantenerse alejado(a) de algo; **to turn a.** apartar *or* desviar la mirada

(**b**) *(not at school, work)* **to be a.** estar fuera

(**c**) *(in time)* **right a.** inmediatamente; **Christmas is only two weeks a.** sólo quedan dos semanas para la Navidad

**awe** [ɔː] *n* sobrecogimiento *m*, temor *m*; **to be in a. of sb/sth** estar intimidado(a) ante alguien/algo

**awe-inspiring** ['ɔːɪnspaɪərɪŋ] *adj* sobrecogedor(ora)

**awesome** ['ɔːsəm] *adj (incredible)* sobrecogedor(ora); *US Fam (wonderful)* flipante, alucinante

**awful** ['ɔːfʊl] *adj (death, weather)* horrible, espantoso(a); *Fam* **an a. lot** muchísimo, un montón; **an a. lot of people** un montón de gente

**awfully** ['ɔːflɪ] *adv (a) (very badly)* fatal, espantosamente (**b**) *(very)* tremendamente; *Fam* **I'm a. sorry/glad** lo siento/me alegro muchísimo; **she's an a. good player** es una jugadora buenísima

**awhile** [ə'waɪl] *adv* **wait a.** espera un poco

**awkward** ['ɔːkwəd] *adj (a) (clumsy)* torpe (**b**) *(inconvenient) (moment, time)* inoportuno(a); *(silence, situation)* incómodo(a), embarazoso(a); *(location, person)* difícil; *Fam* **he's an a. customer** es un tipo difícil

**awl** [ɔːl] *n* lezna *f*

**awning** ['ɔːnɪŋ] *n (of shop)* toldo *m*

**awoke** [ə'wəʊk] *pt of* **awake**

**awoken** [ə'wəʊkən] *pp of* **awake, awaken**

**AWOL** ['eɪwɒl] *adj Mil (abbr* **absent without leave)** **to be A.** estar ausente sin permiso; *Fig* **to go A.** desaparecer así como así

**awry** [ə'raɪ] *adv* **to go a.** salir mal

**axe,** *US* **ax** [æks] **1** *n* hacha *f*; *Fig* **to have an a. to grind** tratar de barrer para dentro; *Fam* **two hospitals have been given the a.** van a cerrar dos hospitales

**2** *vt Fam (jobs, project)* suprimir; *(spending, costs)* recortar

**axiom** ['æksɪəm] *n* axioma *m*

**axiomatic** [æksɪə'mætɪk] *adj* axiomático(a), incontrovertible

**axis** ['æksɪs] (*pl* **axes** ['æksiːz]) *n Math* eje *m*; *Hist* **the A. powers** las potencias del Eje

**axle** ['æksəl] *n* eje *m*

**azalea** [ə'zeɪlɪə] *n* azalea *f*

**Azerbaijan** [æzəbaɪ'dʒɑːn] *n* Azerbaiyán

**Azerbaijani** [æzəbaɪ'dʒɑːnɪ], **Azeri** [ə'zeərɪ] *n & adj* azerbaiyano(a) *m,f*

**Azores** [ə'zɔːz] *npl* **the A.** las Azores

**Aztec** ['æztek] *n & adj* azteca *mf*

**azure** ['eɪʒə(r)] *n & adj* azul *m* celeste, celeste *m*

# B

**B, b** [biː] n (a) (letter) B, b; **B-movie** película f de serie B; Br **B road** carretera f secundaria (b) Mus si m (c) Sch (grade) notable m; **to get a B** sacar un notable

**b** (abbr **born**) nacido(a)

**BA** [biːˈeɪ] n Univ (abbr **Bachelor of Arts**) (qualification) licenciatura f en Filosofía y Letras; (person) licenciado(a) m,f en Filosofía y Letras

**baa** [bɑː] **1** n balido m

**2** vi (pt & pp **baaed** or **baa'd** [bɑːd]) balar

**babble** [ˈbæbəl] **1** n (of voices) parloteo m

**2** vi (a) (of baby) balbucear; (of adult) farfullar; **to b. away** or **on** (about sth) parlotear (sobre algo) (b) (of water) murmurar

**babe** [beɪb] n (a) Literary (child) bebé m; **a b. in arms** un niño de pecho (b) Fam (woman) nena f, bombón m

**baboon** [bəˈbuːn] n babuino m, papión m

**baby** [ˈbeɪbɪ] **1** n (a) (infant) bebé m, Andes, CSur guagua mf; **b. brother** hermanito m; **b. sister** hermanita f; **b. boom** explosión f de la natalidad; US **b. carriage** cochecito m de niño; **b. grand** (piano) piano m de media cola; **b. talk** habla f infantil (b) (idioms) **we have to avoid throwing the b. out with the bathwater** tenemos que evitar dañar lo bueno al eliminar lo malo; **to leave sb holding the b.** endilgar el muerto a alguien

**2** vt mimar, tratar como a un bebé

**baby-faced** [ˈbeɪbɪfeɪst] adj con cara de niño

**babygro** [ˈbeɪbɪɡrəʊ] n pelele m

**babyhood** [ˈbeɪbɪhʊd] n primera infancia f

**babyish** [ˈbeɪbɪʃ] adj Pej infantil

**Babylon** [ˈbæbɪlən] n Babilonia

**baby-minder** [ˈbeɪbɪmaɪndə(r)] n niñera f

**baby-sit** [ˈbeɪbɪsɪt] (pt & pp **baby-sat** [ˈbeɪbɪsæt]) vi hacer de canguro, cuidar a niños; **to b. for sb** cuidar a los niños de alguien

**baby-sitter** [ˈbeɪbɪsɪtə(r)] n canguro mf

**baby-walker** [ˈbeɪbɪwɔːkə(r)] n andador m, tacataca m

**bachelor** [ˈbætʃələ(r)] n soltero m; **b. flat** piso m de soltero; Univ **B. of Arts** (qualification) licenciatura f en Filosofía y Letras; (person) licenciado(a) m,f en Filosofía y Letras; Univ **B. of**

**Science** (qualification) licenciatura f en Ciencias; (person) licenciado(a) m,f en Ciencias

**bacillus** [bəˈsɪləs] (pl **bacilli** [bəˈsɪlaɪ]) n Biol bacilo m

**back** [bæk] **1** n (a) (of person) espalda f; (of animal) lomo m; also Fig **to turn one's b. on sb** volver la espalda a alguien; **to sit/stand with one's b. to sb/sth** dar la espalda a alguien/algo; **b. pain** dolor m de espalda; **to have b. problems** tener problemas de espalda; **b. slapping** (self-congratulation) felicitaciones fpl efusivas

(b) (of page, hand, book) dorso m; (of chair) respaldo m; (of house, car) parte f trasera or de atrás; (of room) fondo m; **at the b. of the book** al final del libro; **the b. of the neck** la nuca, el cogote; **at the b. (of)** (behind) en la parte de atrás (de), detrás (de); (to the rear of) al fondo (de); US **in b. of** (behind) en la parte de atrás (de), detrás (de); (to the rear of) al fondo (de); Br **in the b.,** US **in b.** (of car) atrás, en el asiento trasero; **to have sth at the b. of one's mind** tener algo en la cabeza; **he knows London like the b. of his hand** conoce Londres como la palma de la mano; Fam **at the b. of beyond** en el quinto pino; **b. to front** del revés (con lo de detrás hacia delante)

(c) (in football, rugby) right/left b. defensa mf

(d) (idioms) **to do sth behind sb's b.** hacer algo a espaldas de alguien; **to be glad to see the b. of sb** alegrarse de perder a alguien de vista; **to have one's b. to the wall** estar contra las cuerdas; **put your b. into it!** ¡ponte a hacerlo en serio!; **to break the b. of the work** hacer la parte más dura del trabajo; Fam **the boss was on my b. all day** el jefe estaba todo el día encima de mí; Fam **get off my b.!** ¡déjame en paz!, ¡deja de fastidiarme!; Fam **to put** or **get sb's b. up** hinchar las narices a alguien

**2** adj (a) (in space) (part, wheel) trasero(a), de atrás; Fig **to put sth on the b. burner** dejar algo para más tarde, aparcar algo; **b. door** puerta f trasera or de atrás; Fig **he got it through the b. door** lo consiguió de manera poco ortodoxa; **b. garden** jardín m (en la parte de atrás de una casa); **the b. page** (of newspaper) la contraportada; Euph **b. passage** (rectum) recto m; **b. road** carretera f secundaria; **b. room**

cuarto *m* del fondo, habitación *f* trasera; *Fig* **to take a b. seat** quedarse en segundo plano; **b. yard** *Br (enclosed area)* patio *m* trasero; *US (garden)* jardín *m* trasero

　(b) *(in time)* **b. number** número *m* atrasado; **b. pay** atrasos *mpl*, salario *m* atrasado; **b. rent** alquiler *m* pendiente de pago, atrasos *mpl*

**3** *adv* (a) *(in space)* atrás; **stand b.!** ¡atrás!; **to step b.** dar un paso atrás; **3 kilometres b.** 3 kilómetros atrás

　(b) *(in return, retaliation)* **to get one's own b. (on sb)** tomarse la revancha (contra alguien), desquitarse (de alguien); **to get b. at sb** vengarse de alguien; **to call sb b.** llamar más tarde a alguien; **if you kick me I'll kick you b.** si me pegas una patada, te la devolveré

　(c) *(to original starting point)* **to come/go b.** volver; **when will she be b.?** ¿cuándo estará de vuelta?; **b. in Britain** en Gran Bretaña; **a few pages b.** unas cuantas páginas atrás

　(d) *(in time)* **a few years b.** hace unos cuantos años; **b. when...** cuando..., en el tiempo en que...; **b. in 1982** allá por 1982; **as far b. as 1914** ya en 1914

**4** *vt* (a) *(support)* respaldar, apoyar; *(financially)* financiar, dar respaldo financiero a

　(b) *(bet on)* apostar por

　(c) *(move backwards)* mover hacia atrás; **to b. one's car into the garage** entrar en el garaje (dando) marcha atrás; **he backed his car into a lamppost** dio marcha atrás y chocó contra una farola

**5** *vi (move backwards)* retroceder, ir hacia atrás; *(of car, driver)* recular, dar marcha atrás

▸**back away** *vi* alejarse (retrocediendo) **(from** de)

▸**back down** *vi* echarse atrás

▸**back off** *vi (move back)* echarse atrás; *Fig* **b. off!** *(leave me alone)* ¡déjame en paz!

▸**back on to** *vt insep* dar por la parte de atrás a; **the house backs on to the park** la parte trasera de la casa da al parque

▸**back out** *vi* (a) *(move backwards)* salir de espaldas; *(in car)* salir marcha atrás (b) *(withdraw)* echarse atrás; **to b. out of an agreement** retirarse de un acuerdo

▸**back up 1** *vt sep* (a) *(support)* respaldar (b) *Comptr (file)* hacer una copia de seguridad

**2** *vi* (a) *(move backwards)* retroceder; *(in car)* ir marcha atrás (b) *Comptr* hacer copias de seguridad

**backache** ['bækeɪk] *n* dolor *m* de espalda

**backbencher** ['bæk'bentʃə(r)] *n Br Parl* diputado(a) *m,f* ordinario(a) *(sin cargo en el Gobierno o la oposición)*

**backbiting** ['bækbaɪtɪŋ] *n Fam* chismorreo *m*, murmuración *f*

**backbone** ['bækbəʊn] *n* columna *f* vertebral, espina *f* dorsal; *Fig* **he's got no b.** no tiene agallas

**backbreaking** ['bækbreɪkɪŋ] *adj (work)* extenuante, agotador(ora)

**backchat** ['bæktʃæt] *n Br Fam* impertinencias *fpl*, insolencias *fpl*

**backcloth** ['bækklɒθ] *Br* = **backdrop**

**backdate** ['bækdeɪt] *vt* **the increase will be backdated to 1 July** el aumento tendrá efecto retroactivo a partir del uno de julio

**backdrop** ['bækdrɒp] *n Th* telón *m* de fondo; *Fig* **against a b. of continuing violence** con la violencia como constante telón de fondo

**backer** ['bækə(r)] *n (of political party)* partidario(a) *m,f*; *Fin* fuente *f* de financiación, apoyo *m* económico

**backfire** [bæk'faɪə(r)] *vi (of car)* petardear; *Fig* **it backfired on them** les salió el tiro por la culata

**backgammon** ['bækgæmən] *n* backgammon *m*

**background** ['bækgraʊnd] *n* (a) *(in scene, painting, view)* fondo *m*; **in the b.** al fondo, en el fondo; **to stay in the b.** quedarse en segundo plano; **to push sb into the b.** relegar a alguien a un segundo plano; **b. music** música *f* de fondo; **b. noise** ruido *m* de fondo

　(b) *(social)* origen *m*, extracción *f*; *(educational)* formación *f*; *(professional)* experiencia *f*; **he comes from a disadvantaged b.** procede de un entorno desfavorecido; **we need someone with a b. in computers** necesitamos a alguien con conocimientos de informática

　(c) *(circumstances)* antecedentes *mpl*; **against a b. of unrest** en un contexto de disturbios; **give me some b.** *(information)* ponme en contexto; **b. information** información *f*, antecedentes *mpl*

**backhand** ['bækhænd] *n (in tennis)* revés *m*

**backhanded** [bæk'hændɪd] *adj* equívoco(a), ambiguo(a); **a b. compliment** un cumplido con doble sentido

**backhander** ['bækhændə(r)] *n Fam (bribe)* soborno *m*, *Am* mordida *f*

**backing** ['bækɪŋ] *n (support)* apoyo *m*, respaldo *m*; **financial b.** respaldo *m* financiero; **b. vocals** coros *mpl*

**backlash** ['bæklæʃ] *n (reaction)* reacción *f* violenta

**backlit** ['bæklɪt] *adj Comptr* retroiluminado(a)

**backlog** ['bæklɒg] *n* acumulación *f*; **to clear a b.** ponerse al día con el trabajo; **a b. of work** trabajo *m* atrasado *or* acumulado

**backpack** ['bækpæk] **1** *n* mochila *f*
**2** *vi* viajar con la mochila al hombro; **she**

**backpacked around Europe** recorrió Europa con la mochila al hombro

**backpacker** ['bækpækə(r)] *n* mochilero(a) *m,f*

**back-pedal** ['bæk'pedəl] *vi Fig* dar marcha atrás, echarse atrás

**backrest** ['bækrest] *n* respaldo *m*

**back-seat driver** ['bæksi:t'draɪvə(r)] *n Fam* = pasajero que molesta constantemente al conductor con sus consejos

**backside** [bæk'saɪd] *n Fam* trasero *m*

**backslash** ['bækslæʃ] *n Comptr* barra *f* invertida

**backsliding** ['bækslaɪdɪŋ] *n Fam* recaída *f*, reincidencia *f*

**backspace** ['bækspeɪs] *n Comptr* (tecla *f* de) retroceso *m*

**backstage** [bæk'steɪdʒ] *adv also Fig* entre bastidores; **to go b. after the performance** ir a los camerinos después de la representación

**backstairs** [bæk'steəz] *n* escalera *f* de servicio

**backstitch** ['bækstɪtʃ] *n (in sewing)* pespunte *m*

**backstreet** ['bækstri:t] *n* callejuela *f*; **the backstreets** *(of city)* las zonas deprimidas; **b. abortion** aborto *m* clandestino

**backstroke** ['bækstrəʊk] *n (in swimming)* espalda *f*; **to do** *or* **swim (the) b.** nadar a espalda

**backtalk** ['bæktɔ:k] *n US Fam* impertinencias *fpl*, insolencias *fpl*

**back-to-back** [bæktə'bæk] **1** *adj (in time)* **b. meetings** reuniones *fpl* seguidas

**2** *adv* **(a)** *(physically)* espalda con espalda **(b)** *(consecutively)* sucesivamente; **to watch two films b.** ver dos películas seguidas

**backtrack** ['bæktræk] *vi* **(a)** *(retrace one's steps)* volver atrás, retroceder; **we backtracked to the main road** recorrimos el camino de vuelta hasta la carretera principal **(b)** *(renege)* retractarse, volverse atrás; **to b. on a promise** incumplir una promesa; **to b. on a decision** retractarse de una decisión

**backup** ['bækʌp] *n (support)* apoyo *m*, respaldo *m*; **to call for b.** pedir refuerzos; **the expedition had no technical b.** la expedición no contaba con medios técnicos; *Comptr* **b. copy/file** copia *f* de seguridad; *Comptr* **b. disk** disquete *m* con la copia de seguridad; **b. system** sistema *m* de apoyo; **b. team** equipo *m* técnico

**backward** ['bækwəd] **1** *adj* **(a)** *(direction)* hacia atrás; **b. glance** mirada *f* hacia atrás sin mirar atrás; *Fig* **a b. step** un paso atrás **(b)** *(retarded)* *(child, country)* atrasado(a); *Br Fam* **he isn't b. in coming forward** no se corta

**2** *adv* **= backwards**

**backwardness** ['bækwədnɪs] *n (of child, country)* atraso *m*

**backwards** ['bækwədz] *adv* hacia atrás; **to walk b. and forwards** caminar de un lado para otro; *Fig* **a step b.** un paso atrás; *Fig* **to bend** *or* **lean over b. to help** hacer todo lo posible por ayudar; *Fig* **to know sth b.** conocer algo de pe a pa

**backwash** ['bækwɒʃ] *n (of boat)* estela *f*; *Fig* repercusiones *fpl*

**backwater** ['bækwɔ:tə(r)] *n* **(a)** *(of river)* remanso *m*, aguas *fpl* estancadas **(b)** *(isolated place)* zona *f* estancada, lugar *m* atrasado; **Jibrovia is a cultural b.** Jibrovia está muy atrasado culturalmente

**bacon** ['beɪkən] *n* bacon *m*, beicon *m*; *Fam* **to save sb's b.** salvarle el pellejo a alguien; *Fam* **to bring home the b.** *(succeed)* triunfar; *(earn wages)* ganar el pan

**bacteria** [bæk'tɪərɪə] *npl* bacterias *fpl*

**bacterial** [bæk'tɪərɪəl] *adj* bacteriano(a)

**bacteriological** [bæktɪərɪə'lɒdʒɪkəl] *adj* bacteriológico(a)

**bacteriology** [bæktɪərɪ'ɒlədʒɪ] *n* bacteriología *f*

**bad** [bæd] *(comparative* **worse** [wɜ:s], *superlative* **worst** [wɜ:st]) *adj* **(a)** *(of poor quality)* malo(a); **it's not b.** *(fair)* no está mal; *(good)* no está nada mal; **he's b. at English** se le da mal el inglés; **I'm really b. at cooking** soy un desastre cocinando; **things are going from b. to worse** las cosas van de mal en peor; **it was a b. time to leave** era un mal momento para irse; **to have a b. time** pasarlo mal; *Fin* **b. cheque** cheque *m* sin fondos; *Fin* **b. debts** impagados *mpl*; **in b. faith** de mala fe; **b. feeling** animadversión *f*; **it was a b. idea to invite them** no fue una buena idea invitarles; **to give sth up as a b. job** dejar algo por imposible; **to be a b. loser** ser un mal perdedor; **b. luck** mala suerte *f*

**(b)** *(unpleasant)* malo(a); **b. blood** *(mutual resentment)* mala sangre *f*; **there's b. blood between them** existe una gran hostilidad entre ellos; **to get into sb's b. books** entrar en la lista negra de alguien; **b. manners** mala educación *f*, malos modales *mpl*; **it's b. manners to…** es de mala educación…; **to be in a b. mood** estar de mal humor; *Fig* **she's b. news** no te traerá más que problemas

**(c)** *(unfortunate)* **it's (really) too b.!**, **that's too b.!** ¡es una (verdadera) pena!; **to have a b. effect on sth** perjudicar algo; **he'll come to a b. end** terminará mal

**(d)** *(not healthy)* enfermo(a); **he's got a b. back/heart** está mal de la espalda/del corazón; **smoking/alcohol is b. for you** fumar/el alcohol es perjudicial para la salud; **to be in a**

**b. way** estar muy mal

(e) *(wicked) (person, behaviour)* malo(a); **to use b. language** decir palabrotas; **b. word** palabrota *f*

(f) *(serious) (mistake, illness, accident)* grave; *(pain, headache)* fuerte

(g) *(rotten)* malo(a), podrido(a); **to be b.** estar malo(a) *or* podrido(a); **to go b.** estropearse, echarse a perder; *Fig* **a b. apple** una manzana podrida

(h) *(guilty)* **to feel b. about sth** sentirse mal por algo

**baddie, baddy** ['bædɪ] *n Fam (in film)* **the b.** el malo (de la película); **the goodies and the baddies** *(in conflict, war)* los buenos y los malos

**bade** [bæd, beɪd] *pt of* **bid**

**badge** [bædʒ] *n (bearing coat of arms, logo) & Fig* insignia *f*; *(round, made of metal)* chapa *f*; *(pin)* pin *m*

**badger** ['bædʒə(r)] **1** *n (animal)* tejón *m*

**2** *vt* acosar, importunar; **to b. sb into doing sth** dar la lata a alguien para que haga algo; **she's always badgering me with questions** siempre me está acosando con preguntas

**bad-looking** [bæd'lʊkɪŋ] *adj* he's not b. es bastante guapo

**badly** ['bædlɪ] *adv (comparative* **worse** [wɜːs]*, superlative* **worst** [wɜːst])* **(a)** *(not well)* mal; **to do b.** hacerlo mal; **he didn't do b.** *(in contest)* le fue (bastante) bien; **he took it very b.** se lo tomó muy mal; **we are b. off for money/ time** nos falta dinero/tiempo; **to get on b. (with sb)** llevarse mal (con alguien); **b. dressed** mal vestido(a)

**(b)** *(seriously)* gravemente; **to be b. beaten** recibir una buena paliza; **b. damaged** gravemente dañado(a)

**(c)** *(greatly)* mucho; **to want sth b.** desear algo mucho; **to be b. in need of sth** necesitar algo urgentemente

**bad-mannered** [bæd'mænəd] *adj* maleducado(a)

**badminton** ['bædmɪntən] *n* bádminton *m*

**bad-mouth** ['bædmaʊθ] *vt US Fam* hablar mal de

**badness** ['bædnɪs] *n* **(a)** *(poor quality)* mala calidad *f* **(b)** *(wickedness)* maldad *f*

**bad-tempered** [bæd'tempəd] *adj (remark)* malhumorado(a); **to be b.** *(person) (by nature)* tener mal carácter; *(temporarily)* estar de mal humor; **he made a b. apology** se excusó malhumorado

**BAF** [bi:eɪ'ef] *n Br (abbr* **British Athletics Federation**) = federación británica de atletismo

**baffle** ['bæfəl] *vt (a) (confuse)* desconcertar; **to be baffled** estar desconcertado(a) *or* atónito(a); **I'm baffled as to why she did it** no

logro entender por qué lo hizo **(b)** *(foil) (plot, attempt)* frustrar

**baffling** ['bæfəlɪŋ] *adj* desconcertante, incomprensible

**BAFTA** ['bæftə] *n Br (abbr* **British Academy of Film and Television Arts**) = organización que anualmente concede premios a personalidades del cine y de la televisión británicos

**bag** [bæg] **1** *n (of paper, plastic)* bolsa *f*; *(handbag)* bolso *m*; **to have bags under one's eyes** tener ojeras; *Fam* **to be a b. of bones** estar en los huesos, estar esquelético(a); *Fig* **it's in the b.** *(of deal, victory)* lo tenemos en el bote; *Fig* **he let the secret out of the b.** descubrió el secreto **(b)** *Fam* **bags of** *(lots)* un montón de; **there's bags of room** hay muchísimo sitio **(c)** *Br very Fam Pej (woman)* **old b.** bruja *f*

**2** *vt (pt & pp* **bagged**) **(a)** *(put in bag)* guardar en una bolsa, embolsar **(b)** *(in hunting)* cobrar **(c)** *Fam (claim)* pedirse, pillar; **she always bags the best seat** siempre se pilla el mejor asiento

**bagel** ['beɪgəl] *n* = tipo de rosca de pan

**baggage** ['bægɪdʒ] *n* equipaje *m*; **b. allowance** equipaje *m* permitido; **b. handler** mozo(a) *m,f* de equipajes; **b. reclaim** recogida *f* de equipajes

**baggy** ['bægɪ] *adj (garment)* suelto(a), holgado(a)

**Baghdad** [bæg'dæd] *n* Bagdad

**bagpipes** ['bægpaɪps] *npl* gaita *f*

**baguette** [bæ'get] *n* barra *f* de pan

**bah** [bɑː] *exclam* ¡bah!

**Bahamas** [bə'hɑːməz] *npl* **the B.** las Bahamas

**Bahrain** [bɑː'reɪn] *n* Bahrein

**Bahraini** [bɑː'reɪnɪ] *n & adj* bahreiní *mf*

**bail** [beɪl] *n Law (guarantee)* fianza *f*; **on b.** bajo fianza; **to release sb on b.** poner a alguien en libertad bajo fianza; **to grant b.** conceder la libertad bajo fianza; **to stand b. for sb** pagar la fianza de alguien

▸**bail out** *vt sep Law* **to b. sb out** pagar la fianza de alguien; *Fig* **your parents won't always be there to b. you out!** ¡tus padres no van a estar siempre ahí para sacarte las castañas del fuego!; **to b. a company out** sacar a una empresa del apuro

**bailiff** ['beɪlɪf] *n (a) Law* alguacil *mf* **(b)** *(on estate)* adminis-trador(ora) *m,f*

**bait** [beɪt] **1** *n (for fish)* cebo *m*; *Fig* cebo *m*, anzuelo *m*; *Fig* **to rise to the b.** morder el anzuelo; *Fig* **to swallow** *or* **take the b.** morder el anzuelo, picar

**2** *vt (a) (torment)* hostigar, atormentar **(b)** *(attach bait to)* cebar

**baize** [beɪz] *n* tapete *m*

**bake** [beɪk] **1** *vt (bread, cake)* cocer (al horno), hornear; *(clay)* cocer; *(potatoes)* asar

**2** *vi (of food)* cocerse; *Fam* **I'm baking (hot)** ¡me estoy asando!, ¡estoy asado(a)!

**baked** [beɪkt] *adj* **b. beans** alubias *fpl* con tomate; **b. potato** = patata asada con piel que se suele comer con un relleno

**baker** ['beɪkə(r)] *n* panadero(a) *m,f*; **b.'s (shop)** panadería *f*; **b.'s dozen** docena *f* de fraile *(trece)*

**bakery** ['beɪkərɪ] *n* panadería *f*

**baking** ['beɪkɪŋ] **1** *n* to do the **b.** *(bread)* cocer el pan; *(cakes)* hacer pasteles; **b. powder** levadura *f* (en polvo); **b. sheet** *or* **tray** placa *f* or bandeja *f* de hornear; **b. soda** bicarbonato *m* sódico; **b. tin** molde *m* para hornear

**2** *adj Fam* **it's b. (hot)** hace un calor achicharrante

**balaclava** [bælə'klɑːvə] *n* pasamontañas *m inv*

**balance** ['bæləns] **1** *n* (a) *(equilibrium)* equilibrio *m*; **to keep/lose one's b.** mantener/perder el equilibrio; **to throw sb off b.** hacer que alguien pierda el equilibrio; *Fig* **to catch sb off b.** pillar a alguien desprevenido(a); **the b. of power** el equilibrio de fuerzas; **on b.** en conjunto; **to strike a b.** establecer un equilibrio

(b) *(of bank account)* saldo *m*; *Econ* **b. of trade/payments** balanza *f* comercial/de pagos; **b. sheet** balance *m*

(c) *(for weighing)* balanza *f*; *Fig* **to hang** *or* **be in the b.** *(of decision, result)* estar en el aire

**2** *vt (object)* poner en equilibrio; **she balanced the basket on her head** se puso la cesta en equilibrio sobre la cabeza; **he sought to b. the claims of the two parties** trató de equilibrar las reivindicaciones de ambos bandos; *Fin* **to b. the books** hacer que cuadren las cuentas

**3** *vi* (a) *(physically)* estar *or* mantenerse en equilibrio

(b) *Fin* cuadrar; **she couldn't get the accounts to b.** no consiguió que le cuadraran las cuentas

**balanced** ['bælənst] *adj (unbiased)* objetivo(a), imparcial; **b. diet** dieta *f* equilibrada

**balancing act** ['bælənsɪŋ'ækt] *n Fig* **to do a political b.** hacer malabarismos en política

**balcony** ['bælkənɪ] *n (small)* balcón *m*; *(larger)* terraza *f*; *(in theatre)* anfiteatro *m*

**bald** [bɔːld] *adj* (a) *(person)* calvo(a); *(tyre)* desgastado(a); **to go b.** quedarse calvo(a); *Fam* **as b. as a coot** con la cabeza monda y lironda; **b. eagle** águila *f* calva; **b. patch** calva *f*, claro *m* (b) *(truth)* simple, llano(a); **the report contained a b. statement of the facts** el informe contenía una mera descripción de los hechos

**balderdash** ['bɔːldədæ] *n Fam* bobadas *fpl*, tonterías *fpl*; **b.!** ¡bobadas!; **to talk b.** decir bobadas

**balding** ['bɔːldɪŋ] *adj* medio calvo(a)

**baldly** ['bɔːldlɪ] *adv* francamente, llanamente

**baldness** ['bɔːldnɪs] *n* (a) *(of person)* calvicie *f* (b) *(of statement, demand)* franqueza *f*

**bale** [beɪl] *n (of cloth)* fardo *m*, bala *f*; *(of hay)* paca *f*, bala *f*

▶**bale out** *vi (of pilot)* tirarse *or* lanzarse en paracaídas; *Fig (from difficult situation)* desentenderse, lavarse las manos

**Balearic** [bælɪ'ærɪk] **1** *n* **the Balearics** las (Islas) Baleares

**2** *adj* **the B. Islands** las (Islas) Baleares

**baleful** ['beɪlful] *adj* maligno(a); **she gave me a b. stare** me lanzó una mirada asesina

**Bali** ['bɑːlɪ] *n* Bali

**Balinese** [bɑːlɪ'niːz] *adj* balinés(esa)

**balk = baulk**

**Balkan** ['bɔːlkən] **1** *npl* **the Balkans** los Balcanes

**2** *adj* balcánico(a), de los Balcanes

**ball¹** [bɔːl] *n* (a) *(for cricket, tennis, golf)* pelota *f*; *(of clay, of dough, for billiards)* bola *f*; *(for rugby, basketball, football)* balón *m*, pelota *f*; **to roll sth (up) into a b.** hacer una bola con algo; **a b. of wool** un ovillo de lana; **b. bearing** rodamiento *m* or cojinete *m* de bolas; **b. boy/girl** *(in tennis)* recogepelotas *mf inv*; **b. game** *(in general)* juego *m* de pelota; *US (baseball match)* partido *m* de béisbol; *Fig* **that's a whole new b. game** esa es una historia completamente diferente

(b) *(of foot)* **to stand on the balls of one's feet** estar de puntillas

(c) *Vulg* **balls** *(testicles)* huevos *mpl*, pelotas *fpl*; *(nonsense)* gilipolleces *fpl*; *(courage)* huevos *mpl*, cojones *mpl*; *Fig* **to have sb by the balls** tener a alguien cogido *or* agarrado por los huevos

(d) *(idioms)* **to be on the b.** *(alert)* estar despierto(a); *(knowledgeable)* estar muy enterado(a); **to start the b. rolling** poner las cosas en marcha; **the b. is in your court** te toca dar el siguiente paso; **to play b.** *(co-operate)* cooperar

**ball²** *n (party)* baile *m*; *Fam* **to have a b.** pasárselo en grande; **b. dress** *or* **gown** traje *m* de fiesta

**ballad** ['bæləd] *n* balada *f*

**ball-and-socket joint** [bɔːlənd'sɒkɪt-'dʒɔɪnt] *n* (a) *Tec* junta *f* articulada (b) *Med* enartrosis *f inv*

**ballast** ['bæləst] *n* (a) *Naut* lastre *m* (b) *Rail* balasto *m*

**ballcock** ['bɔːlkɒk] *n* flotador *m*

**ballerina** [bælə'riːnə] *n* bailarina *f*; **prima b.** primera bailarina *f*

**ballet** ['bæleɪ] *n* ballet *m*; **b. dancer** bailarín(ina) *m,f*; **b. shoe** zapatilla *f* de ballet

**ballistic** [bə'lɪstɪk] *adj (missile)* balístico(a); *Fam Fig* **to go b.** ponerse hecho(a) una furia

**ballistics** [bə'lɪstɪks] *n* balística *f*

**balloon** [bə'luːn] **1** *n* **(a)** *(for party, travel)* globo *m*; *Fam Fig* **when the b. goes up** cuando se arme la gorda **(b)** *(in cartoon)* bocadillo *m*

**2** *vi (swell)* hincharse como un globo

**ballooning** [bə'luːnɪŋ] *n* **to go b.** montar en globo

**balloonist** [bə'luːnɪst] *n* piloto *mf* de aerostación

**ballot** ['bælət] **1** *n (process)* votación *f*; *(paper)* voto *m*; **to hold a b.** celebrar una votación; **to put sth to a b.** someter algo a votación; **b. box** urna *f*; **this matter should be decided at the b. box** este asunto habrá que decidirlo en las urnas; **b. paper** papeleta *f* (de voto)

**2** *vt Pol* consultar por votación

**ballpark** ['bɔːlpɑːk] *US* **1** *n* campo *m* de béisbol

**2** *adj* **a b. figure** una cifra aproximada

**ballpoint** ['bɔːlpɔɪnt] *n* **b. (pen)** bolígrafo *m*

**ballroom** ['bɔːlruːm] *n* salón *m* de baile; **b. dancing** baile *m* de salón

►**balls up** *vt sep Br very Fam* **he ballsed up the accounts** armó un despelote con las cuentas

**balls-up** [bɔːlzʌp] *n Br very Fam* **to make a b. of sth** armar un despelote con algo, joder algo

**ballyhoo** [bælɪ'huː] *n Fam* escandalera *f*, alboroto *m*

**balm** [bɑːm] *n* bálsamo *m*

**balmy** ['bɑːmɪ] *adj (weather)* cálido(a), suave

**baloney** [bə'ləʊnɪ] *n Fam (nonsense)* tonterías *fpl*, bobadas *fpl*

**balsa** ['bɔːlsə] *n* **b. (wood)** madera *f* de balsa

**balsam** ['bɔːlsəm] *n* bálsamo *m*

**balti** ['bɔːltɪ] *n Culin* = plato hindú que se come en la misma cazuela en que se prepara

**Baltic** ['bɔːltɪk] **1** *n* **the B.** el (mar) Báltico

**2** *adj* báltico(a); **the B. Sea** el mar Báltico

**balustrade** [bælə'streɪd] *n* balaustrada *f*

**bamboo** [bæm'buː] *n* bambú *m*; **b. shoots** brotes *mpl* de bambú

**bamboozle** [bæm'buːzəl] *vt Fam (confuse)* embarullar; *(trick)* engatusar

**ban** [bæn] **1** *n* prohibición *f*; **to impose a b. on sth** prohibir algo

**2** *vt (pt & pp* **banned)** prohibir; **to b. sb from doing sth** prohibir a alguien hacer algo

**banal** [bə'næl] *adj* banal

**banality** [bə'nælɪtɪ] *n* banalidad *f*

**banana** [bə'nɑːnə] *n* plátano *m*; *Fam* **to be bananas** *(mad)* estar como una cabra; *Fam* **to go bananas** *(angry)* ponerse hecho(a) un basilisco; *Fam* **b. republic** república *f* bananera; **b. skin** *(of fruit)* piel *f* de plátano; *Fig* trampa *f* potencial; **b. split** banana split *m*; **b. tree** platanero *m*, bananero *m*

**band**[1] [bænd] *n* **(a)** *(of metal, cloth)* banda *f*, tira *f*; *(of colour)* raya *f*, franja *f*; *(on hat)* cinta *f*; *(on cigar)* vitola *f* **(b)** *Rad* banda *f* **(c)** *(of age, ability)* franja *f*, banda *f*

**band**[2] *n (of friends)* pandilla *f*, grupo *m*; *(of robbers)* banda *f*; *(of pop musicians)* grupo *m*; *(jazz, brass)* banda *f*

►**band together** *vi* unirse

**bandage** ['bændɪdʒ] **1** *n (fabric)* venda *f*; *(on wound, broken arm)* vendaje *m*, venda *f*

**2** *vt* vendar; **the nurse bandaged his arm** la enfermera le vendó el brazo

►**bandage up** *vt sep* vendar

**Band-Aid**® ['bændeɪd] *n US* tirita® *f*

**bandit** ['bændɪt] *n* bandolero *m*, bandido *m*

**bandmaster** ['bændmɑːstə(r)] *n Mus* director *m (de una banda)*

**bandsman** ['bændzmən] *n Mus* músico *m (de banda)*

**bandstand** ['bændstænd] *n* quiosco *m* de música

**bandwagon** ['bændwægən] *n Fam* **to jump on the b.** subirse al carro

**bandwidth** ['bændwɪdθ] *n Comptr* ancho *m* de banda

**bandy**[1] ['bændɪ] *adj (legs)* arqueado(a) *(hacia afuera)*

**bandy**[2] *vt (words, insults)* intercambiar, cambiar; **his name is being bandied about** se está barajando su nombre

**bandy-legged** [bændɪ'leg(ɪ)d] *adj* estevado(a)

**bane** [beɪn] *n* cruz *f*, perdición *f*; **he's the b. of my life** es mi cruz, es mi ruina

**bang** [bæŋ] **1** *n* **(a)** *(noise)* golpe *m*; *(explosion)* explosión *f*; **the door shut with a b.** la puerta se cerró de un portazo; *Fig* **to go with a b.** *(of party, event)* salir redondo(a) **(b)** *(blow)* golpe *m*; **to get a b. on the head** darse un golpe en la cabeza

**2** *adv* **(a)** **to go b.** explotar ruidosamente; *Fam* **b. went my hopes of a quiet weekend** adiós a mi esperado fin de semana tranquilo **(b)** *Fam (exactly)* **b. in the middle** justo en medio; **b. on time** justo a tiempo

**3** *exclam (sound of gun)* ¡pum!; *(explosion)* ¡boum!

**4** *vt (hit)* golpear; **to b. one's head** golpearse la cabeza

**5** *vi (of door, window)* batir, dar golpes; **the door banged shut** la puerta se cerró de un portazo; **to b. at** *or* **on the door** aporrear la puerta; **to b. into sth** chocar con algo

▸**bang about, bang around** *vi (make noise) (of person)* armar jaleo

▸**bang on** *vi Fam* **to b. on about sth** dar la murga con algo

▸**bang up** *vt sep Br very Fam (imprison)* meter en chirona, enchironar

**banger** ['bæŋə(r)] *n Br* (a) *Fam (sausage)* salchicha *f* (b) *(firework)* petardo *m* (c) *Fam (car)* **old b.** cacharro *m* viejo, carraca *f*

**Bangkok** [bæŋ'kɒk] *n* Bangkok

**Bangladesh** [bæŋglə'deʃ] *n* Bangladesh

**Bangladeshi** [bæŋglə'deʃi] *n & adj* bangladesí *mf*

**bangle** ['bæŋgəl] *n* brazalete *m*, pulsera *f*

**bangs** [bæŋz] *npl US* flequillo *m (corto)*

**banish** ['bæniʃ] *vt (exile)* desterrar; *Fig* **he banished all thought of her from his mind** se la quitó de la cabeza

**banishment** ['bæniʃmənt] *n* destierro *m*

**banister** ['bænistə(r)] *n* barandilla *f*

**banjo** ['bændʒəʊ] *(pl* **banjos**) *n* banjo *m*

**bank¹** [bæŋk] **1** *n* (a) *(of river)* orilla *f*; *(of earth)* terraplén *m* (b) *(of clouds, fog)* banco *m* (c) *(of lights, switches)* batería *f*; **banks of seats** gradas *fpl* con asientos

**2** *vt* flanquear; **the road is banked by trees** la carretera se halla flanqueada por dos filas de árboles

**3** *vi* (a) *(of clouds, mist)* formar bancos; *(of snow)* acumularse (b) *(of plane)* ladearse, escorarse

**bank²** **1** *n* (a) *(financial institution)* banco *m*; **b. account** cuenta *f* bancaria; **b. balance** saldo *m* bancario, haberes *mpl* bancarios; **b. charges** comisión *f* bancaria, gastos *mpl* bancarios; **b. clerk** empleado(a) *m,f* de banca; *Br* **b. holiday** día *m* festivo; **b. loan** préstamo *m* or crédito *m* bancario; **b. manager** director *m* de banco; *Fin* **b. rate** tipo *m* de interés bancario; **b. robber** atracador(ora) *m,f* or ladrón(ona) *m,f* de bancos; **b. statement** extracto *m* or balance *m* de cuenta

(b) *(in gambling)* banca *f*; **to break the b.** hacer saltar la banca; *Fig* **it won't break the b.** no vas a arruinarte por eso

(c) *(store)* **blood/data b.** banco de sangre/datos

**2** *vt (funds)* ingresar (en un banco)

**3** *vi* **to b. with** tener una cuenta en

▸**bank on** *vt insep (outcome, success)* contar con

**bankbook** ['bæŋkbʊk] *n* cartilla *f*, libreta *f*

**banker** ['bæŋkə(r)] *n Fin* banquero *m*; **b.'s draft** giro *m* bancario

**banking** ['bæŋkɪŋ] *n (occupation)* banca *f*, sector *m* bancario; *(activity)* operaciones *fpl* bancarias

**banknote** ['bæŋknəʊt] *n* billete *m (de banco)*

**bankroll** ['bæŋkrəʊl] *vt US (finance)* financiar

**bankrupt** ['bæŋkrʌpt] **1** *n Fin* quebrado(a) *m,f*

**2** *adj* en quiebra, en bancarrota; **to be b.** estar en quiebra; **to go b.** quebrar, ir a la quiebra; *Fig* **to be morally b.** estar en quiebra moral

**3** *vt Law* conducir a la quiebra; *Fig (make poor)* arruinar, dejar en la ruina

**bankruptcy** ['bæŋkrəptsi] *n Law* quiebra *f*, bancarrota *f*; *Fig (poverty)* ruina *f*

**banner** ['bænə(r)] *n (flag)* bandera *f*; *(of trade union, political party)* pancarta *f*; **b. headlines** *(in newspaper)* grandes titulares *mpl*

**bannister** = **banister**

**banns** [bænz] *npl* amonestaciones *fpl*; **to publish the b.** correr las amonestaciones

**banquet** ['bæŋkwit] *n* banquete *m*

**bantam** ['bæntəm] *n* gallina *f* de Bantam

**bantamweight** ['bæntəmweit] *n (in boxing)* peso *m* gallo

**banter** ['bæntə(r)] **1** *n* bromas *fpl*, chanzas *fpl*

**2** *vi* bromear

**bap** [bæp] *n* = panecillo blando redondo

**baptism** ['bæptizəm] *n* bautismo *m*; *Fig* **a b. of fire** un bautismo de fuego

**baptismal** [bæp'tizməl] *adj* **b. certificate** partida *f* de bautismo; **b. font** pila *f* bautismal

**Baptist** ['bæptist] *n* baptista *mf*, bautista *mf*

**baptize** [bæp'taiz] *vt* bautizar

**bar** [bɑː(r)] **1** *n* (a) *(of metal)* barra *f*; *(of soap)* pastilla *f*; *(on window)* barrote *m*; **to be behind bars** estar entre rejas; **chocolate b.** chocolatina *f*; **gold bars** lingotes *mpl* de oro, oro *m* en barras; **a three-b. fire** una estufa (eléctrica) de tres resistencias; **b. chart** gráfico *m* de barras; **b. of chocolate** tableta de chocolate; *Comptr* **b. code** código *m* de barras

(b) *(obstacle)* barrera *f*; **to be a b. to sth** constituir una barrera para algo; **to impose a b. on sth** prohibir algo

(c) *Law* **the B.** la abogacía; **to be called to the B.** obtener el título de abogado(a), ingresar en la abogacía; **the prisoner at the b.** el/la acusado(a)

(d) *(pub, in hotel)* bar *m*; *(pub counter)* barra *f*

(e) *Mus* compás *m*

**2** *vt (pt & pp* **barred**) (a) *(obstruct)* obstruir; **to b. the door against sb** atrancar la puerta para impedir el paso a alguien; **to b. sb's way** obstruir el camino *or* impedir el paso a alguien

(b) *(ban)* **to b. sb from a place** prohibir la entrada de alguien a un lugar; **to b. sb from doing sth** prohibir a alguien hacer algo

**3** *prep* salvo, excepto; **b. none** sin excepción

**barb** [bɑːb] *n* (a) *(on hook)* lengüeta *f* (b) *(remark)* dardo *m*

**Barbadian** [bɑː'beidiən] **1** *n* = habitante *o* nativo de Barbados

**2** *adj* de Barbados

**Barbados** [ba:'beɪdɒs] *n* Barbados

**barbarian** [ba:'beərɪən] *n & adj* bárbaro(a) *m,f*

**barbaric** [ba:'bærɪk] *adj* salvaje

**barbarism** ['ba:bərɪzəm] *n* barbarie *f*

**barbarity** [ba:'bærɪtɪ] *n (act)* barbaridad *f*; *(cruelty)* barbarie *f*

**barbarous** ['ba:bərəs] *adj (act, behaviour)* bárbaro(a)

**barbecue** ['ba:bɪkju:] **1** *n* barbacoa *f*; **to have a b.** hacer una barbacoa; **b. sauce** salsa *f* para barbacoa
**2** *vt* asar en la barbacoa

**barbed** [ba:bd] *adj* **(a)** *(hook)* con lengüeta(s); **b. wire** alambre *m* de espino or de púas **(b)** *(remark, comment)* afilado(a), mordaz

**barber** ['ba:bə(r)] *n* barbero *m*; **to go to the b.'s** ir a la peluquería

**barbershop** ['ba:bəʃɒp] *n US* barbería *f*; **b. quartet** cuarteto *m* de voces masculinas

**barbiturate** [ba:'bɪtjʊreɪt] *n* barbitúrico *m*

**Barcelona** [bæsə'ləʊnə] *n* Barcelona

**bard** [ba:d] *n* bardo *m*, trovador *m*; **the B. =** Shakespeare

**bare** [beə(r)] **1** *adj* **(a)** *(not covered)* desnudo(a); **to strip a house b.** *(of thieves)* llevarse absolutamente todo de una casa; **to fight with one's b. hands** luchar sin armas; **in one's b. feet** descalzo(a); **to lay sth b.** poner algo de manifiesto, descubrir algo
**(b)** *(just sufficient)* **the b. minimum** lo imprescindible, lo indispensable; **the b. bones of the case are...** lo esencial del caso es...; **the b. necessities (of life)** lo indispensable (para vivir); **a b. pass** *(in exam)* un aprobado raspado or por los pelos; **a b. majority** una mayoría por los pelos
**2** *vt* descubrir; **to b. one's head** descubrirse (la cabeza); **to b. one's teeth** enseñar los dientes; **he bared his heart or soul to me** me abrió su corazón or alma

**bareback** ['beəbæk] **1** *adj* **b. rider** jinete *m*/ amazona *f* que monta a pelo
**2** *adv* **to ride b.** montar a pelo

**barefaced** ['beəfeɪst] *adj* descarado(a)

**barefoot(ed)** ['beəfʊt(ɪd)] *adj & adv* descalzo(a); **to be b.** estar descalzo(a)

**bareheaded** [beə'hedɪd] *adj & adv* sin sombrero

**barelegged** [beə'leg(ɪ)d] *adj & adv* con las piernas desnudas

**barely** ['beəlɪ] *adv* **(a)** *(scarcely)* apenas **(b)** *(sparsely)* **b. furnished** amueblado(a) con lo indispensable

**barf** [ba:f] *vi Fam* echar la papa, potar

**bargain** ['ba:gɪn] **1** *n* **(a)** *(agreement)* pacto *m*, trato *m*; **to make or strike a b.** hacer un pacto; **you haven't kept your side or part of the b.** no has cumplido tu parte del trato; **he drives a hard b.** es bueno regateando; **into the b.** *(what's more)* encima, además **(b)** *(good buy)* ganga *f*, chollo *m*; **b. basement** sección *f* de oportunidades; **b. hunter** buscador(ora) *m,f* de gangas; **b. price** precio *m* de saldo
**2** *vi* negociar

▸**bargain away** *vt sep (rights, privileges)* malvender, malbaratar

▸**bargain for** *vt insep* **I hadn't bargained for that** no contaba con eso; **he got more than he bargained for** recibió más de lo que esperaba

▸**bargain on** *vt insep* **I didn't b. on that** no contaba con eso

**barge** [ba:dʒ] *n (boat)* gabarra *f*; *(for parties, river cruises)* = barco para fiestas o pequeñas travesías turísticas

▸**barge in** *vi (enter)* irrumpir en

**bargepole** ['ba:dʒpəʊl] *n* pértiga *f*; **I wouldn't touch it with a b.** no lo tocaría ni con pinzas

**baritone** ['bærɪtəʊn] *n* barítono *m*

**barium** ['beərɪəm] *n Chem* bario *m*; *Med* **b. meal** (papilla *f* de) sulfato *m* de bario

**bark¹** [ba:k] **1** *n (of tree)* corteza *f*
**2** *vt* **to b. one's shins** arañarse or rasguñarse las espinillas

**bark²** **1** *n (of dog)* ladrido *m*; *Fig* **his b. is worse than his bite** perro ladrador, poco mordedor
**2** *vt (order)* gritar
**3** *vi* ladrar; *(of person)* gritar; *Fam Fig* **you're barking up the wrong tree** estás aviado or muy equivocado

**barkeep(er)** ['ba:ki:p(ə(r))] *n US* camarero(a) *m,f*

**barley** ['ba:lɪ] *n* cebada *f*; **b. sugar** azúcar *m or f* cande

**barmaid** ['ba:meɪd] *n Br* camarera *f*

**barman** ['ba:mən] *n* camarero *m*

**barmy** ['ba:mɪ] *adj Br Fam* chiflado(a); **to be b.** estar chiflado(a)

**barn** [ba:n] *n* granero *m*, pajar *m*; **b. dance** baile *m* campestre; **b. owl** lechuza *f*

**barnacle** ['ba:nəkəl] *n* bálano *m*, bellota *f* de mar

**barnstorming** ['ba:nstɔ:mɪŋ] *adj (speech, performance)* apoteósico(a)

**barnyard** ['ba:nja:d] *n* corral *m*

**barometer** [bə'rɒmɪtə(r)] *n* barómetro *m*

**baron** ['bærən] *n* barón *m*; *Fig* **press/oil b.** magnate *m* de la prensa/del petróleo

**baroness** ['bærənes] *n* baronesa *f*

**baronet** ['bærənet] *n* baronet *m (título inglés)*

**baroque** [bə'rɒk] **1** *n* barroco *m*
**2** *adj* barroco(a)

**barrack** ['bærək] *vt (heckle)* abuchear

**barracks** ['bærəks] *npl* cuartel *m*

**barracuda** [bærə'kju:də] *n* barracuda *f*

**barrage** ['bæra:ʒ] **1** *n* (**a**) *(dam)* presa *f* (**b**) *Mil (of artillery fire)* batería *f* de fuego; *Fig (of questions, complaints)* lluvia *f*

**2** *vt* **to b. sb with questions** acribillar a alguien a preguntas

**barrel** ['bærəl] *n* (**a**) *(container)* barril *m*, tonel *m*; *(of oil)* barril *m*; *Fam* **to have sb over a b.** tener a alguien en un puño; *Fam* **the party wasn't exactly a b. of fun** *or* **laughs** la fiesta no fue la más divertida del mundo; **b. organ** organillo *m* (**b**) *(of gun)* cañón *m*

**barren** ['bærən] *adj (land, woman)* yermo(a); *(landscape)* árido(a)

**barrenness** ['bærənnɪs] *n* aridez *f*, esterilidad *f*

**barrette** [bə'ret] *n US* pasador *m*

**barricade** ['bærɪkeɪd] **1** *n* barricada *f*

**2** *vt (door, street)* poner barricadas en; **she had barricaded herself into the room** se había atrincherado en su habitación

**barrier** ['bærɪə(r)] *n also Fig* barrera *f*; **the Great B. Reef** la Gran Barrera de Coral

**barring** ['bɑ:rɪŋ] *prep* salvo, excepto; **b. accidents** salvo imprevistos; **b. a miracle** a menos que ocurra un milagro

**barrister** ['bærɪstə(r)] *n Br Law* abogado(a) *m,f (que ejerce en tribunales superiores)*

**barrow** ['bærəʊ] *n (wheelbarrow)* carretilla *f*; *(in market)* carreta *f*

**bartender** ['bɑ:tendə(r)] *n US* camarero(a) *m,f*

**barter** ['bɑ:tə(r)] **1** *n* trueque *m*

**2** *vt* trocar, cambiar (**for** por)

**3** *vi* hacer trueques, practicar el trueque

**basalt** ['bæsɔ:lt] *n* basalto *m*

**base** [beɪs] **1** *n* (**a**) *(bottom)* base *f*; *Fin* **b. rate** *(interest rate)* tipo *m* de interés básico (**b**) *(for explorers, military forces)* base *f*; **b. camp** campamento *m* base (**c**) *(in baseball)* base *f*; *Fig* **she didn't get past first b.** no llegó a superar la primera etapa

**2** *adj* (**a**) *Formal (motive, conduct)* vil, bajo(a) (**b**) **b. metals** metales *mpl* comunes *or* no preciosos

**3** *vt* basar (**on** en); **to be based on** estar basado(a) en, basarse en; **to be based in Bath** *(of job, operation)* desarrollarse en Bath; *(of troops, company)* estar radicado(a) en Bath

**baseball** ['beɪsbɔ:l] *n* béisbol *m*; **b. cap** gorra *f* de visera

**Basel** ['bɑ:zəl] *n* Basilea

**baseless** ['beɪslɪs] *adj* infundado(a), sin fundamento; **to be b.** carecer de fundamento

**baseline** ['beɪslaɪn] *n (in tennis)* línea *f* de saque *or* de fondo

**basement** ['beɪsmənt] *n* sótano *m*; **b. flat** *(piso m del)* sótano *m*

**bash** [bæʃ] *Fam* **1** *n* (**a**) *(blow)* porrazo *m*, castaña *f*; *Br* **to have a b. at (doing)** sth intentar (hacer) algo (**b**) *(party)* fiesta *f*

**2** *vt* golpear; **to b. one's head** darse una castaña en la cabeza

▸**bash in** *vt sep Br Fam (door)* echar abajo; **I'll b. your face in!** ¡te parto la cara!

▸**bash up** *vt sep Br Fam (person)* dar una paliza a; *(car)* abollar

**bashful** ['bæʃfʊl] *adj* tímido(a)

**bashfulness** ['bæʃfʊlnɪs] *n* timidez *f*

**BASIC** ['beɪsɪk] *n Comptr (abbr* **Beginners' All-purpose Symbolic Instruction Code)** *(lenguaje m)* BASIC *m*

**basic** ['beɪsɪk] **1** *n* **the basics** *(fundamental aspects)* lo esencial; *(of language, science)* fundamentos *mpl*; **let's get down to basics** centrémonos en lo esencial

**2** *adj* básico(a); **I get the b. idea** me hago una idea; **to be b. to sth** ser básico(a) para algo; **b. pay** sueldo *m* base

**basically** ['beɪsɪklɪ] *adv* básicamente, fundamentalmente

**basil** ['bæzəl] *n* albahaca *f*

**basilica** [bə'zɪlɪkə] *n* basílica *f*

**basin** ['beɪsən] *n* (**a**) *(for cooking)* recipiente *m*, bol *m*; *(for washing hands)* lavabo *m*; *(plastic, for washing up)* barreño *m*, palangana *f* (**b**) *Geog* cuenca *f*

**basis** ['beɪsɪs] *(pl* **bases** ['beɪsi:z]) *n* base *f*; **on a weekly b.** semanalmente; **on a monthly b.** mensualmente; **on an informal b.** informalmente; **the accusations have no b. in fact** las acusaciones no se basan en los hechos; **on the b. of...** según...

**bask** [bɑ:sk] *vi* **to b. in the sun** estar tumbado(a) al sol; **to b. in sb's favour** gozar del favor de alguien

**basket** ['bɑ:skɪt] *n* cesta *f*; *(in basketball)* canasta *f*; **wastepaper b.** papelera *f*; *Fam* **to be a b. case** *(person)* estar majareta

**basketball** ['bɑ:skɪtbɔ:l] *n* baloncesto *m*

**basketful** ['bɑ:skɪtfʊl] *n* cesta *f*

**Basle** [bɑ:l] *n* Basilea

**Basque** [bɑ:sk] **1** *n* (**a**) *(person)* vasco(a) *m,f* (**b**) *(language)* vasco *m*, vascuence *m*

**2** *adj* vasco(a); **the B. Country** el País Vasco, Euskadi

**bas-relief** [bɑ:rɪ'li:f] *n Art* bajorrelieve *m*

**bass¹** [bæs] *n (seawater)* lubina *f*, róbalo *m*; *(freshwater)* perca *f*

**bass²** [beɪs] *Mus* **1** *n (voice, singer, guitar)* bajo *m*; *(on amplifier)* graves *mpl*; *(double-bass)* contrabajo *m*; **b. player** bajista *m,f*

**2** *adj (in music)* bajo(a); **b. clef** clave *f* de fa; **b. drum** bombo *m*; **b. guitar** bajo *m*

**basset** ['bæsɪt] *n* **b. (hound)** basset *m*

**bassist** ['beɪsɪst] *n Mus* bajista *mf*

**bassoon** [bə'su:n] *n* fagot *m*

**bastard** ['ba:stəd] **1** *n* **(a)** *(illegitimate child)* hijo(a) *m,f* ilegítimo(a), (hijo(a) *m,f*) bastardo(a) *m,f* **(b)** *Vulg (unpleasant person)* cabrón(ona) *m,f*; **you lucky b.!** ¡qué suerte (tienes), cabrón!; **a b. of a job** un trabajo muy jodido

**2** *adj (child)* bastardo(a)

**baste** [beɪst] *vt (meat)* regar con grasa

**bastion** ['bæstɪən] *n also Fig* bastión *m*, baluarte *m*

**bat¹** [bæt] *n (animal)* murciélago *m*; *Fam* **like a b. out of hell** como alma que lleva el diablo

**bat² 1** *n (for cricket, baseball)* bate *m*; *(for table tennis)* pala *f*; *Fam* **to do sth off one's own b.** hacer algo por cuenta propia

**2** *vt (pt & pp batted) Fig* **he didn't b. an eyelid** ni se inmutó

**3** *vi (in cricket, baseball)* batear

**batch** [bætʃ] *n (of goods, material)* lote *m*, partida *f*; *(of recruits)* tanda *f*; *(of bread)* hornada *f*; *Comptr* **b. file** fichero *m* por lotes; *Comptr* **b. processing** proceso *m* por lotes

**bated** ['beɪtɪd] *adj* **with b. breath** con el alma en vilo

**bath** [ba:θ] **1** *n (action)* baño *m*; *(bathtub)* bañera *f*, *Am* tina *f*; **to take** *or* **have a b.** tomar *or* darse un baño, bañarse; **to give sb a b.** bañar a alguien; *Br* **(swimming) baths** piscina *f*, baños *mpl* públicos; **b. mat** alfombrilla *f* de baño; **b. salts** sales *fpl* de baño; **b. towel** toalla *f* de baño

**2** *vt* bañar

**3** *vi* bañarse

**bathe** [beɪð] **1** *n Old-fashioned* **to go for a b.** ir a bañarse

**2** *vt (wound)* lavar; **she was bathed in sweat** estaba empapada en *or* de sudor

**3** *vi Old-fashioned (swim)* bañarse

**bather** ['beɪðə(r)] *n* bañista *mf*

**bathing** ['beɪðɪŋ] *n* **b. is prohibited** *(sign)* prohibido bañarse; **b. cap** gorro *m* de baño; **b. costume** bañador *m*, traje *m* de baño; **b. trunks** bañador *m* (de hombre)

**bathos** ['beɪθɒs] *n* = paso de lo sublime a lo común

**bathrobe** ['ba:θrəʊb] *n* albornoz *m*

**bathroom** ['ba:θru:m] *n* **(a)** *(with bath)* cuarto *m* de baño; **b. scales** báscula *f* de baño; **b. suite** = conjunto de bañera, lavabo e inodoro **(b)** *(toilet)* servicio *m*, retrete *m*; **to go to the b.** ir al servicio

**bathtub** ['ba:θtʌb] *n* bañera *f*

**batik** [bə'ti:k] *n* batik *m*

**batman** ['bætmən] *n Mil* ordenanza *m*

**baton** ['bætən] *n (in relay race)* testigo *m*; *(of conductor)* batuta *f*; *Br (of policeman)* porra *f*; **b. charge** carga *f* con porras

**batsman** ['bætsmən] *n (in cricket)* bateador *m*

**battalion** [bə'tæljən] *n* batallón *m*

**▸batten down** ['bætən] *vt insep* **to b. down the hatches** *(on ship)* cerrar las escotillas; *Fig (before crisis)* atarse *or* apretarse los machos

**batter¹** ['bætə(r)] *n (in baseball)* bateador(ora) *m,f*

**batter²** *n (in cooking)* pasta *f* para rebozar

**batter³** *vt (beat) (door)* aporrear; *(person)* pegar, maltratar

**battered** ['bætəd] *adj* **(a)** *(person)* maltratado(a) **(b)** *(furniture)* desvencijado(a); *(hat)* ajado(a); *(car)* abollado(a)

**battering ram** ['bætərɪŋ'ræm] *n* ariete *m*

**battery** ['bætərɪ] *(pl* **batteries)** *n* **(a)** *(of radio, clock)* pila *f*; *(of car, video camera)* batería *f*; **to be b. operated** *or* **powered** funcionar a *or* con pilas; **b. charger** cargador *m* de pilas/baterías **(b)** *Mil* batería *f*; *Fig* **a b. of criticism** un aluvión de críticas; *Psy* **a b. of tests** una batería de pruebas **(c)** **b. farming** avicultura *f* intensiva; **b. hen** gallina *f* de granja avícola intensiva

**battle** ['bætəl] **1** *n also Fig* batalla *f*; **to fight a b.** librar una batalla; **to do b. with sb** librar una batalla contra alguien; **a b. of wits** un duelo de ingenio; **that's half the b.** ya está recorrido medio camino; **b. cry** grito *m* de guerra; **b. royal** batalla campal

**2** *vi* batallar, luchar

**battleaxe** ['bætəlæks] *n (weapon)* hacha *f* de guerra; *Fam Pej (woman)* arpía *f*, bruja *f*

**battledress** ['bætəldres] *n* uniforme *m*

**battlefield** ['bætəlfi:ld], **battleground** ['bætəlgraʊnd] *n also Fig* campo *m* de batalla

**battle-hardened** ['bætəl'hɑ:dənd] *adj* curtido(a)

**battlements** ['bætəlmənts] *npl* almenas *fpl*

**battle-scarred** ['bætəl'skɑ:d] *adj (place)* minado(a) por la guerra *or* la batalla

**battleship** ['bætəlʃɪp] *n* acorazado *m*

**batty** ['bætɪ] *adj Fam* pirado(a), chiflado(a); **to be b.** *(of person)* estar chiflado(a) *or* pirado(a); *(of idea)* ser peregrino(a)

**bauble** ['bɔ:bəl] *n (cheap ornament)* chuchería *f*; *(Christmas decoration)* bola *f* de Navidad

**baud** [bɔ:d] *n Comptr* baudio *m*; **b. rate** velocidad *f* de transmisión

**baulk** [bɔ:k] **1** *vt (frustrate, defeat)* frustrar, hacer fracasar

**2** *vi* **to b. at sth** *(of person)* mostrarse reticente *or* echarse atrás ante algo; **he baulked at paying such a price** se mostraba reticente a pagar un precio tan alto

**bauxite** ['bɔ:ksaɪt] *n* bauxita *f*

**Bavaria** [bə'veərɪə] *n* Baviera

**Bavarian** [bə'veərɪən] n & adj bávaro(a) m,f

**bawdy** ['bɔ:dɪ] adj (remark, humour) picante, verde

**bawl** [bɔ:l] **1** vt gritar, proferir; **to b. an order** gritar una orden

**2** vi (**a**) (shout) gritar, vociferar (**b**) (cry) (of baby, child) berrear

▸**bawl out** vt sep (**a**) **to b. out an order** gritar una orden (**b**) Fam (reprimand) **to b. sb out** reñir or regañar a alguien

**bay¹** [beɪ] n (shrub) laurel m; **b. leaf** (hoja f de) laurel m

**bay²** **1** n (pl **bays**) (**a**) (on coastline) bahía f; **the B. of Bengal** el Golfo de Bengala; **the B. of Biscay** el Golfo de Vizcaya (**b**) Archit entrante m, hueco m; **loading b.** zona f de carga y descarga; **parking b.** plaza f de aparcamiento (señalizada); **b. window** ventana f salediza (**c**) **to keep** or **hold sth/sb at b.** tener a raya algo/a alguien

**2** vi (of dog, wolf) aullar

**bayonet** ['beɪənɪt] **1** n bayoneta f

**2** vt **to b. sb to death** matar a alguien a bayonetazos

**bazaar** [bə'zɑ:(r)] n (in Middle East) bazar m; (for charity) mercadillo m

**bazooka** [bə'zu:kə] n bazuca m, bazooka m

**B & B** [bi:ən'bi:] n Br (abbr **bed and breakfast**) (hotel) = hostal familiar en el que el desayuno está incluido en el precio de la habitación; (service) habitación f y desayuno

**BBC** [bi:bi:'si:] n (abbr **British Broadcasting Corporation**) BBC f, = radiotelevisión pública británica

**BC** [bi:'si:] adv (abbr **before Christ**) a.C., antes de Cristo

**BCG** [bi:si:'dʒi:] n Med (abbr **bacillus Calmette-Guérin**) B.C.G. m, = vacuna contra la tuberculosis

**be** [bi:]

En el inglés hablado, y en el escrito en estilo coloquial, el verbo **be** se contrae de forma que **I am** se transforma en **I'm**, **he/she/it is** se transforman en **he's/she's/it's** y **you/we/they are** se transforman en **you're/we're/they're**. Las formas negativas **is not**, **are not**, **was not** y **were not** se transforman en **isn't**, **aren't**, **wasn't** y **weren't**.

(present **I am**, **you/we/they are**, **he/she/it is**; pt **were** [wɜ:(r)]; 1st and 3rd person singular was [wɒz]; pp **been** [bi:n])

**1** vi (**a**) (indicating permanent quality, condition) ser; **sugar is sweet** el azúcar es dulce; **it's two metres wide** tiene dos metros de ancho; **three and two are five** tres y dos (son) cinco; **she is English** es inglesa; **he is clever** es inteligente; **I'm a doctor** soy médico

(**b**) (indicating temporary state) estar; **to be wet/**

**dry** estar seco(a)/mojado(a); **the bottle is empty/full** la botella está vacía/llena; **to be cold/hot** (of person) tener frío/calor; (of thing) estar frío(a)/caliente; **it's cold/hot** (weather) hace frío/calor; **to be hungry/thirsty** tener hambre/sed; **to be right** tener razón; **to be wrong** estar equivocado(a); **to be twenty (years old)** tener veinte años

(**c**) (with time, date) ser; **it's six o'clock** son las seis (en punto); **when is the concert?** ¿cuándo es el concierto?; **today is the tenth** hoy estamos a (día) diez; **what day is it today?** ¿qué día es hoy?; **it's a year since I saw her** hace un año que no la veo

(**d**) (with location) estar; **where is the station?** ¿dónde está la estación?; **is this where you work?** ¿es aquí donde trabajas?; **to be at home** estar en casa; **where was I?** (after digression) ¿por dónde iba?

(**e**) (with cost) ser, costar; **how much are the shoes?** ¿cuánto son or cuestan los zapatos?; **how much is it?** ¿cuánto es?; **how much is a kilo of beef?** ¿a cuánto está el kilo de ternera?

(**f**) (with health) estar; **how are you?** ¿cómo estás?; **I'm fine** estoy bien; **he's better** está mejor

(**g**) (with imperatives) **be good!** ¡sé bueno!; **be still!** ¡estate quieto!; **don't be stupid!** ¡no seas tonto!; **let's be reasonable** seamos razonables

(**h**) (with question tags) **she's beautiful, isn't she?** es guapa ¿verdad?; **they're big, aren't they?** son grandes ¿verdad?; **you aren't from around here, are you?** tú no eres de aquí, ¿no?

(**i**) (as past participle of go) **I have been to London** he estado en Londres

**2** v aux (**a**) (in continuous tenses) estar; **to be doing sth** estar haciendo algo; **she is/was laughing** se está/estaba riendo; **I'm leaving tomorrow** me voy mañana; **I've been waiting for hours** llevo horas esperando

(**b**) (in passives) ser; **six employees were made redundant** fueron despedidos seis empleados; **they have been seen in London** han sido vistos or se les ha visto en Londres; **he was killed** lo mataron; **she is respected by all** todos la respetan

(**c**) (followed by infinitive) **the house is to be sold** la casa se va a vender; **he was never to see them again** nunca volvería a verlos; **you are not to mention this to anyone** no debes decir esto a nadie

**beach** [bi:tʃ] **1** n playa f; **b. ball** balón m or pelota f de playa; **b. hut** caseta f

**2** vt (boat, ship) varar

**beachcomber** ['bi:tʃkəʊmə(r)] n raquero(a) m,f

**beachhead** ['biːtʃhed] *n Mil* cabeza *f* de playa

**beacon** ['biːkən] *n (for plane, ship)* baliza *f*; *(lighthouse)* faro *m*; *(bonfire)* hoguera *f*, *Fig* **a b. of hope** un rayo de esperanza

**bead** [biːd] *n (of glass)* cuenta *f*; *(of dew, sweat)* gota *f*, perla *f*; **a string of beads** unas cuentas ensartadas

**beady** ['biːdɪ] *adj* **he had his b. eyes on it** lo miraba intensamente

**beagle** ['biːgəl] *n* beagle *m*

**beak** [biːk] *n* **(a)** *(of bird)* pico *m*; *Fam (nose)* napias *fpl* **(b)** *Br Fam (magistrate)* juez *m*

**beaker** ['biːkə(r)] *n* vaso *m* (generalmente de plástico)

**be-all and end-all** ['biːɔːlə'nendɔːl] *n Fam* **the b.** lo más importante del mundo

**beam** [biːm] **1** *n* **(a)** *(in building)* viga *f*; *(in gymnastics)* barra *f* de equilibrio **(b)** *(of light)* rayo *f*; *Phys* haz *m* **(c)** *(idioms) Fam* **you're way off b.** te equivocas de medio a medio; *Fam* **broad in the b.** *(of person)* ancho(a) de caderas

**2** *vt (programme)* emitir; *(information)* mandar, enviar

**3** *vi (shine) (of sun, moon)* brillar; **to b. with pride/pleasure** sonreír con orgullo/de placer

**bean** [biːn] *n* **(a)** *(vegetable)* alubia *f*, judía *f*, habichuela *f*; *(of coffee)* grano *m*; **(green) b.** judía *f* verde, *CSur* poroto *m* verde, *Méx* ejote *m*; **b. curd** tofu *m* **(b)** *Fam (idioms)* **to be full of beans** estar lleno(a) de vitalidad; **it isn't worth a b.** no vale un pimiento; **he hasn't a b.** no tiene (ni) un duro

**beanbag** ['biːnbæg] *n (for juggling)* bola *f* de malabares; *(for sitting on)* puf *m* relleno de bolitas

**beanfeast** ['biːnfiːst] *n Br Hum* francachela *f*

**beanpole** ['biːnpəʊl] *n* **(a)** *(stick)* guía *f*, rodrigón *m* **(b)** *Fam (tall, thin person)* larguirucho(a) *m,f*, espagueti *m*

**beansprouts** ['biːnspraʊts] *npl* brotes *mpl* de soja

**beanstalk** ['biːnstɔːk] *n* tallo *m* de judía

**bear¹** [beə(r)] *n (animal)* oso(a) *m,f*; **b. cub** osezno *m*; **to give sb a b. hug** dar un fuerte abrazo a alguien; *Fin* **b. market** mercado *m* a la baja

**bear²** [*pt* bore [bɔː(r)], *pp* borne [bɔːn]) **1** *vt* **(a)** *(carry)* llevar; *(bring)* traer, portar; *(weight, load)* soportar; **to b. sth away** llevarse algo; **to b. sth in mind** tener algo presente or en cuenta; **it bears no relation to...** no tiene nada que ver con...; **we will b. the costs** correremos con los gastos; **to b. the responsibility for sth** cargar con la responsabilidad de algo

**(b)** *(endure)* soportar, aguantar; **I can't b. him** no puedo soportarlo, no lo soporto; **I could b.**
it no longer no podía aguantar más; **it doesn't b. thinking about** no quiero ni pensarlo

**(c)** *(produce)* **she bore him three children** le dio tres hijos; **to b. interest** *(of investment)* devengar intereses; **to b. fruit** *(of tree)* dar fruto, fructificar; *(of effort, plan)* dar fruto(s), ser fructífero(a)

**2** *vi (move)* **to b. (to the) right/left** echarse hacia la derecha/izquierda

▶**bear down (up)on** *vt insep* abalanzarse sobre

▶**bear out** *vt sep (theory)* corroborar, confirmar

▶**bear up** *vi* resistir; **b. up!** ¡ánimo!

▶**bear with** *vt insep* tener paciencia con; **if you could b. with me a minute...** si no le importa esperar un momento...

**bearable** ['beərəbəl] *adj* soportable

**beard** [bɪəd] *n* barba *f*; **to grow/have a b.** dejarse/tener barba

**bearded** ['bɪədɪd] *adj* con barba

**bearer** ['beərə(r)] *n (of news, cheque)* portador(ora) *m,f*; *(of passport)* titular *mf*

**bearing** ['beərɪŋ] *n* **(a)** *(of person)* porte *m* **(b)** *(in mechanism, engine)* cojinete *m*, rodamiento *m* **(c)** *(orientation)* **to find** *or* **get one's bearings** orientarse; **to lose one's bearings** desorientarse **(d)** *(relevance)* relación *f* (**on** con); **it has no b. on the matter** es ajeno al asunto

**beast** [biːst] *n* **(a)** *(animal)* bestia *f*, animal *m*; **b. of burden** bestia de carga *Fam (unpleasant person)* bestia *mf*; **a b. of a job** un trabajo de chinos

**beastly** ['biːstlɪ] *adj Fam (smell, taste)* horroroso(a); **to be b. to sb** portarse como un canalla con alguien; **what b. weather!** ¡qué tiempo tan horrible!

**beat** [biːt] **1** *n* **(a)** *(of heart)* latido *m*; *(in music) (rhythm)* ritmo *m*; *(in bar)* tiempo *m*

**(b)** *Br (of policeman)* ronda *f*; **on the b.** de ronda

**2** *adj Fam (exhausted)* **to be dead b.** estar hecho(a) polvo

**3** *vt (pt* beat, *pp* beaten ['biːtən]) **(a)** *(hit) (person)* golpear *(repetidamente)*; *(eggs)* batir; **to b. a drum** tocar el tambor; **to b. the retreat** batirse en retirada; **to b. a path through the crowd** abrirse camino entre la multitud; *Fam* **b. it!** ¡lárgo!, ¡esfúmate!; **the bird beat its wings** el pájaro batió las alas

**(b)** *(defeat)* ganar; **we beat them easily** les ganamos sin dificultad; **that will take some beating** eso va a ser difícil de mejorar; **I got up early to b. the rush hour** me levanté temprano para adelantarme a la hora punta; **he beat me to it** se me adelantó; **you can't b. a good book** no hay nada mejor que un buen libro; *Prov* **if you can't b. them, join them** si no puedes vencer al enemigo, únete a él; *Fam* **that beats everything!** ¡es lo mejor que he oído en mi vida!; *Fam* **it beats me why he did it** no tengo ni idea de por qué lo hizo

**4** *vi* **(a)** *(of heart)* latir

**(b) to b. about** *or* **around the bush** andarse por las ramas

▸**beat back** *vt sep* rechazar

▸**beat down 1** *vt sep (price)* conseguir una rebaja en; **I b. him down to £40 for the dress** conseguí que me dejara el vestido en 40 libras

**2** *vi (of rain)* caer con fuerza; *(of sun)* caer a plomo

▸**beat off** *vt sep* rechazar

▸**beat out** *vt sep (fire, flames)* apagar

▸**beat up** *vt sep (assault)* dar una paliza a

**beaten** ['biːtən] **1** *adj* **b. earth** tierra *f* batida; *Fig* **off the b. track** retirado(a)

**2** *pp* of **beat**

**beater** ['biːtə(r)] *n* **(a)** *(in hunting)* ojeador(ora) *m,f* **(b)** *(in cookery)* batidora *f*, batidor *m*

**beatification** [biːætɪfɪ'keɪʃən] *n Rel* beatificación *f*

**beating** ['biːtɪŋ] *n (assault, defeat)* paliza *f*; **to give sb a b.** dar una paliza a alguien

**beatitude** [bɪ'ætɪtjuːd] *n Rel* beatitud *f*; **the Beatitudes** *(in the Bible)* las Bienaventuranzas

**beat-up** ['biːtʌp] *adj Fam (car)* desvencijado(a)

**beaut** [bjuːt] *n Fam* **what a b.!** ¡qué preciosidad!

**beautician** [bjuːˈtɪʃən] *n* esteticista *mf*

**beautiful** ['bjuːtɪfʊl] *adj (woman)* bonita, guapa; *(child, animal)* bonito(a), precioso(a); *(music, dress, landscape)* hermoso(a), precioso(a); *(smell, taste)* delicioso(a)

**beautifully** ['bjuːtɪfʊlɪ] *adv* de maravilla

**beautify** ['bjuːtɪfaɪ] *vt* embellecer

**beauty** ['bjuːtɪ] *n (attribute, person)* belleza *f*; *(object)* preciosidad *f*; **that's the b. of it** eso es lo mejor; **b. contest** concurso *m* de belleza; **b. parlour** *or* **salon** salón *m* de belleza; **b. queen** miss *f*; **b. spot** *(on face)* lunar *m*; *(in country)* paraje *m* de gran belleza

**beaver** ['biːvə(r)] *n* castor *m*

▸**beaver away** *vi* afanarse, aplicarse **(at** en)

**becalmed** [bɪ'kɑːmd] *adj* **the ship lay b.** el barco estaba al pairo

**became** [bɪ'keɪm] *pt of* **become**

**because** [bɪ'kɒz] *conj* porque; **why? – just b.** ¿por qué? – porque sí; **b. of** debido a, a causa de

**beck** [bek] *n* **to be at sb's b. and call** estar a (la entera) disposición de alguien

**beckon** ['bekən] **1** *vt* **to b. sb in** hacer a alguien una seña para que entre

**2** *vi* **to b. to sb** hacer una seña a alguien; *Fig* **I can't stay, work beckons** no puedo quedarme, el trabajo me reclama; *Fig* **the beach**

beckoned la playa era una gran tentación; *Fig* **fame beckoned** la fama llamó a mi/su *etc* puerta

**become** [bɪ'kʌm] *(pt* **became** [bɪ'keɪm]*, pp* **become) 1** *vi* **(a)** *(a teacher, a doctor)* hacerse; *(boring, jealous, suspicious)* volverse; *(old, difficult, stronger)* hacerse; *(happy, sad, thin)* ponerse; **to b. angry/interested** enfadarse/interesarse; **to b. king** convertirse en rey; **to b. known** saberse

**(b) what will b. of him?** ¿qué va a ser de él?; **I don't know what has become of her** no sé qué ha sido de ella

**2** *vt Formal (of clothes, colour)* sentar bien a; **such behaviour doesn't b. you** ese comportamiento no es propio *or* digno de ti

**becoming** [bɪ'kʌmɪŋ] *adj (behaviour)* apropiado(a); **green looks very b. on her** le sienta muy bien el verde

**BEd** [biː'ed] *n Univ (abbr* **Bachelor of Education)** *(qualification)* licenciatura *f* en ciencias de la educación; *(person)* licenciado(a) *m,f* en ciencias de la educación

**bed** [bed] **1** *n* **(a)** *(for sleeping)* cama *f*; **to be in b.** estar en la cama; **to go to b.** irse a la cama, acostarse; **to put a child to b.** acostar a un niño; **to go to b. with sb** irse a la cama con alguien; *Fam* **to have got out of b. on the wrong side** haberse levantado con el pie izquierdo; **b. and breakfast** *(hotel)* = hostal familiar en el que el desayuno está incluido en el precio de la habitación; *(service)* habitación *f* y desayuno; **b. linen** ropa *f* de cama

**(b)** *(of river)* lecho *m*, cauce *m*

**(c)** *(of flowers)* macizo *m*

**(d)** *Geol* estrato *m*

**(e)** *(of rice, lettuce)* base *f*, lecho *m*

**2** *vt (pt & pp* **bedded)** *Old-fashioned* acostarse con

▸**bed down** *vi* **to b. down (for the night)** acostarse

**bedbug** ['bedbʌg] *n* chinche *f*

**bedclothes** ['bedkləʊðz] *npl* ropa *f* de cama

**bedding** ['bedɪŋ] *n (sheets, blankets)* ropa *f* de cama

**bedevil** [bɪ'devəl] *(pt & pp* **bedevilled**, *US* **bedeviled)** *vt* **to be bedevilled by problems** tener muchos problemas; **to be bedevilled by bad luck** tener la negra, estar maldito(a)

**bedfellow** ['bedfeləʊ] *n Fig* **they make strange bedfellows** forman una extraña pareja

**bedlam** ['bedləm] *n* jaleo *m*, alboroto *m*

**Bedouin** ['beduːm] *n & adj* beduino(a) *m,f*

**bedpan** ['bedpæn] *n* cuña *f*

**bedpost** ['bedpəʊst] *n* pilar *f* de la cama

**bedraggled** [bɪ'drægəld] *adj* desaliñado(a) y empapado(a)

**bedridden** ['bedrɪdən] *adj* **to be b.** estar postrado(a) en la cama

**bedrock** ['bedrɒk] *n Geol* lecho *m* rocoso; *Fig (of beliefs, faith)* base *f*, fondo *m*

**bedroll** ['bedrəʊl] *n* petate *m*

**bedroom** ['bedru:m] *n* dormitorio *m*, *Am* recámara *f*; *(in hotel)* habitación *f*

**bedside** ['bedsaɪd] *n* **at sb's b.** al lado de la cama de alguien; **b. lamp** lamparita *f* de noche; **b. manner** *(of doctor)* actitud *f* ante el paciente; **b. table** mesilla *f* or mesita *f* (de noche)

**bedsit** ['bedsɪt] *n Br* cuarto *m* de alquiler

**bedsock** ['bedsɒk] *n* calcetín *m* para dormir

**bedsore** ['bedsɔ:(r)] *n* úlcera *f* de decúbito

**bedspread** ['bedspred] *n* colcha *f*

**bedstead** ['bedsted] *n* (armazón *m* or *f* de la) cama *f*

**bedtime** ['bedtaɪm] *n* **it's b.!** ¡es hora de irse a la cama!; **what's your usual b.?** ¿a qué hora te sueles acostar?; **it's past my b.** ya debería estar acostado; **b. story** cuento *m (contado antes de acostarse)*

**bed-wetting** ['bedwetɪŋ] *n* enuresis *f* inv

**bee** [bi:] *n* abeja *f*; *Fam* **to have a b. in one's bonnet about sth** estar obsesionado(a) con algo; *Br Fam* **she thinks she's the b.'s knees** se cree superior al resto de los mortales

**beech** [bi:tʃ] *n* haya *f*

**beechnut** ['bi:tʃnʌt] *n* hayuco *m*

**beef** [bi:f] **1** *n* **(a)** *(meat)* (carne *f* de) vaca *f* or *Am* res; **b. stew** guiso *m* de vaca **(b)** *Fam (strength)* **to have plenty of b.** estar cachas; **give it some b.!** ¡un poco más de esfuerzo! **(c)** *Fam (complaint)* queja *f*
**2** *vi Fam (complain)* quejarse **(about** de)
▸**beef up** *vt sep Fam (text, resources)* ampliar

**beefburger** ['bi:fbɜ:gə(r)] *n* hamburguesa *f*

**Beefeater** ['bi:fi:tə(r)] *n* = guardia de la Torre de Londres

**beefsteak** ['bi:fsteɪk] *n* filete *m*, bistec *m*

**beefy** ['bi:fɪ] *adj Fam (muscular)* muy cachas, fornido(a)

**beehive** ['bi:haɪv] *n* colmena *f*

**beekeeper** ['bi:ki:pə(r)] *n* apicultor(ora) *m,f*, colmenero(a) *m,f*

**beeline** ['bi:laɪn] *n Fam* **to make a b. for sth** ir directamente hacia algo

**been** [bi:n] *pp of* **be**

**beep** [bi:p] **1** *n (sound)* pitido *m*
**2** *vt (page)* llamar *(a un busca)*
**3** *vi* pitar

**beer** [bɪə(r)] *n* cerveza *f*; **to go for a b.** ir a tomar una cerveza; **b. garden** terraza *f* (interior) de un bar; **b. glass** jarra *f* de cerveza

**beery** ['bɪərɪ] *adj (smell, breath, taste)* a cerveza

**beeswax** ['bi:zwæks] *n* cera *f* (de abeja)

**beet** [bi:t] *n* **(a)** *(sugar beet)* remolacha *f* (azucarera) **(b)** *US (beetroot)* remolacha *f*

**beetle** ['bi:təl] *n* escarabajo *m*

**beetroot** ['bi:tru:t] *n* remolacha *f*; *Fam* **to go b.** ponerse colorado(a) como un tomate

**befall** [bɪ'fɔ:l] *(pt* **befell** [bɪ'fel]*, pp* **befallen** [bɪ'fɔ:lən]*) vt Literary* sobrevenir

**befit** [bɪ'fɪt] *(pt & pp* **befitted***) vt* ser digno(a) de

**befitting** [bɪ'fɪtɪŋ] *adj* digno(a)

**before** [bɪ'fɔ:(r)] **1** *prep* **(a)** *(with time)* antes de; **b. Christmas** antes de Navidad; **I got here b. you** he llegado antes que tú; **the day b. the battle** la víspera de la batalla; **b. that,...** antes (de eso)...
**(b)** *(with place)* ante, delante de; **b. my very eyes** ante mis propios ojos; **to appear b. the judge** comparecer ante el juez
**(c)** *(in importance)* **she puts her family b. everything else** su familia es lo primero para ella
**2** *adv* **(a)** *(with time)* antes; **two days b.** dos días antes; **the day/year b.** el día/año anterior; **I have seen him b.** lo he visto antes; **I've told you b.** ya te lo he dicho (otras veces)
**(b)** *(in space)* **this page and the one b.** esta página y la anterior
**3** *conj* antes de que; **come and see me b. you leave** ven a verme antes de marcharte; **b. I forget, will you...** antes de que se me olvide, ¿podrías...?; **give it to her b. she cries** dáselo antes de que empiece a llorar

**beforehand** [bɪ'fɔ:hænd] *adv (in advance)* de antemano; **two hours b.** con dos horas de antelación, dos horas antes; **I must tell you b. that...** debo prevenirte de que...

**befriend** [bɪ'frend] *vt* hacerse amigo(a) de

**befuddled** [bɪ'fʌdəld] *adj (confused)* aturdido(a); **to be b. (with)** estar aturdido(a) (por)

**beg** [beg] *(pt & pp* **begged***)* **1** *vt* **to b. sb to do sth** rogar or suplicar a alguien que haga algo; **to b. a favour of sb** pedir un favor a alguien; **to b. forgiveness** pedir or implorar perdón; **I b. your pardon** *(I apologize)* perdón; *(what did you say?)* ¿cómo dice?; **I b. to differ** me temo que no comparto tu opinión; **this begs the question why** esto nos lleva a preguntarnos el porqué
**2** *vi* **to b. for sth** *(money, food)* mendigar algo; *(help, a chance)* pedir or rogar algo; **to b. for mercy** implorar clemencia; **these jobs are going begging** estos trabajos los hay a patadas

**began** [bɪ'gæn] *pt of* **begin**

**beggar** ['begə(r)] **1** *n* mendigo(a) *m,f*; *Br Fam* **poor b.!** ¡pobre diablo!; *Br Fam* **lucky b.!** ¡qué suertudo(a)!; *Prov* **beggars can't be choosers** a buen hambre no hay pan duro
**2** *vt* **to b. description** *(be impossible to describe)*

resultar indescriptible; *(of sth bad)* no tener nombre; **to b. belief** ser difícil de creer

**begin** [bɪ'gɪn] ( *pt* **began** [bɪ'gæn], *pp* **begun** [bɪ'gʌn]) **1** *vt* empezar, comenzar; **to b. a new job** empezar en un trabajo nuevo; **to b. to do sth, to b. doing sth** empezar *or* comenzar a hacer algo; **I couldn't (even) b. to describe** no sé ni cómo empezar a describir

**2** *vi* empezar, comenzar; **to b. by doing sth** empezar por hacer algo; **to b. again** comenzar de nuevo; **to b. with,...** para empezar,...

**beginner** [bɪ'gɪnə(r)] *n* principiante *mf*

**beginning** [bɪ'gɪnɪŋ] *n* principio *m*, comienzo *m*; **in** *or* **at the b.** al principio; **at the b. of the year/month** a principios de año/mes; **from the b.** desde el principio; **from b. to end** de principio a fin; **the b. of the end** el principio del fin; **the first beginnings of civilization** los orígenes de la civilización; **the problem has its beginnings in...** el problema tiene su origen en...

**begonia** [bɪ'gəʊnɪə] *n* begonia *f*

**begrudge** [bɪ'grʌdʒ] *vt* **(a)** *(resent)* **I b. spending so much money** me duele gastar tanto **(b)** *(envy)* **I don't b. him his success** no le envidio su éxito

**beguile** [bɪ'gaɪl] *vt* **(a)** *(enchant)* seducir **(b)** *(deceive)* engañar; **to b. sb into doing sth** engatusar a alguien para que haga algo; **to b. sb with promises** encandilar a alguien con promesas

**beguiling** [bɪ'gaɪlɪŋ] *adj* seductor(ora)

**begun** [bɪ'gʌn] *pp of* **begin**

**behalf** [bɪ'hɑːf] *n* **on b. of sb, on sb's b.** en nombre de alguien; **don't worry on my b.** no te preocupes por mí

**behave** [bɪ'heɪv] *vi (of person)* portarse, comportarse; *(of car, machine)* funcionar; **to b. (well)** portarse bien; **to b. badly** portarse mal; **what a way to b.!** ¡menudo comportamiento!; **b. (yourself)!** ¡compórtate como es debido!

**behaviour,** *US* **behavior** [bɪ'heɪvjə(r)] *n* comportamiento *m*, conducta *f*; **to be on one's best b.** (com)portarse muy bien

**behavioural,** *US* **behavioral** [bɪ'heɪvjərəl] *adj* del comportamiento, de la conducta

**behaviourism,** *US* **behaviorism** [bɪ'heɪvjərɪzəm] *n Psy* conductismo *m*

**behead** [bɪ'hed] *vt* decapitar

**behest** [bɪ'hest] *n* **at sb's b., at the b. of sb** por orden *or* a instancias de alguien

**behind** [bɪ'haɪnd] **1** *prep* detrás de, tras; **to be b. sb** *(situated)* estar detrás de alguien; *(support)* respaldar a alguien; **to follow close b. sb** seguir de cerca a alguien; **look b. you** mira detrás de ti; **to be b. schedule** ir atrasado(a); **to put**

**sth b. one** dejar algo atrás; **let's put it all b. us** olvidemos todo esto; **she's ten minutes b. the leaders** *(in race)* está a diez minutos de la cabeza de la carrera; **to be b. the times** no andar con los tiempos; **the reasons b. sth** los motivos de algo; **what's b. all this?** ¿qué hay detrás de todo esto?

**2** *adv* atrás; **from b.** *(attack)* por la espalda; **to stay** *or* **remain b.** quedarse; **to leave sth b.** dejarse algo; **to be b. with one's work/with the rent** estar atrasado(a) en el trabajo/en el pago del alquiler; **they are only three points b.** *(in contest)* están a sólo tres puntos

**3** *n Fam (buttocks)* trasero *m*

**behindhand** [bɪ'haɪndhænd] *adv* **to be b. with one's work/with the rent** estar atrasado(a) en el trabajo/en el pago del alquiler

**behold** [bɪ'həʊld] ( *pt & pp* **beheld** [bɪ'held]) *vt Literary* contemplar

**beholden** [bɪ'həʊldən] *adj Formal* **to be b. to sb** estar en deuda con alguien

**beholder** [bɪ'həʊldə(r)] *n Prov* **beauty is in the eye of the b.** sobre gustos no hay nada escrito

**beige** [beɪʒ] *n & adj* beige *m inv*, beis *m inv*

**Beijing** [beɪ'ʒɪŋ] *n* Pekín

**being** ['biːŋ] *n* **(a)** *(creature)* ser *m* **(b)** *(existence)* **to come into b.** nacer; **the company is no longer in b.** la empresa ya no existe; **with all my b.** con todo mi corazón

**Beirut** [beɪ'ruːt] *n* Beirut

**belabour,** *US* **belabor** [bɪ'leɪbə(r)] *vt* apalear; **to b. sb with insults** poner verde a alguien

**Belarus** [belə'ruːs] *n* Bielorrusia

**belated** [bɪ'leɪtɪd] *adj* tardío(a); **wishing you a b. happy birthday** deseándote, con retraso, un feliz cumpleaños

**belch** [beltʃ] **1** *n (burp)* eructo *m*

**2** *vt (smoke, flames)* escupir

**3** *vi (of person)* eructar

**beleaguered** [bɪ'liːgəd] *adj (city, army)* sitiado(a), asediado(a); *(government)* acosado(a); *(person)* atormentado(a)

**Belfast** [bel'fɑːst] *n* Belfast

**belfry** ['belfrɪ] *n* campanario *m*

**Belgian** ['beldʒən] *n & adj* belga *mf*

**Belgium** ['beldʒəm] *n* Bélgica

**Belgrade** [bel'greɪd] *n* Belgrado

**belie** [bɪ'laɪ] *vt* contradecir

**belief** [bɪ'liːf] *n* **(a)** *(conviction)* creencia *f*; **in the b. that...** en el convencimiento de que...; **it is my b. that...** estoy convencido(a) de que...; **it is beyond b.** es imposible de creer **(b)** *(confidence)* confianza *f*, fe *f*; **to have b. in oneself** tener confianza en uno(a) mismo(a)

**believable** [bɪ'liːvəbəl] *adj* verosímil

**believe** [bɪ'liːv] **1** vt creer; **I b. (that) I am right** creo no equivocarme; **I b. him to be alive** creo que está vivo; **she is believed to be here** se cree que está aquí; **I don't b. a word of it** no me creo (ni) una palabra; **I could scarcely b. my eyes** no podía creer lo que veían mis ojos; **I don't b. it!** ¡no me lo puedo creer!; **I can well b. it** no me extrañaría nada

**2** vi **(a)** (have faith) creer; **to b. in God** creer en Dios; **to b. in sb** (have confidence) creer en alguien, tener fe en alguien; **to b. in oneself** tener confianza en uno(a) mismo(a) **(b)** (be in favour) **to b. in sth** ser partidario(a) de algo; **I don't b. in making promises** no soy partidario de las promesas **(c)** (think, suppose) creer; **I b. not** creo que no; **I b. so** así lo creo, creo que sí

**believer** [bɪ'liːvə(r)] n **(a)** (religious person) creyente mf **(b)** (supporter) **to be a b. in sth** ser partidario(a) de algo

**belittle** [bɪ'lɪtəl] vt menospreciar, restar importancia a; **to b. oneself** restarse importancia

**Belize** [be'liːz] n Belice

**bell** [bel] n (of church) campana f; (handbell) campanilla f; (on door, bicycle) timbre m; (on cat, hat) cascabel m; **to ring the b.** (on door) llamar al timbre; Br Fam **to give sb a b.** dar un telefonazo a alguien; **b. jar** campana de cristal; **b. tower** (torre f del) campanario m

**belladonna** [belə'dɒnə] n (plant) belladona f; (poison) atropina f

**bell-bottoms** ['belbɒtəmz] npl pantalones mpl de campana; **a pair of b.** unos pantalones de campana

**bellboy** ['belbɔɪ] n US Fam botones m inv

**belle** [bel] n bella f, belleza f

**bellhop** ['belhɒp] n US Fam botones m inv

**bellicose** ['belɪkəʊs] adj belicoso(a)

**belligerence** [be'lɪdʒərəns] n beligerancia f

**belligerent** [be'lɪdʒərənt] **1** n contendiente m

**2** adj beligerante

**bellow** ['beləʊ] **1** n bramido m

**2** vi bramar

**bellows** ['beləʊz] npl fuelle m; **a pair of b.** un fuelle

**bell-ringer** ['belrɪŋə(r)] n campanero(a) m,f

**belly** ['belɪ] n vientre m, barriga f; **to have a full/an empty b.** tener la barriga llena/vacía; **b. dance** danza f del vientre; **b. laugh** sonora carcajada f

**bellyache** ['belɪeɪk] Fam **1** n dolor m de barriga

**2** vi (complain) quejarse (**about** de)

**bellybutton** ['belɪbʌtən] n Fam ombligo m

**belly-flop** ['belɪflɒp] **1** n to do a b. darse un panzazo or tripazo

**2** vi (pt & pp **belly-flopped**) darse un panzazo or tripazo

**bellyful** ['belɪfʊl] n Fam **I've had a b. of his complaints!** ¡estoy hasta el gorro de sus quejas!

**belong** [bɪ'lɒŋ] vi **(a)** **to b. to** (be property of) pertenecer a; **that book belongs to me** este libro me pertenece **(b)** **to b. to** (be member of) (club) pertenecer a, ser socio(a) de; (party) pertenecer a, estar afiliado(a) a **(c)** (have a proper place) ir; **to put sth back where it belongs** devolver algo a su sitio; **the saucepans don't b. in that cupboard** las ollas no van en esa alacena; **I feel I b. here** aquí me siento (como) en casa; **to feel that one doesn't b.** sentirse un(a) extraño(a)

**belonging** [bɪ'lɒŋɪŋ] n **to have a sense of b.** sentirse (como) en casa

**belongings** [bɪ'lɒŋɪŋz] npl pertenencias fpl; **personal b.** efectos mpl personales

**beloved 1** n [bɪ'lʌvɪd] Literary amado(a) m,f

**2** adj [bɪ'lʌvd] amado(a), querido(a)

**below** [bɪ'ləʊ] **1** prep debajo de, bajo, Am abajo de; **b. the knee** por debajo de la rodilla; **10 degrees b. zero** 10 (grados) bajo cero; **b. sea level** por debajo del nivel del mar; **b. the surface** bajo la superficie

**2** adv abajo; **see b.** (on document) ver más abajo or adelante; **on the floor b.** en el piso de abajo; **it's 10 degrees b.** hace 10 grados bajo cero

**belt** [belt] **1** n **(a)** (for trousers) cinturón m, correa f; Fig **to tighten one's b.** apretarse el cinturón; Fig **now that I've got some experience under my b.** ahora que tengo algo de experiencia a mis espaldas; **to hit sb below the b.** (in boxing) dar un golpe bajo a alguien; Fig **that was a bit below the b.!** (of remark, criticism) ¡eso ha sido un golpe bajo! **(b)** (of machine) correa f **(c)** (of land) franja f, cinturón m **(d)** Fam (blow) golpetazo m; **to give sb a b.** dar a alguien un golpetazo

**2** vt (hit) dar un golpetazo a; (with belt) dar correazos a; (ball) pegar un cañonazo a

**3** vi Fam (move quickly) **to b. along** ir a toda pastilla; **she belted down the stairs** bajó las escaleras a toda pastilla

▶**belt out** vt sep Fam (sing loudly) cantar a grito pelado

▶**belt up** vi Br very Fam (be silent) **b. up!** ¡cierra el pico!

**bemoan** [bɪ'məʊn] vt lamentar, lamentarse de

**bemused** [bɪ'mjuːzd] adj perplejo(a), desconcertado(a); **to be b.** estar perplejo(a) or desconcertado(a)

**bench** [bentʃ] n (seat, work table) banco m; Parl escaños mpl; Br Law **the B.** la magistratura; **to be on the b.** (in football) estar en el banquillo

**benchmark** ['bentʃmɑːk] *n (for comparison)* punto *m* de referencia

**bend** [bend] **1** *n* (a) *(of road, river)* curva *f*; *(of pipe, arm)* codo *m*; *Fam* **to be round the b.** estar pirado(a); *Fam* **to drive sb round the b.** poner a alguien a cien or fuera de sí (b) **the bends** *(decompression sickness)* enfermedad *f* de los buzos; *Med* aeroembolismo *m*

**2** *vt (pt & pp* **bent** [bent]*)* doblar; **to b. one's arm/back** doblar el brazo/la espalda; **do not b.** *(on envelope)* no doblar; **on bended knee** de rodillas; **to b. the rules** ser flexible en la interpretación de las reglas; *Br Fam* **he bent my ear** *(told me his problems)* me contó sus penas

**3** *vi (of road, river)* hacer una curva, girar; **to b. under the strain of sth** ceder bajo la presión de algo

▸**bend down** *vi* agacharse

▸**bend over** *vi* agacharse; **to b. over backwards for sb/to do sth** desvivirse por alguien/por hacer algo

**bender** ['bendə(r)] *n Fam* **to go on a b.** ir de marcha

**beneath** [bɪ'niːθ] **1** *prep* (a) *(physically)* debajo de, bajo (b) *(unworthy of)* **to marry b. one** casarse con alguien de clase social inferior; **she thinks it's b. her to work** cree que trabajar supondría rebajarse; **b. contempt** (completamente) despreciable

**2** *adv* abajo; **from b.** desde abajo

**Benedictine** [benɪ'dɪktɪn] *n & adj Rel* benedictino(a) *m,f*

**benediction** [benɪ'dɪkʃən] *n Rel* bendición *f*

**benefactor** ['benɪfæktə(r)] *n* benefactor *m*

**benefactress** ['benɪfæktrɪs] *n* benefactora *f*

**beneficent** [bɪ'nefɪsənt] *adj* benéfico(a)

**beneficial** [benɪ'fɪʃəl] *adj* beneficioso(a) **(to** para)

**beneficiary** [benɪ'fɪʃərɪ] *n* beneficiario(a) *m,f*

**benefit** ['benɪfɪt] **1** *n* (a) *(advantages)* beneficio *m*, provecho *m*; *(individual advantage)* ventaja *f*; **to have the b. of sth** contar con algo; **to derive b. from** sacar provecho de; **for sb's b.**, **for the b. of sb** en atención a alguien; **that remark was for your b.** ese comentario iba dirigido a ti; **to give sb the b. of the doubt** dar a alguien el beneficio de la duda

(b) *(charity event)* acto *m* benéfico; **b. match** *(in football)* partido *m* benéfico

(c) *(state payment)* prestación *f*, subsidio *m*; **to be on b.** cobrar un subsidio; **social security benefits** prestaciones *fpl* sociales

**2** *vt* beneficiar, favorecer

**3** *vi* **to b. by** *or* **from** beneficiarse de, sacar provecho de

**Benelux** ['benɪlʌks] *n* (el) Benelux; **the B. countries** los países del Benelux

**benevolence** [bɪ'nevələns] *n* benevolencia *f*

**benevolent** [bɪ'nevələnt] *adj* benévolo(a); **b. society** cofradía *f* benéfica

**Bengal** [beŋ'gɔːl] *n* Bengala

**Bengali** [beŋ'gɔːlɪ] **1** *n* (a) *(person)* bengalí *mf* (b) *(language)* bengalí *m*

**2** *adj* bengalí

**benign** [bɪ'naɪn] *adj (attitude, look)* bondadoso(a); *(climate, tumour)* benigno(a)

**Benin** [be'niːn] *n* Benín

**bent** [bent] **1** *n (inclination)* inclinación *f*; **to have a natural b. for music** tener una inclinación natural por la música

**2** *adj* (a) *(curved)* torcido(a), curvado(a) (b) *Fam (dishonest)* corrupto(a); **a b. copper** un policía corrupto (c) *very Fam (homosexual)* maricón(ona) (d) **to be b. on (doing) sth** *(determined)* estar empeñado(a) en hacer algo

**3** *pt & pp* of **bend**

**benzene** ['benziːn] *n Chem* benceno *m*

**benzin(e)** ['benziːn] *n Chem* bencina *f*

**bequeath** [bɪ'kwiːð] *vt Formal* legar

**bequest** [bɪ'kwest] *n Law* legado *m*

**berate** [bɪ'reɪt] *vt Formal* reconvenir, reñir

**Berber** ['bɜːbə(r)] *n & adj* bereber *mf*

**bereaved** [bɪ'riːvd] **1** *npl* **the b.** la familia del (de la) difunto(a)

**2** *adj* privado(a) de un ser querido

**bereavement** [bɪ'riːvmənt] *n* pérdida *f* (de un ser querido); **b. counselling** = atención psicológica prestada a personas que sufren por la pérdida de un ser querido

**bereft** [bɪ'reft] *adj* **to be b. of** estar privado(a) de

**beret** ['bereɪ] *n* boina *f*

**bergamot** ['bɜːgəmɒt] *n* bergamota *f*

**berk** [bɜːk] *n Br Fam* idiota *mf*

**Berlin** [bɜː'lɪn] *n* Berlín; **the B. Wall** el Muro de Berlín

**Berliner** [bɜː'lɪnə(r)] *n* berlinés(esa) *m,f*

**Bermuda** [bə'mjuːdə] *n* (las) Bermudas; **B. shorts** bermudas *fpl*

**Bern(e)** [bɜːn] *n* Berna

**berry** ['berɪ] *n* baya *f*

**berserk** [bə'zɜːk] *adj Fam* **to go b.** volverse loco(a)

**berth** [bɜːθ] **1** *n* (a) *(on train, ship)* litera *f* (b) *(in harbour)* amarradero *m*; *Fig* **to give sb a wide b.** evitar a alguien

**2** *vt & vi Naut* atracar

**beseech** [bɪ'siːtʃ] *(pt & pp* **besought** [bɪ'sɔːt] *or* **beseeched**) *vt Literary* implorar, suplicar

**beseeching** [bɪ'siːtʃɪŋ] *adj* suplicante, implorante

**beset** [bɪ'set] (*pt & pp* **beset**) *vt* acosar; **beset with dangers/difficulties** plagado(a) de peligros/dificultades; **she was beset by doubts** le asaltaron las dudas

**beside** [bɪ'saɪd] *prep* (a) *(next to)* al lado de; **seated b. me** sentado(a) a mi lado; **a house b. the lake** una casa a la orilla del *or* junto al lago; **that's b. the point** eso no viene al caso; **he was b. himself with joy** no cabía en sí de gozo; **he was b. himself with anger** estaba fuera de sí (de ira) (b) *(compared to)* al lado de; **b. him, everyone else appears slow** a su lado todos parecen lentos

**besides** [bɪ'saɪdz] **1** *prep* (a) *(apart from)* además de, aparte de (b) *(in addition to)* además de; **… b. which, she was unwell …** además de lo cual, no se encontraba bien
**2** *adv* además; **many more b.** muchos(as) otros(as)

**besiege** [bɪ'siːdʒ] *vt (castle, town)* asediar, sitiar; *Fig* **to b. sb with complaints/requests** asediar a alguien con quejas/peticiones

**besmirch** [bɪ'smɜːtʃ] *vt Literary (face)* manchar; *(reputation)* mancillar

**besotted** [bɪ'sɒtɪd] *adj* **to be b. with sb/ sth** estar embobado(a) con alguien/algo

**besought** [bɪ'sɔːt] *pt & pp of* **beseech**

**bespatter** [bɪ'spætə(r)] *vt* salpicar (**with** de)

**bespectacled** [bɪ'spektəkəld] *adj* con gafas

**bespoke** [bɪ'spəʊk] *adj (made to measure)* a medida; **b. tailor** sastre *m (que hace trajes a medida)*

**best** [best] *(superlative of* **good, well**) **1** *n* **the b.** el/la/lo mejor; **at b.** en el mejor de los casos; **the b. of it is…** lo mejor del caso es que…; **it's hard enough at the b. of times** incluso en el mejor de los casos ya resulta bastante difícil; **she did her b.** hizo todo lo que pudo; **I'll want to look my b.** tendré que arreglarme lo mejor posible; **he was at his b.** estaba en plena forma; **to bring out the b. in sb** poner de manifiesto lo mejor de alguien; **to get the b. of the bargain** salir ganando en un trato; **to get the b. out of sth** sacar el máximo provecho de algo; **we will have to make the b. of it** nos las tendremos que apañar; **we are the b. of friends** somos muy buenos amigos; **I am in the b. of health** estoy pletórico(a) de salud; **to the b. of my belief** *or* **knowledge** por lo que yo sé; **I will do it to the b. of my ability** lo haré lo mejor que pueda; **he can sing with the b. of them** canta como el mejor; **to hope for the b.** esperar que todo vaya bien; **to have** *or* **get the b. of both worlds** salir ganando por partida doble; *Fam* **all the b.!** ¡te deseo lo mejor!; *(at end of letter)* un saludo
**2** *adj* mejor; **my b. dress** mi mejor vestido; **she is b. at French** *(of group of people)* es la que mejor habla francés; *(French is her best subject)* lo que mejor se le da es el francés; **to put one's b. foot forward** dar lo mejor de sí mismo(a); **it took the b. part of a year** llevó casi todo un año; **to know what is b. for sb** saber lo que le conviene a alguien; **it is b. to…** lo mejor es…; *Com* **b. before…** consumir preferentemente antes de…; **this is a b. case scenario** esto es lo que ocurriría en el mejor de los casos; **b. man** *(at wedding)* padrino *m*; **may the b. man win** *(in contest)* que gane el mejor
**3** *adv* mejor; **I like fish b.** lo que más me gusta es el pescado; **I comforted her as b. I could** la consolé lo mejor que pude; **you know b.** tú sabrás; **do as you think b.** haz lo que te parezca mejor; **the b. dressed man** el hombre mejor vestido; **she came off b.** ella fue la que salió mejor parada
**4** *vt (in contest, argument)* superar

**bestial** ['bestɪəl] *adj* brutal, bestial

**bestiality** [bestɪ'ælɪtɪ] *n* (a) *(cruelty)* brutalidad *f*, bestialidad *f* (b) *(sexual practice)* bestialismo *m*, zoofilia *f*

**bestow** [bɪ'stəʊ] *vt (title)* conceder (**on** a); *(honour)* conferir (**on** a)

**bestseller** [best'selə(r)] *n (book)* éxito *m* de ventas, bestseller *m*

**bestselling** [best'selɪŋ] *adj* **b. novel/ author** novela *f*/escritor(ora) *m,f* de éxito

**bet** [bet] **1** *n* apuesta *f*; **to make** *or* **place a b.** hacer una apuesta; *Fig* **my b. is that he'll come** personalmente, creo que vendrá; *Fig* **your best b. would be to…** lo mejor que puedes hacer es…; *Fig* **it's a safe b.** es casi seguro
**2** *vt (pt & pp* **bet** *or* **betted**) apostar; **I'll b. you £10** te apuesto diez libras; *Fam* **I b. you don't!** ¡a que no!; *Fam Fig* **I b. you she'll win** te apuesto *or* qué te apuestas a que gana ella; *Fam Fig* **I b. you anything he won't do it** te apuesto lo que quieras a que no lo consigue
**3** *vi* **to b. on a horse** apostar a un caballo; *Fig* **I wouldn't b. on it!** yo no me apostaría nada; *Fam* **you b.!** ¡ya lo creo!, ¡por supuesto!; *Fam* **John says he's sorry – I b. he does!** John dice que lo siente – ¡hombre, claro! *or* ¡ya lo creo!

**betel** ['biːtəl] *n* betel *m*; **b. nut** areca *f*

**Bethlehem** ['beθlɪhem] *n* Belén *m*

**betide** [bɪ'taɪd] *vt Literary* **woe b. him/you** pobre de él/ti

**betray** [bɪ'treɪ] *vt* (a) *(person, country)* traicionar; **to b. sb's trust** abusar de la confianza de alguien (b) *(secret, fact)* revelar; **his tone betrayed a lack of conviction** su tono revelaba falta de convicción

**betrayal** [bɪ'treɪəl] *n* (a) *(of person, country)* traición *f*; **a b. of trust** un abuso de confianza (b) *(of secret, fact)* muestra *f*, indicio *m*; **her ex-**

**pression gave no b. of her true feelings** su expresión no permitía adivinar sus verdaderos sentimientos

**betrothal** [bɪ'trəʊðəl] *n Literary* compromiso *m*

**betrothed** [bɪ'trəʊðd] *n & adj Formal* prometido(a) *m,f*

**better** ['betə(r)] (*comparative of* **good, well**) **1** *n* **I expected b. of you** esperaba más de ti; **you should respect your (elders and) betters** deberías guardar respeto a tus mayores; **to change for the b.** cambiar para mejor; **to get the b. of sb** poder con alguien; **his shyness got the b. of him** pudo más su timidez; **the sooner/faster the b.** cuanto antes/más rapido, mejor

**2** *adj* mejor; **to be b.** (*feel well again*) estar mejor; **to get b.** mejorar; **he's b. at tennis than his brother** juega al tenis mejor que su hermano; **she's b. at chemistry than him** se le da mejor la química que a él; **it would be b. for you to go** más vale que te vayas; **that's b.** ¡así está mejor!; **b. luck next time!** ¡a ver si hay más suerte la próxima vez!; **it took the b. part of a week** llevó casi toda una semana; **to have seen b. days** haber visto mejores tiempos; *Br Fam* **my b. half** mi media naranja

**3** *adv* mejor; **I am feeling b.** me siento mejor; **to get to know sb b.** ir conociendo mejor a alguien; **b. and b.** cada vez mejor; **so much the b., all the b.** tanto mejor; **for b. or worse** para bien o para mal; **you had b. not stay** más vale que no te quedes; **to think b. of it** cambiar de idea, pensárselo mejor; **to think b. of sb (for doing sth)** tener mejor concepto de alguien (por haber hecho algo); **to be b. off** estar mejor; (*financially*) tener más dinero

**4** *vt* (*improve*) superar; (*surpass*) mejorar; **she wants to b. herself** quiere mejorar su situación

**betterment** ['betəmənt] *n* mejora *f*

**betting** ['betɪŋ] *n* juego *m*, apuestas *fpl*; *Fam Fig* **the b. is that...** lo más probable es que...; **b. slip** boleto *m* de apuestas; **b. shop** casa *f* de apuestas

**between** [bɪ'twiːn] **1** *prep* entre; **b. eight and nine o'clock** entre (las) ocho y (las) nueve; **b. Edinburgh and London** entre Edimburgo y Londres; **you must choose b. them** tienes que elegir entre ellos; **we bought it b. us** lo compramos entre todos; **this is strictly b. you and me** esto debe quedar entre tú y yo

**2** *adv* (**in**) **b.** en medio; **the trees in b.** los árboles que están en medio

**bevel** ['bevəl] **1** *n* (*on wood, glass*) bisel *m*

**2** *vt* (*pt & pp* **bevelled,** *US* **beveled**) (*wood, glass*) biselar

**beverage** ['bevərɪdʒ] *n* bebida *f*

**bevvy** ['bevɪ] *n Br Fam* **to go for a b.** (*go for a drink*) ir a tomar unas copas

**bevy** ['bevɪ] *n* (*group*) nube *f*, grupo *m*

**bewail** [bɪ'weɪl] *vt* lamentar

**beware** [bɪ'weə(r)] *vi* tener cuidado (**of** con); **b.!** ¡cuidado!; **b. of the dog** (*sign*) cuidado con el perro

**bewilder** [bɪ'wɪldə(r)] *vt* desconcertar

**bewildered** [bɪ'wɪldəd] *adj* desconcertado(a); **I was b. by their lack of interest** me dejó atónito su falta de interés

**bewildering** [bɪ'wɪldərɪŋ] *adj* desconcertante

**bewilderment** [bɪ'wɪldəmənt] *n* desconcierto *m*

**bewitch** [bɪ'wɪtʃ] *vt* (*fascinate*) embrujar, cautivar

**bewitching** [bɪ'wɪtʃɪŋ] *adj* (*smile, beauty*) cautivador(ora)

**beyond** [bɪ'jɒnd] **1** *prep* (**a**) (*in space*) más allá de; **the house is b. the church** la casa está pasada la iglesia

(**b**) (*in time*) **b. a certain date** después de *or* pasada una fecha determinada

(**c**) (*exceeding*) **he lived b. his means** vivió por encima de sus posibilidades; **it's b. me (how they can do it)** no comprendo cómo lo hacen; **due to circumstances b. our control** por circunstancias ajenas a nuestra voluntad; **I am b. caring** ya me trae sin cuidado; **it's b. doubt/question** (**that...**) es indudable/incuestionable (que...); **it's b. a joke** esto ya pasa de castaño oscuro; **to be b. belief** ser difícil de creer; **b. reach** inalcanzable; **b. repair** irreparable

(**d**) (*except*) aparte de, además de; **I have nothing to say b. observing that...** únicamente quisiera hacer notar que...

**2** *adv* más allá

**3** *n* **the b.** el más allá

**Bhutan** [buː'tɑːn] *n* Bután

**bias** ['baɪəs] *n* (**a**) (*prejudice*) prejuicio *m*; (*inclination*) inclinación *f*; **to have a b. towards** sentir inclinación por; **to have a b. against** tener prejuicios contra, estar predispuesto(a) en contra de (**b**) (*in sewing*) bies *m*, sesgo *m*

**2** *vt* (*pt & pp* **biased** *or* **biassed**) influir en; **to b. sb against/for sth** predisponer a alguien en contra/a favor de algo

**bias(s)ed** ['baɪəst] *adj* parcial; (*opinion*) parcial, sesgado(a); **you're b. in her favour** estás predispuesto a favor de ella

**bib** [bɪb] *n* (*for baby*) babero *m*; (*of apron, dungarees*) peto *m*

**bible** ['baɪbəl] *n* biblia *f*; **the B.** la Biblia; *Fig* **this dictionary is his b.** este diccionario es su Biblia; *Fam Pej* **b. basher** *or* **thumper** proselitista *mf* fanático(a); *US* **the B. Belt** = zona integrista protestante en el sur de los Estados Unidos

**biblical** ['bɪblɪkəl] *adj* bíblico(a); *Hum* **to know sb in the b. sense** haberse llevado al huerto a alguien

**bibliography** [bɪblɪ'ɒgrəfɪ] *n* bibliografía *f*

**bibliophile** ['bɪblɪəfaɪl] *n* bibliófilo(a) *m,f*

**bicameral** [baɪ'kæmərəl] *adj Pol* bicameral

**bicarbonate** [baɪ'kɑ:bəneɪt] *n* bicarbonato *m*; **b. of soda** bicarbonato sódico

**bicentenary** [baɪsen'ti:nərɪ], *US* **bicentennial** [baɪsen'tenɪəl] **1** *n* bicentenario *m*
**2** *adj* bicentenario(a)

**biceps** ['baɪseps] *npl Anat* bíceps *m inv*

**bicker** ['bɪkə(r)] *vi* reñir, pelearse

**bickering** ['bɪkərɪŋ] *n* riñas *fpl*, peleas *fpl*

**bicycle** ['baɪsɪkəl] *n* bicicleta *f*; **to ride a b.** montar en bicicleta; **b. clips** = pinzas que ciñen los pantalones a las pantorrillas para montar en bicicleta; **b. kick** *(in football)* tijereta *f*, chilena *f*

**bid**[1] [bɪd] **1** *n* (a) *(offer)* oferta *f*; *(at auction)* puja *f* (b) *(attempt)* tentativa *f*, intento *m*; **a rescue/suicide b.** un intento de rescate/suicidio; **to make a b. for power** intentar conseguir el poder
**2** *vt* (*pt & pp* bid) *(offer)* ofrecer; *(at auction)* pujar (**for** por); **what am I bid for this table?** ¿qué ofrecen por esta mesa?
**3** *vi* *(at auction)* pujar (**for** por)

**bid**[2] (*pt* bade [bæd, beɪd] *or* bid; *pp* bidden ['bɪdən] *or* bid) *vt Literary* (a) *(greet)* **to b. sb welcome** dar la bienvenida a alguien; **to b. sb goodbye** despedir a alguien (b) *(order)* **to b. sb be silent** ordenar callar a alguien

**bidder** ['bɪdə(r)] *n* postor(ora) *m,f*; **the highest b.** el mejor postor

**bidding**[1] ['bɪdɪŋ] *n* *(at auction)* puja *f*; **to start the b. at £5,000** comenzar la puja con 5.000 libras

**bidding**[2] *n Literary (command)* **to do sb's b.** llevar a cabo las órdenes de alguien

**bide** [baɪd] *vt* **to b. one's time** esperar el momento oportuno

**bidet** ['bi:deɪ] *n* bidé *m*

**biennial** [baɪ'enɪəl] **1** *n Bot* planta *f* bienal
**2** *adj* bienal

**bier** [bɪə(r)] *n (for carrying coffin)* andas *fpl*

**biff** [bɪf] *Fam* **1** *n* mamporro *m*
**2** *vt* dar un mamporro a

**bifocal** [baɪ'fəʊkəl] **1** *n* bifocals gafas *fpl* (con lentes) bifocales; **a pair of bifocals** unas (gafas) bifocales
**2** *adj* bifocal

**big** [bɪg] **1** *adj* (a) *(tall, large)* grande; *(before singular nouns)* gran; **a b. problem** un problema grande, un gran problema; **to grow big(ger)** crecer; **my b. brother** mi hermano

mayor; **he's a b. eater** come un montón; **a b. hand for our guest!** ¡un gran aplauso para nuestro invitado!; *Fam* **the B. Apple** *(New York)* Nueva York; **b. business** grandes negocios *mpl*; *Aut* **b. end** cabeza *f* de biela; **b. game** *(in hunting)* caza *f* mayor; **to be a b. spender** gastar mucho; **b. toe** dedo *m* gordo del pie; **b. top** *(of circus)* carpa *f*; **b. wheel** *(at fair)* noria *f*
(b) *(idioms)* **it's her b. day tomorrow** mañana es el gran día para ella; **to have b. ideas** tener grandes ideas; *Fam* **hey, what's the b. idea?** ¡eh!, ¿qué está pasando aquí?; **to earn b. money** ganar millones; **I've got b. plans for you** tengo grandes planes para ti; **to make it b.** triunfar; **she's into computers in a b. way** le van mucho los ordenadores; *Ironic* **that's b. of you!** ¡qué generoso(a)!; **he's getting too b. for his boots** está empezando a darse humos; **the boss is very b. on punctuality** el jefe le da mucha importancia a la puntualidad; **it was b. last year** *(of music, fashion)* hizo furor el año pasado; *Fam* **to have a b. mouth** *(be indiscreet)* ser un/una bocazas; *Fam* **the b. guns** *(important people)* los pesos pesados; **a b. name** una gran figura; *Fam* **b. shot** *or* **noise** pez *m* gordo; **to make** *or* **hit the b. time** conseguir el éxito
**2** *adv* **he always talks b.** se le va siempre la fuerza por la boca; **to think b.** pensar a lo grande

**bigamist** ['bɪgəmɪst] *n* bígamo(a) *m,f*

**bigamous** ['bɪgəməs] *adj* bígamo(a)

**bigamy** ['bɪgəmɪ] *n* bigamia *f*

**biggie, biggy** ['bɪgɪ] *n Fam* **I think this storm's going to be a b.** me parece que ésta va a ser una tormenta de las gordas

**bighead** ['bɪghed] *n Fam* creído(a) *m,f*

**bigheaded** [bɪg'hedɪd] *adj* creído(a), engreído(a); **we don't want him getting b.** no queremos que se vuelva un creído

**big-hearted** [bɪg'hɑ:tɪd] *adj* **to be b.** tener gran corazón

**bigot** ['bɪgət] *n* fanático(a) *m,f*, intolerante *mf*

**bigoted** ['bɪgətɪd] *adj* fanático(a), intolerante

**bigotry** ['bɪgətrɪ] *n* fanatismo *m*, intolerancia *f*

**bigwig** ['bɪgwɪg] *n Fam* pez *m* gordo

**bike** [baɪk] *n Fam (bicycle)* bici *f*; *(motorcycle)* moto *f*; *Br* **on your b.!** *(go away)* ¡largo!, ¡piérdete!; *(don't talk nonsense)* ¡no digas chorradas!; **b. shed** cobertizo *m* para bicicletas

**biker** ['baɪkə(r)] *n Fam* motero(a) *m,f*

**bikini** [bɪ'ki:nɪ] *n* biquini *m*; **b. bottom** parte *f* de abajo del biquini; **b. top** parte *f* de arriba del biquini

**bilateral** [baɪ'lætərəl] *adj* bilateral

**bilberry** ['bɪlbərɪ] *n* arándano *m*

**bile** [baɪl] *n also Fig* bilis *f inv*, hiel *f*

**bilge** [bɪldʒ] *n Fam (nonsense)* tonterías *fpl*, bobadas *fpl*; **to talk (a lot of) b.** no decir más que bobadas

**bilingual** [baɪˈlɪŋgwəl] *adj* bilingüe

**bilious** [ˈbɪlɪəs] *adj* **(a)** *Med* bilioso(a); **b. attack** cólico *m* bilioso; **b. yellow/green** amarillo/verde nauseabundo **(b)** *(bad-tempered)* bilioso(a), atrabiliario(a)

**Bill** [bɪl] *n Br Fam* **the Old B.** *(the police)* la pasma

**bill¹** [bɪl] **1** *n (of bird)* pico *m*
**2** *vi Fam (of lovers)* **to b. and coo** hacerse mimos *or* arrumacos

**bill²** **1** *n* **(a)** *(in restaurant)* cuenta *f*; *(for goods, services)* factura *f*; *Fin* **b. of exchange** letra *f* de cambio
**(b)** *US (banknote)* billete *m*
**(c)** *(notice)* cartel *m*; **(stick) no bills** *(sign)* prohibido fijar carteles; *Th* **to head** *or* **top the b.** estar en cabecera de cartel
**(d)** *(list)* **b. of fare** menú *m*, carta *f*; **the doctor gave me a clean b. of health** el médico me dio el visto bueno; *Fam* **to fit the b.** venir como anillo al dedo
**(e)** *Pol (proposed law)* proyecto *m* de ley; *US Pol* **the B. of Rights** = las diez primeras enmiendas a la constitución estadounidense, relacionadas con la garantía de las libertades individuales
**2** *vt* **(a)** *(give invoice to)* pasar (la) factura a
**(b)** *(publicize)* anunciar; **it was billed as the debate of the decade** fue anunciado como el debate del decenio

**billboard** [ˈbɪlbɔːd] *n* valla *f* publicitaria

**billet** [ˈbɪlɪt] **1** *n Mil* acantonamiento *m*
**2** *vt* acantonar

**billfold** [ˈbɪlfəʊld] *n US* cartera *f*, billetera *f*

**billiard** [ˈbɪljəd] *n* **billiards** billar *m*; **to play billiards** jugar al billar; **b. ball/table** bola *f*/mesa *f* de billar

**billion** [ˈbɪljən] *n* mil millones *mpl*, millardo *m*; *Br Old-fashioned* billón *m*; *Fam* **I've got billions of things to do!** tengo miles de cosas que hacer

**billionaire** [bɪljəˈneə(r)] *n* multimillonario(a) *m,f*

**billow** [ˈbɪləʊ] **1** *n (of smoke)* nube *f*
**2** *vi* ondear

**billowy** [ˈbɪləʊɪ] *adj (dress, sail)* ondeante; *(clouds)* ondulante

**billposter** [ˈbɪlpeʊstə(r)] *n* **billposters will be prosecuted** *(sign)* prohibido fijar carteles (responsable la empresa anunciadora)

**billy-can** [ˈbɪlɪkæn] *n* cazo *m*

**billy-goat** [ˈbɪlɪgəʊt] *n* macho *m* cabrío

**bimbo** [ˈbɪmbəʊ] *n (pl* **bimbos)** *n Fam Pej* = mujer atractiva y de pocas luces

**bin** [bɪn] **1** *n (domestic)* cubo *m*; *(very large)* contenedor *m*; *(for wastepaper, on lamppost)* papelera *f*
**2** *vt (pt & pp* **binned)** tirar (a la papelera)

**binary** [ˈbaɪnərɪ] *adj Math & Comptr* binario(a); **b. code** código *m* binario; **b. number** número *m* binario

**bind** [baɪnd] **1** *n Fam* **to be in a b.** estar en un apuro; **it's a real b. to have to…** es una verdadera lata tener que…
**2** *vt (pt & pp* **bound** [baʊnd]) **(a)** *(tie)* atar; **to b. sb hand and foot** atar a alguien de pies *y* manos; *Fig* **they are bound together by ties of friendship** les unen lazos *or* vínculos de amistad
**(b)** *(bandage)* vendar
**(c)** *(book)* encuadernar
**(d)** *(cause to stick)* unir, ligar; **b. the mixture with egg** ligar la mezcla con huevo
**(e)** *(oblige)* **she bound me to secrecy** me hizo prometer que guardaría el secreto; **you are bound to report any change in your income** tienes obligación de notificar cualquier cambio en tus ingresos; **to be bound by an oath** estar obligado(a) por un juramento
▸**bind over** *vt sep Law* **to b. sb over** obligar judicialmente a alguien
▸**bind up** *vt sep* **(a)** *(cut, wound)* vendar **(b) to be bound up with sth** *(involved)* estar íntimamente relacionado(a) con algo

**binder** [ˈbaɪndə(r)] *n* **(a)** *(for papers)* carpeta *f* **(b)** *(bookbinder)* encuadernador(ora) *m,f* **(c)** *(farm machinery)* empacadora *f*

**binding** [ˈbaɪndɪŋ] **1** *n* cubierta *f*, tapa *f*
**2** *adj* vinculante

**binge** [bɪndʒ] **1** *n Fam (drinking spree)* borrachera *f*; **to go on a b.** ir de jarana *or* marcha; **to go on a shopping b.** ir de compras y traerse media tienda; **a chocolate b.** un atracón de chocolate
**2** *vi* **to b. on sth** darse un atracón de algo

**bingo** [ˈbɪŋgəʊ] **1** *n* bingo *m*; **b. hall** (sala *f* de) bingo *m*
**2** *exclam* ¡ole!, ¡bravo!

**binman** [ˈbɪnmæn] *n Br* basurero *m*

**binoculars** [bɪˈnɒkjʊləz] *npl* prismáticos *mpl*

**biochemic(al)** [baɪəʊˈkemɪk(əl)] *adj* bioquímico(a)

**biochemist** [baɪəʊˈkemɪst] *n* bioquímico(a) *m,f*

**biochemistry** [baɪəʊˈkemɪstrɪ] *n* bioquímica *f*

**biodegradable** [baɪəʊdɪˈgreɪdəbəl] *adj* biodegradable

**biodiversity** [baɪəʊdaɪˈvɜːsɪtɪ] *n* biodiversidad *f*

**biographer** [baɪˈɒgrəfə(r)] *n* biógrafo(a) *m,f*

**biographic(al)** [baɪəˈgræfɪk(əl)] *adj* biográfico(a)

**biography** [baɪˈɒgrəfɪ] *n* biografía *f*

**biological** [baɪəˈlɒdʒɪkəl] *adj* biológico(a); **b. warfare** guerra *f* bacteriológica; **b. washing powder** detergente *m* de *or* con acción biológica

**biologist** [baɪˈɒlədʒɪst] *n* biólogo(a) *m,f*

**biology** [baɪˈɒlədʒɪ] *n* biología *f*

**biopsy** [ˈbaɪɒpsɪ] *n Med* biopsia *f*

**biorhythm** [ˈbaɪərɪðəm] *n* biorritmo *m*

**biosphere** [ˈbaɪəsfɪə(r)] *n* biosfera *f*

**biotechnology** [baɪəʊtekˈnɒlədʒɪ] *n* biotecnología *f*

**bipartisan** [baɪˈpɑːtɪzæn] *adj Pol* bipartito(a)

**biped** [ˈbaɪped] *n & adj* bípedo(a) *m,f*

**biplane** [ˈbaɪpleɪn] *n* biplano *m*

**birch** [bɜːtʃ] **1** *n* abedul *m*; **to give sb the b.** azotar a alguien
**2** *vt (beat)* azotar

**bird** [bɜːd] *n* **(a)** *(in general)* pájaro *m*; *(as opposed to mammals, reptiles etc)* ave *f*; **b. of paradise** ave del paraíso; **b. of prey** (ave) rapaz *f*, ave de presa; **b. sanctuary** refugio *m* de aves; **b. table** comedero *m* de pájaros
**(b)** *Br Fam (woman)* nena *f*, piba *f*
**(c)** *(idioms) Fam* **a little b. told me** me lo ha dicho un pajarito; **the b. has flown** el pájaro ha volado; *Prov* **a b. in the hand is worth two in the bush** más vale pájaro en mano que ciento volando; *Prov* **birds of a feather flock together** Dios los cría y ellos se juntan; **to kill two birds with one stone** matar dos pájaros de un tiro; *Euph* **to tell sb about the birds and the bees** explicar a alguien de dónde vienen los niños

**birdbath** [ˈbɜːdbɑːθ] *n* = especie de pila con agua que se coloca en el jardín para que los pájaros se refresquen

**bird-brained** [ˈbɜːdbreɪnd] *adj Fam* **to be b.** ser un majadero; **a b. idea** una majadería

**birdcage** [ˈbɜːdkeɪdʒ] *n* jaula *f*

**birdie** [ˈbɜːdɪ] *n* **(a)** *Fam (bird)* pajarito *m*; *Fig* **watch the b.!** *(photographer to children)* ¡mira el pajarito! **(b)** *(in golf)* uno *m* bajo par, menos uno *m*

**birdseed** [ˈbɜːdsiːd] *n* alpiste *m*

**bird's-eye view** [ˈbɜːdzaɪˈvjuː] *n* **to have a b.** *(of place)* tener una vista panorámica *(desde arriba)*; *(of situation)* tener una visión de conjunto

**bird-watcher** [ˈbɜːdwɒtʃə(r)] *n* aficionado(a) *m,f* a la observación de aves

**bird-watching** [ˈbɜːdwɒtʃɪŋ] *n* observación *f* de aves

**Birmingham** [ˈbɜːmɪŋəm] *n* Birmingham

**Biro®** [ˈbaɪrəʊ] *(pl Biros) n Br* bolígrafo *m*

**birth** [bɜːθ] *n also Fig* nacimiento *m*; *(delivery)* parto *m*; **to give b. (to sb)** dar a luz (a alguien); **at b.** al nacer; **from b.** de nacimiento; **Irish by b.** irlandés(esa) de nacimiento; **b. certificate** partida *f* de nacimiento; **b. control** control *m* de natalidad; **b. control methods** métodos *mpl* anticonceptivos; *Fig* **b. pangs** dolores *mpl* del parto; **b. rate** índice *m* de natalidad

**birthday** [ˈbɜːθdeɪ] *n* cumpleaños *m inv*; *Fam* **she was in her b. suit** estaba como su madre la trajo al mundo; **b. card** tarjeta *f* de felicitación de cumpleaños; **b. present** regalo *m* de cumpleaños

**birthmark** [ˈbɜːθmɑːk] *n* antojo *m*, mancha *f (en la piel)*

**birthplace** [ˈbɜːθpleɪs] *n* lugar *m* de nacimiento

**birthright** [ˈbɜːθraɪt] *n* derecho *m* natural

**Biscay** [ˈbɪskeɪ] *n* **the Bay of B.** el Golfo de Vizcaya

**biscuit** [ˈbɪskɪt] *n* galleta *f*; *Fam* **that really takes the b.!** ¡esto es el colmo!

**bisect** [baɪˈsekt] *vt Math* bisecar; *(town, area)* dividir por la mitad

**bisexual** [baɪˈseksjʊəl] *n & adj* bisexual *mf*

**bishop** [ˈbɪʃəp] *n* obispo *m*; *(in chess)* alfil *m*

**bishopric** [ˈbɪʃəprɪk] *n* obispado *m*

**bison** [ˈbaɪsən] *n* bisonte *m*

**bistro** [ˈbiːstrəʊ] *(pl bistros) n* restaurante *m* pequeño

**bit¹** [bɪt] *n* **(a)** *(in horseriding)* bocado *m*; *Fig* **to have the b. between one's teeth** haber cogido carrerilla **(b)** *(for drill)* broca *f*

**bit²** *n* **(a)** *(piece)* trozo *m*; **a b. of news** una noticia; **with a b. of luck** con un poco de suerte; **I have done my b.** yo he cumplido con mi parte; *Fam* **she's a b. of all right** está muy buena, no está nada mal; **to have a b. on the side** *(have a lover)* tener un lío, echar una cana al aire
**(b)** *(component part)* **to take sth to bits** desarmar *or* desmontar algo; **to tear/smash sth to bits** hacer añicos algo; **he has eaten every b.** se ha comido hasta el último bocado; **bits and pieces** *or* **bobs** *(personal belongings)* cosas *fpl*, trastos *mpl*
**(c)** *(expressing degree)* **a b. late/heavy/tired** un poco tarde/pesado(a)/cansado(a); **we had a b. of difficulty in finding him** nos costó un poco encontrarlo; **he's a b. of an idiot** es un imbécil; **b. by b.** poco a poco; **not a b. of it!** ¡en absoluto!; **wait a b.!** ¡espera un poco!; **it takes a b. of getting used to** lleva algo de tiempo acostumbrarse; **a good b. older** bastante más viejo(a); **a little b. worried/tired** algo preocupado(a)/cansado(a); **I'm every b. as good as him** no tengo nada que envidiarle; *Fam* **that's a b. much!** ¡eso es pasarse!; **b. part**

*(in play, film)* papel *m* secundario

(d) *Comptr* bit *m*

(e) *Fam (coin)* moneda *f; US* **two bits** 25 centavos

**bit³** *pt of* **bite**

**bitch** [bɪtʃ] **1** *n* (a) *(female dog)* perra *f* (b) *very Fam Pej (woman)* bruja *f,* zorra *f;* **I've had a b. of a day** he tenido un día bien jodido; **life's a b.!** ¡qué vida más perra!

**2** *vi Fam (complain)* dar la tabarra, quejarse; **he's always bitching about his colleagues** siempre está poniendo a parir a sus compañeros

**bitchy** [ˈbɪtʃɪ] *adj Fam* malintencionado(a), malicioso(a)

**bite** [baɪt] **1** *n* (a) *(of person, dog)* mordisco *m; (of insect)* picadura *f; (of snake)* mordedura *f,* picadura *f* (b) *(mouthful)* bocado *m;* **he took a b. out of the apple** dio un bocado a la manzana; **I haven't had a b. to eat all day** no he probado bocado en todo el día (c) *Fig (of speech, article)* chispa *f;* **this mustard has a bit of a b.** esta mostaza está fuertecilla

**2** *vt (pt* **bit** [bɪt], *pp* **bitten** [ˈbɪtən]) (a) *(of person, dog)* morder; *(of insect, snake)* picar; **the dog bit him in the leg** el perro le mordió en la pierna; **to b. one's nails** morderse las uñas (b) *(idioms)* **to b. one's tongue** *(stay silent)* morderse la lengua; *Fam* **to b. the bullet** agarrar el toro por los cuernos; *Fam* **to b. the dust** *(of scheme, plan)* irse al garete; **to b. the hand that feeds you** morder la mano que nos da de comer; *Prov* **once bitten twice shy** gato escaldado del agua fría huye

**3** *vi (of person, dog)* morder; *(of insect, snake)* picar; **to b. into sth** dar un mordisco a algo; *Fig (be felt) (cuts)* hacerse notar; *Fig* **the cost bit into our savings** los gastos supusieron una merma de nuestros ahorros

▶**bite off** *vt sep* arrancar de un mordisco; *Fig* **to b. off more than one can chew** querer abarcar demasiado; *Fam Fig* **there's no need to b. my head off** ¡no hace falta que me contestes así!

**biting** [ˈbaɪtɪŋ] *adj (wind, satire)* penetrante

**bit-mapped** [ˈbɪtmæpt] *adj Comptr* en mapa de bits

**bitten** [ˈbɪtən] *pp of* **bite**

**bitter** [ˈbɪtə(r)] **1** *n Br (beer)* = cerveza británica sin burbujas y de tono castaño

**2** *adj* (a) *(taste)* amargo(a); *Fig* **it was a b. pill to swallow** costó mucho tragar (con) aquello (b) *(wind, opposition)* recio(a); *(struggle)* encarnizado(a); *(tears)* de amargura; **to go on/resist to the b. end** seguir/resistir hasta el final (c) *(resentful) (person)* amargado(a), resentido(a); *(argument, words)* agrio(a); *(experience, memories, disappointment)* amargo(a); **to be b. about sth** estar resentido(a) por algo

**bitterly** [ˈbɪtəlɪ] *adv* (a) *(extremely)* enormemente, terriblemente; **we were b. disappointed** nos llevamos una decepción tremenda; **I b. regretted telling them** me arrepentí enormemente de habérselo dicho; **it was b. cold** hacía un frío horrible (b) *(resentfully)* **to complain b.** quejarse amargamente

**bitterness** [ˈbɪtənɪs] *n* (a) *(taste)* amargor *m* (b) *(resentment)* amargura *f,* amargor *m*

**bittersweet** [ˈbɪtəswiːt] *adj (taste)* agridulce; *Fig* **b. memories** recuerdos entre dulces y amargos

**bitty** [ˈbɪtɪ] *adj Fam (incomplete)* deshilvanado(a)

**bitumen** [ˈbɪtjʊmɪn] *n* betún *m*

**bivouac** [ˈbɪvʊæk] **1** *n* vivac *m,* vivaque *m*

**2** *vi (pt & pp* **bivouacked**) vivaquear

**bi-weekly** [baɪˈwiːklɪ] **1** *adj (fortnightly)* quincenal; *(twice weekly)* bisemanal

**2** *adv (fortnightly)* quincenalmente; *(twice weekly)* dos veces por semana

**bizarre** [bɪˈzɑː(r)] *adj* extraño(a), raro(a)

**blab** [blæb] *(pt & pp* **blabbed**) *Fam* **1** *vt* soltar

**2** *vi (chatter)* parlotear, largar; **someone has blabbed to the newspapers** alguien se lo ha soplado a los periódicos

**black** [blæk] **1** *n* (a) *(colour)* negro *m*

(b) *(person)* negro(a) *m,f*

(c) *(idioms)* **to be in the b.** *(financially)* tener saldo positivo; **it says here in b. and white...** aquí pone claramente que...; **to see everything in b. and white** tener una actitud maniquea

**2** *adj* (a) *(colour)* negro(a); **a b. man** un negro; **a b. woman** una negra; **b. and blue** *(bruised)* amoratado(a); **b. belt** *(in martial arts)* cinturón *m* negro; *Av* **b. box** caja *f* negra; **b. coffee** café *m* solo; **b. eye** ojo *m* morado; *Astron* **b. hole** agujero *m* negro; **b. humour** humor *m* negro; **b. ice** placas *fpl* de hielo; **b. pudding** morcilla *f; Fig* **b. sheep** oveja *f* negra

(b) *(evil, unfavourable)* **to give sb a b. look** lanzar a alguien una mirada asesina; **the future is looking b.** el futuro se presenta muy negro; **it's a b. day for Britain** es un día negro or aciago para Gran Bretaña; **b. magic** magia *f* negra; **that earned him a b. mark** aquello supuso un borrón en su historial; **b. spot** *(for accidents)* punto *m* negro

(c) *(unofficial)* **b. economy** economía *f* sumergida; **b. market** mercado *m* negro

(d) *(in proper names)* **the B. Country** = la región industrial de las Midlands; **the B. Death** la peste negra; **the B. Forest** la Selva Negra; **B. Forest gateau** = tarta de chocolate y guindas; *Br* **B. Maria** *(police van)* coche *m* celular; **the B. Sea** el Mar Negro

**3** *vt* (**a**) *(blacken)* ennegrecer, pintar de negro (**b**) *(boycott) (company)* boicotear

▶**black out 1** *vt sep* (**a**) *(censor) (piece of writing)* borrar, tachar; *(person in photo)* suprimir (**b**) *(city)* dejar a oscuras (**c**) *TV* **industrial action has blacked out this evening's programmes** la huelga ha obligado a suspender los programas de esta noche

**2** *vi (faint)* desmayarse

**black-and-white** [blækən'waɪt] *adj (film, TV, illustration)* en blanco y negro

**blackball** ['blækbɔːl] *vt* vetar, votar en contra de

**blackberry** ['blækbərɪ] *n (bush)* zarzamora *f; (berry)* mora *f*

**blackbird** ['blækbɜːd] *n* mirlo *m*

**blackboard** ['blækbɔːd] *n* pizarra *f*, encerado *m*

**blackcurrant** ['blækkʌrənt] *n (berry)* grosella *f* negra; *(bush)* grosellero *m* (negro)

**blacken** ['blækən] *vt* ennegrecer; *Fig (reputation)* manchar; **clouds blackened the sky** las nubes oscurecían el cielo

**blackguard** ['blægɑːd] *n Old-fashioned* villano *m*, bellaco *m*

**blackhead** ['blækhed] *n* punto *m* negro, barrillo *m*

**blackjack** ['blækdʒæk] *n US* (**a**) *(truncheon)* porra *f* (**b**) *(card game)* veintiuna *f*

**blackleg** ['blækleg] *n Fam (strikebreaker)* esquirol(ola) *m,f*

**blacklist** ['blæklɪst] **1** *n* lista *f* negra

**2** *vt* poner en la lista negra

**blackmail** ['blækmeɪl] **1** *n* chantaje *m*

**2** *vt* hacer chantaje a, chantajear

**blackness** ['blæknɪs] *n (dirtiness)* negrura *f; (darkness)* oscuridad *f*

**blackout** ['blækaʊt] *n* (**a**) *(during air-raid)* apagón *m; Fig* **to impose a news b.** prohibir la cobertura informativa (**b**) *(fainting fit)* desmayo *m*

**blacksmith** ['blæksmɪθ] *n* herrero *m*

**bladder** ['blædə(r)] *n* vejiga *f*

**blade** [bleɪd] *n (of knife, sword)* hoja *f; (of propeller, oar)* pala *f; (of grass)* brizna *f*, hoja *f*

**blame** [bleɪm] **1** *n* culpa *f;* **to put the b. (for sth) on sb** culpar a alguien (de algo), echar la culpa a alguien (de algo); **to take the b. (for sth)** asumir la culpa (de algo)

**2** *vt* culpar, echar la culpa a; **to b. sb for sth, to b. sth on sb** echar la culpa a alguien de algo; **to be to b.** tener la culpa; **I b. myself for what happened** lo que pasó fue culpa mía; **I don't b. you for wanting to leave** no me extraña que quieras marcharte; **she has nobody to b. but herself** ella, y sólo ella, tiene la culpa

**blameless** ['bleɪmlɪs] *adj (person)* inocente; *(conduct, life)* intachable

**blameworthy** ['bleɪmwɜːðɪ] *adj (person)* culpable; *(conduct)* reprobable

**blanch** [blɑːntʃ] **1** *vt Culin* escaldar

**2** *vi (go pale)* palidecer, ponerse pálido(a)

**blancmange** [blə'mɒnʒ] *n* = budín dulce de aspecto gelatinoso a base de leche y maícena

**bland** [blænd] *adj* soso(a), insulso(a); **b. assurances** promesas *fpl* tibias

**blandishments** ['blændɪʃmənts] *npl Formal* halagos *mpl*, lisonjas *fpl*

**blandly** ['blændlɪ] *adv (reply, smile)* tibiamente, con tibieza

**blank** [blæŋk] **1** *n* (**a**) *(space)* espacio *m* en blanco; **my mind is a b.** no recuerdo absolutamente nada; *Fig* **to draw a b.** *(of inquiry)* no sacar nada en claro *or* en limpio (**b**) *(rifle cartridge)* cartucho *m* de fogueo; **to fire blanks** disparar tiros de fogueo; *Fam Fig* ser estéril

**2** *adj (paper, screen)* en blanco; *(face, look)* vacío(a), inexpresivo(a); **he looked b. when I mentioned your name** no dio muestras de reconocer tu nombre cuando lo mencioné; **my mind went b.** se me quedó la mente en blanco; **b. cassette** cinta *f* virgen; **b. cheque** cheque *m* en blanco; *Fig* **to give sb a b. cheque to do sth** dar carta blanca a alguien para hacer algo; **b. verse** *(in poetry)* verso *m* blanco, verso *m* suelto

▶**blank out** *vt sep (erase)* borrar

**blanket** ['blæŋkɪt] **1** *n* manta *f*, *Am* cobija *f*, *Am* frazada *f; Fig (of fog, cloud)* manto *m*

**2** *adj (agreement, ban)* general, total; **the government imposed a b. ban on demonstrations** el gobierno prohibió todas las manifestaciones; **b. term** término *m* general

**blankly** ['blæŋklɪ] *adv (without expression)* inexpresivamente; *(without understanding)* sin comprender; **she stared b. into the distance** tenía la mirada perdida en la distancia

**blare** ['bleə(r)] **1** *n* estruendo *m*

**2** *vi (radio, music)* retumbar

**blarney** ['blɑːnɪ] *n Fam* coba *f*, labia *f*

**blasé** ['blɑːzeɪ] *adj* **she was very b. about the accident** no le dio mayor importancia al accidente

**blaspheme** [blæs'fiːm] *vi* blasfemar

**blasphemer** [blæs'fiːmə(r)] *n* blasfemo(a) *m,f*

**blasphemous** ['blæsfəməs] *adj* blasfemo(a)

**blasphemy** ['blæsfəmɪ] *n* blasfemia *f*

**blast** [blɑːst] **1** *n* (**a**) *(of wind)* ráfaga *f; (of heat)* bocanada *f; (of whistle, horn)* pitido *m;* **at full b.** *(of machines)* a toda máquina; *Fam* **the radio was on full b.** la radio estaba a todo volumen; **b. furnace** alto horno *m*

(**b**) *(explosion)* explosión *f; (shock wave)* onda *f*

expansiva; *Fam* **meeting him was a real b. from the past!** encontrarme con él fue como volver de repente al pasado

(**c**) *US Fam (good time)* pasada *f*; **we had a b.** lo pasamos bomba

**2** *vt* (**a**) *(hole, tunnel)* abrir (con la ayuda de explosivos); **the building had been blasted by a bomb** una bomba había volado el edificio; *Fam* **to b. sb's head off** volarle la cabeza a alguien; *Fam* **to b. sb's hopes** dar al traste con las esperanzas de alguien

(**b**) *Fam (criticize)* machacar, atacar

(**c**) *Fam* **b. (it)!** ¡maldita sea!

▸**blast off** *vi (of space rocket)* despegar

**blast-off** ['blɑːstɒf] *n (of space rocket)* lanzamiento *m*

**blatant** ['bleɪtənt] *adj* descarado(a), manifiesto(a); **a b. lie** una mentira evidente

**blatantly** ['bleɪtəntlɪ] *adv* descaradamente, ostensiblemente; **b. obvious** más que evidente

**blather** ['blæðə(r)] *vi US Fam* desbarrar, decir paridas

**blaze** [bleɪz] **1** *n* (**a**) *(fire) (in hearth)* fuego *m*, hoguera *f*; *(uncontrolled)* fuego *m*, incendio *m* (**b**) *(of colour, light)* explosión *f*; **in a b. of anger** en un ataque de ira; **in a b. of publicity** acompañado(a) de una gran campaña publicitaria; **to go out in a b. of glory** marcharse de forma apoteósica (**c**) *Fam* **what the blazes does he want?** ¿qué diantre(s) quiere?

**2** *vt Fig* **to b. a trail** abrir nuevos caminos

**3** *vi (of fire)* arder; *(of sun)* abrasar; *(of light)* estar encendido(a); **to b. with anger** estar encendido(a) de ira

**blazer** ['bleɪzə(r)] *n* chaqueta *f*, americana *f*

**blazing** ['bleɪzɪŋ] *adj (building)* en llamas; *Fig* **a b. row** una discusión muy violenta

**bleach** [bliːtʃ] **1** *n* lejía *f*

**2** *vt (cloth)* desteñir; **hair bleached by the sun** cabellos descoloridos por el sol

**bleak** [bliːk] *adj (landscape, mountain)* desolado(a); *(weather)* miserable; *(outlook)* desolador(ora)

**bleary** ['blɪərɪ] *adj (eyes)* enrojecido(a)

**bleary-eyed** ['blɪərɪˈaɪd] *adj* **to be b.** tener los ojos enrojecidos

**bleat** [bliːt] **1** *n (of lamb)* balido *m*

**2** *vi (of lamb)* balar; *Fig (complain)* lamentarse (**about** de)

**bleed** [bliːd] *(pt & pp* **bled** [bled]*)* **1** *vt Med* sangrar; *(radiator)* purgar; *Fig* **to b. sb dry** chupar la sangre a alguien

**2** *vi* sangrar; **his nose is bleeding** le sangra la nariz; **to b. to death** morir desangrado(a)

**bleeder** ['bliːdə(r)] *n Br very Fam* imbécil *mf*, soplagaitas *mf inv*; **poor b.** pobre diablo

**bleeding** ['bliːdɪŋ] **1** *n* hemorragia *f*; **has the b. stopped?** ¿te ha dejado de salir sangre?

**2** *adj* (**a**) *(wound)* sangrante (**b**) *Br very Fam (for emphasis)* **you b. liar!** ¡mentiroso de mierda!

**3** *adv Br very Fam (for emphasis)* **it's b. cold/expensive** hace un frío/es caro de la leche; **that was b. stupid !** ¡qué gilipollez!

**bleep** [bliːp] **1** *n* pitido *m*

**2** *vi* pitar

**bleeper** ['bliːpə(r)] *n (pager)* buscapersonas *m inv*, busca *m*

**blemish** ['blemɪʃ] **1** *n (mark)* mancha *f*, marca *f*; *Fig (on reputation)* mancha *f*, mácula *f*

**2** *vt Fig (spoil)* manchar, perjudicar

**blench** [blentʃ] *vi (flinch)* inmutarse

**blend** [blend] **1** *n* mezcla *f*

**2** *vt (styles, ideas)* conjugar (**with** con); *Culin* mezclar; **b. the eggs and butter together** mezclar los huevos y la mantequilla; **blended tea/tobacco** mezcla *f* de tés/tabacos

**3** *vi (mix together)* mezclarse

▸**blend in** *vi (with surroundings)* armonizar (**with** con)

▸**blend into** *vt insep (surroundings)* confundirse con; **to b. into the background** *(go unnoticed)* pasar desapercibido(a)

**blender** ['blendə(r)] *n* batidora *f*

**bless** [bles] *(pt & pp* **blessed** [blest]*)* *vt (say blessing for)* bendecir; **God b. you!** ¡(que) Dios te bendiga!; **b. you!** *(when sb sneezes)* ¡jesús!; **he is blessed with quick wits** tiene la suerte de ser muy espabilado; **they have been blessed with two fine children** han tenido dos hermosos hijos

**blessed** ['blesɪd] *adj* (**a**) *(holy)* sagrado(a), santo(a); **the B. Sacrament** el Santísimo Sacramento (**b**) *Fam (for emphasis)* dichoso(a); **a b. nuisance** una pesadez; **I can't see a b. thing!** ¡no veo un pimiento!

**blessing** ['blesɪŋ] *n* (**a**) *(religious)* bendición *f*; *Fig* **she gave her son/the plan her b.** bendijo a su hijo/el plan (**b**) *(benefit, advantage)* bendición *f*, bondad *f*; **it turned out to be a b. in disguise** a pesar de lo que parecía al principio, resultó ser una bendición; **it was a mixed b.** tuvo sus cosas malas y sus cosas buenas; **to count one's blessings** dar gracias (a Dios) por lo que se tiene

**blether** ['bleðər] *vi Fam (talk rubbish)* desbarrar, decir paridas

**blew** [bluː] *pt of* **blow**

**blight** [blaɪt] **1** *n (crop disease)* mildiu *m*; *Fig* plaga *f*; **potato b.** mildiu *m* de la patata; **to cast a b. on sth** enturbiar algo

**2** *vt Fig* menoscabar, socavar; **to b. sb's hopes** truncar las esperanzas de alguien

**blighter** ['blaɪtə(r)] *n Br Fam Old-fashioned (fellow)* tipo *m*, gachó *m*; **poor b.** pobre diablo *m*; **lucky b.** suertudo(a) *m,f*

**blimey** ['blaɪmɪ] *exclam Br Fam* ¡caray!, ¡caramba!

**blind¹** [blaɪnd] **1** *npl* **the b.** los ciegos; *Fig* **it's like the b. leading the b.** es como un ciego guiando a otro ciego; **b. school** escuela *f* para ciegos

**2** *adj* ciego(a); **to be b.** ser *or* estar ciego(a); **to go b.** quedarse ciego(a); **to be b. to sth** no ver algo; **a b. man** un ciego; **a b. woman** una ciega; **to be b. in one eye** ser tuerto(a); **to be as b. as a bat** ser cegato(a) perdido(a); **to turn a b. eye (to sth)** hacer la vista gorda (con algo); **to be b. with fury** estar ciego de ira; *Fam* **he didn't take a b. bit of notice** no hizo ni caso; **it didn't make a b. bit of difference** no importa lo más mínimo; **b. alley** callejón *m* sin salida; **b. date** cita *f* a ciegas; **b. man's buff** la gallinita ciega; **b. spot** *(for driver)* ángulo *m* muerto

**3** *adv* **to be b. drunk** estar borracho(a) perdido(a)

**4** *vt (deprive of sight, dazzle)* cegar; *Fig* **love blinded her to his faults** el amor le impedía ver sus defectos

**blind²** *n Br* persiana *f*

**blindfold** ['blaɪndfəʊld] **1** *n* venda *f*

**2** *vt* vendar los ojos a

**blinding** ['blaɪndɪŋ] *adj (light)* cegador(ora); *Fig (intensity)* violento(a)

**blindly** ['blaɪndlɪ] *adv Fig (to obey, follow)* ciegamente

**blindness** ['blaɪndnɪs] *n also Fig* ceguera *f*

**blink** [blɪŋk] **1** *n* (a) *(of eyes)* parpadeo *m*, pestañeo *m*; *Br Fam* **the TV is on the b. again** ya se ha vuelto a escacharrar la tele

**2** *vt* **to b. one's eyes** parpadear, pestañear

**3** *vi (of person)* parpadear, pestañear; *(of lights)* parpadear

**blinkered** ['blɪŋkəd] *adj (approach, attitude)* estrecho(a) de miras, cerrado(a)

**blinkers** ['blɪŋkəz] *npl* (a) *(for horse)* anteojeras *fpl*; *Fig* **to be wearing b.** ser estrecho(a) de miras (b) *Fam (indicators)* intermitentes *mpl*

**blinking** ['blɪŋkɪŋ] **1** *adj* (a) *(light)* intermitente (b) *Br Fam (for emphasis)* puñetero(a); **what a b. nuisance!** ¡vaya lata!; **you b. idiot!** ¡idiota de las narices!

**2** *adv (for emphasis)* **it's b. cold/expensive** hace un frío/es caro de narices

**blip** [blɪp] *n (on radar screen)* parpadeo *m*; *Fam (temporary problem)* pequeño problema *m*

**bliss** [blɪs] *n* éxtasis *m inv*; **breakfast in bed – what b.!** el desayuno en la cama, ¡qué maravilla!

**blissful** ['blɪsfʊl] *adj* maravilloso(a), feliz; **to be in b. ignorance** ser felizmente ignorante

**blissfully** ['blɪsfʊlɪ] *adv* felizmente; **b. happy** completamente feliz; **b. ignorant** felizmente ignorante

**blister** ['blɪstə(r)] **1** *n (on feet, skin)* ampolla *f*; *(on paint)* burbuja *f*

**2** *vt (feet, skin)* levantar ampollas en, ampollar; *(paint)* hacer que salgan burbujas en

**3** *vi (of feet, skin)* ampollarse; *(of paint)* hacer burbujas

**blistering** ['blɪstərɪŋ] *adj (sun, heat)* abrasador(ora), achicharrante; *(criticism, attack)* feroz, despiadado(a)

**blithe** ['blaɪð] *adj* alegre

**blithely** ['blaɪðlɪ] *adv* alegremente

**blithering** ['blɪðərɪŋ] *adj* **a b. idiot** un verdadero idiota

**blitz** [blɪts] *n (air bombardment)* bombardeo *m*, ataque *m* aéreo; *Hist* **The B.** = bombardeo alemán de ciudades británicas en 1940-41; *Fam Fig* **let's have a b. on that paperwork** vamos a quitarnos de encima estos papeles

**blizzard** ['blɪzəd] *n* ventisca *f*, tormenta *f* de nieve

**bloated** ['bləʊtɪd] *adj (stomach, budget)* hinchado(a); *(ego)* exagerado(a)

**blob** [blɒb] *n (of cream, jam)* cuajarón *m*; *(of paint)* goterón *m*; *(of ink)* gota *f*

**bloc** [blɒk] *n Pol* bloque *m*

**block** [blɒk] **1** *n* (a) *(of wood, stone)* bloque *m*; *(of butcher, for execution)* tajo *m*; *Fam* **I'll knock your b. off!** ¡te rompo la crisma!; **b. and tackle** *(for lifting)* polipasto *m*, sistema *m* de poleas; **b. capitals** (letras *fpl*) mayúsculas *fpl*; **b. diagram** *(flowchart)* diagrama *m* (de flujo *or* bloques)

(b) *(building)* bloque *m*; *US (group of buildings)* manzana *f*, *Am* cuadra *f*; *Br* **b. of flats** bloque (de pisos)

(c) *(of shares)* paquete *m*; *(of seats, tickets)* grupo *m*, conjunto *m*; *Comptr* **a b. of text** un bloque de texto; **b. booking** reserva *f* de grupo; **b. vote** voto *m* por delegación

**2** *vt* (a) *(pipe, road, proposal)* bloquear; *(toilet, sink)* atascar; *(exit, stairs)* obstruir; **to b. sb's way** cerrar el paso a alguien; **to b. sb's view** no dejar ver a alguien; *Fin* **to b. a cheque** anular un cheque

(b) *Comptr* **to b. text** marcar un bloque de texto

▸**block off** *vt sep (road, exit)* cortar, bloquear

▸**block out** *vt sep (light)* impedir el paso de; *(memory)* enterrar; **she wears ear plugs to b. out the music** se pone tapones en los oídos para no oír la música

▸**block up** *vt sep (door, window)* atrancar; *(hole, entrance)* tapar; **to have a blocked-up nose** tener la nariz taponada

**blockade** [blɒ'keɪd] **1** n bloqueo m, embargo m

**2** vt bloquear

**blockage** ['blɒkɪdʒ] n obstrucción f

**blockbuster** ['blɒkbʌstə(r)] n (success) bombazo m, granéxito m

**blockhead** ['blɒkhed] n Fam tarugo m, zoquete m

**bloke** [bləʊk] n Br Fam tío m, tipo m

**blonde** [blɒnd] **1** n (woman) rubia f; Méx güera f; CAm chela f; Carib catira f

**2** adj rubio(a); Méx güero(a); CAm chele(a); Carib catire(a)

**blood** [blʌd] **1** n (a) sangre f; **to give b.** donar sangre; **b. bank** banco m de sangre; **b. cell** glóbulo m; **b. clot** coágulo m; **b. count** recuento m de células sanguíneas, hemograma m; **b. donor** donante mf de sangre; **b. group** grupo m sanguíneo; **b. poisoning** septicemia f; **b. pressure** tensión f (arterial), presión f sanguínea; **to have high/low b. pressure** tener la tensión alta/baja; **they are b. relations** les unen lazos de sangre; **b. sports** deportes mpl cinegéticos; **b. test** análisis m de sangre; **b. transfusion** transfusión f sanguínea; **b. vessel** vaso m sanguíneo

(**b**) (idioms) **to have b. on one's hands** tener las manos manchadas de sangre; **it makes my b. boil when...** me hierve la sangre cuando...; **it makes my b. run cold** me hiela la sangre; **in cold b.** a sangre fría; **he's after your b.** te tiene ojeriza; **to have sth in one's b.** llevar algo en la sangre; **it's like trying to get b. out of a stone** es como intentar sacar agua de una piedra; Prov **b. is thicker than water** la sangre tira

**2** vt (initiate) (soldier, politician) dar el bautismo de fuego a

**bloodbath** ['blʌdbɑːθ] n baño m de sangre

**bloodcurdling** ['blʌdkɜːdlɪŋ] adj aterrador(ora), horripilante

**bloodhound** ['blʌdhaʊnd] n sabueso m

**bloodless** ['blʌdlɪs] adj (**a**) (without bloodshed) incruento(a), sin derramamiento de sangre; **b. coup** (in country) golpe m incruento; Fig (in company, political party) golpe m de mano (**b**) (pale) pálido(a)

**bloodletting** ['blʌdletɪŋ] n (**a**) Med sangría f (**b**) (slaughter) sangría f, matanza f; (internal feuding) luchas fpl intestinas

**bloodshed** ['blʌdʃed] n derramamiento m de sangre

**bloodshot** ['blʌdʃɒt] adj (eyes) inyectado(a) de sangre

**bloodstain** ['blʌdsteɪn] n mancha f de sangre

**bloodstained** ['blʌdsteɪnd] adj manchado(a) de sangre

**bloodstream** ['blʌdstriːm] n torrente m or flujo m sanguíneo

**bloodsucker** ['blʌdsʌkə(r)] n (mosquito, leech) chupador(ora) m,f de sangre; Fam (person) sanguijuela f, parásito(a) m,f

**bloodthirsty** ['blʌdθɜːstɪ] adj sanguinario(a)

**bloody** ['blʌdɪ] **1** adj (**a**) (bleeding) sanguinolento(a), sangriento(a); (bloodstained) ensangrentado(a); (battle, revolution) sangriento(a); Fig **to give sb a b. nose** poner a alguien en su sitio (**b**) Br very Fam puñetero(a), maldito(a); **a b. liar** un mentiroso de mierda; **b. hell!** ¡mierda!, ¡me cago en la mar!

**2** adv Br very Fam **it's b. hot!** hace un calor de la leche; **not b. likely!** ¡ni de coña!; **he can b. well do it himself!** ¡joder, que lo haga él!

**bloody-minded** [blʌdɪ'maɪndɪd] adj Br terco(a)

**bloom** [bluːm] **1** n flor f; **in (full) b.** en flor, florecido(a); Fig en su apogeo; **in the b. of youth** en la flor de la edad

**2** vi (of garden, flower, talent) florecer; Fig **to b. with health** estar rebosante de salud

**bloomer** ['bluːmə(r)] n (**a**) Fam (mistake) metedura f de pata (**b**) (bread) hogaza f

**bloomers** ['bluːməz] npl pololos mpl

**blooming** ['bluːmɪŋ] Br Fam (for emphasis) **1** adj condenado(a); **you b. idiot!** ¡pedazo de idiota!

**2** adv **b. good** genial; **b. awful** fatal; **he's b. useless!** ¡es un inútil!

**blossom** ['blɒsəm] **1** n flor f; **to be in b.** estar en flor

**2** vi also Fig florecer; Fig **to b. into sth** transformarse en algo

**blot** [blɒt] **1** n (of ink) borrón m, mancha f; Fig tacha f, mácula f; Fig **to be a b. on the landscape** estropear el paisaje

**2** vt (pt & pp blotted) (**a**) (stain) emborronar, manchar; Fig **he had blotted his copybook** había manchado su reputación (**b**) (with blotting paper) secar

▸**blot out** vt sep (sun, light) impedir el paso de; (memory) enterrar

**blotch** [blɒtʃ] n (on skin) mancha f, enrojecimiento m

**blotchy** ['blɒtʃɪ] adj (skin) con manchas

**blotter** ['blɒtə(r)] n (blotting pad) secante m (de rodillo)

**blotting paper** ['blɒtɪŋpeɪpə(r)] n papel m secante

**blotto** ['blɒtəʊ] adj Br Fam (drunk) **to be b.** estar ciego(a) or bolinga

**blouse** [blaʊz] n blusa f

**blow¹** [bləʊ] n (**a**) (hit) golpe m; **to come to blows (over sth)** llegar a las manos (por algo); Fig **to strike a b. for sth** romper una lanza por algo; *Fig* **to soften the b.** para suavizar el golpe (**b**) *(setback)* duro golpe *m*; **this news was a b. to us** la noticia fue un duro golpe para nosotros

**blow²** (*pt* **blew** [bluː], *pp* **blown** [bləʊn]) **1** *vt* (**a**) *(of wind)* **the wind blew down the fence** el viento derribó la valla; **the wind blew the door open** el viento abrió la puerta

(**b**) *(of person) (flute, whistle, horn)* tocar; **to b. glass** soplar vidrio; **to b. the dust off sth** soplar el polvo que hay en algo; **to b. sb a kiss** lanzar un beso a alguien; **to b. bubbles** hacer pompas de jabón; **to b. one's nose** sonarse la nariz; *Fig* **to b. one's own trumpet** echarse flores; *Fig* **to b. the whistle on sth/sb** dar la alarma sobre algo/alguien

(**c**) *Elec* **the hairdryer has blown a fuse** se ha fundido el fusible (del enchufe) del secador; *Fig* **to b. a fuse** *(of person)* ponerse hecho(a) una furia; *Fam Fig* **the Grand Canyon blew my mind** el Gran Cañón me dejó patidifuso(a)

(**d**) *Fam (chance, opportunity)* echar a perder, mandar al garete; **that's blown it!** ¡lo ha estropeado todo!

(**e**) *Fam (money)* fundir; **he blew all his savings on a car** se fundió todos sus ahorros en un coche

**2** *vi* (**a**) *(of wind, person)* soplar; **to b. away** *(of newspaper)* salir volando; **the fence blew down** el viento derribó la valla; **to b. off** *(of hat)* salir volando; **my papers blew out of the window** mis papeles salieron volando por la ventana; **the door blew open/shut** el viento abrió/cerró la puerta; **to b. on one's fingers** calentarse los dedos soplando; *Fig* **he's always blowing hot and cold** está cambiando constantemente de opinión

(**b**) *Elec (of fuse)* fundirse

▶**blow away 1** *vt sep* **the wind blew the newspaper away** el viento se llevó el periódico; *Fam Fig* **to b. sb away** *(shoot dead)* pegar un tiro a alguien; *Fam Fig* **his latest film blew me away** su última película me dejó alucinado

**2** *vi (of paper, hat)* salir volando

▶**blow off 1** *vt sep* **the wind blew her hat off** el viento le quitó el sombrero; *Fam Fig* **to b. sb's head off** volarle la cabeza a alguien

**2** *vi (of hat)* salir volando

▶**blow out** *vt sep (extinguish)* apagar

▶**blow over** *vi (of storm)* amainar; *(of scandal)* calmarse

▶**blow up 1** *vt sep* (**a**) *(inflate) (balloon, tyre)* inflar, hinchar (**b**) *(explode)* explosionar, (hacer) explotar (**c**) *Phot (enlarge)* ampliar; *Fig* **it had been blown up out of all proportion** se sacaron las cosas de quicio

**2** *vi (of bomb)* explotar, hacer explosión; *Fig (lose one's temper)* explotar, ponerse hecho(a) una furia

**blow-by-blow** [bləʊbaɪˈbləʊ] *adj (account)* detallado(a), con todo lujo de detalles

**blow-dry** [ˈbləʊdraɪ] **1** *n* secado *m*
**2** *vt* secar con secador de mano

**blower** [ˈbləʊə(r)] *n Br Fam (telephone)* teléfono *m*

**blowhole** [ˈbləʊhəʊl] *n (of whale)* espiráculo *m*

**blowjob** [ˈbləʊdʒɒb] *n Vulg* mamada *f*; **to give sb a b.** mamársela a alguien

**blowlamp** [ˈbləʊlæmp] *n* soplete *m*

**blown** [bləʊn] *pp of* **blow**

**blow-out** [ˈbləʊaʊt] *n* (**a**) *(of tyre)* reventón *m*, *Am* ponchadura *f* (**b**) *Fam (big meal)* comilona *f*, cuchipanda *f*

**blowpipe** [ˈbləʊpaɪp] *n (weapon)* cerbatana *f*

**blowtorch** [ˈbləʊtɔːtʃ] *n* soplete *m*

**blowzy** [ˈblaʊzɪ] *adj (woman)* desaseada y gorda

**blub** [blʌb] (*pt & pp* **blubbed**) *vi Fam (cry)* lloriquear

**blubber** [ˈblʌbə(r)] **1** *n (fat)* grasa *f*
**2** *vi Fam (cry)* lloriquear

**bludgeon** [ˈblʌdʒən] *vt* apalear; *Fig* **to b. sb into doing sth** forzar a alguien a que haga algo

**blue** [bluː] **1** *n* (**a**) *(colour)* azul *m*; *Fig* **out of the b.** inesperadamente (**b**) *(music)* el blues; *Fam* **to have the blues** *(be depressed)* estar muy depre

**2** *adj* (**a**) *(colour)* azul; **b. with cold** amoratado(a) de frío; *Fam* **she can complain until she's b. in the face** puede quejarse todo lo que quiera; **once in a b. moon** de Pascuas a Ramos; *Fam* **to scream b. murder** poner el grito en el cielo; **b. blood** sangre *f* azul; **b. cheese** queso *m* azul; **b. whale** ballena *f* azul (**b**) *Fam (sad)* **to feel b.** estar depre *or* triste (**c**) *Fam (obscene) (joke)* verde; **to tell b. stories** contar chistes verdes; **a b. film** una película porno

**bluebell** [ˈbluːbel] *n* campanilla *f*

**blueberry** [ˈbluːbərɪ] *n US* arándano *m*

**bluebird** [ˈbluːbɜːd] *n* azulejo *m*

**bluebottle** [ˈbluːbɒtəl] *n* moscarda *f*, mosca *f* azul

**blue-chip** [ˈbluːtʃɪp] *adj Fin (shares, company)* de gran liquidez, puntero(a)

**blue-collar** [ˈbluːkɒlə(r)] *adj* **b. worker** trabajador(ora) *m,f* manual

**blue-eyed** [ˈbluːaɪd] *adj* de ojos azules; *Br Fam* **his mother's b. boy** el niño bonito de mamá

**blueprint** [ˈbluːprɪnt] *n Archit Ind* cianotipo *m*, plano *m*; *Fig (plan)* proyecto *m*

**bluetit** [ˈbluːtɪt] *n* herrerillo *m*, alionín *m*

**bluff¹** [blʌf] **1** *n (pretence)* farol *m*; **to call sb's b.** *(at cards)* ver a alguien con un farol; *(in negotiation)* retar a alguien a que cumpla sus amenazas

**2** *vi (pretend)* fingir, simular; *(in cards)* tirarse un farol

**bluff²** *n (cliff)* despeñadero *m*

**bluff³** *adj (manner)* abrupto(a)

**blunder** ['blʌndə(r)] **1** *n* metedura *f* de pata; *(more serious)* error *m*

**2** *vi* (a) *(make mistake)* meter la pata; *(more seriously)* cometer un error (b) *(move clumsily)* **to b. along** avanzar dando tumbos; **to b. into sb/sth** tropezar con alguien/algo

**blunderbuss** ['blʌndəbʌs] *n* trabuco *m*

**blunt** [blʌnt] **1** *adj* (a) *(blade)* romo(a), desafilado(a); *(pencil)* desafilado(a) (b) *(manner, statement, person)* franco(a); *(refusal)* contundente; **to be b.,...** para ser francos,...

**2** *vt (blade, pencil)* desafilar; *Fig (anger, enthusiasm)* atenuar, templar

**bluntly** ['blʌntlɪ] *adv (frankly)* sin rodeos, claramente

**bluntness** ['blʌntnɪs] *n* (a) *(of blade)* embotadura *f* (b) *(of manner, statement, person)* franqueza *f*, llaneza *f*

**blur** [blɜ:(r)] **1** *n (vague shape)* imagen *f* borrosa; *(unclear memory)* vago recuerdo *m*; **to go by in a b.** *(of time)* pasar sin sentir *or* en un suspiro

**2** *vt* ( *pt & pp* **blurred**) desdibujar

**3** *vi also Fig* desdibujarse

**blurb** [blɜ:b] *n Fam (on book cover)* notas y citas *fpl* promocionales

**blurred** [blɜ:d] *adj* borroso(a)

▶**blurt out** [blɜ:t] *vt sep* soltar

**blush** [blʌʃ] **1** *n* rubor *m*, sonrojo *m*; **to spare sb's blushes** salvar a alguien del bochorno

**2** *vi* ruborizarse, sonrojarse; **I b. to admit it** me da vergüenza confesarlo

**blusher** ['blʌʃə(r)] *n (rouge)* colorete *m*

**bluster** ['blʌstə(r)] **1** *n (protests, threats)* bravuconadas *fpl*, fanfarronadas *fpl*

**2** *vi (protest, threaten)* echar bravatas

**blustery** ['blʌstərɪ] *adj (wind)* tempestuoso(a); **a b. day** un día de vientos tempestuosos

**BMA** [bi:e'meɪ] *n (abbr* **British Medical Association**) = colegio británico de médicos

**BO** [bi:'əʊ] *n Fam (abbr* **body odour**) sobaquina *f*, olor *m* a sudor

**boa** ['bəʊə] *n* **b. (constrictor)** boa *f* (constrictor); **feather b.** boa *m*

**boar** ['bɔ:(r)] *n (male pig)* verraco *m*; *(wild pig)* jabalí *m*

**board** [bɔ:d] **1** *n* (a) *(of wood)* tabla *f*, tablón *m*; *(for notices)* tablón *m*; *(for chess, draughts)* tablero *m*; *(blackboard)* pizarra *f*, encerado *m*; **to go by the b.** *(be abandoned, ignored)* irse a pique; **across the b.** de manera global *or* general; **b. game** juego *m* de mesa

(b) *(group of people)* **b. (of directors)** consejo

*m* de administración; **b. of enquiry** comisión *f* investigadora; *Educ* **b. of examiners** tribunal *m* (de examinadores); *Br* **B. of Trade** = departamento ministerial responsable de la supervisión del comercio y de la promoción de las exportaciones; **b. meeting** reunión *f* del consejo, junta *f*

(c) *(meals)* **half b.** media pensión *f*; **full b.** pensión *f* completa; **b. and lodging** alojamiento *m* y comida

(d) *Naut* **on b.** a bordo; **to go on b.** subir a bordo; *Fig* **to take an idea/a proposal on b.** aceptar una idea/una propuesta

**2** *vt (ship, plane)* embarcar en; *(train, bus)* subir a, montar en

**3** *vi* (a) *(lodge)* alojarse (**with** en casa de); *(at school)* estar interno(a)

(b) *Av* **flight 123 is now boarding** el vuelo 123 está en estos momentos procediendo al embarque

▶**board up** *vt sep (house, window)* cubrir con tablas, entablar

**boarder** ['bɔ:də(r)] *n (lodger)* huésped *mf*; *(at school)* interno(a) *m,f*

**boarding** ['bɔ:dɪŋ] *n* (a) *Av* **b. card** *or* **pass** tarjeta *f* de embarque (b) **b. house** pensión *f*; **b. school** internado *m*

**boardroom** ['bɔ:dru:m] *n* sala *f* de juntas

**boardwalk** ['bɔ:dwɔ:k] *n US* paseo *m* marítimo entarimado

**boast** [bəʊst] **1** *n* jactancia *f*, alarde *m*

**2** *vt* **the school boasts a fine library** el colegio posee una excelente biblioteca

**3** *vi* alardear (**about** de); **it's nothing to b. about!** ¡no es como para estar orgulloso!

**boastful** ['bəʊstfʊl] *adj* jactancioso(a), presuntuoso(a)

**boasting** ['bəʊstɪŋ] *n* jactancia *f*, alardeo *m*

**boat** [bəʊt] *n (in general)* barco *m*; *(small)* barca *f*, bote *m*; *(large)* buque *m*; **I came by b.** vine en barco; *Fig* **we're all in the same b.** estamos todos en el mismo barco; *Fig* **to push the b. out** *(celebrate lavishly)* tirar la casa por la ventana; **the B. race** = carrera anual de barcos de remo que enfrenta en el río Támesis a una embarcación de la universidad de Cambridge con otra de la de Oxford; **b. train** = ferrocarril que enlaza con una línea marítima

**boat-builder** ['bəʊtbɪldə(r)] *n* constructor(ora) *m,f* de barcos

**boater** ['bəʊtə(r)] *n (straw hat)* canotier *m*

**boathouse** ['bəʊthaʊs] *n* cobertizo *m* para barcas

**boating** ['bəʊtɪŋ] *n* paseo *m* en barca; **to go b.** ir a pasear en barca

**boat-load** ['bəʊtləʊd] *n (of cargo, tourists)* cargamento *m*; *Fig* **by the b.** a espuertas

**boatswain** ['bəʊsən] n Naut contramaestre m

**boatyard** ['bəʊtjɑːd] n astillero m

**Bob** [bɒb] n Fam **and B.'s your uncle!** ¡y ya está!

**bob**[1] [bɒb] **1** n (**a**) (curtsey) ligera genuflexión f (a modo de saludo) (**b**) (hairstyle) corte m estilo paje (**c**) (bobsleigh) bobsleigh m, bob m

**2** vt (pt & pp **bobbed**) (**a**) **to b. one's head** hacer un gesto con la cabeza (**b**) **to have one's hair bobbed** cortarse el pelo a lo paje

**3** vi **to b. up and down** moverse arriba y abajo; **to b. about** (on water) mecerse

**bob**[2] (pl **bob**) n Br Old-fashioned Fam (shilling) chelín m; **that must have cost a few b.** debe haber costado un pastón

**bobbin** ['bɒbɪn] n (on machine) canilla f, bobina f; (for thread) carrete m, bobina f

**bobble** ['bɒbəl] n (on hat) borla f

**bobby** ['bɒbɪ] n Br Fam (policeman) poli mf

**bobsled** ['bɒbsled], **bobsleigh** ['bɒbsleɪ] n bobsleigh m, bob m

**bod** [bɒd] n Fam (**a**) Br (person) tío(a) m,f (**b**) (body) cuerpo m; **he's got a nice b.** tiene un cuerpazo

**bode** [bəʊd] vi **this bodes well/ill for the future** es un buen/mal presagio para el futuro

**bodice** ['bɒdɪs] n (**a**) (part of dress) cuerpo m (**b**) (undergarment) corpiño m

**bodily** ['bɒdɪlɪ] **1** adj corporal; **b. functions** funciones fpl fisiológicas; **b. needs** necesidades fpl físicas

**2** adv en volandas; **he was carried b. to the door** lo llevaron en volandas hasta la puerta

**body** ['bɒdɪ] n (**a**) (of person, animal) cuerpo m; (dead) cadáver m; Fig **to have enough to keep b. and soul together** tener lo justo para vivir; Fam **over my dead b.!** ¡por encima de mi cadáver!; **b. bag** = saco de plástico para contener cadáveres; Fig **a b. blow** (severe setback) un duro golpe; **b. builder** culturista mf; **b. building** culturismo m; Mil **b. count** (of casualties) número m de bajas; **b. language** lenguaje m corporal; **b. odour** olor m corporal; **b. piercing** perforaciones fpl en el cuerpo, "piercing" m; **b. warmer** chaleco m acolchado

(**b**) (of hair, wine) cuerpo m

(**c**) (group) grupo m, conjunto m; (organization) entidad f; **public b.** organismo m público; **a large b. of people** un nutrido grupo de gente; **a b. of evidence** un conjunto de pruebas; **the b. politic** el Estado, la nación; **b. of water** masa f de agua

(**d**) (main part) (of car) carrocería f; (of letter, argument) núcleo m; **b. shop** taller m de carrocería

(**e**) (garment) body m; **b. stocking** (leotard) malla f; (women's undergarment) body m

**bodyguard** ['bɒdɪgɑːd] n (person) guardaespaldas mf inv, escolta mf; (group) escolta f

**bodywork** ['bɒdɪwɜːk] n (of car) carrocería f

**Boer** ['bəʊə(r)] n bóer mf; **the B. War** la guerra de los bóers

**boffin** ['bɒfɪn] n Br Fam Hum (scientist) sabio m, lumbrera f

**bog** [bɒg] n (**a**) (marsh) pantano m, ciénaga f (**b**) Br very Fam (toilet) tigre m, váter m; **b. roll** or **paper** papel m higiénico

▸**bog down** vt sep to **get bogged down** (in mud, details) quedarse atascado(a)

**bogey** ['bəʊgɪ] (pl **bogeys**) n (**a**) (cause of fear) pesadilla f (**b**) Fam (snot) moco m

**bogeyman** ['bəʊgɪmæn] n **the b.** el coco, el hombre del saco

**boggle** ['bɒgəl] vi Fam **he boggled at the thought of her reaction** le horripilaba pensar cómo reaccionaría ella; **she boggled at paying such a price** se quedó pasmada de tener que pagar un precio tan alto; **the mind boggles!** no me lo puedo ni imaginar

**Bogota** [bɒgəˈtɑː] n Bogotá

**bogus** ['bəʊgəs] adj falso(a); Fam **he's completely b.** es un farsante

**Bohemian** [bəʊˈhiːmɪən] n & adj also Fig bohemio(a) m,f

**boil**[1] [bɔɪl] n Med forúnculo m, pústula f

**boil**[2] **1** n **to come to the b.** empezar or romper a hervir; **to bring sth to the b.** hacer que algo hierva; Fig **to go off the b.** pasar un mal momento

**2** vt hervir, cocer; **to b. the kettle** poner el agua a hervir; **a boiled egg** un huevo cocido

**3** vi hervir; **the kettle's boiling** el agua está hirviendo; **the kettle boiled dry** el hervidor se quedó sin agua; Fig **to b. with rage** enfurecerse

▸**boil down to** vt insep Fam **it all boils down to...** todo se reduce a...

▸**boil over** vi (of milk, soup) salirse, rebosar; Fig (of situation) estallar

▸**boil up** vt insep (milk, water) (poner a) hervir

**boiler** ['bɔɪlə(r)] n caldera f; **b. maker** calderero m; **b. room** (sala f de) calderas fpl; **b. suit** mono m (de trabajo)

**boiling** ['bɔɪlɪŋ] **1** adj hirviente; Fam **I'm boiling!** ¡me estoy asando!; **b. point** punto m de ebullición; Fig **the situation has reached b. point** la situación está al rojo vivo

**2** adv **it's b. hot** hace un calor abrasador

**boisterous** ['bɔɪstərəs] adj (person) alborotador(ora), bullicioso(a)

**bold** [bəʊld] adj (**a**) (brave) audaz (**b**) (shameless) fresco(a); **to be as b. as brass** tener más cara que espalda (**c**) (striking) marcado(a), acentuado(a); Typ **b. type** negrita f

**boldly** ['bəʊldlɪ] *adv (bravely)* audazmente, con audacia

**boldness** ['bəʊldnɪs] *n* audacia *f*

**Bolivia** [bə'lɪvɪə] *n* Bolivia

**Bolivian** [bə'lɪvɪən] *n & adj* boliviano(a) *m,f*

**bollard** ['bɒləd] *n Naut* bolardo *m*, noray *m*; *Br (traffic barrier)* hito *m*

**bollocking** ['bɒləkɪŋ] *n very Fam* **to give sb a b.** echar a alguien una bronca

**bollocks** ['bɒləks] *npl Vulg (testicles)* cojones *mpl*, pelotas *fpl*; **b.!** *(nonsense)* ¡chorradas!

**Bolshevik** ['bɒlʃəvɪk] *n & adj* bolchevique *mf*

**Bolshevism** ['bɒlʃəvɪzəm] *n* bolchevismo *m*

**bolshie, bolshy** ['bɒlʃɪ] *adj Fam* **to be b.** estar renegón(ona)

**bolster** ['bəʊlstə(r)] **1** *n* almohada *f* cilíndrica

**2** *vt (confidence, pride)* reforzar, fortalecer

**bolt** [bəʊlt] **1** *n* (**a**) *(on door)* cerrojo *m*, pestillo *m*; *(metal fastening)* perno *m*; *Fam* **he has shot his b.** ha quemado sus últimos cartuchos (**b**) *(dash) Fam* **she made a b. for the door** se precipitó hacia la puerta; **b. hole** refugio *m* (**c**) *(of lightning)* rayo *m*; *Fig* **to come like a b. from the blue** ocurrir de sopetón, pillar a todo el mundo por sorpresa

**2** *adv* **b. upright** erguido(a)

**3** *vt* (**a**) *(lock)* **to b. the door/window** cerrar la puerta/ventana con pestillo (**b**) *(attach with bolts)* atornillar (**c**) *(eat)* engullir

**4** *vi (of horse)* salir de estampida; *(of person)* salir huyendo

▸**bolt down** *vt insep (eat quickly)* **to b. sth down** engullir *or* zamparse algo

**bomb** [bɒm] **1** *n* bomba *f*; **to drop/plant a b.** arrojar/colocar una bomba; *Br Fam* **to go like a b.** *(go quickly)* ir como una bala; *Fam* **it cost a b.** costó un ojo de la cara; **b. disposal expert** (experto *m*) artificiero *m*; **b. scare** amenaza *f* de bomba

**2** *vt* bombardear

**3** *vi US (fail)* fracasar (estrepitosamente)

▸**bomb along** *vi Fam (go quickly)* ir a toda pastilla

**bombard** [bɒm'bɑːd] *vt* bombardear; *Fig* **to b. sb with questions** bombardear a alguien con preguntas

**bombardment** [bɒm'bɑːdmənt] *n* bombardeo *m*

**bombast** ['bɒmbæst] *n* ampulosidad *f*, altisonancia *f*

**bombastic** [bɒm'bæstɪk] *adj* ampuloso(a), altisonante

**bomber** ['bɒmə(r)] *n (aircraft)* bombardero *m*; *(person)* terrorista *mf (que coloca bombas)*; **b. jacket** cazadora *f*

**bombing** ['bɒmɪŋ] *n (aerial)* bombardeo *m*; *(by terrorist)* atentado *m* con bomba

**bombshell** ['bɒmʃel] *n* obús *m*; *Fig* **to drop a b.** dejar caer una bomba; *Fam Fig* **a blonde b.** una rubia explosiva

**bombsite** ['bɒmsaɪt] *n* lugar *m* arrasado por un bombardeo; *Fig* **your bedroom is a b.!** ¡tu cuarto está hecho una leonera!

**bona fide** ['bəʊnə'faɪdɪ] *adj* auténtico(a), genuino(a)

**bonanza** [bə'nænzə] *n* filón *m*; **a b. year** un año de grandes beneficios *or* de bonanza

**bonbon** ['bɒnbɒn] *n* caramelo *m*

**bonce** [bɒns] *n Fam (head)* coco *m*, tarro *m*

**bond** [bɒnd] **1** *n* (**a**) *(between materials)* unión *f*; *(between people)* vínculo *m*; **to feel a b. with sb** sentir un vínculo de unión con alguien; *Literary* **bonds** *(ropes, chains)* ataduras *fpl* (**b**) *Fin* bono *m* (**c**) *Law* fianza *f*; *Formal* **my word is my b.** siempre cumplo mi palabra (**d**) *Com* **to be in b.** estar en depósito aduanero

**2** *vt* (**a**) *(stick)* pegar, adherir (**b**) *Fig (unite)* **to b. together** unir

**3** *vi* (**a**) *(stick)* pegar, adherirse (**b**) *Fig (form attachment)* unirse (**with** a)

**bondage** ['bɒndɪdʒ] *n* (**a**) *(slavery)* esclavitud *f*, servidumbre *f* (**b**) *(sexual practice)* = práctica sexual en la que se ata a uno de los participantes

**bonding** ['bɒndɪŋ] *n* (lazos *mpl* de) unión *f*; *Hum* **they're doing a bit of male b.** están haciendo cosas de hombres

**bone** [bəʊn] **1** *n* (**a**) *(of person, animal)* hueso *m*; *(of fish)* espina *f*; **b. china** porcelana *f* fina; **b. meal** harina *f* de hueso (**b**) *(idioms)* **to work one's fingers to the b.** matarse a trabajar; **to be b. idle** *or* **lazy** ser más vago(a) que la chaqueta de un guardia; **I feel it in my bones** tengo una corazonada; **b. of contention** manzana *f* de la discordia; *Fam* **to have a b. to pick with sb** tener que arreglar *or* ajustar cuentas con alguien; **he made no bones about it** no trató de disimularlo; **close to the b.** *(tactless, risqué)* fuera de tono

**2** *vt (chicken)* deshuesar; *(fish)* quitar las espinas a

▸**bone up on** *vt insep Fam* empollarse

**bone-dry** ['bəʊn'draɪ] *adj* completamente seco(a)

**bonfire** ['bɒnfaɪə(r)] *n* hoguera *f*, fogata *f*; *Br* **B. Night** = fiesta del 5 de noviembre en que de noche se hacen hogueras y hay fuegos artificiales

**bongo** ['bɒŋgəʊ] *n Mus* **b. drums, bongos** bongos *mpl*, bongós *mpl*

**bonhomie** ['bɒnɒmiː] *n* camaradería *f*

**bonk¹** [bɒŋk] *vt Fam (hit)* pegar

**bonk²** *Br very Fam* **1** *n (sex)* **to have a b.** chingar, echar un casquete

**2** *vt & vi (have sex)* chingar, echar un casquete

**bonkers** ['bɒŋkəz] *adj Br Fam (mad)* **to be b.** estar majareta *or* chiflado(a)

**Bonn** [bɒn] *n* Bonn

**bonnet** ['bɒnɪt] *n* (a) *(hat)* cofia *f*, papalina *f* (b) *Br (of car)* capó *m*, *CAm, Méx* cofre *m*

**bonny** ['bɒnɪ] *adj Scot* bonito(a), precioso(a)

**bonsai** ['bɒnsaɪ] *n* bonsai *m*

**bonus** ['bəʊnəs] *n* (a) *(for productivity, seniority)* plus *m*; *(in insurance, for investment)* prima *f*; **Christmas b.** aguinaldo *m (dinero)*; **b. number** *(in lottery)* ≃ (número *m*) complementario *m*; **b. scheme** sistema *m* de primas (b) *(advantage)* ventaja *f* adicional

**bony** ['bəʊnɪ] *adj (person, limb)* huesudo(a); *(fish)* con muchas espinas

**boo** [bu:] **1** *n (pl* **boos***)* abucheo *m*
**2** *vt* abuchear
**3** *exclam (of audience, crowd)* ¡buu!; *(to frighten sb)* ¡uuh!; **he wouldn't say b. to a goose** es muy tímido

**boob** [bu:b] *Fam* **1** *n* (a) *Br (mistake)* metedura *f* de pata; **to make a b.** meter la pata (b) *Br* **boobs** *(breasts)* tetas *fpl*; **b. tube** = top ajustado sin mangas ni tirantes; *US (television)* caja tonta
**2** *vi (make mistake)* meter la pata

**booby-prize** ['bu:bɪpraɪz] *n* premio *m* para el farolillo rojo

**booby-trap** ['bu:bɪtræp] **1** *n (explosive device)* bomba *f* trampa *or* camuflada; *(practical joke)* trampa *f*
**2** *vt (pt & pp* **booby-trapped***) (with explosive device)* colocar una bomba trampa; *(as practical joke)* colocar una trampa en

**book** [bʊk] *n* **1** (a) *(in general)* libro *m*; *(of stamps)* librillo *m*; *(of matches)* caja *f* (de solapa); *(of tickets)* talonario *m*; *Fin* **the books** *(of company)* la contabilidad; **b. club** círculo *m* de lectores; **b. end** sujetalibros *m inv*; **b. review** reseña *f* literaria; **b. token** vale *m* para comprar libros
(b) *(idioms)* **physics is a closed b. to me** la física es un misterio para mí; **in my b...** a mi modo de ver...; **to be in sb's good/bad books** estar a buenas/malas con alguien; **to bring sb to b. for sth** obligar a alguien a rendir cuentas por algo; **by** *or* **according to the b.** según las normas; **to throw the b. at sb** castigar a alguien con la máxima severidad
**2** *vt* (a) *(reserve)* reservar; *(performer)* contratar; **to b. sb on a flight** reservarle (plaza en) un vuelo a alguien; **to be fully booked** *(theatre, flight)* estar completo(a); *(person)* tener la agenda completa
(b) *(punish) (for traffic offence)* multar; *(in football match)* amonestar

▸**book in** *vt sep* **to b. sb in** hacer una reserva para alguien

**2** *vi (take a room)* coger una habitación; *(register)* registrarse

▸**book up** *vt sep* **the hotel is fully booked up** el hotel está al completo; **I'm booked up for this evening** ya he quedado para esta noche

**bookable** ['bʊkəbəl] *adj (seat, flight)* que se puede reservar con antelación

**bookbinder** ['bʊkbaɪndə(r)] *n* encuadernador(ora) *m,f*

**bookbinding** ['bʊkbaɪndɪŋ] *n* encuadernación *f*

**bookcase** ['bʊkkeɪs] *n* librería *f*, estantería *f*

**bookie** ['bʊkɪ] *n Fam (in betting)* corredor(ora) *m,f* de apuestas

**booking** ['bʊkɪŋ] *n* (a) *(reservation)* reserva *f*; **to make a b.** hacer una reserva; **b. office** taquilla *f* (b) *(in football)* amonestación *f*; **to receive a b.** ser amonestado(a)

**bookish** ['bʊkɪʃ] *adj (person)* estudioso(a); *Pej (approach, style)* académico(a), sesudo(a)

**bookkeeping** ['bʊkki:pɪŋ] *n Fin* contabilidad *f*

**booklet** ['bʊklɪt] *n* folleto *m*

**bookmaker** ['bʊkmeɪkə(r)] *n (in betting)* corredor(ora) *m,f* de apuestas

**bookmark(er)** ['bʊkmɑ:k(ə(r))] *n* marcador *m*

**bookseller** ['bʊkselə(r)] *n* librero(a) *m,f*

**bookshelf** ['bʊkʃelf] *n (single shelf)* estante *m*; **bookshelves** *(set of shelves)* estantería *f*

**bookshop** ['bʊkʃɒp] *n* librería *f*

**bookstall** ['bʊkstɔ:l] *n* puesto *m or* quiosco *m* de libros

**bookstore** [bʊkstɔ:(r)] *n US* librería *f*

**bookworm** ['bʊkwɜ:m] *n Fig (avid reader)* ratón *m* de biblioteca

**boom¹** [bu:m] *n* (a) *Naut (barrier)* barrera *f*; *(for sail)* botavara *f* (b) *Cin & TV* jirafa *f*

**boom²** **1** *n (economic)* auge *m*, boom *m*; **b. town** ciudad *f* en auge
**2** *vi (of business, trade)* estar en auge, dispararse

**boom³** **1** *n (sound)* estruendo *m*, retumbo *m*
**2** *vi (of thunder, gun)* retumbar

**boomerang** ['bu:məræŋ] *n* bumerán *m*

**booming** ['bu:mɪŋ] *adj (voice)* estruendoso(a), atronador(ora)

**boon** [bu:n] *n* bendición *f*

**boor** ['bʊə(r)] *n* grosero(a) *m,f*, cafre *mf*

**boorish** ['bʊərɪʃ] *adj (person, behaviour)* grosero(a), ordinario(a)

**boost** [bu:st] **1** *n (of rocket)* propulsión *f*; *(of economy)* impulso *m*; **to give sb/sth a b.** dar un impulso a alguien/algo
**2** *vt (rocket)* propulsar; *Tel (signal)* amplificar; *(economy, production)* impulsar, estimular; *(hopes, morale)* levantar

**booster** ['bu:stə(r)] n (a) b. (rocket) (cohete m) propulsor m (b) Elec elevador m de tensión (c) Med revacunación f

**boot** [bu:t] 1 n (a) (footwear) bota f; (anklelength) botín m (b) Br (of car) maletero m, CAm, Méx cajuela f, CSur baúl m (c) (idioms) the b. is on the other foot se ha dado la vuelta a la tortilla; Fam to give sb the b. poner a alguien de patitas en la calle; Fam to get the b. ser despedido(a); Fam to put or stick the b. into sb (beat severely) dar una paliza a alguien; (criticize) ensañarse con alguien; to b. además, por añadidura

2 vt (a) Fam (kick) dar una patada a; to b. sb out poner a alguien en la calle (b) Comptr arrancar

3 vi Comptr to b. (up) arrancar

**bootee** [bu:'ti:] n (child's shoe) patuco m

**booth** [bu:ð] n (at fair) barraca f (de feria); (for telephone, in voting) cabina f; (in restaurant) mesa f (rodeada de asientos corridos fijados al suelo)

**bootlace** ['bu:tleɪs] n cordón m

**bootleg** ['bu:tleg] adj (alcohol) de contrabando; (recording, cassette) pirata

**bootstrap** ['bu:tstræp] n (a) trabilla f, tirante m; Fig he pulled himself up by his bootstraps logró salir adelante por su propio esfuerzo (b) Comptr arranque m; b. routine secuencia f de arranque

**booty** ['bu:tɪ] n (loot) botín m

**booze** [bu:z] Fam 1 n bebida f, priva f

2 vi trincar, empinar el codo

**boozer** ['bu:zə(r)] n Fam (a) (person) bebedor(ora) m,f, esponja f (b) Br (pub) bareto m, bar m

**booze-up** ['bu:zʌp] n Br Fam juerga f

**boozy** ['bu:zɪ] adj Fam (voice, breath) de borracho(a)

**bop**[1] [bɒp] Fam 1 n (dance) baile m

2 vi (pt & pp bopped) (dance) bailotear

**bop**[2] Fam 1 n (blow) golpecito m

2 vt (pt & pp bopped) (hit) dar un golpecito a

**boracic** [bə'ræsɪk] adj Chem bórico(a)

**border** ['bɔ:də(r)] 1 n (a) (edge) borde m; (on clothes) ribete m; (in garden) arriate m (b) (frontier) frontera f; the Borders = región al sureste de Escocia, los Borders; b. guard guardia m fronterizo; b. town ciudad f fronteriza

2 vt bordear; (country) limitar con

▶**border on** vt insep (of country) limitar con; to b. on insanity/the ridiculous bordear la locura/lo ridículo

**borderland** ['bɔ:dəlænd] n frontera f, zona f fronteriza

**borderline** ['bɔ:dəlaɪn] n frontera f, divisoria f; a b. case un caso dudoso

**bore**[1] [bɔ:(r)] 1 n (person) pelma mf, pelmazo(a) m,f; (thing) fastidio m, lata f; what a b.!

¡qué lata or pesadez!

2 vt aburrir

**bore**[2] 1 n (calibre) calibre m

2 vt (with drill) perforar, taladrar; to b. a hole in sth taladrar algo

3 vi to b. for water/minerals hacer perforaciones en busca de agua/mineral

**bore**[3] pt of **bear**[2]

**bored** [bɔ:d] adj aburrido(a); to be b. estar aburrido(a); Fam I was b. stiff or to tears me aburrí como una ostra

**boredom** ['bɔ:dəm] n aburrimiento m

**boring** ['bɔ:rɪŋ] adj aburrido(a); to be b. ser aburrido(a)

**born** [bɔ:n] 1 adj he's a b. storyteller/leader es un narrador/líder nato

2 (pp of **bear** used to form passive) to be b. nacer; I was b. in London/in 1975 nací en Londres/en 1975; Fam I wasn't b. yesterday no me chupo el dedo

**born-again Christian** ['bɔ:nəgen-'krɪstʃən] n Rel = cristiano convertido a un culto evangélico

**borne** [bɔ:n] pp of **bear**[2]

**Borneo** ['bɔ:nɪəʊ] n Borneo

**borough** ['bʌrə] n Br = división administrativa y electoral que comprende un municipio o un distrito urbano

**borrow** ['bɒrəʊ] 1 vt can I b. your pen? ¿me prestas tu boli?; I borrowed his car without him knowing le tomé el coche prestado sin que lo supiera; to b. a book from the library tomar prestado un libro de la biblioteca; to b. money from the bank pedir un crédito al banco; to be living on borrowed time (of ill person, government) tener los días contados

2 vi she's always borrowing from other people siempre está pidiendo cosas prestadas a los demás

**borrower** ['bɒrəʊə(r)] n (from bank) prestatario(a) m,f; (from library) usuario(a) m,f

**borstal** ['bɔ:stəl] n Br Formerly correccional m, reformatorio m

**bosh** [bɒʃ] Fam 1 n palminas fpl, tonterías fpl

2 exclam ¡pamplinas!

**Bosnia(-Herzegovina)** ['bɒznɪə-(hɜ:tsəgə'vi:nə)] n Bosnia(-Herzegovina)

**Bosnian** ['bɒznɪən] 1 n bosnio(a) m,f

2 adj bosnio(a); B. Croat croata mf de Bosnia; B. Muslim musulmán(ana) m,f de Bosnia; B. Serb serbio(a) m,f de Bosnia

**bosom** ['bʊzəm] 1 n (of woman) pecho m; Fig seno m; Fig in the b. of one's family en el seno de la familia

2 adj b. friend amigo(a) m,f del alma

**Bosphorus** ['bɒsfərəs] n the B. el Bósforo

**boss**[1] [bɒs] n (on shield) tachón m

**boss²** *Fam* **1** *n (at work)* jefe(a) *m,f;* **he's his own b.** trabaja por cuenta propia; *Fig* **to show sb who's b.** enseñar a alguien quién manda

**2** *vt* **to b. sb about** *or* **around** dar órdenes a alguien (a diestro y siniestro)

**bossy** ['bɒsɪ] *adj* mandón(ona); *Fam* **a b. boots** un(a) mandón(ona)

**bosun** ['bəʊsən] *n Naut* contramaestre *m*

**botanic(al)** [bə'tænɪk(əl)] *adj* botánico(a); **b. garden(s)** jardín *m* botánico

**botanist** ['bɒtənɪst] *n* botánico(a) *m,f*

**botany** ['bɒtənɪ] *n* botánica *f*

**botch** [bɒtʃ] *Fam* **1** *n* chapuza *f;* **to make a b. of a job/an interview** hacer una chapuza de trabajo/entrevista

**2** *vt* **to b. a job/an interview** hacer una chapuza de trabajo/entrevista

**botched** [bɒtʃt] *adj* chapucero(a); **a b. job** una chapuza

**both** [bəʊθ] **1** *pron* ambos(as), los/las dos; **b. (of them) are dead** los dos *or* ambos están muertos; **b. of us agree** los dos estamos de acuerdo

**2** *adj* ambos(as), los/las dos; **b. (the) brothers** ambos hermanos, los dos hermanos; **to hold sth in b. hands** sostener algo con las dos manos; **b. my brothers** mis dos hermanos; **on b. sides** a ambos lados; **to look b. ways** mirar a uno y otro lado; **you can't have it b. ways** o una cosa o la otra, no puedes tenerlo todo

**3** *adv* **b. you and I** tanto tú como yo; **she is b. intelligent and beautiful** es inteligente y, además, guapa

**bother** ['bɒðə(r)] **1** *n (trouble)* problemas *mpl*, dificultades *fpl; (inconvenience)* molestia *f;* **to go to the b. of doing sth** tomarse la molestia de hacer algo

**2** *vt* **(a)** *(annoy)* molestar; **my back's still bothering me** todavía me molesta la espalda; **I hate to b. you but...** siento tener que molestarte pero... **(b)** *(care about)* **to be bothered about sth** estar preocupado(a) por algo; *Fam* **I can't be bothered** no tengo ganas, paso; *Fam* **I'm not bothered** me da igual

**3** *vi (care)* preocuparse **(about** por); **he didn't even b. to apologize** ni siquiera se molestó en pedir disculpas; **don't b.!** no te molestes

**bothersome** ['bɒðəsəm] *adj* incordiante

**Botswana** ['bɒt'swɑːnə] *n* Botsuana

**bottle** ['bɒtəl] **1** *n* **(a)** *(container)* botella *f; (of medicine)* frasco *m; (for baby)* biberón *m;* **bring your own b.** trae una botella de algo; *Fam* **to take to** *or* **hit the b.** darse a la bebida; **b. bank** contenedor *m* de vidrio; **b. green** verde *m* botella; **b. opener** abrebotellas *m inv;* **b. party** fiesta *f (a la que cada invitado lleva una botella)* **(b)** *Br very Fam (courage)* **to have a lot of b.**

echarle muchas narices, tener muchas agallas

**2** *vt* embotellar

▶**bottle out** *vi Br very Fam* rajarse

▶**bottle up** *vt sep (emotions, anger)* reprimir, contener

**bottled** ['bɒtəld] *adj* embotellado(a); **b. water** agua *f* embotellada

**bottle-feed** ['bɒtəlfiːd] *(pt & pp* **bottle-fed)** *vt* dar el biberón a

**bottleneck** ['bɒtəlnek] *n (in road, traffic)* embotellamiento *m*, estrechamiento *m; (in production)* atasco *m*

**bottom** ['bɒtəm] **1** *n* **(a)** *(lowest part) (of well, corridor, sea)* fondo *m; (of stairs, mountain, page)* pie *m; (of list)* final *m;* **it's in the b. of the cup** está en el fondo de la taza; **at the b. of** *(well, sea)* en el fondo de; *(stairs, mountain, page)* al pie de; **at the b. of the street** al final de la calle; **from the b. of one's heart** de todo corazón; **he's at the b. of the class** es el último de la clase; **to touch b.** *(of boat)* tocar fondo
**(b)** *(underside) (of cup, box)* parte *f* de abajo; *(of shoe)* suela *f; (of ship)* casco *m;* **there's a sticker on the b. of the box** hay una etiqueta en la parte de abajo de la caja
**(c)** *Fam (buttocks)* trasero *m*, culo *m*
**(d)** *(idioms)* **to be at the b. of sth** *(be the cause of)* ser el motivo de algo; **to get to the b. of sth** llegar hasta el fondo de algo; **at b.** *(fundamentally)* en el fondo; **the b. has fallen out of the market** la demanda ha caído en picado; *Fam* **bottoms up!** ¡salud!

**2** *adj* inferior; **the b. layer/drawer** la capa/el cajón de abajo del todo; **b. floor** planta *f* baja; *Fam* **you can bet your b. dollar that...** puedes apostar lo que quieras a que...; **in b. gear** en primera (velocidad); **the b. line** *(financially)* el saldo final; **the b. line is that he is unsuited to the job** la realidad es que no resulta adecuado para el trabajo

▶**bottom out** *vi (of recession, unemployment)* tocar fondo

**bottomless** ['bɒtəmlɪs] *adj (abyss)* sin fondo; *(reserve)* inagotable; *Fig* **a b. pit** un pozo sin fondo

**bottommost** ['bɒtəmməʊst] *adj* de más abajo; **the b. layers of society** los estratos más bajos de la sociedad

**botulism** ['bɒtjʊlɪzəm] *n* botulismo *m*

**boudoir** ['buːdwɑː(r)] *n* tocador *m*

**bouffant** ['buːfɒn] *adj* ahuecado(a)

**bough** [baʊ] *n* rama *f*

**bought** [bɔːt] *pt & pp of* **buy**

**bouillon** ['buːjɒn] *n Culin* caldo *m*

**boulder** ['bəʊldə(r)] *n* roca *f (redondeada)*

**boulevard** ['buːləvɑːd] *n* bulevar *m*

**bounce** [baʊns] **1** *n* **(a)** *(of ball)* rebote *m*, bote *m* **(b)** *Fig (energy)* vitalidad *f*

**2** vt botar; Fig **to b. an idea off sb** preguntar a alguien su opinión acerca de una idea

**3** vi (**a**) (of ball) botar, rebotar; **to b. off the wall** (of ball) rebotar en la pared; Fig **criticism bounces off him** las críticas le resbalan; **to b. into/out of a room** (of person) entrar a/salir de una habitación dando brincos de alegría (**b**) Fam (of cheque) ser rechazado

▸**bounce back** vi (after illness, disappointment) recuperarse, reponerse

**bouncer** ['baʊnsə(r)] n Fam (doorman) gorila m, matón m

**bouncing** ['baʊnsɪŋ] adj (baby) robusto(a)

**bouncy** ['baʊnsɪ] adj (**a**) (ball) que bota bien; (mattress) elástico(a) (**b**) Fig **to be b.** (of person) tener mucha vitalidad

**bound¹** [baʊnd] **1** n (leap) salto m; **at one b.** de un salto

**2** vi (leap) saltar

**bound²** adj (**a**) (destined) **b. for** con destino a; **where are you b. for?** ¿hacia dónde se dirige? (**b**) (certain) **he's b. to come** seguro que viene; **it was b. to happen** tenía que suceder

**bound³** pt & pp of **bind**

**boundary** ['baʊndərɪ] n frontera f, límite m

**bounder** ['baʊndə(r)] n Old-fashioned Fam sinvergüenza m

**boundless** ['baʊndlɪs] adj ilimitado(a)

**bounds** [baʊndz] npl (limit) límites mpl; **to be out of b.** estar vedado(a); **it is (not) beyond the b. of possibility** (no) es del todo imposible; **to know no b.** (of anger, ambition, grief) no conocer límites

**bountiful** ['baʊntɪfʊl] adj abundante, copioso(a)

**bounty** ['baʊntɪ] n (**a**) (reward) recompensa f; **b. hunter** cazarrecompensas mf inv (**b**) (generosity) generosidad f, exuberancia f

**bouquet** [buːˈkeɪ] n (**a**) (of flowers) ramo m (**b**) (of wine) buqué m

**bourbon** ['bɜːbən] n (whisky) whisky m americano, bourbon m

**bourgeois** ['bʊəʒwɑː] adj burgués(esa)

**bourgeoisie** [bʊəʒwɑːˈziː] n burguesía f

**bout** [baʊt] n (**a**) (of illness) ataque m; (of work, activity) período m (**b**) (boxing match) combate m

**boutique** [buːˈtiːk] n boutique f

**bovine** ['bəʊvaɪn] adj bovino(a)

**bow¹** [bəʊ] n (weapon, for violin) arco m (in hair, on dress) lazo m; **b. tie** pajarita f

**bow²** [bəʊ] n (of ship) proa f

**bow³ 1** n (with head) reverencia f; **to take a b.** salir a saludar

**2** vt **to b. one's head** inclinar la cabeza

**3** vi (**a**) (as greeting, sign of respect) inclinar la cabeza; **to b. down** inclinarse; Fig **to b. down before sb** inclinarse ante alguien (**b**)

Fig (yield) **to b. to sb/sth** rendirse ante alguien/algo

▸**bow out** vi (resign) retirarse, hacer mutis (por el foro)

**bowdlerize** ['baʊdləraɪz] vt (text, account) expurgar, censurar

**bowed** [baʊd] adj **with b. head** con la cabeza inclinada; **b. with age** encorvado(a) por la edad

**bowel** ['baʊəl] n intestino m; **bowels** entrañas fpl; Literary **the bowels of the earth** las entrañas de la Tierra; **b. complaint** afección f intestinal

**bower** ['baʊə(r)] n rincón m umbrío

**bowl¹** [bəʊl] n (dish) cuenco m, bol m; **a b. of soup, please** un plato de sopa, por favor; **soup b.** plato m sopero; **salad b.** ensaladera f; **fruit b.** frutero m (**b**) (of toilet) taza f

**bowl² 1** n = juego parecido a la petanca que se juega sobre césped, y en el que las bolas se lanzan a ras de suelo

**2** vi (in cricket) lanzar la bola

▸**bowl along** vi (of car, bicycle) rodar

▸**bowl over** vt sep (knock down) derribar; Fig **she was bowled over by the news** la noticia la dejó pasmada

**bowlegged** [bəʊˈlegɪd] adj con las piernas arqueadas, estevado(a)

**bowler** ['bəʊlə(r)] n (**a**) (hat) sombrero m hongo, bombín m (**b**) (in cricket) lanzador m

**bowling** ['bəʊlɪŋ] n (**a**) (on grass) = **bowls** ver **bowl**; **b. green** = campo de hierba para jugar a los "bowls" (**b**) (in bowling alley) (juego m de) bolos mpl; **b. alley** pista f de bolos; (building) bolera f

**box** [bɒks] **1** n (**a**) (container) caja f; **b. number 12** (postal) apartado m de correos número 12; **b. camera** cámara f de cajón (**b**) (printed, drawn) recuadro m; **tick the b.** ponga una cruz en la casilla; **(penalty) b.** (in football) área f (de castigo) (**c**) Br Fam (television) **the b.** la tele (**d**) (in theatre) palco m

**2** vt (**a**) (place in box) guardar en una caja (**b**) (hit) **to b. sb's ears** abofetear a alguien

**3** vi (fight) boxear

**boxer** ['bɒksə(r)] n (**a**) (fighter) boxeador m; **b. shorts, boxers** (underwear) calzoncillos mpl, boxers mpl (**b**) (dog) bóxer m

**boxing** ['bɒksɪŋ] n boxeo m, CAm, Méx box m; **b. glove** guante m de boxeo; **b. match** combate m de boxeo; **b. ring** ring m

**Boxing Day** ['bɒksɪŋ'deɪ] n Br = San Esteban, el 26 de diciembre, fiesta nacional en Inglaterra y Gales

**box-office** ['bɒksɒfɪs] n taquilla f, Am boletería f; **a b. success** un éxito de taquilla

**boxroom** ['bɒksruːm] *n* = en una vivienda, cuarto pequeño sin ventana que se suele usar como trastero

**boy** [bɔɪ] *n* chico *m*; *(baby)* niño *m*; **one of the boys** uno del grupo, un amigo; *Fam* **oh b.!** vaya; *Fam* **boys will be boys** son como niños; **B. Scout** boy scout *m*, escultista *m*

**boycott** ['bɔɪkɒt] **1** *n* boicot *m*
**2** *vt* boicotear

**boyfriend** ['bɔɪfrend] *n* novio *m*

**boyhood** ['bɔɪhʊd] *n* niñez *f*

**boyish** ['bɔɪɪʃ] *adj* **(a)** *(of man) (looks, grin)* infantil **(b)** *(of woman) (looks, behaviour)* varonil

**bps** [biːpiːˈes] *n Comptr (abbr* **bits per second)** bps

**BR** [biːˈɑː(r)] *n Br Formerly (abbr* **British Rail)** = compañía británica estatal de ferrocarril

**bra** [brɑː] *n* sujetador *m*, sostén *m*

**brace** [breɪs] **1** *n* **(a)** *(on teeth)* aparato *m* (corrector) **(b)** *Br* **braces** *(for trousers)* tirantes *mpl*; **a pair of braces** unos tirantes **(c)** *(pair)* (of birds, pistols) par *m* **(d)** **b. and bit** *(tool)* berbiquí *m*
**2** *vt* **(a)** *(reinforce)* reforzar **(b)** **to b. oneself (for)** prepararse (para)

**bracelet** ['breɪslɪt] *n* pulsera *f*

**bracing** ['breɪsɪŋ] *adj (wind, weather)* vigorizante

**bracken** ['brækən] *n* helechos *mpl*

**bracket** ['brækɪt] **1** *n* **(a)** *(for shelves)* escuadra *f*, soporte *m* **(b)** *(in writing)* paréntesis *m inv*; **in brackets** entre paréntesis **(c)** *(group)* banda *f*, grupo *m*; **age/income b.** banda de edad/de renta; **tax b.** banda impositiva
**2** *vt* **(a)** *(word, phrase)* poner entre paréntesis **(b)** *(classify)* asociar; **bracketed together** asociado(a)

**brackish** ['brækɪʃ] *adj (water)* ligeramente salobre *or* salado(a)

**brag** [bræg] *(pt & pp* **bragged)** *vi* jactarse **(about** de)

**braggart** ['brægət] *n* fanfarrón(ona) *m,f*

**braid** [breɪd] **1** *n* *(of hair)* trenza *f*; *(of thread)* galón *m*
**2** *vt (hair, thread)* trenzar

**Braille** [breɪl] *n* braille *m*

**brain** [breɪn] *n* cerebro *m*; **brains** *(as food)* sesos *mpl*; *Fam* **to have brains** tener cerebro; *Fam* **she's the brains of the business** ella es el cerebro del negocio; *Fam* **to have money/sex on the b.** estar obsesionado(a) con el dinero/sexo; *Med* **to suffer b. damage** sufrir una lesión cerebral; *Med* **b. death** muerte *f* cerebral; **the b. drain** la fuga de cerebros; **b. surgeon** neurocirujano(a) *m,f*; *Med* **b. tumour** tumor *m* cerebral; *Fam* **b. wave** *(brilliant idea)* idea *f* genial
**2** *vt Fam (hit)* descalabrar

**brainbox** ['breɪnbɒks] *n Fam (intelligent person)* cerebro *m*

**brainchild** ['breɪntʃaɪld] *n (idea, project)* idea *f*

**brainless** ['breɪnlɪs] *adj* insensato(a)

**brainpower** ['breɪnpaʊə(r)] *n* capacidad *f* intelectual, intelecto *m*

**brainstorm** ['breɪnstɔːm] *n Fam* **(a)** *Br (mental confusion)* cruce *m* de cables **(b)** *US (brilliant idea)* idea *f* genial

**brainstorming** ['breɪnstɔːmɪŋ] *n* **b. session** = reunión sin orden del día en la que los participantes realizan sugerencias para resolver uno o varios asuntos

**brainwash** ['breɪnwɒʃ] *vt* lavar el cerebro a; **to b. sb into doing sth** lavar el cerebro a alguien para que haga algo

**brainy** ['breɪnɪ] *adj Fam* **to be b.** tener mucho coco

**braise** [breɪz] *vt* estofar

**brake** [breɪk] **1** *n* freno *m*; **to apply the brake(s)** frenar; *Fig* **to put the brakes on a project** frenar un proyecto; **b. fluid** líquido *m* de frenos; **b. lights** luces *mpl* de freno; **b. pedal** (pedal *m* del) freno *m*
**2** *vi* frenar

**braking distance** ['breɪkɪŋ'dɪstəns] *n* distancia *f* de frenado *or* de seguridad

**bramble** ['bræmbəl] *n (plant)* zarza *f*

**bran** [bræn] *n* salvado *m*

**branch** [brɑːntʃ] **1** *n* **(a)** *(of tree, family, subject)* rama *f*; *(of river)* afluente *m*; *(of road, railway)* ramal *m*, derivación *f*; **b. line** *(railway)* línea *f* secundaria, ramal *m* **(b)** *(of bank)* sucursal *f*; *(of shop)* establecimiento *m*
**2** *vi* bifurcarse

▸**branch off** *vi (of discussion)* desviarse

▸**branch out** *vi* ampliar horizontes, diversificarse; **the company has branched out into electronics** la compañía ha ampliado su oferta a productos de electrónica

**brand** [brænd] **1** *n* **(a)** *(of product)* marca *f*; *Fig* **she has her own b. of humour** tiene un humor muy suyo; **b. image** imagen *f* de marca; **b. leader** marca *f* líder (en el mercado); **b. name** marca *f* de fábrica, nombre *m* comercial **(b)** *(on cattle)* hierro *m*
**2** *vt (cattle)* marcar con el hierro; *Fig* **the image was branded on her memory** la imagen se le quedó grabada en la memoria; *Fig* **to b. sb (as) a liar/coward** tildar a alguien de mentiroso/cobarde

**brandish** ['brændɪʃ] *vt* blandir

**brand-new** ['brænd'njuː] *adj* flamante, completamente nuevo(a)

**brandy** ['brændɪ] *n (cognac)* brandy *m*, coñac *m*; *(more generally)* aguardiente *m*; **cherry/plum b.** aguardiente de cerezas/ciruelas

**brash** [bræʃ] *adj (person)* demasiado seguro(a) de sí mismo(a) y chillón(ona)

**brass** [brɑ:s] *n* (**a**) *(metal)* latón *m; Fam* **the top b.** *(in army)* la plana mayor, los peces gordos; *Br Fam* **it's not worth a b. farthing** no vale un pimiento; *Br Fam* **it's b. monkey weather!** ¡hace un frío que pela!; **to get down to b. tacks** ir al grano (**b**) *Mus (brass instruments)* metales *mpl*; **b. band** banda *f* (**c**) *Br Fam (money)* pasta *f, Am* plata *f* (**d**) *Br Fam (cheek, nerve)* cara *f*, caradura *f*; **to have the b. to do sth** tener la caradura de hacer algo; **to have a b. neck** tener más cara que espalda

▶**brass off** *vt sep Br Fam* **to be brassed off** estar hasta la coronilla

**brassière** [ˈbræzɪə(r)] *n* sostén *m*, sujetador *m*

**brassy** [ˈbrɑ:sɪ] *adj Fam (woman)* demasiado segura de sí misma y chillona

**brat** [bræt] *n Pej* niñato(a) *m,f*

**Bratislava** [brætɪˈslɑ:və] *n* Bratislava

**bravado** [brəˈvɑ:dəʊ] *n* fanfarronería *f*, bravuconería *f*

**brave** [breɪv] **1** *n (native American)* guerrero *m* indio

**2** *adj* valiente, valeroso(a); **a b. effort** un intento encomiable; **to put a b. face on it** mostrarse animoso(a) *(ante la dificultad)*

**3** *vt (danger, weather)* encarar, afrontar

**bravely** [ˈbreɪvlɪ] *adv* valientemente, valerosamente

**bravery** [ˈbreɪvərɪ] *n* valentía *f*, valor *m*

**bravo** [brɑːˈvəʊ] *exclam* ¡bravo!

**brawl** [brɔ:l] **1** *n* trifulca *f*, refriega *f*

**2** *vi* pelearse

**brawn** [brɔ:n] *n Fam (strength)* fuerza *f*, músculo *m*; **he's got more b. than brains** tiene más músculo que seso

**brawny** [ˈbrɔ:nɪ] *adj* musculoso(a)

**bray** [breɪ] **1** *n (pl* **brays**) *(of donkey)* rebuzno *m; Fig (laugh)* risotada *f*

**2** *vi (of donkey)* rebuznar; *Fig (laugh)* carcajearse

**brazen** [ˈbreɪzən] *adj* descarado(a)

▶**brazen out** *vt sep* **to b. it out** echarle mucha cara al asunto

**brazier** [ˈbreɪzɪə(r)] *n* brasero *m*

**Brazil** [brəˈzɪl] *n* Brasil

**brazil** [brəˈzɪl] *n* **b. (nut)** coquito *m* del Brasil

**Brazilian** [brəˈzɪlɪən] *n & adj* brasileño(a) *m,f*

**breach** [bri:tʃ] **1** *n* (**a**) *(in wall)* brecha *f*; *Fig* **to step into the b.** *(in emergency)* echar un cable, cubrir el vacío (**b**) *(of agreement, rules)* violación *f*, incumplimiento *m*; *(of trust)* abuso *m*; **b. of discipline** incumplimiento *m* de las normas; *Law* **b. of the peace** alteración *f* del orden público (**c**) *(in friendship)* ruptura *f*

**2** *vt* (**a**) *(defences)* atravesar, abrir brecha en (**b**) *(contract, agreement)* violar, incumplir

**bread** [bred] *n* (**a**) *(food)* pan *m*; **a loaf of b.** un pan; **b. and butter** pan con mantequilla; *Fig* **the customers are our b. and butter** lo que nos da de comer son los clientes; *Fig* **he knows which side his b. is buttered on** él sabe lo que le conviene; **b. bin** panera *f*; **b. knife** cuchillo *m* del pan (**b**) *very Fam (money)* pasta *f, Am* plata *f*

**bread-and-butter** [bredənˈbʌtə(r)] *adj Fam* **b. issues** asuntos *mpl* básicos

**breadbasket** [ˈbredbɑːskɪt] *n* cesta *f* del pan

**breadboard** [ˈbredbɔːd] *n* tabla *f* de cortar el pan

**breadcrumb** [ˈbredkrʌm] *n* miga *f*; **breadcrumbs** *(in recipe)* pan *m* rallado; **fried in breadcrumbs** empanado(a)

**breadline** [ˈbredlaɪn] *n* **on the b.** en la pobreza

**breadth** [bredθ] *n (width)* ancho *m*, anchura *f*; *Fig (of outlook, understanding)* amplitud *f*

**breadwinner** [ˈbredwɪnə(r)] *n* **the b.** el que gana el pan

**break** [breɪk] **1** *n* (**a**) *(fracture) (in bone)* fractura *f*, rotura *f; (in wall, fence)* abertura *f*, hueco *m; (in clouds)* claro *m; (in electric circuit)* corte *m*; **at b. of day** al despuntar el día; *Elec* **b. switch** interruptor *m*

(**b**) *(interval, pause)* descanso *m*, pausa *f; (holiday)* vacaciones *fpl;* **(commercial) b.** *(on TV, radio)* pausa *f* publicitaria, anuncios *mpl;* **to work/talk without a b.** trabajar/hablar sin pausa *or* sin descanso; **a b. in the weather** un período de buen tiempo; *Fam* **give me a b.!** *(leave me alone)* ¡déjame en paz!; *(I don't believe you)* ¡no digas tonterías!

(**c**) *Fam (escape)* fuga *f;* **to make a b. for it** intentar escaparse

(**d**) *Fam (chance)* oportunidad *f;* **to give sb a b.** *(give opportunity)* dar una oportunidad a alguien; **a lucky b.** golpe *m* de suerte; **big b.** gran oportunidad *f*

**2** *vt (pt* **broke** [brəʊk]*, pp* **broken** [ˈbrəʊkən])

(**a**) *(in general)* romper; **she broke the roll in two** partió el panecillo en dos; **to b. one's arm/leg** romperse *or* partirse un brazo/una pierna; **to b. sth into pieces** romper algo en pedazos; **to b. the sound barrier** superar la barrera del sonido; **to b. cover** salir del escondite; *Fig* **to b. the ice** romper el hielo; **to b. one's journey** interrumpir el viaje; **to b. ranks** romper filas; *Fig* **b. a leg!** *(good luck!)* ¡buena suerte!

(**b**) *(soften)* **the undergrowth broke his fall** la maleza amortiguó su caída

(**c**) *(destroy) (person, health, resistance)* acabar con, arruinar; *(strike)* reventar; **to b. sb's heart** romper el corazón a alguien; **to b. sb's spirit** minar la moral a alguien; **to b. the bank** hacer saltar la banca; **to b. sb's serve** *(in tennis)* romper el servicio a alguien

(**d**) *(agreement, promise)* romper; *(law, rules)* violar

(**e**) *(story)* descubrir, revelar (**to** a); **to b. the news of sth to sb** dar la noticia de algo a alguien

**3** *vi* (**a**) *(of glass, machine, bone)* romperse; *(of person's health)* sucumbir; *(of weather)* abrirse; **to b. in two** romperse *or* partirse en dos; **the sea broke against the rocks** el mar rompía contra las rocas; **day was beginning to b.** despuntaba el día

(**b**) *(of news, story)* saltar, estallar

(**c**) *(of voice) (at puberty)* cambiar; **her voice broke with emotion** se quedó con la voz quebrada por la emoción

▸**break away** *vi* (**a**) *(escape)* escapar (**from** de) (**b**) *(from party, country)* separarse (**from** de)

▸**break down** *vt sep* (**a**) *(destroy) (resistance)* vencer (**b**) *(analyze) (argument)* dividir; *(figures)* desglosar

**2** *vi* (**a**) *(of car, machine)* estropearse, averiarse; *(of talks)* romperse; *(of argument)* fallar, desmoronarse; *(of person under pressure)* derrumbarse; **to b. down in tears** romper a llorar

▸**break even** *vi* cubrir gastos, no tener pérdidas

▸**break in 1** *vt sep (horse, new shoes)* domar; *(new recruit)* amoldar

**2** *vi (of burglar)* forzar la entrada *(a una casa o edificio)*

▸**break into** *vt insep* (**a**) *(of burglar) (house)* entrar en (**b**) *(begin suddenly)* **to b. into laughter/ a song/a run** echarse a reír/cantar/correr

▸**break loose** *vi* soltarse

▸**break off 1** *vt sep* (**a**) *(detach) (twig, handle)* partir, desprender (**b**) *(terminate) (relations, engagement)* romper

**2** *vi* (**a**) *(become detached)* partirse, desprenderse (**b**) *(stop talking)* interrumpirse; **to b. off to do sth** parar para hacer algo

▸**break open 1** *vt sep (lock, safe)* forzar; *(door) (kick down)* echar abajo

**2** *vi* romperse, partirse

▸**break out** *vi* (**a**) *(escape)* escaparse (**of** de) (**b**) *(of disease, argument)* desatarse; *(of war)* estallar; **he broke out in a sweat** le entraron sudores; **she broke out in a rash** le salió un sarpullido

▸**break through 1** *vt insep (wall, barrier)* atravesar; *Fig (sb's reserve, shyness)* superar

**2** *vi (of sun)* salir

▸**break up 1** *vt sep* (**a**) *(machine, company)* desmantelar (**b**) *(fight, quarrel)* poner fin a

**2** *vi* (**a**) *(disintegrate)* hacerse pedazos (**b**) *(end) (of meeting, school term)* terminar; *(of marriage, relationship)* romperse, terminar; *(of couple)* separarse; **to b. up with sb** romper con alguien

▸**break with** *vt insep* romper con

**breakable** ['breɪkəbəl] **1** *n* **breakables** objetos *mpl* frágiles

**2** *adj* frágil, rompible

**breakage** ['breɪkɪdʒ] *n* **all breakages must be paid for** *(sign)* el cliente deberá abonar cualquier artículo que resulte roto

**breakaway** ['breɪkəweɪ] *adj* **a. group** un grupo escindido *(del principal)*

**breakdown** ['breɪkdaʊn] *n* (**a**) *(failure) (of car, machine, computer)* avería *f*; *(of talks)* ruptura *f*; *(of communication)* fallo *m*; **(nervous) b.** depresión *f or* crisis *f inv* nerviosa; **he had a b.** *(nervous)* le dio una depresión; **b. truck** grúa *f* (**b**) *(analysis) (of figures, costs)* desglose *m*

**breaker** ['breɪkə(r)] *n (wave)* ola *f* grande

**break-even point** [breɪk'iːvənpɔɪnt] *n Fin* punto *m* de equilibrio, umbral *m* de rentabilidad

**breakfast** ['brekfəst] **1** *n* desayuno *m*; **to have b.** desayunar; **to have sth for b.** desayunar algo; **b. cereal** cereales *mpl* (de desayuno); **b. television** programación *f* matinal

**2** *vi* **to b. (on sth)** desayunar (algo)

**break-in** ['breɪkɪn] *n (burglary)* robo *m* (en el interior de una casa o edificio)

**breaking** ['breɪkɪŋ] *n* (**a**) *Law* **b. and entering** allanamiento *m* de morada (**b**) **b. point** *(of person, patience)* límite *m*

**breakneck** ['breɪknek] *adj* **at b. speed** a una velocidad de vértigo

**break-out** ['breɪkaʊt] *n (from prison)* evasión *f*

**breakthrough** ['breɪkθruː] *n (major advance)* avance *m*, adelanto *m*; **to make a b.** *(in talks)* dar un gran paso adelante

**breakwater** ['breɪkwɔːtə(r)] *n* rompeolas *m inv*

**bream** [briːm] *n (freshwater)* brema *f*; **(sea) b.** besugo *m*

**breast** [brest] *n (of woman)* pecho *m*, seno *m*; *Literary (of man, woman)* pecho *m*; *(of chicken)* pechuga *f*; **to make a clean b. of it** confesarlo todo; **b. cancer** cáncer *m* de mama; **b. pocket** bolsillo *m* superior

**breastbone** ['brestbəʊn] *n* esternón *m*

**breast-feed** ['brestfiːd] *(pt & pp* **breast-fed** ['brestfed]) **1** *vt* dar el pecho a, amamantar

**2** *vi* dar el pecho

**breastplate** ['brestpleɪt] *n (of armour)* peto *m (de armadura)*

**breaststroke** ['brest)strəʊk] *n* braza *f*; **to do** *or* **swim (the) b.** nadar a braza

**breath** [breθ] *n* respiración *f*; **take a deep b.** inspirar profundamente; **to pause for b.** pararse para tomar aliento; **bad b.** mal aliento *m*; **in the same b.** a la vez, al mismo tiempo; **they are not to be mentioned in the same b.** no tienen punto de comparación; **in the next b.** al momento siguiente; *also Fig* **to hold one's b.** contener la respiración; *Fam* **don't hold your b.!** ¡ya puedes esperar sentado(a)!; **to waste one's b.** malgastar saliva; **out of b.** sin aliento, sin respiración; **to get one's b. back** recuperar la respiración; **under one's b.** en voz baja, en un susurro; *Fig* **to take sb's b. away** quitar la respiración a alguien; **a b. of wind** una brisa; **to go out for a b. of fresh air** salir a tomar el aire; *Fig* **she's a real b. of fresh air** es una verdadera bocanada de aire fresco; **b. test** prueba *f* de alcoholemia

**breathalyse, breathalyze** ['breθəlaɪz] *vt (driver)* hacer la prueba de la alcoholemia a

**breathalyser, breathalyzer** ['breθəlaɪzə(r)] *n* alcoholímetro *m*

**breathe** [bri:ð] **1** *vt* (**a**) *(inhale)* respirar, inspirar; *(exhale)* espirar, exhalar; **he breathed alcohol over her** le echó el aliento (con olor) a alcohol (**b**) *(idioms)* **to b. a sigh of relief** dar un suspiro de alivio; *Literary* **to b. one's last** exhalar el último suspiro; **don't b. a word (of it)!** ¡no digas una palabra!; **to b. fire** *(in anger)* echar chispas; **to b. new life into sth** *(project, scheme)* dar vida a algo

**2** *vi* respirar; *Fig* **to b. easily again** volver a respirar tranquilo(a); *Fig* **to b. down sb's neck** pisar los talones a alguien

▶**breathe in** *vt & vi* inspirar, aspirar

▶**breathe out** *vi* espirar

**breather** ['bri:ðə(r)] *n Fam (rest)* respiro *m*; **to take a b.** tomarse un respiro

**breathing** ['bri:ðɪŋ] *n* respiración *f*; **b. apparatus** respirador *m*; *Fig* **b. space** respiro *m*

**breathless** ['breθlɪs] *adj (person)* jadeante; *(calm, silence)* completo(a)

**breathtaking** ['breθteɪkɪŋ] *adj* impresionante, asombroso(a)

**breathy** ['breθɪ] *adj* **to have a b. voice** tener la voz jadeante

**bred** [bred] *pt & pp of* **breed**

**breech** [bri:tʃ] *n* (**a**) *Med* **b. delivery** or **birth** parto *m* de nalgas (**b**) *(of gun)* recámara *f*

**breeches** ['brɪtʃɪz] *npl* (pantalones *mpl*) bombachos *mpl*; **a pair of b.** unos (pantalones) bombachos

**breed** [bri:d] **1** *n (of animal) & Fig* raza *f*; *Fig* **a dying b.** una especie en extinción

**2** *vt* (*pt & pp* **bred** [bred]) *(animals)* criar; *Fig (discontent)* crear, producir

**3** *vi* reproducirse

**breeder** ['bri:də(r)] *n (of animals)* criador(ora) *m,f*; *Phys* **b. reactor** reactor *m* nuclear reproductor

**breeding** ['bri:dɪŋ] *n* (**a**) *(of animals)* cría *f*; **b. ground** criadero *m*; *Fig (of discontent, revolution)* caldo *m* de cultivo (**b**) *(of person)* **(good) b.**

(buena) educación *f*; **to lack b.** no tener educación

**breeze** [bri:z] **1** *n* brisa *f*; *US Fam* **it was a b.** fue coser y cantar

**2** *vi* **to b. in/out** *(casually)* entrar/salir despreocupadamente

**breeze-block** ['bri:zblɒk] *n Br* bloque *m* de cemento ligero

**breezy** ['bri:zɪ] *adj* (**a**) *(weather)* **it's b.** hace aire (**b**) *(person, attitude)* despreocupado(a)

**brethren** ['breðrɪn] *npl Rel* hermanos *mpl*

**Breton** ['bretɒn] *n & adj* bretón(ona) *m,f*

**breviary** ['bri:vɪərɪ] *n Rel* breviario *m*

**brevity** ['brevɪtɪ] *n* brevedad *f*

**brew** [bru:] **1** *n* (**a**) *(beer)* cerveza *f*; *(tea)* té *m*; *(strange mixture)* brebaje *m*

**2** *vt (beer)* elaborar, fabricar; *(tea)* preparar

**3** *vi (of beer)* fermentar; *(tea)* hacerse; **there's a storm brewing** se está preparando una tormenta; *Fig* **there's trouble brewing** se está fraguando *or* cociendo algo

▶**brew up** *vi Br Fam* preparar el té

**brewer** ['bru:ə(r)] *n (firm)* fabricante *mf* de cerveza

**brewery** ['bruərɪ] *n* fábrica *f* de cerveza

**briar** ['braɪə(r)] *n (plant)* brezo *m*; *(pipe)* pipa *f* (de madera) de brezo; **b. rose** escaramujo *m*

**bribe** [braɪb] **1** *n* soborno *m*, *CAm, Méx* mordida *f*, *Andes, CSur* coima *f*

**2** *vt* sobornar; **to b. sb into doing sth** sobornar a alguien para que haga algo

**bribery** ['braɪbərɪ] *n* soborno *m*

**bric-a-brac** ['brɪkəbræk] *n* baratijas *fpl*, chucherías *fpl*

**brick** [brɪk] *n* (**a**) *(for building)* ladrillo *m*; *Fig* **to drop a b.** meter la pata; **b. wall** muro *m* de ladrillo(s); **you're banging your head against a b. wall** te estás esforzando para nada (**b**) *Br Old-fashioned Fam* **he's a b.** es un gran tipo

▶**brick up** *vt sep* tapiar

**brickie** ['brɪkɪ] *n Br Fam* albañil *m*

**bricklayer** ['brɪkleɪə(r)] *n* albañil *m*

**brickwork** ['brɪkwɜːk] *n* albañilería *f*

**bridal** ['braɪdəl] *adj* nupcial; **b. dress** *or* **gown** traje *m* de novia; **b. suite** suite *f* nupcial

**bride** [braɪd] *n* novia *f*; **the b. and groom** los novios

**bridegroom** ['braɪdgruːm] *n* novio *m*

**bridesmaid** ['braɪdzmeɪd] *n* dama *f* de honor

**bridge¹** [brɪdʒ] **1** *n (over river, on ship, of violin, on teeth)* puente *m*; *(of nose)* caballete *m*; *Fig* **we'll cross that b. when we come to it** no adelantemos acontecimientos; *Fig* **a b. building effort** un esfuerzo por tender un puente

**2** *vt (river)* tender un puente sobre; **to b. a gap** llenar un vacío; **to b. the gap between rich**

**and poor** acortar la distancia entre ricos y pobres

**bridge²** *n (cardgame)* bridge *m*

**bridgehead** ['brɪdʒhed] *n Mil* cabeza *f* de puente

**bridging loan** ['brɪdʒɪŋləʊn] *n Fin* crédito *m* de puente

**bridle** ['braɪdəl] **1** *n* brida *f*; **b. path** camino *m* de herradura
 **2** *vt* embridar, poner la brida a
 **3** *vi (with anger)* indignarse (**at** por)

**brief** [bri:f] **1** *n* (**a**) *Law* escrito *m*; *(instructions)* misión *f*; *Fig* **that goes beyond our b.** eso no entra en el ámbito de nuestras competencias (**b**) **in b.** *(briefly)* en suma
 **2** *adj* breve; **a very b. pair of shorts** unos pantalones muy cortos; **to be b.** *(when talking)* ser breve; **to be b...., in b....** en pocas palabras...
 **3** *vt (inform)* informar

**briefcase** ['bri:fkeɪs] *n* maletín *m*, portafolios *m inv*

**briefing** ['bri:fɪŋ] *n (meeting)* sesión *f* informativa; *(information)* información *f*; *(written)* informe *m*

**briefly** ['bri:flɪ] *adv* brevemente; **(put) b....** en pocas palabras...

**briefs** [bri:fs] *npl (underwear) (woman's)* bragas *fpl*; *(man's)* calzoncillos *mpl*

**brier** = **briar**

**brigade** [brɪ'geɪd] *n* brigada *f*

**brigadier** [brɪgə'dɪə(r)] *n* general *m* de brigada

**brigand** ['brɪgənd] *n Literary* malhechor *m*, bandido *m*

**bright** [braɪt] **1** *adj* (**a**) *(sun, light, eyes)* brillante; *(day)* claro(a), luminoso(a); *(colour)* vivo(a); **b. red** rojo *m* vivo; **to go b. red** *(blush)* ruborizarse
 (**b**) *(optimistic) (future, situation)* prometedor(ora); **it was the only b. spot in the day** fue el único momento bueno del día; **to look on the b. side (of things)** fijarse en el lado bueno (de las cosas)
 (**c**) *(cheerful)* jovial
 (**d**) *(clever) (person)* inteligente; *(idea, suggestion)* excelente, brillante; **he's b. at physics** se le da bien la física
 **2** *adv* **b. and early** tempranito

**brighten** ['braɪtən] **1** *vt* (**a**) *(room)* alegrar, avivar (**b**) *(mood)* alegrar, animar
 **2** *vi (of weather, sky)* aclararse; *(of face, eyes, mood)* alegrarse, animarse; *(of prospects)* mejorar
▸**brighten up 1** *vt sep (room, mood)* alegrar
 **2** *vi (of person, face)* animarse; *(of weather, sky)* despejarse

**bright-eyed** ['braɪtaɪd] *adj* con los ojos brillantes; *Fig (enthusiasm)* vivo(a); *Fam* **b. and bushy-tailed** alegre y contento(a)

**brightly** ['braɪtlɪ] *adv (shine)* radiantemente; *(say, smile)* alegremente; **b. coloured** de vivos colores

**brightness** ['braɪtnɪs] *n* (**a**) *(of light, sun)* luminosidad *f*, brillo *m*; *(of colour)* viveza *f*; **b.** (**control**) *(on TV)* (mando *m* del) brillo (**b**) *(cleverness)* inteligencia *f*

**brill** [brɪl] *adj Fam* guay, genial

**brilliance** ['brɪljəns] *n* (**a**) *(of light, colour)* resplandor *m* (**b**) *(of person, idea)* genialidad *f*

**brilliant** ['brɪljənt] *adj* (**a**) *(light, sun, smile)* radiante, resplandeciente (**b**) *(person)* genial; *(future, career)* brillante (**c**) *(excellent)* genial, *Andes, Carib* chévere, *Andes, CSur* macanudo(a), *Méx* padre

**brilliantly** ['brɪljəntlɪ] *adv* (**a**) *(to shine)* radiantemente; **b. lit** muy iluminado(a); **b. coloured** de vivos colores (**b**) *(acted, played)* magníficamente

**brim** [brɪm] **1** *n (of cup, glass)* borde *m*; *(of hat)* ala *f*
 **2** *vi (pt & pp brimmed) (with liquid, enthusiasm)* **to be brimming with** rebosar de; **her eyes brimmed with tears** tenía los ojos anegados de lágrimas
▸**brim over** *vi* rebosar, desbordarse; *Fig* **to be brimming over with health/ideas** estar rebosante de salud/ideas

**brimful** ['brɪmfʊl] *adj* hasta el borde; *Fig* **b. of health/ideas** pletórico(a) de salud/ideas

**brimstone** ['brɪmstəʊn] *n Literary* azufre *m*; **fire and b.** fuego *m* del infierno

**brine** [braɪn] *n (for preserving)* salmuera *f*

**bring** [brɪŋ] *(pt & pp brought* [brɔ:t]*) vt* (**a**) *(take)* traer; **to b. sth to sb's attention** llamar la atención de alguien sobre algo; **what brings you to London?** ¿qué te trae por Londres?; **that brings us to my final point...** esto nos lleva al último punto...; **to b. sth out of a box** sacar algo de una caja; **to b. a child into the world** traer al mundo a un niño; *Law* **to b. an action against sb** interponer una demanda *or* entablar un pleito contra alguien
 (**b**) *(lead to, cause)* traer; **it has brought me great happiness** me ha causado gran alegría; **to b. sb (good) luck/bad luck** traer (buena) suerte/mala suerte a alguien; **the announcement brought an angry reaction** el anuncio produjo una reacción airada; **to b. new hope to sb** infundir nuevas esperanzas a alguien; **to b. tears to sb's eyes** hacer llorar a alguien
 (**c**) *(cause to come to a particular condition)* **to b. sth into disrepute** perjudicar la reputación de *or* desprestigiar algo; **to b. sth into question** poner en duda algo; **to b. sth to the boil**

hacer que algo hierva; **to b. sth to an end** poner fin a algo; **to b. sth to light** sacar algo a la luz; **to b. sth to mind** traer a la memoria algo; **to b. oneself to do sth** resolverse a hacer algo; **I couldn't b. myself to tell her** no pude decírselo

(d) *(be sold for)* **the house won't b. very much** la casa no reportará mucho dinero

▸**bring about** *vt sep (cause)* provocar, ocasionar

▸**bring along** *vt sep* traer

▸**bring back** *vt sep* (a) *(purchase)* devolver; *(person)* traer de vuelta; **to b. sb back to life/ health** devolver la vida/la salud a alguien (b) *(occasion)* recordar; **to b. back memories of sth to sb** traer a alguien recuerdos de algo (c) *(law, punishment)* reinstaurar

▸**bring down** *vt sep* (a) *(from shelf, attic)* bajar (b) *(cause to fall)* (soldier, plane) derribar; *(government)* derrocar; *Fam* **her performance brought the house down** su actuación enfervorizó al público (c) *(price, temperature)* bajar

▸**bring forward** *vt sep* (a) *(proposal, plan)* presentar (b) *(advance time of)* adelantar (c) *Com* pasar a cuenta nueva; **brought forward** saldo anterior

▸**bring in** *vt sep* (a) *(expert, consultant)* contratar los servicios de; **the police brought him in for questioning** la policía lo llevó a comisaría para interrogarlo (b) *(earn)* (of person) ganar; *(of sale, investment)* generar (c) *Pol (law, bill)* introducir (d) *Law (verdict)* pronunciar

▸**bring off** *vt sep (accomplish)* conseguir

▸**bring on** *vt sep* provocar; **you've brought it on yourself** tú te lo has buscado

▸**bring out** *vt sep* (a) *(new product)* sacar (b) *(provoke, elicit)* **to b. out the best/the worst in sb** sacar lo mejor/peor de alguien; **strawberries b. her out in a rash** las fresas le provocan un sarpullido; **to b. sb out of his/her shell** sacar a alguien de su concha

▸**bring round** *vt sep* (a) *(revive)* hacer volver en sí, reanimar (b) *(persuade)* convencer; **she brought him round to her point of view** le convenció (c) *(direct)* **he brought the conversation round to the subject of...** sacó a colación el tema de...

▸**bring to** *vt sep (revive)* hacer volver en sí, reanimar

▸**bring together** *vt sep* reunir

▸**bring up** *vt sep* (a) *(subject)* sacar a colación (b) *(child)* educar; **I was brought up in Spain** fui criado/a en España (c) *(vomit)* vomitar

**bring-and-buy** ['brɪŋən'baɪ] *adj Br* **b. (sale)** = mercadillo benéfico de compra y venta

**brink** [brɪŋk] *n also Fig* borde *m*; **on the b. of** al borde de; *Fig* **to be on the b. of doing sth** estar a punto de hacer algo

**brinkmanship** ['brɪŋkmənʃɪp] *n (in politics, diplomacy)* = política consistente en arriesgarse hasta el límite para obtener concesiones de la parte contraria

**brisk** [brɪsk] *adj* (a) *(weather, wind)* fresco(a), vigorizante (b) *(person, manner)* enérgico(a); **to be b. with sb** *(rude)* ser brusco(a) con alguien (c) *(rapid)* rápido(a); **at a b. pace** a paso ligero; **business is b.** el negocio va muy bien

**briskly** ['brɪsklɪ] *adv* (a) *(efficiently)* enérgicamente; *(dismissively)* bruscamente (b) *(rapidly)* rápidamente

**bristle** ['brɪsəl] **1** *n (of animal, brush)* cerda *f; (on face)* pelo *m* de la barba; *(of plant)* pelo *m*

**2** *vi* (a) *(of animal's fur)* erizarse; *Fig* **to b. (with anger)** enfurecerse (b) *(be full)* **the room was bristling with security men** la habitación estaba repleta de agentes de seguridad; **the situation was bristling with difficulties** la situación estaba erizada de dificultades

**Brit** [brɪt] *n Fam* británico(a) *m,f*

**Britain** ['brɪtən] *n* Gran Bretaña

**British** ['brɪtɪʃ] **1** *npl* **the B.** los británicos

**2** *adj* británico(a); **the B. Isles** las Islas Británicas; **B. Summer Time** = hora oficial de verano en Gran Bretaña

**Briton** ['brɪtən] *n* británico(a) *m,f; Hist* británo(a) *m,f*

**Brittany** ['brɪtənɪ] *n* Bretaña

**brittle** ['brɪtəl] *adj* (a) *(glass, bones)* frágil; *(paper, branches)* quebradizo(a) (b) *(irritable)* **to be b.** *(permanent quality)* ser susceptible; *(temporarily)* estar susceptible

**broach** [brəʊtʃ] *vt (subject, question)* sacar a colación, abordar

**broad**[1] [brɔːd] *adj (wide)* ancho(a); *(smile, sense)* amplio(a); *(accent)* marcado(a); *(humour)* basto(a); *(mind)* abierto(a); **in b. daylight** en pleno día; **to be in b. agreement** estar de acuerdo en líneas generales; *Fig* **the movement was a b. church** el movimiento admitía miembros de diversas tendencias; **b. bean** haba *f;* **a b. hint** una clara indirecta; **b. outline** líneas *fpl* generales

**broad**[2] *n US very Fam* tía *f*, piba *f*

**broadcast** ['brɔːdkɑːst] **1** *n (programme)* emisión *f*

**2** *vt (pt & pp* **broadcast)** transmitir, emitir; *Fam* **don't b. it!** ¡no lo pregones!

**3** *vi (of station)* emitir

**broadcaster** ['brɔːdkɑːstə(r)] *n (person)* presentador(ora) *m,f*

**broadcasting** ['brɔːdkɑːstɪŋ] *n (programmes)* emisiones *fpl*, programas *mpl*; **he works in b.** trabaja en la televisión/radio; **b. station** emisora *f*

**broaden** ['brɔːdən] **1** *vt (road)* ensanchar; **to**

**b. sb's horizons** ampliar los horizontes de alguien

**2** *vi* to **b. (out)** ensancharse, ampliarse

**broadly** ['brɔːdlɪ] *adv (generally)* en general; **to smile b.** esbozar una amplia sonrisa; **b. speaking** en términos generales

**broad-minded** [brɔːd'maɪndɪd] *adj* tolerante, de mentalidad abierta

**broadsheet** ['brɔːdʃiːt] *n (newspaper)* periódico *m* de formato grande *(característico de la prensa británica seria)*

**broad-shouldered** [brɔːd'ʃəʊldəd] *adj* ancho(a) de espaldas

**broadside** ['brɔːdsaɪd] *n also Fig* **to fire a b.** soltar una andanada

**brocade** [brə'keɪd] *n (cloth)* brocado *m*

**broccoli** ['brɒkəlɪ] *n* brécol *m*, brócoli *m*

**brochure** ['brəʊʃə(r)] *n* folleto *m*

**brogue**[1] [brəʊg] *n (shoe)* zapato *m* de vestir *(de cuero calado)*

**brogue**[2] *n (accent)* acento *m (especialmente el irlandés)*

**broil** [brɔɪl] *vt US (grill)* asar a la parrilla

**broke** [brəʊk] **1** *adj Fam* **to be b.** *(penniless)* estar sin blanca; **to go for b.** jugarse el todo por el todo

**2** *pt of* **break**

**broken** ['brəʊkən] **1** *adj (object, bone, promise)* roto(a); *(ground, surface)* accidentado(a); *Fig (person, heart)* destrozado(a); **in a b. voice** con la voz quebrada; **to speak b. English** chapurrear inglés; **b. home** hogar *m* deshecho *or* roto

**2** *pp of* **break**

**broken-hearted** [brəʊkən'hɑːtɪd] *adj* **to be b.** estar desolado(a) *or* desconsolado(a)

**broker** ['brəʊkə(r)] *n Fin* agente *mf*, corredor *m*

**brolly** ['brɒlɪ] *n Br Fam* paraguas *m inv*

**bromide** ['brəʊmaɪd] *n Chem* bromuro *m*; *Fig* fórmula *f* caduca

**bronchial** ['brɒŋkɪəl] *adj Anat* bronquial; **the b. tubes** los bronquios

**bronchitic** [brɒŋ'kɪtɪk] *adj Med* bronquítico(a)

**bronchitis** [brɒŋ'kaɪtɪs] *n* bronquitis *f inv*

**bronze** [brɒnz] **1** *n* bronce *m*; **to win a b.** ganar una medalla de bronce; **the B. Age** la Edad del Bronce

**2** *adj (material)* de bronce; *(colour)* color (de) bronce

**bronzed** [brɒnzd] *adj (tanned)* bronceado(a)

**brooch** [brəʊtʃ] *n* broche *m*

**brood** [bruːd] **1** *n (of baby birds)* nidada *f*; *Hum (of children)* prole *f*, progenie *f*

**2** *vi (of hen)* empollar; *Fig* **to b. over one's mistakes** rumiar los propios errores

**broody** ['bruːdɪ] *adj (hen)* clueca; *Fig (of woman)* **in springtime, I get b.** en primavera me surge el instinto maternal

**brook**[1] [brʊk] *n (stream)* arroyo *m*, riachuelo *m*

**brook**[2] *vt Formal (tolerate)* tolerar, consentir; **he will b. no opposition** no admitirá oposición

**broom** [bruːm] *n* **(a)** *(plant)* retama *f*, escoba *f* **(b)** *(for cleaning)* escoba *f*; *Fig* **a new b.** = jefe recién llegado que quiere cambiar radicalmente las cosas

**broomstick** ['bruːmstɪk] *n* palo *m* de escoba

**Bros** *npl Com (abbr* **Brothers)** Riley B. Hnos. Riley

**broth** [brɒθ] *n (soup) (thin)* sopa *f*, caldo *m*; *(thick)* potaje *m*, sopa

**brothel** ['brɒθəl] *n* burdel *m*

**brother** ['brʌðə(r)] *n* hermano *m*

**brotherhood** ['brʌðəhʊd] *n (feeling)* fraternidad *f*; *Rel* hermandad *f*; **the b. of man** la humanidad

**brother-in-law** ['brʌðərɪnlɔː] *(pl* **brothers-in-law)** *n* cuñado *m*

**brought** [brɔːt] *pt & pp of* **bring**

**brow** [braʊ] *n* **(a)** *(forehead)* frente *f*; *(eyebrow)* ceja *f* **(b)** *(of hill)* cima *f*, cumbre *f*

**browbeat** ['braʊbiːt] *(pt* **browbeat,** *pp* **browbeaten** ['braʊbiːtən]) *vt* intimidar; **to b. sb into doing sth** intimidar a alguien para que haga algo

**brown** [braʊn] **1** *n* marrón *m*; *Am* color *m* café

**2** *adj* marrón; *(hair, eyes)* castaño(a); *(skin)* moreno(a); **b. bread** pan *m* integral; **b. paper** papel *m* de estraza; **b. rice** arroz *m* integral; **b. sugar** azúcar *m or f* moreno(a)

**3** *vt (in cooking)* dorar

**4** *vi (in cooking)* dorarse

**browned-off** ['braʊnd'ɒf] *adj Br Fam* **to be b. (with sb/sth)** estar hasta las narices (de alguien/algo)

**Brownie** ['braʊnɪ] *n (member of girls' organization)* escultista *f*; *Fig* **to win** *or* **get b. points** anotarse tantos

**brownie** ['braʊnɪ] *n US (cake)* bizcocho *m* de chocolate y nueces

**brown-nose** ['braʊnnəʊz] *Vulg vt* lamerle el culo a

**browse** [braʊz] **1** *n* **to have a b.** echar una ojeada

**2** *vi* **(a)** *(in bookshop, magazine)* echar una ojeada; **to b. through sth** *(book, magazine)* hojear algo **(b)** *(of animal)* pacer

**3** *vt Comptr* **to b. the Web** navegar por la Web

**browser** ['braʊzə(r)] *n Comptr* navegador *m*

**bruise** [bruːz] **1** *n (on body)* cardenal *m*, moradura *f*; *(on fruit)* maca *f*, magulladura *f*

**2** *vt (person, sb's arm)* magullar; *Fig (feelings)*

herir; **to b. one's arm** hacerse un cardenal en el brazo

**3** *vi* **to b. easily** *(of fruit)* macarse con facilidad; **he bruises easily** le salen cardenales con facilidad

**bruiser** ['bru:zə(r)] *n Fam* matón *m*

**bruising** ['bru:zɪŋ] **1** *n (bruises)* moratones *mpl*, moraduras *fpl*

**2** *adj (encounter, impact)* duro(a), violento(a)

**Brummie** ['brʌmɪ] **1** *n Fam* = habitante *or* nativo de Birmingham

**2** *adj* de Birmingham

**brunch** [brʌntʃ] *n Fam* desayuno-comida *m*

**Brunei** [bru:'naɪ] *n* Brunei

**brunette** [bru:'net] *n* morena *f*

**brunt** [brʌnt] *n* **she bore the b. of the criticism** recibió la mayor parte de las críticas; **the north of the city bore the b. of the attack** el norte de la ciudad fue la parte más afectada por el ataque

**brush** [brʌʃ] **1** *n* **(a)** *(for clothes, hair)* cepillo *m*; *(for sweeping)* cepillo, escoba *f*; *(for painting pictures)* pincel *m*; *(for house-painting, shaving)* brocha *f*

**(b)** *(action) (to hair, teeth, horse)* cepillado *m*; **to give one's hair a b.** cepillarse el pelo; **to give the floor a b.** barrer el suelo

**(c)** *(light touch)* roce *m*; *Fam* **to have a b. with the law** tener un problemilla con la ley

**(d)** *(of fox)* cola *f*

**(e)** *(undergrowth)* maleza *f*

**2** *vt* **(a)** *(clean)* cepillar; *(floor)* barrer; **to b. one's hair** cepillarse el pelo; **to b. one's teeth** lavarse *or* cepillarse los dientes

**(b)** *(touch lightly)* rozar

**3** *vi* **to b. against sth/sb** rozar algo/a alguien; **to brush past sth/sb** pasar rozando algo/a alguien

▸**brush aside** *vt sep (objection, criticism)* no hacer caso a; *(opponent)* deshacerse de

▸**brush off** *vt sep* **(a)** *(dust, dirt)* sacudir **(b)** *Fam (dismiss)* pasar de, no hacer caso a

▸**brush up** *vt sep* **(a)** *(leaves, crumbs)* barrer **(b)** *Fam (subject, language)* **to b. up (on)** pulir, dar un repaso a

**brushed** [brʌʃt] *adj (cotton, nylon)* afelpado(a)

**brush-off** ['brʌʃɒf] *n Fam* **to give sb the b.** no hacer ni caso a alguien

**brush-up** ['brʌʃʌp] *n* **to have a wash and b.** arreglarse

**brushwood** ['brʌʃwʊd] *n* **(a)** *(as fuel)* leña *f*, broza *f* **(b)** *(undergrowth)* maleza *f*, broza *f*

**brushwork** ['brʌʃwɜ:k] *n Art* pincelada *f*, técnica *f* del pincel

**brusque** [bru:sk] *adj* brusco(a)

**brusquely** ['bru:sklɪ] *adv* bruscamente

**Brussels** ['brʌsəlz] *n* Bruselas; **b. sprouts** coles *fpl* de Bruselas

**brutal** ['bru:təl] *adj* brutal

**brutality** [bru:'tælɪtɪ] *n* brutalidad *f*

**brutalize** ['bru:təlaɪz] *vt (make cruel or insensitive)* embrutecer; *(ill-treat)* tratar con brutalidad

**brutally** ['bru:təlɪ] *adv* brutalmente

**brute** [bru:t] **1** *n* bestia *mf*

**2** *adj* **b. force** *or* **strength** fuerza *f* bruta

**brutish** ['bru:tɪʃ] *adj* brutal

**BSc** [bi:es'si:] *n Univ (abbr* **Bachelor of Science)** *(qualification)* licenciatura *f* en Ciencias; *(person)* licenciado(a) *m,f* en Ciencias

**BSE** [bi:es'i:] *n (abbr* **bovine spongiform encephalopathy)** encefalopatía *f* espongiforme bovina *(enfermedad de las vacas locas)*

**BSI** [bi:es'eɪ] *n Br (abbr* **British Standards Institution)** = asociación británica de normalización, ≃ AENOR

**BST** [bi:es'ti:] *n Br (abbr* **British Summer Time)** = horario británico de verano

**bubble** ['bʌbəl] **1** *n (of air)* burbuja *f*; *(of soap)* pompa *f*; **to blow bubbles** hacer pompas de jabón; *Fig* **the b. has burst** la buena racha ha terminado; **b. bath** *(liquid)* espuma *f* de baño; *(bath)* baño *m* de espuma; **b. gum** chicle *m*; *Comptr* **b. jet (printer)** impresora *f* de inyección

**2** *vi (form bubbles)* burbujear, borbotar

▸**bubble over** *vi (of soup, milk)* salirse, desbordarse; *Fig* **to b. over with joy** rebosar alegría

**bubbly** ['bʌblɪ] **1** *n Fam (champagne)* champán *m*

**2** *adj* **(a)** *(liquid)* espumoso(a) **(b)** *(personality)* alegre, jovial

**bubonic plague** [bju:'bɒnɪk'pleɪg] *n* peste *f* bubónica

**buccaneer** [bʌkə'nɪə(r)] *n* bucanero *m*

**Bucharest** ['bʊkərest] *n* Bucarest

**buck** [bʌk] **1** *n* **(a)** *(deer)* ciervo *m* (macho); *(rabbit)* conejo *m* (macho) **(b)** *US Fam (dollar)* dólar *m*; **to make a fast** *or* **quick b.** hacer dinero fácil **(c)** *Fam (responsibility)* **to pass the b.** escurrir el bulto; **the b. stops here** aquí recae la responsabilidad última

**2** *vt* **to b. the odds** desafiar las leyes de la probabilidad; **to b. the system** oponerse al sistema; **to b. a trend** invertir una tendencia

**3** *vi (of horse)* corcovear

▸**buck up** *Fam* **1** *vt sep (encourage)* animar, entonar; **to b. up one's ideas** espabilarse

**2** *vi (cheer up)* animarse; *(hurry)* espabilarse, aligerar

**bucket** ['bʌkɪt] **1** *n* cubo *m*; *Br Fam* **it's raining buckets** está lloviendo a cántaros; *Fam* **to cry** *or* **weep buckets** llorar a mares; *Fam* **b. shop** *(for air tickets)* agencia *f* de viajes barata

**2** *vi Fam* **it's bucketing (down)** está lloviendo a cántaros

**buckle** ['bʌkəl] **1** *n* hebilla *f*
**2** *vt* (**a**) *(fasten)* abrochar (**b**) *(deform)* combar
**3** *vi* (*deform*) combarse; *(of knees)* doblarse; **he buckled at the knees** se le doblaron las rodillas
▶**buckle down** *vi* poner manos a la obra; **to b. down to a task** ponerse a hacer una tarea
**buckshot** ['bʌkʃɒt] *n* perdigones *mpl*
**buckskin** ['bʌkskɪn] *n* piel *f (de ciervo o cabra)*
**buckteeth** [bʌk'ti:θ] *npl* dientes *mpl* de conejo
**bucktoothed** [bʌk'tu:θt] *adj* con dientes de conejo
**buckwheat** ['bʌkwi:t] *n* alforfón *m*
**bucolic** [bju:'kɒlɪk] *adj Literary* bucólico(a)
**bud** [bʌd] **1** *n (of leaf, branch)* brote *m; (of flower)* capullo *m*
**2** *vi (pt & pp budded)* brotar, salir
**Budapest** ['budəpest] *n* Budapest
**Buddha** ['budə] *n* Buda *m*
**Buddhist** ['budɪst] *n & adj* budista *mf*
**budding** ['bʌdɪŋ] *adj (genius, actor)* en ciernes, incipiente
**buddy** ['bʌdɪ] *n Fam (friend)* colega *mf*
**budge** [bʌdʒ] **1** *vt (move)* mover; *Fig* **I couldn't b. him** *(change his mind)* no conseguí hacerle cambiar de opinión
**2** *vi (move)* moverse; *Fig (yield)* ceder
**budgerigar** ['bʌdʒərɪga:(r)] *n* periquito *m* (australiano)
**budget** ['bʌdʒɪt] **1** *n* presupuesto *m; Br Pol* **the B.** ≃ los Presupuestos Generales del Estado; **to go over b.** salirse del presupuesto; **we are within b.** no nos hemos salido del presupuesto; **b. deficit** déficit *m* presupuestario; **b. surplus** superávit *m* presupuestario
**2** *vt (time, money)* calcular
**3** *vi* **to b. for** *(include in budget)* contemplar en el presupuesto; *Fig* contar con
**budgetary** ['bʌdʒɪtərɪ] *adj Fin* presupuestario(a)
**budgie** ['bʌdʒɪ] *n Fam* periquito *m* (australiano)
**Buenos Aires** ['bwenɒs'aɪrez] *n* Buenos Aires
**buff** [bʌf] **1** *n* (**a**) *(colour)* marrón *m* claro; *Fam* **in the b.** *(naked)* en cueros (**b**) *(enthusiast)* **film b.** cinéfilo(a) *m,f;* **opera b.** entendido(a) en ópera
**2** *adj* marrón claro
**3** *vt (polish)* sacar brillo a
**buffalo** ['bʌfələʊ] *(pl* **buffalo** *or* **buffaloes)** *n* búfalo *m*
**buffer¹** ['bʌfə(r)] *n (on railway track)* tope *m; Comptr* buffer *m;* **to act as a b.** hacer de amortiguador; **b. state** estado *m* barrera; **b. zone** zona *f* de protección
**buffer²** *n Br Fam* **old b.** carcamal *m*

**buffet¹** ['bʌfɪt] *vt (of wind)* zarandear, azotar; *Fig* **he was buffeted by the crowds** le arrolló *or* zarandeó la multitud; *Fig* **to be buffeted by events** verse sacudido(a) por el remolino de los acontecimientos
**buffet²** ['bʊfeɪ] *n* (**a**) *(sideboard)* mostrador *m* de comidas, bufé *m* (**b**) *(meal)* bufé *m;* **b. lunch** *(almuerzo m tipo)* bufé *m* (**c**) *(at station)* cafetería *f;* **b. car** vagón *m* restaurante, bar *m*
**buffeting** ['bʌfɪtɪŋ] *n* **to take a b.** *(of ship)* ser zarandeado(a); *Fig (of person)* recibir muchos golpes
**buffoon** [bə'fu:n] *n* payaso *m*, bufón *m*
**bug** [bʌg] **1** *n* (**a**) *(insect)* bicho *m* (**b**) *Fam (illness)* infección *f;* **there's a b. going round** hay un virus rondando por ahí; *Fig* **the travel b.** el gusanillo de viajar (**c**) *Comptr* error *m* (**d**) *(listening device)* micrófono *m* oculto
**2** *vt (pt & pp bugged)* (**a**) *(telephone)* pinchar, intervenir; *(room)* poner micrófonos en (**b**) *Fam (annoy)* molestar, fastidiar; **stop bugging me about it!** ¡deja de darme la lata con eso!
**bugbear** ['bʌgbeə(r)] *n Fam* tormento *m*, pesadilla *f*
**bug-eyed** ['bʌgeɪd] *adj* con ojos saltones
**bug-free** [bʌg'fri:] *adj Comptr* sin errores
**bugger** ['bʌgə(r)] **1** *n* very *Fam (unpleasant person)* cabrón(ona) *m,f;* **you silly b.** ¡qué tonto(a) eres!; **the poor b.!** ¡pobre desgraciado!; **a b. of a job** una putada de trabajo; **b. all** nada de nada; **he knows b. all about it** no tiene ni puta idea
**2** *vt* (**a**) *(sodomize)* sodomizar (**b**) very *Fam* **b. (it)!** ¡joder!; **I'll be buggered if I'm going to pay for it!** ¡no lo voy a pagar ni de coña!; **I'm buggered if I know** no tengo ni puta idea; **that's really buggered it!** ¡lo ha jodido todo bien!
▶**bugger about, bugger around** very *Fam* **1** *vt sep* **stop buggering me about** *or* **around!** ¡deja de marearme, joder!
**2** *vi* hacer el/la gilipollas
▶**bugger off** *vi* very *Fam* abrirse, pirarse; **b. off!** ¡vete a la mierda!
▶**bugger up** *vt sep* very *Fam* joder
**buggered** ['bʌgəd] *adj* very *Fam* **to be b.** *(broken)* estar jodido(a); *(exhausted)* estar hecho(a) polvo
**buggery** ['bʌgərɪ] *n* (**a**) *Law* sodomía *f* (**b**) very *Fam* **to run like b.** correr a toda hostia
**bugging device** ['bʌgɪŋdɪ'vaɪs] *n (in room)* micrófono *m* oculto; *(in telephone line)* aparato *m* de escucha telefónica
**buggy** ['bʌgɪ] *n* (**a**) *Br (pushchair)* sillita *f* (de niño); *US (pram)* cochecito *m* (de niño) (**b**) *(carriage)* calesa *f*
**bugle** ['bju:gəl] *n* corneta *f*, clarín *m*
**bugler** ['bju:glə(r)] *n* corneta *m*, clarín *m*

**build** [bɪld] **1** n complexión f, constitución f

**2** vt (pt & pp **built** [bɪlt]) construir; **to be built (out)** of sth estar hecho/de algo; **to b. sth into sth** incorporar algo en algo; **they have built their hopes on it** han basado sus esperanzas en ello

▸**build on** vt sep (a) (add) añadir (b) (use as foundation) **she built on their achievements** siguió avanzando a partir de sus logros

▸**build up 1** vt sep (a) (hopes, expectations) alimentar; (resources) aumentar (b) (reputation) crear; **to b. up speed** coger velocidad; **to b. up an immunity (to sth)** hacerse inmune (a algo) (c) (hype) **the press built her up as a future champion** la prensa construyó su imagen de futura campeona

**2** vi (of clouds) formarse; (of tension, pressure) incrementarse, aumentar

**builder** ['bɪldə(r)] n (worker) albañil m; (small businessman) contratista mf de obras

**building** ['bɪldɪŋ] n (a) (structure) edificio m (b) (trade) construcción f; **b. block** (toy) pieza f (de construcción); **b. unit** f básica; **b. site** obra f; Br **b. society** ≃ caja f de ahorros

**build-up** ['bɪldʌp] n (of tension, forces) incremento m, aumento m; (before election, public event) período m previo; **after all the b....** después de toda la expectación creada...

**built** [bɪlt] pt & pp of **build**

**built-in** ['bɪl'tɪn] adj (cupboard) empotrado(a); (included) incorporado(a); Fig (safeguard, obsolescence) inherente

**built-up** ['bɪl'tʌp] adj (area) urbanizado(a)

**bulb** [bʌlb] n (of plant) bulbo m; (lightbulb) bombilla f, CAm, Méx foco m

**bulbous** ['bʌlbəs] adj bulboso(a)

**Bulgaria** [bʌl'geəriə] n Bulgaria

**Bulgarian** [bʌl'geəriən] **1** n (a) (person) búlgaro(a) m,f (b) (language) búlgaro m

**2** adj búlgaro(a)

**bulge** [bʌldʒ] **1** n bulto m, abultamiento m

**2** vi (a) (be full of) estar repleto(a) (**with** de) (b) (swell) abombarse; Fig **his eyes bulged at the sight of all the food** al ver tanta comida parecía que se le iban a salir los ojos de las órbitas

**bulimia** [buːˈlɪmɪə] n Med bulimia f

**bulk** [bʌlk] **1** n (a) (mass) masa f, volumen m; **the b. (of sth)** (most) el grueso (de algo) (b) Com **in b.** a granel; **to buy/sell in b.** comprar/vender al por mayor; **b. purchase** compra f al por mayor

**2** vt **to b. sth out** abultar algo

**3** vi **to b. large** (of problem) tener relieve

**bulkhead** ['bʌlkhed] n Naut mamparo m

**bulky** ['bʌlkɪ] adj (thing) grande, voluminoso(a); (person) corpulento(a)

**bull¹** [bʊl] n (a) (animal) toro m; **b. elephant** elefante m (macho); Fin **b. market** mercado m

al alza (b) very Fam (nonsense) **to talk b.** decir sandeces (c) (idioms) **to take the b. by the horns** coger el toro por los cuernos; **like a b. in a china shop** como un elefante en una cacharrería

**bull²** n Rel bula f

**bulldog** ['bʊldɒg] n bulldog m; **b. clip** pinza f sujetapapeles

**bulldoze** ['bʊldəʊz] vt (flatten) (area, land) allanar, nivelar; (building) demoler; (remove) derribar; Fig **to b. sb into doing sth** forzar or obligar a alguien a hacer algo

**bulldozer** ['bʊldəʊzə(r)] n bulldozer m

**bullet** ['bʊlɪt] n bala f, proyectil m; **b. hole** agujero m de bala; **b. wound** herida f de bala

**bulletin** ['bʊlɪtɪn] n boletín m; US & Comptr **b. board** tablón m de anuncios

**bulletproof** ['bʊlɪtpruːf] adj antibalas inv; **b. vest** chaleco m antibalas

**bullfight** ['bʊlfaɪt] n corrida f de toros

**bullfighter** ['bʊlfaɪtə(r)] n torero m

**bullfighting** ['bʊlfaɪtɪŋ] n toreo m

**bullfinch** ['bʊlfɪntʃ] n camachuelo m

**bullfrog** ['bʊlfrɒg] n rana f toro

**bullion** ['bʊljən] n **gold/silver b.** oro/plata en lingotes or barras

**bullish** ['bʊlɪʃ] adj Fin (market) al alza; Fig (person) optimista

**bullock** ['bʊlək] n buey m

**bullring** ['bʊlrɪŋ] n (building) plaza f de toros; (arena) ruedo m

**bullrush** ['bʊlrʌʃ] n junco m

**bull's-eye** ['bʊlzaɪ] n diana f, blanco m; also Fig **to hit the b.** dar en el blanco or clavo

**bullshit** ['bʊlʃɪt] Vulg **1** n (nonsense) gilipolleces fpl

**2** exclam ¡y un huevo!

**3** vt (pt & pp **bullshitted**) **to b. sb** vacilar a alguien; **she bullshitted her way into the job** consiguió el puesto engañando a todo el mundo

**4** vi (talk nonsense) decir gilipolleces

**bully** ['bʊlɪ] **1** n matón(ona) m,f; (at school) abusón(ona) m,f

**2** exclam Ironic **b. for you!** ¡toma ya!

**3** vt intimidar; **to b. sb into doing sth** intimidar a alguien para que haga algo

**bully-boy** ['bʊlɪbɔɪ] n matón m; **b. tactics** tácticas fpl de intimidación

**bullying** ['bʊlɪɪŋ] **1** n intimidación f

**2** adj intimidatorio(a), amenazador(ora)

**bulrush** ['bʊlrʌʃ] n anea f, espadaña f

**bulwark** ['bʊlwək] n also Fig bastión m (**against** contra)

**bum** [bʌm] Fam **1** n (a) Br (buttocks) trasero m, culo m (b) US (tramp) vagabundo(a) m,f

**2** adj (of poor quality) cutre; **she got a b. deal** la

trataron a patadas

**3** vt ( pt & pp **bummed**) **to b. sth from** or **off sb** gorronearle algo a alguien

▶**bum around** vi Fam (be idle) holgazanear, gandulear; (travel) vagabundear

**bumblebee** ['bʌmbəlbi:] n abejorro m

**bumbling** ['bʌmbəlɪŋ] adj **b. fool** or **idiot** tonto(a) m,f, inútil mf

**bumf** [bʌmf] n Fam papeleos mpl

**bummer** ['bʌmə(r)] n Fam (annoying thing) lata f, petardo m; **what a b.!** ¡qué lata!

**bump** [bʌmp] **1** n (**a**) (jolt) golpe m, sacudida f; Fig **to come back down to earth with a b.** volver a la dura realidad (**b**) (lump) chichón m

**2** vt **to b. one's head against sth** golpearse en la cabeza con algo

▶**bump into** vt insep (collide with) chocarse con; Fam (meet by chance) encontrarse con, toparse con

▶**bump off** vt sep Fam (kill) liquidar, cargarse a

▶**bump up** vt sep Fam (price) subir

**bumper** ['bʌmpə(r)] **1** n Br (of car) parachoques m inv; **b. car** (at fairground) coche m de choque

**2** adj abundante, excepcional; **b. crop** cosecha f excepcional; **b. issue** número m especial

**bumpkin** ['bʌmpkɪn] n (country) **b.** paleto(a) m,f, palurdo(a) m,f

**bump-start** ['bʌmpstɑ:t] vt **to b. a car** arrancar un coche empujando

**bumptious** ['bʌmpʃəs] adj presuntuoso(a), engreído(a)

**bumpy** ['bʌmpɪ] adj (road) lleno(a) de baches, accidentado(a); (journey) incómodo(a), agitado(a); Fam Fig **to have a b. ride** encontrar muchos obstáculos

**bun** [bʌn] n (**a**) (food) bollo m (**b**) (hair) moño m

**bunch** [bʌntʃ] n (of flowers) ramo m, ramillete m; (of bananas, grapes) racimo m; (of keys) manojo m; (of friends) pandilla f; (of people) grupo m; **to wear one's hair in bunches** peinarse con or llevar coletas; **to have a whole b. of things to do** tener un montón de cosas que hacer; **the best** or **the pick of the b.** el mejor de todo el lote

▶**bunch together** vi (of people) apiñarse

**bundle** ['bʌndəl] **1** n (of papers) manojo m; (of banknotes) fajo m; (of straw) haz m, gavilla f; (of clothes) fardo m, hato m; Fam **she's a b. of nerves** es un manojo de nervios; Fam **I don't go a b. on horror films** no me vuelven loco las películas de terror; Fam Ironic **he's a real b. of laughs** es un muermo de tío

**2** vt **to b. sb out of the door** sacar a alguien a empujones por la puerta; **to b. sb into a car** meter a alguien a empujones en un coche

▶**bundle off** vt sep (send) despachar

**bung** [bʌŋ] **1** n (**a**) tapón m (**b**) Br Fam (bribe) soborno m

**2** vt (**a**) (pipe, hole) atascar, taponar (**b**) Fam (put, throw) echar; **b. it there** échalo ahí

▶**bung up** vt sep Fam (pipe, hole) atascar, taponar; **my nose is bunged up** tengo la nariz taponada

**bungalow** ['bʌŋgələʊ] n bungalow m

**bungee jumping** ['bʌndʒi:'dʒʌmpɪŋ] n puenting m

**bunghole** ['bʌŋhəʊl] n agujero m de barril

**bungle** ['bʌŋgəl] **1** vt (job, task) echar a perder, hacer mal; **they bungled their attempt to escape** su intento de fuga les salió mal

**2** vi hacer chapuzas

**bunion** ['bʌnjən] n (on foot) juanete m

**bunk¹** [bʌŋk] n (bed) litera f

**bunk²** n Br Fam **to do a b.** (run away) darse el piro, pirarse

**bunker** ['bʌŋkə(r)] n (**a**) (for coal) carbonera f (**b**) Mil búnker m; **nuclear b.** refugio m antinuclear (**c**) Br (on golf course) búnker m

**bunkum** ['bʌŋkəm] n Fam palabrería f, tonterías fpl

**bunny** ['bʌnɪ] n Fam **b. (rabbit)** conejito m

**Bunsen burner** ['bʌnsən'bɜ:nə(r)] n mechero m Bunsen

**bunting** ['bʌntɪŋ] n (decorations) banderines mpl

**buoy** [bɔɪ] n (pl **buoys**) n boya f

▶**buoy up** vt sep (person) animar, alentar; (prices) mantener estables

**buoyancy** ['bɔɪənsɪ] n (in water) flotabilidad f; Fig (of market) estabilidad f, optimismo m

**buoyant** ['bɔɪənt] adj (in water) flotante; Fig (economy, prices) boyante; Fig (person, mood) optimista, vital

**burble** ['bɜ:bəl] **1** vt (say) farfullar

**2** vi (of stream) borbotar; (of person) mascullar

**burden** ['bɜ:dən] **1** n also Fig carga f; Law **b. of proof** obligación f de probar

**2** vt cargar, sobrecargar (**with** con or de)

**burdensome** ['bɜ:dənsəm] adj pesado(a), molesto(a)

**bureau** ['bjʊərəʊ] (pl **bureaux** ['bjʊərəʊz]) n (**a**) (desk) secreter m, escritorio m; US (chest of drawers) cómoda f (**b**) (office) oficina f, departamento m; US (government department) departamento m

**bureaucracy** [bjʊə'rɒkrəsɪ] n burocracia f

**bureaucrat** ['bjʊərəkræt] n burócrata mf

**bureaucratic** [bjʊərə'krætɪk] adj burocrático(a)

**burgeon** ['bɜ:dʒən] vi (of trade, relationship) florecer; **a burgeoning talent** un talento incipiente

**burger** ['bɜːgə(r)] *n Fam (hamburger)* hamburguesa *f*

**burglar** ['bɜːglə(r)] *n* ladrón(ona) *m,f*; **b. alarm** alarma *f* antirrobo

**burglarize** ['bɜːgləraɪz] *vt US* robar, desvalijar

**burglar-proof** ['bɜːglə'pruːf] *adj* a prueba de ladrones

**burglary** ['bɜːglərɪ] *n* robo *m (en una casa o edificio)*

**burgle** ['bɜːgəl] *vt* robar, desvalijar

**burgundy** ['bɜːgəndɪ] *adj (colour)* (color) burdeos

**burial** ['berɪəl] *n* entierro *m*; **b. ground** cementerio *m*

**Burkina-Faso** [bɜː'kiːnə'fæsəʊ] *n* Burkina Faso

**burlesque** [bɜː'lesk] **1** *n* parodia *f*
   **2** *adj* burlesco(a), paródico(a)

**burly** ['bɜːlɪ] *adj* fornido(a), corpulento(a)

**Burma** ['bɜːmə] *n* Birmania

**Burmese** [bɜː'miːz] **1** *npl (people)* **the B.** los birmanos
   **2** *n (language)* birmano *m*
   **3** *adj* birmano(a)

**burn**[1] **1** *n* quemadura *f*
   **2** *vt (pt & pp burnt* [bɜːnt] *or burned)* **(a)** *(fuel, building)* quemar; **the stove burns wood/coal** la cocina funciona con leña/carbón; **to b. one's hand/finger** quemarse la mano/el dedo; **to b. a hole in sth** hacer un agujero a algo quemándolo
   **(b)** *(idioms)* **to have money to b.** *(rich person)* tener dinero de sobra; **she's just got paid – she's got money to b.** le acaban de pagar y tiene dinero para gastar; **to b. one's boats** *or* **one's bridges** quemar las naves; **to b. the candle at both ends** darse demasiado trote; **to b. the midnight oil** quedarse hasta muy tarde *(estudiando o trabajando)*
   **3** *vi (of fire, fuel, building)* arder; *(of light)* estar encendido(a); *Fig (with desire, anger, enthusiasm)* arder (**with** de); **the fire is burning low** el fuego está bajo
▸**burn down 1** *vt sep* incendiar, quemar
   **2** *vi* quemarse
▸**burn out 1** *vt sep* **to b. itself out** *(of fire)* consumirse, agotarse; *Fig* **to b. oneself out** *(become exhausted)* agotarse
   **2** *vi (of fire)* consumirse; *Fig (of person)* quemarse
▸**burn up 1** *vt sep (energy)* quemar, consumir
   **2** *vi (of rocket)* entrar en combustión

**burn**[2] [bɜːn] *n Scot (stream)* arroyo *m*

**burner** ['bɜːnə(r)] *n* quemador *m*

**burning** ['bɜːnɪŋ] *adj (on fire)* en llamas; *(heat, sun, passion)* abrasador(ora); *(ambition)* irrefrenable; **to be b. hot** abrasar; **a b. issue** un asunto candente

**burnish** ['bɜːnɪʃ] *vt (polish)* bruñir

**burnt** [bɜːnt] **1** *adj* quemado(a); **to be b.** estar quemado(a)
   **2** *pt & pp of* **burn**

**burnt-out** ['bɜːnt'aʊt] *adj (building)* calcinado(a), carbonizado(a); *(volcano)* apagado(a), extinguido(a); *(fuse)* fundido(a); *Fig (person)* quemado(a)

**burp** [bɜːp] **1** *n* eructo *m*
   **2** *vi* eructar

**burr**[1] [bɜː(r)] *n (of plant)* erizo *m*

**burr**[2] *n* **to speak with a b.** hablar arrastrando la "r"

**burrow** ['bʌrəʊ] **1** *n (of animal)* madriguera *f*
   **2** *vi (of animal)* cavar; *Fig* **he burrowed around in his desk** rebuscó en su escritorio

**bursar** ['bɜːsə(r)] *n Univ* tesorero(a) *m,f*

**bursary** ['bɜːsərɪ] *n* beca *f*

**burst** [bɜːst] **1** *n (of applause)* salva *f*; *(of activity, enthusiasm)* arranque *m*; **a b. of gunfire** una ráfaga de disparos; **a b. of laughter** una carcajada; **a b. of speed** un acelerón
   **2** *vt (pt & pp burst) (balloon, tyre)* reventar; **to b. its banks** *(of river)* desbordarse
   **3** *vi (of balloon, tyre, pipe)* reventar; *Fig* **to be bursting with pride/joy** reventar de orgullo/alegría; *Fig* **to be bursting to do sth** morirse de ganas de hacer algo; *Fig* **to be bursting at the seams** *(of room, bus)* estar hasta los topes; *Fam* **I'm bursting for the toilet** (estoy que) me meo
▸**burst into** *vt insep* **(a)** *(enter)* irrumpir en **(b)** *(suddenly start)* **to b. into flames** inflamarse; **to b. into song** ponerse a cantar; **to b. into laughter/tears** echarse a reír/llorar
▸**burst open** *vi (of door, suitcase)* abrirse de golpe; *(plastic bag)* reventar
▸**burst out** *vi* **to b. out laughing** soltar una carcajada; **to b. out crying** echarse a llorar

**Burundi** [bə'rʊndɪ] *n* Burundi

**bury** ['berɪ] *(pt & pp buried) vt (body, treasure)* enterrar; *(of avalanche, mudslide)* sepultar; **she buried the knife in his back** se lo clavó en el cuchillo en la espalda; *Fig* **to b. oneself in the country** retirarse al campo; **to b. one's face in one's hands** esconder la cara en las manos; *Fig* **to b. the hatchet** *(end quarrel)* enterrar el hacha de guerra

**bus** [bʌs] **1** *n* **(a)** autobús *m*, *CAm, Méx* camión *m*, *Ven* microbusete *m*, *Andes* buseta *f*, *Carib* guagua *f*, *CSur* micro *f*; **by b.** en autobús; **b. conductor** cobrador(ora) *m,f* de autobús; **b. driver** conductor(ora) *m,f* de autobús; **b. lane** carril *m* bus; **b. route** línea *f* de autobús; **b. shelter** marquesina *f*; **b. station** estación *f* de autobuses; **b. stop** parada *f* de autobús **(b)** *Comptr* bus *m*

**2** vt (pt & pp **bused** or **bussed**) llevar or transportar en autobús

**bush** [bʊʃ] n (plant) arbusto m, mata f; **the b.** (in Africa, Australia) el monte; Fam **b. telegraph** radio f macuto

**bushed** [bʊʃt] adj Fam (exhausted) **to be b.** estar molido(a) or derrengado(a)

**bushel** ['bʊʃəl] n = medida de áridos (GB = 36,35 litros; US = 35,23 litros); Fig **don't hide your light under a b.** no ocultes tus buenas cualidades

**bushfire** ['bʊʃfaɪə(r)] n incendio m de matorral

**Bushman** ['bʊʃmən] n bosquimano(a) m,f

**bushy** ['bʊʃɪ] adj espeso(a)

**busily** ['bɪzɪlɪ] adv activamente, diligentemente

**business** ['bɪznɪs] n (**a**) (task, concern) asunto m; **it's none of your b.** no es asunto tuyo; **it's not my b. to...** no me corresponde a mí...; **mind your own b.** métete en tus asuntos; **to make it one's b. to do sth** proponerse algo; **I was just going about my b.** yo simplemente iba a lo mío; **to get down to b.** ir a lo esencial, ir a lo importante; **to mean b.** ir en serio; **it's a sad** or **sorry b.** es un asunto lamentable or triste; **I'm sick of the whole b.** estoy harto de todo este asunto; Fam **he was working like nobody's b.** estaba trabajando de lo lindo; Br Fam **it's the b.!** (excellent) ¡es la hostia!
(**b**) (individual company) empresa f; (commercial activity) negocios mpl; **to be in b.** dedicarse a los negocios; **to be in the computing b.** (of person) trabajar en el sector de la informática; **I'm not in the b. of making concessions** no estoy por hacer concesiones; **to go into b.** (**with**) montar un negocio (con); **to go out of b.** quebrar; **to go to London on b.** ir a Londres en viaje de negocios; **how's b.?** ¿cómo van los negocios?; **it's good/bad for b.** es bueno/malo para los negocios; **to talk b.** hablar de negocios; **to do b.** (**with**) hacer negocios (con); Fig **he's a man you can do b. with** es un hombre con el que se puede tratar; Fin **b. account** cuenta f comercial; **b. card** tarjeta f de visita; Av **b. class** clase f preferente; **b. hours** (of company) horario m de trabajo; (of shop) horario m comercial; **b. lunch** comida f de trabajo; **b. management** gestión f or administración f de empresas; **b. park** parque m empresarial; **b. school** escuela f de comercio; **b. studies** empresariales fpl; **b. trip** viaje m de negocios

**businesslike** ['bɪznɪslaɪk] adj eficiente

**businessman** ['bɪznɪsmæn] n (executive, manager) hombre m de negocios, ejecutivo m; (owner of business) empresario m; **to be a good b.** tener cabeza para los negocios

**businesswoman** ['bɪznɪswʊmən] n (executive, manager) mujer f de negocios, ejecutiva f; (owner of business) empresaria f; **to be a good b.** tener cabeza para los negocios

**busk** [bʌsk] vi Br (of street musician) actuar en la calle

**busker** ['bʌskə(r)] n Br (street musician) músico(a) m,f callejero(a)

**busman** ['bʌsmən] n Fam **a b.'s holiday** = tiempo libre que se ocupa con una actividad similar a la del trabajo habitual

**bust¹** [bʌst] n (**a**) (of woman) busto m; **b. measurement** medida f de busto (**b**) (statue) busto m

**bust²** Fam **1** adj (broken) **to be b.** estar escacharrado(a); **to go b.** (bankrupt) quebrar
**2** vt (pt & pp **bust** or **busted**) (**a**) (break) escacharrar (**b**) (arrest) trincar, empapelar
▸**bust out** vi Fam (escape) fugarse, largarse
▸**bust up** vt sep Fam (disrupt) (event) reventar; (friendship, relationship) romper

**bustle** ['bʌsəl] **1** n (activity) bullicio m, trajín m
**2** vi **to b. (about)** trajinar

**bust-up** ['bʌstʌp] n Fam (dispute) bronca f; **to have a b.** tener una bronca

**busy** ['bɪzɪ] **1** adj (**a**) (person) ocupado(a); (day, week) ajetreado(a); **to be b.** (of person) estar ocupado(a); (of day, week) ser ajetreado(a); **to be b. doing sth** estar haciendo algo; **the train was very b.** el tren iba muy lleno; **a b. road** una carretera con mucho tráfico (**b**) US (telephone line) ocupado(a); **the line is b.** (el teléfono) está comunicando
**2** vt **to b. oneself with sth** entretenerse con algo

**busybody** ['bɪzɪbɒdɪ] (pl **busybodies**) n Fam metomentodo mf, entrometido(a) m,f

**but** [bʌt] **1** prep (except) salvo, excepto; **any day b. tomorrow** cualquier día salvo mañana; **it's nothing b. prejudice** no son más que prejuicios; **she is anything b. stupid** es todo menos tonta; **b. for** no ser por, si no es por; **the last b. one** el/la penúltimo(a); **the next b. one** el próximo no, el otro
**2** adv Formal **he is b. a child** no es más que un niño; **had I b. known!** ¡si lo hubiera sabido!; **one can b. try** al menos, se debe intentar
**3** conj (**a**) (in general) pero; **small b. strong** pequeño, pero fuerte; **I told her to do it b. she refused** le dije que lo hiciera, pero se negó; **b. I tell you I saw it!** ¡te aseguro que lo vi!; **what could I do b. invite him?** ¿qué otra cosa podía hacer más que invitarlo? (**b**) (direct contrast) sino; **not once b. twice** no una vez sino dos
**4** n **no buts!** ¡no hay peros que valgan!

**butane** ['bju:teɪn] n butano m

**butch** [bʊtʃ] *Fam adj* **she looks rather b.** tiene pinta de marimacho

**butcher** ['bʊtʃə(r)] **1** *n also Fig* carnicero(a) *m,f*; **the b.'s** *(shop)* la carnicería

**2** *vt also Fig* matar

**butchery** ['bʊtʃərɪ] *n* carnicería *f*; *Fig* carnicería *f*, matanza *f*

**butler** ['bʌtlə(r)] *n* mayordomo *m*

**butt** [bʌt] **1** *n* (**a**) *(of rifle)* culata *f*; *(of cigarette)* colilla *f*; *Fig* **to be the b. of a joke** ser el blanco de una broma (**b**) *US Fam (buttocks)* trasero *m*

**2** *vt (hit with head)* dar *or* arrear un cabezazo a
▸**butt in** *vi (interrupt)* inmiscuirse, entrometerse

**butter** ['bʌtə(r)] **1** *n* mantequilla *f*; *Fig* **she looks as if b. wouldn't melt in her mouth** parece como si no hubiera roto un plato en su vida; **b. bean** = tipo de judía *f* blanca; **b. dish** mantequera *f*; **b. knife** cuchillo *m* de mantequilla

**2** *vt* untar de mantequilla
▸**butter up** *vt sep Fam (flatter)* hacer la rosca a

**buttercup** ['bʌtəkʌp] *n* ranúnculo *m*, botón *m* de oro

**butterfingers** ['bʌtəfɪŋɡəz] *n Fam (clumsy person)* torpe *mf*, manazas *mf inv*

**butterfly** ['bʌtəflaɪ] *n* mariposa *f*; *Fig* **I had butterflies (in my stomach)** me temblaban las rodillas; **b. (stroke)** *(in swimming)* (estilo *m*) mariposa *f*; **to do** *or* **swim (the) b.** nadar a mariposa

**buttermilk** ['bʌtəmɪlk] *n* suero *m* (de leche)

**butterscotch** ['bʌtəskɒtʃ] *n* = dulce de mantequilla y azúcar

**buttock** ['bʌtək] *n* nalga *f*

**button** ['bʌtən] **1** *n* (**a**) *(on shirt, machine)* botón *m*; **b. mushroom** champiñón *m (pequeño)* (**b**) *US (badge)* chapa *f*

**2** *vt (shirt)* abotonar; *Fam* **b. it!** ¡cierra el pico!
▸**button up** *vt sep (shirt, dress)* abotonar; **to b. up one's shirt** abotonarse la camisa

**buttonhole** ['bʌtənhəʊl] **1** *n* ojal *m*

**2** *vt (detain)* agarrar

**buttress** ['bʌtrɪs] **1** *n Archit* contrafuerte *m*; *Fig* apoyo *m*, pilar *m*

**2** *vt Fig (support)* respaldar

**buxom** ['bʌksəm] *adj (full-bosomed)* de amplios senos; *(plump)* de carnes generosas

**buy** [baɪ] **1** *n* compra *f*; **a good/bad b.** una buena/mala compra

**2** *vt (pt & pp bought* [bɔːt]) (**a**) *(purchase)* comprar; **to b. sb sth, to b. sth for sb** comprar algo a *or* para alguien; **to b. sth from sb** comprarle algo a alguien (**b**) *(idioms)* **to b. time** ganar tiempo; *Fam* **he's bought it** *(has died)* la ha palmado; *Fam* **she won't b. that** *(won't believe)* no se lo tragará

▸**buy in** *vt sep (supplies)* aprovisionarse de
▸**buy into** *vt insep (company, scheme)* adquirir una parte *or* acciones de
▸**buy off** *vt sep Fam (opponent)* comprar
▸**buy out** *vt sep Com* comprar la parte de
▸**buy up** *vt sep* acaparar, comprar la totalidad de

**buyer** ['baɪə(r)] *n* comprador(ora) *m,f*; **b.'s market** mercado *m* favorable al comprador

**buy-out** ['baɪaʊt] *n Com* adquisición *f* (de todas las acciones)

**buzz** [bʌz] **1** *n* (**a**) *(noise) (of conversation)* rumor *m*; *(of machine, insects)* zumbido *m*; *Fam* **b. word** palabra *f* de moda (**b**) *Fam (phone call)* **to give sb a b.** dar a alguien un toque *or* un telefonazo (**c**) *Fam (thrill)* **to get a b. out of sth** entusiasmarse con algo

**2** *vt Fam (on intercom)* llamar por el portero electrónico; *(on pager)* llamar a través del busca

**3** *vi (make noise)* zumbar; *Fig* **the whole town was buzzing with excitement** toda la ciudad hervía de animación; *Fam* **my head was buzzing with ideas** las ideas me bullían en la cabeza; **my ears were buzzing** me zumbaban los oídos
▸**buzz off** *vi Br Fam* largarse, pirarse; **b. off!** ¡lárgate!

**buzzard** ['bʌzəd] *n* ratonero *m* común

**buzzer** ['bʌzə(r)] *n (electric bell)* timbre *m*

**buzzing** ['bʌzɪŋ] *n* zumbido *m*

**Bvd** *US (abbr* **Boulevard)** bulevar

**b & w** *Phot & Cin (abbr* **black and white)** b/n, blanco y negro

**by** [baɪ] **1** *prep* (**a**) *(expressing agent)* por; **he was arrested by the police** fue detenido por la policía; **made by hand** hecho a mano; **a play by Shakespeare** una obra de Shakespeare

(**b**) *(close to)* junto a; **by the fire** junto al fuego; **by the side of the road** al borde de la carretera

(**c**) *(via)* por; **to go by the same route** ir por la misma ruta; **by land/sea** por tierra/mar

(**d**) *(with manner, means)* **by rail** en tren; **by car/plane** en coche/avión; **to pay by credit card** pagar con tarjeta de crédito; **he had two children by his first wife** tuvo dos hijos de su primera esposa; **to take sb by the hand/arm** coger a alguien de la mano/del brazo; **to know sb by sight** conocer a alguien de vista; **to earn one's living by teaching** ganarse la vida enseñando; **to go by appearances** fiarse de las apariencias; **to call sb by their first name** llamar a alguien por su nombre (de pila); **what do you mean by that?** ¿qué quieres decir con eso?

(**e**) *(past)* **he walked right by me without stopping** pasó por mi lado sin detenerse; **we drove by the school on the way here** pasamos delante del colegio camino de aquí

**(f)** *(at or before)* **he should be here by now** debería estar ya aquí; **by then it was too late** para entonces ya era demasiado tarde; **by tomorrow** para mañana; **by 1980 they were all dead** en 1980 ya estaban todos muertos

**(g)** *(during)* **by day** de día; **by night** de noche, por la noche

**(h)** *(with measurements, quantities, numbers)* **to divide by three** dividir entre tres; **to multiply by three** multiplicar por tres; **to sell sth by weight** vender algo al peso; **three metres by two** tres por dos metros, tres metros por dos; **one by one** uno(a) a uno(a); **to increase by 50%** aumentar en un 50%

**(i)** *(with reflexive pronouns) see* **myself, himself, yourself** *etc*

**(j)** *(as a result of)* **by chance/mistake** por casualidad/error

**2** *adv* **(a)** **by and by** *(gradually)* poco a poco; *(soon)* dentro de poco; **by and large** en general, por lo general; **by the way,...** a propósito,...

**(b)** *(past)* **to pass by** *(of person)* pasar; *(of time)* transcurrir, pasar; **to drive by** pasar sin detenerse *(en coche)*

**bye** [baɪ] *exclam Fam* ¡adiós!, ¡hasta luego!

**bye-bye** [ˈbaɪˈbaɪ] *exclam Fam* ¡adiós!, ¡hasta luego!

**by-election** [ˈbaɪlekʃən] *n Pol* = elección parcial en una sola circunscripción *(para cubrir un escaño dejado vacante)*

**Byelorussia** [bɪeləʊˈrʌʃə] = **Belarus**

**Byelorussian** [bɪeləʊˈrʌʃən] *n & adj* bielorruso(a) *m,f*

**bygone** [ˈbaɪgɒn] **1** *n* **let bygones be bygones** lo pasado, pasado está

**2** *adj* pasado(a), pretérito(a); **in b. days** en otros tiempos

**by-line** [ˈbaɪlaɪn] *n Journ* pie *m* de autor

**BYOB** *(abbr* **bring your own bottle)** = en invitaciones a una fiesta o en restaurantes, siglas que invitan a llevar bebidas

**bypass** [ˈbaɪpɑːs] **1** *n* **(a)** *(road)* (carretera *f* de) circunvalación *f* **(b)** *(heart operation)* by-pass *m*

**2** *vt* *(of road)* circunvalar; *Fig (difficulty)* evitar, esquivar

**by-product** [ˈbaɪprɒdʌkt] *n (of industrial process)* subproducto *m*; *Fig* consecuencia *f*

**bystander** [ˈbaɪstændə(r)] *n* espectador(ora) *m,f*, transeúnte *mf*

**byte** [baɪt] *n Comptr* byte *m*

**byway** [ˈbaɪweɪ] *n* carretera *f* secundaria

**byword** [ˈbaɪwɜːd] *n* **to be a b. for...** ser sinónimo de...

**Byzantine** [bɪˈzæntaɪn] *n & adj Hist & Fig* bizantino(a) *m,f*

# C

**C, c** [siː] *n* (a) *(letter)* C, c (b) *Mus* do *m* (c) *Sch (grade)* aprobado *m*; **to get a C** *(in exam, essay)* sacar un aprobado

**C** (a) *(abbr* **celsius** *or* **centigrade)** C, centígrado (b) *(abbr* **century)** s., siglo; **C. 16** s. XVI

**c, ca** *(abbr* **circa)** hacia

**CAB** [siː eɪ biː] *n Br (abbr* **Citizens' Advice Bureau)** = oficina de asesoría jurídica para los ciudadanos

**cab** [kæb] *n* (a) *(taxi)* taxi *m*; **c. driver** taxista *mf*; **c. rank** parada *f* de taxis (b) *(of lorry)* cabina *f*

**cabaret** ['kæbəreɪ] *n* cabaret *m*; **c. artist** *(female)* cabaretera *f*; *(male or female)* artista *mf* de variedades

**cabbage** ['kæbɪdʒ] *n* col *f*, repollo *m*; **red c.** lombarda *f*; **c. white** *(butterfly)* mariposa *f* de la col

**cabbie, cabby** ['kæbɪ] *(pl* **cabbies)** *n Fam* taxista *mf*

**cabin** ['kæbɪn] *n* (hut) cabaña *f*; *(of ship)* camarote *m*; *(of plane)* cabina *f*; **c. boy** *(on ship)* grumete *m*; **c. crew** *(on plane)* personal *m* de a bordo, auxiliares *mfpl* de vuelo

**cabinet** ['kæbɪnɪt] *n* (a) *(piece of furniture)* armario *m*; *(with glass front)* vitrina *f* (b) *Pol* Consejo *m* de Ministros; **c. meeting** (reunión *f* del) Consejo *m* de Ministros; **c. minister** ministro(a) *m,f* (con cartera)

**cabinet-maker** ['kæbɪnɪtmeɪkə(r)] *n* ebanista *mf*

**cable** ['keɪbəl] **1** *n* (electrical) cable *m*; *Tel* cable(grama) *m*; **c. car** teleférico *m*, funicular *m*; **c. television** televisión *f* por cable
**2** *vt (message)* cablegrafiar

**caboodle** [kə'buːdəl] *n Fam* **the whole (kit and) c.** toda la pesca

**cacao** [kə'kɑːəʊ] *n (plant)* cacao *m*

**cache** [kæʃ] *n* (a) *(of drugs, arms)* alijo *m* (b) *Comptr* (memoria *f*) caché *f*

**cack-handed** [kæk'hændɪd] *adj Fam* torpe, patoso(a)

**cackle** ['kækəl] **1** *n* (a) *(of hen)* cacareo *m*, cloqueo *m* (b) *Fam (talking)* parloteo *m*; *(laughter)* carcajeo *m*; **cut the c.!** ¡corta el rollo!

**2** *vi* (a) *(of hen)* cacarear, cloquear (b) *Fam (laugh)* carcajearse

**cacophonous** [kə'kɒfənəs] *adj* cacofónico(a)

**cactus** ['kæktəs] *(pl* **cacti** ['kæktaɪ]) *n* cactus *m inv*

**CAD** [siː eɪ diː] *n Comptr (abbr* **computer aided design)** CAD *m*, diseño *m* asistido por ordenador

**cad** [kæd] *n Br Fam Old-fashioned* canalla *m*

**cadaver** [kə'dævə(r)] *n* cadáver *m*

**cadaverous** [kə'dævərəs] *adj* cadavérico(a)

**caddie** ['kædɪ] *n (in golf)* caddie *mf*, ayudante *mf*

**caddy** ['kædɪ] *n (tea) c.* caja *f* para el té

**cadence** ['keɪdəns] *n* cadencia *f*

**cadet** [kə'det] *n Mil* cadete *m*; **c. corps** = organismo que, en algunas escuelas, enseña disciplina militar

**cadge** [kædʒ] *vt Fam* gorronear (**from** *or* **off** a); **can I c. a lift from you?** ¿me puedes llevar?

**cadmium** ['kædmɪəm] *n Chem* cadmio *m*

**caecum,** *US* **cecum** ['siːkəm] *n (intestino m)* ciego *m*

**Caesarean, Caesarian** [sɪ'zeərɪən] *n* **C. (section)** (operación *f* de) cesárea *f*

**café, cafe** ['kæfeɪ] *n* café *m*, cafetería *f*

**cafeteria** [kæfɪ'tɪərɪə] *n* cafetería *f*, cantina *f*

**cafetiere** [kæfə'tjɑː(r)] *n* cafetera *f* (de émbolo)

**caff** [kæf] *n Br Fam* = café barato

**caffeine** ['kæfiːn] *n* cafeína *f*; **c. free** descafeinado(a)

**cage** [keɪdʒ] **1** *n (for bird or animal, of lift)* jaula *f*
**2** *vt* enjaular; **to feel caged in** sentirse enjaulado(a)

**cagey** ['keɪdʒɪ] *adj* **to be c. (about sth)** *(cautious)* andar con tiento (con algo); *(evasive)* salirse por la tangente (en cuanto a algo)

**cagoule** [kə'guːl] *n* chubasquero *m*

**cahoots** [kə'huːts] *npl Fam* **to be in c. (with sb)** estar conchabado(a) (con alguien)

**CAI** [siː eɪ aɪ] *n Comptr (abbr* **computer aided instruction)** enseñanza *f* asistida por ordenador

**cairn** ['keən] *n* hito *m* de piedras

**Cairo** ['kaɪrəʊ] *n* El Cairo

**cajole** [kə'dʒəʊl] *vt* engatusar; **to c. sb into doing sth** engatusar a alguien para que haga algo

**cake** [keɪk] **1** *n* (**a**) *(food)* pastel *m*, tarta *f*; *(small)* pastel *m*; **a birthday c.** una tarta de cumpleaños; **a wedding c.** un pastel de boda; **c. shop** pastelería *f*; **c. tin** molde *m* (**b**) *(of soap)* pastilla *f* (**c**) *(idioms)* **it's a piece of c.** está tirado, es facilísimo; *Prov* **you can't have your c. and eat it** no se puede estar en misa y repicando

**2** *vt* **her shoes were caked with mud** tenía los zapatos llenos de barro seco

**CAL** [kæl] *n Comptr* (*abbr* **computer aided learning**) enseñanza *f* asistida por ordenador

**calamity** [kə'læmɪtɪ] *n* calamidad *f*

**calcium** ['kælsɪəm] *n Chem* calcio *m*

**calculate** ['kælkjʊleɪt] **1** *vt* calcular; **his remark was calculated to shock** pretendió impresionar con el comentario

**2** *vi* **to c. on (doing) sth** contar con (hacer) algo

**calculated** ['kælkjʊleɪtɪd] *adj (intentional)* deliberado(a); **a c. risk** un riesgo calculado

**calculating** ['kælkjʊleɪtɪŋ] *adj (scheming)* calculador(ora)

**calculation** [kælkjʊ'leɪʃən] *n* cálculo *m*; **to upset sb's calculations** desbaratar los cálculos de alguien

**calculator** ['kælkjʊleɪtə(r)] *n (electronic)* calculadora *f*

**calculus** ['kælkjʊləs] *n Math* cálculo *m* (infinitesimal)

**calendar** ['kælɪndə(r)] *n* calendario *m*; **c. month/year** mes *m*/año *m* natural

**calf¹** [kɑːf] *(pl* **calves** [kɑːvz]*)* *n (animal)* becerro(a) *m,f*, ternero(a) *m,f*; **the cow is in** *o* **with c.** la vaca está preñada; *Fig* **to kill the fatted c.** tirar la casa por la ventana

**calf²** *(pl* **calves** [kɑːvz]*)* *n (of leg)* pantorrilla *f*

**calfskin** ['kɑːfskɪn] *n* piel *f* de becerro

**calibrate** ['kælɪbreɪt] *vt (instrument)* calibrar

**calibre** ['kælɪbə(r)] *n (of firearm)* calibre *m*; *Fig (of person)* categoría *f*

**calico** ['kælɪkəʊ] *n* percal *m*, calicó *m*

**California** [kælɪ'fɔːnɪə] *n* California

**Californian** [kælɪ'fɔːnɪən] *n & adj* californiano(a) *m,f*

**call** [kɔːl] **1** *n* (**a**) *(shout) (of person)* llamada *f*, grito *m*; *(of bird)* reclamo *m*

(**b**) *(appeal)* llamamiento *m*, llamada *f*; **a c. for unity/compassion** un llamamiento a la unidad/la compasión; **a c. to arms** una llamada a (tomar) las armas

(**c**) *(on phone)* llamada *f*; **to give sb a c.** llamar a alguien; **to make a c.** hacer una llamada; **to**

**return sb's c.** devolverle la llamada a alguien; **c. girl** prostituta *f* *(que concierta sus citas por teléfono)*

(**d**) *(visit)* visita *f*; **to pay a c. on sb** hacer una visita a alguien

(**e**) *(demand)* demanda *f*; **there are a lot of calls on my time** estoy muy solicitado; **there's not much c. for it** no tiene mucha demanda, no hay mucha demanda de ello; **there's no c. for rudeness!** ¡no hace falta ser grosero!; **to be on c.** *(of doctor)* estar de guardia

(**f**) *(at airport)* aviso *m*, llamada *f*

**2** *vt* (**a**) *(summon) (person)* llamar; *(meeting, strike)* convocar; **he called me over to show me something** me llamó para enseñarme una cosa; **to c. sb's attention to sth** llamar la atención de alguien sobre algo

(**b**) *(on phone)* llamar, telefonear

(**c**) *(name)* llamar; **she is called Teresa** se llama Teresa; **to c. sb names** insultar a alguien; **to c. sb a liar/a thief** llamar a alguien mentiroso/ladrón; **we'll c. it £10** dejémoslo en *o* digamos 10 libras; **do you c. that clean?** ¿llamas limpio a esto?; *Ironic* **c. yourself a computer expert!** ¡vaya un experto en informática (estás hecho)!; **let's c. it a day** ya está bien por hoy

(**d**) **to c. sb's name** llamar a alguien por su nombre

**3** *vi* (**a**) *(to attract sb's attention)* llamar; **to c. for help** pedir ayuda; **he called to his companions** llamó a sus compañeros

(**b**) *(on phone)* llamar; **did anyone c. while I was out?** ¿me llamó alguien mientras no estaba?; **(may I ask) who's calling?** ¿de parte de quién?

(**c**) *(demand)* **to c. for sth** exigir algo

(**d**) *(visit)* **to c. at** pasarse por, hacer una visita a; **this train will c. at York and Peterborough** este tren efectúa parada en York y Peterborough

▸**call back 1** *vt sep* (**a**) *(summon again)* hacer volver; **as I was leaving he called me back** me llamó cuando ya me iba (**b**) *(on phone)* volver a llamar; **could you c. me back later?** ¿podría llamarme más tarde?

**2** *vi (on phone)* volver a llamar

▸**call for** *vt insep (require)* requerir, necesitar; **this calls for a celebration!** ¡esto hay que celebrarlo!; **that wasn't called for!** ¡eso no era necesario!, ¡no había necesidad de eso!

▸**call in 1** *vt sep (doctor, police)* llamar

**2** *vi (visit)* **to c. in on sb** ir a *o* pasarse por casa de alguien

▸**call off** *vt sep* (**a**) *(cancel)* suspender (**b**) *(dogs)* hacer retroceder

▶**call on** vt insep (a) (request) **to c. on sb to do sth** instar a alguien a que haga algo (b) (visit) visitar

▶**call out 1** vt sep (a) (troops) convocar; (doctor) llamar; **the workers were called out on strike** se convocó a los trabajadores a la huelga (b) (shout) gritar

**2** vi (shout out) gritar

▶**call up** vt sep (a) (reinforcements) pedir (b) (on phone) llamar (c) Mil (draft) llamar a filas, reclutar

**callbox** ['kɔːlbɒks] n cabina f telefónica or de teléfono

**caller** [kɔːlə(r)] n (visitor) visita f; (on phone) persona f que llama

**calligraphy** [kə'lɪgrəfɪ] n caligrafía f

**calling** ['kɔːlɪŋ] n (vocation) vocación f

**callipers** ['kælɪpəz] npl (a) (for legs) aparato m ortopédico (b) (measuring device) calibrador m, calibre m

**callisthenics** [kælɪs'θenɪks] n gimnasia f sueca, calistenia f

**callous** ['kæləs] adj cruel, desalmado(a)

**call-up** ['kɔːlʌp] n Mil llamada f a filas, reclutamiento m; **to get one's c. papers** recibir la orden de reclutamiento, ser llamado(a) a filas

**callus** ['kæləs] n callo m, callosidad f

**calm** [kɑːm] **1** n calma f, tranquilidad f; also Fig **the c. before the storm** la calma que precede a la tormenta

**2** adj (person, sea, water) tranquilo(a); (weather) apacible; **to stay c.** mantener la calma; **to become** or **grow calmer** calmarse

**3** vt calmar, tranquilizar

▶**calm down 1** vt sep (person) calmar, tranquilizar

**2** vi (of person) calmarse, tranquilizarse; (of situation) calmarse

**calmly** ['kɑːmlɪ] adv serenamente, tranquilamente

**Calor gas**® ['kælɒgæs] n butano m

**calorie** ['kælərɪ] n caloría f

**calorific** [kælə'rɪfɪk] adj calorífico(a)

**calumny** ['kæləmnɪ] n calumnia f

**calve** [kɑːv] vi (of cow) parir

**calves** [kɑːvz] pl of **calf**

**calypso** [kə'lɪpsəʊ] n Mus calipso m

**CAM** [sɪ'eɪem] n Comptr (abbr **computer aided manufacture**) CAM f, fabricación f asistida por ordenador

**Cambodia** [kæm'bəʊdɪə] n Camboya

**Cambodian** [kæm'bəʊdɪən] n & adj camboyano(a) m,f

**camcorder** ['kæmkɔːdə(r)] n videocámara f (portátil)

**came** [keɪm] pt of **come**

**camel** ['kæməl] n camello m; **c. driver** camellero(a) m,f

**camelhair** ['kæməlheə(r)] n pelo m de camello; **c. coat** abrigo m de pelo de camello

**camellia** [kə'miːlɪə] n camelia f

**cameo** ['kæmɪəʊ] (pl **cameos**) n (a) **c. (brooch)** camafeo m (b) Cin aparición f breve (de un actor famoso)

**camera** ['kæmərə] n (a) (photographic) cámara f (fotográfica); TV & Cin cámara f; **TV off c.** fuera de imagen; TV **on c.** delante de la cámara; TV **c. crew** equipo m de filmación (b) Law **in c.** a puerta cerrada

**cameraman** ['kæmərəmən] n -cámara m, operador m

**Cameroon** [kæmə'ruːn] n Camerún

**camisole** ['kæmɪsəʊl] n combinación f

**camomile** ['kæməmaɪl] n manzanilla f, camomila f; **c. tea** (infusión f de) manzanilla f

**camouflage** ['kæməflɑːʒ] **1** n also Fig camuflaje m

**2** vt also Fig camuflar

**camp**[1] [kæmp] **1** n campamento m; **c. bed** cama f plegable, catre m; **c. site** lugar m de acampada; (commercial) camping m

**2** vi **to c. (out)** acampar

**camp**[2] adj Fam (a) (behaviour, manner) amariposado(a), amanerado(a) (b) (style, taste) hortera

**campaign** [kæm'peɪn] **1** n campaña f

**2** vi **to c. for/against** hacer campaña a favor de/en contra de

**campaigner** [kæm'peɪnə(r)] n defensor(ora) m,f; **to be a c. for/against sth** hacer campaña a favor de/en contra de algo

**camper** ['kæmpə(r)] n (a) (person) campista mf (b) (vehicle) **c. (van)** autocaravana f

**campfire** ['kæmpfaɪə(r)] n fuego m or hoguera f de campamento

**camphor** ['kæmfə(r)] n alcanfor m

**camping** ['kæmpɪŋ] n acampada f; (on commercial camp site) camping m; **to go c.** ir de acampada; (on commercial camp site) ir de camping; **c. site** lugar m de acampada; (commercial) camping

**campus** ['kæmpəs] n campus m inv

**camshaft** ['kæmʃɑːft] n Tech árbol m de levas

**can**[1] [kæn] **1** n (a) (container) lata f, Am tarro m; Fig **to open a c. of worms** sacar a la luz un asunto espinoso; **c. opener** abrelatas m inv (b) US very Fam (toilet) tigre m (c) US very Fam (prison) trullo m

**2** vt (pt & pp **canned**) (a) (fruit, meat) enlatar; Fig **canned laughter** (on radio, TV) risas fpl grabadas (b) US Fam **c. it!** (keep quiet) ¡cállate la boca!

**can**[2] [stressed kæn, unstressed kən]

---

El verbo **can** carece de infinitivo, de gerundio y de participio. En infinitivo o en participio, se empleará la forma correspondiente de **be** able to, por ejemplo: **he wanted to be able to speak English; she has always been able to swim**. En el inglés hablado, y en el escrito en estilo coloquial, la forma negativa **cannot** se transforma en **can't**.

*modal aux v* (**a**) *(be able to)* poder; **I c. go** puedo ir; **c. you help me?** ¿puedes ayudarme?; **we cannot possibly do it** no podemos hacerlo de ninguna manera; **I will come as soon as I c.** iré lo antes posible; **he will do what he c.** hará lo que pueda; **it can't be done** es imposible, no se puede hacer; **we c. but try** habrá que intentarlo

(**b**) *(know how to)* saber; **I c. swim** sé nadar; **she c. play the violin** sabe tocar el violín

(**c**) *(indicating possibility)* poder; **adult animals c. grow to 6 metres** los ejemplares adultos pueden llegar a los 6 metros; **you CAN'T be serious!** ¡no lo dirás en serio!; **what CAN he want now?** ¿pero qué es lo que quiere ahora?

(**d**) *(indicating permission)* poder; **c. I ask you something?** ¿te puedo hacer una pregunta?; **you can't smoke in here** aquí está prohibido fumar

(**e**) *(with* **see**, **hear** *etc: not translated)* **I c. see them** los veo; **I c. see you don't believe me** ya veo que no me crees; **how c. you tell?** ¿cómo lo sabes?

**Canada** ['kænədə] *n* (el) Canadá

**Canadian** [kə'neɪdɪən] *n & adj* canadiense *mf*

**canal** [kə'næl] *n* canal *m*

**Canary** [kə'neərɪ] *n* **the C. Islands, the Canaries** las (Islas) Canarias

**canary** [kə'neərɪ] *n* canario *m*; **c. yellow** amarillo *m* canario

**cancel** ['kænsəl] (*pt & pp* **cancelled**, *US* **canceled**) **1** *vt (match, trip)* suspender; *(flight, train)* suspender, cancelar; *(order, subscription)* anular

**2** *vi* **they were supposed to be playing tonight, but they've cancelled** iban a tocar hoy, pero lo han suspendido

▶**cancel out** *vt sep* **to c. each other out** neutralizarse, contrarrestarse

**cancellation** [kænsə'leɪʃən] *n (of match, trip, flight)* suspensión *f*; *(of order, subscription)* anulación *f*; **c. fee** tarifa *f* de cancelación de reserva

**Cancer** ['kænsə(r)] *n (sign of zodiac)* Cáncer *m*; **to be (a) C.** ser Cáncer; *Geog* **the Tropic of C.** el Trópico de Cáncer

**cancer** ['kænsə(r)] *n (disease)* cáncer *m*; **lung/skin c.** cáncer de pulmón/de piel; **c. research** investigación *f* del cáncer

**cancerous** ['kænsərəs] *adj Med* canceroso(a)

**candelabra** [kændɪ'lɑːbrə] *n* candelabro *m*

**candid** ['kændɪd] *adj* sincero(a), franco(a)

**candidacy** ['kændɪdəsɪ] *n* candidatura *f*

**candidate** ['kændɪdeɪt] *n* (**a**) *(for job, in election)* candidato(a) *m,f*; **to stand as a c.** presentarse como candidato (**b**) *(in exam)* examinando(a) *m,f*, candidato(a) *m,f*

**candidature** ['kændɪdətʃə(r)] = **candidacy**

**candidly** ['kændɪdlɪ] *adv* sinceramente, francamente

**candied** ['kændɪd] *adj* escarchado(a), confitado(a); **c. peel** piel *f* de naranja/limón escarchada

**candle** ['kændəl] *n* (**a**) vela *f* (**b**) *(idioms)* **he can't hold a c. to you** no te llega ni a la suela del zapato; **it's not worth the c.** no merece la pena

**candlelight** ['kændəlaɪt] *n* luz *f* de las velas; **by c.** a la luz de las velas

**candlelit** ['kændəlɪt] *adj (room)* iluminado(a) con velas; **a c. dinner** una cena a la luz de las velas

**candlestick** ['kændəlstɪk] *n* palmatoria *f*

**candour** ['kændə(r)] *n* sinceridad *f*, franqueza *f*

**candy** ['kændɪ] *n US (sweet)* caramelo *m*; *(sweets)* dulces *mpl*, golosinas *fpl*; **c. store** confitería *f*

**candyfloss** ['kændɪflɒs] *n Br* algodón *m* dulce

**cane** [keɪn] **1** *n (of sugar, bamboo)* caña *f*; *(walking stick)* bastón *m*; *(for punishment)* vara *f*, palmeta *f*; **to get the c.** ser castigado(a) con la vara; **c. furniture** muebles *mpl* de mimbre; **c. sugar** azúcar *f* de caña

**2** *vt (beat)* pegar con la vara

**canine** ['keɪnaɪn] **1** *n (dog)* can *m*; *(tooth)* colmillo *m*, canino *m*

**2** *adj* canino(a); **c. tooth** colmillo *m*, (diente *m*) canino *m*

**canister** ['kænɪstə(r)] *n (for tear gas, smoke)* bote *m*; *(for film, oil)* lata *f*

**canker** ['kæŋkə(r)] *n Med* ulceración *f*; *Bot* cancro *m*; *Fig* cáncer *m*

**cannabis** ['kænəbɪs] *n* hachís *m*, cannabis *m*

**cannery** ['kænərɪ] *n* fábrica *f* de conservas

**cannibal** ['kænɪbəl] *n* caníbal *mf*

**cannibalize** ['kænɪbəlaɪz] *vt (machinery, car)* desguazar *(para aprovechar las piezas)*

**cannon** ['kænən] *n* cañón *m*; **c. fodder** carne *f* de cañón

**cannonball** ['kænənbɔːl] *n* bala *f* de cañón

**cannot** ['kænɒt] = **can not**

**canny** ['kænɪ] *adj* astuto(a)

**canoe** [kə'nu:] *n* canoa *f*; *Sport* piragua *f*

**canoeing** [kə'nu:ɪŋ] *n* piragüismo *m*; **to go c.** ir a hacer piragüismo

**canoeist** [kə'nu:ɪst] *n* piragüista *mf*

**canon** ['kænən] *n* Rel **(a)** *(religious decree)* canon *m*; *Fig* **canons of good taste** cánones del buen gusto; **c. law** derecho *m* canónico **(b)** *(priest)* canónigo *m*

**canonize** ['kænənaɪz] *vt* Rel canonizar

**canoodle** [kə'nu:dəl] *vi Hum* hacer mánitas, darse el lote

**canopy** ['kænəpɪ] *n (above bed)* dosel *m*; *(outside shop)* toldo *m*; *(of tree)* copa *f*; **forest c.** fronda *f*, copas *fpl* de los árboles

**cant** [kænt] *n* hipocresías *fpl*, falsedades *fpl*

**can't** [ka:nt] = **can not**

**Cantabria** [kæn'tæbrɪə] *n* Cantabria

**Cantabrian** [kæn'tæbrɪən] *n* **1** *(person)* cántabro(a) *m,f*

**2** *adj* cántabro(a); **the C. Mountains** la Cordillera Cantábrica; **the C. Sea** el (Mar) Cantábrico

**cantaloup(e)** ['kæntəlu:p] *n* **c. (melon)** melón *m* francés

**cantankerous** [kæn'tæŋkərəs] *adj* cascarrabias *inv*, refunfuñón(ona)

**canteen** [kæn'ti:n] *n* **(a)** *(restaurant)* cantina *f*, cafetería *f* **(b)** *(water bottle)* cantimplora *f* **(c)** **a c. of cutlery** una cubertería

**canter** ['kæntə(r)] *n* **1** *(on horse)* medio galope *m*

**2** *vi (of horse)* ir a medio galope; *Fig* **to c. through an exam** pasar un examen con facilidad

**cantilever bridge** ['kæntɪli:və(r)] *n* puente *m* voladizo

**Cantonese** [kæntə'ni:z] **1** *n (language)* cantonés *m*

**2** *adj* cantonés(esa)

**canvas** ['kænvəs] *n* **(a)** *(cloth)* lona *f*; **under c.** *(in tent)* en una tienda de campaña; *Naut* a vela; **c. shoes** zapatillas *fpl* de lona **(b)** *Art* lienzo *m*

**canvass** ['kænvəs] *vt* **1** *Pol* **to c. a street/an area** visitar las casas de una calle/zona haciendo campaña electoral **(b)** *Com (consumers, customers)* encuestar; *Fig* **to c. opinion** hacer un sondeo de opinión informal

**2** *vi* **(a)** *Pol* = hacer campaña electoral hablando directamente con los electores por las casas o en la calle **(b)** *Com* **to c. for customers** tratar de captar clientes

**canvasser** ['kænvəsə(r)] *n Pol* = persona que va de casa en casa tratando de captar votos para un partido

**canyon** ['kænjən] *n* cañón *m*

**CAP** [si:eɪ'pi:] *n (abbr* **Common Agricultural Policy)** PAC *f*

**cap** [kæp] **1** *n* **(a)** *(headgear) (without peak)* gorro *m*; *(with peak)* gorra *f*; *Sport* **to win a c.** entrar en la selección nacional; *Fig* **to go c. in hand to sb** acudir a alguien con actitud humilde; *Prov* **if the c. fits, wear it** quien se pica, ajos come **(b)** *(cover) (of bottle)* tapón *m*; *(for tooth)* funda *f* **(c)** *(for toy gun)* fulminante *m*

**2** *vt (pt & pp* **capped) (a)** *(cover)* **to be capped with** estar cubierto(a) de *or* por **(b)** *(surpass, do better than)* superar; **that caps the lot!** ¡es el colmo!; **to c. it all,...** para colmo,... **(c)** *Sport* **he was capped for England** fue internacional *or* jugó con la selección inglesa

**capability** [keɪpə'bɪlɪtɪ] *n* capacidad *f* (**to do sth** para hacer algo); **it is beyond our capabilities** no entra dentro de nuestras posibilidades

**capable** ['keɪpəbəl] *adj (competent)* capaz, competente; **to be c. of doing sth** *(be able to do)* ser capaz de hacer algo

**capacious** [kə'peɪʃəs] *adj* espacioso(a)

**capacitor** [kə'pæsɪtə(r)] *n Elec* condensador *m*

**capacity** [kə'pæsɪtɪ] *n* **(a)** *(of container, bus, theatre)* capacidad *f*; **a c. crowd** *(in hall, stadium)* un lleno (absoluto) **(b)** *(aptitude)* **to have a c. for sth** tener capacidad para algo; **beyond/within my c.** fuera de/dentro de mis posibilidades **(c)** *(role)* **in my c. as...** en mi calidad de...

**cape¹** [keɪp] *n (cloak)* capa *f*

**cape²** *n Geog* cabo *m*; **the C. of Good Hope** el Cabo de Buena Esperanza; **C. Town** Ciudad del Cabo, El Cabo

**caper¹** ['keɪpə(r)] *n Culin* alcaparra *f*

**caper²** **1** *n* **capers** correrías *fpl*, peripecias *fpl*; **what a c.!** ¡qué aventura!

**2** *vi* **to c. (about)** retozar

**Cape Verde** [keɪpvɜ:d] *n* Cabo Verde

**capillary** [kə'pɪlərɪ] *n & adj* capilar *n*

**capital** ['kæpɪtəl] **1** *n* **(a)** *(letter)* mayúscula *f* **(b)** *(city)* capital *f* **(c)** *Fin* capital *m*; *Fig* **to make c. out of sth** sacar partido de algo; **c. assets** activo *m* fijo, bienes *mpl* de capital; **c. expenditure** inversión *f* en activo fijo; **c. gains tax** impuesto *m* sobre las plusvalías; **c. goods** bienes *mpl* de equipo *or* de producción; **c. investment** inversión *f* (de capital)

**2** *adj* **(a)** *(letter)* mayúscula; **c. T** T mayúscula; *Fam* **he's arrogant with a c. A** es un arrogante de tomo y lomo **(b)** **c. city** capital *f* **(c)** *Law* **c. crime** *or* **offence** delito *m* capital; **c. punishment** pena *f* capital *or* de muerte **(d)** *(important)* capital; **of c. importance** de capital importancia **(e)** *Br Old-fashioned (splendid)* **c.!** ¡excelente!

**capitalism** ['kæpɪtəlɪzəm] *n* capitalismo *m*

**capitalist** ['kæpɪtəlɪst] *n & adj* capitalista *mf*

**capitalization** [kæpɪtəlaɪˈzeɪʃən] n Fin capitalización f

**capitalize** [ˈkæpɪtəlaɪz] vt (a) Fin capitalizar (b) (word, letter) escribir con mayúscula

**►capitalize on** vt insep aprovechar, aprovecharse de

**Capitol** [ˈkæpɪtəl] n US Pol **the C.** el Capitolio

**capitulate** [kəˈpɪtjʊleɪt] vi capitular

**capon** [ˈkeɪpən] n Culin capón m

**caprice** [kəˈpriːs] n capricho m

**capricious** [kəˈprɪʃəs] adj caprichoso(a)

**Capricorn** [ˈkæprɪkɔːn] n (sign of zodiac) Capricornio m; **to be (a) C.** ser Capricornio; Geog **the Tropic of C.** el Trópico de Capricornio

**capsicum** [ˈkæpsɪkəm] n pimiento m

**capsize** [kæpˈsaɪz] vt & vi volcar

**capstan** [ˈkæpstən] n Naut cabrestante m

**capsule** [ˈkæpsjuːl] n cápsula f; **(space)** c. cápsula espacial

**Capt** Mil (abbr **Captain**) Capitán m

**captain** [ˈkæptɪn] **1** n capitán(ana) m,f
**2** vt Sport capitanear

**captaincy** [ˈkæptɪnsɪ] n capitanía f

**caption** [ˈkæpʃən] n (under picture) pie m de foto; (under cartoon) texto m

**captivate** [ˈkæptɪveɪt] vt cautivar, embelesar

**captivating** [ˈkæptɪveɪtɪŋ] adj (smile, manner) cautivador(ora)

**captive** [ˈkæptɪv] **1** n cautivo(a) m,f, prisionero(a) m,f
**2** adj cautivo(a); **he was taken c.** fue hecho prisionero; **he knew he had a c. audience** sabía que su público no tenía elección

**captivity** [kæpˈtɪvɪtɪ] n cautividad f; **in c.** en cautividad

**captor** [ˈkæptə(r)] n captor(ora) m,f

**capture** [ˈkæptjə(r)] **1** vt (person) capturar; (town) tomar; (in chess, draughts) comer; Fig (mood) reflejar
**2** n (of person) captura f; (of town) toma f

**CAR** [siːerˈɑː(r)] n (abbr **Central African Republic**) República f Centroafricana

**car** [kɑː(r)] n (a) (automobile) coche m, automóvil m, Am carro m; **by c.** en coche; **c. bomb** coche m bomba; **c. boot sale** = mercadillo en el que los particulares venden objetos que exponen en el maletero del coche; **c. crash** accidente m de coche; **c. door** puerta f (del coche); Br **c. hire**, US **c. rental** alquiler m de coches; **c. industry** industria f automovilística; Br **c. park** aparcamiento m; **c. phone** teléfono m de coche; **c. pool** parque m móvil; **c. radio** radio f (del coche) (b) US (train carriage) vagón m, coche m

**Caracas** [kəˈrækəs] n Caracas

**carafe** [kəˈræf] n jarra f

**caramel** [ˈkærəməl] n caramelo m

**carat** [ˈkærət] n (of gold) quilate m; **18-c. gold** oro m de 18 quilates

**caravan** [ˈkærəvæn] n (pulled by car, in desert) caravana f; **c. holiday** vacaciones fpl en caravana; **c. site** camping m para caravanas

**caraway** [ˈkærəweɪ] n (plant) alcaravea f; **c. seeds** carvis mpl

**carbohydrate** [kɑːbəʊˈhaɪdreɪt] n hidrato m de carbono, carbohidrato m

**carbolic** [kɑːˈbɒlɪk] adj Chem **c. acid** fenol m, ácido m fénico or carbólico; **c. soap** jabón m (desinfectante) de brea

**carbon** [ˈkɑːbən] n Chem carbono m; **c. copy** copia f en papel carbón; Fig calco m, copia f exacta; **c. dioxide** dióxido m de carbono; **c. monoxide** monóxido m de carbono; **c. paper** papel m carbón or de calco

**carbonated** [ˈkɑːbəneɪtɪd] adj carbónico(a), con gas; **c. water** agua f con gas

**carbonize** [ˈkɑːbənaɪz] vt carbonizar

**carbuncle** [ˈkɑːbʌŋkəl] n Med forúnculo m

**carburettor**, US **carburetor** [ˈkɑːbjʊretə(r)] n carburador m

**carcass** [ˈkɑːkəs] n (of animal) restos mpl, cadáver m; (at butcher's) canal m

**carcinogenic** [kɑːsɪnəʊˈdʒenɪk] adj Med cancerígeno(a), carcinógeno(a)

**card** [kɑːd] n (a) (for game) carta f, naipe m; **to play cards** jugar a las cartas; **c. game** juego m de cartas o naipes; **c. table** mesa f de juego (para las cartas); **c. trick** truco m or juego m de cartas (b) (with printed information) tarjeta f; (for identification) carné m, carnet m; (postcard) (tarjeta) postal f; **birthday c.** tarjeta de felicitación de cumpleaños; **Christmas c.** crismas m inv; **c. index or file** fichero m de tarjetas; Pol **c. vote** votación f por delegación (c) (thin cardboard) cartulina f (d) (idioms) **play your cards right and you could get promoted** si juegas bien tus cartas, puedes conseguir un ascenso; **to put one's cards on the table** poner las cartas sobre la mesa; **to have a c. up one's sleeve** tener un as en la manga; **it is on the cards that…** es más que probable que…; Br Fam **to get one's cards** ser despedido(a)

**cardamom** [ˈkɑːdəməm] n cardamomo m

**cardboard** [ˈkɑːdbɔːd] n cartón m; **c. box** caja f de cartón; **c. city** = lugar donde duermen los vagabundos

**card-carrying** [ˈkɑːdkærɪŋ] adj **c. member** miembro m or socio(a) m,f (de pleno derecho)

**cardiac** [ˈkɑːdɪæk] adj cardíaco(a); **c. arrest** paro m cardíaco

**cardigan** [ˈkɑːdɪgən] n rebeca f, cárdigan m

**cardinal** [ˈkɑːdɪnəl] **1** n Rel cardenal m
**2** adj (importance, significance) capital, cardinal;

**c. number** número *m* cardinal; **c. sins** pecados *mpl* capitales; **c. virtues** virtudes *fpl* cardinales

**cardiograph** ['kɑːdɪəʊgræf] *n* cardiógrafo *m*

**cardiologist** [kɑːdɪ'ɒlədʒɪst] *n* cardiólogo(a) *m,f*

**cardiology** [kɑːdɪ'ɒlədʒɪ] *n* cardiología *f*

**cardiovascular** [kɑːdɪəʊ'væskjʊlə(r)] *adj* cardiovascular

**cardphone** ['kɑːdfəʊn] *n* teléfono *m* que funciona con tarjetas

**cardsharp(er)** ['kɑːdʃɑːp(ə(r))] *n* tahur *m*, fullero(a) *m,f*

**care** [keə(r)] **1** *n* (**a**) *(worry)* preocupación *f*, inquietud *f*; **she doesn't have a c. in the world** no tiene ni una sola preocupación (**b**) *(attention)* cuidado *m*, atención *f*; **medical c.** asistencia *f* médica; **to do sth with great c.** hacer algo con mucho cuidado; **to take c. to do sth** procurar hacer algo; **to take c. of** *(look after)* cuidar de; *(deal with)* ocuparse de; **to take c. of oneself** cuidarse; **it will take c. of itself** se resolverá por sí solo (**c**) *(looking after, maintenance)* cuidado *m*; **to put a child in c.** poner a un niño bajo la tutela del Estado; **to be in** *or* **under sb's c.** estar al cuidado de alguien; **write to me c. of Mrs Wallace** escríbeme a la dirección de la Sra Wallace

**2** *vt* (**a**) *(mind)* **I don't c. what he says** no me importa lo que diga; **I don't c. whether he likes it or not** me da lo mismo que le guste o no (**b**) *(like)* **would you c. to come with me?** ¿te gustaría venir conmigo?

**3** *vi* *(be concerned)* preocuparse (**about** por); **no-one seems to c.** no parece importarle a nadie, nadie parece preocuparse; **that's all he cares about** eso es lo único que le preocupa; **who cares?** ¿qué más da?; **I could be dead for all they c.** por ellos, como si me muero; **I don't c.!** ¡me da igual!, ¡no me importa!

▸**care for** *vt insep* (**a**) *(look after)* cuidar; **well cared for** bien cuidado(a) (**b**) *(like)* **I don't c. for this music** no me gusta esta música; **would you c. for some tea?** ¿te apetece un té?

**career** [kə'rɪə(r)] **1** *n* *(working life, profession)* carrera *f*; **careers officer** asesor(ora) *m,f* de orientación profesional; **careers service** servicio *m* de orientación profesional; **c. diplomat** diplomático(a) *m,f* de carrera; **it was a good c. move** fue bueno para mi/tu/*etc* carrera; **a job with c. prospects** un trabajo con buenas perspectivas profesionales

**2** *vi* **to c. (along)** ir a toda velocidad

**careerist** [kə'rɪərɪst] *n Pej* arribista *mf*

**carefree** ['keəfriː] *adj* despreocupado(a)

**careful** ['keəfʊl] *adj* (**a**) *(taking care)* cuidadoso(a); *(prudent)* cauto(a), precavido(a); (**be**) **c.!**

(ten) cuidado!; **to be c. to do sth** tener cuidado de *or* procurar hacer algo; **she was c. not to mention this** tuvo cuidado de *or* procuró no mencionar esto; **be c. not to drop it** procura que no se te caiga; **be c. what you say** cuidado con lo que dices; **you can't be too c. these days** en estos tiempos que corren toda precaución es poca (**b**) *(thorough)* *(work, inspection)* cuidadoso(a); **after c. consideration** tras mucho reflexionar

**carefully** ['keəfʊlɪ] *adv* *(taking care, thoroughly)* cuidadosamente; *(to think, choose)* con cuidado; *(to drive)* con cuidado, con precaución; **to listen c.** escuchar atentamente

**careless** ['keəlɪs] *adj* *(negligent)* descuidado(a); **he's c. about his appearance** descuida mucho su aspecto; **a c. mistake** un descuido; **a c. remark** una observación inoportuna

**carelessly** ['keəlɪslɪ] *adv* *(negligently)* descuidadamente

**carelessness** ['keəlɪsnɪs] *n* descuido *m*, negligencia *f*

**carer** ['keərə(r)] *n* = persona que cuida de un familiar enfermo o anciano, sin por ello recibir compensación económica

**caress** [kə'res] **1** *n* caricia *f*

**2** *vt* acariciar

**caretaker** ['keəteɪkə(r)] *n* *(of building, school)* conserje *m*; **c. government** gobierno *m* provisional

**careworn** ['keəwɔːn] *adj* agobiado(a); **to be c.** estar agobiado(a)

**cargo** ['kɑːgəʊ] (*pl Br* **cargoes**, *US* **cargos**) *n* cargamento *m*; **c. boat** *or* **ship** barco *m* de carga, carguero *m*; **c. plane** avión *m* de carga

**Caribbean** [kærɪ'biːən, *US* kə'rɪbɪən] **1** *n* **the C.** *(region, sea)* el Caribe

**2** *adj* **the C. islands** las Antillas; **the C. Sea** el (mar) Caribe

**caribou** ['kærɪbuː] *n* caribú *m*

**caricature** ['kærɪkətjə(r)] **1** *n* caricatura *f*

**2** *vt* *(distort)* caricaturizar

**caricaturist** [kærɪkə'tjuːrɪst] *n* caricaturista *mf*

**caries** ['keəriːz] *n Med* caries *f inv*

**caring** ['keərɪŋ] *adj* *(society)* solícito(a), afectuoso(a); **the c. professions** las profesiones relacionadas con la salud y la asistencia social

**carnage** ['kɑːnɪdʒ] *n* matanza *f*

**carnal** ['kɑːnəl] *adj* carnal

**carnation** [kɑː'neɪʃən] *n* clavel *m*

**carnival** ['kɑːnɪvəl] *n* *(funfair)* feria *f*; *(traditional festival)* carnaval *m*

**carnivore** ['kɑːnɪvɔː(r)] *n* carnívoro *m*

**carnivorous** [kɑː'nɪvərəs] *adj* carnívoro(a)

**carob** ['kærəb] *n* *(substance)* extracto *m* de algarroba *(sucedáneo de chocolate)*

**carol** ['kærəl] *n* (**Christmas**) **c.** villancico *m*

**carouse** [kə'rauz] vi estar de parranda

**carousel** [kærə'sel] n (a) US (at fair) tiovivo m (b) (at airport) cinta f transportadora de equipajes (c) (for slides) carro m

**carp¹** [kɑ:p] (pl **carp**) n (fish) carpa f

**carp²** vi quejarse (sin motivo) (**at** de)

**Carpathians** [kɑ:'peɪθɪənz] npl **the C.** los Cárpatos

**carpenter** ['kɑ:pɪntə(r)] n carpintero(a) m,f

**carpentry** ['kɑ:pɪntrɪ] n carpintería f

**carpet** ['kɑ:pɪt] **1** n (a) (rug) alfombra f; (fitted) moqueta f; Fig **a c. of flowers** una alfombra de flores; **c. slippers** zapatillas fpl de (andar por) casa (b) (idioms) **to pull the c. out from under sb** retirarle el apoyo a alguien repentinamente; **c. bombing** bombardeo m de saturación

**2** vt (a) (floor) enmoquetar (b) Fam **to c. sb** echar una bronca a alguien

**carpet-sweeper** ['kɑ:pɪtswi:pə(r)] n cepillo m mecánico (para alfombras)

**carport** ['kɑ:pɔ:t] n Aut aparcamiento m techado

**carriage** ['kærɪdʒ] n (a) (vehicle) carruaje m, coche m (b) Br (of train) vagón m, coche m (c) (of typewriter) carro m (d) Com (transport) transporte m, porte m; (cost) portes mpl; **c. free** franco(a) de porte; **c. forward** porte m debido; **c. paid** porte m pagado (e) (bearing) (of person) porte m

**carriageway** ['kærɪdʒweɪ] n Aut calzada f; **the northbound c.** la calzada en dirección norte

**carrier** ['kærɪə(r)] n (a) (of disease, infection) portador(ora) m,f (b) Com (company) transportista m; (airline) línea f aérea (c) (container) (on bicycle) portaequipaje m, transportín m; **c. (bag)** bolsa f

**carrion** ['kærɪən] n carroña f

**carrot** ['kærət] n zanahoria f; Fig **to hold out a c.** mostrar un señuelo; **to use the c. and stick approach** prometer premios si se trabaja bien y amenazar con castigos si no

**carry** ['kærɪ] **1** vt (a) (transport, convey) llevar, CAm andar; (goods, passengers) transportar; (have on one's person) (gun, money) llevar (encima); **to c. sth away** or **off** llevarse algo; **to be carrying a child** (be pregnant) estar embarazada; Fig **to c. the can** pagar el pato; **to c. oneself well** tener buen porte

(b) (involve) **to c. a fine/a penalty** conllevar una multa/un castigo; **to c. weight/authority** tener peso/autoridad

(c) (take, lead, extend) **to c. sth too far** llevar algo demasiado lejos; **to c. an argument to its logical conclusion** llevar un argumento hasta las últimas consecuencias

(d) (capture, win) **he carried all before him** arrolló, tuvo un éxito arrollador; **his argu-**

**ment carried the day** su argumentación consiguió la victoria

(e) Pol **the bill was carried** se aprobó el proyecto de ley

(f) Com (keep in stock) tener (en almacén); (contain) **to c. an advertisement/article** (of newspaper) publicar un anuncio/artículo

**2** vi (of sound) oírse; **her voice carries well** tiene una voz potente

▸**carry away** vt sep (make excited, overenthusiastic) **to get carried away (by sth)** emocionarse (por or con algo), entusiasmarse (por or con algo)

▸**carry forward** vt sep Fin pasar a nueva columna; **carried forward** suma y sigue

▸**carry off** vt sep (a) (take away) llevarse; **to off a prize** (win) llevarse un premio (b) (do successfully) **she carried it off (well)** salió airosa

▸**carry on 1** vt sep (tradition) seguir; (business, trade) dirigir, gestionar; (correspondence, conversation) mantener

**2** vi (a) (continue) continuar, seguir; **to c. on doing sth** seguir haciendo algo; **c. on!** ¡sigue!, ¡adelante! (b) Fam (behave badly) hacer trastadas; **I don't like the way she carries on** no me gusta su forma de comportarse (c) Fam (have an affair) tener un lío (**with** con)

▸**carry out** vt sep llevar a cabo

**carrycot** ['kærɪkɒt] n moisés m, capazo m

**carry-on** ['kærɪ'ɒn] n Fam bronca f, follón m; **what a c.!** ¡menuda bronca!

**carry-out** ['kærɪ'aʊt] n US & Scot (food) = comida preparada para llevar; (restaurant) = restaurante donde se vende comida para llevar

**carsick** ['kɑ:sɪk] adj **to be c.** estar mareado(a) (en el coche); **to get c.** marearse (en el coche)

**cart** [kɑ:t] **1** n carro m, carreta f; Fig **to put the c. before the horse** empezar la casa por el tejado

**2** vt Fam (carry) cargar con

▸**cart off** vt sep Fam **to c. sb off** llevarse a alguien (a la fuerza)

**carte blanche** ['kɑ:t'blɑ:ʃ] n **to give sb c. (to do sth)** dar a alguien carta blanca (para hacer algo)

**cartel** [kɑ:'tel] n Econ cartel m, cártel m

**carthorse** ['kɑ:θɔ:s] n caballo m de tiro

**cartilage** ['kɑ:tɪlɪdʒ] n cartílago m

**cartographer** [kɑ:'tɒɡrəfə(r)] n cartógrafo(a) m,f

**cartography** [kɑ:'tɒɡrəfɪ] n cartografía f

**carton** ['kɑ:tən] n (for yoghurt, cream) envase m; (for milk) cartón m, tetrabrik® m; **a c. of cigarettes** un cartón de cigarrillos

**cartoon** [kɑ:'tu:n] n (in newspaper) chiste m, viñeta f; (animated film) dibujos mpl animados; **c. strip** tira f cómica

**cartoonist** [kɑːˈtuːnɪst] *n* dibujante *mf* de humor *or* de chistes

**cartridge** [ˈkɑːtrɪdʒ] *n* (**a**) *(for firearm, of film)* cartucho *m; (for pen)* recambio *m;* **c. belt** canana *f*, cartuchera *f* (**b**) **c. paper** papel *m* de dibujo

**cartwheel** [ˈkɑːtwiːl] *n (wheel)* rueda *f* de carro; **to turn cartwheels** hacer la voltereta lateral

**carve** [kɑːv] *vt (wood, stone)* tallar, esculpir; *(meat)* trinchar

▸**carve out** *vt sep Fig* **to c. out a career for oneself** forjarse una carrera

▸**carve up** *vt sep Fig (territory)* repartir, dividir

**carving** [ˈkɑːvɪŋ] *n* (**a**) *Art* talla *f* (**b**) **c. knife** *(for meat)* cuchillo *m* de trinchar

**carwash** [ˈkɑːwɒʃ] *n* lavado *m* de coches

**cascade** [kæsˈkeɪd] **1** *n* cascada *f*

**2** *vi (of water)* caer formando una cascada

**case¹** [keɪs] *n* (**a**) *(instance, situation)* & *Med* caso *m;* **a c. in point** un buen ejemplo, un caso claro; **in c. of emergency/accident** en caso de urgencia/accidente; **in c. he isn't there** en caso de que no esté allí; **just in c.** por si acaso; **in any c.** en cualquier caso; **in that c.** en ese caso; **as the c. may be** según el caso; *Med* **c. history** historial *m* médico, ficha *f;* **c. study** estudio *m* de caso (real) (**b**) *Law* causa *f;* **to bring a c. for sth against sb** entablar un pleito por algo contra alguien; **the c. for the defence** la defensa; **the c. for the prosecution** la acusación; *Fig* **the c. for sth** los argumentos a favor de algo; *Fig* **to have a good c.** estar respaldado(a) por buenos argumentos; **c. law** jurisprudencia *f*

**case²** *n* (**a**) *(container) (for spectacles)* funda *f; (for jewellery)* estuche *m;* **a cigarette c.** una pitillera; **(packing) c.** cajón *m;* **(display or glass) c.** vitrina *f;* **a c. of wine** una caja de vino (**b**) *(suitcase)* maleta *f; (briefcase)* maletín *m*, cartera *f* (**c**) *Typ* **lower/upper c.** caja *f* baja/alta

**casement** [ˈkeɪsmənt] *n (window)* ventana *f* (batiente)

**casework** [ˈkeɪswɜːk] *n* asistencia *f* social en casos individuales

**cash** [kæʃ] **1** *n (coins, banknotes)* (dinero *m* en) efectivo *m; Fam (money in general)* pasta *f;* **to pay (in) c.** pagar en efectivo; **c. and carry** *(shop)* almacén *m* (de venta) al por mayor; **c. in hand** al contado; **c. box** caja *f* (para el dinero); **c. card** tarjeta *f (del cajero automático)* **c. crop** cultivo *m* comercial; **c. desk** (mostrador *m* de) caja *f;* **c. dispenser** *or* **machine** cajero *m* automático; *Fin* **c. flow** flujo *m* de caja, cash-flow *m;* **c. price** precio *m* al contado; **c. register** caja *f* registradora

**2** *vt (cheque, postal order)* hacer efectivo(a)

▸**cash in on** *vt insep Fam* aprovechar, sacar provecho de

**cash-book** [ˈkæʃbʊk] *n* libro *m* de caja

**cashew** [kæˈʃuː] *n* **c. (nut)** anacardo *m*

**cashier¹** [kæˈʃɪə(r)] *n* cajero(a) *m,f*

**cashier²** *vt Mil* destituir

**cashmere** [ˈkæʃmɪə(r)] *n* cachemir *m*

**cashpoint** [ˈkæʃpɔɪnt] *n* cajero *m* automático

**casing** [ˈkeɪsɪŋ] *n Tech (of machine)* cubierta *f*, carcasa *f; (of tyre)* cubierta *f; (of wire, shaft)* revestimiento *m; (of sausage)* piel *f*

**casino** [kəˈsiːnəʊ] *(pl* **casinos)** *n* casino *m*

**cask** [kɑːsk] *n* tonel *m*, barril *m*

**casket** [ˈkɑːskɪt] *n* (**a**) *(for jewellery)* estuche *m* (**b**) *(coffin)* ataúd *m*

**Caspian** [ˈkæspɪən] *adj* **the C. Sea** el mar Caspio

**cassava** [kəˈsɑːvə] *n* mandioca *f*

**casserole** [ˈkæsərəʊl] *n (cooking vessel)* cazuela *f*, cacerola *f; (food)* guiso *m*

**cassette** [kæˈset] *n (audio, video)* cinta *f*, casete *f;* **c. player** casete *m*, magnetófono *m;* **c. recorder** casete *m*, magnetófono *m*

**cassock** [ˈkæsək] *n* sotana *f*

**cast** [kɑːst] **1** *n* (**a**) *(of play, film)* reparto *m* (**b**) *(reproduction)* reproducción *f; (mould)* molde *m;* *Med* **(plaster) c.** escayola *f;* *Fig* **c. of mind** mentalidad *f*

**2** *vt (pt & pp* **cast)** (**a**) *(throw) (stone)* tirar, lanzar; *(shadow)* proyectar, hacer; *(net, line)* lanzar; **to c. one's eyes over sth** echar una ojeada a algo; **to c. doubt on sth** poner en duda algo; *Fig* **to c. light on sth** arrojar luz sobre algo; **to c. one's mind back to sth** remontarse a algo; **to c. its skin** *(of reptile)* mudar de piel *or* camisa; **to c. a spell over sb** hechizar a alguien (**b**) **to c. one's vote** emitir el voto, votar (**c**) *Th & Cin* **to c. a film/play** seleccionar a los actores para una película/una obra; **she was cast in the role of** *or* **as Desdemona** la eligieron para el papel de Desdémona (**d**) *(metal, statue)* fundir

▸**cast about, cast around** *vi* **to c. about** *or* **around for sth** buscar algo

▸**cast aside** *vt sep (idea, prejudice)* abandonar

▸**cast away** *vt sep* **to be cast away** ser un/una náufrago(a)

▸**cast down** *vt sep* **to be cast down** estar deprimido(a), estar abatido(a)

▸**cast off 1** *vt sep (clothes, chains)* deshacerse de

**2** *vi* (**a**) *Naut* soltar amarras (**b**) *(in knitting)* rematar una vuelta

▸**cast on** *vi (in knitting)* engarzar una vuelta

**castanets** [kæstəˈnets] *npl* castañuelas *fpl*

**castaway** [ˈkɑːstəweɪ] *n* náufrago(a) *m,f*

**caste** [kɑːst] *n (social rank)* casta *f*

**caster sugar** ['kɑːstə'ʃugə(r)] *n* azúcar *m or f* extrafino, azúcar *m* molido

**castigate** ['kæstɪgeɪt] *vt Formal (criticize)* reprender

**Castile** [kæ'stiːl] *n* Castilla

**Castilian** [kæs'tɪlɪən] **1** *n* **(a)** *(person)* castellano(a) *m,f* **(b)** *(language)* castellano *m*
  **2** *adj* castellano(a)

**casting** ['kɑːstɪŋ] **1** *n Th & Cin* reparto *m*
  **2** *adj* **c. vote** voto *m* de calidad

**cast-iron** ['kɑːst'aɪən] *n* hierro *m* fundido *or* colado; *Fig* **c. alibi/guarantee** coartada *f*/garantía *f* irrefutable

**castle** ['kɑːsəl] **1** *n (building)* castillo *m*; *(in chess)* torre *f*; *Fig* **to build castles in the air** construir castillos en el aire
  **2** *vi (in chess)* enrocarse

**cast-off** ['kɑːstɒf] **1** *n (garment)* prenda *f* vieja *or* usada; *Fam (person)* persona *f* rechazada
  **2** *adj* **c. clothing** ropa *f* vieja *or* usada

**castor** ['kɑːstə(r)] *n (on furniture)* ruedecita *f*

**castor oil** *n* aceite *m* de ricino

**castrate** [kæs'treɪt] *vt* castrar

**castration** [kæs'treɪʃən] *n* castración *f*

**casual** ['kæʒjʊəl] *adj* **(a)** *(remark, glance)* de pasada, casual **(b)** *(relaxed, informal)* informal; **c. clothes** ropa *f* informal *or* de sport **(c)** *(unconcerned)* despreocupado(a); *(careless)* descuidado(a); **c. sex** relaciones *fpl* sexuales ocasionales **(d)** *(employment, worker)* eventual

**casually** ['kæʒjʊəlɪ] *adv* **she remarked quite c. that...** comentó de pasada que...; **he treated the issue rather c.** se tomó el asunto bastante a la ligera; **to dress c.** vestirse de manera informal, vestirse de sport

**casualty** ['kæʒjʊəltɪ] *n (in accident, earthquake)* víctima *f*; *(in war)* baja *f*; **she was taken to the c. department** la llevaron a urgencias

**CAT** [kæt] *n Med (abbr* **Computerized Axial Tomography)** TAC *f*; **C. scan** escáner *m* (TAC)

**cat** [kæt] *n* **(a)** *(animal)* gato(a) *m,f*; **the big cats** los grandes felinos; **c. burglar** ladrón(ona) *m,f (que entra en las casas escalando)*; **c.'s eye®** *(on road)* = baliza reflectante *(en la calzada)*; **c. flap** gatera *f*; **c. litter** arena *f* para gatos **(b)** *(idioms)* **to fight like c. and dog** llevarse como el perro y el gato; **to play a c.-and-mouse game with sb** jugar al ratón y al gato con alguien; *Fam* **to be like a c. on a hot tin roof** *or* **on hot bricks** estar histérico(a); **to let the c. out of the bag** descubrir el pastel; **to set the c. among the pigeons** sembrar la discordia; *Fam* **there isn't enough room to swing a c.** no se puede uno ni mover; *Fam* **he thinks he's the c.'s whiskers** se lo tiene muy creído

**cataclysm** ['kætəklɪzəm] *n* cataclismo *m*

**Catalan** ['kætəlæn] **1** *n* **(a)** *(person)* catalán(ana) *m,f* **(b)** *(language)* catalán *m*
  **2** *adj* catalán(ana)

**catalogue** ['kætəlɒg] **1** *n* catálogo *m*
  **2** *vt* catalogar

**Catalonia** [kætə'ləʊnɪə] *n* Cataluña

**catalyst** ['kætəlɪst] *n also Fig* catalizador *m*

**catamaran** [kætəmə'ræn] *n* catamarán *m*

**catapult** ['kætəpʌlt] **1** *n (hand-held)* tirachinas *m inv; (mediaeval siege weapon, on aircraft carrier)* catapulta *f*
  **2** *vt* **to be catapulted into the air** salir despedido(a) por los aires; **to c. sb to stardom** lanzar *or* catapultar a alguien al estrellato

**cataract** ['kætərækt] *n (in river) & Med* catarata *f*

**catarrh** [kə'tɑː(r)] *n* catarro *m*

**catastrophe** [kə'tæstrəfɪ] *n* catástrofe *f*

**catastrophic** [kætə'strɒfɪk] *adj* catastrófico(a)

**catatonic** [kætə'tɒnɪk] *adj Med* catatónico(a)

**catcall** ['kætkɔːl] *n* silbido *m*

**catch** [kætʃ] **1** *n* **(a)** *(of ball)* parada *f (sin que la pelota toque el suelo);* **to play c.** *(ball game)* jugar a *(que no caiga)* la pelota; *(chasing game)* jugar al corre-corre-que-te-pillo
  **(b)** *(in fishing)* pesca *f*, captura *f*
  **(c)** *(fastening) (on door, window)* cierre *m*
  **(d)** *(disadvantage)* **where's the c.?** ¿cuál es la pega?; **it's a c.-22 situation** es como la pescadilla que se muerde la cola
  **2** *vt (pt & pp* **caught** [kɔːt]*)* **(a)** *(ball)* coger, atrapar; *(fish)* pescar; *(thief)* atrapar, capturar; **c.!** *(when throwing something)* ¡cógelo!; **to c. sb doing sth** pillar a alguien haciendo algo; **you won't c. me doing that again** no pienso volver a hacerlo; **my bedroom catches the sun** a mi dormitorio le da el sol; **you look as if you've caught the sun** parece que te ha pegado el sol
  **(b)** *(bus, train)* tomar, coger; *(programme, film)* ver, alcanzar a ver
  **(c)** *(hear)* oír, alcanzar a oír
  **(d)** *(manage to find)* pillar, coger; **you've caught me at a bad time** me pillas en un mal momento; **I'll c. you later!** luego te veo
  **(e)** *(trap, entangle)* **I caught my dress on a nail** me enganché el vestido en un clavo; **don't c. your fingers in the door!** ¡no te pilles los dedos con la puerta!; **to c. sb's attention** *or* **eye** llamar la atención de alguien
  **(f)** *(illness)* agarrar, coger; **to c. a cold** coger un resfriado; **I caught this cold from you** tú me pegaste este resfriado; **you'll c. your death out there!** ¡vas a coger un resfriado de muerte ahí fuera!
  **(g)** *(of blow, missile)* **he caught me (a blow)**

on the chest me dio un golpe en el pecho; **the stone caught her on the arm** la piedra le dio en el brazo; *Fam* **you'll c. it!** *(get into trouble)* ¡te la vas a ganar!

**(h)** to c. fire *or* light prenderse

**3** *vi* **(a)** *(of fire)* prender

**(b)** *(in door)* quedarse pillado(a); *(on a nail)* quedarse enganchado(a); **my skirt caught on a nail** se me enganchó la falda en un clavo

**(c)** *(of person)* **to c. at sth** tratar de coger algo

▶**catch on** *vi* **(a)** *(of fashion)* cuajar **(b)** *Fam (understand)* darse cuenta **(to** de), enterarse **(to** de)

▶**catch out** *vt sep* **to c. sb out** pillar a alguien

▶**catch up 1** *vi (close gap, get closer)* **to c. up with sb** alcanzar a alguien; **to c. up with one's work** ponerse al día en el trabajo; **his past has caught up with him** ha salido a relucir su pasado

**2** *vt sep* **(a) to c. sb up** alcanzar a alguien **(b) to get caught up in sth** *(become entangled)* verse envuelto(a) *or* enredarse en algo

**catch-all** ['kætʃɔːl] *adj Fam* **a c. term** un término que vale para todo *or* muy general

**catching** ['kætʃɪŋ] *adj (disease, habit)* contagioso(a)

**catchment area** ['kætʃmənt'eərɪə] *n (of school)* área *f* de cobertura

**catchphrase** ['kætʃfreɪz] *n* coletilla *f*, latiguillo *m*

**catchy** ['kætʃɪ] *adj (tune, slogan)* pegadizo(a)

**catechism** ['kætəkɪzəm] *n* catecismo *m*

**categorical** [kætɪ'gɒrɪkəl] *adj (denial, refusal)* categórico(a)

**categorize** ['kætɪgəraɪz] *vt* clasificar **(as** como)

**category** ['kætɪgərɪ] *n* categoría *f*

**cater** ['keɪtə(r)] *vi* **(a)** *(provide food) (at weddings)* dar *or* organizar banquetes; *(for company, airline)* dar servicio de comidas *or* catering; **we c. for groups of up to 50** *(in restaurant)* servimos a grupos de hasta 50 personas; **parties catered for** *(sign in restaurant)* se organizan banquetes **(b) to c. for** *(needs, requirements)* tener en cuenta; **to c. for all tastes** atender a todos los gustos

**caterer** ['keɪtərə(r)] *n (company)* empresa *f* de hostelería; *(person)* hostelero(a) *m,f*

**catering** ['keɪtərɪŋ] *n (trade)* hostelería *f*; **to do the c.** *(at party)* dar el servicio de comida y bebida; **c. school** escuela *f* de hostelería

**caterpillar** ['kætəpɪlə(r)] *n* oruga *f*; **c. track** *(on tank, tractor)* oruga *f*

**catfish** ['kætfɪʃ] *n* siluro *m*

**cathartic** [kə'θɑːtɪk] *adj* catártico(a)

**cathedral** [kə'θiːdrəl] *n* catedral *f*; **c. town/ city** ciudad *f* catedralicia

**catheter** ['kæθɪtə(r)] *n Med* catéter *m*

**cathode** ['kæθəʊd] *n Elec* cátodo *m*; **c. ray tube** tubo *m* de rayos catódicos

**Catholic** ['kæθlɪk] *n & adj Rel* católico(a) *m,f*

**catholic** ['kæθlɪk] *adj (wide-ranging)* ecléctico(a)

**Catholicism** [kə'θɒlɪsɪzəm] *n* catolicismo *m*

**catkin** ['kætkɪn] *n (on bush, tree)* amento *m*, candelilla *f*

**catnap** ['kætnæp] *n Fam* siestecilla *f*

**catsuit** ['kætsuːt] *n* mallas *fpl*

**cattle** ['kætəl] *npl* ganado *m* (vacuno); **c. breeding** cría *f* de ganado vacuno; **c. market** feria *f* de ganado; **c. truck** vagón *m* de ganado

**cattle-grid** ['kætəlgrɪd] *n* paso *m* canadiense, reja *f (que impide el paso del ganado)*

**catty** ['kætɪ] *adj Fam* avieso(a), malintencionado(a)

**catwalk** ['kætwɔːk] *n* pasarela *f*

**Caucasian** [kɔː'keɪʒən] **1** *n (white person)* blanco(a) *m,f*

**2** *adj (in ethnology)* caucásico(a)

**Caucasus** ['kɔːkəsəs] *n* **the C. (Mountains)** el Cáucaso

**caucus** ['kɔːkəs] *n Br Pol* comité *m*; *US* = congreso de los dos principales partidos de Estados Unidos

**caught** [kɔːt] *pt & pp of* **catch**

**cauldron** ['kɔːldrən] *n* caldero *m*

**cauliflower** ['kɒlɪflaʊə(r)] *n* coliflor *f*; **c. cheese** = coliflor con besamel de queso; **c. ear** *(swollen ear)* oreja *f* hinchada por los golpes

**cause** [kɔːz] **1** *n* **(a)** *(origin)* causa *f*; **c. and effect** causa y efecto **(b)** *(reason)* motivo *m*, razón *f*; **to have good c. for doing sth** tener un buen motivo para hacer algo; **his condition is giving c. for concern** su estado es preocupante **(c)** *(purpose, mission)* causa *f*; **to make common c.** hacer causa común; **it's all in a good c.** es por una buena causa

**2** *vt* causar, provocar; **to c. trouble** crear problemas; **to c. sb to do sth** hacer que alguien haga algo

**causeway** ['kɔːzweɪ] *n* paso *m* elevado *(sobre agua)*

**caustic** ['kɔːstɪk] *adj also Fig (humour, joke)* cáustico(a); **c. soda** sosa *f* cáustica

**cauterize** ['kɔːtəraɪz] *vt Med* cauterizar

**caution** ['kɔːʃən] **1** *n* **(a)** *(prudence)* precaución *f*, cautela *f*; **to exercise c.** actuar con precaución; **to throw c. to the wind(s)** olvidarse de la prudencia **(b)** *(warning)* advertencia *f*; *Law & Sport* **to be given a c.** recibir una advertencia

**2** *vt* **(a)** *(warn)* advertir; **to c. sb against sth** prevenir a alguien contra algo **(b)** *Law (on arrest)* leer los derechos a; *(instead of prosecuting)* amonestar

**cautionary** ['kɔːʃənrɪ] *adj* **a c. tale** un cuento ejemplar

**cautious** ['kɔːʃəs] *adj* cauto(a), prudente

**cautiously** ['kɔːʃəslɪ] *adv* cautelosamente, con prudencia

**cautiousness** ['kɔːʃəsnɪs] *n* cautela *f*, prudencia *f*

**cavalier** [kævə'lɪə(r)] *adj* demasiado despreocupado(a); **to be c. about sth** tomarse algo a la ligera

**cavalry** ['kævəlrɪ] *n* caballería *f*

**cave** [keɪv] *n* cueva *f*, caverna *f*; **c. dweller** cavernícola *mf*; **c. paintings** pinturas *fpl* rupestres

▶**cave in** *vi (of ground, structure)* hundirse, ceder; *Fig (stop resisting)* rendirse, darse por vencido(a)

**caveman** ['keɪvmæn] *n* cavernícola *mf*

**cavern** ['kævən] *n* caverna *f*

**cavernous** ['kævənəs] *adj (room, pit)* cavernoso(a)

**caviar(e)** ['kævɪɑː(r)] *n* caviar *m*

**cavil** ['kævɪl] *(pt & pp* **cavilled,** *US* **caviled)** *vi Literary* poner reparos (**at** a)

**cavity** ['kævɪtɪ] *n (hole)* cavidad *f*; *(of tooth)* caries *f inv*; **c. wall insulation** cámara *f* de aire, aislamiento *m* de doble pared

**cavort** [kə'vɔːt] *vi* retozar, brincar

**caw** [kɔː] **1** *n (of bird)* graznido *m*
  **2** *vi* graznar

**cayenne** [keɪ'en] *n* **c. (pepper)** cayena *f*

**CB** [siː'biː] *n Rad (abbr* **Citizen's Band)** banda *f* ciudadana *or* de radioaficionados

**CBE** [siːbiː'iː] *n Br (abbr* **Commander of the Order of the British Empire)** = condecoración británica al mérito civil

**CBI** [siːbiː'aɪ] *n Br (abbr* **Confederation of British Industry)** = organización empresarial británica, ≃ CEOE *f*

**cc** [siː'siː] *n (abbr* **cubic centimetre(s))** c.c., centímetros *mpl* cúbicos

**CCTV** [siːsiːtiː'viː] *n (abbr* **closed-circuit television)** circuito *m* cerrado de televisión

**CD** [siː'diː] *n* **(a)** *(abbr* **compact disc)** CD *m*, (disco *m*) compacto *m*; **CD player** (lector *m* *or* reproductor *m* de) CD **(b)** *(abbr* **Corps Diplomatique)** CD, cuerpo *m* diplomático

**CDI** [siːdiː'aɪ] *n Comptr (abbr* **compact disc interactive)** CDI *m*

**Cdr** *Mil (abbr* **Commander)** Comandante *m*

**Cdre** *Naut (abbr* **Commodore)** Comodoro *m*

**CD-ROM** [siːdiː'rɒm] *n Comptr (abbr* **compact disc-read only memory)** CD-ROM *m*

**cease** [siːs] **1** *vt* abandonar, suspender; **c. fire!** ¡alto el fuego!
  **2** *vi* cesar; **to c. doing sth** *or* **to do sth** dejar de hacer algo; **it never ceases to amaze me (that…)** no deja de sorprenderme (que…)

**cease-fire** ['siːsfaɪə(r)] *n* alto *m* el fuego, tregua *f*

**ceaseless** ['siːslɪs] *adj* incesante

**ceaselessly** ['siːslɪslɪ] *adv* incesantemente, sin parar

**cecum** *US* = **caecum**

**cedar** ['siːdə(r)] *n (tree, wood)* cedro *m*

**cede** [siːd] *vt Law (territory, property)* ceder

**cedilla** [sɪ'dɪlə] *n* cedilla *f*

**ceilidh** ['keɪlɪ] *n Scot* = fiesta en la que se bailan danzas tradicionales

**ceiling** ['siːlɪŋ] *n (of room)* techo *m*; *Fig* **to reach a c.** tocar techo; **c. price** precio *m* máximo autorizado

**celebrant** ['selɪbrənt] *n Rel* celebrante *mf*

**celebrate** ['selɪbreɪt] **1** *vt* celebrar; *Rel* **to c. mass** decir misa
  **2** *vi* **let's c.!** ¡vamos a celebrarlo!

**celebrated** ['selɪbreɪtɪd] *adj* célebre

**celebration** [selɪ'breɪʃən] *n* celebración *f*; **celebrations** *(of anniversary, victory)* actos *mpl* conmemorativos; **in c.** en celebración; **this calls for a c.!** ¡esto hay que celebrarlo!

**celebrity** [sɪ'lebrɪtɪ] *n* **(a)** *(person)* celebridad *f* **(b)** *(fame)* celebridad *f*, fama *f*

**celery** ['selərɪ] *n* apio *m*

**celestial** [sɪ'lestɪəl] *adj* celeste

**celibacy** ['selɪbəsɪ] *n* celibato *m*

**celibate** ['selɪbət] *adj* célibe

**cell** [sel] *n* **(a)** *(in prison, monastery)* celda *f* **(b)** *Elec* pila *f* **(c)** *Biol Pol* célula *f*

**cellar** ['selə(r)] *n (basement)* sótano *m*; *(for wine)* bodega *f*

**cellist** ['tʃelɪst] *n* violonchelista *mf*

**cello** ['tʃeləʊ] *(pl* **cellos)** *n* violonchelo *m*

**cellophane®** ['seləfeɪn] *n Br* celofán *m*

**cellphone** ['selfəʊn] *n* teléfono *m* celular

**cellular** ['seljʊlə(r)] *adj* celular; **c. phone** teléfono *m* celular

**cellulite** ['seljʊlaɪt] *n* celulitis *f inv*

**celluloid®** ['seljʊlɔɪd] *n* celuloide *m*

**cellulose** ['seljʊləʊs] *n* celulosa *f*

**Celsius** ['selsɪəs] *adj* centígrado(a); **10 degrees C.** 10 grados centígrados

**Celt** [kelt] *n* celta *mf*

**Celtic** ['keltɪk] *adj* celta, céltico(a)

**cement** [sɪ'ment] **1** *n* cemento *m*; **c. mixer** hormigonera *f*
  **2** *vt (glue together)* encolar, pegar; *(cover with cement)* cubrir de cemento; *Fig (friendship)* consolidar

**cemetery** ['semətrɪ] *n* cementerio *m*

**cenotaph** ['senətæf] *n* cenotafio *m*

**censor** ['sensə(r)] **1** n censor(ora) m,f
**2** vt censurar

**censorious** [sen'sɔːrɪəs] adj (person) censurador(ora); (look) reprobatorio(a); **to be c. of** censurar

**censorship** ['sensəʃɪp] n censura f

**censure** ['senʃə(r)] **1** n censura f, crítica f; Pol **vote of c.** moción f de censura
**2** vt censurar, criticar

**census** ['sensəs] n censo m; **to take a c. of** censar

**cent** [sent] n centavo m; US Fam **I haven't got a c.** no tengo ni un céntimo or duro

**centaur** ['sentɔː(r)] n centauro m

**centenarian** [sentɪ'neərɪən] n centenario(a) m,f

**centenary** [sen'tiːnərɪ], US **centennial** [sen'tenɪəl] **1** n centenario m
**2** adj centenario(a)

**center** US = **centre**

**centigrade** ['sentɪgreɪd] adj centígrado(a); **10 degrees c.** 10 grados centígrados

**centigramme**, US **centigram** ['sentɪgræm] n centigramo m

**centilitre**, US **centiliter** ['sentɪliːtə(r)] n centilitro m

**centime** [sɒntiːm] n (subdivision of franc) céntimo m

**centimetre**, US **centimeter** ['sentɪmiːtə(r)] n centímetro m

**centipede** ['sentɪpiːd] n ciempiés m inv

**central** ['sentrəl] adj central; (in convenient location) céntrico(a); (in importance) central, primordial; **it is c. to our plans** es el eje sobre el que giran nuestros planes; **C. London** el centro de Londres; **our hotel is quite c.** nuestro hotel es bastante céntrico; **C. America** Centroamérica, América Central; **C. American** centroamericano(a); **c. bank** banco m central; **c. character** (in book, film) personaje m central, protagonista mf; **C. Europe** Europa Central; **C. European** centroeuropeo(a); **c. government** gobierno m central; **c. heating** calefacción f central; **c. locking** cierre m centralizado; **c. nervous system** sistema m nervioso central; Comptr **c. processing unit** unidad f central de proceso; **c. reservation** (on motorway) mediana f; US **C. Standard Time** hora f oficial del meridiano 90°

**Central African Republic** ['sentrəl-'æfrɪkənrɪ'pʌblɪk] n República f Centroafricana

**centralization** [sentrəlaɪ'zeɪʃən] n centralización f

**centralize** ['sentrəlaɪz] vt centralizar

**centrally** ['sentrəlɪ] adv **c. controlled** de control centralizado; **c. funded** de financiación central; **the flat is c. heated** el piso tiene calefacción central

**centre**, US **center** ['sentə(r)] **1** n centro m; **in the c.** en el centro; Pol **left of c.** de izquierdas; Pol **right of c.** de derechas; **c. of gravity** centro de gravedad; **c. of attraction** foco m or centro de atracción; **c. forward** (in football) delantero m centro
**2** vt (attention, interest) centrar (**on** en)

**centrefold** ['sentəfəʊld] n (in magazine) póster m central

**centrepiece** ['sentəpiːs] n (on table) centro m de mesa; (main element) núcleo m, eje m

**centrifugal** [sentrɪ'fjuːgəl] adj centrífugo(a)

**century** ['sentʃərɪ] n (**a**) (a hundred years) siglo m; **the 19th c.** el siglo XIX (**b**) (in cricket) = cien (o más de cien) carreras

**CEO** [siːiː'əʊ] (pl CEOs) n Com (abbr **chief executive officer**) director(ora) m,f gerente, consejero(a) m,f delegado(a)

**ceramic** [sə'ræmɪk] **1** n cerámica f
**2** adj de cerámica

**ceramics** [sə'ræmɪks] n (art) cerámica f

**cereal** ['sɪərɪəl] n cereal m; (**breakfast**) **c.** cereales mpl (de desayuno)

**cerebellum** [serɪ'beləm] n Anat cerebelo m

**cerebral** ['serɪbrəl] adj (intellectual) & Anat cerebral; Med **c. palsy** parálisis f or cerebral

**cerebrum** ['serɪbrəm] n Anat cerebro m

**ceremonial** [serɪ'məʊnɪəl] **1** n ceremonial m; **ceremonials** ceremoniales mpl
**2** adj ceremonial

**ceremonious** [serɪ'məʊnɪəs] adj ceremonioso(a)

**ceremony** ['serɪmənɪ] n ceremonia f; **the marriage c.** la ceremonia nupcial; **with/ without c.** con/sin ceremonia; Fig **he was sacked without c.** lo despidieron sin ningún miramiento; **there's no need to stand on c.** no hace falta cumplir con formalidades

**cert** [sɜːt] n Fam **it's a (dead) c. to win** no cabe ninguna duda de que ganará

**certain** ['sɜːtən] adj (**a**) (sure) seguro(a); **to be c. of sth** estar seguro(a) de algo; **to make c. of sth** asegurarse de algo; **for c.** con certeza; **he is c. to come** vendrá con toda seguridad (**b**) (particular) cierto(a), determinado(a); **for c. reasons** por ciertos motivos; **a c. person** cierta persona; **a c. Richard Sanders** un tal Richard Sanders

**certainly** ['sɜːtənlɪ] adv (definitely) por supuesto; **c. not!** ¡ni hablar!; **she's c. very clever, but...** sin duda es muy lista, pero...

**certainty** ['sɜːtəntɪ] n certeza f, certidumbre f; **she said it with some c.** lo dijo con certidumbre; **there is no c. that we will win** no es seguro que ganemos; **to know sth for a c.** saber algo a ciencia cierta

**certifiable** ['sɜːtɪfaɪəbəl] adj Fam (mad) **to be c.** estar como para que lo/la encierren

**certificate** [sə'tɪfɪkət] *n* certificado *m; (in education)* título *m;* **marriage/death c.** certificado *or* partida *f* de matrimonio/defunción

**certify** ['sɜ:tɪfaɪ] *vt (confirm)* certificar; **to c. that sth is true** dar fe de que algo es verdad; **this is to c. that...** por la presente certifico que...; **to c. sb insane** declarar demente a alguien

**certitude** ['sɜ:tɪtju:d] *n* certidumbre *f*

**cervical** ['sɜ:vɪkəl] *adj Anat* cervical; **c. cancer** cáncer *m* cervical; **c. smear** frotis *m inv* cervical, citología *f* (cervical)

**cervix** ['sɜ:vɪks] *(pl* **cervices** ['sɜ:vɪsi:z]) *n Anat* cuello *m* del útero

**cessation** [se'seɪʃən] *n* cese *m*

**cesspit** ['sespɪt], **cesspool** ['sespu:l] *n* pozo *m* negro; *Fig* sentina *f*, cloaca *f*

**CET** [si:i:'ti:] *n (abbr* **Central European Time)** = hora de Europa central

**Ceylon** [sɪ'lɒn] *n Formerly* Ceilán *m*

**cf** [si:'ef] *(abbr* **confer, compare)** cf., cfr., compárese

**CFC** [si:ef'si:] *(pl* **CFCs)** *n Chem (abbr* **chlorofluorocarbon)** CFC *m,* clorofluorocarbono *m*

**Chad** [tʃæd] *n* Chad *m*

**chafe** [tʃeɪf] **1** *vt (rub)* rozar, hacer rozadura en
  **2** *vi (rub)* rozar, hacer rozadura; *Fig* **to c. at** *or* **against sth** *(resent)* sentirse irritado(a) por algo

**chaff** [tʃɑ:f] **1** *n* granzas *fpl,* barcia *f; Fig* **to separate the wheat from the c.** separar el grano de la paja
  **2** *vt (tease)* tomar el pelo a

**chaffinch** ['tʃæfɪntʃ] *n* pinzón *m*

**chagrin** ['ʃægrɪn] *n* disgusto *m,* desazón *f;* **much to my/her c.** muy a mi/su pesar

**chain** [tʃeɪn] **1** *n* cadena *f; (of mountains)* cadena *f* montañosa, cordillera *f;* **in chains** encadenado(a); *Fig* **a c. of events** una concatenación de sucesos; **to pull the c.** *(in toilet)* tirar de la cadena; **c. gang** cadena *f* de presidiarios; **c. letter** = carta en la que se pide al destinatario que envíe copias de la misma a otras personas; **c. mail** cota *f* de malla; **c. reaction** reacción *f* en cadena; **c. saw** motosierra *f,* sierra *f* mecánica; **c. store** cadena *f* de tiendas
  **2** *vt* encadenar; **to c. sth to sth** encadenar algo a algo
▸**chain up** *vt sep* encadenar

**chain-smoke** ['tʃeɪnsməʊk] *vi* fumar un cigarrillo tras otro

**chair** [tʃeə(r)] **1** *n* **(a)** *(seat)* silla *f; (armchair)* sillón *m* **(b)** *(chairperson)* presidente(a) *m,f;* **to be in the c.** ocupar la presidencia **(c)** *Univ (of professor)* cátedra *f*
  **2** *vt (meeting)* presidir

**chairlift** ['tʃeəlɪft] *n* telesilla *f*

**chairman** ['tʃeəmən] *n* presidente *m*

**chairmanship** ['tʃeəmənʃɪp] *n* presidencia *f*

**chairperson** ['tʃeəpɜ:sən] *n* presidente(a) *m,f*

**chairwoman** ['tʃeəwʊmən] *n* presidenta *f*

**chalet** ['ʃæleɪ] *n* chalé *m*

**chalice** ['tʃælɪs] *n Rel* cáliz *m*

**chalk** [tʃɔ:k] **1** *n (mineral)* creta *f; (for blackboard)* tiza *f;* **they are as different as c. and cheese** no se parecen ni en el blanco de los ojos; *Fam* **not by a long c.** ni de lejos
  **2** *vt (mark)* trazar *or* marcar con tiza; *(write)* escribir con tiza
▸**chalk up** *vt sep (victory)* apuntarse

**chalkboard** ['tʃɔ:kbɔ:d] *n US* pizarra *f,* encerado *m*

**chalky** ['tʃɔ:kɪ] *adj* calizo(a)

**challenge** ['tʃælɪndʒ] **1** *n* desafío *m,* reto *m;* **to issue/accept a c.** lanzar/aceptar un desafío; **to enjoy a c.** disfrutar con las tareas difíciles; **the job presents a real c.** el trabajo constituye un auténtico reto; **leadership c.** asalto *m* al liderato *or* a la presidencia
  **2** *vt* **(a)** *(to a contest, fight)* desafiar, retar; **to c. sb to do sth** desafiar *or* retar a alguien a hacer algo; **you need a job that will c. you** necesitas un trabajo que represente un reto para ti **(b)** *(statement, authority)* cuestionar, poner en duda; **she challenged his right to decide** puso en duda que él tuviera derecho a decidir **(c)** *Mil* dar el alto a

**challenger** ['tʃælɪndʒə(r)] *n* aspirante *mf*

**challenging** ['tʃælɪndʒɪŋ] *adj (job)* estimulante

**chamber** ['tʃeɪmbə(r)] *n* **(a)** *(hall)* sala *f; Pol* **Lower/Upper C.** cámara *f* alta/baja; **C. of Commerce** cámara *f* de comercio; **c. music** música *f* de cámara; **c. pot** orinal *m* **(b)** *(of heart)* cavidad *f* (cardíaca); *(of revolver)* recámara *f* **(c)** *Law* **chambers** *(of barrister, judge)* despacho *m*

**chambermaid** ['tʃeɪmbəmeɪd] *n* camarera *f* (de hotel)

**chameleon** [kə'mi:lɪən] *n* camaleón *m*

**chamois** *n* **(a)** ['ʃæmwɑ:] *(deer)* rebeco *m,* gamuza *f* **(b)** ['ʃæmɪ] **c. (leather)** *(material)* ante *m; (cloth)* gamuza *f*

**champ¹** [tʃæmp] *n Fam* campeón(ona) *m,f*

**champ²** *vi Fig* **to c. at the bit** hervir de impaciencia

**champagne** [ʃæm'peɪn] *n* champán *m*

**champion** ['tʃæmpɪən] **1** *n* **(a)** *(in sport)* campeón(ona) *m,f;* **world/European c.** campeón(ona) mundial/de Europa **(b)** *(of cause)* abanderado(a) *m,f,* defensor(ora) *m,f*
  **2** *vt* defender, abanderar

**championship** ['tʃæmpɪənʃɪp] *n* campeonato *m*

**chance** [tʃɑːns] **1** n (a) *(luck)* casualidad f, suerte f; **by c.** por casualidad; **to leave nothing to c.** no dejar nada a la improvisación; *Fam* **c. would be a fine thing!** ¡qué más quisiera yo! (b) *(opportunity)* oportunidad f; **to give sb a c.** darle una oportunidad a alguien; **now's your c.!** ¡ésta es la tuya!, ¡ésta es tu oportunidad!; **it's your last c.** es tu última oportunidad; **when I get the c.** en cuanto tenga ocasión *or* oportunidad; *Fam* **to have an eye to the main c.** estar a la que salta (c) *(likelihood)* posibilidad f (of de); **to have** *or* **stand a c.** tener posibilidades; **there's no c. of that happening** es imposible que suceda (d) *(risk)* riesgo m; **to take a c.** correr el riesgo; **it's a c. we'll have to take** es un riesgo que habrá que correr; **I'm taking no chances** no pienso correr riesgos

**2** adj **a c. discovery/meeting** un descubrimiento/encuentro casual

**3** vt **to c. doing sth** arriesgarse a hacer algo; *Fam* **to c. one's arm** arriesgarse, jugársela

**4** vi *(happen)* **to c. to do sth** hacer algo por casualidad

▸**chance on, chance upon** vt insep encontrar por casualidad

**chancellor** [ˈtʃɑːnsələ(r)] n (a) *Univ Br* rector(ora) m,f honorario(a); *US* rector(ora) m,f (b) *Pol (in Austria, Germany)* canciller m; *Br Pol* **C. (of the Exchequer)** ≃ ministro(a) m,f de Hacienda

**chancy** [ˈtʃɑːnsɪ] adj Fam *(risky)* arriesgado(a)

**chandelier** [ʃændəˈlɪə(r)] n araña f *(lámpara)*

**change** [tʃeɪndʒ] **1** n (a) *(alteration)* cambio m; **a c. for the better/worse** un cambio a mejor/peor; **a c. of address** un cambio de domicilio; **a c. of clothes** una muda; **to have a c. of heart** cambiar de parecer; **for a c.** para variar; **that makes a c.** es toda una novedad; **the c. (of life)** *(menopause)* la menopausia
(b) *(money)* cambio m, vuelta f, *CAm, Méx* sencillo m; **small** *or* **loose c.** (dinero m) suelto m; **have you got c. for a £10 note?** ¿tienes cambio de 10 libras?; **keep the c.** quédese con el cambio *or* las vueltas

**2** vt (a) *(transform)* cambiar; **to c. sth into sth** transformar algo en algo; **to c. one's ways** cambiar de comportamiento; **to c. one's mind/the subject** cambiar de opinión/de tema
(b) *(exchange)* cambiar **(for** por); **to c. one thing for another** cambiar una cosa por otra; **to c. hands** *(of money, car)* cambiar de manos; **to c. trains** hacer transbordo; **to c. places with sb** *(in room)* cambiar el sitio con alguien; *(in job)* ponerse en el lugar de alguien; *Fig* **I wouldn't like to c. places with him** no me gustaría estar en su lugar
(c) *(money)* cambiar; **to c. dollars into**

francs cambiar dólares por francos
(d) **to get changed** cambiarse (de ropa)

**3** vi (a) *(alter)* cambiar; **to c. for the better/worse** cambiar a mejor/peor; **to c. into** *(become)* transformarse en
(b) *(put on other clothes)* cambiarse
(c) *(of passenger)* hacer transbordó

▸**change over** vi cambiarse; **to c. over from sth to sth** cambiar de algo a algo; **to c. over from dictatorship to democracy** pasar de la dictadura a la democracia; **to c. over to another channel** cambiar de canal

**changeable** [ˈtʃeɪndʒəbəl] adj *(person, weather)* variable

**changeless** [ˈtʃeɪndʒlɪs] adj invariable

**changeover** [ˈtʃeɪndʒəʊvə(r)] n transición f **(to** a)

**changing** [ˈtʃeɪndʒɪŋ] adj cambiante

**changing room** [ˈtʃeɪndʒɪŋˈruːm] n vestuario m, vestuarios mpl

**channel** [ˈtʃænəl] **1** n c canal m; **c. of communication** canal m de comunicación; **all enquiries must go through the proper channels** todas las consultas han de seguir los trámites *or* cauces apropiados; **the (English) C.** el Canal de la Mancha; **the C. Islands** las Islas del Canal de la Mancha; **the C. Tunnel** el Eurotúnel

**2** vt *(pt & pp* **channelled,** *US* **channeled)** canalizar

**chant** [tʃɑːnt] **1** n (a) *(of demonstrators, crowd)* consigna f; *(at sports matches)* canción f (coreada) (b) *Rel* canto m

**2** vt & vi corear

**chaos** [ˈkeɪɒs] n caos m inv; **there has been c. on the roads today** hoy el tráfico en las carreteras ha sido infernal; **c. theory** teoría f del caos

**chaotic** [keɪˈɒtɪk] adj caótico(a)

**chap** [tʃæp] n Fam *(man)* tío m; **a good c.** un buen tipo

**chapel** [ˈtʃæpəl] n capilla f

**chaperone** [ˈʃæpərəʊn] **1** n carabina f

**2** vt **to c. sb** acompañar a alguien como carabina

**chaplain** [ˈtʃæplɪn] n Rel capellán m

**chaplaincy** [ˈtʃæplɪnsɪ] n capellanía f

**chapped** [tʃæpt] adj *(lips)* cortado(a); *(skin)* agrietado(a)

**chapter** [ˈtʃæptə(r)] n capítulo m; **c. eight** capítulo ocho; **the holiday was a c. of accidents** las vacaciones consistieron en una sucesión de accidentes; *Fig* **to quote c. and verse for sth** dar pelos y señales en relación con algo

**char¹** [tʃɑː(r)] *(pt & pp* **charred)** vt *(burn)* carbonizar, quemar

**char²** *Br Fam* **1** n *(cleaning lady)* señora f de la limpieza

**2** vi (pt & pp **charred**) (clean) **to c. for sb** trabajar como señora de la limpieza para alguien

**char³** n Br Fam (tea) té m

**character** ['kærɪktə(r)] n (a) (in novel, play) personaje m; **c. actor** = actor especializado en personajes poco convencionales; **c. sketch** descripción f de un personaje, semblanza f (b) (personality) carácter m; **to be in/out of c.** ser/no ser típico de él/ella etc; **to have/lack c.** tener/no tener carácter; **a person of good c.** una persona íntegra; **c. assassination** campaña f de desprestigio; **c. reference** (when applying for job) referencias fpl; Law **c. witness** = testigo que declara en favor del buen carácter del acusado (c) (person) personaje m; **he's quite a c.!** es todo un personaje (d) (letter) carácter m; Comptr **c. set** juego m de caracteres

**characteristic** [kærɪktə'rɪstɪk] **1** n característica f

**2** adj característico(a)

**characterization** [kærɪktəraɪ'zeɪʃən] n caracterización f

**characterize** ['kærɪktəraɪz] vt caracterizar; **I would hardly c. him as naive!** ¡yo no lo definiría como ingenuo, ni mucho menos!

**charade** [ʃə'rɑːd] n (farce) farsa f; **charades** (party game) charada f

**charcoal** ['tʃɑːkəʊl] n carbón m vegetal; **c. drawing** dibujo m al carboncillo; **c. grey** gris m marengo

**charge** [tʃɑːdʒ] **1** n (a) (cost) precio m, tarifa f; **free of c.** gratis; **c. account** cuenta f de crédito; **c. card** tarjeta f de compra (b) Law cargo m; **on a c. of...** acusado(a) de...; **to bring a c. against sb** presentar cargos contra alguien; **c. sheet** pliego m de acusaciones, atestado m policial (c) (responsibility) **to take c. (of)** hacerse cargo (de); **to be in c.** estar a cargo, ser el/la encargado(a) (d) (of explosive) carga f

**2** vt (price) cobrar; **c. it to my account** cárguelo a mi cuenta (b) Law acusar; **to c. sb with a crime** acusar a alguien de un delito (c) Mil (attack) cargar contra, atacar (d) Elec cargar; Fig **a highly charged atmosphere** un ambiente muy tenso

**3** vi (rush) cargar; **he charged in** entró apresuradamente

**chariot** ['tʃærɪət] n (in battles) carro m (de caballos); (in ancient Rome) cuadriga f

**charisma** [kæ'rɪzmə] n carisma m

**charismatic** [kærɪz'mætɪk] adj carismático(a)

**charitable** ['tʃærɪtəbəl] adj (person, action) caritativo(a); (organization, work) benéfico(a), de caridad; **it would be c. to call him misguided** decir que anda descaminado sería demasiado generoso

**charity** ['tʃærɪtɪ] n (a) (quality) caridad f; Prov **c. begins at home** la caridad bien entendida empieza por uno mismo (b) (organization) entidad f benéfica; **all proceeds will go to c.** toda la recaudación se dedicará a obras de beneficencia

**charlady** ['tʃɑːleɪdɪ] n Br señora f de la limpieza

**charlatan** ['ʃɑːlətən] n charlatán(ana) m,f, embaucador(ora) m,f

**Charlie** ['tʃɑːlɪ] n Br Fam **to feel a right** or **proper C.** sentirse tonto(a)

**charm** [tʃɑːm] **1** n (a) (attractiveness) encanto m (b) (spell) hechizo m; **to be under a c.** estar hechizado(a); **it worked like a c.** funcionó a las mil maravillas (c) (talisman) **a lucky c.** un amuleto (de la suerte)

**2** vt hechizar, encantar; **she charmed the money out of him** lo cameló para sacarle dinero; **to lead a charmed life** tener buena estrella

**charmer** ['tʃɑːmə(r)] n **to be a real c.** ser todo cumplidos, ser todo gentileza

**charming** ['tʃɑːmɪŋ] adj encantador(ora)

**charred** [tʃɑːd] adj carbonizado(a)

**chart** [tʃɑːt] **1** n (graph) gráfico m; (map) carta f; **the charts** (pop music) las listas (de éxitos)

**2** vt (on map) hacer un mapa de; Fig **the book charts the rise of fascism** el libro describe el auge del fascismo

**charter** ['tʃɑːtə(r)] **1** n (of town) fuero m; (of university, organization) estatutos mpl; **the UN c.** la carta de las Naciones Unidas; **c. flight** vuelo m chárter

**2** vt (plane, ship) fletar

**chartered accountant** ['tʃɑːtəd-ə'kaʊntənt] n contable mf colegiado(a)

**charwoman** ['tʃɑːwʊmən] n Br señora f de la limpieza

**chary** ['tʃeərɪ] adj (cautious) cauteloso(a); **to be c. of doing sth** mostrarse reacio(a) a la hora de hacer algo

**chase** [tʃeɪs] **1** n (pursuit) persecución f; **to give c. to sb** perseguir a alguien

**2** vt (pursue) perseguir

**3** vi **to c. after sb** perseguir a alguien

▶**chase up** vt sep (person) localizar; (report, information) hacerse con

**chaser** [tʃeɪsə(r)] n (drink) = vasito de licor que se bebe después de la cerveza

**chasm** ['kæzəm] n also Fig abismo m

**chassis** ['ʃæsɪ] n (of car) chasis m inv

**chaste** [tʃeɪst] adj casto(a)

**chasten** ['tʃeɪsən] vt aleccionar

**chastise** [tʃæs'taɪz] vt (tell off) reprender

**chastisement** [tʃæs'taɪzmənt] n castigo m

**chastity** ['tʃæstɪtɪ] n castidad f; **c. belt** cinturón m de castidad

**chat** [tʃæt] **1** *n* charla *f*; **to have a c.** charlar; **c. show** *(on TV)* tertulia *f* televisiva

**2** *vi* (*pt & pp* **chatted**) charlar

▶**chat up** *vt sep Fam* intentar ligar con

**chattel** ['tʃætəl] *n Law* **goods and chattels** bienes *mpl* (muebles)

**chatter** ['tʃætə(r)] **1** *n* cháchara *f*

**2** *vi* parlotear; **my teeth were chattering (with cold/fear)** me rechinaban *or* castañeteaban los dientes (de frío/miedo)

**chatterbox** ['tʃætəbɒks] *n Fam* cotorra *f*

**chatty** ['tʃætɪ] *adj (person)* hablador(ora); *(letter)* desenfadado(a)

**chauffeur** ['ʃəʊfə(r)] **1** *n* chófer *m*

**2** *vt* **we were chauffeured to the airport** el chófer nos llevó al aeropuerto

**chauvinism** ['ʃəʊvɪnɪzəm] *n (sexism)* machismo *m*; *(nationalism)* chovinismo *m*

**chauvinist** ['ʃəʊvɪnɪst] *n (sexist)* machista *m*; *(nationalist)* chovinista *mf*

**cheap** [tʃiːp] **1** *n* **to do sth on the c.** hacer algo en plan barato *or* mirando el dinero

**2** *adj* (**a**) *(inexpensive)* barato(a); **c. rate** tarifa *f* reducida (**b**) *(of little value)* **I feel c.** *(of person)* ¡qué bajo he caído!; **c. and nasty** de chichinabo, de chicha y nabo; **a c. joke/remark** *(tasteless)* un chiste/comentario de mal gusto

**3** *adv Fam* **it was going c.** estaba tirado(a) de precio

**cheapen** ['tʃiːpən] *vt* **to c. oneself** rebajarse

**cheaply** ['tʃiːplɪ] *adv* barato; **to live c.** vivir con poco dinero

**cheapskate** ['tʃiːpskeɪt] *n Fam* roñica *mf*

**cheat** [tʃiːt] **1** *n (dishonest person)* tramposo(a) *m,f*; *(deception, trick)* trampa *f*; **that's a c.** eso es trampa

**2** *vt* engañar; **he cheated her out of the money** le estafó todo el dinero

**3** *vi (in game)* hacer trampa; *(in exam)* copiar

▶**cheat on** *vt insep (be unfaithful to)* engañar

**cheating** ['tʃiːtɪŋ] *n (in game)* trampas *fpl*; *(in exam)* copieteo *m*; **that's c.!** ¡eso es trampa!

**check¹** [tʃek] **1** *n* (**a**) *(inspection)* control *m*, inspección *f*; **to keep a c. on sb/sth** llevar un control de alguien/algo; **the police ran a c. on her** la policía investigó sus antecedentes (**b**) *(restraint)* **to keep sth/sb in c.** mantener algo/a alguien a raya *or* bajo control; *Pol* **checks and balances** controles *mpl* (**c**) *(in chess)* jaque *m*; **to put sb in c.** poner en jaque a alguien (**d**) *US (cheque)* cheque *m*; *(restaurant bill)* cuenta *f*

**2** *vt* (**a**) *(verify, examine) (information, statement)* comprobar, verificar; *(passport, ticket)* revisar; **to c. that…** comprobar que… (**b**) *(restrain) (inflation, enemy advance)* frenar; *(emotion, impulse)* contener, reprimir; **to c. oneself** contenerse

**3** *vi (verify)* comprobar; **to c. on sth** compro-

bar algo; **to c. on sb** controlar *or* vigilar a alguien; **to c. with sb** preguntar a alguien

**check²** *n (pattern)* cuadros *mpl*; **a jacket in broad c.** una chaqueta a cuadros grandes

▶**check in 1** *vi (at hotel)* registrarse; *(at airport)* facturar

**2** *vt sep (baggage)* facturar

▶**check out 1** *vt sep (investigate) (person)* investigar; *(information)* comprobar, verificar; *Fam (look at)* mirar, echar un ojo a

**2** *vi (leave hotel)* dejar el hotel

▶**check up** *vi* asegurarse, cerciorarse; **to c. up on sb** hacer averiguaciones sobre alguien

**checkers** ['tʃekəz] *npl US* damas *fpl*

**check-in** ['tʃekɪn] *n Av* facturación *f*; **c. (desk)** mostrador *m* de facturación; **c. time =** hora a la que hay que facturar

**checkmate** ['tʃekmeɪt] **1** *n (in chess)* jaque *m* mate

**2** *vt (in chess)* dar jaque mate a; *Fig (opponent)* poner fuera de combate

**checkout** ['tʃekaʊt] *n (in supermarket)* (mostrador *m* de) caja *f*

**checkpoint** ['tʃekpɔɪnt] *n* control *m*

**checkup** ['tʃekʌp] *n Med* revisión *f* (médica), chequeo *m* (médico)

**cheek** [tʃiːk] **1** *n* (**a**) *(of face)* mejilla *f*; **to dance c. to c.** bailar muy agarrados; **c. by jowl (with sb)** hombro con hombro (con alguien); *Fig* **to turn the other c.** poner la otra mejilla (**b**) *(buttock)* nalga *f* (**c**) *Fam (impudence)* cara *f*, caradura *f*; **he's got a c.!** ¡vaya caradura!

**2** *vt Fam (be impudent to)* ser descarado(a) con

**cheekbone** ['tʃiːkbəʊn] *n* pómulo *m*

**cheeky** ['tʃiːkɪ] *adj Fam* descarado(a)

**cheep** [tʃiːp] *vi (of birds)* piar

**cheer** [tʃɪə(r)] **1** *n* (**a**) *(shout) (of crowd)* ovación *f*; *(of single person)* grito *m* de entusiasmo; **three cheers for Gemma!** ¡tres hurras por Gemma! (**b**) *Fam* **cheers!** *(when drinking)* ¡salud!; *(goodbye)* ¡chao!; *(thanks)* ¡gracias! (**c**) *Literary (mood)* **to be of good c.** estar de buen humor

**2** *vt (applaud)* aclamar, vitorear; *(make happier)* animar

**3** *vi (shout)* lanzar vítores, gritar de entusiasmo

▶**cheer on** *vt sep (support)* animar, vitorear

▶**cheer up 1** *vt sep (person)* animar; *(room)* alegrar

**2** *vi* animarse; **c. up!** ¡anímate!

**cheerful** ['tʃɪəfʊl] *adj* alegre

**cheerfully** ['tʃɪəfʊlɪ] *adv* alegremente; *Fam* **I could c. strangle him!** ¡lo estrangularía con sumo gusto!

**cheerily** ['tʃɪərɪlɪ] *adv* jovialmente

**cheerio** [tʃɪərɪ'əʊ] *exclam* ¡chao!

**cheerleader** ['tʃɪəliːdə(r)] *n* animadora *f*

**cheerless** ['tʃɪəlɪs] *adj* triste, sombrío(a)

**cheery** ['tʃɪərɪ] *adj* jovial, alegre

**cheese** [tʃiːz] *n* queso *m*; *Fam* **(say) c.!** *(for photograph)* ¡di patata!; **c. sandwich/omelette** sandwich *m*/tortilla *f* de queso
▸**cheese off** *vt sep Fam* **to be cheesed off (with)** estar hasta las narices (de)

**cheeseboard** ['tʃiːzbɔːd] *n (selection)* tabla *f* de quesos

**cheeseburger** ['tʃiːzbɜːgə(r)] *n* hamburguesa *f* de *or* con queso

**cheesecake** ['tʃiːzkeɪk] *n* tarta *f* de queso

**cheetah** ['tʃiːtə] *n* guepardo *m*

**chef** [ʃef] *n* chef *m*, jefe(a) *m,f* de cocina

**chemical** ['kemɪkəl] **1** *n* producto *m* químico
**2** *adj* químico(a); **c. warfare** guerra *f* química; **c. weapons** armas *fpl* químicas

**chemist** ['kemɪst] *n* **(a)** *Br (pharmacist)* farmacéutico(a) *m,f*; **c.'s (shop)** farmacia *f* **(b)** *(scientist)* químico(a) *m,f*

**chemistry** ['kemɪstrɪ] *n* química *f*; *Fig* **there was a certain c. between them** entre ambos había una cierta química

**chemotherapy** ['kiːməʊ'θerəpɪ] *n Med* quimioterapia *f*

**cheque** [tʃek] *n Fin* cheque *m*, talón *m*; **to make out** *or* **write a c. (to sb)** extender un cheque *or* talón (a alguien); **a c. for £50** un cheque de 50 libras; **c. card** = tarjeta que avala los cheques

**chequebook** ['tʃekbʊk] *n* talonario *m* (de cheques)

**chequered** ['tʃekəd] *adj (pattern)* a cuadros; *Fig* **she's had a somewhat c. career** su trayectoria ha estado llena de altibajos

**cherish** ['tʃerɪʃ] *vt (person)* querer, tener mucho cariño a; *(possessions)* apreciar; *(hopes, illusion)* albergar; *(memory)* atesorar

**cherry** ['tʃerɪ] *n (fruit)* cereza *f*; **c. orchard** cerezal *m*; **c. tree** cerezo *m*

**cherub** ['tʃerəb] *(pl* **cherubs** *or* **cherubim** ['tʃerəbɪm]) *n* querubín *m*

**chess** [tʃes] *n* ajedrez *m*; **a game of c.** una partida de ajedrez; **c. player** ajedrecista *mf*, jugador(ora) *m,f* de ajedrez

**chessboard** ['tʃesbɔːd] *n* tablero *m* de ajedrez

**chessman** ['tʃesmæn], **chesspiece** ['tʃespiːs] *n* pieza *f* (de ajedrez)

**chest** [tʃest] *n* **(a)** *(of person)* pecho *m*; *Fig* **I needed to get it off my c.** necesitaba desahogarme **(b)** *(box)* baúl *m*; **c. of drawers** cómoda *f*

**chestnut** ['tʃesnʌt] **1** *n (nut)* castaña *f*; *(tree, wood)* castaño *m*; **horse c. (tree)** castaño de Indias; *Fam* **an old c.** un chiste viejísimo
**2** *adj (hair, horse)* castaño(a)

**chew** [tʃuː] *vt* masticar; **to c. one's nails** morderse las uñas
▸**chew over** *vt sep Fam* rumiar

**chewing gum** ['tʃuːɪŋˈɡʌm] *n* chicle *m*

**chewy** ['tʃuːɪ] *adj (meat, bread)* correoso(a); *(sweet)* gomoso(a), correoso(a)

**chic** [ʃiːk] *adj* chic, elegante

**Chicago** [ʃɪ'kɑːgəʊ] *n* Chicago

**Chicana** [tʃɪ'kɑːnə] *n US* chicana *f*

**Chicano** [tʃɪ'kɑːnəʊ] *n US* chicano *m*

**chick** [tʃɪk] *n* **(a)** *(young bird)* polluelo *m*; *(young chicken)* pollito *m* **(b)** *Fam (woman)* nena *f*, piba *f*

**chicken** ['tʃɪkɪn] **1** *n* **(a)** *(bird)* gallina *f*; *(meat)* pollo *m*; *Prov* **don't count your chickens before they are hatched** no cantes victoria antes de tiempo; **c. feed** *(food)* grano *m*; *Fam Fig (insignificant sum)* calderilla *f* **(b)** *Fam (coward)* gallina *mf*
**2** *adj Fam (cowardly) (action)* cobarde; **to be c.** ser un/una gallina
▸**chicken out** *vi Fam* amilanarse, acoquinarse; **to c. out of (doing) sth** amilanarse ante (la idea de hacer) algo

**chickenpox** ['tʃɪkɪnpɒks] *n* varicela *f*

**chickpea** ['tʃɪkpiː] *n* garbanzo *m*

**chicory** ['tʃɪkərɪ] *n* achicoria *f*

**chide** [tʃaɪd] *(pt* **chided** *or* **chid** [tʃɪd], *pp* **chided** *or* **chidden** ['tʃɪdən]) *vt Literary* reprender, regañar

**chief** [tʃiːf] **1** *n (of tribe)* jefe(a) *m,f*; *Fam* **the c.** *(boss)* el/la jefe(a)
**2** *adj (most important)* principal; *Com* **c. executive** director(ora) *m,f* gerente, consejero(a) *m,f* delegado(a)

**chiefly** ['tʃiːflɪ] *adv* principalmente

**chieftain** ['tʃiːftən] *n (of clan)* jefe *m* (del clan)

**chiffon** ['ʃɪfɒn] *n* gasa *f*; **c. scarf** fular *m*

**chihuahua** [tʃɪ'wɑwɑ] *n* (perro *m*) chihuahua *m*

**chilblain** ['tʃɪlbleɪn] *n* sabañón *m*

**child** [tʃaɪld] *(pl* **children** ['tʃɪldrən]) *n* niño(a) *m,f*; *(son)* hijo *m*; *(daughter)* hija *f*; **they have three children** tienen tres hijos; **it's c.'s play** es un juego de niños; **children's literature** literatura *f* infantil; **c. abuse** = malos tratos y/o agresión sexual a menores; **c. benefit** ayuda *f* familiar por hijos; **c. labour** trabajo *m* de menores; **c. minder** niñero(a) *m,f*, canguro *mf*

**child-bearing** ['tʃaɪldbeərɪŋ] *n* maternidad *f*; **of c. age** en edad de tener hijos

**childbirth** ['tʃaɪldbɜːθ] *n* parto *m*; **to die in c.** morir al dar a luz, morir en el parto

**childcare** ['tʃaɪldkeə(r)] *n* cuidado *m* de menores *o* niños

**childhood** ['tʃaɪldhʊd] *n* infancia *f*

**childish** ['tʃaɪldɪʃ] *adj Pej* pueril, infantil

**childless** ['tʃaɪldlɪs] *adj* **to be c.** no tener hijos; **a c. couple** una pareja sin hijos

**childlike** ['tʃaɪldlaɪk] adj (innocence) infantil; (appearance) aniñado(a)

**childproof** ['tʃaɪldpruːf] adj c. bottle = botella que los niños no pueden abrir; c. lock (in car) cierre m de seguridad a prueba de niños

**children** ['tʃɪldrən] pl of child

**Chile** ['tʃɪli] n Chile

**Chilean** ['tʃɪlɪən] n & adj chileno(a) m,f

**chill** [tʃɪl] 1 n (a) Med (cold) resfriado m; to catch a c. coger un resfriado (b) (cold temperature) there's a c. in the air hace bastante fresco; to take the c. off sth templar algo; Fig c. of fear escalofrío m de temor
2 adj frío(a)
3 vt (wine, food) poner a enfriar; serve chilled (on product) sírvase frío; chilled to the bone helado(a) de frío
►chill out vi Fam estar tranqui, relajarse

**chilli** ['tʃɪli] n c. (pepper) guindilla f, chile m, CSur ají m; c. (con carne) = guiso picante de carne picada y alubias rojas; c. powder guindilla or chile en polvo

**chilling** ['tʃɪlɪŋ] adj (frightening) escalofriante

**chilly** ['tʃɪli] adj (a) (cold) frío(a); it's a bit c. out hace bastante fresco fuera (b) (unfriendly) frío(a)

**chime** [tʃaɪm] 1 n (of bells) carillón m; (of clock) campanada f
2 vt the clock chimed nine o'clock el reloj dio las nueve
3 vi (of clock) dar la hora; (of bells) repicar
►chime in vi Fam (in conversation) meter baza; they all chimed in at once se pusieron todos a hablar a la vez

**chimney** ['tʃɪmnɪ] (pl chimneys) n chimenea f; Fam to smoke like a c. (of person) fumar como un carretero; c. sweep deshollinador(ora) m,f

**chimneypot** ['tʃɪmnɪpɒt] n (cañón m exterior de) chimenea f

**chimpanzee** [tʃɪmpæn'ziː], Fam **chimp** [tʃɪmp] n chimpancé m

**chin** [tʃɪn] n mentón m, barbilla f; Fig to keep one's c. up mantener los ánimos

**China** ['tʃaɪnə] n China

**china** ['tʃaɪnə] n porcelana f; c. clay caolín m

**Chinese** [tʃaɪ'niːz] 1 n (a) (person) chino(a) m,f (b) (language) chino m
2 npl the C. los chinos
3 adj chino(a)

**chink**[1] [tʃɪŋk] n (gap) resquicio m; Fig to find a c. in sb's armour encontrar el punto flaco de alguien

**chink**[2] 1 n (sound) tintineo m
2 vt (glasses) entrechocar
3 vi tintinear

**chintz** [tʃɪnts] n (textile) cretona f satinada

**chinwag** ['tʃɪnwæg] n Fam to have a c. charlar

**chip** [tʃɪp] 1 n (a) (of wood) viruta f; (of marble) lasca f; (out of plate, cup) mella f, desportilladura f; chocolate chips trozos mpl de chocolate (b) (food) chips Br patatas fpl fritas; US patatas fpl fritas (de bolsa); Br c. shop = tienda que vende comida para llevar, especialmente pescado frito con patatas fritas (c) (in card games) ficha f (d) Comptr chip m, pastilla f (e) (idioms) he's a c. off the old block de tal palo, tal astilla; to have a c. on one's shoulder (about sth) tener complejo (por algo); Fam when the chips are down en los momentos difíciles; Fam he's had his chips ya ha tenido su oportunidad
2 vt (pt & pp chipped) (a) (cut at) tallar; (damage) (knife) mellar; (plate) mellar, desportillar; (furniture) astillar; to c. one's tooth mellarse un diente (b) (in football) (ball) picar; (in golf) dar un golpe corto con la cucharilla a
3 vi (of plate, cup) mellarse, desportillarse
►chip in vi Fam (in collection of money) poner algo (de dinero); to c. in with a suggestion (in discussion) aportar alguna sugerencia

**chipboard** ['tʃɪpbɔːd] n aglomerado m

**chipmunk** ['tʃɪpmʌŋk] n ardilla f listada

**chiropodist** [kɪ'rɒpədɪst] n podólogo(a) m,f

**chiropody** [kɪ'rɒpədɪ] n podología f

**chirp** [tʃɜːp] 1 n (of birds) trino m; (of grasshopper) chirrido m
2 vi (of bird) trinar; (of grasshopper) chirriar

**chirpy** ['tʃɜːpɪ] adj alegre, jovial

**chirrup** ['tʃɪrəp] n = chirp

**chisel** ['tʃɪzəl] 1 n (for wood) formón m; (for stone) cincel m
2 vt (pt & pp chiselled, US chiseled) (a) (in woodwork, sculpture) tallar (b) very Fam (cheat) to c. sb out of his money estafar a alguien

**chit** [tʃɪt] n (note) nota f

**chitchat** ['tʃɪttʃæt] n Fam charla f, cháchara f

**chivalrous** ['ʃɪvəlrəs] adj (courteous behaviour) caballeroso(a)

**chivalry** ['ʃɪvəlrɪ] n (courteous behaviour) caballerosidad f; Hist caballería f

**chives** [tʃaɪvz] npl cebollinos mpl

**chiv(v)y** ['tʃɪvɪ] vt Br Fam to c. sb into doing sth dar la lata a alguien para que haga algo; to c. sb along meter prisa a alguien

**chloride** ['klɔːraɪd] n Chem cloruro m

**chlorinate** ['klɔːrɪneɪt] vt clorar

**chlorine** ['klɔːriːn] n Chem cloro m

**chloroform** ['klɒrəfɔːm] n Chem cloroformo m

**chlorophyl(l)** ['klɒrəfɪl] n Biol clorofila f

**choc-ice** ['tʃɒkaɪs] n bombón m helado (sin palo)

**chock** [tʃɒk] n (for wheel of car, plane) calzo m

**chock-a-block** ['tʃɒkə'blɒk] *adj Fam* abarrotado(a) (**with** de)

**chocolate** ['tʃɒklət] **1** *n* chocolate *m*; **a c.** *(sweet)* un bombón; **bar of c.** tableta *f* de chocolate; **drinking** *or* **hot c.** chocolate a la taza *or* caliente

**2** *adj (made of chocolate)* de chocolate; **c. (coloured)** marrón oscuro, color chocolate

**choice** [tʃɔɪs] **1** *n* (**a**) *(act, thing chosen)* elección *f*; **to make** *or* **take one's c.** elegir, escoger; **by c.** por (propia) elección (**b**) *(alternative)* alternativa *f*, opción *f*; **you have no c. in the matter** no tienes otra opción; **we had no c. but to do it** no tuvimos más remedio que hacerlo (**c**) *(selection)* selección *f*, surtido *m*; **there isn't much c.** no hay mucho donde elegir; **available in a wide c. of colours** disponible en una amplia gama de colores

**2** *adj* (**a**) *(well chosen)* escogido(a); **she used some c. language** *(offensive)* soltó unas cuantas lindezas (**b**) *(food, wine)* selecto(a)

**choir** ['kwaɪə(r)] *n* coro *m*

**choirboy** ['kwaɪəbɔɪ] *n* niño *m* de coro

**choke** [tʃəʊk] **1** *n Aut* estrangulador *m*, estárter *m*

**2** *vt* (**a**) *(strangle)* ahogar, estrangular (**b**) *(block) (sink)* atascar; **the roads were choked with traffic** las carreteras estaban atascadas *or* colapsadas de tráfico

**3** *vi* ahogarse; **she choked on a fish bone** se atragantó con una espina; **to c. with anger** ponerse rojo(a) de ira

▶**choke back** *vt sep (tears, words, anger)* contener

**cholera** ['kɒlərə] *n* cólera *m*

**cholesterol** [kɒ'lestərɒl] *n* colesterol *m*

**choose** [tʃuːz] (*pt* **chose** [tʃəʊz], *pp* **chosen** ['tʃəʊzən]) **1** *vt* elegir, escoger; **to c. to do sth** decidir hacer algo; **there's not much to c. between them** no es fácil escoger entre los dos

**2** *vi* elegir, escoger; **I'll do as I c.** haré lo que me parezca

**choosy** ['tʃuːzɪ] *adj Fam* exigente (**about** con)

**chop** [tʃɒp] **1** *n* (**a**) *(with axe)* hachazo *m*; *Fam* **she got the c.** *(was sacked)* la pusieron de patitas en la calle (**b**) *(of lamb, pork)* chuleta *f*

**2** *vt* (*pt* & *pp* **chopped**) *(wood)* cortar; *(meat)* trocear; *(vegetables)* picar

**3** *vi* **to c. and change** cambiar de idea continuamente

▶**chop down** *vt sep (tree)* derribar, talar

▶**chop off** *vt sep* cortar; **to c. sb's head off** cortarle a alguien la cabeza

**chopper** ['tʃɒpə(r)] *n* (**a**) *(for meat)* tajadera *f*; *(axe)* hacha *f* pequeña (**b**) *Fam (helicopter)* helicóptero *m*

**chopping** ['tʃɒpɪŋ] *n* **c. block** *(butcher's)* tajo *m*, tajadera *f*; **c. board** tabla *f* (para cortar)

**choppy** ['tʃɒpɪ] *adj (sea, lake)* picado(a); **to be c.** estar picado(a)

**chopsticks** ['tʃɒpstɪks] *npl* palillos *mpl*

**choral** ['kɔːrəl] *adj Mus* coral; **c. society** orfeón *m*, coral *f*

**chord** [kɔːd] *n* (**a**) *Mus* acorde *m*; *Fig* **her speech struck a c. with the electorate** su discurso caló hondo en el electorado (**b**) *Math (of arc)* cuerda *f*

**chore** [tʃɔː(r)] *n* **to do the chores** hacer las tareas; **what a c.!** ¡vaya lata!

**choreograph** ['kɒrɪəgræf] *vt* coreografiar

**choreography** [kɒrɪ'ɒgrəfɪ] *n* coreografía *f*

**chorister** ['kɒrɪstə(r)] *n* orfeonista *mf*, miembro *m* de un coro

**chortle** ['tʃɔːtəl] **1** *n* risa *f* placentera

**2** *vi* reírse con placer

**chorus** ['kɔːrəs] **1** *n* *(of song)* estribillo *m*; *(group of singers, actors)* coro *m*; **in c.** a coro; **a c. of protest** un coro de protestas; **c. girl** corista *f*

**2** *vt* corear, decir a coro

**chose** [tʃəʊz] *pt of* **choose**

**chosen** ['tʃəʊzən] **1** *adj* escogido(a); **the c. few** los elegidos

**2** *pp of* **choose**

**Christ** [kraɪst] *n* Cristo; *very Fam* **C. (Almighty)!** ¡joder!

**christen** ['krɪsən] *vt* bautizar

**christening** ['krɪsənɪŋ] *n* bautizo *m*

**Christian** ['krɪstʃən] **1** *n* cristiano(a) *m,f*

**2** *adj* cristiano(a); **C. name** nombre *m* de pila

**Christianity** [krɪstɪ'ænɪtɪ] *n* cristianismo *m*

**Christmas** ['krɪsməs] *n* Navidad *f*, Navidades *fpl*; **at C.** en Navidad; **Merry** *or* **Happy C.!** ¡Feliz Navidad!; **C. cake** = pastel de Navidad a base de frutas; **C. card** crisma *m*; **C. carol** villancico *m*; **C. Day** día *m* de Navidad; **C. dinner** comida *f* de Navidad; **C. Eve** Nochebuena *f*; **C. present** regalo *m* de Navidad; **C. pudding** = pudin con pasas y otras frutas típico de Navidad; **C. tree** árbol *m* de Navidad

**chrome** [krəʊm] *adj* cromado(a)

**chromium** ['krəʊmɪəm] **1** *n Chem* cromo *m*

**2** *adj* de cromo

**chromosome** ['krəʊməsəʊm] *n Biol* cromosoma *m*

**chronic** ['krɒnɪk] *adj* (**a**) *(invalid, ill-health)* crónico(a); **c. unemployment** desempleo *m* crónico, paro *m* estructural (**b**) *Fam (music, food)* chungo(a), de pena

**chronicle** ['krɒnɪkəl] **1** *n* crónica *f*

**2** *vt* relatar, dar cuenta de

**chronological** [krɒnə'lɒdʒɪkəl] *adj* cronológico(a)

**chronology** [krə'nɒlədʒɪ] *n* cronología *f*

**chrysalis** ['krɪsəlɪs] *n Zool* pupa *f*, crisálida *f*

**chrysanthemum** [krɪ'sænθəməm] n crisantemo m

**chubby** ['tʃʌbɪ] adj rechoncho(a); **c.-cheeked** mofletudo(a)

**chuck** [tʃʌk] vt Fam (a) (throw) tirar (b) (finish relationship with) mandar a paseo

►**chuck away** vt sep Fam tirar (a la basura); Fig (opportunity) desperdiciar

►**chuck out** vt sep Fam (throw away) tirar; (eject from pub, house) echar

**chuckle** ['tʃʌkəl] **1** n risita f
**2** vi reírse por lo bajo

**chuffed** [tʃʌft] adj Fam **to be c. about sth** estar encantado(a) con algo

**chug** [tʃʌg] (pt & pp chugged) vi **the train chugged up the hill** el tren resollaba cuesta arriba; Fam **he's still chugging along in the same job** sigue tirando con el mismo trabajo

**chum** [tʃʌm] n Fam amiguete(a) m,f

**chummy** ['tʃʌmɪ] adj Fam **to be c. with sb** ir de amiguete(a) con alguien

**chump** [tʃʌmp] n Fam (a) (foolish person) zoquete mf (b) **to be off one's c.** estar mal de la azotea

**chunk** [tʃʌŋk] n trozo m

**chunky** ['tʃʌŋkɪ] adj Fam (person) cuadrado(a), robusto(a); **a c. pullover** un jersey grueso or gordo

**church** [tʃɜːtʃ] n iglesia f; **to go to c.** ir a misa; **the C. of England** la Iglesia anglicana; **the C. of Scotland** la Iglesia de Escocia; **c. hall** = sala para actividades parroquiales

**churchgoer** ['tʃɜːtʃgəʊə(r)] n **to be a c.** ser cristiano practicante

**churchyard** ['tʃɜːtʃjɑːd] n (burial ground) cementerio m, camposanto m (de iglesia)

**churlish** ['tʃɜːlɪʃ] adj grosero(a)

**churn** [tʃɜːn] **1** n (for making butter) mantequera f; (for milk) lechera f
**2** vt (butter) batir; **the propeller churned up the water** la hélice agitaba el agua
**3** vi **my stomach's churning** (because of nervousness) tengo un nudo en el estómago

►**churn out** vt sep Fam **he churns out four novels a year** escribe como una máquina cuatro novelas al año

**chute** [ʃuːt] n (a) (for parcels, coal) rampa f; (rubbish) c. colector m de basuras (b) (in swimming pool, playground) tobogán m (c) Fam (parachute) paracaídas m inv

**chutney** ['tʃʌtnɪ] n = salsa agridulce y picante a base de fruta

**CIA** ['siːaɪeɪ] n US (abbr **Central Intelligence Agency**) CIA f, Agencia f Central de Inteligencia

**cicada** [sɪ'kɑːdə] n (insect) cigarra f, chicharra f

**CID** ['siːaɪdiː] n Br (abbr **Criminal Investigation Department**) = policía judicial británica

**cider** ['saɪdə(r)] n sidra f; **c. apple** manzana f sidrera; **c. vinegar** vinagre m de sidra

**cigar** [sɪ'gɑː(r)] n (cigarro m) puro m; **c. butt** colilla f de puro

**cigarette** [sɪgə'ret] n cigarrillo m; **c. ash** ceniza f (de cigarrillo); **c. butt** or **end** colilla f; **c. case** pitillera f; **c. holder** boquilla f; **c. lighter** encendedor m, mechero m; **c. machine** máquina f (expendedora) de tabaco; **c. packet** paquete m de tabaco; **c. paper** papel m de fumar

**C-in-C** [siːɪn'siː] n Mil (abbr **Commander in Chief**) comandante m en jefe

**cinch** [sɪntʃ] n Fam **it's a c.** es pan comido

**cinder** ['sɪndə(r)] n **cinders** cenizas fpl; **burnt to a c.** completamente carbonizado(a)

**Cinderella** [sɪndə'relə] n Cenicienta f

**cine** ['sɪnɪ] pref **c. camera** cámara f de cine; **c. film** película f; **c. projector** proyector m de cine

**cinema** ['sɪnəmə] n cine m

**cinematography** [sɪnəmə'tɒgrəfɪ] n fotografía f

**cinnamon** ['sɪnəmən] n canela f

**cipher** ['saɪfə(r)] n (code) clave f, cifra f; Fig **he's a mere c.** es un don nadie

**circa** ['sɜːkə] prep hacia, circa

**circle** ['sɜːkəl] **1** n (a) (shape) círculo m; **to sit in a c.** sentarse en círculo; Fig **we're going round in circles** estamos dándole vueltas a lo mismo (b) (movement) **to come full c.** volver al punto de partida (c) (in theatre) anfiteatro m; **lower/upper c.** primer/segundo anfiteatro (d) (group) círculo m; **c. of friends** círculo de amistades; **in certain circles** en determinados círculos
**2** vt (a) (go round) girar en torno de (b) (surround) rodear
**3** vi (of plane, birds) volar en círculo, hacer círculos

**circuit** ['sɜːkɪt] n (a) (electric) circuito m; **c. breaker** cortacircuitos m inv (b) (in motor racing) circuito m

**circuitous** [sə'kjuːɪtəs] adj (reasoning) enrevesado(a); **we got there by a c. route** dimos muchos rodeos para llegar

**circular** ['sɜːkjʊlə(r)] **1** n (letter, advertisement) circular f
**2** adj (movement, argument) circular

**circulate** ['sɜːkjʊleɪt] **1** vt hacer circular
**2** vi circular; (at party) alternar

**circulation** [sɜːkjʊ'leɪʃən] n (of air, blood, money) circulación f; (of newspaper) tirada f; **for internal c. only** (on document) para uso interno solamente; Med **to have poor c.** tener mala circulación; *Fig* **to be out of c.** *(of person)* estar fuera de la circulación

**circumcise** ['sɜːkəmsaɪz] *vt* circuncidar

**circumcision** [sɜːkəm'sɪʒən] *n* circuncisión *f*; **female c.** ablación *f* del clítoris

**circumference** [sə'kʌmfərəns] *n* circunferencia *f*

**circumflex** ['sɜːkəmfleks] *n* acento *m* circunflejo

**circumlocution** [sɜːkəmlə'kjuːʃən] *n* circunloquio *m*

**circumnavigate** [sɜːkəm'nævɪgeɪt] *vt* circunnavegar

**circumscribe** ['sɜːkəmskraɪb] *vt (limit)* restringir, circunscribir

**circumspect** ['sɜːkəmspekt] *adj* prudente, comedido(a)

**circumstance** ['sɜːkəmstəns] *n (situation)* circunstancia *f*; **in** *or* **under the circumstances** dadas las circunstancias; **in** *or* **under no circumstances** en ningún caso; **due to circumstances beyond our control** debido a circunstancias ajenas a nuestra voluntad

**circumstantial** [sɜːkəm'stænʃəl] *adj* **c. evidence** prueba *f* indiciaria

**circumvent** [sɜːkəm'vent] *vt* eludir

**circus** ['sɜːkəs] *n* circo *m*

**cirrhosis** [sɪ'rəʊsɪs] *n Med* cirrosis *f inv*; **c. of the liver** cirrosis hepática

**CIS** [siːaːr'es] *n (abbr* **Commonwealth of Independent States)** CEI *f*

**cissy** ['sɪsɪ] *n Fam* mariquita *m*

**cistern** ['sɪstən] *n* cisterna *f*

**citadel** ['sɪtədel] *n* ciudadela *f*

**citation** [saɪ'teɪʃən] *n* **(a)** *(from author)* cita *f* **(b)** *Mil* mención *f* (de honor)

**cite** [saɪt] *vt (quote)* citar

**citizen** ['sɪtɪzən] *n* ciudadano(a) *m,f*; **c.'s band (radio)** (radio *f* de) banda *f* ciudadana *or* de radioaficionados

**citizenship** ['sɪtɪzənʃɪp] *n* ciudadanía *f*

**citric acid** ['sɪtrɪk'æsɪd] *n* ácido *m* cítrico

**citrus** ['sɪtrəs] *n* **c. fruit** cítrico *m*

**city** ['sɪtɪ] *n* ciudad *f*; *Br* **the C.** la City (de Londres), = el barrio financiero y bursátil de Londres; **c. centre** centro *m* urbano

**civic** ['sɪvɪk] *adj* cívico(a); **to do one's c. duty** cumplir con la obligación de uno como ciudadano; **c. centre** centro *m* cívico

**civil** ['sɪvəl] *adj* **(a)** *(of society)* civil; **c. aviation** aviación *f* civil; **c. defence** protección *f* civil; **c. disobedience** desobediencia *f* civil; **c. engineering** ingeniería *f* civil; *Law* **c. law** derecho *m* civil; *Law* **c. rights** derechos *mpl* civiles; **c. servant** funcionario(a) *m,f*; **the c. service** la administración (pública), el funcionariado; **c. war** guerra *f* civil **(b)** *(polite)* cortés

**civilian** [sɪ'vɪljən] *n & adj* civil *mf*

**civility** [sɪ'vɪlɪtɪ] *n* cortesía *f*

**civilization** [sɪvɪlaɪ'zeɪʃən] *n* civilización *f*

**civilize** ['sɪvɪlaɪz] *vt* civilizar

**civilized** ['sɪvɪlaɪzd] *adj* civilizado(a)

**cl** *(abbr* **centilitre)** cl, centilitro *m*

**clad** [klæd] **1** *adj* ataviado(a) **(in** de)
**2** *pt & pp of* **clothe**

**claim** [kleɪm] **1** *n* **(a)** *(for damages, compensation)* reclamación *f* **(for** de); **wage c.** reivindicación *f* salarial; **to make** *or* **put in a c.** hacer *or* presentar una reclamación; **to make a c. on the insurance** dar parte al seguro; **I have many claims on my time** estoy muy ocupado; **he has a c. to the throne of France** tiene derechos sobre el trono de Francia; **his only c. to fame** su único título de gloria **(b)** *(assertion)* afirmación *f*; **she makes no c. to originality** no pretende ser original

**2** *vt* **(a)** *(as a right)* reclamar; **to c. compensation/damages (from sb)** reclamar (a alguien) una compensación/daños y perjuicios; **to c. responsibility for sth** atribuirse la responsabilidad de algo **(b)** *(assert)* **to c. that...** afirmar que...; **he claims to be an expert** asegura ser un experto **(c)** *(baggage)* recoger; *(lost property)* reclamar; **the epidemic claimed thousands of lives** la epidemia segó miles de vidas

**claimant** ['kleɪmənt] *n (to throne)* aspirante *mf*, pretendiente *mf*; *Law (for social security)* solicitante *mf*; *(for insurance)* reclamante *mf*

**clairvoyant** [kleə'vɔɪənt] **1** *n* vidente *mf*
**2** *adj* **to be c.** ser clarividente

**clam** [klæm] *n* almeja *f*
►**clam up** *( pt & pp* **clammed)** *vi Fam* meterse uno en su concha, retraerse

**clamber** ['klæmbər] *vi* trepar **(up** *or* **over** por)

**clammy** ['klæmɪ] *adj (weather)* húmedo(a); **his hands were c.** tenía las manos húmedas y frías

**clamorous** ['klæmərəs] *adj (crowd)* vociferante; *(protest, complaint)* vehemente

**clamour** ['klæmə(r)] **1** *n (noise)* griterío *m*, clamor *m*; *(demands)* demandas *fpl* **(for** de); **a c. of protest** una oleada de protestas
**2** *vi (make noise)* clamar; **to c. for sth** *(demand)* clamar por algo

**clamp** [klæmp] **1** *n (of vice)* mordaza *f*, abrazadera *f*; *Aut* **(wheel) c.** cepo *m*
**2** *vt* sujetar **(to** a); *(car)* poner un cepo a
►**clamp down on** *vt insep Fam (people)* tomar medidas contundentes contra; *(tax evasion, violence)* poner coto a

**clampdown** ['klæmpdaʊn] *n* medidas *fpl* contundentes **(on** contra)

**clan** [klæn] *n* clan *m*

**clandestine** [klæn'destɪn] *adj* clandestino(a)

**clang** [klæŋ] **1** *n* ruido *m* metálico, estrépito *m*
**2** *vi (of bell)* repicar; **the gate clanged shut** la verja se cerró con gran estrépito

**clanger** ['klæŋə(r)] *n Fam* metedura *f* de pata, patinazo *m*; **to drop a c.** meter la pata

**clank** ['klæŋk] **1** *n* sonido *m* metálico
**2** *vi* **the chains clanked** las cadenas produjeron un sonido metálico

**clap** [klæp] **1** *n* (a) *(with hands)* **to give sb a c.** aplaudir a alguien (b) *(noise)* **a c. of thunder** el estampido de un trueno (c) *very Fam (venereal disease)* **the c.** gonorrea *f*
**2** *vt (pt & pp **clapped**)* (a) *(applaud)* aplaudir; **to c. one's hands** dar palmadas; **to c. sb on the back** dar a alguien una palmada en la espalda (b) *(put)* **he clapped his hat on** se encasquetó el sombrero; *Fam* **to c. sb in prison** enchironar a alguien; *Fam* **to c. eyes on sth/sb** ver algo/a alguien
**3** *vi (applaud)* aplaudir

**clapped-out** [klæpt'aʊt] *adj Fam (car, machine)* cascado(a); **to be c.** estar cascado(a)

**clapper** ['klæpə(r)] *n (of bell)* badajo *m*; *Fam* **to run like the clappers** correr como un condenado(a)

**clapping** ['klæpɪŋ] *n (applause)* aplausos *mpl*

**claptrap** ['klæptræp] *n Fam* majaderías *fpl*

**claret** ['klærət] *n* burdeos *m inv* (tinto)

**clarification** [klærɪfɪ'keɪʃən] *n* aclaración *f*

**clarify** ['klærɪfaɪ] *vt* aclarar

**clarinet** [klærɪ'net] *n* clarinete *m*

**clarinettist** [klærɪ'netɪst] *n Mus* clarinetista *mf*

**clarity** ['klærɪtɪ] *n* claridad *f*

**clash** [klæʃ] **1** *n (of opinions)* discrepancia *f*; *(between people)* enfrentamiento *m*, choque *m*; **there have been clashes in the streets** ha habido enfrentamientos callejeros
**2** *vi* (a) *(come into conflict)* enfrentarse (**with** con *or* a) (b) *(of evidence, explanations)* contradecirse; **the wallpaper clashes with the carpet** el papel no pega con la moqueta (c) *(of events)* **to c. with** coincidir con (d) *(of metal objects)* entrechocar

**clasp** [klɑːsp] **1** *n (on necklace, handbag)* broche *m*, cierre *m*; **c. knife** navaja *f*
**2** *vt (grasp)* agarrar; *(embrace)* estrechar; **to c. sb's hand** agarrar a alguien de la mano

**class** [klɑːs] **1** *n (in school, category, social group)* clase *f*; **to be in a c. of one's own** constituir una clase aparte; **to have a lot of c.** tener mucha clase; **c. struggle** lucha *f* de clases
**2** *vt (classify)* clasificar (**as** como)

**classic** ['klæsɪk] **1** *adj* clásico(a); **a c. example** un ejemplo típico

**2** *n* (a) *(book)* clásico *m* (b) *Sch Univ* **classics** (lenguas *fpl*) clásicas *fpl*

**classical** ['klæsɪkəl] *adj* clásico(a); **c. music** música *f* clásica

**classification** [klæsɪfɪ'keɪʃən] *n* clasificación *f*

**classified** ['klæsɪfaɪd] **1** *adj* (a) *(secret)* reservado(a) (b) **c. advertisements** *(in newspaper)* anuncios *mpl* por palabras
**2** *n* **the classifieds** *(in newspaper)* los anuncios por palabras

**classify** ['klæsɪfaɪ] *vt* clasificar

**classmate** ['klɑːsmeɪt] *n* compañero(a) *m,f* de clase

**classroom** ['klɑːsruːm] *n* aula *f*, clase *f*

**classy** ['klɑːsɪ] *adj Fam* con clase, elegante

**clatter** ['klætə(r)] **1** *n* ruido *m*, estrépito *m*
**2** *vi* **he clattered up the stairs** subió las escaleras con estrépito; **to c. about** *(of person)* trastear, trapalear

**clause** [klɔːz] *n (of contract)* cláusula *f*; *(of sentence)* oración *f* (simple), cláusula *f*

**claustrophobia** [klɔːstrə'fəʊbɪə] *n* claustrofobia *f*

**claustrophobic** [klɔːstrə'fəʊbɪk] *adj* claustrofóbico(a)

**clavichord** ['klævɪkɔːd] *n Mus* clavicordio *m*

**clavicle** ['klævɪkəl] *n Anat* clavícula *f*

**claw** [klɔː] **1** *n (of animal, bird)* garra *f*; *(of crab, lobster)* pinza *f*; **c. hammer** martillo *m* de carpintero *or* de oreja
**2** *vt (scratch)* arañar; *Fig* **to c. one's way to the top** lograr abrirse paso hasta la cima del éxito

▸**claw back** *vt (money)* recobrar, recuperar

**clay** [kleɪ] *n* arcilla *f*; *Sport* **c. court** *(for tennis)* pista *f* de tierra batida; **c. pigeon** plato *m*; **c. pigeon shooting** tiro *m* al plato

**clean** [kliːn] **1** *n* **to give sth a c.** limpiar algo
**2** *adj* (a) *(not dirty)* limpio(a); **he keeps his flat very c.** tiene su piso muy limpio; **a c. piece of paper** una hoja (de papel) en blanco; **a c. game** un juego limpio; **c. living** vida *f* sana; **to have a c. driving licence** = no tener puntos de penalización en el carné de conducir (b) *(not obscene) (humour, joke)* sano(a); *(language)* correcto(a), sin tacos; **good c. fun** diversión *f* sana (c) *(clear) (shape, outline)* nítido(a); **to make a c. break with** *(separate completely)* romper radicalmente con
**3** *adv* (a) *(completely)* **to cut c. through sth** hacer un corte a través de algo; *Fam* **I c. forgot** me olvidé completamente (b) *Fam* **to come c. (about sth)** decir la verdad *or* sincerarse (acerca de algo)
**4** *vt* limpiar; **to c. one's teeth/hands** limpiarse los dientes/las manos

▶**clean out** *vt sep* (a) *(cupboard, room)* limpiar de arriba abajo (b) *Fam (leave without money)* desplumar

▶**clean up 1** *vt sep* limpiar

**2** *vi* (a) *(tidy up)* ordenar; *(wash oneself)* lavarse (b) *Fam (win money)* arrasar, ganar un pastón

**clean-cut** ['kli:n'kʌt] *adj (features)* nítido(a)

**cleaner** ['kli:nə(r)] *n (person)* limpiador(ora) *m,f*; *(substance)* producto *m* de limpieza; *Fam* **to take sb to the c.'s** *(cheat)* desplumar a alguien

**cleaning** *n* ['kli:nɪŋ] limpieza *f*; **c. lady** mujer *f* or señora *f* de la limpieza

**cleanliness** ['klenlɪnɪs] *n (of place)* limpieza *f*; *(of person)* higiene *f*

**cleanly** ['kli:nlɪ] *adv* limpiamente

**cleanse** [klenz] *vt* limpiar

**cleanser** ['klenzə(r)] *n* loción *f* limpiadora

**clean-shaven** ['kli:n'ʃeɪvən] *adj (man, face)* (bien) afeitado(a); **to be c.** *(just shaved)* estar bien afeitado(a); *(not having a beard)* no tener barba ni bigote

**cleansing lotion** ['klenzɪŋ'ləʊʃən] *n* loción *f* limpiadora

**clear** [klɪə(r)] **1** *adj* (a) *(liquid, image, explanation)* claro(a); *(sky, road)* despejado(a); **all c.!** ¡no hay peligro!; **to be c.** *(of image, explanation)* ser claro(a); *(of sky, road)* estar despejado(a); **to have a c. conscience** tener la conciencia tranquila; **as c. as a bell** *(of voice, sound)* perfectamente audible; **a c. profit** un beneficio neto; **a c. winner** un claro vencedor

(b) *(obvious)* claro(a); **to make it c. to sb that…** dejar bien claro a alguien que…; **it is c. that…** es evidente or está claro que…; **to make oneself c.** expresarse con claridad or claramente; **I wasn't c. what she meant** no me quedó claro lo que quería decir

(c) *(free)* **c. of** *(not touching)* despegado(a) de; *(at safe distance)* alejado(a) de; **when the plane is c. of the ground** cuando el avión haya despegado; *Fig* **they are six points c. of their nearest rivals** les sacan seis puntos a sus inmediatos perseguidores

**2** *adv* **to steer c. of sth/sb** evitar algo/a alguien; **stand c. of the doors!** ¡apártense de las puertas!

**3** *vt* (a) *(road, area)* despejar; **to c. one's throat** carraspear; **to c. the table** recoger la mesa; **to c. a debt** saldar una deuda; **the police cleared the square of demonstrators** la policía despejó la plaza de manifestantes; *Fig* **to c. the decks** ponerse al día y finalizar los asuntos pendientes; *also Fig* **to c. the way (for sth)** abrir el camino (a algo); *Fig* **to c. the air** disipar los malentendidos

(b) *(exonerate)* eximir; *Law* absolver; **to c. sb of blame** eximir de culpa a alguien; **they campaigned to c. his name** hicieron una

campaña para limpiar su nombre

(c) *(jump over)* **to c. a fence** sortear una valla

(d) *(authorize)* autorizar; *(plan, proposals)* aprobar; **we've been cleared for take-off** nos han dado permiso para el despegue; **I'll need to c. it with the boss** necesito el visto bueno del jefe

**4** *vi* (a) *(of weather, sky)* despejarse

(b) *(of cheque)* **the cheque hasn't cleared yet** el cheque no ha sido compensado todavía

**5** *n* **to be in the c.** *(not under suspicion)* estar fuera de sospecha; *(out of danger)* estar fuera de peligro

▶**clear away** *vt sep* quitar (de en medio)

▶**clear off** *vi Br Fam (leave)* largarse; **c. off!** ¡largo!

▶**clear out 1** *vt sep (empty)* limpiar, ordenar

**2** *vi Fam (leave)* largarse

▶**clear up 1** *vt sep* (a) *(room)* ordenar (b) *(doubt, misunderstanding, problem)* aclarar

**2** *vi (of weather)* despejarse

**clearance** ['klɪərəns] *n* (a) *Com* **reduced for c.** rebajado(a) por liquidación (de existencias); **c. sale** liquidación *f* (de existencias) (b) *(authorization)* autorización *f*; **to get c. to do sth** obtener autorización para hacer algo

**clear-cut** ['klɪə'kʌt] *adj* claro(a), inequívoco(a)

**clear-headed** ['klɪə'hedɪd] *adj* lúcido(a)

**clearing** ['klɪərɪŋ] *n (in forest)* claro *m*

**clearing house** ['klɪərɪŋ'haʊs] *n Fin* cámara *f* de compensación

**clearly** ['klɪəlɪ] *adv* (a) *(to see, explain, write)* claramente, con claridad (b) *(obviously)* claramente; **he is c. wrong** está claramente equivocado; **c.!** ¡sin duda!; **c. not!** ¡en absoluto!

**clearness** ['klɪənɪs] *n* claridad *f*

**clearout** ['klɪəraʊt] *n* **I need to give my desk a c.** tengo que limpiar or ordenar mi escritorio

**clear-sighted** [klɪə'saɪtɪd] *adj (perceptive)* lúcido(a), clarividente

**cleavage** ['kli:vɪdʒ] *n* escote *m*

**cleave** [kli:v] *(pt* cleaved *or* cleft [kleft] *or* clove [kləʊv], *pp* cleaved *or* cleft *or* cloven [kləʊvən]) *vt Literary* hendir, partir en dos

▶**cleave to** *(pt & pp* cleaved) *vt insep Formal* aferrarse a

**cleaver** ['kli:və(r)] *n* cuchillo *m* de carnicero, tajadera *f*

**clef** [klef] *n Mus* clave *f*

**cleft** [kleft] **1** *n* grieta *f*, hendidura *f*

**2** *adj* hendido(a); **to have a c. palate** tener fisura de paladar; **to be caught in a c. stick** *(in awkward situation)* estar entre la espada y la pared

**3** *pt & pp of* **cleave**

**clemency** ['klemənsɪ] *n* clemencia *f*

**clementine** ['klemənti:n] *n* clementina *f*

**clench** [klentʃ] *vt (teeth, fist)* apretar

**clergy** ['klɜ:dʒɪ] *n* clero *m*

**clergyman** ['klɜ:dʒɪmən] *n* clérigo *m*

**cleric** ['klerɪk] *n Rel* clérigo *m*

**clerical** ['klerɪkəl] *adj* (a) *(administrative)* c. assistant auxiliar *mf* administrativo(a); c. work trabajo *m* de oficina (b) *Rel* clerical

**clerk** [klɑ:k, *US* klɜ:rk] *n (in office)* oficinista *mf; (in court)* oficial(ala) *m,f*, secretario(a) *m,f*

**clever** ['klevə(r)] *adj (person, animal)* listo(a); *(plan, idea)* ingenioso(a); **she's very c. at mathematics** se le dan muy bien las matemáticas; **to be c. with one's hands** ser un/una manitas; *Fam* **she's too c. by half** se pasa de lista; *Fam* **a c. Dick** un listillo

**cleverly** ['klevəlɪ] *adv (intelligently)* inteligentemente; *(ingeniously)* ingeniosamente

**cleverness** ['klevənɪs] *n (of person, plan)* inteligencia *f*

**cliché** ['kli:ʃeɪ] *n* tópico *m*

**click** ['klɪk] **1** *n (sound) (of button)* clic *m; (of fingers, tongue)* chasquido *m*

**2** *vt* **to c. one's heels** dar un taconazo; **to c. one's tongue** chasquear la lengua

**3** *vi* (a) *(make a sound)* hacer clic (b) *Fam (idioms)* **suddenly it clicked** *(became obvious to me)* de pronto caí en la cuenta; **they clicked at once** *(got on)* se entendieron desde el primer momento

**client** ['klaɪənt] *n* cliente(a) *m,f*; **c. state** estado *m* satélite

**clientele** [kli:ɒn'tel] *n* clientela *f*

**cliff** [klɪf] *n* acantilado *m*

**cliffhanger** ['klɪfhæŋə(r)] *n* **the film was a real c.** la película tenía mucho suspense

**climactic** [klaɪ'mæktɪk] *adj* culminante

**climate** ['klaɪmət] *n* clima *m*

**climatic** [klaɪ'mætɪk] *adj* climático(a)

**climax** ['klaɪmæks] **1** *n (peak)* clímax *m inv*, momento *m* culminante; *(sexual)* orgasmo *m*

**2** *vi* culminar

**climb** [klaɪm] **1** *n (up hill)* ascensión *f*, subida *f; (of mountaineer)* escalada *f*; **it's quite a c.** hay una buena subida

**2** *vt (tree)* subir a, trepar a; *(mountain)* escalar

**3** *vi (of road, prices)* subir; **to c. over a wall** trepar por un muro

**▸climb down 1** *vt insep (descend)* bajar por

**2** *vi* (a) *(descend)* descender, bajar (b) *Fig (in argument, conflict)* echarse atrás, dar marcha atrás

**climber** ['klaɪmə(r)] *n* (a) *(mountaineer)* alpinista *mf*, escalador(ora) *m,f* (b) *(plant)* (planta *f*) trepadora *f*

**climbing** ['klaɪmɪŋ] **1** *n (mountaineering)* escalada *f*, alpinismo *m*; **c. frame** = en los parques, estructura de hierro o madera para que trepen

los niños

**2** *adj (plant)* trepador(ora)

**clinch** [klɪntʃ] **1** *n (of lovers, fighters)* abrazo *m*; **they were in a c.** estaban abrazados

**2** *vt (settle) (deal)* cerrar; *(argument)* zanjar; **that clinches it!** ¡eso lo resuelve del todo!

**cling** [klɪŋ] *(pt & pp* clung [klʌŋ]) *vi* **to c. to** *(rope, person)* aferrarse a; *Fig* **to c. to an opinion** aferrarse a una idea

**clingfilm** ['klɪŋfɪlm] *n* plástico *m* transparente *(para envolver alimentos)*

**clinic** ['klɪnɪk] *n* clínica *f*

**clinical** ['klɪnɪkəl] *adj* (a) *Med* clínico(a) (b) *(unemotional)* aséptico(a)

**clink**[1] [klɪŋk] **1** *n (sound)* tintineo *m*

**2** *vt* hacer tintinear; **to c. glasses (with sb)** brindar (con alguien)

**3** *vi (of glasses)* tintinear

**clink**[2] *n very Fam (prison)* trullo *m*, chirona *f*

**clip**[1] [klɪp] **1** *n (for paper)* clip *m*, sujetapapeles *m inv*

**2** *vt (pt & pp* clipped) *(attach)* sujetar (con un clip)

**3** *vi* **the two pieces c. together** las dos piezas se acoplan

**clip**[2] **1** *n* (a) *Fam (blow)* **to give sb a c. on the ear** darle a alguien un cachete en la oreja (b) *(of film)* fragmento *m; (of programme)* avance *m*

**2** *(pt & pp* clipped) *vt (hair)* cortar; *(hedge)* podar; *(ticket)* picar; *Fig* **to c. sb's wings** cortar las alas a alguien

**clipboard** ['klɪpbɔ:d] *n* carpeta *f* con sujetapapeles

**clip-on** ['klɪpɒn] *adj* **c. bow tie** pajarita *f* (de broche); **c. earrings** pendientes *mpl* de clip; **c. microphone** micrófono *m* de solapa; **c. sunglasses** suplemento *m* (de sol), = gafas de sol para ponerse sobre las gafas graduadas

**clipped** [klɪpt] *adj (accent, tone)* entrecortado(a)

**clipper** ['klɪpə(r)] *n (ship)* clíper *m*

**clippers** ['klɪpəz] *npl (for hair)* maquinilla *f (para cortar el pelo); (for nails)* cortaúñas *m inv; (for hedge)* podadera *f*, tijeras *fpl* de podar

**clipping** ['klɪpɪŋ] *n (from newspaper)* recorte *m*

**clique** [kli:k] *n* camarilla *f*, círculo *m*

**clitoris** ['klɪtərɪs] *n* clítoris *m inv*

**cloak** [kləʊk] **1** *n* capa *f*; *Fig* **under the c. of darkness** bajo el manto de la oscuridad

**2** *vt Fig* **cloaked in secrecy** rodeado(a) de secreto

**cloak-and-dagger** [kləʊkən'dægər] *adj (film, book)* de intriga; **a c. affair** un asunto lleno de intrigas

**cloakroom** ['kləʊkru:m] *n* guardarropa *m*

**clobber**[1] ['klɒbə(r)] *n Br very Fam (clothes)* trapos *mpl*, ropa *f; (belongings)* trastos *mpl*

**clobber²** vt Fam (hit) sacudir; (defeat) dar una paliza a

**clock** [klɒk] 1 n (a) (for telling the time) reloj m (grande o de pared); **to work round the c.** trabajar día y noche; **a race against the c.** una carrera contrarreloj; **to put the c. forward/back** adelantar/atrasar el reloj; Fig **to turn the c. back** retroceder en el tiempo; **c. radio** radio f despertador (b) Fam (milometer) cuentakilómetros m inv

2 vt (measure speed of) medir la velocidad de; (reach speed of) alcanzar

►**clock in** vi (at work) fichar (a la entrada)

►**clock off** vi (at work) fichar (a la salida)

►**clock on** = **clock in**

►**clock out** = **clock off**

►**clock up** vt sep (votes, profits) registrar; **this car has clocked up 10,000 miles** este coche marca 10.000 millas

**clockmaker** ['klɒkmeɪkə(r)] n relojero(a) m,f

**clockwise** ['klɒkwaɪz] adv en el sentido de las agujas del reloj

**clockwork** ['klɒkwɜːk] 1 n **to go like c.** marchar a la perfección

2 adj (toy) mecánico(a)

**clod** [klɒd] n (of earth) terrón m

**clog** [klɒg] 1 n (shoe) zueco m

2 vt bloquear, atascar

3 vi (pt & pp **clogged**) bloquearse, atascarse

►**clog up 1** vt bloquear, atascar

2 vi bloquearse, atascarse

**cloister** ['klɔɪstə(r)] n claustro m

**cloistered** ['klɔɪstəd] adj **to lead a c. life** no tener mucha relación con el mundo exterior

**clone** [kləʊn] 1 n clon m

2 vt Biol clonar

**close¹** [kləʊs] 1 adj (a) (in distance, time, relationship) cercano(a), próximo(a); (contact, links, cooperation) estrecho(a); **to be c. to** estar cerca de; **in c. proximity to** muy cerca de; **to be in c. contact with sb** tener mucho contacto con alguien; **a c. friend** un amigo íntimo; **a c. relative** un pariente cercano or próximo; **c. combat** combate m cuerpo a cuerpo; **that was a c. call** or **shave** ha faltado un pelo; **at c. quarters** de cerca; **he was shot at c. range** le disparon a quemarropa

(b) (inspection, attention) cuidadoso(a); (observer) atento(a); **to keep a c. watch on sth/sb** vigilar de cerca algo/a alguien

(c) (weather) bochornoso(a); (room) cargado(a)

(d) (contest, election) reñido(a)

2 n (cul-de-sac) callejón m

3 adv (near) cerca; **to hold sb c.** abrazar a alguien fuerte; **c. to** cerca de; **he lives c. to here** vive cerca de aquí; **to be c. to tears/victory** estar a punto de llorar/vencer; **to**

**come c. to death** estar a punto de morir; **to be c. to sb** (of friends) tener mucha confianza con alguien; (of relatives) estar muy unido(a) a alguien; **c. at hand** a mano; **to follow c. behind sb** seguir de cerca a alguien; **to be c. on fifty** estar cerca de los cincuenta

**close²** [kləʊz] 1 n (end) final m; **to draw to a c.** tocar or llegar a su fin; **to bring sth to a c.** poner término a or dar por terminado(a) algo

2 vt (a) (door, eyes, shop) cerrar; Fig **to c. ranks (around sb)** cerrar filas (en torno a alguien) (b) (meeting, debate) terminar; (conference, Olympics) clausurar; (account) cancelar; **to c. a deal** cerrar un trato

3 vi (of shop, door, business) cerrar

►**close down 1** vt sep (production, operations) cesar; (business, factory) cerrar (definitivamente)

2 vi (of business) cerrar (definitivamente); **Channel 6 closes down at midnight** el Canal 6 cierra su emisión a medianoche

►**close in** vi (of night) acercarse; **to c. in on sb** ir cercando a alguien

►**close up 1** vi (a) (of wound, hole) cerrarse (b) (of shopkeeper) cerrar

2 vt sep (hole, shop) cerrar

**close-cropped** ['kləʊs'krɒpt] adj (hair) al rape

**closed** [kləʊzd] adj cerrado(a); **c. circuit television** circuito m cerrado de televisión; **behind c. doors** a puerta cerrada; Ind **c. shop** = centro de trabajo que emplea exclusivamente a trabajadores sindicados

**close-fitting** [kləʊs'fɪtɪŋ] adj ajustado(a)

**close-knit** [kləʊs'nɪt] adj (community, group) muy unido(a)

**closely** ['kləʊslɪ] adv (a) (to examine, watch) de cerca; **to listen c.** escuchar atentamente; **to c. resemble sb** parecerse mucho a alguien; **c. related/connected** íntimamente relacionado(a)/conectado(a); **c. contested** muy reñido(a) (b) (populated) densamente; **c. packed** apiñado(a)

**closeness** ['kləʊsnɪs] n (physical nearness) proximidad f, cercanía f; (of relationship, contact) intimidad f

**close-run** ['kləʊsrʌn] adj (election, race) reñido(a)

**close-set** ['kləʊs'set] adj **to have c. eyes** tener los ojos muy juntos

**closet** ['klɒzɪt] 1 n (cupboard) armario m; Fig **to come out of the c.** declararse homosexual públicamente

2 adj **c. gay** homosexual m no declarado; **she's a c. Julio Iglesias fan** le encanta Julio Iglesias, pero nunca lo confesaría

3 vt **to be closeted with sb** (in meeting) estar encerrado(a) con alguien

**close-up** ['kləʊsʌp] n primer plano m; **in c.** en primer plano

**closing** ['kləʊzɪŋ] n (shutting) cierre m; **c. date** fecha f límite; **c. prices** cotizaciones fpl al cierre; **c. speech/ceremony** discurso m/ ceremonia f de clausura; **c. time** hora f de cierre

**closure** ['kləʊʒə(r)] n (of company, shop) cierre m

**clot** [klɒt] **1** n (a) (of blood) coágulo m (b) Fam (stupid person) memo(a) m,f, lerdo(a) m,f

   **2** vi (pt & pp **clotted**) (of blood) coagularse

**cloth** [klɒθ] n (a) (material) tela f, tejido m; **a man of the c.** un ministro de Dios (b) (individual piece) trapo m

**clothe** [kləʊð] (pt & pp **clad** [klæd] or **clothed**) vt vestir

**clothes** [kləʊðz] npl ropa f; **to put one's c. on** vestirse, ponerse la ropa; **to take one's c. off** quitarse la ropa, desvestirse; **c. brush** cepillo m para la ropa; **c. hanger** percha f; **c. horse** tendedero m (plegable); **c. line** cuerda f de tender la ropa; **c. peg** pinza f de la ropa

**clothing** ['kləʊðɪŋ] n (clothes) ropa f; **an article of c.** una prenda de vestir; **the c. industry** la industria del vestido

**cloud** [klaʊd] **1** n nube f; **to be under a c.** (in disgrace) haber caído en desgracia; **to have one's head in the clouds** estar en Babia; Fam **she is on c. nine** está más contenta que unas castañuelas

   **2** vt (a) (mirror) empañar (b) (obscure) **the news clouded their happiness** las noticias enturbiaron su alegría; **to c. the issue** embrollar las cosas

▸**cloud over** vi (of sky) nublarse

**cloudburst** ['klaʊdbɜːst] n chaparrón m

**cloudless** ['klaʊdlɪs] adj despejado(a)

**cloudy** ['klaʊdɪ] adj (a) (sky, day) nublado(a) (b) (liquid) turbio(a)

**clout** [klaʊt] **1** n (a) Fam (blow) tortazo m, sopapo m; **to give sb a c.** dar a alguien un tortazo or sopapo (b) (power, influence) poder m, influencia f; **to have a lot of c.** ser muy influyente

   **2** vt Fam (hit) sacudir, atizar

**clove**[1] [kləʊv] n (of garlic) diente m de ajo

**clove**[2] n (spice) clavo m

**cloven** ['kləʊvən] **1** adj **c. hoof** pata f hendida

   **2** pp of **cleave**

**clover** ['kləʊvə(r)] n (plant) trébol m; Fig **to be in c.** vivir a cuerpo de rey

**clown** [klaʊn] **1** n (in circus) payaso m; **to act the c.** hacer el payaso

   **2** vi **to c. about** or **around** hacer el payaso

**cloying** ['klɔɪɪŋ] adj (taste, smell) empalagoso(a)

**club** [klʌb] **1** n (a) (society) club m; Fam Fig **join the c.!** ¡ya eres uno más!; **football/tennis c.** club de fútbol/tenis (b) (nightclub) discoteca f, sala f (de fiestas) (c) (weapon) palo m, garrote m (d) (in golf) palo m (e) (in cards) **clubs** tréboles mpl; **ace of clubs** as m de tréboles

   **2** vt (pt & pp **clubbed**) (hit) apalear

▸**club together** vi **to c. together (to buy sth)** poner dinero a escote (para comprar algo)

**clubhouse** ['klʌbhaʊs] n = en unas instalaciones de golf, edificio en el que se encuentran los vestuarios y el bar

**cluck** [klʌk] **1** n cacareo m

   **2** vi cacarear

**clue** [kluː] n (in crime, mystery) pista f; (in crossword) definición f, pregunta f; **to give sb a c.** dar una pista a alguien; **he hasn't got a c.** no tiene ni idea

▸**clue up** vt sep Fam **to be clued up (on sth)** estar muy puesto(a) (en algo)

**clueless** ['kluːlɪs] adj Fam **to be c. (about)** ser (un(a)) negado(a) (para)

**clump** [klʌmp] **1** n (a) (of bushes) mata f, (of people) grupo m (b) (sound) **the c. of her footsteps** el ruido de sus pisotones

   **2** vi **to c. about** andar dando pisotones

**clumsiness** ['klʌmzɪnɪs] n torpeza f

**clumsy** ['klʌmzɪ] adj (person, movement) torpe

**clung** [klʌŋ] pt & pp of **cling**

**cluster** ['klʌstə(r)] **1** n (of flowers) ramo m; (of grapes) racimo m; (of people, islands, houses) grupo m

   **2** vi **to c. round sb/sth** apiñarse en torno a alguien/algo

**clutch**[1] [klʌtʃ] **1** n (a) Aut embrague m; **to let the c. in** pisar el embrague, embragar; **to let the c. out** soltar el embrague, desembragar; **c. pedal** (pedal m de) embrague m (b) (grasp) **she had fallen into his clutches** ella había caído en sus garras

   **2** vt agarrar

   **3** vi **to c. at sth** agarrarse a algo; Fig **to c. at straws** agarrarse a un clavo ardiendo

**clutch**[2] n (of eggs) nidada f

**clutter** ['klʌtə(r)] **1** n desbarajuste m; **in a c.** revuelto(a)

   **2** vt **to be cluttered (up) with sth** estar abarrotado(a) de algo

**cluttered** ['klʌtəd] adj revuelto(a)

**cm** (abbr **centimetre(s)**) cm, centímetro m

**CNAA** [siːenˈeɪ] n Br (abbr **Council for National Academic Awards**) = organismo británico que expide los títulos universitarios

**CND** [siːenˈdiː] n Br (abbr **Campaign for Nuclear Disarmament**) = organización británica en favor del desarme nuclear

**CO** [siːˈəʊ] (pl **COs**) n Mil (abbr **Commanding Officer**) oficial m al mando

**Co, co** [kəʊ] n Com (abbr **company**) cía, compañía f; Fig **Jane and co** Jane y compañía

**c/o** [si:ʹəʊ] (abbr **care of**) en el domicilio de

**coach** [kəʊtʃ] 1 n (a) Br (bus) autocar m, autobús m; (horse-drawn carriage) coche m de caballos, diligencia f; (section of train) vagón m; **c. party** grupo m de viajeros en autocar; **c. trip** excursión f en autocar or autobús (b) (of athlete, team) entrenador(ora) m,f
**2** vt (athlete, team) entrenar; **to c. sb for an exam** ayudar a alguien a preparar un examen

**coachbuilder** [ʹkəʊtʃbɪldə(r)] n Aut carrocero(a) m,f

**coagulant** [kəʊʹægjʊlənt] n Med coagulante m

**coagulate** [kəʊʹægjʊleɪt] vi coagularse

**coal** [kəʊl] n (a) carbón m; **a lump of c.** un trozo de carbón; **c. bunker** carbonera f; **c. merchant** carbonero(a) m,f; **c. mine** mina f de carbón; **c. miner** minero(a) m,f (del carbón); **c. mining** minería f del carbón; **c. tar** alquitrán m mineral (b) (idioms) **to carry coals to Newcastle** ir a vendimiar y llevar uvas de postre; **to haul sb over the coals** echar una bronca a alguien

**coalesce** [kəʊəʹles] vi (views, interests) fundirse; (movements, groups) coaligarse

**coalfield** [ʹkəʊlfiːld] n yacimiento m de carbón; (large region) cuenca f carbonífera

**coalition** [kəʊəʹlɪʃən] n coalición f; **to form a c.** formar una coalición

**coalman** [ʹkəʊlmæn] n carbonero m

**coarse** [kɔːs] adj (a) (person, language) grosero(a), basto(a) (b) (surface, texture) áspero(a); **to have c. hair** tener el pelo basto

**coarsely** [ʹkɔːslɪ] adv (a) (vulgarly) groseramente (b) (roughly) a chopped cortado(a) en trozos grandes; **c. ground** molido(a) grueso(a)

**coarseness** [ʹkɔːsnɪs] n (a) (of person, language) grosería f (b) (of surface, texture) aspereza f

**coast** [kəʊst] 1 n costa f; Fig **the c. is clear** no hay moros en la costa
**2** vi (in car) rodar en punto muerto; (on bicycle) rodar sin pedalear; Fig **she coasted through her exams** pasó sus exámenes con toda facilidad

**coastal** [ʹkəʊstəl] adj costero(a)

**coaster** [ʹkəʊstə(r)] n (a) (ship) buque m de cabotaje (b) (for glass) posavasos m inv

**coastguard** [ʹkəʊstgɑːd] n guardacostas mf inv

**coastline** [ʹkəʊstlaɪn] n costa f, litoral m

**coat** [kəʊt] 1 n (a) (garment) abrigo m; **c. hanger** percha f; **c. hook** colgador m (b) (of dog, horse) pelaje m (c) (of snow, paint) capa f (d) (in heraldry) **c. of arms** escudo m de armas
**2** vt cubrir (**with** de); **coated with mud**

cubierto(a) de barro, embarrado(a); **hazelnuts coated with chocolate** avellanas recubiertas de chocolate

**coating** [ʹkəʊtɪŋ] n (of paint, dust) capa f

**co-author** [kəʊʹɔːθə(r)] 1 n coautor(ora) m,f
**2** vt **to c. a book with sb** escribir un libro conjuntamente con alguien

**coax** [kəʊks] vt persuadir; **to c. sb into doing sth** persuadir a alguien para que haga algo; **to c. sth out of sb** sonsacar algo a alguien

**cob** [kɒb] n (a) (horse) jaca f (b) (of maize) mazorca f

**cobalt** [ʹkəʊbɔːlt] n Chem cobalto m; **c. blue** azul m cobalto

**cobble** [ʹkɒbəl] 1 n adoquín m
**2** vt adoquinar
▸**cobble together** vt sep (make hastily) apañar, improvisar

**cobbled** [ʹkɒbəld] adj (path, street) adoquinado(a)

**cobbler** [ʹkɒblə(r)] n zapatero m (remendón)

**cobblers** [ʹkɒbləz] npl (a) very Fam (nonsense) paridas fpl (b) Br Vulg (testicles) cojones mpl, huevos mpl

**COBOL** [ʹkəʊbɒl] n Comptr (abbr **Common Business Oriented Language**) (lenguaje m) COBOL m

**cobra** [ʹkəʊbrə] n cobra f

**cobweb** [ʹkɒbweb] n telaraña f; Fig **to brush the cobwebs off sth** desempolvar algo

**cocaine** [kəʹkeɪn] n cocaína f

**coccyx** [ʹkɒksɪks] n coxis m

**cock** [kɒk] 1 n (a) (male fowl) gallo m; **c. sparrow** gorrión m macho (b) Vulg (penis) polla f, picha f
**2** vt (gun) montar, amartillar; **to c. a snook at sb** hacer burla a alguien; **to c. its ears** (of horse, dog) aguzar las orejas
▸**cock up** vt sep Br very Fam **to c. sth up** joder algo

**cockade** [kɒʹkeɪd] n escarapela f

**cock-a-doodle-doo** [ʹkɒkəduːdəlʹduː] exclam ¡quiquiriquí!

**cock-a-hoop** [ʹkɒkəʹhuːp] adj **he was c. about the result** estaba encantado con el resultado

**cockatoo** [kɒkəʹtuː] n (pl **cockatoos**) n cacatúa f

**cockcrow** [ʹkɒkkrəʊ] n **at c.** al amanecer

**cocked** [kɒkt] adj **to knock sb into a c. hat** (outclass) dar mil or cien vueltas a alguien

**cockerel** [ʹkɒkərəl] n gallo m joven

**cocker spaniel** [ʹkɒkəʹspænjəl] n cocker mf

**cockeyed** [ʹkɒkaɪd] adj Fam (decision, plan) disparatado(a)

**cockfight** [ʹkɒkfaɪt] n pelea f de gallos

**cockle** ['kɒkəl] *n* (a) *(shellfish)* berberecho *m* (b) *Fam* **it warmed the cockles of his heart** le alegró el corazón

**Cockney** ['kɒknɪ] **1** *n* (*pl* **Cockneys**) *(person)* = habitante de los barrios del este de Londres; *(dialect)* = habla de los barrios del este de Londres
  **2** *adj* = de los barrios del este de Londres

**cockpit** ['kɒkpɪt] *n (of passenger plane)* cabina *f; (of fighter plane)* carlinga *f*

**cockroach** ['kɒkrəʊtʃ] *n* cucaracha *f*

**cocksure** ['kɒk'ʃʊə(r)] *adj (person, manner)* arrogante

**cocktail** ['kɒkteɪl] *n also Fig* cóctel *m;* **c. dress** vestido *m* de noche; **c. lounge** bar *m (de hotel);* **c. party** cóctel *m;* **c. shaker** coctelera *f;* **c. stick** palillo *m*

**cock-up** ['kɒkʌp] *n very Fam* cagada *f;* **it was a c., not a conspiracy** fue un error, no una conspiración

**cocky** ['kɒkɪ] *adj Fam* creído(a)

**cocoa** ['kəʊkəʊ] *n (powder, drink)* cacao *m;* **c. bean** semilla *f or* grano *m* de cacao; **c. butter** crema *f* de cacao

**coconut** ['kəʊkənʌt] *n (fruit)* coco *m;* **c. milk** leche *f* de coco; **c. palm** cocotero *m*

**cocoon** [kə'ku:n] **1** *n* capullo *m*
  **2** *vt* **to be cocooned from the outside world** estar sobreprotegido(a) del mundo exterior

**COD** [si:əʊ'di:] *Com (abbr* **cash on delivery**) entrega *f* contra reembolso

**cod** [kɒd] *n* bacalao *m;* **c. liver oil** aceite *m* de hígado de bacalao

**coddle** ['kɒdəl] *vt (child)* mimar

**code** [kəʊd] **1** *n* (a) *(cipher)* código *m,* clave *f;* **in c.** cifrado(a); **c. book** libro *m* de códigos; **c. name** nombre *m* en clave; **c. number** prefijo *m* (b) *(rules)* código *m;* **c. of conduct** código de conducta; **c. of practice** código de conducta
  **2** *vt (message)* codificar, cifrar

**codeine** ['kəʊdi:n] *n* codeína *f*

**codify** ['kəʊdɪfaɪ] *vt* codificar

**codswallop** ['kɒdzwɒləp] *n Fam* majaderías *fpl,* paparruchas *fpl*

**coeducational** ['kəʊedjʊ'keɪʃənəl] *adj (school)* mixto(a)

**coefficient** [kəʊɪ'fɪʃənt] *n Math* coeficiente *m*

**coerce** [kəʊ'ɜ:s] *vt* coaccionar; **to c. sb into doing sth** coaccionar a alguien para que haga algo

**coercion** [kəʊ'ɜ:ʃən] *n* coacción *f*

**coexist** ['kəʊɪg'zɪst] *vi* convivir, coexistir

**coexistence** ['kəʊɪg'zɪstəns] *n* convivencia *f,* coexistencia *f*

**C of E** [si:ə'vi:] *adj Br (abbr* **Church of England**) anglicano(a)

**coffee** ['kɒfɪ] *n* café *m;* **two coffees, please!** ¡dos cafés, por favor!; **black/white c.** café solo/con leche; **c. bar** café, cafetería *f;* **c. bean** grano *m* de café; **c. break** descanso *m* para el café; **c. cup** taza *f* de café; **c. grinder** molinillo *m* de café; **c. grounds** posos *mpl* del café; **c. machine** cafetera *f;* **c. pot** cafetera *f;* **c. table** mesita *f* baja, mesa *f* de centro; **c. table book** libro de lujo para adornar

**coffer** ['kɒfə(r)] *n (chest)* cofre *m; Fig* **the company's coffers** las arcas de la empresa

**coffin** ['kɒfɪn] *n* ataúd *m,* féretro *m*

**cog** [kɒg] *n* diente *m (en engranaje); Fig* **I'm only a c. in the machinery** no soy más que una pieza del engranaje

**cogent** ['kəʊdʒənt] *adj* poderoso(a), convincente

**cogitate** ['kɒdʒɪteɪt] *Formal vi* meditar, reflexionar

**cognac** ['kɒnjæk] *n* coñá *m,* coñac *m*

**cognition** [kɒg'nɪʃən] *n* cognición *f,* conocimiento *m*

**cohabit** [kəʊ'hæbɪt] *vi* cohabitar, convivir

**cohabitation** [kəʊhæbɪ'teɪʃən] *n* cohabitación *f,* convivencia *f*

**coherence** [kəʊ'hɪərəns] *n* coherencia *f*

**coherent** [kəʊ'hɪərənt] *adj* coherente

**cohesion** [kəʊ'hi:ʒən] *n* cohesión *f*

**cohesive** [kəʊ'hi:sɪv] *adj* cohesivo(a)

**coiffure** [kwɑ:'fjʊə(r)] *n* peinado *m*

**coil** [kɔɪl] **1** *n* (a) *(of rope, wire)* rollo *m; (electrical)* bobina *f; (contraceptive device)* DIU *m,* espiral *f* (b) *(single loop)* bucle *m,* vuelta *f;* **the snake's coils** los anillos de la serpiente
  **2** *vt* enrollar *(round* alrededor de)
  ►**coil up** *vi (of snake)* enrollarse, enroscarse

**coin** [kɔɪn] **1** *n* moneda *f; Fig* **the other side of the c.** la otra cara de la moneda
  **2** *vt* **to c. money** acuñar moneda; *Fam* **he's simply coining it** se está forrando; **to c. a phrase…** por así decirlo…, valga la expresión …

**coinage** ['kɔɪnɪdʒ] *n* (a) *(coins)* monedas *fpl* (b) *(phrase)* **a recent c.** una expresión de nuevo cuño

**coincide** [kəʊɪn'saɪd] *vi* coincidir (**with** con)

**coincidence** [kəʊ'ɪnsɪdəns] *n* coincidencia *f;* **what a c.!** ¡qué coincidencia!

**coincidental** [kəʊɪnsɪ'dentəl] *adj* casual, accidental

**coin-operated** ['kɔɪnɒpəreɪtɪd] *adj* **c. machine** máquina *f* de monedas

**coitus** ['kɔɪtəs] *n Formal* coito *m;* **c. interruptus** coitus *m inv* interruptus

**coke** [kəʊk] *n* (a) *(fuel)* coque *m* (b) *Fam (cocaine)* coca *f*

**Col** *Mil (abbr* **Colonel***)* coronel *m*

**col** *(abbr* **column***)* col., columna *f*

**colander** ['kɒləndə(r)] *n (sieve)* escurridor *m*

**cold** [kəʊld] **1** *n* (a) *(low temperature)* frío *m*; **he doesn't seem to feel the c.** parece que no siente el frío; *Fig* **to be left out in the c.** ser dejado(a) de lado (b) *(illness)* resfriado *m*, catarro *m*; **to have a c.** tener un resfriado, estar acatarrado(a); **to catch a c.** coger un resfriado

**2** *adj* (a) *(in temperature)* frío(a); **to be c.** *(of person)* tener frío; *(of thing)* estar frío(a); **it's c.** hace frío; **to get c.** enfriarse; **to be in a c. sweat** tener sudores fríos; **c. cream** crema *f* de belleza; *Met* **c. front** frente *m* frío; **c. meats** fiambres *mpl* y embutidos; **c. sore** calentura *f*; **c. start** *(of car)* arranque *m* en frío; **c. storage** conservación *f* en cámara frigorífica; **c. war** guerra *f* fría (b) *(person, manner, welcome)* frío(a) (c) *(idioms) Fam* **it leaves me c.** *(doesn't interest or impress me)* me deja frío(a); **in c. blood** a sangre fría; **that's c. comfort** eso no es un consuelo; **to get c. feet** echarse atrás; **to give sb the c. shoulder** dar de lado a alguien

**3** *adv* **to do sth c.** *(without preparation)* hacer algo en frío; *Fam Fig* **to be out c.** estar inconsciente

**cold-blooded** ['kəʊld'blʌdɪd] *adj (animal)* de sangre fría; *Fig (act)* desalmado(a); **to be c.** *(of animal)* tener la sangre fría; *(of person) Fig* ser desalmado(a); **c. murder** asesinato *m* a sangre fría

**cold-hearted** ['kəʊld'hɑːtɪd] *adj (person, decision)* insensible

**coldly** ['kəʊldlɪ] *adv* fríamente, con frialdad

**coldness** ['kəʊldnɪs] *n (of weather, manner)* frialdad *f*

**cold-shoulder** ['kəʊld'ʃəʊldə(r)] *vt* dar de lado a, dar la espalda a

**coleslaw** ['kəʊlslɔː] *n* = ensalada de repollo, zanahoria y cebolla con mayonesa

**colic** ['kɒlɪk] *n* cólico *m*

**collaborate** [kə'læbəreɪt] *vi also Pej* colaborar (**with** con)

**collaboration** [kəlæbə'reɪʃən] *n also Pej* colaboración *f*

**collaborator** [kə'læbəreɪtə(r)] *n* colaborador(ora) *m,f*; *Pej (with the enemy)* colaboracionista *mf*

**collage** ['kɒlɑːʒ] *n (artwork)* collage *m*

**collagen** ['kɒlədʒən] *n* colágeno *m*

**collapse** [kə'læps] **1** *n (of building)* hundimiento *m*, desplome *m*; *(of prices)* caída *f*, desplome *m*; *(of government)* caída *f*, hundimiento *m*; *(of business)* hundimiento *m*

**2** *vi (of person)* desplomarse; *(of building, prices,*

*resistance)* desplomarse, hundirse; *(of government)* caer, hundirse; *(of business)* hundirse

**collapsible** [kə'læpsəbəl] *adj (table, bed)* plegable

**collar** ['kɒlə(r)] **1** *n (of shirt)* cuello *m*; *(for dog)* collar *m*

**2** *vt Fam (seize)* cazar, agarrar

**collarbone** ['kɒləbəʊn] *n* clavícula *f*

**collate** [kɒ'leɪt] *vt* cotejar

**collateral** [kə'lætərəl] **1** *n Fin* garantía *f* (prendaria)

**2** *adj Mil* **c. damage** bajas *fpl* civiles *(en un bombardeo)*

**colleague** ['kɒliːg] *n* colega *mf*, compañero(a) *m,f*

**collect** [kə'lekt] **1** *vt* (a) *(as pastime) (stamps, books)* coleccionar (b) *(gather) (supporters, belongings)* reunir, juntar; *(data, news)* recoger, reunir; *(taxes)* recaudar; **I'll c. you at midday** te recogeré al mediodía (c) *(compose)* **she collected her thoughts** puso en orden sus ideas; **to c. oneself** concentrarse

**2** *vi (of people)* reunirse; *(of things)* acumularse

**3** *adv US* **to call sb c.** llamar a alguien a cobro revertido

**collected** [kə'lektɪd] *adj* (a) *(calm)* sereno(a), entero(a) (b) **the c. works of...** las obras completas de...

**collection** [kə'lekʃən] *n* (a) *(group) (of stamps, paintings)* colección *f*; *(of poems, essays)* recopilación *f*; *(of objects)* montón *m*; *(of people)* grupo *m* (b) *(act of collecting) (of money)* colecta *f*; *(of rubbish)* recogida *f*; *(of taxes)* recaudación *f*; **to make a c.** *(for charity)* hacer una colecta; **c. plate** *(in church)* platillo *m* para las limosnas

**collective** [kə'lektɪv] **1** *n (group)* colectivo *m*; *(farm)* (granja *f*) cooperativa *f*

**2** *adj* colectivo(a); **c. bargaining** negociación *f* colectiva; *Gram* **c. noun** sustantivo *m* colectivo

**collectively** [kə'lektɪvlɪ] *adv* colectivamente; **they are c. known as...** se los/las conoce como...

**collectivize** [kə'lektɪvaɪz] *vt* colectivizar

**collector** [kə'lektə(r)] *n* (a) *(of paintings, stamps)* coleccionista *mf*; **c.'s item** pieza *f* de coleccionista (b) **c. of taxes** recaudador(ora) *m,f* de impuestos

**college** ['kɒlɪdʒ] *n (for adult or further education)* escuela *f*; *(for vocational training)* instituto *m*; *Br (of university)* colegio *m* universitario; **to be at c.** *(be a student)* estar en la universidad; **c. of education** escuela *f* de pedagogía *or* magisterio

**collide** [kə'laɪd] *vi* colisionar, chocar (**with** con *or* contra)

**collie** ['kɒlɪ] *n (dog)* collie *m*

**colliery** ['kɒlıərı] n (coal mine) mina f de carbón

**collision** [kə'lıʒən] n colisión f, choque m; Fig **they are on a c. course** terminarán enfrentándose

**colloquial** [kə'ləukwıəl] adj coloquial

**colloquialism** [kə'ləukwıəlızəm] n voz f or término m coloquial

**collude** [kə'lu:d] vi conspirar, confabularse

**collusion** [kə'lu:ʒən] n connivencia f; **to be in c. with sb** estar en connivencia con alguien

**collywobbles** ['kɒlıwɒbəlz] npl Fam **to have the c.** (be nervous) tener canguelo

**Colombia** [kə'lʌmbıə] n Colombia

**Colombian** [kə'lʌmbıən] n & adj colombiano(a) m,f

**colon** ['kəulən] n (a) Anat colon m (b) (punctuation mark) dos puntos mpl

**colonel** ['kɜ:nəl] n coronel m

**colonial** [kə'ləunıəl] adj colonial

**colonialism** [kə'ləunıəlızəm] n colonialismo m

**colonist** ['kɒlənıst] n colonizador(ora) m,f, colono m

**colonize** ['kɒlənaız] vt colonizar

**colonnade** [kɒlə'neıd] n Archit columnata f

**colony** ['kɒlənı] n colonia f

**color, colored** etc US see **colour, coloured** etc

**colossal** [kə'lɒsəl] adj colosal

**colour,** US **color** ['kʌlə(r)] **1** n (a) color m; **what c. is it?** ¿de qué color es?; **c. bar** (racial discrimination) discriminación f racial; **c. scheme** combinación f de colores; **c. supplement** (of newspaper) suplemento m a color (b) (idioms) **to be off c.** (of person) estar pocho(a); **to give c. to a story** dar colorido a una historia; **let's see the c. of your money** veamós primero el dinero; **to pass with flying colours** aprobar con todos los honores; **to show oneself in one's true colours** quitarse la máscara; **she nailed her colours to the mast** manifestó públicamente su postura

**2** vt (change colour of) colorear; Fig (judgment, view) influir en; **to c. one's hair** teñirse el pelo; **to c. sth blue** pintar or colorear algo de azul

**3** vi (blush) ruborizarse

▸**colour in,** US **color in** vt sep colorear

**colour-blind,** US **color-blind** ['kʌləblaınd] adj daltónico(a)

**colour-coded,** US **color-coded** [kʌlə'kəudıd] adj **the wires are c.** los cables están coloreados de acuerdo con un código

**coloured,** US **colored** ['kʌləd] adj (a) (illustration) coloreado(a); **brightly c.** de colores vivos; Fig **a highly c. narrative** una narrativa llena de colorido (b) (person) de color

**colourful,** US **colorful** ['kʌləful] adj (a) (having bright colours) de colores vivos (b) (interesting, exciting) lleno(a) de colorido; **a c. character** un personaje pintoresco (c) (vivid) (language, description) expresivo(a), vívido(a)

**colouring,** US **coloring** ['kʌlərıŋ] n (a) (in food) colorante m (b) (complexion) tez f; **to have dark/fair c.** ser de tez morena/clara (c) **c. book** libro m para colorear

**colourless,** US **colorless** ['kʌləlıs] adj (a) (clear) incoloro(a) (b) Fig (dull) insulso(a), inexpresivo(a)

**colt** [kəult] n (horse) potro m

**column** ['kɒləm] n (of building, troops, in newspaper) columna f

**columnist** ['kɒləmıst] n (for newspaper, magazine) columnista mf

**coma** ['kəumə] n coma m; **to go into/be in a c.** entrar en/estar en coma

**comatose** ['kəumətəus] adj Med comatoso(a); Fig (exhausted) hecho(a) polvo

**comb** [kəum] **1** n (a) (for hair) peine m; **to run a c. through one's hair, to give one's hair a c.** peinarse (b) (of cock) cresta f

**2** vt (a) (hair) peinar; **to c. one's hair** peinarse (b) (search) (area, town) peinar, rastrear minuciosamente

**combat** ['kɒmbæt] **1** n combate m; **c. jacket** guerrera f; **c. zone** área f de combate

**2** vt (disease, prejudice, crime) combatir

**combatant** ['kɒmbətənt] n & adj combatiente mf

**combination** [kɒmbı'neıʃən] n combinación f; **a c. of circumstances** un cúmulo de circunstancias; **c. lock** cierre m de combinación

**combine 1** n ['kɒmbaın] (a) **c. (harvester)** cosechadora f (b) Econ grupo m empresarial

**2** vt [kəm'baın] combinar; **to c. business with pleasure** combinar los negocios con el placer

**3** vi (of people) unirse; (merge) unirse, combinarse; (of chemical elements) combinarse

**combustible** [kəm'bʌstıbəl] adj combustible

**combustion** [kəm'bʌstʃən] n combustión f; **c. chamber** cámara f de combustión

**come** [kʌm] (pt **came** [keım], pp **come**) vi (a) (in general) venir (**from** de); (arrive) venir, llegar; **to c. from France** ser francés(esa); **to c. from Edinburgh** ser de Edimburgo; **here c. the children** ya llegan or aquí vienen los niños; **c. here!** ¡ven aquí!; **I'll c. and help** iré a ayudar; **coming!** ¡ya voy!; **she always comes to me for help** siempre acude a mí en busca de ayuda; **to c. first/last** (in race, competition) llegar or terminar primero/último; **my name comes before hers on the list** mi nombre está or antes que el de ella en la lista; **the mud came up to our knees el barro nos llegaba a las rodillas; *Fig* **she has come a long way since then** ha progresado mucho desde entonces; *Fam* **I don't know whether I'm coming or going!** ¡no sé dónde tengo la cabeza!; *Fam* **c., c.!** ¡bueno, bueno!, ¡venga ya!; **she won't let anything c. between her and her work** no permite que nada interfiera con su trabajo; **that's surprising coming from him** viniendo de él, es sorprendente; **now that I c. to think of it** ahora que lo pienso; **c. away from there, it's dangerous** quítate de ahí, que es peligroso; **the rain came pouring down** se puso a llover a cántaros; **to c. for sb/sth** venir en busca de alguien/algo; **she came running towards us** vino corriendo hacia nosotros

(**b**) *(in time)* venir; **in the days/years to c.** en días/años venideros; **to take things as they c.** tomarse las cosas como vienen; **what comes next?** ¿qué viene a continuación?; **she will be ten c. January** cumple diez años en enero; **c. what may** suceda lo que suceda; **it came as a relief to me** fue un gran alivio para mí; *Fam* **he had it coming (to him)** se lo estaba buscando

(**c**) *(be available)* **it comes in three sizes** viene en tres tallas; **work of that quality doesn't c. cheap** un trabajo de esa calidad no sale barato; *Fam* **he's as tough as they c.** es duro como el que más; **it's as good as they c.** es de lo mejor que hay

(**d**) *(become)* **to c. loose** aflojarse; **to c. true** cumplirse, hacerse realidad; **to c. of age** hacerse mayor de edad; **how did the door c. to be open?** ¿cómo es que estaba la puerta abierta?

(**e**) *very Fam (have orgasm)* correrse

▸**come about** *vi* ocurrir, suceder; **how did it c. about that…?** ¿cómo fue que…?

▸**come across 1** *vt insep (find)* encontrar, encontrarse con

**2** *vi (make an impression)* **to c. across well/badly** quedar bien/mal, dar buena/mala impresión; **she comes across as a bit arrogant** da la impresión de que es un poco arrogante

▸**come after** *vt insep (chase)* perseguir

▸**come along** *vi* (**a**) *(as exhortation)* **c. along!** ¡venga! (**b**) *(of project, work)* marchar, progresar; **how's the project coming along?** ¿qué tal marcha el proyecto?; **his Spanish is coming along well** su español va mejorando

▸**come at** *vt insep (attack)* ir a por, atacar; **he came at me with a knife** fue a por mí con un cuchillo

▸**come away** *vi (become detached)* soltarse

▸**come back** *vi* volver, regresar; **to c. back to what I was saying…** volviendo a lo que decía antes,…; **it's all coming back to me** ahora me acuerdo de todo

▸**come by 1** *vt insep (acquire)* conseguir; **how did she c. by all that money?** ¿de dónde sacó todo ese dinero?

**2** *vi (visit)* pasarse; **I'll c. by tomorrow** me pasaré mañana (por tu casa)

▸**come down** *vi* (**a**) *(descend)* bajar; *(rain)* caer; *Fig* **to c. down in the world** venir a menos; **to c. down with the flu** coger la gripe (**b**) *(decrease) (of temperature, prices)* bajar, descender (**c**) *(decide)* **to c. down in favour of** decantarse a favor de

▸**come down on** *vt insep (reprimand)* regañar

▸**come down to** *vt insep (be a matter of)* reducirse a, tratarse de

▸**come forward** *vi* presentarse

▸**come in** *vi* (**a**) *(of person)* entrar; *(of tide)* subir; **c. in!** ¡adelante!; **to c. in first/second** llegar en primer/segundo lugar (**b**) *(have a role)* entrar; *Fam* **that's where you c. in** ahí es cuando entras tú; **to c. in handy** *or* **useful** resultar útil, venir bien

▸**come in for** *vt insep* **to c. in for praise/criticism** recibir alabanzas/críticas

▸**come into** *vt insep* (**a**) *(room, city)* entrar en; **to c. into the world** venir al mundo; **to c. into existence** nacer, surgir; **to c. into force** *or* **effect** *(of law, ruling)* entrar en vigor; **luck didn't c. into it** la suerte no tuvo nada que ver (**b**) *(inherit)* heredar

▸**come of** *vi (result from)* **no good will c. of it** no saldrá nada bueno de esto; **that's what comes of being too ambitious** eso es lo que pasa por ser demasiado ambicioso

▸**come off 1** *vt insep* (**a**) *(fall from) (horse, bicycle)* caerse de (**b**) *(c. off it!* ¡anda ya!, ¡venga ya!

**2** *vi* (**a**) *(be removed) (of button)* caerse; *(of paint)* levantarse (**b**) *(succeed) (of plan)* salir; **to c. off well/badly** *(in contest)* quedar bien/mal

▸**come on** *vi* (**a**) *(as exhortation)* **c. on!** ¡venga!, ¡vamos! (**b**) *(make progress)* progresar; **I feel a cold coming on** me estoy resfriando *or* acatarrando

▸**come out** *vi* (**a**) *(of person, sun, magazine)* salir; *(of film)* estrenarse; **the truth will c. out in the end** al final se sabrá la verdad; **to c. out of an affair well/badly** salir bien/mal parado(a) de un asunto; **the photos have c. out well** las fotos han salido bien; **to c. out on strike** declararse en huelga; **she came out in a rash** le salió un sarpullido; **to c. out in favour of/against sth** declararse a favor de/en contra de algo; **to c. out with an opinion** expresar una opinión (**b**) *(of tooth, screw, hair)* caerse; *(of stain)* salir, quitarse (**c**) *(as gay or lesbian)* declararse homosexual

▸**come over 1** *vt insep (affect)* sobrevenir; **a strange feeling came over me** me sobrevino una extraña sensación; **what's come over you?** ¿qué te ha pasado?

**2** vi **(a)** *(make impression)* **to c. over well/badly** quedar bien/mal **(b)** *(feel)* **to c. over all funny** sentirse raro(a); **to c. over all dizzy** marearse **(c)** *(visit)* pasarse; **I'll c. over tomorrow** me pasaré mañana (por tu casa)

▶**come round** vi **(a)** *(visit)* **c. round and see me one day** pásate a verme un día **(b)** *(regain consciousness)* volver en sí **(c)** *(accept)* **to c. round to sb's way of thinking** terminar aceptando la opinión de alguien

▶**come through 1** vi *(of message, news)* llegar

**2** vt insep *(survive)* (war, crisis, illness) sobrevivir a

▶**come to 1** vt insep **(a)** *(amount to)* sumar, alcanzar; **how much does it c. to?** ¿a cuánto asciende?; **the scheme never came to anything** el plan se quedó en nada **(b)** *(reach)* **to c. to a crossroads** llegar a un cruce; **to c. to the end (of sth)** llegar al final (de algo); **to c. to the point** ir al grano; **what is the world coming to?** ¿adónde vamos a ir a parar?; **when it comes to...** en cuestión de...; **if it comes to that, you're not exactly a genius either** si se trata de eso, tú tampoco eres exactamente un genio

**2** vi *(regain consciousness)* volver en sí

▶**come together** vi *(gather)* reunirse

▶**come up 1** vt insep *(stairs, hill)* subir

**2** vi **(a)** *(of sun)* salir; *(of opportunity, problem)* surgir, presentarse; **to c. up against opposition/a problem** enfrentarse con la oposición/un problema; **there are some interesting films coming up on television** van a poner algunas películas interesantes en la televisión; **I'll let you know if anything comes up** te avisaré si surge algo; **the case comes up for trial tomorrow** el caso se verá mañana **(b)** **to c. up with** *(funding, solution)* encontrar; *(idea, theory)* formular

▶**come upon** vt insep *(find)* (person, object) encontrar, encontrarse con

▶**come up to** vt insep **(a)** *(approach)* acercarse a; **a man came up to me and started talking** un hombre se me acercó y comenzó a hablarme; **we're coming up to Christmas** se acerca la Navidad **(b)** *(equal)* estar a la altura de; **the film didn't c. up to my expectations** la película no fue tan buena como yo esperaba

**comeback** ['kʌmbæk] n *(of sportsperson)* vuelta f a la competición; *(of actor)* regreso m; **to make a c.** *(of fashion)* volver; *(of actor)* volver a actuar; *(of sportsperson)* volver a la competición

**COMECON** ['kɒmɪkɒn] n *Formerly* (abbr **Council for Mutual Economic Assistance**) COMECON m, CAME m, Consejo m de Ayuda Mutua Económica

**comedian** [kə'miːdɪən] n humorista mf

**comedienne** [kəmiːdɪ'en] n humorista f

**comedown** ['kʌmdaʊn] n *Fam* degradación f

**comedy** ['kɒmɪdɪ] n *(play, film)* comedia f; *(TV series)* serie f cómica or de humor; *(humorous entertainment)* humor m, humorismo m; **c. show** *(on TV)* programa m de humor

**come-on** ['kʌmɒn] n *Fam* **to give sb the c.** *(sexually)* tirarle los tejos a alguien

**comer** ['kʌmə(r)] n **open to all comers** abierto(a) para todo el mundo

**comet** ['kɒmɪt] n cometa m

**comeuppance** [kʌm'ʌpəns] n *Fam* **he'll get his c.** ya tendrá su merecido

**comfort** ['kʌmfət] **1** n **(a)** *(ease)* comodidad f; **to live in c.** vivir confortablemente; **in the c. of one's own home** en el calor del hogar; **home comforts** las comodidades del hogar; **the bullets were too close for c.** las balas pasaban peligrosamente cerca; *US* **c. station** servicio m, aseos mpl **(b)** *(consolation)* consuelo m; **if it's any c.,...** si te sirve de consuelo,...; **to take c. from** or **in sth** consolarse con algo

**2** vt *(console)* consolar, confortar

**comfortable** ['kʌmfətəbəl] adj **(a)** *(bed, chair)* cómodo(a); **to be c.** *(of person)* estar cómodo(a); **the patient is c.** el paciente no sufre demasiados dolores; **to make oneself c.** ponerse cómodo(a); **to feel c.** sentirse a gusto, sentirse cómodo(a); **I wouldn't feel c. accepting that money** no me sentiría bien si aceptara ese dinero **(b)** *(majority, income)* holgado(a); **to be in c. circumstances** estar en una situación holgada or desahogada

**comfortably** ['kʌmftəblɪ] adv **(a)** *(to sit)* cómodamente **(b)** *(without difficulty)* holgadamente, cómodamente; **to be c. off** estar en una situación holgada or desahogada; **to live c.** vivir sin apuros; **to win c.** ganar holgadamente

**comforter** ['kʌmfətə(r)] n *US* *(baby's dummy)* chupete m

**comforting** ['kʌmfətɪŋ] adj *(news, thought)* reconfortante

**comfy** ['kʌmfɪ] adj *Fam* *(person, place)* cómodo(a)

**comic** ['kɒmɪk] **1** n **(a)** *(performer)* cómico(a) m,f, humorista mf **(b)** **c.** *(book)* *(for children)* tebeo m; *(for adults)* cómic m

**2** adj cómico(a); **c. opera** ópera f cómica; **to provide some c. relief** aliviar la tristeza con un toque de humor; **c. strip** tira f cómica

**comical** ['kɒmɪkəl] adj cómico(a)

**coming** ['kʌmɪŋ] **1** n *(of person)* venida f, llegada f; *(of night)* caída f; **comings and goings** idas fpl y venidas

**2** adj *(year, week)* próximo(a)

**comma** ['kɒmə] n coma f

**command** [kə'mɑːnd] **1** n **(a)** *(order)* orden f; *Comptr* comando m, instrucción f; **to do sth at sb's c.** hacer algo por orden de alguien **(b)**

*(authority, control) (of army, expedition)* mando *m*; **to be in c. (of)** estar al mando (de); **to be in c. of a situation** dominar una situación; **to be at sb's c.** estar a las órdenes de alguien; **he has many resources at his c.** tiene muchos recursos a su disposición; **she has a good c. of English** tiene un buen dominio del inglés; **c. economy** economía *f* dirigida; *Comptr* **c. language** lenguaje *m* de comandos *or* de mando

2 *vt* **(a)** *(order)* mandar, ordenar; **to c. sb to do sth** mandar a alguien que haga algo **(b)** *(ship, regiment)* estar al mando de, mandar **(c)** *(have at one's disposal)* disponer de; **with all the skill he could c.** con toda la habilidad de que disponía **(d)** *(inspire) (respect, admiration)* infundir, inspirar; *(attention)* obtener; **to c. a high price** alcanzar un precio elevado

**commandant** [kɒmən'dænt] *n Mil* comandante *mf*

**commandeer** [kɒmən'dɪə(r)] *vt (requisition)* requisar

**commander** [kə'mɑːndə(r)] *n Mil* comandante *mf*

**commander-in-chief** [kə'mɑːndərɪn'tʃiːf] *n Mil* comandante *mf* en jefe

**commanding** [kə'mɑːndɪŋ] *adj (tone, appearance)* autoritario(a); *(position)* dominante; *(lead)* abrumador(ora); *Mil* **c. officer** oficial *m* al mando

**commandment** [kə'mɑːndmənt] *n Rel* mandamiento *m*

**commando** [kə'mɑːndəʊ] *(pl* **commandos** *or* **commandoes)** *n Mil (soldier)* comando *m*

**commemorate** [kə'meməreɪt] *vt* conmemorar

**commemoration** [kəmemə'reɪʃən] *n* conmemoración *f*; **in c. of** en conmemoración de

**commemorative** [kə'memərətɪv] *adj* conmemorativo(a)

**commence** [kə'mens] *Formal* 1 *vt* comenzar; **to c. doing sth** comenzar a hacer algo
2 *vi* comenzar

**commencement** [kə'mensmənt] *n* **(a)** comienzo *m*, inicio *m* **(b)** *US Univ* ceremonia *f* de licenciatura

**commend** [kə'mend] *vt* **(a)** *(praise)* encomiar, elogiar; **to c. sb for bravery** elogiar la valentía de alguien **(b)** *(recommend)* **highly commended** muy recomendado(a); **the train journey has little to c. it** el viaje en tren tiene poco de recomendable **(c)** *(entrust)* encomendar **(to a)**

**commendable** [kə'mendəbəl] *adj* encomiable

**commendation** [kɒmen'deɪʃən] *n* **to receive a c.** recibir una mención; **worthy of c.** digno(a) de encomio *or* mención

**commensurate** [kə'mensərət] *adj Formal* acorde **(with** con**)**, proporcional **(with** a**)**; **you will receive a salary c. with the position** percibirá un salario adecuado a su puesto

**comment** ['kɒment] 1 *n* comentario *m*; **to make a c. on sth** hacer un comentario acerca de algo; **no c.** sin comentarios
2 *vt* **to c. that…** comentar que…; **"how interesting" he commented** qué interesante, comentó
3 *vi* hacer comentarios; **to c. on sth** comentar algo

**commentary** ['kɒməntərɪ] *n* **(a)** *(on TV, radio)* comentarios *mpl* **(b)** *(on text)* comentario *m*

**commentate** ['kɒmənteɪt] *vi (for TV, radio)* hacer de comentarista; **to c. on a match** ser el comentarista de un partido

**commentator** ['kɒmənteɪtə(r)] *n (on TV, radio)* comentarista *mf*

**commerce** ['kɒmɜːs] *n* comercio *m*

**commercial** [kə'mɜːʃəl] 1 *adj also Pej* comercial; **c. artist** diseñador(ora) *m,f* gráfico(a) de publicidad; *Fin* **c. bank** banco *m* comercial; *TV & Rad* **c. break** pausa *f* publicitaria; **c. law** derecho *m* mercantil; **c. traveller** viajante *mf* de comercio; **c. value** valor *m* comercial; **c. vehicle** vehículo *m* de transporte de mercancías
2 *n (TV, radio advertisement)* anuncio *m* (publicitario)

**commercialism** [kə'mɜːʃəlɪzəm] *n Pej* comercialidad *f*

**commercialize** [kə'mɜːʃəlaɪz] *vt* explotar

**commercially** [kə'mɜːʃəlɪ] *adv* comercialmente

**commie** ['kɒmɪ] *n & adj Fam Pej (communist)* rojo(a) *m,f*

**commiserate** [kə'mɪzəreɪt] *vi* **he commiserated with me** me dijo cuánto lo sentía

**commiseration** [kəmɪzə'reɪʃən] *n* **he offered his commiserations** dijo cuánto lo sentía; **(you have) my commiserations** te compadezco, cuánto lo siento

**commission** [kə'mɪʃən] 1 *n* **(a)** *Com (payment)* comisión *f*; **to charge c.** cobrar comisión **(b)** *(order)* encargo *m* **(c)** *(investigating body)* comisión *f*, comité *m* **(d)** **out of/in c.** *(of ship)* fuera de/en servicio **(e)** *Mil* nombramiento *m*
2 *vt* **(a)** *(order) (person)* encargar; **to c. sb to do sth** encargar a alguien hacer algo **(b)** *Mil* **to be commissioned** ser nombrado(a)

**commissionaire** [kəmɪʃə'neə(r)] *n (at hotel, cinema)* portero *m* de librea

**commissioner** [kə'mɪʃənə(r)] *n* comisario(a) *m,f*; **c. of police** comisario(a) *m,f* de policía; *Law* **c. for oaths** ≈ notario(a) *m,f*

**commit** [kə'mɪt] *vt* **(a)** *(error, crime)* cometer; **to c. suicide** suicidarse **(b)** *(promise)* **to c. one-**

**self** comprometerse; **to c. oneself to (doing) sth** comprometerse a (hacer) algo **(c)** *(entrust)* confiar, encomendar; **to c. sth to writing** *or* **paper** poner algo por escrito; **to c. sth to memory** memorizar algo **(d)** *(confine)* **to c. sb to prison** encarcelar a alguien; **he was committed** *(to mental institution)* fue ingresado en un psiquiátrico **(e)** *Law* **to c. sb for trial** enviar a alguien a un tribunal superior para ser juzgado

**commitment** [kə'mɪtmənt] *n (obligation, loyalty)* compromiso *m*; **to make a c. (to sb/ sth)** comprometerse (con alguien/algo); **she lacks c.** no se compromete lo suficiente; **family commitments** compromisos familiares

**committed** [kə'mɪtɪd] *adj* comprometido(a); **to be c. to an idea** estar comprometido(a) con una idea

**committee** [kə'mɪtɪ] *n* comité *m*, comisión *f*; **to sit** *or* **be on a c.** ser miembro de un comité; **c. meeting** reunión *f* del comité; **c. member** miembro *mf* del comité

**commode** [kə'məʊd] *n* **(a)** *(chest of drawers)* cómoda *f* **(b)** *(toilet)* silla *f* (de) servicio, silla *f* con inodoro

**commodious** [kə'məʊdɪəs] *adj* amplio(a), espacioso(a)

**commodity** [kə'mɒdɪtɪ] *n Econ & Fin* producto *m* básico; *Fig* **a rare c.** un bien muy escaso; **c. market** mercado *m* de productos básicos

**commodore** ['kɒmədɔː(r)] *n Naut* comodoro *m*

**common** ['kɒmən] **1** *n* **(a)** **to have sth in c. (with sb)** tener algo en común (con alguien) **(b)** *(land)* = campo municipal para uso del común, ≃ ejido *m*

**2** *adj* **(a)** *(frequent)* común, frecuente; **in c. use** de uso corriente **(b)** *(shared)* común; **it is by c. consent the best** está considerado por todos como el mejor; **C. Agricultural Policy** Política *f* Agrícola Común; *also Fig* **c. denominator** denominador *m* común; **the c. good** el bien común; *Fig* **c. ground** puntos *mpl* en común; **it's c. knowledge** es de(l) dominio público; **the C. Market** el Mercado Común; *Sch* **c. room** *(for pupils)* sala *f* de alumnos; *(for teachers)* sala *f* de profesores **(c)** *(average, ordinary)* común, corriente; **c. or garden** del montón, normal y corriente; **the c. cold** el resfriado común; **the c. man** el ciudadano medio; **the c. people** la gente corriente; **c. sense** sentido *m* común **(d)** *(vulgar)* ordinario(a)

**commoner** ['kɒmənə(r)] *n* plebeyo(a) *m,f*

**common-law** ['kɒmənlɔː] *adj* **c. marriage** matrimonio *m* or unión *f* de hecho; **c. husband/wife** esposo *m*/esposa *f* de hecho

**commonly** ['kɒmənlɪ] *adv* comúnmente

**commonplace** ['kɒmənpleɪs] **1** *n* tópico *m*, lugar *m* común

**2** *adj* común, habitual

**Commons** ['kɒmənz] *npl* **the (House of) C.** la Cámara de los Comunes

**Commonwealth** ['kɒmənwelθ] *n* **the C.** la Commonwealth, la Comunidad Británica de Naciones

**commotion** [kə'məʊʃən] *n* alboroto *m*, tumulto *m*; **to cause a c.** causar un alboroto

**communal** ['kɒmjʊnəl] *adj* comunal

**commune 1** *n* ['kɒmjuːn] *(collective)* comuna *f*

**2** *vi* [kə'mjuːn] estar en comunión **(with** con)

**communicable** [kə'mjuːnɪkəbəl] *adj (disease)* contagioso(a)

**communicant** [kə'mjuːnɪkənt] *n Rel* comulgante *mf*

**communicate** [kə'mjuːnɪkeɪt] **1** *vt (information, idea)* comunicar **(to** a)

**2** *vi* **(a)** *(of person)* comunicarse **(with** con) **(b)** *(of rooms)* comunicarse

**communication** [kəmjuːnɪ'keɪʃən] *n* comunicación *f*; **to be in c. (with sb)** estar en contacto (con alguien); **radio c.** comunicación *f* por radio; **to pull the c. cord** accionar la alarma *(en los trenes)*; **communications technology** tecnología *f* de las telecomunicaciones

**communicative** [kə'mjuːnɪkətɪv] *adj* comunicativo(a)

**communion** [kə'mjuːnjən] *n Rel* comunión *f*; **to take C.** comulgar

**communism** ['kɒmjʊnɪzəm] *n* comunismo *m*

**communist** ['kɒmjʊnɪst] *n & adj* comunista *mf*

**community** [kə'mjuːnɪtɪ] *n* comunidad *f*; **the Asian c.** la comunidad asiática; **the business c.** el sector empresarial, los empresarios; **c. centre** ≃ centro *m* cívico *or* social; *Formerly* **c. charge** ≃ contribución *f* urbana; **c. service** servicios *mpl* a la comunidad *(impuestos como pena sustitutiva de cárcel)*; **c. spirit** espíritu *m* comunitario

**commute** [kə'mjuːt] **1** *vt Law* conmutar

**2** *vi* **to c. (to work)** viajar diariamente al lugar de trabajo

**commuter** [kə'mjuːtə(r)] *n* = persona que viaja diariamente al trabajo; **c. train** = tren de cercanías que las personas utilizan para desplazarse diariamente al lugar de trabajo

**Comoros** ['kɒmərɒs] *n* **the C. (Islands)** las (Islas) Comores

**compact 1** *n* ['kɒmpækt] **(a)** *(for powder)* polvera *f* **(b)** *(treaty)* pacto *m* **(c)** *US (car)* utilitario *m*

**2** *adj* [kəm'pækt] compacto(a); **c. disc** *(disco m)* compacto *m*; **c. disc player** reproductor *m* de discos compactos

**3** vt [kɒm'pækt] *(scrap metal)* compactar, comprimir

**companion** [kəm'pænjən] *n* (**a**) *(friend)* compañero(a) *m,f;* **a drinking/travelling c.** un compañero de borrachera/viaje (**b**) *(guidebook)* guía *f*

**companionable** [kəm'pænjənəbəl] *adj* sociable

**companionship** [kəm'pænjənʃɪp] *n* compañía *f*

**company** ['kʌmpənɪ] *n* (**a**) *(companionship)* compañía *f;* **in sb's c.** en compañía de alguien; **to keep sb c.** hacer compañía a alguien; **to be good c.** ser buena compañía; **to part c. (with sb)** separarse (de alguien); **to get into bad c.** mezclarse con malas compañías; **you shouldn't pick your nose in c.** no se debe uno meter el dedo en la nariz delante de (la) gente; **we're expecting c.** *(guests)* tenemos invitados; *Prov* **two's c., three's a crowd** dos es compañía, tres es multitud

(**b**) *Com* empresa *f*, compañía *f;* **c. car** coche *m* de empresa; **c. policy** política *f* de empresa; *Com* **c. secretary** jefe(a) *m,f* de administración

(**c**) *(army unit, theatre group)* compañía *f*

(**d**) *Naut* **the ship's c.** la tripulación (del barco)

**comparable** ['kɒmpərəbəl] *adj* comparable

**comparative** [kəm'pærətɪv] **1** *n Gram* comparativo *m*

**2** *adj (cost, comfort, wealth)* relativo(a); *(study, research)* comparado(a)

**compare** [kəm'peə(r)] **1** *n Literary* **beyond c.** incomparable

**2** *vt* comparar (**with** *or* **to** con); **compared with** *or* **to…** comparado(a) con…; *Fig* **to c. notes (with sb)** intercambiar pareceres *or* opiniones (con alguien)

**3** *vi* compararse (**with** con *or* a); **to c. favourably with sth** resultar ser mejor que algo

**comparison** [kəm'pærɪsən] *n* comparación *f;* **in** *or* **by c.** en comparación; **there is no c.** no hay punto de comparación; **to draw** *or* **make a c. between** establecer un paralelismo entre

**compartment** [kəm'pɑːtmənt] *n* compartimento *m*

**compass** ['kʌmpəs] *n* (**a**) *(for finding direction)* brújula *f* (**b**) *Math* **compasses** compás *m;* **a pair of compasses** un compás (**c**) *(range)* ámbito *m*, alcance *m*

**compassion** [kəm'pæʃən] *n* compasión *f*

**compassionate** [kəm'pæʃ(ə)nət] *adj (person, attitude)* compasivo(a); **to be c. towards sb** ser compasivo(a) con alguien; **on c. grounds** por compasión; **c. leave** = permiso por enfermedad grave o muerte de un familiar

**compatibility** [kəmpætə'bɪlɪtɪ] *n* compatibilidad *f*

**compatible** [kəm'pætəbəl] *adj* compatible (**with** con)

**compatriot** [kəm'pætrɪət] *n* compatriota *mf*

**compel** [kəm'pel] *(pt & pp* **compelled***) vt* obligar; **to c. sb to do sth** obligar a alguien a hacer algo; **to c. admiration/respect** inspirar admiración/respeto

**compelling** [kəm'pelɪŋ] *adj (film, performance)* absorbente; *(argument)* poderoso(a), convincente; *(urgency)* apremiante

**compendium** [kəm'pendɪəm] *n* compendio *m*

**compensate** ['kɒmpenseɪt] **1** *vt* compensar, indemnizar (**for** por)

**2** *vi* **to c. for sth** compensar algo

**compensation** [kɒmpen'seɪʃən] *n (reparation)* compensación *f; (money)* indemnización *f*

**compensatory** [kɒmpen'seɪtərɪ] *adj* compensatorio(a)

**compere** ['kɒmpeə(r)] **1** *n* presentador(ora) *m,f*

**2** *vt (programme, show)* presentar

**compete** [kəm'piːt] *vi* competir (**with** con *or* contra); **to c. for a prize** competir por un premio

**competence** ['kɒmpɪtəns] *n* (**a**) *(ability)* competencia *f*, cualidades *fpl* (**b**) *Law* competencia *f*

**competent** ['kɒmpɪtənt] *adj* competente

**competition** [kɒmpɪ'tɪʃən] *n* (**a**) *(contest)* concurso *m; (in sport)* competición *f* (**b**) *(rivalry)* competencia; **to be in c. with sb** competir con alguien; **the c.** *(rivals)* la competencia

**competitive** [kəm'petɪtɪv] *adj* competitivo(a); **c. sports** deportes *mpl* de competición; *Com* **c. tendering** adjudicación *f* por concurso público

**competitor** [kəm'petɪtə(r)] *n* competidor(ora) *m,f*

**compilation** [kɒmpɪ'leɪʃən] *n* recopilación *f*, compilación *f*

**compile** [kəm'paɪl] *vt* recopilar, compilar

**complacency** [kəm'pleɪsənsɪ] *n* autocomplacencia *f*

**complacent** [kəm'pleɪsənt] *adj* autocomplaciente; **to be c. about sth** ser demasiado relajado(a) respecto a algo

**complain** [kəm'pleɪn] *vi* quejarse (**about** de); **to c. of** *(symptoms)* estar aquejado(a) de; **she complained that he had cheated** se quejó de que él había hecho trampa; **I can't c. about the service** no tengo queja alguna del servicio; **how are things? – I can't c.** ¿cómo van las cosas? – no me puedo quejar

**complaint** [kəm'pleɪnt] *n* (**a**) *(grievance)* queja *f;* **to have cause** *or* **grounds for c.** tener motivos de queja; **to lodge** *or* **make a c. (against sb)** presentar una queja (contra alguien) **(b)** *(illness)* afección *f*, problema *m*; **she suffers from a skin c.** tiene un problema de piel

**complement** ['kɒmplɪmənt] **1** *n* **(a)** *Gram* complemento *m* **(b)** *Naut* **the full c.** la dotación, la tripulación; *Fig* **I still have my full c. of teeth** todavía conservo toda mi dentadura
 **2** *vt* complementar

**complementary** [kɒmplɪ'mentərɪ] *adj* complementario(a); **c. medicine** medicina *f* alternativa

**complete** [kəm'pli:t] **1** *adj* **(a)** *(lacking nothing)* completo(a); **the c. works of...** las obras completas de... **(b)** *(entire)* **the c. harvest has been ruined** se ha arruinado la cosecha entera **(c)** *(finished)* terminado(a), acabado(a); **the work is now c.** el trabajo ya está terminado **(d)** *(total, thorough)* total, absoluto(a); **a c. turnaround in the situation** un vuelco total de la situación; **it came as a c. surprise** fue una sorpresa absoluta; **she is a c. fool** es tonta de remate; **he's a c. stranger** es un completo desconocido
 **2** *vt* completar, terminar; **to c. a form** rellenar un impreso

**completely** [kəm'pli:tlɪ] *adv* completamente, totalmente

**completion** [kəm'pli:ʃən] *n* finalización *f*, terminación *f*; **on c.** al terminar; **to be nearing c.** estar próximo a concluir

**complex** ['kɒmpleks] **1** *n (of buildings, psychological)* complejo *m*; **to have a c. about one's weight** tener complejo de gordo(a)
 **2** *adj* complejo(a)

**complexion** [kəm'plekʃən] *n* tez *f*; **to have a dark/fair c.** tener la tez oscura/clara; *Fig* **that puts a different c. on it** eso le da otro color

**complexity** [kəm'pleksɪtɪ] *n* complejidad *f*

**compliance** [kəm'plaɪəns] *n* cumplimiento *m* **(with** de**)**; **in c. with your wishes** en cumplimiento de sus deseos

**compliant** [kəm'plaɪənt] *adj* dócil, sumiso(a)

**complicate** ['kɒmplɪkeɪt] *vt* complicar; **the issue is complicated by the fact that...** el asunto se complica aún más debido al hecho de que...

**complicated** ['kɒmplɪkeɪtɪd] *adj* complicado(a)

**complication** [kɒmplɪ'keɪʃən] *n* complicación *f*; **complications** *(in patient's condition)* complicaciones

**complicity** [kəm'plɪsɪtɪ] *n* complicidad *f*

**compliment** ['kɒmplɪmənt] **1** *n* cumplido *m*; **to pay sb a c.** hacer un cumplido a alguien;

**to return the c.** *also Ironic* devolver el cumplido; **with compliments** con mis mejores deseos; **to send one's compliments to sb** enviar saludos a alguien; **compliments slip** nota *f* de cortesía
 **2** *vt* **to c. sb on sth** felicitar a alguien por algo

**complimentary** [kɒmplɪ'mentərɪ] *adj* **(a)** *(praising)* elogioso(a) **(b)** *(free)* de regalo, gratuito(a); **c. ticket** invitación *f*

**comply** [kəm'plaɪ] *vi* **to c. with** *(rule)* cumplir, ajustarse a; *(order)* cumplir; *(request)* someterse a

**component** [kəm'pəʊnənt] **1** *n* pieza *f*
 **2** *adj* **c. part** pieza *f*

**compose** [kəm'pəʊz] *vt* **(a)** *(music, poetry)* componer **(b)** *(constitute)* **to be composed of** estar compuesto(a) de **(c)** *(calm)* **to c. oneself** serenarse

**composed** [kəm'pəʊzd] *adj* sereno(a)

**composer** [kəm'pəʊzə(r)] *n* *Mus* compositor(ora) *m,f*

**composite** ['kɒmpəzɪt] *adj* compuesto(a)

**composition** [kɒmpə'zɪʃən] *n* *(piece of music, act of composing)* composición *f*; *(essay)* redacción *f*

**compositor** [kəm'pɒzɪtə(r)] *n* *Typ* cajista *mf*

**compost** ['kɒmpɒst] *n* abono *m*; **c. heap** montón *m* de abono

**composure** [kəm'pəʊʒə(r)] *n* compostura *f*; **to lose/recover one's c.** perder/recobrar la compostura

**compound¹** *n* ['kɒmpaʊnd] *Chem & Gram* compuesto *m*
 **2** *adj* compuesto(a); *Math* **c. fraction** fracción *f* mixta; *Med* **c. fracture** fractura *f* abierta; *Fin* **c. interest** interés *m* compuesto
 **3** *vt* [kəm'paʊnd] *(problem)* complicar, empeorar

**compound²** ['kɒmpaʊnd] *n* *(enclosure)* recinto *m*

**comprehend** [kɒmprɪ'hend] *vt* comprender

**comprehensible** [kɒmprɪ'hensəbəl] *adj* comprensible

**comprehension** [kɒmprɪ'henʃən] *n* comprensión *f*; **it is beyond my c.** me resulta incomprensible

**comprehensive** [kɒmprɪ'hensɪv] *adj* *(answer, study, view)* detallado(a), completo(a); *(defeat, victory)* rotundo(a); *Fin* **c. insurance** seguro *m* a todo riesgo; *Br* **c. (school)** ≃ instituto *m* (de enseñanza secundaria) *(no selectiva)*

**compress 1** *n* ['kɒmpres] *Med* compresa *f*, apósito *m*
 **2** *vt* [kəm'pres] *(gas)* comprimir; *Fig (text)* condensar

**compression** [kəm'preʃən] *n* compresión *f*

**compressor** [kəm'presə(r)] *n* compresor *m*

**comprise** [kəm'praɪz] *vt (include)* comprender, incluir; **to be comprised of** constar de

**compromise** ['kɒmprəmaɪz] **1** *n* solución *f* negociada *or* intermedia; **to reach a c.** alcanzar una solución intermedia

**2** *vt* poner en peligro; **to c. oneself** ponerse en un compromiso; **he compromised his principles** traicionó sus principios

**3** *vi* transigir, hacer concesiones

**compromising** ['kɒmprəmaɪzɪŋ] *adj* comprometedor(ora)

**compulsion** [kəm'pʌlʃən] *n (urge)* impulso *m*; *(obligation)* obligación *f*; **under c.** bajo coacción; **to be under no c. to do sth** no estar obligado(a) a hacer algo

**compulsive** [kəm'pʌlsɪv] *adj* compulsivo(a); **it's c. viewing** hay que verlo

**compulsory** [kəm'pʌlsəri] *adj* obligatorio(a); **c. purchase** expropiación *f*; **c. redundancy** despido *m* forzoso

**compunction** [kəm'pʌŋkʃən] *n* reparo *m*; **without c.** sin reparos

**computation** [kɒmpjuˈteɪʃən] *n* cálculo *m*

**compute** [kəm'pjuːt] *vt* calcular

**computer** [kəm'pjuːtə(r)] *n* ordenador *m*, *Am* computadora *f*; **c. game** juego *m* de ordenador; **c. literate** con conocimientos de informática; **c. printout** listado *m*, copia *f* impresa; **c. program** programa *m* informático; **c. programmer** programador(ora) *m,f*; **c. programming** programación *f* (de ordenadores); **c. science** informática *f*; **c. scientist** informático(a) *m,f*; **c. simulation** simulación *f* por ordenador

**computerization** [kəmpjuːtərar'zeɪʃən] *n* informatización *f*

**computerize** [kəm'pjuːtəraɪz] *vt (information, system)* informatizar

**computing** [kəm'pjuːtɪŋ] *n* informática *f*

**comrade** ['kɒmreɪd] *n* camarada *mf*, compañero(a) *m,f*

**comradeship** ['kɒmrədʃɪp] *n* camaradería *f*

**Con** *(abbrev* **Conservative)** conservador(ora)

**con¹** [kɒn] *Fam* **1** *n (swindle)* timo *m*; **what a c.!** ¡menudo timo!; **c. man** timador *m*

**2** *vt (pt & pp* **conned)** *(swindle)* timar; **to c. sth out of sb, to c. sb out of sth** timarle *or* estafarle algo a alguien; **to c. sb into doing sth** embaucar a alguien para que haga algo

**con²** *n Fam (prisoner)* recluso(a) *m,f*, preso(a) *m,f*

**con³** *n (disadvantage)* **the pros and cons** los pros y los contras

**concave** ['kɒnkeɪv] *adj* cóncavo(a)

**conceal** [kənˈsiːl] *vt (object)* ocultar, esconder **(from** de); *(fact)* ocultar **(from** a); **to c. oneself** esconderse, ocultarse

**concede** [kənˈsiːd] **1** *vt (a) (admit)* reconocer, admitir; **to c. defeat** admitir la derrota; **she was forced to c. that he was right** se vio obligada a reconocer que él tenia razón **(b)** *(grant, allow)* conceder **(c)** *Sport* **to c. a goal** encajar un gol

**2** *vi* rendirse

**conceit** [kənˈsiːt] *n (vanity)* engreimiento *m*, presuntuosidad *f*

**conceited** [kənˈsiːtɪd] *adj* engreído(a), presuntuoso(a)

**conceivable** [kənˈsiːvəbəl] *adj* concebible, posible; **it is c. that...** es posible que...

**conceivably** [kənˈsiːvəblɪ] *adv* posiblemente; **she could c. have done it** es posible que lo haya hecho ella

**conceive** [kənˈsiːv] **1** *vt* concebir

**2** *vi* **to c. of** imaginar, concebir

**concentrate** ['kɒnsəntreɪt] **1** *vt* concentrar; **the threat helped to c. their minds** la amenaza les hizo aplicarse

**2** *vi* concentrarse **(on** en)

**3** *n* concentrado *m*

**concentration** [kɒnsən'treɪʃən] *n* concentración *f*; **c. camp** campo *m* de concentración; **c. span** capacidad *f* de concentración

**concentric** [kɒn'sentrɪk] *adj Math* concéntrico(a)

**concept** ['kɒnsept] *n* concepto *m*

**conception** [kən'sepʃən] *n* **(a)** *(of child, idea)* concepción *f* **(b)** *(understanding)* idea *f*; **to have no c. of sth** no tener ni idea de algo

**conceptual** [kən'septjʊəl] *adj* conceptual

**conceptualize** [kən'septjʊəlaɪz] *vt* formarse un concepto de

**concern** [kən'sɜːn] **1** *n* **(a)** *(interest)* interés *m*; **it's no c. of mine/yours** no es de mi/tu incumbencia; **of public c.** de interés público **(b)** *(worry, compassion)* preocupación *f*; **to give cause for c.** dar motivos de preocupación; **there is no cause for c.** no hay motivo de preocupación; **to show c.** mostrar preocupación **(c)** *(company)* empresa *f*

**2** *vt* **(a)** *(affect)* concernir, incumbir; **to c. oneself with** *or* **about sth** preocuparse de algo; **as far as I'm concerned...** por lo que a mí respecta...; **to whom it may c.** a quien pueda interesar **(b)** *(worry)* preocupar **(c)** *(be about)* concernir, atañer; **it concerns your request for a transfer** tiene que ver con tu petición de traslado

**concerned** [kən'sɜːnd] *adj (worried)* preocupado(a) **(about** por)

**concerning** [kən'sɜːnɪŋ] *prep* en relación con *or* a

**concert** ['kɒnsət] *n* (a) *(musical)* concierto *m*; **in c.** en concierto; **c. hall** sala *f* de conciertos; **c. pianist** concertista *mf* de piano (b) *(cooperation)* **in c. with** en colaboración con

**concerted** [kən'sɜːtɪd] *adj* conjunto(a), concertado(a)

**concertina** [kɒnsə'tiːnə] *n* *(musical instrument)* concertina *f*

**concerto** [kən'tʃɜːtəʊ] (*pl* **concertos**) *n* *Mus* concierto *m*; **piano/violin c.** concierto para piano/violín

**concession** [kən'seʃən] *n* (a) *(compromise)* concesión *f*; **to make concessions** hacer concesiones (b) *(discount)* descuento *m*

**concessionary** [kən'seʃənərɪ] *adj* con descuento; *Br* **c. ticket** billete *m* con descuento *(para niños, estudiantes, parados o jubilados)*

**conciliate** [kən'sɪlɪeɪt] *vt* *(appease)* apaciguar; *(reconcile)* conciliar

**conciliation** [kənsɪlɪ'eɪʃən] *n* arbitraje *m*, conciliación *f*; **the dispute went to c.** se recurrió al arbitraje para dirimir el conflicto

**conciliatory** [kən'sɪlɪətərɪ] *adj* conciliador(ora)

**concise** [kən'saɪs] *adj* conciso(a)

**conclude** [kən'kluːd] **1** *vt* (a) *(finish)* concluir; **to c. a treaty** firmar un tratado (b) *(deduce)* **to c. that...** concluir que...

**2** *vi* *(finish)* concluir

**concluding** [kən'kluːdɪŋ] *adj* final

**conclusion** [kən'kluːʒən] *n* (a) *(inference)* conclusión *f*; **to draw a c.** sacar una conclusión; **to come to** *or* **reach a c.** llegar a una conclusión; **to jump to conclusions** sacar conclusiones precipitadas (b) *(end)* conclusión *f*; **in c.** en conclusión, concluyendo

**conclusive** [kən'kluːsɪv] *adj* concluyente

**concoct** [kən'kɒkt] *vt* *(dish)* preparar, confeccionar; *(plan, excuse)* tramar, fraguar

**concoction** [kən'kɒkʃən] *n* poción *f*, brebaje *m*

**concord** ['kɒŋkɔːd] *n* armonía *f*, concordia *f*

**concordance** [kən'kɔːdəns] *n* *(agreement)* consonancia *f*, acuerdo *m*; **to be in c. with...** estar en consonancia con...

**concourse** ['kɒŋkɔːs] *n* *(in airport, railway station)* vestíbulo *m*

**concrete** ['kɒŋkriːt] **1** *n* hormigón *m*; **c. jungle** jungla *f* de(l) asfalto; **c. mixer** hormigonera *f*

**2** *adj* *(definite)* concreto(a); *Gram* **c. noun** sustantivo *m* concreto

**concubine** ['kɒŋkjʊbaɪn] *n* concubina *f*

**concur** [kən'kɜː(r)] (*pt & pp* **concurred**) *vi* *(agree)* coincidir, estar de acuerdo (**with** con)

**concurrent** [kən'kʌrənt] *adj* simultáneo(a)

**concurrently** [kən'kʌrəntlɪ] *adv* simultáneamente

**concuss** [kən'kʌs] *vt* conmocionar

**concussed** [kən'kʌst] *adj* conmocionado(a)

**concussion** [kən'kʌʃən] *n* conmoción *f* cerebral

**condemn** [kən'dem] *vt* (a) *Law (sentence)* condenar (**to** a); **to c. sb to death** condenar a alguien a muerte; **the condemned cell** la celda de los condenados a muerte (b) *(censure)* condenar (c) *(building)* declarar en ruina

**condemnation** [kɒndem'neɪʃən] *n* condena *f*

**condensation** [kɒnden'seɪʃən] *n* *(on glass)* vaho *m*; *(on walls)* condensación *f*, vapor *m* condensado

**condense** [kən'dens] **1** *vt* (a) *(gas, liquid)* condensar; **condensed milk** leche *f* condensada (b) *(text)* condensar

**2** *vi* condensarse

**condenser** [kən'densə(r)] *n* *Tech* condensador *m*

**condescend** [kɒndɪ'send] *vi* **to c. towards sb** tratar a alguien con aires de superioridad; **to c. to do sth** dignarse a *or* tener a bien hacer algo

**condescending** [kɒndɪ'sendɪŋ] *adj* altivo(a)

**condescension** [kɒndɪ'senʃən] *n* altivez *f*

**condiment** ['kɒndɪmənt] *n* condimento *m*

**condition** [kən'dɪʃən] *n* (a) *(state)* condiciones *fpl*, estado *m*; **in good/bad c.** en buen/mal estado; **you're in no c. to drive!** no estás en condiciones de conducir; **to be out of c.** *(of person)* no estar en forma

(b) **conditions** *(circumstances)* circunstancias *fpl*; **working conditions** condiciones *fpl* laborales; **driving conditions** estado *m* de las carreteras; *Law* **conditions of employment** términos *mpl* del contrato

(c) *(requirement)* condición *f*; **on (the) c. that...** con la condición *or* a condición de que...; **on no c.** bajo ningún concepto; **on one c.** con una condición

(d) *Med* enfermedad *f*, afección *f*; **heart c.** afección cardíaca

**2** *vt* (a) *(influence)* condicionar; **we have been conditioned to believe that...** nos han programado para creer que...; *Psy* **a conditioned reflex** un reflejo condicionado

(b) *(hair)* suavizar

**conditional** [kən'dɪʃənəl] **1** *n* *Gram* condicional *m*, potencial *m*

**2** *adj* condicional; **to be c. on sth** depender de algo, tener algo como condición; *Law* **c. discharge** remisión *f* condicional de la pena

**conditionally** [kən'dɪʃənəlɪ] *adv* *(accept, grant)* condicionalmente

**conditioner** [kən'dɪʃənə(r)] *n* *(for hair)* suavizante *m*

**conditioning** [kən'dɪʃənɪŋ] n (psychological) condicionamiento m

**condo** ['kɒndəʊ] (pl condos) n US (apartment) piso m (en propiedad); (building) = bloque de pisos poseídos por diferentes propietarios

**condolences** [kən'dəʊlənsɪz] npl pésame m; to offer sb one's c. dar el pésame a alguien

**condom** ['kɒndəm] n preservativo m, condón m

**condominium** [kɒndə'mɪnɪəm] n US (apartment) piso m (en propiedad); (building) = bloque de pisos poseídos por diferentes propietarios

**condone** [kən'dəʊn] vt justificar; I cannot c. such behaviour no puedo justificar ese tipo de comportamiento

**condor** ['kɒndɔ:(r)] n cóndor m

**conducive** [kən'dju:sɪv] adj to be c. to ser favorable para, facilitar; these conditions are not c. to economic growth estas condiciones no son favorables para el crecimiento de la economía

**conduct 1** n ['kɒndʌkt] (behaviour) conducta f

**2** vt [kən'dʌkt] (a) (business, operations) gestionar, hacer; (campaign, experiment) realizar, hacer; Mus (orchestra) dirigir; to c. oneself comportarse, conducirse (b) (guide) we were conducted round the factory nos llevaron por toda la fábrica; a conducted tour una visita guiada (c) (heat, electricity) conducir

**3** vi Mus dirigir

**conduction** [kən'dʌkʃən] n Phys conducción f

**conductivity** [kɒndʌk'tɪvɪtɪ] n Phys conductividad f

**conductor** [kən'dʌktə(r)] n (a) Br (on bus) revisor m (b) (of orchestra) director(ora) m,f de orquesta (c) Phys conductor m

**conductress** [kən'dʌktrɪs] Br n (on bus) revisora f

**conduit** ['kɒndjʊɪt] n conducto m

**cone** [kəʊn] n (shape) cono m; (of pine) piña f; (for ice cream) cucurucho m; (for traffic) cono m (de tráfico)

**cone-shaped** ['kəʊnʃeɪpt] adj cónico(a)

**confab** ['kɒnfæb] n Fam (discussion) deliberación f; to have a c. about sth deliberar sobre algo

**confectioner** [kən'fekʃənə(r)] n pastelero(a) m,f; Culin c.'s custard crema f pastelera; c.'s (shop) pastelería f

**confectionery** [kən'fekʃənərɪ] n dulces mpl

**confederacy** [kən'fedərəsɪ] n confederación f, liga f

**confederate** [kən'fedərət] **1** n compinche mf, cómplice mf

**2** adj confederado(a)

**confederation** [kənfedə'reɪʃən] n confederación f

**confer** [kən'fɜ:(r)] (pt & pp conferred) **1** vt (title, rank, powers) conferir, otorgar (on a); (degree, diploma) conceder, otorgar (on a)

**2** vi (discuss) deliberar (with con)

**conference** ['kɒnfərəns] n congreso m; Com to be in c. estar reunido(a)

**confess** [kən'fes] **1** vt confesar, admitir; Rel confesar; to c. that... confesar que...

**2** vi confesar; Rel confesarse; to c. to sth confesarse culpable de algo, confesar algo

**confession** [kən'feʃən] n confesión f; Rel to go to c. confesarse

**confessional** [kən'feʃənəl] n Rel confesionario m, confesonario m

**confessor** [kən'fesə(r)] n Rel confesor m

**confetti** [kən'fetɪ] n confeti m

**confidant** [kɒnfɪ'dænt] n confidente m

**confide** [kən'faɪd] **1** vt confiar; to c. sth to sb confiarle algo a alguien

**2** vi to c. in sb confiarse a or confesarse con alguien

**confidence** ['kɒnfɪdəns] n (a) (trust) confianza f; to have c. in sb fiarse de alguien, tener confianza en alguien; to have every c. that... estar completamente seguro(a) de que...; to take sb into one's c. confiarse a alguien; c. trick timo m, estafa f (b) (self-assurance) confianza f (en uno mismo); she's full of c. tiene mucha confianza en sí misma (c) (secret) to exchange confidences intercambiar confidencias; in c. confidencialmente

**confident** ['kɒnfɪdənt] adj seguro(a) de sí mismo(a); to be c. that... estar seguro(a) de que...

**confidential** [kɒnfɪ'denʃəl] adj (secret) confidencial, secreto(a)

**confidentiality** [kɒnfɪdenʃɪ'ælɪtɪ] n confidencialidad f

**confidentially** [kɒnfɪ'denʃəlɪ] adv confidencialmente

**confidently** ['kɒnfɪdəntlɪ] adv con seguridad

**configuration** [kənfɪgjʊ'reɪʃən] n configuración f

**confine** [kən'faɪn] vt (a) (imprison) confinar, recluir; to be confined to bed tener que guardar cama; to be confined to barracks quedarse arrestado(a) en el cuartel; in a confined space en un espacio limitado (b) (limit) to c. oneself to sth limitarse a algo

**confinement** [kən'faɪnmənt] n (a) (in prison) reclusión f, encierro m (b) Old-fashioned Med (birth) parto m

**confines** ['kɒnfaɪnz] npl límites mpl; within the c. of the home en el ámbito del hogar

**confirm** [kən'fɜ:m] vt confirmar

**confirmation** [kɒnfə'meɪʃən] *n also Rel* confirmación *f*

**confirmed** [kən'fɜːmd] *adj (smoker, liar)* empedernido(a)

**confiscate** ['kɒnfɪskeɪt] *vt* confiscar

**confiscation** [kɒnfɪs'keɪʃən] *n* confiscación *f*

**conflagration** [kɒnflə'greɪʃən] *n Formal* incendio *m*

**conflict 1** *n* ['kɒnflɪkt] conflicto *m*; **to come into c. with** entrar en conflicto con; **a c. of interests** un conflicto de intereses

**2** *vi* [kən'flɪkt] *(of evidence, reports)* chocar **(with** con**)**

**conflicting** [kən'flɪktɪŋ] *adj (opinions)* encontrado(a); *(reports, evidence)* contradictorio(a)

**confluence** ['kɒnfluəns] *n* confluencia *f*

**conform** [kən'fɔːm] *vi* **(a)** *(be in keeping with) (laws, standards)* ajustarse **(to** a**)**; *(expectations)* ajustarse *or* responder **(with** a**) (b)** *(behave normally)* ser conformista, actuar como todo el mundo

**conformist** [kən'fɔːmɪst] *n & adj* conformista *mf*

**conformity** [kən'fɔːmɪtɪ] *n* conformidad *f*; **in c. with...** de conformidad con...

**confound** [kən'faʊnd] *vt* **(a)** *(frustrate)* frustrar **(b)** *(surprise)* desconcertar, sorprender **(c)** *Fam* **c. it/him!** ¡maldita sea!

**confront** [kən'frʌnt] *vt (face up to, meet face to face)* enfrentarse a, hacer frente a; **to be confronted by a problem** enfrentarse a un problema; **to c. sb (about sth)** hablar cara a cara con alguien (acerca de algo); **to c. sb with the facts** enfrentar a alguien a los hechos

**confrontation** [kɒnfrʌn'teɪʃən] *n* confrontación *f*

**confuse** [kən'fjuːz] *vt (bewilder)* desconcertar, confundir; *(mix up)* confundir

**confused** [kən'fjuːzd] *adj (person)* confundido(a), desorientado(a); *(mind, ideas, situation)* confuso(a); **to get c.** desorientarse

**confusing** [kən'fjuːzɪŋ] *adj* confuso(a); **Mexican history is very c.** la historia de México es muy complicada

**confusion** [kən'fjuːʒən] *n (of person)* desconcierto *m*; *(disorder)* confusión *f*; **to throw sth into c.** *(country, party)* sumir a algo en el desconcierto; *(plans)* trastocar algo por completo

**congeal** [kən'dʒiːl] *vi (of blood)* coagularse

**congenial** [kən'dʒiːnɪəl] *adj (person)* simpático(a); *(atmosphere)* agradable

**congenital** [kən'dʒenɪtəl] *adj* congénito(a); *Fig* **c. liar** mentiroso(a) *m,f* patológico(a)

**conger** ['kɒŋɡə(r)] *n* **c. (eel)** congrio *m*

**congested** [kən'dʒestɪd] *adj (street, lungs)* congestionado(a)

**congestion** [kən'dʒestʃən] *n (of traffic, lungs)* congestión *f*

**conglomerate** [kən'ɡlɒmərət] *n* **(a)** *Com* conglomerado *m* de empresas **(b)** *Geol* conglomerado *m*

**Congo** ['kɒŋɡəʊ] *n* **the C.** *(country)* el Congo

**Congolese** ['kɒŋɡəliːz] *n & adj* congoleño(a) *m,f*

**congratulate** [kən'ɡrætjʊleɪt] *vt* felicitar; **to c. oneself on (having done) sth** felicitarse por (haber hecho) algo

**congratulations** [kənɡrætjʊ'leɪʃənz] *npl* enhorabuena *f*, felicitaciones *fpl*; **to give** *or* **offer one's c. to sb** dar la enhorabuena a alguien; **c.!** ¡felicidades!

**congratulatory** [kən'ɡrætjʊleɪtərɪ] *adj* de felicitación

**congregate** ['kɒŋɡrɪɡeɪt] *vi* congregarse

**congregation** [kɒŋɡrɪ'ɡeɪʃən] *n (of church)* fieles *mpl*, feligreses *mpl*

**congress** ['kɒŋɡres] *n (conference)* congreso *m*; *US Pol* **C.** el Congreso *(de los Estados Unidos)*

**Congressman** ['kɒŋɡresmæn] *n US Pol* congresista *m*

**Congresswoman** ['kɒŋɡreswʊmən] *n US Pol* congresista *f*

**conical** ['kɒnɪkəl] *adj* cónico(a)

**conifer** ['kɒnɪfə(r)] *n* conífera *f*

**coniferous** [kə'nɪfərəs] *adj* conífero(a)

**conjecture** [kən'dʒektʃə(r)] **1** *n* conjetura *f*; **it's sheer c.** no son más que conjeturas

**2** *vt* conjeturar

**3** *vi* hacer conjeturas

**conjugal** ['kɒndʒʊɡəl] *adj* conyugal

**conjugate** ['kɒndʒʊɡeɪt] *Gram* **1** *vt* conjugar

**2** *vi* conjugarse

**conjugation** [kɒndʒʊ'ɡeɪʃən] *n Gram* conjugación *f*

**conjunction** [kən'dʒʌŋkʃən] *n* conjunción *f*; **in c. with** junto con

**conjunctivitis** [kəndʒʌŋktɪ'vaɪtɪs] *n Med* conjuntivitis *f inv*

**conjure** ['kʌndʒə(r)] *vi (do magic)* hacer juegos de manos; *Fig* **a name to c. with** un nombre ilustre

▶**conjure up** *vt sep* **(a)** *(produce)* hacer aparecer; **she conjured up a meal** preparó una comida prácticamente con nada **(b)** *(call to mind)* evocar

**conjurer** ['kʌndʒərə(r)] *n* mago(a) *m,f*, prestidigitador(ora) *m,f*

**conjuring** ['kʌndʒərɪŋ] *n* magia *f*, prestidigitación *f*; **c. trick** juego *m* de manos

**conjuror = conjurer**

**conk** [kɒŋk] *n Fam (nose)* napias *fpl*

▶**conk out** *vi Fam* **(a)** *(stop working) (of car, TV)* escacharrarse **(b)** *(fall asleep)* quedarse roque

**conker** ['kɒŋkə(r)] n Fam (chestnut) castaña f; Br conkers (game) = juego con castañas ensartadas en cordeles

**conman** ['kɒnmæn] n timador m

**connect** [kə'nekt] **1** vt (a) (pipes, wires, circuits) conectar (**to** con or a), empalmar (**to** con or a); **to c. sth to the mains** enchufar algo, conectar algo a la red

(**b**) (relate) (person, problem) relacionar (**with** con), vincular (**with** con or a); **to be connected with…** estar relacionado(a) con…; **are they connected?** ¿existe algún vínculo or alguna relación entre ellos?; **the two issues are not connected** los dos asuntos no están relacionados; **to be well connected** (socially) estar bien relacionado(a)

(**c**) Tel poner, pasar; **will you c. me with Lost Property, please?** ¿me pone con el departamento de objetos perdidos, por favor?

**2** vi (a) (of wires, roads, pipes) conectarse, empalmarse; **the living room connects with the kitchen** el salón da a la cocina

(**b**) (of train, plane) enlazar (**with** con)

(**c**) (of blow) dar en el blanco

►**connect up** vt sep (pipes, wires) conectar

**connection** [kə'nekʃən] n (a) (link, association) conexión f, vínculo m; **to make a c. between X and Y** relacionar X con Y; **that was when I made the c.** entonces lo relacioné; **in c. with** en relación con; **in this c.** a este respecto (**b**) (acquaintance) contacto m; **she has important connections** está bien relacionada (**c**) (of pipes, wires) conexión f, empalme m (**d**) (train, plane) enlace m; **I missed my c.** he perdido el enlace

**connivance** [kə'naɪvəns] n connivencia f; **to be in c. with sb** estar en connivencia con alguien

**connive** [kə'naɪv] vi (a) (conspire) **to c. with** confabularse con (**b**) (contribute) **to c. at** contribuir a

**conniving** [kə'naɪvɪŋ] adj confabulador(ora)

**connoisseur** [kɒnɪ'sɜː(r)] n entendido(a) m,f (**of** en)

**connotation** [kɒnə'teɪʃən] n connotación f

**conquer** ['kɒŋkə(r)] vt (country, sb's heart) conquistar; (difficulty, one's shyness, fears) vencer

**conquering** ['kɒŋkərɪŋ] adj vencedor(ora)

**conqueror** ['kɒŋkərə(r)] n conquistador(ora) m,f

**conquest** ['kɒŋkwest] n conquista f; **to make a c. of sb** conquistar a alguien

**conscience** ['kɒnʃəns] n conciencia f; **to have a clear c.** tener la conciencia tranquila; **to have a guilty c.** tener sentimiento de culpa; **she had three deaths on her c.** sobre su conciencia pesaban tres muertes; **in all c.** en conciencia

**conscientious** [kɒnʃɪ'enʃəs] adj concienzudo(a); **she's c. about wiping her feet before entering the house** nunca deja de limpiarse los zapatos antes de entrar en casa; **c. objector** objetor(ora) m,f de conciencia

**conscious** ['kɒnʃəs] adj (a) (awake) **to be c.** estar consciente; **to become c.** volver en sí, recobrar la con(s)ciencia (**b**) (aware) **to be c. of** ser consciente de; **to become c. of** cobrar conciencia de, darse cuenta de; **to be c. that…** ser consciente de que…; Psy **the c. mind** la con(s)ciencia, el consciente (**c**) (intentional) consciente, deliberado(a); **to make a c. effort to do sth** hacer un esfuerzo consciente para hacer algo; **to make a c. decision to do sth** tomar conscientemente la decisión de hacer algo

**consciousness** ['kɒnʃəsnɪs] n (a) Med con(s)ciencia f; **to lose c.** quedar inconsciente; **to regain c.** volver en sí (**b**) (awareness) conciencia f, concienciación f; **to raise sb's c. of sth** concienciar a alguien de algo; **c. raising** concienciación f

**conscript 1** n ['kɒnskrɪpt] recluta mf (forzoso)

**2** vt [kən'skrɪpt] reclutar (forzosamente)

**conscription** [kən'skrɪpʃən] n reclutamiento m obligatorio

**consecrate** ['kɒnsɪkreɪt] vt Rel & Fig consagrar (**to** a)

**consecration** [kɒnsɪ'kreɪʃən] n consagración f

**consecutive** [kən'sekjʊtɪv] adj consecutivo(a); **on three c. days** tres días consecutivos

**consensus** [kən'sensəs] n consenso m; **to reach a c.** alcanzar un consenso

**consent** [kən'sent] **1** n consentimiento m

**2** vi **to c. to (do) sth** consentir (en hacer) algo

**consequence** ['kɒnsɪkwəns] n (a) (result) consecuencia f; **as a c.** como consecuencia; **in c.** en consecuencia; **to take the consequences** asumir las consecuencias (**b**) (importance) **of little c.** de poca relevancia; **of no c.** irrelevante

**consequent** ['kɒnsɪkwənt] adj consiguiente; **c. upon sth** resultante de algo

**conservation** [kɒnsə'veɪʃən] n (of the environment) conservación f or protección f del medio ambiente; (of energy, resources) conservación f; **c. area** (of town, city) zona f arquitectónica protegida; (nature reserve) zona f protegida

**conservationist** [kɒnsə'veɪʃənɪst] n ecologista mf

**Conservative** [kən'sɜːvətɪv] Br Pol **1** adj conservador(ora); **the C. Party** el Partido Conservador

**2** n conservador(ora) m,f; **the Conservatives** los conservadores

**conservative** [kən'sɜːvətɪv] *adj* conservador(ora); **a c. estimate** un cálculo prudente *or* por lo bajo

**conservatory** [kən'sɜːvətrɪ] *n* (a) *(room)* = habitación acristalada que da al jardín de una casa (b) *Mus* conservatorio *m*

**conserve 1** *vt* [kən'sɜːv] *(monument)* conservar, preservar; *(water, energy)* reservar
**2** *n* ['kɒnsɜːv] *(jam)* compota *f*

**consider** [kən'sɪdə(r)] *vt* (a) *(think over)* considerar; **to c. doing sth** considerar hacer algo; **to c. whether to do sth** contemplar la posibilidad de hacer algo; **the jury retired to c. its verdict** el jurado se retiró a deliberar; **to c. sb for a job** tener en cuenta a alguien para un puesto (b) *(take into account)* tener en cuenta; **all things considered** mirándolo bien (c) *(regard)* considerar; **c. it done** considéralo hecho; **to c. oneself happy** considerarse feliz

**considerable** [kən'sɪdərəbəl] *adj* considerable; **with c. difficulty** con grandes dificultades

**considerate** [kən'sɪdərət] *adj* considerado(a) **(towards** *or* **to)**

**consideration** [kənsɪdə'reɪʃən] *n* (a) *(deliberation)* **different possibilities are under c.** se están estudiando varias posibilidades; **after due c.** tras las debidas deliberaciones; **to give a proposal some c.** considerar una propuesta; **to take sth into c.** tomar algo en consideración (b) *(factor)* factor *m*; **for a small c.** *(payment)* a cambio de una pequeña retribución (c) *(respect)* consideración *f*; **show some c.!** ¡ten un poco de consideración!; **out of c. for** por consideración hacia

**considering** [kən'sɪdərɪŋ] **1** *prep* considerando, teniendo en cuenta
**2** *conj* considerando que, teniendo en cuenta que; **c. (that) he is so young** teniendo en cuenta su juventud
**3** *adv* it's not so bad, **c.** no está tan mal, después de todo

**consign** [kən'saɪn] *vt* (a) *(entrust)* confiar **(to** a) (b) *(send)* consignar **(to** a), enviar **(to** a)

**consignment** [kən'saɪnmənt] *n* *(of goods)* envío *m*

▸**consist of** [kən'sɪst] *vt insep* consistir en

**consistency** [kən'sɪstənsɪ] *n* (a) *(of substance, liquid)* consistencia *f* (b) *(of actions, arguments)* coherencia *f*, congruencia *f*; **to lack c.** ser incongruente (c) *(of performance, work)* regularidad *f*, constancia *f*

**consistent** [kən'sɪstənt] *adj* *(reasoning, behaviour)* coherente, congruente; *(quality, standard)* invariable, constante; *(refusal, failure)* constante, continuo(a); **c. with** coherente con, consecuente con

**consistently** [kən'sɪstəntlɪ] *adv* *(play, perform)* con regularidad; *(fail, deny, oppose)* constantemente

**consolation** [kɒnsə'leɪʃən] *n* consuelo *m*; **that's one c.** es un consuelo; **if it's any c.** si te sirve de consuelo; **c. prize** premio *m* de consolación

**console¹** ['kɒnsəʊl] *n* *(control panel)* consola *f*

**console²** [kən'səʊl] *vt* consolar

**consolidate** [kən'sɒlɪdeɪt] **1** *vt* consolidar
**2** *vi* consolidarse

**consolidation** [kənsɒlɪ'deɪʃən] *n* consolidación *f*

**consonant** ['kɒnsənənt] **1** *n* consonante *f*
**2** *adj Formal* **c. with** en consonancia con

**consort** ['kɒnsɔːt] *n* *(spouse of monarch)* consorte *mf*

▸**consort with** [kən'sɔːt] *vt insep* asociarse con

**consortium** [kən'sɔːtɪəm] *n Com* consorcio *m*

**conspicuous** [kən'spɪkjʊəs] *adj* *(person)* visible; *(colour)* llamativo(a); *(bravery, intelligence)* notable; **to look c.** resaltar, llamar la atención; **to make oneself c.** hacerse notar; **in a c. position** en un lugar bien visible; **to be c. by one's/its absence** brillar por su ausencia; **c. consumption** ostentación *f* en el consumo

**conspiracy** [kən'spɪrəsɪ] *n* conspiración *f*, conjura *f*; **c. theory** = teoría que sostiene la existencia de una conspiración, generalmente imaginaria

**conspirator** [kən'spɪrətə(r)] *n* conspirador(ora) *m,f*

**conspiratorial** [kənspɪrə'tɔːrɪəl] *adj* conspirador(ora), de conspiración

**conspire** [kən'spaɪə(r)] *vi* *(of person)* conspirar **(against/with** contra/con); *(of events)* obrar; **to c. with sb to do sth** conspirar con alguien para hacer algo; **circumstances conspired against me** las circunstancias obraban en mi contra

**constable** ['kʌnstəbəl, 'kɒnstəbəl] *n Br* policía *mf*; **chief c.** jefe(a) *m,f* de policía

**constabulary** [kən'stæbjʊlərɪ] *n* (cuerpo *m* de) policía *f*

**constant** ['kɒnstənt] **1** *adj* (a) *(unchanging)* *(price, temperature)* constante; *(friend)* leal (b) *(unceasing)* *(attention, questions)* continuo(a), constante; **a c. stream of insults** una sarta de insultos
**2** *n* constante *f*

**constellation** [kɒnstə'leɪʃən] *n* constelación *f*

**consternation** [kɒnstə'neɪʃən] *n* consternación *f*

**constipated** ['kɒnstɪpeɪtɪd] *adj* estreñido(a)

**constipation** [kɒnstɪˈpeɪʃən] *n* estreñimiento *m*

**constituency** [kənˈstɪtjʊənsɪ] *n Pol* circunscripción *f* electoral

**constituent** [kənˈstɪtjʊənt] **1** *n* (a) *Pol* elector(ora) *m,f* (b) *(part)* elemento *m* (constitutivo) **2** *adj* constitutivo

**constitute** [ˈkɒnstɪtjuːt] *vt* constituir

**constitution** [kɒnstɪˈtjuːʃən] *n* (*of state, organization*) constitución *f*; **to have a strong c.** ser de constitución robusta

**constitutional** [kɒnstɪˈtjuːʃənəl] **1** *n* (*walk*) paseo *m*
**2** *adj* (*reform, decision*) constitucional; **c. monarchy** monarquía *f* constitucional

**constrain** [kənˈstreɪn] *vt* restringir, constreñir; **to feel constrained to do sth** sentirse obligado(a) a hacer algo

**constraint** [kənˈstreɪnt] *n* (*restriction*) limitación *f*, restricción *f*; **to place constraints (up)on sb/sth** imponer restricciones a alguien/algo; **to do sth under c.** hacer algo bajo coacción; **to speak without c.** hablar abiertamente; **financial constraints** restricciones económicas

**constrict** [kənˈstrɪkt] *vt* (*blood vessel*) constreñir, contraer; (*person, economy*) constreñir

**constriction** [kənˈstrɪkʃən] *n* (*of person, economy*) constricción *f*; **c. of the blood vessels** vasoconstricción *f*

**construct 1** *n* [ˈkɒnstrʌkt] (*idea*) concepto *m*
**2** *vt* [kənˈstrʌkt] (*build*) construir

**construction** [kənˈstrʌkʃən] *n* (a) (*act of building, thing built*) construcción *f*; **under c.** en construcción; **the c. industry** (el sector de) la construcción; **c. site** obra *f*; **c. workers** obreros *mpl* de la construcción (b) (*interpretation*) **to put a favourable/unfavourable c. on sb's words** darle un sentido bueno/malo a las palabras de alguien

**constructive** [kənˈstrʌktɪv] *adj* (*comment, proposal*) constructivo(a)

**construe** [kənˈstruː] *vt* (*interpret*) interpretar

**consul** [ˈkɒnsəl] *n* cónsul *mf*

**consular** [ˈkɒnsjʊlə(r)] *adj* consular

**consulate** [ˈkɒnsjʊlət] *n* consulado *m*

**consult** [kənˈsʌlt] **1** *vt* consultar
**2** *vi* consultar (**with sb/about sth** con alguien/sobre algo)

**consultancy** [kənˈsʌltənsɪ] *n* (a) (*of medical specialist*) = plaza de especialista hospitalario(a) (b) *Com* asesoría *f*, consultoría *f*

**consultant** [kənˈsʌltənt] *n* (a) (*medical specialist*) médico(a) *m,f* especialista (*en hospital*) (b) *Com* asesor(ora) *m,f*, consultor(ora) *m,f*

**consultation** [kɒnsəlˈteɪʃən] *n* consulta *f*; **to hold a c. (with)** consultar (con); **in c. with sb** con la asesoría de alguien

**consume** [kənˈsjuːm] *vt* (*food, fuel*) consumir; **to be consumed with jealousy/desire** estar consumido(a) por los celos/el deseo

**consumer** [kənˈsjuːmə(r)] *n* (*of product*) consumidor(ora) *m,f*; **the c. society** la sociedad de consumo; **c. durables** bienes *mpl* de consumo duraderos; **c. goods** bienes *mpl* de consumo; *Econ* **c. price index** índice *m* de precios al consumo, IPC *m*; **c. protection** protección *f* del consumidor

**consumerism** [kənˈsjuːmərɪzəm] *n* consumismo *m*

**consummate 1** *adj* [ˈkɒnsjʊmət] (*skilled*) consumado(a)
**2** *vt* [ˈkɒnsəmeɪt] (*marriage, relationship*) consumar

**consumption** [kənˈsʌmpʃən] *n* (a) (*of goods, resources*) consumo *m*; **unfit for human c.** no apto(a) para el consumo humano (b) *Old-fashioned* (*tuberculosis*) tisis *f inv*

**contact** [ˈkɒntækt] **1** *n* contacto *m*; **to be in/come into c. with** estar/ponerse en contacto con; **to make c. with sb** contactar con alguien, ponerse en contacto con alguien; **to lose c. with sb** perder el contacto con alguien; **he has lots of contacts** tiene muchos contactos; **c. lens** lente *f* de contacto; **c. lenses, contacts** lentillas *fpl*
**2** *vt* contactar con, ponerse en contacto con

**contagious** [kənˈteɪdʒəs] *adj* (*disease, laughter*) contagioso(a)

**contain** [kənˈteɪn] *vt* (a) (*hold, include*) contener (b) (*control*) contener; **I could scarcely c. my indignation** apenas podía contener la indignación; **to c. oneself** contenerse

**container** [kənˈteɪnə(r)] *n* (*for storage*) recipiente *m*; (*for transport*) contenedor *m*; **c. lorry** camión *m* de transporte de contenedores; **c. ship** buque *m* de transporte de contenedores; **c. terminal** terminal *f* de contenedores

**contaminate** [kənˈtæmɪneɪt] *vt also Fig* contaminar

**contamination** [kəntæmɪˈneɪʃən] *n* contaminación *f*

**contd** (*abbr* **continued**) cont., continúa, sigue; **c. on page 14** sigue en la página 14

**contemplate** [ˈkɒntəmpleɪt] *vt* (*look at, consider*) contemplar; **to c. doing sth** contemplar (la posibilidad de) hacer algo

**contemplation** [kɒntemˈpleɪʃən] *n* contemplación *f*

**contemplative** [kənˈtemplətɪv] *adj* contemplativo(a)

**contemporary** [kənˈtempərərɪ] *n & adj* contemporáneo(a) *m,f*

**contempt** [kənˈtempt] *n* desprecio *m*, menosprecio *m*; **to hold sb/sth in c.** sentir desprecio por alguien/algo; *Law* **c. of court** desacato *m* (al tribunal)

**contemptible** [kən'temptəbəl] *adj* despreciable

**contemptuous** [kən'temptjʊəs] *adj* despreciativo(a); **to be c. of** mostrar desprecio hacia

**contend** [kən'tend] **1** *vt* **to c. that...** afirmar que..., alegar que...

**2** *vi* (a) *(struggle)* enfrentarse (**with** a *or* con); **the difficulties I have to c. with** las dificultades a las que me tengo que enfrentar (b) *(compete)* **to c. for sth** disputarse algo, competir por algo

**contender** [kən'tendə(r)] *n* contendiente *mf*

**content**[1] ['kɒntent] *n* contenido *m*; **contents** *(of pockets, drawer, house)* contenido *m*; **contents** *(in book)* índice *m*; **high protein/fibre c.** alto contenido en proteínas/fibra

**content**[2] [kən'tent] **1** *adj* **to be c. with sth** estar satisfecho(a) con *or* de algo

**2** *vt* **to c. oneself with (doing) sth** contentarse con (hacer) algo

**contented** [kən'tentɪd] *adj (person, smile)* satisfecho(a) (**with** con *or* de); **to be c. (with)** estar satisfecho(a) (con *or* de)

**contention** [kən'tenʃən] *n* (a) *(dispute)* disputa *f*; **to be in c. (for sth)** tener posibilidades (de ganar algo) (b) *(opinion)* argumento *m*; **my c. is that...** sostengo que...

**contentious** [kən'tenʃəs] *adj (issue, views)* polémico(a); *(person)* que siempre se mete en discusiones

**contentment** [kən'tentmənt] *n* satisfacción *f*

**contest 1** *n* ['kɒntest] *(competition)* concurso *m*; *(in boxing)* combate *m*; **leadership c.** carrera *f* *or* pugna *f* por la jefatura del partido

**2** *vt* [kən'test] *(right, decision)* impugnar, rebatir; **to c. a seat** disputar un escaño; *Pol* **a fiercely contested election** unas elecciones muy reñidas

**contestant** [kən'testənt] *n (in competition, game)* concursante *mf*; *(in sporting competition)* competidor(ora) *m,f*; *(in election)* candidato(a) *m,f*

**context** ['kɒntekst] *n* contexto *m*; **in/out of c.** en/fuera de contexto; **to quote sth out of c.** citar algo fuera de contexto; **to put sth into c.** poner algo en contexto

**continent**[1] ['kɒntɪnənt] *n (landmass)* continente *m*; **(on) the C.** (en) Europa continental

**continent**[2] *adj Med & Formal* continente

**continental** [kɒntɪ'nentəl] *adj* (a) *(in geography)* continental; **c. drift** deriva *f* continental; **c. shelf** plataforma *f* continental (b) *(European)* de la Europa continental; **c. breakfast** desayuno *m* continental; **c. quilt** edredón *m*

**contingency** [kən'tɪndʒənsɪ] *n* contingencia *f*, eventualidad *f*; **to allow for contingencies** tomar precauciones ante cualquier eventualidad; **c. fund** fondo *m* de emergencia; **c. plan** plan *m* de emergencia

**contingent** [kən'tɪndʒənt] **1** *n* contingente *m*

**2** *adj* contingente; **to be c. on sth** depender de algo

**continual** [kən'tɪnjʊəl] *adj* continuo(a)

**continuation** [kəntɪnjʊ'eɪʃən] *n (of story, situation)* continuación *f*; *(of road)* continuación *f*, prolongación *f*

**continue** [kən'tɪnju:] **1** *vt* continuar, seguir; *(after interruption)* reanudar; **to c. doing** *or* **to do sth** continuar *or* seguir haciendo algo; **to be continued** continuará; **continued on page 30** sigue en la página 30

**2** *vi* continuar, seguir; **he continued on his way** siguió su camino; **the situation cannot c.** esto no puede continuar así

**continuity** [kɒntɪ'nju:ɪtɪ] *n* continuidad *f*; **c. announcer** *(on TV)* locutor(ora) *m,f* de continuidad; **c. girl** script *f*, anotadora *f*

**continuous** [kən'tɪnjʊəs] *adj* continuo(a); *Sch Univ* **c. assessment** evaluación *f* continua; *Comptr* **c. paper** *or* **stationery** papel *m* continuo; *Cin* **c. performance** sesión *f* continua

**contort** [kən'tɔ:t] *vt* contorsionar

**contortion** [kən'tɔ:ʃən] *n* contorsión *f*

**contour** ['kɒntʊə(r)] *n* contorno *m*, perfil *m*; **c. (line)** *(on map)* curva *f* de nivel; **c. map** mapa *m* topográfico

**contraband** ['kɒntrəbænd] *n* contrabando *m*; **c. goods** mercancía *f* de contrabando

**contraception** [kɒntrə'sepʃən] *n* anticoncepción *f*

**contraceptive** [kɒntrə'septɪv] **1** *n* anticonceptivo *m*

**2** *adj* **c. method** método *m* anticonceptivo; **c. pill** píldora *f* anticonceptiva

**contract 1** *n* ['kɒntrækt] contrato *m*; **to break one's c.** incumplir el contrato; **to be under c.** estar contratado(a); **to enter into a c.** firmar un contrato; **to take out a c. on sb** *(hire assassin)* contratar a un asesino para matar a alguien; **c. killer** asesino(a) *m,f* a sueldo

**2** *vt* [kən'trækt] *(illness)* contraer; **to c. debts** contraer deudas; **to c. to do sth** firmar un contrato para hacer algo; **to c. sb to do sth** contratar a alguien para hacer algo

**3** *vi (shrink)* contraerse

▸**contract out** *Com* **1** *vt sep* **the cleaning service was contracted out** el servicio de limpieza lo lleva una contrata

**2** *vi* excluirse, optar por salirse (**of** de)

**contraction** [kənˈtrækʃən] *n* contracción *f*; **contractions have begun** *(before childbirth)* han empezado las contracciones

**contractor** [kənˈtræktə(r)] *n* contratista *mf*

**contractual** [kənˈtræktjʊəl] *adj (agreement, obligations)* contractual

**contradict** [kɒntrəˈdɪkt] *vt (disagree with)* contradecir; *(deny)* desmentir; **to c. oneself** contradecirse

**contradiction** [kɒntrəˈdɪkʃən] *n* contradicción *f*; **it's a c. in terms** es una contradicción en sí misma

**contradictory** [kɒntrəˈdɪktərɪ] *adj* contradictorio(a)

**contraflow system** [ˈkɒntrəfləʊˈsɪstəm] *n (on motorway)* habilitación *f* del carril contrario

**contralto** [kənˈtræltəʊ] *(pl* **contraltos***)* n Mus contralto *f*

**contraption** [kənˈtræpʃən] *n Fam* cachivache *m*, artilugio *m*

**contrary** [ˈkɒntrərɪ] **1** *n* **the c.** lo contrario; **on the c.** por el *or* al contrario; **unless you hear to the c.** salvo que te digan lo contrario *or* otra cosa

**2** *adj* **(a)** *(opposite)* contrario(a); **c. to** contrario(a) a; **c. to my expectations** al contrario de lo que esperaba; **c. to popular belief,…** en contra de lo que vulgarmente se cree,… **(b)** [kənˈtreərɪ] *(awkward)* puñetero(a), difícil

**contrast 1** *n* [ˈkɒntrɑːst] contraste *m*; **in c. with** *or* **to** en contraste con

**2** *vt* [kənˈtrɑːst] **to c. sth with sth** contrastar *or* comparar algo con algo *or* algo y algo

**3** *vi* contrastar **(with** con)

**contravene** [kɒntrəˈviːn] *vt* contravenir

**contravention** [kɒntrəˈvenʃən] *n (of law)* contravención *f*; **in c. of…** contraviniendo…

**contribute** [kənˈtrɪbjuːt] **1** *vt* contribuir con, aportar; **to c. an article to a newspaper** escribir una colaboración para un periódico

**2** *vi* contribuir

**contribution** [kɒntrɪˈbjuːʃən] *n* contribución *f*, aportación *f*; *(to charity)* donación *f*; **social security contributions** cotizaciones *fpl* a la seguridad social

**contributor** [kənˈtrɪbjʊtə(r)] *n. (to charity)* donante *mf*; *(to newspaper)* colaborador(ora) *m,f*

**contributory** [kənˈtrɪbjʊtərɪ] *adj (cause, factor)* coadyuvante; *Law* **c. negligence** imprudencia *f or* negligencia *f* (culposa), culpa *f* concurrente

**contrite** [kənˈtraɪt] *adj* arrepentido(a); **to be c.** estar arrepentido(a)

**contrition** [kənˈtrɪʃən] *n* arrepentimiento *m*, contrición *f*

**contrivance** [kənˈtraɪvəns] *n (device)* aparato *m*; *(scheme, plan)* estratagema *f*

**contrive** [kənˈtraɪv] *vt (device, scheme)* idear, inventar; **to c. to do sth** arreglárselas *o* ingeniárselas para hacer algo

**contrived** [kənˈtraɪvd] *adj (words, compliment)* estudiado(a), forzado(a); *(ending, plot)* artificioso(a)

**control** [kənˈtrəʊl] **1** *n* **(a)** *(power, restriction)* control *m*; **to take c.** ponerse al mando, tomar el control; **to have c. over** controlar; **to be in c. of** *(in charge of)* estar al cargo de; **to be back in c.** *(of situation)* volver a controlar la situación; **to get out of c.** descontrolarse; **under c.** bajo control; **to bring a fire under c.** controlar un incendio; **due to circumstances beyond our c.** debido a circunstancias ajenas a nuestra voluntad; **to lose/regain c.** perder/recuperar el control; **he lost c. of himself** perdió el control; **c. group** grupo *m* de control; **c. tower** *(at airport)* torre *f* de control

**(b)** *(of device)* mando *m*; **volume/brightness c.** mando del volumen/brillo; **the controls** los mandos; **to be at the controls** estar a los mandos; **c. panel** tablero *m* de mandos

**2** *vt (pt & pp* **controlled***) (business, production, expenditure)* controlar, regular; *(child, pupils)* controlar, dominar; *(disease)* controlar; *(vehicle)* manejar, controlar; **to c. oneself** controlarse, dominarse; **to c. the traffic** dirigir el tráfico; **she was unable to c. her anger** fue incapaz de dominar su ira

**controlled** [kənˈtrəʊld] *adj (person)* controlado(a), contenido(a); *(experiment)* controlado(a); **c. explosion** explosión *f* controlada

**controlling interest** [kənˈtrəʊlɪŋˈɪntrest] *n Fin* control *m* accionarial, participación *f* mayoritaria

**controversial** [kɒntrəˈvɜːʃəl] *adj* polémico(a), controvertido(a)

**controversy** [ˈkɒntrəvɜːsɪ, kənˈtrɒvəsɪ] *n* polémica *f*, controversia *f*

**conundrum** [kəˈnʌndrəm] *n* enigma *m*

**conurbation** [kɒnɜːˈbeɪʃən] *n* conurbación *f*

**convalesce** [kɒnvəˈles] *vi* convalecer

**convalescence** [kɒnvəˈlesəns] *n* convalecencia *f*

**convalescent** [kɒnvəˈlesənt] *n (patient)* convaleciente *mf*; **c. home** clínica *f* de reposo

**convection** [kənˈvekʃən] *n* convección *f*; **c. heater** calentador *m* de aire

**convene** [kənˈviːn] **1** *vt (meeting)* convocar

**2** *vi (of committee)* reunirse

**convenience** [kənˈviːnɪəns] *n* conveniencia *f*; **at your c.** a su conveniencia, como mejor le convenga; *Formal* **at your earliest c.** en cuanto le sea posible; **(public) c.** *(toilet)* servicio *m* público, aseos *mpl*; **c. food** comida *f* preparada

**convenient** [kən'vi:nɪənt] *adj* (a) *(suitable)* *(arrangement, method)* conveniente, adecuado(a); *(time, place)* oportuno(a); **if it is c. for you** si te viene bien (b) *(handy) (place)* bien situado(a); **c. for** próximo(a) a

**convent** ['kɒnvənt] *n Rel* convento *m*; **c. school** colegio *m* de monjas

**convention** [kən'venʃən] *n* (a) *(conference)* congreso *m* (b) *(agreement)* convención *f*, convenio *m* (c) *(established practice)* convencionalismo *m*, convención *f*; **to go against c.** ir contra las convenciones; **the c. is that...** según la costumbre,...

**conventional** [kən'venʃənəl] *adj* convencional; **the c. wisdom is that...** la sabiduría popular dice que...; **c. warfare** guerra *f* convencional

**converge** [kən'vɜːdʒ] *vi* converger, convergir **(on** con)

**conversant** [kən'vɜːsənt] *adj* **to be c. with sth** estar familiarizado(a) con algo

**conversation** [kɒnvə'seɪʃən] *n* conversación *f*; *CAm, Méx* plática *f*; **to have a c. (with sb)** mantener una conversación (con alguien); **to make c.** dar conversación **(with** a); **c. piece** tema *m* de conversación; **c. stopper** *or* **killer** comentario *m* que corta la conversación

**conversational** [kɒnvə'seɪʃənəl] *adj (tone, style)* coloquial; *Comptr (mode)* conversacional

**conversationalist** [kɒnvə'seɪʃənəlɪst] *n* conversador(ora) *m,f*; **to be a good c.** ser buen conversador

**converse¹** [kən'vɜːs] *vi (talk)* conversar **(about** sobre)

**converse²** ['kɒnvɜːs] *n (opposite)* **the c.** lo contrario, lo opuesto

**conversion** [kən'vɜːʃən] *n* (a) *Rel & Fig* conversión *f* (b) *(alteration)* conversión *f*, transformación *f*; **c. table** *(for measurements)* tabla *f* de conversión *or* de equivalencias (c) *(in rugby)* transformación *f*

**convert 1** *n* ['kɒnvɜːt] *Rel & Fig* converso(a) *m,f* **(to** a)

**2** *vt* [kən'vɜːt] (a) *Rel & Fig* convertir (b) *(alter, adapt)* transformar, convertir **(into** en) (c) *(in rugby)* **to c. a try** transformar un ensayo, realizar la transformación

**3** *vi Rel & Fig* convertirse **(to** a)

**convertible** [kən'vɜːtəbəl] **1** *adj (settee)* convertible; *(car)* descapotable; **c. currency** moneda *f* convertible

**2** *n (car)* descapotable *m*

**convex** ['kɒnveks] *adj* convexo(a)

**convey** [kən'veɪ] *vt* (a) *(communicate)* transmitir (b) *(transport)* transportar

**conveyancing** [kən'veɪənsɪŋ] *n Law* (escrituración *f* de) traspaso *m* de propiedad

**conveyor belt** [kən'veɪə'belt] *n* cinta *f* transportadora

**convict 1** *n* ['kɒnvɪkt] *Hist* convicto(a) *m,f*

**2** [kən'vɪkt] *vt* **to c. sb (of a crime)** declarar a alguien culpable (de un delito), condenar a alguien (por un delito)

**conviction** [kən'vɪkʃən] *n* (a) *Law* condena *f*; **to have no previous convictions** no tener condenas anteriores (b) *(belief)* convicción *f*; **her voice lacked c.** le faltaba convicción en la voz; **to carry c.** ser convincente

**convince** [kən'vɪns] *vt* convencer; **he was convinced he was right** estaba convencido de que tenía razón

**convincing** [kən'vɪnsɪŋ] *adj* convincente

**convivial** [kən'vɪvɪəl] *adj (person)* sociable; *(atmosphere)* agradable

**convoluted** ['kɒnvəlu:tɪd] *adj (argument, explanation)* intrincado(a), enrevesado(a)

**convoy** ['kɒnvɔɪ] *(pl* **convoys)** *n (of ships, lorries)* convoy *m*

**convulse** [kən'vʌls] *vt* convulsionar; **to be convulsed with laughter/pain** retorcerse de risa/dolor

**convulsions** [kən'vʌlʃənz] *npl Med* convulsiones *fpl*; **to be in c.** *(of laughter)* desternillarse de risa

**coo** [ku:] *vi (of dove)* arrullar; **the neighbours came to c. over the baby** los vecinos vinieron a hacer monerías al niño

**cook** [kʊk] **1** *n* cocinero(a) *m,f*; *Prov* **too many cooks spoil the broth** = es difícil obtener un buen resultado cuando hay demasiadas personas trabajando en lo mismo

**2** *vt (prepare) (meal, dish, dinner)* preparar; *(boil, bake, fry)* guisar, cocinar; *Fig* **to c. the books** falsificar las cuentas

**3** *vi (of person)* cocinar; *(of food)* cocinarse, hacerse; *Fam* **what's cooking?** *(what's happening?)* ¿qué se cuece por aquí?

▶**cook up** *vt insep (food)* preparar, cocinar; *Fig* **to c. up an excuse/a story** inventarse una excusa/un cuento

**cookbook** ['kʊkbʊk] *n* libro *m* de cocina

**cooker** ['kʊkə(r)] *n (stove)* cocina *f*; **gas c.** cocina de gas; **electric c.** cocina eléctrica

**cookery** ['kʊkəri] *n* cocina *f*; **c. book** libro *m* de cocina

**cookie** ['kʊki] *n* (a) *US (biscuit)* galleta *f*; *Fam Fig* **that's the way the c. crumbles!** ¡qué se le va a hacer! (b) *Fam (person)* **a smart c.** un/una espabilado(a); **a tough c.** un/una tío(a) duro(a) de pelar

**cooking** ['kʊkɪŋ] *n* cocina *f*; **to do the c.** cocinar; **c. apple** manzana *f* para asar; **c. foil** papel *m* (de) aluminio; **c. time** tiempo *m* de cocción; **c. utensils** utensilios *mpl* de cocina

**cool** [ku:l] **1** *n* (**a**) *(coldness)* fresco *m*; **in the c. of the evening** al fresco de la tarde (**b**) *(calm)* **to keep/lose one's c.** mantener/perder la calma

**2** *adj* (**a**) *(wind, weather) (cold)* fresco(a); *(luke-warm)* tibio(a); **it's c.** hace fresco (**b**) *Fig (person) (calm)* sereno(a); *(unfriendly)* frío(a); **keep c.!** *(stay calm)* ¡mantén la calma!; **to keep a c. head** mantener la cabeza fría; **he's a c. customer!** ¡qué sangre fría tiene!; **as c. as a cucumber** imperturbable, impasible; *Fam* **he lost a c. thousand** *(money)* perdió nada menos que mil libras (**c**) *Fam (trendy) (person)* guay, enrollado(a); *(car, trainers)* molón(ona), guay

**3** *adv Fam* **to play it c.** aparentar calma; **play it c.!** ¡tómatelo con calma!

**4** *vt (make cold)* enfriar; *(make less warm) (air, one's feet)* refrescar; *(food, drink)* enfriar (un poco); *Fam* **c. it!** ¡tranqui!; *Fam* **to c. one's heels** esperar, hacer antesala

**5** *vi (become cold)* enfriarse; *(become less warm) (air)* refrescarse; *(food, drink)* enfriarse (un poco); **his anger soon cooled** pronto se le pasó el enfado

▶**cool down 1** *vt sep* **this will c. you down** *(of cold drink)* esto te refrescará

**2** *vi* (**a**) *(of weather)* refrescar; *(of liquid)* enfriarse (un poco) (**b**) *(become calm)* calmarse, tranquilizarse

▶**cool off** *vi* (**a**) **he had a shower to c. off** se dio una ducha para refrescarse (**b**) *(of affection, enthusiasm)* enfriarse; *(of angry person)* calmarse, tranquilizarse

**coolant** ['ku:lənt] *n (for engine, reactor)* refrigerante *m*

**cool-headed** ['ku:l'hedɪd] *adj* **to be c.** tener la cabeza fría, tener serenidad

**cooling** ['ku:lɪŋ] *adj* refrescante; *Ind* **c. off period** *(before strike)* fase *f* de reflexión; **c. tower** torre *f* de refrigeración

**coop** [ku:p] *n (for chickens)* corral *m*

▶**coop up** *vt sep* encerrar

**co-op** ['kəʊɒp] *n* cooperativa *f*

**cooperate** [kəʊ'ɒpəreɪt] *vi* cooperar (**with** con)

**cooperation** [kəʊɒpə'reɪʃən] *n* cooperación *f*

**cooperative** [kəʊ'ɒpərətɪv] **1** *n* cooperativa *f*

**2** *adj* cooperativo(a)

**coopt** [kəʊ'ɒpt] *vt* **to c. sb onto a committee** nombrar a alguien miembro de una comisión; **to c. sb to do sth** elegir a alguien para que haga algo

**coordinate 1** *n* [kəʊ'ɔ:dɪnət] (**a**) *Math* coordenada *f* (**b**) **co-ordinates** *(clothes)* conjuntos *mpl*

**2** *vt* [kəʊ'ɔ:dɪneɪt] *(campaign, efforts)* coordinar

**coordination** [kəʊɔ:dɪ'neɪʃən] *n* coordinación *f*

**coordinator** [kəʊ'ɔ:dɪneɪtə(r)] *n* coordinador(ora) *m,f*

**co-owner** ['kəʊ'əʊnə(r)] *n* copropietario(a) *m,f*

**cop** [kɒp] *Fam* **1** *n* (**a**) *(policeman)* poli *mf*; **to play cops and robbers** jugar a policías y ladrones (**b**) **it's not much c.** no es nada del otro mundo

**2** *vt (pt & pp* **copped***)* **to c. it** *(be punished)* cargársela; *(die)* palmarla

▶**cop out** *vi Fam* escaquearse; **he copped out of telling her** se escaqueó de decírselo

**cope** [kəʊp] *vi* arreglárselas; **to c. with** hacer frente a, poder con; **he can't c. with his job** su trabajo es demasiado para él; **I just can't c.!** ¡es demasiado para mí!, ¡no puedo con ello!

**Copenhagen** [kəʊpən'hɑ:gən] *n* Copenhague

**copier** ['kɒpɪə(r)] *n (photocopying machine)* fotocopiadora *f*

**copilot** ['kəʊpaɪlət] *n* copiloto *mf*

**copious** ['kəʊpɪəs] *adj* abundante, copioso(a)

**cop-out** ['kɒpaʊt] *n Fam* **to be a c.** ser una forma de escaquearse

**copper** ['kɒpə(r)] **1** *n* (**a**) *(metal)* cobre *m* (**b**) *Fam* **coppers** *(coins)* calderilla *f (sólo monedas de uno y dos peniques)* (**c**) *Fam (policeman)* poli *m*

**2** *adj* **c.(-coloured)** cobrizo(a)

**copperplate** ['kɒpəpleɪt] *n (writing)* letra *f* de caligrafía

**coppice** ['kɒpɪs] *n* arboleda *f*, soto *m*

**coproduction** ·[kəʊprə'dʌkʃən] *n Cin* coproducción *f*

**copse** [kɒps] *n* arboleda *f*, soto *m*

**copulate** ['kɒpjʊleɪt] *vi* copular

**copulation** [kɒpjʊ'leɪʃən] *n* cópula *f*

**copy** ['kɒpɪ] **1** *n* (**a**) *(reproduction)* copia *f* (**b**) *(of letter, document)* copia *f*; **c. typist** mecanógrafo(a) *m,f* (**c**) *(of book, newspaper)* ejemplar *m* (**d**) *Journ* **advertising c.** textos *mpl* publicitarios; **the story made good c.** la noticia dio mucho de sí; **c. editor** corrector(ora) *m,f* de estilo

**2** *vt & vi* copiar

**copybook** ['kɒpɪbʊk] *n* cuaderno *m* de caligrafía; **a c. example** un ejemplo perfecto

**copycat** ['kɒpɪkæt] **1** *n Fam* copión(ona) *m,f*

**2** *adj* **c. crime** = delito inspirado en otro similar

**copyright** ['kɒpɪraɪt] **1** *n* derechos *mpl* de autor, propiedad *f* intelectual; **this book is out of c.** los derechos de autor sobre este libro han vencido

**2** *adj* = protegido(a) por las leyes de la propiedad intelectual

**copywriter** ['kɒpɪraɪtə(r)] n redactor(ora) m,f de publicidad

**coquette** [kɒ'ket] n (mujer f) coqueta f

**coral** ['kɒrəl] n coral m; **c. island** isla f coralina; **c. reef** arrecife m de coral; **C. Sea** Mar del Coral

**cord** [kɔːd] n (a) (string) cuerda f, cordel m; (for curtains, pyjamas) cordón m (b) Elec cable m, cordón m (c) (corduroy) pana f; **a c. jacket/skirt** una chaqueta/falda de pana; **cords** pantalones mpl de pana

**cordial** ['kɔːdɪəl] 1 n (drink) refresco m

2 adj (a) (friendly) cordial (b) (deeply felt) profundo(a)

**cordless** ['kɔːdlɪs] adj **c. kettle** = hervidor eléctrico con soporte independiente enchufado a la red; **c. phone** teléfono m inalámbrico

**cordon** ['kɔːdən] n cordón m

▶**cordon off** vt sep acordonar

**corduroy** ['kɔːdərɔɪ] n pana f; **a c. jacket/skirt** una chaqueta/falda de pana; **c. trousers** pantalones mpl de pana

**core** [kɔː(r)] 1 n (of apple) corazón m; (of earth, nuclear reactor) núcleo m; **a hard c. of support** un núcleo sólido de apoyo; **he's rotten to the c.** está corrompido hasta la médula; Sch **c. curriculum** asignaturas fpl troncales

2 vt (apple) quitar el corazón a

**Corfu** [kɔː'fuː] n Corfú

**coriander** [kɒrɪ'ændə(r)] n cilantro m

**cork** [kɔːk] 1 n (material) corcho m; (stopper) (tapón m de) corcho m

2 vt (bottle) encorchar

**corked** [kɔːkt] adj (wine) agrio(a) (por entrada de aire al descomponerse el corcho)

**corkscrew** ['kɔːkskruː] n sacacorchos m inv

**cormorant** ['kɔːmərənt] n cormorán m

**corn**[1] [kɔːn] n (a) Br (wheat) trigo m (b) US (maize) maíz m; **c. on the cob** mazorca f de maíz cocida; **c. bread** pan m de maíz; **c. meal** harina f de maíz; **c. oil** aceite m de maíz

**corn**[2] n Med callo m; **c. plaster** parche m para callos

**cornea** ['kɔːnɪə] n Anat córnea f

**corned beef** ['kɔːnd'biːf] adj = fiambre de carne de vaca prensado y enlatado

**corner** ['kɔːnə(r)] 1 n (a) (of page, screen, street) esquina f; (of room) rincón m; also Fig **it's just round the c.** está a la vuelta de la esquina; **to turn the c.** doblar la esquina; Fig (of economy, company) empezar a mejorar; **c. shop** = tienda pequeña de barrio que vende productos alimenticios, de limpieza, golosinas, etc.; **from the four corners of the earth** desde todos los rincones de la tierra; **out of the c. of one's eye** con el rabillo del ojo

(b) (bend in road) curva f (cerrada); Fig **to cut corners** hacer las cosas chapuceramente

(c) (in football) **c. (kick)** saque m de esquina, córner m

2 vt (a) (enemy) acorralar, arrinconar

(b) (market) monopolizar, acaparar

3 vi (of car) girar, torcer

**cornerstone** ['kɔːnəstəʊn] n also Fig piedra f angular

**cornet** ['kɔːnɪt, US kɔː'net] n (a) (musical instrument) corneta f (b) (ice-cream) **c.** cucurucho m de helado

**cornfield** ['kɔːnfiːld] n (wheat) trigal m; (maize) maizal m

**cornflakes** ['kɔːnfleɪks] npl copos mpl de maíz

**cornflour** ['kɔːnflaʊə(r)] n Br maicena® f

**cornflower** ['kɔːnflaʊə(r)] n (plant) aciano m; **c. blue** azul m violáceo

**cornice** ['kɔːnɪs] n cornisa f

**Cornish** ['kɔːnɪʃ] 1 npl (people) **the C.** la gente de Cornualles

2 n (language) córnico m

3 adj de Cornualles; Br **C. pasty** empanada f de carne y patatas

**Cornwall** ['kɔːnwəl] n Cornualles

**corny** ['kɔːnɪ] adj Fam (joke) viejo(a), trillado(a); (sentimental) (film, novel) sensiblero(a), cursi

**corollary** [kə'rɒlərɪ] n corolario m

**coronary** ['kɒrənərɪ] 1 n **he had a c.** le dio un infarto (de miocardio)

2 adj Med coronario(a); **c. thrombosis** trombosis f coronaria

**coronation** [kɒrə'neɪʃən] n coronación; f **c. chicken** = pollo con mayonesa aromatizada con curry

**coroner** ['kɒrənə(r)] n Law juez mf de instrucción

**corporal**[1] ['kɔːpərəl] adj corporal; **c. punishment** castigo m corporal

**corporal**[2] n Mil cabo mf

**corporate** ['kɔːpərət] adj Com de empresa, corporativo(a); **c. culture** cultura f empresarial; **c. image** imagen f corporativa or de empresa

**corporation** [kɔːpə'reɪʃən] n (a) Com sociedad f anónima; **c. tax** impuesto m de sociedades (b) (council) consistorio m, ayuntamiento m

**corps** [kɔː(r)] (pl corps [kɔːz]) n Mil cuerpo m; **medical c.** cuerpo m médico

**corpse** [kɔːps] n cadáver m

**corpulent** ['kɔːpjʊlənt] adj obeso(a)

**corpuscle** ['kɔːpʌsəl] n Anat glóbulo m

**corral** [kɒ'rɑːl] n US (for cattle, horses) corral m, cercado m

**correct** [kə'rekt] 1 adj (a) (exact) (amount, change) exacto(a); (information, use, spelling) correcto(a); **do you have the c. time?** ¿sabes qué hora es exactamente?; **he is c.** tiene razón; **that is c.** (eso es) correcto; **to prove c.** resultar (ser) correcto(a) **(b)** *(person, behaviour)* correcto(a)

**2** *vt* corregir; **to c. a misunderstanding** corregir un malentendido; **c. me if I'm wrong, but...** corríjame si me equivoco; **I stand corrected** reconozco mi error

**correction** [kəˈrekʃən] *n* corrección *f*

**correlate** [ˈkɒrɪleɪt] **1** *vt* relacionar **(with con)**

**2** *vi* presentar una correlación **(with con)**

**correlation** [kɒrɪˈleɪʃən] *n* correlación *f*

**correspond** [kɒrɪsˈpɒnd] *vi* **(a)** *(be in accordance, be equivalent)* corresponder **(with or to con or a)**, corresponderse **(with or to con)** **(b)** *(write letters)* mantener correspondencia **(with con)**

**correspondence** [kɒrɪsˈpɒndəns] *n* **(a)** *(relationship)* correspondencia *f*, relación *f* **(between** entre) **(b)** *(letter writing)* correspondencia *f*; **to be in c. with sb** mantener correspondencia con alguien; **c. course** curso *m* por correspondencia

**correspondent** [kɒrɪsˈpɒndənt] *n* *(of newspaper)* corresponsal *mf*; **our Middle East c.** nuestro corresponsal en Oriente Medio

**corresponding** [kɒrɪsˈpɒndɪŋ] *adj* correspondiente

**corridor** [ˈkɒrɪdɔː(r)] *n* pasillo *m*; *Fig* **the corridors of power** las altas esferas

**corroborate** [kəˈrɒbəreɪt] *vt* corroborar

**corroboration** [kərɒbəˈreɪʃən] *n* corroboración *f*

**corrode** [kəˈrəʊd] **1** *vt also Fig* corroer

**2** *vi (of metal)* corroerse

**corrosion** [kəˈrəʊʒən] *n* corrosión *f*

**corrosive** [kəˈrəʊsɪv] *n & adj* corrosivo(a) *m*

**corrugated** [ˈkɒrʊgeɪtɪd] *adj* ondulado(a); **c. iron** chapa *f* ondulada

**corrupt** [kəˈrʌpt] **1** *adj (dishonest)* corrupto(a)

**2** *vt* corromper; *Comptr* introducir errores en; **to c. sb's morals** pervertir a alguien

**corruption** [kəˈrʌpʃən] *n* corrupción *f*

**corset** [ˈkɔːsɪt] *n* corsé *m*

**Corsica** [ˈkɔːsɪkə] *n* Córcega

**Corsican** [ˈkɔːsɪkən] *n & adj* corso(a) *m,f*

**cortege** [kɔːˈteʒ] *n* cortejo *m* (fúnebre)

**cortex** [ˈkɔːteks] *n (pl* **cortices** [ˈkɔːtɪsiːz]) *n* corteza *f*

**cortisone** [ˈkɔːtɪzəʊn] *n* cortisona *f*

**cos¹** [cɒz] *n Math (abbr* **cosine**) cos

**cos²** *conj Fam (because)* porque

**cos³** [kɒs] *n* **c. (lettuce)** lechuga *f* romana

**cosh** [kɒʃ] **1** *Br n* porra *f*

**2** *vt* golpear con una porra

**cosmetic** [kɒzˈmetɪk] **1** *n* cosmético *m*; **cosmetics** cosméticos *mpl*, maquillaje *m*

**2** *adj* cosmético(a); **c. surgery** cirugía *f* estética

**cosmic** [ˈkɒzmɪk] *adj* cósmico(a)

**cosmonaut** [ˈkɒzmənɔːt] *n* cosmonauta *mf*

**cosmopolitan** [kɒzməˈpɒlɪtən] *adj* cosmopolita

**cosmos** [ˈkɒzmɒs] *n* cosmos *m inv*

**cosset** [ˈkɒsɪt] *vt* mimar

**cost** [kɒst] **1** *n* **(a)** *(price)* coste *m*; *Law* **costs** costas *fpl*; **at little c.** a bajo precio; **at great c.** *(financial)* por un precio alto; *Fig* a un alto precio; *Fig* **at the c. of...** a costa de...; *Econ* **c. of living** coste *m* de la vida; *Com* **c. of production** coste *m* de producción; *Fin* **c. accounting** contabilidad *f* de costes; *Econ* **c. benefit analysis** análisis *m inv* de coste-beneficio; *Com* **at c. (price)** a precio de coste *or* costo

**(b)** *(idioms)* **to count the c. of sth** ver las consecuencias de algo; **at all costs** a toda costa, a cualquier precio; **as I found out to my c.** como pude comprobar para mi desgracia

**2** *vt* **(a)** *(pt & pp* **cost)** costar; **how much does it c.?** ¿cuánto cuesta?; **it costs £25** cuesta 25 libras; **whatever it costs** cueste lo que cueste; *Fam* **to c. a fortune** *or* **the earth** costar una fortuna *or* un ojo de la cara; **the attempt cost him his life** el intento le costó la vida

**(b)** *(pt & pp* **costed**) *Com (budget)* presupuestar, calcular el coste de

**co-star** [ˈkəʊstɑː(r)] **1** *n (in film)* coprotagonista *mf*

**2** *vt (pt & pp* **co-starred**) **co-starring...** coprotagonizada por...

**3** *vi* ser el coprotagonista

**Costa Rica** [ˈkɒstəˈriːkə] *n* Costa Rica

**Costa Rican** [ˈkɒstəˈriːkən] *n & adj* costarricense *mf*

**cost-effective** [kɒstɪˈfektɪv] *adj* rentable

**costing** [ˈkɒstɪŋ] *n Com* cálculo *m* de costes

**costly** [ˈkɒstlɪ] *adj* caro(a); **a c. error** *or* **mistake** un error muy caro

**costume** [ˈkɒstjʊm] *n* traje *m*; **(swimming) c.** bañador *m*, traje *m* de baño; **national c.** traje *m* típico; **c. drama** *(TV series, film)* serie *f*/película *f* de época; **c. jewellery** bisutería *f*

**cosy** [ˈkəʊzɪ] *adj* acogedor(ora); **it's c. here** se está bien aquí; **to feel c.** sentirse a gusto; *Fig* **a c. relationship** una relación demasiado estrecha *or* amistosa

**cot** [kɒt] *n Br (for child)* cuna *f*; *US (folding bed)* catre *m*, cama *f* plegable; **c. death** (síndrome *m* de la) muerte *f* súbita *(en la cuna)*

**cottage** [ˈkɒtɪdʒ] *n* casa *f* de campo, chalé *m*; **c. cheese** queso *m* fresco; **c. hospital** hospital *m* rural; **c. industry** industria *f* artesanal; **c. pie** = pastel de carne picada y puré de patata

**cotton** ['kɒtən] *n* algodón *m*; **a c. shirt** una camisa de algodón; **c. bud** bastoncillo *m* (de algodón); *US* **c. candy** algodón dulce; **c. wool** algodón (hidrófilo)

▸**cotton on** *vi Fam* enterarse, coscarse (**to** de)

**couch** [kautʃ] **1** *n* sofá *m*; *Fam Fig* **to be on the c.** *(in psychoanalysis)* estar yendo al psicoanalista; *Fam* **c. potato** = persona que se pasa el día apoltronada viendo la tele

**2** *vt* (express) expresar, formular

**cougar** ['kuːɡə(r)] *n* puma *m*

**cough** [kɒf] **1** *n* tos *f*; **to have a c.** tener tos; **c. drop** pastilla *f* para la tos; **c. mixture** jarabe *m* para la tos

**2** *vi* toser

▸**cough up 1** *vt sep* (a) *(phlegm, blood)* toser (b) *Fam (money)* apoquinar

**2** *vi Fam (pay up)* apoquinar

**could** [kʊd]

> En el inglés hablado, y en el escrito en estilo coloquial, la forma negativa **could not** se transforma en **couldn't**.

*modal aux* v (a) *(was able to: past of* **can***)* I **c. swim well at that age** a esa edad nadaba muy bien; **I c. hear them talking** los oía hablar; **I c. have tried harder** podía haberme esforzado más; **he couldn't have been kinder** fue de lo más amable; **how COULD you!** ¡cómo has podido!; **I c. have hit him!** *(I was so angry)* ¡me dieron ganas de pegarle!; **you c. have warned me!** ¡me podías haber avisado!, ¡haberme avisado!

(b) *(in requests)* **c. you get me some water?** ¿me puedes traer un poco de agua?; **c. you be quiet please?** ¿te podrías callar, por favor?; **c. I borrow your newspaper?** ¿me prestas el periódico?

(c) *(in conditional, suggestions)* **(it) c. be** podría ser; **if I had more money, I c. buy a new car** si tuviera más dinero podría comprarme un coche nuevo; **we c. always telephone** siempre podríamos llamar por teléfono; **you c. go to the beach** podríais ir a la playa

**couldn't** ['kʊdənt] = **could not**

**couldn't-care-less** ['kʊdəntkeəˈles] *adj* **c. attitude** actitud *f* pasota

**council** ['kaunsəl] *n* (a) *(organization)* consejo *m*; **C. of Europe** Consejo *m* de Europa (b) *(local government)* *(of town)* ayuntamiento *m*; *(of region, county)* autoridades *fpl* regionales, ≃ diputación *f* provincial; *Br* **c. house** ≃ vivienda *f* de protección oficial; **c. tax** ≃ contribución *f* urbana

**councillor** ['kaunsɪlə(r)] *n Pol* concejal(ala) *m,f*

**counsel** ['kaunsəl] **1** *n* (a) *(advice)* consejo *m*; **he's someone who keeps his own c.** siempre se reserva su opinión (b) *Law* **c. for the defence** abogado(a) *m,f* defensor(ora); **c. for the prosecution** fiscal *mf*

**2** *vt* (*pt & pp* **counselled,** *US* **counseled**) *(advise)* aconsejar; *(give psychological help to)* proporcionar apoyo psicológico a; **to c. sb to do sth** aconsejar a alguien que haga algo

**counselling** ['kaunsəlɪŋ] *n* apoyo *m* psicológico, orientación *f* psicológica

**counsellor** ['kaunsələ(r)] *n* (a) *(adviser)* consejero(a) *m,f* asesor(ora) *m,f*; *(therapist)* orientador(ora) *m,f* psicológico(a) (b) *US Law* abogado(a) *m,f*

**count¹** [kaunt] *n (nobleman)* conde *m*

**count²** **1** *n* (a) *(calculation)* cuenta *f*, recuento *m*; **at the last c.** según las cifras más recientes; **to keep/loose c.** llevar/perder la cuenta *f* *(in boxing)* cuenta *f* (hasta diez); **to be out for the c.** *(boxer)* estar fuera de combate; *Fig (fast asleep)* estar roque (c) *Law* cargo *m*, acusación *f*; **guilty on both counts** culpable de los dos cargos; *Fig* **on a number of counts** en una serie de puntos

**2** *vt* (a) *(enumerate)* contar; **to c. sheep** *(in order to fall asleep)* contar ovejitas; **counting the dog there were four of us** éramos cuatro, contando al perro (b) *(consider)* considerar; **I c. him as a friend** lo considero un amigo; **c. yourself lucky you weren't killed** considérate afortunado(a) por haber salido con vida

**3** *vi* (a) *(count)* contar; **to c. (up) to ten** contar hasta diez (b) *(be valid)* contar, valer; **that one doesn't c.** ese no cuenta; **it counts as one of my worst holidays** fue una de mis peores vacaciones (c) *(be important)* contar; **every vote counts** todos los votos cuentan *or* son importantes

▸**count against** *vt insep* ir en contra de, perjudicar

▸**count down** *vi* hacer la cuenta atrás; *Fig* **the whole nation is counting down to the elections** toda la nación aguarda con interés el día de las elecciones

▸**count in** *vt sep* **c. me in!** ¡contad conmigo!

▸**count on** *vt insep* contar con; **to c. on sb to do sth** contar con que alguien haga algo

▸**count out** *vt sep* (a) *(money)* contar (b) *(exclude)* dejar fuera, excluir; **c. me out!** ¡no contéis conmigo! (c) *(in boxing)* **to be counted out** quedar fuera de combate (tras la cuenta hasta diez)

▸**count up** *vt sep* contar, hacer la cuenta de

**countable** ['kauntəbəl] *adj* contable

**countdown** ['kauntdaun] *n* cuenta *f* atrás

**countenance** ['kauntɪnəns] *Formal* **1** *n* (a) *(face)* semblante *m* (b) *(support)* **to give c. to**

**sth** dar respaldo a algo

**2** *vt* respaldar

**counter¹** ['kaʊntə(r)] *n* (a) *(in shop)* mostrador *m; (in bank)* ventanilla *f;* **it's available over the c.** *(medicines)* se vende sin receta (médica); **under the c.** bajo cuerda (b) *(token)* ficha *f* (c) *(counting device)* contador *m*

**counter²** **1** *adv* **c. to** en contra de; **to run c. to** estar en contra de

**2** *vt (argument, assertion)* responder a; **to c. that…** replicar que…

**3** *vi* **to c. by doing sth** reaccionar haciendo algo

**counteract** [kaʊntə'rækt] *vt* contrarrestar

**counterattack** ['kaʊntərətæk] **1** *n* contraataque *m*

**2** *vt & vi* contraatacar

**counterbalance** [kaʊntə'bæləns] **1** *n* contrapeso *m; Fig* **to act as a c. (to sth)** contrarrestar (algo)

**2** *vt* contrarrestar

**counter-clockwise** ['kaʊntə'klɒkwaɪz] *US* **1** *adj* **in a c. direction** en sentido opuesto al de las agujas del reloj

**2** *adv* en sentido opuesto al de las agujas del reloj

**counterespionage** [kaʊntər'espɪɑːʒ] *n* contraespionaje *m*

**counterfeit** ['kaʊntəfɪt] **1** *n* falsificación *f*

**2** *adj* falso(a)

**3** *vt* falsificar

**counterfoil** ['kaʊntəfɔɪl] *n* matriz *f*

**counterintelligence** ['kaʊntərɪn-'telɪdʒəns] *n* contraespionaje *m*

**countermand** ['kaʊntəmɑːnd] *vt* revocar

**countermeasure** ['kaʊntəmeʒə(r)] *n* medida *f* en sentido contrario

**counteroffensive** ['kaʊntərə'fensɪv] *n* contraofensiva *f*

**counterpane** ['kaʊntəpeɪn] *n* colcha *f*

**counterpart** ['kaʊntəpɑːt] *n* homólogo(a) *m,f*

**counterpoint** ['kaʊntəpɔɪnt] *n Mus* contrapunto *m*

**counterproductive** ['kaʊntəprə'dʌktɪv] *adj* contraproducente

**counterproposal** ['kaʊntəprə'pəʊzəl] *n* contrapropuesta *f*

**counter-revolution** ['kaʊntərevə'luːʃən] *n* contrarrevolución *f*

**counter-revolutionary** [kaʊntərevə-'luːʃənərɪ] *n & adj* contrarrevolucionario(a) *m,f*

**countersign** ['kaʊntəsaɪn] *vt* refrendar

**counterterrorism** [kaʊntə'terərɪzəm] *n* contraterrorismo *m*

**counterweight** ['kaʊntəweɪt] *n* contrapeso *m;* **to act as a c. (to sth)** servir de contrapeso (a algo), contrarrestar (algo)

**countess** ['kaʊntɪs] *n* condesa *f*

**countless** ['kaʊntlɪs] *adj* innumerables, incontables; **on c. occasions** en innumerables ocasiones

**country** ['kʌntrɪ] *n* (a) *(political entity)* país *m;* **to go to the c.** *(call elections)* convocar elecciones (b) *(as opposed to town)* campo *m;* **in the c.** en el campo; **c. life** vida *f* campestre; **C. and Western music** música *f* country

**countryman** ['kʌntrɪmən] *n* paisano *m;* **a fellow c.** un compatriota

**countryside** ['kʌntrɪsaɪd] *n* campo *m*

**countrywoman** ['kʌntrɪwʊmən] *n* paisana *f;* **a fellow c.** una compatriota

**county** ['kaʊntɪ] *n* condado *m;* **c. council** = órgano de gobierno de un condado; **c. town** capital *f* de condado

**coup** [kuː] *n (surprising achievement)* golpe *m* de efecto; *Pol* **c. (d'état)** golpe *m* de Estado

**couple** ['kʌpəl] **1** *n* (a) *(of things)* par *m;* **a c. of** un par de (b) *(people)* pareja *f*

**2** *vt* (a) *(associate)* relacionar, asociar (b) *(combine)* conjugar, combinar; **coupled with** junto con

**couplet** ['kʌplɪt] *n (in poem)* pareado *m*

**coupon** ['kuːpɒn] *n* cupón *m,* vale *m*

**courage** ['kʌrɪdʒ] *n* valor *m,* coraje *m;* **to have the c. to do sth** tener valor para hacer algo; **he didn't have the c. of his convictions** no tuvo coraje para defender sus convicciones

**courageous** [kə'reɪdʒəs] *adj* valiente

**courageously** [kə'reɪdʒəslɪ] *adv* valientemente

**courgette** [kʊə'ʒet] *n Br* calabacín *m*

**courier** ['kʊrɪə(r)] *n (messenger)* mensajero(a) *m,f; (in tourism)* guía *mf; (drug smuggler)* correo *m,* enlace *m*

**course** [kɔːs] **1** *n* (a) *(of river, illness)* curso *m; (of time, events)* transcurso *m,* curso *m;* **to be on c.** *(ship)* seguir el rumbo; **to be on c. for** *(likely to achieve)* ir camino de; **to be off c.** haber perdido el rumbo; *also Fig* **to change c.** cambiar de rumbo; **in the c. of time** con el tiempo; **a c. of action** una táctica (a seguir); **to be in the c. of doing sth** estar haciendo algo; **in the normal c. of events** normalmente; **to let things take** *or* **run their c.** dejar que las cosas sigan su curso

(b) *of c. (clearly, unsurprisingly)* naturalmente; *(expressing agreement)* **of c. you can come!** ¡pues claro que puedes venir!; **of c. not!** ¡por supuesto que no!

(c) *Educ (as part of degree)* asignatura *f; (self-contained)* curso *m;* **to take a c. in sth** hacer un curso de algo; **(degree) c.** carrera *f;* **a c. of lectures** un ciclo de conferencias

(d) *Med* **c. of treatment** tratamiento *m*

**(e)** *(of meal)* plato *m*; **first c.** primer plato; **main c.** plato principal

**(f)** *(for race)* circuito *m*; *(for golf)* campo *m*; *(for show-jumping)* recorrido *m*

**2** *vi (of liquid)* correr

**court** [kɔ:t] **1** *n* **(a)** *Law* tribunal *m*; **to go to c.** ir a los tribunales *or* a juicio; **to take sb to c.** llevar a alguien a juicio *or* a los tribunales; **to settle a case out of c.** arreglar una disputa sin acudir a los tribunales; **c. of appeal** tribunal *m* de apelación; **c. of inquiry** comisión *f* de investigación; **c. of law** tribunal *m*; **c. appearance** *(of defendant)* comparecencia *f* en un juicio; *Mil* **c. martial** consejo *m* de guerra

**(b)** *(for tennis, basketball, squash)* pista *f*, cancha *f*

**(c)** *(royal)* corte *f*; *Fig* **she held c. in the hotel bar, surrounded by a posse of journalists** entretuvo a un grupo de periodistas en el bar del hotel; **c. shoe** zapato *m* de salón

**2** *vt* **(a)** *Old-fashioned (woo)* cortejar

**(b)** *(seek) (sb's friendship, favour)* intentar ganarse; *(failure)* exponerse a; *(death)* jugar con

**3** *vi* *Old-fashioned* **to be courting** *(of couple)* cortejarse

**courteous** [ˈkɜ:tɪəs] *adj* cortés

**courtesy** [ˈkɜ:təsɪ] *n* cortesía *f*; **do me the c. of listening** ten la cortesía de escucharme; **by c. of**… por cortesía de…; **to exchange courtesies** intercambiar cumplidos; **c. call** visita *f* de cortesía; **c. car** coche *m* gratuito *(cortesía de la empresa)*

**courthouse** [ˈkɔ:thaʊs] *n US* palacio *m* de justicia

**courtier** [ˈkɔ:tɪə(r)] *n* cortesano(a) *m,f*

**court-martial** [ˈkɔ:tˈmɑ:ʃəl] *(pt & pp* **court-martialled,** *US* **court-martialed)** *vt* hacer un consejo de guerra a

**courtroom** [ˈkɔ:tru:m] *n Law* sala *f* de juicios

**courtship** [ˈkɔ:tʃɪp] *n (of people, animals)* cortejo *m*

**courtyard** [ˈkɔ:tjɑ:d] *n* patio *m*

**cousin** [ˈkʌzən] *n* primo(a) *m,f*; **first c.** primo(a) hermano(a); **second c.** primo(a) segundo(a)

**cove** [kəʊv] *n (small bay)* cala *f*, ensenada *f*

**covenant** [ˈkʌvənənt] *Law* **1** *n* pacto *m*, convenio *m*

**2** *vt* pactar, concertar

**Coventry** [ˈkʌvəntrɪ, ˈkɒvəntrɪ] *n Fig* **to send sb to C.** hacer el vacío a alguien

**cover** [ˈkʌvə(r)] **1** *n* **(a)** *(lid)* tapa *f*

**(b)** *(soft covering)* funda *f*, **covers** *(blankets)* mantas *fpl*

**(c)** *(of book)* tapa *f*; *(of magazine)* portada *f*; **front c.** portada *f*; **back c.** contraportada *f*; **to read a book from c. to c.** leerse un libro de principio a fin

**(d)** *(shelter)* protección *f*; **to break c.** ponerse al descubierto; **to take c.** ponerse a cubierto; **under c. of darkness** al amparo de la oscuridad

**(e)** *Fin (in insurance)* cobertura *f*; **full c.** cobertura máxima

**(f)** *(song)* **c. (version)** versión *f (de una canción original)*

**(g)** *(in restaurant)* **c. charge** cubierto *m*

**2** *vt* **(a)** *(person, object)* cubrir; *(with a lid)* tapar; **to c. one's eyes** taparse los ojos; **to c. a wall with paint** recubrir de pintura una pared; **to c. oneself with glory** cubrirse de gloria; **to c. one's costs** cubrir gastos; **to c. a song** *(of musician)* hacer una versión de una canción

**(b)** *(hide) (one's embarrassment, confusion)* ocultar; **to c. one's tracks** no dejar rastro

**(c)** *(travel over)* cubrir, recorrer; **we covered 100 km** cubrimos *or* recorrimos 100 kms; *Fig* **to c. a lot of ground** abarcar mucho

**(d)** *(include, deal with)* cubrir; **to c. a story** *(of journalist)* cubrir una noticia

**(e)** *(protect) Fin (with insurance)* asegurar; *Fig* **to c. oneself** *(take precautions)* cubrirse las espaldas

▸**cover for** *vt insep (replace)* reemplazar *or* sustituir temporalmente; *(provide excuses for)* excusar

▸**cover up 1** *vt sep* **(a)** *(conceal)* ocultar **(b)** *(cover)* cubrir, tapar

**2** *vi (conceal the truth)* encubrir **(for sb** a alguien)

**coverage** [ˈkʌvərɪdʒ] *n (on TV, in newspapers)* cobertura *f* informativa

**covering** [ˈkʌvərɪŋ] *n (on furniture)* funda *f*; *(of snow, dust, chocolate)* capa *f*

**coverlet** [ˈkʌvəlɪt] *n* colcha *f*

**covert** [ˈkʌvət] *adj* encubierto(a)

**cover-up** [ˈkʌvərʌp] *n* encubrimiento *m*

**covet** [ˈkʌvɪt] *vt* codiciar

**covetous** [ˈkʌvɪtəs] *adj* codicioso(a); **to be c.** codiciar

**cow¹** [kaʊ] *n* **(a)** *(animal)* vaca *f*; *(female elephant, whale)* hembra *f*; **till the cows come home** hasta que las ranas críen pelo **(b)** *Pej very Fam (woman)* bruja *f*, pécora *f*

**cow²** *vt* acobardar, intimidar; **to c. sb into submission** reducir a alguien a la obediencia; **to look cowed** parecer intimidado(a)

**coward** [ˈkaʊəd] *n* cobarde *mf*

**cowardice** [ˈkaʊədɪs], **cowardliness** [ˈkaʊədlɪnəs] *n* cobardía *f*

**cowardly** [ˈkaʊədlɪ] *adj* cobarde

**cowboy** [ˈkaʊbɔɪ] *n* **(a)** vaquero *m*; **to play cowboys and indians** jugar a indios y vaqueros **(b)** *Br Fam Pej (careless or dishonest workman)* jeta *m*, sinvergüenza *m*; **a c. company** una empresa de sinvergüenzas

**cower** [ˈkaʊə(r)] *vi* acoquinarse, amilanarse

**cowhide** [ˈkaʊhaɪd] *n* cuero *m*

**cowl** [kaʊl] *n (monk's hood)* capucha *f*; *(on chimney)* sombrerete *m*

**cowshed** ['kaʊʃed] *n* establo *m*

**cox** [kɒks] **1** *n (in rowing)* timonel *mf*
  **2** *vt* llevar el timón de
  **3** *vi* hacer de timonel

**coy** [kɔɪ] *adj (shy)* timorato(a); **to be c. about sth** mostrarse evasivo(a) en relación con algo

**coyote** [kɔɪˈjəʊtɪ] *n* coyote *m*

**Cpl** *Mil (abbr* **Corporal)** cabo *m*

**CPU** [siːpiːˈjuː] *n Comptr (abbr* **central processing unit)** CPU *f*, unidad *f* central de proceso

**Cr** *(abbr* **Crescent)** = calle en forma de media luna

**crab** [kræb] *n (a) (crustacean)* cangrejo *m*; *Am* jaiba *f* **(b)** *Fam (pubic louse)* ladilla *f* **(c) c. apple** *(fruit)* manzana *f* silvestre; *(tree)* manzano *m* silvestre

**crabbed** ['kræbɪd] *adj* **c. writing** letra *f* apretada y difícil de leer

**crabby** ['kræbɪ] *adj Fam (bad-tempered)* gruñón(ona)

**crack** [kræk] **1** *n (a) (in glass, porcelain)* raja *f*; *(in wood, wall, ground, ice)* grieta *f*; **the door was open a c.** la puerta estaba entreabierta; *Fig* **cracks have started to appear in his alibi** su coartada está empezando a hacer agua; **to get up at the c. of dawn** levantarse al amanecer
  **(b)** *(sound)* chasquido *m*; *Fig* **she wasn't given a fair c. of the whip** no tuvo su oportunidad; *Fig* **to have a c. at sth** intentar algo
  **(c)** *(blow)* **a c. on the head** un porrazo en la cabeza
  **(d)** *Fam (joke, insult)* chiste *m*
  **(e)** *very Fam (drug)* crack *m*
  **2** *adj Fam* de primera; **c. troops** tropas *fpl* de élite
  **3** *vt (a) (fracture) (cup, glass)* rajar; *(skin, wood, ground, wall)* agrietar
  **(b)** *(make sound with) (whip)* chasquear; *(fingers)* hacer crujir
  **(c)** *Fam (hit)* **to c. sb over the head** dar a alguien un porrazo en la cabeza; **he cracked his head against the wall** se dio con la cabeza contra la pared
  **(d)** *(solve) (problem)* resolver; *(code)* descifrar
  **(e)** *(break open) (safe)* forzar; *(nut, egg)* cascar
  **(f) to c. a joke** soltar un chiste
  **4** *vi (a) (of cup, glass)* rajarse; *(of skin, wood, ground, wall)* agrietarse
  **(b)** *(of voice) (with emotion)* fallar
  **(c)** *(of person) (under pressure)* venirse abajo, derrumbarse; **his nerve cracked** perdió los nervios
  **(d)** *(make sound)* crujir; *(of whip)* chasquear; *Fam Fig* **get cracking!** ¡manos a la obra!

▶**crack down** *vi* to c. down on sth adoptar medidas severas contra algo

▶**crack up** *Fam* **1** *vt sep* **it's not all it's cracked up to be** no es tan bueno como lo pintan
  **2** *vi (a) (laugh)* partirse de risa, desternillarse **(b)** *(go mad)* empezar a) desvariar

**crackbrained** ['krækbreɪnd] *adj Fam (plan)* descabellado(a)

**crackdown** ['krækdaʊn] *n* medidas *fpl* severas; **a c. on drugs/tax-evasion** medidas severas contra las drogas/la evasión fiscal

**cracked** [krækt] *adj Fam (crazy)* **to be c.** estar chalado(a) *or* chiflado(a)

**cracker** ['krækə(r)] *n (a) (biscuit)* galleta *f* salada, cracker *f* **(b)** *(firework)* petardo *m* **(c)** *Fam (excellent thing, person)* **the first goal was an absolute c.** el primer gol fue de antología; **she's a c.** *(very attractive)* está como un tren **(d)** *Comptr Fam* cracker

**crackers** ['krækəz] *adj Fam (mad)* **to be c.** estar como una cabra; **to go c.** volverse majara

**crackle** ['krækəl] **1** *n (of twigs)* crujido *m*; *(of fire)* crepitación *m*
  **2** *vi (of twigs)* crujir; *(of fire)* crepitar

**crackling** ['kræklɪŋ] *n (pork skin)* cortezas *fpl* de cerdo

**crackpot** ['krækpɒt] *Fam* **1** *n (person)* majara *mf*, majareta *mf*
  **2** *adj (plan)* descabellado(a)

**cradle** ['kreɪdəl] **1** *n (a) (of child, civilization)* cuna *f*; **from the c. to the grave** de la cuna a la sepultura **(b)** *(for cleaning windows)* andamio *m* colgante
  **2** *vt* acunar

**craft**¹ [krɑːft] *n (a) (trade)* oficio *m*; *(skill)* arte *m* **(b)** *(cunning)* maña *f*, astucia *f*

**craft**² *(pl* **craft)** *n (boat)* embarcación *f*

**craftsman** ['krɑːftsmən] *n* artesano *m*

**craftsmanship** ['krɑːftsmənʃɪp] *n* destreza *f*, maestría *f*

**crafty** ['krɑːftɪ] *adj* ladino(a)

**crag** [kræg] *n* peñasco *m*, risco *m*

**craggy** ['krægɪ] *adj (rocky)* escarpado(a); *(features)* marcado(a)

**cram** [kræm] *(pt & pp* **crammed)** **1** *vt (things)* embutir **(into** en); *(people)* apiñar **(into** en); **he crammed the clothes into the suitcase** llenó la maleta de ropa hasta los topes; **to be crammed with sth** estar repleto(a) de algo; **they crammed as much sightseeing as possible into their three days** no pararon de ver monumentos y sitios en los tres días que tenían
  **2** *vi (a)* apiñarse; **we all crammed into the car** nos embutimos todos en el coche **(b)** *Fam (study)* empollar **(for** para)

**cramp** [kræmp] **1** n calambre m

**2** vt (restrict) limitar, coartar; **Fam to c. sb's style** ser un estorbo para or coartar a alguien

**cramped** [kræmpt] adj (room) estrecho(a); **to be c. for space** tener muy poco espacio

**crampon** [ˈkræmpɒn] n crampón m

**cranberry** [ˈkrænbərɪ] n arándano m agrio

**crane** [kreɪn] **1** n (a) (for lifting) grúa f (b) (bird) grulla f; **c. fly** (insect) típula f

**2** vt **to c. one's neck** estirar el cuello

**3** vi **to c. forward** inclinarse hacia delante (estirando el cuello)

**cranium** [ˈkreɪnɪəm] (pl **crania** [ˈkreɪnɪə]) n Anat cráneo m

**crank**[1] [kræŋk] n (gear mechanism) manivela f

**crank**[2] n Fam (eccentric) rarito(a) m,f, maniático(a)

**crankshaft** [ˈkræŋkʃɑːft] n Aut cigüeñal m

**cranky** [ˈkræŋkɪ] adj Fam (eccentric) rarito(a), maniático(a)

**crap** [kræp] **1** n (a) Vulg (excrement) mierda f; **to have** or **take a c.** echar una cagada, cagar (b) very Fam (worthless things) mierdas fpl, porquerías fpl; (nonsense) paridas fpl, chorradas fpl; (disgusting substance) porquería f, guarrería f

**2** adj very Fam (bad) **it's c.!** ¡es una mierda!

**crash** [kræʃ] **1** n (a) (noise) estruendo m (b) choque m, colisión f; (accident) **car/train/plane** c. accidente m de coche/tren/avión; Aut **c. barrier** quitamiedos m inv; Aut **c. helmet** casco m (protector); Av **c. landing** aterrizaje m forzoso or de emergencia (c) (financial) quiebra f (financiera), crac m

**2** adj **c. course** curso m intensivo; **c. diet** dieta f drástica

**3** vt (a) (plane) estrellar; **she crashed the car** chocó con el coche (b) very Fam **to c. a party** colarse en una fiesta

**4** vi (a) (make noise) (of waves) romper; **the bookcase crashed to the ground** la estantería cayó con estruendo (b) (of cars) chocar; **to c. into** estrellarse contra (c) (of business, economy) quebrar (d) Comptr bloquearse, colgarse (e) very Fam (sleep) sobar

▶**crash out 1** vi **he was crashed out on the sofa** estaba sopa en el sofá

**2** vi Fam (go to sleep) quedarse sopa

**crashing** [ˈkræʃɪŋ] adj **a c. bore** un tostón

**crash-land** [ˈkræʃˈlænd] vi realizar un aterrizaje forzoso

**crass** [kræs] adj zafio(a); **c. ignorance/stupidity** ignorancia/estupidez supina

**crate** [kreɪt] n (box) caja f

**crater** [ˈkreɪtə(r)] n cráter m

**cravat** [krəˈvæt] n pañuelo m, fular m

**crave** [kreɪv] **1** vt (affection, a cigarette) ansiar

**2** vi **to be craving for** (affection, a cigarette) ansiar

**craving** [ˈkreɪvɪŋ] n (in general) ansia f (for de); (of pregnant woman) antojo m; **to have a c. for sth** desear vehementemente or ansiar algo

**crawl** [krɔːl] **1** n (a) (slow pace) paso m lento; **the traffic was moving at a c.** el tráfico avanzaba lentamente (b) (swimming stroke) (estilo m) crol m; **to do** or **swim (the) c.** nadar a crol

**2** vi (a) (of person) arrastrarse; (of baby) gatear; (of car) avanzar lentamente (b) Fam (be infested) **the flat was crawling with cockroaches** el piso estaba infestado de cucarachas; **it makes my skin c.** me pone la carne de gallina (c) Fam (be obsequious) **to c. to sb** arrastrarse ante alguien

**crawler** [ˈkrɔːlə(r)] n Fam (obsequious person) pelota mf, adulador(ora) m,f

**crayfish** [ˈkreɪfɪʃ] n cangrejo m de río

**crayon** [ˈkreɪɒn] **1** n (wax) (barra f de) cera f; (pastel) (barra f de) pastel m; (pencil) lápiz m de color

**2** vt pintar

**craze** [kreɪz] n locura f, moda f (for de)

**crazed** [kreɪzd] adj (look, person) demente, delirante

**crazy** [ˈkreɪzɪ] adj (person) loco(a); **to be c.** estar loco(a); **to go c.** volverse loco(a); **to drive sb c.** volver loco(a) a alguien; **she's c. about motorbikes** las motos la vuelven loca; **to be c. about sb** estar loco(a) por alguien; **like c.** (to run, work) como un loco; **c. paving** (on path) pavimento m de formas irregulares

**CRE** [siːɑːˈriː] n Br (abbr **Commission for Racial Equality**) = órgano gubernamental británico contra el racismo

**creak** [kriːk] **1** n (of hinge) chirrido m; (of timber, shoes) chirrido, crujido m

**2** vi (of hinge) chirriar, rechinar; (of timber, shoes) crujir

**creaky** [ˈkriːkɪ] adj (chair) que cruje; Fig **the dialogue is a bit c.** los diálogos chirrían un poco

**cream** [kriːm] **1** n (a) (of milk) nata f; **c. of tomato/chicken soup** crema f de tomate/pollo; **c. cake** pastel m de nata; **c. cheese** queso m blanco para untar (b) Fig **the c.** (best part) la flor y nata (c) (lotion) crema f; **face/hand c.** crema facial/de manos (d) (colour) (color m) crema m

**2** adj **c.(-coloured)** (color) crema

**3** vt Culin (beat) batir

▶**cream off** vt sep seleccionar, quedarse con

**creamy** [ˈkriːmɪ] adj cremoso(a)

**crease** [kriːs] **1** n (in skin, crumpled fabric) arruga f; (in ironed trousers) raya f

**2** vt arrugar; **to c. one's brow** fruncir el ceño

**3** vi (become creased) arrugarse

▶**crease up** vi Fam (laugh) morirse de risa

**create** [krɪ'eɪt] **1** vt crear; **to c. a sensation** causar sensación

**2** vi Fam (get angry, cause fuss) ponerse hecho(a) una furia

**creation** [krɪ'eɪʃən] n creación f

**creative** [krɪ'eɪtɪv] adj creativo(a); **the c. process** el proceso creativo; Fin **c. accounting** maquillaje m de cuentas, artificios mpl contables; **c. writing** creación f literaria

**creativity** [kriːə'tɪvɪtɪ] n creatividad f

**creator** [krɪ'eɪtə(r)] n creador(ora) m,f; Rel **the C.** el Creador

**creature** ['kriːtʃə(r)] n (living being, animal) criatura f; **he's a c. of habit** es un animal de costumbres; **the chairman is a c. of the government** (instrument) el presidente es un títere del Gobierno; **c. comforts** (pequeños) placeres mpl de la vida

**crèche** [kreʃ] n guardería f (infantil)

**credence** ['kriːdəns] n **to give c. to sth** dar crédito a algo

**credentials** [krɪ'denʃəlz] npl (of ambassador) credenciales fpl; Fig **he quickly established his c.** pronto demostró su valía

**credibility** [kredr'bɪlɪtɪ] n credibilidad f; **c. gap** vacío m or falta f de credibilidad

**credible** ['kredɪbəl] adj creíble

**credit** ['kredɪt] **1** n (a) Fin crédito m; **to be in c.** tener saldo positivo; **to give sb c.** conceder un crédito a alguien; **to buy/sell on c.** comprar/vender a crédito; **c. card** tarjeta f de crédito; Econ **c. control** control m crediticio or de crédito; Fin **c. limit** límite m de descubierto or de crédito; Fin **c. note** vale m de compra; Fin **c. rating** clasificación f or grado m de solvencia; Econ **c. squeeze** restricción f de crédito; Fin **c. transfer** transferencia f bancaria

(b) (belief) crédito m; **to give c. to sth** dar crédito a algo; **to gain c.** (of theory) ganar aceptación

(c) (recognition) reconocimiento m; **you'll have to give her c. for that** se lo tendrás que reconocer; **to take the c. for sth** apuntarse el mérito de algo; **c. where c.'s due** las cosas como son; **to her c., she refused** se negó, lo cual dice mucho en su favor; **it does you c.** puedes estar orgulloso(a) de ello; **you're a c. to the school** eres motivo de orgullo para la escuela

(d) (of film) **credits** títulos mpl de crédito

**2** vt (a) (money) abonar; **to c. money to sb's account** abonar dinero en la cuenta de alguien

(b) (attribute) **to c. sb with sth** atribuir algo a alguien; **I credited you with more sense** te consideraba más sensato

(c) (believe) creer; **would you c. it?** ¿te lo quieres creer?

**creditable** ['kredɪtəbəl] adj (praiseworthy) encomiable, digno(a) de encomio

**creditor** ['kredɪtə(r)] n Fin acreedor(ora) m,f

**credulity** [krɪ'djuːlɪtɪ] n credulidad f

**credulous** ['kredjʊləs] adj crédulo(a)

**creed** [kriːd] n also Fig credo m

**creek** [kriːk] n (small bay) cala f; (stream) riachuelo m; Fam Fig **to be up the c. (without a paddle)** tenerlo claro, ir de culo

**creep** [kriːp] **1** n (a) (unpleasant person) asqueroso(a) m,f; (obsequious person) pelota mf (b) **he/it gives me the creeps** (makes me uneasy) me pone la piel de gallina; **I always get the creeps when I'm alone in the house** (get frightened) siempre que me quedo solo(a) en casa me entra el canguelo

**2** vi (pt & pp crept [krept]) (of animal, person) moverse sigilosamente, deslizarse; (of plants) trepar; **to c. in** colarse; **to c. out** escapar (sigilosamente); **a mistake has crept into our calculations** se nos ha colado un error en los cálculos; **old age has crept up on me** los años se me han echado encima; Fam **it makes my flesh c.** me pone la carne de gallina

**creeper** ['kriːpə(r)] n (plant) enredadera f; (in wild) liana f

**creeping** ['kriːpɪŋ] adj (gradual) paulatino(a); **c. privatization** privatización f gradual subrepticia

**creepy** ['kriːpɪ] adj Fam espeluznante

**creepy-crawly** ['kriːpɪ'krɔːlɪ] Fam n bicho m, bicharraco m

**cremate** [krɪ'meɪt] vt incinerar

**cremation** [krɪ'meɪʃən] n incineración f, cremación f

**crematorium** [kremə'tɔːrɪəm] (pl crematoria [kremə'tɔːrɪə]) n crematorio m

**creole** ['kriːəʊl] Ling **1** n criollo m

**2** adj criollo(a)

**creosote** ['kriːəsəʊt] n creosota f

**crêpe** n (a) [kreɪp] (textile) crepé m, crespón m; **c. bandage** venda f; **c. paper** papel m crespón or pinocho; **c.(-rubber) soles** zapatos mpl de suela de goma or de crepé (b) [krep] (pancake) crepe f

**crept** [krept] pt & pp of **creep**

**crescendo** [krɪ'ʃendəʊ] (pl crescendos) n Mus & Fig crescendo m; **to rise to a c.** (of music, complaints) alcanzar el punto culminante

**crescent** ['kresənt] **1** n (shape) medialuna f

**2** adj **c.(-shaped)** en forma de medialuna; **c. moon** cuarto m creciente

**cress** [kres] n berro m

**crest** [krest] n (of bird, wave) cresta f; (of helmet) penacho m; (of hill) cima f; (coat of arms) escudo m; Fig **on the c. of a wave** en la cresta de la ola

**crestfallen** ['krestfɔːlən] adj abatido(a)

**Cretan** ['kriːtən] n & adj cretense mf

**Crete** [kri:t] n Creta

**cretin** ['kretɪn] n Fam cretino(a) m,f

**crevice** ['krevɪs] n grieta f

**crew**[1] [kru:] **1** n (of ship, plane) tripulación f; (of ambulance) personal m de ambulancia; Fam (gang, group) pandilla f; **c. cut** (hairstyle) rapado m, corte m al cero

**2** vt (ship) tripular

**crew**[2] pt of **crow**

**crib** [krɪb] **1** n (a) (cradle) cuna f; (Nativity scene) belén m, pesebre m (b) Fam (at school) (translation) traducción f (que permite entender el original); (in exam) chuleta f

**2** (pt & pp **cribbed**) Fam (at school) copiar

**crick** [krɪk] **1** n (in neck) tortícolis f inv; **to have a c. in one's neck** tener tortícolis

**2** vt **to c. one's neck** hacerse daño en el cuello

**cricket**[1] ['krɪkɪt] n (insect) grillo m

**cricket**[2] n (sport) críquet m; Fig **that's not c.!** ¡eso es juego sucio!; **c. ball** pelota f de críquet; **c. bat** bate m de críquet; **c. pitch** campo m de críquet

**crikey** ['kraɪkɪ] exclam Fam ¡caramba!

**crime** [kraɪm] n (serious criminal act) crimen m; (less serious) delito m; **c. is on the increase** está aumentando la delincuencia; **to commit a c.** cometer un delito, delinquir; Fig **it's a c.** (outrageous) es un crimen; **c. wave** ola f de delincuencia; **c. writer** (of detective novels) escritor(ora) m,f de novela negra

**Crimea** [kraɪ'mɪə] n Crimea

**Crimean** [kraɪ'mɪən] adj de Crimea

**criminal** ['krɪmɪnəl] **1** n (serious) criminal mf; (less serious) delincuente mf

**2** adj delictivo(a), criminal; Fig **a c. waste of money** un despilfarro disparatado; **C. Investigation Department** = policía judicial británica; **c. court** juzgado m de lo penal; **c. law** derecho m penal; **c. lawyer** abogado(a) m,f criminalista, penalista mf; **c. offence** delito m (penal); **to instigate c. proceedings against sb** demandar a alguien ante un juzgado de lo penal; **c. record** antecedentes mpl penales

**criminalize** ['krɪmɪnəlaɪz] vt penalizar

**criminology** [krɪmɪ'nɒlədʒɪ] n criminología f

**crimp** [krɪmp] vt (hair) rizar (con tenacillas)

**crimson** ['krɪmzən] n & adj carmesí m

**cringe** [krɪndʒ] vi (a) (show fear) encogerse (b) (be embarrassed) tener vergüenza ajena, abochornarse; **it makes me c.** me produce vergüenza ajena

**cringing** ['krɪndʒɪŋ] adj (afraid) atemorizado(a); (servile) servil

**crinkle** ['krɪŋkəl] **1** vt (paper) arrugar; **to c. one's nose** arrugar la nariz

**2** vi arrugarse

**crinkly** ['krɪŋklɪ] adj (skin, paper) arrugado(a)

**cripple** ['krɪpəl] **1** n inválido(a) m,f

**2** vt (a) (person) dejar inválido(a), lisiar (b) (industry, system) deteriorar, arruinar

**crippling** ['krɪplɪŋ] adj (a) (illness) incapacitante (b) (taxes, strike) pernicioso(a)

**crisis** ['kraɪsɪs] (pl **crises** ['kraɪsi:z]) n crisis f inv; **in c.** en crisis; **to go through a c.** atravesar una crisis; **c. management** gestión f de crisis

**crisp** [krɪsp] **1** n **crisps** patatas fpl fritas (de bolsa); **burnt to a c.** achicharrado(a)

**2** adj (apple, lettuce) fresco(a); (pastry, bacon) crujiente; (air, breeze) fresco(a); (style) conciso(a); (tone) seco(a)

**crisply** ['krɪsplɪ] adv (say) secamente

**crispy** ['krɪspɪ] adj (bacon, pastry) crujiente

**criss-cross** ['krɪskrɒs] **1** vt entrecruzar

**2** vi entrecruzarse

**criterion** [kraɪ'tɪərɪən] (pl **criteria** [kraɪ'tɪərɪə]) n criterio m

**critic** ['krɪtɪk] n crítico(a) m,f

**critical** ['krɪtɪkəl] adj (a) (negative) crítico(a); **to be c. of** criticar (b) (essay, study) crítico(a); **it was a c. success** fue un éxito de crítica or entre la crítica (c) (decisive) crítico(a), decisivo(a); **she was in a c. condition** (of patient) se encontraba en estado crítico

**criticism** ['krɪtɪsɪzəm] n crítica f

**criticize** ['krɪtɪsaɪz] vt criticar; **to c. sb for (doing) sth** criticar a alguien por (hacer) algo

**critique** [krɪ'ti:k] n crítica f

**croak** [krəʊk] **1** n (of frog) croar m; (of raven) graznido m; (of person) gruñido m

**2** vi (a) (of frog) croar; (of raven) graznar; (of person) gruñir (b) very Fam (die) palmar, espicharla

**Croat** ['krəʊæt] **1** n (a) (person) croata mf (b) (language) croata m

**2** adj croata

**Croatia** [krəʊ'eɪʃə] n Croacia

**Croatian** [krəʊ'eɪʃən] = **Croat**

**crochet** ['krəʊʃeɪ] **1** n ganchillo m; **c. hook** (aguja f de) ganchillo m

**2** vt **to c. sth** hacer algo a ganchillo

**3** vi hacer ganchillo

**crock** [krɒk] n (a) (pot) vasija f de barro (b) Fam **old c.** (person) viejo(a) m,f chocho(a); (car) cacharro m; tartana f

**crockery** ['krɒkərɪ] n vajilla f

**crocodile** ['krɒkədaɪl] n (a) (animal) cocodrilo m; **c. tears** lágrimas fpl de cocodrilo (b) (line of pupils) fila f

**crocus** ['krəʊkəs] n azafrán m

**croft** [krɒft] n Scot granja f pequeña

**crofter** ['krɒftə(r)] n Scot granjero(a) m,f

**croissant** ['krwæsɒŋ] n croissant m

**crone** [krəʊn] n Pej **old c.** bruja f

**crony** ['krəʊnɪ] n amigote m, amiguete(a) m,f

**crook** [krʊk] **1** n (a) *(criminal)* granuja mf, bribón(ona) m,f (b) *(bishop's)* báculo m (c) *(curve)* recodo m; **to hold sth in the c. of one's arm** llevar algo en brazos or en el brazo

**2** vt *(finger, arm)* doblar

**crooked** ['krʊkɪd] adj (a) *(not straight)* torcido(a); *(lane, path)* tortuoso(a) (b) *(dishonest, illegal) (deal)* sucio(a); *(policeman, politician)* corrupto(a)

**croon** [kruːn] vt & vi canturrear

**crop** [krɒp] **1** n (a) *(of fruit, vegetables)* cosecha f; Fig **this year's c. of films** la cosecha de películas de este año (b) *(handle of whip)* (**riding**) **c.** fusta f (c) *(of bird)* buche m

**2** vt *(pt & pp **cropped**)* (a) *(cut) (hair)* cortar; *(photograph)* recortar (b) *(of cattle) (grass)* pacer

▶**crop up** vi *(arise)* surgir

**cropper** ['krɒpə(r)] n Fam **to come a c.** *(fall)* darse un batacazo; Fig *(fail)* pinchar

**croquet** ['krəʊkeɪ] n *(game)* croquet m

**croquette** [krɒ'ket] n Culin croqueta f

**cross** [krɒs] **1** n (a) *(sign, shape)* cruz f; **to make the sign of the c.** *(blessing self)* santiguarse; *(blessing others)* dar la bendición
(b) *(hybrid) (of animals)* cruce m, híbrido m; Fig **to be a c. between A and B** ser una mezcla de A y B
(c) *(in football)* centro m; *(in boxing)* (golpe m) directo m

**2** adj *(annoyed)* enfadado(a); **to be c.** estar enfadado(a); **to get c.** enfadarse

**3** vt (a) *(river, road)* cruzar, atravesar; **to c. sb's path** cruzarse en el camino de alguien; **it crossed my mind that (that…)** se me ocurrió (que…); Fig **we'll c. that bridge when we come to it** no adelantemos acontecimientos
(b) *(place across)* cruzar; **to c. one's legs/arms** cruzar las piernas/los brazos; Fig **to keep one's fingers crossed** cruzar los dedos; **to c. one's eyes** poner los ojos bizcos; Fig **to c. swords (with)** verse las caras or habérselas (con); Fig **we must have got our wires crossed** parece que no nos hemos entendido bien
(c) *(oppose)* oponerse a, contrariar
(d) *(animals, plants)* cruzar (**with** con)
(e) *(cheque)* **to c. a cheque** cruzar un cheque
(f) Rel **to c. oneself** santiguarse; Fam **c. my heart!** ¡te lo juro!

**4** vi (a) *(of roads, lines)* cruzarse; **our letters crossed in the post** nuestras cartas se cruzaron en el correo
(b) *(go across)* cruzar

▶**cross off, cross out** vt sep tachar

**crossbar** ['krɒsbɑː(r)] n *(on bike)* barra f *(de la bicicleta)*; *(of goalposts)* larguero m

**crossbow** ['krɒsbəʊ] n ballesta f

**crossbreed** ['krɒsbriːd] n híbrido m, cruce m

**cross-Channel** ['krɒs'tʃænəl] adj **c. ferry** = transbordador que cruza el Canal de la Mancha; **c. trade** = comercio entre Gran Bretaña y el resto de Europa

**crosscheck** ['krɒs'tʃek] **1** n comprobación f, verificación f

**2** vt comprobar, contrastar

**cross-country** ['krɒs'kʌntrɪ] adj *(vehicle)* todoterreno; **c. runner** corredor(ora) m,f de cross; **c. running** campo m a través, cross m

**cross-examination** ['krɒsɪgzæmɪ'neɪʃən] n interrogatorio m

**cross-examine** ['krɒsɪg'zæmɪn] vt interrogar

**cross-eyed** ['krɒsaɪd] adj bizco(a)

**crossfire** ['krɒsfaɪə(r)] n also Fig fuego m cruzado; **they were caught in the c.** el fuego cruzado los pilló en medio

**crossing** ['krɒsɪŋ] n (a) *(of sea)* travesía f (b) *(in street)* paso m de peatones

**cross-legged** ['krɒs'leg(ɪ)d] adv **to sit c.** sentarse con las piernas cruzadas

**cross-platform** [krɒs'plætfɔːm] adj Comptr multiplataforma inv

**cross-purposes** ['krɒs'pɜːpəsɪz] npl **they were at c. with each other** sin darse cuenta, estaban hablando de cosas distintas

**cross-reference** ['krɒs'refərəns] n referencia f, remisión f

**crossroads** ['krɒsrəʊdz] n also Fig encrucijada f

**cross-section** ['krɒs'sekʃən] n sección f transversal; **a c. of the population** una muestra representativa de la población

**crosswind** ['krɒswɪnd] n viento m lateral

**crossword** ['krɒswɜːd] n **c. (puzzle)** crucigrama m

**crotch** [krɒtʃ] n *(of trousers, person)* entrepierna f

**crotchet** ['krɒtʃɪt] n Mus negra f

**crotchety** ['krɒtʃətɪ] adj *(grumpy)* gruñón(ona)

**crouch** [kraʊtʃ] vi *(of animal)* agazaparse; *(of person)* agacharse

**croupier** ['kruːpɪə(r)] n crupier m

**crouton** ['kruːtɒn] n picatoste m, = dado de pan frito

**crow** [krəʊ] **1** n *(bird)* corneja f; **as the c. flies** en línea recta; **c.'s feet** *(facial lines)* patas fpl de gallo; **c.'s nest** *(on ship)* cofa f

**2** vi *(pt **crowed** or **crew** [kruː], pp **crowed**)* (a) *(of cock)* cantar (b) *(show off)* pavonearse *(about* de)

**crowbar** ['krəʊbɑː(r)] n palanqueta f

**crowd** [kraʊd] 1 n (a) *(large number of people)* muchedumbre f, multitud f; *(at football match)* público m; *Fig* **to stand out from the c.** destacar, sobresalir; *Fig* **to follow the c.** dejarse llevar por la masa; **to be a c. puller** atraer a las masas; **c. scene** *(in film)* escena f de masas (b) *Fam (group)* pandilla f; **the usual c. were there** estaba la gente de siempre, estaban los de siempre

2 *vt* atestar, abarrotar

3 *vi* **to c. (together)** apiñarse, amontonarse; **to c. round sb** apiñarse en torno de alguien

►**crowd out** *vt sep (exclude)* **to c. sb out of a deal/the market** excluir a alguien de un acuerdo/del mercado

**crowded** ['kraʊdɪd] *adj (room, bus)* abarrotado(a), atestado(a); **to be c.** estar abarrotado(a) *or* atestado(a)

**crown** [kraʊn] 1 n (a) *(of monarch)* corona f; **the C.** la Corona; *Br Law* **c. court** = tribunal superior de lo penal; **the c. jewels** las joyas de la corona; **c. prince** príncipe m heredero (b) *(top) (of head)* coronilla f; *(of hat)* copa f; *(of hill)* cima f; *(on tooth)* corona f

2 *vt also Fig* coronar; **to c. sb king** coronar rey a alguien; **to c. a tooth** ponerle una corona a una muela; *Fam Fig* **I'll c. you!** *(hit on the head)* ¡te voy a sacudir!

**crowning** ['kraʊnɪŋ] *adj (achievement)* supremo(a); **c. glory** gloria f suprema

**crucial** ['kru:ʃəl] *adj* (a) *(very important)* crucial (b) *very Fam (very good)* guay, genial

**crucible** ['kru:sɪbəl] n crisol m

**crucifix** ['kru:sɪfɪks] n crucifijo m

**crucifixion** [kru:sɪ'fɪkʃən] n crucifixión f

**crucify** ['kru:sɪfaɪ] *vt also Fig* crucificar

**crude** [kru:d] *adj* (a) *(unsophisticated, unrefined)* burdo(a); **c. (oil)** *(petróleo m)* crudo m (b) *(rude, vulgar)* ordinario(a), grosero(a)

**cruel** ['kru:əl] *adj* cruel; **you have to be c. to be kind** quien bien te quiere te hará llorar

**cruelty** ['kru:əltɪ] n crueldad f

**cruet** ['kru:ɪt] n *Culin* **c. (stand** *or* **set)** vinagreras fpl

**cruise** [kru:z] 1 n *(on ship)* crucero m; **to go on a c.** ir de crucero; **c. missile** misil m de crucero

2 *vi (of ship)* navegar tranquilamente; *(of passengers)* hacer un crucero; *(of car, plane)* ir a velocidad de crucero; *Fam (look for sexual partner)* buscar ligue; **it was cruising at 25 knots** *(of ship)* navegaba a 25 nudos; **cruising speed** *(of ship, plane)* velocidad f de crucero

**cruiser** ['kru:zə(r)] n *(ship)* **(battle) c.** crucero m *(de guerra)*; **(cabin) c.** yate m

**crumb** [krʌm] n *(of bread)* miga f; **my only c. of comfort is...** lo único que me consuela

es...; *Fig* **he was left with the crumbs** no le dejaron más que las migajas

**crumble** ['krʌmbəl] 1 n *(dessert)* = postre al horno a base de compota con masa quebrada dulce por encima

2 *vt (bread)* desmigajar

3 *vi (of stone)* desmenuzarse; *(of bread)* desmigajarse; *Fig (of empire, resistance)* desmoronarse, venirse abajo

**crumbly** ['krʌmblɪ] *adj* **it's very c.** se desmenuza muy fácilmente

**crumpet** ['krʌmpɪt] n (a) *(teacake)* = torta pequeña que se come con mantequilla (b) *very Fam* titis fpl; **a bit of c.** una tía maciza

**crumple** ['krʌmpəl] 1 *vt (material, dress)* arrugar

2 *vi* arrugarse; *Fig (of person)* desplomarse; *(of resistance)* sucumbir

**crunch** [krʌntʃ] 1 n *(sound)* crujido m; *Fig* **when it comes to the c.** a la hora de la verdad

2 *vt (with teeth)* ronzar, machacar con los dientes

3 *vi* crujir

**crunchy** ['krʌntʃɪ] *adj* crujiente

**crusade** [kru:'seɪd] 1 n *also Fig* cruzada f

2 *vi* **to c. for/against** emprender una cruzada a favor de/en contra de

**crusader** [kru:'seɪdə(r)] n *Hist* cruzado m; *Fig* paladín m

**crush** [krʌʃ] 1 n (a) *(crowd)* muchedumbre f, aglomeración f; **c. barrier** barrera f *or* valla f de seguridad (b) *(drink)* **orange c.** naranjada f (c) *Fam (infatuation)* **to have a c. on sb** estar colado(a) por *or* encaprichado(a) de alguien

2 *vt (person, thing)* estrujar, aplastar; *(grapes, garlic)* prensar, aplastar; *Fig (opponent, revolt)* aplastar, destrozar; **to c. sb's hopes** tirar abajo las esperanzas de alguien

3 *vi* **we crushed into the car** nos estrujamos para entrar en el coche

**crushing** ['krʌʃɪŋ] *adj (blow, defeat)* demoledor(ora), aplastante

**crust** [krʌst] n *(of bread, pie, the earth)* corteza f; *Fam* **to earn one's c.** ganarse el pan

**crustacean** [krʌs'teɪʃən] n crustáceo m

**crusty** ['krʌstɪ] *adj* (a) *(bread, roll)* crujiente (b) *(person)* malhumorado(a), gruñón(ona)

**crutch** [krʌtʃ] n (a) *(for walking)* muleta f; *Fig (support)* apoyo m, sostén m; **to be on crutches** ir con muletas (b) *(of trousers, person)* entrepierna f

**crux** [krʌks] n **the c. of the matter** el quid de la cuestión

**cruzado** [kru:'sɑ:dəʊ] n *(pl* **cruzados)** n *(Brazilian currency)* cruzado m

**cry** [kraɪ] 1 n (a) *(call) (of person, animal)* grito m; *(in demonstration)* consigna f; **to give a c.** dar un grito; **a c. of pain** un grito de dolor; *Fig* **a c.**

**for help** una petición de ayuda; **it's a far c. from what was promised** no tiene nada que ver con lo que se prometió (b) *(weeping)* **to have a good c.** llorar abundantemente

**2** *vt (pt & pp* **cried** [kraɪd]) **(a)** *(exclaim)* exclamar (b) *(weep)* **she cried herself to sleep** lloró hasta quedarse dormida

**3** *vi* **(a)** *(weep)* llorar; **to c. over sth** llorar por algo; *Prov* **there's no point in crying over spilt milk** a lo hecho, pecho (b) *(shout, call)* gritar; **to c. for help** gritar pidiendo ayuda

▸**cry off** *vi* volverse atrás

▸**cry out 1** *vt sep* **(a)** *(shout) (name, warning)* gritar (b) *(weep)* **to c. one's eyes** *or* **heart out** llorar a lágrima viva

**2** *vi* *(shout)* gritar; *Fam* **for crying out loud!** ¡por el amor de Dios!; *Fam* **that wall is crying out for a coat of paint** esa pared está pidiendo a gritos una mano de pintura

**crybaby** ['kraɪbeɪbɪ] *n Fam* llorica *mf*

**crying** ['kraɪɪŋ] **1** *n (weeping)* llanto *m*

**2** *adj (need)* acuciante; **it's a c. shame that...** es una auténtica vergüenza que...

**crypt** [krɪpt] *n* cripta *f*

**cryptic** ['krɪptɪk] *adj* críptico(a)

**crystal** ['krɪstəl] **1** *n (glass, mineral)* cristal *m*; **salt/sugar crystals** cristales *mpl* de sal/azúcar

**2** *adj* **(a)** *(clear)* transparente, claro(a) **(b)** *(made of glass)* de cristal; **c. ball** bola *f* de cristal

**crystal-clear** ['krɪstəl'klɪə(r)] *adj (water)* cristalino(a); *(explanation)* clarísimo(a), más claro(a) que el agua

**crystallize** ['krɪstəlaɪz] **1** *vt Chem* cristalizar; **crystallized fruits** frutas *fpl* escarchadas

**2** *vi Chem & Fig* cristalizar

**CSE** [si:es'i:] *n Br Sch Formerly (abbr* **Certificate of Secondary Education)** = certificado de enseñanza secundaria que se obtenía a los 15 o 16 años

**CST** [si:es'ti:] *n US (abbr* **Central Standard Time)** = hora oficial en el centro de los Estados Unidos

**cub** [kʌb] *n (of fox, lion)* cachorro *m*; *(of bear)* osezno *m*; *(of wolf)* lobezno *m*, lobato *m*; **C. (Scout)** lobato *m*, niño *m* explorador

**Cuba** [['kju:bə] *n* Cuba

**Cuban** ['kju:bən] *n & adj* cubano(a) *m,f*

**cubbyhole** ['kʌbɪhəʊl] *n (cupboard)* armario *m* empotrado; *(room)* cuartito *m*

**cube** [kju:b] **1** *n (shape)* cubo *m*; *(of sugar)* terrón *m*; *Math* **c. root** raíz *f* cúbica

**2** *vt Math* elevar al cubo

**cubic** ['kju:bɪk] *adj* cúbico(a); **c. capacity** capacidad *f*, volumen *m*; **c. metre** metro *m* cúbico

**cubicle** ['kju:bɪkəl] *n (in hospital, dormitory)* cubículo *m*; *(in swimming pool)* cabina *f*, vestuario *m*; *(in public toilet)* cubículo *m*

**cubism** ['kju:bɪzəm] *n Art* cubismo *m*

**cuckold** ['kʌkəld] **1** *n* cornudo *m*

**2** *vt* poner los cuernos a

**cuckoo** ['kʊku:] **1** *n (pl* **cuckoos)** cuco *m*; **c. clock** reloj *m* de cuco

**2** *adj Fam (mad)* **to be c.** estar majareta

**cucumber** ['kju:kʌmbə(r)] *n* pepino *m*

**cud** [kʌd] *n* **to chew the c.** rumiar

**cuddle** ['kʌdəl] **1** *n* abrazo *m*; **to give sb a c.** dar un abrazo a alguien

**2** *vt* abrazar

**3** *vi* arrimarse; **to c. up to sb** arrimarse a alguien

**cuddly** ['kʌdlɪ] *adj Fam (child, animal)* tierno(a); **a c. toy** un muñeco de peluche

**cudgel** ['kʌdʒəl] **1** *n* porra *f*, palo *m*; *Fig* **to take up the cudgels on sb's behalf** salir en defensa de alguien

**2** *vt (pt & pp* **cudgelled,** *US* **cudgeled)** **to c. one's brains** estrujarse el cerebro

**cue**¹ [kju:] *n (of actor)* entrada *f*; **to miss one's c.** no oír la entrada; *Fig* **to take one's c. from sb** tomar ejemplo de alguien; **c. card** *(for public speaker)* chuleta *f (en la que están anotados los puntos más importantes)*

**cue**² [kju:] *n (in billiards, pool)* taco *m*; **c. ball** bola *f* jugadora

**cuff**¹ [kʌf] *n (of shirt)* puño *m*; **cuffs** *(handcuffs)* esposas *fpl*; *Fam* **off the c.** improvisadamente; **c. links** gemelos *mpl*

**cuff**² [kʌf] **1** *n (blow)* cachete *m*, cate *m*

**2** *vt (hit)* dar un cachete a

**cuisine** [kwɪ'zi:n] *n* cocina *f*

**cul-de-sac** ['kʌldəsæk] *n* callejón *m* sin salida

**culinary** ['kʌlɪnərɪ] *adj* culinario(a)

**cull** [kʌl] **1** *n (of seals, deer)* sacrificio *m*

**2** *vt* **(a)** *(animals)* sacrificar (b) *(select)* extraer, recoger *(from* de)

**culminate** ['kʌlmɪneɪt] *vi* **to c. in** culminar en

**culmination** [kʌlmɪ'neɪʃən] *n* culminación *f*

**culottes** [kju:'lɒts] *npl* falda pantalón; **a pair of c.** una falda pantalón

**culpable** ['kʌlpəbəl] *adj* culpable; *Scot Law* **c. homicide** homicidio *m* involuntario

**culprit** ['kʌlprɪt] *n* culpable *mf*

**cult** [kʌlt] *n* culto *m*; **he became a c. figure** se convirtió en objeto de culto; **c. film/novel** película *f*/novela *f* de culto

**cultivate** ['kʌltɪveɪt] *vt also Fig* cultivar

**cultivated** ['kʌltɪveɪtɪd] *adj* **(a)** *(land, plant)* cultivado(a) (b) *(educated)* culto(a)

**cultivation** [kʌltɪ'veɪʃən] *n* cultivo *m*

**cultivator** ['kʌltɪveɪtə(r)] *n (machine)* cultivadora *f*; *(person)* cultivador(ora) *m,f*

**cultural** ['kʌltʃərəl] *adj* cultural

**culture** ['kʌltʃə(r)] *n* (a) *(artistic activity, refinement)* cultura *f*; *Hum* c. **vulture** devorador(ora) *m,f* de cultura (b) *(society)* cultura *f*; **c. shock** choque *m* cultural (c) *Biol* cultivo *m*

**cultured** ['kʌltʃəd] *adj (educated)* culto(a)

**cumbersome** ['kʌmbəsəm] *adj* engorroso(a)

**cumin** ['kʌmɪn] *n* comino *m*

**cumulative** ['kju:mjʊlətɪv] *adj* acumulativo(a)

**cunning** ['kʌnɪŋ] **1** *n* astucia *f*

**2** *adj (devious)* astuto(a), artero(a); *(ingenious)* ingenioso(a)

**cunt** [kʌnt] *n Vulg (vagina)* coño *m*; *(as insult)* hijo(a) *m,f* de puta, cabrón(ona) *m,f*

**cup** [kʌp] **1** *n* (a) *(for drinking)* taza *f*; *(measurement)* taza *f*, vaso *m*; **c. of coffee/tea** (taza *f* de) café *m*/té *m*; *Fam Fig* **it's not my c. of tea** no me va mucho; *Fam Fig* **it's not everyone's c. of tea** no (le) gusta a todo el mundo (b) *(trophy)* copa *f*; **c. tie** *(in football)* eliminatoria *f* de copa; **c. final** final *f* de la copa (c) *(of bra)* copa *f*

**2** *vt (pt & pp cupped)* **to c. one's hands round one's mouth** poner las manos en la boca a modo de bocina

**cupboard** ['kʌbəd] *n* armario *m*; *Fam* **it was just c. love** era un amor interesado; **c. space** armarios *mpl*

**cupcake** ['kʌpkeɪk] *n* ≃ magdalena *f*

**Cupid** ['kju:pɪd] *n* Cupido *m*

**cuppa** ['kʌpə] *n Fam* (taza *f* de) té *m*

**curable** ['kjʊərəbəl] *adj* curable

**curate** ['kjʊərət] *n Rel* coadjutor *m*; *Fig* **it's a c.'s egg** tiene alguna que otra cosa buena

**curator** [kjʊə'reɪtə(r)] *n* conservador(ora) *m,f* (de museos)

**curb** [kɜ:b] **1** *n* (a) *(limit)* **to put a c. on sth** poner freno a algo (b) *US (at roadside)* bordillo *m*

**2** *vt (spending)* reducir; *(emotions)* refrenar

**curd** [kɜ:d] *n* **curd(s)** cuajada *f*; **c. cheese** queso *m* blanco

**curdle** ['kɜ:dəl] **1** *vt* cortar; *Fam Fig* **to have a face that would c. milk** tener la cara avinagrada

**2** *vi* cortarse

**cure** [kjʊə(r)] **1** *n* cura *f*; **there is no known c.** no se conoce ninguna cura; **beyond c.** incurable

**2** *vt* (a) *(person) (of illness)* curar, sanar; *Fig (of bad habit)* quitar, curar; **to c. sb of sth** curar a alguien de algo (b) *(preserve) (by salting, drying)* curar; *(hides)* curtir

**cure-all** ['kjʊərɔ:l] *n* panacea *f*

**curfew** ['kɜ:fju:] *n* toque *m* de queda

**curio** ['kjʊərɪəʊ] *(pl curios) n* curiosidad *f*, rareza *f*

**curiosity** [kjʊərɪ'ɒsɪtɪ] *n* curiosidad *f*; *Prov* **c. killed the cat** mejor no te metas donde no te llaman

**curious** ['kjʊərɪəs] *adj (inquisitive, strange)* curioso(a); **to be c. to see/know** tener curiosidad por ver/saber

**curl** [kɜ:l] **1** *n (of hair)* rizo *m*; *(of smoke)* voluta *f*

**2** *vt (hair)* rizar; **to c. one's lip** hacer un gesto de desprecio; **to c. oneself into a ball** enroscarse, hacerse un ovillo

**3** *vi (of hair)* rizarse; *(of paper)* abarquillarse; *(of smoke)* formar volutas

▶**curl up** *vi* (a) *(settle down) (in bed, on sofa)* acurrucarse (b) *(of hedgehog, person)* enroscarse, hacerse un ovillo (c) *(of leaves)* rizarse; *(of paper)* abarquillarse

**curler** ['kɜ:lə(r)] *n (for hair)* rulo *m*

**curlew** ['kɜ:lju:] *n* zarapito *m*

**curling** ['kɜ:lɪŋ] *n* (a) *(sport)* curling *m*, = deporte consistente en el deslizamiento sobre hielo de piedras pulidas lo más cerca posible de una meta (b) **c. tongs** tenacillas *fpl*

**curly** ['kɜ:lɪ] *adj (hair)* rizado(a)

**currant** ['kʌrənt] *n (dried grape)* pasa *f* (de Corinto); **c. bun** bollo *m* de pasas

**currency** ['kʌrənsɪ] *n* (a) *Fin* moneda *f*; **to buy c.** comprar divisas; **foreign c.** divisas *fpl*; **c. market** mercado *m* de divisas (b) *Fig* **to give c. to a rumour** extender un rumor; **to gain c.** *(of idea, belief)* extenderse

**current** ['kʌrənt] **1** *n (of water, electricity, opinion)* corriente *f*; *Fig* **to swim against the c.** ir a *o r* nadar contra corriente

**2** *adj* (a) *(existing, present)* actual; *(common)* corriente; **to be c.** ser corriente; **in c. use** de uso corriente; **c. affairs** (temas *mpl* de) actualidad *f*; **c. issue** *(of magazine)* (último) número *m* (b) *Br Fin* **c. account** cuenta *f* corriente; **c. assets** activo *m* circulante; **c. expenditure** gasto *m* corriente *o r* ordinario; **c. liabilities** pasivo *m* corriente, obligaciones *fpl* a corto plazo

**currently** ['kʌrəntlɪ] *adv* actualmente, en este momento

**curriculum** [kə'rɪkjʊləm] *(pl curricula [kə'rɪkjʊlə]) n Sch* programa *m*, plan *m* de estudios; **c. vitae** currículum *m* (vitae)

**curry¹** ['kʌrɪ] *Culin* **1** *n* curry *m*; **c. powder** curry *m* (especia)

**2** *vt* **curried chicken/lamb** pollo *m*/cordero *m* al curry

**curry²** *vt* **to c. favour with sb** ganarse el favor de alguien con zalamerías

**curse** [kɜ:s] **1** *n (jinx, affliction)* maldición *f*; *(swearword)* maldición *f*, juramento *m*; **to put a c. on sb** echar una maldición a alguien; **a c. on…!** ¡maldito(a) sea…!

**2** *vt* maldecir; **he is cursed with a violent**

**temper** tiene la desgracia de tener mal genio
  **3** *vi* maldecir

**cursor** ['kɜːsə(r)] *n Comptr* cursor *m*; **c. keys** (teclas *fpl* de) flechas *fpl*, teclas *fpl* (de desplazamiento) del cursor

**cursory** ['kɜːsəri] *adj* (glance, examination) somero(a)

**curt** [kɜːt] *adj* brusco(a), seco(a)

**curtail** [kɜː'teɪl] *vt* (shorten) acortar; (limit) restringir, limitar

**curtain** ['kɜːtən] *n* (for window) cortina *f*; (in theatre) telón *m*; **to draw the curtains** (open) descorrer las cortinas; (close) correr *or* echar las cortinas; *Fam Fig* **it's curtains for him** es su final; *Th* **c. call** saludo *m*; **c. raiser** *Th* número *m* introductorio; *Fig* prólogo *m*; **c. rail** *or* **rod** barra *f* para las cortinas; **c. ring** anilla *f* de cortina

▸**curtain off** *vt sep* separar con una cortina

**curts(e)y** ['kɜːtsɪ] **1** *n* reverencia *f*
  **2** *vi* hacer una reverencia

**curvaceous** [kɜː'veɪʃəs] *adj* escultural

**curvature** ['kɜːvətʃə(r)] *n* curvatura *f*; *Med* **c. of the spine** desviación *f* de la columna vertebral

**curve** [kɜːv] **1** *n* curva *f*; *US* (in baseball) **c. ball** bola *f* con mucho efecto
  **2** *vi* (surface) curvarse; (road, river) hacer una curva

**curved** [kɜːvd] *adj* curvo(a), curvado(a)

**cushion** ['kʊʃən] **1** *n* (on chair) cojín *m*, almohadón *m*; (of air) colchón *m*; (on billiard table) banda *f*; *Fig* amortiguador *m* (against para)
  **2** *vt* (blow, impact) amortiguar; **to c. sb against sth** proteger a alguien de algo

**cushy** ['kʊʃɪ] *adj Fam* fácil; **a c. number** un chollo

**custard** ['kʌstəd] *n* natillas *fpl*; **c. pie** (in slapstick comedy) tarta *f* de crema; **c. powder** polvos *mpl* para hacer natillas

**custodial** [kʌ'stəʊdɪəl] *adj Law* **c. sentence** pena *f* de cárcel

**custodian** [kʌ'stəʊdɪən] *n* (of building, library) conservador(ora) *m,f*; (of principles, morals) guardián(ana) *m,f*

**custody** ['kʌstədɪ] *n* (of children) custodia *f*; **to have c. of sb** tener la custodia de alguien; **in safe c.** bien custodiado(a); **to take sb into c.** detener a alguien

**custom** ['kʌstəm] *n* (a) (tradition, practice) costumbre *f*; **it was his c. to rise early** tenía la costumbre de levantarse temprano (b) *Com* clientela *f*; **to lose sb's c.** perder a alguien como cliente; **to take one's c. elsewhere** comprar en otra parte

**customary** ['kʌstəmərɪ] *adj* acostumbrado(a), de costumbre; **it is c. to...** es costumbre...

**custom-built** ['kʌstəmbɪlt] *adj* hecho(a) de encargo

**customer** ['kʌstəmə(r)] *n* (in shop, of business) cliente(a) *m,f*; *Fam* **an awkward c.** un tipo quisquilloso; *Com* **c. care** atención *f* al cliente; *Com* **c. services (department)** (departamento *m* de) atención *f* al cliente

**customize** ['kʌstəmaɪz] *vt* adaptar al gusto del cliente

**custom-made** ['kʌstəm'meɪd] *adj* (equipment) personalizado(a); (clothes) hecho(a) a medida; (musical instrument) de encargo

**customs** ['kʌstəmz] *npl* aduana *f*; **to go through c.** pasar la aduana; **c. declaration** declaración *f* en la aduana; **c. duties** derechos *mpl* de aduana; **c. officer** empleado(a) *m,f* de aduanas

**cut** [kʌt] **1** *n* (a) (in flesh, wood, cloth) corte *m*; *Fig* (in wages, prices) recorte *m*; **a c. of meat** una pieza de carne; *Fig* **a c. of the profits** una tajada de los beneficios; **the c. and thrust of debate** el duelo del debate; *Fig* **to make cuts to** (text, film) cortar; (budget) recortar; *Fam* **to be a c. above sb/sth** ser mejor que *or* estar por encima de alguien/algo
  **(b)** (style) (of clothes, hair) corte *m*

  **2** *adj Fig* **c. and dried** (situation) claro(a), nítido(a); (solution, result) preestablecido(a); **c. flowers** flores *fpl* cortadas; **c. glass** cristal *m* tallado; *Fam* **a c. glass accent** un acento muy afectado

  **3** *vt* (pt & pp **cut**) (a) (in general) cortar; (in slices) rebanar; (wages, prices) recortar; **to c. one's finger** hacerse un corte en un dedo; **to c. one's nails** cortarse las uñas; **to have one's hair cut** (ir a) cortarse el pelo; **to c. sb's hair** cortarle el pelo a alguien; *also Fig* **to c. one's throat** cortarse el cuello; **to c. sth in two** *or* **in half** cortar algo en dos *or* por la mitad; **to c. sth to pieces** cortar algo en pedazos; *Fig* (criticize) poner algo por los suelos; **to c. oneself loose** soltarse; **to c. the cards/deck** cortar la baraja; **to c. a disc** (make recording) grabar un disco
  **(b)** (idioms) **to c. one's losses** cortar por lo sano; **to c. one's teeth on sth** iniciarse con *or* en algo; **to c. sb dead** (ignore) no hacer ni caso a alguien; **it's cutting it** *or* **things (a bit) fine** eso es ir muy justo; **to c. sb short** cortar a alguien; **to c. a speech/a visit short** abreviar un discurso/una visita; **to c. a long story short...** en resumidas cuentas...

  **4** *vi* cortar; *Cin* **c.!** ¡corten!; **that's an argument that cuts both ways** es un arma de doble filo; *Fam* **to c. and run** escabullirse, escaquearse

▸**cut across** *vt insep* (take short cut) atajar por; **this issue cuts across party lines** este tema está por encima de las diferencias entre partidos

▶**cut back 1** *vt sep (bush, tree)* podar; *(costs, production)* recortar

**2** *vi* **to c. back on expenses** recortar gastos; **to c. back on smoking/drinking** fumar/beber menos

▶**cut down 1** *vt sep (tree)* talar, cortar; *(speech, text)* reducir; *(spending, time)* recortar, reducir; **they were cut down by machine-gun fire** los abatió una ráfaga de ametralladora; *Fig* **to c. sb down to size** bajarle los humos a alguien

**2** *vi* **to c. down on sth** reducir algo; **he has cut down on smoking** fuma menos

▶**cut in** *vi (interrupt conversation)* interrumpir; **a van cut in in front of me** una camioneta me cerró el paso

▶**cut into** *vt insep (with knife)* cortar; **the rope was cutting into his wrists** la cuerda se le hincaba en las muñecas; **the work was cutting into her free time** el trabajo estaba interfiriendo en su tiempo libre

▶**cut off** *vt sep (a) (remove)* cortar; **to c. off sb's head** cortarle la cabeza a alguien; *Fig* **to c. off one's nose to spite one's face** tirar piedras contra el propio tejado **(b)** *(disconnect)* cortar; **I've been cut off** *(of electricity, water etc)* me han cortado la luz/el agua/*etc*; **I've been cut off** *(during phone conversation)* se ha cortado la comunicación **(c)** *(isolate)* aislar; **to be cut off (from)** quedar aislado(a) (de)

▶**cut out 1** *vt sep (a) (picture)* recortar; *(tumour)* extirpar; *(from text, film)* eliminar; **to c. out cigarettes** dejar de fumar **(b)** *(idioms)* **to c. sb out of a deal** excluir a alguien de un trato; **to c. sb out of one's will** desheredar a alguien; *Fam* **I've really got my work cut out** lo tengo realmente difícil; **to be cut out for sth** *(suited)* estar hecho(a) para algo; *Fam* **c. it out!** ¡basta ya!

**2** *vi (of engine)* calarse

▶**cut up 1** *vt sep (a) (meat, vegetables)* cortar, trocear; *(paper)* recortar **(b)** *Fam* **to be very cut up (about sth)** *(upset)* estar muy afectado(a) (por algo)

**2** *vi very Fam* **to c. up rough** ponerse hecho(a) una fiera

**cutback** ['kʌtbæk] *n* reducción *f*, recorte *m*

**cute** [kjuːt] *adj* bonito(a), mono(a)

**cuticle** ['kjuːtɪkəl] *n* cutícula *f*

**cutlery** ['kʌtlərɪ] *n* cubiertos *mpl*, cubertería *f*

**cutlet** ['kʌtlɪt] *n (of meat)* chuleta *f*

**cutoff** ['kʌtɒf] *n* **c. date** fecha *f* tope; **c. point** límite *m*, tope *m*

**cutout** ['kʌtaʊt] *n (a) (shape)* figura *f* recortada **(b)** *Elec* cortacircuitos *m inv*

**cut-price** ['kʌt'praɪs] *adj (goods)* rebajado(a)

**cutter** ['kʌtə(r)] *n (ship)* cúter *m*

**cutthroat** ['kʌtθrəʊt] **1** *n* matón *m*, asesino(a) *m,f*

**2** *adj* **c. competition** competencia *f* salvaje *or* sin escrúpulos; **c. razor** navaja *f* barbera

**cutting** ['kʌtɪŋ] **1** *n (a) (of plant)* esqueje *m*; *(newspaper)* **c.** recorte *m* (de periódico) **(b)** *(railway)* **c.** desmonte *m* (para el ferrocarril)

**2** *adj (wind)* cortante; *(remark)* hiriente, cortante; **c. edge** filo *m* cortante; *Fig* **to be at the c. edge of** estar a la vanguardia de

**cuttlefish** ['kʌtəlfɪʃ] *n* sepia *f*, jibia *f*

**CV** [siː'viː] *n (abbr* **curriculum vitae)** CV, currículum *m* vitae

**cwt** *(abbr* **hundredweight) (a)** *(metric)* 50 kg **(b)** *(imperial) Br (112 lb)* = 50,8 kg; *US (100 lb)* = 45,36 kg

**cyanide** ['saɪənaɪd] *n Chem* cianuro *m*

**cybercafe** ['saɪbəkæfeɪ] *n Comptr* cibercafé *m*

**cybernetics** [saɪbə'netɪks] *n Comptr* cibernética *f*

**cyberspace** ['saɪbəspeɪs] *n Comptr* ciberespacio *m*

**cyclamen** ['sɪkləmən] *n* ciclamen *m*, pamporcino *m*

**cycle** ['saɪkl] **1** *n (a) (pattern)* ciclo *m* **(b)** *(bicycle)* bicicleta *f*; **c. lane** *or* **path** carril *m* bici; **c. racing** carreras *fpl* ciclistas

**2** *vi* ir en bicicleta

**cyclic(al)** ['sɪklɪk(əl)] *adj* cíclico(a)

**cycling** ['saɪklɪŋ] *n* ciclismo *m*; **to go on a c. holiday** hacer cicloturismo; **c. track** pista *f* de ciclismo

**cyclist** ['saɪklɪst] *n* ciclista *mf*

**cyclo-cross** ['saɪkləkrɒs] *n* ciclocross *m*

**cyclone** ['saɪkləʊn] *n Met* ciclón *m*

**cygnet** ['sɪgnɪt] *n* cisne *m* joven

**cylinder** ['sɪlɪndə(r)] *n (shape)* cilindro *m*; *(gas container)* bombona *f*; **c. block** bloque *m* (de cilindros); **c. head** culata *f*

**cylindrical** [sɪ'lɪndrɪkəl] *adj* cilíndrico(a)

**cymbal** ['sɪmbəl] *n (musical instrument)* platillo *m*

**cynic** ['sɪnɪk] *n (sceptic)* escéptico(a) *m,f*, descreído(a) *m,f*

**cynical** ['sɪnɪkəl] *adj (shameless)* cínico(a); *(sceptical)* escéptico(a); **to be c. about sth** ser escéptico(a) respecto a algo

**cypress** ['saɪprəs] *n* ciprés *m*

**Cypriot** ['sɪprɪət] *n & adj* chipriota *mf*

**Cyprus** ['saɪprəs] *n* Chipre *m*

**cyst** [sɪst] *n Med* quiste *m*

**cystitis** [sɪs'taɪtɪs] *n Med* cistitis *f inv*

**czar** [zɑː(r)] *n* zar *m*

**Czech** [tʃek] **1** *n (a) (person)* checo(a) *m,f* **(b)** *(language)* checo *m*

**2** *adj* checo(a); **C. Republic** República Checa

**Czechoslovakia** [tʃekəʊslə'vækɪə] *n Formerly* Checoslovaquia

# D

**D, d** [di:] n (a) (letter) D, d (b) Mus re m (c) Sch **to get a D** (in exam, essay) (pass) sacar un aprobado or suficiente bajo; (fail) suspender

**D** US Pol (abbr **Democratic**) demócrata mf

**DA** [di:'eɪ] n US Law (abbr **district attorney**) fiscal mf (del distrito)

**dab** [dæb] **1** n (of paint, glue, perfume) pizca f, toque m; Br very Fam **dabs** (fingerprints) huellas fpl dactilares or digitales; **she's a d. hand at drawing** dibuja que es un alucine

**2** vt (pt & pp **dabbed**) (paint, glue, perfume) aplicar, poner; **she dabbed her eyes with a handkerchief** se secó los ojos delicadamente con un pañuelo

**dabble** ['dæbəl] vi **he dabbles in politics** se entretiene con la política

**dabbler** ['dæblə(r)] n (dilettante) aficionado(a) m,f, diletante mf

**dachshund** ['dækshʊnd] n dachshund m, perro m salchicha

**dad** [dæd] n Fam papá m

**daddy** ['dædɪ] n Fam papi m, papaíto m

**daddy-longlegs** ['dædɪ'lɒŋlegz] n Fam (insect) típula f

**daffodil** ['dæfədɪl] n narciso m

**daft** [dɑ:ft] adj Br (person, idea) tonto(a); **to be d. about sb/sth** estar loco por alguien/algo

**dagger** ['dægə(r)] n (a) daga f, puñal m (b) (idioms) **to be at daggers drawn (with sb)** estar a matar (con alguien); **to look daggers at sb** fulminar a alguien con la mirada

**dago** ['deɪgəʊ] (pl **dagos**) n very Fam = término ofensivo para referirse a españoles, italianos, portugueses o latinoamericanos

**dahlia** ['deɪlɪə] n dalia f

**daily** ['deɪlɪ] **1** n (newspaper) diario m, periódico m

**2** adj diario(a); **on a d. basis** a diario; **our d. bread** el pan nuestro de cada día; Fam **the d. grind** la rutina diaria; **d. paper** diario m, periódico m

**3** adv diariamente; **twice d.** dos veces al día

**dainty** ['deɪntɪ] adj (movement) grácil; (porcelain, lace) delicado(a), fino(a)

**dairy** ['deərɪ] n (shop) lechería f; (factory) central f lechera; **d. cow** vaca f lechera; **d. farm**

vaquería f; **d. farming** industria f lechera; **d. produce** productos mpl lácteos

**dais** ['deɪɪs] n tarima f

**daisy** ['deɪzɪ] n (flower) margarita f; Fam **he's pushing up the daisies** (dead) está criando malvas; **d. chain** guirnalda f de margaritas

**daisywheel** ['deɪzɪwi:l] n (on printer) margarita f

**dale** [deɪl] n valle m

**dalliance** ['dælɪəns] n Formal flirteo m, coqueteo m

**dally** ['dælɪ] vi (dawdle) perder el tiempo; **to d. over a decision** demorarse en tomar una decisión; **to d. with sb** coquetear con alguien

**Dalmatian** [dæl'meɪʃən] n (dog) dálmata m

**dam** [dæm] **1** n (of lake) dique m, presa f

**2** vt (pt & pp **dammed**) (valley) construir una presa en; (river, lake) embalsar

▶**dam up** vt insep (one's feelings) reprimir

**damage** ['dæmɪdʒ] **1** n (to machine, building) daños mpl; (to health, reputation) perjuicio m, daño m; **to do** or **cause d. to sth** ocasionar daños a algo, perjudicar a algo; Law **damages** daños mpl y perjuicios; **the d. is done** el daño ya está hecho; Br Fam **what's the d.?** ¿qué se debe?; **d. limitation** limitación f de daños

**2** vt (machine, building) dañar; (health, reputation) perjudicar, dañar

**damaging** ['dæmɪdʒɪŋ] adj perjudicial

**Damascus** [də'mæskəs] n Damasco

**damask** ['dæməsk] n (cloth) damasco m

**dame** [deɪm] n (a) US Fam (woman) mujer f, tía f (b) Br (in pantomime) = personaje femenino de una vieja interpretado por un actor (c) Br (title) dama f

**damn** [dæm] **1** n very Fam **I don't give a d.** me importa un bledo; **it's not worth a d.** no vale un pimiento; **d.!** ¡mierda!

**2** adj very Fam maldito(a); **you d. fool!** ¡maldito idiota!; **it's a d. nuisance!** ¡qué fastidio!

**3** adv very Fam **d. good** genial, buenísimo(a); **he knows d. all about politics** no tiene ni puñetera idea de política; **you know d. well what I mean!** ¡sabes de sobra lo que quiero decir!

**4** vt (a) (criticize severely) vapulear, criticar duramente (b) very Fam **d. the expense/the**

consequences! ¡a la porra con los gastos/las consecuencias!; *Fam* **well I'll be damned!** ¡que me aspen!, ¡madre mía!

**damnation** [dæm'neɪʃən] *n Rel* condenación *f; Fam* **d.!** ¡maldición!

**damned** [dæmd] **1** *adj very Fam* maldito(a); **you d. fool!** ¡maldito idiota!
**2** *adv very Fam* **d. good** genial, buenísimo(a)
**3** *n* **the d.** los condenados

**damning** ['dæmɪŋ] *adj (admission, revelation)* condenatorio(a)

**damp** [dæmp] **1** *n* humedad *f*
**2** *adj* húmedo(a); *Fig* **a d. squib** un chasco
**3** *vt* **to d. sb's spirits** desanimar a alguien; **d. down a fire** sofocar un fuego

**dampcourse** ['dæmpkɔ:s] *n* aislante *m* hidrófugo

**dampen** ['dæmpən] *vt (make wet)* humedecer; *Fig* **to d. sb's spirits** desanimar a alguien

**damper** ['dæmpə(r)] *n Mus* apagador *m; Fig* **to put a d. on sth** ensombrecer algo

**damsel** ['dæmzəl] *n Literary* doncella *f*, damisela *f; Hum* **a d. in distress** una doncella en apuros

**damson** ['dæmzən] *n (fruit)* ciruela *f* damascena; *(tree)* ciruelo *m* damásceno

**dance** [dɑ:ns] **1** *n* baile *m; Fam* **to lead sb a (merry) d.** traer a alguien al retortero *or* a mal traer; **d. band** orquesta *f* de baile; **d. floor** pista *f* de baile; **d. hall** salón *m* de baile; **d. music** música *f* de baile *or* de discoteca
**2** *vt* bailar; **to d. attendance on sb** atender servilmente a alguien
**3** *vi* bailar; **they danced down the road** bajaron la calle dando brincos

**dancer** ['dɑ:nsə(r)] *n* bailarín(ina) *m,f*

**dancing** ['dɑ:nsɪŋ] *n* baile *m;* **d. shoes** zapatos *mpl* de baile

**dandelion** ['dændɪlaɪən] *n* diente *m* de león

**dander** ['dændə(r)] *n Fam* **to get sb's d. up** *(annoy)* sacar de quicio a alguien

**dandruff** ['dændrəf] *n* caspa *f*

**dandy** ['dændɪ] **1** *n (person)* petimetre *m*, dandi *m*
**2** *adj Fam* genial; **everything's just (fine and) d.** está todo perfecto

**Dane** [deɪn] *n* danés(esa) *m,f*

**danger** ['deɪndʒə(r)] *n* peligro *m;* **in/out of d.** en/fuera de peligro; **to be in d. of doing sth** correr el peligro de hacer algo; **there is no d. that...** no hay peligro de que...; **to be on the d. list** *(of patient)* estar muy grave; **to be off the d. list** *(of patient)* estar fuera de peligro; **d. money** prima *f or* plus *m* de peligrosidad; *Fig* **d. sign** señal *f* de peligro

**dangerous** ['deɪndʒərəs] *adj* peligroso(a)

**dangerously** ['deɪndʒərəslɪ] *adv* peligrosamente; **they came d. close to losing** estuvieron en un tris de caer derrotados

**dangle** ['dæŋgəl] **1** *vt* balancear, hacer oscilar; *Fig* **the company dangled a bonus in front of its workers** la empresa ofreció una paga extra a sus trabajadores como incentivo
**2** *vi* colgar; *Fig* **to keep sb dangling** tener a alguien pendiente

**Danish** ['deɪnɪʃ] **1** *n (language)* danés *m*
**2** *adj* danés(esa); **D. pastry** = pastel dulce de hojaldre

**dank** [dæŋk] *adj (place, atmosphere)* frío(a) y húmedo(a)

**Danube** ['dænju:b] *n* **the D.** el Danubio

**dapper** ['dæpə(r)] *adj* pulcro(a), atildado(a)

**dappled** ['dæpəld] *adj* **the d. light on the forest floor** el lecho del bosque, salpicado de luces y sombras

**dare** ['deə(r)] **1** *n* reto *m*, desafío *m;* **he would do anything for a d.** es capaz de hacer cualquier cosa si le desafían a ello
**2** *vt* **(a) to d. to do sth** atreverse a hacer algo **(b) to d. sb to do sth** retar a alguien a que haga algo; **I d. you to tell her!** ¡a que no se lo dices?, ¿a que no eres capaz de decírselo?
**3** *modal aux v* **to d. do sth** atreverse a hacer algo; **I d. not** *or* **daren't ask him** no me atrevo a preguntarle; **don't you d. tell her!** ¡ni se te ocurra decírselo!; **how d. you!** ¡cómo te atreves!; **I d. say** probablemente

**daredevil** ['deədevəl] *n & adj* temerario(a) *m,f*

**daring** ['deərɪŋ] **1** *n* atrevimiento *m*, osadía *f*
**2** *adj* audaz, atrevido(a)

**dark** [dɑ:k] **1** *n* **(a)** *(darkness)* oscuridad *f;* **before/after d.** antes/después del anochecer; **in the d.** en la oscuridad **(b)** *(idioms)* **to be in the d. (about sth)** estar in albis (sobre algo); **to keep sb in the d. (about sth)** mantener a alguien en la ignorancia (acerca de algo)
**2** *adj* **(a)** *(not light)* oscuro(a); *(skin, hair)* oscuro(a), moreno(a); **it's d. by six o'clock** a las seis ya es de noche; **it's getting d.** está oscureciendo *or* anocheciendo; **d. glasses** gafas *fpl* oscuras; *Fig* **to be a d. horse** *(in competition)* ser quien puede dar la campanada; *(in politics)* ser el/la candidato(a) sorpresa; *(secretive person)* ser un enigma **(b)** *Fig (thought, period)* sombrío(a), oscuro(a); *(look)* siniestro(a); *Hist* **the D. Ages** la Edad Media *(antes del año mil); Fig* **to be in the D. Ages** estar en la prehistoria

**darken** ['dɑ:kən] **1** *vt (sky, colour)* oscurecer; **never d. my door again!** ¡no vuelvas a pisar el umbral de mi casa!
**2** *vi (of sky, colour)* oscurecerse; *(thoughts)* ensombrecerse

**darkness** ['dɑ:knɪs] *n* oscuridad *f*; **in d. a oscuras, en tinieblas**

**darkroom** ['dɑ:kru:m] *n Phot* cuarto *m* oscuro

**dark-skinned** ['dɑ:k'skɪnd] *adj* moreno(a)

**darling** ['dɑ:lɪŋ] **1** *n* encanto *m*; **d.!** ¡querido(a)!; **be a d. and…** sé bueno(a) y…; **she's the d. of the press** es la niña mimada de la prensa

**2** *adj* encantador(ora)

**darn**[1] ['dɑ:n] *vt (mend)* zurcir

**darn**[2] *Fam* **1** *adj* maldito(a); **it's a d. nuisance!** ¡es un verdadero fastidio!

**2** *exclam* **d. (it)!** ¡caramba!

**darning needle** ['dɑ:nɪŋ'ni:dəl] *n* aguja *f* de zurcir

**dart** [dɑ:t] **1** *n* **(a)** *(missile)* dardo *m*; **darts** *(game)* dardos *mpl* **(b)** *(movement)* **to make a d. for sth** salir disparado(a) hacia algo

**2** *vt* **to d. a glance at sb** lanzar una mirada a alguien

**3** *vi (move quickly)* precipitarse; **to d. in/out** entrar/salir precipitadamente

**dartboard** ['dɑ:tbɔ:d] *n* diana *f*

**dash** [dæʃ] **1** *n* **(a)** *(of liquid)* chorrito *m*; *Fig (of humour, colour)* toque *m*, pizca *f* **(b)** *(hyphen, in Morse)* raya *f* **(c)** *(run)* carrera *f*; **to make a d. for it** echar a correr **(d)** *(style)* dinamismo *m*, brío *m*; **to cut a d.** causar sensación

**2** *vt* **(a)** *(throw)* arrojar; **to d. sth to the ground** arrojar algo al suelo **(b)** *(destroy)* **to d. sb's hopes** truncar las esperanzas de alguien; *Fam* **d. (it)!** ¡caramba!

**3** *vi (move quickly)* correr, ir apresuradamente; **to d. in/out** entrar/salir precipitadamente; **to d. about** *or* **around** correr de acá para allá; *Fam* **I must be d.** tengo que salir pitando

▶**dash off 1** *vt sep* **to d. off a letter** escribir a toda prisa una carta

**2** *vi (leave)* salir corriendo

**dashboard** ['dæʃbɔ:d] *n (of car)* salpicadero *m*

**dashing** ['dæʃɪŋ] *adj (person)* imponente; *(appearance)* deslumbrante

**DAT** [di:eɪ'ti:] *n (abbr digital audio tape)* cinta *f* digital de audio, DAT

**data** ['deɪtə] *n* datos *mpl*; **an item** *or* **piece of d.** un dato; **d. bank** banco *m* de datos; *Comptr* **d. processing** proceso *m or* procesamiento *m* de datos; *Comptr* **d. protection** protección *f* de datos

**database** ['deɪtəbeɪs] *n Comptr* base *f* de datos

**date**[1] [deɪt] *n (fruit)* dátil *m*; **d. palm** palmera *f* datilera

**date**[2] **1** *n* **(a)** *(day)* fecha *f*; **d. of birth** fecha de nacimiento; **what's the d. (today)?** ¿a qué (fecha) estamos hoy?, ¿qué fecha es hoy?, *Am*

¿a cómo estamos? **to fix a d. for sth** fijar una fecha para algo; **to have a d. with sb** haber quedado *or* tener una cita con alguien; **to d.** hasta la fecha; **up to d.** al día; **out of d.** anticuado(a), pasado(a) de moda; **d. stamp** sello *m* con la fecha

**(b)** *(with girlfriend, boyfriend)* cita *f*; **d. rape** = violación por una persona a la que se ha conocido de forma circunstancial o en una cita

**(c)** *US (girlfriend, boyfriend)* pareja *f*

**2** *vt* **(a)** *(letter, ticket)* fechar; **that dates you** eso demuestra lo viejo(a) que eres

**(b)** *(go out with)* salir con

**3** *vi* **(a)** **to d. from** *or* **back to** *(of custom, practice)* remontarse a; *(of building)* datar de

**(b)** *(go out of fashion)* pasar de moda

**dateline** [deɪtlaɪn] *n* meridiano *m* de cambio de fecha; *Journ* **d. Tel Aviv** fechado(a) en Tel Aviv

**dating agency** ['deɪtɪŋ'eɪdʒənsɪ] *n* agencia *f* de contactos

**dative** ['deɪtɪv] *n Gram* dativo *m*

**daub** [dɔ:b] *vt (with mud, paint)* embadurnar **(with** de)

**daughter** ['dɔ:tə(r)] *n* hija *f*

**daughter-in-law** ['dɔ:tərɪnlɔ:] *n* nuera *f*

**daunt** [dɔ:nt] *vt* intimidar, acobardar; *Formal* **nothing daunted** sin dejarse arredrar

**daunting** [dɔ:ntɪŋ] *adj* desalentador(ora), desmoralizante; **a d. task** una tarea ingente

**dawdle** ['dɔ:dəl] *vi* perder el tiempo

**dawn** [dɔ:n] **1** *n* amanecer *m*, alba *f*; *Fig (of life, civilization)* albores *mpl*, despertar *m*; **at d.** al alba; **from d. to dusk** de sol a sol; **the d. chorus** el canto de los pájaros al amanecer

**2** *vi* amanecer; *Fig (of life, civilization)* despertar; **the day dawned bright and clear** el día amaneció claro y despejado

▶**dawn on** *vt insep* **the truth finally dawned on him** finalmente vio la verdad; **it dawned on me that…** caí en la cuenta de que…

**day** [deɪ] *n* **(a)** *(period of daylight, 24 hours)* día *m*; *(period of work)* jornada *f*; **once/twice a d.** una vez/dos veces al día; **the d. before yesterday** anteayer; **the d. after tomorrow** pasado mañana; **all d.** todo el día; **d. after d.** día tras día; **from d. to d.** de un día para otro; **one d., one of these days** un día (de estos); **any d. now** cualquier día de estos; **the other d.** el otro día; **every other d.** cada dos días, un día sí y otro no; **a year ago to the d.** hace exactamente un año; **from d. one** desde el primer día; **to take a d. off** tomarse un día libre; **to be paid by the d.** cobrar por día trabajado; **to work d. and night** trabajar día y noche; *Fam* **he's sixty if he's a d.** tiene como mínimo sesenta años; **d. nursery** guardería *f*; **d. pupil**

alumno(a) *m,f* externo(a); **d. release** = sistema que permite a un trabajador realizar cursos de formación continua un día a la semana; **d. return** *(train ticket)* billete *m* de ida y vuelta en el día; **d. school** colegio *m* sin internado; **d. shift** *(in factory)* turno *m* de día; **d. trip** excursión *f* (de un día)

(b) *(era)* **in my d.** en mis tiempos; **in this d. and age** en los tiempos que corren; **Communism has had its d.** el auge del comunismo ya es historia; **in the days of…** en tiempos de…; **these days** hoy (en) día; **in those days** en aquellos tiempos; **those were the days!** ¡aquellos sí que eran buenos tiempos!; **in days to come** más adelante, en el futuro; **he ended his days in poverty** terminó sus días en la pobreza

(c) *(idioms)* **it's all in a d.'s work** son los gajes del oficio; *Fam* **let's call it a d.** dejémoslo por hoy; *Fam* **that'll be the d.!** ¡no lo verán tus ojos!, ¡cuando las ranas críen pelo!; *Fam* **to make sb's d.** alegrarle el día a alguien; **to name the d.** *(of wedding)* fijar la fecha de la boda; **to carry** *or* **win the d.** *(bring victory)* conseguir la victoria

**daybreak** ['deɪbreɪk] *n* amanecer *m*, alba *f*; **at d.** al alba

**daydream** ['deɪdriːm] **1** *n* fantasía *f*
**2** *vi* fantasear, soñar despierto(a); **to d. about sth** fantasear sobre algo

**daylight** ['deɪlaɪt] *n* (luz *f* del) día *m*; **it was still d.** todavía era de día; **d. hours** horas *fpl* de luz; *Fig* **it's d. robbery!** ¡es un atraco a mano armada!

**daytime** ['deɪtaɪm] *n* día *m*; **in the d.** durante el día; **d. TV** programación *f* diurna *or* de día

**day-to-day** ['deɪtə'deɪ] *adj* diario(a), cotidiano(a); **on a d. basis** día a día

**daze** [deɪz] **1** *n* aturdimiento *m*; **to be in a d.** estar aturdido(a)
**2** *vt* aturdir

**dazed** [deɪzd] *adj* aturdido(a)

**dazzle** ['dæzəl] *vt also Fig* deslumbrar

**dazzling** ['dæzlɪŋ] *adj also Fig* deslumbrante

**DC** [diː'siː] *n* (a) *Elec (abbr* **direct current)** corriente *f* continua (b) *(abbr* **District of Columbia)** DC, Distrito de Columbia

**deacon** ['diːkən] *n Rel* diácono *m*

**deaconess** [diːkən'es] *n Rel* diaconisa *f*

**dead** [ded] **1** *adj* (a) *(not alive)* muerto(a); **a d. man** un muerto; **a d. woman** una muerta; **to be d.** estar muerto(a); *Fig* **to be d. to the world** dormir como un tronco; *Fam* **over my d. body!** ¡por encima de mi cadáver!; *Fam* **I wouldn't be seen d. in that dress!** ¡no me pondría ese vestido ni borracha!; *Fam* **as d. as a doornail** *or* **a dodo** muerto(a) y bien muerto(a); *Fig* **d. and buried** finiquitado(a); **half**

**d. with fright** medio muerto(a) de miedo; **d. or alive** vivo(a) o muerto(a); *Fam* **if dad finds out, you're d.** si papá se entera, te mata; **the D. Sea** el Mar Muerto

(b) *(numb)* dormido(a); **my leg went d.** se me durmió la pierna

(c) *(lacking energy) (voice, eyes)* apagado(a); *(battery)* gastado(a), agotado(a); **the phone/line is d.** no hay línea; **this place is d. in winter** este lugar está muerto en invierno; **d. ball situation** *(in football)* jugada *f* a balón parado; *also Fig* **d. end** callejón *m* sin salida; *Fig* **he's a d. weight** es un peso muerto

(d) *(absolute)* **d. calm** calma *f* chicha; **d. heat** *(in race)* empate *m*; *Fam* **it/he was a d. loss** resultó ser un desastre total; *Fam* **to be a d. ringer for sb** ser idéntico(a) a alguien

**2** *adv* (a) *(completely)* **to be d. set against sth** oponerse rotundamente a algo; **to stop d.** pararse en seco; *Fam* **to be d. wrong** equivocarse de medio a medio; *Fam* **d. beat** *or* **tired** hecho(a) polvo, molido(a); **d. slow** *(sign)* muy despacio

(b) *Fam (very)* tela de; **d. easy** facilísimo(a), chupado(a)

(c) *(exactly)* **d. on six o'clock** a las seis en punto

**3 at d. of night** a altas horas de la noche; **in the d. of winter** en pleno invierno

**4** *npl* **the d.** los muertos; **to rise from the d.** resucitar (de entre los muertos)

**deadbeat** ['dedbiːt] *n Fam* vago(a) *m,f*, holgazán(ana) *m,f*

**deaden** ['dedən] *vt (blow, sound, pain)* amortiguar, atenuar; **to become deadened to sth** volverse insensible a algo

**deadline** ['dedlaɪn] *n (day)* fecha *f* tope; *(time)* plazo *m*; **to meet a d.** cumplir un plazo; **to work to a d.** trabajar con un plazo

**deadlock** ['dedlɒk] **1** *n* punto *m* muerto; **to reach (a) d.** llegar a un punto muerto
**2** *vt* **to be deadlocked** *(of talks, negotiations)* estar en un punto muerto

**deadly** ['dedlɪ] **1** *adj* (a) *(poison, blow, enemy)* mortal, mortífero(a); *(weapon)* mortífero(a); *(pallor)* cadavérico(a); *(silence)* sepulcral; **d. nightshade** *(plant)* belladona *f* (b) *Fam (boring)* aburridísimo(a)
**2** *adv (very)* **d. accurate** tremendamente exacto(a); **d. boring** mortalmente aburrido(a); **to be d. serious about sth** decir algo completamente en serio

**deadpan** ['dedpæn] *adj (expression)* inexpresivo(a); *(humour)* socarrón(ona)

**deadwood** ['dedwʊd] *n Fig* there is too much d. in this office en esta oficina sobra mucha gente *or* hay mucha gente que está de más

**deaf** [def] **1** *adj* sordo(a); **to be d.** ser *or* estar sordo(a); **d. and dumb** sordomudo(a); **to go d.** quedarse sordo(a); **to be d. in one ear** ser sordo(a) de un oído; **as d. as a post** sordo(a) como una tapia; **to turn a d. ear to sb** hacer caso omiso de alguien; **the appeal fell on d. ears** la apelación cayó en saco roto

**2** *npl* **the d.** los sordos

**deaf-aid** ['defeid] *n* audífono *m*

**deafen** ['defən] *vt* ensordecer

**deafening** ['defənɪŋ] *adj* ensordecedor(ora)

**deafness** ['defnəs] *n* sordera *f*

**deal**[1] [di:l] *n* *(wood)* madera *f* de conífera, madera *f* blanda

**deal**[2] **1** *n* (a) *(agreement)* acuerdo *m*; *(in business)* trato *m*; **to do a d.** hacer un trato; **it's a d.!** ¡trato hecho!; **to get a good/bad d.** recibir un buen/mal trato; *Ironic Fam* **big d.!** ¡vaya cosa!; *Fam* **it's no big d.** ¡no es nada!, ¡no es para tanto! (b) *(amount)* **a good** *or* **great d.** *(a lot)* mucho; **not a great d.** no mucho; **to have a great d. to do** tener mucho que hacer; **a good** *or* **great d. of my time** gran parte de mi tiempo (c) *(in cards)* **your d.** te toca repartir *or* dar

**2** *vt* *(pt & pp* **dealt** [delt]) (a) *(cards)* repartir, dar (b) **to d. sb/sth a blow** dar un golpe a alguien/algo

**3** *vi* **to d. in leather/shares** comerciar con pieles/acciones; **to d. in drugs** traficar con drogas

▸**deal out** *vt sep (cards, justice)* repartir

▸**deal with** *vt insep (subject)* tratar; *(problem)* ocuparse de; **I know how to d. with him** sé cómo tratarlo

**dealer** ['di:lə(r)] *n* (a) *(in cardgame)* = jugador que reparte (b) *Com* comerciante *mf*; *(in drugs)* traficante *mf*; **art d.** marchante *mf* de arte

**dealings** ['di:lɪŋz] *npl* tratos *mpl*; **to have d. with sb** estar en tratos con alguien

**dealt** [delt] *pt & pp of* **deal**

**dean** [di:n] *n Rel* deán *m*; *Univ* decano(a) *m,f*

**dear** [dɪə(r)] **1** *adj* (a) *(loved)* querido(a); **to hold sth/sb d.** apreciar mucho algo/a alguien; **a d. friend** un amigo muy querido; **my dearest wish is that...** mi mayor deseo es que...; **a place d. to the hearts of...** un lugar muy querido para...; *Fam* **to run for d. life** correr desesperadamente

(b) *(in letter)* **D. Sir** Muy Sr. mío; **D. Madam** Muy Sra. mía; **D. Sir or Madam, D. Sir/ Madam** *(when sex of addressee is unknown)* Muy Sres. míos; **D. Mr Thomas** Estimado Sr. Thomas; **D. Andrew** Querido Andrew; **My dearest Gertrude** Queridísima Gertrude

(c) *(expensive)* caro(a)

(d) *(exclamation)* **oh d.!** ¡vaya!

**2** *n* **poor d.** pobrecito(a); **my d.** cariño mío,

mi amor; **be a d. and...** sé bueno y...; *Fam* **an old d.** una viejecita

**3** *adv (to buy, sell)* caro; *Fig* **it cost me d.** me costó muy caro

**dearly** ['dɪəlɪ] *adv (very much)* **I love him d.** lo quiero muchísimo; **I would d. love to know** me encantaría saberlo; *Fig* **she paid d. for her mistake** pagó muy caro su error

**dearth** [dɜ:θ] *n* escasez *f* *(of de)*

**death** [deθ] *n* (a) *(gen)* muerte *f*; **to put sb to d.** ejecutar a alguien; **a fight to the d.** una lucha a muerte; **d. to traitors!** ¡muerte a *or* mueran los traidores!; **d. camp** campo *m* de exterminio; **d. certificate** certificado *m or* partida *f* de defunción; **d. mask** mascarilla *f*; **d. penalty** pena *f* de muerte; **d. rate** tasa *f* de mortalidad; *US* **d. row** galería *f* de los condenados a muerte; **d. sentence** pena *f* de muerte; **d. squad** escuadrón *m* de la muerte; **d. throes** últimos estertores *mpl*, agonía *f*; **d. toll** número *m or* saldo *m* de víctimas mortales; **d. warrant** orden *f* de ejecución

(b) *(idioms)* **to be sick to d. of sth** estar hasta la coronilla de algo; **to be scared to d.** estar muerto(a) de miedo; **those children will be the d. of her!** esos niños la van a matar (a disgustos); **you'll catch your d. (of cold)!** ¡vas a coger un resfriado de muerte!; **to be at d.'s door** estar a las puertas de la muerte; **to sound the d. knell for sth** asestar el golpe de gracia a algo; **to look like d. warmed up** tener una pinta horrorosa

**deathbed** ['deθbed] *n* lecho *m* de muerte

**deathly** ['deθlɪ] *adj (pallor)* cadavérico(a); *(silence)* sepulcral

**deathtrap** ['deθtræp] *n* **this house/this car is a d.** esta casa/este coche es un auténtico peligro

**deathwatch beetle** ['deθwɒtʃ'bi:təl] *n* carcoma *f*

**debacle** [deɪ'bɑ:kl] *n* desastre *m*, debacle *f*

**debar** [di:'bɑ:(r)] *(pt & pp* **debarred**) *vt (from club, pub)* prohibir la entrada (**from** en); **to d. sb from doing sth** prohibirle a alguien hacer algo

**debase** [dɪ'beɪs] *vt (person, reputation)* degradar; **to d. oneself** degradarse

**debasement** [dɪ'beɪsmənt] *n* degradación *f*

**debatable** [dɪ'beɪtəbəl] *adj* discutible

**debate** [dɪ'beɪt] **1** *n* debate *m*; **after much d.** tras mucho debatir

**2** *vt (issue)* debatir, discutir; **he debated whether to go** se debatía entre ir y no ir

**3** *vi* debatir

**debating society** [dɪ'beɪtɪŋsə'saɪətɪ] *n* = asociación que organiza debates en una universidad o instituto

**debauched** [dɪ'bɔ:tʃt] *adj* depravado(a), degenerado(a)

**debauchery** [dɪ'bɔːtʃərɪ] n libertinaje m, depravación f

**debilitate** [dɪ'bɪlɪteɪt] vt debilitar

**debilitating** [dɪ'bɪlɪteɪtɪŋ] adj debilitador(ora), debilitante

**debility** [dɪ'bɪlɪtɪ] n debilidad f

**debit** ['debɪt] Fin **1** n cargo m, adeudo m; Fig **on the d. side** en el lado negativo

**2** vt cargar, adeudar; **to d. sb with an amount** cargar una cantidad negativa a alguien

**debonair** [debə'neə(r)] adj gallardo(a)

**debrief** [diː'briːf] vt **to d. sb on a mission** pedir a alguien que rinda cuentas sobre una misión

**debriefing** [diː'briːfɪŋ] n interrogatorio m (tras una misión)

**debris** ['debriː] n (of building) escombros mpl; (of plane, car) restos mpl

**debt** [det] n deuda f; **to be in d.** estar endeudado(a); Fig **I shall always be in your d.** siempre estaré en deuda contigo; **to owe sb a d. of gratitude** tener una deuda de gratitud con alguien; **d. collector** cobrador(ora) m,f de morosos

**debtor** ['detə(r)] n deudor(ora) m,f

**debug** [diː'bʌg] (pt & pp **debugged**) vt Comptr (program) depurar, eliminar errores en

**debunk** [diː'bʌŋk] vt Fam (theory, myth) echar por tierra

**debut** ['deɪbjuː] n debut m; **to make one's d.** debutar

**Dec** (abbr **December**) diciembre m

**decade** ['dekeɪd] n decenio m, década f

**decadence** ['dekədəns] n decadencia f

**decadent** ['dekədənt] adj decadente

**decaffeinated** [diː'kæfɪneɪtɪd] adj descafeinado(a)

**decant** [dɪ'kænt] vt (wine) decantar

**decanter** [dɪ'kæntə(r)] n licorera f

**decapitate** [dɪ'kæpɪteɪt] vt decapitar

**decathlon** [dɪ'kæθlɒn] n decatlón m

**decay** [dɪ'keɪ] **1** n (a) (of wood) putrefacción f, descomposición f; (of teeth) caries f inv (b) (decline) declive m, decadencia f; (of building) ruina f

**2** vi (a) (of timber) pudrirse; (of teeth) picarse, cariarse (b) (decline) declinar

**decease** [dɪ'siːs] n Formal fallecimiento m

**deceased** [dɪ'siːst] **1** adj difunto(a)

**2** n **the d.** el/la difunto(a)

**deceit** [dɪ'siːt] n engaño m, mentira f

**deceitful** [dɪ'siːtfʊl] adj (person) mentiroso(a), falso(a); (behaviour) equívoco(a), engañoso(a); **to be d.** ser mentiroso(a)

**deceive** [dɪ'siːv] vt engañar; **to be deceived by appearances** dejarse engañar por las apariencias; **to d. oneself** engañarse; **to d. sb into thinking sth** hacer creer algo a alguien;

**I thought my eyes were deceiving me** no creía lo que veían mis ojos

**decelerate** [diː'seləreɪt] vi decelerar, desacelerar

**December** [dɪ'sembə(r)] n diciembre m; see also **May**

**decency** ['diːsənsɪ] n (of dress, behaviour) decencia f, decoro m; **common d.** (mínima) decencia f; **he didn't even have the d. to tell us first** ni siquiera tuvo la delicadeza de decírnoslo primero

**decent** ['diːsənt] adj (a) (respectable) decente, decoroso(a) (b) (of acceptable quality, size) decente (c) (kind) **a d. chap** un buen tipo; **it's very d. of you** es muy amable de tu parte

**decently** ['diːsəntlɪ] adv (a) (respectably, to an acceptable degree) decentemente; **they pay quite d.** pagan un sueldo bastante decente (b) (kindly) con amabilidad

**decentralization** [diːsentrəlaɪ'zeɪʃən] n descentralización f

**decentralize** [diː'sentrəlaɪz] vt descentralizar

**deception** [dɪ'sepʃən] n engaño m

**deceptive** [dɪ'septɪv] adj engañoso(a)

**deceptively** [dɪ'septɪvlɪ] adv engañosamente; **it looks d. easy** a primera vista parece muy fácil

**decibel** ['desɪbel] n decibelio m

**decide** [dɪ'saɪd] **1** vt decidir; **to d. to do sth** decidir hacer algo; **it was decided to wait for her reply** se decidió esperar su respuesta; **that was what decided me** eso fue lo que me hizo decidirme; **that decides the matter** eso zanja la cuestión

**2** vi decidir; **to d. against doing sth** decidir no hacer algo; **to d. in favour of doing sth** decidir hacer algo

**decided** [dɪ'saɪdɪd] adj (person) decidido(a), resuelto(a); (opinion) tajante; (difference, preference, improvement) claro(a), marcado(a)

**decidedly** [dɪ'saɪdɪdlɪ] adv (a) (to answer, say) categóricamente (b) (very) decididamente; **he was d. unhelpful** no ayudó en lo más mínimo

**decider** [dɪ'saɪdə(r)] n **the d.** (goal, match) el gol/partido/etc decisivo

**deciding** [dɪ'saɪdɪŋ] adj decisivo(a)

**deciduous** [dɪ'sɪdjʊəs] adj de hoja caduca, caducifolio(a)

**decimal** ['desɪməl] **1** n número m decimal

**2** adj decimal; **d. point** coma f (decimal); **correct to five d. places** correcto hasta la quinta cifra decimal

**decimalization** [desɪmələr'zeɪʃən] n conversión f al sistema decimal

**decimate** ['desɪmeɪt] vt diezmar

**decipher** [dɪ'saɪfə(r)] vt descifrar

**decision** [dɪ'sɪʒən] *n* decisión *f*; **to come to** *or* **arrive at** *or* **reach a d.** llegar a una decisión; **to make** *or* **take a d.** tomar una decisión; **to act/speak with d.** actuar/hablar con decisión
**decision-making** [dɪ'sɪʒənmeɪkɪŋ] *n* toma *f* de decisiones
**decisive** [dɪ'saɪsɪv] *adj* decisivo(a)
**deck 1** *n* [dek] **(a)** *(of ship)* cubierta *f*; **on d.** en cubierta; **top/bottom d.** *(of bus)* piso *m* de arriba/abajo; **cassette** *or* **tape d.** pletina *f*; **d. chair** tumbona *f*, hamaca *f* **(b) d. of cards** baraja *f*
**2** *vt* **to d. oneself out in sth** engalanarse con algo
**declaim** [dɪ'kleɪm] **1** *vt* proclamar, pregonar
**2** *vi* pregonar
**declamatory** [dɪ'klæmətərɪ] *adj (style, tone)* declamatorio(a)
**declaration** [deklə'reɪʃən] *n* declaración *f*; *US Hist* **the D. of Independence** la declaración de independencia de los Estados Unidos
**declare** [dɪ'kleə(r)] **1** *vt* declarar; **to d. war (on)** declarar la guerra (a); **to d. sb guilty/innocent** declarar a alguien culpable/inocente; **have you anything to d.?** *(at customs)* ¿(tiene) algo que declarar?
**2** *vi* **to d. for/against sth** declararse a favor de/en contra de algo; *Old-fashioned* **I do d.!** ¡demontre!
**declassify** [diː'klæsɪfaɪ] *vt* desclasificar
**declension** [dɪ'klenʃən] *n Gram* declinación *f*
**decline** [dɪ'klaɪn] **1** *n (of person, empire)* declive *m*; *(decrease, reduction)* descenso *m*, disminución *f*; **to go into d.** decaer, debilitarse; **to be on the d.** estar en declive
**2** *vt* **(a)** *(offer, invitation)* declinar; **to d. to do sth** declinar hacer algo **(b)** *Gram* declinar
**3** *vi* **(a)** *(refuse)* rehusar **(b)** *(of health, influence)* declinar; **to d. in importance** perder importancia
**declining** [dɪ'klaɪnɪŋ] *adj (decreasing)* decreciente; *(deteriorating)* en declive, en decadencia
**decode** [diː'kəʊd] *vt* descodificar, descifrar
**decompose** [diːkəm'pəʊz] *vi* descomponerse
**decomposition** [diːkɒmpə'zɪʃən] *n* descomposición *f*
**decompression** [diːkəm'preʃən] *n* descompresión *f*; **d. chamber** cámara *f* de descompresión; **d. sickness** aeroembolismo *m*
**decongestant** [diːkən'dʒestənt] *n Med* descongestionante *m*
**decontaminate** [diːkən'tæmɪneɪt] *vt* descontaminar
**decor** ['deɪkɔː(r)] *n* decoración *f*
**decorate** ['dekəreɪt] *vt* **(a)** *(cake, room) (with decorations)* decorar, adornar **(with** con) **(b)**

*(room) (with paint)* pintar; *(with wallpaper)* empapelar **(c)** *(with medal)* condecorar
**decoration** [dekə'reɪʃən] *n* **(a)** *(on cake, for party)* decoración *f*; **decorations** adornos *mpl* **(b)** *(of room) (with paint)* pintado *m*; *(with wallpaper)* empapelado *m* **(c)** *(medal)* condecoración *f*
**decorative** ['dekərətɪv] *adj* decorativo(a)
**decorator** ['dekəreɪtə(r)] *n* **(painter and) d.** pintor(ora) *m,f (que también empapela)*
**decorous** ['dekərəs] *adj Formal* decoroso(a)
**decorum** [dɪ'kɔːrəm] *n* decoro *m*
**decoy 1** *n* ('diːkɔɪ] *(pl* decoys*) also Fig* señuelo *m*
**2** *vt* [dɪ'kɔɪ] atraer con un señuelo; **to d. sb into doing sth** lograr que alguien haga algo utilizando un señuelo
**decrease 1** *n* ['diːkriːs] reducción *f* (**in** de); disminución *f* (**in** de); **to be on the d.** estar disminuyendo, decrecer
**2** *vt* [dɪ'kriːs] disminuir, reducir
**3** *vi* disminuir, reducirse
**decreasing** [dɪ'kriːsɪŋ] *adj* decreciente
**decree** [dɪ'kriː] **1** *n* decreto *m*; **to issue a d.** promulgar un decreto; *Law* **d. absolute** sentencia *f* definitiva de divorcio; *Law* **d. nisi** sentencia *f* provisional de divorcio
**2** *vt* decretar
**decrepit** [dɪ'krepɪt] *adj (person)* decrépito(a); *(thing)* ruinoso(a)
**decriminalize** [diː'krɪmɪnəlaɪz] *vt* despenalizar
**decry** [dɪ'kraɪ] *vt* censurar, condenar
**dedicate** ['dedɪkeɪt] *vt* dedicar; **to d. oneself to (doing) sth** consagrarse a (hacer) algo; **she dedicated her life to helping the poor** consagró *or* dedicó su vida a ayudar a los pobres
**dedicated** ['dedɪkeɪtɪd] *adj* **(a)** *(committed)* entregado(a), dedicado(a); **to be d. to sth** estar consagrado(a) a algo **(b)** *Comptr* dedicado(a), especializado(a); **d. word processor** procesador *m* de textos *(ordenador)*
**dedication** [dedɪ'keɪʃən] *n* **(a)** *(of book)* dedicatoria *f* **(b)** *(devotion)* dedicación *f*, entrega *f*
**deduce** [dɪ'djuːs] *vt* deducir (**from** de)
**deduct** [dɪ'dʌkt] *vt* **to d. sth from sth** descontar *or* deducir algo de algo
**deductible** [dɪ'dʌktɪbəl] *adj* deducible; *Fin* **d. for tax purposes** desgravable
**deduction** [dɪ'dʌkʃən] *n* **(a)** *(subtraction)* deducción *f*; **after deductions** después de (hacer las) deducciones **(b)** *(conclusion)* deducción *f*; **by a process of d.** por deducción
**deed** [diːd] *n* **(a)** *(action)* acción *f*, obra *f*; **to do one's good d. for the day** hacer la buena acción *or* obra del día **(b)** *Law (document)* escritura *f*, título *m* de propiedad; **title deeds** *(to property)* escrituras *fpl*, títulos *mpl* de propiedad;

**d. of covenant** = escritura que formaliza el pago de una donación periódica a una entidad, generalmente benéfica, o a un individuo; **to change one's name by d. poll** cambiarse legalmente el nombre

**deem** [di:m] *Formal vt* considerar, estimar

**deep** [di:p] **1** *n Literary* **the d.** las profundidades del mar

**2** *adj* **(a)** *(water, sleep, thinker)* profundo(a); **to be 10 metres d.** tener 10 metros de profundidad; **take a d. breath** respire hondo; *Fig* **to be in d. water** estar en un lío; **d. in debt** endeudado(a) hasta el cuello; **d. in thought** ensimismado(a); **in deepest sympathy** *(on card)* con mi más sincero pésame; **d. end** *(of swimming pool)* parte f profunda; *Fig* **to go off the d. end (at sb)** ponerse hecho(a) un basilisco (con alguien); *Fig* **she was thrown in at the d. end** le hicieron empezar de golpe, sin preparación; **the D. South** *(of USA)* la América profunda de los estados del sur

**(b)** *(colour)* intenso(a); *(sound, voice)* grave

**3** *adv* profundamente; **to walk d. into the forest** internarse en el bosque; **to look d. into sb's eyes** mirar a alguien fijamente a los ojos; **to work d. into the night** trabajar hasta bien entrada la noche; **d. down he's very kind** en el fondo, es muy amable; **mistrust between the two families runs d.** la desconfianza entre las dos familias está profundamente arraigada; **the crowd lining the road was four d.** la gente se agolpaba en cuatro filas a lo largo de la calle

**deepen** ['di:pən] **1** *vt (well, ditch)* profundizar, ahondar; *(sorrow, interest)* acentuar, agudizar; **to d. one's understanding of sth** ahondar en el conocimiento de algo

**2** *vi* **(a)** *(of river, silence, mystery)* hacerse más profundo(a); *(of conviction, belief)* afianzarse; *(of sorrow, interest)* acentuarse, agudizarse **(b)** *(of colour)* intensificarse; *(of sound, voice)* hacerse más grave

**deepfreeze** ['di:p'fri:z] *n* congelador *m*

**deep-fry** ['di:p'fraɪ] *vt* freír (en aceite muy abundante)

**deep-fryer** ['di:p'fraɪə(r)] *n* freidora f

**deep-rooted** ['di:p'ru:tɪd] *adj (prejudice, fear)* muy arraigado(a)

**deep-sea** ['di:p'si:] *adj* **d. diver** buceador(ora) *m,f or* buzo *m* de profundidad; **d. fishing** pesca f de altura

**deep-seated** ['di:p'si:tɪd] *adj* muy arraigado(a)

**deer** ['dɪə(r)] *(pl* deer) *n* ciervo *m*, venado *m*

**deerstalker** ['dɪəstɔ:kə(r)] *n (hat)* gorro *m* de cazador (con orejeras)

**deface** [dɪ'feɪs] *vt* dañar, deteriorar

**de facto** [deɪ'fæktəʊ] *adj & adv* de hecho

**defamation** [defə'meɪʃən] *n* difamación f

**defamatory** [dɪ'fæmətərɪ] *adj (article, remark)* difamatorio(a)

**defame** [dɪ'feɪm] *vt* difamar

**default** [dɪ'fɔ:lt] **1** *n Law & Sport (failure to appear)* incomparecencia f; **to win sth by d.** ganar algo por incomparecencia (del contrario); *Fig* **he became the boss by d.** a falta de otra persona, él terminó por convertirse en el jefe; *Comptr* **d. drive** unidad f (de disco) por defecto *or* omisión; *Comptr* **d. settings** valores *mpl or* configuración f por defecto *or* omisión

**2** *vi Law* **to d. on payments** *(of debt, alimony)* incumplir los pagos

**defaulter** [dɪ'fɔ:ltə(r)] *n (on fine, payment)* moroso(a) *m,f*

**defeat** [dɪ'fi:t] **1** *n* derrota f; **to admit d.** admitir la derrota; **to suffer (a) d.** sufrir una derrota

**2** *vt (army, government, opponent)* derrotar, vencer; *(proposal, bill, motion)* rechazar; **that rather defeats the object of the exercise** eso se contradice con la finalidad de la operación

**defeatism** [dɪ'fi:tɪzəm] *n* derrotismo *m*

**defeatist** [dɪ'fi:tɪst] *n & adj* derrotista *mf*

**defecate** ['defəkeɪt] *vi* defecar

**defect 1** *n* ['di:fekt] defecto *m*

**2** *vi* [dɪ'fekt] desertar *(from* de); **to d. to another party** pasarse a otro partido

**defection** [dɪ'fekʃən] *n* deserción f; *(to another party)* cambio *m* de partido

**defective** [dɪ'fektɪv] *adj (machine)* defectuoso(a); *(reasoning)* erróneo(a)

**defector** [dɪ'fektə(r)] *n* desertor(ora) *m,f*; *(to another party)* tránsfuga *mf*

**defence,** US **defense** [dɪ'fens] *n (of country, in sport, in court case)* defensa f; **defences** *(of country)* defensas *fpl*; **to come to sb's d.** salir en defensa de alguien; *Mil* **Ministry of D.** Ministerio *m* de Defensa; *Law* **d. counsel** abogado(a) *m,f* defensor(ora); **d. mechanism** mecanismo *m* de defensa; **D. Minister** ministro(a) *m,f* de Defensa; **d. spending** gasto *m* de defensa; *Law* **d. witness** testigo *mf* de descargo

**defenceless,** US **defenseless** [dɪ'fensləs] *adj* indefenso(a)

**defend** [dɪ'fend] *vt & vi* defender

**defendant** [dɪ'fendənt] *n Law* acusado(a) *m,f*

**defender** [dɪ'fendə(r)] *n (of country, belief)* defensor(ora) *m,f*; *(in football team)* defensa *mf*

**defending** [dɪ'fendɪŋ] *adj* **the d. champion** el defensor del título, el actual campeón

**defense, defenseless** US = **defence, defenceless**

**defensible** [dɪ'fensəbl] *adj* justificable, defendible

**defensive** [dɪ'fensɪv] **1** *n* **on the d.** a la defensiva

**2** *adj* defensivo(a); **to get d.** ponerse a la defensiva

**defer** [dɪ'fɜ:(r)] *(pt & pp deferred)* **1** *vt (delay, postpone)* aplazar, posponer

**2** *vi* **to d. to** *(person, knowledge)* ceder ante, deferir a

**deference** ['defərəns] *n* deferencia *f*; **in or out of d. to...** por deferencia hacia...

**deferential** [defə'renʃəl] *adj* deferente; **to be d. to sb** mostrar deferencia hacia alguien

**deferment** [dɪ'fɜ:mənt] *n* aplazamiento *m*

**defiance** [dɪ'faɪəns] *n* desafío *m*; **a gesture of d.** un gesto desafiante; **in d. of the law/my instructions** desafiando la ley/mis instrucciones

**defiant** [dɪ'faɪənt] *adj (look, gesture, remark)* desafiante; *(person)* insolente

**deficiency** [dɪ'fɪʃənsɪ] *n* **(a)** *(lack) (of resources)* escasez *f*; *(of vitamins, minerals)* carencia *f*, deficiencia *f* **(b)** *(flaw, defect)* deficiencia *f*, defecto *m*

**deficient** [dɪ'fɪʃənt] *adj (unsatisfactory)* deficiente; **he is d. in vitamin C** anda bajo(a) de or le falta vitamina C

**deficit** ['defɪsɪt] *n Fin* déficit *m*

**defile** [dɪ'faɪl] *vt (memory)* manchar, mancillar; *(sacred place, tomb)* profanar

**definable** [dɪ'faɪnəbəl] *adj* definible

**define** [dɪ'faɪn] *vt* definir

**definite** ['defɪnɪt] *adj* **(a)** *(precise) (plan, date, answer, decision)* claro(a), definitivo(a); *(views)* concluyente **(b)** *(noticeable) (change, advantage, improvement)* claro(a), indudable **(c)** *(sure, certain)* seguro(a); **are you d. about it?** ¿estás seguro (de ello)?, ¿lo tienes claro?; **it's not d. yet** todavía no está claro **(d)** *Gram* **d. article** artículo *m* determinado

**definitely** ['defɪnɪtlɪ] *adv* **(a)** *(certainly)* con certeza; **I'll d. be there** seguro que estaré allí; **are you going? – d.!** ¿vas a ir? – ¡claro!; **d. not!** ¡desde luego que no! **(b)** *(noticeably) (improved, superior)* claramente, sin duda

**definition** [defɪ'nɪʃən] *n* **(a)** *(of word)* definición *f*; **by d.** por definición **(b)** *(of TV, binoculars)* definición *f*

**definitive** [dɪ'fɪnɪtɪv] *adj* definitivo(a)

**deflate** [di:'fleɪt] **1** *vt* **(a)** *(ball, tyre)* deshinchar, desinflar **(b)** *(economy)* producir una deflación en **(c)** *(person)* desanimar; **to d. sb's ego** bajarle los humos a alguien

**2** *vi* **(a)** *(of ball, tyre)* deshincharse, desinflarse **(b)** *(of economy)* sufrir una deflación

**deflated** [di:'fleɪtɪd] *adj* **(a)** *(ball, tyre)* deshinchado(a) **(b)** *(person)* desanimado(a)

**deflation** [di:'fleɪʃən] *n* deflación *f*

**deflationary** [di:'fleɪʃənərɪ] *adj* deflacionario(a)

**deflect** [dɪ'flekt] **1** *vt (bullet, sound)* desviar; *Fig (person)* distraer, desviar **(from** de); **to d. criticism** distraer la atención de los críticos

**2** *vi (of projectile, light)* desviarse

**deflection** [dɪ'flekʃən] *n* desviación *f*

**deforestation** [di:fɒrɪs'teɪʃən] *n* de(s)forestación *f*

**deform** [dɪ'fɔ:m] *vt* deformar

**deformation** [di:fɔ:'meɪʃən] *n* deformación *f*

**deformity** [dɪ'fɔ:mɪtɪ] *n* deformidad *f*; *(in baby, unborn child)* malformación *f* congénita

**defraud** [dɪ'frɔ:d] *vt* defraudar, estafar; **to d. sb of sth** defraudar algo a alguien

**defray** [dɪ'freɪ] *vt Formal* sufragar

**defrost** [di:'frɒst] **1** *vt* descongelar

**2** *vi* descongelarse

**deft** [deft] *adj* diestro(a), hábil

**defunct** [dɪ'fʌŋkt] *adj (person)* difunto(a); *(company, scheme)* ya desaparecido(a)

**defuse** [di:'fju:z] *vt (bomb)* desactivar; *Fig (situation)* calmar, apaciguar

**defy** [dɪ'faɪ] *vt* desafiar; **to d. description** ser indescriptible; **to d. sb to do sth** desafiar a alguien a hacer or a que haga algo

**degenerate 1** *n* [dɪ'dʒenərət] *(person)* degenerado(a) *m,f*

**2** *adj* degenerado(a)

**3** *vi* [dɪ'dʒenəreɪt] degenerar **(into** en)

**degeneration** [dɪdʒenə'reɪʃən] *n* degeneración *f*

**degradation** [degrə'deɪʃən] *n* degradación *f*

**degrade** [dɪ'greɪd] *vt* rebajar, degradar; **I won't d. myself by answering that** no me rebajaré a contestar a eso

**degrading** [dɪ'greɪdɪŋ] *adj* degradante

**degree** [dɪ'gri:] *n* **(a)** *(extent)* grado *m*; **a d. of risk** un cierto riesgo, un elemento de riesgo; **to a d.** hasta cierto punto; **to such a d. that...** hasta tal punto que...; **by degrees** gradualmente

**(b)** *(of temperature, in geometry)* grado *m*; **it's 25 degrees** *(of temperature)* hace 25 grados

**(c)** *(at university) (title)* título *m* universitario, licenciatura; *(course)* carrera *f*; **postgraduate d.** título *m*/curso *m* de posgrado; **to take** or **do a d.** hacer or estudiar una carrera; **to have a d. in physics** ser licenciado (a) en Física

**dehumanize** [di:'hju:mənaɪz] *vt* deshumanizar

**dehumidifier** [di:hju:'mɪdɪfaɪə(r)] *n* deshumidificador *m*

**dehydrate** [di:haɪ'dreɪt] **1** *vt* deshidratar

**2** *vi (of person)* deshidratarse

**dehydrated** [di:haɪ'dreɪtɪd] *adj* deshidratado(a); **to be d.** estar deshidratado(a); **to become d.** deshidratarse

**dehydration** [di:har'drerʃən] *n* deshidratación *f*

**de-icer** [di:'arsə(r)] *n (for car)* descongelador *m* de parabrisas; *(on plane)* dispositivo *m* de descongelación

**deify** ['denfar] *vt* deificar, divinizar

**deign** [dern] *vt* **to d. to do sth** dignarse a hacer algo

**deindustrialization** [di:ɪndʌstrɪəlaɪ-'zeɪʃən] *n* desindustrialización *f*

**deity** ['denti] *n* deidad *f*, divinidad *f*

**dejected** [dɪ'dʒektɪd] *adj* abatido(a), desencantado(a); **to be d.** estar abatido(a) *or* desencantado(a)

**dejection** [dɪ'dʒekʃən] *n* abatimiento *m*, desencanto *m*

**delay** [dɪ'leɪ] **1** *n (pl delays)* retraso *m*; **without d.** sin (mayor) demora; **an hour's d.** un retraso de una hora; **all flights are subject to d.** todos los vuelos llevan retraso

**2** *vt (project, decision, act)* retrasar; *(traffic)* retener, demorar; **to be delayed** *(of train)* llevar retraso; **I don't want to d. you** no te quiero entretener; **delaying tactics** tácticas *fpl* dilatorias

**3** *vi* retrasarse, demorarse; **don't d.!** ¡no deje pasar más tiempo!

**delayed-action** [dɪ'leɪd'ækʃən] *adj (drug, fuse)* de efecto retardado

**delectable** [dɪ'lektəbəl] *adj* delicioso(a)

**delegate 1** *n* ['delɪgət] delegado(a) *m,f*

**2** *vt* ['delɪgeɪt] *(power, responsibility)* delegar (**to** en); **to d. sb to do sth** delegar en alguien para hacer algo

**3** *vi* delegar responsabilidades

**delegation** [delɪ'geɪʃən] *n* delegación *f*

**delete** [dɪ'li:t] *vt* borrar; **d. where inapplicable** táchese lo que no corresponda

**deleterious** [delɪ'tɪərɪəs] *adj Formal* nocivo(a), deletéreo(a)

**deletion** [dɪ'li:ʃən] *n Comptr* supresión *f*, borrado *m*

**deli** ['delɪ] *n Fam (shop)* = tienda de ultramarinos de calidad

**deliberate 1** *adj* [dɪ'lɪbərət] **(a)** *(intentional)* deliberado(a), intencionado(a); **it wasn't d.** fue sin querer **(b)** *(unhurried)* pausado(a)

**2** *vi* [dɪ'lɪbəreɪt] *(think)* reflexionar (**on** sobre); *(discuss)* deliberar (**on** sobre)

**deliberately** [dɪ'lɪbərətlɪ] *adv* **(a)** *(intentionally)* a propósito, deliberadamente **(b)** *(unhurriedly)* pausadamente

**deliberation** [dɪlɪbə'reɪʃən] *n* **(a)** *(thought)* reflexión *f*; *(discussion)* deliberación *f* **(b)** *(unhurriedness)* pausa *f*; **to do sth with d.** hacer algo pausadamente

**delicacy** ['delɪkəsɪ] *n* **(a)** *(of situation)* dificultad *f* **(b)** *(tact)* delicadeza *f*, tacto *m* **(c)** *(food)* esquisitez *f*

**delicate** ['delɪkət] *adj (glass, situation, flavour)* delicado(a); *(health)* frágil, delicado(a)

**delicately** ['delɪkətlɪ] *adv* **(a)** *(finely)* **d. carved** primorosamente tallado(a) **(b)** *(tactfully)* con delicadeza

**delicatessen** [delɪkə'tesən] *n (shop)* = tienda de ultramarinos de calidad

**delicious** [dɪ'lɪʃəs] *adj* delicioso(a)

**delight** [dɪ'laɪt] **1** *n (pleasure)* gusto *m*, placer *m*; **to my/her d.** para mi/su deleite; **he took d. in her failure** se alegró de su fracaso; **to take d. in doing sth** disfrutar haciendo algo; **the car is a d. to drive** conducir ese coche es una delicia; **the delights of Blackpool** los encantos *or* placeres de la ciudad de Blackpool

**2** *vt* deleitar, encantar

**3** *vi* **to d. in doing sth** disfrutar haciendo algo

**delighted** [dɪ'laɪtɪd] *adj* encantado(a); **to be d. (with sth)** estar encantado(a) (con algo); **I'm d. to see you** me alegro mucho de verte

**delightful** [dɪ'laɪtfʊl] *adj (person, smile)* encantador(ora); *(meal, evening)* delicioso(a)

**delightfully** [dɪ'laɪtfʊlɪ] *adv (to sing, write)* maravillosamente

**delimit** [di:'lɪmɪt] *vt* delimitar

**delineate** [dɪ'lɪnɪeɪt] *vt (plan, proposal)* detallar, especificar

**delinquency** [dɪ'lɪŋkwənsɪ] *n* delincuencia *f*

**delinquent** [dɪ'lɪŋkwənt] *n & adj* delincuente *mf*

**delirious** [dɪ'lɪrɪəs] *adj also Fig* delirante; **to be d.** delirar; **to be d. about sth** estar como loco(a) con algo

**deliriously** [dɪ'lɪrɪəslɪ] *adv* **to be d. happy** estar loco(a) de alegría

**delirium** [dɪ'lɪrɪəm] *n also Fig* delirio *m*; *Med* **d. tremens** delírium *m* tremens

**deliver** [dɪ'lɪvə(r)] **1** *vt (letter, parcel)* entregar (**to** a); *(blow)* propinar; *(speech, verdict)* pronunciar; **to d. a service** prestar un servicio; *Fig* **to d. the goods** cumplir (con lo esperado); **to d. a child** traer al mundo a un niño

**2** *vi* repartir; **we d.** repartimos a domicilio; *Fig* **their proposal is impressive, but can they d.?** la propuesta es impresionante, pero ¿podrán llevarla a la práctica?

**deliverance** [dɪ'lɪvərəns] *n Formal* liberación *f*

**delivery** [dɪ'lɪvərɪ] *n* **(a)** *(of letter, parcel)* entrega *f*; **to take d. of sth** recibir algo; **d. date** fecha *f* de entrega; **d. man** repartidor *m*; **d. van** furgoneta *f* de reparto **(b)** *(of child)* parto *m* **(c)** *(style of speaking)* discurso *m*, oratoria *f*

**delta** ['deltə] *n (Greek letter)* delta *f*; *(rivermouth)* delta *m*; **d. wing** *(of plane)* Av ala *f* supercrítica

**delude** [dɪ'luːd] *vt* engañar; **to d. oneself** engañarse

**deluge** ['deljuːdʒ] **1** *n (of water)* diluvio *m*; *Fig (of letters, questions)* avalancha *f*, lluvia *f*
**2** *vt* inundar (**with** de)

**delusion** [dɪ'luːʒən] *n* engaño *m*, ilusión *f*; **to be under a d.** estar engañado(a); **delusions of grandeur** delirios *mpl* de grandeza

**de luxe** [dɪ'lʌks] *adj* de lujo

**delve** [delv] *vi* rebuscar; **to d. into a bag** rebuscar en una bolsa; **to d. into the past** hurgar en el pasado

**demagogue** ['deməgɒg] *n* demagogo(a) *m,f*

**demand** [dɪ'mɑːnd] **1** *n* (**a**) *(request)* exigencia *f*; **to make demands on sb** exigir mucho de alguien (**b**) *(for goods)* demanda *f* (**for** de); **to be in d.** estar muy solicitado(a)
**2** *vt* (**a**) *(request)* exigir (**b**) *(require)* requerir, exigir

**demanding** [dɪ'mɑːndɪŋ] *adj (person)* exigente; **to be d.** *(of job)* exigir mucho (esfuerzo); **he's a d. child** *(trying)* es un niño que da mucho trabajo

**demarcation** [diːmɑː'keɪʃən] *n* demarcación *f*; *Ind* **d. dispute** = enfrentamiento entre grupos sindicales sobre la delimitación de las tareas que sus miembros deben realizar en el trabajo; **d. line** línea *f* de demarcación

**demean** [dɪ'miːn] *vt* **to d. oneself** rebajarse

**demeanour**, *US* **demeanor** [dɪ'miːnə(r)] *n* comportamiento *m*, conducta *f*

**demented** [dɪ'mentɪd] *adj* demente; **to be d. with grief** estar trastornado(a) por el dolor

**dementia** [dɪ'menʃɪə] *n* demencia *f*

**demerara sugar** [demə'reərə'ʃʊɡə(r)] *n* azúcar *m* moreno de caña *(procedente de las Antillas)*

**demigod** ['demɪɡɒd] *n* semidiós *m*

**demilitarize** [diː'mɪlɪtəraɪz] *vt* desmilitarizar

**demise** [dɪ'maɪz] *n* desaparición *f*, extinción *f*

**demister** [diː'mɪstər] *n Br Aut* luneta *f* térmica, dispositivo *m* antivaho

**demo** ['deməʊ] *n (pl demos) n Fam* (**a**) *(protest)* mani *f* (**b**) *(musical)* maqueta *f*

**demob** [diː'mɒb] *(pt & pp demobbed) vt Br Fam (disband troops)* licenciar, desmovilizar

**demobilization** [diːməʊbɪlaɪ'zeɪʃən] *n (of troops)* licencia *f* (absoluta), desmovilización *f*

**demobilize** [diː'məʊbɪlaɪz] *vt (disband troops)* licenciar, desmovilizar

**democracy** [dɪ'mɒkrəsɪ] *n* democracia *f*

**Democrat** ['deməkræt] *n US Pol (politician, voter)* demócrata *m,f*; **the Democrats** *(party)* los demócratas, el partido demócrata

**democrat** ['deməkræt] *n* demócrata *mf*

**democratic** [demə'krætɪk] *adj* democrático(a)

**democratically** [demə'krætɪklɪ] *adv* democráticamente

**demographic** [demə'græfɪk] *adj* demográfico(a)

**demolish** [dɪ'mɒlɪʃ] *vt (building)* demoler, derribar; *Fig (theory)* desbaratar; *(opponent)* aplastar

**demolition** [demə'lɪʃən] *n* demolición *f*, derribo *m*; **d. squad** equipo *m* de demolición

**demon** ['diːmən] *n* demonio *m*; *Fam* **he's a d. tennis player** es un fiera jugando al tenis

**demonic** [dɪ'mɒnɪk] *adj* demoníaco(a)

**demonstrable** [dɪ'mɒnstrəbəl] *adj* demostrable

**demonstrate** ['demənstreɪt] **1** *vt (fact, theory)* demostrar; **to d. how sth works** hacer una demostración de cómo funciona algo
**2** *vi (politically)* manifestarse

**demonstration** [demən'streɪʃən] *n* (**a**) *(of fact, theory, skills)* demostración *f* (**b**) *(political)* manifestación *f*

**demonstrative** [dɪ'mɒnstrətɪv] *adj* (**a**) *(person)* efusivo(a), extravertido(a) (**b**) *Gram* demostrativo(a)

**demonstrator** ['demənstreɪtə(r)] *n (political)* manifestante *mf*

**demoralize** [dɪ'mɒrəlaɪz] *vt* desmoralizar

**demoralizing** [dɪ'mɒrəlaɪzɪŋ] *adj* desmoralizador(ora)

**demote** [dɪ'məʊt] *vt* degradar, relegar (a un puesto más bajo); **two teams were demoted** dos equipos fueron descendidos de categoría

**demotion** [dɪ'məʊʃən] *n (of person)* degradación *f*; *Sport* descenso *m* de categoría

**demur** [dɪ'mɜː(r)] *(pt & pp demurred) vi* objetar; **to d. at a suggestion** poner objeciones a una sugerencia

**demure** [dɪ'mjʊə(r)] *adj* recatado(a)

**demystify** [diː'mɪstɪfaɪ] *vt* aclarar, clarificar

**den** [den] *n* (**a**) guarida *f*; *Fig* **a d. of thieves** una cueva de ladrones; **a d. of iniquity** un antro de depravación (**b**) *(room)* cuarto *m* privado, madriguera *f*

**denationalize** [diː'næʃənəlaɪz] *vt* privatizar, desnacionalizar

**denature** [diː'neɪtʃə(r)] *vt* desnaturalizar

**denial** [dɪ'naɪəl] *n* (**a**) *(of right, request)* denegación *f* (**b**) *(of accusation, guilt)* negación *f*

**denigrate** ['denɪɡreɪt] *vt* denigrar

**denim** ['denɪm] *n* tela *f* vaquera; **denims** *(jeans)* vaqueros *mpl*; **d. skirt/shirt** falda *f*/camisa *f* vaquera

**Denmark** ['denmɑːk] *n* Dinamarca *f*

**denomination** [dɪnɒmɪ'neɪʃən] *n* (**a**) *(religious)* confesión *f* (**b**) *Fin* valor *m* (nominal)

**denominator** [dɪˈnɒmɪneɪtə(r)] n Math denominador m

**denote** [dɪˈnəʊt] vt denotar

**denouement** [deɪˈnuːmɒŋ] n desenlace m

**denounce** [dɪˈnaʊns] vt (a) (inform against) denunciar (b) (criticize publicly) denunciar, condenar

**dense** [dens] adj (a) (smoke, fog) denso(a); (jungle) tupido(a); (crowd) nutrido(a) (b) Fam (stupid) corto(a)

**densely** [ˈdenslɪ] adv densamente; **d. packed** muy apretado(a); **d. populated** densamente poblado(a)

**density** [ˈdensɪtɪ] n densidad f

**dent** [dent] 1 n abolladura f; Fig **the wedding put a d. in his savings** la boda le costó una buena parte de sus ahorros
2 vt (car, bumper) abollar; Fig (confidence, pride) minar

**dental** [ˈdentəl] adj dental; **d. appointment** cita f con el dentista; **d. floss** hilo m (de seda) dental; **d. hygiene** higiene f dental; **d. nurse** enfermera f de dentista; **d. surgeon** odontólogo(a) m,f

**dentist** [ˈdentɪst] n dentista mf; **to go to the d.** ir al dentista

**dentistry** [ˈdentɪstrɪ] n (subject) odontología f

**dentures** [ˈdentʃəz] npl (set of) **d.** dentadura f postiza

**denude** [dɪˈnjuːd] vt **to be denuded of** estar desprovisto(a) de

**denunciation** [dɪnʌnsɪˈeɪʃən] n (a) (accusation) denuncia f (b) (criticism) denuncia f, condena f

**deny** [dɪˈnaɪ] vt (a) (right, request) denegar; **to d. sb his rights** denegar or negar a alguien sus derechos; **to d. oneself sth** privarse de algo (b) (accusation, fact) negar; (rumour) desmentir; **to d. doing sth, d. having done sth** negar haber hecho algo; **there's no denying that...** es innegable que...; **to d. all knowledge of sth** negar tener conocimiento de algo

**deodorant** [diːˈəʊdərənt] n desodorante m

**deodorize** [diːˈəʊdəraɪz] vt desodorizar, eliminar el mal olor de

**dep** Rail (abbr **departure**) salida f

**depart** [dɪˈpɑːt] vi (leave) salir (**from** de); **to d. from** (tradition, subject, truth) desviarse de; **the Glasgow train will d. from Platform 6** el tren con destino a Glasgow efectuará su salida por la vía 6

**department** [dɪˈpɑːtmənt] n (in company, shop) departamento m; (in university) cátedra f, departamento m; (of government) ministerio m; **that's not my d.** eso no es de mi competencia; **d. store** grandes almacenes mpl

**departmental** [diːpɑːˈtmentəl] adj de departamento; **d. head** jefe(a) m,f de departamento

**departure** [dɪˈpɑːtʃə(r)] n (from place) salida f; (from tradition, subject, truth) desviación f; **d. lounge** (in airport) sala f de embarque; **d. time** hora f de salida

**depend** [dɪˈpend] vi depender (**on** de); **that/it depends** depende; **to d. on sb** (be dependent on) depender de alguien; (count on) confiar en alguien; **it depends on how much money I have** depende de cuánto dinero tenga; Ironic **you can d. on him to be late** puedes estar seguro(a) de que llegará tarde

**dependable** [dɪˈpendəbəl] adj fiable

**dependant** [dɪˈpendənt] n **his/her dependants** las personas a su cargo

**dependence** [dɪˈpendəns] n (reliance) dependencia f; (trust) confianza f

**dependency** [dɪˈpendənsɪ] n (territory) dependencia f

**dependent** [dɪˈpendənt] adj dependiente; **to be d. on** depender de

**depending** [dɪˈpendɪŋ] adv **d. on** dependiendo de

**depict** [dɪˈpɪkt] vt (of painting) retratar, plasmar; (of book, piece of writing) describir

**depiction** [dɪˈpɪkʃən] n (picture) representación f; (description) descripción f

**depilatory** [dɪˈpɪlətərɪ] adj depilatorio(a)

**deplete** [dɪˈpliːt] vt mermar

**depletion** [dɪˈpliːʃən] n merma f

**deplorable** [dɪˈplɔːrəbəl] adj deplorable

**deplore** [dɪˈplɔː(r)] vt deplorar

**deploy** [dɪˈplɔɪ] vt desplegar

**deployment** [dɪˈplɔɪmənt] n despliegue m

**depopulate** [diːˈpɒpjʊleɪt] vt despoblar

**depopulation** [diːpɒpjʊˈleɪʃən] n despoblación f

**deport** [dɪˈpɔːt] vt deportar

**deportation** [diːpɔːˈteɪʃən] n deportación f

**deportment** [dɪˈpɔːtmənt] n porte m

**depose** [dɪˈpəʊz] vt deponer

**deposit** [dɪˈpɒzɪt] 1 n (a) (in bank) depósito m; Fin imposición f; **to make a d.** hacer or realizar un ingreso; Br **d. account** cuenta f de depósito or a plazo (b) (returnable) señal f, fianza f; (first payment) entrada f; **to put down a d. (on sth)** pagar la entrada (de algo); Br Pol **to lose one's d.** = perder el dinero depositado al presentarse como candidato por no haber sacado suficientes votos (c) (of minerals) yacimiento m; (of wine) poso m
2 vt depositar; (in bank account) ingresar

**deposition** [diːpəˈzɪʃən] n Law declaración f

**depositor** [dɪˈpɒzɪtə(r)] n Fin depositante m

**depot** ['depǝʊ] n Mil depósito m; Com almacén m; (for keeping and repairing buses) cochera f; US (bus station) estación f or terminal f de autobuses

**depravation** [deprǝ'veɪʃǝn] n depravación f

**depraved** [dɪ'preɪvd] adj depravado(a)

**depravity** [dɪ'prævɪtɪ] n depravación f

**deprecate** ['deprɪkeɪt] vt censurar; **to d. sb's efforts** restar importancia or mérito a los esfuerzos de alguien

**deprecatory** ['deprɪkeɪtǝrɪ] adj de desaprobación; **to be d. about sth/sb** mostrar desaprobación por algo/alguien

**depreciate** [dɪ'priːʃɪeɪt] vi (of value, currency) depreciarse

**depreciation** [dɪpriːʃɪ'eɪʃǝn] n (of value, currency) depreciación f

**depress** [dɪ'pres] vt (person, economy) deprimir; (prices) hacer bajar

**depressed** [dɪ'prest] adj (person, economy) deprimido(a); **to be d.** estar deprimido(a); **to make sb d.** deprimir a alguien

**depressing** [dɪ'presɪŋ] adj deprimente

**depression** [dɪ'preʃǝn] n (a) (of person, economy) depresión f (b) Met depresión f atmosférica, zona f de bajas presiones

**deprivation** [deprɪ'veɪʃǝn] n privación f

**deprive** [dɪ'praɪv] vt **to d. sb of sth** privar a alguien de algo

**deprived** [dɪ'praɪvd] adj (background, area) desfavorecido(a)

**dept** (abbr **department**) dpto., departamento m

**depth** [depθ] n (of water, sleep, feeling) profundidad f; **in d.** (investigate, discuss) a fondo, en profundidad; Fig **she was out of her d. in her new job/in the competition** el nuevo trabajo/el campeonato le venía grande; **in the d. of winter** en pleno invierno; **the depths of despair** la más absoluta desesperación; Mil **d. charge** carga f de profundidad

**deputation** [depjʊ'teɪʃǝn] n delegación f

**depute** [dɪ'pjuːt] vt delegar

**deputize** ['depjʊtaɪz] vi **to d. for sb** suplir a alguien

**deputy** ['depjʊtɪ] n (substitute) sustituto(a) m,f; (political representative) diputado(a) m,f; **d. manager** director(ora) m,f adjunto(a); **d. prime minister** vicepresidente(a) m,f del Gobierno

**derail** [diː'reɪl] **1** vt **to be derailed** (of train) descarrilar; Fig (of project, plan) fracasar
**2** vi (of train) descarrilar

**derailment** [dɪ'reɪlmǝnt] n descarrilamiento m

**deranged** [dɪ'reɪndʒd] adj perturbado(a); **to be d.** estar perturbado(a)

**derby** ['dɑːbɪ] n (football match) derby m

**deregulate** [diː'regjʊlet] vt (economy, market) liberalizar

**deregulation** [diːregjʊ'leɪʃǝn] n Com liberalización f

**derelict** ['derǝlɪkt] adj ruinoso(a), en ruinas

**dereliction** [derɪ'lɪkʃǝn] n ruina f; **d. of duty** incumplimiento m del deber

**deride** [dɪ'raɪd] vt ridiculizar, burlarse de

**derision** [dɪ'rɪʒǝn] n burla f, escarnio m; **to be an object of d.** ser objeto de burla

**derisive** [dɪ'raɪsɪv] adj burlón(ona)

**derisory** [dɪ'raɪsǝrɪ] adj irrisorio(a)

**derivation** [derɪ'veɪʃǝn] n origen m

**derivative** [dɪ'rɪvǝtɪv] **1** n derivado m
**2** adj poco original

**derive** [dɪ'raɪv] **1** vt (pleasure, satisfaction) encontrar (**from** en); (benefit, profit) obtener (**from** de); **to be derived from** (name, behaviour) derivar or provenir de
**2** vi **to d. from** derivar or provenir de

**dermatitis** [dɜːmǝ'taɪtɪs] n Med dermatitis f inv

**dermatology** [dɜːmǝ'tɒlǝdʒɪ] n Med dermatología f

**derogatory** [dɪ'rɒgǝtǝrɪ] adj despectivo(a)

**derrick** ['derɪk] n (in oil industry) torre f de perforación

**derv** [dɜːv] n Br (fuel) gasóleo m, gasoil m

**desalination** [diːsælɪ'neɪʃǝn] n desalinización f, desalación f

**descend** [dɪ'send] **1** vt (a) (hill, stairs) descender por, bajar (b) (be related to) **to be descended from sb** descender de alguien
**2** vi (a) (come down) descender; **darkness descended** cayó la noche; **in descending order** en orden descendente; **a mood of despair descended upon the country** el país quedó sumido en un sentimiento de desesperación; **every summer tourists d. on the town** todos los veranos los turistas invaden la ciudad; Fig **to d. to sb's level** rebajarse al nivel de alguien (b) (be related to) **to d. from sb** (be related to) descender de alguien

**descendant** [dɪ'sendǝnt] n descendiente m

**descent** [dɪ'sent] n (a) (way down) descenso m (b) (ancestry) ascendencia f

**describe** [dɪs'kraɪb] vt (a) (depict verbally) describir; **she describes herself as an artist** se define a sí misma como artista (b) Formal (draw) (circle, line) describir, trazar

**description** [dɪs'krɪpʃǝn] n descripción f; **to give a d. (of)** dar or hacer una descripción (de); **to answer** or **fit the d.** responder a la descripción; **beyond d.** indescriptible; **birds of all descriptions** todo tipo de aves; **she's a journalist of some d.** es periodista o algo así

**descriptive** [dɪs'krɪptɪv] adj descriptivo(a)

**desecrate** ['desɪkreɪt] vt profanar

**desecration** [desɪ'kreɪʃən] n profanación f

**desegregate** [di:'segrɪgeɪt] vt terminar con la segregación racial en

**desert**[1] ['dezət] n desierto m; **d. island** isla f desierta

**desert**[2] [dɪ'zɜ:t] **1** vt (place, family) abandonar; Fig **his courage deserted him** el valor le abandonó

**2** vi (from army) desertar

**deserted** [dɪ'zɜ:tɪd] adj desierto(a)

**deserter** [dɪ'zɜ:tə(r)] n (soldier) desertor(ora) m,f

**desertification** [dɪzɜ:tɪfɪ'keɪʃən] n desertización f

**desertion** [dɪ'zɜ:ʃən] n Law abandono m del hogar; Mil deserción f

**deserts** [dɪ'zɜ:ts] npl **he got his just d.** recibió su merecido

**deserve** [dɪ'zɜ:v] vt merecer, merecerse; **to d. (to do) sth** merecer (hacer) algo; **she got what she deserved** recibió su merecido

**deserving** [dɪ'zɜ:vɪŋ] adj **to be d. of sth** ser digno(a) or merecedor(ora) de algo; **a d. case** un caso merecedor de ayuda

**design** [dɪ'zaɪn] **1** n (a) (in general) diseño m; (decorative pattern) dibujo m, motivo m; **our latest d.** nuestro último diseño (b) (intention) propósito m; **by d.** a propósito; **to have designs on sb/sth** tener las miras puestas en alguien/algo

**2** vt (building, vehicle, clothes) diseñar; **the book is designed for children** el libro está pensado or concebido para los niños; **his remarks were designed to shock** sus comentarios pretendían escandalizar

**designate** ['dezɪgneɪt] **1** vt (person) designar; **to d. sb to do sth** designar a alguien para hacer algo; **he designated her as his successor** la nombró su sucesora; **this area has been designated a national park** esta zona ha sido declarada parque nacional

**2** adj designado(a), nombrado(a)

**designation** [dezɪg'neɪʃən] n (a) (appointment) nombramiento m (b) (title) denominación f

**designer** [dɪ'zaɪnə(r)] n diseñador(ora) m,f; **(set) d.** Th escenógrafo(a) m,f; Cin decorador(ora) m,f; **d. clothes/drugs** ropa f/drogas fpl de diseño

**desirable** [dɪ'zaɪərəbəl] adj (attractive) apetecible; (sexually) deseable; (appropriate) deseable; **a knowledge of French is d.** (in job advert) se valorarán los conocimientos de francés; **d. residence** (in advert) propiedad f impecable

**desire** [dɪ'zaɪə(r)] **1** n deseo m; **I feel no d. to go** no me apetece nada ir

**2** vt desear; **to d. (to do) sth** desear (hacer)

algo; **it leaves a lot to be desired** deja mucho que desear

**desirous** [dɪ'zaɪərəs] adj Formal deseoso(a) (**of** de)

**desist** [dɪ'sɪst] vi Formal desistir (**from** de)

**desk** [desk] n (in school) pupitre m; (in office) mesa f, escritorio m; (in hotel) mostrador m; **d. diary** agenda f; **a d. job** un trabajo de oficina; **d. lamp** lámpara f de mesa or de escritorio

**desktop** ['desktɒp] n Comptr **d. computer** ordenador m de sobremesa; **d. publishing** autoedición f

**desolate** ['desələt] adj (place) desolado(a); (person, look) desolado(a), afligido(a); (future, prospect) desolador(ora)

**desolation** [desə'leɪʃən] n (of landscape, person, defeated country) desolación f

**despair** [dɪs'peə(r)] **1** n desesperación f; **to be in d.** estar desesperado(a); **to drive sb to d.** llevar a alguien a la desesperación

**2** vi desesperarse; **to d. of doing sth** perder la esperanza de hacer algo; **I d. of you** contigo me desespero, no sé qué voy a hacer contigo

**despairing** [dɪ'speərɪŋ] adj de desesperación

**despatch** = **dispatch**

**desperate** ['despərət] adj (person, situation) desesperado(a); **to be d.** (of person) estar desesperado(a); **to be d. to do sth** morirse de ganas de hacer algo; **to be d. for sth, to be in d. need of sth** necesitar algo desesperadamente

**desperately** ['despərətlɪ] adv (to fight, plead) desesperadamente; (in love) perdidamente; **d. ill** gravísimamente enfermo(a); **to be d. sorry about sth** lamentar algo muchísimo

**desperation** [despə'reɪʃən] n desesperación f; **in d.** presa de la desesperación; **she did it in d.** lo hizo por desesperación or a la desesperada

**despicable** [dɪ'spɪkəbəl] adj despreciable

**despise** [dɪ'spaɪz] vt despreciar

**despite** [dɪs'paɪt] prep a pesar de, pese a

**despondency** [dɪs'pɒndənsɪ] n desánimo m, abatimiento m

**despondent** [dɪ'spɒndənt] adj desanimado(a), abatido(a); **to be d.** estar desanimado(a) or abatido(a); **to become d.** desanimarse, abatirse

**despot** ['despɒt] n déspota mf

**despotic** [dɪs'pɒtɪk] adj despótico(a)

**despotism** ['despətɪzəm] n despotismo m

**dessert** [dɪ'zɜ:t] n postre m; **d. wine** vino m dulce

**dessertspoon** [dɪ'zɜ:tspu:n] n cuchara f de postre; (as measurement) cucharada f de las de postre

**destabilize** [di:'steɪbəlaɪz] vt (government, economy) desestabilizar

**destination** [destɪ'neɪʃən] n (lugar m de) destino m; Comptr **d. disk** disco m de destino; **d. drive** unidad f (de disco) de destino

**destine** ['destɪn] vt destinar

**destined** ['destɪnd] adj (a) (meant) destinado(a); **to be d. to do sth** estar destinado a hacer algo (b) (of plane, ship) **d. for** con destino or rumbo a

**destiny** ['destɪnɪ] n destino m, sino m

**destitute** ['destɪtjuːt] adj (needy) indigente; **to be utterly d.** estar en la miseria

**destroy** [dɪs'trɔɪ] vt (a) (damage, ruin) destruir; (health, career, reputation) acabar con, destruir (b) (kill) (sick or unwanted animal) sacrificar; (vermin) acabar con, destruir

**destroyer** [dɪs'trɔɪə(r)] n (ship) destructor m

**destruction** [dɪs'trʌkʃən] n (action) destrucción f; (damage) destrozos mpl

**destructive** [dɪs'trʌktɪv] adj destructivo(a); **d. criticism** crítica f destructiva

**desultory** ['desəltərɪ] adj (attempt, manner) sin convicción, desganado(a); **to have a d. conversation** mantener a desgana una conversación

**detach** [dɪ'tætʃ] vt separar (**from** de); **to d. oneself from sth** distanciarse de algo

**detachable** [dɪ'tætʃəbəl] adj (cover, handle) extraíble; (accessories) desmontable; (hood) de quita y pon

**detached** [dɪ'tætʃt] adj (a) (separate) separado(a); **to become** or **get d. from sth** alejarse or separarse de algo; **to become d. from reality** perder el contacto con la realidad; **d. house** casa f or chalé m individual; Med **d. retina** desprendimiento m de retina (b) (disinterested) **to be d.** (objective) ser imparcial; (cold, distant) ser despegado(a) or distante

**detachment** [dɪ'tætʃmənt] n (a) (military unit) destacamento m (b) (objectivity) imparcialidad f; **with an air of d.** con (aire de) despego or desapego

**detail** ['diːteɪl] 1 n (a) (item of information) detalle m; **to pay attention to d.** prestar atención a los pequeños detalles; **to go into detail(s)** entrar en detalles; **in d.** en or con detalle; **details** (information) detalles mpl; (address and phone number) datos mpl; **minor details** detalles sin importancia (b) Mil (group of soldiers) piquete m, cuadrilla f

2 vt (a) (describe) detallar (b) Mil **to d. sb to do sth** encomendar a alguien hacer algo

**detailed** ['diːteɪld] adj (account, description) detallado(a)

**detain** [dɪ'teɪn] vt (suspect) detener; **such details need not d. us** no deberíamos entretenernos en estos detalles

**detainee** [diːteɪ'niː] n prisionero(a) m,f or preso(a) m,f político(a)

**detect** [dɪ'tekt] vt (of person) percibir; (of machine) detectar; (source of a problem) identificar, hallar

**detection** [dɪ'tekʃən] n (of mines, planes) detección f; (by detective) investigación f; **to escape d.** no ser detectado(a)

**detective** [dɪ'tektɪv] n detective mf; **d. story** relato m detectivesco; **d. work** investigación f

**detector** [dɪ'tektə(r)] n (device) detector m

**détente** [deɪ'tɒnt] n distensión f (entre países)

**detention** [dɪ'tenʃən] n (a) Law detención f, arresto m; **in d.** bajo arresto; **d. centre** centro m de internamiento or reclusión de menores (b) Sch **to get d.** = ser castigado a quedarse en el colegio después de terminadas las clases

**deter** [dɪ'tɜː(r)] (pt & pp deterred) vt disuadir (**from** de); **to d. sb from doing sth** disuadir a alguien de que haga algo

**detergent** [dɪ'tɜːdʒənt] n detergente m

**deteriorate** [dɪ'tɪərɪəreɪt] vi (of situation, health, relations) deteriorarse; (of weather) empeorar

**deterioration** [dɪtɪərɪə'reɪʃən] n (of situation, health, relations) deterioro m; (of weather) empeoramiento m

**determination** [dɪtɜːmɪ'neɪʃən] n (resoluteness) decisión f, determinación f

**determine** [dɪ'tɜːmɪn] vt (a) (decide) decidir, resolver; **to d. to do sth** tomar la determinación de hacer algo (b) (cause, date) determinar

**determined** [dɪ'tɜːmɪnd] adj decidido(a), resuelto(a); **to be d. to do sth** estar decidido(a) a hacer algo

**deterrent** [dɪ'terənt] 1 n elemento m de disuasión; **to act as a d.** tener un efecto disuasorio

2 adj (effect) disuasivo(a), disuasorio(a)

**detest** [dɪ'test] vt detestar

**dethrone** [diː'θrəʊn] vt destronar

**detonate** ['detəneɪt] 1 vt (bomb, explosive) explosionar, hacer explotar

2 vi detonar, explotar

**detonation** [detə'neɪʃən] n detonación f

**detonator** ['detəneɪtə(r)] n detonador m

**detour** ['diːtʊə(r)] n desvío m; **to make a d.** dar un rodeo

**detoxification** [diːtɒksɪfɪ'keɪʃən], Fam **detox** ['diːtɒks] n desintoxicación f; **d. centre/programme** centro m/programa m de desintoxicación

▸**detract from** [dɪ'trækt] vt insep disminuir, mermar; (achievement, contribution) restar importancia or valor a; **the oil refinery detracts from the beauty of the place** la refinería de petróleo resta belleza al lugar

**detractor** [dɪ'træktə(r)] n detractor(ora) m,f

**detriment** ['detrɪmənt] *n* **to the d. of...** en detrimento de...; **without d. to...** sin perjuicio para...

**detrimental** [detrɪ'mentəl] *adj* perjudicial (**to para**); **to have a d. effect on** perjudicar

**detritus** [dɪ'traɪtəs] *n* detrito *m*

**deuce** [dju:s] *n Sport (in tennis)* deuce *m*, cuarenta *m* iguales

**Deutschmark** ['dɔɪtʃmɑːk] *n* marco *m* alemán

**devaluation** [di:vælju'eɪʃən] *n* devaluación *f*

**devalue** [di:'vælju:] *vt* (**a**) *(currency)* devaluar (**b**) *(person, achievements, efforts)* restar mérito a

**devastate** ['devəsteɪt] *vt (crops, village)* devastar; *Fam* **I was devastated by the news** la noticia me dejó consternado(a) *or* desolado(a)

**devastating** ['devəsteɪtɪŋ] *adj (storm, bombardment)* devastador(ora); *(news)* desolador(ora); *(argument, criticism)* demoledor(ora); *(charm, beauty)* arrollador(ora)

**devastation** [devəs'teɪʃən] *n* devastación *f*

**develop** [dɪ'veləp] **1** *vt* (**a**) *(theory, argument, design)* desarrollar; *(skills)* perfeccionar (**b**) *(region)* desarrollar; *(site)* urbanizar; **developed countries** países *mpl* desarrollados (**c**) *(acquire) (infection)* contraer; *(habit)* adquirir; **to d. a liking for sth** tomar afición a algo; **to d. a taste for sth** cogerle el gusto a algo (**d**) *Phot* revelar
**2** *vi* (**a**) *(of body, the faculties, region, trade)* desarrollarse; **to d. into sth** transformarse *or* convertirse en algo (**b**) *(become apparent)* surgir

**developer** [dɪ'veləpə(r)] *n* (**a**) *(builders)* promotor(ora) *m,f* inmobiliario(a) (**b**) *Phot* revelador *m*, líquido *m* de revelado

**developing** [dɪ'veləpɪŋ] *adj (region, country)* en (vías de) desarrollo; *(crisis)* creciente

**development** [dɪ'veləpmənt] *n* (**a**) *(growth, expansion)* desarrollo *m*; **d. aid** ayuda *f* al desarrollo; *Br* **d. area** = área deprimida en la que el gobierno fomenta la creación de nuevas industrias; *Econ* **d. potential** potencial *m* de explotación (**b**) *(progress, change)* cambio *m*, variación *f*; **recent developments in the industry** la evolución reciente de la industria; **there have been some interesting developments** se han dado novedades interesantes; **to await further developments** esperar a ver cómo se desarrolla la situación; **the latest developments in medical research** los últimos avances de la investigación médica

**deviant** ['di:vɪənt] *adj* desviado(a), anómalo(a)

**deviate** ['di:vɪeɪt] *vi* desviarse (**from** de)

**deviation** [di:vɪ'eɪʃən] *n* desviación *f* (**from** de)

**device** [dɪ'vaɪs] *n* (**a**) *(for measuring, processing, cutting)* aparato *m*; *(for safety, security)* dispositivo

*m*; **an explosive d.** un artefacto explosivo (**b**) *(method, scheme)* estratagema *f*; **to leave sb to his own devices** dejar a alguien que se las arregle solo(a)

**devil** ['devəl] *n* (**a**) diablo *m*, demonio *m*; **the D.** el diablo *or* demonio; **poor d.!** ¡pobre diablo!; **you little d.!** *(to child)* ¡granujilla!; **you lucky d.!** ¡qué suerte tienes! (**b**) *Fam (for emphasis)* **what the d. are you doing?** ¿qué diablos *or* demonios estás haciendo?; **how the d....?** ¿cómo diablos *or* demonios...?; **we had a d. of a job moving it** sudamos tinta para moverlo (**c**) *(idioms)* **he's a bit of a d.** *(daring, reckless)* no se corta un pelo; *Fam* **go on, be a d.!** ¡venga pues, date el gusto!; **to be (caught) between the d. and the deep blue sea** estar entre la espada y la pared; **talk of the d....** hablando del rey de Roma...; *Prov* **better the d. you know (than the d. you don't)** más vale lo malo conocido (que lo bueno por conocer); **(to play) d.'s advocate** (hacer de) abogado *m* del diablo

**devilish** ['devəlɪʃ] *adj* diabólico(a)

**devil-may-care** ['devəlmeɪ'keə(r)] *adj* despreocupado(a)

**devious** ['di:vɪəs] *adj (person, mind)* retorcido(a); *(route)* sinuoso(a); **that's a bit d. of you!** ¡qué maquiavélico eres!

**devise** [dɪ'vaɪz] *vt* idear

**devoid** [dɪ'vɔɪd] *adj* desprovisto(a) (**of** de)

**devolution** [di:və'lu:ʃən] *n Pol* transferencia *f* de poder político, traspaso *m* de competencias; **they want d.** quieren la autonomía (política)

**devolve** [dɪ'vɒlv] **1** *vt (functions, powers)* transferir, traspasar
**2** *vi* recaer (**on** en)

**devote** [dɪ'vəʊt] *vt (time, money)* dedicar (**to** a); **to d. oneself to** consagrarse a

**devoted** [dɪ'vəʊtɪd] *adj (father)* muy afectuoso(a); *(admirer)* devoto(a), ferviente; **they are d. to each other** están muy unidos; **after years of d. service** tras años de abnegada dedicación

**devotee** [devəʊ'ti:] *n* (*of person, idea)* adepto(a) *m,f*; *(of sport, music)* fanático(a) *m,f*, entusiasta *mf*

**devotion** [dɪ'vəʊʃən] *n (to friend, family)* devoción *f*; *(to cause, leader of party)* dedicación *f*, entrega *f*; *(to god, saint)* devoción *f*; **devotions** *(prayers)* oraciones *fpl*

**devour** [dɪ'vaʊə(r)] *vt also Fig* devorar

**devout** [dɪ'vaʊt] *adj (person)* devoto(a); *(wish)* sincero(a)

**dew** [dju:] *n* rocío *m*

**dewy-eyed** [dju:'aɪd] *adj (loving)* cándido(a), inocente, sentimental; *(naive)* ingenuo(a), candoroso(a)

**dexterity** [deks'terɪtɪ] n *(mental, physical)* destreza f

**dext(e)rous** ['dekstrəs] adj diestro(a), hábil

**diabetes** [daɪə'biːtiːz] n diabetes f inv

**diabetic** [daɪə'betɪk] **1** n diabético(a) m,f; **d. chocolate** chocolate m para diabéticos

**2** adj diabético(a)

**diabolical** [daɪə'bɒlɪkəl] adj **(a)** *(evil)* diabólico(a), demoníaco(a) **(b)** *Fam (very bad)* espantoso(a)

**diadem** ['daɪədem] n diadema f

**diagnose** ['daɪəgnəʊz] vt *also Fig* diagnosticar

**diagnosis** [daɪəg'nəʊsɪs] *(pl* **diagnoses** [daɪəg'nəʊsiːz]*)* n *Med & Fig* diagnóstico m; **to make** *or* **give a d.** emitir un diagnóstico

**diagnostic** [daɪəg'nɒstɪk] adj diagnóstico(a)

**diagonal** [daɪ'ægənəl] n & adj diagonal f

**diagram** ['daɪəgræm] n diagrama m

**dial** ['daɪəl] **1** n *(of clock)* esfera f; *(of radio)* dial m; *(of phone)* disco m

**2** vt *(pt & pp* **dialled,** *US* **dialed)** *(phone number)* marcar, *Andes, CSur* discar

**dialect** ['daɪəlekt] n dialecto m

**dialectic(al)** [daɪə'lektɪkəl] adj dialéctico(a)

**dialectics** [daɪə'lektɪks] n dialéctica f

**dialling** ['daɪəlɪŋ] n *Br* **d. code** prefijo m *(telefónico)*; **d. tone** tono m *(de marcar)*

**dialogue** ['daɪəlɒg] n diálogo m; *Pol* **to enter into a d.** establecer un diálogo; *Comptr* **d. box** cuadro m de diálogo

**dialysis** [daɪ'ælɪsɪs] n *Med* diálisis f inv

**diameter** [daɪ'æmɪtə(r)] n diámetro m; **the wheel is 60 cm in d.** la rueda tiene 60 cms de diámetro

**diametrically** [daɪə'metrɪklɪ] adv **to be d. opposed to** ser diametralmente opuesto(a) a

**diamond** ['daɪəmənd] n *(gem)* diamante m; *(shape)* rombo m; **diamonds** *(in cards)* diamantes mpl; **d. jubilee** bodas fpl de diamante; **d. necklace** collar m de diamantes; **d. ring** sortija f de diamantes

**diaper** ['daɪəpə(r)] n *US* pañal m

**diaphanous** [daɪ'æfənəs] adj diáfano(a)

**diaphragm** ['daɪəfræm] n diafragma m

**diarrhoea** [daɪə'rɪə] n diarrea f

**diary** ['daɪərɪ] n *(as record)* diario m; *(for appointments)* agenda f; **to keep a d.** llevar un diario

**diatribe** ['daɪətraɪb] n diatriba f *(against* contra *or* en contra de)

**dice** [daɪs] **1** n *(pl* **dice)** *(in game)* dado m; **to play d.** jugar a los dados

**2** vt *(meat, potatoes)* cortar en dados

**3** vi **to d. with death** jugarse la piel

**dicey** ['daɪsɪ] adj *Fam* arriesgado(a)

**dichotomy** [daɪ'kɒtəmɪ] n dicotomía f

**dick** [dɪk] n **(a)** *US Fam (detective)* sabueso(a) m,f **(b)** *Vulg (penis)* picha f, polla f

**dickens** [dɪkɪnz] n **what the d.?** ¿qué diablos?

**dickhead** ['dɪkhed] n *Br Vulg (idiot)* gilipollas mf inv

**dicky** ['dɪkɪ] adj *Br Fam* **to have a d. heart** no estar muy bien del corazón

**dictate 1** n ['dɪkteɪt] **she followed the dictates of her conscience** siguió los dictados de su conciencia

**2** vt [dɪk'teɪt] **(a)** *(letter, passage)* dictar **(b)** *(determine) (choice)* imponer, dictar; *(conditions)* imponer; **circumstances d. that we postpone the meeting** las circunstancias obligan a aplazar la reunión

**3** vi **(a)** *(dictate text)* dictar **(b)** *(give orders)* **to d. to sb** dar órdenes a alguien; **I won't be dictated to!** ¡no voy a permitir que me den órdenes!

**dictation** [dɪk'teɪʃən] n dictado m; **to take d.** escribir al dictado; *Sch* **to do d.** hacer un dictado

**dictator** [dɪk'teɪtə(r)] n dictador(ora) m,f

**dictatorial** [dɪktə'tɔːrɪəl] adj dictatorial

**dictatorship** [dɪk'teɪtəʃɪp] n dictadura f

**diction** ['dɪkʃən] n dicción f

**dictionary** ['dɪkʃənərɪ] n diccionario m

**did** [dɪd] pt of **do**

**didactic** [dɪ'dæktɪk] adj didáctico(a)

**diddle** ['dɪdəl] vt *Fam* tangar, timar; **they diddled him out of the money** le engatusaron para sacarle el dinero

**didn't** ['dɪdənt] = **did not**

**die¹** [daɪ] n **(a)** *(pl* **dice** [daɪs]*)* *(in game)* dado m; *Fig* **the d. is cast** la suerte está echada **(b)** *(pl* **dies** [daɪz]*)* *(mould for casting or stamping)* cuño m, troquel m

**die²** **1** vi morir; **she is dying** se está muriendo; **to d. from** *or* **of one's wounds** morir de las heridas recibidas; **to d. hard** *(of habit, rumour)* ser difícil de eliminar; *Fam* **never say d.!** ¡nunca le des por vencido!; *Fam* **I nearly died laughing/of shame** casi me muero de risa/de vergüenza; *Fam* **to be dying to do sth** morirse de ganas de hacer algo; *Fam* **I'm dying for a cigarette** me muero de ganas de fumar un cigarrillo; **the engine died on me** se me estropeó el motor; **their love died** su amor se extinguió

**2** vt **to d. a natural/violent death** morir de muerte natural/violenta; *Fig* **his proposal died the death** su propuesta no llegó a cuajar

▸**die away** vi *(of sound, voice)* desvanecerse

▸**die down** vi *(of fire)* remitir; *(of wind)* calmarse; *(of sound)* atenuarse; *(of excitement, scandal)* apaciguarse

**▸die off** *vi* **the few remaining veterans were dying off** iban muriendo los pocos veteranos que quedaban

**▸die out** *vi (of family, species)* extinguirse, desaparecer

**die-hard** ['daɪhɑːd] *n & adj* intransigente *mf*

**diesel** ['diːzəl] **1** *n (fuel)* gasoil *m*, gasóleo *m*; *(railway engine)* locomotora *f* diesel; *(car)* coche *m* (de motor) diesel

**2** *adj (engine, train)* diesel; **d. oil** *or* **fuel** gasoil *m*, gasóleo *m*

**diet** ['daɪət] **1** *n (habitual food)* dieta *f*; *(restricted food)* dieta *f*, régimen *m*; **to be/go on a d.** estar/ponerse a dieta *or* régimen

**2** *vi* hacer dieta *or* régimen

**3** *adj (low-calorie)* light, bajo(a) en calorías

**dietary** ['daɪətəri] *adj* dietético(a); **d. fibre** fibra *f* alimenticia

**dietician** [daɪə'tɪʃən] *n* especialista *mf* en dietética

**differ** ['dɪfə(r)] *vi* **(a)** *(be different)* ser distinto(a) *or* diferente **(from** de); **to d. in size/colour** diferenciarse por el tamaño/color **(b)** *(disagree)* discrepar **(with sb/about sth** de alguien/en algo); **I beg to d.** me veo obligado a discrepar; **to agree to d.** reconocer mutuamente las discrepancias

**difference** ['dɪfərəns] *n* **(a)** *(disparity)* diferencia *f* **(between** entre); **that doesn't make any d.** eso no cambia nada; **it makes no d. (to me)** (me) da igual *or* lo mismo; **that makes all the d.** eso cambia mucho las cosas; **a car with a d.** un coche distinto a los demás; **to pay the d.** pagar la diferencia; **a d. of opinion** una diferencia de opiniones **(b)** *(disagreement)* diferencia *f*, discrepancia *f*; **we have to settle our differences** tenemos que resolver nuestras diferencias

**different** ['dɪfərənt] *adj* **(a)** *(not the same)* diferente, distinto(a); **that's quite a d. matter** eso es una cuestión aparte; **she feels a d. person** se siente otra (persona); **he just wants to be d.** sólo busca ser diferente **(b)** *(various)* diferente, distinto(a); **I spoke to d. people about it** he hablado de ello con varias personas

**differential** [dɪfə'renʃəl] **1** *n* **wage** *or* **pay differentials** diferencias *fpl* salariales; *Math* **d. calculus** cálculo *m* diferencial; *Aut* **d. gear** diferencial *m*

**2** *adj* diferencial

**differentiate** [dɪfə'renʃɪeɪt] **1** *vt* diferenciar, distinguir **(from** de)

**2** *vi* diferenciar, distinguir **(between** entre)

**differently** ['dɪfərəntlɪ] *adv* de forma diferente

**difficult** ['dɪfɪkəlt] *adj (task, problem)* difícil; **he's d. to get on with** no es fácil llevarse bien con él; **you're just being d.** no estás siendo

razonable; **to make life d. for sb** complicarle la vida a alguien; **to make things d. for sb** poner las cosas difíciles a alguien

**difficulty** ['dɪfɪkəltɪ] *n* **(a)** *(trouble)* dificultad *f*; **to have d. in doing sth** tener dificultad en hacer algo; **to be in d.** *or* **difficulties** estar en dificultades; **with d.** con dificultad **(b)** *(obstacle, problem)* dificultad *f*, problema *m*; **to make difficulties (for sb)** crear dificultades (a alguien)

**diffidence** ['dɪfɪdəns] *n* pudor *m*, retraimiento *m*

**diffident** ['dɪfɪdənt] *adj* pudoroso(a), retraído(a)

**diffuse 1** *adj* [dɪ'fjuːs] *(light)* difuso(a); *(literary style)* difuso(a), prolijo(a); *(sense of unease)* vago(a), difuso(a)

**2** *vt* [dɪ'fjuːz] difundir

**3** *vi* difundirse

**dig** [dɪg] **1** *n* **(a)** *(in archeology)* excavación *f* **(b)** *(poke)* golpe *m*; **a d. in the ribs** *(with elbow)* un codazo en las costillas **(c)** *(remark)* pulla *f*; **to get a d. in at sb, to have a d. at sb** lanzar una pulla a alguien

**2** *vt (pt & pp dug* [dʌg]*)* **(a)** *(hole, grave)* cavar; *(garden)* cavar en; *(well)* excavar; **the dog dug a hole by the tree** el perro escarbó *or* hizo un agujero junto al árbol; *Fig* **she is digging her own grave** está cavando su propia tumba **(b)** *(thrust)* **to d. sth into sth** clavar algo en algo **(c)** *very Fam (like)* **she really digs that kind of music** ese tipo de música le mola cantidad

**3** *vi* **(a)** *(of person)* cavar **(for** en busca de); *(animal)* escarbar; *(in archeology)* excavar **(b)** *very Fam (understand)* **you d.?** ¿lo pillas?

**▸dig in 1** *vt sep* **to d. one's heels in** emperrarse; **to d. oneself in** *(of soldiers)* atrincherarse

**2** *vi* **(a)** *Fam (start eating)* ponerse a comer; **d. in!** ¡a comer! **(b)** **to d. in** *(of soldiers)* atrincherarse

**▸dig out** *vt sep* **(a)** *(bullet, splinter)* extraer; *(person) (from ruins, snow drift)* rescatar **(b)** *Fam (find) (information)* encontrar; *(thing that has been left unused)* rescatar

**▸dig up** *vt sep* **(a)** *(plant)* arrancar, desarraigar; *(treasure, body)* desenterrar; *(road)* levantar **(b)** *Fam (find) (information)* desenterrar, sacar a la luz; *(person)* sacar

**digest 1** *n* ['daɪdʒest] *(summary)* resumen *m*

**2** *vt* [dɪ'dʒest] *also Fig* digerir

**digestible** [dɪ'dʒestəbəl] *adj* digerible; **to be easily d.** digerirse fácilmente

**digestion** [dɪ'dʒestʃən] *n* digestión *f*

**digestive** [dɪ'dʒestɪv] *adj* digestivo(a); **d. (biscuit)** galleta *f* integral, **d. system** aparato *m* digestivo; **d. tract** tubo *m* digestivo

**digger** ['dɪgə(r)] *n* excavadora *f*

**digit** ['dɪdʒɪt] *n (finger)* dedo *m*; *Math* dígito *m*

**digital** ['dɪdʒɪtəl] *adj (watch, computer)* digital; **d. recording** grabación *f* digital

**dignified** ['dɪgnɪfaɪd] *adj* solemne

**dignify** ['dɪgnɪfaɪ] *vt* dignificar

**dignitary** ['dɪgnɪtərɪ] *n Formal* dignatario(a) *m,f*

**dignity** ['dɪgnɪtɪ] *n* dignidad *f;* **she considered it beneath her d. to respond** le pareció que responder supondría una degradación

**digress** [daɪ'gres] *vi* divagar; **..., but I d. ...,** pero me estoy alejando del tema

**digression** [daɪ'greʃən] *n* digresión *f*

**digs** [dɪgz] *Br npl* habitación *f* or cuarto *m* de alquiler

**dike = dyke**

**dilapidated** [dɪ'læpɪdeɪtɪd] *adj (building)* derruido(a); *(car)* destartalado(a); **to be d.** estar derruido(a)/destartalado(a)

**dilapidation** [dɪlæpɪ'deɪʃən] *n (of building, car)* ruina *f*, grave deterioro *m*

**dilate** [daɪ'leɪt] **1** *vt* dilatar
**2** *vi* dilatarse

**dilation** [daɪ'leɪʃən] *n* dilatación *f*

**dilatory** ['dɪlətərɪ] *adj Formal* dilatorio(a); **to be d. in doing sth** hacer algo con dilación

**dilemma** [daɪ'lemə] *n* dilema *m*, disyuntiva *f;* **to be in a d.** estar en un dilema

**dilettante** [dɪlɪ'tɑ:ntɪ] *n* diletante *mf*

**diligence** ['dɪlɪdʒəns] *n* diligencia *f*

**diligent** ['dɪlɪdʒənt] *adj* diligente

**dill** [dɪl] *n* eneldo *m*

**dilly-dally** ['dɪlɪ'dælɪ] *vi Fam (loiter)* entretenerse; *(hesitate)* titubear, vacilar

**dilute** [daɪ'lu:t] **1** *adj* diluido(a)
**2** *vt (wine, acid)* diluir; *Fig (policy, proposal)* debilitar, restar eficacia a; **d. to taste** diluir al gusto de cada uno

**dilution** [daɪ'lu:ʃən] *n Fig (of policy, proposal)* debilitamiento *m*

**dim** [dɪm] **1** (**a**) *adj (light, outline)* tenue; *(memory)* vago(a); *(eyesight)* débil; *(chance, hope)* remoto(a), lejano(a); **to take a d. view of sth** desaprobar algo (**b**) *(stupid)* tonto(a), corto(a) de alcances
**2** *vt (pt & pp dimmed) (light)* atenuar
**3** *vi (of light)* atenuarse

**dime** [daɪm] *n US* = moneda de diez centavos; *Fam* **it's not worth a d.** no vale un duro; *Fam* **they're a d. a dozen** los hay a patadas

**dimension** [daɪ'menʃən] *n* dimensión *f*

**diminish** [dɪ'mɪnɪʃ] **1** *vt* disminuir; *Law* **diminished responsibility** responsabilidad *f* atenuada
**2** *vi* disminuir

**diminishing** [dɪ'mɪnɪʃɪŋ] *adj* decreciente; **law of d. returns** ley *f* de los rendimientos decrecientes

**diminutive** [dɪ'mɪnjʊtɪv] **1** *n Gram* diminutivo *m*
**2** *adj* diminuto(a), minúsculo(a)

**dimly** ['dɪmlɪ] *adv (remember)* vagamente; *(see)* con dificultad; **d. lit** en penumbra, con luz tenue

**dimmer** ['dɪmə(r)] *n* **d. (switch)** potenciómetro *m*, regulador *m* or modulador *m* de (potencia de) luz

**dimple** ['dɪmpəl] *n* hoyuelo *m*

**dimwit** ['dɪmwɪt] *n Fam* estúpido(a) *m,f*, idiota *mf*

**din** [dɪn] *n (of traffic, machinery)* estrépito; *(of people)* jaleo *m*, alboroto *m*

**dine** [daɪn] *vi* cenar

▶**dine out** *vi* cenar fuera; *Fig* **he'll be able to d. out on that story for weeks!** esa historia le dará tema de conversación para varias semanas

**diner** ['daɪnə(r)] *n* (**a**) *(person)* comensal *mf* (**b**) *US (restaurant)* restaurante *m* barato

**ding-dong** ['dɪŋ'dɒŋ] **1** *n* (**a**) *(sound)* din don *m* (**b**) *Fam (fight)* trifulca *f*
**2** *adj (argument, contest)* reñido(a)

**dinghy** ['dɪŋ(g)ɪ] *n* (**rubber**) **d.** lancha *f* neumática; *(sailing)* **d.** bote *m* de vela

**dingo** ['dɪŋgəʊ] *(pl dingoes)* *n* dingo *m*

**dingy** ['dɪndʒɪ] *adj (room, street)* sórdido(a); *(colour)* sucio(a)

**dining** ['daɪnɪŋ] *n* **d. car** *(on train)* vagón *m* restaurante; **d. hall** *(in school)* comedor *m;* **d. room** comedor *m;* **d. table** mesa *f* de comedor

**dinner** ['dɪnə(r)] *n (midday meal)* comida *f*, almuerzo *m; (evening meal)* cena *f;* **to have d.** *(at midday)* comer, almorzar; *(in evening)* cenar; **what's for d.?** *(midday meal)* ¿qué hay de comida?; *(evening meal)* ¿qué hay de cena?; **d. hour** *(at school)* hora *f* de comer; **d. jacket** esmoquin *m;* **d. lady** camarera *f* en un comedor escolar); **d. party** cena *f* en casa con invitados); **d. service** vajilla *f;* **d. time** *(midday meal)* hora *f* de comer; *(evening meal)* hora *f* de cenar

**dinosaur** ['daɪnəsɔ:(r)] *n also Fig* dinosaurio *m*

**dint** [dɪnt] *n* **by d. of...** a fuerza de...

**diocese** ['daɪəsɪs] *n Rel* diócesis *f inv*

**diode** ['daɪəʊd] *n Elec* diodo *m*

**dioxide** [daɪ'ɒksaɪd] *n Chem* dióxido *m*

**dip** [dɪp] **1** *n* (**a**) *(in road)* bajada *f*, pendiente *f;* *(in prices)* caída *f*, descenso *m* (**b**) *Fam (swim)* chapuzón *m*, baño *m;* **to go for a d.** ir a darse un chapuzón (**c**) *(sauce)* salsa *f* fría *(para mojar aperitivos)*
**2** *vt (pt & pp dipped)* (**a**) *(immerse)* meter **(in(to)** en); *(food)* mojar **(in(to)** en) (**b**) *(lower)* bajar; *Br* **to d. one's headlights** poner las luces de cruce
**3** *vi (of road)* bajar, descender un poco; *(of*

*prices*) caer, descender; **the sun dipped below the horizon** el sol se hundió en el horizonte

►**dip into** *vt insep (savings, capital)* recurrir a, echar mano de; *(book, subject)* echar un vistazo a

**DipEd** ['dɪp'ed] *n Br Educ (abbr* **Diploma in Education**) = diploma de capacitación para la enseñanza, ≃ C.A.P. *m*

**diphtheria** [dɪf'θɪərɪə] *n Med* difteria *f*

**diphthong** ['dɪfθɒŋ] *n Ling* diptongo *m*

**diploma** [dɪ'pləʊmə] *n* diploma *m*, título *m*

**diplomacy** [dɪ'pləʊməsɪ] *n also Fig* diplomacia *f*

**diplomat** ['dɪpləmæt] *n* diplomático(a) *m,f*

**diplomatic** [dɪplə'mætɪk] *adj also Fig* diplomático(a); **d. bag** valija *f* diplomática; **d. corps** cuerpo *m* diplomático; **d. immunity** inmunidad *f* diplomática

**dipper** ['dɪpə(r)] *n* (a) *US (ladle)* cucharón *m*, cazo *m* (b) **the Big D.** *(constellation)* la Osa Mayor; **big d.** *(rollercoaster)* montaña *f* rusa

**dipsomania** [dɪpsə'meɪnɪə] *n* dipsomanía *f*

**dipsomaniac** [dɪpsə'meɪnɪæk] *n* dipsómano(a) *m,f*, dipsomaníaco(a) *m,f*

**dipstick** ['dɪpstɪk] *n* (a) *Aut* varilla *f* del aceite (b) *Fam (idiot)* idiota *mf*, imbécil *mf*

**dire** ['daɪə(r)] *adj (consequences)* terrible; *Fam (bad)* chungo(a); **to be in d. need of sth** tener una necesidad acuciante de algo; **to be in d. straits** estar en un serio apuro

**direct** [dɪ'rekt, daɪ'rekt] **1** *adj* directo(a); **the d. opposite** justamente lo contrario; **to be a d. descendant of sb** ser descendiente directo(a) de alguien; **to score a d. hit** dar en el blanco, hacer diana; *Elec* **d. current** corriente *f* continua; *Fin* **d. debit** domiciliación *f* bancaria *or* de pago; *Com* **d. mail** propaganda *f* por correo, correo *m* directo; *Pol* **d. rule** gobierno *m* directo; *Com* **d. selling** venta *f* directa; *Gram* **d. speech** estilo *m* directo; *Fin* **d. taxation** impuestos *mpl* directos

**2** *adv (travel, write)* directamente; *(broadcast)* en directo

**3** *vt* (a) *(remark, gaze, effort)* dirigir (**at** a); **can you d. me to the station?** ¿podría indicarme cómo llegar a la estación? (b) *(company, traffic, film)* dirigir (c) *(instruct)* **to d. sb to do sth** mandar *or* indicar a alguien que haga algo; **as directed** según las instrucciones

**direction** [dɪ'rekʃən] *n* (a) *(way)* dirección *f*; **in the d. of…** en dirección a…; **in every d., in all directions** en todas direcciones; *Fig* **a step in the right d.** un paso hacia el buen camino *or* en la dirección correcta (b) *(of film, play, project)* dirección *f*; **under the d. of…** dirigido(a) por… (c) **directions** *(to place)* indicaciones *fpl*; **he asked me for directions to the station** me preguntó cómo se llegaba a la estación

**directive** [dɪ'rektɪv] *n* directiva *f*; **an EU d.** una directiva de la UE

**directly** [dɪ'rektlɪ, daɪ'rektlɪ] **1** *adv* (a) *(to go, write)* directamente; **to be d. descended from sb** ser descendiente directo(a) de alguien (b) *(opposite, above)* justo, directamente (c) *(frankly) (to answer, speak)* directamente, abiertamente (d) *(soon)* pronto, en breve; **I'm coming d.** voy ahora mismo

**2** *conj* **I'll come d. I've finished** vendré en cuanto acabe

**director** [dɪ'rektə(r)] *n* *(of company, film)* director(ora) *m,f*; *Law* **d. of public prosecutions** ≃ Fiscal *mf* General del Estado

**directorate** [dɪ'rektər(e)ɪt] *n* *(post)* dirección *f*; *(board)* consejo *m* de administración

**directorship** [dɪ'rektəʃɪp] *n* dirección *f*, puesto *m* de director(ora)

**directory** [dɪ'rektərɪ] *n* *(of phone numbers)* guía *f* (telefónica), listín *m* (de teléfonos); *Comptr* directorio *m*; **(street) d.** callejero *m*

**dirge** [dɜːdʒ] *n Fam (depressing tune)* = canción *f* sombría y aburrida

**dirt** [dɜːt] *n* (a) *(mud, dust)* suciedad *f*; **to treat sb like d.** tratar a alguien como a un trapo; **dog d.** excremento *m* de perro; **d. road** pista *f* de tierra (b) *Fam (scandal)* **to dig for d. on sb** buscar material comprometedor acerca de alguien

**dirt-cheap** ['dɜːt'tʃiːp] *Fam adj & adv* tirado(a) de precio

**dirty** ['dɜːtɪ] **1** *adj* (a) *(unclean)* sucio(a); **to get d.** ensuciarse, mancharse; *also Fig* **to get one's hands d.** mancharse las manos; *Fig* **the party is washing its d. linen in public** el partido está sacando sus propios trapos sucios a la luz pública

(b) *Fig (unprincipled, ruthless)* sucio(a); **it's a d. business** es un asunto sucio; **to give sb a d. look** fulminar a alguien con la mirada; *also Fig* **d. work** trabajo *m* sucio

(c) *(obscene) (film)* pornográfico(a); *(book, language)* obsceno(a), lascivo(a); **to have a d. mind** tener una mente calenturienta; **d. joke** chiste *m* verde; **d. old man** viejo *m* verde; **d. weekend** fin *m* de semana de lujuria; **d. word** palabrota *f*

**2** *adv* (a) *(fight, play)* sucio

(b) *(obscenely)* **to talk d.** decir obscenidades

(c) *Fam (for emphasis)* **a d. big hole** un pedazo de agujero

**3** *vt* ensuciar, manchar

**4** *vt Br Fam* **to do the d. on sb** jugársela a alguien

**disability** [dɪsə'bɪlɪtɪ] *n* discapacidad *f*, minusvalía *f*; **d. allowance** subsidio *m* por discapacidad *or* minusvalía

**disable** [dɪ'seɪbəl] *vt (person)* discapacitar, incapacitar; *(tank, ship)* inutilizar; *(alarm system)* desactivar

**disabled** [dɪ'seɪbəld] **1** *adj* discapacitado(a), minusválido(a); **d. toilet** servicio *m* para minusválidos

**2** *npl* **the d.** los discapacitados *or* minusválidos

**disabuse** [dɪsə'bju:z] *vt Formal* desengañar *(of* de*)*

**disadvantage** [dɪsəd'vɑ:ntɪdʒ] **1** *n* desventaja *f*, inconveniente *m*; **to be at a d.** estar en desventaja; **to put sb at a d.** poner a alguien en desventaja

**2** *vt* perjudicar

**disadvantaged** [dɪsəd'vɑ:ntɪdʒd] *adj* desfavorecido(a)

**disaffected** [dɪsə'fektɪd] *adj* descontento(a)

**disaffection** [dɪsə'fekʃən] *n* descontento *m*, desapego *m*

**disagree** [dɪsə'gri:] *vi* **(a)** *(quarrel)* no estar de acuerdo; **to d. with sb** no estar de acuerdo con alguien **(b)** *(not correspond) (of reports, figures)* no cuadrar, no coincidir **(c)** *(of climate, food)* **to d. with sb** sentarle mal a alguien

**disagreeable** [dɪsə'gri:əbəl] *adj* desagradable

**disagreement** [dɪsə'gri:mənt] *n* **(a)** *(failure to agree)* desacuerdo *m*; **to be in d. with sb** estar en desacuerdo con alguien **(b)** *(quarrel)* discusión *f*; **to have a d. with sb** discutir con alguien **(c)** *(discrepancy)* discrepancia *f*

**disallow** [dɪsə'laʊ] *vt Formal (objection)* rechazar; *(goal)* anular

**disappear** [dɪsə'pɪə(r)] *vi* desaparecer

**disappearance** [dɪsə'pɪərəns] *n* desaparición *f*

**disappoint** [dɪsə'pɔɪnt] *vt (person)* decepcionar, desilusionar; *(hope, ambition)* frustrar, dar al traste con

**disappointed** [dɪsə'pɔɪntɪd] *adj (person)* decepcionado(a), desilusionado(a); *(hope, ambition)* frustrado(a); **to be d.** *(of person)* estar decepcionado(a) *or* desilusionado(a) **she was d. with the book** el libro le decepcionó

**disappointing** [dɪsə'pɔɪntɪŋ] *adj* decepcionante

**disappointment** [dɪsə'pɔɪntmənt] *n* decepción *f*, desilusión *f*; **to be a d.** *(of person, film)* ser decepcionante

**disapproval** [dɪsə'pru:vəl] *n* desaprobación *f*

**disapprove** [dɪsə'pru:v] *vi* estar en contra, mostrar desaprobación; **to d. of sth** desaprobar algo

**disapproving** [dɪsə'pru:vɪŋ] *adj (tone, look)* desaprobatorio(a); **to be d. of sth** desaprobar algo

**disarm** [dɪs'ɑ:m] **1** *vt also Fig* desarmar

**2** *vi* desarmarse

**disarmament** [dɪs'ɑ:məmənt] *n* desarme *m*; **d. talks** conversaciones *fpl* para el desarme

**disarming** [dɪs'ɑ:mɪŋ] *adj (smile)* arrebatador(ora)

**disarray** [dɪsə'reɪ] *n* desorden *m*; **in d.** *(untidy)* en desorden; *(confused)* sumido(a) en el caos

**disaster** [dɪ'zɑ:stə(r)] *n* desastre *m*, catástrofe *f*; **d. area** zona *f* catastrófica; *Cin* **d. movie** película *f* de catástrofes

**disastrous** [dɪ'zɑ:strəs] *adj* desastroso(a), catastrófico(a)

**disband** [dɪs'bænd] **1** *vt* disolver

**2** *vi* disolverse

**disbelief** [dɪsbɪ'li:f] *n* incredulidad *f*; **in d.** con incredulidad

**disbelieve** [dɪsbɪ'li:v] *vt* no creer, dudar de (ora)

**disburse** [dɪs'bɜ:s] *vt Formal* desembolsar

**disbursement** [dɪs'bɜ:smənt] *n Formal* desembolso *m*

**disc** [dɪsk] *n* disco *m*; **d. jockey** pinchadiscos *mf inv*

**discard** [dɪs'kɑ:d] *vt (thing, person)* desechar; *(plan, proposal, possibility)* descartar

**discern** [dɪ'sɜ:n] *vt* distinguir, apreciar

**discernible** [dɪ'sɜ:nɪbəl] *adj* perceptible; **there is no d. difference** no hay una diferencia apreciable

**discerning** [dɪ'sɜ:nɪŋ] *adj (audience, customer)* entendido(a); *(taste)* cultivado(a)

**discharge 1** *n* ['dɪstʃɑ:dʒ] **(a)** *(of patient)* alta *f*, *(of prisoner)* puesta *f* en libertad; *(of soldier)* licencia *f* **(b)** *(of firearm)* descarga *f*, disparo *m* **(c)** *(of gas, chemical)* emisión *f*, *(of pus, fluid)* supuración *f*

**2** *vt* [dɪs'tʃɑ:dʒ] **(a)** *(patient)* dar el alta a; *(prisoner)* poner en libertad; *(employee)* despedir; *(soldier)* licenciar **(b)** *(firearm)* descargar, disparar **(c)** *(gas, chemical)* emitir; *(pus, fluid)* supurar **(d)** *(duty)* cumplir; *(debt)* saldar; *(fine)* abonar

**disciple** [dɪ'saɪpəl] *n* discípulo(a) *m,f*

**disciplinary** ['dɪsɪplɪnərɪ] *adj* disciplinario(a); **to take d. action against sb** abrirle a alguien un expediente disciplinario

**discipline** ['dɪsɪplɪn] **1** *n (control, academic subject)* disciplina *f*; **to keep** *or* **maintain d.** guardar la disciplina

**2** *vt (punish)* castigar; *(train)* disciplinar; **to d. oneself** disciplinarse

**disclaim** [dɪs'kleɪm] *vt (renounce)* renunciar a; *(deny)* negar

**disclaimer** [dɪs'kleɪmə(r)] *n* negación *f* de responsabilidad; **to issue a d.** hacer público un comunicado negando toda responsabilidad

**disclose** [dɪs'kləʊz] *vt* revelar

**disclosure** [dɪs'kləʊʒə(r)] *n* revelación *f*

**disco** ['dɪskəʊ] ( *pl* **discos**) *n* discoteca *f*

**discolour,** *US* **discolor** [dɪs'kʌlə(r)] *vt* *(fade)* decolorar; *(stain)* teñir, manchar

**discomfiture** [dɪs'kʌmfɪtʃə(r)] *n Formal* turbación *f*, desconcierto *m*

**discomfort** [dɪs'kʌmfət] *n (lack of comfort)* incomodidad *f*; *(pain)* molestia *f*, dolor *m*; **to be in d.** sufrir, pasarlo mal

**disconcerting** [dɪskən'sɜːtɪŋ] *adj (causing confusion, embarrassment)* desconcertante; *(causing anxiety)* preocupante

**disconnect** [dɪskə'nekt] *vt (gas, electricity, phone)* cortar, desconectar; *(machine, appliance)* desenchufar, desconectar; **we've been disconnected** nos han cortado el gas/la electricidad/el teléfono

**disconsolate** [dɪs'kɒnsələt] *adj* desconsolado(a) **(at** por); **to be d. (at)** estar desconsolado(a) (por)

**discontent** [dɪskən'tent] *n* descontento *m*

**discontented** [dɪskən'tentɪd] *adj* descontento(a); **to be d.** estar descontento(a)

**discontinue** [dɪskən'tɪnjuː] *vt* suspender, interrumpir; *Com* **discontinued line** restos *mpl* de serie

**discord** ['dɪskɔːd] *n* discordia *f*

**discordant** [dɪs'kɔːdənt] *adj (opinions, sound)* discordante, discorde

**discotheque** ['dɪskətek] *n* discoteca *f*

**discount** **1** *n* ['dɪskaʊnt] descuento *m*, rebaja *f*; **at a d.** con descuento
**2** *vt* **(a)** *(price, goods)* rebajar **(b)** [dɪs'kaʊnt] *(suggestion, possibility)* descartar

**discourage** [dɪs'kʌrɪdʒ] *vt* **(a)** *(dishearten)* desalentar, desanimar **(b)** *(dissuade)* **to d. sb from doing sth** tratar de disuadir a alguien de que haga algo

**discouragement** [dɪs'kʌrɪdʒmənt] *n* **(a)** *(loss of enthusiasm)* desaliento *m*, desánimo *m* **(b)** *(dissuasion)* intento *m* de disuasión

**discouraging** [dɪs'kʌrɪdʒɪŋ] *adj* desalentador(ora)

**discourse** ['dɪskɔːs] *Formal* **1** *n* discurso *m*
**2** *vi* **to d. (up)on a subject** disertar sobre un tema

**discourteous** [dɪs'kɜːtɪəs] *adj* descortés

**discourtesy** [dɪs'kɜːtəsɪ] *n* descortesía *f*

**discover** [dɪs'kʌvə(r)] *vt* descubrir

**discovery** [dɪs'kʌvərɪ] *n* descubrimiento *m*; **to make a d.** realizar un descubrimiento

**discredit** [dɪs'kredɪt] **1** *n* descrédito *m*; **to be a d. to sth/sb** desacreditar algo/a alguien
**2** *vt* desacreditar

**discreet** [dɪs'kriːt] *adj* discreto(a)

**discrepancy** [dɪs'krepənsɪ] *n* discrepancia *f* **(between** entre)

**discretion** [dɪs'kreʃən] *n (tact)* discreción *f*; *(judgement)* criterio *m*; **at your d.** a discreción, a voluntad

**discretionary** [dɪs'kreʃənərɪ] *adj* discrecional

**discriminate** [dɪs'krɪmɪneɪt] **1** *vt* discriminar, distinguir **(from** de)
**2** *vi* **to d. between** discriminar *or* distinguir entre; **to d. against sb** discriminar a alguien; **to d. in favour of** discriminar a favor de

**discriminating** [dɪs'krɪmɪneɪtɪŋ] *adj (audience, customer)* entendido(a); *(taste)* cultivado(a)

**discrimination** [dɪskrɪmɪ'neɪʃən] *n* **(a)** *(bias)* discriminación *f*; **racial/sexual/religious d.** discriminación racial/sexual/religiosa **(b)** *(taste)* buen gusto *m*, refinamiento *m* **(c)** *(differentiation)* distinción *f*, diferenciación *f*

**discriminatory** [dɪs'krɪmɪnətərɪ] *adj* discriminatorio(a)

**discursive** [dɪs'kɜːsɪv] *adj* dilatado(a), con muchas digresiones *o* divagaciones

**discus** ['dɪskəs] *n* disco *m (para lanzamientos)*

**discuss** [dɪs'kʌs] *vt* discutir

**discussion** [dɪs'kʌʃən] *n* discusión *f*; **the matter is under d.** el asunto está siendo discutido

**disdain** [dɪs'deɪn] **1** *n* desdén *m*, desprecio *m*
**2** *vt* desdeñar, despreciar; **to d. to do sth** no dignarse a hacer algo

**disdainful** [dɪs'deɪnful] *adj* desdeñoso(a)

**disease** [dɪ'ziːz] *n* enfermedad *f*

**diseased** [dɪ'ziːzd] *adj (plant, limb)* enfermo(a); **to be d.** estar afectado(a) por una enfermedad

**disembark** [dɪsem'bɑːk] *vt & vi* desembarcar

**disembodied** [dɪsɪm'bɒdɪd] *adj (voice, presence)* inmaterial, incorpóreo(a)

**disenchanted** [dɪsɪn'tʃɑːntɪd] *adj* desencantado(a); **to be d.** estar desencantado(a)

**disenchantment** [dɪsɪn'tʃɑːntmənt] *n* desencanto *m*

**disengage** [dɪsɪn'geɪdʒ] **1** *vt (separate)* soltar; *(gear)* quitar; *(clutch)* soltar; *(embrace, grip)* **to d. oneself from sth** desasirse de algo
**2** *vi* desasirse, soltarse **(from** de); *Mil* retirarse

**disentangle** [dɪsɪn'tæŋgəl] *vt* desenredar

**disfavour** [dɪs'feɪvə(r)] *n* **to be in d.** no ser visto(a) con buenos ojos; **to fall into d.** caer en desgracia

**disfigure** [dɪs'fɪgə(r)] *vt* desfigurar

**disfigurement** [dɪs'fɪgəmənt] *n* desfiguración *f*

**disgorge** [dɪs'gɔːdʒ] *vt (people)* derramar; *(information)* desembuchar

**disgrace** [dɪs'greɪs] **1** *n (shame)* vergüenza *f*; **it's a d.!** ¡es una vergüenza *or* un escándalo!; **he**

**is in d. with the party** el partido está muy disgustado con él; **to resign in d.** dimitir a causa de un escándalo; **he is a d. to his family/country** es una vergüenza or deshonra para su familia/país

**2** vt (person) avergonzar; (family, country) deshonrar

**disgraceful** [dɪsˈgreɪsfʊl] adj vergonzoso(a), indignante; **it's d.!** ¡es una vergüenza!

**disgracefully** [dɪsˈgreɪsfʊlɪ] adv vergonzosamente; **she was d. late** fue vergonzoso lo tarde que llegó

**disgruntled** [dɪsˈgrʌntəld] adj contrariado(a), descontento(a); **to be d.** estar contrariado(a) or descontento(a)

**disguise** [dɪsˈgaɪz] **1** n (costume) disfraz m; **in d.** disfrazado(a)

**2** vt (person) disfrazar (**as** de); (one's feelings, the truth) ocultar, disfrazar; **there is no disguising the fact that...** no se puede ocultar el hecho de que...

**disgust** [dɪsˈgʌst] **1** n asco m, repugnancia f; **to fill sb with d.** dar asco a alguien

**2** vt repugnar

**disgusting** [dɪsˈgʌstɪŋ] adj (revolting) asqueroso(a), repugnante; (disgraceful) vergonzoso(a)

**dish** [dɪʃ] **1** n (bowl) (for serving) fuente f; (for cooking) cazuela f; (food) plato m; **dishes** (crockery) platos mpl; **to do the dishes** lavar los platos, fregar los cacharros

**2** vt Fam **to d. the dirt (on sb)** andar pregonando los trapos sucios (de alguien)

▸**dish out** vt sep (food, money, advice) repartir

▸**dish up** vt sep (meal) servir

**disharmony** [dɪsˈhɑːmənɪ] n discordia f

**dishcloth** [ˈdɪʃklɒθ] n (for washing) bayeta f; (for drying) paño m (de cocina)

**disheartening** [dɪsˈhɑːtənɪŋ] adj descorazonador(ora)

**dishevelled** [dɪˈʃevəld] adj (person, appearance) desaliñado(a); **to be d.** estar desaliñado(a)

**dishonest** [dɪsˈɒnɪst] adj deshonesto(a), poco honrado(a)

**dishonesty** [dɪsˈɒnɪstɪ] n deshonestidad f, falta f de honradez

**dishonour,** US **dishonor** [dɪsˈɒnə(r)] **1** n deshonra f

**2** vt deshonrar

**dishonourable,** US **dishonorable** [dɪsˈɒnərəbəl] adj deshonroso(a)

**dishtowel** [ˈdɪʃtaʊəl] n paño m (de cocina)

**dishwasher** [ˈdɪʃwɒʃə(r)] n (person) lavaplatos mf inv, friegaplatos mf inv; (machine) lavavajillas m inv

**dishwater** [ˈdɪʃwɒtə(r)] n agua f de fregar (los platos), Fig **this coffee is like d.!** ¡este café es puro aguachirle!

**dishy** [ˈdɪʃɪ] adj Br Fam (good-looking) majo(a), de buen ver

**disillusioned** [dɪsɪˈluːʒənd] adj desencantado(a), desilusionado(a); **to be d. (with sb/ sth)** estar desencantado(a) (con alguien/algo)

**disincentive** [dɪsɪnˈsentɪv] n traba f; **it acts as a d. to creativity** constituye una traba para la creatividad

**disinclination** [dɪsɪnklɪˈneɪʃən] n falta f de interés (**to do sth** en hacer algo)

**disinclined** [dɪsɪnˈklaɪnd] adj **to be d. to do sth** no tener ganas de or interés por hacer algo

**disinfect** [dɪsɪnˈfekt] vt desinfectar

**disinfectant** [dɪsɪnˈfektənt] n desinfectante m

**disinformation** [dɪsɪnfəˈmeɪʃən] n desinformación f

**disingenuous** [dɪsɪnˈdʒenjʊəs] adj falso(a), poco sincero(a)

**disinherit** [dɪsɪnˈherɪt] vt desheredar

**disintegrate** [dɪsˈɪntɪgreɪt] vi desintegrarse

**disintegration** [dɪsɪntɪˈgreɪʃən] n desintegración f

**disinterest** [dɪsˈɪntərɪst] n (lack of interest) desinterés m

**disinterested** [dɪsˈɪntərɪstɪd] adj (**a**) (unbiased) desinteresado(a) (**b**) (uninterested) **he was d. in the film** no le interesaba la película

**disinvestment** [dɪsɪnˈvestmənt] n Fin desinversión f

**disjointed** [dɪsˈdʒɔɪntɪd] adj (novel, description) deshilvanado(a)

**disk** [dɪsk] n Comptr disco m; **d. drive** unidad f de disco, disquetera f

**diskette** [dɪsˈket] n Comptr disquete m

**dislike** [dɪsˈlaɪk] **1** n (of things) aversión f (**of** por); (of people) antipatía f (**of** hacia); **my likes and dislikes** las cosas que me gustan y las que me disgustan

**2** vt **I d. him/it** no me gusta; **I don't d. him/ it** no me disgusta; **I d. them** no me gustan; **I don't d. them** no me disgustan

**dislocate** [ˈdɪsləkeɪt] vt (**a**) (shoulder, hip) dislocar; **to d. one's shoulder** dislocarse el hombro (**b**) (plan, timetable) trastocar

**dislocation** [dɪsləˈkeɪʃən] n (**a**) (of shoulder, hip) dislocación f (**b**) (of plan) desbaratamiento m

**dislodge** [dɪsˈlɒdʒ] vt (opponent) desplazar, desalojar; (brick, tile) soltar; (something stuck) sacar

**disloyal** [dɪsˈlɔɪəl] adj desleal

**disloyalty** [dɪsˈlɔɪəltɪ] n deslealtad f

**dismal** [ˈdɪzməl] adj (**a**) (place) sombrío(a), tétrico(a); (weather) muy triste; (future) oscuro(a) (**b**) (failure) horroroso(a); (performance) nefasto(a), fatal

**dismantle** [dɪsˈmæntəl] *vt* desmantelar

**dismay** [dɪsˈmeɪ] **1** *n* consternación *f*; **in d.** con consternación; **(much) to my d.** para mi consternación
  **2** *vt* consternar

**dismember** [dɪsˈmembə(r)] *vt (body)* descuartizar; *(country, company)* desmembrar

**dismiss** [dɪsˈmɪs] *vt* **(a)** *(from job)* despedir **(b)** *(send away)* **to d. sb** dar a alguien permiso para retirarse; *Mil* **d.!** ¡rompan filas! **(c)** *(thought, theory)* descartar; *(proposal, suggestion)* rechazar; *(threat, danger)* no hacer caso de; *Law (case)* sobreseer; *(appeal)* desestimar; **the suggestion was dismissed as being irrelevant** la sugerencia fue rechazada por no venir al caso

**dismissal** [dɪsˈmɪsəl] *n (of employee)* despido *m*; *Law (of case)* sobreseimiento *m*; *(of appeal)* desestimación *f*

**dismissive** [dɪsˈmɪsɪv] *adj* desdeñoso(a), despectivo(a) **(of** hacia *or* respecto a a**); he was very d. of my chances** se mostró escéptico en cuanto a mis posibilidades

**dismount** [dɪsˈmaʊnt] *vi (from horse, bicycle)* desmontar, bajarse **(from** de**)**

**disobedience** [dɪsəˈbiːdɪəns] *n* desobediencia *f*

**disobedient** [dɪsəˈbiːdɪənt] *adj* desobediente

**disobey** [dɪsəˈbeɪ] *vt* desobedecer

**disorder** [dɪsˈɔːdə(r)] *n* **(a)** *(confusion, unrest)* desorden *m*; **in d.** en desorden **(b)** *Med* dolencia *f*; **nervous d.** dolencia *f* nerviosa; **personality d.** trastorno *m* de la personalidad

**disordered** [dɪsˈɔːdəd] *adj (room, mind)* desordenado(a)

**disorderly** [dɪsˈɔːdəlɪ] *adj* **(a)** *(untidy)* desordenado(a) **(b)** *(unruly)* revoltoso(a); *Law* **d. conduct** escándalo *m* público; *Law* **d. house** casa *f* de prostitución

**disorganization** [dɪsɔːɡənaɪˈzeɪʃən] *n* desorganización *f*

**disorganized** [dɪsˈɔːɡənaɪzd] *adj* desorganizado(a)

**disorientate** [dɪsˈɔːrɪənteɪt], **disorient** [dɪsˈɔːrɪənt] *vt* desorientar

**disown** [dɪsˈəʊn] *vt (wife, child)* repudiar; *(country, earlier works)* renegar de; *(statement)* no reconocer como propio(a)

**disparage** [dɪsˈpærɪdʒ] *vt* desdeñar, menospreciar

**disparaging** [dɪsˈpærɪdʒɪŋ] *adj* desdeñoso(a), menospreciativo(a)

**disparate** [ˈdɪspərɪt] *adj* dispar

**disparity** [dɪsˈpærɪtɪ] *n* disparidad *f*

**dispassionate** [dɪsˈpæʃənɪt] *adj* desapasionado(a)

**dispatch** [dɪsˈpætʃ] **1** *n* **(a)** *(of letter, parcel)* envío *m* **(b)** *(message)* despacho *m*; *Mil* **he was**

**mentioned in dispatches** aparecía mencionado en partes de guerra; *Mil* **d. rider** mensajero(a) *m,f* motorizado(a) **(c)** *Formal (promptness)* **with d.** con celeridad *or* prontitud
  **2** *vt* **(a)** *(send)* enviar, mandar **(b)** *(kill)* dar muerte a

**dispel** [dɪsˈpel] *(pt & pp* **dispelled)** *vt (doubt, fear)* disipar

**dispensable** [dɪsˈpensəbəl] *adj* prescindible

**dispensary** [dɪsˈpensərɪ] *n Med* dispensario *m*, botiquín *m*

**dispensation** [dɪspenˈseɪʃən] *n Law Rel (exemption)* dispensa *f* **(from** de**)**

**dispense** [dɪsˈpens] *vt (justice, medication, prescription)* administrar; *(advice)* repartir; *(of vending machine)* expedir

▶**dispense with** *vt insep* prescindir de

**dispensing chemist** [dɪsˈpensɪŋˈkemɪst] *n* farmacéutico(a) *m,f*

**dispersal** [dɪsˈpɜːsəl] *n* dispersión *f*

**disperse** [dɪsˈpɜːs] **1** *vt (seeds, people)* dispersar; *(knowledge, information)* difundir
  **2** *vt (of crowd)* dispersarse; *(of darkness, clouds)* disiparse

**dispirited** [dɪsˈpɪrɪtɪd] *adj* desanimado(a), desalentado(a); **to be d.** estar desanimado(a) *or* desalentado(a)

**displace** [dɪsˈpleɪs] *vt* **(a)** *(shift)* desplazar; **displaced persons** desplazados *mpl* **(b)** *(supplant)* sustituir

**displacement** [dɪsˈpleɪsmənt] *n* **(a)** *(of water, people, ship)* desplazamiento *m* **(b)** *(substitution)* **d. (of A by B)** sustitución *f* (de A por B)

**display** [dɪsˈpleɪ] *(pl* **displays) 1** *n* **(a)** *(of goods)* muestra *f*; *(of handicrafts, paintings)* exposición *f*; **on d.** expuesto(a); **d. cabinet** vitrina *f*; **d. copy** *(of book)* ejemplar *m* de muestra; **d. window** escaparate *m* **(b)** *(of emotion, technique)* demostración *f*; *(of sport)* exhibición *f*; **a fireworks d.** un festival *or* castillo de fuegos artificiales **(c)** *Comptr* pantalla *f*
  **2** *vt* **(a)** *(goods)* disponer; *(on sign, screen)* mostrar **(b)** *(emotion, talent, ignorance)* demostrar, mostrar

**displease** [dɪsˈpliːz] *vt* disgustar, desagradar; **to be displeased with sb/sth** estar disgustado(a) con alguien/algo

**displeasure** [dɪsˈpleʒə(r)] *n* disgusto *m*, desagrado *m*; **to incur sb's d.** provocar el enojo de alguien

**disposable** [dɪsˈpəʊzəbəl] *adj (towel, lighter)* desechable; *(funds)* disponible; **d. income** poder *m* adquisitivo

**disposal** [dɪsˈpəʊzəl] *n* **(a)** *(of rubbish)* eliminación *f* **(b)** *(of property)* venta *f* **(c)** *(availability)* **to have sth at one's d.** disponer de algo

**dispose** [dɪsˈpəʊz] *vt (arrange)* disponer

▶**dispose of** vt insep (a) (get rid of) (rubbish) eliminar; (problem) acabar con (b) (kill) dar muerte a

**disposed** [dɪs'pəʊzd] adj (willing) **to be d. to do sth** estar dispuesto(a) a hacer algo

**disposition** [dɪspə'zɪʃən] n (a) (temperament) carácter m (b) (inclination) **to have a d. to do sth** tener tendencia a hacer algo (c) Formal (arrangement) disposición f

**dispossess** [dɪspə'zes] vt desposeer (**of** de)

**disproportionate** [dɪsprə'pɔ:ʃənət] adj desproporcionado(a)

**disprove** [dɪs'pru:v] (pp **disproved**, Law **disproven** [dɪs'prəʊvən]) vt refutar

**dispute** [dɪs'pju:t] **1** n (debate) discusión f, debate m; (argument) pelea f, disputa f; **the matter in d.** la cuestión debatida; **it's beyond d.** es indiscutible; **it's open to d.** es cuestionable; **(industrial) d.** conflicto m laboral
**2** vt (subject, claim) debatir, discutir; **I'm not disputing that** eso no lo discuto
**3** vi discutir (**about** or **over** sobre)

**disqualification** [dɪskwɒlɪfɪ'keɪʃən] n (from competition) descalificación f; Law **a year's d. from driving** un año de suspensión del permiso de conducir

**disqualify** [dɪs'kwɒlɪfaɪ] vt (from competition) descalificar; **to d. sb from doing sth** incapacitar a alguien para hacer algo; Law **to d. sb from driving** retirar a alguien el permiso de conducir

**disquiet** [dɪs'kwaɪət] n inquietud f, desasosiego m

**disregard** [dɪsrɪ'gɑ:d] **1** n indiferencia f, menosprecio m
**2** vt (warning, fact) no tener en cuenta; (order) desacatar

**disrepair** [dɪsrɪ'peə(r)] n **in (a state of) d.** deteriorado(a); **to fall into d.** deteriorarse

**disreputable** [dɪs'repjʊtəbəl] adj (person, behaviour) poco respetable; (neighbourhood, pub) de mala reputación

**disrepute** [dɪsrɪ'pju:t] n **to bring sth into d.** desprestigiar algo; **to fall into d.** ganar mala fama

**disrespect** [dɪsrɪ'spekt] n irreverencia f, falta f de respeto; **to treat sb with d.** tratar a alguien irrespetuosamente; **I meant no d.** no pretendía faltar al respeto

**disrespectful** [dɪsrɪ'spektfʊl] adj irrespetuoso(a)

**disrupt** [dɪs'rʌpt] vt (traffic) entorpecer, trastornar; (plan) trastornar, trastocar; (meeting) interrumpir, alterar el desarrollo de; (life, routine) alterar

**disruption** [dɪs'rʌpʃən] n (of traffic) entorpecimiento m, trastorno m; (of plan) desbarata-

miento m; (of meeting) interrupción f; (of life, routine) alteración f

**disruptive** [dɪs'rʌptɪv] adj **to be d.** ocasionar trastornos; **to have a d. influence on sb** tener una influencia perjudicial sobre alguien

**dissatisfaction** [dɪsætɪs'fækʃən] n insatisfacción f

**dissatisfied** [dɪ'sætɪsfaɪd] adj insatisfecho(a) (**with** con); **to be d. (with)** estar insatisfecho(a) (con)

**dissect** [dɪ'sekt] vt also Fig diseccionar

**dissemble** [dɪ'sembəl] Formal **1** vt ocultar, disimular
**2** vi disimular

**disseminate** [dɪ'semɪneɪt] **1** vt propagar, difundir
**2** vi propagarse, difundirse

**dissension** [dɪ'senʃən] n Formal disensión f, discordia f

**dissent** [dɪ'sent] **1** n discrepancia f, disconformidad f; **he was booked for d.** fue amonestado por protestar
**2** vi disentir (**from** de)

**dissenter** [dɪ'sentə(r)] n disidente mf

**dissenting** [dɪ'sentɪŋ] adj discrepante

**dissertation** [dɪsə'teɪʃən] n Univ tesina f

**disservice** [dɪs'sɜ:vɪs] n **to do sb a d.** perjudicar a alguien

**dissident** ['dɪsɪdənt] n & adj disidente mf

**dissimilar** [dɪ'sɪmɪlə(r)] adj distinto(a) (**to** de)

**dissipate** ['dɪsɪpeɪt] **1** vt (fears, doubts) disipar; (fortune, one's energy) derrochar
**2** vi (mist, doubts) disiparse

**dissipation** [dɪsɪ'peɪʃən] n (loose living) disipación f

**dissociate** [dɪ'səʊsɪeɪt] vt disociar; **to d. oneself from sb/sth** desmarcarse de alguien/algo

**dissolute** ['dɪsəlu:t] adj disoluto(a)

**dissolve** [dɪ'zɒlv] **1** vt disolver
**2** vi disolverse; **it dissolves in water** es soluble en agua; **to d. into tears** deshacerse en lágrimas

**dissuade** [dɪ'sweɪd] vt **to d. sb from doing sth** disuadir a alguien de hacer algo

**distance** ['dɪstəns] **1** n distancia f; **from a d.** desde lejos; **in the d.** en la lejanía; **at a d. of...** a una distancia de...; **within five minutes walking d.** a cinco minutos a pie; **a short d. away** bastante cerca; **some d. away** bastante lejos; **to keep sb at a d.** guardar las distancias con alguien; **to keep one's d.** mantener las distancias; **at this d. in time...** después de tanto tiempo...; **to go the d.** (in boxing) aguantar todos los asaltos; **d. learning** educación f a distancia

**2** *vt* **to d. oneself from sb/sth** distanciarse de alguien/algo

**distant** ['dɪstənt] *adj* (**a**) *(far-off)* distante, lejano(a); **3 kilometres d.** a 3 kilómetros de distancia; **a d. relative** un pariente lejano; **she had a d. look** tenía la mirada distante *or* perdida; **in the d. past** en el pasado lejano (**b**) *(reserved)* distante

**distantly** ['dɪstəntlɪ] *adv* (**a**) **d. related** lejanamente emparentado(a) (**b**) *(distractedly) (answer, smile)* distraídamente

**distaste** [dɪs'teɪst] *n* desagrado *m* (**for** por)
**distasteful** [dɪs'teɪstfʊl] *adj* desagradable
**distemper**[1] [dɪs'tempə(r)] *n (animal disease)* moquillo *m*
**distemper**[2] *n (paint)* (pintura *f* al) temple *m*
**distend** [dɪs'tend] **1** *vt* hinchar
**2** *vi* hincharse
**distil** [dɪs'tɪl] (*pt & pp* **distilled**) *vt* destilar
**distillery** [dɪs'tɪlərɪ] *n* destilería *f*
**distinct** [dɪs'tɪŋkt] *adj* (**a**) *(different)* distinto(a); **as d. from** a diferencia de (**b**) *(clear) (change, idea, preference)* claro(a) (**c**) *(real) (possibility, feeling)* claro(a)

**distinction** [dɪs'tɪŋkʃən] *n* (**a**) *(difference)* distinción *f*; **to draw a d. between** establecer una distinción entre (**b**) *(honour)* honor *m*; *Ironic* **I had the d. of coming last** me correspondió el honor de ser el último (**c**) *(excellence)* **a writer/scientist of d.** un escritor/científico destacado; **with d.** *(perform, serve)* de manera sobresaliente (**d**) *Sch Univ* sobresaliente *m*

**distinctive** [dɪs'tɪŋktɪv] *adj* característico(a)
**distinctly** [dɪs'tɪŋktlɪ] *adv* (**a**) *(clearly) (speak, hear)* claramente, con claridad; **I d. remember telling you** recuerdo con toda claridad habértelo dicho (**b**) *(decidedly) (better, easier)* claramente; *(stupid, ill-mannered)* verdaderamente

**distinguish** [dɪs'tɪŋgwɪʃ] **1** *vt* (**a**) *(recognize)* distinguir (**b**) *(characterize, differentiate)* distinguir (**from** de); **distinguishing mark** rasgo *m* físico característico (**c**) *(earn praise, honour)* **to d. oneself by...** distinguirse por...
**2** *vi* **to d. between** distinguir entre

**distinguished** [dɪs'tɪŋgwɪʃd] *adj (person, performance, career)* destacado(a); *(air)* distinguido(a)

**distort** [dɪs'tɔːt] *vt (shape)* deformar; *(sound)* distorsionar; *Fig (meaning, facts)* distorsionar, tergiversar

**distorted** [dɪs'tɔːtɪd] *adj (shape)* deformado(a); *(sound, guitar)* distorsionado(a); *Fig (account)* distorsionado(a), tergiversado(a)

**distortion** [dɪs'tɔːʃən] *n (of shape)* deformación *f*; *(of sound)* distorsión *f*; *Fig (of meaning, facts)* distorsión *f*, tergiversación *f*

**distract** [dɪs'trækt] *vt (person, attention)* distraer; **this is distracting us from our main purpose** esto nos está alejando de nuestro objetivo principal; **she is easily distracted** se distrae con facilidad

**distracted** [dɪs'træktɪd] *adj* abstraído(a), ausente; **to be d.** estar abstraído(a) *or* ausente
**distracting** [dɪs'træktɪŋ] *adj* **that noise is very d.** ese ruido distrae mucho

**distraction** [dɪs'trækʃən] *n* (**a**) *(distracting thing)* distracción *f*; **to drive sb to d.** sacar a alguien de quicio (**b**) *(amusement)* entretenimiento *m*, distracción *f*

**distraught** [dɪs'trɔːt] *adj* desconsolado(a), consternado(a); **to be d.** estar desconsolado(a) *or* consternado(a)

**distress** [dɪs'tres] **1** *n* sufrimiento *m*, angustia *f*; **to be in d.** estar sufriendo mucho; *(of ship)* estar en situación de peligro; **d. signal** señal *f* de socorro
**2** *vt (upset)* afligir, angustiar

**distressed** [dɪs'trest] *adj* angustiado(a), afligido(a) **to be d.** estar angustiado(a) *or* afligido(a)

**distressing** [dɪs'tresɪŋ] *adj* angustioso(a); *Fig (worrying)* preocupante

**distribute** [dɪs'trɪbjuːt] *vt* distribuir

**distribution** [dɪstrɪ'bjuːʃən] *n* distribución *f*; **d. of wealth** reparto *m* de la riqueza; *Com* **d. cost** coste *m* de distribución; *Com* **d. network** red *f* de distribución

**distributor** [dɪs'trɪbjʊtə(r)] *n* (**a**) *(person, company)* distribuidor(ora) *m,f* (**b**) *Aut* distribuidor *m*, delco® *m*

**district** ['dɪstrɪkt] *n (of country)* comarca *f*; *(of town, city)* barrio *m*; *US* **d. attorney** fiscal *mf* del distrito; *Br Formerly* **d. council** junta *f* municipal; **d. nurse** = enfermera que visita a los pacientes en sus casas

**distrust** [dɪs'trʌst] **1** *n* desconfianza *f*
**2** *vt* desconfiar de

**distrustful** [dɪs'trʌstfʊl] *adj* desconfiado(a); **to be d. of** desconfiar de

**disturb** [dɪs'tɜːb] *vt* (**a**) *(annoy, interrupt) (person)* molestar; *(sleep, concentration)* perturbar; *Law* **to d. the peace** alterar el orden público (**b**) *(worry)* preocupar (**c**) *(disarrange) (papers, room)* desordenar; *(water surface)* agitar

**disturbance** [dɪs'tɜːbəns] *n* (**a**) *(nuisance)* molestia *f* (**b**) *(atmospheric, emotional)* perturbación *f* (**c**) *(fight, riot)* disturbio *m*; **to cause** *or* **create a d.** provocar disturbios

**disturbed** [dɪs'tɜːbd] *adj (night, sleep)* agitado(a); *(mentally, emotionally)* trastornado(a), perturbado(a); **to be d.** *(mentally, emotionally)* estar trastornado(a) *or* perturbado(a)

**disturbing** [dɪs'tɜːbɪŋ] *adj (worrying)* preocupante

**disunity** [dɪs'juːnɪtɪ] *n* desunión *f*

**disuse** [dɪs'juːs] *n* **to fall into d.** caer en desuso

**ditch** [dɪtʃ] **1** *n* zanja *f*; *(at roadside)* cuneta *f*; *(as defence)* foso *m*

**2** *vt Fam (get rid of) (car, useless object)* deshacerse de; *(girlfriend, boyfriend)* plantar; *(plan, idea)* descartar

**dither** ['dɪðə(r)] *Fam* **1** *n* **to be all of a d., to be in a d.** aturullarse

**2** *vi* vacilar, estar hecho(a) un lío

**ditto** ['dɪtəʊ] *adv* ídem; *Fam* **I'm hungry – d.** tengo hambre – ídem (de ídem)

**ditty** ['dɪtɪ] *n Fam* tonadilla *f*

**diuretic** [daɪjʊ'retɪk] *n & adj* diurético(a)

**divan** [dɪ'væn] *n* diván *m*; **d. bed** cama *f* turca

**dive** [daɪv] **1** *n* **(a)** *(from poolside, diving board)* salto *m* de cabeza; *(of deep-sea diver, submarine)* inmersión *f* **(b)** *Fam Pej (place)* antro *m*

**2** *vi* (*pt US* **dove** [dəʊv]) *(from poolside, diving board)* tirarse de cabeza; *(of scuba-diver)* bucear; *(of deep-sea diver, submarine)* sumergirse; *(of aircraft)* lanzarse en picado; **to d. for cover** ponerse a cubierto

**diver** ['daɪvə(r)] *n (from diving board)* saltador(ora) *m,f*; *(with scuba apparatus)* submarinista *mf*, buzo *m*; *(deep sea)* buzo *m*

**diverge** [daɪ'vɜːdʒ] *vi (of rays)* divergir; *(of roads)* bifurcarse; *(of opinions, persons)* discrepar, divergir

**divergence** [daɪ'vɜːdʒəns] *n* divergencia *f*

**divergent** [daɪ'vɜːdʒənt], **diverging** [daɪ-'vɜːdʒɪŋ] *adj* divergente, discrepante

**diverse** [daɪ'vɜːs] *adj* diverso(a)

**diversification** [daɪvɜːsɪfɪ'keɪʃən] *n Com* diversificación *f*

**diversify** [daɪ'vɜːsɪfaɪ] **1** *vt* diversificar

**2** *vi (of company)* diversificarse

**diversion** [daɪ'vɜːʃən] *n* **(a)** *(of traffic, funds)* desvío *m*; **to create a d.** distraer la atención **(b)** *(amusement)* distracción *f*

**diversity** [daɪ'vɜːsɪtɪ] *n* diversidad *f*

**divert** [daɪ'vɜːt, dɪ'vɜːt] *vt* **(a)** *(traffic, river, attention)* desviar **(b)** *(amuse)* **to d. oneself** distraerse

**divest** [daɪ'vest] *vt Formal* **to d. sb of sth** despojar a alguien de algo

**divide** [dɪ'vaɪd] **1** *n Fig (gulf)* división *f*, separación *f*

**2** *vt* **(a)** *(money, food)* repartir (**between** *or* **among** entre); **to d. sth in two/three** dividir algo en dos/tres partes **(b)** *Math* dividir; **d. 346 by 17** dividir 346 entre 17 **(c)** *(separate)* separar (**from** de); **d. and rule** divide y vencerás

**3** *vi (of road)* bifurcarse; *(of group)* dividirse

▶**divide up** *vt sep (share)* repartir

**divided** [dɪ'vaɪdɪd] *adj* dividido(a); **to be d.** estar dividido(a); **a family d. against itself** una familia dividida

**dividend** ['dɪvɪdend] *n* dividendo *m*; *Fig* **to pay dividends** resultar beneficioso(a)

**dividers** [dɪ'vaɪdəz] *npl (mathematical instrument)* compás *m* de puntas

**dividing** [dɪ'vaɪdɪŋ] *adj* **d. line** línea *f* divisoria; **d. wall** muro *m* divisorio

**divine** [dɪ'vaɪn] **1** *adj (judgement, worship)* divino(a); *Fam* **you look d. in that dress** estás divina con ese vestido

**2** *vt* adivinar

**diving** ['daɪvɪŋ] *n (from poolside, diving board)* salto *m* (de cabeza); *(scuba diving)* submarinismo *m*, buceo *m*; *(deep sea)* buceo *m* en alta mar; **d. bell** campana *f* de buzo; **d. board** trampolín *m*; **d. suit** traje *m* de buceo *or* de hombre rana

**divinity** [dɪ'vɪnɪtɪ] *n* **(a)** *(divine nature, god)* divinidad *f* **(b)** *(subject)* teología *f* **(c)** **the D.** Dios *m*

**divisible** [dɪ'vɪzɪbəl] *adj* divisible

**division** [dɪ'vɪʒən] *n* **(a)** *(separation, in maths)* división *f* **(b)** *(distribution)* reparto *m*; **d. of labour** reparto *m* del trabajo **(c)** *(discord)* discordia *f* **(d)** *(unit)* división *f*; **first/second d.** *(in league)* primera/segunda división

**divisive** [dɪ'vaɪsɪv] *adj* disgregador(ora)

**divorce** [dɪ'vɔːs] **1** *n* divorcio *m*; **to start d. proceedings (against sb)** emprender los trámites de divorcio (contra alguien)

**2** *vt* **(a)** *(spouse)* divorciarse de; **to get divorced (from sb)** divorciarse (de alguien) **(b)** *Fig* separar (**from** de)

**3** *vi (of husband and wife)* divorciarse

**divulge** [daɪ'vʌldʒ] *vt* divulgar, dar a conocer

**DIY** [diːaɪ'waɪ] *(abbr* **do-it-yourself)** bricolaje *m*

**dizzy** ['dɪzɪ] *adj* **(a)** *(unsteady) (because of illness)* mareado(a); *(feeling vertigo)* con vértigo; **to be d.** *(because of illness)* estar mareado(a); *(feeling vertigo)* tener *o* sentir vértigo; *Fig* **to reach the d. heights of government** alcanzar las altas esferas del gobierno; **d. spell** mareo *m* **(b)** *Fam (frivolous)* **a d. blonde** una rubia locuela

**DJ** ['diːdʒeɪ] *n* **(a)** *(abbr* **disc jockey)** pinchadiscos *mf inv* **(b)** *Fam (abbr* **dinner jacket)** esmoquin *m*

**Djibouti** [dʒɪ'buːtɪ] *n* Yibuti

**dl** *(abbr* **decilitres)** dl

**DNA** [diːen'eɪ] *n Chem (abbr* **deoxyribonucleic acid)** ADN *m*, ácido *m* desoxirribonucleico

**do¹** [dəʊ] *n Mus* do *m*

**do²** [duː] **1** *v aux*

En el inglés hablado, y en el escrito en estilo coloquial, las formas negativas **do not, does not** y **did not** se transforman en **don't, doesn't** y **didn't**.

Como verbo transitivo **do**, unido a muchos nombres, expresa actividades, como **to do** the gardening, to do the ironing y to do the shopping. En el presente diccionario, estas estructuras se encuentran bajo los nombres respectivos.

(3rd person singular **does** [dʌz], pt **did** [dɪd], pp **done** [dʌn]) (a) (not translated in negatives and questions) **I don't speak Spanish** no hablo español; **I didn't see him** no lo vi; **do you speak Spanish?** ¿hablas español?; **did you see him?** ¿lo viste?; **don't you speak Spanish?** ¿no hablas español?; **didn't you see him?** ¿no lo viste?

(b) (for emphasis) **she DOES speak Spanish!** ¡sí que habla español!; **I DIDN'T see him!** ¡te digo que no lo vi!

(c) (substituting main verb) **she writes better than I do** escribe mejor que yo; **he has always loved her and still does** siempre la ha querido y todavía la quiere; **if you want to speak to him, do it now** si quieres hablar con él, hazlo ahora; **do you speak Spanish? – no I don't** ¿hablas español? – no; **did you see him? – I did** ¿lo viste? – sí

(d) (in tag questions) **you speak Spanish, don't you?** tú hablas español, ¿no?; **John lives near here, doesn't he?** John vive cerca de aquí, ¿verdad?; **they said they'd come early, didn't they?** dijeron que vendrían pronto, ¿no?; **you didn't see him, did you?** tú no lo viste, ¿verdad?

2 vt (a) (in general) hacer; **what are you doing?** ¿qué haces?, ¿qué estás haciendo?; **what do you do?** (what's your job?) ¿a qué te dedicas?, ¿en qué trabajas?; **what can I do for you?** ¿qué desea?, ¿puedo ayudarle en algo?; **it just isn't done!** (is not acceptable behaviour) ¡eso no se hace!, ¡eso no está bien!; **the car was doing 150 km per hour** el coche iba a 150 kms por hora; **they do good food here** aquí hacen muy buena comida; **that hairstyle does nothing for her** ese peinado no le favorece nada; Fam **this music doesn't do anything for me** esta música no me dice nada; **to do French/physics** (at school, university) estudiar francés/física; **to do the housework** hacer las labores de la casa

(b) **to do one's hair** peinarse, arreglarse el pelo; **to do one's teeth** lavarse los dientes

(c) Fam **to do drugs** tomar drogas

(d) **to be done** (of food) estar hecho(a); **have you done complaining?** ¿has terminado ya de quejarte?; Fam **I've been done!** (cheated) ¡me han tangado or timado!

(e) Fam (prosecute) **he was done for fraud** lo empaparon por fraude

3 vi (a) (perform, act) **she did well/badly** le fue bien/mal; **he does well/badly at school** le va bien/mal en el colegio

(b) (suffice) **it will/won't do** será/no será

suficiente; **that'll do!** ¡ya vale or basta!; **this will never do!** ¡esto es intolerable!; **to make do** arreglárselas, apañárselas

(c) (finish) **hasn't she done yet?** ¿no ha terminado aún?

4 n (a) **do's and don'ts** reglas fpl básicas

(b) Fam (party, celebration) fiesta f

▸**do away with** vt insep (abolish, kill) acabar con

▸**do down** vt sep desacreditar, menospreciar; **to do oneself down** minusvalorarse, infravalorarse

▸**do for** vt insep Fam **he's done for** está perdido, lo tiene crudo or claro

▸**do in** vt sep Fam (a) (murder) cargarse (b) (exhaust) **I'm absolutely done in** estoy hecho(a) migas (c) **to do one's back/knee in** fastidiarse la espalda/rodilla

▸**do out of** vt sep Fam **to do sb out of sth** (deprive) privar a alguien de algo; (cheat) tangar or estafar algo a alguien

▸**do over** vt sep Fam (beat up) **to do sb over** dar una tunda a alguien

▸**do up 1** vt sep (a) (fasten) abrochar; **do your coat up** abróchate el abrigo (b) (wrap) envolver (c) (improve appearance of) remozar, renovar; Fam **to do oneself up** (dress smartly) acicalarse, ponerse guapo(a)

2 vi (of clothes) abrocharse

▸**do with** vt insep (a) (benefit from) **I could do with a cup of tea** no me vendría mal una taza de té (b) (expressing involvement) **I want nothing to do with him** no quiero tener nada que ver con él; **I had nothing to do with it** no tuve nada que ver con eso; **it's nothing to do with you** (not your business) no es asunto tuyo (c) (stop using) **to have done with sth** terminar con algo; **have you done with the scissors yet?** ¿has terminado con las tijeras?

▸**do without** vt insep (manage without) pasar sin; **I could do without your snide remarks** me sobran or puedes ahorrarte tus comentarios sarcásticos

**DOA** [diːəʊˈeɪ] adj Med (abbr **dead on arrival**) = ingresó cadáver

**DOB** (abbr **date of birth**) = fecha de nacimiento

**doc** [dɒk] n Fam doctor(ora) m,f

**docile** ['dəʊsaɪl] adj dócil

**dock**[1] [dɒk] 1 n (for ships) muelle m; **the docks** el puerto; **d. strike** huelga f de estibadores

2 vi (of ship) atracar; (of two spacecraft) acoplarse

**dock**[2] n Law banquillo m (de los acusados)

**dock**[3] vt (a) (tail) recortar (b) (wages) recortar

**docker** ['dɒkə(r)] n estibador m

**dockyard** ['dɒkjaːd] n astillero m

**doctor** ['dɒktə(r)] **1** n (a) (medical) médico(a) m,f; **to go to the d.('s)** ir al médico; Fam Fig **that's just what the d. ordered** me/le/etc viene que ni pintado (b) Univ doctor(ora) m,f

**2** vt (a) Fam (accounts, evidence) amañar (b) (cat) castrar, capar

**doctorate** ['dɒktərət] n Univ doctorado m

**doctrinaire** [dɒktrɪ'neə(r)] adj doctrinario(a)

**doctrinal** [dɒk'traməl] adj doctrinal

**doctrine** ['dɒktrɪn] n doctrina f

**document** ['dɒkjʊmənt] **1** n documento m; Comptr **d. reader** digitalizador m, lector m de documentos

**2** vt documentar; **the first documented case** el primer caso registrado or documentado

**documentary** [dɒkjʊ'mentərɪ] **1** n (TV programme) documental m

**2** adj documental

**documentation** [dɒkjʊmen'teɪʃən] n documentación f

**dodder** ['dɒdə(r)] vi renquear, andar con paso vacilante

**doddering** ['dɒdərɪŋ] adj (walk) renqueante, vacilante; **d. fool** viejo m chocho

**doddle** ['dɒdəl] n Br Fam **it's a d.** es pan comido

**dodge** [dɒdʒ] n **1** (a) (movement) regate m, quiebro m (b) Fam (trick) truco m; **tax d.** trampa f para engañar a Hacienda

**2** vt (blow, person) esquivar; (responsibility, question) eludir

**3** vi apartarse bruscamente

**Dodgems**® ['dɒdʒəmz] npl Br coches mpl or autos mpl de choque

**dodgy** ['dɒdʒɪ] adj Br Fam (situation, deal, brakes) chungo(a); (person) dudoso(a)

**dodo** ['dəʊdəʊ] (pl **dodos** or **dodoes**) n dodo m; (**as**) **dead as a d.** muerto(a) y bien muerto(a)

**DOE** [di:əʊ'i:] n Br (abbr **Department of the Environment**) = ministerio británico del medio ambiente

**doe** [dəʊ] n (deer) cierva f; (rabbit) coneja f

**does** [dʌz] 3rd person singular of **do**

**doesn't** ['dʌzənt] = **does not**

**doff** [dɒf] vt **to d. one's cap to sb** descubrirse ante alguien

**dog** [dɒg] **1** n (a) (animal) perro m; **d. biscuit** galleta f para perros; **d. collar** (of dog) collar m de perro; Fam (of cleric) alzacuello m; **d. food** comida f para perros; **d. handler** adiestrador(ora) m,f de perros; **d. licence** licencia f del perro; **d. paddle** (swimming stroke) estilo m perrito; **d. racing** carreras fpl de galgos; **d. tag** (of dog, soldier) placa f de identificación

(b) Fam (person) **you lucky d.!** ¡qué potra tienes!; **dirty d.** canalla mf, perro(a) m,f asqueroso(a)

(c) Fam Pej (woman) cardo m

(d) (idioms) Fam **to lead a d.'s life** llevar una vida de perros; Fam **to make a d.'s breakfast** or **dinner of sth** hacer una chapuza con algo; Fam **it's a d.-eat-d. world** es un mundo de fieras; Fam **to go to the dogs** irse a pique, hundirse; Fam **to be a d. in the manger** ser como el perro del hortelano, que ni come ni deja comer; Prov **you can't teach an old d. new tricks** a perro viejo no hay tus tus; Prov **every d. has his day** todos tenemos nuestro momento de gloria

**2** vt (pt & pp **dogged**) (follow) perseguir, seguir; **to d. sb's footsteps** seguir los pasos de alguien; **she was dogged by misfortune** le perseguía la mala suerte

**dog-eared** ['dɒgɪəd] adj (book, page) ajado(a), con las esquinas dobladas

**dogfight** ['dɒgfaɪt] n (between planes) combate m aéreo; (between people) lucha f encarnizada

**dogfish** ['dɒgfɪʃ] n lija f, pintarroja f

**dogged** ['dɒgɪd] adj tenaz, perseverante

**doggerel** ['dɒgərəl] n (comical) poesía f burlesca; (bad) ripios mpl

**doggy** ['dɒgɪ] n Fam perrito m; **d. bag** bolsa f con las sobras de la comida

**doghouse** ['dɒghaʊs] n Fam **to be in the d.** haber caído en desgracia

**dogma** ['dɒgmə] n dogma m

**dogmatic** [dɒg'mætɪk] adj dogmático(a)

**do-gooder** ['du:'gʊdə(r)] n Fam Pej buen(ena) samaritano(a) m,f

**dogsbody** ['dɒgzbɒdɪ] n Br Fam burro m de carga

**dog-tired** ['dɒg'taɪəd] adj Fam hecho(a) polvo

**dogwood** ['dɒgwʊd] n cornejo m, cerezo m silvestre (hembra)

**doh** [dəʊ] n Mus do m

**doily** ['dɔɪlɪ] n blonda f

**doing** ['du:ɪŋ] n (a) **this is his d.** esto es obra suya; **it was none of my d.** yo no he tenido nada que ver; **that takes some d.** eso tiene su trabajo or no es ninguna tontería; Fam **to give sb a d.** dar una paliza a alguien (b) **doings** actividades fpl

**do-it-yourself** [du:ɪtjɔ:'self] n bricolaje m; **a d. enthusiast** un amante del bricolaje

**doldrums** ['dɒldrəmz] npl **to be in the d.** (person) estar con la moral baja; (trade, economy) estar estancado(a)

**dole** [dəʊl] n Br Fam (subsidio m de) paro m; **to be on the d.** cobrar el paro; **to join the d. queue** apuntarse al paro

▸**dole out** vt sep Fam repartir

**doleful** ['dəʊlfʊl] adj triste

**doll** [dɒl] *n* muñeca *f*; **d.'s house** casa *f* de muñecas

▸**doll up** *vt sep Fam* **to d. oneself up** emperifollarse

**dollar** ['dɒlə(r)] *n* dólar *m*; **d. bill** billete *m* de un dólar

**dollop** ['dɒləp] *n Fam (of ice cream, mashed potato)* cucharada *f*

**dolly** ['dɒlɪ] *n Fam* muñequita *f*

**dolphin** ['dɒlfɪn] *n* delfín *m*

**dolt** [dəʊlt] *n* estúpido(a) *m,f*, idiota *mf*

**domain** [də'meɪn] *n (lands)* dominios *mpl*; *Comptr* dominio *m*; *Fig (area of influence, expertise)* ámbito *m*, campo *m*; **that is outside my d.** eso queda fuera de mi campo

**dome** [dəʊm] *n* cúpula *f*

**domestic** [də'mestɪk] *adj* (a) *(appliance, pet)* doméstico(a); **d. bliss** felicidad *f* hogareña; *Br* **d. science** *(school subject)* economía *f* doméstica; **d. servant** criado(a) *m,f* (b) *(policy)* interior; *(flight, economy)* nacional

**domesticate** [də'mestɪkeɪt] *vt (animal)* domesticar

**domesticated** [də'mestɪkeɪtɪd] *adj (animal)* domesticado(a); *Fig Hum* **to be d.** *(of person)* estar muy bien enseñado(a)

**domicile** ['dɒmɪsaɪl] *n Law* domicilio *m*

**dominance** ['dɒmɪnəns] *n (in general)* predominio *m*, dominación *f*; *(of gene)* dominancia *f*

**dominant** ['dɒmɪnənt] *adj* dominante

**dominate** ['dɒmɪneɪt] *vt & vi* dominar

**domination** [dɒmɪ'neɪʃən] *n* dominio *m*

**domineering** [dɒmɪ'nɪərɪŋ] *adj* dominante

**Dominica** [də'mɪnɪkə] *n* Dominica

**Dominican** [də'mɪnɪkən] **1** *n (person from Dominican Republic)* dominicano(a) *m,f*
  **2** *adj (of Dominican Republic)* dominicano(a); **the D. Republic** la República Dominicana

**dominion** [də'mɪnjən] *n* dominio *m*

**domino** ['dɒmɪnəʊ] *(pl* **dominoes)** *n* ficha *f* de dominó; **dominoes** dominó *m*; *Pol* **d. effect** efecto *m* dominó

**don¹** [dɒn] *n Br Univ* profesor(ora) *m,f*

**don²** *(pt & pp* **donned)** *vt Formal (hat, clothes)* enfundarse, ponerse

**donate** [də'neɪt] *vt* donar

**donation** [də'neɪʃən] *n* donativo *m*, donación *f*; **to make a d.** hacer un donativo

**done** [dʌn] *pp of* **do**

**donkey** ['dɒŋkɪ] *(pl* **donkeys)** *n (animal)* burro *m*; *(person)* burro(a) *m,f*; *Fam* **I haven't seen him for d.'s years** no lo he visto desde hace siglos; *Fam* **she could talk the hind legs off a d.** hablaba como una cotorra, hablaba por los codos; **d. jacket** chaqueta *f* gruesa de trabajo; *Fam* **d. work** trabajo *m* pesado

**donor** ['dəʊnə(r)] *n* donante *mf*; **d. card** carné *m* de donante

**don't** [dəʊnt] = **do not**

**donut** ['dəʊnʌt] *n US* dónut *m*

**doodle** ['du:dəl] *Fam* **1** *n* garabato *m*
  **2** *vi* garabatear

**doom** [du:m] **1** *n* fatalidad *f*; **it's not all d. and gloom** no todo es tan terrible
  **2** *vt* **to be doomed** *(unlucky)* tener mala estrella; *(about to die)* ir hacia una muerte segura; *(plan, marriage, expedition)* estar condenado(a) al fracaso; **to be doomed to do sth** estar fatalmente predestinado(a) a hacer algo

**doom-laden** ['du:mleɪdən] *adj* funesto(a)

**doomsday** ['du:mzdeɪ] *n* día *m* del Juicio Final; **till d.** hasta el día del Juicio Final

**door** [dɔː(r)] *n* puerta *f*; **to see sb to the d.** acompañar a alguien a la puerta *or* a la salida; **to show sb the d.** *(ask to leave)* echar a alguien; **out of doors** al aire libre; **to shut the d. in sb's face** dar a alguien con la puerta en las narices; **she lives two doors away** vive a dos portales de aquí; *Fig* **to lay sth at sb's d.** achacar algo a alguien; **d. handle** manilla *f*, tirador *m*; **d. knocker** aldaba *f*, llamador *m*

**doorbell** ['dɔːbel] *n* timbre *m*

**doorkeeper** ['dɔːkiːpə(r)] *n* portero(a) *m,f*

**doorknob** ['dɔːnɒb] *n* pomo *m*

**doorman** ['dɔːmən] *n* portero *m*

**doormat** ['dɔːmæt] *n* felpudo *m*; *Fig* **to treat sb like a d.** tratar como un trapo *or* pisotear a alguien

**doorpost** ['dɔːpəʊst] *n* jamba *f*

**doorstep** ['dɔːstep] *n* escalón *m* de entrada; **he stood on the d.** se quedó en el umbral; *Fig* **on one's d.** *(very near)* en la misma puerta

**doorstop** ['dɔːstɒp] *n (fixed)* tope *m*; *(wedge)* cuña *f*

**door-to-door** ['dɔːtə'dɔːr] **1** *adj Pol* **d. canvassing** = campaña electoral en la que los representantes de los partidos van de casa en casa; *Com* **d. salesman** vendedor *m* a domicilio
  **2** *adv* **to sell sth d.** vender algo a domicilio

**doorway** ['dɔːweɪ] *n* puerta *f*, entrada *f*; **in the d.** a *or* en la puerta

**dope** [dəʊp] **1** *n* (a) *very Fam (hashish, cannabis)* costo *m*; *(marijuana)* maría *f* (el término *dope* se refiere a cualquier droga blanda); *Fam* **d. test** *(for athlete)* control *m or* prueba *f* antidoping (b) *Fam (idiot)* tonto(a) *m,f*, bobo(a) *m,f*
  **2** *vt (person, horse)* drogar; *(food, drink)* echar droga en

**dopey** ['dəʊpɪ] *adj Fam (stupid)* tonto(a), bobo(a)

**dorm** [dɔːm] *n Fam (dormitory)* dormitorio *m*

**dormant** ['dɔːmənt] **1** *adj (emotions, ideas)* latente; *(volcano)* inactivo(a)
  **2** *adv* **to lie d.** permanecer latente

**dormitory** ['dɔːmɪtərɪ] n (a) dormitorio m; **d. town** ciudad f dormitorio (b) US Univ ≃ colegio m mayor

**dormouse** ['dɔːmaʊs] (pl **dormice** ['dɔːmaɪs]) n lirón m

**dorsal** ['dɔːsəl] adj dorsal

**DOS** [dɒs] n Comptr (abbr **disk operating system**) DOS m

**dosage** ['dəʊsɪdʒ] n (amount) dosis f; **to increase the d.** aumentar la dosis

**dose** [dəʊs] n **1** dosis f inv; **a d. of flu** una gripe

**2** vt Fam **to d. oneself (up) with pills** tomarse una fuerte dosis de pastillas

**dosh** [dɒʃ] n Br Fam (money) tela f, pasta f

**doss** [dɒs] vi very Fam **to d. (down) in a park** sobar en un parque

**dosser** ['dɒsə(r)] n Br very Fam (tramp) vagabundo(a) m,f; (lazy person) perro(a) m,f or vago(a) m,f del copón

**dossier** ['dɒsɪeɪ] n dossier m, expediente m

**doss-house** ['dɒshaʊs] n Br Fam pensión f de mala muerte

**dot** [dɒt] **1** n punto m; **on the d.** en punto; Comptr **matrix printer** impresora f matricial or de agujas

**2** vt (pt & pp **dotted**) salpicar; **to d. an 'i'** poner el punto sobre una i; **dotted with** salpicado(a) de; Fig **to d. the i's (and cross the t's)** dar los últimos toques; **dotted line** línea f de puntos; **to sign on the dotted line** estampar la firma

**dotage** ['dəʊtɪdʒ] n **to be in one's d.** estar chocho(a), chochear

▶**dote on, dote upon** vt insep mimar, adorar

**dotty** ['dɒtɪ] adj Fam (person) chalado(a); **a d. idea** una chaladura; **to be d.** estar chalado(a); **he's d. about her** se le cae la baba con ella

**double** ['dʌbəl] **1** n (a) (of person) doble mf (b) (hotel room) habitación f doble (c) **doubles** (in tennis) singles mpl; **a doubles match** un partido de dobles (d) **at** or **on the d.** a toda velocidad, corriendo

**2** adj doble; **a d. gin/whisky** una ginebra/un whisky doble; **d. m** (when spelling) doble eme, dos emes; **d. agent** agente mf doble; **d. bass** contrabajo m; **d. bed** cama f de matrimonio; **d. bill** (at cinema) sesión f doble; **d. chin** papada f; **d. cream** nata f líquida enriquecida; Br Fam **to talk d. Dutch** hablar en chino; **d. fault** (in tennis) doble falta f; **d. figures** números mpl de dos cifras; **inflation is now in d. figures** la inflación ha superado la barrera del 10%; **to lead a d. life** llevar una doble vida; **d. meaning** doble sentido m; **d. room** habitación f doble; **d. standard** doble moral f; **to do a d. take** reaccionar un instante más tarde; Br **d.**

**yellow line** = línea doble continua de color amarillo próxima al bordillo que indica prohibición total de estacionamiento

**3** adv **to see d.** ver doble; **to fold sth d.** doblar algo por la mitad; **to be bent d.** estar doblado(a) or agachado(a)

**4** vt (a) (multiply by 2) duplicar (b) (fold) doblar por la mitad

**5** vi (a) (increase) duplicarse (b) **to d. as** (person) hacer también de; (thing) funcionar también como

▶**double back** vi volver (uno) sobre sus pasos

▶**double up** vi (bend) doblarse; **to d. up with pain** retorcerse de dolor; **to d. up with laughter** troncharse de risa

**double-barrelled** ['dʌbəl'bærəld] adj (shotgun) de dos cañones; (surname) compuesto(a)

**double-breasted** ['dʌbəl'brestɪd] adj (jacket, suit) cruzado(a)

**double-check** ['dʌbəl'tʃek] vt & vi comprobar dos veces

**double-cross** ['dʌbəl'krɒs] vt engañar, traicionar

**double-dealing** ['dʌbəl'diːlɪŋ] n doblez f, duplicidad f

**double-decker** ['dʌbəl'dekə(r)] n Br (bus) autobús m de dos pisos

**double-edged** ['dʌbəl'edʒd] adj (blade, remark) de doble filo

**double-glazing** ['dʌbəl'gleɪzɪŋ] n doble acristalamiento m

**double-jointed** ['dʌbəl'dʒɔɪntɪd] adj **to be d.** = tener la articulaciones más flexibles de lo normal de modo que se doblan hacia atrás

**double-lock** ['dʌbəl'lɒk] vt cerrar con dos vueltas (de llave)

**double-park** ['dʌbəl'pɑːk] vt & vi aparcar en doble fila

**double-quick** ['dʌbəl'kwɪk] adv rapidísimamente

**doubly** ['dʌblɪ] adv doblemente, por partida doble

**doubt** [daʊt] **1** n duda f; **to have doubts about sth** tener dudas sobre algo; **to be in d.** (of person) tener dudas; (of outcome) ser incierto(a); **when in d.** en caso de duda; **beyond d.** sin lugar a dudas; **no d.** sin duda; **there is no d. that...** no cabe duda de que...; **there is no d. about her guilt** no hay duda alguna acerca de su culpabilidad; **there is some d. about her guilt** se tienen dudas acerca de su culpabilidad

**2** vt dudar; **I d. it** lo dudo; **I d. whether that is the case** dudo que sea así; **do you d. me?** ¿acaso dudas de mí?

**doubtful** ['daʊtfʊl] adj (a) (uncertain) (person) dubitativo(a); (outcome) incierto(a); **to be d.**

**about sth** tener dudas acerca de algo; **it is d. whether he will succeed** es dudoso que tenga éxito (b) *(questionable)* dudoso(a)

**doubtless** ['daʊtlɪs] *adv* sin duda, indudablemente

**dough** [dəʊ] *n* (a) *(for bread)* masa *f* (b) *very Fam (money)* pasta *f*, pelas *fpl*

**doughnut** ['dəʊnʌt] *n (with hole)* dónut *m*; *(without hole)* buñuelo *m*

**dour** [dʊə(r)] *adj* severo(a), adusto(a)

**Douro** ['dʊərəʊ] *n* the D. el Duero

**douse** [daʊs] *vt* (a) *(soak)* empapar, mojar (b) *(extinguish)* apagar

**dove¹** [dʌv] *n* paloma *f*

**dove²** [dəʊv] *US pt of* **dive**

**dovecote** ['dʌvkɒt] *n* palomar *m*

**dovetail** ['dʌvteɪl] *vi (fit closely)* encajar (**with** en *or* con)

**dowager** ['daʊədʒə(r)] *n* viuda *f (de un noble)*; **d. duchess** duquesa *f* viuda

**dowdy** ['daʊdɪ] *adj* poco atractivo(a)

**dowel** ['daʊəl] *n (in carpentry)* espiga *f*

**down¹** [daʊn] *n (feathers)* plumón *m*

**down²** 1 *prep* **to go d. the street** ir por la calle; **to fall d. the stairs** caerse por las escaleras (abajo); **they sailed d. the river** navegaron río abajo

2 *adv* (a) *(motion)* abajo; **I'll be d. in a minute** bajo enseguida; **d. with traitors!** ¡abajo *or* fuera los traidores!

(b) *(position)* abajo; **d. here/there** aquí/ahí abajo; **further d.** más abajo; **the price is d.** ha bajado el precio; **one d., two to go!** ¡uno menos, ya sólo quedan dos!; **everyone from the boss d.** todos, desde el jefe hacia *or* para abajo

(c) *(idioms)* **to be d. on sb/sth** haber cogido manía a alguien/algo; **it's d. to her** *(her decision)* ella decide; *(her achievement)* es gracias a ella; **I'm d. to my last cigarette** sólo me queda un cigarrillo; *Br Fam* **d. under** = en/a Australia y Nueva Zelanda

(d) *Comptr* **to be d.** no funcionar; **d. time** *(in industry)* paro *m* técnico

3 *adj* (a) *(depressed)* deprimido(a)

(b) **d. payment** entrada *f*, pago *m* inicial; **to make a d. payment (on)** *(car, house, TV)* pagar la entrada (de)

4 *vt* **to d. an aircraft** derribar un avión; **to d. tools** *(of workers)* dejar de trabajar; **he downed his beer and left** se terminó la cerveza de un trago y se fue

5 *n Fam* **to have a d. on sb** haber cogido manía a alguien

**down-and-out** ['daʊnən'aʊt] *Fam* 1 *n (tramp)* vagabundo(a) *m,f*, indigente *mf*

2 *adj* **to be d.** ser indigente

**downbeat** ['daʊnbiːt] *adj* (a) *(gloomy, pessimistic)* triste, pesimista (b) *(restrained)* **to be d. about sth** minimizar algo

**downcast** ['daʊnkɑːst] *adj (eyes)* bajo(a); *(person)* deprimido(a), abatido(a); **to be d.** *(of person)* estar deprimido *or* abatido(a)

**downer** ['daʊnə(r)] *n Fam* (a) *(drug)* calmante *m*, depresor *m* (b) **what a d.!** *(how depressing)* ¡qué muermo!

**downfall** ['daʊnfɔːl] *n (of government)* caída *f*; *(of person)* perdición *f*

**downgrade** ['daʊngreɪd] *vt* degradar, rebajar

**downhearted** [daʊn'hɑːtɪd] *adj* desanimado(a), abatido(a)

**downhill** ['daʊn'hɪl] 1 *adj (road)* cuesta abajo; **d. skiing** *(esquí m de)* descenso *m*

2 *adv also Fig* **to go d.** ir cuesta abajo

**download** ['daʊn'ləʊd] *vt Comptr* bajar, descargar

**down-market** [daʊn'mɑːkɪt] *adj* popular, barato(a)

**downpour** ['daʊnpɔː(r)] *n* aguacero *m*, tromba *f* de agua

**downright** ['daʊnraɪt] 1 *adj (stupidity, dishonesty)* absoluto(a), completo(a); **it's a d. lie!** ¡es completamente falso!

2 *adv (stupid, untrue)* absolutamente, completamente

**downsizing** ['daʊnsaɪzɪŋ] *n* reajuste *m* de plantillas

**Down's Syndrome** ['daʊn'sɪndrəʊm] *n* síndrome *m* de Down

**downstairs 1** ['daʊnsteəz] *adj* del piso de abajo; **the d. flat/bathroom** el piso/cuarto de baño de abajo

2 [daʊn'steəz] *adv* **to come/go d.** bajar (la escalera); **he lives d.** vive en el piso de abajo

**downstream** [daʊn'striːm] *adv* aguas abajo

**downswing** ['daʊnswɪŋ] *n Econ (fase f de)* contracción *f*, bajón *m*

**down-to-earth** ['daʊntə'ɜːθ] *adj* práctico(a), realista

**downtown** ['daʊn'taʊn] *US* **1** *n (city centre)* centro *m* (urbano)

2 *adj* del centro; **d. New York** el centro de Nueva York

3 *adv* **he gave me a lift d.** me llevó al centro; **to live d.** vivir en el centro

**downtrodden** ['daʊntrɒdən] *adj* oprimido(a)

**downturn** ['daʊntɜːn] *n Econ (fase f de)* contracción *f*, bajón *m*

**downward** ['daʊnwəd] *adj (trend)* descendente

**downwards** ['daʊnwədz] *adv* hacia abajo

**dowry** ['daʊrɪ] *n* dote *f*

**doze** [dəʊz] **1** *n* cabezada *f*, sueñecito *m*; **to have a d.** echar una cabezada

**2** *vi* dormitar

▶**doze off** *vi* quedarse traspuesto(a)

**dozen** ['dʌzən] *n* docena *f*; **a d. eggs** una docena de huevos; **half a d. eggs** media docena de huevos; **86 pence a d.** 86 peniques la docena; *Fam* **dozens of times/people** cientos de veces/personas

**dozy** ['dəʊzɪ] *adj Fam (sleepy)* amodorrado(a); *(stupid)* bobo(a), idiota

**Dr** *(abbr* **doctor)** Dr., Dra., doctor(ora) *m,f*

**drab** [dræb] *adj (person)* gris, soso(a); *(colours, clothes)* soso(a), insulso(a); *(atmosphere, city)* anodino(a)

**drachma** ['drækmə] *n (Greek currency)* dracma *m*

**draconian** [drə'kəʊnɪən] *adj* draconiano(a)

**draft** [drɑːft] **1** *n* (a) *(of letter, proposal, novel)* borrador *m* (b) *Fin* letra *f* de cambio, giro *m*; **banker's d.** giro *m* bancario (c) *US (conscription)* llamada *f* a filas, reclutamiento *m*; **d. dodger** = persona que se libra de tener que alistarse en el ejército mediante subterfugios (d) *US* = **draught**

**2** *vt* (a) *(letter, proposal)* hacer un borrador de; **to d. a bill** redactar un anteproyecto de ley (b) *US Mil* llamar a filas a, reclutar

▶**draft in** *vt insep (troops, supporters)* movilizar

**draftsman** *US* = **draughtsman**

**drafty** *US* = **draughty**

**drag** [dræg] **1** *n* (a) *(air resistance)* resistencia *f* del aire; **d. racing** = carreras de aceleración en coches preparados (b) *Fam (person)* plomo *m*, pelma *mf*; *(task)* rollo *m*, lata *f*; **the party was a real d.** la fiesta fue un rollazo (c) *Fam (on cigarette)* calada *f*; **to take a d. on a cigarette** dar una calada a un cigarrillo (d) *(women's clothing)* **he was in d.** iba vestido de mujer; **d. artist** *or* **queen** transformista *m*, travestí *m (que viste espectacularmente)*

**2** *vt (pt & pp* **dragged)** (a) *(pull)* arrastrar; *Fig* **they dragged their feet over the decision** se andaron con muchos rodeos hasta tomar la decisión; *Fig* **we eventually dragged ourselves away from the party** finalmente y a regañadientes nos fuimos de la fiesta (b) *(trawl) (pond, canal)* dragar

**3** *vi (of film, conversation)* resultar pesado(a); **the meeting dragged to a close** la reunión terminó por fin

▶**drag on** *vi (of meeting, film)* durar eternamente

▶**drag out** *vt sep (meeting, speech)* alargar innecesariamente

▶**drag up** *vt (refer to)* sacar a relucir

**dragnet** ['drægnet] *n (in deep-sea fishing)* red *f* de arrastre *or* barredera; *Fig (to catch criminals)* emboscada *f*

**dragon** ['drægən] *n* (a) *(mythological creature)* dragón *m* (b) *Fam (fearsome woman)* ogro *m*, bruja *f*

**dragonfly** ['drægənflaɪ] *n* libélula *f*

**dragoon** [drə'guːn] **1** *n (soldier)* dragón *m*

**2** *vt* **to d. sb into doing sth** obligar a alguien a hacer algo

**drain** [dreɪn] **1** *n* (a) *(for water)* desagüe *m*; *(for sewage)* alcantarilla *f*; *(grating)* sumidero *m*; *Fig* **to go down the d.** *(of money)* echarse a perder; *(of work)* irse al traste (b) *(on strength, resources)* merma *f*, mengua *f* (**on** de); **the space programme is a d. on the country's resources** el programa espacial se lleva muchos de los recursos del país

**2** *vt (liquid)* vaciar, quitar (**from** de); *(sink)* vaciar; *(pond)* desaguar; *(swamp)* drenar; *(pasta, vegetables)* escurrir; *Fig* **to d. wealth from a country** debilitar la economía de un país; *Fig* **to feel drained** estar extenuado(a)

**3** *vi (of liquid)* irse; *(of sink, river)* desaguar; *(of washed dishes)* escurrir; **the colour drained from her face** se puso pálida, empalideció repentinamente

▶**drain away** *vi (of liquid)* irse; *Fig (of strength, enthusiasm)* diluirse, agotarse; *Fig (of fear, tension)* disiparse

**drainage** ['dreɪnɪdʒ] *n (of soil, land)* drenaje *m*

**drainpipe** ['dreɪnpaɪp] *n* tubo *m* de desagüe; **d. trousers, drainpipes** pantalones *mpl* de pitillo

**drake** [dreɪk] *n (male duck)* pato *m*

**dram** [dræm] *n (of whisky)* chupito *m*

**drama** ['drɑːmə] *n* (a) *(art form)* teatro *m*, drama *m*; *(play)* obra *f* de teatro, drama *m*; *Fig* **to make a d. out of sth** hacer una tragedia de algo; **d. school** escuela *f* de arte dramático (b) *(excitement)* dramatismo *m*

**dramatic** [drə'mætɪk] *adj* (a) *Th (actor, work)* dramático(a) (b) *(change, reduction)* drástico(a); *(effect)* dramático(a); *(event, scenery)* espectacular

**dramatist** ['dræmətɪst] *n* dramaturgo(a) *m,f*

**dramatization** [dræmətaɪ'zeɪʃən] *n* dramatización *f*

**dramatize** ['dræmətaɪz] *vt* (a) *(novel)* adaptar para el teatro (b) *(exaggerate)* **to d. a situation** dramatizar una situación

**drank** [dræŋk] *pt of* **drink**

**drape** [dreɪp] **1** *vt (table, coffin)* cubrir (**with** con); **they draped the flag over the coffin** cubrieron el ataúd con la bandera

**2** *n US* **drapes** *(curtains)* cortinas *fpl*

**drastic** ['dræstɪk] *adj* drástico(a)

**drat** [dræt] *exclam Fam* **d. (it)!** ¡caramba!

**draught,** *US* **draft** [drɑːft] *n* (a) *(wind)* corriente *f* (de aire); **d. excluder** burlete *m* (b) *(drink)* trago *m*; **on d.** *(beer)* de barril; **d. beer** cerveza *f* de barril

**draughtboard** ['drɑːftbɔːd] *n* tablero *m* de damas

**draughts** ['drɑːfts] *n (game)* damas *fpl*

**draughtsman,** US **draftsman** ['drɑːftsmən] *n* delineante *mf*

**draughty,** US **drafty** ['drɑːftɪ] *adj* **this room/house is a bit d.** este cuarto/en esta casa hay or hace bastante corriente

**draw** [drɔː] **1** *n* (**a**) *(in football match, argument)* empate *m*
(**b**) *(lottery, for sporting competition)* sorteo *m*
(**c**) *(attraction)* atracción *f*
**2** *vt* (*pt* **drew** [druː], *pp* **drawn** [drɔːn]) (**a**) *(picture, diagram, map)* dibujar; **to d. sb's picture** hacer el retrato de alguien
(**b**) *(pull) (cart)* tirar de; *(person)* llevar (**towards** hacia); **he drew her towards him in a passionate embrace** la atrajo hacia él abrazándola apasionadamente; **to d. the curtains** *(open or shut)* correr las cortinas; **he barely had time to d. breath** apenas tuvo tiempo de respirar
(**c**) *(extract)* (**cork, tooth, nail**) sacar (**from** de); *(pistol)* desenfundar; *(sword)* desenvainar; *Fig (strength, comfort)* hallar (**from** en); **to d. money from the bank** sacar dinero del banco; **to d. a salary** recibir un sueldo; **to d. blood** hacer sangre; **he drew a knife on me** me sacó un cuchillo; **to d. lots** echar a suertes; **to d. a conclusion from sth** sacar una conclusión de algo; **she refused to be drawn on the issue** eludió dar detalles sobre el asunto; **our members are drawn from all walks of life** nuestros socios proceden de diferentes profesiones; **they were drawn against the champions** *(in competition)* les tocó enfrentarse a los campeones
(**d**) *(attract)* atraer; **to d. a crowd** atraer a una multitud; **to feel drawn to sb/sth** sentirse atraído(a)' hacia alguien/algo; *Fig* **to d. sb's fire** suscitar las críticas or iras de alguien
(**e**) *(tie)* **to d. a game with sb** empatar con alguien
**3** *vi* (**a**) *(illustrate)* dibujar
(**b**) *(in game)* empatar (**with** con)
(**c**) *(move)* **to d. ahead of sb** adelantar a alguien; **to d. level with sb** ponerse a la altura de alguien; **to d. to an end** llegar al final; **to d. near** acercarse, aproximarse; **to d. to a halt** detenerse

▸**draw back 1** *vt sep (sheet, veil)* retirar
**2** *vi* echarse atrás

▸**draw in** *vi* **the nights are drawing in** las noches se están alargando

▸**draw on 1** *vt insep (resources, savings, experience)* recurrir a
**2** *vi* **evening was drawing on** caía la tarde

▸**draw out** *vt sep* (**a**) *(encourage to talk)* **to d. sb out** hacer que alguien hable (**b**) *(prolong)* alargar, prolongar

▸**draw up 1** *vt sep* (**a**) *(pull)* **to d. up a chair** acercar una silla; **she drew herself up to her full height** se levantó cuan larga era (**b**) *(plan, document, will)* redactar
**2** *vi (of vehicle)* parar, detenerse

**drawback** ['drɔːbæk] *n* inconveniente *m*

**drawbridge** ['drɔːbrɪdʒ] *n* puente *m* levadizo

**drawer** [drɔː(r)] *n* cajón *m*; **chest of drawers** cómoda *f*

**drawers** [drɔːz] *npl Old-fashioned (for women)* bragas *fpl*; *(for men)* calzoncillos *mpl*

**drawing** ['drɔːɪŋ] *n* (**a**) *(illustration)* dibujo *m*; **d. board** tablero *m* de dibujo; *Fig* **back to the d. board!** ¡hay que volver a empezar desde el principio!; **d. paper** papel *m* de dibujo; **d. pin** chincheta *f* (**b**) **d. power** *(attractive capacity)* poder *m* de convocatoria

**drawing room** ['drɔːɪŋruːm] *n* sala *f* de estar, salón *m*

**drawl** [drɔːl] **1** *n* acento *m* cansino
**2** *vi* arrastrar los sonidos al hablar

**drawn** [drɔːn] **1** *adj* **to look d.** tener aspecto demacrado(a); **d. features** facciones *fpl* demacradas
**2** *pp of* **draw**

**drawstring** ['drɔːstrɪŋ] *n* cordón *m*

**dread** [dred] **1** *n* pavor *m*, terror *m*
**2** *vt* **she dreaded telling him** la idea de decírselo le aterraba; **I d. to think!** ¡me da pavor pensarlo!

**dreaded** ['dredɪd] *adj* temido(a), temible

**dreadful** ['dredfʊl] *adj* (**a**) *(terrible)* espantoso(a), horroroso(a); **to feel d.** sentirse fatal; **to look d.** tener un aspecto terrible (**b**) *Fam (for emphasis)* **it's a d. bore!** ¡es un aburrimiento total!; **it's a d. shame!** ¡es una vergüenza absoluta!

**dreadfully** ['dredfʊlɪ] *adv Fam* (**a**) *(very badly)* fatal, espantosamente (**b**) *(very)* terriblemente

**dreadlocks** ['dredlɒks] *npl* trenzas *fpl* rastafari

**dream** [driːm] **1** *n* sueño *m*; **to have a d.** (**about**) soñar (con); **to have bad dreams** tener pesadillas; **a d. come true** un sueño hecho realidad; **it worked like a d.** salió a la perfección; **my d. house** la casa de mis sueños; **d. world** mundo *m* de ensueño
**2** *vt* (*pt & pp* **dreamt** [dremt] *or* **dreamed**) **to d. that...** soñar que...; *Fig* **I never dreamt you would take me seriously** nunca imaginé que me tomarías en serio
**3** *vi* soñar; **to d. of** *or* **about** soñar con; *Fam* **I wouldn't d. of it!** ¡jamás se me ocurriría!

▸**dream up** *vt (scheme, excuse)* idear, inventarse

**dreamer** ['driːmə(r)] *n* soñador(ora) *m,f*

**dreamlike** ['driːmlaɪk] *adj* onírico(a)

**dreamt** [dremt] *pt & pp of* **dream**

**dreamy** ['dri:mɪ] *adj* soñador(ora)

**dreary** ['drɪərɪ] *adj* deprimente

**dredge** [dredʒ] *vt (canal, harbour)* dragar; *Fig* **she dredged her memory** rebuscó en su memoria

▸**dredge up** *vt* sacar del agua al dragar; *Fig (scandal, memory)* sacar a relucir

**dredger** ['dredʒə(r)] *n (boat)* dragador *m*

**dregs** [dregz] *npl (of drink)* posos *mpl*; *Fig* **the d. of society** la escoria de la sociedad

**drench** [drentʃ] *vt* empapar (**with** *or* **in** con *or* en); **drenched to the skin** calado(a) hasta los huesos

**dress** [dres] **1** *n* (a) *(for woman)* vestido *m* (b) *(clothing)* traje *m*; **to have good/no d. sense** saber/no saber vestirse, tener/no tener estilo para vestir; **d. circle** *(in theatre)* piso *m* principal; **d. rehearsal** *(of play)* ensayo *m* general; **d. shirt** camisa *f* de vestir

**2** *vt* (a) *(person)* vestir; **to d. oneself, to get dressed** vestirse; **to be dressed in black** ir vestido(a) de negro; **well/badly dressed** bien/mal vestido(a) (b) *(wound)* vendar (c) *(salad)* aliñar; **dressed crab** changurro *m*

**3** *vi* vestirse

▸**dress up** *vi (elegantly)* arreglarse, vestirse de etiqueta; *(in fancy dress)* disfrazarse (**as** de)

**dresser** ['dresə(r)] *n* (a) *(in kitchen)* aparador *m* (b) *US (in bedroom)* cómoda *f* (c) *Th* ayudante *mf* de camerino

**dressing** ['dresɪŋ] *n* (a) **d. gown** bata *f*; **d. room** *Th* camerino *m*; *Sport* vestuario *m*; **d. table** tocador *m* (b) *(for wound)* vendaje *m*, gasa *f* (c) *(for salad)* aliño *m*

**dressing down** ['dresɪŋ'daʊn] *n* *Fam* **to give sb a d.** echar un rapapolvo a alguien

**dressmaker** ['dresmeɪkə(r)] *n* modista *f*

**dressmaking** ['dresmeɪkɪŋ] *n* corte *m* y confección

**dressy** [dresɪ] *adj* *Fam* elegante, puesto(a)

**drew** [dru:] *pt of* **draw**

**drib** [drɪb] *n* **in dribs and drabs** poco a poco, con cuentagotas

**dribble** ['drɪbəl] **1** *n* (a) *(saliva)* baba *f*; *(of blood, oil)* reguero *m*

**2** *vi* (a) *(of person)* babear (b) *(of liquid)* gotear; *Fig* **to d. in/out** *(of people)* entrar/salir poco a poco (c) *(of footballer)* llevar el balón controlado; **to d. past a defender** regatear o driblar a un defensa

**drier** ['draɪə(r)] *n (for hair)* secador *m*; *(for clothes)* secadora *f*

**drift** [drɪft] **1** *n* (a) *(of current)* movimiento *m*, arrastre *m*; *(of business, conversation)* tendencia *f*; *(of events)* curso *m*; **d. net** *(for fishing)* red *f* de deriva (b) *(meaning) (of person's words)* sentido *m*, idea *f*; *Fam* **I get the d.** ya veo cuál es la idea (c) *(of snow)* ventisquero *m*

**2** *vi* (a) *(of boat, economy)* ir a la deriva; *(of conversation)* derivar; *(of events)* discurrir; *(of person)* vagar, errar; **to let things d.** dejar que las cosas vayan a la deriva; **people drifted in and out during the speech** durante el discurso, la gente entraba y salía; **to d. apart** irse separando poco a poco; **to d. into war/crime** ir derivando hacia la guerra/la delincuencia (b) *(of sand, snow)* amontonarse

**drifter** ['drɪftə(r)] *n (aimless person)* vagabundo(a) *m,f*

**driftwood** ['drɪftwʊd] *n* madera *f* flotante

**drill** [drɪl] **1** *n* (a) *(electric tool)* taladradora *f*; *(manual tool)* taladro *m* (manual); *(of dentist)* torno *m*; *(pneumatic)* martillo *m* neumático; **d. bit** broca *f*; **d. hole** *(in wood, brick)* taladro *m*; *(for oil well)* perforación *f* (b) *(training)* ejercicio *m*; **fire d.** simulacro *m* de incendio

**2** *vt* (a) *(well, road)* perforar; **to d. a hole in sth** taladrar un agujero en algo (b) *(train) (soldiers)* entrenar; **to d. pupils in pronunciation** hacer practicar la pronunciación a los alumnos; *Fam* **to d. sth into sb** meterle algo en la cabeza a alguien

**3** *vi* (a) **to d. for oil** hacer perforaciones en busca de petróleo (b) *(of troops)* entrenar, practicar

**drink** [drɪŋk] **1** *n* bebida *f*; *(alcoholic)* copa *f*; **to have a d.** beber algo; **to go for a d.** ir a tomar algo; *Fam* **the d.** *(the sea)* el mar; **to take to d.** darse a la bebida; **to have a d. problem** tener un problema con la bebida; **drinks machine** máquina *f* expendedora de bebidas

**2** *vt* (*pt* **drank** [dræŋk], *pp* **drunk** [drʌŋk]) beber; **to d. sb's health** brindar a la salud de alguien; **to d. sb under the table** aguantar bebiendo más que alguien

**3** *vi* beber; **don't d. and drive** si bebes, no conduzcas; **to d. like a fish** beber como un cosaco; **to d. to sb** beber a la salud de alguien; **to d. to sth** brindar por algo; *Fig* **to d. in the atmosphere** empaparse del ambiente

▸**drink up 1** *vt sep* beberse todo

**2** *vi* **d. up!** *(in pub)* ¡vayan terminando!

**drinkable** ['drɪŋkəbəl] *adj (water)* potable; *(wine, beer)* pasable, aceptable

**drink-driving** ['drɪŋk'draɪvɪŋ] *n* **he was arrested for d.** lo detuvieron por conducir en estado de embriaguez

**drinker** ['drɪŋkə(r)] *n* bebedor(ora) *m,f*; **he's a heavy d.** es un bebedor empedernido

**drinking** ['drɪŋkɪŋ] *n* **heavy d. is bad for you** beber mucho es malo; **his d. companions** sus compañeros de borracheras; **d. chocolate** chocolate *m* a la taza; **d. fountain** fuente *f* de agua potable; **d. straw** pajita *f*; **d. water** agua *f* potable

**drip** [drɪp] **1** n (a) (drop) gota f; (sound) goteo m (b) (in hospital) gota a gota m inv; **she's on a d.** le han puesto suero (c) Fam (weak person) sosaina mf

**2** vt (pt & pp **dripped**) gotear

**3** vi gotear; **to be dripping with sweat/blood** estar empapado(a) en sudor/sangre; Fig **to be dripping with jewels** ir cargado(a) de joyas

**drip-dry** ['drɪp'draɪ] adj (shirt, fabric) que no necesita plancha

**dripping** ['drɪpɪŋ] **1** n grasa f

**2** adj **a d. tap** un grifo que gotea

**3** adv **to be d. wet** estar empapado(a)

**drive** [draɪv] **1** n (a) (trip) viaje m (en coche); **it's an hour's d. away** está a una hora en coche; **to go for** or **take a d.** dar una vuelta en coche

(b) Aut (of car) tracción f; **four-wheel d.** (car) cuatro por cuatro m inv, vehículo m con tracción a las cuatro ruedas; (system) tracción a las cuatro ruedas; **left-hand d.** volante m al lado izquierdo

(c) Comptr unidad f de disco

(d) (in golf) golpe m largo, drive m; (in tennis) drive m, golpe m natural

(e) (of house) camino m de entrada

(f) (initiative, energy) brío m, empuje m

(g) (campaign) **sales/membership d.** campaña f de ventas/para captar socios

**2** vt (pt **drove** [drəʊv], pp **driven** ['drɪvən]) (a) (car, train) conducir, Am manejar; **to d. sb somewhere** llevar a alguien a algún sitio en coche

(b) (direct, guide) (cattle, people) conducir, guiar; **to d. sb to do sth** empujar a alguien a que haga algo; **to d. prices up/down** hacer que los precios suban/bajen; **to d. sb mad** volver loco(a) a alguien; **to d. oneself too hard** trabajar demasiado; **to d. a hard bargain** ser un/una duro(a) negociador(ora), no regalar nada a nadie

(c) (machine) impulsar, hacer funcionar; **to be driven by electricity** funcionar con electricidad

**3** vi (in car) conducir, Am manejar; **can you d.?** ¿sabes conducir?; **to d. to work** ir al trabajo en coche

▸**drive at** vi **what are you driving at?** ¿qué estás insinuando?

▸**drive away 1** vt sep (a) (in car) **to d. sb away** llevarse a alguien en un coche (b) (alienate) **to d. sb away** ahuyentar a alguien

**2** vi (in car) irse, marcharse (en coche)

▸**drive off** vt sep (repel) repeler

▸**drive on** vi (in car) seguir adelante

**drive-in** ['draɪvɪn] n **d.** (**cinema**) autocine m; **d.** (**restaurant**) = establecimiento de comida rápida que atiende a los clientes sin que éstos necesiten salir del coche

**drivel** ['drɪvəl] n Fam chorradas fpl; **to talk d.** decir chorradas

**driven** ['drɪvən] pp of **drive**

**driver** ['draɪvə(r)] n (a) (of car, bus) conductor(ora) m,f; (of lorry) camionero(a) m,f; (of taxi) taxista mf; (of train) maquinista mf, Am chofer; US **d.'s licence** carné m de conducir (b) (golf club) driver m

**driveway** ['draɪvweɪ] n camino f de entrada

**driving** ['draɪvɪŋ] **1** n (in car) conducción f; Fig **to be in the d. seat** estar al mando; **d. instructor** profesor(ora) m,f de autoescuela; **d. lessons** clases fpl de conducir; Br **d. licence** carné m de conducir; **d. school** autoescuela f; **d. test** examen m de conducir

**2** adj (rain) torrencial; **d. force** fuerza f motriz

**drizzle** ['drɪzəl] **1** n llovizna f

**2** vi lloviznar, chispear; **it's drizzling** está lloviznando

**drizzly** ['drɪzlɪ] adj (day, weather) **a d. day** un día de llovizna

**droll** [drəʊl] adj gracioso(a); Ironic **oh, very d.!** ¡muy gracioso!

**dromedary** ['drɒmədərɪ] n dromedario m

**drone** [drəʊn] **1** n (a) (bee) zángano m (b) (noise) zumbido m

**2** vi zumbar

▸**drone on** vi **to d. on about sth** soltar una perorata sobre algo

**drool** [dru:l] vi (dribble) babear; Fig **she was drooling at the idea** se le caía la baba con sólo pensarlo

**droop** [dru:p] vi (of head) inclinarse; (of shoulders) encorvarse; (of flower) marchitarse; Fig (of person) desanimarse

**drop** [drɒp] **1** n (a) (of liquid) gota f; **drops** (for eyes, nose) gotas fpl; **you've had a d. too much** (to drink) llevas una copa de más; **I haven't touched a d. since** desde entonces no he bebido ni una gota; Fig **it's only a d. in the ocean** no es más que un grano de arena en el desierto

(b) (fall, decrease) caída f, descenso m (in de); (by parachute) suministro m aéreo; **a d. of 10 metres** una caída de 10 metros; Fig **at the d. of a hat** a la primera or las primeras de cambio

**2** vt (pt & pp **dropped**) (a) (allow to fall) (accidentally) dejar caer; (deliberately) tirar, dejar caer; (bomb) lanzar, tirar; **I've dropped my pen** se me ha caído el boli; Fam **to d. sb a line/a card** mandar unas líneas/una postal a alguien; **I'll d. you at the station** (in car) te dejaré en la estación

(b) (lower) (prices, one's eyes, voice) bajar

(c) (abandon) (subject, idea, plan) dejar; **to d.** (as friend) abandonar or dejar a alguien; **to d.**

**maths/French** dejar las matemáticas/el francés; *Law* **to d. the charges** retirar los cargos

**(d)** *(omit) (letter, syllable)* saltarse, omitir; *(not pronounce)* no pronunciar; **to d. sb from a team** excluir a alguien de un equipo

**(e)** *(lose) (points)* perder

**3** *vi* **(a)** *(of object)* caer, caerse; *(of ground)* caer; **to d. out** *(from pocket, briefcase)* caerse; *Fam* **I'm ready to d.** estoy para el arrastre; *Fam* **people are dropping like flies** la gente está cayendo como moscas; **to d. dead** caerse muerto; *Fam* **d. dead!** ¡muérete!; *Fam* **let it d.!** ¡déjalo ya!

**(b)** *(of prices, temperature, demand, unemployment)* caer, bajar; *(of voice)* bajar; *(of wind)* amainar; *(of speed)* disminuir

▶**drop by** *vi* I thought I'd d. by for a chat se me ocurrió pasarme a charlar un rato

▶**drop in** *vi* **to d. in on sb** pasar a visitar a alguien

▶**drop off 1** *vt sep (person from car)* dejar

**2** *vi* **(a)** *Fam* **to d. off (to sleep)** quedarse traspuesto(a) **(b)** *(of membership, attendance)* bajar, disminuir

▶**drop out** *vi (from a contest)* retirarse; *(from society)* marginarse; **to d. out of university** dejar la universidad

▶**drop round 1** *vt sep (deliver)* **to d. sth round** entregar *or* llevar algo; **I'll d. it round at your place tomorrow** lo dejaré en tu casa mañana

**2** *vi (visit)* pasarse

**droplet** ['droplɪt] *n* gotita *f*

**dropout** ['drɒpaʊt] *n Fam (from society)* marginado(a) *m,f; (from university)* = persona que ha abandonado los estudios; **d. rate** *(from university)* índice *m* de abandono de los estudios

**dropper** ['drɒpə(r)] *n (for medicine)* cuentagotas *m inv*

**droppings** ['drɒpɪŋz] *npl* excrementos *mpl*

**dross** [drɒs] *n Fam (rubbish)* porquería *f*, basura *f*

**drought** [draʊt] *n* sequía *f*

**drove** [drəʊv] **1** *n* **in droves** en manadas
**2** *pt of* **drive**

**drown** [draʊn] **1** *vt* **(a)** *(kill by drowning)* ahogar; **to d. oneself** ahogarse; **to d. one's sorrows (in drink)** ahogar las penas (en alcohol) **(b)** *(make inaudible)* ahogar
**2** *vi (die by drowning)* ahogarse

▶**drown out** *vt sep (sound)* ahogar

**drowse** [draʊz] *vi* dormitar

**drowsy** ['draʊzɪ] *adj (person)* somnoliento(a), soñoliento(a); *(afternoon)* soporífero(a); **to be d.** estar somnoliento(a)

**drudge** [drʌdʒ] *n* = persona que tiene un trabajo pesado y aburrido

**drudgery** ['drʌdʒərɪ] *n* trabajo *m* (duro y) rutinario

**drug** [drʌg] **1** *n (medicine)* medicamento *m*; *(illegal)* droga *f*; **hard/soft drugs** drogas duras/blandas; **to take drugs** drogarse, tomar drogas; **d. abuse** drogadicción *f*; **d. addict** drogadicto(a) *m,f*, toxicómano(a) *m,f*; **d. dealer** *(large-scale)* narcotraficante *m,f*, traficante *mf* de drogas; *(small-scale)* camello *mf*; **d. squad** brigada *f* de estupefacientes

**2** *vt (pt & pp* **drugged)** drogar; **they had drugged his wine/food** le echaron una droga en el vino/la comida

**druggist** ['drʌgɪst] *n US* farmacéutico(a) *m,f*

**drugstore** ['drʌgstɔ:(r)] *n US* = tienda que vende cosméticos, periódicos, medicamentos, etc.

**druid** ['druːɪd] *n* druida *m*

**drum** [drʌm] **1** *n* **(a)** *(musical instrument)* tambor *m*; **d. kit, drums** batería *f* **(b)** *(container)* barril *m*; *(of washing machine)* tambor *m*; *(for oil)* bidón *m*

**2** *vt (pt & pp* **drummed)** she was drumming her fingers on the table** estaba tamborileando en la mesa con los dedos; **to d. sth into sb** meterle algo en la cabeza a alguien

**3** *vi (play drums)* tocar la batería; **the rain was drumming on the window panes** la lluvia golpeaba en los cristales

▶**drum up** *vt (support, enthusiasm)* buscar, reunir

**drummer** ['drʌmə(r)] *n (in pop band)* batería *mf; (in military band)* tamborilero(a) *m,f*

**drumstick** ['drʌmstɪk] *n* **(a)** *(for playing drums)* baqueta *f* **(b)** *(chicken leg)* muslo *m*

**drunk** [drʌŋk] **1** *n* borracho(a) *m,f*
**2** *adj* borracho(a); **to be d.** estar borracho(a); **to get d.** emborracharse; *Law* **d. and disorderly behaviour** estado *m* de embriaguez con conducta violenta; *Fig* **d. with power** ebrio(a) de poder
**3** *pp of* **drink**

**drunkard** ['drʌŋkəd] *n* borracho(a) *m,f*

**drunken** ['drʌŋkən] *adj (person)* borracho(a); *(party, argument)* acalorado(a) por el alcohol; **d. brawl** trifulca *f* de borrachos; **in a d. stupor** aturdido(a) por el alcohol

**dry** [draɪ] **1** *adj* **(a)** *(weather, clothing, wine)* seco(a); **to run** *or* **go d.** secarse; **to be kept d.** *(sign on container)* no mojar; **as d. as a bone** reseco(a); *Naut* **d. dock** dique *m* seco; **d. ice** nieve *f* carbónica, hielo *m* seco; **d. land** tierra *f* firme; **d. rot** putrefacción *f* de la madera; **d. run** ensayo *m* **(b)** *(boring) (prose style, person)* aburrido(a), árido(a) **(c)** *(deadpan) (humour)* lacónico(a)

**2** *vt* secar; **to d. oneself** secarse; **to d. one's**

**hair** secarse el pelo
  **3** *vi* secarse
▸**dry out** *vi* (**a**) *(of alcoholic)* dejar el alcohol (**b**) *(of moisture, wet thing)* secarse
▸**dry up** *vi* (**a**) *(of well, pool)* secarse (**b**) *(of funds, conversation, inspiration)* agotarse (**c**) *(of actor, public speaker)* quedarse en blanco

**dry-clean** [draɪ'kliːn] *vt* limpiar en seco

**dry-cleaner's** [draɪ'kliːnəz] *n* tintorería *f*

**dry-cleaning** [draɪ'kliːnɪŋ] *n (process)* limpieza *f* en seco; *(clothes)* **to collect the d.** recoger la ropa de la tintorería

**dryer** ['draɪə(r)] *n* = **drier**

**DSS** [diːes'es] *n Br (abbr* **Department of Social Security)** = ministerio británico de seguridad social

**DTI** [diːtiː'aɪ] *n Br (abbr* **Department of Trade and Industry)** ≃ Ministerio de Industria

**DTP** [diːtiː'piː] *n Comptr (abbr* **desktop publishing)** autoedición *f*

**DTs** [diː'tiːz] *npl (abbr* **delirium tremens)** delírium tremens *m inv;* **to have the D.** tener un delírium tremens

**dual** ['djʊəl] *adj* doble; **d. carriageway** *(road)* (tramo *m* de) autovía *f;* **to have d. nationality** tener doble nacionalidad; **d. ownership** copropiedad *f*

**dual-purpose** ['djʊəl'pɜːpəs] *adj* de doble uso

**dub** [dʌb] (*pt & pp* **dubbed)** *vt* (**a**) *(film)* doblar (**b**) apodar

**dubbing** ['dʌbɪŋ] *n Cin* doblaje *m*

**dubious** ['djuːbɪəs] *adj* (**a**) *(uncertain)* dudoso(a), inseguro(a); **to be d. (about sth)** no estar convencido(a) (de algo) (**b**) *(questionable) (distinction, honour)* dudoso(a); **a d. character** un tipo sospechoso

**Dublin** ['dʌblɪn] *n* Dublín

**Dubliner** ['dʌblɪnə(r)] *n* dublinés(esa) *m,f*

**duchess** ['dʌtʃɪs] *n* duquesa *f*

**duchy** ['dʌtʃɪ] *n* ducado *m*

**duck** [dʌk] **1** *n* pato *m;* **to take to sth like a d. to water** sentirse en algo como pez en el agua; **criticism runs off him like water off a d.'s back** le resbalan las críticas; **d. pond** estanque *m* de patos
  **2** *vt* (**a**) *(one's head)* agachar; **to d. sb** *(under water)* hacer una ahogadilla a alguien (**b**) *(avoid)* **to d. the issue** eludir el tema
  **3** *vi* *(to avoid being hit)* agacharse; *(under water)* zambullirse
▸**duck out of** *vt insep* **to d. out of sth/doing sth** zafarse de algo/hacer algo

**duck-billed platypus** ['dʌkbɪld'plætɪpəs] *n* ornitorrinco *m*

**duckling** ['dʌklɪŋ] *n* patito *m*

**duct** [dʌkt] *n (for fuel, air, tears)* conducto *m*

**dud** [dʌd] *Fam* **1** *n (person)* mamarracho *m,* desastre *m; (shell)* proyectil *m* que no estalla
  **2** *adj* defectuoso(a); *(banknote)* falso(a)

**dude** [duːd] *n US (man)* tío *m,* tipo *m*

**due** [djuː] **1** *adj* (**a**) *(owed)* pagadero(a); **to fall d.** ser pagadero(a); **are you d. any money from him?** ¿te debe dinero?; **you're d. an apology** mereces una disculpa; **d. to...** *(because of, as result of)* debido a...; *Fin* **d. date** (fecha *f* de) vencimiento *m*
  (**b**) *(merited, proper)* debido(a); **after d. consideration** tras la debida consideración; **with all d. respect,...** con el debido respeto,...; **in d. course** *(when appropriate)* a su debido tiempo; *(eventually)* al final
  (**c**) *(expected)* **the train/he is d. (to arrive) at two o'clock** el tren/él tiene la llegada prevista a las dos; **when is he d.?** ¿cuándo llega?; **she's d. back any minute** volverá en cualquier momento; **when is their baby d.?** ¿para cuándo esperan el niño?; **the film/book is d. out soon** la película/el libro está a punto de aparecer
  **2** *n* (**a**) **to give him his d., he did apologize** para ser justos con él, hay que decir que se disculpó
  (**b**) **dues** *(for membership)* cuota *f*
  **3** *adv* **d. north/south** justo al *or* hacia el norte/sur

**duel** ['djʊəl] **1** *n* duelo *m;* **to fight a d.** batirse en duelo
  **2** *vi* (*pt & pp* **duelled,** *US* **dueled)** batirse en duelo

**duet** [djuː'et] *n Mus* dúo *m;* **to sing/play a d.** cantar/tocar un dúo

**duff** [dʌf] *adj Fam* chungo(a), malo(a)
▸**duff up** *vt sep Fam* dar un paliza a

**duffel** = **duffle**

**duffer** ['dʌfə(r)] *n Fam (incompetent person)* ceporro(a) *m,f,* nulidad *f;* **to be a d. at history/ French** ser una nulidad en historia/francés

**duffle** ['dʌfəl] *n* **d. (coat)** trenca *f;* **d. bag** talega *f* de lona

**dug** [dʌg] *pt & pp* **of dig**

**dugout** ['dʌgaʊt] *n* (**a**) *(canoe)* piragua *f,* canoa *f (hecha con un tronco vaciado)* (**b**) *(shelter)* refugio *m* subterráneo; *Sport* foso *m* (del banquillo)

**duke** [djuːk] *n* duque *m*

**dull** [dʌl] **1** *adj* (**a**) *(boring) (book, film, person)* aburrido(a); *(job, life, party)* insulso(a), soso(a); **to be as d. as ditchwater** ser más soso(a) que la calabaza (**b**) *(not intelligent)* tonto(a), torpe (**c**) *(not sharp) (tool, blade)* romo(a); *(sound, pain)* sordo(a) (**d**) *(not bright) (colour, surface)* mate, apagado(a); *(eyes)* apagado(a); *(weather, sky)* gris, triste
  **2** *vt* (**a**) *(reduce intensity of) (pleasure)* enturbiar; *(the senses)* embotar; *(pain)* mitigar, atenuar;

*(sound)* apagar; *(blade)* desafilar, embotar **(b)** *(make less bright)* *(colours, eyes)* apagar

**duly** ['dju:lı] *adv* **(a)** *(properly)* como corresponde, debidamente; **we were d. worried** estábamos preocupados con razón **(b)** *(as expected)* **he said he'd be punctual and he d. arrived on the stroke of eight** dijo que llegaría puntual y confirmando las previsiones, llegó a las ocho en punto

**dumb** [dʌm] *adj* **(a)** *(unable to speak)* mudo(a); **to be struck d. with astonishment** quedarse mudo(a) de asombro; **d. animals** los animales indefensos **(b)** *Fam (stupid)* *(person, action)* bobo(a), estúpido(a); **d. blonde** rubia *f* sin cerebro

**dumbbell** ['dʌmbel] *n* pesa *f*

**dumbfounded** [dʌm'faʊndıd], **dumb-struck** ['dʌmstrʌk] *adj* boquiabierto(a), pasmado(a)

**dumbwaiter** ['dʌmweıtə(r)] *n (lift)* montaplatos *m inv*

**dummy** ['dʌmı] **1** *n* **(a)** *(in shop window)* maniquí *m*; *(of ventriloquist)* muñeco *m*; *(model of car, plane)* modelo *m*, maqueta *f* **(b)** *(for baby)* chupete *m* **(c)** *Fam (idiot)* idiota *mf*, imbécil *mf*
**2** *adj (fake)* falso(a); **d. run** prueba *f*

**dump** [dʌmp] **1** *n* **(a)** *(for refuse)* vertedero *m*, basurero *m*; *Fam* **what a d.!** ¡qué sitio más cutre!; **d. truck** volquete *m* **(b)** *Mil (store)* depósito *m* **(c)** *Comptr* **(memory** or **storage) d.** volcado *m* de memoria
**2** *vt* **(a)** *(put down)* soltar, dejar; *(unload)* descargar **(b)** *(dispose of)* *(rubbish, old car)* tirar; *(nuclear, toxic waste)* verter; *Fam (lover, boyfriend, girlfriend)* dejar, dar calabazas a **(c)** *Comptr (memory)* volcar

**dumper** ['dʌmpə(r)] *n* **d. (truck)** volquete *m*

**dumping** ['dʌmpıŋ] *n* **(a) no d.** *(sign)* prohibido arrojar basuras; **d. ground** vertedero *m* **(b)** *Econ* dumping *m*

**dumpling** ['dʌmplıŋ] *n (in stew)* = bola de masa hervida; **apple d.** bollo *m* relleno de manzana

**dumps** [dʌmps] *npl Fam* **to be down in the d.** estar con la moral por los suelos

**dumpy** ['dʌmpı] *adj Fam (person, appearance)* rechoncho(a), achaparrado(a)

**dunce** [dʌns] *n (at school)* burro/a *m,f*; **d.'s cap** ≃ orejas *fpl* de burro

**dune** [dju:n] *n* **(sand) d.** duna *f*

**dung** [dʌŋ] *n* estiércol *m*

**dungarees** [dʌŋgə'ri:z] *npl* (pantalón *m* de) peto *m*; **a pair of d.** unos pantalones de peto

**dungeon** ['dʌndʒən] *n* mazmorra *f*

**dunghill** ['dʌŋhıl] *n* estercolero *m*

**dunk** [dʌŋk] *vt* mojar

**duo** ['dju:əʊ] *n (pl* **duos)** *n* dúo *m*

**duodenal** [dju:əʊ'di:nəl] *adj (ulcer)* duodenal

**duodenum** [dju:əʊ'di:nəm] *n* duodeno *m*

**DUP** [di:ju:'pi:] *n Br (abbr* **Democratic Unionist Party)** = Partido Unionista Democrático, que apoya la permanencia de Irlanda del Norte en el Reino Unido

**dupe** [dju:p] **1** *n* primo(a) *m,f*, ingenuo(a) *m,f*
**2** *vt* engañar; **to d. sb into doing sth** engañar a alguien para que haga algo

**duplex** ['dju:pleks] *n & adj* dúplex *m*, duplex *m*

**duplicate** ['dju:plıkət] **1** *n (copy)* duplicado *m*, copia *f*; **in d.** por duplicado
**2** *adj* duplicado(a)
**3** *vt* ['dju:plıkeıt] **(a)** *(copy)* *(document)* duplicar, hacer un duplicado de **(b)** *(repeat)* *(findings, result)* repetir

**duplication** [dju:plı'keıʃən] *n* duplicación *f*

**duplicity** [dju:'plısıtı] *n* duplicidad *f*

**durability** [djʊərə'bılıtı] *n* durabilidad *f*

**durable** ['djʊərəbəl] **1** *adj* duradero(a)
**2** *n* **(consumer) durables** bienes *mpl* de consumo duraderos

**duration** [djʊ'reıʃən] *n* duración *f*; **for the d. (of)** hasta el final (de)

**duress** [djʊ'res] *n* **under d.** bajo coacción

**during** ['djʊərıŋ] *prep* durante

**dusk** [dʌsk] *n* crepúsculo *m*, anochecer *m*; **at d.** al anochecer

**dust** [dʌst] **1** *n* **(a)** *(dirt, powder)* polvo *m*; **d. cover** *(for furniture)* funda *f*; **d. cover** or **jacket** *(for book)* sobrecubierta *f* **(b)** *(action)* **to give sth a d.** quitar el polvo a algo **(c)** *(idioms)* **once the d. has settled** *(when fuss is over)* cuando haya pasado la tormenta; *Fam* **you won't see me for d.!** pondré pies en polvorosa
**2** *vt* **(a)** *(clean)* *(room, furniture)* limpiar el polvo de **(b)** *(sprinkle)* *(with flour, sugar)* espolvorear (with con)
▸**dust down, dust off** *vt sep (furniture)* quitar el polvo a; *Fig (legislation, one's French)* desempolvar

**dustbin** ['dʌstbın] *n* cubo *m* de la basura

**dustcart** ['dʌstkɑ:t] *n* camión *m* de la basura

**duster** ['dʌstə(r)] *n (cloth)* trapo *m* or bayeta *f* del polvo; *(for blackboard)* borrador *m*

**dustman** ['dʌstmən] *n* basurero *m*

**dustpan** ['dʌstpæn] *n* recogedor *m*; **d. and brush** cepillo *m* y recogedor

**dustsheet** ['dʌstʃi:t] *n* guardapolvo *m (funda)*

**dust-up** ['dʌstʌp] *n Fam (brawl)* bronca *f*, trifulca *f*; **to have a d. (with sb)** tener una bronca (con alguien)

**dusty** ['dʌstı] *adj* polvoriento(a); **to get d.** llenarse de polvo

**Dutch** [dʌtʃ] **1** *npl (people)* **the D.** los holandeses
**2** *n (language)* neerlandés *m*

**3** *adj* holandés(esa); **D. cap** *(contraceptive)* diafragma *m*; **D. courage** = valentía que da el alcohol

**4** *adv Fam* **to go D.** pagar a escote

**Dutchman** ['dʌtʃmən] *n* holandés *m*; *Fam* **if that's a real diamond (then) I'm a D.** si esto es un diamante de verdad, que venga Dios y lo vea

**Dutchwoman** ['dʌtʃwʊmən] *n* holandesa *f*

**dutiful** ['djuːtɪfʊl] *adj (son, daughter)* obediente, bien mandado(a)

**duty** ['djuːtɪ] *n* **(a)** *(obligation)* deber *m*; **to do one's d.** cumplir (uno) con su deber; **he failed in his d.** faltó a *or* no cumplió con su deber; **I shall make it my d. to...** yo me ocuparé de...; **it is your d. to...** tu deber es...

(b) *(task)* **duties** tareas *fpl*; **she took up** *or* **assumed her duties** se incorporó a su puesto; **she carried out** *or* **performed her duties well** desempeñó bien su trabajo

(c) *(of soldier, employee)* **to be on d.** estar de servicio; **to be off d.** estar fuera de servicio; *Mil* **tour of d.** destino *m*; **d. roster** rota *f* de guardias

(d) *Fin (tax)* derecho *m*, impuesto *m*; **to pay d. on sth** pagar derechos *or* impuestos por algo

**duty-free** ['djuːtɪ'friː] *adj* exento(a) *or* libre de impuestos; **d. shop** tienda *f* libre de impuestos

**duvet** ['duːveɪ] *n* edredón *m*; **d. cover** funda *f* de edredón

**dwarf** [dwɔːf] **1** *n (pl* **dwarfs** *or* **dwarves** [dwɔːvz])* enano(a) *m,f*

**2** *adj (plant, tree)* enano(a)

**3** *vt* empequeñecer; **the church is dwarfed by the new skyscraper** el nuevo rascacielos hace pequeña a la iglesia

**dwell** [dwel] *(pt & pp* **dwelt** [dwelt]) *vi Literary (live)* morar

▸**dwell on, dwell upon** *vt insep* **why d. on the negative side of things?** ¿para qué fijarse en el lado negativo de las cosas?; **let's not** *or* **don't let's d. on it** no le demos más vueltas al asunto

**dwelling** ['dwelɪŋ] *n Formal* **d. (place)** morada *f*; **d. house** residencia *f*

**dwelt** [dwelt] *pt & pp of* **dwell**

**dwindle** ['dwɪndəl] *vi* disminuir, reducirse; **to d. (away) to nothing** quedar reducido(a) a nada

**dwindling** ['dwɪndəlɪŋ] *adj (funds, membership)* menguante; *(enthusiasm)* decreciente

**dye** [daɪ] **1** *n (for clothes, hair)* tinte *m*

**2** *vt* teñir; **to d. sth black/red** teñir algo de negro/rojo; **to d. one's hair** teñirse el pelo

**dyed-in-the-wool** ['daɪdɪnðə'wʊl] *adj (conservative, Marxist)* acérrimo(a)

**dying** ['daɪɪŋ] **1** *adj (person)* moribundo(a), agonizante; *(industry, tradition)* en vías de desaparición; **to my d. day** hasta el día de mi muerte; **d. wish** última voluntad *f*; **d. words** últimas palabras *fpl*

**2** *npl* **the d.** los moribundos

**dyke** [daɪk] *n* **(a)** *(barrier)* dique *m* **(b)** *very Fam (lesbian)* tortillera *f*

**dynamic** [daɪ'næmɪk] **1** *adj also Fig* dinámico(a)

**2** *n (driving force)* dinámica *f*

**dynamics** [daɪ'næmɪks] *npl (of change, growth)* dinámica *f*

**dynamism** ['daɪnəmɪzəm] *n (of person, society)* dinamismo *m*

**dynamite** ['daɪnəmaɪt] **1** *n* dinamita *f*; *Fig* **his theories were political d.** sus teorías políticas eran pura dinamita; *Fam* **it's d.!** *(marvellous)* ¡es genial!

**2** *vt (building, bridge)* dinamitar

**dynamo** ['daɪnəməʊ] *(pl* **dynamos***) n Elec* dinamo *f*

**dynastic** [dɪ'næstɪk] *adj* dinástico(a)

**dynasty** ['dɪnəstɪ] *n* dinastía *f*

**dysentery** ['dɪsəntrɪ] *n* disentería *f*

**dysfunctional** [dɪs'fʌŋkʃənəl] *adj (family, relationship)* disfuncional

**dyslexia** [dɪs'leksɪə] *n* dislexia *f*

**dyslexic** [dɪs'leksɪk] *adj* disléxico(a)

**dystrophy** ['dɪstrəfɪ] *n Med* distrofia *f*

# E

**E, e** [i:] *n* (**a**) *(letter)* E, e *f* (**b**) *Mus* mi *m* (**c**) *(abbr* **east**) E, este *m* (**d**) *Sch* suspenso *m*; **to get an E** *(in exam, essay)* suspender (**e**) *Fam (abbr* **ecstasy**) *(drug)* éxtasis *m inv*

**each** [i:tʃ] **1** *adj* cada; **e. day** cada día; **e. one of us** todos (y cada uno de) nosotros

**2** *pron* (**a**) *(both, all)* cada uno; **e. of us** cada uno de nosotros; **we e. earn £300** ganamos cada uno 300 libras; **peaches at 25 pence e.** melocotones a 25 peniques la pieza *or* cada uno; **a little of e.** un poco de cada (uno) (**b**) *(reciprocal)* **to hate e. other** odiarse; **to kiss e. other** besarse; **to support e. other** apoyarse mutuamente; **we write to e. other** nos escribimos

**eager** ['i:gə(r)] *adj (look, interest)* ávido(a), ansioso(a); *(supporter)* entusiasta; *(desire, hope)* intenso(a); **to be e. for sth** estar ansioso(a) por *or* ávido(a) de algo; **the audience were e. for more** el público seguía pidiendo más; **to be e. to do sth** estar ansioso por hacer algo; **to be e. to please** estar deseando agradar; **they were e. to learn** estaban ávidos *or* ansiosos por aprender; *Fam* **to be an e. beaver** ser muy aplicado(a)

**eagerly** ['i:gəlɪ] *adv* ansiosamente; **e. awaited** ansiado(a), largamente esperado(a)

**eagerness** ['i:gənɪs] *n (impatience)* avidez *f*, ansia *f*; *(enthusiasm)* entusiasmo *m*; **to show e. in doing sth** hacer algo con entusiasmo

**eagle** ['i:gəl] *n* águila *f*

**eagle-eyed** [i:gə'laɪd] *adj* **to be e.** tener vista de lince

**ear** ['ɪə(r)] *n* (**a**) *(of person, animal) (external part)* oreja *f*; *(internal part)* oído *m*; **to have an e. for music** tener buen oído para la música; **to have an e. for languages** tener aptitudes para los idiomas; *Med* **e., nose and throat specialist** otorrinolaringólogo(a) *m,f*; **e. lobe** lóbulo *m* de la oreja

(**b**) *(of wheat)* espiga *f*

(**c**) *(idioms)* **to play it by e.** ver qué pasa; **he has the boss's e.** goza de la confianza del jefe; **to keep one's e. to the ground** mantenerse al corriente; **to go in one e. and out the other** *(of words, information)* entrar por un oído y salir por el otro; *Fam* **I'm all ears** soy todo

oídos; *Fam* **to be up to one's ears in work/debt** estar hasta las cejas de trabajo/deudas; *Fam* **to be (thrown) out on one's e.** ser puesto(a) de patitas en la calle; **to reach sb's ears** llegar a los oídos de alguien; **the house was falling down around their ears** la casa se les caía encima

**earache** ['ɪəreɪk] *n* dolor *m* de oídos

**eardrum** ['ɪədrʌm] *n* tímpano *m*

**earful** ['ɪəfʊl] *n Fam* **to give sb an e.** *(scold, criticize)* echar un sermón a alguien

**earl** [ɜːl] *n* conde *m*

**earlier** ['ɜːlɪə(r)] **1** *adj* anterior; **I caught an e. train** cogí un tren anterior; **her e. novels** sus novelas anteriores

**2** *adv* **e. (on)** antes; **a few days e.** unos días antes; **no e. than tomorrow** no antes de mañana; **as we saw e.** como vimos anteriormente *or* antes

**earliest** ['ɜːlɪəst] **1** *n* **at the e.** como muy pronto; **the e. I can be there is four o'clock** no podré estar ahí antes de las cuatro

**2** *adj (opportunity, memory)* primero(a); **at the e. possible moment** lo antes posible; **from the earliest times** desde los primeros tiempos

**early** ['ɜːlɪ] **1** *adj* (**a**) *(in the day)* temprano(a); **at this e. hour…** a una hora tan temprana…; **in the e. morning** por la mañana temprano; **in the e. afternoon** a primera hora de la tarde; **to have an e. night** acostarse temprano; **to be an e. riser** ser madrugador(ora); *Prov* **the e. bird catches the worm** a quien madruga, Dios le ayuda

(**b**) *(at beginning of period of time)* temprano(a), primero(a); **an e. goal** un gol temprano *or* temprano; **the e. days/stages of…** los primeros días/las primeras etapas de…; **in e. summer** a principios del verano; **at an e. age** a una edad temprana; **in the e. 1980s** a principios de los ochenta; **an e. example of…** un ejemplo temprano de…

(**c**) *(ahead of time) (arrival)* antes de tiempo; *(breakfast, lunch)* temprano(a); **to be e.** llegar pronto *or* temprano; **I am half an hour e.** llego media hora antes *or* con media hora de adelanto; **an e. death** una muerte prematura; **e. retirement** jubilación *f* anticipada; *Mil* **e.**

**warning system** sistema f de alerta inmediata (d) *(future)* pronto(a); **in e. reply** una pronta respuesta; **at an e. date** en fecha próxima

**2** *adv* (a) *(in the day)* temprano, pronto; **e. in the morning/evening** en las primeras horas de la mañana/tarde; **to get up e.** levantarse temprano; **as e. as possible** lo antes posible, cuanto antes

(b) *(at beginning of period of time)* **e. in the year** a primeros de año; **e. on** temprano; **e. in one's life/career** al principio de la vida/carrera profesional

(c) *(ahead of time)* pronto; **too e.** demasiado pronto; **they left the party e.** se fueron pronto de la fiesta; **to die e.** morir prematuramente; **to retire e.** jubilarse anticipadamente

**earmark** ['ɪəmɑːk] *vt* destinar (**for** a)

**earn** [ɜːn] *vt (money)* ganar; *(rest, respect)* ganarse; **to e. one's living** ganarse la vida

**earner** ['ɜːnə(r)] *n (wage)* **e.** asalariado(a) m,f; **the shop is a nice little e.** la tienda es una buena fuente de ingresos

**earnest** ['ɜːnɪst] **1** *adj* serio(a)

**2** *n* **in e.** en serio

**earnestly** ['ɜːnɪstlɪ] *adv (to speak, discuss, consider)* seriamente, con gravedad; *(to hope, desire, believe)* sinceramente

**earning power** ['ɜːnɪŋ'paʊə(r)] *n* capacidad f de ingresos

**earnings** ['ɜːnɪŋz] *npl (of person)* ingresos mpl; *(of company)* beneficios mpl, ganancias fpl; **e. related** *(pensions, benefits)* proporcional a los ingresos

**earphones** ['ɪəfəʊnz] *npl* auriculares mpl

**earpiece** ['ɪəpiːs] *n (of telephone)* auricular m

**earplug** ['ɪəplʌg] *n* tapón m para los oídos

**earring** ['ɪərɪŋ] *n* pendiente m, Am arete m

**earshot** ['ɪəʃɒt] *n* **within/out of e.** al alcance del/fuera del alcance del oído; **I was within e. of them** yo podía oírles

**ear-splitting** ['ɪəsplɪtɪŋ] *adj* ensordecedor(ora)

**earth** [ɜːθ] **1** *n* (a) *(planet)* **the E.** la Tierra (b) *(soil)* tierra f (c) *Br Elec* toma f de tierra (d) *(idioms)* Fam **where/why on e. ...?** ¿dónde/por qué diablos...?; **to cost the e.** costar un riñón or un ojo de la cara; **to promise sb the e.** prometer a alguien el oro y el moro; *Fig* **to come back to e. (with a bump)** bajarse de la nube, bajar a la tierra

**2** *vt Br Elec* conectar a tierra

**earthenware** ['ɜːθənweə(r)] *n* loza f

**earthling** ['ɜːθlɪŋ] *n* terrícola mf

**earthly** ['ɜːθlɪ] *adj* (a) *(life, existence)* terrenal (b) *Fam (emphatic)* **there's no e. reason** no hay razón alguna; **she hasn't got an e.** *(chance)* no tiene la menor posibilidad; **it's of no e. use** no vale absolutamente para nada

**earthquake** ['ɜːθkweɪk] *n also Fig* terremoto m

**earth-shattering** ['ɜːθʃætərɪŋ] *adj Fam (news, discovery)* extraordinario(a)

**earthworks** ['ɜːθwɜːks] *n* terraplén m

**earthworm** ['ɜːθwɜːm] *n* lombriz f *(de tierra)*

**earthy** ['ɜːθɪ] *adj* (a) *(of or like earth)* terroso(a) (b) *(coarse)* grosero(a); *(uninhibited)* directo(a), campechano(a)

**earwax** ['ɪəwæks] *n* cera f de los oídos, cerumen m

**earwig** ['ɪəwɪg] *n* tijereta f

**ease** [iːz] **1** *n* (a) *(facility)* facilidad f; **with e.** con facilidad (b) *(peace)* **at e.** a gusto; **to put sb at e.** hacer que alguien se sienta a gusto; **to put** or **set sb's mind at e.** tranquilizar a alguien; **a life of e.** una vida desahogada

**2** *vt* (a) *(alleviate) (pain, anxiety)* calmar (b) *(relax) (pressure, tension)* disminuir (c) *(move carefully, slowly)* **she eased the heavy box into the car** despacio y con cuidado, trasladó la pesada caja al interior del coche

**3** *vi (of pain, pressure)* remitir; **the wind/the rain has eased** el viento/la lluvia ha amainado un poco

▸**ease off, ease up** *vi (of pain)* disminuir, remitir; *(of rain)* amainar

**easel** ['iːzəl] *n* caballete m

**easily** ['iːzɪlɪ] *adv* (a) *(without difficulty, probably)* fácilmente; **the information could e. be wrong** la información puede muy bien ser errónea; **e. the best/biggest** sin duda alguna el mejor/mayor; **that's e. said** eso se dice pronto, del dicho al hecho... (b) *(comfortably)* cómodamente, sin dificultad; **he's e. 40** *(at least)* andará por los 40 como poco

**easiness** ['iːzɪnɪs] *n* (a) *(of task)* facilidad f (b) *(of manner)* desenvoltura f

**east** [iːst] **1** *n* **e** este m; **to the e. (of)** al este (de); **the E.** *(Asia)* el Oriente; *(of Europe)* el Este

**2** *adj (side)* oriental, este; **E. Africa** África Oriental; **the E. End** = el barrio este de Londres; *Formerly* **E. Germany** Alemania Oriental or del Este; *Old-fashioned* **the E. Indies** = el archipiélago indonesio, las Indias orientales; **the E. Side** = el barrio este de Manhattan; **e. wind** viento m de levante

**3** *adv (travel, move)* en dirección este, hacia el este; **it's (3 miles) e. of here** está (a 3 millas) al este de aquí; **to face e.** mirar hacia el este

**eastbound** ['iːstbaʊnd] *adj (train, traffic)* en dirección este; **the e. carriageway** el carril que va hacia el este

**Easter** ['iːstə(r)] *n (period)* Semana f Santa; *(festival)* Pascua f; **at E.** en Semana Santa; **E. egg** huevo m de Pascua; **E. Island** la Isla de Pascua; **E. Sunday** Domingo m de Pascua or de Resurrección; **E. week** Semana Santa

**easterly** ['i:stəlɪ] **1** *n (wind)* levante *m*
**2** *adj (direction)* (hacia el) este; **the most e. point** el punto más al este; **e. wind** viento *m* de levante

**eastern** ['i:stən] *adj (region)* del este, oriental; *(religion)* oriental; **E. Europe** Europa Oriental *or* del Este; *US* **E. Standard Time** hora *f* oficial en la costa este de los EE.UU.

**eastward** ['i:stwəd] *adj & adv* hacia el este
**eastwards** ['i:stwədz] *adv* hacia el este

**easy** ['i:zɪ] **1** *adj* **(a)** *(not difficult)* fácil; **e. to please** fácil de contentar; **e. to get on with** tratable; **it's e. to say…** es muy fácil decir…; **that's easier said than done** es muy fácil decirlo, del dicho al hecho (hay mucho trecho); *Fam* **it's as e. as ABC** *or* **as pie** es pan comido; **the e. option** la solución más fácil; *Fam* **e. money** dinero *m* fácil; **e. on the eye** agradable a la vista; *Com* **by e. payments, on e. terms** con facilidades de pago; *Fam* **I'm e.!** *(I don't mind)* ¡por mí es igual!, ¡a mí me da lo mismo!
**(b)** *(comfortable) (pace, life)* cómodo(a), apacible; *(manners, style)* desenvuelto(a); *Fam* **to be on e. street** no tener problemas económicos; **to have an e. time (of it)** tenerlo fácil, no tener que emplearse a fondo; **e. chair** butaca *f*, sillón *m*
**2** *adv* **to go e. on sb** no ser demasiado duro(a) con alguien; **to go e. on sth** no pasarse con algo; **to take things** *or* **it e.** tomarse las cosas con calma, tomárselo con calma; **take it e.!** ¡tranquilo!; **e. come, e. go** tal como viene, se va

**easy-going** ['i:zɪ'gəʊɪŋ] *adj (tolerant)* tolerante; *(calm)* tranquilo(a)

**eat** [i:t] *(pt* **ate** [et, eɪt], *pp* **eaten** ['i:tən]) **1** *vt*
**(a)** comer; **to e. one's breakfast** desayunar
**(b)** *(idioms)* **to e. sb out of house and home** dejarle la nevera *or* la despensa vacía a alguien; *Fam* **I could e. a horse!** ¡tengo un hambre canina!; *Fam* **he won't e. you!** ¡no te va a comer!; *Fam* **what's eating you?** *(worrying you)* ¿qué te preocupa?; **to e. one's words** tragarse (uno) sus propias palabras; *Fam* **if it works, I'll e. my hat** si esto funciona, me meto a monja
**2** *vi* comer; *Fig* **to have sb eating out of one's hand** tener a alguien en el bote
➤**eat away (at)** *vt insep also Fig* erosionar
➤**eat into** *vt insep (erode)* corroer; *Fig (time)* gastar; *(savings)* mermar
➤**eat out** *vi* salir a comer fuera
➤**eat up 1** *vt sep (food)* terminar *(de comer)*; *(petrol, money)* consumir
**2** *vi* **e. up!** ¡termina (de comer)!

**eaten** ['i:tən] *pp of* **eat**

**eater** ['i:tə(r)] *n* **to be a slow/fast e.** comer despacio/deprisa

**eatery** ['i:tərɪ] *n US* restaurante *m*

**eats** [i:ts] *npl Fam* comida *f*, cosas *fpl* de comer

**eau-de-Cologne** ['əʊdəkə'ləʊn] *n* (agua *f* de) colonia *f*

**eaves** [i:vz] *npl (of house)* alero *m*

**eavesdrop** ['i:vzdrɒp] *(pt & pp* **eavesdropped**) *vi* escuchar disimuladamente

**ebb** [eb] **1** *n (of tide)* reflujo *m*; *Fig* **the e. and flow** *(of events)* los vaivenes *mpl*; *Fig* **to be at a low e.** *(of person, spirits)* estar en horas bajas; **e. tide** marea *f* baja, bajamar *f*
**2** *vi (of tide)* bajar
➤**ebb away** *vi (of water)* bajar; *(of strength, enthusiasm)* menguar, disminuir

**ebony** ['ebənɪ] *n* ébano *m*

**ebullience** [ɪ'bʌlɪəns] *n* fogosidad *f*

**ebullient** [ɪ'bʌlɪənt] *adj* fogoso(a)

**EC** [i:'si:] *n Formerly (abbr* **European Community**) CE *f*, Comunidad *f* Europea

**eccentric** [ek'sentrɪk] *n & adj* excéntrico(a) *m,f*

**eccentricity** [eksen'trɪsɪtɪ] *n* excentricidad *f*

**ecclesiastic** [ɪkli:zɪ'æstɪk] **1** *n* clérigo *m*
**2** *adj* eclesiástico(a)

**ECG** [i:si:'dʒi:] *n Med (abbr* **electrocardiogram**) ECG *m*, electrocardiograma *m*

**echelon** ['eʃəlɒn] *n* **the higher echelons** las altas esferas; **the lower echelons** los grados inferiores

**echo** ['ekəʊ] **1** *n (pl* **echoes**) *also Fig* eco *m*
**2** *vt (opinion, words)* repetir, hacerse eco de
**3** *vi* resonar **(with** con)

**éclair** [eɪ'kleə(r)] *n (pastry)* petisú *m*

**eclectic** [ə'klektɪk] *adj* ecléctico(a)

**eclipse** [ɪ'klɪps] **1** *n also Fig* eclipse *m*
**2** *vt also Fig* eclipsar

**eco-friendly** ['i:kəʊfrendlɪ] *adj* ecológico(a)

**ecological** [i:kə'lɒdʒɪkəl] *adj* ecológico(a)

**ecologist** [ɪ'kɒlədʒɪst] *n (scientist)* ecólogo(a) *m,f*

**ecology** [ɪ'kɒlədʒɪ] *n* ecología *f*

**economic** [i:kə'nɒmɪk] *adj* **(a)** *Econ* económico(a) **(b)** *(profitable)* rentable; **it's more e. to buy in bulk** sale más barato *or* económico comprar grandes cantidades

**economical** [i:kə'nɒmɪkəl] *adj (cost-effective)* económico(a); **he was being e. with the truth** no decía toda la verdad

**economically** [i:kə'nɒmɪklɪ] *adv* económicamente

**economics** [i:kə'nɒmɪks] *n* economía *f*; **the e. of a plan** el aspecto económico de un plan

**economist** [ɪ'kɒnəmɪst] *n* economista *mf*

**economize** [ɪ'kɒnəmaɪz] *vi* economizar, ahorrar **(on** en)

**economy** [ɪ'kɒnəmɪ] n economía f; **economies of scale** economías fpl de escala; Av **e. class** clase f turista; **e. drive** (cost-cutting campaign) campaña f de ahorro; **e. measure** medida f de ahorro; **e. size** (of packet) tamaño m económico

**ecosystem** ['i:kəʊsɪstem] n ecosistema m

**ecstasy** ['ekstəsɪ] n (emotional state, drug) éxtasis m inv; **he went into ecstasies over the food** se deshacía en elogios a la comida

**ecstatic** [ek'stætɪk] adj exultante, alborozado(a); **to be e. (about or over sth)** estar exultante de alegría (por algo)

**ECT** [i:si:'ti:] n Med (abbr **electroconvulsive therapy**) electrochoque m

**ECU, ecu** ['ekju:, 'i:kju:] n Fin (abbr **European Currency Unit**) ecu m

**Ecuador** ['ekwədɔ:(r)] n Ecuador

**Ecuadoran** ['ekwədɔ:rən], **Ecuadorian** [ekwə'dɔ:rɪən] n & adj ecuatoriano(a) m,f

**ecumenic(al)** [i:kju'menɪkəl] adj Rel ecuménico(a)

**eczema** ['eksɪmə] n eccema m

**ed** [ed] (a) (abbr **edition**) ed., edición f (b) (abbr **editor**) ed., editor(ora) m,f (c) (abbr **edited**) editado(a)

**eddy** ['edɪ] 1 n remolino m
2 vi arremolinarse

**Eden** ['i:dən] n (jardín m del) Edén m

**edge** [edʒ] 1 n (a) (of table, road, forest) borde m; (of page) margen m; (of coin, book) canto m; **at the water's e.** al borde or a la orilla del agua; Fig **to be on the e. of one's seat** estar (con el alma) en vilo

(b) (of blade, tool) filo m; Fig **to take the e. off sb's hunger** calmar el hambre a alguien; Fig **it took the e. off their victory** deslustró or enturbió su victoria; Fig **to be on e.** (nervous) estar tenso(a) or nervioso(a); Fig **to set sb on e.** (make nervous) poner los nervios de punta a alguien

(c) (advantage) ventaja f; **to have the e. (over sb)** llevar ventaja (a alguien)

2 vt (in sewing) ribetear; **edged with lace** ribeteado(a) con encaje

3 vi (move slowly) **to e. towards sb/sth** acercarse lentamente a alguien/algo; **to e. past sb** pasar deslizándose junto a alguien; **to e. through the crowd** avanzar lentamente entre la multitud

▸**edge out** vt sep (beat narrowly) batir por muy poco a

**edgeways** ['edʒweɪz], **edgewise** ['edʒwaɪz] adv de canto, de lado; Fam **I can't get a word in e.** no me dejan meter baza

**edgy** ['edʒɪ] adj (nervous) nervioso(a); **to be e.** estar nervioso(a)

**edible** ['edɪbəl] adj comestible

**edict** ['i:dɪkt] n Formal edicto m

**edification** [edɪfɪ'keɪʃən] n Formal edificación f, instrucción f

**edifice** ['edɪfɪs] n edificio m

**edify** ['edɪfaɪ] vt edificar

**edifying** ['edɪfaɪɪŋ] adj edificante

**Edinburgh** ['edɪnbrə] n Edimburgo

**edit** [edɪt] vt (a) (rewrite) corregir; Comptr editar (b) (prepare for publication) editar; **edited by...** edición f (a cargo) de... (c) Cin (cut) montar (d) (manage) (newspaper, journal) dirigir

▸**edit out** vt sep eliminar, excluir

**editing** ['edɪtɪŋ] n Cin montaje m

**edition** [ɪ'dɪʃən] n edición f

**editor** ['edɪtə(r)] n (a) (of published writings) editor(ora) m,f (b) (of film) montador(ora) m,f (c) (of newspaper, journal) director(ora) m,f; (newspaper or TV journalist) redactor(ora) m,f (d) Comptr (software) editor m

**editorial** [edɪ'tɔ:rɪəl] 1 n editorial m
2 adj editorial; **e. staff** (equipo m de) redacción f

**EDP** [i:di:'pi:] n Comptr (abbr **electronic data processing**) tratamiento m or procesamiento m electrónico de datos

**educate** ['edjʊkeɪt] vt educar

**educated** ['edjʊkeɪtɪd] adj culto(a); **an e. guess** una suposición bien fundada

**education** [edjʊ'keɪʃən] n (process of learning) educación f, aprendizaje m; (process of teaching) educación f, enseñanza f; (knowledge) educación f, cultura f; **Faculty of E.** facultad f de pedagogía; Fam **it was an e. working over there** trabajar allí fue muy instructivo

**educational** [edjʊ'keɪʃənəl] adj (system, standards, TV programme) educativo(a); (establishment) decente; (experience, visit) instructivo(a); **e. qualifications** títulos mpl académicos

**Edwardian** [ed'wɔ:dɪən] adj (architecture, furniture) = de la época de Eduardo VII (1901-10)

**EEC** [i:i:'si:] n Formerly (abbr **European Economic Community**) CEE f

**eel** [i:l] n anguila f

**eerie** ['ɪərɪ] adj espeluznante, sobrecogedor(ora)

**eerily** ['ɪərɪlɪ] adv de forma espeluznante; **it was e. silent** había un silencio sobrecogedor

**eff** [ef] vi Fam Euph **he was effing and blinding** estaba soltando maldiciones

**efface** [ɪ'feɪs] vt borrar; **to e. oneself** mantenerse en un segundo plano

**effect** [ɪ'fekt] 1 n (a) (result) efecto m; **to have an e. on** tener efecto en or sobre; **to take e.** (drug, medicine) hacer or surtir efecto; (law) entrar en vigor; **to put sth into e.** llevar algo a la práctica; **in e.** de hecho, en la práctica; **or words to that e.** o algo por el estilo (b) (impression) efecto m, impresión f; **for e.** para impresionar (**C**) *Formal* **personal effects** efectos *mpl* personales

**2** *vt Formal (cause) (reconciliation, cure)* efectuar, hacer efectivo(a); **to e. a change** efectuar un cambio; **to e. an entry** entrar, penetrar

**effective** [ɪ'fektɪv] *adj* (**a**) *(efficient, successful)* eficaz (**b**) *(actual, real)* efectivo(a) (**c**) *Law (in force)* **to be e. (from)** entrar en vigor (desde)

**effectively** [ɪ'fektɪvlɪ] *adv* (**a**) *(efficiently)* eficazmente (**b**) *(really)* en realidad, de hecho; **they are e. the same** de hecho vienen a ser lo mismo

**effectiveness** [ɪ'fektɪvnɪs] *n* eficacia *f*

**effeminate** [ɪ'femɪnət] *adj* afeminado(a)

**effervescent** [efə'vesənt] *adj* efervescente

**effete** [ɪ'fiːt] *adj (person, gesture)* afectado(a), refinado(a) en exceso

**efficacious** [efɪ'keɪʃəs] *adj Formal* eficaz

**efficacy** ['efɪkəsɪ] *n Formal* eficacia *f*

**efficiency** [ɪ'fɪʃənsɪ] *n* eficiencia *f*

**efficient** [ɪ'fɪʃənt] *adj* eficiente

**efficiently** [ɪ'fɪʃəntlɪ] *adv* con eficiencia, eficientemente

**effigy** ['efɪdʒɪ] *n (statue)* efigie *f*; *(for ridicule)* monigote *m*; **to burn sb in e.** quemar un monigote de alguien

**effing** ['efɪŋ] *adj very Fam Euph* puñetero(a)

**effluent** ['efluənt] *n* aguas *fpl* residuales

**effort** ['efət] *n* (**a**) *(exertion)* esfuerzo *m*; **to make an e. (to do sth)** hacer un esfuerzo (por hacer algo); **to be worth the e.** valer la pena; **put some e. into it!** ¡podrías hacer un esfuerzo! (**b**) *(attempt)* intento *m*

**effortless** ['efətlɪs] *adj* fácil, cómodo(a)

**effortlessly** ['efətlɪslɪ] *adv* sin esfuerzo, fácilmente

**effrontery** [ɪ'frʌntərɪ] *n* desfachatez *f*, descaro *m*

**effusive** [ɪ'fjuːsɪv] *adj* efusivo(a)

**effusively** [ɪ'fjuːsɪvlɪ] *adv* efusivamente

**EFL** [iːe'fel] *n (abbr* **English as a Foreign Language)** inglés *m* como lengua extranjera

**EFT** [iːef'tiː] *n Comptr (abbr* **electronic funds transfer)** transferencia *f* electrónica de fondos

**EFTA** ['eftə] *n (abbr* **European Free Trade Association)** EFTA *f*, AELC *f*, Asociación *f* Europea de Libre Comercio

**EFTPOS** ['eftpɒs] *n Comptr (abbr* **electronic funds transfer at point of sale)** T.P.V. *f*, transferencia *f* (electrónica de fondos) en el punto de venta

**e.g.** [iː'dʒiː] *abbr* p. ej., por ejemplo

**egalitarian** [ɪgælɪ'teərɪən] **1** *n* partidario(a) *m,f* del igualitarismo

**2** *adj* igualitario(a) *m,f*

**egalitarianism** [ɪgælɪ'teərɪənɪzəm] *n* igualitarismo *m*

**egg** [eg] *n* (**a**) *(of animal, food)* huevo *m*, *CAm, Méx* blanquillo *m*; **e. cup** huevera *f*; **e. timer** reloj *m* de arena (para medir el tiempo que tarda en cocerse un huevo); **e. white** clara *f* (de huevo); **e. yolk** yema *f* (de huevo) (**b**) *(reproductive cell)* óvulo *m* (**c**) *(idioms)* **to be a good/bad e.** *(person)* ser buena/mala gente; **to have e. on one's face** haber quedado en ridículo; *Prov* **don't put all your eggs in one basket** no te lo juegues todo a una sola carta

➤**egg on** *vt sep* **to e. sb on (to do sth)** incitar a alguien (a hacer algo)

**egghead** ['eghed] *n Hum or Pej* lumbrera *f*, cerebrito *m*

**eggplant** ['egplænt] *n US* berenjena *f*

**eggshell** ['egʃel] *n* cáscara *f* (de huevo)

**eggwhisk** ['egwɪsk] *n* batidor *m*, varillas *fpl*

**egis** *US* = **aegis**

**ego** ['iːgəʊ] *(pl* **egos)** *n (self-esteem)* amor *m* propio, autoestima *f*; *Psy* ego *m*, yo *m*; **he has an enormous e.** tiene un ego descomunal, es un presuntuoso; **to boost sb's e.** dar mucha moral a alguien; *Fam* **to be on an e. trip** hacer algo por autocomplacerse

**egocentric** [iːgəʊ'sentrɪk] *adj* egocéntrico(a)

**egoist** ['iːgəʊɪst] *n* egoísta *mf*

**egotism** ['iːgəʊtɪzəm] *n* egocentrismo *m*

**egotist** ['iːgəʊtɪst] *n* egocéntrico(a) *m,f*

**egotistic(al)** [iːgəʊ'tɪstɪk(əl)] *adj* egocéntrico(a)

**Egypt** ['iːdʒɪpt] *n* Egipto

**Egyptian** [ɪ'dʒɪpʃən] *n & adj* egipcio(a) *m,f*

**eiderdown** ['aɪdədaʊn] *n (duvet)* edredón *m*

**eight** [eɪt] **1** *n* ocho *m*; **come at e.** ven a las ocho; **e. and e. are sixteen** ocho y ocho, dieciséis; **there were e. of us** éramos ocho; **all e. of them left** se marcharon los ocho; **the e. of hearts** *(in cards)* el ocho de corazones

**2** *adj* ocho; **they live at number e.** viven en el número ocho; **chapter/page e.** capítulo/página ocho; **e. hundred** ochocientos(as); **e. hundred men** ochocientos hombres; **e. thousand** ocho mil; **to be e. (years old)** tener ocho años (de edad); **it costs e. pounds** cuesta ocho libras; **e. o'clock** las ocho; **it's e. minutes to five** son las cinco menos ocho minutos

**eighteen** [eɪ'tiːn] *n & adj* dieciocho *m*; *see also* **eight**

**eighteenth** [eɪ'tiːnθ] **1** *n* (**a**) *(fraction)* dieciochoavo *m*, decimoctava parte *f* (**b**) *(in series)* decimoctavo(a) *m,f* (**c**) *(of month)* dieciocho *m*

**2** *adj* decimoctavo(a); *see also* **eleventh**

**eighth** [eɪtθ] **1** *n* (**a**) *(fraction)* octavo *m*, octava parte *f* (**b**) *(in series)* octavo(a) *m,f*; **Edward the E.** *(written)* Eduardo VIII; *(spoken)* Eduardo octavo (**C**) *(of month)* ocho *m*; (**on**) **the e. of May** el ocho de mayo; **we're leaving on the e.** nos vamos el (día) ocho

**2** *adj* octavo(a); **the e. century** *(written)* el siglo VIII; *(spoken)* el siglo octavo *or* ocho

**eightieth** ['eɪtɪəθ] *n & adj* octogésimo(a) *m,f*

**eighty** ['eɪtɪ] **1** *n* ochenta *m*; **e.-one** ochenta y uno(a); **he was doing e. (miles an hour)** *(in car)* iba a unos ciento treinta (kilómetros por hora); **in the eighties** *(decade)* en los (años) ochenta; **to be in one's eighties** tener ochenta y tantos años; **the temperature was in the eighties** *(Fahrenheit)* hacía alrededor de 30 grados

**2** *adj* ochenta; **about e. cars/passengers** unos ochenta coches/pasajeros; **e. per cent of the staff** el ochenta por ciento del personal; **she's about e. (years old)** tiene unos ochenta años; **he will be e. tomorrow** mañana cumple ochenta años

**Eire** ['eərə] *n Formerly* Eire *m (hoy la República de Irlanda)*

**either** ['aɪðə(r), 'iːðə(r)] **1** *adj* (**a**) *(one or other)* cualquiera de los/las dos; **e. candidate may win** puede ganar cualquiera de los (dos) candidatos

(**b**) *(each of the two)* **on e. side** a cada lado; **in e. case** en los dos casos, en cualquier caso

**2** *pron* cualquiera; **e. (of them) will do me** sirve cualquiera (de ellos); **I don't believe e. of you** no os creo a ninguno de los dos; **I don't want e. of them** no quiero ninguno

**3** *conj* **e. ... or...** o... o..., (o) bien... o bien...; **e. you or your brother** o tú o tu hermano; **e. come in or go out!** ¡o entras o sales!; **I don't eat e. meat or fish** no como (ni) carne ni pescado

**4** *adv* tampoco; **if you don't go, I won't go e.** si tú no vas, yo tampoco; **he can't sing, and he can't act e.** no sabe cantar ni tampoco actuar

**either-or** ['aɪðərɔː(r)] *adj* **to be in an e. situation** tener que elegir (entre lo uno o lo otro)

**ejaculate** [ɪ'dʒækjʊleɪt] *vi (emit semen)* eyacular

**ejaculation** [ɪdʒækjʊ'leɪʃən] *n* (**a**) *(of semen)* eyaculación *f* (**b**) *Old-fashioned (exclamation)* exclamación *f*

**eject** [ɪ'dʒekt] **1** *vt* expulsar

**2** *vi (from plane)* eyectarse

**ejection** [ɪ'dʒekʃən] *n* expulsión *f*; *Av* eyección *f*

**ejector seat** [ɪ'dʒektəsiːt] *n Av* asiento *m* eyectable *or* eyector

**►eke out** [iːk] *vt sep* **to e. out a living** ganarse la vida a duras penas

**elaborate 1** *adj* [ɪ'læbərət] *(plan, excuse, meal)* elaborado(a); *(drawing, description)* detallado(a)

**2** *vt* [ɪ'læbəreɪt] elaborar

**3** *vi* dar detalles (**on** sobre)

**élan** [eɪ'lɑːn] *n Literary* brío *m*

**elapse** [ɪ'læps] *vi* transcurrir

**elastic** [ɪ'læstɪk] **1** *n* elástico *m*

**2** *adj also Fig* flexible, elástico(a); **e. band** goma *f* (elástica), gomita *f*

**elasticated** [ɪ'læstɪkeɪtɪd] *adj* elástico(a)

**elasticity** [iːlæs'tɪsɪtɪ] *n* elasticidad *f*

**Elastoplast®** [ɪ'læstəplɑːst] *n* tirita *f*

**elated** [ɪ'leɪtɪd] *adj* jubiloso(a), eufórico(a); **to be e. (about sth)** estar jubiloso(a) *or* eufórico(a) (por algo)

**elation** [ɪ'leɪʃən] *n* júbilo *m*, euforia *f*

**elbow** ['elbəʊ] **1** *n* codo *m*; **out at the elbows** *(of pullover, jacket)* con agujeros en los codos; *Fig* **to give sb the e.** *(of employer)* dar la patada a alguien; *(of lover)* mandar a alguien a paseo; *Fig* **put some e. grease into it!** ¡dale fuerte! *(al sacar brillo)*

**2** *vt* **to e. sb in the ribs** dar un codazo a alguien en las costillas; **to e. sb aside** apartar a alguien de un codazo; **to e. one's way through (a crowd)** abrirse paso a codazos (entre una multitud)

**elbowroom** ['elbəʊrʊm] *n Fam Fig (freedom)* **to have enough e.** tener un margen de libertad

**elder¹** ['eldə(r)] **1** *adj* mayor; **my e. brother** mi hermano mayor; **e. statesman** antiguo mandatario *m (que conserva su prestigio)*

**2** *n* (**a**) *(older person)* mayor *mf*; **young people should respect their elders** los jóvenes deberían respetar a sus mayores (**b**) *(of tribe, church)* anciano(a) *m,f*

**elder²** *n (tree)* saúco *m*

**elderberry** ['eldəberɪ] *n (fruit)* baya *f* de saúco

**elderly** ['eldəlɪ] **1** *adj* anciano(a)

**2** *npl* **the e.** los ancianos

**eldest** ['eldɪst] **1** *adj* mayor; **my e. daughter** la mayor de mis hijas, mi hija mayor

**2** *n* **the e.** el/la mayor

**elect** [ɪ'lekt] **1** *adj* electo(a); **the president e.** el presidente electo

**2** *vt* (**a**) *(councillor, MP)* elegir; **to e. sb president, to e. sb to the presidency** elegir a alguien presidente (**b**) *Formal (choose)* **to e. to do sth** elegir hacer algo

**election** [ɪ'lekʃən] *n* elección *f*; **to hold an e.** celebrar unas elecciones; **to stand for e.** presentarse a las elecciones; **e. campaign** campaña *f* electoral

**electioneering** [ɪlekʃə'nɪərɪŋ] *n* electoralismo *m*

**elective** [ɪ'lektɪv] *adj* *(assembly)* electivo(a); *Univ (course)* optativo(a), opcional

**elector** [ɪ'lektə(r)] *n* elector(ora) *m,f*, votante *mf*

**electoral** [ɪ'lektərəl] *adj* *Pol* electoral; **e. reform** reforma *f* electoral; **e. roll** *or* **register** censo *m* electoral

**electorate** [ɪ'lektərət] *n* electorado *m*

**electric** [ɪ'lektrɪk] *adj* eléctrico(a); *Fig* **the atmosphere of the meeting was e.** en la reunión el ambiente estaba electrizado; **e. blanket** manta *f* eléctrica; **e. chair** silla *f* eléctrica; **e. cooker** cocina *f* eléctrica; **e. shock** descarga *f* eléctrica

**electrical** [ɪ'lektrɪkəl] *adj* eléctrico(a); **e. engineering** ingeniería *f* electrónica

**electrically** [ɪ'lektrɪkəlɪ] *adv* **e. powered** *or* **operated** eléctrico(a); **e. charged** con carga eléctrica

**electrician** [ɪlek'trɪʃən] *n* electricista *mf*

**electricity** [ɪlek'trɪsɪtɪ] *n* electricidad *f*

**electrification** [ɪlektrɪfɪ'keɪʃən] *n* electrificación *f*

**electrify** [ɪ'lektrɪfaɪ] *vt* *(supply)* electrificar; *Fig (excite)* electrizar

**electrifying** [ɪ'lektrɪfaɪɪŋ] *adj* *Fig* electrizante

**electrocardiogram** [ɪlektrəʊ'kɑːdɪəʊgræm] *n* *Med* electrocardiograma *m*

**electrocardiograph** [ɪlektrəʊ'kɑːdɪəʊgræf] *n* *Med* electrocardiógrafo *m*

**electrocute** [ɪ'lektrəkjuːt] *vt* electrocutar; **to e. oneself** electrocutarse

**electrocution** [ɪlektrə'kjuːʃən] *n* electrocución *f*

**electrode** [ɪ'lektrəʊd] *n* electrodo *m*

**electrolysis** [ɪlek'trɒlɪsɪs] *n* *Chem* electrólisis *f inv*; *(to remove hair)* depilación *f* eléctrica

**electromagnet** [ɪlektrəʊ'mægnɪt] *n* electroimán *m*

**electron** [ɪ'lektrɒn] *n* electrón *m*; **e. microscope** microscopio *m* electrónico

**electronic** [ɪlek'trɒnɪk] *adj* electrónico(a); *Fin* **e. banking** banca *f* electrónica, (servicio *m* de) telebanco; *Comptr* **e. mail** correo *m* electrónico; *Comptr* **e. office** oficina *f* informatizada *or* electrónica

**electronically** [ɪlek'trɒnɪklɪ] *adv* electrónicamente

**electronics** [ɪlek'trɒnɪks] **1** *n* electrónica *f*; **e. company** casa *f* de electrónica; **the e. industry** el sector de la electrónica
**2** *npl (of machine)* sistema *m* electrónico

**electroplated** [ɪ'lektrəpleɪtɪd] *adj* galvanizado(a)

**electroshock therapy** [ɪlektrəʊ'ʃɒk'θerəpɪ], **electroshock treatment** [ɪlektrəʊ'ʃɒk'triːtmənt] *n* *Med* terapia *f or* tratamiento *m* de electrochoque

**elegance** ['elɪgəns] *n* elegancia *f*

**elegant** ['elɪgənt] *adj* *(appearance, movement)* elegante; *(reasoning)* lúcido(a)

**elegantly** ['elɪgəntlɪ] *adv* *(dress, move)* elegantemente; **e. arranged/proportioned** armoniosamente dispuesto(a)/proporcionado(a)

**elegy** ['elɪdʒɪ] *n* elegía *f*

**element** ['elɪmənt] *n* **(a)** *(constituent part)* elemento *m*, componente *m*; **this film has all the elements of a hit movie** esta película contiene todos los ingredientes del éxito
**(b)** *(factor)* componente *m*, elemento *m*; **the e. of surprise** el factor sorpresa; **the human e.** el factor humano; **an e. of danger** un factor de peligro
**(c)** *(in society)* elemento *m*; **the hooligan e.** los gamberros *(en una multitud, en la sociedad)*
**(d)** *Chem* elemento *m*
**(e)** *(of kettle, electric fire)* resistencia *f*
**(f)** *(force of nature)* **the four elements** los cuatro elementos; **to brave the elements** desafiar a los elementos; **she was in her e.** estaba en su elemento

**elemental** [elɪ'mentəl] *adj* elemental, primario(a)

**elementary** [elɪ'mentərɪ] *adj* elemental, básico(a); **e. algebra** álgebra *f* elemental; *US* **e. school** escuela *f* primaria

**elephant** ['elɪfənt] *n* elefante *m*

**elephantine** [elɪ'fæntaɪn] *adj* *(body, size)* mastodóntico(a); *(steps, movement)* pesado(a), de elefante

**elevate** ['elɪveɪt] *vt* elevar; **to e. sb to the peerage** otorgar a alguien un título nobiliario

**elevated** ['elɪveɪtɪd] *adj* elevado(a); **to have an e. opinion of oneself** tener un concepto demasiado elevado de uno mismo; **e. railway** ferrocarril *m or* tren *m* elevado

**elevation** [elɪ'veɪʃən] *n* **(a)** *(height)* **e. above sea level** altitud *f* (por encima del nivel del mar) **(b)** *(promotion)* ascenso *m*, elevación *f* **(c)** *Archit* alzado *m*

**elevator** ['elɪveɪtə(r)] *n* **(a)** *US (lift)* ascensor *m* **(b)** *(for goods)* montacargas *m inv* **(c)** *(on aeroplane wing)* timón *m* de profundidad

**eleven** [ɪ'levən] **1** *n* once *m*; **the Spanish e.** *(football team)* el once español; *Br Formerly* **e. plus** = prueba selectiva que podían realizar los alumnos británicos a la edad de 11 años para acceder a una "grammar school" y así encaminar su educación secundaria con miras a la universidad
**2** *adj* once; *see also* **eight**

**elevenses** [ɪ'levənzɪz] *npl Br Fam* tentempié *m* (de la mañana)

**eleventh** [ɪ'levənθ] **1** *n* (a) *(fraction)* onceavo *m*, onceava parte *f* (b) *(in series)* undécimo(a) *m,f*; **Louis the E.** *(written)* Luis XI; *(spoken)* Luis once (c) *(in month)* once *m*; **(on) the e. of May** el once de mayo; **we're leaving on the e.** nos vamos el (día) once

**2** *adj* undécimo(a); *Fig* **at the e. hour** en el último momento; **the e. century** *(written)* el siglo XI; *(spoken)* el siglo once

**elf** [elf] ( *pl* **elves** [elvz]) *n* elfo *m*

**elicit** [ɪ'lɪsɪt] *vt (information)* sacar (**from** de), obtener (**from** de); *(reaction, response)* provocar (**from** en)

**eligibility** [elɪdʒɪ'bɪlɪtɪ] *n* elegibilidad *f*; **they questioned his e.** cuestionaron si era apto para presentar su candidatura

**eligible** ['elɪdʒɪbəl] *adj* **to be e. for sth** reunir los requisitos para algo; **an e. bachelor** un buen partido

**eliminate** [ɪ'lɪmɪneɪt] *vt* eliminar

**elimination** [ɪlɪmɪ'neɪʃən] *n* eliminación *f*; **by a process of e.** por (un proceso de) eliminación

**elite** [er'li:t] *n* élite *f*

**elitism** [er'li:tɪzəm] *n* elitismo *m*

**elitist** [er'li:tɪst] *n* & *adj* elitista *mf*

**elixir** [ɪ'lɪksə(r)] *n Literary* elixir *m*

**Elizabethan** [ɪlɪzə'bi:θən] *n* & *adj* isabelino(a) *m,f*

**elk** [elk] *n* alce *m*

**ellipse** [ɪ'lɪps] *n Math* elipse *f*

**ellipsis** [ɪ'lɪpsɪs] ( *pl* **ellipses** [ɪ'lɪpsi:z]) *n Gram* elipsis *f inv*

**elm** [elm] *n* olmo *m*

**elocution** [elə'kju:ʃən] *n* dicción *f*

**elongate** ['i:lɒŋɡeɪt] *vt* alargar

**elope** [ɪ'ləup] *vi* fugarse *(para casarse)*

**eloquence** ['eləkwəns] *n* elocuencia *f*

**eloquent** ['eləkwənt] *adj* elocuente

**else** [els] *adv* **anyone e.** *(any other person)* cualquier otro(a); *(in negative sentences)* nadie más; **would anyone e. like some coffee?** ¿alguien más quiere café?; **someone e.** *(different person)* otra persona; *(additional person)* alguien más; **everyone e.** todos los demás; **no-one e.** nadie más; **anything e.** cualquier otra cosa; *(in negative sentence)* ninguna otra cosa; **can I get you anything e.?** ¿(desean) alguna cosa más *or* algo más?; **something e.** *(different thing)* otra cosa; *(additional thing)* algo más; **everything e.** todo lo demás; **nothing e.** *(nothing different)* ninguna otra cosa; *(nothing additional)* nada más; **somewhere e.** en/a otro sitio; **anywhere e.** (en/a) cualquier otro sitio; **everywhere e.** (en/a) todos los demás sitios; **nowhere e.** (en/a) ningún otro sitio; **who e.**

**was there?** ¿quién más estaba allí?; **who broke it?** – Peter, **who e.?** ¿quién lo rompió? – Peter, ¿quién si no? *or* ¿quién va a ser?; **what e.?** ¿qué más?; **where e.?** ¿en/a qué otro sitio?; **when e.?** ¿en qué otro momento?; **how e.?** ¿cómo si no?; **how e. do you think I did it?** ¿cómo piensas si no que lo hice?; **why e.?** ¿por qué si no?; **why e. would I do that?** ¿por qué iba a hacerlo si no?; **little e.** poca cosa más, poco más; **there isn't much e. we can do** no podemos hacer mucho más; **or e.** de lo contrario, si no; **do what I tell you or e.!** ¡como no hagas lo que te digo, te vas a enterar *or* ya verás!

**elsewhere** ['elsweə(r)] *adv* en otro sitio

**ELT** [i:el'ti:] *n (abbr* **English Language Teaching**) enseñanza *f* del inglés

**elucidate** [ɪ'lu:sɪdeɪt] *vt* aclarar, poner en claro

**elude** [ɪ'lu:d] *vt* eludir; **success has eluded us so far** el éxito nos ha rehuido hasta ahora; **his name eludes me** no consigo recordar su nombre

**elusive** [ɪ'lu:sɪv] *adj (enemy, concept)* escurridizo(a)

**elver** ['elvə(r)] *n* angula *f*

**elves** ['elvz] *pl of* **elf**

**emaciated** [ɪ'meɪsɪeɪtɪd] *adj* esquelético(a), raquítico(a); **to be e.** estar esquelético(a) *or* raquítico(a)

**e-mail** ['i:meɪl] *n* correo *m* electrónico

**emanate** ['eməneɪt] **1** *vt* emanar
**2** *vi* emanar (**from** de)

**emancipate** [ɪ'mænsɪpeɪt] *vt* emancipar

**emancipated** [ɪ'mænsɪpeɪtɪd] *adj* emancipado(a)

**emancipation** [ɪmænsɪ'peɪʃən] *n* emancipación *f*

**emasculate** [ɪ'mæskjuleɪt] *vt Fig (rights, legislation)* desvirtuar; *(group, organization)* debilitar, minar

**embalm** [ɪm'bɑ:m] *vt* embalsamar

**embankment** [ɪm'bæŋkmənt] *n (beside railway)* terraplén *m*; *(alongside river)* dique *m*

**embargo** [em'bɑ:ɡəu] **1** *n* ( *pl* **embargoes**) embargo *m*; **to be under (an) e.** estar sometido(a) a embargo; **to put an e. on** imponer un embargo a
**2** *vt* someter a embargo

**embark** [ɪm'bɑ:k] *vi* embarcar; *Fig* **to e. (up)on** *(adventure)* embarcarse en

**embarrass** [ɪm'bærəs] *vt* avergonzar, abochornar; **to e. the government** poner en apuros al Gobierno

**embarrassed** [ɪmˈbærəst] *adj (ashamed)* avergonzado(a); *(uncomfortable)* azorado(a), violento(a); *(financially)* apurado(a) (de dinero); **to be e.** *(ashamed)* estar avergonzado(a); *(uncomfortable)* estar azorado(a) *or* violento(a)

**embarrassing** [ɪmˈbærəsɪŋ] *adj* embarazoso(a), bochornoso(a); **how e.!** ¡qué vergüenza!

**embarrassment** [ɪmˈbærəsmənt] *n (shame)* vergüenza *f; (discomfort)* apuro *m*, embarazo *m;* **much to my e.** para mi bochorno; **to be an e. to sb** ser motivo de vergüenza para alguien

**embassy** [ˈembəsɪ] *n* embajada *f;* **the Spanish E.** la embajada española *or* de España

**embattled** [ɪmˈbætəld] *adj* acosado(a); **to be e.** estar acosado(a)

**embed** [ɪmˈbed] *(pt & pp embedded) vt* **(a) to be embedded in sth** estar incrustado(a) en algo; **to be embedded in sb's memory** estar grabado(a) en la memoria de alguien **(b)** *Comptr* incrustar

**embellish** [ɪmˈbelɪʃ] *vt (room, account)* adornar **(with** con)

**embers** [ˈembəz] *npl* brasas *fpl*, rescoldos *mpl*

**embezzle** [ɪmˈbezəl] *vt (public money)* malversar; *(private money)* desfalcar

**embezzlement** [ɪmˈbezəlmənt] *n (of public money)* malversación *f; (of private money)* desfalco *m*

**embezzler** [ɪmˈbezlə(r)] *n (of public money)* malversador(ora) *m,f; (of private money)* desfalcador(ora) *m,f*

**embitter** [ɪmˈbɪtə(r)] *vt (person)* amargar

**embittered** [ɪmˈbɪtəd] *adj* amargado(a)

**emblazon** [ɪmˈbleɪzən] *vt (shield)* blasonar; *Fig (name, headline)* estampar con grandes letras

**emblem** [ˈembləm] *n* emblema *m*

**embodiment** [ɪmˈbɒdɪmənt] *n* encarnación *f;* **she seemed the e. of reasonableness** parecía la sensatez personificada

**embody** [ɪmˈbɒdɪ] *vt* encarnar, representar

**embolden** [ɪmˈbəʊldən] *vt* envalentonar

**embolism** [ˈembəlɪzəm] *n Med* embolia *f*

**emboss** [ɪmˈbɒs] *vt (metal, leather)* repujar; *(letter, design)* grabar en relieve; **an embossed letterhead** un membrete en relieve

**embrace** [ɪmˈbreɪs] **1** *n* abrazo *m*
**2** *vt (person, belief)* abrazar; *(include)* abarcar
**3** *vi* abrazarse

**embroider** [ɪmˈbrɔɪdə(r)] *vt (cloth)* bordar; *Fig (account, report)* adornar

**embroidery** [ɪmˈbrɔɪdərɪ] *n* bordado *m*

**embroil** [ɪmˈbrɔɪl] *vt* **to be embroiled in sth** estar enredado(a) en algo; **to get embroiled in a debate with sb** enfrascarse *or* enredarse en una discusión con alguien

**embryo** [ˈembrɪəʊ] *(pl embryos) n* embrión *m; Fig* **in e.** *(of plan, idea)* en estado embrionario

**embryonic** [embrɪˈɒnɪk] *adj Biol* embrionario(a); *(plan, idea)* en estado embrionario

**emend** [ɪˈmend] *vt* corregir

**emendation** [iːmenˈdeɪʃən] *n* corrección *f*

**emerald** [ˈemərəld] *n* esmeralda *f;* **e. (green)** verde *m* esmeralda; **the E. Isle** = Irlanda

**emerge** [ɪˈmɜːdʒ] *vi (from water)* emerger; *(from behind sth)* salir **(from** de); *Fig (of difficulty, truth)* aflorar, surgir; **it later emerged that…** más tarde resultó que…

**emergence** [ɪˈmɜːdʒəns] *n (of facts, from hiding)* aparición *f; (of new state, new leader)* surgimiento *m*

**emergency** [ɪˈmɜːdʒənsɪ] *n* emergencia *f; Med* urgencia *f;* **in an e., in case of e.** en caso de emergencia; **e. exit** salida *f* de emergencia; **e. landing** aterrizaje *m* forzoso; **e. services** *(police, ambulance, fire brigade)* servicios *mpl* de urgencia; **e. stop** parada *f* en seco *or* de emergencia

**emergent** [ɪˈmɜːdʒənt] *adj* pujante; **e. nations** países *mpl* emergentes

**emery board** [ˈemərɪbɔːd] *n* lima *f* de uñas

**emetic** [ɪˈmetɪk] *n* emético *m*, vomitivo *m*

**emigrant** [ˈemɪɡrənt] *n* emigrante *mf*

**emigrate** [ˈemɪɡreɪt] *vi* emigrar

**emigration** [emɪˈɡreɪʃən] *n* emigración *f*

**émigré** [ˈemɪɡreɪ] *n* emigrado(a) *m,f; Pol* exiliado(a) *m,f*

**eminence** [ˈemɪnəns] *n* **(a)** *(importance)* eminencia *f* **(b)** *(title of cardinal)* **Your E.** Su *or* Vuestra Eminencia

**eminent** [ˈemɪnənt] *adj (person)* eminente; *(quality)* notable

**eminently** [ˈemɪnəntlɪ] *adv* sumamente

**emirate** [ˈemɪreɪt] *n* emirato *m*

**emissary** [ˈemɪsərɪ] *n* emisario(a) *m,f*

**emission** [ɪˈmɪʃən] *n* emisión *f*, emanación *f;* **toxic emissions** emanaciones tóxicas

**emit** [ɪˈmɪt] *(pt & pp emitted) vt (heat, light, sound)* emitir; *(smell, gas)* desprender, emanar

**emotion** [ɪˈməʊʃən] *n* emoción *f*

**emotional** [ɪˈməʊʃənəl] *adj (person)* emotivo(a), sensible; *(problem, reaction)* emocional; *(film, farewell)* conmovedor(ora), emotivo(a); **to get** *or* **become e.** emocionarse

**emotionally** [ɪˈməʊʃənəlɪ] *adv* emotivamente; **to be e. involved with sb** tener una relación sentimental con alguien; **e. deprived** privado(a) de cariño

**emotive** [ɪˈməʊtɪv] *adj (words, plea)* emotivo(a); **an e. issue** un asunto que despierta las más encendidas pasiones

**empathize** [ˈempəθaɪz] *vi* identificarse **(with** con)

**empathy** ['empəθɪ] *n* identificación *f*; **to feel e. for sb** identificarse con alguien

**emperor** ['empərə(r)] *n* emperador *m*

**emphasis** ['emfəsɪs] *n* énfasis *m inv*; **to lay or place e. on sth** hacer hincapié en algo; **the e. is on written work** se hace hincapié en el trabajo escrito

**emphasize** ['emfəsaɪz] *vt* **(a)** *(point, fact)* hacer hincapié en, subrayar **(b)** *(word, syllable)* acentuar

**emphatic** [ɪm'fætɪk] *adj (gesture, tone)* enfático(a); *(denial, response)* rotundo(a), categórico(a); *(victory, scoreline)* convincente; **he was quite e. that...** hizo especial hincapié en que...

**emphatically** [ɪm'fætɪkəlɪ] *adv (to say)* enfáticamente; *(to refuse, deny)* categóricamente; **most e.!** ¡absolutamente!

**emphysema** [emfɪ'siːmə] *n* enfisema *m*

**empire** ['empaɪə(r)] *n also Fig* imperio *m*

**empirical** [em'pɪrɪkəl] *adj* empírico(a)

**empiricism** [em'pɪrɪsɪzəm] *n* empirismo *m*

**employ** [ɪm'plɔɪ] **1** *n Formal* **to be in sb's e.** trabajar al servicio or a las órdenes de alguien
**2** *vt* **(a)** *(workers)* emplear; **to e. oneself (by or in doing sth)** ocuparse (en hacer algo) **(b)** *(tool, time, force)* emplear, utilizar

**employee** [em'plɔɪiː] *n* empleado(a) *m,f*; *Com* **e. buyout** = adquisición de una empresa por los empleados

**employer** [ɪm'plɔɪə(r)] *n (person)* empresario(a) *m,f*, patrono(a) *m,f*; *(company)* empresa *f*

**employment** [ɪm'plɔɪmənt] *n* **(a)** *(work)* empleo *m*; **to be in e.** tener un (puesto de) trabajo, estar empleado(a); **to be without e.** no tener empleo, estar desempleado(a); *Com* **e. agency** or **bureau** agencia *f* de colocaciones **(b)** *(use) (of tool, force)* empleo *m*, uso *m*

**empower** [ɪm'paʊə(r)] *vt* **to e. sb to do sth** habilitar or capacitar a alguien para hacer algo

**empress** ['emprɪs] *n* emperatriz *f*

**emptiness** ['emptɪnɪs] *n* vacío *m*

**empty** ['emptɪ] **1** *adj (container, existence)* vacío(a); *(promise, threat)* vano(a); **on an e. stomach** con el estómago vacío
**2** *vt* vaciar
**3** *vi* vaciarse
**4** *n (bottle)* **empties** cascos *mpl*

▶**empty out** *vt sep (pockets)* vaciar

**empty-handed** ['emptɪ'hændɪd] *adv* con las manos vacías

**empty-headed** ['emptɪ'hedɪd] *adj* necio(a), bobo(a); **to be e.** tener la cabeza hueca

**EMS** [iːem'es] *n Fin (abbr* **European Monetary System)** SME *m*, Sistema *m* Monetario Europeo

**EMU** [iːem'juː] *n Fin (abbr* **Economic and Monetary Union)** UEM *f*, Unión *f* Económica y Monetaria

**emu** ['iːmjuː] *n (bird)* emú *m*

**emulate** ['emjʊleɪt] *vt* emular

**emulsion** [ɪ'mʌlʃən] *n (liquid mixture)* emulsión *f*; **e. (paint)** pintura *f* (al temple)

**enable** [ɪ'neɪbl] *vt* **(a)** *(allow)* **to e. sb to do sth** permitir a alguien hacer algo **(b)** *Comptr (function)* ejecutar; *(device)* activar, hacer operativo(a)

**enact** [ɪ'nækt] *vt* **(a)** *(tragedy, play)* interpretar **(b)** *(law)* promulgar

**enamel** [ɪ'næməl] **1** *n* esmalte *m*
**2** *vt (pt & pp* **enamelled,** *US* **enameled)** esmaltar

**enamoured** [ɪ'næməd] *adj* **to be e. of** estar enamorado(a) de; **I'm not greatly e. of the idea** no me entusiasma la idea

**encampment** [ɪn'kæmpmənt] *n Mil* campamento *m*

**encapsulate** [ɪn'kæpsjʊleɪt] *vt (summarize)* sintetizar

**encase** [ɪn'keɪs] *vt (with lining, cover)* revestir; **to be encased in concrete** estar revestido(a) de hormigón

**enchant** [ɪn'tʃɑːnt] *vt* **(a)** *(charm)* cautivar, encantar; **he was less than enchanted by the idea** la idea no le hacía mucha gracia **(b)** *(put under a spell)* hechizar

**enchanting** [ɪn'tʃɑːntɪŋ] *adj* encantador(ora), cautivador(ora)

**enchantment** [ɪn'tʃɑːntmənt] *n* fascinación *f*, encanto *m*

**enchantress** [ɪn'tʃɑːntrɪs] *n (attractive woman)* seductora *f*

**encircle** [ɪn'sɜːkəl] *vt* rodear

**enclave** ['enkleɪv] *n* enclave *m*

**enclose** [ɪn'kləʊz] *vt* **(a)** *(surround)* rodear **(b)** *(include in letter)* adjuntar; **please find enclosed...** le adjunto..., le envío adjunto(a)...

**enclosed** [ɪŋ'kləʊzd] *adj* **(a)** **an e. space** un espacio cerrado **(b)** *(in letter)* adjunto(a)

**enclosure** [ɪn'kləʊʒə(r)] *n* **(a)** *(area)* recinto *m*, cercado *m* **(b)** *(in letter)* documento *m* adjunto

**encode** [en'kəʊd] *vt* cifrar, codificar; *Comptr* codificar

**encompass** [ɪn'kʌmpəs] *vt* abarcar, incluir

**encore** ['ɒŋkɔː(r)] *n (in theatre)* bis *m*; **to call for an e.** pedir un bis; **e.!** ¡otra, otra!

**encounter** [ɪn'kaʊntə(r)] **1** *n (meeting)* encuentro *m*; *(confrontation)* enfrentamiento *m*
**2** *vt (person, difficulty)* encontrarse or toparse con

**encourage** [ɪn'kʌrɪdʒ] vt (person) animar; (growth, belief) promover, impulsar; **to e. sb to do sth** animar a alguien a hacer algo

**encouragement** [ɪn'kʌrɪdʒmənt] n apoyo m, aliento m; **to give** or **offer sb e.** animar or alentar a alguien

**encouraging** [ɪn'kʌrɪdʒɪŋ] adj alentador(ora)

▸**encroach on, encroach upon** vt insep (rights) usurpar; (time, land) invadir

**encrusted** [ɪn'krʌstɪd] adj **e. with diamonds** con diamantes incrustados; **e. with mud** con barro incrustado

**encumber** [ɪn'kʌmbə(r)] vt **to be encumbered by** or **with** estar or verse entorpecido(a) por

**encumbrance** [ɪn'kʌmbrəns] n estorbo m

**encyclical** [ɪn'sɪklɪkəl] n Rel encíclica f

**encyclop(a)edia** [ɪnsaɪklə'piːdɪə] n enciclopedia f

**encyclop(a)edic** [ɪnsaɪklə'piːdɪk] adj enciclopédico(a)

**end** [end] **1** n **(a)** (extremity) extremo m; **from one e. to the other** de un extremo al otro; **at the other e. of the line** al otro lado del teléfono; **the financial e. of the business** el lado or aspecto financiero del negocio; Fig **to come to the e. of the road** or **line** llegar al final; **e. to e.** en hilera; **to stand sth on e.** colocar algo de pie; **the deep/shallow e.** (of swimming pool) el lado más/menos hondo or donde cubre/no cubre

**(b)** (limit in time, quantity) final m, fin m; **for hours/days on e.** por espacio de varias horas/varios días; **to put an e. to sth** poner fin a algo; **to come to an e.** concluir, llegar a su fin; **I am at the e. of my patience** se me está agotando la paciencia; Fig **at the e. of the day** en definitiva, al final; **in the e.** al final; **it's not the e. of the world** no es el fin del mundo; Fam **no e. of…** la mar de…; **e. product** producto m final

**(c)** (aim, purpose) fin m, propósito m; **an e. in itself** un fin en sí mismo; **she attained** or **achieved her end(s)** logró lo que se proponía; **to what e.?** ¿con qué fin or propósito?; **the e. justifies the means** el fin justifica los medios

**(d)** (idioms) Fam **to keep one's e. up** defenderse bien; Fam **this job will be the e. of me!** ¡este trabajo va a acabar conmigo!; Fam **to make ends meet** llegar a fin de mes; Fam **to get hold of the wrong e. of the stick** agarrar el rábano por las hojas; **he can't see beyond the e. of his nose** no ve más allá de sus narices; **we shall never hear the e. of it** nos lo van a recordar mientras vivamos

**2** vt terminar, finalizar; **to e. it all** (commit suicide) quitarse la vida

**3** vi terminar, acabar; **I must e. by thanking…** para terminar, debo dar gracias a…

▸**end up** vi terminar, acabar; **to e. up doing sth** terminar or acabar haciendo algo

**endanger** [ɪn'deɪndʒə(r)] vt poner en peligro; **such work would e. her health** un trabajo así resultaría peligroso para su salud; **an endangered species** una especie amenazada or en peligro de extinción

**endear** [ɪn'dɪə(r)] vt **to e. oneself to sb** hacerse querer por alguien; **her outspokenness did not e. her to her boss** su franqueza no le ganó el favor del jefe

**endearing** [ɪn'dɪərɪŋ] adj encantador(ora)

**endearment** [ɪn'dɪəmənt] n **words of e.** palabras fpl tiernas or cariñosas

**endeavour, US endeavor** [ɪn'devər] **1** n esfuerzo m

**2** vt **to e. to do sth** procurar hacer algo

**endemic** [en'demɪk] adj endémico(a)

**ending** ['endɪŋ] n (of story) final m, desenlace m; (of word) terminación f

**endive** ['endaɪv] n **(a)** (curly) e. escarola f **(b)** US (chicory) endibia f, achicoria f

**endless** ['endlɪs] adj interminable

**endocrine** ['endəʊkraɪn] adj Med endocrino(a); **e. gland** glándula f endocrina

**endocrinology** [endəʊkraɪ'nɒlədʒɪ] n endocrinología f

**endorphin** [en'dɔːfɪn] n endorfina f

**endorse** [ɪn'dɔːs] vt **(a)** (document, cheque) endosar; Br (driving licence) anotar una infracción en **(b)** (approve) (opinion, action) apoyar, respaldar

**endorsement** [ɪn'dɔːsmənt] n **(a)** (on document, cheque) endoso m; Br (on driving licence) infracción f anotada **(b)** (approval) (of action, opinion) apoyo m (of a), respaldo m (of a)

**endow** [ɪn'daʊ] vt dotar (**with de**)

**endowment** [ɪn'daʊmənt] n **(a)** Fin asignación f; **e. mortgage** hipoteca-inversión f, = crédito hipotecario por intereses ligado a un seguro de vida **(b)** (talent) dote f

**endurable** [ɪn'djʊərəbəl] adj soportable

**endurance** [ɪn'djʊərəns] n resistencia f; **beyond e.** a más no poder; **e. test** prueba f de resistencia

**endure** [ɪn'djʊə(r)] **1** vt soportar, aguantar

**2** vi (last) durar

**enduring** [ɪn'djʊərɪŋ] adj duradero(a)

**enema** ['enəmə] n enema m

**enemy** ['enəmɪ] **1** n enemigo(a) m,f; **she's her own worst e.** su peor enemigo es ella misma

**2** adj (country, ship) enemigo(a)

**energetic** [enə'dʒetɪk] adj enérgico(a)

**energetically** [enə'dʒetɪklɪ] *adv* enérgicamente

**energy** ['enədʒɪ] *n* energía *f*; **to save e.** ahorrar energía; **e. crisis** crisis *f* energética

**energy-saving** ['enədʒɪseɪvɪŋ] *adj* que ahorra energía

**enervating** ['enəveɪtɪŋ] *adj* debilitante, enervante

**enfeeble** [ɪn'fi:bəl] *vt* debilitar, enervar

**enfold** [ɪn'fəʊld] *vt* rodear; **he enfolded her in his arms** la rodeó con sus brazos

**enforce** [ɪn'fɔ:s] *vt (law)* hacer cumplir, aplicar; *(rights)* hacer valer

**enforcement** [ɪn'fɔ:smənt] *n* aplicación *f*

**enfranchise** [ɪn'fræntʃaɪz] *vt* otorgar el derecho al voto a

**engage** [ɪn'geɪdʒ] **1** *vt* **(a)** *(employ)* contratar **(b)** *(attention, person)* ocupar; **to e. sb in conversation** entablar conversación con alguien **(c)** *Mil* **to e. the enemy** entrar en liza con el enemigo **(d)** *(cog, gear)* engranar; **to e. the clutch** embragar
**2** *vi* **(a)** **to e. in** *(activity, sport)* dedicarse a **(b)** *(of cog wheel)* engranar

**engaged** [ɪn'geɪdʒd] *adj* **(a)** *(to be married)* prometido(a); **to be e. (to sb)** estar prometido(a) *(a or* con alguien*)* **(b)** *(to be in use)* **to be e.** *Br (phone)* estar comunicando; *(public toilet)* estar ocupado(a); **to be e. in doing sth** estar ocupado(a) haciendo algo

**engagement** [ɪn'geɪdʒmənt] *n* **(a)** *(to be married)* compromiso *m*; *(period)* noviazgo *m*; **e. ring** anillo *m* de pedida *or* de compromiso **(b)** *(appointment)* compromiso *m* **(c)** *(military action)* batalla *f*, combate *m*

**engaging** [ɪn'geɪdʒɪŋ] *adj* atractivo(a)

**engender** [ɪn'dʒendə(r)] *vt* engendrar

**engine** ['endʒɪn] *n* **(a)** *(of car, plane, ship)* motor *m*; **e. room** sala *f* de máquinas; **e. trouble** avería *f (del motor)* **(b)** *Rail* locomotora *f*; **e. driver** maquinista *mf*

**engineer** [endʒɪ'nɪə(r)] **1** *n* ingeniero(a) *mf*; *Naut* maquinista *mf*
**2** *vt (cause, bring about)* urdir

**engineering** [endʒɪ'nɪərɪŋ] *n* ingeniería *f*

**England** ['ɪŋglənd] *n* Inglaterra *f*

**English** ['ɪŋglɪʃ] **1** *n (language)* inglés *m*; **E. class/teacher** clase *f*/profesor(a) *mf* de inglés
**2** *npl (people)* **the E.** los ingleses
**3** *adj* inglés(esa); **the E. Channel** el Canal de la Mancha

**Englishman** ['ɪŋglɪʃmən] *n* inglés *m*

**Englishwoman** ['ɪŋglɪʃwʊmən] *n* inglesa *f*

**engrave** [ɪn'greɪv] *vt* grabar

**engraver** [ɪn'greɪvə(r)] *n* grabador(ora) *m,f*

**engraving** [ɪn'greɪvɪŋ] *n* grabado *m*

**engrossed** [ɪn'grəʊst] *adj* **to be e. (in)** estar absorto(a) (en)

**engrossing** [ɪn'grəʊsɪŋ] *adj* absorbente

**engulf** [ɪn'gʌlf] *vt (of waves, flames)* devorar; **she was engulfed by despair** se sumió en la desesperación

**enhance** [ɪn'hɑːns] *vt (value, chances)* incrementar, aumentar; *(performance, quality)* mejorar; *(beauty, colour)* realzar; *(reputation)* acrecentar, elevar

**enigma** [ɪ'nɪgmə] *n* enigma *m*

**enigmatic** [enɪg'mætɪk] *adj* enigmático(a)

**enjoy** [ɪn'dʒɔɪ] *vt* **(a)** *(take pleasure from)* disfrutar de; **did you e. your meal?** ¿les gustó la comida?; **he enjoys swimming** le gusta nadar; **to e. oneself** divertirse, pasarlo bien **(b)** *(benefit from)* gozar de, disfrutar de

**enjoyable** [ɪn'dʒɔɪəbəl] *adj* agradable

**enjoyment** [ɪn'dʒɔɪmənt] *n (pleasure)* disfrute *m*; **to get e. out of sth** disfrutar con algo

**enlarge** [ɪn'lɑːdʒ] **1** *vt (make larger)* ampliar, agrandar; *(photograph)* ampliar
**2** *vi* ampliarse, agrandarse; **to e. (up)on sth** *(explain in greater detail)* explicar algo más detalladamente

**enlargement** [ɪn'lɑːdʒmənt] *n* ampliación *f*, agrandamiento *m*; *Phot* ampliación *f*

**enlighten** [ɪn'laɪtən] *vt* aclarar; **can somebody e. me as to what is going on?** ¿podría alguien aclararme qué está ocurriendo?

**enlightened** [ɪn'laɪtənd] *adj* ilustrado(a), progresista

**enlightenment** [ɪn'laɪtənmənt] *n (clarification)* aclaración *f*; *Hist* **the E.** la Ilustración

**enlist** [ɪn'lɪst] **1** *vt (support, help)* conseguir; *Mil (soldier)* alistar
**2** *vi Mil* alistarse

**enliven** [ɪn'laɪvən] *vt* animar

**en masse** [ɒn'mæs] *adv* en masa

**enmesh** [ɪn'meʃ] *vt* **to become enmeshed in sth** enredarse en algo

**enmity** ['enmɪtɪ] *n* enemistad *f*

**enormity** [ɪ'nɔːmɪtɪ] *n* magnitud *f*

**enormous** [ɪ'nɔːməs] *adj* enorme, inmenso(a)

**enormously** [ɪ'nɔːməslɪ] *adv* enormemente, inmensamente

**enough** [ɪ'nʌf] **1** *adj* suficiente, bastante; **more than e. money/wine** dinero/vino de sobra *or* más que suficiente
**2** *pron* **will this be e.?** ¿bastará *or* será bastante con esto?; **I haven't got e.** no tengo suficiente; **more than e.** más que suficiente; **that's e.** *(sufficient)* es suficiente; **that's e.!** *(stop doing that)* ¡basta ya!, ¡vale ya!; **e. is e.** ya basta; **e. said!** ¡no me digas más!, ¡ni una palabra más!; **to have e. to live on** tener (lo suficiente) para vivir; **to have had e. of sb/sth** estar har-

to(a) de alguien/algo

**3** *adv* **(a)** *(sufficiently)* suficientemente, bastante; **good e.** suficientemente bueno(a), suficiente; **she is not strong/tall e.** no es lo bastante fuerte/alta

**(b)** *(reasonably)* bastante; **she's a nice e. girl** es una chica bastante maja; **oddly** *or* **strangely e.,...** curiosamente,...

**enquire = inquire**

**enquiry = inquiry**

**enrage** [ɪn'reɪdʒ] *vt* enfurecer, encolerizar

**enrapture** [ɪn'ræptʃə(r)] *vt* embelesar

**enraptured** [ɪn'ræptʃəd] *adj* embelesado(a); **to be e.** estar embelesado(a)

**enrich** [ɪn'rɪtʃ] *vt* enriquecer

**enrol**, *US* **enroll** [ɪn'rəʊl] *(pt & pp* **enrolled) 1** *vt* inscribir

 **2** *vi* inscribirse

**enrolment**, *US* **enrollment** [ɪn'rəʊlmənt] *n* inscripción *f*

**ensconce** [ɪn'skɒns] *vt* **to e. oneself** aposentarse

**ensemble** [ɒn'sɒmbəl] *n* conjunto *m*

**enshrine** [ɪn'ʃraɪn] *vt* **to be enshrined in sth** estar amparado(a) por algo

**ensign** ['ensaɪn] *n* **(a)** *(flag)* bandera *f*, enseña *f* **(b)** *US (naval officer)* alférez *m* de fragata

**enslave** [ɪn'sleɪv] *vt* esclavizar

**ensnare** [ɪn'sneə(r)] *vt (animal, criminal)* capturar

**ensue** [ɪn'sju:] *vi* sucederse, seguir

**ensuing** [ɪn'sju:ɪŋ] *adj* subsiguiente

**en suite bathroom** ['ɒn'swi:t'bɑ:θru:m] *n* cuarto *m* de baño privado(a)

**ensure** [ɪn'ʃʊə(r)] *vt* garantizar

**ENT** [i:en'ti:] *n Med (abbr* **Ear, Nose and Throat)** otorrinolaringología *f*; **E. specialist** otorrinolaringólogo(a) *m,f*

**entail** [en'teɪl] *vt* **to get** *or* **become entangled** *(of wires, animal in net)* enredarse; **to be romantically entangled with sb** tener relaciones amorosas con alguien

**entanglement** [ɪn'tæŋgəlmənt] *n (of wires, cables)* enredo *m*; *(love affair, difficult situation)* lío *m*

**enter** ['entə(r)] **1** *vt* **(a)** *(house, country)* entrar en; *(race)* inscribirse en; *(exam)* presentarse a; *(army, university)* ingresar en; **to e. sb for an exam/a race** inscribir a alguien en un examen/una carrera; **it never entered my head that...** jamás se me pasó por la cabeza que...; **to e. a protest** presentar un escrito de protesta **(b)** *Comptr (data)* introducir

 **2** *vi (go in)* entrar; **to e. for a race** inscribirse en una carrera

**►enter into** *vt insep* **(a)** *(service, dispute, relationship)* empezar, iniciar; **to e. into partnership (with sb)** asociarse (con alguien); **to e. into conversation with sb** entablar conversación con alguien **(b)** *(have a part in)* **money doesn't e. into it** el dinero no tiene nada que ver

**enterprise** ['entəpraɪz] *n* **(a)** *(undertaking)* empresa *f*, iniciativa *f*; *(company)* empresa *f* **(b)** *(initiative)* iniciativa *f*; **to show e.** tener iniciativa

**enterprising** ['entəpraɪzɪŋ] *adj* emprendedor(ora)

**entertain** [entə'teɪn] **1** *vt* **(a)** *(amuse)* entretener, divertir; **to e. guests** tener invitados **(b)** *(consider) (opinion)* considerar; *(fear, suspicion, hope)* albergar

 **2** *vi* recibir (invitados)

**entertainer** [entə'teɪnə(r)] *n* artista *mf* (del espectáculo)

**entertaining** [entə'teɪnɪŋ] **1** *n* **to do a lot of e.** tener a menudo invitados en casa

 **2** *adj* entretenido(a), divertido(a)

**entertainment** [entə'teɪnmənt] *n* **(a)** *(amusement)* entretenimiento *m*, diversión *f*; **much to the e. of the crowd** para regocijo de la multitud; *Com* **e. allowance** gastos *mpl* de representación **(b)** *Th* espectáculo *m*; **the e. business** la industria del espectáculo

**enthral**, *US* **enthrall** [ɪn'θrɔ:l] *(pt & pp* **enthralled)** *vt* cautivar, hechizar

**enthralling** [ɪn'θrɔ:lɪŋ] *adj* cautivador(ora)

**enthuse** [ɪn'θju:z] **1** *vt* entusiasmar

 **2** *vi* entusiasmarse (**about** *or* **over** por)

**enthusiasm** [ɪn'θju:zɪæzəm] *n* entusiasmo *m*

**enthusiast** [ɪn'θju:zɪæst] *n* entusiasta *mf*

**enthusiastic** [ɪnθju:zɪ'æstɪk] *adj (person)* entusiasmado(a); *(praise)* entusiasta; **to be e. (about)** *(of person)* estar entusiasmado(a) (con)

**enthusiastically** [ɪnθju:zɪ'æstɪklɪ] *adv* con entusiasmo

**entice** [ɪn'taɪs] *vt* **to e. sb to do sth** incitar a alguien a hacer algo; **he was enticed away from her** le incitaron a que la abandonara

**enticing** [ɪn'taɪsɪŋ] *adj* tentador(ora), atractivo(a)

**entire** [ɪn'taɪə(r)] *adj (whole, complete)* entero(a); **the e. building/country** el edificio/país entero; **to be in e. agreement (with sb)** estar completamente de acuerdo (con alguien)

**entirely** [ɪn'taɪəlɪ] *adv* completamente, por entero

**entirety** [ɪn'taɪərətɪ] *n* integridad *f*, totalidad *f*; **in its e.** en su totalidad, íntegramente

**entitle** [ɪn'taɪtəl] *vt* (a) *(allow)* to e. sb to do sth autorizar a alguien a hacer algo; **to be entitled to (do) sth** tener derecho a (hacer) algo (b) *(book, song)* titular

**entitlement** [ɪn'taɪtəlmənt] *n* derecho *m*

**entity** ['entɪtɪ] *n* ente *m*, entidad *f*

**entomologist** [entə'mɒlədʒɪst] *n* entomólogo(a) *m,f*

**entomology** [entə'mɒlədʒɪ] *n* entomología *f*

**entourage** [ɒntu:'rɑ:ʒ] *n* séquito *m*, comitiva *f*

**entrails** ['entreɪlz] *npl* entrañas *fpl*

**entrance**¹ ['entrəns] *n* (a) *(way in, act of entering)* entrada *f*; **to gain e. to** lograr acceder a, lograr ingresar en; *Th & Fig* **he made his e.** hizo su aparición *or* entrada (en escena) (b) *(admission)* entrada *f*, ingreso *m*; **e. examination** examen *m* de ingreso

**entrance**² [ɪn'trɑ:ns] *vt (charm)* cautivar, encantar

**entrancing** [ɪn'trɑ:nsɪŋ] *adj* cautivador(ora), encantador(ora)

**entrant** ['entrənt] *n* participante *mf*

**entreat** [ɪn'tri:t] *vt* rogar, suplicar; **to e. sb to do sth** suplicar a alguien que haga algo

**entreaty** [ɪn'tri:tɪ] *n* ruego *m*, súplica *f*

**entrée** ['ɒntreɪ] *n Culin* plato *m* principal

**entrenched** [ɪn'trentʃd] *adj (custom, attitude)* arraigado(a); *(person)* atrincherado(a); **to be e.** *(custom, attitude)* estar arraigado(a); *(person)* estar atrincherado(a)

**entrepreneur** [ɒntrəprə'nɜ:(r)] *n* empresario(a) *m,f*

**entrepreneurial** [ɒntrəprə'nɜ:rɪəl] *adj* empresarial

**entropy** ['entrəpɪ] *n* entropía *f*

**entrust** [ɪn'trʌst] *vt* **to e. sb with sth, to e. sth to sb** confiar algo a alguien

**entry** ['entrɪ] *n* (a) *(way in, act of entering)* entrada *f*; *(into group, organization)* ingreso *m*; **to gain e. to** lograr introducirse en; **she made her e.** hizo su entrada (b) *(of competitor)* participante *mf*; **we had over 1,000 entries for the competition** se recibieron más de 1.000 inscripciones para el concurso; **e. form** (impreso *m* de) inscripción *f* (c) *(in dictionary, encyclopaedia)* entrada *f*

**entryphone** ['entrɪfəʊn] *n* portero *m* automático

**entwine** [ɪn'twaɪn] **1** *vt* entrelazar
**2** *vi* entrelazarse

**enumerate** [ɪ'nju:məreɪt] *vt* enumerar

**enunciate** [ɪ'nʌnsɪeɪt] *vt (sound, word)* articular; *(opinion, view)* enunciar

**envelop** [ɪn'veləp] *vt* envolver

**envelope** ['envələʊp, 'ɒnvələʊp] *n* sobre *m*

**enviable** ['envɪəbəl] *adj* envidiable

**envious** ['envɪəs] *adj* envidioso(a); **to be** *or* **feel e. (of)** tener envidia (de)

**enviously** ['envɪəslɪ] *adv* con envidia

**environment** [ɪn'vaɪrənmənt] *n (surroundings)* entorno *m*; **the e.** el medio ambiente; *Pol* **Department** *or* **Ministry of the E.** ministerio *m* del medio ambiente

**environmental** [ɪnvaɪrən'mentəl] *adj* medioambiental; **e. damage** daños *mpl* medioambientales **e. disaster** catástrofe *f* ecológica; **e. groups** grupos *mpl* ecologistas

**environmentalist** [ɪnvaɪrən'mentəlɪst] *n* ecologista *mf*

**environs** [ɪn'vaɪrənz] *npl* inmediaciones *fpl*, alrededores *mpl*

**envisage** [ɪn'vɪzɪdʒ], *US* **envision** [en-'vɪʒən] *vt (foresee)* prever; *(imagine)* imaginar; **I don't e. any major changes** no preveo ningún cambio importante

**envoy** ['envɔɪ] *(pl* **envoys)** *n (diplomat)* enviado(a) *m,f*

**envy** ['envɪ] **1** *n* envidia *f*; **to be the e. of sb** ser la envidia de alguien
**2** *vt (person)* envidiar; **they envied him his success** tenían envidia de *or* envidiaban su éxito

**enzyme** ['enzaɪm] *n Biol* enzima *m or f*

**EOC** [i:əʊ'si:] *n Br (abbr* **Equal Opportunities Commission)** = organismo público británico que vela por la existencia de igualdad de oportunidades para los diferentes sexos, razas, etc

**eon** *US* = **aeon**

**epaulette,** *US* **epaulet** ['epəlet] *n Mil* charretera *f*

**ephemeral** [ɪ'femərəl] *adj* efímero(a)

**epic** ['epɪk] **1** *n (film)* película *f* épica; *(poem, novel)* epopeya *f*
**2** *adj* épico(a)

**epicentre,** *US* **epicenter** ['epɪsentə(r)] *n* epicentro *m*

**epicurean** [epɪkjʊ'rɪən] *n & adj* epicúreo(a) *m,f*

**epidemic** [epɪ'demɪk] *Med & Fig* **1** *n* epidemia *f*
**2** *adj* epidémico(a)

**epidermis** [epɪ'dɜ:mɪs] *n Anat* epidermis *f inv*

**epidural** [epɪ'djʊərəl] *n Med (anestesia f)* epidural *f*

**epigram** ['epɪɡræm] *n* epigrama *m*

**epilepsy** ['epɪlepsɪ] *n* epilepsia *f*

**epileptic** [epɪ'leptɪk] **1** *n* epiléptico(a) *m,f*
**2** *adj* epiléptico(a); **e. fit** ataque *m* epiléptico

**epilogue** ['epɪlɒɡ] *n* epílogo *m*

**Epiphany** [ɪ'pɪfənɪ] *n* Epifanía *f*

**episcopal** [ɪ'pɪskəpəl] *adj* episcopal

**episcopalian** [ɪpɪskə'peɪlɪən] *n & adj Rel* episcopalista *mf*

**episode** ['epɪsəʊd] *n (part of story, programme)* capítulo *m; (incident)* episodio *m*

**epistle** [ɪ'pɪsəl] *n also Hum* epístola *f*

**epitaph** ['epɪtɑːf] *n* epitafio *m*

**epithet** ['epɪθet] *n* epíteto *m*

**epitome** [ɪ'pɪtəmɪ] *n* vivo ejemplo *m;* **to be the e. of sth** ser el vivo ejemplo de algo

**epitomize** [ɪ'pɪtəmaɪz] *vt* reflejar a la perfección, ser el vivo ejemplo de algo

**epoch** ['iːpɒk] *n* época *f*

**epoch-making** ['iːpɒkmeɪkɪŋ] *adj* **an e. change/event** un cambio/acontecimiento que hace/hizo/*etc* época

**eponymous** [ɪ'pɒnɪməs] *adj* epónimo(a)

**EPS** [iːpiː'es] *n Fin (abbr* **earnings per share)** dividendos *mpl* por acción

**equable** ['ekwəbəl] *adj (person, temper)* ecuánime

**equal** ['iːkwəl] **1** *n* igual *mf;* **to treat sb as an e.** tratar a alguien de igual a igual
**2** *adj* **(a)** *(identical)* igual; **all things being e.** en condiciones normales; **in e. measure** en igual medida; **on e. terms** en igualdad de condiciones; **e. opportunities** igualdad *f* de oportunidades; **e. pay** igualdad *f* de retribuciones; **e. rights** igualdad *f* de derechos **(b)** *(good enough)* **to be e. to (doing) sth** estar capacitado(a) para (hacer) algo
**3** *vt (pt & pp* **equalled,** *US* **equaled)** *(match)* igualar; **four fives equal(s) twenty** cuatro por cinco igual a veinte, cuatro por cinco, veinte

**equality** [ɪ'kwɒlɪtɪ] *n* igualdad *f*

**equalize** ['iːkwəlaɪz] **1** *vt* igualar
**2** *vi Sport* empatar, igualar el marcador

**equalizer** ['iːkwəlaɪzə(r)] *n Elec* ecualizador *m; Sport* tanto *m* del empate

**equally** ['iːkwəlɪ] *adv* **(a)** *(to an equal degree)* igualmente **(b)** *(in equal amounts)* **to share or divide sth e.** dividir algo en partes iguales

**equanimity** [ekwə'nɪmɪtɪ] *n* ecuanimidad *f;* **with e.** ecuánimemente

**equate** [ɪ'kweɪt] *vt* equiparar **(with** con)

**equation** [ɪ'kweɪʒən] *n Math* ecuación *f*

**equator** [ɪ'kweɪtə(r)] *n* ecuador *m*

**equatorial** [ekwə'tɔːrɪəl] *adj* ecuatorial; **E. Guinea** Guinea Ecuatorial

**equestrian** [ɪ'kwestrɪən] **1** *n* caballista *mf*
**2** *adj (statue, ability)* ecuestre

**equidistant** [ekwɪ'dɪstənt] *adj* equidistante

**equilateral** [ekwɪ'lætərəl] *adj* equilátero(a)

**equilibrium** [ekwɪ'lɪbrɪəm] *n* equilibrio *m*

**equinox** ['ekwɪnɒks] *n* equinoccio *m*

**equip** [ɪ'kwɪp] *(pt & pp* **equipped)** *vt* **(a)** *(provide with equipment)* equipar; **to e. sb with sth** equipar a alguien con *or* de algo **(b)** *(prepare)* preparar; **to be equipped for...** estar preparado(a) para...

**equipment** [ɪ'kwɪpmənt] *n (items)* equipo *m;* **e. allowance** gastos *mpl* de equipamiento

**equitable** ['ekwɪtəbəl] *adj* justo(a), equitativo(a)

**Equity** ['ekwɪtɪ] *n Br (actors' union)* = sindicato británico de actores

**equity** ['ekwɪtɪ] *n* **(a)** *(fairness)* justicia *f,* equidad *f* **(b)** *Fin (of shareholders)* fondos *mpl* propios, neto *m* patrimonial; *(of company)* capital *m* escriturado *or* social; **equities** acciones *fpl* ordinarias

**equivalent** [ɪ'kwɪvələnt] **1** *n* equivalente *m*
**2** *adj* equivalente **(to** a)

**equivocal** [ɪ'kwɪvəkəl] *adj* equívoco(a)

**equivocate** [ɪ'kwɪvəkeɪt] *vi* andarse con rodeos

**equivocation** [ɪkwɪvə'keɪʃən] *n* rodeos *mpl,* ambigüedades *fpl*

**ER** [iː'ɑː(r)] *n* **(a)** *US Med (abbr* **Emergency Room)** (sala *f* de) urgencias *fpl* **(b)** *Br (abbr* **Elizabeth Regina)** = emblema de la reina Isabel

**era** ['ɪərə] *n* era *f*

**eradicate** [ɪ'rædɪkeɪt] *vt* erradicar

**erase** [ɪ'reɪz] *vt* borrar

**eraser** [ɪ'reɪzə(r)] *n* goma *f* (de borrar)

**erect** [ɪ'rekt] **1** *adj* erguido(a), erecto(a)
**2** *vt* erigir

**erection** [ɪ'rekʃən] *n* **(a)** *(of building)* erección *f,* construcción *f* **(b)** *(erect penis)* erección *f*

**ergonomic** [ɛːgə'nɒmɪk] *adj* ergonómico(a)

**ergonomics** [ɜːgə'nɒmɪks] *n* ergonomía *f*

**Eritrea** [erɪ'treɪə] *n* Eritrea

**Eritrean** [erɪ'treɪən] *n & adj* eritreo(a) *m,f*

**ERM** [iːɑː'rem] *n Fin (abbr* **Exchange Rate Mechanism)** mecanismo *m* de tipos de cambio

**ermine** ['ɜːmɪn] *n* armiño *m*

**erode** [ɪ'rəʊd] **1** *vt (rock, soil, metal)* erosionar; *(confidence, power)* erosionar, minar; *(savings, income)* mermar
**2** *vi (of rock, soil, metal)* erosionarse; *(of confidence, power)* minarse; *(of savings, income)* mermar

**erogenous** [ɪ'rɒdʒɪnəs] *adj* erógeno(a); **e. zone** zona *f* erógena

**Eros** ['ɪərɒs] *n* Eros

**erosion** [ɪ'rəʊʒən] *n (of rock, soil, metal)* erosión *f; (of confidence, power)* desgaste *m; (of savings, income)* merma *f*

**erotic** [ɪ'rɒtɪk] *adj* erótico(a)

**eroticism** [ɪ'rɒtɪsɪzəm] *n* erotismo *m*

**err** [ɜ:(r)] vi (make mistake) cometer un error, errar; **to e. on the side of caution** pecar de prudente; Prov **to e. is human** errar es humano

**errand** ['erənd] n recado m; **to run errands for sb** hacerle los recados a alguien; **e. boy** chico m de los recados

**erratic** [ɪ'rætɪk] adj (service, performance) desigual, irregular; (course, mood) errático(a)

**erroneous** [ɪ'rəʊnɪəs] adj erróneo(a)

**error** ['erə(r)] n (mistake) error m; **to make an e.** cometer un error, equivocarse; **in e.** por error; **to see the e. of one's ways** darse cuenta de los propios errores

**ersatz** ['ɜːzæts] adj sucedáneo(a)

**erstwhile** ['ɜːstwaɪl] adj Literary antiguo(a), de otros tiempos

**erudite** ['erʊdaɪt] adj erudito(a)

**erudition** [erʊ'dɪʃən] n erudición f

**erupt** [ɪ'rʌpt] vi (volcano) entrar en erupción; Fig estallar, explotar

**eruption** [ɪ'rʌpʃən] n (of volcano) erupción f; (of anger, noise) explosión f, estallido m

**escalate** ['eskəleɪt] vi (of prices) aumentar; **to e. into...** (of conflict) convertirse en...

**escalation** [eskə'leɪʃən] n (of prices, conflict) escalada f

**escalator** ['eskəleɪtə(r)] n escalera f mecánica

**escalope** ['eskəlɒp] n Culin escalope m

**escapade** ['eskəpeɪd] n aventura f, correría f

**escape** [ɪs'keɪp] **1** n (of person) huida f, evasión f; (of gas, fluid) escape m; **to make one's e.** escapar, huir; Com **e. clause** cláusula f de escape or de salvaguardia; **e. route** (from fire) vía f de salida (de emergencia); (of criminal) vía f de escape

**2** vt (danger, punishment) escapar de, librarse de; **to e. sb's notice** pasar inadvertido(a) a alguien; **her name escapes me** ahora no me sale su nombre

**3** vi (of person, gas, fluid) escaparse (**from** de); **to e. from reality** evadirse de la realidad

**escapee** [esker'pi:] n fugitivo(a) m,f

**escapism** [ɪs'keɪpɪzəm] n evasión f de la realidad

**escapist** [ɪs'keɪpɪst] **1** n fantasioso(a) m,f

**2** adj de evasión

**escapologist** [eskə'pɒlədʒɪst] n escapista mf

**escarpment** [ɪs'kɑːpmənt] n escarpa f, escarpadura f

**eschew** [ɪs'tʃuː] vt evitar

**escort 1** [ˈeskɔːt] escolta f; **under e.** escoltado(a); **e. agency** agencia f de contactos; Mil **e. duty** servicio m de escolta

**2** vt [ɪsˈkɔːt] escoltar

**escudo** [e'skuːdəʊ] (pl escudos) n (Portuguese currency) escudo m

**Eskimo** ['eskɪməʊ] (pl Eskimos) n & adj esquimal mf

**ESL** [iːesˈel] n (abbr **English as a Second Language**) = inglés m como segunda lengua

**esophagus** US = **oesophagus**

**esoteric** [esəʊ'terɪk] adj esotérico(a)

**ESP** [iːesˈpiː] n (abbr **extrasensory perception**) percepción f extrasensorial

**espadrille** ['espədrɪl] n alpargata f, zapatilla f de esparto

**especially** [ɪs'peʃəlɪ] adv especialmente; **we were e. lucky with the weather** tuvimos especial suerte con el tiempo

**Esperanto** [espə'ræntəʊ] n esperanto m

**espionage** ['espɪənɑːʒ] n espionaje m

**esplanade** [esplə'neɪd] n paseo m marítimo

**espouse** [ɪs'paʊz] vt patrocinar

**espresso** [es'presəʊ] n café m exprés

**Esq** (abbr **Esquire**) Derek Wilson, E. (Sr.) D. Derek Wilson

**essay** ['eseɪ] (pl essays) n (at school) redacción f; (at university) trabajo m

**essayist** ['eseɪɪst] n ensayista mf

**essence** ['esəns] n (a) (most important part or quality) esencia f; **in e.** esencialmente, en esencia; **the very e. of...** la más pura esencia de...; **time is of the e.** no hay tiempo que perder (b) Culin esencia f; **vanilla/coffee e.** esencia de vainilla/café

**essential** [ɪ'senʃəl] **1** npl **essentials** (basic foodstuffs) productos mpl primarios or de primera necesidad; (basic issues) cuestiones fpl básicas; **just pack a few essentials** guarda sólo lo imprescindible

**2** adj (a) (basic) esencial, básico(a); **e. oil** aceite m esencial (b) (indispensable) esencial, fundamental; **it is e. that...** es fundamental que...

**essentially** [ɪ'senʃəlɪ] adv esencialmente

**EST** [iːesˈtiː] n US (abbr **Eastern Standard Time**) = hora oficial de la costa este de los Estados Unidos

**establish** [ɪs'tæblɪʃ] vt (a) (set up) establecer; **to e. oneself in business** establecerse en el mundo de los negocios; **to e. a reputation** crearse or labrarse una reputación; **they established their right to vote** establecieron su derecho al voto; **the film established her as an important director** la película la consagró como una gran directora (b) (prove) (fact, sb's innocence) determinar

**established** [ɪs'tæblɪʃt] adj (custom, practice) establecido(a); (fact) probado(a); **the e. Church** la religión oficial; **the e. order** el orden establecido

**establishment** [ɪs'tæblɪʃmənt] n (a) the E. (*established order*) el sistema, el orden establecido; (*ruling class*) la clase dominante (b) (*hotel, restaurant*) establecimiento m (c) (*of company*) fundación f; (*of reputation*) establecimiento m; (*of fact*) determinación f

**estate** [ɪs'teɪt] n (a) *Law* (*possessions*) posesiones fpl (b) (*land*) finca f; *Br* (*housing*) e. urbanización f; *Br* e. **agency** (agencia) f inmobiliaria f; *Br* e. **agent** agente m/f inmobiliario(a); *Br* e. (**car**) (coche m) ranchera f

**esteem** [ɪs'tiːm] **1** n estima f; **to hold sb in high/low e.** tener a alguien en gran/poca estima

**2** vt estimar; *Formal* **to e. it an honour that…** considerar un honor que…

**esthetic** [ɪs'θetɪk] adj *US* estético(a)

**estimate 1** n ['estɪmət] (*calculation*) estimación f, cálculo m aproximado; *Com* presupuesto m; **at a rough e.** aproximadamente

**2** vt ['estɪmeɪt] estimar; **an estimated cost/value** un coste/valor estimado

**estimation** [estɪ'meɪʃən] n (a) (*calculation*) cálculo m, estimación f (b) (*judgement*) juicio m, opinión f; **she has gone up/down in my e.** ahora la tengo en más/menos estima

**Estonia** [es'təʊnɪə] n Estonia

**Estonian** [es'təʊnɪən] **1** n (a) (*person*) estonio(a) m,f (b) (*language*) estonio m

**2** adj estonio(a)

**estranged** [ɪs'treɪndʒd] adj separado(a); **to be e. (from)** estar separado(a) (de)

**estrogen** *US* = **oestrogen**

**estuary** ['estjʊərɪ] n estuario m

**ETA** [iːtiː'eɪ] n *Av* (*abbr* **estimated time of arrival**) hora f prevista de llegada

**et al** [et'æl] (*abbr* **et alii**) et al.

**etc** [et'setrə] adv (*abbr* **et cetera**) etc., etcétera

**etch** [etʃ] vt grabar (al aguafuerte); *Fig* **the scene was etched in his memory** tenía la escena grabada en la memoria

**etching** ['etʃɪŋ] n (*picture*) (grabado m al) aguafuerte m

**eternal** [ɪ'tɜːnəl] adj eterno(a)

**eternally** [ɪ'tɜːnəlɪ] adv eternamente; **I shall be e. grateful to you** te estaré eternamente agradecido(a)

**eternity** [ɪ'tɜːnɪtɪ] n eternidad f; *Fam* **I waited an e.** esperé una eternidad

**ether** ['iːθə(r)] n éter m

**ethereal** [ɪ'θɪərɪəl] adj etéreo(a)

**ethical** ['eθɪkəl] adj ético(a)

**ethically** ['eθɪklɪ] adv éticamente

**ethics** ['eθɪks] npl ética f

**Ethiopia** [iːθɪ'əʊpɪə] n Etiopía

**Ethiopian** [iːθɪ'əʊpɪən] n & adj etíope mf

**ethnic** ['eθnɪk] adj étnico(a); **e. cleansing** limpieza f étnica; **e. minority** minoría f étnica

**ethnically** ['eθnɪklɪ] adv étnicamente

**ethnocentric** [eθnəʊ'sentrɪk] adj etnocéntrico(a)

**ethnography** [eθ'nɒɡrəfɪ] n etnografía f

**ethnology** [eθ'nɒlədʒɪ] n etnología f

**ethos** ['iːθɒs] n código m ético, valores mpl (morales)

**etiquette** ['etɪket] n etiqueta f, protocolo m; **professional e.** ética f profesional

**Etruscan** [ɪ'trʌskən] n & adj etrusco(a) m,f

**etymological** [etɪmə'lɒdʒɪkəl] adj etimológico(a)

**etymology** [etɪ'mɒlədʒɪ] n etimología f

**EU** [iː'juː] n (*abbr* **European Union**) UE f

**eucalyptus** [juːkə'lɪptəs] n eucalipto m

**Eucharist** ['juːkərɪst] n the E. la Eucaristía

**eulogize** ['juːlədʒaɪz] vt loar, alabar

**eulogy** ['juːlədʒɪ] n panegírico m

**eunuch** ['juːnək] n eunuco m

**euphemism** ['juːfɪmɪzəm] n eufemismo m

**euphemistic** [juːfɪ'mɪstɪk] adj eufemístico(a)

**euphoria** [juː'fɔːrɪə] n euforia f

**euphoric** [juː'fɔːrɪk] adj eufórico(a); **to be e.** estar eufórico(a)

**Eurasian** [jʊə'reɪʒən] n & adj eur(o)asiático(a) m,f

**EURATOM** [jʊə'rætəm] n (*abbr* **European Atomic Energy Community**) EURATOM f, Comunidad f Europea de la Energía Atómica

**eureka** [jʊə'riːkə] exclam ¡eureka!

**euro** ['jʊərəʊ] (*pl* **euros**) n *Fin* (*European currency*) euro m

**Eurocheque** ['jʊərəʊtʃek] n *Fin* eurocheque m

**Eurodollar** ['jʊərəʊdɒlə(r)] n *Fin* eurodólar m

**Euro-MP** ['jʊərəʊempiː] n eurodiputado(a) m,f

**Europe** ['jʊərəp] n Europa

**European** [jʊərə'piːən] **1** n europeo(a) m,f

**2** adj europeo(a); **E. Commission** Comisión f Europea; **E. Community** Comunidad f Europea; **E. Court of Human Rights** Tribunal m Europeo de Derechos Humanos; **E. Court of Justice** Tribunal m de Justicia Europeo; **E. Currency Unit** unidad f de cuenta europea; **E. Economic Community** Comunidad f Económica Europea; **E. Free Trade Association** Asociación f Europea de Libre Comercio; **E. Monetary System** Sistema m Monetario Europeo; **E. Parliament** Parlamento m Europeo; **E. Union** Unión f Europea

**Eurosceptic** [jʊərəʊ'skeptɪk] *n* euroescéptico(a) *m,f*

**Eustachian tube** [ju:s'teɪʃən'tju:b] *n Anat* trompa *f* de Eustaquio

**euthanasia** [ju:θə'neɪzɪə] *n* eutanasia *f*

**evacuate** [ɪ'vækjʊeɪt] *vt (person, area)* evacuar

**evacuation** [ɪvækjʊ'eɪʃən] *n (of people, area)* evacuación *f*

**evacuee** [ɪvækjʊ'i:] *n* evacuado(a) *m,f*

**evade** [ɪ'veɪd] *vt (pursuer)* burlar; *(blow)* esquivar; *(question)* eludir; **she evaded her responsibilities** rehuyó sus responsabilidades; **to e. tax** evadir impuestos

**evaluate** [ɪ'væljʊeɪt] *vt* evaluar

**evaluation** [ɪvæljʊ'eɪʃən] *n* evaluación *f*

**evangelical** [i:væn'dʒelɪkəl] *n & adj* evangélico(a) *m,f*

**evangelism** [ɪ'vændʒɪlɪzəm] *n* evangelismo *m*

**evangelist** [ɪ'vændʒɪlɪst] *n* evangelista *mf*

**evangelize** [ɪ'vændʒɪlaɪz] *vt & vi* evangelizar

**evaporate** [ɪ'væpəreɪt] **1** *vt* evaporar; **evaporated milk** leche *f* concentrada

**2** *vi (of liquid, enthusiasm)* evaporarse

**evaporation** [ɪvæpə'reɪʃən] *n* evaporación *f*

**evasion** [ɪ'veɪʒən] *n (escape) (of pursuer, question)* evasión *f*; **(tax)** e. evasión fiscal; **I was met with the usual evasions** me dieron las evasivas de costumbre

**evasive** [ɪ'veɪsɪv] *adj (person, reply)* evasivo(a); **to take e. action** quitarse de en medio

**eve** [i:v] *n (day before)* víspera *f*; **on the e. of…** (en) la víspera de…, en vísperas de…

**even** ['i:vən] **1** *adj* **(a)** *(flat) (surface)* llano(a), liso(a)

  **(b)** *(regular) (breathing, pace)* regular, constante; *(temperature)* constante; **to have an e. temper** tener un carácter pacífico; **e. number** número *m* par

  **(c)** *(equal) (contest)* igualado(a); **to have an e. chance (of doing sth)** tener un cincuenta por ciento de posibilidades (de hacer algo); *Fig* **to get e. with sb** *(take revenge on)* vengarse *or* desquitarse de alguien

**2** *adv* **(a)** *incluso*; **e. bigger/more interesting** aún *or* incluso mayor/más interesante; **I never e. saw it** ni siquiera llegué a verlo; **without e. speaking** sin tan siquiera hablar; **e. as I speak** justo a la vez que estoy hablando

  **(b)** *(in phrases)* **e. if** aunque; **e. now** incluso ahora; **e. so** aun así; **e. then** *(still)* ya entonces; *(nevertheless)* aun así; **e. though** aunque, a pesar de que

**3** *vt (make equal)* igualar, equilibrar; **to e. the odds** dar igualdad de oportunidades; **to e. the score** igualar el marcador

▸**even out 1** *vt* **they aim to e. out social inequalities** aspiran a eliminar las desigualdades sociales; **with this account you can e. out payments over the year** con esta cuenta, los pagos se reparten equitativamente a lo largo del año

**2** *vi (of differences, workload)* equilibrarse

▸**even up** *vt sep* **to e. things up** igualar *or* equilibrar las cosas

**even-handed** ['i:vən'hændɪd] *adj* imparcial

**evening** ['i:vnɪŋ] *n (earlier)* tarde *f*; *(later)* noche *f*; **tomorrow e.** mañana por la tarde/noche; **yesterday e.** ayer (por la) tarde/noche; *Fam* **e.!** ¡buenas tardes/noches!; **in the e.** por la tarde/noche; **a musical/cultural e.** una velada musical/cultural; **e. class** clase *f* nocturna; **e. dress** *(for men)* traje *m* de etiqueta; *(for women)* vestido *m* or traje *m* de noche; **e. paper** periódico *m* vespertino *or* de la tarde; **e. performance** *(of play)* sesión *f* de noche

**evenly** ['i:vənlɪ] *adv (uniformly)* uniformemente; *(fairly)* equitativamente; **to breath e.** respirar tranquilamente; **to say sth e.** decir algo en tono neutro; **e. matched** en igualdad de condiciones

**evensong** ['i:vənsɒŋ] *n Rel* vísperas *fpl*

**event** [ɪ'vent] *n* **(a)** *(occurrence)* acontecimiento *m*; **in the course of events** en el transcurso de los acontecimientos; **in any e.** en cualquier caso; **in the e. of fire** en caso de incendio; **in the e. of her resigning…** en caso de que dimita… **(b)** *(in athletics)* prueba *f*

**even-tempered** ['i:vən'tempəd] *adj* ecuánime, sereno(a)

**eventful** [ɪ'ventfʊl] *adj (day, life)* agitado(a), azaroso(a)

**eventual** [ɪ'ventjʊəl] *adj* final

**eventuality** [ɪventjʊ'ælɪtɪ] *n* eventualidad *f*, posibilidad *f*; **in that e.** en ese caso; **to be ready for all eventualities** estar preparado(a) para cualquier eventualidad

**eventually** [ɪ'ventjʊəlɪ] *adv* finalmente, al final

**ever** ['evə(r)] *adv* **(a)** *(always, at any time)* **e. since then/1960** desde entonces/1960; **more than e.** más que nunca; **the worst/best e.** el peor/mejor de todos los tiempos; **all she e. does is criticize** no hace más que criticar; **she was as friendly as e.** estuvo tan amable como siempre; **she's a liar if e. there was one** miente como ella sola, es la más mentirosa del mundo; **she's a genius if e. there was one** es un genio donde los haya; **e. the gentleman**, he opened the door for her caballeroso como siempre, le abrió la puerta

  **(b)** *(with negative sense)* **not e.** nunca; **hardly e.** casi nunca; **nothing e. happens** nunca pasa nada; **I don't know if I'll e. meet him**

**again** no sé si lo volveré a ver (alguna vez); **I seldom if e. see her** apenas la veo

(c) *(in questions)* alguna vez; **have you e. been to Spain?** ¿has estado (alguna vez) en España?

(d) *Fam (intensive)* **e. so pretty** tan guapísima; **e. so expensive** tan carísimo(a); **e. such a lot of money** tantísimo dinero

**evergreen** ['evəgri:n] **1** *n* árbol *m* (de hoja) perenne

**2** *adj* (de hoja) perenne

**everlasting** [evə'lɑːstɪŋ] *adj* eterno(a), perpetuo(a)

**evermore** [evə'mɔː(r)] *adv Formal* por siempre (jamás); **for e.** para siempre

**every** ['evrɪ] *adj* (a) *(each, all)* cada; **at e. opportunity** en toda ocasión; **from e. side** de todas partes; **of e. kind** *or* **sort** de todo tipo; **they hung on his e. word** estaban pendientes de cada una de sus palabras; **e. time** siempre, cada vez; **e. one of us** todos y cada uno de nosotros; **e. man for himself!** ¡sálvese quien pueda!

(b) *(indicating regular occurrence)* **e. week** todas las semanas; **e. day** todos los días; **e. other** *or* **second day** cada dos días; **e. other line/ page** cada dos líneas/páginas; **e. so often, e. now and again** *or* **then** de vez en cuando

(c) *(intensive)* **you have e. right to be angry** tienes todo el derecho a estar enfadado; **e. bit as good/as intelligent as…** exactamente igual de bueno/de inteligente que…; **I shall give you e. assistance** te ayudaré en todo

**everybody** ['evrɪbɒdɪ] *pron* todo el mundo, todos(as); **e. I know was there** toda la gente que conozco estaba allí; **e. else** todos los demás; **e. who is anybody** toda la gente importante

**everyday** ['evrɪdeɪ] *adj (event, expression)* cotidiano(a); **for e. use** para uso cotidiano

**everyone** ['evrɪwʌn] = **everybody**

**everything** ['evrɪθɪŋ] *pron* todo; **e. I did seemed to go wrong** parecía que todo lo hacía mal; **e. possible** todo lo posible; **money isn't e.** el dinero no lo es todo

**everywhere** ['evrɪweə(r)] *adv* por *or* en todas partes; **we looked e.** miramos por todas partes; **e. you go/look** dondequiera que vayas/mires; **e. in France** en toda Francia

**evict** [ɪ'vɪkt] *vt* desahuciar, desalojar

**eviction** [ɪ'vɪkʃən] *n* desahucio *m*, desalojo *m*; **e. order** orden *f* de desahucio *or* desalojo

**evidence** ['evɪdəns] **1** *n* (a) pruebas *fpl*; **to be in e.** ser claramente visible; **to show e. of** demostrar, dar prueba de; **there was no e. of his stay in the house** no había pruebas de su paso por la casa (b) *Law* pruebas *fpl*; **to give e.** testificar, prestar declaración; **to turn** *Br* **King's** *or* **Queen's** *or US* **State's e.** = inculpar

a un cómplice ante un tribunal a cambio de recibir un trato indulgente

**2** *vt Formal* evidenciar, demostrar; **as evidenced by…** como lo demuestra…

**evident** ['evɪdənt] *adj* evidente; **it was e. that…** era evidente que…

**evidently** ['evɪdəntlɪ] *adv* evidentemente

**evil** ['iːvəl] **1** *n* mal *m*; **to speak e. of sb** hablar mal de alguien

**2** *adj (person)* malo(a), malvado(a); *(action, practice)* vil, perverso(a); *(influence, effect)* nocivo(a), perjudicial; *(spirit)* maligno(a)

**evildoer** ['iːvəlduːə(r)] *n Literary* malhechor(ora) *m,f*

**evil-looking** ['iːvəllʊkɪŋ] *adj* de aspecto siniestro

**evil-minded** ['iːvəl'maɪndɪd] *adj* perverso(a)

**evil-smelling** ['iːvəl'smelɪŋ] *adj* maloliente, apestoso(a)

**evince** [ɪ'vɪns] *vt Formal* evidenciar

**evocation** [evə'keɪʃən] *n* evocación *f*

**evocative** [ɪ'vɒkətɪv] *adj* evocador(ora) **(of** de)

**evoke** [ɪ'vəʊk] *vt* evocar

**evolution** [iːvə'luːʃən] *n* evolución *f*

**evolutionary** [iːvə'luːʃənərɪ] *adj* evolutivo(a)

**evolve** [ɪ'vɒlv] **1** *vt* desarrollar

**2** *vi (of species)* evolucionar; *(of situation)* desarrollarse; **to e. from** *(of species)* provenir de; **finding food has evolved into a major problem** encontrar comida se ha convertido en un problema de primer orden

**ewe** [juː] *n* oveja *f (hembra)*

**ex** [eks] *n Fam (former spouse, girlfriend, boyfriend)* ex *mf*

**ex-** [eks] *pref (former)* ex; **ex-minister/ teacher** ex ministro(a)/profesor(ora); **ex-wife/husband** ex mujer/marido, exmujer/exmarido

**exacerbate** [eg'zæsəbeɪt] *vt* exacerbar

**exact** [ɪg'zækt] **1** *adj (number, amount)* exacto(a), preciso(a); **at the e. moment when…** en el preciso momento *or* instante en que…; **those were her e. words** esas fueron exactamente sus palabras; **the e. opposite** exactamente lo contrario; **to be e.** para ser exactos; **an e. science** una ciencia exacta

**2** *vt (promise, apology)* arrancar **(from** a); *(obedience, respect)* imponer **(from** a); *(tax)* imponer el pago de **(from** a)

**exacting** [ɪg'zæktɪŋ] *adj (person)* exigente; *(task)* arduo(a); *(standards)* riguroso(a)

**exactitude** [ɪg'zæktɪtjuːd] *n Formal* exactitud *f*

**exactly** [ɪg'zæktlɪ] *adv* exactamente; **e.!** ¡exacto!; **not e.** *(not very)* no precisamente; *(as a reply)* no exactamente

**exaggerate** [ɪg'zædʒəreɪt] *vt & vi* exagerar

**exaggerated** [ɪg'zædʒəreɪtɪd] *adj* exagerado(a)

**exaggeration** [ɪgzædʒə'reɪʃən] *n* exageración *f*

**exalt** [ɪg'zɔːlt] *vt Formal (praise)* exaltar

**exalted** [ɪg'zɔːltɪd] *adj (high)* elevado(a)

**exam** [ɪg'zæm] *n* examen *m*; **to take** *or* **sit an e.** examinarse, hacer un examen; **e. result** nota *f*, resultado *m*

**examination** [ɪgzæmɪ'neɪʃən] *n (at school, at university, of records)* examen *m*; **to take** *or* **sit an e.** examinarse, hacer un examen; *Educ* **e. board** tribunal *m* (de examen), junta *f* examinadora; *Educ* **e. result** nota *f*, resultado *m*

**examine** [ɪg'zæmɪn] *vt (evidence, student)* examinar; **to e. one's conscience** hacer examen de conciencia

**examinee** [ɪgzæmɪ'niː] *n* examinando(a) *m,f*

**examiner** [ɪg'zæmɪnə(r)] *n* examinador(ora) *m,f*

**example** [ɪg'zɑːmpəl] *n* ejemplo *m*; **for e.** por ejemplo; **to set an e.** dar ejemplo; **to make an e. of sb** imponer un castigo ejemplar a alguien; **to follow sb's e.** seguir el ejemplo de alguien; **to lead by e.** predicar con el ejemplo

**exasperate** [ɪg'zɑːspəreɪt] *vt* exasperar; **to get exasperated** exasperarse

**exasperating** [ɪg'zɑːspəreɪtɪŋ] *adj* exasperante

**exasperation** [ɪgzɑːspə'reɪʃən] *n* exasperación *f*

**excavate** ['ekskəveɪt] *vt* excavar

**excavation** [ekskə'veɪʃən] *n* excavación *f*

**excavator** ['ekskəveɪtə(r)] *n (machine)* excavadora *f*

**exceed** [ɪk'siːd] *vt (amount, number, expectations)* superar, exceder; *(limit)* rebasar

**exceedingly** [ɪk'siːdɪŋlɪ] *adv* sumamente, extremadamente

**excel** [ɪk'sel] *(pt & pp* **excelled)** **1** *vt esp Ironic* **to e. oneself** lucirse
**2** *vi* sobresalir **(at** *or* **in** en)

**excellence** ['eksələns] *n* excelencia *f*

**excellency** ['eksələnsɪ] *n* **Your/His E.** Su Excelencia

**excellent** ['eksələnt] *adj* excelente

**except** [ɪk'sept] **1** *prep* excepto, salvo; **nobody e. him** nadie salvo él; **e. for** a excepción de, exceptuando; **we would have lost, e. for you** de no ser *or* a no ser por ti, habríamos perdido; **the dress is ready e. for the buttons** menos *or* salvo los botones, el vestido está listo; **he's my best friend, e. for you, of course** es mi mejor amigo, aparte de ti, claro está; **e. that** sólo que; **e. when** salvo cuando
**2** *vt* exceptuar, excluir **(from** de); **present company excepted** exceptuando a los aquí presentes; **not excepting...** incluyendo a...

**exception** [ɪk'sepʃən] *n* excepción *f*; **to make an e. of sth/for sb** hacer una excepción con algo/con alguien; **with the e. of...** a excepción (hecha) de...; **without e.** sin excepción; **the e. that proves the rule** la excepción que confirma la regla; **to take e. to sth** *(be offended)* ofenderse por algo; *(object)* censurar algo

**exceptionable** [ɪk'sepʃənəbəl] *adj Formal* inaceptable, censurable

**exceptional** [ɪk'sepʃənəl] *adj* excepcional

**exceptionally** [ɪk'sepʃənəlɪ] *adv* extraordinariamente; **e., more time may be allowed** en casos excepcionales se dará más tiempo

**excerpt** ['eksɜːpt] *n* fragmento *m* **(from** de)

**excess** [ɪk'ses] *n* exceso *m*; **in e. of** más de; **sums in e. of £1,000** sumas superiores a *or* de más de 1.000 libras; **to do sth to e.** hacer algo en exceso; **to lead a life of e.** llevar una vida de excesos; **to pay the e.** *(on ticket)* pagar la diferencia *or* el suplemento; **e. baggage** exceso de equipaje

**excessive** [ɪk'sesɪv] *adj* excesivo(a)

**excessively** [ɪk'sesɪvlɪ] *adv* excesivamente

**exchange** [ɪks'tʃeɪndʒ] **1** *n* **(a)** *(of prisoners, ideas)* intercambio *m*; **in e. (for)** a cambio (de); **there was a heated e.** hubo un acalorado intercambio verbal; *Com* **e. of contracts** acto *m* notarial de compraventa; **e. visit** visita *f* de intercambio
**(b)** *Fin (of currency)* cambio *m*; **e. controls** controles *m* de cambio (monetario); **e. rate** tipo *m* de cambio; **e. rate mechanism** mecanismo *m* de los tipos de cambio
**(c) (Stock) E.** mercado *m* de valores, bolsa *f*
**(d) (telephone) e.** central *f* telefónica, centralita *f*
**2** *vt* intercambiar; *(faulty goods)* descambiar; **to e. sth for sth** cambiar algo por algo; **to e. glances** intercambiar miradas

**exchangeable** [ɪks'tʃeɪndʒəbəl] *adj (voucher, currency)* canjeable

**exchequer** [eks'tʃekə(r)] *n Br* **the E.** ≃ Hacienda *f*, el Tesoro (público); **the Chancellor of the E.** ≃ el ministro de Hacienda

**excise 1** *n* ['eksaɪz] **e. (duties)** *(tax)* impuesto *m* sobre el consumo
**2** *vt* [ɪk'saɪz] *(remove)* extirpar

**excitable** [ɪk'saɪtəbəl] *adj* excitable

**excite** [ɪk'saɪt] *vt (person)* entusiasmar, emocionar; *(feeling, passion)* excitar, estimular; *(envy, interest)* suscitar

**excited** [ɪk'saɪtɪd] *adj* entusiasmado(a), emocionado(a); **to get e. (about)** entusiasmarse *or* emocionarse (con)

**excitedly** [ɪk'saɪtɪdlɪ] *adv* con entusiasmo

**excitement** [ɪk'saɪtmənt] *n* emoción *f*; **to avoid e.** evitar las emociones fuertes; **to cause great e.** provocar un gran revuelo

**exciting** [ɪk'saɪtɪŋ] *adj* emocionante, apasionante

**exclaim** [ɪks'kleɪm] *vt & vi* exclamar

**exclamation** [ɛksklə'meɪʃən] *n* exclamación *f*; *Br* **e. mark** *or* *US* **point** signo *m* de admiración *or* exclamación

**exclamatory** [ɛks'klæmətərɪ] *adj* exclamativo(a)

**exclude** [ɪks'kluːd] *vt* excluir; **excluding...** excluyendo...

**exclusion** [ɪks'kluːʒən] *n* exclusión *f*; **to the e. of...** haciendo caso omiso de...

**exclusive** [ɪks'kluːsɪv] **1** *n* (*in newspaper, on TV*) exclusiva *f*
**2** *adj* exclusivo(a); **e. interview** entrevista *f* en exclusiva
**3** *adv* **e. of** excluyendo

**exclusively** [ɪks'kluːsɪvlɪ] *adv* exclusivamente; (*in newspaper, on TV*) en exclusiva

**excommunicate** [ɛkskə'mjuːnɪkeɪt] *vt* excomulgar

**excommunication** [ɛkskəmjuːnɪ'keɪʃən] *n* excomunión *f*

**excrement** ['ɛkskrɪmənt] *n* excremento *m*

**excrescence** [ɛks'krɛsəns] *n* (*monstrosity*) adefesio *m*

**excrete** [ɪks'kriːt] *Formal vt & vi* excretar

**excruciating** [ɪks'kruːʃɪeɪtɪŋ] *adj* terrible, espantoso(a)

**excruciatingly** [ɪks'kruːʃɪeɪtɪŋlɪ] *adv* terriblemente, espantosamente; **e. painful** terriblemente doloroso(a); *Fam* **e. funny** tremendamente gracioso(a)

**excursion** [ɪks'kɜːʃən] *n* excursión *f*

**excuse 1** [ɪks'kjuːs] *n* excusa *f*; **to make an e., to make excuses** disculparse, excusarse; **a poor e. for a car** una porquería de coche
**2** *vt* [ɪks'kjuːz] (**a**) (*forgive*) disculpar, excusar; **e. me!** (*to attract attention*) ¡perdón!, ¡oiga (por favor)!; (*when trying to get past*) ¿me permite?; **e. me?** (*what did you say?*) ¿cómo? (**b**) (*exempt*) eximir (**from** de) (**c**) **to e. oneself** (*give excuse*) disculparse, excusarse

**ex-directory** [ɛksdɪ'rɛktərɪ] *adj Br* **e. (telephone) number** = número de teléfono que no figura en la guía

**execrable** ['ɛksɪkrəbəl] *adj Formal* execrable

**execute** ['ɛksɪkjuːt] *vt* (*prisoner, command*) ejecutar; (*plan, operation*) llevar a cabo; (*one's duties*) cumplir

**execution** [ɛksɪ'kjuːʃən] *n* (*of order, prisoner*) ejecución *f*; (*of duty*) cumplimiento *m*

**executioner** [ɛksɪ'kjuːʃənə(r)] *n* verdugo *m*

**executive** [ɪg'zɛkjʊtɪv] **1** *n* (*businessman*) ejecutivo(a) *m,f*; (*committee*) ejecutiva *f*
**2** *adj* ejecutivo(a); **an e. car** un coche de lujo; *Br* **e. director** director(ora) *m,f* ejecutivo(a)

**executor** [ɪg'zɛkjʊtə(r)] *n Law* albacea *mf*

**exemplary** [ɪg'zɛmplərɪ] *adj* ejemplar

**exemplify** [ɪg'zɛmplɪfaɪ] *vt* ilustrar

**exempt** [ɪg'zɛmpt] **1** *adj* exento(a) (**from** de)
**2** *vt* eximir (**from** de)

**exemption** [ɪg'zɛm(p)ʃən] *n* exención *f* (**from** de)

**exercise** ['ɛksəsaɪz] **1** *n* (*physical, mental*) ejercicio *m*; (*military*) maniobras *fpl*; **to take e.** hacer ejercicio; **e. bike** bicicleta *f* estática; **e. book** libro *m* de ejercicios
**2** *vt* (**a**) (*body, mind*) ejercitar (**b**) (*right, one's influence*) ejercer; **to e. discretion** ser discreto(a); **to e. restraint** controlarse
**3** *vi* (*physically*) hacer ejercicio

**exert** [ɪg'zɜːt] *vt* (*pressure, influence*) ejercer; **to e. oneself** esforzarse

**exertion** [ɪg'zɜːʃən] *n* esfuerzo *m*

**exhale** [ɛks'heɪl] *vi* espirar

**exhaust** [ɪg'zɔːst] **1** *n* (*on car*) escape *m*; **e. (fumes)** gases *mpl* de la combustión; **e. (pipe)** tubo *m* de escape
**2** *vt* (*person, resources*) agotar

**exhausted** [ɪg'zɔːstɪd] *adj* agotado(a); **to be e.** estar agotado(a)

**exhausting** [ɪg'zɔːstɪŋ] *adj* agotador(ora)

**exhaustion** [ɪg'zɔːstʃən] *n* agotamiento *m*

**exhaustive** [ɪg'zɔːstɪv] *adj* exhaustivo(a)

**exhibit** [ɪg'zɪbɪt] **1** *n* (*in art exhibition*) obra *f* expuesta; (*in court case*) prueba *f* material
**2** *vt* (**a**) (*object*) exhibir (**b**) (*painting in exhibition*) exponer (**c**) (*show*) **to e. signs of stress/wear** mostrar signos de estrés/desgaste

**exhibition** [ɛksɪ'bɪʃən] *n* exposición *f*; *Fam* **to make an e. of oneself** dar el espectáculo, montar el número

**exhibitionist** [ɛksɪ'bɪʃənɪst] *n* exhibicionista *mf*

**exhibitor** [ɪg'zɪbɪtə(r)] *n Art* expositor(ora) *m,f*

**exhilarated** [ɪg'zɪləreɪtɪd] *adj* eufórico(a), enardecido(a)

**exhilarating** [ɪg'zɪləreɪtɪŋ] *adj* vivificante, excitante

**exhort** [ɪg'zɔːt] *vt* exhortar

**exhortation** [ɪgzɔː'teɪʃən] *n* exhortación *f*

**exhume** [ɛks'hjuːm] *vt* exhumar

**exile** ['ɛksaɪl] **1** *n* (**a**) (*banishment*) exilio *m*; **in e.** en el exilio (**b**) (*exiled person*) exiliado(a) *m,f*
**2** *vt* exiliar

**exist** [ɪg'zɪst] *vi* **(a)** *(be in existence)* existir **(b)** *(survive)* sobrevivir **(on** a base de)

**existence** [ɪg'zɪstəns] *n* existencia *f*; **to be in e.** existir; **to come into e.** nacer, ver la luz; **to go out of e.** desaparecer

**existential** [egzɪs'tenʃəl] *adj* existencial

**existentialism** [egzɪs'tenʃəlɪzəm] *n* existencialismo *m*

**existentialist** [egzɪs'tenʃəlɪst] *n & adj* existencialista *mf*

**existing** [ɪg'zɪstɪŋ] *adj* actual, existente

**exit** ['eksɪt] **1** *n* salida *f*; **to make an e.** salir; *Pol* **e. poll** sondeo *m* a la salida de los colegios electorales; **e. visa** visado *m* de salida

  **2** *vi (leave) & Comptr* salir

**exodus** ['eksədəs] *n* éxodo *m*

**ex officio** ['eksə'fɪʃɪəʊ] **1** *adj (member)* en virtud del cargo

  **2** *adv* **to act e.** actuar en virtud del cargo

**exonerate** [ɪg'zɒnəreɪt] *vt* exonerar **(from** *or* **of** de)

**exorbitant** [ɪg'zɔːbɪtənt] *adj* exorbitante, exagerado(a)

**exorcism** ['eksɔːsɪzəm] *n* exorcismo *m*

**exorcist** ['eksɔːsɪst] *n* exorcista *mf*

**exorcize** ['eksɔːsaɪz] *vt* exorcizar

**exotic** [ɪg'zɒtɪk] *adj* exótico(a)

**expand** [ɪks'pænd] **1** *vt (production, output)* ampliar

  **2** *vi (of solid, gas)* dilatarse; *(of company)* expandirse, extenderse

▸**expand on, expand upon** *vt insep (talk, write at greater length about)* desarrollar

**expanded** [ɪks'pændɪd] *adj Comptr* ampliado(a); **e. polystyrene** poliestireno *m* expandido

**expanding** [ɪks'pændɪŋ] *adj (market, company)* en expansión

**expanse** [eks'pæns] *n (of land, water)* extensión *f*

**expansion** [ɪks'pænʃən] *n (of solid, gas)* dilatación *f*; *(of production, output)* ampliación *f*; *(of company)* expansión *f*; *Comptr* **e. card** tarjeta *f* de ampliación (de memoria)

**expansive** [ɪks'pænsɪv] *adj* expansivo(a), comunicativo(a)

**expat** [eks'pæt] *n Br Fam* emigrado(a) *m,f*

**expatriate 1** *n* [eks'pætrɪət] *(voluntary)* emigrado(a) *m,f*; *(exile)* expatriado(a) *m,f*

  **2** *vt* [eks'pætrɪeɪt] expatriar

**expect** [ɪks'pekt] **1** *vt* **(a)** *(anticipate)* esperar; **to e. to do sth** esperar hacer algo; **to e. sb do sth** esperar que alguien haga algo; **I expected as much** ya me lo esperaba; **what do you e. from him?** ¿qué esperas *or* esperabas de él?; **I knew what to e.** ya sabía lo que me esperaba; **to e. the worst** esperarse lo peor; **as one might e.** como era de esperar; **the film was better than I expected** la película era mejor de lo que esperaba; **she's expecting a baby** está esperando un hijo

  **(b)** *(require)* **to e. sb to do sth** esperar de alguien que haga algo; **I e. you to be punctual** confío en que serás puntual; **I don't e. you to be perfect** no pretendo que seas perfecto; **you are expected to answer all the questions** conteste a todas las preguntas; **to e. sth from sb** esperar algo de alguien; **I know what is expected of me** sé qué es lo que se espera de mí; **people e. too much from marriage** la gente espera demasiado del matrimonio

  **(c)** *(suppose)* **to e. (that)...** suponer (que)...; **I e. so/not** supongo que sí/que no

  **2** *vi (be pregnant)* **she's expecting** está en estado

**expectancy** [ɪks'pektənsɪ] *n* expectación *f*; **life e.** esperanza *f* de vida

**expectant** [ɪks'pektənt] *adj (air, crowd)* expectante; **e. mother** futura madre *f*

**expectation** [ekspek'teɪʃən] *n* expectativa *f*; **in (the) e. of sth** en previsión de algo; **to have high expectations of sb/sth** tener muchas esperanzas puestas en alguien/algo; **it came up to/fell short of his expectations** estuvo/no estuvo a la altura de sus expectativas; **contrary to all expectations** contra lo que se esperaba

**expected** [ɪks'pektɪd] *adj* esperado(a), previsto(a)

**expectorant** [ɪks'pektərənt] *n Med* expectorante *m*

**expediency** [ɪks'piːdɪənsɪ] *n* conveniencia *f*

**expedient** [ɪks'piːdɪənt] **1** *n* recurso *m*

  **2** *adj* conveniente, oportuno(a)

**expedite** ['ekspɪdaɪt] *vt Formal* acelerar, apresurar

**expedition** [ekspə'dɪʃən] *n* expedición *f*

**expeditionary force** [ekspə'dɪʃənərɪ'fɔːs] *n Mil* fuerzas *fpl* expedicionarias

**expel** [ɪks'pel] *(pt & pp expelled)* *vt* expulsar

**expendable** [ɪks'pendəbəl] *adj* prescindible

**expenditure** [ɪks'pendɪtʃə(r)] *n (of money, energy)* gasto *m*; **public e.** gasto público

**expense** [ɪks'pens] *n* **(a)** *(cost)* gasto *m*; **at no extra e.** sin coste *or* costo adicional; **at my own e.** a mi costa; **to go to great e.** incurrir en grandes gastos; **no e. was spared to...** no se reparó en gastos para...; **at the e. of one's health/sanity** a costa de perder la salud/cordura; **to make a joke at sb's e.** hacer un chiste a costa de alguien

  **(b)** *Com* **expenses** gastos *mpl*; **to meet** *or* **cover sb's expenses** correr con *or* costear los gastos de alguien; **it's on expenses** corre a cargo de la empresa; **e. account** cuenta *f* de gastos

**expensive** [ɪks'pensɪv] *adj* caro(a), costoso(a); **to have e. tastes** tener gustos caros; **an e. mistake** un error muy caro

**experience** [ɪks'pɪərɪəns] **1** *n* experiencia *f*; **he still lacks e.** todavía le falta experiencia; **to learn from e.** aprender de la experiencia; **in my e.** según mi experiencia; **she had a nasty e.** le pasó una cosa terrible
**2** *vt* experimentar

**experienced** [ɪks'pɪərɪənst] *adj* experimentado(a) (**in** en)

**experiment** [ɪks'perɪmənt] **1** *n* experimento *m*; **to do** *or* **conduct an e.** hacer *or* realizar un experimento; **as an e.** como experimento
**2** *vi* experimentar (**with/on** con)

**experimental** [ɪksperɪ'mentəl] *adj* experimental

**expert** ['eksp3:t] **1** *n* experto(a) *m,f*
**2** *adj* experto(a) (**in** *or* **at** en); **an e. opinion** la opinión de un experto; *Comptr* **e. system** sistema *m* experto; *Law* **e. witness** perito(a) *m,f*

**expertise** [eksp3:'ti:z] *n* destreza *f*, pericia *f*

**expertly** ['eksp3:tlɪ] *adv* diestramente, hábilmente

**expiate** ['ekspɪeɪt] *vt Formal* expiar

**expire** [ɪks'paɪə(r)] *vi* (**a**) *(of law)* caducar; *(of deadline)* expirar, vencer (**b**) *Literary (die)* expirar

**expiry** [ɪks'paɪərɪ] *n* vencimiento *m*; **e. date** fecha *f* de caducidad

**explain** [ɪks'pleɪn] **1** *vt* *(rule, theory)* explicar; **to e. oneself** explicarse
**2** *vi* explicarse

**►explain away** *vt sep* justificar, explicar

**explanation** [eksplə'neɪʃən] *n* explicación *f*; **to give an e. of sth** explicar algo

**explanatory** [ɪks'plænətərɪ] *adj* explicativo(a)

**expletive** [eks'pli:tɪv] *n* taco *m*, palabrota *f*

**explicable** [eks'plɪkəbəl] *adj* explicable

**explicit** [eks'plɪsɪt] *adj* explícito(a)

**explicitly** [eks'plɪsɪtlɪ] *adv* explícitamente

**explode** [ɪks'pləʊd] **1** *vt* *(bomb)* hacer explotar, explosionar; *Fig (idea, theory)* reventar, desbaratar
**2** *vi* *(of bomb)* explotar, estallar; *Fig (with anger)* estallar

**exploit 1** *n* ['eksplɔɪt] hazaña *f*, proeza *f*
**2** *vt* [ɪks'plɔɪt] (**a**) *(take unfair advantage of)* explotar (**b**) *(use)* (resources, sb's talents) aprovechar

**exploitation** [eksplɔɪ'teɪʃən] *n* explotación *f*

**exploration** [eksplə'reɪʃən] *n* exploración *f*

**exploratory** [ɪks'plɔrətərɪ] *adj* exploratorio(a); **e. discussions** *or* **talks** negociaciones *fpl* preliminares; *Med* **e. surgery** cirugía *f* exploratoria

**explore** [ɪks'plɔ:(r)] *vt & vi* explorar

**explorer** [ɪks'plɔrə(r)] *n* explorador(ora) *m,f*

**explosion** [ɪks'pləʊʒən] *n also Fig* explosión *f*, estallido *m*

**explosive** [ɪks'pləʊsɪv] **1** *n* explosivo *m*
**2** *adj* explosivo(a); *Fig* **an e. combination** *(of personalities, factors)* una mezcla explosiva

**exponent** [ɪks'pəʊnənt] *n* (*of theory, art) & Math* exponente *m*; **a leading e. of…** *(supporter)* un destacado defensor de…

**exponential** [ekspəʊ'nenʃəl] *adj* exponencial; **e. growth/increase** crecimiento *m*/aumento *m* exponencial

**export 1** *n* ['ekspɔ:t] (**a**) *(product)* artículo *m* de exportación; **exports** *(of country)* exportaciones *fpl* (**b**) *(exportation)* exportación *f*; **e. duty** derechos *mpl* de exportación; **e. licence** permiso *m* de exportación; **e. trade** comercio *m* de exportación
**2** *vt* [eks'pɔ:t] exportar

**exportation** [ekspɔ:'teɪʃən] *n* exportación *f*

**exporter** [eks'pɔ:tə(r)] *n* exportador(ora) *m,f*

**expose** [ɪks'pəʊz] *vt also Phot* exponer (**to** a); **to be exposed to criticism** estar expuesto(a) a las críticas; **to e. sb as a traitor** revelar que alguien es un traidor; **a man exposed himself to my sister** a mi hermana le salió al paso un exhibicionista

**exposé** [eks'pəʊzeɪ] *n* (*article)* artículo *m* de denuncia *f*; *(TV programme)* programa *m* de denuncia

**exposed** [ɪks'pəʊzd] *adj* expuesto(a); **to be e. (to)** estar expuesto(a) (a)

**exposition** [ekspə'zɪʃən] *n* *(explanation)* exposición *f*

**expostulate** [ɪks'pɒstjʊleɪt] *vi Formal* discutir

**exposure** [ɪks'pəʊʒə(r)] *n* (**a**) *(to air, cold, danger)* exposición *f*; **to die of e.** morir de hipotermia *(a la intemperie)* (**b**) *(publicity)* publicidad *f*; **to get a lot of e.** recibir mucha publicidad (**c**) *(of crime, criminal)* denuncia *f* (**d**) *Phot (time)* (tiempo *m* de) exposición *f*; *(photograph)* foto *f*; **e. meter** fotómetro *m*

**expound** [ɪks'paʊnd] *vt Formal* explicar, dar cuenta de

**express** [ɪks'pres] **1** *n* *(train)* (tren *m*) rápido *m*
**2** *adj* (**a**) *(clear)* (purpose, instruction) expreso(a) (**b**) *(rapid)* **e. letter** carta *f* urgente; **e. train** tren *m* rápido
**3** *adv* **to send a letter e.** enviar una carta urgente
**4** *vt* *(opinion, emotion)* expresar; **to e. oneself** expresarse

**expression** [ɪks'preʃən] *n* *(facial, verbal)* expresión *f*; **freedom of e.** libertad *f* de expresión

**expressionism** [ɪks'preʃənɪzəm] *n* expresionismo *m*

**expressionist** [ɪks'preʃənɪst] n & adj expresionista mf

**expressionless** [ɪks'preʃənlɪs] adj (face, voice) inexpresivo(a)

**expressive** [ɪks'presɪv] adj expresivo(a)

**expressly** [ɪks'preslɪ] adv expresamente

**expresso** [e(k)s'presəʊ] n café m solo

**expropriate** [eks'prəʊprɪeɪt] vt expropiar

**expropriation** [eksprəʊprɪ'eɪʃən] n expropiación f

**expulsion** [ɪks'pʌlʃən] n expulsión f

**expunge** [ɪks'pʌndʒ] vt borrar, eliminar

**expurgate** ['ekspə:geɪt] vt expurgar

**exquisite** ['ekskwɪzɪt] adj exquisito(a)

**exquisitely** [eks'kwɪzɪtlɪ] adv exquisitamente

**extant** [eks'tænt] adj **one of the few e. paintings of that period** una de las pocas pinturas que se conservan de aquel período

**extempore** [ɪks'tempərɪ] **1** adj (speech, speaker) improvisado(a)
**2** adv **to speak e.** hablar improvisando

**extemporize** [ɪks'tempəraɪz] vi improvisar

**extend** [ɪks'tend] **1** vt (**a**) (in space) extender; (frontier, knowledge) ampliar; **to e. a house** ampliar una casa (**b**) (in time) (holiday, contract, deadline) prolongar (**c**) (give, offer) (one's hand) tender; (support, thanks) dar; Fin **to e. credit to sb** conceder un crédito a alguien
**2** vi (**a**) (in space) extenderse (**b**) (in time) prolongarse

**extended family** [ɪks'tendɪd'fæmɪlɪ] n clan m familiar

**extension** [ɪks'tenʃən] n (**a**) (on building) ampliación f; (of deadline) prórroga f, prolongación f; (for essay) aplazamiento m (de la fecha de entrega) (**b**) (for telephone) extensión f (**c**) **e.** (cable) alargador m, alargadera f

**extensive** [ɪks'tensɪv] adj (area, knowledge) extenso(a), amplio(a); (damage, repairs) cuantioso(a); **to make e. use of sth** utilizar algo mucho

**extensively** [ɪks'tensɪvlɪ] adv (to travel, read) mucho, extensamente; **to use sth e.** utilizar algo mucho

**extent** [ɪks'tent] n (of lands) extensión f; (of problem, damage, knowledge) alcance m; **to an e., to a certain e., to some e.** hasta cierto punto, en cierta medida; **to a great e., to a large e.** en gran medida; **to such an e. that...** hasta tal punto que...

**extenuating circumstances** [ɪks-'tenjʊeɪtɪŋ'sə:kəmstænsɪz] npl (circunstancias fpl) atenuantes fpl

**exterior** [ɪks'tɪərɪə(r)] **1** n exterior m; **beneath her calm e. she was extremely nervous** bajo su apariencia tranquila estaba sumamente inquieta
**2** adj externo(a), exterior

**exterminate** [ɪks'tɜ:mɪneɪt] vt exterminar

**extermination** [ɪkstɜ:mɪ'neɪʃən] n exterminio m

**external** [ɪks'tɜ:nəl] adj externo(a); Pol **e. affairs** política f exterior; Univ **e. examiner** examinador(ora) m,f externo(a); **for e. use only** (on medicine) (de) uso tópico

**extinct** [ɪks'tɪŋkt] adj extinto(a), extinguido(a)

**extinction** [ɪks'tɪŋkʃən] n extinción f

**extinguish** [ɪks'tɪŋgwɪʃ] vt extinguir; (light, cigarette) apagar

**extinguisher** [ɪks'tɪŋgwɪʃə(r)] n extintor m

**extirpate** ['ekstɜ:peɪt] vt Formal extirpar, erradicar

**extol**, US **extoll** [ɪks'təʊl] (pt & pp **extolled**) vt ensalzar

**extort** [ɪks'tɔ:t] vt (money) obtener (mediante extorsión)

**extortion** [ɪks'tɔ:ʃən] n extorsión f

**extortionate** [ɪks'tɔ:ʃənɪt] adj (demand, price) abusivo(a)

**extra** ['ekstrə] **1** n (on bill) suplemento m, recargo m; (in film) extra mf
**2** adj (**a**) (additional) adicional; **no e. charge** sin recargo; **e. time** (in football match) prórroga f (**b**) (spare) de repuesto, de sobra
**3** adv **be e. careful with the salt** ten muchísimo cuidado con la sal; **e. fast** superrápido; **e. large** extragrande

**extract 1** n ['ekstrækt] (**a**) (concentrate) extracto m (**b**) (from book, film) fragmento m
**2** vt [ɪks'trækt] extraer, sacar

**extraction** [ɪks'trækʃən] n (removal) extracción f; (social, geographical) origen m; **she is of Danish e.** es de origen danés

**extractor fan** [ɪks'træktə(r)] n extractor m

**extracurricular** ['ekstrəkə'rɪkjʊlə(r)] adj Sch extraescolar

**extradite** ['ekstrədaɪt] vt Law extraditar

**extradition** [ekstrə'dɪʃən] n Law extradición f

**extrajudicial** ['ekstrədʒu:'dɪʃəl] adj extrajudicial

**extramarital** ['ekstrə'mærɪtəl] adj extramarital, adúltero(a)

**extramural** ['ekstrə'mjʊərəl] adj Univ **e. course** = curso universitario para alumnos externos

**extraneous** [ɪks'treɪnɪəs] adj Formal ajeno(a)

**extraordinarily** [ıks'trɔ:dənərılı] *adv* extraordinariamente

**extraordinary** [ıks'trɔ:dənrı] *adj* extraordinario(a); **the e. thing is that...** lo extraordinario es que...; **e. general meeting** junta *f* general extraordinaria; **e. powers** poderes *mpl* or competencias *fpl* extraordinarios(as)

**extrapolate** [ık'stræpəleıt] *vt & vi* extrapolar (**from** a partir de)

**extrapolation** [ıkstræpə'leıʃən] *n* extrapolación *f*

**extrasensory perception** ['ekstrə-'sensərıpə'sepʃən] *n* percepción *f* extrasensorial

**extraterrestrial** ['ekstrətı'restrıəl] *n & adj* extraterrestre *mf*

**extravagance** [ıks'trævəgəns] *n* (a) *(excessive spending)* derroche *m*, despilfarro *m* (b) *(expensive purchase)* dispendio *m*

**extravagant** [ıks'trævəgənt] *adj (person)* derrochador(ora); *(tastes)* caro(a); **an e. purchase** un despilfarro

**extravaganza** [ekstrævə'gænzə] *n* espectáculo *m* fastuoso

**Extremadura** [ekstrəmə'dju:rə] *n* Extremadura

**extreme** [ıks'tri:m] **1** *n* extremo *m*; **to go from one e. to the other** pasar de un extremo al otro; **to go to extremes** recurrir a comportamientos extremos; **extremes of temperature** temperaturas *fpl* extremas; **in the e.** en grado sumo
**2** *adj* extremo(a); *Pol* **the e. left** la extrema izquierda

**extremely** [ıks'tri:mlı] *adv* extremadamente, sumamente

**extremism** [ıks'tri:mızəm] *n* extremismo *m*

**extremist** [ıks'tri:mıst] *n & adj* extremista *mf*

**extremity** [ıks'tremıtı] *n* (a) *(end)* extremo *m* (b) **the extremities** *(of the body)* las extremidades (c) *(of situation)* gravedad *f* extrema; *(extreme measure)* medida *f* extrema

**extricate** ['ekstrıkeıt] *vt* sacar, extraer; **to e. oneself from** *(danger, difficulties)* escapar or librarse de

**extrovert** ['ekstrəvɜ:t] *n & adj* extrovertido(a) *m,f*, extravertido(a) *m,f*

**exuberance** [ıg'zju:bərəns] *n* euforia *f*, exultación *f*

**exuberant** [ıg'zju:bərənt] *adj* eufórico(a), exultante

**exude** [ıg'zju:d] *vt (sweat, odour)* exudar, rezumar; *(health, confidence)* rebosar, rezumar

**exult** [ıg'zʌlt] *vi* alborozarse, exultar (**in** ante)

**exultant** [ıg'zʌltənt] *adj* exultante

**exultation** [egzʌl'teıʃən] *n* júbilo *m*, euforia *f*

**eye** [aı] **1** *n* (a) *(of person, needle)* ojo *m*; **the e. of the storm** el ojo del huracán; **to open/close one's eyes** abrir/cerrar los ojos; **to look sb straight in the e.** mirar a alguien a los ojos; **as far as the e. can see** hasta donde alcanza la vista; **e. contact** contacto *m* visual; **to establish e. contact with sb** mirar a alguien a los ojos, cruzar la mirada con alguien; **e. drops** *(medicine)* colirio *m*; **at e. level** a la altura de los ojos; **e. shadow** sombra *f* de ojos; **e. test** revisión *f* ocular or de la vista

(b) *(idioms)* **in the eye(s) of the law** a (los) ojos de la ley; **to be in the public e.** estar en (el) candelero; **to have an e. for detail/colour** tener buen ojo para los detalles/el color; **to look at sth with a critical e.** mirar algo con ojo crítico; **to look at sth with an experienced e.** mirar algo con ojos de experto; **I don't see e. to e. with my boss** no veo las cosas igual que (las ve) mi jefe; **this is for your eyes only** no se lo enseñas a nadie; **to keep one's eyes and ears open** mantener los ojos y los oídos bien abiertos; **to keep one's eyes peeled** or **skinned** no perder ojo; **to open sb's eyes to sth** abrirle a alguien los ojos en relación con algo, hacer ver algo a alguien; **to shut** or **close one's eyes to sth** negarse a ver algo, no querer ver algo; **to do sth with one's eyes open** hacer algo a sabiendas; **to catch sb's e.** *(attract attention)* llamar la atención de alguien; **to please** or **delight the e.** deleitar la vista; **he has eyes in** or **at the back of his head** se entera de todo; **he has eyes for nobody but her** sólo tiene ojos para ella; **to set** or **lay eyes on sth** ver algo; **I saw it with my own eyes** lo vi con mis propios ojos; **to run** or **cast one's e. over sth** echar una ojeada a algo; **to keep an e. on sth/sb** vigilar algo/a alguien; **I'll keep an e. out for it/him** estaré al tanto de ello/él; **to have one's e. on sth/sb** *(be observing)* estar vigilando algo/a alguien; **to have one's e. on sth** *(be intending to buy)* tenerle el ojo echado a algo; **to have one's eye on sb** *(be attracted to)* haberle echado el ojo a alguien; **to make eyes at sb** echar miradas lánguidas or miraditas a alguien; **with an e. to...** con vistas a...; **to be up to one's eyes in work/debt** estar hasta el cuello de trabajo/deudas; *Fam* **that's one in the e. for him!** ¡le va a sentar como una patada!; **an e. for an e., a tooth for a tooth** ojo por ojo, diente por diente

**2** *vt* observar, mirar

▶**eye up** *vt sep Fam (ogle)* desnudar con la mirada

**eyeball** ['aıbɔ:l] *n* globo *m* ocular

**eyebrow** ['aıbraʊ] *n* ceja *f*; **to raise one's eyebrows** *(in surprise)* arquear las cejas

**eye-catching** ['aıkætʃıŋ] *adj* llamativo(a)

**eyeful** ['aɪful] n Fam **to get an e. of sth** (look at) mirar algo bien

**eyeglass** ['aɪglɑːs] n monóculo m

**eyeglasses** ['aɪglɑːsɪz] npl US (spectacles) gafas fpl

**eyelash** ['aɪlæʃ] n pestaña f

**eyelid** ['aɪlɪd] n párpado m; Fig **she didn't so much as bat an e.** (didn't show surprise) ni se inmutó

**eyeliner** ['aɪlaɪnə(r)] n lápiz m de ojos

**eye-opener** ['aɪəʊpənə(r)] n revelación f

**eyepatch** ['aɪpætʃ] n parche m

**eyeshade** ['aɪʃeɪd] n visera f

**eyesight** ['aɪsaɪt] n vista f; **to have good/bad e.** estar bien/mal de la vista

**eyesore** ['aɪsɔː(r)] n (building) engendro m, adefesio m

**eyestrain** ['aɪstreɪn] n vista f cansada

**eyetooth** ['aɪtuːθ] n colmillo m; **I'd give my eyeteeth to go with them** daría un ojo de la cara por ir con ellos

**eyewash** ['aɪwɒʃ] n (for eye) colirio m, baño m ocular; Fig (nonsense) paparruchas fpl

**eyewitness** ['aɪwɪtnɪs] n testigo mf ocular

**eyrie** ['ɪərɪ] n nido m de águila

# F

**F, f** [ef] *n* (a) *(letter)* F, f *f*; *Br Euph* **the F word**
= eufemismo para referirse a la palabra "fuck"
(b) *Mus* fa *m* (c) *Sch* muy deficiente *m*; **to get
an F** *(in exam, essay)* sacar un muy deficiente

**F** *(abbr* **Fahrenheit)** F, Fahrenheit

**FA** [e'feɪ] *n Br (abbr* **Football Association)** = federación inglesa de fútbol

**fa** [fɑː] *n Mus* fa *m*

**fab** [fæb] *adj Br Fam* chupi

**fable** ['feɪbəl] *n* fábula *f*

**fabled** ['feɪbəld] *adj* legendario(a), fabulo-
so(a)

**fabric** ['fæbrɪk] *n (cloth)* tejido *m*; *Fig* **the f. of
society** el tejido social

**fabricate** ['fæbrɪkeɪt] *vt (story)* inventar; *(evidence)* falsificar

**fabulous** ['fæbjʊləs] *adj* fabuloso(a), magní-
fico(a)

**fabulously** ['fæbjʊləslɪ] *adv (rich)* tremendamente

**façade** [fæ'sɑːd] *n also Fig* fachada *f*

**face** [feɪs] **1** *n* (a) *(of person)* cara *f*, rostro *m*;
*very Fam* **shut your f.!** ¡cierra el pico!; **I told
him to his f.** se lo dije a *or* en la cara; **I shall
never be able to look her in the f. again**
nunca podré volver a mirarla a la cara; **to show
one's f.** dejarse ver, hacer acto de presencia;
**her f. doesn't fit** *(in job, company)* no encaja
bien; **to set one's f. against sth** oponerse
cerrilmente a algo; **in the f. of** *(danger, threat)*
ante; **f. card** *(playing card)* figura *f*; **f. cloth**
toallita *f*; **f. cream** crema *f* facial; **f. pack** mascarilla *f* (facial); **f. powder** polvos *mpl (para la
cara)*

(b) *(expression)* cara *f*; **to make** *or* **pull faces**
hacer muecas, poner caras; **to keep a straight
f.** quedarse serio(a); **to put a brave f. on it**
poner al mal tiempo buena cara

(c) *(appearance)* **on the f. of it** a primera vista;
**to save f.** salvar las apariencias; **to lose f.**
sufrir una humillación; **the changing f. of
Britain** el rostro cambiante de Gran Bretaña;
**to take sth at f. value** aceptar algo sin darle
más vueltas

(d) *(surface)* *(of the earth)* superficie *f*, faz *f*; *(of
clock)* esfera *f*; *(of coin)* cara *f*; *(of cliff)* ladera *f*; **to
disappear off the f. of the earth** desapare-
cer de la faz de la tierra; **f. up/down** boca
arriba/abajo

**2** *vt* (a) *(confront)* *(difficulty, danger)* afrontar,
encarar; **to f. facts** afrontar la realidad; **let's f.
it** no nos engañemos; **to be faced with a
decision** enfrentarse a una decisión; *Fig* **to f.
the music** apechugar con las consecuencias

(b) *(look towards)* mirar a; **to f. the front** mirar
al frente

**3** *vi* **to f. north/south** *(building, window)* estar
orientado(a) hacia el norte/sur

▶**face up to** *vt insep (person, fears)* hacer frente
a

**faceless** ['feɪslɪs] *adj* anónimo(a)

**face-lift** ['feɪslɪft] *n (plastic surgery)* lifting *m*,
estiramiento *m* de piel; *Fig (of building)* lavado *m*
de cara; **to have a f.** hacerse un lifting

**face-saving** ['feɪsseɪvɪŋ] *adj (agreement,
manoeuvre)* para salvar las apariencias

**facet** ['fæsɪt] *n (of gem, situation)* faceta *f*

**facetious** [fə'siːʃəs] *adj* impertinente

**face-to-face** ['feɪstə'feɪs] **1** *adj (meeting)*
cara a cara

**2** *adv* cara a cara, frente a frente; **to meet sb f.**
encontrarse frente a frente con alguien

**facial** ['feɪʃəl] **1** *n* **to have a f.** hacerse una
limpieza de cutis

**2** *adj* facial

**facile** ['fæsaɪl] *adj (argument, remark)* obvio(a),
fácil

**facilitate** [fə'sɪlɪteɪt] *vt* facilitar

**facility** [fə'sɪlɪtɪ] *n* (a) *(ease)* facilidad *f*; **to do
sth with great f.** hacer algo con gran facilidad
(b) **facilities** *(buildings, equipment)* instalaciones *fpl*; *(services)* servicios *mpl*

**facsimile** [fæk'sɪmɪlɪ] *n (copy)* facsímil *m*

**fact** [fækt] *n* hecho *m*; **in f.** de hecho; **to
distinguish f. from fiction** distinguir la realidad de la ficción; **the f. is that...** el hecho es
que...; **it's a f. that...** se sabe que...; **to
know for a f. (that)...** saber a ciencia cierta
(que)...; **it's a f. of life** es una realidad insoslayable *or* un hecho cierto; **the facts of life**
*(sexual)* lo referente al sexo y a la reproducción

**fact-finding** ['fæktfaɪndɪŋ] *adj* de investigación

**faction** ['fækʃən] *n* facción *f*

**factor** ['fæktə(r)] *n* factor *m*

**factory** ['fæktəri] *n* fábrica *f*

**factual** ['fæktʃʊəl] *adj* basado(a) en hechos

**faculty** ['fækəltɪ] *n (of mind, in university)* facultad *f*; **she is still in possession of all her faculties** tiene pleno uso de sus facultades

**fad** [fæd] *n* moda *f* (**for** de)

**fade** [feɪd] **1** *vt* desteñir

**2** *vi (of material)* desteñirse, perder color; *(of flower)* marchitarse; **to f. from memory** desaparecer de la memoria

▸**fade away** *vi (of music, hope)* desvanecerse; *Fig (of person)* evaporarse, desaparecer

▸**fade out** **1** *vt sep Cin* fundir en negro

**2** *vi Cin* fundirse en negro; *(music)* apagarse

**faded** ['feɪdɪd] *adj (flower)* marchito(a); *(photograph, garment)* descolorido(a)

**fading** ['feɪdɪŋ] *adj (light)* mortecino(a)

**faeces** ['fiːsiːz] *npl* heces *fpl*

▸**faff about, faff around** [fæf] *vi Br Fam* enredar

**fag** [fæg] *n* (**a**) *Br Fam (unpleasant job)* lata *f*, rollo *m* (**b**) *US very Fam (homosexual)* = término ofensivo para referirse a los homosexuales, maricón *m* (**c**) *Br Fam (cigarette)* pitillo *m*

**faggot** ['fægət] *n* (**a**) *(firewood)* haz *m* de leña (**b**) *Br (meatball)* albóndiga *f* (**c**) *US very Fam (homosexual)* = término ofensivo para referirse a los homosexuales, maricón *m*

**fah** [fɑː] *n Mus* fa *m*

**Fahrenheit** ['færənhaɪt] *adj* Fahrenheit; **70 degrees** F. 70 grados Fahrenheit, ≃ 21 grados centígrados

**fail** [feɪl] **1** *n* (**a**) *(in exam)* suspenso *m* (**b**) **without f.** sin falta

**2** *vt (exam, candidate)* suspender; **to f. a drugs test** dar positivo en un control antidoping; **words f. me** me faltan las palabras; **his nerve failed him** le fallaron los nervios; **I won't f. you** no te fallaré

**3** *vi (of person, plan, business)* fracasar; *(of health, brakes)* fallar; *(memory, eyesight)* fallar, debilitarse; **the light was failing** se hacía de noche, estaba oscureciendo; **to f. to do sth** no hacer algo; **I f. to see what the problem is** no acabo de ver cuál es el problema; **if all else fails** en último extremo; **he failed in his duty** no cumplió con su obligación; **it never fails** *(strategy, excuse)* nunca falla; **it never fails to surprise me...** nunca deja de sorprenderme...

**failed** [feɪld] *adj (attempt, plan)* fallido(a); *(writer, actor)* fracasado(a)

**failing** ['feɪlɪŋ] **1** *n (fault)* fallo *m*, defecto *m*; **with all her failings** con todos sus fallos

**2** *adj (sight, strength)* debilitado(a)

**3** *prep* a falta de; **f. that** en su defecto; **f. all else** en último extremo

**fail-safe** ['feɪlseɪf] *adj (device)* de seguridad or de bloqueo (en caso de fallo); *Fig (plan, excuse)* infalible

**failure** ['feɪljə(r)] *n (useless person)* inútil *mf*; *(unsuccessful person)* fracasado(a) *m,f*; *(unsuccessful film, lack of success)* fracaso *m*; *(of machine)* fallo *m*; *(of company)* quiebra *f*; **f. to keep a promise** incumplimiento *m* de una promesa; **f. to pay a bill** impago *m* de una factura

**faint** [feɪnt] **1** *n (loss of consciousness)* desmayo *m*

**2** *adj (light, sound, smell)* leve, tenue; *(idea, hope, memory)* vago(a), ligero(a); *(chance, possibility)* remoto(a); *(mark, trace)* ligero(a); *(suggestion)* leve; **I haven't got the faintest idea** no tengo ni la más mínima idea; **to feel f.** *(of person)* sentirse mareado(a)

**3** *vi (lose consciousness)* desmayarse

**faint-hearted** ['feɪnt'hɑːtɪd] *adj* pusilánime

**faintly** ['feɪntlɪ] *adv* (**a**) *(to hear, see)* apenas; *(to shine)* débilmente; *(to remember)* vagamente (**b**) *(slightly) (uneasy, ridiculous)* ligeramente

**fair**¹ [feə(r)] *n* (**a**) *Br (funfair)* feria *f (ambulante)* (**b**) *(trade fair)* feria *f*

**fair**² [feə(r)] **1** *adj* (**a**) *(just)* justo(a); **it's not f.** no es justo; **that's only f., f.'s f.** hay que ser justos; **f. enough!** vale, está bien; **it is only f. to say that...** es justo decir que...; **to be f.,...** para ser justos,...; **by f. means or foul** como sea; *Prov* **all's f. in love and war** en la guerra y en el amor, no hay reglas; *Fam* **to get a f. crack of the whip** tener una oportunidad; **to be f. game** ser un blanco legítimo; **f. play** juego *m* limpio; **they all got their f. share** todos recibieron lo que les correspondía; **we've had our f. share of problems** hemos tenido bastantes problemas

(**b**) *(quite good)* bastante bueno(a); **a f. amount of...** bastante(s)...; **a f. idea** una idea bastante buena; **to f. middling** normal, regular

(**c**) *(attractive)* hermoso(a); *Old-fashioned* **the fair(er) sex** el bello sexo; **f. weather** buen tiempo

(**d**) *(light-coloured) (hair)* rubio(a); *(skin)* claro(a)

**2** *adv (to act)* justamente; **to play/fight f.** jugar/pelear limpio; **you can't say fairer than that** no se puede pedir más; **to beat sb f. and square** derrotar a alguien con todas las de la ley

**fairground** ['feəgraʊnd] *n* feria *f*

**fair-haired** ['feə'heəd] *adj* rubio(a)

**fairly** ['feəlɪ] *adv* (**a**) *(justly)* justamente; **to treat sb f.** tratar justamente a alguien; **to play/fight f.** jugar/pelear limpio; **to come by sth f.** conseguir algo limpiamente (**b**) *(quite)* *(rich, skilful)* bastante; **it is f. certain that...** es bastante probable que...; **he f. lost his temper** perdió por completo los estribos

**fair-minded** ['feə'maɪndɪd] *adj* imparcial, justo(a)

**fairness** ['feənɪs] *n* (a) *(of person)* imparcialidad *f*; *(of decision)* justicia *f*; **in all f.** con toda justicia (b) *(of hair)* color *m* rubio; *(of skin)* claridad *f*

**fair-sized** ['feə'saɪzd] *adj* (de tamaño) considerable

**fairway** ['feəweɪ] *n* calle *f (de campo de golf)*

**fair-weather friend** ['feəweðə'frend] *n* amigo(a) *m,f* sólo para lo bueno

**fairy** ['feərɪ] *n* hada *f*; **f. godmother** hada madrina; **f. lights** lucecitas *fpl* de colores

**fairytale** ['feərɪteɪl] *n* cuento *m* de hadas; *Fig* **a f. ending** un final feliz

**faith** [feɪθ] *n* fe *f*; **an act of f.** un acto de fe; **to be of the Catholic/Jewish f.** profesar la fe católica/judía; **to keep f. with sb** mantenerse fiel a alguien; **in good/bad f.** de buena/mala fe; **f. healer** = persona que pretende curar a la gente gracias a la fe y la oración

**faithful** ['feɪθfʊl] **1** *adj (friend, supporter)* fiel, leal; *(copy, account)* fiel

**2** *npl* **the f.** los fieles

**faithfully** ['feɪθfʊlɪ] *adv (loyally, accurately)* fielmente; **Yours f.** *(in formal letter)* (le saluda) atentamente

**fake** [feɪk] **1** *n (object)* falsificación *f*; *(person)* impostor(ora) *m,f*

**2** *adj (passport, banknote)* falso(a); *(beard)* postizo(a)

**3** *vt (signature, result)* falsificar; *(illness, death)* simular

**falcon** ['fɔːlkən] *n* halcón *m*

**falconry** ['fɔːlkənrɪ] *n* cetrería *f*

**Falkland** ['fɔːlklənd] *n* **the F. Islands, the Falklands** las (Islas) Malvinas

**fall** [fɔːl] **1** *n* (a) *(of person, prices, besieged city)* caída *f*; **to have a f.** sufrir una caída; **a f. in interest rates** una caída de los tipos de interés; **there has been a heavy f. of snow** ha caído una gran nevada; *Fig* **he's heading for a f.** un día de estos se va a pegar un batacazo; *US Fam* **f. guy** chivo *m* expiatorio

(b) *US (autumn)* otoño *m*

(c) **falls** *(waterfall)* cascada *f*, catarata *f*

**2** *vi (pt* **fell** [fel]*, pp* **fallen** ['fɔːlən]) (a) *(of stone, person)* caer; *(of price, temperature)* caer, descender; *(of empire, government)* caer, sucumbir; *(of soldier)* caer, morir; **silence/night fell** se hizo el silencio/de noche; **to f. down a hole** caer por un agujero; **she fell off the ladder** se cayó de la escalera; **Christmas Day falls on a Thursday** el día de Navidad cae en jueves; **my spirits fell** me desmoralicé; **to f. from**

grace caer en desgracia; **to f. into a trap** caer en una trampa; **to f. to pieces** *(of object)* romperse en pedazos; *Fig (of person)* desmoronarse; **to f. flat** *(be disappointing)* no funcionar; **to f. short of doing sth** no llegar a hacer algo; **to f. victim to sth** ser víctima de algo; **the match fell victim to the weather** el partido se suspendió debido al mal tiempo; **the responsibility falls on you** la responsabilidad recae sobre usted; *Formal* **it falls to me to introduce...** es un honor para mí presentarles...

(b) *(become)* **to f. asleep** dormirse; **to f. ill** caer enfermo(a), enfermar; **to f. in love** enamorarse; **to f. silent** quedarse callado(a)

(c) *(be classified)* **to f. into two categories** dividirse en dos categorías; **suddenly everything fell into place** de pronto todo encajaba

▶**fall away** *vi (of ground)* caer, descender; *(of attendance)* declinar

▶**fall back on** *vt insep* **he fell back on his emergency supply** recurrió a sus provisiones de emergencia

▶**fall behind** *vi* quedarse rezagado(a)

▶**fall down** *vi (of person, building)* caerse; *Fig (of argument, plan)* fallar

▶**fall for** *vt insep Fam* (a) *(fall in love with)* enamorarse de (b) *(be deceived by) (story)* tragarse; **to f. for it** picar

▶**fall in** *vi* (a) *(of roof)* hundirse (b) *Mil (of troops)* formar

▶**fall off** *vi (of profits, attendance)* decrecer

▶**fall out** *vi* (a) *(quarrel)* reñir **(with** con), pelearse **(with** con) (b) *Mil* romper filas

▶**fall over 1** *vi* tropezar, caerse

**2** *vt insep (stumble on)* tropezar con; *Fig* **to f. over oneself to do sth** *(be very keen)* desvivirse por hacer algo

▶**fall through** *vi (of plan, deal)* venirse abajo

**fallacious** [fə'leɪʃəs] *adj* falaz

**fallacy** ['fæləsɪ] *n* falacia *f*

**fallen** ['fɔːlən] **1** *npl* **the f.** los caídos

**2** *adj* caído(a); *Old-fashioned* **a f. woman** una mujer perdida

**3** *pp of* **fall**

**fallible** ['fælɪbəl] *adj* falible

**Fallopian tube** [fə'ləʊpɪən'tjuːb] *n Anat* trompa *f* de Falopio

**fallout** ['fɔːlaʊt] *n Phys* lluvia *f* radiactiva; *Fig (from scandal)* secuelas *fpl*

**fallow** ['fæləʊ] **1** *adj (uncultivated)* en barbecho; *Fig* **a f. period** un período improductivo

**2** *adv* **to lie f.** estar en barbecho

**false** [fɔːls] *adj (a) (incorrect)* falso(a); **f. alarm** falsa alarma *f*; **the ceasefire turned out to be a f. dawn** el alto el fuego se convirtió en una esperanza frustrada; **it's a f. economy** es un falso ahorro; **f. friend** *(in foreign language)* falso amigo *m*; **f. modesty** falsa modestia *f*; *Mus &*

*Fig* f. **note** nota *f* falsa; **under f. pretences**
bajo falsas apariencias; **f. start** *(in race)* salida *f*
en falso; **to bear f. witness** presentar falso
testimonio
(b) *(unfaithful)* infiel
(c) *(not real) (beard, nose)* postizo(a); **f. teeth**
dentadura *f* postiza

**falsehood** ['fɔ:lshʊd] *n (lie)* falsedad *f*

**falsely** ['fɔ:lslɪ] *adv (mistakenly)* equivocadamente; *(insincerely)* falsamente

**falsetto** [fɔ:l'setəʊ] *(pl* **falsettos)** *n Mus* falsete *m*

**falsify** ['fɔ:lsɪfaɪ] *vt* (a) *(forge) (records, document)* falsificar (b) *(disprove) (theory)* refutar

**falter** ['fɔ:ltə(r)] *vi* vacilar, titubear

**fame** [feɪm] *n* fama *f*; **to seek f. and fortune**
buscar fama y fortuna

**famed** [feɪmd] *adj* famoso(a), afamado(a)

**familiar** [fə'mɪlɪə(r)] *adj* (a) *(well-known)* familiar; **a f. face** un rostro familiar (b) *(intimate)*
**to be on f. terms with sb** ser íntimo(a) de
alguien; **to get too f. with sb** tomarse demasiada confianza con alguien (c) *(acquainted)* **to
be f. with** estar familiarizado(a) con

**familiarity** [fəmɪlɪ'ærɪtɪ] *n* (a) *(intimacy)* familiaridad *f*, confianza *f*; **f. breeds contempt**
donde hay confianza da asco (b) *(acquaintance)*
familiaridad *f*

**familiarize** [fə'mɪlɪəraɪz] *vt* **to f. oneself
with sth** familiarizarse con algo; **to f. sb with
sth** familiarizar a alguien con algo

**family** ['fæmɪlɪ] *n* familia *f*; **it runs in the f.**
es cosa de familia; **to start a f.** empezar a tener
hijos; **they treat her as one of the f.** la tratan
como si fuera de la familia; *Fam* **she's in the f.
way** está en estado; **f. allowance** ayuda *f* familiar; **f. business** negocio *m* familiar; **f. doctor** médico *m* de familia; **f. life** vida *f* de familia;
**f. man** hombre *m* de familia; **f. name** apellido
*m*; **f. planning** planificación *f* familiar; **f. resemblance** parecido *m* de familia; **f.
tree** árbol *m* genealógico

**famine** ['fæmɪn] *n* hambruna *f*; **f. relief** ayuda *f* humanitaria contra el hambre

**famished** ['fæmɪʃd] *adj* **to be f.** estar muer-
to(a) de hambre

**famous** ['feɪməs] *adj* famoso(a)

**famously** ['feɪməslɪ] *adv Fam* **to get on f.
(with sb)** llevarse genial (con alguien)

**fan¹** [fæn] **1** *n (cooling device) (hand-held)* abanico *m*; *(mechanical)* ventilador *m*; **f. belt** *(of car)*
correa *f* del ventilador; **f. heater** convector *m*

**2** *vt (pt & pp* **fanned)** (a) *(with fan)* abanicar;
**to f. oneself** abanicarse (b) *(fire, passions)* atizar, avivar

**fan²** *n (enthusiast) (of music, art, sport)* fanáti-
co(a) *m,f*; *(of artist, singer)* admirador(ora) *m,f*,
fan *mf*; *Fig* **I'm not a f. of electric cookers**

no soy partidario de las cocinas eléctricas; **football f.** hincha *mf* de fútbol; **f. club** club *m* de
fans; **f. mail** cartas *fpl* de fans *or* de admiradores

▶**fan out** *vi (of police, soldiers)* desplegarse

**fanatic** [fə'nætɪk] *n* fanático(a) *m,f*

**fanatical** [fə'nætɪkəl] *adj* fanático(a)

**fanciful** ['fænsɪfʊl] *adj (unrealistic)* inverosímil

**fancy** ['fænsɪ] **1** *n* (a) *(imagination)* fantasía *f*; **a
flight of f.** un delirio
(b) *(whim)* capricho *m*
(c) *(liking)* **to take a f. to sb/sth** encapricharse de alguien/con algo
**2** *adj (jewels, hat)* de fantasía; *(gadget)* sofistica-
do(a); *(party)* encopetado(a); *(hotel)* lujoso(a);
*(food, decoration)* con muchas florituras; **f. dress**
disfraz *m*; **f. dress party** fiesta *f* de disfraces
**3** *vt* (a) *Fam (want)* **do you f. a drink?** ¿te
apetece algo de beber?; **I didn't f. the idea**
no me atraía la idea
(b) *Br Fam (be attracted by)* **he fancies her** le
gusta ella
(c) *(imagine)* imaginar; **to f. (that)...** imaginar que...; **I f. I have seen her before me**
parece que la he visto antes; *Fam* **f. that!** ¡fíjate!, ¡lo que hay que ver!; **f. meeting you
here!** ¡qué sorpresa encontrarte aquí!
(d) *(have good opinion of)* **he is strongly fancied to win** se cree que tiene muchas posibilidades de ganar; **she fancies herself as a
writer/musician** se las da de buena escri-
tora/música; **he fancies his chances of getting the job** cree que tiene muchas
posibilidades de conseguir el trabajo

**fanfare** ['fænfeə(r)] *n* fanfarria *f*

**fang** [fæŋ] *n* colmillo *m*

**fanny** ['fænɪ] *n* (a) *Br Vulg (vagina)* coño *m*,
chocho *m* (b) *US Fam (bum)* culo *m*; **f. pack**
riñonera *f*

**fantasize** ['fæntəsaɪz] *vi* fantasear (**about**
sobre)

**fantastic** [fæn'tæstɪk] *adj* (a) *Fam (excellent)*
fantástico(a), fabuloso(a) (b) *(enormous) (price,
size)* inmenso(a) (c) *(unbelievable)* absurdo(a)

**fantasy** ['fæntəsɪ] *n* fantasía *f*

**FAO** [efer'əʊ] *n (abbr* **Food and Agriculture Organization)** FAO *f*, Organización *f*
para la Agricultura y la Alimentación

**far** [fɑ:(r)] **1** *adj* lejano(a); **the f. end** el (otro)
extremo; *Pol* **the f. left/right** la extrema iz-
quierda/derecha; **the F. East** el Lejano Oriente
*m*
**2** *adv (comparative* **farther** ['fɑ:ðə(r)] *or*
**further** ['fɜ:ðə(r)], *superlative* **farthest**
['fɑ:ðɪst] *or* **furthest** ['fɜ:ðɪst])** (a) *(distance)* lejos; **how f. is it to Glasgow?** ¿a cuánto estamos de Glasgow?; **f. away** lejos; **f. below/
above** muy abajo/arriba; **to go f.** ir lejos; *Fig*

*(of person)* llegar lejos; *(of money)* dar para mucho; *Fig* **to go so f. as to do sth** llegar al extremo de hacer algo; *Fig* **to go too f.** ir demasiado lejos; *also Fig* **f. from...** lejos de...; *Fig* **f. from it** de eso nada; *Fig* **f. be it from me to criticize, but...** Dios me libre de criticar a nadie, pero...; **f. and wide** *or* **near** por todas partes; *Fig* **as f. as I can see** tal y como yo lo veo; **as f. as I know** que yo sepa; **as f. as I'm concerned** en *or* por lo que a mí respecta; *Fig* **as f. as possible** en la medida de lo posible

**(b)** *(time)* **so f.** hasta el momento; **so f. so good** todo bien de momento; **for as f. back as I can remember** hasta donde alcanzo a recordar; **to work f. into the night** trabajar hasta bien entrada la noche

**(c)** *(much)* **by f.** con diferencia, con mucho; **f. better/worse** mucho mejor/peor; **f. too many** demasiados(as); **f. too much** demasiado; **she's f. too intelligent to do that** es demasiado inteligente para hacer eso; **f. and away the best** el mejor con diferencia

**faraway** ['fɑːrəweɪ] *adj (place)* lejano(a); *(look)* ausente

**farce** [fɑːs] *n also Fig* farsa *f*

**farcical** ['fɑːsɪkəl] *adj* grotesco(a)

**fare** [feər] **1** *n* **(a)** *(for journey)* tarifa *f* **(b)** *(taxi passenger)* pasajero(a) *m,f* **(c)** *Formal (food)* comida *f*

**2** *vi* comportarse; **to f. well/badly** *(of person, team)* hacerlo bien/mal; *(of industry, sector)* comportarse bien/mal; **how did she f.?** ¿cómo le salió?

**farewell** [feə'wel] *n* despedida *f*, adiós *m*; **to bid sb f.** despedirse de alguien; **to say one's farewells** despedirse; **f. dinner** cena *f* de despedida

**far-fetched** [fɑː'fetʃt] *adj (idea, plan)* inverosímil, rebuscado(a)

**far-flung** ['fɑːflʌŋ] *adj* **(a)** *(distant)* remoto(a) **(b)** *(widespread)* amplio(a), vasto(a)

**farm** [fɑːm] **1** *n (small)* granja *f*; *(large)* hacienda *f*, explotación *f* agrícola, *CSur* estancia *f*; **dairy f.** vaquería *f*; **f. animals** animales *mpl* de granja; **f. labourer** trabajador *m* del campo

**2** *vt (land)* cultivar; *(livestock)* criar

**3** *vi (grow crops)* cultivar la tierra

▶**farm out** *vt sep (work)* subcontratar

**farmer** ['fɑːmə(r)] *n (of small farm)* granjero(a) *m,f*; *(of large farm)* agricultor(ora) *m,f*; **cattle f.** ganadero(a) *m,f (de vacuno)*

**farmhouse** ['fɑːmhaʊs] *n* granja *f*, casa *f* de campo

**farming** ['fɑːmɪŋ] *n* agricultura *f*

**farmland** ['fɑːmlænd] *n* terreno *m* agrícola

**farmyard** ['fɑːmjɑːd] *n* corral *m*

**Faroe** ['feərəʊ] *n* **the F. Islands, the Faroes** las islas Feroe

**far-off** ['fɑːrɒf] *adj (place, time)* lejano(a)

**far-out** [fɑː'raʊt] *adj Fam (strange)* raro(a); **f.!** ¡chachi!

**far-reaching** ['fɑː'riːtʃɪŋ] *adj (decision, change)* de gran alcance

**Farsi** ['fɑːsiː] *n (language)* persa *m (moderno)*

**far-sighted** ['fɑːˈsaɪtɪd] *adj (person, decision)* previsor(ora), con visión de futuro

**fart** [fɑːt] *Fam* **1** *n* pedo *m*

**2** *vi* tirarse un pedo, pederse

▶**fart about** *vi Fam (waste time)* perder el tiempo a lo tonto

**farther** ['fɑːðə(r)] = **further**

**farthest** ['fɑːðɪst] = **furthest**

**farthing** ['fɑːðɪŋ] *n Br Hist* cuarto *m* de penique; *Fam* **he doesn't have a (brass) f.** no tiene (ni) un céntimo

**fascinate** ['fæsɪneɪt] *vt* fascinar

**fascinating** ['fæsɪneɪtɪŋ] *adj* fascinante

**fascination** [fæsɪˈneɪʃən] *n* fascinación *f*

**fascism** ['fæʃɪzəm] *n* fascismo *m*

**fascist** ['fæʃɪst] *n & adj* fascista *mf*

**fashion** ['fæʃən] **1** *n* **(a)** *(in clothes)* moda *f*; **in f.** de moda; **out of f.** pasado(a) de moda; **to follow a f.** seguir la moda; **f. designer** modisto(a) *m,f*; **f. house** casa *f* de moda(s); **f. parade** desfile *m* de moda, desfile *m* or pase *m* de modelos **(b)** *(manner)* modo *m*, manera *f*; **after a f.** más o menos

**2** *vt (form)* elaborar **(from** con); **he fashioned a small figure from a block of wood** modeló un figurín a partir de un bloque de madera

**fashionable** ['fæʃənəbəl] *adj* de moda; **to be f.** estar de moda

**fast¹** [fɑːst] **1** *adj* **(a)** *(rapid)* rápido(a); *Fam* **he pulled a f. one on me** me la jugó, me jugó una mala pasada; *Fam Fig* **a f. woman** una mujer casquivana; **f. food** comida *f* rápida; **the f. lane** *(of motorway)* el carril rápido; *Fig* **to live life in the f. lane** llevar un tren de vida frenético **(b)** *(clock, watch)* adelantado(a) **(c)** *(secure)* *(grip)* firme; *(colour)* inalterable, que no destiñe

**2** *adv* **(a)** *(rapidly)* rápido, deprisa; **not so f.!** ¡no tan rápido!; **to play f. and loose with the truth** jugar con la verdad **(b)** *(securely)* firmemente; **to hold f.** sujetarse bien; **f. asleep** profundamente dormido(a)

**fast²** **1** *n* ayuno *m*; **to break one's f.** romper el ayuno; *Rel* **f. day** día *m* de ayuno

**2** *vi* ayunar

**fasten** ['fɑːsən] **1** *vt (attach)* sujetar; *(door, window)* cerrar, echar el cerrojo a; *Fig (eyes, attention)* fijar; **to f. one's belt/buttons** abrocharse el cinturón/los botones

**2** *vi (garment)* abrocharse

**fastener** ['fɑːsənə(r)] *n (of garment)* cierre *m*

**fast-forward** ['fɑːst'fɔːwəd] **1** n avance m rápido

**2** vt (cassette) pasar hacia delante

**fastidious** [fæ'stɪdɪəs] adj (fussy) escrupuloso(a); (meticulous) meticuloso(a)

**fast-moving** ['fɑːst'muːvɪŋ] adj veloz, rápido(a)

**fat** [fæt] **1** n (a) grasa f; **f. content** materia f grasa (b) (idioms) Fam **the f.'s in the fire!** ¡la que se va a armar!; **to live off the f. of the land** vivir a cuerpo de rey; Fam **to chew the f. (with sb)** estar de palique (con alguien)

**2** adj (person) gordo(a); (meat) graso(a); Fam (cheque, salary) jugoso(a); **to get f.** engordar; Fig **to grow f. at the expense of others** (become rich) hacerse rico(a) a costa de los demás; Fam **a f. lot of good that'll do you!** ¡pues sí que te va a servir de mucho!; Fig **f. cat** pez m gordo; Pej **f. cat executive** = alto ejecutivo con un salario desproporcionado; Fam **f. chance!** ¡ni soñarlo!

**fatal** ['feɪtəl] adj fatal

**fatalistic** [feɪtə'lɪstɪk] adj fatalista

**fatality** [fə'tælɪtɪ] n (in accident) víctima f mortal

**fatally** ['feɪtəlɪ] adv (wounded) mortalmente

**fate** [feɪt] n destino m, sino m; **to leave sb to his f.** abandonar a alguien a su suerte; **to suffer/share a similar fate** sufrir/compartir la misma suerte; **a f. worse than death** un sino peor que la muerte

**fated** ['feɪtɪd] adj (destined) predestinado(a)

**fateful** ['feɪtfʊl] adj (words, day) fatídico(a)

**father** ['fɑːðə(r)] **1** n (parent, priest) padre m; **f. of six** padre de seis hijos; **from f. to son** de padre a hijo; **he was like a f. to me** fue como un padre para mí; Prov **like f., like son** de tal palo, tal astilla; **Our F.** Padre Nuestro; **F. Christmas** Papá m Noel; **f. figure** figura f paterna

**2** vt (child) engendrar; Fig (idea, invention) concebir, crear

**fatherhood** ['fɑːðəhʊd] n paternidad f

**father-in-law** ['fɑːðərɪnlɔː] (pl fathers-in-law) n suegro m

**fatherly** ['fɑːðəlɪ] adj paternal

**father-to-be** ['fɑːðətə'biː] (pl fathers-to-be) n futuro padre m

**fathom** ['fæðəm] **1** n (measurement) braza f

**2** vt (mystery) desentrañar; (person) entender

▶**fathom out** vt sep (mystery) desentrañar; (person) entender

**fatigue** [fə'tiːg] **1** n (a) (tiredness) fatiga f, cansancio m; **metal f.** fatiga f del metal (b) Mil **f. (duty)** faena f; **fatigues** (military clothing) traje m de faena

**2** vt (person) fatigar, cansar

**fatso** ['fætsəʊ] (pl fatsos) n very Fam gordinflón(ona) m,f

**fatten** ['fætən] vt engordar, cebar

▶**fatten up** vt sep engordar, cebar

**fatty** ['fætɪ] **1** n Fam gordito(a) m,f

**2** adj graso(a); **f. foods** alimentos mpl grasos; **f. acid** ácido m graso; **f. tissue** tejido m adiposo

**fatuous** ['fætjʊəs] adj fatuo(a), necio(a)

**faucet** ['fɔːsɪt] n US grifo m

**fault** [fɔːlt] **1** n (a) (flaw) (of person, product) defecto m; (of engine) fallo m, avería f; **to find f. with** encontrar defectos a; **she's generous to a f.** se pasa de generosa (b) (guilt) culpa f; **to be at f.** tener la culpa; **whose f. is it?** ¿de quién es la culpa?; **it was my f.** fue culpa mía; **through no f. of mine** sin tener yo la culpa (c) (in tennis) falta f (d) (geological) falla f

**2** vt criticar, poner reparos a; **her attitude can't be faulted** no se puede criticar su actitud

**faultless** ['fɔːltlɪs] adj impecable, intachable

**faulty** ['fɔːltɪ] adj defectuoso(a)

**faun** [fɔːn] n (mythological creature) fauno m

**fauna** ['fɔːnə] n (animal life) fauna f

**favour,** US **favor** ['feɪvə(r)] **1** n favor m; **to be in/out of f. (with)** (of people) ser visto(a) con buenos/malos ojos (por); (of product, method) gozar/no gozar de mucha aceptación (entre); **to look on sth/sb with f.** ser partidario(a) de algo/alguien; **to find favour with sb** encontrar aceptación por parte de alguien; **to ask sb a f., to ask a f. of sb** pedir un favor a alguien; **to do sb a f.** hacer un favor a alguien; Br Fam **do me a f. and shut up!** ¡haz el favor de callarte!; **in f. of...** (in preference to) en favor de...; **to be in f. of sth** estar a favor de algo; **to vote in f. (of)** votar a favor (de); **that's a point in her f.** eso es un punto a su favor; Fin **balance in your f.** saldo a su favor

**2** vt (a) (approve of) estar a favor de, ser partidario(a) de (b) (bestow favour on) favorecer

**favourable,** US **favorable** ['feɪvərəbəl] adj favorable; **in a f. light** desde una óptica favorable

**favourite,** US **favorite** ['feɪvərɪt] n & adj favorito(a) m,f

**favouritism,** US **favoritism** ['feɪvərɪtɪzəm] n favoritismo m

**fawn**[1] [fɔːn] **1** n (a) (deer) cervatillo m (b) (colour) beige m

**2** adj (colour) beige

**fawn**[2] vi adular (**on** a)

**fax** [fæks] **1** n (machine) fax m, telefax m; (message) fax m; **f. number** número m de fax

**2** vt mandar por fax; **to f. sb** mandar un fax a alguien

**faze** [feɪz] vt Fam desconcertar

**FBI** [efbi:'aɪ] *n US (abbr* **Federal Bureau of Investigation)** FBI *m*

**fear** [fɪə(r)] **1** *n* miedo *m*, temor *m*; **to be** *or* **go in f. of** tener miedo de; **she was in f. of her life** temía por su vida; *Fam* **to put the f. of God into sb** meter a alguien el miedo en el cuerpo; **for f. of** por miedo a; *Fam* **no f.!** ¡ni pensarlo!

**2** *vt* temer; **to f. that...** temer(se) que...; **I f. so** me temo que sí; **I f. not** me temo que no; **to f. the worst** temerse lo peor

**3** *vi* temer **(for** por)

**fearful** ['fɪəfʊl] *adj* **(a)** *(pain, consequence)* terrible, espantoso(a) **(b)** *Fam (noise, expense)* tremendo(a) **(c)** *(person)* temeroso(a); **to be f. of...** tener miedo de...

**fearless** ['fɪəlɪs] *adj* valiente, arrojado(a)

**fearsome** ['fɪəsəm] *adj* terrible, espantoso(a)

**feasibility** [fi:zə'bɪlɪtɪ] *n* viabilidad *f*; **f. study** estudio *m* de viabilidad

**feasible** ['fi:zəbəl] *adj* factible, viable

**feast** [fi:st] **1** *n* banquete *m*, festín *m*; *Rel* **f. day** fiesta *f* de guardar

**2** *vt* **to f. one's eyes on sth** recrear la vista en algo

**3** *vi* darse un banquete **(on** *or* **upon** de)

**feat** [fi:t] *n* hazaña *f*

**feather** ['feðə(r)] **1** *n* pluma *f*; **you could have knocked me down with a f.** me quedé de piedra; *Fig* **that's a f. in her cap** es un triunfo personal para ella; *Fig* **to make the feathers fly** armar un buen revuelo; **f. bed** colchón *m* de plumas

**2** *vt Fig* **to f. one's nest** hacer el agosto

**featherweight** ['feðəweɪt] *n –fin boxing)* peso *m* pluma

**feature** ['fi:tʃə(r)] **1** *n* **(a)** *(of face)* rasgo *m*, facción *f*; **features** *(face)* facciones *fpl* **(b)** *(of system, machine)* característica *f* **(c) f. (film)** largometraje *m* **(d)** *(in newspaper, on television, radio)* reportaje *m*; **f. writer** articulista *mf*

**2** *vt* **a film featuring...** una película en la que figura...

**3** *vi (appear)* figurar, aparecer

**featureless** ['fi:tʃəlɪs] *adj* uniforme, monótono(a)

**Feb** *(abbr* **February)** febrero *m*

**febrile** ['fi:braɪl] *adj Formal (atmosphere, state)* febril

**February** ['febrʊərɪ] *n* febrero *m*; *see also* **May**

**feckless** ['feklɪs] *adj* inepto(a)

**fed** [fed] *pt & pp of* **feed**

**federal** ['fedərəl] *adj* federal

**federalism** ['fedərəlɪzəm] *n* federalismo *m*

**federalist** ['fedərəlɪst] *n & adj* federalista *mf*

**federation** [fedə'reɪʃən] *n* federación *f*

**fed up** [fed'ʌp] *adj Fam* **to be f. (with)** estar harto(a) (de)

**fee** [fi:] *n (of lawyer, doctor)* minuta *f*, honorarios *mpl; (for entrance)* (precio *m* de) entrada *f; (for membership)* cuota *f*

**feeble** ['fi:bəl] *adj (person, light)* débil; *(argument, excuse)* flojo(a), pobre

**feeble-minded** ['fi:bəl'maɪndɪd] *adj* lelo(a)

**feebly** ['fi:blɪ] *adv* débilmente

**feed** [fi:d] **1** *n* **(a)** *(animal food)* pienso *m* **(b)** *(for baby) (from breast, bottle)* toma *f*

**2** *vt (pt & pp* **fed** [fed]) **(a)** *(give food to)* alimentar, dar de comer a; *(baby) (from breast)* amamantar, dar de mamar a; *(from bottle)* dar el biberón a; *(plant)* echar fertilizante a; **we were well fed** nos dieron muy bien de comer; **to f. one's family** dar de comer a la familia **(b)** *(supply)* to **f. a fire** alimentar un fuego; **to f. coins into a machine** introducir monedas en una máquina; **to f. sb with information** proporcionar información a alguien

**3** *vi* alimentarse **(on** de)

**feedback** ['fi:dbæk] *n Elec* realimentación *f; (on guitar, microphone)* acoplamiento *m*, feedback *m; Fig (response)* reacción *f*

**feel** [fi:l] **1** *n* **(a)** *(sense of touch)* tacto *m*

**(b)** *(sensation)* sensación *f*; **the f. of silk against her skin** el roce de la seda contra su piel; **the film has an authentic f. to it** la película da sensación de autenticidad

**(c)** *(knack)* **she has a real f. for languages** tiene un don especial para los idiomas; **he soon got the f. for it** enseguida cogió el tranquillo

**2** *vt (pt & pp* **felt** [felt]) **(a)** *(touch with hand)* tocar, palpar; **to f. one's way** *(in darkness)* andar a tientas; *Fig (in new situation)* familiarizarse

**(b)** *(be physically conscious of)* notar; **I felt the floor tremble** *or* **trembling** noté que el suelo temblaba

**(c)** *(experience) (pain, despair)* sentir; **to f. the cold** ser friolero(a); **I f. it in my bones** *(have intuition)* lo presiento, me da en la nariz

**(d)** *(believe)* creer, pensar; **I f. (that)...** me parece que...

**3** *vi* **(a)** *(physically) (of person)* **to f. ill/tired** sentirse enfermo(a)/cansado(a); **to f. hot/cold** tener calor/frío; **to f. hungry/thirsty** tener hambre/sed; **my foot feels better** ya me gejor el pie; **how do you f.?** ¿cómo te encuentras?; **not to f. oneself** no sentirse muy bien; **to f. up to doing sth** *(well enough)* sentirse con fuerzas para hacer algo; *(competent enough)* sentirse capaz de hacer algo

**(b)** *(mentally)* **to f. strongly about sth** tener convicciones muy arraigadas sobre algo; **to f. sure (that)...** estar seguro(a) (de que)...; **to f. bad about sth** sentirse mal por algo; **how would you f. if...?** ¿cómo te sentirías si...?;

**I f. as if...** me da la sensación de que...; **to f. (like) a new man/woman** sentirse otro/otra; **I felt (like) an idiot** me sentí como un/una idiota; **to f. like doing sth** tener ganas de hacer algo; **I feel like... (would like)** me apetece...

**(c)** *(feel sympathy for)* **to f. for sb** sentirlo por alguien; **I really felt for his wife** me daba mucha pena su mujer

**(d)** *(of things)* **to f. hard/soft** ser duro(a)/blando(a) al tacto; **it feels soft now** ahora está blando(a); **to f. hot/cold** estar caliente/frío(a); **it feels like (it's going to) rain** parece que va a llover; **it feels strange/good** es extraño/agradable

**(e)** *(touch with hands)* **to f. in one's pockets** hurgarse or mirarse en los bolsillos; **he felt on the ground for the key** buscó la llave a tientas por el suelo

**feeler** ['fi:lə(r)] *n (of insect)* antena *f; (of snail)* cuerno *m; Fig* **to put out feelers** tantear el terreno

**feeling** ['fi:lɪŋ] *n* **(a) (sense of)** f. sensibilidad *f;* **to have no f. in one's arm** tener un brazo insensible

**(b)** *(sensation) (of cold, pain)* sensación *f*

**(c)** *(emotion)* sentimiento *m;* **a f. of joy/anger** un sentimiento de alegría/ira; **to speak with f.** hablar apasionadamente; **I know the f.!** ¡sé cómo te sientes!; **I had a f. I might find you here** me daba la sensación *or* tenía la impresión de que te encontraría aquí; **his feelings towards me** sus sentimientos hacia mí; **to hurt sb's feelings** herir los sentimientos de alguien; **to have no feelings** no tener sentimientos; **feelings were running high (about)** estaban los ánimos revueltos (en cuanto a); *Fam* **no hard feelings!** ¡estamos en paz!

**(d)** *(opinion)* opinión *f;* **there is a general f. that...** la impresión general es que...; **my f. is that...** pienso *or* creo que...

**(e)** *(sensitivity)* sensibilidad *f;* **to have a f. for sth** tener sensibilidad para algo

**feet** [fi:t] *pl of* **foot**

**feign** [feɪn] *vt (anger, surprise)* simular

**feint** [feɪnt] **1** *n* amago *m,* finta *f*
  **2** *vi* **to f. to the left/right** hacer una finta *or* amagar a la izquierda/derecha

**felicitous** [fɪ'lɪsɪtəs] *adj (choice, expression)* feliz, acertado(a)

**feline** ['fi:laɪn] **1** *n* felino *m,* félido *m*
  **2** *adj* felino(a)

**fell¹** [fel] *vt (tree)* talar; *(opponent)* derribar

**fell²** *adj* **at one f. swoop** de un golpe

**fell³** *n (hill)* monte *m*

**fell⁴** *pt of* **fall**

**fellow** ['feləʊ] *n* **(a)** *(comrade)* compañero(a) *m,f,* camarada *mf;* **f. citizen** conciudadano(a) *m,f;* **f. countryman/countrywoman** compatriota *mf;* **f. feeling** (sentimiento *m* de) solidaridad *f;* **f. passenger/student/worker** compañero(a) *m,f* de viaje/de estudios/de trabajo; *Fig* **f. traveller** *(in politics)* simpatizante *mf* **(b)** *(at university)* profesor(ora) *m,f; (of academy, society)* miembro *m* **(c)** *Fam (man)* tío *m*

**fellowship** ['feləʊʃɪp] *n* **(a)** *(friendship)* compañerismo *m,* camaradería *f* **(b)** *(association)* sociedad *f,* asociación *f* **(c)** *(at university)* beca *f* de investigación

**felon** ['felən] *n Law* criminal *mf*

**felony** ['felənɪ] *n Law* crimen *m,* delito *m* grave

**felt¹** [felt] *n (fabric)* fieltro *m*

**felt²** *pt & pp of* **feel**

**felt-tip** ['felt'tɪp] *n* **f. (pen)** rotulador *m*

**female** ['fi:meɪl] **1** *n (person)* mujer *f; (animal, plant)* hembra *f*
  **2** *adj (person)* femenino(a); *(animal, plant)* hembra

**feminine** ['femɪnɪn] **1** *n Gram* femenino *m*
  **2** *adj* femenino(a)

**femininity** [femɪ'nɪnɪtɪ] *n* femin(e)idad *f*

**feminism** ['femɪnɪzəm] *n* feminismo *m*

**feminist** ['femɪnɪst] *n & adj* feminista *mf*

**femur** ['fi:mə(r)] *n Anat* fémur *m*

**fen** [fen] *n (marshy land)* pantano *m,* ciénaga *f;* **the Fens** = tierras bajas del este de Inglaterra, especialmente Norfolk y Cambridgeshire

**fence** [fens] **1** *n* **(a)** *(barrier)* valla *f,* cerca *f; Fig* **to sit on the f.** no pronunciarse, nadar entre dos aguas; *Fig* **to get off the f.** pronunciarse **(b)** *Fam (receiver of stolen property)* perista *mf*
  **2** *vi (as sport)* hacer esgrima

▶**fence off** *vt sep* vallar, cercar

**fencing** ['fensɪŋ] *n (sport)* esgrima *f*

**fend** [fend] *vi* **to f. for oneself** valerse por sí mismo

▶**fend off** *vt sep (attack)* rechazar; *(blow)* atajar, parar; *(question)* eludir

**fender** ['fendə(r)] *n* **(a)** *US (of car)* aleta *f* **(b)** *(for fireplace)* pantalla *f* (de chimenea), parachispas *m inv*

**fennel** ['fenəl] *n* hinojo *m*

**ferment 1** *n* ['fɜ:ment] *(commotion)* agitación *f;* **in a (state of) f.** agitado(a)
  **2** *vi* [fə'ment] *(of alcoholic drink)* fermentar

**fermentation** [fɜ:men'teɪʃən] *n* fermentación *f*

**fern** [fɜ:n] *n* helecho *m*

**ferocious** [fə'rəʊʃəs] *adj* feroz

**ferocity** [fə'rɒsɪtɪ] *n* ferocidad *f*

**ferret** ['ferɪt] **1** *n* hurón *m*
  **2** *vi Fam* **to f. (about) for sth** rebuscar algo

▶**ferret out** vt sep (object, information) encontrar, dar con

**ferris wheel** ['ferɪs'wiːl] n noria f

**ferrous** ['ferəs] adj ferroso(a)

**ferry** ['ferɪ] **1** n transbordador m, ferry m

**2** vt a f. sth/sb across a river pasar algo/a alguien al otro lado de un río; **the injured were ferried to hospital in taxis** los heridos fueron transportados al hospital en taxis

**ferryman** ['ferɪmən] n barquero m

**fertile** ['fɜːtaɪl] adj also Fig fértil

**fertility** [fɜ'tɪlɪtɪ] n fertilidad f; **f. symbol** símbolo m de fertilidad; Med **f. treatment** tratamiento m de fertilidad

**fertilize** ['fɜːtɪlaɪz] vt (animal, plant, egg) fecundar; (land) fertilizar

**fertilizer** ['fɜːtɪlaɪzə(r)] n fertilizante m

**fervent** ['fɜːvənt] adj ferviente

**fervour**, US **fervor** ['fɜːvə(r)] n fervor m

**fester** ['festə(r)] vi also Fig enconarse

**festival** ['festɪvəl] n **(a)** (of arts, music, drama) festival m **(b)** (public holiday) festividad f

**festive** ['festɪv] adj festivo(a); **in f. mood** con ganas de fiesta; **the f. season** (Christmas) la época navideña

**festivity** [fes'tɪvɪtɪ] n regocijo m; **the festivities** la celebración, las fiestas

**festoon** [fes'tuːn] vt festonear (**with** con), engalanar (**with** con)

**fetal** ['fiːtəl] US fetal; **f. position** posición f fetal

**fetch** [fetʃ] **1** vt **(a)** (bring) (object, liquid) ir a por, traer; (person) ir a recoger a; **f.!** (to dog) ¡busca! (to be sold for) alcanzar; **it should f. at least £50,000** debería venderse al menos por 50.000 libras

**2** vi to f. and carry for sb ser el criado de alguien

▶**fetch up** vi (end up) ir a parar

**fetching** ['fetʃɪŋ] adj atractivo(a)

**fête** [feɪt] **1** n = fiesta benéfica al aire libre con mercadillo, concursos, actuaciones etc.

**2** vt festejar, agasajar

**fetid** ['fetɪd] adj fétido(a)

**fetish** ['fetɪʃ] n fetiche m

**fetishism** ['fetɪʃɪzəm] n fetichismo m

**fetter** ['fetə(r)] **1** vt poner grilletes a; Fig encadenar, atar

**2** npl **fetters** (on slave, prisoner) grilletes mpl; Fig (on rights, freedom) cadenas fpl, ataduras fpl

**fettle** ['fetəl] n **in good** or **fine f.** en plena forma

**fetus** ['fiːtəs] n US feto m

**feud** [fjuːd] **1** n disputa f

**2** vi estar enemistado(a) (**with** con)

**feudal** ['fjuːdəl] adj feudal

**feudalism** ['fjuːdəlɪzəm] n feudalismo m

**fever** ['fiːvə(r)] n also Fig fiebre f; **to have a f.** tener fiebre; **excitement had risen to f. pitch** los ánimos estaban muy exaltados

**feverish** ['fiːvərɪʃ] adj (patient) con fiebre, febril; Fig (excitement, atmosphere) febril

**few** [fjuː] **1** n **the f. who came** los pocos que vinieron

**2** adj **(a)** (not many) pocos(as); **his visits are f. and far between** sólo viene muy de vez en cuando; **every f. minutes/days** cada pocos minutos/días; **he gave too f. examples** dio muy pocos ejemplos; **as f. as a dozen finished the race** tan sólo una docena terminó la carrera; **f. people knew who she was** pocos sabían quién era

**(b)** (some) **a f.** unos(as) pocos(as), algunos(as); **a good f.** unos cuantos; **quite a f.** bastantes; **in the next f. days** en los próximos días

**3** pron **(a)** (not many) pocos(as); **there are very/too f. of us** somos muy/demasiado pocos; **f. (of them) could speak French** pocos (de ellos) hablaban francés; **f., if any** pocos(as) o ninguno(a), apenas alguno(a)

**(b)** (some) **a f.** algunos(as); **a f. of the survivors** algunos supervivientes; **a f. of us** algunos de nosotros

**fewer** ['fjuːə(r)] (comparative of few) **1** adj menos; **no f. than thirty** no menos de treinta; **f. and f. people** cada vez menos gente

**2** pron menos mpl, fpl; **there are f. (of them) than I thought** hay menos de lo que creía

**fewest** ['fjuːɪst] (superlative of few) **1** adj **that hospital reported the f. cases** ese hospital es el que menos casos registró; **take the road which has the f. curves** ve por la carretera que tenga menos curvas

**2** pron **we received the f.** nosotros somos los que menos recibimos

**fiancé** [fɪ'ɒnseɪ] n prometido m, novio m

**fiancée** [fɪ'ɒnseɪ] n prometida f, novia f

**fiasco** [fɪ'æskəʊ] n (pl Br **fiascos**, US **fiascoes**) n fiasco m

**fib** [fɪb] Fam **1** n trola f, bola f; **to tell a f.** meter una bola

**2** vi (pt & pp **fibbed**) meter una bola

**fibber** ['fɪbə(r)] n Fam trolero(a) m,f

**fibre**, US **fiber** ['faɪbə(r)] n fibra f; **f. optics** transmisión f por fibra óptica

**fibreglass**, US **fiberglass** ['faɪbəglɑːs] n fibra f de vidrio

**fibrous** ['faɪbrəs] adj fibroso(a)

**fickle** ['fɪkəl] adj inconstante, voluble

**fiction** ['fɪkʃən] n (sth invented) ficción f; (short stories, novels) (literatura f de) ficción f; **a work of f.** una obra de ficción

**fictional** ['fɪkʃənəl] adj (character) de ficción; (scene, account) novelado(a)

**fictitious** [fɪk'tɪʃəs] adj ficticio(a)

**fiddle** ['fɪdəl] **1** *n* (a) *(violin)* violín *m (en música folk)* (b) *Br Fam (swindle)* timo *m*; **to be on the f.** dedicarse a hacer chanchullos

**2** *vt Br Fam (cheat)* amañar; **to f. the accounts** amañar la contabilidad

**3** *vi* (a) *(play violin)* tocar el violín *(en música folk)* (b) *(fidget)* **to f. (about** or **around) with** sth juguetear or enredar con algo

**fiddler** ['fɪdlə(r)] *n* violinista *mf (en música folk)*

**fiddlesticks** ['fɪdəlstɪks] *exclam* Old-fashioned ¡paparruchas!

**fiddly** ['fɪdlɪ] *adj Fam* complicado(a)

**fidelity** [fɪ'delɪtɪ] *n* fidelidad *f*

**fidget** ['fɪdʒɪt] **1** *n (person)* enredador(ora) *m,f*, trasto *m*

**2** *vi* enredar, trastear

**fidgety** ['fɪdʒɪtɪ] *adj* inquieto(a)

**field** [fi:ld] *n* (a) *(of crops, for sport) & Comptr* campo *m*; *(of oil, coal)* yacimiento *m*; **she's an expert in her f.** es una experta en su campo; **to work in the f.** *(not in office)* hacer trabajo de campo, trabajar in situ; **f. of vision** campo visual; **f. events** *(in athletics)* pruebas *fpl* de salto y lanzamiento; *US* **f. hockey** hockey *m* sobre hierba; **f. study** *(scientific)* estudio *m* de campo; *Sch & Univ* **f. trip** viaje *m* or salida *f* para (realizar) trabajo de campo; **f. work** *(scientific)* trabajo *m* de campo

(b) *Mil* **in the f.** en el campo de batalla; *Fig* **the press had a f. day** la prensa se puso las botas; **f. glasses** prismáticos *mpl*, gemelos *mpl*; **f. gun** cañón *m* de campaña; **f. hospital** hospital *m* de campaña; **f. marshal** mariscal *m* de campo

(c) **the f.** *(in race, contest)* los participantes; *also Fig* **to lead the f.** ir en cabeza

**2** *vt* (a) *(team)* poner a jugar; *(candidates)* presentar

(b) **to f. a question** contestar con destreza a una pregunta

**fieldmouse** ['fi:ldmaʊs] *(pl* **fieldmice** ['fi:ldmaɪs]) *n* ratón *m* de campo

**fiend** [fi:nd] *n (demon)* demonio *m*; **my boss is a f. for punctuality** mi jefe está obsesionado con la puntualidad

**fiendish** ['fi:ndɪʃ] *adj (evil, difficult)* endiablado(a), endemoniado(a)

**fiendishly** ['fi:ndɪʃlɪ] *adv (difficult, clever)* endiabladamente, endemoniadamente

**fierce** [fɪəs] *adj (animal, look)* fiero(a); *(heat)* abrasador(ora); *(contest, argument, competition)* feroz; *(loyalty)* fervoroso(a)

**fiercely** ['fɪəslɪ] *adv (to glare)* fieramente; *(to fight)* ferozmente; *(to condemn, defend)* vehementemente, apasionadamente; *(to resist)* con furia

**fiery** ['faɪərɪ] *adj (heat)* achicharrante, abrasador(ora); *(red, sky)* encendido(a); *(taste)* muy picante; *(person, character)* fogoso(a), ardiente

**FIFA** ['fi:fə] *n (abbr* **Fédération Internationale de Football Association)** FIFA *f*

**fifteen** [fɪf'ti:n] **1** *n* quince *m*; *Sport (rugby team)* equipo *m*

**2** *adj* quince; *see also* **eight**

**fifteenth** [fɪf'ti:nθ] **1** *n* (a) *(fraction)* quinceavo *m*, quinceava parte *f* (b) *(in series)* decimoquinto(a) *m,f* (c) *(of month)* quince *m*

**2** *adj* decimoquinto(a); *see also* **eleventh**

**fifth** [fɪfθ] **1** *n* (a) *(fraction)* quinto *m*, quinta parte *f* (b) *(in series)* quinto(a) *m,f* (c) *(of month)* cinco *m*

**2** *adj* quinto(a); *Pol* **f. column** quinta columna *f*; *see also* **eighth**

**fiftieth** ['fɪftɪəθ] *n & adj* quincuagésimo(a) *m,f*

**fifty** ['fɪftɪ] *n & adj* cincuenta *m*; *see also* **eighty**

**fig¹** [fɪg] *n (fruit)* higo *m*; *Fam* **he doesn't give** or **care a f.** le importa un rábano; **f. leaf** *(in art)* hoja *f* de parra; *Fig* **it's just a f. leaf** no es más que una tapadera; **f. tree** higuera *f*

**fig²** *(abbr* **figure)** fig., figura *f*

**fight** [faɪt] **1** *n* (a) *(physical, verbal)* pelea *f*; *(contest, battle)* lucha *f*; *(boxing match)* combate *m*; **to start a f. (with sb)** pelearse (con alguien); **to get into a f. (with sb)** pelearse (con alguien); **to give in without a f.** ceder sin oponer resistencia; **to put up a good f.** oponer resistencia (b) *(spirit)* **to show some f.** demostrar espíritu de lucha; **there was no f. left in him** no le quedaban arrestos (c) *(struggle)* lucha *f* (por por); **the f. against cancer** la lucha contra el cáncer

**2** *vt (pt & pp* **fought** [fɔ:t]) *(person, enemy, rivals)* luchar contra; *(disease, poverty, fire)* luchar contra, combatir; *(temptation, desire, decision)* luchar contra; *(war, battle)* librar; *Law* **she fought her case** defendió su caso *(en un juicio)*; **to f. an election** presentarse a unas elecciones; *Fig* **to f. sb's battles for them** dar la cara por alguien; **to f. one's way through a crowd** abrirse paso entre una multitud

**3** *vi* (a) *(physically)* luchar, pelearse; *(verbally)* pelearse, discutir; **to go down fighting** luchar hasta el final; **to f. fair** pelear limpio; **to f. shy of sth** evitar algo (b) *(struggle)* luchar; **to f. for breath** luchar por respirar

▸**fight back 1** *vi (retaliate)* responder

**2** *vt sep* **to f. back one's tears** tratar de contener las lágrimas

▸**fight off** *vt sep (enemy, attack)* rechazar, ahuyentar; *(illness)* librarse de

**fighter** ['faɪtə(r)] *n (in fight)* combatiente *mf*, contendiente *mf*; *(for cause)* luchador(ora) *m,f*; **f. pilot** piloto *m* de caza; **f. (plane)** caza *m*; **f. squadron** escuadrón *m* de cazas

**fighting** ['faɪtɪŋ] **1** n peleas fpl; Mil luchas fpl **2** adj **to have a f. chance** tener posibilidad de ganar; **to be f. fit** estar en plena forma; **f. forces** fuerzas fpl de combate

**figment** ['fɪgmənt] n **it's a f. of your imagination** es producto de tu imaginación

**figurative** ['fɪgərətɪv] adj figurado(a)

**figuratively** ['fɪgərətɪvlɪ] adv en sentido figurado

**figure** ['fɪgə(r), US 'fɪgjə(r)] **1** n **(a)** (number) cifra f; **there must be a mistake in the figures** debe de haber un error en los números; **she's good at figures** se le dan bien los números; **to reach double/three figures** alcanzar valores de dos/tres cifras **(b)** (body shape) figura f; **to have a good f.** tener buena figura; **a fine f. of a man** un hombre muy bien plantado; **to cut a sorry f.** tener un aspecto lamentable **(c)** (person) figura f; **a leading f. in local politics** una figura destacada de la política local; **a distinguished f.** una personalidad distinguida **(d)** (illustration) figura f, ilustración f; **see f. 21 b** ver figura 21 b **(e)** (expression) **f. of speech** figura f retórica; **I didn't mean it like that, it was just a f. of speech** no quería decir eso, era sólo una manera or forma de hablar **2** vt US pensar, figurarse; **I f. (that) it will take three years** calculo que llevará tres años **3** vi **(a)** (appear) (in list, book) figurar **(b)** Fam (make sense) **that figures!** (es) normal or lógico

▸**figure on** vt insep Fam **to f. on doing sth** contar con hacer algo

▸**figure out** vt sep Fam (amount) calcular; (problem) solventar; **she can't f. you out at all** ¡no te entiende en absoluto!

**figurehead** ['fɪgəhed] n (on ship) mascarón m de proa; Fig (of country, party) testaferro m

**Fiji** ['fi:dʒi:] n (las islas) Fidji or Fiji

**Fijian** ['fi:dʒi:ən] **1** n fidjiano(a) m,f, fiji mf **2** adj de Fiji

**filament** ['fɪləmənt] n Elec filamento m

**filch** [fɪltʃ] vt Fam mangar

**file**[1] [faɪl] **1** n (tool) lima f **2** vt (metal) limar; **to f. one's nails** limarse las uñas

**file**[2] **1** n **(a)** (folder) carpeta f; (box) archivo m; (documents) expediente m, ficha f; **to keep** or **have a f. on sb/sth** tener una ficha or un expediente de alguien/algo; **to have sth on f.** tener algo archivado **(b)** Comptr archivo m, fichero m; **f. manager** administrador m de archivos; **f. server** servidor m de ficheros or archivos **2** vt **(a)** (store) (documents, letters) archivar **(b)** **to f. a claim** presentar una demanda **3** vi **to f. for divorce** presentar una demanda de divorcio

**file**[3] **1** n (line) fila f; **in single f.** en fila india **2** vi **to f. past** (sth/sb) desfilar (ante algo/alguien); **to f. in/out** entrar/salir en fila

**filial** ['fɪlɪəl] adj filial

**filigree** ['fɪlɪgri:] n filigrana f

**Filipino** [fɪlɪ'pi:nəʊ] **1** n (pl **Filipinos**) filipino(a) m,f **2** adj filipino(a)

**fill** [fɪl] **1** n **to eat one's f.** comer hasta reventar; Fig **to have had one's f. of sth** estar harto(a) de algo **2** vt **(a)** (container) llenar (**with** de); (gap, hole) rellenar; **to f. sb's glass** llenar el vaso a alguien; **to be filled with admiration/hope** estar lleno(a) de admiración/esperanza; **to f. a vacancy** (of employer) cubrir una vacante; **I had a tooth filled** me hicieron un empaste **(b)** (occupy) (time) ocupar **3** vi (become full) llenarse (**with** de or con); **her eyes filled with tears** se le llenaron los ojos de lágrimas

▸**fill in 1** vt sep **(a)** (hole, space, form) rellenar; **to f. in time** matar el tiempo **(b)** Fam (inform) **to f. sb in (on sth)** poner a alguien al tanto (de algo) **2** vi **to f. in for sb** sustituir a alguien

▸**fill out 1** vt sep (form, application) rellenar **2** vi (of person) engordar

▸**fill up 1** vt sep (glass) llenar (hasta el borde); Fam **f. her up!** (with petrol) ¡lleno, por favor! **2** vi (of tank, container) llenarse

**fillet** ['fɪlɪt] **1** n (of fish) filete m; **f. steak** filete m **2** vt (fish) cortar en filetes

**filling** ['fɪlɪŋ] **1** n **(a)** (in tooth) empaste m **(b)** (in sandwich, pie) relleno m **(c)** **f. station** gasolinera f, estación f de servicio **2** adj **a f. meal** una comida que llena mucho

**filly** ['fɪlɪ] n (horse) potra f

**film** [fɪlm] **1** n **(a)** (at cinema, layer) película f; **a (roll of) f.** (for camera) un carrete; **a f. of ice** una capa de hielo; **f. actor/actress** actor m/ actriz f de cine; **f. critic** crítico(a) m,f de cine; **f. director** director(ora) m,f de cine, cineasta mf; **the f. industry** la industria cinematográfica; **f. script** guión m de cine; **f. star** estrella f de cine; **f. studio** estudio m cinematográfico **2** vt (person, event) filmar, rodar **3** vi rodar

**filter** ['fɪltə(r)] **1** n **(a)** (for liquids, on cigarette) & Phot filtro m; **f. coffee** café m de filtro; **f. paper** papel m de filtro **(b)** Aut **f. lane** carril m de giro a la derecha/izquierda; **f. signal** (on traffic light) señal f de giro a la derecha/izquierda **2** vt filtrar **3** vi **(a)** (of liquid, light) filtrarse (**through** a través de); **the news soon filtered through**

la noticia se filtró rápidamente (**b**) *Aut (of traffic)* **to f. to the right/left** girar a la derecha/izquierda *(según la indicación del semáforo)*

**filth** [fɪlθ] *n (dirt)* porquería *f*; **to talk f.** decir cochinadas

**filthy** ['fɪlθɪ] **1** *adj* (**a**) *(very dirty)* asqueroso(a) (**b**) *(very bad)* **to be in a f. temper** tener un humor de perros; **he gave me a f. look** me atravesó con la mirada; *Br* **f. weather** tiempo *m* de perros (**c**) *(obscene)* obsceno(a)

**2** *adv Fam* **f. rich** asquerosamente rico(a)

**FIMBRA** ['fɪmbrə] *n Br Fin (abbr Financial Intermediaries, Managers and Brokers Regulatory Association)* = asociación reguladora de los intermediarios financieros, directores y agentes de cambio y bolsa, ≃ CNMV

**fin** [fɪn] *n (of fish, aeroplane)* aleta *f*

**final** ['faɪnl] **1** *n* (**a**) *(of competition)* final *f*; **to be through to the finals** haber llegado a la final (**b**) *Univ* **finals** *Br* exámenes *mpl* de fin de carrera; *US* exámenes *mpl* finales

**2** *adj* (**a**) *(last)* último(a); **the f. whistle** el pitido final; **the f. stages** las etapas finales, las últimas etapas; *Fin* **f. demand** último aviso *m* de pago; **f. warning** última advertencia *f* (**b**) *(definitive)* definitivo(a); **the umpire's decision is f.** la decisión del árbitro es definitiva; **and that's f.!** ¡y no hay más que hablar!

**finale** [fɪ'nɑːlɪ] *n (of concert, play)* final *m*; **grand f.** gran final; **there was a grand f. to the match** el partido tuvo un final apoteósico

**finalist** ['faɪnəlɪst] *n* finalista *mf*

**finalize** ['faɪnəlaɪz] *vt* ultimar

**finally** ['faɪnəlɪ] *adv* (**a**) *(lastly)* por último, finalmente; **and f.,...** y por último,... (**b**) *(at last)* por fin, finalmente; **she had f. met him** por fin lo había conocido (**c**) *(irrevocably)* definitivamente; **it hasn't been decided f. yet** todavía no se ha tomado la decisión definitiva

**finance** [faɪ'næns, fɪ'næns] **1** *n* (**a**) *(subject)* finanzas *fpl*; *Br* **company** *or* **house** compañía *f* financiera (**b**) **finances** *(funds)* finanzas *fpl*; **his finances are low** se encuentra en una mala situación financiera

**2** *vt* financiar

**financial** [faɪ'nænʃəl, fɪ'nænʃəl] *adj* financiero(a); **f. adviser** asesor(ora) *m,f* financiero(a); **f. control** control *m* financiero; **f. management** gestión *f* financiera; **f. market** mercado *m* financiero; **f. planning** planificación *f* financiera; **f. statement** balance *m* (general); *Br* **f. year** *(for budget)* ejercicio *m* (económico); *(for tax)* año *m* fiscal

**financially** [faɪ'nænʃəlɪ, fɪ'nænʃəlɪ] *adv* económicamente

**financier** [faɪ'nænsɪə(r)] *n* financiero(a) *m,f*

**finch** [fɪntʃ] *n* pinzón *m*

**find** [faɪnd] **1** *n* hallazgo *m*

**2** *vt (pt & pp* **found** [faʊnd]) (**a**) *(discover by chance)* encontrar, hallar; **to f. sb at home** *or* **in** encontrar a alguien en casa; **I found her waiting in the hall** la encontré esperando en la entrada; **leave everything as you found it** deja todo tal y como lo encontraste; **I often f. myself wondering...** a menudo me sorprendo preguntándome...; **they found an unexpected supporter in Richard Sanders** recibieron el inesperado apoyo de Richard Sanders; **you will f. that I am right** te darás cuenta de que tengo razón; **I was surprised to f. that...** me sorprendió enterarme de que...

(**b**) *(discover by searching)* encontrar, hallar; **to try to f. sth** tratar de encontrar algo; **to f. an answer/a solution** hallar una respuesta/una solución; **the money has been found** han encontrado el dinero; **she was nowhere to be found** no la encontraron por ninguna parte; **to f. a job for sb** encontrarle un trabajo a alguien; **he found something for me to do** me encontró algo que hacer; **he couldn't f. it in his heart to tell her** no halló fuerzas para decírselo; **to f. one's way** orientarse, encontrar el camino; **this leaflet somehow found its way into my bag** no sé cómo ha venido a parar a mi bolso este folleto; **to f. a way to do sth** encontrar la manera de hacer algo; **to f. oneself** *(spiritually)* encontrarse a uno mismo

(**c**) *(experience)* **they will f. it easy/difficult** les resultará *or* lo encontrarán fácil/difícil; **she found it impossible to understand him** le resultó imposible entenderle; **he found it necessary to remind her of her duty** consideró necesario recordarle su obligación; **how did you f. the meal/the exam?** ¿qué te pareció la comida/el examen?; **I found her charming** me pareció muy simpática

(**d**) *Law* **to f. sb guilty/innocent** declarar a alguien culpable/inocente

**3** *vi Law* **to f. for/against sb** fallar a favor de/en contra de alguien

▸**find out 1** *vt sep* (**a**) *(discover)* averiguar, descubrir; **we found out that she was French** descubrimos que era francesa (**b**) *(see through)* **to f. sb out** descubrir a alguien; **we've been found out** nos han descubierto

**2** *vi* **to f. out about sth** enterarse de algo

**finder** ['faɪndə(r)] *n* **the f. of the money should contact the police** quien encuentre el dinero ha de llamar a la policía; *Fam* **finders keepers** = si yo lo encontré, es para mí

**findings** ['faɪndɪŋz] *npl* conclusiones *fpl*

**fine¹** [faɪn] **1** *n Law* multa *f*

**2** *vt Law* multar, poner una multa a; **to f. sb £100** poner a alguien una multa de 100 libras

**fine²** 1 *adj* (a) *(excellent) (food, performance)* excelente exquisito(a); *(weather)* bueno(a); **to appeal to sb's finer feelings** apelar a los más nobles sentimientos de alguien; **she's a f. woman** es una mujer extraordinaria; **the f. arts** las bellas artes; **she's got it down to a f. art** lo hace con los ojos cerrados, lo tiene muy controlado (b) *(satisfactory)* bien; **she's f.** está bien; **everything is f.** todo está bien; **that's f. by me** ¡por mí, vale!, ¡me parece bien! (c) *Ironic* **you're a f. one to talk!** ¡mira quién fue a hablar!; **this is another f. mess you've got us into!** ¡en menudo lío nos has vuelto a meter!; **he was in a f. (old) temper!** estaba de un humor de perros (d) *(subtle, delicate)* fino(a); **f. distinction** distinción *f* sutil; **not to put too f. a point on it** hablando en plata; **there's a f. line between eccentricity and madness** la frontera entre la excentricidad y la locura es muy tenue

2 *adv* bien; **she's getting on** *or* **doing f.** le va bien; **they get on f.** se llevan bien

**finely** ['faɪnlɪ] *adv (skilfully)* acertadamente, hábilmente; **f. balanced** *(contest)* muy equilibrado(a); **f. chopped** picado(a) muy fino; **f. tuned** *(engine)* a punto

**finery** ['faɪnərɪ] *n* galas *fpl*

**finesse** [fɪ'nes] *n* finura *f*; **he handled the matter with great f.** llevó el asunto con mucha mano izquierda *or* delicadeza

**fine-tune** ['faɪn'tjuːn] *vt* poner a punto

**finger** ['fɪŋɡə(r)] 1 *n* (a) *(of hand, glove)* dedo *m*; *Fig* **to keep one's fingers crossed** cruzar los dedos; **f. bowl** bol *m or* cuenco *m* para las manos; **f. food** *(snacks)* cosas *fpl* de picar

(b) *(measure)* **a f. of brandy** un dedo de coñac

(c) *(idioms)* **he's got them (wrapped) round his little f.** los tiene a sus pies; **to have a f. in every pie** estar metido(a) en todo; **don't you dare lay a f. on him** no te atrevas a tocarle un pelo; **she wouldn't lift a f. to help you** no levantaría *or* movería un dedo por ayudarte; **I can't quite put my f. on it** no consigo dar con ello; **to get one's fingers burnt** salir escaldado *or* escarmentado; *Br very Fam* **get** *or* **pull your f. out!** ¡mueve el culo!

2 *vt* (a) *(feel)* tocar

(b) *very Fam (inform on)* dar el soplo acerca de

**fingernail** ['fɪŋɡəneɪl] *n* uña *f*

**fingerprint** ['fɪŋɡəprɪnt] 1 *n* huella *f* digital *or* dactilar

2 *vt (person)* tomar las huellas digitales *or* dactilares a

**fingertip** ['fɪŋɡətɪp] *n* punta *f* del dedo; **to have sth at one's fingertips** *(facts, information)* tener algo al alcance de la mano; *(subject)* conocer algo al dedillo

**finicky** ['fɪnɪkɪ] *adj (fussy)* quisquilloso(a); *(complicated)* trabajoso(a), entretenido(a)

**finish** ['fɪnɪʃ] 1 *n* (a) *(end) (of day, meeting)* fin *m*; *(of race)* meta *f*; **to be in at the f.** seguir estando hasta el final (b) *(surface) (of furniture, metalwork)* acabado *m*

2 *vt* (a) *(end)* terminar, acabar; **to f. doing sth** terminar de hacer algo; **you didn't let me f. (what I was saying)** no me dejaste terminar (lo que estaba diciendo) (b) *(ruin, kill) (person)* acabar con

3 *vi* terminar, finalizar; **to f. on an optimistic note** finalizar con una nota de optimismo; **to f. fourth** *(in race, contest)* quedar en cuarto lugar, terminar cuarto(a)

▶**finish off** *vt sep* (a) *(complete) (task, book)* terminar (del todo) (b) *(use up)* acabar (con) (c) *Fam (kill)* terminar con

2 *vi* terminar

**finished** ['fɪnɪʃt] *adj* (a) *(completed)* terminado(a), acabado(a); **the job isn't f. yet** el trabajo no está terminado aún; *Fam* **he's f.!** ¡está acabado! (b) *(of high quality)* elaborado(a)

**finishing** ['fɪnɪʃɪŋ] *adj* **to put the f. touches to sth** dar los últimos (re)toques a algo; **f. line** línea *f* de meta; **f. school** = escuela privada de etiqueta para señoritas

**finite** ['faɪnaɪt] *adj* finito(a); *Gram (verb)* conjugado(a)

**Finland** ['fɪnlənd] *n* Finlandia

**Finn** [fɪn] *n (person)* finlandés(esa) *m,f*

**Finnish** ['fɪnɪʃ] 1 *n (language)* finés *m*, finlandés *m*

2 *adj* finlandés(esa)

**fir** [fɜː(r)] *n* **f. (tree)** abeto *m*; **f. cone** piña *f*

**fire** ['faɪə(r)] 1 *n* (a) *(element, in hearth)* fuego *m*; *(large, destructive)* incendio *m*; *(heater)* estufa *f*; *Fig (enthusiasm)* pasión *f*; **on f.** en llamas, ardiendo; **to cause** *or* **start a f.** provocar un incendio; **to catch f.** prender; **to set f. to sth, to set sth on f.** prender fuego a algo; **f.!** ¡fuego!; *Fig* **to play with f.** jugar con fuego; *Fig* **we'll have to fight f. with f.** a grandes males, grandes remedios; **electric/gas f.** estufa *f* eléctrica/de gas; **f. alarm** alarma *f* contra incendios; *Br* **f. brigade**, *US* **f. department** (cuerpo *m* de) bomberos *mpl*; **f. door** puerta *f* contra incendios; **f. drill** simulacro *m* de incendio; **f. engine** coche *m* de bomberos; **f. escape** escalera *f* de incendios; **f. exit** salida *f* de incendios; **f. extinguisher** extintor *m*; **f. fighter** bombero *m*; **f. hazard** = objeto que supone peligro de incendio; **f. hydrant** boca *f* de incendios; **f. insurance** seguro *m* contra incendios; **f. regulations** *(laws)* normativa *f* contra incendios; *(in building)* procedimiento *m* en caso de incendio; **f. sale** venta *f* de objetos dañados en un incendio; **f. station** parque *m* de bomberos (**b**) *(of rifle, artillery)* fuego *m*; **to open f.** abrir fuego; **to hold one's f.** dejar de disparar; **to come under f.** caer bajo el fuego enemigo; *Fig* **to be** *or* **come under f.** *(be criticized)* recibir muchas críticas; **f. power** capacidad *f* ofensiva

**2** *vt* (**a**) *(rifle, bullet, missile)* disparar (**at** contra); **to f. a shot** disparar; *Fig* **to f. a question at sb** lanzar una pregunta a alguien

(**b**) *Fam (dismiss)* despedir; **you're fired!** ¡quedas despedido!

(**c**) **oil-/gas-fired central heating** calefacción *f* central de petróleo/gas; *Fig* **to f. sb with enthusiasm** hacer a alguien arder de entusiasmo; *Fig* **the film fired his imagination** la película despertó su imaginación

(**d**) *(pottery)* cocer

**3** *vi* (**a**) *(with gun)* disparar; **f.!** ¡fuego!; *Fam Fig* **f. away!** *(to questioner)* ¡adelante!

(**b**) *(of engine)* encenderse

**firearm** ['faɪɑːm] *n* arma *f* de fuego

**firebrand** ['faɪəbrænd] *n (torch)* antorcha *f*; *Fig (agitator)* agitador(ora) *m,f*

**firecracker** ['faɪəkrækə(r)] *n* petardo *m*

**fire-fighting** ['faɪəfaɪtɪŋ] *adj* **f. equipment** equipo *m* contra incendios

**firefly** ['faɪəflaɪ] *n* luciérnaga *f*

**fireguard** ['faɪəgɑːd] *n* pantalla *f* (de chimenea), parachispas *m inv*

**firelight** ['faɪəlaɪt] *n* luz *f* del fuego

**firelighter** ['faɪəlaɪtə(r)] *n* pastilla *f* para (encender) el fuego

**fireman** ['faɪəmən] *n* bombero *m*

**fireplace** ['faɪəpleɪs] *n* chimenea *f*

**fireproof** ['faɪəpruːf] *adj (clothing, material)* ignífugo(a), incombustible

**fireside** ['faɪəsaɪd] *n* **by the f.** junto a la chimenea

**firewall** ['faɪəwɔːl] *n Comptr* cortafuegos *m inv*

**firewood** ['faɪəwʊd] *n* leña *f*

**firework** ['faɪəwɜːk] *n* fuego *m* de artificio; **fireworks** fuegos *mpl* artificiales; *Fig* **there'll be fireworks** se va a armar una buena; **f. display** *(castillo m de)* fuegos *mpl* artificiales

**firing** ['faɪərɪŋ] *n* disparos *mpl*; *Fig* **to be in the f. line** *(be blamed, criticized)* estar en la línea de fuego or en el punto de mira; **f. squad** pelotón *m* de ejecución *or* de fusilamiento

**firm**[1] [fɜːm] *n (company)* empresa *f*

**firm**[2] **1** *adj* (**a**) *(steady, definite)* firme; **the f. favourite** el gran favorito; **it is my f. belief that...** creo firmemente que... (**b**) *(strict)* firme, estricto(a); **to be f. with sb** ser estricto(a) con alguien; **she was polite but f.** se mostró educada, pero firme

**2** *adv* **to stand f.** mantenerse firme; **she held f. to her principles** se mantuvo firme en sus principios

**firmly** ['fɜːmlɪ] *adv (securely, resolutely)* con firmeza, firmemente; **I f. believe that...** creo firmemente que...

**first** [fɜːst] **1** *n* (**a**) *(in series)* primero(a) *m,f*; **we were the f.** to arrive fuimos los primeros en llegar; **it's the f.** I've heard of it es la primera noticia que tengo (de ello), ahora me entero; **Edward the F.** *(written)* Eduardo I; *(spoken)* Eduardo primero

(**b**) *(of month)* uno *m*; **the f. of May** *(labour holiday)* el primero de mayo; **we're leaving on the f.** nos vamos el (día) uno

(**c**) *(beginning)* **from f. to last** de principio a fin; **from the f.** desde el principio; **at f.** al principio

(**d**) *Univ* **to get a F.** sacar una matrícula de honor

(**e**) *(first gear)* primera *f*; **to put the car into f.** meter la primera

(**f**) *(unique event)* **it was a f.** fue un acontecimiento sin precedentes

**2** *adj* primero(a); **the f. century** el siglo uno *or* primero; **for the f. time** por primera vez; **at f. hand** de primera mano; **f. things f.!** lo primero es lo primero; **I don't know the f. thing about motorbikes** no tengo ni idea de motos; **f. thing in the morning** a primera hora de la mañana; **at f. light** al alba; **at f. sight** a primera vista; **in the f. place** en primer lugar; **on the f. floor** *Br* en el primer piso; *US* en la planta baja; **the F. World War** la Primera Guerra Mundial; **f. aid** *(skill)* socorrismo *m*; *(treatment)* primeros auxilios *mpl*; **f. cousin** primo(a) *m,f* carnal; **f. edition** primera edición *f*; *Aut* **f. gear** primera *f*; *US* **the F. Lady** la primera dama; *Naut* **f. mate** segundo *m* de a bordo; **f. name** nombre *m* (de pila); **f. night** *(of play)* (noche *f* del) estreno *m*; *Law* **f. offence** primer delito *m*; *Law* **f. offender** delincuente *mf* sin antecedentes

**3** *adv* (**a**) *(firstly)* primero; **f. and foremost** ante todo; **f. of all** antes de nada, en primer lugar

(**b**) *(for the first time)* por primera vez; **I f. met her in London** la conocí en Londres

(**c**) *(before others)* primero, antes; **you go f.!** *(in queue)* usted está antes; **to come f.** *(in race, contest)* terminar primero; *(in importance)* ser lo primero; **f. come, f. served** por orden de llegada; **ladies f.!** las señoras primero; **to fall head f.** caer de cabeza; **I'd resign f.** *(rather than do sth)* antes dimito

**first-aid** [fɜːst'eɪd] *adj* **f. certificate** título *m* de primeros auxilios; **f. box** *or* **kit** botiquín *m* de primeros auxilios

**first-born** ['fɜːstbɔːn] *n & adj Literary* primogénito(a) *m,f*

**first-class** ['fɜːstklɑːs] **1** *adj (compartment, ticket)* de primera (clase); *Univ* **f. honours**

**(degree)** matrícula *f* de honor; **f. stamp** sello *m* de primera clase *(para expedición urgente)*

**2** *adv* **to travel f.** viajar en primera (clase); **to send a letter f.** enviar una carta urgente

**first-degree** ['fɜːstɪ'griː] *adj* **(a)** *Med (burns)* de primer grado **(b)** *US Law (murder)* en primer grado

**first-hand** ['fɜːsthænd] **1** *adj* de primera mano

**2** *adv* de primera mano; **he heard it f.** se lo dijeron a él mismo

**firstly** ['fɜːstlɪ] *adv* en primer lugar

**first-past-the-post** ['fɜːstpɑːstðə'pəʊst] *adj Pol* **f. system** sistema *m* de elección por mayoría simple

**first-rate** [fɜːst'reɪt] *adj* excelente, de primera clase

**first-time buyer** ['fɜːstaɪm'baɪə(r)] *n* = persona que compra una vivienda por primera vez

**fiscal** ['fɪskəl] *adj* fiscal; **f. policy** política *f* fiscal; **f. year** año *m* fiscal

**fish** [fɪʃ] **1** *n (pl* **fish** or **fishes) (a)** *(animal)* pez *m; (food)* pescado *m; Br* **f. and chips** = pescado frito con patatas fritas; *Br* **f.-and-chip shop** = tienda de "fish and chips"; **f. cake** pastelillo *m* de pescado; **f. farm** piscifactoría *f;* **f. fingers,** *US* **f. sticks** palitos *mpl* or barritas *fpl* de pescado; **f. knife** cuchillo *m* or paleta *f* de pescado; **f. slice** pala *f* or espátula *f* (de cocina); **f. tank** acuario *m*

**(b)** *(idioms)* **there are plenty more f. in the sea** con él/ella no se acaba el mundo; **to have other f. to fry** tener algo más importante que hacer; **she felt like a f. out of water** no se sentía en su elemento; **at school/work, he was a big f. in a small pond** le venía pequeña la escuela/la empresa; **neither f. nor fowl** ni chicha ni limoná

**2** *vt* **(a)** *(river)* pescar en

**(b)** *(remove)* **to f. sth from somewhere** retirar algo de un lugar

**3** *vi* **(a)** *(for fish)* pescar

**(b)** *Fam* **to f. for compliments** tratar de atraer elogios; **she fished around in her pocket for some change** rebuscó en el bolsillo a ver si tenía monedas

**fisherman** ['fɪʃəmən] *n* pescador *m*

**fish-hook** ['fɪʃhʊk] *n* anzuelo *m*

**fishing** ['fɪʃɪŋ] *n* pesca *f;* **to go f.** ir de pesca or a pescar; **f. boat** barco *m* pesquero; **f. grounds** caladeros *mpl;* **f. line** sedal *m;* **f. net** red *f* de pesca; **f. port** puerto *m* pesquero; **f. rod** caña *f* de pescar

**fishmonger** ['fɪʃmʌŋgə(r)] *n (person)* pescadero(a) *m,f;* **the f.'s** la pescadería

**fishnet** ['fɪʃnet] *adj* **f. stockings** or **tights** medias *fpl* de red or de malla

**fishy** ['fɪʃɪ] *adj* **(a)** *(smell, taste)* a pescado **(b)** *Fam (suspicious)* sospechoso(a); **there's something f. going on here** aquí hay gato encerrado

**fission** ['fɪʃən] *n* fisión *f*

**fissure** ['fɪʃə(r)] *n (in mountain, rock)* grieta *f; Med* fisura *f*

**fist** [fɪst] *n* puño *m;* **to shake one's f. at sb** amenazar a alguien con el puño; *Fig* **to make a (good) f. of it** hacerlo bastante bien

**fistful** ['fɪstfʊl] *n* puñado *m*

**fisticuffs** ['fɪstɪkʌfs] *npl* pelea *f* a puñetazos

**fit¹** [fɪt] *n* ataque *m,* crisis *f* inv; **(epileptic) f.** ataque *m* de epilepsia, crisis epiléptica; **a f. of coughing** un acceso de tos; *Fam Fig* **to have a f.** *(get angry)* ponerse hecho(a) una furia; **in a f. of temper** en un arrebato de ira; **a f. of crying** un ataque de llanto; **to have sb in fits (of laughter)** hacer que alguien se muera de risa; **to do sth by fits and starts** hacer algo a trompicones

**fit²** **1** *adj* **(a)** *(appropriate)* adecuado(a), apto(a); **f. to eat** comestible; **f. to drink** potable; **a meal f. for a king** una comida digna de un rey; **do as you see** or **think f.** haz lo que creas conveniente; **this is no f. way to behave** esta no es manera de comportarse; **that's all he's f. for** no vale para más; **she worked until she was f. to drop** trabajó hasta caer rendida

**(b)** *(healthy)* en forma; **to get/keep f.** ponerse/mantenerse en forma; **he is not yet f. to go back to work** todavía no está en condiciones de volver a trabajar; *Fam* **to be as f. as a fiddle** estar en plena forma

**(c)** *Fam (attractive)* **to be f.** estar como un tren

**2** *vt (pt & pp* **fitted) (a)** *(match)* ajustarse a, adecuarse a; **to make the punishment f. the crime** imponer un castigo proporcional al delito

**(b)** *(be the right size for)* **it fits me** me sirve, me queda or me va bien; **this key fits the lock** esta llave entra (bien) en la cerradura

**(c)** *(install)* colocar, poner; **to f. a carpet** colocar una moqueta; **the car is fitted with an alarm** el coche viene equipado con alarma

**(d)** *(insert)* **to f. sth into sth** introducir or encajar algo en algo; **to f. sth onto sth** colocar algo sobre algo; **we can f. another two people inside** podemos meter a dos personas más

**3** *vi* **(a)** *(of lid, key, plug)* encajar; **to f. (together)** encajar; **to f. into sth** caber en algo

**(b)** *(of clothes)* quedar bien (de talla)

**4** *n* **the jacket is a good/bad f.** la chaqueta está bien/mal de talla

▸**fit in 1** *vt sep (in timetable)* **to f. sb in** hacer un hueco a alguien

**2** *vi* **(a)** *(go into place)* encajar **(b)** *(of person)* **he just didn't f. in** simplemente no encajaba bien (en aquel ambiente)

▶**fit up** vt sep very Fam (frame) **to f. sb up** hacer una declaración falsa or un montaje contra alguien

**fitful** ['fitful] adj (sleep) intermitente; **to make f. progress** ir progresando por rachas

**fitness** ['fitnıs] n (a) (health) buena forma f (b) (suitability) aptitud f

**fitted** ['fitıd] adj **f. carpet** moqueta f; **f. kitchen** cocina f amueblada a medida

**fitting** ['fitıŋ] **1** n (a) (of clothes) prueba f; **f. room** probador m (b) **fittings** (of office) equipamiento m; (of bathroom) accesorios mpl

**2** adj apropiado(a)

**five** [faıv] **1** n cinco m; **f.-o'clock shadow** sombra f de barba

**2** adj cinco; see also **eight**

**five-a-side** ['faıvəsaıd] adj **f. football** fútbol m sala

**fiver** ['faıvə(r)] n Fam cinco libras fpl

**fix** [fiks] **1** n (a) Fam (difficulty) **to be in a f.** estar en un lío; **to get into a f.** meterse en un lío

(b) very Fam (of drug) chute m, pico m; Fig **my daily f. of television news** mi dosis diaria de noticias

(c) Fam (set-up) **the match/quiz was a f.** el partido/concurso estaba amañado

**2** vt (a) (attach securely) fijar; **to f. sth in one's memory** fijar algo en la memoria; **to f. one's attention on sth** fijar la atención en algo; **to f. one's eyes on sb** fijar la mirada en alguien

(b) (decide, limit, price) fijar; **nothing is fixed yet** no hay nada fijo todavía

(c) (repair) arreglar

(d) (arrange) (meeting) organizar; **just wait while I f. my hair** espera mientras me peino; Fam **I'll f. him!** ¡se va a enterar!

(e) Fam (rig) (election, contest) amañar

(f) **to f. sb breakfast/a drink** preparar el desayuno/una bebida a alguien

▶**fix up** vt sep (meeting) preparar; **it's all fixed up** está todo dispuesto; **I've fixed you up with a date** te he buscado a alguien para que salgáis juntos

**fixation** [fik'seıʃən] n fijación f; **to have a f. about sth** tener una fijación con algo

**fixed** [fikst] adj (a) (price) fijo(a); **f. assets** activo m fijo or inmovilizado; **f. costs** costes mpl fijos; **f. expenses** gastos mpl fijos; **f. income** renta f fija (b) (definite) **to have f. ideas** tener ideas fijas; **to have no f. plans** no tener planes definidos (c) Fam **how are you f. for money/time?** ¿qué tal andas de dinero/tiempo? (d) Fam (election, contest) amañado(a)

**fixer** ['fiksə(r)] n Fam negociador(ora) m,f

**fixture** ['fikstʃə(r)] n (a) **bathroom fixtures and fittings** saneamientos mpl or sanitarios mpl y accesorios; Fam **she was**

**something of a f. at his parties** asistía invariablemente a todas sus fiestas (b) Br (in football) encuentro m

**fizz** [fiz] **1** n (a) (sound) burbujeo m (b) Fam (soft drink) refresco m; (champagne) champán m

**2** vi burbujear

▶**fizzle out** vi Fam (of plan) quedarse en agua de borrajas; (of enthusiasm, interest) disiparse

**fizzy** ['fizı] adj (wine) espumoso(a); (soft drink) con gas, con burbujas

**fjord** [fjɔːd] n fiordo m

**flab** [flæb] n Fam (fat) grasa f

**flabbergast** ['flæbəgɑːst] vt Fam alucinar, flipar; **I was flabbergasted** aluciné, flipé

**flabby** ['flæbı] adj (person) fofo(a); Fig (argument, reasoning) flojo(a)

**flaccid** ['flæsıd] adj flác(c)ido(a)

**flag** [flæg] **1** n bandera f; (on boat) pabellón m, bandera f; **F. Day** (in United States) = día de la bandera en Estados Unidos, 14 de junio; **f. day** (for charity) día m de la banderita, día m de cuestación

**2** vt (pt & pp flagged) **to f. (down) a taxi** llamar or parar a un taxi; **to f. a mistake** señalar un error

**3** vi (of person) desfallecer; (of conversation, interest) decaer; (of strength) flaquear

**flagellate** ['flædʒəleıt] vt flagelar

**flagpole** ['flægpəʊl] n asta f (de bandera)

**flagrant** ['fleıgrənt] adj flagrante

**flagrantly** ['fleıgrəntlı] adv flagrantemente

**flagship** ['flægʃıp] n (of fleet) buque m insignia; Fig (of range of products, policies) estandarte m

**flagstone** ['flægstəʊn] n losa f

**flail** [fleıl] **1** n (agricultural implement) mayal m

**2** vt agitar; **she flailed her fists at him** trató inútilmente de golpearle

**3** vi agitarse; **I managed to avoid his flailing fists** conseguí evitar sus puñetazos

▶**flail about, flail around** vi (of arms, legs) moverse descontroladamente

**flair** [fleə(r)] n don m, dotes fpl; **to have a f. for sth** tener dotes para algo; **to do sth with f.** hacer algo con estilo or elegancia

**flak** [flæk] n fuego m antiaéreo; Fig **she got a lot of f. for her decision** su decisión recibió duras críticas; **f. jacket** chaleco m antifragmentación

**flake** [fleık] **1** n (of snow, cereal) copo m; (of skin, soap) escama f; (of paint) desconchón m

**2** vi (of skin) descamarse; (of paint) desconcharse

▶**flake out** vi Fam (fall asleep) quedarse roque

**flaky** ['fleıkı] adj (a) (surface) desconchado(a); (skin) con escamas; **f. pastry** hojaldre m (b) US Fam (eccentric) raro(a)

**flamboyant** [flæm'bɔıənt] adj extravagante

**flame** [fleɪm] **1** n llama f; **to go up in flames** ser pasto de las llamas; **to burst into flames** incendiarse; Fam **he's an old f. of mine** es un antiguo amor

**2** vi (of fire) llamear

**flameproof** ['fleɪmpruːf] adj resistente al fuego

**flamethrower** ['fleɪmθrəʊə(r)] n lanzallamas m inv

**flaming** ['fleɪmɪŋ] **1** adj **(a)** (burning) en llamas; **in a f. temper** enfurecido(a) **(b)** Br Fam (for emphasis) maldito(a); **he's got a f. cheek** ¡vaya jeta que tiene el tío!

**2** adv Br Fam **don't be so f. stupid** ¡mira que eres bobo!; **it was f. expensive** fue caro del copón

**flamingo** [fləˈmɪŋgəʊ] (pl **flamingos**) n flamenco m

**flammable** ['flæməbəl] adj inflamable

**flan** [flæn] n tarta f

**Flanders** ['flɑːndəz] n Flandes

**flange** [flændʒ] n pestaña f

**flank** [flæŋk] **1** n (of person, animal) costado m; (of beef, mutton) falda f; (of mountain) ladera f; (of army) flanco m

**2** vt flanquear

**flannel** ['flænəl] n **(a)** (fabric) franela f **(b)** Br (face-cloth) toallita f **(c)** Br Fam (wordy talk) palabrería f

**flannels** ['flænəlz] npl (trousers) pantalones mpl de franela; **a pair of f.** unos pantalones de franela

**flap** [flæp] **1** n **(a)** (of envelope, book cover) solapa f; (of tent) puerta f; (of aeroplane) alerón m **(b)** Fam (panic) **to get into a f.** ponerse hecho(a) un manojo de nervios

**2** vt (pt & pp **flapped**) (wings) batir; **she flapped her arms excitedly** agitó los brazos con excitación

**3** vi (of wings) aletear; (of flag) ondear

**flapjack** ['flæpdʒæk] n **(a)** Br (biscuit) galleta f de avena **(b)** US (pancake) crepe f, hojuela f

**flare** [fleə(r)] **1** n (signal) bengala f

**2** vt **to f. one's nostrils** hinchar las aletas de la nariz

**3** vi (of fire, flame) llamear; (of temper, trouble) estallar

▸**flare up** vi (of fire) llamear; (of medical condition) exacerbarse; (of anger, trouble) estallar

**flares** [fleəz] npl (trousers) pantalones mpl de campana; **a pair of f.** unos pantalones de campana

**flash** [flæʃ] **1** n **(a)** (of light) destello m; **a f. of lightning** un relámpago; **a f. of wit** una ocurrencia; **a f. of inspiration** una inspiración súbita; **in a f.** (very quickly) en un abrir y cerrar de ojos; Fig **a f. in the pan** un éxito aislado; **f. flood** riada f; **f. point** (of situation) momento m

de máxima tensión; (region) zona f conflictiva **(b)** (in photography) flash m

**2** adj Br Fam (showy) llamativo(a), ostentoso(a)

**3** vt (smile, look) lanzar (**at** a); (card, badge) mostrar, exhibir; **to f. one's headlights at sb** darle las luces a alguien, hacerle señales con los faros a alguien

**4** vi **(a)** (of light) destellar; **his eyes flashed with anger** sus ojos lanzaban destellos de ira **(b)** (move quickly) **to f. past** pasar a toda velocidad; **it flashed across my mind that...** se me ocurrió de pronto que...; **my life flashed before me** en un instante vi mi vida entera

**flashback** ['flæʃbæk] n (in novel, film) escena f retrospectiva

**flasher** ['flæʃə(r)] n Br Fam exhibicionista m

**flashing** ['flæʃɪŋ] adj (light) intermitente

**flashlamp** ['flæʃlæmp], US **flashlight** ['flæʃlaɪt] n linterna f

**flashy** ['flæʃɪ] adj Pej llamativo(a), ostentoso(a)

**flask** [flɑːsk] n (in chemistry) matraz m; **(hip) f.** petaca f; **(thermos) f.** termo m

**flat** [flæt] **1** n **(a)** Br (apartment) piso m, Am departamento m

**(b)** Fam (flat tyre) rueda f desinflada

**(c)** mud flats marismas fpl; salt flats salinas fpl

**2** adj **(a)** (surface) llano(a), liso(a), plano(a); (landscape, region) llano(a); (roof) liso(a), plano(a); (nose) chato(a); **to be as f. as a pancake** estar liso(a) como un plato; Fam (flat-chested) estar plana como una tabla; **f. cap** = gorra de tela, generalmente a cuadros; **to have f. feet** tener los pies planos; **f. racing** carrera f de caballos (sin obstáculos); **f. rate** tarifa f única; **f. tyre** rueda f desinflada

**(b)** (refusal) rotundo(a)

**(c)** (existence, atmosphere) gris, monótono(a); (voice) monótono(a); (battery) descargado(a); **this beer is f.** esta cerveza ha perdido el gas or no tiene fuerza

**(d)** Mus (a semitone lower) bemol; (out of tune) desafinado(a); B **f.** si m bemol

**3** adv **(a)** **he lay f. on the floor** estaba tumbado en el suelo; **to fall f. on one's face** caer de bruces; Fig **the joke fell f.** el chiste no hizo mucha gracia

**(b)** (completely) **to turn sb down f.** rechazar a alguien de plano; **in twenty seconds f.** en veinte segundos justos; **to work f. out** trabajar a tope; Fam **to be f. broke** estar sin un duro

**flat-chested** ['flæt'tʃestɪd] adj plana (de pecho)

**flatfish** ['flætfɪʃ] n pez m (de cuerpo) plano

**flat-footed** ['flæt'fʊtɪd] adj **to be f.** tener (los) pies planos

**flatly** ['flætlɪ] *adv (refuse, deny)* rotundamente, de plano

**flatmate** ['flætmeɪt] *n Br* compañero(a) *m,f* de piso

**flatten** ['flætən] *vt (make flat)* aplastar; *(ground)* allanar; *(paper)* alisar; *(building, area)* arrasar; *Fam (in fight)* tumbar

**flatter** ['flætə(r)] *vt (of person)* halagar, adular; *(of clothes)* favorecer; **I felt flattered** me sentí halagado; **to f. oneself** engañarse a sí mismo(a); **she flatters herself that she's a good cook** se piensa que es una buena cocinera; *Fam* **don't f. yourself!** ¡no te engañes!

**flattering** ['flætərɪŋ] *adj (words)* halagador(ora); *(clothes, colour)* favorecedor(ora)

**flattery** ['flætərɪ] *n* halagos *mpl*

**flatulence** ['flætjʊləns] *n Med* flatulencia *f*

**flaunt** [flɔːnt] *vt* hacer ostentación de

**flautist** ['flɔːtɪst] *n Mus* flautista *mf*

**flavour,** *US* **flavor** ['fleɪvə(r)] **1** *n (of food)* & *Fig* sabor *m*; **her stories have a Mediterranean f.** sus relatos tienen un sabor mediterráneo

**2** *vt (food)* condimentar; **vanilla flavoured** con sabor a vainilla

**flavouring,** *US* **flavoring** ['fleɪvərɪŋ] *n* aromatizante *m*

**flavourless,** *US* **flavorless** ['fleɪvəlɪs] *adj* insípido(a)

**flaw** [flɔː] *n (in diamond, plan, personality)* fallo *m*, defecto *m*

**flawed** [flɔːd] *adj* defectuoso(a)

**flawless** ['flɔːlɪs] *adj* impecable

**flax** [flæks] *n (plant)* lino *m*

**flay** [fleɪ] *vt (flog, criticize)* despellejar, desollar

**flea** [fliː] *n (insect)* pulga *f*; *Fam* **to send sb away with a f. in his ear** echarle a alguien una buena bronca; **f. market** mercadillo *m* callejero, rastro *m*

**fleabite** ['fliːbaɪt] *n* picadura *f* de pulga

**flea-bitten** ['fliːbɪtən] *adj Fam (shabby)* mugriento(a)

**fleck** [flek] **1** *n* mota *f*

**2** *vt* motear **(with** de); **flecked with paint** con gotas de pintura

**fled** [fled] *pt* & *pp of* **flee**

**fledgling** ['fledʒlɪŋ] **1** *n (young bird)* polluelo *m*

**2** *adj Fig (person)* novato(a); *(company, state)* naciente

**flee** [fliː] *(pt* & *pp* **fled** [fled]) *vi* huir **(from** de)

**fleece** [fliːs] **1** *n (of sheep)* vellón *m*

**2** *vt Fam (cheat)* desplumar

**fleecy** ['fliːsɪ] *adj* algodonoso(a)

**fleet** [fliːt] *n (of ships)* flota *f*; *(of taxis, buses)* flota *f*, parque *m (móvil)*

**fleet-footed** ['fliːt'fʊtɪd] *adj Literary* de pies ligeros, veloz

**fleeting** ['fliːtɪŋ] *adj* fugaz

**Flemish** ['flemɪʃ] **1** *n (language)* flamenco *m*

**2** *adj* flamenco(a)

**flesh** [fleʃ] *n (of person)* carne *f*; *(of fruit)* pulpa *f*; **in the f.** en persona; **to make sb's f. creep** *or* **crawl** darle escalofríos a alguien; **his own f. and blood** los de su misma sangre; **f. wound** herida *f* superficial

▸**flesh out** *vt sep (plan, remarks)* definir, precisar

**fleshy** ['fleʃɪ] *adj (limb, fruit)* carnoso(a)

**flew** [fluː] *pt of* **fly**

**flex** [fleks] **1** *n Br (cable)* cable *m*, cordón *m*

**2** *vt* flexionar; *Fig* **they are flexing their muscles** están haciendo una demostración de fuerza

**flexibility** [fleksɪ'bɪlɪtɪ] *n* flexibilidad *f*

**flexible** ['fleksɪbəl] *adj* flexible; **f. working hours** horario *m* de trabajo flexible

**flexitime** ['fleksɪtaɪm] *n* horario *m* flexible

**flick** [flɪk] **1** *n* **(a)** *(movement) (of finger)* toba *f*; **a f. of the wrist** (in tennis) un golpe de muñeca; **f. knife** navaja *f* automática **(b)** *Br Fam Old-fashioned* **the flicks** *(cinema)* el cine

**2** *vt (with finger)* dar una toba a; *(with hands, tail)* sacudir; **to f. a switch** pulsar un interruptor; **he flicked the cigarette ash onto the carpet** tiró la ceniza del cigarrillo en la moqueta

▸**flick through** *vt insep (book, magazine)* hojear

**flicker** ['flɪkə(r)] **1** *n* parpadeo *m*; **a f. of hope** un rayo de esperanza; **a f. of interest** un atisbo de interés

**2** *vi (of flame)* parpadear

**flier** ['flaɪə(r)] *n (pilot)* piloto *mf*

**flight** [flaɪt] *n* **(a)** *(act of flying)* vuelo *m*; **it's two hours' f. from Edinburgh** está a dos horas de vuelo desde Edimburgo; *Fig* **a f. of fancy** un vuelo de la imaginación; *Av* **f. attendant** auxiliar *mf* de vuelo; *Av* **f. deck** *(of plane)* cabina *f* del piloto; *Av* **f. path** ruta *f* de vuelo; *Av* **f. recorder** caja *f* negra; *Av* **f. simulator** simulador *m* de vuelo **(b)** *(group of birds)* bandada *f*; *Fig* **in the top f.** con los mejores, entre la élite **(c)** **f. (of stairs)** tramo *m* (de escalera); **two flights up from me** dos pisos más arriba **(d)** *(escape)* huida *f*, fuga *f*; **to put sb to f.** poner a alguien en fuga

**flightless** ['flaɪtlɪs] *adj* no volador(ora)

**flighty** ['flaɪtɪ] *adj (fickle)* inconstante, voluble

**flimsy** ['flɪmzɪ] *adj (structure, fence)* endeble; *(dress)* ligero(a); *(excuse, evidence)* débil, flojo(a)

**flinch** [flɪntʃ] *vi (with pain)* encogerse; **to f. from (doing) sth** *(shy away)* echarse atrás a la hora de (hacer) algo

**fling** [flɪŋ] **1** *n Fam (affair)* aventura *f*

**2** *vt (pt & pp flung* [flʌŋ]*)* arrojar; **to f. one's arms around sb** abrazar fuertemente a alguien; *Fig* **to f. oneself into a campaign** meterse de lleno en una campaña

▶**fling out** *vt sep (object)* tirar; *(person)* echar

**flint** [flɪnt] *n (stone)* sílex *m inv*; pedernal *m*; *(of lighter)* piedra *f*

**flip** [flɪp] **1** *Fam* **the f. side** *(of record)* la cara B; *Fig (of situation)* la otra cara de la moneda

**2** *vt (pt & pp flipped)* **to f. the switch** dar al interruptor; **to f. a coin** lanzar una moneda al aire; *Fam* **he's flipped his lid** se ha vuelto majareta

**3** *vi Fam (get angry)* cabrearse; *(go mad)* volverse majara

▶**flip through** *vt insep (book, magazine)* hojear, echar un vistazo a

**flip-flop** ['flɪpflɒp] *n* chancleta *f*, chancla *f*

**flippant** ['flɪpənt] *adj* frívolo(a)

**flipper** ['flɪpə(r)] *n* aleta *f*

**flirt** [flɜːt] **1** *n (man)* ligón *m*, mariposón *m*; *(woman)* ligona *f*, coqueta *f*

**2** *vi* flirtear **(with** con), coquetear **(with** con); *Fig* **to f. with danger/an idea** coquetear con el peligro/una idea

**flirtatious** [flɜː'teɪʃəs] *adj* coqueto(a)

**flit** [flɪt] **1** *n Br Fam* **to do a moonlight f.** *(move house)* mudarse de casa a escondidas

**2** *vi (pt & pp flitted)* **to f. about** *(of bird)* revolotear; *Fig* **to f. from one thing to another** saltar de una cosa a otra

**float** [fləʊt] **1** *n* **(a)** *(on fishing line, net)* flotador *m*, corcho *m*; *(as swimming aid)* flotador *m* **(b)** *(vehicle in procession)* carroza *f*; *Br* **milk f.** = furgoneta (eléctrica) de reparto de leche

**2** *vt* **(a)** *(ship)* flotar **(b)** *(idea, proposal)* lanzar; **they decided to f. the company** *(on Stock Exchange)* decidieron que la empresa comenzara a cotizar en bolsa

**3** *vi (in water, air)* flotar; *Fig* **she floated out of the room** se deslizó fuera de la habitación

**floating** ['fləʊtɪŋ] *adj (object, exchange rate)* flotante; *(population)* fluctuante, flotante; *Pol (voter)* indeciso(a)

**flock** [flɒk] **1** *n (of sheep)* rebaño *m*; *(of birds)* bandada *f*; *Rel (congregation)* rebaño *m*, grey *f*; **a f. of tourists** un grupo multitudinario de turistas

**2** *vi (gather)* acudir en masa

**flog** [flɒg] *(pt & pp flogged) vt* **(a)** *(beat)* azotar; *Fam Fig* **you're flogging a dead horse** te estás esforzando inútilmente; *Fam* **to f. a subject to death** agotar completamente un tema **(b)** *Br Fam (sell)* enchufar, vender

**flood** [flʌd] **1** *n* inundación *f*; **the F.** *(in the Bible)* el diluvio (universal); **floods of tears** un mar de lágrimas

**2** *vt (land, the bathroom, market)* inundar; **to be flooded with complaints/telephone calls** recibir un aluvión de quejas/llamadas telefónicas

**3** *vi (of river)* desbordarse; **the sun's rays came flooding through the window** el sol entraba a raudales por la ventana; **the spectators flooded out of the stadium** los espectadores salían en masa del estadio; **money flooded out of the country** el dinero salió a raudales del país

**floodgate** ['flʌdgeɪt] *n Fig* **to open the floodgates to sth** abrir las puertas a algo

**flooding** ['flʌdɪŋ] *n* inundaciones *fpl*

**floodlight** ['flʌdlaɪt] **1** *n* foco *m*

**2** *vt (pt & pp floodlit* ['flʌdlɪt]*) or flood-lighted)* iluminar con focos

**floodlit** ['flʌdlɪt] *adj* iluminado(a) con focos

**floor** [flɔː(r)] **1** *n* **(a)** *(of room, forest)* suelo *m*; *(of Stock Exchange)* parquet *m*; *(of ocean)* fondo *m*; **to give sb the f.** *(in debate)* pasar *or* dar la palabra a alguien; **f. show** espectáculo *m* de variedades **(b)** *(storey) (of building)* piso *m*, planta *f*

**2** *vt (knock down)* derribar; *Fig* **the question floored him** la pregunta lo dejó perplejo

**floorboard** ['flɔːbɔːd] *n* tabla *f* del suelo *(de tarima)*

**floozie, floozy** ['fluːzɪ] *n very Fam* putón *m* (verbenero)

**flop** [flɒp] **1** *n (failure)* fracaso *m*

**2** *vi (pt & pp flopped)* **(a)** *(fall)* dejarse caer **(b)** *(fail)* fracasar

**floppy** ['flɒpɪ] **1** *adj (ears)* caído(a); *(garments)* flojo(a); *Comptr* **f. disk** disquete *m*

**2** *n Comptr* disquete *m*

**flora** ['flɔːrə] *n (plant life)* flora *f*

**floral** ['flɔːrəl] *adj* floral; **f. tribute** *(at funeral)* corona *f* de flores

**Florence** ['flɒrəns] *n* Florencia

**florid** ['flɒrɪd] *adj (style)* florido(a); *(complexion)* colorado(a)

**florist** ['flɒrɪst] *n* florista *mf*; **f.'s (shop)** floristería *f*

**floss** [flɒs] **1** *n (dental)* **f.** hilo *m* dental

**2** *vt* **to f. one's teeth** limpiarse los dientes con hilo dental

**flotation** [fləʊ'teɪʃən] *n Com (of company)* emisión *f* de títulos

**flotsam** ['flɒtsəm] *n* **f. (and jetsam)** desechos *mpl* arrojados por el mar; *Fig* **the f. of the war/of society** los desechos de la guerra/de la sociedad

**flounce** [flaʊns] **1** *n (in sewing)* volante *m*

**2** *vi* **to f. in/out/off** entrar/salir/irse haciendo aspavientos

**flounder** ['flaʊndə(r)] **1** *n (fish)* platija *f*

**2** *vi (in water, mud)* debatirse

**flour** ['flaʊə(r)] **1** n harina f
**2** vt enharinar

**flourish** ['flʌrɪʃ] **1** n (gesture) ademán m florituresco; (musical, in writing) floritura f; (in signature) rúbrica f
**2** vt (brandish) blandir
**3** vi (thrive) (of plant, person) crecer con vigor; (of business, arts) florecer

**flourishing** ['flʌrɪʃɪŋ] adj (plant) vigoroso(a), lozano(a); (business) próspero(a), floreciente

**flout** [flaʊt] vt (rule, sb's authority) desobedecer

**flow** [fləʊ] **1** n (of liquid) flujo m; Fig the speaker was interrupted in full f. el orador fue interrumpido en pleno discurso; Fig to follow the f. of an argument seguir el hilo de un razonamiento; Fig to go with the f. seguir la corriente; f. chart organigrama m
**2** vi (a) (of water) correr, fluir; Fig (of ideas, conversation) fluir; to f. into the sea (of river) desembocar en el mar (b) to f. from (be the result of) derivarse de

**flower** ['flaʊə(r)] **1** n flor f; Fig in the first f. of youth en la flor de la juventud; f. arranging arte m or decoración f floral; f. garden jardín m floral; f. girl = dama de honor de corta edad que lleva un ramo de flores en una boda; f. show exposición f de flores
**2** vi (of plant) florecer

**flowerbed** ['flaʊəbed] n parterre m

**flowerpot** ['flaʊəpɒt] n tiesto m, maceta f

**flowery** ['flaʊərɪ] adj (fabric, dress) floreado(a); Fig (prose, compliments) florido(a)

**flowing** ['fləʊɪŋ] adj (hair, movement) suelto(a)

**flown** [fləʊn] pp of **fly**

**flu** [fluː] n gripe f; a dose of the f. una gripe

**fluctuate** ['flʌktjʊeɪt] vi fluctuar

**fluctuation** [flʌktjʊ'eɪʃən] n fluctuación f

**flue** [fluː] n (of heater, chimney) salida f de humos

**fluency** ['fluːənsɪ] n fluidez f; f. in French required (in job advert) se requiere dominio del francés

**fluent** ['fluːənt] adj he is f. in French, he speaks f. French habla francés con soltura

**fluently** ['fluːəntlɪ] adv con soltura

**fluff** [flʌf] **1** n pelusa f
**2** vt Fam (botch) hacer muy mal; (lines) decir mal

**fluffy** ['flʌfɪ] adj esponjoso(a)

**fluid** ['fluːɪd] **1** n fluido m
**2** adj. fluido(a); a f. situation una situación inestable; f. ounce onza f líquida (Br 28,4 ml; US 29,6 ml)

**fluidity** [fluː'ɪdɪtɪ] n fluidez f

**fluke** [fluːk] n Fam (stroke of luck) chiripa f; by a f. de chiripa

**fluk(e)y** ['fluːkɪ] adj Fam (lucky) suertudo(a)

**flume** [fluːm] n tobogán m

**flummox** ['flʌməks] vt Fam desconcertar

**flung** [flʌŋ] pt & pp of **fling**

**flunk** [flʌŋk] vt & vi Fam catear

**flunkey** ['flʌŋkɪ] n (pl flunkeys) n Fam Pej lacayo m

**fluorescent** [flʊə'resənt] adj fluorescente; f. light (luz f) fluorescente m

**fluoride** ['flʊəraɪd] n fluoruro m

**flurry** ['flʌrɪ] n also Fig torbellino m

**flush** [flʌʃ] **1** n (a) (beginning) in the first f. of youth en la primera juventud; in the first f. of enthusiasm en el primer momento de entusiasmo (b) (redness of face) rubor m, sonrojo m (c) (in cards) color m
**2** adj (a) (even) the door is f. with the wall la puerta no sobresale de la pared (b) Fam to be f. (with money) (of person) estar forrado(a) (de dinero)
**3** vt (toilet) to f. the toilet tirar de la cadena
**4** vi (a) (of person) ruborizarse, sonrojarse (b) the lavatory isn't flushing properly la cisterna (del váter) no funciona bien
▸**flush out** vt sep (force to emerge) hacer salir

**flushed** [flʌʃd] adj (face) ruborizado(a); f. with (joy, pride) rebosante de; (success) enardecido(a) por

**fluster** ['flʌstə(r)] **1** vt poner nervioso(a), alterar
**2** vi ponerse nervioso(a), alterarse

**flute** [fluːt] n (musical instrument) flauta f

**flutter** ['flʌtə(r)] **1** n (a) (of wings) aleteo m; (of eyelids) parpadeo m; Fig in a f. of excitement en un revuelo de emoción (b) Br Fam (bet) apuesta f; to have a f. hacer una pequeña apuesta
**2** vt to f. its wings (of bird) batir las alas; she fluttered her eyelashes at him lo miró pestañeando con coquetería
**3** vi (of birds, insects) aletear

**flux** [flʌks] n in a state of f. en constante cambio

**fly¹** [flaɪ] n (a) f. or flies (of trousers) bragueta f (b) f. sheet (of tent) doble techo m

**fly²** Br Fam adj (cunning) astuto(a), listo(a)

**fly³** n (insect) mosca f; he wouldn't hurt a f. es incapaz de matar una mosca; they were dropping like flies caían como moscas; Fig a f. in the ointment una pequeña pega; Fam Fig there are no flies on him se las sabe todas; I wish I could be a f. on the wall (at interview, meeting) me encantaría espiar por un agujerito

**fly⁴** (pt flew [fluː], pp flown [fləʊn]) **1** vt (a) (plane) pilotar; (goods) mandar por avión; (route, distance) cubrir; to f. Air India volar con Air India
(b) (kite) volar; the ship/town hall was flying the Polish flag la bandera polaca ondea-

ba en el barco/ayuntamiento; *Fig* **to f. the flag**
*(be patriotic)* defender el pabellón *(del propio país)*

(c) *(flee)* huir de, escapar de; *Fig* **to f. the nest**
*(of child)* volar del nido

**2** *vi* (a) *(of bird, plane)* volar; *(of passenger)* ir en
avión, volar; **to f. over London** sobrevolar
Londres; **to f. across the Atlantic** cruzar el
Atlántico en avión

(b) *(of flag, hair)* ondear

(c) *(move quickly)* ir volando; **I must f.** tengo
que salir volando; **the door flew open** la
puerta se abrió de golpe; **to f. into a rage**
enfurecerse; **to f. at sb** *(attack)* lanzarse sobre
alguien; *Fam* **to send sth/sb flying** mandar
algo/a alguien por los aires; **to f. in the face of
reason** ir en contra de la razón

▸**fly away** *vi (of bird)* salir volando; *(of papers)*
volarse

▸**fly in 1** *vt sep (transport by aircraft)* traer en
avión

**2** *vi (arrive by aircraft)* llegar en avión

**fly-by-night** ['flaɪbaɪnaɪt] *adj Fam Pej (company)* nada fiable

**flyer** ['flaɪə(r)] *n* (a) *(pilot)* piloto *mf* (b) *(leaflet)*
hoja *f* de propaganda

**flying** ['flaɪɪŋ] **1** *n* **she loves f.** le encanta
volar; **f. club** aeroclub *m*; **f. lessons** lecciones
*fpl* de vuelo; **f. time** horas *fpl* de vuelo

**2** *adj* (a) *(bird)* volador(ora); **to pass an exam
with f. colours** aprobar un examen con muy
buena nota; *Av* **f. boat** hidroavión *m*; **f. doctor**
= médico que hace uso del avión o del helicóptero para visitar a pacientes en zonas remotas o
de difícil acceso; **f. fish** pez *m* volador; **f. saucer** platillo *m* volante (b) *(visit)* breve

**flyleaf** ['flaɪliːf] *(pl* **flyleaves** ['flaɪliːvz]) *n (of
book)* guarda *f*

**flyover** ['flaɪəʊvə(r)] *n Br Aut* paso *m* elevado

**flypaper** ['flaɪpeɪpə(r)] *n* papel *m* atrapamos-
cas

**fly-past** ['flaɪpɑːst] *n Av* desfile *m* aéreo

**flyweight** ['flaɪweɪt] *n (in boxing)* peso *m*
mosca

**FM** [e'fem] *n Rad (abbr* **frequency
modulation)** FM *f*, frecuencia *f* modulada

**FO** [e'fəʊ] *n Br Pol (abbr* **Foreign Office)** =
Ministerio *m* de Asuntos Exteriores, ≃ Mº
AA EE

**foal** [fəʊl] **1** *n (horse)* potro *m*, potrillo *m*

**2** *vi* parir

**foam** [fəʊm] **1** *n* espuma *f*; **f. rubber** gomaespuma *f*

**2** *vi (of sea, beer)* hacer espuma; **to f. at the
mouth** echar espuma por la boca

**foamy** ['fəʊmɪ] *adj* espumoso(a)

**fob** [fɒb] *n* cadena *f* (de reloj), leontina *f*; **f.
watch** reloj *m* de bolsillo

▸**fob off** *(pt & pp* **fobbed)** *vt sep Fam* **to f. sb
off with sth** quitarse a alguien de encima con
algo; **to f. sth off on sb** colocarle *or* endilgarle
algo a alguien

**focal** ['fəʊkəl] *adj* focal; **f. point** núcleo *m*,
foco *m* de atención

**focus** ['fəʊkəs] **1** *n (pl* **focuses** or **foci**
['fəʊkaɪ]) *(of lens, discontent, interest)* foco *m*; **in
f.** enfocado(a); **out of f.** desenfocado(a)

**2** *vt (pt & pp* **focussed** or **focused)** *(rays of
light)* enfocar; *(one's interest, energy)* concentrar
(on en); **all eyes were focused on him** todas
las miradas estaban centradas en él

**3** *vi (with eyes)* enfocar la vista (on en); *Fig* **to f.
on sth** *(of debate, speaker)* centrarse en algo

**fodder** ['fɒdə(r)] *n (for animal)* forraje *m*

**foe** [fəʊ] *n* enemigo(a) *m,f*

**foetal**, *US* **fetal** ['fiːtəl] *adj* fetal; **f. position** posición *f* fetal

**foetus**, *US* **fetus** ['fiːtəs] *n* feto *m*

**fog** [fɒg] *n* niebla *f*; *Fig* **to be in a f.** *(confused)*
estar hecho(a) un lío; *Aut* **f. lamp** *or* **light** faro
*m* antiniebla

▸**fog up** *(pt & pp* **fogged)** *vi (of windows)* empañarse

**fogbound** ['fɒgbaʊnd] *adj (port, airport)*
paralizado(a) por la niebla

**fogey** ['fəʊgɪ] *(pl* **fogeys)** *n Fam* **old f.** carroza *mf*, carcamal *mf*

**foggy** ['fɒgɪ] *adj* neblinoso(a); **a f. day** un día
de niebla; **it's f.** hay (mucha) niebla; *Fam* **I
haven't (got) the foggiest (idea)!** no tengo
ni la menor idea

**foghorn** ['fɒghɔːn] *n (on ship)* sirena *f* de niebla; **a voice like a f.** una voz estridente, un
vozarrón

**fogy** = **fogey**

**foible** ['fɔɪbəl] *n* manía *f*

**foil** [fɔɪl] **1** *n* (a) *(metal paper)* papel *m* de aluminio (b) **to act as a f.** **(to** or **for)** servir de
contrapunto (a or para) (c) *(sword)* florete *m*

**2** *vt (thwart)* frustrar, malograr

**foist** [fɔɪst] *vt* imponer **(on** a)

**fold¹** [fəʊld] *n (sheep)* **f.** redil *m*

**fold²** **1** *n* pliegue *m*

**2** *vt (cloth, paper)* doblar; *(chair, table)* plegar; **to
f. sth in two** *or* **in half** doblar algo por la
mitad; **to f. one's arms** cruzarse de brazos

**3** *vi* (a) *(of chair, table)* plegarse (b) *Fam (of
business)* quebrar

▸**fold up 1** *vt sep* doblar

**2** *vi (of map, chair)* plegarse

**folder** ['fəʊldə(r)] *n (file, document wallet)* carpeta *f*; *(ring binder)* carpeta *f* de anillas

**folding** ['fəʊldɪŋ] *adj (chair, table)* plegable; **f.
doors** puertas *fpl* plegables

**foliage** ['fəʊlɪɪdʒ] *n* follaje *m*

**folio** ['fəʊlɪəʊ] *(pl* **folios)** *n* folio *m*

**folk** [fəuk] **1** *npl Fam (people)* gente *f*; **the f. I work with** la gente con la que trabajo; **my/your folks** *(family)* mi/tu familia, mi/tu gente; *US (parents)* mis/tus padres

**2** *adj (traditional)* **f. dance** baile *m* popular *or* regional; **f. (music)** música *f* folk *or* popular; **f. singer** cantante *mf* de folk; **f. song** canción *f* folk; **f. tale** cuento *m* popular

**folklore** ['fəuklɔ:(r)] *n* folclor *m*, folclore *m*

**follicle** ['fɒlɪkəl] *n* folículo *m*

**follow** ['fɒləu] **1** *vt* **(a)** *(person, path, route)* seguir; **I think we're being followed** creo que nos están siguiendo; **the road follows the coast** la carretera va a lo largo de la costa; **to f. one's nose** *(go straight ahead)* seguir todo recto; *(act instinctively)* guiarse por el instinto; **to f. suit** seguir el ejemplo

**(b)** *(example, pattern, fashion, instructions)* seguir; *(career)* seguir

**(c)** *(understand)* seguir; **I don't quite f. you** no te sigo bien

**(d)** *(pay attention to)* seguir

**2** *vi* **(a)** *(come after)* seguir; **proceed as follows** proceda de la siguiente forma

**(b)** *(result)* **it follows that...** se sigue *or* deduce que...; **it follows from X that Y** de X se deduce que Y

**(c)** *(understand)* entender; **I don't f.** no (lo) entiendo

▶**follow on** *vi* continuar, seguir; **to f. on from my earlier remarks...** a lo anteriormente dicho quisiera añadir...

▶**follow through 1** *vt sep* **to f. a project through (to the end)** llevar a cabo un proyecto (hasta el final)

**2** *vi* llegar hasta el final

▶**follow up** *vt sep (advantage, success)* acrecentar; *(contact, job opportunity)* hacer un seguimiento de; **to f. up a clue** seguir una pista

**follower** ['fɒləuə(r)] *n* seguidor(ora) *m,f*

**following** ['fɒləuɪŋ] **1** *n (of team)* seguidores *mpl*; *(of politician, political party)* partidarios *mpl*; *(of TV programme)* audiencia *f*; *(of novelist, pop group)* admiradores *mpl*

**2** *pron* **the f. is the full list** a continuación figura la lista completa

**3** *adj* siguiente; **on the f. day** al día siguiente; **a f. wind** un viento favorable *or* a favor

**follow-up** ['fɒləuʌp] *n Com* seguimiento *m*

**folly** ['fɒlɪ] *n* locura *f*

**foment** [fə'ment] *vt (unrest, ill-feeling)* fomentar

**fond** [fɒnd] *adj* **(a)** **to be f. of sb** *(like)* tenerle cariño a alguien; **to become f. of sb** encariñarse con alguien; **she was f. of the occasional whisky** le gustaba tomarse un whisky

de vez en cuando **(b)** *(loving)* cariñoso(a); **f. memories** recuerdos *mpl* entrañables **(c)** *(hope, belief)* vano(a)

**fondle** ['fɒndəl] *vt* acariciar

**fondly** ['fɒndlɪ] *adv* **(a)** *(lovingly)* cariñosamente **(b)** *(naively)* **to f. imagine that...** creer ingenuamente que...

**fondness** ['fɒndnɪs] *n* **(a)** *(affection)* cariño *m* **(for** por), afecto *m* **(for** por) **(b)** *(liking)* afición *f* **(for** a), gusto *m* **(for** por)

**fondue** ['fɒndu:] *n* fondue *f*

**font** [fɒnt] *n* **(a)** *Rel* pila *f* bautismal **(b)** *Typ & Comptr* fuente *f*

**food** [fu:d] *n* comida *f*; **f. and drink** comida y bebida; **to be off one's f.** andar desganado(a); **to give sb f. for thought** servir a alguien como materia de reflexión; *Biol* **f. chain** cadena *f* alimentaria; **f. industry** industria *f* alimentaria; **f. poisoning** intoxicación *f* alimentaria; **f. processor** robot *m* de cocina

**foodstuffs** ['fu:dstʌfs] *npl* alimentos *mpl*

**fool** [fu:l] **1** *n (stupid person)* idiota *mf*; *(jester)* bufón *m*; **to play** *or* **act the f.** hacer el tonto; **to make a f. of sb** poner a alguien en ridículo; **to make a f. of oneself** hacer el ridículo; **(the) more f. you!** ¡peor para ti!; **I felt such a f.** me sentí como un tonto; **she's no** *or* **nobody's f.** no tiene un pelo de tonta; **they're living in a f.'s paradise** viven en las nubes

**2** *vt (deceive)* engañar; **to f. sb into doing sth** engañar a alguien para que haga algo; **you can't f. me** a mí no me engañas; **he's an expert? you could have fooled me!** ¿que es un experto? ¡quién lo hubiera dicho!

**3** *vi (act foolishly)* hacer el tonto *or* el indio; **stop fooling!** ¡deja de hacer el tonto!; **I was only fooling** estaba de broma

▶**fool about, fool around** *vi* **(a)** *(act foolishly)* hacer el tonto *or* el indio; **to f. about** *or* **around with sth** enredar con algo **(b)** *(waste time)* perder el tiempo **(c)** *(have affair)* tener un lío **(with** con)

**foolhardy** ['fu:lhɑ:dɪ] *adj* temerario(a)

**foolish** ['fu:lɪʃ] *adj (stupid)* tonto(a); *(imprudent)* absurdo(a), imprudente; **to do sth f.** hacer una tontería; **to make sb look f.** dejar a alguien en ridículo

**foolishly** ['fu:lɪʃlɪ] *adv (act)* irreflexivamente

**foolproof** ['fu:lpru:f] *adj (method, plan)* infalible

**foot** [fut] *(pl* **feet** [fi:t]) **1** *n* **(a)** *(of person)* pie *m*; *(of animal, chair)* pata *f*; **to put one's feet up** *(rest)* descansar; **to set f. in/on** poner los pies en; **she is on her feet all day** se pasa el día entero de pie; **to be on one's feet again** *(after illness)* estar recuperado(a); **on f.** a pie, andando; **it was wet under f.** el suelo estaba mojado; *Mil* **f. patrol** patrulla *f* de infantería; **f.**

**pump** bomba f de pie; **f. soldier** soldado mf de infantería

(**b**) *(lower part) (of mountain, stairs, page)* pie m

(**c**) *(in poetry)* pie m

(**d**) *(measurement)* pie m *(30,48 cm)*; **three f. or feet six (inches)** tres pies y seis pulgadas *(1,06 m)*; **at 2,000 feet** a dos mil pies *(609,6 m)*

(**e**) *(idioms)* **to have one's feet firmly on the ground** tener los pies en la tierra; **to have one f. in the grave** tener un pie en la tumba; **she hasn't put a f. wrong** no ha cometido un solo error; **to put one's f. down** *(be firm)* ponerse serio(a); *(refuse)* negarse en redondo; *Fam* **to put one's f. in it** meter la pata; **to find one's feet** *(in new surroundings, activity)* familiarizarse; **the job's not much, but it's a f. in the door** el trabajo no es gran cosa, pero supone un primer paso; **to have feet of clay** tener (los) pies de barro; *Fam* **my f.!** ¡y un jamón!

**2** vt **to f. the bill** pagar la cuenta

**footage** ['futɪdʒ] n *Cin* secuencias fpl

**foot-and-mouth disease** [futən'mauθ] n glosopeda f, fiebre f aftosa

**football** ['futbɔːl] n *(sport)* fútbol m; *(ball)* balón m (de fútbol); **f. club** club m (de fútbol); **f. fan** hincha mf, forofo(a) m,f; **f. ground** estadio m de fútbol; **f. hooligan** hincha m violento; **f. pitch** campo m de fútbol; **f. player** futbolista mf; *Br* **f. pools** quiniela f; **f. supporter** hincha mf, forofo(a) m,f

**footballer** ['futbɔːlə(r)] n futbolista mf

**footbridge** ['futbrɪdʒ] n puente m peatonal

**foothills** ['futhɪlz] npl estribaciones fpl

**foothold** ['futhəuld] n punto m de apoyo; *Fig* **to gain a f.** afianzarse

**footing** ['futɪŋ] n (**a**) **to lose one's f.** *(on hill, ladder)* perder el equilibrio (**b**) **on an equal f.** de igual a igual; **to be on a friendly f. with sb** tener relaciones amistosas con alguien

**footlights** ['futlaɪts] npl *Th* candilejas fpl

**footloose** ['futluːs] adj libre de ataduras; **to be f. and fancy-free** ser libre como el viento

**footman** ['futmən] n lacayo m

**footnote** ['futnəut] n nota f a pie de página

**footpath** ['futpɑːθ] n sendero m, senda f

**footprint** ['futprɪnt] n huella f, pisada f

**footrest** ['futrest] n *(under desk, on motorcycle)* reposapiés m inv

**footsie** ['futsɪ] n *Fam* **to play f. with sb** = acariciar a alguien con el pie por debajo de la mesa

**footsore** ['futsɔː(r)] adj con los pies doloridos

**footstep** ['futstep] n paso m; *Fig* **to follow in sb's footsteps** seguir los pasos de alguien

**footwear** ['futweə(r)] n calzado m

**footwork** ['futwɜːk] n *(in dancing, sports)* juego m de piernas; *Fig* **fancy f.** *(in difficult situation)* malabarismos mpl

**fop** [fɒp] n *Pej* petimetre m

**foppish** ['fɒpɪʃ] adj peripuesto(a)

**for** [fɔː(r)] unstressed [fə(r)] **1** prep (**a**) *(reason)* por; **they chose him f. his looks** lo eligieron por su aspecto; **she couldn't sleep f. the pain** no pudo dormir a causa del dolor

(**b**) *(purpose, destination)* para; **to leave f. France** salir hacia or para Francia; **there's no time f. that** no hay tiempo para eso; **it's f. you** es para ti; **what's it f.?** ¿para qué es?; **can you give me something f. the pain?** ¿me puede dar algo para el dolor?

(**c**) *(in exchange for)* **I bought it f. £10** lo compré por 10 libras; **you get a lot f. your money** el dinero te da mucho de sí

(**d**) *(with regard to)* para; **he is big f. his age** es grande para su edad; **as f. him/that,...** en cuanto a él/eso,...; **they sell ten red bikes f. every black one** se venden diez bicicletas de color rojo por cada una de color negro

(**e**) *(representing)* **A f. Andrew** A de Andrés; **what's the Russian f. "book"?** ¿cómo se dice "book" en ruso?

(**f**) *(duration)* durante; **I was there f. a month** pasé un mes allí; **I've been here f. a month** llevo un mes aquí; **I will be here f. a month** voy a pasar un mes aquí; **I haven't been there f. a month** hace un mes que no voy (por allí); **we have enough food f. two days** tenemos comida suficiente para dos días

(**g**) *(point in time)* **f. the first/last time** por primera/última vez; **I need it f. Friday** lo necesito (para) el viernes; **can you do it f. next Monday?** ¿lo puedes hacer para el lunes que viene?

(**h**) *(in favour of)* **to be f. sth** estar absolutamente a favor de algo; *Fam* **I'm all f. it!** ¡estoy absolutamente a favor!

(**i**) *(introducing an infinitive clause)* **it is too early f. me to decide** es demasiado pronto para decidirme; **it will be difficult/easy f. her to come** lo va a tener difícil/fácil para venir; **it took an hour f. us to get there** tardamos una hora en llegar

(**j**) *(in phrases)* *Fam* **he's f. it!** ¡se la va a cargar!; **f. all the good it will do!** ¡para lo que va a servir!; **f. all his wealth, he was still unhappy** a pesar de todo su dinero, no era feliz; **that's men f. you!** ¡los hombres, ya se sabe!

**2** conj *Literary (because)* dado que

**forage** ['fɒrɪdʒ] **1** n *(animal food)* forraje m; *Mil* **f. cap** gorra f militar

**2** vi **to f. for** buscar

**foray** ['fɒreɪ] *(pl* forays*)* n incursión f **(into** en)

**forbear** [fɔːˈbeə(r)] (*pt* **forbore** [fɔːˈbɔː(r)], *pp* **forborne** [fɔːˈbɔːn]) *vi Formal* **to f. from doing sth** abstenerse de hacer algo, contenerse para no hacer algo

**forbearance** [fɔːˈbeərəns] *n* paciencia *f*, tolerancia *f*

**forbid** [fəˈbɪd] (*pt* **forbade** [fəˈbæd, fəˈbeɪd], *pp* **forbidden** [fəˈbɪdən]) *vt* prohibir; **to f. sb to do sth** prohibir a alguien que haga algo; **God f.!** ¡Dios no lo quiera!

**forbidden** [fəˈbɪdən] *adj* prohibido(a); **smoking/talking (is) f.** (está) prohibido fumar/hablar

**forbidding** [fəˈbɪdɪŋ] *adj* (*appearance, look*) severo(a); (*sky*) amenazador(ora); (*landscape*) agreste; (*task*) dificultoso(a)

**force** [fɔːs] **1** *n* (a) (*strength, violence*) fuerza *f*; **to use f.** emplear la fuerza; **by sheer** *or* **brute f.** por la fuerza

(b) (*power, influence*) fuerza *f*; **the forces of Nature** las fuerzas de la naturaleza; **a f. for good** una fuerza del bien; **f. of circumstance(s)** causas *fpl* de fuerza mayor; **the f. of gravity** la fuerza de la gravedad; **f. of habit** la fuerza de la costumbre; **various forces conspired to bring about his downfall** diversas causas contribuyeron a su caída

(c) *Mil* fuerza *f*; **the (armed) forces** las fuerzas armadas; **the police f.** la policía, el cuerpo de policía; **to join forces (to do sth)** unir fuerzas (para hacer algo); **they turned out in (full) f.** se presentaron en gran número

(d) (*of law*) **to come into f.** entrar en vigor

**2** *vt* (a) (*compel*) **to f. sb to do sth** *or* **into doing sth** forzar a alguien a hacer algo; **they forced the enemy back** obligaron a retroceder al enemigo; **to f. sth on sb** imponer algo a alguien

(b) (*use force on*) (*door, lock*) forzar; **to f. the issue** acelerar las cosas; **to f. sb's hand** forzar a alguien a tomar una decisión; **to f. a car off the road** obligar a un coche a salirse de la carretera; **to f. one's way through a crowd** abrirse paso a través de una multitud; **to f. oneself on sb** (*sexually*) intentar forzar a alguien

▶**force open** *vt sep* forzar

**forced** [fɔːst] *adj* (*manner, laugh*) forzado(a); **f. labour** trabajos *mpl* forzados; *Av* **f. landing** aterrizaje *m* forzoso; *Mil* **f. march** marcha *f* forzada

**force-feed** [ˈfɔːsˈfiːd] (*pt & pp* **force-fed** [ˈfɔːsˈfed]) *vt* dar de comer a la fuerza

**forceful** [ˈfɔːsfʊl] *adj* (*person, argument*) poderoso(a)

**forceps** [ˈfɔːseps] *npl Med* fórceps *m inv*

**forcible** [ˈfɔːsɪbəl] *adj* (*reminder*) contundente; *Law* **f. entry** allanamiento *m* de morada

**forcibly** [ˈfɔːsɪblɪ] *adv* (a) (*by force*) por la fuerza (b) (*convincingly*) de manera contundente

**ford** [fɔːd] **1** *n* vado *m*
**2** *vt* vadear

**fore** [fɔː(r)] **1** *n* **to come to the f.** cobrar importancia
**2** *adv Naut* **they searched the ship f. and aft** registraron el barco de proa a popa

**forearm** [ˈfɔːrɑːm] *n* antebrazo *m*

**forebear** [ˈfɔːbeə(r)] *n* antepasado(a) *m,f*, ancestro *m*

**foreboding** [fɔːˈbəʊdɪŋ] *n* presentimento *m* ominoso

**forecast** [ˈfɔːkɑːst] **1** *n* pronóstico *m*; *Com* previsión *f*; **the (weather) f.** (*prediction*) el pronóstico meteorológico; (*programme*) el parte meteorológico, el tiempo
**2** *vt* (*pt & pp* **forecast(ed)**) pronosticar

**foreclose** [fɔːˈkləʊz] *vt Fin* **to f. a mortgage** ejecutar una hipoteca

**forecourt** [ˈfɔːkɔːt] *n* (*of petrol station*) = explanada *f* delantera

**forefathers** [ˈfɔːfɑːðəz] *npl* ancestros *mpl*

**forefinger** [ˈfɔːfɪŋɡə(r)] *n* (dedo *m*) índice *m*

**forefront** [ˈfɔːfrʌnt] *n* **to be in the f. (of)** estar a la vanguardia (de)

**forego** [fɔːˈɡəʊ] (*pt* **forwent** [fɔːˈwent], *pp* **forgone** [fɔːˈɡɒn]) *vt* renunciar a

**foregone** [ˈfɔːɡɒn] *adj* **the result was a f. conclusion** el resultado ya se conocía de antemano

**foreground** [ˈfɔːɡraʊnd] **1** *n* primer plano *m*; **in the f.** (*in picture*) en primer plano; (*issue, person*) en primer plano de actualidad, en el candelero
**2** *vt* poner de relieve

**forehand** [ˈfɔːhænd] *n* (*tennis stroke*) derecha *f*

**forehead** [ˈfɔrɪd, ˈfɔːhed] *n* frente *f*

**foreign** [ˈfɒrɪn] *adj* (a) (*from another country*) extranjero(a); **f. aid** (*to another country*) ayuda *f* al exterior; (*from another country*) ayuda *f* extranjera *or* del exterior; *Pol* **f. affairs** política *f* exterior, asuntos *mpl* exteriores; *Journ* **f. correspondent** corresponsal *mf* (en el extranjero); *Econ* **f. debt** deuda *f* exterior *or* externa; *Mil* **F. Legion** legión *f* extranjera; *Pol* **F. Minister**, *Br* **F. Secretary** ministro(a) *m,f* de Asuntos Exteriores; *Br Pol* **F. Office** ministerio *m* de Asuntos Exteriores; *Econ* **f. trade** comercio *m* exterior (b) (*not characteristic of*) ajeno(a); *Med* **f. body** cuerpo *m* extraño

**foreigner** [ˈfɒrɪnə(r)] *n* extranjero(a) *m,f*

**foreleg** [ˈfɔːleg] *n* pata *f* delantera

**foreman** [ˈfɔːmən] *n Ind* encargado *m*; (*of jury*) presidente *m*, portavoz *m*

**foremost** [ˈfɔːməʊst] *adj* principal

**forename** [ˈfɔːneɪm] *n* nombre *m* (de pila)

**forensic** [fə'rensɪk] *adj Law* forense; **f. evidence** pruebas *fpl* forenses; **f. medicine** medicina *f* forense; **f. scientist** forense *mf*

**foreplay** ['fɔːpleɪ] *n* juego *m* amoroso *(antes del coito)*

**forerunner** ['fɔːrʌnə(r)] *n* predecesor(ora) *m,f*

**foresee** [fɔː'siː] *(pt* **foresaw** [fɔː'sɔː], *pp* **foreseen** [fɔː'siːn]) *vt* prever

**foreseeable** [fɔː'siːəbəl] *adj* previsible; **in the f. future** en un futuro próximo *or* no muy lejano

**foreshadow** [fɔː'ʃædəʊ] *vt* presagiar, anunciar

**foresight** ['fɔːsaɪt] *n* previsión *f*; **lack of f.** falta *f* de previsión

**foreskin** ['fɔːskɪn] *n Anat* prepucio *m*

**forest** ['fɒrɪst] *n* bosque *m*; **f. fire** incendio *m* forestal

**forestall** [fɔː'stɔːl] *vt (attempt, criticism, rivals)* anticiparse a, adelantarse a

**forester** ['fɒrɪstə(r)] *n* guardabosque *mf*, guarda *mf* forestal

**forestry** ['fɒrɪstrɪ] *n* silvicultura *f*; *Br* **the F. Commission** = organismo oficial británico dedicado al cuidado y explotación forestales; **f. worker** trabajador(ora) *m,f* forestal

**foretaste** ['fɔːteɪst] *n* anticipo *m*

**foretell** [fɔː'tel] *(pt & pp* **foretold** [fɔː'təʊld]) *vt* predecir

**forethought** ['fɔːθɔːt] *n* previsión *f*

**forever** [fə'revə(r)] **1** *n* **to take f. (to do sth)** tardar una eternidad (en hacer algo)
**2** *adv (until end of time)* para siempre; *(repeatedly)* constantemente; **he was f. changing his mind** siempre estaba cambiando de opinión

**forewarn** [fɔː'wɔːn] *vt* advertir; *Prov* **forewarned is forearmed** hombre prevenido vale por dos

**foreword** ['fɔːwɜːd] *n* prólogo *m*

**forfeit** ['fɔːfɪt] **1** *n* **(in game)** prenda *f*; *Law* sanción *f*
**2** *vt (right, property, sb's respect)* renunciar a, sacrificar

**forgave** [fə'geɪv] *pt of* **forgive**

**forge** [fɔːdʒ] **1** *n (factory)* fundición *f*; *(of blacksmith)* forja *f*, fragua *f*
**2** *vt* **(a)** *(metal, alliance)* forjar **(b)** *(counterfeit)* falsificar
▸**forge ahead** *vi (make progress)* progresar a pasos agigantados; *(in competition)* tomar la delantera

**forged** [fɔːdʒd] *adj (banknote, letter)* falso(a), falsificado(a)

**forgery** ['fɔːdʒərɪ] *n* falsificación *f*; **it's a f.** es una falsificación

**forget** [fə'get] *(pt* **forgot** [fə'gɒt], *pp* **forgotten** [fə'gɒtən]) **1** *vt* olvidar; **to f. to do sth** olvidarse de hacer algo; **to f. how to do sth** olvidar cómo se hace algo; **to be forgotten (by)** caer en el olvido (de); *Fam* **f. it!** *(in reply to apology)* olvídalo; *(in reply to thanks)* no hay de qué; *(stop talking about it)* dejémoslo; *Fam* **you can f. the holiday** ya puedes decir adiós a las vacaciones
**2** *vi* olvidarse **(about** de); **before I f.** antes de que se me olvide; **let's f. about it** olvidémoslo

**forgetful** [fə'getfʊl] *adj* olvidadizo(a)

**forget-me-not** [fə'getmɪnɒt] *n* nomeolvides *m inv*

**forgivable** [fə'gɪvəbəl] *adj* perdonable

**forgive** [fə'gɪv] *(pt* **forgave** [fə'geɪv], *pp* **forgiven** [fə'gɪvən]) **1** *vt* perdonar; **to f. sb (for sth)** perdonar (algo) a alguien
**2** *vi* **to f. and forget** perdonar y olvidar

**forgiven** [fə'gɪvən] *pp of* **forgive**

**forgiveness** [fə'gɪvnɪs] *n* perdón *m*; **to ask (sb) for f.** pedir perdón (a alguien)

**forgiving** [fə'gɪvɪŋ] *adj* indulgente

**forgo** = **forego**

**forgot** [fə'gɒt] *pt of* **forget**

**forgotten** [fə'gɒtən] *pp of* **forget**

**fork** [fɔːk] **1** *n* **(a)** *(for food)* tenedor *m* **(b)** *(for lifting hay)* horca *f* **(c)** *(in road)* bifurcación *f*; **take the left f.** tomar el desvío a *or* de la izquierda
**2** *vi (of road)* bifurcarse
▸**fork out** *Fam* **1** *vt sep (money)* aflojar, apoquinar
**2** *vi* **to f. (out)** pagar

**forked** [fɔːkt] *adj (tongue)* bífido(a); *(stick)* bifurcado(a); **f. lightning** relámpagos *mpl (bifurcados)*

**fork-lift truck** ['fɔːklɪft'trʌk] *n* carretilla *f* elevadora

**forlorn** [fə'lɔːn] *adj (place)* abandonado(a); *(look)* desamparado(a); *(belief, attempt)* desesperado(a); **in the f. hope that...** con la vana esperanza de que...

**form** [fɔːm] **1** *n* **(a)** *(shape)* forma *f*; **in the f. of...** en forma de...; **to take the f. of...** consistir en...; **f. and content** forma y fondo *or* contenido
(**b)** *(type)* **it's a f. of madness** es una forma de locura; **a f. of address** una fórmula de tratamiento
(**c)** *(formality)* **as a matter of f., for f.'s sake** por guardar las formas; **it's good/bad f.** es de buena/mala educación
(**d)** *(for applications, orders)* impreso *m*, formulario *m*; **to fill in** *or* **out a f.** rellenar un impreso
(**e)** *(condition)* forma *f* (física); **to be in (good) f.** estar en (buena) forma
(**f)** *(performance) (in horseracing)* reciente

historial *m*, últimas marcas *fpl*; **on present f.** de seguir así; **to be on (good) f.** estar en plena forma

**(g)** *Br Sch (class)* clase *f*; *(year)* curso *m*

**2** *vt (in general)* formar; *(relationship, friendship)* establecer; *(plan)* concebir; *(obstacle)* constituir; **to f. an idea/opinion** formarse una idea/una opinión; **to f. part of sth** formar parte de algo

**3** *vi* formarse

**formal** ['fɔːməl] *adj (manner, offer)* formal; **f. dress** traje *m* de etiqueta; **f. education** formación *f* académica

**formality** [fɔː'mælɪtɪ] *n* formalidad *f*

**formalize** ['fɔːməlaɪz] *vt* formalizar

**formally** ['fɔːməlɪ] *adv (with formality)* formalmente; *(officially)* oficialmente

**format** ['fɔːmæt] **1** *n* formato *m*

**2** *vt ( pt & pp* **formatted)** *Comptr* formatear

**formation** [fɔː'meɪʃən] *n (act, arrangement)* formación *f*; **f. flying** vuelo *m* en formación

**formative** ['fɔːmətɪv] *adj* formativo(a); **the f. years** el periodo en que se forja la personalidad

**former** ['fɔːmə(r)] **1** *adj (pupil, colleague)* antiguo(a); **in a f. life** en una vida anterior; **he is a mere shadow of his f. self** no es más que una sombra de lo que fue

**2** *pron* **the f.** el/la primero(a); *(plural)* los/las primeros(as)

**formerly** ['fɔːməlɪ] *adv* antiguamente

**formidable** ['fɔːmɪdəbəl] *adj (opponent, difficulty)* terrible; *(performance, talent)* formidable

**formula** ['fɔːmjʊlə] *( pl* **formulas** *or* **formulae** ['fɔːmjʊliː]) *n (a) (in general)* fórmula *f*; **the f. for success** la clave del éxito; **a peace/pay f.** una fórmula para la paz/de pago; *Sport* **F. One** fórmula *f* uno **(b)** *US (baby food)* leche *f* maternizada

**formulate** ['fɔːmjʊleɪt] *vt* formular

**fornication** [fɔːnɪ'keɪʃən] *n Formal* fornicación *f*

**forsake** [fə'seɪk] *( pt* **forsook** [fə'sʊk], *pp* **forsaken** [fə'seɪkən]) *vt Literary* abandonar

**forswear** [fɔː'sweə(r)] *( pt* **forswore** [fɔː'swɔː(r)], *pp* **forsworn** [fɔː'swɔːn]) *vt Formal* renunciar a

**fort** [fɔːt] *n Mil* fortaleza *f*, fuerte *m*; *Fig* **to hold the f.** quedarse al cargo

**forte** ['fɔːtɪ] *n* fuerte *m*; **punctuality is not his f.** la puntualidad no es su fuerte

**forth** [fɔːθ] *adv* **to go f.** partir; **and so f.** y así sucesivamente; **to walk back and f.** ir de aquí para allá; **from that day f.** a partir de ese día

**forthcoming** [fɔːθ'kʌmɪŋ] *adj (a) (imminent) (election)* próximo(a); *(book)* de próxima aparición **(b)** *(available)* **no money/help was f.** no había dinero/ayuda disponible **(c)** *(informative)* comunicativo(a)

**forthright** ['fɔːθraɪt] *adj* directo(a), franco(a)

**forthwith** [fɔːθ'wɪθ] *adv Formal* en el acto

**fortieth** ['fɔːtɪəθ] *n & adj* cuadragésimo(a) *m,f*

**fortification** [fɔːtɪfɪ'keɪʃən] *n* fortificación *f*

**fortified** ['fɔːtɪfaɪd] *adj* **(a)** *(town)* fortificado(a) **(b) f. wine** = vino fuerte tipo Oporto o Jerez

**fortify** ['fɔːtɪfaɪ] *vt Mil* fortificar; **to f. oneself** fortalecerse

**fortitude** ['fɔːtɪtjuːd] *n* fortaleza *f*, entereza *f*

**fortnight** ['fɔːtnaɪt] *n Br* quincena *f*; **a f. today** en quince días; **a f.'s holiday** quince días de vacaciones

**fortnightly** ['fɔːtnaɪtlɪ] *Br* **1** *adj* quincenal

**2** *adv* quincenalmente, cada quince días

**fortress** ['fɔːtrɪs] *n* fortaleza *f*

**fortuitous** [fɔː'tjuːɪtəs] *adj* casual, fortuito(a)

**fortunate** ['fɔːtʃənət] *adj* afortunado(a); **to be f. enough to do sth** tener la suerte de hacer algo

**fortunately** ['fɔːtʃənətlɪ] *adv* afortunadamente

**fortune** ['fɔːtʃən] *n* **(a)** *(riches)* fortuna *f*; **to make a** *or* **one's f.** hacer una fortuna; **Fam it cost me a (small) f.** me ha costado una fortuna **(b)** *(luck)* suerte *f*, fortuna *f*; **good/bad f.** buena/mala suerte; **the changing fortunes of…** los avatares de…; **to tell sb's f.** decir a alguien la buenaventura

**fortune-teller** ['fɔːtʃəntelə(r)] *n* adivino(a) *m,f*

**forty** ['fɔːtɪ] **1** *n* cuarenta *m*

**2** *adj* cuarenta; *Fam* **to have f. winks** echarse una siestecita; *see also* **eighty**

**forum** ['fɔːrəm] *n* foro *m*; **a f. for debate** un foro de debate

**forward** ['fɔːwəd] **1** *n Sport* delantero(a) *m,f*

**2** *adj* **(a)** *(position)* delantero(a); *(movement)* hacia delante; **f. planning** planificación *f* (de futuro); *Fin* **f. market** mercado *m* de futuros **(b)** *(impudent, bold)* atrevido(a)

**3** *adv* **(a)** *(of time)* **from this/that day f.** desde este/ese día en adelante; **to put the clocks f.** adelantar los relojes **(b)** *(of direction)* hacia delante **(c)** *(of position)* delante; **we're too far f.** estamos demasiado delante

**4** *vt* **(a)** *(letter)* reexpedir, remitir; **to f. sth to sb** enviar algo a alguien **(b)** *(one's career, interests)* promover

**forwarding agent** ['fɔːwədɪŋ'eɪdʒənt] *n Com* transitario *m*

**forward-looking** ['fɔːwədlʊkɪŋ] *adj* con visión de futuro, progresista

**forwards** ['fɔːwədz] *adv* = **forward**

**fossil** ['fɒs(ɪ)l] *n* fósil *m; Fam* **an old f.** *(person)* un (viejo) carcamal; **f. fuel** combustible *m* fósil

**fossilized** ['fɒsɪlaɪzd] *adj also Fig* fosilizado(a)

**foster** ['fɒstə(r)] **1** *adj* **f. child** niño(a) *m,f* en régimen de acogida; **f. parents** familia *f* de acogida; **f. home** hogar *m* de acogida

**2** *vt* (a) *(child)* adoptar (temporalmente), acoger (b) *(idea, hope, friendship)* fomentar

**fought** [fɔːt] *pt & pp of* **fight**

**foul** [faʊl] **1** *n Sport* falta *f*

**2** *adj* (a) *(disgusting) (smell, taste)* asqueroso(a); *(weather)* espantoso(a); **to be in a f. temper** estar de un humor de perros; **to be f. to sb** tratar fatal a alguien; **f. air** aire *m* viciado; **f. breath** aliento *m* fétido; **f. language** lenguaje *m* soez (b) *(illegal) Sport* **f. play** juego *m* sucio; *Law* **f. play is not suspected** no hay sospecha de que exista un acto delictivo

**3** *adv* (a) **to smell/taste f.** oler/saber asqueroso(a) *or* fatal (b) **to fall f. of the law** tener problemas con la ley

**4** *vt* (a) *(make dirty)* ensuciar; *(pollute)* contaminar (b) *(entangle)* **weeds had fouled the propeller** unas algas atascaron la hélice (c) *Sport* **to f. sb** hacerle (una) falta a alguien

▶**foul up** *vt sep Fam (ruin)* echar a perder, estropear

**foul-mouthed** ['faʊl'maʊðd] *adj* grosero(a), soez

**found¹** [faʊnd] *vt* (a) *(city, organization)* fundar (b) *(suspicions, hope)* fundar, basar (**on** en); **the story is founded on fact** la historia se basa en hechos reales

**found²** *pt & pp of* **find**

**foundation** [faʊn'deɪʃən] *n* (a) *(act of founding, institution)* fundación *f* (b) *(basis) (of theory, belief)* fundamento *m*; **the rumour is without f.** el rumor no tiene fundamento (c) *Constr* **the foundations** los cimientos; *Fig* **the foundations of modern society** los pilares de la sociedad moderna; **f. stone** primera piedra *f* (d) *(make-up)* **f. (cream)** (crema *f* de) base *f*

**founder¹** ['faʊndə(r)] *n (of hospital, school)* fundador(ora) *m,f*; **f. member** miembro *mf* fundador(ora)

**founder²** *vi (of project, talks)* irse a pique (**on** en)

**founding father** ['faʊndɪŋ'fɑːðə(r)] *n* padre *m* fundador

**foundling** ['faʊndlɪŋ] *n Old-fashioned* expósito(a) *m,f*

**foundry** ['faʊndrɪ] *n* fundición *f*

**fount** [faʊnt] *n Literary & Fig* fuente *f*

**fountain** ['faʊntɪn] *n* fuente *f*; **f. pen** pluma *f* (estilográfica)

**four** [fɔː(r)] **1** *n* cuatro *m*; **on all fours** a gatas, a cuatro patas

**2** *adj* cuatro; **the f. winds** los cuatro vientos; **to the f. corners of the earth** a todos los rincones del orbe; *see also* **eight**

**four-door** ['fɔːdɔː(r)] *n* de cuatro puertas; **f. saloon** berlina *f*; **f. hatchback** cinco puertas *m*

**four-eyes** ['fɔːraɪz] *n Fam* cuatro ojos *mf inv*

**four-figure** ['fɔːfɪgə(r)] *adj* de cuatro cifras; **a f. sum** una suma de dinero de cuatro cifras

**fourfold** ['fɔːfəʊld] **1** *adj* **a f. increase (in)** cuatro veces más (de)

**2** *adv* cuatro veces

**four-legged** ['fɔː'legɪd] *adj* cuadrúpedo(a); *Hum* **f. friend** amigo *m* cuadrúpedo

**four-letter word** ['fɔːletə'wɜːd] *n* palabrota *f*, taco *m*

**four-poster** ['fɔː'pəʊstə(r)] *n* **f. (bed)** cama *f* de dosel

**foursome** ['fɔːsəm] *n* grupo *m* de cuatro; *(for tennis match, card game)* dos parejas *fpl*

**fourteen** ['fɔː'tiːn] *n & adj* catorce *m*; *see also* **eight**

**fourteenth** [fɔː'tiːnθ] **1** *n* (a) *(fraction)* catorceavo *m*, catorceava parte *f* (b) *(in series)* decimocuarto(a) *m,f* (c) *(of month)* catorce *m*

**2** *adj* decimocuarto(a); *see also* **eleventh**

**fourth** [fɔːθ] **1** *n* (a) *(in series)* cuarto(a) *m,f* (b) *(of month)* cuatro *m*

**2** *adj* cuarto(a); *see also* **eighth**

**fourthly** ['fɔːθlɪ] *adv* en cuarto lugar

**four-wheel drive** ['fɔːwiːl'draɪv] *n* tracción *f* a las cuatro ruedas

**fowl** [faʊl] *n (pl* **fowl)** *n* ave *f* de corral

**fox** [fɒks] **1** *n* zorro *m*; *Fig* **a sly old f.** *(cunning person)* un viejo zorro; **f. cub** cría *f* de zorro; **f. hunt** caza *f* del zorro

**2** *vt Fam (perplex)* dejar pasmado(a); *(deceive)* burlar, engañar

**foxglove** ['fɒksglʌv] *n* digital *f*, dedalera *f*

**fox-hunting** ['fɒkshʌntɪŋ] *n* caza *f* del zorro

**foxtrot** ['fɒkstrɒt] **1** *n* foxtrot *m*

**2** *vi (pt & pp* **foxtrotted)** bailar el foxtrot

**foxy** ['fɒksɪ] *adj* (a) *Fam* astuto(a), zorro (b) *US Fam* sexy

**foyer** ['fɔɪeɪ] *n* vestíbulo *m*

**fractal** ['fræktəl] *n* fractal *m*

**fraction** ['frækʃən] *n Math* fracción *f*, quebrado *m*; *Fig (small part)* fracción *f*; **a f. too small/large** un poquitín pequeño/grande

**fractional** ['frækʃənəl] *adj (very small)* ínfimo(a); *(decline, hesitation)* mínimo(a), ligero(a)

**fractious** ['frækʃəs] *adj* irritable

**fracture** ['fræktʃə(r)] **1** *n* fractura *f*

**2** *vt* fracturar

**3** *vi* fracturarse

**fragile** ['frædʒaɪl] *adj* frágil

**fragility** [frə'dʒɪlɪtɪ] *n* fragilidad *f*

**fragment 1** *n* ['frægmənt] *(of object, story)* fragmento *m*
**2** [fræg'ment] *vi (of object)* romperse; *(of organization)* fragmentarse

**fragrance** ['freɪgrəns] *n* fragancia *f*

**fragrant** ['freɪgrənt] *adj* fragante

**frail** [freɪl] *adj (person)* delicado(a), frágil; *(object, beauty, happiness)* frágil

**frailty** ['freɪltɪ] *n* fragilidad *f*

**frame** [freɪm] **1** *n* (a) *(of picture, door)* marco *m*; *(of person, animal)* cuerpo *m*; *(of building, bridge)* estructura *f*; *(of bicycle)* cuadro *m*; *(of spectacles)* montura *f* (b) Fig **f. of mind** humor *m*, estado *m* de ánimo; **f. of reference** marco *m* de referencia
**2** *vt* (a) *(picture) also Fig* enmarcar (b) *(answer, legislation)* formular (c) *Fam (falsely incriminate)* tender una trampa a

**framework** ['freɪmwɜːk] *n (of structure)* estructura *f*; Fig *(for talks)* marco *m*

**franc** [fræŋk] *n (currency)* franco *m*; **Belgian/French/Swiss f.** franco *m* belga/francés/suizo

**France** [frɑːns] *n* Francia *f*

**franchise** ['fræntʃaɪz] **1** *n* (a) Com franquicia *f* (b) Pol sufragio *m*
**2** *vt* Com franquiciar

**Franciscan** [fræn'sɪskən] *n & adj* franciscano(a) *m,f*

**francophile** ['fræŋkəʊfaɪl] *n* francófilo(a) *m,f*

**francophone** ['fræŋkəʊfəʊn] *n & adj* francófono(a) *m,f*

**frank** [fræŋk] **1** *adj (person, answer)* franco(a); **to be f.,...** francamente,...
**2** *vt (letter)* franquear

**Frank** [fræŋk] *n Hist* franco(a) *m,f*

**Frankfurt** [fræŋkfɑːt] *n* Fráncfort

**frankfurter** ['fræŋkfɜːtə(r)] *n (sausage)* salchicha *f* de Fráncfort

**frankincense** ['fræŋkɪnsens] *n* incienso *m*

**frankly** ['fræŋklɪ] *adv* francamente; **f., I couldn't care less** la verdad, me da igual

**frantic** ['fræntɪk] *adj (rush, pace)* frenético(a); **f. with worry** angustiado(a)

**frantically** ['fræntɪklɪ] *adv* frenéticamente

**fraternal** [frə'tɜːnəl] *adj* fraterno(a), fraternal

**fraternity** [frə'tɜːnɪtɪ] *n* (a) *(brotherliness)* fraternidad *f*; *(religious group)* hermandad *f*, cofradía *f*; **the medical/banking f.** el gremio médico/de la banca (b) US Univ = asociación de estudiantes que suele funcionar como club social; **f. house** = residencia perteneciente a dicha asociación

**fraternize** ['frætənaɪz] *vi* confraternizar (**with** con)

**fraud** [frɔːd] *n* (a) *(person)* impostor(ora) *m,f* (b) *(deception)* fraude *m*; **to obtain sth by f.** conseguir algo por medios fraudulentos; **f. squad** brigada *f* de delitos económicos, brigada anticorrupción

**fraudulent** ['frɔːdjʊlənt] *adj* fraudulento(a)

**fraught** [frɔːt] *adj (person, situation)* tenso(a), tirante; **f. with danger/emotion** cargado(a) de peligro/emoción

**fray¹** [freɪ] *n (brawl)* contienda *f*, combate *m*; **to enter the f.** entrar en liza

**fray² 1** *vt (material)* deshilachar
**2** *vi (of material)* deshilacharse; *(of nerves, tempers)* crisparse

**frazzle** ['fræzəl] *n* **to be burnt to a f.** estar (totalmente) carbonizado(a)

**frazzled** ['fræzəld] *adj Fam (worn out)* **to be f.** estar hecho(a) migas

**freak** [friːk] **1** *n* (a) *(strange being)* engendro *m*, monstruo *m*; **by a f. of fortune** por un capricho del destino; **f. show** = espectáculo que consiste en exhibir a personas con extrañas anomalías físicas; **f. storm** tormenta *f* inesperada (b) *(enthusiast)* fanático(a) *mf*; Fam **jazz/film f.** fanático(a) del jazz/cine
**2** *vi* = **freak out**

▶**freak out** *Fam* **1** *vt sep (shock)* alucinar; *(scare)* meter canguelo a
**2** *vi (become angry)* ponerse hecho(a) una furia; **I freaked out** *(panicked)* me entró la neura

**freckle** ['frekəl] *n* peca *f*

**free** [friː] **1** *adj* (a) *(unrestricted)* libre (**from** or of de); **to be f. to do sth** ser libre para hacer algo; **to set sb f.** liberar a alguien; **f. and easy** relajado(a); **feel f. to borrow the car** coge el coche cuando quieras; **feel f. to help yourself to tea** sírvete té si quieres; **she didn't feel f. to...** no se atrevía a...; **as f. as a bird** libre como el viento; **to be a f. agent** *(in general)* poder obrar a su antojo; *(of sports player)* tener la carta de libertad; Fig **to have a f. hand** *(to make decisions)* tener carta blanca; Econ **f. enterprise** empresa *f* libre; **f. fall** *(of parachutist)* caída *f* libre; *(of economy)* caída *f* en picado; **f. kick** *(in football)* golpe *m* franco; Econ **f. market** libre mercado *m*; **f. speech** libertad *f* de expresión; **f. trade** librecambio *m*; **f. verse** verso *m* libre; **f. will** *(generally)* propia voluntad *f*; *(in philosophy, theology)* libre albedrío *m*
(b) *(unoccupied)* libre; **I am f. tomorrow** mañana estoy libre; **is this seat f.?** ¿está libre este asiento?; **f. time** tiempo *m* libre
(c) *(without charge)* gratuito(a), gratis; **f. gift** obsequio *m* (promocional)
(d) *Ironic (generous)* **he is very f. with his advice** es demasiado pródigo a la hora de dar consejo

**2** *adv (without charge)* gratis, gratuitamente; **for f.** gratis

**3** *vt (pt & pp* **freed** [fri:d]*) (prisoner, funds, mechanism)* liberar (**from** de); *(time, place)* desocupar; *(something stuck)* soltar; **to f. oneself from** *or* **of sth** librarse de algo

**freedom** ['fri:dəm] *n* libertad *f;* **to have the f. to do sth** tener libertad para hacer algo; **f. of information/speech/worship** libertad de información/expresión/culto; **f. of the press** libertad *f* de prensa; **to give sb the f. of the city** entregar la llave de la ciudad a alguien; **f. fighter** luchador(ora) *m,f* por la libertad

**free-for-all** ['fri:fərɔ:l] *n Fam (fight, discussion)* cisco *m,* gresca *f;* **it turned into a f.** degeneró en un cisco *or* una gresca

**freehold** ['fri:həʊld] *n Law* propiedad *f* absoluta

**freeholder** ['fri:həʊldə(r)] *n* propietario(a) *m,f* absoluto(a)

**freelance** ['fri:lɑ:ns] **1** *n* (trabajador(ora) *m,f)* autónomo(a) *m,f,* free-lance *mf*
**2** *adj* autónomo(a), free-lance
**3** *adv* **to work f.** trabajar como autónomo(a) *or* free-lance
**4** *vi* trabajar como autónomo(a) *or* free-lance

**freeloader** ['fri:ləʊdə(r)] *n Fam* gorrón(ona) *m,f*

**freely** ['fri:lɪ] *adv (to give, speak)* libremente; **to be f. available** encontrarse fácilmente

**freemason** ['fri:meɪsən] *n* masón *m,* francmasón *m*

**freemasonry** ['fri:meɪsənrɪ] *n* masonería *f,* francmasonería *f*

**Freepost** ['fri:pəʊst] *n Br* franqueo *m* pagado

**free-range** ['fri:'reɪndʒ] *adj (egg, chicken)* de corral

**freestyle** ['fri:staɪl] *n (in swimming)* estilo *m* libre

**freethinker** [fri:'θɪŋkə(r)] *n* librepensador(ora) *m,f*

**freeway** ['fri:weɪ] *n US* autopista *f*

**freewheel** [fri:'wi:l] *vi (bicycle)* ir sin pedalear; *(car)* ir en punto muerto

**freeze** [fri:z] **1** *n (in weather)* helada *f;* **price/ wage f.** congelación *f* de los precios/los salarios
**2** *vt (pt* **froze** [frəʊz]*, pp* **frozen** [frəʊzən]*) (food, prices)* congelar
**3** *vi* **(a)** *(of weather)* **it's freezing** *(very cold)* hace un frío espantoso; **it may f. tonight** puede que hiele esta noche **(b)** *(of liquid)* congelarse; **to f. to death** morirse de frío; *Fam* **I'm freezing!** ¡me estoy congelando! **(c)** *(of person) (stand still)* quedarse paralizado(a); **f.!** ¡quieto(a)!

▸**freeze out** *vt sep Fam* **to f. sb out of the conversation** excluir a alguien de la conversación

▸**freeze over** *vi (of pond, river)* helarse

▸**freeze up** *vi (of pond, mechanism)* helarse

**freeze-dried** ['fri:z'draɪd] *adj (coffee, herbs)* liofilizado(a)

**freeze-frame** ['fri:z'freɪm] *n Cin* imagen *f* congelada

**freezer** ['fri:zə(r)] *n* congelador *m*

**freezing** ['fri:zɪŋ] *adj (room)* helado(a); *(weather, temperature)* muy frío(a); **f. cold** helado(a)

**freight** [freɪt] *Com* **1** *n (transport)* transporte *m or* flete *m* de mercancías; *(goods)* flete *m,* carga *f;* *(price)* flete *m,* porte *m;* **f. train** tren *m* de mercancías
**2** *vt (transport)* fletar, transportar; **we'll f. it to you tomorrow** se lo fletaremos mañana

**freighter** ['freɪtə(r)] *n (ship)* carguero *m*

**French** [frentʃ] **1** *npl (people)* **the F.** los franceses
**2** *n (language)* francés *m; Hum* **excuse my F.** *(after swearing)* con perdón; **F. class/teacher** clase *f*/profesor *m* de francés
**3** *adj* francés(esa); **F. fries** patatas *fpl* fritas; *Mus* **F. horn** trompa *f;* **F. kiss** beso *m* de tornillo; *Br Old-fashioned* **F. letter** condón *m;* **F. loaf** *or* **stick** barra *f* de pan; **F. window** (puerta *f)* cristalera *f*

**Frenchman** ['frentʃmən] *n* francés *m*

**French-speaking** ['frentʃ'spi:kɪŋ] *adj* francófono(a)

**Frenchwoman** ['frentʃwʊmən] *n* francesa *f*

**frenetic** [frə'netɪk] *adj* frenético(a)

**frenzied** ['frenzɪd] *adj* frenético(a); **f. with rage** fuera de sí (de ira); **f. with worry** angustiado(a)

**frenzy** ['frenzɪ] *n* frenesí *m;* **to work oneself into a f.** ponerse frenético(a)

**frequency** ['fri:kwənsɪ] *n* frecuencia *f; Rad* **f. band** banda *f* de frecuencia

**frequent 1** *adj* ['fri:kwənt] frecuente
**2** *vt* [frɪ'kwent] frecuentar

**frequently** ['fri:kwəntlɪ] *adv* con frecuencia

**fresco** ['freskəʊ] *(pl* **frescos** *or* **frescoes)** *n* fresco *m*

**fresh** [freʃ] **1** *adj* **(a)** *(food, air)* fresco(a); **it is still f. in my mind** todavía lo tengo fresco en la memoria; **as f. as a daisy** *(fresco(a))* como una rosa; **to get some f. air** tomar un poco de aire fresco; **f. troops** tropas *f* de refresco; **f. water** *(not salty)* agua *f* dulce
**(b)** *(page, attempt, drink)* nuevo(a); **to make a f. start** empezar de nuevo
**(c)** *(original) (approach, writing)* novedoso(a), original

**(d)** US Fam (cheeky) fresco(a); **to get f. with sb** (sexually) propasarse con alguien

**2** adv **f. from...** recién salido(a) de...; **we're f. out of lemons** se nos acaban de terminar los limones

**freshen** ['freʃən] vi (of wind, weather) refrescar
▶**freshen up** vi (wash) refrescarse

**fresher** ['freʃər] n Br Univ novato(a) m,f; **freshers' week** = semana previa al inicio de las clases universitarias con actividades organizadas para los estudiantes de primero

**freshly** ['freʃlɪ] adv recién; **f. baked/made/ painted** recién horneado/hecho/pintado

**freshman** ['freʃmən] n Univ novato(a) m,f

**freshness** ['freʃnɪs] n (of food) frescura f

**freshwater** ['freʃwɔːtə(r)] adj (fish) de agua dulce

**fret**[1] [fret] (pt & pp **fretted**) vi (worry) ponerse nervioso(a)

**fret**[2] n Mus (on guitar) traste m

**fretful** ['fretfʊl] adj (anxious) inquieto(a)

**Freudian** ['frɔɪdɪən] adj freudiano(a); **F. slip** lapsus m inv (linguae)

**FRG** [efɑː'dʒiː] n (abbr **Federal Republic of Germany**) RFA f, República f Federal de Alemania

**Fri** (abbr **Friday**) viernes m inv

**friar** ['fraɪə(r)] n fraile m; **F. Edmund** Fray Edmund

**fricassee** [frɪkə'siː] n fricasé m

**friction** ['frɪkʃən] n (rubbing, disagreement) fricción f; Phys rozamiento m

**Friday** ['fraɪdɪ] n viernes m inv; **F. the 13th** ≃ martes y trece; see also **Saturday**

**fridge** [frɪdʒ] n nevera f, frigorífico m

**fridge-freezer** ['frɪdʒ'friːzə(r)] n combi m, frigorífico-congelador m

**fried** [fraɪd] adj frito(a)

**friend** [frend] n amigo(a) m,f; **to be friends with sb, to be sb's f.** ser amigo de alguien; **to make friends with sb** hacerse amigo de alguien; **to be a f. to sb** ser amigo de alguien, ser un amigo para alguien; **that's what friends are for** para eso están los amigos; **we're just good friends** sólo somos buenos amigos; **he's no f. of mine** no es amigo mío; **to have friends in high places** tener amigos influyentes; **to be a f. of the arts** ser un mecenas de las artes; Prov **a f. in need is a f. indeed** en la adversidad se conoce al amigo

**friendless** ['frendlɪs] adj **to be f.** no tener amigos; **a f. childhood** una infancia sin amigos

**friendly** ['frendlɪ] **1** n Sport partido m amistoso
**2** adj (person) agradable, amable; (greeting, place) amistoso(a); **to be f. with sb** llevarse bien con alguien; **they became f.** se hicieron amigos(as); **to be on f. terms with sb** llevarse bien con alguien; Mil **f. fire** fuego m del propio bando

**friendship** ['frendʃɪp] n amistad f; **to form a f. with sb** forjar una amistad con alguien; **to lose sb's f.** perder la amistad de alguien

**fries** [fraɪz] npl US (**French**) **f.** patatas fpl fritas

**frieze** [friːz] n Art & Archit friso m

**frigate** ['frɪgət] n fragata f

**fright** [fraɪt] n susto m; **to take f.** asustarse; **to get a f.** darse un susto, asustarse; **to give sb a f.** dar un susto a alguien; Fam **to look a f.** estar horroroso(a)

**frighten** ['fraɪtən] **1** vt asustar; **to f. sb into doing sth** atemorizar a alguien para que haga algo; Fam **to f. the life** or **the wits out of sb** dar a alguien un susto de muerte
**2** vi **I don't f. easily** no me asusto fácilmente

**frightened** ['fraɪtənd] adj asustado(a) (**of** de); **to be f. to do sth** tener miedo de hacer algo

**frightening** ['fraɪtənɪŋ] adj escalofriante, aterrador(ora)

**frightful** ['fraɪtfʊl] adj espantoso(a)

**frightfully** ['fraɪtfʊlɪ] adv tremendamente, terriblemente

**frigid** ['frɪdʒɪd] adj (smile, atmosphere) glacial; (sexually) frígida

**frill** [frɪl] n volante m; Fig **without frills** (of ceremony) sin florituras

**frilly** ['frɪlɪ] adj **f. shirt/skirt** camisa f/falda f de volantes

**fringe** [frɪndʒ] n (a) (on clothes, lampshade) flecos mpl (b) (of hair) flequillo m (c) (edge) extremo m, borde m; **to be on the fringes of society** ser un/una marginado(a), vivir en la marginalidad; **f. benefits** ventajas fpl adicionales or extras; Pol **f. group** grupo m marginal; **f. theatre** teatro m experimental

**frisk** [frɪsk] **1** vt (search) cachear, registrar
**2** vi **to f. about** retozar, corretear

**frisky** ['frɪskɪ] adj (person) lleno(a) de vitalidad; (animal) retozón(ona), saltarín(ina); **to be f.** (of person) estar lleno(a) de vitalidad

**fritter** ['frɪtə(r)] n Culin buñuelo m; **banana f.** plátano rebozado y frito
▶**fritter away** vt sep (money) despilfarrar; (time) desperdiciar

**frivolity** [frɪ'vɒlɪtɪ] n frivolidad f

**frivolous** ['frɪvələs] adj frívolo(a)

**frizzy** ['frɪzɪ] adj ensortijado(a)

**fro** [frəʊ] adv **to go to and f.** ir y venir (de un lado para otro)

**frock** [frɒk] n (dress) vestido m; **f. coat** levita f

**frog** [frɒg] n (a) *(animal)* rana f; *Fam* **to have a f. in one's throat** tener carraspera (b) *Br very Fam* **F.** *(French person)* = término ofensivo para referirse a los franceses, gabacho(a) m,f, franchute mf

**frogman** ['frɒgmən] n hombre m rana

**frogmarch** ['frɒgmɑ:tʃ] vt llevar por la fuerza

**frogspawn** ['frɒgspɔ:n] n huevos mpl de rana

**frolic** ['frɒlɪk] vi retozar

**from** [frɒm] *unstressed* [frəm] *prep* (a) *(expressing place)* de; *(expressing specific location or origin)* desde; **f. above/the outside** desde arriba/fuera; **there's a great view f. the top** desde la cima la vista es magnífica; **to travel f. Edinburgh to Madrid** viajar de Edimburgo a Madrid; **the train f. Manchester** el tren *(procedente)* de Manchester; **10 km f. Barcelona** a 10 km de Barcelona

(b) *(expressing time)* desde; **f. then (on)** desde entonces; **f. tomorrow** a partir de mañana; **f. morning to** *or* **till night** de la mañana a la noche; **f. the beginning** desde el principio; **f. six to seven (o'clock)** de (las) seis a (las) siete; **five years f. now** de aquí a cinco años; **to be blind f. birth** ser ciego(a) de nacimiento

(c) *(expressing range, change)* **f. ... to... de... a...;** **for children f. seven to nine (years)** para niños de siete a nueve años; **wine f. £4 a bottle** vinos desde 4 libras la botella

(d) *(expressing source)* de; **I bought it f. a friend** se lo compré a un amigo; **where are you f.?, where do you come f.?** ¿de dónde eres?; **she's f. Portugal** es portuguesa *or* de Portugal; **to drink f. a cup** beber de una taza *or* en taza; **a quotation f. the Bible** una cita de la Biblia; **made f. rubber** hecho(a) de goma

(e) *(expressing removal)* **to take sth f. sb** quitar algo a alguien; **he was banned f. the club** fue expulsado del club

(f) *(on the basis of)* **f. what I heard/saw...** (a juzgar) por lo que yo he oído/visto...; **to act f. conviction** actuar por convicción

**frond** [frɒnd] n *(of fern)* fronda f; *(of palm)* (hoja f de) palma f

**front** [frʌnt] **1** n (a) *(not back)* parte f delantera; *(of building)* fachada f; *(cover of book)* portada f; **on the f. of the book** en la portada del libro; **at the f. of the book** al principio del libro; **I sat in (the) f.** *(of car)* me senté delante; *Br* **the f.** *(at seaside)* el paseo marítimo

(b) *(outward appearance)* fachada f; **his kindness is only a f.** su amabilidad no es más que fachada; **the company is a f. for their arms dealing** la empresa es una tapadera para el tráfico de armas; *Fam* **f. man** *(of TV, radio programme)* presentador m; *(of pop group)* líder m; *(of organization)* cabeza f visible

(c) *Mil, Pol & Met* frente m; *Fig* **to make progress on all fronts** hacer progresos en todos los frentes; *Met* **warm/cold f.** frente cálido/frío

(d) **in f.** *(in race, contest)* en cabeza, por delante; **in f. of** *(in queue, opposite)* delante de; *(in presence of)* delante de, en presencia de

(e) *Fam* **up f.** *(money)* por adelantado; **to be up f. about sth** ser claro(a) en cuanto a algo

**2** adj delantero(a); *Br Parl* **f. bench** = cada una de las dos primeras filas de escaños ocupados por los ministros y sus homólogos en la oposición; *Rail* **f. carriage** vagón m delantero; **f. cover** *(of magazine, book)* portada f; **f. door** puerta f principal; **f. garden** jardín m delantero; *Mil* **f. line** frente m *(de batalla)*; **f. page** *(of newspaper)* portada f, primera plana f; **f. room** salón m, sala f de estar; **in the f. row** en la primera fila; *Th* **to have a f. row seat** tener asiento de primera fila; *Fig* ser espectador privilegiado; **f. seat** *(in car)* asiento m delantero; **f. teeth** palas fpl; **f. view** vista f frontal

**3** vt *(government)* encabezar; *(TV programme)* presentar; *(organization)* dirigir; *(pop group)* liderar

**4** vi *(of building)* **the house fronts onto the river** la casa da al río

**frontage** ['frʌntɪdʒ] n fachada f

**frontal** ['frʌntəl] adj *Anat & Mil* frontal

**frontier** ['frʌntɪə(r)] n frontera f; **the frontiers of human knowledge** los límites del conocimiento humano; **f. guard** *(person)* guardia mf fronterizo(a); **f. town** ciudad f fronteriza

**frontispiece** ['frʌntɪspiːs] n frontispicio m

**frontrunner** ['frʌntrʌnə(r)] n favorito(a) m,f

**frost** [frɒst] n escarcha f; **there was a f.** cayó una helada

▸**frost over, frost up** vi *(of window)* cubrirse de escarcha

**frostbite** ['frɒstbaɪt] n congelación f

**frostbitten** ['frɒstbɪtən] adj *(fingers, toes)* con síntomas de congelación; *Fig (very cold)* congelado(a); **his fingers were f.** sus dedos mostraban síntomas de congelación

**frosted** ['frɒstɪd] adj *(glass)* esmerilado(a)

**frosting** ['frɒstɪŋ] n *US (on cake)* glaseado m

**frosty** ['frɒstɪ] adj *(night, air)* gélido(a), helado(a); *Fig (welcome, smile)* glacial

**froth** [frɒθ] **1** n *(foam)* espuma f

**2** vi hacer espuma; **he was frothing at the mouth** *(with rage)* echaba espuma por la boca

**frothy** ['frɒθɪ] adj espumoso(a)

**frown** [fraʊn] **1** n **a disapproving f.** el ceño fruncido en señal de desaprobación

**2** vi fruncir el ceño

▸**frown on, frown upon** vt insep *(disapprove of)* desaprobar

**froze** [frəʊz] pt of **freeze**

**frozen** ['frəʊzən] **1** adj congelado(a); **to be f.** estar congelado(a)

**2** pp of **freeze**

**fructose** ['frʌktəʊs] n fructosa f

**frugal** ['fruːgəl] adj frugal

**fruit** [fruːt] n (for eating) fruta f; (on plant) fruto m; **to bear f.** also Fig dar fruto; **f. bowl** frutero m; **f. juice** zumo m de frutas; Br **f. machine** (máquina f) tragaperras f inv; **f. salad** macedonia f (de frutas); **f. tree** (árbol m) frutal m

**fruitcake** ['fruːtkeɪk] n bizcocho m de frutas; Fam (mad person) chalado(a) m,f

**fruitful** ['fruːtfʊl] adj (discussion, meeting) fructífero(a)

**fruition** [fruːˈɪʃən] n **to come to f.** (of plan, effort) fructificar

**fruitless** ['fruːtlɪs] adj infructuoso(a)

**fruity** ['fruːtɪ] adj (taste) afrutado(a); Fam (voice) profundo(a)

**frump** [frʌmp] n Fam **she's a f.** es muy rancia en la manera de vestir

**frumpish** ['frʌmpɪʃ], **frumpy** ['frʌmpɪ] adj Fam **to be f.** ser rancia en la manera de vestir

**frustrate** [frʌsˈtreɪt] vt (person, plan) frustrar

**frustrated** [frʌsˈtreɪtɪd] adj frustrado(a); **to be f.** estar frustrado(a)

**frustrating** [frʌsˈtreɪtɪŋ] adj frustrante

**frustration** [frʌsˈtreɪʃən] n (emotion) frustración f

**fry** [fraɪ] **1** vt freír

**2** vi freírse

**frying** ['fraɪɪŋ] n fritura f; **f. pan** sartén f; **to jump out of the f. pan into the fire** ir de Guatemala a Guatepeor

**ft** (abbr **foot** or **feet**) pie m (30,48 cm); **20 ft** 20 pies

**FTP** [eftiːˈpiː] n Comptr (abbr **File Transfer Protocol**) FTP m, protocolo m de transferencia de ficheros

**fuchsia** ['fjuːʃə] n (plant) fucsia f

**fuck** [fʌk] Vulg **1** n **(a)** (intercourse) polvo m; **to have a f.** echar un polvo, follar **(b)** (other uses) **f.!** ¡joder!; **I don't give a f.** me importa un huevo; **what the f….?** ¿qué coño…?, ¿qué cojones…?; **shut the f. up!** ¡cállate de una puta vez!; **he's as stupid/rich as f.** es más bobo/rico que la hostia; **f. knows why he came!** ¡para qué cojones habrá venido!; **get to f.!** ¡vete a tomar por (el) culo!

**2** vt follarse; **f. it!** ¡joder!; **f. you!** ¡que te den por culo!

**3** vi follar

▸**fuck about**, **fuck around** Vulg **1** vt sep **to f. sb about** or **around** joder a alguien

**2** vi hacer el gilipollas (**with** con)

▸**fuck off** vi Vulg (go away) darse el piro, abrirse; **f. off!** ¡vete a tomar por (el) culo!

▸**fuck up** vt sep Vulg **to f. sth up** (bungle) joder bien algo

**fuck-all** ['fʌkˈɔːl] n Vulg (nothing) **he's done f. this week** se ha tocado los huevos toda la semana; **to know f. about sth** no tener ni puta idea de algo

**fucked** [fʌkt] adj Vulg **to be f.** (exhausted) estar follado(a) or hecho(a) una braga; (broken) estar jodido(a)

**fucking** ['fʌkɪŋ] Vulg **1** adj **he's a f. idiot!** ¡es un gilipollas!; **where's the f. car?** ¿dónde está el puto coche?

**2** adv **it's f. cold!** ¡hace un frío de cojones!; **it's f. brilliant!** ¡está de puta madre!

**fuddy-duddy** ['fʌdɪdʌdɪ] n Fam **an old f.** un carcamal

**fudge** [fʌdʒ] **1** n (sweet) = dulce de azúcar, leche y mantequilla

**2** vt (avoid) **to f. an issue** eludir un asunto

**3** vi **stop fudging!** ¡déjate de evasivas!

**fuel** ['fjʊəl] **1** n combustible m; Fig **to add f. to the flames** (of situation, crisis) echar leña al fuego; **f. bill** factura f del gas y la electricidad; Aut **f. consumption** consumo m de combustible; Aut **f. gauge** indicador m del nivel de gasolina; Aut **f. injection** inyección f (de combustible); **f. pump** bomba f de (la) gasolina; **f. tank** depósito m de combustible

**2** vt Fig (argument, hatred) dar pábulo a, avivar

**fug** [fʌg] n Br Fam ambiente m cargado, aire m viciado

**fugitive** ['fjuːdʒɪtɪv] n fugitivo(a) m,f

**fugue** [fjuːg] n Mus fuga f

**fulcrum** ['fʌlkrəm] n fulcro m, punto m de apoyo

**fulfil**, US **fulfill** [fʊlˈfɪl] (pt & pp **fulfilled**) vt (plan, condition, ambition) cumplir; (dream, task) realizar, cumplir; (need, requirement) satisfacer; (function, role) desempeñar; **to feel fulfilled** (of person) sentirse realizado(a)

**fulfilment**, US **fulfillment** [fʊlˈfɪlmənt] n (of plan, condition) cumplimiento m; (of ambition, dream, task) realización f, cumplimiento; (of need, requirement) satisfacción f; (of function, role) desempeño m; **to find** or **achieve f.** realizarse, hallar satisfacción

**full** [fʊl] **1** adj **(a)** (container, room) lleno(a); (day) completo(a); **to be f. of** estar lleno(a) de; **f. of holes** lleno(a) de agujeros; **to be f. of praise for sb** no tener más que elogios para alguien; **to be f. of oneself** tenérselo muy creído; **f. to the brim** (lleno(a)) hasta el borde; **don't speak with your mouth f.** no hables con la boca llena; **to be f. (up)** (of person) estar lleno(a); **on a f. stomach** con el estómago lleno **(b)** (complete) (amount, support) total; (explanation, recovery) completo(a); **to take f. responsibility for sth** asumir plena responsabilidad por algo; **she gave me the f. story** me lo contó todo; **the f. horror** todo el horror; **the f. implications** todas las implicaciones; **to lead a f. life** llevar una vida plena; **I waited two f. hours** *or* **a f. two hours** esperé dos horas enteras; **to ask for fuller information about sth** pedir más información acerca de algo; **to be in f. bloom** estar reventón(ona) *or* en pleno florecimiento; **in f. flow** *(of speaker)* en pleno discurso; **to be in f. swing** *(of party)* estar en pleno apogeo; **in f. view** completamente a la vista; **f. board** pensión *f* completa; *Phot* **in f. colour** a todo color; *Rail* **f. fare** precio *m* or tarifa *f* normal; **f. house** *(in theatre)* lleno *m*; *(in cards)* full *m*; **f. member** miembro *m* de pleno derecho; **f. moon** luna *f* llena; **f. name** nombre *m* y apellidos; *Th* **f. price** precio *m* completo; **f. stop** *(punctuation)* punto *m* (y seguido); **f. time** *(in football match)* final *m* del tiempo reglamentario

(c) *(maximum)* **at f. blast** *(heater, air conditioning)* a plena potencia; *(radio, TV)* a todo volumen; **at f. pelt** *or* **tilt** a toda pastilla *or* marcha; **(at) f. speed** a toda velocidad; **at f. stretch** a pleno rendimiento; **f. marks** *(in exam)* nota *f* or puntuación *f* máxima

(d) *(skirt, sleeve)* largo(a); **a f. figure** *(of woman)* una figura de formas bien contorneadas; **f. lips** labios *mpl* carnosos

**2** *n* **to pay in f.** pagar el total; **name in f.** nombre *m* y apellidos; **to live life to the f.** disfrutar la vida al máximo

**3** *adv* **I know it f. well** lo sé perfectamente; **it hit him f. in the face** le dió en plena cara

**fullback** ['fʊlbæk] *n (in football)* (defensa *m*) lateral *m*; *(in rugby)* defensa *m* de cierre, zaguero *m*

**full-blown** ['fʊl'bləʊn] *adj (war, scandal)* declarado(a); *(argument)* verdadero(a); **to have f. AIDS** haber desarrollado la enfermedad del SIDA (por completo)

**full-bodied** ['fʊl'bɒdɪd] *adj (wine)* con cuerpo

**full-grown** ['fʊl'grəʊn] *adj* plenamente desarrollado(a); **to be f.** estar plenamente desarrollado(a)

**full-length** ['fʊl'leŋθ] *adj (portrait, mirror)* de cuerpo entero; **f. film** largometraje *m*

**fullness** ['fʊlnɪs] *n* **in the f. of time** en su momento

**full-page** ['fʊl'peɪdʒ] *adj (advert, illustration)* a toda página

**full-scale** ['fʊl'skeɪl] *adj* (a) *(model)* (de) tamaño natural (b) *(search)* exhaustivo(a); **f. war** guerra *f* a gran escala

**full-time** ['fʊl'taɪm] **1** *adj (job, employment)* a tiempo completo; *(teacher, housewife)* con dedicación exclusiva, de plena dedicación; *Fig* look-

ing after the baby is a f. job cuidar del bebé es un trabajo de plena dedicación

**2** *adv (work)* a tiempo completo

**full-timer** ['fʊl'taɪmər] *n* trabajador(ora) *m,f* *or* empleado(a) *m,f* a tiempo completo

**fully** ['fʊlɪ] *adv* (a) *(completely)* completamente; **f. grown** hecho(a) y derecho(a) (b) *(at least)* **it takes f. two hours** lleva dos horas largas

**fully-fledged** ['fʊlɪ'fledʒd] *adj Br Fig* hecho(a) y derecho(a)

**fulminate** ['fʌlmɪneɪt] *vi* tronar, arremeter **(against** contra)

**fulness = fullness**

**fulsome** ['fʊlsəm] *adj* excesivo(a), exagerado(a); **to be f. in one's praise of sth/sb** alabar algo/a alguien con exceso

**fumble** ['fʌmbəl] **1** *vt* **the goalkeeper fumbled the ball** al portero se le escapó la pelota de las manos

**2** *vi* rebuscar; **to f. for words** no encontrar las palabras adecuadas, titubear; **he fumbled with the controls** trató torpemente de accionar los mandos

**fume** [fjuːm] **1** *n* **fumes** humos *mpl*

**2** *vi* (a) *(give off fumes)* despedir humo (b) *(be angry)* **to be fuming** echar humo (por las orejas)

**fumigate** ['fjuːmɪgeɪt] *vt* fumigar

**fun** [fʌn] *n* diversión *f*; **to have f.** divertirse; **it was great f.** fue muy divertido(a); **there'll be f. and games** *(trouble)* se va a armar una buena; **to make f. of, to poke f. at** burlarse de; **to say sth in f.** decir algo en broma; **to do sth for f.,** to do sth for the f. of it hacer algo para divertirse; **to join in the f.** unirse a la diversión; **what f.!** ¡qué divertido!

**function** ['fʌŋkʃən] **1** *n* (a) *(of machine, person, institution) & Math* función *f*; **my f. in life is to...** mi papel consiste en...; *Comptr* **f. key** tecla *f* de función (b) *(celebration)* celebración *f*; *(official occasion)* acto *m*

**2** *vi* funcionar; **to f. as** servir de, hacer de

**functional** ['fʌŋkʃənəl] *adj* (a) *(practical)* funcional (b) *(operational)* **to be f.** estar en funcionamiento *or* funcionar

**functionary** ['fʌŋkʃənərɪ] *n* funcionario(a) *m,f*

**fund** [fʌnd] **1** *n* (a) *(of money)* fondo *m*; **funds** fondos *mpl*, *Fin* **f. manager** gestor(ora) *m,f* financiero(a) *or* de fondos (b) *(of information, jokes)* fuente *f*

**2** *vt Fin* financiar

**fundamental** [fʌndə'mentəl] **1** *adj* fundamental; **her f. honesty** su honradez inherente

**2** *n* **fundamentals** principios *mpl* básicos, fundamentos *mpl*

**fundamentalist** [fʌndə'mentəlɪst] n Rel integrista mf, fundamentalista mf

**fundamentally** [fʌndə'mentəlɪ] adv básicamente, fundamentalmente

**funding** ['fʌndɪŋ] n fondos mpl, financiación f

**fund-raiser** ['fʌndreɪzə(r)] n (person) recaudador(ora) m,f de fondos; (event) acto m para recaudar fondos

**funeral** ['fju:nərəl] n funeral m; Fam that's your f.! ¡eso es cosa tuya or tu problema!; f. director encargado m,f de la funeraria; Mus f. march marcha f fúnebre; f. parlour funeraria f; f. procession cortejo m fúnebre; f. service funeral m, honras fpl fúnebres

**funfair** ['fʌnfeə(r)] n feria f (ambulante)

**fungus** ['fʌŋgəs] (pl fungi ['fʌŋgaɪ]) n (mushroom, toadstool) hongo m; (on walls) & Med hongos mpl

**funk** [fʌŋk] n (a) Fam Old-fashioned (fright) to be in a f. estar muerto(a) de miedo; he got into a f. le entró mieditis (aguditis) (b) (music) funk m, funky m

**funky** ['fʌŋkɪ] adj very Fam (clothing, music, suggestion) guay, muy guapo(a)

**funnel** ['fʌnəl] 1 n (a) (of locomotive, steamship) chimenea f (b) (for filling bottle) embudo m
2 vt (pt & pp funnelled, US funneled) (direct) canalizar

**funnily** ['fʌnɪlɪ] adv (strangely) de forma rara; f. enough... curiosamente..., por raro que parezca...

**funny** ['fʌnɪ] adj (a) (amusing) divertido(a); are you trying to be f.? ¿te estás haciendo el gracioso?; Ironic very f.! ¡muy gracioso!; f. bone hueso m de la risa
(b) (strange) curioso(a), raro(a); I feel a bit f. (ill) no me siento muy allá; (that's) f., I thought I'd locked the door qué curioso, creía que había cerrado la puerta con llave; (it's) f. you should say that es curioso que digas eso; this butter tastes/smells f. esta mantequilla sabe/huele raro; he went a bit f. in his old age (eccentric) se volvió un poco raro(a) con los años; Fam I don't want any f. business! ¡nada de trucos!; Fam f. farm frenopático m

**fur** [fɜ:(r)] n (a) (hair) pelo m; (animal skin) piel f; Fig the f. was flying se armó la marimorena; f. coat abrigo m de piel; f. trade comercio m de pieles (b) (in kettle, boiler, on tongue) sarro m

**furious** ['fjʊərɪəs] adj furioso(a); to be f. estar furioso(a); to be f. with oneself tirarse de los pelos; at a f. speed a una velocidad de vértigo

**furiously** ['fjʊərɪəslɪ] adv con furia; the fire was blazing f. el fuego ardía con furia

**furlong** ['fɜ:lɒŋ] n (measurement) = 201 metros (unidad utilizada en las carreras de caballos)

**furnace** ['fɜ:nɪs] n horno m

**furnish** ['fɜ:nɪʃ] vt (a) (house, flat) amueblar (b) Formal (provide) proporcionar, suministrar; to f. sb with sth proporcionar algo a alguien

**furnished** ['fɜ:nɪʃt] adj (flat, room) amueblado(a); to be f. estar amueblado(a); f. accommodation viviendas fpl amuebladas

**furnishings** ['fɜ:nɪʃɪŋz] npl (furniture, fittings) mobiliario m, muebles mpl; soft f. tapicería f

**furniture** ['fɜ:nɪtʃə(r)] n muebles mpl, mobiliario m; a piece of f. un mueble; f. polish abrillantador m de muebles; f. remover empleado(a) m,f de una empresa de mudanzas; f. shop tienda f de muebles; f. van camión m de mudanzas

**furore, US furor** ['fjʊərɔ:(r)] n (uproar) revuelo m, escándalo m; to cause a f. levantar un gran revuelo

**furrow** ['fʌrəʊ] 1 n (in field, on face) surco m
2 vt Literary his brow was furrowed with worry arrugaba la frente con preocupación

**furry** ['fɜ:rɪ] adj (animal) peludo(a); (toy) de peluche; to have a f. tongue tener la lengua llena de sarro

**further** ['fɜ:ðə(r)] (comparative of far) 1 adv (a) más lejos; I can go no f. no puedo seguir; this mustn't go any f. (don't tell anyone else) esto no debe salir de aquí; I didn't question him any f. no le pregunté más; to go no f. into the matter no profundizar más en el asunto; by being careful he made his money go f. siendo cuidadoso pudo sacar más partido a su dinero; that doesn't get us much f. eso no nos ayuda mucho; f. back (in space) más atrás; (in time) antes
(b) Formal (moreover) además; f. to your recent letter... en respuesta a su última carta...
2 adj (a) (more distant) más alejado(a)
(b) (additional) nuevo(a), adicional; upon f. consideration tras considerarlo de nuevo; until f. notice hasta nuevo aviso; without f. warning sin más aviso; Br f. education = enseñanza no universitaria para adultos, ≃ formación f continua
3 vt promover

**furthermore** [fɜ:ðə'mɔ:(r)] adv Formal es más

**furthermost** ['fɜ:ðəməʊst] adj Literary último(a), más alejado

**furthest** ['fɜ:ðɪst] (superlative of far) 1 adj the f. el/la más alejado(a), el/la más distante
2 adv más lejos

**furtive** ['fɜ:tɪv] adj furtivo(a)

**fury** ['fjʊərɪ] n (of person, storm) furia f; **to be in a f.** estar furioso(a); Fam **to work like f.** trabajar como loco(a)

**fuse,** US **fuze** [fju:z] **1** n (a) Elec fusible m; Fam Fig **she blew a f.** (became angry) se puso como una fiera; **f. box** cuadro m eléctrico, caja f de fusibles; **f. wire** fusible m (b) (for dynamite) mecha f; (in bomb) espoleta f; Fam Fig **to have a short f.** (be short-tempered) saltar a la mínima

**2** vt (a) (join, melt) fundir (b) Br Elec **a surge of power fused the lights** se fundieron los plomos y se fue la luz por una subida de corriente

**3** vi (a) (of metals) fundirse (b) (of organizations, parties) fusionarse (c) Br Elec **the lights have fused** se han fundido los plomos y se ha ido la luz

**fused** [fju:zd] adj Elec (plug, appliance) provisto(a) de fusible

**fuselage** ['fju:zəlɑ:ʒ] n fuselaje m

**fusillade** [fju:zɪ'leɪd] n (of bullets) descarga f cerrada; Fig (of criticism, questions) lluvia f

**fusion** ['fju:ʒən] n fusión f

**fuss** [fʌs] **1** n alboroto m, escándalo m; **a lot of f. about** or **over nothing** mucho ruido y pocas nueces; **I don't see what all the f. is about** no veo a qué viene tanto alboroto; **to make** or Fam **kick up a f.** armar un alboroto or un escándalo; **he always makes a f. of his grandchildren** se deshace en atenciones cada vez que está con sus nietos

**2** vt Fam **I'm not fussed** (I don't mind) me da lo mismo

**3** vi **to f.** (about or around) estar inquieto(a); **stop fussing!** ¡estate quieto(a)!

**fusspot** ['fʌspɒt] n Fam quisquilloso(a) m,f

**fussy** ['fʌsɪ] adj (a) (person) quisquilloso(a), tiquismiquis; **I'm not f.** (I don't mind) me da lo mismo (b) (dress, decor) recargado(a)

**futile** ['fju:taɪl] adj (attempt, protest) inútil, vano(a); (remark, suggestion) fútil

**futility** [fju:'tɪlɪtɪ] n (of attempt, protest) inutilidad; (of remark, suggestion) futilidad f

**futon** ['fu:tɒn] n futón m

**future** ['fju:tʃə(r)] **1** n (a) also Gram futuro m; **in (the) f.** en el futuro; **in the near/distant f.** en un futuro próximo/lejano; **she has a job with a (good) f.** tiene un trabajo con (mucho) futuro (b) Fin **futures** futuros mpl; **futures market** mercado m de futuros

**2** adj futuro(a); **at some f. date** en una fecha futura; **for f. reference** para consultar en el futuro

**futuristic** ['fju:tʃə'rɪstɪk] adj futurista

**fuze** US = **fuse**

**fuzz** [fʌz] n (a) (on peach, skin) pelusa f (b) very Fam **the f.** (the police) la pasma

**fuzzy** ['fʌzɪ] adj (outline) borroso(a); (idea) vago(a); (hair) crespo(a)

# G

**G, g** [dʒiː] n (**a**) (letter) G f, g f (**b**) Mus sol m

**g** (abbr **gramme**) g

**gab** [gæb] Fam **1** n **to have the gift of the g.** tener un pico de oro

  **2** vi (pt & pp **gabbed**) (talk, gossip) darle al pico; (to police, press) dar el soplo

**gabardine** [gæbəˈdiːn] n (coat, material) gabardina f

**gabble** [ˈgæbəl] **1** n vocerío m, alboroto m

  **2** vi farfullar

**gable** [ˈgeɪbəl] n (of house) hastial m, gablete m; **g. end** hastial m

**Gabon** [ˈgæbən] n Gabón

**Gabonese** [gæbəˈniːz] n & adj gabonés(esa) m,f

**▶gad about** [gæd] vi Fam pendonear, zascandilear

**gadfly** [ˈgædflaɪ] n (insect) tábano m; Fig (person) provocador(ora) m,f

**gadget** [ˈgædʒɪt] n artilugio m

**Gael** [geɪl] n = persona de origen celta oriunda de Irlanda o el Noroeste de Escocia

**Gaelic** [ˈgeɪlɪk, ˈgælɪk] **1** n (language) gaélico m

  **2** adj gaélico(a); Sport **G. football** fútbol m gaélico, = deporte irlandés a medio camino entre el fútbol y el rugby

**gaff** [gæf] n (**a**) (in fishing) garfio m (**b**) Br Fam (home) quel(i) f (**c**) Fam **to blow the g. (on)** descubrir el pastel (acerca de)

**gaffe** [gæf] n (blunder) desliz m, metedura f de pata; **to make a g.** cometer un desliz

**gaffer** [ˈgæfə(r)] n Br Fam (boss) mandamás m; (football manager) míster m

**gag** [gæg] **1** n (**a**) (on mouth) mordaza f (**b**) Fam (joke) chiste m

  **2** vt (pt & pp **gagged**) (silence) (person, the press) amordazar

  **3** vi (retch) tener arcadas; **to make sb g.** provocar arcadas a alguien

**gaga** [ˈgɑːgɑː] adj Fam chocho(a)

**gage** US = **gauge**

**gaggle** [ˈgægəl] n (of geese) bandada f; Fig **a g. of journalists** una manada de periodistas

**gaiety** [ˈgeɪətɪ] n regocijo m, alegría f

**gaily** [ˈgeɪlɪ] adv alegremente, con alegría

**gain** [geɪn] **1** n (**a**) (profit) beneficio m, ganancia f; **for personal g.** en beneficio propio (**b**) (increase) aumento m (**in** de)

  **2** vt (**a**) (advantage, reputation) cobrar, ganar; (victory) obtener; (sympathy) granjearse, ganarse; **to g. access to** (of burglar) lograr acceder or acceso a; **he gained the impression that...** le dio la impresión de que... (**b**) (increase) ganar; **to g. weight** ganar peso; **to g. ground on** ganar terreno a; **to g. speed** cobrar velocidad; **to g. time** ganar tiempo

  **3** vi (**a**) (benefit) **to g. by sth** beneficiarse de algo (**b**) (increase) **to g. in confidence** cobrar or ganar confianza; **to g. in popularity** hacerse cada vez más popular (**c**) (of clock) adelantar

**▶gain on** vt insep **to g. on one's competitors** ganar terreno a los competidores

**gainful** [ˈgeɪnfʊl] adj remunerado(a)

**gainfully** [ˈgeɪnfʊlɪ] adv **to be g. employed** tener un empleo remunerado

**gainsay** [geɪnˈseɪ] (pt & pp **gainsaid** [geɪnˈsed]) vt Formal negar

**gait** [geɪt] n paso m, manera f de andar

**gal** [gæl] n Old-fashioned Fam moza f

**gala** [ˈgɑːlə] n gala f; **swimming g.** concurso m de natación; **g. evening** noche f de gala; **g. performance** (actuación f de) gala

**galactic** [gəˈlæktɪk] adj galáctico(a)

**Galapagos** [gəˈlæpəgəs] npl **the G. (Islands)** las (Islas) Galápagos

**galaxy** [ˈgæləksɪ] n galaxia f; Fig **a g. of stars** un elenco de estrellas

**gale** [geɪl] n (strong wind) vendaval m; Fig **a g. of laughter** un torrente de carcajadas

**Galicia** [gəˈlɪsɪə] n (in Spain) Galicia

**Galician** [gəˈlɪsɪən] n & adj (from Spain) gallego(a) m,f

**gall** [gɔːl] **1** n (**a**) Med bilis f inv; **g. bladder** vesícula f biliar (**b**) (impudence) insolencia f; **she had the g. to...** tuvo la insolencia de...

  **2** vt (annoy) irritar, dar rabia a

**gallant** [ˈgælənt] adj (brave) valiente, intrépido(a); (attentive) galante

**gallantry** [ˈgæləntrɪ] n (attentiveness) galantería f; (bravery) valentía f, intrepidez f

**galleon** [ˈgælɪən] n galeón m

**gallery** ['gælərı] n (a) (art) g. (for sale) galería f de arte; (for exhibition) museo m (de arte) (b) (in theatre) galería f, paraíso m; Fig to play to the g. (of politician) actuar para la galería

**galley** ['gælı] (pl galleys) n (a) (ship) galera f; g. slave galeote m (b) (ship's kitchen) cocina f (c) Typ g. (proof) galerada f

**Gallic** ['gælɪk] adj (French) galo(a); Hist (of Gaul) galo(a), gálico(a)

**gallicism** ['gælɪsɪzəm] n Ling galicismo m

**galling** ['gɔːlɪŋ] adj irritante, mortificante

▸**gallivant about, gallivant around** [gælɪvænt] vi pendonear

**gallon** ['gælən] n galón m (GB= 4,546 litros; EU= 3,785 litros)

**gallop** ['gæləp] 1 n galope m; at a g. al galope 2 vi galopar; Fig she galloped through her work despachó rápidamente su trabajo

**gallows** ['gæləʊz] npl patíbulo m, horca f; g. humour humor m negro or macabro

**gallstone** ['gɔːlstəʊn] n cálculo m biliar

**galore** [gə'lɔː(r)] adv Fam a montones, a patadas

**galvanize** ['gælvənaɪz] vt galvanizar; to g. sb into action mover a alguien a la acción

**galvanized** ['gælvənaɪzd] adj galvanizado(a); g. steel acero m galvanizado

**Gambia** ['gæmbɪə] n the G. Gambia

**Gambian** ['gæmbɪən] n & adj gambiano(a), m,f; gambio(a) m,f

**gambit** ['gæmbɪt] n (in chess) gambito m; (in negotiation, diplomacy) jugada f, maniobra f; opening g. (in negotiation, diplomacy) primer envite m

**gamble** ['gæmbəl] 1 n riesgo m; to take a g. arriesgarse
2 vt jugarse; to g. one's future on sth jugarse el porvenir por algo
3 vi jugar, apostar dinero; to g. on sth (bet money on) apostar a algo; (take risk on) jugársela confiando en algo, apostar por algo

**gambler** ['gæmblə(r)] n jugador(ora) m,f

**gambling** ['gæmblɪŋ] n juego m; g. debts deudas fpl de juego; g. den timba f, garito m

**gambol** ['gæmbəl] (pt & pp gambolled, US gamboled) vi (of lamb, children) retozar

**game** [geɪm] 1 n (a) (activity, sport, in tennis) juego m; (of cards, chess) partida f; (match) (of football, tennis, golf) partido m; g., set, and match (in tennis) juego, set y partido; games Br (school subject) deportes mpl; (sporting event) juegos mpl; politics is just a g. to them la política no es más que un juego para ellos; g. show concurso m televisivo
(b) (in hunting) caza f; g. reserve coto m de caza
(c) (idioms) to play the g. jugar limpio; two can play at that g. donde las dan las toman;

to beat sb at his own g. vencer a alguien con sus propias armas; to play games with sb jugar con alguien; to give the g. away desvelar el secreto; what's his g.? ¿qué pretende?; I know what your g. is sé a qué estás jugando; the g.'s up for him para él se acabó lo que se daba; I've been in this g. a long time llevo mucho tiempo metido en esto; Br Fam to be on the g. (of a prostitute) hacer la calle
2 adj (a) (brave) valiente; to be g. (to do sth) (willing) estar dispuesto(a) (a hacer algo)
(b) Fam a g. leg una pata chula

**gamekeeper** ['geɪmkiːpə(r)] n guarda mf de caza

**gamely** ['geɪmlɪ] adv valientemente

**gamma** ['gæmə] n (Greek letter) gamma f; Phys g. rays rayos mpl gamma

**gammon** ['gæmən] n jamón m; g. steak = loncha de jamón a la plancha

**gammy** ['gæmɪ] adj Fam a g. leg una pata chula

**gamut** ['gæmət] n gama f; to run the g. of pasar por toda la gama de

**gamy** ['geɪmɪ] adj (of flavour) de or a caza

**gander** ['gændə(r)] n (a) (male goose) ganso m (b) Br very Fam to take a g. (at) (look) echar un ojo or un vistazo (a)

**gang** [gæŋ] n (of criminals) banda f; (of children, friends) pandilla f; (of workers) cuadrilla f

▸**gang up** vi to g. up on sb/with sb confabularse contra/con alguien

**gangbang** ['gæŋ'bæŋ] n very Fam (group rape) violación f colectiva

**Ganges** ['gændʒiːz] n the G. el Ganges

**gangland** ['gæŋlænd] n (underworld) hampa f; a g. killing un ajuste de cuentas entre gángsters

**gangling** ['gæŋlɪŋ] adj larguirucho(a)

**ganglion** ['gæŋlɪən] (pl ganglia ['gæŋglɪə]) n Anat ganglio m

**gangplank** ['gæŋplæŋk] n Naut pasarela f, plancha f

**gangrene** ['gæŋgriːn] n gangrena f

**gangrenous** ['gæŋgrɪnəs] adj gangrenoso(a); to go g. gangrenarse

**gangster** ['gæŋstə(r)] n gángster m; g. film película f de gángsters

**gangway** ['gæŋweɪ] n Th (passage) pasillo m; Naut (gangplank) pasarela f, plancha f; g.! ¡paso!

**gannet** ['gænɪt] n (bird) alcatraz m; Fig (greedy person) glotón(ona) m,f

**gantry** ['gæntrɪ] n (for crane) pórtico m; (for rocket) torre f de lanzamiento; (for theatre lighting) pasarela f de focos or luces, rejilla f de iluminación; (in pub) botellero m

**gaol** [dʒeɪl] Br 1 n cárcel f, prisión f; to be in g. estar en la cárcel; to go to g. ir a la cárcel
2 vt encarcelar

**gap** [gæp] n (physical opening) hueco m; (in mountains) desfiladero m, paso m; (in time) intervalo m; (in age, ability) diferencia f; (in knowledge) laguna f; (in text) espacio m en blanco; **the g. between rich and poor** la brecha entre ricos y pobres; **his death leaves a g. in all of our lives** su muerte deja un vacío en la vida de todos nosotros; Com **a g. in the market** un hueco en el mercado

**gape** [geɪp] vi (a) (stare) **to g. (at sth/sb)** mirar (algo/a alguien) con los ojos desorbitados (b) **to g. (open)** abrirse

**gaping** ['geɪpɪŋ] adj (hole, chasm) enorme

**garage** ['gærɑːʒ, 'gærɪdʒ] n (for storing cars) garaje m; (where petrol is sold) gasolinera f, estación f de servicio; (for repairing cars) taller m (de reparaciones)

**garb** [gɑːb] n Literary atuendo m, atavío m

**garbage** ['gɑːbɪdʒ] n (a) US (household waste) basura f; Méx cochera f; **g. can** cubo m de la basura; **g. heap** montón m de basura; **g. man** basurero m (b) Fam (nonsense) bobadas fpl, chorradas fpl; **he's talking g.** está diciendo bobadas

**garbled** ['gɑːbəld] adj confuso(a)

**garden** ['gɑːdən] 1 n jardín m; **back/front g.** jardín trasero/delantero; **g. centre** centro m de jardinería; **g. flat** piso m (en planta baja) con jardín; **g. furniture** mobiliario m de jardín; **g. party** recepción f al aire libre; Fig **to lead sb up the g. path** (mislead) engatusar a alguien; **g. suburb** = urbanización con grandes zonas ajardinadas; **g. tools** útiles mpl de jardinería
2 vi cuidar el jardín, trabajar en el jardín

**gardener** ['gɑːdnə(r)] n jardinero(a) m,f

**gardening** [gɑːdnɪŋ] n jardinería f; **to do the g.** cuidar el jardín

**gargantuan** [gɑːˈgæntjʊən] adj (in general) colosal; (meal) pantagruélico(a)

**gargle** ['gɑːgəl] vi hacer gárgaras

**gargoyle** ['gɑːgɔɪl] n gárgola f

**garish** ['geərɪʃ] adj (clothes, colour) chillón(ona), estridente; (light) deslumbrante

**garland** ['gɑːlənd] 1 n guirnalda f
2 vt adornar con guirnaldas

**garlic** ['gɑːlɪk] n ajo m; **g. bread** pan m de ajo; **g. butter** mantequilla f aromatizada con ajo; **g. sausage** embutido m al ajo

**garment** ['gɑːmənt] n prenda f (de vestir)

**garnet** ['gɑːnɪt] n granate m

**garnish** ['gɑːnɪʃ] 1 n Culin guarnición f
2 vt guarnecer, adornar (**with** con)

**garret** ['gærət] n (attic) buhardilla f

**garrison** ['gærɪsən] 1 n guarnición f; **g. town** ciudad f con guarnición
2 vt (troops) acuartelar

**garrotte** [gəˈrɒt] 1 n garrote m vil
2 vt dar garrote vil a

**garrulous** ['gærʊləs] adj gárrulo(a)

**garter** ['gɑːtə(r)] n (for stockings) liga f; Br **the Order of the G.** la Orden de la Jarretera; US **g. belt** liguero m; **g. snake** culebra f de jaretas

**gas** [gæs] 1 n (a) gas m; **to have g.** (as anaesthetic) recibir anestesia gaseosa; **g. bill** factura f del gas; **g. chamber** cámara f de gas; **g. cooker** cocina f de gas; **g. cylinder** bombona f de gas; **g. fire** estufa f de gas; **g. lamp** lámpara f de gas; **g. mask** máscara f antigás (b) US (gasoline) gasolina f, Fam **to step on the g.** (accelerate) pisar el acelerador; **g. station** gasolinera f, estación f de servicio; **g. tank** depósito m de la gasolina (c) Fam **what a g.!** ¡qué divertido!
2 vt (pt & pp gassed) gasear
3 vi Fam (chat) estar de palique or cháchara

**gasbag** ['gæsbæg] n Fam charlatán(ana) m,f, cotorra f

**gaseous** ['geɪsɪəs] adj gaseoso(a)

**gash** [gæʃ] 1 n (wound) herida f (profunda), corte m (profundo); (in wood, metal) brecha f
2 vt hacerse una herida en

**gasket** ['gæskɪt] n Aut junta f; Fam Fig **he blew a g.** (lost his temper) se salió de sus casillas

**gasoline** ['gæsəliːn] n US gasolina f

**gasometer** [gæˈsɒmɪtə(r)] n gasómetro m

**gasp** [gɑːsp] 1 n (of surprise) grito m ahogado; **to be at one's last g.** estar en las últimas
2 vi lanzar un grito ahogado (**with** or **in** de); **to make sb g.** dejar boquiabierto a alguien; **she gasped for breath** or **for air** luchaba por respirar; **to be gasping for a cigarette/a drink** morirse por un cigarrillo/algo de beber

**gassy** ['gæsɪ] adj (beer) con burbujas

**gastric** ['gæstrɪk] adj gástrico(a); **g. flu** gripe f gastrointestinal; **g. juices** jugos mpl gástricos; **g. ulcer** úlcera f de estómago

**gastritis** [gæsˈtraɪtɪs] n gastritis f inv

**gastroenteritis** [gæstrəʊəntəˈraɪtɪs] n gastroenteritis f inv

**gastronomic** [gæstrəˈnɒmɪk] adj gastronómico(a)

**gastronomy** [gæsˈtrɒnəmɪ] n gastronomía f

**gasworks** ['gæswɜːks] n fábrica f de gas

**gate** [geɪt] n (a) (entrance) puerta f; (made of metal) verja f; **g. (number) 15** (in airport) puerta número 15 (b) Sport (spectators) entrada f; (takings) recaudación f

**gâteau** ['gætəʊ] n pastel m, tarta f

**gatecrash** ['geɪtkræʃ] Fam 1 vt **to g. a party** colarse en una fiesta
2 vi colarse

**gatecrasher** ['geɪtkræʃə(r)] n Fam intruso(a) m,f

**gatehouse** ['geɪthaʊs] *n (of park, castle)* casa *f* del guarda; *(of house, estate)* casa *f* del portero

**gatekeeper** ['geɪtki:pə(r)] *n (of park, castle)* guarda *mf; (of house, estate)* portero(a) *m,f*

**gatepost** ['geɪtpəʊst] *n* poste *m* (de la verja)

**gateway** ['geɪtweɪ] *n* entrada *f; Fig* **the g. to the East** la vía de entrada a Oriente; *Fig* **the g. to success** la clave del éxito

**gather** ['gæðə(r)] **1** *vt* **(a)** *(collect)* reunir; *(fruit, flowers)* recoger; **to g. the harvest** recoger la cosecha, cosechar; **he gathered his thoughts** puso en orden sus ideas; **to g. all one's strength to do sth** hacer acopio de fuerzas para hacer algo; **we are gathered here to-day...** estamos hoy aquí reunidos...; **he gathered her in his arms** la tomó entre sus brazos **(b)** *(accumulate) (dirt, dust)* acumular; *Fig* **to be gathering dust** estar arrinconado(a); **to g. speed** ganar velocidad **(c)** *(conclude, understand)* **to g. that...** deducir que..., entender que...; **as you may already have gathered,...** como probablemente ya habrás deducido,...; **so I g.** eso parece

**2** *vi (of people)* reunirse, congregarse; *(of things)* acumularse; **a storm is gathering** se está formando una tormenta; **to g. round the fire/ the radio** reunirse en torno al fuego/a la radio

▸**gather round** *vi* formar corro, agruparse

▸**gather together 1** *vt sep (belongings, evidence)* reunir

**2** *vi (of people)* reunirse

▸**gather up** *vt sep* recoger; **he gathered her up in his arms** la tomó en sus brazos

**gathering** ['gæðərɪŋ] **1** *n (group)* grupo *m* de personas; *(meeting)* reunión *f*

**2** *adj (darkness, speed)* creciente; *also Fig* **the g. storm** la tormenta que se viene preparando

**GATT** [gæt] *n (abbr* **General Agreement on Tariffs and Trade)** GATT *m*

**gauche** [gəʊʃ] *adj* torpe, desmañado(a)

**gaudily** ['gɔːdɪlɪ] *adv* con colores chillones

**gaudy** ['gɔːdɪ] *adj* chillón(ona), llamativo(a)

**gauge,** *US* **gage** [geɪdʒ] **1** *n* **(a)** *(size) (of screw, wire, gun)* calibre *m; (of railway track)* ancho *m* de vía **(b)** *(measuring device)* calibrador *m;* **fuel g.** indicador *m* del nivel de gasolina; **pressure g.** manómetro *m;* **the poll is a useful g. of public opinion** los sondeos son un útil indicador de la opinión pública

**2** *vt (amount, difficulty)* calcular, precisar

**Gaul** [gɔːl] *n Hist* **(a)** *(region)* Galia *f* **(b)** *(inhabitant)* galo(a) *m,f*

**gaunt** [gɔːnt] *adj (person, features)* demacrado(a)

**gauntlet** ['gɔːntlɪt] *n (glove)* guante *m* (largo); *Hist* guantelete *m,* manopla *f; Fig* **to throw** *or* **fling down the g.** *(challenge)* arrojar el guante;

*Fig* **to take up the g.** recoger el guante, aceptar el reto; *Fig* **to run the g. of sth** exponerse a algo

**gauze** [gɔːz] *n* gasa *f*

**gave** [geɪv] *pt of* **give**

**gavel** ['gævəl] *n* martillo *m,* maceta *f (de subastador, juez)*

**gawk** = **gawp**

**gawky** ['gɔːkɪ] *adj Fam* desgarbado(a)

**gawp** [gɔːp] *vi Fam* quedarse papando moscas; **to g. at sth/sb** mirar boquiabierto(a) algo/a alguien

**gay** [geɪ] **1** *adj* **(a)** *(homosexual)* homosexual, gay; **g. rights** derechos *mpl* de los homosexuales **(b)** *esp Old-fashioned (happy)* alegre; **with g. abandon** con alegre despreocupación

**2** *n (man)* homosexual *m,* gay *m; (woman)* lesbiana *f*

**Gaza** [gɑːzə] *n* Gaza; **the G. Strip** la Franja de Gaza

**gaze** [geɪz] **1** *n* mirada *f* (fija); **to meet** *or* **return sb's g.** devolver la mirada a alguien

**2** *vi* **to g. at** mirar fijamente *or* embobadamente; **to g. into space** *or* **the middle distance** mirar al vacío

**gazelle** [gə'zel] *n* gacela *f*

**gazette** [gə'zet] *n (official journal)* boletín *m* oficial

**gazetteer** [gæzɪ'tɪə(r)] *n (book)* diccionario *m* geográfico

**gazump** [gə'zʌmp] *vt Br Fam* = en una compraventa de una propiedad, retractarse el vendedor de un precio acordado verbalmente para obtener otro mayor de otro comprador

**GB** [dʒiː'biː] *n (abbr* **Great Britain)** GB, Gran Bretaña

**GBH** [dʒiːbiː'eɪtʃ] *n Law (abbr* **grievous bodily harm)** lesiones *fpl* graves

**GC** [dʒiː'siː] *n (abbr* **George Cross)** = condecoración civil concedida por actos de heroísmo

**GCE** [dʒiːsiː'iː] *n Br Sch Formerly (abbr* **General Certificate of Education)** = certificado de enseñanza secundaria

**GCHQ** [dʒiːsiːeɪtʃ'kjuː] *n Br (abbr* **Government Communications Headquarters)** = servicio británico de espionaje electrónico

**GCSE** [dʒiːsiːes'iː] *n Br Sch (abbr* **General Certificate of Secondary Education)** = certificado de enseñanza secundaria

**Gdns** *(abbr* **Gardens)** Jardines *(en direcciones)*

**GDP** [dʒiːdiː'piː] *n Econ (abbr* **gross domestic product)** PIB *m*

**GDR** [dʒiːdiːɑː(r)] *n Formerly (abbr* **German Democratic Republic)** RDA *f*

**gear** [gɪə(r)] *n* (a) *(on car, bicycle)* *(speed)* marcha *f*, velocidad *f*; *(mechanism)* engranaje *m*; *Fig* to put sb's plans out of g. desbaratar los planes de alguien; first/second g. primera *f*/segunda *f* (marcha *or* velocidad); *Aut* g. lever palanca *f* de cambios (b) *Fam (equipment)* equipo *m*; *(in kitchen)* aparatos *mpl*; *(belongings)* bártulos *mpl* (c) *Fam (clothes)* ropa *f*

▸gear to *vt sep* to g. sth to sth adaptar algo a algo

▸gear towards *vt sep* to be geared towards sth/sb estar dirigido(a) *or* orientado(a) a algo/alguien

**gearbox** ['gɪəbɒks] *n* caja *f* de cambios

**gearstick** ['gɪəstɪk] *n* palanca *f* de cambios

**gee** [dʒiː] *exclam* (a) *(to horse)* g. up! ¡arre! (b) *US* g. (whizz)! ¡anda!, ¡caramba!

**gee-gee** ['dʒiːdʒiː] *n Fam (in children's language)* caballito *m*

**geese** [giːs] *pl of* **goose**

**geezer** ['giːzə(r)] *n Br very Fam* tío *m*; **old g.** tarra *m*, vejestorio *m*

**Geiger counter** ['gaɪgə(r)] *n* contador *m* Geiger

**gel** [dʒel] **1** *n (for shower)* gel *m*; *(for hair)* gomina *f*
**2** *vi (pt & pp* **gelled)** *(of liquid)* aglutinarse; *Fig (of ideas, plans, team)* cuajar

**gelatin(e)** [dʒelə'tiːn] *n* gelatina *f*

**gelatinous** [dʒɪ'lætɪnəs] *adj* gelatinoso(a)

**gelding** ['geldɪŋ] *n* caballo *m* castrado

**gelignite** ['dʒelɪgnaɪt] *n* gelignita *f* (explosiva)

**gem** [dʒem] *n (precious stone)* gema *f*; *Fig* he's an absolute g. es una verdadera joya

**Gemini** ['dʒemɪnaɪ] *n (sign of zodiac)* Géminis *m inv*; to be (a) G. ser Géminis

**gemstone** ['dʒemstəʊn] *n* piedra *f* preciosa, gema *f*

**gen** [dʒen] *n Br Fam (information)* información *f*, datos *mpl*

**gender** ['dʒendə(r)] *n* (a) *Gram* género *m* (b) *(sex)* sexo *m*

**gene** [dʒiːn] *n Biol* gen *m*; to have sth in one's genes *(talent, trait)* llevar algo en los genes *or* en la sangre

**genealogy** [dʒiːnɪ'ælədʒɪ] *n* genealogía *f*

**general** ['dʒenərəl] **1** *n* (a) in g. en general (b) *Mil* general *m*
**2** *adj* general; as a g. rule por norma *or* regla general; in g. terms en términos generales; g. anaesthetic anestesia *f* general; G. Assembly *(of United Nations)* Asamblea *f* General; g. election elecciones *fpl* generales; g. knowledge cultura *f* general; g. manager director(ora) *m,f* general; g. meeting asamblea *f* general; *Med* g. practice medicina *f* general; *Med* g. practitioner médico(a) *m,f* de

cabecera *or* de familia; the g. public el gran público, el público en general; *US* g. store tienda *f (que vende de todo)*; g. strike huelga *f* general

**generality** [dʒenə'rælɪtɪ] *n* generalidad *f*

**generalization** [dʒenərəlaɪ'zeɪʃən] *n* generalización *f*

**generalize** ['dʒenərəlaɪz] **1** *vt* to become generalized *(of practice, belief)* generalizarse
**2** *vi* generalizar

**generally** ['dʒenrəlɪ] *adv (taken overall)* en general; *(as a general rule)* generalmente, por lo general; g. speaking en términos generales

**generate** ['dʒenəreɪt] *vt (electricity, income)* generar; *(reaction, interest)* provocar

**generation** [dʒenə'reɪʃən] *n* (a) *(of people, computers)* generación *f*; from g. to g. de generación en generación; the younger/older g. la generación joven/vieja; g. gap conflicto *m* generacional (b) *(production) (of electricity)* producción *f*

**generator** ['dʒenəreɪtə(r)] *n Elec* generador *m*

**generic** [dʒɪ'nerɪk] *adj* genérico(a)

**generosity** [dʒenə'rɒsɪtɪ] *n* generosidad *f*

**generous** ['dʒenərəs] *adj* generoso(a)

**generously** ['dʒenərəslɪ] *adv* generosamente

**genesis** ['dʒenɪsɪs] *n* génesis *f inv*, origen *m*; (the Book of) G. (el Libro *m* del) Génesis *m*

**genetic** [dʒɪ'netɪk] *adj* genético(a); g. code código *m* genético; g. engineering ingeniería *f* genética; g. fingerprinting identificación *f* genética

**genetically** [dʒɪ'netɪklɪ] *adv* genéticamente

**genetics** [dʒɪ'netɪks] *n* genética *f*

**Geneva** [dʒɪ'niːvə] *n* Ginebra; Lake G. el Lago Leman; the G. Convention la Convención de Ginebra

**genial** ['dʒiːnɪəl] *adj* cordial, amable

**geniality** [dʒiːnɪ'ælɪtɪ] *n* cordialidad *f*, amabilidad *f*

**genially** ['dʒiːnɪəlɪ] *adv* cordialmente, amablemente

**genie** ['dʒiːnɪ] *n (pl* **genii** ['dʒiːnɪaɪ]) *n* duende *m*, genio *m*

**genital** ['dʒenɪtəl] **1** *adj* genital
**2** *npl* **genitals** (órganos *mpl*) genitales *mpl*

**genitive** ['dʒenɪtɪv] *Gram* **1** *n* genitivo *m*
**2** *adj* genitivo(a); g. case (caso *m*) genitivo *m*

**genius** ['dʒiːnɪəs] *n (person)* genio *m*; *(aptitude)* genio *m*, don *m*; to have a g. for... tener un don *(natural)* para...; man/work of g. hombre *m*/obra *f* genial

**Genoa** ['dʒenəʊə] *n* Génova

**genocide** ['dʒenəsaɪd] *n* genocidio *m*

**genre** ['ʒɒnrə] *n (of film, novel)* género *m*

**gent** [dʒent] *n Br Fam* **(a)** *(gentleman)* caballero *m*, señor *m*; **gents' footwear** calzado *m* de caballero **(b) the gents** *(toilets)* el servicio de caballeros

**genteel** [dʒen'tiːl] *adj (delicate)* fino(a); *Pej* afectado(a); *(respectable)* respetable

**Gentile** ['dʒentaɪl] *n* gentil *mf*, no judío(a) *m,f*

**gentle** ['dʒentəl] *adj (person, manner)* tierno(a), afectuoso(a); *(push, breeze, slope, exercise)* suave; *(hint)* discreto(a); *(rise, fall)* leve; **to be g. with sb/sth** tener cuidado con alguien/algo

**gentleman** ['dʒentəlmən] *n* caballero *m*; **he's a real g.** es todo un caballero; **a g.'s agreement** un pacto entre caballeros; **Ladies and Gentlemen!** ¡señoras y señores!

**gentlemanly** ['dʒentəlmənlɪ] *adj* caballeroso(a), cortés

**gentleness** ['dʒentəlnɪs] *n (of person, nature)* ternura *f*, afectuosidad

**gently** ['dʒentlɪ] *adv (to treat)* con ternura, afectuosamente; *(to move, touch)* con suavidad; *(slowly)* despacio, poco a poco

**gentrification** [dʒentrɪfɪ'keɪʃən] *n Br* aburguesamiento *m (de barrio obrero)*

**gentry** ['dʒentrɪ] *npl* alta burguesía *f*

**genuflect** ['dʒenjʊflekt] *vi* hacer una genuflexión

**genuine** ['dʒenjʊɪn] *adj* **(a)** *(authentic) (manuscript, painting)* genuino(a), auténtico(a) **(b)** *(sincere)* sincero(a); **a g. mistake** un error no intencionado

**genuinely** ['dʒenjʊɪnlɪ] *adv (sincerely)* realmente

**genus** ['dʒiːnəs] (*pl* **genera** ['dʒenərə]) *n Biol* género *m*

**geo-** ['dʒiːəʊ] *pref* geo-

**geographer** [dʒɪ'ɒɡrəfə(r)] *n* geógrafo(a) *m,f*

**geographic(al)** [dʒɪə'ɡræfɪk(əl)] *adj* geográfico(a)

**geography** [dʒɪ'ɒɡrəfɪ] *n* geografía *f*

**geologic(al)** [dʒɪə'lɒdʒɪk(əl)] *adj* geológico(a)

**geologist** [dʒɪ'ɒlədʒɪst] *n* geólogo(a) *m,f*

**geology** [dʒɪ'ɒlədʒɪ] *n* geología *f*

**geometric(al)** [dʒɪə'metrɪk(əl)] *adj* geométrico(a)

**geometry** [dʒɪ'ɒmɪtrɪ] *n* geometría *f*

**geophysics** [dʒɪəʊ'fɪzɪks] *n* geofísica *f*

**geopolitics** [dʒɪəʊ'pɒlɪtɪks] *n* geopolítica *f*

**Geordie** ['dʒɔːdɪ] **1** *n Br Fam* = natural o habitante de la región de Tyneside

**2** *adj* de la región de Tyneside

**Georgia** ['dʒɔːdʒɪə] *n (country, US state)* Georgia

**Georgian** ['dʒɔːdʒɪən] **1** *n* **(a)** *(person)* georgiano(a) *m,f* **(b)** *(language)* georgiano *m*

**2** *adj* **(a)** *(of country, US state)* georgiano(a) **(b)** *Br (architecture, furniture)* georgiano(a)

**geothermal** [dʒiːəʊ'θɜːməl] *adj* geotérmico(a)

**geranium** [dʒə'reɪnɪəm] *n* geranio *m*

**gerbil** ['dʒɜːbɪl] *n* jerbo *m*, gerbo *m*

**geriatric** [dʒerɪ'ætrɪk] **1** *n Med* anciano(a) *m,f*; *Fam Pej* vejestorio *mf*

**2** *adj* geriátrico(a)

**geriatrics** [dʒerɪ'ætrɪks] *n* geriatría *f*

**germ** [dʒɜːm] *n* **(a)** *Med (micro-organism)* germen *m*, microbio *m*; **g. warfare** guerra *f* bacteriológica **(b)** *Bot & Fig* germen

**German** ['dʒɜːmən] **1** *n* **(a)** *(person)* alemán(ana) *m,f* **(b)** *(language)* alemán *m*; **G. class/teacher** clase *f*/profesor(ora) *m,f* de alemán

**2** *adj* alemán(ana); **G. measles** rubeola *f*; **G. shepherd** pastor *m* alemán

**germane** [dʒɜː'meɪn] *adj Formal* pertinente; **that's not entirely g. to the matter** eso no concierne mucho al asunto

**Germanic** [dʒɜː'mænɪk] *adj* germánico(a)

**Germany** ['dʒɜːmənɪ] *n* Alemania

**germinate** ['dʒɜːmɪneɪt] *vi* germinar

**germination** [dʒɜːmɪ'neɪʃən] *n* germinación *f*

**gerrymander** ['dʒerɪmændə(r)] *vt Pol* = alterar los límites de un distrito electoral para que un partido obtenga mejores resultados

**gerund** ['dʒerənd] *n Gram* gerundio *m*

**gestation** [dʒes'teɪʃən] *n Med & Fig* gestación *f*; **g. period** período *m* de gestación

**gesticulate** [dʒes'tɪkjʊleɪt] *vi* gesticular

**gesture** ['dʒestʃə(r)] **1** *n also Fig* gesto *m*; *Fig* **as a g. of friendship** en señal de amistad; *Fig* **a hollow or empty g.** un gesto vacuo or para guardar las apariencias

**2** *vi (single action)* hacer un gesto; *(repeatedly)* gesticular, hacer gestos; **to g. towards sth** *(point)* señalar or indicar hacia algo

**get** [get] (*pt & pp* **got** [gɒt], *US pp* **gotten** ['gɒtən]) **1** *vt*

En las expresiones que aparecen bajo **(l)** y **(m)**, **get** suele ser opcional. Cuando se omite **get**, **have** no se contrae. Para los casos en que se puede omitir, véase **have**.

**(a)** *(obtain)* conseguir; *(buy)* comprar; **could you g. me some crisps from the shop?** ¿me traes unas patatas fritas de la tienda?; **I can g. you a new video for just £30** te puedo conseguir un vídeo nuevo por sólo 30 libras; **to g. a job** encontrar trabajo; **to g. the right/wrong answer** dar la respuesta correcta/equivocada

**(b)** *(receive) (present, reply, shock)* recibir; **we**

can't g. BBC2 here aquí no recibimos or no llega la BBC2; **I got the idea from a book** saqué la idea de un libro; **to g. £18,000 a year** ganar 18.000 libras anuales; **we don't g. many visitors here** no viene mucha gente por aquí

**(c)** *(catch) (person, disease)* coger; *Am* agarrar; *(train, bus)* coger, tomar; *Am* agarrar; *Fam* **I'll g. you for that!** ¡me las pagarás!

**(d)** *(fetch)* **to g. sth for sb** traerle algo a alguien; **g. me the hammer** tráeme el martillo; **go and g. a doctor** ve a buscar a un médico

**(e)** *Fam (annoy)* **what gets me is that…** lo que me saca de quicio es que…

**(f)** *Fam (understand)* **now I g. you!** ¡ahora te entiendo!; **I don't g. your meaning** no pillo or no cojo lo que quieres decir; **to g. a joke** coger un chiste

**(g)** *(send)* **to g. sth to sb** mandar or enviar algo a alguien; **I got a message to them** les mandé or envié un mensaje

**(h)** *(cause to be in a certain state)* **to g. sth dry/wet** secar/mojar algo; **to g. sth dirty** ensuciar algo; **she got her work finished** terminó su trabajo; **to g. sth fixed** arreglar algo; **you've got him worried** lo has dejado preocupado; **to g. the children to bed** acostar a los niños

**(i)** *(cause to do)* **she got me to help her** me pidió que la ayudara; **why don't you g. your mother to do it?** ¿por qué no le pides a tu madre que lo haga ella?; **I finally got my mother to do it** por fin conseguí que lo hiciera mi madre; **you can g. them to wrap it for you** puedes pedir que te lo envuelvan; **I can't g. the car to start** no consigo que arranque el coche

**(j)** *(do gradually)* **to g. to know sb** llegar a conocer a alguien; **you'll g. to like him** te llegará a gustar; **she soon got to thinking that…** pronto empezó a pensar que…

**(k)** *(have opportunity)* **to g. to do sth** llegar a or tener la ocasión de hacer algo; **you g. to travel a lot in this job** en este trabajo se viaja mucho; **I finally got to see her** por fin pude or conseguí verla

**(l)** *(possess) (with* **have***)* **they've got a big house** tienen una casa grande; **she hasn't got a car** no tiene coche; **she's got measles/AIDS** tiene (el) sarampión/sida; **we've got a choice** tenemos una alternativa; **I've got something to do** tengo algo que hacer; **what's that got to do with it?** ¿qué tiene eso que ver?

**(m)** *(must) (with* **have***)* **I've got to go** me tengo que ir; **have you got to work?** ¿tienes que trabajar?; **it's got to be done** hay que hacerlo

**2** *vi* **(a)** *(arrive)* llegar; **to g. home** llegar a casa;

**how do you g. there?** ¿cómo se llega?; **he got as far as Chapter Five** llegó hasta el quinto capítulo

**(b)** *(move)* **to g. in the way** ponerse en medio; **to g. in the way of sb, to g. in sb's way** ponerse delante de alguien; **she got over the wall** sorteó or pasó el muro

**(c)** *(become)* **to g. angry** enfadarse; **to g. better** mejorar; **to g. drunk** emborracharse; **to g. old** envejecer

**(d)** *(in passive-type constructions)* **to g. broken** romperse; **to g. stolen** ser robado(a)

**(e)** *(in reflexive-type constructions)* **to g. dressed** vestirse; **to g. married** casarse

**(f)** *(start)* **to g. going** *(leave)* irse, marcharse; *(start working)* empezar a funcionar; **to g. talking with sb** empezar a hablar con alguien
▸**get about** *vi (of person)* moverse; *(of news, rumour)* difundirse, trascender

▸**get across** *vt sep* **to g. an idea/a message across** hacer entender una idea/un mensaje; **to g. sth across to sb** hacer que alguien entienda algo

▸**get ahead** *vi* abrirse paso or camino

▸**get along** *vi* **(a)** *(leave)* marcharse, irse **(b)** *(progress)* **how are you getting along in your new job?** ¿cómo te va en el nuevo trabajo?; **we can g. along without them** podemos seguir sin ellos **(c)** *(have good relationship)* llevarse bien

▸**get around** *vt insep (avoid)* eludir

**2** *vi =* **get about**

▸**get around to** *vt insep* **to g. around to doing sth** sacar tiempo para hacer algo

▸**get at** *vt insep* **(a)** *(gain access to)* acceder a, llegar a; *(reach)* alcanzar; **to g. at the truth** dar con la verdad **(b)** *(imply)* **what are you getting at?** ¿qué (es lo que) quieres decir? **(c)** *Fam (criticize unfairly) (person)* meterse con, chinchar

▸**get away** *vi (escape)* irse, escaparse; *(have a holiday)* tomarse unas vacaciones; *Fam* **g. away!** *(expressing disbelief)* ¡anda or venga ya!

▸**get away with** *vt insep (crime)* salir impune de; **I don't know how you g. away with speaking to your mother like that** no entiendo cómo tu madre te permite que le hables así; **he got away with a small fine** sólo le han puesto una pequeña multa; *Fig* **that child gets away with murder!** ¡ese niño se sale siempre con la suya!

▸**get back 1** *vt sep (recover)* recuperar

**2** *vi (return)* volver, regresar

▸**get back at** *vt insep* **to g. back at sb (for sth)** vengarse de alguien (por algo)

▸**get behind 1** *vt insep (support)* apoyar

**2** *vi (become delayed)* atrasarse, quedarse atrás

▸**get by** *vi (manage)* arreglárselas; **to g. by in Spanish** defenderse en español

▸**get down 1** *vt sep* **(a)** *(reduce) (weight)* bajar; *(costs, temperature)* reducir **(b)** *(depress)* **to g. sb**

**down** desanimar or deprimir a alguien

**2** vi (descend) bajarse (**from** de)

▶**get down to** vt insep ponerse a; **to g. down to doing sth** ponerse a hacer algo; **to g. down to work** poner manos a la obra; **to g. down to the facts** ir (directamente) a los hechos; **when you g. down to it...** en el fondo...

▶**get in 1** vt sep (a) (bring inside) (washing) meter; (harvest) recoger (**b**) **I couldn't g. a word in** (in conversation) no pude meter baza (**c**) (stock up with) (food, coal) hacer acopio de

**2** vi (**a**) (arrive) (of train, person) llegar (**b**) (be elected) salir elegido(a), ganar las elecciones

▶**get into** vt insep (**a**) (house, car) entrar en; **to g. into Parliament** salir elegido(a) parlamentario(a); **to g. into trouble** meterse en un lío; Fam **I don't know what's got into her** no sé qué mosca le ha picado (**b**) (clothes, boots) ponerse (**c**) Fam **I really got into it** (book, activity) me enganchó muchísimo

▶**get in with** vt insep (ingratiate oneself with) congraciarse con

▶**get off 1** vt sep (**a**) (save from punishment) **to g. sb off** librar or salvar a alguien (**b**) **to g. the children off to school** mandar a los niños al colegio; **to g. a baby off to sleep** dormir a un niño

**2** vt insep (bus, train) bajarse de

**3** vi (**a**) (descend from vehicle) bajarse, apearse; Fig **I told him where to g. off** (rebuked him) lo mandé a paseo (**b**) (go unpunished) librarse (**c**) (begin) **to g. off (to sleep)** dormirse, quedarse dormido(a); **to g. off to a good/bad start** empezar con buen/mal pie

▶**get off on** vt insep very Fam **she really gets off on ordering people about** realmente le mola eso de mandar

▶**get off with** vt insep Br Fam **to g. off with sb** enrollarse or ligar con alguien

▶**get on 1** vt sep **to g. one's clothes/trousers on** ponerse la ropa/los pantalones

**2** vt insep (board) (train, bus, plane) montar en, subir a

**3** vi (**a**) (board) montarse, subirse (**b**) (succeed, progress) **how are you getting on?** ¿cómo te va?; **I'm getting on well/badly** me va bien/mal; **you'll never g. on in life or in the world with that attitude!** ¡con esa actitud nunca llegarás a ninguna parte! (**c**) (have good relationship) llevarse bien; **to g. on well/badly with sb** llevarse bien/mal con alguien (**d**) **to be getting on (in years)** ser bastante mayor

▶**get on for** vt insep **he must be getting on for fifty** debe de tener cerca de los cincuenta; **it was getting on for midnight** era cerca de medianoche

▶**get onto** vt insep (**a**) (contact) ponerse en contacto con (**b**) (move onto subject of) pasar a (hablar de); **they eventually got onto (the subject**

**of) money** finalmente pasaron a hablar de (asuntos de) dinero

▶**get out 1** vt sep (tools, books) sacar; (nail, splinter) sacar, extraer; (stain) quitar

**2** vi (**a**) (leave) salir (**b**) (of news) filtrarse; **the secret got out** se descubrió el secreto

▶**get out of** vt insep (car) salir or bajar de; (the way) apartarse de; **to g. out of doing sth** librarse de hacer algo

▶**get over 1** vt sep (communicate) hacer llegar, transmitir

**2** vt insep (**a**) (cross) (road, river) cruzar; (wall, fence) franquear (**b**) (recover from) (illness, trauma) recuperarse de

▶**get over with** vt sep **to g. sth over with** terminar con algo

▶**get round 1** vt insep (avoid) eludir

**2** vi = **get about**

▶**get round to** = **get around to**

▶**get through 1** vt sep (communicate) **to g. sth through to sb** hacer ver algo a alguien

**2** vt insep (**a**) (pass through) (hole, roof) entrar por (**b**) (survive) (test, interview) pasar, superar; (period of time) superar, aguantar (**c**) (finish) (work) terminar, acabar (**d**) (consume) (food, drink) consumir; (money) gastar

**3** vi (**a**) (arrive) (of news, messenger) llegar (**b**) **to g. through to sb** (on telephone) (lograr) comunicarse con alguien; Fig (communicate with) conectar con alguien; **the idea had finally got through to him** la idea le entró por fin en la cabeza

▶**get together 1** vt sep **to g. some money together** juntar algo de dinero; **let me g. my thoughts together** déjame poner en claro mis ideas

**2** vi (of people) quedar, verse

▶**get up 1** vt sep (**a**) (rouse) **to g. sb up** levantar or despertar a alguien (**b**) (dress up) **he got himself up in his best clothes** se puso sus mejores ropas; **to g. oneself up as sb/sth** disfrazarse de alguien/algo (**c**) very Fam **he couldn't g. it up** (achieve erection) no se le empinaba

**2** vt insep Fig **to g. up sb's nose** (annoy) tocar a alguien las narices

**3** vi (**a**) (rise) levantarse

▶**get up to** vt insep **what have you been getting up to recently?** ¿qué has estado haciendo últimamente?; **to g. up to mischief** hacer de las suyas; **he's been getting up to his old tricks** ha vuelto a las andadas

**getaway** ['getweɪ] n fuga f, huida f; **to make one's g.** fugarse, escaparse; **g. car** vehículo m utilizado en la fuga

**get-rich-quick** ['get'rɪt['kwɪk] adj Fam **a g. scheme** un proyecto para enriquecerse rápidamente

**get-together** ['getˈtəgeðə(r)] *n Fam* reunión *f*

**get-up** ['getʌp] *n Fam (clothes)* indumentaria *f*; *(fancy dress)* disfraz *m*

**get-up-and-go** [getʌpəndˈgəʊ] *n Fam (energy)* dinamismo *m*, iniciativa *f*

**get-well card** ['getˈwelˈkɑːd] *n* = tarjeta con que se desea a un enfermo su mejoría

**geyser** ['giːzə(r)] *n Geog* géiser *m*

**Ghana** ['gɑːnə] *n* Ghana

**Ghanaian** [gɑːˈneɪən] *n & adj* ghanés(esa) *m,f*

**ghastly** ['gɑːstlɪ] *adj (terrible)* horrible, horroroso(a); **it was all a g. mistake** todo fue un tremendo error; **he looked g.** tenía un aspecto horrible

**gherkin** ['gɜːkɪn] *n* pepinillo *m*

**ghetto** ['getəʊ] *(pl* **ghettos**) *n* gueto *m*; **g. blaster** *(cassette player)* radiocasete *m* portátil *(de gran tamaño)*

**ghost** [gəʊst] **1** *n* fantasma *m*; *Fig* **the g. of a smile** la sombra de una sonrisa; *Fig* **she doesn't have the g. of a chance** no tiene ni la más remota posibilidad; *Rel* **the Holy G.** el Espíritu Santo; **to give up the g.** pasar a mejor vida; **g. story** relato *m* de fantasmas; **g. town** ciudad *f*/pueblo *m* fantasma

**2** *vt* **to g. a book for sb** escribir anónimamente un libro para alguien

**ghostly** ['gəʊstlɪ] *adj* fantasmal

**ghostwrite** ['gəʊstraɪt] *vt* **to g. a book for sb** escribir anónimamente un libro para alguien

**ghostwriter** ['gəʊstraɪtə(r)] *n* negro(a) *m,f*, escritor(ora) *m,f* anónimo(a)

**ghoul** [guːl] *n (evil spirit)* espíritu *m* maligno; *Fig (morbid person)* espíritu *m* macabro

**ghoulish** ['guːlɪʃ] *adj (humour, remark)* macabro(a)

**GHQ** [dʒiːeɪtʃˈkjuː] *n Mil (abbr* **General Headquarters)** cuartel *m* general

**GI** [dʒiːˈaɪ] *n US Fam* soldado *m* raso

**giant** ['dʒaɪənt] **1** *n* gigante(a) *m,f*; **g. killer** *(in sport)* matagigantes *mf inv*

**2** *adj* colosal, gigantesco(a)

**gibber** ['dʒɪbər] *vi (talk incoherently)* farfullar; *(of monkey)* parlotear

**gibbering** ['dʒɪbərɪŋ] *adj* incoherente, desvariado(a); *Fam* **a g. idiot** un perfecto idiota

**gibberish** ['dʒɪbərɪʃ] *n (unintelligible speech, writing)* galimatías *m inv*; *(nonsense)* tonterías *fpl*, memeces *fpl*; **to talk g.** decir tonterías *or* memeces

**gibbet** ['dʒɪbɪt] *n* horca *f*

**gibbon** ['gɪbən] *n* gibón *m*

**gibe** [dʒaɪb] **1** *n* burla *f*

**2** *vi* **to g. at sb** hacer burla de alguien

**giblets** ['dʒɪblɪts] *npl* menudillos *mpl*

**Gibraltar** [dʒɪˈbrɔːltə(r)] *n* Gibraltar

**giddiness** ['gɪdɪnɪs] *n (dizziness)* mareo *m*; *(from height)* vértigo *m*

**giddy** ['gɪdɪ] *adj (dizzy)* **to be g.** estar mareado(a); *(from height)* tener vértigo; **g. heights** alturas *fpl*, cumbre *f*

**GIF** [dʒɪf] *n Comptr (abbr* **Graphics Interchange Format)** GIF *m*, formato *m* de intercambio de gráficos

**gift** [gɪft] *n* **(a)** *(present)* regalo *m*, obsequio *m*; *Prov* **never look a g. horse in the mouth** a caballo regalado no le mires el diente; **g. shop** tienda *f* de artículos de regalo; **g. token** vale *m* de regalo **(b)** *(talent)* don *m*; **to have a g. for mathematics** tener un don para las matemáticas; **to have the g. of the gab** tener un pico de oro

**gifted** ['gɪftɪd] *adj (talented)* dotado(a); *(unusually talented)* superdotado(a)

**giftwrapped** ['gɪftræpt] *adj* envuelto(a) para regalo

**gig** [gɪg] *n* **(a)** *(carriage)* calesa *f* **(b)** *Fam (pop concert)* actuación *f*, concierto *m*

**gigabyte** ['dʒɪgəbaɪt] *n Comptr* gigabyte *m*

**gigantic** [dʒaɪˈgæntɪk] *adj* gigantesco(a)

**giggle** ['gɪgəl] **1** *n* risita *f*, risa *f* floja; **to have (a fit of) the giggles** tener un ataque de risa tonta; *Fam* **to do sth for a g.** hacer algo de broma

**2** *vi* soltar risitas

**giggly** ['gɪgəlɪ] *adj* **two g. girls at the back of the class** dos niñas soltando risitas al fondo de la clase

**gigolo** ['dʒɪgələʊ] *(pl* **gigolos)** *n* gigoló *m*

**gild** [gɪld] *(pt & pp* **gilded** *or* **gilt** [gɪlt]) *vt* dorar; *Fig* **to g. the lily** rizar el rizo

**gill¹** [gɪl] *n* gills *(of fish)* branquias *fpl*; *Fig* **to be green about the gills** *(look unwell)* estar pálido(a)

**gill²** [dʒɪl] *n (liquid measure)* cuarto *m* de pinta *(0,142 litros)*

**gilt** [gɪlt] **1** *n (baño m)* dorado *m*; *Fin* **gilts** valores *mpl* del Estado

**2** *adj* dorado(a)

**3** *pt & pp* of **gild**

**gilt-edged** ['gɪltˈedʒd] *adj Fin* **g. securities** *or* **stock** valores *mpl* del Estado

**gimlet** ['gɪmlɪt] *n (tool)* barrena *f*; **his g. eyes** su mirada *f* penetrante

**gimme** ['gɪmi] *Fam* = **give me**

**gimmick** ['gɪmɪk] *n* truco *m*, reclamo *m*

**gimmicky** ['gɪmɪkɪ] *adj* artificioso(a)

**gin** [dʒɪn] *n* ginebra *f*; **g. and tonic** gin-tonic *m*

**ginger** ['dʒɪndʒə(r)] **1** *n* jengibre *m*; **g. ale** ginger ale *m*; **g. beer** = cerveza de baja graduación o sin alcohol con sabor a jengibre

**2** *adj (hair)* pelirrojo(a)

▸**ginger up** *vt sep Fam* animar

**gingerbread** ['dʒɪndʒəbred] *n* pan *m* de jengibre; *(biscuit-like)* galleta *f* de jengibre

**gingerly** ['dʒɪndʒəlɪ] *adv* con mucho tiento

**gingham** ['gɪŋəm] *n* guinga *f*, = tela de algodón a cuadros

**gingivitis** [dʒɪndʒɪ'vaɪtɪs] *n Med* gingivitis *f inv*

**ginormous** [dʒaɪ'nɔːməs] *adj Fam* descomunal, gigantesco(a)

**ginseng** ['dʒɪnsen] *n* ginseng *m*

**gipsy** ['dʒɪpsɪ] *n* gitano(a) *m,f*; **g. caravan** carromato *m* de gitanos

**giraffe** [dʒɪ'rɑːf] *n* jirafa *f*

**gird** [gɜːd] *(pt & pp* **girded** or **girt** [gɜːt]) *vt Literary* **to g. one's loins** armarse para la batalla

**girder** ['gɜːdə(r)] *n* viga *f*

**girdle** ['gɜːdəl] **1** *n (corset)* faja *f*
**2** *vt Literary* ceñir

**girl** [gɜːl] *n (child, baby)* niña *f*; *(young woman)* chica *f*; **that's my g.!** *(well done)* ¡buena chica!; *Br* **G. Guide** scout *f*, escultista *f*

**girlfriend** ['gɜːlfrend] *n (of boy, man)* novia *f*; *(of girl, woman)* amiga *f*

**girlhood** ['gɜːlhʊd] *n* niñez *f*

**girlie** ['gɜːlɪ] *n Fam* **g. mag** revista *f* porno

**girlish** ['gɜːlɪʃ] *adj (of girl, young woman)* de niña **(b)** *(man)* afeminado(a)

**giro** ['dʒaɪrəʊ] *(pl* **giros**) *n Br* **(a)** *Fin* **g. account** cuenta *f* de giros postales **(b)** *Fam (unemployment cheque)* cheque *m* del paro

**girt** [gɜːt] *pt & pp of* **gird**

**girth** [gɜːθ] *n (of tree)* contorno *m*; *(of person)* barriga *f*

**gist** [dʒɪst] *n* esencia *f*; **to get the g. (of sth)** entender el sentido general (de algo)

**git** [gɪt] *n Br very Fam* capullo(a) *m,f*, cabrito(a) *m,f*

**give** [gɪv] **1** *vt (pt* **gave** [geɪv], *pp* **given** ['gɪvən]) **(a)** *(in general)* dar; *(as present)* regalar; **to g. sth to sb, to g. sb sth** dar algo a alguien; *(as present)* regalar algo a alguien; **to g. sb sth to eat** dar algo de comer a alguien; **to g. a child a name** ponerle nombre a un niño; **to g. sb an illness** contagiarle *or* pegarle una enfermedad a alguien; **he was given ten years** le cayeron diez años; **he was given a fine** le pusieron una multa; **g. her my love** dale recuerdos de mi parte; **to g. sb a choice** dar a alguien una alternativa; **given the chance again** si se presentara de nuevo la ocasión; **he gave his age as twenty** declaró que tenía veinte años; **she gave me to understand that…** me dio a entender que…; **g. or take a few minutes/pesetas** minuto/peseta arriba o abajo

**(b)** *(with noun, to form verbal expressions)* **to g. a laugh** soltar una carcajada; **to g. sb a smile** sonreírle a alguien; **to g. sb a fright** dar un susto a alguien; **she gave me a strange look** me lanzó una extraña mirada; **he gave his face a wash** se lavó la cara; **she gave the soup a stir** removió *or* revolvió la sopa

**2** *vi* **(a)** *(donate)* hacer donativos; **please g. generously** por favor, sea generoso en sus donativos; **he gave of his free time to the cause** dedicó gran parte de su tiempo libre a la causa

**(b)** *(bend, stretch)* dar de sí; *(break)* ceder, romperse; **she refused to g. on the question of money** se negó a ceder en la cuestión del dinero

**(c)** *US Fam* **what gives?** ¿qué pasa?

**3** *n* elasticidad *f*

▸**give away** *vt sep* **(a)** *(give for nothing)* regalar **(b)** *(prize)* repartir; **to g. the bride away** llevar a la novia al altar **(c)** *(betray, reveal)* traicionar; **to g. away a secret** revelar un secreto; **his accent gave him away** su acento lo delató

▸**give back** *vt sep* devolver

▸**give in 1** *vt sep (hand over)* entregar
**2** *vi (surrender)* rendirse **(to** a); *(admit defeat)* rendirse, darse por vencido(a)

▸**give off** *vt sep (smell, heat)* despedir

▸**give onto** *vt insep (of window, door)* dar a

▸**give out 1** *vt sep* **(a)** *(money, food)* repartir; *(information)* divulgar **(b)** *(noise, heat)* emitir
**2** *vi (of supplies, patience)* agotarse; *(of luck)* acabarse

▸**give over 1** *vt sep (money, objects)* entregar
**2** *vi Fam (stop)* **g. over, will you?** déjalo ya, ¿quieres?

▸**give up 1** *vt sep (possessions, activity, hope)* abandonar, renunciar a; **to g. up smoking** dejar de fumar; **to g. up one's job** dejar el trabajo; **to g. sb up for dead** dar a alguien por muerto(a)
**2** *vi (stop trying)* rendirse, darse por vencido(a); **to g. up on sth/sb** *(lose faith, hope in)* dejar algo/a alguien por imposible

▸**give way** *vi* **(a)** *(collapse)* ceder, hundirse **(b)** *(yield)* *(in argument)* ceder **(to** ante); *(in car)* ceder el paso **(to** a); **g. way** *(sign)* ceda el paso **(c)** *(be superseded)* verse desbancado(a) **(to** por); **her tears gave way to laughter** las lágrimas dieron paso a la risa

**give-and-take** ['gɪvən'teɪk] *n* toma y daca *m*

**giveaway** ['gɪvəweɪ] *n Fam* **(a)** *(revelation)* señal *f* reveladora; **it was a dead g.** estaba más claro que el agua **(b)** *(free gift)* obsequio *m*; **g. price** precio *m* de saldo

**given** ['gɪvən] **1** *adj* **(a)** *(specific) (time, place)* dado(a), determinado(a); **at a g. point** en un momento dado; **g. name** nombre *m* (de pila) **(b)** *(apt, likely)* **to be g. to** ser dado(a) *or* propenso(a) a

**2** conj (considering) dado(a); **g. the nature of the case** dada la naturaleza del caso

**3** pp of **give**

**gizmo** ['gɪzməʊ] (pl **gizmos**) n US Fam chisme m, aparato m

**gizzard** ['gɪzəd] n molleja f

**glacé** ['glæsɪ] adj Culin confitado(a), escarchado(a); **g. cherries** cerezas fpl confitadas

**glacial** ['gleɪsɪəl] adj also Fig glacial

**glacier** ['glæsɪə(r)] n glaciar m

**glad** [glæd] adj alegre, contento(a); **to be glad about sth** estar alegre or contento por algo; **to be g. of sth** (grateful for) agradecer algo; **to be g. to do sth** estar encantado(a) de hacer algo; Literary **g. tidings** buenas nuevas fpl; Fam **g. rags** ropa f elegante

**gladden** ['glædən] vt alegrar, llenar de contento

**glade** [gleɪd] n Literary calvero m, claro m

**gladiator** ['glædɪeɪtə(r)] n gladiador m

**gladiolus** [glædɪ'əʊləs] (pl **gladioli** [glædɪ'əʊlaɪ]) n gladiolo m

**gladly** ['glædlɪ] adv con mucho gusto

**glamor** US = **glamour**

**glamorize** ['glæməraɪz] vt hacer atractivo(a)

**glamorous** ['glæmərəs] adj atractivo(a)

**glamour, US glamor** ['glæmə(r)] n atractivo m, encanto m; Fam **g. girl** cara f bonita

**glance** [glɑːns] **1** n vistazo m, ojeada f; **at a g.** de un vistazo; **at first g.** a primera vista

**2** vi **to g. at** echar una mirada or un vistazo a; **to g. through** (book, magazine) ojear

▸**glance off** vt insep (of blow, missile) rebotar en

**glancing** ['glɑːnsɪŋ] adj (blow) de lado, de refilón

**gland** [glænd] n glándula f

**glandular** ['glændjʊlə(r)] adj glandular; Med **g. fever** mononucleosis f inv infecciosa

**glare** [gleə(r)] **1** n (a) (angry stare) mirada f feroz (b) (bright light) resplandor m; Fig **in the full g. of publicity** en el punto de mira de toda la gente

**2** vi (stare angrily) **to g. at sth/sb** mirar algo/a alguien con furia

**glaringly** ['gleərɪŋlɪ] adv **g. obvious** clarísimo(a), de una claridad meridiana

**Glasgow** ['glɑːzgəʊ] n Glasgow

**glass** [glɑːs] n (a) (material) vidrio m, cristal m; (vessel) vaso m; (with stem) copa f; (glassware) cristalería f; **a g. of wine** un vaso de vino; **g. bottle** botella f de vidrio or cristal; **g. case** vitrina f; **g. eye** ojo m de cristal; **g. wool** lana f de vidrio

**glass-blower** ['glɑːsbləʊə(r)] n soplador(ora) m,f de vidrio

**glass-blowing** ['glɑːsbləʊɪŋ] n soplado m del vidrio

**glasses** ['glɑːsɪz] npl (spectacles) gafas fpl

**glassful** ['glɑːsfʊl] n vaso m

**glasshouse** ['glɑːshaʊs] n Br invernadero m

**glasspaper** ['glɑːspeɪpə(r)] n papel m de lija

**glassware** ['glɑːsweə(r)] n cristalería f

**glassworks** ['glɑːswɜːks] n fábrica f de vidrio

**glassy** ['glɑːsɪ] adj (water, lake) cristalino(a); (surface) vítreo(a), bruñido(a); **a g. look** una mirada vidriosa

**Glaswegian** [glæs'wiːdʒɪən] **1** n = natural o habitante de Glasgow

**2** adj de Glasgow

**glaucoma** [glɔː'kəʊmə] n glaucoma m

**glaze** [gleɪz] **1** n (on pottery) vidriado m; (on pastry) glaseado m

**2** vt (a) (window) acristalar (b) (pottery) vidriar; (pastry) glasear

▸**glaze over** vi (of eyes) velarse

**glazed** [gleɪzd] adj (a) (roof, door) acristalado(a) (b) (pottery) vidriado(a)

**glazier** ['gleɪzɪə(r)] n cristalero m, vidriero m

**gleam** [gliːm] **1** n (of light) destello m

**2** vi resplandecer, relucir

**gleaming** ['gliːmɪŋ] adj resplandeciente, reluciente

**glean** [gliːn] vt (information) averiguar; **to g. information from sth** extraer información de algo

**glee** [gliː] n (delight) regocijo m, contento m; (malicious pleasure) regodeo m

**gleeful** ['gliːfʊl] adj (happy) regocijado(a); **to be g.** (to be maliciously happy) regodearse

**glen** [glen] n Scot cañada f

**glib** [glɪb] adj (salesman, politician) con mucha labia; (talk) simplista; (excuse, answer) fácil

**glibly** ['glɪblɪ] adv con labia

**glide** [glaɪd] vi (slide) deslizarse; Av planear

**glider** ['glaɪdə(r)] n Av planeador m

**gliding** ['glaɪdɪŋ] n Av vuelo m sin motor

**glimmer** ['glɪmə(r)] **1** n brillo m tenue; Fig **g. of hope** resquicio m de esperanza; **not the slightest g. of intelligence** ni el más mínimo atisbo de inteligencia

**2** vi (of light) brillar tenuemente; (of water, metal) relucir

**glimpse** [glɪmps] **1** n vistazo m fugaz, atisbo m; **to catch a g. of** vislumbrar, entrever; **a g. of the future** un atisbo del futuro

**2** vt vislumbrar, entrever

**glint** [glɪnt] **1** n centelleo m, destello m; **with a g. in her eye** con un brillo en los ojos

**2** vi centellear, lanzar destellos

**glisten** ['glɪsən] vi relucir, brillar

**glitter** ['glɪtə(r)] **1** n (sparkle) brillo m, resplandor m; Fig (of occasion) esplendor m, brillantez f

**2** vi lanzar destellos; **her eyes glittered with**

**excitement** le brillaban los ojos de emoción; *Prov* **all that glitters is not gold** no es oro todo lo que reluce

**glittering** ['glɪtərɪŋ] *adj (jewels)* brillante, resplandeciente; *Fig (occasion, career)* rutilante

**glitz** [glɪts] *n* boato *m*, pompa *f*

**glitzy** ['glɪtsɪ] *adj Fam (party)* espectacular, despampanante

**gloat** [gləʊt] *vi (at one's own success)* alardear (**at** *or* **about** de), presumir (**at** *or* **about** de); *(about someone else's misfortune)* regodearse (**about** *or* **over** con *or* de)

**global** ['gləʊbəl] *adj (comprehensive)* global; *(worldwide)* mundial, global; **the g. village** la aldea global; **g. warming** cambio *m* climático, calentamiento *m* global

**globally** ['gləʊbəlɪ] *adv* globalmente

**globe** [gləʊb] *n (sphere)* esfera *f*, bola *f*; *(with map)* globo *m* terráqueo, bola *f* del mundo; **the g.** *(the Earth)* el globo, el planeta; **to travel the g.** viajar por todo el mundo

**globetrotter** ['gləʊbtrɒtə(r)] *n Fam* trotamundos *mf inv*

**globule** ['glɒbjuːl] *n* gota *f*

**gloom** [gluːm] *n* **(a)** *(darkness)* oscuridad *f*, tinieblas *fpl* **(b)** *Fig (melancholy)* abatimiento *m*, tristeza *f*; *Fig* **to cast** *or* **throw a g. over sth** enturbiar algo **(c)** *Fig (pessimism)* pesimismo *m*

**gloomily** ['gluːmɪlɪ] *adv (unhappily)* sombríamente, tenebrosamente

**gloomy** ['gluːmɪ] *adj* **(a)** *(dark)* oscuro(a); **weather** tiempo *m* gris **(b)** *(melancholy)* abatido(a), decaído(a); **g. thoughts** pensamientos *mpl* sombríos **(c)** *(pessimistic)* pesimista; *Fig* **to paint a g. picture (of sth)** hacer un retrato sombrío (de algo), pintar (algo) muy negro

**glorify** ['glɔːrɪfaɪ] *vt (extol, glamorize)* glorificar, ensalzar; *Rel* **to g. God** alabar a Dios

**glorious** ['glɔːrɪəs] *adj* **(a)** *(reign, victory)* glorioso(a) **(b)** *(view, weather)* espléndido(a), magnífico(a)

**gloriously** ['glɔːrɪəslɪ] *adv* espléndidamente

**glory** ['glɔːrɪ] *n* **(a)** *(honour)* gloria *f*; **to live on past glories** vivir de glorias pasadas **(b)** *(splendour)* esplendor *m*

▸**glory in** *vt insep* deleitarse *or* regocijarse con

**gloss**[1] [glɒs] **1** *n (in text)* glosa *f*

**2** *vt (text)* glosar, explicar

**gloss**[2] *n (of paint, finish)* & *Fig* lustre *m*, brillo *m*; **to take the g. off sth** deslucir algo; **g. paint** pintura *f* (con acabado) brillo

▸**gloss over** *vt insep (difficulty, mistake)* mencionar muy de pasada

**glossary** ['glɒsərɪ] *n* glosario *m*

**glossy** ['glɒsɪ] *adj* brillante; **a g. brochure** un folleto en papel cuché; **g. magazine** revista *f* de lujo a todo color; **g. paper** papel *m* cuché

**glottal stop** ['glɒtəl'stɒp] *n* oclusión *f* glotal

**glove** [glʌv] *n* guante *m*; *Fig* **the gloves are off** se ha desatado la lucha; *Aut* **g. compartment** guantera *f*; **g. puppet** marioneta *f* de guiñol

**glow** [gləʊ] **1** *n (light)* brillo *m*, resplandor *m*; *(on cheeks)* rubor *m*; *Fig* **to have a healthy g.** *(of person)* tener buen color; *Fig* **he had a g. of pride/satisfaction** se le iluminaba la cara de orgullo/satisfacción

**2** *vi (of light, fire)* brillar; *Fig* **to be glowing with health** tener un color muy saludable; *Fig* **he was glowing with pride/pleasure** la cara se le iluminaba de orgullo/placer

**glower** ['glaʊə(r)] *vi* **to g. at sb** mirar con furia a alguien

**glowing** ['gləʊɪŋ] *adj (cigarette, coal)* encendido(a); *Fig (report)* encendido(a), entusiasta; *Fig* **to paint sth in g. colours** pintar algo de color de rosa

**glow-worm** ['gləʊwɜːm] *n* luciérnaga *f*

**glucose** ['gluːkəʊs] *n* glucosa *f*

**glue** [gluː] **1** *n (in general)* pegamento *m*; *(thicker, for wood, metal)* cola *f*

**2** *vt (in general)* pegar; *(wood, metal)* encolar; *Fig* **to be glued to the television** estar pegado(a) a la televisión

**glue-sniffing** ['gluːsnɪfɪŋ] *n* inhalación *f* de pegamento

**glum** [glʌm] *adj* abatido(a), triste; **to be g.** estar abatido *or* triste

**glut** [glʌt] **1** *n Com* saturación *f*

**2** *vt (pt & pp glutted)* **(a)** *Com* saturar **(b)** **to g. oneself (on)** saciarse (de), hartarse (de)

**glutinous** ['gluːtɪnəs] *adj (substance)* viscoso(a), glutinoso(a); *(rice)* apelmazado(a)

**glutton** ['glʌtən] *n (greedy person)* glotón(ona) *m,f*; *Fig* **she's a g. for work** nunca se harta de trabajar; *Fig* **you're a g. for punishment** eres masoquista

**gluttony** ['glʌtənɪ] *n* gula *f*, glotonería *f*

**glycerin** ['glɪsərɪn], **glycerine** ['glɪsəriːn], **glycerol** ['glɪsərɒl] *n* glicerina *f*

**GMT** [dʒiːem'tiː] *n (abbr* **Greenwich Mean Time)** hora *f* del meridiano de Greenwich

**gnarled** [nɑːld] *adj (tree)* retorcido(a) y nudoso(a); *(hands)* deformado(a)

**gnash** [næʃ] *vt* **to g. one's teeth** hacer rechinar los dientes

**gnat** [næt] *n* mosquito *m*

**gnaw** [nɔː] **1** *vt (of animal)* roer

**2 (a)** *(of animal)* **to g. through sth** roer algo **(b)** *Fig (of doubt)* **to g. away at sb** corroer a alguien

**gnome** [nəʊm] *n* gnomo *m*

**GNP** [dʒiːenˈpiː] *n Econ* (*abbr* **Gross National Product**) PNB *m*

**gnu** [nuː] *n* ñu *m*

**go** [gəʊ] **1** *n* (*pl* **goes**) (**a**) (*energy*) **to be full of go** estar lleno(a) de vitalidad

(**b**) (*turn*) turno *m*; (**it's**) **your go!** ¡te toca a ti!; **to have a go at doing sth** probar a *or* intentar hacer algo; *Fam* **let's have a go!** ¡probemos!, ¡intentémoslo!; (*let me try*) ¡déjame probar!; *Fam* **she had a go at me** me echó la bronca; **at one go** de una vez; **this ride is £1 a go** (esta atracción es) a una libra el viaje

(**c**) (*idioms*) **on the go** (*active*) en marcha; **she had three boyfriends on the go at the same time** tenía tres novios al mismo tiempo; **it's all go** hay mucha actividad; **from the word "go"** desde el principio, desde el primer momento; **to make a go of sth** (*succeed*) tener éxito con algo

**2** *vi* (3rd person singular **goes** [gəʊz], *pt* **went** [went], *pp* **gone** [gɒn]) (**a**) (*in general*) ir; **to go home** irse a casa; **to go to Spain/the doctor** ir a España/al médico; **the proceeds will go to charity** las ganancias se destinarán a obras de beneficencia; *Mil* **who goes there?** ¿quién va?; *Fig* **where do we go from here?** (*what do we do next?*) y ahora, ¿qué hacemos?; **to go hunting/skiing** ir de caza/a esquiar

(**b**) (*leave*) (*person*) irse, marcharse; (*train, bus*) salir; **that dog will have to go!** ¡tenemos que librarnos de ese perro!; **we'd better get going** deberíamos irnos *or* salir ya; *Euph* **when I am gone** cuando yo falte

(**c**) (*extend*) **the garden goes down to the river** el jardín llega *or* se extiende hasta el río; **this path goes down to the beach** el camino lleva hasta la playa

(**d**) (*function*) funcionar; (*bell*) sonar; **to keep the conversation going** mantener viva la conversación

(**e**) (*progress*) ir; **to go well/badly** ir bien/mal; **to go wrong** ir mal, *Am* descomponerse, *Andes* malograrse; *Fam* **how's it going?** ¿qué tal?; **if all goes well** si todo va bien; **how does the tune/story go?** ¿cómo es *or* dice la canción/historia?

(**f**) (*of time*) **the time went quickly** el tiempo pasó muy rápido; **it has just gone eight** acaban de dar las ocho; **there are only five minutes to go** sólo quedan cinco minutos

(**g**) (*disappear, deteriorate*) desaparecer; **her sight is going** está perdiendo la vista; **the fuse has gone** se ha fundido el fusible; **the batteries are going** se están acabando las pilas; **most of my money goes on food** la mayor parte del dinero se me va en comida

(**h**) (*forming future*) **to be going to do sth** ir a hacer algo; **I was going to walk there** iba a ir andando; **it's going to rain** va a llover; **I'm**

**going to be a doctor** voy a ser médico

(**i**) (*match*) ir bien, pegar (**with** con); **these colours go/don't go** estos colores pegan/no pegan

(**j**) (*be available*) **there's a job going at the factory** hay una (plaza) vacante en la fábrica; **is there any wine going?** ¿hay vino?; **it went for £12** se vendió por 12 libras

(**k**) (*fit*) caber; **the piano won't go through the door** el piano no cabe por la puerta; **four into three won't go** tres no es divisible entre cuatro, tres entre cuatro no cabe

(**l**) (*become*) **to go crazy** volverse loco(a); **to go bad** echarse a perder; **to go red** enrojecer, ponerse rojo(a); **to go cold** enfriarse

(**m**) (*be the rule*) **what she says goes** ella es la que manda

(**n**) *Fam* (*urinate*) hacer sus necesidades, hacer pipí

(**o**) *US* **to go** (*to take away*) para llevar

**3** *vt* **to go it alone** montárselo por su cuenta; **to go one better than sb** superar a alguien; *Fam* **I could really go a beer!** ¡me tomaría una cerveza ahora mismo!

▸**go about 1** *vi* (*circulate*) (*of person*) ir por ahí; (*of rumour*) correr; **there's a bug going about** hay un virus por ahí suelto

**2** *vt insep* (**a**) (*travel*) (*country*) viajar por (**b**) (*tackle*) (*task*) abordar; **to go about doing sth** (*start*) ponerse a hacer algo; **how do I go about getting a licence?** ¿qué hay que hacer para conseguir un permiso?

▸**go across 1** *vt insep* cruzar, atravesar

**2** *vi* **to go across to the States** ir a los Estados Unidos

▸**go after** *vt insep* (*pursue*) ir tras; *Fig* (*job, prize, person*) ir a por, estar detrás de

▸**go against** *vt insep* (**a**) (*conflict with*) (*principles, instincts*) ir (en) contra de; **he went against my wishes** actuó en contra de mis deseos (**b**) (*be unfavourable to*) **the decision went against him** la decisión le fue desfavorable

▸**go ahead** *vi* (**a**) (*proceed*) seguir adelante; **to go ahead with sth** seguir (adelante) con algo; **may I say something? - go ahead** ¿puedo hablar? – adelante (**b**) (*go in front*) ir delante

▸**go along** *vi* (*proceed*) avanzar; **to do sth as one goes along** hacer algo sobre la marcha

▸**go along with** *vt insep* estar de acuerdo con, aceptar; **she wouldn't go along with it** no quiso tomar parte en ello

▸**go at** *vt insep* (*person*) atacar; (*task*) emprender

▸**go away** *vi* (*leave*) irse; (*disappear*) desaparecer; **go away!** ¡vete!; **to go away on business** irse en viaje de negocios; **to go away for the weekend** irse a pasar el fin de semana fuera

▸**go back** *vi* (**a**) (*return*) volver; **to go back to doing sth** volver a hacer algo; **to go back to one's old ways** volver a las andadas (**b**) (*date* *back)* **to go back to** remontarse a, datar de; *Fam* **we go back a long way** nos conocemos desde hace mucho tiempo

▸**go back on** *vt insep (promise, one's word)* faltar a

▸**go before 1** *vi (precede)* preceder

**2** *vt insep* **to go before the court** *(of defendant)* comparecer ante el juez, ir a juicio; *(of case)* verse

▸**go by 1** *vi* (a) *(pass)* pasar; **to watch people going by** mirar a la gente que pasa (b) *(elapse) (of time)* pasar, transcurrir

**2** *vt insep* (a) *(be guided by)* guiarse por; **to go by appearances** fiarse de las apariencias; **to go by the rules** seguir las reglas (b) *(be known by)* **to go by the name of...** ser conocido(a) con el nombre de...

▸**go down 1** *vt insep (descend) (hill, ladder)* bajar por

**2** *vi* (a) *(descend)* bajar; *(of sun)* ponerse; *(of ship)* hundirse; **to go down on one's knees** arrodillarse, ponerse de rodillas; *Fam* **to go down with an illness** coger una enfermedad (b) *(be defeated)* perder (**to** contra), caer (**to** ante); **I'm not going to go down without a fight** no voy a rendirme sin luchar (c) *(decrease) (of flood, temperature, prices)* descender; *(of tyre, balloon)* desinflarse (d) *(be received)* **to go down well/badly (with sb)** ser bien/mal acogido(a) (por alguien); **he went down in history as a tyrant** pasó a la historia como un tirano

▸**go for** *vt insep* (a) *(attack)* lanzarse contra, atacar; **if you really want the job, go for it!** si realmente te interesa el trabajo, ¡(ve) a por él! (b) *(like)* **she goes for strong types** le van los tipos fuertes (c) *(choose)* escoger, elegir (d) **he has got a lot going for him** tiene mucho a su favor (e) *(apply to)* valer para; **the same goes f. you** lo mismo te digo a ti *or* vale para ti

▸**go in** *vi (enter)* entrar; *(fit)* caber; **the sun has gone in** se ha nublado

▸**go in for** *vt insep* (a) *(competition)* tomar parte en (b) **she doesn't go in for cooking/sports** no le atrae la cocina/el deporte

▸**go into** *vt insep* (a) *(enter) (place)* entrar en; *(hospital)* ingresar en; *(career)* entrar en, meterse en (b) *(examine) (question)* tratar; **to go into detail** entrar en detalle

▸**go off 1** *vi* (a) *(leave)* marcharse, irse; **to go off with sb** *(elope)* escaparse con alguien; **to go off with sth** irse con algo, llevarse algo (b) *(of milk, meat, fish)* echarse a perder (c) *(of gun)* dispararse; *(of bomb)* explotar; *(of alarm)* saltar, sonar (d) **to go off well** *or* **smoothly** *(of event)* salir bien (e) *(be disconnected)* **the lights went off** se fue la luz

**2** *vt insep (lose liking for)* **I've gone off the idea** me ha dejado de gustar la idea

▸**go on 1** *vi* (a) *(continue)* seguir (**with** con), continuar (**with** con); **as time went on...** a medida que pasaba el tiempo... (b) *(proceed)* **to go on to sth/to do sth** pasar a algo/a hacer algo (c) *(talk excessively)* hablar sin parar, enrollarse; **to go on about sth** no parar de hablar de algo, enrollarse con algo; **to go on at sb** dar la lata a alguien (d) *(happen)* pasar, ocurrir; **what's going on here?** ¿qué pasa aquí? (e) *(of electricity, light, heating)* encenderse

**2** *vt insep* (a) *(enter) (boat, train)* subir a (b) *(be guided by)* guiarse por; **the police have nothing to go on** la policía carece de pistas (c) *(approach)* **she's two going on three** tiene dos años, casi tres

▸**go out** *vi* (a) *(leave)* salir; **to go out for a meal** salir a comer fuera; **to go out on strike** ponerse *or* declararse en huelga (b) *(date)* salir; **to go out with sb** salir con alguien (c) *(of fire, light)* apagarse (d) *(become unfashionable)* pasar de moda (e) *Sport (be eliminated)* quedar eliminado(a) (f) *TV & Rad (programme)* emitirse

▸**go over 1** *vi* (a) *(cross)* **to go over to sb** aproximarse a alguien, acercarse hasta alguien (b) *(switch)* **to go over to a different system** cambiar de sistema; **to go over to the enemy** pasarse a las filas del enemigo (c) *(be received)* **to go over well/badly** tener buena/mala acogida

**2** *vt insep* (a) *(road, bridge)* cruzar (b) *(examine) (accounts, report)* estudiar, examinar; **to go over sth in one's mind** repasar algo mentalmente

▸**go round** *vi* (a) *(visit)* **I said I'd go round (and see her)** dije que me pasaría (a visitarla); **she's gone round to a friend's** ha ido a casa de un amigo (b) *(circulate) (of rumour, cold, flu)* circular (c) *(suffice) (of food, drink)* llegar, alcanzar; **there should be enough money to go round** debería llegarnos el dinero

**2** *vt insep* **to go round town/the shops** recorrer la ciudad/las tiendas

▸**go through 1** *vi (be completed) (of bill)* aprobarse; *(of deal, divorce)* consumarse

**2** *vt insep* (a) *(penetrate)* atravesar (b) *(suffer)* pasar (por), atravesar; **in spite of all she had gone through** a pesar de todo lo que había pasado (c) *(complete) (formalities)* cumplir con (d) *(examine) (document, accounts)* estudiar, examinar; *(search) (suitcase, house, pockets)* registrar (e) *(use up) (money, food)* acabar con, gastar; **we've gone through six bottles of milk** hemos gastado seis botellas de leche

▸**go through with** *vt insep (carry out)* llevar a término

▸**go together** *vi (harmonize)* pegar, ir bien

**►go under** *vi (of drowning man)* hundirse; *(of ship)* naufragar; *(go bankrupt)* quebrar, ir a la quiebra

**►go up** *vi (a) (climb, rise)* subir; *Th (curtain)* levantarse; **to go up to bed** subir a acostarse; **a shout went up from the crowd** se elevó un grito desde la multitud; *Fig* **to go up in the world** subir peldaños, prosperar **(b)** *(of prices, temperature)* subir; **to go up in sb's estimation** crecer *or* aumentar en la estima de alguien **(c)** *(explode)* estallar; **to go up in flames** ser pasto de las llamas

**►go up to** *vt insep (a) (approach)* acercarse a, aproximarse a **(b)** *(reach)* **the book only goes up to the end of the war** el libro sólo llega hasta el final de la guerra

**►go with** *vt insep (a) (accompany)* ir con; **a company car goes with the job** el puesto lleva aparejado coche de empresa **(b)** *(harmonize with)* pegar con

**►go without 1** *vi* pasar privaciones; **they haven't got any, so we'll just have to go without** no les quedan, así que habrá que apañárselas (sin ellos)

**2** *vt insep (not have)* prescindir de, quedarse sin

**goad** [gəʊd] **1** *n Fig (remark, criticism)* acicate *m*

**2** *vt Fig (sb's curiosity, interest)* suscitar; **to g. sb into doing sth** pinchar a alguien para que haga algo; **he was goaded by these remarks** estos comentarios le sirvieron de acicate

**►goad on** *vt sep* **to g. sb on** *(motivate)* espolear *or* acicatear a alguien

**go-ahead** ['gəʊəhed] **1** *n* **to give sb/sth the g.** dar luz verde a alguien/algo

**2** *adj (enterprising)* dinámico(ca)

**goal** [gəʊl] *n (a) (aim)* objetivo *m*, meta *f*; **to achieve a g.** alcanzar un objetivo **(b)** *(in football) (point)* gol *m*; *(goalmouth)* portería *f*; **g. kick** saque *m* de puerta; **g. line** línea *f* de fondo *or* de meta; **g. scorer** goleador(ora) *m,f*

**goalkeeper** ['gəʊlkiːpə(r)], *Fam* **goalie** ['gəʊli] *n* portero(a) *m,f*, guardameta *mf*

**goalless** ['gəʊllɪs] *adj (in football)* **g. draw** empate *m* a cero

**goalmouth** ['gəʊlmaʊθ] *n (in football)* portería *f*

**goalpost** ['gəʊlpəʊst] *n (in football)* poste *m*; **the goalposts** la portería, la meta; *Fig* **to move** *or* **shift the goalposts** cambiar las reglas del juego

**goat** [gəʊt] *n* cabra *f*; **g.'s milk** leche *f* de cabra; *Fam* **it really gets my g.!** ¡me pone negro(a) *or* a cien!; **to act** *or* **play the g.** hacer el indio, hacer el ganso

**goatee** [gəʊˈtiː] *n* perilla *f*

**goatherd** ['gəʊthɜːd] *n* cabrero(a) *m,f*

**goatskin** ['gəʊtskɪn] *n* piel *f* de cabra

**gob** [gɒb] *Br very Fam* **1** *n (mouth)* pico *m*; **shut your g.!** ¡cierra el pico!

**2** *vi (pt & pp* **gobbed***) (spit)* escupir, echar lapos

**gobble** ['gɒbəl] **1** *vt (eat)* engullir

**2** *vi (of turkey)* gluglutear

**►gobble up** *vt sep* engullir; **to g. up one's food** engullir la comida; **to g. up money/resources** *(of project)* consumir mucho dinero/muchos recursos

**gobbledygook** ['gɒbldɪguːk] *n Fam* jerigonza *f*, galimatías *m inv*

**go-between** ['gəʊbɪtwiːn] *n* mediador(ora) *m,f*; **to act** *or* **serve as a g.** actuar como mediador, mediar

**goblet** ['gɒblɪt] *n* copa *f*

**goblin** ['gɒblɪn] *n* duende *m*

**gobsmacked** ['gɒbsmækt] *adj Br very Fam* **I was g.** me quedé flipado(a)

**go-cart** ['gəʊkɑːt] *n (child's toy)* coche *m* de juguete; *Sport* kart *m*; **g. racing** carreras *fpl* de karts

**God** [gɒd] *n (a)* Dios *m*; **G. forbid!** ¡Dios no lo quiera!; **G. willing** si Dios quiere; **I wish to G....** ojalá...; **in G.'s name** por el amor de Dios; *Fam* **oh G.!, my G.!** ¡Dios mío!; *Fam* **for G.'s sake!** ¡por (el amor de) Dios!; *Fam* **G. knows** sabe Dios; *Fam* **he thinks he's G.'s gift to women** se cree irresistible para las mujeres **(b)** *Th Fam* **the gods** *(gallery)* el gallinero

**godchild** ['gɒdtʃaɪld] *n* ahijado(a) *m,f*

**goddaughter** ['gɒddɔːtə(r)] *n* ahijada *f*

**goddess** ['gɒdɪs] *n* diosa *f*

**godfather** ['gɒdfɑːðə(r)] *n* padrino *m*

**god-fearing** ['gɒdfɪrɪŋ] *adj* temeroso(a) de Dios

**godforsaken** ['gɒdfəseɪkən] *adj* dejado(a) de la mano de Dios

**godless** ['gɒdlɪs] *adj (person, action)* pecaminoso(a)

**godmother** ['gɒdmʌðə(r)] *n* madrina *f*

**godparent** ['gɒdpeərənt] *n* padrino *m*, madrina *f*; **my godparents** mis padrinos

**godsend** ['gɒdsend] *n* regalo *m* del cielo; **this money is a g. to him** este dinero le viene como llovido del cielo

**godson** ['gɒdsʌn] *n* ahijado *m*

**go-getter** ['gəʊgetə(r)] *n Fam* **he's a real g.** es ambicioso y decidido

**goggle** ['gɒgəl] *vi* mirar con ojos desorbitados; **to g. at sth/sb** mirar algo/a alguien con los ojos como platos

**goggle-eyed** ['gɒgəlaɪd] *adv Fam* con ojos como platos

**goggles** ['gɒgəlz] *npl* gafas *fpl (para esquí, natación)*; **safety g.** gafas protectoras

**go-go dancer** ['gəʊ'gəʊ'dɑːnsə(r)] *n* gogó *f*

**going** ['gəʊɪŋ] **1** *n* (a) *(progress)* that's very good g.! ¡es un buen ritmo!; **it's slow g.** es muy trabajoso(a) (b) *(condition of path)* camino *m*; *(in horseracing)* terreno *m*; *Fig* **heavy g.** *(film, book)* pesado(a); *Fig* **to get out while the g. is good** retirarse mientras las cosas van bien **2** *adj* (a) *(functioning)* **a g. concern** *(successful business)* un negocio en marcha y rentable (b) *(current)* **the g. price** *or* **rate** la tasa *or* el precio vigente

**going-away** ['gəʊɪŋə'weɪ] *adj* **a g. party/present** una fiesta/un regalo de despedida

**going-over** ['gəʊɪŋ'əʊvə(r)] *n Fam* **to give sb a g.** *(beating)* dar una tunda a alguien; *(criticism)* echar un broncazo a alguien; **the auditors gave the accounts a thorough g.** los auditores miraron las cuentas de arriba abajo *or* con lupa

**goings-on** ['gəʊɪŋzɒn] *npl Fam* asuntos *mpl* turbios, tejemanejes *mpl*

**goitre,** *US* **goiter** ['gɔɪtə(r)] *n* bocio *m*

**go-kart** ['gəʊkɑːt] *n* kart *m*; **g. racing** carreras *fpl* de karts

**gold** [gəʊld] **1** *n* oro *m*; **g. bullion** lingotes *mpl* de oro; **g. dust** oro *m* en polvo; **tickets are like g. dust** las entradas están muy solicitadas; **g. leaf** *or* **foil** pan *m* de oro, oro batido; *Sport* **g. medal** medalla *f* de oro; *also Fig* **g. mine** mina *f* de oro; *Fin* **g. reserves** reservas *fpl* de oro **2** *adj* *(of gold)* de oro; *(colour)* dorado(a)

**gold-digger** ['gəʊld'dɪgə(r)] *n Fam Fig (mercenary woman)* cazafortunas *f inv*

**golden** ['gəʊldən] *adj (made of gold)* de oro; *(gold-coloured)* dorado(a); **a g. opportunity** una oportunidad de oro; **the g. boy/girl of...** el chico/la chica de oro de...; **the g. age** la edad de oro; **g. eagle** águila *f* real; **the G. Fleece** el Vellocino de Oro; **g. handshake** *(retirement bonus)* gratificación *f* voluntaria por jubilación; **g. jubilee** quincuagésimo aniversario *m* (de un reinado); *Fin* **g. share** acción *f* de oro, participación *f* de control; **g. wedding** bodas *fpl* de oro

**goldfield** ['gəʊldfiːld] *n* yacimiento *m* de oro

**goldfinch** ['gəʊldfɪntʃ] *n* jilguero *m*

**goldfish** ['gəʊldfɪʃ] *n* pez *m* de colores; **g. bowl** pecera *f*; **it's like living in a g. bowl** es como estar expuesto(a) en un escaparate

**gold-plated** ['gəʊld'pleɪtɪd] *adj* bañado(a) en oro

**goldsmith** ['gəʊldsmɪθ] *n* orfebre *mf*

**golf** [gɒlf] *n* golf *m*; **g. ball** pelota *f* de golf; **g. club** *(stick)* palo *m* de golf; *(association)* club *m* de golf; **g. course** campo *m* de golf

**golfer** ['gɒlfə(r)] *n* jugador(ora) *m,f* de golf, golfista *mf*; **to be a good g.** jugar bien al golf

**golfing** ['gɒlfɪŋ] *n* **g. holiday** = vacaciones dedicadas a jugar al golf

**golly** ['gɒlɪ] *exclam Fam Old-fashioned* ¡caramba!

**gondola** ['gɒndələ] *n* góndola *f*

**gondolier** [gɒndə'lɪə(r)] *n* gondolero *m*

**gone** [gɒn] **1** *adj* (a) *(past)* **it's g. ten o'clock** son las diez pasadas (b) *Fam* **to be six months g.** *(pregnant)* estar (embarazada) de seis meses; *Fam* **to be pretty far g.** *(drunk)* estar como una cuba; *Fam* **to be g. on sb** *(infatuated)* estar colado(a) por alguien **2** *pp of* **go**

**goner** ['gɒnə(r)] *n Fam* **I thought she was a g.** *(thought she would die)* la vi con un pie en la tumba; **I'm a g. if she finds out** *(will be in trouble)* si se entera, me mata

**gong** [gɒŋ] *n* gong *m*; *Br Fam (medal)* medalla *f*

**gonna** ['gɒnə] *Fam* = **going to**

**gonorrhoea,** *US* **gonorrhea** [gɒnə'rɪə] *n* gonorrea *f*

**goo** [guː] *n Fam* (a) *(sticky substance)* pringue *f* (b) *(sentimentality)* cursiladas *fpl*

**good** [gʊd] **1** *n* (a) *(in general)* bien *m*; **to do g.** hacer el bien; **he's up to no g.** está tramando algo malo; **to see the g. in sb/sth** ver el lado bueno de alguien/algo

(b) *(benefit)* bien *m*; **I did it for your own g.** lo hice por tu bien; **it was all to the g.** todo ha sido para bien; **for the g. of his health** por motivos de salud; **for the common g.** por el bien de todos; **it will do you g.** te sentará bien, te vendrá bien; **it won't do any g.** no va a hacer ningún bien; **what's the g. of that?** ¿para qué sirve eso?; **it's no g. complaining** quejarse no sirve de nada; **he's no g.** *(incompetent)* no sirve para nada; *(morally bad)* no es bueno

(c) **for g.** *(permanently)* para siempre

**2** *adj* *(comparative* **better** ['betə(r)], *superlative* **best** [best]) (a) *(of positive quality)* bueno(a); **it looks g. on you** te queda bien; **she looks g. in that hat** le queda muy bien ese sombrero; **to sound/taste g.** sonar/saber bien; **g. to eat** comestible; **it's g. to see you** me alegro de verte; *Fam* **that's a g. one!** *(I don't believe you)* ¡no me digas!, ¡venga ya!; **I suppose he thinks he's too g. for us** debe pensar que es más que nosotros; **if it's g. enough for you, it's g. enough for me** si a ti te vale, a mí también; **to earn g. money** ganar un buen sueldo; **you've got a g. chance** tienes bastantes posibilidades; **to be on to a g. thing** tener entre manos algo bueno; **to have a g. time** pasarlo bien; **to show sb a g. time** sacar a alguien a divertirse por ahí; **all in g. time** todo llegará; **too g. to be true** demasiado bueno para ser verdad; **it's as g. as new** está como nuevo; **he as g. as called me a liar** prácticamente me llamó mentiroso; **the g. old days**

los viejos tiempos; **g. afternoon!** ¡buenas tardes!; **the G. Book** la Biblia; **he's a g. friend** es un buen amigo; **G. Friday** Viernes *m inv* Santo; *Fam* **g. grief!** ¡madre mía!; **the g. life** la buena vida; *Fam* **g. Lord!, g. heavens!, g. gracious!** ¡madre mía!, ¡santo cielo!; **g. morning!** ¡buenos días!; **g. news** buenas noticias *fpl*; **g. night!** ¡buenas noches!, ¡hasta mañana!; **the G. Samaritan** el buen samaritano

(b) *(advantageous, appropriate)* bueno(a); **a g. opportunity** una buena ocasión; **to be in a g. position to do sth** estar en una buena posición para hacer algo; **things are looking g.** la cosa tiene buena pinta

(c) *(beneficial)* bueno(a); **this medicine is very g. for coughs** este medicamento es muy bueno para la tos; **he doesn't know what's g. for him** no sabe lo que le conviene; **to be g. for business** ser bueno para el negocio; **it's a g. thing we were here** menos mal que estábamos aquí; **g. riddance!** ¡ya era hora de que desapareciera!

(d) *(skilful)* bueno(a); **she is g. at chemistry** se le da bien la química; **he is g. at languages** se le dan bien los idiomas; **to be g. with one's hands** ser muy manitas; **she is g. with children** se le dan bien los niños; **to be g. in bed** ser bueno(a) en la cama

(e) *(well-behaved)* bueno(a); **be g.!** *(to child)* ¡sé bueno!, ¡pórtate bien!; **g. conduct** *or* **behaviour** buena conducta, buen comportamiento; **to be as g. as gold** ser más bueno(a) que el pan; **to lead a g. life** llevar una vida ejemplar

(f) *(kind)* amable; **that's very g. of you** es muy amable de tu parte; **he was very g. about it** fue muy comprensivo al respecto; **to do sb a g. turn** hacer un favor a alguien

(g) *(valid)* **a g. reason** una buena razón; **I have g. reason to believe that…** tengo buenas razones para creer que…; **there is no g. reason why…** no hay razón alguna por la que…; **he's g. for £25,000** *(has in credit)* tiene un activo de 25.000 libras; *(will contribute)* aportará 25.000 libras

(h) *(thorough)* bueno(a); **to have a g. look (at sb/sth)** echar una buena ojeada (a alguien/algo); **to have a g. cry (about)** llorar a gusto *or* echarse una buena llantina (por)

(i) **to make g.** *(of person)* prosperar; **he was ordered to make g. the company's losses** fue condenado a indemnizar a la empresa por las pérdidas; **to make g. one's promise** hacer uno una buena su promesa; **he made g. his escape** consiguió escapar

(j) *(at least)* **a g. two hours** dos horas largas, por lo menos dos horas; **a g. deal of** mucho(s), mucha(s); **a g. many** muchos(as)

**3** *adv* (a) *(for emphasis)* bien, muy; **a g. long time** un tiempo bien largo, mucho tiempo; **I'll do it when I'm g. and ready** lo haré cuando crea conveniente

(b) *(as comment, answer)* bien, estupendo; **I feel better today – g.** hoy me encuentro mejor – estupendo

**goodbye** ['gʊd'baɪ] *n* despedida *f*, adiós *m*; **g.!** ¡adiós!; **to say g.** despedirse; **to say g. to sb** decir adiós a alguien, despedir a alguien; **he can say g. to his chances of winning** puede despedirse del triunfo, puede decir adiós al triunfo

**good-for-nothing** ['gʊdfənʌθɪŋ] **1** *n* inútil *mf*

**2** *adj* *(person)* inútil

**good-humoured,** US **good-humored** [gʊd'hju:məd] *adj* jovial, distendido(a)

**good-looking** ['gʊdlʊkɪŋ] *adj* guapo(a)

**good-natured** ['gʊd'neɪtʃəd] *adj* bondadoso(a)

**goodness** ['gʊdnɪs] *n* (a) *(of person)* bondad *f* (b) *(of food)* **if you boil it, you lose all the g.** si lo hierves, pierde todas sus propiedades (c) *(in exclamations)* **g. (me)!** ¡santo cielo!; **thank g.!** ¡gracias a Dios!; **for g. sake, be quiet!** ¡por el amor de Dios, cállate!

**goodnight** [gʊd'naɪt] *n* buenas noches *fpl*; **to say g. (to sb)** dar las buenas noches (a alguien)

**goods** [gʊdz] *npl* (a) *Law* bienes *mpl* (b) *(articles)* productos *mpl*, artículos *mpl*; **leather g.** marroquinería *f*, artículos *mpl* de cuero; *Fig* **to deliver the g.** *(keep one's promise)* cumplir (lo prometido); *Fig* **to come up with the g.** cumplir; **g. depot** almacén *m* de mercancías; **g. train** tren *m* de mercancías

**good-tempered** [gʊd'tempəd] *adj* afable

**goodwill** ['gʊd'wɪl] *n* (a) *(benevolence, willingness)* buena voluntad *f*; **to retain sb's g.** conservar el favor de alguien (b) *Com* fondo *m* de comercio

**goody** ['gʊdɪ] *Fam* **1** *n* (a) *(person)* buenazo(a) *m,f*; **the goodies and the baddies** los buenos y los malos (b) *(food)* golosinas *fpl*

**2** *exclam* **g.!** ¡viva!, ¡qué chupi!

**goody-goody** ['gʊdɪgʊdɪ] *n Fam Pej* niño(a) *m,f* modelo

**gooey** ['gu:ɪ] *adj Fam* (a) *(sticky)* pegajoso(a) (b) *(sentimental)* empalagoso(a), sentimentaloide

**goof** [gu:f] *US Fam* **1** *n* (a) *(blunder)* metedura *f* de pata, patinazo *m* (b) *(idiot)* bobo(a) *m,f*

**2** *vi* meter la pata

▸**goof about, goof around** *vi US Fam (mess around)* hacer el bobo

▸**goof off** *US Fam* **1** *vi insep* **to g. off work** escaquearse

**2** *vi* gandulear, holgazanear

**goofy** ['gu:fi] *adj Fam* **(a)** *(stupid)* bobalicón(ona) **(b)** *Br (buck-toothed)* dentón(a), dentudo(a)

**goolies** ['gu:lɪz] *npl Br Vulg (testicles)* pelotas *fpl*, huevos *mpl*

**goon** [gu:n] *n Fam* **(a)** *Br (stupid person)* bobo(a) *m,f*, lerdo(a) *m,f* **(b)** *US (thug)* matón *m*

**goose** [gu:s] *(pl* **geese** [gi:s]*) n (bird)* ganso *m*, oca *f*; *Fig* **his g. is cooked** se va a caer con todo el equipo; **to kill the g. that lays the golden egg** matar la gallina de los huevos de oro; *Br* **g. pimples,** *US* **g. bumps** carne *f* de gallina

**gooseberry** ['ɡʊzbərɪ] *n* grosella *f*; *Br Fam* **to play g.** hacer de carabina *or* de sujetavelas; **g. bush** grosellero *m*

**gooseflesh** ['gu:sfleʃ] *n* carne *f* de gallina

**goose-step** ['gu:sstep] **1** *n* paso *m* de la oca **2** *vi (pt & pp* **goose-stepped***)* marchar al paso de la oca

**gopher** ['ɡəʊfə(r)] *n (ground squirrel)* ardilla *f* de tierra

**gore** [ɡɔ:(r)] **1** *n (blood)* sangre *f* (derramada) **2** *vt (of bull)* cornear, empitonar

**gorge** [ɡɔ:dʒ] **1** *n* **(a)** *(valley)* garganta *f*, desfiladero *m* **(b)** *(throat)* **it makes my g. rise** me revuelve el estómago **2** *vt* **to g. oneself (on)** hartarse (de), atiborrarse (de) **3** *vi* hartarse, atiborrarse **(on** de)

**gorgeous** ['ɡɔ:dʒəs] *adj (beautiful) (colours, day, sunset)* precioso(a); *(weather)* maravilloso(a); *(woman, baby)* precioso(a); *(man)* guapísimo; *(very good)* buenísimo(a)

**gorilla** [ɡə'rɪlə] *n* gorila *m*

**gormless** ['ɡɔ:mlɪs] *adj Br Fam (person, expression)* idiota, memo(a); **a g. idiot** un completo idiota

**gorse** [ɡɔ:s] *n* tojo *m*, aulaga *f*

**gory** ['ɡɔ:rɪ] *adj (film, crime)* sangriento(a); *(covered in blood)* ensangrentado(a); *Fig & Hum* **in g. detail** con todo lujo de detalles, con pelos y señales

**gosh** [ɡɒʃ] *exclam Fam* ¡jolines!, ¡vaya!

**goshawk** ['ɡɒshɔ:k] *n* azor *m*

**gosling** ['ɡɒzlɪŋ] *n* ansarón *m*

**go-slow** ['ɡəʊ'sləʊ] *n Br* huelga *f* de celo

**gospel** ['ɡɒspəl] *n* evangelio *m*; **St Mark's G., the G. according to St Mark** el evangelio según San Marcos; **to take sth as g.** tomarse algo como si fuera el evangelio; **g. (music)** *(música f)* gospel *m*; **g. singer** cantante *mf* (de) gospel

**gossamer** ['ɡɒsəmə(r)] *n* **(a)** *(spider's thread)* (hilos *mpl* de) telaraña *f* **(b)** *(fabric)* gasa *f*

**gossip** ['ɡɒsɪp] **1** *n* **(a)** *(person)* cotilla *mf*, chismoso(a) *m,f* **(b)** *(talk)* cotilleo *m*, chismorreo *m*; **to have a g. (about)** cotillear (sobre); **g. column** *(in newspaper)* ecos *mpl* de sociedad **2** *vi* cotillear, chismorrear

**gossipy** ['ɡɒsɪpɪ] *adj* **he's very g.** es muy cotilla; **a g. letter** una carta llena de cotilleos

**got** [ɡɒt] *pt & pp of* **get**

**Gothic** ['ɡɒθɪk] **1** *n (artistic style, language)* gótico *m* **2** *adj* gótico(a); **g. novel** novela *f* gótica

**gotta** ['ɡɒtə] *Fam* = **got to**

**gotten** ['ɡɒtən] *US pp of* **get**

▸**gouge out** *vt sep (eye)* arrancar; *(hole)* cavar

**goulash** ['gu:læʃ] *n* gulach *m*

**gourd** ['ɡʊəd] *n (vegetable, container)* calabaza *f*

**gourmet** ['ɡʊəmeɪ] *n* gastrónomo(a) *m,f*, gourmet *mf*; **g. cooking** alta *or* buena cocina *f*

**gout** [ɡaʊt] *n (illness)* gota *f*

**Gov (a)** *(abbr* **government***)* gobierno *m* **(b)** *(abbr* **governor***)* gobernador(ora) *m,f*

**govern** ['ɡʌvən] *vt (state, country)* gobernar; *(of scientific law)* regir, determinar; *(emotions)* dominar; **her behaviour was governed by a desire for revenge** le movía el deseo de venganza

**governess** ['ɡʌvənɪs] *n* institutriz *f*

**governing** ['ɡʌvənɪŋ] *adj (party, coalition)* gobernante; *(concept, principle)* rector(a); **g. body** órgano *m* rector

**government** ['ɡʌvənmənt] *n* gobierno *m*; **to form a g.** formar gobierno; **g. policy** la política gubernamental

**governmental** [ɡʌvən'mentəl] *adj* gubernamental, gubernativo(a)

**governor** ['ɡʌvənə(r)] *n (of colony, central bank)* gobernador(ora) *m,f*; *(of prison)* director(ora) *m,f*; *Br Fam* **the g.** *(boss)* el/la mandamás; **g. general** gobernador general

**governorship** ['ɡʌvənəʃɪp] *n* gobernación *f*

**Govt** *(abbr* **government***)* gobierno *m*

**gown** [ɡaʊn] *n (of woman)* vestido *m* (largo); *(of magistrate, academic)* toga *f*

**GP** [dʒi:'pi:] *n Br (abbr* **general practitioner***)* médico(a) *m,f* de familia *or* de cabecera

**GPO** [dʒi:pi:'əʊ] *n Br Formerly (abbr* **General Post Office***)* ≃ (Administración *f* Central de) Correos *mpl*

**gr** *(abbr* **gramme(s)***)* g

**grab** [ɡræb] **1** *n (movement)* **to make a g. at** *or* **for sth** tratar de agarrar algo; *Fam* **to be up for grabs** estar a disposición de cualquiera **2** *vt (pt & pp* **grabbed***)* **to g. (hold of) sth/sb** agarrar algo/a alguien; **to g. sth off sb** arrebatar algo a alguien; *Fam* **how does that g. you?** ¿qué te parece?; *Fam* **the idea doesn't**

g. me no me entusiasma la idea

**3** vi **to g. at sth/sb** tratar de agarrar algo/a alguien

**grace** [greɪs] **1** n (a) *(of movement, dancer, language)* gracia f, elegancia f

(b) *(of manners)* **to do sth with (a) good/bad g.** hacer algo de buena/mala gana; **to have the (good) g. to do sth** tener la delicadeza de hacer algo

(c) *(favour)* **to be in/get into sb's good graces** gozar del/ganarse el favor de alguien

(d) *Rel* **in a state of g.** en estado de gracia; **to fall from g.** caer en desgracia; **the g. of God** la gracia de Dios; **there, but for the g. of God, go I** siento mucho lo que le ha pasado, nos podría haber pasado a cualquiera

(e) *(for payment of a bill)* **to give a debtor seven days' g.** conceder a un moroso una prórroga de siete días

(f) *(prayer before meal)* **to say g.** bendecir la mesa

(g) *(form of address)* **Your G.** (bishop) (Su) Ilustrísima; *(duke, duchess)* (Su) Excelencia

**2** vt (a) *(honour)* honrar

(b) *(ornament)* adornar

**graceful** ['greɪsfʊl] adj *(person, movement)* airoso(a), elegante; *(speech, style)* elegante

**gracefully** ['greɪsfʊlɪ] adv con elegancia; **to accept/decline g.** aceptar/declinar cortésmente

**graceless** ['greɪslɪs] adj (a) *(inelegant) (person, movement)* falto(a) de gracia, ordinario(a) (b) *(rude) (apology, behaviour)* grosero(a)

**gracious** ['greɪʃəs] adj (a) *(kind, polite)* amable, atento(a); *(in victory)* caballeroso(a) (b) *(elegant)* elegante, lujoso(a) (c) *(exclamation)* **g. (me)!, good(ness) g.!** ¡santo cielo!, ¡Dios bendito!

**graciously** ['greɪʃəslɪ] adv *(kindly)* amablemente, cortésmente

**gradation** [grə'deɪʃən] n gradación f

**grade** [greɪd] **1** n (a) *(rank)* grado m, rango m (b) *(quality)* clase f, calidad f; **to make the g.** *(be good enough)* dar la talla (c) *US Sch (mark)* nota f (d) *US (year at school)* curso m; **g. school** escuela f primaria

**2** vt (a) *(classify)* clasificar (b) *US* **to g. essays** calificar los trabajos

**gradient** ['greɪdɪənt] n (a) *(of slope)* pendiente f; **a g. of 1 in 4, a 1 in 4 g.** una pendiente del 25% (b) *(of temperature)* gradiente m, curva f de temperaturas

**gradual** ['grædjʊəl] adj gradual

**gradualism** ['grædjʊəlɪzəm] n transformación f gradual

**gradually** ['grædjʊəlɪ] adv gradualmente

**graduate 1** n ['grædjʊət] *Br Univ* licenciado(a) m,f; *US (from high school)* ≃ bachiller mf

**2** adj *US (postgraduate)* **g. studies** estudios mpl de posgrado

**3** vi ['grædjʊeɪt] *Br Univ* licenciarse; *US (from high school)* ≃ sacar el bachillerato; *Fig* **she learnt on a cheap violin before graduating to a better instrument** aprendió con un violín corriente antes de pasar a tocar con uno mejor

**graduated** ['grædjʊeɪtɪd] adj *(thermometer)* graduado(a); **g. income tax** impuesto m sobre la renta progresivo

**graduation** [grædjʊ'eɪʃən] n *(from school, university)* graduación f; **g. ceremony** ceremonia f de graduación

**graffiti** [grə'fiːtiː] n *(slogans)* pintadas fpl; *(art)* graffiti mpl

**graft¹** [grɑːft] **1** n *(of skin, plant)* injerto m

**2** vt *(skin, plant)* injertar *(onto* en); *Fig (idea, method)* implantar *(onto* en)

**graft²** *Fam* **1** n (a) *Br (work)* **the job involves a lot of hard g.** en ese trabajo hay que currar mucho (b) *US (bribery)* corruptelas fpl

**2** vi *Br (work hard)* currar a tope

**grafter** ['grɑːftə(r)] n *Br Fam* currante mf

**grain** [greɪn] n (a) *(of wheat, pepper, salt, sand)* grano m; **a g. of truth** una pizca de verdad (b) *(of photo)* grano m; *(of wood, meat)* veta f; *Fig* **it goes against the g. for me to do it** hacer eso va contra mi naturaleza

**grainy** ['greɪnɪ] adj *Phot* granuloso(a), con mucho grano

**gram** [græm] n gramo m

**grammar** ['græmə(r)] n gramática f; **g. (book)** (método m de) gramática f; *Br* **g. school** instituto m de enseñanza secundaria *(al que sólo se accede después de superar un examen de ingreso)*

**grammarian** [grə'meərɪən] n gramático(a) m,f

**grammatical** [grə'mætɪkəl] adj gramatical

**grammatically** [grə'mætɪklɪ] adv gramaticalmente

**gramme** [græm] n gramo m

**gramophone** ['græməfəʊn] n *Br Old-fashioned* gramófono m

**gran** [græn] n *Br Fam (grandmother)* yaya f, abuelita f

**granary** ['grænərɪ] n granero m; *Br* **g. bread** pan m de semillas

**grand** [grænd] **1** adj (a) *(imposing)* grandioso(a), imponente; *(plan, scheme)* ambicioso(a); **on a g. scale** a gran escala; **g. finale** final m apoteósico, apoteosis f inv final; *US* **g. jury** jurado m de acusación; **g. master** *(in chess)* gran maestro(a) m,f; **the G. National** el Grand National, ≃ carrera hípica de obstáculos que se celebra anualmente en Aintree, Gran Bretaña; **g. piano** piano *m* de cola; **g. slam** *(in rugby)* Gran Slam *m*, = conseguir derrotar a los otros cuatro países en el Torneo de las Cinco Naciones; **a g. total of £5,000** una suma total de 5.000 libras

**(b)** *Fam (excellent)* estupendo(a)

**2** *n Fam (thousand pounds)* mil libras *fpl; (thousand dollars)* mil dólares *mpl*

**grandchild** ['grænt∫aɪld] *n* nieto(a) *m,f*

**gran(d)dad** ['grændæd] *n Fam* yayo *m*, abuelito *m*

**grandaddy** ['grændædɪ] *n Fam* yayo *m*, abuelito *m*

**granddaughter** ['grændɔ:tə(r)] *n* nieta *f*

**grandeur** ['grændjə(r)] *n (of place, building)* grandiosidad *f; (personal status)* grandeza *f*

**grandfather** ['grænfɑ:ðə(r)] *n* abuelo *m*; **g. clock** reloj *m* de pie

**grandiloquent** [græn'dɪləkwənt] *adj* grandilocuente

**grandiose** ['grændɪəʊs] *adj* grandioso(a)

**grandly** ['grændlɪ] *adv (impressively)* grandiosamente, majestuosamente; *(pompously)* solemnemente

**grandma** ['grænmɑ:] *n Fam* yaya *f*, abuelita *f*

**grandmother** ['grænmʌðə(r)] *n* abuela *f*

**grandpa** ['grænpɑ:] *n Fam* yayo *m*, abuelito *f*

**grandparent** ['grænpeərənt] *n* abuelo(a) *m,f*; **grandparents** abuelos *mpl*

**grandson** ['grænsʌn] *n* nieto *m*

**grandstand** ['grænstænd] *n (in stadium)* tribuna *m*; **to have a g. view of sth** presenciar algo desde una posición privilegiada

**granite** ['grænɪt] *n* granito *m*

**grannie, granny** ['grænɪ] *n Fam* yaya *f*, abuelita *f*; **g. knot** nudo *m* mal hecho

**grant** [grɑ:nt] **1** *n (financial aid)* subvención *f; (for student)* beca *f*

**2** *vt* **(a)** *(allow) (permission, request)* conceder; **to take sth for granted** dar algo por supuesto or por sentado; **she felt that she was being taken for granted** sentía que no la apreciaban debidamente **(b)** *(award) (money, subsidy)* conceder **(c)** *(admit)* reconocer, admitir; **I g. that he's talented, but...** admito que tiene talento, pero...

**granular** ['grænjʊlə(r)] *adj (surface, texture)* granuloso(a)

**granulated sugar** ['grænjʊleɪtɪd'∫ʊgə(r)] *n* azúcar *m* or *f* granulado(a)

**granule** ['grænjʊl] *n* gránulo *m*

**grape** [greɪp] *n* uva *f*; **g. harvest** vendimia *f*; **g. juice** mosto *m*, zumo *m* de uva; **g. picker** vendimiador(ora) *m,f*

**grapefruit** ['greɪpfru:t] *n* pomelo *m, Am* toronja *f*; **g. juice** zumo *m* de pomelo

**grapevine** ['greɪpvaɪn] *n* vid *f; (climbing)* parra *f; Fam* **I heard on the g. that...** me ha dicho un pajarito que...

**graph** [grɑ:f] *n* gráfico *m*, gráfica *f*; **g. paper** papel *m* cuadriculado

**graphic** ['græfɪk] *adj* **(a)** *(description, language)* gráfico(a) **(b)** *Art* gráfico(a); **g. artist** artista *mf* gráfico(a); **g. arts** artes *fpl* gráficas; **g. designer** diseñador(ora) *m,f* gráfico(a), grafista *mf*; **g. novel** novela *f* ilustrada **(c)** *Elec* **g. equalizer** ecualizador *m* gráfico

**graphically** ['græfɪklɪ] *adv (to describe, portray)* gráficamente

**graphics** ['græfɪks] **1** *n Art* diseño *m* gráfico, grafismo *m*

**2** *npl Comptr* gráficos *mpl*

**graphite** ['græfaɪt] *n* grafito *m*

**graphology** [græ'fɒlədʒɪ] *n* grafología *f*

**grapnel** ['græpnəl] *n Naut* rezón *m*

**grapple** ['græpəl] *vi (fight)* forcejear; **to g. with a problem** debatirse or batallar con un problema

**grappling hook** ['græplɪŋ'hʊk], **grappling iron** ['græplɪŋ 'aɪən] *n Naut* rezón *m*

**grasp** [grɑ:sp] **1** *n* **(a)** *(hold)* asimiento *m*; **to wrest sth from sb's g.** arrancar algo de las manos de alguien; *Fig* **to have sth within one's g.** tener algo al alcance de la mano; *Fig* **the opportunity had slipped from her g.** había dejado escapar la oportunidad **(b)** *(understanding)* comprensión *f*; **to have a good g. of modern history** comprender or dominar muy bien la historia moderna

**2** *vt* **(a)** *(hold firmly)* agarrar, asir; *Fig* **to g. the opportunity** aprovechar la oportunidad **(b)** *(understand)* comprender

**grasping** ['grɑ:spɪŋ] *adj* avaricioso(a)

**grass** [grɑ:s] **1** *n* **(a)** *(plant)* hierba *f; Fig* **she doesn't let the g. grow under her feet** *(is very decisive)* no se dedica a perder el tiempo; *Fig* **the g. roots** *(of organization)* las bases; **g. roots support/opposition** apoyo *m*/oposición *f* de las bases; **g. snake** culebra *f* de agua; **g. widow** = mujer cuyo marido se encuentra ausente

**(b)** *(lawn)* césped *m*, hierba *f*; **keep off the g.** *(en letrero)* prohibido pisar el césped; **g. court** *(in tennis)* pista *f* de hierba

**(c)** *(pasture)* pasto *m; Fig* **to put sb out to g.** = despedir a alguien por ser demasiado mayor para el trabajo

**(d)** *very Fam (marijuana)* maría *f*, hierba *f*

**(e)** *Br very Fam (informer)* soplón(a) *m,f*, chivato(a) *m,f*

**2** *vi Br very Fam (inform)* cantar; **to g. on sb** delatar a alguien, dar el soplo sobre alguien

**grasshopper** ['grɑ:shɒpə(r)] *n* saltamontes *m inv*

**grassland** ['grɑːslænd] *n* pradera *f*, pastizal *m*

**grassroots** ['græs'ruːts] *adj* bases *fpl*; **g. opinion** la opinión de las bases

**grassy** ['grɑːsɪ] *adj* poblado(a) de hierba

**grate¹** [greɪt] *n (of hearth)* parrilla *f*, rejilla *f*

**grate²** 1 *vt (cheese, nutmeg)* rallar

2 *vi (of machinery)* chirriar, rechinar; **to g. on the ear** *(of voice, sound)* chirriar al oído; **it really grates on my nerves** me ataca los nervios

**grateful** ['greɪtful] *adj* agradecido(a); **to be g.** estar agradecido(a); **I'm g. for all you've done** te agradezco todo lo que has hecho; **I would be g. if you could let me know as soon as possible** le agradecería que me lo comunicara lo antes posible

**gratefully** ['greɪtfulɪ] *adv* agradecidamente, con agradecimiento

**grater** ['greɪtə(r)] *n (for cheese, nutmeg)* rallador *m*

**gratification** [grætɪfɪ'keɪʃən] *n* satisfacción *f*

**gratified** ['grætɪfaɪd] *adj* **to be g.** estar satisfecho(a) *or* complacido(a)

**gratify** ['grætɪfaɪ] *vt* satisfacer, complacer

**gratifying** ['grætɪfaɪɪŋ] *adj* satisfactorio(a), gratificante

**grating¹** ['greɪtɪŋ] *adj (noise)* chirriante; *(voice)* chillón(ona)

**grating²** *n (grille)* reja *f*

**gratis** ['grɑːtɪs] *adv* gratis

**gratitude** ['grætɪtjuːd] *n* gratitud *f*

**gratuitous** [grə'tjuːɪtəs] *adj (unnecessary)* gratuito(a), arbitrario(a)

**gratuitously** [grə'tjuːɪtəslɪ] *adv* gratuitamente, arbitrariamente

**gratuity** [grə'tjuːɪtɪ] *n Formal (tip)* propina *f*, gratificación *f*

**grave** [greɪv] 1 *n* (a) tumba *f*, sepultura *f* (b) *(idioms)* **to make sb turn in his g.** hacer que alguien se revuelva en su sepultura; **to have one foot in the g.** estar con un pie en la tumba

2 *adj (manner, voice, situation, mistake)* grave

**gravedigger** ['greɪvdɪgə(r)] *n* sepulturero(a) *m,f*

**gravel** ['grævəl] *n* grava *f*, gravilla *f*; **g. path** camino *m* de grava; **g. pit** yacimiento *m* de grava, gravera *f*

**gravelly** ['grævəlɪ] *adj (sand, soil)* pedregoso(a); **a g. voice** una voz cavernosa

**gravely** ['greɪvlɪ] *adv* gravemente

**graven** ['greɪvən] *adj (in the Bible)* **g. image** ídolo *m*

**graveside** ['greɪvsaɪd] *n* pie *m* de la sepultura

**gravestone** ['greɪvstəʊn] *n* lápida *f*

**graveyard** ['greɪvjɑːd] *n* cementerio *m*

**gravitate** ['grævɪteɪt] *vi* **to g. towards** verse atraído(a) por; *Fig* **most of the guests had gravitated towards the bar** casi todos los invitados se habían ido desplazando hacia el bar

**gravitational** [grævɪ'teɪʃənəl] *adj (force, field)* gravitatorio(a); **g. pull** atracción *f* gravitatoria

**gravity** ['grævɪtɪ] *n also Fig* gravedad *f*

**gravy** ['greɪvɪ] *n* jugo *m* de carne; **g. boat** salsera *f*; *Fam* **to be on the g. train** estar apuntado(a) al chollo de la temporada

**gray, gray-haired** *etc US* = **grey, grey-haired** *etc*

**graze¹** [greɪz] 1 *vt (of farmer) (cattle, herd)* apacentar

2 *vi (of cattle)* pastar, pacer

**graze²** 1 *n* rasguño *m*, arañazo *m*

2 *vt (scrape)* arañar; *(touch lightly)* rozar; **to g. one's knee** hacerse un arañazo en la rodilla

**grease** [griːs] 1 *n (in cooking, for machine)* grasa *f*; **g. gun** pistola *f* engrasadora

2 *vt (machine)* engrasar, lubricar; *(cake tin)* engrasar; **to g. back one's hair** engominarse el pelo; *Fam* **to g. sb's palm** *(bribe)* untar a alguien; *Fam* **to move like greased lightning** moverse con la velocidad del rayo

**greasepaint** ['griːspeɪnt] *n Th* maquillaje *m* de teatro

**greaseproof paper** ['griːspruːf'peɪpə(r)] *adj* papel *m* de cera

**greasy** ['griːsɪ] *adj* (a) *(containing, covered in grease)* grasiento(a); *(hair)* graso(a); *(greasestained)* manchado(a) de grasa (b) *Fam (manner)* adulador(ora), untuoso(a)

**great** [greɪt] 1 *adj* (a) *(large, important)* grande, gran *(before singular noun)*; **a g. deal of…** un montón de…, muchísimo(a)…; **to reach a g. age** llegar a una edad avanzada; **to take g. care** poner mucho cuidado; **they are g. friends** son muy buenos amigos; **a g. artist** un/una gran artista; **to be the greatest** ser el mejor

(b) *(in proper names)* **G. Britain** Gran Bretaña; **G. Dane** gran danés *m*; **the G. Lakes** los Grandes Lagos; **Greater London** el área metropolitana de Londres; *Hist* **the G. War** la Primera Guerra Mundial, la guerra del 14

(c) *Fam (very good)* estupendo(a), fenomenal, *Méx* padre, *Andes, Carib* chévere, *Andes, CSur* macanudo(a); **to have a g. time** pasarlo muy bien; **(that's) g!** ¡estupendo!; **he's a g. guy** es un tipo excelente

(d) *(enthusiastic)* **she's a g. hillwalker** es muy aficionada al montañismo; **he's a g. one for having everything planned in advance** nadie como él para tener todo planeado de antemano

**2** *n* grande *mf*

**3** *adv Fam* (a) *(well)* estupendamente; **I feel g.!** ¡me siento estupendamente!; **he's doing g.** *(in health)* se está recuperando muy bien

(b) *(for emphasis)* **a g. big dog** un perrazo enorme; **you g. fat slob!** ¡so gandulazo!

**great-aunt** ['greɪt'ɑ:nt] *n* tía *f* abuela

**greatcoat** ['greɪtkəʊt] *n* abrigo *m*, gabán *m*

**great-grandchild** ['greɪt'grænt∫aɪld] *n* bisnieto(a) *m,f*

**great-granddaughter** ['greɪt'grænˌdɔ:tə(r)] *n* bisnieta *f*

**great-grandfather** ['greɪt'grænfɑ:ðə(r)] *n* bisabuelo *m*

**great-grandmother** ['greɪt'grænmʌðə(r)] *n* bisabuela *f*

**great-grandparents** ['greɪt'grænpeərənts] *npl* bisabuelos *mpl*

**great-grandson** ['greɪt'grænsʌn] *n* bisnieto *m*

**greatly** ['greɪtlɪ] *adv (when modifying adjective)* muy; *(when modifying verb)* mucho; **he was g. influenced by his father** estaba muy influenciado por su padre

**greatness** ['greɪtnɪs] *n* (a) *(of person)* talla *f*, grandeza *f*; *(of action)* grandeza *f*; **to achieve g.** *(of writer, politician)* alcanzar una gran notoriedad (b) *(of thing, problem)* magnitud *f*

**great-uncle** ['greɪt'ʌŋkəl] *n* tío *m* abuelo

**grebe** [gri:b] *n* somormujo *m*

**Grecian** ['gri:∫ən] *adj* helénico(a), griego(a)

**Greece** [gri:s] *n* Grecia

**greed** [gri:d] *n (for food)* glotonería *f*, gula *f*; *(for material things)* codicia *f* **(for** de), avidez *f* **(for** de); *(for fame, power)* ambición *f* **(for** de), avidez *f* **(for** de)

**greedily** ['gri:dɪlɪ] *adv (to eat)* con glotonería; *(to eye, behave)* con avidez

**greediness** ['gri:dɪnɪs] = **greed**

**greedy** ['gri:dɪ] *adj (for food)* glotón(a); *(for material things)* codicioso(a), ávido(a); **to be g. for sth** *(knowledge, success)* estar ávido de algo; *Fam* **g. guts** tragón(ona) *m,f*

**Greek** [gri:k] **1** *n* (a) *(person)* griego(a) *m,f* (b) *(language)* griego *m*; **modern G.** griego moderno; *Fam* **it's all G. to me** me suena a chino

**2** *adj* griego(a)

**green** [gri:n] **1** *n* (a) *(colour)* verde *m*

(b) **greens** *(vegetables)* verdura *f*

(c) *(grassy area)* *(in golf)* green *m*; **village g.** = en los pueblos, zona de césped de uso público

(d) *Pol (person)* ecologista *mf*, verde *mf*

**2** *adj* (a) *(colour)* verde; **to go** *or* **turn g.** *(traffic lights)* cambiar a *or* ponerse verde; **to be g. with envy** estar muerto(a) de envidia; *Fig* **to give sb the g. light (to do sth)** dar a alguien luz verde (para hacer algo); **g. beans** judías *fpl* verdes; **g. belt** *(around city)* cinturón *m* verde,

pulmón *m*; *US* **g. card** permiso *m* de trabajo; **to have g. fingers** tener buena mano con las plantas; **g. pepper** pimiento *m* verde; **the g. revolution** la revolución verde; **g. salad** ensalada *f* verde

(b) *(young, inexperienced)* novato(a); *(naive)* ingenuo(a)

(c) *(environmentalist)* ecologista, verde; **the G. Party** el partido ecologista *or* de los verdes

**greenback** ['gri:nbæk] *n US Fam* billete *m* *(dólar estadounidense)*

**greenery** ['gri:nərɪ] *n* vegetación *f*

**green-eyed** ['gri:naɪd] *adj* de ojos verdes; *Literary* **the g. monster** *(jealousy)* los celos

**greenfield** ['gri:nfi:ld] *n* **g. site** *(for factory, houses)* terreno *m* edificable *(fuera del casco urbano)*

**greenfly** ['gri:nflaɪ] *n* pulgón *m*

**greengage** ['gri:ngeɪdʒ] *n (fruit)* ciruela *f* claudia

**greengrocer** ['gri:ngrəʊsə(r)] *n Br* verdulero(a) *m,f*; **g.'s (shop)** verdulería *f*

**greenhouse** ['gri:nhaʊs] *n* invernadero *m*; **the g. effect** el efecto invernadero

**Greenland** ['gri:nlənd] *n* Groenlandia

**Greenlander** ['gri:nləndə(r)] *n* groenlandés(esa) *m,f*

**Greenwich Mean Time** ['grenɪt∫'mi:ntaɪm] *n* tiempo *m* universal, hora *f* del meridiano cero *or* de Greenwich

**greet** [gri:t] *vt (say hello to)* saludar; *(welcome) (person, idea)* recibir, acoger

**greeting** ['gri:tɪŋ] *n* saludo *m*; **to send greetings to sb** enviar saludos a alguien; **New Year/birthday greetings** *fpl* de Año Nuevo/cumpleaños; **greetings card** tarjeta *f* de felicitación

**gregarious** [grɪ'geərɪəs] *adj* sociable

**gremlin** ['gremlɪn] *n Fam* duende *m*

**Grenada** [grə'neɪdə] *n* Granada *(país)*

**grenade** [grə'neɪd] *n (small bomb)* granada *f*

**grenadier** [grenə'dɪə(r)] *n (soldier)* granadero *m*

**grenadine** ['grenədi:n] *n (drink)* granadina *f*

**grew** ['gru:] *pt of* **grow**

**grey, *US* gray** [greɪ] **1** *n (colour)* gris *m*

**2** *adj* gris; *(hair)* cano(a), gris; *Fig (boring)* gris; **to go g.** *(hair)* encanecer; *Fig* **a g. area** *(unclear)* una cuestión poco clara; **g. hairs** canas *fpl*; **g. matter** *(brain)* materia *f* gris; **g. squirrel** ardilla *f* gris

**3** *vi (of hair)* encanecer

**grey-haired, *US* gray-haired** ['greɪ'heəd] *adj* canoso(a)

**greyhound** ['greɪhaʊnd] *n (dog)* galgo *m*; **g. stadium** canódromo *m*

**greying**, US **graying** ['greɪɪŋ] adj (hair) encanecido(a); (population) envejecido(a)

**grid** [grɪd] n (a) (bars) reja f (b) (on map) cuadrícula f; (g. layout (of town) trazado m cuadricular, planta f cuadriculada; **g. reference** coordenadas fpl (c) (for electricity) red f eléctrica

**griddle** ['grɪdəl] n (for cooking) plancha f

**gridiron** ['grɪdaɪən] n (a) (for cooking) parrilla f (b) US (American football) fútbol m americano; (field) campo m de fútbol americano

**gridlock** ['grɪdlɒk] n US (traffic jam) atasco m, embotellamiento m

**grief** [griːf] n dolor m, aflicción f; **to come to g.** venirse abajo; Fam **good g.!** ¡santo Dios!; Fam **to give sb g. (about sth)** (hassle) dar la vara or la lata a alguien (con algo)

**grief-stricken** ['griːfstrɪkən] adj afligido(a); **to be g.** estar afligido(a)

**grievance** ['griːvəns] n (a) (resentment) (sentimiento m de) agravio m (b) (complaint) motivo m de queja; Ind **g. procedure** juicio m de faltas

**grieve** [griːv] 1 vt **it grieves me to have to tell you that...** lamento tener que decirle que...
2 vi sufrir de aflicción; **to g. for** or **over sb** llorar la muerte de alguien

**grieving** ['griːvɪŋ] adj desconsolado(a)

**grievous** ['griːvəs] adj Formal grave; Law **g. bodily harm** lesiones fpl graves

**grievously** ['griːvəslɪ] adv Formal (seriously) seriamente; **to be g. wounded** estar gravemente herido(a); **you are g. mistaken** estás en un grave error

**griffin** ['grɪfɪn] n (mythological creature) grifo m

**grill** [grɪl] 1 n Br (on cooker) grill m; (for open fire) parrilla f; (food) parrillada f; **a mixed g.** una parrillada de carne
2 vt (a) Br (cook) asar (a la parrilla); **grilled meat** carne f a la parrilla (b) Fam (interrogate) acribillar a preguntas

**grille** [grɪl] n (bars) reja f; Aut **(radiator) g.** rejilla f del radiador

**grilling** ['grɪlɪŋ] n Fam (interrogation) **to give sb a g.** acribillar a alguien a preguntas

**grim** [grɪm] adj (account, news, prospects) desolador(ora); (reality) duro(a); (mood) desolado(a); (face) severo(a); (landscape) lúgubre; **he showed g. determination** se mostró completamente resuelto; **to hold on like g. death** agarrarse como si le fuera a una la vida en ello; **to look g.** (serious) tener cara de pocos amigos; (ill) tener muy mala cara; Fam **how do you feel? – pretty g.!** ¿cómo te sientes? – ¡fatal!

**grimace** [grɪˈmeɪs] 1 n mueca f
2 vi (once) hacer una mueca; (more than once) hacer muecas

**grime** [graɪm] n mugre f, porquería f

**grimly** ['grɪmlɪ] adv (to fight, hold on) con determinación

**grimy** ['graɪmɪ] adj mugriento(a)

**grin** [grɪn] 1 n (smile) (amplia) sonrisa f
2 vi (smile) sonreír abiertamente; Fig **to g. and bear it** poner al mal tiempo buena cara

**grind** [graɪnd] 1 n Fam (work) **the daily g.** la rutina diaria; **what a g.!** ¡qué rollo de trabajo!
2 vt (pt & pp **ground** [graʊnd]) (a) (grain, coffee) moler; Fig **to g. sth/sb under one's heel** hacer añicos algo/a alguien; **to g. one's teeth** hacer rechinar los dientes (b) (polish) (glass) pulir
3 vi (of wheels, gears) chirriar; **to g. to a halt** (of vehicle, machine) detenerse con estrépito; (of project) acabar estancado(a)
▸**grind down** vt sep Fig (opposition) desgastar, minar
▸**grind on** vi (proceed relentlessly) proseguir machaconamente
▸**grind out** vt sep **to g. out a novel/an essay** escribir con gran dificultad una novela/un ensayo

**grinder** ['graɪndə(r)] n (for coffee, pepper) molinillo m; (crusher) trituradora f; (for polishing) pulidora f; (for sharpening) afilador m

**grinding** ['graɪndɪŋ] adj (boredom, worry) insufrible, insoportable; **to come to a g. halt** (of car, machine) pararse en seco; (of project) acabar estancado(a); **g. poverty** pobreza f absoluta

**grindstone** ['graɪndstəʊn] n muela f, piedra f de afilar; Fig **to keep one's nose to the g.** trabajar como un negro

**gringo** ['grɪŋgəʊ] (pl **gringos**) n US Fam gringo(a) m,f

**grip** [grɪp] 1 n (a) (hold, grasp) sujeción f; (in tennis, golf) sujeción f, forma f de sujetar; **to have a strong g.** agarrar con fuerza; **to get a g. on sth** (rope, handle) agarrar algo; Fig **to get to grips with** (situation) asimilar; (subject, method) llegar a comprender; Fig **to get a g. on oneself** dominarse, contenerse; Fig **get a g.!** (control yourself) ¡no desvaríes!; Fig **to have a firm g. on a situation** ejercer un fuerte control sobre una situación; **to lose one's g. (on sth)** (on rope) perder el control (de algo); Fig **to lose one's g. on reality** perder el contacto con la realidad; Fig **to be in the g. of a disease/a crisis** ser presa de una enfermedad/una crisis
(b) (handle) (of oar, handlebars) mango m
(c) (hair) g. horquilla f
(d) US (bag) bolsa f de viaje
2 vt (pt & pp **gripped**) (seize) agarrar, coger; (hold) sujetar; **tyres that g. the road** neumáticos que se adhieren (bien) a la carretera; Fig **to be gripped by panic/fear** ser presa del páni-

co/miedo; *Fig* **the play gripped the audience** la obra tuvo en vilo al público

**3** *vi (of tyre)* adherirse

**gripe** [graɪp] **1** *n* (**a**) *Fam (complaint)* queja *f*; **what's your g.?** ¿qué tripa se te ha roto? (**b**) **g. water** (medicamento *m*) carminativo *m*, agua *f* de anís

**2** *vi Fam (complain)* quejarse (**about** de)

**gripping** ['grɪpɪŋ] *adj (book, story)* apasionante

**grisly** ['grɪzlɪ] *adj* espeluznante, horripilante

**grist** [grɪst] *n* **it's all g. to his mill** todo lo aprovecha

**gristle** ['grɪsəl] *n* ternilla *f*

**gristly** ['grɪslɪ] *adj (meat)* lleno(a) de nervios

**grit** [grɪt] **1** *n* (**a**) *(gravel)* gravilla *f* (**b**) *(courage, determination)* coraje *m*; **to have a lot of g.** tener mucho coraje

**2** *vt (pt & pp gritted)* (**a**) *(put grit on)* **to g. a road** echar gravilla en una carretera (**b**) *(clench)* **to g. one's teeth** apretar los dientes

**gritter** ['grɪtə(r)] *n Br (lorry)* = camión que va esparciendo gravilla por la carretera cuando está resbaladiza por el hielo o la nieve

**gritty** ['grɪtɪ] *adj* (**a**) *(sandy)* arenoso(a); **g. soil** guijarral *m* (**b**) *(determined)* valiente, audaz (**c**) **g. realism** realismo *m* descarnado

**grizzle** ['grɪzəl] *vi (complain)* refunfuñar

**grizzled** ['grɪzəld] *adj (hair, person) (grey)* canoso(a); *(greyish)* entrecano(a)

**grizzly** ['grɪzlɪ] **1** *n* **g. (bear)** oso *m* pardo *(norteamericano)*

**2** *adj (hair, person)* canoso(a)

**groan** [grəʊn] **1** *n (of pain, dismay)* gemido *m*; *(of chair, floor)* crujido *m*

**2** *vi (in pain, dismay)* gemir; **to g. inwardly** ahogar un gemido; **the shelves groaned under the weight of the books** la estantería estaba hasta arriba de libros

**grocer** ['grəʊsə(r)] *n* tendero(a) *m,f*; **g.'s (shop)** tienda *f* de comestibles *or* de ultramarinos, *Andes, CSur* bodega *f*, *CAm, Méx* (tienda *f* de) abarrotes *mpl*, *CSur* pulpería *f*

**groceries** ['grəʊsərɪz] *npl (shopping)* comestibles *mpl*, ultramarinos *mpl*

**grocery** ['grəʊsərɪ] *n (shop)* tienda *f* de comestibles *or* de ultramarinos, *Andes, CSur* bodega *f*, *CAm, Méx* (tienda *f* de) abarrotes *mpl*, *CSur* pulpería *f*

**grog** [grɒg] *n Fam (drink)* grog *m*, ponche *m*

**groggy** ['grɒgɪ] *adj Fam* atontado(a), aturdido(a); **to be g.** estar atontado(a) *or* aturdido(a)

**groin** [grɔɪn] *n* ingle *f*

**groom** [gruːm] **1** *n* (**a**) *(of horse)* mozo *m* de cuadra (**b**) *(at wedding)* novio *m*

**2** *vt (horse)* almohazar; *Fig (candidate)* preparar

**groove** [gruːv] *n (slot)* ranura *f*; *(of record)* surco *m*

**groovy** ['gruːvɪ] *adj Fam* genial, enrollante

**grope** [grəʊp] **1** *vt* (**a**) **to g. one's way forward** avanzar a tientas (**b**) *very Fam (sexually)* magrear, sobar

**2** *vi* **to g. (about) for sth** buscar algo a tientas

**gross** [grəʊs] **1** *n (quantity)* gruesa *f*, doce docenas *fpl*; **two g.** dos gruesas

**2** *adj* (**a**) *(fat)* muy gordo(a) (**b**) *(blatant) (error, ignorance)* craso(a); *(stupidity, indecency, incompetence)* tremendo(a); *Law* **g. negligence** negligencia *f* grave (**c**) *(vulgar) (joke, person)* basto(a), grosero(a) (**d**) *(profit, income)* bruto(a); *Econ* **g. domestic product** producto *m* interior bruto; *Econ* **g. national product** producto nacional bruto; **g. weight** peso *m* bruto (**e**) *Fam (disgusting)* asqueroso(a)

**3** *vt (profit)* ganar en bruto; **she grosses £40,000 a year** gana 40.000 libras brutas al año

**grossly** ['grəʊslɪ] *adv (exaggerated, negligent)* tremendamente, enormemente

**grotesque** [grəʊ'tesk] *adj* grotesco(a)

**grotto** ['grɒtəʊ] *(pl* **grottoes** *or* **grottos)** *n* gruta *f*

**grotty** ['grɒtɪ] *adj Br Fam (house, job)* cutre; **to feel g.** sentirse fatal

**grouch** [graʊtʃ] *Fam* **1** *n* (**a**) *(person)* gruñón(ona) *m,f* (**b**) *(complaint)* queja *f*

**2** *vi* refunfuñar

**grouchy** ['graʊtʃɪ] *adj Fam* **(to be) g.** *(inherent quality)* (ser) refunfuñón(ona); *(temporary mood)* (estar) enfurruñado(a)

**ground** [graʊnd] *n* (**a**) *(earth)* suelo *m*, tierra *f*; **to sit on the g.** sentarse en el suelo; **above g.** sobre la tierra; **to come above g.** salir a la superficie; **below g.** bajo tierra; **burnt to the g.** completamente destruido(a) por el fuego; *Fig* **to get off the g.** *(of project)* ponerse en marcha; *Fig* **to work oneself into the g.** matarse a trabajar; **to go to g.** ocultarse, desaparecer de la circulación; **to run sb to g.** dar por fin con alguien; *Av* **g. control** control *m* de tierra; *Av* **g. crew** personal *m* de tierra; *Br* **g. floor** planta *f* baja; *Fig* **to get in on the g. floor** *(of project)* estar metido(a) desde el principio; *Mil* **g. forces** ejército *m* de tierra; **g. frost** escarcha *f*; **at g. level** a ras de tierra; **to establish the g. rules** establecer las normas básicas; **g. staff** personal *m* de mantenimiento *(del campo de juego)*

(**b**) *(land)* terreno *m*; *Fig* **to find common g. for negotiations** hallar un terreno común para las negociaciones; *Fig* **to be on firm g.** pisar terreno firme; **he's very sure of his g.** está muy seguro de lo que hace/dice; *Fig* **to be on shaky g.** pisar un terreno resbaladizo; *Fig* **to change** *or* **shift one's g.** cambiar la línea de argumentación; *Fig* **to break new** *or* **fresh g.**

abrir nuevas vías or nuevos caminos; *Fig* **to cover a lot of g.** *(of book, lecture)* abarcar mucho; *Fig* **to gain g. on sb** ganarle terreno a alguien; *Fig* **to lose g. to sb** perder terreno ante alguien; *Fig* **to stand** or **hold one's g.** mantenerse firme; **g. rent** = alquiler que se paga al dueño del solar donde está edificada una vivienda

**(c) grounds** *(of school, hospital)* terrenos *mpl*; *(of country house)* jardines *mpl*

**(d)** *(reason)* **grounds** motivo *m*, razón *f*; **to have (good) g.** or **grounds for doing sth** tener (buenos) motivos para hacer algo; **g.** or **grounds for complaint** motivo de queja; **on grounds of ill-health** por motivos de salud; *Law* **grounds for divorce** motivo de divorcio

**2** *adj (coffee, pepper)* molido(a); *US* **g. meat** carne *f* picada

**3** *vt* **(a)** *(base)* fundamentar, basar; **their argument is not grounded in fact** su argumento no se basa en hechos reales

**(b) to g. sb in a subject** *(educate)* enseñar a alguien los principios de una materia

**(c)** *US Elec (current)* conectar a tierra

**(d)** *Av* **the plane was grounded by bad weather** el avión no salió a causa del mal tiempo

**(e)** *(prevent from going out)* **her parents grounded her** sus padres la castigaron a quedarse en casa

**4** *pt & pp of* **grind**

**groundhog** ['graʊndhɒg] *n* marmota *f*

**grounding** ['graʊndɪŋ] *n* **(a)** *(basis)* fundamento *m*, base *f* **(b)** *(basic knowledge)* nociones *fpl* elementales, rudimentos *mpl*

**groundless** ['graʊndlɪs] *adj (suspicion, fear)* infundado(a), inmotivado(a)

**groundnut** ['graʊndnʌt] *n Br* cacahuete *m*; **g. oil** aceite *m* de cacahuete

**groundsheet** ['graʊndʃiːt] *n (of tent)* suelo *m*

**groundsman** ['graʊndzmən] *n* encargado(a) *m,f* del mantenimiento del campo de juego

**groundswell** ['graʊndswel] *n* oleada *f*

**groundwork** ['graʊndwɜːk] *n* **to do** or **lay the g.** allanar el camino

**group** [gruːp] **1** *n* grupo *m*; **g. decision** decisión *f* colectiva; **g. dynamics** dinámica *f* de grupo; **g. photograph** fotografía *f* de grupo; **g. therapy** terapia *f* de grupo

**2** *vt* agrupar

**3** *vi* agruparse

**groupie** ['gruːpɪ] *n Fam* groupie *mf*, grupi *mf*

**grouping** ['gruːpɪŋ] *n* agrupación *f*, grupo *m*

**grouse¹** [graʊs] *(pl* **grouse)** *n (bird)* urogallo *m*

**grouse²** *Fam* **1** *n (complaint)* queja *f*

**2** *vi* quejarse **(about** de)

**grout** [graʊt] *n (for tiles)* lechada *f*

**grove** [grəʊv] *n (of trees)* arboleda *f*

**grovel** ['grɒvəl] *(pt & pp* **grovelled,** *US* **groveled)** *vi (physically)* andar a gatas, gatear; *Fig* **to g. to sb** arrastrarse ante alguien

**grovelling,** *US* **groveling** ['grɒvəlɪŋ] *adj (tone, remark)* servil

**grow** [grəʊ] *(pt* **grew** [gruː]*, pp* **grown** [grəʊn]) **1** *vt (roses, vegetables)* cultivar; **to g. a beard** dejarse (crecer la) barba; **I've decided to g. my hair long** he decidido dejarme el pelo largo

**2** *vi* **(a)** *(increase in size)* crecer; *Fam* **it'll g. on you** *(of music, book)* te irá gustando con el tiempo; **his influence grew** su influencia se acrecentó; **to g. in wisdom/beauty** ganar en sabiduría/belleza **(b)** *(become)* hacerse; **to g. old** envejecer; **to g. big** or **bigger** crecer; **to g. angry** enfadarse **(c)** *(come eventually)* **they grew to like the house** les llegó a gustar la casa

▸**grow apart** *vi (of people)* distanciarse

▸**grow out of** *vt insep* **(a)** *(become too large for)* **he's grown out of his shoes** se le han quedado pequeños los zapatos **(b)** *(become too old for)* **she grew out of her dolls** dejó de jugar con muñecas al hacerse mayor

▸**grow up** *vi (become adult)* crecer; **I want to be a doctor when I g. up** de mayor quiero ser médico; **we didn't have television when I was growing up** cuando era pequeño no teníamos televisión; *Fam* **g. up!** ¡no seas crío!

**grower** ['grəʊə(r)] *n (person)* cultivador(ora) *m,f*

**growing** ['grəʊɪŋ] **1** *adj (child)* en edad de crecer; *(town, population)* creciente, en crecimiento; *(debt, discontent)* creciente; **there was a g. fear that…** se extendía el temor de que…

**2** *n Fig* **g. pains** *(of firm, country)* dificultades *fpl* del desarrollo

**growl** [graʊl] **1** *n (of dog)* gruñido *m*

**2** *vi (of dog, person)* gruñir **(at** a)

**growling** ['graʊlɪŋ] *n (of dog)* gruñidos *mpl*

**grown** [grəʊn] **1** *adj* adulto(a); **a g. woman** una mujer adulta; **fully g.** completamente desarrollado(a)

**2** *pp of* **grow**

**grown-up 1** *n* ['grəʊnʌp] adulto(a) *m,f*; **the grown-ups** los adultos, los mayores

**2** *adj* [grəʊn'ʌp] *(person, attitude)* maduro(a); **he was very g. about it** reaccionó con mucha madurez

**growth** [grəʊθ] *n* **(a)** *(increase in size)* crecimiento *m*; **a week's g. of beard** una barba de una semana; **a g. area** un área de crecimiento; **g. industry** industria *f* en expansión **(b)** *(lump)* bulto *m*

**grub** [grʌb] *n* (a) *(larva)* larva *f*, gusano *m* (b) *Fam (food)* manduca *f*; **g.'s up!** ¡a comer!

**▶grub about, grub around** *vi (search)* rebuscar **(for sth** algo)

**grubby** ['grʌbɪ] *adj* sucio(a), mugriento(a)

**grudge** [grʌdʒ] **1** *n* rencor *m*, resentimiento *m*; **to bear sb a g.** guardar rencor *or* resentimiento a alguien

**2** *vt* **he paid, but he grudged them every penny** les pagó, pero escatimándoles cada penique; **she grudges him his success** reconoce su éxito a regañadientes

**grudging** ['grʌdʒɪŋ] *adj* **he felt g. respect for her** sentía respeto por ella a pesar de sí mismo; **to be g. in one's praise** ser reacio(a) a alabar

**grudgingly** ['grʌdʒɪŋlɪ] *adv* de mala gana, a regañadientes

**gruel** ['gruːəl] *n (thin porridge)* gachas *fpl* (de avena)

**gruelling,** US **grueling** ['gruːəlɪŋ] *adj (journey, experience)* agotador(ora)

**gruesome** ['gruːsəm] *adj* horripilante, espantoso(a); **in g. detail** sin ahorrar detalles truculentos

**gruesomely** ['gruːsəmlɪ] *adv* horripilantemente, espantosamente

**gruff** [grʌf] *adj (tone, manner)* seco(a), hosco(a); *(voice)* áspero(a)

**gruffly** ['grʌflɪ] *adv* secamente, bruscamente

**grumble** ['grʌmbəl] **1** *n* queja *f*; **she obeyed without so much as a g.** obedeció sin rechistar

**2** *vi (of person)* quejarse **(about** de); *(of stomach)* gruñir

**grumbler** ['grʌmblə(r)] *n* quejica *mf*, gruñón(ona) *m,f*

**grumbling** ['grʌmblɪŋ] **1** *n* quejas *fpl*

**2** *adj* quejumbroso(a); *Med* **g. appendix** dolores *mpl* intermitentes de apéndice

**grump** [grʌmp] *n Fam (person)* gruñón(ona) *m,f*

**grumpily** ['grʌmpɪlɪ] *adv* malhumoradamente

**grumpy** ['grʌmpɪ] *adj* malhumorado(a)

**grunge** [grʌndʒ] *n (music)* (música *f*) grunge *m*

**grunt** [grʌnt] **1** *n (of pig, person)* gruñido *m*; **to give a g.** dar un gruñido

**2** *vi (of pig, person)* gruñir

**guarantee** [gærən'tiː] **1** *n (assurance, document)* garantía *f*; **she gave me her g. that it wouldn't happen again** me aseguró que no volvería a pasar; *Com* **under g.** en garantía

**2** *vt* garantizar; **the watch is guaranteed for two years** el reloj tiene una garantía de dos años; *Fin* **to g. sb against loss** ofrecer a alguien una garantía contra posibles pérdidas

**guaranteed** [gærən'tiːd] *adj* garantizado(a)

**guarantor** [gærən'tɔː(r)] *n* avalista *mf*, garante *mf*

**guard** [gɑːd] **1** *n* (a) *(readiness)* **to be on one's g.** estar en guardia; **to put sb on his g.** poner en guardia a alguien; **to put sb off his g.** desarmar a alguien; **to catch sb off his g.** coger a alguien desprevenido(a)

(b) *(supervision)* **under g.** bajo custodia; **to be on g. duty** estar de guardia; **g. dog** perro *m* guardián

(c) *(sentry)* guardia *mf*; *(on train)* jefe *m* de tren; *US (in prison)* funcionario(a) *m,f* de prisiones, guardián(ana) *m,f*; *Mil (body of sentries)* guardia *f*; **g. of honour** guardia de honor; *Br* **g.'s van** *(on train)* furgón *m* de cola

(d) *(device) (on machine)* protección *f*; **as a g. against...** como protección contra...

(e) *(in basketball)* escolta *mf*

**2** *vt* (a) *(protect)* guardar; **a closely guarded secret** un secreto muy bien guardado

(b) *(supervise)* vigilar

**▶guard against** *vt insep* evitar

**guarded** ['gɑːdɪd] *adj (cautious)* cauteloso(a), cauto(a)

**guardedly** ['gɑːdɪdlɪ] *adv* con cautela, cautamente

**guardhouse** ['gɑːdhaʊs] *n Mil* cuerpo *m* de guardia; *(prison)* prisión *f* militar

**guardian** ['gɑːdɪən] *n (of standards)* guardián(ana) *m,f*; *Law (of minor)* tutor(ora) *m,f*; **g. angel** ángel *m* custodio *or* de la guarda

**guardianship** ['gɑːdɪənʃɪp] *n Law* tutela *f*

**guardrail** ['gɑːdreɪl] *n* barandilla *f*

**guardroom** ['gɑːdruːm] *n (guardhouse)* cuerpo *m* de guardia

**guardsman** ['gɑːdzmən] *n Br Mil* = miembro del regimiento de guardias reales

**Guatemala** [gwætɪ'mɑːlə] *n* Guatemala

**Guatemalan** [gwætɪ'mɑːlən] *n & adj* guatemalteco(a) *m,f*

**guava** ['gwɑːvə] *n (fruit)* guayaba *f*; **g. tree** guayabo *m*

**guerrilla** [gə'rɪlə] *n* guerrillero(a) *m,f*; **g. warfare** guerra *f* de guerrillas

**guess** [ges] **1** *n* conjetura *f*, suposición *f*; **to have *or* make a g.** intentar adivinar; **at a g.** a ojo (de buen cubero); **it was a lucky g.** lo he adivinado por casualidad; **it's anybody's g.** no se sabe

**2** *vt* (a) *(estimate)* adivinar; **g. who I saw!** ¡adivina a quién he visto!; **you've guessed it!** ¡has acertado! (b) *(suppose)* suponer; **I g. you're right** supongo que tienes razón

**3** *vi* adivinar; **to g. right** acertar; **to g. wrong** equivocarse, no acertar; **to keep sb guessing** tener a alguien en vilo; **to g. at sth** hacer suposiciones *or* conjeturas acerca de algo

**guessing game** ['gesɪŋ'geɪm] *n* (juego *m* de las) adivinanzas *fpl*

**guesstimate** ['gestɪmɪt] *n Fam* cálculo *m* a ojo

**guesswork** ['geswɜːk] *n* conjeturas *fpl*; **it's pure** *or* **sheer g.** son sólo conjeturas

**guest** [gest] *n (at home, on TV programme)* invitado(a) *m,f*; *(at hotel)* huésped *mf*; **be my g.!** ¡por favor!, ¡no faltaba más!; **a g. appearance by...** una aparición como artista invitado(a) de...; **g. artist** artista *mf* invitado(a); **g. room** habitación *f* de los invitados; **g. speaker** orador(ora) *m,f* invitado(a)

**guesthouse** ['gesthaʊs] *n (hotel)* casa *f* de huéspedes

**guff** [gʌf] *n very Fam* paparruchas *fpl*

**guffaw** [gʌ'fɔː] **1** *n* carcajada *f*
**2** *vi* carcajearse

**GUI** ['guːi] *n Comptr (abbr* **Graphical User Interface)** interfaz *f* gráfica

**Guiana** [gaɪ'ɑːnə] *n* (la) Guayana, las Guayanas

**guidance** ['gaɪdəns] *n* orientación *f*; **under the g. of...** bajo la dirección de...; **for your g.** para su información

**guide** [gaɪd] **1** *n* **(a)** *(person)* guía *mf*; **Girl G.** scout *f*, escultista *f*; **g. dog** perro *m* lazarillo **(b)** *(book)* guía *f* (to de) **(c)** *(indication)* guía *f*; **as a g.** como guía
**2** *vt* guiar; **I will be guided by your advice** me guiaré por tus consejos

**guidebook** ['gaɪdbʊk] *n* guía *f*

**guided** ['gaɪdɪd] *adj* **g. missile** misil *m* teledirigido; **g. tour** visita *f* guiada

**guideline** ['gaɪdlaɪn] *n (indication)* directriz *f*, línea *f* general; **guidelines** directrices *fpl*; **as a general g.** como orientación general

**guiding** ['gaɪdɪŋ] *adj* **the g. principle of his life** el principio que rige su vida; *Fig* **g. light** guía *mf*

**guild** [gɪld] *n (of craftsmen, merchants)* gremio *m*

**guilder** ['gɪldə] *n (Dutch currency)* florín *m*

**guile** [gaɪl] *n* astucia *f*

**guileless** ['gaɪlɪs] *adj* ingenuo(a), cándido(a)

**guillemot** ['gɪlɪmɒt] *n* arao *m* común

**guillotine** ['gɪləti:n] **1** *n* guillotina *f*; *Br Parl* **to put a g. on a bill** = limitar el tiempo de discusión de un proyecto de ley
**2** *vt* guillotinar

**guilt** [gɪlt] *n* **(a)** *(blame)* culpa *f*; **an admission of g.** una declaración de culpabilidad **(b)** *(emotion)* culpabilidad *f*, culpa *f*; **to feel g.** tener sentimientos de culpabilidad; **g. complex** complejo *m* de culpabilidad

**guiltily** ['gɪltɪlɪ] *adv* con aire culpable

**guiltless** ['gɪltlɪs] *adj* inocente

**guilty** ['gɪltɪ] *adj* **(a)** *(of crime)* culpable; **to find sb g./not g.** declarar a alguien culpable/inocente **(b)** *(emotionally)* **to feel g.** sentirse culpable; **g. conscience** remordimientos *mpl* de conciencia; **a g. secret** un secreto vergonzante

**Guinea** ['gɪnɪ] *n* Guinea

**guinea** ['gɪnɪ] *n* **(a)** *Br (coin)* guinea *f (moneda equivalente a 21 chelines)* **(b)** **g. fowl** gallineta *f*, gallina *f* de Guinea; **g. pig** cobaya *m or f*, conejillo *m* de Indias; *Fig* **to be a g. pig** *(for new idea)* hacer de conejillo de Indias

**Guinea-Bissau** ['gɪnɪbɪ'saʊ] *n* Guinea-Bissau

**Guinean** [gɪ'neɪən] *n & adj* guineano(a) *m,f*

**guise** [gaɪz] *n* apariencia *f*; **in** *or* **under the g. of...** bajo la apariencia de...; **in a different g.** con una apariencia diferente

**guitar** [gɪ'tɑː(r)] *n* guitarra *f*

**guitarist** [gɪ'tɑːrɪst] *n* guitarrista *mf*

**gulch** [gʌltʃ] *n US (valley)* garganta *f*, hoz *f*

**gulf** [gʌlf] *n* **(a)** *(bay)* golfo *m*; **the (Persian) G.** el Golfo (Pérsico); **the G. of Mexico** el Golfo de México; **the G. Stream** la corriente del Golfo; **the G. War** la guerra del Golfo **(b)** *(between people, ideas)* brecha *f*, abismo *m*

**gull** [gʌl] *n* gaviota *f*

**gullet** ['gʌlɪt] *n* esófago *m*

**gullibility** [gʌlɪ'bɪlɪtɪ] *n* credulidad *f*, ingenuidad *f*

**gullible** ['gʌlɪbəl] *adj* crédulo(a), ingenuo(a)

**gully** ['gʌlɪ] *n* barranco *m*

**gulp** [gʌlp] **1** *n* trago *m*; **in** *or* **at one g.** de un trago; **"what money?" he said, with a g.** "¿qué dinero?" dijo, tragando saliva
**2** *vt (swallow)* tragar, engullir
**3** *vi (with surprise)* tragar saliva

▶**gulp down** *vt sep (swallow)* tragar, engullir

**gum** [gʌm] **1** *n* **(a)** *(in mouth)* encía *f*; **g. disease** gingivitis *f inv* **(b)** *(adhesive)* pegamento *m*, goma *f* **(c)** *(chewing)* **g.** chicle *m* **(d)** *(resin)* **g. arabic** goma *f* arábiga; **g. tree** eucalipto *m*; *Fig* **to be up a g. tree** estar metido(a) en un buen lío
**2** *vt (pt & pp gummed)* *(stick)* pegar

▶**gum up** *vt sep (mechanism)* pegar

**gumboot** ['gʌmbuːt] *n* bota *f* de goma

**gummed** [gʌmd] *adj (label)* engomado(a)

**gumption** ['gʌmʃən] *n Fam (common sense)* sensatez *f*, sentido *m* común; *(courage)* narices *fpl*, agallas *fpl*

**gumshield** ['gʌmʃiːld] *n Sport* protector *m* bucal

**gun** [gʌn] **1** *n* **(a)** *(pistol)* pistola *f*; *(rifle)* rifle *m*; *(artillery piece)* cañón *m*; **g. carriage** cureña *f*; **g. dog** perro *m* de caza; **g. laws** legislación *f* sobre armas de fuego; **g. licence** licencia *f* de armas **(b)** *(idioms) Fam* **big g.** *(important person)* pez *m* gordo; **to be going great guns** ir a pedir de boca; **to stick to one's guns** no dar el brazo a torcer; **to jump the g.** precipitarse

**2** *vt* (*pt & pp* **gunned**) **to g. the engine** dar acelerones

▶**gun down** *vt sep* (*kill*) matar a tiros

▶**gun for** *vt insep* **he's gunning for us** la tiene tomada con nosotros; **he's gunning for the heavyweight title** aspira al título de los pesos pesados; **she's gunning for my job** tiene las miras puestas en mi trabajo

**gunboat** ['gʌnbəʊt] *n* cañonera *f*; **g. diplomacy** la diplomacia de los cañones

**gunfight** ['gʌnfaɪt] *n* tiroteo *m*

**gunfire** ['gʌnfaɪə(r)] *n* disparos *mpl*, tiros *mpl*

**gunge** [gʌndʒ] *n Fam* pringue *f*, porquería *f*

**gung-ho** [gʌŋhəʊ] *adj* (*enthusiastic*) exaltado(a); (*eager for war*) belicoso(a); **to be g. about sth** lanzar las campanas al vuelo con relación a algo

**gunk** [gʌŋk] *n Fam* pringue *f*

**gunman** ['gʌnmən] *n* hombre *m* armado

**gunner** ['gʌnə(r)] *n* artillero *m*

**gunpoint** ['gʌnpɔɪnt] *n* **at g.** a punta de pistola

**gunpowder** ['gʌnpaʊdə(r)] *n* pólvora *f*

**gunrunner** ['gʌnrʌnə(r)] *n* contrabandista *mf* de armas

**gunrunning** ['gʌnrʌnɪŋ] *n* contrabando *m* de armas

**gunship** ['gʌnʃɪp] *n* (**helicopter**) **g.** helicóptero *m* de combate

**gunshot** ['gʌnʃɒt] *n* disparo *m*, tiro *m*; **g. wound** herida *f* de bala

**gunsmith** ['gʌnsmɪθ] *n* armero *m*

**gunwale** ['gʌnəl] *n Naut* borda *f*, regala *f*

**gurgle** ['gɜːgəl] **1** *n* (*of liquid*) borboteo *m*, gorgoteo *m*; (*of baby*) gorjeo *m*; **a g. of delight** un gorjeo de placer

**2** *vi* (*of liquid*) borbotear, gorgotear; (*of baby*) gorjear; **to g. with delight** gorjear de placer

**guru** ['gʊruː] *n also Fig* gurú *m*

**gush** [gʌʃ] **1** *n* (*of spring, fountain*) chorro *m*; **a g. of words** un torrente de palabras

**2** *vi* (**a**) (*spurt, pour*) manar, correr; **tears gushed from her eyes** derramaba lágrimas a mares (**b**) *Pej* (*talk effusively*) **to g. about sth** hablar con excesiva efusividad de algo

**gushing** ['gʌʃɪŋ] *adj Pej* (*person, praise*) excesivamente efusivo(a)

**gusset** ['gʌsɪt] *n* (*of tights, underwear*) escudete *m*

**gust** [gʌst] **1** *n* (*of wind, rain, air*) ráfaga *f*

**2** *vi* (*of wind*) soplar racheado *or* en ráfagas

**gusto** ['gʌstəʊ] *n* entusiasmo *m*, ganas *fpl*; **with g.** con muchas ganas

**gusty** ['gʌstɪ] *adj* (*wind*) racheado(a); **a g. day/weather** un día/tiempo con viento racheado

**gut** [gʌt] **1** *n* (**a**) (*intestine*) intestino *m*; *Fam* **guts** (*of person, machine*) tripas *fpl*; *Fam* **to sweat** *or* **work one's guts out** dejarse la piel; *Fam* **she hates my guts** no me puede ver ni en pintura; *Fam* **I'll have his guts for garters** lo haré picadillo; **a g. feeling** (*intuition*) una intuición, una corazonada; **I have a g. feeling that…** tengo la intuición *or* corazonada de que…; **g. reaction** (*intuitive*) reacción *f* instintiva

(**b**) *Fam* **guts** (*courage*) agallas *fpl*, arrestos *mpl*; **I didn't have the guts to tell them** no tuve agallas para decírselo

**2** *vt* (*pt & pp* **gutted**) (**a**) (*fish*) limpiar

(**b**) (*building*) **the house had been gutted by the fire** el fuego destruyó por completo el interior de la casa; **she gutted the house and completely redecorated it** despojó la casa de todos sus enseres y la decoró de nuevo por completo

**gutless** ['gʌtlɪs] *adj* cobarde

**gutsy** ['gʌtsɪ] *adj Fam* (*brave*) corajudo(a)

**gutted** ['gʌtɪd] *adj Br Fam* (*disappointed*) **to be g.** llevarse un chasco enorme, quedarse hecho(a) polvo

**gutter** ['gʌtə(r)] **1** *n* (*in street*) cuneta *f*; (*on roof*) canalón *m*; *Fig* **to end up in the g.** terminar en el arroyo; *Fig* **to drag oneself out of the g.** salir del arroyo; *Fam Pej* **g. press** prensa *f* amarilla *or* sensacionalista

**2** *vi* (*of flame*) parpadear

**guttural** ['gʌtərəl] *adj* gutural

**guy**¹ [gaɪ] *n Fam* (*man*) tipo *m*, tío *m*; **a great g.** un gran tipo; **a tough g.** un tipo duro; **hi guys!** ¡hola, gente!

**guy**² *n* **g.** (**rope**) (*for tent*) viento *m*

**Guyana** [gaɪˈænə] *n* Guyana

**Guyanese** [gaɪəˈniːz] *n & adj* guyanés(esa) *m,f*

**Guy Fawkes Night** ['gaɪˈfɔːksˌnaɪt] *n Br* = fiesta del 5 de noviembre en la que se lanzan fuegos artificiales en recuerdo del fracaso del intento de voladura del Parlamento por Guy Fawkes en 1605

**guzzle** ['gʌzəl] *Fam vt* (*food*) engullir

**gym** [dʒɪm] *n* (*gymnasium*) gimnasio *m*; (*gymnastics*) gimnasia *f*; **g. shoes** zapatillas *fpl* de gimnasia *or* de deporte

**gymkhana** [jɪŋˈkɑːnə] *n* gincana *f* hípica

**gymnasium** [dʒɪmˈneɪziəm] *n* gimnasio *m*

**gymnast** ['dʒɪmnæst] *n* gimnasta *mf*

**gymnastic** [dʒɪmˈnæstɪk] *adj* gimnástico(a)

**gymnastics** [dʒɪmˈnæstɪks] **1** *n* gimnasia *f*

**2** *npl Fig* **mental g.** gimnasia *f* mental

**gynaecological,** *US* **gynecological** [gaɪnɪkə'lɒdʒɪkəl] *adj* ginecológico(a)

**gynaecologist,** *US* **gynecologist** [gaɪnɪ'kɒlədʒɪst] *n* ginecólogo(a) *m,f*

**gynaecology,** *US* **gynecology** [gaɪnɪ'kɒlədʒɪ] *n* ginecología *f*

**gyp** [dʒɪp] *n Br Fam* **my tooth/leg is giving me g.** la muela/pierna me está matando; **he's been giving me g. about my decision** no para de darme la barrila por mi decisión

**gypsum** ['dʒɪpsəm] *n* yeso *m*

**gypsy** = **gipsy**

**gyrate** [dʒaɪ'reɪt] *vi* rotar, girar

**gyration** [dʒaɪ'reɪʃən] *n* rotación *f*, giro *m*

**gyroscope** ['dʒaɪrəskəʊp] *n* giróscopo *m*, giroscopio *m*

# H

**H, h** [eɪtʃ] n (letter) H, h f; **H bomb** bomba f H

**habeas corpus** ['heɪbɪəs'kɔ:pəs] n Law habeas corpus

**haberdashery** ['hæbədæʃərɪ] n (a) Br (sewing items, shop) mercería f (b) US (men's clothes) ropa f de caballero; (shop) tienda f de confección de caballero

**habit** ['hæbɪt] n (a) (custom, practice) hábito m, costumbre f; **to be in the h. of doing sth** tener la costumbre de hacer algo; **to get into the h. of doing sth** adquirir el hábito de hacer algo; **you must get out of the h. of always blaming other people** tienes que dejar de echar siempre la culpa a los demás; **don't make a h. of it** que no se convierta en una costumbre; **from force of h.** por la fuerza de la costumbre; **a bad/good h.** una mala/buena costumbre

(b) Fam (addiction) (to cocaine, heroin) vicio m, hábito m; **to kick the h.** dejar el vicio

(c) (costume) hábito m

**habitable** ['hæbɪtəbəl] adj habitable

**habitat** ['hæbɪtæt] n hábitat m

**habitation** [hæbɪ'teɪʃən] n (a) (occupation) habitación f; **there were few signs of h.** había pocos rastros de habitantes; **fit/unfit for h.** apto/no apto para su uso como vivienda (b) (dwelling place) vivienda f

**habitual** [həˈbɪtjʊəl] adj (generosity, rudeness) habitual, acostumbrado(a); (liar, drunk) habitual

**habitually** [həˈbɪtjʊəlɪ] adv habitualmente

**habituate** [həˈbɪtjʊeɪt] vt habituar (**to** a); **to become habituated to sth** habituarse a algo

**hack¹** [hæk] **1** vt (a) (cut) cortar; **to h. sth/sb to pieces** despedazar algo/a alguien a golpes de cuchillo; **to h. one's way through the jungle** abrirse paso a machetazos por la jungla (b) (in football) dar un hachazo a (c) very Fam (cope with) **he can't h. it** no puede con ello

**2** vi (a) (cut) **to h. at sth** dar machetazos a algo (b) (cough) toser con fuerza (c) Comptr **to h. into a computer system** introducirse ilegalmente en un sistema informático

**hack²** n (a) Fam Pej (journalist) gacetillero(a) m,f; (political activist) militante mf, activista mf (b) (horseride) **to go for a h.** ir a dar un paseo a caballo

▸**hack down** vt sep (tree) talar, cortar

▸**hack off** vt sep (a) (chop off) (branch, limb) cortar (b) Fam **to be hacked off (with sb/sth)** estar rebotado(a) or mosqueado(a) (con alguien/por algo)

**hacker** ['hækə(r)] n Comptr pirata mf informático(a), hacker mf

**hacking jacket** ['hækɪŋ'dʒækɪt] n chaqueta f de montar

**hackles** ['hækəlz] npl (of dog) pelo m del cuello; Fig **to make sb's h. rise** (make sb angry) enfurecer a alguien

**hackney cab** ['hæknɪ'kæb], **hackney carriage** ['hæknɪ'kærɪdʒ] n Formal taxi m

**hackneyed** ['hæknɪd] adj (language, argument) manido(a), trillado(a)

**hacksaw** ['hæksɔː] n sierra f para metales

**had** [hæd] pt & pp of **have**

**haddock** ['hædək] n eglefino m

**hadn't** ['hædənt] = **had not**

**haemoglobin,** US **hemoglobin** [hiːməʊ'gləʊbɪn] n hemoglobina f

**haemophilia,** US **hemophilia** [hiːməʊ'fɪlɪə] n hemofilia f

**haemophiliac,** US **hemophiliac** [hiːməʊ'fɪlɪæk] n hemofílico(a) m,f

**haemorrhage,** US **hemorrhage** ['hemərɪdʒ] **1** n (bleeding) hemorragia f; Fig (of people, resources) fuerte pérdida f

**2** vi Med sangrar, sufrir una hemorragia; Fig (of support, funds) decrecer por momentos

**haemorrhoids,** US **hemorrhoids** ['hemərɔɪdz] npl Med hemorroides fpl

**hag** [hæg] n Pej (old woman) bruja f, arpía f

**haggard** ['hægəd] adj marcado(a) por el cansancio y/o el dolor

**haggis** ['hægɪs] n = plato típico escocés a base de asaduras de cordero embutidas en una tripa

**haggle** ['hægəl] vi regatear; **to h. about** or **over the price of sth** regatear el precio de algo

**hagiography** [hægɪ'ɒgrəfɪ] n hagiografía f

**Hague** [heɪg] n **the H.** La Haya

**hail¹** [heɪl] **1** n (hailstones) granizo m; Fig (of blows, bullets, insults) lluvia f

**2** vi **it's hailing** está granizando

**hail²** vt (a) *(attract attention of)* llamar (b) *(acclaim)* aclamar (**as** como); **she has been hailed as the greatest novelist of the century** la han ensalzado diciendo que era la mejor novelista del siglo

▶**hail from** vt insep proceder de

**hailstone** ['heɪlstəʊn] n (piedra f de) granizo m

**hailstorm** ['heɪlstɔːm] n granizada f

**hair** [heə(r)] n *(of head)* pelo m, cabello m; *(of body)* vello m; *(of animal)* pelo m; **to have long h.** tener el pelo largo; **to do one's h.** peinarse; **to brush/comb one's h.** cepillarse/peinarse el pelo; **to have** or **get one's h. cut** cortarse el pelo; **if you harm** or **touch a h. on that child's head…** como le toques un solo pelo a ese niño…; **to make sb's h. stand on end** ponerle a alguien los pelos de punta; *Fam* **keep your h. on!** ¡no te sulfures!; *Fam* **to get in sb's h.** dar la lata a alguien; *Fig* **to let one's h. down** *(lose inhibitions)* soltarse el pelo; *Fam* **h. of the dog** *(for hangover)* = algo de alcohol para quitar la resaca; **h. gel** gomina f; *Br* **h. slide** pasador m (para el pelo)

**hairband** ['heəbænd] n cinta f (para el pelo)

**hairbrush** ['heəbrʌʃ] n cepillo m

**hairclip** ['heəklɪp] n clip m para el pelo, horquilla f

**haircut** ['heəkʌt] n corte m de pelo; **to have a h.** cortarse el pelo

**hairdo** ['heəduː] n *(pl* **hairdos***)* n *Fam* peinado m

**hairdresser** ['heədresə(r)] n peluquero(a) m,f; **h.'s** peluquería f

**hairdressing** ['heədresɪŋ] n peluquería f; **h. salon** salón m de peluquería

**hairdryer** ['heədraɪə(r)] n secador m (de pelo)

**hairgrip** ['heəgrɪp] n horquilla f

**hairless** ['heəlɪs] adj sin pelo; *(face)* lampiño(a); *(infant, puppy)* pelón(ona)

**hairline** ['heəlaɪn] n (a) *(of person)* nacimiento m del pelo; **to have a receding h.** tener entradas (b) **h. crack** *(in pipe, wall)* fisura f muy pequeña; **h. fracture** *(of bone)* fisura f (de hueso)

**hairnet** ['heənet] n redecilla f para el pelo

**hairpiece** ['heəpiːs] n peluquín m

**hairpin** ['heəpɪn] n horquilla f; **h. bend** *(on road)* curva f muy cerrada

**hair-raising** ['heəreɪzɪŋ] adj espeluznante

**hair's-breadth** ['heəzbredθ] n **by a h.** por un pelo; **to be within a h. of** estar al borde de

**hairspray** ['heəspreɪ] n laca f (de pelo)

**hairstyle** ['heəstaɪl] n peinado m

**hairy** ['heəri] adj (a) *(hair-covered)* velludo(a), peludo(a) (b) *Fam (scary)* peliagudo(a)

**Haiti** ['heɪti] n Haití

**Haitian** ['heɪʃən] n & adj haitiano(a) m,f

**hake** [heɪk] n merluza f

**halcyon days** ['hælsɪən'deɪz] npl *Literary* días mpl felices

**hale** [heɪl] adj sano(a); **to be h. and hearty** estar como una rosa

**half** [hɑːf] **1** n *(pl* **halves** [hɑːvz]*)* (a) *(in general)* mitad f; **h. an hour** media hora f; **h. past twelve, h. twelve** las doce y media; *Sport* **first/second h.** primera/segunda parte f; **to fold/cut sth in h.** doblar/cortar algo por la mitad; **h. a dozen** media docena f; **h. of them** la mitad (de ellos); **to have h. a mind to do sth** estar tentado(a) de hacer algo; *Hum* **my better** or **other h.** mi media naranja; **she is too clever/arrogant by h.** se pasa de lista/arrogante; **she doesn't do things by halves** no le gusta hacer las cosas a medias; **to go halves with sb** pagar or ir a medias con alguien

(b) *(fraction)* medio m; **three and a h.** tres y medio

(c) *(ticket) (for child)* billete m de niño

(d) *Br (half pint)* media pinta f

**2** adj medio(a); **h. board** media pensión f; **h. day** media jornada f; **h. hour** media hora f; **every h. hour** cada media hora; **at h. price** a mitad de precio

**3** adv a medias; **to h. do sth** hacer algo a medias; **the bottle was h. full/empty** la botella estaba medio llena/vacía; **you're h. right** tienes razón a medias; *Br Fam* **not h.!** ¡y que lo digas!; *Br Fam* **it isn't h. cold!** ¡menudo frío (que hace)!, ¡no hace frío ni nada!

**half-** [hɑːf] pref **h.-naked/asleep/dead** medio desnudo/dormido/muerto(a)

**half-baked** [hɑːf'beɪkt] adj *Fam (theory, plan)* mal concebido(a)

**halfbreed** ['hɑːfbriːd] n mestizo(a) m,f

**half-brother** ['hɑːfbrʌðə(r)] n hermanastro m

**half-caste** ['hɑːfkɑːst] n & adj mestizo(a) m,f

**half-cock** ['hɑːfkɒk] n *Fam Fig* **to go off at h.** *(of plan, event)* fracasar *(por falta de preparación)*

**half-hearted** ['hɑːf'hɑːtɪd] adj *(effort, performance)* desganado(a); *(belief, support)* tibio(a)

**half-heartedly** ['hɑːf'hɑːtɪdlɪ] adv sin (muchas) ganas

**half-hourly** [hɑːf'aʊəlɪ] adv cada media hora

**half-life** ['hɑːflaɪf] n *Phys* media vida f

**half-mast** ['hɑːf'mɑːst] n *Br* **at h.** a media asta

**half-sister** ['hɑːf'sɪstə(r)] n hermanastra f

**half-size** ['hɑːf'saɪz] n *(for clothing)* talla f intermedia; *(for shoes)* número m intermedio

**half-term** ['hɑːf'tɜːm] n Br **h. (holiday)** vacaciones fpl de mitad de trimestre

**half-time** ['hɑːf'taɪm] n (of match) descanso m

**half-truth** ['hɑːf'truːθ] n verdad f a medias

**halfway** ['hɑːf'weɪ] **1** adj (point, stage) intermedio(a); **h. line** (on football pitch) línea f divisoria or de medio campo
**2** adv a mitad de camino; Fig **to meet sb h.** (compromise) llegar a una solución de compromiso con alguien

**halfwit** ['hɑːf'wɪt] n bobo(a) m,f, lerdo(a) m,f

**halfwitted** [hɑːf'wɪtɪd] adj (person) idiota, memo(a); **a h. idea** una memez

**half-yearly** ['hɑːf'jɪəlɪ] adj semestral, bianual

**halibut** ['hælɪbət] n fletán m

**halitosis** [hælɪ'təʊsɪs] n Med halitosis f inv

**hall** [hɔːl] n **(a)** (entrance room) vestíbulo m; (corridor) pasillo m **(b)** (for concerts, meetings) (large room) salón m de actos; (building) auditorio m **(c)** Br Univ **h. of residence** residencia f de estudiantes

**hallmark** ['hɔːlmɑːk] n (on silver) contraste m; Fig (of idea, plan) sello m característico

**hallo = hello**

**hallowed** ['hæləʊd] adj sagrado(a)

**Hallowe'en** [hæləʊ'iːn] n = víspera de Todos los Santos en la que los niños se disfrazan de brujas y fantasmas

**hallucinate** [hə'luːsɪneɪt] vi alucinar, sufrir alucinaciones

**hallucination** [həluːsɪ'neɪʃən] n alucinación f

**hallucinatory** [hə'luːsɪnətərɪ] adj alucinatorio(a)

**hallucinogen** [hə'luːsɪnədʒən] n alucinógeno m

**hallucinogenic** [həluːsɪnəʊ'dʒenɪk] adj alucinógeno(a)

**hallway** ['hɔːlweɪ] n (entrance room) vestíbulo m; (corridor) pasillo m

**halo** ['heɪləʊ] (pl halos or haloes) n halo m

**halogen** ['hælədʒən] n halógeno(a); **h. lamp** lámpara f halógena

**halt** [hɔːlt] **1** n alto m, parada f; **to come to a h.** detenerse; **to bring sth to a h.** paralizar algo; **to call a h. to sth** interrumpir algo
**2** vt detener
**3** vi detenerse

**halter** ['hɔːltə(r)] n (for horse) ronzal m

**halterneck** ['hɔːltənek] adj (dress, top) sujeto(a) al cuello

**halting** ['hɔːltɪŋ] adj (voice, progress) vacilante, titubeante

**halve** [hɑːv] vt **(a)** (divide in two) dividir (en dos); (cake, fruit) partir por la mitad **(b)** (reduce by half) reducir a la mitad

**halves** [hɑːvz] pl of **half**

**ham** [hæm] **1** n **(a)** (meat) jamón m **(b)** Fam (actor) actor m exagerado, actriz f exagerada; **h. acting** sobreactuación f, histrionismo m
**2** vt (pt & pp hammed) Fam (of actor) **to h. it up** sobreactuar

**Hamburg** ['hæmbɜːg] n Hamburgo

**hamburger** ['hæmbɜːgə(r)] n hamburguesa f

**ham-fisted** ['hæm'fɪstɪd] adj Fam (person) manazas; (workmanship, attempt) torpe

**hamlet** ['hæmlɪt] n aldea f

**hammer** ['hæmə(r)] **1** n (tool) & Sport martillo m; **to come under the h.** (be auctioned) salir a subasta; **to go at it h. and tongs** (argue) tener una acalorada discusión; (try hard) poner mucho empeño or esfuerzo; **the h. and sickle** la hoz y el martillo
**2** vt **(a)** (hit with hammer) martillear; (hit with fist) dar puñetazos a; **to h. a nail into sth** clavar un clavo en algo; **to h. home** (nail, argument) remachar; **she hammered home her advantage** se aseguró su ventaja **(b)** (defeat) vapulear, machacar
▸**hammer away at** vt insep Fig **to h. away at a problem** ponerse en serio con un problema
▸**hammer out** vt sep Fig (agreement) alcanzar, llegar a

**hammering** ['hæmərɪŋ] n **(a)** (noise) martilleo m **(b)** (defeat) paliza f

**hammock** ['hæmək] n hamaca f

**hamper** ['hæmpə(r)] **1** n (for food) cesta f, cesto m; **(Christmas) h.** cesta de Navidad
**2** vt (hinder) entorpecer

**hamster** ['hæmstə(r)] n hámster m

**hamstring** ['hæmstrɪŋ] **1** n tendón m de la corva
**2** vt (pt & pp hamstrung ['hæmstrʌŋ]) (incapacitate) incapacitar, paralizar

**hand** [hænd] **1** n **(a)** (part of body) mano f; (of clock, watch) manecilla f; **to hold hands** cogerse de las manos; **h. in h.** (cogidos) de la mano; **to hold sth in one's h.** sostener algo en la mano; **to take sb by the h.** coger a alguien de la mano; **on one's hands and knees** a cuatro patas; **by h.** (make, wash) a mano; (on envelope) en propia mano; **hands off!** ¡las manos fuera!; **hands up!** ¡manos arriba!; **h. basin** lavabo m; **h. cream** crema f de manos; **h. grenade** granada f de mano; **h. luggage** equipaje m de mano
**(b)** (worker) brazo m; **to be an old h. at sth** ser veterano(a) en algo
**(c)** (handwriting) **in his own h.** de su puño y letra

**(d)** *(in cards)* mano *f*; *Fig* **to show one's h.** poner las cartas boca arriba *or* sobre la mesa

**(e)** *(idioms)* **at** *or* **on h.** a mano; **to have sth to h.** tener algo a mano; **to ask for sb's h. (in marriage)** pedir la mano de alguien; **to be in good hands** estar en buenas manos; **to fall into the wrong hands** caer en malas manos; **it's out of my hands** no está en mi mano; **to change hands** *(of money, car)* cambiar de mano; **I had a h. in designing the course** tuve que ver *or* puse de mi parte en el diseño del curso; **to go h. in h. with sth** estar asociado(a) a algo; **to try one's h. at sth** intentar algo alguna vez; **to turn one's h. to sth** dedicarse a algo; **to give** *or* **lend sb a h.** echar una mano a alguien; **to give sb a big h.** *(applaud)* dar un gran aplauso a alguien; **to suffer at sb's hands** sufrir a manos de alguien; **on the one h.** por una parte; **on the other h.** por otra parte; **to have time on one's hands** tener tiempo libre; **to have a situation in h.** tener una situación bajo control; **to take sb in h.** hacerse cargo de alguien; **to get out of h.** escaparse de las manos; **the children got out of h.** los niños se desmandaron; **to dismiss a suggestion out of h.** rechazar una sugerencia sin más ni más; **to have one's hands full** estar completamente ocupado(a); **to have one's hands tied** tener las manos atadas; **to be h. in glove with sb** colaborar estrechamente con alguien; **to live from h. to mouth** vivir de forma precaria; **to lose money h. over fist** perder dinero a raudales; **to make money h. over fist** ganar dinero a espuertas; **to win hands down** ganar con comodidad

**2** *vt* pasar; **to h. sth to sb** pasar algo a alguien; *Fig* **to h. sth to sb on a plate** ponerle algo a alguien en bandeja; *Fig* **you've got to h. it to him** tienes que reconocérselo

▸**hand back** *vt sep (return)* devolver

▸**hand down** *vt sep (bequeath)* dejar en herencia

▸**hand in** *vt sep (give)* entregar; *(resignation)* presentar

▸**hand on** *vt sep* traspasar, transferir

▸**hand out** *vt sep (distribute)* repartir

▸**hand over** *vt sep (give)* dar, entregar; *Fig (control, responsibility)* ceder

▸**hand round** *vt sep (circulate)* pasar

**handbag** ['hændbæg] *n* bolso *m*

**handball** ['hændbɔːl] **1** *(game)* balonmano *m* **(b)** ['hænd 'bɔːl] *(offence in football)* mano *f*

**handbook** ['hændbʊk] *n* manual *m*

**handbrake** ['hændbreɪk] *n (of car)* freno *m* de mano

**handclap** ['hændklæp] *n* **a slow h.** = palmas lentas de desaprobación

**handcuff** ['hændkʌf] *vt* esposar

**handcuffs** ['hændkʌfs] *npl* esposas *fpl*

**handful** ['hændfʊl] *n (of sand, rice, people)* puñado *m*; *Fig* **that child is a real h.** ese niño es un terremoto

**handgun** ['hændgʌn] *n* pistola *f*

**handicap** ['hændɪkæp] **1** *n (disadvantage)* desventaja *f*, hándicap *m*; *(disability)* discapacidad *f*, minusvalía *f*; *(in golf, horseracing)* hándicap *m*

**2** *vt (pt & pp* **handicapped)** suponer una desventaja para; **to be handicapped by...** verse perjudicado(a) por...

**handicapped** ['hændɪkæpt] **1** *adj* discapacitado(a), minusválido(a)

**2** *npl* **the h.** los discapacitados *or* minusválidos

**handicraft** ['hændɪkrɑːft] *n (skill)* artesanía *f*; *(object)* objeto *m* de artesanía

**handiwork** ['hændɪwɜːk] *n (craftwork)* trabajos *mpl* manuales, manualidades *fpl*; *Ironic* **this mess looks like Clara's h.!** este desorden parece obra de Clara

**handkerchief** ['hæŋkətʃɪf] *n* pañuelo *m*

**handle** ['hændəl] **1** *n (of broom, umbrella, gun, knife)* mango *m*; *(of racket, bat)* empuñadura *f*; *(of suitcase, cup)* asa *f*; *(of door)* manilla *f*; *Fig* **to fly off the h.** *(lose one's temper)* perder los estribos; *Fig* **to get a h. on sth** *(understand)* hacerse una idea clara de algo

**2** *vt* **(a)** *(touch, hold)* manejar, manipular; **h. with care** *(sign)* frágil; **to h. the ball** *(in football)* hacer (falta con la) mano **(b)** *(cope with) (situation, crisis)* hacer frente a, afrontar **(c)** *Com (business, contract, client)* encargarse de

**3** *vi* **to h. well** *(of car, boat)* responder bien

**handlebars** ['hændəlbɑːz] *npl (of bicycle, motorbike)* manillar *m*

**handmade** ['hændmeɪd] *adj* hecho(a) a mano; **to be h.** estar hecho(a) a mano

**hand-me-downs** ['hændmɪdaʊnz] *npl Fam* **he wore his brother's h.** llevaba ropa heredada de su hermano

**handout** ['hændaʊt] *n* **(a)** *(donation)* donativo *m*, limosna *f* **(b)** *(leaflet)* hoja *f* informativa

**handover** ['hændəʊvə(r)] *n* entrega *f*

**hand-picked** ['hænd'pɪkt] *adj (person, team)* cuidadosamente seleccionado(a)

**handrail** ['hændreɪl] *n* barandilla *f*

**handset** ['hændset] *n (of telephone)* auricular *m*

**handshake** ['hændʃeɪk] *n* apretón *m* de manos

**hands-off** ['hæn'zɒf] *adj (approach, style)* no intervencionista

**handsome** ['hænsəm] *adj* **(a)** *(man)* guapo, atractivo; *(woman)* distinguida; *(animal)* hermoso(a), bello(a); *(building)* elegante, bello(a) **(b)** *(praise)* generoso(a); *(price, profit)* considerable

**handsomely** ['hænsəmlı] *adv* (a) *(dressed, furnished)* elegantemente (b) *(praised, paid)* generosamente

**hands-on** ['hæn'zɒn] *adj* **he has a h. management style** le gusta implicarse en todos los aspectos del negocio; **h. training** formación f práctica

**handstand** ['hændstænd] *n* **to do a h.** hacer el pino

**hand-to-hand** ['hæntə'hænd] *adj* **h. combat** combate *m* cuerpo a cuerpo

**hand-to-mouth** ['hæntə'maʊθ] **1** *adj* **a h. existence** una existencia precaria
**2** *adv* **to live h.** vivir de forma precaria

**handwriting** ['hændraɪtɪŋ] *n* letra f, caligrafía f

**handwritten** ['hænd'rɪtən] *adj* manuscrito(a), escrito(a) a mano

**handy** ['hændɪ] *adj* (a) *(useful)* práctico(a), útil; **to come in h.** venir bien (b) *(conveniently situated)* bien situado(a); **the flat is very h. for the shops** el piso queda muy cerca de las tiendas (c) *(within reach)* a mano; **have you got a pen h.?** ¿tienes un bolígrafo a mano? (d) *(skilful)* habilidoso(a); **he's very h. in the kitchen** se le da muy bien la cocina *or* cocinar; **she's very h. with a paintbrush** es muy hábil con la brocha

**handyman** ['hændɪmæn] *n (person good at odd jobs)* manitas *mf inv*

**hang** [hæŋ] **1** *n Fam* **to get the h. of sth** pillarle el truco *or* el tranquillo a algo
**2** *vt (pt & pp* hung [hʌŋ]) (a) *(suspend)* colgar (b) **to h. one's head** bajar la cabeza; **he hung his head in shame** bajó la cabeza avergonzado (c) *(pt & pp* hanged) *(criminal)* ahorcar, colgar *(for* por)
**3** *vi* (a) *(be suspended)* colgar; **she hung on his every word** estaba totalmente pendiente de sus palabras (b) *(be executed)* ser ahorcado(a) *or* colgado(a) (c) *(of material, clothes)* caer, colgar
▸**hang about, hang around** *vi Fam (wait)* esperar; **he kept me hanging about for hours** me tuvo esperando horas
▸**hang back** *vi (hesitate)* dudar, titubear
▸**hang in** *vi Fam (persevere)* aguantar; **h. in there!** ¡resiste!, ¡aguanta!
▸**hang on 1** *vi* (a) *Fam (wait)* esperar (b) *(survive)* resistir, aguantar
**2** *vt insep (depend on)* depender de; **everything hangs on his answer** todo depende de su respuesta
▸**hang on to** *vt insep (keep)* conservar; **I'd rather on to those documents if I were you** yo, en tu lugar, me quedaría con esos documentos
▸**hang out 1** *vt sep (washing)* tender
**2** *vi* (a) **his tongue/shirt was hanging out** tenía la lengua/camisa fuera (b) *Fam* **to h. out**

**with one's friends** andar por ahí con los amigos; **he usually hangs out in the Bronx Café** normalmente va por el Café Bronx
▸**hang together** *vi (of argument, statements)* encajar, concordar
▸**hang up 1** *vt sep (suspend) (hat, picture)* colgar
**2** *vi (on telephone)* colgar; **to h. up on sb** colgarle (el teléfono) a alguien

**hangar** ['hæŋə(r)] *n Av* hangar *m*

**hangdog** ['hæŋdɒg] *adj* **a h. look** una expresión avergonzada

**hanger** ['hæŋə(r)] *n (for clothes)* percha f

**hanger-on** [hæŋə'rɒn] *(pl* hangers-on) *n* parásito(a) *m,f*, adlátere *mf*

**hang-glider** ['hæŋglaɪdə*r*] *n* ala f delta

**hang-gliding** ['hæŋglaɪdɪŋ] *n* **to go h.** hacer ala delta

**hanging** ['hæŋɪŋ] *n (execution)* ahorcamiento *m*, ejecución f en la horca

**hangman** ['hæŋmən] *n* verdugo *m*

**hangnail** ['hæŋneɪl] *n* padrastro *m*

**hang-out** ['hæŋaʊt] *n Fam* guarida f, sitio *m* predilecto

**hangover** ['hæŋəʊvə(r)] *n* (a) *(from drinking)* resaca f (b) *(practice, belief)* vestigio *m*

**hang-up** ['hæŋʌp] *n Fam (complex)* complejo *m*, paranoia f; **to have a h. about sth** estar acomplejado(a) por algo

**hanker** ['hæŋkə(r)] *vi* **to h. after** *or* **for sth** anhelar algo

**hankering** ['hæŋkərɪŋ] *n* **to have a h. for sth** sentir anhelo de algo

**hankie, hanky** ['hæŋkɪ] *n Fam* pañuelo *m*

**hanky-panky** ['hæŋkɪ'pæŋkɪ] *n Fam* (a) *(sexual activity)* magreo *m*, guarrindonguerías *fpl* (b) *(underhand behaviour)* chanchullos *mpl*, tejemanejes *mpl*

**Hanover** ['hænəʊvər] *n* Hanover

**haphazard** [hæp'hæzəd] *adj (choice, decision)* arbitrario(a), incoherente; *(attempt)* desorganizado(a)

**haphazardly** [hæp'hæzədlı] *adv* a la buena de Dios, descuidadamente

**hapless** ['hæplɪs] *adj* infortunado(a)

**happen** ['hæpən] *vi (take place)* pasar, ocurrir, suceder; **it happened ten years ago** pasó hace diez años; **as it happens,...** precisamente..., casualmente...; **what has happened to him?** ¿qué le ha pasado?; **to h. to meet sb** encontrarse con alguien por casualidad; **I h. to know that...** resulta que sé que...
▸**happen on, happen upon** *vt insep* encontrarse con

**happening** ['hæpənɪŋ] *n* suceso *m*

**happily** ['hæpɪlı] *adv* (a) *(with pleasure)* alegremente; **they lived h. ever after** fueron felices y comieron perdices (b) *(fortunately)* afortunadamente, por suerte

**happiness** ['hæpɪnɪs] n felicidad f

**happy** ['hæpɪ] adj (a) (in a state of contentment) feliz; (pleased) contento(a); (cheerful) alegre, feliz; **to be h. with sth** estar contento con algo; **to be h. to do sth** hacer algo con mucho gusto; **to make sb h.** hacer feliz a alguien; **a h. ending** un final feliz; **a h. medium** un (satisfactorio) término medio; **h. birthday/Christmas/New Year!** ¡feliz cumpleaños/Navidad/Año Nuevo! (b) (fortunate) (choice, phrase) afortunado(a), acertado(a)

**happy-go-lucky** ['hæpɪgəʊ'lʌkɪ] adj despreocupado(a)

**Hapsburg** ['hæpsbɜːg] n **the Hapsburgs** los Habsburgo, los Austrias

**harangue** [hə'ræŋ] **1** n arenga f
**2** vt arengar, soltar una arenga a; **to h. sb into doing sth** acosar a alguien para que haga algo

**harass** [hə'ræs, 'hærəs] vt acosar, hostigar; **to h. sb into doing sth** acosar a alguien para que haga algo

**harassed** [hə'ræst, 'hærəst] adj agobiado(a)

**harassment** [hə'ræsmənt, 'hærəsmənt] n acoso m

**harbour**, US **harbor** ['hɑːbə(r)] **1** n puerto m
**2** vt (fugitive) acoger, proteger; (hope, suspicion) albergar; **to h. a grudge against sb** guardar rencor a alguien

**hard** [hɑːd] **1** adj (a) (substance) duro(a); (fact, evidence) concreto(a), real; Fig **to be as h. as nails** (unfeeling) ser muy borde or un hueso; (tough) ser duro(a) de pelar; **in h. cash** en metálico; Comptr **h. copy** copia f impresa, listado m; **h. court** (for tennis) pista f de superficie dura; Comptr **h. disk** disco m duro; **h. drugs** drogas fpl duras; Pol **h. left** izquierda f radical; Comptr **h. return** retorno m manual; Aut **h. shoulder** arcén m
(b) (difficult) difícil; **it's h. to say…** no es fácil decir…; **to be h. to please** ser muy exigente; **to learn the h. way** aprender a base de equivocarse; **h. of hearing** duro(a) de oído
(c) (harsh) (person, conditions, life) duro(a); **to be h. on sb** ser (muy) duro con alguien; **to give sb a h. time** hacérselo pasar mal a alguien; **a h. winter** un invierno muy duro; Fam **no h. feelings?** ¿no me guardas rencor?; **to take a h. line on sth** ponerse duro(a) con (respecto a) algo; Fam **h. luck!, h. cheese!** ¡mala pata or suerte!
(d) (intense) **to be a h. worker** ser muy trabajador(ora); Law **h. labour** trabajos mpl forzados; Com **h. sell** venta f agresiva
(e) (water) duro(a)
**2** adv (a) (to work) duro, duramente; (to think, consider) detenidamente; (to push, hit) fuerte; **to try h.** esforzarse; **to look h. at sb** mirar fija-

mente a alguien; **to be h. at work** estar muy metido(a) en el trabajo; **it's raining h.** está lloviendo mucho; **to feel h. done by** sentirse injustamente tratado(a); Fam **h. up** en apuros
(b) (near) **h. by** muy cerca de; **to follow h. upon** or **behind sb** seguir a alguien muy de cerca

**hard-and-fast** ['hɑːdən'fɑːst] adj **there are no h. rules** no hay reglas fijas

**hardback** ['hɑːdbæk] n (book) edición f de pasta dura

**hard-bitten** [hɑːd'bɪtən] adj curtido(a)

**hardboard** ['hɑːdbɔːd] n aglomerado m, conglomerado m

**hard-boiled** [hɑːd'bɔɪld] adj (egg) duro(a), cocido(a); Fig (person) (tough) duro(a), curtido(a)

**hard-core** ['hɑːdkɔː(r)] adj (support) incondicional, acérrimo(a); **h. porn(ography)** porno m duro

**hard-earned** [hɑːd'ɜːnd] adj ganado(a) con mucho esfuerzo

**harden** ['hɑːdən] **1** vt endurecer; **to h. oneself to sth** insensibilizarse a algo
**2** vi (of substance, attitude) endurecerse

**hardened** ['hɑːdənd] adj (steel) endurecido(a), templado(a); (drinker) empedernido(a); (sinner) impenitente; **a h. criminal** un delincuente habitual

**hard-fought** ['hɑːd'fɔːt] adj (election, contest) (muy) reñido(a), (muy) disputado(a)

**hard-headed** ['hɑːd'hedɪd] adj pragmático(a)

**hard-hearted** ['hɑːd'hɑːtɪd] adj duro(a), insensible

**hard-hitting** [hɑːd'hɪtɪŋ] adj (criticism, report) contundente

**hardliner** [hɑːd'laɪnə(r)] n (politician, activist) intransigente mf, partidario(a) m,f de la línea dura

**hardly** ['hɑːdlɪ] adv (scarcely) apenas; **h. ever** casi nunca; **h. anyone/anything** casi nadie/nada; **I can h. believe it** me cuesta creerlo

**hardness** ['hɑːdnɪs] n (a) (of substance) dureza f (b) (of problem) dificultad f

**hard-on** ['hɑːdɒn] n Vulg **to have a h.** estar empalmado; **to get a h.** empalmarse

**hard-pressed** [hɑːd'prest], **hard-pushed** [hɑːd'pʊʃt] adj **to be h. to do sth** tenerlo difícil para hacer algo; **to be h. for time/money** estar (muy) apurado(a) de tiempo/dinero

**hardship** ['hɑːdʃɪp] n (suffering) sufrimiento m; (deprivation) privación f; **to live in h.** vivir en la miseria

**hardware** ['hɑːdweə(r)] n (a) (tools) ferretería f; (military) **h.** (weapons) armamento m; US **h. store** (ironmonger's) ferretería f (b) Comptr hardware m, soporte m físico

**hard-wearing** [hɑːd'weərɪŋ] *adj* resistente

**hard-won** [hɑːd'wʌn] *adj* ganado(a) a pulso

**hard-working** [hɑːd'wɜːkɪŋ] *adj* trabajador(ora)

**hardy** ['hɑːdɪ] *adj (person)* recio(a); *(plant)* resistente (al frío); **a h. perennial** una planta vivaz

**hare** [heə(r)] **1** *n (animal)* liebre *f*
**2** *vi* **to h. off** salir disparado(a)

**harebrained** ['heəbremd] *adj* disparatado(a)

**harelip** ['heəlɪp] *n* labio *m* leporino

**harem** [hɑː'riːm] *n* harén *m*

**haricot** ['hærɪkəʊ] *n* **h. (bean)** alubia *f*, judía *f* blanca

**hark** [hɑːk] *exclam Literary* ¡escucha!; *Fam* **h. at him!** ¿has oído lo que dice?
▶**hark back** *vi* **to h. back to sth** recordar algo; **he's always harking back to his youth** siempre está recordando su juventud

**harlot** ['hɑːlət] *n Literary* ramera *f*, meretriz *f*

**harm** [hɑːm] **1** *n* daño *m*; **to do sb h.** hacer daño a alguien; **to do oneself h.** hacerse daño; **it will do more h. than good** hará más mal que bien; **I see no h. in it** no veo que tenga nada de malo; **there's no h. in trying** no se pierde nada por intentarlo; **you will come to no h.** no sufrirás ningún daño; **out of h.'s way** en lugar seguro
**2** *vt (person, animal)* hacer daño a; *(reputation, image, quality)* dañar; *(chances, interests, business)* perjudicar

**harmful** ['hɑːmfʊl] *adj* perjudicial, dañino(a)

**harmless** ['hɑːmlɪs] *adj* inofensivo(a)

**harmonica** [hɑː'mɒnɪkə] *n* armónica *f*

**harmonious** [hɑː'məʊnɪəs] *adj* armonioso(a)

**harmonization** [hɑːmənar'zeɪʃən] *n* armonización *f*

**harmonize** ['hɑːmənaɪz] *vt & vi* armonizar

**harmony** ['hɑːmənɪ] *n also Fig* armonía *f*; **in h. with** en armonía con; **to live in h. (with)** vivir en armonía or en paz (con)

**harness** ['hɑːnɪs] **1** *n* **(a)** *(of horse)* arreos *mpl*; *(for safety, of parachute)* arnés *m* **(b)** *(idioms)* **to work in h. with sb** trabajar hombro con hombro con alguien; **to die in h.** morir antes de jubilarse
**2** *vt (horse)* arrear, aparejar; *(resources)* emplear, hacer uso de

**harp** [hɑːp] **1** *n* arpa *f*
**2** *vi Fam* **to h. on about sth** dar la matraca con algo

**harpist** ['hɑːpɪst] *n* arpista *mf*

**harpoon** [hɑː'puːn] **1** *n* arpón *m*
**2** *vt* arponear

**harpsichord** ['hɑːpsɪkɔːd] *n* clave *m*, clavicémbalo *m*

**harpy** ['hɑːpɪ] *n* arpía *f*

**harrow** ['hærəʊ] *n (farm equipment)* grada *f*

**harrowing** ['hærəʊɪŋ] *adj (experience, sight)* angustioso(a)

**harry** ['hærɪ] *vt* acosar

**harsh** [hɑːʃ] *adj (voice, sound)* áspero(a); *(climate, treatment)* duro(a)

**harshly** ['hɑːʃlɪ] *adv (to answer, speak)* con aspereza; **to treat sb h.** tratar a alguien con dureza

**harvest** ['hɑːvɪst] **1** *n* cosecha *f*; **h. festival** = fiesta con que se celebra la recogida de la cosecha
**2** *vt* cosechar

**has** [hæz] *3rd person singular of* **have**

**has-been** ['hæzbiːn] *n Fam Pej* vieja gloria *f*

**hash** [hæʃ] *n* **(a)** *(stew)* estofado *m* de carne con patatas; *US* **h. browns** = fritura de patata y cebolla **(b)** *very Fam (hashish)* costo *m* **(c)** *(idioms) Fam* **to make a h. of sth** hacer algo muy mal

**hashish** ['hæʃɪʃ] *n* hachís *m*

**hasn't** ['hæznt] = **has not**

**hassle** ['hæsəl] *Fam* **1** *n* lío *m*, follón *m*; **it's too much h.** es demasiado lío; **it's a real h. buying a house** comprarse una casa es un follón *or* lío de aquí te espero; **to give sb h.** dar la lata a alguien
**2** *vt* dar la lata a

**haste** [heɪst] *n* prisa *f*; **in h.** a toda prisa; **to make h.** apresurarse; *Prov* **more h. less speed** vísteme despacio que tengo prisa

**hasten** ['heɪsən] **1** *vt* acelerar; **to h. sb's departure** apresurar *or* acelerar la partida de alguien
**2** *vi* apresurarse; **I h. to add** me apresuro a añadir

**hastily** ['heɪstɪlɪ] *adv (quickly)* deprisa, apresuradamente; *(rashly)* precipitadamente, apresuradamente; **to judge sth h.** juzgar algo a la ligera

**hastiness** ['heɪstɪnɪs] *n (speed)* celeridad *f*; *(rashness)* precipitación *f*

**hasty** ['heɪstɪ] *adj* apresurado(a); **to jump to a h. conclusion** sacar conclusiones apresuradas

**hat** [hæt] *n* sombrero *m*; *also Fig* **to take one's h. off to sb** descubrirse ante alguien; *Fig* **to pass the h. round** *(collect money)* pasar la gorra; *Fig* **to throw one's h. in the ring** *(enter contest)* echarse al ruedo; *Fam Fig* **to keep sth under one's h.** no decir ni media de algo a nadie; **h. stand** perchero *m*; **h. trick** *(of goals)* tres goles *mpl* (en el mismo partido); *(of victories)* tres victorias *fpl* consecutivas

**hatch¹** [hætʃ] *n (covering opening)* escotilla *f*; *Fam* **down the h.!** ¡salud!; *(serving)* **h.** ventanilla *f*

**hatch²** 1 *vt (eggs)* incubar; **to h. a plot** urdir un plan

2 *vi* **the egg hatched** el pollo salió del cascarón

**hatchback** ['hætʃbæk] *n (car) (3-door)* tres puertas *m inv; (5-door)* cinco puertas *m inv*

**hatchet** ['hætʃɪt] *n* hacha *f (pequeña); Fam* **to do a h. job on sb/sth** *(of critic, reviewer)* ensañarse con alguien/algo; *Fam* **h. man** = encargado del trabajo sucio

**hate** [heɪt] 1 *n (hatred)* odio *m;* **h. mail** = cartas que contienen amenazas o fuertes críticas

2 *vt* odiar, detestar; **he hates to be contradicted** no soporta que le contradigan; *Fam* **I h. to admit it but I think he's right** me cuesta admitirlo, pero creo que tiene razón

**hateful** ['heɪtfʊl] *adj* odioso(a), detestable

**hatpin** ['hætpɪn] *n* alfiler *m* (de sombrero)

**hatred** ['heɪtrɪd] *n* odio *m*

**haughty** ['hɔːtɪ] *adj* altanero(a)

**haul** [hɔːl] 1 *n* **(a)** *(fish caught)* captura *f; (loot, of stolen goods)* botín *m; (of drugs)* alijo *m* **(b)** *Fam (journey)* **it's a long h.** hay un tirón

2 *vt* **(a)** *(pull)* arrastrar; *Fam* **he was hauled in for questioning** se lo llevaron para interrogarlo; *Fam Fig* **to h. sb over the coals** *(reprimand)* echar una bronca a alguien; **she was hauled up before the headmaster** la llevaron al despacho del director **(b)** *(transport)* transportar

**haulage** ['hɔːlɪdʒ] *n (transportation)* transporte *m* (de mercancías); *(costs)* portes *mpl;* **h. firm** empresa *f* de transportes, transportista *m*

**haulier**, *US* **hauler** ['hɔːlə(r)] *n (company)* empresa *f* de transportes, transportista *m*

**haunch** [hɔːntʃ] *n (of person)* trasero *m; (of meat)* pierna *f;* **to sit** *or* **squat on one's haunches** ponerse en cuclillas

**haunt** [hɔːnt] 1 *n (favourite place)* lugar *m* predilecto

2 *vt* **(a)** *(of ghost) (house)* aparecerse en; *(person)* aparecerse a **(b)** *(of thought, memory)* asaltar; **he was haunted by the fear that…** le asaltaba el temor de que… **(c)** *(frequent)* frecuentar

**haunted** ['hɔːntɪd] *adj (castle, room)* encantado(a); *Fig* **he has a h. look** tiene una mirada atormentada

**haunting** ['hɔːntɪŋ] *adj* obsesivo(a)

**Havana** [hə'vænə] *n* La Habana; **H. cigar** (puro *m*) habano *m*

**have** [hæv]

En el inglés hablado, y en el escrito en estilo coloquial, el verbo auxiliar **have** se contrae de forma que **I have** se transforma en **I've**, **he/she/it** se transforman en **he's/she's/it's** y **you/we/they have** se transforman en **you've/we've/they've**. Las formas de pasado **I/you/he** *etc* **had** se transforman en **I'd**, **you'd**, **he'd** *etc*. Las formas negativas

has not, have not y had not se transforman en hasn't, haven't y hadn't.

1 *n* **the haves and the have-nots** los ricos y los pobres

2 *vt (3rd person singular* **has** [hæz], *pt & pp* **had** [hæd]) **(a)** *(in general)* tener; **they've got** *or* **they h. a big house** tienen una casa grande; **she hasn't got** *or* **doesn't h. a cat** no tiene gato; **I've got** *or* **I h. something to do** tengo algo que hacer; **which one will you h.?** ¿cuál prefieres?; **she's got** *or* **she has measles/ AIDS** tiene (el) sarampión/el sida; **she's got** *or* **she has blue eyes** tiene los ojos azules; **can I h. a beer and a brandy, please?** ¿(me das) una cerveza y un coñac, por favor?; **I'll h. the soup** yo tomaré una sopa; **we've got** *or* **we h. a choice** tenemos una alternativa; **what's that got to do with it?** ¿qué tiene que ver eso?; **he had me by the throat** me tenía sujeto *or* cogido por el cuello; **he had them in his power** los tenía en su poder; **there were no tickets to be had** no quedaban entradas; **I h. it on good authority that…** sé por fuentes fidedignas que…; **you shall h. it back tomorrow** te lo devolveré mañana; **I'll h. you know that…!** ¡entérate de que…!, ¡has de saber que…!; *Fam* **I've had it if she finds out!** ¡si se entera, me la cargo!; *Fam* **this coat has had it** este abrigo está para el arrastre; *Fam* **you've been had!** *(you've been cheated)* ¡te han timado!; *Fam* **you've got** *or* **you h. me there!** *(I don't know)* ¡ahí me has pillado!

**(b)** *(with noun, to denote activity)* **to h. a bath** darse un baño; **to h. a shave** afeitarse; **to h. a wash** lavarse; **to h. breakfast** desayunar; **to h. lunch** comer; **to h. dinner** cenar

**(c)** *(experience)* pasar; **to h. an accident** tener *or* sufrir un accidente; **to h. a good/bad time** pasarlo bien/mal; **I had a pleasant evening** pasé una agradable velada

**(d)** *(causative)* **I had him do it again** le hice repetirlo; **I'm having my record player repaired** me están arreglando el tocadiscos

**(e)** *(in passive-type constructions)* **to h. one's hair cut** cortarse el pelo; **I had my watch stolen** me robaron el reloj

**(f)** *(allow)* **I will not h. such conduct!** ¡no toleraré ese comportamiento!; **I won't h. you causing trouble!** ¡no permitiré que crees problemas!

**(g)** *(be compelled)* **to h. to do sth** tener que hacer algo; **I h.** *or* **I've got to go** me tengo que ir; **do you h. to work?**, **h. you got to work?** ¿tienes que trabajar?; **it's got** *or* **it has to be done** hay que hacerlo

3 *v aux* haber; **I/you/they h. seen it** lo he/has/hemos/han visto; **he/she/it has seen it** lo ha visto; **I h. worked here for three years** llevo tres años trabajando aquí;

**he has been in prison before – no he hasn't!** ha estado ya antes en la cárcel – ¡no!; **you have told him, haven't you?** se lo has dicho, ¿no? *or* ¿verdad?; **you haven't forgotten, have you?** no te habrás olvidado, ¿no? *or* ¿verdad?

▸**have in** *vt sep Fam* **to h. it in for sb** tenerla tomada con alguien

▸**have off** *vt sep Br very Fam (have sexual intercourse)* **to h. it off (with sb)** echar un polvo (con alguien), hacérselo (con alguien)

▸**have on** *vt sep* (a) *(wear)* llevar puesto; **they had nothing on** estaban desnudos (b) *Fam (fool)* **to h. sb on** tomarle el pelo *or* vacilar a alguien; **you're having me on!** ¡me estás tomando el pelo *or* vacilando! (c) *(have arranged)* **he has a lot on this week** esta semana tiene mucho que hacer; **I haven't got anything on on Tuesday** el martes lo tengo libre

▸**have out** *vt sep* (a) *(have extracted)* **I had a tooth out** me sacaron una muela (b) *(resolve)* **to h. it out with sb** poner las cosas en claro con alguien

▸**have up** *vt sep* **to be had up (for sth)** tener que ir a juicio (por algo)

**haven** ['heɪvən] *n* refugio *m*

**haven't** ['hævnt] = **have not**

**haversack** ['hævəsæk] *n* mochila *f*

**havoc** ['hævək] *n* estragos *mpl*; **to cause** *or* **wreak h.** hacer estragos; **to play h. with** hacer estragos en

**Hawaii** [həˈwaɪiː] *n* Hawai

**Hawaiian** [həˈwaɪən] *n & adj* hawaiano(a) *m,f*

**hawk¹** [hɔːk] *n* (a) *(bird)* halcón *m*; **to watch sth/sb like a h.** mirar algo/a alguien con ojos de lince (b) *Pol* halcón *m*, partidario(a) *m,f* de la línea dura *(en política exterior)*

**hawk²** *vt* **to h. one's wares** hacer venta ambulante

**hawk-eyed** ['hɔːkaɪd] *adj* con ojos de lince

**hawkish** ['hɔːkɪʃ] *adj Pol* partidario(a) de la línea dura *(en política exterior)*

**hawser** ['hɔːzə(r)] *n* cable *m*, estacha *f*

**hawthorn** ['hɔːθɔːn] *n* espino *m* (albar)

**hay** [heɪ] *n* heno *m*; **to make h.** dejar secar la paja; *Prov* **make h. while the sun shines** aprovecha mientras puedas

**hayfever** ['heɪfiːvə(r)] *n* fiebre *f* del heno, alergia *f* al polen

**hayloft** ['heɪlɒft] *n* henal *m*, henil *m*

**haystack** ['heɪstæk] *n* almiar *m*

**haywire** ['heɪwaɪə(r)] *adv Fam* **to go h.** (of plan) desbaratarse; *(of mechanism)* volverse loco(a)

**hazard** ['hæzəd] **1** *n (danger)* peligro *m*, riesgo *m*; **a health h.** un peligro para la salud; **a fire h.** una causa potencial de incendio; *Aut* **h. lights**

luces *fpl* de emergencia

**2** *vt (one's life, fortune)* arriesgar, poner en peligro; *(opinion, guess)* aventurar

**hazardous** ['hæzədəs] *adj* peligroso(a)

**haze** [heɪz] *n (of mist)* neblina *f*; *(of doubt, confusion)* nube *f*; **my mind was in a h.** tenía la mente nublada

**hazel** ['heɪzəl] *n (colour)* color *m* avellana; **h. (tree)** avellano *m*

**hazelnut** ['heɪzəlnʌt] *n* avellana *f*

**hazily** ['heɪzɪlɪ] *adv (remember)* vagamente

**hazy** ['heɪzɪ] *adj (weather)* neblinoso(a); *(image, memory)* vago(a), confuso(a); **to be h. about sth** no tener algo nada claro

**he** [hiː] **1** *pron* él; *(usually omitted in Spanish, except for contrast)* **he's Scottish** es escocés; **HE hasn't got it!** ¡él no lo tiene!; *Formal* **he who believes that...** quien se crea *or* aquel que se crea esto...

**2** *n* **it's a he** *(of animal)* es macho

**head** [hed] **1** *n* (a) *(of person)* cabeza *f*; **a fine h. of hair** una buena cabellera; **to be a h. taller than sb** sacar una cabeza a alguien; **from h. to foot** *or* **toe** de la cabeza a los pies; **to stand on one's h.** hacer el pino (con la cabeza sobre el suelo); *Fig* **to stand a situation on its h.** trastornar completamente una situación; **to win by a h.** *(of horse)* ganar por una cabeza; *Fig* **she's h. and shoulders above the other candidates** *(much better than)* está muy por encima de los demás candidatos; *Med* **h. cold** catarro *m*; **h. start** *(advantage)* ventaja *f*

(b) *(intellect, mind)* **to do sums in one's h.** sumar mentalmente; **to have a good h. on one's shoulders** tener la cabeza sobre los hombros; **to have a good h. for business/figures** tener (buena) cabeza para los negocios/los números; **to have a (good) h. for heights** no tener vértigo; **he has taken it into his h. that...** se le ha metido en la cabeza que...; **it never entered my h. that...** nunca se me pasó por la cabeza que...; **to put ideas into sb's h.** meter ideas a alguien en la cabeza; *Fam* **he's not right in the h.** no está bien de la cabeza

(c) *(of pin, hammer, garlic, list)* cabeza *f*; *(of arrow)* punta *f*; *(of page, stairs)* parte *f* superior; *(of bed, table)* cabecera *f*; *(on beer)* espuma *f*; *(on tape recorder)* cabeza *f* (magnética), cabezal *m*; **a h. of lettuce** una lechuga; **a h. of cabbage** un repollo; **to be at the h. of a list/queue** encabezar una lista/cola; **heads or tails?** *(when tossing coin)* ¿cara o cruz?; **to build up a h. of steam** *(of person, campaign)* tomar ímpetu; **to come to a h.** *(of conflict, situation)* alcanzar un punto crítico

(d) *(person in charge)* *(of family, the Church)*

cabeza *mf*; *(of business)* jefe(a) *m,f*; *Br Sch* **h. (teacher)** director(ora) *m,f*; *Br Sch* **h. boy** delegado *m* de toda la escuela; *Br Sch* **h. girl** delegada *f* de toda la escuela; **h. office** sede *f*, central *f*; **h. of state** jefe *m* de Estado; **h. waiter** maître *m*

(e) *(unit)* **to pay £10 per** *or* **a h.** pagar 10 libras por cabeza; **six h. of cattle** seis cabezas de ganado, seis reses

(f) *(idioms)* **we put our heads together** entre todos nos pusimos a pensar; **they'll have your h. (on a plate) for this** vas a pagar con el pellejo por esto; **to bury** *or* **have one's h. in the sand** adoptar la estrategia del avestruz; **to give sb his h.** *(allow to take decisions)* dar libertad a alguien; **on your own h. be it** allá tú con lo que haces; **to go over sb's h.** *(appeal to higher authority)* pasar por encima de alguien; *Fam* **to shout one's h. off** desgañitarse, vociferar; **the wine/the praise went to his h.** se le subió a la cabeza el vino/tanto halago; *Prov* **two heads are better than one** dos mentes discurren más que una sola; **off the top of one's h.** sin pararse a pensar; **it was** *or* **went over my h.** no me enteré de nada de eso; **I can't make h. or tail of this** no le encuentro ni pies ni cabeza a esto; *Fam* **to lose one's h.** perder la cabeza *or* los nervios; *Fam* **to keep one's h.** mantener la cabeza en su sitio; *Fam* **to be off one's h.** estar mal de la cabeza *or* como un cencerro; *(list, procession)* encabezar

2 *vt* **(a)** *(lead) (organization, campaign)* estar a la cabeza de; *(list, procession)* encabezar

**(b)** *(direct)* conducir; **one of the locals headed me in the right direction** un lugareño me indicó el camino

**(c)** *(put a title on) (page, chapter)* encabezar, titular

**(d)** *(in football)* **to h. the ball** cabecear el balón, darle al balón de cabeza

3 *vi (move)* dirigirse; **they were heading out of town** salían de la ciudad

▸**head for** *vt insep* dirigirse a; **you're heading for trouble/disaster** te estás buscando problemas/la ruina

▸**head off 1** *vt sep (prevent)* eludir, evitar

2 *vi (depart)* marcharse

**headache** ['hedeɪk] *n* dolor *m* de cabeza; *Fig (problem)* quebradero *m* de cabeza

**headband** ['hedbænd] *n* cinta *f* para la cabeza

**headboard** ['hedbɔːd] *n (of bed)* cabecero *m*

**headbutt** ['hedbʌt] *vt* dar un cabezazo a

**headcase** ['hedkeɪs] *n Fam (lunatic)* chiflado(a) *m,f*

**headdress** ['heddres] *n* tocado *m*

**headed** ['hedɪd] *adj* **h. (note)paper** papel *m* con membrete

**header** ['hedə(r)] *n* **(a)** *Typ* encabezamiento *m* **(b)** *(in football)* cabezazo *m*

**headfirst** ['hedfɜːst] *adv* de cabeza

**headgear** ['hedgɪə(r)] *n* tocado *m*

**head-hunt** ['hedhʌnt] *vt Com* captar, cazar *(altos ejecutivos)*

**head-hunter** ['hedhʌntə(r)] *n Com* cazatalentos *mf inv*

**heading** ['hedɪŋ] *n (of chapter, article)* encabezamiento *m*; **it comes** *or* **falls under the h. of...** entra dentro de la categoría de...

**headlamp** ['hedlæmp] *n (on car)* faro *m*

**headland** ['hedlənd] *n* promontorio *m*

**headlight** ['hedlaɪt] *n (on car)* faro *m*

**headline** ['hedlaɪn] **1** *n (of newspaper, TV news)* titular *m*; **to hit the headlines** saltar a los titulares; **to be h. news** ser noticia de portada

2 *vt (article, story)* titular

**headlong** ['hedlɒŋ] *adv* de cabeza; **there was a h. rush for the bar** se produjo una estampida hacia el bar

**headmaster** [hed'mɑːstə(r)] *n Sch* director *m*

**headmistress** [hed'mɪstrɪs] *n Sch* directora *f*

**head-on** ['hedɒn] **1** *adj* de frente; **a h. collision** un choque frontal

2 *adv* de frente; **to meet sb h.** encontrarse con alguien de frente

**headphones** ['hedfəʊnz] *npl* auriculares *mpl*

**headquarters** [hed'kwɔːtəz] *npl (of organization)* sede *f*, central *f*; *Mil* cuartel *m* general

**headrest** ['hedrest] *n* reposacabezas *m inv*

**headroom** ['hedruːm] *n (under bridge)* gálibo *m*; *(inside car)* altura *f* de la cabeza al techo

**headscarf** ['hedskɑːf] *n* pañuelo *m (para la cabeza)*

**headset** ['hedset] *n (earphones)* auriculares *mpl*, cascos *mpl*

**headstone** ['hedstəʊn] *n (on grave)* lápida *f*

**headstrong** ['hedstrɒŋ] *adj* testarudo(a), cabezota

**headway** ['hedweɪ] *n* **to make h.** avanzar

**headwind** ['hedwɪnd] *n* viento *m* de cara

**heady** ['hedɪ] *adj (drink, feeling)* embriagador(ora); *(atmosphere, experience, days)* emocionante

**heal** [hiːl] **1** *vt (wound)* curar; *Fig (differences)* subsanar; *Fig* **wounds which only time would h.** heridas que sólo el tiempo podría cerrar

2 *vi (of wound)* **to h. (up** *or* **over)** curarse, sanar

**health** [helθ] *n* salud *f*; **to be in good/poor h.** estar bien/mal de salud; **the economy is in good h.** la economía goza de buena salud; **the Department of H.** el Ministerio de Sanidad; **to drink (to) sb's h.** brindar a la salud de alguien, brindar por alguien; **h. care** atención *f* sanitaria; *Br* **h. centre** centro *m* de salud, ambulatorio *m*; *Fin* **h. cover** cobertura *f* sanitaria; **h. farm** clínica *f* de adelgazamiento; **h. food** comida *f* integral; **h. hazard** *or* **risk** peligro *m* para la salud; *Fin* **h. insurance** seguro *m* de enfermedad; **h. resort** centro *m* de reposo; *Br* **H. Service** sistema *m* de sanidad pública británico; **h. visitor** enfermero(a) *m,f* visitante

**healthy** ['helθɪ] *adj* (*person, climate*) sano(a), saludable; **a h. appetite** un apetito sano; **it is a h. sign that...** es un buen síntoma que...; **he has a h. disrespect for authority** demuestra una saludable falta de respeto ante la autoridad

**heap** [hi:p] **1** *n* montón *m*; *Fig* **people at the top/bottom of the h.** los de arriba/abajo; *Fam* **we've got heaps of time** tenemos un montón de tiempo; *Fam* **she had heaps of children** tenía montones de hijos

**2** *vt* amontonar; **his plate was heaped with food** tenía el plato lleno hasta arriba de comida; **a heaped spoonful** (*in recipe*) una cucharada colmada; **to h. riches/praise/insults on sb** colmar a alguien de riquezas/alabanzas/insultos

**hear** [hɪə(r)] (*pt & pp* **heard** [hɜːd]) **1** *vt* (a) (*perceive*) oír; **to h. sb speak** oír hablar a alguien; **I could hardly h. myself speak** apenas se oía; **she was struggling to make herself heard over the noise** se esforzaba por hacerse oír en medio del ruido; **let's h. it for...** aplaudamos a...; *Fam* **I've heard that one before!** ¡a otro perro con ese hueso!

(b) (*listen to*) escuchar; **h. me out** escúchame antes; **h.! h.!** (*at meeting*) ¡sí señor!, ¡eso es!; *Law* **to h. a case** ver un caso

(c) (*find out*) oír; **I heard that she was in Spain** he oído (decir) que estaba en España; **I h. you're getting married** tengo entendido que te vas a casar

**2** *vi* **I can't h. properly** no oigo bien; **to h. from sb** tener noticias de alguien, saber de alguien; **you'll be hearing from my lawyer!** ¡mi abogado se pondrá en contacto con usted!; **to h. about sth** saber de algo; **they were never heard of again** nunca se supo nada más de ellos; **that's the first I've heard of it!** es la primera noticia que tengo; **I've never heard of such a thing!** ¡nunca he oído hablar de nada semejante!; **I won't h. of it!** ¡no quiero ni oír hablar de ello!

**hearing** ['hɪərɪŋ] *n* (a) (*sense*) oído *m*; **h. aid** audífono *m* (b) (*earshot*) **to be within/out of h.** estar/no estar lo suficientemente cerca

como para oír (c) (*chance to explain*) **to give sb a fair h.** dejar a alguien que se explique; **to condemn sb without a h.** condenar a alguien sin haberlo escuchado antes (d) *Law (enquiry)* vista *f*

**hearsay** ['hɪəseɪ] *n* rumores *mpl*; *Law* **h. evidence** pruebas *fpl* basadas en rumores

**hearse** [hɜːs] *n* coche *m* fúnebre

**heart** [hɑːt] *n* (a) (*organ*) corazón *m*; **to have h. trouble, to have a weak** *or* **bad h.** tener problemas cardíacos *or* de corazón; **h. attack** ataque *m* al corazón; **h. disease** cardiopatía *f*; **h. failure** paro *m* cardíaco; **h. surgery** cirugía *f* cardíaca; **h. transplant** transplante *m* de corazón

(b) (*seat of the emotions*) corazón *m*; **to have a big h.** tener un gran corazón; **a h. of gold** un corazón de oro; **a h. of stone** un corazón duro; **have a h.!** ¡no seas cruel!; **her h.'s in the right place** tiene un gran corazón; **with a heavy h.** con aflicción; **my h. sank at the news** la noticia me dejó hundido; **to have one's h. in one's mouth** tener el corazón en un puño; **to break sb's h.** romperle el corazón a alguien; **to wear one's h. on one's sleeve** no ocultar tus sentimientos; **affairs** *or* **matters of the h.** asuntos *mpl* *or* cosas *fpl* del corazón; *esp Ironic* **my h. bleeds for you** ¡qué pena me das!; **in my h. of hearts** en el fondo (de mi corazón); **from the bottom of one's h.** (*thank, congratulate*) de todo corazón; **he loved her with all his h.** la amaba con toda su alma; **at h.** en el fondo; **to have sb's welfare/interests at h.** preocuparse de veras por el bienestar/los intereses de alguien; **to take sth to h.** tomarse algo a pecho; **he had set his h. on it** lo deseaba con toda el alma; **he's a man after my own h.** es uno de los míos; **to one's h.'s content** hasta saciarse

(c) (*enthusiasm, courage*) **to take/lose h.** animarse/desanimarse; **he tried to convince them but his h. wasn't in it** trató de convencerlos, pero sin mucho empeño; **I didn't have the h. to tell him** no tuve coraje para decírselo

(d) (*memory*) **by h.** de memoria

(e) (*centre*) **the h. of the matter** el meollo del asunto; **in the h. of the forest** en el corazón del bosque

(f) (*in cards*) **hearts** corazones *mpl*

**heartache** ['hɑːteɪk] *n* dolor *m*, tristeza *f*

**heartbeat** ['hɑːtbiːt] *n* latido *m* (del corazón)

**heartbreaking** ['hɑːtbreɪkɪŋ] *adj* desgarrador(ora)

**heartbroken** ['hɑːtbrəʊkən] *adj* abatido(a), descorazonado(a)

**heartburn** ['hɑːtbɜːn] *n* (*indigestion*) acidez *f* (de estómago), ardor *m* de estómago

**hearten** ['hɑːtən] *vt* alentar

**heartening** ['hɑːtənɪŋ] *adj* alentador(ora)

**heartfelt** ['hɑːtfelt] *adj* sincero(a)

**hearth** [hɑːθ] *n* (a) *(fireplace)* chimenea *f* (b) *(home)* hogar *m*

**heartily** ['hɑːtɪlɪ] *adv* de todo corazón; **to be h. sick of sth** estar hasta las narices de algo

**heartlands** ['hɑːtlænd] *npl* núcleo *m*; **Britain's industrial h. were devastated by the depression** la recesión asoló el núcleo *or* el corazón industrial de Gran Bretaña

**heartless** ['hɑːtlɪs] *adj* inhumano(a), despiadado(a)

**heart-rending** ['hɑːtrendɪŋ] *adj* desgarrador(ora)

**heart-searching** ['hɑːtsɜːtʃɪŋ] *n* **after much h.** tras un profundo examen de conciencia

**heartstrings** ['hɑːtstrɪŋz] *npl* **to tug at sb's h.** tocar la fibra sensible de alguien

**heart-throb** ['hɑːtθrɒb] *n Fam* ídolo *m*

**heart-to-heart** ['hɑːtəˈhɑːt] *n* **to have a h. with sb** tener una charla íntima con alguien

**heart-warming** ['hɑːtwɔːmɪŋ] *adj* conmovedor(ora)

**hearty** ['hɑːtɪ] *adj* (a) *(person, laugh)* jovial; *(approval)* caluroso(a); *(dislike)* profundo(a); *(welcome)* cordial; **my heartiest congratulations** felicidades de todo corazón (b) *(substantial) (meal)* copioso(a); *(appetite)* voraz

**heat** [hiːt] **1** *n* (a) *(high temperature)* calor *m*; **to cook at a high/moderate/low h.** cocinar a fuego vivo/moderado/lento; **to turn up the h.** *(on cooker)* subir el fuego; *Fam Fig* **to turn up the h. on sb** presionar a alguien; **h. exhaustion** colapso *m* por exceso de calor; **h. haze** calima *f*; **h. loss** pérdida *f* de calor; **h. rash** sarpullido *m (por el calor)*; *Med* **h. treatment** termoterapia *f*

(b) *(passion)* calor *m*; **in the h. of the moment/of the argument** con el acaloramiento del momento/de la pelea

(c) *(of female animal)* **in h.** en celo

(d) *(in sport)* serie *f*, eliminatoria *f*

**2** *vt* calentar

▶**heat up 1** *vt sep* calentar

**2** *vi* calentarse; *Fig (of argument, contest)* subir de tono, acalorarse

**heated** ['hiːtɪd] *adj* (a) *(room, building)* caldeado(a); *(swimming pool)* climatizado(a) (b) *(argument)* acalorado(a); **to become h.** *(of person)* acalorarse

**heater** ['hiːtə(r)] *n (radiator)* radiador *m*; *(electric, gas)* estufa *f*

**heath** [hiːθ] *n* brezal *m*, páramo *m*

**heathen** ['hiːðən] *n* bárbaro(a) *m,f*

**heather** ['heðə(r)] *n* brezo *m*

**heating** ['hiːtɪŋ] *n* calefacción *f*

**heatproof** ['hiːtpruːf] *adj* termorresistente, refractario(a)

**heatstroke** ['hiːtstrəʊk] *n Med* insolación *f*

**heatwave** ['hiːtweɪv] *n* ola *f* de calor

**heave** [hiːv] **1** *vt (pull)* tirar de; *(push)* empujar; *(lift)* subir; **she heaved herself out of her chair** se levantó de la silla con dificultad; **to h. a sigh of relief** exhalar un suspiro de alivio

**2** *vi* (a) **they heaved on the rope** tiraron de la cuerda (b) *(of deck, ground)* subir y bajar; *(of bosom)* palpitar (c) *(retch)* tener arcadas; *(vomit)* vomitar (d) *Naut (pt hove [həʊv])* **to h. into view** *(of ship)* aparecer; *Fig Hum (of person)* aparecer por el horizonte

**3** *n (pull)* tirón *m*; *(push)* empujón *m*

▶**heave to** *(pp hove [həʊv])* *vi Naut (of ship)* ponerse al pairo

**heaven** ['hevən] *n* cielo *m*; **in h.** en el cielo; *Fig (overjoyed)* en la gloria; **to go to h.** ir al cielo; **this is h.!** ¡esto es la gloria!; **to move h. and earth to do sth** mover *or* remover Roma con Santiago para hacer algo; **the heavens opened** cayó un aguacero; *Fam* **it stinks to high h.** ¡huele que apesta!; **(good) heavens!, heavens above!** ¡madre mía!, ¡Dios mío!; **thank h. (for that)!** ¡gracias a Dios!; **h. knows!** ¡sabe Dios!; **for h.'s sake!** ¡por el amor de Dios!; **h. forbid!** ¡Dios no lo quiera!

**heavenly** ['hevənlɪ] *adj* (a) **h. body** cuerpo *m* celeste (b) *Fam (weather, food)* celestial

**heaven-sent** ['hevənsent] *adj* como caído(a) del cielo; **a h. opportunity** una ocasión de oro

**heavily** ['hevɪlɪ] *adv (to fall, walk, sleep)* pesadamente; **to drink/smoke h.** beber/fumar mucho; **it was raining h.** llovía a cántaros, llovía con fuerza; **to rely** *or* **depend h.** on **sth** depender mucho de algo; **to be h. defeated** perder estrepitosamente; **to be h. taxed** estar sometido(a) a fuertes impuestos

**heavy** ['hevɪ] **1** *adj* (a) *(in weight)* pesado(a); *(food)* pesado(a); **how h. is it?** ¿cuánto pesa?; **a h. blow** un golpe fuerte; **h. goods vehicle** vehículo *m* pesado; **h. industry** industria *f* pesada; **h. metal** *Chem* metal *m* pesado; *(music)* rock *m* duro, heavy metal *m*

(b) *(large, thick) (coat, shoes)* grueso(a)

(c) *(intense) (fighting)* enconado(a); *(rain, showers)* fuerte; *(drinker, smoker)* empedernido(a); **h. losses** grandes pérdidas; **a h. cold** *(illness)* un fuerte resfriado; **to be a h. sleeper** dormir profundamente; *Fig* **to come under h. fire** recibir una lluvia de críticas; **the traffic was very h.** había mucho tráfico

(d) *(oppressive) (smell)* fuerte; *(sky)* cargado(a), plomizo(a); *(fine, sentence)* duro(a); **h. responsibility** gran responsabilidad

(e) *(hard) (work, day)* duro(a); *(breathing)* pesado(a); **the book was h. going** el libro era muy denso; **h. seas** mar f gruesa

(**f**) *very Fam (threatening) (situation)* chungo(a), fuerte

**2** *n Fam* gorila *m*, matón *m*

**heavy-duty** [hevɪ'dju:tɪ] *adj* resistente

**heavy-handed** [hevɪ'hændɪd] *adj* (**a**) *(clumsy)* torpe (**b**) *(harsh)* de *or* con mano dura

**heavyweight** ['hevɪweɪt] *n (in boxing) & Fig* peso *m* pesado

**Hebrew** ['hi:bru:] **1** *n (language)* hebreo *m*

**2** *adj* hebreo(a); **H. script** escritura f hebrea

**Hebrides** ['hebrɪdi:z] *npl* the H. las Hébridas

**heck** [hek] *n Fam* **h.!** ¡vaya, hombre!; **what the h. are you doing here?** ¿qué narices haces aquí?; **what the h.!** *(when taking risk)* ¡qué demonios!; **a h. of a lot** un montón; **not a h. of a lot** no mucho

**heckle** ['hekəl] *vt & vi* interrumpir (con comentarios impertinentes)

**heckler** ['heklə(r)] *n* espectador *m* molesto

**heckling** ['heklɪŋ] *n* interrupciones *fpl* impertinentes

**hectare** ['hekta:(r)] *n* hectárea f

**hectic** ['hektɪk] *adj* ajetreado(a)

**hector** ['hektə(r)] *vt* intimidar; **she tried to h. me into agreeing** trató de intimidarme para que accediera

**hectoring** ['hektərɪŋ] *adj* intimidante, intimidatorio(a)

**he'd** [hi:d] = **he had, he would**

**hedge** [hedʒ] **1** *n* (**a**) *(in field, garden)* seto *m* (**b**) *(protection)* **a h. against inflation** una protección contra la inflación

**2** *vt* (**a**) *(field)* cercar con un seto (**b**) **to h. one's bets** cubrirse las espaldas

**3** *vi (in discussion)* responder con evasivas

**hedgehog** ['hedʒhɒg] *n* erizo *m*

**hedgerow** ['hedʒrəʊ] *n* seto *m*

**hedonism** ['hedənɪzəm] *n* hedonismo *m*

**heed** [hi:d] **1** *vt (warning, advice)* prestar atención a, escuchar

**2** *n* to pay h. to, to take h. of hacer caso de *or* a; **to pay no h. to, to take no h. of** hacer caso omiso de

**heedless** ['hi:dlɪs] *adj* **to be h. of** hacer caso omiso de

**heel** [hi:l] **1** *n (of foot, sock)* talón *m*; *(of shoe)* tacón *m*; **high heels** *(shoes)* zapatos *mpl* de tacón alto; **he had the police at his heels** la policía le venía pisando los talones; **to take to one's heels** poner pies en polvorosa; **to turn on one's h.** dar media vuelta; *Fam* **to cool or kick one's heels** *(wait)* quedarse esperando un largo rato; *Fig* **to bring sb to h.** meter a alguien en cintura

**2** *vt (shoe)* poner un tacón nuevo a

**hefty** ['heftɪ] *adj Fam (person)* robusto(a), fornido(a); *(suitcase, box)* pesado(a); *(bill, fine)* cuantioso(a)

**heifer** ['hefə(r)] *n (young cow)* novilla f, vaquilla f

**height** [haɪt] *n (of building, mountain)* altura f; *(of person)* estatura f, altura f; **what h. are you?** ¿cuánto mides?; **to gain/lose h.** *(of plane)* ganar/perder altura; **to be afraid of heights** tener vértigo; **she's at the h. of her powers** está en plenas facultades; **she's at the h. of her career** está en la cumbre de su carrera; **the h. of fashion** el último grito; **it's the h. of madness!** ¡es el colmo de la locura!

**heighten** ['haɪtən] *vt (intensify)* intensificar, aumentar

**heinous** ['heɪnəs] *adj Formal (crime)* execrable, infame

**heir** [eə(r)] *n* heredero *m*; **to be h. to sth** ser heredero de algo; **the h. to the throne** el heredero al trono; **h. apparent** heredero *m* forzoso; *Fig* heredero *m* natural

**heiress** ['eərɪs] *n* heredera f

**heirloom** ['eəlu:m] *n* reliquia f familiar

**heist** [haɪst] *n US Fam* golpe *m*, robo *m*

**held** [held] *pt & pp of* **hold**

**helicopter** ['helɪkɒptə(r)] *n* helicóptero *m*

**heliport** ['helɪpɔ:t] *n* helipuerto *m*

**helium** ['hi:lɪəm] *n Chem* helio *m*

**hell** [hel] *n* (**a**) infierno *m*; *Fam* **h.!** *(expressing annoyance)* ¡mierda!

(**b**) *Fam (in phrases)* **it was h.** *(very difficult or unpleasant)* fue un infierno; **to feel like h.** sentirse fatal *or* muy mal; **to make sb's life h.** amargarle a alguien la vida; **these shoes are giving me h.** estos zapatos me están matando; **all h. broke loose** se armó la marimorena; **there'll be h. to pay if…** alguien lo va a pasar muy mal si…; **go to h.!** ¡vete a la mierda!; **to run like h.** correr como alma que lleva el diablo; **like h. (I will)!** ¡ni de coña!; **you can wait till h. freezes over** puedes esperar hasta que las ranas críen pelo; **come h. or high water** pase lo que pase; **to go h. for leather** ir a toda mecha; **to do sth for the h. of it** hacer algo porque sí

(**c**) *Fam (as intensifier)* **a h. of a price** un precio altísimo; **he put up a h. of a fight** opuso muchísima resistencia; **to have a h. of a time** *(good)* pasárselo como Dios; *(bad)* pasarlas moradas; **a h. of a lot of…** una porrada de…; **he's one or a h. of a guy** es una pasada de tío; **what the h. do you think you're doing?** ¿me quieres decir qué demonios estás haciendo?; **who the h. are you?** ¿y tú quién leches eres?

**he'll** [hi:l] = **he will, he shall**

**hellbent** ['helbent] *adj Fam* **to be h. on doing sth** tener entre ceja y ceja hacer algo

**hellhole** ['helhəʊl] *n Fam (place)* infierno *m*, agujero *m* infecto

**hellish** ['helɪʃ] *adj Fam* infernal, horroroso(a)

**hello** [he'ləʊ] *exclam* ¡hola!; *(on phone) (when answering)* ¿sí?, ¿diga?, *Am* ¿aló?, *Méx* ¿bueno?, *CSur* ¿hola?, *Carib* ¿oigo?; *(when calling)* ¡hola!; **to say h. to sb** saludar a (alguien); **h., what's this?** *(indicating surprise)* caramba, ¿qué es esto?

**hell-raiser** ['helreɪzə(r)] *n Fam* camorrista *mf*

**helm** [helm] *n (of ship)* timón *m*; *Fig* **to be at the h.** *(of party, country)* estar al frente

**helmet** ['helmɪt] *n* casco *m*

**helmsman** ['helmzmən] *n (on ship)* timonel *m*

**help** [help] **1** *n* **(a)** *(aid)* ayuda *f*; **h.!** ¡socorro!; **to be of h. to sb** ser de ayuda para alguien; **thank you, you've been a great h.** gracias, has sido de gran ayuda; **with the h. of sb, with sb's h.** con la ayuda de alguien; **to be beyond h.** no tener remedio; **there was no h. for it** no había más remedio **(b)** *(cleaning woman)* asistenta *f*

**2** *vt* **(a)** *(aid)* ayudar; **to h. sb (to) do sth** ayudar a alguien a hacer algo; **to h. sb on/off with his coat** ayudar a alguien a ponerse/quitarse el abrigo; **can I h. you?** *(in shop)* ¿en qué puedo servirle?; **to h. one another** ayudarse mutuamente, ayudarse el uno al otro; **to h. oneself to sth** servirse algo; **h. yourself** sírvete **(b)** *(prevent)* **I can't h. it** no lo puedo evitar; **it can't be helped** no queda otro remedio; **I can't h. laughing** no puedo evitar reírme; **she couldn't h. overhearing** no pudo evitar oír (la conversación); **not if I can h. it!** ¡no, si lo puedo evitar!

**3** *vi* ayudar; **can I h.?** ¿puedo ayudar?

▸**help out** *vt sep* **to h. sb out** ayudar a alguien

**helper** ['helpə(r)] *n* ayudante *mf*

**helpful** ['helpfʊl] *adj (person) (willing to help)* servicial; *(advice, book)* útil, provechoso(a); **you've been very h.** nos has sido de gran ayuda

**helpfully** ['helpfʊlɪ] *adv* "**have you tried asking Sue?**" **he suggested h.** "¿has probado a preguntar a Sue?" sugirió, tratando de ser útil; **a translation is h. provided** como ayuda se incluye una traducción

**helping** ['helpɪŋ] **1** *n (portion)* ración *f*; **I had a second h. of spaghetti** repetí (de) espagueti

**2** *adj* **to lend a h. hand** echar una mano

**helpless** ['helplɪs] *adj (powerless)* impotente; *(defenceless)* indefenso(a); **we were h. to prevent it** no pudimos evitarlo; **to be h. with laughter** no poder dejar de reír

**helplessly** ['helplɪslɪ] *adv* impotentemente, sin poder hacer nada

**helpline** ['helplaɪn] *n* teléfono *m* de asistencia or ayuda

**Helsinki** [hel'sɪŋkɪ] *n* Helsinki

**helter-skelter** ['heltə'skeltə(r)] **1** *n (at fairground)* tobogán *m*

**2** *adv (in disorder)* atropelladamente, a lo loco

**hem** [hem] **1** *n* dobladillo *m*

**2** *vt (pt & pp* **hemmed)** hacer el dobladillo a

▸**hem in** *vt sep (surround)* cercar, rodear

**he-man** ['hi:mæn] *n Fam* hombretón *m*, machote *m*

**hemisphere** ['hemɪsfɪə(r)] *n* hemisferio *m*

**hemline** ['hemlaɪn] *n* bajo *m*

**hemlock** ['hemlɒk] *n* cicuta *f*

**hemoglobin, hemophilia** *etc US =* **haemoglobin, haemophilia** *etc*

**hemp** [hemp] *n* cáñamo *m*

**hen** [hen] *n* gallina *f*; *Fam* **h. party** *(before wedding)* despedida *f* de soltera

**hence** [hens] *adv (thus)* de ahí; **h. his anger** de ahí su enfado **(b)** *(from now)* desde aquí; **five years h.** de aquí a cinco años

**henceforth** [hens'fɔ:θ] *adv Formal* en lo sucesivo, de ahora/ahí en adelante

**henchman** ['henʃmən] *n Pej* sicario *m*, secuaz *m*

**hencoop** ['henku:p] *n* gallinero *m*

**henhouse** ['henhaʊs] *n* gallinero *m*

**henna** ['henə] *n* henna *f*

**henpecked** ['henpekt] *adj* calzonazos *inv*

**hepatitis** [hepə'taɪtɪs] *n Med* hepatitis *f inv*

**heptagon** ['heptəgɒn] *n* heptágono *m*

**her** [*unstressed* hə(r), *stressed* hɜ:(r)] **1** *pron* **(a)** *(direct object)* la; **I hate h.** la odio; **I can forgive her son but not HER** puedo perdonar a su hijo, pero no a ella

**(b)** *(indirect object)* le; **I gave h. the book** le di el libro; **I gave it to h.** se lo di

**(c)** *(after preposition)* ella; **I talked to h.** hablé con ella; **her mother lives near h.** su madre vive cerca de ella

**(d)** *(as complement of verb* **to be)** ella; **it's h.!** ¡es ella!; **it was h. who did it** lo hizo ella

**2** *possessive adj* **(a)** *(singular)* su; *(plural)* sus; **I took h. car** cogí su coche; *(contrasting with his or theirs)* cogí el coche de ella

**(b)** *(for parts of body, clothes)* **h. eyes are blue** tiene los ojos azules; **she hit h. head** se dio un golpe en la cabeza; **she put h. hands in h. pockets** se metió las manos en los bolsillos

**herald** ['herəld] **1** *n* heraldo *m*

**2** *vt* anunciar

**heraldry** ['herəldrɪ] *n* heráldica *f*

**herb** [hɜ:b] *n* hierba *f*

**herbal** ['hɜːbəl] *adj* de hierbas; **h. remedies** = remedios a base de hierbas medicinales; **h. tea** infusión *f*

**herbalist** ['hɜːbəlɪst] *n* herbolario(a) *m,f*

**herbicide** ['hɜːbɪsaɪd] *n* herbicida *m*

**herbivore** ['hɜːbɪvɔː(r)] *n* herbívoro *m*

**herbivorous** [hɜːˈbɪvərəs] *adj* herbívoro(a)

**herd** [hɜːd] **1** *n* (*of cattle, sheep*) rebaño *m*; (*of horses, elephants*) manada *f*; (*of people*) rebaño *m*, manada *f*; **the h. instinct** el instinto gregario
**2** *vt* (*cattle, people*) conducir

**herdsman** ['hɜːdzmən] *n* vaquero(a) *m,f*

**here** [hɪə(r)] **1** *n* the **h. and now** el aquí y ahora
**2** *adv* aquí; **over h.** (por) aquí; **h. it/he is** aquí está; **h.!** (*at roll call*) ¡presente!; **come h.!** ¡ven aquí!; **h.!, come and look at this** ¡ven! echa un vistazo a esto; **she's not h.** no está aquí; **h. she comes** aquí viene; **h. and now** aquí y ahora; **h. and there** aquí y allá; *Fig* **that's neither h. nor there** eso es irrelevante; **what have we h.?** ¿qué es esto?, ¿qué tenemos aquí?; **h.'s what you have to do** esto es lo que tienes que hacer; **h. you are!** (*when giving something*) ¡aquí tienes!; **h. goes!** ¡vamos allá!; **h.'s to the future!** ¡por el futuro!

**hereafter** [hɪərˈɑːftə(r)] **1** *adv Formal* en adelante, en lo sucesivo
**2** *n Literary* the **h.** el más allá

**hereby** [hɪəˈbaɪ] *adv Formal* (*in writing*) por la presente; (*in speech*) por el presente acto

**hereditary** [hɪˈredɪtərɪ] *adj* hereditario(a)

**heredity** [hɪˈredɪtɪ] *n* herencia *f*

**heresy** ['herəsɪ] *n* herejía *f*

**heretic** ['herətɪk] *n* hereje *mf*

**heretical** [hɪˈretɪkəl] *adj* herético(a)

**heritage** ['herɪtɪdʒ] *n* patrimonio *m*

**hermaphrodite** [hɜːˈmæfrədaɪt] *n & adj* hermafrodita *mf*

**hermetic** [hɜːˈmetɪk] *adj* hermético(a)

**hermetically** [hɜːˈmetɪklɪ] *adv* herméticamente

**hermit** ['hɜːmɪt] *n* ermitaño(a) *m,f*; **h. crab** cangrejo *m* ermitaño

**hernia** ['hɜːnɪə] *n* hernia *f*

**hero** ['hɪərəʊ] (*pl* **heroes**) *n* héroe *m*; **h. worship** idolatría *f*

**heroic** [hɪˈrəʊɪk] *adj* heroico(a)

**heroically** [hɪˈrəʊɪklɪ] *adv* heroicamente

**heroics** [hɪˈrəʊɪks] *npl* heroicidades *fpl*

**heroin** ['herəʊɪn] *n* (*drug*) heroína *f*; **h. addict** heroinómano(a) *m,f*

**heroine** ['herəʊɪn] *n* (*female hero*) heroína *f*

**heroism** ['herəʊɪzəm] *n* heroísmo *m*

**heron** ['herən] *n* garza *f*

**hero-worship** ['hɪərəʊwɜːʃɪp] (*pt & pp* **hero-worshipped**) *vt* idolatrar

**herpes** ['hɜːpiːz] *n* herpes *m inv*

**herring** ['herɪŋ] *n* arenque *m*

**hers** [hɜːz] *possessive pron* (**a**) (*singular*) el suyo *m*, la suya *f*; (*plural*) los suyos *mpl*, las suyas *fpl*; (*to distinguish*) el/la/los/las de ella; **my house is big but h. is bigger** mi casa es grande, pero la suya es mayor; **he didn't have a copy, so I gave him h.** no tenía copia, así que le di la de ella
(**b**) (*used attributively*) (*singular*) suyo(a); (*plural*) suyos(as); **this book is h.** este libro es suyo; **a friend of h.** un amigo suyo

**herself** [hɜːˈself] *pron* (**a**) (*reflexive*) se; **she hurt h.** se hizo daño
(**b**) (*emphatic*) ella misma; **she did all the work h.** hizo todo el trabajo ella misma *or* ella sola; **she told me h.** me lo dijo ella misma; **she's not h. today** hoy está un poco rara
(**c**) (*after preposition*) ella; **she lives by h.** vive sola; **she bought it for h.** se lo compró para ella; **she talks to h.** habla sola

**he's** [hiːz] = **he is, he has**

**hesitancy** ['hezɪtənsɪ] *n* duda *f*, vacilación *f*

**hesitant** ['hezɪtənt] *adj* indeciso(a); (*speaker, smile, gesture*) vacilante; **to be h. about doing sth** tener dudas a la hora de algo; **I would be h. to…** no me atrevería a…

**hesitate** ['hezɪteɪt] *vi* dudar, vacilar

**hesitation** [hezɪˈteɪʃən] *n* vacilación *f*, titubeo *m*; **without h.** sin vacilar

**heterogeneous** [hetərəˈdʒiːnɪəs] *adj* heterogéneo(a)

**heterosexual** [hetərəʊˈseksjʊəl] *n & adj* heterosexual *mf*

**het up** ['hetʌp] *adj Br Fam* (*angry*) mosqueado(a); (*tense*) nervioso(a); **to get h.** (*about sth*) (*angry*) mosquearse (por algo); (*tense*) ponerse nervioso (por algo)

**heuristics** [hjuːˈrɪstɪks] *npl* heurística *f*

**hew** [hjuː] (*pp* **hewn** [hjuːn] *or* **hewed**) *vt* (*cut down*) cortar; (*shape*) tallar

**hexagon** ['heksəgən] *n* hexágono *m*

**hexagonal** [hekˈsægənəl] *adj* hexagonal

**hey** [heɪ] *exclam* ¡eh!; **h. presto!** ¡ale-hop!

**heyday** ['heɪdeɪ] *n* apogeo *m*; **in his/its h.** en su apogeo

**HGV** [eɪtʃdʒiːˈviː] *n Br* (*abbr* **heavy goods vehicle**) vehículo *m* de carga pesada

**hi** [haɪ] *exclam Fam* ¡hola!

**hiatus** [haɪˈeɪtəs] *n* (*interruption*) interrupción *f*; (*blank space*) laguna *f*

**hibernate** ['haɪbəneɪt] *vi* hibernar

**hibernation** [haɪbəˈneɪʃən] *n* hibernación *f*

**hiccup** ['hɪkʌp] **1** *n* hipo *m*; *Fig* (*minor problem*) traspié *m*, desliz *m*; **to have (the) hiccups** tener hipo
**2** *vi* (*pt & pp* **hiccuped**) (*repeatedly*) tener hipo; (*once*) hipar

**hick** [hɪk] n US Fam paleto(a) m,f, pueblerino(a) m,f

**hickory** ['hɪkərɪ] n (tree, wood) nogal m americano

**hid** [hɪd] pt of **hide**

**hidden** ['hɪdən] 1 adj oculto(a); **to be h.** estar oculto(a); **h. agenda** objetivo m secreto
2 pp of **hide**

**hide¹** [haɪd] 1 n (for birdwatching) puesto m de observación
2 vt (pt hid [hɪd], pp hidden ['hɪdən]) esconder (from de); (emotions, truth) ocultar; **to have nothing to h.** no tener nada que ocultar; **to h. oneself** esconderse
3 vi esconderse (from de)

**hide²** n (a) (skin) piel f (b) (idioms) **to save one's h.** salvar el pellejo; **I haven't seen h. nor hair of her** no le he visto el pelo

**hide-and-seek** [haɪdən'siːk] n escondite m; **to play h.** jugar al escondite

**hidebound** ['haɪdbaʊnd] adj (person, attitude) rígido(a), inflexible

**hideous** ['hɪdɪəs] adj espantoso(a)

**hideously** ['hɪdɪəslɪ] adv espantosamente

**hide-out** ['haɪdaʊt] n guarida f, escondite m

**hiding¹** ['haɪdɪŋ] n **to be in h.** estar en la clandestinidad; **to go into/come out of h.** pasar a/salir de la clandestinidad; **h. place** escondite m

**hiding²** n Fam (beating) paliza f; **to give sb a h.** dar una paliza a alguien; Fig **to be on a h. to nothing** no tener nada que hacer, estar perdiendo el tiempo

**hierarchical** [haɪə'rɑːkɪkəl] adj jerárquico(a)

**hierarchy** ['haɪərɑːkɪ] n jerarquía f

**hieroglyphics** [haɪərə'glɪfɪks] npl jeroglíficos mpl

**hi-fi** ['haɪfaɪ] n alta fidelidad f, (stereo system) equipo m de alta fidelidad

**higgledy-piggledy** ['hɪɡəldɪ'pɪɡəldɪ] adv Fam de cualquier manera, a la buena de Dios

**high** [haɪ] 1 n (a) (peak) punto m álgido; **to reach a new h.** (in career, performance) alcanzar nuevas cotas de éxito; (of unemployment, inflation) alcanzar un nuevo máximo or récord; **to be on a h.** (from drugs) estar colocado(a); (from success) estar ebrio(a) de triunfo; **highs and lows** altibajos mpl
(b) Met anticiclón m
2 adj (a) (mountain, building) alto(a); **it's 2 metres h.** tiene dos metros de altura; Fam **to be left h. and dry** quedarse en la estacada; **h. jump** salto m de altura; Fig **you'll be for the h. jump** (will be punished) te vas a enterar de lo que vale un peine; **h. jumper** saltador(ora) m,f de altura; **h. tide** marea f alta; **h. wire** cuerda f floja

(b) (price, speed, standards) alto(a), elevado(a); **to have a h. opinion of sb** tener una buena opinión de alguien; **h. explosive** explosivo m de gran potencia; **h. point** momento m culminante; **in h. spirits** muy animado(a); Law **h. treason** alta traición f; **h. winds** viento m fuerte

(c) (rank, position) elevado(a), alto(a); **to act all h. and mighty** comportarse de forma arrogante; Mil **h. command** alto mando m; **H. Commission** = embajada de un país de la Commonwealth en otro; **H. Court** Tribunal m Supremo; **H. Mass** misa f solemne; **h. school** instituto m de enseñanza secundaria; **h. society** alta sociedad f

(d) (in tone, pitch) agudo(a); Fig **h. note** (of career, performance) punto m culminante

(e) (of time) **it's h. time you got yourself a job** ya es hora de que te busques un trabajo; **h. noon** mediodía m; **h. summer** pleno verano m; Br **h. tea** merienda f cena

(f) (meat) pasado(a)

(g) Fam **to be h.** (on drugs) estar colocado(a); Fig (on success, excitement) estar eufórico(a) (**on** de)

3 adv (to aim, jump) alto; **to hunt h. and low for sth** buscar algo por todas partes; **feelings were running h.** los ánimos estaban exaltados or caldeados

**highbrow** ['haɪbraʊ] adj (tastes, interests) intelectual, culto(a)

**highchair** ['haɪtʃeə(r)] n trona f

**Higher** ['haɪə(r)] n Scot Sch = examen final de los estudios preuniversitarios

**higher education** ['haɪərədjʊ'keɪʃən] n enseñanza f superior

**high-flier, high-flyer** ['haɪ'flaɪə(r)] n (successful person) persona f brillante y ambiciosa

**high-flying** ['haɪ'flaɪɪŋ] adj brillante y ambicioso(a)

**high-frequency** [haɪ'friːkwənsɪ] adj de alta frecuencia

**high-handed** [haɪ'hændɪd] adj despótico(a)

**high-heeled** ['haɪ'hiːld] adj de tacón alto

**highland** ['haɪlənd] adj de montaña

**Highlander** ['haɪləndə(r)] n (Scottish) habitante mf de las Tierras Altas de Escocia

**Highlands** ['haɪləndz] npl **the H.** (of Scotland) las Tierras Altas de Escocia; **the Kenyan/Guatemalan H.** las zonas montañosas de Kenia/Guatemala

**high-level** ['haɪlevəl] adj (talks, delegation) de alto nivel

**highlight** ['haɪlaɪt] 1 n (a) (of performance, career) momento m cumbre; **highlights** (of match) (repetición f de las) jugadas fpl más interesantes, mejores momentos mpl (b) (in hair)

**highlights** reflejos *mpl*, mechas *fpl*
  **2** *vt (problem, difference)* destacar; *(with pen)* resaltar *(con rotulador fluorescente)*

**highlighter** ['haɪlaɪtə(r)] *n (pen)* rotulador *m* fluorescente

**highly** ['haɪlɪ] *adv* (a) *(very)* muy; **h. paid** (muy) bien pagado(a); **h. seasoned** muy condimentado(a); **to be h. strung** ser muy nervioso(a) (b) **to think h. of sb** tener buena opinión de alguien

**high-minded** ['haɪ'maɪndɪd] *adj* noble, elevado(a)

**Highness** ['haɪnɪs] *n* **His/Her Royal H.** Su Alteza Real

**high-pitched** ['haɪpɪtʃt] *adj* agudo(a)

**high-powered** ['haɪ'paʊəd] *adj (engine, car, telescope)* potente, de gran potencia; *(person, job)* de altos vuelos

**high-pressure** ['haɪ'preʃə(r)] *adj (substance, container)* a gran presión

**high-profile** ['haɪ'prəʊfaɪl] *adj (person)* prominente, destacado(a); *(campaign)* de gran alcance

**high-rise** ['haɪraɪz] **1** *n (block of flats)* bloque *m*, torre *f*
  **2** *adj* **h. building** bloque *m*, torre *f*

**high-risk** ['haɪrɪsk] *adj (strategy, investment)* de alto riesgo

**highroad** ['haɪrəʊd] *n Old-fashioned* carretera *f* principal; *Fig* **the h. to success** la vía directa hacia el éxito

**high-speed** ['haɪ'spiːd] *adj* de alta velocidad

**high-spirited** ['haɪ'spɪrɪtɪd] *adj* radiante, exultante

**high-tech** ['haɪ'tek] *adj* de alta tecnología

**high-up** ['haɪʌp] *adj Fam* importante

**highway** ['haɪweɪ] *n* autovía *f*; *(motorway)* autopista *f*; **H. Code** código *m* de la circulación

**highwayman** ['haɪweɪmən] *n* bandolero *m*, salteador *m* de caminos

**hijack** ['haɪdʒæk] *vt* secuestrar

**hijacker** ['haɪdʒækə(r)] *n* secuestrador(ora) *m,f*

**hike** [haɪk] **1** *n* (a) *(walk)* excursión *f*, caminata *f*; **to go on** *or* **for a h.** darse una caminata; *Fig* **go take a h.!** ¡vete a paseo! (b) *(in prices)* subida *f*
  **2** *vi (walk)* caminar
  **3** *vt (prices)* subir

**hiker** ['haɪkə(r)] *n* excursionista *mf*, senderista *mf*

**hiking** ['haɪkɪŋ] *n* senderismo *m*; **to go h.** hacer senderismo; **h. boots** botas *fpl* de excursionismo

**hilarious** [hɪ'leərɪəs] *adj* divertidísimo(a), tronchante

**hilariously** [hɪ'leərɪəslɪ] *adv* **h. funny** divertidísimo(a), tronchante

**hilarity** [hɪ'lærɪtɪ] *n* hilaridad *f*

**hill** [hɪl] *n* (a) *(small mountain)* colina *f*, monte *m*; *Fig* **to be over the h.** *(past one's best)* no estar ya para muchos trotes (b) *(slope)* cuesta *f*; **to go down/up the h.** ir cuesta abajo/arriba

**hillbilly** ['hɪlbɪlɪ] *n US Pej* palurdo(a) *m,f* de la montaña

**hillock** ['hɪlək] *n* cerro *m*, collado *m*

**hillside** ['hɪlsaɪd] *n* ladera *f*

**hilltop** ['hɪltɒp] *n* cima *f*, cumbre *f*

**hill-walker** ['hɪlwɔːkə(r)] *n* senderista *mf*

**hill-walking** ['hɪlwɔːkɪŋ] *n* senderismo *m*

**hilly** ['hɪlɪ] *adj* con muchas colinas

**hilt** [hɪlt] *n (of sword, dagger)* puño *m*, empuñadura *f*; **to back sb to the h.** *(support)* apoyar sin reservas a alguien

**him** [hɪm] *pron* (a) *(direct object)* lo; **I hate h.** lo odio; **I can forgive his son but not HIM** puedo perdonar a su hijo, pero no a él (b) *(indirect object)* le; **I gave h. the book** le di el libro; **I gave it to h.** se lo di (c) *(after preposition)* él; **I talked to h.** hablé con él; **his mother lives near h.** su madre vive cerca de él (d) *(as complement of verb to be)* él; **it's h.!** ¡es él!; **it was h. who did it** es él el que lo hizo

**Himalayan** [hɪmə'leɪən] *adj* himalayo(a)

**Himalayas** [hɪmə'leɪəz] *npl* **the H.** el Himalaya

**himself** [hɪm'self] *pron* (a) *(reflexive)* se; **he hurt h.** se hizo daño (b) *(emphatic)* él mismo; **he did all the work h.** hizo todo el trabajo él mismo *or* él solo; **he told me h.** me lo dijo él mismo; **he's not h. today** hoy está un poco raro (c) *(after preposition)* él; **he lives by h.** vive solo; **he bought it for h.** se lo compró para él; **he talks to h.** habla solo

**hind** [haɪnd] *adj* trasero(a), de atrás; **h. legs** patas *fpl* traseras

**hinder** ['hɪndə(r)] *vt (person)* estorbar; *(movements, operation, negotiations)* entorpecer; **his shyness hindered him from making friends** su timidez le impedía hacer amigos

**Hindi** ['hɪndɪ] *n (language)* hindi *m*

**hindquarters** ['haɪndkwɔːtəz] *npl* cuartos *mpl* traseros

**hindrance** ['hɪndrəns] *n (person)* estorbo *m*; *(thing)* impedimento *m*, traba *f*

**hindsight** ['haɪndsaɪt] *n* retrospección *f*; **with the benefit of h.** con la ventaja que proporciona una mirada retrospectiva

**Hindu** ['hɪnduː] *n & adj* hindú *mf*

**Hinduism** ['hɪnduːɪzəm] *n* hinduismo *m*

**hinge** [hɪndʒ] *n* bisagra *f*
  ▸**hinge on, hinge upon** *vt insep (depend on)* depender de

**hint** [hɪnt] **1** n (a) (allusion) indirecta f, insinuación f; **to give** or **drop sb a h.** lanzar a alguien una indirecta; **to be able to take a h.** saber coger una indirecta (b) (sign) rastro m; **not a h. of surprise** ni un asomo de sorpresa; **a h. of garlic** un ligero gusto a ajo (c) (piece of advice) consejo m; **to give sb a h.** dar a alguien una pista

**2** vt **to h. that...** insinuar que...

▸**hint at** vt insep aludir a, hacer alusión a

**hinterland** ['hɪntəlænd] n región f interior

**hip¹** [hɪp] n cadera f; **h. flask** petaca f; **h. joint** articulación f de la cadera; **h. pocket** bolsillo m trasero

**hip²** adj Fam (trendy) moderno(a), a la última

**hippo** ['hɪpəʊ] (pl **hippos**) n Fam hipopótamo m

**hippopotamus** [hɪpə'pɒtəməs], (pl**hippopotami** [hɪpə'pɒtəmaɪ]) n hipopótamo m

**hippy** ['hɪpɪ] n hippy mf

**hire** [haɪə(r)] **1** n Br (of car, room) alquiler m; **for h.** (taxi) libre; **bicycles for h.** (en letrero) se alquilan bicicletas; **h. car** coche m de alquiler

**2** vt (car, room) alquilar; (lawyer, worker) contratar

▸**hire out** vt sep Br (boat, bicycle) alquilar; (one's services) ofrecer

**hired** ['haɪəd] adj (car, suit) alquilado(a); **h. hand** (on farm) jornalero(a) m,f

**hire-purchase** ['haɪə'pɜːtʃɪs] n Com compra f a plazos; **h. agreement** contrato m de compra a plazos

**hirsute** ['hɜːsjuːt] adj Literary hirsuto(a)

**his** [hɪz] **1** possessive adj (a) (singular) su; (plural) sus; **I took h. car** tomé su coche; (contrasting with hers or theirs) tomé el coche de él

(b) (for parts of body, clothes) **h. eyes are blue** tiene los ojos azules; **he hit h. head** se dio un golpe en la cabeza; **he put h. hands in h. pockets** se metió las manos en los bolsillos

**2** possessive pron (a) (singular) el suyo m, la suya f; (plural) los suyos mpl, las suyas fpl; (to distinguish) el/la/los/las de él; **my house is big but h. is bigger** mi casa es grande, pero la suya es mayor; **she didn't have a book so I gave her h.** ella no tenía libro, así que le di el de él

(b) (used attributively) (singular) suyo(a); (plural) suyos(as); **this book is h.** este libro es suyo; **a friend of h.** un amigo suyo

**Hispanic** [hɪs'pænɪk] **1** n US hispano(a) m,f

**2** adj hispánico(a), hispano(a)

**Hispanist** ['hɪspənɪst], **Hispanicist** [hɪs'pænɪsɪst] n hispanista mf

**Hispanophile** [hɪs'pænəfaɪl] n hispanófilo(a) m,f

**hiss** [hɪs] **1** n (sound) silbido m; (to express disapproval) siseo m

**2** vt sisear

**3** vi (a) (expressing disapproval) chistar (b) (of snake, steam) silbar

**histogram** ['hɪstəgræm] n histograma m

**historian** [hɪs'tɔːrɪən] n historiador(ora) m,f

**historic** [hɪs'tɒrɪk] adj histórico(a)

**historical** [hɪs'tɒrɪkəl] adj histórico(a); **h. novel** novela f histórica

**historically** [hɪs'tɒrɪklɪ] adv históricamente

**history** ['hɪstərɪ] n historia f; **to go down in h. as...** pasar a (los anales de) la historia como...; Fig **that's h.** eso pasó a la historia; Med **to have a h. of...** tener un historial de...; **h. book** libro m de historia; **h. teacher** profesor(ora) m,f de historia

**histrionic** [hɪstrɪ'ɒnɪk] adj Pej histriónico(a), teatral

**histrionics** [hɪstrɪ'ɒnɪks] npl Pej histrionismo m, teatralidad f

**hit** [hɪt] **1** n (a) (blow) golpe m; (in shooting) impacto m; **to score a direct h.** dar de lleno en el blanco; **h. list** (of assassination targets) lista f negra; **h. man** asesino m a sueldo

(b) (success) éxito m; **h. (record)** (disco m de) éxito m

**2** adj (successful) de mucho éxito

**3** vt (pt & pp **hit**) (a) (of person) golpear; (of car) (tree, bus) chocar contra; Comptr (key) pulsar; **to h. one's hand (on sth)** darse un golpe en la mano (con algo); **the bullet hit him in the leg** la bala le dio en or le alcanzó la pierna; Fig **it suddenly hit me that...** de repente me di cuenta de que...; Fig **he didn't know what had hit him** no le dio tiempo ni a reaccionar

(b) (reach) **to h. a note** llegar a or dar una nota; **to h. 90 (miles an hour)** alcanzar las noventa millas por hora; **to have hit an all-time low** (of investment) haber alcanzado un mínimo histórico; Fig (of relationship) estar por los suelos

(c) (affect) afectar; **to be hard hit by...** verse muy afectado(a) por...

(d) (arrive at) (barrier, difficulty) toparse or encontrarse con; **the circus hits town tomorrow** el circo llega mañana a la ciudad; **it hits the shops next week** estará a la venta la próxima semana; Fam **to h. the road** (leave) ponerse en marcha, largarse

**4** vi golpear

▸**hit back 1** vt sep **to h. sb back** devolver el golpe a alguien

**2** vi (return blow) devolver el golpe; Fig (with answer, accusation, criticism) responder

▸**hit off** vt sep Fam **to h. it off** caerse bien

▸**hit on** vt insep (idea, solution) dar con

▶**hit out** vi (physically) lanzar golpes (**at** contra); (verbally) lanzar ataques (**at** contra)

▶**hit upon** = **hit on**

**hit-and-run** ['hɪtən'rʌn] adj he was knocked down in a h. accident lo atropelló un coche que se dio a la fuga; a h. driver = conductor que huye tras atropellar a alguien

**hitch** [hɪtʃ] **1** n (a) (difficulty) contratiempo m; **without a h.** sin ningún contratiempo (b) (knot) nudo m
**2** vt (a) (attach) enganchar (**to** a); Fam Fig **to get hitched** (marry) casarse (b) Fam **to h. a lift to…** ir en autostop a…
**3** vi Fam hacer autostop

**hitch up** vt sep (trousers, skirt) subirse

**hitchhike** ['hɪtʃhaɪk] vi hacer autostop

**hitchhiker** ['hɪtʃhaɪkə(r)] n autoestopista mf

**hi-tech** ['haɪ'tek] adj de alta tecnología

**hither** ['hɪðə(r)] adv Literary acá; **h. and thither** de acá para allá

**hitherto** ['hɪðə'tuː] adv hasta ahora, hasta la fecha

**hit-or-miss** ['hɪtɔ'mɪs] adj azaroso(a), al tuntún

**HIV** [eɪtʃaɪ'viː] n (abbr **human immunodeficiency virus**) VIH m, virus m inv de la inmunodeficiencia humana; **to be H. positive/negative** ser/no ser seropositivo(a)

**hive** [haɪv] n colmena f; Fig **a h. of activity** un hervidero de actividad

▶**hive off** vt sep (sell) desprenderse de

**HMG** [eɪtʃem'dʒiː] n Br (abbr **Her/His Majesty's Government**) el Gobierno de Su Majestad

**HMI** [eɪtʃem'aɪ] n Br Educ Formerly (abbr **Her/His Majesty's Inspectorate**) = organismo británico de inspección de enseñanza; (abbr **Her/His Majesty's Inspector**) inspector(ora) m,f de enseñanza

**HMS** [eɪtʃem'es] n Br Naut (abbr **Her/His Majesty's Ship**) = título que precede a los nombres de buques de la marina británica

**HMSO** [eɪtʃemes'əʊ] n Br (abbr **Her/His Majesty's Stationery Office**) imprenta f del Estado

**HNC** [eɪtʃen'siː] n Br Educ (abbr **Higher National Certificate**) = título de escuela técnica de grado medio (un año)

**HND** [eɪtʃen'diː] n Br Educ (abbr **Higher National Diploma**) = título de escuela técnica de grado superior (dos años)

**hoard** [hɔːd] n **1** (of food) provisión f; (of money) montón m
**2** vt (food) hacer acopio de; (money) atesorar

**hoarder** ['hɔːdə(r)] n acaparador(ora) m,f

**hoarding** ['hɔːdɪŋ] n (a) (of food, money) acaparamiento m, acopio m (b) (display board) valla f publicitaria

**hoarfrost** ['hɔːfrɒst] n escarcha f

**hoarse** [hɔːs] adj ronco(a); **to be h.** quedarse ronco(a)

**hoary** ['hɔːrɪ] adj (old) viejo(a)

**hoax** [həʊks] **1** n engaño m; **to play a h. on sb** engañar a alguien; **h. caller** = persona que realiza falsas alarmas por teléfono
**2** vt engañar

**hob** [hɒb] n (on electric cooker) placa f, fuego m; (on hearth) plancha f

**hobble** ['hɒbəl] vi cojear

**hobby** ['hɒbɪ] n afición f, hobby m

**hobbyhorse** ['hɒbɪhɔːs] n (toy) caballito m de juguete; Fig (favourite subject) tema m favorito

**hobnail boot** ['hɒbneɪl'buːt] n bota f de suela claveteada

**hobnob** ['hɒbnɒb] (pt & pp **hobnobbed**) vi Fam **to h. with sb** codearse con alguien

**hock¹** [hɒk] n (wine) = vino blanco alemán del valle del Rin

**hock²** Fam **1** n **in h.** empeñado(a); **to be in h. to the bank** tener una deuda con el banco
**2** vt empeñar

**hockey** ['hɒkɪ] n Br (on grass) hockey m (sobre hierba); US (on ice) hockey (sobre hielo); **h. pitch** campo m de hockey; **h. stick** stick m, palo m de hockey

**hocus-pocus** ['həʊkəs'pəʊkəs] n camelo m, embaucamiento m

**hoe** [həʊ] **1** n azada f, azadón m
**2** vt remover con la azada

**hog** [hɒg] **1** n (a) (pig) cerdo m, puerco m; **to go the whole h.** (be extravagant) tirar la casa por la ventana (b) (glutton) glotón(ona) m,f
**2** vt (pt & pp **hogged**) Fam acaparar

**Hogmanay** ['hɒgmə'neɪ] n Scot Nochevieja f

**hogwash** ['hɒgwɒʃ] n Fam sandeces fpl, tonterías fpl

**hoist** [hɔɪst] **1** n (device) aparejo m para izar
**2** vt (equipment, person) subir, izar; (flag, sail) izar; Fig **she was hoist with her own petard** le salió el tiro por la culata

**hoity-toity** ['hɔɪtɪ'tɔɪtɪ] adj altivo(a), engreído(a)

**hold** [həʊld] **1** n (a) (grip) **to have h. of sth** tener algo cogido or Am agarrado; **to catch** or **take h. of** agarrarse a; **to let go one's h. on sth** soltar algo; Fig **to get h. of sb** (make contact with) localizar a alguien; Fig **to get h. of sth** (obtain) hacerse con algo; **to lose one's h. on reality** perder el contacto con la realidad; Fig **to have a h. on** or **over sb** tener poder sobre alguien
(b) (in wrestling) llave f; Fig **no holds barred** sin límites
(c) **to put sth on h.** suspender algo temporalmente; Tel **to put sb on h.** poner a alguien a la espera

**(d)** *(of ship)* bodega *f*

**2** *vt* (*pt & pp* **held** [held]) **(a)** *(grip)* coger, sujetar, *Am* agarrar; *(embrace)* abrazar; **h. this!** ¡sujeta esto!; **to h. sth/sb tight** coger *or* sujetar algo/a alguien fuerte; **they held hands** estaban agarrados(as) de la mano; **to h. sth in position** sujetar algo sin que se mueva; **to h. sb prisoner** retener a alguien como prisionero; **the police are holding him for questioning** la policía lo tiene retenido para interrogarlo; **to h. sb's interest/attention** mantener el interés/la atención de alguien; **to h. sb to his promise** hacer que alguien cumpla su promesa; **to h. one's breath** contener el aliento; **there's no holding him** no hay quien lo pare; **h. your tongue!** ¡cierra la boca!; *Fam* **h. it!, h. your horses!** ¡para el carro!; *Mus* **to h. a note** sostener una nota; *Tel* **h. the line** espere un momento, no cuelgue

**(b)** *(keep)* *(ticket, room)* guardar, reservar; **to h. a town** tener tomada una ciudad; **to h. one's position** mantener la posición; *Fig* **to h. one's ground** mantenerse en sus trece; **to h. one's own** resistir, mantenerse; **to h. one's own against sb** no desmerecer frente a alguien

**(c)** *(carry)* **to h. one's head high** llevar la cabeza bien alta; **to h. oneself well** mantenerse erguido(a)

**(d)** *(contain)* contener; **the stadium holds over 20,000** el estadio tiene capacidad *or* cabida para más de 20.000 espectadores; *Fig* **to h. water** *(of theory, story)* no hacer agua; **nobody knows what the future holds** nadie sabe lo que deparará el futuro; **it holds no interest for me** no tiene ningún interés para mí

**(e)** *(conduct)* *(negotiations, meeting)* llevar a cabo; *(conversation)* mantener

**(f)** *(possess)* *(title, rank)* poseer; *(job, position)* ocupar; *(opinion)* mantener; *(record)* ostentar; **she had held office before** ya antes había ocupado un cargo

**(g)** *(consider)* **to h. sb responsible** hacer a alguien responsable; **to be held in respect** ser respetado(a); **to h. that…** sostener que…

**3** *vi* **(a)** *(of rope)* resistir, aguantar; **h. tight!** ¡agárrate bien!

**(b)** *(of agreement, weather)* mantenerse; **if your luck holds** si sigues teniendo suerte; **the same holds (true) for everyone** lo mismo es válido para todos

▸**hold against** *vt sep* **to h. sth against sb** tener algo contra alguien

▸**hold back 1** *vt sep* *(person, emotion)* contener; *(progress, project)* impedir el avance de; **he's holding something back** se está guardando algo

**2** *vi* *(refrain)* contenerse; **to h. back from doing sth** abstenerse de hacer algo

▸**hold down** *vt sep* **(a)** *(restrain)* *(person)* sujetar; *(taxes, prices)* mantener a un nivel bajo

**(b)** **to h. down a job** conservar un trabajo

▸**hold forth** *vi* explayarse

▸**hold off 1** *vt sep* *(keep at bay)* rechazar; **she held off making a decision until she had more information** pospuso su decisión hasta disponer de más datos

**2** *vi* *(delay)* **the rain is holding off** no se decide a llover

▸**hold on** *vi* **(a)** *(endure)* resistir, aguantar **(b)** *(wait)* esperar; **h. on (a minute)!** ¡espera (un momento)! **(c)** **h. on (tight)!** ¡agárrate (fuerte)!

▸**hold on to** *vt insep* **(a)** *(grip tightly)* *(to stop something from falling)* agarrarse a; *(to stop something from falling)* agarrar; *Fig* *(idea, hope)* aferrarse a **(b)** *(keep)* guardar, conservar

▸**hold out 1** *vt sep* *(one's hand)* tender; *(hope, opportunity)* ofrecer; **I don't h. out much hope that…** tengo pocas esperanzas de que…

**2** *vi* **(a)** *(resist)* resistir; **to h. out for a better offer** aguantar a la espera de una oferta mejor **(b)** *(of supplies)* durar

▸**hold over** *vt sep* diferir, posponer

▸**hold together 1** *vt sep* *(party, marriage, alliance)* mantener unido(a); *(with glue, string, rope)* sujetar

**2** *vi* *(party, marriage, alliance)* mantenerse unido(a)

▸**hold up 1** *vt sep* **(a)** *(support)* soportar, aguantar **(b)** *(raise)* levantar, alzar; *Fig* **to h. sb up as an example** poner a alguien como ejemplo **(c)** *(delay)* retrasar **(d)** *(rob)* atracar

**2** *vi* *(of theory, alibi)* tenerse en pie; *(of good weather)* aguantar; **she's holding up well under the pressure** está aguantando bien las presiones

▸**hold with** *vt insep* *(behaviour)* aprobar; **I don't h. with his opinions** no estoy de acuerdo con sus opiniones

**holdall** ['hǝuldɔ:l] *n* bolsa *f* *(de viaje o de deporte)*

**holder** ['hǝuldǝ(r)] *n* **(a)** *(of record, trophy, ticket)* poseedor(ora) *m,f*; *(of passport, licence, permit)* titular *mf*; *(of belief, opinion)* defensor(ora) *m,f* **(b)** *(device)* soporte *m*

**holding** ['hǝuldɪŋ] *n* **(a)** *(property)* propiedad *f*; *(of shares)* participación *f*; *Com* **h. company** holding *m* **(b)** *Mil* **h. operation** maniobra *f* de contención

**hold-up** ['hǝuldʌp] *n* **(a)** *(delay)* *(in plan)* retraso *m*; *(of traffic)* retención *f* **(b)** *(armed robbery)* atraco *m*

**hole** [hǝul] **1** *n* **(a)** *(in roof, clothing)* agujero *m*; *(in ground)* hoyo *m*, agujero *m*; *(animal's burrow)* madriguera *f*; *(in golf)* hoyo *m*; **to make a h. in sth** hacer un agujero en algo; **the holiday made a h. in their savings** las vacaciones dejaron maltrecha su economía; *Fig* **to pick holes in sth** *(in argument, theory)* encontrar defectos en *or* a algo; *Fig* a h. **in the law** un vacío legal; **h. in one** *(in golf)* hoyo *m* en uno; *Fam Fig* **to be in a h.** *(in difficulty)* estar en un brete

(b) *Fam Fig (room, house)* cuchitril *m*; *(town)* lugar *m* de mala muerte

**2** vt (a) *(make a hole in)* agujerear

(b) *(in golf)* **to h. a shot** embocar la bola

▸**hole up** vi *Fam (hide)* esconderse

**holiday** ['hɒlɪdeɪ] **1** n (a) *Br (vacation)* vacaciones *fpl*; **to go on h.** irse de vacaciones; **h. camp** centro *m* turístico, colonia *f* turística; **h. home** segunda residencia *f*, casa *f* para las vacaciones; **h. season** temporada *f* de vacaciones

(b) *(day off)* (día *m* de) fiesta *f*

**2** vi pasar las vacaciones; *(in summer)* veranear

**holidaymaker** ['hɒlɪdeɪˌmeɪkə(r)] n turista *mf*; *(in summer)* veraneante *mf*

**holiness** ['həʊlɪnɪs] n santidad *f*; **Your H.** Su Santidad

**holistic** [həʊ'lɪstɪk] adj holístico(a)

**Holland** ['hɒlənd] n Holanda

**holler** ['hɒlə(r)] vi *Fam* gritar, dar voces

**hollow** ['hɒləʊ] **1** n hueco *m*; *(in ground)* depresión *f*

**2** adj (a) *(container, log)* hueco(a); *(cheek, eyes)* hundido(a) (b) *(sound)* hueco(a), resonante; **in a h. voice** con voz hueca; **a h. laugh** una risa sardónica (c) *(promise, guarantee)* vacío(a); **h. victory** victoria *f* deslucida

**3** adv (a) **to sound h.** sonar a hueco (b) *Fam* **to beat sb h.** dar una (buena) paliza a alguien

▸**hollow out** vt sep ahuecar, vaciar

**holly** ['hɒli] n acebo *m*

**hollyhock** ['hɒlihɒk] n malvarrosa *f*

**holocaust** ['hɒləkɔːst] n holocausto *m*

**hologram** ['hɒləgræm] n holograma *m*

**holster** ['həʊlstə(r)] n pistolera *f*

**holy** ['həʊli] adj santo(a); **the H. Bible** la Sagrada Biblia; *Fam* **h. cow** *or* **smoke** *or* **mackerel!** ¡madre del amor hermoso!; **H. Communion** la comunión; **the H. Father** el Santo Padre; **the H. Ghost** *or* **Spirit** el Espíritu Santo; *Fam Pej* **H. Joe** meapilas *mf inv*; **the H. Land** Tierra Santa; **h. orders** sagradas órdenes *fpl*; **h. war** guerra *f* santa; **h. water** agua *f* bendita; **H. Week** Semana *f* Santa

**homage** ['hɒmɪdʒ] n homenaje *m*; **to pay h. to sth/sb** rendir homenaje a algo/alguien

**home** [həʊm] **1** n (a) *(house)* casa *f*; *(of animal, plant)* hábitat *m*; *(family)* hogar *m*; **at h.** en casa; **to feel at h.** sentirse como en casa; **make yourself at h.** estás en tu casa, ponte cómodo; **to leave h.** *(in the morning)* salir de casa; *(one's parents' home)* independizarse, irse de casa; **to be away from h.** estar fuera (de casa); *Sport* **to be** *or* **play at h.** jugar en casa; **to have a h. of one's own** tener casa propia; **it's a h. from h.** es como estar en casa; **to make one's h. in…**

asentarse en…; **children's/old people's h.** residencia *f* infantil/de ancianos; **h. address** domicilio *m*; **h. banking** telebanco *m*; **h. brew** cerveza *f* casera; **h. cooking** cocina *f* casera; *Br* **the H. Counties** = los condados de alrededor de Londres; **h. economics** *(school subject)* economía *f* doméstica; **h. help** ayuda *f* doméstica; **h. life** vida *f* doméstica; *Fin* **h. loan** crédito *m* hipotecario, hipoteca *f*; **h. movie** vídeo *m* casero *or* doméstico; **h. owner** propietario(a) *m,f* de vivienda; *Comptr* **h. page** portada *f* de página Web, página *f* inicial *or* de inicio; *US Sch* **h. room** = aula donde cada alumno debe presentarse todas las mañanas; **h. run** *(in baseball)* carrera *f* completa, home run *m*; **the h. straight** *(in athletics)* la recta final; **h. town** ciudad *f*/pueblo *m* natal; **to tell sb a few h. truths** decirle a alguien cuatro verdades

(b) *(country, region)* tierra *f*; **at h. and abroad** nacional e internacionalmente; **an example nearer h.** un ejemplo más cercano; **Milan, the h. of fashion** Milán, la meca *or* la cuna de la moda; **h. front** frente *m* civil; *TV & Journ* **h. news** noticias *fpl* nacionales; *Pol* **H. Office** Ministerio *m* del Interior; *Pol* **h. rule** autonomía *f*, autogobierno *m*; *Br Pol* **the H. Secretary** el ministro del Interior

**2** adv (a) *(in general)* a casa; **to go/come h.** ir/venir a casa; **to be h.** estar en casa; **to send sb h.** mandar a alguien a casa

(b) *(all the way)* **he drove the knife h.** hundió el cuchillo hasta el fondo; **to bring sth h. to sb** dejar bien claro algo a alguien

▸**home in on** vt insep *(on target)* apuntar a, dirigirse a; *(on mistake, evidence)* señalar, concentrarse en

**homecoming** ['həʊmkʌmɪŋ] n regreso *m* a casa, recepción *f*

**home-grown** ['həʊm'grəʊn] adj *(from own garden)* de cosecha propia; *Fig (not imported)* del país

**homeland** ['həʊmlænd] n tierra *f* natal, país *m*

**homeless** ['həʊmlɪs] **1** adj sin techo, sin hogar

**2** npl **the h.** las personas sin techo, los sin techo

**homely** ['həʊmli] adj (a) *Br (welcoming)* *(person, atmosphere)* hogareño(a) (b) *US (ugly)* feúcho(a)

**home-made** ['həʊm'meɪd] adj casero(a)

**homeopath** ['həʊmɪəʊpæθ] n homeópata *mf*

**homeopathic** [həʊmɪəʊ'pæθɪk] adj homeopático(a)

**homeopathy** [həʊmɪ'ɒpəθɪ] n homeopatía *f*

**homesick** ['həʊmsɪk] adj nostálgico(a); **to be** *or* **feel h. (for)** tener morriña (de)

**homesickness** ['həʊmsɪknɪs] n morriña f

**homespun** ['həʊmspʌn] adj Fig (wisdom, advice) de andar por casa

**homestead** ['həʊmsted] n finca f, hacienda f

**homeward** ['həʊmwəd] 1 adj de vuelta a casa

2 adv a casa; **to be h. bound** estar de regreso a casa

**homewards** ['həʊmwədz] adv = **homeward**

**homework** ['həʊmwɜ:k] n Sch deberes mpl; also Fig **to do one's h.** hacer los deberes

**homicidal** [hɒmɪ'saɪdəl] adj homicida

**homicide** ['hɒmɪsaɪd] n homicidio m

**homily** ['hɒmɪlɪ] n Rel homilía f; Fig sermón m

**homing** ['həʊmɪŋ] adj **h. device** (of missile) sistema m de guiado pasivo; **h. pigeon** paloma f mensajera

**homogeneous** [hɒmə'dʒi:nɪəs, hə'mɒdʒɪnəs] adj homogéneo(a)

**homogenize** [hɒ'mɒdʒənaɪz] vt homogeneizar

**homonym** ['hɒmənɪm] n homónimo m

**homophobia** [hɒmə'fəʊbɪə] n homofobia f

**homosexual** [hɒmə'seksjʊəl] n & adj homosexual mf

**homosexuality** [hɒməseksjʊ'ælɪtɪ] n homosexualidad f

**Hon** Br Parl (abbr **the Honourable**) the H. **member (for...)** el/la señor(ora) diputado(a) (por...)

**honcho** ['hɒntʃəʊ] n Fam the head h. el/la mandamás

**Honduran** [hɒn'djʊərən] n & adj hondureño(a) m,f

**Honduras** [hɒn'djʊərəs] n Honduras

**hone** [həʊn] vt afilar

**honest** ['ɒnɪst] adj (trustworthy) honrado(a); (truthful) sincero(a); **he has an h. face** tiene aspecto de honrado; **the h. truth** la pura verdad; **I don't think he was being h. with me** creo que no me estaba diciendo la verdad; **to be h., I don't know** la verdad es que no lo sé; **to earn an h. living** ganarse honradamente la vida; esp Hum **to make an h. woman of sb** (marry) llevar a alguien al altar

**honestly** ['ɒnɪstlɪ] adv (a) (legitimately) honradamente; **to obtain sth h.** conseguir algo honradamente

(b) (sincerely) sinceramente; **I can h. say that...** puedo decir sin faltar a la verdad que...; **h., I'm fine/it doesn't matter** en serio que estoy bien/no importa; **I can't h. remember** la verdad es que no me acuerdo

(c) (expressing indignation) **well h.!** ¡desde luego!, ¡hay que ver!; **h.! some people!** ¡desde luego, hay cada uno por ahí!

**honesty** ['ɒnɪstɪ] n (trustworthiness) honradez f; (truthfulness) sinceridad f; **in all h.** con toda sinceridad; Prov **h. is the best policy** lo mejor es decir la verdad

**honey** ['hʌnɪ] n (a) (food) miel f (b) US Fam (term of endearment) cariño m, cielo m

**honeycomb** ['hʌnɪkəʊm] 1 n panal m

2 vt **the mountain is honeycombed with tunnels** el interior de la montaña es un entramado de túneles

**honeymoon** ['hʌnɪmu:n] 1 n luna f de miel, viaje m de novios; Fig **the h. is over** se acabó el periodo de gracia

2 vi pasar la luna de miel, estar de viaje de novios

**honeysuckle** ['hʌnɪsʌkəl] n madreselva f

**Hong Kong** ['hɒŋ'kɒŋ] n Hong Kong

**honk** [hɒŋk] 1 n (of goose) graznido m; (of car horn) bocinazo m

2 vi (of goose) graznar; (of car driver) tocar la bocina or el claxon, dar bocinazos

**honky** ['hɒŋkɪ] n US very Fam = término ofensivo para referirse a un blanco

**honor, honorable** etc US = **honour, honourable** etc

**honorary** ['ɒnərərɪ] adj honorífico(a), honorario(a); Univ **h. degree** título m honoris causa

**honour,** US **honor** ['ɒnə(r)] 1 n (a) (respect) honor m; (pride) honor f; **in h.** of en honor de; **this is a great h.** es un gran honor; **to have the h. of doing sth** tener el honor de hacer algo; Hum **to what do I owe this h.?** ¿a qué debo semejante honor o privilegio?; **Your H.** (judge) Señoría

(b) (good name) honor m, honra f; **to feel h. bound to do sth** sentirse moralmente obligado(a) a hacer algo; **on my (word of) h.!** ¡palabra de honor!; Prov **(there is) h. among thieves** hasta los ladrones tienen sus reglas

(c) (award, distinction) **honours list** relación f de condecorados; **honours degree** licenciatura f (necesaria para realizar un máster); **he was buried with full military honours** fue enterrado con todos los honores militares; Hum **to do the honours** (serve food or drink) hacer los honores

2 vt (a) (person) honrar; **I felt honoured that they had invited me** me honró mucho su invitación

(b) (fulfil) (commitment, obligation) cumplir; (debt, cheque) pagar

**honourable,** US **honorable** ['ɒnərəbəl] adj honorable; Br Parl **the H. member for Caithness** el señor diputado por Caithness; **h. mention** mención f honorífica

**honourably,** US **honorably** ['ɒnərəblɪ] adv honorablemente

**hooch** [hu:tʃ] n US Fam (liquor) alcohol m (destilado clandestinamente)

**hood** [hʊd] n (a) (of coat, cloak) capucha f; Br (of car, pram) capota f; US (car bonnet) capó m; (over cooker, fireplace) campana f (extractora) (b) US Fam (gangster) matón m

**hoodlum** ['hu:dləm] n Fam matón m

**hoodwink** ['hʊdwɪŋk] vt Fam timar, engañar

**hoof** [hu:f] 1 n (pl hooves [hu:vz]) (of horse) casco m; (of cattle, deer, sheep) pezuña f
 2 vt Fam to h. it ir a pata

**hoo-ha** ['hu:hɑ:] n Fam (fuss) jaleo m, alboroto m

**hook** [hʊk] 1 n (a) (in general) gancho m; (for coats) colgador m; (on dress) corchete m; (for fishing) anzuelo m; (for hanging pictures) escarpia f, alcayata f; **to leave the phone off the** h. dejar el teléfono descolgado; Fam Fig **to get sb off the** h. (get out of trouble) sacar a alguien del apuro; Fam **he swallowed it** h., **line and sinker** (believed it) se tragó el anzuelo; Fam **by h. or by crook** sea como sea (b) (in boxing) gancho m
 2 vt enganchar; **to** h. **one's legs around sth** rodear algo con las piernas; **to** h. **a fish** pescar un pez (con anzuelo)

▶**hook up 1** vt sep TV & Comptr conectar
 2 vi (of dress) abrocharse (b) Comptr conectar (**with** con or a)

**hooked** [hʊkt] adj (a) h. **nose** nariz f aguileña (b) Fam **to be** h. **on sth** estar enganchado(a) a algo

**hooker** ['hʊkər] n (a) Br (in rugby) talon(e)ador m (b) US Fam (prostitute) fulana f, puta f

**hooky** ['hʊkɪ] n US Fam **to play** h. hacer novillos

**hooligan** ['hu:lɪgən] n gamberro(a) m,f, vándalo(a) m,f

**hooliganism** ['hu:lɪgənɪzəm] n gamberrismo m, vandalismo m

**hoop** [hu:p] n aro m; Fig **to put sb through the hoops** (test thoroughly) poner a alguien a prueba

**hooray** [hʊ'reɪ] exclam ¡hurra!

**hoot** [hu:t] 1 n (a) (of owl) ululato m; (of horn, factory whistle) bocinazo m; **hoots of laughter** risotadas fpl; Fam Fig **I don't give a** h. or **two hoots** me importa un bledo (b) Fam **he's a** h.! ¡es un cachondo!; **it was a** h.! ¡fue un cachondeo!
 2 vi (of owl) ulular; (of car) dar bocinazos; (of train) pitar; **to** h. **with laughter** reírse a carcajadas

**hooter** ['hu:tə(r)] n Br (a) (of ship, factory) sirena f; (of car) bocina f, claxon m (b) Fam (nose) napias fpl

**hoover**® ['hu:və(r)] 1 n aspiradora f, aspirador m
 2 vt (room) aspirar, pasar la aspiradora por

**hooves** [hu:vz] pl of **hoof**

**hop** [hɒp] 1 n (jump) salto m, brinco m; Fam (on plane) vuelo m corto; Fam (dance) baile m; Fam Fig **to catch sb on the** h. coger desprevenido(a) a alguien
 2 vt (pt & pp hopped) Fam h. **it!** ¡lárgate!
 3 vi (jump) saltar, brincar; **to** h. **out of bed** salir de la cama de un salto; Fam h. **in!** (to car) ¡sube!

▶**hop off** vi Fam largarse

**hope** [həʊp] 1 n esperanza f; **in the** h. **of (doing) sth** con la esperanza de (hacer) algo; **in the** h. **that...** con la esperanza de que...; **there is little** h. **(of)** hay pocas esperanzas (de); **there is no** h. **(of)** no hay esperanza(s) (de); **to have (high) hopes of doing sth** tener (grandes) esperanzas de hacer algo; **to get one's hopes up** hacerse ilusiones; **to raise (sb's) hopes** dar esperanzas a alguien; **she hasn't got a** h. **of winning** no tiene posibilidad alguna de ganar; Ironic **what a** h.!, **some** h.! ¡no caerá esa breva!; **we live in** h.! la esperanza es lo último que se pierde
 2 vt **to** h. **to do sth** esperar hacer algo; **I** h. **to see you again** espero volverte a ver; **I** h. **(that) your brother is better** espero que tu hermano esté mejor; **I** h. **you are right** ojalá tengas razón; **we** h. **and pray that...** ojalá que...; **I** h. **so** eso espero; **I** h. **not** espero que no
 3 vi esperar; **don't** h. **for too much** no esperes demasiado; **to** h. **for the best** esperar (que pase) lo mejor; **we must** h. **against** h. no debemos perder la esperanza

**hopeful** ['həʊpfʊl] 1 n Fam **a young** h. un/una joven con aspiraciones
 2 adj (situation) prometedor(ora); **we are** h. **that...** esperamos que...

**hopefully** ['həʊpfʊlɪ] adv (a) (in a hopeful manner) esperanzadamente (b) (it is to be hoped) h. **not** esperemos que no; h. **we will have found him by then** con un poco de suerte, para entonces ya le habremos encontrado

**hopeless** ['həʊplɪs] adj (a) (without hope) (person) desesperanzado(a), sin esperanza; (situation) desesperado(a); **it's** h.! ¡es inútil!; **a** h. **cause** una causa perdida (b) Fam (very bad) malísimo(a); **to be** h. **at maths/cooking** ser un(a) negado(a) para las matemáticas/la cocina

**hopelessly** ['həʊplɪslɪ] adv (a) (inconsolably) desesperadamente (b) (completely) totalmente; **he was** h. **in love with her** estaba desesperadamente enamorado de ella

**hopping** ['hɒpɪŋ] adv Fam **to be** h. **mad** estar hecho(a) un basilisco

**hops** [hɒps] *npl* lúpulo *m*

**hopscotch** ['hɒpskɒtʃ] *n* tejo *m*, rayuela *f*

**horde** [hɔːd] *n* horda *f*

**horizon** [ha'raizən] *n* horizonte *m*; **there is a general election on the h.** hay elecciones generales a la vista

**horizontal** [hɒrɪ'zɒntəl] **1** *n* horizontal *f*
**2** *adj* horizontal

**horizontally** [hɒrɪ'zɒntəlɪ] *adv* horizontalmente

**hormonal** [hɔː'məʊnəl] *adj* hormonal

**hormone** ['hɔːməʊn] *n* hormona *f*; *Med* **h. replacement therapy** terapia *f* hormonal sustitutiva

**horn** [hɔːn] *n* (a) *(of animal)* cuerno *m* (b) *(musical instrument)* trompa *f*; *(on car)* bocina *f*, claxon *m*; **to sound one's h.** *(in car)* tocar la bocina *or* el claxon (c) *(idioms)* **to be on the horns of a dilemma** estar entre la espada y la pared

**horned** [hɔːnd] *adj* con cuernos

**hornet** ['hɔːnɪt] *n* avispón *m*; *Fig* **to stir up a h.'s nest** remover un avispero

**hornpipe** ['hɔːnpaɪp] *n (dance, music)* aire *m* marinero

**horn-rimmed** ['hɔːnrɪmd] *adj* **h. spectacles** *or* **glasses** gafas *fpl* de (montura de) concha

**horny** ['hɔːnɪ] *adj* (a) *(hands)* calloso(a), encallecido(a) (b) *very Fam (sexually aroused)* cachondo(a), calentorro(a); *US (sexually attractive)* buenorro(a)

**horoscope** ['hɒrəskəʊp] *n* horóscopo *m*

**horrendous** [hɒ'rendəs] *adj* horrendo(a), espantoso(a)

**horrendously** [hɒ'rendəslɪ] *adv Fam (expensive, complicated)* terriblemente

**horrible** ['hɒrəbəl] *adj* (a) *(unpleasant)* horrible; **how h.!** ¡qué horror! (b) *(unkind)* antipático(a); **to be h. to sb** ser muy antipático(a) con alguien

**horribly** ['hɒrɪblɪ] *adv* espantosamente, horriblemente

**horrid** ['hɒrɪd] *adj* (a) *(unpleasant)* espantoso(a) (b) *(unkind)* antipático(a); **to be h. to sb** ser muy antipático con alguien

**horrific** [hɒ'rɪfɪk] *adj* horrible, espantoso(a)

**horrify** ['hɒrɪfaɪ] *vt* horrorizar

**horrifying** ['hɒrɪfaɪɪŋ] *adj* horroroso(a)

**horror** ['hɒrə(r)] *n (feeling, terrifying thing)* horror *m*; **to my h. I saw that…** me horroricé al ver que…; **to have a h. of sth** tener pánico *or* horror a algo; *Fam* **that child's a little h.** ese niño es un monstruo; **h. film** película *f* de terror; **h. story** cuento *m* de terror

**horror-stricken** ['hɒrəstrɪkən], **horror-struck** ['hɒrəstrʌk] *adj* horrorizado(a)

**horse** [hɔːs] *n* (a) *(animal, gym apparatus)* caballo *m*; **h. chestnut** *(tree)* castaño *m* de Indias; **h. racing** carreras *fpl* de caballos; **I like h. riding** me gusta montar a caballo; *Fig* **h. trading** negociaciones *fpl* entre bastidores (b) *(idioms)* **to eat like a h.** comer como una lima; **to get up on one's high h.** darse ínfulas; **to hear sth from the h.'s mouth** haber oído algo de boca del propio interesado

▸**horse about, horse around** *vi* hacer el indio

**horseback** ['hɔːsbæk] *n* **on h.** a caballo

**horsebox** ['hɔːsbɒks] *n* remolque *m* para caballos

**horse-drawn** ['hɔːsdrɔːn] *adj* de tiro, de caballos

**horsefly** ['hɔːsflaɪ] *n* tábano *m*

**horsehair** ['hɔːsheə(r)] *n* crin *f*, crines *fpl*; **h. mattress** colchón *m* de crin

**horseman** ['hɔːsmən] *n* jinete *m*

**horsemanship** ['hɔːsmənʃɪp] *n* equitación *f*, manejo *m* del caballo

**horseplay** ['hɔːspleɪ] *n* retozo *m*, jugueteo *m*

**horsepower** ['hɔːspaʊə(r)] *n Tech* caballos *mpl* de vapor

**horseradish** ['hɔːsrædɪʃ] *n* rábano *m* silvestre

**horseshoe** ['hɔːsʃuː] *n* herradura *f*

**horsewhip** ['hɔːswɪp] **1** *n* fusta *f*
**2** *vt (pt & pp horsewhipped)* azotar

**horsewoman** ['hɔːswʊmən] *n* amazona *f*

**horsy, horsey** ['hɔːsɪ] *adj* (a) *(horse-like)* caballuno(a) (b) *(keen on horses)* aficionado(a) a los caballos (c) *Br Fam (upper class)* pijo(a)

**horticultural** [hɔːtɪ'kʌltʃərəl] *adj* hortícola

**horticulture** ['hɔːtɪkʌltʃə(r)] *n* horticultura *f*

**hose** [həʊz] **1** *n (pipe)* manguera *f*
**2** *vt* regar con manguera

▸**hose down** *vt sep* limpiar con manguera

**hosepipe** ['həʊzpaɪp] *n* manguera *f*

**hosiery** ['həʊzɪərɪ] *n* calcetines *mpl* y medias

**hospice** ['hɒspɪs] *n (for the terminally ill)* hospital *m* para enfermos terminales

**hospitable** [hɒs'pɪtəbəl] *adj* hospitalario(a)

**hospitably** [hɒs'pɪtəblɪ] *adv* hospitalariamente

**hospital** ['hɒspɪtəl] *n* hospital *m*; **h. bed** cama *f* de hospital; **h. care** atención *f* hospitalaria

**hospitality** [hɒspɪ'tælɪtɪ] *n* hospitalidad *f*

**hospitalize** ['hɒspɪtəlaɪz] *vt* hospitalizar

**host**[1] [həʊst] **1** *n* (a) *(at home, party)* anfitrión *m*; *(on TV)* presentador(ora) *m,f*; **h. country** país *m* anfitrión *or* organizador (b) *Biol (of parasite)* huésped *m*
**2** *vt (party)* dar; *(TV show)* presentar

**host²** n (great number) **a whole h. of** un sinfín de

**host³** n Rel (consecrated bread) hostia f

**hostage** ['hɒstɪdʒ] n rehén m; **to take/hold sb h.** tomar/tener a alguien como rehén; Fig **that's offering a h. to fortune** eso supone hipotecar el futuro

**hostel** ['hɒstəl] n residencia f; **youth h.** albergue m juvenil

**hostelling**, US **hosteling** ['hɒstəlɪŋ] n **to go h.** ir de albergues

**hostess** ['həʊstɪs] n (in private house) anfitriona f; (on TV) azafata f; (air) **h.** azafata f

**hostile** ['hɒstaɪl, US 'hɒstəl] adj hostil (**to a, con**); **to be h. to** ser hostil a, mostrarse hostil ante

**hostility** [hɒs'tɪlɪtɪ] n hostilidad f; **hostilities** (war) hostilidades fpl

**hot** [hɒt] adj (**a**) (having high temperature) caliente; (day, summer, climate) caluroso(a); **to be h.** (of person) tener calor; (of thing) estar caliente; **it's h.** (of weather) hace calor; Med **h. flushes** sofocos mpl; US **h. tub** jacuzzi® m; **h. water bottle** bolsa f de agua caliente

(**b**) (spicy) picante

(**c**) (close) **you're getting h.** (in guessing game) caliente, caliente; **to be h. on sb's/sth's trail** estar pisando los talones a alguien/algo

(**d**) Fam (good) **to be h. on sth** (be knowledgeable about) estar muy puesto(a) en algo; (attach importance to) ser muy quisquilloso(a) con algo; **it wasn't such a h. idea** no fue una idea tan buena; **how are you? – not so h.** ¿qué tal? – regular

(**e**) Fam (sexy) caliente

(**f**) Fam (stolen) afanado(a), chorizado(a)

(**g**) (idioms) **h. from the press** (of news) caliente; (of book) recién salido(a) (de la imprenta); **too h. to handle** (issue) demasiado comprometido(a); **to have a h. temper** tener mal genio; **to get h. under the collar** (become indignant) acalorarse; Fam **h. air** (meaningless talk) palabras fpl vanas; **Fam it's all h. air** no son más que fanfarronadas; **they're selling like h. cakes** se venden como churros; **a h. favourite** (in race) un/una gran favorito(a); **h. gossip** cotilleo m jugoso; Fam **h. line** línea f directa; **h. news** noticias fpl frescas; Fam **h. potato** (controversial issue) patata f caliente, asunto m espinoso; **to be in the h. seat** ser el responsable; **h. spot** (trouble spot) zona f conflictiva; Fam **to be in h. water** (in difficult situation) estar en apuros

▸**hot up** (pt & pp **hotted**) vi Fam (of situation, contest) calentarse

**hot-air balloon** ['hɒteəb'luːn] n globo m de aire caliente, aerostato m

**hotbed** ['hɒtbed] n **a h. of rebellion/intrigue** un foco de rebelión/intrigas

**hot-blooded** ['hɒt'blʌdɪd] adj (**a**) (passionate) ardiente (**b**) (excitable) irascible

**hotchpotch** ['hɒtʃpɒtʃ] n Fam batiburrillo m, revoltijo m

**hotdog** ['hɒtdɒg] n perrito m caliente

**hotel** [həʊ'tel] n hotel m; **h. room** habitación f (de hotel); **h. manager** director(ora) m,f de hotel

**hotelier** [həʊ'teljər] n hotelero(a) m,f

**hotfoot** ['hɒt'fʊt] Fam **1** adv a la carrera, zumbando

**2** vt **to h. it** ir a la carrera, ir zumbando

**hothead** ['hɒthed] n impulsivo(a) m,f, impetuoso(a) m,f

**hot-headed** ['hɒt'hedɪd] adj impulsivo(a), impetuoso(a)

**hothouse** ['hɒthaʊs] n (glasshouse) invernadero m; Fig hervidero m

**hotly** ['hɒtlɪ] adv (to reply, protest) acaloradamente; **h. contested** reñidamente disputado(a)

**hotplate** ['hɒtpleɪt] n (on cooker) placa f; (for keeping food warm) = placa para mantener la comida caliente

**hotpot** ['hɒtpɒt] n (stew) estofado m

**hots** [hɒts] npl very Fam **she had the h. for him** le ponía a cien or muy caliente

**hotshot** ['hɒtʃɒt] n Fam (expert) as m, hacha m

**hot-tempered** ['hɒt'tempəd] adj enfadadizo(a), con mal genio

**hot-water** ['hɒt'wɔːtə(r)] adj de agua caliente; **h. bottle** bolsa f de agua caliente

**hound** [haʊnd] **1** n (dog) perro m de caza

**2** vt (persecute) acosar; **she was hounded by the press** la prensa la acosaba

**hour** ['aʊə(r)] n (**a**) (period of time) hora f; **an h. and a half** una hora y media; **half an h.** media hora; **to pay sb by the h.** pagar a alguien por horas; **to take hours over sth** tardar horas en algo; **we've been waiting for hours** llevamos horas esperando; **to work long hours** trabajar muchas horas; **to keep late hours** acostarse muy tarde; **h. hand** (of watch, clock) manecilla f de las horas

(**b**) (time of day) **at this h.!** ¡a estas horas!; **till all hours** hasta las tantas; **where were you in my h. of need?** ¿dónde estabas cuando te necesitaba?; **his h. has come** ha llegado su hora

**hourglass** ['aʊəglɑːs] n reloj m de arena; **an h. figure** una cintura de avispa

**hourly** ['aʊəlɪ] **1** adj **at h. intervals** con intervalos de una hora

**2** adv (every hour) cada hora; (at any time) en cualquier momento

**house 1** *n* [haʊs] **(a)** *(dwelling)* casa *f*, *Fig* **to set one's h. in order** poner uno sus cosas en orden; **to get on like a h. on fire** llevarse estupendamente; **the h. of God** la casa del Señor; **the H. of Commons/Lords** la cámara de los comunes/lores; **the Houses of Parliament** el Parlamento británico; **the H. of Representatives** la cámara de representantes; **the H. of Stuart/Bourbon** la casa de los Estuardo/los Borbones; *Law* **h. arrest** arresto *m* domiciliario; **h. guest** huésped *mf*, invitado(a) *m,f*; **h. martin** avión *m* común; **h. painter** pintor(ora) *m,f* de brocha gorda; **h. party** fiesta *f* (*en una casa de campo*); **h. plant** planta *f* de interior; **h. surgeon** (*in hospital*) cirujano(a) *m,f* residente

**(b)** *(music)* (música *f*) house *m*

**(f)** *Br Sch* = división que se hace de los alumnos de cada curso para la realización de actividades no académicas

**2** *vt* [haʊz] (*person, collection, mechanism*) alojar

**houseboat** ['haʊsbəʊt] *n* barco-vivienda *m*

**housebound** ['haʊsbaʊnd] *adj* **to be h.** estar confinado(a) en casa

**housebreaker** ['haʊsbreɪkə(r)] *n* ladrón(ona) *m,f*

**housebreaking** ['haʊsbreɪkɪŋ] *n* allanamiento *m* de morada

**housecoat** ['haʊskəʊt] *n* bata *f* de (estar en) casa

**housefly** ['haʊsflaɪ] *n* mosca *f* (doméstica)

**household** ['haʊshəʊld] *n* hogar *m*; **h. appliance** electrodoméstico *m*; **h. chores** tareas *fpl* domésticas; **to be a h. name** (*of famous person*) ser un nombre conocidísimo

**householder** ['haʊshəʊldə(r)] *n* ocupante *mf* de vivienda

**househusband** ['haʊshʌzbənd] *n* amo *m* de casa

**housekeeper** ['haʊskiːpə(r)] *n* ama *f* de llaves

**housekeeping** ['haʊskiːpɪŋ] *n* **h. (money)** dinero *m* para los gastos domésticos

**housemaid** ['haʊsmeɪd] *n* doncella *f*, criada *f*; **h.'s knee** (*inflammation*) bursitis *f inv* de rodilla

**houseman** ['haʊsmən] *n* *Br Med* médico(a) *m,f* interno(a) residente

**housemaster** ['haʊsmɑːstə(r)] *n* *Br Sch* = profesor a cargo de una "house" (división para actividades no académicas)

**housemistress** ['haʊsmɪstrɪs] *n* *Br Sch* = profesora a cargo de una "house" (división para actividades no académicas)

**house-proud** ['haʊspraʊd] *adj* **she's very h.** es una mujer muy de su casa

**houseroom** ['haʊsruːm] *n* **I wouldn't give it h.** (*of theory, suggestion*) yo no lo aceptaría

**house-to-house** ['haʊstə'haʊs] *adj* (*search*) de casa en casa

**house-trained** ['haʊstreɪnd] *adj* (*dog*) = que ya ha aprendido a no hacer sus necesidades en casa; *Hum* (*husband*) bien enseñado

**house-warming** ['haʊswɔːmɪŋ] *n* **h. (party)** fiesta *f* de inauguración (*de un piso, de una casa*)

**housewife** ['haʊswaɪf] *n* ama *f* de casa

**housework** ['haʊswɜːk] *n* tareas *fpl* domésticas

**housing** ['haʊzɪŋ] *n* vivienda *f*; *Br* **h. association** cooperativa *f* de viviendas; *Br* **h. benefit** = subsidio para el pago del alquiler; *Br* **h. estate** (*public housing*) ≃ viviendas *fpl* de protección oficial; (*private housing*) urbanización *f*; **h. market** mercado *m* inmobiliario; *US* **h. project** ≃ viviendas *fpl* de protección oficial

**hovel** ['hɒvəl] *n* chabola *f*, chozo *m*

**hover** ['hɒvə(r)] *vi* **(a)** (*of bird*) cernerse, cernirse; (*of aircraft*) permanecer inmóvil en el aire **(b)** (*of person*) rondar; **she hovered between life and death** se debatía entre la vida y la muerte

**hovercraft** ['hɒvəkrɑːft] *n* aerodeslizador *m*, hovercraft *m*

**how** [haʊ] *adv* **(a)** (*in what way, by what means*) cómo; **h. did they find out?** ¿cómo lo averiguaron?; **h. do you pronounce this word?** ¿cómo se pronuncia esta palabra?; **tell me h. he did it** dime cómo lo hizo; *Fam* **h. come?** ¿cómo es eso?; *Fam* **and h.!** ¡y cómo!

**(b)** (*to what extent*) **h. much** cuánto; **h. many** cuántos(as); **h. many times?** ¿cuántas veces?; **h. often?** ¿con qué frecuencia?; **h. old are you?** ¿cuántos años tienes?; **h. big is it?** ¿cómo es de grande?; **h. long have you been here?** ¿cuánto tiempo llevas aquí?; **you know h. useful he is to me** sabes lo útil que me resulta; **h. interested are you in politics?** ¿hasta qué punto te interesa la política?

**(c)** (*greetings, enquiries after health*) **h. are you?** ¿cómo estás?, ¿qué tal estás?; *Fam* **h. are things?** ¿qué tal?; **h.'s business?** ¿qué tal el negocio?

**(d)** (*in exclamations*) qué; **h. pretty she is!** ¡qué guapa es!; **h. disgusting!** ¡qué asqueroso(a)!; **h. she has changed!** ¡cómo ha cambiado!

**(e)** (*in suggestions*) **h. about a game of cards?** ¿te apetece jugar a las cartas?; **h. about going**

**out for a meal?** ¿te apetece salir a comer?; **h. about it?** ¿qué te parece?; **h. about you?** ¿y tú?

**however** [haʊˈevə(r)] **1** adv **(a)** (to whatever degree) **h. clever she is** por muy lista que sea; **h. hard she tried, she couldn't do it** por mucho que lo intentaba no podía hacerlo **(b)** (in whatever way) **h. you look at it,...** se mire como se mire,...; **h. did she find out?** pero, ¿cómo se pudo enterar?
**2** conj sin embargo, no obstante

**howl** [haʊl] **1** n (of animal, person) aullido m
**2** vi (of animal, person) aullar; **to h. with laughter** desternillarse de risa
▸**howl down** vt sep (silence by shouting) acallar con gritos

**howler** [ˈhaʊlə(r)] n Fam (mistake) error m de bulto

**howling** [ˈhaʊlɪŋ] **1** n aullidos mpl
**2** adj (wolf) aullador(ora); (gale, wind) violento(a), salvaje; Fam **it wasn't exactly a h. success** no fue un éxito clamoroso, que digamos

**HP, hp** [eɪtʃˈpiː] n **(a)** Tech (abbr **horse-power**) C.V. **(b)** Com (abbr **hire-purchase**) compra f a plazos

**HQ** [eɪtʃˈkjuː] n (abbr **headquarters**) sede f, central f

**hr** (abbr **hour**) h., hora f

**HRH** [eɪtʃɑːˈreɪtʃ] n Br (abbr **Her/His Royal Highness**) S.A.R.

**HRT** [eɪtʃɑːˈtiː] n Med (abbr **hormone replacement therapy**) terapia f hormonal sustitutiva

**HTML** [eɪtʃtiːemˈel] n Comptr (abbr **Hyper Text Markup Language**) HTML m

**HTTP** [eɪtʃtiːtiːˈpiː] n Comptr (abbr **Hyper Text Transfer Protocol**) HTTP m

**hub** [hʌb] n **(a)** (of wheel) cubo m **(b)** (of community) centro m

**hubbub** [ˈhʌbʌb] n griterío m, algarabía f

**hubby** [ˈhʌbɪ] n Fam (husband) maridito m

**hubcap** [ˈhʌbkæp] n (of wheel) tapacubos m inv

**huddle** [ˈhʌdəl] **1** n (of people, houses) piña f
**2** vi acurrucarse
▸**huddle together, huddle up** vi apiñarse

**Hudson Bay** [hʌdsənˈbeɪ] n la bahía de Hudson

**hue¹** [hjuː] n (colour) tonalidad f

**hue²** n and **cry** n revuelo m tremendo; **to raise a h. and cry about sth** poner el grito en el cielo por algo

**huff** [hʌf] **1** n Fam **to be in a h.** estar mosqueado(a)
**2** vi **to h. and puff** (blow) resoplar; Fig (show annoyance) refunfuñar

**huffy** [ˈhʌfɪ] adj Fam (sulky) refunfuñón(ona)

**hug** [hʌg] **1** n abrazo m; **to give sb a h.** dar un abrazo a alguien
**2** vt (pt & pp **hugged**) **(a)** (embrace) abrazar; **she hugged the child to her** abrazó al niño; **her dress hugged her figure** el vestido se ceñía a su cuerpo **(b)** Fig (ground, shore) no alejarse de

**huge** [hjuːdʒ] adj enorme, inmenso(a)

**hugely** [ˈhjuːdʒlɪ] adv enormemente

**hulk** [hʌlk] n **(a)** (of ship) casco m, carcasa f **(b)** (large thing) armatoste m; (large person) mole f, mastodonte m

**hulking** [ˈhʌlkɪŋ] adj descomunal, mastodóntico(a)

**hull** [hʌl] **1** n **(a)** (of ship) casco m **(b)** (of pea) vaina f
**2** vt (peas) desgranar

**hullabaloo** [hʌləbəˈluː] n Fam jaleo m, alboroto m

**hullo** = **hello**

**hum** [hʌm] **1** n zumbido m
**2** vt (pt & pp **hummed**) (tune) tararear, canturrear
**3** vi **(a)** (make noise) (of person) tararear; (of insect, engine) zumbar; **to h. and haw** titubear, vacilar; **to h. with activity** bullir de actividad **(b)** Fam (smell) apestar

**human** [ˈhjuːmən] **1** n ser m humano
**2** adj humano(a); **h. being** ser m humano; **h. error** error m humano; **h. nature** la naturaleza humana; **h. resources** recursos mpl humanos; **h. rights** derechos mpl humanos

**humane** [hjuːˈmeɪn] adj humano(a)

**humanely** [hjuːˈmeɪnlɪ] adv humanamente

**humanism** [ˈhjuːmənɪzəm] n humanismo m

**humanistic** [hjuːməˈnɪstɪk] adj humanístico(a)

**humanitarian** [hjuːmænɪˈteərɪən] **1** n persona f humanitaria
**2** adj humanitario(a)

**humanity** [hjuːˈmænɪtɪ] n humanidad f; Univ **the humanities** humanidades fpl, letras fpl

**humanize** [ˈhjuːmənaɪz] vt humanizar

**humankind** [hjuːmənˈkaɪnd] n humanidad f, raza f humana

**humanly** [ˈhjuːmənlɪ] adv humanamente; **to do everything h. possible** hacer todo lo humanamente posible

**humble** [ˈhʌmbəl] **1** adj (meek, unpretentious) humilde; **in my h. opinion** en mi humilde opinión; Fig **to eat h. pie** (admit one was wrong) tragarse (uno) sus palabras
**2** vt (defeat) humillar, poner en su sitio; **to be humbled (by sth)** sacar una lección de humildad (de algo)

**humbling** [ˈhʌmbəlɪŋ] adj **a h. experience** una lección de humildad

**humbly** [ˈhʌmblɪ] adv humildemente

**humbug** ['hʌmbʌg] n (a) (nonsense) tonterías fpl (b) (hypocrite) embaucador(ora) m,f (c) Br (sweet) caramelo m de menta

**humdinger** ['hʌmdɪŋə(r)] n Fam a h. of a film una película bestial or morrocotuda

**humdrum** ['hʌmdrʌm] adj anodino(a)

**humerus** ['hju:mərəs] n Anat húmero m

**humid** ['hju:mɪd] adj húmedo(a)

**humidifier** [hju'mɪdɪfaɪə(r)] n humidificador m

**humidity** [hju'mɪdɪtɪ] n humedad f

**humiliate** [hju'mɪlɪeɪt] vt humillar

**humiliating** [hju'mɪlɪeɪtɪŋ] adj humillante

**humiliation** [hjumɪlɪ'eɪʃən] n humillación f

**humility** [hju'mɪlɪtɪ] n humildad f

**hummingbird** ['hʌmɪŋbɜːd] n colibrí m

**humor, humorless** US = **humour, humourless**

**humorous** ['hju:mərəs] adj (person, remark) gracioso(a); (play, magazine) humorístico(a)

**humorously** ['hju:mərəslɪ] adv con humor, con gracia

**humour,** US **humor** ['hju:mə(r)] 1 n (in general) humor m; (of a situation, a story) gracia f; **sense of h.** sentido m del humor; Formal **to be in good/bad h.** estar de buen/mal humor
2 vt (indulge) complacer

**humourless,** US **humorless** ['hju:məlɪs] adj serio(a), con poco sentido del humor

**hump** [hʌmp] 1 n (on back) joroba f; (on road) bache m (convexo)
2 vt (a) Fam (carry) acarrear (b) Vulg (have sex with) tirarse a

**humpback** ['hʌmpbæk] n h. **bridge** puente m peraltado; h. **whale** yubarta f

**humus** ['hju:məs] n (in soil) humus m inv

**hunch** [hʌntʃ] 1 n (intuition) presentimiento m, corazonada f
2 vt **to h. one's back** encorvar la espalda, encorvarse

**hunchback** ['hʌntʃbæk] n (person) jorobado(a) m,f

**hundred** ['hʌndrəd] 1 n (in general and before "thousand", "million", etc) cien m; (before other numbers) ciento m; **one** or **a h.** cien; **one** or **a h. thousand** cien mil; **a h. and twenty-five books** ciento veinticinco libros; **two h. books** doscientos libros; Fig **a h. and one details** mil y un detalles; **to live to be a h.** vivir hasta los cien años; **I've told you hundreds of times** te lo he dicho cientos de veces
2 adj cien; **a h. kilometres an hour** cien kilómetros por hora; **one** or **a h. per cent** cien por cien, ciento por ciento; **to be a h. per cent certain** estar seguro(a) al cien por cien; **I'm not feeling a h. per cent** no me encuentro al

todo bien; **the h. metres** (in athletics) los cien metros (lisos); **the H. Years' War** la guerra de los Cien Años

**hundredfold** ['hʌndrədfəʊld] adv **to increase a h.** multiplicar por cien

**hundredth** ['hʌndrədθ] 1 n (a) (fraction) centésimo m, centésima parte f (b) (in series) centésimo(a) m,f
2 adj centésimo(a); Fam **for the h. time, no!** por enésima vez, ¡no!

**hundredweight** ['hʌndrədweɪt] n (a) (metric) 50 kg (b) (imperial) Br = 50,8 kg; US = 45,36 kg

**hung** [hʌŋ] 1 adj h. **jury** jurado m dividido; h. **parliament** parlamento m sin mayoría
2 pt & pp of **hang**

**Hungarian** [hʌŋ'geərɪən] 1 n (a) (person) húngaro(a) m,f (b) (language) húngaro m
2 adj húngaro(a)

**Hungary** ['hʌŋgərɪ] n Hungría

**hunger** ['hʌŋgə(r)] n hambre f; h. **strike** huelga f de hambre
▸**hunger after, hunger for** vt insep ansiar

**hungrily** ['hʌŋgrɪlɪ] adv (eat) vorazmente; (stare) con avidez

**hungry** ['hʌŋgrɪ] adj hambriento(a); **to be h.** tener hambre; **to be as h. as a wolf** tener un hambre canina; **to be h. for knowledge** tener ansias de conocimiento

**hunk** [hʌŋk] n (a) (large piece of bread, meat) pedazo m, trozo m (b) Fam (attractive man) tío m bueno

**hunky** ['hʌŋkɪ] adj Fam (man) cachas inv

**hunt** [hʌnt] 1 n (for animals) caza f; (for person, work) búsqueda f, caza f
2 vt (fox, deer) cazar; **to h. a criminal** ir tras la pista de un delincuente
3 vi (a) (search) **to h. for** ir en busca de (b) (kill animals) cazar
▸**hunt down** vt sep (animal) cazar; (person) atrapar, capturar; (information) conseguir
▸**hunt out** vt sep (find) (person) dar con, lograr encontrar; (look for) (thing) buscar

**hunted** ['hʌntɪd] adj (look, appearance) angustiado(a)

**hunter** ['hʌntə(r)] n cazador(ora) m,f

**hunting** ['hʌntɪŋ] n caza f; h. **ground** terreno m de caza; h. **lodge** refugio m de cazadores

**huntsman** ['hʌntsmən] n (hunter) cazador m

**hurdle** ['hɜːdəl] 1 n (in race) valla f; Fig (obstacle) obstáculo m; Fig **to overcome a h.** vencer un obstáculo
2 vt (obstacle) saltar

**hurdler** ['hɜːdlə(r)] n Sport vallista mf

**hurdling** ['hɜːdlɪŋ] n Sport carreras fpl de vallas

**hurl** [hɜːl] *vt (thing)* lanzar; *(insults)* proferir; **to h. oneself at sb** lanzarse contra alguien; **she hurled herself off the bridge** se tiró desde el puente

**hurling** ['hɜːlɪŋ] *n (Irish game)* = hockey irlandés

**hurly-burly** ['hɜːlɪ'bɜːlɪ] *n Fam* tumulto *m*, barullo *m*

**hurrah** [hʊ'rɑː], **hurray** [hʊ'reɪ] *exclam* ¡hurra!

**hurricane** ['hʌrɪkən, *US* 'hʌrɪkeɪn] *n* huracán *m*; **h. lamp** farol *m*

**hurried** ['hʌrɪd] *adj* apresurado(a); **to be h.** tener prisa

**hurriedly** ['hʌrɪdlɪ] *adv* apresuradamente

**hurry** ['hʌrɪ] **1** *n* prisa *f*; **to be in a h. (to do sth)** tener prisa *or Am* apuro (por hacer algo); **to do sth in a h.** hacer algo deprisa; **to leave in a h.** marcharse apresuradamente; **I won't do that again in a h.** no lo volveré a hacer con prisas; **there's no h.** no hay prisa, no corre prisa; **what's the h.?** ¿a qué tanta prisa?

**2** *vt (person)* meter prisa a, apremiar; *(work, decision)* apresurar, realizar con prisas; **she was hurried to hospital** la llevaron apresuradamente al hospital

**3** *vi* apresurarse **(to do sth** a hacer algo), *Am* apurarse **(to do sth** a hacer algo); **to h. into a room** entrar apresuradamente en una habitación; **to h. out of a room** salir apresuradamente de una habitación

▸**hurry along** *vt sep (person)* meter prisa a

**2** *vi* irse rápido; **to h. along towards** precipitarse hacia

▸**hurry back** *vi* volver corriendo

▸**hurry on 1** *vt sep (person)* hacer irse con rapidez; *(work)* acelerar

**2** *vi (proceed quickly) (of person)* seguir sin pararse; **to h. on with sth** continuar algo deprisa

▸**hurry up 1** *vt sep (person)* meter prisa a; *(work)* acelerar

**2** *vi* apresurarse, darse prisa; **h. up!** ¡date prisa!

**hurt** [hɜːt] **1** *n (emotional)* dolor *m*

**2** *adj (emotionally)* dolido(a); *(look)* dolorido(a); *(feelings)* herido(a)

**3** *vt ( pt & pp* **hurt)** **(a)** *(physically)* hacer daño a; *Fig (chances, prospects)* perjudicar; **to h. oneself** hacerse daño; **to h. one's foot** hacerse daño en un pie; **to get hurt** hacerse daño; **are you h.?** *(after falling)* ¿te has hecho daño?; *(wounded)* ¿estás herido?; *Fig* **it wouldn't h. him to have to wait** no le va a pasar nada por que espere **(b)** *(emotionally)* herir; **to h. sb's feelings** herir los sentimientos de alguien

**4** *vi* **(a)** *(cause pain)* doler; **it hurts** me duele; **where does it h.?** ¿dónde te duele?; **my foot hurts** me duele el pie **(b)** *(emotionally)* resultar doloroso(a), doler

**hurtful** ['hɜːtfʊl] *adj (remark)* hiriente

**hurtle** ['hɜːtəl] *vi* **to h. along** pasar zumbando; **to h. down the street** bajar por la calle a todo correr; **to h. towards** precipitarse hacia

**husband** ['hʌzbənd] **1** *n* marido *m*; **h. and wife** marido y mujer

**2** *vt Formal (one's resources)* economizar

**husbandry** ['hʌzbəndrɪ] *n* agricultura *f*; **animal h.** ganadería *f*

**hush** [hʌʃ] **1** *n (quiet)* silencio *m*; **h.!** ¡silencio!

**2** *vt* acallar

▸**hush up** *vt sep (scandal)* echar tierra a

**hushed** [hʌʃt] *adj* susurrado(a)

**hush-hush** ['hʌʃhʌʃ] *adj Fam* secreto(a)

**husk** [hʌsk] **1** *n (of seed)* cáscara *f*

**2** *vt (grain)* pelar

**huskiness** ['hʌskɪnɪs] *n (of voice, sound) (hoarse)* aspereza *f*; *(attractive)* tonalidad *f* grave

**husky**[1] ['hʌskɪ] *adj (voice)* áspero(a); *(attractive)* grave

**husky**[2] *n (dog)* perro *m* esquimal

**hussar** [hʊ'zɑː(r)] *n Mil* húsar *m*

**hussy** ['hʌsɪ] *n Old-fashioned or Hum* fresca *f*, pelandusca *f*

**hustings** ['hʌstɪŋz] *npl* mítines *mpl* electorales

**hustle** ['hʌsəl] **1** *n* agitación *f*, bullicio *m*; **h. and bustle** ajetreo *m*, bullicio *m*

**2** *vt (shove, push)* empujar; **I was hustled into a small room** me metieron a empujones en un cuartito

**hustler** ['hʌslə(r)] *n US Fam (swindler)* timador(ora) *m,f*, fullero(a) *m,f*

**hut** [hʌt] *n (shed)* cobertizo *m*; *(dwelling)* cabaña *f*, choza *f*

**hutch** [hʌtʃ] *n (for rabbit)* jaula *f* para conejos

**hyacinth** ['haɪəsɪnθ] *n* jacinto *m*

**hybrid** ['haɪbrɪd] **1** *n* híbrido *m*

**2** *adj* híbrido(a)

**hydrangea** [haɪ'dreɪndʒə] *n* hortensia *f*

**hydrant** ['haɪdrənt] *n* boca *f* de incendio *or* de riego

**hydraulic** [haɪ'drɔːlɪk] *adj* hidráulico(a)

**hydraulics** [haɪ'drɔːlɪks] *npl* hidráulica *f*

**hydrocarbon** [haɪdrəʊ'kɑːbən] *n* hidrocarburo *m*

**hydrochloric acid** [haɪdrəʊ'klɒrɪk'æsɪd] *n* ácido *m* clorhídrico

**hydroelectric** [haɪdrəʊɪ'lektrɪk] *adj* hidroeléctrico(a); **h. power** energía *f* hidroeléctrica

**hydroelectricity** [haɪdrəʊɪlek'trɪsɪtɪ] *n* hidroelectricidad *f*

**hydrofoil** ['haɪdrəfɔɪl] *n* barco *m* con hidroala

**hydrogen** ['haɪdrədʒən] *n Chem* hidrógeno *m*; **h. bomb** bomba *f* de hidrógeno

**hydrolysis** [haɪ'drɒlɪsɪs] *n* hidrólisis *f inv*

**hydrophobia** [haɪdrə'fəʊbɪə] *n Med (rabies)* hidrofobia *f*, rabia *f*

**hydroplane** ['haɪdrəpleɪn] *n* planeadora *f*, hidroplano *m*

**hydroxide** [haɪ'drɒksaɪd] *n* hidróxido *m*

**hyena** [haɪ'iːnə] *n* hiena *f*

**hygiene** ['haɪdʒiːn] *n* higiene *f*

**hygienic** [haɪ'dʒiːnɪk] *adj* higiénico(a)

**hymen** ['haɪmen] *n Anat* himen *m*

**hymn** [hɪm] *n* himno *m*; **h. book** libro *m* de himnos, himnario *m*

**hymnal** ['hɪmnəl] *n Rel* himnario *m*, libro *m* de himnos

**hype** [haɪp] *Fam* **1** *n (publicity)* bombo *m*, revuelo *m* publicitario

**2** *vt (publicize)* dar mucho bombo a

►**hype up** *vt sep* (**a**) *(publicize)* dar mucho bombo a (**b**) **to be hyped up** *(excited)* estar hecho(a) un manojo de nervios

**hyper** ['haɪpə(r)] *adj Fam (overexcited)* acelerado(a)

**hyperactive** [haɪpə'ræktɪv] *adj* hiperactivo(a)

**hyperbola** [haɪ'pɜːbələ] *n Math* hipérbola *f*

**hyperbole** [haɪ'pɜːbəlɪ] *n* hipérbole *f*

**hypercritical** [haɪpə'krɪtɪkəl] *adj* criticón(ona)

**hypermarket** ['haɪpəmɑːkɪt] *n* hipermercado *m*

**hypersensitive** [haɪpə'sensɪtɪv] *adj* hipersensible, muy susceptible

**hypertension** [haɪpə'tenʃən] *n Med* hipertensión *f*

**hypertext** ['haɪpətekst] *n Comptr* hipertexto *m*

**hyphen** ['haɪfən] *n* guión *m*

**hyphenate** ['haɪfəneɪt] *vt (word)* escribir con guión

**hypnosis** [hɪp'nəʊsɪs] *n* hipnosis *f inv*

**hypnotic** [hɪp'nɒtɪk] *adj* hipnótico(a)

**hypnotism** ['hɪpnətɪzəm] *n* hipnotismo *m*

**hypnotist** ['hɪpnətɪst] *n* hipnotizador(ora) *m,f*

**hypnotize** ['hɪpnətaɪz] *vt* hipnotizar

**hypoallergenic** [haɪpəʊælə'dʒenɪk] *adj* hipoalergénico(a)

**hypochondria** [haɪpə'kɒndrɪə] *n Med* hipocondría *f*

**hypochondriac** [haɪpə'kɒndrɪæk] *n* hipocondríaco(a) *m,f*

**hypocrisy** [hɪ'pɒkrɪsɪ] *n* hipocresía *f*

**hypocrite** ['hɪpəkrɪt] *n* hipócrita *mf*

**hypocritical** [hɪpə'krɪtɪkəl] *adj* hipócrita

**hypodermic** [haɪpə'dɜːmɪk] **1** *n (jeringuilla f)* hipodérmica *f*

**2** *adj* hipodérmico(a)

**hypotenuse** [haɪ'pɒtənjuːz] *n Math* hipotenusa *f*

**hypothermia** [haɪpəʊ'θɜːmɪə] *n Med* hipotermia *f*

**hypothesis** [haɪ'pɒθəsɪs] *n* hipótesis *f inv*

**hypothesize** [haɪ'pɒθəsaɪz] **1** *vt* plantear como hipótesis, conjeturar

**2** *vi* plantear hipótesis, conjeturar

**hypothetical** [haɪpə'θetɪkəl] *adj* hipotético(a)

**hysterectomy** [hɪstə'rektəmɪ] *n Med* histerectomía *f*

**hysteria** [hɪs'tɪərɪə] *n* (**a**) *(panic)* histeria *f*, histerismo *m* (**b**) *(laughter)* grandes carcajadas *fpl*, hilaridad *f*

**hysterical** [hɪs'terɪkəl] *adj* (**a**) *(uncontrolled)* histérico(a) (**b**) *(very funny)* graciosísimo(a), divertidísimo(a); **h. laughter** grandes carcajadas *fpl*, hilaridad *f*

**hysterically** [hɪs'terɪklɪ] *adv* (**a**) *(uncontrolledly)* histéricamente (**b**) **h. funny** para morirse de risa

**hysterics** [hɪs'terɪks] *npl* (**a**) *(panic)* ataque *m* de histeria; **to go into** *or* **have h.** tener un ataque de histeria (**b**) *(laughter)* **we were in h.** nos desternillábamos de risa

**Hz** *Elec (abbr* **Hertz***)* Hz

**I, i**¹ [aɪ] *n (letter)* I, i *f*

**I**² *pron* yo *(usually omitted, except for contrast)*; **I'm Scottish** soy escocés; **I haven't got it!** ¡yo no lo tengo!; *Formal* **it was I who did it** yo fui el que lo hizo

**IAAF** [aɪdʌˈbəliːˈef] *n (abbr* **International Amateur Athletics Federation***)* IAAF *f*

**IAEA** [aɪeiːˈeɪ] *n (abbr* **International Atomic Energy Agency***)* AIEA *f*

**IBA** [aɪbiːˈeɪ] *n Br (abbr* **Independent Broadcasting Authority***)* = organismo regulador de las cadenas privadas de radio y televisión británicas

**Iberian** [aɪˈbɪːrɪən] *adj* ibérico(a); **the I. peninsula** la península Ibérica

**ibex** [ˈaɪbeks] *n* íbice *m*, cabra *f* montés

**ibid** [ˈɪbɪd] *adv (abbr* **ibidem***)* ibíd., ib.

**IBM** [aɪbiːˈem] *n Mil (abbr* **intercontinental ballistic missile***)* misil *m* balístico intercontinental

**IBRD** [aɪbiːɑːˈdiː] *n (abbr* **International Bank for Reconstruction and Development***)* BIRD *m*, Banco *m* Mundial

**ice** [aɪs] **1** *n* **(a)** *(frozen water)* hielo *m*; **i. age** glaciación *f*; **i. (cream)** helado, *Am* sorbete; **i. cube** cubito *m* de hielo; **i. floe** témpano *m (de* hielo); **i. hockey** hockey *m* sobre hielo; **i. lolly** polo *m*; **i. pack** bolsa *f* de hielo; **i. pick** pico *m* para el hielo; **i. rink** pista *f* de hielo **(b)** *(idioms)* **to put a project on i.** aparcar un proyecto; **to break the i.** *(socially)* romper el hielo; **to be skating on thin i.** estar jugándosela; **that cuts no i. with me** eso no me deja frío

**2** *vt (cake)* glasear

▸**ice over** *vi (pond)* cubrirse de hielo, helarse

▸**ice up** *vi* helarse

**iceberg** [ˈaɪsbɜːg] *n* iceberg *m*; **i. lettuce** lechuga *f* iceberg *or* repolluda; *Fig* **that's just the tip of the i.** eso es sólo la punta del iceberg

**icebound** [ˈaɪsbaʊnd] *adj (ship, port)* bloqueado(a) por el hielo

**icebox** [ˈaɪsbɒks] *n Br (in fridge)* congelador *m*; *US (fridge)* nevera *f*

**icebreaker** [ˈaɪsbreɪkə(r)] *n (ship)* rompehielos *m inv*; *Fig* **this game's a good i.** este juego viene muy bien para romper el hielo

**icecap** [ˈaɪskæp] *n (at poles)* casquetes *mpl* polares *or* glaciares

**ice-cold** [ˈaɪsˈkəʊld] *adj* helado(a)

**iced** [aɪst] *adj* **(a)** **i. water** agua *f* con hielo **(b)** *(cake)* glaseado(a)

**Iceland** [ˈaɪslənd] *n* Islandia

**Icelander** [ˈaɪsləndə(r)] *n* islandés(esa) *m,f*

**Icelandic** [aɪsˈlændɪk] **1** *n (language)* islandés *m*

**2** *adj* islandés(esa)

**ice-skate** [ˈaɪsˈskeɪt] **1** *n* patín *m (de hielo)*

**2** *vi* patinar sobre hielo

**ice-skating** [ˈaɪsˈskeɪtɪŋ] *n* patinaje *m* sobre hielo

**icicle** [ˈaɪsɪkəl] *n* carámbano *m*

**icing** [ˈaɪsɪŋ] *n (on cake)* glaseado *m*; *Fig* **the i. on the cake** la guinda; **i. sugar** azúcar *m* de lustre

**icon** [ˈaɪkɒn] *n Art, Comptr & Fig* icono *m*

**iconoclastic** [aɪkɒnəʊˈklæstɪk] *adj* iconoclasta

**ICRC** [aɪsiːɑːˈsiː] *n (abbr* **International Committee of the Red Cross***)* CICR *m*

**icy** [ˈaɪsɪ] *adj* **(a)** *(road)* con hielo; *(wind)* helado(a) **(b)** *Fig (expression, reply)* frío(a)

**ID** [ˈaɪdiː] *n (abbr* **identification***)* documentación *f*; **ID card** carné *m* de identidad, ≃ DNI *m*

**I'd** [aɪd] = **I had, I would**

**idea** [aɪˈdɪə] *n* **(a)** *(individual notion)* idea *f*; **what a good i.!** ¡qué buena idea!; **what put that i. into your head?** ¿qué te metió esa idea en la cabeza?; **the very i.!** ¡es el colmo!, ¡vaya ideas!; *Fam* **what's the big i.?** ¿a qué viene esto?

**(b)** *(concept)* idea *f*, concepto *m*; **to have an i. that...** tener la sensación de que...; **her i. of a joke is...** su idea de una broma es...; **I had no i. that...** no tenía ni idea de que...; **can you give me an i. of how much it will cost?** ¿puede darme una idea de cuánto va a costar?; **I thought the i. was for them to come here** creí que la idea era que ellos vinieran aquí; **the general i. is to...** la idea general es...

**ideal** [aɪˈdɪəl] *n & adj* ideal *m*

**idealism** [aɪˈdɪəlɪzəm] *n* idealismo *m*

**idealist** [aɪˈdɪəlɪst] *n* idealista *mf*

**idealistic** [aɪdɪəˈlɪstɪk] *adj* idealista

**idealize** [aɪˈdɪəlaɪz] *vt* idealizar

**ideally** [aɪˈdiːəlɪ] *adv* **i., we should all be there** lo ideal sería que estuviéramos todos; **they're i. matched** están hechos el uno para el otro; **i. situated** en una posición ideal

**identical** [aɪˈdentɪkəl] *adj* idéntico(a); **i. twins** gemelos(as) *mfpl* idénticos(as) *or* mono-cigóticos(as)

**identifiable** [aɪdentɪˈfaɪəbəl] *adj* identifica-ble; **it was not easily i.** no se podía identificar fácilmente

**identification** [aɪdentɪfɪˈkeɪʃən] *n* (**a**) *(of body, criminal)* identificación *f* (**b**) *(documents)* documentación *f*

**identify** [aɪˈdentɪfaɪ] **1** *vt* identificar; **to i. sth with sth** identificar algo con algo

**2** *vi* **to i. with sb/sth** identificarse con al-guien/algo

**identifying mark** [aɪˈdentɪfaɪɪŋ ˈmɑːk] *n* seña *f* de identidad

**Identikit**® [aɪˈdentɪkɪt] *n* **i. (picture)** retra-to *m* robot

**identity** [aɪˈdentɪtɪ] *n* identidad *f*; **a case of mistaken i.** un caso de identificación errónea; **i. card** carné *m* de identidad, ≃ DNI *m*; **i. crisis** crisis *f inv* de identidad; **i. parade** rueda *f* de identificación

**ideological** [aɪdɪəˈlɒdʒɪkəl] *adj* ideológi-co(a)

**ideology** [aɪdɪˈɒlədʒɪ] *n* ideología *f*

**idiocy** [ˈɪdɪəsɪ] *n* idiotez *f*, estupidez *f*

**idiom** [ˈɪdɪəm] *n (expression)* modismo *m*, giro *m*; *(dialect)* lenguaje *m*

**idiomatic** [ɪdɪəˈmætɪk] *adj* **his English isn't very i.** su inglés no suena muy natural; **i. expression** modismo *m*, giro *m*

**idiosyncrasy** [ɪdɪəʊˈsɪŋkrəsɪ] *n* peculiaridad *f*, particularidad *f*

**idiosyncratic** [ɪdɪəʊsɪŋˈkrætɪk] *adj* pecu-liar, particular

**idiot** [ˈɪdɪət] *n* idiota *mf*, estúpido(a) *m,f*; **you i.!** ¡idiota!, ¡imbécil!

**idiotic** [ɪdɪˈɒtɪk] *adj* idiota, estúpido(a)

**idle** [ˈaɪdəl] **1** *adj* (**a**) *(unoccupied) (person)* ocio-so(a), desocupado(a); *(factory, machine)* inacti-vo(a); **an i. moment** un momento libre (**b**) *(lazy)* vago(a) (**c**) *(futile) (threat, boast)* vano(a); *(gossip, rumour)* frívolo(a); **i. curiosity** mera curiosidad

**2** *vi (of engine)* estar en punto muerto

▸**idle away** *vt sep* pasar ociosamente

**idleness** [ˈaɪdəlnɪs] *n* (**a**) *(inaction)* ociosidad *f* (**b**) *(laziness)* vagancia *f*

**idler** [ˈaɪdlə(r)] *n (lazy person)* vago(a) *m,f*

**idly** [ˈaɪdlɪ] *adv* (**a**) *(inactively)* ociosamente; **to stand i. by** estar sin hacer nada (**b**) *(casually)* despreocupadamente

**idol** [ˈaɪdəl] *n* ídolo *m*

**idolatry** [aɪˈdɒlətrɪ] *n* idolatría *f*

**idolize** [ˈaɪdəlaɪz] *vt* idolatrar

**idyll** [ˈɪdɪl] *n* idilio *m*

**idyllic** [ɪˈdɪlɪk] *adj* idílico(a)

**i.e.** [ˈaɪˈiː] *(abbr* **id est)** i.e., es decir

**if** [ɪf] *n* **ifs and buts** pegas *fpl*; **it's a big if** es un gran condicionante

**2** *conj* (**a**) *(conditional)* si; **if I were rich** si fuese rico; **if I were you** yo en tu lugar; **if the weather's good** si hace buen tiempo

(**b**) *(conceding)* si bien; **the film was good, if rather long** la película fue buena, si bien un poco larga; **if anything it's better** en todo caso, es mejor

(**c**) *(whether)* si; **I asked if it was true** pre-gunté si era verdad

(**d**) *(in phrases)* **if not** si no; **if so** en ese caso; **if only!** ¡ojalá!; **if only I had more money!** ¡ojalá tuviera más dinero!; **if and when...** en caso de que...; **he sees them rarely, if at all** *or* **if ever** apenas los ve

**iffy** [ˈɪfɪ] *adj Fam (doubtful)* dudoso(a)

**igloo** [ˈɪgluː] *n (pl* **igloos)** iglú *m*

**ignite** [ɪgˈnaɪt] **1** *vt (fire, conflict)* prender, en-cender

**2** *vi (of fire, conflict)* prender, encenderse

**ignition** [ɪgˈnɪʃən] *n Aut* encendido *m*, con-tacto *m*; **i. key** llave *f* de contacto

**ignoble** [ɪgˈnəʊbəl] *adj* innoble, indigno(a)

**ignominious** [ɪgnəˈmɪnɪəs] *adj* ignominio-so(a)

**ignominy** [ˈɪgnəmɪnɪ] *n* ignominia *f*

**ignoramus** [ɪgnəˈreɪməs] *n* ignorante *mf*

**ignorance** [ˈɪgnərəns] *n* ignorancia *f*; **out of** *or* **through i.** por ignorancia

**ignorant** [ˈɪgnərənt] *adj* ignorante; **to be i. of sth** ignorar algo

**ignore** [ɪgˈnɔː(r)] *vt (person)* no hacer caso a, ignorar; *(warning, advice)* no hacer caso de, ignorar; **just i. him!** ¡no le hagas caso!

**iguana** [ɪgˈwɑːnə] *n* iguana *f*

**ilk** [ɪlk] *n* **of that i.** por el estilo

**ill** [ɪl] **1** *npl* **ills** males *mpl*

**2** *adj* (**a**) *(unwell)* enfermo(a); **to be i.** estar enfermo(a) *or* malo(a); **to fall** *or* **be taken i.** caer enfermo(a) *or* malo(a) (**b**) *(bad, poor)* **i. ef-fects** efectos *mpl* indeseables; **i. feeling** rencor *m*; **i. fortune** mala suerte *f or* fortuna *f*; **to be in i. health** tener mala salud; **to be** *or* **feel i. at ease** no sentirse a gusto; **a house of i. repute** *(brothel)* una casa de prostitución; **i. will** rencor *m*

**3** *adv* mal; **I can i. afford it** me lo puedo permitir a duras penas; **to speak/think i. of sb** hablar/pensar mal de alguien

**ill.** (*abbr* **illustration**) ilustración *f*

**I'll** [aɪl] = **I will, I shall**

**ill-advised** ['ɪləd'vaɪzd] *adj* imprudente, desacertado(a); **you'd be i. to complain** harías mal en quejarte

**ill-bred** ['ɪl'bred] *adj* maleducado(a)

**ill-concealed** ['ɪlkən'siːld] *adj* (*disappointment, disgust*) mal disimulado(a)

**ill-considered** ['ɪlkən'sɪdəd] *adj* (*remark, decision*) irreflexivo(a), precipitado(a)

**ill-disposed** ['ɪldɪs'pəuzd] *adj* **to be i. towards sb** tener mala disposición hacia alguien

**illegal** [ɪ'liːgəl] *adj* ilegal

**illegality** [ɪlɪ'gælɪtɪ] *n* ilegalidad *f*

**illegible** [ɪ'ledʒɪbəl] *adj* ilegible

**illegitimate** [ɪlɪ'dʒɪtɪmət] *adj* ilegítimo(a)

**ill-equipped** ['ɪlɪ'kwɪpd] *adj* mal equipado(a); *Fig* **to be i. to do sth** (*lack skill, experience*) no estar preparado(a) para hacer algo

**ill-fated** ['ɪl'feɪtɪd] *adj* (*day, occasion*) aciago(a); (*enterprise*) infausto(a), desdichado(a)

**ill-founded** ['ɪl'faundɪd] *adj* infundado(a)

**ill-gotten gains** ['ɪlgɒtn'geɪnz] *npl* ganancias *fpl* obtenidas por medios ilícitos

**illiberal** [ɪ'lɪbərəl] *adj* (*narrow-minded*) intolerante

**illicit** [ɪ'lɪsɪt] *adj* ilícito(a)

**ill-informed** [ɪlɪn'fɔːmd] *adj* mal informado(a)

**ill-intentioned** ['ɪlɪn'tenʃənd] *adj* malintencionado(a)

**illiteracy** [ɪ'lɪtərəsɪ] *n* analfabetismo *m*

**illiterate** [ɪ'lɪtərət] **1** *adj* (*unable to read or write*) analfabeto(a); (*usage, style*) analfabeto(a), ignorante

**2** *n* analfabeto(a) *m,f*

**ill-mannered** ['ɪl'mænəd] *adj* maleducado(a)

**ill-natured** ['ɪl'neɪtʃəd] *adj* malhumorado(a)

**illness** ['ɪlnɪs] *n* enfermedad *f*

**illogical** [ɪ'lɒdʒɪkəl] *adj* ilógico(a)

**ill-suited** ['ɪl'suːtɪd] *adj* (*not appropriate*) inadecuado(a) (**to** para)

**ill-tempered** ['ɪl'tempəd] *adj* (*person*) malhumorado(a); (*meeting, exchange*) agrio(a); (*match, occasion*) brusco(a), áspero(a)

**ill-timed** ['ɪl'taɪmd] *adj* inoportuno(a)

**ill-treat** ['ɪl'triːt] *vt* maltratar

**illuminate** [ɪ'luːmɪneɪt] *vt* (**a**) (*light up*) iluminar (**b**) (*clarify*) ilustrar

**illuminating** [ɪ'luːmɪneɪtɪŋ] *adj* ilustrativo(a), iluminador(ora)

**illumination** [ɪlʊmɪ'neɪʃən] *n* iluminación *f*; *Fig* **his answer provided little i.** su respuesta no resultó muy ilustrativa; **illuminations** (*decorative lights*) iluminación

**ill-use 1** ['ɪl'juːs] maltrato *m*

**2** *vt* ['ɪl'juːz] maltratar; **to feel ill-used** sentirse maltratado(a)

**illusion** [ɪ'luːʒən] *n* ilusión *f*; **to be under the i. that…** hacerse la ilusión de que…; **I was under no illusions about the risk** no me engañaba en lo referente al peligro

**illusory** [ɪ'luːsərɪ] *adj* ilusorio(a)

**illustrate** ['ɪləstreɪt] *vt also Fig* ilustrar

**illustration** [ɪləs'treɪʃən] *n* (*picture, example*) ilustración *f*

**illustrator** ['ɪləstreɪtə(r)] *n* ilustrador(ora) *m,f*

**illustrious** [ɪ'lʌstrɪəs] *adj* ilustre, insigne

**ILO** [aɪɛ'ləʊ] *n* (*abbr* **International Labour Organization**) OIT *f*, Organización *f* Internacional del Trabajo

**I'm** [aɪm] = **I am**

**image** ['ɪmɪdʒ] *n* imagen *f*; **he's the i. of his father** es la viva imagen *or* el vivo retrato de su padre

**imagery** ['ɪmɪdʒərɪ] *n* imágenes *fpl*

**imaginable** [ɪ'mædʒɪnəbəl] *adj* imaginable; **the best/worst thing i.** lo mejor/peor del mundo

**imaginary** [ɪ'mædʒɪnərɪ] *adj* imaginario(a), ficticio(a)

**imagination** [ɪmædʒɪ'neɪʃən] *n* imaginación *f*; **to have no i.** no tener imaginación

**imaginative** [ɪ'mædʒɪnətɪv] *adj* imaginativo(a)

**imagine** [ɪ'mædʒɪn] *vt* (**a**) (*mentally picture*) imaginar, imaginarse; **to i. sb doing sth** imaginarse a alguien haciendo algo; **you're imagining things** son imaginaciones tuyas; **you must have imagined it** debes de haberlo imaginado (**b**) (*suppose*) imaginar, imaginarse; **I i. that you must be very tired** (me) imagino que debes de estar muy cansado

**imbalance** [ɪm'bæləns] *n* desequilibrio *m*

**imbecile** ['ɪmbɪsiːl] *n* imbécil *mf*, idiota *mf*

**imbibe** [ɪm'baɪb] *vt Formal* (*drink*) ingerir, beber; *Fig* (*knowledge, ideas*) absorber, embeber

**imbue** [ɪm'bjuː] *vt Formal* **to i. sb with sth** inculcar algo a alguien; **to be imbued with sth** estar imbuido(a) de algo

**IMF** [aɪɛ'mef] *n* (*abbr* **International Monetary Fund**) FMI *m*

**imitate** ['ɪmɪteɪt] *vt* imitar

**imitation** [ɪmɪ'teɪʃən] *n* (*action, copy*) imitación *f*; **in i. of** a imitación de, imitando a; **i. jewellery** bisutería *f*; **i. leather** piel *f* sintética

**imitative** ['ɪmɪtətɪv] *adj* imitativo(a)

**imitator** [ˈɪmɪteɪtə(r)] *n* imitador(ora) *m,f*

**immaculate** [ɪˈmækjʊlət] *adj (very clean, tidy)* inmaculado(a); *(performance, rendition, taste)* impecable; *Rel* the I. **Conception** la Inmaculada Concepción

**immaterial** [ɪməˈtɪərɪəl] *adj* irrelevante; **that's quite i.** eso no tiene ninguna importancia

**immature** [ɪməˈtjʊə(r)] *adj* inmaduro(a)

**immaturity** [ɪməˈtjʊərɪtɪ] *n* inmadurez *f*

**immeasurable** [ɪˈmeʒərəbəl] *adj* inconmensurable

**immediacy** [ɪˈmiːdɪəsɪ] *n* inmediatez *f*, proximidad *f*

**immediate** [ɪˈmiːdɪət] *adj* inmediato(a); **in the i. future** en un futuro inmediato; **the i. family** la familia más cercana; **in the i. vicinity** en las inmediaciones

**immediately** [ɪˈmiːdɪətlɪ] **1** *adv* inmediatamente

**2** *conj* **i. I saw her I knew…** en cuanto la vi supe…

**immemorial** [ɪmɪˈmɔːrɪəl] *adj* **from time i.** desde tiempo(s) inmemorial(es)

**immense** [ɪˈmens] *adj* inmenso(a)

**immensely** [ɪˈmenslɪ] *adv* inmensamente

**immensity** [ɪˈmensɪtɪ] *n* inmensidad *f*

**immerse** [ɪˈmɜːs] *vt also Fig* sumergir **(in** en); **to i. oneself in sth** sumergirse en algo

**immigrant** [ˈɪmɪgrənt] *n & adj* inmigrante *mf*

**immigrate** [ˈɪmɪgreɪt] *vi* inmigrar

**immigration** [ɪmɪˈgreɪʃən] *n* inmigración *f*; **to go through i.** pasar por el control de pasaportes; **i. control** control *m* de pasaportes; **i. officer** agente *mf* de inmigración

**imminent** [ˈɪmɪnənt] *adj* inminente

**immobile** [ɪˈməʊbaɪl] *adj* inmóvil

**immobilize** [ɪˈməʊbɪlaɪz] *vt* inmovilizar

**immoderate** [ɪˈmɒdərət] *adj* desmedido(a)

**immodest** [ɪˈmɒdɪst] *adj (vain)* inmodesto(a), vanidoso(a); *(indecent)* deshonesto(a), impúdico(a)

**immoral** [ɪˈmɒrəl] *adj* inmoral; *Law* **i. earnings** ganancias *fpl* procedentes del proxenetismo

**immorality** [ɪməˈrælɪtɪ] *n* inmoralidad *f*

**immortal** [ɪˈmɔːtəl] *adj & n* inmortal *mf*

**immortality** [ɪmɔːˈtælɪtɪ] *n* inmortalidad *f*

**immortalize** [ɪˈmɔːtəlaɪz] *vt* inmortalizar

**immovable** [ɪˈmuːvəbəl] *adj (object)* inamovible, fijo(a); *Fig (opposition)* inflexible

**immune** [ɪˈmjuːn] *adj* inmune; **to be i. to a disease** ser inmune a una enfermedad; *Fig* **i. to criticism** inmune a la crítica; *Med* **i. system** sistema *m* inmunológico

**immunity** [ɪˈmjuːnɪtɪ] *n Med* inmunidad *f*; *Law* **i. (from prosecution)** inmunidad *f* (procesal)

**immunization** [ɪmjʊnərˈzeɪʃən] *n Med* inmunización *f*, vacunación *f*

**immunize** [ˈɪmjʊnaɪz] *vt Med* inmunizar

**immunodeficiency** [ɪmjʊnəʊdəˈfɪʃənsɪ] *n* inmunodeficiencia *f*

**immunology** [ɪmjʊˈnɒlədʒɪ] *n* inmunología *f*

**immutable** [ɪˈmjuːtəbəl] *adj* inmutable

**imp** [ɪmp] *n* diablillo *m*

**impact 1** *n* [ˈɪmpækt] impacto *m*; **on i.** en el momento del impacto; *Fig* **to make an i. on sb/sth** causar (un) gran impacto en algo/alguien

**2** *vt* [ɪmˈpækt] *(collide with)* impactar en, chocar con; *(influence)* repercutir en

**impacted** [ɪmˈpæktɪd] *adj* **to have i. wisdom teeth** tener las muelas del juicio impactadas *or* incluidas

**impair** [ɪmˈpeə(r)] *vt (sight, hearing)* dañar, estropear; *(relations, chances)* perjudicar

**impaired** [ɪmˈpeəd] *adj* defectuoso(a)

**impale** [ɪmˈpeɪl] *vt* clavar **(on** en)

**impart** [ɪmˈpɑːt] *vt Formal (heat, light)* desprender; *(quality)* conferir; *(knowledge)* impartir; *(news)* revelar

**impartial** [ɪmˈpɑːʃəl] *adj* imparcial

**impartiality** [ɪmpɑːʃɪˈælɪtɪ] *n* imparcialidad *f*

**impassable** [ɪmˈpɑːsəbəl] *adj (river, barrier)* infranqueable; *(road)* intransitable

**impasse** [ˈæmpɑːs] *n* punto *m* muerto, callejón *m* sin salida

**impassioned** [ɪmˈpæʃənd] *adj* apasionado(a)

**impassive** [ɪmˈpæsɪv] *adj* impasible, impertérrito(a)

**impassively** [ɪmˈpæsɪvlɪ] *adv* impasiblemente

**impatience** [ɪmˈpeɪʃəns] *n* impaciencia *f*

**impatient** [ɪmˈpeɪʃənt] *adj* impaciente; **to be i. (to do sth)** estar impaciente (por hacer algo); **to get i. (with sb)** impacientarse (con alguien); **to be i. for change** esperar con impaciencia el cambio

**impatiently** [ɪmˈpeɪʃəntlɪ] *adv* impacientemente

**impeach** [ɪmˈpiːtʃ] *vt US Law* acusar de prevaricación a

**impeccable** [ɪmˈpekəbəl] *adj* impecable

**impede** [ɪmˈpiːd] *vt* dificultar

**impediment** [ɪmˈpedɪmənt] *n* impedimento *m*; *(speech)* **i.** defecto *m* del habla, trastorno *m* del lenguaje

**impel** [ɪmˈpel] *(pt & pp* **impelled)** *vt* impulsar

**impending** [ɪm'pendɪŋ] *adj* inminente
**impenetrable** [ɪm'penɪtrəbəl] *adj (defences, mystery)* impenetrable
**imperative** [ɪm'perətɪv] **1** *n Gram* imperativo *m*
**2** *adj* (a) *(need)* imperioso(a), acuciante; **it is i. that he should come** es imprescindible que venga (b) *(tone) & Gram* imperativo(a)
**imperceptible** [ɪmpə'septɪbəl] *adj* imperceptible
**imperfect** [ɪm'pɜːfɪkt] **1** *n Gram* imperfecto *m*
**2** *adj (not perfect) & Gram* imperfecto(a)
**imperfection** [ɪmpə'fekʃən] *n* imperfección *f*
**imperial** [ɪm'pɪərɪəl] *adj* (a) *(of empire)* imperial (b) *(weights and measures)* británico(a), imperial *(que utiliza pesos y medidas anglosajones: la pulgada, la libra, el galón, etc)*
**imperialism** [ɪm'pɪərɪəlɪzəm] *n* imperialismo *m*
**imperialist** [ɪm'pɪərɪəlɪst] *n & adj* imperialista *mf*
**imperil** [ɪm'perɪl] *(pt & pp* **imperilled**, US **imperiled)** *vt* poner en peligro
**imperious** [ɪm'pɪərɪəs] *adj* imperioso(a), autoritario(a)
**impermanent** [ɪm'pɜːmənənt] *adj* provisional, pasajero(a)
**impersonal** [ɪm'pɜːsənəl] *adj* impersonal
**impersonate** [ɪm'pɜːsəneɪt] *vt (pretend to be)* hacerse pasar por; *(do impression of)* imitar, hacer una imitación de
**impersonation** [ɪmpɜːsə'neɪʃən] *n (impression)* imitación *f;* **he was sent to prison for i. of a diplomat** fue encarcelado por hacerse pasar por un diplomático
**impersonator** [ɪm'pɜːsəneɪtə(r)] *n (impostor)* impostor(ora) *m,f; (impressionist)* imitador(ora) *m,f*
**impertinence** [ɪm'pɜːtɪnəns] *n* impertinencia *f*
**impertinent** [ɪm'pɜːtɪmənt] *adj* impertinente
**imperturbable** [ɪmpə'tɜːbəbəl] *adj* imperturbable
**impervious** [ɪm'pɜːvɪəs] *adj (to water)* impermeable; *(to threats, persuasion)* insensible; **she is i. to reason** es imposible que razone
**impetuous** [ɪm'petjʊəs] *adj* impetuoso(a)
**impetus** ['ɪmpɪtəs] *n* ímpetu *m,* impulso *m*
▸**impinge on** [ɪm'pɪndʒ] *vt insep* influir en, repercutir en
**impious** ['ɪmpɪəs] *adj* impío(a)
**impish** ['ɪmpɪʃ] *adj* travieso(a)
**implacable** [ɪm'plækəbəl] *adj* implacable

**implant 1** *n* ['ɪmplɑːnt] *Med* implante *m*
**2** *vt* [ɪm'plɑːnt] (a) *Med* implantar (b) *(opinion, belief)* inculcar
**implausible** [ɪm'plɔːzɪbəl] *adj* poco convincente
**implement 1** *n* ['ɪmplɪmənt] utensilio *m*
**2** *vt* ['ɪmplɪment] *(plan, agreement, proposal)* poner en práctica, llevar a cabo
**implementation** [ɪmplɪmen'teɪʃən] *n (of plan, agreement, proposal)* puesta *f* en práctica
**implicate** ['ɪmplɪkeɪt] *vt* implicar
**implication** [ɪmplɪ'keɪʃən] *n (effect)* consecuencia *f; (inference)* insinuación *f;* **by i.** indirectamente, implícitamente
**implicit** [ɪm'plɪsɪt] *adj* implícito(a); **it was i. in his remarks** estaba implícito en sus comentarios; **i. faith** fe *f* inquebrantable
**implied** [ɪm'plaɪd] *adj* implícito(a)
**implore** [ɪm'plɔː(r)] *vt* implorar; **to i. sb to do sth** implorar a alguien que haga algo
**imploring** [ɪm'plɔːrɪŋ] *adj* implorante
**imply** [ɪm'plaɪ] *vt* (a) *(insinuate)* insinuar (b) *(involve)* implicar
**impolite** [ɪmpə'laɪt] *adj* maleducado(a)
**impoliteness** [ɪmpə'laɪtnɪs] *n* mala educación *f*
**imponderable** [ɪm'pɒndərəbəl] **1** *n* (factor *m*) imponderable *m*
**2** *adj* imponderable
**import 1** *n* ['ɪmpɔːt] (a) *(item, activity)* importación *f;* **i. duty** derechos *mpl* de importación or de aduana (b) *Formal (importance)* significación *f,* importancia *f*
**2** *vt* [ɪm'pɔːt] *(goods)* importar
**importance** [ɪm'pɔːtəns] *n* importancia *f;* **it is of no great** i. no tiene mucha importancia; **to attach i. to sth** dar importancia a algo; **to be full of one's own i.** darse aires, estar pagado(a) de sí mismo(a)
**important** [ɪm'pɔːtənt] *adj* importante; **it's not i.** no tiene importancia
**importantly** [ɪm'pɔːtəntlɪ] *adv (speak)* dándose importancia; **but, more i…** pero, lo que es más importante…
**importation** [ɪmpɔː'teɪʃən] *n (of goods)* importación *f*
**importer** [ɪm'pɔːtə(r)] *n* importador(ora) *m,f*
**import-export** ['ɪmpɔːt'ekspɔːt] *n* **i. (trade)** importación *f* y exportación, comercio *m* exterior
**importune** [ɪm'pɔːtjuːn] *vt Formal* importunar
**impose** [ɪm'pəʊz] *vt (silence, one's will, restrictions)* imponer **(on** a); **to i. a tax on sth** gravar algo con un impuesto; **to i. a fine on sb** poner or imponer a alguien una multa
▸**impose on, impose upon** *vt insep (take advantage of)* abusar de

**imposing** [ɪmˈpəʊzɪŋ] *adj* imponente

**imposition** [ɪmpəˈzɪʃən] *n* (a) *(of tax, fine)* imposición *f* (b) *(unfair demand)* abuso *m*

**impossibility** [ɪmpɒsɪˈbɪlɪtɪ] *n* imposibilidad *f*; **it's a physical i.** es físicamente imposible

**impossible** [ɪmˈpɒsɪbəl] **1** *n* **the i.** lo imposible; **to ask the i.** pedir lo imposible; **to attempt the i.** intentar lo imposible

**2** *adj* imposible; **an i. position/situation** una posición/situación insostenible; **to make it i. for sb to do sth** imposibilitar a alguien hacer algo; **it's not i. that...** no es imposible que...; **it's i. to say when we'll finish** es imposible saber cuándo terminaremos; **you're i.!** ¡eres imposible!

**impossibly** [ɪmˈpɒsɪblɪ] *adv* increíblemente; **he's i. stupid** es increíblemente estúpido; **to behave i.** portarse de forma insoportable

**impostor** [ɪmˈpɒstə(r)] *n* impostor(ora) *m,f*

**impotence** [ˈɪmpətəns] *n* impotencia *f*

**impotent** [ˈɪmpətənt] *adj* impotente

**impound** [ɪmˈpaʊnd] *vt Law* embargar; *(car)* trasladar al depósito municipal por infracción; **his car has been impounded** se le ha llevado el coche la grúa

**impoverish** [ɪmˈpɒvərɪʃ] *vt* empobrecer

**impoverished** [ɪmˈpɒvərɪʃd] *adj* empobrecido(a); **to be i.** estar empobrecido(a)

**impracticable** [ɪmˈpræktɪkəbəl] *adj* irrealizable, impracticable

**impractical** [ɪmˈpræktɪkəl] *adj* *(person, suggestion)* poco práctico(a)

**imprecise** [ɪmprɪˈsaɪs] *adj* impreciso(a)

**imprecision** [ɪmprɪˈsɪʒən] *n* imprecisión *f*

**impregnable** [ɪmˈpregnəbəl] *adj* *(fortress)* inexpugnable; *Fig (argument)* incontestable

**impregnate** [ˈɪmpregneɪt] *vt* (a) *(fertilize)* fecundar (b) *(soak)* impregnar **(with** de)

**impresario** [ɪmprɪˈsɑːrɪəʊ] *(pl* **impresarios)** *n* empresario(a) *m,f* or organizador(ora) *m,f* de espectáculos

**impress** [ɪmˈpres] *vt* (a) *(make an impression on)* impresionar; **she was impressed with** or **by it** aquello la impresionó; **to i. sb favourably/unfavourably** causar buena/mala impresión a alguien (b) *(emphasize to sb)* **to i. sth on sb** recalcarle a alguien la importancia de algo (c) *(imprint)* **to i. sth on sth** imprimir algo en algo; **to i. sth on sb's mind** imprimir algo en la mente de alguien

**impression** [ɪmˈpreʃən] *n* (a) *(effect)* impresión *f*; **to make a good/bad i.** dar buena/mala impresión; **to create a false i.** dar una impresión falsa; **to be under the i. that...** tener la impresión de que...; **to give the i. that...** dar la impresión de que... (b) *(imprint)*

*(in wax, snow)* marca *f*, impresión *f* (c) *(of book)* impresión *f*, tirada *f* (d) *(imitation)* imitación *f*; **to do impressions** hacer imitaciones

**impressionable** [ɪmˈpreʃənəbəl] *adj* impresionable

**impressionism** [ɪmˈpreʃənɪzəm] *n Art* impresionismo *m*

**impressionist** [ɪmˈpreʃənɪst] **1** *n* (a) *Art* impresionista *mf* (b) *(impersonator)* imitador(ora) *m,f*

**2** *adj Art* impresionista

**impressionistic** [ɪmpreʃəˈnɪstɪk] *adj* impresionista

**impressive** [ɪmˈpresɪv] *adj* impresionante

**imprint 1** *n* [ˈɪmprɪnt] (a) *(of seal)* marca *f*; *(of feet)* huella *f* (b) *(of publisher)* pie *m* de imprenta

**2** *vt* [ɪmˈprɪnt] marcar **(on** en), grabar **(on** en); **her words were imprinted on my memory** sus palabras se me quedaron grabadas en la memoria

**imprison** [ɪmˈprɪzən] *vt* encarcelar

**imprisonment** [ɪmˈprɪzənmənt] *n* encarcelamiento *m*

**improbability** [ɪmprɒbəˈbɪlɪtɪ] *n* *(unlikelihood)* improbabilidad *f*; *(strangeness)* inverosimilitud *f*

**improbable** [ɪmˈprɒbəbəl] *adj* *(unlikely)* improbable; *(strange, unusual)* inverosímil

**impromptu** [ɪmˈprɒmptjuː] **1** *adj* *(speech, party)* improvisado(a)

**2** *adv* *(unexpectedly)* de improviso; *(ad lib)* improvisadamente

**improper** [ɪmˈprɒpə(r)] *adj* *(use, purpose)* impropio(a), incorrecto(a); *(suggestion, behaviour)* indecoroso(a); *Law* **i. practices** actuaciones *fpl* irregulares

**impropriety** [ɪmprəˈpraɪətɪ] *n* *(inappropriateness)* impropiedad *f*, incorrección *f*; *(indecency)* falta *f* de decoro; *(unlawfulness)* irregularidad *f*

**improve** [ɪmˈpruːv] **1** *vt* mejorar; **to i. a property** hacer mejoras en un inmueble; **she was eager to i. her mind** estaba ansiosa por ampliar sus conocimientos

**2** *vi* mejorar; **to i. with time** mejorar con el tiempo

▸**improve on, improve upon** *vt insep* mejorar, superar

**improved** [ɪmˈpruːvd] *adj* *(system, design)* mejorado(a); **he is much i.** ha mejorado mucho

**improvement** [ɪmˈpruːvmənt] *n* *(in situation, quality, behaviour)* mejora *f*; *(in health)* mejoría *f*; **to be an i. on** ser mejor que; **there's room for i.** se puede mejorar; **to make improvements (to)** *(home)* hacer reformas (en)

**improvident** [ɪmˈprɒvɪdənt] *adj Formal* poco previsor(ora), imprudente

**improvisation** [ɪmprəvaɪˈzeɪʃən] n improvisación f

**improvise** [ˈɪmprəvaɪz] vt & vi improvisar

**imprudent** [ɪmˈpruːdənt] adj imprudente

**impudence** [ˈɪmpjʊdəns] n desvergüenza f, insolencia f

**impudent** [ˈɪmpjʊdənt] adj desvergonzado(a), insolente

**impugn** [ɪmˈpjuːn] vt Formal poner en tela de juicio, cuestionar

**impulse** [ˈɪmpʌls] n impulso m; **to do sth on i.** hacer algo guiado(a) por un impulso; **i. buying** compra f impulsiva

**impulsive** [ɪmˈpʌlsɪv] adj impulsivo(a)

**impunity** [ɪmˈpjuːnɪtɪ] n impunidad f; **with i.** impunemente

**impure** [ɪmˈpjʊə(r)] adj impuro(a)

**impurity** [ɪmˈpjʊərɪtɪ] n impureza f

**impute** [ɪmˈpjuːt] vt Formal **to i.** sth to sb imputar or achacar algo a alguien

**in**[1] (abbr **inch** or **inches**) pulgada f (2,54 cm)

**in**[2] [ɪn] **1** prep (a) (with place) en; **in Spain** en España; **to arrive in Spain** llegar a España; **it was cold in the bar** dentro del bar or en el bar hacía frío; **those records in the corner are mine** los discos del rincón son míos; **in the rain** bajo la lluvia; **in the sun** al sol; **in bed** en la cama; **in hospital** en el hospital; **in here** aquí dentro; **in there** allí dentro

(b) (with expressions of time) en; **in 1927/ April/spring** en 1927/abril/primavera; **he did it in three hours** lo hizo en tres horas; **he'll be here in three hours** llegará dentro de tres horas; **in the morning/afternoon** por la mañana/tarde; **at three o'clock in the afternoon** a las tres de la tarde; **for the first time in years** por primera vez en años or desde hace años; **I haven't seen her in years** hace años que no la veo

(c) (expressing manner) **in Spanish** en español; **to write in pen/pencil** escribir con bolígrafo/a lápiz; **in a loud/quiet voice** en voz alta/baja; **in this way** de este modo, de esta manera; **dressed in white** vestido(a) de blanco; **in horror/surprise** con horror/sorpresa

(d) (expressing quantities, denominations, ratios) **in twos** de dos en dos; **one in ten** uno de cada diez; **2 metres in length/height** dos metros de longitud/altura; **in small/large quantities** en poca/gran cantidad; **in dollars** en dólares; **he's in his forties** anda por los cuarenta; **the temperature was in the nineties** ≃ hacía (una temperatura de) treinta y tantos grados

(e) (with gerund) **he had no difficulty in doing it** no tuvo dificultad en hacerlo; **in saying this, I don't mean to imply that…** no quiero dar a entender con esto que…

(f) (with field of activity) **to be in insurance/ marketing** dedicarse a los seguros/al marketing

(g) (in phrases) Fam **I didn't think she had it in her (to…)** no la creía capaz (de…)

**2** adv (a) (inside) dentro; **to go in** entrar

(b) (not out) **is your mother in?** ¿está tu madre (en casa)?; **to stay in** quedarse en casa, no salir

(c) (of train, plane) **is the train in yet?** ¿ha llegado ya el tren?

(d) (fashionable) de moda; **mini-skirts are in** se llevan las minifaldas

(e) **in that…** en el sentido de que…

(f) (idioms) **she is in for a surprise** le espera una sorpresa; Fam **he's got it in for me** la tiene tomada conmigo; **to be in on a plan** estar al corriente de un plan; **he's in for it** se va a enterar de lo que vale un peine

**3** adj **the in crowd** la gente selecta

**4** n **the ins and outs** los pormenores

**inability** [ɪnəˈbɪlɪtɪ] n incapacidad f (**to do sth** para hacer algo)

**inaccessibility** [ɪnæksesɪˈbɪlɪtɪ] n inaccesibilidad f

**inaccessible** [ɪnækˈsesɪbəl] adj inaccesible

**inaccuracy** [ɪnˈækjʊrəsɪ] n inexactitud f, imprecisión f; **the report was full of inaccuracies** el informe estaba lleno de imprecisiones

**inaccurate** [ɪnˈækjʊrət] adj inexacto(a), impreciso(a)

**inaction** [ɪnˈækʃən] n pasividad f, inactividad f

**inactive** [ɪnˈæktɪv] adj inactivo(a)

**inactivity** [ɪnækˈtɪvɪtɪ] n inactividad f

**inadequacy** [ɪnˈædɪkwəsɪ] n (of person) incapacidad f; (of explanation, measures) insuficiencia f

**inadequate** [ɪnˈædɪkwət] adj (a) (insufficient) insuficiente (b) (not capable) incapaz, inepto(a); **I feel i.** siento que no doy la talla

**inadmissible** [ɪnədˈmɪsɪbəl] adj Law (evidence) inadmisible

**inadvertent** [ɪnədˈvɜːtənt] adj fortuito(a), intencionado(a)

**inadvertently** [ɪnədˈvɜːtəntlɪ] adv sin querer

**inadvisable** [ɪnədˈvaɪzəbəl] adj poco aconsejable

**inalienable** [ɪnˈeɪlɪənəbəl] adj Formal inalienable

**inane** [ɪˈneɪn] adj necio(a), estúpido(a)

**inanimate** [ɪnˈænɪmət] adj inanimado(a)

**inanity** [ɪˈnænɪtɪ] n necedad f, estupidez f

**inapplicable** [ɪnˈæplɪkəbəl] adj inaplicable (**to** a); **delete where i.** táchese lo que no proceda

**inappropriate** [ɪnəˈprəʊprɪət] *adj (behaviour, remark)* inadecuado(a), improcedente; *(dress)* inadecuado(a), impropio(a); *(present, choice)* inapropiado(a); *(time, moment)* inoportuno(a)

**inapt** [ɪnˈæpt] *adj* inapropiado(a)

**inarticulate** [ɪnɑːˈtɪkjʊlɪt] *adj (sound)* inarticulado(a); **to be i.** *(of person)* expresarse mal; **she was i. with rage** estaba tan enfadada que no podía ni hablar

**inasmuch as** [ɪnəzˈmʌtʃəz] *conj Formal* por cuanto

**inattention** [ɪnəˈtenʃən] *n* falta *f* de atención

**inattentive** [ɪnəˈtentɪv] *adj* distraído(a); **to be i. to** no poner suficiente atención a *or* en

**inaudible** [ɪnˈɔːdɪbəl] *adj* inaudible

**inaugural** [ɪˈnɔːgjʊrəl] *adj* inaugural

**inaugurate** [ɪˈnɔːgjʊreɪt] *vt (event, scheme)* inaugurar; **the President will be inaugurated in January** el presidente tomará posesión de su cargo en enero

**inauguration** [ɪnɔːgjʊˈreɪʃən] *n (of event, scheme)* inauguración *f*; *(of president)* toma *f* de posesión

**inauspicious** [ɪnɔːˈspɪʃəs] *adj (circumstances)* desafortunado(a); *(start, moment)* aciago(a)

**inauthentic** [ɪnɔːˈθentɪk] *adj* no auténtico(a), falso(a)

**in-between** [ɪnbɪˈtwiːn] *adj* intermedio(a)

**inborn** [ˈɪnbɔːn] *adj* innato(a)

**inbred** [ˈɪnbred] *adj* **(a)** *(animals, people)* endogámico(a) **(b)** *(innate)* innato(a)

**in-built** [ˈɪnbɪlt] *adj (tendency, weakness)* inherente; *(feature)* incorporado(a); **his height gives him an i. advantage** su altura le proporciona una ventaja de entrada

**Inc** [ɪŋk] *adj Com (abbr* **Incorporated)** ≃ S.A.

**Inca** [ˈɪŋkə] **1** *n* inca *mf* **2** *adj* incaico(a), inca

**incalculable** [ɪnˈkælkjʊləbəl] *adj* incalculable

**incandescent** [ɪnkænˈdesənt] *adj* incandescente; *Fig* **to be i. with rage** estar rojo(a) de ira

**incantation** [ɪnkænˈteɪʃən] *n* conjuro *m*

**incapable** [ɪnˈkeɪpəbəl] *adj* incapaz **(of doing sth** de hacer algo); **she is i. of kindness/deceit** es incapaz de ser amable/engañar a nadie

**incapacitate** [ɪnkəˈpæsɪteɪt] *vt* incapacitar

**incapacity** [ɪnkəˈpæsɪtɪ] *n* incapacidad *f*

**incarcerate** [ɪnˈkɑːsəreɪt] *vt Formal* encarcelar, recluir

**incarceration** [ɪnkɑːsəˈreɪʃən] *n Formal* encarcelamiento *m*, reclusión *f*

**incarnate** [ɪnˈkɑːneɪt] *adj* personificado(a); **beauty i.** la belleza personificada; **the devil i.** el diablo en persona

**incarnation** [ɪnkɑːˈneɪʃən] *n* encarnación *f*

**incautious** [ɪnˈkɔːʃəs] *adj* incauto(a)

**incendiary** [ɪnˈsendɪərɪ] **1** *n (arsonist)* incendiario(a) *m,f*; *(bomb)* bomba *f* incendiaria **2** *adj (bomb, device, remarks)* incendiario(a)

**incense¹** [ˈɪnsens] *n* incienso *m*

**incense²** [ɪnˈsens] *vt (anger)* encolerizar, enfurecer

**incensed** [ɪnˈsenst] *adj* enfurecido(a); **to get** *or* **become i.** enfurecerse

**incentive** [ɪnˈsentɪv] *n (stimulus, payment)* incentivo *m*; **i. scheme** plan *m* de incentivos

**inception** [ɪnˈsepʃən] *n* comienzo *m*, inicio *m*

**incessant** [ɪnˈsesənt] *adj* incesante, continuo(a)

**incest** [ˈɪnsest] *n* incesto *m*

**incestuous** [ɪnˈsestjʊəs] *adj (sexually)* incestuoso(a); *Fig (environment, group)* endogámico(a)

**inch** [ɪntʃ] *n* **(a)** pulgada *f (2,54 cm)*; **i. by i.** palmo a palmo; **the car missed me by inches** el coche no me atropelló por cuestión de centímetros **(b)** *(idioms)* **I know every i. of the town** me conozco la ciudad como la palma de la mano; **he's every i. the gentleman** es todo un caballero; **to be within an i. of doing sth** estar en un tris de hacer algo; **she won't give an i.** no cederá ni un ápice; **give her an i. and she'll take a mile** dale la mano y se tomará el brazo

▸**inch along, inch forward** *vi* avanzar lentamente

**incidence** [ˈɪnsɪdəns] *n* incidencia *f* **(of** de)

**incident** [ˈɪnsɪdənt] *n* incidente *m*

**incidental** [ɪnsɪˈdentəl] *adj* incidental, accesorio(a); **i. expenses** gastos *mpl* imprevistos; *Cin Th* **i. music** música *f* de acompañamiento

**incidentally** [ɪnsɪˈdentəlɪ] *adv (by the way)* por cierto

**incinerate** [ɪnˈsɪnəreɪt] *vt* incinerar

**incineration** [ɪnsɪnəˈreɪʃən] *n* incineración *f*

**incinerator** [ɪnˈsɪnəreɪtə(r)] *n* incineradora *f*

**incipient** [ɪnˈsɪpɪənt] *adj Formal* incipiente

**incision** [ɪnˈsɪʒən] *n* incisión *f*

**incisive** [ɪnˈsaɪsɪv] *adj (comment, analysis)* agudo(a), incisivo(a); *(mind)* sagaz, incisivo(a)

**incisor** [ɪnˈsaɪzə(r)] *n* incisivo *m*

**incite** [ɪnˈsaɪt] *vt* incitar; **to i. sb to do sth** incitar a alguien a que haga algo

**incitement** [ɪnˈsaɪtmənt] *n* incitación *f*

**incivility** [ɪnsɪˈvɪlɪt] *n Formal* descortesía *f*

**incl** (a) *(abbr* **including)** incl. **(b)** *(abbr* **inclusive)** incl.

**inclement** [ɪnˈklemənt] *adj Formal (weather)* inclemente

**inclination** [ɪnklɪ'neɪʃən] *n (desire, angle)* inclinación *f*; **to have no i. to do sth** no sentir ninguna inclinación por *or* a hacer algo; **by i.** por naturaleza

**incline 1** *n* ['ɪnklaɪn] *(slope)* cuesta *f*, pendiente *f*

**2** *vt* [ɪn'klaɪn] **(a)** *(motivate, cause)* inclinar; **her remarks don't i. me to be sympathetic** sus comentarios no me mueven a ser comprensivo **(b)** *(lean)* inclinar; **she inclined her head towards him** inclinó la cabeza hacia él **(c)** *(tend)* **to be inclined to do sth** tener tendencia a *or* tender a hacer algo; **I'm inclined to agree with you** soy de tu misma opinión

**3** *vi* **(a)** *(lean)* inclinarse **(b)** *(tend)* **to i. to** *or* **towards** inclinarse a; **to i. to the belief that…** inclinarse a pensar que…

**include** [ɪn'klu:d] *vt* incluir; *(in letter)* adjuntar; **my name was not included on the list** mi nombre no figuraba en la lista; **the price does not i. accommodation** el alojamiento no está incluido en el precio

**including** [ɪn'klu:dɪŋ] *prep* contando, incluyendo; **not i.** sin contar, sin incluir; **£4.99 i. postage and packing** 4,99 libras incluyendo gastos de envío

**inclusion** [ɪn'klu:ʒən] *n* inclusión *f*

**inclusive** [ɪn'klu:sɪv] *adj* **an i. price/sum** un precio/una cifra con todo incluido; **i. of** incluido(a), incluido; **i. of VAT** IVA incluido; **from the 4th to the 12th February i.** del 4 al 12 de febrero, ambos inclusive

**incognito** [ɪnkɒg'ni:təʊ] *adv* de incógnito

**incoherence** [ɪnkəʊ'hɪərəns] *n* incoherencia *f*

**incoherent** [ɪnkəʊ'hɪərənt] *adj* incoherente; **he was i. with rage** estaba tan furioso que le fallaban las palabras

**income** ['ɪnkʌm] *n (of person) (from work)* ingresos *mpl; (from shares, investment)* rendimientos *mpl*, réditos *mpl; (from property)* renta *f; (in accounts)* ingresos *mpl; Br* **i. support** = ayuda gubernamental a personas con muy bajos ingresos o desempleadas pero sin derecho al subsidio de desempleo; **i. tax** impuesto *m* sobre la renta

**incoming** ['ɪnkʌmɪŋ] *adj (government, president)* entrante; *(tide)* ascendente; **i. flights** vuelos *mpl* de llegada; **the i. missile** el misil que se aproximaba; **i. mail** correo *m* recibido; **i. calls** llamadas *fpl* de fuera

**incommensurate** [ɪnkə'menʃərɪt] *adj* desproporcionado(a) **(with** con relación a, en relación con)

**incommunicado** [ɪnkəmju:nɪ'kɑ:dəʊ] *adv* **to be held i.** estar incomunicado(a)

**in-company** ['ɪnkʌmpəni] *adj* **i. training** formación *f* en el lugar de trabajo

**incomparable** [ɪn'kɒmpərəbəl] *adj* incomparable

**incompatible** [ɪnkəm'pætɪbəl] *adj* incompatible **(with** con)

**incompetence** [ɪn'kɒmpɪtəns] *n* incompetencia *f*

**incompetent** [ɪn'kɒmpɪtənt] *adj* incompetente

**incomplete** [ɪnkəm'pli:t] *adj* incompleto(a)

**incomprehensible** [ɪnkɒmprɪ'hensɪbəl] *adj* incomprensible

**incomprehension** [ɪnkɒmprɪ'henʃən] *n* incomprensión *f*

**inconceivable** [ɪnkən'si:vəbəl] *adj* inconcebible

**inconclusive** [ɪnkən'klu:sɪv] *adj (evidence, investigation)* no concluyente; **the meeting was i.** la reunión no sirvió para aclarar las cosas

**incongruity** [ɪnkɒŋ'gru:ɪtɪ] *n* incongruencia *f*

**incongruous** [ɪn'kɒŋgrʊəs] *adj* incongruente

**inconsequential** [ɪnkɒnsɪ'kwenʃəl] *adj* trivial, intrascendente

**inconsiderate** [ɪnkən'sɪdərɪt] *adj* desconsiderado(a)

**inconsistency** [ɪnkən'sɪstənsɪ] *n (lack of logic, illogical statement)* contradicción *f*, incongruencia *f; (uneven quality)* irregularidad *f*

**inconsistent** [ɪnkən'sɪstənt] *adj (contradictory)* contradictorio(a), incongruente; *(uneven)* irregular; **his words are i. with his conduct** sus palabras no están en consonancia con sus actos

**inconsolable** [ɪnkən'səʊləbəl] *adj* inconsolable

**inconspicuous** [ɪnkən'spɪkjʊəs] *adj* discreto(a); **to be i.** pasar desapercibido(a)

**incontestable** [ɪnkən'testəbəl] *adj* incontestable, indiscutible

**incontinence** [ɪn'kɒntɪnəns] *n* incontinencia *f*

**incontinent** [ɪn'kɒntɪnənt] *adj* incontinente

**incontrovertible** [ɪnkɒntrə'vɜ:tɪbəl] *adj* incontrovertible, indiscutible

**inconvenience** [ɪnkən'vi:njəns] **1** *n (difficulty)* molestia *f; (problem, drawback)* inconveniente *m*; **we apologize for any i.** disculpen las molestias; **to be an i. to sb** suponer una molestia para alguien

**2** *vt* causar molestias a

**inconvenient** [ɪnkən'vi:njənt] *adj (time, request)* inoportuno(a); *(place)* mal situado(a); **I'm afraid 4.30 would be i.** (me temo que) las cuatro y media no me viene bien *or* no es buena hora

**incorporate** [ɪn'kɔ:pəreɪt] *vt* incorporar

**incorrect** [ɪnkə'rekt] *adj* incorrecto(a)

**incorrigible** [ɪn'kɒrɪdʒɪbəl] *adj* incorregible

**incorruptible** [ɪnkə'rʌptɪbəl] *adj* incorruptible

**increase 1** *n* ['ɪnkri:s] aumento *m* (**in** de); *(in price, temperature)* subida *f* (**in** de); **to be on the i.** ir en aumento

**2** *vt* [ɪn'kri:s] aumentar; **to i. one's efforts** esforzarse más; **to i. one's speed** acelerar, aumentar la velocidad

**3** *vi* aumentar; **to i. in price** subir de precio; **to i. in value** aumentar de valor

**increasing** [ɪn'kri:sɪŋ] *adj* creciente

**increasingly** [ɪn'kri:sɪŋlɪ] *adv* cada vez más

**incredible** [ɪn'kredɪbəl] *adj* (**a**) *(unbelievable)* increíble (**b**) *Fam (excellent)* increíble, extraordinario(a)

**incredibly** [ɪn'kredɪblɪ] *adv* increíblemente; *Fam* **i. good** increíblemente bueno(a)

**incredulity** [ɪnkrɪ'dju:lɪtɪ] *n* incredulidad *f*

**incredulous** [ɪn'kredjʊləs] *adj* incrédulo(a)

**increment** ['ɪnkrɪmənt] *n* incremento *m*

**incriminate** [ɪn'krɪmɪneɪt] *vt* incriminar

**incriminating** [ɪn'krɪmɪneɪtɪŋ] *adj* incriminador(ora)

**incubate** ['ɪnkjʊbeɪt] *vt* incubar

**incubation** [ɪnkjʊ'beɪʃən] *n* incubación *f*; *Med* **i. period** *(of disease)* período *m* de incubación

**incubator** ['ɪnkjʊbeɪtə(r)] *n (for eggs, babies)* incubadora *f*

**inculcate** ['ɪnkʌlkeɪt] *vt Formal* **to i. sth in sb, to i. sb with sth** inculcar algo en alguien

**incumbent** [ɪn'kʌmbənt] **1** *n* titular *mf*

**2** *adj* **to be i. on sb to do sth** incumbir *or* corresponder a alguien hacer algo

**incur** [ɪn'kɜ:(r)] *(pt & pp* **incurred)** *vt (blame, expense)* incurrir en; *(sb's anger)* provocar, incurrir en; *(debt)* contraer

**incurable** [ɪn'kjʊərəbəl] *adj (disease)* incurable; *(optimist, bigot)* incorregible

**incurious** [ɪn'kjʊərɪəs] *adj* poco curioso(a)

**incursion** [ɪn'kɜ:ʃən] *n Formal* incursión *f*

**indebted** [ɪn'detɪd] *adj (financially)* endeudado(a); **to be i. to sb** *(financially)* estar endeudado(a) con alguien; *(for help, advice)* estar en deuda con alguien

**indebtedness** [ɪn'detɪdnɪs] *n (financial)* endeudamiento *m*; *(for help, advice)* deuda *f* (**to** con), agradecimiento *m* (**to** a)

**indecency** [ɪn'di:sənsɪ] *n* indecencia *f*

**indecent** [ɪn'di:sənt] *adj* indecente, indecoroso(a); **to do sth with i. haste** apresurarse descaradamente a hacer algo; *Law* **i. assault** abusos *mpl* deshonestos; *Law* **i. exposure** exhibicionismo *m*

**indecipherable** [ɪndɪ'saɪfərəbəl] *adj* indescifrable

**indecision** [ɪndɪ'sɪʒən] *n* indecisión *f*

**indecisive** [ɪndɪ'saɪsɪv] *adj (person)* indeciso(a); *(battle, election)* no concluyente

**indecorous** [ɪn'dekərəs] *adj Formal* indigno(a), indecoroso(a)

**indeed** [ɪn'di:d] *adv* (**a**) *(used with "very")* **very happy i.** contentísimo(a); **I am very glad i.** me alegro muchísimo; **thank you very much i.** muchísimas gracias (**b**) *(in confirmation)* efectivamente, ciertamente; **yes i.!** ¡ciertamente!; **i. not!** ¡por supuesto que no!; **you've been to Venice, haven't you? – i. I have!** has estado en Venecia, ¿verdad? – ¡ya lo creo! (**c**) *(what is more)* es más; **I think so, i. I am sure of it** creo que sí, es más, estoy seguro (**d**) *(expressing ironic surprise)* **have you i.?** ¿ah, sí?, ¿no me digas?

**indefatigable** [ɪndɪ'fætɪgəbəl] *adj Formal* infatigable, incansable

**indefensible** [ɪndɪ'fensɪbəl] *adj* indefendible, injustificable

**indefinable** [ɪndɪ'faɪnəbəl] *adj* indefinible

**indefinite** [ɪn'defɪnɪt] *adj* (**a**) *(period of time, number)* indefinido(a) (**b**) *(ideas, promises)* indefinido(a), vago(a) (**c**) *Gram* indeterminado(a), indefinido(a)

**indefinitely** [ɪn'defɪnɪtlɪ] *adv* indefinidamente

**indelible** [ɪn'delɪbəl] *adj* indeleble, imborrable

**indelicate** [ɪn'delɪkət] *adj* poco delicado(a), indelicado(a)

**indemnify** [ɪn'demnɪfaɪ] *vt* **to i. sb for sth** *(compensate)* indemnizar a alguien por algo; **to i. sb against sth** *(give security)* asegurar a alguien contra algo

**indemnity** [ɪn'demnɪtɪ] *n (guarantee)* indemnidad *f*; *(money)* indemnización *f*

**indent** *Typ* **1** *n* ['ɪndent] sangrado *m*

**2** *vt* [ɪn'dent] sangrar

**indentation** [ɪnden'teɪʃən] *n (on edge)* muesca *f*; *(dent)* abolladura *f*; *Typ* sangrado *m*

**independence** [ɪndɪ'pendəns] *n* independencia *f*

**independent** [ɪndɪ'pendənt] *adj* independiente; **to be i. of** ser independiente de; *Br* **i. school** colegio *m* privado

**independently** [ɪndɪ'pendəntlɪ] *adv* independientemente (**of** de)

**in-depth** ['ɪn'depθ] *adj* a fondo, exhaustivo(a)

**indescribable** [ɪndɪs'kraɪbəbəl] *adj (pain, beauty)* indescriptible

**indestructible** [ɪndɪs'trʌktəbəl] *adj* indestructible

**indeterminate** [ɪndɪ'tɜːmɪnət] *adj* indeterminado(a)

**index** ['ɪndeks] **1** *n (of book, in library, financial)* índice *m*; **i. finger** (dedo *m*) índice *m*

**2** *vt* **(a)** *(book)* indizar **(b)** *Fin (wages)* ajustar según el IPC

**index-linked** ['ɪndeks'lɪŋkt] *adj Fin (wages, pension)* ajustado(a) al IPC

**India** ['ɪndɪə] *n* (la) India

**Indian** ['ɪndɪən] **1** *n (native of India)* indio(a) *m,f*, hindú *mf*; *(Native American)* indio(a) *m,f*, *Am* indígena *mf*

**2** *adj (from India)* indio(a), hindú; *(Native American)* indio(a), *Am* indígena; **I. elephant** elefante *m* asiático; **I. file** fila *f* india; **the I. Ocean** el Océano Índico; **I. summer** veranillo *m* de San Martín

**indicate** ['ɪndɪkeɪt] **1** *vt* **(a)** *(point to)* indicar, señalar **(b)** *(show)* demostrar **(c)** *(state)* manifestar

**2** *vi (of car-driver)* poner el intermitente

**indication** [ɪndɪ'keɪʃən] *n* indicación *f*; **she gave no i. of her feelings** no manifestó sus sentimientos; **there is every i. that he was speaking the truth** todo parece indicar que dijo la verdad; **all the indications are that...** todo indica que...

**indicative** [ɪn'dɪkətɪv] **1** *n Gram* indicativo *m*

**2** *adj* indicativo(a) **(of** de); *Gram* **i. mood** modo *m* indicativo

**indicator** ['ɪndɪkeɪtə(r)] *n* **(a)** *(sign)* indicador *m*; **economic indicators** indicadores *mpl* económicos; *Rail* **i. board** panel *m* de información **(b)** *Br Aut* intermitente *m*

**indict** [ɪn'daɪt] *vt Law* acusar **(for** de)

**indictable** [ɪn'daɪtəbəl] *adj Law* **i. offence** delito *m* procesable

**indictment** [ɪn'daɪtmənt] *n Law* acusación *f*; *Fig* **it is an i. of our society** pone en tela de juicio a nuestra sociedad

**indie** ['ɪndɪ] *adj Fam (music, band)* independiente, indie

**indifference** [ɪn'dɪfərəns] *n* indiferencia *f*; **it's a matter of complete i. to me** es un asunto que me trae sin cuidado

**indifferent** [ɪn'dɪfərənt] *adj* **(a)** *(not interested)* indiferente **(b)** *(mediocre)* mediocre, regular

**indigenous** [ɪn'dɪdʒɪnəs] *adj* indígena **(to** de)

**indigestible** [ɪndɪ'dʒestɪbəl] *adj* indigerible

**indigestion** [ɪndɪ'dʒestʃən] *n* indigestión *f*

**indignant** [ɪn'dɪgnənt] *adj* indignado(a); **to get i. about sth** indignarse por algo

**indignation** [ɪndɪg'neɪʃən] *n* indignación *f*

**indignity** [ɪn'dɪgnɪtɪ] *n* indignidad *f*

**indigo** ['ɪndɪgəʊ] *n & adj* añil *m*

**indirect** [ɪndɪ'rekt] *adj* indirecto(a); *Com* **i. costs** costes *mpl* indirectos; *Gram* **i. object** complemento *m or* objeto *m* indirecto; *Gram* **i. speech** estilo *m* indirecto; **i. tax** impuesto *m* indirecto

**indirectly** [ɪndɪ'rektlɪ] *adv* indirectamente

**indiscernible** [ɪndɪ'sɜːnɪbəl] *adj* indiscernible

**indiscipline** [ɪn'dɪsɪplɪn] *n* indisciplina *f*

**indiscreet** [ɪndɪs'kriːt] *adj* indiscreto(a)

**indiscretion** [ɪndɪs'kreʃən] *n* indiscreción *f*

**indiscriminate** [ɪndɪs'krɪmɪnət] *adj* indiscriminado(a); **to be i. in one's praise** hacer elogios indiscriminadamente

**indispensable** [ɪndɪs'pensəbəl] *adj* indispensable, imprescindible

**indisposed** [ɪndɪs'pəʊzd] *adj Formal (ill)* indispuesto(a); **to be i.** hallarse indispuesto

**indisputable** [ɪndɪs'pjuːtəbəl] *adj* indiscutible

**indissoluble** [ɪndɪ'sɒljʊbəl] *adj Formal* indisoluble

**indistinct** [ɪndɪs'tɪŋkt] *adj* indistinto(a), impreciso(a)

**indistinguishable** [ɪndɪs'tɪŋgwɪʃəbəl] *adj* indistinguible **(from** de)

**individual** [ɪndɪ'vɪdjʊəl] **1** *n (person)* individuo *m*

**2** *adj* **(a)** *(of or for one person)* individual; **the i. hospitals are responsible for running their own affairs** cada hospital lleva sus propios asuntos **(b)** *(characteristic)* personal

**individualist** [ɪndɪ'vɪdjʊəlɪst] *n* individualista *mf*

**individuality** [ɪndɪvɪdjʊ'ælɪtɪ] *n* individualidad *f*

**individually** [ɪndɪ'vɪdjʊəlɪ] *adv* individualmente; **he spoke to us all i.** nos habló a todos uno por uno

**indivisible** [ɪndɪ'vɪzɪbəl] *adj* indivisible

**Indochina** [ɪndəʊ'tʃaɪnə] *n* Indochina

**indoctrinate** [ɪn'dɒktrɪneɪt] *vt* adoctrinar; **he indoctrinated his pupils with his prejudices** inculcó sus prejuicios a sus alumnos

**indoctrination** [ɪndɒktrɪ'neɪʃən] *n* adoctrinamiento *m*

**indolent** ['ɪndələnt] *adj Formal* indolente

**indomitable** [ɪn'dɒmɪtəbəl] *adj Formal* indómito(a)

**Indonesia** [ɪndəʊ'niːzɪə] *n* Indonesia

**Indonesian** [ɪndəʊ'niːʒən] **1** *n* **(a)** *(person)* indonesio(a) *m,f* **(b)** *(language)* indonesio *m*

**2** *adj* indonesio(a)

**indoor** ['ɪndɔː(r)] *adj (plant, photography)* de interior; **i. athletics** atletismo *m* en pista cubierta; **i. (swimming) pool** piscina *f* cubierta

**indoors** [ɪn'dɔːz] *adv* dentro (de casa); **to go i.** entrar en casa

**induce** [ɪn'djuːs] *vt* (a) *(persuade)* inducir; **to i. sb to do sth** inducir a alguien a hacer algo (b) *(cause)* provocar; *Med* **to i. labour** provocar *or* inducir el parto

**inducement** [ɪn'djuːsmənt] *n (incentive)* aliciente *m*, incentivo *m*

**induction** [ɪn'dʌkʃən] *n Med (of labour)* inducción *f*; **i. course** *(to new job)* cursillo *m* introductorio

**inductive** [ɪn'dʌktɪv] *adj (reasoning)* inductivo(a)

**indulge** [ɪn'dʌldʒ] **1** *vt* consentir; **they indulged his every whim** le consentían todos los caprichos; **to i. oneself** darse un capricho *or* un gusto

     **2** *vi* **to i. in alcohol** darse a la bebida; **to i. in idle speculation** entregarse a especulaciones vanas

**indulgence** [ɪn'dʌldʒəns] *n* indulgencia *f*; **I allow myself the occasional i.** de vez en cuando me permito algún vicio

**indulgent** [ɪn'dʌldʒənt] *adj* indulgente (**to** con)

**industrial** [ɪn'dʌstrɪəl] *adj* industrial; **i. action** huelga *f* (obrera); **to take i. action** declararse en huelga; **i. disease** enfermedad *f* laboral; **i. dispute** conflicto *m* laboral; **i. espionage** espionaje *m* industrial; *Br* **i. estate** polígono *m* industrial; **i. injury** accidente *m* laboral; **i. park** polígono *m* industrial; **i. relations** relaciones *fpl* laborales; *Hist* **the I. Revolution** la Revolución Industrial; *Law* **i. tribunal** magistratura *f* de trabajo; **i. unrest** conflictividad *f* laboral; **i. waste** residuos *mpl* industriales

**industrialist** [ɪn'dʌstrɪəlɪst] *n* industrial *mf*

**industrialization** [ɪndʌstrɪəlaɪ'zeɪʃən] *n* industrialización *f*

**industrialize** [ɪn'dʌstrɪəlaɪz] *vt* industrializar

**industrious** [ɪn'dʌstrɪəs] *adj (pupil, worker)* aplicado(a); *(research)* minucioso(a)

**industry** ['ɪndʌstrɪ] *n* (a) *(economic)* industria *f*; **heavy/light i.** industria pesada/ligera; **aircraft/mining/shipping i.** industria aeronáutica/minera/naviera; **tourist i.** sector *m* turístico; **entertainment i.** industria *or* sector del espectáculo (b) *(hard work)* aplicación *f*

**inebriated** [ɪn'iːbrɪeɪtɪd] *adj Formal* ebrio(a); **to be i.** estar ebrio(a)

**inedible** [ɪn'edɪbəl] *adj (not edible)* incomestible; *(unpalatable)* incomible

**ineffable** [ɪn'efəbəl] *adj Formal* inefable, indescriptible

**ineffective** [ɪnɪ'fektɪv] *adj* ineficaz

**ineffectual** [ɪnɪ'fektjʊəl] *adj (person)* inepto(a); *(measure)* ineficaz

**inefficiency** [ɪnɪ'fɪʃənsɪ] *n* ineficiencia *f*

**inefficient** [ɪnɪ'fɪʃənt] *adj* ineficiente

**inelastic** [ɪnɪ'læstɪk] *adj (material, principles)* rígido(a)

**inelegant** [ɪn'elɪgənt] *adj* vulgar, poco elegante

**ineligible** [ɪn'elɪdʒɪbəl] *adj* **to be i. for sth** no tener derecho a algo

**inept** [ɪn'ept] *adj* inepto(a) (**at** para)

**ineptitude** [ɪn'eptɪtjuːd] *n* ineptitud *f*

**inequality** [ɪnɪ'kwɒlɪtɪ] *n* desigualdad *f*

**inequitable** [ɪn'ekwɪtəbəl] *adj Formal* injusto(a), no equitativo(a)

**inert** [ɪ'nɜːt] *adj (motionless)* inmóvil; *Chem* **i. gas** gas *m* noble *or* inerte

**inertia** [ɪ'nɜːʃɪə] *n* inercia *f*

**inescapable** [ɪnɪ'skeɪpəbəl] *adj* inevitable, ineludible

**inessential** [ɪnɪ'senʃə] *adj* prescindible

**inestimable** [ɪn'estɪməbəl] *adj* inestimable, inapreciable

**inevitability** [ɪnevɪtə'bɪlɪtɪ] *n* inevitabilidad *f*

**inevitable** [ɪn'evɪtəbəl] *adj* inevitable

**inevitably** [ɪn'evɪtəblɪ] *adv* inevitablemente

**inexact** [ɪnɪg'zækt] *adj* inexacto(a)

**inexcusable** [ɪnɪks'kjuːzəbəl] *adj* inexcusable, injustificable

**inexhaustible** [ɪneg'zɔːstɪbəl] *adj* inagotable

**inexorable** [ɪn'eksərəbəl] *adj* inexorable

**inexpensive** [ɪnɪks'pensɪv] *adj* económico(a), barato(a)

**inexperience** [ɪnɪks'pɪərɪəns] *n* inexperiencia *f*

**inexperienced** [ɪnɪks'pɪərɪənst] *adj* inexperto(a); **to the i. eye/ear** para el ojo/oído inexperto; **he's i. in handling staff** no tiene experiencia en cuestiones de personal

**inexplicable** [ɪnɪks'plɪkəbəl] *adj* inexplicable

**inexpressible** [ɪnɪks'presɪbəl] *adj* indescriptible, indecible

**inexpressive** [ɪnɪks'presɪv] *adj* inexpresivo(a)

**inextricably** [ɪneks'trɪkəblɪ] *adv* inseparablemente

**infallibility** [ɪnfælɪ'bɪlɪtɪ] *n* infalibilidad *f*

**infallible** [ɪn'fælɪbəl] *adj* infalible

**infamous** ['ɪnfəməs] *adj* infame; **to be i. for sth** ser tristemente famoso(a) por algo

**infamy** ['ɪnfəmɪ] *n Formal* infamia *f*

**infancy** ['ɪnfənsɪ] *n (childhood)* infancia *f*; *Fig* **when medicine was still in its i.** cuando la medicina daba sus primeros pasos

**infant** ['ɪnfənt] n (baby) bebé m; (small child) niño(a) m,f pequeño(a); **i. class** clase f de párvulos; Med **i. mortality** mortalidad f infantil; **i. school** colegio m de párvulos, escuela f infantil

**infanticide** [ɪn'fæntɪsaɪd] n infanticidio m

**infantile** ['ɪnfəntaɪl] adj Pej pueril, infantil

**infantry** ['ɪnfəntrɪ] n infantería f

**infantryman** ['ɪnfəntrɪmən] n soldado m de infantería, infante m

**infatuated** [ɪn'fætjʊeɪtɪd] adj to be i. with estar prendado(a) or encaprichado(a) de

**infatuation** [ɪnfætjʊ'eɪʃən] n encaprichamiento m (amoroso)

**infect** [ɪn'fekt] vt (with disease) infectar; (with prejudice) emponzoñar; **to become infected** (of wound) infectarse; **to i. sb with sth** contagiar algo a alguien; **her enthusiasm infected us all** nos contagió a todos su entusiasmo

**infection** [ɪn'fekʃən] n Med infección f

**infectious** [ɪn'fekʃəs] adj (a) (disease) infeccioso(a) (b) (laughter, enthusiasm) contagioso(a)

**infer** [ɪn'fɜ:(r)] (pt & pp inferred) vt (deduce) inferir (from de), deducir (from de)

**inference** ['ɪnfərəns] n inferencia f, deducción f; **by i.** por deducción

**inferior** [ɪn'fɪərɪə(r)] **1** n to be sb's i. ser inferior a alguien
**2** adj (in status, quality) inferior (**to** a)

**inferiority** [ɪnfɪərɪ'ɒrɪtɪ] n inferioridad f; **i. complex** complejo m de inferioridad

**infernal** [ɪn'fɜ:nəl] adj (diabolical) infernal, diabólico(a); Fam **that i. little man!** ¡esa peste de hombre!

**inferno** [ɪn'fɜ:nəʊ] (pl infernos) n infierno m

**infertile** [ɪn'fɜ:taɪl] adj (land) yermo(a); (person) estéril

**infertility** [ɪnfɜ:'tɪlɪtɪ] n esterilidad f

**infest** [ɪn'fest] vt infestar; **to be infested with** or **by sth** estar infestado(a) de algo

**infidelity** [ɪnfɪ'delɪtɪ] n infidelidad f

**infield** ['ɪnfi:ld] n US Sport (in baseball) diamante m (interior)

**infielder** ['ɪnfi:ldə(r)] n US Sport (in baseball) jugador m (del diamante) interior

**infighting** ['ɪnfaɪtɪŋ] n lucha f interna

**infiltrate** ['ɪnfɪltreɪt] **1** vt infiltrar; **the organization had been infiltrated by spies** se habían infiltrado espías en la organización
**2** vi infiltrarse

**infiltration** [ɪnfɪl'treɪʃən] n infiltración f

**infinite** ['ɪnfɪnɪt] **1** n **the i.** el infinito
**2** adj infinito(a); Rel or Hum **in his i. wisdom** en su infinita sabiduría

**infinitely** ['ɪnfɪnɪtlɪ] adv infinitamente

**infinitesimal** [ɪnfɪnɪ'tesɪməl] adj infinitesimal

**infinitive** [ɪn'fɪnɪtɪv] n Gram infinitivo m; **in the i.** en infinitivo

**infinity** [ɪn'fɪnɪtɪ] n infinito m

**infirm** [ɪn'fɜ:m] adj achacoso(a)

**infirmary** [ɪn'fɜ:mərɪ] n (hospital) hospital m, clínica f; (in school, prison) enfermería f

**infirmity** [ɪn'fɜ:mɪtɪ] n (weakness) debilidad f; **the infirmities of old age** los achaques de la edad

**inflame** [ɪn'fleɪm] vt (**a**) (desire, curiosity) despertar; (crowd) enardecer (**b**) (of wound) **to become inflamed** inflamarse

**inflammable** [ɪn'flæməbəl] adj (substance) inflamable; Fig (situation) explosivo(a)

**inflammation** [ɪnflə'meɪʃən] n inflamación f

**inflammatory** [ɪn'flæmətrɪ] adj (speech) incendiario(a)

**inflatable** [ɪn'fleɪtəbəl] **1** n (rubber dinghy) barca f hinchable
**2** adj hinchable

**inflate** [ɪn'fleɪt] **1** vt (**a**) (tyre) inflar, hinchar; (sail) hinchar (**b**) (prices) inflar
**2** vi hincharse, inflarse

**inflated** [ɪn'fleɪtɪd] adj (balloon, tyre) inflado(a), hinchado(a); (prices, salary) desorbitado(a); **she has an i. opinion of herself** se cree mejor de lo que es

**inflation** [ɪn'fleɪʃən] n Econ inflación f; **i.-proof pension** pensión f revisable de acuerdo con la inflación

**inflationary** [ɪn'fleɪʃənrɪ] adj Econ inflacionista

**inflect** [ɪn'flekt] **1** vt (voice) modular
**2** vi Gram (of verb) conjugarse; (of noun) declinarse

**inflection** [ɪn'flekʃən] n (of word) flexión f, terminación f; (in voice) inflexión f

**inflexibility** [ɪnfleksɪ'bɪlɪtɪ] n rigidez f, inflexibilidad f

**inflexible** [ɪn'fleksɪbəl] adj (material, principles) rígido(a), inflexible

**inflict** [ɪn'flɪkt] vt (suffering, punishment, defeat) infligir (**on** a); **he was inflicting himself on us** teníamos que estar aguantando su presencia

**in-flight** ['ɪnflaɪt] adj **i. entertainment** distracciones fpl ofrecidas durante el vuelo; **i. meal** comida f (servida) a bordo

**influence** ['ɪnflʊəns] **1** n influencia f; **to be a good/bad i. on sb** tener una buena/mala influencia en alguien; **to have i. over/with sb** tener influencia sobre/con alguien; **a man of i.** un hombre influyente; **under the i. (of drink)** bajo los efectos del alcohol
**2** vt influir en, influenciar; **he is easily influenced** se deja influir fácilmente

**influential** [ɪnflʊ'enʃəl] adj influyente

**influenza** [ɪnflʊ'enzə] n gripe f

**influx** ['ınflʌks] n afluencia f

**info** ['ınfəu] n Fam información f

**inform** [ın'fɔ:m] 1 vt informar (**of/about** de/sobre); **keep me informed of what is happening** manténme informado de lo que pase
 2 vi **to i. on sb** delatar a alguien

**informal** [ın'fɔ:məl] adj (dress, manner) informal; (word, language) familiar; (meeting, talks) extraoficial, informal

**informality** [ınfɔ:'mælıtı] n informalidad f

**informally** [ın'fɔ:məlı] adv (hold talks, inform) extraoficialmente; (dress, behave) informalmente, de manera informal

**informant** [ın'fɔ:mənt] n (for police) confidente mf; (for study) informante mf

**information** [ınfə'meıʃən] n (a) (news, facts) información f; **a piece of i.** una información, un dato; **for your i.** para tu información; **i. bureau** oficina f de información; **i. desk** mostrador m de información (b) Comptr **i. processing** proceso m de datos; **i. retrieval** recuperación f de la información; **i. science** informática f; **i. society** sociedad f de la información; **i. superhighway** autopista f de la información; **i. technology** informática f

**informative** [ın'fɔ:mətıv] adj informativo(a)

**informed** [ın'fɔ:md] adj (person) informado(a); **an i. guess/decision** una conjetura/decisión bien fundada

**informer** [ın'fɔ:mə(r)] n confidente mf

**infra dig** ['ınfrə'dıg] adj Fam cutre

**infrared** [ınfrə'red] adj Phys infrarrojo(a)

**infrastructure** ['ınfrəstrʌktʃə(r)] n infraestructura f

**infrequent** [ın'fri:kwənt] adj infrecuente

**infringe** [ın'frındʒ] vt (rule) infringir; (right) violar, vulnerar

▸**infringe on** vt insep infringir

**infringement** [ın'frındʒmənt] n (of rule, law) infracción f; (of right) violación f, vulneración f

**infuriate** [ın'fjʊərıeıt] vt exasperar, enfurecer

**infuriating** [ın'fjʊərıeıtıŋ] adj exasperante

**infuse** [ın'fju:z] vt infundir (**into** en)

**infusion** [ın'fju:ʒən] n (a) (drink) infusión f (b) (of money, high spirits) inyección f

**ingenious** [ın'dʒi:nıəs] adj ingenioso(a)

**ingenuity** [ındʒɪ'nju:ıtı] n ingenio m

**ingenuous** [ın'dʒenjuəs] adj ingenuo(a)

**inglorious** [ın'glɔ:rıəs] adj vergonzoso(a)

**ingot** ['ıŋgɒt] n lingote m

**ingrained** [ın'greınd] adj (dirt) incrustado(a); (prejudice, belief) arraigado(a)

**ingratiate** [ın'greıʃıeıt] vt **to i. oneself (with sb)** congraciarse (con alguien)

**ingratiating** [ın'greıʃıeıtıŋ] adj obsequioso(a)

**ingratitude** [ın'grætıtju:d] n ingratitud f

**ingredient** [ın'gri:dıənt] n also Fig ingrediente m; Fig **the missing i.** lo que falta

**ingrowing toenail** ['ıŋgrəuıŋ'təuneıl], **ingrown toenail** ['ıŋgrəun'təuneıl] n Med uña f encarnada

**inhabit** [ın'hæbıt] vt habitar

**inhabitable** [ın'hæbıtəbəl] adj habitable

**inhabitant** [ın'hæbıtənt] n habitante mf

**inhabited** [ın'hæbıtıd] adj habitado(a)

**inhale** [ın'heıl] 1 vt (gas, fumes) inhalar; (cigarette smoke) aspirar
 2 vi inspirar; (when smoking) tragarse el humo

**inhaler** [ın'heılə(r)] n (for asthmatics) inhalador m

**inherent** [ın'herənt] adj inherente (**in** a)

**inherit** [ın'herıt] vt heredar (**from** de)

**inheritance** [ın'herıtəns] n herencia f; **i. tax** impuesto m sobre sucesiones

**inhibit** [ın'hıbıt] vt (progress, growth) impedir, coartar; (breathing) inhibir; (feeling, person) cohibir, inhibir

**inhibited** [ın'hıbıtıd] adj cohibido(a)

**inhibition** [ını'bıʃən] n inhibición f; **to lose one's inhibitions** dejar de sentirse cohibido(a); **to have no inhibitions about doing sth** no sentir ninguna vergüenza a la hora de hacer algo

**inhospitable** [ınhɒ'spıtəbəl] adj (person) inhospitalario(a); (town, climate) inhóspito(a)

**in-house** ['ın'haus] 1 adj **i. staff** personal m en plantilla; **i. training** formación f en el lugar de trabajo
 2 adv **the work was done i.** el trabajo se hizo en la misma empresa

**inhuman** [ın'hju:mən] adj inhumano(a)

**inhumane** [ınhju:'meın] adj inhumano(a)

**inhumanity** [ınhju:'mænıtı] n falta f de humanidad

**inimical** [ı'nımıkəl] adj adverso(a) (**to** a)

**inimitable** [ı'nımıtəbəl] adj inimitable

**iniquitous** [ı'nıkwıtəs] adj inicuo(a)

**iniquity** [ı'nıkwıtı] n iniquidad f

**initial** [ı'nıʃəl] 1 n inicial f; **initials** iniciales fpl
 2 adj inicial
 3 vt (pt & pp **initialled**, US **initialed**) poner las iniciales en

**initially** [ı'nıʃəlı] adv inicialmente

**initiate** [ı'nıʃıeıt] vt (a) Formal (begin) iniciar; Law **to i. proceedings (against sb)** emprender una acción legal (contra alguien) (b) (to secret society, gang) iniciar (**into** en)

**initiation** [ınıʃı'eıʃən] n iniciación f; **i. ceremony** ceremonia f iniciática or de iniciación

**initiative** [ı'nıʃıtıv] n iniciativa f; **to take the i.** tomar la iniciativa; **on one's own i.** por iniciativa propia; **she lacks i.** le falta iniciativa

**inject** [ɪnˈdʒekt] vt (drug, money) inyectar (**into** en); **to i. sb with a drug** inyectar un medicamento a alguien; Fig **to i. sb with enthusiasm** infundir entusiasmo a alguien; Fig **to i. new life into sth** infundir nueva vida a algo

**injection** [ɪnˈdʒekʃən] n inyección f; **to give sb an i.** poner una inyección a alguien

**injudicious** [ɪndʒʊˈdɪʃəs] adj imprudente, poco juicioso(a)

**injunction** [ɪnˈdʒʌŋkʃən] n Law requerimiento m judicial

**injure** [ˈɪndʒə(r)] vt (person) herir, lesionar; (feelings) herir; (reputation, interests) dañar, perjudicar; **to i. oneself** lesionarse; **to i. one's leg** lesionarse una pierna

**injured** [ˈɪndʒəd] **1** npl **the i.** los heridos
**2** adj also Fig herido(a); (tone, voice) resentido(a); Law **the i. party** la parte perjudicada

**injurious** [ɪnˈdʒʊrɪəs] adj perjudicial (**to** para)

**injury** [ˈɪndʒərɪ] n (open wound) herida f; (broken bone, damaged muscle) lesión f; (harm) lesiones fpl; **to do oneself an i.** hacerse daño; Sport **i. time** tiempo m de descuento

**injustice** [ɪnˈdʒʌstɪs] n injusticia f; **you do her an i.** estás siendo injusto con ella

**ink** [ɪŋk] n tinta f; Comptr **i. jet** (printer) impresora f de chorro de tinta; **i. pad** tampón m

**inkling** [ˈɪŋklɪŋ] n **to have an i. of sth** tener una ligera idea de algo; **she had no i. of what they were up to** no tenía ni idea de lo que estaban tramando

**inkwell** [ˈɪŋkwel] n tintero m

**inky** [ˈɪŋkɪ] adj (a) (stained with ink) manchado(a) de tinta (b) **i. (black)** negro(a) (como el carbón)

**inlaid** [ɪnˈleɪd] adj (with wood) taraceado(a); (with jewels) incrustado(a)

**inland** [ˈɪnlænd] **1** adj interior, del interior; Br **the I. Revenue** la Agencia Tributaria or la Hacienda británica
**2** adv (travel) al interior; (live) en el interior

**in-laws** [ˈɪnlɔːz] npl familia f política

**inlet** [ˈɪnlet] n (a) (of sea) ensenada f (b) (of pipe, machine) entrada f

**inmate** [ˈɪnmeɪt] n (in prison) recluso(a) m,f; (in mental hospital) paciente mf

**inn** [ɪn] n mesón m, posada f

**innards** [ˈɪnədz] npl tripas fpl

**innate** [ɪˈneɪt] adj innato(a)

**inner** [ˈɪnə(r)] adj (a) (chamber, lining) interior; **i. city** = área céntrica y degradada de una ciudad; Anat **i. ear** oído m interno; **i. tube** cámara f (de aire) (b) (thought, feeling) íntimo(a); **i. peace** paz f interior

**innermost** [ˈɪnəməʊst] adj **i. part** parte f más interior; **i. thoughts** pensamientos mpl más íntimos

**innings** [ˈɪnɪŋz] n (in cricket) turno m para batear; Fig **she had a good i.** (a long life) tuvo una vida larga y plena

**innkeeper** [ˈɪnkiːpə(r)] n mesonero(a) m,f, posadero(a) m,f

**innocence** [ˈɪnəsəns] n inocencia f

**innocent** [ˈɪnəsənt] adj (not guilty, naive) inocente

**innocuous** [ɪˈnɒkjʊəs] adj inocuo(a)

**innovate** [ˈɪnəveɪt] vi innovar

**innovation** [ɪnəˈveɪʃən] n innovación f

**innovative** [ˈɪnəveɪtɪv], **innovatory** [ˈɪnəveɪtərɪ] adj innovador(ora)

**innovator** [ˈɪnəveɪtə(r)] n innovador(ora) m,f

**innuendo** [ɪnjʊˈendəʊ] (pl **innuendos**) n indirecta f, insinuación f; (in jokes) doble sentido m, juegos mpl de palabras (sobre sexo)

**innumerable** [ɪˈnjuːmərəbəl] adj innumerable

**inoculate** [ɪˈnɒkjʊlet] vt inocular; **to i. sb with sth** inocularle algo a alguien; **to i. sb against sth** vacunar a alguien de algo

**inoculation** [ɪnɒkjʊˈleɪʃən] n (action) vacunación f

**inoffensive** [ɪnəˈfensɪv] adj inofensivo(a)

**inoperable** [ɪnˈɒpərəbəl] adj Med **to be i.** no ser operable

**inoperative** [ɪnˈɒpərətɪv] adj (rule) inoperante; **to be i.** (of machine) no funcionar

**inopportune** [ɪnˈɒpətjuːn] adj inoportuno(a)

**inordinate** [ɪnˈɔːdɪnət] adj desmesurado(a)

**inorganic** [ɪnɔːˈgænɪk] adj inorgánico(a)

**in-patient** [ˈɪnpeɪʃənt] n paciente mf interno(a)

**input** [ˈɪnpʊt] **1** n Elec entrada f; Comptr input m, entrada f (de información); (to project) aportación f, aporte m
**2** vt Comptr **to i. data** introducir datos

**inquest** [ˈɪnkwest] n Law investigación f; (in politics, business) análisis m inv, evaluación f; **to hold an i.** Law (of coroner) determinar las causas de la muerte; (in politics, business) hacer un análisis

**inquire** [ɪnˈkwaɪə(r)] vi preguntar; **to i. as to or about...** informarse sobre...; **he inquired why I was there** me preguntó por qué estaba allí; **i. within** (sign) razón aquí
▸**inquire after** vt insep preguntar por
▸**inquire into** vt insep investigar, indagar

**inquiring** [ɪnˈkwaɪrɪŋ] adj (mind) inquisitivo(a); (look) de interrogación

**inquiry** [ɪnˈkwaɪrɪ] n (a) (official investigation) investigación f (oficial); **to hold an i.** (into sth) realizar una investigación (sobre algo) (b) (request for information) consulta f; **to make.in-**

**quiries (about sth)** consultar *or* informarse (sobre algo); **i. desk** (mostrador *m* de) información *f*

**inquisition** [ɪnkwɪˈzɪʃən] *n Hist* **the Spanish I.** la (Santa) Inquisición

**inquisitive** [ɪnˈkwɪzɪtɪv] *adj* (*person*) curioso(a); (*mind*) inquisitivo(a); (*look*) de curiosidad

**inroads** [ˈɪnrəʊdz] *npl* **I had to make i. into my savings** tuve que recurrir a mis propios ahorros; **to make i. into the market** penetrar en el mercado; **the Nationalists had made i. into the Labour vote** los nacionalistas se habían hecho con parte del voto laborista

**insane** [ɪnˈseɪn] *adj* (*person*) demente, loco(a); *Fam* (*desire, scheme*) demencial, descabellado(a); **to be i.** (*of person*) estar loco(a); **to go i.** trastornarse, volverse loco(a); **to drive sb i.** volver loco(a) a alguien; **to be i. with grief/jealousy** enloquecer de dolor/celos

**insanely** [ɪnˈseɪnlɪ] *adv* disparatadamente; **i. jealous** loco(a) de celos

**insanitary** [ɪnˈsænɪtrɪ] *adj* antihigiénico(a)

**insanity** [ɪnˈsænɪtɪ] *n* (*of person*) demencia *f*, locura *f*; *Fam* (*of desire, scheme*) demencialidad *f*, locura *f*

**insatiable** [ɪnˈseɪʃəbəl] *adj* insaciable

**inscribe** [ɪnˈskraɪb] *vt* (*write, engrave*) inscribir

**inscription** [ɪnˈskrɪpʃən] *n* (*on stone, coin*) inscripción *f*; (*in book*) dedicatoria *f*

**inscrutable** [ɪnˈskruːtəbəl] *adj* inescrutable

**insect** [ˈɪnsekt] *n* insecto *m*; **i. bite** picadura *f* de insecto; **i. repellent** repelente *m* contra insectos

**insecticide** [ɪnˈsektɪsaɪd] *n* insecticida *m*

**insecure** [ɪnsɪˈkjʊə(r)] *adj* inseguro(a)

**insecurity** [ɪnsɪˈkjʊərɪtɪ] *n* inseguridad *f*

**insemination** [ɪnsemɪˈneɪʃən] *n* inseminación *f*

**insensible** [ɪnˈsensɪbəl] *adj* (a) (*unconscious*) inconsciente; **to be i.** estar inconsciente (b) (*unaware*) **to be i. of sth** no ser consciente de algo

**insensitive** [ɪnˈsensɪtɪv] *adj* insensible

**insensitivity** [ɪnsensɪˈtɪvɪtɪ] *n* insensibilidad *f*

**inseparable** [ɪnˈsepərəbəl] *adj* inseparable

**insert 1** *n* [ˈɪnsɜːt] (*in magazine*) encarte *m*

**2** *vt* [ɪnˈsɜːt] (*key, finger, coin*) introducir (**into** en); (*clause, advertisement*) insertar (**in** en)

**insertion** [ɪnˈsɜːʃən] *n* inserción *f*

**inset** [ˈɪnset] *n* (*in map, picture*) recuadro *m*

**inshore** [ɪnˈʃɔː(r)] **1** *adj* (*navigation*) costero(a); (*fishing*) de bajura **2** *adv* (*to sail, blow*) hacia la costa

**inside 1** *n* [ˈɪnsaɪd] (a) (*of house*) interior *m*; **on/from the i.** en/desde el interior; **to overtake on the i.** (*in Britain*) adelantar por la izquierda; (*in Europe, USA*) adelantar por la derecha

(b) *Fam* **insides** (*internal organs*) tripas *fpl*

(c) (*in phrases*) **his shirt is i. out** lleva la camisa del revés; *Fig* **to know sth i. out** saberse algo al dedillo

**2** *adj* [ˈɪnsaɪd] interior; **to have i. information/help** tener información/ayuda confidencial; **to know the i. story** conocer la historia de cerca *or* de primera mano; *Fam* **it must have been an i. job** (*robbery, fraud*) debe de haber sido un trabajo realizado desde dentro; **i. lane** (*in Britain*) carril *m* de la izquierda; (*in Europe, USA*) carril de la derecha; **i. left/right** (*in football*) interior *m* izquierdo/derecho

**3** *adv* (a) (*be, stay*) dentro; (*look, run*) adentro; **they painted the house i. and out** pintaron la casa por dentro y por fuera; **come i.!** (*to guest*) ¡pasa!; (*to children playing outside*) ¡vamos para dentro!

(b) (*within oneself*) **i. she was angry** por dentro estaba enfadada

(c) *Fam* (*in prison*) en chirona

**4** *prep* [ɪnˈsaɪd] (a) (*place*) dentro de

(b) (*with time*) **i. (of) a week/hour** en el espacio de una semana/hora

**insider** [ɪnˈsaɪdə(r)] *n* = persona que cuenta con información confidencial; *Fin* **i. dealing, i. trading** uso *m* de información privilegiada

**insidious** [ɪnˈsɪdɪəs] *adj* insidioso(a), larvado(a)

**insight** [ˈɪnsaɪt] *n* (a) (*perspicacity*) perspicacia *f*, penetración *f* (b) (*understanding*) idea *f* (**into** de); (*revealing comment*) revelación *f*, aclaración *f* (**into** sobre); **to get an i. into sth** hacerse una idea de algo

**insignia** [ɪnˈsɪgnɪə] *npl* insignias *fpl*

**insignificance** [ɪnsɪgˈnɪfɪkəns] *n* insignificancia *f*; **my problems pale into i. beside yours** mis problemas son insignificantes comparados con los tuyos

**insignificant** [ɪnsɪgˈnɪfɪkənt] *adj* insignificante

**insincere** [ɪnsɪnˈsɪə(r)] *adj* falso(a), insincero(a)

**insincerity** [ɪnsɪnˈserɪtɪ] *n* falsedad *f*, insinceridad *f*

**insinuate** [ɪnˈsɪnjʊeɪt] *vt* (*hint*) insinuar; **to i. oneself into sb's favour** ganarse arteramente el favor de alguien

**insinuation** [ɪnsɪnjʊˈeɪʃən] *n* insinuación *f*

**insipid** [ɪnˈsɪpɪd] *adj* insípido(a)

**insist** [ɪnˈsɪst] **1** *vt* **to i. that...** insistir en que...

**2** *vi* insistir; **to i. on sth** (*demand*) exigir algo; (*emphasize*) insistir en algo; **to i. on doing sth** insistir en hacer algo

**insistence** [ɪn'sɪstəns] *n* insistencia *f*; **at her i.** ante su insistencia

**insistent** [ɪn'sɪstənt] *adj (person, demand)* insistente; **to be i. about sth** insistir sobre *or* en algo

**insofar as** ['ɪnsəʊ'fɑ:rəz] *adv* en la medida en que

**insole** ['ɪnsəʊl] *n (of shoe)* plantilla *f*

**insolence** ['ɪnsələns] *n* insolencia *f*

**insolent** ['ɪnsələnt] *adj* insolente

**insoluble** [ɪn'sɒljʊbəl] *adj* **(a)** *(substance)* insoluble, indisoluble **(b)** *(problem)* irresoluble

**insolvency** [ɪn'sɒlvənsɪ] *n Fin* insolvencia *f*

**insolvent** [ɪn'sɒlvənt] *adj Fin* insolvente

**insomnia** [ɪn'sɒmnɪə] *n* insomnio *m*

**insomniac** [ɪn'sɒmnɪæk] *n* insomne *mf*

**inspect** [ɪn'spekt] *vt (passport, luggage, picture)* examinar, inspeccionar; *(school, factory)* inspeccionar; *(troops)* pasar revista a

**inspection** [ɪn'spekʃən] *n (of passport, luggage, picture)* examen *m*, inspección *f*; *(of school, factory)* inspección *f*; *(of troops)* revista *f*; **on closer i.** tras un examen más detallado

**inspector** [ɪn'spektə(r)] *n (of schools, factories)* inspector(ora) *m,f*; *Br (on train, bus)* revisor(ora) *m,f*; *Br* **(police) i.** inspector(ora) de policía; *Br* **tax i.** inspector(ora) de Hacienda

**inspiration** [ɪnspɪ'reɪʃən] *n* inspiración *f*; **to be an i. to sb** servir una fuente de inspiración para alguien; **to draw i. from sth** inspirarse en algo

**inspire** [ɪn'spaɪə(r)] *vt* inspirar; **to i. sb to do sth** inspirar a alguien para hacer algo; **to i. confidence in sb, to i. sb with confidence** inspirar confianza a alguien

**inspired** [ɪn'spaɪəd] *adj* inspirado(a)

**inspiring** [ɪn'spaɪərɪŋ] *adj* estimulante

**instability** [ɪnstə'bɪlɪtɪ] *n* inestabilidad *f*

**install,** *US* **instal** [ɪn'stɔ:l] *vt* instalar; **to i. sb in a post** colocar a alguien en un puesto; **to i. oneself in an armchair** instalarse en una butaca

**installation** [ɪnstə'leɪʃən] *n* instalación *f*

**instalment,** *US* **installment** [ɪn'stɔ:lmənt] *n* **(a)** *(part payment)* plazo *m*; **to pay by instalments** pagar a plazos **(b)** *(of radio, TV programme)* episodio *m*; **to publish sth in instalments** publicar algo por entregas

**instance** ['ɪnstəns] *n (example)* caso *m*; **for i.** por ejemplo; **in the first i.** en primer lugar

**instant** ['ɪnstənt] **1** *n (moment)* instante *m*; **do it this i.!** ¡hazlo ahora mismo!; **not an i. too soon** justo a tiempo; **in an i.** en un instante; **the i. I saw him** en cuanto lo vi

**2** *adj* instantáneo(a); *TV* **i. replay** repetición *f* (a cámara lenta)

**instantaneous** [ɪnstən'teɪnɪəs] *adj* instantáneo(a)

**instantly** ['ɪnstəntlɪ] *adv* al instante

**instead** [ɪn'sted] *adv* **she couldn't come so he came i.** como ella no podía venir, vino él en su lugar; **I was going to buy the green one but I bought the blue one i.** iba a comprar el verde, pero al final compré el azul; **i. of** en vez de, en lugar de; **i. of doing sth** en lugar *or* vez de hacer algo

**instep** ['ɪnstep] *n* empeine *m*

**instigate** ['ɪnstɪgeɪt] *vt (strike, unrest, violence)* instigar; *(inquiry, search, changes)* iniciar

**instigation** ['ɪnstɪgeɪʃən] *n (of strike, unrest, violence)* instigación *f*; **at sb's i.** a instancias de alguien

**instigator** ['ɪnstɪgeɪtə(r)] *n (of strike, unrest, violence)* instigador(ora) *m,f*; *(of inquiry, search, changes)* iniciador(ora) *m,f*

**instil,** *US* **instill** [ɪn'stɪl] *(pt & pp* **instilled)** *vt* inculcar **(in en)**

**instinct** ['ɪnstɪŋkt] *n* instinto *m*; **to have an i. for sth** tener buen olfato para algo

**instinctive** [ɪn'stɪŋktɪv] *adj* instintivo(a)

**institute** ['ɪnstɪtju:t] **1** *n* instituto *m*

**2** *vt (system, procedure)* instaurar; *(search)* emprender; *Law (enquiry)* emprender; *Law* **to i. proceedings (against sb)** emprender una acción legal (contra alguien)

**institution** [ɪnstɪ'tju:ʃən] *n* **(a)** *(organization)* institución *f*; *Fig* **to become a national i.** *(of event, TV programme)* convertirse en una institución (nacional) **(b)** *(mental hospital)* (hospital *m*) psiquiátrico *m*; *(old people's home)* residencia *f* de ancianos, asilo *m*; *(children's home)* centro *m* de menores

**institutional** [ɪnstɪ'tju:ʃənəl] *adj* institucional

**institutionalize** [ɪnstɪ'tju:ʃənəlaɪz] *vt* **(a)** *(put in a home)* internar en un asilo/psiquiátrico; **to become institutionalized** desarrollar una fuerte dependencia institucional *(de la vida carcelaria, hospitalaria, etc)* **(b)** *(turn into an institution)* institucionalizar

**instruct** [ɪn'strʌkt] *vt* **(a)** *(teach)* instruir **(in en) (b)** *(command)* dar instrucciones a; **to i. sb to do sth** ordenar a alguien que haga algo

**instruction** [ɪn'strʌkʃən] *n* **(a)** *(training)* instrucción *f*, adiestramiento *m*; **we received i. in using the machines** nos enseñaron cómo utilizar las máquinas **(b)** *instructions* instrucciones *fpl*; **instructions for use** instrucciones de uso; **i. manual** manual *m* de instrucciones

**instructive** [ɪn'strʌktɪv] *adj* instructivo(a)

**instructor** [ɪn'strʌktə(r)] *n (teacher)* instructor(ora) *m,f*; *US (university lecturer)* profesor(ora) *m,f* de universidad; **driving i.** profesor de autoescuela; **ski i.** monitor(ora) *m,f* de esquí

**instrument** ['ɪnstrʊmənt] *n Mus Med* instrumento *m*; *Av* **i. board** or **panel** tablero *m* de mandos, panel *m* de instrumentos

**instrumental** [ɪnstrʊ'mentəl] **1** *n Mus* (pieza *f*) instrumental *m*

**2** *adj* (a) fundamental; **she was i. in negotiating the agreement** desempeñó un papel fundamental en la negociación del acuerdo (b) *Mus* instrumental

**instrumentalist** [ɪnstrʊ'mentəlɪst] *n (musician)* instrumentista *mf*

**instrumentation** [ɪnstrʊmen'teɪʃən] *n* instrumentación *f*

**insubordinate** [ɪnsə'bɔːdɪnət] *adj* insubordinado(a)

**insubordination** [ɪnsəbɔːdɪ'neɪʃən] *n* insubordinación *f*

**insubstantial** [ɪnsəb'stænʃəl] *adj (structure, argument)* endeble; *(meal)* poco sustancioso; *(book)* intrascendente, insustancial

**insufferable** [ɪn'sʌfrəbəl] *adj* insufrible, insoportable

**insufficient** [ɪnsə'fɪʃənt] *adj* insuficiente

**insular** ['ɪnsjʊlə(r)] *adj (people, views)* provinciano(a)

**insulate** ['ɪnsjʊleɪt] *vt (wire, pipe)* aislar; *Fig* **insulated from the outside world** aislado(a) del mundo exterior

**insulating tape** [ɪnsjʊleɪtɪŋ'teɪp] *n* cinta *f* aislante

**insulation** [ɪnsjʊleɪʃən] *n* aislamiento *m*

**insulin** [ɪnsjʊlɪn] *n* insulina *f*

**insult 1** *n* ['ɪnsʌlt] *(words, action)* insulto *m*; **to add i. to injury...** para colmo...

**2** *vt* [ɪn'sʌlt] insultar

**insulting** [ɪn'sʌltɪŋ] *adj* insultante

**insuperable** [ɪn'suːpərəbəl] *adj* insuperable, infranqueable

**insurance** [ɪn'ʃʊərəns] *n* seguro *m*; **to take out i.** hacerse un seguro, asegurarse; **i. broker** agente *mf* libre de seguros; **i. claim** reclamación *f* al seguro; **i. company** aseguradora *f*, compañía *f* de seguros; **i. policy** póliza *f* de seguros; **i. premium** prima *f* (del seguro)

**insure** [ɪn'ʃʊə(r)] *vt* asegurar **(against** contra**); to i. one's life** hacerse un seguro de vida

**insured** [ɪn'ʃʊəd] *adj* asegurado(a); **to be i.** estar asegurado(a); **i. value** valor *m* asegurado

**insurer** [ɪn'ʃʊərə(r)] *n* asegurador(ora) *m,f*

**insurgent** [ɪn'sɜːdʒənt] *n* insurgente *mf*

**insurmountable** [ɪnsə'maʊntəbəl] *adj* insuperable, insalvable

**insurrection** [ɪnsə'rekʃən] *n* insurrección *f*

**intact** [ɪn'tækt] *adj* intacto(a); **to be i.** estar intacto(a)

**intake** ['ɪnteɪk] *n (of alcohol, calories)* ingestión *f*; *(of pupils, recruits)* remesa *f*

**intangible** [ɪn'tændʒɪbəl] *adj* intangible

**integer** ['ɪntɪdʒə(r)] *n Math* (número *m*) entero *m*

**integral** ['ɪntɪɡrəl] *adj (essential)* esencial; **to be** or **form an i. part of sth** formar parte integrante de algo; *Math* **i. calculus** cálculo *m* integral

**integrate** ['ɪntɪɡreɪt] **1** *vt* integrar **(into** en)

**2** *vi* integrarse

**integrated** ['ɪntɪɡreɪtɪd] *adj* integrado(a)

**integration** [ɪntɪ'ɡreɪʃən] *n* integración *f*

**integrity** [ɪn'teɡrɪtɪ] *n* integridad *f*

**intellect** ['ɪntɪlekt] *n* intelecto *m*

**intellectual** [ɪntɪ'lektjʊəl] *n & adj* intelectual *mf*

**intelligence** [ɪn'telɪdʒəns] *n* (a) *(faculty)* inteligencia *f*; *Psy* **i. quotient** cociente *m* intelectual; **i. test** test *m* de inteligencia (b) *(information)* información *f* secreta; **i. officer** agente *mf* de los servicios de inteligencia; **i. service** servicio *m* de inteligencia

**intelligent** [ɪn'telɪdʒənt] *adj* inteligente

**intelligentsia** [ɪntelɪ'dʒensɪə] *n* intelectualidad *f*

**intelligible** [ɪn'telɪdʒɪbəl] *adj* inteligible

**intemperate** [ɪn'tempərət] *adj (climate)* riguroso(a); *(person, behaviour)* inmoderado(a)

**intend** [ɪn'tend] *vt* **to i. to do sth** tener la intención de hacer algo; **to i. sth for sb** *(plan to give to)* tener pensado dar algo a alguien; **those comments were intended for you** esos comentarios iban por ti or destinados a ti; **was that intended?** ¿ha sido a propósito?; **it was intended as a joke/a compliment** pretendía ser una broma/un cumplido; **I told her to do it, and I i. to be obeyed** le dije que lo hiciera sin rechistar; **I didn't i. her to see it yet** no quería que ella lo viera todavía; **a film intended for children** una película para niños or dirigida a los niños

**intended** [ɪn'tendɪd] **1** *n Old-fashioned* or *Hum (future spouse)* prometido(a) *m,f*

**2** *adj (consequence, outcome)* deseado(a); *(insult, mistake)* intencionado(a)

**intense** [ɪn'tens] *adj* intenso(a); *(person)* muy serio(a)

**intensely** [ɪn'tenslɪ] *adv (strongly, deeply)* intensamente; *(highly, extremely)* enormemente

**intensify** [ɪn'tensɪfaɪ] **1** *vt* intensificar

**2** *vi* intensificarse

**intensity** [ɪn'tensɪtɪ] *n* intensidad *f*

**intensive** [ɪn'tensɪv] *adj* intensivo(a); *Med* **i. care** cuidados *mpl* intensivos

**intent** [ɪn'tent] **1** *n* intención *f*; **to all intents and purposes** a todos los efectos

**2** *adj (look, expression)* intenso(a), concentrado(a); **to be i. on doing sth** estar empeñado(a) en hacer algo

**intention** [ɪnˈtenʃən] n intención f; **to have no i. of doing sth** no tener ninguna intención de hacer algo; **to have every i. of doing sth** tener toda la intención de hacer algo

**intentional** [ɪnˈtenʃənəl] adj intencionado(a)

**intentionally** [ɪnˈtenʃənəlɪ] adv adrede, a propósito

**intently** [ɪnˈtentlɪ] adv (to listen) atentamente; (to look at) intensamente

**inter** [ɪnˈtɜ:(r)] (pt & pp **interred**) vt enterrar

**interact** [ɪntəˈrækt] vi (of people) interrelacionarse (**with** con); (of factors, events) combinarse (**with** con); Comptr interactuar (**with** con)

**interaction** [ɪntəˈrækʃən] n interacción f

**interactive** [ɪntəˈræktɪv] adj interactivo(a); Comptr **i. CD** CD m interactivo; Comptr **i. video** vídeo m interactivo

**intercede** [ɪntəˈsi:d] vi interceder (**with/for** ante/por)

**intercept** [ɪntəˈsept] vt interceptar

**interception** [ɪntəˈsepʃən] n interceptación f

**intercession** [ɪntəˈseʃən] n intercesión f

**interchange 1** n [ˈɪntətʃeɪndʒ] (exchange) intercambio m; (on motorway) enlace m, nudo m de carreteras
**2** vt [ɪntəˈtʃeɪndʒ] intercambiar

**interchangeable** [ɪntəˈtʃeɪndʒəbəl] adj intercambiable

**intercity** [ˈɪntəˈsɪtɪ] adj intercity

**intercom** [ˈɪntəkɒm] n interfono m

**interconnect** [ɪntəkəˈnekt] vt interconectar

**intercontinental** [ɪntəkɒntɪˈnentəl] adj intercontinental; Mil **i. ballistic missile** misil m balístico intercontinental

**intercourse** [ˈɪntəkɔ:s] n (a) (sexual) **i.** coito m, cópula f (b) Formal (dealings) trato m; **social i.** relaciones fpl sociales

**interdependent** [ˈɪntədɪˈpendənt] adj interdependiente

**interest** [ˈɪntrest] 1 n (a) (curiosity) interés m; (hobby) afición f; **of i.** de interés; **to be of i. to sb** interesar a alguien; **to take an i. in sth** interesarse por algo; **to lose i. (in sth)** perder el interés (por algo)
(b) (stake) interés m; **to have an i. in sth** (in general) tener interés en or por algo; Fin tener intereses or participación en algo
(c) (benefit) **to act in sb's interests** obrar en interés de alguien; **the public i.** el interés general or público; **it's in my i. to do it** me interesa hacerlo; **in the interests of...** en pro de...
(d) Fin (on investment) interés m; **i. rate** tipo m de interés

**2** vt interesar; **to i. sb in sth** interesar a alguien en algo; **to be interested in sth** estar interesado(a) en algo, interesarse por algo

**interested** [ˈɪntrestɪd] adj interesado(a)

**interest-free** [ˈɪntrestˈfri:] adj (loan) sin intereses

**interesting** [ˈɪntrestɪŋ] adj interesante

**interface** [ˈɪntəfeɪs] n Comptr interface m, interfaz f

**interfere** [ɪntəˈfɪə(r)] vi interferir, entrometerse (**in/with** en); **to i. with a child** (sexually) realizar abusos deshonestos a un menor; **he's always interfering** siempre está metiéndose donde no le importa; **don't i. with my papers** no enredes en mis papeles; **to i. with sth** (hinder) interferir en or afectar a algo

**interference** [ɪntəˈfɪərəns] n (a) (meddling) intromisión f (b) Rad TV interferencia f

**interfering** [ɪntəˈfɪərɪŋ] adj entrometido(a)

**interim** [ˈɪntərɪm] 1 n **in the i.** entre tanto, en el ínterin
**2** adj (agreement, report) provisional

**interior** [ɪnˈtɪərɪə(r)] 1 n interior m
**2** adj interior; **i. decorator** interiorista mf

**interject** [ɪntəˈdʒekt] vt interponer

**interjection** [ɪntəˈdʒekʃən] n interjección f

**interlocking** [ɪntəˈlɒkɪŋ] adj interconectado(a)

**interlocutor** [ɪntələˈkju:tə(r)] n Formal interlocutor(ora) m,f

**interloper** [ˈɪntələʊpə(r)] n intruso(a) m,f

**interlude** [ˈɪntəlu:d] n Th intermedio m; Fig intervalo m

**intermarriage** [ɪntəˈmærɪdʒ] n matrimonio m mixto (entre personas de distintas razas, religiones o comunidades)

**intermarry** [ɪntəˈmærɪ] vi casarse (personas de diferente raza, religión o comunidad); **Catholics and Protestants rarely intermarried** católicos y protestantes raras veces se casaban entre sí

**intermediary** [ɪntəˈmi:dɪərɪ] n intermediario(a) m,f, mediador(ora) m,f

**intermediate** [ɪntəˈmi:dɪət] adj intermedio(a)

**interminable** [ɪnˈtɜ:mɪnəbəl] adj interminable

**intermingle** [ɪntəˈmɪŋgəl] 1 vt mezclar (**with** con)
**2** vi mezclarse (**with** con)

**intermission** [ɪntəˈmɪʃən] n Cin Th intermedio m, descanso m

**intermittent** [ɪntəˈmɪtənt] adj intermitente

**intern 1** n [ˈɪntɜ:n] US Med médico(a) m,f interno(a) residente
**2** vt [ɪnˈtɜ:n] recluir

**internal** [ɪnˈtɜːnəl] *adj* interno(a); *Fin* **i. audit** auditoría *f* interna; *Tech* **i. combustion engine** motor *m* de combustión interna

**internalize** [ɪnˈtɜːnəlaɪz] *vt* interiorizar

**internally** [ɪnˈtɜːnəlɪ] *adv* internamente; **not to be taken i.** *(on medicine container)* para uso externo

**international** [ɪntəˈnæʃənəl] **1** *n Sport (player)* (jugador(ora) *m,f*) internacional *mf*; *(match)* partido *m* internacional

**2** *adj* internacional; **I. Date Line** línea *f* de cambio de fecha; **i. law** derecho *m* internacional; *Fin* **I. Monetary Fund** Fondo *m* Monetario Internacional

**internee** [ɪntɜːˈniː] *n* recluso(a) *m,f*

**Internet** [ˈɪntənet] *n Comptr* **the I.** Internet

**internment** [ɪnˈtɜːnmənt] *n* reclusión *f*

**interpersonal** [ɪntəˈpɜːsənəl] *adj* interpersonal

**interplay** [ˈɪntəpleɪ] *n* interacción *f* (**of** de)

**Interpol** [ˈɪntəpɒl] *n* Interpol *f*

**interpolate** [ɪnˈtɜːpəleɪt] *vt* interpolar

**interpose** [ɪntəˈpəʊz] *vt* interponer (**between** entre)

**interpret** [ɪnˈtɜːprɪt] *vt & vi* interpretar

**interpretation** [ɪntɜːprɪˈteɪʃən] *n* interpretación *f*

**interpreter** [ɪnˈtɜːprɪtə(r)] *n* intérprete *mf*

**interracial** [ɪntəˈreɪʃəl] *adj* interracial

**interrelated** [ɪntərɪˈleɪtɪd] *adj* interrelacionado(a)

**interrogate** [ɪnˈterəgeɪt] *vt* interrogar

**interrogation** [ɪnterəˈgeɪʃən] *n* interrogatorio *m*

**interrogative** [ɪnteˈrɒgətɪv] **1** *n Gram (voice)* forma *f* interrogativa; *(word)* interrogativo *m*

**2** *adj (look, tone) & Gram* interrogativo(a)

**interrogator** [ɪnˈterəgeɪtə(r)] *n* interrogador(ora) *m,f*

**interrupt** [ɪntəˈrʌpt] *vt & vi* interrumpir

**interruption** [ɪntəˈrʌpʃən] *n* interrupción *f*

**intersect** [ɪntəˈsekt] **1** *vt (of street)* cruzar, atravesar

**2** *vi* cruzarse

**intersection** [ɪntəˈsekʃən] *n (of roads)* cruce *m*, intersección *f*

**intersperse** [ɪntəˈspɜːs] *vt* **to be interspersed with sth** estar salpicado(a) de algo

**interstate** [ɪntəˈsteɪt] **1** *n US* autopista *f (que une un estado con otro)*

**2** *adj* entre estados

**intertwine** [ɪntəˈtwaɪn] *vt* entrelazar (**with** con), entretejer (**with** con); **his fate seemed to be intertwined with hers** sus destinos parecían estar entrelazados

**interval** [ˈɪntəvəl] *n (time, space) & Mus* intervalo *m*; *(at theatre)* intermedio *m*, descanso *m*; **at regular intervals** a intervalos regulares; **rainy weather with sunny intervals** tiempo lluvioso con intervalos soleados

**intervene** [ɪntəˈviːn] *vi (of person)* intervenir; *(of event)* sobrevenir

**intervening** [ɪntəˈviːnɪŋ] *adj (years, months)* mediante, transcurrido(a); *(miles)* intermedio(a); **in the i. period** en el ínterin

**intervention** [ɪntəˈvenʃən] *n* intervención *f*

**interview** [ˈɪntəvjuː] **1** *n* entrevista *f*

**2** *vt* entrevistar

**interviewee** [ɪntəvjuːˈiː] *n* entrevistado(a) *m,f*

**interviewer** [ˈɪntəvjuːə(r)] *n* entrevistador(ora) *m,f*

**intestate** [ɪnˈtesteɪt] *adv Law* **to die i.** morir intestado(a)

**intestinal** [ɪntesˈtaɪnəl] *adj* intestinal

**intestine** [ɪnˈtestaɪn] *n Anat* intestino *m*; **large/small i.** intestino grueso/delgado

**intimacy** [ˈɪntɪməsɪ] *n (of relationship, atmosphere)* intimidad *f*; *Euph (sexual)* relaciones *fpl* (sexuales)

**intimate 1** *n* [ˈɪntɪmət] *(close friend, associate)* íntimo(a) *m,f*, allegado(a) *m,f*

**2** *adj* [ˈɪntɪmət] *(friend, restaurant)* íntimo(a); **to be i. with sb** *(friendly)* ser amigo(a) íntimo(a) de alguien; *Euph (sexually)* tener relaciones (sexuales) con alguien; **to have an i. knowledge of sth** conocer algo a fondo

**3** *vt* [ˈɪntɪmeɪt] *Formal* dar a entender, sugerir

**intimately** [ˈɪntɪmətlɪ] *adv* íntimamente

**intimidate** [ɪnˈtɪmɪdeɪt] *vt* intimidar; **to i. sb into doing sth** intimidar a alguien para que haga algo

**intimidation** [ɪntɪmɪˈdeɪʃən] *n* intimidación *f*

**into** [ɪntʊ] *prep* **(a)** *(with motion, direction)* en, dentro de; **to go i. a house** entrar en una casa; **to get i. a car** subirse a un coche; **she fell i. the water** cayó al agua; **the car crashed i. a tree** el coche chocó contra un árbol

**(b)** *(with change)* en; **to change i. sth** convertirse en algo; **to grow i. a man** hacerse un hombre; **to translate sth i. English** traducir algo al inglés; **to break sth i. pieces** romper algo en pedazos

**(c)** *(regarding)* en relación con; **an inquiry i. the accident** una investigación sobre el accidente

**(d)** *(with time)* **rain continued to fall well i. the summer** siguió lloviendo hasta bien entrado el verano

**(e)** *Math* **three i. six goes twice** seis entre tres cabe a dos

**(f)** *Fam* **she's really i.** jazz es muy aficionada al jazz; **he's really i. my sister** le mola un montón mi hermana

**intolerable** [ɪn'tɒlərəbəl] *adj (heat, conditions)* insoportable; *(price, behaviour)* intolerable

**intolerance** [ɪn'tɒlərəns] *n* intolerancia *f*

**intolerant** [ɪn'tɒlərənt] *adj* intolerante **(of** con)

**intonation** [ɪntə'neɪʃən] *n* entonación *f*

**intone** [ɪn'təʊn] *vt* decir solemnemente

**intoxicated** [ɪn'tɒksɪkeɪtɪd] *adj (drunk)* **to be i.** estar embriagado(a) *or* ebrio(a); *Fig* **i. with power** ebrio de poder

**intoxication** [ɪntɒksɪ'keɪʃən] *n* embriaguez *f*, ebriedad *f*

**intractable** [ɪn'træktəbəl] *adj (person)* intratable; *(problem)* arduo(a)

**intransigence** [ɪn'trænzɪdʒəns] *n Formal* intransigencia *f*

**intransigent** [ɪn'trænzɪdʒənt] *adj Formal* intransigente

**intransitive** [ɪn'trænzɪtɪv] *adj Gram* intransitivo(a)

**intrauterine device** ['ɪntrə'juːtəraɪndɪ'vaɪs] *n Med* dispositivo *m* intrauterino, DIU *m*

**intravenous** ['ɪntrə'viːnəs] *adj Med* **i. drip** gota a gota *m*; **i. injection** inyección *f* intravenosa

**in-tray** ['ɪntreɪ] *(pl* **in-trays)** *n* = bandeja de trabajos pendientes

**intrepid** [ɪn'trepɪd] *adj* intrépido(a)

**intricacy** ['ɪntrɪkəsɪ] *n* complejidad *f*, complicación *f*; **the intricacies of...** los entresijos de...

**intricate** ['ɪntrɪkət] *adj* intrincado(a), complicado(a)

**intrigue 1** *n* ['ɪntriːg] intriga *f*
**2** *vt* [ɪn'triːg] *(interest)* intrigar
**3** *vi (conspire)* intrigar, conspirar **(against** contra)

**intrinsic** [ɪn'trɪnsɪk] *adj* intrínseco(a)

**introduce** [ɪntrə'djuːs] *vt* **(a)** *(person)* presentar; **to i. oneself** presentarse; **allow me to i. you to Mr Black** permítame presentarle al Sr. Black; **to i. sb to sth** introducir *or* iniciar a alguien en algo **(b)** *(reform, practice)* introducir; **this custom was introduced by missionaries** esta costumbre la trajeron los misioneros

**introduction** [ɪntrə'dʌkʃən] *n* **(a)** *(in general)* introducción *f* **(b)** *(of person)* presentación *f*; **to make the introductions** hacer las presentaciones

**introductory** [ɪntrə'dʌktərɪ] *adj* introductorio(a); *Com* **i. price/offer** precio *m*/oferta *f* de lanzamiento

**introspection** [ɪntrə'spekʃən] *n* introspección *f*

**introspective** [ɪntrə'spektɪv] *adj* introspectivo(a)

**introvert** ['ɪntrəvɜːt] *n* introvertido(a) *m,f*

**introverted** [ɪntrə'vɜːtɪd] *adj* introvertido(a)

**intrude** [ɪn'truːd] *vi* **(a)** *(impose oneself)* **to i. on sb** molestar *or* importunar a alguien; **I hope I'm not intruding** espero no molestar **(b)** *(interfere)* **her work intrudes on her family life** el trabajo invade su vida familiar; **to i. on sb's privacy** perturbar *or* invadir la intimidad de alguien

**intruder** [ɪn'truːdə(r)] *n* intruso(a) *m,f*

**intrusion** [ɪn'truːʒən] *n* intromisión *f*

**intrusive** [ɪn'truːsɪv] *adj* molesto(a), importuno(a)

**intuition** [ɪntjuː'ɪʃən] *n* intuición *f*

**intuitive** [ɪn'tjuːɪtɪv] *adj* intuitivo(a)

**Inuit** ['ɪnʊɪt] *n & adj* inuit *mf*, esquimal *mf*

**inundate** ['ɪnʌndeɪt] *vt also Fig* inundar **(with** de)

**invade** [ɪn'veɪd] *vt* invadir; **to i. sb's privacy** perturbar *or* invadir la intimidad de alguien

**invader** [ɪn'veɪdə(r)] *n* invasor(ora) *m,f*

**invalid¹** [ɪn'vælɪd] *adj (document, argument)* nulo(a)

**invalid²** ['ɪnvəlɪd] *n (disabled person)* inválido(a) *m,f*; **I'm not an i.!** ¡no soy ningún inválido!

**invalidate** [ɪn'vælɪdeɪt] *vt (theory)* invalidar; *(document, contract)* anular, invalidar

**invaluable** [ɪn'væljʊəbəl] *adj* inestimable, inapreciable; **to be i. for sth/to sb** ser de gran valor para algo/para alguien

**invariable** [ɪn'veərɪəbəl] *adj* invariable

**invariably** [ɪn'veərɪəblɪ] *adv* invariablemente

**invasion** [ɪn'veɪʒən] *n* invasión *f*

**invective** [ɪn'vektɪv] *n* invectivas *fpl*

**inveigh** [ɪn'veɪ] *vi Formal* **to i. against** lanzar invectivas contra

**inveigle** [ɪn'veɪgəl] *vt* **to i. sb into doing sth** engatusar a alguien para que haga algo

**invent** [ɪn'vent] *vt* inventar

**invention** [ɪn'venʃən] *n* **(a)** *(action)* invención *f*; *(thing invented)* invento *m*, invención *f*; *(lie)* invención *f* **(b)** *(creativity)* inventiva *f*

**inventive** [ɪn'ventɪv] *adj (creative)* inventivo(a), imaginativo(a); *(ingenious)* ingenioso(a)

**inventiveness** [ɪn'ventɪvnəs] *n* inventiva *f*

**inventor** [ɪn'ventə(r)] *n* inventor(ora) *m,f*

**inventory** ['ɪnventərɪ] *n (list)* inventario *m*; *(stock)* existencias *fpl*

**inverse** [ɪn'vɜːs] *adj* inverso(a)

**invert** [ɪn'vɜːt] *vt* invertir

**invertebrate** [ɪn'vɜːtɪbrɪt] **1** *n* invertebrado *m*
**2** *adj* invertebrado(a)

**inverted** [ɪnˈvɜːtɪd] *adj* invertido(a); **i. commas** comillas *fpl*; **in i. commas** entre comillas; **i. snob** = persona que rechaza la ostentación y el lujo y busca lo más sencillo

**invest** [ɪnˈvest] **1** *vt* (**a**) *(money, time)* invertir (**in** en) (**b**) *Formal (confer on)* **to i. sb with sth** investir a alguien con algo
**2** *vi* invertir (**in** en)

**investigate** [ɪnˈvestɪɡeɪt] *vt* investigar

**investigation** [ɪnvestɪˈɡeɪʃən] *n* investigación *f*

**investigative** [ɪnˈvestɪɡətɪv] *adj* de investigación, investigador(ora); **i. journalism** periodismo *m* de investigación

**investigator** [ɪnˈvestɪɡeɪtə(r)] *n* investigador(ora) *m,f*

**investment** [ɪnˈvestmənt] *n Fin* inversión *f*; **i. account** cuenta *f* de inversiones; **i. analyst** analista *mf* financiero(a) *or* de inversiones; **i. bank** banco *m* de inversiones; **i. income** rendimientos *mpl (de una inversión)*; **i. trust** sociedad *f or* fondo *m* de inversión

**investor** [ɪnˈvestə(r)] *n* inversor(ora) *m,f*

**inveterate** [ɪnˈvetərɪt] *adj (gambler, smoker, reader)* empedernido(a); *(liar)* redomado(a)

**invidious** [ɪnˈvɪdɪəs] *adj (choice, comparison)* odioso(a); **to be in an i. position** estar en una posición ingrata

**invigilate** [ɪnˈvɪdʒɪleɪt] *vt & vi Br* vigilar

**invigilator** [ɪnˈvɪdʒɪleɪtə(r)] *n Br (in exam)* vigilante *mf*

**invigorating** [ɪnˈvɪɡəreɪt] *adj (bath, air)* tonificante; *(walk)* vigorizante

**invincible** [ɪnˈvɪnsɪbəl] *adj* invencible

**inviolable** [ɪnˈvaɪələbəl] *adj Formal* inviolable

**inviolate** [ɪnˈvaɪələt] *adj Formal* inviolado(a)

**invisible** [ɪnˈvɪzɪbəl] *adj* invisible; *Fin* **i. assets** activos *mpl* invisibles *or* intangibles; *Fin* **i. earnings** (ganancias *fpl*) invisibles *mpl*; **i. ink** tinta *f* simpática *or* invisible

**invitation** [ɪnvɪˈteɪʃən] *n* invitación *f*

**invite 1** *vt* [ɪnˈvaɪt] (**a**) *(guest)* invitar; **to i. sb in/up** invitar a alguien a entrar/subir (**b**) *(request)* **to i. sb to do sth** invitar a alguien a que haga algo; **applications are invited for the post of...** se admiten candidaturas para el puesto de... (**c**) *(trouble, criticism)* buscarse, provocar
**2** *n* [ˈɪnvaɪt] *Fam* invitación *f*

**inviting** [ɪnˈvaɪtɪŋ] *adj* atractivo(a); *(meal)* apetecible, apetitoso(a)

**in vitro fertilization** [ɪnˈviːtrəʊfɜːtɪlaɪˈzeɪʃən] *n* fertilización *f or* fecundación *f* in vitro

**invoice** [ˈɪnvɔɪs] *Com* **1** *n* factura *f*; **to make out an i.** extender *or* hacer una factura
**2** *vt (goods)* facturar; *(person, company)* mandar la factura a

**invoke** [ɪnˈvəʊk] *vt Formal* invocar

**involuntary** [ɪnˈvɒlʌntərɪ] *adj* involuntario(a)

**involve** [ɪnˈvɒlv] *vt* (**a**) *(implicate, concern)* **to i. sb in sth** implicar *or* involucrar a alguien en algo; **this doesn't i. you** esto no tiene nada que ver contigo (**b**) *(entail) (work, expense)* entrañar, implicar

**involved** [ɪnˈvɒlvd] *adj* (**a**) *(implicated)* **to be i. in sth** *(crime, affair)* estar implicado(a) *or* involucrado(a) en algo; **to be i. in an accident** verse envuelto(a) en un accidente; **to be i. in teaching/banking** dedicarse a la enseñanza/la banca (**b**) *(emotionally)* **to be/get i. with sb** tener una relación (sentimental) con alguien (**c**) *(engrossed)* **to get i. in a book/film** enfrascarse en un libro/una película (**d**) *(complicated)* complicado(a), embrollado(a)

**involvement** [ɪnˈvɒlvmənt] *n* (**a**) *(participation)* participación *f* (**in** en); *(role)* relación *f* (**in** con) (**b**) *(commitment)* implicación *f*, compromiso *m*

**invulnerable** [ɪnˈvʌlnərəbəl] *adj* invulnerable

**inward** [ˈɪnwəd] **1** *adj (thoughts)* interno(a), interior; *(motion)* hacia dentro; *Econ* **i. investment** inversión *f* del exterior
**2** *adv* = **inwards**

**inward-looking** [ɪnwədˈlʊkɪŋ] *adj (person)* introvertido(a); *(community)* cerrado(a)

**inwards** [ˈɪnwədz] *adv* hacia dentro

**IOC** [aɪəʊˈsiː] *n (abbr* **International Olympic Committee)** COI *m*, Comité *m* Olímpico Internacional

**iodine** [ˈaɪədiːn] *n Chem* yodo *m*

**ion** [ˈaɪən] *n* ion *m*

**Ionian** [aɪˈəʊnɪən] *n* **the I. (Sea)** el mar Jónico

**ionize** [ˈaɪənaɪz] *vt* ionizar

**iota** [aɪˈəʊtə] *n* ápice *m*; **not an i. of truth** ni un ápice de verdad

**IOU** [aɪəʊˈjuː] *n (= I owe you)* pagaré *m*

**IP** [aɪˈpiː] *n Comptr (abbr* **Internet Protocol)** IP address dirección *f* IP

**IPA** [aɪpiːˈeɪ] *n Ling (abbr* **International Phonetic Alphabet)** AFI *m*, Alfabeto *m* Fonético Internacional

**IQ** [aɪˈkjuː] *n Psy (abbr* **intelligence quotient)** cociente *m* intelectual

**IR** *Br Fin (abbr* **Inland Revenue)** Agencia *f* Tributaria *or* Hacienda *f* británica

**IRA** [aɪˈɑːˈreɪ] *n Br (abbr* **Irish Republican Army)** IRA *m*, Ejército *m* Republicano Irlandés

**Iran** [ɪˈrɑːn] *n* Irán

**Iranian** [ɪˈreɪnɪən] *n & adj* iraní *mf*

**Iraq** [ɪˈrɑːk] *n* Iraq, Irak

**Iraqi** [ɪˈrɑːkɪ] *n & adj* iraquí *mf*, irakí *mf*

**irascible** [ɪˈræsɪbəl] *adj* irascible

**irate** [aɪˈreɪt] adj airado(a), furioso(a)

**ire** [ˈaɪə(r)] n Literary ira f

**Ireland** [ˈaɪələnd] n Irlanda

**iridium** [ɪˈrɪdɪəm] n Chem iridio m

**iris** [ˈaɪrɪs] n (of eye) iris m inv; (flower) lirio m

**Irish** [ˈaɪrɪʃ] **1** npl (people) the I. los irlandeses
**2** n (language) irlandés m
**3** adj irlandés(esa); I. coffee café m irlandés; the I. Sea el Mar de Irlanda; I. stew guiso m de carne con patatas

**Irishman** [ˈaɪrɪʃmən] n irlandés m

**Irishwoman** [ˈaɪrɪʃwʊmən] n irlandesa f

**irk** [ɜːk] vt fastidiar, irritar; I was irked by his attitude me fastidiaba or irritaba su actitud

**irksome** [ˈɜːksəm] adj molesto(a), irritante

**iron** [ˈaɪən] **1** n (a) (metal) hierro m; made of i. de hierro; the i. and steel industry la industria siderúrgica; he has an i. constitution está hecho(a) un roble; a will of i. una voluntad de hierro; i. discipline disciplina f férrea; the I. Age la Edad del Hierro; the I. Curtain el telón de acero; Med i. lung pulmón m de acero; i. ore mineral m or mena f de hierro (b) (for clothes) plancha f; Fig to have several irons in the fire andar metido(a) en muchos asuntos (c) (golf) hierro m
**2** vt & vi (clothes) planchar
▶**iron out** vt sep (problem, difficulty) allanar, solventar

**ironic(al)** [aɪˈrɒnɪk(əl)] adj irónico(a)

**ironing** [ˈaɪənɪŋ] n planchado m; to do the i. planchar; i. board tabla f de planchar

**ironmonger** [ˈaɪənmʌŋɡə(r)] n Br ferretero(a) m,f; i.'s (shop) ferretería f

**irony** [ˈaɪrənɪ] n ironía f; the i. is that... lo paradójico del asunto es que...

**irrational** [ɪˈræʃənəl] adj irracional

**irreconcilable** [ɪrekənˈsaɪləbəl] adj irreconciliable

**irredeemable** [ɪrɪˈdiːməbəl] adj (fault, situation) irremediable

**irrefutable** [ɪrɪˈfjuːtəbəl] adj irrefutable

**irregular** [ɪˈreɡjʊlə(r)] adj irregular

**irregularity** [ɪreɡjʊˈlærɪtɪ] n irregularidad f

**irrelevance** [ɪˈreləvəns], **irrelevancy** [ɪˈreləvənsɪ] n falta f de pertinencia

**irrelevant** [ɪˈreləvənt] adj carente de pertinencia; an i. objection/remark una objeción/un comentario que no viene al caso; that's i. eso no viene al caso

**irreligious** [ɪrɪˈlɪdʒəs] adj irreligioso(a), impío(a)

**irremediable** [ɪrɪˈmiːdɪəbəl] adj Formal irreparable, irremediable

**irreparable** [ɪˈrepərəbəl] adj irreparable

**irreplaceable** [ɪrɪˈpleɪsəbəl] adj irreemplazable

**irrepressible** [ɪrɪˈpresəbəl] adj irreprimible

**irreproachable** [ɪrɪˈprəʊtʃəbəl] adj irreprochable, intachable

**irresistible** [ɪrɪˈzɪstɪbəl] adj irresistible

**irresolute** [ɪˈrezəluːt] adj Formal irresoluto(a)

**irrespective of** [ɪrɪˈspektɪvəv] adv independientemente de

**irresponsible** [ɪrɪˈspɒnsɪbəl] adj irresponsable

**irretrievable** [ɪrɪˈtriːvəbəl] adj (loss, money) irrecuperable; (mistake, situation, damage) irreparable, irremediable

**irreverent** [ɪˈrevərənt] adj irreverente

**irreversible** [ɪrɪˈvɜːsɪbəl] adj (decision, process) irreversible

**irrevocable** [ɪˈrevəkəbəl] adj irrevocable

**irrigate** [ˈɪrɪɡeɪt] vt regar

**irrigation** [ɪrɪˈɡeɪʃən] n riego m, irrigación f; i. canal or ditch acequia f

**irritable** [ˈɪrɪtəbəl] adj irritable; Med i. bowel syndrome colon m irritable

**irritant** [ˈɪrɪtənt] n (to eyes, skin) agente m irritante; (to person, government) molestia f

**irritate** [ˈɪrɪteɪt] vt (annoy) irritar, fastidiar; Med irritar

**irritating** [ˈɪrɪteɪtɪŋ] adj irritante, exasperante

**irritation** [ɪrɪˈteɪʃən] n irritación f; I discovered, to my intense i., that... me irritó profundamente descubrir que...

**IRS** [aɪɑːˈres] US (abbr Internal Revenue Service) the I. la Agencia Tributaria or la Hacienda (estadounidense)

**is** [ɪz] 3rd person singular of be

**ISBN** [aɪesbiːˈen] n (abbr International Standard Book Number) ISBN m

**Islam** [ˈɪzlɑːm] n (el) Islam

**Islamic** [ɪzˈlæmɪk] adj islámico(a)

**island** [ˈaɪlənd] n (in sea, river) isla f; (in road) isleta f

**islander** [ˈaɪləndə(r)] n isleño(a) m,f

**isle** [aɪl] n isla f; the I. of Man la isla de Man; the I. of Wight la isla de Wight

**isn't** [ˈɪzənt] = is not

**ISO** [aɪesˈəʊ] n (abbr International Standards Organization) ISO f, Organización f Internacional de Normalización

**isobar** [ˈaɪsəʊbɑː(r)] n isobara f

**isolate** [ˈaɪsəleɪt] vt aislar (from de)

**isolated** [ˈaɪsəleɪtɪd] adj aislado(a); to be i. (from) estar aislado (de)

**isolation** [aɪsəˈleɪʃən] n aislamiento m; to deal with sth in i. tratar algo aisladamente; Med i. ward pabellón m de enfermedades infecciosas

**isosceles** [aɪˈsɒsɪliːz] *adj* isósceles; **i. triangle** triángulo *m* isósceles

**isotope** [ˈaɪsəʊtəʊp] *n Phys* isótopo *m*

**Israel** [ˈɪzreɪəl] *n* Israel

**Israeli** [ɪzˈreɪlɪ] *n & adj* israelí *mf*

**Israelite** [ˈɪzrəlaɪt] *n Hist* israelita *mf*

**issue** [ˈɪʃuː] **1** *n* (a) *(topic)* tema *m*, cuestión *f*; **the issues of the day** los temas de actualidad; **that's not the i.** no se trata de eso; **to avoid the i.** evitar el tema; **to confuse the i.** complicar el asunto; **to make an i. of sth** sacar algo de quicio; **at i.** en cuestión; **to take i. with sb** discrepar de alguien (b) *(of banknotes, stamps)* emisión *f* (c) *(of magazine)* número *m* (d) *Formal (offspring)* descendencia *f*; *Law* **to die without i.** morir sin dejar descendencia

**2** *vt (banknote, stamp)* emitir, poner en circulación; *(order)* dar; **to i. sb with sth** proporcionar algo a alguien; **to i. a statement** emitir un comunicado; *Law* **to i. a summons** enviar una citación judicial

**3** *vi Formal (of blood)* manar **(from** de); *(of noise)* surgir **(from** de); *(of smoke)* brotar **(from** de)

**Istanbul** [ɪstænˈbʊl] *n* Estambul

**isthmus** [ˈɪsməs] *n* istmo *m*

**IT** [aɪˈtiː] *n Comptr (abbr* **information technology)** informática *f*

**it** [ɪt] *pron* (a) *(subject) (usually omitted in Spanish)* **it is red** es rojo(a); **it escaped** se escapó (b) *(direct object)* lo *m*, la *f*; **I don't want it** no lo/la quiero; **give it to him** dáselo (c) *(indirect object)* le; **give it something to eat** dale algo de comer (d) *(prepositional object) (masculine)* él; *(feminine)* ella; *(referring to uncountable nouns)* ello; **from it** de él/ella/ello; **with it** con él/ella/ello; **I don't want to talk about it** no quiero hablar de ello; **put some newspaper under it** pon papel de periódico debajo (e) *(impersonal subject)* **it's raining** está lloviendo, llueve; **it's ten o'clock** son las diez (en punto); **it's cold today** hoy hace frío (f) *(as complement of verb to be)* **who is it?** ¿quién es?; **that's it for today** eso es todo por hoy

**Italian** [ɪˈtæljən] **1** *n* (a) *(person)* italiano(a) *m,f* (b) *(language)* italiano *m*; **I. class/teacher** clase *f*/profesor(ora) *m,f* de italiano

**2** *adj* italiano(a)

**italic** [ɪˈtælɪk] *n Typ* italic(s) cursiva *f*; **in italics** en cursiva

**Italy** [ˈɪtəlɪ] *n* Italia

**itch** [ɪtʃ] **1** *n* picor *m*; *Fig* **to have an i. to do sth** tener muchas ganas de hacer algo

**2** *vi* picar; **my leg is itching** me pica la pierna; *Fig* **to be itching to do sth** tener muchas ganas de hacer algo

**itchy** [ˈɪtʃɪ] *adj* **I've got an i. hand, my hand's i.** me pica la mano; *Fig* **to have i. feet** tener muchas ganas de viajar

**it'd** [ˈɪtəd] = **it would, it had**

**item** [ˈaɪtəm] *n (in collection)* artículo *m*; *(on list, agenda)* punto *m*; *Journ* noticia *f*; **an i. of clothing** una prenda de vestir; **personal items** objetos *mpl* personales; *Fam* **they're an i.** llevan un montón de tiempo (saliendo) juntos

**itemize** [ˈaɪtəmaɪz] *vt (contents)* hacer una lista de; *(bill)* detallar

**iterative** [ˈɪtərətɪv] *adj Comptr* iterativo(a)

**itinerant** [ɪˈtɪnərənt] *adj* ambulante, itinerante

**itinerary** [aɪˈtɪnərərɪ] *n* itinerario *m*

**it'll** [ˈɪtəl] = **it will**

**ITN** [aɪtiːˈen] *n Br (abbr* **Independent Television News)** = servicio de noticias del canal privado de televisión ITV

**its** [ɪts] *possessive adj* (a) *(singular)* su; *(plural)* sus; **the lion returned to i. den** el león volvió a su guarida

(b) *(for parts of body, clothes)* **the bear hurt i. paw** el oso se hizo daño en la zarpa; **the plane lost one of i. engines** el avión perdió uno de los motores

**it's** [ɪts] = **it is, it has**

**itself** [ɪtˈself] *pron* (a) *(reflexive)* se; **the dog hurt i.** el perro se hizo daño

(b) *(emphatic)* **this method is simplicity i.** este método es la sencillez misma; **the town i. isn't very interesting** la ciudad en sí (misma) no es muy interesante

(c) *(after preposition)* **by/in i.** por/en sí mismo(a)

**ITV** [aɪtiːˈviː] *n Br (abbr* **Independent Television)** = canal privado de televisión británico

**IUD** [aɪjuːˈdiː] *n Med (abbr* **intra-uterine device)** DIU *m*, dispositivo *m* intrauterino

**I've** [aɪv] = **I have**

**IVF** [aɪviːˈef] *n Med (abbr* **in vitro fertilization)** fertilización *f* in vitro

**ivory** [ˈaɪvərɪ] *n (substance)* marfil *m*; *(colour)* color *m* marfil; **the I. Coast** la Costa de Marfil; *Fig* **i. tower** torre *f* de marfil

**ivy** [ˈaɪvɪ] *n (plant)* hiedra *f*; *US* **I. League** = grupo de universidades de gran prestigio del nordeste de Estados Unidos

# J

**J, j** [dʒeɪ] *n* (*letter*) J, j *f*

**J** *Elec* (*abbr* **Joule(s)**) J

**jab** [dʒæb] **1** *n* (**a**) (*with elbow*) codazo *m*; (*with finger*) movimiento *m* seco; (*in boxing*) golpe *m* corto (**b**) *Br Fam* (*injection*) inyección *f*, pinchazo *m*

**2** *vt* (*pt & pp* **jabbed**) **he jabbed her in the leg with a pencil** le clavó un lápiz en la pierna; **to j. a finger at sb** señalar a alguien con el dedo

**jabber** ['dʒæbə(r)] *vi Fam* parlotear

**Jack** [dʒæk] *n* (*diminutive of* **John**) J. Frost la escarcha, la helada; *Br Fam* **an "I'm all right, J." attitude** una actitud de "ande yo caliente…"

**jack** [dʒæk] *n* (**a**) (*person*) **every man j. of them** todo quisque; **he is a j. of all trades** hace *or* sabe hacer un poco de todo (**b**) (*for car*) gato *m* (**c**) (*in cards*) jota *f*; (*in Spanish cards*) sota *f* (**d**) *Elec* (*plug*) clavija *f*; (*socket*) clavijero *m*

▸**jack in** *vt sep Br Fam* (*job*) dejar

▸**jack up** *vt sep Fam* (*price, salaries*) subir

**jackal** ['dʒækəl] *n* chacal *m*

**jackass** ['dʒækæs] *n* (**a**) (*male donkey*) burro *m*, asno *m* (**b**) *Fam* (*person*) burro(a) *m,f*, animal *mf*

**jackboot** ['dʒækbuːt] *n* bota *f* militar; *Fig* **under the j. of a military dictatorship** bajo el yugo de una dictadura militar

**jackdaw** ['dʒækdɔː] *n* grajilla *f*

**jacket** ['dʒækɪt] *n* (**a**) (*coat*) (*formal*) chaqueta *f*, americana *f*, *Am* saco *m*; (*casual*) cazadora *f*; **j. potatoes** patatas *fpl* asadas (*con piel*) (**b**) (*of book*) sobrecubierta *f* (**c**) (*of boiler*) funda *f*

**jackhammer** ['dʒækhæmə(r)] *n* martillo *m* neumático

**jack-in-the-box** ['dʒækɪnðəbɒks] *n* caja *f* sorpresa

**jackknife 1** ['dʒæknaɪf] *n* navaja *f*

**2** *vi* (*of articulated lorry*) hacer la tijera, derrapar por el remolque

**jack-o'-lantern** ['dʒækə'læntən] *n US* (*Hallowe'en lantern*) = farolillo hecho con una calabaza hueca y una vela dentro

**jackpot** ['dʒækpɒt] *n* (*in lottery*) (premio *m*) gordo *m*; **he hit *or* won the j.** le tocó el gordo

**jack rabbit** *n* (*North American hare*) liebre *f* americana

**Jacobean** [dʒækə'bɪən] *adj* jacobino(a), = relativo al periodo del reinado de Jacobo I de Inglaterra (1603-1625)

**Jacobite** ['dʒækəbaɪt] *n & adj* jacobita *mf*

**Jacuzzi** ® [dʒə'kuːzɪ] *n* jacuzzi *m*

**jade** [dʒeɪd] **1** *n* (*stone*) jade *m*; (*colour*) verde *m* jade

**2** *adj* (*colour*) verde jade

**jaded** ['dʒeɪdɪd] *adj* (*tired*) agotado(a); (*bored*) harto(a), hastiado(a)

**jag** [dʒæg] *n Fam* (**a**) **to go on a (drinking) j.** ir de borrachera; **he had a crying j.** le dio la llorera (**b**) *Br* (*injection*) pinchazo *m*

**jagged** ['dʒægɪd] *adj* (*coastline*) accidentado(a); (*crest*) escarpado(a); (*blade*) dentado(a)

**jaguar** *Br* ['dʒægjʊə(r), *US* 'dʒægwɑː(r)] *n* jaguar *m*

**jail** [dʒeɪl] **1** *n* cárcel *f*; **to be in j.** estar en la cárcel; **to go to j.** ir a la cárcel

**2** *vt* encarcelar

**jailbird** ['dʒeɪlbɜːd] *n Fam* preso(a) *m,f* reincidente

**jailbreak** ['dʒeɪlbreɪk] *n* fuga *f*, evasión *f*

**jailer** ['dʒeɪlə(r)] *n* carcelero(a) *m,f*; (*of hostages*) captor(ora) *m,f*

**jailhouse** ['dʒeɪlhaʊs] *n US* cárcel *f*

**jailor** = **jailer**

**Jakarta** [dʒə'kɑːtə] *n* Yakarta

**jalop(p)y** [dʒə'lɒpɪ] *n Fam* cacharro *m*, cafetera *f*

**jam¹ 1** [dʒæm] *n* (**a**) (*crowd*) (*of people*) muchedumbre *f*, multitud *f*; **traffic j.** atasco *m*, embotellamiento *m* (**b**) *Fam* (*difficult situation*) **to be in/get into a j.** estar/meterse en un aprieto (**c**) (*improvised performance*) **j. (session)** jamsession *f*

**2** *vt* (*pt & pp* **jammed**) (**a**) (*pack tightly*) (*objects*) embutir (**into** en); (*container*) atestar (**with** de); **traffic jammed the streets** el tráfico colapsaba las calles (**b**) (*block*) (*radio broadcast, station*) provocar interferencias en; (*switchboard*) bloquear; **the drawer is jammed** el cajón se ha atascado; **he jammed the window open** atrancó la ventana para que se quedara abierta

**3** vi (**a**) (of drawer) atascarse; **people jammed into the hall** la gente abarrotaba la sala (**b**) Mus improvisar (con un grupo)

**jam²** n (fruit preserve) mermelada f; **j. tart** pastel m de confitura

▸**jam on** vt sep **to j. on the brakes** frenar en seco

**Jamaica** [dʒə'meɪkə] n Jamaica

**Jamaican** [dʒə'meɪkən] n & adj jamaicano(a) m,f

**jamb** [dʒæm] n (side post of door) jamba f

**jamboree** [dʒæmbə'riː] n (scouts' meeting) encuentro m de boy-scouts; Fam (celebration) jolgorio m, fiesta f

**jamming** ['dʒæmɪŋ] n Rad interferencias fpl

**jammy** ['dʒæmɪ] adj (**a**) (covered with jam) cubierto(a) de mermelada (**b**) Br Fam (lucky) suertudo(a)

**jam-packed** ['dʒæm'pækd] adj **to be j. (with)** estar atestado(a) or abarrotado(a) (de)

**Jan** (abbr **January**) ene., enero m

**jangle** ['dʒæŋgəl] **1** n (of keys, chain) tintineo m
**2** vt (keys, chain) hacer tintinear
**3** vi (of keys, chain) tintinear; Fig **her voice made his nerves j.** su voz le ponía los nervios de punta

**janitor** ['dʒænɪtə(r)] n US Scot (caretaker) conserje m, bedel m

**January** ['dʒænjʊərɪ] n enero m; see also **May**

**Jap** [dʒæp] n very Fam = término ofensivo para referirse a los japoneses

**Japan** [dʒə'pæn] n Japón

**Japanese** [dʒæpə'niːz] **1** n (**a**) (person) japonés(esa) m,f (**b**) (language) japonés m; **J. class/teacher** clase f/profesor(ora) m,f de japonés
**2** npl **the J.** los japoneses
**3** adj japonés(esa)

**jape** [dʒeɪp] n broma f

**jar¹** [dʒɑːr] (**1**) n (jolt, shock) sacudida f; **the news gave him a nasty j.** la noticia supuso una desagradable sorpresa para él
**2** vt (pt & pp **jarred**) (knock) sacudir, golpear; Fig (surprise) alterar, sacudir
**3** vi (make unpleasant sound) rechinar; **to j. on the ears** rechinar en los oídos; **to j. on the nerves** crispar los nervios; **to j. (with each other)** (of colours) desentonar; (of ideas) chocar (entre sí)

**jar²** n (container) tarro m; Br Fam (beer) **to have a j.** tomarse una birra

**jargon** ['dʒɑːgən] n Pej jerga f

**jarring** ['dʒɑːrɪŋ] adj (noise, voice) estridente; (blow) contundente

**jasmine** ['dʒæzmɪn] n (plant) jazmín m

**jaundice** ['dʒɔːndɪs] n Med icteria f

**jaundiced** ['dʒɔːndɪst] adj (attitude, opinion) resentido(a)

**jaunt** [dʒɔːnt] n excursión f

**jauntiness** ['dʒɔːntɪnɪs] n desenfado m

**jaunty** ['dʒɔːntɪ] adj desenfadado(a)

**Java** ['dʒɑːvə] n Java

**javelin** ['dʒævlɪn] n jabalina f

**jaw** [dʒɔː] **1** n mandíbula f; **jaws** (of animal) fauces fpl; (of vice) mordaza f; **the jaws of death** las garras de la muerte
**2** Fam vi (chat) charlar

**jawbone** ['dʒɔːbəʊn] n maxilar m inferior

**jawbreaker** ['dʒɔːbreɪkə(r)] n Fam (unpronounceable word, name) trabalenguas m inv

**jay** [dʒeɪ] n arrendajo m

**jaywalker** ['dʒeɪwɔːkə(r)] n peatón(ona) m,f imprudente

**jaywalking** ['dʒeɪwɔːkɪŋ] n imprudencia f peatonal

**jazz** [dʒæz] n jazz m; Fam **and all that j.** y otras cosas por el estilo

▸**jazz up** vt sep Fam (enliven) animar

**jazzy** ['dʒæzɪ] adj (tune) jazzístico(a); (clothes, pattern) llamativo(a)

**jealous** ['dʒeləs] adj (**a**) (envious) envidioso(a); **to be j. of sb** tener envidia de alguien (**b**) (possessive) celoso(a)

**jealously** ['dʒeləslɪ] adv (**a**) (enviously) con envidia (**b**) (possessively) celosamente; **a j. guarded secret** un secreto celosamente guardado

**jealousy** ['dʒeləsɪ] n (**a**) (envy) envidia f (**b**) (possessiveness) celos mpl

**jeans** [dʒiːnz] npl (pantalones mpl) vaqueros mpl; **a pair of j.** unos (pantalones) vaqueros

**jeep** [dʒiːp] n todoterreno m, jeep m

**jeer** [dʒɪə(r)] **1** n (boo) abucheo m; (derision) burla f
**2** vt (boo) abuchear; (mock) burlarse de
**3** vi (boo) abuchear (at a); (mock) burlarse (at de)

**jeering** ['dʒɪərɪŋ] **1** n (booing) abucheo m; (mocking) burlas fpl
**2** adj burlón(ona)

**jeez** [dʒiːz] exclam Fam ¡caray!

**Jehovah** [dʒɪ'həʊvə] n Jehová; **J.'s Witness** testigo mf de Jehová

**jell** [dʒel] vi (of liquid) aglutinarse; Fig (of ideas, plans, team) cuajar

**jelly** ['dʒelɪ] n (dessert) gelatina f, jalea f; (jam) mermelada f, confitura f; Br **j. baby** = gominola en forma de bebé

**jellybean** ['dʒelɪbiːn] n pastilla f de goma, gominola f

**jellyfish** ['dʒelɪfɪʃ] n medusa f

**jemmy** ['dʒemɪ] n Br palanqueta f

**jeopardize** ['dʒepədaɪz] vt poner en peligro

**jeopardy** ['dʒepədɪ] n **in j.** en peligro; **to put sth/sb in j.** poner en peligro algo/a alguien

**jerk¹** [dʒɜːk] **1** n *(sudden movement)* sacudida f; *(pull)* tirón m; **to give sth a j.** sacudir algo
**2** vt *(move suddenly)* sacudir; *(pull) (once)* dar un tirón a; *(in order to move)* mover a tirones
**3** vi **to j. forward** *(of car)* dar una sacudida hacia delante; *(of head)* caer hacia delante; **to j. to a halt** detenerse con una sacudida

**jerk²** n Fam *(person)* majadero(a) m,f
**▸jerk off** vi Vulg *(masturbate)* hacerse una paja
**jerkily** [dʒɜːkɪlɪ] adv a trompicones
**jerky** [dʒɜːkɪ] adj *(movement)* brusco(a)
**jerrican** [dʒerɪkæn] n bidón m
**jerry-built** [dʒerɪbɪlt] adj chapucero(a)
**Jersey** [dʒɜːzɪ] n *(island)* Jersey; **J. (cow)** vaca f de Jersey
**jersey** [dʒɜːzɪ] *(pl* **jerseys)** n *(garment)* jersey m
**Jerusalem** [dʒəˈruːsələm] n Jerusalén; **J. artichoke** aguaturma f, cotufa f
**jest** [dʒest] **1** n **in j.** en broma, de broma; **(only) half in j.** *(to speak)* medio en broma medio en serio
**2** vi bromear
**jester** [dʒestə(r)] n bufón m
**jesting** [dʒestɪŋ] adj *(remark, tone)* de broma
**Jesuit** [dʒezjʊɪt] n jesuita m
**Jesuitical** [dʒezjʊˈɪtɪkəl] adj Pej *(argument, reasoning)* retorcido(a), sibilino(a)
**Jesus** [dʒiːzəs] n Jesús m; **J. Christ** Jesucristo m; very Fam **J. (Christ)!** ¡joder!, ¡(la) hostia!
**jet¹** [dʒet] **1** n **(a)** *(plane)* reactor m, avión m a reacción; **j. engine** reactor m; **j. fighter** caza m; **j. lag** desfase m horario, jet lag m; **j. propulsion** propulsión f a reacción or a chorro; **the j. set** la jet (set) **(b)** *(of liquid, steam)* chorro m **(c)** *(nozzle)* boquilla f
**2** vi *(pt & pp* **jetted)** Fam *(travel by plane)* **to j. in/off** llegar/salir en avión
**jet²** **1** n *(stone)* azabache m
**2** adj **j. (black)** (negro) azabache m
**jet-lagged** [dʒetlægd] adj afectado(a) por el desfase horario, con jet lag
**jet-powered** [dʒetˈpaʊəd], **jet-propelled** [dʒetprəˈpeld] adj a reacción
**jettison** [dʒetɪsən] vt also Fig tirar or echar por la borda
**jetty** [dʒetɪ] n malecón m
**Jew** [dʒuː] n judío(a) m,f; **J.'s harp** birimbao m, guimbarda f
**jewel** [dʒuːəl] n *(gem, piece of jewellery)* joya f, alhaja f; Fig *(person)* joya f
**jeweller,** US **jeweler** [dʒuːələ(r)] n joyero(a) m,f; **j.'s (shop)** joyería f
**jewellery,** US **jewelry** [dʒuːəlrɪ] n joyas fpl, alhajas fpl
**Jewess** [dʒuːes] n Old-fashioned judía f
**Jewish** [dʒuːɪʃ] adj judío(a)

**Jewry** [dʒuːərɪ] n British **J.** la comunidad judía británica
**jib¹** [dʒɪb] n *(sail)* foque m; *(of crane)* aguilón m
**jib²** *(pt & pp* **jibbed)** vi **to j. at doing sth** resistirse a hacer algo
**jibe** [dʒaɪb] **1** n burla f
**2** vi **to j. at sb** hacer burla de alguien
**jiffy** [dʒɪfɪ] n Fam **in a j.** en un segundo
**jig** [dʒɪg] **1** n *(dance, music)* giga f, jiga f
**2** vi *(pt & pp* **jigged)** *(dance)* bailar (a ritmo ligero)
**jigger** [dʒɪgə(r)] vt Fam *(damage)* descuajaringar, escacharrar
**jiggered** [dʒɪgəd] adj Fam *(TV, microwave)* descuajaringado(a), escacharrado(a); *(back, knee)* descoyuntado(a)
**jiggery-pokery** [dʒɪgərɪˈpəʊkərɪ] n Br Fam tejemanejes mpl
**jiggle** [dʒɪgəl] **1** vt menear
**2** vi menearse
**▸jiggle about, jiggle around** vt sep & vi = **jiggle**
**jigsaw** [dʒɪgsɔː] n **(a)** *(saw)* sierra f de calar or de vaivén, caladora f **(b)** *(game)* **j. (puzzle)** rompecabezas m inv, puzzle m
**jihad** [dʒɪˈhæd] n guerra f santa, yihad f (islámica)
**jilt** [dʒɪlt] vt *(lover, girlfriend)* dejar plantado(a)
**jingle** [dʒɪŋgəl] **1** n *(of bells, keys)* tintineo m; Rad & TV melodía f (de un anuncio), sintonía f
**2** vt *(bells, keys)* hacer tintinear
**3** vi tintinear
**jingoism** [dʒɪŋgəʊɪzəm] n Pej patrioterismo m
**jingoistic** [dʒɪŋgəʊˈɪstɪk] adj Pej patriotero(a)
**jinx** [dʒɪŋks] Fam **1** n *(spell, curse)* gafe m; **to put a j. on sth/sb** gafar algo/a alguien
**2** vt **to be jinxed** tener el gafe, estar gafado(a)
**JIT** [dʒɪt] adj Ind *(abbr* **just in time) J. production** producción f "justo a tiempo" *(con minimización de stocks)*
**jitters** [dʒɪtəz] npl Fam **the j.** *(anxiety)* canguelo m; **I got the j.** me entró canguelo
**jittery** [dʒɪtərɪ] adj Fam *(anxious)* histérico(a); **to be/get j.** estar/ponerse histérico
**jive** [dʒaɪv] **1** n *(music, dance)* swing m
**2** vi *(dance)* bailar el swing
**Jnr** *(abbr* **Junior) Nigel Molesworth, J.** Nigel Molesworth, hijo
**job** [dʒɒb] n **(a)** *(employment)* trabajo m, empleo m; *(post)* (puesto m de) trabajo m, empleo m; **to be out of a j.** estar sin trabajo or empleo; Br Fam **jobs for the boys** enchufismo m, amiguismo m; **j. creation** creación f de empleo; **j. description** responsabilidades fpl del puesto; **to go j. hunting** ponerse a buscar empleo; **j. losses** despidos mpl; **j. offer** oferta f de em-

pleo; **j. opportunities** ofertas *fpl* de empleo; **j. satisfaction** satisfacción *f* laboral; **j. security** seguridad *f* en el trabajo; **j. sharing** empleo compartido; **j. title** cargo *m*, nombre *m* del puesto

(b) *(piece of work, task)* tarea *f*; **to do a good j.** hacer un buen trabajo; *Fig* **to do the j.** *(serve purpose)* servir, funcionar; **it was quite a j. getting her to come** me costó mucho convencerla para que viniera; *Com* **j. lot** lote *m* de saldos

(c) *(responsibility, duty)* tarea *f*; **I have (been given) the j. of writing the report** me han encargado redactar el informe

(d) *Fam (crime)* **to do a j.** dar un golpe

(e) *(idioms) Br* **it's a good j. (that)...!** ¡menos mal que...!; **that's just the j.!** ¡eso viene que ni pintado!

**jobbing** ['dʒɒbɪŋ] *Br adj (carpenter, electrician)* a destajo

**Jobcentre** ['dʒɒbsentə(r)] *n Br* oficina *f* de empleo

**jobless** ['dʒɒblɪs] **1** *npl* **the j.** los desempleados, los parados

**2** *adj* parado(a), desempleado(a)

**job-share** ['dʒɒbʃeə(r)] **1** *n* empleo *m* compartido

**2** *vi* compartir un empleo

**jobsworth** ['dʒɒbzwɜːθ] *n Fam* **he's a real j.** es muy cuadriculado en su trabajo

**jockey** ['dʒɒkɪ] **1** *n (pl* **jockeys)** jockey *m*, jinete *m*

**2** *vi* **to j. for position** luchar por tomar posiciones

**jockstrap** ['dʒɒkstræp] *n* suspensorio *m*

**jocular** ['dʒɒkjʊlə(r)] *adj* jocoso(a)

**jodhpurs** ['dʒɒdpəz] *npl* pantalones *mpl* de montar

**Joe** [dʒəʊ] *n US Fam* **he's an ordinary J.** es un tipo del montón; *Br* **J. Bloggs, J. Public** el ciudadano de a pie

**jog** [dʒɒg] **1** *n* (a) *(push)* empujoncito *m*; **to give sb's memory a j.** refrescar la memoria de alguien (b) *(run)* trote *m*; **to break into a j.** echar a correr lentamente; **to go for a j.** ir a hacer footing or jogging, ir a correr

**2** *vt (pt & pp* **jogged)** *(push)* empujar; **to j. sb's memory** refrescar la memoria a alguien

**3** *vi Sport* hacer footing or jogging, correr; **to go jogging** ir a hacer footing or jogging, ir a correr

▶**jog along** *vi (run)* correr lentamente; *Fig (in job)* seguir apalancado(a)

**jogger** ['dʒɒgə(r)] *n* corredor(ora) *m,f* de footing or jogging

**jogging** ['dʒɒgɪŋ] *n* footing *m*, jogging *m*; **to go j.** ir a hacer footing or jogging; **j. bottoms** pantalones *mpl* de chándal

**joggle** ['dʒɒgəl] *vt* menear

**Johannesburg** [dʒəʊ'hænɪzbɜːg] *n* Johan(n)esburgo

**john** [dʒɒn] *n US Fam* **the j.** *(lavatory)* el váter

**John Bull** ['dʒɒn'bʊl] *n (Englishman)* el inglés de a pie; *(England)* = la personificación de Inglaterra

**join** [dʒɔɪn] **1** *n* juntura *f*, unión *f*; *(in sewing)* costura *f*

**2** *vt* (a) *(unite, connect)* unir; **to j. two things/ places together** unir dos cosas/lugares; **to j. battle** entablar batalla; **we joined forces with them** unimos nuestras fuerzas con ellos or a las de ellos

(b) *(become a member of) (club)* ingresar en; *(political party, union)* afiliarse a; *(army)* alistarse en; *(discussion, game)* unirse a; **to j. the queue** ponerse a la cola; **may I j. you?** *(to sb at table)* ¿puedo sentarme contigo?; **to j. sb for a drink** tomarse una copa con alguien

(c) *(of river, road)* desembocar en; **where the river joins the sea** en la desembocadura del río

**3** *vi* (a) *(of pipes, roads, rivers)* juntarse, unirse

(b) *(enrol) (in club)* ingresar; *(in political party, union)* afiliarse

▶**join in 1** *vt insep (game, discussion)* participar en

**2** *vi* participar

▶**join up** *vi Mil* alistarse

**joiner** ['dʒɔɪnə(r)] *n Br (carpenter)* carpintero(a) *m,f*

**joint** [dʒɔɪnt] **1** *n* (a) *Anat* articulación *f*; **out of j.** dislocado(a); *Br Fig* **to put sb's nose out of j.** *(upset)* desairar a alguien (b) *(in woodwork)* junta *f*, juntura *f* (c) *(of meat) (raw)* pieza *f*; *(roasted)* asado *m* (d) *Fam (nightclub, restaurant)* garito *m*, local *m* (e) *Fam (cannabis cigarette)* porro *m*, canuto *m*

**2** *adj* conjunto(a); *Fin* **j. account** cuenta *f* indistinta or conjunta; **j. ownership** copropiedad *f*; **j. stock company** sociedad *f* anónima; **j. venture** empresa *f* conjunta or común

**3** *vt (chicken)* trinchar

**jointly** ['dʒɔɪntlɪ] *adv* conjuntamente

**joist** [dʒɔɪst] *n (beam)* viga *f*

**joke** [dʒəʊk] **1** *n* (a) *(funny remark)* broma *f*, chiste *m*; *(funny story)* chiste *m*; *(prank, trick)* broma; **to tell** or **crack a j.** contar un chiste; **to make a j. about sth** hacer una broma or bromear sobre algo; **to make a j. of sth** pretender que algo era en broma; **to say/do sth for a j.** decir/hacer algo en or de broma; **to play a j. on sb** gastar una broma a alguien; **the j. was on him when he had to...** la broma le salió rana cuando tuvo que...; **she can't take a j.** no sabe aguantar una broma; **that's** or **it's no j.!** ¡no es cosa de broma!; **it's getting beyond a j.** esto ya pasa de castaño oscuro (b) *Fam* **to**

**be a j.** *(of person)* ser un/una inútil, no valer un duro; *(of thing)* ser de chiste

**2** *vi* bromear; **to j. about sth** bromear acerca de algo; **to j. with sb** bromear con alguien; **I'm not joking** (hablo) en serio; **I was only joking** estaba de broma; **you're joking!, you must be joking!** *(expressing surprise)* ¡no hablarás en serio!; *(expressing refusal)* ¡ni hablar!; **joking apart...** bromas aparte..., fuera de broma...

**joker** ['dʒəʊkə(r)] *n* **(a)** *(clown)* bromista *mf*, gracioso(a) *m,f*; *(incompetent person)* inútil *mf* **(b)** *(in cards)* comodín *m*; *Fig* **the j. in the pack** la gran incógnita

**jokily** ['dʒəʊkɪlɪ] *adv* en tono de broma

**jokingly** ['dʒəʊkɪŋlɪ] *adv* en broma

**joky** ['dʒəʊkɪ] *adj* jocoso(a)

**jolly** ['dʒɒlɪ] **1** *adj (cheerful)* alegre; **the J. Roger** la bandera pirata

**2** *adv Br Fam (very)* bien; **j. good!** ¡estupendo!; **it serves him j. well right!** ¡se lo tiene bien merecido!; **yes, I j. well DID do it!** sí, fui yo ¿qué pasa?

**3** *vt* **to j. sb into doing sth** animar a alguien a hacer algo; **to j. sb along** animar a alguien

**jolt** [dʒəʊlt] **1** *n (shake)* sacudida *f*; *(shock, surprise)* susto *m*; **it gave me a bit of a j.** me dio un buen susto

**2** *vt (shake)* sacudir; *(shock, surprise)* sacudir, alterar; **to j. sb into action** empujar a alguien a actuar; **to j. sb out of a depression** hacer salir a alguien de una depresión

**3** *vi (shake)* dar sacudidas; **to j. along** *(of vehicle)* avanzar a tirones; **to j. to a stop** *(of vehicle)* pararse en seco

**Jordan** ['dʒɔ:dən] *n (country)* Jordania; **the (River) J.** el Jordán

**Jordanian** [dʒɔ:'deɪnɪən] *n & adj* jordano(a) *m,f*

**josh** [dʒɒʃ] *vt Fam (tease)* tomar el pelo a

**joss stick** ['dʒɒsstɪk] *n* pebete *m*, varilla *f* aromática

**jostle** [dʒɒsəl] **1** *vt* empujar; **to j. sb out of the way** quitar a alguien de en medio a empujones

**2** *vi (push)* empujarse; **to j. for position** *(in contest, job)* luchar por tomar posiciones

**jot** [dʒɒt] *n Fam* **not a j.** ni pizca; **he doesn't care a j.** le importa un comino; **there isn't a j. of truth in what you say** no hay ni un ápice de verdad en lo que dices

▸**jot down** *vt sep* apuntar, anotar

**jotter** ['dʒɒtə(r)] *n* libreta *f*

**jottings** ['dʒɒtɪŋz] *npl* anotaciones *fpl*

**joule** [dʒu:l] *n Phys* julio *m*

**journal** ['dʒɜ:nəl] *n (publication)* revista *f (especializada)*, boletín *m*; *(diary)* diario *m*; **to keep a j.** llevar or escribir un diario

**journalese** [dʒɜ:nə'li:z] *n Fam Pej* jerga *f* periodística

**journalism** ['dʒɜ:nəlɪzəm] *n* periodismo *m*

**journalist** ['dʒɜ:nəlɪst] *n* periodista *mf*

**journalistic** [dʒɜ:nə'lɪstɪk] *adj* periodístico(a)

**journey** ['dʒɜ:nɪ] **1** *n (pl journeys)* viaje *m*; **a train/plane/boat j.** un viaje en tren/avión/barco; **to make a j.** hacer un viaje; **to set off** *or* **out on a j.** salir de viaje; **to go (away) on a j.** ir(se) de viaje; **to get to** *or* **reach the end of one's j.** llegar al final del viaje

**2** *vi* viajar

**joust** [dʒaʊst] *vi Hist* justar; *(compete)* pugnar, estar en liza

**jovial** ['dʒəʊvɪəl] *adj* jovial

**jovially** ['dʒəʊvɪəlɪ] *adv* jovialmente

**jowl** [dʒaʊl] *n (jaw)* mandíbula *f*; *(cheek)* carrillo *m*, mejilla *f*

**joy** [dʒɔɪ] *n* **(a)** *(happiness)* alegría *f*, gozo *m*; **to wish sb j.** desear a alguien lo mejor **(b)** *(pleasure)* placer *m*, maravilla *f*; **she's a j. to be with** su compañía es muy placentera; **he's a j. to work for** es una maravilla de jefe **(c)** *Br Fam (success)* **(did you have** *or* **get) any j.?** ¿hubo suerte?; **I didn't get any j.** no conseguí nada

**joyful** ['dʒɔɪfʊl] *adj* alegre

**joyfully** ['dʒɔɪfəlɪ] *adv* alegremente

**joyless** ['dʒɔɪlɪs] *adj* triste

**joyous** ['dʒɔɪəs] *adj* jubiloso(a)

**joyride** ['dʒɔɪraɪd] *n (in stolen car)* **to go for a j.** ir a dar una vuelta en un coche robado

**joyrider** ['dʒɔɪraɪdə(r)] *n* = persona que roba coches para darse una vuelta por diversión

**joystick** ['dʒɔɪstɪk] *n Av* palanca *f* de mando; *Comptr* joystick *m*

**JP** [dʒeɪ'pi:] *n Br Law (abbr* **justice of the peace)** juez *mf* de paz

**Jr** *(abbr* **Junior) Nigel Molesworth, Jr** Nigel Molesworth, hijo

**jubilant** ['dʒu:bɪlənt] *adj (shouts, expression)* de júbilo; *(person, celebration)* jubiloso(a); **to be j. (at** *or* **about** *or* **over sth)** estar encantado(a) (con algo)

**jubilation** [dʒu:bɪ'leɪʃən] *n* júbilo *m*

**jubilee** ['dʒu:bɪli:] *n* aniversario *m*; **silver/golden j.** vigésimo quinto/quincuagésimo aniversario

**Judaic** [dʒu:'deɪɪk] *adj* judaico(a)

**Judaism** ['dʒu:deɪɪzəm] *n* judaísmo *m*

**Judas** ['dʒu:dəs] *n (traitor)* judas *mf*

**judder** [dʒʌdə(r)] *vi Br* dar sacudidas; **to j. to a halt** pararse en seco

**judge** [dʒʌdʒ] **1** *n Law* juez *mf*, jueza *f*; *(in competition)* jurado *m*, juez *m*; **to be a good/poor j. of sth** tener buen ojo para (juzgar) algo;

**I will be the j. of that** lo juzgaré por mí mismo

**2** *vt* **(a)** *Law Sport (try, give decision about)* juzgar; **to j. a case** juzgar un caso **(b)** *(assess critically)* juzgar, calificar; **to j. sb by** *or* **on sth** juzgar a alquien por algo; **to j. sth/sb a success/failure** calificar algo/a alguien de éxito/fracaso; **to j. it necessary to do sth** juzgar necesario hacer algo **(c)** *(estimate)* estimar, calcular

**3** *vi Law Rel* juzgar; **to j. by appearances** juzgar por las apariencias; **as far as I can j.** en mi opinión; **j. for yourself** júzgalo tú mismo, juzga por ti mismo; **judging by...** a juzgar por...

**judg(e)ment,** *US* **judgment** ['dʒʌdʒmənt] *n* **(a)** *(decision)* juicio *m*; *(of judge, in court)* fallo *m*; *Law* **to sit in j.** deliberar; *Law* **to pass j.** pronunciar *or* emitir el veredicto; *Fig* **to sit in** *or* **pass j. on sb** emitir juicios sobre alguien; *Rel* **J. Day** el día del Juicio Final

**(b)** *(opinion)* juicio *m*, parecer *m*; **she gave her j. on the performance** dio su parecer acerca de la actuación; **to form a j.** formarse un juicio **(c)** *(discernment)* juicio *m*; **good j.** buen juicio; **to show poor j.** demostrar tener poco juicio; **to trust sb's j.** fiarse (del juicio) de alguien; **in my j.** a mi juicio; **against my better j.** a pesar de no estar plenamente convencido(a)

**judg(e)mental** [dʒʌdʒ'mentəl] *adj* **to be j.** hacer juicios a la ligera

**judicial** [dʒu:'dɪʃəl] *adj* judicial

**judiciary** [dʒu:'dɪʃərɪ] *n (judges)* judicatura *f*, magistratura *f*; *(branch of authority)* poder *m* judicial

**judicious** [dʒu:'dɪʃəs] *adj* juicioso(a)

**judiciously** [dʒu:'dɪʃəslɪ] *adv* juiciosamente

**judiciousness** [dʒu:'dɪʃəsnɪs] *n* buen juicio *m*

**judo** ['dʒu:dəʊ] *n* judo *m*

**jug** [dʒʌg] *n* **(a)** *(for wine, water)* jarra *f* **(b)** *very Fam (prison)* **in the j.** en chirona, en el trullo

**juggernaut** ['dʒʌgənɔ:t] *n Br* camión *m* grande, tráiler *m*

**juggle** ['dʒʌgəl] **1** *vt (balls, figures)* hacer malabarismos *or* juegos malabares con

**2** *vi* hacer malabarismos, hacer juegos malabares

**juggler** ['dʒʌglə(r)] *n* malabarista *mf*

**jugular** ['dʒʌgjʊlə(r)] **1** *n* yugular *f*; *Fig* **to go for the j.** *(in argument)* entrar a degüello

**2** *adj* yugular

**juice** [dʒu:s] *n* **(a)** *(of fruit)* zumo *m*, *Am* jugo *m*; *(of meat)* jugo *m* **(b)** *US Fam (petrol)* caldo *m*, gasofa *f*

**juicy** ['dʒu:sɪ] *adj also Fig* jugoso(a)

**jukebox** ['dʒu:kbɒks] *n* máquina *f* de discos

**Jul** *(abbr* **July)** julio *m*

**July** [dʒu:'laɪ] *n* julio *m*; *see also* **May**

**jumble** ['dʒʌmbəl] **1** *n (of things, ideas, words)* revoltijo *m*, batiburrillo *m*; **in a j.** *(papers)* revueltos; *(ideas)* confusas; *Br* **j. sale** rastrillo *m* benéfico

**2** *vt (things, ideas, words)* revolver

**jumbo** ['dʒʌmbəʊ] *adj* gigante; **j. sized** *(de tamaño)* gigante; **j. jet** jumbo *m*

**jump** [dʒʌmp] **1** *n* **(a)** *(leap)* salto *m*; *Fig* **go take a j.!** ¡vete a freír espárragos!; *Fig* **to be one j. ahead** ir (un paso) por delante; *Av* **j. jet** reactor *m* de despegue vertical; *Br Aut* **j. leads** pinzas *fpl or* cables *mpl* (de arranque) de batería; **j. suit** mono *m (de vestir)*

**(b)** *(rise)* salto *m* **(in** en)

**(c)** *(fence on racecourse)* obstáculo *m*

**2** *vt (hedge, ditch)* saltar; *(word, paragraph, page)* saltarse; **to j. sb** *(attack)* asaltar a alguien; **to j. bail** huir durante la libertad bajo fianza; **to j. the gun** *(in race)* hacer una salida en falso; *Fig* precipitarse; **to j. the lights** *(in car)* saltarse un semáforo; *Br* **to j. the queue** colarse; **to j. ship** desertar, abandonar el barco

**3** *vi* **(a)** *(leap) (of person, animal)* saltar, brincar; **to j. to one's feet** ponerse en pie de un salto; **to j. for joy** saltar de alegría; **to j. on a train/bus** coger *or* tomar un tren/un autobús; **to j. into a taxi** montar en un taxi; **to j. from a train** tirarse de un tren; **to j. (down) from a wall/tree** dejarse caer desde (lo alto de) un muro/árbol; **to j. out of bed** tirarse de la cama, levantarse (de la cama) de un salto; **to j. to conclusions** sacar conclusiones precipitadas; *Fig* **let's wait and see which way she jumps** esperemos a ver por dónde sale; *Fam* **to j. down sb's throat** echarse encima de alguien con una furia con alguien; *Fig* **to j. out at sb** *(of mistake, surprising detail)* saltarle a alguien a la vista

**(b)** *(go directly)* **to j. from one subject to another** saltar de un tema a otro; **the film then jumps to the present** luego la película da un salto hasta el presente

**(c)** *(rise rapidly) (of unemployment)* dispararse, ascender rápidamente

**(d)** *(make a sudden movement)* dar un salto, saltar; **my heart jumped** me dio un vuelco el corazón; **we nearly jumped out of our skins** nos dimos un susto de muerte

▸**jump at** *vt insep* **to j. at an offer/a chance** no dejar escapar una oferta/una oportunidad

▸**jump on** *vt insep Fam (reprimand)* **to j. on sb (for doing sth)** echarse encima de alguien (por haber hecho algo)

**jumped-up** [dʒʌmp'ʌp] *adj Br Fam Pej (recently promoted, arrogant)* advenedizo(a)

**jumper** ['dʒʌmpə(r)] *n Br (sweater)* jersey *m*; *US (sleeveless dress)* pichi *m*

**jumping-off place** ['dʒʌmpɪŋ'ɒf pleɪs], **jumping-off point** ['dʒʌmpɪŋ'ɒf pɔɪnt] *n* punto *m* de partida

**jump-start** ['dʒʌmpstɑ:t] vt (car) arrancar empujando

**jumpy** ['dʒʌmpɪ] adj nervioso(a); **to be j.** estar nervioso(a)

**Jun** (abbr **June**) junio m

**junction** ['dʒʌŋkʃən] n (of roads, railway lines) cruce m, nudo m; Elec **j. box** caja f de empalmes

**juncture** ['dʒʌŋktʃə(r)] n coyuntura f; **at this j.** en esta coyuntura

**June** [dʒu:n] n junio m; see also **May**

**jungle** ['dʒʌŋgəl] n (forest) selva f, jungla f; Fig jungla f

**junior** ['dʒu:njə(r)] **1** adj **(a)** (in age) **to be j. to sb** ser más joven que alguien; **Nigel Molesworth J.** Nigel Molesworth hijo; US **j. high (school)** (between 11 and 15) escuela f secundaria; Br **j. school** (between 7 and 11) escuela f primaria **(b)** (in rank) de rango inferior; **to be j. to sb** tener un rango inferior al de alguien; Br Univ **j. common room** sala f de estudiantes; Br Parl **j. minister** ≃ secretario(a) m,f de Estado

**2** n **(a)** (in age) **to be sb's j.** ser más joven que alguien; **he's three years my j.** es tres años menor que yo **(b)** (in rank) subalterno(a) m,f

**juniper** ['dʒu:nɪpə(r)] n **j. (tree)** enebro m; **j. berry** enebrina f, baya f de enebro

**junk¹** [dʒʌŋk] **1** n (unwanted objects) trastos mpl; Fin **j. bond** bono m basura; Pej **j. food** comida f basura; Pej **j. mail** propaganda f (postal); **j. shop** cacharrería f, baratillo m

**2** vt Fam (discard) deshacerse de

**junk²** n (boat) junco m

**junket** ['dʒʌŋkɪt] n **(a)** (food) cuajada f **(b)** Pej (trip by public official) = viaje pagado con dinero del contribuyente

**junkie, junky** ['dʒʌŋkɪ] n Fam (drug addict in general) drogota mf; (heroin addict) yonqui mf; **a game-show j.** un adicto a los concursos

**junkyard** ['dʒʌŋkjɑ:d] n (for metal) chatarrería f, depósito m de chatarra

**junta** ['dʒʌntə] n Pej junta f militar

**Jupiter** ['dʒu:pɪtə(r)] n (planet, god) Júpiter m

**jurisdiction** [dʒʊərɪs'dɪkʃən] n jurisdicción f; **to have j. over** tener jurisdicción sobre; **within** or **under the j. of...** bajo la jurisdicción de...

**jurisprudence** [dʒʊərɪs'pru:dəns] n jurisprudencia f

**jurist** ['dʒʊərɪst] n Formal (legal expert) jurista mf

**juror** ['dʒʊərə(r)] n Law (miembro m del) jurado m

**jury** ['dʒʊərɪ] n Law jurado m; **to be** or **serve on the j.** ser miembro del jurado; Fig **the j. is still out on the reforms** aún está por ver la conveniencia de las reformas; **j. box** tribuna f del jurado; **to do j. service** formar parte de un jurado (popular)

**just** [dʒʌst] **1** adj (fair) justo(a); **it's only j. that...** es justo que...; **he got his j. deserts** recibió su merecido

**2** adv **(a)** (exactly) justamente, justo; **that's j. what I told her** eso es exactamente or justo lo que le dije; **that's j. the point!** ¡de eso se trata, precisamente!; **isn't that j. my luck!** ¡vaya mala suerte que tengo!; **it's j. as good/difficult as...** es tan bueno/difícil como...; **j. then** justo entonces; **he's busy j. now** está ocupado en este (preciso) momento; **j. as I was leaving...** justo en el momento en que me iba...; **I can j. see her as a doctor** me imagino perfectamente como médica

**(b)** (only) sólo, solamente; **she's j. a baby** no es más que una niña; **it costs j. £10** sólo cuesta 10 libras

**(c)** (barely) justo; **j. before/after** justo antes/ después; **j. over/under £50** poco más/menos de 50 libras; **j. in time** justo a tiempo; **it's only j. big enough** tiene el tamaño justo; **it's j. enough to live on** llega justo para vivir; **they j. caught/missed the train** cogieron/ perdieron el tren por los pelos

**(d)** (recently) **to have j. done sth** acabar de hacer algo; **I saw him j. now** lo acabo de ver; **j. yesterday** ayer mismo; **j. last year** tan sólo el año pasado

**(e)** (simply) **it was j. wonderful/dreadful!** ¡fue sencillamente maravilloso/horroroso!; **he j. refuses to listen!** ¡es que se niega a escuchar!; **j. ask if you need money** si necesitas dinero, no tienes más que pedirlo

**(f)** (in threats, exhortations) **j. (you) try/wait!** ¡inténtalo/espera y verás!; **(that's) j. as well!** ¡menos mal!

**(g)** (in phrases) **j. about** (almost) casi; **they're j. about the same** son casi iguales; **I can j. about manage** me las puedo arreglar más o menos; **to be j. about to do sth** estar a punto de hacer algo

**justice** ['dʒʌstɪs] n **(a)** (power of law) justicia f; **to bring sb to j.** llevar a alguien a los tribunales **(b)** (fairness) justicia f; **this photograph doesn't do him j.** esta fotografía no le hace justicia; **not to do oneself j.** no dar lo mejor de sí mismo(a) **(c)** Law (judge) juez mf, jueza f; Br **J. of the Peace** juez de paz

**justifiable** ['dʒʌstɪfaɪəbəl] adj justificable; Law **j. homicide** homicidio m justificado

**justifiably** ['dʒʌstɪfaɪəblɪ] adv justificadamente

**justification** [dʒʌstɪfɪ'keɪʃən] n justificación f; **in j. of** para justificar

**justify** ['dʒʌstɪfaɪ] vt **(a)** (explain) justificar; **to**

**be justified in doing sth** tener justificación para hacer algo (**b**) *Typ & Comptr* justificar

**justly** ['dʒʌstlɪ] *adv (fairly, rightly)* justamente, con justicia; **j. famous** justamente *or* merecidamente famoso(a)

▸**jut out** [dʒʌt] **1** *vt sep (chin)* sacar
  **2** *vi (of balcony, rock)* sobresalir

**jute** [dʒuːt] *n (plant, fibre)* yute *m*

**juvenile** ['dʒuːvɪnaɪl] **1** *adj* (**a**) *(for young people)* juvenil; *Law* **j. court** tribunal *m* (tutelar) de menores; **j. delinquent** delincuente *mf* juvenil (**b**) *Pej (childish)* infantil, pueril
  **2** *n Law* menor *mf*

**juxtapose** [dʒʌkstə'pəʊz] *vt* yuxtaponer

**juxtaposition** [dʒʌkstəpə'zɪʃən] *n* yuxtaposición *f*

# K

**K, k** [keɪ] *n* **(a)** *(letter)* K, k *f* **(b)** *(thousand)* **he earns 30K** gana treinta mil

**Kabul** ['kɑ:bʊl] *n* Kabul

**Kaffir** ['kæfə(r)] *n very Fam* = término ofensivo para referirse a los negros, negraco(a) *m,f*, moreno(a) *m,f*

**kaftan** ['kæftæn] *n* caftán *m*

**kale** [keɪl] *n* col *f* rizada

**kaleidoscope** [kə'laɪdəskəʊp] *n* calidoscopio *m*

**kamikaze** [kæmɪ'kɑ:zɪ] *n & adj also Fig* kamikaze *mf*

**Kampuchea** [kæmpʊ'tʃɪə] *n Formerly* Kampuchea

**kangaroo** [kæŋgə'ru:] *n* (*pl* **kangaroos**) *n* canguro *m*; *Pej* **k. court** tribunal *m* irregular

**kaput** [kə'pʊt] *adj Fam* **to be k.** estar cascado(a)

**karaoke** [kærɪ'əʊkɪ] *n* karaoke *m*

**karate** [kə'rɑ:tɪ] *n* kárate *m*; **k. chop** golpe *m* de kárate

**Kashmir** [kæʃ'mɪə(r)] *n* Cachemira

**Kashmiri** [kæʃ'mɪərɪ] **1** *n* = habitante *or* nativo(a) de Cachemira
 **2** *adj* de Cachemira

**Katmandu** [kætmæn'du:] *n* Katmandú

**kayak** ['kaɪæk] *n* canoa *f*, kayak *m*

**Kazak(h)stan** [kæzæk'stɑ:n] *n* Kazajistán

**kebab** [kə'bæb] *n* brocheta *f*, pincho *m* moruno

**kedgeree** [kedʒə'ri:] *n* = plato especiado de arroz, pescado y huevo duro

**keel** [ki:l] *n Naut* quilla *f*; *Fig* **to be on an even k.** *(of business, economy)* estar en equilibrio
**▶keel over** *vi* *(of boat)* volcar; *Fam (of person)* derrumbarse

**keen** [ki:n] *adj* **(a)** *(enthusiastic)* entusiasta; **to be k. to do sth** tener muchas ganas de hacer algo; **to be k. for sth to happen** tener muchas ganas de que ocurra algo; **she's k. on Patrick** le gusta Patrick; **he wasn't k. on the idea** no le entusiasmaba la idea; *Fam* **to be as k. as mustard** estar entusiasmadísimo(a); **to take a k. interest in sth** mostrar gran interés por algo
 **(b)** *(acute, perceptive) (mind)* penetrante; *(eye-*

*sight)* agudo(a); *(sense of smell)* fino(a); **to have a k. eye for detail** tener buen ojo para el detalle; **to have a k. awareness of sth** ser profundamente consciente de algo
 **(c)** *(sharp, intense) (sorrow, regret)* profundo(a); **a k. appetite** un apetito voraz; **a k. blade** una hoja afilada; **k. competition** competencia *f* feroz; *Br Com* **k. prices** precios *mpl* competitivos; **a k. wind** un viento cortante

**keenly** ['ki:nlɪ] *adv* *(enthusiastically)* con entusiasmo; *(intensely)* profundamente; **a k. contested election** unas elecciones muy reñidas

**keep** [ki:p] **1** *n* **(a)** *(maintenance)* **to pay for one's k.** pagarse la manutención; **to earn one's k.** ganarse el sustento
 **(b)** *(of castle)* torre *f* del homenaje
 **(c)** *Fam* **for keeps** para siempre

 **2** *vt* (*pt & pp* **kept** [kept]) **(a)** *(retain)* quedarse con, guardar; *(store)* guardar; **to k. sth for sb** guardar algo para alguien; **to k. sth from sb** *(information)* ocultar algo a alguien; **to k. one's job** conservar el trabajo; **to k. its shape** *(of garment)* no deformarse; **to k. its colour** *(of garment)* no desteñir; **to k. sb's attention** mantener la atención de alguien; **k. the change** quédese con el cambio
 **(b)** *(maintain)* **to k. a diary** llevar un diario; **to k. a note of sth** llevar cuenta de algo; **to k. order** mantener el orden; **to k. a record of sth** registrar algo; **to k. a secret** guardar un secreto
 **(c)** *(maintain in a certain condition)* mantener; **to k. sth clean/secret** mantener algo limpio/en secreto; **to k. sb awake** mantener *or* tener despierto(a) a alguien; **to k. sb waiting** tener a alguien esperando
 **(d)** *(look after) (animals, shop)* tener; *(mistress)* mantener; **a kept woman** una mujer mantenida; **I've got a family to k.** tengo una familia que mantener
 **(e)** *(detain)* entretener, parar; **what kept you?** ¿qué fue lo que te retrasó?
 **(f)** *(observe) (promise)* cumplir; **to k. late hours** trasnochar; **she kept her word** mantuvo su palabra

 **3** *vi* **(a)** *(remain, stay)* mantenerse; **to k. well** mantenerse bien; **how are you keeping?** ¿qué tal estás?; **to k. quiet** estar callado(a)

**(b)** *(continue)* **to k. doing sth** *(continue doing)* seguir haciendo algo; **he kept getting into trouble** siempre se estaba metiendo en líos; **to k. straight on** seguir todo recto; **k. (to the) left/right** circular por la izquierda/derecha; **I wish you wouldn't k. saying that** me gustaría que no dijeras eso todo el tiempo

**(c)** *(of food)* conservarse; *Fig* **it will k.** *(of problem)* puede esperar

▸**keep away 1** *vt sep* **to k. sb away from sth** mantener a alguien alejado(a) de algo; **k. that dog away from me!** ¡no me acerques ese perro!

**2** *vi* **to k. away from** mantenerse alejado(a) de

▸**keep back 1** *vt sep* **(a)** *(crowd, tears)* contener; **to k. sth back from sb** ocultarle algo a alguien **(b)** *(delay)* entretener; **he was kept back by his lack of qualifications** su falta de titulación le impidió progresar

**2** *vi (not approach)* no acercarse

▸**keep down 1** *vt sep* **(a) to k. one's voice down** hablar bajo; **to k. one's head down** *(physically)* mantener la cabeza agachada; *Fig* esconder la cabeza; **I can't k. my food down** vomito todo lo que como **(b)** *(repress)* reprimir; *(prices)* mantener bajos

**2** *vi (not stand up)* mantenerse cuerpo a tierra

▸**keep from** *vt sep* **to k. sb from doing sth** impedir que alguien haga algo; **to k. sb from his work** no dejar trabajar a alguien

▸**keep in** *vt sep (pupil)* castigar sin salir; **they decided to k. her in overnight** *(in hospital)* decidieron dejarla ingresada hasta el día siguiente

▸**keep in with** *vt insep Fam* **to k. in with sb** cultivar la amistad de alguien

▸**keep off 1** *vt sep* **k. your hands off that!** ¡no toques eso!; **k. your hands off me!** ¡no me toques!

**2** *vt insep* **k. off the grass!** *(sign)* prohibido pisar el césped

**3** *vi (stay away)* mantenerse al margen

▸**keep on 1** *vt sep (not take off)* dejarse puesto(a); *(not switch off)* dejar encendido(a); *(continue to employ)* mantener en el puesto; *Fam* **k. your hair on!** ¡no te sulfures!

**2** *vi* continuar, seguir; **to k. on doing sth** *(continue doing)* seguir haciendo algo; **she kept on getting into trouble** siempre se estaba metiendo en líos; **to k. on about sth** insistir sobre algo

▸**keep on at** *vt insep Fam* **to k. on at sb (to do sth)** dar la lata a alguien (para que haga algo)

▸**keep out 1** *vt sep (intruders, foreign imports)* impedir el paso a

**2** *vi (avoid, stay away from)* **to k. out of sth** no meterse en algo; **to k. out of trouble** no meterse en líos; **to k. out of an argument** mantenerse al margen de una discusión; **k. out** *(sign)* prohibida la entrada, prohibido el paso

▸**keep to 1** *vt sep* **(a)** *(hold)* **to k. sb to a promise** hacer que alguien cumpla una promesa; **to k. delays/costs to a minimum** reducir al mínimo *or* minimizar los retrasos/costes **(b)** *(not reveal)* **to k. sth to oneself** no contar algo; **to k. oneself to oneself** mantenerse apartado(a) del resto

**2** *vt insep (promise)* cumplir; **to k. to a subject** ceñirse a un tema; **she kept to her room** se quedó encerrada en su habitación

▸**keep up 1** *vt sep* **(a)** *(custom)* mantener; **to k. up the payments** llevar al día los pagos; **k. it up!** ¡sigue así!; **k. up the good work!** ¡sigue así!; **to k. up appearances** guardar las apariencias **(b)** *(keep awake)* tener en vela

**2** *vi* **(a)** *(of rain, snow)* continuar **(b)** *(remain level, go at same speed)* no quedarse atrás; **to k. up with sb** seguir el ritmo de alguien; **to k. up with the Joneses** no ser menos que el vecino; **to k. up with events** mantenerse informado(a); **to k. up with the times** adaptarse a los tiempos

**keeper** ['ki:pə(r)] *n (in zoo, park)* guarda *mf*; *(in museum)* conservador(ora) *m,f*; *(gamekeeper)* guardabosque *m*; *Fam (goalkeeper)* portero *m*, guardameta *m*

**keep-fit** ['ki:p'fɪt] *n* **k. class** clase *f* de mantenimiento, clase *f* de gimnasia; **k. fanatic** = persona obsesionada por mantenerse en forma

**keeping** ['ki:pɪŋ] *n* **to have sth/sb in one's k.** tener algo/a alguien bajo la custodia de uno; **in k. with...** de acuerdo con...; **out of k. with...** en desacuerdo con...

**keepsake** ['ki:pseɪk] *n* recuerdo *m*

**keg** [keg] *n* barrica *f*, barrilete *m*

**ken** [ken] *n* **to be beyond sb's k.** estar fuera del alcance de alguien

**kennel** ['kenəl] *n* caseta *f* (del perro); **to put a dog into kennels** dejar a un perro en una residencia canina

**Kenya** ['kenjə, 'ki:njə] *n* Kenia

**Kenyan** ['kenjən] *n & adj* keniano(a) *m,f*, keniata *mf*

**kept** [kept] *pt & pp of* **keep**

**kerb** [kɜːb] *n Br* bordillo *m* (de la acera)

**kerbcrawler** ['kɜːbkrɔːlə(r)] *n* = persona que busca prostitutas conduciendo lentamente junto a la acera

**kerbcrawling** ['kɜːbkrɔːlɪŋ] *n* = conducir despacio en busca de prostitutas

**kerbstone** ['kɜːbstəʊn] *n Br* adoquín *m* (del bordillo)

**kerfuffle** [kə'fʌfəl] *n Fam* jaleo *m*, follón *m*

**kernel** ['kɜːnəl] *n (of nut)* pepita *f*, fruto *m*; *(of grain)* grano *m*; *Fig (of problem)* núcleo *m*

**kerosene** ['kerəsi:n] *n US* queroseno *m*; **k. lamp** lámpara *f* de queroseno

**kestrel** ['kestrəl] *n* cernícalo *m*

**ketchup** ['ketʃəp] n (tomato) k. ketchup m, catchup m

**kettle** [ketəl] n (for boiling water) (on stove) tetera f; (electric) hervidor m (eléctrico); **I'll put the k. on** pondré el agua a hervir; Fam **that's a different k. of fish** eso es harina de otro costal

**kettledrum** ['ketəldrʌm] n timbal m

**key** [ki:] 1 n (pl **keys**) (a) (of door) llave f; (of clock, mechanical toy) cuerda f; (of piano, typewriter) tecla f; (to problem, situation) clave f, llave f; **the k. to happiness/success** la clave de la felicidad/del éxito (b) (answers, guide) (of map) clave f; (to exercises) respuestas fpl (c) Mus tono m; **major/minor k.** tono mayor/menor; **the k. of C** la clave de do; **to be off k.** estar desafinado(a)

2 adj (most important) clave

▶**key in** vt sep Comptr teclear

**keyboard** ['ki:bɔ:d] n (of piano, computer) teclado m; Mus **keyboards** teclado m, teclados mpl; **k. player** teclista mf

**keyhole** ['ki:həʊl] n (ojo m de la) cerradura f; **k. surgery** cirugía f endoscópica

**keynote** ['ki:nəʊt] 1 n nota f dominante

2 adj (speech, speaker) principal

**keypad** ['ki:pæd] n Comptr teclado m numérico

**keyring** ['ki:rɪŋ] n llavero m

**keystone** ['ki:stəʊn] n Archit clave f (de un arco); Fig piedra f angular

**keystroke** ['ki:strəʊk] n Comptr pulsación f

**kg** (abbr **kilogram**) kg m

**KGB** [keɪdʒi:'bi:] n Formerly KGB m

**khaki** ['kɑ:kɪ] 1 n caqui m

2 adj caqui inv; **k. shorts** pantalones mpl cortos caqui

**Khartoum** [kɑ:'tu:m] n Jartum f

**kHz** Elec (abbr **kilohertz**) kHz m

**kibbutz** [kɪ'bʊts] (pl **kibbutzim** [kɪbʊt-'si:m]) n kibutz m

**kibosh** ['kaɪbɒʃ] n Fam **to put the k. on sth** echar algo a pique

**kick** [kɪk] 1 n (a) (with foot) patada f, puntapié m; (of horse) coz f; (of gun) retroceso m; **to have a k.** (of drink) estar fuerte (aunque entre bien); **to give sth/sb a k.** dar una patada a algo/alguien; Fam Fig **she needs a k. up the backside** necesita una buena patada en el trasero; Fig **that was a k. in the teeth for him** le sentó como una patada en la boca

(b) (thrill) **to get a k. out of sth** disfrutar con algo; **to get a k. out of doing sth** disfrutar haciendo algo; **to do sth for kicks** hacer algo por gusto, regodearse haciendo algo

2 vt (once) dar una patada a; (several times) dar patadas a; **to get kicked** (once) recibir una patada, (several times) recibir patadas; very Fam **to**

**k. the bucket** estirar la pata; Fig **to k. a man when he's down** atacar a alguien cuando ya está derrotado; **I could have kicked myself** me hubiera dado de bofetadas, era para tirarme de los pelos; Fam **to k. the habit** (stop taking drugs) dejar las drogas

3 vi (once) dar una patada; (several times) dar patadas; (of animal) dar coces; (of gun) hacer retroceso; Fam **to k. against sth** (rebel against) patalear contra algo

▶**kick about, kick around 1** vt sep **to k. a ball about** or **around** pelotear, dar patadas a un balón; Fam **to k. an idea about** or **around** darle vueltas a una idea; **don't let them k. you about** or **around** no dejes que te traten a patadas

2 vi Fam andar por ahí

▶**kick in** vt sep (door) abrir de una patada; Fam **to k. sb's head in** romperle la cabeza a alguien

▶**kick off** vi (in football) hacer el saque inicial; Fam Fig (in meeting, debate) empezar

▶**kick out** vt sep Fam **he was kicked out** (of job, house) lo echaron, le dieron la patada

▶**kick up** vt sep Fam **to k. up a fuss** montar or armar un alboroto; **to k. up a row** or **a racket** montar or armar una bronca

**kickback** ['kɪkbæk] n Fam (payment) **he got a k. for doing it** le untaron para que lo hiciera

**kick-off** ['kɪkɒf] n (in football) saque m inicial; Fam Fig **for a k.** (to start with) para empezar

**kick-start** ['kɪkstɑːt] vt (motorbike, engine) arrancar a patada (con el pedal); Fig (economy) reactivar

**kid** [kɪd] 1 n (a) Fam (child) crío(a) m,f, niño(a) m,f, Arg pibe(a) m,f, CAm chavalo(a) m,f, Chile cabro(a) m,f, Méx chavo(a) m,f; **my k. brother** mi hermano pequeño; **it's k.'s stuff** (easy, childish) eso es cosa de niños (b) (young goat) cabrito m; (skin) cabritilla f; **k. gloves** guantes mpl de cabritilla; Fig **to handle sb with k. gloves** tratar a alguien con mucho tacto

2 vt (pt & pp **kidded**) Fam (fool) quedarse con, vacilar; **to k. oneself** engañarse

3 vi Fam **to be kidding** estar bromeando; **no kidding!** ¿en serio?

**kidnap** ['kɪdnæp] vt (pt & pp **kidnapped**) secuestrar, raptar

**kidnapper** ['kɪdnæpə(r)] n secuestrador(ora) m,f, raptor(ora) m,f

**kidnapping** ['kɪdnæpɪŋ] n secuestro m, rapto m

**kidney** ['kɪdnɪ] (pl **kidneys**) n riñón m; **k. beans** judías fpl, alubias fpl; Am frijoles mpl, CSur porotos mpl; **k. donor** donante mf de riñón; **k. machine** riñón artificial, aparato m de diálisis

**kill** [kɪl] **1** n *(animals killed)* presas *fpl*, caza *f*; *Fig* **to be in at the k.** no perderse el desenlace

**2** vt **(a)** *(person, animal)* matar; **twelve people were killed** resultaron muertas doce personas; **to k. oneself** matarse; *Fam* **to k. oneself laughing** morirse de risa; *Ironic* **don't k. yourself!** *(to sb not working very hard)* ¡cuidado, no te vayas a herniar!; *Fam* **this one'll k. you** *(of joke)* este es buenísimo; **to k. two birds with one stone** matar dos pájaros de un tiro; *Fam* **my feet/these shoes are killing me** los pies/estos zapatos me están matando

**(b)** *(pain)* acabar con; *(sound)* amortiguar; **the speech killed his chances of promotion** el discurso acabó con sus posibilidades de ascenso; *Journ* **to k. a story** = interrumpir la difusión de una noticia; **to k. time** matar el tiempo

►**kill off** vt sep acabar con; **to k. off a character** *(in novel, TV series)* matar a un personaje

**killer** ['kɪlə(r)] n asesino(a) *m,f*; *Fam Fig* **those steps were a k.!** ¡esos escalones me han dado muerto!; *Fam Fig* **this one's a k.** *(joke)* este es buenísimo; *Fig* **he lacks the k. instinct** *(of sportsman)* le falta garra para terminar con su contrincante; **k. whale** orca *f*

**killing** ['kɪlɪŋ] **1** n *(of person)* asesinato *m*; *(of animals)* matanza *f*; *Fam* **to make a k.** *(on Stock Exchange)* forrarse de dinero

**2** adj **(a)** *Fam (exhausting)* matador(ora) **(b)** *Fam (very amusing)* desternillante

**killjoy** ['kɪldʒɔɪ] *(pl* **killjoys)** n aguafiestas *mf inv*

**kiln** [kɪln] n horno *m (para cerámica, ladrillos)*

**kilo** ['kiːləʊ] *(pl* **kilos)** n kilo *m*

**kilobyte** ['kɪləbaɪt] n *Comptr* kilobyte *m*

**kilocalorie** ['kɪləkælərɪ] n kilocaloría *f*

**kilogram(me)** ['kɪləɡræm] n kilogramo *m*

**kilohertz** ['kɪləhɜːts] n kilohercio *m*, kilohertz *m*

**kilometre,** *US* **kilometer** ['kɪləmiːtə(r), kɪ'lɒmiːtə(r)] n kilómetro *m*

**kilowatt** ['kɪləwɒt] n kilovatio *m*; **k.-hour** kilovatio-hora *m*

**kilt** [kɪlt] n falda *f* escocesa

**kilter** ['kɪltə(r)] n *Fam* **out of k.** *(of machine part)* changado(a), escacharrado(a); *(of schedule)* manga por hombro

**kimono** [kɪ'məʊnəʊ] *(pl* **kimonos)** n quimono *m*, kimono *m*

**kin** [kɪn] n *Formal* parientes *mpl*, familiares *mpl*; **next of k.** pariente *mf* más cercano(a)

**kind¹** [kaɪnd] n (a) *(class, sort)* clase *f*, tipo *m*; **all kinds of...** toda clase *or* todo tipo de...; **something of the k.** algo así; **nothing of the k.** nada por el estilo; **in a k. of a way** en cierto sentido; **well, it's coffee of a k., I suppose** supongo que debe de ser café, pero no lo parece; **we're two of a k.** estamos hechos de la misma pasta; **it's the only one of its k.** es único en su género; **he's that k. of person** es de esa clase de personas; **this is my k. of party!** ¡este es el estilo de fiestas que me gusta!; **is this the k. of thing you're looking for?** ¿estás buscando algo así?

**(b) in k.** *(payment)* en especie

**(c)** *Fam* **you look k. of tired** pareces como cansado; **I k. of expected this** me esperaba algo así, me lo temía; **do you like it? – k. of** ¿te gusta? – vaya *or* más o menos; **it was a k. of saucer-shaped thing** era una especie de objeto con forma de plato

**kind²** adj amable; **to be k. to sb** ser amable con alguien; **it's very k. of you (to do sth)** es muy amable de tu parte (hacer algo); *Formal* **would you be k. enough to** *or* **so k. as to...?** ¿le importaría...?; **k. to the skin** *(on detergent, soap package)* no irrita la piel; **by k. permission of...** con el consentimiento de...; **k. words** palabras *fpl* amables

**kinda** ['kaɪndə] *very Fam* = **kind of**

**kindergarten** ['kɪndəɡɑːtən] n jardín *m* de infancia, guardería *f*

**kind-hearted** ['kaɪnd'hɑːtɪd] adj bondadoso(a)

**kindle** ['kɪndəl] vt *(flame, fire)* encender; *Fig (emotions)* despertar

**kindling** ['kɪndlɪŋ] n leña *f* (menuda)

**kindly** ['kaɪndlɪ] **1** adv amablemente; *(nobly)* generosamente; **to speak k. of sb** hablar bien de alguien; *Formal* **(would you) k. be quiet!** ¿serías tan amable de callarte?; **she didn't take k. to being criticized** no se tomaba bien las críticas

**2** adj amable

**kindness** ['kaɪndnɪs] n amabilidad *f*; **to show k. to sb** mostrarse amable con alguien; **to do sb a k.** hacer un favor a alguien; *Formal* **would you have the k. to...?** ¿tendría la bondad de...?; **she did it out of the k. of her heart** lo hizo desinteresadamente

**kindred** ['kɪndrɪd] adj por el estilo; **k. spirits** almas *fpl* gemelas

**kinetic** [kɪ'netɪk] adj cinético(a)

**king** [kɪŋ] n rey *m*; **the three Kings** *(in the Bible)* los Reyes Magos; **the k. of the beasts** el rey de la selva

**kingdom** ['kɪŋdəm] n reino *m*; **the k. of Heaven** el Reino de los Cielos; **the animal/plant k.** el reino animal/vegetal; *Fam* **till k. come** hasta el día del Juicio Final; *Fam* **to send sb to k. come** mandar a alguien al otro mundo

**kingfisher** ['kɪŋfɪʃə(r)] n martín *m* pescador

**kingpin** ['kɪŋpɪn] n *(of organization, company)* eje *m*

**king-size(d)** ['kɪŋ'saɪz(d)] adj (de) tamaño gigante; *(cigarette)* extralargo(a)

**kink** [kɪŋk] *n (in wire, rope)* retorcimiento *m; (in hair)* rizo *m; (in character)* manía *f*

**kinky** ['kɪŋkɪ] *adj* (**a**) *(hair)* rizado(a) (**b**) *Fam (person)* aberrante, pervertido(a); *(erotic, pornographic)* erótico(a)

**kinship** ['kɪnʃɪp] *n (family relationship)* parentesco *m; (affinity)* afinidad *f*

**kinsman** ['kɪnzmən] *n Literary* pariente *m*

**kinswoman** ['kɪnzwʊmən] *n Literary* pariente *f*

**kiosk** ['ki:ɒsk] *n* quiosco *m*, kiosco *m*

**kip** [kɪp] *Br Fam* **1** *n (sleep)* sueño *m;* **to have a k.** echar un sueño

**2** *vi (pt & pp kipped) (sleep)* dormir

**kipper** ['kɪpə(r)] *n* arenque *m* ahumado

**Kirg(h)izia** [kɜː'gɪzɪə], **Kirg(h)izstan** [kɜːgɪz'stæn] *n* Kirguizistán

**Kiribati** [kɪrɪ'bætɪ] *n* Kiribati

**kirk** [kɜːk] *n Scot* iglesia *f;* **the K.** la Iglesia de Escocia

**kiss** [kɪs] **1** *n* beso *m;* **to give sb a k.** dar un beso a alguien; **to give sb the k. of life** hacer el boca a boca a alguien; *Fig* **the news was the k. of death for the project** la noticia dio el golpe de gracia al proyecto; **k. curl** caracolillo *m (en la frente o la mejilla)*

**2** *vt* besar; **to k. sb goodbye/goodnight** dar un beso de despedida/de buenas noches a alguien; **you can k. your chances of promotion goodbye** ya puedes despedirte de tu ascenso

**3** *vi* besarse; **to k. and make up** reconciliarse; **to k. and tell** = tener un lío con un/una famoso(a) y luego contárselo a la prensa

**kissogram** ['kɪsəgræm] *n* = servicio en el que se contrata a una persona para que felicite a otra dándole un beso

**kit** [kɪt] *n* (**a**) *Mil (equipment)* equipo *m* (**b**) *(sports clothes)* equipo *m* (**c**) *(for assembly)* kit *m*, modelo *m* para armar; **to make sth from a k.** montar algo; **in k. form** para montar

▸**kit out** *vt sep* equipar (**with** con)

**kitbag** ['kɪtbæg] *n* petate *m*

**kitchen** ['kɪtʃɪn] *n* cocina *f;* **k. knife** cuchillo *m* de cocina; **k. sink** fregadero *m; Fam* **he took everything but the k. sink** se llevó hasta el colchón; **k. roll** (rollo *m* de) papel *m* de cocina; **k. unit** módulo *m* de cocina

**kitchenette** [kɪtʃɪ'net] *n* pequeña cocina *f*

**kitchenware** ['kɪtʃɪnweə(r)] *n* menaje *m*

**kite** [kaɪt] *n* (**a**) *(toy)* cometa *f; Fig* **to fly a k.** lanzar un globo sonda (para tantear el terreno); *Fam* **go fly a k.!** ¡vete a hacer gárgaras!; *Fam* **to be as high as a k.** ir como una moto (**b**) *(bird)* milano *m*

**kith** [kɪθ] *n Literary* **k. and kin** parientes y amigos *mpl*

**kitsch** [kɪtʃ] *n* kitsch *m*

**kitten** ['kɪtən] *n (young cat)* gatito(a) *m,f; Fig* **she had kittens** *(was shocked)* le dio un soponcio

**kitty** ['kɪtɪ] *n* (**a**) *Fam (cat)* gatito(a) *m,f*, minino(a) *m,f* (**b**) *(for bills)* fondo *m or* caja *f* común; *(in cards)* posturas *fpl*, puesta *f*

**kiwi** ['ki:wi:] *n* (**a**) *(bird)* kiwi *m;* **k. fruit** kiwi *m* (**b**) *Fam (New Zealander)* **K.** neozelandés(esa) *m,f*

**kleptomania** [kleptə'meɪnɪə] *n* cleptomanía *f*

**kleptomaniac** [kleptə'meɪnɪæk] *n* cleptómano(a) *m,f*

**km** *(abbr* **kilometre**) km *m*

**kmph, km/h** *(abbr* **kilometres per hour**) km/h *mpl*

**knack** [næk] *n* habilidad *f*, maña *f;* **to have the k. of** *or* **a k. for doing sth** tener habilidad *or* darse maña para hacer algo; **to get the k. of sth** cogerle el tranquillo a algo

**knacker** ['nækə(r)] *n* matarife *m* de caballos; **k.'s yard** matadero *m* de caballos

**knackered** ['nækəd] *adj Br Fam* **to be k.** *(tired)* estar hecho(a) polvo *or* reventado(a); *(broken, damaged)* estar hecho(a) polvo

**knapsack** ['næpsæk] *n* mochila *f*

**knave** [neɪv] *n* (**a**) *(in cards) (English pack)* jota *f; (Spanish pack)* sota *f* (**b**) *Literary (scoundrel)* villano *m*

**knead** [ni:d] *vt (dough)* amasar; *(muscles)* masajear, dar un masaje a

**knee** [ni:] **1** *n* rodilla *f;* **to go down on one's knees** arrodillarse, ponerse de rodillas; *Fig* **to bring sb to his knees** hacer que alguien hinque la rodilla *or* se arrodille

**2** *vt (hit with knee)* dar un rodillazo a

**kneecap** ['ni:kæp] **1** *n* rótula *f*

**2** *vt (pt & pp kneecapped)* **to k. sb** = dispararle una bala en la rodilla a alguien como castigo

**knee-deep** ['ni:'di:p] *adj* **she was k. in water** le llegaba el agua por la rodilla; *Fig* **she was k. in work** estaba hasta el cuello de trabajo

**knee-high** ['ni:'haɪ] *adj* hasta (la altura de) la rodilla; *Fam* **when I was k. to a grasshopper** cuando era canijo

**kneejerk** ['ni:dʒɜːk] *adj (reaction, response)* reflejo(a)

**kneel** [ni:l] *(pt & pp knelt* [nelt]) *vi (go down on one's knees)* arrodillarse, ponerse de rodillas; *(be on one's knees)* estar de rodillas

**knee-length** ['ni:leŋθ] *adj* hasta la rodilla

**knees-up** ['ni:zʌp] *n Br Fam* fiestorro *m*, juerga *f*

**knell** [nel] *n Literary* tañido *m* fúnebre, toque *m* de difuntos; *Fig* **to toll the (death) k. for sb/ sth** suponer el (principio del) fin para alguien/ algo

**knelt** [nelt] *pt & pp of* **kneel**

**knew** [nju:] *pt of* **know**

**knickerbockers** ['nɪkəbɒkəz], US **knickers** ['nɪkəz] *npl* bombachos *mpl*

**knickers** ['nɪkəz] *npl* (a) *(underwear)* bragas *fpl*, braga *f*; *Br Fam* **he got his k. in a twist** se salió de sus casillas (b) *US (breeches)* = **knick-erbockers**

**knick-knack** ['nɪknæk] *n Fam* chuchería *f*, baratija *f*

**knife** [naɪf] **1** *n (pl* **knives** [naɪvz]) cuchillo *m*; *Fig* **the knives are out for the Prime Minister** el primer ministro tiene los días contados; **k. sharpener** afilador *m* de cuchillos; **k. wound** puñalada *f*, cuchillada *f*

**2** *vt (stab)* apuñalar, acuchillar

**knife-edge** ['naɪfedʒ] *n Fig* **he has been on a k. all day** *(nervous)* ha estado todo el día con los nervios de punta; *Fig* **the situation/game is balanced on a k.** la situación/el partido pende de un hilo

**knife-point** ['naɪfpɔɪnt] *n* **to be robbed at k.** ser robado(a) a punta de cuchillo

**knifing** ['naɪfɪŋ] *n* apuñalamiento *m*, acuchillamiento *m*

**knight** [naɪt] **1** *n (person)* caballero *m*; *(in chess)* caballo *m*

**2** *vt* ordenar caballero a

**knighthood** ['naɪthʊd] *n (title)* título *m* de caballero

**knit** [nɪt] *(pt & pp* **knitted** or **knit**) **1** *vt (sweater)* tejer; **to k. one's brows** fruncir el ceño

**2** *vt* hacer punto

►**knit together** *vi (of broken bones)* soldarse

**knitted** ['nɪtəd] *adj* de punto

**knitting** ['nɪtɪŋ] *n (item produced)* (labor *f* de) punto *m*, calceta *f*; **have you finished your k.?** ¿has terminado de hacer punto?; **k. machine** tricotosa *f*; **k. needle** aguja *f* de punto

**knitwear** ['nɪtweə(r)] *n* prendas *fpl* de punto

**knob** [nɒb] *n (on a cane)* empuñadura *f*, puño *m*; *(on banisters, door, drawer)* pomo *m*; *(on radio)* botón *m*, mando *m*; **a k. of butter** una nuez de mantequilla

**knobbly** ['nɒblɪ] *adj* nudoso(a); **k. knees** rodillas *fpl* huesudas

**knock** [nɒk] **1** *n (blow)* golpe *m*; *(to sb's pride, chances)* revés *m*; **there was a k. at the door** se oyó un golpe en la puerta

**2** *vt* (a) *(hit)* golpear; **to k. sb to the ground** tumbar a alguien *(a golpes)*; **to k. sb unconscious** dejar a alguien inconsciente; **to k. one's head against sth** golpearse la cabeza contra algo; **to k. a hole in sth** abrir un agu-

jero de un golpe en algo; **to k. holes in an argument** echar por tierra un argumento; **to k. some sense into sb** meter un poco de sentido común en la cabeza a alguien; *Fig* **to k. sth/sb into shape** poner algo/a alguien a punto

(b) *Fam (criticize)* poner peros a, criticar

**3** *vi* (a) *(hit)* dar golpes; **to k. at the door** llamar a la puerta (con los nudillos); **to k. against sth** chocar con or contra algo; **his knees were knocking** le temblaban las rodillas

(b) *(of engine)* golpetear

►**knock about, knock around 1** *vt sep* (a) *(person)* maltratar, pegar; **the furniture has been badly knocked about** or **around** los muebles están muy maltratados (b) *Fam (idea, suggestion)* dar vueltas a

**2** *vt insep Fam* **she's been knocking about** or **around Glasgow for years** se ha movido por Glasgow durante años

**3** *vi Fam* **to k. about** or **around with sb** ir or andar con alguien; **they knocked about** or **around together at school** en la escuela iban juntos; **has anyone seen my keys knocking about** or **around?** ¿ha visto alguien mis llaves por ahí?

►**knock back** *vt sep Fam* (a) **to k. back a drink** atizarse una copa (b) *(idea, proposal)* rechazar

►**knock down** *vt sep* (a) *(pedestrian)* atropellar (b) *(building)* derribar

►**knock off 1** *vt sep* (a) *(cause to fall off)* tirar; **he was knocked off his bike by a car** un coche lo tiró de la bicicleta; *Fam* **to k. sb's head** or **block off** romperle la cabeza a alguien; *Fam* **I managed to get something knocked off the price** conseguí que me rebajaran algo el precio

(b) *very Fam (steal)* mangar

(c) *Fam (kill)* despachar, cepillarse a

(d) *Fam* **k. it off!** *(stop it)* ¡para ya!

(e) *Fam (produce quickly) (letter, report, song)* despachar

**2** *vi (finish work)* terminar de trabajar

►**knock out** *vt sep* (a) *(make unconscious)* dejar sin sentido; *(in boxing match)* dejar fuera de combate; *Fam* **to k. sb's brains/teeth out** partirle la cabeza/la boca a alguien (b) *(eliminate from competition)* eliminar

►**knock over** *vt sep (person)* derribar; *(container)* volcar

►**knock up** *vt sep* (a) *(make hastily)* improvisar (b) *very Fam (make pregnant)* dejar preñada a

**knockdown price** ['nɒkdaʊnpraɪs] *n Fam* **at a k.** a un precio de risa

**knocker** ['nɒkə(r)] *n* (a) *(on door)* llamador *m*, aldaba *f* (b) *very Fam* **knockers** *(breasts)* melones *mpl*, domingas *fpl*

**knocking** ['nɒkɪŋ] n (at door) golpes mpl; (of engine) golpeteo m

**knock-kneed** ['nɒk'niːd] adj patizambo(a)

**knock-on effect** ['nɒkɒnɪ'fekt] n efecto m dominó

**knockout** ['nɒkaʊt] **1** n **(a)** (in boxing) K.O. m, fuera de combate m; Fig (to chances) golpe m de gracia **(b)** Fam he's/she's a k. (attractive) está imponente

**2** adj **(a)** k. blow (in boxing) golpe m que pone fuera de combate; Fig to deliver the k. blow (to chances) asestar el golpe de gracia **(b)** (in sport) a k. competition una competición por eliminatorias

**knot** [nɒt] **1** n **(a)** (in rope, string) nudo m; (in ribbon) lazo m, lazada f; **to tie/untie a k.** atar/desatar un nudo, hacer/deshacer un nudo; Fam Fig **to tie the k.** (get married) casarse **(b)** (in wood) nudo m **(c)** Naut (unit of speed) nudo m; Fam **at a rate of knots** a toda máquina **(d)** (group of people) corro m

**2** vt (pt & pp **knotted**) (piece of string) anudar, atar; Br very Fam **get knotted!** ¡que te den!, ¡vete al cuerno!

**knotty** ['nɒtɪ] adj Fam (problem) espinoso(a)

**know** [nəʊ] **1** n Fam **to be in the k.** estar enterado(a), estar en el ajo

**2** vt (pt knew [njuː], pp known [nəʊn]) **(a)** (be acquainted with) conocer; **to get to k. sb** conocer a alguien; **she had long hair when I first knew her** cuando la conocí tenía el pelo largo; **I've never known anything like it** nunca he visto nada igual; **I k. him to say hello to** lo conozco de hola y adiós nada más; **knowing HIM…** conociéndolo…

**(b)** (have knowledge of) saber; **to k. that…** saber que…; **to k. the answer** saber la respuesta; **to k. Spanish** saber español; **to k. a lot/a little about sth** saber mucho/poco de algo; **she knows what she is talking about** sabe de lo que está hablando; **to k. how to do sth** saber hacer algo; Fam **to k. a thing or two** saber alguna que otra cosa, saber un rato; **to k. one's own mind** tener las ideas claras; **heaven or God knows!** ¡sabe Dios!

**(c)** (recognize, distinguish) distinguir, reconocer; **I knew her by her walk** la distinguí or la reconocí por su forma de andar; **he knows a good business opportunity when he sees one** sabe reconocer un buen negocio (cuando lo tiene delante); **to k. right from wrong** distinguir lo bueno de lo malo

**3** vi saber; **to k. about sth** saber de algo; **to get to k. of sth** enterarse de algo; **as far as I k.** que yo sepa; **how should I k.?** ¿cómo voy a saberlo yo?; **you never k.** nunca se sabe; **not that I k. of** que yo sepa, no; **you should k. better than that by now!** ¡a estas alturas ya podías saber que eso no se hace!; Fam **it**

wasn't, you k., quite what I was expecting en fin, no era lo que me esperaba; **James, you k., my cousin…** James, sí hombre, mi primo…

**know-all** ['nəʊːl] n Fam sabihondo(a) m,f, sabelotodo mf

**know-how** ['nəʊhaʊ] n Fam conocimientos mpl prácticos; Com técnica f, conocimientos mpl técnicos

**knowing** ['nəʊɪŋ] **1** n **there's no k.** no hay manera de saber

**2** adj (look, smile) cómplice, de complicidad

**knowledge** ['nɒlɪdʒ] n **(a)** (awareness) conocimiento m; **(not) to my k.** que yo sepa(, no); **I had no k. of it** no tenía conocimiento de ello; **to have full k. of sth** saber algo perfectamente; **it is common k. that…** todo el mundo sabe que…, de todos es sabido que…; Formal **it has come to our k. that…** ha llegado a nuestro conocimiento que…

**(b)** (learning) conocimientos mpl; **to have a k. of several languages** saber varios idiomas; **her k. is immense** tiene unos grandes conocimientos; Prov **k. is power** el poder llega por el conocimiento; Comptr **k.-based system** sistema m experto

**knowledgeable** ['nɒlɪdʒəbəl] adj entendido(a); **to be k. about sth** ser un (gran) entendido en algo

**known** [nəʊn] **1** adj conocido(a)

**2** pp of **know**

**knuckle** ['nʌkəl] n nudillo m

▸**knuckle down** vi Fam **to k. down (to sth)** ponerse (a algo) en serio

▸**knuckle under** vi Fam pasar por el aro, rendirse

**knuckle-duster** ['nʌkəldʌstə(r)] n puño m americano

**KO** ['keɪ'əʊ] Fam **1** n (pl KO's ['keɪ'əʊz]) (in boxing) K.O. m

**2** vt (pp & pt KO'd ['keɪ'əʊd]) (in boxing) dejar fuera de combate, noquear

**koala** [kəʊ'ɑːlə] n **k. (bear)** koala m

**kopek** ['kəʊpek] n (subdivision of rouble) kopek m, copec m

**Koran** [kə'rɑːn] n **the K.** el Corán

**Koranic** [kə'rænɪk] adj coránico(a)

**Korea** [kə'rɪə] n Corea; **North/South K.** Corea del Norte/del Sur

**Korean** [kə'rɪən] **1** n **(a)** (person) coreano(a) m,f **(b)** (language) coreano m

**2** adj coreano(a); **the K. War** la guerra de Corea

**kosher** ['kəʊʃə(r)] adj **(a)** (in Judaism) kosher, conforme a la ley judaica; **k. meat** carne f kosher **(b)** Fam (legitimate) legal

**kowtow** ['kaʊ'taʊ] vi also Fig **to k. to sb** inclinarse ante alguien

**Kraut** [kraʊt] *n very Fam* = término despectivo para referirse a los alemanes, cabeza cuadrada *mf*

**krona** ['kreʊnə] *n (Swedish currency)* corona *f* (sueca)

**krone** ['kreʊnə] *n (Danish/Norwegian currency)* corona *f* (danesa/noruega)

**kudos** ['kjuːdɒs] *n* gloria *f*, renombre *m*

**Kurd** [kɜːd] *n & adj* kurdo(a) *m,f*

**Kurdish** ['kɜːdɪʃ] **1** *n (language)* kurdo *m*
**2** *adj* kurdo(a)

**Kurdistan** [kɜːdɪˈstæn] *n* Kurdistán

**Kuwait** [kʊˈweɪt] *n* Kuwait

**Kuwaiti** [kʊˈweɪtɪ] *n & adj* kuwaití *mf*

**kW** *Elec (abbr* **kilowatt***)* kW *m*

**kWh** *(abbr* **kilowatt-hour***)* kWh

**Kyoto** [kiˈəʊtəʊ] *n* Kioto

# L

**L** [el] n (a) (letter) L, l f (b) Br Aut **L-plate** placa f de la "L"

**l** (abbr **litre(s)**) l, litro(s) m(pl)

**LA** [el'eɪ] n (abbr **Los Angeles**) Los Ángeles

**la** [lɑ:] n Mus la

**Lab** Br Pol (abbr **Labour**) laborista

**lab** [læb] n Fam (abbr **laboratory**) laboratorio m

**label** ['leɪbəl] **1** n (a) also Fig etiqueta f (b) (of record company) casa f discográfica, sello m discográfico

**2** vt (pt & pp **labelled**, US **labeled**) (parcel, bottle) etiquetar; (describe) tildar de; **the bottle was labelled "poison"** la botella tenía una etiqueta que decía "veneno"; **to l. sb a liar** tildar a alguien de mentiroso(a)

**labor, labored** etc US = **labour, laboured** etc

**laboratory** [lə'bɒrətrɪ] n laboratorio m; **l. assistant** ayudante mf de laboratorio

**laborious** [lə'bɔ:rɪəs] adj (work, explanation) laborioso(a), arduo(a)

**laboriously** [lə'bɔ:rɪəslɪ] adv laboriosamente, arduamente

**labour,** US **labor** ['leɪbə(r)] **1** n (a) (work) trabajo m; **l. camp** campo m de trabajo (b) (workers) mano f de obra, trabajadores mpl; **l. costs** costes mpl de mano de obra; **l. dispute** conflicto m laboral; Br Formerly **l. exchange** bolsa f de trabajo; **l. force** mano f de obra; **l. market** mercado m laboral or de trabajo; **l. shortage** escasez f de mano de obra (c) Pol **L., the L. Party** el partido laborista (d) (task) esfuerzo m, tarea f; **a l. of love** un trabajo hecho por amor al arte (e) (childbirth) parto m; **to be in l.** estar de parto; **l. pains** dolores mpl del parto

**2** vt **to l. a point** repetir lo mismo una y otra vez

**3** vi (a) (of person) trabajar afanosamente (at or over en); **to l. in vain** trabajar en vano; **to be labouring under a misapprehension/a delusion** tener un malentendido/una falsa ilusión (b) (of engine) funcionar con dificultad

**laboured,** US **labored** ['leɪbəd] adj (breathing) fatigoso(a), trabajoso(a); (style) farragoso(a); (joke) pesado(a)

**labourer,** US **laborer** ['leɪbərə(r)] n obrero(a) m,f

**labouring,** US **laboring** ['leɪbərɪŋ] adj **he did a number of l. jobs** trabajó de obrero en varias ocasiones

**labour-intensive,** US **labor-intensive** ['leɪbərɪn'tensɪv] adj que absorbe mucha mano de obra

**labour-saving device,** US **labor-saving device** ['leɪbəseɪvɪŋdɪ'vaɪs] n aparato m que permite ahorrarse trabajo

**labrador** ['læbrədɔ:(r)] n (dog) terranova m, labrador m

**laburnum** [lə'bɜ:nəm] n codeso m

**labyrinth** ['læbərɪnθ] n laberinto m

**labyrinthine** [læbe'rɪnθaɪn] adj laberíntico(a)

**lace** [leɪs] **1** n (a) (cloth) encaje m; **l. handkerchief** pañuelo m de encaje (b) (of shoe) cordón m

**2** vt (a) (shoes) atar (los cordones de) (b) **to l. a drink** rociar una bebida (con unas gotas de algo fuerte); Fig **he laced his story with salacious details** aderezó el relato con detalles obscenos

▶**lace up 1** vt sep **to l. one's shoes up** atarse los zapatos

**2** vi (of shoes, corset) atarse

**lacerate** ['læsəreɪt] vt lacerar

**laceration** [læsə'reɪʃən] n laceración f

**lace-up** ['leɪsʌp] **1** n (shoe) zapato m de cordones

**2** adj (shoe) de cordones

**lachrymose** ['lækrɪməʊs] adj Literary lacrimoso(a)

**lack** [læk] **1** n falta f (**of** de), carencia f (**of** de); **for l. of...** por falta de...

**2** vt carecer de

**3** vi **time was lacking** faltaba tiempo; **she is lacking in confidence/experience** le falta confianza/experiencia; **they l. for nothing** no les falta de nada

**lackadaisical** [lækə'deɪzɪkəl] adj dejado(a)

**lackey** ['lækɪ] (pl **lackeys**) n Pej lacayo m

**lacklustre** ['læklʌstə(r)] adj (mediocre) deslucido(a)

**laconic** [lə'kɒnɪk] adj lacónico(a)

**lacquer** ['lækə(r)] **1** n laca f
**2** vt (wood) lacar, laquear; (hair) aplicar laca a

**lacrosse** [lə'krɒs] n Sport lacrosse m

**lacuna** [lə'kju:nə] (pl **lacunae** [lə'kju:ni:] or **lacunas**) n laguna f

**lad** [læd] n Fam (young man) tío m; (boy) chaval m, chavalillo m; **come on, lads!** ¡vamos, tíos!; **he's a bit of a l.** es un golfete

**ladder** ['lædə(r)] **1** n (a) escalera f; **the social l.** la escala social; Fig **to get one's foot on the l.** dar el primer paso; Fig **to reach the top of the l.** llegar a la cumbre (b) (in stocking) carrera f
**2** vt (stocking) hacer una carrera en
**3** vi (of stocking) hacerse una carrera

**laddie** ['lædɪ] n Fam chavalín m, muchacho m

**laden** ['leɪdən] adj cargado(a) (with de)

**la-di-da** [lɑ:dɪ'dɑ:] adj Fam (accent, manner) pijo(a)

**ladle** ['leɪdəl] n cucharón m, cazo m
►**ladle out** vt sep (soup) servir (con el cucharón); Fig (sympathy, praise) prodigar

**lady** ['leɪdɪ] n (a) (woman) señora f; (in literature, of high status) dama f; **a young l.** (unmarried) una señorita; (married) una (señora) joven; **an old l.** una señora mayor; **ladies and gentlemen!** ¡señoras y señores!; **he's a ladies' man** es un mujeriego; **the l. of the house** la señora de la casa; **ladies' room** servicio m de señoras; **l. friend** querida f, amiga f (b) Our L. Nuestra Señora (c) (title) L. Browne Lady Browne; **L. Luck** la diosa Fortuna; Fam **she's acting like L. Muck** se porta como una señoritinga

**ladybird** ['leɪdɪbɜ:d] n mariquita f

**lady-in-waiting** ['leɪdɪn'weɪtɪŋ] n dama f de honor

**lady-killer** ['leɪdɪkɪlə(r)] n Fam castigador m, casanova m

**ladylike** ['leɪdɪlaɪk] adj femenino(a), propio(a) de una señorita

**ladyship** ['leɪdɪʃɪp] n her/your L. su señoría

**lag** [læg] **1** n (a) (gap) intervalo m, lapso m (b) very Fam (prisoner) **old l.** presidiario m
**2** vt (pt & pp **lagged**) (pipes, boiler) revestir con un aislante
**3** vi **to l. (behind)** quedarse atrás

**lager** ['lɑ:gə(r)] n cerveza f (rubia); Fam **l. lout** borracho m gamberro

**laggard** ['lægəd] n rezagado(a) m,f

**lagoon** [lə'gu:n] n laguna f

**lah-di-dah** = **la-di-da**

**laid** [leɪd] pt & pp of **lay**

**laid-back** [leɪd'bæk] adj Fam tranquilo(a), cachazudo(a)

**lain** [leɪn] pp of **lie²**

**lair** [leə(r)] n guarida f

**laird** [leəd] n Scot terrateniente m

**laisser-faire** [leseɪ'feə(r)] **1** n Econ liberalismo m
**2** adj (in general) permisivo(a); Econ liberal

**laity** ['leɪtɪ] n **the l.** el sector laico, los seglares

**lake** [leɪk] n lago m; **L. Geneva** el Lago Leman; **the L. District, the Lakes** la Región de los Lagos (en el noroeste de Inglaterra)

**lamb** [læm] n cordero m; Rel **L. (of God)** Cordero de Dios; **poor l.!** ¡pobrecillo!; **like lambs to the slaughter** como ovejas al matadero; **l. chop** chuleta f de cordero

**lambast** ['læmbæst] vt vapulear

**lambing** ['læmɪŋ] n (tiempo m del) nacimiento m de los corderos

**lambskin** ['læmskɪn] n piel f de cordero

**lambswool** ['læmswʊl] **1** n lana f de cordero
**2** adj de lana de cordero

**lame** [leɪm] **1** adj (a) (person, animal) cojo(a); **to be l.** (permanently) ser cojo(a); (temporarily) estar cojo(a); **to go l.** quedarse cojo(a) (b) (excuse, argument) endeble, pobre
**2** vt dejar cojo(a)

**lamé** ['lɑ:meɪ] n lamé m

**lamely** ['leɪmlɪ] adv (to apologize) sin convicción

**lament** [lə'ment] **1** n lamento m; Mus canto m elegíaco, treno m
**2** vt lamentar; **the late lamented Mr Jones** el llorado difunto Sr. Jones
**3** vi lamentarse (over de)

**lamentable** [lə'mentəbəl] adj lamentable

**lamentably** [lə'mentəblɪ] adj lamentablemente

**lamentation** [læmən'teɪʃən] n lamentación f

**laminate** ['læmɪneɪt] n laminado m

**laminated** ['læmɪneɪtɪd] adj (a) (glass) laminado(a); **the wood is laminated with plastic** la madera está laminada en plástico (b) (paper, identity card) plastificado(a)

**lamp** [læmp] n lámpara f

**lamplight** ['læmplaɪt] n luz f de una lámpara

**lampoon** [læm'pu:n] **1** n sátira f
**2** vt satirizar

**lamppost** ['læmppəʊst] n farola f

**lamprey** ['læmprɪ] (pl **lampreys**) n lamprea f

**lampshade** ['læmpʃeɪd] n pantalla f (de lámpara)

**lampstand** ['læmpstænd] n pie m de lámpara

**LAN** [eleɪ'en] n Comptr (abbr **local area network**) red f de área local

**lance** [lɑ:ns] **1** n (weapon) lanza f
**2** vt Med sajar, abrir con una lanceta

**lance corporal** ['lɑ:ns'kɔ:pərəl] n Mil soldado mf de primera

**lancer** ['lɑ:nsə(r)] *n (soldier)* lancero *m*

**lancet** ['lɑ:nsɪt] *n* lanceta *f*

**land** [lænd] **1** *n* (a) *(in general)* tierra *f*; **on l.** en tierra; **to live off the l.** vivir de la tierra; *Literary* **he came from a distant l.** venía de una tierra lejana; **he's still in the l. of the living** todavía está en el reino de los vivos; *Mil* **l. forces** ejército *m* de tierra; *Mil* **l. mine** mina *f* terrestre; **l. reform** reforma *f* agraria **(b)** *(property)* tierras *fpl*, terrenos *mpl*; **get off my l.!** ¡fuera de mi propiedad!

**2** *vt* **(a)** *(passengers)* desembarcar; *(cargo)* descargar **(b)** *(plane)* hacer aterrizar **(c)** *(fish)* capturar; *Fam* **he's just landed a good job** acaba de conseguir un buen trabajo; *Fam* **that will l. you in prison** eso hará que des con tus huesos en la cárcel; *Fam* **he was landed with the problem** le endosaron el problema **(d)** *Fam (hit)* **I landed him one** le di un buen tortazo

**3** *vi* **(a)** *(of aircraft, pilot)* aterrizar, tomar tierra; **we landed in New York** aterrizamos en Nueva York **(b)** *(of gymnast, somebody falling)* caer; *Fig* **to l. on one's feet** caer de pie

▶**land up** *vi* ir a parar **(in** a)

**landed** [lændəd] *adj* **l. gentry** aristocracia *f* terrateniente; **l. proprietor** terrateniente *mf*

**landfall** ['lændfɔ:l] *n Naut* **to make l.** arribar a tierra

**landfill site** ['lændfɪl'saɪt] *n* = vertedero donde se entierran basuras

**landing** [lændɪŋ] *n* **(a)** *Naut* desembarco *m*; **l. card** tarjeta *f* de inmigración; **l. craft** lancha *f* de desembarco; **l. stage** desembarcadero *m* **(b)** *Av* aterrizaje *m*; **l. gear** tren *m* de aterrizaje; **l. lights** luces *fpl* de aterrizaje; **l. strip** pista *f* de aterrizaje **(c)** *(of staircase)* descansillo *m*, rellano *m*

**landlady** ['lændleɪdɪ] *n* **(a)** *(owner of rented accommodation)* casera *f*, dueña *f* **(b)** *(woman who runs boarding house, pub)* patrona *f*

**landlocked** ['lændlɒkt] *adj (country)* sin salida al mar, interior

**landlord** ['lændlɔ:d] *n* **(a)** *(owner of rented accommodation)* casero *m*, dueño *m* **(b)** *(man who runs pub)* patrón *m* **(c)** *(landowner)* terrateniente *m*

**landmark** ['lændmɑ:k] *n (distinctive feature)* punto *m* de referencia, lugar *m* señero; *Fig (in history)* hito *m*

**landmass** ['lændmæs] *n* masa *f* terrestre

**landmine** ['lændmaɪn] *n* mina *f* terrestre

**landowner** ['lændəʊnə(r)] *n* terrateniente *mf*

**landowning** ['lændəʊnɪŋ] *adj* **the l. classes** la clase terrateniente

**landscape** ['lændskeɪp] **1** *n (land, painting)* paisaje *m*; **l. design** paisajismo *m*; **l. gardener** paisajista *mf*; *Comptr* **l. (orientation)** formato *m* apaisado; **l. painter** paisajista *mf*

**2** *vt* ajardinar

**landslide** ['lændslaɪd] *n* desprendimiento *m* or corrimiento *m* de tierras; *Pol* **to win by a l.** ganar por una mayoría abrumadora

**landslip** ['lændslɪp] *n* desprendimiento *m* or corrimiento *m* de tierras

**landward** ['lændwəd] *adj Naut* más cercano(a) a (la) tierra

**lane** [leɪn] *n* **(a)** *(in country)* vereda *f*, camino *m*; *(in town)* callejón *m* **(b)** *(on road)* carril *m*; **traffic is reduced to two lanes** se ha limitado el tráfico a dos carriles **(c)** *(for runner, swimmer)* calle *f*

**language** ['læŋgwɪdʒ] *n* **(a)** *(of a people)* idioma *m*, lengua *f*; *Fam Fig* **we don't talk the same l.** no hablamos el mismo idioma; **l. laboratory** laboratorio *m* de idiomas; **l. learning** aprendizaje *m* de idiomas; **l. teaching** enseñanza *f* de idiomas **(b)** *(style of speech or writing)* lenguaje *m*; **you should have heard the l. they were using!** ¡tenías que haber oído el lenguaje que empleaban!

**languid** ['læŋgwɪd] *adj* lánguido(a)

**languidly** ['læŋgwɪdlɪ] *adv* lánguidamente

**languish** ['læŋgwɪʃ] *vi* languidecer; **to l. in prison** pudrirse en la cárcel

**languor** ['læŋgə(r)] *n* languidez *f*

**languorous** ['læŋgərəs] *adj* lánguido(a)

**lank** [læŋk] *adj (hair)* lacio(a)

**lanky** ['læŋkɪ] *adj* larguirucho(a)

**lanolin(e)** ['lænəlɪn] *n* lanolina *f*

**lantern** ['læntən] *n* farol *m*; **l. jawed** demacrado(a)

**Laos** [laʊs] *n* Laos

**Laotian** ['laʊʃən] *n & adj* laosiano(a) *m,f*

**lap**[1] [læp] *n* regazo *m*; **to sit on sb's l.** sentarse en el regazo de alguien; *Fig* **it's in the l. of the gods** está en el aire; *Fig* **he expects everything to fall into his l.** espera que todo le llueva del cielo; *Fig* **to live in the l. of luxury** vivir a cuerpo de rey

**lap**[2] **1** *n (in race)* vuelta *f*; **l. of honour** vuelta de honor

**2** *vt (overtake)* doblar

**lap**[3] *(pt & pp lapped)* *vi (of animal)* beber a lengüetadas; **to l. against sth** *(of waves)* lamer algo

▶**lap up** *vt sep (drink)* beberse a lengüetadas; *Fam Fig (enjoy)* tragarse

**lapdog** ['læpdɒg] *n* perrito *m* faldero

**lapel** [lə'pel] *n* solapa *f*

**Lapland** ['læplænd] *n* Laponia

**Laplander** ['læplændə(r)] *n* lapón(ona) *m,f*

**Lapp** [læp] *n & adj* lapón(ona) *m,f*

**lapse** [læps] **1** *n* (a) *(of time)* lapso *m* (b) *(in behaviour)* desliz *m*; *(in standards)* bajón *m*; **a l. in concentration** un momento de distracción

**2** *vi* (a) *(err)* tener un desliz; *(morally)* reincidir; **to l. into silence** sumirse en el silencio; **he soon lapsed back into his old ways** pronto volvió a las andadas (b) *(of permit, membership)* caducar, vencer

**lapsed** [læpst] *adj* *Rel* **a l. Catholic** un/una católico(a) no practicante

**laptop** ['læptɒp] *n* *Comptr* ordenador *m* portátil

**lapwing** ['læpwɪŋ] *n* avefría *f*

**larceny** ['lɑːsənɪ] *n* *Law* (delito *m* de) robo *m* or latrocinio *m*

**larch** [lɑːtʃ] *n* alerce *m*

**lard** [lɑːd] **1** *n* *(fat)* manteca *f* de cerdo

**2** *vt* *Fam Fig* **he larded his writings with quotations** sus escritos estaban recargados de citas

**larder** ['lɑːdə(r)] *n* despensa *f*

**large** [lɑːdʒ] **1** *n* **to be at l.** andar suelto(a); **people/the public at l.** la gente/el público en general

**2** *adj* (a) *(in size)* grande; **to grow** or **get larger** crecer; **to make sth larger** agrandar algo; **as l. as life** en persona; **larger than life** singular, que se sale de la norma (b) *(extensive, significant)* **to a l. extent** en gran medida; **a l. part of my job involves...** gran parte de mi trabajo implica...

**3** *adv* **by and l.** en general

**largely** ['lɑːdʒlɪ] *adv* *(to a great extent)* en gran medida; *(mostly)* principalmente

**large-scale** ['lɑːdʒ'skeɪl] *adj* a gran escala

**largesse** [lɑː'ʒes] *n* magnanimidad *f*

**lark**[1] [lɑːk] *n* *(bird)* alondra *f*; **to be up/rise with the l.** levantarse con el gallo

**lark**[2] *n* *(joke)* broma *f*; **to do sth for a l.** hacer algo por diversión; **what a l.!** ¡qué divertido!; **I don't like this fancy dress l.** no me gusta este asunto de la fiesta de disfraces

▸**lark about, lark around** *vi* trastear, jugar

**larva** ['lɑːvə] *(pl* **larvae** ['lɑːviː]*) n* larva *f*

**laryngitis** [lærɪn'dʒaɪtɪs] *n* laringitis *f inv*

**larynx** ['lærɪŋks] *n* laringe *f*

**lasagne** [lə'sænjə] *n* lasaña *f*

**lascivious** [lə'sɪvɪəs] *adj* lascivo(a)

**laser** ['leɪzə(r)] *n* láser *m*; **l. beam** rayo *m* láser; *Comptr* **l. printer** impresora *f* láser; *Med* **l. surgery** cirugía *f* con láser

**lash** [læʃ] **1** *n* (a) *(eyelash)* pestaña *f* (b) *(blow with whip)* latigazo *m*

**2** *vt* (a) *(with whip)* azotar; **to l. (against) sth** *(of rain, waves)* azotar algo (b) *(tie)* amarrar **(to** a)

**3** *vi* **the rain** or **it was lashing down** caían chuzos de punta

▸**lash out** *vi* (a) **to l. out at sb** *(physically)* atacar or agredir a alguien; *(verbally)* arremeter contra alguien (b) *Fam (spend extravagantly)* tirar la casa por la ventana

**lashings** ['læʃɪŋz] *npl* *Fam Old-fashioned (lots)* **l. of** un montón de

**lass** [læs] *n* chica *f*, muchacha *f*

**lassitude** ['læsɪtjuːd] *n* lasitud *f*

**lasso** [læ'suː] **1** *(pl* **lassos** or **lassoes**) lazo *m*

**2** *vt* capturar con lazo

**last**[1] [lɑːst] **1** *n* the **l.** el/la último(a); **the l. but one** el/la penúltimo(a); **we'll never hear the l. of it** nos lo recordará eternamente; **I don't think we've heard the l. of him** creo que volveremos a oír hablar de él; **that's the l. I saw of him** fue la última vez que lo vi; **that's the l. of the wine** es lo último que queda de vino; **to** or **till the l.** hasta el fin; **at (long) l.** por fin

**2** *adj* (a) *(final)* último(a); **this is your l. chance** es tu última oportunidad; **you are my l. hope** eres mi última esperanza; **to have the l. word** tener la última palabra; **the l. word in comfort** el no va más en comodidad; **at the l. moment** or **minute** en el último momento or minuto; **l. thing at night** lo último antes de acostarse; **to be on one's l. legs** estar en las últimas; **he's the l. person I'd ask to help me** es la última persona a la que pediría ayuda; **that's the l. thing I'd do in your position** eso es lo último que haría si estuviera en tu lugar; **as a l. resort** como último recurso; *Rel* the **L. Judgment** el Juicio Final; **l. name** apellido *m*; *Rel* **l. rites** extremaunción *f*; **the l. straw** la gota que colma el vaso

(b) *(most recent)* pasado(a), último(a); **the l. time I saw him** la última vez que lo vi; **l. January** en enero pasado; **l. night** anoche; **l. Tuesday** el martes pasado; **l. week** la semana pasada

**3** *adv* **when I l. saw him** la última vez que lo vi; **to come l.** llegar en último lugar; **to finish l.** terminar el último; *(in race)* llegar en último lugar; **l. but not least** por último, pero no por ello menos importante

**last**[2] *n (for shoe)* horma *f*

**last**[3] **1** *vt* durar; **it will l. me a lifetime** me durará toda la vida; **it has lasted him well** le ha durado bastante

**2** *vi* durar; **it's too good to l.** es demasiado bueno para que dure; **he won't l. long in that job** no durará mucho en ese trabajo; **she won't l. the night** no llegará a mañana

▸**last out 1** *vt sep* **to l. the year/the weekend out** llegar a fin de año/al fin de semana

**2** *vi (of person)* aguantar, resistir; *(of supplies)* durar

**last-ditch** [lɑ:st'dɪtʃ] *adj* último(a), desesperado(a)

**lasting** ['lɑ:stɪŋ] *adj* duradero(a)

**lastly** ['lɑ:stlɪ] *adv* por último

**last-minute** [lɑ:st'mɪnɪt] *adj* de última hora

**lat** *Geog* (*abbr* **latitude**) lat., latitud *f*

**latch** [lætʃ] *n* picaporte *m*, pestillo *m*; **to be on the l.** = tener sólo el pestillo echado, no la llave
▶**latch onto** *vt insep Fam* (**a**) (*attach oneself to*) **to l. onto sb** pegarse a alguien; *Fig* **to l. onto an idea** meterse una idea en la cabeza (**b**) (*understand*) **to l. onto sth** enterarse de algo

**latchkey** ['lætʃki:] (*pl* **latchkeys**) *n* llave *f* (*de la puerta de entrada*); **l. kid** = niño que llega a casa antes que sus padres, que están trabajando

**late** [leɪt] **1** *adj* (**a**) (*not on time*) retrasado(a); **to be l. (for sth)** llegar tarde, *Am* demorarse; **the train is ten minutes l.** el tren tiene *or* lleva diez minutos de retraso
(**b**) (*far on in time*) tarde; **it is getting l.** se está haciendo tarde; **to keep l. hours** trasnochar; **in the l. afternoon** al final de la tarde; **in l. summer** al final del verano; **in l. March** a últimos de marzo; *Fig* **it's a bit l. in the day to...** ya es un poco tarde para...; **to be in one's l. thirties** tener treinta y muchos años; **in the l. eighties** a finales de los ochenta
(**c**) (*dead*) difunto(a); **my l. husband** mi difunto marido
**2** *adv* (**a**) (*in general*) tarde; **to arrive too l.** llegar demasiado tarde; **he came home very l.** llegó a casa muy tarde; **to work l.** trabajar hasta tarde; **this l. in the day** a estas alturas; **to go to bed/get up l.** acostarse/levantarse tarde; **l. into the night** hasta (altas horas de la madrugada; **l. in the year** a finales de año; **l. in life** hacia el final de la vida; *Prov* **better l. than never** más vale tarde que nunca
(**b**) (*recently*) **as l. as last week** incluso la semana pasada; **of l.** recientemente

**latecomer** ['leɪtkʌmə(r)] *n* rezagado(a) *m,f*

**lately** ['leɪtlɪ] *adv* recientemente, últimamente; **until l.** hasta hace poco

**lateness** ['leɪtnɪs] *n* (*of person, train*) retraso *m*; **the l. of the hour** lo avanzado de la hora

**latent** ['leɪtənt] *adj* (*disease, tendency*) latente; **l. period** periodo *m* de incubación

**later** ['leɪtə(r)] **1** *adj* posterior; **I caught a l. train** cogí otro tren más tarde; **his l. novels** sus novelas posteriores; **in l. life** en la madurez
**2** *adv* **l. (on)** más tarde; **a few days l.** unos días más tarde; **no l. than tomorrow** mañana como muy tarde; **as we shall see l.** como veremos más adelante; *Fam* **see you l.!** ¡hasta luego!

**lateral** ['lætərəl] *adj* lateral; **l. thinking** pensamiento *m* lateral, = capacidad para darse cuenta de aspectos no inmediatamente evidentes de los problemas

**latest** ['leɪtɪst] **1** *n* **at the l.** como muy tarde; **the l. I can stay is four o'clock** sólo puedo quedarme hasta las cuatro; **have you heard the l.?** ¿has oído las últimas noticias?
**2** *adj* último(a); **her l. work** su última obra; **the l. news** las últimas noticias; **the l. edition** la última edición; **the l. fashions** la última moda

**latex** ['leɪteks] *n* látex *m*

**lathe** [leɪð] *n* torno *m*

**lather** ['læðə(r)] **1** *n* espuma *f*; *Fam* **to work oneself into a l.** ponerse histérico(a)
**2** *vt* enjabonar; **to l. one's face** enjabonarse la cara

**Latin** ['lætɪn] **1** *n* (**a**) (*language*) latín *m* (**b**) (*person*) latino(a) *m,f*
**2** *adj* latino(a)

**Latin America** ['lætɪnə'merɪkə] *n* Latinoamérica *f*

**Latin American** ['lætɪnə'merɪkən] *n & adj* latinoamericano(a) *m,f*

**latitude** ['lætɪtju:d] *n* (**a**) *Geog* latitud *f* (**b**) (*freedom*) libertad *f*

**latrine** [lə'tri:n] *n* letrina *f*

**latter** ['lætə(r)] **1** *adj* (**a**) (*of two*) último(a), segundo(a) (**b**) (*last*) último(a); **the l. half** *or* **part of June** la segunda mitad de junio
**2** *n* (*of two*) **the former...**, **the l....** aquél..., éste...; el primero..., el segundo...

**latter-day** ['lætə'deɪ] *adj* moderno(a), de hoy; *Rel* **the L. Saints** los Mormones

**latterly** ['lætəlɪ] *adv* recientemente, últimamente

**lattice** ['lætɪs] *n* celosía *f*; **l. window** vidriera *f* de celosía

**latticework** ['lætɪswɜ:k] *n* celosía *f*, enrejado *m*

**Latvia** ['lætvɪə] *n* Letonia

**Latvian** ['lætvɪən] **1** *n* (**a**) (*person*) letón(ona) *m,f* (**b**) (*language*) letón *m*
**2** *adj* letón(ona)

**laudable** ['lɔ:dəbəl] *adj* loable

**laudanum** ['lɔ:dənəm] *n* láudano *m*

**laugh** [lɑ:f] **1** *n* risa *f*; *Fam* **to do sth for a l.** hacer algo para divertirse *or* por diversión; *Ironic* **that's a l.!** ¡no me hagas reír!; *Fam* **he's a good l.** es muy divertido; **to have the last l.** ser el último en reír
**2** *vi* reírse (**at** de); *Fam* **don't make me l.!** ¡no me hagas reír!; **he'll be laughing on the other side of his face when...** se llevará un buen chasco cuando...; *Fam* **to l. all the way to the bank** hacer el agosto; *Prov* **he who laughs last laughs longest** el que ríe el último ríe mejor
**3** *vt* **you'll be laughed out of court** se te reirán en la cara; *Fam* **to l. one's head off**, **to l. oneself silly** partirse de risa

▶**laugh off** *vt sep* tomarse a risa

**laughable** ['lɑːfəbəl] *adj* ridículo(a), risible; *(sum)* irrisorio(a)

**laughing** ['lɑːfɪŋ] 1 *n* risa *f*

2 *adj (eyes)* risueño(a); **it's no l. matter** no es ninguna tontería; **l. gas** gas *m* hilarante; **l. stock** hazmerreír *m*

**laughter** ['lɑːftə(r)] *n* risa *f*

**launch** [lɔːntʃ] 1 *n* (a) *(boat)* lancha *f* (b) *(act of launching) (of ship)* botadura *f*; *(of rocket, product)* lanzamiento *m*; **l. pad** plataforma *f* de lanzamiento

2 *vt (ship)* botar; *(rocket, product)* lanzar; *(business, enquiry)* emprender; **to l. sb on a career** *(of event)* marcar el inicio de la carrera de alguien

▶**launch into** *vt insep (attack, story)* emprender; *(complaint)* embarcarse en

**launching pad** ['lɔːntʃɪŋ'pæd] *n* plataforma *f* de lanzamiento

**launder** ['lɔːndə(r)] *vt (clothes)* lavar (y planchar); *Fig (money)* blanquear

**laund(e)rette** [lɔːn'dret] *n Br* lavandería *f*

**laundry** ['lɔːndrɪ] *n (dirty clothes)* ropa *f* sucia; *(clean clothes)* colada *f*; **to do the l.** hacer la colada; **l. basket** cesto *m* de la ropa sucia

**laurel** ['lɒrəl] *n (tree)* laurel *m*; *Fig* **to rest on one's laurels** dormirse en los laureles; **l. wreath** corona *f* de laurel

**lava** ['lɑːvə] *n* lava *f*

**lavatory** ['lævətrɪ] *n (room)* cuarto *m* de baño, servicio *m*; *(receptacle)* váter *m*, retrete *m*; **to go to the l.** ir al baño; **public l.** servicios *mpl or* aseos *mpl* públicos; **l. paper** papel *m* higiénico

**lavender** ['lævɪndə(r)] 1 *n (shrub)* espliego *m*, lavanda *f*; **l. water** agua *f* de lavanda

2 *adj (colour)* lila *inv*, violeta *inv*

**lavish** ['lævɪʃ] 1 *adj* (a) *(person)* generoso(a), espléndido(a) (**with** con) (b) *(expenditure, decor)* espléndido(a)

2 *vt* **to l. gifts/praise on sb** colmar de regalos/alabanzas a alguien

**lavishly** ['lævɪʃlɪ] *adv* espléndidamente

**law** [lɔː] *n* (a) *(rule)* ley *f*; **there's no l. against it** no hay ninguna ley que lo prohíba; **the laws of gravity** la ley de la gravedad; **she is a l. unto herself** hace lo que le viene en gana *or* lo que le da la gana; **there's one l. for the rich and another for the poor** hay una ley para el rico y otra para el pobre

(b) *(set of rules)* ley *f*; **it's the l.** es la ley; **to break the l.** quebrantar la ley; **to be above the l.** estar por encima de la ley; **you can't take the l. into your own hands** no te puedes tomar la justicia por tu mano; **l. and order** el orden público; **the problem of l. and order** la inseguridad ciudadana; **l. firm** bufete *m* de abogados

(c) *(system of justice, subject)* derecho *m*; **to practise l.** ejercer la abogacía

(d) *Fam* **the l.** *(police)* la poli

**law-abiding** ['lɔːəbaɪdɪŋ] *adj* respetuoso(a) con la ley

**lawbreaker** ['lɔːbreɪkə(r)] *n* delincuente *mf*

**lawcourt** ['lɔːkɔːt] *n* juzgado *m*

**lawful** ['lɔːfʊl] *adj (legal)* legal; *(rightful)* legítimo(a); *(not forbidden)* lícito(a)

**lawless** ['lɔːlɪs] *adj* sin ley; **a l. mob** una muchedumbre anárquica

**lawlessness** ['lɔːlɪsnɪs] *n* anarquía *f*

**lawmaker** ['lɔːmeɪkə(r)] *n* legislador(ora) *m,f*

**lawn** [lɔːn] *n* césped *m*; **l. tennis** tenis *m* en pista de hierba

**lawnmower** ['lɔːnməʊə(r)] *n* cortadora *f* de césped, cortacésped *m or f*

**lawsuit** ['lɔːs(j)uːt] *n* pleito *m*

**lawyer** ['lɔːjə(r)] *n* abogado(a) *m,f*

**lax** [læks] *adj (morals, discipline)* relajado(a), laxo(a); *(person)* negligente, poco riguroso(a); *(security, standards)* descuidado(a), poco riguroso(a)

**laxative** ['læksətɪv] 1 *n* laxante *m*

2 *adj* laxante

**laxity** ['læksɪtɪ], **laxness** ['læksnɪs] *n (of morals, discipline)* relajo *m*, laxitud *f*; *(of person)* negligencia *f* (**in doing sth** al hacer algo); *(of security, standards)* falta *f* de rigor

**lay¹** [leɪ] *adj Rel* laico(a), lego(a); **l. preacher** predicador *m* laico

**lay²** 1 *vt* (*pt & pp* **laid** [leɪd]) (a) *(place)* dejar, poner; **to l. a book on the table** dejar un libro encima de la mesa; **to l. sb flat** *(hit)* tumbar a alguien (de un golpe); **to l. sth flat** extender algo; **to l. sb to rest** *(bury)* dar sepultura a alguien; **to l. one's hands on sth** *(find)* dar con algo; **she reads everything she can l. her hands on** lee todo lo que cae en sus manos; **if you l. a finger on her...** como le pongas un solo dedo encima...; **to have nowhere to l. one's head** no tener donde caerse muerto; **to l. eyes on sth/sb** ver algo/a alguien; **to l. emphasis on sth** hacer hincapié en algo; **to l. the facts before sb** exponer los hechos a alguien; **to l. claim to sth** reclamar algo; **to l. a curse on sb** echar una maldición a alguien; **to l. the blame on sb** echar la culpa a alguien; **this decision lays bare her true intentions** esta decisión deja claro cuáles son sus verdaderas intenciones; **to l. oneself open to criticism** exponerse a (las) críticas; **to l. sb's fears to rest** apaciguar los temores de alguien

(b) *(foundations, carpet, mine)* colocar, poner; *(cable, trap)* tender; *Br* **to l. the table** poner la mesa

(c) *(egg)* poner

**(d) to l. a bet** hacer una apuesta

**(e)** *very Fam* **to get laid** echar un polvo

**2** *vi (of bird)* poner (huevos)

**3** *pt of* **lie²**

▶**lay aside** *vt sep* **(a)** *(money)* reservar, apartar **(b)** *(prejudices, doubt)* dejar a un lado

▶**lay by** *vt sep (money)* ahorrar, guardar

▶**lay down** *vt sep* **(a) to l. down one's arms** dejar *or* deponer las armas; **he laid down his life for his beliefs** dio su vida por sus creencias **(b)** *(principle, rule)* establecer; **she's always laying down the law** siempre está dando órdenes

▶**lay in** *vt sep (supplies, food)* abastecerse de

▶**lay into** *vt insep Fam (attack, criticize)* arremeter contra

▶**lay off 1** *vt sep (make redundant)* despedir *(por reducción de plantilla)*

**2** *vt insep Fam (abstain from)* dejar; **to l. off drink** dejar la bebida

**3** *vi Fam* **l. off!** ¡déjame en paz!

▶**lay on** *vt sep (food, drink)* preparar; *(party, entertainment)* organizar, preparar

▶**lay out** *vt sep* **(a)** *(arrange, display)* colocar, disponer; *(dead body)* amortajar **(b)** *(plan) (road)* trazar; *(town)* diseñar el trazado de

**layabout** ['leɪəbaʊt] *n Fam* holgazán(ana) *m,f*, gandul(ula) *m,f*

**lay-by** ['leɪbaɪ] *(pl* **lay-bys)** *n* área *f* de descanso

**layer** ['leɪə(r)] **1** *n (of paint, chocolate)* capa *f; (of rock)* estrato *m*

**2** *vt* **to have one's hair layered** cortarse el pelo a capas

**layman** ['leɪmən] *n Rel* laico *m*, lego *m; (non-specialist)* profano *m*, lego *m*

**lay-off** ['leɪɒf] *(pl* **lay-offs)** *n* despido *m (por reducción de plantilla)*

**layout** ['leɪaʊt] *n (of town)* trazado *m; (of house)* disposición *f; (of text)* composición *f*

**laywoman** ['leɪwʊmən] *n Rel* laica *f*, lega *f; (non-specialist)* profana *f*, lega *f*

**laze** [leɪz] *vi* **to l. (about/around)** holgazanear, gandulear

**laziness** ['leɪzɪnɪs] *n* pereza *f*

**lazy** ['leɪzɪ] *adj (person)* perezoso(a); *(afternoon)* ocioso(a)

**lazybones** ['leɪzɪbəʊnz] *n Fam* holgazán(ana) *m,f*

**lb** *(abbr* **pound)** libra *f (= 0,45 kg )*

**LCD** [elsi:'di:] *n Elec & Comptr (abbr* **liquid crystal display)** LCD, pantalla *f* de cristal líquido

**LDC** [eldi:'si:] *n Econ (abbr* **less-developed country)** país *m* menos desarrollado

**LEA** [eli:'eɪ] *n Br Pol (abbr* **Local Education Authority)** = organismo local encargado de la enseñanza, ≃ consejería *f* de educación

**lead¹** [led] *n* **(a)** *(metal)* plomo *m*; **l. poisoning** saturnismo *m* **(b)** *(for pencil)* mina *f* **(c)** *(idioms)* **to go down like a l. balloon** fracasar estrepitosamente; *Fam* **they filled him full of l.** le llenaron el cuerpo de plomo; *Fam* **to swing the l.** escurrir el bulto

**lead²** [li:d] **1** *n* **(a)** *(advantage)* ventaja *f*; **to be in the l.** ir *or* estar a la cabeza *or* en cabeza; **to take** *or* **go into the l.** ponerse a la *or* en cabeza; *Ind* **l. time** *(for production)* tiempo *m or* período *m* de producción; *(for delivery)* tiempo *m* de entrega

**(b)** *(example)* ejemplo *m*; **to give sb a l.** dar un ejemplo a alguien; **to follow sb's l.** seguir el ejemplo de alguien

**(c)** *(clue)* pista *f*

**(d)** *(in cardgame)* mano *f*; **it's your l.** tú eres mano, tú llevas la mano

**(e)** *Th & Cin* papel *m* protagonista

**(f)** *(for dog)* correa *f*

**(g)** *(cable)* cable *m*

**2** *vt (pt & pp* **led** [led]) **(a)** *(show the way to)* llevar, conducir; **to l. the way** mostrar el camino; **to l. the conversation away from a subject** llevar la conversación hacia otro tema; **to be easily led** dejarse influir con facilidad; **that leads me to believe that…** eso me hace creer que…

**(b)** **to l. a happy/sad life** tener *or* llevar una vida feliz/triste

**(c)** *(team, attack, troops)* dirigir

**(d)** *(be ahead of)* **to l. the field** estar *or* ir a la cabeza; *Fig* **to l. the field in sth** estar a la cabeza *or* a la vanguardia en algo; **to l. sb by eight points** llevar a alguien ocho puntos de ventaja

**3** *vi* **(a)** *(of road)* conducir, llevar

**(b)** **to l. to sth** *(cause)* llevar a algo

**(c)** *(in competition, race)* ir en cabeza; *(in cardgame)* salir; **you l. and I'll follow** tú vas delante y yo te sigo

▶**lead away** *vt sep* **to l. sb away** llevarse a alguien

▶**lead off** *vi* **(a)** *(road, corridor)* salir, bifurcarse *(from de)* **(b)** *(in discussion)* comenzar, empezar

▶**lead on** *vt sep (deceive, seduce)* tomar el pelo a

▶**lead up to** *vt insep (subject, event)* llevar a, conducir a; *(of person)* ir a referirse a; **the period leading up to the war** el periodo previo *or* que precedió a la guerra; **what are you leading up to?** ¿a dónde quieres ir a parar (con todo esto)?

**leaded** ['ledɪd] *adj* **l. window** vidriera *f* (emplomada); **l. petrol** gasolina *f* con plomo

**leaden** ['ledən] *adj (heavy)* pesado(a), plúmbeo(a); **a l. sky** un cielo plomizo

**leader** ['li:də(r)] *n* (a) *(of group, in race)* líder *mf*; **to be a born l.** ser un líder nato (b) *(in newspaper)* editorial *m*

**leadership** ['li:dəʃɪp] *n* *(people in charge)* dirección *f*; *(position)* liderato *m*, liderazgo *m*; *(quality)* capacidad *f* de liderazgo, dotes *fpl* de mando

**lead-free** [led'fri:] *adj* *(petrol, paint)* sin plomo

**lead-in** ['li:dɪn] *n TV & Rad* presentación *f*

**leading** ['li:dɪŋ] *adj* (a) *(best, most important)* principal, destacado(a); **one of Europe's l. electronics firms** una de las principales empresas europeas de electrónica; **a l. authority in the field** una destacada autoridad en la materia; *Journ* **l. article** editorial *m*; **l. light** *(in politics, society)* figura *f* prominente; **l. question** *(seeking to elicit answer)* pregunta *f* capciosa; *Cin & Th* **l. role** papel *m* protagonista (b) *(team, runner)* líder

**leaf** [li:f] *(pl* **leaves** [li:vz]*)* *n* (a) *(of plant, book)* hoja *f*; *Fig* **to turn over a new l.** hacer borrón y cuenta nueva; *Fig* **to take a l. out of sb's book** seguir el ejemplo de alguien (b) *(of table)* hoja *f* abatible

▸**leaf through** *vt insep (book, magazine)* hojear

**leaflet** ['li:flɪt] **1** *n* folleto *m*; *(political)* octavilla *f*; *(folded)* díptico *m*, panfleto *m*

**2** *vt* **to l. an area** repartir folletos en una zona

**leafy** ['li:fɪ] *adj (tree)* frondoso(a); **l. suburb** zona *f* residencial con arbolado

**league** [li:g] *n* liga *f*; **l. champions** *(in football)* campeón *m* de liga; **to be in l. with sb** estar coaligado(a) con alguien; *Fig* **to be in a different l.** estar a otro nivel

**leak** [li:k] **1** *n* (a) *(in bucket)* agujero *m*; *(in pipe)* fuga *f*, escape *m*; *(in roof)* gotera *f*; *(in ship)* vía *f* de agua; *very Fam* **to take or have a l.** echar una meadilla (b) *(of liquid, gas)* fuga *f*, escape *m*; *(of information)* filtración *f*

**2** *vt (liquid, gas)* tener una fuga *or* un escape de; *(information)* filtrar

**3** *vi* (a) *(of pipe)* tener una fuga *or* un escape; *(of roof)* tener goteras; *(of shoe)* calar; *(of ship)* hacer agua; **this bucket's leaking** este cubo pierde (b) *(of liquid, gas)* salirse, escaparse; *(of information)* filtrarse

**leakage** ['li:kɪdʒ] *n (of liquid, gas)* fuga *f*, escape *m*; *(of information)* filtración *f*

**leaky** ['li:kɪ] *adj (bucket)* con agujeros; *(pipe)* con fugas *or* escapes; *(roof)* con goteras; *(shoe)* que cala; *(ship)* que hace agua; *(tap)* que gotea

**lean**¹ [li:n] *adj* (a) *(person)* delgado(a); *(meat)* magro(a) (b) *(year)* de escasez; *(harvest)* escaso(a)

**lean**² *(pt & pp* **leant** [lent] *or* **leaned**) **1** *vt* **to l. sth against sth** apoyar algo contra algo

**2** *vi (of building)* inclinarse; **to l. on/against sth** apoyarse en/contra algo; *Fig* **to l. on sb**

*(rely on)* apoyarse en alguien; *(pressurize)* presionar a alguien; **to l. out of the window** asomarse a la ventana

▸**lean back** *vi* reclinarse

▸**lean over** *vt insep* **he leaned over the fence** se asomó por encima de la valla

**leaning** ['li:nɪŋ] *n (tendency)* inclinación *f*, tendencia *f*; **to have artistic leanings** tener tendencias *or* inclinaciones artísticas

**leant** [lent] *pt & pp of* **lean**

**lean-to** ['li:ntu:] *n (pl* **lean-tos**) *(shack)* cobertizo *m*

**leap** [li:p] **1** *n* salto *m*, brinco *m*; *Fig* **to take a l. in the dark** dar un salto al vacío; *Fig* **to advance by leaps and bounds** avanzar a pasos agigantados; **l. year** año *m* bisiesto

**2** *vt (pt & pp* **leapt** [lept] *or* **leaped***)* saltar

**3** *vi* saltar; **to l. to one's feet** ponerse en pie de un salto; **to l. at the chance** no dejar escapar la oportunidad; **to l. for joy** dar saltos de alegría

**leapfrog** ['li:pfrɒg] **1** *n* **to play l.** jugar a pídola

**2** *vt (pt & pp* **leapfrogged***)* saltar por encima de

**3** *vi Fig* **to l. over** *(rivals)* pasar por encima de

**leapt** [lept] *pt & pp of* **leap**

**learn** [lɜ:n] *(pt & pp* **learnt** [lɜ:nt] *or* **learned***)* **1** *vt* (a) *(language, skill)* aprender; *Fig* **he has learnt his lesson** ha aprendido la lección (b) *(find out about)* enterarse de; **we are sorry to l. that…** sentimos mucho haber sabido que…

**2** *vi* (a) *(acquire knowledge)* aprender (b) *(find out)* enterarse; **to l. of** *or* **about sth** enterarse de algo

**learned** ['lɜ:nɪd] *adj* erudito(a); *Br Law* **my l. friend** mi colega

**learner** ['lɜ:nə(r)] *n (beginner)* principiante *mf*; *(student)* estudiante *mf*; **to be a quick l.** aprender deprisa; **to be a slow l.** ser lento(a) *(para aprender)*; *Aut* **l. driver** conductor(ora) *m,f* en prácticas

**learning** ['lɜ:nɪŋ] *n (process)* aprendizaje *m*; *(knowledge)* conocimientos *mpl*; **l. curve** curva *f* de aprendizaje

**learnt** [lɜ:nt] *pt & pp of* **learn**

**lease** [li:s] **1** *n Law* (contrato *m* de) arrendamiento *m*; *Fig* **to give sb a new l. of life** dar a alguien una nueva inyección de vida

**2** *vt* arrendar *(from/to* de/a*)*

**leasehold** ['li:shəʊld] *n* arriendo *m*; **l. property** propiedad *f* arrendada

**leaseholder** ['li:shəʊldə(r)] *n* arrendatario(a) *m,f*

**leash** [li:ʃ] *n (for dog)* correa *f*; *Fig* **to keep sb on a tight l.** atar corto a alguien

**leasing** ['li:sɪŋ] *n Com* leasing *m*, arrendamiento *m*

**least** [li:st] **1** *n* the l. lo menos; **it's the l. I can do** es lo menos que puedo hacer; **that's the l. of my worries** eso es lo que menos me preocupa; **to say the l.** por no decir otra cosa; **at l.** por lo menos; **at l. as old/expensive as...** por lo menos tan viejo/caro como...; **at the very l. they should pay your expenses** como mínimo deberían pagar tus gastos; **he's leaving, at l. that's what I've heard** se marcha, o al menos eso he oído; **not in the l.** en absoluto; **it doesn't matter in the l.** no tiene la menor importancia

**2** *adj* (superlative of little) (smallest) menor; **the l. thing annoys her** la menor cosa le molesta

**3** *adv* menos; **the l. interesting/difficult** el menos interesante/difícil; **l. of all her** mucho menos ella; **when I was l. expecting it** cuando menos lo esperaba

**least-cost** ['li:st'kɒst] *n* Com coste *m* mínimo

**leather** ['leðə(r)] **1** *n* piel *f*, cuero *m*

**2** *vt* Fam (beat) zurrar

**leather-bound** ['leðəbaʊnd] *adj* (book) encuadernado(a) en piel

**leathery** ['leðərɪ] *adj* (face, skin) curtido(a); (meat) correoso(a)

**leave** [li:v] **1** *n* (a) (permission, holiday) permiso *m*; **to be on l.** estar de permiso; **to ask l. to do sth** pedir permiso para hacer algo; **to grant** or **give sb l. to do sth** conceder or dar permiso a alguien para hacer algo; **l. of absence** permiso *m*

(b) (farewell) **to take one's l. (of sb)** despedirse (de alguien); **to take l. of one's senses** perder el juicio

**2** *vt* (pt & pp **left** [left]) (a) (depart from) (place) irse de, marcharse de; (room) salir de; (person) dejar; **he has left London** se ha ido de Londres; **to l. the table** levantarse de la mesa; **to l. one's job** dejar el trabajo; **the car left the road** el coche salió de la carretera; **his eyes never left her** sus ojos no se apartaban de ella

(b) (abandon) abandonar, dejar; **he left his wife** dejó a su mujer

(c) (put, deposit) **to l. sth somewhere** (deliberately) dejar algo en algún sitio; (by mistake) dejarse algo en algún sitio; **take it or l. it** lo tomas o lo dejas; **to l. a message for sb** dejar un recado or mensaje para alguien

(d) (allow to remain) dejar; **to l. the door open** dejar la puerta abierta; **to l. oneself open to criticism** exponerse a las críticas; **to l. sth unfinished** dejar algo sin terminar; **to l. sb to do sth** dejar a alguien hacer algo; **l. it to me** déjamelo a mí; **it leaves much to be desired** deja mucho que desear; **let's l. it at that** vamos a dejarlo aquí; **I think we should l. (it) well alone** creo que sería mejor no me-

terse or dejar las cosas como están; **l. me alone!** ¡déjame en paz!

(e) (bequeath) legar, dejar; **he leaves a wife and three children** deja mujer y tres hijos

(f) (remain) **to be left** quedar; **how many are there left?** ¿cuántos quedan?; **three from seven leaves four** siete menos tres son cuatro

**3** *vi* (depart) salir; (go away) irse, marcharse

▶**leave behind** *vt sep* **to l. sth behind** dejarse algo; **to l. sb behind** dejar a alguien

▶**leave off 1** *vt insep* **to l. off doing sth** dejar de hacer algo; **to l. off work** dejar el trabajo

**2** *vi* **where did we l. off?** ¿dónde lo dejamos?

▶**leave on** *vt sep* **to l. the light/TV on** dejar la luz/televisión encendida

▶**leave out** *vt sep* (a) (omit) omitir (b) (not involve) **to l. sb out of sth** dejar a alguien al margen de algo; **to feel left out** sentirse excluido(a) (c) (leave ready, available) **I'll l. your dinner out on the table for you** te dejaré la cena encima de la mesa; **l. the disks out where I can see them** deja los disquetes donde pueda verlos (d) (not put away) **we l. the car out on the street** dejamos el coche en la calle; **who left the milk out?** ¿quién ha dejado la leche fuera? (e) Fam **l. it out!** (stop it) ¡vale ya!

▶**leave over** *vt sep* **to be left over** (of food, money) sobrar

**leaven** ['levən] *n* Culin & Fig fermento *m*

**leave-taking** ['li:vteɪkɪŋ] *n* despedida *f*

**Lebanese** [lebə'ni:z] **1** *npl* (people) **the L.** los libaneses

**2** *n & adj* libanés(esa) *m,f*

**Lebanon** ['lebənən] *n* el Líbano

**lecher** ['letʃə(r)] *n* sátiro *m*, obseso *m*

**lecherous** ['letʃərəs] *adj* lascivo(a), lujurioso(a)

**lechery** ['letʃərɪ] *n* lascivia *f*, lujuria *f*

**lectern** ['lektən] *n* atril *m*

**lecture** ['lektʃə(r)] **1** *n* (a) (public speech) conferencia *f*; (university class) clase *f*; **l. theatre** (in university) aula *f*; (in conference centre) sala *f* de conferencias (b) Fam (reprimand) sermón *m*; **to give sb a l.** echarle un sermón a alguien, sermonear a alguien

**2** *vt* Fam (reprimand) echar un sermón a, sermonear

**3** *vi* (give public lectures) dar conferencias; (at university) dar clases

**lecturer** ['lektʃərə(r)] *n* Univ profesor(ora) *m,f* de universidad

**LED** [eli:'di:] *n* Elec (abbr **light-emitting diode**) LED *m*, diodo *m* emisor de luz

**led** [led] *pt & pp* of **lead**

**ledge** [ledʒ] *n* (shelf) repisa *f*; (on cliff) saliente *m*; (of window) alféizar *m* (exterior); (on building) cornisa *f*

**ledger** ['ledʒə(r)] *n* libro *m* mayor

**lee** [li:] *n* socaire *m*

**leech** [li:tʃ] *n* (a) *(animal)* sanguijuela *f*; **to cling to sb like a l.** pegarse a alguien como una lapa (b) *Pej (parasitical person)* sanguijuela *f*, chupóptero(a) *m,f*

**leek** [li:k] *n* puerro *m*

**leer** ['lɪə(r)] **1** *n* mirada *f* impúdica *or* obscena
**2** *vi* **to l. at sb** mirar impúdicamente a alguien

**lees** [li:z] *npl (of wine)* madre *f*, heces *fpl*

**leeward** ['li:wəd] **1** *n* sotavento *m*
**2** *adj* de sotavento; **the L. Islands** las Islas de Sotavento

**leeway** ['li:weɪ] *n (freedom)* margen *m* de maniobra

**left¹** [left] **1** *n* izquierda *f*; **on** *or* **to the l.** a la izquierda; **on my l.** a mano izquierda
**2** *adj* izquierdo(a); **the l. wing** *(of party)* la izquierda
**3** *adv* a la izquierda

**left²** *pt & pp of* **leave**

**left-field** ['left'fi:ld] *adj US Fam (bizarre)* raro(a), extravagante

**left-hand** ['left'hænd] *adj* de la izquierda; **on the l. side** a la izquierda

**left-handed** [left'hændɪd] **1** *adj* zurdo(a)
**2** *adv* con la izquierda *or* zurda

**left-hander** [left'hændə(r)] *n (person)* zurdo(a) *m,f*

**left luggage office** ['left'lʌgɪdʒ'ɒfɪs] *n* consigna *f*

**leftover** ['leftəʊvə(r)] **1** *npl* **leftovers** *(food)* sobras *fpl*
**2** *adj (food, paint)* sobrante

**left-wing** ['leftwɪŋ] *adj* izquierdista, de izquierdas

**left-winger** ['left'wɪŋə(r)] *n Pol* izquierdista *mf*

**leg** [leg] **1** *n* (a) *(of person)* pierna *f*; *(of animal, table, chair)* pata *f*; *(of trousers)* pernera *f*; *Culin (of lamb)* pierna *f*; *Culin (of chicken)* muslo *m* (b) *(stage) (of journey, race)* etapa *f* (c) *(idioms)* **to pull sb's l.** tomar el pelo a alguien; **shake a l.!** ¡muévete!; **to show a l.** *(get up)* levantarse; **you don't have a l. to stand on** no tienes a qué agarrarte; **he was given a l. up** *(was helped)* le echaron una mano *or* un cable; *very Fam* **to get one's l. over** *(have sex)* echar un polvo
**2** *vt (pt & pp* **legged)** *Fam* **to l. it** *(hurry)* salir zumbando

**legacy** ['legəsɪ] *n* legado *m*; **to come into a l.** recibir una herencia

**legal** ['li:gəl] *adj* legal; **to take l. action (against sb)** presentar una demanda (contra alguien); **l. advice** asesoría *f* jurídica *or* legal; **l.**

**aid** asistencia *f* jurídica de oficio; **the l. profession** la profesión jurídica; **l. tender** moneda *f* de curso legal

**legality** [lɪ'gælɪtɪ] *n* legalidad *f*

**legalization** [li:gəlaɪ'zeɪʃən] *n* legalización *f*

**legalize** ['li:gəlaɪz] *vt* legalizar

**legally** ['li:gəlɪ] *adv* legalmente

**legate** ['legɪt] *n Rel* nuncio *m*

**legation** [lɪ'geɪʃən] *n (diplomatic mission)* legación *f*

**legend** ['ledʒənd] *n* leyenda *f*; **to be a l. in one's own lifetime** ser una leyenda viva

**legendary** ['ledʒəndərɪ] *adj* legendario(a)

**leggings** ['legɪŋz] *npl (of woman)* mallas *fpl*; *(of cowboy)* antiparas *fpl*, polainas *fpl*

**leggy** ['legɪ] *adj (person)* patilargo(a)

**legible** ['ledʒɪbəl] *adj* legible

**legion** ['li:dʒən] *n* legión *f*

**legionary** ['li:dʒənərɪ] *n* legionario *m*

**legionnaire** [li:dʒə'neə(r)] *n* legionario *m*; *Med* **l.'s disease** enfermedad *f* del legionario, legionel(l)a *f*

**legislate** ['ledʒɪsleɪt] *vi* legislar **(against** en contra de)

**legislation** [ledʒɪs'leɪʃən] *n* legislación *f*

**legislative** ['ledʒɪslətɪv] *adj* legislativo(a)

**legislator** ['ledʒɪsleɪtə(r)] *n* legislador(ora) *m,f*

**legislature** ['ledʒɪslətjə(r)] *n* legislativo *m*, asamblea *f* legislativa

**legitimacy** [lɪ'dʒɪtɪməsɪ] *n* legitimidad *f*

**legitimate 1** *adj* [lɪ'dʒɪtɪmət] legítimo(a)
**2** *vt* [lɪ'dʒɪtɪmeɪt] legitimar

**legitimately** [lɪ'dʒɪtɪmətlɪ] *adv* legítimamente

**legitimize** [lɪ'dʒɪtɪmaɪz] *vt* legitimizar

**legless** ['legləs] *adj Fam (drunk)* mamado(a), pedo

**legroom** ['legrʊm] *n* espacio *m* para las piernas *(en vehículo, en el cine)*

**legume** ['legju:m] *n Bot* legumbre *f*

**legwarmers** ['legwɔ:məz] *npl* calentadores *mpl*, calientapiernas *mpl*

**leisure** ['leʒə(r), *US* 'li:ʒər] *n* ocio *m*; **take these leaflets and read them at your l.** llévate estos folletos y tómate tu tiempo para leerlos; **a life of l.** una vida de ocio; **l. activities** actividades *fpl* para el tiempo libre; **l. centre** centro *m* recreativo *or* de ocio

**leisurely** ['leʒəlɪ, *US* 'li:ʒərlɪ] *adj (unhurried)* pausado(a), lento(a); *(relaxed)* tranquilo(a), relajado(a)

**lemming** ['lemɪŋ] *n* lemming *m*; **they followed him like lemmings** le siguieron ciegamente

**lemon** ['lemən] **1** n (a) (fruit) limón m; (colour) amarillo m limón; **l. curd** crema f de limón; **l. sole** mendo m limón, = pescado similar al lenguado y al gallo; **l. squeezer** exprimidor m, exprimelimones m inv; **l. tea** té m con limón; **l. tree** limonero m (b) Fam **I felt like a real l.** me sentí como un verdadero merluzo

**2** adj **l. (coloured)** (color) amarillo limón

**lemonade** [lemə'neɪd] n (fizzy) gaseosa f; (still) limonada f

**lemur** ['liːmə(r)] n lémur m

**lend** [lend] (pt & pp **lent** [lent]) vt (money, book, pen) prestar; (dignity, support, credibility) proporcionar, prestar (**to** a); **to l. sb a (helping) hand** echar una mano a alguien; **to l. an ear** or **one's ear to...** escuchar de buena gana a...; **her work doesn't l. itself to dramatization** su obra no se presta a la dramatización

**lender** ['lendə(r)] n Fin prestamista mf

**lending** ['lendɪŋ] n Fin préstamos mpl, créditos mpl; **l. library** biblioteca f de préstamo; Fin **l. rate** tipo m de interés de los préstamos or créditos

**length** [leŋθ] n (a) (in space) longitud f; **it's 4.50m in length** tiene 4,5 m de longitud; **to wander the l. and breadth of the country** vagabundear a lo largo y ancho del país (b) (in time) duración f; **at (great) l.** extensamente, dilatadamente; **a great l. of time** un largo periodo de tiempo; **l. of service** antigüedad f en la empresa (c) **to go to the l. of doing sth** llegar incluso a hacer algo; **to go to great lengths to do sth** tomarse muchas molestias para hacer algo; **he would go to any lengths (to do sth)** estaría dispuesto a cualquier cosa (con tal de hacer algo) (d) (piece) (of wood, string) trozo m, pedazo m (e) (of swimming pool) largo m

**lengthen** ['leŋθən] **1** vt alargar

**2** vi alargarse

**lengthily** ['leŋθɪlɪ] adv extensamente, dilatadamente

**lengthways** ['leŋθweɪz], **lengthwise** ['leŋθwaɪz] adv a lo largo

**lengthy** ['leŋθɪ] adj largo(a), extenso(a)

**lenient** ['liːnɪənt] adj indulgente, benévolo(a)

**Leningrad** ['lenɪngræd] n Formerly Leningrado

**lens** [lenz] n (of glasses) cristal m, lente f; (of camera) objetivo m, lente f; (of eye) cristalino m; (contact) lenses lentes fpl, lentes fpl de contacto; **l. cap** tapa f del objetivo

**Lent** [lent] n Rel Cuaresma f

**lent** [lent] pt & pp of **lend**

**lentil** ['lentɪl] n lenteja f

**Leo** ['liːəʊ] n (sign of zodiac) Leo m; **to be (a) L.** ser Leo

**leopard** ['lepəd] n leopardo m

**leotard** ['liːətɑːd] n malla f

**leper** ['lepə(r)] n leproso(a) m,f; **l. colony** prosería f, lazareto m

**leprechaun** ['leprəkɔːn] n (Irish fairy) duende m

**leprosy** ['leprəsɪ] n lepra f

**lesbian** ['lezbɪən] **1** n lesbiana f

**2** adj lésbico(a), lesbiano(a)

**lesion** ['liːʒən] n lesión f

**Lesotho** [lɪ'suːtuː] n Lesoto

**less** [les] **1** adj (comparative of little) menos; **it's l. than a week's work** es menos de una semana de trabajo; **the distance is l. than we thought** la distancia es menor de lo que pensábamos

**2** prep menos; **a year l. two days** un año menos dos días; **I've got £50, l. what I spent on the train ticket** tengo 50 libras, menos lo que me he gastado en el billete de tren

**3** pron menos; **I don't think any (the) l. of you** no pienso peor de ti; **I see l. of her nowadays** la veo menos ahora; **in l. than an hour** en menos de una hora; **the l. said about it the better** cuanto menos se hable de ello, mejor; Fam **l. of that!** ¡basta ya!

**4** adv menos; **l. and l.** cada vez menos; **no more, no l.** ni más ni menos; **still l., even l.** todavía menos; **nothing l. than** nada menos que; **she was driving a Rolls, no l.** conducía nada menos que un Rolls; **I expected no l. from you** no esperaba menos de ti; **they haven't got a fridge, much l. a freezer** no tienen nevera y mucho menos congelador

**lessen** ['lesən] **1** vt reducir

**2** vi disminuir, reducirse

**lesser** ['lesə(r)] adj menor; **the l. of two evils** el mal menor; **to a l. extent** or **degree** en menor medida

**lesson** ['lesən] n clase f, lección f; Fig **he has learnt his l.** ha aprendido la lección; Fig **to teach sb a l.** dar una lección a alguien

**lest** [lest] conj Formal para que no, por si; **l. we forget...** para que no olvidemos, ...

**let**¹ [let] n (in tennis) servicio m nulo

**let**² **1** n (of property) short/long **l.** alquiler m por un periodo corto/largo

**2** vt (pt & pp **let**) (rent out) alquilar; **to l.** (sign) se alquila

**let**³ **1** vt (pt & pp **let**) (a) (allow) **to l. sb do sth** dejar a alguien hacer algo; **to l. sb know sth** decir algo a alguien; **l. me see** (when answering) veamos, a ver; (show me) déjame ver; **to l. sth pass** (not criticize, comment on) dejar pasar algo, pasar algo por alto; **to l. go of sth**, **to l. sth go** soltar algo; **to l. oneself go** (lose restraint) soltarse el pelo; (stop caring for one's appearance) abandonarse; **I'm afraid we'll have to l. you go** (on making somebody redundant) me temo que vamos a tener que prescindir de usted; **don't l. it get to you** or **get you down** no dejes que eso pueda contigo; **can you l. me have it back tomorrow?** ¿me lo puedes devolver mañana?; **don't l. me see you here again!** ¡que no te vuelva a ver por aquí!; *Math* **l. AB be equal to CD** sea AB igual a CD

**(b)** *(with suggestions)* **l.'s go!** ¡vamos!; **l.'s hurry!** ¡deprisa!; **l.'s not have an argument about it!** ¡no nos peleemos por eso!; **now, don't l.'s have any nonsense!** ¡bueno, y nada de tonterías!

**2** conj **l. alone** mucho menos, menos aún
▶**let by** vt sep *(allow to pass)* **to l. sb by** dejar pasar a alguien
▶**let down** vt sep **(a)** *(hem)* bajar; *(tyre)* deshinchar, desinflar; *Fig* **to l. one's hair down** soltarse el pelo **(b)** *Fam (disappoint, fail)* **to l. sb down** fallar a alguien; **the car let us down again** el coche nos dejó tirados otra vez
▶**let in** vt sep **(a)** *(allow to enter)* dejar pasar; **to l. oneself in** *(to house)* entrar; **to l. in the light** dejar que entre la luz; **my shoes are letting in water** me están calando los zapatos **(b)** *to* **l. sb in on a secret/a plan** contar a alguien un secreto/un plan **(c)** *Fam* **do you know what you are letting yourself in for?** ¿tienes idea de en qué te estás metiendo?
▶**let into** vt sep **who let them into the house?** ¿quién los dejó entrar en la casa?; **I'll let you into a secret** te cuento un secreto
▶**let off** vt sep **(a)** *(bomb, firework)* hacer explotar; *Fig* **to l. off steam** desfogarse **(b)** *(excuse)* perdonar; **they l. him off with a fine** sólo le pusieron una multa
▶**let on** vi *Fam* **don't l. on that I was there** no digas que estuve allí; **he was more ill than he let on** estaba más enfermo de lo que decía
▶**let out** vt sep **(a)** *(release)* dejar salir; **to l. out the air from sth** desinflar or deshinchar algo; **to l. out a yell** soltar un grito **(b)** *(jacket, trousers)* agrandar **(c)** *(rent out)* alquilar
▶**let up** vi *(weather)* amainar; **once he's started he never lets up** una vez que empieza ya no se detiene
**let-down** ['letdaʊn] n *Fam* chasco m, desilusión f
**lethal** ['li:θəl] adj letal, mortal; *Fam* **that vodka's l.!** ¡ese vodka es fortísimo!; **l. dose** dosis f inv letal; **l. weapon** arma f mortífera
**lethargic** [lɪˈθɑːdʒɪk] adj *(drowsy)* aletargado(a); *(inactive)* apático(a)
**lethargy** ['leθədʒɪ] n *(drowsiness)* sopor m, letargo m; *(inactivity)* apatía f
**let-out** ['letaʊt] n *Fam (from obligation)* salida f
**letter** ['letə(r)] n **(a)** *(written message)* carta f; **l. of acknowledgement** carta de acuse de recibo; *Com* **l. of credit** carta de crédito; *Com* **l. of exchange** letra f de cambio; **l. bomb** carta bomba; **l. box** buzón m; **l. opener** abrecartas

m inv **(b)** *(of alphabet)* letra f; **the l. of the law** la interpretación literal de la ley; **to obey to the l.** obedecer al pie de la letra **(c)** **man of letters** hombre m de letras
**letterhead** ['letəhed] n membrete m
**lettuce** ['letɪs] n lechuga f
**let-up** ['letʌp] n *Fam* tregua f, descanso m; **they worked fifteen hours without a l.** trabajaron quince horas sin descanso
**leukaemia** [luːˈkiːmɪə] n leucemia f
**level** ['levəl] **1** n nivel m; **at eye l.** a la altura de los ojos; **to be on a l. with** estar al mismo nivel or a la misma altura que; *Fam* **on the l.** honrado(a); **to come down to sb's l.** ponerse al nivel de alguien; **to sink to sb's l.** rebajarse al nivel de alguien; **at ministerial/international l.** a nivel ministerial/internacional
**2** adj **(a)** *(not sloping)* nivelado(a), liso(a), horizontal; *Fig* **a l. playing field** igualdad f de condiciones
**(b)** **l. with...** a la altura de...; **to draw l. with...** *(in race)* alcanzar, ponerse a la altura de; *(in match)* conseguir el (gol del) empate contra; **she did her l. best** hizo todo lo que estaba en su mano; **the two parties are l. pegging** los dos partidos están empatados; **a l. spoonful** una cucharada rasa; *Rail* **l. crossing** paso m a nivel
**(c)** *(voice, tone)* neutro(a), desapasionado(a); **to keep a l. head** mantener la cabeza fría
**3** vt *(pt & pp* **levelled***, US* **leveled)** **(a)** *(make level)* nivelar; *(raze)* arrasar
**(b)** *(aim)* **to l. a blow at sb** propinar or asestar un golpe a alguien; **to l. criticism at sb** dirigir críticas a alguien; **to l. accusations at sb** lanzar acusaciones contra alguien
**4** vi *Fam* **to l. with sb** ser franco(a) con alguien
▶**level off, level out** vi *(ground)* nivelarse, allanarse; *(prices, demand)* estabilizarse; *Av* enderezarse
**level-headed** ['levəl'hedɪd] adj ecuánime
**lever** ['liːvə(r), US levə(r)] **1** n palanca f
**2** vt **to l. a box open** abrir una caja haciendo palanca
**leverage** ['liːvərɪdʒ] n *Tech* apalancamiento m; *Fig* **to bring l. to bear on** *(pressurize)* ejercer presión sobre
**leveraged buyout** ['liːvərɪdʒd'baɪaʊt] n *Fin* compra f apalancada
**levitate** ['levɪteɪt] vi levitar
**levitation** [levɪˈteɪʃən] n levitación f
**levity** ['levɪtɪ] n frivolidad f
**levy** ['levɪ] **1** n *(tax)* impuesto m, tasa f (**on** sobre)
**2** vt *(tax)* aplicar (**on** a)
**lewd** [luːd] adj obsceno(a)
**lexical** ['leksɪkəl] adj léxico(a)

**lexicographer** [leksɪ'kɒɡrəfə(r)] n lexicógrafo(a) m,f

**liability** [laɪə'bɪlɪtɪ] n (a) Law (responsibility) responsabilidad f (for de); Fin liabilities pasivo m, deudas fpl (b) (disadvantage) estorbo m

**liable** ['laɪəbəl] adj (a) Law (responsible) responsable (for de) (b) (to tax, fine) sujeto(a) (to a) (c) (likely) propenso(a) (to a); it is l. to explode puede que explote

**liaise** [li:'eɪz] vi to l. with sb (about sth) trabajar en cooperación con alguien (para algo)

**liaison** [lɪ'eɪzɒn] n (a) (cooperation) coordinación f; Mil l. officer oficial m de enlace (b) (love affair) relación f (amorosa)

**liar** ['laɪə(r)] n mentiroso(a) m,f

**libel** ['laɪbəl] Law 1 n libelo m; l. action juicio m por libelo; l. laws legislación f sobre el libelo
2 vt (pt & pp libelled, US libeled) calumniar

**libellous**, US **libelous** ['laɪbələs] adj calumnioso(a)

**liberal** ['lɪbərəl] 1 n Pol L. liberal mf
2 adj (a) (tolerant) liberal; l. education educación f liberal (b) (generous) desprendido(a), generoso(a) (with con) (c) (abundant) abundante, generoso(a) (d) Pol L. liberal

**liberalism** ['lɪbərəlɪzəm] n liberalismo m

**liberalize** ['lɪbərəlaɪz] vt liberalizar

**liberally** ['lɪbərəlɪ] adv generosamente

**liberate** ['lɪbəreɪt] vt liberar

**liberated** ['lɪbəreɪtɪd] adj liberado(a); a l. woman una mujer liberada

**liberation** [lɪbə'reɪʃən] n liberación f; l. movement movimiento m de liberación; l. theology teología f de la liberación

**liberator** ['lɪbəreɪtə(r)] n libertador(ora) m,f, liberador(ora) m,f

**Liberia** [laɪ'bɪərɪə] n Liberia

**Liberian** [laɪ'bɪərɪən] n & adj liberiano(a) m,f

**libertarian** [lɪbə'teərɪən] n & adj libertario(a) m,f

**liberty** ['lɪbətɪ] n libertad f; at l. (free) en libertad; to be at l. to do sth tener libertad para hacer algo; to take the l. of doing sth tomarse la libertad de hacer algo; to take liberties with tomarse (excesivas) libertades con; what a l.! ¡qué cara más dura!

**libido** [lɪ'bi:dəʊ] (pl libidos) n libido f

**Libra** ['li:brə] n (sign of zodiac) Libra m; to be (a) L. ser Libra

**librarian** [laɪ'breərɪən] n bibliotecario(a) m,f

**library** ['laɪbrərɪ] n biblioteca f; film l. filmoteca f; music l. fonoteca f; l. book libro m de biblioteca; l. card carné m de biblioteca

**libretto** [lɪ'bretəʊ] (pl librettos or libretti [lɪ'breti:]) n Mus libreto m

**Libya** ['lɪbɪə] n Libia

**Libyan** ['lɪbɪən] n & adj libio(a) m,f

**lice** [laɪs] pl of **louse**

**licence** ['laɪsəns] Br n (a) (permit) licencia f, permiso m; Com under l. bajo licencia, con autorización; (driving) l. carné m or permiso m de conducir; TV l. fee = tarifa de la licencia de uso de la televisión; Aut l. number (of car) (número m de) matrícula f (b) (freedom) licencia f, (excessive freedom) libertinaje m

**license** ['laɪsəns] 1 US n (a) (permit) licencia f, permiso m; Com under l. bajo licencia, con autorización; (driver's) l. carné m or permiso m de conducir; Aut l. number (of car) (número m de) matrícula f; Aut l. plate (placa f de) matrícula f (b) (freedom) licencia f, (excessive freedom) libertinaje m
2 vt Com autorizar; to be licensed to carry a gun tener permiso or licencia de armas

**licensed** ['laɪsənst] adj l. premises = establecimiento donde se pueden vender bebidas alcohólicas; l. restaurant = restaurante con licencia para vender bebidas alcohólicas

**licensing** ['laɪsənsɪŋ] n l. hours = horario en el que está permitido servir bebidas alcohólicas; l. laws = legislación f sobre la venta de bebidas alcohólicas

**licentious** [laɪ'senʃəs] adj licencioso(a)

**lichen** ['laɪkən] n liquen m

**lick** [lɪk] 1 n (a) (with tongue) lametazo m, lamedura f; a l. of paint una mano de pintura (b) Fam at a great l. a toda pastilla
2 vt (a) (with tongue) lamer; Fig to l. one's lips (in anticipation) relamerse; Fig to l. one's wounds lamerse las heridas; Fam Fig to l. sb's boots darle coba a alguien; Vulg to l. sb's arse lamerle el culo a alguien; Fam to l. sth/sb into shape poner algo/a alguien a punto (b) very Fam (defeat) hacer trizas a

**licorice** ['lɪkərɪs] n regaliz m

**lid** [lɪd] n (a) (of pot, jar) tapa f (b) (idioms) to take the l. off sth destapar algo; to keep the l. on sth mantener oculto algo

**lie¹** [laɪ] 1 n mentira f; to tell a l. decir una mentira, mentir; to give the l. to sth desmentir algo; l. detector detector m de mentiras
2 vi mentir; to l. through one's teeth mentir descaradamente

**lie²** 1 n the l. of the land (in politics, business) el estado de las cosas
2 vi (pt lay [leɪ], pp lain [leɪn]) (a) (of person, animal) (be still) estar tumbado(a) or acostado(a); (get down) tumbarse, acostarse; here lies... (on gravestone) aquí yace...; to l. in bed estar en la cama; I lay awake all night permanecí despierto toda la noche; to l. in wait for sb permanecer or estar a la espera de alguien; Fig to l. low permanecer en un segundo plano
(b) (of object) estar; a vast plain lay before us ante nosotros se extendía una vasta llanura; to

**l. in ruins** *(of building)* quedar en ruinas; *(of career, hopes)* quedar arruinado(a); **the obstacles that l. in our way** los impedimentos que obstaculizan nuestro camino; **the snow did not l.** la nieve no cuajó

**(c)** *(of abstract thing)* **the responsibility lies with the author** la responsabilidad recae sobre el autor; **they know where their true interests l.** saben dónde se hallan sus verdaderos intereses; **the difference lies in that...** la diferencia radica en que...; **a brilliant future lies before her** tiene ante sí un brillante futuro; **what lies behind this uncharacteristic generosity?** ¿qué hay detrás de esta inusual generosidad?

▸**lie about** *vi (of person, thing)* estar tirado(a); **she had left her papers lying about** había dejado sus papeles tirados

▸**lie back** *vi* recostarse

▸**lie down** *vi* echarse, acostarse; *Fig* **I'm not going to take this lying down** no voy a quedarme de brazos cruzados ante esto

▸**lie in** *vi* quedarse en la cama hasta tarde

**Liechtenstein** ['lɪktenstaɪn] *n* Liechtenstein

**lie-down** ['laɪˈdaʊn] *n* **to have a l.** echarse un rato

**lie-in** ['laɪ'ɪn] *n* **to have a l.** quedarse en la cama hasta tarde

**lieu** [ljuː, luː] *n* **in l. of...** en lugar de...

**lieutenant** [lefˈtenənt] *n Mil* teniente *m*; *Naut* teniente *m* de navío; *US (police officer)* oficial *mf* de policía; *Fig (helper)* lugarteniente *mf*; *Mil* **l. colonel** teniente *m* coronel

**life** [laɪf] *(pl* **lives** [laɪvz]*)* *n* **(a)** *(existence)* vida *f*; **to take sb's l.** quitar la vida a alguien; **to take one's own l.** quitarse la vida; **to bring sb back to l.** devolver la vida a alguien; **a matter of l. and death** una cuestión de vida o muerte; **l. after death** la vida después de la muerte; **to risk one's l., to risk l. and limb** arriesgar la vida; **to escape with one's l.** salir con vida; **to lose one's l.** perder la vida; **no lives were lost** no hubo que lamentar víctimas *or* ninguna muerte; **he held on to the rope for dear l.** se aferró a la cuerda con todas sus fuerzas; **run for your lives!** ¡sálvese quien pueda!; *Fam* **not on your l.!** ¡ni en broma!, ¡ni soñarlo!; *Fam* **I couldn't for the l. of me remember** por más que lo intentaba, no conseguía recordar; **from l.** *(to draw, paint)* del natural; **bird l.** avifauna *f*; **plant l.** flora *f*; **l. belt** flotador *m*, salvavidas *m inv*; **l. cycle** ciclo *m* vital; **l. force** fuerza *f* vital; **l. form** forma *f* de vida; **l. jacket** chaleco *m* salvavidas; **l. sciences** ciencias *fpl* naturales *or* biológicas

**(b)** *(period of existence)* vida *f*; **she worked all her l.** trabajó toda su vida; **never in (all) my l.** (nunca) en mi vida...; **a l. of Tolstoy** una biografía de Tolstói; **to be given a l. sentence,** *Fam* **to get l.** ser condenado(a) a cadena perpetua; *Fin* **l. annuity** renta *f* anual, anualidad *f* vitalicia; *Med* **l. expectancy** esperanza *f* de vida; *Law* **l. imprisonment** cadena *f* perpetua; *Fin* **l. insurance** seguro *m* de vida; **l. member** socio(a) *m,f* vitalicio(a); *Br Pol* **l. peer** = noble que ostenta la dignidad de par a título personal no hereditario; *Fin* **l. pension** pensión *f* vitalicia; **l. span** vida; **l. story** biografía *f*; **l. subscription** suscripción *f* vitalicia

**(c)** *(mode of existence)* vida *f*; *Fam* **to live** *or* **lead the l. of Riley** vivir como un rajá; **to make a new l. for oneself** construirse una nueva vida; **the man/woman in your l.** el hombre/la mujer que hay en tu vida; **way of l.** modo *m* de vida; **he makes her l.** a misery le amarga la vida; **to make l. worth living** hacer que la vida merezca la pena; *Fam* **how's l.?** ¿qué tal te va la vida?; *Fam* **what a l.!** ¡qué vida estal; *Fam* **such is l.!, that's l.!** ¡así es la vida!, ¡la vida es así!; *Fam* **this is the l.!** ¡esto sí vida!; *Fam* **get a l.!** colega, ¿no tienes nada mejor que hacer?

**(d)** *(liveliness)* **to come to l.** animarse, cobrar vida; **to bring sb to l.** dar vida a alguien; **to breathe new l. into** *(person, company)* dar nuevos bríos a; **the l. and soul of the party** el alma de la fiesta; **there's l. in the old dog yet** todavía le queda mucha cuerda

**lifeblood** ['laɪfblʌd] *n (blood)* sangre *f*; *Fig (key part)* alma *f*

**lifeboat** ['laɪfbəʊt] *n* **(a)** *(from coast)* lancha *f* de salvamento **(b)** *(on ship)* bote *m* salvavidas

**life-giving** ['laɪfgɪvɪŋ] *adj* salvador(ora)

**lifeguard** ['laɪfgɑːd] *n* socorrista *mf*

**lifeless** ['laɪflɪs] *adj* sin vida

**lifelessly** ['laɪflɪslɪ] *adv* sin vida

**lifelike** ['laɪflaɪk] *adj* realista

**lifeline** ['laɪflaɪn] *n Fig* tabla *f* de salvamento

**lifelong** ['laɪflɒŋ] *adj* de toda la vida

**lifer** ['laɪfə(r)] *n Fam (prisoner)* condenado(a) *m,f* a cadena perpetua

**life-saver** ['laɪfseɪvə(r)] *n Fam Fig* **to be a l.** *(provide relief)* salvar la vida

**life-saving** ['laɪfseɪvɪŋ] *adj* **a l. drug** un medicamento que salva muchas vidas; **he had a l. operation** la operación le salvó la vida

**life-size(d)** ['laɪfsaɪz(d)] *adj* (de) tamaño natural

**lifestyle** ['laɪfstaɪl] *n* estilo *m* de vida

**life-support system** ['laɪfsəpɔːˈsɪstəm], **life-support machine** ['laɪfsəpɔːˈməʃiːn] *n Med* equipo *m* de ventilación *or* respiración asistida

**life-threatening** ['laɪfθretnɪŋ] adj Med **1. condition** or **disease** enfermedad f mortífera or que puede ocasionar la muerte; **l. situation** situación f de peligro mortal

**lifetime** ['laɪftaɪm] n vida f; **in my l.** durante mi vida; **it's the chance** or **opportunity of a l.** es la oportunidad de mi/tu/su etc vida; **the holiday of a l.** las vacaciones de mi/tu/su etc vida

**lift** [lɪft] **1** n (a) Br (elevator) ascensor m; **l.* attendant** ascensorista mf; **l. shaft** hueco m del ascensor (b) (car ride) **to give sb a l.** llevar a alguien (en el coche); **could you give me a l. to the station?** ¿puedes llevarme or acercarme a la estación? (c) Fam **that really gave me a l.!** (cheered me up) ¡eso me levantó muchísimo los ánimos! (d) Av sustentación f
   **2** vt (a) (one's head, eyes, arm) levantar; **he won't l. a finger to help** no moverá un dedo para ayudar; **to l. sb (up)** (after fall) levantar a alguien; **to l. a child up** coger a un niño en brazos (b) Fam (take, steal) birlar; (arrest) trincar, emplumar (c) (remove) (restrictions, siege) levantar
   **3** vi (mist, fog) disiparse

▸**lift off** vi (of rocket) despegar

**liftoff** ['lɪftɒf] n (of rocket) despegue m

**ligament** ['lɪgəmənt] n ligamento m

**light**[1] [laɪt] **1** n (a) (illumination) luz f; **artificial/electric l.** luz artificial/eléctrica; **by the l. of the moon** a la luz de la luna; **things will look different in the cold l. of day** las cosas se ven distintas a la luz del día; **to be in sb's l.** taparle la luz a alguien; Comptr **l. pen** lápiz m óptico; Astron **l. year** año m luz
   (b) (lamp) luz f; **to put** or **turn on the l.** encender la luz; **to put** or **turn off the l.** apagar la luz; Fam **to go out like a l.** (fall asleep) quedarse traspuesto(a); **(traffic) lights** semáforo m; **l. bulb** bombilla f
   (c) (fire) **to set l. to sth** prender fuego a algo; **have you got a l.?** ¿tienes fuego?
   (d) (idioms) **the l. at the end of the tunnel** la luz al final del túnel; **to throw** or **cast l. on sth** arrojar luz sobre algo; **to bring sth to l.** sacar algo a la luz; **to come to l.** salir a la luz; **to see sth/sb in a new** or **different l.** ver algo/a alguien desde un punto de vista diferente; **in a positive** or **favourable l.** desde una óptica positiva or favorable; **in the l. of...** (considering) a la luz de..., en vista de...
   **2** adj (a) (room) luminoso(a); **it will soon be l.** pronto será de día
   (b) (hair, complexion, colour) claro(a)
   **3** vt (pt & pp **lit** [lɪt]) (a) (fire) prender, encender; (cigarette) encender
   (b) (room, street) iluminar

**light**[2] **1** adj (a) (not heavy) ligero(a); **to be l. on one's feet** tener los pies ligeros; **to have a l. meal** tomar una comida ligera; **to be a l. sleeper** tener el sueño ligero; **to have a l. touch** tener delicadeza; Av **l. aircraft** avioneta f; Mil **l. artillery** artillería f ligera; Mil **l. infantry** infantería f ligera (b) (not strenuous) (job, work) ligero(a); (rain) fina; **a l. sentence** una sentencia benévola (c) (not serious) alegre; **to make l. of sth** no dar importancia a algo; **l. entertainment** espectáculo m de entretenimiento; **l. reading** lectura f ligera; **l. verse** poesía f ligera
   **2** adv **to travel l.** viajar ligero(a) de equipaje

▸**light on** (pt & pp **lighted**) vt insep dar con; **his eyes lighted on the picture** su mirada se posó en el cuadro

▸**light up 1** vt sep (a) (house, room) iluminar (b) (cigarette) encender
   **2** vi (a) (of sky) iluminarse; **his eyes lit up** se le encendieron los ojos (b) Fam (of smoker) encender un cigarrillo

**lighten**[1] ['laɪtən] **1** vt (colour, hair) aclarar
   **2** vi (of sky) aclararse

**lighten**[2] ['laɪtən] vt (make less heavy) aligerar; Fig **to l. sb's load** aligerar la carga de alguien

▸**lighten up** vi Fam **l. up!** ¡no te pongas así!

**lighter** ['laɪtə(r)] n mechero m, encendedor m; **l. fluid** gas m (licuado) para mecheros

**light-fingered** [laɪt'fɪŋgəd] adj Fam largo(a) de manos

**light-headed** [laɪt'hedɪd] adj **to feel l.** (dizzy) estar mareado(a); (with excitement) estar exaltado(a)

**light-hearted** [laɪt'hɑːtɪd] adj alegre

**lighthouse** ['laɪthaʊs] n faro m; **l. keeper** farero(a) m,f

**lighting** ['laɪtɪŋ] n (act, system) iluminación f; **street l.** alumbrado m público

**lighting-up time** ['laɪtɪŋ'ʌptaɪm] n (for cars) = hora de encender los faros

**lightly** ['laɪtlɪ] adv ligeramente; **to sleep l.** tener el sueño ligero; **to get off l.** salir bien parado(a); **to speak l. of sth/sb** hablar a la ligera de algo/alguien; **it was not a decision she took l.** no tomó la decisión a la ligera

**lightness** ['laɪtnɪs] n (a) (brightness) claridad f (b) (in weight) ligereza f

**lightning** ['laɪtnɪŋ] n (a) (bolt) rayo m; (sheet) relámpago m; **l. conductor** pararrayos m inv (b) (idioms) **as quick as l., with l. speed** como el rayo; **l. attack** ataque m relámpago; **l. strike** huelga f relámpago or sin previo aviso; **l. visit** visita f relámpago

**lightweight** ['laɪtweɪt] **1** n (in boxing) peso m ligero; Fig Pej **an intellectual l.** un personaje de poca talla intelectual
   **2** adj (garment) ligero(a)

**lignite** ['lɪgnaɪt] *n* lignito *m*

**like¹** [laɪk] **1** *n* he and his l. él y los de su clase; **it's not for the likes of me** no es para gente como yo; **music, painting and the l.** música, pintura y cosas así; **I've never seen the l. (of it)** nunca he visto nada parecido *or* nada igual

**2** *adj* parecido(a), similar; **they are of l. temperament** tienen un temperamento parecido; **they are as l. as two peas (in a pod)** son como dos gotas de agua

**3** *prep* **(a)** *(similar to)* como; **to be l. sb/sth** ser como alguien/algo; **to taste l. sth** saber a algo; **to look l. sb/sth** parecerse a alguien/algo; **what's the weather l.?** ¿qué tiempo hace?; **people l. you** la gente como tú; **you know what she's l.** ya sabes cómo es; **it costs something l. £10** cuesta unas 10 libras; **that's more l. it** eso está mejor; **we don't have anything l. as many as that** no tenemos tantos, ni muchísimo menos; **there's nothing l. it!** ¡no hay nada igual!; **she is nothing l. as intelligent as you** no es ni mucho menos tan inteligente como tú; **that's not l. him** no es su estilo; **that's just l. him!** ¡es típico de él!; *Prov* l. **father l. son** de tal palo tal astilla

**(b)** *(in the manner of)* como; **just l. anybody else** como todo el mundo; *Fam* **to run l. blazes** *or* **mad** correr como alma que lleva el diablo; *Fam* **don't be l. that** no seas así; **l. this?** ¿así?

**(c)** *(such as)* como (por ejemplo); **take more exercise, l. jogging** haz más ejercicio, como (por ejemplo) correr

**4** *adv Fam* **as l. as not** casi seguro, seguramente

**5** *conj Fam* **do it l. I said** hazlo como te dije; **he looked l. he'd seen a ghost** parecía que *or* como si hubiera visto una aparición; **it's not l. he's ill or anything** no es que esté enfermo

**like²** **1** *n* **likes** preferencias *fpl*; **likes and dislikes** preferencias y aversiones *fpl*

**2** *vt* **(a)** *(in general)* **she likes him/it** le gusta; **she likes them** le gustan; **she likes John** *(as friend)* le cae bien John; *(is attracted to)* le gusta John; **I don't l. him/it** no me gusta; **I don't l. them** no me gustan; **they l. him/it** les gusta; **they l. each other** se gustan; **do you l. Italian food?** ¿te gusta la comida italiana?; **she likes reading** le gusta leer; **she is well liked** es muy querida (por todo el mundo); **I l. to think my father would have agreed** me gusta pensar que mi padre habría estado de acuerdo; **he doesn't l. people to talk about it** no le gusta que la gente hable de ello; *Fam Ironic* **well, I l. that!** ¡qué te parece?, ¡tiene gracia la cosa!

**(b)** *(want)* querer; **what would you l.?** ¿qué

quieres?, *Am* ¿qué se te antoja? **would you l. a cigarette?** ¿quieres un cigarrillo?; **I would very much l. to go** me encantaría ir; **I would l. to know whether...** me gustaría saber si...; **I would l. nothing better than...** nada me gustaría más que...; **you can't always do just as you l.!** ¡no puedes hacer siempre lo que te dé la gana!; **he thinks he can do anything he likes** se cree que puede hacer lo que quiera; **if you l.** si quieres; **when you l.** cuando quieras; **as much/often/many as you l.** tanto/tan a menudo/tantos como quieras; **I didn't l. to mention it** no quise mencionarlo

**likeable** ['laɪkəbəl] *adj* simpático(a)

**likelihood** ['laɪklɪhʊd] *n* probabilidad *f*; **in all l.** con toda probabilidad; **there is little l. of finding it** hay pocas probabilidades de encontrarlo; **the l. is that...** lo más probable es que...

**likely** ['laɪklɪ] **1** *adj* **(a)** *(probable)* probable; **a l. outcome** un resultado probable; **it's not very l.** no es muy probable; **it's more than l.** es más que probable; **it's l. to rain** lo más probable es que llueva; **she is l. to come** lo más probable es que venga; *Ironic* **a l. story!** ¡y yo me lo creo! **(b)** *(suitable)* apropiado(a), adecuado(a)

**2** *adv* **very l.** muy probablemente; **as l. as not** casi seguro, seguramente; *Fam* **not l.!** ¡ni hablar!

**like-minded** [laɪk'maɪndɪd] *adj* de mentalidad similar

**liken** ['laɪkən] *vt* comparar **(to** a *or* con)

**likeness** ['laɪknɪs] *n* **(a)** *(similarity)* parecido *m*; **a close l.** un parecido muy marcado; **family l.** parecido familiar **(b)** *(portrait)* retrato *m*

**likewise** ['laɪkwaɪz] *adv* *(similarly)* también, asimismo; **to do l.** hacer lo mismo

**liking** ['laɪkɪŋ] *n* **it's too sweet for my l.** es demasiado dulce para mi gusto; **is it to your l.?** ¿es de su agrado?; **to have a l. for sth** ser aficionado(a) a algo; **to take a l. to sth** aficionarse a algo; **to take a l. to sb** coger simpatía a alguien

**lilac** ['laɪlək] **1** *n* *(tree)* lilo *m*, lila *f*; *(flower)* lila *f*; *(colour)* lila *m*

**2** *adj* lila

**Lilo**® ['laɪləʊ] *(pl* **Lilos***)* *n* colchoneta *f* (inflable)

**lilt** [lɪlt] *n* modulación *f*, entonación *f*

**lilting** ['lɪltɪŋ] *adj* melodioso(a)

**lily** ['lɪlɪ] *n* lirio *m*; **l. of the valley** lirio de los valles

**lily-livered** ['lɪlɪlɪvəd] *adj* cobarde, pusilánime

**Lima** ['liːmə] *n* Lima

**lima bean** ['li:mə'bi:n] *n* judía *f* blanca (limeña)

**limb** [lɪm] *n* (**a**) *(of body)* miembro *m*; **to tear sb l. from l.** descuartizar a alguien (**b**) *(of tree)* rama *f*; *Fig* **to be out on a l.** quedarse más solo(a) que la una

**limber** ['lɪmbə(r)] *adj* flexible

▸**limber up** *vi* precalentar, hacer precalentamiento

**limbo** ['lɪmbəʊ] *n Rel* limbo *m*; *Fig* **to be in l.** *(person)* estar perdido(a); *(negotiations, project)* estar en el aire

**lime¹** [laɪm] *n (fruit)* lima *f*; *(citrus tree)* lima *f*, limero *m*; *(linden tree)* tilo *m*; **l. juice** zumo *m* de lima; **l. green** verde *m* lima

**lime²** *n Chem* cal *f*

**limelight** ['laɪmlaɪt] *n Fig* **to be in the l.** estar en el candelero

**limerick** ['lɪmərɪk] *n* = estrofa humorística de cinco versos

**limestone** ['laɪmstəʊn] *n (roca f)* caliza *f*

**limey** ['laɪmɪ] *(pl* **limeys)** *n US Fam (British person)* = término peyorativo para referirse a un británico

**limit** ['lɪmɪt] **1** *n* límite *m*; **within limits** dentro de un límite; **to be off limits** estar en una zona de acceso prohibido; **the limits of decency** los límites de la decencia; **to know no limits** no conocer límites; **he's/that's the l.!** ¡es el colmo!
  **2** *vt* limitar; **to l. oneself to sth** limitarse a algo

**limitation** [lɪmɪ'teɪʃən] *n* limitación *f*; **I know my limitations** conozco mis limitaciones

**limited** ['lɪmɪtɪd] *adj* limitado(a); *Com* **l. company** sociedad *f* (de responsabilidad) limitada; **l. edition** edición *f* limitada; *Law* **l. liability** responsabilidad *f* limitada

**limitless** ['lɪmɪtlɪs] *adj* ilimitado(a)

**limo** ['lɪməʊ] *(pl* **limos)** *n Fam* limusina *f*

**limousine** [lɪmə'zi:n] *n* limusina *f*

**limp¹** [lɪmp] **1** *n* cojera *f*; **to have a l.** cojear
  **2** *vi* cojear

**limp²** *adj (handshake, body)* lánguido(a), flojo(a); *(lettuce)* mustio(a); **to go l.** relajarse

**limpet** ['lɪmpɪt] *n* lapa *f*; **to stick like a l.** pegarse como una lapa; *Mil* **l. mine** mina *f* lapa, mina *f* magnética

**limpid** ['lɪmpɪd] *adj* límpido(a), cristalino(a)

**limply** ['lɪmplɪ] *adv (weakly)* lánguidamente, débilmente

**linchpin** ['lɪntʃpɪn] *n Fig (of team, policy)* pieza *f* clave

**linctus** ['lɪŋktəs] *n* jarabe *m* para la tos

**linden** ['lɪndən] *n* **l. (tree)** tilo *m*

**line¹** [laɪn] **1** *n* (**a**) *(in general)* línea *f*; *(on face)* arruga *f*; *Fig* **to draw the l. at doing sth** no estar dispuesto(a) a hacer algo; **l. drawing** dibujo *m (sin sombreado)*
  (**b**) *(row of people or things)* fila *f*; **to stand in a l.** formar una fila; *US* **to stand in l.** *(queue)* hacer cola; *Fig* **to get out of l.** *(be disobedient)* saltarse las normas; **to be in l. with sth** estar de acuerdo con algo; *Fig* **she is in l. for promotion** la van a ascender; *Fig* **to be on the l.** *(of job, reputation)* correr peligro; *Com Ind* **l. manager** gerente *mf* or jefe(a) *m,f* de línea
  (**c**) *(rope, for washing)* cuerda *f*; *(for fishing)* sedal *m*; *(telephone line)* línea *f*
  (**d**) *(railway track)* vía *f*; *(railway route)* línea *f*
  (**e**) *(direction)* **l. of argument** hilo *m* argumental; **l. of attack** línea or plan *m* de ataque; **l. of fire** *also Fig* línea de fuego; **on the same lines as** en la misma línea que; **to be on the right/wrong lines** estar en el buen/mal camino; **along the lines of…** en la (misma) línea que…
  (**f**) *(policy)* línea *f*, política *f*; **the party l.** la línea del partido; **to take a firm l. with sb** tener mano dura con alguien
  (**g**) *(of text)* línea *f*; *(of poem, song)* verso *m*; **to drop sb a l.** mandar unas letras or escribir a alguien; *Fig* **to learn one's lines** aprenderse el papel; *Fig* **to read between the lines** leer entre líneas
  (**h**) *(family)* línea *f*; **male/female l.** línea paterna/materna; **in (a) direct l.** por línea directa
  (**i**) *Fam (job)* especialidad *f*; **what l. (of business) are you in?** ¿a qué te dedicas?
  (**j**) *Com (of goods)* línea *f*
  **2** *vt (border)* bordear; **the crowd lined the street** la muchedumbre bordeaba la calle

**line²** *vt (provide with lining)* forrar; *Fig* **to l. one's pockets** *(enrich oneself)* forrarse

▸**line up 1** *vt sep* (**a**) *(form into a line)* alinear (**b**) *(prepare)* **have you got anyone lined up for the job?** ¿tienes algún candidato firme or a alguien pensado para el trabajo?; **have you got anything lined up for this evening?** ¿tienes algo pensado para esta noche?
  **2** *vi (form a line)* alinearse

**lineage** ['lɪnɪɪdʒ] *n* linaje *m*

**linear** ['lɪnɪə(r)] *adj* lineal; *Math* **l. equation** ecuación *f* lineal; *Comptr* **l. programming** programación *f* lineal

**lined¹** [laɪnd] *adj (paper)* de rayas, pautado(a); *(face)* arrugado(a)

**lined²** *adj (coat)* forrado(a) **(with)** de

**linen** ['lɪnɪn] *n* (**a**) *(fabric)* lino *m* (**b**) *(clothes)* ropa *f* blanca; *Fig* **dirty l.** trapos *mpl* sucios; **l. basket** cesto *m* de la ropa sucia

**liner** ['laɪnə(r)] *n (ship)* transatlántico *m*

**linesman** ['laɪnzmən] *n* juez *m* de línea, linier *m*

**line-up** ['laɪnʌp] *n (of team)* alineación *f*

**linger** ['lɪŋgə(r)] *vi (of person)* entretenerse; *(of smell, custom)* persistir; **to l. behind** rezagarse; **to l. over doing sth** quedarse haciendo algo

**lingerie** ['lɔ:nʒərɪ] *n* lencería *f*, ropa *f* interior femenina

**lingo** ['lɪŋgəʊ] *n Fam (language)* idioma *m*; *(jargon)* jerga *f*

**lingua franca** ['lɪŋgwə'fræŋkə] *n* lengua *f* or lingua *f* franca

**linguist** ['lɪŋgwɪst] *n (specialist in linguistics)* lingüista *mf*; *(polyglot)* políglota *mf*

**linguistic** [lɪŋ'gwɪstɪk] *adj* lingüístico(a)

**linguistics** [lɪŋ'gwɪstɪks] *n* lingüística *f*

**lining** ['laɪnɪŋ] *n (of coat)* forro *m*; *(of brakes, stomach)* revestimiento *m*

**link** [lɪŋk] **1** *n* **(a)** *(of chain)* eslabón *m*; *(connection)* conexión *f*, nexo *m* **(between** entre); *(between countries, people)* lazo *m*, vínculo *m*; *(road, railway line)* enlace *m*; *Fig* **the weak l.** *(in argument, team)* el punto débil **(b) links** *Sport* campo *m* de golf *(cerca del mar)*
**2** *vt (places)* enlazar, comunicar; *(facts, events, situations)* relacionar; *(computers, radio stations)* conectar; **she has been linked to** or **with the mafia** ha sido asociada con la mafia; **to l. hands** enlazar las manos
▶**link up 1** *vt Comptr* conectar
**2** *vi (of roads, travellers)* encontrarse **(with** con)

**lino** ['laɪnəʊ] *n Fam* linóleo *m*, sintasol® *m*

**linoleum** [lɪ'nəʊlɪəm] *n* linóleo *m*, sintasol® *m*

**linseed** ['lɪnsi:d] *n* linaza *f*; **l. oil** aceite *m* de linaza

**lintel** ['lɪntəl] *n* dintel *m*

**lion** ['laɪən] *n* león *m*; **the l.'s share** la mejor parte; **l. cub** cachorro *m* de león; **l. tamer** domador(ora) *m,f* de leones

**lioness** ['laɪənes] *n* leona *f*

**lion-hearted** ['laɪənhɑ:tɪd] *adj* valeroso(a), valiente

**lip** [lɪp] *n* **(a)** *(of mouth)* labio *m*; **to read sb's lips** leer los labios a alguien; **the government is only paying l. service to fighting crime** el Gobierno dice luchar or defiende que lucha contra la delincuencia **(b)** *(of jug)* pico *m* **(c)** *Fam (impudence)* **less of your l.!** ¡no seas impertinente!

**liposuction** ['lɪpəʊsʌkʃən] *n* liposucción *f*

**lip-read** ['lɪpri:d] *vi* leer los labios

**lipstick** ['lɪpstɪk] *n (substance)* carmín *m*, pintalabios *m inv*; *(stick)* barra *f* de labios

**liquefy** ['lɪkwɪfaɪ] **1** *vt* licuar
**2** *vi* licuarse

**liqueur** [lɪ'kjʊə(r)] *n* licor *m*

**liquid** ['lɪkwɪd] **1** *n* líquido *m*
**2** *adj* líquido(a); *Fin* **l. assets** activo *m* líquido or disponible; **l. crystal display** pantalla *f* de cristal líquido

**liquidate** ['lɪkwɪdeɪt] *vt (kill)* & *Fin* liquidar

**liquidation** [lɪkwɪ'deɪʃən] *n Fin* liquidación *f*; **to go into l.** *(of company)* ir a la quiebra

**liquidity** [lɪ'kwɪdɪtɪ] *n Fin* liquidez *f*; **l. ratio** coeficiente *m* or ratio *m* or *f* de liquidez

**liquidize** ['lɪkwɪdaɪz] *vt* licuar

**liquidizer** ['lɪkwɪdaɪzə(r)] *n* licuadora *f*

**liquor** ['lɪkə(r)] *n US* bebida *f* alcohólica, alcohol *m*; **l. store** tienda *f* de bebidas alcohólicas

**liquorice** ['lɪkərɪs] *n* regaliz *m*

**lira** ['lɪrə] *(pl* **lire** ['lɪrə]*) n (Italian, Turkish currency)* lira *f*

**Lisbon** ['lɪzbən] *n* Lisboa

**lisp** [lɪsp] **1** *n* ceceo *m*; **to have a l.** cecear
**2** *vi* cecear

**list¹** [lɪst] **1** *n* lista *f*
**2** *vt (enter in list)* **his phone number isn't listed in the directory** su número de teléfono no aparece or figura en la guía; **to l. names in alphabetical order** poner nombres en orden alfabético; **he listed his demands** enumeró sus exigencias; *Archit* **listed building** edificio *m* de interés histórico-artístico

**list²** [lɪst] *Naut* **1** *n* escora *f*
**2** *vi (of ship)* escorarse

**listen** ['lɪsən] *vi* escuchar; **to l. to sth/sb** escuchar algo/a alguien; **to l. for sth** estar pendiente or a la escucha de algo; **to l. to reason** atender a razones; **he wouldn't l.** no hizo (ningún) caso
▶**listen in** *vi* escuchar; **to l. in on/to sth** escuchar algo

**listener** ['lɪsnə(r)] *n* **(a) to be a good l.** saber escuchar **(b)** *(to radio programme)* oyente *mf*

**listeria** [lɪ'stɪərɪə] *n Med (illness)* listeriosis *f inv*; *(bacteria)* listeria *f*

**listing** ['lɪstɪŋ] *n (list)* listado *m*, lista *f*; **listings** *(in newspaper)* cartelera *f*; **listings magazine** = guía de espectáculos y actividades de ocio

**listless** ['lɪstlɪs] *adj* desfallecido(a), desmayado(a); **to be l.** estar desfallecido(a) or sin fuerzas

**lit** [lɪt] *pt* & *pp of* **light**

**litany** ['lɪtənɪ] *n (of complaints)* letanía *f*

**liter** *US =* **litre**

**literacy** ['lɪtərəsɪ] *n* alfabetización *f*; **l. rate** índice *m* de alfabetización

**literal** ['lɪtərəl] *adj* literal

**literally** ['lɪtərəlɪ] *adv* literalmente; **to take sth l.** tomar algo al pie de la letra; **it was l. this big!** ¡era sin exagerar así de grande!

**literary** ['lɪtərərɪ] *adj* literario(a)

**literate** ['lɪtərɪt] *adj (style)* culto(a); **to be l.** *(able to read and write)* saber leer y escribir

**literature** ['lɪtərɪtʃə(r)] *n (fiction, poetry)* literatura *f; (of academic subject)* bibliografía *f;* **Com** *(leaflets)* folletos *mpl,* prospectos *mpl*

**lithe** [laɪð] *adj* ágil

**lithium** ['lɪθɪəm] *n* **Chem** litio *m*

**lithograph** ['lɪθəgræf] *n* litografía *f*

**Lithuania** [lɪθjʊ'eɪnɪə] *n* Lituania

**Lithuanian** [lɪθjʊ'eɪnɪən] **1** *n* **(a)** *(person)* lituano(a) *m,f* **(b)** *(language)* lituano *m*
**2** *adj* lituano(a)

**litigant** ['lɪtɪgənt] *n* **Law** litigante *mf,* pleiteante *mf*

**litigate** ['lɪtɪgeɪt] *vi* **Law** litigar, pleitear

**litigation** [lɪtɪ'geɪʃən] *n* **Law** litigio *m,* pleito *m*

**litmus** ['lɪtməs] *n* **l. paper** papel *m* de tornasol; *Fig* **l. test** prueba *f* definitiva

**litre,** *US* **liter** ['liːtə(r)] *n* litro *m*

**litter** ['lɪtə(r)] **1** *n* **(a)** *(rubbish)* basura *f;* **l. bin** cubo *m* de basura; *Fam* **l. lout** = persona que arroja desperdicios en la vía pública **(b)** *(of animal)* camada *f* **(c)** *(for cat)* arena *f* absorbente; **l. tray** cama *for* bandeja *f* para la arena del gato
**2** *vt* **to be littered with** estar sembrado(a) *or* cubierto(a) de

**litterbug** ['lɪtəbʌg] *n* **Fam** = persona que arroja desperdicios en la vía pública

**little** ['lɪtəl] **1** *n* poco *m;* **a l. (bit)** un poco; **to eat l. or nothing** apenas comer; **he knows very l.** no sabe casi nada; **a l. issue** un tema candente **(b)** *(TV, radio broadcast)* en directo; **l. more** un poco más; **a l. hot/slow** un poco caliente/lento(a); **l. by l.** poco a poco; **every l. helps** todo cuenta aunque sea poco
**2** *adj* **(a)** *(small)* pequeño(a); **a l. girl** una niña pequeña; **a l. house** una casita; **wait a l. while!** ¡espera un poco!; **l. finger** (dedo *m*) meñique *m* **(b)** *(comparative* **less,** *superlative* **least)** *(not much)* poco(a); **a l. money/luck** un poco de dinero/suerte; **there is l. hope/doubt...** quedan pocas esperanzas/dudas...; **it makes l. sense** no tiene mucho sentido
**3** *adv (comparative* **less,** *superlative* **least)** poco; **l. known** poco conocido; **l. more than an hour ago** hace poco más de una hora; **that's l. short of bribery** eso es poco menos que un soborno; **l. did I think that...** poco me podía imaginar que...

**littoral** ['lɪtərəl] *n & adj* **Geog** litoral *m*

**liturgy** ['lɪtədʒɪ] *n* liturgia *f*

**live¹** [laɪv] **1** *adj* **(a)** *(person, animal)* vivo(a); *Fam* **a real l. filmstar** un estrella de carne y hueso; **a l. issue** un tema candente **(b)** *(TV, radio broadcast)* en directo; **l. performance** actuación *f* en vivo **(c)** *(ammunition) (unused)* sin utilizar; *(not blank)* real **(d)** **Elec** **l. wire** cable *m*

con corriente; *Fig* **she's a l. wire** rebosa energía
**2** *adv (to broadcast, perform)* en directo

**live²** [lɪv] **1** *vi* vivir; **to l. a happy/long life** vivir una vida feliz/larga; **it makes life worth living** hace que merezca la pena vivir; **to l. a lie** vivir en la mentira
**2** *vi* vivir; **to l. with sb** vivir con alguien; **as long as I l.** mientras viva; **I want to l. a little** quiero disfrutar un poco de la vida; **he lives by his writing** vive de lo que escribe; **l. and let l.** vive y deja vivir; **you l. and learn** ¡vivir para ver!

▸**live down** *vt sep (mistake, one's past)* relegar al olvido, enterrar; **I'll never l. it down** nunca lograré que se olvide

▸**live off** *vt insep (depend on)* vivir de

▸**live on 1** *vt insep (depend on)* vivir de; **it's not enough to l. on** no da para vivir
**2** *vi (continue to live) (of person)* sobrevivir, vivir; *(of memory)* perdurar

▸**live out** *vt sep* **she lived out her life** *or* **days in poverty/sadness** acabó sus días sumida en la pobreza/la tristeza; **to l. out a fantasy** vivir *or* realizar una fantasía

▸**live through** *vt insep (war, hard times)* sobrevivir a

▸**live together** *vi* vivir juntos(as)

▸**live up** *vt sep* **Fam** **to l. it up** pasarlo bien, divertirse

▸**live up to** *vt insep (expectations)* responder a, satisfacer; **to fail to l. up to expectations** no responder a las expectativas; **he lives up to his principles** vive de acuerdo con sus principios

**live-in** ['lɪvɪn] *adj (chauffeur, nanny)* interno(a); **she has a l. lover** su amante vive con ella

**livelihood** ['laɪvlɪhʊd] *n* sustento *m;* **to earn one's l.** ganarse la vida

**liveliness** ['laɪvlɪnɪs] *n (of person)* vivacidad *f,* viveza *f; (of place, debate)* animación *f*

**lively** ['laɪvlɪ] *adj (person, place, debate)* animado(a); *(interest)* vivo(a); **a l. mind** una mente despierta; *Fam* **to make things l. for sb** poner las cosas difíciles a alguien; *Fam* **look l.!** ¡vamos, muévete!

▸**liven up** ['laɪvən] **1** *vt sep* animar
**2** *vi* animarse

**liver** ['lɪvə(r)] *n* hígado *m*

**Liverpool** ['lɪvəpuːl] *n* Liverpool

**Liverpudlian** [lɪvə'pʌdlɪən] **1** *n* = natural *or* habitante de Liverpool
**2** *adj* de Liverpool

**livery** ['lɪvərɪ] *n* librea *f*

**livestock** ['laɪvstɒk] *n* ganado *m*

**livid** ['lɪvɪd] *adj* **(a)** *(angry)* **to be l. (with rage)** estar colérico(a) *or* enfurecido(a) **(b)** *(bluish-grey)* lívido(a), amoratado(a)

**living** ['lɪvɪŋ] **1** n (a) (way of life) vida f; **to be fond of good l.** ser aficionado a la buena vida; **l. conditions** condiciones fpl de vida; **l. expenses** gastos mpl (cotidianos); **l. room** sala f de estar, salón m (b) (livelihood) sustento m; **to earn one's l.** ganarse la vida; **what does he do for a l.?** ¿a qué se dedica?
**2** adj vivo(a); **she is our finest l. artist** es nuestra mejor artista viva; **there is not a l. soul to be seen** no se ve ni un alma; **the best/worst within l. memory** lo mejor/peor que se recuerda; Fam **to scare the l. daylights out of sb** dar un susto de muerte a alguien; Fam **to beat the l. daylights out of sb** dar una buena tunda a alguien

**lizard** ['lɪzəd] n (small) lagartija f; (large) lagarto m

**llama** ['lɑ:mə] n (animal) llama f

**lo** [ləʊ] exclam **lo and behold...** hete aquí que...

**load** [ləʊd] **1** n (a) (burden) carga f; **to share/spread the l.** compartir/repartir el trabajo; **that's a l. off my mind!** ¡me quito un peso de encima! (b) Fam (lot) **a l. of, loads of** un montón de; **it's a l. of rubbish!** (nonsense) ¡no son más que tonterías!; (very bad) ¡es nefasto(a) or de pena!; **we've got loads of time** tenemos tiempo de sobra
**2** vt & vi cargar
▸**load up** vt sep & vi cargar

**loaded** ['ləʊdɪd] adj (a) (lorry, gun) cargado(a); (dice) trucado(a); **to be l.** (of gun) estar cargado(a); **a l. question** una pregunta capciosa (b) Fam (rich) **to be l.** estar forrado(a)

**loading** ['ləʊdɪŋ] n (of lorry) carga f; **l. bay** zona f de carga y descarga

**loaf** [ləʊf] n (pl **loaves** [ləʊvz]) n pan m; **a l. of bread** (in general) un pan; (brick-shaped) un pan de molde; (round and flat) una hogaza de pan; Fig **use your l.!** ¡utiliza la mollera!
▸**loaf about, loaf around** vi haraganear, gandulear

**loafer** ['ləʊfə(r)] n (a) (person) haragán(ana) m,f, gandul(ula) m,f (b) US (shoe) mocasín m

**loam** [ləʊm] n humus m, mantillo m

**loan** [ləʊn] **1** n préstamo m; **to give sb a l. of sth** prestar algo a alguien; Fin **to take out a l.** obtener un préstamo o crédito; Fam **l. shark** usurero(a) m,f
**2** vt prestar

**loath** [ləʊθ] adj **to be l. to do sth** ser reacio(a) a hacer algo

**loathe** [ləʊð] vt odiar, detestar; **to l. doing sth** detestar hacer algo

**loathing** ['ləʊðɪŋ] n odio m, aborrecimiento m

**loathsome** ['ləʊðsəm] adj (person, character, behaviour) detestable, odioso(a)

**lob** [lɒb] **1** n (in tennis) globo m, lob m
**2** vt (pt & pp **lobbed**) (in tennis) hacer un globo or lob a

**lobby** ['lɒbɪ] **1** n (a) (of hotel) vestíbulo m (b) (pressure group) grupo m de presión, lobby m
**2** vt **to l. an MP** presionar a un diputado
**3** vi cabildear, presionar; **to l. for/against sth** hacer presión a favor de/en contra de algo

**lobbyist** ['lɒbɪɪst] n Pol miembro m de un lobby or grupo de presión

**lobe** [ləʊb] n (of ear, brain) lóbulo m

**lobotomy** [ləʊ'bɒtəmɪ] n lobotomía f

**lobster** ['lɒbstə(r)] n (with pincers) bogavante m; (spiny) l. langosta f; **he was as red as a l.** (sunburnt) estaba rojo como un cangrejo; **l. pot** nasa f

**local** ['ləʊkəl] **1** n (a) (person) **the locals** los lugareños, los paisanos (b) Fam (pub) bar m habitual
**2** adj local; **l. anaesthetic** anestesia f local; **l. government** gobierno m or administración f municipal; **l. newspaper** periódico m local

**locale** [ləʊ'kɑ:l] n emplazamiento m, lugar m

**locality** [ləʊ'kælɪtɪ] n vecindad f, zona f

**locally** ['ləʊkəlɪ] adv **I live/work l.** vivo/trabajo cerca

**locate** [ləʊ'keɪt] **1** vt (find) localizar; (situate) emplazar, ubicar
**2** vi (of company) instalarse, ubicarse

**location** [ləʊ'keɪʃən] n (a) (place) emplazamiento m, ubicación f; Cin **on l.** en exteriores; Cin **l. shot** toma f de exteriores (b) (act of finding) localización f

**loch** [lɒx] n Scot (lake) lago m; (inlet) ría f

**lock¹** [lɒk] **1** n (a) (on door) cerradura f; **to be under l. and key** estar encerrado(a) bajo siete llaves; Fig **l., stock and barrel** (in its entirety) íntegramente (b) (in wrestling) llave f, inmovilización f (c) (on canal) esclusa f
**2** vt (door, padlock) cerrar; **they were locked in each other's arms** estaban fundidos en un fuerte abrazo; Fig **to l. horns with sb** enzarzarse en una disputa con alguien
**3** vi (of door) cerrar; (of car-wheels) bloquearse
▸**lock in** vt sep encerrar
▸**lock out** vt sep dejar fuera; **I locked myself out of my flat** me dejé las llaves dentro de casa
▸**lock up 1** vt sep (person) encerrar; (valuables) guardar bajo llave; (house) cerrar or dejar cerrado(a) (con llave)
**2** vi cerrar (con llave)

**locker** ['lɒkə(r)] n (for luggage, in school) taquilla f; US **l. room** vestuarios mpl

**locket** ['lɒkɪt] n guardapelo m

**lockjaw** ['lɒkdʒɔː] n Old-fashioned tétanos m

**lockout** ['lɒkaʊt] n cierre m patronal

**locksmith** ['lɒksmɪθ] *n* cerrajero *m*

**lockup** ['lɒkʌp] *n* (a) *Br (for storage)* garaje *m* (b) *Fam (police cells)* calabozo *m*

**locomotion** [ləʊkə'məʊʃən] *n* locomoción *f*

**locomotive** [ləʊkə'məʊtɪv] 1 *n (train)* locomotora *f*
   2 *adj* locomotor(ora)

**locum** ['ləʊkəm] *n Br (doctor, vet)* suplente *mf*, sustituto(a) *m,f*

**locust** ['ləʊkəst] *n* langosta *f*

**locution** [ləʊ'kjuːʃən] *n* locución *f*

**lodge** [lɒdʒ] 1 *n (of porter)* garita *f*, portería *f*; *(of gatekeeper)* garita *f*, casa *f* del guarda; *(of beaver)* madriguera *f*; *(of masons)* logia *f*
   2 *vt (a) (accommodate)* hospedar, alojar (b) *Law* **to l. an appeal** presentar una apelación, apelar
   3 *vi (a) (live)* hospedarse, alojarse (b) *(become fixed)* alojarse; **the bullet had lodged in his lung** la bala se le había alojado en el pulmón; **the name had lodged in her memory** el nombre se le quedó grabado en la memoria

**lodger** ['lɒdʒə(r)] *n* huésped *mf*, huéspeda *f*

**lodging** ['lɒdʒɪŋ] *n* alojamiento *m*; **to take up lodgings** instalarse; **l. house** casa *f* de huéspedes

**loft** [lɒft] *n (attic)* buhardilla *f*, ático *m*

**lofty** ['lɒftɪ] *adj (aim, desire)* noble, elevado(a)

**log** [lɒg] 1 *n (a) (tree-trunk)* tronco *m*; *(firewood)* leño *m*; **to sleep like a l.** dormir como un tronco; **l. cabin** cabaña *f*; **l. fire** fuego *m* de leña (b) *(record)* registro *m*; *(of ship, traveller)* diario *m* de a bordo
   2 *vt (pt & pp* **logged)** *(record)* registrar
▸**log in** *vi Comptr* entrar
▸**log off** *vi Comptr* salir
▸**log on** = **log in**
▸**log out** = **log off**

**logarithm** ['lɒgərɪðəm] *n* logaritmo *m*

**logbook** ['lɒgbʊk] *n Naut* cuaderno *m* de bitácora

**loggerheads** ['lɒgəhedz] *n Fam* **to be at l. with sb** andar a la greña con alguien

**logic** ['lɒdʒɪk] *n* lógica *f*

**logical** ['lɒdʒɪkəl] *adj* lógico(a)

**logically** ['lɒdʒɪklɪ] *adv* lógicamente

**logistic(al)** [lɒ'dʒɪstɪk(əl)] *adj* logístico(a)

**logistics** [lɒ'dʒɪstɪks] *npl* logística *f*

**logjam** ['lɒgdʒæm] *n (in negotiations)* punto *m* muerto

**logo** ['ləʊgəʊ] *(pl* **logos)** *n* logotipo *m*

**loin** [lɔɪn] *n (a) (of person)* **loins** pubis *m inv*, bajo vientre *m* (b) *(of meat)* lomo *m*

**loincloth** ['lɔɪnklɒθ] *n* taparrabos *m inv*

**loiter** ['lɔɪtə(r)] *vi (delay)* entretenerse; *(suspiciously)* merodear; *Law* **to l. (with intent)** merodear

**lollipop** ['lɒlɪpɒp] *n (disc)* piruleta *f*; *(ball)* chupachúps® *m inv*; *Br Fam* **l. man/lady** = persona encargada de ayudar a cruzar la calle a los colegiales

**lollop** ['lɒləp] *vi Fam* **to l. along** avanzar con paso desgarbado

**lolly** ['lɒlɪ] *n Fam (a) (ice)* **l.** polo *m* (b) *(lollipop) (disc)* piruleta *f*; *(ball)* chupachúps® *m inv* (c) *Br (money)* pasta *f*

**London** ['lʌndən] 1 *n* Londres
   2 *adj* londinense

**Londoner** ['lʌndənə(r)] *n* londinense *mf*

**lone** [ləʊn] *adj (solitary)* solitario(a); **l. parent** madre *f* soltera, padre *m* soltero; **the L. Ranger** el Llanero Solitario; *Fig* **a l. wolf** una persona solitaria

**loneliness** ['ləʊnlɪnɪs] *n* soledad *f*

**lonely** ['ləʊnlɪ] *adj* solitario(a); **to feel very l.** sentirse muy solo(a); **l. hearts club** club *m* de contactos; *Journ* **l. hearts column** sección *f* de contactos

**loner** ['ləʊnə(r)] *n* solitario(a) *m,f*

**lonesome** ['ləʊnsəm] 1 *n Fam* **to be on one's l.** estar solito
   2 *adj US* solitario(a); **to be l.** *(of person)* estar solo(a)

**long¹** [lɒŋ] 1 *n* **the l. and the short of it is that…** el caso es que…
   2 *adj (a) (in size)* largo(a); **how l. is the table?** ¿cuánto mide *or* tiene la mesa de largo?; **it's 4 metres l.** mide *or* tiene cuatro metros de largo; **to go the l. way (round)** ir por el camino más largo; *Fig* **the best by a l. way** con mucho *or* de lejos el/la mejor; *Fig* **she'll go a l. way** llegará lejos; *Fig* **to go a l. way towards doing sth** contribuir mucho a hacer algo; *Fam* **to be l. on charm/good ideas** andar sobrado(a) de encanto/buenas ideas; **the l. arm of the law** el largo brazo de la ley; *Fig* **to have/pull a l. face** tener/poner cara triste; **it's a l. shot, but it's our only hope** es difícil que funcione, pero es nuestra única esperanza; **not by a l. shot** *or* **chalk** ni muchísimo menos; **l. johns** calzoncillos *mpl* largos; **l. jump** salto *m* de longitud
   (b) *(in time)* largo(a); **a l. time ago** hace mucho tiempo; **it's been a l. day** ha sido un día muy largo; **the days are getting longer** se están alargando los días; **three days at the longest** tres días como mucho; **it looks like being a l. job** parece que el trabajo va a llevar mucho tiempo; **to take a l. look at sth** mirar algo largamente; **in the l. term** *or* **run** a largo plazo, a la larga; **to have a l. memory** no olvidar con facilidad; **l. weekend** fin de semana *m* largo, puente *m* (corto)
   3 *adv (a) (for a long period)* durante mucho tiempo, mucho; **I didn't wait l.** no esperé

mucho; **I won't stay for l.** no me voy a quedar mucho tiempo; **it won't take l.** no llevará mucho tiempo; **she won't be l.** no tardará mucho; **l. live the King/Queen!** ¡viva el Rey/la Reina!; **as l. as** (providing) mientras, siempre que; **as l. as he is alive,...** mientras viva,...; **to think l. and hard (about sth)** reflexionar profundamente (sobre algo); **I have l. been convinced of it** llevo mucho tiempo convencido de ello; **how l. have you known her?** ¿cuánto (tiempo) hace que la conoces?; Fam **so l.!** ¡hasta luego!; **l. before/after** mucho antes/después; **l. ago** hace mucho (tiempo)

(b) (for the duration of) **all day/winter l.** todo el día/el invierno, el día/el invierno entero

(c) (idioms) **I could no longer hear him** ya no lo oía; **I couldn't wait any longer** no podía esperar más; **five minutes longer** cinco minutos más

**long²** vi **to l. to do sth** desear or anhelar hacer algo; **to l. for the day when...** desear que llegue el día en que...; **to l. for sth to happen** desear que ocurra algo; **a longed-for holiday** unas ansiadas vacaciones

**long³** Geog (abbr **longitude**) long., longitud f

**longboat** ['lɒŋbəʊt] n Hist chalupa f, lancha f de remos

**longbow** ['lɒŋbəʊ] n arco m

**long-distance** ['lɒŋ'dɪstəns] **1** adj **a l. (telephone) call** una conferencia; Br **l. lorry driver** camionero(a) m,f (que hace viajes largos); **a l. race** carrera f de fondo; **l. runner** corredor(ora) m,f de fondo

**2** adv **to telephone l.** poner una conferencia

**longevity** [lɒn'dʒevɪtɪ] n longevidad f

**long-forgotten** ['lɒŋfə'gɒtən] adj olvidado(a)

**longhaired** ['lɒŋ'heəd] adj de pelo largo

**longhorn** ['lɒŋhɔ:n] n US buey m colorado de Tejas

**longing** ['lɒŋɪŋ] n (in general) deseo m (**for** de), anhelo m (**for** de); (for home, family, old days) añoranza f (**for** de)

**longingly** ['lɒŋɪŋlɪ] adv con deseo, anhelantemente

**longitude** ['lɒndʒɪtju:d] n longitud f (coordenada)

**longitudinal** [lɒndʒɪ'tju:dɪnəl] adj longitudinal

**long-life** ['lɒŋ'laɪf] adj (battery, milk) de larga duración

**long-lost** ['lɒŋ'lɒst] adj perdido(a) tiempo atrás; **his l. brother returned** regresó su hermano al que no veía desde hacía mucho tiempo

**long-range** ['lɒŋ'reɪndʒ] adj (missile) de largo alcance; (forecast) a largo plazo

**longshoreman** [lɒŋ'ʃɔ:mən] n US estibador m

**long-sighted** [lɒŋ'saɪtɪd] adj hipermétrope

**long-sleeved** [lɒŋ'sli:vd] adj de manga larga

**long-standing** [lɒŋ'stændɪŋ] adj (arrangement, friendship) antiguo(a), viejo(a)

**long-suffering** [lɒŋ'sʌfərɪŋ] adj sufrido(a)

**long-term** ['lɒŋtɜ:m] adj a largo plazo; **the l. unemployed** los parados de larga duración; **l. planning** planificación f a largo plazo

**long-winded** [lɒŋ'wɪndɪd] adj prolijo(a)

**loo** [lu:] (pl **loos**) n Br Fam baño m, váter m; **l. paper** papel m higiénico or del váter

**loofah** ['lu:fə] n esponja f vegetal

**look** [lʊk] **1** n (a) (act of looking) **to have** or **take a l. at sth** mirar algo; **to have a l. for sth** buscar algo; **let me have a l.** déjame ver; **to have a l. round the town** (ir a) ver la ciudad; **to have a l. through some magazines** ojear unas revistas

(b) (glance) mirada f; **a suspicious/angry l.** una mirada recelosa/de enfado; **we got some very odd looks** nos miraron con cara rara; **if looks could kill...** si las miradas mataran...

(c) (appearance) aspecto m; Fig **I don't like the l. of this at all!** no me gusta nada el cariz or la pinta que tiene esto; Fig **I don't like the l. of him** me da mala espina; **I don't like the l. of those clouds** no me gusta la pinta de esas nubes; **by the l. of it** por lo que parece

(d) (personal appearance) (good) **looks** atractivo m, guapura f; **looks don't matter** la belleza no es lo principal

**2** vt **I can never l. him in the face again** nunca podré volver a mirarlo a la cara; **to l. sb up and down** mirar a alguien de arriba abajo; **l. what you've done!** ¡mira lo que has hecho!; **l. where you're going!** ¡mira por dónde vas!

**3** vi (a) (in general) mirar, Am ver; **to l. at sth/sb** mirar algo/a alguien; **he's not much to l. at** no es gran cosa, es del montón; Fig **to l. the other way** hacer la vista gorda; **I'm just looking, thank you** (in shop) sólo estoy mirando; **to l. on the bright side** mirar el lado bueno (de las cosas); **to l. to the future** mirar al futuro; **l. here!** ¡mire usted!; **(now) l.!** ¡mira!; **I don't l. at it that way** yo no lo miro de esa manera; Prov **l. before you leap** hay que pensar las cosas dos veces (antes de hacerlas)

(b) (search) **to l. for sth/sb** buscar algo/a alguien; **we've looked everywhere** hemos buscado por todas partes

(c) (seem, appear) parecer; **to l. old/ill** parecer viejo/enfermo; **she looks tired** parece cansada; **things are looking good/bad** las cosas van bien/mal; **he doesn't l. his age** no aparenta la edad que tiene; **to l. the part** dar la talla; **what does she l. like?** ¿cómo es?, ¿qué aspecto tiene?; **to l. like sb** parecerse a alguien; **it looks like** or **as if...** parece que or como si...; **it looks like rain** parece que va a llover; **you l. as if you've slept badly** tienes aspecto de haber dormido mal

▸**look after** vt insep (person, property, possessions) cuidar; (process, arrangements, finances) hacerse cargo de

▸**look around** vi **I went into the centre of town to l. around** fui al centro a dar una vuelta; **I've been looking around for something better** he estado buscando para ver si encontraba algo mejor

▸**look back** vi (a) (in space) mirar atrás, volver la vista atrás (b) (in time) **to l. back on sth** recordar algo; **he has never looked back since that day** desde ese día no ha hecho más que progresar

▸**look down** vi (from above) mirar hacia abajo; (lower one's eyes) bajar la mirada or la vista; Fig **to l. down on sb** desdeñar a alguien

▸**look forward** vt insep **to l. forward to sth** (party, event) estar deseando que llegue algo; **I was looking forward to my holidays/a good breakfast** tenía muchas ganas de coger las vacaciones/de un buen desayuno; **I really looking forward to this film** creo que esta película va a ser muy buena; **I'm looking forward to our next meeting in April** confío en que nuestra próxima reunión de abril será de sumo interés; **I'm sure we're all looking forward to a productive couple of days' work** seguro que vamos a disfrutar de dos días de fructífero trabajo; **to l. forward to doing sth** estar deseando hacer algo, tener muchas ganas de hacer algo; **I l. forward to hearing from you** (in letter) quedo a la espera de recibir noticias suyas

▸**look in** vi **to l. in (on sb)** (visit) hacer una visita (a alguien)

▸**look into** vt insep (investigate) investigar, examinar

▸**look on 1** vt insep (consider) considerar; **to l. on sth/sb as...** considerar algo/a alguien...; **I l. on her as a friend** la considero una amiga
   **2** vi quedarse mirando

▸**look out 1** vt sep **to l. sth out for sb** encontrar algo para or a alguien
   **2** vi mirar; **to l. out of the window** mirar por la ventana; **l. out!** (be careful) ¡cuidado!

▸**look out for** vt insep (a) (look for) buscar (b) (be on guard for) estar al tanto de

▸**look over** vt insep mirar por encima, repasar

▸**look round = look around**

▸**look through** vt (a) (inspect) examinar (b) (not see) **she looked straight through me** miró hacia mí, pero no me vio

▸**look to** vt insep (a) (rely on) **to l. to sb (for sth)** dirigirse a alguien (en busca de algo) (b) **we must l. to the future** debemos mirar hacia el futuro

▸**look up 1** vt sep (in dictionary, address book) buscar; **to l. sb up** (visit) visitar a alguien
   **2** vi (from below) mirar hacia arriba; (raise one's eyes) levantar la mirada or la vista; Fig **things are looking up** las cosas están mejorando

▸**look upon** vt insep (consider) considerar

▸**look up to** vt insep admirar

**lookalike** ['lʊkəlaɪk] n doble mf

**look-in** ['lʊkɪn] n Fam (chance) **he won't get a l.** no tendrá ninguna oportunidad

**looking-glass** ['lʊkɪŋɡlɑːs] n Old-fashioned espejo m

**lookout** ['lʊkaʊt] n (person) centinela mf, vigilante mf; **to keep a l. for sth/sb** estar alerta por si se ve algo/a alguien; **to be on the l. for sth/sb** estar buscando algo/a alguien; Fam **that's your l.!** ¡allá tú!; **l. post** puesto m de vigilancia; **l. tower** atalaya f

**loom¹** [luːm] n (for making cloth) telar m

**loom²** vi cernerse, cernirse; **dangers l. ahead** los peligros nos acechan; **to l. large** cobrar relevancia; **with the elections/exams looming large,...** con las elecciones/los exámenes a la vuelta de la esquina,...

**loony** ['luːnɪ] Fam **1** n chalado(a) m,f, lunático(a) m,f; **l. bin** frenopático m, loquero m
   **2** adj (person) chalado(a), lunático(a); (idea) disparatado(a)

**loop** [luːp] **1** n bucle m
   **2** vt (string) enrollar; **to l. sth around sth** enrollar algo alrededor de algo; Av **to l. the loop** rizar el rizo

**loophole** ['luːphəʊl] n (in law) resquicio m legal

**loopy** ['luːpɪ] adj Fam (person) majareta, chiflado(a); (idea) disparatado(a); **to be l.** (of person) estar majareta or chiflado(a)

**loose** [luːs] **1** n **to be on the l.** andar suelto(a)
   **2** adj (tooth, animal, connection) suelto(a); (piece of clothing) suelto(a), holgado(a); (skin) colgante; (alliance, network) informal; (translation) poco exacto(a); (morals, lifestyle) disoluto(a); (sweets, olives) suelto(a), a granel; **to come l.** aflojarse; **to let sb l. on sth** dar rienda suelta a alguien en algo; **don't let him l. in the kitchen!** ¡no lo dejes suelto en la cocina!; **they let the riot police l. on the crowd** soltaron a los antidisturbios entre la multitud; **to let l. a torrent of abuse** soltar una sarta de improperios; **l. change** (dinero m) suelto m; **to be at a l. end** no tener nada que hacer; Fig **to tie up the l. ends** (in investigation) atar cabos sueltos; **l. living** vida f disoluta or disipada; **l. talk**

indiscreciones *fpl*; **a l. woman** una mujer fácil

**3** *vt Literary (arrow)* disparar

**4** *adv* **to buy sth l.** comprar algo a granel

▶**loose off** *vt (fire)* disparar

**loose-fitting** ['luːsfɪtɪŋ] *adj* suelto(a), holgado(a)

**loose-leaf** ['luːsliːf] *adj* **l. binder** *or* **folder** cuaderno *m* *or* carpeta *f* de anillas

**loose-limbed** ['luːslɪmd] *adj* suelto(a)

**loosely** ['luːslɪ] *adv* **(a) l. attached** flojo(a), **l. packed** *(snow, earth)* suelto(a) **(b)** *(roughly)* aproximadamente, vagamente; **l. speaking** hablando en términos generales; **l. translated** traducido(a) muy libremente

**loosen** ['luːsən] **1** *vt (screw, knot, belt)* aflojar; *(restrictions)* suavizar; **to l. one's grip** soltar, aflojar la presión; **to l. sb's tongue** soltar la lengua a alguien

**2** *vi* aflojarse

▶**loosen up** *vi (relax)* relajarse

**loot** [luːt] **1** *n (booty)* botín *m*; *Fam (money)* pasta *f*

**2** *vt* saquear

**looter** ['luːtə(r)] *n* saqueador(ora) *m,f*

**looting** ['luːtɪŋ] *n* saqueo *m*, pillaje *m*

**lopsided** [lɒp'saɪdɪd] *adj* torcido(a); **a l. grin** una sonrisa torcida

**loquacious** [lɒ'kweɪʃəs] *adj* locuaz

**lord** [lɔːd] **1** *n* **(a)** *(aristocrat)* señor *m*, lord *m*; *Br* **the (House of) Lords** la cámara de los lores; **the l. Mayor** el alcalde *(en Londres y en algunos otros municipios)* **(b)** *Rel* **the L.** el Señor; **the L.'s Prayer** el padrenuestro; *Fam* **good L.!** ¡Dios mío!; *Fam* **L. knows if…** sabe Dios si…

**2** *vt* **to l. it over sb** tratar despóticamente a alguien

**lordly** ['lɔːdlɪ] *adj* altanero(a)

**lordship** ['lɔːdʃɪp] *n* señoría *f*; **Your L.** (su) Señoría

**lore** [lɔː(r)] *n* tradición *f*

**lorry** ['lɒrɪ] *n Br* camión *m*; *Fam Euph* **it fell off the back of a l.** *(was stolen)* es de trapicheo; **l. driver** camionero(a) *m,f*

**Los Angeles** [lɒs'ændʒəliːz] *n* Los Ángeles

**lose** [luːz] *(pt & pp* **lost** [lɒst]) **1** *vt* **(a)** *(accidentally)* perder; **you have nothing to l.** no tienes nada que perder; **to l. one's voice** quedarse afónico(a); **he had lost interest in his work** había perdido el interés por su trabajo; **it loses something in translation** al traducirlo, pierde algo; **to be lost at sea** desaparecer *o* morir en el mar; **the joke/the irony was lost on him** no entendió el chiste/la ironía; **my watch loses five minutes a day** mi reloj se atrasa cinco minutos al día; **that mistake lost him the match** ese error hizo que perdiera el partido; **to l. one's way, to get lost** perderse; *Fam* **get lost!** ¡lárgate!, ¡piérdete!; **to l. one's**

**balance** perder el equilibrio; **to l. sight of sth/sb** perder algo/a alguien de vista; *Fam Fig* **you've lost me!** *(I don't understand)* no te sigo

**(b)** *(deliberately)* **to l. weight** adelgazar, perder peso; **we lost him in the crowd** le dimos esquinazo entre la multitud; **she had lost herself in a book/in her work** se quedó absorta en la lectura de un libro/en su trabajo

**2** *vi (in contest)* perder; **to l. in value** perder valor

▶**lose out** *vi* salir perdiendo **(to** en beneficio de**); to l. out on sth** salir perdiendo en algo

**loser** ['luːzə(r)] *n (in contest)* perdedor(ora) *m,f*; **to be a good/bad l.** ser buen/mal perdedor(ora); **he's a (born) l.** es un fracasado

**losing** ['luːzɪŋ] *adj* **to fight a l. battle** luchar por una causa perdida; **the l. side** los vencidos

**loss** [lɒs] *n* **(a)** *(in general)* pérdida *f*; **there was great l. of life** hubo muchas víctimas mortales; **to suffer heavy losses** *(casualties)* sufrir muchas bajas (mortales); **it's no great l.** no es una gran pérdida; **without l. of face** sin perder la dignidad; **to be at a l. to explain…** no saber cómo explicar…; **she's never at a l. for an answer** siempre sabe qué contestar

**(b)** *(financial)* **losses** pérdidas *fpl*; **to make a l.** tener pérdidas; **to sell at a l.** vender con pérdidas; **to cut one's losses** reducir pérdidas; **l. leader** reclamo *m* de ventas

**loss-making** ['lɒsmeɪkɪŋ] *adj* con pérdidas

**lost** [lɒst] **1** *adj* perdido(a); **to be l.** estar perdido(a); **to seem** *or* **look l.** *(confused)* tener un aire perdido(a); **to give sth/sb up for l.** dar algo/a alguien por perdido(a); **l. cause** causa *f* perdida; **l. property** objetos *mpl* perdidos; **l. property office** oficina *f* de objetos perdidos

**2** *pt & pp of* **lose**

**lot** [lɒt] **1** *n* **(a)** *(large quantity)* **a l.** *(singular)* mucho; *(plural)* muchos(as); **a l. of** *(singular)* mucho(a); *(plural)* muchos(as); **a l.** *or* **lots of questions** muchas preguntas; **a l.** *or* **lots of people** mucha gente; **I saw quite a l. of her in Paris** la vi mucho en París; **we had a l.** *or* **lots of fun** nos divertimos mucho; **the l.** todo; **I bought the l.** lo compré todo; *Fam* **listen, you l.!** ¡oíd, vosotros!; *Fam* **that l. next door** los de al lado; *Fam* **he's a bad l.** es un mal bicho

**(b)** *(destiny)* fortuna *f*, suerte *f*; **to draw** *or* **cast lots for sth** echar algo a suertes; **he was happy with his l.** estaba contento con su suerte; **to throw in one's l. with** compartir la suerte de alguien, unir (uno) su suerte a la de alguien

**(c)** *(piece of land)* terreno *m*; *(at auction)* lote *m*; **in lots** por lotes

**2** *adv* **a l.** mucho; **a l. bigger** mucho más grande; **thanks a l.** muchas gracias

**lotion** ['ləʊʃən] *n* loción *f*

**lottery** ['lɒtərɪ] n lotería f; Fig **it's a l.** es una lotería; Br **the National L.** ≃ la lotería primitiva; **l. ticket** billete m de lotería

**lotto** ['lɒtəʊ] n (game) = juego parecido al bingo

**lotus** ['ləʊtəs] n loto m; **l. position** posición f del loto

**loud** [laʊd] **1** adj **(a)** (noise, bang, explosion) fuerte; (voice, music, radio) alto(a); Pej (person) escandaloso(a); **to be l. in one's praise/condemnation of sth** elogiar/condenar algo rotundamente **(b)** (colour, clothes) chillón(ona)
**2** adv alto; **to think out l.** pensar en alto; **louder!** ¡más alto!; **l. and clear** alto y claro

**loudhailer** [laʊd'heɪlə(r)] n megáfono m

**loudly** ['laʊdlɪ] adv alto

**loud-mouth** ['laʊdmaʊθ] n Fam **to be a l.** ser un/una bocazas

**loud-mouthed** ['laʊdmaʊðd] adj Fam bocazas (inv)

**loudness** ['laʊdnɪs] n (of noise, bang, explosion) fuerza f, intensidad f; (of voice, music, radio) volumen m (alto)

**loudspeaker** [laʊd'spiːkə(r)] n altavoz m

**lounge** [laʊndʒ] **1** n (in house, hotel) salón m; (in airport) sala f (de espera); **l. bar** bar m (de categoría); **l. suit** traje m de calle
**2** vi holgazanear, gandulear
►**lounge about, lounge around** vi holgazanear, gandulear

**louse** [laʊs] n (pl lice [laɪs]) n (a) (insect) piojo m **(b)** Fam (person) sinvergüenza mf, rufián m

**lousy** ['laʊzɪ] adj Fam pésimo(a), horroroso(a); **to feel l.** sentirse fatal; **a l. trick** una jugarreta; **we had a l. time on holiday** lo pasamos fatal or de pena durante las vacaciones

**lout** [laʊt] n gamberro m

**loutish** ['laʊtɪʃ] adj gamberro(a), grosero(a)

**louvred door** ['luːvəˈdɔː(r)] n puerta f (tipo) persiana or de listones

**lovable** ['lʌvəbəl] adj adorable, encantador(ora)

**love** [lʌv] **1** n (a) (between lovers or members of a family) amor m; **to fall in l. with sb** enamorarse de alguien; **to be in l. with sb** estar enamorado(a) de alguien; **to make l. with** or **to sb** (have sex) hacer el amor con or a alguien; Old-fashioned **to make l. to sb** (court) cortejar a alguien; **the l. of my life** el amor de mi vida; **it was l. at first sight** fue un flechazo; **(my) l.** (term of endearment) mi amor; **a l.-hate relationship** una relación de amor y odio; **l. affair** aventura f (amorosa); Euph **l. child** hijo(a) m,f natural; **l. letter** carta f de amor; **l. life** vida f amorosa; **l. match** matrimonio m por amor; **l. nest** nido m de amor; **l. song** canción f de amor; **l. story** historia f de amor
**(b)** (affection) cariño m; **l. of one's country**

cariño por el propio país; **give my l. to your parents** saluda a tus padres de mi parte; **with l. from…** (at end of letter) con cariño,…; **Bill sends his l.** Bill manda recuerdos; **there's no l. lost between them** se llevan mal; **I wouldn't do it for l. or money** no lo haría por nada del mundo
**(c)** (liking, interest) afición f (**of** or **for** a or por); **to do sth for the l. of it** hacer algo por gusto or afición
**(d)** (in tennis) nada, cero
**2** vt amar, querer; **I l. you** te quiero; **I l. Chinese food** me encanta la comida china; **they l. to go for walks, they l. going for walks** les encanta ir de paseo; **I'd l. to come** me encantaría ir

**lovebird** ['lʌvbɜːd] n Fam **a pair of lovebirds** un par de tórtolos

**lovebite** ['lʌvbaɪt] n chupetón m, señal f (de un mordisco)

**loveless** ['lʌvlɪs] adj sin amor, carente de amor

**lovely** ['lʌvlɪ] adj (weather, idea, smell) estupendo(a), fabuloso(a); (curtains, room, garden) precioso(a), Am lindo(a); (person) encantador(ora); **to have a l. time** pasárselo estupendamente; Fam **it's l. and warm** hace un tiempo fabuloso; **Clara's coming – oh l.!** viene Clara – ¡estupendo!

**lovemaking** ['lʌvmeɪkɪŋ] n relaciones fpl sexuales; **a night of passionate l.** una noche de pasión

**lover** ['lʌvə(r)] n (of person) amante mf; (of nature, good food) amante mf, aficionado(a) mf

**lovesick** ['lʌvsɪk] adj con mal de amores, enfermo(a) de amor

**lovey-dovey** ['lʌvɪ'dʌvɪ] adj Fam almibarado(a)

**loving** ['lʌvɪŋ] adj cariñoso(a), afectuoso(a)

**low¹** [ləʊ] **1** n (a) Met zona f de bajas presiones
**(b)** (minimum) mínimo m; **to reach a new l.** (of price, popularity) alcanzar un nuevo mínimo; (of country, reputation) caer aún más bajo; **an all-time l.** un mínimo histórico
**2** adj (a) (not high, not loud) bajo(a); **fuel is getting l.** nos estamos quedando sin combustible; **our stock of food is rather l.** nos queda bastante poca comida; **to cook sth over a l. heat** cocinar algo a fuego lento; **a l. bow** una reverencia profunda; **of l. birth** de baja extracción; **the lower classes** las clases bajas; Mil **lower ranks** soldados mpl rasos or de rango inferior; **to have a l. opinion of sb** tener mala opinión de alguien; Fig **a l. blow** un golpe bajo; **the L. Countries** los Países Bajos; **a l. neckline** un escote amplio; **l. tide** marea f baja
**(b)** (depressed) **to feel l.** estar un poco deprimi-

do(a)

**(c)** *(ignoble)* **the lowest of the l.** lo más bajo; **that's a l. trick!** ¡eso es una mala pasada!

**3** *adv (to hang, aim)* bajo; **to bow l.** hacer una reverencia profunda; **to fly l.** volar bajo; **the l. paid** los que perciben salarios bajos; **turn the music/the lights down l.** baja la música/las luces; **we're running l. on fuel/food** nos estamos quedando sin combustible/comida

**low²** [lɔʊ] *vi (of cattle)* mugir

**lowbrow** ['lɔʊbraʊ] *adj (tastes, interests)* vulgar, de las masas; **l. novelist** novelista *mf* populachero(a)

**low-budget** [lɔʊ'bʌdʒɪt] *adj (film, holiday)* de bajo presupuesto

**low-calorie** [lɔʊ'kælərɪ] *adj* bajo(a) en calorías

**low-cost** [lɔʊ'kɒst] *adj* de bajo coste

**low-cut** [lɔʊ'kʌt] *adj (dress)* escotado(a)

**low-down** ['lɔʊdaʊn] *Fam n* **to give sb the l. on sth** explicar de pe a pa a alguien los pormenores de algo

**lower¹** ['lɔʊə(r)] *vt (in general)* bajar; *(flag, sail)* arriar; **to l. one's guard** bajar la guardia; **he lowered his voice** bajó la voz; **to l. oneself into sth** entrar en algo; **to l. oneself onto sth** bajar hasta algo; *Fig* **to l. oneself to do sth** rebajarse a hacer algo

**lower²** ['lɑʊə(r)] *vi (of person)* mirar amenazadoramente; *(of sky)* estar tormentoso(a)

**low-flying** ['lɔʊ'flaɪŋ] *adj* que vuela bajo

**low-grade** ['lɔʊ'greɪd] *adj (in quality)* de baja calidad

**low-key** [lɔʊ'kiː] *adj* discreto(a)

**lowlands** ['lɔʊlənd] *npl* tierras *fpl* bajas; **the L.** *(of Scotland)* las Tierras Bajas de Escocia

**low-level** ['lɔʊ'levəl] *adj* **(a)** *(discussion)* de bajo nivel **(b)** **l. radiation** radiación *f* de baja intensidad

**lowly** ['lɔʊlɪ] *adj* humilde

**low-lying** ['lɔʊ'laɪŋ] *adj (area, mist)* bajo(a)

**low-spirited** ['lɔʊ'spɪrɪtɪd] *adj* desanimado(a)

**low-tech** ['lɔʊtek] *adj* rudimentario(a), elemental

**loyal** ['lɔɪəl] *adj* leal, fiel

**loyalist** ['lɔɪəlɪst] *n & adj (to government, party)* leal *mf*, adicto(a) *m,f*; *Br Pol (in Northern Ireland)* lealista *mf*

**loyally** ['lɔɪəlɪ] *adv* lealmente, fielmente

**loyalty** ['lɔɪəltɪ] *n* lealtad *f*, fidelidad *f*; **you'll have to decide where your loyalties lie** tienes que decidir con quién estás; **she had divided loyalties** sus lealtades estaban divididas; **l. card** tarjeta *f* or carné *m* de cliente

**lozenge** ['lɒzɪndʒ] *n (shape)* rombo *m*; *(cough sweet)* pastilla *f* para la tos

**LP** [el'piː] *n (abbr* **long player)** LP *m*, elepé *m*

**LSD** [eles'diː] *n (abbr* **lysergic acid diethylamide)** LSD *m*

**Lt** *Mil (abbr* **Lieutenant)** Tte., teniente *m*

**lt** *(abbr* **litres)** l.

**Ltd** *Br Com (abbr* **limited)** S.L.

**lubricant** ['luːbrɪkənt] *n* lubricante *m*

**lubricate** ['luːbrɪkeɪt] *vt* lubricar

**lubrication** [luːbrɪ'keɪʃən] *n* lubricación *f*

**lucid** ['luːsɪd] *adj* lúcido(a)

**luck** [lʌk] *n (chance)* suerte *f*; **(good) l.** (buena) suerte; **bad l.** mala suerte; **he couldn't believe his l.** no podía creerse la suerte que tenía; **to bring sb good/bad l.** traer buena/mala suerte a alguien; **good l.!** ¡(buena) suerte!; **to wish sb l.** desear suerte a alguien; **to be in l.** estar de suerte; **to be out of l.** no tener suerte; **to be down on one's l.** no estar de suerte; **to try one's l.** probar suerte; **to push one's l.** tentar a la suerte; **don't push your l.!** *(said in annoyance)* ¡no me busques las cosquillas!; **some people have all the l.** hay quien nace con estrella; **just my l.!** ¡qué mala suerte!; **no such l.!** ¡ojalá!; **with any l. he'll still be there** con un poco de suerte, todavía estará allí

**luckily** ['lʌkɪlɪ] *adv* por suerte, afortunadamente

**lucky** ['lʌkɪ] *adj (person)* afortunado(a); **to be l.** tener suerte; **to make a l. guess** adivinarlo por casualidad; *Fam* **(you) l. devil!, (you) l. beggar!** ¡qué suertudo(a)!; *Ironic* **you'll be l.!** ¡ni lo sueñes!; **it's l. you came when you did** fue una suerte que llegaras en ese momento; **she's l. to be alive** tiene suerte de estar con vida; **my l. number** mi número de la suerte; **it's not my l. day** hoy no es mi día de suerte; **that was l.** ¡qué suerte!; **to strike it l.** tener suerte; **l. charm** amuleto *m*; *Br* **l. dip** caja *f* de sorpresas; **you can thank your l. stars she didn't see you!** ¡da gracias al cielo porque no te vio!

**lucrative** ['luːkrətɪv] *adj* lucrativo(a)

**lucre** ['luːkə(r)] *n Pej or Hum (money)* vil metal *m*; **to do sth for filthy l.** hacer algo por el vil metal

**ludicrous** ['luːdɪkrəs] *adj* ridículo(a)

**lug** [lʌg] *(pt & pp* **lugged)** *vt Fam* arrastrar, cargar con

**luggage** ['lʌgɪdʒ] *n* equipaje *m*; **a piece of l.** un bulto (de equipaje); **l. label** etiqueta *f* identificativa del equipaje; **l. locker** taquilla *f* (para el equipaje); **l. rack** *(in train, bus)* portaequipajes *m inv*; *(on car)* baca *f*; *Br* **l. van** *(on train)* furgón *m* de equipajes

**lughole** ['lʌghəʊl] *n Br very Fam* oreja *f*

**lugubrious** [luː'guːbrɪəs] *adj* lúgubre

**lukewarm** ['luːkwɔːm] *adj (water, response)* tibio(a); **she was rather l. about my suggestion** recibió mi sugerencia con bastante tibieza

**lull** [lʌl] **1** *n (in conflict)* tregua *f*; *(in conversation)* pausa *f*; *Fig* **the l. before the storm** la calma que precede a la tormenta

**2** *vt* **to l. sb to sleep** dormir a alguien; **to l. sb into a false sense of security** dar a alguien una falsa sensación de seguridad

**lullaby** ['lʌləbaɪ] *n* nana *f*, canción *f* de cuna

**lumbago** [lʌm'beɪɡəʊ] *n* lumbago *m*

**lumbar** ['lʌmbə(r)] *adj Anat* lumbar

**lumber** ['lʌmbə(r)] **1** *n* (a) *Br (junk)* trastos *mpl* (viejos); **l. room** trastero *m* (b) *US (wood)* madera *f*, maderos *mpl*

**2** *vt* **to l. sb with sth** hacerle a alguien cargar con algo; **I got lumbered with a huge bill** me hicieron pagar una factura enorme

**3** *vi* **to l. about** *or* **around** caminar pesadamente

**lumbering** ['lʌmbərɪŋ] *adj (walk)* pesado(a)

**lumberjack** ['lʌmbədʒæk] *n* leñador(ora) *m,f*

**luminary** ['luːmɪnərɪ] *n* figura *f*, lumbrera *f*

**luminous** ['luːmɪnəs] *adj (in general)* luminoso(a); *(strip, roadsign)* reflectante; *(colour, socks)* fluorescente, fosforito(a)

**lump** [lʌmp] **1** *n* (a) *(of earth, sugar)* terrón *m*; *(of stone, coal)* trozo *m*; *(in sauce)* grumo *m*; *(on head)* chichón *m*; *(on breast)* bulto *m*; *Fig* **it brought a l. to my throat** *(made me sad)* me hizo sentir un nudo en la garganta; *Fin* **l. sum** pago *m* único, suma *f* global (b) *Fam (person)* zoquete *m*, tarugo *m*

**2** *vt* (a) *(group)* **all such payments were lumped under "additional expenses"** todos esos pagos estaban agrupados bajo el epígrafe de "gastos adicionales"; **you shouldn't l. them together just because they're brothers** no deberías tratarlos de la misma manera sólo porque sean hermanos (b) *Fam (endure)* **you'll just have to (like it or) l. it!** ¡no te queda más remedio que aguantar!

**lumpy** ['lʌmpɪ] *adj (sauce)* grumoso(a), lleno(a) de grumos; *(mattress)* lleno(a) de bultos

**lunacy** ['luːnəsɪ] *n* locura *f*, demencia *f*; *Fam* **it's sheer l.** ¡es demencial!

**lunar** ['luːnə(r)] *adj* lunar; **l. eclipse** eclipse *m* de luna; **l. landing** alunizaje *m*

**lunatic** ['luːnətɪk] **1** *n* loco(a) *m,f*, lunático(a) *m,f*; **l. asylum** manicomio *m*

**2** *adj (idea, behaviour)* demencial; **the l. fringe** el sector fanático *or* intransigente

**lunch** [lʌntʃ] **1** *n* comida *f*, almuerzo *m*; **to have l.** comer, almorzar; *Fam* **to be out to l.** *(be crazy)* estar chalado(a); **l. hour** hora *f* de comer

**2** *vi* comer, almorzar

**luncheon** ['lʌntʃən] *n* (a) *Formal* almuerzo *m*, comida *f* (b) **l. meat** fiambre *m* de lata; **l. voucher** vale *m* de comida

**lung** [lʌŋ] *n* pulmón *m*; **to shout at the top of one's lungs** gritar a pleno pulmón; **l. cancer** cáncer *m* de pulmón

**lunge** [lʌndʒ] **1** *n* embestida *f*, acometida *f*; **to make a l. for sb/sth** embestir contra alguien/algo

**2** *vi* **to l. at sb (with sth)** embestir contra alguien (con algo)

**lupin** ['luːpɪn] *n* altramuz *m*

**lurch** [lɜːtʃ] **1** *n (of ship, car)* bandazo *m*; **a l. to the right/left** *(of politician, party)* un giro brusco a la derecha/izquierda; *Fam* **to leave sb in the l.** dejar a alguien en la estacada

**2** *vi (of ship, car)* dar bandazos; *(of person)* tambalearse; **to l. to the left/right** *(of politician, party)* dar un giro brusco a la izquierda/derecha

**lure** ['lʊə(r)] **1** *n (attraction)* atractivo *m*; **she was drawn by the l. of the big city** la sedujo el reclamo de la gran ciudad

**2** *vt (into trap, ambush)* atraer (**into** hasta); **nothing could l. her away from the computer** nada conseguía alejarla del ordenador

**lurid** ['lʊərɪd] *adj* (a) *(sensational)* provocador(ora); *(shocking)* espeluznante; **in l. detail** con macabra precisión (b) *(gaudy)* chillón(ona)

**lurk** [lɜːk] *vi* estar al acecho; **a doubt still lurked in his mind** su mente todavía albergaba una duda

**luscious** ['lʌʃəs] *adj (woman)* voluptuoso(a); *(fruit)* jugoso(a)

**lush** [lʌʃ] *adj (vegetation, garden)* exuberante; *(offices, furniture)* lujoso(a)

**lust** [lʌst] *n (sexual)* lujuria *f*; *Fig (for power, knowledge)* sed *f*, ansia *f* (**for** de)

►**lust after** *vt insep* **to l. after sb** beber los vientos por alguien; **to l. after sth** desvivirse por *or* ansiar algo

**luster** *US* = **lustre**

**lustful** ['lʌstfʊl] *adj* lujurioso(a)

**lustre**, *US* **luster** ['lʌstə(r)] *n* lustre *m*

**lustrous** ['lʌstrəs] *adj* lustroso(a)

**lusty** ['lʌstɪ] *adj (person)* lozano(a), vigoroso(a); *(cry)* sonoro(a)

**lute** [luːt] *n* laúd *m*

**Lutheran** ['luːθərən] *n & adj* luterano(a) *m,f*

**Luxemb(o)urg** ['lʌksəmbɜːɡ] *n* Luxemburgo

**Luxemburger** ['lʌksəmbɜːɡər] *n* luxemburgués(esa) *m,f*

**luxuriant** [lʌɡ'zjʊərɪənt] *adj* exuberante

**luxuriate** [lʌɡ'zjʊərɪeɪt] *vi* deleitarse (**in** con)

**luxurious** [lʌɡ'zjʊərɪəs] *adj* lujoso(a)

**luxury** ['lʌkʃərɪ] **1** *n* lujo *m*; **a life of l.** una vida llena de lujos

**2** *adj (car, flat)* de lujo

**LW** *Rad* (*abbr* **Long Wave**) LW, OL
**lychee** [lar'tʃi:] *n* lichi *m*
**lying** ['laɪŋ] **1** *n* mentiras *fpl*
  **2** *adj* mentiroso(a), embustero(a)
**lymph** [lɪmf] *n Anat* linfa *f*; **l. node** ganglio *m* linfático
**lynch** [lɪntʃ] *vt* linchar
**lynching** ['lɪntʃɪŋ] *n* linchamiento *m*

**lynx** [lɪŋks] *n* lince *m*
**lyre** ['laɪə(r)] *n* (*musical instrument*) lira *f*
**lyric** ['lɪrɪk] *adj* lírico(a)
**lyrical** ['lɪrɪkəl] *adj* lírico(a)
**lyricism** ['lɪrɪsɪzəm] *n* lirismo *m*
**lyricist** ['lɪrɪsɪst] *n* letrista *mf*
**lyrics** ['lɪrɪks] *npl* letra *f*

# M

**M¹, m** [em] *n (letter)* M, m *f*

**M²** *Br Aut (abbr* **motorway***)* A, autopista *f*

**m³** (**a**) *(abbr* **metre(s)***)* m, metro *m* (**b**) *(abbr* **mile(s)***)* milla *f*

**MA** [em'eɪ] *n Univ (abbr* **Master of Arts***)* máster *m (de Humanidades)*; **to have an MA in linguistics** tener un máster en Lingüística; **Frederick Watson, MA** Frederick Watson, licenciado con máster (en letras)

**ma** [mɑː] *n Fam* mamá *f*

**ma'am** [mɑːm] *n Old-fashioned* señora *f*

**mac** [mæk] *n Fam (raincoat)* impermeable *m*, gabardina *f*

**macabre** [mə'kɑːbə(r)] *adj* macabro(a)

**macaroni** [mækə'rəʊnɪ] *n* macarrones *mpl*; **m. cheese** macarrones con queso

**macaroon** [mækə'ruːn] *n* mostachón *m*

**macaw** [mə'kɔː] *n* guacamayo *m*

**Mace®** [meɪs] *n (spray)* aerosol *m* antivioladores

**mace¹** [meɪs] *n (weapon, symbol of office)* maza *f*

**mace²** *n (spice)* macis *f inv*

**Macedonia** [mæsə'dəʊnɪə] *n* Macedonia

**Macedonian** [mæsə'dəʊnɪən] **1** *n* (**a**) *(person)* macedonio(a) *m,f* (**b**) *(language)* macedonio *m*
**2** *adj* macedonio(a)

**Mach** [mæk] *n Phys* **M. (number)** *(número m de)* Mach *m*

**machete** [mə'ʃetɪ] *n* machete *m*

**Machiavellian** [mækɪə'velɪən] *adj* maquiavélico(a)

**machinations** [mæʃɪ'neɪʃənz] *npl* maquinaciones *fpl*

**machine** [mə'ʃiːn] **1** *n* máquina *f*; **he's a m.!** ¡es (como) una máquina!; **party/propaganda m.** aparato *m* del partido/propagandístico; *Comptr* **m. code** código *m* máquina; **m. gun** ametralladora *f*; *Comptr* **m. language** lenguaje *m* máquina; **m. shop** taller *m* de máquinas; **m. tool** máquina *f* herramienta
**2** *vt* (**a**) *Ind* producir a máquina (**b**) *(with sewing machine)* coser a máquina

**machine-gun** [mə'ʃiːngʌn] *(pt & pp* **machine-gunned***) vt* ametrallar

**machine-readable** [mə'ʃiːn'riːdəbəl] *adj Comptr* legible para el ordenador

**machinery** [mə'ʃiːnərɪ] *n also Fig* maquinaria *f*

**machinist** [mə'ʃiːnɪst] *n (operator)* operario(a) *m,f*

**machismo** [mæ'tʃɪzməʊ] *n* machismo *m*

**macho** ['mætʃəʊ] *adj (remark, attitude)* muy de macho; **to be m.** *(of person)* (presumir de) ser muy macho

**macintosh = mackintosh**

**mackerel** ['mækrəl] *n* caballa *f*

**mackintosh** ['mækɪntɒʃ] *n* impermeable *m*, gabardina *f*

**macro** ['mækrəʊ] *(pl* **macros***) n Comptr* macro *m or f*

**macrobiotic** [mækrəʊbaɪ'ɒtɪk] *adj* macrobiótico(a); **a m. diet** una dieta macrobiótica

**macrobiotics** ['mækrəʊbaɪ'ɒtɪks] *n* macrobiótica *f*

**macroeconomics** ['mækrəʊiːkə'nɒmɪks] *n (subject)* macroeconomía *f*

**mad** [mæd] *adj* (**a**) *(insane) (person)* loco(a); *(idea)* disparatado(a); *(dog)* rabioso(a); **to be m.** *(of person)* estar loco(a); **to go m.** volverse loco(a); **as m. as a hatter** más loco(a) que una cabra; **m. with fear** aterrorizado(a); **there was a m. rush for the door** la gente se precipitó como loca hacia la puerta; *Fam* **to run/shout/work like m.** correr/gritar/trabajar como (un/una) loco(a); *Fam* **m. cow disease** el mal *or* la enfermedad de las vacas locas
(**b**) *Fam (enthusiastic)* **to be m. about sth** estar loco(a) por algo
(**c**) *Fam (angry)* enfadado(a); **to be m. with** *or* **at sb** estar muy enfadado(a) con alguien

**Madagascan** [mædə'gæskən] *n & adj* malgache *mf*

**Madagascar** [mædə'gæskə(r)] *n* Madagascar

**madam** ['mædəm] *n (as form of address)* señora *f*; *Br Fam* **she's a proper little m.** *(of child)* es una señoritinga

**madcap** ['mædkæp] *adj (scheme, idea)* disparatado(a)

**madden** ['mædən] *vt* sacar de quicio, exasperar

**maddening** ['mædənɪŋ] *adj* irritante, exasperante

**made** [meɪd] *pt & pp of* **make**

**Madeira** [mə'dɪərə] *n (island)* (la isla de) Madeira; *(wine)* (vino *m* de) Madeira

**made-to-measure** ['meɪdtə'meʒə(r)] *adj* a medida

**made-up** [meɪ'dʌp] *adj* (a) *(story, excuse)* inventado(a) (b) *(lips)* pintado(a); *(face)* maquillado(a); **to be heavily m.** ir muy maquillado(a)

**madhouse** ['mædhaʊs] *n Fam (lunatic asylum)* manicomio *m*, casa *f* de locos; *Fig* **this place is a m.!** ¡esto es una casa de locos!

**madly** ['mædlɪ] *adv* (a) *(insanely)* enloquecidamente (b) *(desperately) (to rush, struggle)* como loco(a) (c) *Fam (extremely)* tremendamente; **m. in love** locamente enamorado(a)

**madman** ['mædmən] *n* loco *m*, demente *m*

**madness** ['mædnɪs] *n* locura *f*, demencia *f*; **it's sheer m.!** ¡es una locura!

**Madrid** [mə'drɪd] *n* Madrid

**madwoman** ['mædwʊmən] *n* loca *f*, demente *f*

**maelstrom** ['meɪlstrəm] *n also Fig* torbellino *m*

**maestro** ['maɪstrəʊ] *(pl* **maestros**) *n* maestro *m*

**mafia** ['mæfɪə] *n* mafia *f*

**mag** [mæg] *n Fam* revista *f*

**magazine** [mægə'ziːn] *n* (a) *(publication)* revista *f*; **m. programme** *(on radio, TV)* magazine *m*, programa *m* de variedades (b) *(for gun)* recámara *f*; *(ammunition store)* polvorín *m*

**magenta** [mə'dʒentə] *n & adj* magenta *m*

**maggot** ['mægət] *n* larva *f*, gusano *m*

**Maghreb** [mæ'greb] *n* **the M.** el Magreb

**Maghrebi** [mæ'grebɪ] *n & adj* magrebí *mf*

**Magi** ['meɪdʒaɪ] *npl* **the M.** los Reyes Magos

**magic** ['mædʒɪk] **1** *n* magia *f*; **as if by m.** como por arte de magia; **black/white m.** magia negra/blanca
**2** *adj* (a) mágico(a); **m. wand** varita *f* mágica (b) *Fam (excellent)* genial

▶**magic away** *(pt & pp* **magicked**) *vt sep* hacer desaparecer

**magical** ['mædʒɪkəl] *adj* mágico(a)

**magician** [mə'dʒɪʃən] *n* mago(a) *m,f*

**magisterial** [mædʒɪs'tɪərɪəl] *adj (domineering)* autoritario(a); *(authoritative)* magistral

**magistrate** ['mædʒɪstreɪt] *n Law* juez *mf* de primera instancia; **magistrates' court** juzgado *m* de primera instancia

**magnanimity** [mægnə'nɪmɪtɪ] *n* magnanimidad *f*

**magnanimous** [mæg'nænɪməs] *adj* magnánimo(a)

**magnate** ['mægneɪt] *n* magnate *mf*

**magnesium** [mæg'niːzɪəm] *n Chem* magnesio *m*

**magnet** ['mægnɪt] *n* imán *m*; *Fig (for tourists, investors)* foco *m* de atracción

**magnetic** [mæg'netɪk] *adj (force, pole)* magnético(a); *Fig (personality)* cautivador(ora); **m. compass** brújula *f*

**magnetism** ['mægnɪtɪzəm] *n also Fig* magnetismo *m*

**magnification** [mægnɪfɪ'keɪʃən] *n* ampliación *f*; **a lens with a m. of 7** una lente de siete aumentos

**magnificence** [mæg'nɪfɪsəns] *n* magnificencia *f*

**magnificent** [mæg'nɪfɪsənt] *adj* magnífico(a)

**magnify** ['mægnɪfaɪ] *vt (of lens, telescope)* ampliar, aumentar; *(exaggerate)* magnificar, desorbitar

**magnifying glass** ['mægnɪfaɪɪŋ'glɑːs] *n* lupa *f*

**magnitude** ['mægnɪtjuːd] *n* magnitud *f*; **a problem of the first m.** un problema de primer orden

**magnolia** [mæg'nəʊlɪə] *n* magnolia *f*

**magnum** ['mægnəm] *n* = botella de vino o champán de 1,5 litros

**magpie** ['mægpaɪ] *n* urraca *f*; *Fig* **he's a bit of a m.** parece un trapero

**mahogany** [mə'hɒgənɪ] **1** *n (wood)* caoba *f*; *(colour)* (color *m*) caoba *m*
**2** *adj* de caoba

**maid** [meɪd] *n* (a) *(servant)* sirvienta *f*; **m. of honour** dama *f* de honor (b) *Literary (girl)* doncella *f*

**maiden** ['meɪdən] **1** *n Literary (girl)* doncella *f*
**2** *adj (flight)* inaugural; **m. aunt** tía *f* soltera; **m. name** apellido *m* de soltera; *Parl* **m. speech** primer discurso *m* como parlamentario(a)

**mail¹** [meɪl] **1** *n (postal system)* correo *m*; *(letters or parcels received)* correspondencia *f*; **it came in the m.** vino en el correo; *Comptr* **m. merge** fusión *f* de correo; *Com* **m. order** venta *f* por correo; **m. train** tren *m* correo
**2** *vt* enviar *or* mandar (por correo)

**mail²** *n (armour)* malla *f*

**mailbag** ['meɪlbæg] *n* saca *f* de correos; **she gets a huge m.** *(of celebrity, politician)* recibe muchísimas cartas

**mailbox** ['meɪlbɒks] *n US* buzón *m* (de correos); *Comptr* buzón *m*

**mailing** ['meɪlɪŋ] *n (mailshot)* mailing *m*; **m. list** lista *f* de direcciones *(para envío de publicidad)*

**mailshot** ['meɪlʃɒt] *n (leaflet)* carta *f* publicitaria; *(campaign)* mailing *m*

**maim** [meɪm] *vt* lisiar

**main** [meɪn] **1** *n* (a) *(pipe)* tubería *f* general *f*; *(cable)* cable *m* principal; **the mains** *(water, gas)* la (tubería) general; *(electricity)* la red eléctrica **(b)** in the m. *(generally)* en general

**2** *adj* principal; **the m. thing is to...** lo principal es...; **m. entrance** entrada *f* principal; *Gram* **m. clause** oración *f* principal; **m. course** plato *m* principal; *Rail* **m. line** línea *f* principal; **m. road** carretera *f* general; **m. street** calle *f* principal

**mainframe** ['meɪnfreɪm] *n Comptr* ordenador *m* central

**mainland** ['meɪnlænd] *n* tierra *f* firme; **m. Europe** la Europa continental; **on the m.** en tierra firme; **he escaped from Mull to the Scottish m.** escapó de la isla de Mull hacia tierra firme escocesa

**mainline** ['meɪnlaɪn] *vi very Fam (inject drugs)* picarse, chutarse

**mainly** ['meɪnlɪ] *adv* principalmente; **the accident was caused m. by carelessness** la imprudencia fue la principal causa del accidente; **the passengers were m. Spanish** los pasajeros eran en su mayoría españoles

**mainspring** ['meɪnsprɪŋ] *n (of clock, watch)* muelle *m* real, resorte *m* principal; *Fig (of change, revolution)* móvil *m* principal

**mainstay** ['meɪnsteɪ] *(pl* **mainstays**) *n (of economy, philosophy)* pilar *m* fundamental

**mainstream** ['meɪnstriːm] **1** *n* corriente *f* principal *or* dominante

**2** *adj (politics, ideas, tastes)* convencional; *(movie, literature)* comercial

**maintain** [meɪn'teɪn] *vt* mantener; **to m. (that)...** mantener *or* sostener que...

**maintenance** ['meɪntənəns] *n* **(a)** *(of car, equipment, roads)* mantenimiento *m;* **m. costs** costes *mpl* de mantenimiento **(b)** *Law (alimony)* pensión *f* (alimenticia)

**maisonette** [meɪzə'net] *n* dúplex *m inv*

**maize** [meɪz] *n* maíz *m,* *Am* elote *m,* *CSur* choclo *m*

**Maj (a)** *Mil (abbr* **Major)** comandante *m* **(b)** *Mus (abbr* **Major)** mayor

**majestic** [mə'dʒestɪk] *adj* majestuoso(a)

**majesty** ['mædʒəstɪ] *n* majestuosidad *f;* **His/Her/Your M.** Su Majestad

**major** ['meɪdʒə(r)] **1** *n* **(a)** *Mil* comandante *m;* **m. general** general *m* de división **(b)** *US Univ (subject)* especialidad *f*

**2** *adj* **(a)** *(important)* importante, de primer orden; **of m. importance** de enorme importancia **(b)** *Mus* mayor

**3** *vi US Univ* **to m. in** *(subject)* especializarse en

**Majorca** [mə'jɔːkə] *n* Mallorca

**Majorcan** [mə'jɔːkən] *n & adj* mallorquín(ina) *m,f*

**majority** [mə'dʒɒrɪtɪ] *n* **(a)** *(in vote)* mayoría *f;* **to be in a** *or* **the m.** ser mayoría; **m. decision** decisión *f* por mayoría; *Fin* **m. interest** partici-

pación *f* mayoritaria; *Pol* **m. rule** gobierno *m* mayoritario; *Law* **m. verdict** veredicto *m* mayoritario; *Pol* **m. vote** votación *f* por mayoría **(b)** *Law (age)* mayoría *f* de edad

**make** [meɪk] **1** *n* **(a)** *(brand)* marca *f*

**(b)** *Fam* **to be on the m.** *(financially)* buscar sólo el propio beneficio; *(sexually)* ir a ligar

**2** *vt* *(pt & pp* **made** [meɪd]) **(a)** *(produce, prepare, perform)* hacer; *(payment, transaction)* realizar, efectuar; *(speech)* pronunciar; *(decision)* tomar; *(mistake)* cometer; **to m. a promise** hacer una promesa; **made in Spain** fabricado(a) en España; **made from** *or* **out of...** hecho con *or* de...; *Fam* **I'll show them what I'm made of** les voy a demostrar quién soy yo; *Fam* **I'm not made of money!** ¡que no soy millonario(a) *or* de oro!; **to m. something of oneself** convertirse en una persona de provecho; **two and two m. four** dos y dos son cuatro; **to m. a choice** elegir; **to m. a difference** cambiar mucho las cosas (a mejor); **it doesn't m. any difference** da lo mismo; **to m. a noise** hacer ruido; **to m. trouble** crear problemas

**(b)** *(earn) (money)* ganar; **to m. a living** ganarse la vida; **to m. a name for oneself** crearse *or* labrarse una reputación

**(c)** *(cause to be successful)* **to m. it** *(be successful)* tener éxito, llegar a la cima; **you've got it made** lo tienes todo hecho; **this book made her** este libro le dio la fama; **it's m. or break** es la hora de la verdad; **it made my day** me alegró el día

**(d)** *(cause to be)* hacer; **to m. sb happy** hacer feliz a alguien; **to m. sb sad** entristecer a alguien; **to m. sb hungry** dar hambre a alguien; **to m. sb tired** cansar a alguien; **that made me angry** eso me enfadó; **to m. sb a present of sth** regalar algo a alguien

**(e)** *(compel)* **to m. sb do sth** hacer que alguien haga algo; **they made us wear suits** nos obligaron a llevar traje; **don't m. me laugh!** ¡no me hagas reír!

**(f)** *(estimate, calculate)* **what time do you m. it?** ¿qué hora tienes?; **I m. it £50 in total** calculo un total de 50 libras

**(g)** *(reach) Fam* **to m. it** *(arrive in time)* llegar (a tiempo); *(finish in time)* terminar a tiempo; **to m. the charts** *(of record)* llegar a las listas de éxitos; **to m. the first team** *(be selected)* conseguir entrar en el primer equipo

**(h)** *(become, be)* ser; **he'll m. a good doctor/singer** será un buen médico/cantante

**(i)** *(manage to attend) (show, meeting)* llegar a; **I can m. 2 o'clock** puedo estar allí para las dos

**3** *vi* **(a)** *(act)* **to m. as if** *or* **as though to do sth** hacer como si se fuera a hacer algo

**(b)** **to m. do** arreglárselas; **to m. believe (that)...** imaginarse que...

(c) **to m. sure** or **certain (of sth)** asegurarse (de algo)

▶**make after** vt insep **to m. after sb** (chase) salir en persecución de alguien

▶**make for** vt insep (a) (head towards) dirigirse hacia (b) (contribute to) facilitar, contribuir a

▶**make of** vt sep what do you m. of the new manager? ¿qué te parece el nuevo jefe?; I don't know what to m. of that remark no sé cómo interpretar ese comentario

▶**make off** vi Fam (leave) largarse

▶**make off with** vt insep Fam (steal) largarse con, llevarse

▶**make out 1** vt sep (a) (write) (list) elaborar, hacer; (cheque) extender (b) Fam (claim) **to m. out (that)...** decir or pretender que... (c) (understand, decipher) entender; (see) distinguir; (hear) oír

**2** vi US Fam (sexually) meterse mano, darse el lote

▶**make over** vt sep she has made the estate over to her granddaughter ha nombrado a su nieta heredera de sus propiedades

▶**make up 1** vt sep (a) (story, excuses) inventar

(b) (deficit, loss) enjugar, recuperar; I'll m. it up to you later, I promise te prometo que te recompensaré (por ello) más adelante

(c) (complete) (team, amount) completar

(d) (form) formar, componer; **the community is made up primarily of old people** la comunidad se compone principalmente de ancianos; **to m. up one's mind** decidirse

(e) (put together) (list) elaborar, hacer; (parcel, bed) hacer; (prescription) preparar

(f) (apply make-up to) **to m. oneself up** maquillarse

**2** vi (end quarrel) reconciliarse

▶**make up for** vt insep (losses) compensar; (lost time) recuperar

**make-believe** ['meɪkbɪliːv] **1** n **to live in the land of m.** vivir en un mundo de fantasías

**2** adj ficticio(a)

**makeover** ['meɪkəʊvə(r)] n renovación f or cambio m de imagen

**maker** ['meɪkə(r)] n (a) (manufacturer) fabricante mf (b) **to meet one's M.** entregar el alma a Dios

**makeshift** ['meɪkʃɪft] adj improvisado(a)

**make-up** ['meɪkʌp] n (a) (cosmetics) maquillaje m; **m. artist** maquillador(ora) m,f; **m. bag** bolsa f del maquillaje; **m. remover** desmaquillador m (b) (composition) (of team, group) composición f; (of person) temperamento m, carácter m

**making** ['meɪkɪŋ] n (of goods) fabricación f, manufactura f; **the film was three years in the m.** llevó tres años realizar la película; **this is history in the m.** se está haciendo historia (aquí y ahora); **a musician in the m.** un músico en ciernes; **the problem is of her own m.** el problema se lo ha buscado ella; **he has the makings of an actor** tiene madera de actor

**maladjusted** [mælə'dʒʌstɪd] adj inadaptado(a)

**maladroit** [mælə'drɔɪt] adj torpe, desacertado(a)

**malady** ['mælədɪ] n mal m

**Malaga** ['mæləgə] n Málaga

**Malagasy** ['mæləgæsɪ] **1** n (language) malgache m

**2** adj malgache

**malaise** [mæ'leɪz] n malestar m

**malaria** [mə'leərɪə] n malaria f

**Malawi** [mə'lɑːwɪ] n Malaui

**Malawian** [mə'lɑːwɪən] n & adj malauita mf

**Malay** [mə'leɪ] n & adj malayo(a) m,f

**Malaysia** [mə'leɪzɪə] n Malaisia

**Malaysian** [mə'leɪzən] n & adj malaisio(a) m,f

**Maldives** ['mɔːldiːvz] npl **the M.** las Maldivas

**male** [meɪl] **1** n (person) varón m, hombre m; (animal) macho m

**2** adj (person) masculino(a); (animal) macho; **m. chauvinism** machismo m; **m. nurse** enfermero m

**malefactor** ['mælɪfæktə(r)] n Literary malhechor(ora) m,f

**malevolence** [mə'levələns] n malevolencia f

**malevolent** [mə'levələnt] adj malévolo(a)

**malformed** [mæl'fɔːmd] adj (organ, baby) con malformación, deforme

**malfunction** [mæl'fʌŋkʃən] **1** n mal funcionamiento m

**2** vi averiarse

**Mali** ['mɑːlɪ] n Mali

**malice** ['mælɪs] n malicia f; Law **with m. aforethought** con premeditación y alevosía

**malicious** [mə'lɪʃəs] adj malicioso(a)

**maliciously** [mə'lɪʃəslɪ] adv maliciosamente

**malign** [mə'laɪn] **1** adj perjudicial, pernicioso(a)

**2** vt difamar

**malignant** [mə'lɪgnənt] adj (person, tumour) maligno(a)

**malinger** [mə'lɪŋgə(r)] vi fingir una enfermedad (para no ir a trabajar)

**malingerer** [mə'lɪŋgərə(r)] n = persona que se finge enferma (para no ir a trabajar)

**mall** [mɔːl] n US centro m comercial

**mallard** ['mælɑːd] n ánade m real

**malleable** ['mælɪəbəl] adj (person, metal) maleable

**mallet** ['mælɪt] n mazo m

**mallow** ['mæləʊ] n (plant) malva f

**malnutrition** [mælnjuːˈtrɪʃən] *n* desnutrición *f*

**malpractice** [mælˈpræktɪs] *n* negligencia *f* (*profesional*)

**malt** [mɔːlt] *n* malta *f*; **m. vinegar** vinagre *m* de malta; **m. whisky** whisky *m* de malta

**Malta** [ˈmɔːltə] *n* Malta

**Maltese** [mɔːlˈtiːz] **1** *n* (**a**) (*person*) maltés(esa) *m,f* (**b**) (*language*) maltés *m*
**2** *npl* (*people*) **the M.** los malteses
**3** *adj* maltés(esa); **M. cross** cruz *f* de Malta

**maltreat** [mælˈtriːt] *vt* maltratar

**maltreatment** [mælˈtriːtmənt] *n* maltrato *m*, malos tratos *mpl*

**mammal** [ˈmæməl] *n* mamífero *m*

**mammary** [ˈmæmərɪ] *adj Anat* mamario(a); **m. glands** mamas *fpl*, glándulas *fpl* mamarias

**mammography** [mæˈmɒgrəfɪ] *n Med* mamografía *f*

**mammoth** [ˈmæməθ] **1** *n* (*animal*) mamut *m*
**2** *adj* (*huge*) gigantesco(a), enorme; (*task*) ingente

**mammy** [ˈmæmɪ] *n Fam* mamá *f*

**man** [mæn] **1** *n* (*pl* **men** [men]) (**a**) (*adult male*) hombre *m*; *Fam* **hey m.!** ¡oye, tío!; **a m.'s jacket/bicycle** una cazadora/bicicleta de hombre; **the army will make a m. of him** el ejército lo hará un hombre; **he took it like a m.** lo aceptó como un hombre; **this will separate the men from the boys** así se verá quién vale de verdad; **to be m. enough to do sth** tener el valor suficiente para hacer algo; **to talk to sb m. to m.** hablar con alguien de hombre a hombre; **he's just the m. for the job** es el hombre indicado (para el trabajo); **to be one's own m.** ser dueño de sí mismo; **he's a m.'s m.** le gustan las cosas de hombres; **the m. in the street** el hombre de la calle; **a m. of God** un clérigo; **a m. of the world** un hombre de mundo
(**b**) (*individual, person*) persona *f*, hombre *m*; **any m.** cualquiera; **few men** pocos, pocas personas; **they replied as one m.** respondieron como un solo hombre; **they were patriots to a m.** hasta el último de ellos era un patriota
(**c**) (*husband*) marido *m*; **to live as m. and wife** vivir como marido y mujer
(**d**) (*humanity*) el hombre
(**e**) (*employee*) (*in factory*) empleado(a) *m,f*; (*servant*) criado *m*; (*soldier*) hombre *m*; **our m. in Rome** (*spy*) nuestro agente en Roma; (*diplomat*) nuestro representante en Roma; (*reporter*) nuestro corresponsal en Roma
(**f**) (*in chess*) pieza *f*; (*in draughts*) ficha *f*
**2** *vt* (*pt & pp* **manned**) (*machine*) manejar; (*plane, boat*) tripular; (*phone, reception desk*) atender; **a manned flight** un vuelo tripulado

**manacles** [ˈmænəkəlz] *npl* (*for hands*) esposas *fpl*; (*for feet*) grilletes *mpl*

**manage** [ˈmænɪdʒ] **1** *vt* (**a**) (*company, hotel, project*) dirigir; (*the economy, resources*) gestionar, administrar; (*shop*) llevar (**b**) (*deal with*) (*situation*) manejar, tratar; **to m. to do sth** conseguir hacer algo; **to know how to m. sb** saber cómo tratar a alguien; **I can't m. three suitcases** no puedo con tres maletas; **£100 is the most that I can m.** no puedo dar más de 100 libras; **can you m. dinner on Thursday?** ¿puedes venir el jueves a cenar?
**2** *vi* (*cope*) arreglárselas; **to m. without sb/sth** arreglárselas sin alguien/algo; **he'll never m. on his own** no lo podrá hacer él solo

**manageable** [ˈmænɪdʒəbəl] *adj* (*object, hair*) manejable; (*level, proportions*) razonable; (*task*) realizable, factible

**management** [ˈmænɪdʒmənt] *n* (**a**) (*activity*) (*of company, project*) dirección *f*, gestión *f*; (*of economy, resources*) gestión *f*, administración *f*; **m. consultant** consultor(ora) *m,f* en administración de empresas; **m. studies** estudios *mpl* de gestión empresarial *o* administración de empresas; **m. style** estilo *m* de dirección·
(**b**) (*managers, employers*) **the m.** la dirección; **under new m.** (*sign*) nuevos propietarios; **m. and unions** la patronal y los sindicatos; **m. buyout** = adquisición de una empresa por sus directivos; **m. team** equipo *m* de dirección

**manager** [ˈmænɪdʒə(r)] *n* (*of bank, company*) director *m*; (*of shop, bar*) encargado *m*; (*of boxer, singer*) representante *mf*, manager *mf*; (*of football team*) entrenador(ora) *m,f*

**manageress** [mænɪdʒəˈres] *n* (*of bank, company*) directora *f*; (*of shop, bar*) encargada *f*

**managerial** [mænɪˈdʒɪərɪəl] *adj* de gestión, directivo(a); **m. skills** capacidad *f* de gestión; **m. staff** directivos *mpl*

**managing director** [ˈmænɪdʒɪŋdaɪˈrektə(r)] *n* director(ora) *m,f* gerente

**Manchester** [ˈmæntʃestə(r)] *n* Manchester

**Mancunian** [mæŋˈkjuːnɪən] **1** *n* = natural o habitante de Manchester
**2** *adj* de Manchester

**Mandarin** [ˈmændərɪn] *n* (*language*) mandarín *m*

**mandarin** [ˈmændərɪn] *n* (**a**) (*official*) mandarín *m* (**b**) (*fruit*) mandarina *f*

**mandate** [ˈmændeɪt] *n* mandato *m*; **to have a m. to do sth** tener autoridad para hacer algo; **to obtain/give a m.** obtener/conferir autoridad *o* permiso

**mandatory** [ˈmændətərɪ] *adj* obligatorio(a)

**mandible** [ˈmændɪbəl] *n* mandíbula *f*

**mandolin** [ˈmændəlɪn] *n* mandolina *f*

**mane** [meɪn] *n* (*of lion*) melena *f*; (*of horse*) crines *fpl*

**man-eater** ['mæni:tə(r)] n (a) *(animal)* devorador(ora) *m,f* de hombres (b) *Fig (woman)* devoradora *f* de hombres

**man-eating** ['mæni:tɪŋ] adj devorador(ora) de hombres

**maneuverable, maneuver** *US* = **manoeuvrable, manoeuvre**

**manfully** ['mænfʊlɪ] adv con hombría

**manganese** [mæŋɡə'ni:z] n *Chem* manganeso *m*

**mange** [meɪndʒ] n *(animal disease)* sarna *f*

**manger** ['meɪndʒə(r)] n pesebre *m*

**mangle** ['mæŋɡəl] **1** n *(for clothes)* escurridor *m* de rodillos *(para ropa)*
  **2** vt *(body, text, truth)* mutilar

**mango** ['mæŋɡəʊ] *(pl* mangos *or* mangoes*)* n mango *m*

**mangrove** ['mæŋɡrəʊv] n mangle *m*; **m. swamp** manglar *m*

**mangy** ['meɪndʒɪ] adj *(animal)* sarnoso(a); *(carpet, coat)* raído(a)

**manhandle** ['mænhændəl] vt **they manhandled him into the car** lo metieron en el coche a empujones; **they manhandled the piano down the stairs** acarrearon a duras penas el piano escaleras abajo

**manhole** ['mænhəʊl] n *(boca f de)* alcantarilla *f*; **m. cover** tapa *f* de alcantarilla

**manhood** ['mænhʊd] n (a) *(maturity)* madurez *f*; **to reach m.** alcanzar la madurez (b) *(masculinity)* hombría *f*; **he proved his m.** demostró su hombría (c) *(men collectively)* **Scottish m.** los hombres escoceses

**man-hour** ['mænaʊə(r)] n *Econ* hora-hombre *f*

**manhunt** ['mænhʌnt] n caza *f* del hombre

**mania** ['meɪnɪə] n *(strong interest)* pasión *f* **(for** por); **to have a m. for doing sth** tener pasión por hacer algo

**maniac** ['meɪnɪæk] n maníaco(a) *m,f*; **to drive like a m.** conducir como un loco

**manic** ['mænɪk] adj *(person)* histérico(a)

**manic-depressive** ['mænɪkdɪ'presɪv] n & adj *Psy* maníacodepresivo(a) *m,f*

**manicure** ['mænɪkjʊə(r)] **1** n manicura *f*
  **2** vt **to m. one's nails** hacerse la manicura

**manifest** ['mænɪfest] **1** n *(of ship, aircraft)* manifiesto *m*
  **2** adj manifiesto(a), patente
  **3** vt manifestar

**manifestation** [mænɪfes'teɪʃən] n manifestación *f*

**manifestly** ['mænɪfestlɪ] adv manifiestamente

**manifesto** [mænɪ'festəʊ] *(pl* manifestos *or* manifestoes*)* n *Pol* manifiesto *m*

**manifold** ['mænɪfəʊld] adj *(numerous)* múltiple

**Manila** [mə'nɪlə] n Manila

**mani(l)la envelope** [mə'nɪlə'envələʊp] n sobre *m* marrón de papel manila

**manipulate** [mə'nɪpjʊleɪt] vt *(controls, people, statistics)* manipular

**manipulation** [mənɪpjʊ'leɪʃən] n *(of controls, people, statistics)* manipulación *f*

**manipulative** [mə'nɪpjʊlətɪv] adj *Pej* manipulador(ora)

**mankind** [mæn'kaɪnd] n la humanidad

**manliness** ['mænlɪnɪs] n hombría *f*, virilidad *f*

**manly** ['mænlɪ] adj viril

**man-made** ['mænmeɪd] adj *(fabric, product)* sintético(a), artificial; *(lake, beach)* artificial; **m. disaster** catástrofe *f* provocada por el hombre

**mannequin** ['mænɪkɪn] n *(person)* modelo *mf*, maniquí *mf*; *(dummy)* maniquí *m*

**manner** ['mænə(r)] n (a) *(way, method, style)* manera *f*, modo *m*; **in a m. of speaking** en cierto modo
  (b) *(etiquette)* **(good) manners** buenos modales *mpl*; **bad manners** malos modales; **it's bad manners to…** es de mala educación…; **he's got no manners** no tiene modales, es un maleducado
  (c) *(type)* **all m. of…** toda clase de…; **by no m. of means, not by any m. of means** en absoluto
  (d) *(attitude, behaviour)* actitud *f*; **I don't like his m.** no me gusta su actitud; **she's got a very unpleasant m.** es muy arisca

**mannered** ['mænəd] adj afectado(a), amanerado(a)

**mannerism** ['mænərɪzəm] n tic *m*, peculiaridad *f*

**manoeuvrable,** *US* **maneuverable** [mə'nu:vrəbəl] adj manejable

**manoeuvre,** *US* **maneuver** [mə'nu:və(r)] **1** n *also Fig* maniobra *f*; *Fig* **there wasn't much room for m.** no había mucho margen de maniobra; *Mil* **to be on manoeuvres** estar de maniobras
  **2** vt **we manoeuvred the piano up the stairs** subimos el piano con cuidado por la escalera; **she manoeuvred the car into the space** maniobró para meter el coche en el hueco
  **3** vi maniobrar

**manor** ['mænə(r)] n *(estate)* señorío *m*; **m. (house)** casa *f* solariega

**manpower** ['mænpaʊə(r)] n mano *f* de obra

**mansion** ['mænʃən] n mansión *f*

**manslaughter** ['mænslɔ:tə(r)] n *Law* homicidio *m* (involuntario)

**mantelpiece** ['mæntəlpi:s] *n* repisa *f* (de la chimenea)

**mantis** ['mæntɪs] *n US* mantis *f* inv religiosa

**mantle** ['mæntəl] *n (of lava, snow)* manto *m*, capa *f*; *(of gas lamp)* camisa *f*, manguito *m* incandescente; *(cloak)* capa *f*; *Fig* **to take on the m. of office** asumir las responsabilidades del puesto

**man-to-man** [mæntʊ'mæn] *adj & adv* de hombre a hombre

**manual** ['mænjʊəl] **1** *n (handbook)* manual *m*
**2** *adj* manual

**manually** ['mænjʊəlɪ] *adv* a mano, manualmente

**manufacture** [mænjʊ'fæktʃə(r)] **1** *n (act)* fabricación *f*, manufactura *f*; **manufactures** *(products)* productos *mpl* manufacturados
**2** *vt (cars, clothes)* fabricar; *Fig (excuse)* inventarse; *(evidence)* sacarse de la manga; **to m. an opportunity to do sth** crear *or* generar la oportunidad para hacer algo

**manufacturer** [mænjʊ'fæktʃərə(r)] *n Ind* fabricante *m,f*

**manufacturing** [mænjʊ'fæktʃərɪŋ] *n Ind* fabricación *f*; **m. capacity** capacidad *f* de fabricación; **m. industries** industrias *fpl* manufactureras *or* de transformación

**manure** [mə'njʊə(r)] **1** *n* estiércol *m*, abono *m*
**2** *vt* abonar, estercolar

**manuscript** ['mænjʊskrɪpt] *n* manuscrito *m*

**many** ['menɪ] **1** *adj (comparative* **more**, *superlative* **most)** muchos(as); **m. people** mucha gente; **m. times** muchas veces; **there weren't m. houses** no había muchas casas, había pocas casas; **in m. ways** de muchas maneras; **not in so m. words** no exactamente; **so m.** tantos(as); **so m. people** tanta gente; **too m.** demasiados(as); **too m. people** demasiada gente; **how m. times?** ¿cuántas veces?; **I have as m. books as you** tengo tantos libros como tú; **m.'s the time I've done that** lo he hecho muchas veces; *Prov* **m. hands make light work** cuanta más gente, más llevadero es el trabajo
**2** *pron* muchos(as); **m. of us** muchos de nosotros; **not (very) m.** no muchos(as); **how m.?** ¿cuántos(as)?; **as m. as you like** todos los que quieras; **too m.** demasiados(as); **one of the m. I have known** uno de los muchos que he conocido; *Fam* **to have had one too m.** llevar una copa de más, haber bebido más de la cuenta

**many-coloured** ['menɪ'kʌləd] *adj* multicolor

**Maori** ['maʊrɪ] *n & adj* maorí *mf*

**map** [mæp] **1** *n* mapa *m*; *Fig* **this will put Stonybridge on the m.** esto dará a conocer a Stonybridge; **m. reference** coordenadas *fpl*

**2** *vt (pt & pp* **mapped)** *(region)* trazar un mapa de
▸**map out** *vt sep (route)* indicar en un mapa; *(plan, programme)* proyectar; **she had her career all mapped out** tenía su carrera profesional planeada paso por paso

**maple** ['meɪpəl] *n (tree, wood)* arce *m*; **m. leaf** hoja *f* de arce; **m. syrup** jarabe *m* de arce

**Mar** *(abbr* **March)** marzo *m*

**mar** [mɑː(r)] *(pt & pp* **marred)** *vt* deslucir, empañar

**maracas** [mə'rækəz] *npl Mus* maracas *fpl*

**marathon** ['mærəθən] *n* maratón *m*; **a m. speech** un discurso maratoniano; **m. runner** corredor(ora) *m,f* de maratón

**marauder** [mə'rɔːdə(r)] *n* merodeador(ora) *m,f*

**marauding** [mə'rɔːdɪŋ] *adj (gangs, people)* merodeador(ora); **m. animals** animales *mpl* en busca de su presa

**marble** ['mɑːbəl] *n* **(a)** *(stone)* mármol *m* **(b)** *(glass ball)* canica *f*; **to play marbles** jugar a las canicas; *Fam Fig* **to lose one's marbles** *(go mad)* volverse majara

**marbled** ['mɑːbəld] *adj (paper)* jaspeado(a)

**March** [mɑːtʃ] *n* marzo *m*; *see also* **May**

**march** [mɑːtʃ] **1** *n (of soldiers, demonstrators)* marcha *f*; *Fig (of time, events)* transcurso *m*; **on the m.** en marcha; **m.** past desfile *m*
**2** *vt* hacer marchar; **he was marched off to prison** le llevaron (por la fuerza) a la cárcel
**3** *vi (of soldiers, demonstrators)* marchar; **to m. off** marcharse; **to m. by** *or* **past (sb/sth)** desfilar (ante alguien/algo)

**marcher** ['mɑːtʃə(r)] *n (demonstrator)* manifestante *mf*

**marching orders** ['mɑːtʃɪŋ'ɔːdəz] *npl Fam* **to give sb his m.** dar boleto *or* mandar a paseo a alguien

**mare** [meə(r)] *n* yegua *f*

**margarine** [mɑːdʒə'riːn], *Fam* **marge** [mɑːdʒ] *n* margarina *f*

**margin** ['mɑːdʒɪn] *n also Com* margen *m*; **on the margin(s) of society** en la marginación; **to win by a narrow/an enormous m.** ganar por un estrecho/un amplio margen; **m. of error** margen de error

**marginal** ['mɑːdʒɪnəl] **1** *n Br Pol (constituency)* = circunscripción electoral con mayoría muy estrecha
**2** *adj* **(a)** *(improvement, increase)* marginal **(b)** *(note)* al margen, marginal **(c)** *Br Pol (seat, constituency)* muy reñido(a)

**marginalize** ['mɑːdʒɪnəlaɪz] *vt* marginar

**marginally** ['mɑːdʒɪnəlɪ] *adv* ligeramente

**marigold** ['mærɪɡəʊld] *n* caléndula *f*

**marihuana, marijuana** [mærɪ'hwɑːnə] *n* marihuana *f*

**marina** [mə'ri:nə] *n* puerto *m* deportivo

**marinade** [mærɪ'neɪd] *Culin* **1** *n* adobo *m*

**2** *vi* = **marinate**

**marinate** ['mærɪneɪt] *vi Culin* adobar

**marine** [mə'ri:n] **1** *n* (*soldier*) marine *m,f*; *US Fam* (*go*) **tell it to the marines!** ¡eso cuénta-selo a tu abuela!

**2** *adj* (*life, biology*) marino(a); **m. engineering** ingeniería *f* naval

**mariner** ['mærɪnə(r)] *n Literary* marinero *m*

**marionette** [mærɪə'net] *n* marioneta *f*

**marital** ['mærɪtəl] *adj* marital; **m. status** es-tado *m* civil

**maritime** ['mærɪtaɪm] *adj* marítimo(a)

**marjoram** ['mɑ:dʒərəm] *n* mejorana *f*

**mark¹** [mɑ:k] *n* (*German currency*) marco *m* (alemán)

**mark²** **1** *n* (a) (*scratch, stain, symbol*) marca *f*
(b) (*sign, proof*) signo *m*, señal *f*; **as a m. of respect** en señal de respeto; **years of im-prisonment had left their m. on him** había quedado marcado por años de reclusión; **to make one's m.** (*succeed*) dejar huella, hacerse famoso(a)
(c) (*target*) **his comments hit the m.** dio en el blanco con sus comentarios; **unemploy-ment has passed the three million m.** el número de desempleados ha rebasado la ba-rrera de los tres millones; **her accusation was wide of the m.** su acusación estaba lejos de ser cierta; **he's not up to the m.** no está a la altura de las circunstancias
(d) *Sch* (*score*) nota *f*, calificación *f*; (*point*) punto *m*; **to get good** *or* **high marks** sacar buenas notas; **full marks** nota *f* máxima, sobresa-liente *m*; **full marks for observation!** no se te escapa una, ¿eh?
(e) (*in race*) **on your marks! get set! go!** preparados, listos, ¡ya!; **to be quick/slow off the m.** (*in race*) salir rápidamente/lentamente; *Fig* reaccionar con rapidez/lentitud
(f) (*of machine*) **m. II/III** versión *f* II/III
(g) (*on cooker*) **cook at (gas) m. 4** cocínese con el mando en el 4

**2** *vt* (a) (*scratch, stain*) marcar
(b) (*homework, exam*) corregir, calificar; **to m. sth right/wrong** dar/no dar algo por bue-no(a); **it's marked out of ten** está puntua-do(a) sobre diez
(c) (*indicate*) marcar; **this decision marks a change in policy** esta decisión marca un cam-bio de política; **to m. time** (*of musician*) marcar el compás; *Fig* (*wait*) hacer tiempo
(d) (*characterize*) marcar, caracterizar; **his comments were marked by their sarcasm** sus comentarios se caracterizaban por el sarcas-mo
(e) (*in sport*) (*opponent*) marcar

(f) (*pay attention to*) **m. my words** fíjate en lo que te digo

▸**mark down** *vt sep* (a) (*make note of*) anotar, apuntar; **they had him marked down as a troublemaker** lo tenían fichado como alboro-tador (b) *Com* rebajar

▸**mark off** *vt sep* (a) (*line, road*) delimitar (b) (*tick off*) poner una marca en

▸**mark out** *vt sep* **to m. sb out** distinguir a al-guien

▸**mark up** *vt sep* (*price*) subir; (*goods*) subir de precio

**marked** [mɑ:kt] *adj* (a) (*difference*) marca-do(a); (*improvement*) notable (b) **m. cards** car-tas *fpl* marcadas; **to be a m. man** tener los días contados

**markedly** ['mɑ:kɪdlɪ] *adv* notablemente, con-siderablemente

**marker** ['mɑ:kə(r)] *n* (a) (*of essay, exam*) examinador(ora) *m,f*, corrector(ora) *m,f* de exá-menes; **he's a hard m.** es muy severo al corre-gir (b) **m. (pen)** rotulador *m* (c) (*indicator*) se-ñal *f*

**market** ['mɑ:kɪt] **1** *n* mercado *m*, *CSur* feria *f*, *CAm, Méx* tianguis *m*; **to put sth on the m.** sacar algo al mercado; *Fin* **m. analyst** analista *mf* de mercados; **m. day** día *m* de mercado; *Econ* **(free) m. economy** economía *f* de (libre) mer-cado; *Econ* **m. forces** fuerzas *fpl* del mercado; **m. garden** huerto *m*; (*larger*) huerta *f*; *Com* **m. leader** líder *mf* del mercado; *Econ* **m. price** precio *m* de mercado; *Com* **m. research** estu-dio *m* *or* investigación *f* de mercado; *Com* **m. share** cuota *f* de mercado; **m. square** (plaza *f* del) mercado *m*; *Com* **m. survey** estudio *m* de mercados; **m. town** localidad *f* con mercado

**2** *vt* comercializar

**marketable** ['mɑ:kɪtəbəl] *adj* comerciali-zable

**marketing** ['mɑ:kɪtɪŋ] *n Com* (*study, theory*) marketing *m*, mercadotecnia *f*; (*promotion*) co-mercialización *f*; **m. campaign** campaña *f* de marketing *or* de publicidad; **m. department** departamento *m* de marketing; **m. manager** director(ora) *m,f* comercial, director(ora) *m,f* de marketing; **m. strategy** estrategia *f* de market-ing

**marketplace** ['mɑ:kətpleɪs] *n also Econ* mer-cado *m*

**marking** ['mɑ:kɪŋ] *n* (a) **markings** (*on ani-mal*) marcas *fpl*, manchas *fpl*; (*on plane*) distinti-vo *m*; **m. ink** tinta *f* indeleble (b) (*of essay, exam*) corrección *f*; **I've got a lot of m. to do** tengo que corregir muchos exámenes

**markka** ['mɑ:kə] *n* (*Finnish currency*) marco *m* finlandés

**marksman** ['mɑ:ksmən] *n* tirador *m*

**mark-up** ['mɑ:kʌp] *n* (*on price*) recargo *m*

**marmalade** ['mɑːməleid] n mermelada f (de naranja)

**maroon¹** [mə'ruːn] n (a) (colour) granate m (b) (firework) bengala f de auxilio (en el mar)

**maroon²** vt (sailor) abandonar; Fig **we were marooned by the floods** nos quedamos aislados or incomunicados por la inundación

**marquee** [mɑː'kiː] n Br (tent) carpa f; US (of building) marquesina f

**marquis** ['mɑːkwɪs] n marqués m

**Marrakesh** ['mærəkeʃ] n Marraquech

**marriage** ['mærɪdʒ] n (wedding) boda f; (institution, period, relationship) matrimonio m; Fig (of ideas, organizations) unión f; **m. of convenience** matrimonio m de conveniencia; **uncle by m.** tío m político; Fig **a m. of minds** una perfecta sintonía; **m. certificate** certificado m or partida f de matrimonio; **m. guidance counsellor** consejero(a) m,f matrimonial; **m. vows** votos mpl matrimoniales

**marriageable** ['mærɪdʒəbəl] adj **a girl of m. age** una muchacha casadera

**married** ['mærɪd] adj casado(a); **to be m.** estar casado(a); **to get m.** casarse; **a m. couple** un matrimonio; **m. life** vida f matrimonial; **m. name** apellido m de casada; Mil **m. quarters** = residencia para oficiales casados y sus familias

**marrow** ['mærəʊ] n (a) (of bone) médula f; **to be frozen to the m.** estar helado(a) hasta la médula or hasta los tuétanos (b) (vegetable) = especie de calabacín de gran tamaño

**marrowbone** ['mærəʊbəʊn] n hueso m de caña

**marrowfat pea** ['mærəʊfæt'piː] n = tipo de guisante grande

**marry** ['mærɪ] 1 vt (a) (get married to) casarse con; (of priest, parent) casar; **will you m. me?** ¿te quieres casar conmigo?; Fig **he's married to his job** es esclavo de su trabajo (b) (combine) casar, combinar; **a style which marries the traditional and the modern** un estilo que combina lo tradicional con lo moderno
2 vi casarse

►**marry off** vt sep casar

**Mars** [mɑːz] n (planet, god) Marte m

**Marseilles** [mɑː'saɪ] n Marsella

**marsh** [mɑːʃ] n pantano m, ciénaga m

**marshal** ['mɑːʃəl] 1 n (a) (army officer) mariscal m (b) (at race, demonstration) miembro m del servicio de orden
2 vt (pt & pp marshalled, US marshaled) (people, troops) dirigir; (arguments, thoughts) poner en orden

**marshland** ['mɑːʃlænd] n ciénaga f, zona f pantanosa

**marshmallow** [mɑː'ʃmæləʊ] n (a) (food) = dulce de consistencia esponjosa (b) (plant) malvavisco m

**marshy** ['mɑːʃɪ] adj pantanoso(a)

**marsupial** [mɑː'suːpɪəl] n & adj marsupial m

**martial** ['mɑːʃəl] adj marcial; **m. arts** artes fpl marciales; **to declare m. law** declarar la ley marcial

**Martian** ['mɑːʃən] n & adj marciano(a) m,f

**martyr** ['mɑːtə(r)] 1 n mártir mf; Fig **to be a m. to rheumatism** estar martirizado(a) por el reúma; Fig **to make a m. of oneself** hacerse el/la mártir
2 vt martirizar, hacer mártir

**martyrdom** ['mɑːtədəm] n martirio m

**marvel** ['mɑːvəl] 1 n maravilla f; **to work marvels** hacer maravillas; **if we survive this it'll be a m.** si salimos de ésta será un milagro; Fam **you're a m.!** ¡eres un genio!
2 vi (pt & pp marvelled, US marveled) maravillarse (at de), asombrarse (at de)

**marvellous**, US **marvelous** ['mɑːvələs] adj maravilloso(a)

**Marxism** ['mɑːksɪzəm] n marxismo m

**Marxist** ['mɑːksɪst] n & adj marxista mf

**marzipan** ['mɑːzɪpæn] n mazapán m

**mascara** [mæs'kɑːrə] n rímel m

**mascot** ['mæskət] n mascota f

**masculine** ['mæskjʊlɪn] 1 n Gram (género m) masculino m
2 adj masculino(a)

**masculinity** [mæskjʊ'lɪnɪtɪ] n masculinidad f

**mash** [mæʃ] 1 n (a) Fam (mashed potato) puré m de patatas (b) (for pigs, poultry) frangollo m
2 vt (squash, crush) machacar; (vegetables) majar, hacer puré de

**mashed potatoes** [mæʃtpə'teɪtəʊz] npl puré m de patatas

**mask** [mɑːsk] 1 n máscara f, careta f; Fig **his m. had slipped** se le había caído la máscara
2 vt (conceal) enmascarar

**masked** [mɑːskt] adj enmascarado(a)

**masking tape** ['mɑːskɪŋteɪp] n cinta f adhesiva de pintor

**masochism** ['mæsəkɪzəm] n masoquismo m

**masochist** ['mæsəkɪst] n masoquista mf

**masochistic** [mæsə'kɪstɪk] adj masoquista

**mason** ['meɪsən] n (a) (builder) cantero(a) m,f, picapedrero(a) m,f (b) (freemason) masón m

**masonry** ['meɪsənrɪ] n (stonework) albañilería f, obra f; **she was hit by a piece of falling m.** le cayó encima un cascote que se había desprendido del edificio

**masquerade** [mæskə'reɪd] 1 n mascarada f
2 vi **to m. as** hacerse pasar por

**mass¹** [mæs] **1** n (a) (large number) sinnúmero m; Fam **I've got masses (of things) to do** tengo un montón de cosas que hacer; Fam **there's masses of room** hay muchísimo espacio; **m. grave** fosa f común; **m. hysteria** histeria f colectiva; **m. media** medios mpl de comunicación (de masas); **m. meeting** mítin m multitudinario; **m. murderer** asesino(a) m,f múltiple; **m. production** fabricación f en serie; **m. unemployment** desempleo m generalizado or masivo

(b) (shapeless substance) masa f

(c) Pol **the masses** las masas

(d) Phys masa f

**2** vi (of troops, people) congregarse, concentrarse; (of clouds) acumularse

**mass²** n Rel misa f

**massacre** ['mæsəkə(r)] **1** n masacre f; Fam Fig **it was a m.** (in sport, election) fue una auténtica paliza

**2** vt also Fig masacrar; Fam Fig **they were massacred** (in sport, election) les dieron un palizón

**massage** ['mæsɑ:ʒ] **1** n masaje m

**2** vt (body, scalp) dar un masaje a, masajear; Fig **to m. the figures** maquillar las cifras

**masseur** [mæ'sɜ:(r)] n masajista m

**masseuse** [mæ'sɜ:z] n masajista f

**massive** ['mæsɪv] adj enorme, inmenso(a); (heart attack, stroke) muy grave

**mass-produce** [mæsprə'dju:s] vt Ind fabricar en serie

**mast** [mɑ:st] n (of ship) mástil m; (of radio, TV transmitter) torre f

**mastectomy** [mæs'tektəmɪ] n Med mastectomía f

**master** ['mɑ:stə(r)] **1** n (a) (of servants) señor m; (of ship) patrón m; **the m. of the house** el señor de la casa; **to be one's own m.** ser dueño(a) de sí mismo(a); **to be m. of the situation** ser dueño(a) de la situación; **m. of ceremonies** maestro m de ceremonias; **m. bedroom** dormitorio m principal; **m. copy** original m; **m. key** llave f maestra; **m. plan** plan m maestro; **m. race** raza f superior

(b) (skilled person) maestro(a) m,f; Univ **M. of Arts/Science** (degree) máster m en humanidades/ciencias; (person) licenciado(a) m,f con máster en humanidades/ciencias; **m. carpenter/builder** maestro carpintero/albañil; Mus **m. class** clase f magistral; **m.'s (degree)** máster m; **she has a m.'s (degree) in economics** tiene un máster en o de Economía

(c) (instructor) **fencing/dancing m.** maestro m de esgrima/ de danza; **French/Geography m.** profesor m de francés/geografía

(d) Old-fashioned (young boy) **M. David Thomas** señorito David Thomas

(e) Art **an old m.** (painter, painting) un clásico de la pintura antigua

**2** vt (one's emotions, foreign language, violin) dominar

**masterful** ['mɑ:stəfʊl] adj autoritario(a)

**masterly** ['mɑ:stəlɪ] adj magistral

**mastermind** ['mɑ:stəmaɪnd] **1** n cerebro m

**2** vt (project, plot) dirigir

**masterpiece** ['mɑ:stəpi:s] n obra f maestra

**masterstroke** ['mɑ:stəstrəʊk] n golpe m maestro

**mastery** ['mɑ:stərɪ] n (of territory, subject matter) dominio m

**mastiff** ['mæstɪf] n mastín m

**mastitis** [mæs'taɪtɪs] n Med mastitis f inv

**masturbate** ['mæstəbeɪt] **1** vt masturbar

**2** vi masturbarse

**masturbation** [mæstə'beɪʃən] n masturbación f

**mat** [mæt] **1** n (on floor) alfombrilla f; (at door) felpudo m; (table) **m.** salvamanteles m inv; (drink) **m.** posavasos m inv

**2** vi (pt & pp matted) (of hair, fibres) enredarse

**match¹** [mætʃ] n cerilla f

**match²** [mætʃ] **1** n (a) (in sport) partido m; **m. point** (in tennis) punto m de partido (b) (in design, ability) **they're a good m.** (of clothes) pegan, combinan bien; **to be no m. for sb** no ser rival para alguien; **he had met his m.** había encontrado la horma de su zapato (c) (marriage) **to make a good m.** casarse bien

**2** vt (equal in quality, performance) igualar, llegar a la altura de; (pair up) emparejar; (of colours, clothes) pegar con, combinar con; (of description, account) coincidir con; **we can't m. their prices** no podemos igualar sus precios; **to m. sb against sb** enfrentar a alguien con alguien; **m. your skill against the experts** mide tu habilidad con los expertos; **to be well matched** (of teams, players) estar muy igualados(as); **to be a well-matched couple** hacer buena pareja

**3** vi (of colours, clothes) pegar, combinar; (descriptions, stories) coincidir

▶**match up 1** vt sep (colours, clothes) pegar, combinar

**2** vi (of clothes, colours) pegar, combinar; (of explanations) coincidir; **to m. up to sb's expectations** estar a la altura de las expectativas de alguien

**matchbox** ['mætʃbɒks] n caja f de cerillas

**matching** ['mætʃɪŋ] adj a juego

**matchless** ['mætʃlɪs] adj sin par, sin igual

**matchmaker** ['mætʃmeɪkə(r)] n (arranger of marriages) casamentero(a) m,f

**matchstick** ['mætʃstɪk] n cerilla f; **m. man or figure** monigote m (dibujo hecho con palotes)

**mate**[1] [meɪt] **1** n (a) *(male animal)* macho m; *(female animal)* hembra f; *(person)* pareja f (b) Br Fam *(friend)* colega mf (c) *(assistant)* aprendiz(iza) m,f (d) *(on ship)* oficial mf; **(first) m.** primer oficial m
**2** vt *(animals)* aparear
**3** vi *(of animals)* aparearse

**mate**[2] *(in chess)* **1** n jaque m mate
**2** vt dar jaque mate a

**material** [məˈtɪərɪəl] **1** n (a) *(in general)* material m; **he isn't officer m.** no tiene madera de oficial (b) *(for book)* documentación f, material m; **reading m.** (material m de) lectura f, lecturas fpl; **she writes all her own m.** *(of singer, musician)* ella sola compone toda su música (c) *(cloth)* tejido m, tela f (d) *(equipment)* **building materials** material m de construcción; **cleaning materials** productos mpl de limpieza; **writing materials** objetos mpl de papelería or escritorio
**2** adj (a) *(physical)* material (b) *(important)* sustancial, relevante; **the point is m. to my argument** es un punto pertinente para mi razonamiento

**materialism** [məˈtɪərɪəlɪzəm] n materialismo m

**materialistic** [mətɪərɪəˈlɪstɪk] adj materialista

**materialize** [məˈtɪərɪəlaɪz] vi *(of hope, something promised)* materializarse; *(of spirit)* aparecer

**materially** [məˈtɪərɪəlɪ] adv (a) *(in money, goods)* materialmente (b) *(appreciably)* sustancialmente

**maternal** [məˈtɜːnəl] adj *(feelings, instinct, love)* maternal; *(relative, genes)* materno(a)

**maternity** [məˈtɜːnɪtɪ] n maternidad f; **m. dress** vestido m premamá; **m. hospital** (hospital m de) maternidad f; **m. leave** baja f por maternidad; **m. ward** pabellón m de maternidad

**matey** [ˈmeɪtɪ] Fam **1** n listen, **m.** mira, colega
**2** adj **he's been very m. with the boss recently** se ha hecho muy colega del jefe últimamente

**math** [mæθ] n US matemáticas fpl

**mathematical** [mæθəˈmætɪkəl] adj matemático(a)

**mathematician** [mæθəməˈtɪʃən] n matemático(a) m,f

**mathematics** [mæθəˈmætɪks] n *(subject)* matemáticas fpl; **the m. of the problem is quite complex** el problema entraña una complicada aritmética

**maths** [mæθs] n matemáticas fpl

**matinée** [ˈmætɪneɪ] n *(of play)* función f de tarde; *(of film)* sesión f de tarde, primera sesión f

**mating** [ˈmeɪtɪŋ] n apareamiento m; **m. call** llamada f nupcial; **m. season** época f de celo or apareamiento

**matriarch** [ˈmeɪtrɪɑːk] n matriarca f

**matriarchal** [meɪtrɪˈɑːkəl] adj matriarcal

**matriarchy** [ˈmeɪtrɪɑːkɪ] n matriarcado m

**matriculate** [məˈtrɪkjʊleɪt] vi *(enrol)* matricularse

**matriculation** [mətrɪkjʊˈleɪʃən] n *(enrolment)* matrícula f

**matrimonial** [mætrɪˈməʊnɪəl] adj matrimonial

**matrimony** [ˈmætrɪmənɪ] n matrimonio m

**matrix** [ˈmeɪtrɪks] *(pl* **matrixes** [ˈmeɪtrɪksɪz], **matrices** [ˈmeɪtrɪsiːz]*)* n matriz f

**matron** [ˈmeɪtrən] n (a) *(in school)* = mujer a cargo de la enfermería; *(in hospital)* enfermera f jefe (b) *(older woman)* matrona f

**matt** [mæt] adj *(colour, finish)* mate

**matted** [ˈmætɪd] adj *(hair)* enredado(a), apelmazado(a)

**matter** [ˈmætə(r)] **1** n (a) *(substance)* materia f (b) *(affair, issue)* asunto m, cuestión f; **that's a m. of opinion/taste** es una cuestión de opinión/gustos; **it's no easy m.** no es asunto fácil; **that's quite another m.** eso es otra cuestión; **within a m. of hours** en cuestión de horas; **he doesn't like it and nor do I for that m.** a él no le gusta y a mí de hecho tampoco; **as a m. of course** automáticamente; **as a m. of fact** de hecho, en realidad; **as matters stand** tal como están las cosas; **to make matters worse...** para colmo de males...; **military/business matters** cuestiones fpl militares/de negocios
(c) *(problem)* **what's the m.?** ¿qué pasa?; **what's the m. with you?** ¿qué (es lo que) te pasa?; **there's something the m.** hay algo que no va bien
(d) *(with no)* **no m.!** ¡no importa!; **no m. who/where** quien/donde sea; **no m. how hard I push...** por muy fuerte que empuje...; **no m. who I ask...** pregunte a quien pregunte...; **no m. where I look for it...** por mucho que lo busque...; **no m. what I do...** haga lo que haga...
**2** vi importar (**to** a); **it doesn't m.** no importa; **nothing else matters** lo demás no importa; **it doesn't m. to me/her** no me/le importa

**matter-of-fact** [ˈmætərəˈfækt] adj *(tone, voice)* pragmático(a); **he was very m. about it** se lo tomó como si tal cosa

**matting** [ˈmætɪŋ] n estera f

**mattress** [ˈmætrɪs] n colchón m

**mature** [məˈtjʊə(r)] **1** adj *(person)* maduro(a); *(wine)* de crianza; *(cheese)* curado(a); Br Univ **m. student** ≃ estudiante mf mayor de 25 años

**2** vt madurar; (wine) criar

**3** vi (of person) madurar; (of wine) envejecer, criarse; Fin (of investment) vencer

**maturity** [mə'tjʊərɪtɪ] n madurez f; Fin vencimiento m

**maudlin** ['mɔ:dlɪn] adj llorón(ona), lacrimoso(a); **to be m.** estar llorón(ona) or lacrimoso(a)

**maul** [mɔ:l] vt **he was mauled by a tiger...** fue gravemente herido por un tigre...; Fig **the book was mauled by the critics** los críticos destrozaron el libro

**Mauritania** [mɒrɪ'teɪnɪə] n Mauritania

**Mauritanian** [mɒrɪ'teɪnɪən] n & adj mauritano(a) m,f

**Mauritian** [mə'rɪʃən] n & adj mauriciano(a) m,f

**Mauritius** [mə'rɪʃəs] n (isla) Mauricio

**mausoleum** [mɔ:sə'li:əm] n mausoleo m

**mauve** [məʊv] n & adj malva m

**maverick** ['mævərɪk] n & adj inconformista mf, disidente mf

**mawkish** ['mɔ:kɪʃ] adj Pej empalagoso(a)

**max** [mæks] n (abbr **maximum**) máx., máximo m

**maxim** ['mæksɪm] n máxima f

**maximize** ['mæksɪmaɪz] vt elevar al máximo, maximizar

**maximum** ['mæksɪməm] **1** n (pl maxima ['mæksɪmə]) máximo m; **to the m.** al máximo; **at the m.** como máximo

**2** adj máximo(a); **m. speed** velocidad f máxima

**May** [meɪ] n mayo m; **in M.** en mayo; **at the beginning/end of M.** a principios/finales de mayo; **during M.** en mayo; **each** or **every M.** todos los meses or cada mes de mayo; **in the middle of M.** a mediados de mayo; **last/next M.** el mayo pasado/próximo; **(on) the first/sixteenth of M.** el uno/dieciséis de mayo; **she was born on the 22nd of M. 1953** nació el 22 de mayo de 1953; **M. Day** el Primero or Uno de Mayo

**may** [meɪ]

En las expresiones del apartado (**a**), puede utilizarse **might** sin que se altere apenas el significado.

v aux (3rd person singular **may**, pt **might** [maɪt])

(**a**) (expressing possibility) **he m. return at any moment** puede volver de un momento a otro; **I m. tell you and I m. not** puede que te lo diga o puede que no; **he m. have lost it** puede que lo haya perdido; **it m. be that...** podría ser que...; **you m. well ask!** ¡eso quisiera saber yo!; **we m. as well go** ya puestos, podíamos ir; **shall we go? – we m. as well...** ¿vamos? – bueno or vale...

(**b**) Formal (asking for or giving permission) **m. I come in?** ¿se puede?, ¿puedo pasar?; **if I m. say so** si se me permite hacer una observación; **m. I?** (when borrowing sth) ¡con permiso!, ¿me permite?

(**c**) (expressing wishes, fears, purpose) **m. she rest in peace** que en paz descanse; **m. the best man win!** ¡que gane el mejor!; **I fear you m. be right** me temo que tengas razón; **they work long hours so their children m. have a better future** trabajan mucho para que sus hijos tengan un futuro mejor

(**d**) (conceding a fact) **he m. be very rich, but I still don't like him** tendrá mucho dinero, pero sigue sin caerme bien; **be that as it m., that's as m. be** en cualquier caso

**Maya** ['maɪə], **Mayan** ['maɪən] n & adj maya mf

**maybe** ['meɪbi:] adv quizá(s), tal vez; **m. she won't accept** quizá no acepte

**Mayday** ['meɪdeɪ] n Av Naut (distress signal) SOS m, señal f de socorro; **M.!** ¡SOS!

**mayhem** ['meɪhem] n alboroto m

**mayonnaise** [meɪə'neɪz] n mayonesa f

**mayor** ['meə(r)] n alcalde m

**mayoress** ['meəres] n alcaldesa f

**maypole** ['meɪpəʊl] n mayo m (poste)

**maze** [meɪz] n also Fig laberinto m

**MBA** [embi:'eɪ] n Univ (abbr **Master of Business Administration**) máster m en administración de empresas

**MBE** [embi:'i:] n Br (abbr **Member of the Order of the British Empire**) miembro mf de la Orden del Imperio Británico

**MBO** [embi:'əʊ] (pl **MBOs**) n Com (abbr **management buyout**) = adquisición de una empresa por sus directivos

**MC** [em'si:] n (abbr **Master of Ceremonies**) maestro m de ceremonias

**MD** [em'di:] n (**a**) Med (abbr **Doctor of Medicine**) doctor(ora) m,f en medicina (**b**) Com (abbr **Managing Director**) director(ora) m,f gerente

**ME** [em'i:] Med (abbr **myalgic encephalomyelitis**) encefalomielitis f inv miálgica

**me** unstressed [mɪ], stressed [mi:] pron (**a**) (object) me; **she hates me** me odia; **she forgave my brother but not ME** perdonó a mi hermano, pero no a mí; **she gave me the book** me dio el libro

(**b**) (after preposition) mí; **with me** conmigo

(**c**) (as complement of verb to be) yo; **it's me!** ¡soy yo!

(**d**) (in interjections) **who, me?** ¿quién, yo?; **silly me!** ¡qué bobo soy!

**meadow** ['medəʊ] n prado m, pradera f

**meagre**, US **meager** ['mi:gə(r)] adj exiguo(a), escaso(a)

**meal¹** [mi:l] *n* comida *f*; **midday m.** comida *f*, almuerzo *m*; **evening m.** cena *f*; *Fig* **to make a m. of sth** *(make a fuss)* hacer de algo un mundo; *(take too long)* entretenerse un montón con algo

**meal²** *n (flour)* harina *f*

**mealtime** ['mi:ltaɪm] *n* hora *f* de comer

**mealy** ['mi:lɪ] *adj* harinoso(a)

**mealy-mouthed** [mi:lɪ'maʊðd] *adj Pej* evasivo(a); **to be m.** andarse con rodeos

**mean¹** [mi:n] **1** *n (average)* media *f*
  **2** *adj (average)* medio(a)

**mean²** *adj* **(a)** *(miserly)* tacaño(a) **(b)** *(nasty)* malo(a), mezquino(a); **she has a m. streak** a veces tiene muy mala uva; **that was a m. thing to do/say** hacer/decir eso estuvo fatal; **a m. trick** una jugarreta **(c)** *(poor)* **she's no m. photographer** es muy buena fotógrafa; **it was no m. feat** fue una gran proeza **(d)** *US Fam (good)* genial, guay; **he plays a m. game of pool** juega al billar de vicio

**mean³** *[pt & pp* **meant** [ment]*] vt* **(a)** *(signify) (of word, event)* significar; *(person)* querer decir; **what does the word "tacky" m.?** ¿qué significa *o* qué quiere decir la palabra "tacky"?; **this is Tim, I m. Tom** éste es Tim, digo Tom; **what do you m.?** ¿qué quieres decir?; **it doesn't m. anything** no quiere decir *o* significa nada
  **(b)** *(speak sincerely)* hablar en serio; **I m. it** lo digo en serio; **you don't m. it!** ¡no lo dirás en serio!
  **(c)** *(be of importance)* significar **(to** para); **the price means nothing to him** el precio no le preocupa; **it means a lot to me** significa mucho para mí
  **(d)** *(imply, involve)* significar, suponer; **it would m. having to give up smoking** significaría tener que dejar de fumar
  **(e)** *(intend)* **to m. to do sth** tener (la) intención de hacer algo; **she means well** lo hace con buena intención; **I m. him no harm** no pretendo hacerle ningún daño; **I m. to succeed** me he propuesto triunfar; **you were meant to ring me first** se suponía que primero me tenías que telefonear; **it's meant to be a good film** (se supone que) tiene que ser una buena película; **she meant you to have this ring** quería que esta sortija fuera para ti; **it was meant as a joke/a compliment** pretendía ser una broma/un cumplido; **the bomb was meant for you** la bomba iba destinada a ti; **this portrait is meant to be of the duke** este cuadro pretende ser un retrato del duque; **we were meant for each other** estábamos hechos el uno para el otro

**meander** [mɪ'ændə(r)] **1** *n* meandro *m*
  **2** *vi (of river, road)* serpentear; *(of person)* vagar, callejear

**meaning** ['mi:nɪŋ] *n* significado *m*, sentido *m*; **to understand sb's m.** entender lo que alguien quiere decir; *Fam* **if you get my m.** sabes por dónde voy ¿no?; **what's the m. of this?** *(expressing indignation)* ¿qué significa esto?; **the m. of life** el sentido de la vida

**meaningful** ['mi:nɪŋfʊl] *adj* significativo(a); **to be m.** tener sentido; **it no longer seemed m. to her** ya no parecía tener sentido para ella

**meaningless** ['mi:nɪŋlɪs] *adj* sin sentido; **to be m.** no tener sentido

**meanness** ['mi:nnɪs] *n* **(a)** *(miserliness)* tacañería *f* **(b)** *(nastiness)* maldad *f*

**means** [mi:nz] **1** *n (method)* medio *m*; **by m. of...** mediante..., por medio de...; **there is no m. of escape** no hay forma de escapar; **by some m. or other** de un modo u otro; **a m. to an end** un medio para conseguir un (determinado) fin; **to use every possible m. to do sth** utilizar cualquier medio para hacer algo; **by all m.** por supuesto; **by no m.** de ningún modo, en absoluto; **m. of production** medios *mpl* de producción; **m. of transport** medio *m* de transporte
  **2** *npl (income, wealth)* medios *mpl*; **a man of m.** un hombre acaudalado *o* de posibles; **I live beyond/within my m.** vivo por encima de/de acuerdo con mis posibilidades; **m. test** *(for benefits)* estimación *f* de ingresos *(para la concesión de un subsidio)*

**meant** [ment] *pt & pp* **of mean**

**meantime** ['mi:ntaɪm], **meanwhile** ['mi:nwaɪl] **1** *n* **in the m.** mientras tanto
  **2** *adv* mientras tanto

**measles** ['mi:zəlz] *n* sarampión *m*

**measly** ['mi:zlɪ] *adj Fam* ridículo(a), irrisorio(a)

**measurable** ['meʒərəbəl] *adj* apreciable

**measure** ['meʒə(r)] **1** *n* **(a)** *(measurement, quantity)* medida *f*; *(means of estimating)* indicador *m*, índice *m*; **this was a m. of how serious the situation was** esto era una muestra *o* un indicador de la gravedad de la situación; **a m. of...** cierto grado de...; **there was a m. of bravado in his words** había cierta fanfarronería en sus palabras; **to get the m. of sb** tomar la medida a alguien; **for good m.** por añadidura; **for good m., he called me a liar** no contento con ello, me llamó mentiroso
  **(b)** *(degree)* **in some m.** en cierta medida, hasta cierto punto; **beyond m.** increíblemente; **she has tried my patience beyond m.** ya ha acabado con mi paciencia
  **(c)** *(action, step)* medida *f*; **to take measures** tomar medidas
  **2** *vt & vi* medir

▸**measure up** *vi* dar la talla (**to** para)

**measured** ['meʒəd] *adj (movement, step)* medido(a), pausado(a); *(tone, response)* comedido(a), mesurado(a)

**measurement** ['meʒəmənt] *n (quantity, length)* medida *f*

**measuring** ['meʒərɪŋ] *n* **m. jug** recipiente *m* graduado; **m. spoon** cuchara *f* dosificadora; **m. tape** cinta *f* métrica

**meat** [miːt] *n* **(a)** *(food)* carne *f*; *Fig* **it was m. and drink to them** era algo que les entusiasmaba **(b)** *Fig (substantial content)* miga *f*

**meatball** ['miːtbɔːl] *n* albóndiga *f*

**meaty** ['miːtɪ] *adj (taste)* a carne; *(fleshy)* carnoso(a); *Fig (book, film)* con mucha miga, sustancioso(a)

**Mecca** ['mekə] *n* La Meca; *Fig* meca *f*

**mechanic** [mɪ'kænɪk] *n* mecánico(a) *m,f*

**mechanical** [mɪ'kænɪkəl] *adj also Fig* mecánico(a); **m. engineer** ingeniero(a) *m,f* industrial; **m. engineering** ingeniería *f* industrial

**mechanics** [mɪ'kænɪks] **1** *n* **(a)** *(science)* mecánica *f* **(b)** *(working parts)* mecanismo *m*, mecánica *f*

**2** *npl Fig* **the m. of the electoral system** la mecánica del sistema electoral

**mechanism** ['mekənɪzəm] *n* mecanismo *m*

**mechanize** ['mekənaɪz] *vt* mecanizar

**mechanized** ['mekənaɪzd] *adj* **m. industry** industria *f* mecanizada; **m. troops** tropas *fpl* mecanizadas

**MEd** [e'med] *n Univ (abbr* **Master of Education)** *(title)* máster *m* en Pedagogía

**medal** ['medəl] *n* medalla *f*

**medalist** *US* = **medallist**

**medallion** [mɪ'dælɪən] *n* medallón *m*

**medallist,** *US* **medalist** ['medəlɪst] *n* medallista *mf*, ganador(ora) *m,f* de medalla; **gold/silver m.** medalla *mf* de oro/plata

**meddle** ['medəl] *vi* entrometerse **(in** en)

**meddler** ['medlə(r)] *n* entrometido(a) *m,f*

**meddlesome** ['medəlsəm] *adj* entrometido(a)

**media** ['miːdɪə] *n* **(a)** *(TV, press)* medios *mpl* de comunicación; **m. coverage** cobertura *f* informativa; **m. studies** ciencias *fpl* de la información **(b)** *pl of* **medium**

**mediaeval** = **medieval**

**median** ['miːdɪən] *Math* **1** *n* mediana *f*

**2** *adj* mediano(a)

**mediate** ['miːdɪeɪt] *vi* mediar **(in/between** en/entre)

**mediation** [miːdɪ'eɪʃən] *n* mediación *f*

**mediator** ['miːdɪeɪtə(r)] *n* mediador(ora) *m,f*

**medic** ['medɪk] *n (student)* estudiante *mf* de medicina; *(doctor)* médico(a) *m,f*

**medical** ['medɪkəl] **1** *n (physical examination)* reconocimiento *m or* examen *m* médico; **to**

**pass/fail a m.** pasar/no pasar un reconocimiento médico

**2** *adj (record, treatment, profession)* médico(a); *(book, student)* de medicina; **m. advice** consejo *m* médico; **m. insurance** seguro *m* médico *or* de enfermedad; **m. practitioner** facultativo(a) *m,f*, médico(a) *m,f*

**medicated** ['medɪkeɪtɪd] *adj* medicinal

**medication** [medɪ'keɪʃən] *n* medicamento *m*, medicina *f*; **to be on m.** tomar medicación

**medicinal** [me'dɪsɪnəl] *adj* medicinal

**medicine** ['medsɪn] *n* **(a)** *(science)* medicina *f*; **to practise m.** ejercer la medicina; **to study m.** estudiar medicina **(b)** *(drugs)* medicina *f*, medicamento *m*; *Fig* **to give sb a taste of his own m.** pagar a alguien con su misma moneda; **m. chest** *or* **cabinet** (armario *m* del) botiquín *m*; **m. man** *(traditional healer)* hechicero *m* (de la tribu), chamán *m*

**medieval** [medɪ'iːvəl] *adj* medieval

**mediocre** [miːdɪ'əʊkə(r)] *adj* mediocre

**mediocrity** [miːdɪ'ɒkrɪtɪ] *n* mediocridad *f*

**meditate** ['medɪteɪt] *vi (spiritually)* meditar; *(reflect)* reflexionar, meditar **(on** sobre)

**meditation** [medɪ'teɪʃən] *n (spiritual)* meditación *f*; *(reflection)* reflexión *f*

**Mediterranean** [medɪtə'reɪnɪən] **1** *n* **the M.** el Mediterráneo

**2** *adj* mediterráneo(a); **the M. Sea** el (mar) Mediterráneo

**medium** ['miːdɪəm] **1** *n* **(a)** *(pl* **media** ['miːdɪə] *or* **mediums )** *(means of expression, communication)* medio *m*; **through the m. of the press** a través de la prensa; *Art* **mixed media** técnica *f* mixta **(b)** *(in spiritualism)* médium *mf*

**2** *adj* medio(a); **of m. height** de estatura mediana; **in the m. term** a medio plazo; **m. dry** *(wine)* semiseco(a); *Culin* **m. rare** poco hecho(a); *Rad* **m. wave** onda *f* media

**medley** ['medlɪ] *n (pl* **medleys)** *n (mixture)* mezcla *f*; *Mus* popurrí *m*

**meek** [miːk] *adj* manso(a), dócil; **to be m. and mild** ser manso como un corderito

**meekly** ['miːklɪ] *adv* dócilmente

**meet** [miːt] *(pt & pp* **met** [met]) **1** *vt* **(a)** *(encounter) (by accident)* encontrar, encontrarse con; *(by arrangement)* encontrarse con, reunirse con; **to m. sb in the street** encontrarse con alguien en la calle; **to arrange to m. sb** quedar con alguien; **to go to m. sb** ir a encontrarse con alguien; **to m. sb at the station** ir a buscar a alguien a la estación; **his eyes met mine** nuestras miradas se encontraron; **a remarkable sight met our eyes** nos topamos con una vista extraordinaria; **there's more to this than meets the eye** es más complicado de lo que parece

**(b)** *(become acquainted with)* conocer; **m. Mr**

Jones le presento al señor Jones; **have you met my husband?** ¿conoces a mi marido?

(**c**) *(join with)* unirse con, juntarse con; **where East meets West** donde se encuentran el Oriente y el Occidente

(**d**) *(satisfy) (demand, need, condition)* satisfacer; *(objection, criticism)* responder a; *(cost, expense)* cubrir; *(order)* servir, cumplir; **to m. a deadline** cumplir (con) un plazo

(**e**) *(encounter) (danger, difficulties)* encontrar, encontrarse con; **to m. one's death** encontrar la muerte

**2** *vi* (**a**) *(by accident)* encontrarse; *(by arrangement)* quedar, encontrarse; **where shall we m.?** ¿dónde quedamos?; **our eyes met** nuestras miradas se encontraron

(**b**) *(become acquainted)* conocerse

(**c**) *(of society, assembly)* reunirse; **the club meets every Tuesday** el club se reúne todos los martes

(**d**) *(of rivers, continents)* encontrarse, unirse

►**meet up** *vi* encontrarse, quedar (**with** con)

►**meet with** *vt insep (danger, difficulty)* encontrarse con; *(success)* tener; *(accident)* sufrir; **to m. with failure** resultar un fracaso; **to m. with refusal** ser recibido(a) con rechazo

**meeting** ['miːtɪŋ] *n* (**a**) *(encounter) (by chance)* encuentro *m*; *(prearranged)* cita *f*; **m. place** lugar *m* or punto *m* de encuentro (**b**) *(of committee, delegates)* reunión *f*; **she's in a m.** está en una reunión; **to hold a m.** celebrar una reunión

**megabyte** ['megəbaɪt] *n Comptr* megabyte *m*, mega *m*

**megahertz** ['megəhɜːts] *n Elec* megahercio *m*

**megalomania** [megələʊ'meɪnɪə] *n* megalomanía *f*

**megalomaniac** [megələʊ'meɪnɪæk] *n* megalómano(a) *m,f*

**megaphone** ['megəfəʊn] *n* megáfono *m*

**megaton** ['megətʌn] *n* megatón *m*

**megawatt** ['megəwɒt] *n Elec* megavatio *m*

**melancholy** ['melənkəlɪ] **1** *n* melancolía *f*

**2** *adj* melancólico(a)

**melee** ['meleɪ] *n (excited crowd)* turba *f*, enjambre *m*; *(fight)* riña *f*, tumulto *m*

**mellifluous** [me'lɪfluəs] *adj* melifluo(a)

**mellow** ['meləʊ] **1** *adj (flavour)* delicado(a); *(wine)* añejo(a); *(voice, colour)* suave; *(person)* apacible, sosegado(a)

**2** *vi (of flavour)* ganar (con el tiempo); *(of wine)* añejarse; *(of voice, light)* suavizarse; *(of person)* serenarse, sosegarse

**melodic** [mɪ'lɒdɪk] *adj* melódico(a)

**melodious** [mɪ'ləʊdɪəs] *adj* melodioso(a)

**melodrama** ['melədrɑːmə] *n* melodrama *m*

**melodramatic** [melədrə'mætɪk] *adj* melodramático(a)

**melody** ['melədɪ] *n* melodía *f*

**melon** ['melən] *n (honeydew)* melón *m*; *(watermelon)* sandía *f*

**melt** [melt] **1** *vt* derretir, fundir; *Fig (sb's resistance)* vencer

**2** *vi* derretirse, fundirse; **it melts in the mouth** se funde en la boca; **to m. into thin air** esfumarse

►**melt away** *vi (of snow)* derretirse; *(of crowd)* dispersarse, disgregarse; *(of objections, opposition)* disiparse, desvanecerse

►**melt down** *vt sep (metal)* fundir

**meltdown** ['meltdaʊn] *n Phys (process)* = fusión accidental del núcleo de un reactor; *(leak)* fuga *f* radiactiva

**melting** ['meltɪŋ] *n* **m. point** punto *m* de fusión; *Fig* **m. pot** crisol *m*

**member** ['membə(r)] **1** *n* (**a**) *(of family, group)* miembro *m*; *(of club)* socio(a) *m,f*; *(of union, party)* afiliado(a) *m,f*, militante *mf*; *Br Pol* **M. of Parliament** diputado(a) *m,f* (**b**) *(limb, penis)* miembro *m*

**2** *adj* **m. country/state** país *m*/estado *m* miembro

**membership** ['membəʃɪp] *n* (**a**) *(state of being a member) (of club)* calidad *f* de socio; *(of party, union)* afiliación *f*; **to renew one's m.** *(of club)* renovar el carné de socio; *(of party, union)* renovar la afiliación; **m. card** carné *m* de socio/afiliado; **m. fee** cuota *f* de socio/afiliado (**b**) *(members) (of club)* socios *mpl*; *(of union, party)* afiliación *f*, afiliados(as) *mfpl*; **a large/small m.** un elevado/escaso número de socios/afiliados

**membrane** ['membreɪn] *n* membrana *f*

**memento** [mɪ'mentəʊ] *n (pl mementos or mementoes)* recuerdo *m*

**memo** ['meməʊ] *n (pl memos)* memorándum *m*; *(within office)* nota *f*; **m. pad** bloc *m* de notas

**memoir** ['memwɑː(r)] *n (biography)* biografía *f*; *(essay)* memoria *f*; **she's writing her memoirs** está escribiendo sus memorias

**memorable** ['memərəbəl] *adj* memorable

**memorandum** [memə'rændəm] *n (pl memorandums or memoranda* [memə'rændə]) *n* memorándum *m*; *(within office)* nota *f*

**memorial** [mɪ'mɔːrɪəl] **1** *n (monument)* monumento *m* conmemorativo

**2** *adj* conmemorativo(a)

**memorize** ['meməraɪz] *vt* memorizar

**memory** ['memərɪ] *n* (**a**) *(faculty) & Comptr* memoria *f*; **to have a good/bad m.** tener buena/mala memoria; **if my m. serves me right** si la memoria no me engaña; **from m.** de memoria; **to commit sth to m.** memorizar algo; **there has been famine here within living m.** aquí todavía se recuerdan épocas de hambre; **m. loss** pérdida *f* de memoria

**(b)** *(thing remembered)* recuerdo *m*; **good/bad memories (of sth)** buenos/malos recuerdos (de algo); **my earliest memories** mis primeros recuerdos; **to have no m. of sth** no recordar algo; **in m. of...** en memoria de...; **to take a trip down m. lane** volver al pasado

**men** [men] *pl of* **man**

**menace** ['menis] **1** *n (threat)* amenaza *f*; *(danger)* peligro *m*; *Fam* **that kid's a m.** este niño es un demonio
**2** *vt* amenazar

**menacing** ['menəsiŋ] *adj* amenazador(ora)

**menagerie** [mɪ'nædʒərɪ] *n* colección *f* de animales *(privada)*

**mend** [mend] **1** *n Fam* **she's on the m.** se está recuperando
**2** *vt (repair)* arreglar; *(garment)* coser, remendar; **to m. one's ways** corregirse
**3** *vi (of broken bone)* soldarse

**menfolk** ['menfəuk] *npl* **the m.** los hombres

**menial** ['mi:nɪəl] **1** *n Pej* lacayo(a) *m,f*
**2** *adj* ingrato(a), penoso(a)

**meningitis** [menɪn'dʒaɪtɪs] *n* meningitis *f inv*

**menopause** ['menəpɔ:z] *n* menopausia *f*

**menstrual** ['menstruəl] *adj* menstrual; **m. cycle** ciclo *m* menstrual

**menstruate** ['menstrueɪt] *vi* tener la menstruación, menstruar

**menstruation** [menstru'eɪʃən] *n* menstruación *f*

**menswear** ['menzweə(r)] *n* ropa *f* de caballero *or* hombre; **m. department** departamento *m or* sección *f* de caballeros

**mental** ['mentəl] *adj* **(a)** *(state, age)* mental; **to make a m. note of sth/to do sth** tratar de acordarse de algo/de hacer algo; **to have a m. block about sth** tener un bloqueo mental con algo; **m. arithmetic** cálculo *m* mental; **to have a m. breakdown** sufrir un ataque de enajenación mental; **m. health** salud *f* mental; **m. hospital** hospital *m* psiquiátrico; **m. illness** enfermedad *f* mental
**(b)** *very Fam (mad)* zumbado(a), pirado(a); **to be m.** estar como una chota *or* mal de la azotea; **he went m. when I told him** *(angry)* se puso cabreado como una mona cuando se lo conté

**mentality** [men'tælɪt] *n* mentalidad *f*

**mentally** ['mentəlɪ] *adv* mentalmente; **to be m. handicapped** tener una minusvalía psíquica; **to be m. ill** tener una enfermedad mental

**menthol** ['menθɒl] *n* mentol *m*; **m. cigarettes** cigarrillos *mpl* mentolados

**mention** ['menʃən] **1** *n* mención *f*; **to make m. of sth** hacer mención de algo
**2** *vt* mencionar; **to m. sb in one's will** mencionar *or* incluir a alguien en el testamento; **not to m. ...** por no mencionar...; **now that you**

**m. it** ahora que lo dices; **don't m. it!** ¡no hay de qué!

**mentor** ['mentɔ:(r)] *n* mentor(ora) *m,f*

**menu** ['menju:] *n (list of dishes) (at restaurant)* carta *f*, menú *m*; *(for a particular meal)* menú *m*; *Comptr* menú *m*

**MEP** [emi:'pi:] *n Br Pol (abbr* **Member of the European Parliament)** eurodiputado(a) *m,f*

**mercantile** ['mɜ:kəntaɪl] *adj* mercantil

**mercenary** ['mɜ:smərɪ] *n & adj* mercenario(a) *m,f*

**merchandise** ['mɜ:tʃəndaɪz] **1** *n* mercancías *fpl*, géneros *mpl*
**2** *vt* comercializar

**merchandising** ['mɜ:tʃəndaɪzɪŋ] *n Com* artículos *mpl* de promoción *or* promocionales

**merchant** ['mɜ:tʃənt] *n* comerciante *m,f*; **m. bank** banco *m* mercantil *or* de negocios; **m. navy** marina *f* mercante; **m. seaman** marino *m* mercante; **m. ship** buque *m or* barco *m* mercante

**merchantman** ['mɜ:tʃəntmən] *n (ship)* buque *m or* barco *m* mercante

**merciful** ['mɜ:sɪfʊl] *adj* compasivo(a), clemente

**mercifully** ['mɜ:sɪfʊlɪ] *adv (showing mercy)* con compasión; *(fortunately)* afortunadamente

**merciless** ['mɜ:sɪlɪs] *adj* despiadado(a)

**mercurial** [mɜ:'kjuərɪəl] *adj* voluble, veleidoso(a)

**Mercury** ['mɜ:kjʊrɪ] *n (planet, god)* Mercurio *m*

**mercury** ['mɜ:kjʊrɪ] *n Chem* mercurio *m*

**mercy** ['mɜ:sɪ] *n* compasión *f*, clemencia *f*; **to have m. on sb** tener compasión *or* apiadarse de alguien; **to beg for m.** suplicar clemencia; **to be at the m. of** estar a merced de; **we should be thankful for small mercies** habría que dar gracias de que las cosas no vayan aún peor; **m. killing** eutanasia *f*

**mere** [mɪə(r)] *adj* simple, mero(a); **a m. 10% of the candidates passed the test** tan sólo un 10% de los aspirantes superaron la prueba; **the m. mention/presence of...** la sola *or* mera mención/presencia de...; **there was the merest hint of irony in his voice** en su voz había un matiz casi imperceptible de ironía

**merely** ['mɪəlɪ] *adv* meramente, simplemente

**merge** [mɜ:dʒ] **1** *vt (in general)* fundir; *(companies, organizations)* fusionar; *Comptr (files)* fusionar, unir
**2** *vi (in general)* fundirse **(into/with** con); *Com Fin (of companies, banks)* fusionarse; **to m. into the background** perderse de vista

**merger** ['mɜ:dʒə(r)] *n Com* fusión *f*

**meridian** [mə'rɪdɪən] *n Geog Astron* meridiano *m*

**meringue** [mə'ræŋ] n Culin merengue m

**merit** ['merɪt] **1** n (advantage, worth) mérito m; **the merits of peace** las ventajas de la paz; **to judge sth on its merits** juzgar algo por sus méritos; **in order of m.** según los méritos

**2** vt merecer; **we hardly m. a mention in the report** apenas nos mencionan en el informe

**meritocracy** [merɪ'tɒkrəsɪ] n meritocracia f

**meritorious** [merɪ'tɔːrɪəs] adj Formal meritorio(a)

**mermaid** ['mɜːmeɪd] n sirena f

**merrily** ['merɪlɪ] adv alegremente

**merriment** ['merɪmənt] n alegría f, regocijo m

**merry** ['merɪ] adj (a) (happy) alegre; **to make m.** festejar; **M. Christmas!** ¡Feliz Navidad!; **the more the merrier** cuantos más, mejor (b) (slightly drunk) alegre, piripi

**merry-go-round** ['merɪgəʊraʊnd] n tiovivo m

**mesh** [meʃ] **1** n (of net, sieve) malla f, red f

**2** vi (a) (of gears) engranarse (b) (of proposals) estar de acuerdo; (of ideas, characters) encajar

**mesmerize** ['mezməraɪz] vt cautivar

**mess** [mes] **1** n (a) (disorder) lío m, desorden m; **the kitchen's a m.** la cocina está toda revuelta; **you look a m.!** ¡estás hecho un desastre!; **to be in a m.** (of room) estar todo(a) revuelto(a); Fig (of person) estar en un lío o aprieto; Fig **to make a m. of sth** (bungle) hacer algo desastrosamente. (b) (dirt) porquería f; **the dog's done a m. on the carpet** el perro ha hecho caca en la alfombra (c) Mil comedor m; **m. tin** plato m de campaña or del rancho

**2** vi Fam (of dog, cat) hacer caca

➤**mess about, mess around** Fam**1** vt sep (treat badly) traer a maltraer

**2** vi (a) (fool about, waste time) hacer el tonto (b) (tinker) **to m. about** or **around with sth** enredar con algo

➤**mess up** vt sep Fam (room) desordenar; (hair) revolver; (plan) estropear

**message** ['mesɪdʒ] n mensaje m; **to leave a m. for sb** dejar un recado a o para alguien; Fam **to get the m.** enterarse

**messenger** ['mesɪndʒə(r)] n mensajero(a) m,f; **m. boy** chico m de los recados

**Messiah** [mɪ'saɪə] n Rel Mesías m inv

**messianic** [mesɪ'ænɪk] adj mesiánico(a)

**messily** ['mesɪlɪ] adv **to eat m.** ponerse perdido(a) comiendo; Fig **to end m.** (of relationship) terminar mal

**Messrs** ['mesəz] npl (abbr **Messieurs**) Sres., señores mpl

**mess-up** ['mesʌp] n Fam lío m, desastre m

**messy** ['mesɪ] adj (a) (dirty) sucio(a); **to be m.** (place) estar sucio(a); (person) ser sucio(a) (b) (untidy) (room) desordenado(a); (hair) revuel-

to(a); (appearance) desastroso(a); (handwriting) malo(a); (person) desaliñado(a) (c) (unpleasantly complex) lioso(a)

**met** [met] pt & pp of **meet**

**metabolic** [metə'bɒlɪk] adj metabólico(a)

**metabolism** [mɪ'tæbəlɪzəm] n metabolismo m

**metal** ['metəl] **1** n metal m; **m. detector** detector m de metales; **m. polish** abrillantador m de metales

**2** adj metálico(a)

**metalled road** ['metəld'rəʊd] n carretera f de grava

**metallic** [mɪ'tælɪk] adj (sound, voice, taste) metálico(a); (paint) metalizado(a)

**metallurgy** [me'tælədʒɪ] n metalurgia f

**metalwork** ['metəlwɜːk] n (craft) trabajo m del metal, metalistería f; (articles) objetos mpl de metal

**metamorphosis** [metə'mɔːfəsɪs] (pl **metamorphoses** [metə'mɔːfəsiːz]) n metamorfosis f sing

**metaphor** ['metəfə(r)] n metáfora f

**metaphoric(al)** [metə'fɒrɪk(əl)] adj metafórico(a)

**metaphysical** [metə'fɪzɪkəl] adj metafísico(a)

**metaphysics** [metə'fɪzɪks] n (subject) metafísica f

➤**mete out** [miːt] vt sep (punishment) imponer; (justice) aplicar (to a)

**meteor** ['miːtɪə(r)] n meteoro m, bólido m

**meteoric** [miːtɪ'ɒrɪk] adj meteórico(a); Fig **a m. rise** un ascenso meteórico

**meteorite** ['miːtɪəraɪt] n meteorito m

**meteorological** [miːtɪərə'lɒdʒɪkəl] adj meteorológico(a)

**meteorology** [miːtɪə'rɒlədʒɪ] n meteorología f

**meter** ['miːtə(r)] n (a) (device) contador m; (gas/electricity) m. contador (del gas/de la electricidad); (parking) m. parquímetro m; **m. reading** lectura f del contador (b) US = **metre**

**methadone** ['meθədəʊn] n metadona f

**methane** ['miːθeɪn] n Chem metano m

**method** ['meθəd] n método m; **there's m. in his madness** no está tan loco como parece; Th & Cin **m. acting** interpretación f según el método de Stanislavski

**methodical** [mɪ'θɒdɪkəl] adj metódico(a)

**Methodism** ['meθədɪzəm] n Rel metodismo m

**Methodist** ['meθədɪst] n Rel metodista mf

**methodology** [meθə'dɒlədʒɪ] n metodología f

**methylated spirits** ['meθɪleɪtɪd'spɪrɪts], *Fam* **meths** [meθs] *n Br* alcohol *m* desnaturalizado *(con metanol)*, alcohol *m* de quemar

**meticulous** [mɪ'tɪkjʊləs] *adj* meticuloso(a)

**metre¹** ['mi:tə(r)] *n (of poetry)* metro *m*

**metre²**, *US* **meter** *n (measurement)* metro *m*

**metric** ['metrɪk] *adj (system)* métrico(a)

**metronome** ['metrənəʊm] *n Mus* metrónomo *m*

**metropolis** [mɪ'trɒpəlɪs] *n* metrópolis *f inv*

**metropolitan** [metrə'pɒlɪtən] *adj* metropolitano(a); **the M. Police** la policía de Londres

**mettle** ['metəl] *n (courage)* valor *m*, ánimo *m*; **you'll have to be on your m.** tendrás que dar el do de pecho; **she showed her m.** demostró de lo que era capaz

**mew** [mju:] **1** *n* maullido *m*
**2** *vi* maullar

**mews** [mju:z] *n Br (backstreet)* = plazoleta o callejuela formada por antiguos establos convertidos en viviendas o garajes; **m. cottage** = antiguo establo reconvertido en apartamento de lujo

**Mexican** ['meksɪkən] **1** *n* mejicano(a) *m,f*, mexicano(a) *m,f*
**2** *adj* mejicano(a), mexicano(a); **M. wave** *(in stadium)* ola *f* (mejicana)

**Mexico** ['meksɪkəʊ] *n* Méjico, México; **M. City** Ciudad de Méjico *or* México

**mezzanine** ['metsəni:n] *n* **m. (floor)** entreplanta *f*

**mg** [em'dʒi:] *n (abbr* **milligram(s))** mg, miligramo *m*

**Mgr** *Rel (abbr* **monsignor)** Mons., monseñor *m*

**MHz** *Elec (abbr* **megahertz)** Mhz, megahercio *m*

**mi** [mi:] *n Mus* mi *m*

**MI5** [emaɪ'faɪv] *n Br (abbr* **Military Intelligence Section 5)** = servicio británico de espionaje interior

**MI6** [emaɪ'sɪks] *n Br (abbr* **Military Intelligence Section 6)** = servicio británico de espionaje exterior

**miaow** [mɪ'aʊ] **1** *n* maullido *m*; **m.!** ¡miau!
**2** *vi* maullar

**mica** ['maɪkə] *n* mica *f*

**mice** [maɪs] *pl of* **mouse**

**mickey** ['mɪkɪ] *n Br Fam* **to take the m. (out of sb)** tomar el pelo (a alguien)

**Mickey Mouse** ['mɪkɪ'maʊs] *adj Fam Pej (job, qualification)* de tres al cuarto

**micro** ['maɪkrəʊ] *(pl* **micros)** *n Comptr* microordenador *m*

**microbe** ['maɪkrəʊb] *n* microbio *m*

**microbiology** [maɪkrəʊbaɪ'ɒlədʒɪ] *n* microbiología *f*

**microchip** ['maɪkrəʊtʃɪp] *n Comptr* microchip *m*

**microcomputer** ['maɪkrəʊkəm'pju:tə(r)] *n Comptr* microordenador *m*

**microcosm** ['maɪkrəʊkɒzəm] *n* microcosmos *m inv*

**microfiche** ['maɪkrəʊfi:ʃ] *n* microficha *f*

**microfilm** ['maɪkrəʊfɪlm] **1** *n* microfilm *m*
**2** *vt* microfilmar

**micrometer** [maɪ'krɒmɪtə(r)] *n* micrómetro *m*

**microorganism** ['maɪkrəʊ'ɔ:rgənɪzəm] *n* microorganismo *m*

**microphone** ['maɪkrəfəʊn] *n* micrófono *m*

**microprocessor** ['maɪkrəʊ'prəʊsesə(r)] *n Comptr* microprocesador *m*

**microscope** ['maɪkrəskəʊp] *n* microscopio *m*

**microscopic** [maɪkrə'skɒpɪk] *adj* microscópico(a)

**microsurgery** [maɪkrəʊ'sɜ:dʒərɪ] *n* microcirugía *f*

**microwave** ['maɪkrəʊweɪv] **1** *n Phys* microonda *f*; **m. (oven)** microondas *m inv*
**2** *vt* cocinar en el microondas

**mid** [mɪd] *adj in* **m. ocean** en medio del océano; **in m. June** a mediados de junio; **she stopped in m. sentence** se detuvo a mitad de la frase

**midair** [mɪd'eə(r)] **1** *n Fig* **to leave sth in m.** dejar algo en el aire
**2** *adj (collision, explosion)* en pleno vuelo

**mid-Atlantic accent** [mɪdət'læntɪk'æksent] *n* = acento a medio camino entre el británico y el americano

**midday** ['mɪd'deɪ] *n* mediodía *m*; **at m.** a mediodía; **m. meal** comida *f*, almuerzo *m*

**middle** ['mɪdəl] **1** *n* **(a)** *(in general)* medio *m*; **in the m. of the room** en medio de la habitación; **to be in the m. of doing sth** estar ocupado(a) haciendo algo; **he was in the m. of an important conversation** estaba en mitad de una importante conversación; **in the m. of the month** a mediados de mes; **in the m. of the night** en plena noche, en mitad de la noche; *Fig* **to split sth down the m.** dividir algo por la mitad; **in the m. of nowhere** en un lugar dejado de la mano de Dios
**(b)** *(waist)* cintura *f*
**2** *adj (in the middle)* del medio; **m. age** edad *f* madura, madurez *f*; *Hist* **the M. Ages** la Edad Media; *Mus* **m. C** do *m* central; **the m. class(es)** la clase media; *Fig* **to steer a m. course** *(in politics, diplomacy)* tomar la vía intermedia; **in the m. distance** a media distancia; **the M. East** Oriente *m* Medio; **M. Eastern** de Oriente Medio; *Pol* **the m. ground** el centro; **m. management** mandos *mpl* intermedios;

**m. name** segundo nombre *m*; *Fam* **"generosity" isn't exactly his m. name!** no destaca precisamente por su generosidad

**middle-aged** [mɪdəl'eɪdʒd] *adj* de mediana edad

**middlebrow** ['mɪdəlbrəʊ] *adj (tastes, interests)* del público medio; **a m. novelist** un/una novelista para el público medio

**middle-class** [mɪdəl'klɑ:s] *adj* de clase media

**middleman** ['mɪdəlmæn] *n* intermediario *m*

**middle-of-the-road** ['mɪdləvðə'rəʊd] *adj (policy)* moderado(a); *(music)* convencional

**middle-sized** ['mɪdəl'saɪzd] *adj* mediano(a)

**middleweight** ['mɪdəlweɪt] *n (in boxing)* peso *m* medio

**middling** ['mɪdlɪŋ] *adj* regular

**midfield** [mɪd'fi:ld] *n (in football)* media *f*, centro *m* del campo; **m. player** centrocampista *mf*

**midfielder** [mɪd'fi:ldə(r)] *n (in football)* centrocampista *mf*

**midge** [mɪdʒ] *n* mosquito *m*

**midget** ['mɪdʒɪt] **1** *n (small person)* enano(a) *m,f*
**2** *adj* en miniatura

**midi system** ['mɪdɪ'sɪstəm] *n (stereo)* minicadena *f*

**Midlands** ['mɪdləndz] *npl* **the M.** = la región central de Inglaterra

**midlife crisis** ['mɪdlaɪf'kraɪsɪs] *n* crisis *f inv* de los cuarenta

**midmorning** [mɪd'mɔ:nɪŋ] *n* media mañana *f*

**midnight** ['mɪdnaɪt] *n* medianoche *f*; **to burn the m. oil** quedarse hasta muy tarde *(estudiando o trabajando)*

**midriff** ['mɪdrɪf] *n* diafragma *m*

**midshipman** ['mɪdʃɪpmən] *n* guardia *m* marina, guardiamarina *m*

**midst** [mɪdst] *n* **in the m. of** en medio de; **in our/their m.** entre nosotros/ellos

**midstream** [mɪd'stri:m] *n* **in m.** por el centro del río; *Fig (when speaking)* en mitad del discurso; **to interrupt sb in m.** interrumpir a alguien en plena conversación

**midsummer** ['mɪdsʌmə(r)] *n* pleno verano *m*; **M.'s Day** el 24 de junio, San Juan

**midterm** ['mɪd'tɜ:m] *n* **(a)** *Pol Br* **m. by-election** = elecciones parciales a mitad de legislatura; *US* **m. elections** = elecciones a mitad del mandato presidencial **(b)** *Sch Univ* de mitad de trimestre; **m. break** = vacaciones de mitad de trimestre

**midway** ['mɪdweɪ] **1** *adj* medio(a)
**2** *adv. (in space)* a mitad de camino, a medio camino; *(in time)* hacia la mitad

**midweek** [mɪd'wi:k] *adv* a mediados de semana; **m. show/flight** representación *f*/vuelo *m* de mitad de semana

**Mid-West** ['mɪd'west] *n* Medio Oeste *m* (de Estados Unidos)

**Mid-Western** [mɪd'westən] *adj* del Medio Oeste (de Estados Unidos)

**midwife** ['mɪdwaɪf] *n* comadrona *f*

**midwifery** [mɪd'wɪfərɪ] *n* obstetricia *f*

**midwinter** ['mɪd'wɪntə(r)] *n* pleno invierno *m*

**might¹** [maɪt] *n (strength)* fuerza *f*, poder *m*; **with all his m.** *(to work, push)* con todas sus fuerzas; *Prov* **m. is right** quien tiene la fuerza tiene la razón

**might²**

En el inglés hablado, y en el escrito en estilo coloquial, la forma negativa **might not** se transforma en **mightn't**. La forma **might have** se transforma en **might've**. Cuando expresa posibilidad (ver (a)), puede utilizarse **may** sin que se altere apenas el significado.

*v aux* **(a)** *(expressing possibility)* **it m. be difficult** puede que sea o puede ser difícil; **I m. go if I feel like it** puede que vaya si tengo ganas; **it m. be better to ask permission first** sería mejor pedir permiso primero; **you m. want to…** tal vez podrías…; **shall we go? – we m. as well** ¿nos vamos? – bueno, vale; **I wonder what I m. have done to offend him** me pregunto qué le habré hecho para que se ofenda; **I m. as well be talking to myself!** ¡es como si hablara con la pared!

**(b)** *(as past form of* may*)* **I knew he m. be angry** ya sabía que se podía enfadar; **I was afraid she m. have killed him** tenía miedo de que (ella) lo hubiera matado; **he said he m. be late** dijo que quizá se retrasaría

**(c)** *Formal (asking for permission)* **m. I have a word with you?** ¿podría hablar un momento con usted?

**(d)** *(with concessions)* **it might not be the fastest car in the world, but…** no será el coche más rápido del mundo, pero…

**mightily** ['maɪtɪlɪ] *adv* **(a)** *(powerfully)* con fuerza **(b)** *Fam* cantidad de, muy; **to be m. relieved** quedarse aliviadísimo(a)

**mightn't** ['maɪtənt] = **might not**

**might've** ['maɪtəv] = **might have**

**mighty** ['maɪtɪ] **1** *adj* **(a)** *(powerful)* fuerte, poderoso(a) **(b)** *(large, imposing)* grandioso(a)
**2** *adv US Fam* cantidad de, muy

**migraine** ['mi:greɪn] *n* migraña *f*

**migrant** ['maɪgrənt] **1** *n (person)* emigrante *m,f*; *(bird)* ave *f* migratoria
**2** *adj* migratorio(a); **m. worker** trabajador(ora) *m,f* inmigrante

**migrate** [maɪ'greɪt] vi migrar, emigrar

**migration** [maɪ'greɪʃən] n migración f, emigración f

**migratory** ['maɪgrətrɪ] adj migratorio(a)

**mike** [maɪk] n Fam (microphone) micro m, micrófono m

**Milan** [mɪ'læn] n Milán

**mild** [maɪld] **1** adj (person, remark) apacible, afable; (food) suave; (punishment, illness, criticism) leve; (climate) benigno(a), suave; (displeasure, amusement) ligero(a)
  **2** n Br (beer) cerveza f tostada (suave)

**mildew** ['mɪldju:] n moho m; (on plants) añublo m

**mildly** ['maɪldlɪ] adv (a) (to say) con suavidad (b) (moderately) ligeramente; **to put it m.** por no decir algo peor

**mildness** ['maɪldnɪs] n (of person) afabilidad f; (of weather) suavidad f; (of criticism) comedimiento m; (of punishment) levedad f

**mile** [maɪl] n (distance) milla f (= 1,6 km); **miles per hour** millas por hora; **he lives miles away** vive a kilómetros de distancia; Fam Fig **to be miles away** (be daydreaming) estar en Babia; Fam **miles better** muchísimo mejor; Fam **it sticks** or **stands out a m.** se ve a la legua

**mileage** ['maɪlɪdʒ] n (a) (distance travelled) ≃ kilómetros mpl (recorridos); **m. allowance** ≃ (dieta f de) kilometraje m (b) (rate of fuel consumption) consumo m (de millas por galón de gasolina); Fig **to get a lot of m. out of sth** sacarle mucho partido a algo

**milestone** ['maɪlstəʊn] n (on road) mojón m; Fig (in career, history) hito m

**milieu** ['mi:ljɜ:] n entorno m, medio m

**militant** ['mɪlɪtənt] **1** n militante mf, activista mf
  **2** adj militante

**militarism** ['mɪlɪtərɪzəm] n militarismo m

**military** ['mɪlɪtrɪ] **1** n **the m.** el ejército
  **2** adj militar; **m. academy** academia f militar; **m. man** militar m; **m. police** policía f militar; **m. service** servicio m militar

**militate** ['mɪlɪteɪt] vi (of fact, reason) obrar (**against** en contra de)

**militia** [mɪ'lɪʃə] n milicia f

**milk** [mɪlk] **1** n leche f; **the m. of human kindness** el don de la amabilidad; **m. of magnesia** magnesia f; **m. bottle** botella f de leche; **m. chocolate** chocolate m con leche; **m. churn** lechera f; **m. float** = camioneta eléctrica para el reparto de leche; **m. jug** jarra f de leche; **m. round** = ruta de reparto de leche; **m. shake** batido m; **m. tooth** diente m de leche
  **2** vt (cow) ordeñar; Fam Fig **to m. sb dry** (exploit) exprimir a alguien hasta la última gota; Fig

**they milked the story for all it was worth** le sacaron todo el jugo posible a la noticia

**milking** ['mɪlkɪŋ] n ordeño m; **m. machine** ordeñadora f

**milkman** ['mɪlkmən] n lechero m

**milky** ['mɪlkɪ] adj (containing too much milk) con demasiada leche; (containing a lot of milk) con mucha leche; (colour) lechoso(a); **the M. Way** la Vía Láctea

**mill** [mɪl] **1** n (a) (grinder) molinillo m; (for flour) molino m; Fam **to put sb through the m.** hacérselas pasar moradas a alguien (b) (textile factory) fábrica f de tejidos
  **2** vt (grain) moler; (metal) fresar
  ▸**mill about, mill around** vi (of crowd) pulular

**millennium** [mɪ'lenɪəm] n milenio m

**miller** ['mɪlə(r)] n molinero(a) m,f

**millet** ['mɪlɪt] n mijo m

**milligram(me)** ['mɪlɪɡræm] n miligramo m

**millilitre** ['mɪlɪli:tə(r)] n mililitro m

**millimetre** ['mɪlɪmi:tə(r)] n milímetro m

**milliner** ['mɪlɪnə(r)] n sombrerero(a) m,f

**million** ['mɪljən] n millón m; **two m. men** dos millones de hombres; Fam **I've told him a m. times** se lo he dicho millones de veces; Fam **thanks a m.!** ¡un millón de gracias!; Fam **she's one in a m.** es única

**millionaire** [mɪljə'neə(r)] n millonario(a) m,f

**millionairess** [mɪljə'neərɪs] n millonaria f

**millionth** ['mɪljənθ] **1** n (a) (fraction) millonésimo m (b) (in series) millonésimo(a) m,f
  **2** adj millonésimo(a)

**millipede** ['mɪlɪpi:d] n milpiés m inv

**millpond** ['mɪlpɒnd] n **as calm as a m.** (of water) como una balsa de aceite, totalmente en calma

**millstone** ['mɪlstəʊn] n muela f, rueda f de molino; Fig **it's a m. round my neck** es una cruz que llevo encima

**milometer** [maɪ'lɒmɪtə(r)] n (in car) cuentakilómetros m inv

**mime** [maɪm] **1** n (performance) mimo m, pantomima f; **m. artist** mimo m
  **2** vt representar con gestos
  **3** vi hacer mimo

**mimic** ['mɪmɪk] **1** n imitador(ora) m,f
  **2** vt (pt & pp **mimicked**) imitar

**mimicry** ['mɪmɪkrɪ] n imitación f

**Min** Mus (abbr **Minor**) menor

**min** (a) (abbr **minute(s)**) min., minuto m
(b) (abbr **minimum**) mín., mínimo m

**minaret** [mɪnə'ret] n alminar m, minarete m

**mince** [mɪns] **1** n Br carne f picada; **m. pie** (containing meat) = especie de empanada de carne picada; (containing fruit) = pastel navideño a base de fruta escarchada, frutos secos y especias

**2** vt (chop up) picar; Fig **she doesn't m. her words** no tiene pelos en la lengua

**3** vi (walk) caminar con afectación

**mincemeat** ['mɪnsmiːt] n (meat) carne f picada; (fruit) = relleno a base de fruta escarchada, frutos secos, especias, zumo de limón y grasa animal; Fam Fig **to make m. of sb** hacer picadillo a alguien

**mincer** ['mɪnsə(r)] n picadora f (de carne)

**mincing** ['mɪnsɪŋ] adj (walk, voice) afectado(a)

**mind** [maɪnd] **1** n **(a)** (thoughts) mente f; **to see sth in one's m.'s eye** hacerse una imagen mental de algo; **to bear** or **keep sth in m.** tener algo en cuenta; **it went completely** or **clean out of my m.** se me fue por completo de la cabeza; **to have sth on one's m.** tener algo en la cabeza; **to put** or **set sb's m. at rest** tranquilizar a alguien; **to take sb's m. off sth** quitarle a alguien algo de la cabeza, hacer que alguien olvide algo; **I couldn't get it off my m.** no podía quitármelo de la cabeza; **it puts me in m. of…** me recuerda…

**(b)** (opinion) **to my m.** en mi opinión; **to speak one's m.** hablar sin rodeos; **to change one's m. (about sth)** cambiar de opinión (acerca de algo); Fam **I gave him a piece of my m.** le canté las cuarenta; **to be of one m., to be of the same m.** ser de la misma opinión; **to keep an open m. (about sth)** no formarse ideas preconcebidas (respecto a algo)

**(c)** (will, wants) **she knows her own m.** sabe bien lo que quiere; **to have a m. of one's own** ser capaz de pensar or decidir por sí mismo(a); **to make up one's m.** decidirse; **to be in two minds (about sth)** estar indeciso(a) (acerca de algo); **I've a good m. to do it** me estoy planteando seriamente or tengo en mente hacerlo; **I've half a m. to tell his parents** me entran ganas de decírselo a sus padres; **this computer has a m. of its own** este ordenador hace lo que le da la gana; **to have sth/sb in m.** estar pensando en algo/alguien

**(d)** (attention) **to keep one's m. on sth** mantenerse concentrado(a) en algo; **your m. is not on the job** no estás concentrado en el trabajo; **I'm sure if you put your m. to it you could do it** estoy seguro de que podrías hacerlo si pusieses tus cinco sentidos (en ello)

**(e)** (way of thinking) **to have the m. of a three-year-old** tener la mentalidad de un niño de tres años; **you've got a dirty/nasty m.!** ¡qué ideas más cochinas/desagradables tienes!

**(f)** (reason) **to be out of one's m.** (mad) haber perdido el juicio; **to be bored out of one's m.** estar más aburrido(a) que una ostra; **to be worried out of one's m.** estar muerto(a) de preocupación; **no-one in his right m….** nadie en su sano juicio…; **his m. is going** se le va

la cabeza

**(g)** (person) **one of the finest minds of this century** una de las mentes más insignes de este siglo; Prov **great minds think alike** los genios siempre tenemos las mismas ideas

**2** vt **(a)** (pay attention to) **m. you don't fall!** ¡ten cuidado no te caigas or no te vayas a caer!; **mind you're not late!** ¡ten cuidado de no llegar tarde!; **m. the step!** ¡cuidado con el escalón!; **m. your language!** ¡vaya lenguaje!, ¡no digas tacos!

**(b)** (concern oneself with) preocuparse de or por; **never m. the car/money** no te preocupes por el coche/dinero; **m. you, I've always thought that…** fíjate, yo siempre he pensado que…

**(c)** (object to) **I don't m. the cold** el frío no me importa or no me molesta; **what I mind is…** lo que me molesta es…; **I don't m. trying** no me importa intentarlo; **if you don't m. my asking,…** si no te importa que te lo pregunte; **would you m. not doing that?** ¿te importaría no hacer eso?; **I wouldn't m. a cup of tea** me gustaría tomar una taza de té

**(d)** (look after) (children) cuidar; (house, shop) atender

**3** vi **(a)** (object) **do you m.!** (how dare you) ¡oiga usted!; **do you m. if I smoke?** ¿le importa or molesta que fume?; **I don't m.** no me importa; **I don't m. if I do** (accepting sth offered) ¿por qué no?

**(b)** (trouble oneself) **never m.!** ¡es igual!; **never m. about that now** olvídate de eso ahora; Fam **never you m.!** (it's none of your business) ¡no es asunto tuyo!

►**mind out** vi Br **m. out!** ¡cuidado!

**mind-boggling** ['maɪndbɒglɪŋ], **mind-blowing** ['maɪndbləʊɪŋ] adj Fam alucinante

**minded** ['maɪndɪd] adj **if you were so m.** si te pusieras (a hacerlo); **he is commercially/mechanically m.** se le da muy bien el comercio/la mecánica

**minder** ['maɪndə(r)] n Fam (bodyguard) guardaespaldas mf inv; (child or baby) **m.** canguro mf

**mindful** ['maɪndfʊl] adj **to be m. of sth** ser consciente de algo

**mindless** ['maɪndlɪs] adj (destruction, violence) gratuito(a), absurdo(a); (task, job) mecánico(a)

**mind-reader** ['maɪndriːdə(r)] n adivinador(-ora) m,f del pensamiento; Fam Hum **I'm not a m.!** ¡yo no soy ningún adivino!

**mine¹** [maɪn] **1** n **(a)** (for coal, tin, diamonds) mina f; Fig **a m. of information** una mina or un filón de información; **m. shaft** pozo m de extracción **(b)** (bomb) **m.** mina f; **m. detector** detector m de minas

**2** vt **(a)** (coal, gold) extraer **(b)** (place explosive *mines in)* minar

**3** *vi* **to m. for coal/gold** extraer carbón/oro

**mine²** *possessive pron* (**a**) *(singular)* el mío *m*, la mía *f*; *(plural)* los míos *mpl*, las mías *fpl*; **her house is big but m. is bigger** su casa es grande, pero la mía es mayor

(**b**) *(used attributively) (singular)* mío(a); *(plural)* míos(as); **this book is m.** este libro es mío; **a friend of m.** un amigo mío

**minefield** ['maɪnfiːld] *n* campo *m* de minas; *Fig (in law, politics)* campo *m* minado, polvorín *m*

**miner** ['maɪnə(r)] *n* minero(a) *m,f*

**mineral** ['mɪnərəl] *n* mineral *m*; **m. deposits** depósitos *mpl* minerales; **m. water** agua *f* mineral

**minesweeper** ['maɪnswiːpə(r)] *n (ship)* dragaminas *m inv*

**mingle** ['mɪŋɡəl] **1** *vt* mezclar

**2** *vi (of things)* mezclarse; *(of person)* alternar; **to m. with the crowd** mezclarse con la multitud

**mini** ['mɪnɪ] *n (miniskirt)* mini *f*, minifalda *f*

**miniature** ['mɪnɪtʃə(r)] **1** *n* miniatura *f*

**2** *adj* en miniatura

**miniaturize** ['mɪnɪtʃəraɪz] *vt* miniaturizar

**minibus** ['mɪnɪbʌs] *n* microbús *m*

**minicab** ['mɪnɪkæb] *n* radiotaxi *m*

**minim** ['mɪnɪm] *n Mus* blanca *f*

**minimal** ['mɪnɪməl] *adj* mínimo(a)

**minimize** ['mɪnɪmaɪz] *vt* minimizar, reducir al mínimo

**minimum** ['mɪnɪməm] **1** *n* mínimo *m*; **to keep sth to a m.** reducir algo al mínimo

**2** *adj* mínimo(a); *Fin* **m. lending rate** tipo *m* activo mínimo de interés; **m. wage** salario *m* mínimo (interprofesional)

**mining** ['maɪnɪŋ] *n* minería *f*; **m. area** cuenca *f* minera; **m. engineer** ingeniero(a) *mf* de minas; **the m. industry** el sector minero

**minion** ['mɪnjən] *n* lacayo *m*, subordinado(a) *m,f*

**miniskirt** ['mɪnɪskɜːt] *n* minifalda *f*

**minister** ['mɪnɪstə(r)] **1** *n* (**a**) *Pol* ministro(a) *m,f*; *Br* **M. of Defence/Health** ministro de Defensa/Sanidad (**b**) *Rel* ministro *m* de la Iglesia

**2** *vi* **to m. to sb** ocuparse de alguien; **to m. to sb's needs** atender las necesidades de alguien

**ministerial** [mɪnɪ'stɪərɪəl] *adj Pol* ministerial

**ministry** ['mɪnɪstrɪ] *n* (**a**) *Pol* ministerio *m*; *Br* **the M. of Defence/Transport** el Ministerio de Defensa/Transportes (**b**) *Rel* **to enter the m.** hacerse sacerdote

**mink** [mɪŋk] *n* visón *m*; **a m. coat** un abrigo de visón

**minnow** ['mɪnəʊ] *n (fish)* alevín *m*; *Fig (team, company)* comparsa *mf*

**minor** ['maɪnə(r)] **1** *n Law* menor *mf* (de edad)

**2** *adj (lesser)* menor; *(unimportant) (injury, illness)* leve; *(role, problem)* menor; *(detail, repair)* pequeño(a); **of m. importance** de poca importancia; *Mus* **m. key** tono *m* menor; *Med* **m. operation** operación *f* sencilla; **m. roads** carreteras *fpl* secundarias

**Minorca** [mɪ'nɔːkə] *n* Menorca

**Minorcan** [mɪ'nɔːkən] *adj* menorquín(ina)

**minority** [maɪ'nɒrɪtɪ] *n* (**a**) *(of total number)* minoría *f*; **to be in a** *or* **the m.** ser minoría; *Fin* **m. interest** participación *f* minoritaria; **m. opinion** opinión *f* de la minoría; **m. party/ government** partido *m*/gobierno *m* minoritario (**b**) *Law (age)* minoría *f* de edad

**minstrel** ['mɪnstrəl] *n* juglar *m*

**mint¹** [mɪnt] *n (plant)* menta *f*; *(sweet)* caramelo *m* de menta; **m. sauce** salsa *f* de menta; **m. tea** *(herbal tea)* poleo *m*

**mint²** **1** *n* **the (Royal) M.** ≃ la Fábrica Nacional de Moneda y Timbre; *Fam* **to make a m.** montarse en el dólar; **in m. condition** como nuevo(a)

**2** *vt (coins)* acuñar

**minuet** [mɪnjʊ'et] *n Mus* minué *m*, minueto *m*

**minus** ['maɪnəs] **1** *n (sign)* (signo *m*) menos *m*; *(negative aspect)* desventaja *f*, punto *m* negativo

**2** *adj (quantity, number)* negativo(a); *Sch* **B m.** notable *m* bajo; **the m. side** la parte negativa; **m. sign** signo *m* menos

**3** *prep* **ten m. eight leaves two** diez menos ocho igual a dos; **it's m. 12 degrees** hace 12 grados bajo cero; **he managed to escape, but m. his luggage** consiguió escapar, pero sin el equipaje

**minuscule** ['mɪnəskjuːl] *adj* minúsculo(a), diminuto(a)

**minute¹** ['mɪnɪt] **1** *n* (**a**) *(of time)* minuto *m*; **it's ten minutes to three** son las tres menos diez; **it's ten minutes past three** son las tres y diez; **wait a m.!** ¡espera un momento!; **just a m.** un momento; **go downstairs this m.!** ¡baja ahora mismo!; **the m. my back was turned she...** en cuanto me di la vuelta, ella...; **he'll be here any m.** llegará en cualquier momento; **it'll be ready in a m.** estará listo en un minuto *or* momento; **I've just popped in for a m.** sólo me quedaré un momento; **until/at the last m.** hasta/en el último momento; **m. hand** *(of watch)* minutero *m*; **m. steak** filete *m* muy fino

(**b**) *(note)* nota *f*; **minutes** *(of meeting)* acta *f*, actas *fpl*

**2** *vt (make note of)* hacer constar en acta; **the meeting will be minuted** se levantará acta de la reunión

**minute²** [mar'nju:t] *adj* **(a)** *(small)* diminuto(a), minúsculo(a); *(increase, improvement)* mínimo(a) **(b)** *(detailed) (examination)* minucioso(a)

**minutely** [mar'nju:tlɪ] *adv (to examine)* minuciosamente

**mips** *Comptr (abbr* **million instructions per second)** millón *m* de instrucciones por segundo

**miracle** ['mɪrəkəl] *n* milagro *m*; **to perform** *or* **work miracles** hacer milagros; **by a** *or* **some m.** de milagro, milagrosamente; **it's a m. that...** es un milagro que...; **m. cure** cura *f* milagrosa; **m. worker** persona *f* que hace milagros

**miraculous** [mɪ'rækjʊləs] *adj* milagroso(a)

**mirage** ['mɪrɑ:ʒ] *n also Fig* espejismo *m*

**MIRAS** ['mærəs] *n (abbr* **Mortgage Interest Relief at Source)** = desgravación fiscal de intereses por adquisición o reforma de vivienda habitual

**mire** [maɪə(r)] *n* lodo *m*, fango *m*

**mirror** ['mɪrə(r)] **1** *n* espejo *m*; *Fig* **to hold a m. (up) to sth** dar un fiel reflejo de algo; **m. image** *(exact copy)* reflejo *m* exacto; *(reversed image)* imagen *f* invertida
   **2** *vt also Fig* reflejar

**mirth** [mɜ:θ] *n* regocijo *m*

**misadventure** [mɪsəd'ventʃə(r)] *n* desventura *f*; *Law* **death by m.** muerte *f* accidental

**misanthropic** [mɪzən'θrɒpɪk] *adj* misantrópico(a)

**misanthropist** [mɪ'zænθrəpɪst] *n* misántropo(a) *m,f*

**misapprehension** [mɪsæprɪ'henʃən] *n* malentendido *m*, equívoco *m*; **to be (labouring) under a m.** albergar una falsa impresión

**misappropriation** ['mɪsəprəʊprɪ'eɪʃən] *n (of private funds)* apropiación *f* indebida; *(of public funds)* malversación *f* (de fondos públicos)

**misbehave** [mɪsbɪ'heɪv] *vi* (com)portarse mal

**misbehaviour,** *US* **misbehavior** [mɪsbɪ'heɪvjə(r)] *n* mala conducta *f*, mal comportamiento *m*

**misc** *(abbr* **miscellaneous)** varios

**miscalculate** [mɪs'kælkjʊleɪt] *vt & vi* calcular mal

**miscalculation** [mɪskælkjʊ'leɪʃən] *n* error *m* de cálculo

**miscarriage** [mɪs'kærɪdʒ] *n* **(a)** *Med* aborto *m* (natural *or* espontáneo); **to have a m.** abortar de forma natural **(b)** *Law* **m. of justice** error *m* judicial

**miscarry** [mɪs'kærɪ] *vi* **(a)** *(of pregnant woman)* abortar de forma natural **(b)** *Fig (of plan)* fracasar

**miscast** [mɪs'kɑ:st] *vt* **to m. an actor** dar a un actor un papel poco apropiado

**miscellaneous** [mɪsə'leɪnɪəs] *adj* diverso(a)

**miscellany** [mɪ'selənɪ] *n* miscelánea *f*

**mischief** ['mɪstʃɪf] *n* **(a)** *(naughtiness)* travesura *f*; **to be full of m.** ser un/una travieso(a); **to get up to m.** hacer travesuras; **to keep sb out of m.** evitar que alguien haga de las suyas **(b)** *(trouble)* problemas *mpl*; **to make m. (for sb)** crear problemas (a alguien) **(c)** *Fam (injury)* **to do oneself a m.** hacerse daño

**mischievous** ['mɪstʃɪvəs] *adj (naughty)* travieso(a); *(malicious)* malicioso(a)

**misconception** [mɪskən'sepʃən] *n* idea *f* equivocada *or* errónea

**misconduct** [mɪs'kɒndʌkt] *n* conducta *f* poco ética

**misconstrue** [mɪskən'stru:] *vt* malinterpretar

**misdemeanour,** *US* **misdemeanor** [mɪsdɪ'mi:nə(r)] *n Law* falta *f*

**misdiagnose** [mɪsdaɪəg'nəʊz] *vt Med* diagnosticar erróneamente

**misdirect** [mɪsdɪ'rekt] *vt* **(a)** *(person)* dar indicaciones equivocadas a; *Law* **to m. the jury** dar instrucciones erróneas al jurado **(b)** *(letter)* mandar a una dirección equivocada

**miser** ['maɪzə(r)] *n* avaro(a) *m,f*

**miserable** ['mɪzərəbəl] *adj* **(a)** *(unhappy)* triste, infeliz; **to be m.** estar triste, ser infeliz; **to make sb's life m.** amargar la vida a alguien **(b)** *(unpleasant)* lamentable; *(weather)* horroroso(a) **(c)** *(wretched)* miserable; **I only got a m. £70** sólo me dieron 70 miserables libras

**miserably** ['mɪzərəblɪ] *adv* **(a)** *(unhappily)* tristemente **(b)** *(wretchedly)* miserablemente **(c)** *(very badly)* lamentablemente

**miserly** ['maɪzəlɪ] *adj* avariento(a)

**misery** ['mɪzərɪ] *n* **(a)** *(unhappiness)* tristeza *f*, infelicidad *f*; **to make sb's life a m.** amargar la vida a alguien; **to put an animal out of its m.** terminar con los sufrimientos de un animal; *Hum* **put him out of his m.!** *(by telling him sth)* ¡acaba de una vez con sus sufrimientos! **(b)** *Br Fam (person)* amargado(a) *m,f*

**misery-guts** ['mɪzərɪgʌts] *n Fam* amargado(a) *m,f*

**misfire** [mɪs'faɪə(r)] *vi (of gun)* encasquillarse; *(of plan)* fallar

**misfit** ['mɪsfɪt] *n (person)* inadaptado(a) *m,f*

**misfortune** [mɪs'fɔ:tʃən] *n* desgracia *f*

**misgiving** [mɪs'gɪvɪŋ] *n* recelo *m*, duda *f*; **to have misgivings (about sth)** tener recelos (sobre algo); **to have misgivings about doing sth** tener reparos en hacer algo

**misgovern** [mɪs'gʌvən] *vt* gobernar mal

**misguided** [mɪs'gaɪdɪd] *adj (person)* confundido(a), equivocado(a); *(advice, decision, attempt)* desacertado(a), desafortunado(a); *(energy, belief, idealism)* mal encaminado(a); **to be m.** *(of per-*

*son*) estar confundido(a) *or* equivocado(a); *(of advice, decision, attempt)* ser desacertado(a) *or* desafortunado(a); *(of energy, belief, idealism)* ir mal encaminado(a)

**mishandle** [mɪsˈhændəl] *vt (device)* manejar mal; *(situation)* encauzar mal

**mishap** [ˈmɪshæp] *n* contratiempo *m*; **without m.** sin ningún contratiempo

**mishear** [mɪsˈhɪə(r)] *(pt & pp misheard* [mɪsˈhɜːd]*) vt & vi* entender mal

**mishmash** [ˈmɪʃmæʃ] *n Fam* batiburrillo *m*

**misinterpret** [mɪsɪnˈtɜːprɪt] *vt* malinterpretar

**misjudge** [mɪsˈdʒʌdʒ] *vt (distance)* calcular mal; *(person, situation)* juzgar mal

**misjudg(e)ment** [mɪsˈdʒʌdʒmənt] *n* error *m* de apreciación

**mislay** [mɪsˈleɪ] *(pt & pp mislaid* [mɪsˈleɪd]*) vt* extraviar, perder

**mislead** [mɪsˈliːd] *(pt & pp misled* [mɪsˈled]*) vt* engañar; **they misled him into thinking that...** le hicieron creer que...

**misleading** [mɪsˈliːdɪŋ] *adj* engañoso(a)

**mismanage** [mɪsˈmænɪdʒ] *vt* administrar *or* gestionar mal

**mismanagement** [mɪsˈmænɪdʒmənt] *n* mala administración *f*, mala gestión *f*

**misnomer** [mɪsˈnəʊmə(r)] *n* denominación *f* impropia

**misogynist** [mɪˈsɒdʒɪnɪst] *n* misógino(a) *m,f*

**misplace** [mɪsˈpleɪs] *vt (book, umbrella)* extraviar; *(trust, confidence)* depositar equivocadamente

**misprint** [ˈmɪsprɪnt] *n* errata *f* (de imprenta)

**mispronounce** [mɪsprəˈnaʊns] *vt* pronunciar mal

**mispronunciation** [mɪsprənʌnsɪˈeɪʃən] *n* pronunciación *f* incorrecta

**misquote** [mɪsˈkwəʊt] *vt* **(a)** *(accidentally)* citar equivocadamente **(b)** *(deliberately) (person)* tergiversar las palabras de; *(words)* tergiversar

**misread** [mɪsˈriːd] *(pt & pp misread* [mɪsˈred]*) vt* **(a)** *(notice, timetable)* leer mal **(b)** *(misinterpret)* malinterpretar

**misrepresent** [mɪsreprɪˈzent] *vt (person)* tergiversar las palabras de; *(words, facts)* deformar, tergiversar

**misrepresentation** [mɪsreprɪzənˈteɪʃən] *n* deformación *f*, tergiversación *f*

**misrule** [mɪsˈruːl] *n* desgobierno *m*

**Miss** [mɪs] *n* señorita *f*; **M. Jones** la señorita Jones; **M. World** Miss Mundo

**miss** [mɪs] **1** *n* fallo *m*; *Fam* **I think I'll give the cake/film a miss** creo que voy a pasar de tomar tarta/ver la película

**2** *vt* **(a)** *(target)* no acertar en; *(shot)* fallar; *(bus, train, chance)* perder; *(film, TV programme)* per-

derse; *Fig* **to m. the boat** *(miss opportunity)* perder el tren; **you've just missed him** se acaba de marchar; **you haven't missed much!** no te has perdido mucho; **you can't m. the house** la casa no tiene pérdida; **you can't m. the turning** *(in city)* no puedes confundirte de bocacalle; **the boss doesn't m. a thing** al jefe no se le pasa *or* escapa nada

**(b)** *(not hear) (question, remark)* no oír, perderse; **to m. the point** no entender bien

**(c)** *(omit) (word, line)* saltarse

**(d)** *(avoid)* **the car just missed me** el coche no me pilló por poco; **she just missed being killed** por poco se mata

**(e)** *(feel lack of)* echar de menos; **I m. you** te echo de menos

**(f)** *(lack)* **the table's missing one of its legs** a la mesa le falta una pata

**3** *vi* **(a)** *(miss target)* fallar

**(b)** *(be absent)* **to be missing** faltar; **nothing is missing** no falta nada

**▸miss out 1** *vt sep (omit)* pasar por alto, omitir

**2** *vi (not benefit)* **to m. out on sth** perderse algo

**missal** [ˈmɪsəl] *n Rel* misal *m*

**misshapen** [mɪsˈʃeɪpən] *adj* deforme

**missile** [ˈmɪsaɪl, *US* ˈmɪsəl] *n (rocket)* misil *m*; *(object thrown)* proyectil *m*; **m. launcher** lanzamisiles *m inv*

**missing** [ˈmɪsɪŋ] *adj (lost)* perdido(a); *(absent)* ausente; **to be m.** *(of person, thing)* faltar; **find the m. word** encontrar la palabra que falta; **m. link** eslabón *m* perdido; **m. person** desaparecido(a) *m,f*

**mission** [ˈmɪʃən] *n* **(a)** *(task)* misión *f*; *Com* **m. statement** declaración *f* de (la) misión, misión *f* **(b)** *(delegation)* delegación *f* **(c)** *Rel* misión *f*; **m. station** misión *f*

**missionary** [ˈmɪʃənərɪ] *n Rel* misionero(a) *m,f*; **m. position** *(sexual)* postura *f* del misionero

**missive** [ˈmɪsɪv] *n Formal* misiva *f*

**misspell** [ˈmɪsˈspel] *(pt & pp misspelt* [ˈmɪsˈspelt]*) vt* escribir incorrectamente

**misspent** [ˈmɪsˈspent] *adj* **a m. youth** una juventud malgastada *or* desaprovechada

**missus** [ˈmɪsɪz] *n Fam (wife)* **the m.** la parienta

**mist** [mɪst] *n (fog)* neblina *f*; *(condensation)* vaho *m*; **sea m.** bruma *f*; **the mists of time** la noche de los tiempos

**▸mist over** *vi (of mirror, eyes)* empañarse

**▸mist up** *vi (of mirror, glasses)* empañarse

**mistake** [mɪsˈteɪk] **1** *n* error *m*, equivocación *f*; **to make a m.** cometer un error; **make no m.** puedes estar seguro(a); **by m.** por error *or* equivocación; *Fam* **this is hard work and no m.!** no cabe duda de que es un trabajo duro

**2** *vt (pt mistook* [mɪsˈtʊk]*, pp mistaken*

[mɪs'teɪkən]) (a) *(misunderstand)* interpretar mal; **I mistook her intentions** interpreté mal sus intenciones (b) *(confuse)* confundir (for con); **I mistook him for someone else** lo confundí con otra persona; **there's no mistaking a voice like that!** ¡esa voz es inconfundible!

**mistak(e)able** [mɪs'teɪkəbəl] *adj* confundible (for por)

**mistaken** [mɪs'teɪkən] *adj (belief, impression)* equivocado(a), erróneo(a); **to be m.** *(of person)* estar equivocado(a)

**Mister** ['mɪstə(r)] *n* señor *m*; **M. Jones** el señor Jones

**mistime** [mɪs'taɪm] *vt* **to m. sth** hacer algo a destiempo

**mistletoe** ['mɪsəltəʊ] *n* muérdago *m*

**mistranslation** [mɪstræns'leɪʃən] *n* error *m* de traducción, mala traducción *f*

**mistreat** [mɪs'triːt] *vt* maltratar

**mistress** ['mɪstrɪs] *n* (a) *(of servant, house)* señora *f*, ama *f* (b) *(woman teacher) (in primary school)* señorita *f*, maestra *f*; *(in secondary school)* profesora *f* (c) *(lover)* querida *f*, amante *f*

**mistrial** [mɪs'traɪəl] *n Law* juicio *m* nulo

**mistrust** [mɪs'trʌst] **1** *n* desconfianza *f*
**2** *vt* desconfiar de

**mistrustful** [mɪs'trʌstfʊl] *adj* desconfiado(a); **to be m. of...** desconfiar de...

**misty** ['mɪstɪ] *adj (place, weather)* neblinoso(a); *(at sea or seaside)* brumoso(a); *(form)* borroso(a)

**misunderstand** [mɪsʌndə'stænd] ( *pt & pp* **misunderstood** [mɪsʌndə'stʊd]) *vt & vi* entender mal

**misunderstanding** [mɪsʌndə'stændɪŋ] *n* (a) *(misconception)* malentendido *m*, confusión *f*; **there's been a m. about the time** ha habido un malentendido con la hora (b) *(disagreement)* desacuerdo *m*, diferencias *fpl*

**misuse 1** *n* [mɪs'juːs] uso *m* indebido
**2** *vt* [mɪs'juːz] usar indebidamente

**mite** [maɪt] *n* (a) *(bug)* ácaro *m* (b) *Fam (child)* criatura *f*; **poor little m.!** ¡pobre criaturita! (c) *Fam (a little bit)* **it's a m. expensive** es un pelín caro

**miter** *US* = **mitre**

**mitigate** ['mɪtɪgeɪt] *vt (effect, suffering)* atenuar, mitigar; *(pain)* aliviar, mitigar; *Law* **mitigating circumstances** circunstancias *fpl* atenuantes

**mitigation** [mɪtɪ'geɪʃən] *n* atenuación *f*; *Law* **in m.** como atenuante

**mitre, US miter** ['maɪtə(r)] *n Rel* mitra *f*

**mitt** [mɪt] *n* (a) *(mitten)* manopla *f*; *US* **baseball m.** guante *m* de béisbol (b) *Fam (hand)* **mitts** zarpas *fpl*

**mitten** ['mɪtən] *n (glove)* manopla *f*; *(fingerless)* mitón *m*

**mix** [mɪks] **1** *n also Mus* mezcla *f*
**2** *vt* mezclar; *(drink)* preparar; **to m. business with pleasure** mezclar el placer con los negocios
**3** *vi* (a) *(blend)* mezclarse; *(combine well)* compaginar bien (b) *(socially)* relacionarse (with con)
▶**mix up** *vt sep* (a) *(ingredients)* mezclar (b) *(confuse) (one's papers)* revolver, desordenar; *(people, dates)* confundir (c) *Fam (in situation, relationship)* **to be mixed up in sth** andar metido(a) en algo; **to get mixed up with sb** liarse con alguien

**mixed** ['mɪkst] *adj (assorted)* variado(a); **it was a m. blessing** tuvo su lado bueno y su lado malo; *Fam* **it was a m. bag** había de todo; **to have m. feelings (about sth)** tener sentimientos contradictorios (respecto a algo); **m. doubles** *(in tennis)* dobles *mpl* mixtos; **m. grill/salad** parrillada *f*/ensalada *f* mixta; **m. marriage** = matrimonio entre personas de distintas razas o religiones; **m. school** *(coeducational)* colegio *m* mixto

**mixed-up** [mɪks'tʌp] *adj Fam (person)* desorientado(a), confuso(a)

**mixer** ['mɪksə(r)] *n* (a) *(for cooking)* batidora *f* (b) *(in drink)* refresco *m* *(para mezcla alcohólica)* (c) *(socially)* **to be a good m.** ser muy abierto(a) con la gente (d) *Br* **m. tap** (grifo *m*) monomando *m*

**mixing bowl** ['mɪksɪŋ'bəʊl] *n* cuenco *m*, bol *m*

**mixture** ['mɪkstʃə(r)] *n* mezcla *f*

**mix-up** ['mɪksʌp] *n* confusión *f*; **there was a m. over the dates** hubo una confusión con las fechas

**mktg** *Com (abbr* **marketing***)* marketing *m*

**ml** *(abbr* **millilitre(s)***)* ml, mililitro *m*

**MLR** [emel'ɑː(r)] *n Fin (abbr* **minimum lending rate***)* tipo *m* activo mínimo de interés

**mm** *(abbr* **millimetre(s)***)* mm, milímetro *m*

**mnemonic** [nɪ'mɒnɪk] *n* recurso *m* mnemotécnico

**moan** [məʊn] **1** *n* (a) *(sound)* gemido *m* (b) *(complaint)* queja *f*
**2** *vi* (a) *(make sound)* gemir (b) *(complaint)* quejarse (about de)

**moat** [məʊt] *n* foso *m*

**mob** [mɒb] **1** *n (crowd)* turba *f*, horda *f*; *Fam* **the M.** *(the Mafia)* la Mafia; **m. rule** la ley de la calle
**2** *vt* ( *pt & pp* **mobbed***)* **to be mobbed by fans** ser asediado(a) por una multitud de admiradores

**mobile** ['məʊbaɪl] **1** *n* (a) *(hanging ornament)* móvil *m* (b) *Fam (mobile phone)* (teléfono *m*) móvil *m*
**2** *adj* móvil; **m. home** *(caravan)* caravana *f*; **m. phone** teléfono *m* móvil

**mobility** [məʊ'bɪlɪtɪ] *n* movilidad *f*

**mobilize** ['məʊbɪlaɪz] vt (troops, support) movilizar

**mobster** ['mɒbstə(r)] n US Fam gángster m

**moccasin** ['mɒkəsɪn] n mocasín m

**mock** [mɒk] **1** adj fingido(a), simulado(a); **m. battle** simulacro m de batalla; Br Sch **m. examination** examen m de prueba
  **2** vt (ridicule) burlarse de

**mockery** ['mɒkərɪ] n (a) (ridicule) burlas fpl (b) (travesty) farsa f; **to make a m. of sth/sb** poner algo/a alguien en ridículo

**mockingbird** ['mɒkɪŋbɜːd] n sinsonte m

**mock-up** ['mɒkʌp] n reproducción f, modelo m (de tamaño natural)

**MOD** [eməʊ'di:] n Br (abbr **Ministry of Defence**) Ministerio m de Defensa

**mod cons** ['mɒd'kɒnz] npl Fam **with all m.** con todas las comodidades

**modal** ['məʊdəl] **1** n verbo m modal
  **2** adj **m. verb** verbo m modal

**mode** [məʊd] n (a) (manner) modo m; **m. of transport** medio m de transporte (b) Comptr Tech modalidad f, función f (c) Math moda f

**model** ['mɒdəl] **1** n (a) (small version) maqueta f; **m. aircraft** maqueta de avión; **m. kit** kit m de montaje (b) (example) modelo m; **this is our latest m.** este es nuestro último modelo (c) (paragon) modelo m; **to take sb as one's m.** tomar a alguien como modelo; **m. pupil** alumno(a) m,f modélico(a) or modelo (d) (person) (fashion model, for artist) modelo mf
  **2** vt (pt & pp **modelled**, US **modeled** (a) **to m. oneself on sb** seguir el ejemplo de alguien (b) Comptr simular por ordenador
  **3** vi (of artist's model) posar; (of fashion model) hacer or trabajar de modelo

**modem** ['məʊdem] n Comptr módem m

**moderate** ['mɒdərɪt] **1** n Pol moderado(a) m,f
  **2** adj moderado(a); **to be a m. drinker** beber moderadamente
  **3** vt ['mɒdəreɪt] (one's demands, zeal) moderar
  **4** vi Formal (at meeting) moderar, hacer de moderador

**moderately** ['mɒdərɪtlɪ] adv (to eat, drink) moderadamente, con moderación; (reasonably) medianamente, moderadamente

**moderation** [mɒdə'reɪʃən] n moderación f; **in m.** con moderación

**modern** ['mɒdən] adj moderno(a); **m. languages** lenguas fpl modernas

**modernism** ['mɒdənɪzəm] n modernismo m

**modernization** [mɒdənaɪ'zeɪʃən] n modernización f

**modernize** ['mɒdənaɪz] **1** vt modernizar
  **2** vi modernizarse

**modest** ['mɒdɪst] adj (a) (not boastful) modesto(a) (b) (moderate) (requirement, increase) modesto(a), moderado(a) (c) (chaste) recatado(a)

**modestly** ['mɒdɪstlɪ] adv (a) (not boastfully) modestamente (b) (moderately) moderadamente (c) (chastely) recatadamente

**modesty** ['mɒdɪstɪ] n (a) (humility) modestia f; **false m.** falsa modestia (b) (moderation) (of requirement, increase) modestia f, moderación f (c) (chastity) recato m

**modicum** ['mɒdɪkəm] n **a m. of...** un mínimo de...

**modification** [mɒdɪfɪ'keɪʃən] n modificación f; **to make modifications to sth** modificar algo

**modify** ['mɒdɪfaɪ] vt modificar

**modular** ['mɒdjʊlə(r)] adj por módulos

**modulate** ['mɒdjʊleɪt] vt modular

**modulation** [mɒdjʊ'leɪʃən] n modulación f

**module** ['mɒdju:l] n módulo m

**mogul** ['məʊgəl] n Fig (magnate) magnate m,f

**mohair** ['məʊheə(r)] n mohair m; **m. sweater** jersey m de mohair

**Mohammed** [məʊ'hæmɪd] n Mahoma

**moist** [mɔɪst] adj húmedo(a)

**moisten** ['mɔɪsən] vt humedecer

**moisture** ['mɔɪstʃə(r)] n humedad f

**moisturize** ['mɔɪstʃəraɪz] vt (skin) hidratar

**moisturizer** ['mɔɪstʃəraɪzə(r)] n crema f hidratante

**molar** ['məʊlə(r)] n muela f, molar m

**molasses** [mə'læsɪz] n melaza f

**mold, molder** etc US = **mould, moulder** etc

**Moldavia** [mɒl'deɪvɪə], **Moldova** [mɒl-'dəʊvə] n Moldavia

**Moldavian** [mɒl'deɪvɪən], **Moldovan** [mɒl'dəʊvən] n & adj moldavo(a) m,f

**mole**[1] ['məʊl] n (birthmark) lunar m

**mole**[2] n (animal, spy) topo m

**molecular** [mə'lekjʊlə(r)] adj molecular

**molecule** ['mɒlɪkju:l] n molécula f

**molehill** ['məʊlhɪl] n topera f

**molest** [mə'lest] vt (pester) molestar, importunar; (sexually) abusar (sexualmente) de

**mollify** ['mɒlɪfaɪ] vt apaciguar

**mollusc**, US **mollusk** ['mɒləsk] n molusco m

**mollycoddle** ['mɒlɪkɒdəl] vt Fam mimar

**molten** ['məʊltən] adj fundido(a)

**mom** [mɒm] n US Fam mamá f, mami f

**moment** ['məʊmənt] n (a) (instant) momento m; **a m. ago** hace un momento; **at the m.** (right now) en este momento; (these days) actualmente; **at the last m.** en el último momento; **for the m.** por el momento; **in a m.** enseguida; **at any m.** en cualquier momento; **wait a m.!, one m.!** ¡espera un momento!; **I haven't a m. to spare** no tengo ni un minuto; **tell him the m. he arrives** díselo en cuanto llegue; **without a**

m.'s hesitation sin dudarlo un momento; to live for the m. vivir el presente; **the man of the m.** el hombre del momento; **the m. of truth** la hora de la verdad; **he has his moments** tiene sus buenos golpes; **the book has its moments** el libro tiene sus (buenos) momentos

(b) *(importance)* **of great/little m.** de mucha/poca importancia

**momentary** ['məʊməntəri] *adj* momentáneo(a)

**momentous** [məʊ'mentəs] *adj* muy importante, trascendental

**momentum** [məʊ'mentəm] *n Phys* momento *m* (lineal); **to gather/lose m.** *(of car, campaign)* cobrar/perder impulso

**Mon** *(abbr* **Monday)** lunes *m inv*

**Monaco** [mə'nɑːkəʊ] *n* Mónaco

**monarch** ['mɒnək] *n* monarca *mf*

**monarchist** ['mɒnəkɪst] *n* monárquico(a) *m,f*

**monarchy** ['mɒnəkɪ] *n* monarquía *f*

**monastery** ['mɒnəstrɪ] *n* monasterio *m*

**monastic** [mə'næstɪk] *adj* monástico(a)

**Monday** ['mʌndɪ] *n* lunes *m inv; see also* **Saturday**

**monetarism** ['mʌnɪtərɪzəm] *n* monetarismo *m*

**monetarist** ['mʌnɪtərɪst] *n & adj* monetarista *mf*

**monetary** ['mʌnɪtərɪ] *adj* monetario(a); **m. policy** política *f* monetaria

**money** ['mʌnɪ] *n* dinero *m;* **to do sth for m.** hacer algo por dinero; **to make m.** *(of person)* ganar or hacer dinero; *(of business)* dar dinero; **to be worth a lot of m.** *(of thing)* valer mucho dinero; *(of person)* tener mucho dinero; **there's no m. in it** no es un buen negocio; *Fam* **to be in the m.** haberse hecho con un montón de pasta; **we really got our m.'s worth** desde luego, valía la pena pagar ese dinero; *Fam* **it was m. for old rope** era dinero fácil; **the Government must put its m. where its mouth is** el Gobierno debe demostrar con hechos lo que mantiene; *Fam* **to spend m. like water** gastar dinero a espuertas; *Fam* **m. doesn't grow on trees!** el dinero no cae del cielo; **for my m....** para mí..., en mi opinión...; *Fin* **m. market** mercado *m* monetario; *Econ* **m. supply** oferta *f or* masa *f* monetaria

**moneybags** ['mʌnɪbægz] *n Fam (person)* ricachón(ona) *m,f*

**moneybox** ['mʌnɪbɒks] *n* hucha *f*

**moneyed** ['mʌnɪd] *adj* adinerado(a), pudiente

**moneylender** ['mʌnɪlendə(r)] *n* prestamista *mf*

**moneymaker** ['mʌnɪmeɪkə(r)] *n (shop, business, product)* negocio *m* rentable

**moneymaking** ['mʌnɪmeɪkɪŋ] *adj* rentable, lucrativo(a)

**Mongol** ['mɒŋgəl] *Hist* 1 *n* mongol(ola) *m,f* 2 *adj* mongol(ola); **the M. Hordes** las hordas mongolas

**mongol** ['mɒŋgəl] *n Old-fashioned (person with Down's Syndrome)* mongólico(a) *m,f*

**Mongolia** [mɒŋ'gəʊlɪə] *n* Mongolia

**Mongolian** [mɒŋ'gəʊlɪən] *n & adj* mongol(ola) *m,f*

**mongoose** [mɒŋ'guːs] *n* mangosta *f*

**mongrel** ['mʌŋgrəl] *n (dog)* perro *m* cruzado

**monitor** ['mɒnɪtə(r)] 1 *n* (a) *(supervisor)* supervisor(ora) *m,f* (b) *TV* pantalla *f; Comptr* monitor *m*
2 *vt* controlar

**monk** [mʌŋk] *n* monje *m*

**monkey** ['mʌŋkɪ] *(pl* monkeys) *n* (a) *(animal)* mono *m; Fam* **to make a m. out of sb** tomarle el pelo a alguien; *very Fam* **I don't give a m.'s** me la trae floja; *Fam* **m. business** bribonadas *fpl;* **m. nut** cacahuete *m;* **m. puzzle tree** araucaria *f; US* **m. wrench** llave *f* inglesa (b) *(naughty child)* diablillo *m*

▶**monkey about, monkey around** *vi Fam (fool around)* hacer el indio (**with** con)

**monkfish** ['mʌŋkfɪʃ] *n* rape *m*

**mono** ['mɒnəʊ] **n in m.** *(of sound recording)* en mono(aural)

**monochrome** ['mɒnəkrəʊm] *adj Art* monocromo(a), monocromático(a); *Phot* en blanco y negro

**monocle** ['mɒnəkəl] *n* monóculo *m*

**monogamous** [mɒ'nɒgəməs] *adj* monógamo(a)

**monogamy** [mɒ'nɒgəmɪ] *n* monogamia *f*

**monogram** ['mɒnəgræm] *n* monograma *m*

**monograph** ['mɒnəgræf] *n* monografía *f*

**monolingual** [mɒnəʊ'lɪŋgwəl] *adj* monolingüe

**monolithic** [mɒnə'lɪθɪk] *adj* monolítico(a)

**monologue** ['mɒnəlɒg] *n* monólogo *m*

**monopolize** [mə'nɒpəlaɪz] *vt* monopolizar; *Fig* **she monopolized him for the evening** lo acaparó *or* monopolizó toda la noche

**monopoly** [mə'nɒpəlɪ] *n also Fig* monopolio *m;* **to have a m. on sth** tener el monopolio *or* la exclusiva de algo

**monorail** ['mɒnəʊreɪl] *n* monorraíl *m*

**monosyllabic** [mɒnəʊsɪ'læbɪk] *adj (word)* monosílabo(a), monosilábico(a); *(person, reply)* lacónico(a)

**monosyllable** [mɒnəʊ'sɪləbəl] *n* monosílabo *m*

**monotone** ['mɒnətəʊn] *n* **to speak in a m.** hablar con voz monótona

**monotonous** [mə'nɒtənəs] *adj* monótono(a)

**monotony** [mə'nɒtənɪ] *n* monotonía *f*

**Monsignor** [mɒn'si:njə(r)] *n* monseñor *m*

**monsoon** [mɒn'su:n] *n* monzón *m*

**monster** ['mɒnstə(r)] **1** *n* monstruo *m*

**2** *adj Fam (enormous)* monstruoso(a)

**monstrosity** [mɒn'strɒsɪtɪ] *n* monstruosidad *f*

**monstrous** ['mɒnstrəs] *adj (repugnant, enormous)* monstruoso(a); **it is m. that...** es una monstruosidad que...

**montage** ['mɒntɑ:ʒ] *n Cin Phot* montaje *m*

**month** [mʌnθ] *n* mes *m*; **in the m. of August** en el mes de agosto; **in the summer/winter months** en los meses de verano/invierno; **a m. ago** hace un mes; **a ten-m.-old baby** un bebé de diez meses; **once a m.** una vez al mes; *Fam* **never in a m. of Sundays** ni aunque viva cien años

**monthly** ['mʌnθlɪ] **1** *n (magazine)* revista *f* mensual

**2** *adj* mensual; **m. instalment** plazo *m* mensual; **m. payment** mensualidad *f*

**3** *adv* mensualmente

**Montreal** [mɒntrɪ'ɔ:l] *n* Montreal

**Montserrat** [mɒntsə'ræt] *n* (la isla de) Montserrat

**monument** ['mɒnjʊmənt] *n* monumento *m*

**monumental** [mɒnjʊ'mentəl] *adj (large, impressive)* monumental; **of m. significance** de enorme trascendencia; **m. ignorance** ignorancia *f* supina

**moo** [mu:] **1** *n (pl* **moos)** mugido *m*; **m.!** ¡mu!

**2** *vi* mugir

▸**mooch about, mooch around** *vi Fam* zascandilear, zangolotear

**mood** [mu:d] *n* **(a)** *(state of mind)* humor *m*; **the m. of the public/electorate** el sentir del gran público/del electorado; **to be in a good/bad m.** estar de buen/mal humor; **she's in one of her moods** está otra vez de mal humor; **I'm not in the m. (for)** no estoy de humor (para); **he's in no m. for jokes** no está de humor para chistes **(b)** *Gram* modo *m*

**moodily** ['mu:dɪlɪ] *adv* malhumoradamente

**moody** ['mu:dɪ] *adj* **(a)** *(sulky)* malhumorado(a); **to be m.** *(permanently)* tener mal humor; *(temporarily)* estar malhumorado(a) *or* de mal humor **(b)** *(changeable)* voluble, variable

**moon** [mu:n] **1** *n* luna *f*; **the M.** la Luna; *Fam* **to ask for the m.** pedir la luna; *Fam* **to promise sb the m.** prometer a alguien el oro y el moro; *Fam* **to be over the m.** estar encantado(a); **m. landing** alunizaje *m*

**2** *vi Fam (expose one's buttocks)* enseñar el culo

▸**moon about, moon around** *vi* vagar, andar mirando a las musarañas

**moonbeam** ['mu:nbi:m] *n* rayo *m* de luna

**moonlight** ['mu:nlaɪt] **1** *n* luz *f* de la luna; **in the m., by m.** a la luz de la luna; *Fam* **to do a m. flit** escaparse de noche

**2** *vi Fam (work illegally)* estar pluriempleado(a)

**moonlighting** ['mu:nlaɪtɪŋ] *n Fam* pluriempleo *m*

**moonlit** ['mu:nlɪt] *adj* iluminado(a) por la luna

**moonshine** ['mu:nʃaɪn] *n Fam* **(a)** *(nonsense)* sandeces *fpl* **(b)** *US (illegal alcohol)* = alcohol destilado ilegalmente

**Moor** [mʊə(r)] *n* moro(a) *m,f*

**moor¹** [mʊə(r)] *n (heath)* páramo *m*

**moor²** *vt (ship)* atracar

**mooring** ['mʊərɪŋ] *n (place)* atracadero *m*; **moorings** amarras *fpl*

**Moorish** ['mʊərɪʃ] *adj* moro(a)

**moorland** ['mʊələnd] *n* páramo *m*

**moose** [mu:s] *n (pl* **moose** ) *n (elk)* alce *m*

**moot** [mu:t] *adj* **it's a m. point** es discutible

**2** *vt (propose, suggest)* **it was mooted that...** se sugirió que...

**mop** [mɒp] **1** *n (for floor)* fregona *f*; *Fam* **a m. of hair** una mata de pelo

**2** *vt (pt & pp* **mopped)** **to m. the floor** fregar el suelo, pasarle la fregona al suelo; **to m. one's brow** enjugarse la frente

▸**mop up** *vt sep (liquid)* limpiar, enjugar; *Fig (enemy forces)* terminar con

▸**mope about, mope around** *vi* andar como alma en pena

**moped** ['məʊped] *n (motorbike)* ciclomotor *m*

**moral** ['mɒrəl] **1** *n* **(a)** *(of story)* moraleja *f* **(b)** **morals** moral *f*, moralidad *f*

**2** *adj* moral; **to give sb m. support** dar apoyo moral a alguien; **he is lacking in m. fibre** carece de solidez *or* talla moral; **m. victory** victoria *f* moral

**morale** [mɒ'rɑ:l] *n* moral *f*; **his m. is very low/high** tiene la moral muy baja/alta; **to be good/bad for m.** ser bueno/malo para la moral

**moralistic** [mɒrə'lɪstɪk] *adj* moralista

**morality** [mə'rælɪtɪ] *n* moralidad *f*

**moralize** ['mɒrəlaɪz] *vi* moralizar

**morally** ['mɒrəlɪ] *adv* moralmente; **m. right/wrong** moralmente aceptable/inaceptable

**morass** [mə'ræs] *n (marsh)* pantano *m*, cenagal *m*; *Fig (of detail, despair)* marasmo *m*, laberinto *m*

**moratorium** [mɒrə'tɔ:rɪəm] *n* moratoria *f* **(on** en)

**morbid** ['mɔ:bɪd] *adj* morboso(a)

**morbidly** ['mɔ:bɪdlɪ] *adv* morbosamente

**mordant** ['mɔːdənt] *adj Formal (sarcasm, wit)* mordaz

**more** [mɔː(r)] *(comparative of* **many, much)** 1 *pron* más; **there are m. of us** nosotros somos más; **there's no m.** ya no hay *or* queda más; **do you want (any *or* some) m.?** ¿quieres más?; **what m. can I say?** ¿qué más puedo decir?; **he knows m. than you (do)** él sabe más que tú; **we should see m. of each other** deberíamos vernos más; **it's just m. of the same** es más de lo mismo; **what is m.,…** lo que es más,…; **let us say no m. about it** el asunto queda olvidado; **the m. I hear about this, the less I like it** cuanto más sé del asunto, menos me gusta

**2** *adj* más; **m. water/children** más agua/niños; **m. than 100 people** más de 100 personas; **one m. week** una semana más; **is there any m. bread?** ¿hay *or* queda más pan?; **to have some m. wine** tomar un poco más de vino; **I have no m. money** no me queda dinero; **there are m. and m. accidents** cada vez hay más accidentes; **there are two m. questions to go** quedan dos preguntas (más)

**3** *adv* **(a)** *(to form comparative of adjective or adverb)* más; **m. interesting (than)** más interesante (que); **he became m. and m. drunk** cada vez estaba más borracho; **this made things all the m. difficult** esto ponía las cosas aún más difíciles; **m. easily** más fácilmente **(b)** *(with verbs) (to eat, exercise)* más; **I would think m. of her if…** tendría mejor opinión de ella si…; **(the) m.'s the pity** es una lástima; **he was m. surprised than annoyed** más que molesto estaba sorprendido; **I'm m. than satisfied** estoy más que satisfecho; **I like her m. than I used to** me cae mejor que antes; **that's m. like it!** ¡eso está mejor!; **m. or less** más o menos

**(c)** *(in time)* **once m.** una vez más, otra vez; **he doesn't drink any m.** ha dejado la bebida; *Euph* **he is no m.** ha pasado a mejor vida

**moreover** [mɔː'rəʊvə(r)] *adv* además, (lo que) es más

**mores** ['mɔːreɪz] *npl Formal* costumbres *fpl*

**morgue** [mɔːg] *n* depósito *m* de cadáveres; *Fig* **this place is like a m.** este sitio parece un entierro

**moribund** ['mɒrɪbʌnd] *adj* agonizante, moribundo(a)

**Mormon** ['mɔːmən] *n Rel* mormón(ona) *m,f*

**morning** ['mɔːnɪŋ] *n* mañana *f*; **this m.** esta mañana; **tomorrow m.** mañana por la mañana; **yesterday m.** ayer por la mañana; **the next m., the m. after** la mañana siguiente; **the m. before** la mañana anterior; **the m. after (the night before)** la resaca (de la noche anterior); **m., noon and night** (mañana,) día y noche; **(early) in the m.** por la mañana

(temprano); **on Wednesday m.** el miércoles por la mañana; **good m.!,** *Fam* **m.!** ¡buenos días!; **m. dress** chaqué *m*; **m. sickness** náuseas *fpl* matutinas del embarazo; **m. star** lucero *m* del alba

**morning-after pill** ['mɔːnɪŋ'ɑːftə'pɪl] *n* píldora *f* del día siguiente

**Moroccan** [mə'rɒkən] *n & adj* marroquí *mf*

**Morocco** [mə'rɒkəʊ] *n* Marruecos

**moron** ['mɔːrɒn] *n Fam* zote *mf*, subnormal *mf*

**moronic** [mə'rɒnɪk] *adj Fam (person)* zote; *(expression, play, behaviour)* memo(a); **a m. comment** una memez

**morose** [mə'rəʊs] *adj* hosco(a), huraño(a)

**morphine** ['mɔːfiːn] *n* morfina *f*

**Morse** [mɔːs] *n* in M. en (código) morse; **M. code** código *m* morse

**morsel** ['mɔːsəl] *n* pedacito *m*

**mortal** ['mɔːtəl] 1 *n* mortal *mf*; *Ironic* **he doesn't speak to mere mortals like us!** ¡no habla con los simples mortales como nosotros!

**2** *adj* mortal; **m. enemy** enemigo *m* mortal; **m. remains** restos *mpl* mortales; **m. sin** pecado *m* mortal; **m. wound** herida *f* mortal

**mortality** [mɔː'tælɪtɪ] *n (of person, death rate)* mortalidad *f*

**mortally** ['mɔːtəlɪ] *adv* **m. wounded** herido(a) de muerte; **m. offended** ultrajado(a)

**mortar** ['mɔːtə(r)] *n* **(a)** *(in construction)* argamasa *f*, mortero *m* **(b)** *(for grinding)* **pestle and m.** almirez *m*, mortero *m* **(c)** *(missile)* mortero *m*

**mortgage** ['mɔːgɪdʒ] 1 *n* hipoteca *f*; **m. (re)payments** plazos *mpl* de la hipoteca; **m. rate** tipo *m* (de interés) hipotecario

**2** *vt (property, one's future)* hipotecar

**mortician** [mɔː'tɪʃən] *n US (undertaker)* encargado(a) *m,f* de funeraria

**mortification** [mɔːtɪfɪ'keɪʃən] *n Rel* mortificación *f*; *Fig (embarrassment)* bochorno *m*

**mortify** ['mɔːtɪfaɪ] *vt Rel* mortificar; **I was mortified** me sentí abochornado

**mortise** ['mɔːtɪs] *n (in carpentry)* muesca *f*, mortaja *f*; **m. lock** cerradura *f* embutida *or* de pestillo

**mortuary** ['mɔːtjʊərɪ] *n* depósito *m* de cadáveres

**mosaic** [məʊ'zeɪɪk] *n* mosaico *m*

**Moscow** ['mɒskəʊ] *n* Moscú

**Moses** ['məʊzɪz] *n* Moisés

**Moslem** ['mɒzlem] *n & adj* musulmán(ana) *m,f*

**mosque** [mɒsk] *n* mezquita *f*

**mosquito** [məs'kiːtəʊ] *(pl* **mosquitoes)** *n* mosquito *m*, *Am* zancudo *m*; **m. bite** picadura *f* de mosquito; **m. net** mosquitera *f*, mosquitero *m*

**moss** [mɒs] n musgo m

**most** [məʊst] (*superlative of* **many, much**) **1** *pron* m. of my friends la mayoría de *or* casi todos mis amigos; **m. of the time** la mayor parte del *or* casi todo el tiempo; **at m., at the (very) m.** como mucho; **to make the m. of an opportunity** aprovechar al máximo una oportunidad; **he is more interesting than m.** es más interesante que la mayoría; **he earns the m.** él es el que más (dinero) gana

**2** *adj* (a) *(the majority of)* la mayoría de; **m. women** la mayoría de las mujeres

(b) *(greatest amount of)* **the m.** más; **he has (the) m. money** él es el que más dinero tiene; **for the m. part** en su mayor parte

**3** *adv* (a) *(to form superlative of adjectives and adverbs)* el/la más; **the m. beautiful woman** la mujer más bella; **the m. interesting book** el libro más interesante; **these are the m. expensive** éstos son los más caros; **those who have answered m. accurately** los que mejor hayan contestado

(b) *(with verbs)* **the one who works m. is...** el/la que trabaja más es...; **who do you like m.?** ¿quién te cae mejor?; **what I want m.** lo que más deseo; **that's what worries me (the) m.** eso es lo que más me preocupa

(c) *(very)* muy, sumamente; **m. unhappy** muy desgraciado(a)

**mostly** ['məʊstlɪ] *adv* (a) *(in the main)* principalmente, sobre todo (b) *(most often)* casi siempre

**MOT** [eməʊ'tiː] n *Aut* ≃ ITV f, ≃ Inspección f Técnica de Vehículos

**motel** [məʊ'tel] n motel m

**moth** [mɒθ] n polilla f

**mothball** ['mɒθbɔːl] n bola f de naftalina; *Fig* **to put a project in mothballs** aparcar un proyecto

**moth-eaten** ['mɒθiːtən] *adj* apolillado(a)

**mother** ['mʌðə(r)] **1** n madre f; **m. of six** madre de seis hijos; **M.'s Day** Día m de la Madre; **m. country** madre patria f; **M. Nature** la madre naturaleza; *Rel* **M. Superior** madre superiora; **m. tongue** lengua f materna

**2** *vt* mimar

**motherboard** ['mʌðəbɔːd] n *Comptr* placa f madre

**motherhood** ['mʌðəhʊd] n maternidad f

**mother-in-law** ['mʌðərɪnlɔː] n suegra f

**motherland** ['mʌðəlænd] n tierra f natal

**mother-of-pearl** ['mʌðərəv'pɜːl] n nácar m

**mother-to-be** ['mʌðətə'biː] n futura madre f

**motif** [məʊ'tiːf] n motivo m

**motion** ['məʊʃən] **1** n (a) *(movement)* movimiento m; **to set sth in m.** poner algo en marcha; *Fig* **to go through the motions** ha-

cer las cosas mecánicamente; **to go through the motions of doing sth** cumplir con el formulismo de hacer algo; *US* **m. picture** película f (b) *(in meeting, debate)* moción f; **to propose/second a m.** proponer/apoyar una moción; **the m. was carried** la moción fue aprobada (c) *(of bowel) Formal* deposición f, evacuación f

**2** *vt* **to m. sb to do sth** indicar a alguien (con un gesto) que haga algo

**3** *vi* **to m. to sb to do sth** indicar a alguien (con un gesto) que haga algo

**motionless** ['məʊʃənlɪs] *adj* inmóvil; **to remain m.** permanecer inmóvil

**motivate** ['məʊtɪveɪt] *vt* motivar

**motivation** [məʊtɪ'veɪʃən] n motivación f

**motive** ['məʊtɪv] **1** n *(reason)* motivo m, razón f; *Law* móvil m

**2** *adj* **m. force** fuerza f motriz

**motley** ['mɒtlɪ] *adj* heterogéneo(a), abigarrado(a); **m. crew** grupo m heterogéneo

**motocross** ['məʊtəkrɒs] n motocross m

**motor** ['məʊtə(r)] **1** n *(engine)* motor m; *Fam (car)* coche m; **m. industry** sector m automovilístico; **m. insurance** seguro m de automóviles; **m. racing** carreras fpl de coches; **m. show** salón m del automóvil; **the m. trade** el sector de compraventa de automóviles; **m. vehicle** vehículo m de motor

**2** *vi* viajar en coche; *Fam* **he was really motoring** *(going fast)* iba a toda mecha

**motorbike** ['məʊtəbaɪk] n moto f

**motorboat** ['məʊtəbəʊt] n (lancha f) motora f

**motorcade** ['məʊtəkeɪd] n desfile m de coches

**motorcar** ['məʊtəkɑː(r)] n *Br* automóvil m, coche m

**motorcycle** ['məʊtəsaɪkəl] n motocicleta f

**motorcyclist** ['məʊtəsaɪklɪst] n motociclista mf

**motoring** ['məʊtərɪŋ] n automovilismo m; **school of m.** autoescuela f; **m. offence** infracción f de tráfico

**motorist** ['məʊtərɪst] n conductor(ora) m,f, automovilista mf

**motorize** ['məʊtəraɪz] *vt* motorizar

**motorized** ['məʊtəraɪzd] *adj* *Mil* motorizado(a)

**motorway** ['məʊtəweɪ] n *Br* autopista f; **m. services** área f de servicios

**mottled** ['mɒtəld] *adj* *(complexion)* con manchas rojizas; *(coat, surface)* moteado(a)

**motto** ['mɒtəʊ] *(pl* **mottoes)** n lema m

**mould**[1], *US* **mold** [məʊld] n *(fungus)* moho m

**mould**[2], *US* **mold 1** n *(in art, cooking)* molde m; *Fig* **cast in the same m.** cortado(a) por el mismo patrón; *Fig* **a star in the John Wayne m.** un actor del estilo de John Wayne; *Fig* **to break the m.** romper moldes *or* el molde

**2** *vt (plastic, person's character)* moldear

**moulder,** *US* **molder** ['məʊldə(r)] *vi* desmoronarse

**moulding,** *US* **molding** ['məʊldɪŋ] *n Archit* moldura *f*

**mouldy,** *US* **moldy** ['məʊldɪ] *adj* mohoso(a)

**moult** [məʊlt] *vi (of animal)* mudar el pelo; *(of bird)* mudar el plumaje

**mound** [maʊnd] *n (hill)* colina *f*; *(of earth, sand)* montículo *m*

**mount¹** [maʊnt] *n (mountain)* monte *m*; **M. Sinai** el Monte Sinaí; **M. Vesuvius** el Vesubio

**mount²** [maʊnt] **1** *n* **(a)** *(for painting, colour slide)* soporte *m* **(b)** *(horse)* montura *f*

**2** *vt* **(a)** *(bicycle, horse)* montar en, subirse a; *(stairs, ladder)* subir **(b)** *(photograph, gun)* montar; **to m. an exhibition** montar una exposición; **to m. an offensive** realizar una ofensiva; **to m. guard** montar guardia

**3** *vi* **(a)** *(get onto horse)* montar, montarse **(b)** *(of opposition, tension)* aumentar, crecer

▶**mount up** *vi (of cost, debts)* aumentar, crecer

**mountain** ['maʊntɪn] *n* montaña *f*; *Fig* **a m. of work** una montaña de trabajo; **EC butter m.** toneladas *fpl* de excedentes comunitarios de mantequilla; **to make a m. out of a molehill** hacer una montaña de un grano de arena; **m. bike** bicicleta *f* de montaña; **m. climbing** alpinismo *m*, montañismo *m*; **m. lion** puma *m*; **m. range** cadena *f* montañosa, cordillera *f*; **m. rescue team** equipo *m* de rescate de montaña; *US* **M. Standard Time** = hora oficial en la zona de las Montañas Rocosas en los Estados Unidos

**mountaineer** [maʊntɪ'nɪə(r)] *n* alpinista *mf*, montañero(a) *m,f*

**mountaineering** [maʊntɪ'nɪərɪŋ] *n* alpinismo *m*, montañismo *m*

**mountainous** ['maʊntɪnəs] *adj* montañoso(a)

**mounted** ['maʊntɪd] *adj* montado(a); **the m. police** la policía montada

**mounting** ['maʊntɪŋ] **1** *n (for engine, gun)* soporte *m*

**2** *adj (cost, opposition)* creciente

**mourn** ['mɔːn] **1** *vt* llorar la muerte de

**2** *vi* **to m. for sb** llorar la muerte de alguien

**mourner** ['mɔːnə(r)] *n* doliente *mf*

**mournful** ['mɔːnfʊl] *adj* fúnebre, lúgubre

**mourning** ['mɔːnɪŋ] *n* duelo *m*, luto *m*; **to be in m. (for sb)** guardar luto (por alguien); **to go into m.** ponerse de luto

**mouse** [maʊs] *(pl mice* [maɪs]) *n also Comptr* ratón *m*; **m. mat** alfombrilla *f*

**mousetrap** ['maʊstræp] *n* ratonera *f*

**mousse** [muːs] *n (dessert)* mousse *m or f*; *(for hair)* espuma *f*

**moustache** [mə'stɑːʃ], *US* **mustache** ['mʌstæʃ] *n* bigote *m*

**mousy** ['maʊsɪ] *adj* **(a)** *(hair)* parduzco(a) **(b)** *(person, manner)* apocado(a), tímido(a)

**mouth 1** *n* [maʊθ] *(of person, animal, tunnel)* boca *f*; *(of river)* desembocadura *f*; **we have seven mouths to feed** tenemos siete bocas que alimentar; *Fam* **keep your m. shut about this** no digas ni pío de esto; *Fam* **to have a big m.** ser un/una bocazas; *Fam* **he's all m.** todo lo hace de boquilla; **to put words into sb's m.** poner palabras en boca de alguien; **m. organ** armónica *f*

**2** *vt* [maʊð] *(without sincerity)* decir mecánicamente; *(silently)* decir moviendo sólo los labios

**mouthful** ['maʊθfʊl] *n (of food)* bocado *m*; *(of drink)* trago *m*; *Fam* **to give sb a m.** poner a alguien de vuelta y media; *Fam Fig* **that's quite a m.!** *(of long name, word)* ¡menudo trabalenguas!

**mouthpiece** ['maʊθpiːs] *n* **(a)** *(of musical instrument)* boquilla *f*; *(of telephone)* micrófono *m* **(b)** *(of government, political party)* portavoz *mf*

**mouth-to-mouth** ['maʊθtə'maʊθ] *adj* **m. resuscitation** (respiración *f*) boca a boca *m*; **to give sb m. resuscitation** hacer el boca a boca a alguien

**mouthwash** ['maʊθwɒʃ] *n* elixir *m* (bucal)

**mouthwatering** ['maʊθwɔːtərɪŋ] *adj* muy apetecible

**movable** ['muːvəbəl] *adj* móvil; *Rel* **a m. feast** fiesta *f* movible

**move** [muːv] **1** *n* **(a)** *(motion)* movimiento *m*; **we must make a m.** debemos irnos; **to make a m. towards sb/sth** hacer amago de dirigirse hacia alguien/algo; **on the m.** *(travelling)* de viaje; *(active, busy)* en marcha, en movimiento; *Fam* **get a m. on!** ¡date prisa!

**(b)** *(action, step)* paso *m*; **to make the first m.** dar el primer paso

**(c)** *(from home)* mudanza *f*, traslado *m*; *(in job)* cambio *m*

**(d)** *(in games)* movimiento *m*, jugada *f*; **(it's) your m.** te toca (jugar), tú mueves

**2** *vt* **(a)** *(shift) (person, object, chesspiece)* mover; *(employee)* trasladar; *(postpone)* trasladar; **could you m. your bag out of the way?** ¿puedes quitar tu bolsa de en medio?; **m. your chair a bit closer** acerca la silla un poco; **to m. house** mudarse de casa; **to m. jobs** *(within company, sector)* cambiar de trabajo; *Fam* **m. yourself! we're going to be late!** ¡muévete, que vamos a llegar tarde!

**(b)** *(influence)* **I won't be moved** no voy a cambiar de opinión; **I felt moved to protest**

me sentí impulsado a protestar **(c)** *(affect emotionally)* conmover; **to m. sb to anger** enfurecer a alguien; **to m. sb to tears** hacer saltar las lágrimas a alguien

**(d)** *(in debate) (resolution)* proponer; **I m. that...** propongo que...

**3** *vi* **(a)** *(change position)* moverse; *(progress, advance)* avanzar; **to get things moving** poner las cosas en marcha; **don't m.!** ¡no te muevas!; **I can't m.** *(I'm stuck)* ¡no puedo moverme!; **could you m., please?** ¿podría apartarse, por favor?; *Fam* **come on, m.!** ¡venga, muévete!

**(b)** *(act)* moverse, actuar; **to m. to do sth** moverse *or* actuar para hacer algo

**(c)** *(to new home, office)* mudarse; **to m. to another job** cambiar de trabajo; **to m. to the country** irse a vivir al campo

**(d)** *(in games)* mover

►**move about**, **move around 1** *vt sep (furniture)* mover; *(employee)* trasladar

**2** *vi* moverse; **I heard somebody moving about upstairs** oí a alguien trajinar arriba; **he moves around a lot** *(in job)* se mueve mucho

►**move along** ⇒ **move on**

►**move away 1** *vt sep* apartar, retirar

**2** *vi (from window, person)* apartarse, retirarse; *(from house)* mudarse

►**move back 1** *vt sep (further away)* hacer retroceder; *(to former position)* devolver a su sitio

**2** *vi (retreat)* retirarse; *(to former position)* volver

►**move forward 1** *vt sep (meeting)* adelantar

**2** *vi (of person, car)* avanzar

►**move in** *vi (take up residence)* instalarse, mudarse; **to m. in with sb** irse a vivir con alguien

►**move off** *vi (person)* marcharse, irse; *(car, train, procession)* partir

►**move on 1** *vt sep (crowd)* dispersar; **he was moved on by the police** la policía lo echó de allí

**2** *vi (a) (of person, queue)* avanzar; **time's moving on** no queda mucho tiempo; **it's time we were moving on** es hora de marcharse; **things have moved on since then** las cosas han cambiado mucho desde entonces **(b)** *(change subject)* cambiar de tema; **to m. on to** pasar a (hablar de)

►**move out** *vi (move house)* mudarse; **my boyfriend moved out last week** mi novio me dejó y se fue de casa la semana pasada

►**move over** *vi (make room)* echarse a un lado, correrse; **to m. over to a new system** pasar a un nuevo sistema; **m. over!** ¡apártate!, ¡córrete!

►**move up** *vi* **(a)** *(make room)* echarse a un lado, correrse **(b)** *(be promoted)* ascender

**moveable** ['mu:vəbəl] = **movable**

**movement** ['mu:vmənt] *n also Mus* movimiento *m*; **free m. of people, goods,...** la libre circulación de personas, mercancías,...;

**to watch sb's movements** seguir los movimientos de alguien; **the armour made m. very difficult** la armadura dificultaba el movimiento; **a political m.** un movimiento político; **(bowel) m.** evacuación *f* (del vientre)

**mover** ['mu:və(r)] *n (a) (in debate)* ponente *mf*; **the movers and shakers** *(in politics)* los que mueven los hilos **(b)** **he's a beautiful m.** *(of dancer, footballer)* se mueve con mucha elegancia

**movie** ['mu:vɪ] *n US* película *f*; **to go to the movies** ir al cine; **she's in the movies** es actriz de cine; **m. actor/actress** actor *m*/actriz *f* de cine; **m. camera** cámara *f* cinematográfica *or* de cine; **m. industry** industria *f* cinematográfica *or* del cine; **m. star** estrella *f* de cine

**moviegoer** ['mu:vɪɡəʊə(r)] *n US* asiduo(a) *m,f* al cine

**moving** ['mu:vɪŋ] *adj (a) (train, vehicle)* en movimiento; **m. staircase** escalera *f* mecánica **(b)** *(causing motion)* **the m. spirit** la fuerza impulsora **(c)** *(description, story)* conmovedor(ora)

**mow** [məʊ] *vt (pp mown* [məʊn]*) (lawn)* cortar; *(hay)* segar

►**mow down** *vt sep (slaughter)* segar la vida de

**mown** [məʊn] *pp of* **mow**

**Mozambican** [məʊzæm'bi:kən] *n & adj* mozambiqueño(a) *m,f*

**Mozambique** [məʊzæm'bi:k] *n* Mozambique

**MP** [em'pi:] *n (a) Br Pol (abbr* **Member of Parliament)** diputado(a) *m,f* **(b)** *Mil (abbr* **Military Police(man))** P.M., policía *f* militar

**mpg** [empi:'dʒi:] *n Aut (abbr* **miles per gallon)** ≃ litros *mpl* a los cien; = consumo del coche medido en millas por galón de combustible

**mph** [empi:'eɪtʃ] *n (abbr* **miles per hour)** millas *fpl* por hora

**Mr** ['mɪstə(r)] *n (abbr* **Mister)** Sr., señor *m*; **Mr Jones** el Sr. Jones; **Mr Right** *(ideal man)* hombre ideal

**Mrs** ['mɪsɪz] *n (abbr* **Missus)** Sra., señora *f*; **Mrs Jones** la Sra. Jones

**MS** *(abbr* **manuscript)** ms., manuscrito *m*

**Ms** [mɪz]

Ms es el equivalente femenino de **Mr**, y se utiliza para dirigirse a una mujer sin precisar su estado civil.

*n (non-specific as to marital status)* Sra.

**ms** *(abbr* **milliseconds)** ms, milisegundos *mpl*

**MSc** [emes'si:] *n Univ (abbr* **Master of Science)** máster *m* en Ciencias; **to have an M. in chemistry** tener un máster en Química; **Fiona Watson, M.** Fiona Watson, licenciada con máster en Ciencias

**MSG** [emes'dʒi:] n (abbr **monosodium glutamate**) glutamato m monosódico

**MST** [emes'ti:] n US (abbr **Mountain Standard Time**) = hora oficial en la zona de las Montañas Rocosas en los Estados Unidos

**Mt** (abbr **Mount**) monte m

**much** [mʌtʃ] (comparative **more**, superlative **most**) **1** pron **there is not m.** left no queda mucho; **it's not worth m.** no vale mucho, no tiene mucho valor; **m. has happened since you left** han pasado muchas cosas desde que te fuiste; **she made m. of the fact that...** le dio mucha importancia al hecho de que...; **I'll say this m. for him, he's very polite** tengo que admitir que es muy amable; **I don't think m. of him** no lo tengo en gran estima; **it didn't come as m. of a surprise** no fue ninguna sorpresa; **she isn't m. of a singer** no es gran cosa como cantante; **in the end it cost as m. again** al final costó el doble; **twice as m.** el doble; **I thought/expected as m.** era lo que pensaba/me esperaba; **as m. as possible** todo lo posible; **it was as m. as we could do to stand upright** apenas podíamos mantenernos en pie; **he left without so m. as saying goodbye** se marchó sin siquiera decir adiós; **he has drunk so m. that...** ha bebido tanto que...; **so m. the better** tanto mejor; **so m. so that...** tanto es así que...; **so m. for her promises of help!** ¡y me había prometido su ayuda!; **I've got too m.** tengo demasiado; Fam **that's a bit m.!** ¡eso es pasarse!

**2** adj

> Normalmente, sólo se usa en estructuras negativas e interrogativas, salvo en lenguaje formal.

mucho(a); **how m. money?** ¿cuánto dinero?; **there isn't m. traffic** no hay mucho tráfico; **too m. time** demasiado tiempo; **so m. time** tanto tiempo; **as m. time as you like** tanto tiempo como quieras, todo el tiempo que quieras; Formal **m. work still needs to be done** aún queda mucho trabajo por hacer

**3** adv mucho; **I don't like it m.** no me gusta mucho; **m. as I'd like to, I can't go** por mucho que quiera, no puedo ir; **m. better/worse** mucho mejor/peor; **m. the best/largest** con mucho el mejor/más grande; **thank you very m.** muchas gracias; **it's/he's m. the same (as before)** no ha cambiado mucho; **m. to my astonishment** para mi estupefacción; **m. too good** demasiado bueno; **m. as I like him, I don't really trust him** aunque me cae muy bien, no me fío de él; **the result was m. as I expected** resultó más o menos como esperaba; **so m.** tanto; **too m.** demasiado; **they charged me £10 too m.** me

cobraron 10 libras de más; **this is too m.!** ¡esto ya es el colmo!

**muchness** ['mʌtʃnɪs] n Fam **they're much of a m.** son prácticamente iguales

**muck** [mʌk] n (dirt) mugre f, porquería f; (manure) estiércol m; Fam (bad food) bazofia f
▸**muck about, muck around** Br Fam **1** vt sep (treat badly) traer a maltraer
**2** vi (a) (fool about, waste time) hacer el tonto (b) (tinker) **to m. about** or **around with sth** enredar con algo
▸**muck in** vi Br Fam (help) arrimar el hombro
▸**muck out** vt sep (stables) limpiar
▸**muck up** vt sep Fam (make dirty) ensuciar; (spoil) echar a perder

**muckraking** ['mʌkreɪkɪŋ] n Fam (in journalism) búsqueda f del escándalo

**mucky** ['mʌkɪ] adj Br Fam mugriento(a)

**mucous** ['mju:kəs] adj mucoso(a)

**mucus** ['mju:kəs] n mocos mpl, mucosidad f

**mud** [mʌd] n barro m; Fig **to throw m. at sb** difamar or desacreditar a alguien; Fam **his name is m.** tiene muy mala fama; **m. hut** choza f de barro

**mudbank** ['mʌdbæŋk] n barrizal m, cenagal m

**mudflat** ['mʌdflæt] n marisma f

**muddle** ['mʌdəl] **1** n (a) (mess) lío m; **to be in a m.** (of things, person) estar hecho(a) un lío; **to get into a m.** (of things) liarse; (of person) hacerse un lío; **there was a m. over the dates** hubo un lío con las fechas
**2** vt (a) (put in disorder) desordenar; (mix up) confundir (b) (bewilder) liar; **to get muddled** hacerse un lío
▸**muddle along** vi ir tirando
▸**muddle through** vi arreglárselas; **we'll m. through somehow** ya nos las arreglaremos
▸**muddle up** vt sep (a) (put in disorder) desordenar; (mix up) confundir (b) (bewilder) liar; **to get muddled up** hacerse un lío

**muddleheaded** [mʌdəl'hedɪd] adj (person, decision) atolondrado(a)

**muddy** ['mʌdɪ] **1** adj (path) embarrado(a), enfangado(a); (water) turbio(a); (jacket, hands) lleno(a) de barro; (colour, complexion) terroso(a)
**2** vt manchar de barro; Fig **to m. the waters** enturbiar el asunto

**mudguard** ['mʌdgɑ:d] n guardabarros m inv

**mudpack** ['mʌdpæk] n mascarilla f de barro

**mudslinging** ['mʌdslɪŋɪŋ] n Fam **the debate degenerated into m.** el debate degeneró en meras descalificaciones

**muesli** ['mju:zlɪ] n muesli m

**muff**[1] [mʌf] vt Br Fam (one's lines) meter la pata en; (catch) fallar; (chance, opportunity) echar a perder; (job, task) hacer de pena

**muff**[2] n (for hands) manguito m

**muffin** ['mʌfɪn] *n Br (teacake)* tortita *f; US* ≃ magdalena *f*

**muffle** ['mʌfəl] *vt* (a) *(deaden sound of)* amortiguar (b) **to m. oneself up** abrigarse bien

**muffled** ['mʌfəld] *adj (sound, footstep)* apagado(a)

**muffler** ['mʌflə(r)] *n* (a) *(scarf)* bufanda *f* (b) *US (of car)* silenciador *m*

**mufti** ['mʌftɪ] *n very Fam* **in m.** *(of soldier)* de paisano

**mug** [mʌg] **1** *n* (a) *(cup)* taza *f* alta (b) *Fam (face)* jeta *f;* **m. shot** foto *f* para ficha policial (c) *Br Fam (gullible person)* primo(a) *m,f,* bobo(a) *m,f;* **it's a m.'s game** eso es cosa de tontos
**2** *vt ( pt & pp* **mugged)** *(attack)* atracar

▸**mug up** *vi Br Fam (study)* **to m. up on sth** empollar algo

**mugger** ['mʌgə(r)] *n* atracador(ora) *m,f*

**mugging** ['mʌgɪŋ] *n* atraco *m*

**muggins** ['mʌgɪnz] *n Br Fam* **I suppose m. will have to do it!** supongo que tendrá que hacerlo un servidor *or* mi menda, como siempre

**muggy** ['mʌgɪ] *adj* bochornoso(a); **it's m.** hace mucho bochorno

**mulatto** [mjuː'lætəʊ] *n (pl* **mulattos** *or* **mulattoes)** *n* mulato(a) *m,f*

**mulberry** ['mʌlbərɪ] *n (fruit)* mora *f; (tree)* morera *f*

**mule** [mjuːl] *n* mulo(a) *m,f*

▸**mull over** [mʌl] *vt sep (consider)* **to m. sth over** darle vueltas a algo

**mulled wine** ['mʌld'waɪn] *n* = vino con azúcar y especias que se toma caliente

**mullet** ['mʌlɪt] *n* **grey m.** mújol *m;* **red m.** salmonete *m*

**multi-access** ['mʌltɪ'ækses] *adj Comptr* multiusuario *inv,* de acceso múltiple

**multicoloured** ['mʌltɪkʌləd] *adj* multicolor

**multicultural** [mʌltɪ'kʌltʃərəl] *adj* multicultural

**multifarious** [mʌltɪ'feərɪəs] *adj* múltiple

**multi-functional** [mʌltɪ'fʌŋkʃənəl] *adj* multifuncional

**multilateral** [mʌltɪ'lætərəl] *adj* multilateral

**multimedia** [mʌltɪ'miːdɪə] **1** *n* multimedia *f*
**2** *adj* multimedia *inv*

**multimillionaire** [mʌltɪmɪljə'neə(r)] *n* multimillonario(a) *m,f*

**multinational** [mʌltɪ'næʃənəl] *n & adj* multinacional *f*

**multiparty** [mʌltɪ'pɑːtɪ] *adj* **m. democracy/system** democracia *f*/sistema *m* pluripartidista

**multiple** ['mʌltɪpəl] **1** *n* (a) *Math* múltiplo *m* (b) *Com (chain store)* cadena *f* (de tiendas)
**2** *adj* múltiple; *Med* **m. sclerosis** esclerosis *f inv* múltiple

**multiple-choice** ['mʌltɪpl'tʃɔɪs] *adj* **m. exam/question** examen *m*/pregunta *f* (de) tipo test

**multiplex** ['mʌltɪpleks] *n* multicine *m*

**multiplication** [mʌltɪplɪ'keɪʃən] *n* multiplicación *f;* **m. table** tabla *f* de multiplicar

**multiplicity** [mʌltɪ'plɪsɪtɪ] *n* multiplicidad *f,* diversidad *f*

**multiply** ['mʌltɪplaɪ] **1** *vt* multiplicar (**by** por)
**2** *vi (reproduce)* multiplicarse

**multipurpose** [mʌltɪ'pɜːpəs] *adj* multiuso *inv*

**multiracial** [mʌltɪ'reɪʃəl] *adj* multirracial

**multistorey,** *US* **multistory** [mʌltɪ'stɔːrɪ] *adj* de varios pisos *or* plantas; **m. car-park** aparcamiento *m* de varias plantas

**multitude** ['mʌltɪtjuːd] *n (large number, crowd)* multitud *f;* **a m. of** multitud de

**mum** [mʌm] *Fam* **1** *n Br (mother)* mamá *f;* **m.'s the word!** ¡de esto ni mu!
**2** *adv* **to keep m. (about sth)** no decir ni pío *or* ni mu (sobre algo)

**mumble** ['mʌmbəl] **1** *n* murmullo *m*
**2** *vt & vi* murmurar, musitar

**mumbo jumbo** ['mʌmbəʊ'dʒʌmbəʊ] *n (nonsense)* palabrería *f,* monsergas *fpl; (jargon)* jerigonza *f,* jerga *f*

**mummify** ['mʌmɪfaɪ] *vt* momificar

**mummy**[1] ['mʌmɪ] *n (embalmed body)* momia *f*

**mummy**[2] *n Br Fam (mother)* mamá *f;* **m.'s boy** niño *m* de mamá

**mumps** [mʌmps] *n (illness)* paperas *fpl*

**munch** [mʌntʃ] *vt* ronzar, mascar

**munchies** ['mʌntʃɪz] *npl Fam* (a) *(snacks)* cosillas *fpl* de picar (b) *(desire to eat)* **to have the m.** tener un poquillo de gusa

**mundane** [mʌn'deɪn] *adj* banal

**municipal** [mjuː'nɪsɪpəl] *adj* municipal

**municipality** [mjuː'nɪsɪ'pælɪtɪ] *n* municipio *m*

**munitions** [mjuː'nɪʃənz] *npl* municiones *fpl,* armamento *m*

**mural** ['mjʊərəl] *n* mural *m*

**Murcian** ['mɜːsɪən] *n & adj* murciano(a) *m,f*

**murder** ['mɜːdə(r)] **1** *n* (a) *(killing)* asesinato *m; Fig* **she gets away with m.** se le consiente cualquier cosa; **m. case** causa *f* de *or* juicio *m* por asesinato; **m. inquiry** investigación *f* de un asesinato (b) *Fam Fig (difficult task)* tortura *f;* **finding a parking place on a Saturday is m.** buscar aparcamiento en sábado es una tortura
**2** *vt* (a) *(kill)* asesinar; *Fam Fig* **I'll m. you (for that)!** ¡te voy a matar!; *Fam* **I could m. a beer/a pizza!** ¡me muero por una cerveza/ una pizza! (b) *Fig (destroy) (song, tune)* destrozar

**murderer** ['mɜːdərə(r)] *n* asesino(a) *m,f*

**murky** ['mɜːkɪ] *adj (weather, sky)* oscuro(a), sombrío(a); *(details, past)* tenebroso(a)

**murmur** ['mɜːmə(r)] **1** *n* murmullo *m*; **to do sth without a m.** hacer algo sin rechistar

**2** *vi* murmurar

**muscle** ['mʌsəl] *n* músculo *m*; **she didn't move a m.** no movió un solo músculo; *Fig* **political m.** pujanza *f* política

▶**muscle in** *vi* entrometerse (**on** en)

**muscleman** ['mʌsəlmæn] *n* forzudo *m*, hércules *m inv*

**Muscovite** ['mʌskəvaɪt] *n & adj* moscovita *mf*

**muscular** ['mʌskjʊlə(r)] *adj (tissue)* muscular; *(person)* musculoso(a); *Med* **m. dystrophy** distrofia *f* muscular

**Muse** [mjuːz] *n* musa *f*

**muse** [mjuːz] *vi* reflexionar, cavilar (**on** or **about** sobre)

**museum** [mjuː'zɪəm] *n* museo *m*

**mush** [mʌʃ] *n* (**a**) *(pulp)* masa *f*, puré *m* (**b**) *Fig (sentimentality)* ñoñeces *fpl*, sensiblerías *fpl*

**mushroom** ['mʌʃrʊm] **1** *n Bot* hongo *m*, seta *f*; *Culin (wild mushroom)* seta *f*; *(button mushroom)* champiñón *m*; **m. cloud** hongo *m* atómico

**2** *vi (of costs, prices)* dispararse; *(of town)* expandirse, extenderse

**mushy** ['mʌʃɪ] *adj (pulpy)* blando(a), pastoso(a); *Fig (sentimental)* ñoño(a), sensiblero(a)

**music** ['mjuːzɪk] *n* música *f*; **to set words to m.** poner música a la letra; *Fig* **those words were m. to her ears** esas palabras le sonaban a música celestial; **m. box** caja *f* de música; **m. stand** atril *m*; **m. teacher** profesor(ora) *m,f* de música

**musical** ['mjuːzɪkəl] **1** *n (show, film)* musical *m*

**2** *adj (tuneful)* musical; *(musically gifted)* con talento musical; **m. chairs** juego *m* de las sillas; *Fig* **to play m. chairs** andar constantemente cambiando de puesto; **m. instrument** instrumento *m* musical

**musician** [mjuː'zɪʃən] *n* músico(a) *m,f*

**musicologist** [mjuːzɪ'kɒlədʒɪst] *n* musicólogo(a) *m,f*

**musings** ['mjuːzɪŋz] *npl* reflexiones *fpl*, cavilaciones *fpl*

**musk** [mʌsk] *n* almizcle *m*

**musket** ['mʌskɪt] *n* mosquete *m*

**musketeer** [mʌskɪ'tɪə(r)] *n* mosquetero *m*

**muskrat** ['mʌskræt] *n* rata *f* almizclada

**Muslim** ['mʌzlɪm] *n & adj* musulmán(ana) *m,f*

**muslin** ['mʌzlɪn] *n* muselina *f*

**mussel** ['mʌsəl] *n* mejillón *m*; **m. bed** vivero *m* de mejillones

**must** [mʌst] **1** *Fam* (**a**) *(necessity)* **to be a m.** ser imprescindible

(**b**) *(thing not to be missed)* **this film's a m.** esta

película hay que verla *or* no hay que perdérsela

**2** *modal aux v* (**a**) *(expressing obligation)* tener que, deber; **you m. do it** tienes que hacerlo, debes hacerlo; **you m. be ready at four o'clock** tienes que estar listo a las cuatro; **you mustn't tell anyone** no se lo digas a nadie; **this plant m. be watered daily** esta planta hay que regarla todos los días; **I m. say I thought it was rather good** la verdad es que me pareció bastante bueno; **will you come with me? – if I m.** ¿vendrás conmigo? – si no queda más remedio; **take it if you m.** cógelo si tanta falta te hace; **m. you be so silly?** ¡mira que eres tonto!

(**b**) *(suggesting, inviting)* tener que; **you m. come and visit us** tienes que venir a vernos; **we m. go out for a drink sometime** tenemos que quedar algún día para tomar algo

(**c**) *(expressing probability)* deber de; **you m. be hungry** debes de tener hambre; **it m. be interesting working there** debe de ser interesante trabajar allí; **I m. have made a mistake** debo de haberme equivocado; **you m. be joking!** ¡no lo dirás en serio!

**mustache** *US* = **moustache**

**mustard** ['mʌstəd] *n* mostaza *f*; *US Fam Fig* **she couldn't cut the m.** no consiguió dar la talla; **m. gas** gas *m* mostaza

**muster** ['mʌstə(r)] **1** *n Fig* **it was good enough to pass m.** era pasable

**2** *vt (gather)* reunir; **to m. one's strength/courage** hacer acopio de fuerzas/valor

**musty** ['mʌstɪ] *adj* **to have a m. smell** *(of room)* oler a cerrado; *(of clothes)* oler a humedad

**mutant** ['mjuːtənt] *n & adj* mutante *mf*

**mutate** [mjuː'teɪt] *vi* mutarse (**into** en), transformarse (**into** en)

**mutation** [mjuː'teɪʃən] *n* mutación *f*

**mute** [mjuːt] **1** *n* (**a**) *(person)* mudo(a) *m,f* (**b**) *Mus* sordina *f*

**2** *adj (silent)* mudo(a)

**muted** ['mjuːtɪd] *adj (sound)* apagado(a); *(protest, criticism)* débil

**mutilate** ['mjuːtɪleɪt] *vt* mutilar

**mutilation** [mjuːtɪ'leɪʃən] *n* mutilación *f*

**mutineer** [mjuːtɪ'nɪə(r)] *n* amotinado(a) *m,f*

**mutinous** ['mjuːtɪnəs] *adj (rebellious)* rebelde; *(taking part in mutiny)* amotinado(a)

**mutiny** ['mjuːtɪnɪ] **1** *n* motín *m*

**2** *vi* amotinarse

**mutt** [mʌt] *n Fam (dog)* chucho *m*

**mutter** ['mʌtə(r)] **1** *n* murmullo *m*

**2** *vt & vi* murmurar

**mutton** ['mʌtən] *n (meat of sheep)* carnero *m*; *Fam* **m. dressed as lamb** una mujer ya carroza con pintas de jovencita

**mutual** ['mju:tʃʊəl] *adj (reciprocal)* mutuo(a); *(shared)* común; **the feeling is m.** el sentimiento es mutuo; **a m. friend** un amigo común

**mutually** ['mju:tʃʊəlɪ] *adv* mutuamente; **to be m. exclusive** excluirse mutuamente

**muzzle** ['mʌzəl] **1** *n* (**a**) *(dog's snout)* hocico *m*; *(device for dog)* bozal *m* (**b**) *(of gun)* boca *f*

**2** *vt (dog)* poner un bozal a; *Fig (person, press)* amordazar

**MW** (**a**) *Rad (abbr* **Medium Wave**) OM, onda *f* media (**b**) *Elec (abbr* **Megawatts**) MW, megavatio *m*

**my** [maɪ] *possessive adj* (**a**) *(singular)* mi; *(plural)* mis; **my dog** mi perro; **my parents** mis padres; **it wasn't MY idea!** ¡no fue idea mía!

(**b**) *(for parts of body, clothes) (translated by definite article)* **my eyes are blue** tengo los ojos azules; **I hit my head** me di un golpe en la cabeza; **I put my hands in my pockets** me metí las manos en los bolsillos

(**c**) **(oh) my!** ¡madre mía!, ¡jesús!

**Myanmar** [maɪæn'mɑ:(r)] *n (official name of Burma)* Myanmar

**mynah** ['maɪna] *n* **m. (bird)** miná *f*, = estornino hablador de la India

**myopia** [maɪ'əʊpɪə] *n also Fig* miopía *f*

**myopic** [maɪ'ɒpɪk] *adj* miope; *Fig* corto(a) de miras

**myriad** ['mɪrɪəd] *adj Literary* **there are m. examples** hay una miríada *or* un sinnúmero de ejemplos

**myrrh** [mɜ:(r)] *n* mirra *f*

**myrtle** ['mɜ:təl] *n (shrub)* mirto *m*, arrayán *m*

**myself** [maɪ'self] *pron* (**a**) *(reflexive)* me; **I hurt m.** me hice daño

(**b**) *(emphatic) (male)* yo mismo; *(female)* yo misma; **I did all the work m.** yo mismo *or* yo solo hice todo el trabajo; **I told her m.** se lo dije yo mismo; **I'm not quite m. today** hoy no estoy muy allá

(**c**) *(after preposition)* mí; **I bought it for m.** lo compré para mí; **I live by m.** vivo solo; **I realized I was talking to m.** me di cuenta de que estaba hablando solo

**mysterious** [mɪs'tɪərɪəs] *adj* misterioso(a); **to be m. about sth** andarse con muchos misterios acerca de algo

**mysteriously** [mɪs'tɪərɪəslɪ] *adv* misteriosamente

**mystery** ['mɪstərɪ] **1** *n* misterio *m*; **it's a m. to me** es un misterio para mí; **m. tour** = excursión organizada con un destino sorpresa

**2** *adj (guest, prize)* sorpresa *inv*; *(benefactor, witness)* anónimo(a), desconocido(a)

**mystic** ['mɪstɪk] *n* místico(a) *m,f*

**mystical** ['mɪstɪkəl] *adj* místico(a)

**mysticism** ['mɪstɪsɪzəm] *n* misticismo *m*

**mystify** ['mɪstɪfaɪ] *vt* dejar estupefacto(a) *or* perplejo(a), desconcertar; **I was mystified** me quedé estupefacto

**mystique** [mɪs'ti:k] *n* aureola *f* de misterio

**myth** [mɪθ] *n* mito *m*

**mythical** ['mɪθɪkəl] *adj* mítico(a)

**mythological** [mɪθə'lɒdʒɪkəl] *adj* mitológico(a)

**mythology** [mɪ'θɒlədʒɪ] *n* mitología *f*

**myxomatosis** [mɪksəmə'təʊsɪs] *n* mixomatosis *f inv*

# N

**N, n** [en] *n* (**a**) *(letter)* N, n *f* (**b**) *(abbr* **north**) N

**NAACP** [eneıeısı:'pi:] *n US (abbr* **National Association for the Advancement of Colored People**) = asociación americana para la defensa de los derechos de la gente de color

**naan** [na:n] *n* **n. (bread)** = clase de pan indio en forma de hogaza aplanada

**nab** [næb] *(pt & pp* **nabbed**) *vt Fam* (**a**) *(catch, arrest)* trincar, pescar (**b**) *(steal)* birlar

**nadir** ['neıdıə(r)] *n Astron* nadir *m; Fig* **to reach a n.** *(of party, career)* tocar fondo

**naff** [næf] *adj Br Fam (tasteless)* hortera, cutre; *(insensitive)* de mal gusto; **a n. remark** una bordería

▶**naff off** *vi Br Fam* **n. off!** ¡que te den!

**nag¹** [næg] *n Fam (horse)* rocín *m*, jamelgo *m*

**nag²** **1** *n (person)* pesado(a) *m,f*, latoso(a) *m,f*

**2** *vt (pt & pp* **nagged**) *(of person)* fastidiar, dar la lata a; *(of doubt)* asaltar; **to n. sb into doing sth** dar la lata a alguien para que haga algo

**3** *vi* fastidiar, dar la lata a; **to n. at sb to do sth** dar la lata a alguien para que haga algo; **her conscience was nagging at her to go to the police** tenía remordimientos de conciencia que le impulsaban a acudir a la policía

**nagging** ['nægıŋ] **1** *n* regañinas *fpl*

**2** *adj* persistente

**nail** [neıl] **1** *n* (**a**) *(in carpentry)* clavo *m; Fig* **it was another n. in his coffin** era otro clavo más en su ataúd; *Fig* **to hit the n. on the head** dar en el clavo (**b**) *(of finger, toe)* uña *f;* **n. file** lima *f* de uñas; **n. scissors** tijeras *fpl* de manicura; **n. varnish** *or* **polish** laca *f or* esmalte *m* de uñas; **n. varnish remover** quitaesmaltes *m inv*

**2** *vt* (**a**) *clavar;* **he nailed the lid shut** fijó la tapa con clavos; *Fig* **he stood nailed to the spot** se quedó clavado (**b**) *(idioms) Fam* **to n. sb for a crime** emplumar *or* empapelar a alguien por un delito; *Fam* **to n. a lie** desterrar una falsedad

▶**nail down** *vt sep (fasten)* fijar con clavos; *Fam Fig* **to n. sb down to a date/price** hacer que alguien se comprometa a dar una fecha concreta/un precio concreto

**nail-biting** ['neılbaıtıŋ] *adj Fam (contest, finish)* de infarto, emocionantísimo(a); **after a n. few hours, the hostages were released** después de varias horas de tensa espera liberaron a los rehenes

**nailbrush** ['neılbrʌʃ] *n* cepillo *m* de uñas

**naive** [naɪ'i:v] *adj* ingenuo(a)

**naively** [naɪ'i:vlı] *adv* ingenuamente

**naivety** [naɪ'i:vətı] *n* ingenuidad *f*

**naked** ['neıkıd] *adj* desnudo(a); **to be n.** estar desnudo(a); **a n. flame** una llama (sin protección); **n. aggression** agresión *f* abierta *or* alevosa; **visible to the n. eye** visible a simple vista

**namby-pamby** ['næmbı'pæmbı] *n & adj* ñoño(a) *m,f*

**name** [neım] **1** *n* (**a**) *(of person)* nombre *m;* **my name is...** me llamo...; **what's your n.?** ¿cómo te llamas?; **to mention sb by n.** mencionar a alguien por su nombre; **to take sb's n.** *(note down)* anotar *or* tomar el nombre de alguien; **a big n. in the theatre** una figura del teatro; **to put one's n. down (for sth)** apuntarse (a algo); **to go by** *or* **under the n. of...** ser conocido(a) como...; **in the n. of...** en nombre de...; **in the n. of God** *or* **Heaven!, in God's** *or* **Heaven's n.!** ¡por el amor de Dios!; **he was President in all but n.** él era el Presidente de hecho; **to call sb names** poner verde *or* insultar a alguien; **he hasn't got a penny to his n.** no tiene ni un duro; **last n.** apellido *m*

(**b**) *(reputation)* nombre *m*, reputación *f;* **she has a good/bad n.** tiene buena/mala fama; **to have a n. for prompt and efficient service** tener fama de ofrecer un servicio bueno y rápido; **to make a n. for oneself (as)** hacerse un nombre (como)

**2** *vt* (**a**) *(give name to)* poner nombre a, bautizar; **they named her Paula** le pusieron *or* llamaron Paula; **to n. sb after** *or US* **for sb** poner a alguien el nombre de alguien

(**b**) *(appoint)* nombrar

(**c**) *(designate, identify)* nombrar; **to n. names** dar nombres concretos; **n. your price** di *or* pon un precio

**name-calling** ['neɪmkɔːlɪŋ] *n* improperios *mpl*, insultos *mpl*

**name-dropper** ['neɪmdrɒpə(r)] *n Fam* **she's a terrible n.** se las da de conocer a muchos famosos

**name-dropping** ['neɪmdrɒpɪŋ] *n Fam* **there was a lot of n. in his speech** en el discurso se las daba de conocer a muchos famosos

**nameless** ['neɪmlɪs] *adj (person)* anónimo(a); **someone who shall remain n.** alguien que permanecerá en el anonimato

**namely** ['neɪmlɪ] *adv* a saber, es decir

**nameplate** ['neɪmpleɪt] *n* placa *f* con el nombre

**namesake** ['neɪmseɪk] *n* tocayo(a) *m,f*

**Namibia** [nə'mɪbɪə] *n* Namibia

**Namibian** [nə'mɪbɪən] *n & adj* namibio(a) *m,f*

**nancy** ['nænsɪ] *n very Fam* **n. (boy)** *(homosexual)* mariquita *m*, marica *m; (effeminate man)* mariposón *m*

**nanny** ['nænɪ] *n* **(a)** *(nursemaid)* niñera *f* **(b)** **n. goat** cabra *f*

**nanosecond** ['nænəʊsekənd] *n Phys* nanosegundo *m*

**nap¹** [næp] **1** *n (sleep)* cabezada *f*, siesta *f*; **to take** *or* **have a n.** echar una cabezada *or* una siesta

**2** *vi (pt & pp napped)* echar una cabezada *or* una siesta; *Fig* **they were caught napping** los cogieron desprevenidos

**nap²** *n (of cloth)* pelusa *f*, lanilla *f*

**napalm** ['neɪpɑːm] *n* napalm *m*

**nape** [neɪp] *n* **n. (of the neck)** nuca *f*

**naphthalene** ['næfθəliːn] *n* naftalina *f*

**napkin** ['næpkɪn] *n* **(a)** *(table)* **n.** servilleta *f*; **n. ring** servilletero *m (aro)* **(b)** *US (sanitary towel)* compresa *f*

**Naples** ['neɪpəlz] *n* Nápoles

**Napoleonic** [nəpəʊlɪ'ɒnɪk] *adj* napoleónico(a); **the N. Wars** las guerras napoleónicas

**nappy** ['næpɪ] *n Br* pañal *m*; **n. rash** escoceduras *fpl or* eritema *m* del pañal

**narc** [nɑːk] *n US Fam* estupa *mf (agente de la brigada de estupefacientes)*

**narcissus** [nɑː'sɪsəs] *(pl* **narcissi** [nɑː'sɪsaɪ]*) n (flower)* narciso *m*

**narcosis** [nɑː'kəʊsɪs] *n Med* narcosis *f inv*

**narcotic** [nɑː'kɒtɪk] **1** *n* narcótico *m*, estupefaciente *m*; *US* **narcotics agent** agente *mf (de la brigada)* de estupefacientes

**2** *adj* narcótico(a), estupefaciente

**nark** [nɑːk] *n Br Fam* **(a)** *(informer)* soplón(ona) *m,f* **(b)** *(irritable person)* picajoso(a) *m,f*, malaleche *mf*

**narky** ['nɑːkɪ] *adj Br Fam* **to be n.** *(by nature)* ser picajoso(a); *(temporarily)* estar picajoso(a); **he's a n. git** es un susceptible

**narrate** [nə'reɪt] *vt* narrar

**narrative** ['nærətɪv] **1** *n (story)* narración *f*

**2** *adj* narrativo(a)

**narrator** [nə'reɪtə(r)] *n* narrador(ora) *m,f*

**narrow** ['nærəʊ] **1** *adj* estrecho(a); *(majority)* escaso(a); **to grow** *or* **become n.** estrecharse, angostarse; **to have a n. mind** ser estrecho(a) de miras; **to have a n. escape** librarse por los pelos; **by a n. margin** *(to win, lose)* por un estrecho margen; **in the narrowest sense** en el sentido mas estricto; **to take a n. view of sth** enfocar algo desde un punto de vista muy limitado

**2** *vt* **to n. one's eyes** *(in suspicion, anger)* entornar los ojos *or* la mirada

**3** *vi (of road)* estrecharse

▶**narrow down** *vt sep (choice, possibilities)* limitar, reducir

**narrowly** ['nærəʊlɪ] *adv* **(a)** *(to interpret)* estrictamente, al pie de la letra **(b)** *(only just)* por poco

**narrow-minded** [nærəʊ'maɪndɪd] *adj* estrecho(a) de miras

**NASA** ['næsə] *n US (abbr* **National Aeronautics and Space Administration***)* la NASA, = agencia aeroespacial norteamericana

**nasal** ['neɪzəl] *adj* nasal; **to have a n. voice** tener la voz nasal

**nastily** ['nɑːstɪlɪ] *adv (to act, behave, remark)* con mala intención, desagradablemente; **to fall n.** tener una mala caída

**nastiness** ['nɑːstɪnɪs] *n (of person, remark)* mala intención *f*

**nasturtium** [nə'stɜː∫əm] *n* capuchina *f*

**nasty** ['nɑːstɪ] *adj (taste, experience, person)* desagradable; *(remark)* malintencionado(a); *(book, film, crime)* repugnante; *(shock)* desagradable; *(problem)* espinoso(a), peliagudo(a); **a n. accident** un accidente grave; **a n. cut** una herida muy fea; **a n. fall** una mala caída; **to be n. to sb** ser antipático(a) con alguien; **to turn n.** *(of situation, weather)* ponerse feo(a); **hiding her clothes was a really n. thing to do** esconderle la ropa fue una broma demasiado pesada; *Fig* **his behaviour left (me with) a n. taste in the mouth** su comportamiento me dejó muy mal sabor de boca; **you've got a n. mind!** ¡qué mal pensado eres!; **he's a n. piece of work** es un elemento de cuidado

**nation** ['neɪ∫ən] *n* nación *f*

**national** ['næ∫ənəl] *n* **(a)** *(person)* ciudadano(a) *m,f*, súbdito(a) *m,f* **(b)** *(newspaper)* periódico *m* (de ámbito) nacional

**2** *adj* nacional; **n. anthem** himno *m* nacional;

**the n. debt** la deuda pública; **the n. grid** la red eléctrica nacional; *Br* **N. Health Service** = la sanidad pública británica; **n. insurance** seguridad *f* social; **n. park** parque *m* nacional; **n. service** *(in army)* servicio *m* militar; **National Trust** ≃ Patrimonio *m* Nacional, = organismo estatal británico encargado de la conservación de edificios y parajes de especial interés

**nationalism** ['næʃənəlɪzəm] *n* nacionalismo *m*

**nationalist** ['næʃənəlɪst] *n & adj* nacionalista *mf*

**nationalistic** [næʃənə'lɪstɪk] *adj* nacionalista

**nationality** [næʃə'nælɪtɪ] *n* nacionalidad *f*

**nationalization** [næʃənəlaɪ'zeɪʃən] *n* nacionalización *f*

**nationalize** ['næʃənəlaɪz] *vt* nacionalizar

**nationally** ['næʃənəlɪ] *adv* en el ámbito nacional; **to be n. renowned** ser conocido(a) en todo el país

**nationwide** ['neɪʃənwaɪd] **1** *adj* de ámbito nacional

**2** *adv* en todo el país; **to be broadcast n.** ser transmitido(a) a todo el país

**native** ['neɪtɪv] **1** *n (of country, town)* natural *mf*, nativo(a) *m,f*; **I am a n. of Edinburgh** soy natural de Edimburgo; **the koala is a n. of Australia** el koala es originario de Australia; **she speaks English like a n.** su inglés es perfecto

**2** *adj* natal, nativo(a); **he returned to his n. London** regresó a su Londres natal; **N. American** indio(a) *m,f* americano(a); **n. land** tierra *f* natal; **n. language** lengua *f* materna; **n. speaker** hablante *mf* nativo(a); **I'm not a n. speaker of Spanish** mi lengua materna no es el español

**Nativity** [nə'tɪvɪtɪ] *n Rel* **the N.** la Natividad; **N. play** auto *m* navideño *or* de Navidad

**Nato, NATO** ['neɪtəʊ] *n (abbr* **North Atlantic Treaty Organization)** OTAN *f*

**natter** ['nætə(r)] *Br Fam* **1** *n* charla *f*; **to have a n.** charlar, darle a la lengua

**2** *vi* charlar, darle a la lengua

**natty** ['nætɪ] *adj Fam (person, dress)* fino(a), elegante

**natural** ['nætʃərəl] **1** *n* **he's a n. as an actor** es un actor nato

**2** *adj* **(a)** *(colour, taste)* natural; **death from n. causes** muerte *f* natural; **n. childbirth** parto *m* natural; **n. disaster** catástrofe *f* natural; **n. gas** gas *m* natural; **n. history** historia *f* natural; **n. mother** madre *f* biológica; **n. resources** recursos *mpl* naturales; **n. sciences** ciencias *fpl* naturales

**(b)** *(normal, to be expected)* natural, lógico(a); **it's only n. that you should want to be here** es natural que quieras estar aquí; **one's**

*or* **the n. reaction is to…** la reacción más normal es…; *Ind* **n. wastage** amortización *f* de puestos de trabajo por jubilación

**(c)** *(unaffected)* natural, espontáneo(a)

**naturalism** ['nætʃərəlɪzəm] *n* naturalismo *m*

**naturalist** ['nætʃərəlɪst] *n* naturalista *mf*

**naturalistic** ['nætʃərəlɪstɪk] *adj* naturalista

**naturalization** [nætʃərəlaɪ'zeɪʃən] *n* naturalización *f*

**naturalize** ['nætʃərəlaɪz] *vt* naturalizar, nacionalizar

**naturally** ['nætʃərəlɪ] *adv (obviously, logically)* naturalmente; *(in one's nature)* por naturaleza; *(unaffectedly)* con naturalidad; **to come n. to sb** ser innato(a) en alguien

**nature** ['neɪtʃə(r)] *n* **(a)** *(the natural world)* naturaleza *f*; **to let n. take its course** dejar que la naturaleza siga su curso; **n. lover** amante *mf* de la naturaleza; **n. reserve** reserva *f* natural; **n. trail** senda *f* natural, ruta *f* ecológica

**(b)** *(character) (of thing)* naturaleza *f*; *(of person)* naturaleza *f*, carácter *m*; **to have a jealous n.** tener un carácter celoso; **it's not in her n.** no es su carácter, no es propio de ella; **to be shy by n.** ser tímido(a) por naturaleza

**(c)** *(sort)* género *m*, clase *f*; **problems of this n.** problemas de este género; *Formal* **what is the n. of your complaint?** ¿cuál es el motivo de su queja?

**naught** [nɔːt] *n* **(a)** *Literary (nothing)* nada *f*; **his plans came to n.** sus planes (se) quedaron en nada **(b)** *US* = **nought**

**naughtily** ['nɔːtɪlɪ] *adv* **to behave n.** portarse mal

**naughty** ['nɔːtɪ] *adj (child)* malo(a), travieso(a); *(word, picture, magazine)* picante

**Naúru** ['naʊruː] *n* Nauru

**nausea** ['nɔːzɪə] *n* náuseas *fpl*

**nauseate** ['nɔːzɪeɪt] *vt* dar *or* provocar náuseas a

**nauseating** ['nɔːzɪeɪtɪŋ] *adj* nauseabundo(a)

**nauseous** ['nɔːzɪəs] *adj* nauseabundo(a); **to feel n.** sentir *or* tener náuseas

**nautical** ['nɔːtɪkəl] *adj* náutico(a); **n. mile** milla *f* marina *or* náutica

**naval** ['neɪvəl] *adj* naval; **n. battle** batalla *f* naval; **n. officer** oficial *mf* de marina

**Navarre** [nə'vɑː] *n* Navarra

**Navarrese** [nævə'riːz] *adj* navarro(a)

**nave** [neɪv] *n Archit (of church)* nave *f* central

**navel** ['neɪvəl] *n* ombligo *m*

**navigable** ['nævɪgəbəl] *adj* navegable

**navigate** ['nævɪgeɪt] **1** *vt (seas)* surcar, navegar por; *(ship)* gobernar, pilotar

**2** *vi* navegar; **I'll drive if you n.** *(in car)* yo conduzco si tú haces de copiloto

**navigation** [nævɪ'geɪʃən] *n* navegación *f*

**navigational** [nævɪˈgeɪʃənəl] *adj* n. **equipment** equipo *m* de navegación

**navigator** [ˈnævɪgeɪtə(r)] *n Naut* oficial *m* de derrota; *Av* piloto *m* navegante

**navvy** [ˈnævɪ] *n Br* peón *m*

**navy** [ˈneɪvɪ] *n* marina *f*, armada *f*; n. **(blue)** azul *m* marino

**Nazi** [ˈnɑːtsɪ] *n & adj* nazi *mf*

**Nazism** [ˈnɑːtsɪzəm] *n* nazismo *m*

**NB** [enˈbiː] *(abbr* **nota bene)** N.B.

**NBA** [enbiːˈeɪ] *US (abbr* **National Basketball Association)** NBA *f*

**NCO** [ensiːˈəʊ] *(pl* NCOs*) n Mil (abbr* **non-commissioned officer)** suboficial *mf*

**NE** *(abbr* **north east)** NE

**Neanderthal** [nɪˈændətɑːl] **1** *n* (a) hombre *m* de Neanderthal (b) *Fig (coarse person)* troglodita *mf*

**2** *adj* (a) **N. man** el hombre de Neanderthal (b) *Fig (attitude, behaviour)* cavernícola

**Neapolitan** [niːəˈpɒlɪtən] *n & adj* napolitano(a) *m,f*

**near** [nɪə(r)] **1** *adj* cercano(a), próximo(a); **to the nearest metre** en número redondo de metros; **in the n. future** en un futuro próximo; **it was a n. thing** poco faltó; **this is the nearest thing we have to a conference room** esto es lo más parecido que tenemos a una sala de reuniones; **the N. East** (el) Oriente Próximo

**2** *adv* cerca; **to be n.** estar cerca; **n. at hand** *(of thing)* a mano; *(of event)* cercano(a); **they were n. to giving up** estuvieron a punto de abandonar; **n. to tears** a punto de (echarse a) llorar; **n. to despair** próximo(a) a la desesperación; **she's nowhere n. finished** le falta mucho para terminar; **a n. total failure** un fracaso casi absoluto

**3** *prep* cerca de; **n. Madrid/the town centre** cerca de Madrid/del centro; **her birthday is n. Christmas** su cumpleaños cae por Navidad; **he came n. (to) being run over** estuvo a punto de ser atropellado; **nobody comes anywhere n. her** *(in skill, performance)* nadie se le puede comparar; **he's nowhere n. it!** *(with guess)* ¡no tiene ni idea!

**4** *n* **my nearest and dearest** mis (parientes) más allegados

**5** *vt* acercarse a, aproximarse a; **to be nearing completion** estar próximo(a) a finalizarse

**nearby 1** [ˈnɪəbaɪ] *adj* cercano(a)

**2** [nɪəˈbaɪ] *adv* cerca

**nearly** [ˈnɪəlɪ] *adv (almost)* casi; **we're n. there** *(finished)* ya casi hemos terminado; *(at destination)* ya casi hemos llegado; **he very n. died** estuvo a punto de morir; **not n. enough money/time** muy poco dinero/tiempo; **it's not n. so beautiful as I remember** no es ni de lejos tan bonito como lo recuerdo

**nearly-new** [ˈnɪəlɪˈnjuː] *adj* casi como nuevo(a)

**nearside** [ˈnɪəsaɪd] *Aut* **1** *n* lado *m* del copiloto

**2** *adj* del lado del copiloto

**near-sighted** [nɪəˈsaɪtɪd] *adj* corto(a) de vista, miope

**neat** [niːt] *adj* (a) *(person) (in habits)* ordenado(a); *(in appearance)* aseado(a), pulcro(a); *(room, house)* pulcro(a), ordenado(a); *(handwriting)* claro(a), nítido(a); *(solution)* certero(a), hábil; **he's a n. worker** es un trabajador esmerado (b) *(whisky, vodka)* seco(a), solo(a) (c) *US Fam (good)* genial, fenomenal

▸**neaten up** [ˈniːtən] *vt sep (hair, garden)* arreglar

**neatly** [ˈniːtlɪ] *adv* (a) *(carefully)* cuidadosamente, con esmero (b) *(skilfully)* **she n. avoided the subject** eludió hábilmente el tema

**neatness** [ˈniːtnɪs] *n (of appearance)* pulcritud *f*; *(of work)* esmero *m*; *(of solution)* acierto *m*, habilidad *f*; *(of handwriting)* nitidez *f*; *(of room, house)* pulcritud *f*

**nebula** [ˈnebjʊlə] *n Astron* nebulosa *f*

**nebulous** [ˈnebjʊləs] *adj (vague)* nebuloso(a)

**necessarily** [nesɪˈserɪlɪ] *adv* necesariamente; **it's not n. the case** no tiene por qué ser necesariamente así

**necessary** [ˈnesɪsərɪ] **1** *n Fam* **the n.** *(thing, action required)* lo necesario; *(money)* el dinero

**2** *adj (indispensable)* necesario(a), preciso(a); **it is n. to remind them** hay que recordárselo; **to do what is n.** hacer lo necesario; **if n.** si es preciso *or* necesario; **when(ever) n.** cuando sea necesario *or* preciso; **a n. evil** un mal necesario

**necessitate** [nɪˈsesɪteɪt] *vt Formal* hacer necesario(a), precisar

**necessity** [nɪˈsesɪtɪ] *n (need)* necesidad *f*; **of n.** por fuerza, necesariamente; **necessities** *(things needed)* necesidades *fpl*; *Prov* **n. is the mother of invention** la necesidad aviva el ingenio

**neck** [nek] **1** *n* (a) *(of person, dress, bottle)* cuello *m*; *(of animal)* pescuezo *m*; *(of guitar)* mástil *m*; *(of violin)* mango *m*; *(of land)* istmo *m*; **n. of lamb/beef** cuello *m or* cogote *m* de cordero/vaca; **high n.** *(of dress)* cuello alto; **low n.** *(of dress)* escote *m*

(b) *(idioms) Fam* **to risk one's n.** jugarse el pellejo; *Fam* **he got it in the n.** *(was severely punished)* se le cayó el pelo; *Fam* **he's in it up to his n.** está metido hasta el cuello; **to finish n. and n.** llegar igualados(as); *Fam* **to stick one's n. out** *(take risk)* arriesgarse; *Fam* **what are you doing in this n. of the woods?** ¿qué haces tú por estos andurriales?

**2** vi Fam (of couple) morrear

**necklace** ['neklɪs] n collar m

**neckline** ['neklaɪn] n escote m

**necromancy** ['nekrəʊmænsɪ] n Formal nigromancia f, necromancia f

**nectar** ['nektə(r)] n néctar m

**nectarine** ['nektəri:n] n nectarina f

**née** [neɪ] adj de soltera; **Mrs Gutteridge, n. Bard** la Sra. Gutteridge, de soltera Bard

**need** [ni:d] **1** n necesidad f (for de); **to attend to sb's needs** atender las necesidades de alguien; **there is no n. to...** no hace falta...; **if n. be, in case of n.** si fuera necesario; **to be in n.** (poor, destitute) estar necesitado(a); **to be in n. of sth** necesitar algo; **in time of n.** en los momentos de necesidad; **their n. is greater than mine** ellos están más necesitados que yo

**2** vt (of person) necesitar; **to n. to do sth** tener que hacer algo; **you'll n. to take more money** te hará falta más dinero; **I didn't n. to be reminded of it** no hizo falta que nadie me lo recordara; **his hair needs cutting** le hace falta un corte de pelo; **the torch needs a new battery** hay que cambiarle la pila a la linterna; **this work needs a lot of patience** este trabajo requiere mucha paciencia; Ironic **that's all I n.!** ¡sólo me faltaba eso!

**3** modal aux v

> Cuando se emplea como verbo modal sólo existe una forma, y los auxiliares **do/does** no se usan: **he need only worry about himself; need she go?; it needn't matter**.

**you needn't worry, I'll be fine!** no te preocupes, no me va a pasar nada; **you needn't wait** no hace falta me esperes; **n. I say more?** no hace falta decir más, ya se sabe

**needful** ['ni:dfʊl] n Fam **to do the n.** hacer lo necesario

**needle** ['ni:dəl] **1** n (for sewing, of compass, of pine-tree) aguja f; **it's like looking for a n. in a haystack** es como buscar una aguja en un pajar; Fam Fig **to give sb the n.** (annoy) fastidiar a alguien; Fam **n. match** (in football) partido m a muerte or con tintes revanchistas

**2** vt Fam pinchar, picar

**needlecraft** ['ni:dəlkrɑ:ft] n costura f

**needless** ['ni:dlɪs] adj innecesario(a); **n. to say,...** ni que decir tiene que..., huelga decir que...

**needlessly** ['ni:dlɪslɪ] adv innecesariamente

**needlework** ['ni:dəlwɜ:k] n (sewing) costura f; (embroidery) bordado m

**need-to-know** [ni:dtə'nəʊ] adj **information is given on a n. basis** se proporciona la información sólo a las personas que se considere que la necesitan

**needy** ['ni:dɪ] **1** npl **the n.** los necesitados

**2** adj (person) necesitado(a); **to be n.** estar necesitado(a)

**nefarious** [nɪ'feərɪəs] adj infame

**negate** [nɪ'geɪt] vt (work, effect) invalidar, anular

**negation** [nɪ'geɪʃən] n negación f

**negative** ['negətɪv] **1** n (a) Gram negación f, forma f negativa; **to answer in the n.** dar una respuesta negativa (b) Phot negativo m

**2** adj negativo(a); **don't be so n.** ¡no seas tan negativo!; Fin **n. cash flow** cash flow m or flujo m de caja negativo; Fin **n. equity** = depreciación del valor de mercado de una propiedad por debajo de su valor en hipoteca

**negatively** ['negətɪvlɪ] adv negativamente

**negativity** [negə'tɪvɪtɪ] n negatividad f

**neglect** [nɪ'glekt] **1** n (of garden, person, machine) abandono m, descuido m; (of duty, responsibilities) incumplimiento m; **from** or **through n.** por negligencia

**2** vt (a) (not care for) (child, one's health) descuidar, desatender; **to n. oneself** descuidarse (b) (ignore) (duty, responsibilities) incumplir; (post) abandonar; (one's work) tener abandonado(a); **to n. to do sth** dejar de hacer algo

**neglectful** [nɪ'glektfʊl] adj descuidado(a), negligente; **to be n. of sth/sb** descuidar or desatender algo/a alguien

**negligée** ['neglɪʒeɪ] n salto m de cama, negligé m

**negligence** ['neglɪdʒəns] n negligencia f

**negligent** ['neglɪdʒənt] adj negligente

**negligently** ['neglɪdʒəntlɪ] adv negligentemente

**negligible** ['neglɪdʒɪbəl] adj insignificante

**negotiable** [nɪ'gəʊʃəbəl] adj (demand, salary) negociable; **not n.** (obstacle) infranqueable; (path) intransitable; (demand) no negociable, innegociable

**negotiate** [nɪ'gəʊʃɪeɪt] **1** vt (a) (price, treaty) negociar; **price to be negotiated** precio a convenir (b) (obstacle) salvar, franquear

**2** vi negociar

**negotiation** [nɪgəʊʃɪ'eɪʃən] n negociación f; **under n.** en proceso de negociación; **negotiations** negociaciones

**negotiator** [nɪ'gəʊʃɪeɪtə(r)] n negociador(ora) m,f

**Negress** ['ni:grɪs] n Old-fashioned negra f

**Negro** ['ni:grəʊ] Old-fashioned **1** n (pl **Negroes**) negro(a) m,f

**2** adj negro(a); **N. spiritual** (song) espiritual m negro

**neigh** [neɪ] **1** n relincho m

**2** vi relinchar

**neighbour,** US **neighbor** ['neɪbə(r)] n vecino(a) m,f; **to be a good n.** ser un buen vecino; *Rel* **love thy n. as thyself** ama a tu prójimo como a ti mismo

**neighbourhood,** US **neighborhood** ['neɪbəhʊd] *n* (**a**) *(district)* barrio *m*; *(people)* vecindario *m*; *Br* **n. watch** vigilancia *f* vecinal (**b**) *(vicinity)* cercanías *fpl*; **to live in the (immediate) n.** **of...** vivir en las cercanías de...; **a figure in the n. of £2,000** una cantidad que ronda las 2.000 libras

**neighbouring,** US **neighboring** ['neɪbərɪŋ] *adj* vecino(a)

**neighbourliness,** US **neighborliness** ['neɪbəlɪnɪs] *n* buena vecindad *f*

**neighbourly,** US **neighborly** ['neɪbəlɪ] *adj (person)* amable (con los vecinos); **to be n.** ser buen(a) vecino(a)

**neither** ['naɪðə(r), 'niːðə(r)] **1** *adv* **n. ... nor...** ni... ni...; **n. (the) one nor the other** ni uno ni otro; **that's n. here nor there** eso no viene al caso

**2** *conj* **n. do I** yo tampoco; **if you don't go n. shall I** si tú no vas, yo tampoco; **the money wasn't available and n. were the facilities** no había ni dinero ni instalaciones

**3** *adj* ninguno(a); **n. driver was injured** ninguno de los conductores resultó herido

**4** *pron* ninguno(a); **which do you want? - n. (of them)** ¿cuál quieres? - ninguno; **n. of my brothers can come** no puede venir ninguno de mis hermanos

**neo-** ['niːəʊ] *pref* neo-

**neoclassical** [niːəʊ'klæsɪkəl] *adj* neoclásico(a)

**neofascist** [niːəʊ'fæʃɪst] *n & adj* neofascista *mf*

**neolithic** [niːəʊ'lɪθɪk] *adj* neolítico(a)

**neologism** [nɪ'ɒlədʒɪzəm] *n* neologismo *m*

**neon** ['niːɒn] *n Chem* neón *m*; **n. light** luz *f* de neón; **n. sign** letrero *m or* rótulo *m* de neón

**Nepal** [nɪ'pɔːl] *n* Nepal

**Nepalese** [nepə'liːz], **Nepali** [ne'pɔːlɪ] **1** (**a**) *(person)* nepalés(esa) *m,f*, nepalí *mf* (**b**) *(language)* nepalés *m*, nepalí *m*

**2** *adj* nepalés(esa), nepalí

**nephew** ['nefjuː] *n* sobrino *m*

**nepotism** ['nepətɪzəm] *n* nepotismo *m*

**Neptune** ['neptjuːn] *n (planet, god)* Neptuno

**nerd** [nɜːd] *n Fam* (**a**) *(boring person)* petardo(a) *m,f*, plasta *mf*; **a computer n.** un tipo raro obsesionado con los ordenadores (**b**) *(as insult)* bobo(a) *m,f*, gil *mf*

**nerve** [nɜːv] **1** *n* (**a**) *Anat* nervio *m*; *Fam* **she gets on my nerves!** ¡me saca de quicio!; **her nerves were in a terrible state** tenía los nervios destrozados; *Anat* **n. cell** neurona *f*, *Fig* **n. centre** *(of organization)* centro *m* neurálgico; **n. gas** gas *m* nervioso

(**b**) *(courage)* sangre *f* fría; **to have nerves of**

steel tener nervios de acero; **to keep/lose one's n.** mantener/perder la calma

(**c**) *Fam (cheek)* cara *f* dura, descaro *m*; **what a n.!** ¡qué cara más dura!; **you've got a n.!** ¡qué cara tienes!

**2** *vt* **to n. oneself to do sth** templar los nervios para hacer algo

**nerve-(w)racking** ['nɜːvrækɪŋ] *adj* angustioso(a)

**nervous** ['nɜːvəs] *adj* (**a**) *(apprehensive)* inquieto(a), nervioso(a); **to be n.** *(by nature)* ser nervioso; *(temporarily)* estar nervioso; **he was n. about (doing) it** le ponía nervioso (hacerlo) (**b**) **n. breakdown** crisis *f inv* nerviosa; **n. energy** nervio *m*; **n. exhaustion** agotamiento *m* nervioso; **n. system** sistema *m* nervioso

**nervously** ['nɜːvəslɪ] *adv* nerviosamente

**nervousness** ['nɜːvəsnɪs] *n (of speaker, performer)* nerviosismo *m*

**nervy** ['nɜːvɪ] *adj Fam (tense)* nervioso(a); **to be n.** estar nervioso(a)

**nest** [nest] **1** *n (of bird, bandits)* nido *m*; *(of ants)* hormiguero *m*; *(of wasps)* avispero *m*; *Fig* **to fly the n.** dejar el nido, irse de casa; **n. of tables** mesas *fpl* nido; *Fig* **n. egg** ahorrillos *mpl*

**2** *vi* anidar

**nestle** ['nesəl] *vi (of person)* acomodarse; **to n. up to sb** recostarse en alguien

**nestling** ['neslɪŋ] *n (young bird)* polluelo *m*

**Net** [net] *n Fam Comptr (Internet)* **the N.** la Red

**net¹** [net] **1** *n* red *f*; *Fig* **to slip through the n.** *(of mistake)* colarse; *(of criminal)* escaparse; **n. curtain** visillo *m*

**2** *vt (pt & pp netted) (capture) (animals)* capturar, apresar; *(drugs)* incautarse de; *(donations)* recoger; *(reward)* embolsarse

**net²** **1** *adj (weight, price, profit)* neto(a)

**2** *vt (pt & pp netted) (earn)* **to n. £2,000 pounds** ganar 2.000 libras netas *or* limpias

**netball** ['netbɔːl] *n* nétbol *m*, = modalidad de baloncesto para mujeres

**Netherlands** ['neðələndz] *npl* **the N.** los Países Bajos

**netting** ['netɪŋ] *n* red *f*, malla *f*

**nettle** ['netəl] **1** *n (plant)* ortiga *f*

**2** *vt (irritate)* irritar, fastidiar

**network** ['netwɜːk] **1** *n also Comptr* red *f*; *TV* cadena *f*

**2** *vi (establish contacts)* establecer contactos

**networking** ['netwɜːkɪŋ] *n Com* establecimiento *m* de contactos profesionales

**neural** ['njʊərəl] *adj Anat* neural

**neuralgia** [njʊ'rældʒə] *n Med* neuralgia *f*

**neurologist** [njʊə'rɒlədʒɪst] *n Med* neurólogo(a) *m,f*

**neurology** [njʊə'rɒlədʒɪ] *n Med* neurología *f*

**neuron** ['njʊərɒn] *n Anat* neurona *f*

**neurosis** [nju'rəusɪs] (*pl* **neuroses** [nju-'rəusi:z]) *n* neurosis *f inv*

**neurosurgery** [njuərəu'sɜ:dʒərɪ] *n Med* neurocirugía *f*

**neurotic** [nju'rɒtɪk] **1** *n* neurótico(a) *m,f*
**2** *adj* neurótico(a), paranoico(a); **to be/get n. about sth** estar/ponerse neurótico *or* paranoico por algo

**neuter** ['nju:tə(r)] **1** *n Gram* (género *m*) neutro *m*
**2** *adj Gram* neutro(a)
**3** *vt (animal)* castrar

**neutral** ['nju:trəl] **1** *n* **(a)** *(country)* nación *f* neutral; **to be a n.** ser neutral **(b)** *Aut* **in n.** en punto muerto
**2** *adj* **(a)** *Pol* neutral **(b)** *(colour)* neutro(a); **n. shoe polish** crema *f* (de calzado) incolora

**neutrality** [nju:'trælɪt] *n* neutralidad *f*

**neutralize** ['nju:trəlaɪz] *vt* neutralizar

**neutrino** [nju'tri:nəu] *n Phys* neutrino *m*

**neutron** ['nju:trɒn] *n Phys* neutrón *m*; **n. bomb** bomba *f* de neutrones

**never** ['nevə(r)] *adv* nunca; **n. again!** ¡nunca más!; **n. mind!** ¡no importa!; **she n. said a word** no dijo ni una palabra; **I've n. met him** no lo conozco de nada; **I n. expected this** jamás hubiera esperado esto; **he n. even congratulated me** ni siquiera me felicitó; *Fam* **well I n.!** ¡no me digas!

**never-ending** [nevər'endɪŋ] *adj* interminable

**never-never** [nevə'nevə(r)] *n Br Fam* **to buy sth on the n.** comprar algo a plazos

**nevertheless** [nevəðə'les] *adv (however)* no obstante, sin embargo; *(despite everything)* de todas maneras, a pesar de todo

**new** [nju:] *adj* nuevo(a); **we need a n. dishwasher** nos hace falta otro lavavajillas *or* un lavavajillas nuevo; **what's n.?** ¿qué tal?; **that's nothing n.!** no es ninguna novedad; **she's n. to this work** es la primera vez que trabaja en esto; **to be n. to a town** ser nuevo en *or* acabar de mudarse a una ciudad; **N. Age** *(music)* New Age; **N. Delhi** Nueva Delhi; **N. England** Nueva Inglaterra; **N. Guinea** Nueva Guinea; **n. man** hombre *m* moderno *(que ayuda en casa, etc)*; **N. Mexico** Nuevo México; **n. moon** luna *f* nueva; **N. Orleans** Nueva Orleans; **N. South Wales** Nueva Gales del Sur; **the N. Testament** el Nuevo Testamento; **n. town** = ciudad satélite de nueva planta creada para descongestionar un núcleo urbano; **the N. World** el Nuevo Mundo; **N. Year** año *m* nuevo; **N. Year's Day** día *m* de año nuevo; **N. Year's Eve** Nochevieja *f*; **N. Year's resolutions** = buenos propósitos para el año nuevo; **N. York** Nueva York; **N. Yorker** neoyorquino(a) *m,f*

**newborn** ['nju:bɔ:n] *adj* recién nacido(a); **n. baby** (bebé *m*) recién nacido *m*

**newcomer** ['nju:kʌmə(r)] *n* recién llegado(a) *m,f* (to a)

**newfangled** ['nju:fæŋgəld] *adj Pej* moderno(a); **I don't hold with those n. ideas** yo no comulgo con esas moderneces

**Newfoundland** ['nju:fəndlænd] *n* Terranova

**newly** ['nju:lɪ] *adv* recién, recientemente; *Econ* **n. industrialized country** país *m* de reciente industrialización

**newlyweds** ['nju:lɪwedz] *npl* recién casados *mpl*

**newness** ['nju:nɪs] *n (of design)* novedad *f*; **because of her n. to the job** por ser nueva en el trabajo

**news** [nju:z] *n* noticias *fpl*; *(TV programme)* telediario *m*; **a piece of n.** una noticia; **to be in the n.** ser noticia; **good/bad n.** buenas/malas noticias; *Fam* **he's bad n.** es un tipo de cuidado, tiene mucho peligro; *Fam* **that's n. to me!** ¡(pues) ahora me entero!; *Prov* **no n. is good n.** si no hay noticias, es que todo va bien; **n. agency** agencia *f* de noticias; **n. bulletin** boletín *m* de noticias; **n. conference** rueda *f* de prensa; **n. item** noticia *f*

**newsagent** ['nju:zeɪdʒənt] *n Br* vendedor(ora) *m,f* de periódicos; **n.'s (shop)** = tienda que vende prensa así como tabaco, chucherías e incluso artículos de papelería

**newscaster** ['nju:zka:stə(r)] *n* locutor(ora) *m,f or* presentador(ora) *m,f* de informativos

**newsflash** ['nju:zflæʃ] *n* noticia *f* de última hora *or* de alcance

**newsgroup** ['nju:zgru:p] *n Comptr* grupo *m* de noticias

**newsletter** ['nju:zletə(r)] *n* boletín *m* informativo

**newspaper** ['nju:zpeɪpə(r)] *n* periódico *m*; *(daily)* periódico, diario *m*; **wrapped in n.** envuelto(a) en papel de periódico; **n. report** artículo *m* periodístico

**newspaperman** ['nju:zpeɪpəmæn] *n (reporter)* periodista *m*, hombre *m* de prensa; *(proprietor)* propietario *m* de un periódico, hombre *m* de prensa

**newsprint** ['nju:zprɪnt] *n* papel *m* de periódico

**newsreader** ['nju:zri:də(r)] *n Rad TV* locutor(ora) *m,f or* presentador(ora) *m,f* de informativos

**newsreel** ['nju:zri:l] *n* noticiario *m* cinematográfico, ≃ nodo *m*

**newsroom** ['nju:zru:m] *n* (sala *f* de) redacción *f*

**newsstand** ['nju:zstænd] *n* quiosco *m*, puesto *m* de periódicos

**newsworthy** ['nju:zwɜ:ðɪ] *adj* de interés periodístico

**newt** [nju:t] *n* tritón *m*

**New Zealand** ['nju:'zi:lənd] *n* Nueva Zelanda

**New Zealander** ['nju:'zi:ləndə(r)] *n* neozelandés(esa) *m,f*, neocelandés(esa) *m,f*

**next** [nekst] **1** *adj* (a) *(in space)* siguiente; *(room, house)* de al lado; **n. door** (en la casa de) al lado (b) *(in time, order)* siguiente, próximo(a); **n. week/month** la semana/el mes que viene; **the n. chapter/page** el capítulo/la página siguiente; **the n. time I see him** la próxima vez que lo vea; **the year after n.** el año siguiente al que viene; **it's the n. station** es la próxima estación; **the n. turning on the right** el primer desvío a la derecha; **your name is n. on the list** tu nombre es el siguiente de la lista; **your train is the n. but one** tu tren no es el siguiente, sino el otro; **ask the n. person you meet** pregunta a la primera persona que te encuentres; **(the) n. to arrive was Carmen** la siguiente en llegar fue Carmen; **who's n.?**, **whose turn is it n.?** ¿quién es el siguiente?, ¿a quién le toca?; **n. please!** ¡el siguiente, por favor!; **the n. size up/down** la siguiente talla más grande/más pequeña

**2** *adv* (a) *(in space)* **to be n. to** estar al lado de; **I can't bear wool n. to my skin** no soporto el contacto de la lana (en la piel) (b) *(in time, order)* después, luego; **what shall we do n.?** ¿qué hacemos ahora?; **what did you do n.?** ¿qué hiciste después *or* a continuación?; **she'll be asking me to give up my job n.!** ¡ya sólo falta que me pida que deje el trabajo!; **when shall we meet n.?** ¿cuándo nos volveremos a ver?; **n. to my dog I like my sister best** después de mi perro, a quien más quiero es a mi hermana; **if we can't do that, the n. best thing would be to...** si eso no se puede hacer, siempre podríamos...; **the n. fastest after the Ferrari was...** el (siguiente) más rápido después del Ferrari fue...; **who is the n. oldest/youngest after Mark?** ¿quién es el más viejo/joven después de Mark?; **I got it for n. to nothing** lo compré por casi nada; **there is n. to no evidence** no hay apenas pruebas; **in n. to no time** en un abrir y cerrar de ojos

**next-door** ['neks'dɔ:(r)] *adj* de al lado; **n. neighbours** los vecinos de al lado

**next-of-kin** [nekstəv'kɪn] *n* familiar *m or* pariente *m* más próximo

**NFL** [enef'el] *n US (abbr* **National Football League)** = una de las dos ligas nacionales de fútbol americano

**NGO** [endʒi:'əʊ] *(pl* **NGOs)** *n (abbr* **non-governmental organization)** ONG *f*, organización *f* no gubernamental

**NHS** [eneɪtʃ'es] *n Br (abbr* **National Health Service)** = la sanidad pública británica

**NI** [en'aɪ] *n Br (abbr* **National Insurance)** SS, seguridad *f* social

**nib** [nɪb] *n (of pen)* plumilla *f*

**nibble** ['nɪbəl] **1** *n* **to have a n. at sth** dar un mordisquito a *or* mordisquear algo; **nibbles** *(snacks)* cosillas *fpl* de picar

**2** *vt* mordisquear

**Nicaragua** [nɪkə'rægjʊə] *n* Nicaragua

**Nicaraguan** [nɪkə'rægjʊən] *n & adj* nicaragüense *mf*

**nice** [naɪs] *adj* (a) *(pleasant)* agradable; *(good)* bueno(a); *(attractive)* bonito(a); *(friendly)* simpático(a), majo(a); **to be n. to sb** ser amable con alguien; **to have a n. time** pasarlo bien; **have a n. day!** ¡adiós, buenos días!, ¡que pase un buen día!; **it was n. of her to...** fue muy amable de su parte...; *Ironic* **we ARE in a n. mess!** ¡nos hemos metido en un buen lío!; *Ironic* **that's a n. way to behave!** ¡bonita manera de comportarse! (b) *(intensive)* **n. and easy** muy fácil; **n. and handy** muy conveniente; **a n. warm bath** un buen baño calentito

**nice-looking** ['naɪslʊkɪŋ] *adj* guapo(a)

**nicely** ['naɪslɪ] *adv* (a) *(politely) (to behave)* bien, correctamente; *(to ask)* con educación (b) *(well)* bien; **to be doing n.** ir bien; **she has done very n. (for herself)** le han ido muy bien las cosas

**nicety** ['naɪsɪtɪ] *n* **niceties** detalles *mpl*, sutilezas *fpl*

**niche** [ni:ʃ] *n* hornacina *f*, nicho *m*; *Com* **n. market** mercado *m* especializado

**nick** [nɪk] **1** *n* (a) *(in wood)* muesca *f*; *(on face)* corte *m* (b) **in the n. of time** justo a tiempo (c) *Fam (condition)* **in good/bad n.** en buen/mal estado (d) *Br Fam (prison)* trullo *m*; *(police station)* comisaría *f*

**2** *vt* (a) *(cut) (object)* hacer un corte *or* una muesca en; **to n. one's face** cortarse la cara (b) *Br Fam (arrest)* trincar (c) *Br Fam (steal)* mangar

**nickel** ['nɪkəl] *n (metal)* níquel *m*; *US (coin)* moneda *f* de cinco centavos

**nickname** ['nɪkneɪm] **1** *n* apodo *m*, mote *m*

**2** *vt* apodar; **he was nicknamed "Tank"** lo apodaron "Tank"

**nicotine** ['nɪkəti:n] *n* nicotina *f*

**niece** [ni:s] *n* sobrina *f*

**niff** [nɪf] *Br Fam* **1** *n (bad smell)* tufo *m*, peste *f*

**2** *vi (smell bad)* atufar, apestar

**nifty** ['nɪftɪ] *adj Fam* (a) *(clever) (idea, device)* ingenioso(a) (b) *(agile) (person, footwork)* ágil

**Niger** ['naɪdʒə] *n* Níger

**Nigeria** [naɪ'dʒɪərɪə] *n* Nigeria

**Nigerian** [naɪˈdʒɪərɪən] *n & adj* nigeriano(a) *m,f*

**niggardly** [ˈnɪɡədlɪ] *adj* mísero(a)

**nigger** [ˈnɪɡə(r)] *n very Fam* = término ofensivo para referirse a un negro

**niggle** [ˈnɪɡəl] **1** *vt* incomodar, fastidiar; **there is still something that is niggling me** todavía hay algo que me provoca desazón

**2** *vi (be overfussy)* **to n. about details** ser muy quisquilloso(a); **to n. (away) at sb** dar la tabarra a alguien

**niggling** [ˈnɪɡəlɪŋ] *adj (details)* de poca monta, insignificante; *(pain)* molesto(a); *(doubt)* inquietante

**nigh** [naɪ] *adv* (a) *Literary* cerca; **the end is n.!** ¡el fin está cerca! (b) **well n. impossible** *(almost)* casi *or* prácticamente imposible

**night** [naɪt] *n* noche *f*; **at n.** por la noche; **late at n.** bien entrada la noche; **all n.** toda la noche; **last n.** anoche; **tomorrow n.** mañana por la noche; **on Thursday n.** el jueves por la noche; **good n.!** ¡buenas noches!; **to have a n. out** salir por la noche; **to make a n. of it** salir toda la noche; *Fig* **n. bird** noctámbulo(a) *m,f*, trasnochador(ora) *m,f*; **n. flight** vuelo *m* nocturno; *Fig* **n. owl** noctámbulo(a) *m,f*, trasnochador(ora) *m,f*; **n. school** escuela *f* nocturna; **n. shift** turno *m* de noche

**nightcap** [ˈnaɪtkæp] *n* (a) *(hat)* gorro *m* de dormir (b) *(drink)* copa *f* antes de acostarse

**nightclub** [ˈnaɪtklʌb] *n* sala *f* de fiestas, discoteca *f*

**nightdress** [ˈnaɪtdres] *n* camisón *m*

**nightfall** [ˈnaɪtfɔːl] *n* anochecer *m*; **at n.** al anochecer

**nightgown** [ˈnaɪtɡaʊn] *n* camisón *m*

**nightie** [ˈnaɪtɪ] *n Fam* camisón *m*

**nightingale** [ˈnaɪtɪŋɡeɪl] *n* ruiseñor *m*

**nightjar** [ˈnaɪtdʒɑː(r)] *n (bird)* chotacabras *m inv*

**nightlife** [ˈnaɪtlaɪf] *n* vida *f* nocturna, ambiente *m* nocturno

**nightlong** [ˈnaɪtlɒŋ] *adj* **n. celebrations/ vigil** fiesta *f*/vigilia *f* durante toda la noche

**nightly** [ˈnaɪtlɪ] **1** *adj* **his n. stroll** su paseo de cada noche; **twice n. flights** dos vuelos cada noche

**2** *adv* todas las noches

**nightmare** [ˈnaɪtmeə(r)] *n also Fig* pesadilla *f*

**nightmarish** [ˈnaɪtmeərɪʃ] *adj* de pesadilla

**nightshirt** [ˈnaɪtʃɜːt] *n* camisa *f* de dormir

**night-time** [ˈnaɪttaɪm] **1** *n* noche *f*; **at n.** por la noche, durante la noche

**2** *adj* nocturno(a)

**nihilistic** [naɪ(h)ɪˈlɪstɪk] *adj* nihilista

**nil** [nɪl] *n* cero *m*; **to win two/three n.** ganar (por) dos/tres a cero

**Nile** [naɪl] *n* **the N.** el Nilo

**nimble** [ˈnɪmbəl] *adj* ágil; **to have n. feet** *(footballer)* tener un buen juego de piernas

**nimbly** [ˈnɪmblɪ] *adv* con agilidad

**nincompoop** [ˈnɪŋkəmpuːp] *n Fam* bobo(a) *m,f*, percebe *mf*

**nine** [naɪn] **1** *n* nueve *m*; **a n.-to-five job** un trabajo de oficina *(de nueve a cinco)*; *Fam* **to be dressed up to the nines** ir de punta en blanco

**2** *adj* nueve; *Fig* **n. times out of ten** la mayoría de las veces; **to have n. lives** tener siete vidas (como los gatos); *see also* **eight**

**nineteen** [naɪnˈtiːn] **1** *n* diecinueve *m*; *Br Fam* **to talk n. to the dozen** hablar por los codos

**2** *adj* diecinueve; *see also* **eight**

**nineteenth** [naɪnˈtiːnθ] **1** *n* (a) *(fraction)* diecinueveavo *m*, diecinueveava parte *f* (b) *(in series)* decimonoveno(a) *m,f* (c) *(of month)* diecinueve *m*

**2** *adj* decimonoveno(a); *Fam* **the n. hole** *(of golf course)* el bar; *see also* **eleventh**

**ninetieth** [ˈnaɪntɪθ] *n & adj* nonagésimo(a) *m,f*

**ninety** [ˈnaɪntɪ] **1** *n* noventa *m*

**2** *adj* noventa; **n. nine times out of a hundred** el noventa y nueve por ciento de las veces; *see also* **eighty**

**ninth** [naɪnθ] **1** *n* (a) *(fraction)* noveno *m*, novena parte *f* (b) *(in series)* noveno(a) *m,f* (c) *(of month)* nueve *m*

**2** *adj* noveno(a); *see also* **eighth**

**nip** [nɪp] **1** *n* (a) *(pinch)* pellizco *m*; *(with teeth)* bocado *m*, mordisquillo *m* (b) **there's a n. in the air** hace fresco (c) *Fam (of brandy)* chupito *m*, copita *f*

**2** *vt (pt & pp nipped)* (a) *(pinch)* pellizcar; *(with teeth)* mordisquear; *Fam Fig* **to n. sth in the bud** cortar algo de raíz (b) *(of cold, frost)* helar

**3** *vi (sting)* escocer

▸**nip out** *vi Br Fam (go out)* salir (un momento); **I'll n. out and buy a paper** salgo un momento a comprar el periódico

**nipper** [ˈnɪpə(r)] *n Br Fam (child)* chavalín(ina) *m,f*, chiquillo(a) *m,f*

**nipple** [ˈnɪpəl] *n (female)* pezón *m*; *(male)* tetilla *f*; *(on baby's bottle)* tetilla *f*, tetina *f*

**nippy** [ˈnɪpɪ] *adj Fam* (a) *(quick)* ligero(a), rápido(a) (b) *(cold)* fresco(a); **it's a bit n. today** hoy hace un poco de fresco

**nit** [nɪt] *n* (a) *(insect)* piojo *m*; *(insect's egg)* liendre *f* (b) *Br Fam (person)* idiota *mf*, bobo(a) *m,f*

**nit-picker** [ˈnɪtpɪkə(r)] *n Fam* quisquilloso(a) *m,f*

**nit-picking** [ˈnɪtpɪkɪŋ] *Fam* **1** *n* puñetería *f*, critiqueo *m* por nimiedades

**2** *adj* quisquilloso(a)

**nitrate** ['naɪtreɪt] n nitrato m

**nitric** ['naɪtrɪk] adj nítrico(a)

**nitrogen** ['naɪtrədʒən] n Chem nitrógeno m

**nitroglycerine** [naɪtrəʊ'glɪsəriːn] n nitroglicerina f

**nitrous** ['naɪtrəs] adj nitroso(a)

**nitty-gritty** ['nɪtɪ'grɪtɪ] n Fam meollo m; **to get down to the n.** ir al grano, ir al meollo del asunto

**nitwit** ['nɪtwɪt] n Fam idiota mf, bobo(a) m,f

**NNE** (abbr **north-northeast**) NNE, nornordeste

**NNW** (abbr **north-northwest**) NNO, nornoroeste

**No, no** (abbr **number**) nº, núm., número

**no** [nəʊ] **1** adv (a) (interjection) no; **to say no** decir que no; **she won't take no for an answer** no para hasta salirse con la suya (b) no; **he's no cleverer than her** no es más listo que ella; **no more/less than £100** no más/menos de 100 libras

**2** adj **there is no bread** no hay pan; **he's no friend of mine** no es amigo mío; **I am in no way surprised** no me sorprende en absoluto; **there's no denying it** no se puede negar; **there's no pleasing him** no hay forma de agradarle; **no smoking** (sign) prohibido fumar; Fam **no way!** ¡de eso nada!, ¡ni hablar!

**3** n (pl **noes**) Pol **ayes and noes** votos a favor y en contra

**Noah's ark** ['nəʊə'zɑːk] n el arca de Noé

**nobble** ['nɒbəl] vt Br Fam (a) (bribe) untar, sobornar (b) (waylay) pillar por banda

**Nobel Prize** ['nəʊbel'praɪz] n Premio m Nobel

**nobility** [nəʊ'bɪlɪtɪ] n nobleza f

**noble** ['nəʊbəl] **1** n noble mf

**2** adj (birth, person) noble; (sentiment, act) noble, magnánimo(a); (building, sight) grandioso(a)

**nobleman** ['nəʊbəlmən] n noble m

**noble-minded** [nəʊbəl'maɪndɪd] adj noble

**noblewoman** ['nəʊbəlwʊmən] n noble f

**nobly** ['nəʊblɪ] adv generosamente, noblemente

**nobody** ['nəʊbədɪ] **1** n **he's/she's a n.** es un/una don nadie

**2** pron nadie; **n. spoke to me** nadie me dirigió la palabra; **n. else** nadie más; **he is n.'s fool** no tiene un pelo de tonto; **if you don't have money, you're n.** si no tienes dinero, no eres nadie

**no-claims bonus** ['nəʊ'kleɪmz'bəʊnəs] n descuento m por no siniestralidad

**nocturnal** [nɒk'tɜːnəl] adj nocturno(a)

**nod** [nɒd] **1** n (greeting) saludo m (con la cabeza); (in agreement) señal f de asentimiento (con la cabeza); **to give sb/sth the n.** dar el consentimiento a alguien/para algo

**2** vt (pt & pp **nodded**) **to n. one's head** (in assent) asentir con la cabeza; (in greeting) saludar con la cabeza; (as signal) hacer una señal con la cabeza; **to n. one's approval** dar la aprobación con una inclinación de cabeza

**3** vi **to n. in agreement** asentir con la cabeza

▸**nod off** vi Fam quedarse dormido(a), dormirse

**node** [nəʊd] n nudo m; Med nodo m, nódulo m

**nodule** ['nɒdjuːl] n nódulo m

**no-frills** [nəʊ'frɪlz] adj sin florituras

**no-go area** ['nəʊ'gəʊ'eərɪə] n zona f prohibida

**no-good** ['nəʊgʊd] Fam adj inútil

**no-hoper** [nəʊ'həʊpə(r)] n inútil mf

**noise** [nɔɪz] n ruido m; **to make a n.** (individual sound) hacer un ruido; (racket) hacer ruido; **to make noises about doing sth** andar diciendo que uno va a hacer algo; Fig **a big n.** un pez gordo

**noiselessly** ['nɔɪzlɪslɪ] adv silenciosamente

**noisily** ['nɔɪzɪlɪ] adv ruidosamente

**noisy** ['nɔɪzɪ] adj ruidoso(a)

**nomad** ['nəʊmæd] n & adj nómada mf

**nomadic** [nəʊ'mædɪk] adj nómada

**no man's land** ['nəʊmænzlænd] n also Fig tierra f de nadie

**nomenclature** [nəʊ'menklətʃə(r)] n nomenclatura f

**nominal** ['nɒmɪnəl] adj nominal; (price, amount) simbólico(a)

**nominally** ['nɒmɪnəlɪ] adv nominalmente

**nominate** ['nɒmɪneɪt] vt (propose) proponer; (appoint) nombrar

**nomination** [nɒmɪ'neɪʃən] n (proposal) nominación f; (appointment) nombramiento m

**nominative** ['nɒmɪnətɪv] **1** n nominativo m

**2** adj nominativo(a)

**nominee** [nɒmɪ'niː] n candidato(a) m,f

**non-** [nɒn] pref no

**non-aggression pact** [nɒnə'greʃənpækt] n Pol pacto m de no agresión

**non-alcoholic** [nɒnælkə'hɒlɪk] adj sin alcohol

**nonaligned** [nɒnə'laɪnd] adj Pol no alineado(a)

**nonattendance** [nɒnə'tendəns] n ausencia f

**nonchalance** ['nɒnʃələns] n indiferencia f, despreocupación f

**nonchalant** ['nɒnʃələnt] adj indiferente, despreocupado(a)

**nonchalantly** [nɒnʃə'læntlɪ] adv con indiferencia or despreocupación

**noncombatant** [nɒn'kɒmbətənt] n & adj Mil no combatiente mf

**noncommissioned officer** ['nɒnkəmɪʃənd'ɒfɪsə(r)] n Mil suboficial mf

**noncommittal** [nɒnkə'mɪtəl] *adj (answer)* evasivo(a); **to be n.** responder con evasivas

**nonconformist** [nɒnkən'fɔːmɪst] *n & adj* inconformista *mf*

**nondescript** ['nɒndɪskrɪpt] *adj* anodino(a)

**none** [nʌn] **1** *pron (not any)* nada; *(not one)* ninguno(a); **n. of you/them** ninguno de vosotros/ellos; **n. of this** concerns me nada de esto me concierne; **it was n. other than the President** no era otro que el propio Presidente; **there was n. left** no quedaba nada; **there were n. left** no quedaba ninguno; *Fam* **we'll have n. of that!** ¡eso no te lo consiento!

**2** *adv* **his answer left me n. the wiser** su respuesta no me aclaró nada; **she was n. too happy about the situation** la situación no le hacía ninguna gracia; **n. too soon** justo a tiempo

**nonentity** [nɒ'nentɪtɪ] *n* nulidad *f*

**nonessential** [nɒnɪ'senʃəl] **1** *n* nonessentials lo accesorio

**2** *adj* accesorio(a), prescindible

**nonetheless** [nʌnðə'les] *adv (however)* no obstante, sin embargo; *(despite everything)* de todas maneras, a pesar de todo

**non-event** [nɒnɪ'vent] *n* chasco *m*; **the party turned out to be a bit of a n.** al final la fiesta no fue nada especial

**nonexecutive director** [nɒnɪg'zekjʊtɪvdaɪ'rektə(r)] *n* director(ora) *m,f* no ejecutivo(a)

**nonexistent** [nɒnɪg'zɪstənt] *adj* inexistente

**non-fiction** [nɒn'fɪkʃən] *n* no ficción *f*

**nonflammable** [nɒn'flæməbəl] *adj* incombustible, ininflamable

**non-linear** [nɒn'lɪnɪə(r)] *adj Comptr* **n. programming** programación *f* no lineal

**non-negotiable** [nɒnnɪ'gəʊʃɪəbəl] *adj* no negociable

**non-nuclear** [nɒn'njuːklɪə(r)] *adj (war)* convencional; *(energy)* no nuclear; *(country)* sin armamento nuclear

**no-no** ['nəʊnəʊ] *n Fam* **that's a n.** eso ni se te ocurra

**no-nonsense** [nəʊ'nɒnsəns] *adj (approach)* serio(a) y directo(a); *(implement, gadget)* práctico(a), funcional

**non-partisan** [nɒn'pɑːtɪzæn] *adj* imparcial

**non-payment** [nɒn'peɪmənt] *n* impago *m*

**non-person** ['nɒn'pɜːsən] *n* **politically, she became a n.** políticamente hablando, dejó de existir

**nonplussed** [nɒn'plʌst] *adj* perplejo(a), anonadado(a)

**non-profit(-making)** [nɒn'prɒfɪt(meɪkɪŋ)] *adj* sin ánimo de lucro

**non-racist** [nɒn'reɪsɪst] *adj* no racista

**nonresident** [nɒn'rezɪdənt] *n (of country, hotel)* no residente *mf*

**non-returnable** [nɒnrɪ'tɜːnəbəl] *adj* no retornable

**nonsense** ['nɒnsəns] *n* tonterías *fpl*, disparates *mpl*; **n.!** ¡tonterías!; **to talk (a lot of) n.** decir (muchos) disparates; **to make a n. of sth** echar por tierra algo

**nonsensical** [nɒn'sensɪkəl] *adj* absurdo(a), disparatado(a)

**non sequitur** [nɒn'sekwɪtə(r)] *n* incongruencia *f*

**non-sexist** [nɒn'seksɪst] *adj* no sexista

**non-smoker** [nɒn'sməʊkə(r)] *n* no fumador(ora) *m,f*

**non-specialist** [nɒn'speʃəlɪst] **1** *n* profano(a) *m,f*

**2** *adj* no especializado(a)

**nonstarter** [nɒn'stɑːtə(r)] *n* **the project's a n.** es un proyecto inviable

**nonstick** ['nɒn'stɪk] *adj* antiadherente

**non-stop** ['nɒn'stɒp] **1** *adj (journey, flight)* directo(a), sin escalas **2** *adv* sin parar, ininterrumpidamente; *(fly)* directo

**non-tariff barrier** ['nɒn'tærɪf bærɪə(r)] *n Econ* barrera *f* no arancelaria

**nontransferable** ['nɒntræns'fɜːrəbəl] *adj* intransferible

**nonverbal** [nɒn'vɜːbəl] *adj* no verbal; **n. communication** comunicación *f* no verbal

**nonviolent** [nɒn'vaɪələnt] *adj* no violento(a)

**noodles** ['nuːdəlz] *npl* tallarines *mpl*

**nook** [nʊk] *n* rincón *m*, recoveco *m*; **nooks and crannies** recovecos *mpl*

**nooky, nookie** ['nʊkɪ] *n Fam* marcha *f* para el cuerpo, ñacañaca *m*; **to get one's n.** echar un polvete *or* casquete

**noon** [nuːn] *n* mediodía *m*; **at n.** al mediodía

**noonday** ['nuːndeɪ] *n* **the n. sun** el sol del mediodía

**no-one** ['nəʊwʌn] = **nobody**

**noose** [nuːs] *n (loop)* nudo *m* corredizo; *(rope)* soga *f*; *Fig* **to put one's head in a n.** meterse en la boca del lobo

**nope** [nəʊp] *adv Fam* no

**nor** [nɔː(r)] *conj* ni; **neither... n.** ni... ni; **he neither drinks n. smokes** ni fuma ni bebe; **n. do I** yo tampoco, ni yo

**Nordic** ['nɔːdɪk] *adj* nórdico(a)

**norm** [nɔːm] *n* norma *f*; **to deviate from the n.** salirse de la norma

**normal** ['nɔːməl] **1** *n above/below n. (temperature, rate)* por encima/por debajo de lo normal; **things quickly got back to n. after the strike** las cosas volvieron pronto a la normalidad después de la huelga

**2** *adj* normal

**normality** [nɔː'mælɪtɪ], *US* **normalcy** ['nɔːməlsɪ] *n* normalidad *f*

**normalization** [nɔːməlaɪˈzeɪʃən] *n* normalización *f*

**normalize** [ˈnɔːməlaɪz] **1** *vt* normalizar
**2** *vi* normalizarse

**normally** [ˈnɔːməlɪ] *adv* normalmente

**Norman** [ˈnɔːmən] *n & adj* normando(a) *m,f*

**Normandy** [ˈnɔːməndɪ] *n* Normandía

**north** [nɔːθ] **1** *n* norte *m*; **to the n. (of)** al norte (de)

**2** *adj (direction, side)* norte; **n. London** el norte de Londres; **n. wind** viento *m* del norte; **N. Africa** África del Norte; **N. African** norteafricano(a) *m,f*; **N. America** Norteamérica; **N. American** norteamericano(a); **N. Carolina** Carolina del Norte; **N. Dakota** Dakota del Norte; **the N. Pole** el Polo Norte; **the N. Sea** el Mar del Norte

**3** *adv* al norte; **to face n.** estar orientado(a) al norte; **to go n.** ir hacia el norte

**northbound** [ˈnɔːθbaʊnd] *adj (train, traffic)* en dirección norte; **the n. carriageway** el carril que va hacia el norte

**northeast** [nɔːˈθiːst] **1** *n* nordeste *m*, noreste *m*

**2** *adj (side)* nordeste, noreste; **n. wind** viento *m* del nordeste

**3** *adv (to go, move)* hacia el nordeste; *(to be situated, face)* al nordeste

**northeasterly** [nɔːˈθiːstəlɪ] **1** *n (wind)* viento *m* del nordeste

**2** *adj (direction)* nordeste; **n. wind** viento *m* del nordeste

**northeastern** [nɔːˈθiːstən] *adj (region)* del nordeste

**northerly** [ˈnɔːðəlɪ] **1** *n (wind)* viento *m* del norte

**2** *adj (direction)* norte; **the most n. point** el punto más septentrional; **n. wind** viento *m* del norte

**northern** [ˈnɔːðən] *adj (region, accent)* del norte, norteño(a); **n. Spain** el norte de España; **n. hemisphere** hemisferio *m* norte; **N. Ireland** Irlanda del Norte; **N. Irish** norirlandés(esa); **n. lights** aurora *f* boreal

**northerner** [ˈnɔːðənə(r)] *n* norteño(a) *m,f*

**north-facing** [ˈnɔːθˈfeɪsɪŋ] *adj* orientado(a) al norte

**North Korea** [nɔːθkəˈriːə] *n* Corea del Norte

**North Korean** [nɔːθkəˈriːən] *n & adj* norcoreano(a) *m,f*

**north-northeast** [nɔːθnɔːˈθiːst] *adv* en dirección nornordeste

**north-northwest** [nɔːθnɔːˈθwest] *adv* en dirección nornoroeste

**northward** [ˈnɔːθwəd] *adj & adv* hacia el norte

**northwards** [ˈnɔːθwədz] *adv* hacia el norte

**northwest** [nɔːˈθwest] **1** *n* noroeste *m*

**2** *adj (side)* noroeste; **n. wind** viento *m* del noroeste

**3** *adv (to go, move)* hacia el noroeste; *(to be situated, face)* al noroeste

**northwesterly** [nɔːˈθwestəlɪ] **1** *n (wind)* viento *m* del noroeste

**2** *adj (direction)* noroeste; **n. wind** viento *m* del noroeste

**northwestern** [nɔːˈθwestən] *adj (region)* del noroeste

**Norway** [ˈnɔːweɪ] *n* Noruega

**Norwegian** [nɔːˈwiːdʒən] **1** *n* **(a)** *(person)* noruego(a) *m,f* **(b)** *(language)* noruego *m*

**2** *adj* noruego(a)

**nose** [nəʊz] *n* **(a)** *(of person)* nariz *f*; *(of animal)* hocico *m*; **her n. is bleeding** está sangrando por la nariz; **to blow one's n.** sonarse la nariz; **to hold one's n.** taparse la nariz; **to have a n. job** *(cosmetic surgery)* operarse la nariz

**(b)** *(of vehicle, plane, missile)* morro *m*; **the traffic was n. to tail** había caravana (de coches)

**(c)** *(idioms)* **it's right under your n.** lo tienes delante de las narices; **to turn one's n. up at sth** hacerle ascos a algo; **she walked by with her n. in the air** pasó con gesto engreído; **to look down one's n. at sb** mirar a alguien por encima del hombro; **she paid through the n. for it** le costó un ojo de la cara; **to put sb's n.** poner negro(a) a alguien; **they are leading them by the n.** les están manejando a su antojo; **to keep one's n. clean** no meterse en líos; **to have a n. for sth** tener olfato para algo; **to poke one's n. into other people's business** meter las narices en los asuntos de otros; **to put sb's n. out of joint** hacerle un feo a alguien

▸**nose about, nose around** *vi Fam* curiosear

**nosebleed** [ˈnəʊzbliːd] *n* **to have a n.** sangrar por la nariz

**nose-dive** [ˈnəʊzdaɪv] **1** *n (of plane)* picado *m*; *(of prices)* caída *f* en picado

**2** *vi (of plane)* hacer un picado; *(of prices)* caer en picado

**nosey** [ˈnəʊzɪ] *adj Fam* entrometido(a); *Br* **n. parker** metomentodo *mf*

**nosh** [nɒʃ] *Fam* **1** *n (food)* manduca *f*

**2** *vi (eat)* manducar

**no-show** [nəʊˈʃəʊ] *n (for flight)* pasajero *m* (con reserva) no presentado; *(at theatre)* reserva *f* no cubierta

**nosiness** [ˈnəʊzɪnɪs] *n* curiosidad *f*, entrometimiento *m*

**no-smoking** [nəʊˈsməʊkɪŋ] *adj (carriage, area)* de or para no fumadores

**nostalgia** [nɒsˈtældʒɪə] *n* nostalgia *f* **(for** de)

**nostalgic** [nɒsˈtældʒɪk] *adj* nostálgico(a)

**nostalgically** [nɒsˈtældʒɪklɪ] *adv* con nostalgia

**nostril** [ˈnɒstrɪl] *n* orificio *m* nasal, ventana *f* de la nariz

**nosy = nosey**

**not** [nɒt]

> En el inglés hablado, y en el escrito en estilo coloquial, **not** se contrae después de verbos modales y auxiliares.

*adv* no; **n. me/him** yo/él no; **I don't know** no sé; **don't move!** ¡no te muevas!; **whether she likes it or n.** le guste o no; **I think/hope n.** creo/espero que no; **she asked me n. to tell him** me pidió que no se le dijera; **n. wishing to cause an argument,** he said nothing como no deseaba provocar una discusión, no dijo nada; **you understand, don't you?** entiendes, ¿no?; **n. at all** en absoluto; **thank you so much! - n. at all!** ¡muchísimas gracias! - ¡de nada! *or* ¡no hay de qué!; **n. always** no siempre; **n. any more** ya no; **n. even** ni siquiera; **n. only... but also...** no sólo... sino también...; **n. yet** todavía no, aún no; **n. that I minded** no es que me importara; **n. that it matters** no es que importe

**notable** [ˈnəʊtəbəl] *adj* notable; **to be n. for sth** destacar por algo

**notably** [ˈnəʊtəblɪ] *adv (especially)* en particular, en especial; *(noticeably)* notablemente

**notary** [ˈnəʊtərɪ] *n Law* **n. (public)** notario(a) *m,f*

**notation** [nəʊˈteɪʃən] *n* notación *f*

**notch** [nɒtʃ] **1** *n* **(a)** *(in stick)* muesca *f* **(b)** *(grade, level)* punto *m*, grado *m*; **she's a n. above the rest** está por encima de los demás
**2** *vt (once)* hacer una muesca en; *(several times)* hacer muescas en
▸**notch up** *vt sep (victory, sale)* apuntarse

**note** [nəʊt] **1** *n* **(a)** *(short letter, at foot of page, record)* nota *f*; **(lecture) notes** apuntes *mpl* de clase; **to take** *or* **make a n. of sth** tomar nota de algo; **to take n. of sb/sth** *(notice)* fijarse en alguien/algo **(b)** *(musical)* nota *f*; *Fig (of doubt, anger)* nota *f*, tono *m*; **on a lighter n.** pasando a cosas menos serias **(c)** *(banknote)* billete *m* **(d)** **of n.** excepcional, destacable
**2** *vt (notice)* notar; *(mention)* señalar; *(error, mistake)* advertir; *(fact)* darse cuenta de; **please n. that...** tenga en cuenta que...
▸**note down** *vt sep* anotar, apuntar

**notebook** [ˈnəʊtbʊk] *n* libreta *f*; *(bigger)* cuaderno *m*; *Comptr* ordenador *m* portátil

**noted** [ˈnəʊtɪd] *adj* destacado(a); **to be n. for sth** destacar por algo

**notepad** [ˈnəʊtpæd] *n* bloc *m* de notas

**notepaper** [ˈnəʊtpeɪpə(r)] *n* papel *m* de carta

**noteworthy** [ˈnəʊtwɜːðɪ] *adj* digno(a) de mención

**nothing** [ˈnʌθɪŋ] **1** *pron* nada; **n. happened** no pasó nada; **say n. about it** no digas nada (de esto); **to say n. of...** por no hablar de...; **he was n. if not discreet** desde luego fue muy discreto; **n. new/remarkable** nada nuevo/especial; **n. else** nada más; **n. but** tan sólo; **you've caused me n. but trouble** no me has traído (nada) más que problemas; **buy n. but the best** compre sólo lo mejor; **n. much** no mucho, poca cosa; **there is n. more to be said** no hay (nada) más que decir; **there's n. like a nice steak!** ¡no hay nada como un buen filete!; **as a pianist he has n. on his brother** como pianista, no tiene ni punto de comparación con su hermano; **there's n. in it** *(it's untrue)* es falso; **he thinks n. of telling lies to get what he wants** no le importa mentir para conseguir sus propósitos; *Fam* **there's n. to it** no tiene ningún misterio; **£1,000 is n. to her** para ella 1.000 libras no son nada; **I have n. to do** no tengo nada que hacer; **to have n. to do with sb/sth** no tener nada que ver con alguien/algo; **we have n. to do with the neighbours** no tenemos trato con los vecinos; **that's n. to do with you** no tiene nada que ver contigo; **to get angry/worried for** *or* **about n.** enfadarse/preocuparse por nada; **to do sth for n.** *(in vain)* hacer algo para nada; *(with no reason)* hacer algo porque sí; *(free of charge)* hacer algo gratis
**2** *n* **to come to n.** quedar en nada; **a hundred pounds? - a mere n.!** ¿cien libras? - ¡una bagatela!
**3** *adv* **she looks n. like her sister** no se parece en nada a su hermana; **it was n. like as difficult as they said** no era ni mucho menos tan difícil como decían

**notice** [ˈnəʊtɪs] **1** *n* **(a)** *(warning)* aviso *m*; **to give sb n. of sth** avisar a alguien de algo, notificar algo a alguien; **without (prior) n.** sin previo aviso; **until further n.** hasta nuevo aviso; **at short n.** en poco tiempo, con poca antelación; **at a moment's n.** enseguida; **to give** *or* **hand in one's n.** *(resign)* presentar la dimisión, despedirse; **to give sb their n.** *(make redundant)* despedir a alguien; **to give sb a month's n.** *(of redundancy)* comunicarle a alguien el despido con un mes de antelación; *(to move out)* darle a alguien un plazo de un mes para abandonar el inmueble
**(b)** *(attention)* **to take n. of sb/sth** prestar atención a alguien/algo; **to take no n. (of)** no hacer caso (de); **to attract n.** llamar la atención; **the fact escaped everyone's n.** el hecho pasó inadvertido a todo el mundo; **it has come to my n. that...** ha llegado a mi conocimiento que...

**(c)** *(sign)* cartel *m*, letrero *m*
**(d)** *Th* crítica *f*, reseña *f*
**2** *vt (realize)* darse cuenta de; *(sense)* notar; *(observe)* fijarse en; **I noticed he was uncomfortable** me di cuenta de que estaba incómodo; **have you noticed anything strange in her behaviour?** ¿has notado algo extraño en su comportamiento?; **I noticed a man yawning at the back** me fijé en un hombre al fondo que bostezaba; **to be noticed, to get oneself noticed** llamar la atención
**3** *vi* darse cuenta

**noticeable** ['nəʊtɪsəbəl] *adj (change, difference)* apreciable, notable; **barely n.** apenas perceptible; **it was very n. that...** se notaba claramente que...

**noticeably** ['nəʊtɪsəblɪ] *adv* claramente, notablemente

**noticeboard** ['nəʊtɪsbɔːd] *n* tablón *m* de anuncios

**notification** [nəʊtɪfɪ'keɪʃən] *n* notificación *f*; **to give sb n. of sth** notificar algo a alguien

**notify** ['nəʊtɪfaɪ] *vt* notificar; **to n. sb of sth** notificar algo a alguien

**notion** ['nəʊʃən] *n* idea *f*, noción *f*; **to have no n. of sth** no tener noción de algo; **I have a n. that...** me parece que...; **to have a n. to do sth** tener el capricho de hacer algo

**notoriety** [nəʊtə'raɪətɪ] *n* mala fama *f*

**notorious** [nəʊ'tɔːrɪəs] *adj Pej* tristemente famoso(a) *or* célebre

**notoriously** [nəʊ'tɔːrɪəslɪ] *adv* **it is n. difficult/bad** es de sobra conocido lo difícil/malo que es

**notwithstanding** [nɒtwɪθ'stændɪŋ] *Formal* **1** *prep* a pesar de, pese a
**2** *adv* no obstante, sin embargo

**nougat** ['nuːgɑː] *n* = tipo de dulce con frutos secos

**nought,** *US* **naught** [nɔːt] *n* cero *m*; **noughts and crosses** *(game)* tres en raya *m*

**noun** [naʊn] *n Gram* sustantivo *m*, nombre *m*; **proper n.** nombre propio

**nourish** ['nʌrɪʃ] *vt (person, animal)* nutrir, alimentar; *(feeling, hope)* abrigar, albergar; **to be well nourished** estar bien alimentado(a)

**nourishing** ['nʌrɪʃɪŋ] *adj* nutritivo(a)

**nourishment** ['nʌrɪʃmənt] *n (food)* alimentos *mpl*; *(nourishing quality)* alimento *m*, alimentación *f*

**nous** [naʊs] *n Br Fam (common sense)* seso *m*

**Nov** *(abbr* **noviembre)** noviembre *m*

**Nova Scotia** ['nəʊvə'skəʊʃə] *n* Nueva Escocia

**novel** ['nɒvəl] **1** *n* novela *f*
**2** *adj (original)* novedoso(a), original

**novelist** ['nɒvəlɪst] *n* novelista *mf*

**novelty** ['nɒvəltɪ] *n (newness)* novedad *f*; *(cheap toy)* baratija *f*; **the n. will soon wear off** pronto dejará de ser una novedad; **it has a certain n. value** tiene un cierto atractivo por ser nuevo

**November** [nəʊ'vembə(r)] *n* noviembre *m*; *see also* **May**

**novice** ['nɒvɪs] *n (beginner)* principiante *mf*, novato(a) *m,f*; *Rel* novicio(a) *m,f*

**now** [naʊ] **1** *adv* **(a)** *(at this moment)* ahora; *(these days)* hoy (en) día; **what shall we do n.?** ¿y ahora qué hacemos?; *Fam* **it's n. or never** ahora o nunca; **that'll do for n.** ya basta por ahora *or* por el momento; **it's two years n. since his mother died** hace dos años que murió su madre; **he won't be long n.** no tardará mucho; **n. is the time to...** ahora es el momento de...; **any minute n.** en cualquier momento; **any day n.** cualquier día de estos; **right n.** ahora mismo; **(every) n. and then, (every) n. and again** de vez en cuando; **up to** *or* **until n.** hasta ahora; **from n. on** a partir de ahora; **in three days from n.** de aquí a tres días; **he ought to be here by n.** ya debería haber llegado; **and n. for some music** y a continuación, un poco de música
**(b)** *(to introduce statement, question)* **n., there are two ways of interpreting this** ahora bien, lo podemos interpretar de dos maneras; **well n., what's happened here?** vamos a ver, ¿qué ha pasado?
**(c)** *(as reproof)* **come n.!** ¡venga, hombre/mujer!; **n., n.! stop quarrelling!** ¡hala, hala! ¡basta de peleas!
**2** *conj* **n. (that) I'm older I think differently** ahora que soy más viejo, ya no pienso igual; **n. (that) you mention it,...** ahora que lo dices,...

**nowadays** ['naʊədeɪz] *adv* hoy (en) día, actualmente

**nowhere** ['nəʊweə(r)] **1** *n* **in the middle of n.** en un lugar dejado de la mano de Dios; **he came from n. to win the race** remontó desde atrás y ganó la carrera
**2** *adv (posición)* en/a ningún lugar, en/a ninguna parte; **n. else** en/a ningún otro lugar; **she was n. to be found** no se la podía encontrar por ninguna parte; **qualifications alone will get you n.** sólo con los estudios no irás a ninguna parte; **it's n. near the shopping centre** no queda nada cerca del centro comercial; **the rest were n.** *(in contest)* los demás quedaron muy por detrás; *Fam* **we're getting n. fast** estamos perdiendo el tiempo

**noxious** ['nɒkʃəs] *adj* nocivo(a)

**nozzle** ['nɒzəl] *n* boquilla *f*

**nr** *(abbr* **near)** cerca de

**NRA** [enɑː'reɪ] *n US* (*abbr* **National Rifle Association**) = asociación estadounidense que se opone a cualquier restricción en el uso de armas de fuego

**NSPCC** [enespiːsiː'siː] *n Br* (*abbr* **National Society for the Prevention of Cruelty to Children**) = sociedad protectora de la infancia

**nth** [enθ] *adj Fam* enésimo(a); **for the n. time** por enésima vez

**nuance** ['njuːɒns] *n* matiz *m*

**nub** [nʌb] *n* **the n. of the matter** *or* **issue** el quid de la cuestión

**nubile** ['njuːbaɪl] *adj* (*attractive*) de buen ver

**nuclear** ['njuːklɪə(r)] *adj* nuclear; **n. disarmament** desarme *m* nuclear; **n. energy** energía *f* nuclear; **n. family** familia *f* nuclear; **n. physics** física *f* nuclear; **n. power** energía *f* nuclear *or* atómica; **n. power station** central *f* nuclear; **n. war(fare)** guerra *f* nuclear *or* atómica; **n. warhead** cabeza *f* nuclear; **n. waste** residuos *mpl* nucleares; **n. weapon** arma *f* nuclear *or* atómica; **n. winter** invierno *m* nuclear

**nuclear-free zone** [njuːklɪə'friːzəʊn] *n* zona *f* desnuclearizada

**nucleus** ['njuːklɪəs] (*pl* **nuclei** ['njuːklɪaɪ]) *n also Fig* núcleo *m*

**nude** [njuːd] **1** *n* desnudo *m*; **in the n.** desnudo(a)
**2** *adj* desnudo(a); **to be in n.** estar desnudo(a)

**nudge** [nʌdʒ] **1** *n* (*push*) empujón *m*; (*with elbow*) codazo *m*
**2** *vt* (*push*) dar un empujón a; (*elbow*) dar un codazo a

**nudist** ['njuːdɪst] *n* nudista *mf*; **n. camp/colony** campamento *m*/colonia *f* nudista

**nudity** ['njuːdɪtɪ] *n* desnudez *f*

**nugatory** ['njuːgətɒrɪ] *adj* fútil

**nugget** ['nʌgɪt] *n* (*of gold*) pepita *f*; *Fig* **a few useful nuggets of information** unas cuantas informaciones útiles

**nuisance** ['njuːsəns] *n* (*annoying thing*) pesadez *f*, molestia *f*; (*annoying person*) pesado(a) *m,f*; **to make a n. of oneself** dar la lata; **what a n.!, that's a n.!** ¡qué contrariedad!; **n. call** llamada *f* (telefónica) molesta

**nuke** [njuːk] *vt Fam* atacar con armas nucleares

**null** [nʌl] *adj* nulo(a); **n. and void** nulo y sin valor

**nullify** ['nʌlɪfaɪ] *vt* anular, invalidar

**NUM** [enjuː'em] *n Br* (*abbr* **National Union of Mineworkers**) = sindicato minero británico

**numb** [nʌm] **1** *adj* entumecido(a); **to be n.** estar entumecido(a); **to go n.** entumecerse; **n. with cold** entumecido(a) por el frío; **n. with fear** paralizado(a) por el miedo
**2** *vt* (*of cold, grief*) entumecer; (*of terror*) paralizar

**number** ['nʌmbə(r)] **1** *n* (**a**) número *m*; **a large n. of** gran número de; **their supporters were present in small/great numbers** un pequeño/gran número de sus partidarios hizo acto de presencia; **I live at n. 40** vivo en el (número) 40; (**telephone**) **n.** número (de teléfono); *Comptr* **n. crunching** cálculos *mpl*; **to be n. one** ser el número uno; *Fam* **to look after n. one** cuidarse de los propios intereses; *Br* **N. Ten** = la residencia oficial del primer ministro británico
(**b**) (*song*) tema *m*, canción *f*
(**c**) (*idioms*) **he's my n. two** (*of subordinate*) es mi segundo (de a bordo); *Fam* **I've got your n.!** ¡te tengo calado!; *Fam* **his n.'s up** le ha llegado la hora; *Fam* **that car/dress is a nice little n.** ¡vaya cochazo/modelito!; *Fam* **she's got a nice little n. there** (*situation*) ha conseguido un buen chollo
**2** *vt* (**a**) (*assign number to*) numerar
(**b**) (*count*) contar; (*amount to*) sumar; **his days are numbered** tiene los días contados; **he numbers her among his friends** la cuenta entre sus amigos

**numberplate** ['nʌmbəpleɪt] *n Br* (*on car*) (placa *f* de la) matrícula *f*

**numbly** ['nʌmlɪ] *adv* (*answer, stare*) sin poder reaccionar

**numbness** ['nʌmnɪs] *n* (*of fingers*) entumecimiento *m*; (*from grief*) aturdimiento *m*; (*from fear*) parálisis *f inv*

**numbskull** ['nʌmskʌl] *n Fam* majadero(a) *m,f*, idiota *mf*

**numeracy** ['njuːmərəsɪ] *n* conocimiento *m* de aritmética

**numeral** ['njuːmərəl] *n* número *m*

**numerate** ['njuːmərət] *adj* **to be n.** tener un conocimiento básico de aritmética

**numerator** ['njuːməreɪtə(r)] *n Math* numerador *m*

**numerical** [njuː'merɪkəl] *adj* numérico(a)

**numerically** [njuː'merɪklɪ] *adv* en número, numéricamente

**numerous** ['njuːmərəs] *adj* numeroso(a); **on n. occasions** en numerosas ocasiones

**nun** [nʌn] *n* monja *f*

**nunnery** ['nʌnərɪ] *n* convento *m*

**nuptial** ['nʌpʃəl] **1** *npl* **nuptials** boda *f*, esponsales *mpl*
**2** *adj* nupcial

**nurse** [nɜːs] **1** *n* (**a**) (*medical*) enfermera *f*; (**male**) **n.** enfermero *m* (**b**) (*looking after children*) niñera *f*
**2** *vt* (*look after*) cuidar, atender; (*suckle*) amamantar, dar de mamar a; *Fig* (*feeling, hope*) guardar, abrigar; **she nursed him back to health** lo cuidó hasta que se restableció; *Fig* **to n. a grievance** guardar rencor

**nursery** ['nɜːsərɪ] n (a) (establishment) guardería f; (room in house) cuarto m de los niños; **n. education** educación f preescolar; **n. rhyme** poema m or canción f infantil; **n. school** centro m de preescolar, parvulario m; **n. slopes** (in skiing) pistas fpl para principiantes (b) (for plants) vivero m, semillero m

**nursing** ['nɜːsɪŋ] n (profession) enfermería f; (care given by a nurse) cuidados mpl, atención f sanitaria; **n. home** (where children are born) maternidad f; (for old people, war veterans) residencia f; **n. staff** personal m sanitario

**nurture** ['nɜːtʃə(r)] vt (a) (feed) (children, plants) nutrir, alimentar; (plan, scheme) alimentar (b) (bring up) criar

**NUS** [enjuː'es] n Br (abbr **National Union of Students**) = sindicato nacional de estudiantes británico

**NUT** [enjuː'tiː] n Br (abbr **National Union of Teachers**) = sindicato británico de profesores

**nut** [nʌt] n (a) (food) fruto m seco, nuez f; **nuts and raisins** frutos secos; Fig **a hard** or **tough n.** (person) un hueso (duro de roer); Fig **a tough** or **hard n. to crack** (problem) un hueso duro de roer

(b) Fam (head) coco m; **to be off one's n.** estar mal de la azotea; Br **he'll do his n. when he finds out!** ¡se va a cabrear cuando se entere!

(c) Fam (mad person) chalado(a) m,f; **a jazz/tennis n.** un loco del jazz/tenis

(d) (for fastening bolt) tuerca f; Fig **the nuts and bolts** los aspectos prácticos

(e) very Fam (testicle) **nuts** huevos mpl

**nutcase** ['nʌtkeɪs] n Fam chalado(a) m,f

**nutcrackers** ['nʌtkrækəz] npl cascanueces m inv; **a pair of n.** un cascanueces

**nuthouse** ['nʌthaʊs] n Fam manicomio m, frenopático m

**nutmeg** ['nʌtmeg] n nuez f moscada

**nutrient** ['njuːtrɪənt] **1** n **nutrients** sustancias fpl nutritivas
**2** adj nutritivo(a)

**nutrition** [njuː'trɪʃən] n nutrición f

**nutritional** [njuː'trɪʃənəl] adj nutritivo(a)

**nutritious** [njuː'trɪʃəs] adj nutritivo(a), alimenticio(a)

**nuts** [nʌts] adj Fam (mad) majara, chiflado(a); **to be n.** estar majara or chiflado; **to be n. about** (be very keen on) estar loco(a) por

**nutshell** ['nʌtʃel] n cáscara f (de fruto seco); Fig **in a n....** en una palabra...

**nutter** ['nʌtə(r)] n Br Fam (mad person) chalado(a) m,f

**nutty** ['nʌtɪ] adj (a) (in taste) **to have a n. taste** saber a avellana/nuez/etc (b) Fam (mad) chiflado(a), chalado(a); **to be n.** estar chiflado(a) or chalado(a)

**nuzzle** ['nʌzəl] **1** vt (of dog, cat) acariciar con el morro or hocico; (of person) acurrucarse contra
**2** vi **to n. against sb** (of person) acurrucarse contra

**NW** (abbr **north west**) NO

**NY** [en'waɪ] n US (abbr **New York**) Nueva York

**nylon** ['naɪlɒn] n (textile) nylon m, nailon m

**nylons** ['naɪlɒnz] npl (stockings) medias fpl de nylon; **a pair of nylons** unas medias de nylon

**nymph** [nɪmf] n ninfa f

**nymphomania** [nɪmfəʊ'meɪnɪə] n ninfomanía f

**nymphomaniac** [nɪmfəʊ'meɪnɪæk] n ninfómana f

**NZ** (abbr **New Zealand**) Nueva Zelanda

# O

**O, o** [əʊ] *n* (**a**) *(letter)* O, o *f; Br Sch Formerly* **O-level** = examen o diploma de una asignatura, de orientación académica, que se realizaba normalmente a los 16 años (**b**) *(zero)* cero *m*

**oaf** [əʊf] *n* tarugo *m*, zote *m*

**oak** [əʊk] *n* roble *m*; **o. apple** agalla *f* de roble

**OAP** [əʊer'piː] *n Br (abbr* **old age pensioner**) pensionista *mf*, jubilado(a) *m,f*

**oar** [ɔː(r)] *n* remo *m; Fig* **to put** *or* **stick one's o. in** meter las narices

**oarsman** ['ɔːzmən] *n* remero *m*

**OAS** [əʊer'es] *n (abbr* **Organization of American States**) OEA *f*, Organización *f* de Estados Americanos

**oasis** [əʊ'eɪsɪs] *(pl* **oases** [əʊ'eɪsiːz]) *n* oasis *m inv; Fig* **an o. of calm** un oasis de tranquilidad

**oatcake** ['əʊtkeɪk] *n* galleta *f* de avena

**oath** [əʊθ] *n* (**a**) *(pledge)* juramento *m*; **o. of allegiance** juramento de adhesión; **to take** *or* **swear an o.** prestar juramento, jurar; *Law* **on** *or* **under oath** bajo juramento (**b**) *(swearword)* juramento *m*, palabrota *f*

**oatmeal** ['əʊtmiːl] *n* harina *f* de avena

**oats** [əʊts] *npl (plant)* avena *f; (food)* copos *mpl* de avena; *Br very Fam* **to get one's o.** echar el polvo de costumbre

**OAU** [əʊer'juː] *n (abbr* **Organization of African Unity**) OUA *f*, Organización *f* para la Unidad Africana

**obdurate** ['ɒbdjʊrɪt] *adj* obstinado(a)

**OBE** [əʊbiː'iː] *n Br (abbr* **Officer of the Order of the British Empire**) título de miembro de la Orden del Imperio Británico, otorgado por servicios a la comunidad

**obedience** [ə'biːdɪəns] *n* obediencia *f*

**obedient** [ə'biːdɪənt] *adj* obediente

**obelisk** ['ɒbəlɪsk] *n* obelisco *m*

**obese** [əʊ'biːs] *adj* obeso(a)

**obesity** [əʊ'biːsɪtɪ] *n* obesidad *f*

**obey** [ə'beɪ] **1** *vt (person, order)* obedecer; **to o. the law** obedecer las leyes
**2** *vi* obedecer

**obfuscation** [ɒbfʌ'skeɪʃən] *n* oscurecimiento *m*

**obituary** [ə'bɪtjʊərɪ] *n* nota *f* necrológica, necrología *f*; **o. column** sección *f* de necrológicas; **o. notice** nota necrológica

**object** ['ɒbdʒɪkt] **1** *n* (**a**) *(thing)* objeto *m* (**b**) *(focus)* **he was the o. of their admiration** él era el objeto de su admiración; *Fig* **to give sb an o. lesson in sth** dar a alguien una lección magistral de algo
(**c**) *(purpose, aim)* objeto *m*, propósito *m*; **the o. of the exercise is to...** el ejercicio tiene por objeto...
(**d**) *(obstacle)* **expense is no o.** el gasto no es ningún inconveniente
(**e**) *Gram* **direct/indirect o.** complemento *m or* objeto *m* directo/indirecto
**2** [əb'dʒekt] *vi* oponerse (**to** a); **I o. to doing that** me indigna tener que hacer eso

**objection** [əb'dʒekʃən] *n* objeción *f*, reparo *m*; **to raise objections** poner objeciones *or* reparos; **I see no o.** no veo ningún inconveniente

**objectionable** [əb'dʒekʃənəbəl] *adj (behaviour)* reprobable; **he made himself thoroughly o.** se puso muy desagradable

**objective** [əb'dʒektɪv] **1** *n (aim, goal)* objetivo *m*
**2** *adj (impartial)* objetivo(a)

**objectively** [əb'dʒektɪvlɪ] *adv* objetivamente

**objectivity** [ɒbdʒek'tɪvɪtɪ] *n* objetividad *f*

**obligation** [ɒblɪ'geɪʃən] *n* obligación *f*; **to be under an o. to sb** tener una obligación para con alguien; **to be under an o. to do sth** estar obligado(a) a hacer algo

**obligatory** [ɒ'blɪgətərɪ] *adj* obligatorio(a)

**oblige** [ə'blaɪdʒ] *vt* (**a**) *(compel)* obligar; **to be obliged to do sth** estar obligado(a) a hacer algo (**b**) *(do a favour for)* hacer un favor a (**c**) **to be obliged to sb** *(be grateful)* estarle agradecido(a) a alguien; **I would be obliged if you would...** te estaría muy agradecido si...; **much obliged** muy agradecido(a)

**obliging** [ə'blaɪdʒɪŋ] *adj* atento(a)

**oblique** [ə'bliːk] *adj (line, angle)* oblicuo(a); *(reference, hint)* indirecto(a)

**obliterate** [ə'blɪtəreɪt] *vt* (**a**) *(erase)* borrar; *Fig (the past)* suprimir (**b**) *(destroy)* asolar, arrasar

**oblivion** [ə'blɪvɪən] *n* olvido *m*; **to sink into o.** caer en el olvido

**oblivious** [ə'blɪvɪəs] *adj* inconsciente; **o. to the pain/risks** ajeno(a) al dolor/a los riesgos; **I was o. of** *or* **to what was going on** no era consciente de lo que estaba pasando

**oblong** ['ɒblɒŋ] **1** *n* rectángulo *m*
**2** *adj* rectangular

**obnoxious** [əb'nɒkʃəs] *adj (person, action)* perverso(a)

**oboe** ['əʊbəʊ] *n* oboe *m*

**oboist** ['əʊbəʊɪst] *n Mus* oboe *mf*

**obscene** [əb'siːn] *adj (indecent)* obsceno(a); *Fig (profits, prices)* escandaloso(a)

**obscenely** [əb'siːnlɪ] *adv* obscenamente; **o. rich** escandalosamente rico(a)

**obscenity** [əb'senɪtɪ] *n* obscenidad *f*

**obscure** [əb'skjʊə(r)] **1** *adj (author, book, background)* oscuro(a); *(remark, argument)* oscuro(a), enigmático(a); *(feeling, sensation)* vago(a), oscuro(a)
**2** *vt* **(a)** *(hide from view)* ocultar **(b)** *(make unclear)* oscurecer

**obscurity** [əb'skjʊərɪtɪ] *n* oscuridad *f*

**obsequious** [əb'siːkwɪəs] *adj* obsequioso(a)

**observable** [əb'zɜːvəbəl] *adj* observable, apreciable

**observance** [əb'zɜːvəns] *n (of law, custom)* observancia *f*, acatamiento *m*; **religious observances** prácticas *fpl* religiosas

**observant** [əb'zɜːvənt] *adj* observador(ora)

**observation** [ɒbzə'veɪʃən] *n* **(a)** *(act of observing)* observación *f*; *(by police)* vigilancia *f*; *also Med* **to keep sb under o.** tener a alguien en o bajo observación; **to escape o.** pasar inadvertido(a); *Mil* **o. post** puesto *m* de observación **(b)** *(remark)* observación *f*, comentario *m*; **to make an o.** hacer una observación *or* un comentario

**observatory** [əb'zɜːvətərɪ] *n* observatorio *m*

**observe** [əb'zɜːv] *vt* **(a)** *(watch)* observar **(b)** *(notice)* advertir **(c)** *(say)* **to o. that…** señalar *or* observar que… **(d)** *(law, customs)* observar, acatar; **to o. the Sabbath** guardar el descanso sabático

**observer** [əb'zɜːvə(r)] *n* observador(ora) *m,f*

**obsess** [əb'ses] *vt* obsesionar; **to be obsessed with** *or* **by sb/sth** estar obsesionado(a) con *or* por alguien/algo

**obsession** [əb'seʃən] *n* obsesión *f*

**obsessive** [əb'sesɪv] *adj* obsesivo(a)

**obsolescence** [ɒbsə'lesəns] *n* obsolescencia *f*

**obsolete** ['ɒbsəliːt] *adj* obsoleto(a)

**obstacle** ['ɒbstəkəl] *n* obstáculo *m*; **to put obstacles in sb's way** ponerle a alguien obstá-

culos en el camino; *also Fig* **o. course** carrera *f* de obstáculos

**obstetrician** [ɒbste'trɪʃən] *n Med* obstetra *mf*, tocólogo(a) *m,f*

**obstetrics** [ɒb'stetrɪks] *n Med* obstetricia *f*, tocología *f*

**obstinacy** ['ɒbstɪnəsɪ] *n* obstinación *f*, terquedad *f*

**obstinate** ['ɒbstɪnɪt] *adj (person)* obstinado(a), terco(a); *(resistance)* tenaz, obstinado(a); *(illness)* pertinaz; **to be o. about sth** obstinarse en algo

**obstreperous** [əb'strepərəs] *adj* alborotado(a); **to get o. (about sth)** alborotarse (por algo)

**obstruct** [əb'strʌkt] *vt* **(a)** *(block) (road, pipe)* obstruir, bloquear; *(view)* impedir **(b)** *(hinder)* obstaculizar, entorpecer; *(in football, rugby)* obstruir; *Parl* **to o. a bill** entorpecer la aprobación de un proyecto de ley; *Law* **to o. the course of justice** obstaculizar *or* entorpecer la acción de la justicia

**obstruction** [əb'strʌkʃən] *n* **(a)** *(action) (of street)* obstrucción *f*; *(in football, rugby)* obstrucción *f* **(b)** *(blockage)* atasco *m*; **to cause an o.** *(on road)* provocar un atasco

**obstructive** [əb'strʌktɪv] *adj (behaviour, tactics)* obstruccionista; **to be o.** *(person)* poner impedimentos

**obtain** [əb'teɪn] **1** *vt (information, money)* obtener, conseguir
**2** *vi Formal (of practice, rule)* prevalecer

**obtainable** [əb'teɪnəbəl] *adj* **easily o.** fácilmente obtenible; **only o. on prescription** sólo disponible con receta médica

**obtrusive** [əb'truːsɪv] *adj* **(a)** *(person)* entrometido(a); *(behaviour)* molesto(a) **(b)** *(smell)* penetrante

**obtuse** [əb'tjuːs] *adj* **(a)** *Math* obtuso(a) **(b)** *(person, mind)* obtuso(a), duro(a) de mollera; **you're being deliberately o.** no estás queriendo entender

**obverse** ['ɒbvɜːs] **1** *n (of medal)* anverso *m*; *Fig* **the o. is sometimes true** a veces se da el caso contrario
**2** *adj* opuesto(a)

**obviate** ['ɒbvɪeɪt] *vt Formal (difficulty, danger)* evitar; **this would obviate the need to…** esto evitaría la necesidad de…

**obvious** ['ɒbvɪəs] **1** *n* **to state the o.** constatar lo evidente
**2** *adj* obvio(a), evidente; **it was the o. thing to do** hacer eso era lo más lógico

**obviously** ['ɒbvɪəslɪ] *adv* **(a)** *(in an obvious way)* obviamente, evidentemente; **she o. likes you** está claro que le gustas **(b)** *(of course)* desde luego, por supuesto; **o. not** claro que no

**occasion** [ə'keɪʒən] **1** n **(a)** *(time)* ocasión f; **on one o.** en una ocasión; **on several occasions** en varias ocasiones; **on o.** *(occasionally)* en ocasiones

**(b)** *(event)* acontecimiento m; **on the o. of...** con ocasión de...; **a sense of o.** un ambiente de gala

**(c)** *(opportunity)* ocasión f, oportunidad f; **on the first o.** a la primera oportunidad; **I'd like to take this o. to...** me gustaría aprovechar esta oportunidad para...

**(d)** *Formal (cause)* motivo m; **to have o. to do sth** tener motivos para hacer algo; **o. for complaint** motivo de queja

**2** vt *Formal (fear, surprise)* ocasionar, causar

**occasional** [ə'keɪʒənəl] *adj* ocasional, esporádico(a); **o. showers** chubascos ocasionales; **o. table** mesita f auxiliar

**occasionally** [ə'keɪʒənəlɪ] *adv* ocasionalmente, de vez en cuando

**occidental** [ɒksɪ'dentəl] *adj* occidental

**occult** [ɒ'kʌlt] **1** n **the o.** lo oculto
**2** *adj* oculto(a)

**occupant** ['ɒkjʊpənt] n *(of house, car)* ocupante mf; *(of job)* titular mf

**occupation** [ɒkjʊ'peɪʃən] n **(a)** *(profession)* profesión f, ocupación f **(b)** *(pastime)* pasatiempo m **(c)** *(of house, land)* ocupación f

**occupational** [ɒkjʊ'peɪʃənəl] *adj* profesional, laboral; **o. disease** enfermedad f profesional; **o. hazard** gaje m del oficio; **o. therapy** terapia f ocupacional

**occupied** ['ɒkjʊpaɪd] *adj* **(a)** *(house)* ocupado(a) **(b)** *(busy)* ocupado(a), atareado(a); **to be o. with sth** estar ocupado(a) con algo; **to keep sb o.** tener ocupado(a) a alguien

**occupier** ['ɒkjʊpaɪə(r)] n *(of house)* ocupante mf

**occupy** ['ɒkjʊpaɪ] vt *(house, sb's attention)* ocupar; **she occupies her time in studying** ocupa su tiempo estudiando, dedica su tiempo a estudiar

**occur** [ə'kɜː(r)] *(pt & pp* **occurred***)* vi **(a)** *(of event)* suceder, ocurrir; *(opportunity)* darse, surgir; **his name occurs several times in the report** su nombre aparece varias veces en el informe **(b)** *(of idea)* **when did the idea o. to you?** ¿cuándo se te ocurrió esa idea?

**occurrence** [ə'kʌrəns] n **(a)** *(event)* suceso m **(b)** *(incidence) (of disease)* incidencia f; **to be of frequent o.** ocurrir con frecuencia

**ocean** ['əʊʃən] n océano m; *Fam* **oceans of** la mar de

**ocean-going** ['əʊʃəngəʊɪŋ] *adj (vessel)* marítimo(a)

**Oceania** [əʊʃɪ'emɪə] n Oceanía

**oceanic** [əʊʃɪ'ænɪk] *adj* oceánico(a)

**ocelot** ['ɒsəlɒt] n ocelote m

**ochre,** *US* **ocher** ['əʊkə(r)] n & adj ocre m

**o'clock** [ə'klɒk] *adv* **(it's) one o.** (es) la una; **(it's) two/three o.** (son) las dos/tres; **at four o.** a las cuatro

**OCR** [əʊsiː'ɑː(r)] n *Comptr (abbr* **optical character reader***)* lector m óptico de caracteres; *(abbr* **optical character recognition***)* reconocimiento m óptico de caracteres

**Oct** *(abbr* **October***)* octubre m

**octagon** ['ɒktəgən] n octógono m, octágono m

**octagonal** [ɒk'tægənəl] *adj* octogonal, octagonal

**octane** ['ɒkteɪn] n *Chem* octano m; **o. number** octanaje m

**octave** ['ɒktɪv] n *Mus* octava f

**October** [ɒk'təʊbə(r)] n octubre m; *see also* **May**

**octogenarian** [ɒktədʒɪ'neərɪən] n & adj octogenario(a) m,f

**octopus** ['ɒktəpəs] n pulpo m

**OD** [əʊ'diː] *(pt & pp* **OD'd, OD'ed***)* vi *Fam* meterse una sobredosis; *Fig* **I think I've rather OD'd on pizza** creo que me he pasado con la pizza

**odd** [ɒd] **1** *adj* **(a)** *(strange)* raro(a), extraño(a) **(b)** *Math (number)* impar; **to be the o. man out** ser el bicho raro **(c)** *(one of a pair)* **an o. sock** un calcetín desparejado **(d)** *(occasional)* ocasional; **I smoke the o. cigarette** me fumo un cigarrillo de cuando en cuando; **you've made the o. mistake** has cometido algún que otro error; **o. jobs** chapuzas fpl, trabajillos mpl (caseros)

**2** *adv* **a hundred o. sheep** ciento y pico ovejas; **twenty o. pounds** veintitantas libras

**oddball** ['ɒdbɔːl] *Fam* **1** n excéntrico(a) m,f, raro(a) m,f

**2** *adj* excéntrico(a), raro(a)

**oddity** ['ɒdɪtɪ] n **(a)** *(strangeness)* rareza f **(b)** *(person)* bicho m raro; *(thing)* rareza f; **it's just one of his little oddities** no es más que otra de sus rarezas

**oddly** ['ɒdlɪ] *adv* extrañamente, de manera rara; **o. enough** aunque parezca raro

**oddness** ['ɒdnɪs] n *(strangeness)* rareza f

**odds** [ɒdz] *npl* **(a)** *(probability)* probabilidades fpl; *(in betting)* apuestas fpl; **this horse has o. of 7-1** las apuestas para este caballo están en *or* son de 7 a 1; **the o. are that... / it's more probable es que...; **the o. are against him** tiene pocas posibilidades; **the o. are in his favour** tiene muchas posibilidades; **to succeed against the o.** triunfar a pesar de las dificultades; **to pay over the o. (for sth)** pagar más de lo que vale (por algo); *Fam* **it makes no o.** da igual

**(b)** **to be at o. with sb** *(disagree)* estar peleado(a) con alguien

(C) *Fam* **o. and ends, o. and sods** cosillas *fpl*, chismes *mpl*

**odds-on** [ɒd'zɒn] *adj (horse)* **o. favourite** favorito(a) *m,f* claro(a) *or* indiscutible; *Fam* **it's o. that…** es casi seguro que…

**ode** [əʊd] *n* oda *f*

**odious** ['əʊdɪəs] *adj* odioso(a), aborrecible

**odium** ['əʊdɪəm] *n* odio *m*, aborrecimiento *m*

**odour,** *US* **odor** ['əʊdə(r)] *n (smell)* olor *m*; *(unpleasant smell)* mal olor *m*, tufo *m*; *Fig* **to be in good/bad o. with sb** estar a bien/mal con alguien

**odourless,** *US* **odorless** ['əʊdəlɪs] *adj* in-odoro(a)

**Odyssey** ['ɒdɪsɪ] *n* odisea *f*

**OECD** [əʊiːsiː'diː] *n (abbr* **Organization for Economic Co-operation and Development)** OCDE *f*, Organización *f* para la Cooperación y el Desarrollo Económico

**Oedipal** ['iːdɪpəl] *adj* edípico(a)

**oesophagus,** *US* **esophagus** [iː-'sɒfəgəs] *(pl* **oesophagi,** *US* **esophagi** [iː'sɒfəgaɪ]) *n Anat* esófago *m*

**oestrogen,** *US* **estrogen** ['iːstrədʒen] *n Biol Chem* estrógeno *m*

**of** [ɒv] *unstressed* [əv] *prep* de; **made of wood** de madera; **to be guilty/capable of…** ser culpable/capaz de…; **to be proud/tired of…** estar orgulloso(a)/cansado(a) de…; **a bag of potatoes** una bolsa de patatas; **a bottle of wine** una botella de vino; **a friend of mine** un amigo mío; **a car of her own** su propio coche; **the two of us** los dos, nosotros dos; **how much of it do you want?** ¿cuánto quiere?; **a drop of 20 per cent** una bajada del 20 por ciento; **there were four of us** éramos cuatro; **he of all people should know that…** él más que nadie debería saber que…; **it was clever of her to do it** fue muy lista en hacerlo; **the husband of the Prime Minister** el marido de la primera ministra; **the University of Manchester** la Universidad de Manchester; **a girl of ten** una niña de diez años; **fear of spiders** miedo a las arañas; **it was very kind of you** fue muy amable de tu parte; **the 4th of October** el 4 de octubre; **of an evening** por la noche; *US* **a quarter of one** la una menos cuarto

**off** [ɒf] **1** *adv* **(a)** *(away)* **the meeting is only two weeks o.** sólo quedan dos semanas para la reunión; **five miles o.** a cinco millas (de distancia); **I must be o.** tengo que irme; **I'm o. to London** me voy a Londres; **o. you go!** ¡andando!

**(b)** *(indicating removal)* **to take o. one's coat** quitarse el abrigo; **the handle has come o.** se ha soltado el asa; **the light/TV is o.** la luz/tele está apagada

**(c)** *(with prices)* **20%/£5 o.** una rebaja del 20%/de 5 libras

**(d)** *(away from work, school)* **to have time o.** tener tiempo libre

**2** *prep* **(a)** *(away from)* **o. the coast** cerca de la costa; **a street o. the main road** una calle que sale de la principal; **o. the record** extraoficialmente

**(b)** *(indicating removal from)* **to fall/jump o. sth** caerse/saltar de algo; **the handle has come o. the saucepan** se ha desprendido el mango de la cacerola

**(c)** *(with prices)* **20%/£5 o. the price** una rebaja del 20%/de 5 libras

**(d)** *(absent from)* **to be o. work/school** faltar al trabajo/colegio; **Jane's o. work today** Jane no viene hoy a trabajar

**(e)** *(not liking)* **she's been o. her food lately** últimamente no está comiendo bien *or* anda desganada

**(f)** *Fam (from)* **to buy/borrow sth o. sb** comprar/pedir prestado algo a alguien; **I got some useful advice o. him** me dio algunos consejos útiles

**3** *adj* **(a)** *(not functioning) (light, TV)* apagado(a); *(water, electricity)* desconectado(a); **o. and on, on and o.** *(intermittently)* a intervalos, intermitentemente

**(b)** *(cancelled)* **the wedding is o.** se ha cancelado la boda; **the deal is o.** el acuerdo se ha roto

**(c)** *(absent from work, school)* **to be o.** faltar; **Jane's o. today** Jane no viene hoy a trabajar *or* a clase

**(d)** *(food, milk)* echado(a) a perder, pasado(a)

**(e)** *(unsuccessful)* **to have an o. day** tener un mal día

**(f)** *(in tourism)* **the o. season** la temporada baja

**(g)** *(describing situation)* **to be well/badly o.** tener mucho/poco dinero; **you'd be better o. staying where you are** será mejor *or* más vale que te quedes donde estás

**(h)** *(unpleasant)* **that comment was a bit o.** ese comentario estaba de más

**offal** ['ɒfəl] *n Culin* asaduras *fpl*

**offbeat** [ɒf'biːt] *adj Fam (unconventional)* inusual, original

**off-chance** ['ɒftʃɑːns] *n* **on the o.** por si acaso

**off-colour,** *US* **off-color** [ɒf'kʌlə(r)] *adj* **(a)** *Br (unwell)* indispuesto(a) **(b)** *(joke)* fuera de tono

**offcut** ['ɒfkʌt] *n (of wood)* recorte *m*; *(of cloth)* retal *m*; *(of carpet)* retazo *m*

**off-duty** ['ɒf'djuːtɪ] *adj (soldier)* de permiso; *(policeman)* fuera de servicio

**offence,** *US* **offense** [ə'fens] *n* **(a)** *Law* delito *m*, infracción *f*; **petty** *or* **minor o.**

infracción leve **(b)** *(annoyance, displeasure)* ofensa *f*; **to cause o.** ofender; **to take o.** sentirse ofendido(a) **(at** por), ofenderse **(at** por) .

**offend** [ə'fend] **1** *vt* ofender; **to be offended (at** *or* **by sth)** ofenderse *or* sentirse ofendido(a) (por algo)

**2** *vi Law* delinquir; **to o. against good taste** atentar contra el buen gusto

**offended** [ə'fendɪd] *adj (insulted)* ofendido(a)

**offender** [ə'fendə(r)] *n Law* delincuente *mf*

**offending** [ə'fendɪŋ] *adj (causing a problem)* enojoso(a)

**offense** *US* = **offence**

**offensive** [ə'fensɪv] **1** *n Mil & Fig* ofensiva *f*; **to take the o.** pasar a la ofensiva; **to be on the o.** estar en plena ofensiva

**2** *adj (word, action)* ofensivo(a); **to be o. to sb** mostrarse ofensivo(a) con alguien

**offer** ['ɒfə(r)] **1** *n* oferta *f*; **to make sb an o. (for sth)** hacer a alguien una oferta (por algo); **on o.** *(reduced)* de oferta; *(available)* disponible; **o. of marriage** propuesta *f* de matrimonio

**2** *vt* ofrecer; **to o. sb sth, to o. sth to sb** ofrecer algo a alguien; **to o. to do sth** ofrecerse a hacer algo; *Law* **to o. a plea of guilty/innocent** declararse culpable/inocente

▶**offer up** *vt sep (prayers)* ofrecer

**offering** ['ɒfərɪŋ] *n* entrega *f*; *Rel* ofrenda *f*

**offhand** [ɒf'hænd] **1** *adj* frío(a); **to be o. (with sb)** mostrarse indiferente (con alguien)

**2** *adv (immediately)* **I don't know o.** ahora mismo, no lo sé

**office** ['ɒfɪs] *n* **(a)** *(place)* oficina *f*; **the manager's o.** el despacho *or* la oficina del jefe; **o. boy** chico *m* de los recados; **o. building** bloque *m* de oficinas; **o. hours** horas *fpl or* horario *m* de oficina; **o. work** trabajo *m* de oficina; **o. worker** oficinista *mf*

**(b)** *Pol (position)* cargo *m*; **to hold o.** ocupar un cargo; **to be out of o.** *(of political party)* estar en la oposición

**(c) I got the flat through the good offices of Philip** conseguí el piso gracias a los buenos oficios de Philip

**officeholder** ['ɒfɪshəʊldə(r)] *n* alto cargo *m*

**officer** ['ɒfɪsə(r)] *n (army)* oficial *mf*; *(police)* agente *mf*; *(in local government)* inspector(ora) *m,f*

**official** [ə'fɪʃəl] **1** *n (in public sector)* funcionario(a) *m,f*; *(in trade union)* representante *mf*

**2** *adj* oficial; *Br* **O. Secrets Act** ≃ ley de secretos oficiales *or* de Estado

**officialdom** [ə'fɪʃəldəm] *n Pej (bureaucracy)* los funcionarios, la administración

**officialese** [əfɪʃə'liːz] *n Pej* jerga *f* administrativa

**officially** [ə'fɪʃəlɪ] *adv* oficialmente

**officiate** [ə'fɪʃɪeɪt] *vi Rel* celebrar (el oficio) **(at** en)

**officious** [ə'fɪʃəs] *adj* excesivamente celoso(a) *or* diligente

**officiously** [ə'fɪʃəslɪ] *adv* con excesiva diligencia

**offing** ['ɒfɪŋ] *n* **(to be) in the o.** (ser) inminente

**off-key** ['ɒf'kiː] *Mus* **1** *adj* desafinado(a)

**2** *adv* desafinadamente

**off-licence** ['ɒflaɪsəns] *n Br* tienda *f* de bebidas alcohólicas *or* de licores

**off-line** ['ɒflaɪn] *adj Comptr (processing)* fuera de línea; *(printer)* desconectado(a)

**off-load** ['ɒfləʊd] *vt (surplus goods)* colocar; **to o. sth onto sb** colocarle algo a alguien; **to o. blame onto sb** descargar la culpa en alguien

**off-peak** ['ɒf'piːk] *adj (electricity, travel)* en horas valle; *(holidays)* en temporada baja; *(phonecall)* en horas de tarifa reducida

**offprint** ['ɒfprɪnt] *n Typ* separata *f*

**off-putting** ['ɒfpʊtɪŋ] *adj* desagradable; **I find his manner rather o.** sus modales me resultan desagradables

**off-sales** ['ɒfseɪlz] *n Br* = venta de bebidas alcohólicas para llevar

**off-season** ['ɒfsiːzən] *adj (rate)* de temporada baja

**offset** ['ɒfset] **1** *n Typ (process)* offset *m*

**2** *vt (pt & pp* **offset)** compensar

**offshoot** ['ɒfʃʊt] *n (of tree)* vástago *m*; *(of family)* rama *f*; *(of political party, artistic movement)* ramificación *f*

**offshore** ['ɒfʃɔː(r)] **1** *adv* cerca de la costa

**2** *adj (island)* cercano(a) a la costa; **o. oil rig** plataforma *f* petrolífera *(en el mar)*; *Fin* **o. investment** inversión *f* en un paraíso fiscal

**offside** ['ɒfsaɪd] **1** *n Aut* lado *m* del conductor

**2** *adj* **(a)** *Aut* al lado del conductor **(b)** ['ɒf'saɪd] *(in football, rugby)* (en) fuera de juego

**offspring** ['ɒfsprɪŋ] *npl (young of an animal)* crías *fpl*; *(children)* hijos *mpl*, descendencia *f*

**offstage** [ɒf'steɪdʒ] *Th* **1** *adv* fuera del escenario

**2** *adj* de fuera del escenario

**off-the-cuff** [ɒfðə'kʌf] *adj (remark)* espontáneo(a), improvisado(a)

**off-the-peg** [ɒfðə'peg] *adj* de confección; **an o. suit** un traje de confección

**off-the-record** [ɒfðə'rekɔːd] *adj* extraoficial, oficioso(a)

**off-the-wall** [ɒfðə'wɔːl] *adj Fam* estrafalario(a)

**off-white** ['ɒf'waɪt] **1** *n* tono *m* blancuzco, blanco *m* marfil

**2** *adj* blancuzco(a)

**OFGAS** ['ɒfgæs] *n Br (abbr* **Office of Gas Supply)** = organismo regulador del suministro de gas en Gran Bretaña

**OFSTED** ['ɒfsted] *n Br (abbr* **Office for Standards in Education**) = organismo responsable de la supervisión del sistema educativo británico

**OFTEL** ['ɒftel] *n Br (abbr* **Office of Tele-communications**) = organismo regulador de las telecomunicaciones en Gran Bretaña

**often** ['ɒfən, 'ɒftən] *adv* a menudo, frecuentemente; **how o.?** *(how many times)* ¿cuántas veces?; *(how frequently)* ¿cada cuánto tiempo?, ¿con qué frecuencia?; **as o. as not** la mitad de las veces; **more o. than not** muchas veces; **every so o.** de vez en cuando, cada cierto tiempo

**OFWAT** ['ɒfwɒt] *n Br (abbr* **Office of Water Services**) = organismo regulador del suministro de agua en Gran Bretaña

**ogle** ['əʊgəl] *vt* **to o. sb** comerse a alguien con los ojos

**ogre** ['əʊgə(r)] *n also Fig* ogro *m*

**ogress** ['əʊgrɪs] *n (frightening woman)* ogro *m*

**oh** [əʊ] *exclam (expressing surprise)* ¡oh!; **oh no!** ¡oh, no!

**ohm** [əʊm] *n Elec* ohmio *m*

**OHMS** [əʊeɪtʃem'es] *Br (abbr* **On Her/His Majesty's Service**) = siglas que aparecen en documentos emitidos por el gobierno británico indicando su carácter oficial

**oho** [əʊ'həʊ] *exclam (expressing triumph, surprise)* ¡ajajá!

**oil** [ɔɪl] **1** *n (for cooking, lubricating)* aceite *m*; *(petroleum)* petróleo *m*; *Fig* **to pour o. on troubled waters** calmar los ánimos; **o. company** compañía *f* petrolera; **o. drum** bidón *m* de petróleo; **o. lamp** lámpara *f* de aceite; **o. paint** pintura *f* al óleo; **o. painting** óleo *m*; *Fig Hum* **he's/she's no o.** painting no es ninguna belleza; **o. refinery** refinería *f* de petróleo; **o. rig** plataforma *f* petrolífera; **o. slick** marea *f* negra; **o. tanker** petrolero *m*; **o. well** pozo *m* petrolífero or de petróleo

**2** *vt (machine)* engrasar, lubricar; *Fig* **to o. the wheels** allanar el terreno

**oilcan** ['ɔɪlkæn] *n (for applying oil)* aceitera *f*; *(large container)* lata *f* de aceite

**oilfield** ['ɔɪlfiːld] *n* yacimiento *m* petrolífero

**oil-fired** ['ɔɪlfaɪəd] *adj* **o. central heating** calefacción *f* central de petróleo

**oilskin** ['ɔɪlskɪn] *n (fabric)* hule *m*; **oilskins** chubasquero *m*, impermeable *m*

**oily** ['ɔɪlɪ] *adj* **(a)** *(hands, rag)* grasiento(a); *(skin, hair)* graso(a); *(food)* grasiento(a), aceitoso(a) **(b)** *Pej (manner)* empalagoso(a)

**oink** [ɔɪŋk] *vi (of pig)* gruñir

**ointment** ['ɔɪntmənt] *n* ungüento *m*, pomada *f*

**O.K., okay** ['əʊ'keɪ] **1** *exclam* vale, de acuerdo; **O.K., O.K.! I'll do it now** ¡bueno, vale! ya lo hago

**2** *adj* bien; **that's O.K. by** *or* **with me** (a mí) me parece bien; **is it O.K. to wear jeans?** ¿está bien si voy con vaqueros?; **no, it is NOT O.K.!** no, no está bien; **it's more than O.K.** está pero que muy bien; *Fam* **she was O.K. about it** *(didn't react badly)* se lo tomó bastante bien; *Fam* **he's an O.K. sort of guy** es un buen tipo; **are we O.K. for time?** ¿vamos bien de tiempo?

**3** *n* **to give (sb) the O.K.** dar permiso (a alguien)

**4** *vt (pt & pp* **O.K.'d** *or* **okayed**) *Fam (proposal, plan)* dar el visto bueno a

**okra** ['ɒkrə] *n* quingombó *m*, okra *f*

**old** [əʊld] **1** *npl* **the o.** los ancianos, las personas mayores

**2** *adj* **(a)** *(not young, not new) (person)* anciano(a), viejo(a), *Am* grande; *(furniture, car, custom)* viejo(a); **an o. man** un anciano, un viejo; **an o. woman** una anciana, una vieja; **o. people, o. folk(s)** los ancianos, las personas mayores; **to go over o. ground** volver sobre un asunto muy trillado; **to be an o. hand at sth** tener larga experiencia en algo; *Fam* **to be o. hat** estar muy visto(a); *Fig* **he's one of the o. school** es de la vieja escuela; **o. age** la vejez; **o. age pension** pensión *f* de jubilación; **o. age pensioner** pensionista *mf*, jubilado(a) *m,f*; **the O. Testament** el Antiguo Testamento; **o. wives' tale** cuento *m* de viejas

**(b)** *(referring to person's age)* **how o. are you?** ¿cuántos años tienes?; **to be five years o.** tener cinco años; **at six years o.** a los seis años (de edad); **a two-year-o. (child)** un niño de dos años; **to grow** *or* **get older** hacerse mayor; **when you're older** cuando seas mayor; **you're o. enough to do that yourself** ya eres mayorcito para hacerlo tú mismo

**(c)** *(former)* antiguo(a); **in the o. days** antes, antiguamente; **o. boy/girl** *(of school)* antiguo(a) alumno(a) *m,f*; **o. boy network** = red de contactos entre antiguos compañeros de los colegios privados y universidades más selectos; **an o. flame** un antiguo amor

**(d)** *(long-standing)* **an o. friend (of mine)** un viejo amigo (mío); **o. habits die hard** es difícil abandonar las costumbres de toda la vida

**(e)** *Fam (intensifier)* **any o. how** de cualquier manera; **any o. thing** cualquier cosa

**(f)** *Fam (affectionate)* **o. Fred** el bueno de Fred; **o. fellow** *or* **boy** *(addressing sb)* muchacho; **my** *or* **the o. man** *(father)* mi *or* el viejo; *(husband)* mi *or* el pariente; **my** *or* **the o. woman** *or* **lady** *(wife)* mi *or* la parienta

**old-fashioned** [əʊld'fæʃənd] *adj (outdated)* anticuado(a); *(from former times)* tradicional, antiguo(a); **the o. way** a la antigua

**old-timer** [əʊld'taɪmə(r)] *n Fam* **(a)**

*(experienced person)* veterano(a) *m,f* **(b)** *US (form of address)* abuelo(a) *m,f*

**old-world** ['əʊld'wɜːld] *adj (courtesy, charm)* del pasado, de antes

**oleander** [əʊlɪ'ændə(r)] *n* adelfa *f*

**olfactory** [ɒl'fæktərɪ] *adj Anat* olfativo(a)

**oligarchy** ['ɒlɪgɑːkɪ] *n* oligarquía *f*

**olive** ['ɒlɪv] **1** *n (fruit)* aceituna *f*; *(tree)* olivo *m*; *Fig* **to hold out the o. branch** hacer un gesto de paz; **o. grove** olivar *m*; **o. oil** aceite *m* de oliva

**2** *adj (skin)* aceitunado(a); **o. (green)** verde oliva

**Olympic** [ə'lɪmpɪk] **1** *npl* **the Olympics** las Olimpíadas, los Juegos Olímpicos

**2** *adj* olímpico(a); **the O. Games** los Juegos Olímpicos

**Oman** [əʊ'mɑːn] *n* Omán

**Omani** [əʊ'mɑːnɪ] *n & adj* omaní *mf*

**ombudsman** ['ɒmbʊdzmən] *n* defensor(ora) *m,f* del pueblo

**omelette, US omelet** ['ɒmlɪt] *n* tortilla *f*, *Am* tortilla *f* francesa; **ham/cheese o.** tortilla de jamón/queso

**omen** ['əʊmen] *n* presagio *m*, augurio *m*

**ominous** ['ɒmɪnəs] *adj* siniestro(a); **an o.-looking sky** un cielo amenazador; **an emergency meeting? – that sounds o.** ¿una reunión de emergencia? – eso no presagia nada bueno

**ominously** ['ɒmɪnəslɪ] *adv* siniestramente, amenazadoramente

**omission** [ə'mɪʃən] *n* omisión *f*

**omit** [əʊ'mɪt] *(pt & pp* **omitted)** *vt* omitir; **to o. to do sth** no hacer algo

**omnibus** ['ɒmnɪbəs] *n* **(a)** *(book)* recopilación *f*, antología *f* **(b)** *Old-fashioned (bus)* ómnibus *m inv*

**omnipotence** [ɒm'nɪpətəns] *n* omnipotencia *f*

**omnipotent** [ɒm'nɪpətənt] *adj* omnipotente

**omnipresent** [ɒmnɪ'prezənt] *adj* omnipresente

**omniscient** [ɒm'nɪsɪənt] *adj* omnisciente

**omnivorous** [ɒm'nɪvərəs] *adj* omnívoro(a); *Fig (reader)* insaciable

**on** [ɒn] **1** *prep* **(a)** *(position)* en; **on the table** encima de *or* sobre la mesa, en la mesa; **on the second floor** en el segundo piso; **on the wall** en la pared; **on page 4** en la página 4; **on the right/left** a la derecha/izquierda; **on bicycle** en bicicleta; **on foot** a pie; **on horseback** a caballo; **on (the) television** en la televisión; **to be on a committee** formar parte de un comité; **I haven't got any money on me** no llevo nada de dinero encima

**(b)** *(direction)* **to fall on sth** caerse encima de *or* sobre algo

**(c)** *(time)* **on the 15th** el día 15; **on Sunday** el domingo; **on Christmas Day** el día de Navidad; **on that occasion** en aquella ocasión

**(d)** *(about)* sobre, acerca de; **a book on France** un libro sobre Francia

**(e)** *(introducing a gerund)* **on completing the test, you should…** después de terminar la prueba, tienes que…; **on discovering the corpse, she screamed** al descubrir el cadáver, dio un grito

**(f)** *(indicating use, support)* **to live on £200 a week** vivir con 200 libras a la semana; **it runs on lead-free petrol** usa *or* lleva gasolina sin plomo; **to play sth on the guitar** tocar algo a la guitarra; **the drinks are on me** las bebidas corren de mi cuenta; **I'm on antibiotics** estoy tomando antibióticos; **to be on drugs** tomar drogas

**2** *adv* **(a)** *(in operation) (light, television, engine)* encendido(a); **in the 'on' position** en posición de encendido

**(b)** *(taking place)* **what's on?** *(on TV)* ¿qué hay en la tele?; *(at cinema)* ¿qué película echan?; **is the meeting still on?** ¿sigue en pie lo de la reunión?; **I've got a lot on at the moment** *(am very busy)* ahora estoy muy ocupado; **on and off** *(intermittently)* a intervalos, intermitentemente

**(c)** *(on duty)* de servicio; **who's on this evening?** ¿quién está de servicio esta noche?

**(d)** **she had a red dress on** llevaba un vestido rojo; **he had nothing on** estaba desnudo; **to put sth on** ponerse algo

**(e)** *(in time)* **earlier on** antes; **later on** más tarde; **from that day on** desde aquel día, a partir de aquel día

**(f)** *(expressing continuation)* **to read/work on** seguir leyendo/trabajando; **he went on and on about it** no dejaba de hablar de ello

**(g)** *(in phrases) Fam* **it's not on** *(is unacceptable)* eso no está bien; **I've been on at him to get it fixed** le he estado dando la lata para que lo arregle

**once** [wʌns] **1** *adv* **(a)** *(on one occasion)* una vez; **more than o.** más de una vez; **o. a week** una vez a la semana; **o. or twice** una o dos veces; **o. in a while** de vez en cuando; **o. more, o. again** otra vez, una vez más; **you've called me stupid o. too often** ya me has llamado estúpido demasiadas veces; **o. and for all** de una vez por todas; **a o.-in-a-lifetime opportunity** una ocasión única, una ocasión que sólo se presenta una vez en la vida

**(b)** *(formerly)* una vez, en otro tiempo; **o. upon a time there was a princess** érase una vez una princesa

**(c)** **at o.** *(immediately)* inmediatamente, ahora mismo; *(at the same time)* al mismo tiempo, a la vez

**2** *conj* una vez que; **o. he reached home, he collapsed** una vez en casa, se derrumbó; **o. he finishes we can leave** cuando termine, nos podremos marchar

**once-over** ['wʌnsəʊvə(r)] *n Fam* **to give sth the o.** dar a algo un repaso; **to give sb the o.** mirar a alguien de arriba a abajo

**oncoming** ['ɒnkʌmɪŋ] *adj (traffic)* en dirección contraria

**one** [wʌn] **1** *n* uno(a) *m,f*; **there's only o. left** sólo queda uno; **the guests arrived in ones and twos** poco a poco fueron llegando los invitados; **to be at o. with sb** coincidir plenamente con alguien; **o. for the road** *(final drink)* la espuela; **to have o. too many** *(drink)* tomar una copa de más; *Fam* **to get o. up on sb** quedar por encima de alguien

**2** *pron* **(a)** *(identifying)* **this o.** éste(a); **that o.** ése(a), aquél(élla); **these ones** éstos(as); **those ones** ésos(as), aquéllos(as); **which o. do you want?** ¿cuál quieres?; **the o. I told you about** el/la que te dije; **the big/red o.** el grande/rojo; **the ones with the long sleeves** los/las de manga larga; **the last but o.** el/la penúltimo(a); **that's a difficult o.!** ¡qué difícil!

**(b)** *(indefinite)* **I haven't got a pencil, have you got o.?** no tengo lápiz, ¿tienes tú (uno)?; **he is o. of us** es uno de los nuestros; **she is o. of the family** es de la familia; **o. of my friends** uno de mis amigos; **o. of these days** un día de estos; **any o. of us** cualquiera de nosotros; **it is just o. of those things** son cosas que pasan; **o. after the other** uno tras otro; **o. at a time** de uno en uno; **o. by o.** de uno en uno, uno por uno

**(c)** *(particular person)* **to act like o. possessed** actuar como un/una poseso(a); **I, for o., do not believe it** yo, desde luego, no me lo creo; **I'm not o. to complain** yo no soy de los que se quejan; **he's not a great o. for parties** no le van mucho las fiestas

**(d)** *(impersonal)* **o. never knows** nunca se sabe; **it is enough to make o. weep** basta para hacerle llorar a uno(a)

**3** *adj* **(a)** *(number)* uno(a); **chapter o.** capítulo *m* primero; **page o.** primera página *f*; **to be o. (year old)** tener un año; **they live at number o.** viven en el número uno; **o. o'clock** la una; **come at o.** ven a la una; **o. or two people** una o dos personas; **o. stormy evening in January** una tarde tormentosa de enero; **o. day we shall be free** algún día seremos libres; **for o. thing,...** para empezar,...

**(b)** *(single)* un/una único(a), un/una solo(a); **he did it with o. end in mind** lo hizo con un solo propósito; **her o. worry** su única preocupación; **my o. and only suit** mi único

traje; **they are o. and the same thing** son una *or* la misma cosa; **we'll manage o. way or another** nos las arreglaremos de una forma u otra; **as o. man** como un solo hombre; *Fam* **it's all o. to me** me da igual

**one-armed** ['wʌnɑːmd] *adj (person)* manco(a); *Br Fam* **o. bandit** (máquina *f*) tragaperras *f inv*

**one-eyed** ['wʌnaɪd] *adj* tuerto(a)

**one-horse town** ['wʌnhɔːrs'taʊn] *n Fam* pueblo *m* de mala muerte

**one-legged** [wʌn'legɪd] *adj* cojo(a)

**one-liner** [wʌn'laɪnə(r)] *n Fam (joke)* golpe *m*

**one-man** ['wʌnmæn] *adj (job)* individual, de una sola persona; **o. band** hombre *m* orquesta; **o. show** espectáculo *m* en solitario; *Fig* **this company/team is a o. show** el funcionamiento de esta empresa/de este equipo gira en torno a un solo hombre

**one-night stand** ['wʌnnaɪt'stænd] *n Fam (of performer)* representación *f* única; *(of musician)* concierto *m* único; *(sexual encounter)* ligue *m* de una noche

**one-off** ['wʌnɒf] *Br n Fam* **it was a o.** *(mistake, success)* fue una excepción *or* un hecho aislado; **a o. job** un trabajo aislado

**one-parent family** ['wʌnpeərənt'fæmɪlɪ] *n* familia *f* monoparental

**one-party** ['wʌn'pɑːtɪ] *adj* unipartidista

**one-piece swimsuit** ['wʌnpiːs'swɪmsuːt] *n* bañador *m* de una pieza

**onerous** ['əʊnərəs] *adj* oneroso(a)

**oneself** [wʌn'self] *pron* **(a)** *(reflexive)* **to look after o.** cuidarse; **to trust o.** confiar en uno mismo; **to feel o. again** volver a sentirse el/la de siempre **(b)** *(emphatic)* uno(a) mismo(a), uno(a) solo(a); **to do sth all by o.** hacer algo uno solo; **to see (sth) for o.** ver (algo) uno(a) mismo(a)

**one-sided** [wʌn'saɪdɪd] *adj* **(a)** *(unequal)* desnivelado(a), desigual **(b)** *(biased)* parcial

**one-time** ['wʌntaɪm] *adj* antiguo(a); **her o. lover** su ex amante

**one-to-one** ['wʌntə'wʌn] *adj (discussion)* cara a cara; **o. tuition** clases *fpl* particulares

**one-track** ['wʌntræk] *adj* **to have a o. mind** *(be obsessed with one thing)* estar obsesionado(a) con una cosa, no pensar más que en una cosa; *(be obsessed with sex)* no pensar más que en el sexo

**one-upmanship** [wʌn'ʌpmənʃɪp] *n Fam* **it was pure o.** todo era por quedar por encima de los demás

**one-way** ['wʌnweɪ] *adj (ticket)* de ida; *(street, traffic)* de sentido único

**ongoing** ['ɒngəʊɪŋ] *adj* en curso

**onion** ['ʌnjən] n cebolla f; Br Fam **she knows her onions** sabe lo que se trae entre manos; **o. soup** sopa f de cebolla

**on-line** ['ɒn'laɪn] adj Comptr en línea, on line; **to be o.** (person) estar conectado(a) (a Internet)

**onlooker** ['ɒnlʊkə(r)] n curioso(a) m,f

**only** ['əʊnlɪ] **1** adj único(a); **o. child** hijo(a) m,f único(a); **you are not the o. one** no eres el único; **the o. thing that worries me is…** lo único que me preocupa es…

**2** adv solamente, sólo; **I o. touched it** no hice más que tocarlo; **it's o. natural** es (más que) natural; **I shall be o. too pleased to come** me encantará acudir; **if o. they knew!**, **if they o. knew!** ¡si ellos supieran!; **not o.…, but also…** no sólo… sino también…; **I saw her o. yesterday** la vi ayer mismo; **I o. just managed it** por poco no lo consigo; **it's o. me** (sólo) soy yo

**3** conj sólo que, pero; **I would do it o. I haven't the time** lo haría, sólo que no tengo tiempo

**o.n.o** [əʊen'əʊ] adv Com (abbr **or nearest offer**) £300 o. 300 libras negociables

**on-off switch** ['ɒn'ɒfswɪtʃ] n interruptor m

**onomatopoeia** [ɒnəmætə'piːə] n onomatopeya f

**onomatopoeic** [ɒnəmætə'piːɪk] adj onomatopéyico(a)

**onrush** ['ɒnrʌʃ] n (of emotions) arrebato m; (of people) oleada f

**onset** ['ɒnset] n irrupción f; **the o. of a disease** el desencadenamiento or inicio de una enfermedad; **the o. of war** el estallido de la guerra

**on-site** ['ɒn'saɪt] adj & adv in situ

**onslaught** ['ɒnslɔːt] n acometida f

**onto** ['ɒntʊ] unstressed ['ɒntə] prep sobre, encima de; **to jump o. sth** saltar sobre algo; **to fall o. sth** caerse encima de algo; **to get o. sb** (contact) ponerse en contacto con alguien; **to be o. a good thing** habérselo montado bien; **I think the police are o. us** creo que la policía anda detrás de nosotros

**onus** ['əʊnəs] n responsabilidad f; **the o. is on the government to resolve the problem** la resolución del problema es incumbencia del Gobierno; Law **o. of proof** peso m de la prueba, onus probandi m

**onward** ['ɒnwəd] **1** adj (motion) hacia delante
**2** adv = **onwards**

**onwards** ['ɒnwədz] adv **from tomorrow o.** a partir de mañana; **from this time o.** (de ahora) en adelante

**onyx** ['ɒnɪks] n ónice m

**oodles** ['uːdəlz] npl Fam **o. of time/money** una porrada de tiempo/dinero

**oomph** [ʊmf] n Fam (energy) gancho m, garra f

**oops** [uːps] exclam (to child) ¡aúpa!; (after mistake) ¡uy!, ¡oh!

**ooze** [uːz] **1** n (a) (mud) fango m (b) (flow) flujo m

**2** vt (liquid) rezumar; **to o. charm** rezumar encanto; **to o. confidence** rebosar confianza

**3** vi rezumar, brotar; **to o. with confidence** rebosar confianza

**op** [ɒp] n Fam (medical operation) operación f

**opal** ['əʊpəl] n ópalo m

**opaque** [əʊ'peɪk] adj (glass) opaco(a); Fig (difficult to understand) oscuro(a), poco claro(a)

**op cit** [ɒp'sɪt] n (abbr **opere citato**) op. cit., en la obra citada

**OPEC** ['əʊpek] n (abbr **Organization of Petroleum-Exporting Countries**) OPEP f, Organización f de Países Exportadores de Petróleo

**open** ['əʊpən] **1** n (a) **in the o.** (outside) al aire libre; (not hidden) a la vista; **to bring sth out into the o.** (problem, disagreement) sacar a relucir algo; **to come out into the o. about sth** desvelar algo

(b) (sporting competition) open m, abierto m

**2** adj (a) (in general) abierto(a); **to be o.** estar abierto(a); **o. from nine to five** abierto(a) de nueve a cinco; **o. to the public** abierto(a) al público; **o. all night** abierto(a) toda la noche or las 24 horas; **o. late** abierto(a) hasta tarde; **let's leave the matter o.** dejemos el asunto ahí pendiente de momento; **a career o. to very few** una profesión reservada a unos pocos; **o. to traffic** abierto(a) al tráfico; **membership is o. to people over eighteen** pueden hacerse socios los mayores de dieciocho años; **two possibilities are o. to us** tenemos dos opciones; **o. to the elements** expuesto(a) a las inclemencias del tiempo; **to be o. to doubt** ser dudoso(a) or cuestionable; **to be o. to ridicule** exponerse a quedar en ridículo; **to be o. to suggestions** estar abierto(a) a sugerencias; **in the o. air** al aire libre; **to welcome sb with o. arms** recibir a alguien con los brazos abiertos; **o. country** campo m abierto; Law **in o. court** en juicio público, en vista pública; Br **o. day**, US **o. house** jornada f de puertas abiertas; **o. invitation** (to guests) invitación f permanente; Fig (to thieves) invitación clara; Econ **o. market** mercado m libre; **to keep an o. mind (on sth)** mantenerse libre de prejuicios (acerca de algo); **o. prison** cárcel f de régimen abierto; **o. sandwich** = una rebanada de pan con algo de comer encima; **the o. sea** mar m abierto; **o. season** (for hunting) temporada f (de caza); Fig **to declare o. season on sb/sth** abrir la veda de or contra alguien/algo; **o. spaces** (parks) zonas fpl verdes; **o. ticket** billete m abierto; Br **O. University** ≃ Universidad Nacional de Educación a Distancia; Law **o. verdict** = declaración de

que se ha producido una muerte sin esclarecimiento de las causas; **o. wound** herida *f* abierta

 **(b)** *(person, manner)* abierto(a); *(preference, dislike)* claro(a), manifiesto(a); *(conflict)* abierto(a);
**to be o. with sb** ser franco(a) con alguien; **to
be o. about sth** ser muy claro(a) *or* sincero(a)
con respecto a algo; **o. letter** *(in newspaper)*
carta *f* abierta; **o. secret** secreto *m* a voces

**3** *adv* **to cut sth o.** abrir algo de un corte; **the
door flew o.** la puerta se abrió con violencia

**4** *vt (in general)* abrir; *(negotiations, conversation)*
entablar, iniciar; **to o. a hole in sth** abrir *or*
practicar un agujero en algo; **to o. fire (on sb)**
hacer *or* abrir fuego (sobre alguien); **he opened
his heart to her** se sinceró con ella

**5** *vi (of door, window, flower)* abrirse; *(of shop,
bank)* abrir; *(of meeting, negotiations)* abrirse, dar
comienzo; **to o. late** *(of shop)* abrir hasta tarde;
**the kitchen opens onto the garden** la cocina da al jardín; **the play opens with a death
scene** la obra comienza con una escena de
muerte; **the film opens next week** la película se estrena la semana que viene; **o. wide!** *(at
dentist's)* ¡abre bien la boca!

▶**open out 1** *vt sep (sheet of paper)* abrir, desdoblar

**2** *vi (of flower)* abrirse; *(of view, prospects)* abrirse,
extenderse *(of road, valley)* ensancharse, abrirse

▶**open up 1** *vt sep (new shop, business)* abrir; **to
o. up opportunities for** abrir las puertas a,
presentar nuevas oportunidades para

**2** *vi (of shopkeeper, new shop)* abrir; *(of flower, new
market)* abrirse; *Fig (of person)* abrirse, sincerarse;
**this is the police – o. up!** ¡policía, abran la
puerta!

**open-air** [əʊpə'neə(r)] *adj (restaurant, market)*
al aire libre

**open-and-shut case** ['əʊpənən'ʃʌt'keɪs]
*n* un caso elemental *or* claro

**opencast** ['əʊpən'kɑːst] *adj (mine)* a cielo
abierto

**open-door policy** ['əʊpən'dɔːpɒlɪsɪ] *n* política *f* permisiva *or* de puertas abiertas

**open-ended** ['əʊpən'endɪd] *adj (contract)* in-
definido(a); *(question)* abierto(a); *(discussion)* sin
restricciones

**open-heart surgery** ['əʊpən'hɑːt-
sɜːdʒərɪ] *n* cirugía *f* a corazón abierto

**opening** ['əʊpənɪŋ] **1** *n* **(a)** *(of play, new era)*
principio *m*; *(of negotiations)* apertura *f*; *(of parliament)* sesión *f* inaugural **(b)** *(gap)* abertura *f*,
agujero *m* **(c)** *(of cave, tunnel)* entrada *f* **(d)** *(opportunity)* oportunidad *f*; *(job)* puesto m vacante

**2** *adj* **o. address** *or* **speech** *(in court case)* presentación *f* del caso; **o. batsman** *(in cricket)*
bateador *m* inicial; **o. ceremony** ceremonia *f*
inaugural *or* de apertura; **o. gambit** *(in chess)*
gambito *m* de salida; *(in conversation, negotiation)*

táctica *f* inicial; **o. hours** horario *m* de apertura;
*Br* **o. time** *(of pub)* hora *f* de abrir

**openly** ['əʊpənlɪ] *adv* abiertamente

**open-minded** [əʊpə'maɪndɪd] *adj* de mentalidad abierta

**open-mouthed** [əʊpən'maʊðd] *adj* bo-
quiabierto(a)

**openness** ['əʊpənnɪs] *n (frankness)* franqueza *f*

**open-plan** ['əʊpənplæn] *adj (office)* diáfa-
no(a)

**opera** ['ɒpərə] *n* ópera *f*; **o. glasses** prismáticos *mpl*, gemelos *mpl (de teatro)*; **o. house** *(teatro m de la)* ópera; **o. singer** cantante *mf* de
ópera

**operable** ['ɒpərəbəl] *adj Med* operable

**operate** ['ɒpəreɪt] **1** *vt (machine)* manejar, hacer funcionar; *(brakes)* accionar; *(service)* proporcionar; **to be operated by electricity**
funcionar con electricidad

**2** *vi* **(a)** *(of machine)* funcionar; *(company)* actuar, operar; **we operate in most of the
North of Scotland** desarrollamos nuestra actividad en la mayor parte del norte de Escocia
**(b)** *Med* operar; **to o. on sb (for)** operar a
alguien (de); **to be operated on** ser opera-
do(a)

**operatic** [ɒpə'rætɪk] *adj* operístico(a)

**operating** ['ɒpəreɪtɪŋ] *adj* **o. costs** costes
*mpl* de explotación; *Comptr* **o. system** sistema
*m* operativo; *Med* **o. table** mesa *f* de operaciones; *Br* **o. theatre**, *US* **o. room** quirófano *m*

**operation** [ɒpə'reɪʃən] *n* **(a)** *(of machine)* funcionamiento *m*; **to be in o.** *(of machine)* estar
funcionando; *(of system, law)* estar en vigor; **to
come into o.** *(of law)* entrar en vigor **(b)** *(process)* tarea *f*, operación *f*; **a firm's operations**
las operaciones *or* actividades de una empresa
**(c)** *Med* operación *f*; **to have an o. (for sth)**
operarse (de algo) **(d)** *Mil* operación *f*; **operations room** centro *m* de control

**operational** [ɒpə'reɪʃənəl] *adj* operativo(a);
**it should be o. next year** debería entrar en
funcionamiento el año que viene

**operative** ['ɒpərətɪv] **1** *n (manual worker)*
operario(a) *m,f*; *(spy)* agente *mf*

**2** *adj (law, rule)* vigente; **to become o.** *(of law)*
entrar en vigor; **the o. word** la palabra clave

**operator** ['ɒpəreɪtə(r)] *n* **(a)** *(of machine)*
operario(a) *m,f* **(b)** *Tel* telefonista *mf*, opera-
dor(ora) *m,f* **(c)** *Fam* **he's a pretty smooth
o.** *(with women)* se las lleva de calle; *(in business)*
es un lince *or* un hacha para los negocios

**operetta** [ɒpə'retə] *n Mus* opereta *f*

**ophthalmology** [ɒfθæl'mɒlədʒɪ] *n Med* oftalmología *f*

**opinion** [ə'pɪnjən] *n* opinión *f*; **in my o.** en mi
opinión; **to be of the o. that…** ser de la opi-

nión de que…; **to ask sb's o.** pedir la opinión de alguien; **to form an o. of sb/sth** formarse una opinión sobre alguien/algo; **to have a high/low o. of sb** tener (una) buena/mala opinión de alguien; **what is your o. of him?** ¿qué opinas de él?; **o. poll** *or* **survey** sondeo *m* de opinión, encuesta *f*

**opinionated** [ə'pɪnjəneɪtɪd] *adj* dogmático(a); **to be o.** creer a toda costa que uno lleva la razón

**opium** ['əʊpɪəm] *n* opio *m*; **o. addict** adicto(a) *m,f* al opio; **o. den** fumadero *m* de opio

**Oporto** [ɒ'pɔːtəʊ] *n* Oporto

**opossum** [ə'pɒsəm] *n* zarigüeya *f*

**opp** (*abbr* **opposite**) en la página opuesta

**opponent** [ə'pəʊnənt] *n* (*in game, politics*) adversario(a) *m,f*, oponente *mf*; (*of policy, system*) opositor(ora) *m,f*

**opportune** ['ɒpətjuːn] *adj* oportuno(a)

**opportunism** [ɒpə'tjuːnɪzəm] *n* oportunismo *m*

**opportunist** [ɒpə'tjuːnɪst] *n & adj* oportunista *mf*

**opportunistic** [ɒpətjʊ'nɪstɪk] *n* oportunista; *Med* **o. infection** infección *f* oportunista

**opportunity** [ɒpə'tjuːnɪtɪ] *n* oportunidad *f*, ocasión *f*; **to have the o. of doing sth** *or* **to do sth** tener la oportunidad *or* ocasión de hacer algo; **at every o.** a la mínima oportunidad; **at the first** *or* **earliest o.** a la primera oportunidad; **if I get an o.** si tengo ocasión *or* oportunidad; **the o. of a lifetime** una oportunidad única en la vida; **a job with opportunities** un trabajo con buenas perspectivas

**oppose** [ə'pəʊz] *vt* oponerse a; **to be opposed to sth** estar en contra de algo; **we should act now as opposed to waiting till later** deberíamos actuar ya en lugar de esperar más; **I'm referring to my real father as opposed to my stepfather** me refiero a mi verdadero padre y no a mi padrastro

**opposing** [ə'pəʊzɪŋ] *adj* opuesto(a), contrario(a)

**opposite** ['ɒpəzɪt] **1** *n* **the o. of…** lo contrario de…

**2** *adj* (**a**) (*page, shore*) opuesto(a); **the o. side of the street** el otro lado de la calle (**b**) (*opinion*) contrario(a); **in the o. direction** en dirección contaria; **the o. sex** el sexo opuesto

**3** *adv* enfrente; **the house o.** la casa de enfrente

**4** *prep* enfrente de

**opposition** [ɒpə'zɪʃən] *n* (**a**) (*resistance*) oposición *f*; **to meet with o.** encontrar oposición (**b**) (*contrast*) **to act in o. to…** actuar en contra de… (**c**) (*opponents*) **the o.** los contrincantes, los adversarios; *Br Pol* **the O.** la oposición; *Pol* **to be in o.** estar en la oposición

**oppress** [ə'pres] *vt* (*treat cruelly*) oprimir

**oppressed** [ə'prest] **1** *npl* **the o.** los oprimidos

**2** *adj* (*people, nation*) oprimido(a)

**oppression** [ə'preʃən] *n* (**a**) (*of a people*) opresión *f* (**b**) (*of the mind*) agobio *m*, desasosiego *m*

**oppressive** [ə'presɪv] *adj* (**a**) (*law, regime*) opresor(ora), opresivo(a) (**b**) (*atmosphere*) agobiante; (*heat*) sofocante

**opt** [ɒpt] **1** *vi* **to o. to do sth** optar por hacer algo

**2** *vi* **to o. for…** optar por…

▸**opt out** *vi* **they opted out of the project** decidieron no participar en el proyecto; **to o. out of local authority control** (*of school, hospital*) decidir no continuar bajo el control de las autoridades locales

**optic** ['ɒptɪk] *adj* óptico(a); **o. nerve** nervio *m* óptico

**optical** ['ɒptɪkəl] *adj* óptico(a); *Comptr* **o. character reader** lector *m* óptico de caracteres; *Comptr* **o. character recognition** reconocimiento *m* óptico de caracteres; *Comptr* **o. disk** disco *m* óptico; **o. fibre** fibra *f* óptica; **o. illusion** ilusión *f* óptica

**optician** [ɒp'tɪʃən] *n* óptico(a) *m,f*

**optics** ['ɒptɪks] *n* (*subject*) óptica *f*

**optimism** ['ɒptɪmɪzəm] *n* optimismo *m*

**optimist** ['ɒptɪmɪst] *n* optimista *mf*

**optimistic** [ɒptɪ'mɪstɪk] *adj* optimista

**optimize** ['ɒptɪmaɪz] *vt* optimizar

**optimum** ['ɒptɪməm] **1** *n* nivel *m* óptimo

**2** *adj* óptimo(a)

**option** ['ɒpʃən] *n* (**a**) (*choice*) opción *f*; **to have the o. of doing sth** tener la opción de hacer algo; **to have no o.** no tener opción; **a soft** *or* **easy o.** una opción cómoda *or* fácil; **to leave** *or* **keep one's options open** dejar abiertas varias opciones (**b**) *Fin* opción *f* (**c**) *Sch Univ* (*asignatura f*) optativa *f*

**optional** ['ɒpʃənəl] *adj* optativo(a); **o. extras** accesorios *mpl* opcionales; *Sch* **o. subject** asignatura *f* optativa

**opt-out** ['ɒptaʊt] **1** *n* autoexclusión *f*

**2** *adj* **o. clause** cláusula *f* de exclusión *or* de no participación

**opulent** ['ɒpjʊlənt] *adj* opulento(a)

**or** [ɔː(r)] *unstressed* [ə(r)] *conj* (**a**) o; (*before o or ho*) u; **an hour or so** alrededor de una hora; **did she do it or not?** ¿lo hizo o no?; **keep still or I'll shoot!** ¡quieto o disparo!; **snow or no snow, she was determined to go** con nieve o sin ella, estaba decidida a ir (**b**) (*with negative*) ni; **she didn't write or phone** no escribió ni llamó

**oracle** ['ɒrəkəl] *n* oráculo *m*

**oral** ['ɔːrəl] **1** *n (exam)* (examen *m*) oral *m*
**2** *adj (tradition, history, skills)* oral; *(agreement)* verbal; *Sch* **o. examination** examen *m* oral; **o. sex** sexo *m* oral

**orally** ['ɔːrəlɪ] *adv* oralmente; **to take medicine o.** tomar un medicamento por vía oral

**orange** ['ɒrɪndʒ] **1** *n (fruit)* naranja *f*; *(colour)* naranja *m*; **o. blossom** flor *f* de azahar; **o. grove** naranjal *m*; **o. juice** zumo *m* de naranja; **o. peel** peladura *f* de naranja; **o. squash** naranjada *f*; **o. tree** naranjo *m*
**2** *adj (colour)* naranja, anaranjado(a)

**orang-outan(g)** [əˈræŋəˈtæŋ] *n* orangután *m*

**oration** [ɔːˈreɪʃən] *n* alocución *f*, discurso *m*

**orator** ['ɒrətə(r)] *n* orador(ora) *m,f*

**oratory¹** ['ɒrətərɪ] *n (art of speaking)* oratoria *f*

**oratory²** *n Rel (chapel)* oratorio *m*, capilla *f*

**orb** [ɔːb] *n Literary* esfera *f*

**orbit** ['ɔːbɪt] **1** *n (a) (of planet)* órbita *f*; **in o.** en órbita; **to go into o.** entrar en órbita **(b)** *(scope)* órbita *f*, ámbito *m*
**2** *vt* girar alrededor de
**3** *vi* estar en órbita

**orchard** ['ɔːtʃəd] *n* huerto *m* (de frutales); **(apple) o.** huerto de manzanos, manzanal *m*

**orchestra** ['ɔːkɪstrə] *n* orquesta *f*; *Th* **o. pit** orquesta, foso *m*

**orchestral** [ɔːˈkestrəl] *adj* orquestal

**orchestrate** ['ɔːkɪstreɪt] *vt also Fig* orquestar

**orchid** ['ɔːkɪd] *n* orquídea *f*

**ordain** [ɔːˈdeɪn] *vt* **(a)** *Formal (decree)* decretar, disponer; **fate ordained that we should meet** el destino dispuso que nos encontráramos **(b)** *Rel (priest)* ordenar

**ordeal** [ɔːˈdiːl] *n* calvario *m*

**order** ['ɔːdə(r)] **1** *n* **(a)** *(instruction)* orden *f*; **to give sb an o.** dar una orden a alguien; **to obey** *or* **follow orders** obedecer *or* cumplir órdenes; **to be under orders (to do sth)** tener órdenes (de hacer algo); **I don't take orders from you/anyone** yo no acepto órdenes tuyas/de nadie; *Fin* **pay to the o. of L. Black** páguese a L. Black
**(b)** *Com* pedido *m*; **to place an o. (with sb)** hacer un pedido (a alguien); **to have sth on o.** haber hecho un pedido de algo; **to make sth to o.** hacer algo por encargo; **o. book** libro *m* de pedidos; **o. form** hoja *f* de pedido
**(c)** *(peace, tidiness)* orden *m*; **to restore o.** restablecer el orden; *Fig* **to set one's own house in o.** poner (uno) orden en su vida
**(d)** *(condition)* **out of o.** averiado(a), estropeado(a); **in (good) working** *or* **running o.** en buen estado de funcionamiento
**(e)** *(in meeting)* **to call sb to o.** llamar a alguien al orden; **to rule a question out of o.** declarar improcedente una pregunta; *Fam* **that's**

**out of o.!** ¡eso no está bien!, ¡eso no es de recibo!; *Fig* **I think a celebration is in o.** creo que se impone celebrarlo; *Rel* **o. of service** orden *m* ritual *or* litúrgico; *Parl* **o. paper** orden *m* del día
**(f)** *(system)* orden *m*; **the new world o.** el nuevo orden mundial
**(g)** *(sequence)* orden *m*; **in the right/wrong o.** bien/mal ordenado(a); **in o.** en orden; **out of o.** desordenado(a); **in o. of age/size** por orden de edad/tamaño
**(h)** *(degree)* orden *m*; **of the highest o.** de primer orden; **in the o. of…** del orden de…; **the higher/lower orders** *(social classes)* las capas altas/bajas de la sociedad
**(i)** *Rel* orden *f*; **to take holy orders** ordenarse sacerdote
**(j)** **in o. to do sth** para hacer algo; **in o. that they understand** para que comprendan
**2** *vt* **(a)** *(instruct)* **to o. sb to do sth** mandar *or* ordenar a alguien hacer algo; *Law* **he was ordered to pay costs** el juez le ordenó pagar las costas
**(b)** *Com* pedir, encargar; *(in restaurant)* pedir
**(c)** *(arrange)* ordenar, poner en orden; **to o. sth according to size/age** ordenar algo de acuerdo con el tamaño/la edad
**3** *vi (in restaurant)* pedir
▸**order about, order around** *vt sep* **to o. sb about** *or* **around** mangonear a alguien, no parar de dar órdenes a alguien
▸**order in** *vt sep (supplies)* encargar; *(troops)* solicitar el envío de

**ordered** ['ɔːdəd] *adj (organized)* ordenado(a)

**orderly** ['ɔːdəlɪ] **1** *n* celador(ora) *m,f*
**2** *adj* **(a)** *(tidy, methodical)* ordenado(a) **(b)** *(well-behaved)* formal; **in an o. fashion** de forma ordenada

**ordinal** ['ɔːdɪnəl] *n & adj* ordinal *m*

**ordinance** ['ɔːdɪnəns] *n Formal (decree)* ordenanza *f*, decreto *m*

**ordinarily** [ɔːdɪnərɪlɪ] *adv* normalmente

**ordinary** ['ɔːdɪnərɪ] **1** *n* **out of the o.** fuera de lo normal
**2** *adj (normal)* normal; *(mediocre)* común, ordinario(a); **an o. Englishman** un inglés medio; **she was just an o. tourist** no era más que una simple turista; **this is no o. car** es un coche fuera de lo normal; **in the o. course of events** si las cosas siguen su curso normal; *Br Naut* **o. seaman** marinero *m*; *Br Fin* **o. share** acción *f* ordinaria

**ordination** [ɔːdɪˈneɪʃən] *n Rel* ordenación *f*

**ordnance** ['ɔːdnəns] *n Mil (supplies)* pertrechos *mpl*; *(guns)* armamento *m*; **o. factory** fábrica *f* de armamento; *Br* **O. Survey** = instituto británico de cartografía

**ore** [ɔː(r)] *n* mineral *m*; **iron/aluminium o.** mineral de hierro/aluminio

**oregano** [ɒrɪˈgɑːnəʊ] *n* orégano *m*

**organ** [ˈɔːgən] *n* (a) *Anat & Mus* órgano *m*; **o. donor** donante *mf* de órganos; **o. transplant** transplante *m* de órganos (b) *(newspaper, journal)* órgano *m* (de difusión)

**organ-grinder** [ˈɔːgəngraɪndə(r)] *n* organillero(a) *m,f*

**organic** [ɔːˈgænɪk] *adj (disease, function)* orgánico(a); *(farming, gardening)* biológico(a), ecológico(a)

**organism** [ˈɔːgənɪzəm] *n* organismo *m*

**organist** [ˈɔːgənɪst] *n* organista *mf*

**organization** [ɔːgənaɪˈzeɪʃən] *n* organización *f*

**organize** [ˈɔːgənaɪz] **1** *vt* organizar; **they organized accommodation for me** se encargaron de buscarme alojamiento

**2** *vi (of workers)* organizarse; *(form union)* constituirse en sindicato

**organizer** [ˈɔːgənaɪzə(r)] *n* (a) *(person)* organizador(ora) *m,f* (b) *(diary)* agenda *f*

**orgasm** [ˈɔːgæzəm] *n* orgasmo *m*; **to have an o.** tener un orgasmo

**orgy** [ˈɔːdʒɪ] *n* orgía *f*; *Fig* **an o. of violence** una masacre

**orient** [ˈɔːrɪənt] **1** *n* **the O.** (el) Oriente

**2** *vt* = **orientate**

**oriental** [ɔːrɪˈentəl] **1** *n Old-fashioned (person)* **an O.** un/una oriental

**2** *adj* oriental

**orientate** [ˈɔːrɪənteɪt] *vt* orientar; **to o. one-self** orientarse

**orientation** [ɔːrɪənˈteɪʃən] *n* orientación *f*; **o. course** curso *m* orientativo

**orienteering** [ɔːrɪənˈtɪərɪŋ] *n* orientación *f (deporte de aventura)*

**orifice** [ˈɒrɪfɪs] *n* orificio *m*

**origin** [ˈɒrɪdʒɪn] *n* origen *m*; **country of o.** país *m* de origen; **Greek o.** de origen griego

**original** [əˈrɪdʒɪnəl] **1** *n (painting, document)* original *m*; **to read Tolstoy in the o.** leer a Tolstói en el idioma original

**2** *adj (first, innovative)* original; *Rel* **o. sin** pecado *m* original

**originality** [ərɪdʒɪˈnælɪtɪ] *n* originalidad *f*

**originally** [əˈrɪdʒɪnəlɪ] *adv* (a) *(initially)* originariamente, en un principio; **where do you come from o.?** ¿cuál es tu lugar de origen? (b) *(in an innovative way)* originalmente, de forma original

**originate** [əˈrɪdʒɪneɪt] **1** *vt* crear, promover

**2** *vi* originarse; **to o. from...** *(of person)* proceder de...; **to o. in...** *(of river)* nacer en; *(of custom)* proceder o surgir de

**Orkney** [ˈɔːknɪ] *n* **the O. Islands, the Orkneys** las (Islas) Órcadas

**ornament 1** *n* [ˈɔːnəmənt] adorno *m*

**2** *vt* [ˈɔːnəment] *(room)* decorar; *(style)* adornar

**ornamental** [ɔːnəˈmentəl] *adj* ornamental, decorativo(a); **purely o.** meramente decorativo(a)

**ornate** [ɔːˈneɪt] *adj (building, surroundings)* ornamentado(a); *(style)* recargado(a)

**ornithology** [ɔːnɪˈθɒlədʒɪ] *n* ornitología *f*

**orphan** [ˈɔːfən] **1** *n* huérfano(a) *m,f*; **to be left an o.** quedar huérfano(a)

**2** *adj* **an o. child** un niño huérfano

**3** *vt* **to be orphaned** quedar huérfano(a)

**orphanage** [ˈɔːfənɪdʒ] *n* orfanato *m*

**orthodontics** [ɔːθəˈdɒntɪks] *n* ortodoncia *f*

**orthodontist** [ɔːθəˈdɒntɪst] *n* ortodontista *mf*

**orthodox** [ˈɔːθədɒks] *adj* ortodoxo(a)

**orthodoxy** [ˈɔːθədɒksɪ] *n* ortodoxia *f*

**orthopaedic**, *US* **orthopedic** [ɔːθəˈpiːdɪk] *adj Med* ortopédico(a)

**orthopaedics**, *US* **orthopedics** [ɔːθəˈpiːdɪks] *n Med* ortopedia *f*

**oscillate** [ˈɒsɪleɪt] *vi* oscilar; **he oscillated between hope and despair** pasaba de la esperanza a la desesperación

**Oslo** [ˈɒzləʊ] *n* Oslo

**osmosis** [ɒzˈməʊsɪs] *n also Fig* ósmosis *f inv*, osmosis *f inv*

**osprey** [ˈɒspreɪ] *(pl* **ospreys***) n* águila *f* pescadora

**ossify** [ˈɒsɪfaɪ] *vi Anat* osificarse; *Fig (of person, system)* anquilosarse

**ostensible** [ɒsˈtensɪbəl] *adj* aparente

**ostensibly** [ɒsˈtensɪblɪ] *adv* aparentemente

**ostentation** [ɒstenˈteɪʃən] *n* ostentación *f*

**ostentatious** [ɒstenˈteɪʃəs] *adj* ostentoso(a)

**osteoarthritis** [ɒstɪəʊɑːˈθraɪtɪs] *n Med* osteoartritis *f inv*, artritis *f inv* ósea

**osteopath** [ˈɒstɪəpæθ] *n Med* osteópata *mf*

**ostracism** [ˈɒstrəsɪzəm] *n* ostracismo *m*

**ostracize** [ˈɒstrəsaɪz] *vt* aislar, condenar al ostracismo

**ostrich** [ˈɒstrɪtʃ] *n* avestruz *m*

**OTC** [əʊtiːˈsiː] *n Br (abbr* **Officers' Training Corps***)* = unidad de adiestramiento de futuros oficiales del ejército británico provenientes de la universidad

**other** [ˈʌðə(r)] **1** *adj* otro(a); **the o. one** el otro/la otra; **every o. day/week** cada dos días/semanas; **I work every o. day/month** trabajo un día/mes sí, un día/mes no **the o. day** el otro día; **the o. four** los otros cuatro; **o. people seem to like it** parece que a otros les gusta; **o. people's property** propiedad ajena; **any o. book** cualquier otro libro; **somebody o. than me should do it** debería hacerlo alguien que no sea yo

**2** *pron* **the o.** el otro/la otra; **one after the o.** uno tras otro; **(the) others** (los) otros; **some laughed, others wept** unos reían y otros lloraban; **one or o. of us will be there** alguno de nosotros estará allí; **somewhere or o.** en algún sitio; **someone or o.** no sé quién, alguien; **some woman or o.** no sé qué mujer, una mujer; **something or o.** no sé qué, algo; **somehow or o.** de la manera que sea, sea como sea; **somehow or o., we arrived on time** nos las arreglamos para llegar a tiempo

**3** *adv* **the colour's odd – o. than that, it's perfect** el color es un poco raro, pero, por lo demás, resulta perfecto; **she never speaks of him o. than admiringly** siempre habla de él con admiración

**otherwise** ['ʌðəwaɪz] **1** *adv* **(a)** *(differently)* de otra manera; **he could not do o.** no pudo hacer otra cosa; **to think o.** pensar de otra manera; **to be o. engaged** tener otros asuntos que resolver; **except where o. stated** excepto donde se indique lo contrario **(b)** *(apart from that)* por lo demás

**2** *conj* si no, de lo contrario

**other-worldly** [ʌðə'wɜːldlɪ] *adj (person)* místico(a); *(religion, experience)* sobrenatural

**OTT** [əʊtiː'tiː] *adj Fam (abbr* **over the top)** exagerado(a); **to be O.** pasarse un pelín

**Ottawa** ['ɒtəwə] *n* Ottawa

**otter** ['ɒtə(r)] *n* nutria *f*

**Ottoman** ['ɒtəmən] *Hist n & adj* otomano(a) *m,f*

**ottoman** ['ɒtəmən] *n (piece of furniture)* canapé *m*, otomana *f*

**OU** [əʊ'juː] *n Br (abbr* **Open University)** ≃ UNED *f*, Universidad *f* Nacional de Educación a Distancia

**ouch** [aʊtʃ] *exclam (expressing pain)* ¡ay!

**ought** [ɔːt]

En el inglés hablado, y en el escrito en estilo coloquial, la forma negativa **ought not** se transforma en **oughtn't**.

*v aux* **(a)** *(expressing obligation, desirability)* deber, tener que; **I o. to be going** tendría que irme ya; **you oughtn't to worry so much** no deberías preocuparte tanto; **I thought I o. to let you know about it** me pareció que deberías saberlo; **he had drunk more than he o. to** había bebido más de la cuenta; **this o. to have been done before** esto se tenía que haber hecho antes; **they o. not to have waited** no tenían que haber esperado **(b)** *(expressing probability)* **they o. to be in Paris by now** a estas horas tendrían que estar ya en París; **you o. to be able to get £150 for the painting** deberías conseguir al menos 150 libras por el cuadro

**oughtn't** ['ɔːtənt] = **ought not**

**ounce** [aʊns] *n (measurement)* onza *f*; **if you had an o. of sense** si tuvieras dos dedos de frente

**our** ['aʊə(r)] *possessive adj* **(a)** *(singular)* nuestro(a); *(plural)* nuestros(as) **(b)** *(for parts of body, clothes) (translated by definite article)* **someone stole o. clothes** nos robaron la ropa

**ours** ['aʊəz] *possessive pron* **(a)** *(singular)* el nuestro *m*, la nuestra *f*; *(plural)* los nuestros *mpl*, las nuestras *fpl*; **their house is big but o. is bigger** su casa es grande, pero la nuestra es mayor **(b)** *(used attributively) (singular)* nuestro *m*, nuestra *f*; *(plural)* nuestros *mpl*, nuestras *fpl*; **this book is o.** este libro es nuestro; **a friend of o.** un amigo nuestro

**ourselves** [aʊə'selvz] *pron* **(a)** *(reflexive)* nos; **we both hurt o.** los dos nos hicimos daño **(b)** *(emphatic)* nosotros mismos *or* solos *mpl*, nosotras mismas *or* solas *fpl*; **we did all the work o.** hicimos todo el trabajo nosotros solos; **we o. do not believe it** nosotros mismos no nos lo creemos **(c)** *(after preposition)* nosotros *mpl*, nosotras *fpl*; **we shouldn't talk about o.** no deberíamos hablar sobre nosotros; **we shouldn't fight among o.** no deberíamos pelearnos entre nosotros; **we were all by o.** estábamos nosotros solos

**oust** [aʊst] *vt* desbancar; **to o. sb from his post** destituir a alguien, separar a alguien de su cargo

**out** [aʊt] **1** *adv* **(a)** *(outside, not in, not at home)* fuera; **he's o.** está fuera; **I was only o. for a minute** sólo salí un momento; **o. here** aquí fuera; **it's cold o. there** hace frío (ahí) fuera; **to go o.** salir; **to stay o. late** salir hasta muy tarde; **the tide is o.** la marea está baja; **o.!** *(in tennis)* ¡out! **(b)** *(not concealed)* **the secret is o.** se ha desvelado el secreto; **he's o.** *(openly gay)* es homosexual declarado; **the sun is o.** ha salido el sol, hace sol; **the tulips are o. early this year** los tulipanes han salido *or* florecido muy pronto este año **(c)** *(published)* **to come o.** salir; **her new book will be o. next week** la semana que viene sale su nuevo libro **(d)** *(not in fashion)* **to be o.** no llevarse **(e)** *(indicating intention)* **to be o. to do sth** pretender hacer algo; **to be o. for money/a good time** ir en busca de dinero/diversión; *Fam* **to be o. to get sb** ir a por alguien, ir detrás de alguien **(f)** *(unconscious, asleep)* **to be o. cold** *or Fam* **for the count** *(unconscious)* estar K.O.; *(asleep)* estar roque; *Fam* **I was o. like a light** caí redondo en la cama **(g)** *(extinguished) (fire, light)* apagado(a) **(h)** *(incorrect)* equivocado(a); **I was £50 o.** me equivocaba en 50 libras; **the calculations were o.** los cálculos no eran correctos

**(i) to be o. (on strike)** estar en huelga

**(j)** *(indicating completion)* **before the week is o.** antes de que termine la semana

**(k)** *Law* **the jury is o.** el jurado está deliberando

**(l)** *(unacceptable)* **that's o.** eso es imposible

**(m)** *(in phrases with* **of)** *(outside)* **to go o. of the office** salir de la oficina; **to throw sth o. of the window** tirar algo por la ventana; **keep o. of direct sunlight** manténgase a resguardo de los rayos del sol; **to be o. of the country** estar fuera del país; **o. of danger** fuera de peligro; **to be o. of power** estar en la oposición

**(n)** *(in phrases with* **of)** *(lacking)* **I'm o. of cash/ideas** me he quedado sin dinero/ideas

**(o)** *(in phrases with* **of)** *(from)* **to get sth o. of sth/sb** sacar algo de algo/a alguien; **three days o. of four** tres días de cada cuatro; **twenty v. of twenty** *(mark)* veinte sobre *or* de veinte; **he built a hut o. of sticks** construyó una choza con palos; **it's made o. of plasticine** está hecho de plastilina; **she paid for it o. of her own money** lo pagó de *or* con su dinero; **o. of friendship/curiosity** por amistad/curiosidad

**(p)** *(in phrases with* **of)** *Fam* **to be o. of it** *(dazed)* estar atontado(a); **to feel o. of it** *(excluded)* no sentirse integrado(a)

**2** *prep (through)* **to look o. the window** mirar por la ventana

**3** *vt* revelar la homosexualidad de

**out-and-out** [autə'naut] *adj (villain, reactionary)* consumado(a), redomado(a); *(success, failure)* rotundo(a), absoluto(a)

**outback** ['autbæk] *n* **the o.** el interior despoblado de Australia

**outbid** [aut'bɪd] *(pt & pp* **outbid)** *vt* sobrepasar *(en una puja);* **to o. sb** sobresar la puja de alguien

**outboard** ['autbɔːd] **1** *n (motor)* fueraborda *m*
**2** *adj* **o. motor** motor *m* (de) fueraborda

**outbreak** ['autbreɪk] *n (of hostilities)* ruptura *f; (of epidemic, violence)* brote *m; (of war, conflict)* estallido *m*

**outbuilding** ['autbɪldɪŋ] *n* dependencia *f*

**outburst** ['autbɜːst] *n* arrebato *m,* arranque *m*

**outcast** ['autkɑːst] *n* paria *mf,* marginado(a) *m,f*

**outclass** [aut'klɑːs] *vt* superar (ampliamente)

**outcome** ['autkʌm] *n* resultado *m*

**outcrop** ['autkrɒp] *n (of rock)* afloramiento *m*

**outcry** ['autkraɪ] *n (protest)* protesta *f;* **to raise an o. (against)** protestar (en contra de)

**outdated** [aut'deɪtɪd] *adj* anticuado(a)

**outdistance** [aut'dɪstəns] *vt* dejar atrás

**outdo** [aut'duː] *(pt* **outdid** [aut'dɪd], *pp* **outdone** [aut'dʌn]) *vt (person)* superar, sobrepasar; **not to be outdone,...** para no ser menos,...

**outdoor** ['autdɔː(r)] *adj* al aire libre; **she's an o. person** le gusta salir al aire libre; **the o. life** la vida al aire libre; **o. swimming pool** piscina *f* descubierta

**outdoors** [aut'dɔːz] **1** *n* **the great o.** la naturaleza, el campo

**2** *adv* fuera; **the wedding will be held o.** la boda se celebrará al aire libre; **to sleep o.** dormir al raso

**outer** ['autə(r)] *adj* exterior; **o. door** puerta exterior; **o. London** la periferia londinense; **O. Mongolia** Mongolia Exterior; **o. space** el espacio exterior

**outermost** ['autəməust] *adj (layer)* exterior

**outfit** ['autfɪt] *n* **(a)** *(clothes)* traje *m* **(b)** *Fam (organization)* grupo *m*

**outflank** [aut'flæŋk] *vt Mil* sorprender por la espalda; *Fig (outmanoeuvre)* superar

**outflow** ['autfləu] *n (of liquid, currency)* salida *f,* fuga *f*

**outgoing** [aut'gəuɪŋ] *adj* **(a)** *(departing)* saliente **(b)** *(sociable)* abierto(a), extrovertido(a)

**outgoings** ['autgəuɪŋz] *npl Fin* gastos *mpl*

**outgrow** [aut'grəu] *(pt* **outgrew** [aut'gruː], *pp* **outgrown** [aut'grəun]) *vt (toys)* hacerse demasiado mayor para; **he's outgrown the jacket** se le ha quedado pequeña la chaqueta; **he should have outgrown that habit by now** ya no tiene edad para esas cosas; **to have outgrown one's friends** tener ya poco en común *or* poco que ver con los amigos

**outhouse** ['authaus] *n* dependencia *f*

**outing** ['autɪŋ] *n* **(a)** *(excursion)* excursión *f* **(b)** *(of homosexual)* = hecho de revelar la homosexualidad de alguien, generalmente un personaje célebre

**outlandish** [aut'lændɪʃ] *adj* estrafalario(a), extravagante

**outlast** [aut'lɑːst] *vt* sobrevivir a

**outlaw** ['autlɔː] **1** *n* proscrito(a) *m,f*
**2** *vt (custom)* prohibir; *(person)* proscribir

**outlay** ['autleɪ] *(pl* **outlays)** *n (expense)* desembolso *m*

**outlet** ['autlet] *n* **(a)** *(for water)* desagüe *m; (for steam)* salida *f; (for talents, energy)* válvula *f* de escape **(b)** *(shop)* punto *m* de venta

**outline** ['autlaɪn] **1** *n* **(a)** *(shape)* silueta *f,* contorno *m; (drawing)* esbozo *m,* bosquejo *m; (of play, novel)* resumen *m; (of plan, policy)* líneas *fpl* maestras; **a rough o.** *(of plan, proposal)* un esbozo, una idea aproximada; **in o.** a grandes rasgos

**2** *vt (shape)* perfilar; *(plot of novel)* resumir; *(plan, policy)* exponer a grandes rasgos

**outlive** [aʊt'lɪv] *vt* sobrevivir a; **to have out-lived its usefulness** *(of machine, theory)* haber dejado de ser útil *or* de servir

**outlook** ['aʊtlʊk] *n* (a) *(prospect)* perspectiva *f*; *(of weather)* previsión *f*; **the o. is gloomy** *(for economy)* las previsiones son muy malas (b) *(attitude)* punto *m* de vista, visión *f*; **o. on life** visión *f* de la vida

**outlying** ['aʊtlaɪɪŋ] *adj* periférico(a)

**outmanoeuvre**, *US* **outmaneuver** [aʊtmə'nuːvə(r)] *vt* Mil superar a base de estrategia; *(in politics, sport)* superar

**outmoded** [aʊt'məʊdɪd] *adj* anticuado(a)

**outnumber** [aʊt'nʌmbə(r)] *vt* (the enemy) superar en número; **we were outnumbered** eran más que nosotros

**out-of-doors** [aʊtəv'dɔːz] *adv* fuera; **to sleep o.** dormir al raso

**out-of-pocket expenses** ['aʊtəv-'pɒkɪt'spensɪz] *npl* gastos *mpl* extras

**out-of-the-way** [aʊtəvðə'weɪ] *adj* (remote) apartado(a), remoto(a); *(unusual)* fuera de lo común

**outpatient** ['aʊtpeɪʃənt] *n* paciente *mf* externo(a)

**outplacement** ['aʊtpleɪsmənt] *n* recolocación *f*, = asesoramiento dirigido a facilitar la recolocación de empleados, generalmente subvencionado por la empresa que los despide

**outpost** ['aʊtpəʊst] *n* Mil enclave *m*; Fig **the last o. of civilization** el último baluarte de la civilización

**output** ['aʊtpʊt] **1** *n* (of goods, of author) producción *f*; *(of data, information)* información *f* producida; *(of generator)* potencia *f* (de salida)
**2** *vt* *(pt & pp* output) producir

**outrage** ['aʊtreɪdʒ] **1** *n* (a) *(act)* ultraje *m*; **it's an o.!** ¡es un escándalo! (b) *(indignation)* indignación *f*
**2** *vt* (make indignant) indignar, ultrajar; **I am outraged** estoy indignado

**outrageous** [aʊt'reɪdʒəs] *adj* (cruelty) atroz; *(price, conduct)* escandaloso(a); *(clothes, haircut)* estrambótico(a)

**outrageously** [aʊt'reɪdʒəslɪ] *adv* (cruel) espantosamente, terriblemente; *(expensive, to behave)* escandalosamente; *(to dress)* estrambóticamente

**outreach worker** ['aʊtriːtʃ'wɜːkə(r)] *n* = trabajador social que presta asistencia a personas que pudiendo necesitarla no la solicitan

**outright 1** *adv* [aʊt'raɪt] (a) *(completely)* (ban, win) completamente; **to buy sth o.** comprar algo (con) dinero en mano; **he was killed o.** murió en el acto (b) *(bluntly)* **I told him o. what I thought of him** le dije claramente lo que pensaba de él; **to refuse o.** negarse rotundamente

**2** *adj* ['aʊtraɪt] total, absoluto(a); **an o. fail-ure** un fracaso total, un rotundo fracaso; **the o. winner** el campeón absoluto

**outrun** [aʊt'rʌn] *(pt* outran [aʊt'ræn], *pp* outrun) *vt* (run faster than) correr más rápido que

**outsell** [aʊt'sel] *vt* superar en ventas

**outset** ['aʊtset] *n* principio *m*; **at the o.** al principio; **from the o.** desde el principio

**outshine** [aʊt'ʃaɪn] *(pt & pp* outshone [aʊt'ʃɒn]) *vt* (surpass) eclipsar

**outside** ['aʊtsaɪd, aʊt'saɪd] **1** *n* (of book, building) exterior *m*; **on the o.** por fuera; **from the o.** desde fuera; **at the o.** (of estimate) a lo sumo
**2** *adj* (help, influence, world) exterior; Rad TV **o. broadcast** emisión *f* desde fuera del estudio; **o. lane** carril *m* de fuera *or* de adelantamiento; **there's an o. chance** existe una posibilidad remota
**3** *adv* fuera; **to go o.** salir afuera; **from o.** desde fuera
**4** *prep* (a) *(physically)* fuera de; **I'll meet you o. the cinema** nos vemos a la entrada del cine; **o. office hours** fuera de horas de oficina (b) *(apart from)* aparte de; **o. (of) a few friends** aparte de unos pocos amigos

**outsider** [aʊt'saɪdə(r)] *n* (a) *(socially)* extraño(a) *m,f* (b) *(in election, race, competition)* **he's an o.** no figura entre los favoritos

**outsize** ['aʊtsaɪz] *n* Com (large size) talla *f* (grande) especial

**outsize(d)** ['aʊtsaɪz(d)] *adj* (clothes) de talla especial; *(appetite, ego)* desmedido(a)

**outskirts** ['aʊtskɜːts] *npl* (of city) afueras *fpl*

**outsmart** [aʊt'smɑːt] *vt* superar en astucia, burlar

**outsourcing** ['aʊtsɔːsɪŋ] *n* Com subcontratación *f*, contratación *f* externa

**outspend** [aʊt'spend] *vt* gastar más que

**outspoken** [aʊt'spəʊkən] *adj* abierto(a), directo(a)

**outstanding** [aʊt'stændɪŋ] *adj* (a) *(remark-able)* (feature, incident) notable, destacado(a); *(person)* excepcional (b) *(unresolved, unpaid)* pendiente

**outstay** [aʊt'steɪ] *vt* **to o. one's welcome** abusar de la hospitalidad, quedarse más tiempo del apropiado

**outstretched** ['aʊtstretʃt] *adj* extendido(a), estirado(a); **with o. arms** con los brazos extendidos

**outstrip** [aʊt'strɪp] *(pt & pp* outstripped) *vt* superar, aventajar

**out-tray** ['aʊttreɪ] *(pl* out-trays) *n* bandeja *f* de trabajos terminados

**outward** ['aʊtwəd] **1** *adj* (a) **o. voyage** *or* **journey** viaje *m* de ida (b) *(external)* externo(a)
**2** *adv* = **outwards**

**outwardly** ['aʊtwədlɪ] *adv* aparentemente, en apariencia; **o. calm** aparentemente tranquilo

**outwards** ['aʊtwədz] *adv* hacia fuera

**outweigh** [aʊt'weɪ] *vt (be more important than)* tener más peso que

**outwit** [aʊt'wɪt] (*pt & pp* **outwitted**) *vt* ser más astuto(a) que, burlar

**outworker** ['aʊtwɜːkə(r)] *n* trabajador(ora) *m,f* a domicilio *or* externo(a)

**outworn** [aʊt'wɔːn] *adj (theories, ideas)* anticuado(a)

**oval** ['əʊvəl] **1** *n* óvalo *m*
 **2** *adj* oval, ovalado(a)

**ovarian** [əʊ'veərɪən] *adj Anat* ovárico(a); **o. cancer** cáncer *m* de ovario

**ovary** ['əʊvərɪ] *n Anat* ovario *m*

**ovation** [əʊ'veɪʃən] *n* ovación *f*; **the audience gave her a standing o.** el público puesto en pie le dedicó una calurosa ovación

**oven** ['ʌvən] *n* horno *m*; **electric/gas o.** horno eléctrico/de gas; **o. gloves** manoplas *fpl* de cocina

**oven-proof** ['ʌvənpruːf] *adj* refractario(a)

**oven-ready** ['ʌvənredɪ] *adj (chicken)* listo(a) para hornear

**ovenware** ['ʌvənweə(r)] *n* accesorios *mpl* para el horno

**over** ['əʊvə(r)] **1** *n (in cricket)* = serie de seis lanzamientos en la misma dirección
 **2** *prep* **(a)** *(above, on top of)* sobre, encima de; **to put a blanket o. sb** cubrir a alguien con una manta; **all o. Spain** por toda España; **all o. the world** por todo el mundo; **to throw sth o. the wall** tirar algo por encima de la tapia; **to read o. sb's shoulder** leer por encima del hombro de alguien; **directly o. our heads** justo encima de nosotros; *Fig* **the lecture was way o. my head** no me enteré de nada de la conferencia; **I couldn't hear her o. the noise** no podía oírla por el ruido; *Fam Fig* **o. the top** *(excessive)* exagerado(a)
 **(b)** *(across)* **to go o. the road** cruzar la calle; **to live o. the road** vivir al otro lado de la calle; **o. the border** al otro lado de la frontera; **the bridge o. the river** el puente sobre el río
 **(c)** *(about)* **to laugh o. sth** reírse de algo; **to fight o. sth** pelear por algo; **we had trouble o. the tickets** tuvimos problemas con las entradas
 **(d)** *(in excess of)* más de; **o. and above** además de, más allá de; **he's o. fifty** tiene más de cincuenta años; **children o. five** los niños mayores de cinco años
 **(e)** *(during)* durante; **o. Christmas/the weekend** durante la Navidad/el fin de semana; **o. the last three years** (durante) los tres últimos años; **to discuss sth o. lunch** hablar de algo durante la comida

**(f)** *(recovered from)* **I'm o. the flu/the disappointment** ya se me ha pasado la gripe/la desilusión
 **3** *adv* **(a)** *(across)* **o. here/there** aquí/allí; **he led me o. to the window** me llevó hasta la ventana; **to cross o.** *(the street)* cruzar; **I asked him o.** **(to my house)** lo invité a mi casa
 **(b)** *(down)* **to fall o.** caerse; **to bend o.** agacharse; **to push sth o.** tirar algo
 **(c)** *(everywhere)* **famous the world o.** famoso(a) en el mundo entero
 **(d)** *(indicating repetition)* **three times o.** tres veces; **o. and o. again** una y otra vez; **all o. again** otra vez desde el principio
 **(e)** *(in excess)* **children of five and o.** niños mayores de cinco años; **there was £5 left o.** sobraron *or* quedaron 5 libras; *Fam* **I wasn't o. happy about it** no estaba demasiado contento
 **(f)** *(on radio)* **o. (and out)** cambio (y corto)
 **4** *adj (finished)* **it is (all) o.** todo ha terminado; **the danger is o.** ha pasado el peligro; **to get sth o. (and done) with** terminar algo de una vez por todas

**overabundant** [əʊvərə'bʌndənt] *adj* superabundante

**overact** [əʊvə'rækt] *vi* sobreactuar

**overactive** [əʊvər'æktɪv] *adj* hiperactivo(a)

**overall** ['əʊvərɔːl] **1** *adj* total, global
 **2** *adv* en general; **England came third o.** Inglaterra quedó tercera en la clasificación general

**overalls** ['əʊvərɔːlz] *npl* mono *m* (de trabajo)

**overanxious** [əʊvər'æŋkʃəs] *adj* excesivamente preocupado(a)

**overawe** [əʊvə'rɔː] *vt* intimidar, cohibir; **to be overawed by sb/sth** quedarse anonadado(a) por alguien/algo

**overbalance** [əʊvə'bæləns] *vi* perder el equilibrio

**overbearing** [əʊvə'beərɪŋ] *adj* imperioso(a), despótico(a)

**overblown** [əʊvə'bləʊn] *adj* exagerado(a)

**overboard** ['əʊvəbɔːd] *adv* por la borda; **to fall o.** caer por la borda, caer al agua; **man o.!** ¡hombre al agua!; *Fig* **to go o. (about)** entusiasmarse mucho (con)

**overbook** ['əʊvə'bʊk] *vt (flight, holiday)* = aceptar un número de reservas mayor que el de plazas disponibles; **they've overbooked this flight** este vuelo tiene overbooking

**overbooking** [əʊvə'bʊkɪŋ] *n* overbooking *m*, = venta de más plazas de las disponibles

**overcapacity** ['əʊvəkə'pæsɪtɪ] *n Ind* capacidad *f* excesiva de producción

**overcast** ['əʊvəkɑːst] *adj (sky, day)* nublado(a); **to be o.** estar nublado(a)

**overcautious** [əʊvə'kɔːʃəs] *adj* demasiado cauteloso(a)

**overcharge** [əʊvə'tʃɑːdʒ] *vt* (**a**) *(for goods, services)* **to o. sb (for sth)** cobrar de más a alguien (por algo); **he overcharged me by £5** me cobró cinco libras de más (**b**) *Elec (battery)* sobrecargar

**overcoat** ['əʊvəkəʊt] *n* abrigo *m*

**overcome** [əʊvə'kʌm] (*pt* **overcame** [əʊvə'keɪm], *pp* **overcome**) *vt (defeat) (an opponent, one's fears)* vencer; *(problem, obstacle)* superar; **to be o. with** *or* **by grief** sucumbir al dolor; **I was quite overcome** estaba totalmente abrumado(a), me embargaba la emoción

**overcompensate** [əʊvə'kɒmpenseɪt] *vi* **to o. for sth** compensar algo en exceso

**overconfident** [əʊvə'kɒnfɪdənt] *adj* demasiado confiado(a)

**overcook** [əʊvə'kʊk] *vt* cocinar demasiado, pasar mucho

**overcrowded** [əʊvə'kraʊdəd] *adj (room)* atestado(a); *(area, region)* superpoblado(a); **the problem of o. classrooms** el problema de la masificación de las aulas

**overcrowding** [əʊvə'kraʊdɪŋ] *n (of slums, prisons)* hacinamiento *m*; *(of classrooms)* masificación *f*; *(of city, region)* superpoblación *f*

**overdeveloped** [əʊvədɪ'veləpt] *adj* hiperdesarrollado(a); *Phot* sobrerrevelado(a)

**overdo** [əʊvə'duː] (*pt* **overdid** [əʊvə'dɪd], *pp* **overdone** [əʊvə'dʌn]) *vt* (**a**) *(exaggerate)* exagerar; **to o. it** *(work too hard)* trabajar demasiado (**b**) *(do or have too much of)* pasarse con; **to o. the salt/make-up** pasarse con la sal/el maquillaje

**overdone** ['əʊvədʌn] *adj (food)* demasiado hecho(a), pasado(a)

**overdose** ['əʊvədəʊs] **1** *n* sobredosis *f inv*
**2** *vi* tomar una sobredosis; **to o. on drugs** tomar una sobredosis de drogas; *Fig* **to o. on chocolate** darse un atracón de chocolate

**overdraft** ['əʊvədrɑːft] *n Fin (amount borrowed)* saldo *m* negativo *or* deudor; **to arrange an o.** acordar un (límite de) descubierto

**overdrawn** [əʊvə'drɔːn] *adj Fin (account)* en descubierto; **to be £100 o.** tener un descubierto de 100 libras

**overdressed** ['əʊvədrest] *adj* demasiado trajeado(a)

**overdrive** ['əʊvədraɪv] *n Fig* **to go into o.** entregarse a una actividad frenética

**overdue** [əʊvə'djuː] *adj* **to be o.** *(person, train)* retrasarse, venir con retraso; *(bill)* estar sin pagar; *(library book)* haber rebasado el plazo de préstamo; **this measure is long o.** esta medida debía haberse adoptado hace tiempo

**overeat** [əʊvə'riːt] (*pt* **overate** [əʊvə'ret], *pp* **overeaten** [əʊvə'riːtən]) *vi* comer demasiado

**overemphasize** [əʊvər'emfəsaɪz] *vt* hacer excesivo hincapié en, recalcar en exceso

**overenthusiastic** [əʊvərɪnθjuːzɪ'æstɪk] *adj* excesivamente entusiasta

**overestimate** [əʊvə'restɪmeɪt] *vt* sobreestimar

**overexcited** [əʊvərɪk'saɪtɪd] *adj* sobreexcitado(a)

**overexpose** [əʊvərɪks'pəʊz] *vt Phot* sobreexponer

**overextended** [əʊvərɪk'stendɪd] *adj Fin* insolvente, con alto grado de pasivo

**overflow 1** *n* ['əʊvəfləʊ] *(of population)* exceso *m* de población; **o. (pipe)** rebosadero *m*, desagüe *m*
**2** *vi* [əʊvə'fləʊ] *(of river)* desbordarse; *(of liquid, cup)* rebosar; **to o. with joy** estar rebosante de felicidad

**overfull** [əʊvə'fʊl] *adj* repleto(a), saturado(a)

**overgrown** [əʊvə'grəʊn] *adj* **o. with weeds** *(garden)* invadido(a) por las malas hierbas; **he's like an o. schoolboy** es como un niño grande

**overhang 1** *n* ['əʊvəhæŋ] *(of roof)* alero *m*, voladizo *m*; *(on mountain)* saliente *m*
**2** *vt* [əʊvə'hæŋ] (*pt* & *pp* **overhung** [əʊvə'hʌŋ]) *(of balcony, rocks)* colgar sobre

**overhaul 1** *n* ['əʊvəhɔːl] *(of machine, policy)* revisión *f*
**2** *vt* [əʊvə'hɔːl] (**a**) *(machine, policy)* revisar (**b**) *(overtake)* adelantar

**overhead 1** *adj* ['əʊvəhed] *(cable)* aéreo(a); **o. projector** retroproyector *m*, proyector *m* de transparencias
**2** *adv* [əʊvə'hed] *(por)* arriba; **a plane flew o.** un avión sobrevoló nuestras cabezas
**3** *n* ['əʊvəhed] *Com US* = **overheads**

**overheads** ['əʊvəhedz] *npl Br Com* gastos *mpl* generales

**overhear** [əʊvə'hɪə(r)] (*pt* & *pp* **overheard** [əʊvə'hɜːd]) *vt* oír *or* escuchar casualmente

**overheat** [əʊvə'hiːt] *vi (of engine, economy)* recalentarse

**overindulge** [əʊvərɪn'dʌldʒ] **1** *vt (child)* consentir; **to o. oneself** *(drink, eat to excess)* atiborrarse, empacharse
**2** *vi* atiborrarse, empacharse

**overjoyed** [əʊvə'dʒɔɪd] *adj* contentísimo(a); **to be o. at sth** estar contentísimo(a) con algo; **he was o. to hear that they were coming** le encantó saber que venían

**overkill** ['əʊvəkɪl] *n* **there's a danger of o.** se corre el peligro de caer en el exceso; **media o.** *(on TV, in newspapers)* cobertura *f* informativa exagerada

**overland 1** [əʊvə'lænd] *adv* por tierra
**2** ['əʊvəlænd] *adj* terrestre

**overlap 1** n ['əʊvəlæp] (of planks, tiles) superposición f, solapamiento m; (between two areas of work, knowledge) coincidencia f

**2** vi [əʊvə'læp] (pt & pp **overlapped**) (of planks, tiles) superponerse or solaparse (**with** con); (of categories, theories) tener puntos en común (**with** con); (of periods of time) coincidir (**with** con)

**overleaf** [əʊvə'li:f] adv al dorso; **see o.** véase al dorso

**overload 1** n ['əʊvələʊd] Elec sobrecarga f

**2** vt [əʊvə'ləʊd] (machine, person) sobrecargar

**overlong** [əʊvə'lɒŋ] adj demasiado largo(a)

**overlook** [əʊvə'lʊk] vt (**a**) (look out over) dar a; **the town is overlooked by the castle** el castillo domina la ciudad (**b**) (fail to notice) pasar por alto, no darse cuenta de (**c**) (disregard) pasar por alto, no tener en cuenta

**overly** ['əʊvəlɪ] adv excesivamente, demasiado; **not o.** no excesivamente, no demasiado

**overmanning** [əʊvə'mænɪŋ] n Ind exceso m de empleados

**overmuch** [əʊvə'mʌtʃ] adv en exceso

**overnight 1** adv [əʊvə'naɪt] (**a**) (during the night) durante la noche; **to stay o.** quedarse a pasar la noche (**b**) (suddenly) de la noche a la mañana, de un día para otro

**2** adj ['əʊvənaɪt] (**a**) (for one night) de una noche; **o. bag** bolso m de viaje; **o. train/flight** tren m/vuelo m nocturno; **o. stay** estancia f de una noche (**b**) (sudden) repentino(a)

**overoptimistic** [əʊvərɒptɪ'mɪstɪk] adj demasiado optimista

**overpaid** [əʊvə'peɪd] adj **to be o.** ganar demasiado (dinero), estar demasiado bien pagado(a)

**overpass** ['əʊvəpɑ:s] n paso m elevado

**overpayment** [əʊvə'peɪmənt] n (of taxes, employee) pago m excesivo

**overpopulation** [əʊvəpɒpjʊ'leɪʃən] n superpoblación f

**overpower** [əʊvə'paʊə(r)] vt vencer, dominar

**overpowering** [əʊvə'paʊərɪŋ] adj (emotion, heat) tremendo(a), desmesurado(a); (smell, taste) fortísimo(a), intensísimo(a); (desire) irrefrenable, irreprimible

**overpriced** [əʊvə'praɪst] adj excesivamente caro(a)

**overproduction** [əʊvəprə'dʌkʃən] n Econ superproducción f

**overrated** [əʊvə'reɪtɪd] adj sobrevalorado(a)

**overreach** [əʊvə'ri:tʃ] vt **to o. oneself** extralimitarse

**overreact** [əʊvərɪ'ækt] vi reaccionar exageradamente

**override** [əʊvə'raɪd] (pt **overrode** [əʊvə'rəʊd], pp **overridden** [əʊvə'rɪdən]) vt (**a**) (objections, wishes, regulations) hacer caso omiso de (**b**) (take precedence over) anteponerse a; Tech (controls) anular

**overriding** [əʊvə'raɪdɪŋ] adj primordial

**overrule** [əʊvə'ru:l] vt (opinion) desautorizar; Law (decision) anular, invalidar; **she was overruled by her boss** su jefe la desautorizó

**overrun 1** n ['əʊvərʌn] Com (cost) o. costes mpl superiores a los previstos

**2** vt [əʊvə'rʌn] (pt **overran** [əʊvə'ræn], pp **overrun**) (**a**) (country) invadir; **the house was overrun with mice** los ratones habían invadido la casa (**b**) (allotted time) rebasar, excederse de; **to o. a budget** salirse del presupuesto

**3** vi (exceed allotted time) alargarse más de la cuenta, rebasar el tiempo previsto

**overseas 1** adj ['əʊvəsi:z] extranjero(a); (trade, debt) exterior; **o. possessions** territorios mpl de ultramar

**2** adv [əʊvə'si:z] fuera del país

**oversee** [əʊvə'si:] (pt **oversaw** [əʊvə'sɔ:], pp **overseen** [əʊvə'si:n]) vt supervisar

**overseer** ['əʊvəsɪə(r)] n Old-fashioned supervisor(ora) m,f

**oversensitive** [əʊvə'sensɪtɪv] adj susceptible

**oversexed** [əʊvə'sekst] adj libidinoso(a), lujurioso(a)

**overshadow** [əʊvə'ʃædəʊ] vt (person, success) eclipsar; (occasion) deslucir

**overshoe** ['əʊvəʃu:] n US chanclo m

**overshoot** [əʊvə'ʃu:t] (pt & pp **overshot** [əʊvə'ʃɒt]) vt pasar de largo, pasarse; Av **to o. the runway** salirse de la pista

**oversight** ['əʊvəsaɪt] n descuido m, omisión f; **through** or **by an o.** por descuido

**oversimplify** [əʊvə'sɪmplɪfaɪ] vt simplificar en exceso

**oversized** ['əʊvəsaɪzd] adj enorme

**oversleep** [əʊvə'sli:p] (pt & pp **overslept** [əʊvə'slept]) vi quedarse dormido(a)

**overspend** [əʊvə'spend] (pt & pp **overspent** [əʊvə'spent]) **1** vt **to o. one's budget** salirse del presupuesto

**2** vi gastar de más; **to o. by £100** gastar cien libras de más

**overspill** ['əʊvəspɪl] n (of population) exceso m de población

**overstaffing** [əʊvə'stɑ:fɪŋ] n exceso m de personal

**overstate** [əʊvə'steɪt] vt exagerar

**overstay** [əʊvə'steɪ] vt **to o. one's welcome** abusar de la hospitalidad, quedarse más tiempo del apropiado

**overstep** [əʊvə'step] vt traspasar, saltarse; Fig **to o. the mark** (exceed one's powers) pasarse de la raya

**oversubscribed** [əʊvəsəb'skraɪbd] *adj Fin* **the share offer was (five times) o.** la demanda superó (en cinco veces) la oferta de venta de acciones

**overt** [əʊ'vɜːt] *adj* claro(a), ostensible; **do you have to be so o. about it?** ¿tienes que mostrarlo tan a las claras?

**overtake** [əʊvə'teɪk] (*pt* **overtook** [əʊvə'tʊk], *pp* **overtaken** [əʊvə'teɪkən]) **1** *vt (car)* adelantar; *(competitor in race)* rebasar; **they had been overtaken by events** se habían visto superados por los acontecimientos
**2** *vi (in car)* adelantar

**overthrow 1** *n* ['əʊvəθrəʊ] derrocamiento *m*
**2** *vt* [əʊvə'θrəʊ] (*pt* **overthrew** [əʊvə'θruː], *pp* **overthrown** [əʊvə'θrəʊn]) derrocar

**overtime** ['əʊvətaɪm] *Ind* **1** *n* horas *fpl* extraordinarias *or* extras
**2** *adv* **to work o.** hacer horas extras; *Fig* **your imagination is working o.** se te está disparando la imaginación

**overtly** [əʊ'vɜːtlɪ] *adv* abiertamente, claramente

**overtone** ['əʊvətəʊn] *n (of sadness, bitterness)* tinte *m*, matiz *m*

**overture** ['əʊvətjʊə(r)] *n Mus* obertura *f*; *Fig* **to make overtures to sb** hacer proposiciones a *or* tener contactos con alguien

**overturn** [əʊvə'tɜːn] **1** *vt (table, boat)* volcar; *(government)* derribar; *(bill)* rechazar
**2** *vi* volcar

**overuse 1** *n* [əʊvə'juːs] uso *m* excesivo, abuso *m*
**2** *vt* [əʊvə'juːz] abusar de

**overvalue** [əʊvə'væljuː] *vt Com* sobrevalorar; *(person's abilities)* sobreestimar

**overview** ['əʊvəvjuː] *n* visión *f* general

**overweight** [əʊvə'weɪt] *adj* **to be o.** tener exceso de peso; **to be 10 kilos o.** tener 10 kilos de más

**overwhelm** [əʊvə'welm] *vt (enemy, opponent)* arrollar; **to be overwhelmed with joy** no caber en sí de alegría; **overwhelmed by grief/with work** abrumado(a) por la pena/el trabajo

**overwhelming** [əʊvə'welmɪŋ] *adj (need, desire)* acuciante; *(pressure)* abrumador(ora); *(defeat, majority)* aplastante

**overwhelmingly** [əʊvə'welmɪŋlɪ] *adv* **to vote o. in favour of sth** aprobar algo por mayoría aplastante

**overwork** [əʊvə'wɜːk] **1** *n* exceso *m* de trabajo
**2** *vt (person)* hacer trabajar en exceso
**3** *vi* trabajar en exceso

**overwrite** *Comptr* **1** *n* ['əʊvəraɪt] **o. mode** función *f* de "sobreescribir"
**2** *vt* [əʊvə'raɪt] sobreescribir

**overwrought** [əʊvə'rɔːt] *adj* muy alterado(a), muy nervioso(a); **to get o. (about sth)** alterarse mucho (por algo)

**ovulate** ['ɒvjʊleɪt] *vi Biol* ovular

**ovulation** [ɒvjʊ'leɪʃən] *n Biol* ovulación *f*

**ovum** ['əʊvəm] (*pl* **ova** ['əʊvə]) *n Biol* óvulo *m*

**ow** [aʊ] *exclam* ¡ay!

**owe** [əʊ] *vt* deber; **to o. sb sth, to o. sth to sb** deber algo a alguien; **to o. sb an apology** deber disculpas a alguien; **to o. it to oneself to do sth** deber hacer algo, tener merecido hacer algo; **I o. my life to you** te debo la vida

**owing** ['əʊɪŋ] *adj* **the money o. to me** el dinero que se me adeuda; **o. to** *(because of)* debido a

**owl** [aʊl] *n* **(short-eared) o.** búho *m*, *CAm, Méx* tecolote *m*; **(barn) o.** lechuza *f*

**own** [əʊn] **1** *adj* propio(a); **her o. money** su propio dinero; **I saw it with my o. eyes** lo vi con mis propios ojos; **I do my o. accounts** llevo mi propia contabilidad; **in one's o. right** por derecho propio; **o. goal** *(in football)* gol *m* en propia meta; *Fig* **to score an o. goal** tirar piedras contra el propio tejado
**2** *pron* **(a)** *(of possession)* **my o.** el/la mío(a); **it's my o.** es mío(a); **I have money of my o.** tengo dinero propio; **a child of his o.** un hijo suyo; **he made that expression/paper his o.** hizo suya esa expresión/suyo ese papel; **she has a copy of her o.** tiene un ejemplar para ella; **for reasons of his o.** por razones privadas
**(b)** *(idioms)* **to do sth on one's o.** *(without company)* hacer algo solo(a); *(on one's own initiative)* hacer algo por cuenta propia; **I am (all) on my o.** estoy solo; **you're on your o.!** *(I won't support you)* ¡conmigo no cuentes!; **he has come into his o. since being promoted** desde que lo ascendieron ha demostrado su verdadera valía *or* sus verdaderas posibilidades; **to get one's o. back (on sb)** vengarse (de alguien), tomarse la revancha (contra alguien); **he looks after his o.** *(friends, relatives)* cuida de los suyos; **she managed to hold her o.** consiguió defenderse
**3** *vt* **(a)** *(property)* poseer; **who owns this land?** ¿de quién es esta tierra?, ¿quién es el propietario de esta tierra?; **he behaves as if he owned the place** se comporta como si fuera el dueño
**(b)** *(admit)* Old-fashioned **to o. (that)…** reconocer que…
▸**own up** *vi (confess)* **to o. up (to sth)** confesar (algo)

**own-brand** ['əʊn'brænd] *adj Com* = de la marca del supermercado que vende el producto

**owner** ['əʊnə(r)] *n* dueño(a) *m,f*, propietario(a) *m,f*; **cars parked here at owners' risk**

*(sign)* aparcamiento permitido bajo responsabilidad del propietario

**owner-occupier** [ˈəʊnərˈɒkjʊpaɪə(r)] *n* propietario(a) *m,f* de la vivienda que habita

**ownership** [ˈəʊnəʃɪp] *n* propiedad *f*; **under new o.** *(sign)* nuevos propietarios; **to be in private/public o.** ser de propiedad privada/pública

**ox** [ɒks] (*pl* **oxen** [ˈɒksən]) *n* buey *m*

**Oxbridge** [ˈɒksbrɪdʒ] *n* = las universidades de Oxford y Cambridge

**oxide** [ˈɒksaɪd] *n Chem* óxido *m*

**oxidize** [ˈɒksɪdaɪz] *Chem* **1** *vt* oxidar
**2** *vi* oxidarse

**oxtail** [ˈɒksteɪl] *n* rabo *m* de buey

**oxyacetylene** [ˈɒksɪəˈsetɪliːn] *n Chem* oxiacetileno *m*; **o. torch** soplete *m* (oxiacetilénico)

**oxygen** [ˈɒksɪdʒən] *n Chem* oxígeno *m*; **o. bottle** *or* **cylinder** bombona *f* de oxígeno; **o. mask** mascarilla *f* de oxígeno

**oyster** [ˈɔɪstə(r)] *n* ostra *f*; *Fig* **the world is your o.** el mundo es tuyo, te vas a comer el mundo; **o. bed** criadero *m* de ostras

**oystercatcher** [ˈɔɪstəkætʃə(r)] *n (bird)* ostrero *m*

**Oz** [ɒz] *n Fam* Australia

**oz** (*abbr* **ounce(s)**) onza(s) *f(pl)*

**ozone** [ˈəʊzəʊn] *n Chem* ozono *m*; **o. layer** capa *f* de ozono

**ozone-friendly** [ˈəʊzəʊnˈfrendlɪ] *adj* no perjudicial para la capa de ozono

# P

**P, p** [pi:] *n (letter)* P, p *f*; *Fam* **to mind one's P's and Q's** comportarse (con educación)

**p** [pi:] *n Br (abbr* **penny***)* penique *m*; *(abbr* **pence***)* peniques *mpl*

**p & p** [pi:ən'pi:] *n Br (abbr* **postage and packing***)* gastos *mpl* de envío

**PA** [pi:'ei] *n* (a) *(abbr* **public address***)* megafonía *f*; **a message came over the PA (system)** dieron un mensaje por megafonía (b) *Com (abbr* **personal assistant***)* secretario(a) *m,f* personal

**pa** [pɑ:] *n US Fam (dad)* papá *m*

**p.a.** *(abbr* **per annum***)* anual, al año

**PAC** [pi:ei'si:] *n US Pol (abbr* **Political Action Committee***)* = grupo de presión estadounidense para el apoyo de causas políticas

**pace** [peis] **1** *n* (a) *(step)* paso *m*; *Fig* **to put sb through his paces** poner a alguien a prueba (b) *(speed)* ritmo *m*, paso *m*; **at a slow p.** lentamente; **at a fast p.** rápidamente; **to set the p.** marcar el paso, imponer el ritmo; **to force the p.** forzar el ritmo; **to keep pace with sb** seguirle el ritmo a alguien

**2** *vt (room, street)* caminar por; **to p. oneself** controlar el ritmo

**3** *vi* caminar; **to p. up and down** caminar de un lado a otro

**pacemaker** ['peismeikə(r)] *n* (a) *Sport* liebre *f* (b) *(for heart)* marcapasos *m inv*

**Pacific** [pə'sifik] *adj* **the P. (Ocean)** el (océano) Pacífico; **the P. Rim** = los países que bordean el Pacífico, sobre todo los asiáticos; *US* **P. Standard Time** = hora oficial de la costa del Pacífico en Estados Unidos

**pacifier** ['pæsifaiə(r)] *n US (baby's dummy)* chupete *m*

**pacifism** ['pæsifizəm] *n* pacifismo *m*

**pacifist** ['pæsifist] *n & adj* pacifista *mf*

**pacify** ['pæsifai] *vt (country)* pacificar; *(person)* apaciguar

**pack** [pæk] **1** *n* (a) *(rucksack)* mochila *f*; **p. animal** bestia *f* de carga

(b) *(small box) (of cigarettes)* paquete *m*; *(of playing cards)* baraja *f*

(c) *(group) (of thieves, photographers)* pandilla *f*; *(of runners, cyclists)* pelotón *m*; *(in rugby)* delanteros *mpl*; *(of wolves)* manada *f*; **a p. of lies** una

sarta de mentiras; **p. ice** banco *m* de hielo

**2** *vt* (a) *(put into box)* empaquetar; *(items for sale)* envasar; *(in cotton wool, newspaper)* envolver; **did you pack my toothbrush?** ¿metiste mi cepillo de dientes (en la maleta)?

(b) *(cram) (earth into hole)* meter; *(passengers into bus, train)* apiñar; **we were packed in like sardines** estábamos como sardinas en lata

(c) *(fill) (hole, box)* llenar (**with** de); **to p. one's suitcase** hacer la maleta; *Fig* **to p. one's bags** *(leave)* hacer las maletas

(d) **to p. a punch** *(of fighter, drink)* pegar duro

**3** *vi* (a) *(prepare luggage)* hacer el equipaje; *Fam Fig* **to send sb packing** *(send away)* mandar a alguien a paseo

(b) *(cram)* **to p. into a room** apiñarse en una habitación

▶**pack in** *Fam* **1** *vt (job, course)* dejar; **p. it in!** *(stop complaining)* ¡deja de protestar *or* de dar la murga!

**2** *vi (of car, computer)* escacharrarse

▶**pack off** *vt sep Fam (send)* mandar

▶**pack up 1** *vt sep (belongings)* recoger

**2** *vi (before moving house)* embalar, preparar la mudanza; *(finish work)* dejarlo, parar de trabajar

**package** ['pækidʒ] **1** *n (parcel)* paquete *m*; *(pay deal, contract)* paquete *m*; *Com* **p. deal** acuerdo *m* global; **p. holiday** paquete *m* turístico, viaje *m* organizado

**2** *vt (goods)* envasar; *Fig* **to p. sb** *(pop star, politician)* vender a alguien

**packaging** ['pækidʒiŋ] *n (for transport, freight)* embalaje *m*; *(of product)* envasado *m*

**packed** ['pækt] *adj* (a) *(crowded)* abarrotado(a) (b) **p. lunch** comida *f* preparada de casa *(para excursión, trabajo, colegio)*

**packer** ['pækə(r)] *n* empaquetador(ora) *m,f*, embalador(ora) *m,f*

**packet** ['pækit] *n* (a) *(of tea, cigarettes)* paquete *m*; *(bag)* bolsa *f*; **p. soup** sopa *f* de sobre (b) *Fam (lot of money)* **to make** *or* **earn a p.** ganar una millonada; **that'll cost a p.** costará un riñón

**packhorse** ['pækhɔ:s] *n* caballo *m* de carga

**packing** ['pækiŋ] *n* (a) *(packing material)* embalaje *m*; **p. case** cajón *m* (b) *(for holiday)* **to do one's p.** hacer el equipaje

**pact** [pækt] *n* pacto *m*; **to make a p. with sb** hacer un pacto con alguien

**pad** [pæd] **1** *n* (**a**) *(for protection, of dog's feet)* almohadilla *f*; *(of cotton wool)* tampón *m*; *(for helicopters)* plataforma *f*; **(writing) pad** bloc *m* (**b**) *very Fam (home)* queli *f*, choza *f*

**2** *vt* *(pt & pp* **padded***) (stuff)* acolchar *or* almohadillar **(with** con)

**3** *vi* **to p. about** caminar con suavidad

▶**pad out** *vt sep (speech, essay)* rellenar

**padded** ['pædɪd] *adj (door, wall)* acolchado(a), almohadillado(a); *(shoulders of jacket)* con hombreras; **p. cell** celda *f* acolchada

**padding** ['pædɪŋ] *n (material)* relleno *m*; *(of cotton)* guata *f*; *Fig (in speech, essay)* paja *f*, relleno *m*

**paddle** ['pædəl] **1** *n* (**a**) *(for canoe)* canalete *m*, remo *m*; *(of paddle boat)* pala *f*; **p. boat** barco *m* (de vapor) de ruedas (**b**) *(walk in water)* **to go for a p.** dar un paseo por el agua *or* la orilla

**2** *vt (canoe)* remar en; *Fig* **to p. one's own canoe** arreglárselas solo(a)

**3** *vi* (**a**) *(in canoe)* remar; *(of duck)* nadar (**b**) *(walk in water)* dar un paseo por el agua *or* la orilla

**paddling pool** ['pædlɪŋ'puːl] *n (inflatable)* piscina *f* hinchable; *(in park)* piscina *f* para niños

**paddock** ['pædək] *n (field)* cercado *m*, potrero *m*

**Paddy** ['pædɪ] *n Fam* irlandés *m*

**paddy** ['pædɪ] *n* **p. (field)** arrozal *m*

**padlock** ['pædlɒk] **1** *n* candado *m*

**2** *vt* cerrar con candado

**padre** ['pɑːdreɪ] *n Fam (military chaplain)* capellán *m*

**paediatric,** *US* **pediatric** [piːdɪˈætrɪk] *adj Med* pediátrico(a)

**paediatrician,** *US* **pediatrician** [piːdɪəˈtrɪʃən] *n Med* pediatra *mf*

**paediatrics,** *US* **pediatrics** [piːdɪˈætrɪks] *n Med* pediatría *f*

**paedophile,** *US* **pedophile** ['piːdəʊfaɪl] *n* pedófilo(a) *m,f*

**paedophilia,** *US* **pedophilia** [piːdəˈfɪlɪə] *n* pederastia *f*

**pagan** ['peɪɡən] *n & adj* pagano(a) *m,f*

**paganism** ['peɪɡənɪzəm] *n* paganismo *m*

**page¹** [peɪdʒ] *n* página *f*; **on p. 6** en la página 6; *Fig* **a glorious p. in our history** una página gloriosa de nuestra historia

**page²** [peɪdʒ] **1** *n (servant, at wedding)* paje *m*

**2** *vt (call) (by loudspeaker)* avisar por megafonía; *(by electronic device)* llamar por el busca *or* buscapersonas

**pageant** ['pædʒənt] *n (procession)* desfile *m*, procesión *f*; *(of historical events)* representación *f* de escenas históricas

**pageantry** ['pædʒəntrɪ] *n* pompa *f*, esplendor *m*

**pageboy** ['peɪdʒbɔɪ] *n (servant, at wedding)* paje *m*; **p. (haircut)** *(hairstyle)* corte *m* estilo paje

**pager** ['peɪdʒə(r)] *n* busca *m*, buscapersonas *m inv*

**pagination** [pædʒɪˈneɪʃən] *n Typ* paginación *f*

**pagoda** [pəˈɡəʊdə] *n* pagoda *f*

**paid** [peɪd] **1** *adj* (**a**) *(person, work)* remunerado(a); **p. holidays** vacaciones *fpl* pagadas (**b**) **to put p. to sb's chances/hopes** truncar las posibilidades/esperanzas de alguien

**2** *pt & pp* of **pay**

**paid-up** ['peɪdʌp] *adj (member)* con las cuentas al día

**pail** [peɪl] *n (bucket)* cubo *m*

**pain** [peɪn] **1** *n* (**a**) *(physical)* dolor *m*; *(mental)* sufrimiento *m*, pena *f*; **to cause sb p.** *(physical)* dolerle a alguien; *(mental)* afligir *or* hacer sufrir a alguien; **to be in p.** estar sufriendo; **I have a p. in my leg** me duele una pierna (**b**) *(trouble)* **to take pains to do sth, to be at great pains to do sth** tomarse muchas molestias para hacer algo; **for my pains** por mi esfuerzo (**c**) *Formal* **on p. of death** so pena de muerte (**d**) *(idioms) Fam* **he's a p. (in the neck)** es un pelmazo; *very Fam* **it's a p. in the arse** es un coñazo; *Fam* **cooking can be a p.** a veces resulta una lata cocinar

**2** *vt* afligir, hacer sufrir

**pained** [peɪnd] *adj (look, expression)* afligido(a), de pena

**painful** ['peɪnfʊl] *adj (physically, mentally)* doloroso(a); *(part of body)* dolorido(a); **is it p. here?** ¿te duele aquí?; **it's p. to watch them** resulta penoso mirarlos

**painfully** ['peɪnfʊlɪ] *adv (walk, move)* con dolor; *Fig (extremely)* tremendamente; **she fell p.** tuvo una caída dolorosa

**painkiller** ['peɪnkɪlə(r)] *n* analgésico *m*

**painless** ['peɪnlɪs] *adj (not painful)* indoloro(a); *Fig (easy)* fácil, muy llevadero(a)

**painstaking** ['peɪnzteɪkɪŋ] *adj (person, research)* meticuloso(a), concienzudo(a); *(care)* esmerado(a)

**paint** [peɪnt] **1** *n* pintura *f*; **wet p.** *(sign)* recién pintado; **p. gun** pistola *f (para pintar)*; **p. remover** decapante *m*

**2** *vt (picture, person, room)* pintar; *Fam* **to p. one's face** *(put on make-up)* pintarse; **to p. one's nails** pintarse las uñas; *Fig* **to p. a favourable picture (of)** dar una visión favorable (de); *Fig* **to p. the town red** irse de juerga

**3** *vi* pintar

**paintbox** ['peɪntbɒks] *n* caja *f* de acuarelas

**paintbrush** ['peɪntbrʌʃ] *n (of artist)* pincel *m*; *(of decorator)* brocha *f*

**painter** ['peɪntə(r)] n (artist) pintor(ora) m,f; (decorator) pintor(ora) m,f (de brocha gorda)

**painting** ['peɪntɪŋ] n (picture) cuadro m, pintura f; (activity) pintura f; **p. and decorating** pintura y decoración

**paintwork** ['peɪntwɜːk] n (of car, room) pintura f

**pair** [peə(r)] **1** n (of shoes, gloves) par m; (of people, cards) pareja f; **a p. of glasses** unas gafas; **a p. of scissors** unas tijeras; **a p. of trousers** unos pantalones

**2** vt (people, animals) emparejar (**with** con)

►**pair off 1** vt sep (people) emparejar

**2** vi (of people) emparejarse

►**pair up** vi hacer pareja, emparejarse

**pajamas** US = **pyjamas**

**Pakistan** [pɑːkɪˈstɑːn] n Paquistán

**Pakistani** [pɑːkɪˈstɑːnɪ] n & adj paquistaní mf

**PAL** [pæl] n TV (abbr **phase alternation line**) (sistema m) PAL m

**pal** [pæl] n Fam amiguete(a) m,f, colega mf; **look here, p.!** ¡mira, tío!

**palace** ['pælɪs] n palacio m

**palatable** ['pælətəbəl] adj (food) apetitoso(a); Fig (suggestion) aceptable

**palate** ['pælɪt] n (in mouth) paladar m

**palatial** [pəˈleɪʃəl] adj suntuoso(a), señorial

**palaver** [pəˈlɑːvə(r)] n Fam (fuss) jaleo m, follón m; **what a p.!** ¡vaya jaleo!

**pale¹** [peɪl] **1** adj (skin) pálido(a); (colour) claro(a); **to turn p. (with fright)** palidecer (de miedo); Fig **a p. imitation of sth** un pálido remedo de algo; Br **p. ale** = cerveza del tipo "bitter" pero más rubia

**2** vi (of person) palidecer; **to p. into insignificance** reducirse hasta la insignificancia

**pale²** n (of fence) estaca f; Fig **to be/go beyond the p.** pasarse de la raya

**paleness** ['peɪlnɪs] n palidez f

**Palestine** ['pælɪstaɪn] n Palestina

**Palestinian** [pælɪˈstɪnɪən] n & adj palestino(a) m,f

**palette** ['pælɪt] n Art paleta f; **p. knife** espátula f

**paling** ['peɪlɪŋ] n (for fence) cerca f, estacada f

**palisade** [pælɪˈseɪd] n (fence) empalizada f

**pall¹** [pɔːl] n (of smoke) cortina f, manto m

**pall²** vi (become uninteresting) decaer

**pallbearer** ['pɔːlbeərə(r)] n portador(ora) m,f del féretro

**pallet¹** ['pælɪt] n (bed) jergón m

**pallet²** n Ind (wooden platform) palet m, palé m

**palliative** ['pælɪətɪv] n paliativo m

**pallid** ['pælɪd] adj pálido(a)

**pallor** ['pælə(r)] n lividez f

**pally** ['pælɪ] adj Fam **to be p. with sb** comportarse amistosamente con alguien

**palm¹** [pɑːm] n **p. (tree)** palmera f; **p. (leaf)** palma f; **P. Sunday** Domingo m de Ramos

**palm²** n (of hand) palma f; Fig **to have sb in the p. of one's hand** tener a alguien en el bolsillo

►**palm off** vt sep **to p. sth off onto sb** endilgar algo a alguien

**palmistry** ['pɑːmɪstrɪ] n quiromancia f

**palomino** [pæləˈmiːnəʊ] n (horse) = caballo alazán de crin y cola blancas

**palpable** ['pælpəbəl] adj palpable

**palpate** ['pælpeɪt] vt Med explorar

**palpitate** ['pælpɪteɪt] vi (of heart) palpitar; **to p. with fear/excitement** estar estremecido(a) de miedo/emoción

**palpitations** [pælpɪˈteɪʃənz] npl palpitaciones fpl

**paltry** ['pɔːltrɪ] adj miserable

**pamper** ['pæmpə(r)] vt (person) mimar, consentir; **to p. oneself** darse lujos

**pamphlet** ['pæmflɪt] n (informative) folleto m; (controversial) panfleto m

**pan¹** [pæn] **1** n (for cooking) cacerola f, cazuela f; (frying pan) sartén f; (of scales) platillo m; (of lavatory) taza f; Fam Fig **to go down the p.** echarse a perder, irse al garete

**2** vi (pt & pp **panned**) **to p. for gold** extraer oro

**pan²** (pt & pp **panned**) vt Fam (criticize) vapulear, poner por los suelos

►**pan out** vi Fam (turn out) salir; **let's see how things p. out** a ver cómo salen las cosas

**panacea** [pænəˈsɪə] n panacea f

**panache** [pəˈnæʃ] n gracia f, garbo m

**Pan-African** [pænˈæfrɪkən] adj panafricano(a)

**Panama** ['pænəmɑː] n Panamá f; **the P. Canal** el canal de Panamá; **P. (hat)** (sombrero m) panamá m

**Panamanian** [pænəˈmeɪnɪən] n & adj panameño(a) m,f

**Pan-American** [pænəˈmerɪkən] adj panamericano(a)

**pancake** ['pænkeɪk] n crepe f, torta f; **P. Day** or **Tuesday** Martes m inv de Carnaval

**pancreas** ['pæŋkrɪəs] n Anat páncreas m inv

**panda** ['pændə] n (oso m) panda m; Br **p. car** coche m patrulla

**pandemonium** [pændɪˈməʊnɪəm] n **there was p., p. broke out** se armó un auténtico pandemónium; **to cause p.** sembrar el caos

**pander** ['pændə(r)] vi **to p. to sb** complacer a alguien; **to p. to sb's views** someterse a la opinión de alguien

**pane** [peɪn] n **p. (of glass)** hoja f de vidrio or cristal

**panel** ['pænəl] n (a) (on wall, of door) panel m; (of switches, lights) panel m, tablero m; **p. beater** (in car industry) chapista mf (b) (at interview, of experts) panel m, equipo m; **p. discussion** debate m, mesa f redonda

**panelling**, US **paneling** ['pænəlɪŋ] n (on wall) paneles mpl

**panellist**, US **panelist** ['pænəlɪst] n (on radio, TV programme) participante mf (en un debate)

**pang** [pæŋ] n (of hunger, jealousy) punzada f

**panic** ['pænɪk] 1 n pánico m; **in a p.** aterrorizado(a); **to get into a p. (over sth)** aterrorizarse (por algo); **the crowd was thrown into a p.** cundió el pánico entre la multitud; **p. attack** ataque m de pánico; **p. button** botón m de alarma; Fin **p. buying/selling** compra f/ venta f provocada por el pánico; Fam **it was p. stations** cundió el pánico

2 vt (pt & pp **panicked**) aterrorizar; **to p. sb into doing sth** aterrorizar a alguien para que haga algo

3 vi aterrorizarse; **don't p.!** ¡que no cunda el pánico!

**panicky** ['pænɪkɪ] adj Fam (reaction) de pánico; **she got p.** le entró el pánico

**panic-stricken** ['pænɪkstrɪkən] adj aterrorizado(a); **to be p.** estar aterrorizado(a)

**pannier** ['pænɪə(r)] n (on animal, bicycle) alforja f

**panoply** ['pænəplɪ] n boato m

**panorama** [pænə'rɑːmə] n panorama m

**panoramic** [pænə'ræmɪk] adj panorámico(a)

**panpipes** ['pænpaɪps] npl Mus siringa f, flauta f de Pan

**pansy** ['pænzɪ] n (a) (flower) pensamiento m (b) Fam (effeminate man) mariposón m, mariquita m

**pant** [pænt] vi jadear; **to p. for breath** resollar (intentando recobrar el aliento)

**panther** ['pænθə(r)] n pantera f

**panties** ['pæntɪz] npl braga f, bragas fpl

**pantomime** ['pæntəmaɪm] n Br Th = obra de teatro musical para niños basada en un cuento de hadas y representada en Navidad

**pantry** ['pæntrɪ] n despensa f

**pants** [pænts] npl (a) Br (men's underwear) calzoncillos mpl; (women's underwear) bragas fpl (b) US (trousers) pantalones mpl; Fam **to scare the p. off sb** hacer que a alguien le entre el canguelo

**pantyhose, pantihose** ['pæntɪhəʊz] n US medias fpl, pantis mpl

**pap** [pæp] n Fam Pej (nonsense) bobadas fpl

**papa** [pə'pɑː] n Old-fashioned papá m

**papacy** ['peɪpəsɪ] n papado m

**papal** ['peɪpəl] adj papal

**paper** ['peɪpə(r)] 1 n (a) (material) papel m; **a piece of p.** un papel; Fig **on p.** (in theory) sobre el papel; **p. aeroplane** avión m de papel; **p. bag** bolsa f de papel; **p. cup** vaso m de papel; Comptr **p. feed** sistema m de alimentación de papel; **p. mill** fábrica f de papel, papelera f; **p. money** papel m moneda; **p. towel** toallita f de papel; Comptr **p. tray** bandeja f del papel

(b) **papers** (documents) papeles mpl, documentación f

(c) (examination) examen m

(d) (scholarly study, report) estudio m, trabajo m; **to read** or **give a p.** leer or presentar una ponencia

(e) (newspaper) periódico m; **p. boy/girl** repartidor(ora) m,f de periódicos; **to do a p. round** hacer el reparto de periódicos a domicilio; **p. shop** ≃ quiosco m de periódicos

2 vt (wall, room) empapelar

▸**paper over** vt sep Fig **to p. over the cracks** poner parches

**paperback** ['peɪpəbæk] n libro m or edición f en rústica

**paperclip** ['peɪpəklɪp] n clip m

**paperknife** ['peɪpənaɪf] n abrecartas m inv

**paperweight** ['peɪpəweɪt] n pisapapeles m inv

**paperwork** ['peɪpəwɜːk] n papeleo m

**papery** ['peɪpərɪ] adj apergaminado(a)

**papier-mâché** ['pæpjeɪ'mæʃeɪ] n cartón m piedra

**paprika** ['pæprɪkə] n pimentón m, paprika f

**Papuan** ['pæpjʊən] n & adj papú mf, papúa mf

**Papua New Guinea** ['pæpjʊə'njuː'gɪnɪ] n Papúa Nueva Guinea

**papyrus** [pə'paɪrəs] n papiro m

**par** [pɑː(r)] n (a) (equality) **to be on a p. with** estar al mismo nivel que (b) (in golf) par m; **a p.-three (hole)** un (hoyo de) par tres; Fig **that's about p. for the course** es lo que cabe esperar (c) Fin **above p.** sobre la par; **below p.** bajo par; Fig **to feel below p.** no encontrarse muy allá

**parable** ['pærəbəl] n parábola f

**parabola** [pə'ræbələ] n parábola f

**parabolic** [pærə'bɒlɪk] adj parabólico(a)

**paracetamol** [pærə'siːtəmɒl] n paracetamol m

**parachute** ['pærəʃuːt] 1 n paracaídas m inv; **p. jump** salto m en paracaídas

2 vt (person, supplies) lanzar en paracaídas

3 vi saltar en paracaídas

**parachuting** ['pærəʃuːtɪŋ] n paracaidismo m; **to go p.** hacer paracaidismo

**parachutist** ['pærəʃuːtɪst] n paracaidista mf

**parade** [pə'reɪd] 1 n (procession) desfile m; **on p.** (of troops) pasando revista; **a p. of shops** una hilera de tiendas; **p. ground** plaza f de armas

**2** vt (troops) pasar revista a; (riches, knowledge) ostentar

**3** vi (of troops) desfilar; **to p. about** or **around** desfilar

**paradigm** ['pærədaɪm] n paradigma m

**paradise** ['pærədaɪs] n paraíso m; **bird of p.** ave f del Paraíso

**paradox** ['pærədɒks] n paradoja f

**paradoxical** [pærə'dɒksɪkəl] adj paradójico(a)

**paraffin** ['pærəfɪn] n queroseno m; **p. heater** estufa f de petróleo; **p. lamp** lámpara f de queroseno; **p. wax** parafina f

**paragon** ['pærəgɒn] n dechado m; **a p. of virtue** un dechado de virtudes

**paragraph** ['pærəgræf] n párrafo m

**Paraguay** ['pærəgwaɪ] n Paraguay

**Paraguayan** [pærə'gwaɪən] n & adj paraguayo(a) m,f

**parakeet** ['pærəki:t] n periquito m

**parallel** ['pærəlel] **1** n Math (línea f) paralela f; Geog paralelo m; Fig (analogy) paralelismo m; **to draw a p. between two things** establecer un paralelismo entre dos cosas; **without p.** sin parangón

**2** adj paralelo(a); **to be** or **run p. to sth** ser or ir paralelo a algo; **p. bars** barras fpl paralelas; **p. circuits** circuitos mpl en paralelo; **p. lines** líneas fpl paralelas; Comptr **p. processing** procesado m en paralelo

**3** vt (be similar to) asemejarse a

**parallelogram** [pærə'leləgræm] n paralelogramo m

**paralyse**, US **paralyze** ['pærəlaɪz] vt paralizar; **to be paralysed by fear** estar paralizado(a) por el miedo

**paralysis** [pə'ræləsɪs] n parálisis f inv

**paralytic** [pærə'lɪtɪk] adj Med paralítico(a); Fam **to be p.** (very drunk) estar como una cuba

**paralyze** US = **paralyse**

**paramedic** [pærə'medɪk] n auxiliar mf sanitario(a)

**parameter** [pə'ræmɪtə(r)] n parámetro m

**paramilitary** [pærə'mɪlɪtrɪ] adj paramilitar

**paramount** ['pærəmaʊnt] adj primordial, vital; **it is of p. importance** es de capital or suma importancia

**paranoia** [pærə'nɔɪə] n paranoia f

**paranoid** ['pærənɔɪd] adj paranoico(a) (**about** por or con)

**paranormal** [pærə'nɔ:məl] **1** n **the p.** lo paranormal

**2** adj paranormal

**parapet** ['pærəpet] n parapeto m

**paraphernalia** [pærəfə'neɪlɪə] npl parafernalia f

**paraphrase** ['pærəfreɪz] **1** n paráfrasis f inv

**2** vt parafrasear

**paraplegic** [pærə'pli:dʒɪk] n & adj parapléjico(a) m,f

**parasite** ['pærəsaɪt] n also Fig parásito m

**parasitic** [pærə'sɪtɪk] adj also Fig parásito(a)

**parasol** ['pærəsɒl] n sombrilla f

**paratrooper** ['pærətru:pə(r)] n (soldado m) paracaidista m

**parboil** ['pɑ:bɔɪl] vt cocer a medias, sancochar

**parcel** ['pɑ:səl] n (package) paquete m; (of land) parcela f; **p. bomb** paquete m bomba; **p. post** (servicio m de) paquete m postal

▸**parcel out** vt sep (land) parcelar; (money) dividir en lotes

▸**parcel up** vt sep (wrap up) embalar, empaquetar

**parchment** ['pɑ:tʃmənt] n pergamino m; **p. paper** papel m pergamino

**pardon** ['pɑ:dən] **1** n (forgiveness) perdón m; Law indulto m; (**I beg your) p.?** (what did you say?) ¿cómo dice?; **I beg your p.!** (in apology) ¡discúlpeme!

**2** vt (action, person) perdonar, excusar; Law indultar; **p. me?** (what did you say?) ¿cómo dice?; **p. me!** (in apology) ¡discúlpeme!

**pardonable** ['pɑ:dənəbəl] adj (mistake, behaviour) perdonable, excusable

**pare** [peə(r)] vt (vegetable) pelar; (nails) cortar; (expenses) recortar

▸**pare down** vt sep (expenses) recortar

**parent** ['peərənt] n (father) padre m; (mother) madre f; **parents** padres mpl; **p. company** empresa f matriz; **p.-teacher association** = asociación de padres de alumnos y profesores, ≃ APA

**parentage** ['peərəntɪdʒ] n origen m, familia f

**parental** [pə'rentəl] adj de los padres

**parenthesis** [pə'renθəsɪs] (pl **parentheses** [pə'renθəsi:z]) n paréntesis m inv; **in parentheses** entre paréntesis

**parenthood** ['peərənthʊd] n (fatherhood) paternidad f; (motherhood) maternidad f; **the joys of p.** las satisfacciones que trae tener hijos

**parenting** ['peərəntɪŋ] n **p. skills** capacidad f para cuidar de los hijos

**pariah** [pə'raɪə] n paria mf

**Paris** ['pærɪs] n París

**parish** ['pærɪʃ] n parroquia f, feligresía f; **p. church** parroquia, iglesia f parroquial; **p. council** concejo m

**parishioner** [pə'rɪʃənə(r)] n feligrés(esa) m,f, parroquiano(a) m,f

**Parisian** [pə'rɪzɪən] n & adj parisino(a) m,f

**parity** ['pærɪtɪ] n paridad f; **to achieve p.** (of pay, output) equipararse

**park** [pɑːk] **1** n parque m; **p. keeper** guarda m, guardesa f

**2** vt aparcar, estacionar; Fam **to p. oneself in front of the TV** apoltronarse enfrente de la televisión

**3** vi aparcar, estacionar, Am estacionarse

**parka** ['pɑːkə] n parka f

**parking** ['pɑːkɪŋ] n aparcamiento m, estacionamiento m; **no p.** (sign) prohibido aparcar, estacionamiento prohibido; **p. attendant** vigilante mf de aparcamiento; **p. bay** plaza f de aparcamiento; **p. lights** (on car) luces fpl de estacionamiento; US **p. lot** aparcamiento m, Am playa f de estacionamiento; **p. meter** parquímetro m; **p. space** aparcamiento m, sitio m or hueco m para aparcar; **p. ticket** multa f de estacionamiento

**Parkinson's disease** ['pɑːkɪnsənzdɪ'ziːz] n (síndrome m de) Parkinson m

**parkland** ['pɑːklænd] n zonas fpl verdes, parque m

**parkway** ['pɑːkweɪ] n US bulevar m, avenida f

**parlance** ['pɑːləns] n **in scientific/political p.** en la jerga científica/política; **in common p.** en el habla común

**parley** [pɑːlɪ] vi parlamentar (**with** con)

**parliament** ['pɑːləmənt] n **(a)** (law-making body) parlamento m **(b)** (period between elections) legislatura f

**parliamentarian** [pɑːləmen'teərɪən] n parlamentario(a) m,f

**parliamentary** [pɑːlə'mentərɪ] adj parlamentario(a); **P. privilege** inmunidad f parlamentaria

**parlour,** US **parlor** ['pɑːlə(r)] n (in house) salón m; **beauty p.** salón m de belleza

**Parmesan** [pɑːmɪ'zæn] n & **P. (cheese)** queso m parmesano

**parochial** [pə'rəʊkɪəl] adj Rel parroquial; Fig Pej (narrow-minded) provinciano(a), corto(a) de miras

**parody** ['pærədɪ] **1** n parodia f (**of** de)

**2** vt parodiar

**parole** [pə'rəʊl] **1** n Law libertad f bajo palabra; **to be (out) on p.** estar en libertad bajo palabra; **p. officer** = asistente social que supervisa a un preso en libertad bajo palabra y ante quien se presenta periódicamente

**2** vt Law poner en libertad bajo palabra

**paroxysm** ['pærəksɪzəm] n (of anger, guilt, jealousy) arrebato m, ataque m; **to be in paroxysms of laughter** tener un ataque de risa

**parquet** ['pɑːkeɪ] n **p. (floor)** (suelo m de) parqué m

**parrot** ['pærət] **1** n loro m

**2** vt repetir como un loro

**parrot-fashion** ['pærətfæʃən] adv (repeat, learn) como un loro

**parry** ['pærɪ] vt (blow) parar, desviar; (question) esquivar, eludir

**parsimonious** [pɑːsɪ'məʊnɪəs] adj (mean) tacaño(a), mísero(a)

**parsley** ['pɑːslɪ] n perejil m

**parsnip** ['pɑːsnɪp] n pastinaca f, chirivía f

**parson** ['pɑːsən] n párroco m

**parsonage** ['pɑːsənɪdʒ] n casa f parroquial

**part** [pɑːt] **1** n **(a)** (portion, element) parte f; (of machine) pieza f; **the parts of the body** las partes del cuerpo; **parts of speech** categorías fpl gramaticales; **(spare) parts** recambios mpl, piezas fpl de recambio, Am refacciones fpl; **p. two** (of TV, radio series) segunda parte; **in that p. of the world** en esa parte del mundo; **in these parts** por aquí; **good in parts** bueno(a) a ratos; **the worst p. was when she started laughing** lo peor fue cuando empezó a reírse; **the difficult p. is remembering** lo difícil es acordarse; **for the best** or **greater p. of five years** durante casi cinco años; **the greater p. of the population** la mayor parte de la población; **to be** or **form p. of sth** ser or formar parte de algo; **it's all p. of growing up** forma parte del proceso de crecimiento; **it is p. and parcel of...** es parte integrante de...; **in p.** en parte, parcialmente; **for the most p.** en su mayor parte; **in p. exchange** como parte del pago; **p. owner** copropietario(a) m,f

**(b)** (role) papel m; Th **to play a p.** interpretar un papel; **to take p. (in sth)** participar or tomar parte (en algo); **to have** or **play a large p. in sth** tener un papel importante en algo; **I want no p. of** or **in it** no quiero tener nada que ver con eso

**(c)** (side) **to take sb's p.** tomar partido por or ponerse de parte de alguien; **on the p. of...** por parte de...; **for my p.** por mi parte

**2** adv **she's p. Spanish** es medio española; **it's p. silk, p. cotton** es de seda y algodón

**3** vt (fighters, lovers) separar; (curtains) abrir, descorrer; **to p. one's hair** hacerse raya (en el pelo); **to p. company** separarse

**4** vi (separate) separarse; **to p. (as) friends** quedar como amigos; **to p. with sth** desprenderse de algo

**partake** [pɑː'teɪk] (pt **partook** [pɑː'tʊk], pp **partaken** [pɑː'teɪkən]) vi Formal **(a)** (drink) **to p. of** tomar, ingerir **(b)** (have quality) **to p. of** participar de, tener parte de

**partial** ['pɑːʃəl] adj **(a)** (incomplete, biased) parcial **(b)** (fond) **she is p. to wine** le gusta el vino

**partially** ['pɑːʃəlɪ] adv (in part, with bias) parcialmente

**participant** [pɑː'tɪsɪpənt] n & adj participante mf

**participate** [pɑː'tɪsɪpeɪt] vi participar (**in** en)

**participation** [pɑːtɪsɪˈpeɪʃən] *n* participación *f* (**in** en)

**participle** [ˈpɑːtɪsɪpəl] *n Gram* participio *m*; **past p.** participio pasado *or* pasivo; **present p.** participio de presente *or* activo

**particle** [ˈpɑːtɪkəl] *n* partícula *f*

**particular** [pəˈtɪkjʊlə(r)] **1** *n* detalle *m*, pormenor *m*; **in p.** *(specifically)* en particular; **I didn't notice anything in p.** no noté nada de particular; **alike in every p.** iguales en todos los aspectos; **to go into particulars** entrar en detalles; **to take down sb's particulars** tomar los datos de alguien

**2** *adj* **(a)** *(specific)* particular, específico(a); **which p. person did you have in mind?** ¿en quién pensabas en concreto?; **for no p. reason** por ninguna razón en particular *or* en especial **(b)** *(special)* particular, especial; **he is a p. friend of mine** es un amigo mío muy querido; **to take p. care over sth** tener especial cuidado con algo **(c)** *(exacting)* exigente; **to be p. about sth** ser exigente con algo; **I'm not p.** me da lo mismo

**particularly** [pəˈtɪkjʊləlɪ] *adv (especially)* particularmente, especialmente; **not p.** no especialmente; **it's cold here, p. at night** aquí hace frío, sobre todo por la noche

**parting** [ˈpɑːtɪŋ] *n* **(a)** *(leave-taking)* despedida *f*, partida *f*; **they had come to the p. of the ways** había llegado la hora de despedirse *or* el momento de la despedida; **p. shot** = comentario hiriente a modo de despedida; **p. words** palabras *fpl* de despedida **(b)** *(in hair)* raya *f*

**partisan** [pɑːtɪˈzæn] **1** *n (during 2nd World War)* partisano(a) *m,f; (supporter)* partidario(a) *m,f* (**of** de)

**2** *adj (biased)* parcial

**partition** [pɑːˈtɪʃən] **1** *n (in room)* tabique *m*

**2** *vt (country)* dividir

▸**partition off** *vt sep (room)* dividir con un tabique *or* con tabiques

**partly** [ˈpɑːtlɪ] *adv* en parte, parcialmente

**partner** [ˈpɑːtnə(r)] **1** *n (in company)* socio(a) *m,f; (in tennis)* compañero(a) *m,f; (in dancing)* pareja *f; (lover)* compañero(a) *m,f*, pareja *f*; **p. in crime** cómplice *mf*

**2** *vt (in games, in dancing)* hacer pareja con

**partnership** [ˈpɑːtnəʃɪp] *n* asociación *f*, sociedad *f*; **to enter** *or* **go into p. (with sb)** formar sociedad *or* asociarse (con alguien)

**partridge** [ˈpɑːtrɪdʒ] *n* perdiz *f*

**part-time** [pɑːtˈtaɪm] *adj & adv* a tiempo parcial

**part-timer** [pɑːtˈtaɪmə(r)] *n* trabajador(ora) *m,f* a tiempo parcial

**partway** [ˈpɑːtweɪ] *adv* **I'm p. through it** *(of book, task)* voy por la mitad; **this will go p.**

towards covering the costs esto sufragará parte de los gastos

**party** [ˈpɑːtɪ] **1** *n* **(a)** *(political)* partido *m*; **a p. member, a member of the p.** un miembro del partido; **to follow** *or* **toe the p. line** seguir la línea del partido; **p. political broadcast** espacio *m* televisivo/radiofónico asignado a un partido

**(b)** *(celebration)* fiesta *f*; **to have** *or* **throw a p.** dar *or* celebrar una fiesta; *Fig* **the p.'s over** se acabó la fiesta; *Fam* **p. animal** fiestero(a) *m,f*; **p. piece** numerito *m* habitual *(para entretener a la gente)*

**(c)** *(group)* grupo *m*; *Tel* **p. line** línea *f* compartida, party-line *f*; **p. wall** *(in house)* pared *f* medianera

**(d)** *Law (participant)* parte *f*; **I would never be p. to such a thing** nunca tomaría parte en algo semejante

**2** *vi Fam (celebrate)* estar de marcha

**pass¹** [pɑːs] *n (over mountains)* paso *m*, desfiladero *m*

**pass²** **1** *n* **(a)** *(permit)* pase *m*; **rail/bus p.** abono *m* de tren/autobús

**(b)** *(in examination)* **to obtain** *or* **get a p.** aprobar; **p. mark** nota *f* mínima para aprobar

**(c)** *(in sport)* pase *m*

**(d) the aircraft made two low passes over the village** el avión pasó dos veces sobre el pueblo a baja altura; *Fam* **to make a p. at sb** tirar los tejos a alguien

**2** *vt* **(a)** *(go past) (person)* pasar junto a; *(destination)* pasarse, saltarse; *(frontier)* pasar; *(car, runner)* pasar, adelantar; **I often p. him in the street** me cruzo con él a menudo en la calle

**(b)** *(exam, candidate, bill)* aprobar

**(c)** *(give) & Sport* pasar; **p. me the salt, please** ¿me pasas la sal?

**(d) to p. the time** *(of person)* pasar el tiempo; **it passes the time** sirve para matar el tiempo

**(e)** *Law* **to p. sentence** dictar sentencia; **to p. judgement on sb** juzgar a alguien

**(f) to p. water** orinar; **to p. wind** ventosear, expulsar ventosidades

**3** *vi* **(a)** *(go past)* pasar; *(overtake)* adelantar, pasar; **to let sb p., to allow sb to p.** dejar pasar a alguien; **to p. from one person to another** pasar de una persona a otra; **to p. unobserved** pasar desapercibido(a); **let it p.!** ¡no hagas caso!; **p.!** *(when answering question)* ¡paso!; **I think I'll p. on the potatoes** no voy a tomar patatas

**(b)** *(of time)* pasar, transcurrir

**(c)** *(go away)* pasar

**(d)** *Literary (take place)* **it came to p. that...** aconteció que...

**(e)** *(in exam)* aprobar

▸**pass away** *vi Euph* fallecer

**▸pass down** *vt sep (knowledge, tradition)* pasar, transmitir

**▸pass for** *vt insep* pasar por

**▸pass off 1** *vt sep* **to p. sth off as sth** hacer pasar algo por algo; **to p. oneself off as** hacerse pasar por; **he tried to p. it off as a joke** intentó hacer ver que había sido una broma

**2** *vi* **everything passed off well** todo fue bien

**▸pass on 1** *vt sep (object)* pasar, hacer circular; *(news, information)* pasar, transmitir; *(disease)* contagiar

**2** *vi Euph* fallecer

**▸pass out** *vi* **(a)** *(faint)* desvanecerse, desmayarse **(b)** *(of military cadet)* graduarse

**▸pass over** *vt sep* **to p. sb over (for promotion)** olvidar a alguien (para el ascenso)

**▸pass through** *vt insep (city, area)* pasar por

**2** *vi* **I was just passing through** pasaba por aquí

**▸pass up** *vt sep (opportunity)* dejar pasar

**passable** ['pɑːsəbəl] *adj* **(a)** *(of acceptable quality)* pasable, aceptable **(b)** *(road, bridge)* practicable, transitable

**passage** ['pæsɪdʒ] *n* **(a)** *(journey)* viaje *m*, travesía *f*; **the p. of time** el paso del tiempo; **to work one's p.** *(on ship)* = costearse el pasaje trabajando durante la travesía **(b)** *(corridor)* corredor *m*, pasillo *m*; *(alley)* pasaje *m*, callejón *m* **(c)** *(from book, piece of music)* pasaje *m*

**passageway** ['pæsɪdʒweɪ] *n (corridor)* corredor *m*, pasillo *m*; *(alley)* pasaje *m*, callejón *m*

**passé** [pɑː'seɪ] *adj* pasado(a) de moda

**passenger** ['pæsɪndʒə(r)] *n* pasajero(a) *m,f*; **p. seat** asiento *m* del copiloto

**passer-by** ['pɑːsə'baɪ] *n* viandante *mf*

**passing** ['pɑːsɪŋ] **1** *n* **(a)** *(going past)* paso *m*; **in p.** de pasada; **p. place** *(on road)* apartadero *m* *(en la carretera)* **(b)** *(of time)* paso *m*, transcurso *m* **(c)** *(death)* fallecimiento *m*

**2** *adj (car)* que pasa; *(remark)* de pasada; *(whim, fancy)* pasajero(a)

**passion** ['pæʃən] *n (emotion, desire)* pasión *f*; *(anger, vehemence)* ira *f*; **to have a p. for sth** sentir pasión por algo; **in a fit of p.** *(anger)* en un arrebato de ira; **she hates him with a p.** lo odia con toda su alma; *Law* **crime of p.** crimen *m* pasional; *Rel* **the P. (of Christ)** la Pasión (de Cristo); **p. fruit** granadilla *f*, fruta *f* de la pasión

**passionate** ['pæʃənɪt] *adj (lover, embrace)* apasionado(a); *(speech, advocate)* vehemente, apasionado(a)

**passive** ['pæsɪv] **1** *n Gram* (voz *f*) pasiva *f*

**2** *adj* pasivo(a); **p. resistance** resistencia *f* pasiva; **p. smoking** el fumar pasivamente

**passively** ['pæsɪvlɪ] *adv* pasivamente

**passkey** ['pɑːskiː] *(pl* **passkeys)** *n* llave *f* maestra

**Passover** ['pɑːsəʊvə(r)] *n Rel* Pascua *f* judía

**passport** ['pɑːspɔːt] *n* pasaporte *m*

**password** ['pɑːswɜːd] *n Mil & Comptr* contraseña *f*

**past** [pɑːst] **1** *n* pasado *m*; **in the p.** en el pasado; *Gram* en pasado; **it is a thing of the p.** es (una) cosa del pasado; **to live in the p.** vivir en el pasado

**2** *adj* pasado(a); **those days are p.** esos días han pasado; **in times p.** en otros tiempos, en tiempos pasados; **to be a p. master at sth** ser un/una maestro(a) consumado(a) en algo; **the p. week** la última semana; *Gram* **p. participle** participio *m* pasado *or* pasivo

**3** *prep (beyond)* **a little p. the bridge** poco después del puente, justo pasado el puente; **to walk p. the house** pasar por delante de la casa; **it is p. four (o'clock)** son más de las cuatro; **half p. four** las cuatro y media; **a quarter p. four** las cuatro y cuarto; **twenty p. four** las cuatro y veinte; **I'm p. caring** ya me trae sin cuidado; *Fam* **to be p. it** estar para el arrastre; *Fam* **I wouldn't put it p. her** ella es muy capaz (de hacerlo)

**4** *adv* **to walk** *or* **go p.** pasar (caminando); **to run p.** pasar corriendo

**pasta** ['pæstə] *n* pasta *f*

**paste** [peɪst] **1** *n* **(a)** *(smooth substance)* pasta *f*, crema *f* **(b)** *(pâté)* paté *m* **(c)** *(glue) (for paper)* pegamento *m*; *(for wallpaper)* engrudo *m*, cola *f*

**2** *vt (glue)* pegar

**pastel** ['pæstəl] **1** *n (crayon)* pastel *m*; *(drawing)* dibujo *m* al pastel

**2** *adj* pastel

**pasteurize** ['pæstəraɪz] *vt* pasteurizar; **pasteurized milk** leche *f* pasteurizada

**pastiche** [pæ'stiːʃ] *n* pastiche *m*

**pastille** ['pæstɪl] *n* pastilla *f*

**pastime** ['pɑːstaɪm] *n* pasatiempo *m*, afición *f*

**pasting** ['peɪstɪŋ] *n Fam (beating)* paliza *f*, tunda *f*; **to give sb a p.** dar una paliza a alguien

**pastor** ['pɑːstə(r)] *n Rel* pastor *m*

**pastoral** ['pɑːstərəl] *adj* **(a)** *(rural)* pastoril, pastoral **(b)** *(work, activities)* pastoral; **p. care** tutoría y orientación *f* individual

**pastry** ['peɪstrɪ] *n (dough)* masa *f*; *(cake)* pastel *m*; **p. cook** pastelero(a) *m,f*

**pasture** ['pɑːstʃə(r)] *n* pasto *m*; *Fig* **to put sb out to p.** jubilar a alguien; *Fig* **to move on to pastures new** ir en busca de nuevos horizontes

**pasty** ['peɪstɪ] *adj (face, complexion)* pálido(a), descolorido(a); **p.-faced** pálido

**pat** [pæt] **1** *n* **(a)** *(tap)* palmadita *f*; *Fig* **to give sb a p. on the back** felicitar a alguien **(b)** *(of butter)* porción *f*

**2** *adj (answer, explanation)* fácil, rápido(a)

**3** *adv* **to know** *or* **have sth off p.** saber algo

de memoria; **his answer came p.** respondió sin vacilar

**4** *vt* (*pt & pp* **patted**) *(tap)* **to p. sb on the head** dar palmaditas a alguien en la cabeza; *Fig* **to p. sb on the back** dar a alguien unas palmaditas en la espalda

**Patagonia** [pætə'geʊnɪə] *n* la Patagonia

**patch** [pætʃ] **1** *n* (**a**) *(of cloth)* remiendo *m*; **(eye) p.** parche *m* (en el ojo); *Fam* **his last novel isn't a p. on the others** su última novela no le llega ni a la suela de los zapatos a las anteriores (**b**) *(of colour, light)* mancha *f*; **a p. of blue sky** un claro; *Fam Fig* **to be going through a bad p.** estar pasando por un bache (**c**) *(of land)* parcela *f*, terreno *m*; *(of prostitute, salesperson)* zona *f*; *Fam* **keep off my p.!** ¡fuera de mi territorio!

**2** *vt (hole, garment)* remendar, poner un parche en

▸**patch up** *vt sep Fam (wounded person)* hacer una cura de urgencia a; *(marriage, friendship)* arreglar; **we've patched things up** *(after quarrel)* hemos hecho las paces

**patchwork** ['pætʃwɜːk] *n (in sewing)* labor *f* de retazo, patchwork *m*; *(of ideas, policies)* mosaico *m*; **p. quilt** edredón *m* de retazos *or* de patchwork

**patchy** ['pætʃɪ] *adj (novel, economic recovery)* desigual

**pâté** ['pæteɪ] *n* paté *m*

**patent** ['peɪtənt] **1** *n* patente *f*; **to take out a p. on sth** patentar algo; *Com* **p. applied for, p. pending** patente solicitada, en espera de patente

**2** *adj* (**a**) *(patented)* patentado(a); **p. leather** charol *m*; **p. medicine** específico *m*, especialidad *f* farmacéutica (**b**) *(evident)* patente, evidente

**3** *vt* patentar

**patently** ['peɪtəntlɪ] *adv* evidentemente, patentemente

**paternal** [pə'tɜːnəl] *adj (feelings)* paternal; *(duty, responsibilities)* paterno(a)

**paternally** [pə'tɜːnəlɪ] *adv* paternalmente

**paternity** [pə'tɜːnɪtɪ] *n* paternidad *f*; *Law* **p. suit** juicio *m* para determinar la paternidad

**path** [pɑːθ] *n (route)* camino *m*, sendero *m*; *(of rocket, planet, bird)* trayectoria *f*; *(of inquiry, to success)* vía *f*, camino *m*; **he killed everyone in his p.** mató a todo el que encontró a su paso; **their paths had crossed before** sus caminos ya se habían cruzado antes

**pathetic** [pə'θetɪk] *adj (feeble)* penoso(a); *(touching)* patético(a), conmovedor(ora)

**pathetically** [pə'θetɪklɪ] *adv (feebly)* penosamente, lastimosamente; *(touchingly)* patéticamente, conmovedoramente; **p. bad** penoso(a)

**pathological** [pæθə'lɒdʒɪkəl] *adj* patológico(a)

**pathologist** [pə'θɒlədʒɪst] *n (forensic scientist)* forense *mf*, médico(a) *m,f* forense

**pathology** [pə'θɒlədʒɪ] *n* patología *f*

**pathos** ['peɪθɒs] *n* patetismo *m*

**pathway** ['pɑːθweɪ] *n* camino *m*

**patience** ['peɪʃəns] *n* (**a**) *(quality)* paciencia *f*; **to try** *or* **tax sb's p.** poner a prueba la paciencia de alguien; **to exhaust sb's p.** acabar con *or* agotar la paciencia de alguien; **to lose one's p. (with sb)** perder la paciencia con alguien; **I've no p. with him** me exaspera (**b**) *(card-game)* solitario *m*; **to play p.** hacer un solitario

**patient** ['peɪʃənt] **1** *n* paciente *mf*

**2** *adj* paciente; **to be p. with sb** ser paciente con alguien, tener paciencia con alguien

**patiently** ['peɪʃəntlɪ] *adv* pacientemente

**patio** ['pætɪəʊ] *(pl* **patios**) *n* = área pavimentada contigua a una casa, utilizada para solazarse o comer al aire libre

**patriarch** ['peɪtrɪɑːk] *n* patriarca *m*

**patriarchal** [peɪtrɪ'ɑːkəl] *adj* patriarcal

**patriarchy** ['peɪtrɪɑːkɪ] *n* patriarcado *m*

**patrimony** ['pætrɪmənɪ] *n* patrimonio *m*

**patriot** ['pætrɪət, 'peɪtrɪət] *n* patriota *mf*

**patriotic** [pætrɪ'ɒtɪk, peɪtrɪ'ɒtɪk] *adj* patriótico(a)

**patriotism** ['pætrɪətɪzəm, 'peɪtrɪətɪzəm] *n* patriotismo *m*

**patrol** [pə'trəʊl] **1** *n* patrulla *f*; **to be on p.** patrullar; **p. car** coche *m* patrulla

**2** *vt (pt & pp* **patrolled**) *(area, border)* patrullar

**3** *vi* patrullar; **to p. up and down** ir y venir

**patrolman** [pə'trəʊlmæn] *n US* patrullero(a) *m,f*, policía *mf*

**patron** ['peɪtrən] *n* (**a**) *(of artist)* mecenas *mf inv*; *(of charity)* patrocinador(ora) *m,f*; **p. saint** patrón(ona) *m,f*, santo(a) *m,f* patrón(ona) (**b**) *(of shop)* cliente(a) *m,f*

**patronage** ['pætrənɪdʒ] *n* (**a**) *(of arts)* mecenazgo *m*; *(of charity)* patrocinio *m*; **under the p. of...** bajo *or* con el patrocinio de... (**b**) *Pej* clientelismo *m*; **political p.** clientelismo político

**patronize** ['pætrənaɪz] *vt* (**a**) *(artist)* patrocinar; *(shop, restaurant)* frecuentar (**b**) *(treat condescendingly)* tratar con condescendencia *or* paternalismo

**patronizing** ['pætrənaɪzɪŋ] *adj* condescendiente, paternalista

**patter¹** ['pætə(r)] **1** *n (of footsteps)* correteo *m*; *(of rain)* repiqueteo *m*

**2** *vi (of rain)* repiquetear, tamborilear; **he pattered along the corridor** pasó correteando por el pasillo

**patter²** *n Fam (talk)* charla *f*

**pattern** ['pætən] **1** n (a) *(design)* dibujo m; *(on dress, cloth)* estampado m, dibujo m; **p. book** muestrario m (b) *(of events)* evolución f; *(of behaviour)* pauta f; **the evening followed the usual p.** la noche transcurrió como de costumbre (c) *(in sewing, knitting)* patrón m (d) *(norm)* pauta f, norma f; **to set a p.** marcar la pauta

**2** vt *(model)* **to p. sth on sth** imitar algo tomando algo como modelo

**patterned** ['pætənd] adj estampado(a)

**paunch** [pɔːntʃ] n barriga f, panza f; **to have a p.** tener barriga

**pauper** ['pɔːpə(r)] n indigente mf; **p.'s grave** fosa f común

**pause** [pɔːz] **1** n *(in music, conversation)* pausa f; *(rest)* pausa f, descanso m

**2** vi *(when working)* parar, descansar; *(when speaking)* hacer una pausa; **to p. for breath** hacer una pausa or detenerse para tomar aliento

**pave** [peɪv] vt *(road)* pavimentar; *Fig* **to p. the way for sb/sth** preparar el terreno para alguien/algo

**pavement** ['peɪvmənt] n *Br (beside road)* acera f; *US (roadway)* calzada f; **p. artist** = dibujante que pinta con tiza sobre la acera; **p. cafe** café m con terraza

**pavilion** [pə'vɪliən] n pabellón m

**paving** ['peɪvɪŋ] n *(surface)* pavimento m; **p. stone** losa f

**paw** [pɔː] **1** n *(of cat, lion, bear)* garra f, pata f; *(of dog)* pata f; *Fam* **paws off!** ¡no se toca!

**2** vt *(of animal)* tocar con la pata; **to p. the ground** piafar

**pawn¹** [pɔːn] **1** n **to put sth in p.** empeñar algo; **p. ticket** resguardo m de la casa de empeños

**2** vt empeñar

**pawn²** n *(chesspiece)* peón m; *Fig* títere m

**pawnbroker** ['pɔːnbrəʊkə(r)] n prestamista mf *(de casa de empeños)*

**pawnshop** ['pɔːnʃɒp] n casa f de empeños

**pay** [peɪ] **1** n sueldo m, paga f; **the p.'s good/bad** el sueldo es bueno/malo; **to be in sb's p.** estar a sueldo de alguien; **p. cheque** cheque m del sueldo; **p. packet** sobre m de la paga; **p. phone** teléfono m de monedas; **p. rise** aumento m de sueldo; **p. slip** nómina f *(documento)*; **p. talks** negociación f salarial

**2** vt *(pt & pp* **paid** [peɪd]*)* (a) *(person, money, bill)* pagar; **I paid £5 for it** me costó 5 libras; **to be well/badly paid** estar bien/mal pagado(a); **I wouldn't do it if you paid me** no lo haría ni aunque me pagaras; **he insisted on paying his way** se empeñó en pagarlo de su propio dinero or costeárselo él mismo; **to p. cash** pagar en efectivo; **to p. money into sb's account** ingresar dinero en la cuenta de alguien (b) *(give)* **to p. attention** prestar atención; **to**

**p. sb a compliment** hacerle un cumplido a alguien; **to p. sb a visit** hacer una visita a alguien; **to p. homage to sb** rendir homenaje a alguien; **she paid her respects to the President** presentó sus respetos al presidente (c) *(profit)* **it will p. you to do it** te conviene hacerlo

**3** vi (a) *(give payment)* pagar; **to p. for sth** pagar algo; **to p. through the nose** pagar un riñón; **who's paying?** ¿quién paga?; **to p. by cheque** pagar con un cheque (b) *(be profitable)* **it wouldn't p.** no sería rentable, no merecería la pena; **it pays to be honest** conviene ser honrado

▸**pay back** vt sep *(person)* devolver el dinero a; *(money)* devolver; *(loan)* amortizar; *Fig* **I'll p. you back for this!** *(take revenge)* ¡me las pagarás por esto!

▸**pay in** vt *(cheque, money)* ingresar

▸**pay off 1** vt sep (a) *(debt)* saldar, liquidar; *(mortgage)* amortizar, redimir; *Fam* **to p. sb off** *(bribe)* untar a alguien; *(worker)* hacer el finiquito a

**2** vi *(of efforts)* dar fruto

▸**pay out 1** vt sep (a) *(money)* gastar (b) *(pt* **payed**) *(rope)* soltar poco a poco

**2** vi pagar

▸**pay up** vi pagar

**payable** ['peɪəbəl] adj pagadero(a); **to make a cheque p. to sb** extender un cheque a favor de alguien

**pay-as-you-earn** [peɪæzjuː'ɜːn] n retención f del impuesto sobre la renta

**payday** ['peɪdeɪ] n día m de pago

**PAYE** [piːeɪwɑːˈiː] n *Br (abbr* **pay-as-you-earn**) retención f del impuesto sobre la renta

**payee** [peɪˈiː] n beneficiario(a) m,f

**paying** ['peɪɪŋ] adj **p. guest** huésped(eda) m,f de pago

**payload** ['peɪləʊd] n *(of vehicle, spacecraft)* carga f útil; *(of missile)* carga f explosiva

**paymaster** ['peɪmɑːstə(r)] n oficial m pagador; **the terrorists' p.** la mano negra que financia a los terroristas

**payment** ['peɪmənt] n *(act of paying, amount paid)* pago m; **to make a p.** efectuar un pago; **to stop p. on a cheque** revocar un cheque; **non p.** impago m; **on p. of £100** previo pago de 100 libras; **p. by instalments** pago a plazos; **p. in full** liquidación f

**payoff** ['peɪɒf] n *Fam* (a) *(bribe)* soborno m (b) *(reward)* compensación f

**payroll** ['peɪrəʊl] n *Com* plantilla f, nómina f *(de empleados)*; **to be on the p.** estar en plantilla or nómina

**PC** ['piːˈsiː] **1** n (a) *Br (abbr* **Police Constable**) agente mf de policía (b) *(abbr* **personal computer**) PC m, ordenador m personal

**2** *adj* (*abbr* **politically correct**) políticamente correcto(a)

**pc** (*abbr* **postcard**) (tarjeta *f*) postal *f*

**PDQ** [pi:di:'kju:] *adv Fam* (*abbr* **Pretty Damn Quick**) por la vía rápida, rapidito

**PE** ['pi:'i:] *n Sch* (*abbr* **physical education**) educación *f* física

**pea** [pi:] *n* guisante *m*, *CAm, Méx* chícharo *m*, *CSur* arveja *f*; **like two peas in a pod** como dos gotas de agua

**peace** [pi:s] *n* paz *f*; **at p.** en paz; **to make (one's) p. with sb** hacer las paces con alguien; **p. and quiet** paz y tranquilidad; **for the sake of p. and quiet** para tener la fiesta en paz; **p. of mind** tranquilidad *f* de espíritu, sosiego *m*; *Law* **to keep/disturb the p.** mantener/alterar el orden (público); **p. campaigner** pacifista *mf*; **P. Corps** = organización gubernamental estadounidense de ayuda al desarrollo con cooperantes sobre el terreno; **p. movement** pacifismo *m*, movimiento *m* pacifista; **p. negotiations** negociaciones *fpl* de paz; **p. offering** oferta *f* de paz; **p. talks** conversaciones *fpl* de paz; **p. treaty** tratado *m* de paz

**peaceable** ['pi:səbəl] *adj* pacífico(a)

**peaceful** ['pi:sfʊl] *adj* (*calm*) tranquilo(a), sosegado(a); (*non-violent*) pacífico(a)

**peacekeeping** ['pi:ski:pɪŋ] *n* mantenimiento *m* de la paz; **p. forces** fuerzas *fpl* de pacificación *or* interposición

**peace-loving** ['pi:slʌvɪŋ] *adj* amante de la paz

**peacetime** ['pi:staɪm] *n* tiempo *m* de paz

**peach** [pi:tʃ] *n* (*fruit*) melocotón *m*, *Am* durazno *m*; *Fam* **she's a p.** es monísima; **p. melba** copa *f* Melba; = postre a base de melocotón, helado de vainilla y jarabe de frambuesa; **p. tree** melocotonero *m*

**peacock** ['pi:kɒk] *n* pavo *m* real

**peak** [pi:k] **1** *n* (a) (*summit of mountain*) cima *f*, cumbre *f*; (*mountain*) pico *m* (b) (*of price, inflation, success*) punto *m* máximo, (máximo) apogeo *m*; **in p. condition** en condiciones óptimas; **p. period** horas *fpl* punta; **p. season** temporada *f* alta (c) (*of cap*) visera *f*

**2** *vi* alcanzar el punto máximo

**peaky** ['pi:kɪ] *adj Fam* pachucho(a); **to be p.** estar pachucho

**peal** [pi:l] *n* (*of bells*) repique *m*; **p. of thunder** trueno *m*; **peals of laughter** risotadas *fpl*, carcajadas *fpl*

▸**peal out** *vi* (*of bells*) repicar

**peanut** ['pi:nʌt] *n* cacahuete *m*, *CAm, Méx* cacahuate *m*, *Andes, CSur* maní *m*; *Fam* **peanuts** (*small sum of money*) calderilla *f*; **p. butter** mantequilla *f or* crema *f* de cacahuete; **p. oil** aceite *m* de cacahuete

**pear** [peə(r)] *n* (*fruit*) pera *f*; **p. tree** peral *m*

**pearl** [pɜːl] *n* (a) perla *f*; **p. diver** pescador(ora) *m,f* de perlas; **p. necklace** collar *m* de perlas (b) (*idioms*) **pearls of wisdom** perlas de sabiduría; **I was casting pearls before swine** no está la miel hecha para la boca del asno

**pearly** ['pɜːlɪ] *adj* perlado(a); **the P. Gates** las puertas del cielo

**peasant** ['pezənt] *n* campesino(a) *m,f*, *Pej* (*uncultured person*) cateto(a) *m,f*, paleto(a) *m,f*

**peashooter** ['pi:ʃu:tə(r)] *n* cerbatana *f*

**peat** [pi:t] *n* turba *f*; **p. bog** turbera *f*

**pebble** ['pebəl] *n* guijarro *m*; **p. beach** playa *f* pedregosa

**pebbledash** ['pebəldæʃ] *n* enguijarrado *m* (*mampostería*)

**pebbly** ['peblɪ] *adj* pedregoso(a)

**pecan** ['pi:kən] *n* pacana *f*

**peccary** ['pekərɪ] *n* pecarí *m*

**peck** [pek] **1** *n* (a) (*of bird*) picotazo *m* (b) *Fam* (*kiss*) besito *m*; **to give sb a p. on the cheek** dar un besito a alguien en la mejilla

**2** *vt* (a) (*of bird*) picotear (b) *Fam* (*kiss*) **to p. sb on the cheek** dar un besito a alguien en la mejilla

**peckish** ['pekɪʃ] *adj Fam* **to be p.** tener un poco de gusa *or* hambre

**pecs** [peks] *npl Fam* (*pectoral muscles*) pectorales *mpl*

**pectin** ['pektɪn] *n Chem* pectina *f*

**pectoral** ['pektərəl] *Anat* **1** *npl* **pectorals** pectorales *mpl*

**2** *adj* pectoral

**peculiar** [pɪ'kju:lɪə(r)] *adj* (a) (*strange*) raro(a); **how p.!** ¡qué raro!; **she is a little p.** es un poco rara; **to feel p.** (*unwell*) sentirse mal (b) (*particular*) **p. to** característico(a) *or* peculiar de; **this species is p. to Spain** es una especie autóctona de España

**peculiarity** [pɪkju:lɪ'ærɪtɪ] *n* (*strangeness*) rareza *f*; (*unusual characteristic*) peculiaridad *f*

**peculiarly** [pɪ'kju:lɪəlɪ] *adv* (a) (*strangely*) extrañamente (b) (*especially*) particularmente

**pecuniary** [pɪ'kju:nɪərɪ] *adj Formal* pecuniario(a)

**pedagogic(al)** [pedə'gɒdʒɪk(əl)] *adj* pedagógico(a)

**pedagogy** ['pedəgɒdʒɪ] *n* pedagogía *f*

**pedal** ['pedəl] **1** *n* pedal *m*; **p. bin** cubo *m* (de basura) con pedal

**2** *vt* (*pt & pp* **pedalled**, *US* **pedaled**) **to p. a bicycle** dar pedales a la bicicleta

**3** *vi* pedalear

**pedalo** ['pedələʊ] (*pl* **pedalos**) *n* patín *m*, hidropatín *m*

**pedant** ['pedənt] *n* puntilloso(a) *m,f*, = persona excesivamente preocupada por los detalles

**pedantic** [pɪ'dæntɪk] *adj* puntilloso(a), = excesivamente preocupado por los detalles

**pedantry** ['pedəntrɪ] *n* escrupulosidad *f*, meticulosidad *f* exagerada

**peddle** ['pedəl] *vt (goods)* vender de puerta en puerta; *(ideas, theories)* difundir; **to p. drugs** trapichear con drogas

**peddler** ['pedlə(r)] *n (of goods)* vendedor(ora) *m,f* ambulante, mercachifle *mf*; *(of ideas, theories)* divulgador(ora) *m,f*, propagador(ora) *m,f*; *(of drugs)* camello *m*

**pederast** ['pedəræst] *n Formal* pederasta *m*

**pedestal** ['pedɪstəl] *n* pedestal *m*; *Fig* **to put sb on a p.** poner a alguien en un pedestal; **p. lamp** lámpara *f* de pie

**pedestrian** [pɪ'destrɪən] **1** *n* peatón(ona) *m,f*; **p. crossing** paso *m* de peatones; **p. precinct** zona *f* peatonal

**2** *adj (unimaginative)* prosaico(a), pedestre

**pedestrianize** [pɪ'destrɪənaɪz] *vt* **to p. a road** hacer peatonal una calle

**pediatric, pediatrician** *etc US* = **paediatric, paediatrician** *etc*

**pedicure** ['pedɪkjʊə(r)] *n* pedicura *f*; **to have a p.** hacerse la pedicura

**pedigree** ['pedɪgriː] **1** *n (of dog) & Fig* pedigrí *m*; *(ancestry)* linaje *m*; *Fig* **his p. as a democrat is open to question** su pedigrí democrático es discutible

**2** *adj (dog)* con pedigrí

**pedlar** ['pedlə(r)] *n* vendedor(ora) *m,f* ambulante, mercachifle *mf*

**pedophile, pedophilia** *US* = **paedophile, paedophilia**

**pee** [piː] *Fam* **1** *n* pis *m*; **to have a p.** hacer pis, mear

**2** *vi* hacer pis, mear

**peek** [piːk] **1** *n* vistazo *m*, ojeada *f*; **to take** *or* **have a p. (at sth)** echar un vistazo *or* una ojeada (a algo)

**2** *vi* echar un vistazo *or* una ojeada **(at a)**

**peel** [piːl] **1** *n (on fruit, vegetable)* piel *f*; *(after peeling)* monda *f*, peladura *f*

**2** *vt (fruit, vegetable)* pelar; **to keep one's eyes peeled** tener los ojos bien abiertos

**3** *vi (of paint)* levantarse; *(of sunburnt skin, person)* pelarse

▸**peel off 1** *vt sep (skin of fruit, vegetable)* pelar; *(one's clothes)* quitarse, despojarse de

**2** *vi (of paint)* levantarse; *(of sunburnt skin)* pelarse

**peelings** ['piːlɪŋz] *npl (of potato, carrot)* mondas *fpl*, peladuras *fpl*

**peep¹** [piːp] **1** *n (furtive glance)* vistazo *m*, ojeada *f*; **to have** *or* **take a p. at sth** echar un vistazo *or* una ojeada a algo

**2** *vi* echar una ojeada **(at a)**; **to p. through the keyhole** mirar *or* espiar por el ojo de la cerradura; **to p. out from behind sth** asomar por detrás de algo

**peep²** *n (sound)* pitido *m*; *Fam* **I don't want to hear another p. out of you** no quiero volver a oírte decir ni pío

**peephole** ['piːphəʊl] *n* mirilla *f*

**Peeping Tom** ['piːpɪŋ'tɒm] *n Fam* mirón(ona) *m,f*

**peer¹** [pɪə(r)] *n* **(a)** *(equal)* igual *m*; *Formal* **without p.** sin igual, sin par; **he started smoking because of p. pressure** empezó a fumar por influencia de la gente de su entorno; **his p. group** (la gente de) su entorno **(b)** *Br (noble)* par *m*

**peer²** *vi* **to p. at sth/sb** mirar con esfuerzo algo/a alguien; **to p. over a wall** atisbar por encima de un muro

**peerage** ['pɪərɪdʒ] *n Br (rank)* título *m* de par; **the p.** *(peers)* los pares

**peerless** ['pɪəlɪs] *adj* sin igual, sin par

**peeve** [piːv] *vt Fam* fastidiar; **to be peeved about sth** estar fastidiado(a) *or* molesto(a) por algo

**peevish** ['piːvɪʃ] *adj* irritable, malhumorado(a)

**peewit** ['piːwɪt] *n* avefría *f*

**peg** [peg] **1** *n (pin for fastening)* clavija *f*; *(for coat, hat)* colgador *m*; *(clothes)* p. pinza *f*; *(tent)* p. clavija *f*, estaquilla *f*; **to buy clothes off the p.** comprar ropa prêt-à-porter; **to take sb down a p. (or two)** bajarle a alguien los humos

**2** *vt (pt & pp pegged)* **(a)** *(fasten)* **to p. sth in place** fijar algo con clavijas; **to p. the washing on the line** tender la ropa (con pinzas) **(b)** *(prices)* fijar; **to p. sth to the rate of inflation** ajustar algo al índice de inflación

▸**peg out** *vi very Fam (die)* estirar la pata

**pejorative** [pɪ'dʒɒrətɪv] *adj* peyorativo(a)

**Pekinese** [piːkɪ'niːz] *n (perro m)* pequinés *m*

**Peking** [piː'kɪŋ] *n* Pekín

**pelican** ['pelɪkən] *n (bird)* pelícano *m*; *Br* **p. crossing** = paso de peatones con semáforo accionado mediante botón

**pellet** ['pelɪt] *n (of paper, bread, clay)* bolita *f*; *(for gun)* perdigón *m*

**pell-mell** ['pel'mel] *adv* desordenadamente, en tropel

**pelmet** ['pelmɪt] *n (of wood)* galería *f* (para cortinas); *(of cloth)* cenefa *f*

**pelt¹** [pelt] *n (animal skin)* piel *f*, pellejo *m*

**pelt²** **1** *vt* **to p. sb with stones** lanzar a alguien una lluvia de piedras, apedrear a alguien

**2** *vi* **(a)** *Fam (rain)* **it was pelting down** caían chuzos de punta **(b)** *(go fast)* ir disparado(a); **he came pelting along the corridor** venía disparado por el pasillo

**pelvic** ['pelvɪk] *adj* pélvico(a)

**pelvis** ['pelvɪs] *n* pelvis *f inv*

**pen¹** [pen] **1** *n (for writing)* pluma *f* (estilográfica); *(ballpoint)* bolígrafo *m*; **to put p. to paper** ponerse a escribir; **p. friend** *or* **pal** amigo(a) *m,f* por correspondencia; **p. name** seudónimo *m*

  **2** *vt (pt & pp penned)* escribir

**pen²** *n (for sheep)* redil *m*; *(for cattle)* corral *m*

**pen³** *n US Fam (prison)* trena *f*

▸**pen in** *vt sep (animals, people)* encerrar

**penal** ['pi:nəl] *adj* penal; **p. code** código *m* penal; **p. colony** colonia *f* penitenciaria; **p. servitude** trabajos *mpl* forzados

**penalize** ['pi:nəlaɪz] *vt* penalizar; **to p. sb for doing sth** penalizar a alguien por hacer algo

**penalty** ['penltɪ] *n* **(a)** *(punishment) (fine)* sanción *f*; *(for serious crime)* pena *f*, castigo *m*; **to impose a p. on sb** imponer un castigo a alguien; **on** *or* **under p. of death** so pena de muerte; **to pay the p.** pagar las consecuencias; *Com* **p. clause** cláusula *f* de penalización **(b)** *(in football)* penalty *m*; *Sport* **p. area** área *f* de castigo; *Sport* **p. kick** (lanzamiento *m* de) penalty *m*; *Sport* **p. shootout** lanzamiento *m* *or* tanda *f* de penaltys

**penance** ['penəns] *n also Fig* penitencia *f*; **to do p. (for sth)** hacer penitencia (por algo)

**pence** [pens] *pl of* **penny**

**penchant** ['pɒnʃɒn] *n* inclinación *f*, propensión *f*; **to have a p. for (doing) sth** tener propensión a (hacer) algo

**pencil** ['pensəl] **1** *n* lápiz *m*; **p. case** plumier *m*; **p. drawing** dibujo *m* a lápiz; **p. sharpener** sacapuntas *m inv*

  **2** *vt (pt & pp pencilled, US penciled) (draw)* dibujar a lápiz; *(write)* redactar *(con lápiz)*

▸**pencil in** *vt sep (provisionally decide)* apuntar provisionalmente

**pendant** ['pendənt] *n* colgante *m*

**pending** ['pendɪŋ] **1** *adj (unresolved)* pendiente; **to be p.** estar pendiente

  **2** *prep* a la espera de; **p. the outcome** a la espera del resultado

**pendulum** ['pendjʊləm] *n* péndulo *m*

**penetrate** ['penɪtreɪt] **1** *vt* **(a)** *(object, body, wall)* penetrar; *(area, market, group)* penetrar en, adentrarse en **(b)** *(enemy, rival group)* infiltrarse en

  **2** *vi* penetrar

**penetrating** ['penɪtreɪtɪŋ] *adj (sound, voice, cold)* penetrante; *(mind)* perspicaz, penetrante

**penetration** [penɪ'treɪʃən] *n* penetración *f*

**penguin** ['peŋgwɪn] *n* pingüino *m*

**penicillin** [penɪ'sɪlɪn] *n* penicilina *f*

**peninsula** [pɪ'nɪnsjʊlə] *n* península *f*

**peninsular** [pɪ'nɪnsjʊlə(r)] *adj* peninsular; *Hist* **the P. War** la Guerra de la Independencia (española)

**penis** ['pi:nɪs] *n* pene *m*

**penitence** ['penɪtəns] *n* arrepentimiento *m*

**penitent** ['penɪtənt] *n & adj* arrepentido(a) *m,f*

**penitentiary** [penɪ'tenʃərɪ] *n US* prisión *f*, cárcel *f*

**penknife** ['pennaɪf] *n* navaja *f*, cortaplumas *m inv*

**pennant** ['penənt] *n* banderín *m*

**penniless** ['penɪlɪs] *adj* **to be p.** estar sin un duro *or* sin blanca

**Pennsylvania** [pensɪl'veɪnɪə] *n* Pensilvania

**penny** ['penɪ] *n* **(a)** *Br (coin)* *(pl* **pence** [pens]*)* penique *m*; **a ten/fifty pence piece** una moneda de diez/cincuenta peniques; **it was worth every p.** valía (realmente) la pena *(el precio pagado)*; **it didn't cost them a p.** no les costó ni un duro; **p. farthing** velocípedo *m*; **p. pinching** tacañería *f*; **p. whistle** flautín *m* **(b)** *US (cent)* centavo *m* **(c)** *(idioms)* **they haven't a p. to their name** no tienen ni un duro *or* una perra gorda; **she didn't get the joke at first, but then the p. dropped** al principio no entendió el chiste, pero más tarde cayó; **they're ten a p.** los hay a patadas; **a p. for your thoughts** dime en qué estás pensando; **he keeps turning up like a bad p.** no hay forma de perderlo de vista *or* de quitárselo de encima

**penny-pinching** ['penɪpɪntʃɪŋ] *adj (person)* agarrado(a), tacaño(a); *(ways, habits)* mezquino(a)

**pension** ['penʃən] *n* pensión *f*; **to be on a p.** cobrar una pensión; **p. fund** fondo *m* de pensiones; **p. scheme** plan *m* de jubilación *or* de pensiones

▸**pension off** *vt sep* jubilar

**pensionable** ['penʃənəbəl] *adj* **of p. age** en edad de jubilación

**pensioner** ['penʃənə(r)] *n* pensionista *mf*, jubilado(a) *m,f*

**pensive** ['pensɪv] *adj* pensativo(a); **to be p.** estar pensativo

**pensively** ['pensɪvlɪ] *adv* pensativamente

**pentagon** ['pentəgən] *n* pentágono *m*; **the P.** *(building)* el Pentágono

**pentathlon** [pen'tæθlən] *n* pentatlón *m* (moderno)

**Pentecost** ['pentɪkɒst] *n Rel* Pentecostés *m*

**penthouse** ['penthaʊs] *n* ático *m*

**pent-up** [pen'tʌp] *adj* contenido(a)

**penultimate** [pe'nʌltɪmɪt] *adj* penúltimo(a)

**penury** ['penjʊrɪ] *n* miseria *f*, penuria *f*

**peony** ['pi:ənɪ] *n* peonía *f*

**people** ['pi:pəl] **1** *npl* (a) *(plural of* **person***) (as group)* gente *f*; *(as individuals)* personas *fpl*; **other p.** otras personas; **most p.** la mayoría de la gente; **old p.** las personas mayores; **young p.** los jóvenes; **there were five p. in the room** había cinco personas en la habitación; **he's one of those p. who...** es una de esas personas que...; **p. say that...** se dice que... (b) *(citizens)* pueblo *m*, ciudadanía *f*; **the common p.** la gente corriente *or* común; **a man of the p.** un hombre del pueblo; **p. power** poder *m* popular; **P.'s Republic** República *f* Popular (c) *Fam (family)* **my/his p.** mi/su gente

**2** *n (nation)* pueblo *m*; **the Scottish p.** el pueblo escocés

**3** *vt* poblar

**PEP** [pep] *n Fin (abbr* **personal equity plan***)* = plan personal de inversión en valores de renta variable fiscalmente incentivado por el Gobierno

**pep** [pep] *n Fam* ánimo *m*, energía *f*; **p. pill** estimulante *m*; **she gave us a p. talk** nos dirigió unas palabras de ánimo

▶**pep up** *(pt & pp* **pepped)** *vt sep Fam (person, event)* animar; *(dish)* alegrar

**pepper** ['pepə(r)] **1** *n (spice)* pimienta *f*; *(vegetable)* pimiento *m*; **black/white p.** pimienta negra/blanca; **green/red p.** pimiento verde/rojo; **p. mill** molinillo *m* de pimienta; **p. pot** pimentero *m*

**2** *vt (in cooking)* sazonar con pimienta; *Fig* **to p. sth with bullets** acribillar a balazos algo

**peppercorn** ['pepəkɔ:n] *n* grano *m* de pimienta

**peppermint** ['pepəmɪnt] *n (plant)* hierbabuena *f*; *(flavour)* menta *f*; *(sweet)* caramelo *m* de menta

**peppery** ['pepərɪ] *adj* (a) *(spicy)* **to be too p.** tener demasiada pimienta (b) *(irritable)* picajoso(a), irascible

**peptic ulcer** ['peptɪk'ʌlsə(r)] *n Med* úlcera *f* gastroduodenal

**per** [pɜ:(r)] *prep* por; **p. day** al día, por día; **100 km p. hour** 100 kms por hora; *Formal* **as p. your instructions** según sus instrucciones; **as p. usual** como de costumbre; **p. annum** al año, por año; **p. capita** per cápita; **p. se** en sí, per se

**perceive** [pə'si:v] *vt* (a) *(notice) (sound, light, smell)* percibir; *(difference)* apreciar, distinguir (b) *(understand) (truth, importance)* apreciar, entender (c) *(view)* **to perceive sth/sb as...** ver *or* juzgar algo/a alguien como...

**per cent, percent** [pə'sent] **1** *n* porcentaje *m*, tanto *m* por ciento; **forty p. of women** el cuarenta por ciento de las mujeres; **a ten p.**

**increase** un aumento del diez por ciento

**2** *adv* por ciento

**percentage** [pə'sentɪdʒ] *n* porcentaje *m*, tanto *m* por ciento; **to receive a p. on all sales** percibir un tanto por ciento de todas las ventas

**perceptible** [pə'septɪbəl] *adj* perceptible

**perceptibly** [pə'septɪblɪ] *adv* sensiblemente

**perception** [pə'sepʃən] *n* (a) *(with senses)* percepción *f* (b) *(of difference, importance, facts)* apreciación *f* (c) *(discernment)* perspicacia *f*

**perceptive** [pə'septɪv] *adj* atinado(a), perspicaz

**perch**[1] [pɜ:tʃ] **1** *n (for bird)* percha *f*; *Fam (seat, position)* atalaya *f*; *Fam Fig* **to knock sb off his p.** bajarle los humos a alguien

**2** *vi (of bird)* posarse; **he perched on the edge of the table** *(of person)* se sentó en el borde de la mesa

**perch**[2] *n (fish)* perca *f*

**percolate** ['pɜ:kəleɪt] **1** *vt (coffee)* hacer *(con la cafetera)*; **percolated coffee** café *m* de cafetera

**2** *vi* filtrarse

**percolator** ['pɜ:kəleɪtə(r)] *n* cafetera *f* (de filtro)

**percussion** [pə'kʌʃən] *n Mus* percusión *f*; **p. instruments** instrumentos *mpl* de percusión

**percussionist** [pə'kʌʃənɪst] *n Mus* percusionista *mf*

**peregrine falcon** ['perɪgrɪn'fɔ:lkən] *n* halcón *m* peregrino

**peremptory** [pə'remptərɪ] *adj (person, manner, voice)* imperioso(a); *(command)* perentorio(a)

**perennial** [pə'renɪəl] **1** *n Bot* planta *f* perenne

**2** *adj (plant)* (de hoja) perenne; *(problems, beauty)* eterno(a)

**perfect 1** *adj* ['pɜ:fɪkt] (a) *(excellent, flawless)* perfecto(a); **no one's p.** nadie es perfecto; **Tuesday would be p.** el martes me vendría muy bien; *Mus* **to have p. pitch** tener una entonación perfecta (b) *(complete)* **it makes p. sense** es del todo razonable; **he's a p. stranger to me** no lo conozco de nada; **he's a p. fool** es un perfecto idiota; **he's a p. gentleman** es un perfecto caballero (c) *Gram* perfecto(a); **future p.** futuro *m* perfecto; **past p.** pretérito *m* pluscuamperfecto

**2** *vt* [pə'fekt] perfeccionar

**perfection** [pə'fekʃən] *n* perfección *f*

**perfectionist** [pə'fekʃənɪst] *n* perfeccionista *mf*

**perfectly** ['pɜ:fɪktlɪ] *adv (faultlessly)* perfectamente; *(absolutely)* completamente; **it's p. obvious** resulta totalmente evidente; **she's p. right** tiene toda la razón

**perfidious** [pə'fɪdɪəs] *adj Literary* pérfido(a)

**perforate** ['pɜ:fəreɪt] *vt* perforar

**perforated** ['pɜːfəreɪtɪd] *adj* perforado(a); **p. line** línea *f* perforada; *Med* **p. ulcer** úlcera *f* perforada

**perforation** [pɜːfə'reɪʃən] *n* (*hole, on stamp*) perforación *f*

**perform** [pə'fɔːm] **1** *vt* (*miracle, operation, service*) realizar, efectuar; (*one's duty*) cumplir; (*play*) representar; (*role, piece of music*) interpretar

**2** *vi* (*of actor*) actuar; (*of singer*) interpretar, cantar; (*of machine, car*) funcionar, comportarse

**performance** [pə'fɔːməns] *n* (**a**) (*of task*) realización *f*, ejecución *f*; (*of duty*) cumplimiento *m*; **p. appraisal** evaluación *f* del rendimiento (**b**) (*of actor, sportsperson*) actuación *f*; (*of pupil, economy*) comportamiento *m*; (*of machine, car*) rendimiento *m*, prestaciones *fpl* (**c**) (*of play*) representación *f*; *Fig* **to make a p.** (*fuss*) montar un cacao

**performer** [pə'fɔːmə(r)] *n* intérprete *mf*

**performing** [pə'fɔːmɪŋ] *adj* (*dog, seal*) amaestrado(a); **p. arts** artes *fpl* interpretativas

**perfume 1** *n* ['pɜːfjuːm] (*of flowers*) aroma *m*, fragancia *f*; (*for person*) perfume *m*; **p. counter** sección *f* de perfumería

**2** *vt* [pə'fjuːm] perfumar

**perfumed** ['pɜːfjuːmd] *adj* perfumado(a)

**perfunctory** [pə'fʌŋktərɪ] *adj* (*glance, smile*) rutinario(a), superficial; (*letter, instructions, examination*) somero(a)

**perhaps** [pə'hæps] *adv* quizá, quizás, tal vez; **p. so/not** quizá sí/no; **p. she'll come** quizá venga

**peril** ['perɪl] *n* peligro *m*, riesgo *m*; **in p. of her life** a riesgo de (perder) su vida; **at your p.** por tu cuenta y riesgo

**perilous** ['perɪləs] *adj* peligroso(a)

**perilously** ['perɪləslɪ] *adv* peligrosamente; **we came p. close to a collision** estuvimos en un tris de chocar

**perimeter** [pə'rɪmɪtə(r)] *n* perímetro *m*; **p. fence** valla *f* exterior

**period** ['pɪərɪəd] *n* (**a**) (*stretch of time*) período *m*, periodo *m*; **for a p. of three months** durante un período de tres meses; **within the agreed p.** dentro del plazo acordado; **sunny periods** intervalos *mpl* de sol (**b**) *Sch* clase *f*; **a French p.** una clase de francés (**c**) (*menstruation*) período *m*, regla *f*; **to have one's p.** tener el período *or* la regla; **p. pains** dolores *mpl* menstruales (**d**) (*historical age*) época *f*, período *m*; **p. dress/furniture** traje *m*/muebles *mpl* de época; *TV* **p. drama** drama *m* (televisivo) de época (**e**) *US* (*full stop*) punto *m*

**periodic** [pɪərɪ'ɒdɪk] *adj* periódico(a); *Chem* **p. table** tabla *f* periódica

**periodical** [pɪərɪ'ɒdɪkəl] *n* publicación *f* periódica, boletín *m*

**periodically** [pɪərɪ'ɒdɪklɪ] *adv* periódicamente

**peripheral** [pə'rɪfərəl] **1** *n pl Comptr* **peripherals** periféricos *mpl*

**2** *adj* (*area, vision*) periférico(a); (*issue, importance*) secundario(a)

**periphery** [pə'rɪfərɪ] *n* periferia *f*

**periscope** ['perɪskəʊp] *n* periscopio *m*

**perish** ['perɪʃ] *vi* (**a**) (*of person*) perecer; **p. the thought!** ¡Dios no lo quiera! (**b**) (*of rubber, leather*) estropearse

**perishable** ['perɪʃəbəl] **1** *n pl* **perishables** productos *mpl* perecederos

**2** *adj* perecedero(a)

**perishing** ['perɪʃɪŋ] *adj Fam* (*very cold*) **it's p.** ¡hace un frío que pela!

**peritonitis** [perɪtə'naɪtɪs] *n Med* peritonitis *f inv*

**perjure** ['pɜːdʒə(r)] *vt Law* **to p. oneself** perjurar

**perjury** ['pɜːdʒərɪ] *n Law* perjurio *m*; **to commit p.** cometer perjurio

**perk** [pɜːk] *n Br Fam* ventaja *f* extra, remuneración *f* en especie

▶**perk up** *Fam* **1** *vt sep* animar, levantar el ánimo a

**2** *vi* animarse

**perky** ['pɜːkɪ] *adj Fam* animado(a); **to be p.** estar animado(a)

**perm** [pɜːm] **1** *n* (*hairdo*) permanente *f*; **to have a p.** llevar una permanente

**2** *vt* **to have one's hair permed** hacerse la permanente

**permanence** ['pɜːmənəns] *n* permanencia *f*

**permanent** ['pɜːmənənt] *adj* permanente; (*employee, job*) fijo(a); **p. address** domicilio *m* fijo, residencia *f* habitual; **p. wave** (*hairdo*) permanente *f*

**permeate** ['pɜːmɪeɪt] **1** *vt* impregnar

**2** *vi* **to p. through sth** (*of liquid*) filtrarse a través de algo; (*of fear, suspicion*) extenderse por algo

**permissible** [pə'mɪsɪbəl] *adj* admisible, permisible

**permission** [pə'mɪʃən] *n* permiso *m*; **to ask for p. to do sth** pedir permiso para hacer algo; **to give sb p. to do sth** dar a alguien permiso para hacer algo; **with your p.** con (su) permiso

**permissive** [pə'mɪsɪv] *adj* permisivo(a)

**permit 1** *n* ['pɜːmɪt] (*for fishing, imports, exports*) licencia *f*; (*for parking, work, residence*) permiso *m*; **p. holders only** (*sign*) estacionamiento reservado

**2** *vt* [pə'mɪt] (*pt & pp* **permitted**) permitir; **to p. sb to do sth** permitir a alguien hacer algo

**3** *vi* **weather permitting** si el tiempo lo permite

**permutation** [pɜ:mjʊ'teɪʃən] *n* permutación *f*

**pernicious** [pə'nɪʃəs] *adj* pernicioso(a)

**pernickety** [pə'nɪkɪtɪ] *adj Fam (person)* quisquilloso(a); *(task)* engorroso(a)

**peroxide** [pə'rɒksaɪd] *n Chem* peróxido *m*; **p. blonde** *(woman)* rubia *f* de bote, rubia oxigenada

**perpendicular** [pɜ:pən'dɪkjʊlə(r)] **1** *n* perpendicular *f*
**2** *adj* perpendicular

**perpetrate** ['pɜ:pɪtreɪt] *vt (crime, deception)* perpetrar

**perpetrator** ['pɜ:pɪtreɪtə(r)] *n* autor(ora) *m,f*

**perpetual** [pə'petjʊəl] *adj (eternal)* perpetuo(a); *(constant)* continuo(a), constante; *Phys* **p. motion** movimiento *m* perpetuo

**perpetually** [pə'petjʊəlɪ] *adv (eternally)* perpetuamente; *(constantly)* continuamente, constantemente

**perpetuate** [pə'petjʊeɪt] *vt Formal* perpetuar

**perpetuity** [pɜ:pɪ'tjuːɪtɪ] *n Formal* **in p. a** perpetuidad

**perplex** [pə'pleks] *vt* dejar perplejo(a)

**perplexing** [pə'pleksɪŋ] *adj* desconcertante

**perplexity** [pə'pleksɪtɪ] *n* perplejidad *f*, desconcierto *m*

**persecute** ['pɜ:sɪkjuːt] *vt (for political, religious reasons)* perseguir; *(harass)* acosar, atormentar

**persecution** [pɜ:sɪ'kjuːʃən] *n* persecución *f*; *Psy* **p. complex** manía *f* persecutoria

**persecutor** ['pɜ:sɪkjuːtə(r)] *n* perseguidor(ora) *m,f*

**perseverance** [pɜ:sɪ'vɪərəns] *n* perseverancia *f*

**persevere** [pɜ:sɪ'vɪə(r)] *vi* perseverar **(with** en); **to p. in doing sth** seguir haciendo algo con perseverancia

**Persia** ['pɜ:ʒə] *n Formerly* Persia

**Persian** ['pɜ:ʒən] **1** *n* **(a)** *(person)* persa *mf* **(b)** *(language)* persa *m*
**2** *adj* persa; **the P. Gulf** el Golfo Pérsico

**persimmon** ['pɜ:sɪmən] *n* caqui *m (fruta)*

**persist** [pə'sɪst] *vi (of person)* persistir, perseverar; *(of fog, fever)* persistir; *(of belief)* persistir, subsistir; **to p. in doing sth** empeñarse en hacer algo; **to p. in one's belief that...** empeñarse en creer que...; **to p. in one's efforts (to do sth)** no cejar en el empeño (de hacer algo)

**persistence** [pə'sɪstəns] *n (of person)* empeño *m*, persistencia *f*; *(of pain, belief, rumours)* persistencia *f*

**persistent** [pə'sɪstənt] *adj (person)* persistente, insistente; *(rain, pain)* pertinaz; *(doubts, rumours)* persistente; **p. offender** delincuente *mf* habitual

**persistently** [pə'sɪstəntlɪ] *adv (constantly)* constantemente; *(repeatedly)* repetidamente

**person** ['pɜ:sən] *(pl* **people** ['piːpəl], *Formal* **persons)** *n* persona *f*; **in p.** en persona; **to have sth on one's p.** llevar algo encima; *Gram* **in the first/second/third p.** en primera/segunda/tercera persona; *Law* **by a p. or persons unknown** por uno o varios desconocidos

**personable** ['pɜ:sənəbəl] *adj* agradable

**personage** ['pɜ:sənɪdʒ] *n* personaje *m*

**personal** ['pɜ:sənəl] *adj* personal; **to make a p. appearance** hacer acto de presencia; **for p. reasons** por motivos personales; **don't be p., don't make p. remarks** no hagas comentarios de índole personal; **it's nothing p. but...** no es nada personal, pero...; **she's a p. friend of the president** es amiga personal del presidente; **p. ad** *(in newspaper, magazine)* anuncio *m* personal (por palabras); **p. assistant** secretario(a) *m,f* personal; **p. best** *(in sport)* plusmarca *f* (personal), récord *m* personal; **p. column** *(in newspaper, magazine)* sección *f* de anuncios personales *or* de contactos; *Comptr* **p. computer** ordenador *m* personal; **p. effects** efectos *mpl* personales; **p. growth** desarrollo *m* personal; **p. hygiene** aseo *m* personal; **p. loan** préstamo *m or* crédito *m* personal; **p. organizer** agenda *f*; *Gram* **p. pronoun** pronombre *m* personal; **p. stereo** walkman® *m*

**personality** [pɜ:sə'nælɪtɪ] *n* personalidad *f*; **p. cult** culto *m* a la personalidad; *Psy* **p. disorder** trastorno *m* de la personalidad

**personally** ['pɜ:sənəlɪ] *adv (in my opinion)* personalmente; *(to visit, talk to, know)* en persona; **p., I think...** personalmente, creo...; **don't take it p.** no te lo tomes como algo personal; **I will hold you p. responsible if she gets hurt** si se hace daño te pediré cuentas a ti personalmente

**personification** [pɜ:sɒnɪfɪ'keɪʃən] *n* personificación *f*; **to be the p. of meanness** ser la tacañería personificada

**personify** [pɜ:'sɒnɪfaɪ] *vt* personificar

**personnel** [pɜ:sə'nel] *n* personal *m*; **p. (department)** departamento *m* de personal; **p. manager** director(ora) *m,f or* jefe(a) *m,f* de personal

**perspective** [pə'spektɪv] *n* perspectiva *f*; **to see things in p.** ver las cosas con perspectiva; **to put sth into p.** ver algo con perspectiva

**perspicacious** [pɜ:spɪ'keɪʃəs] *adj Formal* perspicaz

**perspiration** [pɜ:spə'reɪʃən] *n* transpiración *f*, sudor *m*

**perspire** [pə'spaɪə(r)] *vi* transpirar, sudar

**persuade** [pə'sweɪd] *vt* persuadir; **to p. sb to do sth** persuadir a alguien para que haga algo;

**to p. sb not to do sth** disuadir a alguien de que haga algo

**persuasion** [pə'sweɪʒən] *n* (a) *(act, ability)* persuasión *f*; **powers of p.** poder *m* de persuasión (b) *(beliefs)* convicciones *fpl*

**persuasive** [pə'sweɪzɪv] *adj (person, argument)* persuasivo(a)

**persuasively** [pə'sweɪzɪvlɪ] *adv* persuasivamente

**pert** [pɜːt] *adj* (a) *(cheeky)* pizpireta (b) *(nose, breasts, bottom)* respingón(ona)

**pertain** [pə'teɪn] *vi Formal* **to p. to** *(be relevant to)* concernir a; *(belong to)* pertenecer a

**pertinent** ['pɜːtɪnənt] *adj* pertinente; **to be p. to** concernir a

**perturb** [pə'tɜːb] *vt* inquietar, perturbar

**Peru** [pə'ruː] *n* Perú

**perusal** [pə'ruːzəl] *n Formal* lectura *f*

**peruse** [pə'ruːz] *vt (read carefully)* leer con detenimiento; *(read quickly)* ojear

**Peruvian** [pə'ruːvɪən] *n & adj* peruano(a) *m,f*

**pervade** [pɜː'veɪd] *vt* impregnar

**pervasive** [pɜː'veɪsɪv] *adj (smell)* penetrante; *(influence)* poderoso(a)

**perverse** [pə'vɜːs] *adj* (a) *(contrary)* aberrante; *(stubborn)* terco(a), cabezota; **he's just being p.** simplemente está llevando la contraria; **she takes a p. delight in causing harm** disfruta de lo lindo haciendo daño (b) *(sexually deviant)* pervertido(a)

**perversely** [pə'vɜːslɪ] *adv (contrarily)* por llevar la contraria

**perversion** [pə'vɜːʃən] *n (sexual)* perversión *f*; *(of the truth)* deformación *f*, tergiversación *f*; *(of justice)* distorsión *f*, corrupción *f*

**pervert 1** *n* ['pɜːvɜːt] *(sexual)* **p.** pervertido(a) *m,f* *(sexual)*

**2** *vt* [pə'vɜːt] *(corrupt)* pervertir; *(distort)* tergiversar; *Law* **to p. the course of justice** obstaculizar el curso de la justicia

**peseta** [pə'seɪtə] *n (Spanish currency)* peseta *f*

**pesky** ['peskɪ] *adj US* molesto(a)

**peso** ['peɪseʊ] *(pl pesos) n (Argentinian, Mexican currency)* peso *m*

**pessary** ['pesərɪ] *n Med* pesario *m*

**pessimism** ['pesɪmɪzəm] *n* pesimismo *m*

**pessimist** ['pesɪmɪst] *n* pesimista *mf*

**pessimistic** [pesɪ'mɪstɪk] *adj* pesimista

**pest** [pest] *n* (a) *(vermin, insects)* plaga *f*; **p. control** métodos *mpl* para combatir las plagas (b) *Fam (nuisance)* latazo *m*

**pester** ['pestə(r)] *vt* incordiar; **to p. sb to do sth** incordiar a alguien para que haga algo; **to p. sb into doing sth** conseguir que alguien haga algo a fuerza de incordiarle

**pesticide** ['pestɪsaɪd] *n* pesticida *m*

**pestilence** ['pestɪləns] *n Literary* pestilencia *f*, peste *f*

**pestilential** [pestɪ'lenʃəl] *adj Literary* pestilente

**pestle** ['pesəl] *n* mano *f* del mortero; **p. and mortar** mortero *m*, almirez *m*

**pet** [pet] **1** *n* (a) *(animal)* animal *m* doméstico or de compañía; **p. food** comida *f* para animales domésticos; **p. shop** pajarería *f* (b) *(favourite)* **mother's/teacher's p.** preferido(a) *m,f* de mamá/del profesor; **my p.!** ¡mi tesoro!; **my p. hate** lo que más odio; **p. name** *(diminutive)* apelativo *m* or nombre *m* cariñoso; **p. subject** tema *m* favorito

**2** *vt (pt & pp petted) (stroke, pat) (person, dog)* acariciar

**3** *vi Fam (sexually)* hacer manitas

**petal** ['petəl] *n* pétalo *m*

▸**peter out** ['piːtə] *vi (of conversation, enthusiasm)* decaer, declinar; *(of path, stream)* extinguirse, desaparecer

**petite** [pə'tiːt] *adj* menudo(a)

**petition** [pɪ'tɪʃən] **1** *n (request, document)* petición *f*, súplica *f*; *(list of names)* lista *f* de firmas recogidas; *Law* **p. for a divorce** demanda *f* de divorcio

**2** *vt (court, sovereign)* presentar una petición a

**3** *vi* **to p. for sth** solicitar algo; *Law* **to p. for divorce** presentar una demanda de divorcio

**petitioner** [pɪ'tɪʃənə(r)] *n* peticionario(a) *m,f*

**petrify** ['petrɪfaɪ] *vt Geol* petrificar; *(with fear)* petrificar, paralizar

**petrochemical** [petrəʊ'kemɪkəl] **1** *npl* **petrochemicals** productos *mpl* petroquímicos

**2** *adj* petroquímico(a)

**petrol** ['petrəl] *n Br* gasolina *f*, *Andes* bencina *f*, *CSur* nafta *f*; **p. bomb** bomba *f* incendiaria, cóctel *m* Molotov; **p. can** lata *f* de gasolina; **p. pump** surtidor *m* de gasolina; **p. station** gasolinera *f*, estación *f* de servicio, *Andes* grifo *m*; **p. tank** depósito *m* de gasolina or del combustible

**petroleum** [pə'trəʊlɪəm] *n* petróleo *m*; **p. jelly** vaselina *f*

**petticoat** ['petɪkəʊt] *n (from waist down)* enaguas *fpl*; *(full-length)* combinación *f*

**petty** ['petɪ] *adj* (a) *(insignificant)* insignificante; **p. cash** caja *f* para gastos menores; **p. crime** delitos *mpl* menores; *Naut* **p. officer** suboficial *mf* de marina (b) *(small-minded)* mezquino(a)

**petulance** ['petjʊləns] *n* **a fit of p.** una rabieta

**petulant** ['petjʊlənt] *adj (person)* caprichoso(a); **with a p. gesture** con un gesto de niño caprichoso

**petunia** [pɪ'tjuːnɪə] *n* petunia *f*

**pew** [pjuː] *n* banco *m*; *Fam* **take a p.!** ¡siéntate!

**pewter** ['pjuːtə(r)] *n* peltre *m*

**pfennig** ['fenɪɡ] *n (subdivision of mark)* pfennig *m*, = céntimo del marco alemán

**PG** [pi:'dʒi:] *n Br Cin (abbr* **parental guidance**) = para menores de 15 años acompañados

**PGA** [pi:dʒi:'eɪ] *n (abbr* **Professional Golfers' Association**) PGA *f*, asociación *f* de golfistas profesionales

**pH** [pi:'eɪtʃ] *n Chem* pH *m*

**phalanx** ['fælæŋks] *n Mil Hist* falange *f*; *Fig (of officials, journalists)* pelotón *m*

**phallic** ['fælɪk] *adj* fálico(a); **p. symbol** símbolo *m* fálico

**phallus** ['fæləs] *n* falo *m*

**phantom** ['fæntəm] *n* fantasma *m*; **p. pregnancy** embarazo *m* psicológico

**Pharaoh** ['feərəʊ] *n* faraón *m*

**pharmaceutical** [fɑːmə'sju:tɪkəl] **1** *npl* **pharmaceuticals** productos *mpl* farmacéuticos
  **2** *adj* farmacéutico(a)

**pharmacist** ['fɑːməsɪst] *n* farmacéutico(a) *m,f*

**pharmacology** [fɑːmə'kɒlədʒɪ] *n* farmacología *f*

**pharmacy** ['fɑːməsɪ] *n* farmacia *f*

**pharynx** ['færɪŋks] *n* faringe *f*

**phase** [feɪz] *n* fase *f*, etapa *f*; **it's just a p. (he's going through)** ya se le pasará; **out of p.** desfasado(a)
**▸phase in** *vt sep* introducir gradualmente *or* escalonadamente
**▸phase out** *vt sep* eliminar gradualmente *or* escalonadamente

**phased** [feɪzd] *adj (gradual)* gradual; *(in stages)* escalonado(a)

**PhD** [pi:eɪtʃ'di:] *n Univ (abbr* **Doctor of Philosophy**) *(person)* doctor(ora) *m,f*; *(degree)* doctorado *m*

**pheasant** ['fezənt] *n* faisán *m*

**phenomenal** [fɪ'nɒmɪnəl] *adj* fenomenal, extraordinario(a)

**phenomenally** [fɪ'nɒmɪnəlɪ] *adv* fenomenalmente, extraordinariamente

**phenomenon** [fɪ'nɒmɪnən] *(pl* **phenomena** [fɪ'nɒmɪnə]*) n* fenómeno *m*

**pheromone** ['ferəməʊn] *n* feromona *f*

**phew** [fju:] *exclam* ¡uf!

**phial** ['faɪəl] *n* ampolla *f*, vial *m*

**Philadelphian** [fɪlə'delfɪən] **1** *n* = habitante o nativo de Filadelfia
  **2** *adj* de Filadelfia

**philanderer** [fɪ'lændərə(r)] *n Pej* donjuán *m*

**philanthropic** [fɪlən'θrɒpɪk] *adj* filantrópico(a)

**philanthropist** [fɪ'lænθrəpɪst] *n* filántropo(a) *m,f*

**philanthropy** [fɪ'lænθrəpɪ] *n* filantropía *f*

**philately** [fɪ'lætəlɪ] *n* filatelia *f*

**philharmonic** [fɪlə'mɒnɪk] *Mus* **1** *n* filarmónica *f*
  **2** *adj* filarmónico(a)

**Philippines** ['fɪlɪpi:nz] *npl* **the P.** las Filipinas

**philology** [fɪ'lɒlədʒɪ] *n* filología *f*

**philosopher** [fɪ'lɒsəfə(r)] *n* filósofo(a) *m,f*

**philosophic(al)** [fɪlə'sɒfɪk(əl)] *adj (person, attitude)* filosófico(a); **to be p. about sth** tomarse algo con filosofía

**philosophize** [fɪ'lɒsəfaɪz] *vi* filosofar

**philosophy** [fɪ'lɒsəfɪ] *n* filosofía *f*; **my p. is...** mi filosofía es...

**phlegm** [flem] *n (mucus, composure)* flema *f*

**phlegmatic** [fleɡ'mætɪk] *adj* flemático(a)

**phobia** ['fəʊbɪə] *n* fobia *f*

**phoenix** ['fi:nɪks] *n* fénix *m inv*; **to rise like a p.** renacer de las propias cenizas

**phone** [fəʊn] **1** *n* teléfono *m*; **to be on the p.** *(talking)* estar al teléfono; *(have a telephone)* tener teléfono; **to give sb a p.** llamar a alguien (por teléfono); **p. bill** factura *f* del teléfono; **p. book** guía *f* de teléfonos; **p. box/booth** cabina *f* telefónica; **p. call** llamada *f* telefónica; **p. number** número *m* de teléfono
  **2** *vt* **to p. sb** telefonear a alguien, llamar a alguien (por teléfono)
  **3** *vi* telefonear, llamar (por teléfono); **to p. home** llamar a casa (por teléfono)

**phonecard** ['fəʊnkɑːd] *n* tarjeta *f* telefónica

**phone-in** ['fəʊnɪn] *n Rad & TV* **p. (programme)** = programa con llamadas de los televidentes/oyentes

**phoneme** ['fəʊni:m] *n Ling* fonema *m*

**phonetic** [fə'netɪk] *adj Ling* fonético(a)

**phonetics** [fə'netɪks] *n Ling* fonética *f*

**phoney,** *US* **phony** ['fəʊnɪ] *Fam* **1** *n (pl* **phoneys,** *US* **phonies)** *(person)* falso(a) *m,f*, farsante *mf*
  **2** *adj* falso(a)

**phosphate** ['fɒsfeɪt] *n* fosfato *m*

**phosphorescent** [fɒsfə'resənt] *adj* fosforescente

**phosphorus** ['fɒsfərəs] *n Chem* fósforo *m*

**photo** ['fəʊtəʊ] *(pl* **photos)** *n* foto *f*; **p. album** álbum *m* de fotos; **p. finish** *(in race)* fotofinish *f*; **p. opportunity** = ocasión de aparecer fotografiado dando una buena imagen

**photocopier** ['fəʊtəʊkɒpɪə(r)] *n* fotocopiadora *f*

**photocopy** ['fəʊtəʊkɒpɪ] **1** *n* fotocopia *f*
  **2** *vt* fotocopiar

**photoelectric** [fəʊtəʊɪ'lektrɪk] *adj* fotoeléctrico(a); **p. cell** célula *f* fotoeléctrica

**photogenic** [fəʊtə'dʒenɪk] *adj* fotogénico(a)

**photograph** ['fəʊtəgræf] **1** *n* fotografía *f*; **to take sb's p.** sacarle una fotografía a alguien; **p. album** álbum *m* de fotografías

**2** *vt* fotografiar

**photographer** [fə'tɒgrəfə(r)] *n* fotógrafo(a) *m,f*

**photographic** [fəʊtə'græfɪk] *adj* fotográfico(a); **to have a p. memory** tener memoria fotográfica

**photography** [fə'tɒgrəfɪ] *n* fotografía *f*

**photosensitive** [fəʊtəʊ'sensɪtɪv] *adj* fotosensible

**Photostat®** ['fəʊtəʊstæt] *n* (fotocopia *f* de) fotostato *m*

**photosynthesis** [fəʊtəʊ'sɪnθɪsɪs] *n Bot* fotosíntesis *f inv*

**photosynthesize** [fəʊtəʊ'sɪnθɪsaɪz] *vt Bot* fotosintetizar

**phrasal verb** ['freɪzəl'vɜːb] *n Gram* verbo *m* regido por preposición/adverbio

**phrase** [freɪz] **1** *n* frase *f*; **p. book** manual *m* or guía *f* de conversación

**2** *vt* expresar; *Mus* frasear

**phraseology** [freɪzɪ'ɒlədʒɪ] *n* fraseología *f*

**physical** ['fɪzɪkəl] **1** *n* (*examination*) chequeo *m*, examen *m* or reconocimiento *m* médico

**2** *adj* físico(a); **p. education** educación *f* física; **p. exercise** or **training** ejercicios *mpl* físicos; **p. fitness** buena forma *f* física; **p. geography** geografía *f* física; **a p. impossibility** una imposibilidad física or material; **p. sciences** ciencias *fpl* físicas

**physically** ['fɪzɪklɪ] *adv* físicamente; **p. fit** en buena forma física; **p. handicapped** discapacitado(a) *m,f* físico(a)

**physician** [fɪ'zɪʃən] *n* médico(a) *m,f*

**physicist** ['fɪzɪsɪst] *n* físico(a) *m,f*

**physics** ['fɪzɪks] *n* física *f*

**physiognomy** [fɪzɪ'ɒnəmɪ] *n Formal* fis(i)onomía *f*

**physiological** [fɪzɪə'lɒdʒɪkəl] *adj* fisiológico(a)

**physiology** [fɪzɪ'ɒlədʒɪ] *n* fisiología *f*

**physiotherapist** [fɪzɪəʊ'θerəpɪst] *n* fisioterapeuta *mf*

**physiotherapy** [fɪzɪəʊ'θerəpɪ] *n* fisioterapia *f*

**physique** [fɪ'ziːk] *n* físico *m*

**pianist** ['pɪənɪst] *n* pianista *mf*

**piano** [pɪ'ænəʊ] *n* (*pl* **pianos**) *n* piano *m*; **p. concerto** concierto *m* para piano y orquesta; **p. stool** escabel *m*, taburete *m* de piano; **p. tuner** afinador(ora) *m,f* de pianos

**piccolo** ['pɪkələʊ] *n* (*pl* **piccolos**) *n* flautín *m*, piccolo *m*

**pick** [pɪk] **1** *n* (**a**) (*tool*) pico *m* (**b**) (*choice*) **we had first p.** nos dejaron elegir los primeros;

take your p.** escoge a tu gusto; **the p. of the bunch** el/la mejor de todos(as)

**2** *vt* (**a**) (*choose*) escoger, elegir; (*team*) seleccionar; **to p. a fight with sb** buscar pelea con alguien

(**b**) (*flowers, fruit*) coger, recoger

(**c**) (*other uses*) **to p. a lock** forzar una cerradura; **to p. a guitar** puntear; **to p. one's nose** meterse el dedo en or hurgarse la nariz; **to p. one's teeth** escarbarse los dientes; **to p. a spot/a scab** arrancarse un grano/una costra; **to p. sb's pocket** robar algo del bolsillo de alguien; **she picked a hole in her jumper** se hizo un punto en el jersey (tirando); *Fig* **to p. holes in sth** (*in argument, theory*) sacar fallos a algo; **to p. sb's brains** aprovechar los conocimientos de alguien; **to have a bone to p. with sb** tener que ajustar cuentas con alguien

**3** *vi* **we can't afford to p. and choose** no podemos andar eligiendo

▶**pick off** *vt sep* (*remove*) retirar; (*of gunman, sniper*) ir abatiendo (uno por uno)

▶**pick on** *vt insep* tomarla con

▶**pick out** *vt sep* (**a**) (*remove*) quitar (**b**) (*select*) elegir, escoger (**c**) (*recognize*) reconocer

▶**pick up 1** *vt sep* (**a**) (*lift up*) recoger; **to p. up the phone** descolgar el teléfono; **to p. up survivors** rescatar supervivientes; *Fig* **to p. oneself up** (*after defeat*) recuperarse; *Fig* **to p. up the pieces** empezar de nuevo (*tras un fracaso*); *Fig* **to p. up the bill** pagar la cuenta

(**b**) (*collect*) recoger; (*arrest*) detener

(**c**) (*acquire, learn*) aprender; **to p. up speed** ganar velocidad

(**d**) (*radio station*) sintonizar; (*message*) captar, recibir

(**e**) (*notice*) percatarse de

(**f**) (*discussion*) reanudar

(**g**) (*make better*) **that will p. you up** eso te reconfortará

(**h**) *Fam* **to p. sb up** (*find sexual partner*) ligar con alguien

**2** *vi* (**a**) (*improve*) mejorar; **business is picking up** el negocio se va animando

(**b**) (*continue*) **let's p. up where we left off** vamos a seguir por donde estábamos

**pickaxe** ['pɪkæks] *n* pico *m*

**picket** ['pɪkɪt] **1** *n* (**a**) (*in strike, of guards*) piquete *m*; **p. line** piquete *m* (**b**) (*stake*) estaca *f*; **p. fence** cerca *f*, estacada *f*

**2** *vt* (*during strike*) hacer piquetes en

**pickings** ['pɪkɪŋz] *npl* botín *m*; **rich p.** pingües beneficios *mpl*

**pickle** ['pɪkəl] **1** *n* = salsa agridulce a base de trocitos de fruta y verduras; **pickles** variantes *mpl*, encurtidos *mpl*; *Fam Fig* **to be in a bit of a p.** estar en un buen lío

**2** *vt* encurtir; **pickled cabbage/onions** col *f*/cebolletas *fpl* en vinagre

**pick-me-up** ['pɪkmiʌp] n Fam reconstituyente m, tónico m

**pickpocket** ['pɪkpɒkɪt] n carterista mf

**pick-up** ['pɪkʌp] n (a) **p. (arm)** (on record player) brazo m del tocadiscos; **p. (truck)** camioneta f; **p. point** (for goods, passengers) lugar m de recogida (b) Fam (improvement) recuperación f

**picky** ['pɪkɪ] adj Fam exigente, escrupuloso(a)

**picnic** ['pɪknɪk] 1 n picnic m, comida f campestre; **to go on a p.** ir de picnic; Fam Fig **it was no p.** (wasn't easy) tuvo bemoles, se las trajo; **p. basket** or **hamper** cesta f de merienda
2 vi (pt & pp **picnicked**) ir de picnic

**picnicker** ['pɪknɪkə(r)] n excursionista mf

**Pict** [pɪkt] n Hist picto(a) m,f

**pictorial** [pɪk'tɔːrɪəl] adj gráfico(a), ilustrado(a)

**picture** ['pɪktʃə(r)] 1 n (a) (painting) cuadro m, pintura f; (drawing) dibujo m; (in book) ilustración f; (photograph) fotografía f; (on TV, in mind) imagen f; **he's the p. of health** es la viva imagen de la salud; **his face was a p.** puso una cara digna de verse; Fig **the political/economic p.** el panorama político/económico; Fig **to put sb in the p.** poner a alguien al tanto or en situación; Fam Fig **I get the p.** ya veo, ya entiendo; **p. book** libro m ilustrado; **p. frame** marco m; **p. gallery** pinacoteca f; **p. postcard** postal f; **p. window** ventanal m (b) Fam (film) película f; Br **to go to the pictures** ir al cine
2 vt (a) (imagine) imaginarse; **I can't p. him as a teacher** no me lo imagino (trabajando) de profesor (b) (represent, portray) retratar

**picturesque** [pɪktʃə'resk] adj pintoresco(a)

**pidgin** ['pɪdʒɪn] n lengua f híbrida, (lengua f) pidgin m; **p. English** = mezcla de inglés con un idioma local

**pie** [paɪ] n (of meat, fish) empanada f, pastel m; (of fruit) tarta f; Fam **p. in the sky** castillos mpl en el aire; **p. chart** gráfico m de sectores

**piece** [piːs] n (a) (of paper, meat, cake) trozo m, pedazo m; (of cloth, music) pieza f; (newspaper article) artículo m; **a p. of advice** un consejo; Fig **it was a p. of cake** (very easy) estaba tirado or chupado; **a p. of carelessness** un descuido; **a p. of clothing** una prenda (de vestir); **a p. of furniture** un mueble; **a p. of land** un terreno; **that was a p. of (good) luck!** ¡fue (una) suerte!; **a p. of luggage** un bulto (de equipaje); **a p. of news** una noticia; **p. rate** (pay) tarifa f a destajo
(b) (in games, of jigsaw puzzle) pieza f; (in dominoes, draughts) ficha f
(c) (coin) **five/fifty pence p.** moneda f de cinco/cincuenta peniques
(d) (of artillery) pieza f; (firearm) arma f (de fuego)

(e) (idioms) **they are all of a p.** están cortados por el mismo patrón; **to be still in one p.** estar sano y salvo; **to give sb a p. of one's mind** cantar las cuarenta a alguien; **he said his p.** dijo lo que pensaba; **p. by p.** paso por paso, poco a poco; Fig **to go to pieces** derrumbarse; **to fall to pieces** caerse a pedazos; **to take sth to pieces** desmontar algo

▸**piece together** vt sep (parts) montar; (broken object) recomponer; (facts) reconstruir; (evidence) componer

**piecemeal** ['piːsmiːl] 1 adj deslavazado(a), poco sistemático(a) 2 adv deslavazadamente, desordenadamente

**piecework** ['piːswɜːk] n Ind (trabajo m a) destajo m

**pier** [pɪə(r)] n (landing stage) muelle m, embarcadero m; (with seaside amusements) malecón m; (of bridge) pilar m

**pierce** [pɪəs] vt perforar; **to have one's ears pierced** hacerse agujeros en las orejas

**piercing** ['pɪəsɪŋ] adj (voice, sound, look) penetrante; (wind) cortante

**piety** ['paɪətɪ] n piedad f

**pig** [pɪg] 1 n (a) (animal) cerdo m, puerco m, Am chancho m (b) Fam (greedy person) comilón(ona) m,f, glotón(ona) m,f; (unpleasant person) cerdo(a) m,f, asqueroso(a) m,f (c) very Fam (policeman) madero m (d) Fam (idioms) **to buy a p. in a poke** recibir gato por liebre; **to make a p.'s ear of sth** hacer un desaguisado con algo; **to make a p. of oneself** ponerse hasta las orejas de comida; **pigs might fly!** ¡y yo soy la reina de los mares!, ¡que te crees tú eso!
2 vt (pt & pp **pigged**) Fam **to p. oneself** ponerse las botas (comiendo)

▸**pig out** vi Fam ponerse las botas (comiendo)

**pigeon** ['pɪdʒɪn] n paloma f

**pigeonhole** ['pɪdʒɪnhəʊl] 1 n casillero m, casilla f
2 vt encasillar

**piggy** ['pɪgɪ] Fam 1 n cerdito(a) m,f; **p. bank** hucha f en forma de cerdito
2 adj **p. eyes** ojillos mpl de cerdo

**piggyback** ['pɪgɪbæk] n **to give sb a p.** llevar a alguien a cuestas

**pigheaded** [pɪg'hedɪd] adj cabezota, testarudo(a)

**piglet** ['pɪglɪt] n cochinillo m, cerdito m

**pigment** ['pɪgmənt] n pigmento m

**pigmentation** [pɪgmən'teɪʃən] n pigmentación f

**pigmy** ['pɪgmɪ] n pigmeo(a) m,f

**pigsty** ['pɪgstaɪ] n also Fig pocilga f

**pigtail** ['pɪgteɪl] n (plaited) trenza f; (loose) coleta f

**pike**[1] [paɪk] n (weapon) pica f

**pike**[2] n (fish) lucio m

**pilchard** ['pɪltʃəd] n sardina f

**pile** [paɪl] **1** n (a) (heap) pila f, montón m; **to put in(to) a p., to make a p. of** apilar; Fam **she made her p. in property** se forró con el negocio inmobiliario; Fam **to have piles of** or **a p. of work to do** tener un montón de trabajo que hacer; Fam Fig **to be at the top/bottom of the p.** estar en lo más alto/bajo de la escala **(b)** (of carpet) pelo m **(c)** Phys **(atomic) p.** pila f atómica **(d)** (building) mansión f; (column, pillar) pilar m

**2** vt amontonar, apilar; **they piled food onto my plate** me llenaron el plato de comida

**3** vi Fam **to p. into a car** meterse atropelladamente en un coche

▶**pile in** vi meterse atropelladamente

▶**pile on** vt sep **to p. on the pressure** aumentar la presión al máximo

▶**pile out** vi salir atropelladamente

▶**pile up** vi (of dirty clothes, work) acumularse, apilarse

**pile-driver** ['paɪldraɪvə(r)] n (tool) martinete m

**piles** [paɪlz] npl (haemorrhoids) almorranas fpl

**pile-up** ['paɪlʌp] n Fam (of cars) choque m masivo

**pilfer** ['pɪlfə(r)] vt & vi hurtar, sisar

**pilgrim** ['pɪlgrɪm] n peregrino(a) m,f

**pilgrimage** ['pɪlgrɪmɪdʒ] n peregrinación f, peregrinaje m; **to go on a p., to make a p.** hacer una peregrinación

**pill** [pɪl] n pastilla f, píldora f; **the p.** (contraceptive) la píldora; **to be on the p.** tomar la píldora

**pillage** ['pɪlɪdʒ] **1** n pillaje m, saqueo m

**2** vt & vi saquear

**pillar** ['pɪlə(r)] n (of building) pilar m; (of fire) columna f; Fig **a p. of society/the Church** uno de los pilares de la sociedad/la Iglesia; **from p. to post** de la Ceca a la Meca; **to be a p. of strength** ser como una roca; **p. box** buzón m (de correos)

**pillion** ['pɪljən] **1** n p. (seat) asiento m trasero

**2** adv **to ride p.** ir de paquete

**pillock** ['pɪlək] n very Fam gilipollas

**pillory** ['pɪlərɪ] **1** n picota f

**2** vt (ridicule) poner en la picota

**pillow** ['pɪləʊ] n almohada f

**pillowcase** ['pɪləʊkeɪs], **pillowslip** ['pɪləʊslɪp] n funda f de almohada

**pilot** ['paɪlət] **1** n (of plane, ship) piloto mf; TV **p. (programme)** programa m piloto; **p. light** piloto m; **p. scheme/study** proyecto m/estudio m piloto

**2** vt (plane, ship) pilotar

**pimp** [pɪmp] n chulo m

**pimple** ['pɪmpəl] n grano m

**pimply** ['pɪmplɪ] adj lleno(a) de granos

**PIN** [pɪn] n Fin (abbr **personal identification number**) PIN m, número m secreto

**pin** [pɪn] **1** n (for sewing) alfiler m; (bolt) clavija f; Med clavo m; Elec **two/three p. plug** enchufe m de dos/tres clavijas; **you could have heard a p. drop** se oía el vuelo de una mosca; Fam **pins and needles** hormigueo m; **(firing) p.** percutor m; **(safety) p.** (for fastening clothes) imperdible m, Am seguro m; (of grenade) seguro m; **p. money** dinero m extra

**2** vt (pt & pp **pinned**) (fasten with pin) clavar; (hold still) sujetar, atrapar; **to p. sb against** or **to a wall** atrapar a alguien contra una pared; **to p. the blame on sb** cargar la culpa a alguien; **he pinned his hopes on them** puso or cifró sus esperanzas en ellos

▶**pin down** vt sep **(a)** (trap) atrapar, sujetar **(b)** (identify) identificar **(c)** (force to be definite) **we tried to p. him down to a date** intentamos que se comprometiera a dar una fecha

▶**pin up** vt sep (notice) clavar; (hair) recoger; (hem) coger or prender con alfileres

**pinafore** ['pɪnəfɔː(r)] n (apron) delantal m; **p. dress** pichi m

**pinball** ['pɪnbɔːl] n **to play p.** jugar a la máquina or al flíper; **p. machine** máquina f de bolas, flíper m

**pincer** ['pɪnsə(r)] n (of crab, insect) pinza f; Mil **p. movement** movimiento m de tenaza

**pincers** ['pɪnsəz] npl (tool) tenazas fpl

**pinch** [pɪntʃ] **1** n **(a)** (action) pellizco m; (small amount) pizca f, pellizco m; **to give sb a p.** dar un pellizco a alguien **(b)** (idioms) **to feel the p.** pasar estrecheces; **at a p.** haciendo un esfuerzo; **to take sth with a p. of salt** no tomarse algo muy en serio, no dar demasiado crédito a algo

**2** vt **(a)** (nip) pellizcar; **these shoes p. my feet** estos zapatos me aprietan **(b)** Fam (steal) mangar

**3** vi (of shoes) apretar

**pincushion** ['pɪnkʊʃən] n acerico m, alfiletero m

**pine¹** [paɪn] n (tree, wood) pino m; **p. cone** piña f; **p. forest** pinar m; **p. needle** aguja f de pino; **p. nut** piñón m

**pine²** vi **to p. for sth/sb** echar de menos or añorar algo/a alguien

▶**pine away** vi consumirse de pena

**pineapple** ['paɪnæpəl] n piña f

**ping** [pɪŋ] **1** n sonido m metálico

**2** vi sonar

**ping-pong** ['pɪŋpɒŋ] n pimpón m, ping-pong m

**pinhead** ['pɪnhed] n Fam (stupid person) majadero(a) m,f

**pinion** ['pɪnjən] **1** *n (cogwheel)* piñón *m*
**2** *vt (restrain)* inmovilizar, sujetar; **to p. sb to the ground** inmovilizar a alguien en el suelo

**pink** [pɪŋk] **1** *n* **(a)** *(color m)* rosa *m*; *Fam* **to be in the p.** *(be well)* estar como una rosa **(b)** *(flower)* clavel *m*
**2** *adj* rosa; **to turn p.** sonrojarse; **p. gin** pink gin *m*, ginebra *f* con angostura

**pinkeye** ['pɪŋkaɪ] *n US* conjuntivitis *f inv*

**pinkie** ['pɪŋkɪ] *n US & Scot* (dedo *m*) meñique *m*

**pinnacle** ['pɪnəkəl] *n (of mountain, fame, career)* cima *f*, cumbre *f*

**pinpoint** ['pɪnpɔɪnt] *vt* señalar, precisar

**pinprick** ['pɪnprɪk] *n* pinchazo *m*

**pinstripe** ['pɪnstraɪp] *adj* de milrayas; **p. suit** (traje *m*) milrayas *m inv*

**pint** [paɪnt] *n (measurement)* pinta *f (0,57 litros)*; *Br* **a p.** *(of beer)* una pinta (de cerveza); **I'm going for a p.** voy a tomarme una cerveza

**pinto bean** ['pɪntəʊ'biːn] *n* alubia *f* or judía *f* pinta

**pint-size(d)** ['paɪntsaɪz(d)] *adj Fam* diminuto(a), pequeñajo(a)

**pin-up** ['pɪnʌp] *n Fam* **(a)** *(poster)* pin-ups posters *mpl* de chicas ligeritas de ropa **(b)** *(woman)* modelo *f* de revista (erótica)

**pioneer** [paɪə'nɪə(r)] **1** *n also Fig* pionero(a) *m,f*
**2** *vt* iniciar, promover

**pioneering** [paɪə'nɪərɪŋ] *adj* pionero(a)

**pious** ['paɪəs] *adj* pío(a), piadoso(a); **a p. hope** una vana ilusión

**piously** ['paɪəslɪ] *adv* piadosamente

**pip** [pɪp] **1** *n* **(a)** *(of fruit)* pepita *f* **(b)** *(on card, die)* punto *m; (on uniform)* estrella *f* **(c)** *(sound)* **the pips** *(on radio)* las señales horarias; *(on public telephone)* la señal *or* los tonos de fin de llamada **(d)** *Fam* **it/he gives me the p.!** ¡me pone enfermo!
**2** *vt (pt & pp pipped) Fam* **he was pipped at the post** lo superaron en el último momento

**pipe** [paɪp] **1** *n* **(a)** *(tube)* tubería *f; (musical instrument)* flauta *f;* **the pipes** *(bagpipes)* la gaita; **p. band** grupo *m* de gaiteros **(b)** *(for smoking)* pipa *f;* **to smoke a p.** fumarse una pipa; *Fam Fig* **put that in your p. and smoke it!** ¡toma del frasco, Carrasco!; **p. cleaner** limpiapipas *m inv;* **p. dream** sueño *m* imposible
**2** *vt (water, oil)* conducir mediante tuberías; *Fam* **piped music** hilo *m* musical
▸**pipe down** *vi Fam* cerrar el pico, callarse
▸**pipe up** *vi* hacerse oír

**pipeline** ['paɪplaɪn] *n* tubería *f*, conducto *m;* **oil p.** oleoducto *m; Fig* **there are several projects in the p.** hay en preparación varios proyectos

**piper** ['paɪpə(r)] *n (bagpipe player)* gaitero(a) *m,f; Prov* **he who pays the p. calls the tune** el que paga, manda

**pipette** [pɪ'pet] *n* pipeta *f*

**piping** ['paɪpɪŋ] **1** *n* **(a)** *(pipes)* tuberías *fpl*, tubos *mpl* **(b)** *(sound of bagpipes)* (sonido *m* de) gaitas *fpl* **(c)** *(on uniform)* ribetes *mpl*
**2** *adj (sound)* agudo(a); **a p. voice** una voz de pito
**3** *adv* **p. hot** caliente, calentito(a)

**pipsqueak** ['pɪpskwiːk] *n Fam* pelagatos *mf inv*

**piquant** ['piːkənt] *adj* fuerte, picante

**pique** [piːk] **1** *n* rabia *f;* **in a fit of p.** en una rabieta
**2** *vt* molestar

**piracy** ['paɪrəsɪ] *n also Com* piratería *f*

**piranha** [pɪ'rɑːnə] *n* piraña *f*

**pirate** ['paɪrɪt] *n* pirata *mf;* **p. edition** edición *f* pirata; **p. radio** radio *f* pirata

**pirouette** [pɪruː'et] **1** *n* pirueta *f*
**2** *vi* hacer piruetas

**Pisa** ['piːzə] *n* Pisa

**Pisces** ['paɪsiːz] *n (sign of zodiac)* Piscis *m inv;* **to be (a) P.** ser Piscis

**piss** [pɪs] *very Fam* **1** *n (urine)* meada *f;* **to have a p.** mear, echar una meada; *Fig* **to take the p. out of sb/sth** cachondearse de alguien/algo; **p. artist** borrachuzo(a) *m,f*, privota *mf*
**2** *vt* **to p. oneself, to p. one's pants** mearse encima, mearse en los pantalones
**3** *vi* mear
▸**piss about, piss around** *vi very Fam (behave foolishly)* hacer el gilipollas; *(waste time)* tocarse los huevos
▸**piss off** *very Fam* **1** *vt sep (annoy)* cabrear, joder; **to be pissed off** estar cabreado
**2** *vi (go away)* largarse; **p. off!** ¡vete al carajo!

**pissed** [pɪst] *adj very Fam* **(a)** *Br (drunk)* pedo, ciego(a); **to be p.** estar pedo or ciego(a); **to get p.** agarrarse un pedo **(b)** *US (angry)* cabreado(a); **to be p.** estar cabreado

**piss-up** ['pɪsʌp] *n very Fam* **to have a p.** privar como cosacos, ponerse ciegos a privar

**pistachio** [pɪ'stɑːʃɪəʊ] *(pl pistachios) n (nut)* pistacho *m; (tree)* alfóncigo *m*, pistachero *m*

**pistol** ['pɪstəl] *n (gun)* pistola *f;* **p. shot** disparo *m* (de pistola), pistoletazo *m*

**piston** ['pɪstən] *n* émbolo *m*, pistón *m*

**pit¹** [pɪt] *n* **(a)** *(hole in ground)* hoyo *m; (coal mine)* mina *f;* **the news hit him in the p. of his stomach** la noticia le dolió en lo más profundo; *US Fam* **it's/he's the pits!** ¡es penoso! **(b)** *Th* foso *m* (de la orquesta); **the pits** *(in motor racing)* los boxes **(c)** *(on metal, glass)* marca *f; (on skin)* picadura *f*

**pit²** *n (of cherry)* hueso *m*, pipo *m*

**pit³** (*pt & pp* **pitted**) *vt* **to p. sb against sb** enfrentar a alguien con alguien; **to p. oneself against sb** enfrentarse con alguien; **she pitted her wits against them** midió su ingenio con el de ellos

**pit-a-pat** ['pɪtə'pæt] **1** *n (of rain)* tamborileo *m*, repiqueteo *m; (of feet, heart)* golpeteo *m*
**2** *adv* **to go p.** *(of rain)* repiquetear; *(of feet, heart)* golpetear

**pitch¹** *n (tar)* brea *f*

**pitch²** [pɪtʃ] **1** *n* (**a**) *Br (for market stall)* puesto *m* (**b**) *(for sport)* campo *m* (**c**) *Mus (of note)* tono *m; Fig* **to reach such a p. that…** llegar a tal punto que…; **p. pipes** diapasón *m* (**d**) *(talk)* **(sales) p.** charla *f* para vender (**e**) *(slope) (of roof, ceiling)* pendiente *f*
**2** *vt* (**a**) *(throw)* lanzar (**b**) *(aim)* **our new model is pitched to appeal to executives** nuestro nuevo modelo está diseñado para atraer a ejecutivos; **he pitched the talk at the right level** le imprimió a la charla el tono *or* nivel apropiado (**c**) *(set up) (tent)* montar
**3** *vi (of ship, plane)* cabecear, tambalearse
▸**pitch in** *vi* colaborar, echar una mano

**pitch-black** [pɪtʃ'blæk] *adj* oscuro(a) como boca de lobo

**pitched** [pɪtʃt] *adj* (**a**) *(sloping)* en pendiente (**b**) **p. battle** batalla *f* campal

**pitcher¹** ['pɪtʃə(r)] *n (jug)* jarra *f; (large and made of clay)* cántaro *m*

**pitcher²** *n US (in baseball)* lanzador(ora) *m,f*

**pitchfork** ['pɪtʃfɔːk] *n* horca *f*

**piteous** ['pɪtɪəs] *adj* penoso(a), patético(a)

**pitfall** ['pɪtfɔːl] *n (danger)* peligro *m*, riesgo *m*

**pith** [pɪθ] *n (of orange)* piel *f* blanca; *(of argument, idea)* meollo *m;* **p. helmet** salacot *m*

**pithy** ['pɪθɪ] *adj (style, story)* sustancioso(a), enjundioso(a)

**pitiable** ['pɪtɪəbəl] *adj* lamentable

**pitiful** ['pɪtɪfʊl] *adj (arousing pity)* lastimoso(a); *(deplorable)* lamentable, deplorable

**pitifully** ['pɪtɪfʊlɪ] *adv (arousing pity)* lastimosamente; *(deplorably)* deplorablemente, lamentablemente

**pitiless** ['pɪtɪlɪs] *adj* despiadado(a)

**pitta bread** ['pɪtəbred] *n* pan *m* (de) pitta, = pan hindú sin levadura

**pittance** ['pɪtəns] *n* miseria *f*

**pituitary gland** [pɪ'tjuːɪtərɪ'glænd] *n Anat* hipófisis *f inv*, glándula *f* pituitaria

**pity** ['pɪtɪ] **1** *n* (**a**) *(compassion)* piedad *f*, compasión *f;* **to take** *or* **have p. (on sb)** apiadarse *or* compadecerse (de alguien); **to show no p.** no mostrar compasión; **for p.'s sake!** ¡por el amor de Dios! (**b**) *(misfortune)* **it's a p. that…** es una lástima *or* una pena que…; **what a p.!** ¡qué penal, ¡qué lástima!; **more's the p.** por

desgracia
**2** *vt* compadecer

**pitying** ['pɪtɪɪŋ] *adj* compasivo(a)

**pivot** ['pɪvət] **1** *n (of turning mechanism)* eje *m*, pivote *m; (key person)* eje *m*
**2** *vi (of turning mechanism)* pivotar (**on** sobre); *(of plan)* girar (**on** *or* **around** en torno a)

**pivotal** ['pɪvətəl] *adj* crucial

**pixel** ['pɪksəl] *n Comptr* píxel *m*, elemento *m* de imagen

**pixie** ['pɪksɪ] *n* duende *m*

**pizza** ['piːtsə] *n* pizza *f;* **p. parlour** pizzería *f*

**Pk** *(abbr* **Park**) parque *m*

**pkt** *(abbr* **packet**) paquete *m*

**Pl** *(abbr* **Place**) C/, calle *f*

**placard** ['plækɑːd] *n* pancarta *f*

**placate** [plə'keɪt] *vt* aplacar

**place** [pleɪs] **1** *n* (**a**) *(location)* lugar *m*, sitio *m; (in street names)* calle *f;* **to move from one p. to another** ir de un lugar a otro; **a good p. to meet people** un buen sitio para conocer (a) gente; **I'm looking for a p. to live** estoy buscando casa; **can you recommend a p. to eat?** ¿me puedes recomendar un restaurante?; **this is no p. for you** este no es lugar para ti; **I can't be in two places at once!** ¡no puedo estar en dos sitios a la vez!; *Fam* **she has worked all over the p.** ha trabajado en mil sitios; *Fig* **his explanation was all over the p.** su explicación fue muy liosa; *Fam* **my hair is all over the p.** llevo el pelo hecho un desastre; **at the interview he was all over the p.** en la entrevista no dio una a derechas; *Fam Fig* **to go places** *(be successful)* llegar lejos; **p. of birth/death** lugar de nacimiento/defunción; **p. name** topónimo *m;* **p. of work/residence** lugar de trabajo/residencia; **p. of worship** templo *m*
(**b**) *(assigned to person)* puesto *m; (assigned to thing)* sitio *m; (at university, on course)* plaza *f;* **to find a p. for sb** *(job)* encontrar colocación a alguien; **there's a time and a p. for everything** cada cosa a su tiempo; **to hold sth in p.** sujetar algo; **he had lost his p.** *(in a book)* había perdido la página por la que iba; **to take p.** tener lugar; **to take sb's p.** ocupar el puesto de alguien; *Fig* **out of p.** *(person, remark)* fuera de lugar
(**c**) *Fam (residence)* casa *f;* **a little p. in the country** una casita en el campo; **your p. or mine?** ¿en tu casa o en la mía?
(**d**) *(seat)* sitio *m*, asiento *m;* **to keep sb's p. in a queue** guardarle a alguien el sitio en una cola; **to set** *or* **lay an extra p. at table** poner un cubierto *or* servicio más en la mesa; **to change places with sb** cambiarle el sitio a alguien; *Fig* cambiarse por alguien; *Fig* **put yourself in my p.** ponte en mi lugar; **p. mat** mantel *m* indivi-

dual

**(e)** *(in competition, society)* puesto *m*, lugar *m*; **in first/second p.** en primer/segundo lugar; **in the first p.…** en primer lugar…; **in the second p.…** en segundo lugar…; **I don't know why they gave him the job in the first p.** no sé cómo se les ocurrió darle el trabajo; **you have to know your p.** hay que saber estar (en su sitio); **to put sb in his p.** poner a alguien en su sitio

**(f)** *Math* **to three decimal places** con tres (cifras) decimales

**2** *vt* **(a)** *(put)* colocar, poner; **the house is well placed** la casa está bien situada; **to be well placed to do sth** estar en una buena posición para hacer algo; **I know his face but I can't p. him** conozco su cara, pero no sé de qué

**(b)** *Com & Fin* **to p. an order (with sb)** hacer un pedido (a alguien); **to p. a contract with sb** conceder un contrato a alguien; **to p. a bet (on sth)** hacer una apuesta (por algo)

**(c)** *(find a job for)* colocar

**(d)** *(classify)* situar, colocar; **to be placed third** clasificarse en tercer lugar

**placebo** [plæ'si:bəʊ] *(pl placebos)* *n also Fig* placebo *m*

**placement** ['pleɪsmənt] *n (for trainee, student)* colocación *f* en prácticas

**placenta** [plə'sentə] *n* placenta *f*

**placid** ['plæsɪd] *adj* plácido(a)

**plagiarism** ['pleɪdʒərɪzəm] *n* plagio *m*

**plagiarize** ['pleɪdʒəraɪz] *vt* plagiar

**plague** [pleɪg] **1** *n (disease)* peste *f*; *(of insects, frogs)* plaga *f*; **to avoid sb like the p.** huir de alguien como de la peste

**2** *vt (of person)* molestar, fastidiar; *(of problem)* fastidiar; **to p. sb with questions** asediar a alguien a *or* con preguntas

**plaice** [pleɪs] *n (fish)* solla *f*, platija *f*

**plaid** [plæd] *n (fabric)* tela *f* escocesa

**plain** [pleɪn] **1** *n* llanura *f*

**2** *adj* **(a)** *(clear, unambiguous)* claro(a); **to make sth p. to sb** dejar claro algo a alguien; **I'll be quite p. with you** voy a ser claro con usted; *Fam* **it's as p. as the nose on your face** está más claro que el agua; **in p. English** en lenguaje llano; **a p. answer** una respuesta clara or clara; *Fig* **it was p. sailing** fue pan comido; **p. speaking** franqueza *f*; **the p. truth** la verdad pura y simple **(b)** *(simple) (style, garment)* sencillo(a); *Fam* **that's just p. foolishness** es pura tontería; **one p., one purl** *(in knitting)* uno del derecho, uno del revés; **p. chocolate** chocolate *m* amargo; **in p. clothes** *(of policeman)* de paisano; **p. flour** harina *f* sin levadura **(c)** *(not beautiful)* feo(a); **a p. Jane** un patito feo

**plainly** ['pleɪnlɪ] *adv* **(a)** *(clearly)* claramente; **to speak p.** hablar con franqueza **(b)** *(simply) (to live, dress)* con sencillez

**plain-spoken** [pleɪn'spəʊkən] *adj* franco(a), directo(a)

**plaintiff** ['pleɪntɪf] *n Law* demandante *mf*

**plaintive** ['pleɪntɪv] *adj* lastimero(a)

**plaintively** ['pleɪntɪvlɪ] *adv* lastimosamente

**plait** [plæt] **1** *n* trenza *f*

**2** *vt* trenzar

**plan** [plæn] **1** *n* **(a)** *(proposal, intention)* plan *m*; **a change of p.** un cambio de planes; **everything went according to p.** todo fue según lo previsto; **the best p. would be to…** lo mejor sería…; **what are your plans for the summer?** ¿qué planes tienes para el verano?; **to have other plans** tener otras cosas que hacer **(b)** *(of building, town)* plano *m*; *(of essay, novel)* esquema *m*

**2** *vt (pt & pp planned)* **(a)** *(arrange)* planear; **to p. to do sth** planear hacer algo; **it all went as planned** todo fue según lo previsto **(b)** *(design) (building)* proyectar; *(economy)* planificar

**3** *vi* hacer planes; **to p. for the future** hacer planes para el futuro

▸**plan out** *vt sep* planificar

**plane¹** [pleɪn] *n (surface, level)* plano *m*

**plane²** *n (aeroplane)* avión *m*; **by p.** en avión; **p. ticket** billete *m* de avión

**plane³** *n (tool)* cepillo *m*

**2** *vt* cepillar

**plane⁴** *n* **p. (tree)** plátano *m*

**planet** ['plænɪt] *n* planeta *m*

**planetarium** [plænɪ'teərɪəm] *n* planetario *m*

**planetary** ['plænɪtərɪ] *adj* planetario(a)

**plank** [plæŋk] *n (of wood)* tablón *m*; *Fig (central element)* punto *m* principal

**plankton** ['plæŋktən] *n* plancton *m*

**planner** ['plænə(r)] *n* encargado(a) *m,f* de la planificación; *(town planner)* urbanista *mf*

**planning** ['plænɪŋ] *n* planificación *f*; *(town planning)* urbanismo *m*; **it's still at the p. stage** aún está en fase de estudio; **p. permission** licencia *f* de obras

**plant** [plɑ:nt] **1** *n* **(a)** *(living thing)* planta *f*; **p. life** flora *f* **(b)** *Ind (equipment)* maquinaria *f*; *(factory)* fábrica *f*, planta *f*; *Ind* **p. hire** alquiler *m* de equipo; *Ind* **p. maintenance** mantenimiento *m* de la planta

**2** *vt (tree, flower)* plantar; *(crops, field)* sembrar; *(bomb)* colocar; **to p. an idea in sb's mind** inculcar una idea a alguien; *Fam* **to p. sth on sb** endosar algo a alguien

**plantain** ['plæntɪn] *n* **(a)** *(wild plant)* llantén *m* **(b)** *(similar to banana) (fruit)* plátano *m*; *(tree)* platanero *m*

**plantation** [plæn'teɪʃən] *n* plantación *f*

**planter** ['plɑ:ntə(r)] n (person) plantador(ora) m,f; (machine) sembradora f

**plaque** [plɑ:k] n (a) (bronze, marble) placa f (b) (on teeth) placa f dental (bacteriana)

**plasma** ['plæzmə] n plasma m

**plaster** ['plɑ:stə(r)] 1 n (a) (on wall) yeso m; **p. of Paris** escayola f; **to put a leg in p.** escayolar una pierna; **p. cast** escayola (b) Br (sticking) **p.** tirita f

2 vt (a) (wall) enyesar, enlucir (b) (cover) cubrir (with de); **plastered with mud** embarrado(a), cubierto(a) de barro; **his name was plastered over the front pages** su nombre aparecía en los titulares de todas las portadas

**plasterboard** ['plɑ:stəbɔ:d] n pladur® m

**plastered** ['plæstəd] adj very Fam (drunk) mamado(a), pedo; **to be p.** estar mamado or pedo

**plasterer** ['plɑ:stərə(r)] n enlucidor(ora) m,f

**plastic** ['plæstɪk] 1 n plástico m

2 adj (cup, bag) de plástico; **p. bullet** bala f de goma; **p. explosive** (explosivo m) plástico m; **p. surgeon** cirujano(a) m,f plástico(a); **p. surgery** cirugía f plástica

**plate** [pleɪt] 1 n (a) (for food) plato m; (for church offering) platillo m; Fam Fig **she's got a lot on her p.** tiene un montón de cosas entre manos; Fam Fig **to hand sth to sb on a p.** poner algo en bandeja a alguien; **p. rack** escurreplatos m inv (b) (sheet of metal, glass, plastic) placa f; **gold/silver p.** oro m/plata f chapado(a); **p. glass** vidrio m para cristaleras

2 vt (with gold) dorar; (with silver) platear

**plateau** ['plætəʊ] n Geog meseta f; Fig **to reach a p.** (of career, economy) estabilizarse

**platform** ['plætfɔ:m] n (a) (raised flat surface) plataforma f; (in train station) (where passengers stand) andén m; (where train stops) vía f; Rail **p. 4** vía 4; **p. shoes** zapatos mpl de plataforma (b) (at meeting) tribuna f; (political programme) programa m

**platinum** ['plætɪnəm] n Chem platino m; **p. blond hair** pelo m rubio platino

**platitude** ['plætɪtju:d] n tópico m, trivialidad f

**platonic** [plə'tɒnɪk] adj platónico(a)

**platoon** [plə'tu:n] n Mil pelotón m

**platter** ['plætə(r)] n (serving plate) fuente f

**platypus** ['plætɪpəs] n ornitorrinco m

**plausible** ['plɔ:zəbəl] adj (excuse, argument) plausible

**play** [pleɪ] 1 n (a) (drama) obra f (de teatro)
(b) (of children) juego m; **at p.** jugando; **to make great p. of sth** sacarle mucho juego a algo; **p. on words** juego de palabras
(c) (in sport) juego m; **p. began at one o'clock** el juego comenzó a la una; **in p.** en juego; **out of p.** fuera del campo; Fig **to come into p.** entrar en juego; Fig **to make a p. for sth** tratar de conseguir algo

(d) Tech juego m

2 vt (a) (game, sport) jugar a; (opponent) jugar contra; **to p. centre forward** jugar de delantero centro; **to p. football/chess** jugar al fútbol/ajedrez; **to p. sb at sth** jugar contra alguien a algo; **he decided not to p. Sanders** decidió no sacar a Sanders; **to p. a shot** (in snooker, pool) dar un golpe, hacer un tiro; **to p. a card** jugar una carta; Fig **stop playing games!** ¡basta ya de juegos!; Fig **to p. ball** (cooperate) cooperar; **to p. the Stock Exchange** jugar a la bolsa; **to p. a joke** or **a trick on sb** gastarle una broma a alguien

(b) (in play, film) interpretar; **to p. Macbeth** interpretar a Macbeth; Fig **to p. an important part (in sth)** desempeñar un papel importante (en algo); Fig **to p. no part in sth** (of person) no tomar parte en algo; (of thing, feeling) no tener nada que ver con algo; Fig **to p. the fool** hacer el tonto

(c) (musical instrument, piece) tocar; (record, CD, tape) poner

3 vi (a) (of children) jugar; (of animals) retozar; **to p. with sth** (pen, hair) juguetear con algo; Fig **to p. with an idea** darle vueltas a una idea; Fig **to p. with fire** jugar con fuego; Fam Fig **what's she playing at?** ¿a qué juega?

(b) (of sportsperson) jugar; **to p. fair/dirty** jugar limpio/sucio; **to p. for money** jugar por or con dinero; Fig **to p. for time** intentar ganar tiempo; Fig **to p. into sb's hands** hacerle el juego a alguien, facilitarle las cosas a alguien; Fig **to p. safe** ir a lo seguro, no arriesgarse

(c) (of musical instrument) sonar; (of musician) tocar

(d) (of actor) actuar; (of film) exhibirse; (of play) representarse

▶**play about, play around** vi juguetear, jugar

▶**play along** vi seguir la corriente (**with** a)

▶**play back** vt sep **to p. back a recording** reproducir una grabación

▶**play down** vt sep restar importancia a

▶**play off** vt sep **she played her two enemies off against each other** enfrentó a sus dos enemigos entre sí

▶**play on 1** vt insep (exploit) (feelings, fears) aprovecharse de

2 vi (continue to play) (of musician) seguir tocando; (of sportsperson) seguir jugando

▶**play out** vt sep **the drama being played out before them** la tragedia que se desarrolla ante sus ojos

▶**play up** vi Br Fam (of car, child, injury) dar guerra

**play-acting** ['pleɪæktɪŋ] n teatro m, cuento m

**playboy** ['pleɪbɔɪ] n vividor m, playboy m

**player** ['pleɪə(r)] n (sportsperson) jugador(ora) m,f; (musician) intérprete mf; (actor) actor m, actriz f, intérprete mf

**playful** ['pleɪfʊl] *adj (person, animal, mood)* juguetón(ona); *(remark)* de or en broma

**playground** ['pleɪgraʊnd] *n (at school)* patio *m* de recreo; *(in park)* zona *f* de juegos

**playgroup** ['pleɪgruːp] *n* escuela *f* infantil, guardería *f*

**playhouse** ['pleɪhaʊs] *n (theatre)* teatro *m*

**playing** ['pleɪɪŋ] *n* **p. card** carta *f*, naipe *m*; **p. field** campo *m* de juegos

**playmate** ['pleɪmeɪt] *n* compañero(a) *m,f* de juegos

**play-off** ['pleɪɒf] *n Sport* (partido *m* de) desempate *m*

**playpen** ['pleɪpen] *n* parque *m*, corral *m*

**playroom** ['pleɪruːm] *n* cuarto *m* de juegos

**playschool** ['pleɪskuːl] *n* escuela *f* infantil, guardería *f*

**plaything** ['pleɪθɪŋ] *n* juguete *m*

**playtime** ['pleɪtaɪm] *n (at school)* recreo *m*

**playwright** ['pleɪraɪt] *n* dramaturgo(a) *m,f*, autor(ora) *m,f* teatral

**plaza** ['plɑːzə] *n US (shopping centre)* centro *m* comercial

**PLC, plc** [piːel'siː] *n Br Com (abbr* **public limited company)** S.A., sociedad *f* anónima

**plea** [pliː] *n* **(a)** *(appeal)* petición *f*, súplica *f*; **to make a p. for sth** suplicar algo **(b)** *(excuse)* excusa *f*; **on the p. that...** alegando que... **(c)** *Law* declaración *f*; **to enter a p. of guilty/not guilty** declararse culpable/inocente; *US* **p. bargaining** = negociación extrajudicial entre el abogado y el fiscal por la que el acusado acepta su culpabilidad en cierto grado a cambio de no ser juzgado por un delito más grave

**plead** [pliːd] *(US pt & pp* **pled)** **1** *vt Law* **to p. sb's case** *(of lawyer)* defender a alguien; *Law* **to p. insanity** alegar enajenamiento de las facultades mentales; **to p. ignorance** alegar desconocimiento

**2** *vi* **to p. with sb (to do sth)** implorar a alguien (que haga algo); *Law* **to p. guilty/not guilty** declararse culpable/inocente

**pleasant** ['plezənt] *adj (remark, place, weather)* agradable; *(person)* agradable, simpático(a); *(surprise)* grato(a), agradable

**pleasantly** ['plezəntli] *adv (smile, behave)* con simpatía; **to be p. surprised** estar gratamente sorprendido(a)

**pleasantry** ['plezəntri] *n (joke)* broma *f*; **to exchange pleasantries** *(polite remarks)* intercambiar cumplidos

**please** [pliːz] **1** *adv* por favor; **p. don't cry** no llores, por favor; **p. tell me...** dime...; **may I? – p. do** ¿puedo? – por favor or no faltaba más; **p. sit down** tome asiento, por favor; **p. don't interrupt!** ¡no interrumpas!;

**yes, p.!** ¡sí!

**2** *vt (give pleasure to)* complacer, agradar; **you can't p. everybody** no se puede complacer a todo el mundo; **p. yourself!** ¡como quieras!; **to be easy/hard to p.** ser fácil/difícil de complacer; **p. God!** ¡ojalá!

**3** *vi* **(a)** *(like)* **he does as he pleases** hace lo que quiere; **this way, if you p.** por aquí, por favor; **and then, if you p., he blamed me for it!** ¡y luego, por si fuera poco, me echó la culpa a mí! **(b)** *(give pleasure)* agradar, complacer; **to be eager to p.** estar ansioso(a) por agradar

**pleased** [pliːzd] *adj (happy)* contento(a); **to be p.** *(happy)* estar contento(a); **to be p. with sth/sb** *(satisfied)* estar satisfecho(a) or contento(a) con algo/alguien; **to be p. to do sth** alegrarse de hacer algo; **to be p. for sb** alegrarse por alguien; **he was as p. as Punch** estaba encantado de la vida; **he's very p. with himself** está muy satisfecho or pagado de sí mismo; **p. to meet you** encantado(a) de conocerle); **I'm p. to say that...** tengo el gusto de comunicarles que...

**pleasurable** ['pleʒərəbəl] *adj* agradable, grato(a)

**pleasure** ['pleʒə(r)] *n* **(a)** *(contentment)* satisfacción *f*, placer *m*; **he took p. in informing them that they had been sacked** disfrutó mucho comunicándoles que habían sido despedidos; **it gave me great p.** fue un auténtico placer para mí; **with p.** con (mucho) gusto; **(it's) my pleasure!** ¡no hay de qué!; *Formal* **I have p. in informing you that...** tengo el gusto de or me complace informarles de que... **(b)** *(enjoyment)* placer *m*; **p. boat** barco *m* de recreo; **p. trip** viaje *m* de placer **(c)** *(will)* voluntad *f*; **at sb's p.** según disponga alguien; *Law* **to be detained at or during Her Majesty's p.** ser encarcelado(a) a discreción del Estado

**pleat** [pliːt] *n (in sewing)* pliegue *m*

**pleated** ['pliːtɪd] *adj (skirt)* plisado(a)

**plebeian** [plə'biːən] *n & adj* plebeyo(a) *m,f*

**plebiscite** ['plebɪsɪt] *n* plebiscito *m*

**plectrum** ['plektrəm] *n Mus* púa *f*, plectro *m*

**pled** [pled] *US pt & pp of* **plead**

**pledge** [pledʒ] **1** *n* **(a)** *(promise)* promesa *f* **(b)** *(token)* prenda *f*

**2** *vt (promise)* prometer; **to p. one's allegiance to the king** jurar fidelidad al rey; **to p. money** *(in radio, television appeal)* prometer hacer un donativo (de dinero)

**plenary** ['pliːnərɪ] *adj* plenario(a); **p. assembly** asamblea *f* plenaria; **p. (session)** sesión *f* plenaria

**plenipotentiary** [plenɪpə'tenʃərɪ] **1** *n* embajador(ora) *m,f* plenipotenciario(a)

**2** *adj* plenipotenciario(a)

**plentiful** ['plentɪfʊl] *adj* abundante

**plenty** ['plentɪ] **1** *n* abundancia *f*; **land of p.** tierra *f* de la abundancia

**2** *pron* **p. of time/money** mucho tiempo/dinero; **p. of food** mucha comida; **p. of books** muchos libros; **that's p.** es (más que) suficiente

**3** *adv Fam* **it's p. big enough** es grande más que de sobra

**plethora** ['pleθərə] *n* plétora *f*

**pleurisy** ['plʊərɪsɪ] *n* pleuresía *f*

**pliable** ['plaɪəbəl] *adj (wood, plastic)* flexible; *(person)* influenciable

**pliers** ['plaɪəz] *npl* alicates *mpl*; **a pair of p.** unos alicates

**plight** [plaɪt] *n* trance *m*, situación *f* comprometida

**plimsolls** ['plɪmsəlz] *npl* playeras *fpl*

**plinth** [plɪnθ] *n* pedestal *m*

**PLO** [piːˈel̩əʊ] *n (abbr* **Palestine Liberation Organization)** OLP *f*

**plod** [plɒd] ( *pt & pp* **plodded**) *vi* (a) *(walk)* caminar con paso lento; **to p. on** seguir caminando *(con lentitud o esfuerzo)* (b) *(work)* **to p. (away)** trabajar pacientemente

**plonk¹** [plɒŋk] **1** *n (sound)* golpe *m* (seco), ruido *m* (sordo)

**2** *vt Fam* **to p. sth down** dejar *or* poner algo de golpe; **to p. oneself down in an armchair** dejarse caer (de golpe) en una butaca

**plonk²** *n Br Fam (cheap wine)* vino *m* peleón

**plonker** ['plɒŋkə(r)] *n* (a) *Vulg (penis)* polla *f* (b) *very Fam (idiot)* gilipollas

**plop** [plɒp] **1** *n* glu(p) *m*, = sonido de algo al hundirse en un líquido

**2** *vi (pt & pp* **plopped**) caer haciendo glup

**plot** [plɒt] **1** *n* (a) *(conspiracy)* trama *f*, complot *m* (b) *(of play, novel)* trama *f*, argumento *m*; *Fig* **the p. thickens** el asunto se complica (c) *(land)* terreno *m*; **(vegetable) p.** huerta *f*, huerto *m*

**2** *vt (pt & pp* **plotted**) (a) *(plan)* tramar, planear; **to p. to do sth** tramar *or* planear hacer algo; **to p. a film/novel** trazar el argumento de una película/novela (b) *(draw) (curve)* trazar; *(progress, development)* representar; **to p. a course** planear *or* trazar una ruta (en el mapa)

**3** *vi (conspire)* confabularse, conspirar

**plotter** ['plɒtə(r)] *n (conspirator)* conspirador(ora) *m,f*

**plough,** *US* **plow** [plaʊ] **1** *n* arado *m*; **the P.** *(constellation)* la Osa Mayor

**2** *vt (field, furrow)* arar, labrar; *Fig* **to p. profits back into a company** reinvertir beneficios en una empresa

**3** *vi* arar, labrar; *Fig* **to p. through sth** *(work, reading)* tomarse el trabajo de hacer algo; *Fig* **to p. into sth** *(of vehicle)* chocar contra algo

▸**plough on** *vi* esforzarse en seguir adelante (**with** con)

▸**plough up** *vt sep (field)* roturar; **the park had been ploughed up by vehicles** los vehículos dejaron el parque lleno de surcos

**ploughman** ['plaʊmən] *n* labrador *m*; **p.'s lunch** = almuerzo a base de pan, queso, ensalada y encurtidos

**plover** ['plʌvə(r)] *n* chorlito *m*

**plow** *US* = **plough**

**ploy** [plɔɪ] *(pl* **ploys**) *n* estratagema *f*

**pluck** [plʌk] **1** *n (courage)* coraje *m*, valor *m*

**2** *vt (hair, feathers)* arrancar; *(flower)* coger; *(chicken)* desplumar; **to p. one's eyebrows** depilarse las cejas; **they were plucked from danger by a helicopter** un helicóptero les sacó del peligro; **to p. a guitar** puntear (a la guitarra)

**3** *vi* **to p. at sb's sleeve** tirar a alguien de la manga

▸**pluck up** *vt sep* **to p. up the courage to do sth** armarse de valor para hacer algo

**plucky** ['plʌkɪ] *adj* valiente

**plug** [plʌg] **1** *n* (a) *(for sink)* tapón *m* (b) *(electrical)* enchufe *m*; *Aut (spark)* **p.** bujía *f*; *Comptr* **p. and play** plug and play; *Fam Fig* **to pull the p. on sth** acabar con algo (c) *(of tobacco)* rollo *m* (de tabaco de mascar) (d) *Fam (publicity)* publicidad *f*; **to give sth a p.** hacer publicidad de *or* promocionar algo

**2** *vt (pt & pp* **plugged**) (a) *(block)* tapar, taponar; **to p. a leak** tapar una fuga (b) *Fam (promote)* hacer publicidad de, promocionar

▸**plug away** *vi Fam* trabajar con tesón (**at** en)

▸**plug in** *vt sep* enchufar

**plughole** ['plʌghəʊl] *n* desagüe *m*; *Fam Fig* **to go down the p.** echarse a perder

**plug-in** ['plʌgɪn] *n Comptr* dispositivo *m* opcional

**plum** [plʌm] **1** *n (fruit)* ciruela *f*; **p. pudding** = pudín con pasas y otras frutas típico de Navidad; **p. tree** ciruelo *m*

**2** *adj* (a) *(colour)* morado(a) (b) *Fam (very good)* **a p. job** un chollo (de trabajo)

**plumage** ['pluːmɪdʒ] *n* plumaje *m*

**plumb** [plʌm] **1** *n* **p. (line)** plomada *f*; **out of p.** torcido(a)

**2** *adv (exactly)* de lleno, directamente; **p. in the centre** en todo *or* justo en el centro

**3** *vt (sea)* sondear; *Fig* **to p. the depths of** abismarse *or* sumergirse en las profundidades de

▸**plumb in** *vt sep* **to p. in a washing machine** instalar una lavadora (en la red de agua)

**plumber** ['plʌmə(r)] *n* fontanero(a) *m,f*

**plumbing** ['plʌmɪŋ] *n* (a) *(job)* fontanería *f* (b) *(system)* cañerías *fpl*

**plume** [pluːm] *n (single feather)* pluma *f*; *(on hat)* penacho *m*; *(of smoke)* nube *f*, penacho *m*

**plummet** ['plʌmɪt] vi also Fig desplomarse, caer en picado

**plummy** ['plʌmɪ] adj Fam (voice, accent) engolado(a) (propio de la clase alta británica)

**plump** [plʌmp] **1** adj rechoncho(a)

  **2** vt **to p. oneself into an armchair** dejarse caer en una butaca

▸**plump down** vt sep dejar or poner de golpe; **she plumped herself down on the sofa** se dejó caer en el sofá

▸**plump for** vt insep Fam (choose) decidirse por

**plunder** ['plʌndə(r)] **1** n (action) saqueo m, pillaje m; (loot) botín m

  **2** vt saquear, expoliar

**plunge** [plʌndʒ] **1** n (dive) zambullida f; Fig (decrease) desplome m; Fam Fig **to take the p.** dar el paso (decisivo)

  **2** vt sumergir (**into** en); **to p. a knife into sb's back** hundir a alguien un cuchillo en la espalda; **to p. sb into despair** sumir a alguien en la desesperación

  **3** vi (into water) zambullirse (**into** en); Fig (decrease) desplomarse; **she plunged to her death** murió tras caer al vacío

**plunger** ['plʌndʒə(r)] n (of syringe) émbolo m; (for clearing sink) desatascador m

**plunging** ['plʌndʒɪŋ] adj (prices) en picado; **p. neckline** escote m pronunciado

**pluperfect** ['pluːpɜːfɪkt] n Gram pluscuamperfecto m

**plural** ['plʊərəl] n & adj Gram plural m

**pluralism** ['plʊərəlɪzəm] n pluralismo m

**plurality** [plʊə'rælɪtɪ] n pluralidad f

**plus** [plʌs] **1** n (pl **plusses** ['plʌsɪz]) (a) (sign) signo m más (b) (advantage) ventaja f

  **2** adj **on the p. side the bicycle is light** esta bicicleta tiene la ventaja de ser ligera; **fifteen p.** de quince para arriba, más de quince; **I got a C p.** saqué un aprobado alto

  **3** prep más; **seven p. nine** siete más nueve; **two floors p. an attic** dos pisos y una buhardilla

**plush** [plʌʃ] **1** n Tex felpa f

  **2** adj Fam lujoso(a), muy puesto(a)

**Pluto** ['pluːtəʊ] n (planet, god) Plutón m

**plutonium** [pluː'təʊnɪəm] n Chem plutonio m

**ply**[1] [plaɪ] n **three-p.** (wood, paper handkerchief) de tres capas

**ply**[2] [plaɪ] vt **to p. one's trade** ejercer su oficio; **to p. sb with questions** acribillar a alguien a preguntas; **to p. sb with drink** ofrecer bebida insistentemente a alguien

  **2** vi **to p. between** cubrir la ruta entre

**plywood** ['plaɪwʊd] n contrachapado m

**PM** [piː'em] n (abbr **Prime Minister**) primer(era) ministro(a) m,f

**p.m.** ['piːem] adv (abbr **post meridiem**) p.m., post meridiem; **6 p.m.** las 6 de la tarde

**PMT** [piːem'tiː] n Med (abbr **premenstrual tension**) (síndrome m de) tensión f premenstrual

**pneumatic** [njuː'mætɪk] adj neumático(a); **p. drill** martillo m neumático; **p. tyre** neumático m

**pneumonia** [njuː'məʊnɪə] n pulmonía f, neumonía f

**PO** [piː'əʊ] n (a) Br (abbr **Post Office**) oficina f de correos; **PO Box** apartado m de correos (b) (abbr **postal order**) giro m postal

**poach**[1] [pəʊtʃ] vt Culin (eggs) escalfar; (fish) cocer; **poached eggs** huevos mpl escalfados

**poach**[2] vt (a) (catch illegally) **to p. fish/game** cazar/pescar furtivamente (b) (employee) robar

**poacher** ['pəʊtʃə(r)] n (of fish) pescador m furtivo; (of game) cazador m furtivo

**pocket** ['pɒkɪt] n (a) (in trousers, jacket) bolsillo m; **to go through sb's pockets** buscar en los bolsillos de alguien; **prices to suit every p.** precios para todos los bolsillos; **to be out of p.** haber perdido dinero; **I paid for the presents out of my own p.** pagué los regalos de mi propio bolsillo; Fig **to line one's pockets** llenarse los bolsillos, forrarse; Fig **to have sb in one's p.** tener a alguien metido en el bolsillo; **p. calculator** calculadora f de bolsillo; **p. money** (for buying things) dinero m para gastos; (given by parents) paga f, propina f (b) (in snooker, pool) agujero m, tronera f (c) (of air, gas) bolsa f; (of resistance, rebellion) foco m

  **2** vt (put in pocket) meter en el bolsillo; Fam (steal) embolsarse

**pocketbook** ['pɒkɪtbʊk] n US (wallet) cartera f; (handbag) bolso m

**pocketknife** ['pɒkɪtnaɪf] n navaja f, cortaplumas m inv

**pockmarked** ['pɒkmɑːkt] adj (face) picado(a) (de viruelas); (surface) acribillado(a)

**pod** [pɒd] n (of plant) vaina f

**podgy** ['pɒdʒɪ] adj gordinflón(ona)

**podiatrist** [pə'daɪətrɪst] n US podólogo(a) m,f

**podium** ['pəʊdɪəm] n podio m

**poem** ['pəʊɪm] n poema m

**poet** ['pəʊɪt] n (male) poeta m; (female) poetisa f, poeta f

**poetic** [pəʊ'etɪk] adj poético(a); **it was p. justice that she should be replaced by someone she herself had sacked** fue una ironía del destino que la reemplazaran por alguien a quien ella había despedido anteriormente; **p. licence** licencia f poética

**poetical** [pəʊ'etɪkəl] adj poético(a)

**poetry** ['pəʊɪtrɪ] n poesía f; **p. in motion** poesía en movimiento; **p. reading** recital m de poesía

**poignancy** ['pɔɪnjənsɪ] n patetismo m

**poignant** ['pɔɪnjənt] *adj* patético(a), conmovedor(ora)

**point** [pɔɪnt] **1** *n* (a) *(in space)* punto *m*; **p. of contact** punto de contacto; **p. of sale** punto de venta; **p. of view** punto de vista

(b) *(in time)* instante *m*, momento *m*; **at this p. in time** en este preciso instante; **at this p. the phone rang** en ese instante sonó el teléfono; **to be on the p. of doing sth** estar a punto de hacer algo; **to reach the p. of no return** llegar a un punto irreversible; **outspoken to the p. of rudeness** franco(a) hasta lindar con la grosería

(c) *(of argument, discussion)* punto *m*, asunto *m*; **the p. is,...** la cuestión es que...; **I take your p.** estoy de acuerdo con lo que dices; **she has a p.** no le falta razón; **he made several interesting points** hizo varias observaciones *or* puntualizaciones muy interesantes; **to get to the p.** ir al grano; **that's beside the p.** eso no viene al caso; **that's not the p.** no es esa la cuestión; **what's the p.?** ¿para qué?; **to make a p. of doing sth** preocuparse de *or* procurar hacer algo; **there is no p. in waiting any longer** no vale la pena seguir esperando; **in p. of fact** en realidad; **her remarks were very much to the p.** sus comentarios fueron muy pertinentes; **it has its good points** tiene sus cosas buenas; **up to a p.** hasta cierto punto; **not to put too fine a p. on it...** hablando en plata...; **a p. of grammar/law** una cuestión gramatical/legal; **p. of order** cuestión *f* de procedimiento *or* de forma

(d) *(punctuation mark)* punto *m*; Math **(decimal) p.** coma *f* (decimal); **three p. five** tres coma cinco

(e) *(in game)* punto *m*, tanto *m*; *(in exam)* punto *m*; **to win on points** ganar por puntos

(f) *(on compass, thermometer)* grado *m*; Fin *(on stockmarket)* entero *m*, punto *m*

(g) *(of needle, pencil, sword)* punta *f*; **to end in a p.** acabar en punta

(h) *(electric socket)* toma *f* de corriente

(i) *(of land)* punta *f*, cabo *m*

(j) Rail **points** agujas *fpl*

**2** *vt (aim)* dirigir; **to p. a gun at sb** apuntar con un arma a alguien; *Fig* **to p. the finger at sb** *(accuse)* señalar (con el dedo) a alguien; *Fam* **just p. me in the right direction** *(show how to do)* basta con que me digas cómo hacerlo más o menos; **to p. the way** indicar el camino; *Fig* indicar el rumbo a seguir

**3** *vi* **to p. at sth/sb** *(with finger)* señalar algo/a alguien; **to p. north** señalar al norte; **the hour hand is pointing to ten** la manecilla horaria indica las diez; **to be pointing towards sth** estar mirando hacia algo, estar en dirección a algo; **this points to the fact that...** esto nos lleva al hecho de que...; **all the evidence**

**points to suicide** todas las pruebas sugieren que se trata de un suicidio

▶**point out** *vt sep (error)* hacer notar, indicar; *(fact)* recalcar; **to p. sth/sb out (to sb)** señalar algo/a alguien (a alguien); **to p. out to sb the advantages of sth** mostrar a alguien las ventajas de algo; **might I p. out that...?** ¿puedo hacer notar que...?

▶**point up** *vt sep (highlight)* subrayar

**point-blank** ['pɔɪnt'blæŋk] **1** *adj (refusal, denial)* rotundo(a), tajante; **at p. range** a bocajarro, a quemarropa

**2** *adv (fire)* a bocajarro, a quemarropa; **he asked me p. whether...** me preguntó de sopetón si...; **to deny sth p.** negar algo en redondo; **to refuse p.** negarse en redondo *or* de plano

**pointed** ['pɔɪntɪd] *adj* (a) *(sharp)* puntiagudo(a) (b) *(remark)* intencionado(a)

**pointedly** ['pɔɪntɪdlɪ] *adv* intencionadamente, con intención

**pointer** ['pɔɪntə(r)] *n* (a) *(indicator)* indicador *m*; *(stick)* puntero *m* (b) *Fam (advice)* indicación *f* (c) *(dog)* perro *m* de muestra, pointer *m*

**pointless** ['pɔɪntlɪs] *adj* sin sentido; **to be p.** no tener sentido

**poise** [pɔɪz] *n (balance)* equilibrio *m*; *(composure)* compostura *f*, aplomo *m*

**poised** [pɔɪzd] *adj* (a) *(composed)* equilibrado(a) (b) *(ready)* **to be p. to do sth** estar preparado(a) para hacer algo (c) *(suspended)* suspendido(a)

**poison** ['pɔɪzən] **1** *n* veneno *m*; *Fam* **what's your p.?** ¿qué tomas?; **p. gas** gas *m* tóxico; **p. ivy** zumaque *m*; **p. pen letter** anónimo *m* malicioso

**2** *vt* (a) *(person, food) (intentionally)* envenenar; *(accidentally)* intoxicar; **to p. sb's mind (against sb)** enemistar *or* encizañar a alguien (con alguien) (b) *(pollute)* contaminar

**poisoning** ['pɔɪzənɪŋ] *n* (a) *(of person, food) (intentional)* envenenamiento *m*; *(accidental)* intoxicación *f*; **to die of p.** *(intentional)* morir envenenado(a); *(accidental)* morir por intoxicación (b) *(pollution)* contaminación *f*

**poisonous** ['pɔɪzənəs] *adj (snake, plant, mushroom)* venenoso(a); *(chemical, fumes)* tóxico(a); *(remark)* envenenado(a); *(rumour, doctrine)* nocivo(a), dañino(a)

**poke** [pəʊk] **1** *n* golpe *m* *(con la punta de un objeto)*; **she gave him a p. with her umbrella** le dio con la punta del paraguas

**2** *vt* **to p. sb with one's finger/a stick** dar a alguien con la punta del dedo/de un palo; **to p. sb in the ribs** *(with elbow)* dar a alguien un codazo en las costillas; **to p. a hole in sth** hacer un agujero en algo; **to p. the fire** atizar el fuego; *Fig* **to p. one's nose into other**

**people's business** meter las narices en asuntos ajenos; **to p. fun at sb/sth** reírse de alguien/algo

**3** *vi* **to p. at sth (with one's finger/a stick)** dar un golpe a algo (con la punta del dedo/de un palo)

▸**poke about, poke around** *vi (search)* rebuscar; *(be nosy)* fisgonear, fisgar

▸**poke out 1** *vt sep* **to p. one's head out (of) the window** asomar la cabeza por la ventana; **to p. one's tongue out** sacar la lengua; **be careful! you nearly poked my eye out!** ¡ten cuidado! ¡casi me sacas un ojo!

**2** *vi (protrude)* asomar, sobresalir

**poker¹** ['pəʊkə(r)] *n (for fire)* atizador *m*

**poker²** *n (cardgame)* póquer *m*

**poker-faced** ['pəʊkəfeɪst] *adj* con cara de póquer

**poky** ['pəʊkɪ] *adj* **a p. room** un cuchitril, un cuartucho

**Poland** ['pəʊlənd] *n* Polonia

**polar** ['pəʊlə(r)] *adj* polar; **p. bear** oso *m* polar *or* blanco

**polarity** [pəʊ'lærɪtɪ] *n* polaridad *f*

**polarization** [pəʊlərar'zeɪʃən] *n* polarización *f*

**polarize** ['pəʊləraɪz] **1** *vt* polarizar
**2** *vi* polarizarse

**Polaroid®** ['pəʊlərɔɪd] *n (camera)* polaroid® *f*; *(photo)* foto *f* instantánea

**Pole** [pəʊl] *n* polaco(a) *m,f*

**pole¹** [pəʊl] *n (for supporting)* poste *m*; *(for jumping, punting)* pértiga *f*; *(for flag, tent)* mástil *m*; *Sport* **p. vault** salto *m* con pértiga

**pole²** *n Elec & Geog* polo *m*; **North/South P.** Polo Norte/Sur; *Fig* **to be poles apart** estar en polos opuestos; **P. Star** estrella *f* polar

**poleax(e)** ['pəʊlæks] *vt (physically)* noquear, tumbar de un golpe; *(emotionally)* dejar anonadado(a)

**polecat** ['pəʊlkæt] *n* turón *m*

**polemic** [pə'lemɪk] *n (controversy)* polémica *f*; *(speech, article)* diatriba *f*

**polemical** [pə'lemɪkəl] *adj* polémico(a)

**police** [pə'liːs] **1** *npl* **the p.** la policía; **200 p.** 200 policías; **p. car** coche *m* de policía; **p. constable** (agente *mf* de) policía *mf*; *US* **p. department** jefatura *f* de policía; **p. dog** perro *m* policía; **p. force** cuerpo *m* de policía; **p. officer** (agente *mf* de) policía *mf*; **p. record** antecedentes *mpl* policiales; **p. state** estado *m* policial; **p. station** comisaría *f* de policía

**2** *vt* vigilar, custodiar; *Fig* vigilar, supervisar; **the streets are not properly policed these days** no hay suficientes policías en la calle hoy en día

**policeman** [pə'liːsmən] *n* policía *m*

**policewoman** [pə'liːswʊmən] *n* (mujer *f*) policía *f*

**policy** ['pɒlɪsɪ] *n* **(a)** *(of government, personal)* política *f*; **foreign p.** política exterior; **it's a matter of p.** es una cuestión de política; **it's a good/bad p.** es/no es conveniente; **p. statement** declaración *f* de principios **(b)** *Fin* **(insurance) p.** póliza *f* (de seguros); **p. holder** asegurado(a) *m,f*

**polio** ['pəʊlɪəʊ] *n* poliomielitis *f inv*, polio *f*

**Polish** ['pəʊlɪʃ] **1** *n (language)* polaco *m*
**2** *adj* polaco(a)

**polish** ['pɒlɪʃ] **1** *n* **(a)** *(finish, shine)* brillo *m*; **to give sth a p.** dar *or* sacar brillo a algo **(b)** *(for shoes)* betún *m*, crema *f* (para calzado); *(for furniture, floors)* cera *f*; *(for metal)* abrillantador *m*; *(for nails)* esmalte *m*, laca *f* **(c)** *(refinement)* acabado *m*, refinamiento *m*

**2** *vt* **(a)** *(wood, metal, stone)* pulir; *(shoes)* dar brillo a, limpiar; *(floor)* encerar **(b)** *(improve)* pulir, perfeccionar

▸**polish off** *vt sep Fam (food)* zamparse; *(drink)* pimplarse; *(work, opponent)* cepillarse

**polished** ['pɒlɪʃt] *adj (wood, metal, stone)* pulido(a); *(shoes)* brillante, limpio(a); *(floor)* encerado(a); *(manners)* refinado(a); *(style)* acabado(a), pulido(a)

**polite** [pə'laɪt] *adj* educado(a), cortés; **to be p. to sb** ser amable *or* educado(a) con alguien; **it's not p. to...** no es de buena educación...; **in p. society** entre gente educada

**politely** [pə'laɪtlɪ] *adv* educadamente, cortésmente

**politeness** [pə'laɪtnɪs] *n* educación *f*, cortesía *f*

**politic** ['pɒlɪtɪk] *adj Formal* prudente

**political** [pə'lɪtɪkəl] *adj* político(a); **he isn't very p.** no le va mucho la política; **p. asylum** asilo *m* político; **p. prisoner** preso(a) *m,f* político(a); **p. science** ciencias *fpl* políticas, politología *f*

**politically** [pə'lɪtɪklɪ] *adv* políticamente; **p. motivated** por motivos políticos; **p. correct** políticamente correcto(a)

**politician** [pɒlɪ'tɪʃən] *n* político(a) *m,f*

**politicize** [pə'lɪtɪsaɪz] *vt* politizar

**politics** ['pɒlɪtɪks] **1** *n* política *f*
**2** *npl* **(a)** *(views)* ideas *fpl* políticas **(b)** **office p.** intrigas *fpl* de oficina

**polka** ['pɒlkə] *n* polca *f*; **a p. dot tie** una corbata de lunares

**poll** [pəʊl] **1** *n (voting)* votación *f*; **(opinion) p.** *(survey)* sondeo *m or* encuesta *f* (de opinión); **to go to the polls** acudir a las urnas; **p. tax** = impuesto directo, individual y de tarifa única pagado por los inscritos en el censo electoral para financiar la administración local

**2** *vt (votes)* obtener; *(people)* sondear

**pollen** ['pɒlən] *n* polen *m*; **p. count** concentración *f* de polen en el aire

**pollinate** ['pɒlɪneɪt] *vt* polinizar

**polling** ['pəʊlɪŋ] *n* votación *f*; **p. booth** cabina *f* electoral; **p. day** jornada *f* electoral; **p. station** colegio *m* electoral

**pollster** ['pəʊlstə(r)] *n* encuestador(ora) *m,f*

**pollutant** [pə'lu:tənt] *n* (sustancia *f*) contaminante *m*

**pollute** [pə'lu:t] *vt* contaminar

**polluter** [pə'lu:tə(r)] *n* (*company*) empresa *f* contaminante; (*industry*) industria *f* contaminante

**pollution** [pə'lu:ʃən] *n* contaminación *f*

**polo** ['pəʊləʊ] *n* (*sport*) polo *m*; **p. neck (sweater)** jersey *m* de cuello alto

**poltergeist** ['pɒltəgaɪst] *n* espíritu *m* or fuerza *f* paranormal, poltergeist *m*

**poly** ['pɒlɪ] *n Br Fam* (*polytechnic*) (escuela *f*) politécnica *f*

**poly bag** ['pɒlɪ'bæg] *n Fam* bolsa *f* de plástico

**polyester** [pɒlɪ'estə(r)] *n* poliéster *m*

**polygamy** [pə'lɪgəmɪ] *n* poligamia *f*

**polyglot** ['pɒlɪglɒt] *n & adj* políglota(a) *m,f*

**polygon** ['pɒlɪgən] *n* polígono *m*

**polymer** ['pɒlɪmə(r)] *n Chem* polímero *m*

**Polynesia** [pɒlɪ'ni:zɪə] *n* Polinesia

**Polynesian** [pɒlɪ'ni:zɪən] *n & adj* polinesio(a) *m,f*

**polyp** ['pɒlɪp] *n Med* pólipo *m*

**polyphonic** [pɒlɪ'fɒnɪk] *adj Mus* polifónico(a)

**polystyrene** [pɒlɪ'staɪri:n] *n* poliestireno *m*

**polytechnic** [pɒlɪ'teknɪk] *n Br* (escuela *f*) politécnica *f*

**polythene** ['pɒlɪθi:n] *n* polietileno *m*; **p. bag** bolsa *f* de plástico

**polyunsaturated** [pɒlɪʌn'sætʃʊreɪtɪd] *adj* poliinsaturado(a)

**polyurethane** [pɒlɪ'jʊərɪθeɪn] *n* poliuretano *m*

**pom** [pɒm] = **pommie**

**pomegranate** ['pɒmɪgrænɪt] *n* (*fruit*) granada *f*; **p. (tree)** granado *m*

**pommie, pommy** ['pɒmɪ] *n Fam Pej* = término utilizado en Australia para referirse a los ingleses

**pomp** [pɒmp] *n* pompa *f*, boato *m*; **p. and circumstance** pompa y circunstancia

**pompom** ['pɒmpɒm] *n* (*on hat*) pompón *m*

**pomposity** [pɒm'pɒsɪtɪ] *n* pretenciosidad *f*, pedantería *f*

**pompous** ['pɒmpəs] *adj* (*person*) pretencioso(a), pedante; (*language, remark*) altisonante, grandilocuente; (*style, speech*) pomposo(a), altisonante

**ponce** [pɒns] *n* (a) *very Fam* (*effeminate man*) marica *m* (b) (*pimp*) chulo *m*

▶**ponce about, ponce around** *vi Fam* (a) (*waste time*) perder el tiempo (b) (*of effeminate man*) hacer el mariquita

**poncho** ['pɒntʃəʊ] *n* (*pl* **ponchos**) *n* poncho *m*

**pond** [pɒnd] *n* estanque *m*

**ponder** ['pɒndə(r)] **1** *vt* considerar

**2** *vi* **to p. over** or **on sth** reflexionar sobre algo

**ponderous** ['pɒndərəs] *adj* (*person, movement*) pesado(a), cansino(a); (*progress*) ralentizado(a), muy lento(a); (*piece of writing*) cargante, pesado(a)

**pong** [pɒŋ] *Fam* **1** *n* (*smell*) tufo *m*, peste *f*

**2** *vi* atufar, apestar

**pontiff** ['pɒntɪf] *n* pontífice *m*

**pontificate¹** [pɒn'tɪfɪkət] *n Rel* pontificado *m*

**pontificate²** [pɒn'tɪfɪkeɪt] *vi* pontificar

**pontoon¹** [pɒn'tu:n] *n* (*float*) pontón *m*; **p. bridge** puente *m* de pontones

**pontoon²** *n* (*card game*) veintiuna *f*

**pony** ['pəʊnɪ] *n* poni *m*; **to go p. trekking** hacer recorridos en poni

**ponytail** ['pəʊnɪteɪl] *n* (*hairstyle*) coleta *f*

**poo** [pu:] *n* (*pl* **poos**) *n Fam* caca *f*; **to do** or **have a p.** hacer caca

**poodle** ['pu:dəl] *n* caniche *m*

**poof** [pʊf], **poofter** ['pʊftə(r)] *n very Fam* maricón *m*, marica *m*

**pooh¹** [pu:] *exclam* (*at a smell*) ¡puaj!; (*scornful*) ¡bah!

**pooh²** = **poo**

**pooh-pooh** ['pu:'pu:] *vt* **to p. a suggestion** despreciar una sugerencia

**pool¹** [pu:l] *n* (*pond*) charca *f*; (*puddle, of blood*) charco *m*; (**swimming**) **p.** piscina *f*

**pool²** **1** *n* (a) (*group*) conjunto *m*; (*of money*) fondo *m* común; **car p.** parque *m* móvil, flota *f* de automóviles (b) **the pools** las quinielas; **to do the (football) pools** jugar a las quinielas (de fútbol)

**2** *vt* (*ideas, resources*) poner en común

**pool³** *n* (*game*) billar *m* americano; **p. table** mesa *f* de billar americano

**pooped** [pu:pt] *adj Fam* hecho(a) migas or polvo

**poor** [pʊə(r)] **1** *npl* **the p.** los pobres

**2** *adj* (a) (*not rich*) pobre; **the abacus is the p. man's calculator** el ábaco es la calculadora de los pobres (b) (*inferior*) malo(a); (*chances, reward*) escaso(a); **to be in p. health** estar mal de salud; **to have a p. memory** tener mala memoria; **to be p. at maths** no ser bueno(a) en matemáticas; **to be a p. sailor** marearse siempre en los barcos; **the light is p.** hay poca luz; **to be a p. loser** ser un/una mal perdedor(ora); **in p. taste** de mal gusto (c) (*expres-*

*sing pity)* **p. creature** *or* **thing!** ¡pobrecillo(a)!; **p. (old) Tim!** ¡pobre Tim!

**poorly** ['pʊəlɪ] **1** *adv* mal; **p. dressed** mal vestido(a); **to be p. off** ser pobre

**2** *adj* enfermo(a); **to be p.** estar enfermo

**pop¹** [pɒp] **1** *n (music)* (música *f*) pop *m*

**2** *adj* **p. art** arte *m* pop; **p. group** grupo *m* (de música) pop; **p. music** música *f* pop; **p. singer** cantante *mf* pop; **p. song** canción *f* pop

**pop²** *n US (father)* papá *m*

**pop³ 1** *n* **(a)** *(sound)* pequeño estallido *m* **(b)** *Fam (fizzy drink)* gaseosa *f*

**2** *vt (pt & pp* **popped)** **(a)** *(burst)* hacer explotar **(b)** *Fam (put quickly)* **to p. sth into a drawer** poner *or* echar algo en un cajón; **to p. one's head out of the window** asomar la cabeza por la ventana; *Fam* **he decided to p. the question** decidió pedirle que se casara con él; **to p. pills** atiborrarse de pastillas

**3** *vi* **(a)** *(burst)* estallar, explotar; *(of cork)* saltar; **my ears popped** se me destaponaron los oídos **(b)** *Fam (go quickly)* **we popped over to France for the weekend** el fin de semana hicimos una escapada a Francia

▸**pop in** *vi Fam* pasarse un momento *(por casa de alguien)*

▸**pop off** *vi very Fam (die)* irse al otro barrio

▸**pop out** *vi Fam (go out)* salir

**pop.** *(abbr* **population)** población *f*

**popcorn** ['pɒpkɔ:n] *n* palomitas *fpl* de maíz

**pope** [pəʊp] *n* papa *m*

**pop-eyed** ['pɒpaɪd] *adj Fam* de ojos saltones

**popgun** ['pɒpgʌn] *n* pistola *f* de juguete *(de aire comprimido)*

**poplar** ['pɒplə(r)] *n* álamo *m*

**poplin** ['pɒplɪn] *n (cloth)* popelina *f*, popelín *m*

**popper** ['pɒpə(r)] *n Br Fam (fastener)* automático *m*, corchete *m*

**poppet** ['pɒpɪt] *n Old-fashioned Fam* **she's a p.** es una ricura; **my p.!** ¡mi tesoro!, ¡mi vida!

**poppy** ['pɒpɪ] *n* amapola *f*; **p. seed** semilla *f* de amapola

**poppycock** ['pɒpɪkɒk] *n Fam (nonsense)* majaderías *fpl*

**populace** ['pɒpjʊləs] *n Formal* **the p.** el pueblo, la plebe

**popular** ['pɒpjʊlə(r)] *adj (in general)* popular; *(newspapers, TV programmes)* de masas; **you won't make yourself very p. doing that** no va a sentar nada bien que hagas eso; **she is p. with her colleagues** cae bien a sus compañeros; **by p. demand** a petición popular *or* del público; **contrary to p. belief** en contra de lo que comúnmente se cree

**popularity** [pɒpjʊ'lærɪtɪ] *n* popularidad *f*; **p. rating** índice *m* de popularidad

**popularize** ['pɒpjʊləraɪz] *vt (make popular)* popularizar; *(make easy to understand)* divulgar

**popularly** ['pɒpjʊləlɪ] *adv* comúnmente, popularmente; **it is p. believed that...** todo el mundo cree que...

**populate** ['pɒpjʊleɪt] *vt* poblar; **sparsely populated** *(region)* poco poblado(a)

**population** [pɒpjʊ'leɪʃən] *n* población *f*; **p. explosion** explosión *f* demográfica

**populist** ['pɒpjʊlɪst] *n & adj* populista *mf*

**populous** ['pɒpjʊləs] *adj* populoso(a)

**porcelain** ['pɔ:slɪn] *n* porcelana *f*; **p. ware** porcelana

**porch** [pɔ:tʃ] *n Br (entrance)* zaguán *m*; *US (veranda)* porche *m*

**porcupine** ['pɔ:kjʊpaɪn] *n* puerco *m* espín

**pore** [pɔ:r] *n* poro *m*

▸**pore over** *vt insep* leer atentamente, estudiar con detenimiento

**pork** [pɔ:k] *n (carne f de)* cerdo *m or Am* chancho *m*; **p. chop** chuleta *f* de cerdo; **p. pie** empanada *f* de carne de cerdo

**porn** [pɔ:n] *n Fam* porno *m*; **soft/hard p.** porno blando/duro

**pornographic** [pɔ:nə'græfɪk] *adj* pornográfico(a)

**pornography** [pɔ:'nɒgrəfɪ] *n* pornografía *f*

**porous** ['pɔ:rəs] *adj* poroso(a)

**porpoise** ['pɔ:pəs] *n* marsopa *f*

**porridge** ['pɒrɪdʒ] *n* gachas *fpl* de avena; **p. oats** copos *mpl* de avena

**port¹** [pɔ:t] *n (harbour, town)* puerto *m*; **in p.** en puerto; *also Fig* **p. of call** escala *f*; *Prov* **any p. in a storm** en casos extremos, se olvidan los remilgos; **P. of Spain** Puerto España

**port²** *n Naut (left-hand side)* babor *m*

**port³** *n (drink)* (vino *m* de) oporto *m*

**port⁴** *n Comptr* puerto *m*; **parallel/serial p.** puerto paralelo/(en) serie

**portable** ['pɔ:təbəl] *adj* portátil

**Port-au-Prince** [pɔ:təʊ'prɛs] *n* Puerto Príncipe

**portcullis** [pɔ:t'kʌlɪs] *n* rastrillo *m (reja)*

**portend** [pɔ:'tend] *vt Formal* augurar

**portent** ['pɔ:tent] *n Formal (omen)* augurio *m*

**portentous** [pɔ:'tentəs] *adj Formal (significant)* decisivo(a), relevante; *(threatening)* de mal agüero

**porter** ['pɔ:tə(r)] *n (at station)* mozo *m* de equipaje; *(at hotel)* portero(a) *m,f*, conserje *mf*; *(in hospital)* celador(ora) *m,f*

**portfolio** [pɔ:t'fəʊlɪəʊ] *(pl* **portfolios)** *n (for documents, drawings)* cartera *f*; *(of person's work)* carpeta *f*; *Fin* **share p.** cartera de valores

**porthole** ['pɔ:thəʊl] *n Naut* portilla *f*, ojo *m* de buey

**portion** ['pɔ:ʃən] *n (share)* parte *f*, porción *f*; *(of food)* ración *f*, porción *f*

▸**portion out** *vt sep* repartir

**portly** ['pɔ:tlɪ] *adj* corpulento(a)

**portrait** ['pɔ:treɪt] *n also Fig* retrato *m*; **he had his p. painted** le pintaron un retrato; **p. gallery** galería *f* de retratos; *Comptr* **p. (orientation)** formato *m* vertical *or* de retrato; **p. painter** retratista *mf*

**portray** [pɔ:'treɪ] *vt (of painting, writer, book)* retratar, describir; *(of actor)* interpretar (el papel de)

**portrayal** [pɔ:'treɪəl] *n (description)* descripción *f*, representación *f*; *(by actor)* interpretación *f*

**Portugal** ['pɔ:tjʊgəl] *n* Portugal

**Portuguese** [pɔ:tjʊ'gi:z] **1** *n* (a) *(pl* **Portuguese)** *(person)* portugués(esa) *m,f* (b) *(language)* portugués *m*
**2** *adj* portugués(esa)

**POS** [pi:əʊ'es] *n Com (abbr* **point of sale)** punto *m* de venta

**pose** [pəʊz] **1** *n* (a) *(position)* postura *f*, posición *f* (b) *Pej (affectation)* pose *f*; **it's just a p.** no es más que una pose
**2** *vt (problem, question)* plantear; *(danger, threat)* suponer
**3** *vi (for portrait)* posar; *Pej (behave affectedly)* tomar *or* hacer poses; **to p. as** *(pretend to be)* hacerse pasar por

**poser** ['pəʊzə(r)] *n Fam* (a) *Pej (affected person)* afectado *m,f* (b) *(difficult question)* rompecabezas *m inv*

**posh** [pɒʃ] *Br* **1** *adj (person, accent)* pijo(a); *(restaurant, area, clothes)* elegante
**2** *adv* **to talk p.** hablar con acento pijo

**position** [pə'zɪʃən] **1** *n* (a) *(physical posture)* posición *f*; **in a horizontal/vertical p.** en posición horizontal/vertical; **in the on/off p.** *(of switch, lever)* (en la posición de) encendido/apagado
(b) *(opinion)* postura *f*, posición *f*
(c) *(place)* posición *f*, lugar *m*; *(in sport)* posición *f*; **in p.** en su sitio; **out of p.** fuera de su sitio
(d) *(situation)* posición *f*, situación *f*; **to be in a strong p.** estar en una buena posición; **put yourself in my p.** ponte en mi lugar *or* situación; **to be in a p. to do sth** estar en condiciones de hacer algo; **to be in no p. to do sth** no estar en condiciones de hacer algo
(e) *Formal (job)* puesto *m*, empleo *m*; **a p. of responsibility** un puesto de responsabilidad
**2** *vt (place) (object)* colocar, situar; *(troops)* apostar; **to p. oneself** colocarse, situarse; **to be well/poorly positioned to do sth** estar en una buena/mala posición para hacer algo

**positioning** [pə'zɪʃənɪŋ] *n Com* posicionamiento *m*

**positive** ['pɒzɪtɪv] *adj* (a) *(answer)* afirmativo(a); *(evidence, proof)* concluyente; *Med* **the test was p.** la prueba ha dado positivo; **on**

**the p. side** como aspecto positivo (b) *(constructive) (person, philosophy)* positivo(a); **p. discrimination** discriminación *f* positiva; **p. thinking** actitud *f* positiva (c) *(certain)* (completamente) seguro(a); **to be p. about sth** estar completamente seguro de algo (d) *(for emphasis)* **it's a p. disgrace** es una verdadera desgracia (e) *Math & Elec* positivo(a)

**positively** ['pɒzɪtɪvlɪ] *adv* (a) *(answer)* afirmativamente; *(think, react)* positivamente (b) *(for emphasis)* verdaderamente, realmente; *Fam* **p. not** de ninguna manera

**posse** ['pɒsɪ] *n (to catch criminal)* partida *f or* cuadrilla *f* (de persecución); *Fig (group)* banda *f*, cuadrilla *f*

**possess** [pə'zes] *vt* (a) *(property, quality, faculty)* poseer (b) **possessed by fear/rage** embargado(a) por el miedo/la rabia; **what possessed you to do that?** ¿qué te impulsó a hacer eso?

**possession** [pə'zeʃən] *n (ownership, thing possessed)* posesión *f*; **to be in p. of sth** estar en posesión de algo; **in full p. of his senses** *or* **faculties** en plena posesión de sus facultades (mentales)

**possessive** [pə'zesɪv] **1** *n Gram* posesivo *m*
**2** *adj (parent, lover) & Gram* posesivo(a); **to be p. of** *or* **about sb/sth** ser posesivo con alguien/algo

**possessor** [pə'zesə(r)] *n* poseedor(ora) *m,f*

**possibility** [pɒsɪ'bɪlɪtɪ] *n* posibilidad *f*; **to be within/outside the bounds of p.** entrar/no entrar dentro de lo posible; **that is a distinct p.** es una posibilidad real; **to allow for all possibilities** prepararse para cualquier eventualidad

**possible** ['pɒsɪbəl] **1** *n (person)* candidato(a) *m,f* posible
**2** *adj* posible; **to make sth p.** hacer posible algo; **if p.** si es posible; **it is p. that he will come** es posible que venga; **as much as p.** cuanto sea posible; **I want you to try, as much as p., to behave** quiero que, en la medida de lo posible, intentes portarte bien; **as soon as p.** cuanto antes; **whenever/wherever p.** cuando/donde sea posible; **anything's p.** todo es posible

**possibly** ['pɒsɪblɪ] *adv* (a) *(perhaps)* posiblemente; **will you go? – p.** ¿irás? – puede *or* quizá; **p. not** puede que no (b) *(for emphasis)* **I can't p. do it** me resulta de todo punto imposible hacerlo; **I'll do all I p. can** haré todo lo que esté en mi mano; **how could you p. do such a thing?** ¿cómo se te ocurrió hacer semejante cosa?

**post¹** [pəʊst] **1** *n* (a) *(wooden stake)* poste *m* (b) *(job, military position)* puesto *m*; **to be/die at**

one's p. estar/morir al pie del cañón

  2 vt Mil (assign) destinar

**post²** vt (affix) poner, pegar; **p. no bills** (sign) prohibido fijar carteles

**post³** Br 1 n (mail) correo m; **by p.** por correo; **the first p.** el correo de (primera hora de) la mañana; **to miss the p.** llegar tarde para la recogida del correo; **it's in the p.** ha sido enviado por correo; **p. office** oficina f de correos; **the P. Office** (government department) Correos m

  2 vt (letter) enviar or mandar (por correo); Fam Fig **I'll keep you posted** te mantendré informado(a)

**postage** ['pəʊstɪdʒ] n franqueo m; **p. and packing** gastos mpl de envío; **p. paid** franqueo pagado; **p. stamp** sello m (de correos)

**postal** ['pəʊstəl] adj postal; **p. order** giro m postal; **p. vote** voto m por correo

**postbag** ['pəʊstbæg] n Br (bag) saca f de correos

**postbox** ['pəʊstbɒks] n Br buzón m (de correos)

**postcard** ['pəʊstkɑːd] n (tarjeta f) postal f

**postcode** ['pəʊstkəʊd] n Br código m postal

**postdate** [pəʊst'deɪt] vt extender con fecha posterior

**poster** ['pəʊstə(r)] n (for advertising) cartel m, póster m; (of painting, pop group) póster m; **p. paint** témpera f

**posterior** [pɒs'tɪərɪə(r)] n Hum (buttocks) trasero m, posaderas fpl

**posterity** [pɒs'terɪtɪ] n posteridad f

**postgraduate** [pəʊst'grædjʊɪt] 1 n estudiante mf de posgrado

  2 adj de posgrado; **p. studies** estudios mpl de posgrado

**posthaste** ['pəʊst'heɪst] adv a toda prisa

**posthumous** ['pɒstjʊməs] adj póstumo(a)

**posthumously** ['pɒstjʊməslɪ] adv póstumamente

**posting** ['pəʊstɪŋ] n Mil destino m

**postman** ['pəʊstmən] n Br cartero m

**postmark** ['pəʊstmɑːk] n matasellos m inv

**postmaster** ['pəʊstmɑːstə(r)] n funcionario m de correos

**postmistress** ['pəʊstmɪstrɪs] n funcionaria f de correos

**postmodernist** [pəʊst'mɒdənɪst] n & adj posmoderno(a) m,f

**postmortem** [pəʊst'mɔːtəm] n autopsia f

**postnatal** [pəʊst'neɪtəl] adj Med posparto, puerperal; **p. depression** depresión f puerperal or posparto

**post-operative** [pəʊst'ɒpərətɪv] adj Med pos(t)operatorio(a)

**postpone** [pəʊst'pəʊn] vt aplazar, posponer

**postponement** [pəʊst'pəʊnmənt] n aplazamiento m

**postscript** ['pəʊsskrɪpt] n posdata f

**postulate** ['pɒstjʊleɪt] vt postular

**posture** ['pɒstʃə(r)] 1 n postura f; **to have good/bad p.** tener (una) buena/mala postura

  2 vi tomar or hacer poses

**postwar** ['pəʊst'wɔː(r)] adj de posguerra; **the p. period** la posguerra

**posy** ['pəʊzɪ] n ramillete m, ramo m

**pot** [pɒt] 1 n (a) (container) bote m; (for cooking) cacerola f, olla f; (for tea) tetera f; (for coffee) cafetera f; **pots and pans** cazos mpl y ollas; **I'd like a p. of tea** quiero un té (de tetera); Fam **pots of money** montones de dinero; Fam **to go to p.** irse al garete; **to take a p. shot at sth** disparar al tuntún a algo; **p. plant** planta f de interior (b) very Fam (marijuana) maría f

  2 vt (pt & pp potted) (a) (butter, meat) envasar; (plant) plantar (en tiesto) (b) (in snooker) meter

**potash** ['pɒtæʃ] n potasa f

**potassium** [pə'tæsɪəm] n potasio m

**potato** [pə'teɪtəʊ] (pl potatoes) n patata f, papa f; Br **p. crisps,** US **p. chips** patatas fpl fritas (de bolsa); **p. peeler** pelapatatas m inv; **p. salad** ensalada f de patatas

**potbellied** [pɒt'belɪd] adj (from over-eating) barrigón(ona); (from malnourishment) con el vientre hinchado

**potency** ['pəʊtənsɪ] n potencia f

**potent** ['pəʊtənt] adj potente

**potentate** ['pəʊtənteɪt] n soberano m absoluto

**potential** [pə'tenʃəl] 1 n potencial m; **to have p.** tener potencial; **she failed to fulfil her p.** no llegó a explotar todo su potencial

  2 adj potencial

**potentially** [pə'tenʃəlɪ] adv en potencia

**pothole** ['pɒthəʊl] n (cave) cueva f; (in road) bache m

**potholer** ['pɒthəʊlə(r)] n espeleólogo(a) m,f

**potholing** ['pɒthəʊlɪŋ] n espeleología f; **to go p.** hacer espeleología

**potion** ['pəʊʃən] n poción f

**potluck** ['pɒt'lʌk] n Fam **to take p.** aceptar lo que haya

**potpourri** [pəʊ'pʊərɪ] n (of flowers, music) popurrí m

**potted** ['pɒtɪd] adj (a) (food) en conserva (b) **a p. version** una versión condensada

**potter¹** ['pɒtə(r)] n alfarero(a) m,f, ceramista mf; **p.'s wheel** torno m (de alfarero)

**potter²** vi Br **to p. about** or **around** entretenerse

**pottery** ['pɒtərɪ] n (art, place) alfarería f; (objects) cerámica f, alfarería f

**potty**[1] ['pɒtɪ] *n* orinal *m*; **p. training** = proceso de enseñar a un niño a usar el orinal

**potty**[2] *adj Br Fam (mad)* majareta, chalado(a); **to be p.** estar majareta *or* chalado(a); **to go p.** volverse majareta; **to be p. about sb/sth** estar loco(a) por alguien/algo

**potty-trained** ['pɒtɪtreɪnd] *adj* **he/she is p.** ya no necesita pañales

**pouch** [paʊtʃ] *n* **(a)** *(for money)* saquito *m*; *(for tobacco)* petaca *f*; *(for ammunition)* cebador *m* **(b)** *(of marsupial)* marsupio *m*

**pouf(fe)** [pu:f] *n* puf *m*

**poulterer** ['pəʊltərə(r)] *n* pollero(a) *m,f*

**poultice** ['pəʊltɪs] *n* cataplasma *f*

**poultry** ['pəʊltrɪ] *n (birds)* aves *fpl* de corral; *(meat)* carne *f* de ave *or* pollería; **p. farm** granja *f* avícola; **p. farmer** avicultor(ora) *m,f*

**pounce** [paʊns] *vi* abalanzarse **(on** sobre)

**pound**[1] [paʊnd] *n* **(a)** *(unit of weight)* libra *f* *(= 0,454 kg)* **(b)** *(British currency)* libra *f* (esterlina); **p. coin** moneda *f* de una libra; **p. sign** símbolo *m* de la libra; **p. sterling** libra esterlina

**pound**[2] *n (for dogs)* perrera *f*; *(for cars)* depósito *m* de coches

**pound**[3] **1** *vt (crush)* machacar; *(with artillery)* atacar; **to p. sth to pieces** destrozar algo a golpes; **to p. sb into submission** someter a alguien por la fuerza

**2** *vi (of drum)* redoblar; *(of heart)* latir, palpitar; **to p. at** *or* **on sth** aporrear algo; **my head is pounding** tengo la cabeza a punto de estallar

**pounding** ['paʊndɪŋ] *n* **to give sb a p.** dar una buena tunda a alguien

**pour** [pɔ:(r)] **1** *vt* verter **(into** en); **to p. sb a drink** servir una bebida a alguien; **to p. money into a project** invertir un dineral en un proyecto

**2** *vi* brotar, fluir; **it's pouring (with rain)** llueve a cántaros; **sweat was pouring off him** le chorreaba el sudor; **tourists were pouring into the palace** entraban al palacio turistas a espuertas

▸**pour in 1** *vt sep (liquid)* verter

**2** *vi (of liquid)* entrar a raudales; *(of people, letters)* llegar a raudales

▸**pour out 1** *vt sep (tea, coffee)* servir; *Fig (anger, grief)* desahogar

**2** *vi (of liquid)* salirse; *Fig (of people)* salir a raudales

**pouring** ['pɔ:rɪŋ] *adj (rain)* torrencial

**pout** [paʊt] **1** *n (in annoyance)* mohín *m*; *(seductive)* mueca *f* seductora (con los labios)

**2** *vi (in annoyance)* hacer un mohín, ponerse de morros; *(seductively)* fruncir los labios con aire seductor

**poverty** ['pɒvətɪ] *n* pobreza *f*; *Fig (of ideas)* escasez *f*, pobreza *f*; **to live in p.** vivir en la pobreza; **p. line** umbral *m* de pobreza

**poverty-stricken** ['pɒvətɪstrɪkən] *adj* empobrecido(a), depauperado(a)

**POW** [pi:əʊ'dʌbəlju:] *n (abbr* **prisoner of war***)* prisionero(a) *m,f* de guerra

**powder** ['paʊdə(r)] **1** *n* polvo *m*; *(face)* **p.** polvos *mpl*; *Fig* **p. keg** polvorín *m*; **p. puff** borla *f*; **p. room** *(toilet)* servicios *mpl* de señoras

**2** *vt* **to p. sth with sugar** espolvorear azúcar sobre algo; **to p. one's face** empolvarse la cara; *Euph* **to p. one's nose** ir al tocador

**powdered** ['paʊdəd] *adj (milk)* en polvo

**powdery** ['paʊdərɪ] *adj (substance)* arenoso(a); *(snow)* en polvo; *(apple, potato)* harinoso(a)

**power** ['paʊə(r)] **1** *n* **(a)** *(authority)* poder *m*; **to come to p.** subir al poder; **to be in/out of p.** estar/no estar en el poder; **to be in sb's p.** estar en poder de alguien; **he had them in his p.** los tenía en su poder; **p. base** bastión *f* de popularidad; **p. struggle** lucha *f* por el poder **(b)** *(capacity)* capacidad *f*, facultad *f*; **to have the p. to do sth** tener la facultad de hacer algo; **she did everything in her p. to help** hizo todo lo que estuvo en su mano para ayudar; **it is beyond my p.** no está en mi mano; **to be at the height** *or* **peak of one's powers** estar en plenas facultades; *Fam* **that'll do you a p. of good** eso te sentará estupendamente; **powers of concentration** capacidad *f* de concentración; **powers of persuasion** poder *m* de persuasión; **the p. of speech** la facultad del habla; **p. of life and death over sb** poder para decidir sobre la vida de alguien

**(c)** *(physical strength)* potencia *f*; *Aut* **p. steering** dirección *f* asistida, servodirección *f*

**(d)** *(powerful person)* autoridad *f*; *(powerful group, nation)* potencia *f*; **the great powers** las grandes potencias; *Fig* **the p. behind the throne** el/la que maneja los hilos; **the powers that be** las autoridades

**(e)** *Law* competencia *f*; **p. of attorney** poder *m* (notarial)

**(f)** *(electricity)* electricidad *f*; *(energy)* energía *f*; **wind p.** energía eólica; **p. cut** corte *m* de corriente *or* del fluido eléctrico; **p. pack** alimentador *m* de corriente; **p. plant** *or* **station** central *f* eléctrica; **p. point** toma *f* de corriente

**(g)** *Math* potencia *f*; **three to the p. of ten** tres elevado a diez

**2** *vt (provide with power)* propulsar; **powered by two engines** con dos motores

**power-assisted steering** ['paʊər-əsɪstɪd'stɪərɪŋ] *n Aut* dirección *f* asistida

**powerful** ['paʊəfʊl] *adj (muscles, engine, voice)* potente; *(country, politician)* poderoso(a); *(drug, smell)* fuerte; *(speech, image)* conmovedor(ora)

**powerhouse** ['pauəhaus] *n Fam (person)* motor *m*

**powerless** ['pauəlıs] *adj* impotente; **to be p. to react** no tener capacidad para *or* no ser capaz de reaccionar

**PR** [pi:'ɑ(r)] *n* (a) (*abbr* **public relations**) relaciones *fpl* públicas (b) *Pol* (*abbr* **proportional representation**) representación *f* proporcional

**practicable** ['præktıkəbəl] *adj* factible, viable

**practical** ['præktıkəl] **1** *n (lesson)* (clase *f*) práctica *f*; *(exam)* examen *m* práctico

**2** *adj* (a) *(mind, solution)* práctico(a); **he's very p.** es muy práctico; **for all p. purposes** a efectos prácticos; **p. joke** broma *f* (pesada); **to play a p. joke on sb** gastar una broma a alguien (b) *(virtual)* **it's a p. certainty** es prácticamente seguro

**practicality** [præktı'kælıtı] *n (of suggestion, plan)* viabilidad *f*; **practicalities** aspectos *mpl* prácticos

**practically** ['præktıklı] *adv* prácticamente

**practice** ['præktıs] **1** *n* (a) *(action, exercise)* práctica *f*; *(in sport)* entrenamiento *m*; **in p.** en la práctica; **to put an idea into p.** poner en práctica una idea; **to be out of p.** estar desentrenado(a); *Prov* **p. makes perfect** se aprende a base de práctica; **p. match** partido *m* de entrenamiento (b) *(of profession)* ejercicio *m*, práctica *f*; **medical p.** *(place)* consulta *f* médica, consultorio *m* médico; *(group of doctors)* = grupo de médicos que comparten un consultorio; **legal p.** *(place, legal firm)* bufete *m* de abogados (c) *(custom)* práctica *f*; **to make a p. of doing sth** tomar por costumbre hacer algo; **it's the usual p.** es el procedimiento habitual; **to be good/bad p.** ser una buena/mala costumbre

**2** *vt & vi US* = **practise**

**practiced, practicing** *US* = **practised, practising**

**practise, *US* practice** ['præktıs] **1** *vt* (a) *(musical instrument, language)* practicar (b) *(medicine, law)* ejercer (c) *(religion, custom)* practicar; **to p. what one preaches** predicar con el ejemplo

**2** *vi* (a) *(of musician)* practicar; *(of sportsperson)* entrenar (b) *(of doctor, lawyer)* ejercer

**practised, *US* practiced** ['præktıst] *adj* experto(a) (**at** en)

**practising, *US* practicing** ['præktısıŋ] *adj (doctor, lawyer)* en ejercicio, en activo; *(Christian)* practicante

**pragmatic** [præg'mætık] *adj* pragmático(a)

**pragmatism** ['prægmətızəm] *n* pragmatismo *m*

**pragmatist** ['prægmətıst] *n* pragmático(a) *m,f*

**Prague** [prɑːg] *n* Praga

**prairie** ['preərı] *n* pradera *f*; **p. dog** perro *m* de las praderas; *US* **p. schooner** = carromato típico de los colonos del oeste americano

**praise** [preız] **1** *n* elogio *m*, alabanza *f*; **in p. of** en alabanza de; **to sing the praises of** prodigar alabanzas a; **I have nothing but p. for him** no tengo más que elogios para él

**2** *vt* elogiar, alabar; **to p. God** alabar a Dios; **to p. sb to the skies** poner a alguien por las nubes

**praiseworthy** ['preızwɜːðı] *adj* encomiable

**pram** [præm] *n Br* cochecito *m* de niño, carricoche *m*

**prance** [prɑːns] *vi (of horse)* encabritarse; *(of person)* dar brincos, brincar; **to p. in/out** entrar/salir dando brincos

**prank** [præŋk] *n* broma *f* (pesada), jugarreta *f*; **to play a p. on sb** gastarle una broma a alguien

**prat** [præt] *n Br Fam* tonto(a) *m,f* del culo, soplagaitas *mf inv*

**prate** [preıt] *vi Formal* perorar

**prattle** ['prætəl] **1** *n* charla *f*, parloteo *m*

**2** *vi* charlar, parlotear (**about** de *or* acerca de)

**prawn** [prɔːn] *n* gamba *f*; **p. cocktail** cóctel *m* de gambas; **p. cracker** corteza *f* de gambas, = especie de corteza ligera y crujiente con sabor a marisco

**pray** [preı] *vi* rezar, orar; **to p. to God** rezar a Dios; **to p. for sb/sth** rezar por alguien/algo; *Fig* **to p. for good weather/rain** rezar para que haga buen tiempo/llueva

**prayer** [preə(r)] *n* oración *f*; **to say one's prayers** rezar las oraciones; **to say a p.** rezar una oración; **her p. had been answered** sus súplicas habían sido atendidas; *Fam Fig* **he doesn't have a p.** *(has no chance)* no tiene ninguna posibilidad, no tiene nada que hacer; **p. beads** rosario *m*; **p. book** devocionario *m*; **p. mat** = esterilla que utilizan los musulmanes para el rezo; **p. meeting** = reunión de creyentes, generalmente protestantes, para rezar en grupo

**praying mantis** ['preıŋ'mæntıs], *US* **mantis** ['mæntıs] *n* mantis *f inv* religiosa

**preach** [priːtʃ] **1** *vt* predicar

**2** *vi* predicar; *Fig* **you're preaching to the converted** estás evangelizando en un convento

**preacher** ['priːtʃə(r)] *n* predicador(ora) *m,f*

**preamble** ['priːæmbəl] *n Formal* preámbulo *m*

**prearranged** [priːə'reındʒd] *adj* acordado(a) de antemano

**precarious** [prı'keərıəs] *adj* precario(a)

**precariously** [prı'keərıəslı] *adv* precariamente; **p. balanced** *(object, situation)* en equilibrio precario

**precaution** [prı'kɔːʃən] *n* precaución *f*; **to take precautions** tomar precauciones; *(use* *contraceptive)* usar anticonceptivos; **as a p.** como (medida de) precaución

**precautionary** [prɪˈkɔːʃənərɪ] *adj* preventivo(a)

**precede** [prɪˈsiːd] *vt (in time, space, importance)* preceder a; **in the weeks preceding her departure** durante las semanas previas a su partida

**precedence** [ˈpresɪdəns] *n* prioridad *f*, precedencia *f*; **in order of p.** por orden de precedencia; **to take p. over** tener prioridad sobre

**precedent** [ˈpresɪdənt] *n* precedente *m*; **to create** *or* **set a p.** sentar (un) precedente; **without p.** sin precedentes

**preceding** [prɪˈsiːdɪŋ] *adj* precedente, anterior

**precept** [ˈpriːsept] *n* precepto *m*

**precinct** [ˈpriːsɪŋkt] *n* **(a)** *Br (area)* **(shopping) p.** zona *f* comercial; **within the precincts of** dentro de los límites de **(b)** *US (administrative, police division)* distrito *m*

**precious** [ˈpreʃəs] **1** *n (term of endearment)* **my p.!** ¡mi cielo!
**2** *adj* **(a)** *(valuable)* precioso(a), valioso(a); *(secret, possession)* preciado(a); **this photo is very p. to me** esta foto tiene mucho valor para mí; *Ironic* **you and your p. books!** ¡tú y tus dichosos libros! **(b)** *Pej (affected)* afectado(a)
**3** *adv Fam (for emphasis)* **p. little** poquísimo(a); **p. few** poquísimos(as)

**precipice** [ˈpresɪpɪs] *n* precipicio *m*

**precipitate 1** *n* [prɪˈsɪpɪtɪt] *Chem* precipitado *m*
**2** *adj Formal* precipitado(a)
**3** *vt* [prɪˈsɪpɪteɪt] *(hasten)* precipitar

**precipitately** [prɪˈsɪpɪtətlɪ] *adv* precipitadamente

**precipitation** [prɪsɪpɪˈteɪʃən] *n Met* precipitaciones *fpl*; **annual p.** pluviosidad *f* anual

**precipitous** [prɪˈsɪpɪtəs] *adj (steep)* empinado(a)

**précis** [ˈpreɪsiː] *(pl* **précis** [ˈpreɪsiːz]) *n* resumen *m*

**precise** [prɪˈsaɪs] *adj* **(a)** *(exact)* preciso(a); **to be p.** para ser exactos; **at the p. moment when…** en el preciso momento en que… **(b)** *(meticulous)* meticuloso(a)

**precisely** [prɪˈsaɪslɪ] *adv* precisamente; **at six (o'clock) p.** a las seis en punto; **p.!** ¡exactamente!

**precision** [prɪˈsɪʒən] *n* precisión *f*; *Mil* **p. bombing** bombardeo *m* de precisión; **p. instrument** instrumento *m* de precisión

**preclude** [prɪˈkluːd] *vt* excluir; **to p. sb from doing sth, to p. sb's doing sth** impedir a alguien hacer algo

**precocious** [prɪˈkəʊʃəs] *adj* precoz

**precociousness** [prɪˈkəʊʃəsnɪs], **precocity** [prɪˈkɒsɪtɪ] *n* precocidad *f*

**preconceived** [priːkənˈsiːvd] *adj (idea)* preconcebido(a)

**preconception** [priːkənˈsepʃən] *n* idea *f* preconcebida; *(prejudice)* prejuicio *m*

**precondition** [priːkənˈdɪʃən] *n* condición *f* previa

**precooked** [priːˈkʊkt] *adj* precocinado(a)

**precursor** [prɪˈkɜːsə(r)] *n* precursor(ora) *m,f*

**predate** [priːˈdeɪt] *vt* **(a)** *(precede)* preceder a, anteceder a **(b)** *(put earlier date on)* antedatar

**predator** [ˈpredətə(r)] *n (animal)* predador(ora) *m,f*, depredador(ora) *m,f*; *(person)* aprovechado(a) *m,f*, buitre *mf*

**predatory** [ˈpredətərɪ] *adj (animal)* predador(ora), depredador(ora); *(person)* aprovechado(a)

**predecessor** [ˈpriːdɪsesə(r)] *n* predecesor(ora) *m,f*

**predestination** [priːdestɪˈneɪʃən] *n* predestinación *f*

**predestine** [priːˈdestɪn] *vt* predestinar; **to be predestined to do sth** estar predestinado(a) a hacer algo

**predetermine** [priːdɪˈtɜːmɪn] *vt* predeterminar

**predicament** [prɪˈdɪkəmənt] *n (unpleasant situation)* aprieto *m*, apuro *m*; *(difficult choice)* dilema *m*, conflicto *m*; **to be in an awkward p.** estar en un brete

**predicate 1** *n* [ˈpredɪkət] *Gram* predicado *m*
**2** *vt* [ˈpredɪkeɪt] **to be predicated on sth** fundarse *or* basarse en algo

**predict** [prɪˈdɪkt] *vt* predecir

**predictable** [prɪˈdɪktəbəl] *adj* predecible, previsible; *(unoriginal)* poco original; *Fam* **you're so p.!** ¡siempre estás con lo mismo!

**predictably** [prɪˈdɪktəblɪ] *adv* previsiblemente; **p., he arrived an hour late** como era de prever, llegó con una hora de retraso

**prediction** [prɪˈdɪkʃən] *n* predicción *f*

**predispose** [priːdɪsˈpəʊz] *vt* predisponer; **I was not predisposed to believe her** no estaba predispuesto a creerla

**predisposition** [priːdɪspəˈzɪʃən] *n* predisposición *f* **(to** *or* **towards** a)

**predominance** [prɪˈdɒmɪnəns] *n* predominio *m*

**predominant** [prɪˈdɒmɪnənt] *adj* predominante

**predominantly** [prɪˈdɒmɪnəntlɪ] *adv* predominantemente

**predominate** [prɪˈdɒmɪneɪt] *vi* predominar

**pre-eminence** [prɪˈemɪnəns] *n* preeminencia *f*

**pre-eminent** [prɪˈemɪnənt] *adj* preeminente

**pre-empt** [prɪˈempt] *vt* adelantarse a; **he was pre-empted by a rival** se le adelantó uno de sus rivales

**pre-emptive** [prɪˈemptɪv] *adj Fin* **p. bid** licitación *f* or oferta *f* preferente; *Mil* **p. strike** ataque *m* preventivo

**preen** [priːn] *vt* **to p. itself** *(of bird)* atusarse las plumas; **to p. oneself** *(of person)* acicalarse

**pre-established** [priːɪsˈtæblɪʃt] *adj* preestablecido(a)

**prefab** [ˈpriːfæb] *n Fam (house)* casa *f* prefabricada

**prefabricated** [priːˈfæbrɪkeɪtɪd] *adj* prefabricado(a)

**preface** [ˈprefɪs] **1** *n (of book)* prefacio *m*, prólogo *m*; *(to speech)* preámbulo *m*
**2** *vt* **she prefaced her speech with an anecdote** abrió su discurso con una anécdota

**prefect** [ˈpriːfekt] *n Sch* monitor(ora) *m,f*

**prefer** [prɪˈfɜː(r)] *(pt & pp preferred) vt* **(a)** *(favour)* preferir; **I p. wine to beer** prefiero el vino a la cerveza; **I p. her to her sister** me cae mejor ella que su hermana; **I would p. to stay at home** preferiría quedarme en casa **(b)** *Law* **to p. charges** presentar cargos

**preferable** [ˈprefərəbəl] *adj* preferible

**preferably** [ˈprefərəblɪ] *adv* preferiblemente

**preference** [ˈprefərəns] *n* preferencia *f*; **to give sb p., to give p. to sb** dar preferencia a alguien; **I have no p.** me da lo mismo; **in p. to…** antes que…, en lugar de…; **in order of p.** por orden de preferencia

**preferential** [prefəˈrenʃəl] *adj* preferente

**preferred** [prɪˈfɜːd] *adj* preferido(a), favorito(a)

**prefigure** [priːˈfɪɡə(r)] *vt* prefigurar

**prefix** [ˈpriːfɪks] *n* prefijo *m*

**pregnancy** [ˈpreɡnənsɪ] *n* embarazo *m*; **p. test** prueba *f* de embarazo

**pregnant** [ˈpreɡnənt] *adj* **(a)** *(woman)* embarazada; *(animal)* preñada; **to be p.** *(of woman)* estar embarazada; *(of animal)* estar preñada; **she's three months p.** está (embarazada) de tres meses **(b)** *Fig* **p. with** *(situation, remark)* preñado(a) *or* cargado(a) de; **a p. silence** un silencio significativo

**preheat** [priːˈhiːt] *vt* precalentar

**prehensile** [prɪˈhensaɪl] *adj* prensil

**prehistoric** [priːhɪsˈtɒrɪk] *adj* prehistórico(a)

**prehistory** [priːˈhɪstərɪ] *n* prehistoria *f*

**prejudge** [priːˈdʒʌdʒ] *vt* prejuzgar

**prejudice** [ˈpredʒʊdɪs] **1** *n* **(a)** *(bias)* prejuicio *m* **(b)** *Law* **without p. to** sin perjuicio *or* menoscabo de
**2** *vt* **(a)** *(bias)* predisponer **(against/in favour of** en contra de/a favor de) **(b)** *(harm)*. perjudicar

**prejudiced** [ˈpredʒʊdɪst] *adj* **to be p.** tener prejuicios; **to be p. against/in favour of** estar predispuesto(a) en contra de/a favor de

**prejudicial** [predʒʊˈdɪʃəl] *adj* perjudicial **(to** para)

**preliminary** [prɪˈlɪmɪnərɪ] **1** *n* preludio *m*; **preliminaries** *(to investigation, meeting)* preliminares *mpl*
**2** *adj* preliminar

**prelude** [ˈpreljuːd] *n* preludio *m* (**to** de *or* a)

**premarital** [priːˈmærɪtəl] *adj* prematrimonial

**premature** [ˈpremətjʊə(r)] *adj* prematuro(a); *Fam* **you're being a bit p.!** ¡te estás adelantando un poco!; **p. ejaculation** eyaculación *f* precoz

**prematurely** [ˈpremətjʊəlɪ] *adv* prematuramente

**premeditated** [priːˈmedɪteɪtɪd] *adj* premeditado(a)

**premenstrual** [priːˈmenstrʊəl] *adj Med* **p. syndrome** síndrome *m* premenstrual; **p. tension** tensión *f* premenstrual

**premier** [ˈpremɪə(r)] **1** *n (prime minister)* jefe(a) *m,f* del Gobierno, primer(era) ministro(a) *m,f*
**2** *adj* primero(a)

**premiere** [ˈpremɪeə(r)] *n (of play, film)* estreno *m*

**premise** [ˈpremɪs] **1** *n (of argument, theory)* premisa *f*
**2** *vt* **to be premised on…** partir del supuesto *or* de la premisa de que…

**premises** [ˈpremɪsɪz] *npl (of factory)* instalaciones *fpl*; *(of shop)* local *m*, locales *mpl*; **business p.** locales comerciales; **on/off the p.** dentro/fuera del establecimiento; **to see sb off the p.** sacar a alguien del establecimiento

**premium** [ˈpriːmɪəm] *n* **(a)** *Fin (for insurance)* prima *f*; *(additional sum)* recargo *m*; **to sell sth at a p.** vender algo por encima de su valor; *Fin* **p. bonds** = cupón numerado emitido por el Gobierno británico, cuyo comprador entra en un sorteo mensual de premios en metálico otorgados al azar por un ordenador **(b)** *(idioms)* **to be at a p.** *(be scarce)* estar muy cotizado(a); **to put a p. on sth** conceder una importancia especial a algo

**premonition** [priːməˈnɪʃən] *n* presentimiento *m*, premonición *f*; **to have a p. that…** tener el presentimiento de que…

**prenatal** [priːˈneɪtəl] *adj* prenatal

**preoccupation** [priːɒkjʊˈpeɪʃən] *n* preocupación *f* (**with** por)

**preoccupied** [priːˈɒkjʊpaɪd] *adj* preocupado(a); **to be p. with** *or* **by sth** estar preocupado(a) por algo

**preoccupy** [priːˈɒkjʊpaɪ] *vt* preocupar

**prep** [prep] *n Br Fam (schoolwork)* deberes *mpl*; **p. school** = colegio privado para alumnos de entre 7 y 13 años

**prepaid** [priːˈpeɪd] *adj (envelope)* franqueado(a), con franqueo pagado

**preparation** [prepəˈreɪʃən] *n* (**a**) *(act of preparing)* preparación *f*; **preparations** *(for ceremony, party)* preparativos *mpl* (**b**) *(medicine)* preparado *m*

**preparatory** [prɪˈpærətərɪ] *adj* preparatorio(a); *Formal* **p. to (doing) sth** antes de (hacer) algo; **p. school** *Br* = colegio privado para alumnos de entre 7 y 13 años; *US* = escuela privada de enseñanza secundaria y preparación para estudios superiores

**prepare** [prɪˈpeə(r)] **1** *vt* preparar
**2** *vi* prepararse (**for** para); **to p. to do sth** prepararse para hacer algo

**prepared** [prɪˈpeəd] *adj* (**a**) *(willing)* **to be p. to do sth** estar dispuesto(a) a hacer algo (**b**) *(ready)* **to be p. for sth** estar preparado(a) para algo (**c**) *(made in advance)* **a p. statement** una declaración preparada (de antemano)

**prepayment** [priːˈpeɪmənt] *n* pago *m* (por) adelantado

**preponderance** [prɪˈpɒndərəns] *n* preponderancia *f*, predominio *m*

**preposition** [prepəˈzɪʃən] *n* preposición *f*

**prepositional** [prepəˈzɪʃənəl] *adj* preposicional

**prepossessing** [priːpəˈzesɪŋ] *adj* atractivo(a), agradable

**preposterous** [prɪˈpɒstərəs] *adj* absurdo(a), ridículo(a)

**preppy** [ˈprepɪ] *adj US Fam* pijo(a)

**preprogrammed** [priːˈprəʊɡræmd] *adj Comptr* preprogramado(a)

**prerecorded** [priːrɪˈkɔːdɪd] *adj* pregrabado(a)

**prerequisite** [priːˈrekwɪzɪt] *n* requisito *m* previo (**of/for** para)

**prerogative** [prɪˈrɒɡətɪv] *n* prerrogativa *f*

**presage** [ˈpresɪdʒ] *Literary* **1** *n* presagio *m*
**2** *vt* presagiar

**Presbyterian** [prezbɪˈtɪərɪən] *n & adj* presbiteriano(a) *m,f*

**presbytery** [ˈprezbɪt(ə)rɪ] *n* presbiterio *m*

**preschool** [priːˈskuːl] *adj* preescolar

**prescribe** [prɪˈskraɪb] *vt* (**a**) *(medicine)* recetar (**b**) *(punishment, solution)* prescribir; **in the prescribed manner** de la forma prescrita

**prescription** [prɪˈskrɪpʃən] *n* receta *f*; **available only on p.** sólo con receta médica; **p. charge** precio *m* de un medicamento con receta

**presence** [ˈprezəns] *n* presencia *f*; **in the p. of** en presencia de; **to have p.** tener mucha presencia; **she made her p. felt** hizo sentir su presencia; **p. of mind** presencia de ánimo

**present¹** [ˈprezənt] **1** *n* **the p.** el presente; **up to the p.** hasta la fecha, hasta ahora; **at p.** *(now)* en estos momentos; *(these days)* actualmente; **for the p.** de momento, por el momento
**2** *adj* (**a**) *(in attendance)* presente; **to be p. (at)** estar presente (en); **those p.** los presentes (**b**) *(current)* actual; **at the p. time** *or* **moment** en estos momentos; **in the p. case** en este caso; *Gram* **the p. tense** el (tiempo) presente; **p. participle** participio *m* de presente *or* activo

**present²** [ˈprezənt] *n (gift)* regalo *m*; **to give sb a p.** regalar algo a alguien; **birthday/Christmas p.** regalo de cumpleaños/Navidad
**2** *vt* [prɪˈzent] (**a**) *(introduce, put forward)* presentar; **if the opportunity presents itself** si se presenta la ocasión (**b**) *(give)* entregar; **to p. sth to sb, to p. sb with sth** *(gift)* regalar algo a alguien; *(award, certificate)* otorgar *or* entregar algo a alguien (**c**) *Mil* **p. arms!** ¡presenten armas!

**presentable** [prɪˈzentəbəl] *adj* presentable; **to make oneself p.** ponerse presentable

**presentation** [prezənˈteɪʃən] *n* (**a**) *(of person)* presentación *f* (**b**) *(of gift, award)* entrega *f*; **to make a p. to sb** *(give present)* hacer (entrega de) un obsequio a alguien; *(give award)* otorgar *or* entregar un premio a alguien (**c**) *(formal talk)* **to give a p.** hacer una exposición, dar una charla *(con la ayuda de gráficos, diapositivas, etc)* (**d**) **on p. of** *(passport, coupon)* con la presentación de, presentando

**present-day** [ˈprezəntˈdeɪ] *adj* actual

**presenter** [prɪˈzentə(r)] *n (on radio, TV)* presentador(ora) *m,f*

**presentiment** [prɪˈzentɪmənt] *n* premonición *f*, presentimiento *m*

**presently** [ˈprezəntlɪ] *adv* (**a**) *(soon)* pronto; *(soon afterwards)* poco después (**b**) *US (now)* actualmente

**preservation** [prezəˈveɪʃən] *n* (**a**) *(maintenance)* conservación *f*, mantenimiento *m* (**b**) *(protection) (of species, building)* conservación *f*, protección *f*; **p. order** orden *f* de conservación *(de un monumento o edificio de valor histórico-artístico)*

**preservative** [prɪˈzɜːvətɪv] *n* conservante *m*

**preserve** [prɪˈzɜːv] **1** *n* (**a**) *(jam)* confitura *f*, mermelada *f* (**b**) *(in hunting)* coto *m* de caza (**c**) *(area of dominance)* territorio *m*; **engineering is no longer a male p.** la ingeniería ya no es un reducto masculino
**2** *vt* (**a**) *(maintain)* conservar, mantener (**b**) *(leather, wood)* conservar (**c**) *(fruit)* confitar, poner en conserva (**d**) *(protect)* conservar, proteger (**from** de); **saints p. us!** ¡que Dios nos proteja *or* ampare!

**preshrunk** [priːˈʃrʌŋk] *adj* lavado(a) previamente

**preside** [prɪ'zaɪd] *vi* presidir; **to p. over a meeting** presidir una reunión; **he presided over the decline of the empire** él estuvo al mando durante el declive del imperio

**presidency** ['prezɪdənsɪ] *n* presidencia *f*

**president** ['prezɪdənt] *n (of country, company)* presidente(a) *m,f*

**presidential** [prezɪ'denʃəl] *adj* presidencial

**press** [pres] **1** *n* (**a**) *(act of pushing)* **at the p. of a button...** al pulsar un botón...; *Hist* **p. gang** = grupo de marineros que se encargaba de reclutar por la fuerza a gente para la Armada; **p. stud** automático *m*, corchete *m*
(**b**) *(newspapers)* **the p.** la prensa; **to get a good/bad p.** tener buena/mala prensa; **p. agency** agencia *f* de noticias; **p. box** tribuna *f* de prensa or periodistas; **p. conference** rueda *f* or conferencia *f* de prensa; **p. cutting** recorte *m* de prensa; **p. officer** jefe(a) *m,f* de prensa; **p. photographer** fotógrafo(a) *m,f* de prensa; **p. release** comunicado *m* or nota *f* de prensa
(**c**) *(machine)* prensa *f*; **(printing) p.** imprenta *f*; **to go to p.** *(of newspaper)* entrar en prensa
**2** *vt* (**a**) *(button, switch)* apretar; *(into clay, cement)* presionar (**into** sobre); **he pressed the note into my hand** me puso el billete en la mano
(**b**) *(squeeze)* apretar; *(juice, lemon)* exprimir; *(grapes, olives, flowers)* prensar
(**c**) *(iron)* planchar
(**d**) *(pressurize)* presionar; **to p. sb to do sth** presionar a alguien para que haga algo; **to be pressed for time/money** estar apurado(a) de tiempo/dinero
(**e**) *(force)* **to p. sth on sb** obligar a alguien a aceptar algo; **to p. home one's advantage** sacar (uno) el máximo partido a su ventaja; **to p. one's attentions on sb** prodigar excesivas atenciones a alguien
(**f**) *Law* **to p. charges (against sb)** presentar cargos (contra alguien)
**3** *vi (push)* empujar; *(of crowd)* apelotonarse

▸**press ahead** = **press on**

▸**press for** *vt insep (demand)* exigir

▸**press on** *vi* seguir adelante

**press-gang** ['presgæŋ] *vt* **to p. sb into doing sth** forzar a alguien a hacer algo

**pressing** ['presɪŋ] *adj (urgent)* apremiante

**pressman** ['presmən] *n Br* periodista *m*

**press-up** ['presʌp] *n (exercise)* flexión *f* (de brazos); **to do press-ups** hacer flexiones

**pressure** ['preʃə(r)] **1** *n* presión *f*; **to put p. on sb (to do sth)** presionar a alguien (para que haga algo); **to be under p.** estar presionado(a); **p. of work** estrés *m* laboral; **p. cooker** olla *f* a presión; **p. gauge** manómetro *m*; **p. group** grupo *m* de presión; *Med* **p. point** punto *m* de presión

**2** *vt* **to p. sb to do sth** presionar a alguien para que haga algo

**pressurize** ['preʃəraɪz] *vt* (**a**) *Tech (container)* presurizar (**b**) *(person)* **to p. sb (into doing sth)** presionar a alguien (para que haga algo)

**prestige** [pres'ti:ʒ] *n* prestigio *m*

**prestigious** [pres'tɪdʒəs] *adj* prestigioso(a)

**presumably** [prɪ'zju:məblɪ] *adv* presumiblemente, según cabe suponer; **p. she'll come** cabe suponer que vendrá

**presume** [prɪ'zju:m] **1** *vt* (**a**) *(suppose)* suponer; **I p. so** supongo (que sí) (**b**) **to p. to do sth** tomarse la libertad de hacer algo

**2** *vi (be cheeky)* pasarse de listo(a); **I don't want to p. on you** no quiero abusar de su generosidad

**presumption** [prɪ'zʌmpʃən] *n* (**a**) *(assumption)* suposición *f*, supuesto *m*; *Law* **p. of innocence** presunción *f* de inocencia (**b**) *(arrogance)* presunción *f*, osadía *f*

**presumptuous** [prɪ'zʌmptjʊəs] *adj* presuntuoso(a), osado(a)

**presuppose** [pri:sə'pəʊz] *vt* presuponer

**presupposition** [pri:sʌpə'zɪʃən] *n* supuesto *m*, suposición *f*

**pretence** [prɪ'tens] *n* fingimiento *m*; **he says... but it's all a p.** dice que... pero es mentira; **to make a p. of doing sth** aparentar hacer algo; **he made no p. of his scepticism** no trató de ocultar su escepticismo

**pretend** [prɪ'tend] **1** *vt* (**a**) *(feign)* fingir, simular; **to p. to be ill** fingir que se está enfermo(a); **to p. to do sth** fingir hacer algo; **they pretended that nothing had happened** hicieron como si no hubiera pasado nada (**b**) *(claim)* pretender

**2** *vi (put on an act)* fingir

**3** *adj Fam* de mentira; **p. money** dinero *m* de mentira; **a p. slap** un amago de bofetada

**pretension** [prɪ'tenʃən] *n* pretensión *f*

**pretentious** [prɪ'tenʃəs] *adj* pretencioso(a)

**pretentiousness** [prɪ'tenʃəsnəs] *n* pretenciosidad *f*

**preterite** ['pretərɪt] *n Gram* **the p.** el pretérito

**pretext** ['pri:tekst] *n* pretexto *m*; **under** *or* **on the p. of doing sth** con el pretexto de hacer algo

**Pretoria** [prɪ'tɔ:rɪə] *n* Pretoria

**pretty** ['prɪtɪ] **1** *adj (person, thing)* bonito(a); **it's not a p. sight** es un espectáculo lamentable; *Fam* **to cost a p. penny** costar un riñón

**2** *adv* (**a**) *(fairly)* bastante; **they're p. much the same** son poco más o menos lo mismo (**b**) *Fam* **to be sitting p.** encontrarse en una situación ventajosa

**pretzel** ['pretzəl] *n* palito *m* salado *(alargado o en forma de 8)*

**prevail** [prɪ'veɪl] *vi* (**a**) *(be successful)* prevalecer (over sobre); **let us hope that justice prevails** esperemos que se imponga la justicia (**b**) *(persuade)* **to p. upon sb to do sth** convencer a alguien para que haga algo (**c**) *(predominate)* predominar; **in the conditions now prevailing** en las circunstancias actuales

**prevailing** [prɪ'veɪlɪŋ] *adj* predominante

**prevalent** ['prevələnt] *adj* frecuente, corriente

**prevaricate** [prɪ'værɪkeɪt] *vi* dar rodeos, andar con evasivas

**prevarication** [prɪværɪ'keɪʃən] *n* rodeos *mpl*, evasivas *fpl*

**prevent** [prɪ'vent] *vt* evitar, impedir; **to p. sb from doing sth** evitar *or* impedir que alguien haga algo; **to p. sth from happening** evitar *or* impedir que pase algo

**preventable** [prɪ'ventəbəl] *adj* evitable

**preventative** [prɪ'ventətɪv] = **preventive**

**prevention** [prɪ'venʃən] *n* prevención *f*; *Prov* **p. is better than cure** más vale prevenir que curar

**preventive** [prɪ'ventɪv] *adj* **p. medicine** medicina *f* preventiva; **p. measures** medidas *fpl* preventivas

**preview** ['pri:vju:] **1** *n* (*of play, film*) preestreno *m*; (*of TV programme*) avance *m*; (*of new product*) presentación *f*
**2** *vt* **the film was previewed** hubo un preestreno de la película

**previous** ['pri:vɪəs] **1** *adj* previo(a), anterior; **the p. day** el día anterior; **p. engagement** compromiso *m* previo; *Law* **p. convictions** antecedentes *mpl* penales
**2** *adv* **p. to** con anterioridad a

**previously** ['pri:vɪəslɪ] *adv* anteriormente; **three days p.** tres días antes

**prewar** ['pri:'wɔ:(r)] *adj* de preguerra

**prey** [preɪ] *n* presa *f*; *Fig* **to be a p. to** ser presa (fácil) para *or* de; **to fall p. to** caer *or* ser víctima de

▶**prey on, prey upon** *vt insep* (*of animal*) alimentarse de; (*of opportunist*) aprovecharse de, cebarse en; **something is preying on his mind** está atormentado por algo

**price** [praɪs] **1** *n* precio *m*; **to rise** *or* **increase in p.** subir de precio; **at any p.** a toda costa; **not at any p.** por nada del mundo; *Fig* **to pay the p. (for sth)** pagar el precio (de algo); *Fig* **it's too high a p. (to pay)** es un precio demasiado alto *or* caro; **to put** *or* **set a p. on sb's head** poner precio a la cabeza de alguien; *Fig* **everyone has his p.** todos tienen un precio; *Fam* **what p. patriotism now?** ¿de qué ha servido tanto patriotismo?; **p. cut** reducción *f* de precios; **p. freeze** congelación *f* de precios;

**p. increase** subida *f* de precios; **p. index** índice *m* de precios; **p. list** lista *f* de precios; **p. range** escala *f* de precios; **that's outside my p. range** eso no está a mi alcance; **p. tag** etiqueta *f* del precio; **p. war** guerra *f* de precios
**2** *vt* (*decide cost of*) poner precio a; **the toy is priced at £10** el precio del juguete es de 10 libras; **to p. oneself out of the market** perder mercado por pedir precios demasiado elevados

**price-cutting** ['praɪskʌtɪŋ] *n Com* reducción *f* de precios

**price-fixing** ['praɪsfɪksɪŋ] *n Com* fijación *f* de precios

**priceless** ['praɪslɪs] *adj* (**a**) *(invaluable)* de valor incalculable (**b**) *Fam (funny)* graciosísimo(a)

**pricey** ['praɪsɪ] *adj Fam* carillo(a)

**prick** [prɪk] **1** *n* (**a**) *(of needle)* pinchazo *m*; **pricks of conscience** remordimientos *mpl* de conciencia (**b**) *Vulg (penis)* polla *f*, picha *f*; *(person)* gilipollas *mf inv*
**2** *vt (make holes in)* pinchar; **to p. one's finger** pincharse el dedo; **to p. a hole in sth** hacer un agujero en algo

▶**prick up** *vt sep* **to p. up one's ears** *(of dog)* aguzar las orejas; *(of person)* aguzar el oído *or* los oídos

**prickle** ['prɪkəl] **1** *n* (**a**) *(of hedgehog)* púa *f*; *(of plant)* espina *f*, pincho *m* (**b**) *(sensation)* hormigueo *m*
**2** *vi (of skin)* hormiguear

**prickly** ['prɪklɪ] *adj* (**a**) *(animal)* cubierto(a) de púas; *(plant)* espinoso(a); *Fig (person)* susceptible, irritable; **p. pear** *(tree)* chumbera *f*; *(fruit)* higo *m* chumbo (**b**) *(sensation)* hormigueante; **p. heat** = erupción cutánea producida por el calor

**pride** [praɪd] **1** *n* (**a**) *(satisfaction)* orgullo *m*; *(self-esteem)* amor *m* propio; *Pej (vanity)* soberbia *f*, orgullo *m*; **to take p. in sth** enorgullecerse de algo (**b**) *(person, thing)* **he is the p. of the family** es el orgullo de la familia; **the p. of my collection** la joya de mi colección; **she's his p. and joy** ella es su mayor orgullo; **to have p. of place** ocupar el lugar preferente (**c**) *(of lions)* manada *f*
**2** *vt* **to p. oneself on sth** enorgullecerse de algo

**priest** [pri:st] *n* sacerdote *m*

**priestess** ['pri:stɪs] *n* sacerdotisa *f*

**priesthood** ['pri:sthʊd] *n* sacerdocio *m*; **to enter the p.** ordenarse sacerdote

**prig** [prɪg] *n* puritano(a) *m,f*, mojigato(a) *m,f*

**priggish** ['prɪgɪʃ] *adj* puritano(a), mojigato(a)

**prim** [prɪm] *adj* **p. (and proper)** remilgado(a)

**primacy** ['praɪməsɪ] *n* primacía *f*

**prima facie** ['praɪmə'feɪʃɪ] **1** *adj Law* **p. case** caso *m* prima facie
**2** *adv* a primera vista

**primarily** [praɪˈmərɪlɪ] *adv* principalmente

**primary** [ˈpraɪmərɪ] **1** *n (election)* elecciones *fpl* primarias

**2** *adj* (**a**) *(main)* principal; **p. colours** colores *mpl* primarios (**b**) *(initial)* **p. education** enseñanza *f* primaria; **p. school** escuela *f* primaria

**primate** [ˈpraɪmeɪt] *n* (**a**) *(animal)* primate *m* (**b**) *Rel* primado *m*

**prime** [praɪm] **1** *n (best time)* **the p. of life** la flor de la vida; **she was in her p.** estaba en sus mejores años; **she is past her p.** su mejor momento ha pasado

**2** *adj* (**a**) *(principal)* principal, primordial; *(importance)* capital; **p. minister** primer(era) ministro(a) *m,f*; *Math* **p. number** número *m* primo; **p. time** *(on TV)* franja *f* (horaria) de máxima audiencia (**b**) *(excellent)* óptimo(a), excelente; **a p. example (of)** un ejemplo palmario (de); **p. quality** calidad *f* suprema

**3** *vt* (**a**) *(prepare) (engine, pump)* cebar; *(surface)* imprimar (**b**) *(provide with information)* **to p. sb for sth** preparar *ór* instruir a alguien para algo

**primer**¹ [ˈpraɪmə(r)] *n (paint)* tapaporos *m inv*

**primer**² *n (textbook)* texto *m* elemental

**primeval** [praɪˈmiːvəl] *adj* primigenio(a), primitivo(a); **p. forests** bosques *mpl* vírgenes

**primitive** [ˈprɪmɪtɪv] *adj* primitivo(a)

**primly** [ˈprɪmlɪ] *adv* con remilgo

**primordial** [praɪˈmɔːdɪəl] *adj* primigenio(a), primitivo(a); **p. soup** sustancia *f* primigenia

**primrose** [ˈprɪmrəʊz] *n (plant)* primavera *f*; **p. yellow** amarillo *m* claro

**primula** [ˈprɪmjʊlə] *n* prímula *f*

**primus (stove)** [ˈpraɪməs('stəʊv)] *n* infiernillo *m*, camping-gas *m inv*

**prince** [prɪns] *n* príncipe *m*; **the P. of Wales** el Príncipe de Gales; **P. Charming** príncipe *m* azul

**princely** [ˈprɪnslɪ] *adj (splendid)* magnífico(a); *also Ironic* **a p. sum** una bonita suma

**princess** [prɪnˈses] *n* princesa *f*; *Br* **the P. Royal** = hija mayor del monarca

**principal** [ˈprɪnsɪpəl] **1** *n (of school)* director(ora) *m,f*; *(of university)* rector(ora) *m,f*

**2** *adj* principal

**principality** [prɪnsɪˈpælɪtɪ] *n* principado *m*; **the P.** Gales

**principle** [ˈprɪnsɪpəl] *n* principio *m*; **in p.** en principio; **on p.** por principios

**principled** [ˈprɪnsɪpəld] *adj (person, behaviour)* ejemplar, de grandes principios

**print** [prɪnt] **1** *n* (**a**) *(of fingers, feet)* huella *f* (**b**) *(printed matter)* **in p.** impreso(a); **out of p., no longer in p.** agotado(a); **to appear in p.** aparecer impreso(a) (**c**) *(characters)* caracteres *mpl*; *Fig* **the small p.** *(in contract)* la letra pequeña (**d**) *(engraving)* grabado *m*; *(photographic copy)* copia *f*; *(textile)* estampado *m*

**2** *vt* (**a**) *(book)* imprimir; *(newspaper)* publicar; **the image had printed itself on her memory** se le quedó la imagen grabada en la memoria (**b**) *(write clearly)* escribir claramente *(con las letras separadas)* (**c**) *(in photography)* **to p. a negative** sacar copias de un negativo

**3** *vi (write clearly)* escribir con claridad

▸**print out** *vt sep Comptr* imprimir

**printed** [ˈprɪntɪd] *adj* impreso(a); *Elec* **p. circuit** circuito *m* impreso; **p. matter** impresos *mpl*

**printer** [ˈprɪntə(r)] *n (person)* impresor(ora) *m,f*; *(machine)* impresora *f*

**printing** [ˈprɪntɪŋ] *n (process, action)* impresión *f*; *(industry)* imprenta *f*, artes *fpl* gráficas; **first/second p.** primera/segunda impresión; **p. error** errata *f* (de imprenta); **p. press** imprenta

**printout** [ˈprɪntaʊt] *n Comptr* listado *m*, copia *f* en papel

**prior**¹ [ˈpraɪə(r)] **1** *adj* previo(a); **to have p. knowledge of sth** tener conocimiento previo de algo

**2** *adv* **p. to** con anterioridad a

**prior**² *n Rel* prior *m*

**prioritize** [praɪˈɒrɪtaɪz] *vt* dar prioridad a

**priority** [praɪˈɒrɪtɪ] *n* prioridad *f*; **to have** *or* **take p. over sb/sth** tener prioridad respecto a alguien/algo; **we need to get our priorities right** tenemos que establecer un orden de prioridades; **you should get your priorities right!** ¡tienes que darte cuenta de lo que es verdaderamente importante!

**priory** [ˈpraɪərɪ] *n Rel* priorato *m*

**prise** [praɪz] *vt* **to p. sth off** arrancar algo; **to p. sth open** forzar algo; **to p. sth out of sb** *(secret, truth)* arrancarle algo a alguien

**prism** [ˈprɪzəm] *n* prisma *m*

**prison** [ˈprɪzən] *n* cárcel *f*, prisión *f*; **p. camp** campo *m* de prisioneros; **p. officer** funcionario(a) *m,f* de prisiones

**prisoner** [ˈprɪzənə(r)] *n (in jail)* recluso(a) *m,f*; *(captive)* prisionero(a) *m,f*; **to hold/take sb p.** tener/hacer prisionero(a) a alguien; *Fig* **to take no prisoners** no andarse con chiquitas; **p. of war** prisionero de guerra

**prissy** [ˈprɪsɪ] *adj Fam* remilgado(a)

**pristine** [ˈprɪstiːn] *adj* prístino(a), inmaculado(a)

**privacy** [ˈprɪvəsɪ, ˈpraɪvəsɪ] *n* intimidad *f*; **in the p. of one's own home** en la intimidad del hogar

**private** [ˈpraɪvɪt] **1** *n* (**a**) **in p.** en privado (**b**) *(soldier)* soldado *m* raso

**2** *adj* (**a**) *(personal)* privado(a), personal; **p. life** vida *f* privada; *Parl* **p. member's bill** = proyecto de ley propuesto de forma independiente por un diputado; *Fam* **p. parts** partes *fpl* pudendas

(b) *(secret)* privado(a); **p. and confidential** privado y confidencial; **can we go somewhere p.?** ¿podemos ir a un lugar donde estemos a solas?

(c) *(for personal use)* particular; **a p. house** una casa particular; **p. lessons** clases *fpl* particulares; *Tel* **p. line** línea *f* privada; **p. office** oficina *f* particular; **p. secretary** secretario(a) *m,f* personal

(d) *(not state-run)* privado(a); **p. detective** or **investigator** or *Fam* **eye** detective *mf* or investigador(ora) *m,f* privado(a); **p. education** enseñanza *f* privada; **p. enterprise** empresa *f* privada; **p. school** colegio *m* privado

(e) *(not for the public)* **a p. party** una fiesta particular or privada; **p. property** propiedad *f* privada; **p. road** carretera *f* particular

**privately** ['praɪvɪtlɪ] *adv (in private)* en privado; **she was p. educated** fue a un colegio privado; **p. owned** en manos privadas

**privation** [praɪ'veɪʃən] *n* privación *f*

**privatization** [praɪvɪtaɪ'zeɪʃən] *n* privatización *f*

**privatize** ['praɪvɪtaɪz] *vt* privatizar

**privet** ['prɪvɪt] *n* alheña *f*

**privilege** ['prɪvɪlɪdʒ] **1** *n* privilegio *m*; **to have the p. of doing sth** tener el privilegio de hacer algo

**2** *vt* **to be privileged to do sth** tener el privilegio de hacer algo

**privy** ['prɪvɪ] **1** *n Old-fashioned (toilet)* retrete *m*, excusado *m*

**2** *adj* (a) *Formal* **to be p. to sth** estar enterado(a) de algo (b) *Br Pol* **the P. Council** el consejo privado del monarca, = grupo formado principalmente por ministros y antiguos ministros del gabinete que asesora al monarca

**prize¹** [praɪz] **1** *n (award)* premio *m*; **to win a p.** ganar un premio; *Fig* **no prizes for guessing who did it** es evidente quién lo hizo; **p. day** día *m* de la entrega de premios; **p. draw** rifa *f*; **p. money** *(dinero m del)* premio; **he won p. money of £60,000** ganó un premio en metálico de 60.000 libras

**2** *vt (value)* apreciar

**prize²** = **prise**

**prizefight** ['praɪzfaɪt] *n* combate *m* profesional de boxeo

**prizefighter** ['praɪzfaɪtə(r)] *n* boxeador *m* profesional

**prizegiving** ['praɪzgɪvɪŋ] *n* entrega *f* de premios

**prizewinner** ['praɪzwɪnə(r)] *n* premiado(a) *m,f*

**pro¹** [prəʊ] *(pl* **pros)** *n Fam (professional)* profesional *mf*

**pro²** **1** *n (pl* **pros) the pros and cons** los pros y los contras

**2** *prep* **to be p. sth** estar a favor de algo

**proactive** [prəʊ'æktɪv] *adj* **to be p.** tomar la iniciativa

**pro-am** ['prəʊ'æm] *n Sport* torneo *m* abierto para profesionales y aficionados

**probability** [probə'bɪlɪtɪ] *n* probabilidad *f*; **in all p.** con toda probabilidad

**probable** ['probəbəl] *adj* probable

**probably** ['probəblɪ] *adv* probablemente

**probation** [prə'beɪʃən] *n (in job)* período *m* de prueba; *Law* libertad *f* condicional; **on p.** *(in job)* a prueba; *Law* en libertad condicional; **p. officer** = asistente social que ayuda y supervisa a un preso en libertad condicional

**probationary** [prə'beɪʃənərɪ] *adj* de prueba

**probationer** [prə'beɪʃənə(r)] *n (in job)* trabajador(ora) *m,f* en período de prueba

**probe** [prəʊb] **1** *n* (a) *(instrument)* sonda *f*; **(space) p.** sonda espacial (b) *Fam (enquiry)* investigación *f*

**2** *vt* (a) *Med* sondar; *(feel)* tantear (b) *(investigate)* investigar

**3** *vi* **to p. into** *(past, private life)* escarbar en

**probity** ['prəʊbɪtɪ] *n Formal* probidad *f*

**problem** ['probləm] *n* problema *m*; **he's a p.** es problemático; *Fam* **no p.!** ¡claro (que sí)!; **p. area** *(in town)* zona *f* problemática; *(in project)* asunto *m* problemático; **p. child** niño(a) *m,f* problemático(a) or difícil; **p. page** consultorio *m* sentimental

**problematic(al)** [problɪ'mætɪk(əl)] *adj* problemático(a)

**procedure** [prə'siːdʒə(r)] *n* procedimiento *m*

**proceed** [prə'siːd] **1** *vi* **to p. to do sth** proceder a hacer algo, ponerse a hacer algo

**2** *vi* (a) *(go on)* proseguir; **to p. with sth** seguir adelante con algo; **to p. with caution** proceder con cautela; **how shall we p.?** ¿cómo hemos de proceder? (b) *(result)* **to p. from** proceder de

**proceedings** [prə'siːdɪŋz] *npl* (a) *(events)* acto *m* (b) *Law* proceso *m*, pleito *m*; **to start p. against sb** entablar un pleito contra alguien

**proceeds** ['prəʊsiːdz] *npl* recaudación *f*

**process¹** ['prəʊses] **1** *n* proceso *m*; **by a p. of elimination** por eliminación; **he failed, and lost all his money in the p.** al fracasar, perdió todo su dinero; **to be in the p. of doing sth** estar haciendo algo

**2** *vt (raw material, waste, information)* procesar; *(request)* tramitar; *(film)* revelar; **processed food** alimentos *mpl* manipulados or procesados

**process²** [prə'ses] *vi (walk in procession)* desfilar

**processing** ['prəʊsesɪŋ] *n (of raw material, waste, information)* procesamiento *m*; *(of request)* tramitación f; *(of photographs)* revelado m; *Comptr* **p. language** lenguaje m de programación; *Comptr* **p. speed** velocidad f de proceso

**procession** [prə'seʃən] n procesión f; **in p.** en fila

**processor** ['prəʊsesə(r)] n *Comptr* procesador m

**pro-choice** ['prəʊtʃɔɪs] *adj* = en favor del derecho de la mujer a decidir en materia de aborto

**proclaim** [prə'kleɪm] vt *(one's innocence, guilt)* proclamar; **to p. a state of emergency** declarar el estado de emergencia

**proclamation** [prɒklə'meɪʃən] n proclamación f

**proclivity** [prəʊ'klɪvɪtɪ] n *Formal* propensión f, proclividad f **(for** a)

**procrastinate** [prəʊ'kræstɪneɪt] vi andarse con dilaciones, retrasar las cosas

**procrastination** [prəʊkræstɪ'neɪʃən] n dilaciones fpl, demora f

**procreate** ['prəʊkrɪeɪt] vi reproducirse, procrear

**procreation** [prəʊkrɪ'eɪʃən] n procreación f

**procure** [prə'kjʊə(r)] vt obtener, conseguir; **to p. sth for sb** procurarle algo a alguien; **to p. sth for oneself** hacerse con algo

**procurement** [prə'kjʊəmənt] n obtención f

**prod** [prɒd] **1** n **to give sb/sth a p.** dar un empujón a alguien/algo; *Fig* **he needs a p.** necesita que lo espoleen

**2** vt *(pt & pp prodded)* *(poke)* empujar; *Fig* **to p. sb into doing sth** espolear a alguien para que haga algo

**prodigal** ['prɒdɪgəl] *adj* pródigo(a)

**prodigious** [prə'dɪdʒəs] *adj* prodigioso(a)

**prodigy** ['prɒdɪdʒɪ] n prodigio m

**produce 1** n ['prɒdjuːs] *(food)* productos mpl del campo; **agricultural/dairy p.** productos mpl agrícolas/lácteos; **p. of Spain** producto de España

**2** vt [prə'djuːs] **(a)** *(create)* *(food, goods)* producir; *(effect, reaction)* producir, provocar **(b)** *(present)* *(ticket, passport)* presentar, mostrar; *(documents, alibi)* presentar; **she produced a £10 note** sacó un billete de 10 libras **(c)** *(play)* montar; *(film, radio, TV programme)* producir

**producer** [prə'djuːsə(r)] n **(a)** *(of crops, goods)* productor(ora) m,f **(b)** *(of film, play, radio or TV programme)* productor(ora) m,f

**product** ['prɒdʌkt] n producto m; *Com* **p. development** desarrollo m del producto

**production** [prə'dʌkʃən] n **(a)** *Ind (manufacture)* producción f; **to go into p.** empezar a fabricarse; **it went out of p. years ago** hace años que dejó de fabricarse; **p. costs** costes mpl de producción; **p. line** cadena f de producción; **p. manager** jefe(a) m,f de producción; **p.**

**process** proceso m de producción; **p. target** objetivo m de producción **(b)** *(of document, ticket)* presentación f; **on p. of one's passport** al presentar el pasaporte **(c)** *(play)* montaje m; *(film, radio or TV programme)* producción f

**productive** [prə'dʌktɪv] *adj* productivo(a)

**productivity** [prɒdʌk'tɪvɪtɪ] n *Ind* productividad f; **p. agreement** acuerdo m sobre productividad; **p. bonus** plus m de productividad; **p. drive** campaña f de productividad

**Prof** *(abbr* **Professor)** catedrático(a) m,f

**profane** [prə'feɪn] **1** *adj (language)* blasfemo(a) **(b)** *Rel (secular)* profano(a)

**2** vt profanar

**profanity** [prə'fænɪtɪ] n **(a)** *(oath)* blasfemia f **(b)** *(blasphemous nature)* grosería f

**profess** [prə'fes] vt **(a)** *(declare)* manifestar **(b)** *(claim)* proclamar; **he professes to be a socialist** se dice socialista; **I don't p. to be an expert, but...** no pretendo ser un experto, pero...

**professed** [prə'fest] *adj* **(a)** *(self-declared)* declarado(a) **(b)** *(pretended)* supuesto(a), pretendido(a)

**profession** [prə'feʃən] n **(a)** *(occupation)* profesión f; **by p.** de profesión; **the teaching p.** el profesorado **(b)** *(declaration)* manifestación f

**professional** [prə'feʃənəl] **1** n profesional mf

**2** *adj (paid, competent)* profesional; *(soldier)* de carrera; *(army)* profesional; **they made a very p. job of the repair** hicieron la reparación con gran profesionalidad; **to turn or go p.** *(of sportsperson)* hacerse profesional; **to take p. advice on sth** pedir asesoramiento sobre algo a un profesional; **p. misconduct** violación f de la ética profesional

**professionalism** [prə'feʃənəlɪzəm] n **(a)** *(professional approach)* profesionalidad f **(b)** *(in sports)* profesionalismo m

**professor** [prə'fesə(r)] n *Univ Br* catedrático(a) m,f; *US* profesor(ora) m,f

**proffer** ['prɒfə(r)] vt *Formal (advice)* brindar; *(opinion)* ofrecer, dar; *(thanks)* dar; *(hand, object)* tender

**proficiency** [prə'fɪʃənsɪ] n competencia f **(in** or **at** en), aptitud f **(in** or **at** para)

**proficient** [prə'fɪʃənt] *adj* competente **(in** or **at** en)

**profile** ['prəʊfaɪl] **1** n **(a)** *(side view, outline)* perfil m; **to keep a low p.** mantenerse en un segundo plano **(b)** *(description)* retrato m

**2** vt *(describe)* retratar

**profit** ['prɒfɪt] **1** n **(a)** *(of company, on deal)* beneficio m; **at a p.** con beneficios; **to make a p.** obtener o sacar beneficios; **p. and loss account** cuenta f de pérdidas y ganancias; **p. margin** margen m de beneficios **(b)** *(advantage)*

provecho *m*
**2** *vi* **to p. by** *or* **from** sacar provecho de
**profitability** [prɒfɪtə'bɪlɪtɪ] *n* rentabilidad *f*
**profitable** ['prɒfɪtəbəl] *adj (company, deal)* rentable; *(experience)* provechoso(a)
**profitably** ['prɒfɪtəblɪ] *adv (trade, operate)* con beneficios; *(use one's time)* provechosamente
**profiteer** [prɒfɪ'tɪə(r)] *Pej* **1** *n* desaprensivo(a) *m,f*, especulador(ora) *m,f*
**2** *vi* especular
**profit-making** ['prɒfɪtmeɪkɪŋ] *adj* con ánimo de lucro, lucrativo(a)
**profit-sharing** ['prɒfɪt'ʃeərɪŋ] *n Com* participación *f* en los beneficios
**profligate** ['prɒflɪgət] *adj Formal* derrochador(ora)
**profound** [prə'faʊnd] *adj* profundo(a)
**profundity** [prə'fʌndɪtɪ] *n* profundidad *f*
**profuse** [prə'fju:s] *adj* profuso(a); **he offered p. apologies/thanks** se prodigó en disculpas/agradecimientos
**profusely** [prə'fju:slɪ] *adv (apologize, thank)* cumplidamente; *(sweat, bleed)* profusamente
**profusion** [prə'fju:ʒən] *n* profusión *f*
**progeny** ['prɒdʒɪnɪ] *n Formal* progenie *f*, prole *f*
**prognosis** [prɒg'nəʊsɪs] *(pl* **prognoses** [prɒg'nəʊsi:z]) *n Med & Fig* pronóstico *m*
**program¹** ['prəʊgræm] *Comptr* **1** *n* programa *m*
**2** *vt & vi (pt & pp* **programmed**) programar
**program²** *US =* **programme**
**programmable** [prəʊ'græməbəl] *adj* programable; **p. calculator** calculadora *f* programable
**programme,** *US* **program** ['prəʊgræm] **1** *n* (on TV, for play, of political party) programa *m*; **what's the p. for today?** ¿qué programa tenemos para hoy?; **p. seller** vendedor(ora) *m,f* de programas
**2** *vt* programar; **to p. sth to do sth** programar algo para que haga algo
**programmed** ['prəʊgræmd] *n Educ* **p. instruction** *or* **learning** enseñanza *f* programada
**programmer** ['prəʊgræmə(r)] *n Comptr* programador(ora) *m,f*
**progress 1** *n* ['prəʊgres] **(a)** *(improvement)* progreso *m*; **to make p. (in sth)** hacer progresos (en algo) **(b)** *(movement)* avance *m*, progreso *m*; **in p.** en curso; **a p. report on the project** un informe sobre la marcha del proyecto
**2** *vi* [prə'gres] **(a)** *(improve)* progresar; **the patient is progressing satisfactorily** el paciente evoluciona satisfactoriamente **(b)** *(advance)* avanzar
**progression** [prə'greʃən] *n* evolución *f*, progresión *f*

**progressive** [prə'gresɪv] **1** *n* progresista *mf*
**2** *adj* **(a)** *(increasing)* progresivo(a); **p. disease** enfermedad *f* degenerativa **(b)** *(forward-looking)* progresista
**progressively** [prə'gresɪvlɪ] *adv* progresivamente
**prohibit** [prə'hɪbɪt] *vt (forbid)* prohibir; **to p. sb from doing sth** prohibir a alguien que haga algo; **smoking prohibited** *(sign)* prohibido fumar; **it is prohibited by law** lo prohíbe la ley
**prohibition** [prəʊɪ'bɪʃən] *n* prohibición *f*; *Hist* **P.** la Ley Seca
**prohibitive** [prə'hɪbɪtɪv] *adj* prohibitivo(a)
**prohibitively** [prə'hɪbɪtɪvlɪ] *adv* **p. expensive** de precio prohibitivo
**project 1** *n* ['prɒdʒekt] *(undertaking, plan)* proyecto *m*; *(at school, university)* trabajo *m*; *Com* **p. manager** jefe(a) *m,f* de proyecto
**2** *vt* [prə'dʒekt] **(a)** *(plan)* proyectar, planear **(b)** *(propel)* proyectar; **to p. one's voice** proyectar la voz
**3** *vi (protrude)* sobresalir, proyectarse
**projectile** [prə'dʒektaɪl] *n* proyectil *m*
**projection** [prə'dʒekʃən] *n* **(a)** *(of film, in mapmaking, psychological)* proyección *f*; *Cin* **p. room** sala *f* de proyección **(b)** *(prediction)* estimación *f*, pronóstico *m* **(c)** *(protruding part)* proyección *f*, saliente *m*
**projectionist** [prə'dʒekʃənɪst] *n* proyeccionista *mf*
**projector** [prə'dʒektə(r)] *n* proyector *m*
**prolapse** ['prəʊlæps] *n Med* prolapso *m*
**proletarian** [prəʊlɪ'teərɪən] *n & adj* proletario(a) *m,f*
**proletariat** [prəʊlɪ'teərɪət] *n* proletariado *m*
**pro-life** [prəʊ'laɪf] *adj* pro vida, antiabortista
**proliferate** [prə'lɪfəreɪt] *vi* proliferar
**proliferation** [prəlɪfə'reɪʃən] *n* proliferación *f*
**prolific** [prə'lɪfɪk] *adj* prolífico(a)
**prolix** ['prəʊlɪks] *adj Formal* prolijo(a)
**prologue** ['prəʊlɒg] *n* prólogo *m*
**prolong** [prə'lɒŋ] *vt* prolongar
**prom** [prɒm] *n* **(a)** *Br Fam (at seaside)* paseo *m* marítimo **(b)** *Br Fam (concert)* = concierto sinfónico en el que parte del público está de pie **(c)** *US (school dance)* baile *m* de fin de curso
**promenade** ['prɒmənɑːd] **1** *n Br (at seaside)* paseo *m* marítimo; **p. deck** *(on ship)* cubierta *f* de paseo
**2** *vi* pasear
**prominence** ['prɒmɪnəns] *n* **(a)** *(of land, physical feature)* prominencia *f* **(b)** *(of issue, person)* relevancia *f*, importancia *f*; **to give sth p.** destacar algo; **to come to p.** empezar a descollar *or* sobresalir; **to occupy a position of some p.** ocupar un puesto de cierto relieve

**prominent** ['prɒmɪnənt] *adj* (a) *(projecting)* prominente (b) *(conspicuous)* visible, destacado(a); *(important)* renombrado(a), prominente

**prominently** ['prɒmɪntlɪ] *adv* visiblemente; **to figure p. in sth** tener un papel relevante *or* destacar en algo

**promiscuity** [prɒmɪs'kjuːɪtɪ] *n* promiscuidad *f*

**promiscuous** [prə'mɪskjʊəs] *adj* promiscuo(a)

**promise** ['prɒmɪs] 1 *n* (a) *(pledge)* promesa *f*; **to make a p.** hacer la promesa; **to keep/break one's p.** mantener/romper la promesa (b) *(potential)* buenas perspectivas *fpl*; **to show p.** ser prometedor(ora); **she never fulfilled her early p.** nunca llegó tan lejos como parecía prometer

2 *vt* prometer; **to p. to do sth** prometer hacer algo; **to p. sth to sb, to p. sb sth** prometerle algo a alguien; **he promised me he'd do it** me prometió que lo haría; **it promises to be hot** promete hacer calor

**promising** ['prɒmɪsɪŋ] *adj* prometedor(ora)

**promontory** ['prɒməntərɪ] *n* promontorio *m*

**promote** [prə'məʊt] *vt* (a) *(raise in rank)* ascender; **to be promoted** *(of officer, employee)* ser ascendido(a); *(of football team)* ascender (b) *(encourage)* fomentar, promover; **to p. sb's interests** favorecer los intereses de alguien (c) *Com* promocionar

**promoter** [prə'məʊtə(r)] *n* (of theory, cause, boxing match) promotor(ora) *m,f*; (of show) organizador(ora) *m,f*

**promotion** [prə'məʊʃən] *n* (a) *(of employee, officer, football team)* ascenso *m* (b) *(of product, plan)* promoción *f*

**promotional** [prə'məʊʃənəl] *adj* (literature, campaign) promocional

**prompt** [prɒmpt] 1 *n* (a) **to give an actor a p.** dar el pie a un actor (b) *Comptr (short phrase)* mensaje *m* (al usuario); **return to the C:\ p.** volver a C:\

2 *adj (swift)* rápido(a); **p. payment** pronto pago *m* (b) *(punctual)* puntual

3 *adv* **at three o'clock p.** a las tres en punto

4 *vt* (a) *(cause)* provocar, suscitar; **to p. sb to do sth** provocar que alguien haga algo, impulsar a alguien a hacer algo (b) *Th* apuntar (c) *(encourage) (interviewee)* ayudar a seguir

**prompter** ['prɒmptə(r)] *n Th* apuntador(ora) *m,f*

**promptly** ['prɒmptlɪ] *adv (rapidly)* sin demora; *(punctually)* con puntualidad; *(immediately)* inmediatamente

**prone** [prəʊn] *adj* (a) *(inclined)* **to be p. to sth/to do sth** ser propenso(a) a algo/a hacer algo (b) *Formal (lying face down)* boca abajo

**prong** [prɒŋ] *n (of fork)* diente *m*

**pronghorn** ['prɒŋhɔːn] *n US* antílope *m* americano

**pronoun** ['prəʊnaʊn] *n Gram* pronombre *m*

**pronounce** [prə'naʊns] 1 *vt* (a) *(word)* pronunciar; **this letter is not pronounced** esta letra no se pronuncia (b) *(declare) (opinion)* manifestar; **to p. that...** manifestar que...; **to p. oneself for/against sth** pronunciarse a favor de/en contra de algo; **he was pronounced dead/innocent** fue declarado muerto/inocente; *Law* **to p. sentence** dictar sentencia

2 *vi* **to p. on** pronunciarse sobre; **to p. for/against sb** emitir un dictamen a favor de/en contra de alguien

**pronounced** [prə'naʊnst] *adj* pronunciado(a), acusado(a)

**pronouncement** [prə'naʊnsmənt] *n Formal* declaración *f*, manifestación *f*

**pronto** ['prɒntəʊ] *adv Fam* enseguida, ya

**pronunciation** [prənʌnsɪ'eɪʃən] *n* pronunciación *f*

**proof** [pruːf] 1 *n* (a) *(evidence)* prueba *f*; **to give p. of sth** probar algo; **p. of identity** documento *m* de identidad; **p. of purchase** tíquet *m or* justificante *m* de compra; **to put sth to the p.** poner algo a prueba; *Prov* **the p. of the pudding is in the eating** el movimiento se demuestra andando (b) *Typ* prueba *f* (c) *(of alcohol)* **40 degrees p.** de 40 grados

2 *adj (resistant)* **to be p. against sth** ser resistente a algo

**proofread** ['pruːfriːd] *vt Typ* corregir pruebas de

**proofreader** ['pruːfriːdə(r)] *n Typ* corrector(ora) *m,f* de pruebas

**prop** [prɒp] 1 *n* (a) *(physical support)* puntal *m*; *(emotional support)* apoyo *m*, sostén *m* (b) *(in theatre)* accesorio *m*; **props** atrezo *m*

2 *vt (pt & pp* **propped**) apoyar (**against** contra)

▸**prop up** *vt sep (building, tunnel)* apuntalar; *Fig (economy, regime)* apoyar; **to p. sth up against sth** apoyar algo contra *or* en algo

**propaganda** [prɒpə'gændə] *n* propaganda *f*

**propagate** ['prɒpəgeɪt] 1 *vt (plant, theory)* propagar

2 *vi (of plant)* propagarse

**propagation** [prɒpə'geɪʃən] *n* propagación *f*

**propane** ['prəʊpeɪn] *n Chem* propano *m*

**propel** [prə'pel] *(pt & pp* **propelled**) *vt* propulsar; **to p. sth/sb along** propulsar algo/a alguien; **propelled by ambition** impulsado(a) por la ambición

**propellant, propellent** [prə'pelənt] *n (for rocket)* propulsante *m*, combustible *m*; *(for aerosol)* propelente *m*

**propeller** [prə'pelə(r)] *n* hélice *f*

**propelling pencil** [prə'pelɪŋ'pensəl] *n* portaminas *m inv*

**propensity** [prə'pensɪtɪ] *n* tendencia *f*, propensión *f*

**proper** ['prɒpə(r)] *adj* (a) *(correct)* correcto(a); *(real)* verdadero(a); **he isn't a p. doctor** no es médico de verdad; **to get a p. night's sleep** dormir bien toda la noche; **we're still not in London p.** todavía no estamos en Londres propiamente dicho; *Gram* **p. noun** nombre *m* propio (b) *(appropriate) (time, place)* adecuado(a), apropiado(a) (c) *(characteristic)* **p. to** propio(a) de (d) *Br Fam (for emphasis)* **we're in a p. mess** estamos en un buen lío; **he's a p. fool** es un idiota de tomo y lomo

**properly** ['prɒpəlɪ] *adv* (a) *(correctly)* bien (b) *(suitably)* apropiadamente

**property** ['prɒpətɪ] *n* (a) *(possessions)* propiedades *fpl*; *(land, house)* propiedad *f*, inmueble *m*; **p. developer** promotor(ora) *m,f* inmobiliario(a); **p. market** mercado *m* inmobiliario; **p. tax** impuesto *m* sobre el patrimonio (b) *(quality)* propiedad *f*

**prophecy** ['prɒfɪsɪ] *n* profecía *f*

**prophesy** ['prɒfɪsaɪ] *vt* profetizar

**prophet** ['prɒfɪt] *n* profeta *m*

**prophetic** [prə'fetɪk] *adj* profético(a)

**prophylactic** [prɒfɪ'læktɪk] *Med* **1** *n* profiláctico *m*; *(condom)* preservativo *m*, profiláctico *m*
**2** *adj* profiláctico(a)

**propitiate** [prə'pɪʃɪeɪt] *vt Formal* propiciar

**propitious** [prə'pɪʃəs] *adj Formal* propicio(a)

**proportion** [prə'pɔːʃən] **1** *n* (a) *(relationship)* proporción *f*; **in p.** proporcionado(a); **out of p.** desproporcionado(a); **in p. to...** en proporción a...; **the payment is out of all p. to the work involved** lo que se paga no es proporcional al trabajo que supone; **to lose all sense of p.** perder el sentido de la medida; **to get sth out of p.** exagerar algo (b) *(part, amount)* proporción *f*, parte *f* (c) **proportions** *(dimensions)* proporciones *fpl*
**2** *vt* proporcionar

**proportional** [prə'pɔːʃənəl] *adj* proporcional (**to** a); *Pol* **p. representation** representación *f* proporcional

**proportionate** [prə'pɔːʃənɪt] *adj* proporcional (**to** a)

**proposal** [prə'pəʊzəl] *n* *(offer)* propuesta *f*; *(plan)* proyecto *m*; **p. (of marriage)** propuesta *or* proposición *f* de matrimonio

**propose** [prə'pəʊz] **1** *vt* proponer; **to p. to do sth, to p. doing sth** *(suggest)* proponer hacer algo; *(intend)* proponerse hacer algo; **to p. a toast** proponer un brindis
**2** *vi* **he proposed to her** le pidió que se casara con él

**proposition** [prɒpə'zɪʃən] **1** *n* (a) *(offer)* propuesta *f*; *Fam* **it's not a paying p.** no es rentable (b) *(in logic, argument)* proposición *f*
**2** *vt* hacer proposiciones a

**propound** [prə'paʊnd] *vt Formal* exponer

**proprietary** [prə'praɪətrɪ] *adj* *(air, attitude)* de propietario(a), posesivo(a); *Com (brand)* registrado(a)

**proprietor** [prə'praɪətə(r)] *n* propietario(a) *m,f*

**propriety** [prə'praɪətɪ] *n* decoro *m*; **the proprieties** *(etiquette)* las convenciones

**propulsion** [prə'pʌlʃən] *n* propulsión *f*

**pro rata** ['prəʊ'rɑːtə] **1** *adj* prorrateado(a)
**2** *adv* de forma prorrateada

**prosaic** [prəʊ'zeɪɪk] *adj* prosaico(a)

**proscribe** [prəʊ'skraɪb] *vt* proscribir, excluir

**prose** [prəʊz] *n* prosa *f*; *(translation in exam)* (prueba *f* de) traducción *f* inversa

**prosecute** ['prɒsɪkjuːt] *Law* **1** *vt* procesar
**2** *vi (of lawyer)* ejercer de acusación

**prosecution** [prɒsɪ'kjuːʃən] *n Law (proceedings)* proceso *m*, juicio *m*; **the p.** la acusación

**prosecutor** ['prɒsɪkjuːtə(r)] *n Law* fiscal *mf*; **public p.** fiscal *mf* (del Estado)

**prospect 1** *n* ['prɒspekt] (a) *(expectation, thought)* perspectiva *f* (b) *(chance, likelihood)* posibilidad *f*; **there is very little p. of it** es muy poco probable; **there is no p. of agreement** no hay posibilidad *or* perspectivas de acuerdo; **future prospects** perspectivas *fpl* de futuro; **a job with prospects** un trabajo con buenas perspectivas (de futuro) (c) *(view)* vista *f*, panorámica *f*
**2** *vi* [prə'spekt] **to p. for gold** hacer prospecciones en busca de oro

**prospective** [prə'spektɪv] *adj* *(future)* futuro(a); *(potential)* posible, potencial

**prospector** [prə'spektə(r)] *n* **oil/gold p.** buscador(ora) *m,f* de petróleo/oro

**prospectus** [prə'spektəs] *n* folleto *m*, prospecto *m*

**prosper** ['prɒspə(r)] *vi* prosperar

**prosperity** [prɒs'perɪtɪ] *n* prosperidad *f*

**prosperous** ['prɒspərəs] *adj* próspero(a)

**prostate** ['prɒsteɪt] *n Anat* **p. (gland)** próstata *f*

**prosthesis** ['prɒs'θiːsɪs] *(pl* **prostheses** [prɒs'θiːsiːz]) *n* prótesis *f inv*

**prosthetic** [prɒs'θetɪk] *adj* artificial; **p. limb** prótesis *f*

**prostitute** ['prɒstɪtjuːt] **1** *n* prostituta *f*; **male p.** prostituto *m*
**2** *vt also Fig* **to p. oneself** prostituirse

**prostitution** [prɒstɪ'tjuːʃən] *n* prostitución *f*

**prostrate 1** *adj* ['prɒstreɪt] *(lying down)* postrado(a), tendido(a) boca abajo; *Fig* **with**

**grief** postrado(a) por el dolor

**2** vt [prəˈstreɪt] **to p. oneself (before)** postrarse (ante)

**protagonist** [prəˈtægənɪst] n (main character) protagonista mf; (of idea, theory) abanderado(a) m,f, promotor(ora) m,f

**protect** [prəˈtekt] vt proteger (**from** or **against** de or contra)

**protection** [prəˈtekʃən] n protección f; **p. money** extorsión f or impuesto m (a cambio de protección); **p. racket** red f de extorsión

**protectionism** [prəˈtekʃənɪzəm] n Econ proteccionismo m

**protective** [prəˈtektɪv] adj protector(ora); **p. custody** detención f cautelar (para protección del detenido)

**protector** [prəˈtektə(r)] n (device) protector m; (person) protector(ora) m,f

**protégé** [ˈprɒteʒeɪ] n protegido(a) m,f

**protein** [ˈprəʊtiːn] n proteína f

**protest 1** [ˈprəʊtest] protesta f; **to make a p.** protestar; **to do sth under p.** hacer algo de mal grado; **she resigned in p.** dimitió en señal de protesta; **p. song** canción f protesta; **p. vote** voto m de castigo

**2** vt [prəˈtest] (a) US (protest against) protestar en contra de (b) (one's innocence, love) declarar, manifestar; **to p. that...** declarar or manifestar que...

**3** vi protestar (**about/against** por/en contra de)

**Protestant** [ˈprɒtɪstənt] n & adj protestante mf

**Protestantism** [ˈprɒtɪstəntɪzəm] n protestantismo m

**protestation** [prɒtesˈteɪʃən] n declaración f, manifestación f

**protester** [prəˈtestə(r)] n manifestante mf

**protocol** [ˈprəʊtəkɒl] n protocolo m

**proton** [ˈprəʊtɒn] n Phys protón m

**prototype** [ˈprəʊtətaɪp] n prototipo m

**protracted** [prəˈtræktɪd] adj prolongado(a)

**protractor** [prəˈtræktə(r)] n transportador m

**protrude** [prəˈtruːd] vi sobresalir

**protruding** [prəˈtruːdɪŋ] adj (ledge) saliente; (jaw, teeth) prominente

**protuberance** [prəˈtjuːbərəns] n protuberancia f

**proud** [praʊd] **1** adj (in general) orgulloso(a); (arrogant) orgulloso(a), soberbio(a); (noble) orgulloso(a), digno(a); **to be p. of (having done) sth** estar orgulloso(a) de (haber hecho) algo; **a p. moment** un momento de gran satisfacción; **to be as p. as a peacock** estar orgullosísimo(a)

**2** adv **you've done us p.** lo has hecho muy bien; **to do oneself p.** hacerlo muy bien

**proudly** [ˈpraʊdlɪ] adv orgullosamente, con orgullo; (arrogantly) con soberbia

**prove** [pruːv] (pp **proven** [ˈpruːvən, ˈprəʊvən] or **proved**) **1** vt (demonstrate) demostrar, probar; **to p. sb wrong/guilty** demostrar que alguien está equivocado(a)/es culpable; **she wanted a chance to p. herself** quería una oportunidad para demostrar su valía

**2** vi **to p. (to be) correct** resultar (ser) correcto(a)

**proverb** [ˈprɒvɜːb] n refrán m, proverbio m

**proverbial** [prəˈvɜːbɪəl] adj proverbial

**provide** [prəˈvaɪd] vt (a) (supply) suministrar, proporcionar; (service, support) prestar, proporcionar; **to p. sb with sth** suministrar or proporcionar algo a alguien (b) (stipulate) establecer

▸**provide against** vt insep (danger, possibility) prepararse para

▸**provide for** vt insep (a) (support) mantener (b) Formal (allow for) prever

**provided** [prəˈvaɪdɪd] conj **p. (that)** siempre que, a condición de que

**providence** [ˈprɒvɪdəns] n providencia f

**providential** [prɒvɪˈdenʃəl] adj providencial

**provider** [prəˈvaɪdə(r)] n proveedor(ora) m,f, abastecedor(ora) m,f

**providing** [prəˈvaɪdɪŋ] conj **p. (that)** siempre que, a condición de que

**province** [ˈprɒvɪns] n (a) (of country) provincia f; **in the provinces** en provincias (b) Fig (domain) terreno m, campo m de acción

**provincial** [prəˈvɪnʃəl] adj provincial; Pej (parochial) provinciano(a)

**provision** [prəˈvɪʒən] n (a) **provisions** (supplies) provisiones fpl (b) (supplying) (of money, water) suministro m, abastecimiento m; (of services) prestación f (c) (allowance) **to make p. for sth** prever algo, tener en cuenta algo; **the law makes no p. for a case of this kind** la ley no contempla un caso de este tipo (d) (in treaty, contract) estipulación f, disposición f

**provisional** [prəˈvɪʒənəl] adj provisional

**provisionally** [prəˈvɪʒənəlɪ] adv provisionalmente

**proviso** [prəˈvaɪzəʊ] (pl **provisos**, US **provisoes**) n condición f; **with the p. that...** a condición de que...

**provocation** [prɒvəˈkeɪʃən] n provocación f; **at the slightest p.** a la menor provocación; **without p.** sin mediar provocación

**provocative** [prəˈvɒkətɪv] adj (polemical) provocador(ora); (sexually) provocativo(a)

**provoke** [prəˈvəʊk] vt (incite) provocar; **to p. sb into doing sth** empujar a alguien a hacer algo; **to p. sb to anger** provocar la ira de alguien

**provoking** [prə'vəʊkɪŋ] *adj (irritating)* irritante, enojoso(a)

**provost** ['prɒvəst] *n* (**a**) *Br Univ (head of college)* decano(a) *m,f* (**b**) *Scot (mayor)* alcalde(esa) *m,f*

**prow** [praʊ] *n (of ship)* proa *f*

**prowess** ['praʊɪs] *n (skill)* proezas *fpl*

**prowl** [praʊl] **1** *n* to be on the p. *(person, animal)* merodear; **to be on the p. for sth** andar a la caza de algo
**2** *vt (streets, area)* merodear por
**3** *vi* merodear

**prowler** ['praʊlə(r)] *n* merodeador(ora) *m,f*

**proximity** [prɒk'sɪmɪtɪ] *n* cercanía *f*, proximidad *f*; **in close p. to** muy cerca de

**proxy** ['prɒksɪ] *n (person)* apoderado(a) *m,f*; *(power)* poder *m*; **to vote by p.** votar por poderes

**prude** [pru:d] *n* mojigato(a) *m,f*

**prudence** ['pru:dəns] *n* prudencia *f*

**prudent** ['pru:dənt] *adj* prudente

**prudish** ['pru:dɪʃ] *adj* mojigato(a), pacato(a)

**prune¹** [pru:n] *n (fruit)* ciruela *f* pasa

**prune²** *vt (bush, tree)* podar; *Fig (article)* recortar

**prurient** ['prʊərɪənt] *adj* procaz, lascivo(a)

**Prussia** ['prʌʃə] *n* Prusia

**Prussian** ['prʌʃən] *n & adj* prusiano(a) *m,f*

**pry** [praɪ] *vi* entrometerse, husmear; **to p. into sth** entrometerse en algo

**prying** ['praɪɪŋ] *adj* entrometido(a)

**PS** ['pi:es] *n (abbr* **postscript**) P.D.

**psalm** [sɑ:m] *n* salmo *m*

**pseud** [sju:d] *n Fam* pretencioso(a) *m,f*

**pseudo-** ['sju:dəʊ] *pref* seudo-, pseudo-

**pseudonym** ['sju:dənɪm] *n* seudónimo *m*

**psoriasis** [sə'raɪəsɪs] *n* soriasis *f*

**PST** [pi:es'ti:] *n US (abbr* **Pacific Standard Time**) = hora oficial de la costa del Pacífico en Estados Unidos

**psyche** ['saɪkɪ] *n* psique *f*, psiquis *f inv*
▶**psyche out** [saɪk] *vt sep Fam (unnerve)* hacer guerra psicológica a, poner nervioso(a)
▶**psyche up** *vt sep Fam* **to p. sb up** mentalizar a alguien; **to p. oneself up (for sth)** mentalizarse (para algo)

**psychedelic** [saɪkə'delɪk] *adj* psicodélico(a)

**psychiatric** [saɪkɪ'ætrɪk] *adj* psiquiátrico(a)

**psychiatrist** [saɪ'kaɪətrɪst] *n* psiquiatra *mf*

**psychiatry** [saɪ'kaɪətrɪ] *n* psiquiatría *f*

**psychic** ['saɪkɪk] **1** *n* médium *mf inv*
**2** *adj (phenomena, experiences)* paranormal, extrasensorial; *(person)* vidente; **to have p. powers** tener poderes paranormales; *Fam* **I'm not p.!** ¡no soy un adivino!

**psycho** ['saɪkəʊ] *(pl* **psychos**) *n Fam (crazy person)* colgado(a) *m,f*

**psychoanalysis** [saɪkəʊə'nælɪsɪs] *n* psicoanálisis *m inv*

**psychoanalyst** [saɪkəʊ'ænəlɪst] *n* psicoanalista *mf*

**psychoanalyze** [saɪkəʊ'ænəlaɪz] *vt* psicoanalizar

**psychological** [saɪkə'lɒdʒɪkəl] *adj* psicológico(a); **p. warfare** guerra *f* psicológica

**psychologist** [saɪ'kɒlədʒɪst] *n* psicólogo(a) *m,f*

**psychology** [saɪ'kɒlədʒɪ] *n* psicología *f*

**psychometric** [saɪkə'metrɪk] *adj* **p. test** prueba *f* psicométrica

**psychopath** ['saɪkəʊpæθ] *n* psicópata *mf*

**psychosis** [saɪ'kəʊsɪs] *(pl* **psychoses** [saɪ'kəʊsi:z]) *n* psicosis *f inv*

**psychosomatic** [saɪkəʊsə'mætɪk] *adj* psicosomático(a)

**psychotherapist** [saɪkəʊ'θerəpɪst] *n* psicoterapeuta *mf*

**psychotherapy** [saɪkəʊ'θerəpɪ] *n* psicoterapia *f*

**psychotic** [saɪ'kɒtɪk] *n & adj* psicótico(a) *m,f*

**PT** [pi:'ti:] *n (abbr* **physical training**) educación *f* física

**PTA** [pi:ti:'eɪ] *n Sch (abbr* **Parent-Teacher Association**) = asociación de padres de alumnos y profesores, ≃ APA *f*

**ptarmigan** ['tɑ:mɪgən] *n* perdiz *f* nival

**Pte** *Mil (abbr* **private**) soldado *m* raso

**PTO** [pi:ti:'əʊ] *(abbr* **please turn over**) sigue

**pub** [pʌb] *n Br* = típico bar de las islas Británicas donde se suele consumir cerveza y licores, estos servidos en medidas estrictamente dosificadas, y que a veces sirve comidas simples

**pub-crawl** ['pʌbkrɔ:l] *n Br Fam* to go on a p. ir de copas

**puberty** ['pju:bətɪ] *n* pubertad *f*

**pubic** ['pju:bɪk] *adj* pubiano(a)

**public** ['pʌblɪk] **1** *n* the (general) p. el público en general, el gran público; **in p.** en público
**2** *adj* público(a); **to go p.** *(of company)* pasar a cotizar en Bolsa; **to go p. with sth** *(reveal information)* manifestar públicamente algo; **to make sth p.** hacer público algo; **to make a p. appearance** hacer *or* efectuar una aparición pública; **to be in the p. domain** ser del dominio público; **at p. expense** con dinero público; **to be in the p. eye** estar expuesto(a) a la opinión pública; **in the p. interest** en favor del interés general; **p. address system** (sistema *m* de) megafonía *f*; **p. call box** cabina *f* telefónica; **p. convenience** servicios *mpl or* aseos *mpl* públicos; *Com* **p. enterprise** empresa *f* pública; **p. holiday** día *m* festivo; **p. house** = pub; **p. limited company** sociedad *f* anónima;

opinion opinión f pública; Law **p. prosecutor** fiscal mf (del Estado); **p. relations** relaciones fpl públicas; **p. school** Br colegio m privado; US colegio m público; **p. sector** sector m público; **p. spending** gasto m público; **p. transport** transporte m público; Com **p. utility** (empresa f de) servicio m público

**publican** ['pʌblɪkən] n dueño(a) m,f de un "pub"

**publication** [pʌblɪ'keɪʃən] n publicación f

**publicity** [pʌb'lɪsɪtɪ] n publicidad f; **p. campaign** campaña f publicitaria or de publicidad; **p. stunt** artimaña f publicitaria

**publicize** ['pʌblɪsaɪz] vt hacer público(a); **a much publicized dispute** un enfrentamiento muy aireado por los medios de comunicación

**publicly** ['pʌblɪklɪ] adv públicamente; **p. owned** de titularidad pública

**public-spirited** ['pʌblɪkspɪrɪtɪd] adj cívico(a)

**publish** ['pʌblɪʃ] vt publicar

**publisher** ['pʌblɪʃə(r)] n (person) editor(ora) m,f; (company) editorial f

**publishing** ['pʌblɪʃɪŋ] n industria f editorial; **p. house** editorial f

**pucker** ['pʌkə(r)] **1** vt **to p. one's lips** fruncir los labios
**2** vi (of face) arrugarse; (lips) fruncirse

**pudding** ['pʊdɪŋ] n (**a**) (dessert) postre m; **what's for p.?** ¿qué hay de postre? (**b**) (dish) (sweet) budín m, pudín m; (savoury) pastel m; **p. basin** or **bowl** bol m

**puddle** ['pʌdəl] n charco m

**pudgy** ['pʌdʒɪ] adj rechoncho(a), regordete(a)

**puerile** ['pjʊəraɪl] adj Pej pueril

**Puerto Rican** [pweətəʊ'riːkən] n & adj puertorriqueño(a) m,f

**Puerto Rico** [pweətəʊ'riːkəʊ] n Puerto Rico

**puff** [pʌf] **1** n (of breath) bocanada f; (of air) soplo m; (of smoke) nube f; (of cigarette) calada f, chupada f; Fam **to be out of p.** resoplar, estar sin aliento; **p. pastry** hojaldre m
**2** vt **to p. smoke into sb's face** echar una bocanada de humo a la cara de alguien
**3** vi (of person) resoplar, jadear; **to p. along** (of steam engine) avanzar echando humo; **to p. on a cigarette** dar caladas or chupadas a un cigarrillo
▶**puff out** vt sep (cheeks, chest) inflar, hinchar
▶**puff up** vt sep (cheeks) inflar, hinchar; **he was puffed up with pride** no cabía en sí de orgullo

**puffin** ['pʌfɪn] n frailecillo m

**puffy** ['pʌfɪ] adj hinchado(a)

**pug** [pʌg] n (dog) dogo m; **p.-nosed** chato(a)

**pugnacious** [pʌg'neɪʃəs] adj combativo(a)

**puke** [pjuːk] Fam **1** n papa f, vomitona f
**2** vt devolver
**3** vi echar la papa, devolver

**pull** [pʊl] **1** n (**a**) (act of pulling) tirón m; (of water current) fuerza f; **to give sth a p.** dar un tirón a algo; **to take a p. at a bottle** echar un trago de una botella
(**b**) Fam (influence) influencia f; **to have a lot of p.** ser muy influyente
**2** vt (**a**) (tug) tirar de; (trigger) apretar; **to p. sth open/shut** abrir/cerrar algo de un tirón; **to p. a muscle** sufrir un tirón en un músculo; Fig **she's not pulling her weight** no arrima el hombro (como los demás); also Fig **to p. sth to pieces** hacer trizas algo; Fam Fig **to p. sb's leg** tomarle el pelo a alguien; Fam Fig **p. the other one! (it's got bells on!)** ¡venga ya!, ¡a otro perro con ese hueso!
(**b**) (attract) atraer
(**c**) (extract) (tooth, cork) sacar; Fam Fig **talking to her is like pulling teeth** hay que sacarle las cosas con sacacorchos; **to p. a pint** tirar or servir una cerveza (de barril); **to p. a gun on sb** sacar un arma y apuntar a alguien
(**d**) very Fam (sexually) **to p. sb** ligarse or tirarse a alguien
(**e**) (idioms) **to p. a face** hacer una mueca; Fam **to p. a bank job** atracar un banco; Fam **to p. a fast one on sb** hacer una jugarreta or engañar a alguien
**3** vi tirar (on de); **to p. clear of sth** dejar algo atrás
▶**pull about** vt sep (handle roughly) zarandear, maltratar
▶**pull ahead** vi (in race, election) tomar la delantera, ponerse en cabeza
▶**pull apart** vt sep also Fig hacer trizas
▶**pull away** vi (from station) alejarse; (from kerb, embrace) apartarse
▶**pull back 1** vt sep (curtains) descorrer
**2** vi (of person) echarse atrás; (of troops) retirarse
▶**pull down** vt sep (demolish) demoler, derribar
▶**pull in 1** vt sep (**a**) (rope, fishing line) recoger (**b**) (money) sacar; **to p. sb in for questioning** detener a alguien para interrogarlo (**c**) (attract) atraer
**2** vt (**a**) (of car) parar; (of train, bus) llegar
▶**pull off** vt sep (**a**) (clothes) quitarse; **she pulled off her jumper** se quitó el jersey (**b**) Fam (succeed in doing) sacar adelante; **he pulled it off** lo consiguió
▶**pull on** vt sep (clothes) ponerse
▶**pull out 1** vt sep (tooth) sacar, arrancar; Fam Fig **to p. out all the stops** tocar todos los registros
**2** vi (**a**) (of train) salir; **he pulled out into the stream of traffic** se incorporó al tráfico (**b**) (of race, agreement) **to p. out (of sth)** retirarse (de algo)
▶**pull over** vi (of driver) parar en el arcén
▶**pull through** vi (recover) recuperarse, salir adelante

▶**pull together 1** *vt sep* **to p. oneself to-gether** serenarse
**2** *vi* juntar esfuerzos
▶**pull up 1** *vt sep Fig* **to p. one's socks up** espabilar; **to p. sb up (short)** parar a alguien en seco
**2** *vi (of car)* parar
**pull-down menu** ['pʊldaʊn'menjuː] *n Comptr* menú *m* desplegable
**pullet** ['pʊlɪt] *n* polla *f*, gallina *f* joven
**pulley** ['pʊlɪ] *(pl pulleys)* *n* polea *f*
**pull-out** ['pʊlaʊt] *n (in newspaper, magazine)* suplemento *m*
**pullover** ['pʊləʊvə(r)] *n* jersey *m*
**pulmonary** ['pʌlmənərɪ] *adj* pulmonar
**pulp** [pʌlp] **1** *n (of fruit)* pulpa *f*, carne *f*; **to reduce sth to (a) p.** reducir algo a (una) pasta; *Fam* **to beat sb to a p.** hacer picadillo *or* papilla a alguien; **p. fiction** literatura *f* barata *or* de baja estofa, novelas *fpl* de tiros
**2** *vt* hacer pasta de papel con
**pulpit** ['pʊlpɪt] *n* púlpito *m*
**pulsate** [pʌl'seɪt] *vi* palpitar
**pulse¹** [pʌls] *n (of blood)* pulso *m*; *(of light, sound)* impulso *m*; **to feel** *or* **take sb's p.** tomar el pulso a alguien
**pulse²** *n (pea, bean, lentil)* legumbre *f*
**pulverize** ['pʌlvəraɪz] *vt* pulverizar; *Fam Fig* **to p. sb** *(beat up, defeat heavily)* dar una paliza a alguien
**puma** ['pjuːmə] *n* puma *m*
**pumice** ['pʌmɪs] *n* **p. (stone)** piedra *f* pómez
**pummel** ['pʌməl] *(pt & pp* **pummelled,** *US* **pummeled)** *vt* aporrear
**pump¹** [pʌmp] *n (flat shoe)* zapato *m* de salón; *(ballet shoe)* zapatilla *f* de ballet; *(plimsoll)* playera *f*
**pump²** **1** *n (machine)* bomba *f*; *(at petrol station)* surtidor *m*
**2** *vt* bombear; **to p. sb's stomach** hacer un lavado de estómago a alguien; *Fig* **to p. money into sth** inyectar una gran cantidad de dinero en algo; *Fam* **to p. sb for information** sonsacar a alguien; **to p. sb's hand** dar un enérgico apretón de manos a alguien; *Fam* **to p. iron** *(do weightlifting)* hacer pesas
**3** *vi (of heart, machine)* bombear
▶**pump out** *vt sep (music, information)* emitir
▶**pump up** *vt sep* inflar
**pumpkin** ['pʌmpkɪn] *n* calabaza *f*
**pun** [pʌn] *n* juego *m* de palabras
**punch¹** [pʌntʃ] **1** *n (tool)* punzón *m*; **(ticket) p.** canceladora *f* de billetes
**2** *vt (metal)* perforar; *(ticket)* picar
**punch²** **1** *n* **(a)** *(blow)* puñetazo *m*; *Fig* **he didn't pull his punches** no tuvo pelos en la lengua, se despachó a gusto **(b)** *(energy)* garra *f*; **p. line** final *m* del chiste *m*, golpe *m*; **he**

had forgotten the **p. line** había olvidado cómo acababa el chiste
**2** *vt (hit)* dar *or* pegar un puñetazo a; **to p. sb in the face/on the nose** pegarle a alguien un puñetazo en la cara/en la nariz
**punch³** *n (drink)* ponche *m*
**Punch and Judy show** ['pʌntʃən-'dʒuːdɪˈʃəʊ] *n* = espectáculo de títeres de la cachiporra representado en una feria o junto al mar
**punchbag** ['pʌntʃbæg] *n* saco *m* (de boxeo)
**punchball** ['pʌntʃbɔːl] *n* punching-ball *m*
**punch-drunk** ['pʌntʃdrʌŋk] *adj (dazed)* aturdido(a); *(boxer)* sonado(a)
**punch-up** ['pʌntʃʌp] *n Fam* pelea *f*
**punchy** ['pʌntʃɪ] *adj Fam* con garra
**punctilious** [pʌŋk'tɪlɪəs] *adj* puntilloso(a)
**punctual** ['pʌŋktjʊəl] *adj* puntual
**punctuality** [pʌŋktjʊˈælɪtɪ] *n* puntualidad *f*
**punctually** ['pʌŋktjʊəlɪ] *adv* puntualmente
**punctuate** ['pʌŋktjʊeɪt] *vt (sentence, writing)* puntuar; *Fig* **her speech was punctuated with applause** su discurso se vio interrumpido en ocasiones por aplausos
**punctuation** [pʌŋktjʊˈeɪʃən] *n* puntuación *f*; **p. mark** signo *m* de puntuación
**puncture** ['pʌŋktʃə(r)] **1** *n (in tyre)* pinchazo *m*; *(in skin)* punción *f*; *(in metal)* perforación *f*; **to have a p.** tener un pinchazo
**2** *vt (tyre)* pinchar, *Am* ponchar; *(metal, lung)* perforar; *(blister, abscess)* punzar
**pundit** ['pʌndɪt] *n* experto(a) *m,f*
**pungent** ['pʌndʒənt] *adj (smell, taste)* acre; *(style, wit)* mordaz
**punish** ['pʌnɪʃ] *vt* castigar; **to p. sb for doing sth** castigar a alguien por hacer algo
**punishment** ['pʌnɪʃmənt] *n* castigo *m*; **to make the p. fit the crime** hacer que el castigo guarde proporción con el delito; **to take a lot of p.** *(of boxer)* recibir muchos golpes; *(of clothing, paint)* aguantar mucho trote
**punitive** ['pjuːnɪtɪv] *adj* de castigo, punitivo(a)
**punk** [pʌŋk] *n* punk *mf*, punki *mf*; **p. (rock)** *(música f)* punk *m*
**punnet** ['pʌnɪt] *n* cestita *f (para fresas, bayas)*
**punt¹** [pʌnt] **1** *n* batea *f (impulsada con pértiga)*
**2** *vi* **to go punting** pasear en batea por un río
**punt²** *n (Irish currency)* libra *f* irlandesa
**punter** ['pʌntə(r)] *n (gambler)* apostante *mf*; *Fam* **the punters** *(the public)* el personal, el público; *(regulars in bar)* los parroquianos
**puny** ['pjuːnɪ] *adj* enclenque
**pup** [pʌp] *n (of dog)* cachorro *m*; *(of seal)* cría *f*
**pupil¹** ['pjuːpəl] *n (student)* alumno(a) *m,f*
**pupil²** *n (of eye)* pupila *f*

**puppet** ['pʌpɪt] n also Fig títere m, marioneta f; Fig **p. government** gobierno m títere; **p. show** (espectáculo m de) guiñol m

**puppy** ['pʌpɪ] n cachorro m; **p. fat** obesidad f infantil; **p. love** amor m de adolescente

**purchase** ['pɜːtʃɪs] 1 n (a) (action, thing bought) adquisición f, compra f; **p. price** precio m de compra (b) (grip) **to get a p. on sth** agarrarse o asirse a algo
  2 vt adquirir, comprar

**purchaser** ['pɜːtʃəsə(r)] n comprador(ora) m,f

**purchasing** ['pɜːtʃəsɪŋ] n **p. manager** jefe(a) m,f de compras; **p. power** poder m adquisitivo

**pure** [pjʊə(r)] adj puro(a); **p. silk** pura seda; **p. wool** pura lana f virgen; **p. mathematics** matemáticas fpl puras

**purebred** ['pjʊəbred] adj (dog) de raza; (horse) purasangre

**purée** ['pjʊəreɪ] 1 n puré m
  2 vt hacer puré

**purely** ['pjʊəlɪ] adv puramente; **p. by chance** por pura casualidad; **p. and simply** lisa y llanamente

**purgatory** ['pɜːgətərɪ] n Rel purgatorio m

**purge** [pɜːdʒ] 1 n purga f
  2 vt purgar

**purification** [pjʊərɪfɪ'keɪʃən] n purificación f; (of water) depuración f

**purify** ['pjʊərɪfaɪ] vt purificar; (water) depurar

**purist** ['pjʊərɪst] n purista mf

**puritan** ['pjʊərɪtən] n puritano(a) m,f

**puritanical** [pjʊərɪ'tænɪkəl] adj puritano(a)

**purity** ['pjʊərɪtɪ] n pureza f

**purl** [pɜːl] 1 n punto m del revés
  2 vi hacer punto del revés

**purloin** [pɜː'lɔɪn] vt sustraer

**purple** ['pɜːpəl] 1 n morado m
  2 adj morado(a); **to turn** o **go p.** (with embarrassment, anger) enrojecer; **p. prose** prosa f recargada

**purport** Formal 1 n ['pɜːpɔːt] sentido m, significado m
  2 vt [pɜː'pɔːt] **to p. to be sth** pretender ser algo

**purpose** ['pɜːpəs] n (a) (object, aim) propósito m, objeto m; **on p.** adrede, a propósito; **to be to no p.** ser en vano; **what is the p. of your visit?** ¿cuál es el objeto de su visita?; **they have a real sense of p.** saben lo que quieren (conseguir) (b) (use) finalidad f; **to serve a p.** tener una utilidad o finalidad; **to serve no p.** no servir para nada; **to serve sb's purpose(s)** ser útil a los propósitos de alguien; **for all practical purposes** a efectos prácticos; **for the purposes of** a efectos de

**purpose-built** ['pɜːpəs'bɪlt] adj construido(a) al efecto

**purposeful** ['pɜːpəsfʊl] adj decidido(a)

**purposely** ['pɜːpəslɪ] adv adrede, a propósito

**purr** [pɜː(r)] 1 n (of cat) ronroneo m; (of machine) rumor m, zumbido m
  2 vi (of cat) ronronear

**purse** [pɜːs] 1 n Br (wallet) monedero m; US (handbag) bolso m; **the public p.** el erario público; Fig **to hold the p. strings** llevar las riendas del gasto
  2 vt **to p. one's lips** fruncir los labios

**pursue** [pə'sjuː] vt (a) (person, animal) perseguir; (pleasure, knowledge, happiness) buscar (b) (studies, enquiry) proseguir, continuar; (course of action) seguir; (profession) ejercer

**pursuer** [pə'sjuːə(r)] n perseguidor(ora) m,f

**pursuit** [pə'sjuːt] n (a) (of person, animal) persecución f; (of pleasure, knowledge, happiness) busca f, búsqueda f; **to be in p. of** ir en busca de; **he came with two policemen in hot p.** venía con dos policías pisándole los talones (b) (activity) ocupación f; (leisure) **pursuits** aficiones fpl

**purveyor** [pə'veɪə(r)] n Formal proveedor(ora) m,f

**pus** [pʌs] n pus m

**push** [pʊʃ] 1 n (a) (act of pushing) empujón m; **to give sth/sb a p.** dar un empujón a algo/alguien; Fam **to give sb the p.** (of employer) poner en la calle a alguien; (of lover) dejar a alguien; Fam **at a p.** apurando mucho; Fam **when p. comes to shove…, if it comes to the p.…** a la hora de la verdad…
  (b) Mil (attack) ofensiva f; **sales p.** campaña f de ventas; **to make a p. for sth** tratar de conseguir algo
  2 vt (a) (in general) empujar; (button) apretar, pulsar; **to p. the door shut/open** cerrar/abrir la puerta empujándola; **P.** (sign) empujar, empuje; **to p. sb out of the way** apartar a alguien de un empujón; **to p. one's way through the crowd** abrirse paso a empujones entre la gente; Fig **don't p. yourself too hard** no te pases en el esfuerzo; Fig **to p. sb into doing sth** forzar a alguien a hacer algo; **to p. one's luck** tentar a la suerte; **don't p. your luck!** (said in annoyance) ¡no me busques las cosquillas!; **to be pushed for time** estar apurado(a) de tiempo
  (b) (sell, promote) (goods) promocionar; (theory) defender
  (c) Fam (drugs) pasar, trapichear con
  (d) Fam **he's pushing sixty** ronda los sesenta
  3 vi (in general) empujar; (move forward) avanzar (a empujones); **he pushed past me** se me coló a empujones; **to p. forward** empujar hacia delante

▶**push about, push around** vt sep Fam Fig (bully) abusar de

▶**push ahead** vi seguir adelante (**with** con)

▶**push aside** vt sep apartar (de un empujón); Fig (reject) dejar a un lado

▶**push in** vi (in queue) colarse

▶**push off** vi Fam **p. off!** ¡lárgate!

▶**push on** vi (continue) seguir, continuar; **to p. on with sth** seguir adelante con algo

▶**push over** vt sep derribar

▶**push through** vt sep (reform, law) hacer aprobar (con urgencia)

**push-bike** ['pʊʃbaɪk] n Fam bici f, bicicleta f

**push-button** ['pʊʃ'bʌtən] adj de teclas, de botones

**pushchair** ['pʊʃtʃeə(r)] n (for baby) silla f or sillita f de niño

**pusher** ['pʊʃə(r)] n Fam (drug) p. camello m

**pushover** ['pʊʃəʊvə(r)] n Fam **it's a p.** es pan comido; **I'm a p.** no sé decir que no

**push-up** ['pʊʃʌp] n flexión f (de brazos)

**pushy** ['pʊʃɪ] adj Fam avasallador(ora)

**puss** [pʊs] n Fam (cat) gatito m, minino m

**pussy** ['pʊsɪ] n Fam **p. (cat)** gatito m, minino m; **p. willow** sauce m blanco

**pussyfoot** ['pʊsɪfʊt] vi Fam **to p. around** or **about** andarse con rodeos

**pustule** ['pʌstjuːl] n pústula f

**put** [pʊt] (pt & pp put) **1** vt (**a**) (place) poner; (carefully) colocar; **to p. sth into sth** meter algo en algo; **to p. one's arms around sth/sb** rodear algo/a alguien con los brazos; **she put her head round the door** asomó la cabeza por la puerta; **to p. a man on the moon** enviar un hombre a la Luna; **to p. a limit on sth** poner un límite a algo; Fam **p. it there!** (shake hands) ¡choca esos cinco!, ¡chócala!; Fig **to p. oneself into sb's hands** ponerse en manos de alguien; Fig **to p. sb in his place** poner a alguien en su sitio; Fig **p. yourself in my position** ponte en mi lugar; **to p. a matter right** arreglar una cuestión; **to p. money on a horse** apostar a un caballo; **to p. a lot of work into sth** trabajar intensamente en algo; **to p. a stop to sth** poner fin a algo; **to p. a child to bed** acostar a un niño; **to p. sb to the test** poner a alguien a prueba; Fam Fig **I didn't know where to p. myself** no sabía dónde meterme

(**b**) (present) **to p. a question to sb** hacer una pregunta a alguien; **to p. a proposal to sb** presentar una propuesta a alguien; **I p. it to you that...** (in court case) ¿no es cierto que...?

(**c**) (express) **to p. sth well/badly** expresar algo bien/mal; **I couldn't have put it better myself** nadie le hubiera dicho mejor; **to p. it bluntly** hablando claro; **to p. it mildly** por no decir otra cosa; **how shall I p. it?** ¿cómo lo

diría?

(**d**) (estimate) calcular (**at** en); **I would p. her age at forty** yo diría que tiene unos cuarenta años

**2** vi **to p. to sea** zarpar

▶**put about 1** vt sep (rumour) difundir; **to p. it about that...** difundir el rumor de que...

**2** vi (of ship) cambiar de rumbo

▶**put across** vt sep (message, idea) transmitir, hacer llegar; **to p. oneself across well/badly** hacerse entender bien/mal

▶**put aside** vt sep (**a**) (reserve) apartar; **we'll p. it aside for you** (in shop) se lo dejamos apartado (**b**) (save) (money) ahorrar (**c**) (problem, fact) dejar a un lado

▶**put away** vt sep (**a**) (tidy away) ordenar, recoger; **p. your money/wallet away** guarda tu dinero/cartera (**b**) Fam (imprison) encerrar (**c**) Fam (eat, drink) **he can really p. it away!** ¡cómo traga!

▶**put back** vt sep (**a**) (replace) devolver a su sitio (**b**) (postpone) aplazar, posponer; (clock) retrasar, atrasar; (schedule) retrasar; Fig **that puts the clock back ten years** esto nos devuelve a la misma situación de hace diez años

▶**put by** vt sep (save) ahorrar

▶**put down** vt sep (**a**) (set down) dejar; **I couldn't p. it down** (book) no me podía despegar del libro

(**b**) (revolt, opposition) reprimir, ahogar

(**c**) (write) poner por escrito; **to p. sth down in writing** poner algo por escrito; **to p. one's name down for sth** apuntarse a or inscribirse en algo

(**d**) (attribute) **to p. sth down to sth** achacar or atribuir algo a algo

(**e**) (animal) sacrificar; **to have a cat/dog put down** sacrificar a un gato/perro

(**f**) (criticize) **to p. sb down** dejar a alguien en mal lugar; **to p. oneself down** menospreciarse

▶**put forward** vt sep (**a**) (plan, theory, candidate) proponer; (proposal) presentar (**b**) (clock, time of meeting) adelantar

▶**put in 1** vt sep (**a**) (install) poner, instalar (**b**) (claim, protest) presentar; **to p. in a (good) word for sb** decir algo en favor de alguien (**c**) (time, work) invertir, dedicar

**2** vi (of ship) atracar, hacer escala

▶**put off** vt sep (**a**) (postpone) aplazar, posponer; **to p. off doing sth** dejar algo para más tarde

(**b**) (cause to dislike) desagradar, resultar desagradable a; **that meal p. me off seafood** después de aquella comida dejó de gustarme el marisco

(**c**) (distract) distraer

(**d**) (discourage) **to p. sb off doing sth** quitarle a alguien las ganas de hacer algo

(**e**) (make wait) tener esperando

▶**put on** *vt sep* (a) *(clothes)* ponerse; **he put his trousers on** se puso el pantalón; **to p. on one's make-up** ponerse el maquillaje, maquillarse; **to p. on an act** fingir; **to p. on an accent** poner *or* simular un acento; **to p. on weight** engordar (b) *(light, TV, heating)* encender; *(music, videotape)* poner; **to p. the kettle on** poner el agua a hervir *(en el hervidor de agua)* (c) *(play, show)* representar, hacer

▶**put out** *vt sep* (a) *(fire, light)* apagar
  (b) *(place outside)* sacar
  (c) *(extend)* **to p. out one's hand** tender la mano
  (d) *(arrange for use)* dejar preparado(a)
  (e) *(report, statement)* emitir
  (f) *(annoy)* **to be put out** estar disgustado(a)
  (g) *(inconvenience)* molestar; **to p. oneself out (for sb)** molestarse (por alguien)
  (h) *(dislocate)* **to p. one's shoulder/knee out** dislocarse el hombro/la rodilla

▶**put through** *vt sep* (a) *(on phone)* **to p. sb through to sb** poner *or* pasar a alguien con alguien; *(subject to)* **to p. sb through sth** someter a alguien a algo; **he put her through hell** le ha hecho pasar las de Caín

▶**put together** *vt sep (machine, furniture)* montar; *(file, report, meal, team)* confeccionar; **she's more intelligent than the rest of them put together** ella es más lista que todos los demás juntos; *Fig* **to p. two and two together** atar cabos

▶**put up** *vt sep* (a) *(ladder)* situar; *(tent)* montar; *(building, barricade, fence)* levantar, construir; *(painting, notice)* colocar, poner; *(statue)* erigir, poner; *(umbrella)* abrir; **to p. up one's hand** levantar la mano; **to p. one's hair up** recogerse el pelo (b) *(increase)* elevar, subir (c) *(provide accommodation for)* alojar (d) *(provide) (money)* aportar; *(candidate)* presentar; **to p. sth up for sale** poner algo a la venta; **to p. up a fight *or* struggle** ofrecer resistencia

▶**put upon** *vt insep* **to feel put upon** sentirse utilizado(a)

▶**put up to** *vt sep* **to p. sb up to doing sth** animar a alguien a hacer algo

▶**put on with** *vt insep* aguantar, soportar

**putative** ['pju:tətɪv] *adj Formal* presunto(a), supuesto(a); *Law (father)* putativo(a)

**put-down** ['pʊtdaʊn] *n Fam* desaire *m*

**putrefy** ['pju:trɪfaɪ] *vi* pudrirse

**putrid** ['pju:trɪd] *adj* putrefacto(a), pútrido(a)

**putsch** [pʊtʃ] *n* pronunciamiento *m* (militar)

**putt** [pʌt] **1** *n (in golf)* golpe *m* corto *(con el putter)*
  **2** *vi (in golf)* golpear en corto *(con el putter)*

**putter** ['pʌtə(r)] *n (golf club)* putter *m*

**putty** ['pʌtɪ] *n* masilla *f; Fig* **he's p. in her hands** hace lo que quiere con él

**put-up job** ['pʊtʌp'dʒɒb] *n Fam* pufo *m*, apaño *m*

**puzzle** ['pʌzl] **1** *n* (a) *(game)* rompecabezas *m inv; (mental)* acertijo *m;* **p. book** libro *m* de pasatiempos (b) *(mystery)* enigma *m*
  **2** *vt (person)* desconcertar, dejar perplejo(a)

▶**puzzle out** *vt sep* desentrañar

▶**puzzle over** *vt insep* dar vueltas a

**puzzled** ['pʌzld] *adj* perplejo(a)

**puzzling** ['pʌzlɪŋ] *adj* desconcertante

**PVC** [pi:vi:'si:] *n (abbr* **polyvinyl chloride)** PVC *m*

**pygmy** ['pɪgmɪ] *n* pigmeo(a) *m,f*

**pyjamas,** *US* **pajamas** [pə'dʒɑ:məz] *npl* pijama *m;* **a pair of p.** un pijama

**pylon** ['paɪlən] *n* torre *f* (de alta tensión)

**pyramid** ['pɪrəmɪd] *n* pirámide *f*

**pyre** ['paɪə(r)] *n* pira *f*

**Pyrenean** [pɪrə'nɪən] *adj* pirenaico(a)

**Pyrenees** [pɪrə'ni:z] *npl* **the P.** los Pirineos

**Pyrex®** ['paɪreks] *n* pyrex® *m;* **P. dish** fuente *f* de pyrex

**pyromaniac** [paɪrəʊ'meɪnɪæk] *n* pirómano(a) *m,f*

**pyrotechnics** [paɪrəʊ'teknɪks] **1** *n (science)* pirotecnia *f*
  **2** *npl (fireworks display)* fuegos *mpl* artificiales; *Fig (in speech, writing)* malabarismos *mpl*, virguerías *fpl*

**python** ['paɪθən] *n* (serpiente *f*) pitón *m or f*

# Q

**Q, q** [kjuː] *n (letter)* Q, q *f*

**Qatar** [kæ'tɑː(r)] *n* Qatar

**Qatari** [kæ'tɑːrɪ] **1** *n* = habitante o nativo de Qatar
  **2** *adj* de Qatar

**QC** [kjuː'siː] *n Br Law (abbr* **Queen's Counsel***)* = título honorífico que la Reina concede a algunos abogados eminentes

**QED** [kjuːiː'diː] *(abbr* **quod erat demonstrandum***)* QED, lo que había que demostrar

**qty** *Com (abbr* **quantity***)* cantidad *f*

**quack¹** [kwæk] **1** *n (of duck)* graznido *m*
  **2** *vi (of duck)* graznar

**quack²** *n Pej or Hum (doctor)* matasanos *m inv*

**quad** [kwɒd] *n Fam (of school, college)* patio *m*

**quadrangle** ['kwɒdræŋɡəl] *n* **(a)** *(shape)* cuadrilátero *m*, cuadrángulo *m* **(b)** *(of school, college)* patio *m*

**quadrant** ['kwɒdrənt] *n* cuadrante *m*

**quadraphonic** [kwɒdrə'fɒnɪk] *adj* cuadrafónico(a)

**quadratic equation** [kwɒ'drætɪkɪ'kweɪʒən] *n Math* ecuación *f* de segundo grado

**quadrilateral** [kwɒdrɪ'lætərəl] **1** *n* cuadrilátero *m*
  **2** *adj* cuadrilátero(a)

**quadriplegic** [kwɒdrɪ'pliːdʒɪk] *n & adj* tetrapléjico(a) *m,f*

**quadruped** ['kwɒdrʊped] *n* cuadrúpedo *m*

**quadruple** [kwɒ'druːpəl] **1** *adj* cuádruple, cuádruplo(a)
  **2** *vt* cuadruplicar
  **3** *vi* cuadruplicarse

**quadruplet** [kwɒ'druːplɪt] *n* cuatrillizo(a) *m,f*

**quaff** [kwɒf] *vt Literary* trasegar, ingerir a grandes tragos

**quagmire** ['kwæɡmaɪə(r)] *n (bog)* barrizal *m*, lodazal *m*; *Fig (difficult situation)* atolladero *m*

**quail¹** [kweɪl] *(pl* **quail***) n (bird)* codorniz *f*

**quail²** *vi (of person)* amedrentarse, amilanarse

**quaint** [kweɪnt] *adj (picturesque)* pintoresco(a); *(old-fashioned)* anticuado(a) y singular

**quaintly** ['kweɪntlɪ] *adv (in a picturesque way)* pintorescamente; *(in an old-fashioned way)* de forma anticuada y singular

**quake** [kweɪk] **1** *n Fam (earthquake)* terremoto *m*
  **2** *vi* temblar, estremecerse; **to q. in one's boots** temblar de miedo

**Quaker** ['kweɪkə(r)] *n Rel* cuáquero(a) *m,f*

**qualification** [kwɒlɪfɪ'keɪʃən] *n* **(a)** *(diploma)* título *m*; *(skill)* aptitud *f*, capacidad *f* **(b)** *(completion of studies)* **after q.** después de obtener el título **(c)** *(modification)* condición *f*, reserva *f* **(d)** *(for competition)* clasificación *f*

**qualified** ['kwɒlɪfaɪd] *adj* **(a)** *(having diploma)* titulado(a); *(competent)* capaz, capacitado(a); **to be q. to do sth** *(have diploma)* tener el título exigido para hacer algo; *(be competent)* estar capacitado(a) para hacer algo **(b)** *(modified)* limitado(a), parcial

**qualifier** ['kwɒlɪfaɪə(r)] *n* **(a)** *(person, team)* clasificado(a) *m,f*; *(match)* partido *m* de clasificación, eliminatoria *f* **(b)** *Gram* calificador *m*, modificador *m*

**qualify** ['kwɒlɪfaɪ] **1** *vt* **(a)** *(make competent)* **to q. sb to do sth** capacitar a alguien para hacer algo **(b)** *(modify)* matizar
  **2** *vi* **(a)** *(in competition)* clasificarse **(b)** *(complete studies)* **to q. as a doctor** obtener el título de médico(a) **(c)** *(be eligible)* **to q. for sth** tener derecho a algo

**qualifying** ['kwɒlɪfaɪɪŋ] *adj* **(a)** *(round, match)* eliminatorio(a) **(b)** *(exam)* de ingreso

**qualitative** ['kwɒlɪtətɪv] *adj* cualitativo(a)

**quality** ['kwɒlɪtɪ] *n* **(a)** *(excellence, standard)* calidad *f*; **of good/poor q.** de buena/mala calidad; **q. of life** calidad de vida; **q. circle** círculo *m* de calidad; **q. control** control *m* de calidad; **q. goods** artículos *mpl* de calidad; *Br* **q. newspapers** prensa *f* no sensacionalista **(b)** *(characteristic, feature)* cualidad *f*

**qualm** [kwɑːm] *n* escrúpulo *m*, reparo *m*; **to have no qualms about doing sth** no tener ningún escrúpulo *or* reparo en hacer algo

**quandary** ['kwɒndərɪ] *n* dilema *m*; **to be in a q. (about sth)** estar en un dilema (acerca de algo)

**quango** ['kwæŋɡəʊ] *(pl* **quangos***) n Br Admin (abbr* **quasi-autonomous non-governmental organization***)* = organismo público semiindependiente

**quantifiable** [kwɒntɪˈfaɪəbəl] *adj* cuantificable; **a q. amount** una cantidad cuantificable

**quantifier** [ˈkwɒntɪfaɪə(r)] *n Math* cuantificador *m*

**quantify** [ˈkwɒntɪfaɪ] *vt* cuantificar

**quantitative** [ˈkwɒntɪtətɪv] *adj* cuantitativo(a)

**quantity** [ˈkwɒntɪtɪ] *n* cantidad *f*; **q. surveyor** aparejador(ora) *m,f*

**quantum** [ˈkwɒntəm] *n Phys* cuanto *m*; *Fig* **q. leap** paso *m* de gigante; **q. mechanics** mecánica *f* cuántica; **q. theory** teoría *f* cuántica

**quarantine** [ˈkwɒrəntiːn] **1** *n* cuarentena *f*; **to be in q.** estar en cuarentena
  **2** *vt* poner en cuarentena

**quark** [kwɑːk] *n Phys* quark *m*

**quarrel** [ˈkwɒrəl] **1** *n* (**a**) *(argument)* pelea *f*, discusión *f*; **to have a q.** pelearse; **to pick a q. with sb** buscar pelea con alguien (**b**) *(disagreement)* discrepancia *f*, desacuerdo *m*; **to have no q. with sb** no tener discrepancia alguna con alguien
  **2** *vi* (*pt & pp* **quarrelled**, *US* **quarreled**) (**a**) *(argue)* pelearse, discutir (**with** con) (**b**) *(disagree)* **to q. with sth** discrepar de algo

**quarrelling**, *US* **quarreling** [ˈkwɒrəlɪŋ] *n* peleas *fpl*, discusiones *fpl*

**quarrelsome** [ˈkwɒrəlsəm] *adj* peleón(ona)

**quarry¹** [ˈkwɒrɪ] *n* *(prey) & Fig* presa *f*

**quarry²** **1** *n* *(for stone)* cantera *f*
  **2** *vt* *(hill)* excavar; *(stone)* extraer

**quart** [kwɔːt] *n (liquid measurement)* cuarto *m* de galón *(UK = 1,136 litros; US = 0,946 litros)*

**quarter** [ˈkwɔːtə(r)] **1** *n* (**a**) *(fraction, of orange, of moon)* cuarto *m*; **he ate a q. of the cake** se comió una *or* la cuarta parte del pastel; **a q. of a century** un cuarto de siglo; **a q. of an hour** un cuarto de hora; **a q. (of a pound)** un cuarto de libra *(= 113,5 grs)*; **three quarters** tres cuartos; **three quarters of all women** las tres cuartas partes de las mujeres; **three and a q. (litres)** tres (litros) y cuarto; **the bottle was still a q. full** quedaba aún un cuarto de botella (**b**) *(in telling time) Br* **it's/at a q. to six**, *US* **it's/at a q. of six** son/a las seis menos cuarto; **it's a q. to six** son menos cuarto; *Br* **it's/at a q. past six**, *US* **it's/at a q. after six** son/a las seis y cuarto; **it's a q. past** son y cuarto
  (**c**) *(three-month period)* trimestre *m*
  (**d**) *(area)* barrio *m*
  (**e**) *(group)* **in some quarters** en algunos círculos; **help came from an unexpected q.** la ayuda llegó por el lado que menos se esperaba
  (**f**) *Mil* **quarters** *(lodgings)* alojamiento *m*; **officer quarters** residencia *f* de oficiales
  (**g**) *(mercy)* **to give no q.** no dar cuartel
  (**h**) *US (coin)* cuarto *m* de dólar

  **2** *vt* (**a**) *(divide into four)* dividir en cuatro partes
  (**b**) *Mil (troops)* acantonar, alojar

**quarterback** [ˈkwɔːtəbæk] *n US* quarterback *m (en fútbol americano, jugador que dirige el ataque)*

**quarterdeck** [ˈkwɔːtədek] *n (of ship)* alcázar *m*, cubierta *f* de popa

**quarterfinal** [kwɔːtəˈfaɪnəl] *n (match)* enfrentamiento *m* de cuartos de final; **the quarterfinals** los cuartos de final

**quarterly** [ˈkwɔːtəlɪ] **1** *n* publicación *f* trimestral
  **2** *adj* trimestral
  **3** *adv* trimestralmente

**quartermaster** [ˈkwɔːtəmɑːstə(r)] *n Mil* oficial *m* de intendencia

**quartet** [kwɔːˈtet] *n* cuarteto *m*

**quarto** [ˈkwɔːtəʊ] *n (pl* **quartos***)* pliego *m* en cuarto

**quartz** [kwɔːts] *n* cuarzo *m*; **q. watch** reloj *m* de cuarzo

**quasar** [ˈkweɪzɑː(r)] *n Astron* cuásar *m*, quasar *m*

**quash** [kwɒʃ] *vt (revolt)* sofocar; *(objection)* acallar; *Law (sentence)* revocar, anular

**quaver** [ˈkweɪvə(r)] **1** *n* (**a**) *Mus* corchea *f* (**b**) *(in voice)* temblor *m*
  **2** *vi (of voice)* temblar

**quay** [kiː] *n* muelle *m*

**quayside** [ˈkiːsaɪd] *n* muelles *mpl*

**queasy** [ˈkwiːzɪ] *adj* **to feel q.** estar mareado(a), tener mal cuerpo

**Quebec** [kwɪˈbek] *n (provincia f de)* Quebec *m*; **Q. City** Quebec *(capital)*

**queen** [kwiːn] *n* (**a**) *(of country)* reina *f*; *(in cards, chess)* dama *f*, reina *f*; **Q.'s Counsel** = título honorífico que la Reina concede a algunos abogados eminentes; **the Q.'s English** el inglés estándar; **the Q. Mother** la reina madre (**b**) *very Fam Pej (homosexual)* marica *m*, maricón *m*

**queer** [ˈkwɪə(r)] **1** *n very Fam (male homosexual)* marica *m*, maricón *m*
  **2** *adj* (**a**) *(strange)* raro(a), extraño(a) (**b**) *(suspicious)* raro(a), sospechoso(a) (**c**) *Fam (unwell)* **to feel q.** encontrarse mal; **to come over** *or* **to be taken q.** ponerse malo(a) (**d**) *very Fam (homosexual)* marica, maricón
  **3** *vt Fam* **to q. sb's pitch** aguarle la fiesta a alguien

**quell** [kwel] *vt (revolt)* sofocar; *(doubt, worry, passion)* apagar

**quench** [kwentʃ] *vt (thirst, fire)* apagar

**querulous** [ˈkwerʊləs] *adj* lastimero(a), quejumbroso(a)

**query** [ˈkwɪərɪ] **1** *n* duda *f*, pregunta *f*; *(on phone line, to expert, at information desk)* consulta *f*; **to raise a q. about sth** *(call into question)* poner en duda algo

**2** *vt (question) (invoice)* reclamar contra; *(decision)* cuestionar; **to q. if** *or* **whether...** poner en duda si...

**quest** [kwest] *Literary* **1** *n* búsqueda *f* (**for** de); **to go** *or* **be in q. of sth** ir en busca de algo

**2** *vi* **to q. after** *or* **for sth** ir en busca de algo, buscar algo

**question** ['kwestʃən] **1** *n* (**a**) *(interrogation)* pregunta *f*; **to ask (sb) a q.** hacer una pregunta (a alguien); **q. mark** signo *m* de interrogación; *Fig* **a q. mark hangs over the future of the project** el futuro del proyecto está en el aire; *Br Pol* **q. time** = sesión de control parlamentario en la que los ministros responden a las preguntas de los diputados

(**b**) *(doubt)* duda *f*; **there is no q. about it** no cabe duda (al respecto); **to call sth into q.** poner algo en duda; **beyond q.** fuera de (toda) duda; **to be open to q.** ser cuestionable; **without q.** sin duda

(**c**) *(matter)* cuestión *f*; **it is a q. of...** se trata de...; **there is no q. of our agreeing to that** en ningún caso vamos a estar conformes con eso; **that's out of the q.!** ¡de eso ni hablar!; **it's only a q. of time** sólo es cuestión de tiempo; **the matter/person in q.** el asunto/individuo en cuestión

**2** *vt* (**a**) *(ask questions to) (for inquiry)* interrogar; *(for survey)* encuestar; **she was questioned on her views** *(in interview)* le pidieron su opinión

(**b**) *(cast doubt on)* cuestionar, poner en duda

**questionable** ['kwestʃənəbəl] *adj* cuestionable, dudoso(a)

**questioning** ['kwestʃənɪŋ] **1** *n (interrogation)* interrogatorio *m*; **he was held for q. by the police** la policía lo detuvo para interrogarlo

**2** *adj (look, mind)* inquisitivo(a)

**questionnaire** [kwestʃə'neə(r)] *n* cuestionario *m*

**queue** [kju:] **1** *n* cola *f*; **to form a q.** hacer cola; **to jump the q.** colarse

**2** *vi* hacer cola

**queue-jump** ['kju:dʒʌmp] *vi* colarse, saltarse la cola

**quibble** ['kwɪbəl] **1** *n* pega *f* insignificante, pequeñez *f*

**2** *vi* poner pegas (**about** *or* **over** a); **let's not q.** no vamos a discutir por una tontería

**quiche** [ki:ʃ] *n* quiche *m* or *f*

**quick** [kwɪk] **1** *n* **to bite one's nails to the q.** morderse las uñas hasta hacerse daño; *Fig* **to cut sb to the q.** herir a alguien en lo más profundo

**2** *adj* (**a**) *(rapid)* rápido(a); **to have a q. bath** darse un baño rápido; **to have a q. drink** tomarse algo rápidamente; **that was q.!** ¡qué rápido!; **be q.!** ¡date prisa!; **as q. as a flash** como una exhalación; **to be q. to do sth** no

tardar en hacer algo; **to be q. to criticize** apresurarse a criticar; **to be q. off the mark** *(to act)* no perder el tiempo; *(to understand)* ser muy espabilado(a); **to have a q. temper** tener mal genio (**b**) *(clever)* listo(a), despierto(a)

**3** *adv Fam (run, talk, think)* rápido

**quicken** ['kwɪkən] **1** *vt* (**a**) *(make faster)* acelerar; **to q. one's pace** apretar *or* acelerar el paso (**b**) *(imagination)* estimular; *(interest)* despertar

**2** *vi* (**a**) *(of pace)* acelerarse; **his pulse quickened** se le aceleró el pulso (**b**) *(of imagination)* estimularse; *(of interest)* despertarse

**quickfire** ['kwɪkfaɪə(r)] *adj* rápido(a)

**quickie** ['kwɪkɪ] *Fam* **1** *n* **to have a q.** *(drink)* tomar una copa rápida; *(sex)* echar uno rápido

**2** *adj* **q. divorce** divorcio *m* por la vía rápida

**quicklime** ['kwɪklaɪm] *n* cal *f* viva

**quickly** ['kwɪklɪ] *adv* rápidamente, rápido, deprisa; **I q. realized that...** enseguida me di cuenta de que...

**quickness** ['kwɪknɪs] *n (speed)* rapidez *f*; *(of mind)* agudeza *f*

**quicksand** ['kwɪksænd] *n* arenas *fpl* movedizas

**quicksilver** ['kwɪksɪlvə(r)] *n Old-fashioned (mercury)* azogue *m*

**quick-tempered** ['kwɪk'tempəd] *adj* irascible, enfadadizo(a); **to be q.** tener mal genio

**quick-witted** ['kwɪk'wɪtɪd] *adj* agudo(a)

**quid** [kwɪd] *n (pl* quid*) n Br Fam (pound)* libra *f*

**quiescent** [kwɪ'esənt] *adj Formal* inactivo(a), pasivo(a)

**quiet** ['kwaɪət] **1** *n* silencio *m*, tranquilidad *f*; **the q. of the countryside** la paz del campo; *Fam* **to do sth on the q.** hacer algo a escondidas *or* a la chita callando

**2** *adj* (**a**) *(not loud) (person, music)* tranquilo(a); *(voice)* bajo(a); *(engine)* silencioso(a); **to keep sb q.** hacer callar a alguien; **to keep q.** *(make no noise)* no hacer ruido; *(say nothing)* estar callado(a); **to keep q. about sth** guardar silencio *or* no decir nada sobre algo; **to keep sth q.** mantener algo en secreto; **be q.!** ¡cállate!; **q. please!** ¡silencio, por favor!; **as q. as a mouse** *(person)* callado(a) como un muerto

(**b**) *(discreet)* discreto(a); **to have a q. laugh at sb/sth** reírse para sus adentros de alguien/algo

(**c**) *(peaceful)* tranquilo(a); **a q. wedding** una boda íntima *or* discreta

(**d**) *(business, market)* inactivo(a), poco animado(a)

▸**quiet down** = **quieten down**

**quieten** ['kwaɪətən] *vt* tranquilizar

▸**quieten down 1** *vt sep (make silent)* hacer callar; *(make calm)* tranquilizar, calmar

**2** *vi (become silent)* callarse; *(become calm)* tranquilizarse, calmarse

**quietly** ['kwaɪətlɪ] *adv* (**a**) *(silently)* silenciosamente, sin hacer ruido (**b**) *(discreetly)* discretamente; **to be q. determined** estar interiormente resuelto(a); **to be q. confident** estar íntimamente convencido(a)

**quietness** ['kwaɪətnɪs] *n (of place)* silencio *m*, calma *f*; *(of person, manner)* tranquilidad *f*

**quiff** [kwɪf] *n (of hair)* tupé *m*

**quill** [kwɪl] *n (feather, pen)* pluma *f*; *(of porcupine)* púa *f*

**quilt** [kwɪlt] **1** *n* edredón *m*
**2** *vt (garment)* acolchar; **quilted jacket** chaqueta *f* acolchada

**quince** [kwɪns] *n* membrillo *m*; **q. jelly** dulce *m* de membrillo

**quinine** [kwɪ'niːn] *n* quinina *f*

**quintessential** [kwɪntɪ'senʃəl] *adj Formal* arquetípico(a), prototípico(a); **Holmes is the q. Englishman** Holmes es el inglés por excelencia, Holmes es la quintaesencia de lo inglés

**quintessentially** [kwɪntɪ'senʃəlɪ] *adv Formal* prototípicamente, esencialmente

**quintet** [kwɪn'tet] *n* quinteto *m*

**quintuplet** [kwɪn'tjuːplɪt] *n* quintillizo(a) *m,f*

**quip** [kwɪp] **1** *n* broma *f*, chiste *m*
**2** *vi (pt & pp quipped)* bromear

**quirk** [kwɜːk] *n (a) (of character)* manía *f* (**b**) *(of fate, nature)* capricho *m*; **by a q. of fate** por un capricho del destino

**quirky** ['kwɜːkɪ] *adj* peculiar

**quisling** ['kwɪzlɪŋ] *n* traidor(ora) *m,f*

**quit** [kwɪt] **1** *vt (pt & pp* **quit** *or* **quitted**) *(person, place)* abandonar, dejar; *Comptr* salir de; **to q. one's job** dejar el trabajo; **to q. doing sth** dejar de hacer algo
**2** *vi (give up)* abandonar; *(resign)* dimitir; *Comptr* salir
**3** *adj* **to be q. of** librarse *or* deshacerse de

**quite** [kwaɪt] *adv (a) (entirely)* completamente, totalmente; **that's not q. true** no es del todo cierto; **I'm not q. ready** no estoy del todo listo; **it's not q. what I wanted** no es exactamente lo que yo quería; **I can't q. see what you mean** no alcanzo a ver qué quieres decir; **q. enough** más que suficiente; **that's q. enough of that!** ¡ya es más que suficiente!; **q. apart from the fact that...** sin mencionar el hecho de que...; **q.!** ¡efectivamente!; **that's q. all right** *(it doesn't matter)* no importa; *(you're welcome)* no hay de qué; **you know q. well what I mean!** ¡sabes muy bien lo que quiero decir!; **I q. understand** lo entiendo perfectamente
(**b**) *(fairly)* bastante; **I q. like him** me gusta bastante; **q. a lot of problems** bastantes problemas
(**c**) *(for emphasis)* **it was q. a surprise** fue toda una sorpresa; **it's been q. a day!** ¡menudo día!; **that film is q. something** ¡menuda película!

**quits** [kwɪts] *adj* **to be q. (with sb)** estar en paz (con alguien); **let's call it q.** vamos a dejarlo así

**quiver¹** ['kwɪvə(r)] *n (for arrows)* carcaj *m*, aljaba *f*

**quiver²** **1** *n (tremble)* estremecimiento *m*
**2** *vi (tremble)* estremecerse (**with** de)

**quivering** ['kwɪvərɪŋ] *adj* tembloroso(a), trémulo(a)

**quixotic** [kwɪk'sɒtɪk] *adj* quijotesco(a)

**quiz** [kwɪz] **1** *n (pl* **quizzes**) concurso *m*; **q. (show)** programa *m* concurso
**2** *vt (pt & pp* **quizzed**) interrogar

**quizzical** ['kwɪzɪkəl] *adj (look, air)* interrogador(ora), de interrogación

**quorum** ['kwɔːrəm] *n* quórum *m inv*

**quota** ['kwəʊtə] *n (share)* cupo *m*, cuota *f*

**quotation** [kwəʊ'teɪʃən] *n (a) (from author)* cita *f*; **q. marks** comillas *fpl* (**b**) *Com (for work)* presupuesto *m*

**quote** [kwəʊt] **1** *n Fam (a) (from author)* cita *f*; **in quotes** *(in quotation marks)* entre comillas (**b**) *Com (for work)* presupuesto *m*
**2** *vt (a) (author, passage)* citar; **he was quoted as saying that...** se le atribuye haber dicho que...; **in reply please q. this number** en su contestación por favor indique este número (**b**) *Com (price)* dar un presupuesto de; **he quoted me a price of £100** me dio un presupuesto de 100 libras, fijó un precio de 100 libras; *Fin* **quoted company** empresa *f* cotizada en Bolsa

**quotient** ['kwəʊʃənt] *n Math* cociente *m*

# R

**R, r** [ɑː(r)] *n (letter)* R, r *f; Fam* **the three R's**
lectura, escritura y aritmética

**R** *US Pol (abbr* **Republican**) republicano(a)

**RA** [ɑːˈreɪ] *n Br (abbr* **Royal Academy**) =
academia británica de las artes

**rabbi** [ˈræbaɪ] *n Rel* rabino *m*

**rabbit** [ˈræbɪt] *n* conejo *m*; **r. hole** madriguera
*f*; **r. hutch** conejera *f*

▸**rabbit on** *vi Fam* parlotear, cascar

**rabble** [ˈræbəl] *n* multitud *f*; **r. rouser** agita-
dor(ora) *m,f* (de masas)

**rabid** [ˈræbɪd] *adj* (a) *(animal)* rabioso(a) (b)
*Fig (person, emotion)* furibundo(a)

**rabies** [ˈreɪbiːz] *n* rabia *f*, hidrofobia *f*

**RAC** [ɑːreɪˈsiː] *n (abbr* **Royal Automobile.
Club**) = organización británica de ayuda al
automovilista, ≃ RACE *m*

**raccoon** [rəˈkuːn] *n* mapache *m*

**race¹** [reɪs] **1** *n (contest)* carrera *f*; **the hundred metres r.** los cien metros lisos; *Fig* **a r.
against time** una carrera contrarreloj; **the
races** *(horseraces)* las carreras; **a r. meeting** *(for
horseraces)* concurso *m* de carreras de caballos

**2** *vt* (a) *(athlete)* correr con *or* contra; **I'll r. you
home!** ¡te echo una carrera hasta casa! (b)
*(horse)* hacer correr (en carreras)

**3** *vi* (a) *(of athlete, horse)* correr, competir (b)
*(move quickly)* correr; **to r. in/out** entrar/salir
corriendo; **to r. down the street** correr calle
abajo; **to r. by** *(of time)* pasar volando (c) *(of
engine)* acelerarse; *(of pulse, heart)* palpitar ace-
leradamente

**race²** *n (of people, animals)* raza *f*; **the human
r.** la raza humana; **r. relations** relaciones *fpl*
interraciales

**racecourse** [ˈreɪskɔːs] *n* hipódromo *m*

**racehorse** [ˈreɪshɔːs] *n* caballo *m* de carreras

**racer** [ˈreɪsə(r)] *n (person)* corredor(ora) *m,f*;
*(bicycle)* bicicleta *f* de carreras

**racetrack** [ˈreɪstræk] *n (for athletes)* pista *f*;
*(for cars)* circuito *m*; *US (for horses)* hipódromo *m*

**racial** [ˈreɪʃəl] *adj* racial; **r. discrimination**
discriminación *f* racial

**racing** [ˈreɪsɪŋ] **1** *n* carreras *fpl*

**2** *adj* **r. bicycle/car** bicicleta *f*/coche *m* de
carreras

**racism** [ˈreɪsɪzəm] *n* racismo *m*

**racist** [ˈreɪsɪst] *n & adj* racista *mf*

**rack** [ræk] **1** *n* (a) *(for bottles)* botellero *m*; *(for
plates)* escurreplatos *m inv*; *(for magazines)* revistero *m*; *(for goods in shop)* expositor *m*; *(for luggage)* portaequipajes *m inv*; *Tech* **r. and pinion**
engranaje *m* de piñón y cremallera (b) *(for torture)* potro *m*; *Fig* **to be on the r.** estar contra
las cuerdas (c) *(idioms)* **to go to r. and ruin**
venirse abajo

**2** *vt (torment)* torturar, atormentar; **to be
racked with pain** estar atormentado(a) por
el dolor; **to r. one's brains** devanarse los sesos

**racket¹** [ˈrækɪt] *n (for tennis)* raqueta *f*

**racket²** *n* (a) *Fam (noise)* jaleo *m*, estruendo *m*;
**to make a r.** armar jaleo *or* alboroto (b) *(criminal activity)* negocio *m* mafioso; *(swindling)* estafa *f*

**racketeer** [rækɪˈtɪə(r)] *n (criminal)* mafioso(a)
*m,f*; *(swindler)* estafador(ora) *m,f*

**racketeering** [rækɪˈtɪərɪŋ] *n* negocios *mpl*
mafiosos; *(swindling)* estafas *fpl*

**racquet** [ˈrækɪt] *n (for tennis)* raqueta *f*

**racy** [ˈreɪsɪ] *adj (risqué)* atrevido(a); *(lively)* vívi-
do(a)

**RADA** [ˈrɑːdə] *n Br (abbr* **Royal Academy
of Dramatic Art**) = academia británica de
arte dramático

**radar** [ˈreɪdɑː(r)] *n* radar *m*; **r. operator** ope-
rador(ora) *m,f* de radar; **r. screen** pantalla *f* de
radar

**radial** [ˈreɪdɪəl] **1** *n (tyre)* neumático *m* (de cubierta) radial

**2** *adj* radial

**radiance** [ˈreɪdɪəns] *n (of light)* resplandor *m*;
*(of person, smile)* esplendor *m*

**radiant** [ˈreɪdɪənt] *adj (light, person, smile)* radiante, resplandeciente; **to be r. (with)** *(of person, smile)* estar radiante (de)

**radiate** [ˈreɪdɪeɪt] **1** *vt (heat, light)* irradiar; *Fig
(happiness, enthusiasm)* irradiar; *(health)* rebosar

**2** *vi* irradiar **(from** de *or* desde)

**radiation** [reɪdɪˈeɪʃən] *n* radiación *f*

**radiator** [ˈreɪdɪeɪtə(r)] *n (heater)* radiador *m*

**radical** [ˈrædɪkəl] *n & adj* radical *mf*

**radicalism** [ˈrædɪkəlɪzəm] *n* radicalismo *m*

**radio** [ˈreɪdɪəʊ] **1** *n (pl* **radios**) radio *f*; **r. cassette (recorder** *or* **player)** radiocasete *m*; **r.**

**station** emisora *f* de radio

  **2** *vt* (*information*) transmitir por radio; (*person*) comunicar por radio con

  **3** *vi* to r. for help pedir ayuda por radio

**radioactive** [reɪdɪəʊˈæktɪv] *adj* radiactivo(a); **r. waste** residuos *mpl* radiactivos

**radioactivity** [reɪdɪəʊæˈtɪvɪtɪ] *n* radiactividad *f*

**radio-controlled** [reɪdɪəʊkənˈtrəʊld] *adj* teledirigido(a)

**radiograph** [ˈreɪdɪəʊgrɑːf] *n* radiografía *f*

**radiographer** [reɪdɪˈɒgrəfə(r)] *n* técnico(a) *m,f* especialista en rayos X

**radiography** [reɪdɪˈɒgrəfɪ] *n* radiografía *f*

**radiologist** [reɪdɪˈɒlədʒɪst] *n* radiólogo(a) *m,f*

**radiology** [reɪdɪˈɒlədʒɪ] *n* radiología *f*

**radiotherapy** [reɪdɪəʊˈθerəpɪ] *n* radioterapia *f*

**radish** [ˈrædɪʃ] *n* rábano *m*

**radium** [ˈreɪdɪəm] *n* Chem radio *m*

**radius** [ˈreɪdɪəs] (*pl* **radii** [ˈreɪdɪaɪ]) *n* radio *m*; **within a r. of** en un radio de

**radon** [ˈreɪdɒn] *n* Chem radón *m*

**RAF** [ɑːrˈeɪˈef] *n* (*abbr* **Royal Air Force**) RAF *f*, fuerzas *fpl* aéreas británicas

**raffia** [ˈræfɪə] *n* rafia *f*

**raffish** [ˈræfɪʃ] *adj* pícaro(a)

**raffle** [ˈræfəl] **1** *n* rifa *f*; **r. ticket** boleto *m* de rifa

  **2** *vt* rifar

**raft** [rɑːft] *n* balsa *f*

**rafter** [ˈrɑːftə(r)] *n* viga *f* (de tejado); Constr cabrio *m*

**rafting** [ˈrɑːftɪŋ] *n* rafting *m*; **to go r.** hacer rafting

**rag¹** [ræg] *n* (**a**) (*piece of cloth*) trapo *m*; **rags** (*clothes*) harapos *mpl*; **to go from rags to riches** salir de la miseria y pasar a la riqueza; **r. doll** muñeca *f* de trapo; Fam **the r. trade** la industria de la moda (**b**) Fam Pej (*newspaper*) periodicucho *m*

**rag²** **1** *n* Old-fashioned (*prank*) broma *f*; Univ **r. week** = semana en que los estudiantes colectan dinero para obras de caridad

  **2** *vt* (*pt & pp* **ragged**) Old-fashioned (*tease*) pitorrearse de

**ragamuffin** [ˈrægəmʌfɪn] *n* golfillo(a) *m,f*, pilluelo(a) *m,f*

**rag-and-bone man** [rægənˈbəʊnmæn] *n* trapero(a) *m,f*

**ragbag** [ˈrægbæg] *n* batiburrillo *m*

**rage** [reɪdʒ] **1** *n* (**a**) (*fury*) cólera *f*, ira *f*; **to be in a r.** estar hecho(a) una furia (**b**) Fam (*fashion*) **to be all the r.** (*of music, style*) hacer furor

  **2** *vi* (**a**) **to r. about sth** despotricar contra algo; **to r. against** *or* **at sb/sth** encolerizarse

con alguien/algo (**b**) (*of sea*) embravecerse, encresparse; (*of epidemic, war*) recrudecerse

**ragged** [ˈrægɪd] *adj* (*clothes*) raído(a); (*edge*) irregular; (*person*) andrajoso(a); Fam **she had run herself r.** se había quedado molida

**raging** [ˈreɪdʒɪŋ] *adj* (**a**) (*person*) furioso(a); **to be in a r. temper** estar hecho(a) una furia (**b**) (*sea*) embravecido(a), encrespado(a); (*fire*) pavoroso(a); (*fever, thirst, headache*) atroz

**ragwort** [ˈrægwɜːt] *n* hierba *f* cana

**raid** [reɪd] **1** *n* (*on bank*) atraco *m*; (*by army*) incursión *f*; (*by police*) redada *f*

  **2** *vt* (*of robbers*) atracar, asaltar; (*of army*) hacer una incursión en; (*of police*) hacer una redada en; Fig **to r. the fridge** saquear la nevera

**raider** [ˈreɪdə(r)] *n* (*criminal*) atracador(ora) *m,f*

**rail¹** [reɪl] *n* (**a**) (*of stairway, balcony*) pasamanos *m inv*, barandilla *f* (**b**) (*train system*) ferrocarril *m*, tren *m*; (*track*) riel *m*, carril *m*; **by r.** en tren; Fig **to go off the rails** (*of person, economy*) desencaminarse, perder el norte; **r. network** red *f* ferroviaria; **r. strike** huelga *f* ferroviaria *or* de trenes

**rail²** *vi* **to r. at** *or* **against sth** protestar airadamente contra algo

**railcar** [ˈreɪlkɑː(r)] *n* US vagón *m*

**railcard** [ˈreɪlkɑːd] *n* Br **family/young person's r.** = tarjeta familiar/juvenil para obtener billetes de tren con descuento

**railings** [ˈreɪlɪŋz] *npl* verja *f*

**railroad** [ˈreɪlrəʊd] **1** *n* US (*system*) (red *f* de) ferrocarril *m*; (*track*) vía *f* férrea

  **2** *vt* Fam **to r. sb into doing sth** avasallar a alguien para que haga algo; **to r. a bill through Parliament** utilizar el rodillo parlamentario para que se apruebe un proyecto de ley

**railway** [ˈreɪlweɪ] *n* Br (*system*) (red *f* de) ferrocarril *m*; (*track*) vía *f* férrea; **r. carriage** vagón *m* (de tren); **r. line** (*track*) vía *f* (férrea); (*route*) línea *f* de tren; **r. network** *or* **system** red *f* ferroviaria; **r. station** estación *f* de trenes *or* de ferrocarril

**railwayman** [ˈreɪlweɪmən] *n* ferroviario *m*

**rain** [reɪn] **1** *n* lluvia *f*; **in the r.** bajo la lluvia; **it looks like r.** parece que va a llover; **the rains** las lluvias; **come r. or shine** (*whatever the weather*) llueva o truene; (*whatever the circumstances*) sea como sea, pase lo que pase; **r. cloud** nube *f* de lluvia, nubarrón *m*; **r. dance** danza *f* de la lluvia

  **2** *vt* **to r. blows/gifts on sb** hacer llover los golpes/los regalos sobre alguien

  **3** *vi* llover; **it's raining** está lloviendo; Br Fam **it's raining cats and dogs** está lloviendo a cántaros *or* a mares; Prov **it never rains but it pours** las desgracias nunca vienen solas

**rainbow** ['reɪnbəʊ] *n* arco *m* iris; **r. coalition** = coalición de partidos minoritarios; **r. trout** trucha *f* arco iris

**raincoat** ['reɪnkəʊt] *n* impermeable *m*

**raindrop** ['reɪndrɒp] *n* gota *f* de lluvia

**rainfall** ['reɪnfɔːl] *n* pluviosidad *f*

**rainforest** ['reɪnfɒrɪst] *n* selva *f* tropical

**rainproof** ['reɪnpruːf] *adj* impermeable

**rainstorm** ['reɪnstɔːm] *n* aguacero *m*

**rainwater** ['reɪnwɔːtə(r)] *n* agua *f* de lluvia

**rainy** ['reɪnɪ] *adj* lluvioso(a); *Fig* **to save sth for a r. day** guardar algo para cuando haga falta; **the r. season** la estación de las lluvias

**raise** [reɪz] **1** *n US (pay increase)* aumento *m* (de sueldo)

**2** *vt* (a) *(lift)* levantar; **to r. one's voice** alzar *or* levantar la voz; **to r. one's glass to one's lips** llevarse el vaso a los labios; *Fig* **to r. one's hat to sb** quitarse el sombrero ante alguien; *Fig* **the audience raised the roof** *(in theatre)* el teatro (literalmente) se vino abajo

(b) *(price, standard)* aumentar, elevar; *Fig* **to r. the stakes** forzar la situación

(c) *(problem, subject)* plantear

(d) *(smile, laugh)* provocar; *(fears, doubts)* levantar, sembrar; **I don't want to r. your hopes** no quisiera darte falsas esperanzas; **to r. the alarm** dar la voz de alarma; **to r. hell** *or* **Cain** poner el grito en el cielo

(e) *(money)* reunir, recaudar

(f) *(children, cattle)* criar; *(crops)* cultivar

(g) *(blockade, embargo)* levantar

(h) *(statue)* erigir

**raisin** ['reɪzən] *n* (uva *f*) pasa *f*

**rake** [reɪk] **1** *n* (a) *(garden tool)* rastrillo *m*; **to be as thin as a r.** estar en los huesos (b) *(dissolute man)* crápula *m*, calavera *m*

**2** *vt (leaves, soil)* rastrillar; **to r. one's memory** escarbar en la memoria

▸**rake about, rake around** *vi (search)* rebuscar

▸**rake in** *vt sep Fam (money)* amasar; **she's raking it in!** ¡se está forrando!

▸**rake off** *vt sep Fam (money)* llevarse

▸**rake over** *vt sep (subject, the past)* remover

**rakish** ['reɪkɪʃ] *adj (dissolute)* licencioso(a), disoluto(a); *(charm, smile)* desenvuelto(a); **to wear one's hat at a r. angle** llevar el sombrero ladeado con un aire de desenfado

**rally** ['rælɪ] **1** *n* (a) *(protest gathering)* concentración *f* (de protesta) (b) *(in tennis)* intercambio *m* de golpes, peloteo *m* (c) *(car race)* rally *m*; **r. driver** piloto *m* de rallys

**2** *vt (troops)* reagrupar; *(support)* reunir, recabar; **to r. sb's spirits** elevar el ánimo a alguien; **rallying cry** consigna *f*, grito *m* de guerra

**3** *vi (recover)* recuperarse; **to r. to sb's defence** salir en defensa de alguien

▸**rally round 1** *vt insep* agruparse en torno a

**2** *vi* agruparse

**RAM** [ræm] *n Comptr (abbr* **random access memory)** (memoria *f*) RAM *f*, memoria *f* de acceso aleatorio

**ram** [ræm] **1** *n* (a) *(animal)* carnero *m* (b) *(implement)* **(battering) r.** ariete *m*

**2** *vt (pt & pp* **rammed)** (a) *(crash into)* embestir; *(of ship)* abordar (b) *(force into place)* embutir, apretar; *Fam* **she's always ramming her views down my throat** siempre está tratando de inculcarme a la fuerza sus ideas

**Ramadan** [ˌræmə'dæn] *n Rel* ramadán *m*

**ramble** ['ræmbəl] **1** *n (walk)* excursión *f*, caminata *f*

**2** *vi* (a) *(walk)* caminar, marchar (b) *(digress)* divagar

▸**ramble on** *vi* divagar constantemente; **to r. on about sth** divagar sobre algo

**rambler** ['ræmblə(r)] *n (walker)* excursionista *mf*, senderista *mf*

**rambling** ['ræmblɪŋ] **1** *n* (a) *(walking)* **to go r.** ir de excursión, hacer senderismo (b) **ramblings** *(words)* divagaciones *fpl*, digresiones *fpl*

**2** *adj* (a) *(letter, speech)* inconexo(a) (b) *(house)* laberíntico(a); **r. rose** rosal *m* trepador

**ramification** [ræmɪfɪ'keɪʃən] *n* ramificación *f*

**ramp** [ræmp] *n* rampa *f*; *(to plane)* escalerilla *f*; *(on road)* resalto *m*, bache *m* (de moderación de velocidad)

**rampage 1** ['ræmpeɪdʒ] **to go on the r.** ir arrasando con todo

**2** *vi* [ræm'peɪdʒ] **to r. about** ir en desbandada

**rampant** ['ræmpənt] *adj* incontrolado(a)

**rampart** ['ræmpɑːt] *n* muralla *f*

**ramrod** ['ræmrɒd] *n (for rifle)* baqueta *f*; *Fig* **r. straight** con la espalda recta

**ramshackle** ['ræmʃækəl] *adj* destartalado(a)

**ran** [ræn] *pt of* **run**

**ranch** [rɑːntʃ] *n* rancho *m*

**rancher** ['rɑːntʃə(r)] *n* ranchero(a) *m,f*

**rancid** ['rænsɪd] *adj* rancio(a); **to go r.** ponerse rancio(a)

**rancour** ['ræŋkə(r)] *n* acritud *f*, resentimiento *m*

**rand** [rænd] *n* rand *m*

**random** ['rændəm] **1** *n* **at r.** al azar

**2** *adj (choice, sample)* al azar; *Comptr* **r. access memory** memoria *f* de acceso aleatorio; **r. sampling** muestreo *m* aleatorio, pruebas *fpl* aleatorias

**randy** ['rændɪ] *adj Br Fam* cachondo(a), calentorro(a)

**rang** [ræŋ] *pt of* **ring**²

**range** [reɪndʒ] **1** *n* (a) *(of weapon, telescope, hearing)* alcance *m*; *(of ship, plane)* autonomía *f*; **out of r.** fuera del alcance; **within r.** al alcance (**b**) *(of prices, colours, products)* gama *f*; *(of instrument, voice)* registro *m*; *(of knowledge)* amplitud *f*; *(of research)* ámbito *m* (**c**) *(of hills, mountains)* cordillera *f* (**d**) *(practice area)* (**shooting**) **r.** campo *m* de tiro (**e**) *(cooker)* fogón *m*, cocina *f* de carbón

**2** *vt* (**a**) *(arrange in row) (troops, books)* alinear; **to r. oneself with/against sb** alinearse con/en contra de alguien (**b**) *(travel)* recorrer

**3** *vi* (**a**) *(extend)* **ages ranging from ten to ninety** edades comprendidas entre los diez y los noventa años; **during the summer temperatures r. from 21 to 30 degrees** durante el verano las temperaturas oscilan entre los 21 y los 30 grados (**b**) **to r. over** *(include)* abarcar, comprender

**rangefinder** ['reɪndʒfaɪndə(r)] *n* telémetro *m*

**ranger** ['reɪndʒə(r)] *n (in forest)* guardabosques *mf inv; US Mil* comando *m*

**Rangoon** [ræn'guːn] *n* Rangún

**rangy** ['reɪndʒɪ] *adj (limb)* largo(a); *(person)* patilargo(a)

**rank**[1] [ræŋk] **1** *n* (**a**) *(status)* rango *m*; *Fig* **she pulled r. on him** le recordó quién mandaba (allí) (**b**) *(row)* fila *f*; *Mil* **the ranks** la tropa; *Fig* **to rise from the ranks** ascender de soldado a oficial; *Fig* **the ranks of the unemployed** las filas del paro; *Fig* **to break ranks (with)** desmarcarse (de); *Fig* **to close ranks** cerrar filas; (**taxi**) **r.** parada *f* de taxis

**2** *vt* clasificar (**among** entre *or* dentro de); **to r. sth/sb as** catalogar algo/a alguien como

**3** *vi* figurar (**among** entre *or* dentro de); **that ranks as one of the best films I've seen** es una de las mejores películas que he visto; **to r. above/below sb** tener un rango superior/inferior al de alguien; **this ranks as a major disaster** esto constituye un desastre de primer orden

**rank**[2] *adj* (**a**) *(foul-smelling)* pestilente (**b**) *(absolute)* total; **she's a r. outsider** no es más que una comparsa, no tiene muchas posibilidades

**rank-and-file** [ræŋkən'faɪl] *n* **the r.** *(in army)* la tropa; *(of political party)* las bases

**ranking** ['ræŋkɪŋ] *n (classification)* clasificación *f*

**rankle** ['ræŋkəl] *vi* **to r. with sb** dolerle *or* escocerle a alguien

**ransack** ['rænsæk] *vt (house, desk)* revolver, poner patas arriba; *(shop, town)* saquear

**ransom** ['rænsəm] **1** *n* rescate *m*; **to hold sb to r.** pedir un rescate por alguien; *Fig* **to be held to r. by sb** estar a merced de alguien

**2** *vt* rescatar, pagar el rescate de

**rant** [rænt] *vi Fam* despotricar (**about/at** acerca de/contra); **to r. and rave (about sth/at sb)** poner el grito en el cielo (por algo/ante alguien)

**rap** [ræp] *n* **1** (**a**) *(sharp blow)* golpe *m*; *Fig* **to give sb a r. over the knuckles** echar un rapapolvo a alguien; *Fam Fig* **to take the r. for sth** pagar el pato por algo (**b**) *(music)* rap *m*

**2** *vt* *(pt & pp* **rapped**) *(strike)* dar un golpe a; *Fig* **to r. sb's knuckles, to r. sb over the knuckles** echar un rapapolvo a alguien

**rapacious** [rə'peɪʃəs] *adj* rapaz

**rape**[1] [reɪp] **1** *n (crime)* violación *f*; *Fig (of countryside, environment)* destrucción *f*

**2** *vt* violar

**rape**[2] *n (crop)* colza *f*

**rapid** ['ræpɪd] *adj* rápido(a); **r. reaction force** fuerza *f* de intervención rápida

**rapidity** [rə'pɪdɪtɪ] *n* rapidez *f*, celeridad *f*

**rapidly** ['ræpɪdlɪ] *adv* rápidamente

**rapids** ['ræpɪdz] *npl (in river)* rápidos *mpl*

**rapier** ['reɪpɪə(r)] *n* estoque *m*

**rapist** ['reɪpɪst] *n* violador *m*

**rapper** ['ræpə(r)] *n* rapero(a) *m,f*

**rapport** [ræ'pɔː(r)] *n* buena relación *f*; **to have a good r. (with sb)** entenderse *or* llevarse muy bien (con alguien)

**rapt** [ræpt] *adj (attention, look)* extasiado(a); **to be r. in contemplation** estar absorto(a) en la contemplación

**rapture** ['ræptʃə(r)] *n* gozo *m*; **to be in raptures** estar encantado(a); **to go into raptures over** estar embelesado(a) con

**rapturous** ['ræptʃərəs] *adj (cries, applause)* arrebatado(a); *(reception, welcome)* clamoroso(a)

**rare** [reə(r)] *adj* (**a**) *(uncommon)* raro(a); **to have a r. gift (for sth)** tener un don especial (para algo) (**b**) *(steak)* muy poco hecho(a)

**rarefied** ['reərɪfaɪd] *adj (air, gas)* rarificado(a), enrarecido(a); *Fig (atmosphere, ideas)* exclusivista, encopetado(a)

**rarely** ['reəlɪ] *adv* raras veces, raramente

**raring** ['reərɪŋ] *adj* **to be r. to do sth** estar deseando hacer algo; **to be r. to go** estar deseando empezar

**rarity** ['reərɪtɪ] *n* rareza *f*; **to be/become a r.** ser/convertirse en una rareza *or* un caso especial; **r. value** rareza

**rascal** ['rɑːskəl] *n (child)* pillo(a) *m,f*; *Old-fashioned or Hum (scoundrel)* bribón(ona) *m,f*

**rash**[1] [ræʃ] *n* (**a**) *(on skin)* erupción *f*, sarpullido *m* (**b**) *(of complaints, letters)* alud *f*, avalancha *f*

**rash**[2] *adj (person)* impulsivo(a); *(action, remark)* imprudente

**rasher** ['ræʃə(r)] *n Br* **r. (of bacon)** loncha *f* de bacon

**rashly** ['ræʃlɪ] *adv* impulsivamente, precipitadamente

**rasp** [rɑːsp] **1** *n* (**a**) *(tool)* lima *f* gruesa, escofina *f* (**b**) *(sound)* chirrido *m*

**2** *vt (say hoarsely)* bufar, carraspear

**raspberry** ['rɑːzbərɪ] n (fruit) frambuesa f; (plant) frambueso m; Fam Fig to blow a r. at sb hacerle una pedorreta a alguien; **r. jam** mermelada f de frambuesa

**rat** [ræt] **1** n (a) (animal) rata f; **r. poison** matarratas m inv, raticida m; **r. trap** ratonera f, trampa f para ratas (b) Fam (scoundrel) miserable mf, canalla mf (c) (idioms) **I smell a r.** aquí hay gato encerrado; **to get out of the r. race** huir de la lucha frenética por escalar peldaños en la sociedad

**2** vi (pt & pp **ratted**) Fam (inform) cantar; **to r. on sb** delatar a alguien

**ratchet** ['rætʃɪt] n trinquete m; **r. (wheel)** rueda f de trinquete

**rate** [reɪt] **1** n (a) (of inflation, crime, divorce, unemployment) índice m, tasa f; (of interest) tipo m; Fin **r. of return** tasa f de rentabilidad (b) (speed) ritmo m; **at this r.** a este paso; **at any r.** (anyway) en cualquier caso; (at least) por lo menos (c) (price, charge) tarifa f (d) Br Formerly **rates** (local tax) (impuesto m de) contribución f urbana

**2** vt (a) (classify) clasificar (**among** entre or dentro de); **to r. sth/sb as** catalogar algo/a alguien como; **to r. sb/sth highly** tener una buena opinión de alguien/algo; **I don't really r. their chances** no les doy muchas posibilidades (b) (deserve) merecer; **to r. a mention** ser digno(a) de mención

**3** vi **to r. as** figurar como

**rateable value** ['reɪtəbəl'væljuː] n Br Formerly ≃ valor m catastral

**ratepayer** ['reɪtpeɪə(r)] n Br Formerly contribuyente mf (de impuestos municipales)

**rather** ['rɑːðə(r)] adv (a) (preferably) **I'd r. stay** preferiría quedarme; **I'd r. not go** preferiría no ir; **r. you than me!** ¡no quisiera estar en tu lugar!

(b) (more exactly) más bien; **he seemed tired or, r., bored** parecía cansado o, más bien, aburrido

(c) (quite) bastante; (very) muy; **I r. liked it** me gustó mucho

(d) (instead of) **r. than him** en vez or lugar de él; **r. than staying** en vez or lugar de quedarse

**ratification** ['rætɪfɪkeɪʃən] n ratificación f

**ratify** ['rætɪfaɪ] vt ratificar

**rating** ['reɪtɪŋ] n (classification) puesto m, clasificación f; **the ratings** (for TV, radio) los índices de audiencia

**ratio** ['reɪʃɪəʊ] (pl **ratios**) n proporción f, razón f; **in a r. of four to one** en una proporción de cuatro a uno

**ration** ['ræʃən, US 'reɪʃən] **1** n ración f; **rations** (supplies) (raciones fpl de) víveres mpl; **r. book** cartilla f de racionamiento

**2** vt racionar

**rational** ['ræʃənəl] adj (sensible) racional; (sane) lúcido(a)

**rationalism** ['ræʃənəlɪzəm] n racionalismo m

**rationalist** ['ræʃənəlɪst] n racionalista mf

**rationalization** [ræʃənəlaɪ'zeɪʃən] n racionalización f

**rationalize** ['ræʃənəlaɪz] vt racionalizar

**rationally** ['ræʃənəlɪ] adv (sensibly) racionalmente; (sanely) lúcidamente

**rationing** [ræʃənɪŋ] n racionamiento m

**rattle** ['rætəl] **1** n (a) (for baby) sonajero m (b) (noise) (of train) traqueteo m; (of gunfire) tableteo m; (of chains) crujido m; (of glass, coins, keys) tintineo m; (of door, window) golpeteo m

**2** vt (a) (chains, keys) hacer entrechocar; (door, window) sacudir (b) Fam (make nervous) **to be rattled by sth** perder la calma a causa de algo

**3** vi (of chains) crujir; (of glass, keys, coins) tintinear; (of door, window) golpetear

▸**rattle off** vt sep Fam (say quickly) soltar de un tirón; (write quickly) garabatear

▸**rattle on** vi Fam cascar, parlotear

▸**rattle through** vt insep Fam (work, book) despachar, terminar rápidamente

**rattlesnake** ['rætəlsneɪk] n serpiente f de cascabel

**ratty** ['rætɪ] adj Br Fam (annoyed) mosqueado(a); (irritable) susceptible, picajoso(a)

**raucous** ['rɔːkəs] adj (hoarse) ronco(a); (rowdy) ruidoso(a)

**raunchy** ['rɔːntʃɪ] adj Fam (lyrics, film, novel) picante, procaz; (dress) provocativo(a), sexy

**ravage** [rævɪdʒ] **1** npl **ravages** estragos mpl

**2** vt arrasar

**rave** [reɪv] **1** n (party) macrofiesta f (tecno)

**2** adj **r. notice** or **review** (for play) crítica f entusiasta

**3** vi (deliriously) desvariar; **to r. about sb/sth** (enthusiastically) deshacerse en elogios sobre alguien/algo

**raven** ['reɪvən] **1** n (bird) cuervo m

**2** adj (colour) azabache

**ravenous** ['rævənəs] adj (animal, person) hambriento(a) m,f; **to be r.** tener un hambre canina

**raver** ['reɪvə(r)] n Br Fam (who goes to lots of parties) juerguista mf; (who goes to raves) aficionado(a) m,f al bakala

**rave-up** ['reɪvʌp] n Br Fam farra f, juerga f

**ravine** [rə'viːn] n barranco m

**raving** ['reɪvɪŋ] adj (a) (delirious) **to be r. mad** estar como una cabra; **a r. lunatic** un loco de atar (b) (success) clamoroso(a); (beauty) arrebatador(ora)

**ravish** ['rævɪʃ] vt (a) Literary (delight) deslumbrar, cautivar (b) Old-fashioned (rape) forzar, violar

**ravishing** ['rævɪʃɪŋ] *adj* deslumbrante, cautivador(ora); **she's a r. beauty** es de una belleza deslumbrante

**raw** [rɔ:] *adj* (a) *(food, silk)* crudo(a); *(sugar)* sin refinar; *(statistics)* en bruto; **to be r.** *(of meat, vegetables)* estar crudo(a); **r. materials** materias *fpl* primas; **r. recruit** recluta *m* novato (b) *(skin)* agrietado(a); *Fig* **to get a r. deal** ser tratado(a) injustamente; *Fig* **to touch a r. nerve** dar en lo más vivo (c) *(weather, wind)* crudo(a)

**ray**¹ [reɪ] *n* *(of light, sun)* rayo *m*; **a r. of hope** un rayo de esperanza

**ray**² *n* *(fish)* raya *f*

**rayon** ['reɪɒn] *n* *(fabric)* rayón *m*

**raze** [reɪz] *vt* arrasar; **to r. sth to the ground** arrasar totalmente algo

**razor** ['reɪzə(r)] *n* navaja *f* de afeitar; *(electric)* maquinilla *f* de afeitar; **r. blade** cuchilla *f* de afeitar

**razor-sharp** ['reɪzəʃɑ:p] *adj* *(knife)* muy afilado(a); *Fig (intelligence)* agudo(a); *(wit)* afilado(a)

**razor-shell** ['reɪzəʃel] *n* navaja *f* (molusco)

**razzmatazz** ['ræzmətæz] *n* *Fam* oropel *m*, fastuosidad *f*

**RC** [ɑ:'si:] *n & adj* *(abbr* **Roman Catholic**) católico(a) *m,f* romano(a)

**Rd** *(abbr* **Road**) C/, calle *f*

**R & D** [ɑ:rən'di:] *n* *Com (abbr* **research and development**) I+D, investigación *f* y desarrollo

**RDA** [ɑ:di:'eɪ] *n* *(abbr* **recommended daily allowance**) cantidad *f* diaria recomendada

**RE** [ɑ:'ri:] *n* *(abbr* **Religious Education**) (asignatura *f* de) religión *f*

**re**¹ [ri:] *prep* con referencia a; **re your letter…** con referencia a *or* en relación con su carta…; **re: 1997 sales figures** REF: cifras de ventas de 1997

**re**² [reɪ] *n* *Mus* re *m*

**reach** [ri:tʃ] **1** *n* (a) *(accessibility)* alcance *m*; **within r.** al alcance; **out of r.** fuera del alcance (b) **the upper reaches of a river** la cabecera *or* el curso alto de un río; **the further reaches of the empire** los últimos confines del imperio

**2** *vt* (a) *(manage to touch)* alcanzar; *(conclusion, decision, destination)* llegar a; *(agreement, stage, level)* alcanzar, llegar a; **the news didn't r. him** no le llegó la noticia (b) *(contact)* *(by phone)* contactar con; **to r. a wider audience** llegar a un público más amplio (c) *(stretch as far as)* *(one's shoulder, waist)* llegar a

**3** *vi (of forest, property)* extenderse; *(of noise, voice)* oírse; **to r. for sth** (tratar de) alcanzar algo; *Fig* **to r. for the sky** *or* **the stars** apuntar a lo más alto

▸**reach out** *vi* **to r. out for sth** extender el brazo para coger algo

**reachable** ['ri:tʃəbəl] *adj* *(place)* accesible; *(goal, objective)* asequible, alcanzable

**react** [rɪ'ækt] *vi* reaccionar (**against/to** contra/ante)

**reaction** [rɪ'ækʃən] *n* reacción *f*

**reactionary** [rɪ'ækʃənərɪ] *n & adj* reaccionario(a) *m,f*

**reactivate** [rɪ'æktɪveɪt] *vt* reactivar

**reactor** [rɪ'æktə(r)] *n* reactor *m*

**read** [ri:d] **1** *n* **to have a r. of sth** leer algo; **this book's a good r.** este libro se lee muy bien *or* es muy entretenido

**2** *vt* *(pt & pp* **read** [red]) (a) *(book, newspaper, letter)* leer; **to r. Italian** leer en italiano; **do you r. me?** *(on radio)* ¿me recibes?; *Fig* **to take sth as read** dar por hecho *or* por sentado algo (b) *(interpret)* interpretar; **to r. sb's mind** adivinar los pensamientos a alguien; **it can be read in two ways** tiene una doble lectura; **to r. the future** adivinar el futuro (c) *(say aloud)* *(letter, poem)* leer (en voz alta) (d) *Br Univ (study)* estudiar (e) *(of dial, thermometer)* marcar; **the sign read "No Entry"** el letrero decía "prohibida la entrada"

**3** *vi* (a) *(of person)* leer; **to r. aloud** leer en alto *or* en voz alta; *Fig* **to r. between the lines** leer entre líneas (b) *(of text)* **to r. well/badly** estar bien/mal escrito(a)

▸**read out** *vt sep* leer (en voz alta)

▸**read up on** *vt insep* empaparse de, leer mucho sobre

**readable** ['ri:dəbəl] *adj* *(book)* ameno(a); *(handwriting)* legible

**reader** ['ri:də(r)] *n* (a) *(person)* lector(ora) *m,f* (b) *(reading book)* libro *m* de lectura

**readily** ['redɪlɪ] *adv* *(willingly)* de buena gana; *(easily)* fácilmente

**reading** ['ri:dɪŋ] *n* (a) *(action, pastime)* lectura *f*; **r. glasses** *fpl* gafas *fpl* para leer (b) *(measurement)* **to take a r. from the gas meter** leer el contador del gas (c) *(interpretation)* interpretación *f*, lectura *f*

**readjust** [ri:ə'dʒʌst] **1** *vt* reajustar; *(clothing, device, object)* ajustar

**2** *vi* adaptarse de nuevo

**readjustment** [ri:ə'dʒʌstmənt] *n* reajuste *m*

**readmit** [ri:əd'mɪt] *vt* readmitir (**to** en)

**read-only memory** ['ri:d'əʊnlɪ'memərɪ] *n* *Comptr* memoria *f* sólo de lectura

**readvertise** [ri:'ædvətaɪz] *vt* **to r. a post** volver a anunciar una oferta de empleo

**ready** ['redɪ] **1** *n* (a) **at the r.** a mano (b) *Fam* **readies** *(cash)* dinero *m* contante y sonante

**2** *adj* (a) *(prepared)* listo(a), preparado(a); **to**

be r. (to do sth) estar listo(a) or preparado(a) (para hacer algo); **we were r. to give up** estuvimos a punto de darnos por vencidos; **to get r.** (prepared) prepararse; (smarten up) arreglarse; **to get sth r.** preparar algo; **r.!, steady!, go!** preparados, listos, ¡ya!; **r. cash** dinero m en efectivo

(b) (willing) dispuesto(a); **to be r. to do sth** estar dispuesto(a) a hacer algo

(c) (quick) rápido(a); **to have a r. wit** ser muy despierto(a)

**3** vt (prepare) preparar; **to r. oneself for action** prepararse para la acción

**ready-made** [redɪ'meɪd] adj **r. food** platos mpl precocinados; **a r. phrase** una frase hecha

**reaffirm** [riːə'fɜːm] vt reafirmar

**reafforestation** [riːəfɒrɪ'steɪʃən] n reforestación f, repoblación f forestal

**real** [rɪəl] **1** adj (a) (danger, fear, effort) real; (authentic) (gold, leather) auténtico(a); **r. flowers** flores fpl naturales; **the r. reason** el verdadero motivo; **a r. friend** un amigo de verdad; **r. ale** = cerveza tostada de elaboración tradicional y con presión natural

(b) (actual) real; **the r. world** el mundo real; **what does that mean in r. terms?** ¿qué significado tiene a efectos prácticos?; Com **r. estate** bienes mpl inmuebles

(c) (for emphasis) **a r. idiot** un tonto de remate; **a r. disaster** un perfecto desastre

**2** adv US Fam (very) muy; **it's r. good** es superbueno(a)

**realism** ['rɪəlɪzəm] n realismo m

**realist** ['rɪəlɪst] n realista mf

**realistic** [rɪə'lɪstɪk] adj realista

**reality** [rɪ'ælɪtɪ] n realidad f; **in r.** en realidad

**realization** [rɪəlaɪ'zeɪʃən] n **this r.** frightened her al darse cuenta se asustó; **the r. of what he meant was slow in coming** tardó en darse cuenta de lo que quería decir

**realize** ['rɪəlaɪz] vt (a) (become aware of) darse cuenta de; **I r. he's busy, but…** ya sé que está ocupado, pero… (b) (ambition, dream) realizar; **our fears were realized** nuestros temores se vieron confirmados

**really** ['rɪəlɪ] adv (truly) de verdad; (very) realmente, verdaderamente; **is it r. true?** ¿es eso verdad or cierto?; **r.?** ¿de verdad?, ¿en serio?; **this is r. not all that bad** esto no está pero que nada mal

**realm** [relm] n (a) (kingdom) reino m (b) (field) ámbito m, dominio m; **within/beyond the realms of possibility** dentro de/fuera de lo posible

**realtor** ['rɪəltə(r)] n US agente mf inmobiliario(a)

**ream** [riːm] n (of paper) resma f; Fig **reams of** toneladas fpl de

**reanimate** [riː'ænɪmeɪt] vt reanimar

**reap** [riːp] vt recolectar, cosechar; **to r. the benefits (of)** cosechar los beneficios (de)

**reaper** ['riːpə(r)] n (machine) cosechadora f

**reappear** [riːə'pɪə(r)] vi reaparecer

**reappearance** [riːə'pɪərəns] n reaparición f

**reapply** [riːə'plaɪ] vi (for job) volver a presentar solicitud or presentarse

**reappraise** [riːə'preɪz] vt reconsiderar

**rear¹** [rɪə(r)] n (a) (back part) parte f trasera; (of military column) retaguardia f; **at the r. of** (inside) al fondo de; (behind) detrás de; **in the r.** detrás, en la parte de atrás; **to bring up the r.** (in race) ser el farolillo rojo; **r. admiral** contralmirante m; **r. entrance** puerta f trasera; **r. legs** (of animal) patas fpl traseras; **r. lights** (of car) luces fpl traseras; **r. window** (of car) luneta f, ventana f trasera (b) Fam (buttocks) trasero m

**rear²** vt (a) (child, livestock) criar (b) (one's head) levantar; **fascism has reared its ugly head** el fascismo ha levantado su repugnante cabeza

▸**rear up** vi (of horse) encabritarse

**rearguard** ['rɪəgɑːd] n Mil retaguardia f; Fig **to fight a r. action** emprender un último intento a la desesperada

**rearm** [riː'ɑːm] **1** vt rearmar

**2** vi rearmarse

**rearmament** [riː'ɑːməmənt] n rearme m

**rearrange** [riːə'reɪndʒ] vt (books, furniture) reordenar; (appointment) cambiar

**rear-view mirror** ['rɪəvjuː'mɪrə(r)] n (espejo m) retrovisor m

**reason** ['riːzən] **1** n (a) (cause, motive) razón f, motivo m (for de); **for reasons of health** por razones de salud; **for one r. or another** por un motivo u otro; **for no particular r.** sin or por ningún motivo en especial; **that's no r. for giving up!** ¡eso no es motivo para darse por vencido!; **I don't know the r. why** no sé por qué; Ironic **for reasons best known to himself** por razones que a mí se me escapan; **give me one good r. why I should!** ¿por qué razón debería hacerlo? (b) (sanity, common sense) razón f; **to listen to** or **see r.** atender a razones; **it stands to r.** es lógico or evidente; **within r.** dentro de lo razonable

**2** vt to r. that… argumentar que…

**3** vi razonar (about sobre) **to r. with sb** razonar con alguien

**reasonable** ['riːzənəbəl] adj (fair, sensible, moderate) razonable; (acceptable) aceptable, razonable; **the weather/meal was r.** el tiempo/la comida fue aceptable; **be r.!** ¡sé razonable!

**reasonably** ['riːzənəblɪ] adv (a) (behave, act) razonablemente (b) (quite) bastante, razonablemente

**reasoning** ['riːzənɪŋ] n (thinking) razonamiento m

**reassemble** [riːəˈsembəl] **1** vt (people) reagrupar; (machine) volver a montar

**2** vi (of people) reagruparse

**reassess** [riːəˈses] vt (a) (policy, situation) replantearse (b) Fin (tax) revisar; (property) volver a tasar

**reassurance** [riːəˈʃʊərəns] n (comfort) consuelo m; (guarantee) garantía f

**reassure** [riːəˈʃʊə(r)] vt confortar, tranquilizar; **to feel reassured** sentirse más tranquilo(a); **he reassured them that he would be there** les aseguró que estaría allí

**reassuring** [riːəˈʃʊərɪŋ] adj tranquilizador(ora), confortante

**reawaken** [riːəˈweɪkən] **1** vt volver a despertar

**2** vi (of person) volver a despertarse

**rebate** [ˈriːbeɪt] n Fin (refund) devolución f, reembolso m; (discount) bonificación f

**rebel** **1** n [ˈrebəl] rebelde mf; **r. leader** cabecilla mf rebelde or de la rebelión

**2** vi [rɪˈbel] (pt & pp **rebelled**) rebelarse (**against** contra)

**rebellion** [rɪˈbeljən] n rebelión f

**rebellious** [rɪˈbeljəs] adj rebelde

**rebirth** [riːˈbɜːθ] n (renewal) resurgimiento m

**reboot** [riːˈbuːt] vt & vi Comptr reinicializar

**reborn** [riːˈbɔːn] adj **to be r.** renacer

**rebound** **1** n [ˈriːbaʊnd] (of ball) rebote m; Fig **she married him on the r.** se casó con él después de una decepción amorosa

**2** vi [rɪˈbaʊnd] (of ball) rebotar; Fig **to r. on sb** (of joke, lie) volverse en contra de alguien

**rebuff** [rɪˈbʌf] **1** n (slight) desaire m, desplante m; (rejection) rechazo m; **to meet with a r.** (of person, suggestion) ser rechazado(a)

**2** vt (slight) desairar; (reject) rechazar

**rebuild** [riːˈbɪld] (pt & pp **rebuilt** [riːˈbɪlt]) vt reconstruir

**rebuke** [rɪˈbjuːk] **1** n reprensión f, reprimenda f

**2** vt reprender

**rebut** [rɪˈbʌt] (pt & pp **rebutted**) vt refutar

**rebuttal** [rɪˈbʌtəl] n refutación f

**recalcitrant** [rɪˈkælsɪtrənt] adj recalcitrante

**recall** **1** n [ˈriːkɔːl] (memory) memoria f; **lost beyond r.** perdido(a) irremisiblemente

**2** vt [rɪˈkɔːl] (a) (remember) recordar; **to r. doing sth** recordar haber hecho algo (b) (defective goods) retirar del mercado; (library book) reclamar; Br Pol **to r. Parliament** convocar un pleno extraordinario del Parlamento (fuera del período de sesiones)

**recant** [rɪˈkænt] **1** vt (opinion) retractarse de

**2** vi (change opinion) retractarse; Rel abjurar

**recap** [ˈriːkæp] **1** n (summary) recapitulación f

**2** vi (pt & pp **recapped**) recapitular

**recapitulate** [riːkəˈpɪtjʊleɪt] vt & vi recapitular

**recapture** [riːˈkæptʃə(r)] **1** n (of criminal) nueva captura f, segunda detención f; (of town, territory) reconquista f; **he escaped r. for nearly a year** no lo volvieron a capturar hasta pasado casi un año

**2** vt (a) (criminal) volver a detener; (town, territory) reconquistar (b) Fig (memory, atmosphere) recuperar; (one's youth) revivir

**recede** [rɪˈsiːd] vi (of tide, coastline) retroceder; **to have a receding chin** tener la barbilla hundida; **to have a receding hairline** tener entradas

**receipt** [rɪˈsiːt] n (a) (act of receiving) recibo m; **to be in r. of sth** haber recibido algo (b) (proof of payment) recibo m; **receipts** (at box office) recaudación f

**receive** [rɪˈsiːv] vt recibir; **to r. stolen goods** comerciar con or receptar bienes robados; **it was well/badly received** (of film, proposal) fue bien/mal acogido(a); **to r. sb into the Church** recibir a alguien en el seno de la Iglesia

**received** [rɪˈsiːvd] adj (idea, opinion) común, aceptado(a); **r. pronunciation** pronunciación f estándar (del inglés)

**receiver** [rɪˈsiːvə(r)] n (a) (of stolen goods) perista mf; Jur receptador(ora) m,f (b) (of telephone) auricular m; **to pick up the r.** descolgar el teléfono; **to replace the r.** colgar el teléfono (c) (of radio set) receptor m (d) Fin **to call in the receivers** declararse en quiebra, poner la empresa en manos de la administración judicial

**receivership** [rɪˈsiːvəʃɪp] n Fin **to go into r.** declararse en quiebra

**receiving** [rɪˈsiːvɪŋ] **1** n (of stolen goods) receptación f

**2** adj Fam **to be on the r. end (of sth)** ser la víctima (de algo)

**recent** [ˈriːsənt] adj reciente; **in r. months** en los últimos meses; **in r. times** recientemente; **her most r. novel** su última or su más reciente novela

**recently** [ˈriːsəntlɪ] adv recientemente, hace poco; **as r. as yesterday** ayer sin ir más lejos; **until quite r.** hasta hace muy poco

**receptacle** [rɪˈseptəkəl] n receptáculo m

**reception** [rɪˈsepʃən] n (a) (of guests, new members) recibimiento m; (of announcement, new film) recibimiento m, acogida f; **to get a warm r.** ser acogido(a) calurosamente; **r. centre** (for refugees) centro m de acogida (b) (party) recepción f; (wedding) r. banquete m de boda (c) (in hotel) **r. (desk)** recepción f (d) (of radio, TV programme) recepción f

**receptionist** [rɪˈsepʃənɪst] n recepcionista mf

**receptive** [rɪˈseptɪv] adj receptivo(a)

**recess** ['ri:ses] n (**a**) (of Parliament) período m vacacional; (in trial) descanso m (**b**) (in wall) hueco m; (of mind, past) recoveco m (**c**) US Sch (between classes) recreo m

**recession** [rɪ'seʃən] n Econ recesión f

**recharge** [ri:'tʃɑ:dʒ] vt (battery) recargar; Fig **to r. one's batteries** recargar las baterías

**rechargeable** [ri:'tʃɑ:dʒəbəl] adj recargable

**recidivism** [rɪ'sɪdɪvɪzəm] n Law reincidencia f

**recipe** ['resɪpɪ] n also Fig receta f; **a r. for disaster/success** la receta para el desastre/el éxito; **r. book** recetario m (de cocina)

**recipient** [rɪ'sɪpɪənt] n (of gift, letter) destinatario(a) m,f; (of cheque, award, honour) receptor(ora) m,f

**reciprocal** [rɪ'sɪprəkəl] adj recíproco(a)

**reciprocate** [rɪ'sɪprəkeɪt] **1** vt corresponder a
**2** vi corresponder

**recital** [rɪ'saɪtəl] n (of poetry, music) recital m; (of facts) perorata f

**recitation** [resɪ'teɪʃən] n (of poem) recitación f

**recite** [rɪ'saɪt] **1** vt (poem) recitar; (complaints, details) enumerar
**2** vi recitar

**reckless** ['reklɪs] adj (decision, behaviour) imprudente; (driving) temerario(a); **r. driver** conductor(ora) m,f temerario(a)

**reckon** ['rekən] **1** vt (**a**) (consider) considerar; **he is reckoned to be…** está considerado como… (**b**) (calculate) calcular (**c**) Fam (think) **to r. (that)** creer que
**2** vi calcular

▸**reckon on** vt insep contar con; **you should r. on there being about thirty people there** debes contar con que habrá por lo menos treinta personas

▸**reckon up** vt sep (figures, cost) calcular; **to r. up a bill** calcular el importe de una factura

▸**reckon with** vt insep contar con; **she's someone to be reckoned with** es una mujer de armas tomar

**reckoning** ['rekənɪŋ] n **by my r.** según mis cálculos; **day of r.** hora f de la verdad

**reclaim** [rɪ'kleɪm] vt (lost property, expenses) reclamar; (waste materials) recuperar; **to r. land from the sea** ganar terreno al mar

**reclamation** [reklə'meɪʃən] n (of waste materials) recuperación f; **land r. project** proyecto m para ganar terreno al mar

**recline** [rɪ'klaɪn] vi reclinarse

**reclining** [rɪ'klaɪnɪŋ] adj **in a r. position** reclinado(a); **r. seat** asiento m reclinable

**recluse** [rɪ'klu:s] n solitario(a) m,f

**recognition** [rekəg'nɪʃən] n reconocimiento m; **to have changed beyond** or **out of all r.** estar irreconocible; **in r. of** en reconocimiento a

**recognizable** [rekəg'naɪzəbəl] adj reconocible

**recognize** ['rekəgnaɪz] vt reconocer

**recognized** ['rekəgnaɪzd] adj (government) legítimo(a); (method) reconocido(a); (qualification) homologado(a); **to be a r. authority (on sth)** ser una autoridad reconocida (en algo)

**recoil 1** n ['ri:kɔɪl] (of gun) retroceso m
**2** vi [rɪ'kɔɪl] (of gun, person) retroceder

**recollect** [rekə'lekt] vt recordar

**recollection** [rekə'lekʃən] n recuerdo m; **to the best of my r.** en lo que alcanzo a recordar

**recommend** [rekə'mend] vt (**a**) (praise) recomendar; **to r. sth to sb** recomendar algo a alguien; **the proposal has a lot to r. it** la propuesta presenta muchas ventajas (**b**) (advise) recomendar, aconsejar; **to r. sb to do sth** recomendar a alguien hacer algo; Com **recommended retail price** precio m recomendado de venta al público

**recommendation** [rekəmen'deɪʃən] n recomendación f; **on my/her r.** recomendado(a) por mí/por ella

**recompense** ['rekəmpens] **1** n recompensa f; **in r. for** como recompensa por
**2** vt recompensar (**for** por)

**reconcile** ['rekənsaɪl] vt (**a**) (people) reconciliar; **to be reconciled with sb** reconciliarse con alguien; **to be reconciled to sth** estar resignado(a) a algo (**b**) (facts, differences, opinions) conciliar

**reconciliation** [rekənsɪlɪ'eɪʃən] n (**a**) (of people) reconciliación f (**b**) (of differences, opinions) conciliación f

**reconditioned** [ri:kən'dɪʃənd] adj (TV, washing machine) reparado(a)

**reconnaissance** [rɪ'kɒnɪsəns] n Mil reconocimiento m; **r. flight** vuelo m de reconocimiento

**reconquer** [ri:'kɒŋkə(r)] vt reconquistar

**reconquest** [ri:'kɒŋkwest] n reconquista f

**reconsider** [ri:kən'sɪdə(r)] vt reconsiderar

**reconstitute** [ri:'kɒnstɪtju:t] vt (organization, committee) reconstituir; (dried food) rehidratar

**reconstruct** [ri:kən'strʌkt] vt reconstruir

**reconstruction** [ri:kən'strʌkʃən] n reconstrucción f

**record** ['rekɔ:d] **1** n (**a**) (account) registro m; **to keep a r. of sth** anotar algo; **to put sth on r.** dejar constancia (escrita) de algo; **the coldest winter on r.** el invierno más frío del que se tiene constancia; **to be on r. as saying that…** haber declarado públicamente que…; **off the r.** (say) confidencialmente; **(just) for the r.** para que conste; **to put** or **set the r. straight** poner las cosas en claro or en su sitio; **r. office** (oficina f del) registro m

(b) *(personal history)* historial m; *(of criminal)* antecedentes mpl penales; **to have a good/ bad safety r.** tener un buen/mal historial en materia de seguridad; **he has a r.** *(of criminal)* tiene antecedentes; **academic r.** expediente m académico; *Med* **case r.** historial m (clínico)

(c) *(musical)* disco m; **to make a r.** grabar un disco; **r. company** compañía f discográfica; **r. player** tocadiscos m inv

(d) *(best performance)* récord m; **to set a r.** establecer un récord; **to hold the r.** tener el récord; **to break** or **beat the r.** batir el récord

(e) *Comptr* registro m

**2** adj **in r. time** en tiempo récord; **unemployment is at a r. high/low** el desempleo ha alcanzado un máximo/mínimo histórico

**3** vt [rɪ'kɔːd] (a) *(on video, cassette)* grabar

(b) *(write down)* anotar; **recorded delivery** *(of parcel, letter)* correo m certificado

**record-breaking** ['rekɔːdbreɪkɪŋ] adj récord inv; **to have r. sales** batir todos los récords de ventas

**recorder** [rɪ'kɔːdə(r)] n (a) **(tape) r.** grabadora f, magnetófono m (b) *(musical instrument)* flauta f dulce, flauta f de pico

**record-holder** ['rekɔːdhəʊldə(r)] n plusmarquista mf

**recording** [rɪ'kɔːdɪŋ] n *(on tape)* grabación f; **r. studio** estudio m de grabación

**recount** [rɪ'kaʊnt] vt *(relate)* relatar

**re-count** ['riːkaʊnt] n *(in election)* segundo recuento m

**recoup** [rɪ'kuːp] vt recuperar, resarcirse de

**recourse** [rɪ'kɔːs] n recurso m; **to have r. to** recurrir a

**recover** [rɪ'kʌvə(r)] **1** vt *also Comptr* recuperar

**2** vi *(from illness, setback)* recuperarse

**recoverable** [rɪ'kʌvərəbəl] adj recuperable

**recovery** [rɪ'kʌvərɪ] n (a) *(of lost object)* recuperación f; **r. vehicle** (vehículo m) grúa f (b) *(from illness, of economy)* recuperación f; **to make a r.** recuperarse

**re-create** [riːkrɪ'eɪt] vt recrear

**recreation** [rekrɪ'eɪʃən] n *(leisure)* ocio m, esparcimiento m; *Sch (break)* recreo m; **to do sth for r.** hacer algo como pasatiempo; **r. ground** patio m (de recreo); **r. room** sala f de recreo

**recreational** [rekrɪ'eɪʃənəl] adj recreativo(a); **r. drug** = droga de consumo esporádico y por diversión

**recrimination** [rɪkrɪmɪ'neɪʃən] n recriminación f, reproche m

**recruit** [rɪ'kruːt] **1** n *(soldier)* recluta mf; *(new employee, member)* nuevo miembro m

**2** vt *(soldier)* reclutar; *(employee)* contratar; *(member)* enrolar, reclutar

**recruitment** [rɪ'kruːtmənt] n *(of soldier)* reclutamiento m; *(of employee)* contratación f; *(of new member)* enrolamiento m, reclutamiento m

**rectangle** ['rektæŋgəl] n rectángulo m

**rectangular** [rek'tæŋgjʊlə(r)] adj rectangular

**rectify** ['rektɪfaɪ] vt rectificar

**rectitude** ['rektɪtjuːd] n Formal rectitud f, integridad f

**rector** ['rektə(r)] n (a) Rel párroco m (b) Scot Univ rector(ora) m,f; Scot Sch (headmaster) director(ora) m,f

**rectory** ['rektərɪ] n Rel rectoría f

**rectum** ['rektəm] n Anat recto m

**recumbent** [rɪ'kʌmbənt] adj Formal yacente

**recuperate** [rɪ'kuːpəreɪt] **1** vt *(one's strength, money)* recuperar

**2** vi *(of person)* recuperarse

**recuperation** [rɪkuːpə'reɪʃən] n recuperación f

**recur** [rɪ'kɜː(r)] *(pt & pp recurred)* vi *(of event, problem)* repetirse; *(of illness)* reaparecer

**recurrence** [rɪ'kʌrəns] n *(of event, problem)* repetición f; *(of illness)* reaparición f

**recurrent** [rɪ'kʌrənt] adj recurrente

**recurring** [rɪ'kɜːrɪŋ] adj *(problem)* recurrente, reiterativo(a); *Math* **six point six r.** seis coma seis período or periódico (puro); **a r. nightmare** una pesadilla recurrente

**recycle** [riː'saɪkəl] vt reciclar; **recycled paper/glass** papel m/vidrio m reciclado

**recycling** [riː'saɪklɪŋ] n reciclaje m, reciclado m; **r. plant** planta f de reciclaje

**red** [red] **1** n *(colour)* rojo m; *Fam Fig* **to see r.** *(become angry)* ponerse hecho(a) una furia; **to be in the r.** *(be in debt)* estar en números rojos

**2** adj rojo(a); **to have r. hair** ser pelirrojo(a); **to turn** or **go r.** *(of sky)* ponerse rojo; *(of person)* ponerse colorado(a); **to be as r. as a beetroot** estar más rojo que un tomate; **r. alert** alerta f roja; *Formerly* **the R. Army** el Ejército Rojo; **r. card** tarjeta f roja; **to be shown the r. card** ser expulsado(a) del campo; *Fig* **to roll out the r. carpet for sb** recibir a alguien con todos los honores; **R. Cross** Cruz f Roja; *Fig* **r. herring** *(distraction)* señuelo m *(para desviar la atención)*; *(misleading clue)* pista f falsa; *Old-fashioned* **R. Indian** (indio(a) m,f) piel roja mf; **r. light** semáforo m (en) rojo; **to go through a r. light** saltarse un semáforo en rojo; **r.-light district** barrio m chino; **r. meat** carne f roja; **r. pepper** pimiento m rojo or colorado; **mentioning her name to him was like a r. rag to a bull** la sola mención de su nombre le ponía hecho una furia; **(Little) R. Riding Hood** Caperucita f Roja; **the R. Sea** el Mar Rojo; **r. tape** burocracia f, papeleo m (burocrático); **r. wine** vino m tinto

**red-blooded** [red'blʌdɪd] *adj* a r. male un macho de pelo en pecho

**redbrick** ['redbrɪk] *adj (building)* de ladrillo rojo; r. university = por oposición a Oxford y Cambridge, universidad construida en alguna gran urbe británica, aparte de Londres, a finales del XIX o principios del XX

**redcurrant** ['redkʌrənt] *n* grosella *f* (roja)

**redden** ['redən] **1** *vt* enrojecer

**2** *vi (of sky)* ponerse rojo(a); *(of person)* ponerse colorado(a)

**reddish** ['redɪʃ] *adj (light, colour)* rojizo(a)

**redecorate** [riː'dekəreɪt] *vt (repaint)* pintar de nuevo; *(repaper)* empapelar de nuevo

**redeem** [rɪ'diːm] *vt* **(a)** *(pawned item)* desempeñar; *(promise)* cumplir; *(gift token, coupon)* canjear; **to r. a mortgage** amortizar una hipoteca **(b)** *(sinner)* redimir; *Fig* **he redeemed himself by scoring the equalizer** subsanó su error al marcar el gol del empate

**Redeemer** [rɪ'diːmə(r)] *n Rel* **the R.** el Redentor

**redeeming** [rɪ'diːmɪŋ] *adj* **he has no r. features** no se salva por ningún lado, no tiene nada que lo salve

**redemption** [rɪ'dempʃən] *n Rel* redención *f*; *also Fig* **to be beyond** *or* **past r.** no tener salvación

**redeploy** [riːdɪ'plɔɪ] *vt (troops, resources)* redistribuir, reorganizar

**redeployment** [riːdɪ'plɔɪmənt] *n* redistribución *f*, reorganización *f*

**redevelop** [riːdɪ'veləp] *vt (land)* reconvertir; *(town)* reedificar

**red-faced** ['red'feɪst] *adj (naturally)* sonrosado(a); *(with anger)* sulfurado(a); *(with embarrassment)* ruborizado(a)

**red-handed** ['red'hændɪd] *adv* **he was caught r.** lo cogieron con las manos en la masa

**redhead** ['redhed] *n* pelirrojo(a) *m,f*

**red-hot** [red'hɒt] *adj* **(a)** *(very hot)* al rojo vivo, candente **(b)** *Fam* **to be r. (on sth)** *(very good)* ser un hacha (en algo); **r. news** noticias *fpl* de candente actualidad

**redirect** [riːdɪ'rekt, riːdaɪ'rekt] *vt (letter)* reexpedir; *(plane, traffic)* desviar; **to r. one's energies (towards sth)** reorientar los esfuerzos (hacia algo)

**rediscover** [riːdɪs'kʌvə(r)] *vt* redescubrir

**redistribute** [riːdɪ'strɪbjuːt] *vt* redistribuir

**red-letter day** ['red'letədeɪ] *n* jornada *f* memorable

**redo** [riː'duː] *(pt* **redid** [riː'dɪd]*, pp* **redone** [riː'dʌn]*) vt* rehacer

**redolent** ['redələnt] *adj* **to be r. of** *(smell of)* oler a; *(be suggestive of)* tener reminiscencias de

**redouble** [riː'dʌbəl] *vt* redoblar; **to r. one's efforts** redoblar los esfuerzos

**redraft** [riː'drɑːft] *vt* redactar de nuevo, reescribir

**redress** [rɪ'dres] **1** *n (of grievance)* reparación *f*; **to seek r.** exigir reparación

**2** *vt (injustice, grievance)* reparar; **to r. the balance** reestablecer el equilibrio

**redskin** ['redskɪn] *n Old-fashioned* piel roja *mf*

**reduce** [rɪ'djuːs] *vt* **(a)** *(make smaller, lower)* reducir; *(price, product)* rebajar; **to r. a sauce** reducir una salsa; **to r. speed** reducir la velocidad **(b)** *(bring to a certain state)* reducir; **to r. sth to ashes/dust** reducir algo a cenizas/polvo; **to r. sb to silence** reducir a alguien al silencio; **his words reduced her to tears** sus palabras le hicieron llorar; **to be reduced to doing sth** no tener más remedio que hacer algo

**reduced** [rɪ'djuːst] *adj (smaller)* reducido(a); **on a r. scale** a escala reducida; **at r. prices** a precios reducidos; **to live in r. circumstances** haber venido a menos

**reduction** [rɪ'dʌkʃən] *n* reducción *f*; *(of price, product)* rebaja *f*

**redundancy** [rɪ'dʌndənsɪ] *n (dismissal)* despido *m* (por reducción de plantilla); **r. notice** notificación *f* de despido; **r. pay** indemnización *f* por despido

**redundant** [rɪ'dʌndənt] *adj* **(a)** *Ind* **to make sb r.** despedir a alguien; **to be made r.** ser despedido(a) **(b)** *(superfluous)* superfluo(a), innecesario(a); *(words, information)* redundante

**reed** [riːd] *n* **(a)** *(plant)* caña *f* **(b)** *Mus (of instrument)* lengüeta *f*

**reef** [riːf] *n* arrecife *m*

**reek** [riːk] **1** *n* peste *f*, tufo *m*

**2** *vi also Fig* apestar **(of** a)

**reel** [riːl] **1** *n* **(a)** *Br (for thread, fishing line)* carrete *m*; *(of cinema film)* rollo *m* **(b)** *(dance, music)* danza escocesa o irlandesa

**2** *vi (sway)* tambalearse; **my head is reeling** me da vueltas la cabeza

▸**reel off** *vt sep (names, statistics)* soltar de un tirón

**re-elect** [riːɪ'lekt] *vt Pol* reelegir

**re-election** [riːɪ'lekʃən] *n* reelección *f*

**re-enact** [riːɪ'nækt] *vt (crime, battle)* reconstruir

**re-enter** [riː'entə(r)] **1** *vt (room, country)* volver a entrar en; **to r. the job market** reinsertarse en el *or* reincorporarse al mercado de trabajo

**2** *vi* volver a entrar; **to r. for an examination** volver a examinarse

**re-establish** [riːɪ'stæblɪʃ] *vt* restablecer

**re-examine** [riːɪg'zæmɪn] *vt* reexaminar

**ref** [ref] *n* **(a)** *(abbr* **reference)** r. number no ref., número *m* de referencia **(b)** *Fam (referee)* árbitro *m*

**refectory** [rɪ'fektərɪ] n (at university, school) comedor m; (in monastery) refectorio m

**refer** [rɪ'fɜː(r)] (pt & pp **referred**) vt remitir; **to r. a matter to sb** remitir un asunto a alguien; **to r. a patient to a specialist** enviar a un paciente al especialista

►**refer to** vt insep (a) (consult) consultar (b) (allude to, mention) referirse a; **who are you referring to?** ¿a quién te estás refiriendo?; **referred to as...** conocido(a) como...; **he never refers to it** nunca hace referencia al asunto (c) (apply to) referirse a, ser aplicable a

**referee** [refə'riː] 1 n (a) (in sport) árbitro m (b) (for job) **please give the names of two referees** por favor dé los nombres de dos personas que puedan proporcionar referencias suyas
2 vt & vi arbitrar

**reference** ['refərəns] n (a) (consultation) consulta f; (source) referencia f; **for r. only** (book) para consulta en sala; **to keep sth for future r.** guardar algo para su posterior consulta; **r. book/work** libro m/obra f de consulta; **r. number** número m de referencia; **r. point, point of r.** punto m de referencia (b) (allusion) referencia f, alusión f; **with r. to...** con referencia a... (c) (from employer) informe m, referencia f

**referendum** [refə'rendəm] n referéndum m; **to hold a r.** celebrar un referéndum

**refill 1** n ['riːfɪl] (for notebook, pen) recambio m; **would you like a r.?** (of drink) ¿quieres otra copa?
2 vt [riː'fɪl] (glass) volver a llenar; (lighter, pen) recargar

**refine** [rɪ'faɪn] vt (sugar, petroleum) refinar; (technique, machine) perfeccionar

**refined** [rɪ'faɪnd] adj (a) (petroleum, sugar) refinado(a) (b) (person, taste) refinado(a), sofisticado(a)

**refinement** [rɪ'faɪnmənt] n (a) (of manners, taste, person) refinamiento m (b) (of technique) sofisticación f; **to make refinements to sth** perfeccionar algo

**refinery** [rɪ'faɪnərɪ] n refinería f

**refit** ['riːfɪt] 1 n (of ship) reparación f
2 vt [riː'fɪt] (pt & pp **refitted**) (ship) reparar

**reflate** [riː'fleɪt] vt Econ reflacionar

**reflation** [riː'fleɪʃən] n Econ reflación f

**reflect** [rɪ'flekt] 1 vt (a) (image, light) reflejar; **to be reflected** reflejarse (b) Fig (portray) reflejar (c) (think) **to r. that...** considerar que...
2 vi (a) (think) reflexionar (**on** sobre) (b) **to r. well/badly on sb** dejar en buen/mal lugar a alguien

**reflection** [rɪ'flekʃən] n (a) (reflected image) reflejo m; Fig **an accurate r. of the situation** un fiel reflejo de la situación; Fig **the termination of the project is no r. on your own performance** la cancelación del proyecto no significa que tú no lo hayas hecho bien (b) (thought) reflexión f; **on r.** después de pensarlo

**reflective** [rɪ'flektɪv] adj (a) (surface) reflectante (b) (person) reflexivo(a)

**reflector** [rɪ'flektə(r)] n (on bicycle, vehicle) reflectante m, catadióptrico m

**reflex** ['riːfleks] 1 n reflejo m
2 adj reflejo(a); **r. action** acto m reflejo; **r. camera** (cámara f) réflex f inv

**reflexive** [rɪ'fleksɪv] adj reflexivo(a); **r. verb** verbo m reflexivo

**reforestation** [riːfɒrɪ'steɪʃən] n reforestación f, repoblación f forestal

**reform** [rɪ'fɔːm] 1 n reforma f
2 vt (improve) reformar; **he's a reformed character** se ha reformado completamente
3 vi reformarse

**re-form** ['riː'fɔːm] vi (of organization, pop group) volver a unirse

**reformat** ['riː'fɔːmæt] (pt & pp **reformatted**) vt Comptr (disk) volver a formatear

**reformation** [refə'meɪʃən] n reforma f; Hist **the R.** la Reforma

**reformatory** [rɪ'fɔːmətərɪ] n reformatorio m

**reformer** [rɪ'fɔːmə(r)] n reformador(ora) m,f

**reformist** [rɪ'fɔːmɪst] n & adj reformista mf

**refract** [rɪ'frækt] vt (light) refractar

**refrain** [rɪ'freɪn] 1 n (musical) estribillo m; Fig (repeated comment) cantinela f
2 vi abstenerse (**from** de); **to r. from comment** abstenerse de hacer comentarios; **please r. from talking/smoking** (sign) se ruega guardar silencio/no fumar

**re-freeze** [riː'friːz] vt volver a congelar

**refresh** [rɪ'freʃ] vt refrescar; Comptr regenerar; **to r. oneself** refrescarse; **to r. one's memory** refrescar la memoria; **to r. sb's glass** (top up) llenarle el vaso a alguien

**refreshing** [rɪ'freʃɪŋ] adj (breeze, drink) refrescante

**refreshments** [rɪ'freʃmənts] npl refrigerio m

**refrigerate** [rɪ'frɪdʒəreɪt] vt refrigerar, conservar en (el) frigorífico

**refrigeration** [rɪfrɪdʒə'reɪʃən] n **keep under r.** manténgase en el frigorífico

**refrigerator** [rɪ'frɪdʒəreɪtə(r)] n (domestic) nevera f, frigorífico m; (industrial) cámara f frigorífica m

**refuel** [riː'fjʊəl] 1 vt (ship, aircraft) repostar combustible a
2 vi (of ship, aircraft) repostar

**refuge** ['refjuːdʒ] n (from danger, weather) refugio m; **to seek r.** buscar refugio; **to take r.** refugiarse

**refugee** [refjʊ'dʒiː] *n* refugiado(a) *m,f*; **r. camp** campo *m* de refugiados

**refund 1** *n* ['riːfʌnd] reintegro *m*, reembolso *m*
**2** *vt* [riːˈfʌnd] reembolsar

**refurbish** [riːˈfɜːbɪʃ] *vt (flat, restaurant)* remodelar

**refusal** [rɪˈfjuːzəl] *n* negativa *f*; **to give a flat r.** negarse rotundamente; **to meet with a r.** ser rechazado(a); **that's its third r.** *(of horse)* ha rehusado por tercera vez; **to have first r. (on sth)** tener opción de compra (sobre algo)

**refuse¹** ['refjuːs] *n (rubbish)* basura *f*; **r. collection** recogida *f* de basuras; **r. disposal** eliminación *f* de basuras; **r. dump** vertedero *m* (de basuras)

**refuse²** [rɪˈfjuːz] **1** *vt (invitation, offer, request)* rechazar; **to r. to do sth** negarse a hacer algo; **to r. sb sth** denegar algo a alguien
**2** *vi (of person)* negarse; *(of horse)* rehusar

**refute** [rɪˈfjuːt] *vt (argument, theory)* refutar; *(allegation)* desmentir, negar

**regain** [rɪˈgeɪn] *vt* (a) *(get back)* recuperar; **to r. consciousness** recobrar *or* recuperar el conocimiento; **to r. the lead** *(in contest)* volver a ponerse en cabeza (b) *(reach again) (shore, seat)* volver a alcanzar

**regal** ['riːgəl] *adj* regio(a)

**regale** [rɪˈgeɪl] *vt* divertir, entretener (**with** con)

**regalia** [rɪˈgeɪlɪə] *npl* galas *fpl*; **in full r.** con toda la parafernalia

**regard** [rɪˈgɑːd] **1** *n* (a) *(admiration)* admiración *f*, estima *f*; **to hold sb in high/low r.** tener mucha/poca estima a alguien (b) *(consideration)* consideración *f*; **out of r. for** por consideración hacia; **without r. to** *(safety, rules)* sin (ninguna) consideración por; *(gender, race)* independientemente de; **don't pay any r. to what she says** no hagas caso de lo que diga (c) *(connection)* **in this r.** en este sentido; **in all regards** en todos los sentidos *or* aspectos; **with r. to** en cuanto a, con respecto a (d) **regards** *(good wishes)* saludos *mpl*; **give her my regards** salúdala de mi parte
**2** *vt* (a) *(admire, respect)* **I r. him highly** tengo un alto concepto de él (b) *(consider)* **to r. sth/sb as...** considerar algo/a alguien...; **to r. sth/sb with suspicion** tener recelo de algo/alguien (c) *(concern)* concernir; **as regards...** en lo referente *or* concerniente a...

**regarding** [rɪˈgɑːdɪŋ] *prep* con respecto a, en cuanto a

**regardless** [rɪˈgɑːdlɪs] *adv* (a) *(despite everything)* a pesar de todo (b) **r. of** *(without considering)* sin tener en cuenta; **r. of the expense** cueste lo que cueste

**regatta** [rɪˈgætə] *n* regata *f*

**regency** ['riːdʒənsɪ] *n* regencia *f*

**regenerate** [rɪˈdʒenəreɪt] **1** *vt* regenerar
**2** *vi* regenerarse

**regeneration** [rɪdʒenəˈreɪʃən] *n* regeneración *f*

**regent** ['riːdʒənt] *adj* regente

**reggae** ['regeɪ] *n Mus* reggae *m*

**regime** [reɪˈʒiːm] *n (political)* régimen *m*

**regiment** ['redʒɪmənt] **1** *n (in army)* regimiento *m*
**2** *vt* someter a severa disciplina

**regimental** [redʒɪˈmentəl] *adj (band, flag)* de regimiento

**regimentation** [redʒɪmenˈteɪʃən] *n* severa disciplina *f*

**region** ['riːdʒən] *n* región *f*; **in the r. of** *(approximately)* alrededor de, del orden de

**regional** ['riːdʒənəl] *adj* regional

**regionalism** ['riːdʒənəlɪzəm] *n* regionalismo *m*

**register** ['redʒɪstə(r)] **1** *n (record) & Mus, Ling* registro *m*; *Sch* **to take the r.** pasar lista; **r. of births, marriages and deaths** registro *m* civil; **r. of voters** censo *m* electoral; *(cash)* **r. office** registro *m* civil
**2** *vt* (a) *(record) (member)* inscribir; *(student)* matricular; *(birth, marriage, death)* registrar; *(complaint, protest)* presentar (b) *(show) (temperature, speed)* registrar; *(astonishment, displeasure)* denotar, mostrar (c) *(realize) (fact, problem)* darse cuenta de, enterarse de (d) *(achieve) (progress)* realizar
**3** *vi* (a) *(for course)* matricularse; *(at hotel)* inscribirse, registrarse; *(of voter)* inscribirse (en el censo) (b) *Fam (of fact)* **it didn't r. with him** no se enteró

**registered** ['redʒɪstɜːd] *adj* **r. letter** carta *f* certificada; **r. trademark** marca *f* registrada

**registrar** ['redʒɪstrɑː(r)] *n* (a) *(record keeper)* registrador(ora) *m,f* (b) *Univ* secretario(a) *m,f* (c) *(in hospital)* doctor(ora) *m,f*, médico(a) *m,f*

**registration** [redʒɪsˈtreɪʃən] *n (of student)* matriculación *f*; *(of voter)* inscripción *f* (en el censo); *(of birth, death, marriage)* registro *m*; *Aut* **r. number** (número *m* de) matrícula *f*

**registry office** ['redʒɪstrɪˈɒfɪs] *n* registro *m* civil

**regress** [rɪˈgres] *vi* involucionar, sufrir una regresión

**regression** [rɪˈgreʃən] *n* regresión *f*

**regressive** [rɪˈgresɪv] *adj* regresivo(a)

**regret** [rɪˈgret] **1** *n (remorse)* remordimiento *m*; *(sadness)* pesar *m*; **she sent her regrets** mandó sus disculpas *or* excusas
**2** *vt (pt & pp regretted)* sentir, lamentar; **to r. doing** *or* **having done sth** arrepentirse de *or* lamentar haber hecho algo; **I r. to (have to) inform you that...** siento (tener que) comunicarte que...

**regretful** [rɪˈgretfʊl] *adj (remorseful)* arrepentido(a); *(sad)* apesadumbrado(a), pesaroso(a)

**regrettable** [rɪˈgretəbəl] *adj* lamentable

**regroup** [riːˈgruːp] **1** *vt* reagrupar
**2** *vi* reagruparse

**regular** [ˈregjʊlə(r)] **1** *n (in bar, restaurant)* habitual *mf*, parroquiano(a) *m,f*
**2** *adj* **(a)** *(features, pulse, verb)* regular; **on a r. basis** con regularidad, regularmente; **as r. as clockwork** como un reloj, con una regularidad cronométrica **(b)** *(normal, habitual)* habitual; *(in size)* normal, mediano(a) **(c)** *(army, soldier)* profesional **(d)** *Fam (for emphasis)* verdadero(a), auténtico(a)

**regularity** [regjʊˈlærɪtɪ] *n* regularidad *f*

**regulate** [ˈregjʊleɪt] *vt* regular

**regulation** [regjʊˈleɪʃən] **1** *n* **(a)** *(action)* regulación *f* **(b)** *(rule)* regla *f*, norma *f*; **regulations** reglamento *m*, normas *fpl*
**2** *adj (size, dress)* reglamentario(a)

**regulator** [ˈregjʊleɪtə(r)] *n (device)* regulador *m*; *(regulatory body)* organismo *m* regulador

**regulatory** [regjʊˈleɪtərɪ] *adj* regulador(ora)

**regurgitate** [rɪˈgɜːdʒɪteɪt] *vt* regurgitar

**rehabilitate** [riːhəˈbɪlɪteɪt] *vt* rehabilitar

**rehabilitation** [riːhəbɪlɪˈteɪʃən] *n* rehabilitación *f*

**rehash 1** [ˈriːhæʃ] *n* refrito *m*
**2** *vt* [riːˈhæʃ] hacer un refrito con

**rehearsal** [rɪˈhɜːsəl] *n* ensayo *m*

**rehearse** [rɪˈhɜːs] *vt & vi* ensayar

**rehouse** [riːˈhaʊz] *vt* realojar

**reign** [reɪn] **1** *n* reinado *m*
**2** *vi* reinar

**reigning** [ˈreɪnɪŋ] *adj (monarch)* reinante; *(champion)* actual

**reimburse** [riːɪmˈbɜːs] *vt* reembolsar

**rein** [reɪn] *n also Fig* rienda *f*; *Fig* **to give sb free r. to do sth** dar carta blanca a alguien para hacer algo; *Fig* **to give free r. to one's imagination** dar rienda suelta a la imaginación; *Fig* **to keep a tight r. on sth** llevar algo muy controlado; **to keep a tight r. on sb** atar corto a alguien

**reincarnate** [riːɪnˈkɑːneɪt] *vt* **to be reincarnated** reencarnarse

**reincarnation** [riːɪnkɑːˈneɪʃən] *n* reencarnación *f*

**reindeer** [ˈreɪndɪə(r)] *n* reno *m*

**reinforce** [riːɪnˈfɔːs] *vt* reforzar; **reinforced concrete** hormigón *m* armado

**reinforcement** [riːɪnˈfɔːsmənt] *n* refuerzo *m*; *Mil* **reinforcements** refuerzos *mpl*

**reinsert** [riːɪnˈsɜːt] *vt* volver a introducir

**reinstate** [riːɪnˈsteɪt] *vt (person in job)* restituir (en el puesto); *(clause)* reincorporar; *(law, practice)* reinstaurar

**reinsurance** [riːɪnˈʃʊərəns] *n* reaseguro *m*

**reinsure** [riːɪnˈʃʊə(r)] *vt* reasegurar

**reinvent** [riːɪnˈvent] *vt* **to r. the wheel** reinventar la rueda, = perder el tiempo haciendo algo que ya está hecho

**reinvest** [riːɪnˈvest] *vt* reinvertir

**reissue** [riːˈɪʃuː] **1** *n (of book, record)* reedición *f*; *(of bank note)* nueva emisión *f*
**2** *vt (book, record)* reeditar; *(bank note)* emitir de nuevo

**reiterate** [riːˈɪtəreɪt] *vt* reiterar

**reiteration** [riːɪtəˈreɪʃən] *n* reiteración *f*

**reject 1** [ˈriːdʒekt] *n (object)* artículo *m* con tara o defectuoso; *Fam (person)* inútil *mf*, inepto(a) *m,f*
**2** *vt* [rɪˈdʒekt] rechazar; **to feel rejected** sentirse rechazado(a)

**rejection** [rɪˈdʒekʃən] *n* rechazo *m*; **to meet with r.** ser rechazado(a)

**rejoice** [rɪˈdʒɔɪs] *vi* alegrarse

**rejoicing** [rɪˈdʒɔɪsɪŋ] *n* regocijo *m*, alegría *f*

**rejoin¹** [riːˈdʒɔɪn] *vt* **(a)** *(join again) (party, firm)* reincorporarse a **(b)** *(meet again)* reunirse con

**rejoin²** [rɪˈdʒɔɪn] *vt & vi (retort)* replicar

**rejoinder** [rɪˈdʒɔɪndə(r)] *n* réplica *f*

**rejuvenate** [rɪˈdʒuːvɪneɪt] *vt* rejuvenecer

**rekindle** [riːˈkɪndəl] *vt (fire, enthusiasm, hope)* reavivar

**relapse** *Med* **1** [ˈriːlæps] *n* recaída *f*
**2** *vi* [rɪˈlæps] recaer, sufrir una recaída

**relate** [rɪˈleɪt] **1** *vt* **(a)** *(narrate)* relatar, narrar **(b)** *(connect) (two facts, ideas)* relacionar
**2** *vi* **(a)** **to r. to** *(be relevant to)* estar relacionado(a) con **(b)** **to r. to** *(understand)* comprender, entender; **she doesn't r. to other children very well** no se entiende mucho con los demás niños

**related** [rɪˈleɪtɪd] *adj (linked)* relacionado(a); **to be r. to sb** *(of same family)* ser pariente de alguien

**relation** [rɪˈleɪʃən] *n* **(a)** *(relative)* pariente *mf* **(b)** *(connection)* relación *f*; **to bear no r. to** no guardar relación con; **in r. to** en relación a

**relationship** [rɪˈleɪʃənʃɪp] *n* **(a)** *(between people, countries)* relación *f*; *(kinship)* parentesco *m*; **to have a good/bad r. with sb** llevarse bien/mal con alguien **(b)** *(connection)* relación *f*

**relative** [ˈrelətɪv] **1** *n (person)* pariente *mf*
**2** *adj (comparative)* relativo(a); **r. to** con relación a; *Gram* **r. clause** oración *f* relativa

**relatively** [ˈrelətɪvlɪ] *adv* relativamente

**relativity** [reləˈtɪvɪtɪ] *n Phys* relatividad *f*

**relax** [rɪˈlæks] **1** *vt (person, muscles, discipline)* relajar; **to r. one's grip** dejar de apretar
**2** *vi (of person, muscles, discipline)* relajarse; **r.!** *(calm down)* ¡tranquilízate!

**relaxation** [ri:læk'seɪʃən] n (of person, muscles, discipline) relajación f; **a form of** r. una forma de relajarse

**relaxed** [rɪ'lækst] adj (atmosphere, person) relajado(a)

**relaxing** [rɪ'læksɪŋ] adj relajante

**relay** n ['ri:leɪ] (of workers) relevo m, turno m; **to work in relays** trabajar por turnos; r. **(race)** carrera f de relevos; Rad & TV r. **station** repetidor m
**2** vt [rɪ'leɪ] Rad TV retransmitir; (information) pasar

**release** [rɪ'li:s] **1** n **(a)** (of prisoner) liberación f; (of gas) emisión f; (from care, worry) alivio m **(b)** (of book, record) publicación f; (of film) estreno m; **new releases** (records) novedades fpl (discográficas); **to be on general** r. (of film) estar en cartel
**2** vt **(a)** (prisoner) liberar, soltar; (gas, fumes) desprender, emitir; (balloon, bomb) soltar; (brake) soltar; (funds) desbloquear; **to r. sb from an obligation** liberar a alguien de una obligación; **to r. sb's hand** soltar la mano a alguien **(b)** (book, record) publicar; (film) estrenar; (news, information) hacer público(a)

**relegate** ['relɪgeɪt] vt relegar; **United were relegated** el United bajó de categoría or descendió

**relegation** [relɪ'geɪʃən] n (of person) relegación f; (of team) descenso m

**relent** [rɪ'lent] vi (of storm, wind) amainar; (of person) ceder, ablandarse

**relentless** [rɪ'lentlɪs] adj implacable

**relevance** ['reləvəns] n pertinencia f; **to have no r. to sth** no tener nada que ver con algo

**relevant** ['reləvənt] adj pertinente; **that's not r.** eso no viene al caso; **the r. chapters** los capítulos correspondientes; **the r. facts** los hechos que vienen al caso; **the r. authorities** la autoridad competente; **her ideas are still r. today** sus ideas siguen teniendo vigencia

**reliability** [rɪlaɪə'bɪlɪtɪ] n fiabilidad f

**reliable** [rɪ'laɪəbəl] adj (person, machine) fiable; (information) fidedigno(a), fiable; **from a r. source** de fuentes fidedignas

**reliably** [rɪ'laɪəblɪ] adv **to be r. informed that…** saber de buena fuente que…

**reliance** [rɪ'laɪəns] n (dependence) dependencia f (on de); (trust) confianza f (on en)

**reliant** [rɪ'laɪənt] adj **to be r. on** depender de

**relic** ['relɪk] n Rel & Fig reliquia f

**relief** [rɪ'li:f] n **(a)** (in general) alivio m; **to bring r. to sb** aliviar a alguien; **that's a r.!** ¡qué alivio! **much to my r.** para mi tranquilidad **(b)** (help) ayuda f, auxilio m; r. **fund** fondo m de ayuda **(c)** (replacement) relevo m **(d)** (of besieged city, troops) liberación f **(e)** Art relieve m;

**in r.** en relieve; **to throw sth into r.** poner algo de relieve; r. **map** mapa m de relieve

**relieve** [rɪ'li:v] vt **(a)** (alleviate) (pain, anxiety, problem) aliviar; (tension, boredom) atenuar, mitigar; **to feel relieved** sentirse aliviado(a); Euph **he relieved himself** hizo sus necesidades **(b)** (replace) relevar **(c)** (liberate) (city) liberar; **to r. sb from a duty** liberar a alguien de una obligación; Hum **to r. sb of his wallet** birlarle a alguien la cartera

**religion** [rɪ'lɪdʒən] n religión f

**religious** [rɪ'lɪdʒəs] adj religioso(a)

**religiously** [rɪ'lɪdʒəslɪ] adv also Fig religiosamente

**relinquish** [rɪ'lɪŋkwɪʃ] vt renunciar a; **to r. one's hold on sth** renunciar a algo

**relish** ['relɪʃ] **1** n **(a)** (pleasure) deleite m, goce m; **to do sth with r.** hacer algo con gran deleite **(b)** (pickle) salsa f condimentada
**2** vt gozar con, deleitarse en; **I didn't r. the idea** no me entusiasmaba la idea

**relive** [ri:'lɪv] vt revivir

**relocate** [ri:ləʊ'keɪt] **1** vt trasladar
**2** vi mudarse, trasladarse

**relocation** [ri:ləʊ'keɪʃən] n traslado m

**reluctance** [rɪ'lʌktəns] n resistencia f, reticencia f; **to do sth with r.** hacer algo a regañadientes

**reluctant** [rɪ'lʌktənt] adj reacio(a), reticente; **to be r. to do sth** ser reacio(a) a hacer algo

**►rely on, rely upon** [rɪ'laɪ] vt insep **(a)** (count on) contar con; **I'm relying on you to do it** cuento con que vas a hacerlo **(b)** (be dependent on) depender de

**REM** [a:ri:'em] n (abbr **rapid eye movement**) (fase f) REM m, movimientos mpl oculares rápidos

**remain** [rɪ'meɪn] vi **(a)** (stay behind) permanecer, quedarse **(b)** (be left) quedar; **it remains to be seen** queda or está por ver **(c)** (continue to be) seguir siendo; **to r. silent** permanecer callado(a); **to r. faithful to** permanecer fiel a

**remainder** [rɪ'meɪndə(r)] n resto m

**remaindered** [rɪ'meɪndəd] adj r. **books** libros mpl de saldo

**remaining** [rɪ'meɪnɪŋ] adj restante

**remains** [rɪ'meɪnz] npl (of meal) sobras fpl, restos mpl; (of civilization, fortune) restos mpl; (of old building) ruinas fpl; (of person) restos mpl (mortales); **human r.** restos mpl humanos

**remake** ['ri:meɪk] n (of film) nueva versión f

**remand** [rɪ'mɑ:nd] **1** n Law **to be on r.** (in custody) estar en prisión preventiva; r. **home** = centro de reclusión para delincuentes juveniles a la espera de juicio; r. **prisoner** preso(a) m,f preventivo(a)
**2** vt Law **to r. sb in custody** poner a alguien en prisión preventiva

**remark** [rɪ'mɑ:k] **1** *n (comment)* comentario *m*; **to make** *or* **pass a r.** hacer un comentario **2** *vt* comentar, observar

**remarkable** [rɪ'mɑ:kəbəl] *adj (impressive)* notable, excepcional; *(surprising)* insólito(a), sorprendente

**remarkably** [rɪ'mɑ:kəblɪ] *adv (impressively)* excepcionalmente, extraordinariamente; *(surprisingly)* curiosamente, sorprendentemente

**remarry** [ri:'mærɪ] *vi* volver a casarse

**remedial** [rɪ'mi:dɪəl] *adj* correctivo(a); **r. education** educación *f* especial; **r. teacher** profesor(ora) *m,f* de educación especial

**remedy** ['remɪdɪ] **1** *n* remedio *m*; **it's past r.** ya no tiene remedio **2** *vt* poner remedio a, remediar

**remember** [rɪ'membə(r)] **1** *vt* (a) *(recall)* recordar, acordarse de; **to r. doing sth** recordar haber hecho algo; **to r. to do sth** acordarse de hacer algo; **to r. that...** recordar que...; **a night to r.** una noche inolvidable; **r. me to your father!** dale recuerdos a tu padre de mi parte (b) *(commemorate)* recordar **2** *vi* recordar, acordarse; **as far as I r.** según recuerdo, por lo que yo recuerdo

**remembrance** [rɪ'membrəns] *n Formal (memory)* recuerdo *m*; **in r. of** en recuerdo *or* conmemoración de; **R. Day** día *m* de homenaje a los caídos *(en las guerras mundiales)*

**remind** [rɪ'maɪnd] *vt* recordar (**of** a); **to r. sb to do sth** recordar a alguien que haga algo; **that reminds me – did you get the cheese?** eso me recuerda *or* ahora que recuerdo... ¿has comprado el queso?

**reminder** [rɪ'maɪndə(r)] *n* aviso *m*

**reminisce** [remɪ'nɪs] *vi* **to r. about sth** rememorar algo

**reminiscence** [remɪ'nɪsəns] *n* rememoración *f*, remembranza *f*

**reminiscent** [remɪ'nɪsənt] *adj* **to be r. of** evocar, tener reminiscencias de

**remiss** [rɪ'mɪs] *adj* negligente, descuidado(a); **it was very r. of him** fue muy descuidado por su parte

**remission** [rɪ'mɪʃən] *n* (a) *Law* reducción *f* de la pena (b) *(of disease)* **to be in r.** haber remitido

**remit 1** *n* ['ri:mɪt] cometido *m*; **that goes beyond/comes within our r.** eso está fuera de/dentro de nuestro ámbito de actuación **2** *vt* [rɪ'mɪt] *(pt & pp* **remitted**) *(payment)* remitir, girar

**remittance** [rɪ'mɪtəns] *n Fin* giro *m*, envío *m* de dinero

**remnant** ['remnənt] *n (of banquet, building)* resto *m*; *(of civilization, dignity)* vestigio *m*; *(of cloth)* retal *m*

**remonstrate** ['remənstreɪt] *vi* quejarse, protestar; **to r. with sb** tratar de hacer entrar en razón a alguien; **she remonstrated with him over his decision** trató de convencerle de que cambiara su decisión

**remorse** [rɪ'mɔ:s] *n* remordimientos *mpl*; **without r.** sin remordimientos; **to feel r.** tener remordimientos

**remorseful** [rɪ'mɔ:sfʊl] *adj* lleno(a) de remordimientos; **to be r.** tener remordimientos

**remorseless** [rɪ'mɔ:slɪs] *adj (merciless)* despiadado(a); *(relentless)* implacable

**remote** [rɪ'məʊt] *adj* (a) *(far-off)* remoto(a), lejano(a); **r. control** telemando *m*, mando *m* a distancia (b) *(aloof)* distante (c) *(slight) (chance, possibility)* remoto(a); **I haven't the remotest idea** no tengo ni la más remota idea

**remote-controlled** [rɪ'məʊtkən'trəʊld] *adj* teledirigido(a)

**remotely** [rɪ'məʊtlɪ] *adv* (a) *(distantly)* remotamente, lejanamente (b) *(slightly)* remotamente; **not r.** ni remotamente, ni de lejos

**remould** ['ri:məʊld] *n Aut* neumático *m* recauchutado

**removal** [rɪ'mu:vəl] *n* (a) *(of politician, official)* destitución *f*; *(of control, doubt, threat, stain)* eliminación *f* (b) *(moving house)* mudanza *f*; **r. van** camión *m* de mudanzas

**remove** [rɪ'mu:v] *vt* (a) *(take away) (thing)* quitar, retirar; *(doubt)* despejar; *(control, threat)* eliminar; *(stain)* quitar; *(politician, official)* destituir; **to r. a child from school** no llevar más a un niño al colegio (b) *(take off) (coat, hat)* quitarse; *(tyre)* quitar

**remover** [rɪ'mu:və(r)] *n* (a) **paint r.** decapante *m*; **nail varnish r.** quitaesmaltes *m inv* (b) *(furniture)* **removers** *(people)* empleados *mpl* de mudanzas; *(firm)* (empresa *f* de) mudanzas *fpl*

**remunerate** [rɪ'mju:nəreɪt] *vt Formal* remunerar, retribuir

**remuneration** [rɪmju:nə'reɪʃən] *n Formal* remuneración *f*, retribución *f*

**remunerative** [rɪ'mju:nərətɪv] *adj Formal* remunerado(a)

**renaissance** [rɪ'neɪsəns] *n* renacimiento *m*; **the R.** el Renacimiento

**renal** ['ri:nəl] *adj Anat* renal

**rename** [ri:'neɪm] *vt* cambiar el nombre a

**rend** [rend] *(pt & pp* **rent** [rent]) *vt Literary (tear)* desgarrar; **the country was rent by civil war** el país quedó destrozado por la guerra civil

**render** ['rendə(r)] *vt* (a) *Formal (give)* **to r. homage to sb** rendir homenaje a alguien; **for services rendered** por los servicios prestados (b) *(cause to be)* dejar; **the news rendered her speechless** la noticia la dejó sin habla (c) *(translate)* traducir; **to r. sth into French** traducir algo al francés

**rendezvous** ['rɒndɪvuː] **1** *n* (*pl* **rendezvous** ['rɒndɪvuːz]) (*meeting*) cita *f*; (*meeting place*) lugar *m* de encuentro

**2** *vi* encontrarse, reunirse

**rendition** [ren'dɪʃən] *n* versión *f*

**renegade** ['renɪgeɪd] *n* renegado(a) *m,f*

**renege** [rɪ'neɪg] *vi* **to r. on a promise** incumplir una promesa

**renew** [rɪ'njuː] *vt* (*passport, membership*) renovar; (*attempts, calls, attacks*) renovar, reanudar; (*relations, friendship*) reanudar

**renewable** [rɪ'njuːəbəl] *adj* renovable; **r. energy source** fuente *f* de energía renovable

**renewal** [rɪ'njuːəl] *n* (*of passport, membership*) renovación *f*; (*of attempts, calls, attacks*) reanudación *f*

**rennet** ['renɪt] *n Culin* cuajo *m*

**renounce** [rɪ'naʊns] *vt* renunciar a

**renovate** ['renəveɪt] *vt* renovar, restaurar

**renovation** [renə'veɪʃən] *n* renovación *f*, restauración *f*

**renown** [rɪ'naʊn] *n* fama *f*, renombre *m*

**renowned** [rɪ'naʊnd] *adj* célebre, renombrado(a)

**rent**¹ [rent] **1** *n* (*on flat, house*) alquiler *m*; **for r.** en alquiler; **how much r. do you pay?** ¿cuánto pagas de alquiler?; *Br Fam* **r. boy** (*male prostitute*) chapero *m*

**2** *vt* (*flat, video, car*) alquilar, *Am* rentar

**rent**² *pt & pp of* **rend**

**rental** ['rentəl] *n* alquiler *m*

**rent-free** [rent'friː] **1** *adj* exento(a) del pago de alquiler

**2** *adv* sin pagar alquiler

**reopen** [riː'əʊpən] **1** *vt* (*frontier, investigation*) reabrir; (*talks*) reanudar; *Fig* **to r. old wounds** abrir viejas heridas

**2** *vi* (*of shop, theatre*) volver a abrir; **school reopens on the 21st of August** las clases se reanudan el 21 de agosto

**reorder** [riː'ɔːdə(r)] *vt Com* pedir de nuevo

**reorganize** [riː'ɔːgənaɪz] *vt* reorganizar

**reorganization** [riːɔːgənaɪ'zeɪʃən] *n* reorganización *f*

**rep** [rep] *n Fam* (*salesman*) representante *mf*, comercial *mf*

**repaint** [riː'peɪnt] *vt* repintar

**repair** [rɪ'peə(r)] **1** *n* reparación *f*; (*of shoes, clothes*) arreglo *m*; **to be beyond r.** no poderse arreglar; **to be in good/bad r.** estar en buen/mal estado; **to be under r.** estar en reparación; **r. shop** taller *m*

**2** *vt* (*watch, car, machine*) reparar; (*shoes, clothes, road*) arreglar

**repairman** [rɪ'peəmæn] *n* técnico *m*

**reparation** [repə'reɪʃən] *n* (**a**) *Formal* compensación *f*, reparación *f*; **to make r. for sth** compensar por algo (**b**) (*after war*) **reparations** indemnizaciones *fpl* (de guerra)

**repartee** [repɑː'tiː] *n* pulso *m* verbal a base de agudezas

**repast** [rɪ'pɑːst] *n Literary* colación *f*, comida *f*

**repatriate** [riː'pætrɪeɪt] *vt* repatriar

**repatriation** [riːpætrɪ'eɪʃən] *n* repatriación *f*

**repay** [riː'peɪ] (*pt & pp* **repaid** [riː'peɪd]) *vt* (**a**) (*money*) devolver; (*person*) pagar; (*debt*) saldar (**b**) (*person for kindness, help*) recompensar; (*kindness, loyalty*) pagar

**repayable** [riː'peɪəbəl] *adj* (*loan*) pagadero(a), a devolver (**over** en)

**repayment** [riː'peɪmənt] *n* pago *m*, devolución *f*; **r. plan** plan *m* de amortización

**repeal** [rɪ'piːl] *vt* (*law, regulation*) derogar, abrogar

**repeat** [rɪ'piːt] **1** *n* (*of event, TV programme*) repetición *f*

**2** *vt* repetir; **to r. oneself** repetirse; **don't r. this, but...** no se lo cuentes a nadie, pero...

**repeated** [rɪ'piːtɪd] *adj* repetido(a)

**repeatedly** [rɪ'piːtɪdlɪ] *adv* repetidas veces, repetidamente

**repel** [rɪ'pel] (*pt & pp* **repelled**) *vt* (*throw back*) repeler, rechazar; (*disgust*) repeler, repugnar

**repellent** [rɪ'pelənt] **1** *n* (*for insects*) repelente *m* (antiinsectos)

**2** *adj* repelente

**repent** [rɪ'pent] **1** *vt* arrepentirse de

**2** *vi* arrepentirse (**of** de)

**repentance** [rɪ'pentəns] *n* arrepentimiento *m*

**repentant** [rɪ'pentənt] *adj* arrepentido(a); **to be r.** estar arrepentido(a)

**repercussion** [riːpə'kʌʃən] *n* repercusión *f*

**repertoire** ['repətwɑː(r)] *n* repertorio *m*

**repertory** ['repətərɪ] *n Th* **r. company** compañía *f* de repertorio

**repetition** [repɪ'tɪʃən] *n* repetición *f*

**repetitious** [repɪ'tɪʃəs] *adj* repetitivo(a)

**repetitive** [rɪ'petɪtɪv] *adj* (*style, job*) repetitivo(a)

**rephrase** [riː'freɪz] *vt* reformular, expresar de forma diferente

**replace** [rɪ'pleɪs] *vt* (**a**) (*put back*) volver a poner, devolver; **to r. the receiver** colgar (el teléfono) (**b**) (*substitute for*) sustituir, reemplazar (**with/by** por); (*tyre, broken part*) (re)cambiar

**replacement** [rɪ'pleɪsmənt] *n* (**a**) (*act of putting back*) devolución *f*; (*act of substituting*) sustitución *f*; (*of tyre, broken part*) (re)cambio *m*; *Fin* **r. cost** coste *m* de sustitución; **r. parts** piezas *fpl* de recambio; **r. value** valor *m* de reposición (**b**) *(for person)* sustituto(a) *m,f*

**replay 1** *n* ['ri:pleɪ] *(of football match)* repetición *f* (del partido); (**action**) **r.** *(on TV)* repetición *f* (de la jugada)

**2** *vt* [ri:'pleɪ] *(match)* jugar de nuevo

**replenish** [rɪ'plenɪʃ] *vt (cup, tank)* rellenar; **to r. one's supplies** surtirse de provisiones

**replete** [rɪ'pli:t] *adj Formal* repleto(a) (**with** de)

**replica** ['replɪkə] *n* réplica *f*

**replicate** ['replɪkeɪt] *vt* reproducir

**reply** [rɪ'plaɪ] **1** *n* respuesta *f*, contestación *f*; **in r.** en *or* como respuesta; **there was no r.** *(to telephone)* no contestaban, no había nadie

**2** *vi* responder, contestar; **to r. to a letter** contestar a una carta

**report** [rɪ'pɔːt] **1** *n* (**a**) *(account)* informe *m*; *(in newspaper, on radio, television)* reportaje *m*; **there are reports that…** circula el rumor *or* corre la voz de que…; *Sch* **r.** *(card)* boletín *m* de evaluación (**b**) *(sound)* estallido *m*, explosión *f*

**2** *vt (information)* informar de; *(accident, theft)* dar parte de; **the incident was reported in the local press** la prensa local informó del incidente; **it is reported that the Prime Minister is about to resign** se ha informado de la inminente dimisión del primer ministro; **to r. sb missing** denunciar la desaparición de alguien; **to r. sb to the police** denunciar a alguien a la policía; **she reported her findings to him** le informó de *or* le dio a conocer sus hallazgos

**3** *vi* (**a**) *(present oneself)* presentarse; **to r. for duty** presentarse para el servicio (**b**) *(give account)* informar; *(of journalist)* informar (**on** sobre); **she reported to her boss** informó a su jefe (**c**) *(be accountable)* **to r. to sb** ser responsable ante alguien

**reportedly** [rɪ'pɔːtɪdlɪ] *adv* según se dice; **he is r. resident in Paris** según se dice, reside en París

**reporter** [rɪ'pɔːtə(r)] *n* reportero(a) *m,f*

**repose** [rɪ'pəʊz] *Formal* **1** *n* reposo *m*

**2** *vi* reposar

**repository** [rɪ'pɒzɪtərɪ] *n (for books, furniture)* depósito *m*; *(of knowledge)* arsenal *m*, depositario(a) *m,f*

**repossess** [ri:pə'zes] *vt Fin* embargar (definitivamente)

**reprehensible** [reprɪ'hensɪbəl] *adj* censurable, recriminable

**represent** [reprɪ'zent] *vt (depict, symbolize)* representar; *(describe)* presentar, describir; **to r. a company** representar a una empresa; **this represents a great improvement** esto representa una gran mejora

**representation** [reprɪzen'teɪʃən] *n (of facts, in Parliament)* representación *f*; *Formal* **to make representations (to sb)** presentar una protesta (ante alguien)

**representative** [reprɪ'zentətɪv] **1** *n* representante *mf*

**2** *adj* representativo(a)

**repress** [rɪ'pres] *vt* reprimir

**repressed** [rɪ'prest] *adj* **to be r.** estar reprimido(a)

**repression** [rɪ'preʃən] *n* represión *f*

**repressive** [rɪ'presɪv] *adj* represivo(a)

**reprieve** [rɪ'priːv] **1** *n Law* indulto *m*; *Fig* **to win a r.** *(of project, company)* salvarse de momento

**2** *vt Law* indultar; *Fig (project, company)* salvar de momento

**reprimand** ['reprɪmɑːnd] **1** *n* reprimenda *f*

**2** *vt* reprender

**reprint 1** *n* ['riːprɪnt] reimpresión *f*

**2** *vt* [riː'prɪnt] reimprimir

**reprisal** [rɪ'praɪzəl] *n* represalia *f*; **to take reprisals** tomar represalias; **in r. for** en represalia por

**reproach** [rɪ'prəʊtʃ] **1** *n* reproche *m*; **beyond** *or* **above r.** irreprochable, intachable

**2** *vt* hacer reproches a; **to r. sb for (doing) sth** reprochar (el haber hecho) algo a alguien; **to r. oneself for sth** reprocharse algo

**reproachful** [rɪ'prəʊtʃfʊl] *adj (tone, look)* de reproche

**reprobate** ['reprəbeɪt] *n* granujilla *mf*, tunante *mf*

**reproduce** [ri:prə'djuːs] **1** *vt* reproducir

**2** *vi* reproducirse

**reproduction** [ri:prə'dʌkʃən] *n* reproducción *f*; **r. furniture** reproducciones *fpl* de muebles antiguos

**reproductive** [ri:prə'dʌktɪv] *adj Biol* reproductor(ora); **r. organs** órganos *mpl* reproductores

**reproof** [rɪ'pruːf] *n Formal* reprobación *f*, desaprobación *f*

**reprove** [rɪ'pruːv] *vt Formal* recriminar, reprobar

**reproving** [rɪ'pruːvɪŋ] *adj Formal* de reprobación, reprobatorio(a)

**reptile** ['reptaɪl] *n* reptil *m*

**reptilian** [rep'tɪlɪən] *adj also Fig* de reptil

**republic** [rɪ'pʌblɪk] *n* república *f*

**republican** [rɪ'pʌblɪkən] *n & adj* republicano(a) *m,f*

**repudiate** [rɪ'pjuːdɪeɪt] *vt Formal (offer)* rechazar; *(rumour, remark)* desmentir

**repudiation** [rɪpjuːdɪ'eɪʃən] *n (of offer)* rechazo *m*; *(of rumour, remark)* desmentido *m*

**repugnant** [rɪ'pʌɡnənt] *adj* repugnante

**repulse** [rɪ'pʌls] vt *(army, attack)* rechazar; **I am repulsed by your heartlessness** me repulsa tu crueldad

**repulsive** [rɪ'pʌlsɪv] *adj* repulsivo(a)

**reputable** ['repjʊtəbəl] *adj* reputado(a), acreditado(a)

**reputation** [repjʊ'teɪʃən] *n (of person, shop)* reputación *f*; **to have a good/bad r.** tener buena/mala reputación *or* fama; **to have a r. for frankness** tener fama de franco(a); **they lived up to their r.** hicieron honor a su reputación

**repute** [rɪ'pjuːt] **1** *n Formal* reputación *f*, fama *f*; **of r.** de prestigio; **to be held in high r.** estar muy bien considerado(a)

**2** vt **to be reputed to be wealthy/a genius** tener fama de rico/de ser un genio; **the reputed author of the work** el supuesto autor de la obra

**reputedly** [rɪ'pjuːtɪdlɪ] *adv* según parece, según se dice

**request** [rɪ'kwest] **1** *n* petición *f*, solicitud *f*; **to make a r. (for sth)** hacer una petición (de algo); **available on r.** disponible mediante solicitud; **by popular r.** a petición del público; **r. stop** *(for bus)* parada *f* discrecional

**2** vt pedir, solicitar; **to r. sb to do sth** pedir *or* solicitar a alguien que haga algo; **passengers are requested not to smoke** se ruega a los señores pasajeros se abstengan de fumar; **as requested** como se solicitaba

**requiem** ['rekwɪəm] *n Mus* réquiem *m*; *Rel* **r. (mass)** misa *f* de difuntos

**require** [rɪ'kwaɪə(r)] vt requerir, necesitar; **you are required to…** se le pide que…; **if required** si es necesario; **when required** cuando sea necesario

**requirement** [rɪ'kwaɪəmənt] *n* requisito *m*

**requisite** ['rekwɪzɪt] **1** *npl* **requisites** *(necessary conditions)* requisitos *mpl*; *(objects)* accesorios *mpl*, artículos *mpl*

**2** *adj* necesario(a), requerido(a); **without the r. care** sin el debido cuidado

**requisition** [rekwɪ'zɪʃən] vt *(supplies)* requisar

**rerun** ['riːrʌn] *n (on TV)* reposición *f*; *(of situation, conflict)* repetición *f*

**resale** [riːˈseɪl] *n* reventa *f*

**reschedule** [riːˈʃedjuːl] vt *(meeting, flight)* volver a programar; *(debt)* renegociar

**rescind** [rɪ'sɪnd] vt *Law (law)* derogar; *(contract)* rescindir

**rescue** ['reskjuː] **1** *n* rescate *m*; **to come to sb's r.** acudir al rescate de alguien; **r. services** servicios *mpl* de salvamento

**2** vt rescatar

**rescuer** ['reskjuːə(r)] *n* salvador(ora) *m,f*

**research** [rɪ'sɜːtʃ] **1** *n* investigación *f*; **to do r. into sth** investigar algo; **r. and development** investigación y desarrollo; **r. assistant** ayudante *mf* de investigación; **r. laboratory** laboratorio *m* de investigación

**2** vt investigar; **a well researched book** un libro muy bien documentado

**3** vi investigar; **to r. into sth** investigar algo

**researcher** [rɪ'sɜːtʃə(r)] *n* investigador(ora) *m,f*

**resemblance** [rɪ'zembləns] *n* parecido *m*, similitud *f*; **to bear a r. to sb/sth** guardar parecido con alguien/algo

**resemble** [rɪ'zembəl] vt parecerse a

**resent** [rɪ'zent] vt sentirse molesto(a) por; **I r. his interference** me parece mal que se entrometa; **I r. being treated like an idiot** me molesta que me traten como a un imbécil; **I r. that!** ¡eso no me parece nada bien!; **they obviously resented my presence** evidentemente, les molestaba mi presencia

**resentful** [rɪ'zentfʊl] *adj* resentido(a); **to be** *or* **feel r.** estar resentido(a)

**resentment** [rɪ'zentmənt] *n* resentimiento *m*; **to feel r. towards sb** tener resentimiento hacia alguien

**reservation** [rezə'veɪʃən] *n* **(a)** *(booking)* reserva *f*; **to make a r.** hacer una reserva; **r. desk** mostrador *m* de reservas **(b)** *(doubt)* reserva *f*; **without r.** sin reservas **(c)** *(Indian)* **r.** reserva *f* india

**reserve** [rɪ'zɜːv] **1** *n* **(a)** *(supply)* reserva *f*; **to keep sth in r.** reservar algo, tener algo en reserva; **he drew on his reserves** echó mano de sus reservas **(b)** *Sport* reserva *mf*; *Mil* **the reserves** la reserva **(c)** *(for birds, game)* reserva *f*; **game r.** coto *m* de caza; **nature r.** reserva natural **(d)** *(reticence)* reserva *f*; **without r.** sin reservas

**2** vt *(book, keep)* reservar; **to r. the right to do sth** reservarse el derecho a hacer algo; **to r. one's strength** ahorrar *or* reservar fuerzas; **to r. judgement (on sth)** reservarse la opinión (sobre algo)

**reserved** [rɪ'zɜːvd] *adj* reservado(a)

**reservist** [rɪ'zɜːvɪst] *n Mil* reservista *mf*

**reservoir** ['rezəvwɑː(r)] *n (lake)* embalse *m*, pantano *m*; *Fig (of strength, courage)* reserva *f*, cúmulo *m*

**reset** [riː'set] *( pt & pp* **reset)** vt *(watch)* ajustar; *(counter)* poner a cero; *Med (bone)* colocar en su sitio; *Comptr* **r. button** *or* **switch** botón *m* para reinicializar

**reshape** [riːˈʃeɪp] vt *(plans, future)* rehacer, reorganizar; *(party, industry)* reestructurar, remodelar

**reshuffle** [ˈriːʃʌfəl] n Pol (Cabinet) r. reajuste m or remodelación f del Gabinete (ministerial)

**reside** [rɪˈzaɪd] vi (a) (of person) residir (b) (of power, quality) **to r. in** residir en, radicar en

**residence** [ˈrezɪdəns] n (a) (stay) estancia f; **she took up r. in London** fijó su residencia en Londres; **place of r.** lugar m de residencia; **r. permit** permiso m de residencia (b) Formal (home) residencia f (c) Br Univ **(hall of) r.** colegio m mayor

**resident** [ˈrezɪdənt] **1** n (of country, street) residente mf; (of hotel) residente mf, huésped mf; **residents' association** asociación f de vecinos

**2** adj residente; **to be r. in Manchester** residir en Manchester

**residential** [rezɪˈdenʃəl] adj residencial

**residual** [rɪˈzɪdjʊəl] adj residual

**residue** [ˈrezɪdjuː] n (remainder) resto m, residuo m; Chem residuo m

**resign** [rɪˈzaɪn] **1** vt (job, position) dimitir de, renunciar a; **to r. oneself to (doing) sth** resignarse a (hacer) algo

**2** vi dimitir

**resignation** [rezɪɡˈneɪʃən] n (a) (from job) dimisión f; **to hand in one's r.** presentar la dimisión (b) (attitude) resignación f

**resilience** [rɪˈzɪliəns] n (of material, metal) elasticidad f; (of person) capacidad f de recuperación

**resilient** [rɪˈzɪliənt] adj (material, metal) elástico(a); **to be r.** (of person, economy) tener capacidad de recuperación

**resin** [ˈrezɪn] n resina f

**resist** [rɪˈzɪst] **1** vt resistir; Law **to r. arrest** resistirse a la autoridad; **I couldn't r. telling him** no pude resistir la tentación de decírselo; **I can't r. chocolates** los bombones me resultan irresistibles

**2** vi resistir

**resistance** [rɪˈzɪstəns] n resistencia f; **to put up** or **offer r.** oponer or ofrecer resistencia; **to meet with no r.** no encontrar resistencia; **to take the line of least r.** tomar el camino más fácil; **r. fighter** miembro m de la resistencia

**resistant** [rɪˈzɪstənt] adj **to be r. to sth** (change, suggestion) mostrarse remiso(a) a aceptar algo, mostrar resistencia a algo; (disease) ser resistente a algo

**resistor** [rɪˈzɪstə(r)] n Elec resistencia f (componente)

**resit** [riːˈsɪt] (pt & pp **resat** [riːˈsæt]) vt (exam, driving test) presentarse de nuevo a

**resolute** [ˈrezəluːt] adj resuelto(a), decidido(a)

**resolution** [rezəˈluːʃən] n (a) (decision) (of individual) determinación f; (of committee) resolu-

ción f (b) (firmness) resolución f, decisión f (c) (solution) resolución f, solución f

**resolve** [rɪˈzɒlv] **1** n determinación f; **to make a firm r. to do sth** resolver firmemente hacer algo

**2** vt (a) (decide) **to r. to do sth** resolver hacer algo (b) (solve) resolver, solucionar

**3** vi **to r. on/against doing sth** tomar la resolución de hacer/no hacer algo

**resonance** [ˈrezənəns] n (of voice) resonancia f

**resonant** [ˈrezənənt] adj resonante

**resonate** [ˈrezəneɪt] vi resonar

**resort** [rɪˈzɔːt] **1** n (a) (recourse) recurso m; **to have r. to sth** recurrir a algo; **as a last r.** como último recurso (b) (holiday place) centro m turístico, lugar m de veraneo

**2** vi **to r. to** recurrir a

**resound** [rɪˈzaʊnd] vi (of voice) resonar, retumbar; **the stadium resounded with applause** los aplausos resonaban en el estadio, el estadio resonaba con aplausos

**resounding** [rɪˈzaʊndɪŋ] adj (crash) estruendoso(a); (applause) sonoro(a), clamoroso(a); (success, failure) clamoroso(a), sonado(a)

**resource** [rɪˈzɔːs] **1** n recurso m; **to be left to one's own resources** tener que arreglárselas solo(a); **r. management** gestión f de recursos

**2** vt (project) financiar

**resourceful** [rɪˈzɔːsfʊl] adj ingenioso(a), lleno(a) de recursos

**respect** [rɪˈspekt] **1** n (a) (admiration, consideration) respeto m; **to have r. for sth/sb** respetar algo/a alguien; **out of r. for...** por respeto hacia...; **to treat mountains with r.** respetar la montaña; **with all due r...** con el debido respeto...; **to pay one's last respects** decir el último adiós (b) (aspect) sentido m, aspecto m; **in some/certain respects** en algunos/ciertos aspectos; **in all respects, in every r.** en todos los sentidos; **with r. to, in r. of** con respecto a

**2** vt respetar

**respectability** [rɪspektəˈbɪlɪti] n respetabilidad f

**respectable** [rɪˈspektəbəl] adj (a) (honourable, decent) respetable (b) (fairly large) considerable, respetable; (fairly good) decente

**respectably** [rɪˈspektəbli] adv (a) (in a respectable manner) respetablemente (b) (fairly well) decentemente, pasablemente

**respectful** [rɪˈspektfʊl] adj respetuoso(a)

**respective** [rɪˈspektɪv] adj respectivo(a)

**respectively** [rɪˈspektɪvli] adv respectivamente

**respiration** [respɪˈreɪʃən] n respiración f

**respiratory** [rɪˈspɪrɪtəri] adj Anat respiratorio(a)

**respite** ['respait] *n* respiro *m*, tregua *f*; **to work without r.** trabajar sin tregua; **they gave her no r.** no le concedieron un momento de respiro, no le dieron cuartel

**resplendent** [rɪ'splendənt] *adj* resplandeciente; **to be r.** estar resplandeciente

**respond** [rɪ'spɒnd] *vi* responder; *Med* **to r. to treatment** responder al tratamiento

**respondent** [rɪ'spɒndənt] *n* (a) *Law* demandado(a) *m,f* (b) *(to questionnaire)* encuestado(a) *m,f*

**response** [rɪ'spɒns] *n* respuesta *f*; **in r. to** en respuesta a; **r. time** tiempo *m* de respuesta

**responsibility** [rɪspɒnsɪ'bɪlɪtɪ] *n* responsabilidad *f* (**for** de); **to take** *or* **accept full r. for sth** asumir toda la responsabilidad de algo; **answering the phone is his r., not mine** contestar el teléfono le corresponde a él, no a mí

**responsible** [rɪ'spɒnsɪbəl] *adj (trustworthy, accountable)* responsable; **to be r.** ser responsable de; **to hold sb r.** considerar a alguien responsable; **a r. job** un puesto de responsabilidad

**responsive** [rɪ'spɒnsɪv] *adj* **to be r.** *(to criticism, praise, idea, suggestion)* ser receptivo(a), responder bien; *(willing to participate)* demostrar interés; **to be r. to treatment** responder (bien) al tratamiento

**rest**[1] [rest] **1** *n* (a) *(repose)* descanso *m*; **to have** *or* **take a r.** descansar, tomarse un descanso; *Euph* **to be at r.** *(be dead)* descansar en paz; **to put** *or* **set sb's mind at r.** tranquilizar a alguien; *Fam* **give it a r., will you!** ¿quieres parar de una vez?; **to come to r.** detenerse (b) *(support)* soporte *m*, apoyo *m* (c) *Mus (pause)* silencio *m*

**2** *vt* (a) *(cause to repose)* **to r. one's eyes/legs** descansar los ojos/las piernas; **God r. his soul!** ¡Dios lo tenga en su gloria! (b) *(lean)* apoyar (**on** en) (c) *(base) (argument, theory)* apoyar (**on** en), basar (**on** en); *(one's hopes, confidence)* depositar (**on** en); *Fig* **I r. my case!** ¡he dicho!

**3** *vi* (a) *(relax)* descansar; **I won't r. until…** no descansaré hasta…; **to r. on** *(of structure, argument)* descansar en *or* sobre, apoyarse en *or* sobre; **r. in peace** *(on gravestone)* descanse en paz (b) *(remain)* **there the matter rests** así ha quedado la cosa; **I won't let it r. at that** esto no va a quedar así; **r. assured (that)** puedes estar seguro(a) (de que); **to r. with sb** *(of decision, responsibility)* corresponderle a alguien

**rest**[2] *n* **the r.** *(remainder)* el resto; *(others)* el resto, los demás; **the r. of us** los demás

**restaurant** ['restrɒnt] *n* restaurante *m*; **r. car** *(in train)* coche *m or* vagón *m* restaurante

**restful** ['restfʊl] *adj* tranquilo(a), reposado(a)

**restive** ['restɪv] *adj* inquieto(a), nervioso(a)

**restless** ['restlɪs] *adj (fidgety)* inquieto(a), agitado(a); *(dissatisfied)* descontento(a); **I've had a r. night** he pasado una noche agitada

**restoration** [restə'reɪʃən] *n (of building, furniture, monarchy)* restauración *f*; *(of communications, law and order)* restablecimiento *m*; *(of lost property, fortune)* restitución *f*

**restore** [rɪ'stɔː(r)] *vt (building, furniture, monarchy)* restaurar; *(communications, law and order)* restablecer; *(confidence)* devolver; *(property, fortune)* restituir; **to r. sb to health/strength** devolver la salud/la fuerza a alguien

**restrain** [rɪ'streɪn] *vt (person, crowd, dog, one's curiosity)* contener; *(passions, anger)* reprimir, dominar; **to r. sb from doing sth** impedir a alguien que haga algo; **to r. oneself** contenerse, controlarse

**restrained** [rɪ'streɪnd] *adj (person)* comedido(a); *(response, emotion)* contenido(a)

**restraint** [rɪ'streɪnt] *n* (a) *(moderation)* dominio *m* de sí mismo(a), comedimiento *m*; **to urge r.** pedir moderación (b) *(restriction)* restricción *f*, limitación *f*; **without r.** sin restricciones

**restrict** [rɪ'strɪkt] *vt (person, freedom)* restringir, limitar; **to r. oneself to…** limitarse a…

**restricted** [rɪ'strɪktɪd] *adj* restringido(a), limitado(a); **r. area** zona *f* de acceso restringido; **r. document** documento *m* confidencial

**restriction** [rɪ'strɪkʃən] *n* restricción *f*, limitación *f*; **to place restrictions on sth** poner trabas a algo

**restrictive** [rɪ'strɪktɪv] *adj* restrictivo(a); *Ind* **r. practices** prácticas *fpl* restrictivas

**restroom** ['restruːm] *n US* servicios *mpl*, aseo *m*

**restructure** [riː'strʌktʃə(r)] *vt* reestructurar

**restructuring** [riː'strʌktʃərɪŋ] *n Ind* reestructuración *f*, reconversión *f*

**result** [rɪ'zʌlt] **1** *n* resultado *m*; **as a r.** como consecuencia *or* resultado; **as a r. of…** como consecuencia *or* resultado de…; **the r. is that…** el caso es que…; **to yield** *or* **show results** dar resultado

**2** *vi* **to r. from** resultar de; **to r. in sth** tener algo como resultado

**resultant** [rɪ'zʌltənt] *adj* resultante

**resume** [rɪ'zjuːm] **1** *vt (relations, work)* reanudar

**2** *vi* continuar

**résumé** ['rezjʊmeɪ] *n (summary)* resumen *m*; *US (curriculum vitae)* currículum (vitae) *m*

**resumption** [rɪ'zʌmpʃən] *n* reanudación *f*

**resurface** [riː'sɜːfɪs] **1** *vt (road)* rehacer el firme de

**2** *vi (of submarine)* volver a la superficie; *Fig (of person)* reaparecer

**resurgence** [rɪ'sɜːdʒəns] *n* resurgimiento *m*

**resurgent** [rɪ'sɜ:dʒənt] *adj* renaciente, resurgente

**resurrect** [rezə'rekt] *vt (the dead, fashion, argument)* resucitar

**resurrection** [rezə'rekʃən] *n (of conflict, accusation)* reavivamiento *m*; *Rel* **the R.** la Resurrección

**resuscitate** [rɪ'sʌsɪteɪt] *vt (person)* reanimar, hacer revivir; *(scheme, career)* resucitar

**retail** ['ri:teɪl] **1** *n Com (selling, trade)* venta *f* al por menor, *Am* menoreo *m*; **r. outlet** punto *m* de venta; **r. price** precio *m* de venta (al público); *Econ* **r. price index** índice *m* de precios al consumo
**2** *vt (goods)* vender al por menor; *(gossip)* contar
**3** *vi* **it retails at £9,995** su precio de venta al público es 9.995 libras

**retailer** ['ri:teɪlə(r)] *n Com* minorista *mf*

**retain** [rɪ'teɪn] *vt* **(a)** *(keep)* conservar; *(heat)* retener **(b)** *(hold in place)* sujetar; **retaining wall** muro *m* de contención **(c)** *(remember)* retener

**retainer** [rɪ'teɪnə(r)] *n* **(a)** *(fee)* anticipo *m* **(b)** *(servant)* criado(a) *m,f* (de toda la vida)

**retaliate** [rɪ'tælɪeɪt] *vi* desquitarse, tomarse la revancha

**retaliation** [rɪtælɪ'eɪʃən] *n* represalias *fpl*; **in r. (for sth)** como represalia (por algo)

**retard** [rɪ'tɑ:d] *vt (delay)* retrasar

**retarded** [rɪ'tɑ:dɪd] *adj* **to be (mentally) r.** ser retrasado(a) mental

**retch** [retʃ] *vi* tener arcadas

**retention** [rɪ'tenʃən] *n (of custom, practice)* conservación *f*, preservación *f*; *(of fact, impression)* retención *f*

**retentive** [rɪ'tentɪv] *adj (memory, person)* retentivo(a)

**rethink 1** *n* ['ri:θɪŋk] **to have a r. (about sth)** hacerse un replanteamiento (de algo)
**2** *vt* [ri:'θɪŋk] *(pt & pp* **rethought** [ri:'θɔ:t]*)* replantear(se)

**reticent** ['retɪsənt] *adj* reservado(a)

**retina** ['retɪnə] *n Anat* retina *f*

**retinue** ['retɪnju:] *n* comitiva *f*, séquito *m*

**retire** [rɪ'taɪə(r)] **1** *vt* jubilar
**2** *vi* **(a)** *(of employee)* jubilarse **(b)** *(withdraw)* retirarse **(c)** *Formal (to bed)* retirarse (a descansar)

**retired** [rɪ'taɪəd] *adj (from job)* jubilado(a); *(from military)* retirado(a); **to be r.** *(from job)* estar jubilado(a)

**retirement** [rɪ'taɪəmənt] *n (act)* jubilación *f*; *(period)* retiro *m*; **to take early r.** tomar la jubilación anticipada; **he came out of r.** salió de su retiro; **(of) r. age** (en) edad *f* de jubilación; **r. pension** pensión *f* de jubilación

**retiring** [rɪ'taɪərɪŋ] *adj* **(a)** *(reserved)* retraído(a), reservado(a) **(b)** *(official)* saliente *(por jubilación)*

**retort** [rɪ'tɔ:t] **1** *n (answer)* réplica *f*
**2** *vt & vi* replicar

**retrace** [rɪ'treɪs] *vt* **they retraced their steps** volvieron sobre sus pasos

**retract** [rɪ'trækt] **1** *vt* **(a)** *(statement, offer)* retractarse de **(b)** *(claws)* retraer; *(undercarriage)* replegar
**2** *vi* **(a)** *(of person)* retractarse **(b)** *(of claws)* retraerse; *(of undercarriage)* replegarse

**retractable** [rɪ'træktəbəl] *adj (antenna, tip of instrument)* retráctil; *(undercarriage)* replegable

**retrain** [ri:'treɪn] **1** *vt (employee)* reciclar
**2** *vi (of employee)* reciclarse

**retraining** [ri:'treɪnɪŋ] *n* reciclaje *m* profesional

**retread** ['ri:tred] *n Aut* neumático *m* recauchutado

**retreat** [rɪ'tri:t] **1** *n (withdrawal)* retirada *f*; **to beat a r.** batirse en retirada **(b)** *(place)* retiro *m*, refugio *m*
**2** *vi* retirarse

**retrial** [ri:'traɪəl] *n Law* nuevo juicio *m*

**retribution** [retrɪ'bju:ʃən] *n* represalias *fpl*

**retrieve** [rɪ'tri:v] *vt also Comptr* recuperar

**retriever** [rɪ'tri:və(r)] *n (dog)* perro *m* cobrador

**retro** ['retrəʊ] *adj* retro

**retroactive** [retrəʊ'æktɪv] *adj Formal* retroactivo(a)

**retrograde** ['retrəgreɪd] *adj (movement, step)* retrógrado(a)

**retrospect** ['retrəspekt] *n* **in r.** retrospectivamente

**retrospective** [retrə'spektɪv] **1** *n (exhibition)* retrospectiva *f*
**2** *adj* retrospectivo(a)

**return** [rɪ'tɜ:n] **1** *n* **(a)** *(of person, peace, season)* vuelta *f*, regreso *m*; *Com (of goods)* devolución *f*; *(of tennis service)* resto *m*; **on my r.** a mi vuelta or regreso; **by r. of post** a vuelta de correo; **in r.** a cambio; **to do sth in r.** corresponder con algo; **many happy returns of the day!** ¡felicidades!, ¡feliz cumpleaños!; **r. journey** viaje *m* de vuelta; **r. match** partido *m* de vuelta; **r. ticket** billete *m* de ida y vuelta
**(b)** *Fin (profit)* rendimiento *m*; **to bring a good r.** proporcionar buenos dividendos; **r. on investment** rendimiento de las inversiones
**2** *vt* **(a)** *(give or send back)* devolver; **to r. a favour** devolver un favor; **to r. sb's love** corresponder al amor de alguien; **r. to sender** *(on letter)* devolver al remitente; **to r. service** *(in tennis)* restar, devolver el servicio; **to r. a call** devolver una llamada; *Law* **to r. a verdict of**

**guilty/not guilty** pronunciar un veredicto de culpable/inocente

(**b**) *Com & Fin (profit)* rendir, proporcionar

**3** *vi (come or go back)* volver, regresar; **to r. to work** volver al trabajo

**returnable** [rɪˈtɜːnəbəl] *adj (bottle)* retornable; **sale items are not r.** no se admite la devolución de artículos rebajados

**reunification** [riːjuːnɪfɪˈkeɪʃən] *n* reunificación *f*

**reunify** [riːˈjuːnɪfaɪ] *vt* reunificar

**reunion** [riːˈjuːnɪən] *n* reunión *f*

**reunite** [riːjuːˈnaɪt] **1** *vt* reunir; **to be re-united (with sb)** reencontrarse *or* volver a reunirse (con alguien)

**2** *vi* reunirse

**reusable** [reˈjuːzəbəl] *adj* reutilizable

**reuse** [riːˈjuːz] *vt* volver a utilizar, reutilizar

**rev** [rev] *Aut* **1** *n* **r. counter** cuentarrevoluciones *m inv*

**2** *vt (pt & pp* **revved**) **to r. the engine** revolucionar *or* acelerar el motor

**Rev** *n Rel (abbr* **Reverend**) **R. Gray** el reverendo Gray

**revalue** [riːˈvæljuː] *vt Fin* revalorizar

**revamp** [riːˈvæmp] *vt Fam* renovar

**reveal** [rɪˈviːl] *vt* revelar; **it has been re-vealed that…** se ha dado a conocer que…

**revealing** [rɪˈviːlɪŋ] *adj (sign, comment)* revelador(ora); *(dress)* insinuante

**revel** [ˈrevəl] *(pt & pp* **revelled**) *vi* estar de juerga; **to r. in sth** deleitarse con algo

**revelation** [revəˈleɪʃən] *n* revelación *f*; **(the Book of) Revelations** el Apocalipsis

**reveller** [ˈrevələ(r)] *n* juerguista *mf*

**revenge** [rɪˈvendʒ] **1** *n* venganza *f*; **to take r. (on sb)** vengarse (de alguien); **to do sth out of r.** hacer algo por venganza; *Prov* **r. is sweet** la venganza es un placer de dioses

**2** *vt* **to be revenged** vengarse

**revenue** [ˈrevənjuː] *n Fin* ingresos *mpl*

**reverberate** [rɪˈvɜːbəreɪt] *vi* (**a**) *(of sound)* reverberar; **the stadium reverberated with applause** el estadio resonaba con los aplausos (**b**) *(of news, rumour)* repercutir

**reverberation** [rɪvɜːbəˈreɪʃən] *n* (**a**) *(sound)* reverberación *f* (**b**) *(news, rumour)* repercusión *f*

**revere** [rɪˈvɪə(r)] *vt* reverenciar, venerar

**reverence** [ˈrevərəns] *n* reverencia *f*, veneración *f*

**Reverend** [ˈrevərənd] *Rel n* reverendo *m*; **Right R.** reverendísimo

**reverential** [revəˈrenʃəl] *adj* reverente

**reverie** [ˈrevərɪ] *n* ensoñación *f*

**reversal** [rɪˈvɜːsəl] *n (of opinion, policy, roles)* inversión *f*; *Law (of decision)* revocación *f*; **to suffer a r.** sufrir un revés

**reverse** [rɪˈvɜːs] **1** *n* (**a**) *(opposite)* **the r.** lo contrario; **quite the r.!** ¡todo lo contrario! (**b**) *(other side) (of coin)* reverso *m*; *(of fabric)* revés *m*; *(of sheet of paper)* dorso *m* (**c**) *(defeat, misfortune)* revés *m* (**d**) *Aut (gear)* marcha *f* atrás; **he put the car into r.** puso *or* metió la marcha atrás

**2** *adj* contrario(a), inverso(a); **in r. order** en orden inverso; **the r. side** *(of fabric)* el revés; *(of sheet of paper)* el dorso; *Br* **r.-charge call** llamada *f* a cobro revertido; *Aut* **r. gear** marcha *f* atrás

**3** *vt (order, situation, trend)* invertir; **the roles are reversed** se han invertido los papeles; **she reversed the car into the road** salió a la carretera marcha atrás

**reversible** [rɪˈvɜːsəbəl] *adj* (**a**) *(jacket)* reversible (**b**) *(decree, decision)* revocable; *(surgery)* reversible; **the decision is not r.** la decisión es irrevocable

**revert** [rɪˈvɜːt] *vi* (**a**) *(return)* volver; **he soon reverted to type** pronto volvió a su antiguo ser (**b**) *Law (of property)* revertir

**review** [rɪˈvjuː] **1** *n* (**a**) *(of policy, situation)* revisión *f*; **to be under r.** estar siendo revisado(a) (**b**) *(of book, play, film)* crítica *f*, reseña *f* (**c**) *Mil* revista *f*

**2** *vt* (**a**) *(policy, situation)* revisar (**b**) *(book, play, film)* hacer una crítica de, reseñar (**c**) *Mil (troops)* pasar revista a

**reviewer** [rɪˈvjuːə(r)] *n (of book, play, film)* crítico(a) *m,f*

**revile** [rɪˈvaɪl] *vt Formal* denigrar, vilipendiar

**revise** [rɪˈvaɪz] **1** *vt* (**a**) *(text, law)* revisar; **to r. one's opinion of sb** cambiar de opinión sobre alguien (**b**) *(for exam) (subject, notes)* repasar

**2** *vi (for exam)* repasar

**revision** [rɪˈvɪʒən] *n* (**a**) *(of text)* revisión *f* (**b**) *(for exam)* **to do some r.** repasar

**revisionism** [rɪˈvɪʒənɪzəm] *n Pol* revisionismo *m*

**revisionist** [rɪˈvɪʒənɪst] *n & adj* revisionista *mf*

**revisit** [rɪˈvɪzɪt] *vt* volver a visitar

**revitalize** [rɪˈvaɪtəlaɪz] *vt* reanimar, revitalizar

**revival** [rɪˈvaɪvəl] *n (of person)* reanimación *f*; *(of industry)* reactivación *f*; *(of hope)* recuperación *f*; *(of custom, fashion)* resurgimiento *m*; *(of play)* reposición *f*, nuevo montaje *m*

**revive** [rɪˈvaɪv] **1** *vt (person)* reanimar; *(industry)* reactivar; *(hopes)* recuperar; *(custom, fashion)* hacer resurgir

**2** *vi (of person)* reanimarse; *(of industry)* reactivarse; *(of hopes)* renacer; *(of custom, fashion)* revivir

**revoke** [rɪˈvəʊk] *vt (law)* derogar; *(decision, privilege)* revocar

**revolt** [rɪ'vəʊlt] **1** n rebelión f; **to be in r.** rebelarse
**2** vt (disgust) repugnar; **to be revolted by sth** sentir asco por algo
**3** vi (rebel) rebelarse

**revolting** [rɪ'vəʊltɪŋ] adj (disgusting) repugnante

**revolution** [revə'lu:ʃən] n (a) (radical change) revolución f (b) (turn) vuelta f, giro m

**revolutionary** [revə'lu:ʃənərɪ] n & adj revolucionario(a) m,f

**revolutionize** [revə'lu:ʃənaɪz] vt revolucionar

**revolve** [rɪ'vɒlv] vi girar (**around** en torno a)

**revolver** [rɪ'vɒlvə(r)] n revólver m

**revolving** [rɪ'vɒlvɪŋ] adj giratorio(a)

**revue** [rɪ'vju:] n Th revista f

**revulsion** [rɪ'vʌlʃən] n repugnancia f

**reward** [rɪ'wɔ:d] **1** n recompensa f
**2** vt recompensar

**rewarding** [rɪ'wɔ:dɪŋ] adj gratificante

**rewind** [ri:'waɪnd] (pt & pp **rewound** [ri:'waʊnd]) vt (tape, film) rebobinar

**rewire** [ri:'waɪə(r)] vt (house) renovar la instalación eléctrica de

**reword** [ri:'wɜ:d] vt reformular, expresar de otra manera

**rework** [ri:'wɜ:k] vt (idea, text) rehacer, reelaborar

**rewrite** [ri:'raɪt] (pt **rewrote** [ri:'rəʊt], pp **rewritten** [ri:'rɪtən]) vt reescribir

**Reykjavik** ['rekjəvɪk] n Reikiavik

**RFU** [ɑ:ref'ju:] n Br (abbr **Rugby Football Union**) = federación inglesa de "rugby union"

**rhapsodic(al)** [ræp'sɒdɪk(əl)] adj (prose, description) enardecido(a)

**rhapsodize** ['ræpsədaɪz] vi deshacerse en elogios (**over** or **about** sobre)

**rhapsody** ['ræpsədɪ] n Mus rapsodia f; **to go into rhapsodies over sth** deshacerse en elogios sobre algo

**rhesus** ['ri:səs] n (a) Med **r. factor** factor m Rh; **r. positive/negative** Rh m positivo/negativo (b) **r. monkey** macaco m (de la India)

**rhetoric** ['retərɪk] n also Fig retórica f

**rhetorical** [rɪ'tɒrɪkəl] adj retórico(a); **r. question** pregunta f retórica

**rheumatic** [ru:'mætɪk] adj Med reumático(a); **r. fever** fiebre f reumática

**rheumatism** ['ru:mətɪzəm] n reumatismo m, reúma m

**rheumatoid arthritis** ['ru:mətɔɪdɑ:'θraɪtɪs] Med n artritis f inv reumatoide

**Rhine** [raɪn] n the R. el Rin

**rhinestone** ['raɪnstəʊn] n diamante m de imitación

**rhino** ['raɪnəʊ] (pl **rhinos**) n Fam rinoceronte m

**rhinoceros** [raɪ'nɒsərəs] n rinoceronte m

**rhizome** ['raɪzəʊm] n Bot rizoma m

**Rhodes** [rəʊdz] n Rodas

**rhododendron** [rəʊdə'dendrən] n rododendro m

**rhomboid** ['rɒmbɔɪd] n romboide m

**rhombus** ['rɒmbəs] n rombo m

**Rhone** [rəʊn] n the R. el Ródano

**rhubarb** ['ru:bɑ:b] n ruibarbo m; **r. jam** confitura f de ruibarbo

**rhyme** [raɪm] **1** n rima f; **to speak in r.** hablar en verso; **without r. or reason** sin venir a cuento
**2** vi rimar

**rhythm** ['rɪðəm] n ritmo m; **r. method** (of contraception) método m (de) Ogino

**rhythmic(al)** ['rɪðmɪk(əl)] adj rítmico(a)

**rib** [rɪb] **1** n (a) (of person, animal) costilla f (b) (of umbrella) varilla f
**2** vt (pt & pp **ribbed**) Fam (tease) tomar el pelo a

**ribald** ['rɪbəld, 'raɪbəld] adj (joke, song) procaz; (language) grosero(a)

**ribbed** [rɪbd] adj (pullover) acanalado(a)

**ribbon** ['rɪbən] n (for hair, typewriter) cinta f; (of land) franja f, faja f; **torn to ribbons** hecho(a) jirones

**ribcage** ['rɪbkeɪdʒ] n caja f torácica

**riboflavin(e)** [raɪbəʊ'fleɪvɪn] n Chem riboflavina f, vitamina f $B_2$

**rice** [raɪs] n arroz m; **r. field** or **paddy** arrozal m; **r. pudding** arroz con leche

**rich** [rɪtʃ] **1** npl **the r.** los ricos; **riches** riquezas fpl
**2** adj (person, country) rico(a); (food) sustancioso(a); (chocolate) extrafino(a); (soil) fértil; (harvest, supply) abundante; (colour, voice) profundo(a); **to become r.** hacerse rico; **to be r. in...** ser rico en...; I'll only have a small piece, this cake's very r. sólo tomaré un trocito de pastel porque llena mucho; Fam **that's a bit r.!** ¡esa sí que es buena!

**richly** ['rɪtʃlɪ] adv (furnished, ornamented) lujosamente; **r. deserved** merecidísimo(a)

**Richter Scale** ['rɪktə'skeɪl] n escala f de Richter

**rick¹** [rɪk] n (of hay, straw) almiar m

**rick²** vt **to r. one's neck** torcerse el cuello; **to r. one's back** hacerse daño en la espalda

**rickets** ['rɪkɪts] npl Med raquitismo m

**rickety** ['rɪkɪtɪ] adj Fam (furniture, staircase) desvencijado(a); (alliance, alibi) precario(a)

**ricochet** ['rɪkəʃeɪ] **1** n bala f rebotada
**2** vi (pt **ricochetted** ['rɪkəʃeɪd]) rebotar

**rid** [rɪd] (*pt & pp* **rid**) *vt* **to r. sb of sth** librar a alguien de algo; **to r. oneself of sth, to get r. of sth** deshacerse de algo

**riddance** ['rɪdəns] *n Fam* **good r.!** ¡ya era hora (de que se fuera)!

**ridden** ['rɪdən] *pp of* **ride**

**riddle** ['rɪdəl] **1** *n* (*puzzle*) acertijo *m*, adivinanza *f*; (*mystery*) enigma *m*

**2** *vt* **to r. sb with bullets** acribillar a alguien a balazos; **riddled with mistakes** plagado(a) de errores

**ride** [raɪd] **1** *n* (**a**) (*on bicycle, in car, on horse*) paseo *m*; **to give sb a r.** (*in car*) llevar a alguien (en coche); **to go for a r.** ir a dar una vuelta (en coche/en bicicleta/a caballo); **it's only a short r. away** está a poca distancia; *Fig* **she was given a rough r.** (*by interviewer, critics*) se las hicieron pasar moradas; *Fig* **to take sb for a r.** engañar a alguien como a un chino, tomar a alguien el pelo (**b**) (*attraction at funfair*) atracción *f*

**2** *vt* (*pt* **rode** [rəʊd], *pp* **ridden** ['rɪdən]) (*horse*) montar a; (*bicycle*) montar en; *US* (*bus, train*) viajar en

**3** *vi* (*on horse, bicycle*) **can you r.?** ¿sabes montar?; **I rode into town** fui a la ciudad en bicicleta/a caballo; *Fig* **to be riding high** atravesar un buen momento; *Fig* **to let sth r.** dejar pasar algo

▸**ride out** *vt sep* (*problem, crisis*) soportar, aguantar; **to r. out the storm** capear el temporal

**rider** ['raɪdə(r)] *n* (**a**) (*on horse*) (*man*) jinete *m*; (*woman*) amazona *f*; (*on bicycle*) ciclista *mf*; (*on motorbike*) motorista *mf* (**b**) *Law* (*to document, treaty*) cláusula *f* adicional

**ridge** [rɪdʒ] *n* (*of mountain*) cresta *f*; (*of roof*) caballete *m*, cumbrera *f*; (*on surface*) rugosidad *f*; *Met* **r. of high pressure** zona *f* de altas presiones

**ridicule** ['rɪdɪkjuːl] **1** *n* burlas *fpl*, mofa *f*; **to hold sth/sb up to r.** poner algo/a alguien en ridículo

**2** *vt* ridiculizar, poner en ridículo

**ridiculous** [rɪ'dɪkjʊləs] *adj* ridículo(a); **to make sb look r.** poner en ridículo or ridiculizar a alguien; **to make oneself r.** hacer el ridículo

**riding** ['raɪdɪŋ] *n* equitación *f*, monta *f*; **r. boots** botas *fpl* de montar; **r. crop** or **whip** fusta *f*; **r. school** escuela *f* hípica

**rife** [raɪf] *adj* **to be r.** reinar, imperar; **the text is r. with errors** el texto está plagado de errores

**riffraff** ['rɪfræf] *n* gentuza *f*

**rifle**[1] ['raɪfəl] *n* rifle *m*, fusil *m*; **r. range** campo *m* de tiro; **r. shot** disparo *m* de rifle

**rifle**[2] *vt* (*house, office*) revolver (*en busca de algo*); (*pockets, drawer*) rebuscar en

**rifleman** ['raɪfəlmən] *n* fusilero *m*

**rift** [rɪft] *n* (*in earth, rock*) grieta *f*, brecha *f*; (*in relationship*) desavenencia *f*; (*in political party*) escisión *f*

**rig** [rɪg] **1** *n* (**a**) (*of ship*) aparejo *m* (**b**) (*oil*) **r.** (*on land*) torre *f* de perforación (petrolífera); (*at sea*) plataforma *f* petrolífera (**c**) *Fam* (*outfit*) vestimenta *f*

**2** *vt* (*pt & pp* **rigged**) (**a**) (*ship*) aparejar (**b**) *Fam* (*election*) amañar

▸**rig out** *vt sep Fam* **to be rigged out in...** estar vestido(a) con...

▸**rig up** *vt sep* improvisar, apañar

**Riga** ['riːgə] *n* Riga

**rigging** ['rɪgɪŋ] *n Naut* jarcias *fpl*, cordaje *m*

**right** [raɪt] **1** *n* (**a**) (*morality*) bien *m*; **to know r. from wrong** distinguir lo que está bien de lo que está mal; **to be in the r.** tener razón; **to set things to rights** poner las cosas en orden (**b**) (*entitlement*) derecho *m*; **to have the r. to do sth** tener derecho a hacer algo; **to be within one's rights to do sth** tener todo el derecho a hacer algo; **by rights** en justicia; **by r.** por derecho propio; **to be famous in one's own r.** ser famoso(a) por méritos propios or por derecho propio; **the r. to vote** el derecho al voto; **r. of way** (*on land*) derecho de paso; (*on road*) prioridad *f* (**c**) (*right-hand side*) derecha *f*; **on** or **to the r.** a la derecha; **on my r.** a mi derecha; *Pol* **the r.** la derecha; **a r. to the jaw** (*in boxing*) un derechazo en la mandíbula

**2** *adj* (**a**) (*correct*) correcto(a); **that was the r. thing to do** eso es lo que había que hacer; **are you sure that's the r. time?** ¿seguro que es ésa la hora?; **my watch is r.** mi reloj va bien; **to be r.** (*of person*) tener razón; **you were r. not to say anything** hiciste bien en no decir nada; **to stay on the r. side of sb** seguir a buenas con alguien; **to be on the r. lines** ir bien encaminado(a) (**b**) (*morally good*) **it's not r.** no está bien; **to do the r. thing** hacer lo (que es) debido (**c**) (*appropriate*) (*place, time, action*) apropiado(a); **to wait for the r. moment** esperar el momento oportuno; **to know the r. people** tener buenos contactos; **to be in the r. place at the r. time** estar en el lugar y en el momento adecuados (**d**) (*mentally, physically well*) **I'm not feeling quite r.** no me siento muy bien; **to be as r. as rain** estar como una rosa; **no one in his r. mind...** nadie en su sano juicio...; **he's not quite r. in the head** no está muy bien de la cabeza (**e**) *Fam* (*as intensifier*) **I felt a r. fool** me sentí como un tonto de remate; **the place was in a r. mess** el lugar estaba todo desordenado (**f**) (*righthand*) derecho(a); **on the r. side** a la derecha; **r. hand** mano *f* derecha; *Pol* **the**

wing la derecha
  (g) *Math* **r. angle** ángulo *m* recto
  **3** *adv* (**a**) *(straight)* directamente; **he drove r. into the wall** chocó de frente *or* directamente contra la pared; **to put things r.** arreglar las cosas; **to put sb r.** sacar a alguien de su error
  (**b**) *(immediately)* **r. away** en seguida, inmediatamente, *CAm, Méx* ahorita, *CSur* al tiro; **I'll be r. back** vuelvo en seguida; **r. now** ahora mismo
  (**c**) *(completely)* **the bullet went r. through his arm** la bala le atravesó el brazo de parte a parte; **to go r. up to sb** acercarse justo hasta donde está alguien; **he turned r. round** se dio media vuelta; **r. at the top/back** arriba/detrás del todo
  (**d**) *(exactly)* **r. here/there** aquí/ahí mismo; **r. behind/in the middle** justo detrás/en medio; *Fig* **to be r. behind sb** *(support)* apoyar plenamente a alguien
  (**e**) *(to answer, guess)* correctamente, bien; **to understand/remember r.** entender/recordar bien
  (**f**) *(well)* **I'm sure it'll all come r. for you** estoy seguro de que todo te saldrá bien; **to see sb r.** asegurar el futuro de alguien; **it was a mistake, r. enough** de acuerdo, fue un error
  (**g**) *(to look, turn)* a la derecha; *Fig* **left, r. and centre** por todas partes
  **4** *vt* (**a**) *(put upright) (boat, car)* enderezar, poner derecho(a)
  (**b**) *(redress)* **to r. a wrong** terminar con una injusticia

**right-angled** ['raɪtæŋgəld] *adj (triangle)* rectángulo(a); *(corner, bend)* en ángulo recto

**righteous** ['raɪtʃəs] *adj (person)* virtuoso(a); *(indignation)* justo(a)

**rightful** ['raɪtfʊl] *adj* legítimo(a)

**right-hand** ['raɪthænd] *adj* **on the r. side** a la derecha; *Aut* **r. drive** *(vehicle)* vehículo *m* con el volante a la derecha; **to be sb's r. man** ser la mano derecha de alguien

**right-handed** [raɪt'hændɪd] **1** *adj* diestro(a)
  **2** *adv* con la mano derecha

**right-hander** [raɪt'hændə(r)] *n (person)* diestro(a) *m,f*

**rightly** ['raɪtlɪ] *adv* correctamente; **I don't r. know why…** no sé muy bien por qué…; **r. or wrongly** para bien o para mal; **…and r. so** …y con razón; **he was r. angry** se enfadó y con razón

**right-minded** [raɪt'maɪndɪd], **right-thinking** [raɪt'θɪŋkɪŋ] *adj* **any r. person would have done the same** cualquier persona de bien hubiera hecho lo mismo

**right-wing** [raɪt'wɪŋ] *adj Pol* derechista, de derechas

**right-winger** [raɪt'wɪŋə(r)] *n Pol* derechista *mf*

**rigid** ['rɪdʒɪd] *adj* rígido(a); **she's very r. in her ideas** es de ideas muy rígidas; *Br* **to be bored r.** aburrirse como una ostra

**rigidity** [rɪ'dʒɪdɪtɪ] *n* rigidez *f*

**rigmarole** ['rɪgmərəʊl] *n Fam (process)* engorro *m*, latazo *m*; *(speech)* rollo *m*, galimatías *m inv*

**rigor mortis** ['rɪgə'mɔːtɪs] *n Med* rigidez *f* cadavérica, rigor *m* mortis

**rigorous** ['rɪgərəs] *adj* riguroso(a)

**rigour** ['rɪgə(r)] *n* rigor *m*

**rigout** ['rɪgaʊt] *n Fam (outfit)* vestimenta *f*

**rile** [raɪl] *vt Fam (annoy)* fastidiar, irritar

**rim** [rɪm] *n (of cup, bowl)* borde *m*; *(of wheel)* llanta *f*; *(of spectacles)* montura *f*

**rind** [raɪnd] *n (of fruit)* cáscara *f*; *(of cheese, bacon)* corteza *f*

**ring¹** [rɪŋ] **1** *n* (**a**) *(for finger)* anillo *m*; *(with gem)* sortija *f*; *(for keys)* llavero *m*; *(plain metal band)* aro *m*; *(for can of drink, bird, curtains)* anilla *f*; **the rings** *(in gymnastics)* las anillas; **r. binder** archivador *m or* carpeta *f* de anillas; **r. finger** *(dedo m)* anular *m* (**b**) *(of people, chairs)* corro *m*, círculo *m*; *(on stove)* fuego *m*, quemador *m*; *(stain)* cerco *m*; **to have rings under one's eyes** tener ojeras; *Fig* **to run rings round sb** darle mil vueltas a alguien; **r. road** carretera *f* de circunvalación (**c**) *(for boxing, wrestling)* cuadrilátero *m*, ring *m* (**d**) *(of spies, criminals)* red *f*
  **2** *vt (surround)* rodear

**ring²** **1** *n (sound) (of bell)* timbrazo *m*; *(of small bell, coins)* tintineo *m*; **there was a r. at the door** sonó el timbre de la puerta; *Fam* **to give sb a r.** *(phonecall)* dar un telefonazo a alguien; **to have the r. of truth** ser verosímil; **the name has a familiar r. to it** el nombre me suena
  **2** *vt (pt* **rang** [ræŋ], *pp* **rung** [rʌŋ]) (**a**) *(bell, alarm)* hacer sonar; *Fig* **that rings a bell** *(sounds familiar)* eso me suena (**b**) *(on phone)* llamar (por teléfono) a, telefonear a
  **3** *vi* (**a**) *(of bell, telephone)* sonar; **to r. at the door** llamar al timbre de la puerta; *Fig* **to r. true/false** tener pinta de ser verdad/mentira (**b**) *(on phone)* llamar (por teléfono), telefonear (**c**) *(resonate) (of street, room)* resonar; **my ears were ringing** me zumbaban los oídos
  ▸**ring back** *vt sep (on phone)* llamar más tarde
  ▸**ring off** *vi (on phone)* colgar
  ▸**ring out** *vi (voice, shout)* resonar
  ▸**ring up** *vt sep* (**a**) *(on phone)* llamar (por teléfono) a, telefonear a (**b**) *(on cash register)* teclear; **the concert rang up a profit of…** el concierto recaudó unos beneficios de…

**ringleader** ['rɪŋliːdə(r)] *n* cabecilla *mf*

**ringlet** ['rɪŋlɪt] *n* tirabuzón *m*

**ringmaster** ['rɪŋmɑːstə(r)] *n* director *m* de circo

**ring-pull** ['rɪŋpʊl] *n* anilla *f (de lata)*

**ringside** ['rɪŋsaɪd] *n* a r. seat *(in boxing)* un asiento de primera fila; *Fig (close view)* una visión muy cercana

**ringworm** ['rɪŋwɜːm] *n Med* tiña *f*

**rink** [rɪŋk] *n* pista *f* de patinaje

**rinse** [rɪns] **1** *n* to give sth a r. aclarar algo
   **2** *vt (clothes, dishes)* aclarar; **to r. one's hands** enjuagarse las manos
▸**rinse out** *vt sep (cup)* enjuagar; *(clothes)* aclarar; **to r. out one's mouth** enjuagarse la boca

**Rio (de Janeiro)** ['riːəʊ(dɪdʒə'neəreʊ)] *n* Río de Janeiro

**riot** ['raɪət] **1** *n (uprising)* disturbio *m*, algarada *f*; **a r. of colour** una explosión de colores; **the children ran r. while their parents were away** los niños se desmandaron cuando no estaban sus padres; **her imagination was running r.** su imaginación se había desbocado; **to read sb the r. act** llamar a alguien al orden; **r. police** policía *f* antidisturbios
   **2** *vi (of crowd)* causar *or* provocar disturbios; *(of prisoners)* amotinarse

**rioter** ['raɪətə(r)] *n* alborotador(ora) *m,f*

**riotous** ['raɪətəs] *adj (party, occasion, living)* desenfrenado(a); **a r. success** un éxito arrasador

**RIP** [ɑːraɪ'piː] *n (abbr* **Rest In Peace)** R.I.P., Q.E.P.D.

**rip** [rɪp] **1** *n (in cloth, paper)* desgarrón *m*, rasgadura *f*
   **2** *vt (pt & pp* **ripped)** *(cloth, paper)* rasgar; **to r. sth to pieces** hacer jirones algo; *Fig (performance, argument)* hacer añicos algo
   **3** *vi* **(a)** *(of cloth, paper)* rasgarse **(b)** *Fam* **to let r.** *(while driving)* pisar a fondo; *(in performance)* darlo todo, entregarse; **to let r. (at sb)** *(shout at)* echar una bronca (a alguien)
▸**rip off** *vt sep* **(a)** *(tear)* arrancar; **he ripped off his shirt** se desembarazó de su camisa **(b)** *Fam (swindle)* **to r. sb off** timar *or* clavar a alguien; **that sketch was ripped off from another comedian** ese sketch está copiado de otro humorista
▸**rip open** *vt sep* abrir de un tirón

**ripe** [raɪp] *adj (fruit)* maduro(a); *(cheese)* curado(a); **to be r.** estar maduro(a); **to live to a r. old age** vivir hasta una edad avanzada; **the time is r. for…** ha llegado el momento de…

**ripen** ['raɪpən] *vi* madurar

**rip-off** ['rɪpɒf] *n Fam* timo *m*; **what a r.!** ¡menudo robo!

**riposte** [rɪ'pɒst] *n (reply)* réplica *f*

**ripple** [rɪpl] **1** *n (on water)* onda *f*, ondulación *f*; *(of excitement)* asomo *m*; *(of applause)* murmullo *m*

-2 *vi (of water)* ondular; *(of laughter, applause)* extenderse

**rise** [raɪz] **1** *n* **(a)** *(in price, temperature, pressure)* aumento *m or* subida *f* (in de); *(pay)* r. aumento (de sueldo); **to be on the r.** ir en aumento; **the r. and fall** el ascenso y la caída, el esplendor y la decadencia
   **(b)** *(of leader, party)* ascenso *m*; **her r. to power** su ascenso *or* acceso al poder; **to give r. to sth** dar pie a algo; *Fam* **to get a r. out of sb** conseguir mosquear a alguien
   **(c)** *(in ground)* subida *f*, cuesta *f*
   **2** *vi (pt* **rose** [rəʊz], *pp* **risen** ['rɪzən]) **(a)** *(get up)* levantarse; **to r. early/late** levantarse temprano/tarde; *Fam* **r. and shine!** ¡arriba!
   **(b)** *(of road, ground)* subir, elevarse; *(of smoke, balloon)* ascender, subir; *(of sun, moon)* salir; *(in society)* ascender; **a murmur rose from the crowd** un murmullo se elevó entre la multitud; **to r. to the occasion** estar a la altura de las circunstancias; **to r. to power** ascender *or* acceder al poder; **to r. in sb's esteem** ganarse la estima de alguien
   **(c)** *(of temperature, price)* aumentar, subir; *(of voice)* elevarse, subir; *(of hope)* aumentar; *(of dough)* fermentar, subir; **my spirits rose** se me levantó el ánimo
   **(d)** *(revolt)* levantarse; **to r. in arms** levantarse en armas; **to r. in protest (against sth)** alzarse en protesta (contra algo)
▸**rise above** *vt insep (problem, criticism)* remontar, superar; **he rose above his limitations** superó sus limitaciones
▸**rise up** *vi (revolt)* levantarse; **to r. up in arms** levantarse en armas; **to r. up in protest (against sth)** alzarse en protesta (contra algo)

**risen** ['rɪzən] *pp of* **rise**

**risible** ['rɪzɪbəl] *adj* risible

**rising** ['raɪzɪŋ] **1** *n (revolt)* revuelta *f*, levantamiento *m*
   **2** *adj (sun)* naciente; *(prices, temperature)* en aumento, ascendente; *(artist, politician)* en alza; *Fig* **r. star** valor *m* en alza, estrella *f* en ciernes

**risk** [rɪsk] **1** *n* riesgo *m*, peligro *m*; **at r.** en peligro; **at the r. of…** a riesgo de…; **to run the r. of…** correr el riesgo de…; **to take risks** arriesgarse, correr riesgos; **r. assessment** evaluación *f* de riesgos; *Fin* **r. capital** capital *m* (de) riesgo; **r. management** gestión *f* de riesgos
   **2** *vt* poner en peligro; **to r. one's neck** jugarse el cuello; **we can't r. it** no podemos correr ese riesgo; **to r. defeat** correr el riesgo de *or* arriesgarse a ser derrotado(a)

**risky** ['rɪski] *adj* arriesgado(a)

**risotto** [rɪ'zɒtəʊ] *(pl* **risottos)** *n* risotto *m*, = guiso italiano a base de arroz, verduras, etc.

**risqué** [rɪs'keɪ] *adj (humour)* atrevido(a), subido(a) de tono

**rissole** ['rɪsəʊl] $n$ = pequeña masa frita, generalmente redonda, de carne o verduras

**rite** [raɪt] $n$ *Rel* rito $m$; **the last rites** la extremaunción

**ritual** ['rɪtjʊəl] **1** $n$ ritual $m$
**2** *adj* ritual

**ritzy** ['rɪtsɪ] *adj Fam* lujoso(a)

**rival** ['raɪvəl] **1** $n$ & *adj* rival $mf$
**2** $vt$ (*pt* & *pp* **rivalled**, *US* **rivaled**) rivalizar con

**rivalry** ['raɪvəlrɪ] $n$ rivalidad $f$

**river** ['rɪvə(r)] $n$ río $m$; **a r. of blood** un río de sangre; **r. traffic** tráfico $m$ fluvial

**riverbed** ['rɪvəbed] $n$ lecho $m$ (del río)

**riverside** ['rɪvəsaɪd] $n$ ribera $f$, orilla $f$ (del río); **r. villa** mansión $f$ a la orilla del río

**rivet** ['rɪvɪt] **1** $n$ remache $m$
**2** $vt$ remachar; **to be absolutely riveted** *(fascinated)* estar completamente fascinado(a); *Fig* **to be riveted to the spot** quedarse clavado(a)

**riveting** ['rɪvɪtɪŋ] *adj (fascinating)* fascinante

**RN** [ɑː'ren] *Br (abbr* **Royal Navy**) armada $f$ británica

**RNA** [ɑːen'eɪ] *Biol (abbr* **ribonucleic acid**) ARN $m$, ácido $m$ ribonucleico

**RNLI** [a:renel'aɪ] $n$ *Br (abbr* **Royal National Lifeboat Institution**) = organización británica de voluntarios para operaciones marítimas de salvamento

**roach** [rəʊtʃ] $n$ **(a)** *(fish)* rubio $m$, rutilo $m$ **(b)** *US Fam (cockroach)* cucaracha $f$

**road** [rəʊd] $n$ *(in general)* carretera $f$; *(in town)* calle $f$; *(path, track)* camino $m$; **they live across** *or* **over the r.** viven al otro lado de la calle, viven enfrente; **by r.** por carretera; **to be off the r.** *(of vehicle)* estar averiado(a); **the r. is up** la calle está en obras; **down** *or* **up the r.** un poco más lejos, por *or* en la misma calle; **a few years down the r.** dentro de unos años; **after three hours on the r.** después de tres horas en la carretera *or* de camino; **to be on the r.** *(of salesman)* estar de viaje (de ventas); *(pop group)* estar de gira; *also Fig* **somewhere along the r.** en algún punto *or* momento; *Fam* **let's have one for the r.** vamos a tomar la última *or* la espuela; **to be on the r. to recovery** estar en vías de recuperación; **to be on the right r.** ir por (el) buen camino; *Fam* **let's get this show on the r.!** ¡en marcha!, ¡vamos allá!; **to come to the end of the r.** *(of relationship)* acabar; **r. accident** accidente $m$ de carretera; **r. conditions** estado $m$ de las carreteras; *Fam* **r. hog** conductor(ora) $m,f$ temerario(a), loco(a) $m,f$ del volante; **r. map** mapa $m$ de carreteras; **r. rage** violencia $f$ en carretera *or* al volante; **r. sign** señal $f$ de tráfico; **r. tax** impuesto $m$ de circulación; **r. works** *or* **repairs** obras *fpl* (en la calzada)

**roadblock** ['rəʊdblɒk] $n$ control $m$ de carretera

**roadside** ['rəʊdsaɪd] $n$ borde $m$ de la carretera; **r. bar/hotel** bar $m$/hotel $m$ de carretera

**road-test** ['rəʊdtest] $vt$ *(car)* probar en carretera

**roadway** ['rəʊdweɪ] $n$ calzada $f$

**roadworthy** ['rəʊdwɜːðɪ] *adj (vehicle)* en condiciones de circular

**roam** [rəʊm] **1** $vt$ *(streets, the world)* vagar por, recorrer
**2** $vi$ **to r. (about)** vagar

**roar** [rɔː(r)] **1** $n$ *(of person)* grito $m$, rugido $m$; *(of animal, sea, wind, crowd)* rugido $m$; *(of traffic, engine)* estruendo $m$
**2** $vi$ *(in general)* rugir; *(of person)* vociferar, rugir; **to r. with laughter** reírse a carcajadas

**roaring** ['rɔːrɪŋ] *adj* **a r. fire** un fuego muy vivo; **the shop was doing a r. trade** el negocio iba viento en popa; **it was a r. success** fue un éxito clamoroso

**roast** [rəʊst] **1** $n$ *(piece of meat)* asado $m$
**2** *adj* asado(a)
**3** $vt$ **(a)** *(meat)* asar; *(nuts, coffee)* tostar **(b)** *Fam (criticize)* desollar

**roasting** ['rəʊstɪŋ] *Fam* **1** $n$ **to give sb a r.** *(tell off)* echar un broncazo a alguien; *(criticize)* poner a parir a alguien
**2** *adj* **r.(-hot)** abrasador(ora), achicharrante; **it's r. in here** aquí te achicharras

**rob** [rɒb] *(pt* & *pp* **robbed**) $vt$ *(person, bank)* atracar; *(house)* robar; **to r. sb of sth** robar algo a alguien

**robber** ['rɒbə(r)] $n$ atracador(ora) $m,f$

**robbery** ['rɒbərɪ] $n$ atraco $m$

**robe** [rəʊb] $n$ *(of priest)* sotana $f$; *(of judge)* toga $f$; *US (dressing gown)* bata $f$, batín $m$

**robin** ['rɒbɪn] $n$ petirrojo $m$

**robot** ['rəʊbɒt] $n$ robot $m$

**robotics** [rəʊ'bɒtɪks] $n$ robótica $f$

**robust** [rəʊ'bʌst] *adj (person)* robusto(a); *(material, suitcase)* resistente; *(defence, speech)* enérgico(a)

**rock** [rɒk] **1** $n$ **(a)** *(substance, large stone)* roca $f$; *Fig* **to be on the rocks** *(of marriage, company)* estar al borde del naufragio; **on the rocks** *(whisky)* con hielo; **to reach** *or* **hit r. bottom** tocar fondo; **the R. (of Gibraltar)** el Peñón (de Gibraltar); **r. climbing** escalada $f$; **r. face** pared $f$ (de roca); **r. garden** jardín $m$ de rocalla; **r. pool** charca $f$ *(en las rocas de la playa)*; **r. salt** sal $f$ gema; **r. solid** *(support, morale)* inquebrantable
**(b)** *Br* **stick of r.** = barra de caramelo de menta que se vende sobre todo en localidades costeras y lleva el nombre del lugar impreso
**(c)** *(rocking motion)* **to give sth a r.** mecer algo
**(d)** *(music)* rock $m$; **r. and roll** rock and roll $m$;

**r. concert** concierto *m* de rock; **r. group** grupo *m* de rock; **r. singer** cantante *mf* de rock

**2** *vt (boat, cradle)* mecer, balancear; *(building) (of earthquake, explosion)* sacudir; **to r. a baby to sleep** mecer a un niño hasta que se quede dormido; *Fig* **to r. the boat** *(create problems)* complicar el asunto; **the country was rocked by these revelations** estas revelaciones conmocionaron al país

**3** *vi (sway)* balancearse; *(building)* estremecerse; **to r. (backwards and forwards) in one's chair** mecerse en la silla; **to r. with laughter** reírse a carcajadas

**rock-bottom** ['rɒkbɒtəm] *adj (prices)* mínimo(a)

**rocker** ['rɒkə(r)] *n* **(a)** *(chair)* mecedora *f*; *Fam* **she's off her r.** le falta un tornillo **(b)** *(musician, fan)* roquero(a) *m,f*

**rockery** ['rɒkərɪ] *n (in garden)* jardín *m* de rocalla

**rocket** ['rɒkɪt] **1** *n* cohete *m*; *Fig* **to give sb a r.** *(reprimand)* echar una bronca a alguien; **r. launcher** lanzacohetes *m inv*

**2** *vi (of prices)* dispararse

**rockfall** ['rɒkfɔːl] *n* desprendimiento *m* (de piedras)

**rock-hard** [rɒk'hɑːd] *adj* duro(a) como una piedra

**Rockies** ['rɒkɪz] *npl* **the R.** las Montañas Rocosas

**rocky** ['rɒkɪ] *adj* **(a)** *(path, soil)* pedregoso(a); **the R. Mountains** las Montañas Rocosas **(b)** *Fig (marriage, relationship, economy)* inestable

**rod** [rɒd] *n (wooden)* vara *f*; *(metal)* barra *f*; *(for fishing)* caña *f* (de pescar); *Fig* **to rule with a r. of iron** gobernar con mano de hierro; *Fig* **to make a r. for one's own back** cavarse la propia tumba

**rode** [rəʊd] *pt of* **ride**

**rodent** ['rəʊdənt] *n* roedor *m*

**rodeo** ['rəʊdɪəʊ] *n* rodeo *m*

**roe**[1] [rəʊ] *n* **r. (deer)** corzo *m*

**roe**[2] *n (of fish)* huevas *fpl*

**roger**[1] ['rɒdʒə(r)] *exclam* **r.!** *(in radio message)* ¡recibido!

**roger**[2] *vt very Fam* tirarse a, echar un polvo a

**rogue** [rəʊg] *n (dishonest)* granuja *mf*, bribón(ona) *m,f*; *(mischievous)* truhán(ana) *m,f*; **r. elephant** elefante *m* solitario

**roguish** ['rəʊgɪʃ] *adj (smile, look)* pícaro(a), picarón(ona)

**role** [rəʊl] *n Cin, Th & TV* papel *m*; *Fig* **to play an important r.** desempeñar un papel importante; **r. model** ejemplo *m*, modelo *m* a seguir

**role-playing** ['rəʊlpleɪɪŋ] *n* juego *m* de roles

**roll** [rəʊl] **1** *n* **(a)** *(of paper, film)* rollo *m*; *(of fat)* michelín *m*; *(of banknotes)* fajo *m*

**(b)** *(bread)* panecillo *m*, *Méx* bolillo *m*; **ham/cheese r.** bocadillo *m* de jamón/queso

**(c)** *(noise) (of drum)* redoble *m*; *(of thunder)* retumbo *m*

**(d)** *(movement) (of ship)* balanceo *m*; *Fam* **to be on a r.** llevar una buena racha

**(e)** *(list)* lista *f*; **to take a r. call** pasar lista; *Mil* **r. of honour** lista de los caídos en la guerra

**2** *vt* **(a)** *(ball)* hacer rodar; **to r. sth along the ground** hacer rodar algo por el suelo; **to r. one's eyes** poner los ojos en blanco; **to r. one's r's** marcar las erres al hablar; **the animal rolled itself into a ball** el animal se hizo una bola or se enroscó

**(b)** *(road, lawn)* apisonar; *(metal)* laminar

**(c)** *(cigarette)* liar; *(paper, carpet)* enrollar

**3** *vi* **(a)** *(of ball)* rodar; *(of ship)* balancearse; *(of cine camera)* rodar; *Fig* **heads will r.** van a rodar cabezas; *Fam* **to be rolling in money, to be rolling in it** nadar en la abundancia, estar montado(a) en el dólar; *Fig* **to start the ball rolling** poner las cosas en marcha

**(b)** *(of thunder)* retumbar

▸**roll back** *vt sep* **to r. back the enemy** hacer retroceder al enemigo

▸**roll on** *vi Fam* **r. on Friday/Christmas!** ¡que llegue el viernes/la Navidad!

▸**roll over** *vi (several times)* dar vueltas; *(once) (of person)* darse la vuelta; *(of car)* dar una vuelta (de campana)

▸**roll up 1** *vt sep (map)* enrollar; *(trousers)* remangar, arremangar; *(blind, car window)* subir; **to r. sth up in paper** envolver algo con papel; **to r. up one's sleeves** remangarse or arremangarse la camisa

**2** *vi Fam (arrive)* llegar; **r. up!, r. up!** ¡acérquense!, ¡vengan todos!

**rolled-up** [rəʊl'dʌp] *adj (sleeves, trousers)* remangado(a), arremangado(a); *(umbrella)* cerrado(a); *(newspaper)* enrollado(a)

**roller** ['rəʊlə(r)] *n (for paint, garden, in machine)* rodillo *m*; *(for hair)* rulo *m*; **r. blades** patines *mpl* en línea; **r. coaster** montaña *f* rusa; **r. skates** patines *mpl* (de ruedas)

**roller-blading** ['rəʊləbleɪdɪŋ] *n* **to go r.** patinar *(con patines en línea)*

**roller-skate** ['rəʊləskeɪt] *vi* patinar (sobre ruedas)

**roller-skating** ['rəʊləskeɪtɪŋ] *n* **to go r.** ir a patinar (sobre ruedas)

**rolling** ['rəʊlɪŋ] *adj (hills, fields)* ondulado(a); *(sea, waves)* ondulante; *(thunder)* retumbante; **r. mill** *(for steel)* laminadora *f*; **r. pin** rodillo *m* (de cocina); *Rail* **r. stock** material *m* móvil or rodante

**rollneck** ['rəʊlnek] *adj (sweater)* de cuello vuelto

**roll-on** ['rəʊlɒn] *adj* **(a)** **r. (deodorant)** desodorante *m* de bola **(b)** *Naut* **r.-roll-off ferry**

transbordador *m*, ferry *m* (*con trasbordo horizontal*)

**roll-top desk** ['rəʊltɒp'desk] *n* buró *m*

**roll-up** ['rəʊlʌp] *n Fam* (*cigarette*) pitillo *m* (liado a mano)

**roly-poly** ['rəʊlɪ'pəʊlɪ] *adj Fam* (*plump*) rechoncho(a)

**ROM** [rɒm] *n Comptr* (*abbr* **read only memory**) (memoria *f*) ROM *f*

**Roman** ['rəʊmən] **1** *n* romano(a) *m,f*
  **2** *adj* romano(a); *Rel* **R. Catholic** católico(a) (romano(a)); **R. nose** nariz *f* aguileña; **R. numerals** números *mpl* romanos

**roman** ['rəʊmən] *n Typ* (*caracteres mpl* en) redonda *f*

**romance** ['rəʊmæns, rə'mæns] *n* (**a**) (*book*) novela *f* rosa; (*film*) película *f* romántica *or* de amor (**b**) (*love affair*) romance *m*, aventura *f* (amorosa) (**c**) (*charm*) encanto *m*

**Romania** [rə'meɪnɪə] *n* Rumanía

**Romanian** [rə'meɪnɪən] **1** *n* (**a**) (*person*) rumano(a) *m,f* (**b**) (*language*) rumano *m*
  **2** *adj* rumano(a)

**romantic** [rə'mæntɪk] *n & adj* romántico(a) *m,f*

**romanticism** [rəʊ'mæntɪsɪzəm] *n* (*of person, in art*) romanticismo *m*

**romanticize** [rə'mæntɪsaɪz] *vt* (*idea, incident*) idealizar; **to r. war** rodear la guerra de un halo romántico

**Romany** ['rəʊmənɪ] **1** *n* (**a**) (*person*) romaní *mf*, gitano(a) *m,f* (**b**) (*language*) romaní *m*; (*in Spain*) caló *m*
  **2** *adj* romaní, gitano(a)

**Rome** [rəʊm] *n* Roma; *Prov* **R. wasn't built in a day** no se ganó Zamora en una hora; *Prov* **when in R., (do as the Romans do)** (allá) donde fueres haz lo que vieres

**romp** [rɒmp] **1** *n* to have a r. juguetear; **the play is an enjoyable r.** la obra es un divertimiento agradable
  **2** *vi* **to r. (about** *or* **around)** juguetear; **to r. through an examination** sacar un examen con toda facilidad

**romper** ['rɒmpə(r)] *n* **r. suit, rompers** pelele *m*

**roof** [ru:f] **1** *n* (*of building*) tejado *m*; (*of car, tunnel, cave*) techo *m*; **to have a r. over one's head** tener un techo *or* sitio donde dormir; **to live under one** *or* **the same r.** vivir bajo el mismo techo; *Fam* **to hit the r.** (*of person*) ponerse hecho(a) una furia; *Fam* **to go through the r.** (*of inflation, prices*) ponerse por las nubes; **the r. of the mouth** el paladar, el cielo de la boca; **r. garden** azotea *f* con jardín *or* ajardinada; *Aut* **r. rack** baca *f*
  **2** *vt* techar, cubrir

**roofing** ['ru:fɪŋ] *n* **r. material** (*for making roofs*) techumbre *f*; (*for covering roofs*) revestimiento *m* de tejados

**rooftop** ['ru:ftɒp] *n* tejado *m*; *Fig* **to shout sth from the rooftops** proclamar algo a los cuatro vientos

**rook** [rʊk] *n* (*bird*) grajo *m*; (*in chess*) torre *f*

**rookery** ['rʊkərɪ] *n* colonia *f* de grajos

**rookie** ['rʊkɪ] *n US Fam* novato(a) *m,f*

**room** [ru:m] *n* (**a**) (*in house*) habitación *f*, cuarto *m*; (*in hotel*) habitación *f*; (*bedroom*) dormitorio *m*; (*large, public*) sala *f*; **double/single r.** habitación doble/individual; **r. and board** pensión *f* completa; **r. service** servicio *m* de habitaciones (**b**) (*space*) espacio *m*, sitio *m*; **there's no r.** no hay sitio; **to make r. (for sb)** hacer sitio (para *or* a alguien); **is there r. for one more?** ¿cabe uno más?; **there's no r. for doubt** no hay lugar a dudas; **there is r. for improvement** se puede mejorar

**roomy** ['ru:mɪ] *adj* espacioso(a)

**roost** [ru:st] **1** *n* percha *f*, palo *m*; **to rule the r.** manejar el cotarro
  **2** *vi* estar posado(a) (*para dormir*); *Fig* **his actions have come home to r.** ahora está sufriendo las consecuencias de sus actos

**rooster** ['ru:stə(r)] *n* gallo *m*

**root** [ru:t] **1** *n* (**a**) (*of plant, tooth, word*) raíz *f*; **to pull sth up by the roots** arrancar algo de raíz; **to take r.** (*of plant, idea*) arraigar; **they destroyed the party r. and branch** destrozaron el partido por completo; *Fig* **to put down roots** echar raíces; *Fig* **to get back to one's roots** volver a las raíces; *US* **r. beer** = bebida gaseosa sin alcohol elaborada con extractos de plantas; **r. crops** tubérculos *mpl* (comestibles); **r. vegetables** tubérculos *mpl* (**b**) (*origin*) raíz *f*; **the conflict has its roots in the past** el conflicto hunde sus raíces en el pasado; *Prov* **money is the r. of all evil** el dinero es la raíz de todos los males
  **2** *vt* **to be rooted to the spot** quedarse de una pieza
  **3** *vi* (**a**) **to r. about** *or* **around (for sth)** rebuscar (algo) (**b**) *US* **to r. for sb** apoyar a alguien

▶**root out** *vt sep* (*racism, crime*) cortar de raíz

**rope** [rəʊp] **1** *n* (**a**) (*thick, for hanging*) soga *f*; (*thinner*) cuerda *f*; *Naut* cabo *m*, maroma *f*; (*of pearls*) sarta *f*; **r. ladder** escalera *f* de cuerda (**b**) (*idioms*) **to be on the ropes** estar contra las cuerdas; **to learn the ropes** ponerse al tanto (*con un trabajo*); **to show sb the ropes** poner a alguien al tanto; **to give sb plenty of r.** dar gran libertad de movimientos a alguien
  **2** *vt* (*fasten*) atar (**to** a); **they roped themselves together** (*for climbing*) se encordaron

▶**rope in** *vt sep Fam* **to r. sb in (to doing sth)** liar a alguien (para hacer algo)

▶**rope off** *vt sep* acordonar

**rop(e)y** ['rəʊpɪ] *adj Fam (unreliable)* flojo(a); *(ill)* pachucho(a)

**rosary** ['rəʊzərɪ] *n Rel* rosario *m*; **to say one's r.** rezar el rosario

**rose** [rəʊz] **1** *n* (a) *(flower)* rosa *f*; *(on watering can, shower)* alcachofa *f*; **r. (bush)** rosal *m*; **r. bed** macizo *m* de rosas; **r. garden** rosaleda *f*, jardín *m* de rosas; **r. grower** cultivador(ora) *m,f* de rosas; *Archit* **r. window** rosetón *m* (b) *(idioms)* **life is not a bed of roses** la vida no es un lecho *or* camino de rosas; **to come up roses** salir a pedir de boca

**2** *adj (colour)* rosa

**3** *pt of* **rise**

**rosé** ['rəʊzeɪ] *n (wine)* rosado *m*

**rosebud** ['rəʊzbʌd] *n* capullo *m* de rosa

**rose-coloured** ['rəʊzkʌləd], **rose-tinted** ['rəʊztɪntɪd] *adj* rosado(a), color de rosa; **to see things through r. glasses** *or* **spectacles** ver las cosas de color de rosa

**rosehip** ['rəʊzhɪp] *n* escaramujo *m*

**rosemary** ['rəʊzmərɪ] *n* romero *m*

**rosette** [rəʊ'zet] *n (badge of party, team)* escarapela *f*

**rose-water** ['rəʊzwɔːtə(r)] *n* agua *f* de rosas

**rosewood** ['rəʊzwʊd] *n* palo *m* de rosa

**roster** ['rɒstə(r)] *n* lista *f*

**rostrum** ['rɒstrəm] *n* estrado *m*

**rosy** ['rəʊzɪ] *adj (pink)* rosa, rosado(a); *(cheeks, complexion)* sonrosado(a); *Fig (future)* (de) color de rosa

**rot** [rɒt] **1** *n* (a) *(in house, wood)* podredumbre *f*; *Fig* **the r. has set in** el mal ha empezado a arraigar; *Fig* **to stop the r.** impedir que la situación siga degenerando (b) *Fam (nonsense)* bobadas *fpl*, sandeces *fpl*

**2** *vt (pt & pp* **rotted)** pudrir

**3** *vi* pudrirse; **to r. in prison** pudrirse en la cárcel

**rota** ['rəʊtə] *n* horario *m* con los turnos

**rotary** ['rəʊtərɪ] **1** *n US (roundabout)* rotonda *f*

**2** *adj (movement)* rotatorio(a), giratorio(a); **r. pump** bomba *f* rotatoria

**rotate** [rəʊ'teɪt] **1** *vt* (a) *(turn)* hacer girar (b) *(alternate) (duties, crops)* alternar

**2** *vi* (a) *(turn)* girar (b) *(in job)* turnarse, rotar

**rotation** [rəʊ'teɪʃən] *n* (a) *(circular movement)* rotación *f* (b) *(in job)* rotación *f*, alternancia *f*; **by** *or* **in r.** por turno (rotatorio); **crop r.** rotación de cultivos

**rote** [rəʊt] *n* **r. learning** aprendizaje *m* memorístico; **to learn sth by r.** aprender algo de memoria *or* de corrido

**rotor** ['rəʊtə(r)] *n* rotor *m*

**rotten** ['rɒtən] *adj* (a) *(wood, egg, fruit)* podrido(a); **to be r.** estar podrido (b) *(bad, of poor quality)* malísimo(a); **I feel r.** *(ill)* me siento fatal *or* muy mal; **I feel r. about what happened** *(sorry)* siento en el alma lo que pasó; **what r. luck!** ¡qué mala pata!; **a r. trick** una canallada

**rotter** ['rɒtə(r)] *n Fam Old-fashioned* miserable *mf*, rufián *m*

**rotund** [rəʊ'tʌnd] *adj* orondo(a), rollizo(a)

**rouble** ['ruːbəl] *n (Russian currency)* rublo *m*

**rouge** [ruːʒ] *n* colorete *m*

**rough** [rʌf] **1** *n* (a) *(in golf)* matojos *mpl* (b) *Fam Old-fashioned (hooligan)* matón *m* (c) *(difficulty)* **to take the r. with the smooth** estar a las duras y a las maduras

**2** *adj* (a) *(surface, skin)* áspero(a); *(terrain)* accidentado(a)

(b) *(unrefined) (manners, speech)* tosco(a); *Fig* **she is a r. diamond** vale mucho, aunque no tenga muchos modales; **r. draft** borrador *m*; **r. sketch** bosquejo *m*

(c) *(violent, not gentle)* bruto(a); **to receive r. treatment** ser maltratado(a); **a r. crossing** una travesía difícil; **r. sea(s)** mar *f* brava, mar *m* embravecido

(d) *(harsh) (voice)* ronco(a); *(wine)* peleón(ona); *(spirits)* de garrafa; *Fam* **it was r. on her** fue muy duro para ella; **r. justice** injusticia *f*

(e) *(approximate) (calculation, estimate)* aproximado(a); **at a r. guess** a ojo; **I've got a r. idea of what he wants** tengo una vaga idea de *or* sé más *o* menos lo que quiere

(f) *Fam (ill)* **to feel r.** sentirse mal; **to look r.** tener mal aspecto

**3** *adv* **to play r.** jugar duro; *Fam* **to sleep r.** dormir al raso *or* a la intemperie

**4** *vt Fam* **we had to r. it** nos las apañamos como pudimos

▶**rough up** *vt sep Fam* **to r. sb up** dar a alguien una paliza

**roughage** ['rʌfɪdʒ] *n* fibra *f*

**rough-and-ready** [rʌfən'redɪ] *adj* rudimentario(a); *(person)* basto(a), tosco(a)

**rough-and-tumble** [rʌfən'tʌmbəl] *n* riña *f*, rifirrafe *m*; **the r. of politics** la brega de la política

**roughly** ['rʌflɪ] *adv* (a) *(violently)* brutalmente; **to treat sb r.** tratar a alguien con brutalidad (b) *(crudely)* groseramente (c) *(approximately)* aproximadamente; **r. (speaking)** aproximadamente

**roughness** ['rʌfnɪs] *n* (a) *(of surface, skin)* aspereza *f* (b) *(of sea)* embravecimiento *m*, agitación *f* (c) *(violent behaviour)* brutalidad *f*

**roughshod** ['rʌfʃɒd] *adv* **to ride r. over sth** pisotear algo

**rough-spoken** [rʌf'spəʊkən] *adj* malhablado(a)

**roulette** [ruː'let] *n (game)* ruleta *f*; **r. table** mesa *f* de ruleta; **r. wheel** ruleta *f*

**round** [raʊnd] **1** *n* (a) *(slice) (of bread)* rebanada *f*; **a r. of sandwiches** un sándwich *(cortado en dos o en cuatro)*

(b) *(stage of match, tournament)* vuelta *f*, ronda *f* (eliminatoria); *(in boxing)* asalto *m*, round *m*; *(of golf)* recorrido *m* (del campo); **the first r. of the elections** la primera vuelta de las elecciones; **to get through to the next r.** pasar a la siguiente ronda

(c) *(of talks, visits, drinks)* ronda *f*; **it's my r.** me toca pagar esta ronda; **a r. of applause** una ovación

(d) **to do one's rounds** *(of doctor) (visit patients at home)* hacer las visitas (a los pacientes); *(in hospital)* hacer la ronda de visitas en sala; **the daily r.** *(of tasks)* las tareas cotidianas; **one of the rumours doing the rounds** uno de los rumores que corren

(e) *Mil (bullet)* bala *f*

(f) *Mus* canon *m*

**2** *adj* (a) *(in shape)* redondo(a); **to have r. shoulders** tener las espaldas cargadas; **r. table** *(conference)* mesa *f* redonda; **r. trip** viaje *m* de ida y vuelta

(b) *(number)* redondo(a); **a r. dozen** una docena justa; **in r. figures** en números redondos

**3** *adv (surrounding)* **all (the) year r.** durante todo el año; **all r., it was a good result** en conjunto, fue un buen resultado; **to be the wrong/right way r.** *(of jumper, book)* estar del revés/del derecho; **to do sth the wrong/right way r.** hacer algo al revés/bien; **the other way r.** al revés; **to go r. to sb's house** ir a casa de alguien; **to invite sb r.** invitar a alguien a casa

**4** *prep* (a) *(position)* alrededor de; **r. the table** en torno a la mesa; **r. here** por aquí

(b) *(motion)* **to look r. the room** mirar por toda la habitación; **to travel r. the world** viajar por todo el mundo; **to go r. an obstacle** rodear un obstáculo; **to go r. the corner** doblar la esquina; **it's just r. the corner** está a la vuelta de la esquina; *Fig* **to drive *or* send sb r. the bend** volver loco(a) a alguien

(c) *(approximately)* **r. about** alrededor de, aproximadamente; **r. about midday** a eso del mediodía

**5** *vt* (a) *(make round)* redondear

(b) *(move round) (obstacle)* rodear; *(corner)* doblar

(c) *(figures)* **to r. up/down** redondear al alza/a la baja

▸**round off** *vt sep (conclude)* rematar, concluir

▸**round up** *vt sep (cattle)* recoger; *(criminals, suspects)* detener

**roundabout** ['raʊndəbaʊt] **1** *n* (a) *(at fairground)* tiovivo *m* (b) *(for cars)* rotonda *f*

**2** *adj (approach, route)* indirecto(a); **to lead up to a question in a r. way** preguntar algo después de un largo preámbulo

**rounders** ['raʊndəz] *n (game)* = juego similar al béisbol

**roundly** ['raʊndlɪ] *adv (praise, condemn)* con rotundidad

**round-trip** ['raʊnd'trɪp] *adj US (ticket)* de ida y vuelta

**round-up** ['raʊndʌp] *n (of criminals)* redada *f*; *(on TV, radio)* resumen *m*

**rouse** [raʊz] *vt (from sleep)* despertar; *(make more active)* incitar; **to r. oneself (to do sth)** animarse (a hacer algo); **to r. sb to action** empujar a alguien a la acción; **to r. sb to anger** encolerizar a alguien

**rousing** ['raʊzɪŋ] *adj (music, speech)* estimulante; *(welcome, send-off, cheers)* entusiasta

**rout** [raʊt] **1** *n* derrota *f* aplastante

**2** *vt* arrollar, aplastar

**route** [ruːt] **1** *n (of traveller)* ruta *f*, itinerario *m*; *(of plane, ship)* ruta *f*; *(of parade)* itinerario *m*; *(to failure, success)* vía *f* (**to** hacia); **bus r.** línea *f* de autobús

**2** *vt* hacer pasar, dirigir; **the train was routed through Birmingham** hicieron pasar el tren por Birmingham

**routine** [ruː'tiːn] **1** *n* (a) *(habit)* rutina *f*; **the daily r.** la rutina diaria (b) *(of performer, comedian)* número *m*; *Fam Fig* **don't give me that r.** no me vengas con ese cuento (c) *Comptr* rutina *f*

**2** *adj* (a) *(normal)* habitual; **r. enquiries** investigación *f* rutinaria (b) *(dull)* rutinario(a), monótono(a)

**routinely** [ruː'tiːnlɪ] *adv* habitualmente

**rove** [rəʊv] **1** *vt* vagar por

**2** *vi* vagar; **his eyes roved around the room** sus ojos recorrieron la habitación

**row**[1] [rəʊ] *n* hilera *f*; *(of seats)* fila *f*; **in a r.** en hilera, en fila; **two Sundays in a r.** dos domingos seguidos; **in the front r.** *(of seats)* en primera fila

**row**[2] [rəʊ] **1** *n (in boat)* paseo *m* en barca; **to go for a r.** darse un paseo en barca

**2** *vt* **to r. a boat** llevar una barca remando; **he rowed us across the river** nos llevó al otro lado del río en barca

**3** *vi* remar

**row**[3] [raʊ] **1** *n* (a) *(noise)* jaleo *m*, alboroto *m*; *(protest)* escándalo *m* (b) *(quarrel)* bronca *f*, trifulca *f*; **to have a r. (with sb)** tener una bronca (con alguien)

**2** *vi* discutir

**rowan** ['raʊən] *n* serbal *m*

**rowboat** ['rəʊbəʊt] *n US* bote *m or* barca *f* de remos

**rowdy** ['raʊdɪ] **1** *n* alborotador(ora) *m,f*

**2** *adj* (*noisy*) ruidoso(a); (*disorderly*) alborotador(ora)

**rower** ['rəʊə(r)] *n* remero(a) *m,f*

**rowing** ['rəʊɪŋ] *n* remo *m*; **r. boat** bote *m* or barca *f* de remos; **r. machine** banco *m* de remo

**royal** ['rɔɪəl] **1** *n Fam* **the Royals** la familia real

**2** *adj* real; (*splendid*) magnífico(a); **His/Her R. Highness** Su Alteza Real; **r. blue** azul *m* real (*intenso y más claro que el marino*); **the R. Family** la Familia Real; **r. jelly** jalea *f* real

**royalist** ['rɔɪəlɪst] *n & adj* monárquico(a) *m,f*

**royally** ['rɔɪəlɪ] *adv* (*entertain, welcome*) con magnificencia

**royalty** ['rɔɪəltɪ] *n* (*a*) (*rank, position*) realeza *f* (*b*) **royalties** (*for author, singer*) derechos *mpl* de autor

**RP** [ɑːˈpiː] *n Ling* (*abbr* **received pronunciation**) pronunciación *f* estándar (*del inglés*)

**RPI** [ɑːpiːˈaɪ] *n Econ* (*abbr* **retail price index**) IPC *m*, Índice *m* de Precios al Consumo

**RPM** [ɑːpiːˈem] *n Econ* (*abbr* **resale price maintenance**) mantenimiento *m or* fijación *f* del precio de venta al público

**rpm** [ɑːpiːˈem] *n Aut* (*abbr* **revolutions per minute**) rpm, revoluciones *fpl* por minuto

**R & R** [ɑːrənˈɑː(r)] *n Mil* (*abbr* **rest and recreation**) permiso *m*

**RRP** *Com* (*abbr* **recommended retail price**) P.V.P. *m* recomendado, precio *m* de venta al público recomendado

**RS** [ɑːˈres] *n Br* (*abbr* **Royal Society**) ≃ academia británica de las ciencias

**RSA** [ɑːresˈeɪ] *n abbr* **Republic of South Africa** República *f* de Sudáfrica

**RSPB** [ɑːrespiːˈbiː] *n Br* (*abbr* **Royal Society for the Protection of Birds**) = sociedad protectora de las aves, ≃ SEO *f*

**RSPCA** [ɑːrespiːsiːˈeɪ] *n Br* (*abbr* **Royal Society for the Prevention of Cruelty to Animals**) = sociedad protectora de animales

**RSVP** [ɑːresviːˈpiː] (*abbr* **répondez s'il vous plaît**) (*on invitation*) se ruega contestación

**Rt Hon** *Br Parl* (*abbr* **Right Honourable**) = tratamiento que se da a los diputados en el Parlamento británico, ≃ su señoría

**rub** [rʌb] **1** *n* **to give sth a r.** frotar algo; *Fig* **there's the r.!** ¡ahí está el problema!

**2** *vt* (*pt & pp* **rubbed**) frotar; **to r. one's hands together** frotarse las manos; *Fig* **to r. shoulders with** codearse con; *Fam* **to r. sb up the wrong way** caer mal a alguien; *Fam* **there's no need to r. it in!** ¡no tienes por qué restregármelo por las narices!

**3** *vi* (*of straps, shoes*) rozar (**against** contra)

▸**rub along** *vi Fam* (*a*) (*manage*) apañarse, defenderse (*b*) (*get on*) llevarse bien (**with** con)

▸**rub off 1** *vt sep* (*dirt, stains*) limpiar, eliminar (*frotando*); (*writing*) borrar

**2** *vi borrarse*; *Fig* **to r. off on sb** (*of manners, enthusiasm*) influir en or contagiarse a alguien

▸**rub out** *vt sep* (*a*) (*erase*) borrar (*b*) *Fam* (*murder*) cepillarse, cargarse

**rubber** ['rʌbə(r)] *n* (*a*) (*substance*) goma *f*, *Am* hule *m*; **r. ball** pelota *f* de goma; **r. band** goma (elástica); **r. dinghy** lancha *f* neumática; **r. gloves** guantes *mpl* de goma; **r. plant** ficus *m* *inv*; **r. ring** (*swimming aid*) flotador *m* (*aro*); **r. stamp** tampón *m* de goma (*b*) (*eraser*) goma *f* (de borrar); (*for blackboards*) borrador *m* (*c*) *US Fam* (*condom*) goma *f*

**rubber-stamp** [rʌbəˈstæmp] *vt Fig* (*approve*) dar el visto bueno a

**rubbery** ['rʌbərɪ] *adj* correoso(a)

**rubbish** ['rʌbɪʃ] **1** *n* (*a*) (*refuse, junk*) basura *f*; **r. bin** cubo *m* de la basura; **r. collection** recogida *f* de basuras; **r. dump** vertedero *m* (de basura); *Fig* **to throw sth/sb on the r. heap** desahuciar algo/a alguien (*b*) (*nonsense*) tonterías *fpl*, bobadas *fpl*; **to talk r.** decir tonterías; **that book is a load of r.** ese libro es una porquería

**2** *vt Fam* (*book, plan*) poner por los suelos

**rubble** ['rʌbəl] *n* escombros *mpl*

**rubella** [ruːˈbelə] *n Med* rubeola *f*

**rubric** ['ruːbrɪk] *n* (*set of instructions*) directrices *fpl*, normas *fpl*

**ruby** ['ruːbɪ] **1** *n* rubí *m*

**2** *adj* (*colour*) rojo(a) intenso(a) *or* rubí

**ruck¹** [rʌk] *n* (*in rugby*) melé *f* espontánea

**ruck²** *n* (*in cloth*) arruga *f*

▸**ruck up** *vi* (*of sheet, dress*) arrugarse

**rucksack** ['rʌksæk] *n* macuto *m*, mochila *f*

**ructions** ['rʌkʃənz] *npl Fam* bronca *f*, jaleo *m*; **there'll be r.** se va a armar la gorda

**rudder** ['rʌdə(r)] *n* (*on boat, plane*) timón *m*

**ruddy** ['rʌdɪ] *adj* (*a*) (*complexion*) rubicundo(a); (*sky*) rojizo(a), arrebolado(a) (*b*) *Br Fam* (*euphemism for* **bloody**) condenado(a); **the r. fool!** ¡el/la muy estúpido(a)!

**rude** [ruːd] *adj* (*a*) (*impolite*) maleducado(a), grosero(a) (*b*) (*indecent*) de mal gusto, ordinario(a); **a r. joke** un chiste verde (*c*) (*primitive*) tosco(a) (*d*) (*shock, surprise*) duro(a); **to receive a r. awakening** llevarse una desagradable sorpresa (*e*) (*vigorous*) **to be in r. health** estar rebosante de salud

**rudeness** ['ruːdnɪs] *n* (*a*) (*impoliteness*) mala educación *f*, grosería *f* (*b*) (*indecency*) (*of joke, story*) ordinariez *f*, mal gusto *m*

**rudimentary** [ruːdɪˈmentərɪ] *adj* rudimentario(a)

**rudiments** ['ru:dɪmənts] *npl* rúdimentos *mpl*, fundamentos *mpl*

**rue** [ru:] *vt Formal* lamentar, deplorar

**rueful** ['ru:fʊl] *adj* compungido(a)

**ruff** [rʌf] *n (on costume)* golilla *f*

**ruffian** ['rʌfɪən] *n Old-fashioned* rufián *m*

**ruffle** ['rʌfəl] *vt (disturb) (water surface)* rizar; *(hair)* despeinar; **to r. sb's feathers** hacer enfadar a alguien; **to r. sb's composure** hacer perder la calma a alguien

**rug** [rʌg] *n* (a) *(carpet)* alfombra *f*; *Fig* **to pull the r. from under sb's feet** dejar a alguien en la estacada (b) *(blanket)* manta *f*

**rugby** ['rʌgbɪ] *n* rugby *m*; **r. league** = modalidad de rugby con trece jugadores; **r. union** rugby *(de quince jugadores)*; **r. tackle** placaje *m*

**rugby-tackle** ['rʌgbɪ'tækəl] *vt* **to r. sb** hacer un placaje a alguien, atrapar a alguien por las piernas

**rugged** ['rʌgɪd] *adj* (a) *(ground, country)* irregular, accidentado(a); **r. features** rasgos *mpl* recios (b) *(manner)* rudo(a), tosco(a)

**rugger** ['rʌgə(r)] *n Fam (rugby)* rugby *m*

**ruin** ['ru:ɪn] **1** *n* ruina *f*; **to fall into ruin(s)** quedar en ruinas; **it will be the r. of him** será su ruina; **r. is staring us in the face** estamos a punto de perderlo todo
**2** *vt* arruinar; **to r. one's health/eyesight** arruinarse la salud/la vista; **we're ruined** estamos arruinados; **the meal's ruined** se ha echado a perder la comida; **tourism has ruined the town** el turismo ha echado a perder la ciudad

**ruined** ['ru:ɪnd] *adj (building)* en ruinas

**ruinous** ['ru:ɪnəs] *adj (expense)* ruinoso(a); **in a r. condition** en un estado ruinoso

**rule** [ru:l] **1** *n* (a) *(principle, regulation)* regla *f*, norma *f*; **as a r.** por norma, por regla general; **to make it a r. to do sth** tener por costumbre *or* norma hacer algo; **rules and regulations** normativa *f*, reglamento *m*; *Ind* **to work to r.** hacer huelga de celo; **it's against the rules** va contra las normas; **as a r. of thumb** por regla general; **r. book** reglamento *m*
(b) *(government)* gobierno *m*; **under British r.** bajo dominio *or* gobierno británico; **the r. of law** el imperio de la ley
(c) *(for measuring)* regla *f*
**2** *vt* (a) *(country, people)* gobernar; **don't let him r. your life** no le dejes que gobierne *or* controle tu vida
(b) *(decide, decree)* decretar, determinar
(c) *(paper)* rayar; **ruled paper** papel *m* rayado *or* pautado
**3** *vi* (a) *(of monarch)* reinar
(b) *(of judge)* decidir, fallar; **to r. in favour of/against sb** fallar a favor de/en contra de alguien

▶**rule out** *vt sep* descartar, excluir

**ruler** ['ru:lə(r)] *n* (a) *(of country)* gobernante *mf* (b) *(for measuring)* regla *f*

**ruling** ['ru:lɪŋ] **1** *n (of judge, umpire)* fallo *m*, decisión *f*
**2** *adj (passion, consideration)* predominante, primordial; *(party)* gobernante, en el poder; **the r. classes** las clases dirigentes

**rum¹** [rʌm] *n (drink)* ron *m*

**rum²** *adj Fam (strange)* raro(a)

**Rumania = Romania**

**Rumanian = Romanian**

**rumble** ['rʌmbəl] **1** *n (of thunder, gunfire)* rugido *m*, retumbo *m*; *(of cart)* fragor *m*, estrépito *m*; *(of stomach)* gruñido *m*; **rumbles of discontent** murmullos *mpl* de insatisfacción
**2** *vt Fam (see through)* pillar, descubrir (el juego a); **we've been rumbled** nos han pillado
**3** *vi (of thunder)* retumbar; *(of stomach)* gruñir; **to r. past** pasar rugiendo

**rumbustious** [rʌm'bʌstjəs] *adj* bullicioso(a)

**ruminant** ['ru:mɪnənt] *n Zool* rumiante *m*

**ruminate** ['ru:mɪneɪt] *vi Formal* **to r. about** *or* **on sth** meditar acerca de algo

**rummage** ['rʌmɪdʒ] *vi* **he rummaged through my suitcase** rebuscó en *or* revolvió mi maleta

**rumour** ['ru:mə(r)] **1** *n* rumor *m*; **r. has it that...** según los rumores,...; **there's a r. going round that...** corren rumores de que...
**2** *vt* **it is rumoured that...** se rumorea que...; **he is rumoured to be about to resign** se rumorea que está a punto de dimitir

**rump** [rʌmp] *n* (a) *(of animal)* cuartos *mpl* traseros; *Fam (of person)* trasero *m*; **r. steak** filete *m* de lomo (b) *(of political party, assembly)* resto *m* *(tras escisión)*

**rumple** ['rʌmpəl] *vt (crease)* arrugar; *(hair)* despeinar

**rumpus** ['rʌmpəs] *n Fam (noise)* follón *m*, jaleo *m*; **to kick up** *or* **cause a r.** armar un jaleo *or* un follón

**run** [rʌn] **1** *n* (a) *(act of running)* carrera *f*; **at a r.** corriendo; **to go for a r.** ir a correr; **to be on the r.** *(of prisoner, suspect)* estar fugado(a) *or* en fuga; *Fig* **we've got them on the r.** los tenemos contra las cuerdas; **to give sb the r. of the house** poner la casa a disposición de alguien; *Fam* **to make a r. for it** salir corriendo *or* por piernas; *Fam* **to give sb a r. for his money** hacer sudar (la camiseta) a alguien; *Fam* **to have the runs** estar suelto(a), tener cagalera
(b) *(trip) (in car)* vuelta *f*; **to go for a r.** ir a dar una vuelta (en coche)
(c) *Com (of book)* tirada *f*; *(of product)* partida *f*,

tanda f

(**d**) *(sequence, series)* serie f; *(in cards)* escalera f; **a r. of good/bad luck** una racha de buena/mala suerte; **in the long r.** a la larga, a largo plazo; **in the short r.** a corto plazo; **in the ordinary r. of things** en condiciones normales

(**e**) *Fin (on bank, stock exchange)* retirada f masiva de fondos; **a r. on the dollar** una fuerte presión sobre el dólar

(**f**) *(in cricket)* carrera f

(**g**) *(in stocking)* carrera f

(**h**) *(for skier)* pista f

(**i**) *(for chickens, rabbits)* corral m

(**j**) *Mus* carrerilla f

**2** vt *(pt* **ran** [ræn], *pp* **run**) (**a**) *(distance)* correr, recorrer; **to r. a race** correr (en) una carrera; **to r. an errand** hacer un recado; **to allow things to r. their course** dejar que las cosas sigan su curso; **to r. sb close** quedarse a un paso de vencer a alguien; *Fam* **we were run off our feet** no tuvimos ni un momento de descanso

(**b**) *(drive)* **to r. sb to the airport** llevar a alguien al aeropuerto

(**c**) *(smuggle) (drugs, arms)* pasar de contrabando

(**d**) *(operate) (machine, car)* hacer funcionar; *(tests)* hacer, efectuar; *Comptr (program)* ejecutar; **this car is expensive to r.** este coche consume mucho

(**e**) *(manage) (business, hotel)* dirigir, llevar; **stop trying to r. my life for me!** ¡deja de dirigir mi vidal; *Fig* **who's running the show?** ¿quién está a cargo de esto?

(**f**) *(pass) (cables, pipes)* hacer pasar; **to r. one's fingers over sth** acariciar algo; **he ran his fingers through his hair** se pasó los dedos entre los cabellos; **she ran her eye over the page** echó una ojeada a la página

(**g**) *(water)* dejar correr; **to r. a bath** preparar un baño

(**h**) **to r. a temperature** tener fiebre; **to r. a deficit** tener déficit; **to r. an article** publicar un artículo

**3** vi (**a**) *(of person)* correr; **to r. up/down the street** subir/bajar la calle corriendo; **to r. about** correr de acá para allá; **I'll just r. across** or **round to the shop** voy en un momento a la tienda; **to r. after sb** correr detrás de alguien; **to r. for help** correr en busca de ayuda; **to r. out** *(exit)* salir corriendo; *Fig* **to r. out on sb** abandonar a alguien

(**b**) *(flee)* escapar corriendo; **r. for it!** ¡huye!, ¡corre!

(**c**) *(compete in race)* correr; **to r. for Parliament** presentarse a las elecciones parlamentarias

(**d**) *(flow)* correr; **the river runs into a lake** el río desemboca en un lago; **my nose is running** me moquea la nariz, tengo mocos; **my blood ran cold** se me heló la sangre en las venas

(**e**) **to r. aground** *(of ship)* encallar, embarrancar; *Fig (of project, economy)* irse al traste, malograrse

(**f**) *(last, extend) (contract, lease)* durar; *(play)* estar en cartel; **it runs in the family** es cosa de familia; **a murmur ran through the crowd** se extendió un murmullo entre la multitud; **that song keeps running through my head** no se me va esa canción de la cabeza; **the total ran to £2,000** el total ascendió a 2.000 libras

(**g**) *(of bus, train)* circular; **to be running late** *(of bus, person)* ir con retraso

(**h**) *(operate) (of machine)* funcionar (**on** con); **the engine's running** el motor está en marcha; **the software won't r. on this machine** el programa no funciona en este ordenador; **to r. off the mains** funcionar conectado(a) a la red; **things are running smoothly** las cosas marchan bien

(**i**) *(pass) (of road, railway)* ir; **the line runs along the coast** la línea de tren discurre paralela a la costa

(**j**) *(feelings* or *tempers are running high* los ánimos están revueltos; **supplies are running low** se están agotando las reservas; **the river had run dry** el río se había secado

(**k**) *(of colour, dye)* desteñir

▶**run away** vi *(of person)* escapar, huir; **to r. away from home** escaparse de casa; *Fig* **to r. away from the facts** no querer ver los hechos; *Fig* **don't r. away with the idea that...** no vayas a pensar que...

▶**run down 1** vt sep (**a**) *(in car)* atropellar (**b**) *(find)* localizar, encontrar (**c**) *(criticize)* menospreciar, criticar (**d**) *(reduce) (production, stocks)* reducir, disminuir; *(industry, factory)* desmantelar

**2** vi *(of battery)* agotarse

▶**run in** vt sep (**a**) *Fam (arrest)* detener (**b**) *(engine)* rodar

▶**run into** vt insep (**a**) *(collide with)* chocar con or contra; **to r. into difficulties** tropezar con problemas (**b**) *(meet by chance)* encontrarse con

▶**run off 1** vt sep *(print)* tirar

**2** vi echar a correr, salir corriendo; **to r. off with the cash** escapar con el dinero; **to r. off with sb** escaparse con alguien

▶**run on** vi *(of meeting)* continuar; *Fam (talk a lot)* hablar sin parar

▶**run out** vi *(of lease, contract)* vencer, cumplirse; *(of money, supplies)* agotarse; **to r. out of sth** quedarse sin algo; *Fig* **to r. out of steam** *(of person)* quedarse sin fuerzas; *(of project)* perder empuje

►**run over 1** *vt sep (in car)* atropellar

**2** *vt insep (rehearse, check)* ensayar, repasar

**3** *vi (of speech, TV programme)* durar demasiado

►**run to** *vt insep* poder permitirse; **I'm afraid we don't r. to that kind of thing** me temo que el dinero no nos da para algo así

►**run up** *vt sep* (**a**) *(debts)* acumular (**b**) *(flag)* izar (**c**) *(clothes)* hacerse, coser

**run-around** ['rʌnəraʊnd] *n Fam* **to give sb the r.** enredar a alguien

**runaway** ['rʌnəweɪ] **1** *n* fugitivo(a) *m,f*

**2** *adj (prisoner, slave)* fugitivo(a); *(train, lorry)* incontrolado(a); *(inflation)* galopante; *(victory, success)* apabullante

**rundown** ['rʌndaʊn] *n (summary)* resumen *m*, informe *m*; **to give sb a r.** poner a alguien al tanto

**run-down** [rʌn'daʊn] *adj (building)* ruinoso(a); *(person)* pachucho(a), débil

**rung** [rʌŋ] **1** *n (of ladder)* peldaño *m*, escalón *m*; *Fig* **the bottom r.** *(in organization)* el escalón más bajo

**2** *pp of* **ring²**

**run-in** ['rʌnɪn] *n Fam* **to have a r. with sb** tener una pelea *or* una riña con alguien

**runner** ['rʌnə(r)] *n* (**a**) *(athlete)* corredor(ora) *m,f*; *(messenger)* mensajero(a) *m,f*, recadero(a) *m,f* (**b**) **r. bean** judía *f* verde (**c**) *(on sleigh)* patín *m* (**d**) *(carpet)* alfombra *f* estrecha (para escaleras) (**e**) *Fam* **to do a r.** salir por piernas

**runner-up** [rʌnə'rʌp] *n (pl* **runners-up)** *n* subcampeón(ona) *m,f*

**running** ['rʌnɪŋ] **1** *n* (**a**) *(competition, race)* **to be out of/in the r.** no tener/tener posibilidades de ganar; **to make all the r.** *(in contest)* ocupar el primer puesto desde el principio; *US Pol* **r. mate** candidato(a) *m,f* a la vicepresidencia; **r. shoe** zapatilla *f* deportiva; **r. track** pista *f* (de atletismo)

(**b**) *(operation) (of machine, car)* funcionamiento *m*; **r. costs** costes *mpl* de mantenimiento

(**c**) *(management) (of hotel, restaurant)* dirección *f*, gestión *f*

**2** *adj (battle, feud)* continuo(a), constante; *Fam* **he told them to take a r. jump** los mandó a freír espárragos; *Aut* **r. board** estribo *m*; **r. commentary** comentario *m* en directo; **r. repairs** arreglos *mpl* (momentáneos); **r. sore** llaga *f* supurante; **r. total** total *m* actualizado; **r. water** agua *f* corriente

**runny** ['rʌnɪ] *adj (sauce, custard)* demasiado líquido(a); *(honey)* fluido(a); **to have a r. nose** tener mocos, moquear

**run-off** ['rʌnɒf] *n* desempate *m*

**run-of-the-mill** [rʌnəvðə'mɪl] *adj* corriente y moliente

**runt** [rʌnt] *n* (**a**) *(of litter)* cachorro *m* más pequeño (**b**) *(weak person)* enano(a) *m,f*, pigmeo(a) *m,f*

**run-up** ['rʌnʌp] *n (before jump)* carrerilla *f*; *(before event)* período *m* previo

**runway** ['rʌnweɪ] *n (for takeoff)* pista *f* de despegue; *(for landing)* pista *f* de aterrizaje

**rupee** [ru:'pi:] *n (Indian currency)* rupia *f*

**rupture** ['rʌptʃə(r)] **1** *n (breaking)* ruptura *f*; *Med* hernia *f*

**2** *vt (relations, container)* romper; *Med* **to r. oneself** herniarse

**3** *vi (of container, pipeline)* romperse

**rural** ['rʊərəl] *adj* rural

**ruse** [ru:z] *n* artimaña *f*, ardid *m*

**rush¹** [rʌʃ] *n (plant)* rushes juncos *mpl*; **r. matting** estera *f* de junco

**rush²** **1** *n* (**a**) *(hurry)* prisa *f*; **to be in a r.** tener prisa; **there's no r.** no hay prisa; **to make a r. for sth** apresurarse a alcanzar algo; **to make a r. at sb** abalanzarse hacia alguien; **the r. hour** la hora punta; **a r. job** una chapuza (**b**) *(surge) (of air)* ráfaga *f*; *(of water)* chorro *m*; *(of requests)* ola *f* (**c**) *(demand)* demanda *f*; **there's been a r. on sugar** ha habido una fuerte demanda de azúcar (**d**) *Cin* **rushes** primeras pruebas *fpl*

**2** *vt (hurry) (task)* realizar a toda prisa; *(person)* apresurar; **don't r. me!** ¡no me metas prisa!; **to r. sb into doing sth** meter prisa a alguien para que haga algo; **to be rushed off one's feet** no tener un momento de descanso (**b**) *(transport quickly)* llevar apresuradamente; **she was rushed to hospital** la llevaron al hospital a toda prisa (**c**) *(attack)* arremeter contra

**3** *vi (move fast)* precipitarse; *(hurry)* apresurarse, precipitarse; **I must r.** (me voy que) tengo mucha prisa; **the blood rushed to his cheeks** se le subieron los colores; **she rushed into marriage** casó demasiado apresuradamente

►**rush about, rush around** *vi* trajinar (de acá para allá)

►**rush in** *vi (enter)* entrar a toda prisa

►**rush off** *vi (flee)* irse corriendo

►**rush out 1** *vt sep (book)* sacar a toda prisa

**2** *vi (exit)* salir apresuradamente

►**rush through 1** *vt sep* **to r. a bill/decision through** aprobar un proyecto de ley/tomar una decisión a toda prisa

**2** *vt insep (book, meal, work)* despachar con rapidez

**rusk** [rʌsk] *n* = galleta dura y crujiente para niños que comienzan a masticar

**russet** ['rʌsɪt] **1** *n (colour)* castaño *m* rojizo

**2** *adj* rojizo(a)

**Russia** ['rʌʃə] *n* Rusia

**Russian** ['rʌʃən] **1** *n* (**a**) *(person)* ruso(a) *m,f* (**b**) *(language)* ruso *m*; **R. class/teacher** clase _f_ / profesor(ora) _m,f_ de ruso

  **2** _adj_ ruso(a); **R. roulette** ruleta _f_ rusa

**rust** [rʌst] **1** _n_ óxido _m_, herrumbre _f_

  **2** _adj (colour)_ color teja _inv_

  **3** _vi_ oxidarse

**rustic** ['rʌstɪk] _adj_ rústico(a)

**rustle¹** ['rʌsəl] **1** _n (of leaves)_ susurro _m; (of paper)_ crujido _m_

  **2** _vt (leaves)_ hacer susurrar; _(paper)_ hacer crujir

  **3** _vi (of leaves)_ susurrar; _(of paper)_ crujir

**rustle²** _vt (cattle)_ robar

▸**rustle up** _vt sep Fam (meal, snack)_ apañar, improvisar; **to r. up support** reunir apoyo

**rustler** ['rʌslə(r)] _n (cattle thief)_ cuatrero(a) _m,f_, ladrón(ona) _m,f_ de ganado

**rustproof** ['rʌstpruːf] _adj_ inoxidable

**rusty** ['rʌstɪ] _adj_ **(a)** _(metal)_ oxidado(a); _Fig_ **my French is a bit r.** hace mucho que no practico mi francés **(b)** _(colour)_ color teja _inv_

**rut¹** [rʌt] _n (groove)_ rodada _f; Fig_ **to be in a r.** _(routine)_ estar apalancado(a) _or_ estancado(a)

**rut²** **1** _n (of stag)_ celo _m_

  **2** _vi ( pt & pp_ **rutted**) _(of stag)_ estar en celo

**ruthless** ['ruːθlɪs] _adj_ despiadado(a); **with r. efficiency** con rigurosa eficacia

**Rwanda** [rəˈwændə] _n_ Ruanda

**Rwandan** [rəˈwændən] _n & adj_ ruandés(esa) _m,f_

**rye** [raɪ] _n_ centeno _m;_ **r. bread** pan _m_ de centeno

# S

**S, s** [es] *n* (**a**) *(letter)* S, s *f* (**b**) *(abbr* **south**) S

**Sabbath** ['sæbəθ] *n* *(Jewish)* Sabbat *m*, sábado *m* judío; *(Christian)* domingo *m*; **(witches') S.** aquelarre *m*; **S. day observance** cumplimiento *m* del descanso sabático/dominical

**sabbatical** [sə'bætɪkəl] *Univ* **1** *n* **to be on s.** estar en excedencia
**2** *adj* **s. year/term** año *m*/trimestre *m* sabático *or* de excedencia

**sable** ['seɪbəl] **1** *n* *(animal)* marta *f* cebellina; **s. coat** abrigo *m* de marta
**2** *adj Literary (black)* prieto(a), negro(a)

**sabotage** ['sæbətɑːʒ] **1** *n* sabotaje *m*
**2** *vt* sabotear

**saboteur** [sæbə'tɜː(r)] *n* saboteador(ora) *m,f*

**sabre** ['seɪbə(r)] *n* sable *m*

**sac** [sæk] *n Biol* bolsa *f*, saco *m*

**saccharin** ['sækərɪn] *n* sacarina *f*

**saccharine** ['sækərɪn] *adj Pej (smile, film)* empalagoso(a)

**sachet** ['sæʃeɪ] *n* sobrecito *m*

**sack**¹ [sæk] **1** *n* (**a**) *(bag)* saco *m*; *Fam* **to hit the s.** *(go to bed)* irse a la piltra, meterse en el sobre (**b**) *Fam (dismissal)* **to give sb the s.** echar a alguien; **he got the s.** lo echaron
**2** *vt Fam (dismiss from job)* echar, despedir

**sack**² **1** *n (plundering)* saqueo *m*
**2** *vt (town)* saquear

**sacking** ['sækɪŋ] *n* (**a**) *(textile)* arpillera *f*, tela *f* de saco (**b**) *Fam (dismissal)* despido *m*

**sacrament** ['sækrəmənt] *n Rel* sacramento *m*; **to take** *or* **receive the sacraments** tomar *or* recibir los sacramentos

**sacred** ['seɪkrɪd] *adj (place, book)* sagrado(a); *(duty, vow)* solemne; **s. to the memory of...** consagrado(a) a la memoria de...; **is nothing s.?** ¿es que ya no se respeta nada?; *Fig* **to be a s. cow** ser sacrosanto(a)

**sacrifice** ['sækrɪfaɪs] **1** *n (act, offering)* sacrificio *m*; **to make sacrifices** sacrificarse, hacer sacrificios
**2** *vt* sacrificar; **to s. oneself** sacrificarse

**sacrificial** [sækrɪ'fɪʃəl] *adj* de sacrificio; *Fig* **s. lamb** *or* **victim** chivo *m* expiatorio

**sacrilege** ['sækrɪlɪdʒ] *n also Fig* sacrilegio *m*

**sacrilegious** [sækrɪ'lɪdʒəs] *adj* sacrílego(a)

**sacristan** ['sækrɪstən] *n Rel* sacristán *m*

**sacrosanct** ['sækrəʊsæŋkt] *adj* sacrosanto(a)

**SAD** [sæd] *n Med (abbr* **Seasonal Affective Disorder)** trastorno *m* afectivo estacional

**sad** [sæd] *adj* (**a**) *(unhappy, depressing)* triste; **to become s.** entristecerse; **to make sb s.** entristecer a alguien (**b**) *Fam (pathetic)* lamentable, penoso(a)

**sadden** ['sædən] *vt* entristecer

**saddle** ['sædəl] **1** *n (on horse)* silla *f* (de montar); *(on bicycle)* sillín *m*; **in the s.** a caballo; *Fig* **to be in the s.** *(be in charge)* llevar las riendas
**2** *vt (horse)* ensillar; *Fam Fig* **to s. sb with sth** endilgar algo a alguien

**saddlebag** ['sædəlbæg] *n (for horse)* alforja *f*; *(for bicycle)* cartera *f*

**sadism** ['seɪdɪzəm] *n* sadismo *m*

**sadist** ['seɪdɪst] *n* sádico(a) *m,f*

**sadistic** [sə'dɪstɪk] *adj* sádico(a)

**sadly** ['sædlɪ] *adv (to reply, smile)* tristemente; **you're s. mistaken** estás muy equivocado(a); **he is s. missed** lo echamos mucho de menos; **s., this is so** así es, por desgracia

**sadness** ['sædnɪs] *n* tristeza *f*

**sadomasochism** [seɪdəʊ'mæsəkɪzəm] *n* sadomasoquismo *m*

**sadomasochist** [seɪdəʊ'mæsəkɪst] *n* sadomasoquista *mf*

**SAE** [eseɪ'iː] *n (abbr* **stamped addressed envelope)** sobre *m* franqueado con la dirección

**safari** [sə'fɑːrɪ] *n* safari *m*; **on s.** de safari; **s. jacket** sahariana *f*; **s. park** safari *m* park

**safe** [seɪf] **1** *n (for money)* caja *f* fuerte
**2** *adj (house, activity)* seguro(a); *(choice, topic of conversation)* prudente; **s. from sth** a salvo de algo; **s. and sound** sano(a) y salvo(a); **as s. as houses** completamente seguro; **it is s. to say that...** se puede decir sin temor a equivocarse que...; **it's a pretty s. assumption** *or* **bet that...** es prácticamente seguro que...; **at a s. distance** a una distancia prudencial; **in s. hands** en buenas manos; **to wish sb a s. journey** desear a alguien un feliz viaje *or* un viaje sin percances; **to be on the s. side** para mayor

seguridad; *Prov* **better s. than sorry** más vale prevenir (que curar); **s. house** piso *m* franco; **s. seat** *(in parliament)* escaño *m* seguro; **s. sex** sexo *m* seguro or sin riesgo

**3** *adv* **to play (it) s.** ser precavido(a)

**safe-conduct** [seɪf'kɒndʌkt] *n* salvoconducto *m*

**safeguard** ['seɪfɡɑːd] **1** *n* salvaguardia *f*, garantía *f*

**2** *vt (sb's interests, rights)* salvaguardar

**3** *vi* **to s. against sth** salvaguardarse or protegerse de algo

**safe-keeping** [seɪf'kiːpɪŋ] *n* **in s.** bajo custodia

**safely** ['seɪflɪ] *adv (without risk)* sin riesgos; **once we're s. home** cuando estemos tranquilos en casa; **drive s.!** ¡conduce con cuidado!; **to arrive s.** llegar sano(a) y salvo(a) **(b)** *(with certainty)* con certeza; **I can s. say that...** puedo decir sin temor a equivocarme que...

**safety** ['seɪftɪ] *n* seguridad *f*; **for s.'s sake** para mayor seguridad; **she's very s. conscious** tiene muy en cuenta la seguridad; *Prov* **there's s. in numbers** en compañía está uno más seguro; **s. belt** cinturón *m* de seguridad; **s. catch** *(on gun)* seguro *m*; **s. glass** vidrio *m* de seguridad; **s. matches** cerillas *fpl* de seguridad; **s. measures** medidas *fpl* de seguridad; **s. net** red *f* (de seguridad); *Fig* red *f* asistencial (del Estado); *Fig* **to fall through the s. net** quedar excluido(a) de la red asistencial; **s. pin** imperdible *m*; *also Fig* **s. valve** válvula *f* de escape

**saffron** ['sæfrən] **1** *n* azafrán *m*

**2** *adj* (de color) azafrán

**sag** [sæɡ] (*pt & pp* **sagged**) *vi (of roof, bridge)* hundirse, ceder; *(of flesh, rope)* colgar; *(of confidence, support)* decaer

**saga** ['sɑːɡə] *n (story)* saga *f*; *Fig* **a s. of corruption** una historia interminable de corrupción

**sagacious** [sə'ɡeɪʃəs] *adj Formal* sagaz

**sagacity** [sə'ɡæsɪtɪ] *n Formal* sagacidad *f*

**sage**[1] [seɪdʒ] **1** *n (wise man)* sabio *m*

**2** *adj (person, conduct)* sabio(a)

**sage**[2] *n (herb)* salvia *f*

**Sagittarius** [sædʒɪ'teərɪəs] *n (sign of zodiac)* Sagitario *m*; **to be (a) S.** ser Sagitario

**Sahara** [sə'hɑːrə] *n* **the S. (Desert)** el (desierto del) Sahara

**said** [sed] *pt & pp of* **say**

**sail** [seɪl] **1** *n (on boat)* vela *f*; *(of windmill)* aspa *f*; **to set s. (for)** zarpar (con rumbo a); **to go for a s.** hacer una excursión en velero

**2** *vi (of ship, person)* navegar; *(start voyage)* zarpar; **the clouds sailed by** las nubes avanzaban suavemente; *Fig* **to s. close to the wind** adentrarse en terreno peligroso; **his book sailed out of the window** su libro salió volando por la ventana; *Fam* **to s. through an examination** pasar un examen con la gorra

**sailing** ['seɪlɪŋ] *n (activity)* (navegación *f* a) vela *f*; *(departure)* salida *f*; *Br* **s. boat/ship** (barco *m*/buque *m*) velero *m*

**sailor** ['seɪlə(r)] *n* marinero *m*; **to be a bad s.** no soportar bien los viajes por mar; **s. suit** traje *m* de marinero

**saint** [seɪnt] *n* santo(a) *m,f*; **All Saints' (Day)** día *m* de Todos los Santos; **S. Bernard** *(dog)* San Bernardo *m*

**saintly** ['seɪntlɪ] *adj* santo(a)

**sake** [seɪk] *n* **for the s. of sb, for sb's s.** por (el bien de) alguien; **for God's** or **goodness'** or **heaven's s.** por (el amor de) Dios; **for the s. of peace** para que haya paz; **for old times's.** por los viejos tiempos; **this is talking for talking's s.** es hablar por hablar; **for the s. of argument...** como hipótesis...

**salacious** [sə'leɪʃəs] *adj* salaz

**salad** ['sæləd] *n* ensalada *f*; **s. bowl** ensaladera *f*; *Br* **s. cream** = especie de mayonesa un poco dulce para ensaladas; *Fig* **s. days** tiempos *mpl* mozos; **s. dressing** aliño *m* para la ensalada

**salamander** ['sæləmændə(r)] *n* salamandra *f*

**salami** [sə'lɑːmɪ] *n* salami *m*

**salaried** ['sælərɪd] *adj* asalariado(a)

**salary** ['sælərɪ] *n* salario *m*, sueldo *m*; **s. earner** asalariado(a) *m,f*; **s. grade** nivel *m* or grado *m* salarial; **s. scale** escala *f* salarial

**sale** [seɪl] *n* **(a)** *(action of selling)* venta *f*; **for s.** *(available)* en venta; *(sign)* se vende; **to put sth up for s.** poner algo en venta; **on s.** a la venta; *Br* **sales assistant** dependiente(a) *m,f*; **sales department** departamento *m* de ventas; **sales drive** promoción *f* de ventas; **sales force** personal *m* de ventas; **sales manager** jefe(a) *m,f* de ventas; **sales pitch** estrategia *f* de ventas **(b)** *(turnover)* **sales** ventas *fpl*; **sales forecast** previsión *f* de ventas; **sales target** objetivo *m* de ventas **(c)** *(auction)* subasta *f*; **book s.** mercadillo *m* de libros **(d)** *(with reduced prices)* rebajas *fpl*; **the sales** las rebajas; **s. price** precio *m* rebajado; **there's a s. on at Woolworths** están de rebajas en Woolworths

**saleable** ['seɪləbəl] *adj* vendible

**saleroom** ['seɪlruːm] *n (for auctions)* sala *f* de subastas

**salesclerk** ['seɪlzklɑːk] *n US* dependiente(a) *m,f*, vendedor(ora) *m,f*

**salesgirl** ['seɪlzɡɜːl] *n* dependienta *f*

**salesman** ['seɪlzmən] *n (for company)* comercial *m*, vendedor *m*; *(in shop)* dependiente *m*, vendedor *m*

**salesmanship** ['seɪlzmənʃɪp] *n* habilidad *f* para vender

**salesperson** ['seɪlzpɜ:sən] *n (for company)* comercial *mf*, vendedor(ora) *m,f*; *(in shop)* dependiente(a) *m,f*, vendedor(ora) *m,f*

**saleswoman** ['seɪlzwʊmən] *n (for company)* comercial *f*, vendedora *f*; *(in shop)* dependienta *f*, vendedora *f*

**salient** ['seɪlɪənt] *adj (feature, fault)* relevante, sobresaliente; **s. points** puntos *mpl* más sobresalientes

**saline** ['seɪlaɪn] *adj* salino(a); *Med* **s. drip** gota a gota *m* de suero (fisiológico); **s. solution** solución *f* salina

**saliva** [sə'laɪvə] *n* saliva *f*

**salivate** ['sælɪveɪt] *vi* salivar, segregar saliva; *Fig* he was salivating se le hacía la boca agua

**sallow** ['sæləʊ] *adj (complexion)* amarillento(a), demacrado(a)

▸**sally forth** ['sælɪ] *vi Literary* partir con determinación

**salmon** ['sæmən] *n* salmón *m*; **s. (pink)** color *m* salmón; **s. trout** trucha *f* asalmonada

**salmonella** [sælmə'nelə] *n (bacteria)* salmonella *f*; *(illness)* salmonelosis *f inv*

**salon** ['sælɒn] *n* **(beauty) s.** salón *m* de belleza; **(hairdressing) s.** (salón *m* de) peluquería *f*

**saloon** [sə'lu:n] *n* **(a)** *(room)* sala *f*, salón *m*; *US (bar)* bar *m* **(b)** *Br* **s. (car)** turismo *m*

**SALT** [sɔːlt] *n (abbr* **Strategic Arms Limitation Talks)** SALT *fpl*, negociaciones *fpl* para la limitación de armas estratégicas

**salt** [sɔːlt] **1** *n* **(a)** *(substance)* sal *f*; **(bath) salts** sales *fpl* de baño; **s. mine** mina *f* de sal, salina *f* **(b)** *Fam (sailor)* **an old s.** un lobo de mar **(c)** *(idioms)* **to take a story with a pinch** *or* **grain of s.** no creerse del todo una historia; **no journalist worth his s. ...** ningún periodista que se precie...; **to rub s. in sb's wounds** removerle la herida a alguien; **the s. of the earth** la sal de la tierra

**2** *adj* **s. beef** salazón *f* de ternera; **s. cod** bacalao *m* (salado); **s. water** agua *f* salada

**3** *vt (food)* salar; *(roads)* esparcir sal en

▸**salt away** *vt sep (money)* ahorrar *or* guardar en secreto

**saltcellar** ['sɔːltselə(r)] *n* salero *m*

**salt-free** ['sɔːltfri:] *adj* sin sal

**saltpetre** [sɒlt'pi:tə(r)] *n* salitre *m*

**saltwater** [sɔːltwɔ:tə(r)] *adj* **s. lake** lago *m* de agua salada; **s. fish** pez *m* de agua salada

**salty** ['sɔːltɪ] *adj* salado(a)

**salubrious** [sə'lu:brɪəs] *adj Formal (hygienic)* salubre; *(respectable)* acomodado(a), respetable

**salutary** ['sæljʊtərɪ] *adj* saludable; **to have a s. effect on sb** tener un efecto saludable sobre alguien

**salute** [sə'lu:t] **1** *n* saludo *m*; **a ten gun s.** una salva de diez cañonazos; **to take the s.** pasar revista a las tropas (en desfile)

**2** *vt* saludar; *Fig* **to s. sb's achievements** rendir homenaje a los logros de alguien

**3** *vi* saludar

**salvage** ['sælvɪdʒ] **1** *n* **(a)** *(of ship)* rescate *m*, salvamento *m*; *(of waste material)* recuperación *f*; **s. vessel** buque *m* de salvamento **(b)** *(objects salvaged)* material *m* rescatado

**2** *vt also Fig* salvar, rescatar

**salvation** [sæl'veɪʃən] *n* salvación *f*; **S. Army** Ejército *m* de Salvación

**salve** [sælv] *vt* **to s. one's conscience** descargar la conciencia

**salver** ['sælvə(r)] *n (tray)* bandeja *f*, fuente *f*

**salvo** ['sælvəʊ] *(pl* **salvos** *or* **salvoes)** *n also Fig* salva *f*

**Samaritan** [sə'mærɪtən] *n* **the Good S.** el Buen Samaritano; **to phone the Samaritans** ≃ llamar al teléfono de la esperanza

**same** [seɪm] **1** *adj* **the s. man** el mismo hombre; **the s. woman** la misma mujer; **the s. children** los mismos niños; **the s. one** el (la) mismo(a); **the house isn't the s. without her** la casa no es la misma sin ella; **in the s. way** del mismo modo, de igual forma; **to go the s. way** ir por el mismo camino; **the** *or* **that very s. day** el *or* ese mismo día; **it all amounts** *or* **comes to the s. thing** todo viene a ser lo mismo; **at the s. time** *(simultaneously)* al mismo tiempo; *(nevertheless)* sin embargo

**2** *pron* **s.** lo mismo; **it's the s. everywhere** es igual en todas partes; **if it's all the s. to you** si no te importa; *Fam* **(the) s. again?** *(in pub)* ¿(otra de) lo mismo?; *Fam* **s. here!** *(I agree)* estoy de acuerdo; *(I did the same thing)* yo también; **(the) s. to you!** ¡igualmente!; **I would have done the s.** yo hubiera hecho lo mismo

**3** *adv* **to think/taste the s.** pensar/saber igual; **all the s.** *(nevertheless)* de todas maneras

**sameness** ['seɪmnɪs] *n* uniformidad *f*

**Samoa** [sə'məʊə] *n* Samoa

**Samoan** [sə'məʊən] **1** *n* **(a)** *(person)* samoano(a) *m,f* **(b)** *(language)* samoano *m*

**2** *adj* samoano(a)

**sample** ['sɑ:mpəl] **1** muestra *f*; *Med* **to take a s.** tomar una muestra

**2** *vt (public opinion)* sondear; *(food, experience)* probar

**sanatorium** [sænə'tɔ:rɪəm] *(pl* **sanatoria** [sænə'tɔ:rɪə]) *n* sanatorio *m*

**sanctify** ['sæŋ(k)tɪfaɪ] *vt* santificar

**sanctimonious** [sæŋ(k)tɪ'məʊnɪəs] *adj* mojigato(a)

**sanction** ['sæŋ(k)ʃən] **1** *n* **(a)** *(penalty)* sanción *f*; **(economic) sanctions** sanciones *fpl*

económicas **(b)** *Formal (consent)* sanción *f*
　**2** *vt Formal (authorize)* sancionar, autorizar

**sanctity** ['sæŋ(k)tɪtɪ] *n (of life)* carácter *m* sagrado; *(of home)* santidad *f*

**sanctuary** ['sæŋ(k)tj(ʊ)ərɪ] *n Rel* santuario *m*; *(for fugitive, refugee)* asilo *m*, refugio *m*; *(for birds, wildlife)* santuario *m*; **to seek s.** buscar refugio

**sand** [sænd] **1** *n* arena *f*; **s. castle** castillo *m* de arena; **s. dune** duna *f*
　**2** *vt* **(a)** *(smooth with sandpaper)* lijar **(b)** *(cover with sand)* enarenar

**sandal** ['sændəl] *n* sandalia *f*, *Andes, CAm* ojota *f*, *Méx* guarache *m*

**sandbag** ['sændbæg] *n* saco *m* terrero

**sandbank** ['sændbæŋk] *n* banco *m* de arena

**sandblast** ['sændblɑːst] *vt* limpiar con chorro de arena

**sander** ['sændə(r)] *n* acuchillador(ora) *m,f* de suelos

**sandpaper** ['sændpeɪpə(r)] **1** *n* (papel *m* de) lija *f*
　**2** *vt* lijar

**sandpit** ['sændpɪt] *n (for children)* recinto *m* de arena

**sandstone** ['sændstəʊn] *n* arenisca *f*

**sandstorm** ['sændstɔːm] *n* tormenta *f* de arena

**sandwich** ['sændwɪtʃ] **1** *n* sándwich *m*; *Educ* **s. course** curso *m* teórico-práctico; **s. filling** relleno *m*
　**2** *vt* intercalar; **to be sandwiched (between)** estar encajonado(a) (entre)

**sandy** ['sændɪ] *adj* **(a)** *(earth, beach)* arenoso(a) **(b)** *(hair)* rubio(a) rojizo(a)

**sane** [seɪn] *adj (not mad)* cuerdo(a); *(sensible)* juicioso(a)

**San Franciscan** ['sænfrən'sɪskən] **1** *n* = habitante o nativo de San Francisco
　**2** *adj* de San Francisco

**San Francisco** ['sænfrən'sɪskeʊ] *n* San Francisco

**sang** [sæŋ] *pt of* **sing**

**sanguine** ['sæŋgwɪn] *adj Formal (optimistic)* optimista

**sanitary** ['sænɪtərɪ] *adj (clean)* higiénico(a); *(relating to hygiene)* sanitario(a); *Br* **s. towel** compresa *f*

**sanitation** [sænɪ'teɪʃən] *n* saneamiento *m*, instalaciones *fpl* sanitarias

**sanitize** ['sænɪtaɪz] *vt (document, biography)* mutilar, meter la tijera a; **a sanitized account of events** un relato de los hechos demasiado aséptico

**sanity** ['sænɪtɪ] *n* cordura *f*

**sank** [sæŋk] *pt of* **sink**

**San Marino** [sænmə'riːnəʊ] *n* San Marino

**Santa (Claus)** ['sæntə('klɔːz)] *n* Papá *m* Noel

**Santiago** [sæntɪɑ'geʊ] *n* Santiago de Chile

**Sao Tomé and Principe** ['saʊtə'meɪən'prɪnsɪpeɪ] *n* Santo Tomé y Príncipe

**sap¹** [sæp] *n (of plant)* savia *f*

**sap²** *n Fam (gullible person)* pardillo(a) *m,f*, papanatas *mf inv*

**sap³** (*pt & pp* **sapped**) *vt (undermine) & Fig* minar, debilitar

**sapling** ['sæplɪŋ] *n* pimpollo *m*, árbol *m* joven

**sapper** ['sæpə(r)] *n Mil* zapador *m*

**sapphire** ['sæfaɪə(r)] *n (precious stone)* zafiro *m*; *(colour)* azul *m* zafiro

**Saragossa** [særə'gɒsə] *n* Zaragoza

**Sarajevo** [særə'jerveʊ] *n* Sarajevo

**sarcasm** ['sɑːkæzm] *n* sarcasmo *m*

**sarcastic** [sɑː'kæstɪk] *adj* sarcástico(a)

**sarcastically** [sɑː'kæstɪklɪ] *adv* sarcásticamente

**sarcophagus** [sɑː'kɒfəgəs] (*pl* **sarcophagi** [sɑː'kɒfəgaɪ]) *n* sarcófago *m*

**sardine** [sɑː'diːn] *n* sardina *f*; **packed in like sardines** como sardinas en lata

**Sardinia** [sɑː'dɪnɪə] *n* Cerdeña

**Sardinian** [sɑː'dɪnɪən] *n & adj* sardo(a) *m,f*

**sardonic** [sɑː'dɒnɪk] *adj* sardónico(a)

**sari** ['sɑːrɪ] *n* sari *m*

**sartorial** [sɑː'tɔːrɪəl] *adj Formal* del vestir; **s. elegance** elegancia *f* en el vestir

**SAS** [eser'es] *n Br (abbr* **Special Air Service***)* = comando de operaciones especiales del ejército británico; ≃ GEO *m*

**sash** [sæʃ] *n (on dress)* faja *f*, fajín *m*; **s. cord** cordón *m* (de las ventanas de guillotina); **s. window** ventana *f* de guillotina

**Sassenach** ['sæsənæx] *n Scot Pej* = término peyorativo para referirse a un inglés

**SAT** [sæt] **(a)** *Br (abbr* **standard assessment task***)* = tarea de la que se examina a un alumno para determinar si ha alcanzado el nivel de conocimientos correspondiente a su edad **(b)** *US (abbr* **scholastic aptitude test***)* = examen que realizan al final de la enseñanza secundaria los alumnos que quieren ir a la universidad

**Sat** *(abbr* **Saturday***)* sábado *m*

**sat** [sæt] *pt & pp of* **sit**

**Satan** ['seɪtən] *n* Satanás *m*, Satán *m*

**satanic** [sə'tænɪk] *adj* satánico(a)

**satchel** ['sætʃəl] *n* cartera *f* (de colegial)

**sate** [seɪt] *vt Formal* saciar

**satellite** ['sætəlaɪt] *n* satélite *m*; **s. dish** (antena *f*) parabólica *f*; **s. (state)** estado *m* satélite; **s. television** televisión *f* vía satélite; **s. (town)** ciudad *f* satélite

**satiate** ['seɪʃɪeɪt] *vt Formal* saciar

**satin** ['sætɪn] *n (cloth)* satén *m*; **s. finish** *(of paper, paint)* (acabado *m*) satinado *m*

**satire** ['sætaɪə(r)] *n* sátira *f*

**satirical** [sə'tɪrɪkəl] *adj* satírico(a)

**satirist** ['sætɪrɪst] *n* escritor(ora) *m,f* de sátiras

**satirize** ['sætɪraɪz] *vt* satirizar

**satisfaction** [sætɪs'fækʃən] *n* satisfacción *f*; **it gives me great s. to know that…** me satisface enormemente saber que…

**satisfactory** [sætɪs'fæktərɪ] *adj (result, standard, condition)* satisfactorio(a); *Sch* **I got "s." for my work** saqué un aprobado en el trabajo

**satisfied** ['sætɪsfaɪd] *adj* satisfecho(a); **to be s.** estar satisfecho

**satisfy** ['sætɪsfaɪ] *vt (person, curiosity)* satisfacer; *(condition)* satisfacer, cumplir; **to s. the examiners** aprobar el examen; **I am satisfied that he is telling the truth** ahora estoy convencido de que dice la verdad

**saturate** ['sætʃəreɪt] *vt (soak)* empapar; *Fig* saturar; **to s. the market** saturar el mercado; **saturated fats** grasas *fpl* saturadas

**saturation** [sætʃə'reɪʃən] *n (soaking)* empapamiento *m*; *Fig* saturación *f*; *Mil* **s. bombing** bombardeo *m* intensivo; **to reach s. point** llegar al punto de saturación

**Saturday** ['sætədɪ] *n* sábado *m*; **this S.** este sábado; **on S.** el sábado; **on S. morning/night** el sábado por la mañana/por la noche; **on S. afternoon/evening** el sábado por la tarde/noche; **on Saturdays** los sábados; **every S.** todos los sábados; **every other S.** cada dos sábados, un sábado sí y otro no; **last S.** el sábado pasado; **the S. before last** hace dos sábados; **next S.** el sábado que viene; **the S. after next, a week on S., S. week** dentro de dos sábados, del sábado en ocho días; **the following S.** el sábado siguiente; **the S.'s paper** el periódico del sábado; **the S. film** la película del sábado

**Saturn** ['sætɜːn] *n (planet, god)* Saturno *m*

**sauce** [sɔːs] *n* (a) *(for food)* salsa *f*; **tomato/cheese s.** salsa de tomate/queso; **s. boat** salsera *f* (b) *Fam (impudence)* descaro *m*

**saucepan** ['sɔːspən] *n* cazo *m*

**saucer** ['sɔːsə(r)] *n* platillo *m*

**saucy** ['sɔːsɪ] *adj Fam (impertinent)* descarado(a); *(risqué)* picante, subido(a) de tono

**Saudi** ['saʊdɪ] **1** *n (person)* saudí *mf*; *Fam (country)* Arabia Saudí
**2** *adj* saudí

**Saudi Arabia** ['saʊdɪə'reɪbɪə] *n* Arabia Saudí

**Saudi Arabian** ['saʊdɪə'reɪbɪən] *n & adj* saudí *mf*

**sauna** ['sɔːnə] *n* sauna *f*

**saunter** ['sɔːntə(r)] **1** *n* paseo *m* (con aire desenfadado)
**2** *vi* **to s. (along)** pasear (con aire desenfadado)

**sausage** ['sɒsɪdʒ] *n* salchicha *f*; *(cured)* ≃ salchichón *m*, ≃ chorizo *m*; *Fam* **not a s.** *(nothing)* nada de nada; *Hum* **you silly s.!** ¡mira que eres tontorrón(ona)!; *Fam* **s. dog** perro *m* salchicha; **s. meat** carne *f* de embutido; *Br* **s. roll** salchicha *f* envuelta en hojaldre

**sauté** ['saʊteɪ] *Culin* **1** *adj* salteado(a)
**2** *vt* saltear

**savage** ['sævɪdʒ] **1** *n Old-fashioned* salvaje *mf*
**2** *adj (animal, person)* salvaje; *(attack)* salvaje, feroz; *(criticism)* virulento(a)
**3** *vt (attack physically)* atacar salvajemente; *Fig (criticize)* criticar con saña *or* virulencia

**savagely** ['sævɪdʒlɪ] *adv (beat, attack)* salvajemente; *(criticize)* con virulencia

**savanna(h)** [sə'vænə] *n* sabana *f*

**save¹** [seɪv] *prep Formal (except)* salvo, a excepción de

**save²** [seɪv] *vt* (a) *(rescue) (person, animal)* salvar; **to s. sb's life** salvarle la vida a alguien; *Fam* **she can't sing to s. her life** no tiene ni idea de cantar; *Fam* **to s. one's (own) neck** *or* **skin** salvar el pellejo; **to s. sb from falling** evitar que alguien se caiga; **to s. a shot** parar un disparo; **to s. the situation** salvar la situación; **to s. one's soul** salvar el alma; **God save the King/the Queen!** ¡Dios salve al Rey/a la Reina!
(b) *(keep for future)* guardar; *(money)* ahorrar; *Comptr* guardar, salvar; *(on screen)* archivar, guardar; **to s. oneself for sth** reservarse para algo; **I am saving my strength** estoy ahorrando fuerzas
(c) *(not waste) (time, money, space)* ahorrar; **this will s. us having to do it again** esto nos evitará *or* ahorrará tener que hacerlo de nuevo; **s. your breath** no te esfuerces, ahórrate las palabras; **I saved £10 by buying it there** me ahorré 10 libras por comprarlo ahí
**2** *vi* **to s. for sth** ahorrar para algo; **s. on heating costs by insulating your house** aísle su casa y ahorre en calefacción
**3** *n (of goalkeeper)* parada *f*; **to make a s.** hacer una parada

▸**save up** *vi* ahorrar **(for** para)

**saver** ['seɪvə(r)] *n Fin* ahorrador(ora) *m,f*

**saving** ['seɪvɪŋ] **1** *n* (a) *(economy)* ahorro *m*; **to make savings** ahorrar, economizar (b) *Fin* **savings** ahorros *mpl*; **she lived off her savings** vivía de sus ahorros; **savings account** cuenta *f* de ahorros; **savings bank** caja *f* de ahorros
**2** *adj* **her s. grace** lo único que la salva

**saviour** ['seɪvjə(r)] *n* salvador(ora) *m,f*

**savour** ['seɪvə(r)] **1** n (interest, enjoyment) sabor m

**2** vt saborear

**3** vi **to s. of** oler a

**savoury** ['seɪvərɪ] adj (a) (food) (appetizing) sabroso(a); (not sweet) salado(a) (b) (conduct) **not very s.** no muy edificante

**saw¹ 1** n (tool) sierra f

**2** vt (pp **sawn** [sɔːn] or **sawed**) serrar

▸**saw off** vt sep serrar, cortar (con sierra)

▸**saw up** vt sep serrar en trozos

**saw²** [sɔː] pt of **see**

**sawdust** ['sɔːdʌst] n serrín m

**sawmill** ['sɔːmɪl] n aserradero m, serrería f

**sawn** [sɔːn] pp of **saw**

**sawn-off shotgun** ['sɔːnɒf'ʃɒtɡʌn] n escopeta f de cañones recortados, recortada f

**sax** [sæks] n Fam (saxophone) saxo m

**Saxon** ['sæksən] **1** n (a) (person) sajón(ona) m,f (b) (language) sajón m

**2** adj sajón(ona)

**Saxony** ['sæksənɪ] n Sajonia

**saxophone** ['sæksəfəʊn] n saxofón m; **s. player** saxofonista mf

**saxophonist** [sæk'sɒfənɪst] n saxofonista mf

**say** [seɪ] **1** n he wasn't allowed to have his s. no le dejaron expresar su opinión; **I had no s. in the matter** no tuve ni voz ni voto en el asunto

**2** vt (pt & pp **said** [sed]) decir; **to s. sth to sb** decir algo a alguien; **to s. sth again** repetir algo; **to s. mass** decir misa; **to s. a prayer** rezar una oración; **it says...** (of text, sign) dice..., pone...; **my watch says four o'clock** en mi reloj pone las cuatro en punto; **good morning, she said** "buenos días" dijo; **he said that you were here** dijo que estabas aquí; **to s. hello (to sb)** saludar (a alguien); **to s. goodbye (to sb)** despedirse (de alguien); **to s. yes to an offer/a proposal** aceptar una oferta/una propuesta; **to s. no to an offer/a proposal** rechazar una oferta/una propuesta; **I wouldn't s. no to a cup of tea** me tomaría un té; **he didn't s. a word** no dijo nada; **it's (not) for him to s.** (no) le corresponde a él decidir; **there's no saying what might happen if...** es imposible decir lo que ocurriría si...; **what have you got to s. for yourself?** ¿qué tienes que decir a tu favor?; **there's a lot to be said for...** hay mucho que decir a favor de...; **you're honest, I'll s. that for you** eres honrado, eso sí o eso hay que reconocerlo; **it says a lot about her that...** dice mucho de ella que...; **don't s. you've forgotten already!** ¡no me digas que ya te has olvidado!; **you can s. that again!** ¡y que lo digas!; **need I s. more?** está claro ¿no?; **they s. that..., it is**

said that... dicen que..., se dice que...; **it is difficult to s. (when/where/which...)** es difícil decir (cuándo/dónde/cuál...); **if I had s., £100,000** si yo tuviera, digamos, 100.000 libras; **countries such as Germany, s., or France** países como Alemania, por poner un caso o ejemplo, o Francia

**3** vi **I'm not saying** no te lo digo; **as they s., as people s.** como se dice, como dice la gente; **I s.!** (expressing surprise) ¡caramba!; (to attract attention) ¡oiga!; **I'll s.!** ¡ya lo creo!; Fam **you don't s.!** ¡no me digas!

**saying** ['seɪɪŋ] n dicho m; **as the s. goes** como dice el refrán

**scab** [skæb] n (a) (on skin) costra f, postilla f (b) Fam (strikebreaker) esquirol m

**scabbard** ['skæbəd] n vaina f

**scabies** ['skeɪbiːz] n sarna f

**scaffold** ['skæfəld] n (outside building) andamio m; (for execution) patíbulo m

**scaffolding** ['skæfəldɪŋ] n andamiaje m

**scald** [skɔːld] **1** n escaldadura f

**2** vt escaldar

**scalding** ['skɔːldɪŋ] adj **to be s. (hot)** estar ardiendo, escaldar

**scale¹** [skeɪl] **1** n (on fish, reptile) escama f; (in pipes, kettle) incrustación f (de cal)

**2** vt (fish) escamar, descamar; (teeth) limpiar, quitar el sarro a; (boiler, pipe) desincrustar

**scale²** n (a) (of instrument, pay rates) escala f; **on a s. of one to ten** en una escala de uno a diez (b) (of problem, changes) escala f, magnitud f; (of map, drawing) escala f; **to s. a escala**; **s. model** modelo m a escala, maqueta f

**scale³** vt (climb) escalar

▸**scale down** vt sep (demands, expectations) reducir

▸**scale up** vt sep (prices, demands) aumentar

**scales** [skeɪlz] npl balanza f; **a pair or set of (kitchen) s.** una balanza (de cocina); **(bathroom) s.** báscula f (de baño)

**scallop** ['skæləp, 'skɒləp] n (a) (shellfish) vieira f (b) (in sewing) festón m

**scallywag** ['skælɪwæɡ] n Fam granuja mf

**scalp** [skælp] **1** n (skin of head) cuero m cabelludo; (as war trophy) cabellera f

**2** vt (in war) cortar la cabellera a

**scalpel** ['skælpəl] n Med bisturí m

**scaly** ['skeɪlɪ] adj (fish) con escamas; (skin) escamoso(a)

**scam** [skæm] n Fam pufo m

**scamp** [skæmp] n (rascal) granuja mf

**scamper** ['skæmpə(r)] vi ir dando brincos

▸**scamper away, scamper off** vi salir dando brincos

**scampi** ['skæmpɪ] n gambas fpl rebozadas

**scan** [skæn] **1** vt (pt & pp **scanned**) (a) (examine closely) (face, crowd, newspaper) escrutar, escudriñar; *(the horizon)* otear, escudriñar; *Med* hacer un escáner a **(b)** *(glance at) (newspaper, list)* ojear

**2** *n Med* escáner *m*

**scandal** ['skændəl] *n* **(a)** *(outrage)* escándalo *m*; **sex/financial/political s.** escándalo sexual/financiero/político; **it's a s.!** ¡es un escándalo!; **to create** *or* **cause a s.** provocar *or* ocasionar un escándalo **(b)** *(gossip)* cotilleo *m*

**scandalize** ['skændəlaɪz] *vt* escandalizar

**scandalous** ['skændələs] *adj* escandaloso(a)

**Scandinavia** [skændɪ'neɪvɪə] *n* Escandinavia

**Scandinavian** [skændɪ'neɪvɪən] *n & adj* escandinavo(a) *m,f*

**scanner** ['skænə(r)] *n Comptr & Med* escáner *m*

**scant** [skænt] *adj* escaso(a)

**scantily** ['skæntɪlɪ] *adv* apenas; **s. dressed** *or* **clad** ligero(a) de ropa

**scanty** ['skæntɪ] *adj (dress)* exiguo(a); *(information)* escaso(a)

**scapegoat** ['skeɪpgəʊt] *n* chivo *m* expiatorio

**scar** [skɑː(r)] **1** *n* cicatriz *f*; *Fig (emotional)* cicatriz *f*, huella *f*; **s. tissue** tejido *m* cicatrizal

**2** *vt (pt & pp scarred)* dejar cicatrices en; *also Fig* **to be scarred for life** quedar marcado(a) de por vida

**3** *vi (of wound)* cicatrizar

**scarce** ['skeəs] *adj* escaso(a); *Fam* **to make oneself s.** esfumarse, poner (los) pies en polvorosa

**scarcely** ['skeəslɪ] *adv* apenas; **she could s. speak** apenas podía hablar; **s. ever/any/anyone** casi nunca/ninguno/nadie; **it is s. likely that...** es muy improbable que...

**scarcity** ['skeəsɪtɪ], **scarceness** ['skeəsnɪs] *n* escasez *f*

**scare** ['skeə(r)] **1** *n* **a safety/pollution s.** una alarma (social) por razones de seguridad/contaminación; **you gave me an awful s.** me has dado un susto tremendo

**2** *vt* asustar; *Fam* **to s. the life out of sb, to s. the living daylights out of sb** pegarle un susto de muerte a alguien

**3** *vi* asustarse

▶**scare away, scare off** *vt sep* ahuyentar

**scarecrow** ['skeəkrəʊ] *n* espantapájaros *m inv*

**scared** [skeəd] *adj* asustado(a); **to be s.** estar asustado(a); **to be s. of** tener miedo de; **to be s. stiff, to be s. to death** estar muerto(a) de miedo

**scaremongering** ['skeəmʌŋgərɪŋ] *n* alarmismo *m*

**scarf** [skɑːf] *(pl* **scarves** [skɑːvz]*)* *n (woollen)* bufanda *f*; *(of silk, for head)* pañuelo *m*

**scarlet** ['skɑːlɪt] **1** *n (color m)* escarlata *m*

**2** *adj* escarlata; *Fig* **to go** *or* **turn s.** *(with anger, embarrassment)* ponerse colorado(a); **s. fever** escarlatina *f*

**scarper** ['skɑːpə(r)] *vi Br Fam* abrirse, darse el piro

**scary** ['skeərɪ] *adj Fam (noise, situation)* aterrador(ora), espantoso(a); *(film, book)* de miedo

**scat** [skæt] *exclam Fam* ¡largo!

**scathing** ['skeɪðɪŋ] *adj (remark, sarcasm)* mordaz, cáustico(a); **she was s. about the security arrangements** criticó con mordacidad las medidas de seguridad

**scatological** [skætə'lɒdʒɪkəl] *adj* escatológico(a)

**scatter** ['skætə(r)] **1** *vt (clouds, demonstrators)* dispersar; *(corn, seed)* esparcir; **to s. crumbs/papers all over the place** dejar todo lleno *or* sembrado de migas/papeles

**2** *vi (of crowd)* dispersarse

**scatterbrain** ['skætəbreɪn] *n Fam* despistado(a) *m,f*

**scatty** ['skætɪ] *adj Br Fam* despistado(a)

**scavenge** ['skævɪndʒ] **1** *vt* rebuscar (entre los desperdicios)

**2** *vi* **to s. for sth** rebuscar algo entre los desperdicios; **to s. in the dustbins** rebuscar en los cubos de basura

**scavenger** ['skævɪndʒə(r)] *n (animal)* (animal *m*) carroñero *m*

**scenario** [sɪ'nɑːrɪəʊ] *(pl* **scenarios** *n* **(a)** *(of film)* argumento *m* **(b)** *(situation)* situación *f* hipotética; **a likely s. is...** puede muy bien ocurrir que...

**scene** [siːn] *n* **(a)** *Th Cin* escena *f*; *also Fig* **a touching/terrifying s.** una escena conmovedora/aterradora; **Fig behind the scenes** entre bastidores; *Th* **s. shifter** tramoyista *mf*

**(b)** *(of event)* escenario *m*; **a change of s. would do him good** un cambio de aires le vendría bien; **to arrive** *or* **come on the s.** aparecer (en escena); **the s. of the crime/accident** el escenario *or* lugar del crimen/accidente; **the political/sporting s.** el panorama político/deportivo; **a s. of devastation** una escena de destrucción; **I can picture the s.** me puedo imaginar la escena; *Fam* **it's not my s.** no me va mucho

**(c)** *(fuss)* **to make a s.** montar un número, hacer una escena

**scenery** ['siːnərɪ] *n* **(a)** *(in play)* decorado *m* **(b)** *(landscape)* paisaje *m*; *Fam* **you need a change of s.** necesitas un cambio de aires

**scenic** ['siːnɪk] *adj (picturesque)* pintoresco(a); **s. railway** *(train)* tren *m* turístico; **s. route** ruta *f* turística

**scent** [sent] **1** *n* **(a)** *(smell)* aroma *m*, olor *m* **(b)** *(perfume)* perfume *m* **(c)** *(in hunting)* rastro *m*; **to pick up the s.** seguir el rastro; **to be on the s. of** seguir el rastro de; **to lose the s.** perder el rastro; **he threw his pursuers off the s.** despistó a sus perseguidores

**2** *vt* **(a)** *(smell)* olfatear, localizar el rastro de; *Fig* **to s. danger** olerse el peligro **(b)** *(perfume)* perfumar

**sceptic** ['skeptɪk] *n* escéptico(a) *m,f*

**sceptical** ['skeptɪkəl] *adj* escéptico(a)

**sceptically** ['skeptɪklɪ] *adv* escépticamente, con escepticismo

**scepticism** ['skeptɪsɪzəm] *n* escepticismo *m*

**sceptre** ['septə(r)] *n* cetro *m*

**schedule** [*'*ʃedjuːl, *US* 'skedjuːl] **1** *n* **(a)** *(plan)* programa *m*, plan *m*; **on s.** *(train, bus)* de acuerdo con el horario previsto; **behind/ ahead of s.** detrás de/por delante de lo programado *or* previsto; **everything went according to s.** todo fue según las previsiones; **I work to a very tight s.** tengo que cumplir unos plazos muy estrictos **(b)** *Com (list of prices)* lista *f or* catálogo *m* de precios

**2** *vt* programar; **we're scheduled to arrive at 21.45** está previsto que lleguemos a las 21:45

**scheduled** [*'*ʃedjuːld, *US* 'skedjuːld] *adj (services)* programado(a); **s. flight** vuelo *m* regular; **at the s. time** a la hora prevista

**schematic** [skɪ'mætɪk] *adj* esquemático(a)

**scheme** [skiːm] **1** *n (arrangement, system)* sistema *m*, método *m*; *(plan)* plan *m*, proyecto *m*; *(plot)* intriga *f*; **in the (greater) s. of things** desde una perspectiva general, en un plano global; **(housing) s.** plan *m* de vivienda

**2** *vi Pej* intrigar

**schilling** ['ʃɪlɪŋ] *n (Austrian currency)* chelín *m*

**schism** ['s(k)ɪzəm] *n* cisma *m*

**schizoid** ['skɪtsɔɪd] *n & adj* esquizoide *mf*

**schizophrenia** [skɪtsəʊ'friːnɪə] *n* esquizofrenia *f*

**schizophrenic** [skɪtsəʊ'frenɪk] *n & adj* esquizofrénico(a) *m,f*

**schmaltzy** [*'*ʃmɔːltsɪ] *adj Fam* sensiblero(a)

**scholar** ['skɒlə(r)] *n (learned person)* erudito(a) *m,f*

**scholarly** ['skɒləlɪ] *adj* erudito(a)

**scholarship** ['skɒləʃɪp] *n* **(a)** *(learning)* erudición *f* **(b)** *Educ (grant)* beca *f*

**scholastic** [skə'læstɪk] *adj Formal* académico(a)

**school¹** [skuːl] **1** *n* **(a)** *(for children) (up to 14)* colegio *m*, escuela *f*; *(from 14 to 18)* instituto *m*; *(of dance, languages etc) (private)* escuela *f*, academia *f*; **to go to s.** ir al colegio; **I went to s. with him** fuimos juntos al colegio; **there is no s. tomorrow** mañana no hay colegio *or*

clase; **when does s. start?** ¿cuándo empiezan las clases?; **s. of art, art s.** escuela de arte; **of s. age** en edad escolar; *Br* **s. board** consejo *m* escolar; **s. book** libro *m* de texto (escolar); **s. day** día *m* de colegio; **s. friend** amigo(a) *m,f* del colegio; **s. leaver** = alumno que ha finalizado sus estudios; **s. uniform** uniforme *m* escolar; **s. year** año *m* escolar *or* académico

**(b)** *US (college, university)* universidad *f*

**(c)** *(university department)* facultad *f*

**(d)** *(of artists, thinkers)* escuela *f*; **s. of thought** corriente *f or* escuela de pensamiento; *Fig* **he's one of the old s.** es de la vieja escuela

**2** *vt (educate)* educar; *(train) (child, mind)* instruir, adiestrar; **to s. sb in sth** instruir a alguien en algo

**school²** *n (of fish)* banco *m*

**schoolboy** ['skuːlbɔɪ] *n* colegial *m*

**schoolchild** ['skuːltʃaɪld] *n* colegial(ala) *m,f*

**schoolfellow** ['skuːlfeləʊ] *n* compañero(a) *m,f* de colegio

**schoolgirl** ['skuːlgɜːl] *n* colegiala *f*

**schooling** ['skuːlɪŋ] *n* enseñanza *f or* educación *f* escolar

**schoolmaster** ['skuːlmɑːstə(r)] *n Formal (primary)* maestro *m*; *(secondary)* profesor *m*

**schoolmate** ['skuːlmeɪt] *n* compañero(a) *m,f* de colegio

**schoolmistress** ['skuːlmɪstrɪs] *n Formal (primary)* maestra *f*; *(secondary)* profesora *f*

**schoolroom** ['skuːlruːm] *n* aula *f*, clase *f*

**schoolteacher** ['skuːltiːtʃə(r)] *n (primary)* maestro(a) *m,f*; *(secondary)* profesor(ora) *m,f*

**schooner** ['skuːnə(r)] *n* **(a)** *(ship)* goleta *f* **(b)** *(glass)* catavino *m*, copa *f* (de jerez)

**sciatic** [saɪ'ætɪk] *adj* ciático(a); **s. nerve** nervio *m* ciático

**sciatica** [saɪ'ætɪkə] *n Med* ciática *f*

**science** ['saɪəns] *n* ciencia *f*; **s. class** clase *f* de ciencias; **s. fiction** ciencia ficción; **s. teacher** profesor(ora) *m,f* de ciencias

**scientific** [saɪən'tɪfɪk] *adj* científico(a)

**scientist** ['saɪəntɪst] *n* científico(a) *m,f*

**sci-fi** ['saɪfaɪ] *Fam* **1** *n* ciencia *f* ficción

**2** *adj* de ciencia ficción

**Scilly** ['sɪlɪ] *n* **the S. Isles, the Scillies** las Islas Scilly *or* Sorlingas

**scimitar** ['sɪmɪtə(r)] *n* cimitarra *f*

**scintillating** ['sɪntɪleɪtɪŋ] *adj (conversation)* chispeante; *(performance)* brillante

**scissors** ['sɪzəz] *npl* tijeras *fpl*; **a pair of s.** una tijeras

**sclerosis** [sklɪə'rəʊsɪs] *n Med* esclerosis *f inv*

**scoff** [skɒf] **1** *vt Br Fam (eat)* zamparse

**2** *vi (mock)* mofarse (**at** de)

**scold** [skəʊld] *vt* reñir, regañar

**scone** [skɒn, skəʊn] n = bollo pequeño, redondo y bastante seco, a veces con pasas

**scoop** [sku:p] 1 n (a) (utensil) (for flour, mashed potato) paleta f; (for ice cream) pinzas fpl de cuchara; (for sugar) cucharilla f plana (b) (portion) (of ice cream) bola f; (of mashed potato) paletada f (c) Journ primicia f
  2 vt to s. a story obtener una primicia
▸**scoop up** vt sep (with hands) recoger ahuecando las manos; (with spoon) tomar una cucharada de; **he scooped up the papers in his arms** recogió los papeles entre sus brazos

**scoot** [sku:t] vi Fam **to s. (off** or **away)** salir disparado(a)

**scooter** ['sku:tə(r)] n (for child) patinete m; (motor) s. escúter m, Vespa® f

**scope** [skəʊp] n ámbito m, alcance m; **to give s. for…** (interpretation, explanation) permitir (la posibilidad de)…; **to give free s. to one's imagination** dar rienda suelta a la imaginación

**scorch** [skɔ:tʃ] 1 n s. **(mark)** (marca f de) quemadura f
  2 vt chamuscar; **scorched earth policy** (of retreating army) política f de tierra quemada

**scorcher** ['skɔ:tʃə(r)] n Fam (hot day) día m (de calor) abrasador

**scorching** ['skɔ:tʃɪŋ] adj abrasador(ora)

**score** [skɔ:(r)] 1 n (a) (total) (in sport) resultado m; (in quiz) puntuación f; **there was still no s.** no se había movido el marcador; **what's the s.?** ¿cómo van?; **to keep the s.** llevar el tanteo; Fam Fig **to know the s.** conocer el percal
  (b) (line) arañazo m
  (c) (quarrel) **to have a s. to settle with sb** tener una cuenta que saldar con alguien
  (d) (reason, grounds) **don't worry on that s.** no te preocupes en ese aspecto; **on that s. alone** sólo por eso
  (e) Mus partitura f; (for film) banda f sonora original
  (f) Old-fashioned (twenty) **a s.** una veintena; Fam **scores** (a lot) montones mpl
  2 vt (a) (in sport) (goal) marcar; (point, run) anotar; Fig (success, victory) apuntarse; **to s. a hit** (hit target) hacer blanco; Fig (of person, film) acertar; Fig **to s. points off sb** (in debate) anotarse puntos a costa de alguien
  (b) (cut line in) marcar con una raya or estría; **she scored her name on a tree** grabó su nombre en un árbol
  (c) very Fam (buy) **to s. drugs** pillar droga
  3 vi (a) (get a goal) marcar; Fig **her proposal scores on cost** el punto fuerte de su propuesta son los costes
  (b) very Fam (have sex) echar un polvo, mojar; (buy drugs) pillar droga
▸**score off** vt sep (delete) tachar

▸**score out** vt sep (delete) tachar

**scoreboard** ['skɔ:bɔ:d] n marcador m

**scorecard** ['skɔ:kɑ:d] n tarjeta f de puntuación

**scorer** ['skɔ:rə(r)] n (in football) goleador(ora) m,f

**scorn** [skɔ:n] 1 n desprecio m, desdén m; **to pour s. on sth** hablar de algo con desdén
  2 vt despreciar, desdeñar; **to s. to do sth** no dignarse a hacer algo

**scornful** ['skɔ:nfʊl] adj despreciativo(a), desdeñoso(a); **to be s. of sth** despreciar or desdeñar algo

**Scorpio** ['skɔ:pɪəʊ] n (sign of zodiac) Escorpio m, Escorpión m; **to be (a) S.** ser Escorpio or Escorpión

**scorpion** ['skɔ:pɪən] n escorpión m, alacrán m

**Scot** [skɒt] n escocés(esa) m,f

**scotch** [skɒtʃ] vt (rumour) desmentir

**Scotch** [skɒtʃ] 1 n (whisky) whisky m escocés
  2 adj S. **broth** = caldo típico escocés; US S. **tape®** celo m; S. **whisky** whisky m escocés

**scot-free** ['skɒt'fri:] adj Fam **to get off s.** quedar impune

**Scotland** ['skɒtlənd] n Escocia

**Scots** [skɒts] 1 n (dialect) (dialecto m) escocés m
  2 adj escocés(esa)

**Scotsman** ['skɒtsmən] n escocés m

**Scotswoman** ['skɒtswʊmən] n escocesa f

**Scottie dog** ['skɒtɪ'dɒg] n Fam terrier m escocés

**Scottish** ['skɒtɪʃ] adj escocés(esa); S. **terrier** terrier m escocés

**scoundrel** ['skaʊndrəl] n (wicked person) bellaco(a) m,f, canalla mf; Fam (rascal) granujilla mf

**scour** ['skaʊə(r)] vt (a) (pot, surface) restregar (b) (area) peinar; (house) registrar, rebuscar en

**scourer** ['skaʊərə(r)] n estropajo m

**scourge** [skɜ:dʒ] n azote m

**scout** [skaʊt] 1 n (a) Mil (person) explorador(ora) m,f; (boy) s. boy-scout m, escultista m; (talent) s. cazatalentos mf inv (b) (action) **to have a s. around (for sth)** buscar (algo)
  2 vi **to s. ahead** reconocer el terreno; **to s. for talent** ir a la caza de talentos

**scoutmaster** ['skaʊtmɑ:stə(r)] n jefe m de exploradores or boy-scouts

**scowl** [skaʊl] 1 n ceño m
  2 vi fruncir el ceño or el ceño

**scrabble** ['skræbəl] vi **to s. about** or **around for sth** buscar algo a tientas

**scraggy** ['skrægɪ] adj raquítico(a), esquelético(a)

**scram** [skræm] (pt & pp **scrammed**) vi Fam largarse, pirarse; **s.!** ¡largo!

**scramble** ['skræmbəl] **1** *n (rush)* desbandada *f; (struggle)* lucha *f* (**for** por); **it was a short s. to the top** para alcanzar la cumbre había que trepar un poco
**2** *vt Tel (signal)* codificar
**3** *vi* **to s. for sth** luchar por algo; **to s. up a hill** trepar por una colina

**scrambled eggs** ['skræmbəld'egz] *npl* huevos *mpl* revueltos

**scrap**[1] [skræp] **1** *n* (**a**) *(of material)* trozo *m; (of information)* fragmento *m; (of evidence)* indicio *m;* **to tear sth into scraps** hacer trizas algo; **scraps** *(of food)* sobras *fpl;* **there isn't a s. of truth in what she says** no hay ni rastro de verdad en lo que dice; **s. paper** papel *m* usado (**b**) **s. (metal)** chatarra *f;* **to sell sth for s.** vender algo para chatarra; **s. merchant** *or* **dealer** chatarrero(a) *m,f*
**2** *vt (pt & pp **scrapped**) (car)* mandar a la chatarra; *(submarine, missile)* desmantelar; *(project)* descartar, abandonar

**scrap**[2] *Fam* **1** *n (fight)* bronca *f*, pelea *f;* **to have a s.**, **to get into a s.** pelearse
**2** *vi (pt & pp **scrapped**) (fight)* pelearse

**scrapbook** ['skræpbʊk] *n* álbum *m* de recortes

**scrape** [skreɪp] **1** *n* (**a**) *(action)* rascada *f; (mark)* arañazo *m; (on skin)* arañazo *m*, rasguño *m; (sound)* chirrido *m;* **to give sth a s.** rascar algo (**b**) *Fam* **to get into a s.** meterse en un fregado
**2** *vt* (**a**) *(scratch) (side of car)* rayar, arañar; *(dirt, wallpaper)* raspar, arrancar; *(vegetables)* raspar; **to s. one's knee** arañarse *or* rasguñarse la rodilla; **to s. one's shoes** restregar los zapatos; **to s. one's plate clean** rebañar el plato; *Fig* **to s. the bottom of the barrel** tener que recurrir a lo peor (**b**) *(barely obtain)* **I just s. a living** me gano la vida como puedo; **to s. a pass** *(in exam)* aprobar por los pelos
**3** *vi* (**a**) *(make sound)* chirriar; **she was scraping away on her fiddle** rascaba el violín con un sonido chirriante (**b**) *(barely manage)* **to s. home** *(in contest)* ganar a duras penas; **to s. into college** entrar en la universidad por los pelos
▸**scrape through** *vt insep (exam)* aprobar por los pelos
▸**scrape together** *vt sep (money, resources)* reunir a duras penas

**scraper** ['skreɪpə(r)] *n (tool)* rasqueta *f*

**scrapheap** ['skræphiːp] *n* montón *m* de chatarra; *Fig* **to be on the s.** *(person)* estar excluido(a) del mundo laboral; *(idea)* quedar descartado(a)

**scrappy** ['skræpɪ] *adj (knowledge, performance)* deslavazado(a)

**scratch** [skrætʃ] **1** *n* (**a**) *(on skin, record, furniture)* arañazo *m;* **it's just a s.** no es más

que un rasguño *or* arañazo; **he came out of it without a s.** salió sin un rasguño (**b**) *(action)* **to give one's nose a s.** rascarse la nariz (**c**) *Fam (idioms)* **to start from s.** partir de cero; **to come up to s.** dar la talla; **to bring sth/sb up to s.** poner algo/a alguien a punto
**2** *adj (meal, team)* improvisado(a), de circunstancias
**3** *vt* (**a**) *(skin)* arañar; *(glass, record)* rayar; **to s. oneself** rascarse; **to s. one's nose** rascarse la nariz; **he scratched his name on the card** garabateó su nombre en la tarjeta; *Fig* **you s. my back and I'll s. yours** hoy por ti y mañana por mí; *Fig* **we've only scratched the surface of the problem** no hemos hecho más que empezar a tratar el problema (**b**) *(remove)* **to s. sb's name from a list** quitar a alguien de una lista
**4** *vi (oneself)* rascarse; *(of thorns)* picar; *(of new clothes)* rascar, raspar; **the dog was scratching at the door** el perro estaba arañando la puerta
▸**scratch out** *vt sep (number, name)* tachar; *Fig* **to s. sb's eyes out** arrancarle a alguien los ojos

**scratchy** ['skrætʃɪ] *adj (garment, towel)* áspero(a); *(record)* con muchos arañazos

**scrawl** [skrɔːl] **1** *n* garabatos *mpl*
**2** *vt* garabatear
**3** *vi* hacer garabatos

**scrawny** ['skrɔːnɪ] *adj* esquelético(a), raquítico(a)

**scream** [skriːm] **1** *n* (**a**) *(of person)* grito *m*, chillido *m;* **to let out a s.** soltar un grito; **screams of laughter** carcajadas *fpl* (**b**) *Fam (good fun)* **it was a s.** fue para mondarse; **he's a s.** es la monda
**2** *vt* gritar; **to s. abuse** lanzar improperios o insultos; **the headlines screamed "guilty"** los titulares clamaban "culpable"
**3** *vi* gritar, chillar; **jets screamed overhead** los reactores pasaron con estruendo; **to s. in pain** gritar de dolor; **to s. with laughter** reírse a carcajadas

**screamingly** ['skriːmɪŋlɪ] *adv Fam* **s. funny** divertidísimo(a), para mondarse de risa

**scree** [skriː] *n* pedruscos *mpl*

**screech** [skriːtʃ] **1** *n (of bird, person)* chillido *m; (of brakes)* chirrido *m;* **a s. of laughter** una carcajada
**2** *vt* chillar; **to s. an order** dar una orden con un chillido
**3** *vi (of bird, person)* chillar; *(of brakes)* chirriar, rechinar; **the car screeched to a halt** el coche se detuvo chirriando

**screen** [skriːn] **1** *n* (**a**) *(barrier)* mampara *f; (folding)* biombo *m* (**b**) *(of TV, cinema, computer)* pantalla *f;* **the big/small s.** la gran/pequeña pantalla; **s. actor/actress** actor *m*/actriz *f* de cine; *Cin* **s. test** prueba *f* (de cámara)

**2** *vt* **(a)** *(protect)* proteger; **to s. sth from view** ocultar algo a la vista **(b)** *(show) (film)* proyectar **(c)** *(filter) (staff, applicants)* examinar, controlar; *(information)* filtrar

**screening** ['skri:nɪŋ] *n* **(a)** *Cin* proyección *f*; **first s.** estreno *m* **(b)** *(of staff, applicants)* examen *m*, control *m*

**screenplay** ['skri:npleɪ] *n Cin* guión *m*

**screensaver** ['skri:nseɪvə(r)] *n Comptr* salvapantallas *m*

**screenwriter** ['skri:nraɪtə(r)] *n Cin* guionista *mf*

**screw** [skru:] **1** *n* **(a)** *(for fixing)* tornillo *m*; *Fam Fig* **she has a s. loose** le falta un tornillo; *Fam Fig* **to put the screws on sb** apretar las clavijas a alguien; **s. top** *(of bottle, jar)* tapón *m* de rosca **(b)** *(propeller)* hélice *f* **(c)** *very Fam (prison officer)* boqueras *m inv (carcelero)* **(d)** *Vulg (sexual intercourse)* polvo *m*; **to have a s.** echar un polvo

**2** *vt* **(a)** *(fix)* atornillar **(on** *or* **onto** a); **to s. one's face into a smile** sonreír forzadamente; *Fam* **they'll s. you for every penny you've got** van a sacarte hasta el último céntimo **(b)** *Vulg (have sex with)* tirarse, follarse; **go and s. yourself!** ¡vete a tomar por culo!

**3** *vi Vulg (have sex)* follar, joder

▸**screw around** *vi Vulg* follar a diestro y siniestro

▸**screw on 1** *vt sep (with screw)* atornillar; *(lid, top)* enroscar; *Fam* **he's got his head screwed on** tiene la cabeza en su sitio

**2** *vi (of lid, top)* enroscarse

▸**screw up 1** *vt sep* **(a)** **to s. up a piece of paper** arrugar un trozo de papel; **to s. up one's face** contraer *or* arrugar la cara; **to s. up one's courage** armarse de valor **(b)** *very Fam (spoil)* jorobar; **his parents really screwed him up** sus padres lo dejaron bien tarado

**2** *vi very Fam (fail)* **don't s. up this time** no la cagues esta vez

**screwdriver** ['skru:draɪvə(r)] *n* destornillador *m*

**scribble** ['skrɪbəl] **1** *n* garabatos *mpl*; **I can't read this s.** no entiendo estos garabatos

**2** *vt* **to s. sth (down)** garabatear algo

**3** *vi* hacer garabatos

**scribe** [skraɪb] *n* escribano(a) *m,f*, amanuense *mf*

**scrimmage** ['skrɪmɪdʒ] *n* tumulto *m*, alboroto *m*

**scrimp** [skrɪmp] *vi* **to s. (and save)** economizar, hacer economías

**script** [skrɪpt] *n* **(a)** *(for play, film)* guión *m*; *(in exam)* ejercicio *m* (escrito), examen *m* **(b)** *(handwriting)* caligrafía *f*, letra *f*

**scriptural** ['skrɪptʃərəl] *adj* bíblico(a)

**Scripture** ['skrɪptʃə(r)] *n* **(Holy) S., the Scriptures** la Sagrada Escritura

**scriptwriter** ['skrɪptraɪtə(r)] *n TV & Cin* guionista *mf*

**scroll** [skrəʊl] **1** *n* **(a)** *(of paper, parchment)* rollo *m* **(b)** *Archit* voluta *f*

**2** *vi Comptr* desplazar el cursor

▸**scroll down** *vi Comptr* bajar el cursor

▸**scroll up** *vi Comptr* subir el cursor

**scrotum** ['skrəʊtəm] *n* escroto *m*

**scrounge** [skraʊndʒ] *Fam* **1** *n* **to be on the s.** gorronear

**2** *vt* **to s. sth from** *or* **off sb** gorronearle algo a alguien

**3** *vi* **to s. off sb** vivir de alguien por la gorra

**scrounger** ['skraʊndʒə(r)] *n Fam* gorrón(ona) *m,f*

**scrub** [skrʌb] **1** *n* **(a)** *(bushes)* maleza *f*, matorral *m* **(b)** *(wash)* **to give sth a (good) s.** fregar (bien) algo

**2** *vt (pt & pp* **scrubbed)** **(a)** *(floor, pots)* fregar; **to s. one's hands** lavarse bien las manos **(b)** *Fam (cancel)* borrar

▸**scrub up** *vi Med* lavarse bien las manos

**scrubber** ['skrʌbə(r)] *n (for dishes)* estropajo *m*

**scrubbing brush** ['skrʌbɪŋ'brʌʃ] *n* cepillo *m* de fregar

**scrubland** ['skrʌblænd] *n* monte *m* bajo, matorral *m*

**scruff** [skrʌf] *n* **(a)** **the s. of the neck** el cogote **(b)** *Fam (unkempt person)* andrajoso(a) *m,f*, zarrapastroso(a) *m,f*

**scruffily** ['skrʌfɪlɪ] *adv* **to be s. dressed** vestir andrajosamente *or* con desaliño

**scruffy** ['skrʌfɪ] *adj (person)* desaliñado(a), zarrapastroso(a); *(clothes)* andrajoso(a)

**scrum** [skrʌm] *n (in rugby)* melé *f*; *Fig* **there was a s. at the door** hubo apretujones en la puerta; **s. half** medio melé *m*

**scrumptious** ['skrʌm(p)ʃəs] *adj Fam (food)* riquísimo(a), de chuparse los dedos

**scrunch** [skrʌn(t)ʃ] **1** *vt (paper)* estrujar; *(can)* aplastar

**2** *vi (make sound)* crujir

**scruple** ['skru:pəl] **1** *n* escrúpulo *m*; **to have no scruples** no tener escrúpulos

**2** *vi* **not to s. to do sth** no tener escrúpulos en hacer algo

**scrupulous** ['skru:pjʊləs] *adj* escrupuloso(a)

**scrupulously** ['skru:pjʊləslɪ] *adv* escrupulosamente

**scrutineer** [skru:tɪ'nɪə(r)] *n Pol* escrutador(ora) *m,f*

**scrutinize** ['skru:tɪnaɪz] *vt (document, votes)* escrutar

**scrutiny** ['skruːtɪnɪ] n (of document, votes) escrutinio m; **to come under s.** ser cuidadosamente examinado(a)

**scuba** ['skjuːbə] n **s. diver** submarinista mf, buceador(ora) m,f; **s. diving** buceo m or submarinismo m con botellas de oxígeno

**scuff** [skʌf] **1** n **s. mark** rozadura f, rasguño m
**2** vt rozar

**scuffle** ['skʌfəl] **1** n riña f, reyerta f
**2** vi reñir, pelear

**scullery** ['skʌlərɪ] n Br fregadero m, trascocina f

**sculpt** [skʌlpt] vt & vi esculpir

**sculptor** ['skʌlptə(r)] n escultor(ora) m,f

**sculpture** ['skʌlptʃə(r)] **1** n escultura f
**2** vt esculpir

**scum** [skʌm] n **(a)** (layer of dirt) capa f de suciedad; (froth) espuma f **(b)** (worthless people) escoria f; **the s. of the earth** la escoria de la sociedad

**scupper** ['skʌpə(r)] vt (ship, project) hundir

**scurrilous** ['skʌrɪləs] adj ultrajante, denigrante

**scurry** ['skʌrɪ] vi (dash) corretear apresuradamente
▸**scurry away, scurry off** vi escabullirse

**scurvy** ['skɜːvɪ] n Med escorbuto m

**scuttle**[1] ['skʌtəl] **1** n (coal) **s.** cajón m para el carbón
**2** vt (ship) barrenar, taladrar; (plan) hundir

**scuttle**[2] vi (run) corretear
▸**scuttle away, scuttle off** vi escabullirse

**scythe** [saɪð] **1** n guadaña f
**2** vt segar

**SDLP** [esdiːelˈpiː] n Br (abbr **Social Democratic Labour Party**) = partido norirlandés que propugna la reintegración en la República de Irlanda por medios pacíficos

**SDP** [esdiːˈpiː] n Br Formerly (abbr **Social Democratic Party**) = partido creado en 1981 a raíz de la escisión de una rama moderada del partido laborista y posteriormente fundido con el Partido Liberal

**SE** [eˈsiː] n (abbr **south east**) SE

**sea** [siː] n mar m or f; **by the s.** junto al mar; **to go by s.** ir en barco; **to go to s.** (become a sailor) enrolarse de marinero; Fig **a s. of people** un mar de gente; **heavy or rough seas** mar f gruesa; **on the high seas, out at s.** en alta mar; **to find or get one's s. legs** acostumbrarse al mar (no marearse); Fig **to be all at s.** estar totalmente perdido(a), no saber uno por dónde anda; **s. air** aire m del mar; **s. anemone** anémona f de mar; **s. battle** batalla f naval; **s. breeze** brisa f marina; Fam **(old) s. dog** (viejo) lobo m de mar; Naut **s. lane** ruta f marítima; **s. level** nivel m del mar; **s. lion** león m marino; **s. monster** monstruo m marino; **s. power** (country) potencia f naval; **s. salt** sal f marina; **s. urchin** erizo m de mar; **s. voyage** travesía f, viaje m por mar

**seaboard** ['siːbɔːd] n litoral m, costa f

**seaborne** ['siːbɔːn] adj marítimo(a)

**seafarer** ['siːfeərə(r)] n marino(a) m,f, marinero(a) m,f

**seafaring** ['siːfeərɪŋ] adj marinero(a)

**seafood** ['siːfuːd] n marisco m

**seafront** ['siːfrʌnt] n paseo m marítimo

**seagoing** ['siːɡəʊɪŋ] adj marítimo(a)

**seagull** ['siːɡʌl] n gaviota f

**seahorse** ['siːhɔːs] n hipocampo m, caballito m de mar

**seal**[1] [siːl] n (animal) foca f

**seal**[2] **1** n **(a)** (stamp) sello m; **to give one's s. of approval to sth** dar el visto bueno a algo; **to set the s. on sth** (alliance, friendship, defeat) sellar algo; (fate) determinar algo **(b)** (on machine, pipes, connection) junta f; (on bottle, box, letter) precinto m
**2** vt (with official seal) sellar; (close) (envelope, frontier) precintar, cerrar; (jar, joint) precintar, cerrar herméticamente; (fate) determinar; **my lips are sealed** soy una tumba
▸**seal in** vt sep encerrar
▸**seal off** vt sep impedir el paso a

**sealing wax** n ['siːlɪŋ wæks] lacre m

**sealskin** ['siːlskɪn] n piel f de foca

**seam** [siːm] n **(a)** (of garment) costura f; (in metalwork) unión f, juntura f; **to be coming apart at the seams** (of clothing) estar descosiéndose; Fig (of plan, organization) estar desmoronándose **(b)** (of coal) filón m, veta f

**seaman** ['siːmən] n Naut marino m

**seamanship** ['siːmənʃɪp] n Naut náutica f, navegación f

**seamstress** ['semstrɪs] n costurera f

**seamy** ['siːmɪ] adj sórdido(a)

**seance** ['seɪɒns] n sesión f de espiritismo

**seaplane** ['siːpleɪn] n hidroavión m

**seaport** ['siːpɔːt] n puerto m de mar

**sear** [sɪə(r)] vt (skin) quemar, abrasar; Fig **the image was seared on his memory** la imagen le quedó grabada a fuego en la memoria

**search** [sɜːtʃ] **1** n búsqueda f; **to be in s. of** in busca de; **to make a s. of** rastrear; Comptr **to do a s.** hacer una búsqueda; **s. party** equipo m de búsqueda; Law **s. warrant** orden f de registro
**2** vt (person, place) registrar; Comptr (file, directory) buscar en; Fam **s. me!** ¡ni idea!, ¡yo qué sé!
**3** vi buscar; **to s. after or for sth** buscar algo; Comptr **s. and replace** buscar y reemplazar

**searching** ['sɜːtʃɪŋ] adj (question) penetrante; (gaze) escrutador(ora)

**searchlight** ['sɜ:tʃlaɪt] n reflector m

**searing** ['sɪərɪŋ] adj (pain) punzante; (heat) abrasador(ora); (criticism, indictment) incisivo(a)

**seascape** ['si:skeɪp] n Art marina f

**seashell** ['si:ʃel] n concha f

**seashore** ['si:ʃɔ:(r)] n orilla f del mar

**seasick** ['si:sɪk] adj **to be s.** estar mareado(a); **to get s.** marearse

**seasickness** ['si:sɪknɪs] n mareo m (en barco)

**seaside** ['si:saɪd] n playa f; **at the s.** en la playa; **s. resort** centro m turístico costero

**season¹** ['si:zən] n (period of year) estación f; (of football, cricket) temporada f; (of films) ciclo m; **S.'s Greetings** Felices Fiestas; **in s.** (of food) en temporada; **the high s.** (for tourism) la temporada alta; **s. ticket** (for train, football team) abono m

**season²** vt (a) (dish) condimentar, sazonar (b) (wood) curar

**seasonable** ['si:zənəbəl] adj (a) **s. weather** tiempo m propio de la época (b) (help, advice) oportuno(a)

**seasonal** ['si:zənəl] adj (changes) estacional; (commerce) de temporada; **s. worker** temporero(a) m,f, trabajador(ora) m,f temporero(a)

**seasoned** ['si:zənd] adj (a) (food) condimentado(a), sazonado(a) (b) (wood) curado(a) (c) (person) experimentado(a); **a s. soldier** un soldado veterano

**seasoning** ['si:zənɪŋ] n Culin condimento m

**seat** [si:t] n 1 (a) (chair, on bus, train, plane) asiento m; (in theatre, cinema) butaca f; (in stadium) localidad f, asiento m; (in Parliament) escaño m; **to take a s.** tomar asiento, sentarse; **s. belt** cinturón m de seguridad (b) (part) (of chair, toilet) asiento m; (of trousers) parte f del trasero (c) (centre) (of government) sede f; **a s. of learning** un centro de enseñanza; **country s.** (of aristocrat) casa f de campo

2 vt (a) (cause to sit) sentar; **to remain seated** permanecer sentado(a); Formal **please be seated** por favor, tome asiento (b) (accommodate) **the bus seats thirty** el autobús tiene capacidad or cabida para treinta pasajeros sentados; **this table seats twelve** en esta mesa caben doce personas

**seating** ['si:tɪŋ] n (seats) asientos mpl; **s. capacity** (at cinema, stadium) aforo m (de personas sentadas); (on bus, plane) número m de plazas (sentadas)

**SEATO** ['si:təʊ] n (abbr **Southeast Asia Treaty Organization**) OTASE f, Organización f del Tratado del Sudeste Asiático

**seaway** ['si:weɪ] n ruta f marítima

**seaweed** ['si:wi:d] n algas fpl marinas; **a piece of s.** un alga

**seaworthy** ['si:wɜ:ðɪ] adj (ship) en condiciones de navegar

**sebaceous** [sɪ'beɪʃəs] adj sebáceo(a)

**sec¹** (abbr **seconds**) s., segundos mpl

**sec²** [sek] n Fam (moment) **just a s.!** ¡un momentín!

**secateurs** [sekə'tɜ:z] npl podadera f, tijeras fpl de podar

**secede** [sɪ'si:d] vi escindirse, separarse (**from** de)

**secession** [sɪ'seʃən] n secesión f, escisión f

**secluded** [sɪ'klu:dɪd] adj apartado(a), retirado(a)

**seclusion** [sɪ'klu:ʒən] n retiro m; **to live in s.** vivir recluido(a)

**second¹** ['sekənd] n (of time) segundo m; **I won't be a s.** no tardo nada; **just a s.** un momento, un segundo; **s. hand** (of clock) segundero m

**second²** 1 n (a) (in series) segundo(a) m,f; **Edward the S.** (written) Eduardo II; (spoken) Eduardo segundo; **she was s.** quedó (en) segunda (posición); **s. in command** segundo de a bordo

(b) (of month) **the s. of May** el dos de mayo; **we're leaving on the s.** nos marchamos el (día) dos

(c) Com **seconds** (defective goods) artículos mpl defectuosos

(d) (in duel) padrino m; (in boxing) ayudante m del preparador

(e) Br Univ **to get a s.** (in degree) ≃ licenciarse con una media de notable

(f) **s.** (gear) segunda f

(g) Fam (at meal) **anyone for seconds?** ¿alguien quiere repetir?

2 adj segundo(a); **the s. century** el siglo dos or segundo; **twenty-s.** vigésimo segundo(a), vigésimosegundo(a); Fig **to take s. place** (to sb) quedar por debajo (de alguien); **to be s. to none** no tener rival; **the s. largest city in the world** la segunda ciudad más grande del mundo; **a s. Picasso/Churchill** un nuevo Picasso/Churchill; **on s. thoughts** pensándolo bien; **to have s. thoughts (about sth)** tener alguna duda (sobre algo); Fig **to play s. fiddle to sb** hacer de comparsa de alguien; **lying is s. nature to her** las mentiras le salen automáticamente; **she got her s. wind** le entraron energías renovadas, se recuperó; **s. chance** segunda oportunidad f; **s. childhood** senilidad f; **s. class** (on train) segunda f (clase f); Rel **the S. Coming** el Segundo Advenimiento; **s. cousin** primo(a) m,f segundo(a); **s. floor** Br segundo piso m; US primer piso m; **s. language** segunda lengua f; **s. name** apellido m; Law **s. offence** reincidencia f; **s. opinion** segunda opinión f; Gram (**in the**) **s. person** (en) segunda persona

**f**; **s. rate** de segunda (categoría); **s. sight** clarividencia f; **s. violin** segundo violín m; **the S. World War** la Segunda Guerra Mundial

**second³** vt (motion, speaker) secundar

**second⁴** [sɪ'kɒnd] vt (officer, employee) trasladar temporalmente; **to be seconded** ser trasladado(a)

**secondary** ['sekəndərɪ] adj secundario(a); Educ **s. education** enseñanza f secundaria; Educ **s. school** instituto m (de enseñanza secundaria)

**second-best** ['sekənd'best] **1** n segunda opción f; **to be content with s.** conformarse con una segunda opción
**2** adv **to come off s.** caer derrotado(a)

**second-class** ['sekənd'klɑːs] **1** adj (ticket, carriage) de segunda (clase); **s. citizen** ciudadano(a) m,f de segunda (clase); Br Univ **to get a s. degree** ≃ licenciarse con una media de notable; **s. mail** correo m ordinario
**2** adv **to travel s.** viajar en segunda

**seconder** ['sekəndə(r)] n **the s. of a motion** la persona que secunda una moción

**second-guess** ['sekənd'ges] vt predecir, anticiparse a

**second-hand** ['sekənd'hænd] **1** adj (car, clothes) de segunda mano
**2** adv (to buy) de segunda mano; **to hear news s.** enterarse de una noticia a través de terceros

**secondly** ['sekəndlɪ] adv en segundo lugar

**secondment** [sɪ'kɒndmənt] n **to be on s.** estar trasladado(a) temporalmente; (in civil service, government department) estar en comisión de servicios

**secrecy** ['siːkrɪsɪ] n confidencialidad f; **in s.** en secreto; **to swear sb to s.** hacer jurar a alguien que guardará el secreto

**secret** ['siːkrɪt] **1** n secreto m; **to do sth in s.** hacer algo en secreto; **I make no s. of it** no pretendo que sea un secreto; **to let sb into a s.** revelar or contar un secreto a alguien
**2** adj secreto(a); **to keep sth s. from sb** ocultar algo a alguien; **s. agent** agente mf secreto(a); **s. police** policía f secreta; **the S. Service** los servicios secretos; also Fig **s. weapon** arma f secreta

**secretarial** ['sekrə'teərɪəl] adj (work) administrativo(a); **s. college** escuela f de secretariado; **s. course** curso m de secretariado

**secretariat** [sekrə'teərɪət] n Pol secretaría f

**secretary** ['sekrətərɪ] n (a) (in office) secretario(a) m,f (b) Pol ministro(a) m,f; US **S. of State** secretario(a) m,f de Estado; Br **the S. for...** el ministro de...

**secretary-general** ['sekrətərɪ'dʒenərəl] n Pol secretario(a) m,f general

**secrete** [sɪ'kriːt] vt (a) (discharge) secretar, segregar (b) (hide) ocultar

**secretion** [sɪ'kriːʃən] n secreción f

**secretive** ['siːkrɪtɪv] adj reservado(a); **to be s. about sth** ser reservado(a) respecto a algo

**secretly** ['siːkrɪtlɪ] adv en secreto

**sect** [sekt] n secta f

**sectarian** [sek'teərɪən] adj sectario(a)

**sectarianism** [sek'teərɪənɪzəm] n sectarismo m

**section** ['sekʃən] **1** n sección f; Mus **the brass/string s.** la sección de metal/cuerda; **all sections of society** todos los sectores de la sociedad
**2** vt (cut) seccionar

**sectional** ['sekʃənəl] adj (a) (interests, rivalries) particular (b) **a s. drawing** una sección, un corte

**sector** ['sektə(r)] n sector m; **public/private s.** sector m público/privado

**secular** ['sekjʊlə(r)] adj (history, art) secular; (music) profano(a); (education) laico(a)

**secure** [sɪ'kjʊə(r)] **1** adj (a) (free from anxiety) seguro(a); **s. in the knowledge that...** con la conciencia tranquila sabiendo que... (b) (investment, place, foothold) seguro(a); (foundations) firme, seguro(a); **to make sth s.** asegurar algo
**2** vt (a) (make safe) (region) proteger; (future) asegurar (b) (fasten) (load) asegurar, afianzar; (door, window) cerrar bien (c) (obtain) (support, promise, loan) conseguir

**securely** [sɪ'kjʊəlɪ] adv (a) (safely) a buen recaudo (b) (firmly) firmemente; **the door was s. fastened** la puerta estaba firmemente cerrada

**security** [sɪ'kjʊərɪtɪ] n (a) (stability, safety) seguridad f; **s. of tenure** cargo m vitalicio; **S. Council** Consejo m de Seguridad; **s. forces** fuerzas fpl de seguridad; **s. guard** guarda mf jurado(a); **s. officer** agente mf de seguridad; **s. risk** peligro m para la seguridad del Estado (persona) (b) Fin (for loan) garantía f, aval m (c) Fin **securities** valores mpl

**sedan** [sɪ'dæn] n (a) US Aut turismo m (b) **s. chair** silla f de manos

**sedate** [sɪ'deɪt] **1** adj sosegado(a), sereno(a)
**2** vt sedar

**sedately** [sɪ'deɪtlɪ] adv sosegadamente

**sedation** [sɪ'deɪʃən] n **under s.** sedado(a)

**sedative** ['sedətɪv] n sedante m

**sedentary** ['sedəntrɪ] adj sedentario(a)

**sediment** ['sedɪmənt] n sedimento m

**sedition** [sɪ'dɪʃən] n sedición f

**seditious** [sɪ'dɪʃəs] adj sedicioso(a)

**seduce** [sɪ'djuːs] vt (sexually) seducir; Fig **to s. sb into doing sth** inducir a alguien a hacer algo

**seducer** [sɪ'djuːsə(r)] n seductor(ora) m,f

**seduction** [sɪ'dʌkʃən] n seducción f

**seductive** [sɪ'dʌktɪv] *adj* seductor(ora); **a s. offer** una oferta tentadora

**see¹** [si:] *n Rel* sede *f* (episcopal)

**see²** [si:], (*pt* **saw** [sɔː], *pp* **seen** [si:n]) **1** *vt* (**a**) *(with eyes, perceive)* ver; **to s. sb** *or* **doing sth** ver a alguien hacer algo; **did you s. that programme last night?** ¿viste anoche ese programa?; **now s. what you've done!** ¡mira lo que has hecho!; **to s. the sights** hacer turismo; **s. page 50** ver *or* véase pág. 50; **to be seeing things** *(hallucinate)* ver visiones; **it has to be seen to be believed** hay que verlo para creerlo; **I can't s. a way out of this problem** no le veo solución a este problema; **could you s. your way to lending me your car?** ¿crees que podrías prestarme el coche?; **to s. sense** *or* **reason** atender a razones; **these years saw many changes** estos años fueron testigos de muchos cambios; **I don't know what you s. in her** no sé qué ves en ella; **it remains to be seen whether...** está por ver si...; **I can't s. any** *or* **the sense in continuing this discussion** creo que no tiene sentido continuar esta discusión; **this is how I s. it** yo lo veo así

(**b**) *(understand)* ver, entender; **I s. what you mean** ya veo lo que quieres decir; **I don't s. the need for...** no veo qué necesidad hay de...; **I don't s. the point** no creo que tenga sentido

(**c**) *(envisage, imagine)* creer, imaginarse; **what do you s. happening next?** ¿qué crees que ocurrirá a continuación?; **I can't s. them accepting this** no creo que vayan a aceptar esto; **I can't s. you as a boxer** no te imagino como *or* de boxeador

(**d**) *(investigate, enquire)* **I'll s. what I can do** veré qué puedo hacer; **let's s. what happens if...** veamos qué ocurre si...

(**e**) *(make sure)* **I shall s. (to it) that he comes** me encargaré de que venga; **s. (to it) that you don't miss the train!** ¡asegúrate de no perder el tren!; *Fam* **he'll s. you (all) right** él te echará una mano

(**f**) *(meet)* *(person)* ver; *(doctor, solicitor)* ver, visitar; **I'm seeing Bill tomorrow** mañana voy a ver a Bill; **s. you soon!** ¡hasta pronto!

(**g**) *(escort, accompany)* acompañar; **to s. sb home/to the door** acompañar a alguien a casa/a la puerta

**2** *vi* (**a**) *(with eyes)* ver; **as far as the eye can s.** hasta donde alcanza la vista; **s. for yourself** míralo tú mismo; **we shall s.** ya veremos

(**b**) *(understand)* entender, ver; **as far as I can s.** a mi entender; **ah, I s.!** ¡ah, ya veo!

(**c**) *(imagine, consider)* **let me s., let's s.** veamos; **can we go to the beach? – we'll s.** ¿podemos ir a la playa? – ya veremos

(**d**) *(find out)* **I'll go and s.** voy a ver

▸**see about** *vt insep* (**a**) *(deal with)* encargarse

or ocuparse de (**b**) *(consider)* ver, pensar; *Fam* **we'll (soon) s. about that!** ¡eso está por ver!

▸**see in** *vt sep* **to s. the New Year in** recibir el Año Nuevo

▸**see off** *vt sep* (**a**) *(say goodbye to)* despedir (**b**) *(in fight)* deshacerse de

▸**see out** *vt sep* *(escort to door)* acompañar a la puerta; **I'll s. myself out** ya conozco el camino (de salida), gracias

▸**see through** *vt sep* *(project, policy)* **to s. sth through** sacar algo adelante

**2** *vt insep* *(not be deceived by)* *(person)* ver las intenciones de; *(plan, lies)* percatarse de

▸**see to** *vt insep* *(deal with)* ocuparse de; **to get sth seen to** hacer que alguien se ocupe de algo; **I'll s. to it that you're not disturbed** me aseguraré *or* encargaré de que nadie te moleste

**seed** [si:d] **1** *n* (**a**) *(for sowing)* semilla *f*; *(of fruit)* pepita *f*; **to go** *or* **run to s.** *(of plant)* granar; *Fig* **to sow (the) seeds of discord/doubt** sembrar la discordia/la duda; **s. corn** simiente *f* de trigo; *Fig* inversión *f* de futuro; **s. merchant** vendedor *m* de semillas; **s. potatoes** patatas *fpl* de siembra (**b**) *Literary (semen)* semilla *f*, semen *m* (**c**) *Sport (in tournament)* cabeza *mf* de serie

**2** *vt* (**a**) *(remove seeds from)* despepitar (**b**) *Sport (in tournament)* **seeded players/teams** jugadores *mpl*/equipos *mpl* seleccionados como cabezas de serie; **he's seeded 5th** es el cabeza de serie número 5

**3** *vi* *(of plant)* dar semilla, granar

**seedless** ['si:dlɪs] *adj* sin pepitas

**seedling** ['si:dlɪŋ] *n* plantón *m*

**seedy** ['si:dɪ] *adj* (**a**) *(shabby)* *(person, appearance, hotel)* miserable, cutre (**b**) *Fam (unwell)* **to feel s.** estar pachucho(a)

**seeing** ['si:ɪŋ] **1** *n* **s. is believing** ver para creer

**2** *conj* **s. that** *or* **how...** en vista de que..., ya que...; **s. it's so simple, why don't you do it yourself?** ya que es tan sencillo, ¿por qué no lo haces tú mismo?

**seek** [si:k] (*pt & pp* **sought** [sɔːt]) *vt* (**a**) *(look for)* *(thing lost, job)* buscar; *(friendship, promotion)* tratar de conseguir; **to s. one's fortune** buscar fortuna (**b**) *(request)* **to s. sth from sb** pedir algo a alguien; **to s. sb's help/advice** pedir ayuda/consejo a alguien (**c**) *(try)* **to s. to do sth** procurar hacer algo

▸**seek after** *vt insep* **to be much sought after** estar muy solicitado(a)

▸**seek out** *vt sep (person)* ir en busca de

**seem** [si:m] *vi* parecer; **s. tired** parecer cansado(a); **do what seems best** haz lo que te parezca mejor; **it seemed like a dream** parecía un sueño; **it doesn't s. right** no me parece bien; **I s. to have dropped your vase** creo que he tirado tu jarrón; **I can't s. to get it right** no consigo que me salga bien; **it seems**

(that)..., it would s. (that)... parece que...; it seems likely that... parece probable que...; it seems to me that... me parece que...; it seems or would s. so parece que sí; it seems or would s. not parece que no

**seeming** ['si:mɪŋ] *adj* aparente

**seemingly** ['si:mɪŋlɪ] *adv* aparentemente

**seemly** ['si:mlɪ] *adj Formal* correcto(a), apropiado(a)

**seen** [si:n] *pp of* **see**

**seep** [si:p] *vi* to s. into sth filtrarse en algo

**seepage** ['si:pɪdʒ] *n* filtración *f*

**seer** [sɪə(r)] *n Literary* adivino(a) *m,f*, profeta *m*

**seesaw** ['si:sɔ:] **1** *n* balancín *m (columpio)*
**2** *vi Fig (of prices, mood)* fluctuar

**seethe** [si:ð] *vi (of liquid)* borbotar; to be seething (with anger) estar a punto de estallar (de cólera)

**see-through** ['si:θru:] *adj* transparente

**segment 1** *n* ['segmənt] *(of circle, worm)* segmento *m*; *(of orange)* gajo *m*
**2** *vt* [seg'ment] segmentar

**segmentation** [segmen'teɪʃən] *n Econ* segmentación *f*

**segregate** ['segrɪgeɪt] *vt* segregar (from de)

**segregation** [segrɪ'geɪʃən] *n* segregación *f*

**Seine** [seɪn] *n* the S. el Sena

**seismic** ['saɪzmɪk] *adj* sísmico(a)

**seismograph** ['saɪzməgræf] *n* sismógrafo *m*

**seismology** [saɪz'mɒlədʒɪ] *n* sismología *f*

**seize** [si:z] *vt* **(a)** *(grab)* agarrar, coger; to s. hold of sth agarrar algo; to s. the opportunity of doing sth aprovechar la oportunidad de hacer algo **(b)** *(take for oneself) (city, territory)* tomar; *Law (drugs, stolen goods)* incautarse de
▸**seize on, seize upon** *vt insep* aprovecharse de
▸**seize up** *vi (of engine, machine)* atascarse

**seizure** ['si:ʒə(r)] *n* **(a)** *(of land, city)* toma *f*; *Law (of property, goods)* incautación *f* **(b)** *Med* ataque *m*

**seldom** ['seldəm] *adv* rara vez, raras veces

**select** [sɪ'lekt] **1** *adj* selecto(a); **s. committee** comisión *f* parlamentaria
**2** *vt* seleccionar

**selected** [sɪ'lektɪd] *adj* seleccionado(a); **s. works** obras *fpl* escogidas

**selection** [sɪ'lekʃən] *n* **(a)** *(act of choosing)* selección *f*; to make a s. realizar una selección **(b)** *(range)* gama *f* **(c)** *(thing chosen)* elección *f*

**selective** [sɪ'lektɪv] *adj* selectivo(a); to be s. (about sth) ser selectivo (con algo)

**selector** [sɪ'lektə(r)] *n (of team)* miembro *m* del comité seleccionador

**self** [self] *(pl* **selves** [selvz]) *n* **(a)** he's quite his old s. again ha vuelto a ser él mismo; she

is a shadow of her former s. no es ni sombra de lo que era; she was her usual cheerful s. se mostró alegre como siempre **(b)** *Psy* the s. el yo, el ser

**self-addressed envelope** ['selfə'drest-'envələup] *n* sobre *m* dirigido a uno mismo

**self-appointed** ['selfə'pɔɪntɪd] *adj* autodesignado(a), autoproclamado(a)

**self-assured** ['selfə'ʃuəd] *adj* seguro(a) de sí mismo(a); to be s. estar seguro de sí mismo

**self-catering** ['self'keɪtərɪŋ] *adj (holiday, accommodation)* sin servicio de comidas

**self-centred** ['self'sentəd] *adj* egoísta

**self-confessed** ['selfkən'fest] *adj* confeso(a)

**self-confidence** ['self'kɒnfɪdəns] *n* confianza *f* en sí mismo(a)

**self-confident** ['self'kɒnfɪdənt] *adj* lleno(a) de confianza en sí mismo(a)

**self-conscious** ['self'kɒnʃəs] *adj* cohibido(a)

**self-contained** ['selfkən'teɪnd] *adj (person, apartment)* independiente

**self-contradictory** ['selfkɒntrə'dɪktərɪ] *adj* contradictorio(a)

**self-control** ['selfkən'trəul] *n* autocontrol *m*

**self-deception** ['selfdɪ'sepʃən] *n* autoengaño *m*

**self-defeating** ['selfdɪ'fi:tɪŋ] *adj* contraproducente

**self-defence,** *US* **self-defense** ['self-dɪ'fens] *n (judo, karate etc)* defensa *f* personal *(non-violent action)* autodefensa *f*; in s. en defensa propia, en legítima defensa

**self-denial** ['selfdɪ'naɪəl] *n* abnegación *f*

**self-destruct** ['selfdɪ'strʌkt] *vi* autodestruirse

**self-determination** ['selfdɪtɜ:mɪ'neɪʃən] *n* autodeterminación *f*

**self-discipline** ['self'dɪsɪplɪn] *n* autodisciplina *f*

**self-doubt** ['self'daʊt] *n* falta *f* de confianza (en uno mismo)

**self-effacing** ['selfɪ'feɪsɪŋ] *adj* modesto(a), humilde

**self-employed** ['selfɪm'plɔɪd] *adj* autónomo(a)

**self-esteem** [selfɪ'sti:m] *n* to have high/low s. tener mucho/poco amor propio, tener mucha/poca autoestima

**self-evident** ['self'evɪdənt] *adj* evidente, obvio(a)

**self-explanatory** ['selfɪk'splænətərɪ] *adj* to be s. estar muy claro(a), hablar por sí mismo(a)

**self-expression** ['selfik'spreʃən] *n* autoexpresión *f*

**self-government** ['self'gʌvənmənt] *n* autogobierno *m*, autonomía *f*

**self-help** ['self'help] *n* autoayuda *f*; **s. group** grupo *m* de apoyo

**self-important** ['selfim'pɔ:tənt] *adj* presuntuoso(a), engreído(a)

**self-indulgent** ['selfin'dʌldʒənt] *adj* autocomplaciente

**self-inflicted** ['selfin'flɪktɪd] *adj* autoinfligido(a)

**self-interest** ['self'ɪntərɪst] *n* interés *m* propio

**selfish** ['selfɪʃ] *adj* egoísta

**selfishness** ['selfɪʃnɪs] *n* egoísmo *m*

**self-knowledge** ['self'nɒlɪdʒ] *n* conocimiento *m* de sí mismo(a)

**selfless** ['selflɪs] *adj* desinteresado(a), desprendido(a)

**self-made man** ['selfmeɪd'mæn] *n* hombre *m* hecho a sí mismo

**self-pity** ['self'pɪtɪ] *n* autocompasión *f*

**self-portrait** ['self'pɔ:treɪt] *n* autorretrato *m*

**self-possessed** ['selfpə'zest] *adj* sereno(a), dueño(a) de sí mismo(a)

**self-preservation** ['selfprezə'veɪʃən] *n* propia conservación *f*; **instinct for s.** instinto *m* de conservación

**self-raising flour** ['self'reɪzɪŋ'flaʊə(r)], *US* **self-rising flour** ['selfraɪsɪŋ'flaʊə(r)] *n* harina *f* con levadura

**self-reliant** ['selfrɪ'laɪənt] *adj* autosuficiente

**self-respect** ['selfrɪ'spekt] *n* amor *m* propio, dignidad *f*

**self-restraint** ['selfrɪs'treɪnt] *n* autodominio *m*, autocontrol *m*

**self-righteous** ['self'raɪtʃəs] *adj* santurrón(ona)

**self-rising flour** *US* = **self-raising flour**

**selfsame** ['selfseɪm] *adj* mismísimo(a)

**self-satisfied** ['selfsætɪsfaɪd] *adj* satisfecho(a) *or* pagado(a) de sí mismo(a); **to be s.** estar satisfecho *or* pagado de sí mismo

**self-service** ['self'sɜ:vɪs] **1** *n* autoservicio *m*
**2** *adj* de autoservicio

**self-starter** ['self'stɑ:tə(r)] *n* (*person*) persona *f* con iniciativa

**self-styled** ['selfstaɪld] *adj* (*president, king*) autoproclamado(a); (*philosopher, expert*) pretendido(a), sedicente

**self-sufficient** ['selfsə'fɪʃənt] *adj* autosuficiente

**self-taught** ['self'tɔ:t] *adj* autodidacto(a)

**sell** [sell] (*pt & pp* **sold** [səʊld]) **1** *vt* vender; **to s. sb sth, to s. sth to sb** vender algo a alguien; **to s. sth at a loss/a profit** vender algo con pérdida/ganancia; **scandal sells newspapers** las noticias escandalosas venden bien; *Fig* **to s. oneself** venderse; *Fig* **to s. sb an idea** vender una idea a alguien; *Fig* **to s. sb down the river** traicionar *or* vender a alguien
**2** *vi* (*of product*) venderse (**for** a); **to s. like hot cakes** venderse como rosquillas

▶**sell off** *vt sep* (*property, stock*) liquidar

▶**sell out 1** *vt sep* (**a**) **the concert is sold out** no quedan entradas para el concierto (**b**) (*betray*) vender, traicionar
**2** *vi* (**a**) **they have sold out of tickets** se han agotado las entradas (**b**) (*betray beliefs*) venderse

▶**sell up** *vi* (*sell home, business*) venderlo todo

**sell-by date** ['selbaɪdeɪt] *n Com* fecha *f* límite de venta

**seller** ['selə(r)] *n* vendedor(ora) *m,f*; *Econ* **sellers' market** mercado *m* de vendedores

**selling** ['selɪŋ] *n* venta *f*; **s. point** ventaja *f* (*de un producto*); **s. price** precio *m* de venta

**sell-off** ['selɒf] *n* (*of state-owned company*) privatización *f*

**Sellotape®** ['seləteɪp] *n* celo *m*, *CAm, Méx* durex® *m*

**sellout** ['selaʊt] *n* (**a**) (*play, concert*) lleno *m* (**b**) (*betrayal*) traición *f*

**semantic** [sɪ'mæntɪk] *adj* semántico(a)

**semantics** [sɪ'mæntɪks] *n* semántica *f*; *Fig* **let's not worry about s.** dejemos a un lado los matices

**semaphore** ['seməfɔ:(r)] *n* código *m* alfabético de banderas

**semblance** ['sembləns] *n* apariencia *f*

**semen** ['si:men] *n* semen *m*

**semester** [sɪ'mestə(r)] *n Univ* semestre *m*

**semi** ['semɪ] *n Br Fam* (*semi-detached house*) chalet *m* adosado

**semiautomatic** ['semɪɔ:tə'mætɪk] *adj* semiautomático(a)

**semicircle** ['semɪsɜ:kəl] *n* semicírculo *m*

**semicircular** [semɪ'sɜ:kjʊlə(r)] *adj* semicircular

**semicolon** ['semɪ'kəʊlən] *n* punto *m* y coma

**semiconductor** ['semɪkən'dʌktə(r)] *n Elec* semiconductor *m*

**semiconscious** ['semɪ'kɒnʃəs] *adj* semiconsciente

**semi-detached** ['semɪdɪ'tætʃt] **1** *n* (*house*) chalet *m* adosado
**2** *adj* adosado(a)

**semifinal** ['semɪ'faɪnəl] *n* semifinal *f*

**semifinalist** ['semɪ'faɪnəlɪst] *n* semifinalista *mf*

**seminal** ['semɪnəl] *adj* (*very important*) trascendental

**seminar** ['semɪnɑ:(r)] *n* seminario *m*

**seminary** ['semɪnərɪ] n seminario m

**semi-precious** ['semɪ'preʃəs] adj s. stone piedra f fina or semipreciosa

**semiquaver** ['semɪkweɪvə(r)] n Br Mus semicorchea f

**Semite** ['semaɪt] n semita mf

**Semitic** [sɪ'mɪtɪk] adj semita, semítico(a)

**semitone** ['semɪtəʊn] n Br Mus semitono m

**semitropical** ['semɪ'trɒpɪkəl] adj subtropical

**semivowel** [semɪ'vaʊəl] n semivocal f

**semolina** [semə'li:nə] n sémola f

**senate** ['senɪt] n the S. el Senado

**senator** ['senətə(r)] n senador(ora) m,f

**send** [send] (pt & pp sent [sent]) vt (letter, message, person) mandar, enviar; to s. word to sb (that…) mandar el recado a alguien (de que…); to s. sb to prison enviar a alguien a prisión; to s. sb on an errand mandar a alguien a (hacer) un recado; to s. sth/sb flying mandar or lanzar algo/a alguien por los aires; that sent him into fits of laughter aquello le provocó un ataque de risa
▸**send away 1** vt sep to s. sb away mandar a alguien que se marche
**2** vi to s. away for sth pedir algo por correo
▸**send back** vt sep (purchase, order of food) devolver
▸**send down** vt sep Br (a) Univ (expel) expulsar (b) Fam (send to prison) enchironar
▸**send for** vt insep (help, supplies) mandar traer; (doctor) mandar llamar
▸**send in** vt sep (application, troops, supplies) enviar
▸**send off 1** vt sep (a) (letter, order) mandar, enviar (b) Sport expulsar
**2** vi to s. off for sth pedir algo por correo
▸**send on** vt sep (a) (send ahead) we had our belongings sent on enviamos nuestras pertenencias a nuestro destino antes de partir (b) (forward after use) enviar más tarde
▸**send out 1** vt sep (letters, invitations) mandar, enviar; (radio signals) emitir
**2** vi to s. out for sth pedir que traigan algo
▸**send up** vt sep Br Fam (parody) parodiar, remedar

**sender** ['sendə(r)] n remitente mf

**send-off** ['sendɒf] n Fam despedida f

**send-up** ['sendʌp] n Br Fam parodia f, remedo m

**Senegal** [senɪ'gɔ:l] n Senegal

**Senegalese** [senɪgə'li:z] n & adj senegalés(esa) m,f

**senile** ['si:naɪl] adj senil; Med s. dementia demencia f senil

**senility** [sɪ'nɪlɪtɪ] n senilidad f

**senior** ['si:njə(r)] 1 n to be sb's s. (in age) ser mayor que alguien; (in rank) ser el superior de alguien; she is three years his s. ella es tres años mayor que él
**2** adj (a) (in age) mayor; Thomas Smith, S. Thomas Smith, padre; s. citizen persona f de la tercera edad (b) (in rank, position) superior; s. officer oficial m superior; s. partner (in company) socio m principal

**seniority** [si:nɪ'ɒrɪtɪ] n (in age, length of service) antigüedad f; (in rank) rango m, categoría f

**sensation** [sen'seɪʃən] n (a) (feeling) sensación f; burning s. quemazón f (b) (excitement) to be a s. ser todo un éxito; to cause a s. causar sensación

**sensational** [sen'seɪʃənəl] adj (a) (exaggerated) tremendista, sensacionalista (b) (excellent) extraordinario(a), sensacional

**sensationalism** [sen'seɪʃənəlɪzəm] n sensacionalismo m

**sense** [sens] 1 n (a) (faculty) sentido m; to come to one's senses (recover consciousness) recobrar el conocimiento or sentido; (see reason) entrar en razón; s. of smell/hearing sentido del olfato/oído; to lose all s. of time perder la noción del tiempo; s. of direction sentido de la orientación; s. of duty sentido del deber; s. of humour sentido del humor
(b) (feeling) sensación f; a s. of achievement la sensación de haber logrado algo
(c) (rationality, common sense) sensatez f, buen juicio m; good s. buen juicio; there's no s. in staying no tiene sentido quedarse
(d) (meaning) sentido m; to make (no) s. (no) tener sentido; to make s. of sth entender algo; in a s. en cierto sentido; in the s. that… en sentido de que…
**2** vt (perceive) notar, percibir; to s. that… tener la sensación de que…

**senseless** ['senslɪs] adj (a) (unconscious) inconsciente (b) (pointless) absurdo(a)

**sensibilities** [sensɪ'bɪlɪtɪz] npl sensibilidad f; to offend sb's s. herir la sensibilidad de alguien

**sensible** ['sensɪbəl] adj (a) (rational) (person, decision) sensato(a); the s. thing to do lo sensato, lo que tiene sentido (hacer) (b) (practical) (clothes, shoes) práctico(a) (c) Formal (aware) to be s. of sth ser consciente de algo

**sensibly** ['sensɪblɪ] adv (rationally) sensatamente

**sensitive** ['sensɪtɪv] adj (in general) sensible (to a); (touchy) susceptible

**sensitivity** [sensɪ'tɪvɪtɪ] n sensibilidad f

**sensor** ['sensə(r)] n sensor m

**sensory** ['sensərɪ] adj sensorial; s. organs órganos mpl sensoriales

**sensual** ['sensjʊəl] adj sensual

**sensuality** [sensjʊ'ælɪtɪ] n sensualidad f

**sensuous** ['sensjʊəs] adj sensual

**sent** [sent] *pt & pp of* **send**

**sentence** ['sentəns] **1** *n* (a) *Gram* oración *f*, frase *f* (b) *Law* sentencia *f*; **to pass s.** dictar sentencia

**2** *vt Law* sentenciar (**to** a)

**sententious** [sen'tenʃəs] *adj Formal* sentencioso(a)

**sentient** ['sentiənt] *adj* sensitivo(a), sensible

**sentiment** ['sentimənt] *n* (a) *(opinion)* parecer *m*; **public s.** el sentir popular (b) *(sentimentality)* sentimentalismo *m*

**sentimental** [senti'mentəl] *adj* sentimental

**sentimentality** [sentimen'tælɪtɪ] *n* sentimentalismo *m*

**sentry** ['sentrɪ] *n Mil* centinela *m*; **to be on s. duty** estar de guardia; **s. box** garita *f*

**Seoul** [səʊl] *n* Seúl

**Sep** *(abbr* **September)** septiembre *m*

**separable** ['sepərəbəl] *adj* separable

**separate 1** *adj* ['sepərət] *(parts, box, room)* separado(a); *(occasion, attempt)* distinto(a); *(organization)* independiente; **the two issues are quite s.** son dos cuestiones bien distintas; **fish and meat should be kept s.** hay que guardar la carne y el pescado por separado; **to lead s. lives** vivir separados(as); *also Fig* **they went their s. ways** siguieron cada uno su camino

**2** *vt* ['sepəreɪt] separar (**from** de); **he is separated from his wife** está separado de su mujer

**3** *vi* separarse (**from** de)

**separation** [sepə'reɪʃən] *n* separación *f*

**separatist** ['sepərətɪst] *n Pol* separatista *mf*

**sepia** ['si:pɪə] *n (colour)* (color *m*) sepia *m*

**sepsis** ['sepsɪs] *n Med* sepsis *f inv*, infección *f*

**Sept** *(abbr* **September)** septiembre *m*

**September** [sep'tembə(r)] *n* septiembre *m*; *see also* **May**

**septet** [sep'tet] *n Mus* septeto *m*

**septic** ['septɪk] *adj* séptico(a); **to become s.** infectarse; **s. tank** fosa *f* séptica

**septicaemia,** *US* **septicemia** [septɪ'si:mɪə] *n Med* septicemia *f*

**sepulchre,** *US* **sepulcher** ['sepəlkə(r)] *n Formal* sepulcro *m*

**sequel** ['si:kwəl] *n* (a) *(book, film)* continuación *f* (**to** de) (b) *(result)* secuela *f*

**sequence** ['si:kwəns] *n* (a) *(order)* sucesión *f*, secuencia *f*; **in s.** en sucesión *or* orden; **out of s.** desordenado(a) (b) *(of numbers, events)* serie *f*; *(in film)* secuencia *f*

**sequential** [sɪ'kwenʃəl] *adj* secuencial

**sequestrate** ['sekwəstreɪt] *vt Law* embargar

**sequestration** [si:kwe'streɪʃən] *n Law* embargo *m*

**sequin** ['si:kwɪn] *n* lentejuela *f*

**sequoia** [se'kwɔɪə] *n* sec(u)oya *f*

**Serbia** ['sɜ:bɪə] *n* Serbia

**Serb(ian)** ['sɜ:b(ɪən)] *n & adj* serbio(a) *m,f*

**Serbo-Croat** ['sɜ:bəʊ'krəʊæt] *n (language)* serbocroata *m*

**serenade** [serə'neɪd] **1** *n* serenata *f*

**2** *vt* dar una serenata a

**serene** [sɪ'ri:n] *adj* sereno(a)

**serenity** [sɪ'renɪtɪ] *n* serenidad *f*

**serf** [sɜ:f] *n Hist* siervo(a) *m,f* (de la gleba)

**serfdom** ['sɜ:fdəm] *n Hist* servidumbre *f*

**serge** [sɜ:dʒ] *n* sarga *f*

**sergeant** ['sɑ:dʒənt] *n Mil* sargento *mf*; *(in police)* ≃ oficial *mf* de policía

**sergeant-major** [sɑ:dʒənt'meɪdʒə(r)] *n Mil* sargento *mf* primero

**serial** ['sɪərɪəl] **1** *n* *(in magazine)* novela *f* por entregas, folletín *m*; *(on TV)* serial *m*

**2** *adj* en serie; **s. killer** asesino(a) *m,f* en serie; **s. number** número *m* de serie; *Comptr* **s. port** puerto *m* (en) serie

**serialize** ['sɪərɪəlaɪz] *vt (in newspaper, magazine)* publicar por entregas; *(on TV)* emitir en forma de serial

**series** ['sɪəri:z] *n* serie *f*

**serious** ['sɪərɪəs] *adj (person)* serio(a); *(situation, problem, injury)* serio(a), grave; **to be s. about doing sth** estar decidido(a) a hacer algo; **are you s.?** ¿lo dices en serio?; **it wasn't a s. suggestion** no lo decía en serio; *Fam* **s. money** cantidad de dinero

**seriously** ['sɪərɪəslɪ] *adv* (a) *(in earnest)* seriamente, en serio; **to take sth/sb s.** tomar algo/a alguien en serio; **to take oneself too s.** tomarse demasiado en serio (b) *(gravely)* seriamente, gravemente; **s. ill** seriamente *or* gravemente enfermo(a) (c) *Fam (very)* cantidad de

**sermon** ['sɜ:mən] *n also Fig* sermón *m*

**serpent** ['sɜ:pənt] *n Literary* sierpe *f*, serpiente *f*

**serpentine** ['sɜ:pəntaɪn] *adj Literary* serpenteante, serpentino(a)

**SERPS** [sɜ:ps] *n Br Fin (abbr* **State Earnings Related Pension Scheme)** = sistema público de pensiones contributivas

**serrated** [se'reɪtɪd] *adj* dentado(a)

**serum** ['sɪərəm] *n Med* suero *m*

**servant** ['sɜ:vənt] *n (in household)* criado(a) *m,f*, sirviente(a) *m,f*; *(of leader, country)* servidor(ora) *m,f*

**serve** [sɜ:v] **1** *n (in tennis)* servicio *m*; *(it's)* **your s.!** ¡tú sacas!

**2** *vt* (a) *(be faithful to) (master, cause)* servir, estar al servicio de; **to s. one's own interests** actuar en interés propio

(b) *(be useful to)* servir; **it doesn't s. my purpose** no me sirve; **it has served me well** me ha hecho un buen servicio *or* apaño; **if my memory serves me right** si mal no recuerdo

**(c)** *(complete) (prison sentence, term of office)* cumplir; *(apprenticeship)* realizar, hacer

**(d)** *(customer)* atender; **are you being served?** ¿le están atendiendo?

**(e)** *(meal, drink)* servir; **to s. lunch/dinner** servir el almuerzo/la cena; **s. chilled** *(on wine)* sírvase bien frío; **serves four** *(on packet, in recipe)* para cuatro raciones

**(f)** *Law* **to s. sb with a summons** citar a alguien

**(g) it serves her right!** ¡se lo merece!, ¡lo tiene bien merecido!

**3** *vi* **(a)** *(carry out duty)* servir; **to s. in a government** ser miembro de un gobierno

**(b) to s. as...** *(be used as)* servir de...; **to s. as an example** servir de ejemplo

**(c)** *(in shop)* atender, despachar

**(d)** *(in tennis)* servir, sacar

▸**serve up** *vt sep (food)* servir; *Fig* ofrecer

**server** ['sɜ:və(r)] *n* **(a)** *(in tennis)* jugador(ora) *m,f* al servicio **(b)** *(tray)* bandeja *f* **(c)** *Comptr* servidor *m*

**service** ['sɜ:vɪs] **1** *n* **(a)** *(with army, firm)* servicio *m; Mil* **the services** las fuerzas armadas; **to do sb a s.** hacer un favor a alguien; **to be at sb's s.** estar al servicio de alguien; **to be of s. to sb** serle a alguien de utilidad; **he offered his services** ofreció sus servicios

**(b)** *Old-fashioned (of servant)* **to be in s.** servir; **to go into s.** entrar a servir

**(c)** *(in shop, restaurant)* servicio *m*; **s. is included** el servicio está incluido; **s. not included** servicio no incluido; **s. charge** (tarifa *f* por) servicio *m*; **s. industry** industria *f* de servicios; *Br* **s. lift** montacargas *m inv*

**(d)** *(system)* **postal/air/train s.** servicios *mpl* postales/aéreos/de ferrocarril

**(e)** *(maintenance)* revisión *f*; **s. area, services** *(on motorway)* área *f* de servicio; **s. station** *(on motorway)* estación *f* de servicio

**(f)** *Rel* oficio *m*, servicio *m*

**(g)** *(tea/dinner* **s.** servicio *m* de té/de mesa

**(h)** *(in tennis)* saque *m*, servicio *m*; **s. line** línea *f* de saque *or* servicio

**2** *vt (car, computer, TV)* revisar; *Fin (loan, debt)* amortizar los intereses de

**serviceable** ['sɜ:vɪsəbəl] *adj* **(a)** *(in working order)* en buen uso **(b)** *(useful)* útil, práctico(a)

**serviceman** ['sɜ:vɪsmən] *n Mil* militar *m*

**servicewoman** ['sɜ:vɪswʊmən] *n Mil* militar *f*

**serviette** [sɜ:vɪ'et] *n Br* servilleta *f*

**servile** ['sɜ:vaɪl] *adj* servil

**serving** ['sɜ:vɪŋ] *n (portion)* ración *f*; **s. hatch** ventanilla *f* (de cocina)

**servitude** ['sɜ:vɪtju:d] *n* esclavitud *f*

**servo** ['sɜ:vəʊ] **1** *n (pl* **servos)** *Fam (servomechanism)* servomecanismo *m*

**2** *adj Aut* **s. brake** servofreno *m*

**sesame** ['sesəmɪ] *n* **s. oil** aceite *m* de sésamo *or* de ajonjolí; **s. seeds** (semillas *fpl* de) sésamo *m*; **open s.!** ¡ábrete, Sésamo!

**session** ['seʃən] *n* **(a)** *(period of activity)* sesión *f* **(b)** *(meeting)* reunión *f*; **to be in s.** estar reunido(a) **(c)** *Sch & Univ (term)* trimestre *m*; *(year)* curso *m*

**set** [set] **1** *n* **(a)** *(of keys, boxes, chess pieces, pans)* juego *m*; *(of problems, rules, symptoms & Math* conjunto *m*; *(of stamps, picture cards, books)* serie *f*, colección *f*; **s. of teeth** dentadura *f*

**(b)** *(of people)* grupo *m*, círculo *m*

**(c)** *Sch* **top/bottom s.** = grupo de los alumnos más/menos aventajados en cada asignatura a los que se enseña por separado

**(d)** *(TV, radio)* aparato *m*, receptor *m*; **television s.** televisor *m*

**(e)** *Th & TV (scenery)* decorado *m; Cin* plató *m*

**(f)** *(in tennis)* set *m*; **s. point** punto *m* de set

**2** *adj* **(a)** *(fixed) (ideas, price)* fijo(a); **to be s. in one's ways** tener hábitos fijos; **s. lunch** menú *m* (del día); **s. phrase** frase *f* hecha; **s. piece** *(in play, film)* = escena clásica e impactante; *(in sport)* jugada *f* ensayada (a balón parado)

**(b)** *(ready)* **to be (all) s. for sth/to do sth** estar preparado(a) para algo/para hacer algo

**(c)** *(determined)* **to be (dead) s. on doing sth** estar empeñado(a) en hacer algo; **to be (dead) s. against sth** oponerse totalmente a algo

**3** *vt (pt & pp* **set)** **(a)** *(place)* colocar; *(jewel)* engastar; **to s. the table** poner la mesa; **to s. a trap (for sb)** tender una trampa (a alguien); **the novel/film is set in Edinburgh** la novela/película transcurre *or* se desarrolla en Edimburgo

**(b)** *(fix) (date, day, limit, price)* fijar; *(task, problem)* dar, encargar; *(record)* establecer; *(watch, clock)* poner en hora; **to s. a value on sth** poner precio *or* asignar un valor a algo; **s. the alarm clock for 8 a.m.** pon el despertador a las ocho; **to s. the scene for sb** poner a alguien en situación; *Sch* **to s. an essay** mandar (hacer) un trabajo

**(c)** *(cause to start)* **that set me thinking** eso me hizo pensar; **to s. sb free** dejar libre *or* poner en libertad a alguien; **to s. sth on fire** prender fuego a algo; **her performance set people talking** su actuación dio que hablar (a la gente)

**(d)** *Med (bone, fracture)* recomponer

**4** *vi* **(a)** *(of sun, moon)* ponerse; **we saw the sun setting** vimos la puesta de sol

**(b)** *(become firm) (of jelly)* cuajar; *(of concrete)* endurecerse; *(of broken bone)* soldarse

▸**set about** *vt insep* **(a)** *(task, job)* emprender; *(problem, situation)* abordar; **to s. about doing sth** empezar a hacer algo **(b)** *(attack)* atacar

▸**set against** *vt sep* **(a)** *(cause to oppose)* **to s. sb against sb** enemistar a alguien con alguien

(b) *(compare)* **to s. sth against sth** comparar algo con algo (c) *(deduct)* **to s. expenses against tax** deducir gastos de los impuestos

▸**set apart** *vt sep (distinguish)* distinguir **(from** de)

▸**set aside** *vt sep* (a) *(job, task)* dejar (a un lado) (b) *(save) (money)* ahorrar; *(time)* reservar

▸**set back** *vt sep* (a) *(delay)* retrasar (b) *Fam (cost)* costar

▸**set down** *vt sep (put down) (object)* dejar; *(passenger)* dejar (bajar); **to s. sth down in writing** poner algo por escrito

▸**set forth** *vi Literary (depart)* partir

▸**set in** *vi (of fog, winter)* instalarse; *(of night)* caer; *(of mood, infection)* arraigar

▸**set off 1** *vt sep* (a) *(bomb, alarm)* accionar; *(argument, chain of events)* desencadenar (b) *(enhance) (colour, feature)* realzar

2 *vi (depart)* salir

▸**set out 1** *vt sep (arrange)* disponer; *(ideas)* exponer

2 *vi* (a) *(depart)* salir (b) *(in job, task)* empezar, comenzar (c) *(intend)* **to s. out to do sth** pretender hacer algo

▸**set to** *vi* (a) *(start working)* empezar o ponerse a trabajar (b) *Fam (start arguing)* enzarzarse en una pelea

▸**set up 1** *vt sep* (a) *(erect) (statue)* erigir; *(tent, barrier)* montar (b) *(arrange, organize) (meeting, group)* organizar; *(system, company)* establecer; **to s. up house** or **home** instalarse; *Fam* **I've been set up!** *(I've been framed)* ¡me han tendido una trampa!

2 *vi (establish oneself)* establecerse **(as** de o como); **to s. up in business** montar un negocio

▸**set upon** *vt insep (attack)* atacar

**setback** ['setbæk] *n* contratiempo *m*, revés *m*

**set-square** ['setskweə(r)] *n Math (with angles of 45, 45 and 90°)* escuadra *f*; *(with angles of 30, 60 and 90°)* cartabón *m*

**settee** [se'ti:] *n* sofá *m*

**setter** ['setə(r)] *n (dog)* setter *m*

**setting** ['setɪŋ] *n* (a) *(of story, festival)* escenario *m*, marco *m* (b) *(of sun)* puesta *f* (de sol) (c) *(on machine)* posición *f*; **highest s.** máximo *m*; **lowest s.** mínimo *m* (d) **s. lotion** fijador *m*

2 *adj (sun, star)* poniente

**settle** ['setəl] **1** *vt* (a) *(put in place)* colocar, poner; **she had settled herself in an armchair** se había instalado cómodamente en un sillón; **to s. the children for the night** acostar a los niños (b) *(nerves)* calmar; **I took something to s. my stomach** tomé algo que me asentara el estómago (c) *(day, venue)* fijar (d) *(problem, dispute)* resolver; *(account, debt)* liquidar, saldar; **she settled her affairs** resolvió sus asuntos; *Fam* **that settles it!** ¡no se hable más!; *Law* **to s. a matter out of court** llegar a un acuerdo extrajudicial (e) *(colonize)* colonizar

2 *vi* (a) *(of bird, insect, dust)* posarse **(on** en o sobre); *(of liquid, beer)* reposar (b) *(of person, family)* asentarse **(in** en); *(of crowd, situation)* apaciguarse, tranquilizarse; **to s. into an armchair** instalarse en un sillón; *Law* **to s. (out of court)** llegar a un acuerdo extrajudicial

▸**settle down 1** *vt sep* (a) *(make comfortable)* acomodar (b) *(make calm)* calmar, tranquilizar

2 *vi* (a) *(make oneself comfortable)* acomodarse, instalarse; **to s. down to work** concentrarse en el trabajo (b) *(adopt regular life)* sentar la cabeza (c) *(of situation, excitement)* tranquilizarse, calmarse

▸**settle for** *vt insep (accept)* conformarse con

▸**settle in** *vi (become established)* establecerse

▸**settle on** *vt insep (decide on, choose)* decidirse por

▸**settle up** *vi (pay bill, debt)* pagar

**settled** ['setəld] *adj (stable)* estable

**settlement** ['setəlmənt] *n* (a) *(of problem, dispute)* resolución *f*; *Com (of account, debt)* liquidación *f*; **to reach a s.** llegar a un acuerdo (b) *(town, village) (recently built)* asentamiento *m*; *(in isolated area)* poblado *m*

**settler** ['setlə(r)] *n* colono *m*

**set-to** ['set'tu:] *n (pl* **set-tos)** *n Fam (argument, fight)* pelea *f*, trifulca *f*

**setup** ['setʌp] *n Fam (organization, arrangement)* sistema *m*, montaje *m*

**seven** ['sevən] **1** *n* siete *m*

2 *adj* siete; *Rel* **the s. deadly sins** los siete pecados capitales; *Literary* **to sail the s. seas** surcar los siete mares; *see also* **eight**

**seventeen** [sevən'ti:n] *n & adj* diecisiete *m*; *see also* **eight**

**seventeenth** [sevən'ti:nθ] **1** *n* (a) *(fraction)* diecisieteavo *m*, decimoséptima parte *f* (b) *(in series)* decimoséptimo *m*, *f* (c) *(of month)* diecisiete *m*

2 *adj* decimoséptimo(a); *see also* **eleventh**

**seventh** ['sevənθ] **1** *n* (a) *(fraction)* séptimo *m*, séptima parte *f* (b) *(in series)* séptimo(a) *m*, *f* (c) *(of month)* siete *m*

2 *adj* séptimo(a); **to be in s. heaven** estar en el séptimo cielo; *see also* **eighth**

**seventieth** ['sevəntɪθ] *n & adj* septuagésimo(a) *m*, *f*

**seventy** ['sevəntɪ] *n & adj* setenta *m*; *see also* **eighty**

**sever** ['sevə(r)] *vt also Fig* cortar

**several** ['sevərəl] **1** *adj* varios(as)

2 *pron* varios(as) *m*, *fpl*; **s. of us/them** varios de nosotros/ellos

**severance** ['sevərəns] *n* ruptura *f*; *Ind* **s. pay** indemnización *f* por despido

**severe** [sɪ'vɪə(r)] *adj (person, punishment, criticism)* severo(a); *(pain)* fuerte, intenso(a); *(illness)* grave; *(style, architecture)* sobrio(a)

**severity** [sɪ'verɪtɪ] n (of person, punishment, criticism) severidad f; (of pain) intensidad f; (of illness) gravedad f; (of style, architecture) sobriedad f

**Seville** [se'vɪl] n Sevilla

**sew** [səʊ] (pp **sewn** [səʊn]) vt & vi coser

►**sew up** vt sep Fam **it's all sewn up** está todo arreglado

**sewage** ['suːɪdʒ] n aguas fpl residuales; **s. disposal** depuración f de aguas residuales; **s. works** depuradora f; **s. system** alcantarillado m

**sewer** ['suːə(r)] n (pipe) alcantarilla f, cloaca f; **main s.** colector m

**sewn** [səʊn] pp of **sew**

**sex** [seks] n sexo m; **to have s. with sb** hacer el amor con alguien, acostarse con alguien; **s. appeal** atractivo m sexual; **s. education** educación f sexual; **s. life** vida f sexual; **s. maniac** obseso(a) m,f (sexual); **s. shop** sex shop f; **s. symbol** símbolo m sexual, sex symbol mf

**sexagenarian** [seksədʒɪ'neərɪən] n sexagenario(a) m,f

**sexism** ['seksɪzəm] n sexismo m

**sexist** ['seksɪst] n & adj sexista mf

**sexologist** [sek'splədʒɪst] n sexólogo(a) m,f

**sextant** ['sekstənt] n Naut sextante m

**sextet** [seks'tet] n Mus sexteto m

**sexton** ['sekstən] n Rel sacristán m

**sexual** ['seksjʊəl] adj sexual; **s. discrimination** discriminación f sexual; **s. harassment** acoso m sexual; **s. intercourse** relaciones fpl sexuales, el acto sexual; **s. reproduction** reproducción f sexual

**sexuality** [seksjʊ'ælɪtɪ] n sexualidad f

**sexually** ['seksjʊəlɪ] adv sexualmente; **s. transmitted disease** enfermedad f de transmisión sexual

**sexy** ['seksɪ] adj Fam sexy; Fig (car) muy atractivo(a)

**Seychelles** [seɪ'ʃelz] npl **the S.** las (islas) Seychelles

**Sgt** Mil (abbr **Sergeant**) sargento mf

**sh** [ʃ] exclam ¡chsss!, ¡shis(t)!

**shabbily** ['ʃæbɪlɪ] adv (furnished) cochambrosamente; (dressed) desaliñadamente, desastradamente (b) (to behave) ruinmente, con mezquindad; **he was treated very s.** lo trataron fatal

**shabbiness** ['ʃæbɪnɪs] n (a) (of appearance) desaliño m; (of furniture) aspecto m cochambroso (b) (of conduct, treatment) ruindad f, mezquindad f

**shabby** ['ʃæbɪ] adj (a) (clothing) raído(a), desgastado(a); (appearance) desaliñado(a), desastrado(a); (furniture, house) cochambroso(a) (b) (conduct, behaviour) ruin, mezquino(a); **s. trick** mala jugada f or pasada f

**shack** [ʃæk] n choza f

►**shack up** vi very Fam **to s. up with sb** arrejuntarse or vivir arrejuntado(a) con alguien

**shackle** ['ʃækəl] **1** n shackles grilletes mpl

**2** vt (prisoner) poner grilletes a; Fig **to be shackled by convention** ser prisionero(a) de los convencionalismos

**shade** [ʃeɪd] **1** n (a) (shadow) sombra f; **in the s.** a la sombra; Fig **to put sb in the s.** hacer sombra or eclipsar a alguien; **shades of 1968...** (reminders) esto recuerda a 1968... (b) (nuance) (of colour) tono m, tonalidad f; (of opinion) matiz m; **a s. better/longer** ligeramente mejor/más largo(a) (c) Literary (ghost) espíritu m, fantasma m (d) Fam **shades** (sunglasses) gafas fpl de sol

**2** vt (protect from sun) dar sombra a, proteger del sol

►**shade in** vt sep (part of drawing) sombrear

**shaded** ['ʃeɪdɪd] adj sombreado(a)

**shading** ['ʃeɪdɪŋ] n (on drawing, map) sombreado m

**shadow** ['ʃædəʊ] **1** n also Fig sombra f; **to cast a s.** proyectar una sombra; Fig **the news cast a s. over the occasion** la noticia vino a ensombrecer el acto; **without a s. of doubt** sin sombra de duda; **to have shadows under one's eyes** tener ojeras

**2** adj Br Pol **S. Cabinet** gabinete m en la sombra, = el grupo de políticos de la oposición que formarían el gobierno en caso de que su partido estuviera en el poder; **S. Minister** = político de la oposición que probablemente sería ministro en caso de que su partido formara gobierno

**3** vt (follow) seguir

**shadowy** ['ʃædəʊɪ] adj (vague) vago(a), impreciso(a); (dark) oscuro(a), sombrío(a); **a s. form** una figura en la oscuridad

**shady** ['ʃeɪdɪ] adj (a) (garden, lane) sombreado(a), umbrío(a) (b) Fam (suspicious) (person) sospechoso(a), siniestro(a); (transaction) turbio(a), oscuro(a)

**shaft** [ʃɑːft] n (a) (of spear) asta f, vara f; (of golf club) vara f, barra f; (of tool) mango m; (of light) rayo m (b) (of mine) pozo m; (for lift) hueco m (c) (in engine, machine) eje m

**shag¹** [ʃæg] n (tobacco) picadura f

**shag²** Br Vulg **1** n (sexual intercourse) **to have a s.** echar un polvo

**2** vt (pt & pp **shagged**) (have sexual intercourse with) echar un polvo a

**3** vi (have sexual intercourse) echar un polvo

**shaggy** ['ʃægɪ] adj (hairy) peludo(a), lanoso(a); Fam **s. dog story** chiste m interminable (con final flojo)

**shah** [ʃɑː] n sha m

**shake** [ʃeɪk] **1** n (a) (action) sacudida f; **a s. of the head** (to say no) un movimiento negativo de la cabeza; *(with resignation)* un gesto de resignación con la cabeza; *Fam* **he got the shakes** le entró el tembleque; **with a s. in his voice** con la voz temblorosa; *Fam* **in two shakes** en un pispás; *Fam* **to be no great shakes** no ser gran cosa **(b) (milk)** s. batido *m*

**2** *vt (pt* **shook** [ʃʊk]*, pp* **shaken** [ˈʃeɪkən]*) (person, duster)* sacudir; *(branch, box, bottle)* agitar; *(building)* sacudir, hacer temblar; *(shock emotionally)* conmocionar; *Fig* **to s. sb's faith** quebrantar la fe de alguien; **to s. one's head** *(to say no)* negar con la cabeza; *(in disbelief)* hacer un gesto de incredulidad con la cabeza; **to s. one's fist at sb** amenazar a alguien con el puño; **to s. hands with sb** estrechar *or* dar la mano a alguien; **to s. hands on a deal** sellar un trato con un apretón de manos

**3** *vi* **(a)** *(of person, building, voice)* temblar; **to s. with fear/rage** temblar de miedo/rabia; **to be shaking like a leaf** temblar como un flan **(b)** *Fam* **to s. on it** cerrar el trato con un apretón de manos

▸**shake off** *vt sep (illness, depression)* salir de, quitarse de encima; *(pursuer)* librarse de

▸**shake up** *vt sep* **(a)** *(upset)* trastornar **(b)** *(reorganize) (system)* reorganizar

**shaken** [ˈʃeɪkən] *pp of* **shake**

**Shakespearian** [ʃeɪksˈpɪərɪən] *adj* shakespeariano(a)

**shake-up** [ˈʃeɪkʌp] *n Fam (reorganization)* reorganización *f*

**shakily** [ˈʃeɪkɪlɪ] *adv (to walk, write, speak)* temblorosamente

**shaky** [ˈʃeɪkɪ] *adj (table, ladder)* inestable, inseguro(a); *(handwriting, voice)* tembloroso(a); *(health, position)* débil, precario(a); **his English is s.** habla un inglés precario

**shale** [ʃeɪl] *n (rock)* esquisto *m*

**shall** [*stressed* ʃæl, *unstressed* ʃəl]

> En el inglés hablado, y en el escrito en estilo coloquial, el verbo **shall** se contrae de manera que **I/you/he** *etc* **shall** se transforman en **I'll/you'll/he'll** *etc.* La forma negativa **shall not** se transforma en **shan't**.

*modal aux v* **(a)** *(with first person) (expressing intentions, promises, predictions)* **I s. be there if I can** si puedo, estaré allí; **I shan't say this more than once** esto no lo voy a repetir; **we s. take note of your comments** tendremos en cuenta tus comentarios; **as we s. see** como veremos

**(b)** *Formal (with 2nd and 3rd person) (expressing determination)* **you s. pay for this!** ¡me las pagarás *or* vas a pagar!; **they s. not pass** no pasarán

**(c)** *(making suggestions, offers)* **s. I open the window?** ¿abro la ventana?; **s. I make some coffee?** ¿preparo café?

**(d)** *(indicating rule)* **all members s. be entitled to vote** todos los socios tendrán derecho al voto; **the term "company property" s. be understood to include...** se entiende que el término "propiedad de la empresa" comprende...

**shallot** [ʃəˈlɒt] *n* chalota *f*

**shallow** [ˈʃæləʊ] *adj* **(a)** *(water)* poco profundo(a); *(dish)* llano(a) **(b)** *Fig (person, mind)* superficial, poco profundo(a)

**sham** [ʃæm] **1** *n (trial, election)* farsa *f*; *(person)* farsante *mf*

**2** *adj (illness, emotion)* fingido(a)

**3** *vt (pt & pp* **shammed**) *(feign)* fingir, simular

**4** *vi* fingir

**shamble** [ˈʃæmbəl] *vi* **to s. along** caminar arrastrando los pies

**shambles** [ˈʃæmbəlz] *n (disorder)* desastre *m*, desorden *m*; **this place is a s.!** ¡esto es un desorden!; *Fam* **what a s.!** ¡qué desastre!

**shambolic** [ʃæmˈbɒlɪk] *adj Fam* desastroso(a)

**shame** [ʃeɪm] **1** *n* **(a)** *(disgrace, guilt)* vergüenza *f*; **to my s.** para mi vergüenza; **to have no s.** no tener vergüenza; **s. on you!** ¡debería darte vergüenza!; **to put sb to s.** dejar a alguien en mal lugar **(b)** *(pity)* pena *f*; **it would be a s. to...** sería una pena...; **what a s.!** ¡qué pena!

**2** *vt* **(a)** *(cause to feel ashamed)* avergonzar; **to s. sb into doing sth** avergonzar a alguien para que haga algo **(b)** *(bring shame on)* deshonrar, dejar en mal lugar

**shamefaced** [ˈʃeɪmfeɪst] *adj* avergonzado(a)

**shameful** [ˈʃeɪmfʊl] *adj* vergonzoso(a)

**shamefully** [ˈʃeɪmfəlɪ] *adv* vergonzosamente

**shameless** [ˈʃeɪmlɪs] *adj* desvergonzado(a); **he/she is s. about doing it** no le da ninguna vergüenza hacerlo

**shammy** [ˈʃæmɪ] *n* **s. (leather)** gamuza *f*

**shampoo** [ʃæmˈpuː] **1** *n* champú *m*

**2** *vt* **to s. one's hair** lavarse el pelo con champú

**shamrock** [ˈʃæmrɒk] *n* trébol *m*

**shandy** [ˈʃændɪ] *n* clara *f*, cerveza *f* con gaseosa

**shank** [ʃæŋk] *n (of lamb, beef)* pierna *f* (deshuesada)

**shan't** [ʃɑːnt] = **shall not**

**shanty¹** [ˈʃæntɪ] *n (hut)* chabola *f*; **s. town** barrio *m* de chabolas, *Am* barriada *f*, *Chile* callampa *f*, *Carib* ranchería *f*, *Andes* pueblo *m* joven

**shanty²** *n (song)* saloma *f* (marinera)

**shape** [ʃeɪp] **1** *n* **(a)** *(form)* forma *f*; **what is it?** ¿qué forma tiene?; **to be the same s. as...** tener la misma forma que...; **to take s.** *(of* *plan)* tomar forma; **they won't accept change in any s. or form** no aceptarán absolutamente ningún tipo de cambio; *Fig* **in the s. of...** en forma de... **(b)** *(condition)* **to be in good/bad s.** *(person)* estar/no estar en forma; *(company, economy)* estar en buenas/malas condiciones; **to get into/keep in s.** *(of person)* ponerse/mantenerse en forma; **to be out of s.** no estar en forma

**2** *vt* **(a)** *(clay)* modelar, moldear; *(wood)* tallar **(b)** *Fig (character, attitude)* moldear, modelar; *(events)* dar forma a

▶**shape up** *vi* **how is she shaping up in her new job?** ¿qué tal se está adaptando a su nuevo trabajo?; **he is shaping up well** va haciendo progresos

**shapeless** ['ʃeɪplɪs] *adj* informe

**shapely** ['ʃeɪplɪ] *adj* **she's very s.** tiene muy buen tipo

**shard** [ʃɑːd] *n (of pottery)* fragmento *m*; *(of glass)* esquirla *f*

**share** [ʃeə(r)] **1** *n* **(a)** *(portion)* parte *f*; **in equal shares** en *or* a partes iguales; **to have a s. in sth** participar en algo; **he doesn't do his s.** no hace lo que le corresponde; **you've had your fair s. of problems/luck** has tenido bastantes problemas/bastante suerte **(b)** *Fin* acción *f*; **s. capital** capital *m* social; **s. certificate** título *m* de acción

**2** *vt (secret, opinion, profit)* compartir

**3** *vi* compartir; **to s. in sth** participar de algo; **s. and s. alike!** ¡hay que compartir las cosas!

▶**share out** *vt sep* repartir

**shareholder** ['ʃeəhəʊldə(r)] *n Fin* accionista *mf*

**shareholding** ['ʃeəhəʊldɪŋ] *n Fin* participación *f* accionarial

**shark** [ʃɑːk] *n (a) (fish)* tiburón *m* **(b)** *(ruthless person)* buitre *mf*

**sharp** [ʃɑːp] **1** *n (in music)* sostenido *m*

**2** *adj* **(a)** *(knife, point, features)* afilado(a); *(needle, pencil)* puntiagudo(a); **to be s.** *(of knife)* estar afilado

   **(b)** *(angle, bend)* cerrado(a); *(rise, fall)* pronunciado(a); *(outline, focus, photograph)* nítido(a); *(contrast)* acusado(a), fuerte; *(sight, hearing)* agudo(a); *Fig* **to be at the s. end of sth** tener que enfrentarse cara a cara con algo

   **(c)** *(intelligent)* agudo(a), despierto(a)

   **(d)** *(harsh) (retort, words, person)* mordaz, seco(a); **a s. tongue** una lengua afilada *or* viperina

   **(e)** *(taste, sauce)* ácido(a); *(sound, pain)* agudo(a); *(wind, frost)* cortante, intenso(a)

   **(f)** *(in music)* sostenido(a); **C s.** do *m* sostenido

**3** *adv* **(a)** *(punctually)* en punto; **at four o'clock s.** a las cuatro en punto

   **(b)** *(immediately)* **to turn s. left/right** girar

repentinamente a la izquierda/derecha

   **(c)** *(idioms) Fam* **look s.!** ¡espabila!; **to pull up s.** detenerse en seco

**sharpen** ['ʃɑːpən] *vt* **(a)** *(knife, tool)* afilar; *(pencil)* sacar punta a **(b)** *(pain, desire)* aguizar; **to s. one's wits** aguizar el ingenio

**sharpener** ['ʃɑːpənə(r)] *n (for knife)* afilador *m*; *(for pencil)* sacapuntas *m inv*, afilalápices *m inv*

**sharp-eyed** ['ʃɑːpaɪd] *adj* observador(ora)

**sharply** ['ʃɑːplɪ] *adv* **(a)** *(contrast)* acusadamente; **to bring sth s. into focus** enfocar algo nítidamente **(b)** *(rise, fall)* pronunciadamente; *(brake)* en seco

**sharpness** ['ʃɑːpnɪs] *n* **(a)** *(of knife)* agudeza *f* **(b)** *(of contours, photograph)* nitidez *f*; *(of mind, hearing, sight)* agudeza *f* **(c)** *(of voice, words)* mordacidad *f* **(d)** *(of pain)* agudeza *f*; *(of wind)* intensidad *f*

**sharpshooter** ['ʃɑːpʃuːtə(r)] *n* tirador(ora) *m,f* de élite

**sharp-sighted** [ʃɑːp'saɪtɪd] *adj* observador(ora)

**sharp-tongued** [ʃɑːp'tʌŋd] *adj* mordaz

**shat** [ʃæt] *pt & pp of* **shit**

**shatter** ['ʃætə(r)] **1** *vt* **(a)** *(glass, bone)* hacer añicos **(b)** *Fig (hopes)* echar por tierra; *(silence)* romper; *(health, nerves)* destrozar **(c)** *Fam* **to be shattered** *(stunned)* quedarse destrozado(a); *(exhausted)* estar rendido(a) *or* derrengado(a)

**2** *vi (of glass, windscreen)* hacerse añicos

**shattering** ['ʃætərɪŋ] *adj* **(a)** *(blow, defeat, news)* demoledor(ora), devastador(ora) **(b)** *Fam (exhausting)* agotador(ora), matador(ora)

**shatterproof** ['ʃætəpruːf] *adj* inastillable

**shave** [ʃeɪv] **1** *n* afeitado *m*; **to have a s.** afeitarse; *Fig* **that was a close s.!** ¡ha faltado un pelo!

**2** *vt* **(a)** afeitar; **to s. one's face** afeitarse; **to s. one's legs** afeitarse las piernas **(b)** *(wood)* cepillar

**3** *vi* afeitarse

▶**shave off** *vt sep* afeitar; **he shaved his beard off** se afeitó la barba

**shaven** ['ʃeɪvən] *adj* afeitado(a)

**shaver** ['ʃeɪvə(r)] *n* maquinilla *f* de afeitar eléctrica

**shaving** ['ʃeɪvɪŋ] *n* **(a)** **s. brush** brocha *f* de afeitar; **s. foam** espuma *f* de afeitar **(b)** *(piece of wood, metal)* viruta *f*

**shawl** [ʃɔːl] *n* chal *m*, *Am* rebozo *m*

**she** [ʃiː] **1** *pron* ella *(usually omitted in Spanish, except for contrast)*; **she's Scottish** es escocesa; **SHE hasn't got it!** ¡ella no lo tiene!

**2** *n* **it's a s.** *(of animal)* es hembra

**sheaf** [ʃiːf] *n (pl* **sheaves** [ʃiːvz]*) (of corn)* gavilla *f*; *(of papers)* manojo *m*

**shear** [ʃɪə(r)] *(pp* **shorn** [ʃɔːn] *or* **sheared) 1** *vt (sheep)* esquilar; *Fig* **to be shorn of sth** verse despojado(a) de algo

**2** *vi (cut)* **to s. through sth** atravesar *or* cortar algo

**shears** ['ʃɪəz] *npl (for garden)* tijeras *fpl* de podar

**sheath** [ʃi:θ] *n* (**a**) *(for cable, knife)* funda *f*; **s. knife** cuchillo *m* de monte (**b**) *(contraceptive)* condón *m*

**she'd** [ʃi:d] **= she had, she would**

**shed**[1] [ʃed] *n (in garden)* cobertizo *m; (in factory)* nave *f*

**shed**[2] *(pt & pp shed) vt (leaves)* perder; *(tears, blood)* derramar; **to s. light on sth** arrojar luz sobre algo; **to s. its skin** *(of snake)* mudar la piel; **to s. weight** perder peso; **a lorry has shed its load on the motorway** un camión ha perdido su carga por la autopista

**sheen** [ʃi:n] *n* lustre *m*, brillo *m*

**sheep** [ʃi:p] *(pl sheep) n* oveja *f*; **s. farming** ganadería *f* ovina

**sheepdog** ['ʃi:pdɒg] *n* perro *m* pastor

**sheepfold** ['ʃi:pfəʊld] *n* redil *m*

**sheepish** ['ʃi:pɪʃ] *adj* avergonzado(a), azarado(a)

**sheepskin** ['ʃi:pskɪn] *n* piel *f* de oveja; **s. jacket** zamarra *f*

**sheer** [ʃɪə(r)] *adj* (**a**) *(pure, total)* puro(a), verdadero(a); **it's s. madness** es una verdadera locura (**b**) *(steep)* empinado(a), escarpado(a) (**c**) *(stockings, fabric)* fino(a), transparente

**sheet** [ʃi:t] *n (on bed)* sábana *f; (of paper, glass)* hoja *f; (of ice)* capa *f; (of metal)* lámina *f; (of flame)* cortina *f;* **s. lightning** relámpagos *mpl* (difusos); **s. metal** chapa *f* (de metal); **s. music** partituras *fpl* sueltas

**sheetfeed** ['ʃi:tfi:d] *n Comptr* alimentador *m* de hojas sueltas

**sheik(h)** [ʃeɪk] *n* jeque *m*

**shekel** ['ʃekəl] *n (Israeli currency)* shekel *m*

**shelf** [ʃelf] *(pl shelves* [ʃelvz]*) n* (**a**) *(in cupboard, bookcase)* estante *m*, balda *f;* (**set of**) **shelves** estantería *f; Fig* **to be left on the s.** quedarse para vestir santos; *Com* **s. life** *(of goods)* vida *f* útil, vida *f* en estantería *or* expositor (**b**) *(of cliff, rock face)* plataforma *f*, saliente *m*

**shell** [ʃel] *n* (**a**) *(of snail, oyster, on beach)* concha *f; (of lobster, tortoise)* caparazón *m; (of egg, nut)* cáscara *f; Fig* **she soon came out of her s.** rápidamente salió de su concha *or* caparazón; **s. suit** chándal *m* de nylon (**b**) *(of building)* esqueleto *m*, armazón *m or f* (**c**) *(bomb)* proyectil *m;* **s. shock** neurosis *f inv* de guerra

**2** *vt* (**a**) *(nuts, eggs)* pelar; *(peas)* desgranar (**b**) *(bombard)* atacar con fuego de artillería

▸**shell out** *Fam* **1** *vt sep (money)* apoquinar

**2** *vi* apoquinar; **to s. out for sth** pagar por algo

**she'll** [ʃi:l] **= she will, she shall**

**shellfire** ['ʃelfaɪə(r)] *n* fuego *m* de artillería

**shellfish** ['ʃelfɪʃ] *n (crustacean)* crustáceo *m; (mollusc)* molusco *m; (food)* marisco *m*

**shelling** ['ʃelɪŋ] *n* ataque *m* de artillería

**shellshocked** ['ʃelʃɒkt] *adj (soldier)* que sufre neurosis de guerra; *Fig* **to feel s.** sentirse traumatizado(a)

**shelter** ['ʃeltə(r)] **1** *n (place, protection)* refugio *m;* **to take s.** refugiarse

**2** *vt* resguardar (**from** de), refugiar (**from** de)

**3** *vi* resguardarse (**from** de), refugiarse (**from** de)

**sheltered** ['ʃeltəd] *adj* resguardado(a); **he had a s. childhood** fue un niño muy protegido(a); **s. housing** = hogares con atención especial para ancianos

**shelve** [ʃelv] *vt (postpone)* aparcar, posponer

**shelving** ['ʃelvɪŋ] *n* estanterías *fpl*

**shepherd** ['ʃepəd] **1** *n* pastor *m;* **s.'s pie** = pastel de carne picada y puré de patata

**2** *vt (sheep)* pastorear; *Fig (people)* dirigir *(en grupo)*

**shepherdess** [ʃepə'des] *n* pastora *f*

**sherbet** ['ʃɜ:bət] *n Br (powder)* polvos *mpl* para preparar un refresco; *US (sorbet)* sorbete *m*

**sheriff** ['ʃerɪf] *n Br* = representante de la Corona; *Scot* ≃ juez *mf* de primera instancia; *US* sheriff *m*

**sherry** ['ʃerɪ] *n (vino m de)* jerez *m*

**she's** [ʃi:z] **= she is, she has**

**Shetland** ['ʃetlənd] *n* **the S. Islands, the Shetlands** las Islas Shetland; **S. pony** pony *m* de Shetland

**shield** [ʃi:ld] **1** *n (of knight)* escudo *m; (police badge, trophy)* placa *f; Fig (protection)* protección *f*

**2** *vt (protect)* proteger (**from** de); **to s. one's eyes** protegerse los ojos

**shift** [ʃɪft] **1** *n* (**a**) *(change)* cambio *m;* **a s. in meaning** un cambio de significado; **a s. to the right/left** *(in politics)* un desplazamiento hacia la derecha/izquierda; **s. key** *(on typewriter, computer)* tecla *f* de mayúsculas (**b**) *Ind* turno *m;* **to work (in) shifts** trabajar por turnos (**c**) **s.** *(dress)* vestido *m* recto

**2** *vt* (**a**) *(move)* mover; *(stain)* eliminar; **to s. the blame onto sb** echar la culpa a alguien (**b**) *Fam (sell)* vender, despachar

**3** *vi (move)* moverse; *(change)* cambiar; *Fam (move quickly)* ir a toda mecha

**shiftless** ['ʃɪftlɪs] *adj* holgazán(ana)

**shiftwork** ['ʃɪftwɜ:k] *n Ind* trabajo *m* por turnos

**shifty** ['ʃɪftɪ] *adj (person)* sospechoso(a); *(look)* furtivo(a)

**shilling** ['ʃɪlɪŋ] *n* chelín *m*

**shimmer** ['ʃɪmə(r)] **1** *n* brillo *m* trémulo

**2** *vi* rielar

**shimmering** ['ʃɪmərɪŋ] *adj* con brillo trémulo

**shin** [ʃɪn] *n* espinilla *f*; **s. guard** *or* **pad** espinillera *f*

▶**shin up** (*pt & pp* **shinned**) *vt insep* (*climb*) trepar por

**shinbone** [ˈʃɪnbəʊn] *n* espinilla *f*

**shindy** [ˈʃɪndɪ] *n Fam* (*din*) jaleo *m*, follón *m*; **to kick up a s.** armar un jaleo

**shine** [ʃaɪn] **1** *n* (**a**) brillo *m*, lustre *m*; **to give one's shoes a s.** sacar brillo a los zapatos (**b**) (*idioms*) **to take the s. off sth** empañar *or* deslucir algo; *Fam* **to take a s. to sb** tomar cariño a alguien

**2** *vt* (*pt & pp* **shone** [ʃɒn]) (**a**) **to s. a torch on sth** enfocar una linterna hacia algo (**b**) (*pt & pp* **shined** [ʃaɪnd]) (*polish*) lustrar, sacar brillo a

**3** *vi* brillar; *Fig* **to s. at sth** destacar en algo; **her face shone with joy** estaba resplandeciente de alegría

**shiner** [ˈʃaɪnə(r)] *n Fam* (*black eye*) ojo *m* morado *or* a la virulé

**shingle** [ˈʃɪŋɡəl] *n* (**a**) (*wooden tile*) teja *f* de madera (**b**) (*pebbles*) guijarros *mpl*

**shingles** [ˈʃɪŋɡəlz] *n* (*disease*) herpes *m inv*; **to have s.** tener un herpes

**shining** [ˈʃaɪnɪŋ] *adj* brillante , reluciente; *Fig* **a s. example (of)** un ejemplo señero *or* brillante (de)

**shiny** [ˈʃaɪnɪ] *adj* brillante, reluciente

**ship** [ʃɪp] **1** *n* barco *m*, buque *m*; **to go by s.** ir en barco; *Fig* **when my s. comes in** cuando me haga rico(a)

**2** *vt* (*pt & pp* **shipped**) (*transport by sea, rail*) fletar, transportar; (*take on board*) cargar

▶**ship off** *vt sep Fam* mandar

**shipboard** [ˈʃɪpbɔːd] *n Naut* **on s.** a bordo

**shipbuilder** [ˈʃɪpbɪldə(r)] *n* constructor *m* naval *or* de buques

**shipbuilding** [ˈʃɪpbɪldɪŋ] *n* construcción *f* naval; **the s. industry** la industria naval

**shipload** [ˈʃɪpləʊd] *n* cargamento *m*, carga *f*; *Fig* **by the s.** a montones

**shipmate** [ˈʃɪpmeɪt] *n Naut* compañero *m* de tripulación

**shipment** [ˈʃɪpmənt] *n* flete *m*, cargamento *m*

**shipowner** [ˈʃɪpəʊnə(r)] *n* armador(ora) *m,f*, naviero(a) *m,f*

**shipping** [ˈʃɪpɪŋ] *n* (*ships*) navíos *mpl*, buques *mpl*; **s. agent** (*person*) agente *mf* marítimo(a), consignatario(a) *m,f*; (*company*) compañía *f* naviera; **s. lane** ruta *f* de navegación

**shipshape** [ˈʃɪpʃeɪp] *adj* ordenado(a), en perfecto orden

**shipwreck** [ˈʃɪprek] **1** *n* naufragio *m*

**2** *vt* **to be shipwrecked** naufragar

**shipwrecked** [ˈʃɪprekt] *adj* náufrago(a)

**shipwright** [ˈʃɪpraɪt] *n Naut* carpintero *m* de ribera

**shipyard** [ˈʃɪpjɑːd] *n* astillero *m*

**shire** [ˈʃaɪə(r)] *n* condado *m*; **s. horse** (*caballo m*) percherón *m*; **the s. counties** los condados del centro de Inglaterra

**shirk** [ʃɜːk] **1** *vt* (*obligation, task*) eludir

**2** *vi* (*avoid work*) gandulear

**shirker** [ˈʃɜːkə(r)] *n Fam* gandul(ula) *m,f*, vago(a) *m,f*

**shirt** [ʃɜːt] *n* camisa *f*; *Fam* **keep your s. on!** ¡no te sulfures!

**shirtmaker** [ˈʃɜːtmeɪkə(r)] *n* camisero(a) *m,f*

**shirtsleeves** [ˈʃɜːtsliːvz] *npl* **to be in s.** estar en mangas de camisa

**shirt-tail** [ˈʃɜːtteɪl] *n* faldón *m* de la camisa

**shirty** [ˈʃɜːtɪ] *adj Br Fam* **to be s.** estar mosqueado(a) *or* de mala uva; **to get s. (with sb)** mosquearse (con alguien)

**shit** [ʃɪt] *Vulg* **1** *n* (**a**) (*excrement*) mierda *f*; (*mess*) porquería *f*, mierda *f*; **to have a s.** cagar (**b**) (*nasty person*) cabrón(ona) *m,f* (**c**) (*idioms*) **to talk s.** decir gilipolleces; **he's in the s.** se va a cagar, tiene un marrón que te cagas; **he doesn't give a s.** le importa un huevo; **to beat the s. out of sb** inflar a alguien a hostias; **to scare the s. out of sb** acojonar a alguien, hacer que alguien se jiñe (de miedo)

**2** *vt* (*pt & pp* **shitted** *or* **shat** [ʃæt]) **to s. oneself** (*defecate*) cagarse (encima); (*be scared*) jiñarse de miedo

**3** *vi* cagar

**4** *exclam* **s.!** ¡mierda!

**shitless** [ˈʃɪtlɪs] *adj Vulg* **to scare sb s.** acojonar a alguien; **to be scared s.** estar acojonado(a); **to be scared s. (of sb/sth)** acojonarle a uno (algo/alguien)

**shitty** [ˈʃɪtɪ] *adj Vulg* (**a**) (*nappies, trousers*) lleno(a) de mierda, todo cagado(a) (**b**) (*weather, job*) chungo(a), asqueroso(a); (*behaviour, remark*) muy cabrón(ona); **to feel s.** sentirse de puta pena

**shiver** [ˈʃɪvə(r)] **1** *n* (*of cold, fear*) escalofrío *m*; **it sent shivers down my spine** me produjo *or* dio escalofríos

**2** *vi* (*with cold*) tiritar (**with** de); (*with fear*) temblar (**with** de)

**shoal** [ʃəʊl] *n* (*of fish*) banco *m*; *Fig* (*of people*) manada *f*

**shock¹** [ʃɒk] *n* **a s. of hair** una mata de pelo, una pelambrera

**shock²** [ʃɒk] **1** *n* (**a**) (*impact*) sacudida *f*; (*of earthquake*) temblor *m*; **s. absorber** amortiguador *m*; **s. tactics** (*in campaign*) táctica *f* sensacionalista; *Mil* **s. troops** tropas *fpl* de choque; *also Fig* **s. wave** onda *f* expansiva (**b**) (*surprise*) susto *m*; (*emotional blow*) conmoción *f*; **I got a real s. when...** me quedé de piedra cuando...; **to be in s.** estar conmocionado(a) (**c**) (*electric*) calambrazo *m*, descarga *f* (eléctrica); **s. therapy** terapia *f* de electrochoque

**2** vt (surprise, startle) dejar boquiabierto(a), dar un susto a; (scandalize) escandalizar; **to s. sb into doing sth** amedrentar a alguien para que haga algo

**shocked** [ʃɒkt] adj (startled) conmocionado(a), impactado(a); (scandalized) escandalizado(a)

**shocking** ['ʃɒkɪŋ] adj (a) (scandalous) escandaloso(a); **s. pink** rosa m chillón (b) (very bad) (weather) de perros; (pain) insoportable

**shockproof** ['ʃɒkpruːf] adj (watch) antichoque

**shod** [ʃɒd] pt & pp of **shoe**

**shoddy** ['ʃɒdɪ] adj (goods) de pacotilla; (workmanship) chapucero(a); (conduct) miserable

**shoe** [ʃuː] **1** n zapato m; (horseshoe) herradura f; **a pair of shoes** unos zapatos, un par de zapatos; Fig **I wouldn't like to be in his shoes** no me gustaría estar en su pellejo; Fig **put yourself in my shoes** ponte en mi lugar; **s. polish** betún m, crema f (para calzado); **s. shop** zapatería f

**2** vt (pt & pp **shod** [ʃɒd]) (horse) herrar

**shoebrush** ['ʃuːbrʌʃ] n cepillo m (para zapatos)

**shoehorn** ['ʃuːhɔːn] n calzador m

**shoelace** ['ʃuːleɪs] n cordón m (de zapato)

**shoemaker** ['ʃuːmeɪkə(r)] n zapatero(a) m,f

**shoeshine** ['ʃuːʃaɪn] n US (person) limpiabotas mf inv

**shoestring** ['ʃuːstrɪŋ] n (a) Fam **on a s.** (cheaply) con cuatro perras (b) US cordón m (de zapato)

**shone** [ʃɒn] pt & pp of **shine**

**shoo** [ʃuː] exclam **s.!** ¡fuera!

▶**shoo away, shoo off** vt sep espantar

**shook** [ʃʊk] pt of **shake**

**shoot** [ʃuːt] **1** n (a) (of plant) retoño m, vástago m

(b) (hunting party) cacería f

**2** (pt & pp **shot** [ʃɒt]) vt (a) (fire) (bullet) disparar; (arrow) lanzar, tirar; **to s. a glance at sb** lanzar una mirada a alguien

(b) **to s. sb** (wound) disparar a alguien; (kill) matar de un tiro a alguien; (execute) fusilar a alguien; **she was shot in the arm** le dieron un tiro en el brazo; **to s. rabbits/grouse** cazar conejos/urogallos; Fig **to s. oneself in the foot** tirar (uno) piedras contra su propio tejado

(c) (film, TV programme) rodar

(d) (pass rapidly) **to s. the rapids** salvar or atravesar los rápidos; **to s. the lights** (in car) saltarse el semáforo

(e) **to s. dice/pool** jugar a los dados/al billar americano

**3** vi (a) (with gun) disparar (**at** a); (in football) tirar, chutar

(b) (move rapidly) ir a escape, ir como una

exhalación; **he shot into/out of the house** entró en/salió de la casa como una exhalación; **the pain shot up his left side** le daban punzadas de dolor en el costado izquierdo

▶**shoot down** vt sep (person) abatir (a tiros); (plane) derribar

▶**shoot off** vi (leave quickly) salir a escape

▶**shoot out** vi (emerge quickly) aparecer de pronto

▶**shoot up** vi (a) (of plants, children) crecer con rapidez; (of buildings) levantarse con rapidez (b) (of rocket) elevarse a gran velocidad; (of prices) dispararse (c) Fam (with drugs) chutarse

**shooting** ['ʃuːtɪŋ] **1** n (a) (gunfire) tiroteo m; (incident) ataque m con disparos; (killing) asesinato m (con arma de fuego); **s. stick** bastón m asiento (b) (of film, TV programme) rodaje m

**2** adj **s. star** estrella f fugaz

**shoot-out** ['ʃuːtaʊt] n (gunfight) tiroteo m; **penalty s.** lanzamiento m or tanda f de penaltis

**shop** [ʃɒp] **1** n (a) (for goods) tienda f; **s. assistant** dependiente(a) m,f; **s. window** escaparate m (b) Fam **to do a s.** (do shopping) hacer la compra (c) (workshop) taller m; Fig **the s. floor** los trabajadores (d) Fam (idioms) **to talk s.** hablar del curro; **to be all over the s.** ser un caos total

**2** vt (pt & pp **shopped**) Br Fam (betray) chivarse de

**3** vi comprar, hacer compra(s); **to go shopping** ir de compras; **to s. around** comparar precios (en diferentes establecimientos)

**shopgirl** ['ʃɒpgɜːl] n dependienta f

**shopkeeper** ['ʃɒpkiːpə(r)] n tendero(a) m,f

**shoplifter** ['ʃɒplɪftə(r)] n ratero(a) m,f (en comercios)

**shoplifting** ['ʃɒplɪftɪŋ] n hurtos mpl (en comercios)

**shopper** ['ʃɒpə(r)] n comprador(ora) m,f

**shopping** ['ʃɒpɪŋ] n (activity) compra f; (purchases) compras fpl; **to do the s.** hacer la compra; **s. bag** bolsa f de la compra; **s. basket** cesta f de la compra; **s. centre** centro m comercial; **s. list** lista f de la compra; **s. precinct** área f comercial; **s. trolley** carrito m (de la compra)

**shore** [ʃɔː(r)] n (of sea, lake) orilla f; **on s.** en tierra; **to go on s.** (from ship) bajar a tierra

▶**shore up** vt sep also Fig apuntalar

**shoreline** ['ʃɔːlaɪn] n orilla f

**shorn** [ʃɔːn] pp of **shear**

**short** [ʃɔːt] **1** n Fam (a) (short film) corto m, cortometraje m

(b) (drink) chupito m

(c) (short circuit) cortocircuito m

**2** adj (a) (physically) corto(a); (person) bajo(a), Méx chaparro(a); **Bill is s. for William** Bill es el diminutivo de William; **to have a s. temper or fuse** tener el genio muy vivo; **s. story** cuento m

**(b)** *(in time)* corto(a), breve; **in s.** en resumen, en pocas palabras, la respuesta es "no"; **to make s. work of sb/sth** dar buena cuenta de alguien/algo; **s. and sweet** conciso(a) y al grano

**(c)** *(abrupt)* seco(a); **to be s. with sb** ser seco con alguien

**(d)** *(insufficient, lacking)* escaso(a); **to be in s. supply** *(of money, water)* escasear; **to be s. of** andar escaso de; **the change was 50 pence s.** faltaban 50 peniques en las vueltas; **it's little** or **not far s. of...** *(almost)* le falta poco para ser...; **he's not far s. of forty** anda cerca de los cuarenta; **it was little s. of miraculous that she survived** fue poco menos que un milagro que sobreviviera

**3** *adv* **(a)** *(suddenly)* **to stop s.** pararse en seco; **to bring sb up s.** dejar paralizado(a) a alguien

**(b)** *(in length, duration)* **they stopped s. of...** no llegaron a...; **to cut sth/sb s.** interrumpir algo/a alguien

**(c)** *(without)* **to go s.** pasar privaciones; **to go s. of sth** andar escaso(a) de algo

**(d)** *(to express insufficiency)* **we are running s. of coffee** se nos está terminando el café; **to fall s.** quedarse corto(a); **to fall s. of** *(target, standard, expectations)* no alcanzar; *Fig* **to sell sb s.** *(cheat)* estafar a alguien; **I was taken** or **caught s.** me entraron muchas ganas de ir al cuarto de baño

**shortage** ['ʃɔːtɪdʒ] *n* escasez *f*, carestía *f*; **petrol/food s.** escasez de gasolina/alimentos; **he has no s. of ideas** no le faltan ideas

**shortbread** ['ʃɔːtbred], **shortcake** ['ʃɔːtkeɪk] *n* = especie de galleta elaborada con mantequilla, ≃ mantecada *f*

**short-change** ['ʃɔːt(t)ʃeɪndʒ] *vt* *(in shop)* devolver de menos a; *Fig (cheat)* timar

**short-circuit** [ʃɔːt'sɜːkɪt] **1** *n* cortocircuito *m*

**2** *vt (electrical)* producir un cortocircuito en; *Fig (bypass)* saltarse

**3** *vi* tener un cortocircuito

**shortcomings** ['ʃɔːtkʌmɪŋz] *npl* defectos *mpl*

**shortcut** ['ʃɔːtkʌt] *n also Fig* atajo *m*

**shorten** ['ʃɔːtən] *vt (skirt, text)* acortar; *(visit, task)* abreviar

**shortfall** ['ʃɔːtfɔːl] *n* déficit *m*

**shorthaired** ['ʃɔːtheəd] *adj* de pelo corto

**shorthand** ['ʃɔːthænd] *n* taquigrafía *f*; **s. typist** taquimecanógrafo(a) *m,f*

**short-haul** ['ʃɔːthɔːl] *adj* de corto recorrido

**shortlist** ['ʃɔːtlɪst] **1** *n* lista *f* de seleccionados

**2** *vt* **to be shortlisted (for sth)** estar seleccionado(a) (para algo)

**short-lived** [ʃɔːt'lɪvd] *adj (success, rejoicing)* efímero(a)

**shortly** ['ʃɔːtlɪ] *adv* **(a)** *(soon)* en seguida, pronto; **s. after(wards)** poco después **(b)** *(abruptly)* secamente, bruscamente

**short-range** ['ʃɔːtreɪndʒ] *adj (missile)* de corto alcance

**shorts** [ʃɔːts] *npl (short trousers)* pantalones *mpl* cortos

**short-sighted** [ʃɔːt'saɪtɪd] *adj* miope, corto(a) de vista; *Fig* corto(a) de miras

**short-sleeved** ['ʃɔːt'sliːvd] *adj* de manga corta

**shortstop** ['ʃɔːtstɒp] *n US Sport* = jugador que intenta interceptar bolas entre la segunda y tercera base

**short-tempered** [ʃɔːt'tempəd] *adj* **to be s.** tener mal genio

**short-term** ['ʃɔːttɜːm] *adj (solution, loan)* a corto plazo; **s. contract** contrato *m* temporal

**shorty** ['ʃɔːtɪ] *n Fam* canijo(a) *m,f*, retaco(a) *m,f*

**shot** [ʃɒt] **1** *n* **(a)** *(act of firing, sound)* tiro *m*, disparo *m*; **to fire a s.** disparar; *Fig* **like a s.** *(without hesitation)* al instante; *Fig* **my answer was a s. in the dark** respondí al azar or a ciegas; *Fig* **to call the shots** dirigir el cotarro; **s. put** lanzamiento *m* de peso

**(b)** *(marksman)* **he is a good/bad s.** es un buen/mal tirador

**(c)** *(in football)* tiro *m*, chut(e) *m*; *(in basketball)* tiro *m*, lanzamiento *m*

**(d)** *(photograph)* foto *f*; *(of film, TV programme)* toma *f*

**(e)** *Fam (injection)* inyección *f*

**(f)** *(attempt)* intento *m*, intentona *f*; **to have a s. at sth/at doing sth** intentar algo/hacer algo

**(g)** *(drink)* chupito *m*, dedal *m*

**2** *pt & pp of* **shoot**

**shotgun** ['ʃɒtgʌn] *n* escopeta *f*; *Fam* **to have a s. wedding** casarse de penalty

**should** [ʃʊd]

La forma negativa **should not** se transforma en **shouldn't**.

*modal aux v* **(a)** *(expressing obligations, recommendations, instructions)* **you s. do it at once** deberías hacerlo inmediatamente; **you shouldn't laugh at him** no deberías reírte de él; **you s. have come earlier** deberías haber venido antes; **he shouldn't have told them** no debería habérselo dicho; **a present?, oh you shouldn't have!** ¿un regalo? ¡no tenías que haberte molestado!; **you s. have seen the expression on his face!** ¡tendrías que haber visto la cara que puso!; **you s. read the instructions carefully** lea detenidamente las instrucciones

**(b)** *(expressing probability)* **the weather s.**

**improve from now on** a partir de ahora, el tiempo debería mejorar; **she s. have arrived by this time** a estas horas ya debe de haber llegado

(c) *(in exclamations, in rhetorical questions)* **why s. you suspect me?** ¿por qué habrías de sospechar de mí?; **who s. I meet but Martin!** y ¿a quién me encontré? ¡a Martin!; **he apologized – I s. think so, too!** se disculpó – ¡es lo mínimo que podía hacer!

(d) *(in subordinate clauses)* **he ordered that they s. be released** ordenó que los liberaran; **she insisted that he s. wear his hair short** insistió en que llevase el pelo corto

(e) *(in conditional clauses)* **if he s. come** *or Formal* **s. he come, let me know** si viene, avísame; **if you s. have any difficulty, phone this number** si tuviera algún problema, llame a este número

(f) *(expressing opinions, preferences)* **I s. like a drink** me apetecería tomar algo; **we s. want to know if there was anything seriously wrong** si algo va muy mal, nos gustaría saberlo; **I s. imagine he was rather angry!** ¡me imagino que estaría bastante enfadado!; **I shouldn't be surprised if...** no me sorprendería que...

**shoulder** ['ʃəʊldə(r)] **1** *n (of person)* hombro *m*; *(of meat)* paletilla *f*; **s. to s.** hombro con hombro; *Fig* **to rub shoulders with sb** codearse con alguien; *Fig* **to be looking over one's s.** estar inquieto(a); *Fig* **to cry on sb's s.** coger a alguien de paño de lágrimas; **s. bag** bolsa *f* de bandolera; **s. blade** omóplato *m*; **s. pad** hombrera *f*; **s. strap** *(of garment)* tirante *m*; *(of bag)* correa *f*

**2** *vt* (a) *(push)* **to s. one's way through a crowd** abrirse paso a empujones entre la multitud; **to s. sb aside** apartar a alguien de un empujón (del hombro) (b) *(put on shoulder)* echarse al hombro; *Fig (responsibility)* asumir

**shouldn't** ['ʃʊdnt] = **should not**

**shout** [ʃaʊt] **1** *n* grito *m*; **shouts of laughter** carcajadas *fpl*

**2** *vt* gritar; **to s. sth at sb** gritarle algo a alguien

**3** *vi* gritar; **to s. at sb** gritar a alguien; **to s. for help** gritar pidiendo ayuda; *Fig* **to have something to s. about** tener algo que celebrar

▸**shout down** *vt sep* **to s. sb down** impedir con gritos que alguien hable

**shouting** ['ʃaʊtɪŋ] *n* griterío *m*, gritos *mpl*

**shove** [ʃʌv] **1** *n* empujón *m*; **to give sth/sb a s.** dar un empujón a algo/alguien

**2** *vt & vi* empujar

▸**shove around** *vt sep Fam (bully)* abusar de
▸**shove off** *vi Fam (leave)* largarse

**shovel** ['ʃʌvəl] **1** *n* pala *f*

**2** *vt* (*pt & pp* **shovelled**, *US* **shoveled**) echar a paladas; *Fam* **to s. food into one's mouth** atiborrarse de comida

**shovelful** ['ʃʌvəlfʊl] *n* palada *f*

**show** [ʃəʊ] **1** *n* (a) *(exhibition)* exposición *f*, muestra *f*; **to be on s.** exhibirse, estar expuesto(a); **to put sth on s.** exponer algo; **s. house/flat** casa *f*/piso *m* piloto; **s. jumper** jinete *m*/amazona *f* de pruebas de saltos; **s. jumping** prueba *f* de saltos (de equitación); *Pej* **s. trial** juicio *m* ejemplarizante

(b) *(concert, play)* espectáculo *m*; *(on TV, radio)* programa *m*; *Fig* **to run the s.** dirigir el cotarro; **s. business** el mundo del espectáculo; **s. girl** corista *f*; *Fam* **it was a real s. stopper** fue una auténtica sensación

(c) *(act of showing)* demostración *f*; **s. of hands** votación *f* a mano alzada; **it's all s.** es pura fachada; **to do sth for s.** hacer algo por alardear; *Fam* **good s.!** *(well done)* ¡bien hecho!

**2** *vt* (*pp* **shown** [ʃəʊn]) (a) *(display)* mostrar, enseñar; *(picture)* exponer, exhibir; *(courage, talent)* mostrar, demostrar; **to s. sb sth, to s. sth to sb** enseñar *or* mostrar algo a alguien; *Fig* **to s. one's cards** *or* **one's hand** mostrar las verdaderas intenciones; **they had nothing to s. for all their work** trabajaron mucho para nada; **he won't s. his face here again** no volverá a dejarse ver por aquí; **to s. oneself** dejarse ver; **to s. a profit/a loss** registrar *or* arrojar beneficios/pérdidas; **you're showing your age** estás hecho un carcamal; **to s. oneself to be...** demostrar ser...

(b) *(indicate)* mostrar; *(time, temperature)* indicar, señalar

(c) *(prove, demonstrate)* mostrar, demostrar; **it goes to show that...** eso viene a demostrar que...

(d) *(teach)* enseñar; **to s. sb how to do sth** enseñar a alguien a hacer algo

(e) *(film)* proyectar; *(TV programme)* emitir, poner; **they are showing a Clint Eastwood film tonight** esta noche ponen *or* echan una película de Clint Eastwood

(f) *(escort, lead)* **to s. sb the way** mostrar a alguien el camino; **to s. sb to his room** llevar a alguien a su habitación; **to s. sb round the town** enseñarle la ciudad a alguien

**3** *vi* (a) *(be visible)* notarse

(b) *(of film)* **what's showing this week?** ¿qué ponen *or* echan esta semana?; **"now showing at the Odeon"** "en pantalla en el cine Odeon"

▸**show in** *vt sep (escort in)* acompañar hasta dentro

▸**show off 1** *vt sep* alardear de
  **2** *vi* alardear, fanfarronear

▸**show out** *vt sep (escort out)* acompañar hasta la puerta

▶**show up** *vt sep* (a) *(reveal)* descubrir, poner al descubierto (b) *(embarrass)* poner en evidencia

2 *vi* (a) *(stand out)* destacar; **the marks s. up under infra-red light** la luz infrarroja revela las marcas (b) *Fam (arrive)* aparecer, presentarse

**showbiz** ['ʃəʊbɪz] *n Fam* la farándula, el mundo del espectáculo

**showcase** ['ʃəʊkeɪs] *n (for displaying objects)* vitrina *f*; *Fig (for talents, work)* escaparate *m*

**showdown** ['ʃəʊdaʊn] *n* discusión *f* cara a cara

**shower** ['ʃaʊə(r)] 1 *n* (a) *(of rain)* chubasco *m*, chaparrón *m*; *(of stones, insults)* lluvia *f* (b) *(for washing)* ducha *f*, *Am* regadera *f*; **to have** *or* **take a s.** ducharse, darse una ducha; **s. cap** gorro *m* de baño; **s. curtain** cortinas *fpl* de ducha; **s. gel** gel *m* de baño; **s. head** alcachofa *f* (de ducha) (c) *Br Fam (group)* **what a s.!** ¡menuda cuadrilla!

2 *vt* **to s. sb with sth, to s. sth on sb** colmar a alguien de algo

3 *vi (take a shower)* ducharse

**showery** ['ʃaʊərɪ] *adj* lluvioso(a)

**showing** ['ʃəʊɪŋ] *n (exhibition)* exposición *f*, muestra *f*; *(of film)* pase *m*, proyección *f*

**showman** ['ʃəʊmən] *n Fig (entertaining person)* hombre *m* espectáculo

**showmanship** ['ʃəʊmənʃɪp] *n Fig* espectacularidad *f*

**shown** [ʃəʊn] *pp of* **show**

**show-off** ['ʃəʊɒf] *n Fam* fanfarrón(ona) *m,f*, fantasma *mf*

**showpiece** ['ʃəʊpiːs] *n* pieza *f* principal *(de una colección)*

**showroom** ['ʃəʊruːm] *n* sala *f* de exposición

**showy** ['ʃəʊɪ] *adj* llamativo(a)

**shrank** [ʃræŋk] *pt of* **shrink**

**shrapnel** ['ʃræpnəl] *n* metralla *f*

**shred** [ʃred] 1 *n* jirón *m*; **in shreds** hecho(a) jirones; *also Fig* **to tear sth to shreds** hacer trizas algo; *Fig* **there isn't a s. of evidence** no hay ni rastro de pruebas

2 *vt (pt & pp* **shredded***) (documents)* hacer tiras, triturar; *(food)* cortar en tiras

**shredder** ['ʃredə(r)] *n (for paper)* trituradora *f* de documentos

**shrew** [ʃruː] *n* (a) *(animal)* musaraña *f* (b) *(nagging woman)* bruja *f*

**shrewd** [ʃruːd] *adj (person)* astuto(a); *(decision)* inteligente, astuto(a)

**shrewdly** ['ʃruːdlɪ] *adv* astutamente

**shriek** [ʃriːk] 1 *n* alarido *m*, chillido *m*; **shrieks of laughter** carcajadas *fpl*; **to give a s.** soltar un alarido *or* chillido

2 *vi* chillar

3 *vi* chillar; **to s. with laughter** reírse a carcajadas

**shrift** [ʃrɪft] *n* **to give sb short s.** prestar escasa atención a alguien

**shrill** [ʃrɪl] *adj* estridente, agudo(a)

**shrimp** [ʃrɪmp] *n Br* camarón *m*, quisquilla *f*; *US (prawn)* gamba *f*

**shrine** [ʃraɪn] *n (tomb)* sepulcro *m*; *(place) & Fig* santuario *m*

**shrink** [ʃrɪŋk] 1 *n Fam (psychiatrist)* psiquiatra *mf*

2 *vt (pt* **shrank** [ʃræŋk], *pp* **shrunk** [ʃrʌŋk]*)* encoger

3 *vi* (a) *(of material)* encoger(se); *(of income, budget)* reducirse, disminuir (b) *(move back)* **to s. from sth** retroceder ante algo; **to s. from doing sth** no atreverse a hacer algo

**shrinkage** ['ʃrɪŋkɪdʒ] *n (of material)* encogimiento *m*; *Fig (in sales, profits)* reducción

**shrink-wrapped** [ʃrɪŋk'ræpt] *adj* empaquetado(a) con plástico (de polietileno) adherente

**shrivel** ['ʃrɪvəl] *(pt & pp* **shrivelled**, *US* **shriveled***)* 1 *vt* marchitar

2 *vi* marchitarse

▶**shrivel up** *vi* secarse

**shroud** [ʃraʊd] 1 *n* mortaja *f*, sudario *m*; *Fig (of mystery)* halo *m*; *(of darkness)* manto *m*

2 *vt Fig* envolver; **to be shrouded in sth** estar envuelto(a) en algo

**Shrove Tuesday** ['ʃrəʊv'tjuːzdɪ] *n* Martes *m inv* de Carnaval

**shrub** [ʃrʌb] *n* arbusto *m*

**shrug** [ʃrʌg] 1 *n* encogimiento *m* de hombros

2 *vt (pt & pp* **shrugged***)* **to s. one's shoulders** encogerse de hombros

3 *vi* **to s.** encogerse de hombros

▶**shrug off** *vt sep* quitar importancia a

**shrunk** [ʃrʌŋk] *pp of* **shrink**

**shrunken** ['ʃrʌŋkən] *adj* encogido(a)

**shudder** ['ʃʌdə(r)] 1 *n (of person)* estremecimiento *m*; *Fam* **it gives me the shudders** me pone los pelos de punta

2 *vi (of person)* estremecerse; *(of vehicle)* dar una sacudida; **I s. to think of it** me estremezco sólo de pensarlo

**shuffle** ['ʃʌfəl] 1 *n* (a) **to walk with a s.** caminar arrastrando los pies (b) **to give the cards a s.** barajar *or* mezclar las cartas

2 *vt (papers)* revolver; *(cards)* barajar

3 *vi (when walking)* arrastrar los pies

**shun** [ʃʌn] *(pt & pp* **shunned***) vt* rehuir, evitar

**shunt** [ʃʌnt] *vt (train, carriages)* cambiar de vía; *Fam Fig* **we were shunted into another room** nos hicieron pasar a otra habitación

**shush** [ʃʌʃ] 1 *vt* hacer callar

2 *exclam* **s.!** ¡sssh!

**shut** [ʃʌt] 1 *adj* cerrado(a); **to be s.** estar cerrado; *Fam* **to keep one's mouth s.** no decir ni pío

**2** vt (pt & pp **shut**) cerrar; **to s. the door on sb** dar a alguien con la puerta en las narices; **to s. one's finger in the door** pillarse un dedo con la puerta; Fam **s. your mouth!** ¡cierra el pico!

**3** vi (of door) cerrarse; (of shop) cerrar

▸**shut down 1** vt sep cerrar por completo; (production) suspender

**2** vi cerrar por completo

▸**shut in** vt sep (confine) encerrar

▸**shut off** vt sep (a) (electricity, water, funds, flow of arms) cortar; (engine) apagar (b) (road, exit) cortar (c) (isolate) **to s. oneself off (from)** aislarse (de)

▸**shut out** vt sep (a) (exclude) (person) excluir; (light, view) tapar (b) (keep outside) dejar fuera; **to s. oneself out** quedarse fuera sin llaves

▸**shut up 1** vt sep (a) (confine) encerrar (b) (close) cerrar (c) Fam (silence) hacer callar

**2** vi Fam (be quiet) callarse

**shutdown** ['ʃʌtdaʊn] n (of factory) cierre m

**shut-eye** ['ʃʌtaɪ] n Fam **to get some s.** echar un sueñecito or una cabezadita

**shutter** ['ʃʌtə(r)] n (a) (on window) contraventana f; (of shop) persiana f; **to put up the shutters** (of shop) cerrar (b) (of camera) obturador m; **s. speed** tiempo m de exposición

**shuttle** ['ʃʌtəl] **1** n (a) (train, bus) servicio m regular (entre dos puntos); (plane) avión m (de puente aéreo); (space vehicle) transbordador m espacial; **s. service** (of planes) puente m aéreo; (of trains, buses) servicio regular (b) (in badminton) volante m

**2** vt **to s. sb back and forth** trasladar a alguien de acá para allá

**3** vi **to s. between A and B** ir y venir entre A y B

**shuttlecock** ['ʃʌtəlkɒk] n volante m

**shy** [ʃaɪ] **1** adj tímido(a); **to be s. of sb** tener miedo de alguien; **to be s. of doing sth** mostrarse remiso(a) a hacer algo

**2** vi (of horse) asustarse (at de)

▸**shy away** vi **to s. away from doing sth** no atreverse a hacer algo; **to s. away from sth** eludir algo

**shyly** ['ʃaɪlɪ] adv tímidamente, con timidez

**Siamese** [saɪə'miːz] **1** n (pl **Siamese**) (cat) (gato m) siamés m

**2** adj siamés(esa); **S. cat** gato m siamés; **S. twins** hermanos(as) m,fpl siameses(esas)

**Siberia** [saɪ'bɪərɪə] n Siberia

**Siberian** [saɪ'bɪərɪən] adj siberiano(a)

**sibling** ['sɪblɪŋ] n (brother) hermano m; (sister) hermana f; **s. rivalry** rivalidad f entre hermanos

**sic** [sɪk] adv sic

**Sicilian** [sɪ'sɪlɪən] n & adj siciliano(a) m,f

**Sicily** ['sɪsɪlɪ] n Sicilia

**sick** [sɪk] **1** n Fam (vomit) devuelto m, vomitona f

**2** npl **the s.** los enfermos

**3** adj (a) (ill) enfermo(a); **to be s.** (be ill) estar enfermo; (vomit) vomitar, devolver; **to feel s.** sentirse mal; **to make oneself s.** (deliberately) provocarse el vómito; **you're going to make yourself s.!** ¡te vas a empachar!; Fig **it makes me s.!** ¡me pone enfermo(a)!; Fig **to be worried s.** estar muerto(a) de preocupación; **s. bay** enfermería f; **s. leave** baja f por enfermedad; **s. note** certificado m de baja (por enfermedad); **s. pay** paga f por enfermedad

(b) (fed up) **to be s. of sb/sth** estar harto(a) de alguien/algo; **to grow s. of sth** hartarse de algo; **to be s. and tired of sb/sth, to be s. to death of sb/sth** estar hasta la coronilla de alguien/algo

(c) (cruel) (humour, joke) morboso(a), macabro(a); (person) retorcido(a); **to have a s. mind** tener una mente retorcida, ser retorcido

▸**sick up** vt sep Br Fam (vomit) devolver, vomitar

**sicken** ['sɪkən] **1** vt (make ill) (hacer) enfermar; (disgust) poner enfermo(a)

**2** vi ponerse enfermo(a), enfermar; **to be sickening for something** estar empezando a ponerse enfermo

**sickening** ['sɪkənɪŋ] adj (disgusting) repugnante; Fam (annoying) irritante, exasperante

**sickle** ['sɪkəl] n hoz f

**sickly** ['sɪklɪ] adj (a) (person, complexion) enfermizo(a); (plant) marchito(a); (colour, light) pálido(a), desvaído(a); (smile) falso(a) (b) (taste, sentiment) empalagoso(a); **s. sweet** empalagoso(a), dulzarrón(ona)

**sickness** ['sɪknɪs] n (illness) enfermedad f; (nausea) mareo m; **s. benefit** subsidio m por enfermedad

**sickroom** ['sɪkruːm] n habitación f del enfermo

**side** [saɪd] **1** n (a) (of person) costado m; (of animal) ijada f; **by sb's s.** al lado de alguien; **s. by s.** uno al lado del otro; Fam **to split one's sides (laughing)** partirse de risa

(b) (part) (of house, box, triangle, square) lado m; (of river) orilla f, margen m or f; (of road) borde m, margen m or f; (of mountain) ladera f; **on the south s. (of the city)** en la parte sur (de la ciudad); **s. door/entrance** puerta f/entrada f lateral

(c) (of record, paper) cara f

(d) (adjacent area) lado m; **on this/that s. (of)** a este/ese lado (de); **on the other s. (of sth)** al otro lado (de algo); **on both sides** a ambos lados; **on all sides, on every s.** por todos (los) lados; **from all sides, from every s.** desde todas partes; **to move from s. to s.** moverse de un lado a otro; **the left-hand s.** la izquierda; **the right-hand s.** la derecha; **to**

**stand on** or **to one s.** mantenerse al margen; **s. dish** plato m de acompañamiento or guarnición; **s. salad** ensalada f de acompañamiento or guarnición; **s. view** vista f lateral

(e) *(of situation, argument, personality)* lado m, aspecto m; **to look on the bright/gloomy s. (of things)** mirar el lado positivo/negativo (de las cosas); **to hear** or **look at both sides of the question** considerar las dos caras de una situación

(f) *(in game)* equipo m; *(in dispute)* parte f, bando m; **to be on sb's s.** *(defending)* estar de parte de alguien; *(in game)* estar en el equipo de alguien; **to take sides** tomar partido; **he's on our s.** está de nuestro lado; **to change sides** cambiar de bando; **he let the s. down** dejó en mal lugar a los suyos

(g) *(secondary part)* **s. effects** efectos mpl secundarios; **s. issue** cuestión f secundaria; **s. road** carretera f secundaria; **s. street** bocacalle f

(h) *(idioms)* **on his mother's s.** *(of family)* por línea materna; **to put sth to one s.** dejar algo a un lado; **to take sb to one s.** llevar a alguien aparte; **to be on the wrong s. of forty** pasar de los cuarenta; **to get on the right s. of sb** caer en gracia a alguien, complacer a alguien; **to get on the wrong s. of sb** ganarse la antipatía de alguien; **it's a bit on the expensive/long s.** es un poco caro/largo; **he does a bit of gardening on the s.** hace algunos trabajos extras de jardinería; *Fam* **to have a bit on the s.** tener un lío (amoroso)

**2** vi **to s. with** ponerse del lado de; **to s. against** ponerse en contra de

**sideboard** ['saɪdbɔ:d] n aparador m

**sideboards** ['saɪdbɔ:dz] npl *(facial hair)* patillas fpl

**sideburns** ['saɪdbɜ:nz] npl patillas fpl

**sidecar** ['saɪdkɑ:(r)] n sidecar m

**sidekick** ['saɪdkɪk] n *Fam* compinche mf

**sidelight** ['saɪdlaɪt] n *Aut* luz f de posición

**sideline** ['saɪdlaɪn] n (a) *(of football, rugby pitch)* línea f de banda; *Fig* **to sit on the sidelines** quedarse al margen (b) *Com (business)* negocio m subsidiario; *(job)* segundo empleo m

**side-saddle** ['saɪdsædəl] **1** n jamugas fpl, silla f de amazona
**2** adv **to ride s.** montar a mujeriegas

**sideshow** ['saɪdʃəʊ] n (a) *(at fair)* barraca f (de feria); *Fig* cuestión f menor or secundaria

**side-splitting** ['saɪdsplɪtɪŋ] adj *Fam* desternillante, divertidísimo(a)

**sidestep** ['saɪdstep] *(pt & pp sidestepped)* **1** vt *(tackle)* esquivar, evitar; *(player)* regatear; *Fig (question)* soslayar, eludir
**2** vi *(in boxing)* esquivar

**sideswipe** ['saɪdswaɪp] n **to take a s. at sb/sth** meterse de pasada con alguien/algo

**sidetrack** ['saɪdtræk] vt desviar

**sidewalk** ['saɪdwɔ:k] n US acera f

**sideways** ['saɪdweɪz] **1** adj *(look)* de reojo *(movement)* lateral
**2** adv de lado

**siding** ['saɪdɪŋ] n *(on railway)* apartadero m *(not connected to main track)* vía f muerta

**sidle** ['saɪdəl] vi **to s. up to sb** acercarse tím damente a alguien

**siege** [si:dʒ] n asedio m, sitio m; **to lay s. to** town sitiar una ciudad; **under s.** sitiado(a); s mentality manía f persecutoria

**Sierra Leone** [sɪˈerəlɪˈəʊn] n Sierra Leona

**sieve** [sɪv] **1** n *(with coarse mesh)* criba f, cedaza m; *(with fine mesh)* tamiz m; *(in kitchen)* colado m; *Fam* **to have a memory like a s.** tener un memoria pésima or de mosquito
**2** vt *(with coarse mesh)* cribar, cerner; *(with fin mesh)* tamizar; *(in kitchen)* colar

**sift** [sɪft] **1** vt *(flour, sugar)* tamizar
**2** vi *Fig* **to s. through sth** examinar algo con cienzudamente

**sigh** [saɪ] **1** n suspiro m
**2** vi suspirar; *(of wind)* susurrar

**sight** [saɪt] **1** n (a) *(faculty)* vista f; **to lose** one's **s.** perder la vista

(b) *(act of seeing)* **to catch s. of sth/sb** ve algo/a alguien; **to lose s. of sth/sb** perder d vista algo/a alguien; **I hate the s. of him** no puedo ni ver; **I can't stand the s. of blood** n soporto ver la sangre; **to shoot sb on s.** dis parar contra alguien en cuanto se lo ve; **at firs s.** a primera vista; **it was love at first s.** fue un flechazo; **to know sb by s.** conocer a alguien de vista; **to buy sth s. unseen** comprar algo ciegas

(c) *(range of vision)* **to come into s.** aparecer **to be within s. (of)** *(able to see)* estar a la vist (de); *Fig (of victory, the end)* estar a un paso (de) **to keep sb in s.** no perder de vista a alguien; to **put sth out of s.** esconder algo; **to keep ou of s.** no dejarse ver; *Prov* **out of s., out o mind** ojos que no ven, corazón que no siente

(d) *(of instrument)* visor m; *(of gun)* mira f; *Fig* t **have sth/sb in one's sights** tener algo/a al guien en el punto de mira; *Fig* **to have or se one's sights on sth/sb** tener las miras pues tas en algo/alguien

(e) *(spectacle)* espectáculo m; *Fam* **you're/it' a s. for sore eyes!** ¡dichosos los ojos que te/lo ven!; *Fam* **you look a s.!** *(mess)* ¡mira cómo t has puesto!; *(ridiculous)* ¡vaya facha or pinta tienes!; **the sights** *(of city)* los lugares de interés

(f) *Fam (for emphasis)* **a (damn) s. longer/ harder** muchísimo más largo/duro
**2** vt *(see)* avistar, ver

**sighted** ['saɪtɪd] **1** *npl* **the s.** las personas sin discapacidades visuales

**2** *adj (person)* sin discapacidades visuales

**sighting** ['saɪtɪŋ] *n* **several sightings have been reported** ha sido visto(a) en varias ocasiones

**sightless** ['saɪtlɪs] *adj* ciego(a)

**sight-read** ['saɪtriːd] (*pt & pp* **sight-read** ['saɪtred]) *vt & vi* repentizar

**sightseeing** ['saɪtsiːɪŋ] *n* visitas *fpl* turísticas; **to go s.** hacer turismo

**sightseer** ['saɪtsiːə(r)] *n* turista *mf*

**sign** [saɪn] **1** *n* (a) *(gesture)* seña *f*; **to make a s. to sb** hacer una seña a alguien; **s. language** lenguaje *m* por señas

(b) *(indication)* indicio *m*, señal *f*; **it's a sure s. that...** es un indicio inequívoco de que...; **a good/bad s.** una buena/mala señal; **a s. of the times** un signo de los tiempos que corren; **there's no s. of an improvement** no hay indicios de mejoría; **there is no s. of him/it** no hay ni rastro de él/ello; **he gave no s. of having heard** no dio muestras de haberlo oído; **all the signs are that...** todo parece indicar que...; **the equipment showed signs of having been used** el equipo tenía aspecto de haber sido utilizado

(c) *(notice)* cartel *m*; *(of pub, shop)* letrero *m*, rótulo *m*; *(on road)* señal *f* (de tráfico); **follow the signs for Manchester** sigue las indicaciones para Manchester

(d) *(symbol)* signo *m*; **plus/minus s.** signo más/menos; **s. of the zodiac** signo del zodíaco

**2** *vt* (a) *(write signature on)* firmar

(b) *(in sign language)* indicar (con señas)

(c) *(in sport)* fichar

**3** *vi* (a) *(write signature)* firmar

(b) *(in sport)* fichar (**for** por)

▶**sign away** *vt sep (rights)* ceder (por escrito)

▶**sign for** *vt insep (delivery, equipment)* firmar el acuse de recibo de

▶**sign in** *vi (in factory)* fichar; *(in hotel)* registrarse

▶**sign off** *vi* (a) *(of radio, TV presenter)* despedir la emisión (b) *(close letter)* despedirse, terminar

▶**sign on** *vi Fam (for unemployment benefit) (initially)* apuntarse al paro; *(regularly)* sellar la cartilla del paro

▶**sign out 1** *vt sep* **to s. sth out** *(book, equipment)* registrar *or* consignar el préstamo de algo

**2** *vi* firmar a la salida

▶**sign up** *vi* (a) *(register)* apuntarse (**for** a) (b) *(of soldier)* alistarse

**signal** ['sɪgnəl] **1** *n* señal *f*; *Fig* **to send the wrong signals** dar una impresión equivocada; *Rail* **s. box** sala *f* de agujas, puesto *m* de señales;

**2** *vt* (*pt & pp* **signalled**, *US* **signaled**) (a) *(send message to)* indicar (mediante señales); **to s. sb to do sth** hacerle una señal a alguien de *or* para que haga algo (b) *(be sign of)* señalar

**3** *vi* **s. to me if you need help** hazme una seña si necesitas ayuda; **she signalled for the bill** pidió la cuenta con una seña *or* haciendo señas; *Aut* **he didn't s. before he turned** no dio la indicación de que iba a torcer

**signalman** ['sɪgnəlmən] *n Rail* guardavía *m*

**signatory** ['sɪgnətərɪ] *n* signatario(a) *m,f*

**signature** ['sɪgnətʃə(r)] *n* firma *f*; **s. tune** *(of radio, TV programme)* sintonía *f*

**signboard** ['saɪnbɔːd] *n* letrero *m*

**signet ring** ['sɪgnɪt'rɪŋ] *n* sello *m* (sortija)

**significance** [sɪg'nɪfɪkəns] *n* (a) *(importance)* importancia *f*; **of no/of great s.** de ninguna/de gran importancia (b) *(meaning)* significado *m*

**significant** [sɪg'nɪfɪkənt] *adj (important)* considerable, importante; *(meaningful)* significativo(a); **s. other** media naranja *f*

**significantly** [sɪg'nɪfɪkəntlɪ] *adv* (a) *(appreciably)* sensiblemente (b) *(meaningfully)* significativamente; **s., no one mentioned it** es significativo que nadie lo mencionara

**signify** ['sɪgnɪfaɪ] *vt* (a) *(indicate)* señalar; *(constitute)* suponer, representar (b) *(mean)* significar

**signpost** ['saɪnpəʊst] **1** *n also Fig* señal *f*, indicación *f*

**2** *vt* señalizar; *Fig* señalar

**Sikh** [siːk] *n & adj* sij *mf*

**silage** ['saɪlɪdʒ] *n* forraje *m*

**silence** ['saɪləns] **1** *n* silencio *m*; **to listen/watch in s.** escuchar/observar en silencio; *Prov* **s. is golden** en boca cerrada no entran moscas

**2** *vt* hacer callar

**silencer** ['saɪlənsə(r)] *n (on car, gun)* silenciador *m*

**silent** ['saɪlənt] *adj (person, place)* silencioso(a); *(not pronounced) (letter)* mudo(a); **to be s.** *(not talk)* estar callado(a); **she's rather s.** *(by nature)* es muy callada; **to fall s.** quedarse en silencio; **to remain** *or* **keep s.** permanecer callado(a); **s. film** película *f* muda; **the s. majority** la mayoría silenciosa; **s. protest** protesta *f* silenciosa

**silently** ['saɪləntlɪ] *adv (not speaking)* en silencio; *(without noise)* sin hacer ruido, silenciosamente

**silhouette** [sɪlu:'et] **1** *n* silueta *f*

**2** *vt* **she was silhouetted against the light** la luz dibujaba su silueta, su silueta se recortaba al trasluz

**silica** ['sɪlɪkə] *n* sílice *f*

**silicon** ['sɪlɪkən] *n* silicio *m*; **s. chip** chip *m* de silicio

**silk** [sɪlk] *n* seda *f*; **s. screen printing** serigrafía *f*

**silkworm** ['sɪlkwɜːm] *n* gusano *m* de (la) seda

**silky** ['sɪlkɪ] *adj* sedoso(a); *(voice)* meloso(a)

**sill** [sɪl] *n (of window)* alféizar *m*

**silliness** ['sɪlɪnɪs] *n* tontería *f*, estupidez *f*; **stop this s.!** ¡ya basta de tonterías!

**silly** ['sɪlɪ] **1** *adj* tonto(a), estúpido(a); **the s. thing is that...** lo más ridículo es que...; **to make sb look s.** poner a alguien en ridículo; **to say/do something s.** decir/hacer una tontería; **to laugh/worry oneself s.** morirse de la risa/de preocupación; **to knock sb s.** dejar a alguien atontado de un mamporro

**2** *n Fam* idiota *mf*

**silo** ['saɪləʊ] *(pl* **silos)** *n* silo *m*

**silt** [sɪlt] *n* limo *m*, sedimentos *mpl* fluviales

▸**silt up** *vi* encenagarse

**silver** ['sɪlvə(r)] **1** *n* **(a)** *(metal)* plata *f*; *Prov* **every cloud has a s. lining** no hay mal que por bien no venga; **s. haired** con el pelo blanco; **s. (medal)** medalla *f* de plata; **s. paper** papel *m* de plata; **s. plate** *(coating)* baño *m* de plata; *(articles)* objetos *mpl* plateados; **the s. screen** la pantalla grande; **s. wedding** bodas *fpl* de plata **(b)** *Br (coins)* monedas *fpl* plateadas *(de entre 5 y 50 peniques)* **(c)** *(silverware)* (objetos *mpl* de) plata *f*

**2** *adj* **(a)** *(made of silver)* de plata **(b)** **s.(-coloured)** plateado(a)

**silver-plated** ['sɪlvə'pleɪtɪd] *adj* con baño de plata

**silversmith** ['sɪlvəsmɪθ] *n* platero(a) *m,f*

**silverware** ['sɪlvəweə(r)] *n* (objetos *mpl* de) plata *f*

**silverwork** ['sɪlvəwɜːk] *n* (trabajo *m* de) platería *f*

**silvery** ['sɪlvərɪ] *adj (colour)* plateado(a); *(sound)* argentino(a)

**simian** ['sɪmɪən] *adj* simiesco(a)

**similar** ['sɪmɪlə(r)] *adj* parecido(a) **(to** a); **s. in appearance/size** de parecido aspecto/tamaño

**similarity** [sɪmɪ'lærɪtɪ] *n* parecido *m*, similitud *f*

**similarly** ['sɪmɪləlɪ] *adv* **(a)** *(in the same way)* igual, de la misma manera **(b)** *(likewise)* igualmente, del mismo modo

**simile** ['sɪmɪlɪ] *n* símil *m*

**simmer** ['sɪmə(r)] **1** *n* **at a s.** a fuego lento

**2** *vt* cocer a fuego lento

**3** *vi* cocerse a fuego lento; *Fig (of revolt, discontent)* fraguarse; **she was simmering with rage** estaba a punto de explotar

▸**simmer down** *vi* calmarse, tranquilizarse

**simper** ['sɪmpə(r)] *vi* sonreír con afectación

**simple** ['sɪmpəl] *adj* **(a)** *(uncomplicated)* sencillo(a); **it's as s. as that** es así de sencillo; **in s. terms** sencillamente; **the s. truth** la pura ver-

dad **(b)** *(naive)* inocente, cándido(a); **he's a bit s.** es un poco simplón

**simple-minded** ['sɪmpəl'maɪndɪd] *adj (person)* simplón(ona); *(ideas, belief)* ingenuo(a)

**simpleton** ['sɪmpəltən] *n* simple *mf*, papanatas *mf inv*

**simplicity** [sɪm'plɪsɪtɪ] *n* sencillez *f*; **it's s. itself** es de lo más sencillo

**simplification** [sɪmplɪfɪ'keɪʃən] *n* simplificación *f*

**simplify** ['sɪmplɪfaɪ] *vt* simplificar

**simplistic** [sɪm'plɪstɪk] *adj* simplista

**simply** ['sɪmplɪ] *adv* **(a)** *(in simple manner)* con sencillez **(b)** *(absolutely)* sencillamente **(c)** *(just)* sólo; **it's s. a question of time** sólo es una cuestión de tiempo; **she s. had to snap her fingers and...** sólo con chasquear los dedos...

**simulate** ['sɪmjʊleɪt] *vt* simular

**simulated** ['sɪmjʊleɪtɪd] *adj (leather, marble)* de imitación; *(surprise, anger)* fingido(a), simulado(a)

**simulation** [sɪmjʊ'leɪʃən] *n* simulación *f*

**simultaneous** [sɪməl'teɪnɪəs] *adj* simultáneo(a); **s. broadcast** retransmisión *f* simultánea; **s. translation** traducción *f* simultánea

**simultaneously** [sɪməl'teɪnɪəslɪ] *adv* simultáneamente

**sin** [sɪn] **1** *n* pecado *m*; *Old-fashioned or Hum* **to be living in s.** vivir en pecado; *Fam* **it would be a s. to...** sería un pecado...

**2** *vi (pt & pp* **sinned)** pecar

**since** [sɪns] **1** *prep* desde; **s. his death** desde su muerte; **s. June/1993** desde junio/1993; **s. then** desde entonces

**2** *adv* desde entonces; **long s.** hace mucho

**3** *conj* **(a)** *(in time)* desde que; **it's a long time s. I saw her** ha pasado mucho tiempo desde que la vi **(b)** *(because)* ya que

**sincere** [sɪn'sɪə(r)] *adj* sincero(a)

**sincerely** [sɪn'sɪəlɪ] *adv* sinceramente; **Yours s.** *(ending letter)* Atentamente

**sincerity** [sɪn'serɪtɪ] *n* sinceridad *f*; **in all s.** con toda sinceridad

**sinecure** ['saɪnɪkjʊə(r)] *n* sinecura *f*

**sinew** ['sɪnjuː] *n* tendón *m*

**sinewy** ['sɪnjuː] *adj (person, muscles)* fibroso(a); *(hands)* nervudo(a)

**sinful** ['sɪnfʊl] *adj (person)* pecador(ora); *(act, life)* pecaminoso(a); *(waste)* escandaloso(a)

**sing** [sɪŋ] *(pt* **sang** [sæŋ], *pp* **sung** [sʌŋ]) **1** *vt (song)* cantar; **to s. sb to sleep** arrullar a alguien

**2** *vi (of person, bird)* cantar; *(of kettle)* pitar

▸**sing out** *vi (sing loudly)* cantar en voz alta

**Singapore** [sɪŋə'pɔː(r)] *n* Singapur

**Singaporean** [sɪŋə'pɔ:rɪən] *n & adj* singapurense *mf*

**singe** [sɪndʒ] *vt* chamuscar

**singer** ['sɪŋə(r)] *n* cantante *mf*; **s. songwriter** cantautor(ora) *m,f*

**singing** ['sɪŋɪŋ] *n* canto *m*; **his s. is awful** canta fatal; **s. lessons** clases *fpl* de canto; **to have a fine s. voice** tener una buena voz

**single** ['sɪŋgəl] **1** *n* **(a)** *(record)* sencillo *m*, single *m*
 **(b)** *(ticket)* billete *m* sencillo *or* de ida
 **(c)** *(hotel room)* habitación *f* sencilla *or* individual
 **(d) singles** *(in tennis)* (modalidad *f* de) individuales *mpl*
 **2** *adj* **(a)** *(just one)* único(a), solo(a); **every s. day** todos los días; **not a s. one**,ni uno solo; **I haven't seen a s. soul** no he visto ni un alma; **don't say a s. word** no digas ni una (sola) palabra; **s. cream** nata *f* líquida; *Fin* **s. currency** moneda *f* única; *Econ* **s. (European) market** mercado *m* único (europeo)
 **(b)** *(not double)* **in s. figures** por debajo de diez; **in s. file** en fila india; **s. bed** cama *f* individual; **s. room** habitación *f* sencilla *or* individual
 **(c)** *(not married)* soltero(a); **s. mother** madre *f* soltera; **s. parent** padre *m*/madre *f* soltero(a); **s. parent family** familia *f* monoparental

▸**single out** *vt sep* señalar, distinguir; **she was singled out for special praise** fue distinguida con una mención especial

**single-breasted** ['sɪŋgəl'brestɪd] *adj* *(jacket, suit)* recto(a), no cruzado(a)

**single-decker** ['sɪŋgəl'dekə(r)] *n* autobús *m* de un piso

**single-handed** ['sɪŋgəl'hændɪd] *adj & adv* en solitario, sin ayuda

**single-minded** ['sɪŋgəl'maɪndɪd] *adj*, resuelto(a), determinado(a)

**single-sex school** ['sɪŋgəl'seks'sku:l] *n (for girls)* colegio *m* para niñas; *(for boys)* colegio *m* para niños

**singlet** ['sɪŋglɪt] *n* camiseta *f* (de tirantes)

**single-track railway** ['sɪŋgəl'træk-'reɪlweɪ] *n* vía *f* única

**singsong** ['sɪŋsɒŋ] **1** *n* **(a)** *(voice, tone)* **he spoke in a s.** habló con voz cantarina **(b)** *Fam (singing session)* **to have a s.** reunirse para cantar
 **2** *adj (voice, tone)* cantarín(ina)

**singular** ['sɪŋgjʊlə(r)] **1** *n Gram* singular *m*; **in the s.** en singular
 **2** *adj* **(a)** *Gram* singular **(b)** *(remarkable)* singular, excepcional

**singularly** ['sɪŋgjʊləlɪ] *adv* singularmente, excepcionalmente

**Sinhalese** [sɪnə'li:z] **1** *n* **(a)** *(person)* cingalés(esa) *m,f* **(b)** *(language)* cingalés *m*
 **2** *adj* cingalés(esa)

**sinister** ['sɪnɪstə(r)] *adj* siniestro(a)

**sink**[1] [sɪŋk] *n (in kitchen)* fregadero *m*; *(in bathroom)* lavabo *m*

**sink**[2] (*pt* **sank** [sæŋk], *pp* **sunk** [sʌŋk]) **1** *vt* **(a)** *(ship)* hincar; **to be sunk in thought** estar abstraído(a); *Fam Fig* **to be sunk** *(in trouble)* estar perdido(a) **(b)** *(well)* cavar; *(shaft)* excavar; **to s. one's teeth into sth** hundir *or* hincar los dientes en algo; **to s. money into a project** invertir mucho dinero en un proyecto; *Fam* **to s. a pint** pimplarse una pinta (de cerveza)
 **2** *vi (in water, mud)* hundirse; **her heart sank** se le cayó el alma a los pies; **his spirits sank** se desanimó; **to s. into sb's memory** quedar grabado(a) en la memoria de alguien; **to s. into oblivion** sumirse en el olvido; **to s. into a deep sleep** sumirse en un sueño profundo; **to s. into an armchair** hundirse en un sillón; **to s. into the ground** ir cayendo al suelo; **he has sunk in my estimation** ha perdido gran parte de mi estima; **how could you s. so low?** ¿cómo pudiste caer tan bajo?

▸**sink in** *vi (of liquid)* penetrar, calar; *(of information)* calar; *Fig* **it hasn't sunk in yet** todavía no lo he *or* lo tengo asumido

**sinking** ['sɪŋkɪŋ] **1** *n* **(a)** *(of ship)* hundimiento *m* **(b)** *Fin* **s. fund** fondo *m* de amortización
 **2** *adj* **with a s. heart** con creciente desánimo; **to get that s. feeling** empezar a preocuparse

**sinner** ['sɪnə(r)] *n* pecador(ora) *m,f*

**sinuous** ['sɪnjʊəs] *adj* sinuoso(a)

**sinus** ['saɪnəs] *n* seno *m* (nasal); **s. infection** sinusitis

**sinusitis** [saɪnə'saɪtɪs] *n* sinusitis *f inv*

**sip** [sɪp] **1** *n* sorbo *m*; **to take a s. (of sth)** dar un sorbo (a algo)
 **2** *vt (pt & pp* **sipped**) sorber, beber a sorbos
 **3** *vi* **she sipped at her drink** bebió un sorbo

**siphon** ['saɪfən] **1** *n* sifón *m*
 **2** *vt* bombear

▸**siphon off** *vt sep (liquid)* sacar a sifón; *Fig (money, supplies)* desviar

**sir** [sɜ:(r)] *n* **(a)** *(form of address)* señor *m*; **Dear S.** *(in letter)* Estimado señor, Muy señor mío; **Dear Sirs** Estimados señores, Muy señores míos **(b)** *(title)* **S. Cedric** sir Cedric *(título nobiliario masculino)*

**sire** ['saɪə(r)] **1** *n* **(a)** *(of animal)* padre *m* **(b)** *Old-fashioned (address to sovereign)* señor *m*, majestad *m*
 **2** *vt* engendrar

**siren** ['saɪərən] *n* sirena *f*

**sirloin** ['sɜ:lɔɪn] *n* **s. (steak)** solomillo *m*

**sissy** ['sɪsɪ] *n Fam (weak male)* blandengue *m*, llorica *m*; *(effeminate male)* mariquita *m*

**sister** ['sɪstə(r)] *n* (**a**) *(sibling)* hermana *f*; **s. company** empresa *f* asociada; **s. ship** buque *m* gemelo (**b**) *(nun)* hermana *f*; **s. Teresa** sor Teresa, la hermana Teresa (**c**) *(nurse)* enfermera *f* jefe

**sisterhood** ['sɪstəhʊd] *n* (**a**) *(community of nuns)* hermandad *f*, congregación *f* (**b**) *(solidarity)* hermandad *f* (entre mujeres)

**sister-in-law** ['sɪstərɪn'lɔː] (*pl* **sisters-in-law**) *n* cuñada *f*

**sisterly** ['sɪstəlɪ] *adj* de hermana

**sit** [sɪt] (*pt & pp* **sat** [sæt]) **1** *vt* (**a**) **to s. a child on one's knee** sentar a un niño en el regazo (**b**) *Br (exam)* presentarse a
**2** *vi* (**a**) *(of person) (be seated)* estar sentado(a); *(sit down)* sentarse; **s.!** *(to dog)* ¡siéntate!; **don't just s. there!** ¡no te quedes ahí (sentado) sin hacer nada!; *Fam* **to s. tight** quedarse quieto(a) (**b**) *(of assembly, court)* reunirse; **to s. on a jury** formar parte de un jurado (**c**) *(of object)* **to be sitting on the radiator** estar encima del radiador
▸**sit about, sit around** *vi* gandulear, holgazanear
▸**sit back** *vi* (**a**) *(lean back)* **to s. back in one's chair** recostarse en la silla (**b**) *Fam (relax)* relajarse; *(not intervene)* quedarse de brazos cruzados
▸**sit down** *vt sep* **to s. sb down** sentar a alguien; *Fam* **s. yourself down!** ¡siéntate!
**2** *vi* sentarse; **to be sitting down** estar sentado(a)
▸**sit in** *vi* *(at meeting)* estar presente (**on** en) *(como observador)*
▸**sit on** *vt insep Fam* (**a**) *(not deal with)* no tocar (**b**) *(repress)* hacer la vida imposible a
▸**sit out 1** *vt sep (not participate in)* saltarse
**2** *vi (in garden)* sentarse fuera
▸**sit through** *vt insep* aguantar
▸**sit up** *vi* (**a**) *(straighten one's back)* sentarse derecho(a); *(from lying position)* incorporarse; *Fig* **to make sb s. up** hacer reaccionar a alguien (**b**) *(not go to bed)* **to s. up (late)** quedarse levantado(a) hasta tarde

**sitar** ['sɪtɑː(r)] *n Mus* sitar *m*

**sitcom** ['sɪtkɒm] *n TV* telecomedia *f* (de situación)

**site** [saɪt] **1** *n* (**a**) *(position)* lugar *m*; *(archaeological)* yacimiento *m*; *(of monument, building, complex)* emplazamiento *m* (**b**) **(building) s.** obra *f*
**2** *vt* emplazar, ubicar; **to be sited** estar situado(a)

**sit-in** ['sɪtɪn] *n* encierro *m*

**sitting** ['sɪtɪŋ] **1** *n* *(of committee, for portrait)* sesión *f*; *(for meal)* turno *m*; **at one s.** de una sentada; **s. room** *(in house)* salón *m*, sala *f* de

estar
**2** *adj* (**a**) *(seated)* sentado(a); *Fam Fig* **to be a s. duck** *or* **target** ser un blanco fácil (**b**) *(current)* *Parl* **the s. member** el/la actual representante; **s. tenant** inquilino(a) *m,f* titular *or* legal

**situate** ['sɪtjʊeɪt] *vt* situar, ubicar

**situated** ['sɪtjʊeɪtɪd] *adj* situado(a)

**situation** [sɪtjʊ'eɪʃən] *n* (**a**) *(circumstances)* situación *f*; **s. comedy** *(on TV)* telecomedia *f* (de situación) (**b**) *(job)* colocación *f*; **situations vacant/wanted** ofertas *fpl*/demandas *fpl* de empleo (**c**) *(location)* situación *f*, ubicación *f*

**sit-up** ['sɪtʌp] *n* **to do sit-ups** hacer abdominales

**six** [sɪks] **1** *n* seis *m*; *Fam* **it's s. of one and half a dozen of the other** viene a ser lo mismo; **at sixes and sevens** hecho(a) un lío; *Fam* **to knock sb for s.** hacer polvo *or* picadillo a alguien
**2** *adj* seis; *see also* **eight**

**six-figure** ['sɪks'fɪgə(r)] *adj* **a s. sum** una cantidad (de dinero) de seis cifras

**sixpence** ['sɪkspəns] *n Br Formerly* moneda *f* de seis peniques

**six-shooter** ['sɪksʃuːtə(r)] *n* revólver *m* (de seis disparos)

**sixteen** [sɪks'tiːn] *n & adj* dieciséis *m*; *see also* **eight**

**sixteenth** [sɪks'tiːnθ] **1** *n* (**a**) *(fraction)* dieciseisavo *m*, decimosexta parte *f* (**b**) *(in series)* decimosexto(a) *m,f* (**c**) *(of month)* dieciséis *m*
**2** *adj* decimosexto(a); *see also* **eleventh**

**sixth** [sɪksθ] **1** *n* (**a**) *(fraction)* sexto *m*, sexta parte *f* (**b**) *(in series)* sexto(a) *m,f* (**c**) *(of month)* seis *m*
**2** *adj* sexto(a); *Br Sch* **the s. form** = últimos dos cursos del bachillerato británico previos a los estudios superiores; *Br Sch* **s. former** = estudiante de los dos últimos cursos del bachillerato británico; **s. sense** sexto sentido *m*; *see also* **eighth**

**sixtieth** ['sɪkstɪθ] *n & adj* sexagésimo(a) *m,f*

**sixty** ['sɪkstɪ] *n & adj* sesenta *m*; *see also* **eighty**

**size** [saɪz] *n* (**a**) *(of person)* talla *f*, tamaño *m*; *(of place, object)* tamaño *m*; *(of problem, undertaking)* envergadura *f*, dimensiones *fpl*; *Fam* **that's about the s. of it** así están las cosas (**b**) *(of clothes)* talla *f*; *(of shoes)* número *m*; **what s. do you take?, what s. are you?** *(of clothes)* ¿qué talla usas o gastas?; *(of shoes)* ¿qué número calzas?; **s. 10 shoes** ≃ zapatos del número 44; **to try sth (on) for s.** probarse algo para ver qué tal queda de talla
▸**size up** *vt sep (situation)* calibrar; *(person)* analizar

**sizeable** ['saɪzəbəl] *adj* considerable

**sizzle** ['sɪzəl] **1** n crepitación f
  **2** vi crepitar
**skate¹** [skeɪt] n (fish) raya f
**skate²** [skeɪt] n patín m; Fam Fig **to get one's skates on** (hurry) ponerse las pilas, aligerar
  **2** vi patinar; Fig **to s. round sth** evitar algo
▸**skate over** vt insep (deal with superficially) tocar muy por encima
**skateboard** ['skeɪtbɔːd] n monopatín m
**skater** ['skeɪtə(r)] n patinador(ora) m,f
**skating** ['skeɪtɪŋ] n patinaje m; **s. rink** pista f de patinaje
**skeletal** ['skelɪtəl] adj esquelético(a)
**skeleton** ['skelɪtən] **1** n (of person) esqueleto m; (of building) esqueleto m, estructura f; Fig **a s. in the cupboard** or **closet** un secreto vergonzante; **s. crew** tripulación f mínima; **s. key** llave f maestra; **s. staff** personal m mínimo
**sketch** [sketʃ] **1** n **(a)** (drawing, description) esbozo m, bosquejo m; **s. map** esquema m, croquis m inv; **s. pad** bloc m de dibujo **(b)** (on stage, TV) episodio m, sketch m
  **2** vt also Fig esbozar
▸**sketch in** vt sep also Fig esbozar
▸**sketch out** vt sep hacer un esquema de
**sketchbook** ['sketʃbʊk] n cuaderno m de dibujo
**sketchily** ['sketʃɪlɪ] adv someramente, superficialmente
**sketchy** ['sketʃɪ] adj somero(a), vago(a)
**skew** [skjuː] **1** n **on the s.** ladeado(a), torcido(a)
  **2** vt (distort) distorsionar
**skewer** ['skjuːə(r)] **1** n brocheta f
  **2** vt ensartar, espetar
**ski** [skiː] **1** n esquí m; **a pair of skis** unos esquís; **s. boots** botas fpl de esquí; **s. instructor** monitor(ora) m,f de esquí; **s. jump** salto m de esquí; **s. jumper** saltador(ora) m,f de esquí; **s. lift** remonte m, telesquí m; **s. pants** pantalones mpl de esquí; **s. resort** estación f de esquí; **s. run** or **slope** pista f de esquí; **s. stick** bastón m de esquí
  **2** vi (pt & pp skied) esquiar
**skid** [skɪd] **1** n **(a)** (of car) patinazo m; **to go into a s.** patinar **(b)** (idioms) Fam **to put the skids under sth** dar al traste con algo; Fam **to be on the skids** estar yéndose a pique; US Fam **to be on s. row** pordiosear, vivir en la indigencia
  **2** vi (pt & pp skidded) patinar
**skidmark** ['skɪdmɑːk] n marca f de neumáticos
**skier** ['skiːə(r)] n esquiador(ora) m,f
**skiing** ['skiːɪŋ] n esquí m; **to go s.** ir a esquiar; **s. holiday** vacaciones fpl de esquí; **s. instructor** monitor(ora) m,f de esquí
**skilful** ['skɪlfʊl] adj hábil, habilidoso(a)

**skilfully** ['skɪlfʊlɪ] adv hábilmente
**skill** [skɪl] n (ability) destreza f, habilidad f; (talent) talento m, aptitud f; (technique) técnica f, capacidad f
**skilled** [skɪld] adj (person) experto(a), capacitado(a); (work) especializado(a); **she's s. in resolving such problems** se le da muy bien resolver ese tipo de problemas; **s. worker** trabajador(ora) m,f cualificado(a)
**skim** [skɪm] (pt & pp skimmed) **1** vt **(a)** (milk) quitar la nata a; (soup) espumar **(b)** (surface) rozar apenas; **to s. stones (on water)** hacer cabrillas or la rana (en el agua)
  **2** vi **to s. along** or **over the ground** pasar rozando el suelo
▸**skim off** vt sep (fat, cream) retirar; Fig (money) quedarse con
▸**skim through** vt insep (novel, document) echar una ojeada a
**skimmed milk** ['skɪmd'mɪlk], US **skim milk** ['skɪm'mɪlk] n leche f desnatada or descremada
**skimp** [skɪmp] **1** vt escatimar
  **2** vi **to s. on sth** escatimar algo
**skimpy** ['skɪmpɪ] adj (meal) exiguo(a), escaso(a); (clothes) exiguo(a)
**skin** [skɪn] **1** n **(a)** (of person, animal, fruit) piel f; (on milk, sauce) nata f; **to be all s. and bone** estar en los huesos; Fam **I nearly jumped out of my s.** casi me muero del susto; **by the s. of one's teeth** por los pelos; **to save one's (own) s.** salvar el pellejo; Fam **to get under sb's s.** poner histérico(a) a alguien; Fam **it's no s. off my nose** me trae sin cuidado or al fresco; **s. cancer** cáncer m de piel; **s. complaint** afección f cutánea; **s. cream** crema f para la piel; **s. disease** enfermedad f cutánea; **s. diving** buceo m a pulmón libre; US Fam **s. flick** (porn film) película f porno; Med **s. graft** injerto m de piel **(b)** Fam (skinhead) cabeza mf rapada
  **2** vt (pt & pp skinned) (animal) despellejar, desollar; (tomato) pelar; **to s. one's knees** arañarse las rodillas
**skinflint** ['skɪnflɪnt] n Fam rata mf, roñoso(a) m,f
**skinhead** ['skɪnhed] n cabeza mf rapada
**skinny** ['skɪnɪ] adj flaco(a)
**skint** [skɪnt] adj Br Fam **to be s.** estar pelado(a), estar sin blanca
**skintight** ['skɪntaɪt] adj muy ajustado(a)
**skip¹** [skɪp] **1** n brinco m
  **2** vt (pt & pp skipped) (meal, page, stage) saltarse
  **3** vi (of lambs, children) brincar; (with rope) saltar a la comba
**skip²** n (for rubbish) contenedor m

**skipper** ['skɪpə(r)] **1** *n (of ship)* patrón(ona) *m,f*, capitán(ana) *m,f*; *(of team)* capitán(ana) *m,f*
**2** *vt Fam* capitanear

**skipping** ['skɪpɪŋ] *n (saltos mpl a la)* comba *f*; **s. rope** comba

**skirmish** ['skɜːmɪʃ] **1** *n Mil* escaramuza *f*; *Fig* refriega *f*, trifulca *f*
**2** *vi* pelear, luchar

**skirt** [skɜːt] **1** *n* falda *f*, *CAm, CSur* pollera *f*
**2** *vt (village, hill)* bordear, rodear; **to s. round a problem** soslayar un problema

**skirting board** ['skɜːtɪŋbɔːd] *n* zócalo *m*, rodapié *m*

**skit** [skɪt] *n* parodia *f*

**skittish** ['skɪtɪʃ] *adj (person)* locuelo(a), juguetón(ona)

**skittle** ['skɪtəl] *n* bolo *m*

**skive** [skaɪv] *vi Br Fam (avoid work)* escaquearse
▸**skive off** *vi Br Fam (off school)* hacer novillos; *(off work)* escaquearse

**skiver** ['skaɪvə(r)] *n Br Fam* holgazán(ana) *m,f*, gandul(ula) *m,f*

**skivvy** ['skɪvɪ] *n Br Pej* fregona *f*, criada *f*

**skulduggery** [skʌl'dʌgərɪ] *n* tejemanejes *mpl*

**skulk** [skʌlk] *vi (hide)* esconderse; *(move furtively)* merodear

**skull** [skʌl] *n* cráneo *m*; **the s. and crossbones** la calavera y las tibias

**skullcap** ['skʌlkæp] *n* casquete *m*; *(of priest)* solideo *m*

**skunk** [skʌŋk] *n (animal)* mofeta *f*; *Fam Pej (person)* perro *m*, miserable *mf*

**sky** [skaɪ] *n* cielo *m*; *Fam* **the s.'s the limit** podemos conseguir cualquier cosa que nos propongamos; *Fam* **to praise sb to the skies** poner a alguien por las nubes; **s. high** *(price, costs)* altísimo(a)

**sky-blue** [skaɪ'bluː] *adj* azul celeste

**skydiver** ['skaɪdaɪvə(r)] *n* = persona que practica la caída libre (en paracaídas)

**skydiving** ['skaɪdaɪvɪŋ] *n* caída *f* libre (en paracaídas)

**skylark** ['skaɪlɑːk] *n* alondra *f*

**skylight** ['skaɪlaɪt] *n* claraboya *f*

**skyline** ['skaɪlaɪn] *n (horizon)* horizonte *m*; *(of city)* silueta *f*, contorno *m*

**skyscraper** ['skaɪskreɪpə(r)] *n* rascacielos *m inv*

**slab** [slæb] *n (of stone, concrete)* losa *f*; *(of cake, meat)* trozo *m*; *(of chocolate)* tableta *f*; *(in mortuary)* mesa *f* de amortajamiento

**slack** [slæk] **1** *n* **to take up the s.** *(in rope)* tensar la cuerda; *Fig* **I'm fed up with having to take up your s.** estoy harto de tener que encargarme de tu trabajo

**2** *adj* (a) *(not tight)* flojo(a); **to be s.** estar flojo(a); **trade is s.** el negocio está flojo; **s. periods** períodos *mpl* de poca actividad (b) *(careless)* dejado(a)
**3** *vi Fam* vaguear
▸**slack off** *vi (diminish)* aflojar

**slacken** ['slækən] **1** *vt (pace, rope)* aflojar
**2** *vi (of person)* flojear; *(of crowd)* destensarse; *(of speed)* reducirse, disminuir; *(of storm, wind)* amainar, aflojar; *(of energy, enthusiasm)* atenuarse, disminuir
▸**slacken off** *vi (diminish)* aflojar

**slacker** ['slækə(r)] *n Fam* vago(a) *m,f*, gandul(ula) *m,f*

**slackness** ['slæknɪs] *n* (a) *(negligence, laziness)* dejadez *f* (b) *(of rope)* distensión *f* (c) *(of business)* atonía *f*, inactividad *f*

**slacks** [slæks] *npl (trousers)* pantalones *mpl*

**slag** [slæg] *n* (a) *(from coalmine)* escoria *f*; **s. heap** escorial *m* (b) *very Fam Pej (woman)* fulana *f*, cualquiera *f*
▸**slag off** *vt sep Fam (criticize)* poner a caldo or como un trapo

**slain** [sleɪn] **1** *npl* **the s.** las bajas, los fallecidos
**2** *pp of* **slay**

**slake** [sleɪk] *vt Literary* **to s. one's thirst** apagar or calmar la sed

**slalom** ['slɑːləm] *n* eslalon *m*

**slam** [slæm] **1** *n (of door)* portazo *m*
**2** *vt (pt & pp* **slammed)** (a) *(door, lid, drawer)* cerrar de un golpe; **to s. the door in sb's face** dar con la puerta en las narices a alguien; **to s. sth down** dejar caer or estampar algo de un golpe (b) *Fam (criticize)* despellejar, poner verde
**3** *vi (of door)* cerrarse de golpe, dar un portazo; **to s. on the brakes** pisar el freno de golpe

**slander** ['slɑːndə(r)] **1** *n* difamación *f*
**2** *vt* difamar

**slanderous** ['slɑːndərəs] *adj* difamatorio(a)

**slang** [slæŋ] **1** *n* argot *m*
**2** *vt Fam (insult)* poner verde; **slanging match** rifirrafe *m*, intercambio *m* de insultos

**slant** [slɑːnt] **1** *n* (a) *(slope)* inclinación *f* (b) *(emphasis, bias)* sesgo *m*, orientación *f*; **she put a favourable s. on the information** le dio un cariz or sesgo favorable a la información
**2** *vt* (a) *(set at angle)* inclinar (b) *(bias)* enfocar subjetivamente
**3** *vi (slope)* estar inclinado(a)

**slanting** ['slɑːntɪŋ] *adj* inclinado(a)

**slap** [slæp] **1** *n (with hand)* bofetada *f*, cachete *m*; *also Fig* **a s. in the face** una bofetada; *Fig* **a s. on the wrist** *(reprimand)* un tirón de orejas
**2** *adv Fam* **s. (bang) in the middle** en todo el medio
**3** *vt (pt & pp* **slapped)** dar una palmada en; **to s. sb's face, to s. sb in the face** abofetear a

alguien; **to s. sb on the back** dar a alguien una palmada en la espalda; *Fig* **to s. sb down** hacer callar a alguien; **to s. some paint on sth** dar una mano de pintura a algo

**slapdash** ['slæpdæʃ] *adj* chapucero(a)

**slapstick** ['slæpstɪk] *n* **s. (comedy)** = comedia visual facilona

**slap-up** ['slæpʌp] *adj Br Fam* **s. meal** comilona *f*, banquete *m*

**slash** [slæʃ] **1** *n* (**a**) *(cut)* tajo *m*, corte *m* (**b**) *Typ* barra *f* (**c**) *Br very Fam* **to have/go for a s.** echar/ir a echar una meada

**2** *vt (cut)* cortar; *(reduce)* recortar fuertemente; **prices slashed** *(sign)* precios por los suelos

**slat** [slæt] *n* listón *m*, tablilla *f*

**slate** [sleɪt] **1** *n* (**a**) *(stone)* pizarra *f*; *(writing)* **s.** pizarra *f*; **s. grey** gris *m* pizarra; **s. quarry** pizarral *m* (**b**) *(idioms) Fam* **put it on the s.** anótalo en mi cuenta; **to wipe the s. clean** hacer borrón y cuenta nueva

**2** *vt Fam (criticize)* vapulear, poner por los suelos

**slaughter** ['slɔːtə(r)] **1** *n (of animals)* sacrificio *m*; *(of people)* matanza *f*

**2** *vt (animals)* sacrificar; *(people)* matar; *Fam (defeat heavily)* machacar, dar una paliza a

**slaughterhouse** ['slɔːtəhaʊs] *n* matadero *m*

**Slav** [slɑːv] *n* eslavo(a) *m,f*

**slave** [sleɪv] **1** *n* esclavo(a) *m,f*; *Fam Fig* **s. driver** negrero(a) *m,f*, tirano(a) *m,f*; **s. labour** trabajo *m* de esclavos; **s. trade** comercio *m or* trata *f* de esclavos

**2** *vi* trabajar como un negro; **I've been slaving over a hot stove all day!** ¡me he pasado el día bregando en la cocina!

**slaver** ['slævə(r)] *vi* babear

**slavery** ['sleɪvərɪ] *n* esclavitud *f*

**Slavic** ['slɑːvɪk] *adj* eslavo(a)

**slavish** ['sleɪvɪʃ] *adj* servil

**Slavonic** [slə'vɒnɪk] *adj* eslavo(a)

**slay** [sleɪ] *(pt* slew [sluː], *pp* slain [sleɪn]) *vt Literary (kill)* quitar la vida a, matar

**sleaze** [sliːz] *n Fam* corrupción *f*

**sleazy** ['sliːzɪ] *adj Fam (place, bar, hotel)* cutre; *(government, politician)* corrupto(a); *(affair, reputation)* escandaloso(a)

**sledge** [sledʒ], *US* **sled** [sled] **1** *n* trineo *m*

**2** *vi* montar en trineo

**sledgehammer** ['sledʒhæmə(r)] *n* mazo *m*, maza *f*; *Fig* **to use a s. to crack a nut** matar moscas a cañonazos

**sleek** [sliːk] *adj (hair)* liso(a) y brillante; *(manner)* bien plantado(a)

▶**sleek down** *vt sep* **to s. down one's hair** alisarse el pelo

**sleep** [sliːp] **1** *n* (**a**) *(rest)* sueño *m*; **to go to s.** irse a dormir; **to put sb to s.** *(anaesthetize)*

dormir a alguien; **to put an animal to s.** *(kill)* sacrificar a un animal *(para evitar que sufra); Fig* **to send sb to s.** *(bore)* dar sueño *or* aburrir a alguien; **I'm not losing any s. over it** no me quita el sueño; **to walk/talk in one's s.** caminar/hablar en sueños; **my foot has gone to s.** se me ha dormido el pie (**b**) *(in eye)* legañas *fpl*

**2** *vi (pt & pp* slept [slept]) dormir; **s. well!** ¡que duermas bien!, ¡que descanses!; *Euph* **to s. with sb** acostarse con alguien; **I slept through the alarm** no oí el despertador; **I'll s. on it** lo consultaré con la almohada; **to s. rough** dormir a la intemperie

**3** *vt* **the cottage sleeps four** la casa puede albergar a cuatro personas; **I haven't slept a wink all night** no he pegado ojo en toda la noche

▶**sleep around** *vi Fam* acostarse con unos y con otros

▶**sleep in** *vi* quedarse durmiendo hasta tarde

▶**sleep off** *vt sep* **to s. off a hangover** dormir la mona

▶**sleep together** *vi* acostarse juntos

**sleeper** ['sliːpə(r)] *n* (**a**) **to be a light/ heavy s.** tener el sueño ligero/profundo (**b**) *Rail (train)* tren *m* con literas; *Br (on track)* traviesa *f*

**sleepily** ['sliːpɪlɪ] *adv* soñolientamente

**sleeping** ['sliːpɪŋ] **1** *n* **s. arrangements** distribución *f* de (las) camas; **s. bag** saco *m* de dormir; **s. car** *(on train)* coche *m* cama; **s. pill** somnífero *m*, pastilla *f* para dormir

**2** *adj* dormido(a); *Fig* **to let s. dogs lie** no enturbiar las aguas; **s. partner** *(in company)* socio *m* capitalista *or* comanditario; *Br* **s. policeman** *(in road)* resalto *m or* bache *m* (de moderación de velocidad)

**sleepless** ['sliːplɪs] *adj* **to have a s. night** pasar una noche en blanco

**sleepwalk** ['sliːpwɔːk] *vi* caminar dormido(a) *or* sonámbulo(a)

**sleepwalker** ['sliːpwɔːkə(r)] *n* sonámbulo(a) *m,f*

**sleepy** ['sliːpɪ] *adj* adormilado(a), soñoliento(a); **to be *or* feel s.** tener sueño

**sleet** [sliːt] **1** *n* aguanieve *f*

**2** *vi* **it's sleeting** está cayendo aguanieve

**sleeve** [sliːv] *n* (**a**) *(of shirt, jacket)* manga *f*; *Fig* **he's still got something up his s.** aún le queda algo escondido en la manga (**b**) *(of record)* funda *f*

**sleeveless** ['sliːvlɪs] *adj* sin mangas

**sleigh** [sleɪ] *n* trineo *m*

**sleight** [slaɪt] *n* **s. of hand** trucos *mpl*, juegos *mpl* de manos; *Fig* **by s. of hand** con tejemanejes, por arte de birlibirloque

**slender** ['slendə(r)] *adj (person, waist, figure)* esbelto(a) (**b**) *(hope)* remoto(a); *(income, majority)* escaso(a); **of s. means** de pocos recursos

**slept** [slept] *pt & pp of* **sleep**

**sleuth** [slu:θ] *n Fam* sabueso *m*, detective *mf*

**slew** [slu:] *pt of* **slay**

**slice** [slaɪs] **1** *n (of bread)* rebanada *f*; *(of cheese, ham)* loncha *f*; *(of beef)* tajada *f*; *(of salami, cucumber)* rodaja *f*; *(of cake)* trozo *m*, porción *f*; *Fig* **a s. of the profits** una parte de los beneficios

**2** *vt* **(a)** *(bread)* partir en rebanadas; *(cheese, ham)* partir en lonchas; *(beef)* partir; *(salami, cucumber)* partir en rodajas; *(cake)* trocear, dividir; **to s. sth in two** *or* **in half** dividir algo en dos *or* por la mitad **(b)** *(in golf)* golpear mal

▶**slice off** *vt sep* cortar

▶**slice through** *vt insep* atravesar, cortar

▶**slice up** *vt sep* repartir, dividir

**sliced bread** ['slaɪst'bred] *n* pan *m* de molde en rebanadas; *Fam* **it's the best thing since s.** es lo mejor del mundo

**slick** [slɪk] **1** *n (oil)* **s.** marea *f* negra

**2** *adj* **(a)** *(campaign)* hábil; *(performance, production)* perfecto(a) **(b)** *Pej (salesman)* **to be s.** tener mucha labia **(c)** *(surface, tyre)* resbaladizo(a)

▶**slick back** *vt sep* **to s. one's hair back** alisarse el pelo

**slid** [slɪd] *pt & pp of* **slide**

**slide** [slaɪd] **1** *n* **(a)** *(fall) (of land)* desprendimiento *m*, deslizamiento *m*; *(in prices, popularity)* caída *f*, desplome *m* (**in** de); *Math* **s. rule** regla *f* de cálculo **(b)** *(in playground)* tobogán *m* **(c)** *(photographic)* diapositiva *f*, *(for microscope)* portaobjetos *m inv*; **s. projector** proyector *m* de diapositivas **(d)** *Br (for hair)* pasador *m*

**2** *vt* (*pt & pp* **slid** [slɪd]) pasar, deslizar; **to s. the lid off** quitar la tapa corriéndola *or* deslizándola

**3** *vi* **(a)** *(slip)* resbalar; **the door slid open** la puerta se abrió deslizándose; **to s. down a rope** deslizarse por una cuerda; *Fig* **to let things s.** dejar que las cosas vayan a peor **(b)** *(move quietly)* deslizarse

**sliding** ['slaɪdɪŋ] *adj* corredero(a); **s. door** puerta *f* corredera; **s. scale** escala *f* móvil

**slight** [slaɪt] **1** *n (affront)* desaire *m*

**2** *adj* **(a)** *(small, unimportant)* ligero(a), pequeño(a); **not the slightest danger/interest** ni el más mínimo peligro/interés; **not in the slightest** en lo más mínimo **(b)** *(person)* menudo(a)

**3** *vt* desairar

**slightly** ['slaɪtlɪ] *adv* **(a)** *(to a small degree)* ligeramente, un poco **(b)** **s. built** menudo(a)

**slim** [slɪm] **1** *adj (person)* delgado(a); *(book)* fino(a), delgado(a); *(chance, hope)* pequeño(a); *(majority)* escaso(a)

**2** *vi* (*pt & pp* **slimmed**) adelgazar

▶**slim down 1** *vt sep Fig (budget)* reducir, recortar; *(company)* reducir plantilla en

**2** *vi (of person)* adelgazar, perder peso; *Fig (of company)* reducir plantilla

**slime** [slaɪm] *n (mud)* lodo *m*, cieno *m*; *(of snail, slug)* baba *f*

**slimmer** ['slɪmə(r)] *n* persona *f* que está a régimen

**slimming** ['slɪmɪŋ] *n* adelgazamiento *m*; **s. can be bad for you** adelgazar puede ser perjudicial; **s. diet** régimen *m* de adelgazamiento; **s. product** producto *m* para adelgazar

**slimy** ['slaɪmɪ] *adj (frog, snail)* viscoso(a); *(person)* pegajoso(a), empalagoso(a)

**sling** [slɪŋ] **1** *n* **(a)** *(for injured arm)* cabestrillo *m* **(b)** *(weapon)* honda *f*

**2** *vt* (*pt & pp* **slung** [slʌŋ]) *(throw)* lanzar, arrojar; **to s. sth over one's shoulder** echarse algo a la espalda; *Fam Fig* **s. your hook!** ¡piérdete!

▶**sling out** *vt sep Fam (throw away)* tirar; *(person)* echar

**slingshot** ['slɪŋʃɒt] *n US* tirachinas *m inv*

**slink** [slɪŋk] (*pt & pp* **slunk** [slʌŋk]) *vi* **to s. off** *or* **away** marcharse subrepticiamente

**slinky** ['slɪŋkɪ] *adj* **a s. dress** un vestido que marca las curvas

**slip** [slɪp] **1** *n* **(a)** *(fall)* resbalón *m*; *(of land)* corrimiento *m*, deslizamiento *m*; *(in prices, standards)* derrumbamiento *m*, caída *f*

**(b)** *(error)* desliz *m*; **s. of the pen** lapsus *m* *inv* (calami); **s. of the tongue** lapsus *m inv* (linguae)

**(c)** **to give sb the s.** dar esquinazo a alguien

**(d)** *(of paper)* papeleta *f*; *(form)* hoja *f*

**(e)** **a s. of a girl** una chavalina; **a s. of a lad** un chavalín

**(f)** *Br Aut* **s. road** *(into motorway)* carril *m* de incorporación *or* aceleración; *(out of motorway)* carril *m* de salida *or* deceleración

**(g)** *(garment)* combinación *f*; **(pillow) s.** funda *f* (de almohada)

**2** *vt* (*pt & pp* **slipped**) **(a)** *(leave)* **his name has slipped my mind** se me ha ido su nombre de la cabeza; **the ship slipped its moorings** el barco se soltó del amarre

**(b)** *(put)* **he slipped on/off his shoes** se puso/se quitó los zapatos deslizar; **to s. sth into the conversation** deslizar algo en la conversación

**(c)** **to have slipped a disc** tener una vértebra dislocada, tener una hernia discal

**3** *vi* **(a)** *(slide)* resbalar; **his foot slipped** le resbaló un pie; *also Fig* **to s. from sb's hands** *or* **grasp** escapársele de las manos a alguien; *Fig* **to s. through sb's fingers** escapársele de las manos a alguien; **to let one's guard s.** bajar la guardia; **to let one's concentration s.** desconcentrarse

**(b)** *(move quickly)* **to s. into sth** *(bed)* meterse

en algo; *(room)* colarse en algo; *(clothes, shoes)* ponerse algo; **to s. out of sth** *(clothes)* quitarse algo; **I'll just s. round to the post office** voy un momento a correos

  **(c)** *(make mistake)* tener un desliz, cometer un error; **you're slipping** estás fallando

  **(d) she let s. a few swear words** se le escaparon unas cuantas palabrotas; **he let it s. that he would be resigning** se le escapó que iba a dimitir

▸**slip away** *vi (leave)* desaparecer, desvanecerse

▸**slip by** *vi (of time, years)* pasar

▸**slip out** *vi (escape)* escaparse; **to s. out to the shop** salir un momento a la tienda

▸**slip through** *vi (of mistake, saboteur)* colarse

▸**slip up** *vi (make mistake)* tener un desliz, cometer un error

**slip-on** ['slɪpɒn] **1** *n Fam* **slip-ons** zapatos *mpl* sin cordones

  **2** *adj* **s. shoes** zapatos *mpl* sin cordones

**slipper** ['slɪpə(r)] *n* zapatilla *f*

**slippery** ['slɪpərɪ] *adj* resbaladizo(a), escurridizo(a); *(person)* tramposo(a); *Fig* **to be on a s. slope** caer cuesta abajo

**slippy** ['slɪpɪ] *adj* resbaladizo(a), escurridizo(a)

**slipshod** ['slɪpʃɒd] *adj* chapucero(a)

**slipstream** ['slɪpstriːm] *n* estela *f*

**slip-up** ['slɪpʌp] *n* (pequeño) error *m*, desliz *m*

**slipway** ['slɪpweɪ] *n Naut* grada *f*

**slit** [slɪt] **1** *n (below door)* rendija *f*; *(of dress, in paper)* corte *m*, raja *f*

  **2** *vt (pt & pp* **slit**) hacer una abertura en; **to s. sth open** abrir algo rajándolo; **to s. sb's throat** degollar a alguien

**slither** ['slɪðə(r)] *vi* deslizarse

**sliver** ['slɪvə(r)] *n (of ham, cheese)* lonchita *f*; *(of glass)* esquirla *f*

**slob** [slɒb] *n Fam (untidy person)* guarro(a) *m,f*; *(lazy person)* dejado(a) *m,f*, tirado(a) *m,f*

**slobber** ['slɒbə(r)] *vi* babear

**sloe** [sləʊ] *n (fruit)* endrina *f*; **s. gin** licor *m* de endrinas, ≃ pacharán *m*

**slog** [slɒg] *Fam* **1** *n* **it was a bit of a s.** fue un tostonazo *or* palizón (de trabajo); **it's a long s.** *(walk)* hay una buena tirada

  **2** *vi (pt & pp* **slogged**) *(work hard)* trabajar como un/una negro(a), dar el callo

**slogan** ['sləʊgən] *n* eslogan *m*

**sloop** [sluːp] *n (ship)* balandro *m*

**slop** [slɒp] **1** *n* **(a)** *(pig food)* desperdicios *mpl* (para los cerdos); *Pej (bad food)* bazofia *f* **(b)** *Fam (sentimentality)* cursilerías *fpl*

  **2** *vt (pt & pp* **slopped**) derramar

  **3** *vi* derramarse

**slope** [sləʊp] **1** *n* cuesta *f*, pendiente *f*

  **2** *vi* caer, inclinarse

▸**slope off** *vi Fam* escabullirse

**sloping** ['sləʊpɪŋ] *adj (roof, ground)* en cuesta, inclinado(a); *(handwriting)* inclinado(a); *(shoulders)* caído(a)

**sloppy** ['slɒpɪ] *adj* **(a)** *(careless)* descuidado(a) **(b)** *Fam (sentimental)* almibarado(a)

**slosh** [slɒʃ] *vi (of liquid)* chapotear

**sloshed** [slɒʃt] *adj Fam* mamado(a), ciego(a)

**slot** [slɒt] **1** *n (in box, machine, computer)* ranura *f*; *(in schedule, list)* hueco *m*; **s. machine** *(for vending)* máquina *f* expendedora; *(for gambling)* (máquina *f*) tragaperras *f inv*

  **2** *vt (pt & pp* **slotted**) *(part)* introducir

▸**slot in 1** *vt sep (into schedule)* hacer un hueco a

  **2** *vi (of part, into team)* encajar

**sloth** [sləʊθ] *n* **(a)** *(laziness)* pereza *f* **(b)** *(animal)* perezoso *m*

**slothful** ['sləʊθfʊl] *adj* perezoso(a), *m,f*

**slouch** [slaʊtʃ] **1** *n Fam* **he's no s. when it comes to computers** es un hacha con los ordenadores

  **2** *vi (on chair)* repantigarse; **he slouched out of the room** salió de la habitación caminando encorvado; **don't s.!** ¡ponte derecho!

**slough** [slʌf] *vt* **to s. its skin** *(of reptile)* mudar de piel *or* de camisa

**Slovak** ['sləʊvæk] **1** *n* **(a)** *(person)* eslovaco(a) *m,f* **(b)** *(language)* eslovaco *m*

  **2** *adj* eslovaco(a)

**Slovakia** [sləʊ'vækɪə] *n* Eslovaquia

**Slovakian** [sləʊ'vækɪən] *n & adj* eslovaco(a) *m,f*

**Slovene** ['sləʊviːn] **1** *n* **(a)** *(person)* esloveno(a) *m,f* **(b)** *(language)* esloveno *m*

  **2** *adj* esloveno(a)

**Slovenia** [sləʊ'viːnɪə] *n* Eslovenia

**Slovenian** [sləʊ'viːnɪən] = **Slovene**

**slovenly** ['slʌvənlɪ] *adj (untidy)* desastrado(a); *(careless)* descuidado(a)

**slow** [sləʊ] **1** *adj* **(a)** *(not fast)* lento(a); **to be s. to do sth** tardar en hacer algo; **business is s.** el negocio está flojo; **my watch is s.** mi reloj va atrasado; **to be s. off the mark** *(to start)* tardar en arrancar; *(to understand)* ser un poco torpe; *Culin* **in a s. oven** a horno moderado; **we're making s. progress** avanzamos muy poco; **she's a s. worker** trabaja despacio; *Aut* **s. lane** carril *m* lento; *Cin & TV* **(in) s. motion** a cámara lenta; **s. train** tren *m* lento **(b)** *(stupid)* corto(a) *or* lento(a) de entendederas

  **2** *adv* despacio, lentamente

  **3** *vi* aminorar la velocidad; **to s. to a halt** ir aminorando la velocidad hasta detenerse

▸**slow down, slow up 1** *vt sep* retrasar

  **2** *vi* aminorar la velocidad

**slowcoach** ['sləʊkəʊtʃ] *n Br Fam* parsimonioso(a) *m,f*, tortuga *f*

**slowly** ['sləʊlɪ] adv despacio, lentamente; **s. but surely** lento, pero seguro

**slowness** ['sləʊnɪs] n lentitud f

**slowpoke** ['sləʊpəʊk] US = **slowcoach**

**slow-witted** ['sləʊ'wɪtɪd] adj torpe, obtuso(a)

**slow-worm** ['sləʊwɜːm] n lución m

**SLR** [esel'ɑː(r)] n Phot (abbr **single-lens reflex**) (cámara f) réflex f inv monoobjetivo

**sludge** [slʌdʒ] n fango m, lodo m

**slug** [slʌg] **1** n (**a**) (mollusc) babosa f (**b**) Fam (bullet) bala f (**c**) Fam (of drink) trago m
**2** vt (pt & pp **slugged**) Fam (hit) dar un castañazo a

**sluggish** ['slʌgɪʃ] adj (person) indolente, aplatanado(a); (business, market) inactivo(a), flojo(a); **at a s. pace** con paso cansino

**sluice** [sluːs] **1** n (**a**) (channel) canal m (**b**) (sluicegate) esclusa f, compuerta f
**2** vt **to s. sth down** or **out** enjuagar algo

**sluicegate** ['sluːsgeɪt] n esclusa f, compuerta f

**slum** [slʌm] **1** n (district) barrio m bajo; (on outskirts) arrabal m, suburbio m; (house) tugurio m; **s. landlord** casero m que alquila tugurios
**2** vt (pt & pp **slummed**) **to s. it** ir de pobre, llevar vida de pobre

**slumber** ['slʌmbə(r)] **1** n (**a**) Literary sueño m (**b**) US **s. party** = fiesta de adolescentes que se quedan a dormir en casa de quien la organiza
**2** vi dormir

**slump** [slʌmp] **1** n (in prices, sales) desplome m, caída f; (economic depression) crisis f inv, recesión f
**2** vi (of person) caer, desplomarse; (of economy) hundirse; (of prices) desplomarse

**slung** [slʌŋ] pt & pp of **sling**

**slunk** [slʌŋk] pt & pp of **slink**

**slur** [slɜː(r)] **1** n (**a**) (insult) agravio m, injuria f; **to cast a s. on sb's reputation** manchar la reputación de alguien (**b**) (in speech) **there was a s. in her voice** hablaba arrastrando las palabras
**2** vt (pt & pp **slurred**) pronunciar con dificultad

**slurp** [slɜːp] vt & vi sorber

**slush** [slʌʃ] n (**a**) (snow) nieve f sucia (medio derretida) (**b**) Fam Pol **s. fund** fondos mpl para corruptelas (**c**) Fam (sentimentality) sensiblería f

**slut** [slʌt] n Fam (promiscuous woman) puta f

**sluttish** ['slʌtɪʃ] adj (slovenly) desastrado(a)

**sly** [slaɪ] **1** n **on the s.** subrepticiamente, a hurtadillas
**2** adj (**a**) (cunning) astuto(a), artero(a) (**b**) (dishonest) desaprensivo(a) (**c**) (mischievous) malicioso(a)

**S & M** [esən'em] n (abbr **sadomasochism**) SM, sado m

**smack** [smæk] **1** n (**a**) (blow) (on bottom) azote m; (in face) bofetada f; (sound) chasquido m; **a s. in the face** una bofetada (**b**) very Fam (heroin) caballo m
**2** adv Fam **to bump s. into a tree** chocar de lleno con un árbol
**3** vt (hit) (on bottom) dar un azote a; (in face) dar una bofetada a; **to s. one's lips** relamerse
▸**smack of** vt insep (suggest) oler a

**smacker** ['smækə(r)] n Fam (**a**) (big kiss) besazo m (**b**) **fifty smackers** (pounds) cincuenta libras fpl; (dollars) cincuenta dólares mpl

**small** [smɔːl] **1** n (**a**) **the s. of the back** región lumbar, los riñones
(**b**) Fam **smalls** (underwear) ropa f interior
**2** adj (**a**) (not large) pequeño(a), Am chico(a); **to make sth smaller** empequeñecer algo; **it made me feel s.** hizo que me sintiera muy poca cosa o me avergonzara de mí mismo; **to have a s. appetite** tener poco apetito; **the s. hours** la madrugada; Journ **s. ads** anuncios mpl breves or por palabras; **s. arms** armas fpl cortas; **s. business** pequeña empresa f; **s. businessman** pequeño empresario m; **s. letters** (letras fpl) minúsculas fpl; **the s. print** la letra pequeña; **s. talk** charla f insustancial
(**b**) (not important) pequeño(a); **it's s. wonder that...** no es de extrañar que...; **it's no s. achievement** es un logro nada despreciable; **in a s. way** a pequeña escala; Fam **it's s. beer** es una nadería, es cosa de niños; **s. change** cambio m, suelto m; **s. fry** gente f de poca monta
**3** adv (write) con letra pequeña; **to chop sth up s.** cortar algo en trozos pequeños; **to think s.** plantearse las cosas a pequeña escala

**smallholder** ['smɔːlhəʊldə(r)] n minifundista mf

**smallholding** ['smɔːlhəʊldɪŋ] n minifundio m

**small-minded** [smɔːl'maɪndɪd] adj mezquino(a)

**smallness** ['smɔːlnɪs] n pequeñez f, pequeño tamaño m

**smallpox** ['smɔːlpɒks] n viruela f

**small-scale** ['smɔːlskeɪl] adj a pequeña escala

**small-time** ['smɔːltaɪm] adj Fam de poca monta

**smarmy** ['smɑːmɪ] adj Pej zalamero(a)

**smart** [smɑːt] **1** adj (**a**) (clever) inteligente; (sharp) agudo(a), listo(a); **don't try to get s. with me** no te hagas el listo (conmigo); Fam **s. aleck** listillo m,f, sabelotodo mf; **s. bomb** bomba f teledirigida; **s. card** tarjeta f inteligente (**b**) (elegant) elegante; **the s. set** la gente guapa; **to be a s. dresser** vestir elegantemente (**c**) (quick) rápido(a); **look s. (about it)!** ¡date prisa! **(d)** *Fam (excellent)* molón(ona); *(pretty)* mono(a)

**2** *vi (sting) (of wound, graze)* escocer; *(of person)* resentirse, dolerse

▶**smarten up** ['smɑːtən] **1** *vt sep (place)* arreglar; **to s. oneself up** acicalarse

**2** *vi (behave more cleverly)* espabilarse

**smarty-pants** ['smɑːtɪpænts] ( *pl* **smarty-pants**) *n Fam* listillo(a) *m,f*, sabelotodo *mf*

**smash** [smæʃ] **1** *n (blow)* golpe *m*, batacazo *m*; *(noise)* estruendo *m*; *(collision)* choque *m*; *(in tennis)* mate *m*, smash *m*; **s. (hit)** *(record, film)* gran éxito *m*

**2** *vt* **(a) to s. sth (to pieces)** hacer algo pedazos *or* añicos; **to s. sth against sth** destrozar algo contra algo; **to s. sth open** abrir algo de un golpetazo; **to s. down a door** derribar una puerta **(b)** *(ruin) (hopes, chances, resistance)* acabar con; **to s. a drugs ring** desarticular una red de narcotraficantes; **she smashed the world record** pulverizó el récord mundial

**3** *vi* **(a)** *(collide)* **to s. into sth** empotrarse en algo, chocar contra algo **(b) to s. (into pieces)** estallar (en mil pedazos)

▶**smash up** *vt sep* destrozar

**smash-and-grab raid** [smæʃən'græb-'reɪd] *n* = rotura de un escaparate para robar artículos expuestos en él

**smashed** ['smæʃt] *adj Fam (drunk)* mamado(a)

**smasher** ['smæʃə(r)] *n* encanto *m*

**smashing** ['smæʃɪŋ] *adj* **(a)** *(blow)* violento(a), potente **(b)** *Fam (excellent)* genial, estupendo(a); **we had a s. time** nos lo pasamos genial

**smattering** ['smætərɪŋ] *n* nociones *fpl*

**smear** [smɪə(r)] **1** *n* **(a)** *(stain)* mancha *f*; *Med* **s. test** citología *f* **(b)** *(slander)* calumnia *f*; **s. campaign** campaña *f* de difamación

**2** *vt* **(a)** *(stain)* embadurnar, untar; *(smudge)* emborronar **(b)** *(slander)* difamar, calumniar

**smell** [smel] **1** *n* **(a)** *(odour)* olor *m*; **there's a bad s.** huele mal; **to have a s. of sth** oler algo **(b)** *(sense)* olfato *m*

**2** *vt* ( *pt & pp* **smelled** *or* **smelt** [smelt]) oler; *Fig (danger)* oler, presentir; *Fig* **I s. a rat** aquí hay gato encerrado

**3** *vi* oler; *(stink)* apestar; **to s. of sth** oler a algo; **to s. nice/horrible** oler bien/fatal

**smelly** ['smelɪ] *adj* apestoso(a); **to be s.** apestar

**smelt** [smelt] **1** *vt (ore)* fundir

**2** *pt & pp of* **smell**

**smile** [smaɪl] **1** *n* sonrisa *f*; **to give sb a s.** sonreírle a alguien; **she was all smiles** estaba muy contenta; **to take** *or* **wipe the s. off sb's face** borrarle la sonrisa a alguien

**2** *vi* sonreír; **to s. at sb** sonreírle a alguien;

**fortune smiled on them** les sonrió la fortuna; **s.!** *(for photograph)* sonría, por favor

**smiling** ['smaɪlɪŋ] *adj* sonriente

**smirk** [smɜːk] **1** *n* sonrisa *f* complacida *(despreciativa)*

**2** *vi* sonreír con satisfacción *(despreciativa)*

**smite** [smaɪt] ( *pt* **smote** [sməʊt], *pp* **smitten** ['smɪtən]) *vt* **(a)** *Literary (strike)* golpear **(b) they were smitten with terror/remorse** les asaltó el pánico/el remordimiento

**smith** [smɪθ] *n* herrero *m*

**smithereens** [smɪðə'riːnz] *npl* **to smash/blow sth to s.** hacer algo añicos

**smithy** ['smɪðɪ] *n (forge)* fragua *f*

**smitten** ['smɪtən] **1** *adj (in love)* enamorado(a) **(with de)**, colado(a) **(with por)**

**2** *pp of* **smite**

**smock** [smɒk] *n* blusón *m*

**smog** [smɒg] *n* niebla *f* tóxica, hongo *m* de contaminación

**smoke** [sməʊk] **1** *n* humo *m*; **to have a s.** fumarse un cigarrillo; *Fig* **to go up in s.** esfumarse, desvanecerse; *Prov* **there's no s. without fire** cuando el río suena, agua lleva; **s. bomb** bomba *f* de humo; **s. detector** detector *m* de humo; *also Fig* **s. screen** cortina *f* de humo; **s. signals** señales *fpl* de humo

**2** *vt* **(a)** *(cigarette)* fumar; **to s. a pipe** fumar en pipa **(b)** *(meat, fish)* ahumar

**3** *vi* **(a)** *(of person)* fumar **(b)** *(of chimney, oil)* echar humo

▶**smoke out** *vt sep (insects)* ahuyentar con humo; *Fig (rebels)* sacar de su escondite

**smoked** [sməʊkt] *adj* ahumado(a); **s. glass** cristal *m* ahumado

**smokeless** ['sməʊklɪs] *adj* **s. fuel** combustible *m* que no produce humos; **s. zone** = zona con restricción del uso de combustibles que producen humo

**smoker** ['sməʊkə(r)] *n* fumador(ora) *m,f*; **to be a heavy s.** ser un/una fumador(ora) empedernido(a); **s.'s cough** tos *f* de fumador

**smoking** ['sməʊkɪŋ] *n* **s. can damage your health** el tabaco perjudica seriamente la salud; **no s.** *(sign)* prohibido fumar; **s. compartment** compartimento *m* de fumadores; **s. jacket** batín *m*; **s. room** salón *m* de fumar

**smoky** ['sməʊkɪ] *adj (atmosphere, room)* lleno(a) de humo; *(fire, lamp)* humeante; *(surface, taste)* ahumado(a)

**smolder** US = **smoulder**

**smooch** [smuːtʃ] *vi Fam* besuquearse

**smooth** [smuːð] **1** *adj* **(a)** *(not rough) (paper, skin)* liso(a), suave; *(road, surface)* llano(a), liso(a); *(sea)* en calma; *(sauce)* homogéneo(a); *(wine, whisky) (style)* fluido(a); *(flight, crossing)* tranquilo(a), cómodo(a); **a s. shave** un afeitado suave **(b)** *(person, manner)* meloso(a);

**he's a s. talker** tiene el don de la palabra; **to be a s. operator** ser un águila, saber cómo llevarse el gato al agua (**c**) *(without problems)* sin contratiempos

2 *vt* alisar; **to s. the way for sb/sth** allanarle el camino a alguien/algo

▸**smooth back** *vt sep* **to s. back one's hair** alisarse el pelo hacia atrás

▸**smooth down** *vt sep* alisar

▸**smooth out** *vt sep (map, sheets, crease)* estirar, alisar; *Fig (difficulty)* allanar, resolver

▸**smooth over** *vt sep* **to s. over difficulties** mitigar las dificultades; **to s. things over** dulcificar las cosas

**smoothly** ['smu:ðlɪ] *adv* **to go s.** transcurrir sin contratiempos

**smoothness** ['smu:ðnɪs] *n (of paper, skin, wine, whisky)* suavidad *f; (of road, surface)* lisura *f; (of sauce)* homogeneidad *f*

**smooth-talking** ['smu:ð'tɔ:kɪŋ] *n* con mucha labia

**smote** [sməʊt] *pt of* **smite**

**smother** ['smʌðə(r)] *vt* (**a**) *(person)* ahogar, asfixiar; *(fire)* ahogar; *(cry, yawn)* contener, ahogar; **to s. sb with kisses** colmar a alguien de besos (**b**) *(cover)* **to s. sth in sth** cubrir algo de algo

**smoulder,** *US* **smolder** ['sməʊldə(r)] *vi (of fire)* arder con rescoldo; *Fig* **to s. with anger/ passion** arder de ira/pasión

**smudge** [smʌdʒ] **1** *n* mancha *f; (of ink)* borrón *m*

2 *vt (ink, paper)* emborronar; *(lipstick)* correr; *(drawing)* difuminar

3 *vi (of ink, lipstick)* correrse

**smug** [smʌg] *adj* engreído(a)

**smuggle** ['smʌgəl] *vt (arms, drugs)* pasar de contrabando; **to s. sth into/out of the country** introducir/sacar algo del país de contrabando; **to s. sb in/out** meter/sacar a alguien clandestinamente

**smuggler** ['smʌglə(r)] *n* contrabandista *mf*

**smuggling** ['smʌglɪŋ] *n* contrabando *m*

**smut** [smʌt] *n* (**a**) *(soot)* hollín *m*, carbonilla *f* (**b**) *(obscenity)* cochinadas *fpl*

**smutty** ['smʌtɪ] *adj* (**a**) *(dirty)* tiznado(a) (**b**) *(obscene)* verde, cochino(a)

**snack** [snæk] **1** *n* tentempié *m*, piscolabis *m inv, Am* botana *f, CSur* onces *fpl;* **s. bar** cafetería *f*

2 *vi* **to s. (on sth)** tomarse un tentempié *or* piscolabis (de algo)

**snag** [snæg] **1** *n (problem)* problema *m*, inconveniente *m*

2 *vt (pt & pp* **snagged) to s. one's dress on sth** engancharse el vestido en *or* con algo

**snail** [sneɪl] *n* caracol *m;* **at a s.'s pace** a paso de tortuga; *Fam* **s. mail** correo *m* caracol, correo *m* tradicional

**snake** [sneɪk] **1** *n (big)* serpiente *f; (small)* culebra *f; Fig* **a s. in the grass** un judas; **snakes and ladders** ≃ juego *m* de la oca; **s. charmer** encantador(ora) *m,f* de serpientes

2 *vi (of road, river)* serpentear

**snakebite** ['sneɪkbaɪt] *n* (**a**) *(of snake)* mordedura *f* de serpiente (**b**) *(drink)* = cerveza rubia con sidra

**snakeskin** ['sneɪkskɪn] *n* piel *f* de serpiente

**snap** [snæp] **1** *n* (**a**) *(bite)* mordisco *m* al aire (**b**) *(sound)* chasquido *m* (**c**) *(of weather)* **cold s.** ola *f* de frío (**d**) *Fam (photograph)* foto *f* (**e**) *(card game)* = juego de naipes que gana quien dice "snap" primero cuando aparecen dos cartas iguales; *Fam (in identical situation)* **I'm going to Paris – s.!** me voy a París – ¡anda, yo también!

2 *adj (judgement, decision)* en el acto, súbito; **to call a s. election** adelantar las elecciones para aprovechar una circunstancia favorable

3 *vt (pt & pp* **snapped)** (**a**) *(break)* romper, partir; **to s. sth in two** partir algo en dos (**b**) *(make noise with)* **to s. one's fingers** chasquear los dedos (**c**) *(say sharply)* espetar (**d**) *Fam (take photograph of)* fotografiar

4 *vi* (**a**) *(break cleanly)* romperse, partirse; *(break noisily)* quebrarse, romperse (con un chasquido) (**b**) *(bite)* **the dog snapped at him** el perro intentó morderle; **to s. shut** *(of jaws, lid)* cerrarse de golpe (**c**) *(speak abruptly)* **to s. at sb** hablar en mal tono a alguien (**d**) *(idioms)* **to s. out of it** *(of depression, apathy)* recuperar el ánimo; *(of sulk)* **s. out of it!** ¡alegra esa cara!

▸**snap off** *vt sep* (**a**) *(break)* partir, arrancar (**b**) *Fam Fig* **to s. sb's head off** soltarle un bufido a alguien, gruñir a alguien

2 *vi* partirse, desprenderse

▸**snap up** *vt sep* (**a**) *(seize in jaws)* agarrar, morder (**b**) *Fam (buy, take quickly)* pillar, hacerse con

**snapdragon** ['snæpdrægən] *n* (boca *f* de) dragón *m* (planta)

**snappy** ['snæpɪ] *adj (style, prose)* chispeante; *(slogan)* ingenioso(a); **to be a s. dresser** vestirse muy bien; *Fam* **make it s.!** *(be quick)* ¡rapidito!

**snapshot** ['snæpʃɒt] *n Fam (photograph)* foto *f*

**snare** [sneə(r)] **1** *n also Fig* trampa *f;* **s. drum** *(in military band)* tambor *m; (in rock music)* caja *f*

2 *vt (animal)* cazar *(con trampa); Fig* **the police snared the criminals** la policía atrapó a los delincuentes *(tendiéndoles una trampa)*

**snarl** [snɑːl] **1** *n (of dog)* gruñido *m; (of lion, person)* rugido *m*

2 *vi (of dog)* gruñir; *(of lion)* rugir; **to s. at sb** *(of person)* gruñirle a alguien

▸**snarl up** *vi* atascarse

**snarl-up** ['snɑːlʌp] *n (of traffic)* atasco *m*, embotellamiento *m*; *(in system)* lío *m*, jaleo *m*

**snatch** [snætʃ] **1** *n (of music, conversation)* retazo *m*; **to sleep in snatches** dormir a ratos

  **2** *vt* **(a)** *(grab)* **to s. sth (from sb)** arrebatar algo (a alguien); **to s. something to eat** comer algo apresuradamente; **to s. some sleep** aprovechar para dormir un poco **(b)** *(wallet, handbag)* robar (con tirón); *(person)* secuestrar

  **3** *vi* **to s. at sth** intentar coger algo

▸**snatch away** *vt sep* arrebatar

**snazzy** ['snæzɪ] *adj Fam* chulo(a)

**sneak** [sniːk] **1** *n* **(a)** *Fam (telltale)* chivato(a) *m,f* **(b)** **to get a s. preview of sth** tener un anticipo en exclusiva de algo

  **2** *vt (pt & pp* **sneaked**, *US* **snuck** [snʌk]) **to s. sth past sb** pasar algo por delante de alguien sin que se dé cuenta; **to s. sb in/out** introducir/sacar a alguien a hurtadillas; **to s. a glance at sb** mirar furtivamente a alguien; **she sneaked her boyfriend into her bedroom** coló a su novio en su dormitorio

  **3** *vi* **(a)** *Fam (tell tales)* chivarse **(b)** *(move furtively)* deslizarse; **to s. past sb** colarse sin ser visto(a) por alguien; **to s. in/out** entrar/salir a hurtadillas

▸**sneak away, sneak off** *vi* escaparse, escabullirse

**sneaker** ['sniːkə(r)] *n US (running shoe)* playera *f*, zapatilla *f* de deporte

**sneaky** ['sniːkɪ] *adj Fam* ladino(a), artero(a)

**sneer** ['snɪə(r)] **1** *n (expression)* mueca *f* desdeñosa

  **2** *vt* decir con desprecio

  **3** *vi* **to s. at sb/sth** burlarse de alguien/algo

**sneering** ['snɪərɪŋ] **1** *n* burlas *fpl*

  **2** *adj* burlón(ona)

**sneeze** [sniːz] **1** *n* estornudo *m*

  **2** *vi* estornudar; *Fam Fig* **it's not to be sneezed at** no es moco de pavo

**snicker** ['snɪkə(r)] *US* **1** *n* risilla *f* burlona

  **2** *vi* burlarse, reírse

**snide** [snaɪd] *adj* malicioso(a)

**sniff** [snɪf] **1** *n* **to take a s. at sth** olfatear algo; **with a s. of disgust** con un aire disgustado

  **2** *vt* **(a)** *(smell)* oler, olfatear; *(detect)* olfatear, detectar **(b)** *(inhale) (air)* aspirar; *(cocaine, glue)* esnifar

  **3** *vi (inhale)* inspirar; *(disdainfully)* hacer un gesto de desprecio; *Fam* **it's not to be sniffed at** no es moco de pavo

▸**sniff out** *vt sep (of dog)* encontrar olfateando; *Fig (of investigator)* descubrir, dar con

**sniffer dog** ['snɪfədɒg] *n* = perro policía entrenado para detectar drogas o explosivos

**sniffle** ['snɪfəl] **1** *n (slight cold)* **to have the sniffles** tener un ligero resfriado

  **2** *vi* **(a)** *(sniff repeatedly)* sorber **(b)** *(cry quietly)* gimotear

**sniffy** ['snɪfɪ] *adj Fam (disdainful)* desdeñoso(a); **to be s. about sth** tratar algo con desprecio

**snifter** ['snɪftə(r)] *n Fam Old-fashioned (drink)* trago *m*, copita *f*

**snigger** ['snɪgə(r)] **1** *n* risilla *f* burlona

  **2** *vi* reírse burlonamente

**snip** [snɪp] **1** *n* **(a)** *(cut)* corte *m* **(b)** *Br Fam (bargain)* chollo *m*

  **2** *vt (pt & pp* **snipped**) cortar

▸**snip off** *vt sep* cortar

**snipe¹** [snaɪp] *(pl* **snipe**) *n (bird)* agachadiza *f*

**snipe²** *vi (shoot)* disparar *(desde un escondite)*; **to s. at sb** disparar a alguien; *Fig (criticize)* criticar a alguien

**sniper** ['snaɪpə(r)] *n (rifleman)* francotirador(ora) *m,f*

**snippet** ['snɪpɪt] *n (of information, conversation)* retazo *m*; **a s. of news** un fragmento de una noticia

**snitch** [snɪtʃ] *Fam* **1** *n* **(a)** *(informer)* chivato(a) *m,f* **(b)** *(nose)* napias *fpl*

  **2** *vi* **to s. on sb** chivarse de alguien

**snivel** ['snɪvəl] *(pt & pp* **snivelled**, *US* **sniveled**) *vi* lloriquear, gimotear

**snivelling,** *US* **sniveling** ['snɪvəlɪŋ] *adj* llorica

**snob** [snɒb] *n* presuntuoso(a) *m,f*

**snobbery** ['snɒbərɪ] *n* presuntuosidad *f*

**snobbish** ['snɒbɪʃ] *adj* presuntuoso(a)

**snog** [snɒg] *Br Fam* **1** *n* **to have a s.** morrear

  **2** *vi (pt & pp* **snogged**) morrear

**snooker** ['snuːkə(r)] **1** *n (game)* snooker *m*, billar *m* inglés

  **2** *vt* **to s. sb** *(in game)* = dejarle la bola blanca al rival en una posición que impide golpear directamente a la bola; *Fig* acorralar a alguien

**snoop** [snuːp] *Fam* **1** *n* **(a)** *(person)* fisgón(ona) *m,f* **(b)** *(look)* **to have a s. (around)** fisgar, fisgonear

  **2** *vi* fisgar, fisgonear

**snooper** ['snuːpə(r)] *n Fam* fisgón(ona) *m,f*

**snooty** ['snuːtɪ] *adj Fam* presuntuoso(a)

**snooze** [snuːz] *Fam* **1** *n* siestecita *f*; **to have a s.** echarse una siestecita

  **2** *vi* echarse una siestecita

**snore** [snɔː(r)] **1** *n* ronquido *m*

  **2** *vi* roncar

**snoring** ['snɔːrɪŋ] *n* ronquidos *mpl*

**snorkel** ['snɔːkəl] **1** *n* snorkel *m*, tubo *m* para buceo

  **2** *vi (pt & pp* **snorkelled**, *US* **snorkeled**) bucear con tubo *or* snorkel

**snort** [snɔ:t] **1** n (of person, horse) bufido m, resoplido m

**2** vt Fam (drugs) esnifar

**3** vi (of person, horse) resoplar, bufar

**snot** [snɒt] n Fam mocos mpl

**snotty** ['snɒtɪ] adj Fam (**a**) (nose) con mocos (**b**) (arrogant) creído(a), petulante

**snout** [snaʊt] n (of animal) hocico m, morro m; Fam (of person) napias fpl

**snow** [snəʊ] **1** n nieve f; **s. blindness** deslumbramiento m por la nieve; **s. line** límite m de las nieves perpetuas

**2** vi nevar; **it's snowing** está nevando

▸**snow in** vt sep **to be snowed in** estar aislado(a) por la nieve

▸**snow under** vt sep **to be snowed under** (with work) estar desbordado(a); (with invitations, offers) no dar abasto

**snowball** ['snəʊbɔ:l] **1** n bola f de nieve; **s. fight** guerra f de bolas de nieve; Fam **she hasn't a s.'s chance (in hell)** lo tiene muy crudo

**2** vi (problems) multiplicarse; (project) crecer vertiginosamente

**snowboard** ['snəʊbɔ:d] n snowboard m

**snowboarding** ['snəʊbɔ:dɪŋ] n snowboard m; **to go s.** hacer snowboard

**snowbound** ['snəʊbaʊnd] adj aislado(a) a causa de la nieve

**snowcapped** ['snəʊkæpt] adj cubierto(a) de nieve

**snowdrift** ['snəʊdrɪft] n nevero m, ventisquero m

**snowdrop** ['snəʊdrɒp] n (flower) campanilla f de invierno

**snowfall** ['snəʊfɔ:l] n nevada f

**snowflake** ['snəʊfleɪk] n copo m de nieve

**snowman** ['snəʊmæn] n muñeco m de nieve

**snowmobile** ['snəʊməbi:l] n motonieve f, moto f de nieve

**snowplough,** US **snowplow** ['snəʊplaʊ] n quitanieves f inv

**snowshoe** ['snəʊʃu:] n raqueta f (de nieve)

**snowstorm** ['snəʊstɔ:m] n ventisca f, tormenta f de nieve

**snowsuit** ['snəʊsu:t] n traje m de esquí

**Snow White** ['snəʊ'waɪt] n **S. and the Seven Dwarfs** Blancanieves y los siete enanitos

**snowy** ['snəʊɪ] adj (landscape, field) nevado(a); (weather, day) nevoso(a), de nieve

**SNP** [esen'pi:] n (abbr **Scottish National Party**) Partido m Nacionalista Escocés

**Snr** (abbr **Senior**) Ivan Fox S. Ivan Fox padre

**snub** [snʌb] **1** n desaire m

**2** vt (pt & pp **snubbed**) desairar

**snub nose** ['snʌb'nəʊz] n nariz f respingona

**snuck** [snʌk] US pt & pp of **sneak**

**snuff** [snʌf] **1** n rapé m

**2** vt (candle) apagar; Br very Fam **to s. it** (die) estirar la pata

▸**snuff out** vt sep (candle) apagar; (life, opposition) truncar, cercenar

**snuffbox** ['snʌfbɒks] n tabaquera f, caja f para el rapé

**snuffle** ['snʌfəl] **1** n (sniff) resoplido m

**2** vi (sniff) sorber

**snug** [snʌg] adj (**a**) (cosy) **I'm nice and s. by the fire** estoy muy a gusto delante de la chimenea; **this bed's very s.** se está muy a gusto en esta cama (**b**) (tight-fitting) ajustado(a)

▸**snuggle up** ['snʌgəl] vi **to s. up to sb** acurrucarse contra alguien

**snugly** ['snʌglɪ] adv (comfortably) a gusto, confortablemente; **to fit s.** quedar ajustado(a)

**so** [səʊ] **1** adv (**a**) (to such an extent) **it isn't so very old** no es tan viejo; **he's not so clever as she is** él no es tan listo como ella; **so many children** tantos niños; **so much money** tanto dinero; **would you be so kind as to...?** ¿sería tan amable de...?; **it was difficult – so much so that...** ha sido difícil – tanto (es así) que...; **a little girl SO high** una niña así de alta; **I was SO hungry I had three helpings** tenía tantísima hambre que me serví tres veces

(**b**) (intensive) **it's so easy** es facilísimo, es muy fácil; **we enjoyed ourselves SO much!** ¡nos hemos divertido muchísimo!; **I was SO disappointed** me llevé una decepción enorme; **we're SO pleased you could come!** ¡qué bien que hayas podido venir!

(**c**) (expressing agreement) **you're late – so I am!** llegas tarde – ¡pues sí!; **that's Mrs Thatcher! – so it is!** ¡mira, Margaret Thatcher! – ¡anda, es verdad!

(**d**) (referring to statement already mentioned) **I hope/think/suppose so** espero/creo/supongo que sí, eso espero/creo/supongo; **so I believe** eso creo; **I'm not very organized – so I see!** no me organizo muy bien – ¡ya lo veo!; **so be it!** ¡así sea!; **is that so?** ¿ah, sí?, ¿de verdad?; **if so,...** si es así,...

(**e**) (also) **so am I** yo también; **so do we** nosotros también; **so can they** ellos también (pueden); **so is my brother** mi hermano también

(**f**) (in this way) **do it so** hazlo así; **and so on, and so forth** y cosas así, etcétera

**2** conj (**a**) (because of this) así que; **she has a bad temper, so be careful** tiene mal genio, así que ten cuidado; **he wasn't there, so I came back again** como no estaba, me volví

(**b**) (introducing remark) **so that's what it is!** ¡así que es eso!; **so why not coming?** entonces ¿no vienes?; **so what do we do now?** y ahora ¿qué hacemos?; **so (what)?** ¿y (qué)?

(**c**) **so as to** para; **we hurried so as not to be late** nos dimos prisa para no llegar tarde

(**d**) **so that** para que; **she sat down so that I could see better** se sentó para que yo viera mejor; **we hurried so that we wouldn't be late** nos dimos prisa para no llegar tarde

**soak** [səʊk] **1** vt (leave in water) poner en remojo; (make very wet) empapar (**with** or **de**)

**2** vi (of food, clothes) estar en remojo; **to leave sth to s.** dejar algo en remojo

▸**soak in** vi impregnarse

▸**soak up** vt sep (liquid) absorber; Fig **to s. up the sun** tostarse al sol

**soaked** [səʊkt] adj empapado(a); **to be s.** estar empapado(a); **s. to the skin** calado(a) hasta los huesos

**so-and-so** ['səʊənsəʊ] (pl **so-and-sos**) n Fam (**a**) (unspecified person) fulanito(a) m,f; **Mr S.** don fulanito de tal (**b**) (unpleasant person) hijo(a) m,f de mala madre

**soap** [səʊp] **1** n jabón m; **a bar of s.** una pastilla de jabón; **s. (opera)** telenovela f, culebrón m; **s. powder** detergente m en polvo

**2** vt enjabonar

**soapbox** ['səʊpbɒks] n tribuna f improvisada

**soapdish** ['səʊpdɪʃ] n jabonera f

**soapflakes** ['səʊpfleɪks] npl jabón m en escamas

**soapsuds** ['səʊpsʌdz] npl espuma f (de jabón)

**soapy** ['səʊpɪ] adj (water) jabonoso(a); (hands, face) enjabonado(a); (taste, smell) a jabón

**soar** [sɔː(r)] vi (of bird, plane) remontarse, remontar el vuelo; Fig (of building) elevarse, alzarse; Fig (of hopes, prices) desorbitarse, dispararse

**soaring** ['sɔːrɪŋ] adj Fig (hopes, prices) desorbitado(a); (building) altísimo(a)

**sob** [sɒb] **1** n sollozo m; Fam **s. story** dramón m

**2** vi (pt & pp **sobbed**) sollozar

**s.o.b.** [esəʊ'biː] n US very Fam (abbr **son of a bitch**) hijo(a) m,f de puta

**sobbing** ['sɒbɪŋ] n sollozos mpl, llanto m

**sober** ['səʊbə(r)] adj (**a**) (not drunk) sobrio(a), sereno(a) (**b**) (sensible) serio(a)

▸**sober up** vt sep quitar la borrachera a

**2** vi **by the next day he had sobered up** al día siguiente ya se le había pasado la borrachera

**sobering** ['səʊbərɪŋ] adj **it's a s. thought** da mucho que pensar

**sobriety** [səʊ'braɪətɪ] n seriedad f

**Soc** (abbr **society**) asociación f

**so-called** [səʊ'kɔːld] adj (generally known as) (así) llamado(a); (wrongly known) mal llamado(a)

**soccer** ['sɒkə(r)] n fútbol m; **s. match** partido m de fútbol

**sociable** ['səʊʃəbəl] adj sociable

**social** ['səʊʃəl] **1** adj social; **s. class** clase f social; **s. climber** arribista mf; Pol **s. democrat** socialdemócrata mf; **s. life** vida f social; **s. outcast** marginado(a) m,f; **s. sciences** ciencias fpl sociales; **s. security** seguridad f social; **the s. services** los servicios sociales; **s. studies** (ciencias fpl) sociales fpl; **s. work** asistencia f or trabajo m social; **s. worker** asistente mf or trabajador(ora) m, f social

**2** n (party) reunión f, fiesta f

**socialism** ['səʊʃəlɪzəm] n socialismo m

**socialist** ['səʊʃəlɪst] n & adj socialista mf

**socialite** ['səʊʃəlaɪt] n personaje m de la vida mundana

**socialize** ['səʊʃəlaɪz] vi alternar; **to s. with sb** tener trato or alternar con alguien

**socially** ['səʊʃəlɪ] adv socialmente; **we don't see each other s.** no tenemos relación fuera del trabajo

**society** [sə'saɪətɪ] n (in general) sociedad f; (club) asociación f, sociedad f; (**high**) **s.** la alta sociedad

**socioeconomic** [səʊsɪəʊiːkə'nɒmɪk] adj socioeconómico(a)

**sociological** [səʊsɪə'lɒdʒɪkəl] adj sociológico(a)

**sociologist** [səʊsɪ'ɒlədʒɪst] n sociólogo(a) m,f

**sociology** [səʊsɪ'ɒlədʒɪ] n sociología f

**sock** [sɒk] **1** n (**a**) (garment) calcetín m; Br Fam Fig **to pull one's socks up** esforzarse más, aplicarse (**b**) Fam (blow) puñetazo m

**2** vt Fam (hit) dar un puñetazo a; Fig **s. it to them!** ¡a por ellos!, ¡valor y al toro!

**socket** ['sɒkɪt] n (of eye) cuenca f; (for plug) enchufe m (toma de corriente)

**sod¹** [sɒd] n (of earth) tepe m

**sod²** [sɒd] **1** n very Fam (person) mamón(ona) m,f; **poor s.!** ¡pobre diablo!; **I got s. all from them** no me dieron ni la hora; **you've done s. all today** no has dado golpe en todo el día; **S.'s law** la ley de Murphy

**2** vt (pt & pp **sodded**) Vulg **s. it!** ¡joder!; **s. you!** ¡vete a la mierda!; **s. the party, I'm tired** a la mierda la fiesta, yo estoy cansado

▸**sod off** vi Br Vulg abrirse, pirarse; **s. off!** ¡vete a tomar por saco!

**soda** ['səʊdə] n (**a**) **s. water** (agua f de) seltz m, soda f; **s. fountain** sifón m (**b**) US (fizzy drink) refresco m (gaseoso); **s. fountain** puesto m de helados y refrescos (**c**) Chem sosa f

**sodden** ['sɒdən] adj empapado(a); **to be s.** estar empapado(a)

**sodium** ['səʊdɪəm] n Chem sodio m; **s. bicarbonate** bicarbonato m sódico or de sodio; **s. chloride** cloruro m de sodio

**sodomize** ['sɒdəmaɪz] vt sodomizar

**sodomy** ['sɒdəmɪ] n sodomía f

**sofa** ['səʊfə] n sofá m; **s. bed** sofá-cama m

**Sofia** [səʊ'fiə] n Sofía

**soft** [sɒft] adj (a) (in texture) (ground, rock, cheese) blando(a); (pillow, carpet, fabric) suave; **s. furnishings** tapicería f; Anat **s. tissue** tejido m blando; **s. toy** peluche m (muñeco)
(b) (not harsh, not strong) (voice, rain, colour) suave; **s. currency** divisa f débil; **s. drinks** refrescos mpl; **s. drugs** drogas fpl blandas; Phot **in s. focus** ligeramente velado(a) or difuminado(a); Fin **s. loan** crédito m blando; Com **s. sell** venta f no agresiva
(c) (not strict) blando(a); **to have a s. spot for sb** tener debilidad por alguien; **to have a s. heart** ser muy blando(a)
(d) Fam (stupid) tonto(a)
(e) (easy) (job, life) fácil; Fam **to be a s. touch** ser un poco primo(a); **s. option** opción f fácil
(f) Comptr **s. copy** copia f en formato electrónico; **s. return** retorno m automático

**softback** ['sɒftbæk] n libro m de tapa blanda or en rústica

**softball** ['sɒftbɔːl] n = juego parecido al béisbol jugado en un campo más pequeño y con una pelota más blanda

**soft-boiled** ['sɒftbɔɪld] adj (egg) pasado(a) por agua

**soften** ['sɒfən] **1** vt (wax, butter, leather) ablandar, reblandecer; (light, contrast, skin) suavizar; Fig **to s. the blow** amortiguar el golpe
**2** vi (of wax, butter) ablandarse; Fig (of person) ceder, ablandarse; Fig (of opinions, resolve, stance) suavizarse
▸**soften up** vt sep Fam (before attack) debilitar; (before request) ablandar

**softener** ['sɒfənə(r)] n suavizante m

**softhearted** [sɒft'hɑːtɪd] adj bondadoso(a), de buen corazón

**softie** = **softy**

**softly** ['sɒftlɪ] adv (talk) suavemente; (walk) con suavidad; **to be s. lit** tener una iluminación tenue or suave

**softly-softly** ['sɒftlɪ'sɒftlɪ] adj Fam (approach, attitude) cauteloso(a)

**softness** ['sɒftnɪs] n (of ground) blandura f; (of skin, voice, fabric) suavidad f

**soft-pedal** [sɒft'pedəl] (pt & pp **soft-pedalled**, US **soft-pedaled**) vt (minimize) restar importancia a

**soft-soap** ['sɒft'səʊp] vt Fam dar coba a

**soft-spoken** [sɒft'spəʊkən] adj de voz suave

**software** ['sɒftweə(r)] n Comptr soporte m lógico, software m; **s. engineer** ingeniero(a) m,f de programas; **s. package** paquete m de software

**softy** ['sɒftɪ] n Fam (gentle person) buenazo(a) m,f; (coward) gallina mf

**soggy** ['sɒgɪ] adj empapado(a); **to be s.** estar empapado(a)

**soh** [səʊ] n Mus sol m

**soil** [sɔɪl] **1** n (earth) tierra f; **the s.** el suelo, el terreno; **on British s.** en suelo británico
**2** vt (clothes, sheet) manchar, ensuciar; Fig **to s. one's hands** mancharse las manos

**solace** ['sɒləs] n Literary consuelo m

**solar** ['səʊlə(r)] adj (system, energy) solar; **s. eclipse** eclipse m de sol; **s. plexus** plexo m solar

**sold** [səʊld] pt & pp of **sell**

**solder** ['səʊldə(r)] **1** n soldadura f
**2** vt soldar

**soldering iron** ['səʊldərɪŋ'aɪən] n soldador m

**soldier** ['səʊldʒə(r)] **1** n soldado m; **an old s.** un veterano, un excombatiente
**2** vi servir como soldado
▸**soldier on** vi seguir adelante pese a todo

**sole¹** [səʊl] **1** n (of foot) planta f; (of shoe) suela f
**2** vt (shoe) poner suelas a

**sole²** n (fish) lenguado m

**sole³** adj (only) único(a); Com **s. agent** agente mf en exclusiva

**solely** ['səʊllɪ] adv únicamente

**solemn** ['sɒləm] adj solemne

**solemnity** [sə'lemnɪtɪ] n solemnidad f

**sol-fa** [sɒl'fɑː] n Mus solfa f

**solicit** [sə'lɪsɪt] **1** vt Formal (request) solicitar
**2** vi (of prostitute) abordar clientes

**solicitor** [sə'lɪsɪtə(r)] n Br = abogado que hace las veces de notario para contratos de compraventa y testamentos o que actúa de procurador en juzgados administrativos o de primera instancia, pero no más altos; **S. General** Fiscal m General del Estado

**solicitous** [sə'lɪsɪtəs] adj Formal solícito(a)

**solid** ['sɒlɪd] **1** n sólido m; **solids** (food) alimentos mpl sólidos
**2** adj (a) (not liquid) sólido(a); Fig (support) fuerte, sólido(a); Fig **he's a s. worker** es un trabajador de fiar; **s. fuel** combustible m sólido
(b) (not hollow) macizo(a); **s. gold** oro m macizo; **s. silver** plata f maciza
**3** adv **ten hours s.** diez horas sin interrupción; **the hall was packed s.** la sala estaba atestada de gente

**solidarity** [sɒlɪ'dærɪtɪ] n solidaridad f

**solidify** [sə'lɪdɪfaɪ] vi solidificarse

**solidity** [sə'lɪdɪtɪ] n solidez f

**solidly** ['sɒlɪdlɪ] adv (firmly) sólidamente; (without interruption) sin interrupción; (vote) unánimemente

**solid-state** ['sɒlɪd'steɪt] adj Elec de estado sólido, de componentes sólidos

**soliloquy** [sə'lɪləkwɪ] n soliloquio m

**solitaire** [sɒlɪ'teə(r)] n (game, jewellery) solitario m

**solitary** ['sɒlɪtərɪ] adj solitario(a); **s. confinement** aislamiento m, incomunicación f; **to be in s. confinement** estar incomunicado(a)

**solitude** ['sɒlɪtju:d] n soledad f

**solo** ['səʊləʊ] **1** n (pl solos) (musical) solo m
**2** adj (performance) en solitario; **s. flight** vuelo m en solitario
**3** adv en solitario; **to go s.** (of musician) iniciar una carrera en solitario; (of business partner) montar el propio negocio

**soloist** ['səʊləʊɪst] n solista mf

**Solomon Islands** ['sɒləmən'aɪləndz] npl **the S.** las Islas Salomón

**solstice** ['sɒlstɪs] n solsticio m

**soluble** ['sɒljʊbəl] adj soluble

**solution** [sə'lu:ʃən] n solución f

**solve** [sɒlv] vt resolver

**solvency** ['sɒlvənsɪ] n solvencia f

**solvent** ['sɒlvənt] **1** n disolvente m; **s. abuse** inhalación f de disolventes (pegamento y otros)
**2** adj (financially) solvente

**Somali** [sə'mɑ:lɪ] n & adj somalí mf

**Somalia** [sə'mɑ:lɪə] n Somalia

**sombre**, US **somber** ['sɒmbə(r)] adj (colour) oscuro(a); (person, mood) sombrío(a)

**some** [sʌm] **1** pron (a) (people) algunos(as); **s. believe that...** hay quien cree que...; **s. of my friends** algunos amigos míos; **they went off, s. one way, s. another** unos se fueron en una dirección y otros en otra
(b) (a certain number) unos(as), algunos(as); (a certain quantity) algo; **s. are more difficult than others** unos son más difíciles que otros; **there is s. left** queda algo; **there are s. left** quedan algunos; **give me s.** (a few) dame unos(as) cuantos(as); (a bit) dame un poco; **s. of the time** parte del tiempo
**2** adj (a) (certain quantity or number) **there are s. apples in the kitchen** hay manzanas en la cocina; (a few) hay algunas o unas pocas manzanas en la cocina; **to drink s. water** beber agua; **I ate s. fruit** comí fruta; **would you like s. wine?** ¿te apetece vino?; (a bit) ¿quieres un poco de vino?; **I felt s. uneasiness** sentí un cierto malestar; **in s. ways** en cierto modo; **to s. extent** hasta cierto punto
(b) (as opposed to other) **s. people say...** hay quien dice...; **s. mornings I don't feel like getting up** algunas mañanas no me apetece

levantarme
(c) (considerable) **for s. time** durante un buen rato; **s. distance away** bastante lejos; **s. miles away** a bastantes millas
(d) (unspecified) algún(una); **for s. reason or other** por una razón u otra, por alguna razón; **he'll come s. day** algún día vendrá; **at s. time in the future** en algún momento futuro; **in s. book or other** en no sé qué libro, en algún libro; **s. fool left the door open** algún idiota dejó la puerta abierta
(e) Fam (intensive) **that was s. storm/meal!** ¡menuda tormenta/comida!; Ironic **s. hope** or **chance!** ¡ni lo sueñes!
**3** adv (approximately) unos(as); **s. fifteen minutes** unos quince minutos

**somebody** ['sʌmbədɪ] **1** n **she thinks she's s.** se cree alguien; **I want to be s.** quiero ser alguien
**2** pron alguien; **s. told me that...** me dijeron que...; **he's s. you can trust** se puede confiar en él; **s. else** otra persona

**somehow** ['sʌmhaʊ] adv (a) (in some way or other) de alguna manera (b) (for some reason or other) por alguna razón

**someone** ['sʌmwʌn] = **somebody**

**somersault** ['sʌməsɔ:lt] **1** n (of person) salto m mortal
**2** vi (of person) dar un salto mortal/saltos mortales; (of car) dar una vuelta de campana/vueltas de campana

**something** ['sʌmθɪŋ] **1** n **I've brought you a little s.** te he traído una cosilla
**2** pron (a) (in general) algo; **s. or other** alguna cosa; **there's s. about him I don't like** hay algo en él que no me gusta; **s. tells me she'll be there** algo me dice que estará allí; **s. to drink/to read** algo de beber/para leer; **s. to live for** una razón para vivir; **I've got s. else to do after I finish this** aún me queda algo que hacer después de esto; **he's s. in publishing** tiene un puesto importante en el mundo editorial; **in the year eleven hundred and s.** en el año mil ciento y algo; **she's eighty s.** tiene ochenta y tantos años; **at least he apologized – that's s.!** al menos pidió disculpas – ¡eso ya es algo!; **there's s. in what you say** tienes algo de razón; **she has s. to do with what happened** está relacionada con lo que ocurrió; **that was quite s.!** ¡fue impresionante!; **she's got a cold or s.** tiene un resfriado o algo así
(b) (certain degree) **there's been s. of an improvement** se ha producido una cierta mejora; **she's s. of a miser** es un poco tacaña; **it's s. like a guinea pig** es algo así como un conejillo de Indias
**3** adv Fam (intensifying) **it hurt s. awful** dolía horrores, dolía (una) cosa mala

**sometime** ['sʌmtaɪm] *adv* algún día, alguna vez; **see you s.** ya nos veremos; **s. last week** un día de la semana pasada; **s. before Christmas** en algún momento antes de Navidad; **s. soon** un día de estos; **s. or other** tarde o temprano

**sometimes** ['sʌmtaɪmz] *adv* a veces

**somewhat** ['sʌmwɒt] *adv* un poco, un tanto

**somewhere** ['sʌmweə(r)] *adv* (**a**) *(in some place)* en algún sitio, en alguna parte; *(to some place)* a algún sitio, a alguna parte; **it must be s. else** debe de estar en otra parte; **why don't you go s. else?** ¿por qué no te vas a otro sitio?; **s. in Spain** en (algún lugar de) España; **s. or other** en algún sitio; *Fig* **now we're getting s.!** ¡ya parece que las cosas marchan!

(**b**) *(approximately)* **he is s. around fifty** tiene unos cincuenta años; **it costs s. in the region of £500** cuesta alrededor de 500 libras; **s. around four o'clock** a eso de las cuatro

**somnolent** ['sɒmnələnt] *adj Formal* somnoliento(a)

**son** [sʌn] *n* hijo *m*; **youngest/eldest s.** hijo *m* menor/mayor; *US very Fam* **s. of a bitch** hijo *m* de puta, hijoputa *m*

**sonar** ['səʊnɑ:(r)] *n* sonar *m*

**sonata** [sə'nɑ:tə] *n* sonata *f*

**song** [sɒŋ] *n* (**a**) *(song)* canción *f*; **to burst or break into s.** ponerse a cantar; **s. book** libro *m* de canciones (**b**) *(idioms)* **to buy sth for a s.** comprar algo por cuatro perras gordas; **to make a s. and dance (about sth)** montar un número (a cuenta de algo)

**songbird** ['sɒŋbɜːd] *n* pájaro *m* cantor

**songwriter** ['sɒŋraɪtə(r)] *n* compositor(ora) *m,f*; *(of lyrics only)* letrista *mf*

**sonic** ['sɒnɪk] *adj (of sound)* del sonido; *(of speed of sound)* sónico(a); *Av* **s. boom** estampido *m* sónico *(al rebasar la barrera del sonido)*

**son-in-law** ['sʌnɪnlɔː] *n* (*pl* **sons-in-law**) yerno *m*

**sonnet** ['sɒnɪt] *n* soneto *m*

**sonny** ['sʌnɪ] *n Fam* hijo *m*, pequeño(a)

**sonorous** ['sɒnərəs] *adj* sonoro(a)

**soon** [su:n] *adv* (**a**) *(within a short time)* pronto; **it will s. be Friday** pronto será viernes; **see you s.!** ¡hasta pronto!; **s. after(wards)** poco después; **s. after four** poco después de las cuatro; **no sooner had she left than...** en cuanto se fue...

(**b**) *(early)* pronto; **must you leave so s.?** ¿tienes que irte tan pronto?; **it's too s. to tell** aún no se puede saber; **none too s.** en buena hora; **how s. can you get here?** ¿cuánto tardarás en llegar?; **sooner or later** tarde o temprano; **the sooner the better** cuanto antes mejor; **as s. as** tan pronto como; **as s. as possible** lo antes posible

(**c**) *(expressing preference)* **I would just as s. stay** preferiría quedarme; **I would sooner do it alone** preferiría hacerlo yo solo

**soot** [sʊt] *n* hollín *m*

**soothe** [suːð] *vt (pain, burn)* aliviar, calmar; *(person, anger)* calmar

**soothing** ['suːðɪŋ] *adj (relaxing)* relajante, sedante

**soothsayer** ['suːθseɪə(r)] *n* adivino(a) *m,f*

**sooty** ['sʊtɪ] *adj (covered in soot)* tiznado(a); *(black)* negro(a)

**sop** [sɒp] *n (concession)* pequeña concesión *f* (to a)

**sophist** ['sɒfɪst] *n* sofista *mf*

**sophisticated** [sə'fɪstɪkeɪtɪd] *adj* sofisticado(a)

**sophistication** [səfɪstɪ'keɪʃən] *n* sofisticación *f*

**sophistry** ['sɒfɪstrɪ] *n* sofismas *mpl*, sofistería *f*

**sophomore** ['sɒfəmɔː(r)] *n US Univ* = estudiante de segundo curso

**soporific** [sɒpə'rɪfɪk] *adj Formal* soporífero(a)

**sopping** ['ʃɒpɪŋ] *adj* **to be s. (wet)** estar empapado(a)

**soppy** ['sɒpɪ] *adj Fam* ñoño(a), sensiblero(a)

**soprano** [sə'prɑːnəʊ] *(pl* **sopranos** *or* **soprani**) *n (singer)* soprano *mf*; **s. voice** (voz *f* de) soprano *m*

**sorbet** ['sɔːbeɪ] *n* sorbete *m*

**sorcerer** ['sɔːsərə(r)] *n* brujo *m*, hechicero *m*

**sorceress** ['sɔːsərɪs] *n* bruja *f*, hechicera *f*

**sorcery** ['sɔːsərɪ] *n* brujería *f*, hechicería *f*

**sordid** ['sɔːdɪd] *adj* sórdido(a)

**sore** [sɔː(r)] **1** *n (wound)* llaga *f*, úlcera *f*

**2** *adj* (**a**) *(painful)* dolorido(a); **his feet were s.** tenía los pies doloridos; **to have a s. throat** tener dolor de garganta; **I've got a s. leg/back** me duele la pierna/la espalda (**b**) *Fam (annoyed)* enfadado(a) **(about** por), molesto(a) **(about** por); **it's a s. point (with him)** es un tema delicado (para él)

**sorely** ['sɔːlɪ] *adv (greatly)* enormemente; **she will be s. missed** se la echará muchísimo de menos; **to be s. in need of sth** necesitar algo desesperadamente; **s. tempted** enormemente tentado(a)

**sorrow** ['sɒrəʊ] *n* pesar *m*, pena *f*; **to my great s.** con gran pesar mío

**sorrowful** ['sɒrəfʊl] *adj* afligido(a), apenado(a)

**sorry** ['sɒrɪ] *adj* (**a**) *(regretful, disappointed)* **to be s. about sth** lamentar *or* sentir algo; **I'm s.** *(regretful)* lo lamento, lo siento; *(apology)* lo siento; **s. to keep you waiting** siento haberle hecho esperar; **s.!** *(apology)* ¡perdón!; **s.?**

(*what?*) ¿perdón?, ¿cómo dice(s)?; **to say s. (to sb)** pedir perdón (a alguien); **she's s. she did it** siente mucho haberlo hecho; **I'm s. to hear that...** lamento saber que...; *Fam* **you'll be s.!** ¡te arrepentirás!

(**b**) (*sympathetic*) **to feel s. for sb** sentir pena *or* lástima por alguien; **he felt s. for himself** se compadecía de sí mismo

(**c**) (*pathetic*) lamentable; **to be a s. sight** ofrecer un espectáculo lamentable

**sort** [sɔːt] **1** *n* (**a**) (*kind*) clase *f*, tipo *m*; **what s. of tree is it?** ¿qué clase de árbol es éste?; **all sorts of** todo tipo de; **that s. of thing** ese tipo de cosas; **she's that s. of person** ella es así; **something of the s.** algo por el estilo; **did you leave this window open? – I did nothing of the s.!** ¿has dejado la ventana abierta? – ¡qué va!; **he's so arrogant! – he's nothing of the s.!** ¡es tan arrogante! – ¡qué va a ser arrogante!; **it takes all sorts** de todo tiene que haber; *Fam* **she's a good s.** es buena gente; **she's not the s. to give in easily** no es de las que se rinden fácilmente; **we don't want your s. here** no queremos gente como tú por aquí; **to be out of sorts** no encontrarse muy allá; **coffee of a s.** café, por llamarlo de alguna forma; **he's a writer of sorts** se le podría llamar escritor

(**b**) *Fam* **s. of** (*a little*) un poco; (*in a way*) en cierto modo; **this is s. of embarrassing** esto es un poco embarazoso; **I s. of expected it** en cierto modo ya me lo esperaba; **do you like it? – s. of** ¿te gusta? – bueno, más o menos

(**c**) (*to organize*) **to have a s. through sth** revisar algo

**2** *vt* (*classify*) ordenar, clasificar; *Comptr* clasificar

▸**sort out** *vt sep* (**a**) (*organize*) ordenar; **she sorted out the clothes she wanted to keep** separó la ropa que no quería tirar; **to s. oneself out** reorganizar (uno) su vida, aclararse las ideas

(**b**) (*problem*) arreglar; *Fam* **to s. sb out** poner a alguien en su sitio

**sortie** [ˈsɔːtiː] *n Mil & Fig* incursión *f*

**sorting** [ˈsɔːtɪŋ] *n* selección *f*, clasificación *f*; **s. office** oficina *f* de clasificación de correo

**SOS** [esəʊˈes] *n* S.O.S. *m*

**so-so** [ˈsəʊˈsəʊ] *adj* regular; **it was only s.** fue regularcillo

**soufflé** [ˈsuːfleɪ] *n* suflé *m*; **cheese s.** suflé de queso

**sought** [sɔːt] *pt & pp of* **seek**

**sought-after** [ˈsɔːtɑːftə(r)] *adj* solicitado(a)

**soul** [səʊl] *n* (**a**) (*spirit*) alma *f*; **to sell one's s.** venderse, vender el alma; *Fig* **she's the s. of discretion** es la discreción en persona; *Fig* **it lacks s.** le falta gancho *or* garra; **All Souls' Day** el día de (los) difuntos (**b**) (*person*) alma *f*;

**not a s.** ni un alma; **he's a good s.** es (una) buena persona; **poor s.!** ¡pobrecillo! (**c**) (*music*) soul *m*

**soul-destroying** [ˈsəʊldɪstrɔɪŋ] *adj* desmoralizador(ora)

**soulful** [ˈsəʊlfʊl] *adj* emotivo(a), conmovedor(ora)

**soulless** [ˈsəʊllɪs] *adj* (*person*) inhumano(a), desalmado(a); (*place*) impersonal

**soulmate** [ˈsəʊlmeɪt] *n* alma *f* gemela

**soul-searching** [ˈsəʊlsɑːtʃɪŋ] *n* examen *m* de conciencia, reflexión *f*

**sound¹** [saʊnd] **1** *n* (*in general*) sonido *m*; (*individual noise*) ruido *m*; **not a s. could be heard** no se oía nada; **he likes the s. of his own voice** le gusta escucharse a sí mismo; **to turn the s. up/down** (*on TV, radio*) subir/bajar el volumen; *Fig* **I don't like the s. of it** no me gusta nada como suena; **he's angry, by the s. of it** parece que está enfadado; **s. barrier** barrera *f* del sonido; **s. bite** frase *f* lapidaria (*en medios de comunicación*); **s. effects** efectos *mpl* sonoros *or* de sonido; **s. engineer** ingeniero(a) *m,f* de sonido; **s. wave** onda *f* sonora

**2** *vt* (**a**) (*trumpet*) tocar; (*alarm*) hacer sonar; **to s. one's horn** tocar el claxon *or* la bocina; *Fig* **to s. the alarm** dar la voz de alarma (**b**) (*pronounce*) pronunciar; **the "h" is not sounded** la "h" no se pronuncia

**3** *vi* (**a**) (*make sound*) (*of trumpet, bell*) sonar (**b**) (*seem*) parecer; **she sounds French** suena francesa; **that sounds like trouble!** eso suena a que puede haber problemas; **that sounds like a good idea** eso me parece muy buena idea; **he sounds like a nice guy** parece un tipo majo (*por lo que me han dicho de él*); **it sounds like Mozart** suena a *or* parece Mozart; **how does that s. to you?** (*referring to suggestion*) ¿a ti qué te parece?

**sound²** **1** *adj* (**a**) (*healthy*) sano(a); (*solid*) sólido(a); (*in good condition*) en buen estado; **he is of s. mind** tiene pleno uso de sus facultades mentales (**b**) (*argument, reasoning*) sólido(a); **a s. piece of advice** un consejo sensato; **it makes good s. sense** parece lo más razonable (**c**) (*reliable*) (*investment, business*) seguro(a), sólido(a); (*person*) competente

**2** *adv* **to be s. asleep** estar profundamente dormido(a)

▸**sound off** *vi Fam* despotricar (**about** de)

▸**sound out** *vt sep* sondear, tantear (**about** acerca de)

**sounding board** [ˈsaʊndɪŋbɔːd] *n* (*on pulpit, stage*) tornavoz *m*; *Fig* **I used John as a s.** puse a prueba mis ideas contándoselas a John

**soundings** [ˈsaʊndɪŋz] *npl Fig* **to take s.** tantear *or* sondear el terreno

**soundly** ['saʊndlɪ] *adv* (a) *(solidly)* sólidamente (b) *(logically)* razonablemente (c) *(thoroughly)* **to sleep s.** dormir profundamente; **to thrash sb s.** dar a alguien una buena paliza

**soundproof** ['saʊndpruːf] **1** *adj* insonorizado(a)
**2** *vt* insonorizar

**soundtrack** ['saʊndtræk] *n* banda *f* sonora

**soup** [suːp] *n* sopa *f*; *Fam* **Fig to be in the s.** estar en un aprieto; **s. kitchen** comedor *m* popular; **s. ladle** cucharón *m*; **s. plate** plato *m* hondo *or* sopero; **s. spoon** cuchara *f* sopera

▸**soup up** *vt sep Fam (engine)* trucar

**sour** ['saʊə(r)] **1** *adj (fruit, wine)* ácido(a), agrio(a); *(milk)* agrio(a), cortado(a); *Fig (person)* agrio(a), áspero(a); **to turn s.** *(of milk)* cortarse, agriarse; *Fig (of situation, relationship)* agriarse, echarse a perder; **s. cream** nata *f* agria; *Fig* **it's (a case of) s. grapes** es cuestión de despecho
**2** *vt (milk)* cortar, agriar; *Fig (atmosphere, relationship)* agriar, echar a perder
**3** *vi (of milk)* cortarse, agriarse; *Fig (of atmosphere, relationship)* agriarse, echarse a perder

**source** [sɔːs] *n (of river)* nacimiento *m*; *(of light, information)* fuente *f*; *(of infection, discontent)* foco *m*

**sourly** ['saʊəlɪ] *adv* con acritud, agriamente

**souse** [saʊs] *vt* empapar

**south** [saʊθ] **1** *n* sur *m*; **to the s. (of)** al sur (de)
**2** *adj (direction, side)* (del) sur; **s. wind** viento *m* del sur; **S. Africa** Sudáfrica; **S. African** sudafricano(a) *m,f*; **S. America** Sudamérica, América del Sur; **S. American** sudamericano(a) *m,f*; **S. Carolina** Carolina del Sur; **the S. China Sea** el mar de China (meridional); **S. Dakota** Dakota del Sur; **S. Korea** Corea del Sur; **S. Korean** surcoreano(a) *m,f*; **the S. Pole** el Polo Sur
**3** *adv* hacia el sur, en dirección sur; **to face s.** *(of house)* estar orientado(a) al sur

**southbound** ['saʊθbaʊnd] *adj (train, traffic)* en dirección sur; **the s. carriageway** la calzada en dirección sur

**southeast** [saʊθ'iːst] **1** *n* sudeste *m*, sureste *m*
**2** *adj (side)* sudeste; *(wind)* del sudeste
**3** *adv* al sudeste, en dirección sudeste

**southeasterly** [saʊθ'iːstəlɪ] **1** *n (wind)* viento *m* del sudeste
**2** *adj (direction)* sudeste; **s. wind** viento *m* del sudeste

**southeastern** [saʊθ'iːstən] *adj (region)* del sudeste

**southerly** ['sʌðəlɪ] **1** *n (wind)* viento *m* del sur
**2** *adj (direction)* sur; *(wind)* del sur; **the most s. point** el punto más meridional

**southern** ['sʌðən] *adj (region, accent)* del sur, meridional; **s. Spain** el sur de España, la España meridional; **the s. hemisphere** el hemisferio sur

**southerner** ['sʌðənə(r)] *n* sureño(a) *m,f*

**south-facing** ['saʊθˈfeɪsɪŋ] *adj* orientado(a) al sur

**south-southeast** [saʊθsaʊθ'iːst] *adv* con dirección sursudeste

**south-southwest** [saʊθsaʊθ'west] *adv* con dirección sursudoeste

**southward** ['saʊθwəd] *adj & adv* hacia el sur

**southwards** ['saʊθwədz] *adv* hacia el sur

**southwest** [saʊθ'west] **1** *n* sudoeste *m*, suroeste *m*
**2** *adj (side)* sudoeste; *(wind)* del sudoeste
**3** *adv* hacia el sudoeste, en dirección sudoeste

**southwesterly** [saʊθ'westəlɪ] **1** *n (wind)* (viento *m* del) sudoeste *m*
**2** *adj (direction)* sudoeste; *(wind)* del sudoeste
**3** *adv* hacia el sudoeste

**southwestern** [saʊθ'westən] *adj (region)* del sudoeste

**souvenir** [suːvə'nɪə(r)] *n* recuerdo *m*

**sovereign** ['sɒvrɪn] *n & adj* soberano(a) *m,f*

**sovereignty** ['sɒvrəntɪ] *n* soberanía *f*

**Soviet** ['səʊvɪet] **1** *n (person)* soviético(a) *m,f*
**2** *adj* soviético(a); *Formerly* **the S. Union** la Unión Soviética

**sow¹** [səʊ] ( *pt* **sowed** [səʊd], *pp* **sown** [səʊn] *or* **sowed**) *vt (seeds) & Fig* sembrar; **to s. a field with wheat** sembrar trigo en un campo

**sow²** [saʊ] *n (female pig)* cerda *f*, puerca *f*

**sown** [səʊn] *pp of* **sow¹**

**soya** ['sɔɪə] *n* soja *f*

**soy sauce** [sɔɪ'sɔːs] *n* (salsa *f* de) soja *f*

**sozzled** ['sɒzəld] *adj Fam (drunk)* mamado(a), bolinga; **to be s.** estar mamado(a) *or* bolinga; **to get s.** agarrarse una bolinga

**spa** [spɑː] *n* balneario *m*

**space** [speɪs] **1** *n* (a) *(room)* espacio *m*, sitio *m*; **to stare into s.** mirar al vacío; **to take up a lot of s.** ocupar mucho espacio *or* sitio
(b) *(individual place)* sitio *m*; *(on printed form)* espacio *m* (en blanco); **wide open spaces** grandes extensiones *fpl*; **a parking s.** un sitio para aparcar; **s. bar** *(on keyboard)* barra *f* espaciadora
(c) *(period of time)* espacio *m*, intervalo *m*; **in the s. of a year** en el espacio de un año
(d) *(outer space)* espacio *m*; **the s. age** la era espacial; *Fam* **he's a bit of a s. cadet** está un poco colgado, anda siempre como alucinado; **s. rocket** cohete *m* espacial; **s. shuttle** transbordador *m* espacial; **s. suit** traje *m* espacial; **s. travel** viajes *mpl* espaciales

**(e)** *(gap) (in timetable)* hueco *m*
**2** *vt* espaciar
▸**space out** *vt sep (arrange with gaps)* espaciar, separar; *very Fam Fig* **to be spaced out** estar atontado(a)

**space-age** ['speɪseɪdʒ] *adj* de la era espacial

**spacecraft** ['speɪskrɑːft] *n* nave *f* espacial, astronave *f*

**spaceman** ['speɪsmæn] *n* astronauta *m*

**spaceship** ['speɪsʃɪp] *n* nave *f* espacial

**spacing** ['speɪsɪŋ] *n* espacio *m*; *Typ* **double s.** doble espacio

**spacious** ['speɪʃəs] *adj* espacioso(a)

**spade** [speɪd] *n* **(a)** *(tool)* pala *f*; **to call a s. a s.** llamar a las cosas por su nombre, llamar al pan pan y al vino vino **(b)** *(in cards)* **spades** picas *fpl*

**spaghetti** [spə'getɪ] *n* espaguetis *mpl*

**Spain** [speɪn] *n* España

**span¹** [spæn] **1** *n* **(a)** *(of hand)* palmo *m*; *(of wing)* envergadura *f* **(b)** *(of arch)* luz *f*, vano *m*; *(of bridge)* arcada *f*, ojo *m* **(c)** *(of time)* período *m*, lapso *m* **(d)** *(of knowledge, interests)* repertorio *m*, gama *f*
**2** *vt (pt & pp **spanned**) (of bridge)* atravesar, cruzar; *Fig (of life, knowledge)* abarcar

**span²** *pt of* **spin**

**Spanglish** ['spæŋglɪʃ] *n* spanglish *m*

**Spaniard** ['spænɪəd] *n* español(ola) *m,f*

**spaniel** ['spænjəl] *n* spaniel *m*

**Spanish** ['spænɪʃ] **1** *npl (people)* **the S.** los españoles
**2** *n (language)* español *m*, castellano *m*; **S. class/teacher** clase *f*/profesor(ora) *m,f* de español
**3** *adj* español(ola); **the S. Armada** la Armada Invencible; **the S. Civil War** la guerra civil española; **the S. Inquisition** la (Santa) Inquisición; **S. omelette** tortilla *f* española *or* de patatas

**spank** [spæŋk] **1** *n* **to give sb a s.** darle un azote a alguien
**2** *vt* dar unos azotes a, azotar

**spanking** ['spæŋkɪŋ] **1** *n* azotaina *f*, zurra *f*; **to give sb a s.** dar a alguien una azotaina
**2** *adv Fam* **s. new** flamante; **they had a s. good time** se lo pasaron bomba *or* en grande

**spanner** ['spænə(r)] *n Br* llave *f* plana *(herramienta)*; *Fig* **to throw a s. in the works** aguar la fiesta

**spar¹** [spɑː(r)] *n (on ship)* palo *m*, verga *f*

**spar²** *(pt & pp **sparred**) vi* **to s. with sb** *(in boxing)* entrenar con alguien como sparring; *(argue)* discutir en tono cordial con alguien

**spare** ['speə(r)] **1** *n (spare part)* (pieza *f* de) recambio *m or* repuesto *m*; *(tyre)* rueda *f* de repuesto
**2** *adj* **(a)** *(available)* de más; *(surplus)* sobrante; **do you have a s. pen?** ¿tienes un bolígrafo de

sobra?; **to be going s.** sobrar; **a s. moment** un rato libre; **s. parts** recambios *mpl*, piezas *fpl* de recambio; **s. ribs** costillas *fpl* de cerdo; **s. room** habitación *f* de invitados; **s. time** tiempo *m* libre; **s. tyre** rueda *f* de repuesto; *Br Fam Fig (around waist)* michelines *mpl*; **s. wheel** rueda *f* de repuesto
**(b)** *(frugal) (meal, style, room)* sobrio(a), sencillo(a)
**(c)** *Br Fam (angry)* **to go s.** subirse por las paredes
**3** *vt* **(a)** *(go without)* **to have no time to s.** no tener ni un minuto libre, no poder entretenerse; **they arrived with five minutes to s.** llegaron cinco minutos antes; **can you s. the time?** ¿tienes tiempo?; **can you s. me a few moments?** ¿tienes un rato?, ¿me puedes dedicar unos minutos?; **could you s. me some milk?** ¿puedes dejarme un poco de leche?; **to s. a thought for sb** acordarse de alguien
**(b)** *(in negative constructions)* **to s. no expense/effort** no reparar en gastos/esfuerzos
**(c)** *(save)* **to s. sb the trouble of doing sth** ahorrar a alguien las molestias de hacer algo; **s. me the details!** ¡ahórrame los detalles!
**(d)** *(show mercy towards)* apiadarse de; **to s. sb's life** perdonarle la vida a alguien; **to s. sb's feelings** ahorrar sufrimientos a alguien

**sparing** ['speərɪŋ] *adj* parco(a) **(with** en)

**sparingly** ['speərɪŋlɪ] *adv* con moderación, parcamente

**spark** [spɑːk] **1** *n (electrical, from fire)* chispa *f*; *Fig* **sparks flew** salían chispas; *Fig* **he hasn't a s. of imagination** no tiene ni gota *or* chispa de imaginación; *Aut* **s. plug** bujía *f*
**2** *vi* echar chispas
▸**spark off** *vt sep* desencadenar

**sparkle** ['spɑːkəl] **1** *n (of light, eyes, diamond)* destello *m*; *Fig (of person)* chispa *f*; *Fig* **the s. had gone out of their marriage** su matrimonio ya no tenía ninguna chispa
**2** *vi (of light, eyes, diamond)* destellar; *Fig (of person, conversation)* brillar, ser chispeante

**sparkler** ['spɑːklə(r)] *n (firework)* bengala *f*

**sparkling** ['spɑːklɪŋ] *adj (light, eyes, diamond)* centelleante, brillante; *Fig (conversation)* chispeante; **s. wine** vino *m* espumoso

**sparring partner** ['spɑːrɪŋ'pɑːtnə(r)] *n (in boxing)* sparring *m*; *Fig* contertulio(a) *m,f*

**sparrow** ['spærəʊ] *n* gorrión *m*

**sparse** [spɑːs] *adj (population)* disperso(a); *(information)* somero(a), escaso(a); *(hair)* ralo(a)

**sparsely** ['spɑːslɪ] *adv (populated)* poco, dispersamente; *(covered)* escasamente, someramente; **s. furnished** poco amueblado(a)

**Spartan** ['spɑːtən] *n & adj also Fig* espartano(a) *m,f*

**spasm** ['spæzəm] *n Med* espasmo *m*; *Fig (of coughing, jealousy)* acceso *m*; *Fig (of activity)* arranque *m*

**spasmodic** [spæz'mɒdɪk] *adj (irregular)* intermitente, con altibajos; *Med* espasmódico(a)

**spasmodically** [spæz'mɒdɪklɪ] *adv (irregularly)* intermitentemente

**spastic** ['spæstɪk] *n* (a) *Med* enfermo(a) *m,f* de parálisis cerebral (b) *very Fam (idiot)* subnormal *m,f*, inútil *mf*

**spat¹** [spæt] *n Fam (quarrel)* rifirrafe *m*, bronca *f*

**spat²** *pt & pp of* **spit²**

**spate** [speɪt] *n (of letters, crimes)* oleada *f*; **to be in full s.** *(of river)* estar *or* bajar muy crecido; *Fig (of speaker)* estar en plena arenga

**spatial** ['speɪʃəl] *adj* espacial

**spatter** ['spætə(r)] *vt* salpicar (**with** de)

**spatula** ['spætjʊlə] *n* espátula *f*

**spawn** [spɔːn] **1** *n (of frog, fish)* hueva *f*
  **2** *vt (give rise to)* generar
  **3** *vi (of fish)* desovar

**speak** [spiːk] (*pt* **spoke** [spəʊk], *pp* **spoken** ['spəʊkən]) **1** *vt* (a) *(utter)* pronunciar; **she always speaks her mind** siempre dice lo que piensa; **to s. the truth** decir la verdad
  (b) *(language)* hablar; **to s. Spanish** hablar español; **Spanish spoken** *(sign)* se habla español
  **2** *vi* (a) *(talk)* hablar; **to s. to sb (about)** hablar con alguien (de); **they're not speaking** *(to each other)* no se hablan; **I'll s. to him about it** hablaré con él al respecto; **I know her to s. to** la conozco lo bastante como para hablar con ella; **legally/morally speaking** (hablando) en términos legales/morales; **so to s.** por así decirlo; **who's speaking?** *(on phone)* ¿con quién hablo?; **Mr Curry? – yes, speaking** ¿el señor Curry? – sí, soy yo
  (b) *(give a speech)* dar una charla; **he spoke on the subject of…** el tema de su charla fue…
  ▸**speak for** *vt insep* **to s. for sb** *(on behalf of)* hablar en nombre de alguien; **s. for yourself!** ¡no pluralices!, ¡eso lo dices tú!; **the facts s. for themselves** los hechos hablan por sí solos *or* mismos
  ▸**speak out** *vi* hablar abiertamente (**against** en contra de)
  ▸**speak up** *vi* hablar más alto, levantar la voz; **to s. up for sb** hablar en favor de alguien

**speaker** ['spiːkə(r)] *n* (a) *(person) (in conversation, on radio)* interlocutor(ora) *m,f*; *(at meeting)* orador(ora) *m,f*; *(at conference)* conferenciante *mf*, orador(ora) *m,f*; *(of language)* hablante *mf*; **she's a good s.** es (una) buena oradora; *Parl* **the S.** el/la presidente(a) de la Cámara de los Comunes (b) *(loudspeaker)* altavoz *m*

**speaking** ['spiːkɪŋ] *adj (doll, robot)* parlante; **s. clock** información *f* horaria; *Th Cin* **a s. part** un papel con diálogo

**spear** ['spɪə(r)] **1** *n (for thrusting)* lanza *f*; *(for throwing)* jabalina *f*
  **2** *vt (food)* pinchar

**spearhead** ['spɪəhed] **1** *n also Fig* punta *f* de lanza
  **2** *vt (attack, campaign)* encabezar

**spearmint** ['spɪəmɪnt] *n (plant)* hierbabuena *f*; *(flavour)* menta *f*

**spec** [spek] *n Fam* **to do sth on s.** hacer algo por si acaso

**special** ['speʃəl] **1** *n (on menu)* plato *m* del día
  **2** *adj* especial; **it's nothing s.** no es nada del otro mundo; **what's so s. about the 19th of November?** ¿qué tiene de especial el 19 de noviembre?; **s. agent** agente *mf* especial; *Br* **S. Branch** servicio *m* de seguridad del Estado; **s. delivery** envío *m* urgente, ≃ postal exprés *m*; *Cin* **s. effects** efectos *mpl* especiales; **s. needs** necesidades *fpl* educativas especiales; **s. offer** oferta *f* especial; *Pol* **s. powers** competencias *fpl* extraordinarias

**specialist** ['speʃəlɪst] **1** *n* especialista *mf*; *Med* **heart s.** cardiólogo(a) *m,f*; *Med* **cancer s.** oncólogo(a) *m,f*
  **2** *adj (knowledge)* especializado(a); **s. subject** especialidad *f*

**speciality** [speʃɪ'ælɪtɪ] *n* especialidad *f*

**specialization** [speʃəlaɪ'zeɪʃən] *n* especialización *f*

**specialize** ['speʃəlaɪz] *vi* especializarse (**in** en)

**specially** ['speʃəlɪ] *adv (in particular)* especialmente; **they had a cake s. made** les hicieron un pastel para la ocasión

**specialty** ['speʃəltɪ] *n US* especialidad *f*

**species** ['spiːʃiːz] *(pl* **species**) *n* especie *f*

**specific** [spɪ'sɪfɪk] **1** *npl* **specifics** detalles *mpl*
  **2** *adj (case, task, sequence)* específico(a); *(command, instructions)* preciso(a), concreto(a); **to be s.,…** para ser más precisos,…; **to be s. about sth** ser claro(a) respecto a algo; **could you be more s.?** ¿podrías especificar *or* concretar más?; *Phys* **s. gravity** peso *m* específico

**specifically** [spɪ'sɪfɪkəlɪ] *adv* (a) *(expressly)* específicamente (b) *(precisely)* precisamente, concretamente

**specification** [spesɪfɪ'keɪʃən] *n* especificación *f*; **specifications** *(of machine)* especificaciones *fpl or* características *fpl* técnicas

**specify** ['spesɪfaɪ] *vt* especificar

**specimen** ['spesmɪn] *n (of mineral, handwriting, blood)* muestra *f*; *Fam* **he's an odd s.** es un bicho raro; **s. copy** ejemplar *m* de muestra

**specious** ['spi:ʃəs] *adj* engañoso(a), especioso(a)

**speck** [spek] *n (of dust, dirt)* mota *f; (of paint, ink)* gotita *f*

**speckled** ['spekəld] *adj* moteado(a)

**specs** [speks] *npl Fam (spectacles)* gafas *fpl;* **a pair of s.** unas gafas

**spectacle** ['spektəkəl] *n* **(a)** *(show, sight)* espectáculo *m;* **to make a s. of oneself** dar el espectáculo, dar el número **(b) spectacles** gafas *fpl;* **a pair of spectacles** unas gafas; **s. case** *(hard)* estuche *m* de gafas; *(soft)* funda *f* de gafas

**spectacular** [spek'tækjʊlə(r)] **1** *n Th* espectáculo *m* grandioso
**2** *adj* espectacular

**spectator** [spek'teɪtə(r)] *n* espectador(ora) *m,f;* **the spectators** el público, los espectadores; **s. sport** deporte *m* de masas

**spectre** ['spektə(r)] *n* espectro *m*

**spectrum** ['spektrəm] *(pl* **spectra** ['spektrə]) *n also Fig* espectro *m*

**speculate** ['spekjʊleɪt] *vi* especular **(about** sobre)

**speculation** [spekjʊ'leɪʃən] *n* especulación *f*

**speculative** ['spekjʊlətɪv] *adj* especulativo(a)

**speculator** ['spekjʊleɪtə(r)] *n Fin* especulador(ora) *m,f*

**sped** [sped] *pt & pp of* **speed**

**speech** [spi:tʃ] *n* **(a)** *(faculty)* habla *f;* **s. defect** *or* **impediment** defecto *m* del habla *or* de dicción; **s. therapist** logopeda *mf;* **s. therapy** logopedia *f* **(b)** *(language)* habla *f,* lenguaje *m* **(c)** *(of politician, at conference)* discurso *m; Th* parlamento *m;* **to give** *or* **make a s.** dar *or* pronunciar un discurso; *Br Sch* **s. day** ceremonia *f* de fin de curso **(d)** *Gram* **part of s.** categoría *f* gramatical; **direct/indirect s.** estilo *m* directo/indirecto

**speechless** ['spi:tʃlɪs] *adj* sin habla; **to be left s.** quedarse sin habla

**speechwriter** ['spi:tʃraɪtə(r)] *n* redactor(ora) *m,f* de discursos

**speed** [spi:d] **1** *n* **(a)** *(rate of movement)* velocidad *f; (quickness)* rapidez *f;* **the s. of light/of sound** la velocidad de la luz/del sonido; **at s.** a gran velocidad; **to gather** *or* **pick up s.** ganar *or* cobrar velocidad; **to lose s.** perder velocidad; *Fam* **s. cop** policía *mf* de tráfico (en carretera); **s. limit** límite *m* de velocidad; **s. trap** radar *m* (de control de velocidad)
**(b)** *(gear)* marcha *f,* velocidad *f;* **a five-s. gearbox** una caja de cambios de cinco marchas
**(c)** *very Fam (amphetamine)* anfetas *fpl,* speed *m*
**2** *vi* **(a)** *(pt & pp* **sped** [sped] *or* **speeded)** *(go fast)* avanzar rápidamente; *(hurry)* precipitarse
**(b)** *Aut (exceed speed limit)* sobrepasar el límite de velocidad; **I was caught speeding** me

pillaron conduciendo demasiado deprisa
**(c)** *very Fam (be under effect of amphetamines)* **to be speeding** estar *or* ir puesto(a) de speed
▸**speed off** *vi* salir disparado(a)
▸**speed up 1** *vt sep (process)* acelerar; *(person)* apresurar
**2** *vi (car)* acelerar; *(process)* acelerarse; *(person)* apresurarse

**speedboat** ['spi:dbəʊt] *n* motora *f,* planeadora *f*

**speedily** ['spi:dɪlɪ] *adv* rápidamente

**speeding** ['spi:dɪŋ] *n Aut* **I was stopped for s.** me pararon por exceso de velocidad

**speedometer** [spi:'dɒmɪtə(r)] *n Aut* velocímetro *m*

**speedway** ['spi:dweɪ] *n* carreras *fpl* de motos

**speedy** ['spi:dɪ] *adj* rápido(a); **to wish sb a s. recovery** desearle a alguien una pronta recuperación

**spell¹** [spel] *n* hechizo *m,* encantamiento *m;* **to cast a s. over sb** hechizar *or* encantar a alguien; *Fig* **to break the s.** romper la magia del momento; *Fig* **to be under a s.** estar hechizado(a); *Fig* **to be under sb's s.** estar cautivado(a) por alguien

**spell²** *n* **(a)** *(period)* período *m,* temporada *f;* **a cold s.** una ola de frío; **sunny spells** intervalos *mpl* soleados; **a good/bad s.** una buena/mala racha **(b)** *(turn)* turno *m;* **she offered to do a s. at the wheel** se ofreció para conducir un rato

**spell³** *(pt & pp* **spelt** [spelt] *or* **spelled) 1** *vt* **(a)** *(write correctly)* deletrear; **how do you s. it?** ¿cómo se escribe? **(b)** *(signify)* suponer; **to s. disaster** suponer un desastre
**2** *vi* escribir sin faltas; **he can't s.** tiene muchas faltas de ortografía
▸**spell out** *vt sep Fig (explain explicitly)* explicar claramente; **do I have to s. it out for you?** ¿cómo te lo tengo que decir?

**spellbound** ['spelbaʊnd] *adj* hechizado(a)

**spell-checker** ['speltʃekə(r)] *n Comptr* corrector *m* ortográfico

**speller** ['spelə(r)] *n US (book)* manual *m* de ortografía

**spelling** ['spelɪŋ] *n* ortografía *f;* **to be good/bad at s.** tener buena/mala ortografía; **s. mistake** falta *f* de ortografía

**spelt** [spelt] *pt & pp of* **spell³**

**spend** [spend] *(pt & pp* **spent** [spent]) *vt* **(a)** *(money)* gastar **(on** en) **(b)** *(time)* pasar; **to s. time on sth** dedicar tiempo a algo

**spender** ['spendə(r)] *n* **to be a high/low s.** gastar mucho/poco

**spending** ['spendɪŋ] *n* gasto *m;* **consumer s.** gasto *m or* consumo *m* privado; **public s.** gasto *m* público; **s. money** dinero *m* para gastos; **s. power** poder *m* adquisitivo; **to go on a s. spree** salir a gastar a lo loco

**spendthrift** ['spendθrɪft] *n* despilfarrador(ora) *m,f*, manirroto(a) *m,f*

**spent** [spent] **1** *adj (fuel, ammunition)* usado(a); **to be a s. force** ser una fuerza devaluada

**2** *pt & pp of* **spend**

**sperm** [spɜ:m] *n* esperma *m*, semen *m*; **s. bank** banco *m* de semen; **s. donor** donante *m* de semen; **s. whale** cachalote *m*

**spermicide** ['spɜ:mɪsaɪd] *n* espermicida *m*

**spew** [spju:] *vt & vi Fam (vomit)* devolver, vomitar

**sphere** [sfɪə(r)] *n also Fig* esfera *f*; **that's outside my s.** eso está fuera de mi ámbito; **s. of influence** ámbito *m* de influencia

**spherical** ['sferɪkəl] *adj* esférico(a)

**sphincter** ['sfɪŋktə(r)] *n Anat* esfínter *m*

**sphinx** [sfɪŋks] *n* esfinge *f*

**spice** [spaɪs] **1** *n (seasoning)* especia *f*; *Fig* chispa *f*; **s. rack** especiero *m*

**2** *vt (food)* sazonar, especiar

▸**spice up** *vt (make more exciting)* dar chispa a

**spick**[1] [spɪk] *adj* **s. and span** como los chorros del oro, impecable

**spick**[2] *n US very Fam* = término ofensivo para referirse a un latino

**spicy** ['spaɪsɪ] *adj (food) (seasoned with spices)* especiado(a), sazonado(a); *(hot)* picante; *Fig (story, gossip)* jugoso(a), picante

**spider** ['spaɪdə(r)] *n* araña *f*; **s.'s web** tela *f* de araña, telaraña *f*; **s. plant** cinta *f*

**spiel** [spi:l] *n Fam* rollo *m*

**spike** [spaɪk] **1** *n* pincho *m*; **spikes** *(running shoes)* zapatillas *fpl* de clavos

**2** *vt* **to s. sb's guns** *(spoil plans)* chafarle los planes a alguien; **to s. sb's drink** añadir licor a la bebida de alguien

**spiky** ['spaɪkɪ] *adj* espinoso(a); **s. hair** pelo *m* de punta

**spill** [spɪl] **1** *vt (pt & pp* **spilt** [spɪlt] *or* **spilled)** *(liquid, salt)* derramar; *Fig* **to s. the beans** descubrir el pastel

**2** *vi (of liquid)* derramarse

**3** *n* **to take a s.** *(fall)* tener una caída

▸**spill over** *vi (of liquid)* rebosar; *Fig (of conflict)* extenderse **(into** a)

**spillage** ['spɪlɪdʒ] *n* derrame *m*

**spilt** [spɪlt] *pt & pp of* **spill**

**spin** [spɪn] **1** *n (turning movement)* giro *m*; *(on ball)* efecto *m*; **to go into a s.** *(of car)* dar vueltas; *(of plane)* entrar en barrena; **to go for a s.** *(in car)* ir a dar una vuelta; **to put s. on a ball** dar efecto a una pelota; **s. doctor** asesor(ora) *m,f* político(a) *(para dar buena prensa a un partido o político)*

**2** *vt (pt* **span** [spæn], *pp* **spun** [spʌn]) **(a)** *(wool, cotton)* hilar **(b)** *(wheel, top)* (hacer) girar; **to s. a**

**coin** echar a cara o cruz **(c)** *(spin-dry)* centrifugar

**3** *vi (of wheel, spinning top, dancer)* dar vueltas, girar; **my head's spinning** me da vueltas la cabeza; **the room's spinning** todo me da vueltas

▸**spin out** *vt sep (speech, debate)* alargar; *(money)* estirar

**spinach** ['spɪnɪtʃ] *n* espinacas *fpl*

**spinal** ['spaɪnəl] *adj Anat* espinal; **s. column** columna *f* vertebral; **s. cord** médula *f* espinal; *Med* **s. injury** lesión *f* de columna

**spindle** ['spɪndəl] *n* huso *m*

**spindly** ['spɪndlɪ] *adj* larguirucho(a)

**spin-dry** ['spɪn'draɪ] *vt* centrifugar

**spin-dryer** ['spɪn'draɪə(r)] *n* centrifugadora *f*

**spine** [spaɪn] *n* **(a)** *(backbone)* columna *f* vertebral **(b)** *(of book)* lomo *m* **(c)** *(spike) (of plant, fish)* espina *f*

**spineless** ['spaɪnlɪs] *adj (weak)* pusilánime, débil

**spinney** ['spɪnɪ] *n (pl* **spinneys)** *n* bosquecillo *m*, boscaje *m*

**spinning top** ['spɪnɪŋ'tɒp] *n* peonza *f*

**spinning wheel** ['spɪnɪŋ'wi:l] *n* rueca *f*

**spinster** ['spɪnstə(r)] *n* solterona *f*

**spiny** ['spaɪnɪ] *adj* espinoso(a); **s. lobster** langosta *f*

**spiral** ['spaɪərəl] **1** *n* espiral *f*; **s. staircase** escalera *f* de caracol

**2** *vi (pt & pp* **spiralled,** *US* **spiraled)** *(of smoke)* ascender en espiral; *(of prices)* subir vertiginosamente

**spire** ['spaɪə(r)] *n (of church)* aguja *f*

**spirit** ['spɪrɪt] *n* **(a)** *(ghost, person)* espíritu *m*; **the Holy S.** el Espíritu Santo

**(b)** *(mood, attitude)* espíritu *m*; **that was not the s. of the agreement** ese no era el espíritu del acuerdo; **she entered into the s. of the occasion** se puso a tono con la ocasión, participó del acontecimiento; *Fam* **that's the s.!** ¡eso es!

**(c)** *(courage)* valor *m*, coraje *m*; *(energy)* brío *m*; **to show s.** mostrar valor *or* coraje; **to break sb's s.** desmoralizar a alguien; **to be in good/poor spirits** tener la moral alta/baja; **to say sth with s.** decir algo con arrestos

**(d)** **spirits** *(drinks)* licores *mpl*; **s. lamp** lámpara *f* de alcohol; **s. level** *(instrument)* nivel *m* de burbuja

▸**spirit away, spirit off** *vt sep* hacer desaparecer

**spirited** ['spɪrɪtɪd] *adj (person)* valeroso(a), con arrestos; *(defence, reply)* enérgico(a)

**spiritual** ['spɪrɪtjʊəl] **1** *n Mus* **(negro) s.** espiritual *m* negro

**2** adj Rel espiritual; **France is my s. home** Francia es mi patria espiritual

**spiritualism** ['spɪrɪtjʊəlɪzəm] n espiritismo m

**spirituality** [spɪrɪtjʊˈælɪtɪ] n espiritualidad f

**spit**[1] [spɪt] n (**a**) (for cooking) espetón m, asador m (**b**) (of land) lengua f

**spit**[2] **1** n (saliva) saliva f; Fam **s. and polish** limpieza f, pulcritud f

**2** (pt & pp **spat** [spæt], US **spit**) vt escupir

**3** vi (of person, cat) escupir; (of hot fat) saltar; **it's spitting (with rain)** está chispeando

▸**spit out** vt sep escupir; Fam **s. it out!** (say what you want to) ¡suéltalo!

**spite** [spaɪt] **1** n (**a**) (malice) rencor m; **out of s.** por rencor (**b**) **in s. of...** a pesar de...

**2** vt fastidiar

**spiteful** ['spaɪtfʊl] adj rencoroso(a)

**spitting image** ['spɪtɪŋ'ɪmɪdʒ] n Fam **he's the s. of his father** es el vivo retrato de su padre

**spittle** ['spɪtəl] n saliva f, baba f

**spiv** [spɪv] n Br very Fam (flashy person) **he's a s.** tiene pinta de gánster

**splash** [splæʃ] **1** n (**a**) (of liquid) salpicadura f; **there was a loud s.** se oyó un fuerte ruido de algo cayendo al agua; **to fall into the water with a s.** caer al agua salpicando; Fam Fig **to make a s.** causar sensación (**b**) (of colour) mancha f

**2** vt salpicar; **a photo was splashed across the front page** publicaron una gran foto en la portada

**3** vi (of water, waves) salpicar; (of children) chapotear

▸**splash down** vi (of spacecraft) amerizar

**splatter** ['splætə(r)] **1** n salpicadura f

**2** vt **to s. sb with mud** salpicar a alguien de barro

**splay** [spleɪ] vt extender

**spleen** [spliːn] n (**a**) Anat bazo m (**b**) Formal (anger) rabia f, ira f; **she vented her s. on him** descargó toda su rabia sobre él

**splendid** ['splendɪd] adj espléndido(a)

**splendour**, US **splendor** ['splendə(r)] n esplendor m

**splice** [splaɪs] vt (**a**) (rope, tape, film) empalmar (**b**) Fam **to get spliced** (marry) casarse

**splint** [splɪnt] n (for broken limb) tablilla f; **in splints** entablillado(a)

**splinter** ['splɪntə(r)] **1** n (of wood, bone) astilla f; (of glass) esquirla f; Pol **s. group** grupo m disidente

**2** vt astillar

**3** vi astillarse; Fig (of political party) escindirse

**split** [splɪt] **1** n (in wood) grieta f; (in group) escisión f; (in garment) raja f; **to do the splits** abrirse totalmente de piernas

**2** adj partido(a); **s. ends** (in hair) puntas fpl abiertas; **s. peas** guisantes m secos partidos; **s. personality** doble personalidad f; **s. screen** pantalla f partida; **in a s. second** en una fracción de segundo

**3** vt (pt & pp **split**) (wood, cloth) rajar; (amount of money, group) dividir; **to s. one's head open** hacerse una brecha en la cabeza; Fam **to s. one's sides laughing** troncharse de risa; Fig **to s. hairs** buscarle tres pies al gato; **to s. the vote** dividir el voto; **to s. the difference** dejarlo en la mitad

**4** vi (**a**) (of wood, cloth) rajarse; (of political party) escindirse; Fam **my head's splitting** me va a estallar la cabeza (**b**) very Fam (leave) abrirse, pirarse

▸**split up 1** vt sep (money, work) dividir; (couple, people fighting) separar

**2** vi (of couple) separarse

**split-second** ['splɪtsekənd] adj (decision) instantáneo(a); (timing) al milímetro

**splitting** ['splɪtɪŋ] adj (headache) atroz

**splodge** [splɒdʒ] n Fam (stain) manchurrón m

**splutter** ['splʌtə(r)] vi (of person) farfullar; (of engine, candle) chisporrotear

**spoil** [spɔɪl] **1** vt (pt & pp **spoilt** [spɔɪlt] or **spoiled**) (**a**) (ruin) estropear; **to s. sb's fun** aguarle la fiesta a alguien; **to s. sb's appetite** quitarle las ganas de comer a alguien; Pol **spoilt ballot** papeleta f (de voto) nula (**b**) (indulge) (person) mimar, consentir; **a spoilt child** un niño/una niña mimado(a); **to be spoilt for choice** tener mucho donde elegir

**2** vi (**a**) (of fruit, fish) estropearse (**b**) **to be spoiling for a fight** tener ganas de pelea

**spoils** [spɔɪlz] npl (of war, crime) botín m; **to claim one's share of the s.** reclamar una parte del botín

**spoilsport** ['spɔɪlspɔːt] n Fam aguafiestas mf inv

**spoilt** [spɔɪlt] pt & pp of **spoil**

**spoke**[1] [spəʊk] n (of wheel) radio m; Fig **to put a s. in sb's wheel** poner trabas a alguien

**spoke**[2] pt of **speak**

**spoken** ['spəʊkən] pp of **speak**

**spokesman** ['spəʊksmən] n portavoz m

**spokesperson** ['spəʊkspɜːsən] n portavoz mf

**spokeswoman** ['spəʊkswʊmən] n portavoz f

**sponge** [spʌndʒ] **1** n esponja f; Fig **to throw in the s.** tirar la toalla; **s. bag** bolsa f de aseo; **s. cake** bizcocho m; **s. pudding** budín m de bizcocho (al baño María)

**2** vt (**a**) (wash) limpiar (con una esponja) (**b**) Fam (scrounge) **to s. sth off** or **from sb** gorronearle algo a alguien

**3** vi Fam (scrounge) vivir de gorra

▶**sponge down** *vt sep (wash)* lavar *(con una esponja)*

▶**sponge off** *vt insep Fam (scrounge from)* vivir a costa de

**sponger** ['spʌndʒə(r)] *n Fam* gorrón(ona) *m,f*

**spongy** ['spʌndʒɪ] *adj* esponjoso(a)

**sponsor** ['spɒnsə(r)] **1** *n (of team, exhibition)* patrocinador(ora) *m,f*; *(of student, club member) (man)* padrino *m*; *(woman)* madrina *f*
  **2** *vt (team, exhibition)* patrocinar, financiar; *(student)* subvencionar; *(club member)* apadrinar; **sponsored walk** marcha *f* para recaudar fondos

**sponsorship** ['spɒnsəʃɪp] *n (of athlete, team, festival)* patrocinio *m*, financiación *f*; *(of candidate)* apoyo *m* **(of** a**);** **s. deal** *(of athlete, team)* contrato *m* con un patrocinador

**spontaneity** [spɒntə'neɪtɪ] *n* espontaneidad *f*

**spontaneous** [spɒn'teɪnɪəs] *adj* espontáneo(a)

**spoof** [spu:f] *n Fam* **(a)** *(parody)* parodia *f*, burla *f* **(b)** *(hoax)* broma *f*

**spook** [spu:k] *n Fam (ghost)* fantasma *m*

**spooky** ['spu:kɪ] *adj Fam* espeluznante, escalofriante

**spool** [spu:l] *n (of film, thread)* carrete *m*

**spoon** [spu:n] **1** *n* cuchara *f*; *(spoonful)* cucharada *f*
  **2** *vt* **to s. sauce onto sth** rociar salsa sobre algo con una cuchara; **he spooned the soup into the baby's mouth** dio la sopa al bebé con una cuchara

**spoon-feed** ['spu:nfi:d] *(pt & pp* **spoon-fed** ['spu:nfed]*) vt Fig* dar las cosas hechas *or* masticadas a

**spoonful** ['spu:nfʊl] *n* cucharada *f*

**sporadic** [spə'rædɪk] *adj* esporádico(a)

**spore** [spɔ:(r)] *n (of fungus)* espora *f*

**sporran** ['spɒrən] *n Scot* = taleguilla de piel que cuelga por delante de la falda en el traje típico escocés

**sport** [spɔ:t] **1** *n* **(a)** *(activity)* deporte *m*; **to be good at s.** ser buen/buena deportista **(b)** *Fam (person)* **to be a (good) s.** ser un/una tío(a) grande; **to be a bad s.** *(bad loser)* tener mal perder
  **2** *vt (wear)* lucir, llevar

**sporting** ['spɔ:tɪŋ] *adj (related to sport, fair)* deportivo(a); **to give sb a s. chance** dar una oportunidad seria a alguien

**sports** [spɔ:ts] *adj* **s. car** coche *m* deportivo; **s. centre** polideportivo *m*; *Sch* **s. day** día *m* dedicado a competiciones deportivas; **s. ground** campo *m* de deportes; *Br* **s. jacket** chaqueta *f* de sport; *Journ* **s. page** página *f* de deportes; **s. shop** tienda *f* de deportes

**sportsman** ['spɔ:tsmən] *n* deportista *m*

**sportsmanship** ['spɔ:tsmənʃɪp] *n* deportividad *f*

**sportsperson** ['spɔ:tspɜ:sən] *n* deportista *mf*

**sportswoman** ['spɔ:tswʊmən] *n* deportista *f*

**spot** [spɒt] **1** *n* **(a)** *(place)* lugar *m*, sitio *m*; *Fam* **to put sb on the s.** poner a alguien en un aprieto; *Fam* **to be in a (tight) s.** estar en un aprieto; **s. check** inspección *f* al azar; *Fin* **s. price** precio *m* al contado **(b)** *(stain)* mancha *f* **(c)** *(pimple)* grano *m* **(d)** *(on shirt, tie, leopard)* lunar *m* **(e)** *Br Fam (small amount) (of rain, wine)* gota *f*; **a s. of lunch** algo de comer; **a s. of bother** una problemilla **(f)** *Th (spotlight)* foco *m* **(g)** *TV Rad (in schedule)* espacio *m*
  **2** *vt (pt & pp* **spotted***)* **(a)** *(stain, mark)* salpicar **(b)** *(notice) (person, object, mistake)* localizar, ver; **to s. sb doing sth** ver a alguien hacer algo; **well spotted!** ¡buena observación!

**spotless** ['spɒtlɪs] *adj also Fig* inmaculado(a)

**spotlight** ['spɒtlaɪt] *n* foco *m*, reflector *m*; *Fig* **to be in the s.** estar en el candelero

**spot-on** ['spɒt'ɒn] *adj Fam* exacto(a), clavado(a)

**spotter plane** ['spɒtə'pleɪn] *n* avión *m* de reconocimiento

**spotty** ['spɒtɪ] *adj (pimply)* con acné

**spouse** [spaʊz] *n* cónyuge *mf*

**spout** [spaʊt] **1** *n* **(a)** *(of teapot, kettle)* pitorro *m*; *Fam Fig* **to be up the s.** *(of plans, finances)* haberse ido al garete **(b)** *(jet of liquid)* chorro *m*
  **2** *vt (liquid)* chorrear; *Fam Fig (speech, nonsense)* soltar
  **3** *vi (of liquid)* chorrear; *Fam Fig (of person)* largar, enrollarse

**sprain** [spreɪn] **1** *n (injury)* torcedura *f*, esguince *m*
  **2** *vt* **to s. one's ankle/wrist** torcerse el tobillo/la muñeca

**sprang** [spræŋ] *pt of* **spring**

**sprat** [spræt] *n (fish)* espadín *m*

**sprawl** [sprɔ:l] *vi (of person)* despatarrarse; *(of town)* extenderse

**sprawling** ['sprɔ:lɪŋ] *adj (person)* despatarrado(a); *(town)* desperdigado(a)

**spray¹** [spreɪ] *n (of flowers)* ramo *m*

**spray²** [spreɪ] **1** *n* **(a)** *(liquid)* rociada *f*; *(from sea)* rocío *m* del mar, roción *m* **(b)** *(act of spraying)* rociada *f*; **to give sth a s.** *(flowers, crops)* rociar algo; *(room)* rociar algo con ambientador **(c)** *(device)* aerosol *m*, spray *m*; *(for perfume)* atomizador *m*; **s. can** aerosol, spray; **s. gun** *(for paint)* pistola *f* (pulverizadora)
  **2** *vt (liquid, room, crops)* rociar

**spray-paint** ['spreɪ'peɪnt] **1** *n* pintura *f* en aerosol

**2** *vt (with spray can)* pintar con aerosol; *(with spray gun)* pintar a pistola

**spread** [spred] **1** *n* (a) *(of wings, sails)* envergadura *f*
(b) *(of products, ages)* gama *f*
(c) *(of doctrine)* difusión *f*; *(of disease)* propagación *f*
(d) *Fam (big meal)* banquete *m*, comilona *f*
(e) *(in newspaper)* **a full-page s.** una plana entera; **a two-page s.** una página doble
(f) *(paste)* **cheese s.** queso *m* para untar; **chocolate s.** crema *f* de cacao

**2** *vt (pt & pp spread)* (a) *(extend)* **to s. one's arms/legs** extender los brazos/las piernas; *Fig* **to s. one's wings** emprender el vuelo
(b) *(distribute)* (sand, straw) extender, esparcir; *(terror)* sembrar; *(disease)* propagar; *(news, lies)* difundir; **to s. work/payments over several months** distribuir el trabajo/los pagos a lo largo de varios meses
(c) *(apply)* (butter, ointment) untar; **to s. a surface with sth** untar algo en una superficie

**3** *vi (of forest)* extenderse; *(of news)* difundirse; *(of disease)* propagarse

▶**spread out 1** *vt sep (map, newspaper)* desplegar, extender
**2** *vi (of person) (on floor, bed)* estirarse; *(of search party)* desplegarse

**spreadsheet** ['spredʃi:t] *n Comptr* hoja *f* de cálculo

**spree** [spri:] *n Fam* **to go on a s.** *(go drinking)* ir de juerga; **to go on a shopping/spending s.** salir a comprar/gastar a lo loco

**sprig** [sprɪg] *n* ramita *f*

**sprightly** ['spraɪtlɪ] *adj* vivaz, vivaracho(a)

**spring** [sprɪŋ] **1** *n* (a) *(of water)* manantial *m*
(b) *(season)* primavera *f*; **in (the) s.** en primavera; **s. onion** cebolleta *f*; **s. roll** rollo *m* or rollito *m* de primavera; **s. tide** marea *f* viva *(de primavera)* (c) *(leap)* brinco *m*, salto *m* (d) *(elasticity)* elasticidad *f*; **he walked with a s. in his step** caminaba con paso alegre (e) *(device) (in watch)* resorte *m*; *(in car)* ballesta *f*; *(in mattress)* muelle *m*

**2** *vt (pt sprang* [spræŋ], *pp sprung* [sprʌŋ]) (a) *(reveal unexpectedly)* **to spring sth on sb** soltarle algo a alguien (b) *(develop)* **to s. a leak** *(container)* empezar a tener una fuga; *(boat)* empezar a hacer agua (c) *Fam* **to s. sb out of jail** ayudar a alguien a escapar de la cárcel

**3** *vi* (a) *(jump)* brincar, saltar; **to s. to one's feet** levantarse de un brinco; **to s. into action** entrar en acción; **to s. to sb's defence** lanzarse a la defensa de alguien; **the lid sprang open** la tapa se abrió de pronto; **to s. to mind** venir(se) a la cabeza (b) *(originate, come into being)* **to s. from** provenir de, proceder de; **to s. into existence** aparecer de pronto; *Fam*

**where did you s. from?** ¿de dónde has salido?

▶**spring up** *vi* (a) *(jump to one's feet)* levantarse de un brinco (b) *(appear suddenly)* brotar, surgir *(de la noche a la mañana)*

**springboard** ['sprɪŋbɔ:d] *n also Fig* trampolín *m*

**spring-clean** [sprɪŋ'kli:n] **1** *n* limpieza *f* a fondo
**2** *vt (house)* limpiar a fondo

**spring-cleaning** [sprɪŋ'kli:nɪŋ] *n* limpieza *f* a fondo; **to do the s.** hacer una limpieza a fondo

**springtime** ['sprɪŋtaɪm] *n* primavera *f*

**springy** ['sprɪŋɪ] *adj (material)* elástico(a); *(ground, mattress)* mullido(a)

**sprinkle** ['sprɪŋkəl] *vt (with liquid)* rociar **(with** con); *(with salt, flour)* espolvorear **(with** con)

**sprinkler** ['sprɪŋklə(r)] *n (for lawns)* aspersor *m*; *(as fire prevention)* rociador *m* antiincendios

**sprinkling** ['sprɪŋklɪŋ] *n* pizca *f*, poco *m*; **there was a s. of new faces** había unas cuantas caras nuevas

**sprint** [sprɪnt] **1** *n (fast run)* carrera *f*; *(running race)* carrera *f* de velocidad
**2** *vi (run fast)* correr a toda velocidad

**sprinter** ['sprɪntə(r)] *n* velocista *mf*, esprínter *mf*

**sprocket** ['sprɒkɪt] *n* diente *m* (de engranaje); **s. (wheel)** rueda *f* dentada

**sprout** [spraʊt] **1** *n (of plant)* brote *m*; **(Brussels) sprouts** coles *fpl* de Bruselas
**2** *vt Fam* **to s. a moustache/a beard** dejarse crecer el bigote/la barba; **he's starting to s. a beard** *(for first time)* le está saliendo barba
**3** *vi (of leaves, hair)* brotar

▶**sprout up** *vi (of plant, child)* crecer rápidamente; *(of new buildings, towns)* surgir *(de la noche a la mañana)*

**spruce¹** [spru:s] *n (tree)* picea *f*

**spruce²** *adj (tidy)* pulcro(a); *(smart)* elegante

▶**spruce up** *vt sep (room)* adecentar; **to s. oneself up** arreglarse, acicalarse

**sprung** [sprʌŋ] **1** *adj* de muelles
**2** *pp of* **spring**

**spry** [spraɪ] *adj* vivaz, vivaracho(a)

**spud** [spʌd] *n Fam (potato)* papa *f*, patata *f*

**spun** [spʌn] **1** *adj* **s. silk** hilado *m* de seda
**2** *pp of* **spin**

**spunk** [spʌŋk] *n* (a) *Fam (courage)* agallas *fpl*, arrestos *mpl* (b) *Vulg (semen)* lefa *f*, lechada *f*

**spur** [spɜ:(r)] **1** *n* (a) *(for riding)* espuela *f*; *Fig (stimulus)* acicate *m*, incentivo *m*; *Fig* **he won his spurs** demostró su valía; **on the s. of the moment** sin pararse a pensar (b) *(of land, rock)* estribación *f*
**2** *vt (pt & pp spurred)* *(horse)* espolear; *Fig* **to**

**s. sb on (to do sth)** espolear a alguien (para que haga algo); *Fig* **to s. sb into action** hacer que alguien pase a la acción

**spurious** ['spjʊərɪəs] *adj* falso(a), espurio(a)

**spurn** [spɜːn] *vt* desdeñar

**spurt** [spɜːt] **1** *n (of liquid)* chorro *m; (of action, energy)* arranque *m; (of speed)* arrancada *f;* **to put on a s.** acelerar

**2** *vt* lanzar chorros de

**3** *vi (of liquid)* chorrear

**sputter** ['spʌtə(r)] *vi (fire, flame, candle)* crepitar

**spy** [spaɪ] **1** *n* espía *mf;* **s. plane** avión *m* espía *or* de espionaje; **s. ring** red *f* de espionaje; **s. satellite** satélite *m* espía *or* de espionaje

**2** *vt (notice)* ver; **she had spied a flaw in his reasoning** había captado un error en su razonamiento

**3** *vi* espiar; **to s. on sb** espiar a alguien

▸**spy out** *vt sep* **to s. out the land** reconocer el terreno

**Sq** *(abbr* **Square)** Pl., Plaza *f*

**sq** *Math (abbr* **square)** cuadrado(a)

**sq. ft.** *(abbr* **square foot** *or* **feet)** pie(s) *m(pl)* cuadrado(s)

**squabble** ['skwɒbəl] **1** *n* riña *f,* pelea *f*

**2** *vi* reñir, pelear

**squabbling** ['skwɒblɪŋ] *n* riñas *fpl,* peleas *fpl*

**squad** [skwɒd] *n (a) (of workmen)* brigada *f,* cuadrilla *f (b) (of athletes, footballers) (for national team)* lista *f* de convocados; **the first-team s.** el primer equipo **(c)** *(of soldiers)* escuadra *f; (of police force)* brigada *f;* **s. car** coche *m* patrulla

**squadron** ['skwɒdrən] *n Mil (of planes)* escuadrón *m; (of ships)* escuadra *f*

**squalid** ['skwɒlɪd] *adj (dirty)* mugriento(a), inmundo(a); *(sordid)* sórdido(a)

**squall** [skwɔːl] **1** *n (of wind)* turbión *m,* ventarrón *m*

**2** *vi (cry)* berrear

**squalor** ['skwɒlə(r)] *n (dirtiness)* inmundicia *f; (poverty)* miseria *f*

**squander** ['skwɒndə(r)] *vt (money, time, talents)* despilfarrar, malgastar; *(opportunity)* desperdiciar

**square** [skweə(r)] **1** *n (a) (shape)* cuadrado *m; (on chessboard)* casilla *f; (on map)* recuadro *m; Fig* **to be back at s. one** haber vuelto al punto de partida **(b)** *Math* cuadrado *m* **(c)** *(of town, village)* plaza *f; (smaller)* plazoleta *f* **(d)** *Old-fashioned Fam (unfashionable)* carca *mf*

**2** *adj (a) (in shape)* cuadrado(a) **(b)** *(right-angled)* **s. corner** esquina *f* en ángulo recto **(c)** *Math (metre, centimetre)* cuadrado(a); **s. root** raíz *f* cuadrada **(d)** *Old-fashioned Fam (unfashionable)* carca **(e)** *(idioms)* **to be s. with sb** *(honest)* ser claro(a) con alguien; **that's us s.** *(having settled debt)* estamos en paz; **she felt like a s. peg in**

**a round hole** se sentía fuera de lugar; **a s. deal** un trato justo; **a s. meal** una buena comida

**3** *adv* directamente; **she hit him s. on the jaw** le dio de lleno en la mandíbula

**4** *vt (a) (make square)* cuadrar; *Math (number)* elevar al cuadrado; **squared paper** papel *m* cuadriculado **(b)** *(settle)* **to s. accounts with sb** arreglar cuentas con alguien; **how do you s. it with your convictions?** ¿cómo lo haces encajar con tus convicciones?

**5** *vi (agree)* cuadrar, concordar

▸**square up** *vi (a) (settle debts)* hacer *or* saldar cuentas **(b)** *(of fighters)* ponerse en guardia; *Fig* **to s. up to a problem/an opponent** hacer frente a un problema/un adversario

**squarely** ['skweəlɪ] *adv (a) (directly)* directamente **(b)** *(honestly)* con franqueza

**squash**[1] [skwɒʃ] **1** *n (a) (crush)* apretones *mpl;* **it was a s., but everyone got into the car** nos tuvimos que apretar, pero entramos todos en el coche **(b)** *(drink)* **orange/lemon s.** *(bebida f a base de)* concentrado *m* de naranja/limón **(c)** *(sport)* squash *m;* **s. court** pista *f or* cancha *f* de squash

**2** *vt* aplastar

**3** *vi* **to s. into a room/a car** apretujarse en una habitación/un coche

**squash**[2] *n (vegetable)* US calabacera *f,* cucurbitácea *f*

▸**squash up** *vi* apretujarse, apretarse

**squat** [skwɒt] **1** *n (illegally occupied dwelling)* casa *f* ocupada *(ilegalmente)*

**2** *adj (person)* chaparro(a), achaparrado(a); *(object, building)* muy bajo(a)

**3** *vi (pt & pp* **squatted) (a)** *(crouch down)* agacharse, ponerse de cuclillas **(b)** *(occupy dwelling illegally)* ocupar una vivienda ilegalmente

**squatter** ['skwɒtə(r)] *n* ocupante *mf* ilegal

**squaw** [skwɔː] *n* mujer *f* india norteamericana

**squawk** [skwɔːk] **1** *n (of bird)* graznido *m*

**2** *vi (of bird)* graznar; *Fam (of person, baby)* chillar

**squeak** [skwiːk] **1** *n (of animal, person)* chillido *m; (of door, hinges)* chirrido *m; Fam* **I don't want to hear another s. out of you** no quiero oírte decir ni pío

**2** *vi (of animal, person)* chillar; *(of door, wheel)* chirriar, rechinar; *(of shoes)* crujir

**squeaky** ['skwiːkɪ] *adj (voice)* chillón(ona); *(door, wheel)* chirriante; *(shoes)* que crujen; **s. clean** *(person, image)* impoluto(a)

**squeal** [skwiːl] **1** *n* chillido *m*

**2** *vt* chillar

**3** *vi (a)* chillar; *Fam* **to s. about sth** *(complain)* quejarse de algo **(b)** *very Fam (inform)* **to s. (on sb)** dar el soplo (sobre alguien)

**squeamish** ['skwiːmɪʃ] *adj* aprensivo(a), escrupuloso(a); **to be s. about sth** ser (muy) aprensivo(a) con algo; **I'm very s. about blood** la sangre me da mucha aprensión

**squeeze** [skwiːz] *n* apretón *m*, apretujón *m*; **to give sb a s.** *(hug)* dar un achuchón a alguien; **a. s. of lemon** un chorrito de limón; *Fam* **we all got in but it was a tight s.** cupimos todos, pero tuvimos que apretujarnos bastante; *Fam* **to put the s. on sb** *(pressurize)* apretarle las tuercas a alguien

**2** *vt* (**a**) *(in general)* apretar; *(sponge)* estrujar; *(lemon)* exprimir; **to s. sb's hand** dar a alguien un apretón de manos; **to s. sth into a box** meter algo en una caja apretando; **I think we can just s. you in** creo que te podemos hacer un hueco (**b**) *Fig (put pressure on)* presionar

**3** *vi* **to s. into a place** meterse a duras penas en un sitio; **s. up a bit!** ¡apretaos *or* correos un poco más!

▸**squeeze out** *vt sep (juice)* exprimir

**squelch** [skweltʃ] *vi* chapotear; **to s. through the mud** atravesar el lodo chapoteando

**squib** [skwɪb] *n (firework)* petardo *m*; *Fig* **the party was a damp s.** la fiesta resultó decepcionante

**squid** [skwɪd] (*pl* **squid**) *n (animal)* calamar *m*; *(food)* calamares *mpl*

**squiggle** ['skwɪɡəl] *n* garabato *m*

**squint** [skwɪnt] **1** *n* (**a**) *(eye defect)* **to have a s.** tener estrabismo, ser estrábico(a) (**b**) *(quick look)* ojeada *f*, vistazo *m*; **to have a s. at sth** echar una ojeada a algo

**2** *vi* (**a**) *(have an eye defect)* tener estrabismo (**b**) *(narrow one's eyes)* entrecerrar *or* entornar los ojos; **to s. at sth/sb** *(look sideways)* mirar algo/a alguien de reojo

**squire** ['skwaɪə(r)] *n (landowner)* terrateniente *m*; *Hist* escudero *m*

**squirm** [skwɜːm] *vi (wriggle)* retorcerse; *(with embarrassment)* ruborizarse, avergonzarse

**squirrel** ['skwɪrəl] *n* ardilla *f*

**squirt** [skwɜːt] **1** *n* (**a**) *(of liquid)* chorro *m* (**b**) *Fam (insignificant person)* mequetrefe *mf*

**2** *vt (liquid)* lanzar un chorro de

**3** *vi (of liquid)* **to s. out** chorrear

**Sr** *(abbr* **Senior**) Thomas Smith, Sr Thomas Smith, padre

**Sri Lanka** [sriːˈlæŋkə] *n* Sri Lanka

**Sri Lankan** [sriːˈlæŋkən] *n & adj* esrilanqués(esa) *m,f*

**SSE** *(abbr* **south-southeast**) SSE, sursudeste

**SSW** *(abbr* **south-southwest**) SSO, sursudoeste

**St** (**a**) *(abbr* **Street**) c/, calle *f* (**b**) *(abbr* **Saint**) S., San *m*, Santa *f*; **St Kitts and Nevis** *(island group)* San Cristóbal y Nevis; **St Lucia** *(island)* Santa Lucía; **St Vincent and the**

**Grenadines** *(island group)* San Vicente y las Granadinas; **St Petersburg** San Petersburgo

**stab** [stæb] **1** *n (with knife)* cuchillada *f*, puñalada *f*; *Fig (of pain, envy)* punzada *f*; *Fam* **to have a s. at sth/doing sth** intentar algo/hacer algo

**2** *vt* (*pt & pp* **stabbed**) *(with knife)* acuchillar, apuñalar; *(food)* pinchar, ensartar; **to s. sb to death** matar a alguien a puñaladas; *Fig* **to s. sb in the back** darle a alguien una puñalada por la espalda

**stabbing** ['stæbɪŋ] **1** *n (attack)* apuñalamiento *m*

**2** *adj (pain)* punzante

**stability** [stəˈbɪlɪtɪ] *n* estabilidad *f*

**stabilize** ['steɪbɪlaɪz] **1** *vt* estabilizar

**2** *vi* estabilizarse

**stabilizer** ['steɪbɪlaɪzə(r)] *n (on bicycle)* estabilizador *m*, estabilizador *m (para bicicleta infantil)*

**stable¹** ['steɪbəl] **1** *n (for horses)* cuadra *f*, establo *m*; *Fig* **to lock the s. door after the horse has bolted** tomar medidas demasiado tarde

**2** *vt (keep in stable)* guardar en cuadra

**stable²** *adj (marriage, job)* estable; *(person)* equilibrado(a); *(object, structure, instrument)* fijo(a), seguro(a); *(medical condition)* estacionario(a)

**stack** [stæk] **1** *n* (**a**) *(of wood, plates)* pila *f*, montón *m*; *(of hay)* almiar *m*; *Fam* **stacks of time/money** un montón de tiempo/dinero (**b**) *(chimney)* chimenea *f*

**2** *vt (wood, plates)* apilar; **the odds were stacked against them** tenían todo en contra de ellos

**stadium** ['steɪdɪəm] *n* estadio *m*

**staff** [stɑːf] **1** *n* (**a**) *(stick)* bastón *m*; *(of shepherd)* cayado *m* (**b**) *(personnel)* personal *m*, plantilla *f*; **teaching/nursing s.** personal docente/de enfermería; *Mil* **general s.** estado *m* mayor; *Med* **s. nurse** enfermero(a) *m,f*; *Sch* **s. room** sala *f* de profesores (**c**) *Mus* (*pl* **staves** [steɪvz]) pentagrama *m*

**2** *vt* proveer de personal; **the office is staffed by volunteers** la oficina se nutre de personal voluntario; **the desk is staffed at all times** el mostrador está atendido en todo momento

**stag** [stæɡ] *n (animal)* ciervo *m*; **s. beetle** ciervo *m* volante; **s. night** *or* **party** despedida *f* de soltero

**stage** [steɪdʒ] **1** *n* (**a**) *(platform) (in theatre)* escenario *m*; *(more generally)* estrado *m*; **to go on the s.** hacerse actor *m*/actriz *f*; *Fig* **to set the s. for sth** preparar el terreno para algo; **s. directions** acotaciones *fpl*; **s. door** entrada *f* de artistas; **s. fright** miedo *m* escénico; **s. manager** director(ora) *m,f* de escena, regidor(ora) *m,f*; **s. name** nombre *m* artístico; **s. whisper** aparte *m*

(**b**) *(phase)* etapa *f*, fase *f*; **at this s. in...** en esta fase de…; **to do sth in stages** hacer algo por etapas; **s. (coach)** diligencia *f*

**2** *vt (play)* llevar a escena, representar; *Fig (demonstration, invasion)* llevar a cabo

**stagehand** ['steɪdʒhænd] *n Th* tramoyista *mf*, sacasillas *mf inv*

**stage-manage** ['steɪdʒ'mænɪdʒ] *vt Th* dirigir; *Fig (event, demonstration)* orquestar

**stage-struck** ['steɪdʒstrʌk] *adj Th* **to be s.** estar enamorado(a) de las tablas

**stagflation** [stæg'fleɪʃən] *n Econ* estanflación *f*

**stagger** ['stægə(r)] **1** *vt* (a) *(astound)* dejar anonadado(a) (b) *(work, holidays)* escalonar

**2** *vi (stumble)* tambalearse; **to s. along** ir tambaleándose; **to s. to one's feet** levantarse tambaleándose

**stagnant** ['stægnənt] *adj* estancado(a)

**stagnate** [stæg'neɪt] *vi* estancarse

**stagnation** [stæg'neɪʃən] *n* estancamiento *m*

**staid** [steɪd] *adj* formal, estirado(a)

**stain** [steɪn] **1** *n (mark)* mancha *f*; *(dye)* tinte *m*; **s. remover** quitamanchas *m inv*

**2** *vt (mark)* manchar; *(dye)* teñir

**stained-glass** ['steɪndɡlɑːs] *n* vidrio *m* de colores; **s. window** vidriera *f*

**stainless steel** ['steɪnlɪs'stiːl] *n* acero *m* inoxidable

**stair** ['steə(r)] *n (single step)* escalón *m*, peldaño *m*; **stair('s)** escalera(s) *f(pl)*

**staircase** ['steəkeɪs] *n* escalera *f*

**stake** [steɪk] **1** *n* (a) *(piece of wood, metal)* estaca *f*; *(for plant)* guía *f*, rodrigón *m*; **to be burned at the s.** morir quemado(a) en la hoguera (b) *(bet)* apuesta *f*; **to be at s.** estar en juego (c) *(share)* **to have a s. in sth** *(interest)* tener intereses en algo; *(shareholding)* tener una participación (accionaria) en algo

**2** *vt* (a) *(bet) (money)* apostar **(on** a); *Fig (one's reputation, job)* jugarse **(on** en); **I'd s. my life on it** pondría la mano en el fuego por ello (b) **to s. a claim (to sth)** reivindicar el derecho (a algo)

**stakeout** ['steɪkaʊt] *n* **to be on s.** montar vigilancia

**stalactite** ['stæləktaɪt] *n* estalactita *f*

**stalagmite** ['stæləɡmaɪt] *n* estalagmita *f*

**stale** [steɪl] *adj* (a) *(bread)* revenido(a), pasado(a); *(air)* viciado(a); *(smell)* rancio(a) (b) *Fig (ideas, jokes)* manido(a); *(social life, relationship)* anquilosado(a); **to get s.** *(person)* anquilosarse

**stalemate** ['steɪlmeɪt] *n (in chess, negotiations)* tablas *fpl*; **to reach a s.** llegar a un punto muerto

**stalk¹** [stɔːk] **1** *vt (track)* seguir con sigilo; *(obsessively)* acechar

**2** *vi (walk angrily)* **she stalked out of the room** salió enfadada de la habitación

**stalk²** *n (of plant, flower)* tallo *m*; *(of fruit)* rabo *m*

**stalker** ['stɔːkə(r)] *n* = persona que sigue o vigila obsesivamente a otra

**stall** [stɔːl] **1** *n* (a) *(in stable)* casilla *f* (b) *(in market)* puesto *m* (c) *Th* **the stalls** el patio de butacas

**2** *vt (hold off)* retener

**3** *vi* (a) *(of car)* calarse, pararse; *Fig (of campaign)* estancarse, quedarse estancado(a) (b) *(delay)* demorarse; **to s. (for time)** *(intentar)* ganar tiempo

**stallion** ['stæljən] *n (caballo m)* semental *m*

**stalwart** ['stɔːlwət] **1** *n* incondicional *mf*

**2** *adj* enérgico(a)

**stamen** ['steɪmən] *n Bot* estambre *m*

**stamina** ['stæmɪnə] *n* resistencia *f*, aguante *m*

**stammer** ['stæmə(r)] **1** *n* tartamudeo *m*

**2** *vt* balbucir

**3** *vi* tartamudear

▸**stammer out** *vt insep* balbucir, farfullar

**stamp** [stæmp] **1** *n (on letter, mark)* sello *m*, *Am* estampilla *f*, *Méx* timbre *m*; *(device)* tampón *m*; *(on legal documents)* póliza *f*, timbre *m*; *Fig* **to bear the s. of genius** tener el sello *o* la marca inconfundible del genio; *Fig* **s. of approval** aprobación *f*, beneplácito *m*; **s. album** álbum *m* de sellos; **s. collector** coleccionista *mf* de sellos; *Fin* **s. duty** póliza *f* del Estado; **s. machine** máquina *f* expendedora de sellos

**2** *vt* (a) *(put mark on)* estampar; **a stamped addressed envelope** un sobre franqueado y con el domicilio (b) **to s. one's foot** patear

**3** *vi* **to s. upstairs** subir ruidosamente las escaleras; **he stamped off in a rage** se marchó enfadado

▸**stamp out** *vt sep (resistance, dissent)* acabar *or* terminar con

**stampede** [stæm'piːd] **1** *n* estampida *f*, desbandada *f*; **there was a s. for the door** hubo una desbandada hacia la puerta

**2** *vt* lanzar en estampida

**3** *vi* salir de estampida

**stance** [stæns] *n (physical position, view)* postura *f*

**stand** [stænd] **1** *n* (a) *(view)* postura *f*; **to take a s.** adoptar una postura

(b) *(of lamp)* soporte *m*; *(for books, postcards)* expositor *m*

(c) *(stall) (in open air)* puesto *m*, tenderete *m*; *(at exhibition)* stand *m*, puesto *m*; **newspaper s.** quiosco *m* (de periódicos)

(d) *(grandstand)* gradas *fpl*, graderío *m*

(e) *(taxi rank)* parada *f* de taxis

**2** *vt (pt & pp stood* [stʊd]*)* (a) *(place)* colocar; **he stood the ladder against the wall** apoyó la escalera contra la pared

(b) (*endure*) soportar; **he can't s. her** no la soporto; **to s. comparison with** poder compararse con; **to s. one's ground** mantenerse firme

(c) (*pay for*) **to s. sb a drink** invitar a alguien a una copa

(d) (*have*) **to s. a chance (of doing sth)** tener posibilidades (de hacer algo); **he doesn't s. a chance!** ¡no tiene ninguna posibilidad!

(e) *Law* **to s. trial** ser procesado(a)

**3** *vi* (a) (*of person*) (*get up*) ponerse de pie, levantarse; (*be upright*) estar de pie; (*remain upright*) quedarse de pie; **to s. on one's head** hacer el pino; **I could hardly s.** casi no me tenía en pie; **don't just s. there!** ¡no te quedes ahí parado(a)!; **to s. fast** *or* **firm** mantenerse firme; **to s. still** (*of person*) quedarse quieto(a); (*of time*) detenerse

(b) (*of building*) estar situado(a) *or* ubicado(a); (*of object*) estar colocado(a)

(c) (*be in situation*) **the debt/inflation stands at...** la deuda/la inflación asciende *or* se sitúa en...; **to s. in need of...** tener necesidad de...; **you s. in danger of getting killed** corres el peligro de que te maten; **you s. to lose/gain £5,000** puedes perder/ganar 5.000 libras; **it stands to reason that...** se cae por su propio peso que...

(d) (*remain motionless*) (*of liquid*) reposar

(e) (*idioms*) **we're standing right behind you** estamos de tu lado; **to s. on one's own two feet** ser autosuficiente; **I don't know where I s.** no sé a qué atenerme; **to know how things s.** saber cómo están las cosas; **I s. corrected** corrijo lo dicho; **to s. (as candidate) for Parliament** presentarse (como candidato) a las elecciones parlamentarias; **the offer still stands** la oferta sigue en pie

▸**stand aside** *vi* (*move aside*) hacerse a un lado

▸**stand back** *vi* (*move away*) alejarse (**from** de)

▸**stand by 1** *vt insep* (a) (*friend*) apoyar (b) (*promise, prediction*) mantener

**2** *vi* (a) (*be ready*) estar preparado(a) (**for** para) (b) (*not get involved*) mantenerse al margen, quedarse sin hacer nada

▸**stand down** *vi* (*retire*) retirarse

▸**stand for** *vt insep* (a) (*mean*) significar, querer decir; (*represent*) representar (b) (*tolerate*) aguantar, soportar

▸**stand out** *vi* (a) (*be prominent*) destacar; *Fam* **it stands out a mile!** ¡se nota *or* se ve a la legua! (b) **to s. out against sth** (*oppose*) oponerse a algo

▸**stand up 1** *vt sep Fam* **to s. sb up** (*on date*) dar plantón a alguien

**2** *vi* (a) (*get up*) levantarse, ponerse de pie; (*be standing*) estar de pie; *Fig* **to s. up for sth/sb** defender algo/a alguien; *Fig* **to s. up to sb** hacer

frente a alguien (b) (*of argument, theory*) sostenerse; **it'll never s. up in court** eso no serviría como prueba en un juicio

**stand-alone word processor** ['stændələʊn'wɜːdprəʊsesə(r)] *n Comptr* procesador *m* de texto independiente

**standard** ['stændəd] **1** *n* (a) (*for weight, measurement*) norma *f*; (*to judge performance, success*) criterio *m*, patrón *m*; *Fin* **gold/dollar s.** patrón *m* oro/dólar (b) (*required level*) nivel *m*; **to be up to/below s.** estar al nivel/por debajo del nivel exigido; **to have high/low standards** (*at work*) ser muy/poco exigente; (*morally*) tener muchos/pocos principios; **s. of living** nivel *m* de vida (c) (*flag*) estandarte *m*; *also Fig* **s. bearer** abanderado(a) *m,f*

**2** *adj* (a) (*length, width, measure*) estándar; *Math* **s. deviation** desviación *f* típica *or* estándar; **s. lamp** lámpara *f* de pie; **s. size** tamaño *m* estándar *or* normal (b) (*usual*) habitual; **headrests are fitted as s. on this car** en este coche los reposacabezas vienen con el equipamiento de serie; **S. English** inglés *m* normativo; **it is s. practice** es la práctica habitual

**standardization** [stændədaɪ'zeɪʃən] *n* normalización *f*, estandarización *f*

**standardize** ['stændədaɪz] *vt* normalizar, estandarizar

**stand-by** ['stændbaɪ] *n* (a) (*money, fuel, food*) reserva *f*; **to have sth as a s.** tener algo de reserva; **to be on s.** (*of troops, emergency services*) estar en alerta (b) (*for air travel*) **to be on s.** estar en lista de espera; **s. passenger** pasajero(a) *m,f* en lista de espera; **s. ticket** billete *m* de lista de espera

**stand-in** ['stændɪn] *n* suplente *mf*, sustituto(a) *m,f*

**standing** ['stændɪŋ] **1** *n* (a) (*position, status*) posición *f*, reputación *f* (b) **friends of long s.** amigos de hace mucho tiempo; **an agreement of long s.** un acuerdo que viene de lejos

**2** *adj* (a) (*upright*) vertical, derecho(a); **s. ovation** ovación *f* cerrada (del público puesto) en pie; **s. room only** (*on train*) sólo pasajeros de pie (b) (*permanent*) permanente; **s. army** ejército *m* permanente; **you have a s. invitation** estás invitado a venir cuando quieras; **it's a s. joke in the office** es una de las bromas de siempre en la oficina; *Fin* **s. order** domiciliación *f* (bancaria)

**stand-offish** [stænd'ɒfɪʃ] *adj Fam* distante

**standpoint** ['stændpɔɪnt] *n* punto *m* de vista

**standstill** ['stændstɪl] *n* **to be at a s.** estar detenido(a); **to come to a s.** pararse, detenerse; **to bring sth to a s.** paralizar algo

**stank** [stæŋk] *pt of* **stink**

**stanza** ['stænzə] *n* estrofa *f*

**staple¹** ['steɪpəl] **1** n grapa f; **s. gun** grapadora f industrial

**2** vt grapar

**staple²** n (basic food) alimento m básico; Fig **such stories are a s. of the tabloid press** esas historias son el pan de cada día en la prensa amarilla

**stapler** ['steɪplə(r)] n grapadora f

**star** [stɑː(r)] **1** n (a) (heavenly body, famous person) estrella f; **the Stars and Stripes** la bandera americana; **to reach for the stars** (aspire) apuntar al cielo; **to see stars** (after blow to head) ver las estrellas; **film** or **movie s.** estrella de cine; **s. fruit** carambola f (fruto); **s. player** estrella f or figura f del equipo; **s. sign** signo m del zodiaco; **s. turn** atracción f principal, actuación f estelar **(b)** Fam **stars** (horoscope) horóscopo m

**2** vt (pt & pp **starred**) (of film) estar protagonizado(a) por

**3** vi **to s. in a film** protagonizar una película

**starboard** ['stɑːbəd] n Naut estribor m

**starch** [stɑːtʃ] **1** n (for shirts) almidón m; (in food) fécula f

**2** vt (shirt) almidonar

**starchy** ['stɑːtʃɪ] adj **(a)** (food) feculento(a) **(b)** Fam (person, manner) estirado(a), rígido(a)

**stardom** ['stɑːdəm] n estrellato m

**stare** [steə(r)] **1** n mirada f fija

**2** vt **the answer was staring me in the face** tenía la solución delante de las narices

**3** vi **to s.** (at sth/sb) mirar fijamente (algo/a alguien); **to s. into the distance** mirar al vacío; **it's rude to s.** es de mala educación quedarse mirando (con descaro)

**starfish** ['stɑːfɪʃ] n estrella f de mar

**stark** [stɑːk] **1** adj (contrast) claro(a); (light, colours) frío(a); (truth, facts) crudo(a); (landscape) desolado(a)

**2** adv **s. naked** completamente desnudo(a); **s. staring mad** completamente loco(a)

**starkers** ['stɑːkəz] adj Fam en pelotas, en cueros

**starlet** ['stɑːlɪt] n (young actress) actriz f incipiente

**starlight** ['stɑːlaɪt] n luz f de las estrellas

**starling** ['stɑːlɪŋ] n estornino m

**starlit** ['stɑːlɪt] adj iluminado(a) por las estrellas

**starry** ['stɑːrɪ] adj estrellado(a)

**starry-eyed** [stɑːrɪ'aɪd] adj cándido(a), idealista; (lovers) embelesado(a), embobado(a)

**start** [stɑːt] **1** n **(a)** (beginning) principio m, comienzo m; (starting place, of race) salida f; **for a s.** para empezar; **at the s.** al principio; **at the s. of the month** a principios de mes; **from the s.** desde el principio; **from s. to finish** de principio a fin; **to make a s. on sth** empezar

con algo; **he lent her £500 to give her a s.** le prestó 500 libras para ayudarla a empezar; **to give sb a 60 metre(s) s.** (in race) dar a alguien una ventaja de 60 metros

**(b)** (sudden movement) susto m, sobresalto m; **to wake with a s.** despertarse sobresaltado(a); **to give sb a s.** (frighten) sobresaltar a alguien, dar un susto a alguien

**2** vt **(a)** (begin) empezar, comenzar; (conversation, talks) entablar, iniciar; (a fashion, rumour) promover, poner en circulación; (a fire) ocasionar, provocar; (a business) montar; **to s. school** empezar el colegio; **to s. doing sth, to s. to do sth** ponerse or empezar a hacer algo; **it's just started raining** acaba de ponerse or empezar a llover; **to get started** empezar

**(b)** (cause to start) (machine, engine, car) arrancar, poner en marcha

**3** vi **(a)** (begin) empezar, comenzar; **to s. at the beginning** empezar por el principio; **to s. by doing sth** comenzar haciendo algo; **she had started as a doctor** había comenzado trabajando como médica; **to s. with** para empezar; **to s. on sth** empezar algo; **now don't YOU s.!** ¡no empieces!, ¡no empecemos!

**(b)** (be frightened) sobresaltado(a); **to s. out of one's sleep** despertarse sobresaltado(a)

**(c)** (begin journey) salir, partir

**(d)** (of car, engine) arrancar

▶**start off 1** vt sep (argument, debate) suscitar, provocar; **to s. sb off** (in business) dar un primer empujón a alguien; (on a subject) dar cuerda a alguien

**2** vi (begin) empezar, comenzar; (on journey) salir; **to s. off by doing sth** comenzar haciendo algo

▶**start out** vi (begin) empezar; (on journey) salir, partir

▶**start up 1** vt sep (car, machine) arrancar, poner en marcha; (business) montar, poner

**2** vi (of engine) arrancar, ponerse en marcha; **to s. up in business** poner or montar un negocio

**starter** ['stɑːtə(r)] n **(a)** Sport (competitor) competidor(ora) m,f; (official) juez mf de salida **(b)** **to be a late s.** (of child) llevar retraso (en el aprendizaje); **to be a slow s.** tardar en ponerse en marcha **(c)** (device) motor m de arranque **(d)** (in meal) entrada f, primer plato m; **for starters** (in meal) de primero; Fig (for a start) para empezar

**starting** ['stɑːtɪŋ] n Sport **s. block** tacos mpl or puesto m de salida; Sport **s. line** línea f de salida; Sport **s. pistol** (gun) pistola f para dar la salida; **s. point** or **place** punto m de partida; **s. price** (in betting) precio m de las apuestas a la salida; **s. salary** salario m or sueldo m inicial

**startle** ['stɑːtəl] vt sobresaltar

**startling** ['stɑːtlɪŋ] adj (noise) que sobresalta; (news, event) sorprendente

**start-up** ['stɑ:ʌp] *n Com* puesta *f* en marcha; **s. costs** gastos *mpl* de puesta en marcha

**starvation** [stɑ:'veɪʃən] *n* inanición *f*; **to die of s.** morir de inanición; **s. diet** dieta *f* miserable; **s. wages** salario *m* mísero

**starve** [stɑ:v] **1** *vt* privar de alimentos; **to s. sb to death** matar a alguien de inanición; *Fig* **to be starved of sth** estar privado(a) de algo
**2** *vi (lack food)* pasar mucha hambre; **to s. (to death)** morir de inanición; *Fam* **I'm starving** me muero de hambre

**starving** ['stɑ:vɪŋ] *adj* famélico(a), hambriento(a)

**stash** [stæʃ] *Fam* **1** *n* alijo *m*
**2** *vt (hide)* poner a buen recaudo

**state** [steɪt] **1** *n* **(a)** *(condition, situation)* estado *m*; **I am not in a fit s. to travel** no estoy en condiciones de viajar; **a s. of emergency** un estado de emergencia; **s. of health** estado *m* de salud; **s. of mind** estado *m* anímico; **in a s. of terror** aterrorizado(a); **in a s. of shock** en estado de shock; **to be in a terrible s.** estar en un estado terrible; **to lie in s.** *(before funeral)* yacer en la capilla ardiente
**(b)** *(country, administrative region)* estado *m*; *Fam* **the States** *(the USA)* (los) Estados Unidos; **s. control** control *m* estatal; *US Pol* **S. Department** Ministerio *m* de Asuntos Exteriores estadounidense; **s. occasions** ceremonias *fpl* de gala; **s. school** colegio *m* estatal *or* público; **s. secret** secreto *m* de Estado; **s. sector** sector *m* público; **s. visit** viaje *m* oficial *or* de Estado
**2** *vt (declare)* declarar; *(one's name and address)* indicar; *(reasons, demands, objections)* exponer; **to s. the obvious** decir una obviedad; **as stated earlier/above** como se hizo constar antes/más arriba; **at the stated times** a las horas fijadas

**stateless** ['steɪtlɪs] *adj* apátrida

**stately** ['steɪtlɪ] *adj* imponente, majestuoso(a); **s. home** casa *f* solariega

**statement** ['steɪtmənt] *n (of opinion)* declaración *f*; *(from bank)* extracto *m* (bancario); **a s. of the facts** una exposición de los hechos; **to make a s.** *(of spokesperson)* hacer una declaración; *(of witness)* prestar declaración; *Fig of life-style, behaviour)* decir algo de sí mismo(a)

**state-of-the-art** [steɪtəvðɑ:'ɑ:t] *adj* de vanguardia; **s. technology** tecnología *f* punta

**state-owned** ['steɪt'əʊnd] *adj* público(a), estatal

**state-run** ['steɪtrʌn] *adj* estatal

**statesman** ['steɪtsmən] *n* estadista *m*, hombre *m* de Estado

**statesmanlike** ['steɪtsmənlaɪk] *adj (behaviour, speech)* digno(a) de un gran hombre de Estado; **he's not very s.** le falta la gravedad propia de un hombre de Estado

**static** ['stætɪk] **1** *n (electricity)* electricidad *f* estática; *(on radio, TV)* interferencias *fpl*
**2** *adj* estático(a); **s. electricity** electricidad *f* estática

**station** ['steɪʃən] **1** *n* **(a)** *(for trains, buses)* estación *f*; **s. master** jefe *m* de estación; *US* **s. wagon** *(car)* ranchera *f* **(b)** *(post)* puesto *m*; **(police) s.** comisaría *f* (de policía); **(radio) s.** emisora *f* (de radio); **(television) s.** canal *m* (de televisión) **(c)** *(social condition)* posición *f*; **to have ideas above one's s.** tener demasiadas aspiraciones
**2** *vt (person)* colocar; *(soldier, troops)* apostar

**stationary** ['steɪʃənərɪ] *adj (not moving)* inmóvil; **to remain s.** permanecer inmóvil

**stationer** ['steɪʃənə(r)] *n* **s.'s (shop)** papelería *f*

**stationery** ['steɪʃənərɪ] *n (writing materials)* artículos *mpl* de papelería; *(writing paper)* papel *m* de carta

**statistic** [stə'tɪstɪk] *n* estadística *f*, dato *m* estadístico; **statistics** *(facts)* estadísticas *fpl*; *(science)* estadística *f*

**statistical** [stə'tɪstɪkəl] *adj* estadístico(a)

**statistician** [stætɪs'tɪʃən] *n* estadístico(a) *m,f*

**statue** ['stætju:] *n* estatua *f*

**statuesque** [stætju'esk] *adj* escultural

**statuette** [stætju'et] *n* estatuilla *f*

**stature** ['stætʃə(r)] *n (physical build)* estatura *f*; *(reputation)* talla *f*, estatura *f*

**status** ['steɪtəs] *n (in society, profession)* categoría *f*, posición *f*; *(prestige)* categoría *f*, prestigio *m*; *Law* estado *m*; *Comptr* **s. line** línea *f* de estado; **s. report** informe *m* de la situación; **s. symbol** señal *f* de prestigio

**status quo** ['steɪtəs'kwəʊ] *n* statu quo *m*

**statute** ['stætju:t] *n* estatuto *m*; **by s.** por ley; **s. book** legislación *f*, código *m* de leyes

**statutory** ['stætjʊtərɪ] *adj* legal, reglamentario(a); **s. duty** obligación *f* legal; **s. holidays** días *mpl* festivos oficiales

**staunch¹** [stɔːntʃ] *adj (resolute)* fiel, leal

**staunch²** *vt (blood)* cortar; *(wound)* restañar

**staunchly** ['stɔːntʃlɪ] *adv* firmemente, fielmente

**stave** [steɪv] *n* **(a)** *(of barrel)* duela *f* **(b)** *Mus* pentagrama *m*
▸**stave in** *(pt & pp* staved *or* stove [stəʊv]) *vt sep* romper, quebrar
▸**stave off** *vt sep (problem, disaster)* aplazar, retrasar; **to s. off one's hunger** espantar el hambre

**stay** [steɪ] **1** *n* **(a)** *(visit)* estancia *f* **(b)** *Law* **s. of execution** aplazamiento *m* de sentencia
**2** *vt (endure)* **to s. the course** *or* **distance** aguantar hasta el final
**3** *vi* **(a)** *(not move, remain)* permanecer, que-

darse; **s. where you are!** ¡no te muevas de donde estás!; *Fam* **to s. put** no moverse; **to s. still** quedarse quieto(a); **computers are here to s.** los ordenadores son algo ya establecido; **I can't s. long** no puedo quedarme mucho tiempo (**b**) *(reside temporally)* quedarse; **I'm staying at a hotel** estoy (alojado) en un hotel; **to s. with sb** estar (alojado) en casa de alguien (**c**) *Scot (live)* vivir

▸**stay away** *vi* mantenerse alejado(a) **(from de)**

▸**stay in** *vi (not go out)* quedarse en casa

▸**stay on** *vi (remain longer)* quedarse

▸**stay out** *vi* (**a**) *(stay outside)* quedarse *or* permanecer fuera; **to s. out all night** estar fuera toda la noche (**b**) *(of strikers)* permanecer en huelga (**c**) *(not interfere)* **to s. out of sth** mantenerse al margen de algo; **s. out of this!** ¡no te metas en esto!

▸**stay up** *vi (not go to bed)* quedarse levantado(a)

**staying power** ['steɪɪŋ'paʊə(r)] *n* resistencia *f*

**stead** [sted] *n* **it will stand you in good s.** te será de gran utilidad; **in sb's s.** en lugar de alguien

**steadfast** ['stedfɑ:st] *adj* firme

**steadily** ['stedɪlɪ] *adv (change, grow)* constantemente; *(work)* a buen ritmo; *(walk)* con paso firme; *(look)* fijamente; *(breathe)* con regularidad

**steady** ['stedɪ] **1** *adj* (**a**) *(stable)* firme, estable; **in a s. voice** con voz tranquila (**b**) *(regular) (rate, growth, pace)* constante; *(progress)* continuo(a); *(income)* regular; *(pulse)* constante, regular; **s. girlfriend/boyfriend** novia *f*/novio *m* estable; **to have a s. job** tener un trabajo fijo; **to drive at a s. 95 km/h** conducir a una velocidad constante de 95 km/h

**2** *adv* **they are going s.** son novios formales; **s.!** ¡tranquilo!; *Fam* **s. (on)!** ¡calma!

**3** *vt* estabilizar, afianzar; **to s. oneself** *(physically)* afianzarse; *(mentally)* reunir fuerzas; **to s. one's nerves** tranquilizarse

**steak** [steɪk] *n (beef)* filete *m*, bistec *m*, *CSur* bife *m*; *(of fish)* filete *m*; **s. and kidney pie** empanada *f* de ternera y riñones

**steal** [sti:l] (*pt* **stole** [stəʊl], *pp* **stolen** ['stəʊlən]) **1** *vt* (**a**) *(rob)* robar; **to s. sth from sb** robar algo a alguien (**b**) *(idioms)* **to s. a glance at sb** dirigir una mirada furtiva a alguien; **to s. the show** acaparar toda la atención

**2** *vi* (**a**) *(rob)* robar (**b**) *(move quietly)* **to s. away/in/out** alejarse/entrar/salir furtivamente; **to s. up on sb** acercarse furtivamente a alguien; **middle age steals up on you** cuando te quieres dar cuenta, eres una persona de mediana edad

**stealth** [stelθ] *n* sigilo *m*

**stealthily** ['stelθɪlɪ] *adv* subrepticiamente, furtivamente

**stealthy** ['stelθɪ] *adj* subrepticio(a), furtivo(a)

**steam** [sti:m] **1** *n* (**a**) vapor *m*; *(on window, mirror)* vaho *m*; **s. bath** baño *m* de vapor; **s. engine** máquina *f* de vapor; **s. iron** plancha *f* de vapor; **s. shovel** excavadora *f* (**b**) *(idioms)* **to run out of s.** *(lose momentum)* perder fuelle; **to let off s.** desfogarse; **she did it under her own s.** lo hizo por sus propios medios

**2** *vt Culin* cocinar al vapor; **to s. open an envelope** abrir un sobre exponiéndolo al vapor

**3** *vi (give off steam)* despedir vapor

▸**steam up 1** *vt sep* **to get all steamed up (about sth)** *(of person)* acalorarse

**2** *vi (of window, glasses)* empañarse

**steamer** ['sti:mə(r)] *n* (**a**) *(ship)* barco *m* de vapor (**b**) *Culin (pot)* olla *f* para cocinar al vapor

**steamroller** ['sti:mrəʊlə(r)] **1** *n Constr* apisonadora *f*

**2** *vt* **to s. sb into doing sth** forzar a alguien a hacer algo

**steamship** ['sti:mʃɪp] *n* barco *m* de vapor

**steamy** ['sti:mɪ] *adj* (**a**) *(room)* lleno(a) de vapor (**b**) *Fam (novel, film)* erótico(a)

**steel** [sti:l] **1** *n* acero *m*; **nerves of s.** nervios *mpl* de acero; **the s. industry** la industria del acero; **s. band** *(musical)* = grupo de percusión caribeño que utiliza bidones de metal; **s. mill** fundición *f* de acero; **s. wool** estropajo *m* de acero

**2** *vt* **to s. oneself to do sth** armarse de valor para hacer algo; **to s. oneself against sth** armarse de valor para enfrentarse con algo

**steelworker** ['sti:lwɜ:kə(r)] *n* trabajador(ora) *m,f* del acero

**steelworks** ['sti:lwɜ:ks] *n* acería *f*

**steep¹** [sti:p] *adj* (**a**) *(path, hill, climb)* empinado(a); *(rise, fall)* pronunciado(a) (**b**) *Fam (expensive)* abusivo(a)

**steep²** *vt (clothes)* dejar en remojo; *(food)* macerar; **to be steeped in history** rezumar historia

**steeple** ['sti:pəl] *n (of church)* torre *f*

**steeplechase** ['sti:pəltʃeɪs] *n Sport* carrera *f* de obstáculos

**steeplejack** ['sti:pəldʒæk] *n* = persona que arregla torres y chimeneas

**steer¹** [stɪə(r)] **1** *vt (car)* conducir; *(ship)* gobernar; **to s. sb out of trouble** sacar a alguien de un aprieto

**2** *vi (of person)* conducir; *(of ship, car)* manejarse; **to s. for sth** llevar rumbo a algo; **to s. clear of sth/sb** evitar algo/a alguien

**steer²** *n (bull)* buey *m*

**steering** ['stɪərɪŋ] n (mechanism) dirección f; Aut **s. column** columna f de dirección; Pol **s. committee** comisión f directiva; Aut **s. wheel** volante m

**stem** [stem] **1** n (of plant) tallo m; (of glass) pie m; (of tobacco pipe) tubo m; (of word) raíz f

**2** vt (pt & pp **stemmed**) (halt) contener

**3** vi to **s. from** derivarse de

**stench** [stentʃ] n pestilencia f

**stencil** ['stensəl] **1** n (a) Art plantilla f (b) (for typing) cliché m, clisé m

**2** vt (pt & pp **stencilled**, US **stenciled**) estarcir

**stenographer** [stə'nɒɡrəfə(r)] n US taquígrafo(a) m,f

**step** [step] **1** n (a) (movement, sound) paso m; **to take a s.** dar un paso; **at every s.** a cada paso; **s. by s.** paso a paso; also Fig **to watch one's s.** mirar dónde se pone el pie; **every s. of the way** en todo momento; **to keep (in) s.** (in dance) seguir el ritmo; Fig **to be out of s. (with sth)** no estar en consonancia (con algo)

(b) (action, measure) medida f; **to take steps (to do sth)** tomar medidas (para hacer algo); **the next s. is to...** el siguiente paso es...; **a s. in the right direction** un avance, un adelanto

(c) (of staircase) escalón m, peldaño m; (of stepladder) peldaño m; (on outside of building) escalón m; (flight of) **steps** (tramo m de) escalera f; **mind the s.** cuidado con el escalón

(d) (exercise) **steps** step m, aerobic m con escalón; **s. class** clase f de step

**2** vi (pt & pp **stepped**) (take a step) dar un paso; (walk) caminar; **to s. on sb's foot** pisarle un pie a alguien; **s. this way** pasa por aquí; Fam Fig **to s. on it** (hurry up) aligerar, darse prisa

▸**step back** vi **to s. back from a situation** dar un paso atrás para considerar una situación objetivamente

▸**step down** vi (resign) dimitir

▸**step forward** vi (volunteer) presentarse, ofrecerse

▸**step in** vi (of referee, government) intervenir

▸**step up** vt sep (production, pace) aumentar

**stepbrother** ['stepbrʌðə(r)] n hermanastro m

**stepchild** ['steptʃaɪld] n hijastro(a) m,f

**stepdaughter** ['stepdɔ:tə(r)] n hijastra f

**stepfather** ['stepfɑ:ðə(r)] n padrastro m

**stepladder** ['steplædə(r)] n escalera f de tijera

**stepmother** ['stepmʌðə(r)] n madrastra f

**step-parent** ['steppeərənt] n (man) padrastro m; (woman) madrastra f; **step-parents** padrastros mpl

**steppe** [step] n estepa f

**stepsister** ['stepsɪstə(r)] n hermanastra f

**stepson** ['stepsʌn] n hijastro m

**stereo** ['sterɪəʊ] **1** n (pl **stereos**) (equipment) equipo m de música; (sound) estéreo m, sonido m estereofónico; **in s.** en estéreo

**2** adj estéreo, estereofónico(a)

**stereophonic** [sterɪə'fɒnɪk] adj estereofónico(a)

**stereoscopic** [sterɪəʊ'skɒpɪk] adj (vision) estereoscópico(a)

**stereotype** ['sterɪətaɪp] n estereotipo m

**stereotyped** ['sterɪətaɪpt] adj estereotipado(a)

**sterile** ['steraɪl] adj estéril

**sterility** [stə'rɪlɪtɪ] n esterilidad f

**sterilization** [sterɪlaɪ'zeɪʃən] n esterilización f

**sterilize** ['sterɪlaɪz] vt esterilizar

**sterling** ['stɜ:lɪŋ] **1** n (British currency) libra f esterlina

**2** adj (a) (silver) de ley (b) (effort, quality) admirable, excelente

**stern¹** [stɜ:n] adj (person, look) severo(a); **we are made of sterner stuff** somos más duros de pelar de lo que parece

**stern²** n Naut popa f

**sternum** ['stɜ:nəm] n Anat esternón m

**steroid** ['stɪərɔɪd] n esteroide m

**stethoscope** ['steθəskəʊp] n Med fonendoscopio m, estetoscopio m

**stevedore** ['sti:vədɔ:(r)] n estibador m

**stew** [stju:] **1** n Culin guiso m; Fam Fig **to be in a s.** (person) estar hecho(a) un manojo de nervios

**2** vt (meat) guisar, cocer; (fruit) cocer para compota

**3** vi (of meat) guisarse, cocer; Fam **to let sb s. (in his own juice)** dejar a alguien que sufra

**steward** ['stjʊəd] n (on estate) administrador m; (on plane) auxiliar m de vuelo; (on ship) camarero m; (at sporting event, demonstration) auxiliar mf de la organización

**stewardess** [stjʊə'des] n (on plane) azafata f; (on ship) camarera f

**stewed** [stju:d] adj **s. beef** carne f de vaca; **s. fruit** compota f; **this tea is s.** este té ha reposado demasiado

**stick¹** [stɪk] n (a) (of wood) palo m; (for walking) bastón m; (of chewing gum, glue, deodorant) barra f; (of dynamite) cartucho m; (of celery, rhubarb) tallo m, rama f; Fam Fig **to get hold of the wrong end of the s.** coger el rábano por las hojas; Fam **he lives out in the sticks** vive perdido en medio del monte; **s. insect** insecto m palo (b) Fam (criticism) **to give sb s. for sth** poner verde a alguien por algo; **to take a lot of s.** llevarse muchos palos or críticas

**stick²** (pt & pp **stuck** [stʌk]) **1** vt (a) (insert) **to s. sth in(to) sth** clavar algo en algo (b) Fam (put) poner; **s. your things over there** pon tus bártulos por ahí (**c**) *(attach with glue)* pegar (**on** a) (**d**) *Fam (endure)* aguantar, soportar; **I can't s. him** no lo trago

**2** *vi* (**a**) *(adhere)* pegarse; **the name stuck** el nombre tuvo éxito, se quedó con el nombre; *Fig* **to s. to one's guns** mantenerse en sus trece; **to s. to the facts** atenerse a los hechos; **she stuck to her principles** fue fiel a sus principios (**b**) *(become jammed)* atascarse; **it sticks in my throat** se me atraganta

▸**stick around** *vi Fam* quedarse

▸**stick at** *vt insep (persevere with)* perseverar en; **to s. at nothing** no reparar en nada

▸**stick by** *vt insep (friend)* apoyar; *(promise, statement)* mantener

▸**stick out 1** *vt sep* (**a**) *(cause to protrude)* sacar; **she stuck her tongue out at me** me sacó la lengua; *Fam* **to s. one's neck out** arriesgar el pellejo (**b**) *Fam (endure)* **to s. it out** aguantar

**2** *vi* (**a**) *(protrude)* sobresalir (**b**) *(be noticeable)* notarse, resaltar; **it sticks out a mile** se ve a la legua; **it sticks out like a sore thumb** llama la atención, da la nota

▸**stick together 1** *vt sep* pegar

**2** *vi* (**a**) *(with glue)* pegarse (**b**) *(of friends)* apoyarse

▸**stick up 1** *vt sep (sign, poster)* pegar; *Fam* **s. 'em up!** ¡manos arriba!

**2** *vi (point upwards) (of building)* sobresalir; **her hair sticks up** tiene el pelo de punta

▸**stick up for** *vt insep (person, rights)* defender

▸**stick with** *vt insep (not give up)* seguir con

**sticker** ['stɪkə(r)] *n (with information, price)* etiqueta *f*; *(with slogan, picture)* pegatina *f*

**stick-in-the-mud** ['stɪkɪnðəmʌd] *n Fam* carroza *mf*

**stickleback** ['stɪkəlbæk] *n* espinoso *m* (de agua dulce)

**stickler** ['stɪklə(r)] *n* **to be a s. for sth** ser un/una maniático(a) de algo

**stick-on** ['stɪkɒn] *adj* adhesivo(a)

**stick-up** ['stɪkʌp] *n Fam (robbery)* atraco *m* (a mano armada)

**sticky** ['stɪkɪ] *adj* (**a**) *(substance)* pegajoso(a); *(climate, weather)* bochornoso(a); *(label)* adhesivo(a); **s. tape** cinta *f* adhesiva (**b**) *Fig (awkward)* problemático(a); **to come to a s. end** tener un final sangriento; *Fam* **to be on a s. wicket** estar en un atolladero

**stiff** [stɪf] *adj* (**a**) *(rigid)* tieso(a), rígido(a); *(paste)* consistente; **as s. as a board** tieso(a) como un palo; **to be bored/scared/frozen s.** estar muerto(a) de aburrimiento/miedo/frío

(**b**) *(joint)* agarrotado(a), anquilosado(a); **to be s.** *(of person)* tener agujetas; **to have a s. neck** tener tortícolis

(**c**) *(handle, hinge, drawer)* duro(a)

(**d**) *(severe) (fine, competition, prison sentence)* duro(a); *(exam, test)* difícil; *(breeze, drink)* fuerte; **s. resistance** gran resistencia *f*

(**e**) *(formal) (person, manner)* rígido(a), estirado(a); *(smile)* forzado(a)

**stiffen** ['stɪfən] **1** *vt (fabric, paper)* aprestar, endurecer; *(paste)* espesar; *(resolve, resistance)* reforzar

**2** *vi (of limb, joint, person)* agarrotarse; *(opposition)* endurecerse

**stiffly** ['stɪflɪ] *adv (to bow)* con rigidez; *(to answer, greet)* forzadamente

**stifle** ['staɪfəl] *vt (person)* ahogar, asfixiar; *(cries, yawn)* ahogar, reprimir; *(rebellion)* sofocar

**stifling** ['staɪflɪŋ] *adj* sofocante, asfixiante

**stigma** ['stɪgmə] *n (disgrace)* estigma *m*, deshonra *f*

**stigmata** [stɪg'mɑːtə] *npl (of saint)* estigmas *mpl*

**stigmatize** ['stɪgmətaɪz] *vt* estigmatizar

**stile** [staɪl] *n (in fence, hedge)* escalones *mpl*

**stiletto** [stɪ'letəʊ] *(pl* **stilettos**) *n (dagger)* estilete *m*; *(shoe)* zapato *m* de tacón de aguja; **s. heels** tacones *mpl* de aguja

**still¹** [stɪl] **1** *n* (**a**) **in the s. of the night** en el silencio de la noche (**b**) *Cin* fotograma *m*

**2** *adj (motionless)* quieto(a); *(calm)* sereno(a); *(silent)* silencioso(a); *(orange juice)* natural; *(mineral water)* sin gas; *Art* **s. life** naturaleza *f* muerta; *Prov* **s. waters run deep** tras una fachada silenciosa se ocultan fuertes emociones

**3** *adv* **to be/stand s.** estar quieto(a)

**4** *vt (person)* calmar, tranquilizar; **to s. sb's fears** ahuyentar los temores de alguien

**still²** *adv* (**a**) *(up to given point in time)* todavía, aún, *Am* siempre; **I s. think/say that...** sigo creyendo/diciendo que...; **I s. have £50** aún me quedan 50 libras

(**b**) *(even)* todavía, aún; **s. more/better** aún más/mejor

(**c**) *(nonetheless)* de todas formas, aún así

**still³** *n (distilling equipment)* alambique *m*

**stillbirth** ['stɪlbɜːθ] *n* nacimiento *m* de un niño muerto

**stillborn** ['stɪlbɔːn] *adj* **the child was s.** el niño nació muerto

**stillness** ['stɪlnɪs] *n* calma *f*, quietud *f*

**stilt** [stɪlt] *n (for walking)* zanco *m*; *(for building)* poste *m*, pilote *m*

**stilted** ['stɪltɪd] *adj (style, manner)* forzado(a)

**stimulant** ['stɪmjʊlənt] *n* estimulante *m*

**stimulate** ['stɪmjʊleɪt] *vt (person, mind, appetite)* estimular; *(enthusiasm, interest)* suscitar

**stimulating** ['stɪmjʊleɪtɪŋ] *adj* estimulante

**stimulation** [stɪmjʊ'leɪʃən] *n (action)* estimulación *f*; *(result)* estímulo *m*

**stimulus** ['stɪmjʊləs] *(pl* **stimuli** ['stɪmjʊlaɪ]) *n* estímulo *m*

**sting** [stɪŋ] **1** *n* (**a**) *(of bee, scorpion)* *(organ)* aguijón *m; (wound)* picadura *f* (**b**) *(sensation)* escozor *m* (**c**) *(idioms)* **to have a s. in the tail** *(of story)* tener un final sorpresa muy fuerte; **to take the s. out of sth** hacer algo menos traumático(a)

**2** *vt (pt & pp* **stung** [stʌŋ]) *(of bee)* picar; *(of nettle)* pinchar; *Fig (of remark)* herir; *Fig* **to s. sb into action** espolear a alguien para que pase a la acción; *Fam Fig* **they stung him for £10** le clavaron 10 libras

**3** *vi (of eyes, skin)* escocer

**stinging** [ˈstɪŋɪŋ] *adj (pain)* punzante; *(remark, criticism)* hiriente, despiadado(a); **s. nettle** ortiga *f*

**stingray** [ˈstɪŋreɪ] *n* pastinaca *f (pez)*

**stingy** [ˈstɪndʒɪ] *adj (person)* tacaño(a), rácano(a); *(portion)* raquítico(a); **to be s. with food/praise** ser tacaño(a) con la comida/los elogios

**stink** [ˈstɪŋk] **1** *n (smell)* peste *f*, hedor *m; Fig* **to kick up a s.** *(about sth)* montar un escándalo *(por algo)*

**2** *vi (pt* **stank** [stæŋk] *or* **stunk** [stʌŋk], *pp* **stunk**) apestar *(of* a); *Fam* **Fig this film stinks!** ¡esta película no vale un pimiento or es una patata!; *Fam Fig* **to s. of corruption** apestar a corrupción

**stinkbomb** [ˈstɪŋkbɒm] *n* bomba *f* fétida

**stinker** [ˈstɪŋkə(r)] *n Fam (person)* mamón(ona) *m,f*, mal bicho *mf*; **to be a real s.** ser muy chungo(a); *(difficult)* hueso *m*

**stinking** [ˈstɪŋkɪŋ] **1** *adj* apestoso(a); **a s. cold** un resfriado espantoso

**2** *adv Fam* **to be s. rich** estar podrido(a) de dinero

**stint** [stɪnt] **1** *n (period)* período *m*; **to take a s. at the wheel** tomar el relevo al volante; **he had a two-year s. in the army** sirvió por un período de dos años en el ejército

**2** *vt* escatimar; **to s. oneself** privarse de algunas cosas *(en beneficio de otras personas)*

**3** *vi* **to s. on sth** escatimar algo

**stipend** [ˈstaɪpend] *n Rel & Univ* estipendio *m*

**stipulate** [ˈstɪpjʊleɪt] *vt* estipular

**stipulation** [stɪpjʊˈleɪʃən] *n* estipulación *f*

**stir** [stɜ:(r)] **1** *n* (**a**) **to give sth a s.** remover *or* revolver algo (**b**) *Fig* **to cause a s.** causar (un gran) revuelo

**2** *vt (pt & pp* **stirred**) (**a**) *(liquid, mixture)* remover, revolver; *(leaves)* agitar (**b**) *Fig (person)* conmover, emocionar; *(emotion)* provocar; *(curiosity)* despertar; **to s. sb to do sth** mover a alguien a hacer algo; *Fam* **s. yourself!** ¡muévete!; *Fam* **she's just stirring it!** *(making trouble)* ¡está venga a meter cizaña!

**3** *vi (move)* moverse

▸**stir up** *vt sep* (**a**) *(dust, leaves)* levantar (**b**) *Fig (rebellion, dissent, anger)* provocar; *(workers, crowd)* agitar; **to s. things up** solivientar los ánimos

**stir-fry** [ˈstɜ:fraɪ] *Culin* **1** *n* = salteado de (carne y) verduras típico de la cocina china

**2** *vt* saltear, rehogar a fuego vivo

**stirrer** [ˈstɜ:rə(r)] *n Fam (trouble-maker)* cizañero(a) *m,f*

**stirring** [ˈstɜ:rɪŋ] **1** *n* **the first stirrings of…** los primeros indicios de…

**2** *adj (speech, film)* emotivo(a), emocionante

**stirrup** [ˈstɪrəp] *n* estribo *m*

**stitch** [stɪtʃ] **1** *n* (**a**) *(in sewing)* puntada *f; (in knitting)* punto *m; Med* punto *m* (de sutura); *Fam* **she didn't have a s. on** estaba en cueros *or* en pelotas; *Prov* **a s. in time saves nine** una puntada a tiempo ahorra ciento (**b**) *(sharp pain)* **to have a s.** tener flato (**c**) *Fam* **we were in stitches** *(laughing)* nos partíamos (de risa)

**2** *vt (clothing)* coser; *Med* suturar, coser

▸**stitch up** *vt sep Fam (falsely incriminate)* **they stitched him up** hicieron un montaje para que cargara con el muerto

**stoat** [stəʊt] *n* armiño *m*

**stock** [stɒk] **1** *n* (**a**) *(supply)* reservas *fpl; Com* existencias *fpl;* **the red ones are out of s.** los rojos están agotados; **the red ones are in s.** nos quedan rojos en almacén; *Fig* **to take s.** hacer balance; *Com* **s. control** control *m* de existencias; *Com* **s. list** inventario *m*

(**b**) *(livestock)* ganado *m*

(**c**) *Fin (share)* valor *m; (total share value)* (capital *m* en) acciones *fpl;* **stocks and shares** valores *mpl; Fig* **her s. is going up/down** está ganando/perdiendo crédito; **s. exchange** bolsa *f* (de valores); **s. market** mercado *m* de valores

(**d**) *(descent)* ascendencia *f*, origen *m;* **she's of German s.** es de origen alemán

(**e**) *(of rifle)* culata *f*

(**f**) **stocks** *(for punishment)* picota *f*

(**g**) *(in cooking)* caldo *m;* **s. cube** pastilla *f or* cubito *m* de caldo (concentrado)

**2** *adj (argument, excuse)* tópico(a)

**3** *vt* (**a**) *(have in stock) (goods)* tener (existencias de)

(**b**) *(supply) (shop)* surtir *(with* de), abastecer *(with* de); **the shop is well stocked** la tienda está bien surtida

▸**stock up** *vi* aprovisionarse *(with* de)

**stockade** [stɒˈkeɪd] *n* empalizada *f*

**stockbroker** [ˈstɒkbrəʊkə(r)] *n Fin* corredor(ora) *m,f* de Bolsa

**stockholder** [ˈstɒkhəʊldə(r)] *n Fin* accionista *mf*

**Stockholm** [ˈstɒkhəʊm] *n* Estocolmo

**stocking** [ˈstɒkɪŋ] *n* media *f*

**stockist** [ˈstɒkɪst] *n Com* distribuidor(ora) *m,f*

**stockpile** ['stɒkpaɪl] **1** n reservas fpl
**2** vt acumular, hacer acopio de

**stockroom** ['stɒkru:m] n almacén m

**stock-still** ['stɒk'stɪl] adv to stand s. quedarse inmóvil

**stocktaking** ['stɒkteɪkɪŋ] n Com inventario m (de existencias); Fig a s. exercise un balance provisional

**stocky** ['stɒkɪ] adj chaparro(a)

**stodge** [stɒdʒ] n Fam (food) mazacote m

**stodgy** ['stɒdʒɪ] adj (food, book, person) pesado(a)

**stoic** ['stəʊɪk] n estoico(a) m,f

**stoical** ['stəʊɪkəl] adj estoico(a)

**stoicism** ['stəʊɪsɪzəm] n estoicismo m

**stoke** [stəʊk] vt (add fuel to) alimentar

**STOL** [stɒl] n Av (abbr short take-off and landing) despegue m y aterrizaje rápido or en corto

**stole**¹ ['stəʊl] n (garment) estola f

**stole**² pt of **steal**

**stolen** ['stəʊlən] **1** adj (car, property) robado(a)
**2** pp of **steal**

**stolid** ['stɒlɪd] adj imperturbable

**stomach** ['stʌmək] **1** n estómago m; on an empty s. con el estómago vacío; Fig it turns my s. me revuelve el estómago; Fig to have no s. for sth no tener estómago para algo; to have (a) s. ache tener dolor de estómago; Med s. pump sonda f gástrica
**2** vt Fig (tolerate) soportar

**stomp** [stɒmp] vi dar fuertes pisadas; to s. in/out entrar/salir airadamente

**stone** [stəʊn] **1** n (a) (material, piece of rock) piedra f; (on grave) lápida f; Fig to leave no s. unturned remover Roma con Santiago; Fig a s.'s throw from here a un tiro de piedra (de aquí); the S. Age la Edad de Piedra (b) (of fruit) hueso m (c) (unit of weight) = unidad de peso equivalente a 6,35 kg
**2** adj de piedra
**3** vt (a) (fruit) deshuesar (b) (person) apedrear; he was stoned to death murió lapidado

**stone-cold** ['stəʊn'kəʊld] adj helado(a)

**stoned** [stəʊnd] adj very Fam (on drugs) colocado(a); to be s. estar colocado(a)

**stone-dead** ['stəʊn'ded] adj Fam to be s. estar tieso(a) or seco(a); to kill sb s. dejar a alguien tieso(a) or seco(a)

**stone-deaf** ['stəʊn'def] adj Fam sordo(a) como una tapia; to be s. estar sordo(a) como una tapia

**stonemason** ['stəʊnmeɪsən] n cantero(a) m,f (que labra la piedra)

**stonewall** [stəʊn'wɔ:l] vi (in game) jugar a la defensiva; (in inquiry) entorpecer, andarse con evasivas

**stoneware** ['stəʊnweə(r)] n (cerámica f de) gres m

**stonework** ['stəʊnwɜ:k] n obra f de cantería

**stonily** ['stəʊnɪlɪ] adv con frialdad, insensiblemente

**stony** ['stəʊnɪ] adj (ground, beach) pedregoso(a); Fig (look, silence) glacial; Fam Fig to be s. broke estar sin un duro or sin blanca

**stood** [stʊd] pt & pp of **stand**

**stooge** [stu:dʒ] n (comedian's fall-guy) comparsa mf; (minion) títere m, secuaz mf

**stool** [stu:l] n (a) (seat) banqueta f; (with short legs) taburete m; Fig to fall between two stools quedarse nadando entre dos aguas; very Fam s. pigeon soplón(ona) m,f (b) Med (faeces) heces fpl

**stoop**¹ [stu:p] **1** n to have a s. ser cargado(a) de espaldas; to walk with a s. caminar encorvado(a)
**2** vi (bend down) agacharse, agachar el cuerpo; Fig to s. to (doing) sth rebajarse a (hacer) algo; I never thought they'd s. so low as to... nunca pensé que caerían tan bajo como para...

**stoop**² n US (verandah) porche m

**stop** [stɒp] **1** n (a) (halt) parada f; to put a s. to sth poner fin a algo; to come to a s. detenerse; Aut s. sign (señal f de) stop m
(b) (pause) (in work, journey) parada f; (of plane) escala f; to make a s. parar, detenerse; ten minutes' s. una parada de diez minutos
(c) (stopping place) parada f
(d) (full stop) punto m; (in telegram) stop m
(e) Mus (on organ) registro m; Fig to pull out all the stops tocar todos los registros
**2** vt (pt & pp stopped) (a) (halt) (person, vehicle) parar, detener; (conversation) interrumpir; (corruption, abuse) poner fin a; (cheque) bloquear; s., thief! ¡al ladrón!
(b) (cease) parar; to s. doing sth dejar de hacer algo; to s. smoking/drinking dejar de fumar/de beber
(c) (prevent) impedir; to s. sb (from) doing sth impedir que alguien haga algo; I couldn't s. myself no podía parar
(d) (fill in) (hole, gap) taponar
**3** vi (a) (halt) (of moving person, vehicle) parar(se), detenerse
(b) (cease) (of speaker, worker) parar; the rain has stopped ha dejado de llover; the pain has stopped ya no me duele; she did not s. at that no se contentó con eso; he'll s. at nothing no se detendrá ante nada; to s. short or dead pararse en seco
(c) (stay) quedarse

▶**stop by** vi (visit briefly) pasarse; I'll s. by at your place tomorrow me pasaré mañana por tu casa

►**stop off** vi (stay briefly) parar, hacer una parada

►**stop over** vi Av hacer escala

►**stop up** vt sep (hole) taponar, tapar; (sink, pipe) atascar

**stopcock** ['stɒpkɒk] n llave f de paso

**stopgap** ['stɒpgæp] n (thing) recambio m, repuesto m (provisional); (person) sustituto(a) m,f (temporal); **s. measure** medida f provisional

**stoplight** ['stɒplaɪt] n US Aut semáforo m

**stopover** ['stɒpəʊvə(r)] n Av escala f

**stoppage** ['stɒpɪdʒ] n (a) (of flow, traffic) retención f, detención f; (of work) interrupción f; (as protest) paro m (b) Fin (deduction) retención f

**stopper** ['stɒpə(r)] n tapón m

**stop-press** ['stɒppres] adj Journ **s. news** noticias fpl de última hora

**stopwatch** ['stɒpwɒtʃ] n cronómetro m

**storage** ['stɔːrɪdʒ] n almacenamiento m, almacenaje m; **in s.** en almacén; **to put sth into s.** almacenar algo; **s. charges** gastos mpl de almacenaje; **s. heater** acumulador m de calor; **s. space** sitio m or espacio m para guardar cosas; **s. tank** depósito m

**store** [stɔː(r)] **1** n (a) (supply) (of goods) reserva f, provisión f; Fig (of knowledge) caudal m, cúmulo m; **stores** (supplies) reservas fpl

　(b) (warehouse) almacén m

　(c) US (shop) tienda f; also Br **s. detective** vigilante m de paisano (de establecimiento comercial)

　(d) (idioms) **to hold** or **keep sth in s.** tener algo guardado(a) or reservado(a); **I have a surprise in s. for her** le tengo reservada or guardada una sorpresa; **to set** or **lay great s. by sth** dar mucha importancia a algo

**2** vt (put in storage) almacenar; (electricity, heat) acumular; (keep) guardar; **s. in a cool place** consérvese en lugar fresco

►**store up** vt sep acumular

**storehouse** ['stɔːhaʊs] n almacén m

**storeroom** ['stɔːruːm] n (in office, factory) almacén m; (at home) trastero m

**storey**, US **story** ['stɔːrɪ] (pl storeys, US stories) n piso m, planta f; **a four-s. building** un edificio de cuatro plantas

**stork** [stɔːk] n cigüeña f

**storm** [stɔːm] **1** n (a) (bad weather) tormenta f; Fig **a s. in a teacup** una tormenta en un vaso de agua; **s. clouds** nubes fpl de tormenta; **s. door** doble puerta f, contrapuerta f (b) Fig (scandal) tormenta f, (of insults, protest) aluvión m (c) Mil **to take a town/a fortress by s.** tomar una ciudad/una fortaleza por asalto; Fig **he took the audience by s.** tuvo un éxito arrasador entre el público; **s. troops** tropas fpl de asalto

**2** vt (town, fortress) asaltar

**3** vi (of person) enfurecerse; **to s. at sb** echar la bronca a alguien; **to s. in/out** salir/entrar airadamente

**stormy** ['stɔːmɪ] adj also Fig tormentoso(a)

**story¹** ['stɔːrɪ] n (a) (account) (fictional) cuento m; (factual) historia f; Fig **to tell stories** (lie) contar cuentos (b) (plot) (of novel, play) argumento m (c) (in newspaper) artículo m (d) (idioms) **that is quite another s.** eso ya es otra cosa; **it's the same old s.** es la historia de siempre; Fam **it's the s. of my life!** ¡siempre me pasa lo mismo!; **it's a long s.** es muy largo de contar; **to cut a long s. short, ...** para resumir, ...

**story²** US = **storey**

**storybook** ['stɔːrɪbʊk] n libro m de cuentos

**storyteller** ['stɔːrɪtelə(r)] n narrador(ora) m,f

**stout** [staʊt] **1** n (beer) cerveza f negra

**2** adj (a) (fat) (person) rechoncho(a) (b) (solid) (door, shoes) resistente (c) (brave) (person, resistance) valeroso(a)

**stouthearted** [staʊt'hɑːtɪd] adj Literary denodado(a), valeroso(a)

**stoutly** ['staʊtlɪ] adv (resist) denodadamente; (maintain) a toda costa

**stove¹** [staʊv] n (for cooking) cocina f; (for heating) estufa f

**stove²** pt & pp of **stave**

**stow** [staʊ] vt (put away) guardar; Naut estibar

►**stow away** vi (on ship) ir or viajar de polizón

**stowaway** ['staʊəweɪ] n polizón m

**straddle** ['strædəl] vt sentarse a horcajadas en

**strafe** [streɪf] vt Mil ametrallar desde el aire

**straggle** ['strægəl] vi (lag behind) rezagarse; (spread untidily) desparramarse

**straggler** ['stræglə(r)] n rezagado(a) m,f

**straggly** ['stræglɪ] adj (hair) desordenado(a)

**straight** [streɪt] **1** n (a) **to keep to the s. and narrow** seguir por el buen camino

　(b) (in sport) recta f

**2** adj (a) (not curved) (line, back) recto(a); (hair) liso(a); (tie, skirt, picture) derecho(a); **to keep a s. face** contener la sonrisa; **to put things or matters s.** aclarar las cosas; **to put sb s.** aclararle las cosas a alguien

　(b) (consecutive) consecutivo(a); **three s. wins** tres victorias consecutivas; **s. flush** (in cards) escalera f de color

　(c) (honest) (person, answer) franco(a); **to be s. with sb** ser franco(a) con alguien

　(d) (conventional) convencional; Th **s. man** actor m (con papel) serio

　(e) Fam (heterosexual) heterosexual

　(f) (undiluted) solo(a); **to drink s. vodkas** beber vodka a palo seco

**3** adv (a) (in straight line) recto, en línea recta;

**sit up s.!** ¡siéntate derecho!; **to look s. ahead** mirar hacia adelante; **go s. on** sigue todo recto or derecho; **to see/think s.** ver/pensar con claridad; *Fig* **to go s.** *(of criminal)* reformarse

(**b**) *(immediately)* inmediatamente, en seguida; **s. away** or **off** inmediatamente

(**c**) *(directly)* directamente; **to cut s. through sth** atravesar algo; **to come** or **get s. to the point** ir directamente al grano; **to come s. out with sth** decir algo sin rodeos

**straightaway** ['streɪtəweɪ] *adv* inmediatamente, *Méx* ahorita, *Andes, CSur* al tiro

**straighten** ['streɪtən] *vt (bent nail, rod)* enderezar; *(picture, tie)* poner derecho(a); **to s. one's back** enderezar la espalda

▸**straighten out** *vt sep (problem)* resolver; *(one's affairs)* poner en orden

**straight-faced** ['streɪt'feɪst] *adj* con la cara seria

**straightforward** [streɪt'fɔːwəd] *adj* (**a**) *(honest)* franco(a) (**b**) *(simple)* sencillo(a)

**strain**[1] [streɪn] **1** *n* (**a**) *(on rope, beam) (from pressure, pushing)* presión *f*; *(from tension, pulling)* tensión *f*; *(on economy)* tensión *f*; *(on friendship)* tirantez *f*; *(of muscle)* distensión *f*; *(of ankle)* torcedura *f*; **to put a s. on** *(economy, friendship)* crear tensiones en (**b**) *(mental stress)* agobio *m*; **to be under a lot of s.** estar muy agobiado(a)

**2** *vt* (**a**) *(put strain on) (rope)* tensar; *(economy, friendship)* crear tensiones en; **to s. a muscle** distenderse un músculo; **to s. one's ankle** torcerse el tobillo; **to s. one's back** hacerse daño en la espalda; **to s. one's ears** aguzar el oído (**b**) *Culin (liquid)* colar; *(vegetables)* escurrir

**3** *vi* **to s. at a rope/door** tirar de una cuerda/puerta; *Fig* **to be straining at the leash (to do sth)** estar impaciente (por hacer algo)

**strain**[2] *n (variety) (of virus)* cepa *f*; *(of plant)* variedad *f*; **a s. of madness** *(streak)* un toque de locura; **in the same s.** en la misma línea

**strained** [streɪnd] *adj (muscle)* distendido(a); *(atmosphere, conversation, relations)* tenso(a), tirante

**strainer** ['streɪnə(r)] *n* colador *m*

**strait** [streɪt] *n* estrecho *m*; **the Straits of Gibraltar** el estrecho de Gibraltar; *Fig* **to be in dire** or **desperate straits** estar en serios aprietos

**straitlaced** ['streɪt'leɪst] *adj* mojigato(a)

**strand**[1] [strænd] *vt (ship)* varar; **to be stranded** quedar varado(a)

**strand**[2] *n (of rope)* cabo *m*; *(of cotton)* hebra *f*; *(of hair)* pequeño mechón *m*; *Fig (of plot)* hilo *m* (argumental)

**strange** [streɪndʒ] *adj* (**a**) *(odd) (person, behaviour)* raro(a), extraño(a); **it felt s. to be back in Scotland** se hacía raro estar de nuevo en

Escocia (**b**) *(unfamiliar) (person, place)* desconocido(a), extraño(a)

**strangely** ['streɪndʒlɪ] *adv (behave, dress)* de modo extraño; **s. familiar** extrañamente familiar; **s. enough,...** aunque parezca raro or extraño,...

**strangeness** ['streɪndʒnɪs] *n* (**a**) *(oddness)* rareza *f* (**b**) *(unfamiliarity)* lo desconocido

**stranger** ['streɪndʒə(r)] *n (unknown person)* desconocido(a) *m,f*, extraño(a) *m,f*; *(person from other place)* forastero(a) *m,f*

**strangle** ['stræŋgəl] *vt (person, economy)* estrangular

**stranglehold** ['stræŋgəlhəʊld] *n Fig* **to have a s. on sb/sth** tener un control absoluto sobre alguien/algo

**strangulation** [stræŋgjʊ'leɪʃən] *n* estrangulamiento *m*

**strap** [stræp] **1** *n (of watch, handbag, bag)* correa *f*; *(of shoe)* tira *f*; *(on dress, bra)* tirante *m*

**2** *vt (pt & pp* **strapped)** **to s. sth to sth** sujetar algo con correas a algo

▸**strap in** *vt sep* abrocharse; **to s. oneself in** abrocharse or ponerse el cinturón (de seguridad)

**strapless** ['stræplɪs] *adj (dress, bra)* sin tirantes

**strapping** ['stræpɪŋ] *adj* fornido(a)

**Strasbourg** ['stræzbɜːg] *n* Estrasburgo

**strategic** [strə'tiːdʒɪk] *adj* estratégico(a)

**strategist** ['strætədʒɪst] *n* estratega *mf*

**strategy** ['strætɪdʒɪ] *n* estrategia *f*

**stratification** [strætɪfɪ'keɪʃən] *n* estratificación *f*

**stratosphere** ['strætəsfɪə(r)] *n* estratosfera *f*

**stratum** ['strɑːtəm] *(pl* **strata** ['strɑːtə]) *n also Fig* estrato *m*

**straw** [strɔː] *n* paja *f*; *(for drinking)* pajita *f*; *Fig* **to clutch** or **grasp at straws** agarrarse a un clavo ardiendo; *Fig* **that's the last s.** (eso) es la gota que colma el vaso; **s. hat** sombrero *m* de paja; *Fig* **s. man** hombre *m* de paja; **s. poll** sondeo *m* informal

**strawberry** ['strɔːbərɪ] *n* fresa *f*, *Am* frutilla *f*; **s. jam** mermelada *f* de fresa; **s. blonde** rubio(a) bermejo(a)

**straw-coloured** ['strɔːkʌləd] *adj* pajizo(a)

**stray** [streɪ] **1** *n (dog)* perro *m* callejero; *(cat)* gato *m* callejero

**2** *adj (dog, cat)* callejero(a); *(bullet)* perdido(a)

**3** *vi* **to s. from** *(of person)* desviarse de; *(of animal)* descarriarse de; **to s. from the point** divagar

**streak** [striːk] **1** *n (stripe)* raya *f*, lista *f*; *(in hair)* mecha *f*; **a s. of lightning** un rayo; **a s. of luck** una racha de suerte; **winning/losing s.** racha *f* de ganar/de perder; **to have a cruel s.** tener un vena de crueldad

**2** *vt* **streaked with dirt** manchado(a); **streaked with tears** cubierto(a) de lágrimas; **his hair is streaked with silver** tiene mechones grises; **to have one's hair streaked** hacerse mechas en el pelo

**3** *vi* (**a**) *(move quickly)* **to s. off** salir disparado(a); **to s. past** pasar a toda velocidad (**b**) *Fam (run naked)* hacer streaking

**streaker** ['striːkə(r)] *n Fam* persona *f* que hace streaking

**streaky** ['striːkɪ] *adj (surface, pattern)* veteado(a); **s. bacon** bacon *m* entreverado

**stream** [striːm] **1** *n* (**a**) *(brook)* arroyo *m*, riachuelo *m* (**b**) *(of light, blood, water)* chorro *m*; *(of tears, insults)* torrente *m*; *(of people)* oleada *f*; **to come on s.** *(of industrial plant)* entrar en funcionamiento

**2** *vt* (**a**) *(spurt)* chorrear (**b**) *Br Sch* **to s. pupils** dividir en grupos a los alumnos según su capacidad

**3** *vi* (**a**) **the water streamed out** el agua salía a chorros; **people streamed into the stadium** la gente entraba en masa al estadio; **his eyes were streaming** le lloraban los ojos (**b**) *(of hair, banner)* ondear

**streamer** ['striːmə(r)] *n* serpentina *f*

**streamline** ['striːmlaɪn] *vt (vehicle)* hacer más aerodinámico(a); *Fig (system, department)* racionalizar

**streamlined** ['striːmlaɪnd] *adj (vehicle)* aerodinámico(a); *Fig (system, department)* racionalizado(a)

**street** [striːt] *n* (**a**) *(of body)* calle *f*; **on the s.** en la calle; **s. fighting** peleas *fpl* callejeras; **s. lamp** farola *f*; **s. map** plano *m* de calles; *(book)* callejero *m*; **s. market** mercado *m* en la calle; **s. sweeper** barrendero(a) *m,f*; **s. theatre** teatro *m* callejero; **s. value** *(of drugs)* valor *m* en la calle (**b**) *(idioms)* **to walk the streets** *(of prostitute)* hacer la calle; **the man in the s.** el hombre de la calle; *Fam* **to be streets better than** dar mil vueltas a; **that's right up my s.** eso es lo que me va; *Fam* **to have s. cred** tener buena imagen entre la gente

**streetcar** ['striːtkɑː(r)] *n US* tranvía *m*

**streetwalker** ['striːtwɔːkə(r)] *n* prostituta *f*

**streetwise** ['striːtwaɪz] *adj* espabilado(a)

**strength** [streŋθ] *n* (**a**) *(power)* *(of person)* fuerza *f*; *(of nail, rope)* resistencia *f*; *(of currency)* fortaleza *f*; *(of emotion, light, sound)* intensidad *f*; *(of alcohol)* graduación *f*; **to be at full s.** *(of department, regiment)* tener el cupo completo; **to be under s.** *(of department, regiment)* estar debajo del cupo; **in s.** en gran número; **to go from s. to s.** ir cada vez mejor; **on the s. of...** atendiendo a... (**b**) *(strong point)* punto *m* fuerte

**strengthen** ['streŋθən] **1** *vt (wall, building)* reforzar; *(muscles)* fortalecer; *(friendship)* consolidar; *(determination)* reafirmar; *(position)* reforzar, afianzar

**2** *vi (of friendship)* consolidarse; *(of determination)* reafirmarse; *(of currency)* fortalecerse

**strenuous** ['strenjʊəs] *adj (activity, lifestyle)* agotador(ora); *(effort)* denodado(a); *(opposition)* enérgico(a); *(denial)* tajante

**strenuously** ['strenjʊəslɪ] *adv (campaign)* enérgicamente; *(resist)* denodadamente; *(deny)* tajantemente

**stress** [stres] **1** *n* (**a**) *(tension)* *(physical)* presión *f*; *(mental)* estrés *m*; **to be under a lot of s.** estar sometido(a) a mucho estrés; **a s. factor** un factor de estrés (**b**) *(emphasis)* énfasis *m*; *Ling* acento *m*; **to put s. on sth** hacer hincapié en algo

**2** *vt (emphasize)* subrayar, hacer hincapié en

**stressful** ['stresfʊl] *adj* estresante

**stretch** [stretʃ] **1** *n* (**a**) *(of body)* **to have a s.** estirarse; **by no s. of the imagination** de ningún modo; **s. marks** estrías *fpl* (**b**) *(of water, land)* extensión *f*; *(of road)* tramo *m*; *(of time, silence)* período *m*; **at one s.** de una vez (**c**) *(factory)* **at full s.** a pleno rendimiento

**2** *vt* (**a**) *(extend)* *(elastic, belt)* estirar; *(arm, hand)* estirar, extender; **to s. one's legs** estirar las piernas; **to s. the truth** apurar *or* forzar las cosas (**b**) *(put demands on)* *(person)* exigir mucho a; *(resources)* mermar mucho; *(sb's patience)* abusar de; **we're fully stretched at the moment** en este momento estamos trabajando al límite (de nuestras posibilidades) (**c**) *(make last)* *(income, supplies)* estirar

**3** *vi* (**a**) *(of rope, elastic, person)* estirarse (**b**) *(of road, time)* extenderse (**c**) *(of resources, budget)* dar de sí (**to para**)

▸**stretch out 1** *vt sep* (**a**) *(extend)* **to s. out one's arm** estirar el brazo; **to s. out one's hand** tender la mano (**b**) *(resources, budget)* estirar

**2** *vi* (**a**) *(of person)* tenderse (**b**) *(of road, time)* extenderse

**stretcher** ['stretʃə(r)] *n* camilla *f*; **s. bearer** camillero(a) *m,f*

**stretchy** ['stretʃɪ] *adj* elástico(a)

**strew** [struː] *(pp* **strewed** *or* **strewn** [struːn]) *vt (objects)* dispersar (**over** *or* **around** por); *(surface)* cubrir (**with** de)

**stricken** ['strɪkən] *adj (with grief, guilt)* afligido(a) (**with** por); *(with illness, by disaster)* gravemente afectado(a) (**with/by** por)

**strict** [strɪkt] *adj* (**a**) *(person, instruction, discipline)* estricto(a); **s. morals** moral *f* estricta; **a s. Moslem** un musulmán ortodoxo (**b**) *(meaning, minimum)* estricto(a); **in strictest confidence** en el más riguroso secreto

**strictly** ['strıktlı] *adv* (a) *(severely)* estrictamente (b) *(exactly)* rigurosamente; **s. speaking**
en un sentido estricto; **not s. true** no del todo
*or* rigurosamente cierto

**strictness** ['strıktnıs] *n (of discipline, rules)*
rigor *m*

**stride** [straɪd] **1** *n* (a) *zancada f* (b) *(idioms)* **to
make great strides** progresar a pasos agigan-
tados; **to take sth in one's s.** asumir algo
bien; **to get into one's s.** coger el ritmo
**2** *vi (pt* **strode** [strɔ̆ud], *pp* **stridden** ['strıdən])
**to s. in/out/off** entrar/salir/alejarse a
grandes zancadas

**strident** ['straɪdənt] *adj* estridente

**strife** [straɪf] *n* conflictos *mpl*

**strike** [straɪk] **1** *n* (a) *Ind* huelga *f*; **teachers'/miners' s.** huelga de profesores/de
mineros; **to be on s.** estar en huelga; **to go
on s.** declararse en huelga; **s. fund** caja *f* de
resistencia; **s. pay** subsidio *m* de huelga
(b) *(discovery) (of ore, oil)* descubrimiento *m*
(c) *(blow)* golpe *m*; *Mil* ataque *m*
**2** *vt (pt & pp* **struck** [strʌk]) (a) *(hit)* golpear;
**to s. sb in the face** golpear a alguien en la
cara; **to s. sb a blow** pegar un golpe a alguien;
*Fig* **to s. a blow for freedom** romper una
lanza a favor de la libertad; **the clock struck
ten** el reloj dio las diez; *Fig* **to s. the right
note** *(of speech, remark)* calar hondo; *Fig* **to s.
the wrong note** *(of speech, remark)* dar una
nota discordante; **to s. terror into sb** aterrorizar a alguien; **to be struck dumb** quedarse
mudo(a), no poder articular palabra; **he was
struck dead by a heart attack** murió de un
ataque cardíaco; **the child/the tree was
struck by lightning** el niño/el árbol fue alcanzado por un rayo
(b) *(collide with)* chocar contra; **her head
struck the floor** su cabeza chocó contra el
suelo
(c) *(a match)* encender, prender
(d) *(mint) (coin, medal)* acuñar
(e) *(impress, surprise)* chocar, sorprender; **what
struck me was her voice** lo que me chocó
mucho fue su voz
(f) *(occur to)* **it strikes me that...** se me
ocurre que...
(g) *(seem to)* parecer; **it doesn't s. me as
being very difficult** no me parece muy difícil; **he strikes me as a reasonable person**
me da la impresión de que es una persona razonable
(h) *(discover) (gold, oil)* descubrir; *Fam* **to s. it
rich** hacerse rico(a); *Fam* **to s. it lucky** tener
suerte
(i) *(reach)* **to s. a bargain** *or* **deal** hacer un
trato; **to s. a balance** encontrar un equilibrio
**3** *vi* (a) *(attack) (of enemy, criminal)* atacar; *(of
disaster, earthquake)* sobrevenir; *(of clock)* dar las

horas; **s. while the iron is hot** aprovecha
ahora que estás a tiempo .
(b) *(go on strike)* hacer huelga, declararse en
huelga; *(be on strike)* estar en huelga

▶**strike back** *vi (retaliate)* devolver el ataque

▶**strike down** *vt sep (of disease)* abatir, abatirse
sobre; *(of lightning, bullet)* alcanzar

▶**strike off** *vt sep (doctor, lawyer)* expulsar del
colegio profesional

▶**strike out1** *vt sep (delete)* tachar
**2** *vi* (a) *(hit out)* **to s. out at sb** arremeter contra
alguien (b) *(leave)* partir **(for** hacia); **to s. out in
a new direction** tomar un nuevo rumbo; **to s.
out on one's own** independizarse

▶**strike up** *vt sep (song)* arrancar con; *(friendship, conversation)* trabar, iniciar

**strikebreaker** ['straɪkbreɪkə(r)] *n* esquirol
*mf*

**striker** ['straɪkə(r)] *n* (a) *(striking worker)* huelguista *mf* (b) *(in football)* delantero *m*

**striking** ['straɪkıŋ] *adj* (a) *(noticeable, surprising)* chocante, sorprendente; *(impressive)* deslumbrante (b) *(worker)* en huelga

**string** [strıŋ] **1** *n* (a) *(substance)* cuerda *f*; **a
(piece of) s.** una cuerda (b) *(of violin, tennis
racket, bow)* cuerda *f*; *(of puppet)* hilo *m*; *Mus* **the
strings** la sección de cuerda, las cuerdas; *Fig* **to
have more than one s. to one's bow** tener
varios recursos; *Fig* **with no strings attached**
sin compromiso; *Fig* **to pull strings** mover
hilos; *Mus* **s. quartet** cuarteto *m* de cuerda; *Br*
**s. vest** camiseta *f* interior de rejilla; *(of
onions)* ristra *f*; *(of pearls, beads)* sarta *f*; *(of islands)*
rosario *m*; *(of words, shops, defeats)* serie *f*; *Comptr*
cadena *f*
**2** *vt (pp & pt* **strung** [strʌŋ]) (a) *(violin, tennis
racket, bow)* encordar (b) *(pearls, beads)* ensartar

▶**string along** *vt sep Fam* dar falsas esperanzas a

▶**string up** *vt sep Fam (criminal)* ahorcar

**stringed** [strıŋd] *adj (instrument)* de cuerda

**stringent** ['strındʒənt] *adj* riguroso(a), es-
tricto(a)

**strip¹** [strıp] *n* (a) *(of cloth, paper, metal)* tira *f*;
*(of land)* franja *f*; *Fam* **to tear sb off a s.** echar
un rapapolvo a alguien; **s. cartoon** tira *f* cómica; **s. lighting** iluminación *f* con fluorescentes
(b) *(of football team)* indumentaria *f*

**strip²** **1** *n* **to do a s.** *(undress)* hacer un striptease; **s. club** club *m* de striptease; **s. poker**
strip póquer *m*; **s. show** (espectáculo *m* de)
striptease *m*
**2** *vt (pt & pp* **stripped**) *(person)* desnudar;
*(bed)* deshacer; *(paint, wallpaper)* rascar, quitar;
**to s. sb of sth** despojar a alguien de algo
**3** *vi (undress)* desnudarse

▶**strip off 1** vt sep (paint, wallpaper) rascar, quitar

**2** vi (undress) desnudarse, desvestirse

**stripe** [straɪp] n **(a)** (on cloth, animal's coat) raya f, lista f **(b)** (indicating rank) galón m

**striped** [straɪpt] adj a rayas

**stripling** ['strɪplɪŋ] n mozalbete m

**stripper** ['strɪpə(r)] n (striptease artist) artista mf de striptease

**strip-search** ['strɪpsɜːtʃ] **1** n registro m integral

**2** vt to s. sb someter a alguien a un registro integral

**striptease** ['strɪptiːz] n striptease m

**strive** [straɪv] (pt **strove** [strəʊv], pp **striven** ['strɪvən]) vi esforzarse; **to s. to do sth** esforzarse por hacer algo; **to s. for** or **after sth** luchar por algo

**striven** ['strɪvən] pp of **strive**

**strobe** [strəʊb] n Phys estroboscopio m; **s. lighting** luces fpl estroboscópicas (de discoteca)

**strode** [strəʊd] pt of **stride**

**stroke** [strəʊk] **1** n **(a)** (blow, tennis shot) golpe m; (in rowing) palada f; (movement in swimming) brazada f; (swimming style) estilo m; **a brush s.** Art una pincelada; (of decorator) un brochazo; **on the s. of nine** al dar las nueve **(b)** (caress) caricia f; **to give sth/sb a s.** acariciar algo/a alguien **(c)** Med derrame m cerebral, apoplejía f **(d)** (idioms) **she hasn't done a s. of work** no ha dado ni golpe; **a s. of luck** un golpe de suerte; **a s. of genius** una genialidad; **at a s.** de un golpe

**2** vt (caress) acariciar

**stroll** [strəʊl] **1** n paseo m; **to go for a s.** ir a dar un paseo

**2** vi caminar

**strong** [strɒŋ] **1** adj **(a)** (physically or mentally powerful) fuerte; (friendship, argument) sólido(a) **(b)** (intense) (colour, light) intenso(a); (smell, drink) fuerte; (resemblance, accent) marcado(a); (belief, support) firme; (protest, measures, language) fuerte; (possibility) serio(a); **s. point** (punto m) fuerte m **(c)** (durable) (rope, cloth, shoes) fuerte, resistente **(d)** (good) (candidate) firme; (team) fuerte; **she's s. at physics** la física es una de sus fuertes

**2** adv **to be still going s.** estar todavía en forma

**3** npl **the s.** los fuertes

**strong-arm tactics** ['strɒŋɑːm'tæktɪks] npl mano f dura

**strong-box** ['strɒŋbɒks] n caja f fuerte

**stronghold** ['strɒŋhəʊld] n (fortress) fortaleza f; Fig (of political party, religion) baluarte m, bastión m

**strongly** ['strɒŋlɪ] adv (oppose, endorse) rotundamente, fuertemente; (believe) firmemente; **s. built** sólidamente construido(a); **a s. worded letter** una carta escrita en un tono fuerte; **he feels very s. about it** (es un tema que) le preocupa mucho

**strongman** ['strɒŋmæn] n (in circus) forzudo m; Fig (dictator) dictador m

**strong-minded** [strɒŋ'maɪndɪd] adj decidido(a), resuelto(a)

**strongroom** ['strɒŋruːm] n cámara f acorazada

**strong-willed** [strɒŋ'wɪld] adj tenaz, tozudo(a)

**strontium** ['strɒntɪəm] n Chem estroncio m

**stroppy** ['strɒpɪ] adj Br Fam **to be s.** (by nature) tener mala leche; (in a mood) estar de mala leche

**strove** [strəʊv] pt of **strive**

**struck** [strʌk] pt & pp of **strike**

**structural** ['strʌktʃərəl] adj estructural; **s. damage** daños mpl estructurales; **s. survey** peritaje m or tasación f de estructuras

**structurally** ['strʌktʃərəlɪ] adv estructuralmente

**structure** ['strʌktʃə(r)] **1** n **(a)** (in general) estructura f **(b)** (building, monument) construcción f

**2** vt estructurar, articular

**struggle** ['strʌgəl] **1** n (effort) lucha f (for por); (physical fight) forcejeo m; **without a s.** sin oponer resistencia; **life is a s.** la vida es una lucha constante

**2** vi (try hard) luchar (for por); (fight physically) forcejear; **to s. to do sth** luchar por hacer algo; **to be struggling** (of person, company) estar pasándolo muy mal

**strum** [strʌm] (pt & pp **strummed**) vt (guitar) rasguear

**strung** [strʌŋ] pt & pp of **string**

**strut¹** [strʌt] n (for frame) riostra f; Av montante m

**strut²** (pt & pp **strutted**) vi pavonearse; **to s. in/out** entrar/salir pavoneándose

**strychnine** ['strɪkniːn] n estricnina f

**stub** [stʌb] n (of pencil) punta f final; (of cigarette) colilla f; (of cheque) matriz f

**2** vt (pt & pp **stubbed**) **to s. one's toe** (on or against sth) darse un golpe en el dedo gordo (contra algo)

▶**stub out** vt sep (cigarette) apagar, aplastar

**stubble** ['stʌbəl] n **(a)** (in field) rastrojo m **(b)** (on face) barba f de unos días

**stubborn** ['stʌbən] adj (person) testarudo(a), terco(a); (determination, resistance) obstinado(a), pertinaz; (stain, infection) pertinaz; **as s. as a mule** terco(a) como una mula

**stubbornness** ['stʌbənnɪs] n (of person) testarudez f; (of determination, resistance) obstinación f

**stubby** ['stʌbɪ] adj regordete(a)

**stucco** ['stʌkəʊ] n estuco m

**stuck** [stʌk] **1** adj to get s. atascarse; to be s. for sth no tener algo; Fam to be s. with sb/sth tener que cargar con alguien/algo
**2** pt & pp of **stick²**

**stuck-up** ['stʌk'ʌp] adj Fam creído(a), engreído(a)

**stud¹** [stʌd] n (fastener) automático m, corchete m; (for decoration) tachón m; (on football, rugby boots) taco m; (earring) pendiente m

**stud²** n (a) (farm) cuadra f; (stallion) semental m (b) Fam (man) semental m

**student** ['stjuːdənt] n (at university) estudiante mf; (at school) alumno(a) m,f, estudiante mf; law/medical s. estudiante mf de derecho/medicina; s. card carné m de estudiante; s. life la vida estudiantil; s. nurse estudiante mf de enfermería; s. teacher profesor(ora) m,f en prácticas; students' union (association) = en una universidad, asociación que organiza actividades, asesora y representa a los alumnos; (place) = edificio para los alumnos que cuenta con bares, discoteca, servicios y oficinas

**studied** ['stʌdɪd] adj (manner, attitude) estudiado(a)

**studio** ['stjuːdɪəʊ] (pl studios) n (of TV, film company) estudio m, plató m; (of artist, photographer) estudio m; TV s. audience público m en estudio; Br s. flat (apartamento m) estudio m

**studious** ['stjuːdɪəs] adj estudioso(a)

**study** ['stʌdɪ] **1** n (a) (investigation) estudio m, investigación f; to make a s. of sth realizar un estudio sobre algo; s. group grupo m de estudio; s. tour viaje m de estudio (b) (of artist) estudio m (c) (room) (cuarto m de) estudio m
**2** vt & vi estudiar

**stuff** [stʌf] **1** n (a) (substance) cosa f; (objects, possessions) cosas fpl; what's this s.? ¿qué es esto?; he reads all that intellectual s. se dedica a leer todas esas cosas de intelectuales; Fam this wine is good s. es bueno este vino; Fam she writes good s. escribe bien; Fam he knows his s. conoce bien el tema; Fam that's the s.! ¡sí señor!, ¡eso es! (b) (cloth) tejido m
**2** vt (fill) rellenar; (cushion) forrar, rellenar; (pockets) llenar; (dead animal) disecar; to s. sth into sth meter algo dentro de algo; Fam to s. oneself atiborrarse; Br very Fam get stuffed! ¡que te den!

**stuffing** ['stʌfɪŋ] n (for furniture, chicken) relleno m; Fam to knock the s. out of sb dejar la moral por los suelos a alguien

**stuffy** ['stʌfɪ] adj (a) (room) cargado(a) (b) (person) retrógrado(a), anticuado(a)

**stultifying** ['stʌltɪfaɪɪŋ] adj tedioso(a)

**stumble** ['stʌmbl] **1** n tropezón m
**2** vi (when walking) tropezar, toparse; Fig (when speaking) trastabillar

▸**stumble across** vt insep (find) tropezar con, toparse con

**stump** [stʌmp] **1** n (a) (of tree) tocón m; (of arm, leg) muñón m (b) (in cricket) estaca f (c) Fam to be on the s. (of politician) estar de campaña electoral
**2** vt (baffle) dejar perplejo(a); to be stumped for an answer no saber qué contestar

▸**stump up** vi Br Fam (pay) apoquinar

**stumpy** ['stʌmpɪ] adj rechoncho(a)

**stun** [stʌn] (pt & pp stunned) vt (make unconscious) dejar sin sentido; Fig (shock) dejar de piedra

**stung** [stʌŋ] pt & pp of **sting**

**stunk** [stʌŋk] pp of **stink**

**stunning** ['stʌnɪŋ] adj (blow) contundente; (performance) soberbio(a); (woman, outfit) imponente

**stunt¹** [stʌnt] vt (person, growth) atrofiar

**stunt²** n (in film) escena f peligrosa; (for publicity) truco m publicitario; s. man especialista m, doble m

**stupefy** ['stjuːpɪfaɪ] vt (of alcohol, drugs, news) aturdir, ofuscar; (of behaviour) dejar perplejo(a)

**stupefying** ['stjuːpɪfaɪɪŋ] adj (boring) embotante; (amazing) asombroso(a)

**stupendous** [stjuː'pendəs] adj estupendo(a), extraordinario(a)

**stupid** ['stjuːpɪd] adj estúpido(a), idiota; don't be s.! ¡no seas estúpido!; how s. of me! ¡qué tonto/a soy!; what a s. thing to do! ¡menuda estupidez!

**stupidity** [stjuː'pɪdɪtɪ] n estupidez f, imbecilidad f

**stupidly** ['stjuːpɪdlɪ] adv tontamente

**stupor** ['stjuːpə(r)] n aturdimiento m

**sturdy** ['stɜːdɪ] adj (person) robusto(a); (object) resistente; (opposition, resistance) firme, sólido(a)

**sturgeon** ['stɜːdʒən] n esturión m

**stutter** ['stʌtə(r)] **1** n tartamudeo m
**2** vi tartamudear

**sty¹** [staɪ] n (pigsty) & Fig pocilga f

**sty², stye** [staɪ] n Med orzuelo m

**style** [staɪl] **1** n (manner, design, sophistication) estilo m; she has s. tiene estilo; to live in s. vivir con lujo
**2** vt (design) diseñar; (hair) peinar

**stylish** ['staɪlɪʃ] adj elegante

**stylist** ['staɪlɪst] n (hairdresser) peluquero(a) m,f, estilista mf

**stylistic** [staɪ'lɪstɪk] adj estilístico(a)

**stylized** ['staɪəlaɪzd] adj convencional, estereotipado(a)

**stylus** ['staıləs] *n* (*for engraving*) estilo *m*, punzón *m*; (*on record player*) aguja *f*

**stymie** ['staımı] *vt Fam* bloquear

**suave** [swɑ:v] *adj* fino(a), cortés; *Pej* zalamero(a), lisonjero(a)

**sub** [sʌb] *Fam* **1** *n* (**a**) (*abbr* **subscription**) (*to newspaper, magazine*) suscripción *f*; (*to club*) cuota *f* (**b**) (*abbr* **substitute**) suplente *mf* (**c**) (*abbr* **submarine**) submarino *m* (**d**) *Journ* (*abbr* **subeditor**) redactor(ora) *m,f*

**2** *vt* (*pt & pp* **subbed**) *Journ* (*abbr* **subedit**) corregir

**3** *vi* (*abbr* **substitute**) **to s. for sb** reemplazar *or* sustituir a alguien

**subaltern** ['sʌbəltən] *n Mil* (oficial *m*) subalterno *m* (*por debajo de capitán*)

**subcommittee** ['sʌbkəmıtı] *n* subcomité *m*

**subconscious** [sʌb'kɒnʃəs] *n & adj* subconsciente *m*

**subcontinent** [sʌb'kɒntınənt] *n* subcontinente *m*; **the (Indian) S.** el subcontinente asiático *or* indio

**subcontract** *Com* **1** *n* [sʌb'kɒntrækt] subcontrato *m*

**2** *vt* [sʌbkən'trækt] subcontratar

**subcontractor** ['sʌbkəntræktə(r)] *n Com* subcontratista *mf*

**subculture** ['sʌbkʌltʃə(r)] *n* subcultura *f*

**subcutaneous** [sʌbkju'teınıəs] *adj* subcutáneo(a)

**subdivision** ['sʌbdıvıʒən] *n* subdivisión *f*

**subdue** [səb'dju:] *vt* (*enemy*) someter, subyugar; (*resistance*) doblegar; (*emotions*) dominar, controlar

**subdued** [səb'dju:d] *adj* (*person, voice, tone*) apagado(a); (*light, sound*) tenue

**subedit** [sʌb'edıt] *vt Journ* corregir

**subeditor** [sʌb'edıtə(r)] *n Journ* redactor(ora) *n,f*

**subhuman** [sʌb'hju:mən] **1** *n* bestia *mf*

**2** *adj* infrahumano(a)

**subject** ['sʌbdʒıkt] **1** *n* (**a**) (*of conversation, book, painting, photograph*) tema *m*; (*at school, university*) asignatura *f*, materia *f*; **while we are on the s.** ya que hablamos del tema; **to change the s.** cambiar de tema; **s. matter** (*of letter, book*) tema *m*, asunto *m* (**b**) *Gram* sujeto *m* (**c**) (*of monarch*) súbdito(a) *m,f*

**2** *adj* (**a**) (*state, country*) sometido(a) (**b**) (*prone*) **to be s. to illness/jealousy/depression** ser propenso(a) a las enfermedades/los celos/la depresión; **to be s. to delay/a fine of £50** estar sujeto(a) a retrasos/una multa de 50 libras (**c**) **s. to** (*dependent on*) sujeto(a) a

**3** *vt* [səb'dʒekt] (**a**) (*subjugate*) (*people, nation*) someter, subyugar (**b**) (*force to undergo*) **to s. sb to sth** someter a alguien a algo

**subjective** [səb'dʒektıv] *adj* subjetivo(a)

**subjectivity** [sʌbdʒek'tıvıtı] *n* subjetividad *f*

**sub judice** ['sʌb'dʒu:dısı] *adj Law* sub iudice, sub júdice

**subjugate** ['sʌbdʒʊgeıt] *vt* (*people, nation*) someter, subyugar

**subjunctive** [səb'dʒʌŋktıv] *Gram* **1** *n* subjuntivo *m*

**2** *adj* subjuntivo(a)

**sublet** [sʌb'let] (*pt & pp* **sublet**) *vt* subarrendar

**sublimate** ['sʌblımeıt] *vt* sublimar

**sublime** [sə'blaım] **1** *n* **from the s. to the ridiculous** de lo sublime a lo ridículo

**2** *adj* (*beauty*) sublime; *Ironic* (*ignorance*) supino(a), sumo(a)

**subliminal** [sʌb'lımınəl] *adj Psy* subliminal

**submachine gun** [sʌbmə'ʃi:ngʌn] *n* metralleta *f*

**submarine** [sʌbmə'ri:n] *n* submarino *m*

**submerge** [səb'mɜ:dʒ] **1** *vt* (*immerse*) sumergir; (*flood*) inundar; *Fig* **to s. oneself in one's work** encerrarse en el trabajo

**2** *vi* (*of submarine, diver*) sumergirse

**submersion** [səb'mɜ:ʃən] *n* inmersión *f*

**submission** [səb'mıʃən] *n* (**a**) (*to person's will, authority*) sumisión *f*; **to starve sb into s.** someter a alguien dejándole sin comer; **to beat sb into s.** someter a alguien a golpes (**b**) (*of documents*) entrega *f* (**c**) (*report*) ponencia *f*, presentación *f*

**submissive** [səb'mısıv] *adj* sumiso(a)

**submit** [səb'mıt] **1** *vt* presentar; **to s. sth for approval/inspection** presentar algo para su aprobación/inspección

**2** *vi* (*to person, authority*) someterse (**to** a)

**subnormal** [sʌb'nɔːməl] *adj* subnormal

**subordinate** [sə'bɔːdınət] **1** *n* subordinado(a) *m,f*

**2** *adj* (*rank, role*) secundario(a), inferior; **to be s. to sb** estar subordinado(a) a alguien; *Gram* **s. clause** oración *f* subordinada

**3** *vt* [sə'bɔːdıneıt] subordinar

**subordination** [səbɔːdı'neıʃən] *n* subordinación *f*

**subplot** ['sʌbplɒt] *n* trama *f* secundaria

**subpoena** [sə'piːnə] *Law* **1** *n* citación *f*

**2** *vt* citar

**subscribe** [səb'skraıb] *vi* (**a**) **to s. to** (*newspaper, magazine*) suscribirse a; (*to charity*) dar donativos a; (*to telephone, Internet service*) abonarse a (**b**) **to s. to** (*opinion, theory*) suscribir

**subscriber** [səb'skraıbə(r)] *n* (*to newspaper, magazine*) suscriptor(ora) *m,f*; (*to telephone, Internet service*) abonado(a) *m,f*; (*to charity*) donador(ora) *m,f*

**subscript** ['sʌbskrıpt] *n Typ* subíndice *m*; **s. 'a'** "a" escrita como subíndice

**subscription** [sʌb'skrɪpʃən] *n (to newspaper, magazine)* suscripción *f; (to club)* cuota *f; (to charity)* donativo *m*

**subsection** ['sʌbsekʃən] *n* apartado *m*

**subsequent** ['sʌbsɪkwənt] *adj* posterior

**subservient** [sʌb'sɜ:vɪənt] *adj* servil

**subset** ['sʌbset] *n* subconjunto *m*

**subside** [səb'saɪd] *vi (of ground, building)* hundirse; *(of water)* bajar (de nivel); *(of blister, bump)* bajar, deshincharse; *(of storm)* amainar; *(of excitement, fever)* calmarse

**subsidence** [səb'saɪdəns] *n (of ground, building)* hundimiento *m; (of water)* bajada *f*

**subsidiarity** [sʌbsɪdɪ'ærɪtɪ] *n* subsidiariedad *f*

**subsidiary** [sʌb'sɪdɪərɪ] **1** *n (company)* filial *f*
**2** *adj* secundario(a)

**subsidize** ['sʌbsɪdaɪz] *vt* subvencionar

**subsidy** ['sʌbsɪdɪ] *n* subvención *f*

**subsistence** [səb'sɪstəns] *n* subsistencia *f; Com* **s. allowance** dietas *fpl;* **s. wage** salario *m* exiguo

**subspecies** ['sʌbspi:ʃi:z] *n* subespecie *f*

**substance** ['sʌbstəns] *n (a) (matter)* sustancia *f* **(b)** *(essential element) (of article, argument)* esencia *f;* **I agree in s.** esencialmente, estoy de acuerdo **(c)** *(solidity, worth)* consistencia *f;* **the accusations lack s.** las acusaciones son inconsistentes

**substandard** [sʌb'stændəd] *adj* deficiente

**substantial** [səb'stænʃəl] *adj (a) (significant) (progress, difference)* sustancial, significativo(a); *(reason, evidence)* de peso; **a s. number of...** una cantidad considerable de... **(b)** *(meal)* abundante; *(structure)* sólido(a); *(book)* enjundioso(a) **(c)** *(sum of money, profit)* sustancioso(a), considerable

**substantially** [səb'stænʃəlɪ] *adv (a) (considerably) (better, worse)* significativamente, considerablemente **(b)** *(for the most part)* esencialmente **(c)** *(solidly)* firmemente

**substantiate** [səb'stænʃɪeɪt] *vt (statement, claim)* probar

**substantive** ['sʌbstəntɪv] **1** *n Gram* sustantivo *m*
**2** *adj (measures, issue)* significativo(a)

**substitute** ['sʌbstɪtju:t] **1** *n (thing)* sustituto *m; (person)* sustituto(a) *m,f; Sport* suplente *mf;* **coffee s.** sucedáneo *m* de café
**2** *vt* sustituir, reemplazar **(for** por)
**3** *vi* **to s. for sb** sustituir *or* reemplazar a alguien

**substitution** [sʌbstɪ'tju:ʃən] *n* sustitución *f; Sport* sustitución *f,* cambio *m*

**subsume** [sʌb'sju:m] *vt Formal* englobar, incluir

**subterfuge** ['sʌbtəfju:dʒ] *n (trickery)* subterfugios *mpl*

**subterranean** [sʌbtə'reɪnɪən] *adj* subterráneo(a)

**subtitle** ['sʌbtaɪtəl] *TV & Cin* **1** *n* subtítulo *m*
**2** *vt* subtitular

**subtle** ['sʌtəl] *adj* sutil

**subtlety** ['sʌtəltɪ] *n* sutileza *f*

**subtly** ['sʌtlɪ] *adv* sutilmente

**subtotal** ['sʌbtəʊtəl] *n* subtotal *m*

**subtract** [səb'trækt] *vt* restar, sustraer

**subtraction** [səb'trækʃən] *n* resta *f,* sustracción *f*

**subtropical** [sʌb'trɒpɪkəl] *adj* subtropical

**suburb** ['sʌbɜːb] *n* = zona residencial en la periferia de una ciudad; **the suburbs** las zonas residenciales de la periferia

**suburban** [sə'bɜːbən] *adj (attitudes, life)* aburguesado(a); **s. train** tren *m* de cercanías

**suburbia** [sə'bɜːbɪə] *n* zonas *fpl* residenciales de la periferia

**subversion** [səb'vɜːʃən] *n* subversión *f*

**subversive** [səb'vɜːsɪv] *n & adj* subversivo(a) *m,f*

**subvert** [səb'vɜːt] *vt* subvertir

**subway** ['sʌbweɪ] *n (a) Br (underpass)* paso *m* subterráneo **(b)** *US (underground railway)* metro *m, CSur* subte *m*

**sub-zero** [sʌb'zɪərəʊ] *adj* bajo cero

**succeed** [sək'si:d] **1** *vt (follow)* suceder a
**2** *vi (a) (be successful) (of person)* tener éxito; *(of plan)* tener éxito, funcionar; *(in life)* triunfar; **to s. in doing sth** conseguir *or* lograr hacer algo **(b)** **to s. to the throne** suceder al *or* en el trono

**succeeding** [sək'si:dɪŋ] *adj (following)* siguiente

**success** [sək'ses] *n* éxito *m;* **to be a s.** ser un éxito; **without s.** sin éxito; **to meet with s.** tener éxito; **s. story** éxito *m*

**successful** [sək'sesfʊl] *adj (person)* con éxito; *(attempt, negotiations)* fructífero(a); *(project, film novel)* exitoso(a); **one of Britain's most s. authors** uno de los autores británicos de más éxito; **s. applicants** los candidatos elegidos; **to be s.** *(of person, project)* tener éxito; **to be s. in doing sth** conseguir *or* lograr hacer algo

**successfully** [sək'sesfəlɪ] *adv* con éxito

**succession** [sək'seʃən] *n* sucesión *f;* **for two years in s.** dos años consecutivos

**successive** [sək'sesɪv] *adj* sucesivo(a)

**successor** [sək'sesə(r)] *n* sucesor(ora) *m,f*

**succinct** [sʌk'sɪŋkt] *adj* sucinto(a), escueto(a)

**succulent** ['sʌkjʊlənt] **1** *n Bot* planta *f* carnosa *or* suculenta
**2** *adj (delicious)* suculento(a)

**succumb** [sə'kʌm] *vi* sucumbir **(to** a)

**such** [sʌtʃ] **1** *pron* **if s. were the case** en tal caso; **and s.** y otros(as) por el estilo; **s. is life!**

¡así es la vida!; **philosophy as s. is not taught in our schools** la filosofía, como tal (asignatura), no se enseña en nuestros colegios; **the text as s. is fine but...** el texto en sí está bien pero...; **I wasn't scared as s.** asustado, lo que se dice asustado, no estaba

**2** *adj* tal; **s. a man** un hombre así, semejante hombre; **s. ignorance** tamaña *or* semejante ignorancia; **animals s. as the lion or the tiger** animales tales como el león y el tigre; **did you ever see s. a thing!** ¿has visto alguna vez algo parecido *or* semejante?; **do you have s. a thing as a screwdriver?** ¿no tendrás un destornillador?; **how can you tell s. lies?** ¿cómo puedes mentir de esa manera?; **their problems are s. that...** sus problemas son tales *or* de tal calibre que...; **there's the church, s. as it is** ahí está la iglesia, que *or* aunque no es gran cosa; **there is no s. thing** eso no existe; **I said no s. thing** yo no dije tal cosa *or* nada de eso; **on s. and s. a day** tal día; **in s. a way that...** de tal forma *or* forma tal que...; *Formal* **until s. time as may be convenient** en tanto resulte conveniente

**3** *adv* tan; **I had never seen s. a big house** nunca había visto una casa tan grande; **I had never heard s. good music** nunca había escuchado una música tan buena; **it was s. a long time ago** pasó hace tanto tiempo; **we had s. a good time!** ¡nos lo pasamos tan bien!

**suchlike** ['sʌtʃlaɪk] *pron* **and s.** y similares

**suck** [sʌk] **1** *vt* *(lollipop)* chupar; *(liquid)* succionar; *(mother's milk)* mamar; *(air)* aspirar; **to s. one's thumb** chuparse el dedo

**2** *vi US very Fam* **that film/idea sucks!** ¡esa película/idea es una caca!

▸**suck in** *vt sep (gas)* aspirar; *(liquid)* succionar; *Fig* **to get sucked into sth** *(situation)* caer en algo

▸**suck up 1** *vt sep (liquid)* succionar; *(dust)* aspirar

**2** *vi very Fam* **to s. up to sb** hacer la pelota a alguien

**sucker** ['sʌkə(r)] *n* **(a)** *(of octopus)* ventosa *f*; *(of plant)* chupón *m*, vástago *m* **(b)** *Fam (gullible person)* pringado/a *m,f*, primo/a *m,f*; **he's a s. for blondes** las rubias le chiflan

**suckle** ['sʌkəl] **1** *vt (child, young)* amamantar

**2** *vi (of baby, animal)* mamar

**sucrose** ['su:krəʊs] *n* sacarosa *f*

**suction** ['sʌkʃən] *n* succión *f*

**Sudan** [su:'dæn] *n* Sudán

**Sudanese** [su:də'ni:z] *n & adj* sudanés(esa) *m,f*

**sudden** ['sʌdən] *adj* repentino(a), súbito(a); **all of a s.** de repente; **it was all very s.** fue todo muy precipitado; *Fig* **s. death** *(in match, contest)* muerte *f* súbita

**suddenly** ['sʌdənlɪ] *adv* de repente, de pronto

**suddenness** ['sʌdənnɪs] *n* **the s. of her death/decision** lo repentino de su muerte/decisión

**suds** [sʌdz] *npl (of soap)* espuma *f* (de jabón)

**sue** [su:] **1** *vt Law* demandar **(for** por)

**2** *vi* **(a)** *Law* **to s. for divorce** solicitar el divorcio **(b)** **to s. for peace** pedir la paz

**suede** [sweɪd] *n* ante *m*

**suet** ['su:ɪt] *n* sebo *m*, unto *m*

**Suez** ['su:ɪz] *n* **the S. Canal** el Canal de Suez

**suffer** ['sʌfə(r)] **1** *vt* **(a)** *(loss, defeat, consequences)* sufrir; *(pain, sorrow)* sufrir, padecer **(b)** *(tolerate)* aguantar, soportar; **she doesn't s. fools gladly** no les da ningún cuartel a los tontos

**2** *vi* sufrir **(from** de); **your health/work will s.** se resentirá tu salud/trabajo

**sufferance** ['sʌfərəns] *n* **to admit sb on s.** tolerar la presencia de alguien

**sufferer** ['sʌfərə(r)] *n* enfermo(a) *m,f*; **a cancer s.** un enfermo de cáncer

**suffering** ['sʌfərɪŋ] *n* sufrimiento *m*

**suffice** [sə'faɪs] *vi Formal* bastar, ser suficiente

**sufficient** [sə'fɪʃənt] *adj* suficiente; **to be s.** bastar, ser suficiente; **£5 should be s.** debería bastar con 5 libras

**sufficiently** [sə'fɪʃəntlɪ] *adv* suficientemente, bastante; **to be s. big** ser (lo) suficientemente *or* lo bastante grande

**suffix** ['sʌfɪks] *n Gram* sufijo *m*

**suffocate** ['sʌfəkeɪt] **1** *vt* asfixiar; *Fig* sofocar

**2** *vi* asfixiarse

**suffocating** ['sʌfəkeɪtɪŋ] *adj* asfixiante

**suffocation** [sʌfə'keɪʃən] *n* asfixia *f*

**suffrage** ['sʌfrɪdʒ] *n Pol* sufragio *m*, derecho *m* de voto; **universal/women's s.** sufragio *m* universal/femenino

**suffragette** [sʌfrə'dʒet] *n Hist* sufragista *f*

**suffuse** [sə'fju:z] *vt Literary* **suffused with light** bañado/a de luz

**sugar** ['ʃʊgə(r)] **1** *n* **(a)** *(food)* azúcar *m or f*; **two sugars, please** dos (cucharaditas) de azúcar, por favor; **s. almond** peladilla *f*; **s. beet** remolacha *f* (azucarera); **s. bowl** azucarero *m*; **s. cane** caña *f* de azúcar; *Fam* **s. daddy** = hombre maduro que tiene una joven mantenida; **s. lump** terrón *m* de azúcar, azucarillo *m*; **s. plantation** plantación *f* de azúcar; **s. refinery** azucarera *f*, refinería *f* de azúcar **(b)** *Fam (term of address)* cielo *m*, cariño *m*

**2** *vt (coffee, tea)* echar azúcar a; *Fig* **to s. the pill** dorar la píldora

**sugar-coated** [ʃʊgə'kəʊtɪd] *adj (pills, sweets)* azucarado(a); *(almonds)* garrapiñado(a)

**sugar-free** [ʃʊgə'fri:] *adj* sin azúcar

**sugary** ['ʃʊgəri] adj (a) (containing sugar) azucarado(a) (b) Fig (smile, tone) almibarado(a)

**suggest** [sə'dʒest] vt (a) (propose) sugerir; **to s. (that)...** sugerir que...; **I s. (that) we discuss it tomorrow** sugiero que lo discutamos mañana (b) (insinuate, imply) sugerir, denotar; **her expression suggested a lack of interest** su expresión denotaba falta de interés

**suggestible** [sə'dʒestɪbəl] adj sugestionable

**suggestion** [sə'dʒestʃən] n (a) (proposal) sugerencia f; **to make a s.** hacer una sugerencia; **suggestions box** buzón m de sugerencias (b) (insinuation, hint) indicio m; **there is no s. that he might be guilty** no hay indicios de que pueda ser culpable; **she has just a s. of a foreign accent** tiene un ligerísimo acento extranjero

**suggestive** [sə'dʒestɪv] adj (a) (reminiscent, thought-provoking) sugerente; **to be s. of sth** sugerir algo (b) (erotic) insinuante

**suicidal** [sʊɪ'saɪdəl] adj suicida

**suicide** ['sʊɪsaɪd] n suicidio m; **to commit s.** suicidarse; **s. mission** misión f suicida; **s. note** = nota que deja un suicida

**suit** [suːt] 1 n (a) (clothing) traje m, Andes, CSur terno m; **s. of armour** armadura f
(b) (in cards) palo m; Fig **to follow s.** seguir el ejemplo; Fig **politeness is not his strong s.** la amabilidad no es su fuerte
(c) Law pleito m, demanda f
**2** vt (a) (of clothes, colours) sentar bien a; **blue/ this hat suits you** el azul/este sombrero te sienta bien
(b) (of arrangement, time, job) convenir, venir bien a; **to be suited to** or **for sth** (purpose, job) ser indicado(a) para algo; **they are well suited to each other** están hechos el uno para el otro; Fam **that suits me down to the ground** (eso) me viene a pedir de boca; **s. yourself** haz lo que quieras
(c) (adapt) adecuar

**suitability** [suːtə'bɪlɪtɪ] n (of arrangement, comment) conveniencia f

**suitable** ['suːtəbəl] adj adecuado(a), apropiado(a); **the film is not s. for children** la película no es apta para menores

**suitably** ['suːtəblɪ] adv (behave, dress) adecuadamente; **she was s. impressed** estaba impresionada como correspondía

**suitcase** ['suːtkeɪs] n maleta f

**suite** [swiːt] n (a) (of rooms) suite f; **(three-piece) s.** tresillo m, conjunto m de sofá y (dos) sillones (b) Mus suite f

**suitor** ['suːtə(r)] n (a) (admirer) pretendiente m (b) Law demandante mf

**sulfate, sulfide** etc US = **sulphate, sulphide** etc

**sulk** [sʌlk] 1 n to be in a s. estar enfurruñado(a)
**2** vi enfurruñarse

**sulky** ['sʌlkɪ] adj enfurruñado(a)

**sullen** ['sʌlən] adj huraño(a), hosco(a)

**sully** ['sʌlɪ] vt Literary (reputation) manchar; Fig **to s. one's hands (with sth)** mancharse las manos (con algo)

**sulphate, US sulfate** ['sʌlfeɪt] n Chem sulfato m

**sulphide, US sulfide** ['sʌlfaɪd] n Chem sulfuro m

**sulphur, US sulfur** ['sʌlfə(r)] n Chem azufre m; **s. dioxide** dióxido m de azufre

**sulphuric, US sulfuric** [sʌl'fjʊərɪk] adj Chem sulfúrico(a); **s. acid** ácido m sulfúrico

**sultan** ['sʌltən] n sultán m

**sultana** [sʌl'tɑːnə] n pasa f (de color marrón claro y sin pepitas)

**sultry** ['sʌltrɪ] adj (heat, weather) bochornoso(a), sofocante; (look, smile) sensual

**sum** [sʌm] n (amount of money, mathematical problem) suma f; **to do sums** hacer cuentas; **in s.** en suma; **the s. of my efforts** el resultado de mis esfuerzos; **s. total** (suma) total m
▶**sum up** (pt & pp **summed**) 1 vt sep (a) (summarize) resumir (b) (assess quickly) evaluar
**2** vi (summarize) resumir; (in debate, trial) recapitular

**summarily** ['sʌmərɪlɪ] adv sumariamente

**summarize** ['sʌməraɪz] vt resumir

**summary** ['sʌmərɪ] 1 n resumen m; TV & Rad **news s.** resumen m de noticias
**2** adj (brief) sumario(a); **s. dismissal** despido m inmediato

**summer** ['sʌmə(r)] 1 n verano m; **in (the) s.** en verano; **s. holidays** vacaciones fpl de verano; **s. school** escuela f de verano
**2** vi veranear

**summerhouse** ['sʌməhaʊs] n (in garden) glorieta f, cenador m

**summertime** ['sʌmətaɪm] n verano m

**summery** ['sʌmərɪ] adj veraniego(a)

**summing-up** [sʌmɪŋ'ʌp] n Law recapitulación f, conclusiones fpl

**summit** ['sʌmɪt] n (a) (of mountain, career, power) cima f, cumbre f (b) (meeting) cumbre f; **to hold a s.** celebrar una (reunión en la) cumbre

**summon** ['sʌmən] vt (police, doctor) llamar; (help) pedir; (meeting) convocar; Law (witness) citar
▶**summon up** vt sep (courage) armarse de; (support) reunir; **to s. up one's strength** hacer acopio de fuerzas

**summons** ['sʌmənz] 1 n (pl **summonses** ['sʌmənzɪz]) citación f
**2** vt Law citar

**sump** [sʌmp] *n* (a) *Aut* cárter *m* (b) *(cesspool)* pozo *m* negro

**sumptuous** ['sʌm(p)tjʊəs] *adj* suntuoso(a)

**Sun** *(abbr* **Sunday)** domingo *m*

**sun** [sʌn] **1** *n* sol *m*; **in the s.** al sol; **you've caught the s.** te ha dado el sol; **everything under the s.** todo lo habido y por haber; **s. lamp** lámpara *f* de rayos UVA; **s. lotion** loción *f* broncedora; *Aut* **s. shield** *or* **visor** parasol *m*
   **2** *vt (pt & pp* **sunned)** **to s. oneself** tomar el sol

**sunbaked** ['sʌnbeɪkt] *adj* abrasado(a), agostado(a)

**sunbathe** ['sʌnbeɪð] *vi* tomar el sol

**sunbeam** ['sʌnbi:m] *n* rayo *m* de sol

**sunbed** ['sʌnbed] *n* cama *f* de rayos UVA

**sunburn** ['sʌnbɜ:n] *n* quemadura *f* (de sol)

**sunburnt** ['sʌnbɜ:nt], **sunburned** ['sʌnbɜ:nd] *adj* quemado(a) (por el sol)

**sundae** ['sʌndeɪ] *n* helado *m* con fruta y nueces

**Sunday** ['sʌndeɪ] *n* domingo *m*; **S. best** traje *m* de los domingos; **S. paper** periódico *m* dominical or del domingo; *Rel* **S. school** catequesis *f inv* dominical; *see also* **Saturday**

**sundial** ['sʌndaɪəl] *n* reloj *m* de sol

**sundown** ['sʌndaʊn] *n* puesta *f* de sol, atardecer *m*; **at s.** al atardecer

**sun-drenched** ['sʌndrenʃt] *adj* bañado(a) de sol

**sun-dried** ['sʌndraɪd] *adj* secado(a) al sol; **s. tomatoes** tomates *mpl* secos

**sundry** ['sʌndrɪ] **1** *n* (a) **all and s.** todo quisque (b) **sundries** *(items)* artículos *mpl* varios; *(costs)* gastos *mpl* diversos
   **2** *adj* diversos(as)

**sunflower** ['sʌnflaʊə(r)] *n* girasol *m*; **s. oil** aceite *m* de girasol; **s. seeds** *(as snack)* pipas *fpl* (de girasol)

**sung** [sʌŋ] *pp of* **sing**

**sunglasses** ['sʌnglɑ:sɪz] *npl* gafas *fpl* de sol

**sunhat** ['sʌnhæt] *n* pamela *f*

**sunk** [sʌŋk] *pp of* **sink**[2]

**sunken** ['sʌŋkən] *adj (ship, eyes)* hundido(a); *(rock)* sumergido(a)

**sunlight** ['sʌnlaɪt] *n* (luz *f* del) sol *m*; **in the s.** al sol

**sunlit** ['sʌnlɪt] *adj* soleado(a)

**sunny** ['sʌnɪ] *adj* (a) *(day, place)* soleado(a); **it's s.** hace sol (b) *Fig (face, personality)* radiante

**sunray lamp** ['sʌnreɪˈlæmp] *n* lámpara *f* de rayos UVA

**sunrise** ['sʌnraɪz] *n* amanecer *m*; **at s.** al amanecer; *Econ* **s. industry** industria *f* de tecnología punta

**sunroof** ['sʌnru:f] *n Aut* techo *m* solar

**sunset** ['sʌnset] *n* puesta *f* de sol, atardecer *m*; **at s.** al atardecer

**sunshade** ['sʌnʃeɪd] *n (for table)* sombrilla *f*

**sunshine** ['sʌnʃaɪn] *n* sol *m*; **five hours' s.** cinco horas de sol

**sunspot** ['sʌnspɒt] *n* (a) *Astron* mancha *f* solar (b) *Fam (holiday resort)* lugar *m* (costero) de veraneo

**sunstroke** ['sʌnstrəʊk] *n Med* insolación *f*

**suntan** ['sʌntæn] *n* bronceado *m*; **s. lotion** loción *f* bronceadora

**suntrap** ['sʌntræp] *n* solana *f*, solanera *f (lugar)*

**sup** [sʌp] *(pt & pp* **supped)** *vt* beber a sorbos

**super** ['su:pə(r)] **1** *n (petrol)* (gasolina *f*) súper *f*
   **2** *adj Fam (excellent)* estupendo(a), formidable

**superabundant** [su:pərə'bʌndənt] *adj* superabundante

**superannuation** [su:pərænju'eɪʃən] *n Fin* pensión *f* (de jubilación)

**superb** [su:'pɜ:b] *adj* excelente

**supercharger** ['su:pətʃɑ:dʒə(r)] *n Aut & Av* sobrealimentador *m*

**supercilious** [su:pə'sɪlɪəs] *adj* arrogante, altanero(a)

**superconductor** [su:pəkən'dʌktə(r)] *n Phys* superconductor *m*

**super-duper** ['su:pə'du:pə(r)] *adj Fam* estupendo(a), fenomenal

**superego** ['su:pəri:gəʊ] *(pl* **superegos)** *n Psy* superyó *m*, superego *m*

**superficial** [su:pə'fɪʃəl] *adj* superficial

**superficiality** [su:pəfɪʃɪ'ælɪtɪ] *n* superficialidad *f*

**superficially** [su:pə'fɪʃəlɪ] *adv* superficialmente

**superfluous** [su:'pɜ:flʊəs] *adj* superfluo(a)

**superhuman** [su:pə'hju:mən] *adj* sobrehumano(a)

**superimpose** [su:pərɪm'pəʊz] *vt* superponer

**superintend** [su:pərɪn'tend] *vt* supervisar

**superintendent** [su:pərɪn'tendənt] *n (supervisor)* supervisor(ora) *m,f*, director(ora) *m,f*; *(police officer)* inspector(ora) *m,f* jefe

**superior** [su:'pɪərɪə(r)] **1** *n (senior)* superior *m*; **to be sb's s.** ser el superior de alguien
   **2** *adj* (a) *(better, more senior)* superior (b) *(arrogant)* arrogante; **a s. smile** una sonrisa (con aires) de superioridad

**superiority** [su:pɪərɪ'ɒrɪtɪ] *n* superioridad *f*

**superlative** [su:'pɜ:lətɪv] **1** *n Gram* superlativo *m*
   **2** *adj* (a) *(excellent)* excelente (b) *Gram* superlativo(a)

**superman** ['su:pəmæn] *n* superhombre *m*

**supermarket** ['su:pəmɑ:kɪt] *n* supermercado *m*

**supernatural** [su:pə'nætʃərəl] **1** *n* **the s.** lo sobrenatural

**2** *adj* sobrenatural

**superpower** ['su:pəpauə(r)] *n* superpotencia *f*

**superscript** ['su:pəskrɪpt] *n Typ* superíndice *m*; **s. 'a'** "a" escrita como superíndice

**supersede** [su:pə'si:d] *vt* sustituir

**supersonic** [su:pə'sɒnɪk] *adj Av* supersónico(a)

**superstar** ['su:pəstɑ:(r)] *n* superestrella *f*

**superstition** [su:pə'stɪʃən] *n* superstición *f*

**superstitious** [su:pə'stɪʃəs] *adj* supersticioso(a)

**superstore** ['su:pəstɔ:(r)] *n Com* hipermercado *m*, gran superficie *f*

**superstructure** ['su:pəstrʌktʃə(r)] *n* superestructura *f*

**supertanker** ['su:pətæŋkə(r)] *n Naut* superpetrolero *m*

**supervise** ['su:pəvaɪz] *vt* (*children*) vigilar; (*work, workers*) supervisar

**supervision** [su:pə'vɪʒən] *n* (*of children*) vigilancia *f*; (*of work, workers*) supervisión *f*

**supervisor** ['su:pəvaɪzə(r)] *n* supervisor(ora) *m,f*

**supervisory** [su:pə'vaɪzərɪ] *adj* de supervisión; **in a s. capacity** en calidad de supervisor(ora)

**supine** ['su:paɪn] *Formal* **1** *adj* tumbado(a) de espaldas, *Fig* (*inactive*) pasivo(a)

**2** *adv* **to lie s.** yacer de espaldas

**supper** ['sʌpə(r)] *n* (*evening meal*) cena *f*; (*snack before going to bed*) = refrigerio que se toma antes de ir a la cama; **to have s.** cenar; **we had fish for s.** cenamos pescado

**suppertime** ['sʌpətaɪm] *n* hora *f* de cenar

**supplant** [sə'plɑ:nt] *vt* desbancar; **she supplanted her rival** arrebató el puesto a su rival

**supple** ['sʌpəl] *adj* flexible

**supplement** ['sʌplɪmənt] **1** *n Journ* suplemento *m*

**2** *vt* complementar

**supplementary** [sʌplɪ'mentərɪ] *adj* complementario(a), suplementario(a)

**supplication** [sʌplɪ'keɪʃən] *n* súplica *f*

**supplier** [sə'plaɪə(r)] *n* proveedor *m*

**supply** [sə'plaɪ] **1** *n* abastecimiento *m*, suministro *m*; **a week's/a month's s. (of sth)** reservas *fpl* (de algo) para una semana/un mes; **petrol is in short s.** escasean los suministros de gasolina; *Econ* **s. and demand** la oferta y la demanda; *Mil* **s. lines** líneas *fpl* de abastecimiento; *Naut* **s. ship** buque *m* nodriza; *Sch* **s. teacher** profesor(ora) *m,f* suplente *or* interino(a)

**2** *vt* **to s. sb with sth, to s. sth to sb** suministrar algo a alguien; **to s. sb's needs** satisfacer las necesidades de alguien

**support** [sə'pɔ:t] **1** *n* (**a**) (*backing*) apoyo *m*; **to give s. to sth/sb** apoyar algo/a alguien; **in s. of...** en apoyo de...; **my son is my only means of s.** mi hijo es mi único sostén económico (**b**) (*person, thing supporting*) soporte *m*

**2** *vt* (**a**) (*hold up*) sostener, soportar; **I supported him with my arm** lo sujeté con mi brazo (**b**) (*encourage, aid*) apoyar; **to s. a team** ser seguidor(ora) de un equipo; **which team do you s.?** ¿de qué equipo eres? (**c**) (*sustain*) mantener; **to s. oneself** ganarse la vida, mantenerse

**supporter** [sə'pɔ:tə(r)] *n* (*of opinion, party*) partidario(a) *m,f*; (*of team*) seguidor(ora) *m,f*

**supporting** [sə'pɔ:tɪŋ] *adj* **s. band** teloneros *mpl*; *Cin* **s. film** película *f* de acompañamiento; *Cin & Th* **s. cast** actores *mpl* de reparto *or* secundarios

**supportive** [sə'pɔ:tɪv] *adj* **he was s.** apoyó mucho, fue muy comprensivo

**suppose** [sə'pəuz] *vt* suponer; **I s. so** supongo (que sí); **I s. not** supongo que no; **s. or supposing he came back** supongamos *or* suponiendo que volviera; **I don't s. you'd consider sharing it?** ¿considerarías la posibilidad de compartirlo?; **s. we change the subject?** ¿qué te parece si cambiamos de tema?

**supposed** [sə'pəuzd] *adj* (**a**) (*meant*) **to be s. to do sth** tener que hacer algo; **you were s. to wash the dishes** tenías que fregar los platos; **you're not s. to smoke in here** aquí dentro no se puede fumar; **there's s. to be a meeting today** se supone que hoy hay reunión (**b**) (*reputed*) **the film's s. to be very good** se supone que es una película muy buena

**supposition** [sʌpə'zɪʃən] *n* suposición *f*; **on the s. that...** dando por supuesto que...

**suppository** [sə'pɒzɪtrɪ] *n Med* supositorio *m*

**suppress** [sə'pres] *vt* (*revolt*) reprimir, sofocar; (*fact, evidence*) ocultar; (*feelings, emotions, smile*) reprimir; (*cough*) ahogar

**suppressed** [sə'prest] *adj* (*emotion*) reprimido(a)

**suppression** [sə'preʃən] *n* (*of revolt, feelings, emotions*) represión *f*; (*of fact, evidence*) ocultación *f*

**suppurate** ['sʌpjʊreɪt] *vi Med* supurar

**supranational** [su:prə'næʃənəl] *adj* supranacional

**supremacy** [sʊ'preməsɪ] *n* supremacía *f*

**supreme** [sʊ'pri:m] *adj* supremo(a); **to make the s. sacrifice** dar *or* entregar la vida; **to reign s.** (*of person*) no tener rival; (*of justice, ideology*) imperar; *Mil* **S. Commander**

comandante *m* en jefe; *US Law* **S. Court** Tribunal *m* Supremo

**supremely** [sʊ'priːmlɪ] *adv* sumamente

**supremo** [sʊ'priːməʊ] (*pl* **supremos**) *n Fam* mandamás *mf*, jefazo(a) *m,f*

**surcharge** ['sɜːtʃɑːdʒ] **1** *n* recargo *m*

**2** *vt* cobrar con recargo a

**sure** [ʃʊə(r)] **1** *adj* seguro(a); **to be s. of** *or* **about sth** estar seguro(a) de algo; **she is very s. of herself** está muy segura de sí misma; **to make s. of sth** asegurarse de algo; **to make s. (that)...** asegurarse de que...; **she's s. to win** ganará sin duda; **for s.** con (toda) seguridad; *Fam* **s. thing!** ¡desde luego!

**2** *adv* (**a**) *US Fam* (*really*) **it s. is cold** menudo frío que hace; **are you tired? – I s. am** ¿estás cansado? – ya lo creo *or* y tanto (**b**) (*yes*) claro (**c**) **s. enough he was there** efectivamente estaba allí

**surefooted** [ʃʊə'fʊtɪd] *adj* **to be s.** moverse con paso seguro

**surely** ['ʃʊəlɪ] *adv* (**a**) (*certainly*) seguramente, sin duda; **s. you don't believe that!** ¡no me digas que te crees eso!; **s. not!** ¡no me digas! (**b**) (*in a sure manner*) **slowly but s.** lento pero seguro

**surety** ['ʃʊərətɪ] *n Law* (*money*) fianza *f*, garantía *f*; **to stand s. (for sb)** ser fiador(ora) *m,f or* garante *mf* (de alguien)

**surf** [sɜːf] **1** *n* oleaje *m*

**2** *vt Comptr* **to s. the Net** navegar por Internet

**3** *vi Sport* hacer surf

**surface** ['sɜːfɪs] **1** *n* (**a**) (*exterior, face*) superficie *f*; *Fig* **on the s.** a primera vista; **by s. mail** por correo terrestre; *Phys* **s. tension** tensión *f* superficial; **s. water** aguas *fpl* superficiales (**b**) (*area*) área *f*, superficie *f*

**2** *vt* (*road*) pavimentar, revestir

**3** *vi* (*of submarine, whale*) salir a la superficie; *Fig* (*of person, emotion*) surgir, aparecer

**surface-to-air missile** ['sɜːfɪstʊeə-'mɪsaɪl] *n Mil* misil *m* superficie-aire *or* tierra-aire

**surface-to-surface missile** ['sɜːfɪstə-'sɜːfɪs'mɪsaɪl] *n Mil* misil *m* superficie-superficie *or* tierra-tierra

**surfboard** ['sɜːfbɔːd] *n* tabla *f* de surf

**surfeit** ['sɜːfɪt] *n* exceso *m*

**surfer** ['sɜːfə(r)] *n* surfista *mf*

**surfing** ['sɜːfɪŋ] *n* surf *m*

**surge** [sɜːdʒ] **1** *n* (*of electricity*) sobrecarga *f* (*temporal*); (*of enthusiasm, support*) oleada *f*

**2** *vi* (*of electricity*) experimentar una sobrecarga (*temporal*); (*of sea*) encresparse; (*of crowd*) abalanzarse

**surgeon** ['sɜːdʒən] *n* cirujano(a) *m,f*

**surgery** ['sɜːdʒərɪ] *n* (**a**) (*operation*) cirugía *f*; **to perform s. on sb** realizar una operación a alguien (**b**) *Br* (*of doctor*) consulta *f*

**surgical** ['sɜːdʒɪkəl] *adj* quirúrgico(a); *Fig* **with s. precision** con una precisión milimétrica; **s. instruments** instrumental *m* quirúrgico; **s. spirit** alcohol *m* desinfectante; *Mil* **s. strike** ataque *m* controlado (*de objetivos específicos*)

**Surinam** [sʊrɪ'næm] *n* Surinam

**surly** ['sɜːlɪ] *adj* hosco(a), arisco(a)

**surmise** [sə'maɪz] *vt* presumir, figurarse

**surmount** [sə'maʊnt] *vt* (*obstacle, emotion*) vencer, superar

**surname** ['sɜːneɪm] *n* apellido *m*

**surpass** [sə'pɑːs] *vt* (*rival*) aventajar, sobrepasar; (*expectation, record*) superar

**surplice** ['sɜːplɪs] *n Rel* sobrepelliz *f*

**surplus** ['sɜːpləs] **1** *n Econ* (*of goods*) excedente *m*; (*of trade, budget*) superávit *m inv*

**2** *adj* (*items*) excedente; **to be s. to requirements** sobrar

**surprise** [sə'praɪz] **1** *n* sorpresa *f*; **to take sb by s.** coger *or* pillar a alguien por sorpresa; **to give sb a s.** dar una sorpresa a alguien; **what a s.!** ¡qué sorpresa!; **it was no s.** no fue ninguna sorpresa; **to my great s., much to my s.** para mi sorpresa

**2** *adj* (*attack*) (por) sorpresa; (*defeat*) sorpresivo(a); **s. party** fiesta *f* sorpresa

**3** *vt* (**a**) (*astonish*) sorprender; **I was pleasantly surprised** me sorprendió gratamente; **I'm not surprised that...** no me extraña que... (**b**) (*catch unawares*) coger *or* pillar por sorpresa

**surprising** [sə'praɪzɪŋ] *adj* sorprendente

**surprisingly** [sə'praɪzɪŋlɪ] *adv* sorprendentemente; **s. enough** sorprendentemente; **not s.** como era de esperar

**surreal** [sə'rɪəl] *adj* surrealista

**surrealism** [sə'rɪəlɪzəm] *n Art* surrealismo *m*

**surrealist** [sə'rɪəlɪst] *n & adj Art* surrealista *mf*

**surrender** [sə'rendə(r)] **1** *n* (*of army*) rendición *f*; (*of weapons*) entrega *f*; **no s.!** ¡no nos rendiremos!; *Fin* **s. value** valor *m* de rescate

**2** *vt* (*fortress, town*) rendir, entregar; (*right, possessions*) renunciar a; (*advantage*) perder; **to s. control of sth** entregar el control de algo

**3** *vi* rendirse

**surreptitious** [sʌrəp'tɪʃəs] *adj* subrepticio(a), clandestino(a)

**surrogate** ['sʌrəgət] *n* sustituto(a) *m,f*; **s. mother** madre *f* de alquiler

**surround** [sə'raʊnd] **1** *n* marco *m*

**2** *vt* rodear; **surrounded by...** rodeado(a) de *or* por...

**surrounding** [sə'raʊndɪŋ] *adj* circundante

**surroundings** [sə'raʊndɪŋz] *npl* entorno *m*

**surtax** ['sɜːtæks] *Fin* **1** *n* impuesto *m* adicional

**2** *vt* aplicar un impuesto adicional a

**surveillance** [sɜːˈveɪləns] *n* vigilancia *f*; **under s.** bajo vigilancia

**survey 1** *n* ['sɜːveɪ] (*pl* **surveys**) **(a)** (*of subject, situation*) estudio *m*; (*of opinions*) encuesta *f* **(b)** (*of building*) tasación *f*, peritaje *m*; (*of land*) estudio *m* topográfico

**2** *vt* [sɜːˈveɪ] **(a)** (*topic, subject*) estudiar **(b)** (*building*) tasar, peritar; (*land*) medir

**surveying** [sɜːˈveɪɪŋ] *n* (*of building*) tasación *f*, peritaje *m*; (*of land*) agrimensura *f*

**surveyor** [sɜːˈveɪə(r)] *n* (*of building*) tasador(ora) *m,f* *or* perito(a) *m,f* de la propiedad; (*of land*) agrimensor(ora) *m,f*

**survival** [səˈvaɪvəl] *n* **(a)** (*continued existence*) supervivencia *f*; *also Fig* **the s. of the fittest** la supervivencia del más apto; **s. kit** equipo *m* de supervivencia **(b)** (*relic*) vestigio *m*

**survive** [səˈvaɪv] **1** *vt* sobrevivir a

**2** *vi* sobrevivir; **my pay is barely enough to s. on** mi sueldo apenas llega para sobrevivir

**surviving** [səˈvaɪvɪŋ] *adj* superviviente

**survivor** [səˈvaɪvə(r)] *n* superviviente *mf*

**susceptible** [səˈseptɪbəl] *adj* (*to criticism, pressure*) sensible (**to** a); (*to illness*) propenso(a) (**to** a)

**suspect** ['sʌspekt] **1** *n* sospechoso(a) *m,f*

**2** *adj* sospechoso(a)

**3** *vt* [səˈspekt] **(a)** (*person*) sospechar de; **to s. sb of having done sth** sospechar que alguien ha hecho algo **(b)** (*have intuition of*) (*motives*) recelar de; **to s. the truth** sospechar (cuál es la verdad) **(c)** (*consider likely*) **I s. you're right** sospecho que tienes razón; **I suspected as much!** ¡ya me lo imaginaba!

**suspend** [səˈspend] *vt* **(a)** (*hang*) suspender, colgar (**from** de) **(b)** (*service, employee*) suspender; **he was suspended from school** lo expulsaron temporalmente del colegio

**suspended** [səˈspendɪd] *adj* suspendido(a); **s. animation** muerte *f* aparente; *Law* **to give sb a s. sentence** conceder a alguien una suspensión *or* remisión condicional de la pena

**suspender** [səˈspendə(r)] *n* **(a)** *Br* (*for stocking, sock*) liga *f*; **s. belt** liguero *m* **(b)** *US* **suspenders** (*for trousers*) tirantes *mpl*

**suspense** [səˈspens] *n* (*uncertainty*) incertidumbre *f*; (*in film*) suspense *m*; **to keep sb in s.** tener a alguien en suspenso

**suspension** [səˈspenʃən] *n* **(a)** (*of car*) suspensión *f*; **s. bridge** puente *m* colgante **(b)** (*of service, employee*) suspensión *f*; (*from school*) expulsión *f* (*temporal*)

**suspicion** [səˈspɪʃən] *n* **(a)** (*belief of guilt*) sospecha *f*; **to be under s.** estar bajo sospecha; **to be above s.** estar libre de sospecha; **I have my**

suspicions about him tengo mis sospechas sobre él; **to arouse s.** despertar sospechas **(b)** (*small amount*) asomo *m*

**suspicious** [səˈspɪʃəs] *adj* **(a)** (*arousing suspicion*) (*fact, behaviour, circumstances*) sospechoso(a) **(b)** (*having suspicions*) (*person, mind*) receloso(a) (**of** *or* **about** de); **his behaviour made me s.** su comportamiento me hizo sospechar

**suspiciously** [səˈspɪʃəslɪ] *adv* (*behave*) sospechosamente; (*watch, ask*) recelosamente, con suspicacia; **s. similar** sospechosamente similares

▸**suss out** [sʌs] *vt sep Br Fam* (*person*) calar; (*system*) pillar el truco a; **I haven't sussed out how it works yet** todavía no me he coscado de cómo funciona

**sustain** [səˈsteɪn] *vt* **(a)** (*weight, growth, life*) sostener; *Law* **objection sustained** se admite la protesta **(b)** (*loss, attack*) sufrir

**sustainable** [səˈsteɪnəbl] *adj* sostenible; **s. development** desarrollo *m* sostenible

**sustained** [səˈsteɪnd] *adj* continuo(a); **s. applause** aplauso *m* prolongado

**sustenance** ['sʌstɪnəns] *n* sustento *m*; **means of s.** medio *m* de vida

**suture** ['suːtʃə(r)] *n Med* sutura *f*

**SW** *n* **(a)** (*abbr* **south west**) SO, sudoeste *m* **(b)** *Rad* (*abbr* **Short Wave**) SW, OC, onda *f* corta

**swab** [swɒb] **1** *n Med* (*cotton wool*) torunda *f*

**2** *vt* (*pt & pp* **swabbed**) (*clean*) (*wound*) limpiar; (*floor*) fregar

**swag** [swæg] *n Fam* (*of thief*) botín *m*

**swagger** ['swægə(r)] **1** *n* pavoneo *m*

**2** *vi* (*strut*) pavonearse; **to s. in/out** entrar/ salir pavoneándose

**swallow**[1] ['swɒləʊ] **1** *n* (*of drink*) trago *m*; (*of food*) bocado *m*

**2** *vt* **(a)** (*food, drink*) tragar, tragarse; **to s. sth whole** tragar algo sin masticar; *Fig* **to s. one's pride** tragarse el orgullo **(b)** *Fam* (*believe*) tragarse

**3** *vi* tragar; **to s. hard** (*when nervous, afraid*) tragar saliva

**swallow**[2] *n* (*bird*) golondrina *f*; *Prov* **one s. doesn't make a summer** una golondrina no hace verano

▸**swallow up** *vt sep Fig* (*company, country*) absorber

**swam** [swæm] *pt of* **swim**

**swamp** [swɒmp] **1** *n* pantano *m*; **s. fever** (*malaria*) paludismo *m*, malaria *f*

**2** *vt* (*flood*) anegar, inundar; *Fig* **to be swamped with work** estar desbordado(a) de trabajo

**swan** [swɒn] **1** *n* cisne *m*; *Fig* **s. song** canto *m* de cisne

**2** *vi* (*pt & pp* **swanned**) *Fam* **to s. in/out** entrar/salir despreocupadamente

▸**swan about, swan around** *vi Fam* pasearse (por ahí) a la buena de Dios

**swank** [swæŋk] *Fam* **1** *n* (*ostentation*) fanfarronería *f*; (*ostentatious person*) fanfarrón(ona) *m,f*, figurón *m*
**2** *vi* fanfarronear

**swanky** ['swæŋkɪ] *adj Fam* (*person*) fanfarrón(ona); (*restaurant, hotel*) fastuoso(a), pomposo(a)

**swap** [swɒp] **1** *n* trueque *m*, intercambio *m*; **to do a s.** hacer un trueque
**2** *vt* (*pt & pp* **swapped**) **to s. sth for sth** cambiar algo por algo; **to s. places with sb** (*change seat*) cambiarse de sitio con alguien; *Fig* intercambiar papeles con alguien; **to s. insults/ideas** intercambiar insultos/ideas
**3** *vi* hacer un intercambio

**swarm** [swɔːm] **1** *n* (*of bees*) enjambre *m*; (*of people*) nube *f*, enjambre *m*
**2** *vi* (*of bees*) volar en enjambre; (*of people*) apelotonarse, ir en masa; **Oxford was swarming with tourists** Oxford era un hervidero de turistas

**swarthy** ['swɔːðɪ] *adj* moreno(a), atezado(a)

**swashbuckling** ['swɒʃbʌklɪŋ] *adj* (*hero*) intrépido(a); (*film, story*) de espadachines

**swastika** ['swɒstɪkə] *n* esvástica *f*, cruz *f* gamada

**swat** [swɒt] (*pt & pp* **swatted**) *vt* aplastar

**swathe** [sweɪð] **1** *n* faja *f*, banda *f*; *Fig* **the cannons had cut great swathes through the troops** los cañones hicieron estragos en las tropas
**2** *vt* **to s. sth in bandages** vendar algo, envolver algo en vendajes

**sway** [sweɪ] **1** *n* (*a*) (*movement*) vaivén *m*, balanceo *m* (*b*) (*control, power*) dominio *m*; **he was under her s.** estaba bajo la férula o el yugo de ella; **to hold s. over sth** ejercer dominio sobre algo
**2** *vt* (*influence, persuade*) hacer cambiar (de opinión)
**3** *vi* balancearse; **to s. from side to side** balancearse de un lado a otro

**Swazi** ['swɑːzɪ] **1** *n* (*a*) (*person*) suazi *mf* (*b*) (*language*) suazi *m*
**2** *adj* suazi

**Swaziland** ['swɑːzɪlænd] *n* Suazilandia

**swear** [sweə(r)] (*pt* **swore** [swɔː(r)], *pp* **sworn** [swɔːn]) **1** *vt* (*vow*) jurar; **to s. to do sth** jurar hacer algo; *Law* **to s. an oath** prestar juramento
**2** *vi* (*use swearwords*) jurar, decir palabrotas; **to s. at sb** insultar a alguien

▸**swear by** *vt insep* (*have confidence in*) confiar en

▸**swear in** *vt sep Law* (*jury, witness*) tomar juramento a

**swearing** ['sweərɪŋ] *n* palabrotas *fpl*; **s. is naughty** decir palabrotas es de mala educación

**swearword** ['sweəwɜːd] *n* palabrota *f*, taco *m*

**sweat** [swet] **1** *n* (*perspiration*) sudor *m*; *Fig* **to be in a s. about sth** apurarse por algo; *very Fam* **no s.!** ¡no hay problema!; **s. gland** glándula *f* sudorípara
**2** *vt* sudar; *Fam* **to s. buckets** sudar a chorros; *Fig* **to s. blood** sudar tinta
**3** *vi* (*a*) (*perspire*) sudar; *Fam* **to s. like a pig** sudar como un cerdo (*b*) *Fam Fig* (*worry*) sufrir, angustiarse; **I'm going to make him s.** voy a dejarle que sufra

**sweatband** ['swetbænd] *n* (*on head*) banda *f* (*para la frente*); (*on wrist*) muñequera *f*

**sweater** ['swetə(r)] *n* jersey *m*, *Am* suéter *m*, chompa *f*, *CSur* buzo *m*

**sweatshirt** ['swetʃɜːt] *n* sudadera *f*

**sweatshop** ['swetʃɒp] *n* = fábrica donde se explota al trabajador

**sweaty** ['swetɪ] *adj* sudoroso(a); **to be s.** estar sudoroso(a); **s. smell** olor *m* a sudor

**Swede** [swiːd] *n* (*person*) sueco(a) *m,f*

**swede** [swiːd] *n* (*vegetable*) colinabo *m*

**Sweden** ['swiːdən] *n* Suecia

**Swedish** ['swiːdɪʃ] **1** *npl* (*people*) **the S.** los suecos
**2** *n* (*language*) sueco *m*
**3** *adj* sueco(a)

**sweep** [swiːp] **1** *n* (*a*) (*action*) barrido *m*; **to give the floor a s.** barrer el suelo; *Fig* **at one s.** de una pasada; *Fig* **to make a clean s.** (*replace staff*) quitar de en medio personal; (*of prizes*) arrasar (*b*) (*movement*) **with a s. of the arm** moviendo el brazo extendido (*c*) (*extent*) (*of land, knowledge*) extensión *f*; (*of road, river*) curva *f*
**2** *vt* (*pt & pp* **swept** [swept]) (*a*) (*floor, street*) barrer; (*chimney*) deshollinar; **a wave swept him overboard** lo arrastró una ola y cayó al mar (*b*) (*idioms*) **to s. sth under the carpet** soterrar algo; **to s. the board** (*in competition*) arrasar; **the latest craze to s. the country** la última moda que está haciendo furor en todo el país; *Fig* **he swept her off her feet** se enamoró perdidamente de él
**3** *vi* (*a*) (*with broom*) barrer (*b*) (*move rapidly*) **to s. in/out** entrar/salir con gallardía; **to s. to power** subir al poder de forma arrasadora

▸**sweep aside** *vt sep* (*opposition*) barrer; (*criticism*) hacer caso omiso de

▸**sweep away** *vt sep* (*remove*) barrer

▸**sweep up 1** *vt sep* (*dust, leaves*) barrer
**2** *vi* (*clean up*) limpiar

**sweeper** ['swiːpə(r)] n (a) **(carpet)** s. cepillo m mecánico (b) (footballer) líbero m

**sweeping** ['swiːpɪŋ] adj (gesture) amplio(a); (statement) (demasiado) generalizador(ora); (change) radical

**sweepstake** ['swiːpsteɪk] n porra f (juego)

**sweet** [swiːt] **1** n Br (confectionery) dulce m, caramelo m; (dessert) postre m; **s. shop** confitería f

**2** adj (a) (taste, wine) dulce; (smell) fragante; (sound) suave, dulce; **to taste s.** saber dulce; **as s. as honey** dulce como la miel; Fig **the s. smell of success** las mieles del éxito; **to have a s. tooth** ser goloso(a); Bot **s. pea** guisante m de olor; **s. potato** batata f, boniato m, Méx camote m; Bot **s. william** minutisa f (b) (charming) rico(a), mono(a); **that's very s. of you** eres muy amable; **to whisper s. nothings to sb** susurrar palabras de amor a alguien

**sweet-and-sour** ['swiːtən'saʊə(r)] adj agridulce; **s. pork** cerdo m agridulce

**sweetbreads** ['swiːtbredz] npl mollejas fpl

**sweetcorn** ['swiːtkɔːn] n Br maíz m

**sweeten** ['swiːtən] vt (food) endulzar; Fig **to s. sb's temper** aplacar el mal humor de alguien

**sweetener** ['swiːtənə(r)] n (a) (in food) edulcorante m (b) Fam (bribe) propina f

**sweetheart** ['swiːthɑːt] n novio(a) m,f

**sweetie** ['swiːtɪ] n Fam (a) Br (confectionery) golosina f (b) (darling) cariño m; **he's such a s.** es un encanto

**sweetly** ['swiːtlɪ] adv (sing, smile) con dulzura

**sweetness** ['swiːtnɪs] n dulzura f, dulzor m; **to be all s. and light** estar de lo más amable

**sweet-talk** ['swiːttɔːk] vt Fam **to s. sb into doing sth** convencer a alguien con halagos de que haga algo

**sweet-tempered** [swiːt'tempəd] adj apacible

**swell** [swel] **1** vt (pp **swollen** ['swəʊlən] or **swelled**) (numbers, crowd) aumentar

**2** vi (of part of body) hincharse; (of number, crowd) aumentar, crecer; **to s. with pride** henchirse de orgullo

**3** n (of sea) mar m de fondo

**4** adj US Fam (excellent) genial, estupendo(a)

▸**swell up** vi (part of body) hincharse

**swelling** ['swelɪŋ] n hinchazón f

**sweltering** ['sweltərɪŋ] adj asfixiante, sofocante

**swept** [swept] pt & pp of **sweep**

**swerve** [swɜːv] **1** n (of car) giro m or desplazamiento m brusco; (of player) regate m

**2** vi (of car, driver) desplazarse bruscamente; (of player) regatear; (of ball) ir con efecto

**swift** [swɪft] **1** n (bird) vencejo m

**2** adj (runner, horse) veloz, rápido(a); (reaction, reply) rápido(a), pronto(a)

**swift-footed** ['swɪftfʊtɪd] adj rápido(a)

**swiftly** ['swɪftlɪ] adv (move) velozmente, rápidamente; (react) con rapidez, con prontitud

**swiftness** ['swɪftnɪs] n (of movement, reply) rapidez f

**swig** [swɪg] Fam **1** n trago m; **he took a s. from the bottle** dio un trago de la botella

**2** vt (pt & pp **swigged**) pimplar

**swill** [swɪl] **1** n (food) (for pigs) sobras fpl para los cerdos; Pej (for people) bazofia f, bodrio m

**2** vt Fam (drink) trasegar, tragar

▸**swill about, swill around** vi (of liquid) agitarse

▸**swill out** vt sep (rinse) enjuagar, aclarar

**swim** [swɪm] **1** n baño m; **to go for** or **have a s.** ir a nadar, ir a darse un baño

**2** vt (pt **swam** [swæm], pp **swum** [swʌm]) nadar; **to s. the breaststroke** nadar a braza; **to s. the Channel** atravesar el Canal de la Mancha a nado

**3** vi (a) (in water) nadar; **to go swimming** ir a nadar; **to s. across a river** atravesar un río a nado; Fig **to s. with the tide** seguir la corriente (b) (be dizzy) **my head is swimming** me da vueltas la cabeza

**swimmer** ['swɪmə(r)] n nadador(ora) m,f

**swimming** ['swɪmɪŋ] n natación f; **s. costume** bañador m, traje m de baño; **s. lesson** clase f de natación; **s. pool** piscina f, CAm, Méx alberca f, CSur pileta f; **s. trunks** bañador m (de hombre)

**swimmingly** ['swɪmɪŋlɪ] adv Fam como la seda

**swimsuit** ['swɪmsuːt] n bañador m, traje m de baño

**swindle** ['swɪndəl] **1** n timo m, estafa f

**2** vt timar, estafar; **to s. sb out of sth** estafarle algo a alguien

**swindler** ['swɪndlə(r)] n timador(ora) m,f, estafador(ora) m,f

**swine** [swaɪn] (pl **swine**) n (a) Literary (pig) cerdo m, puerco m; **s. fever** peste f porcina (b) Fam (unpleasant person) cerdo(a) m,f, canalla mf

**swing** [swɪŋ] **1** n (a) (movement) (of rope, chain) vaivén m, balanceo m; (of pendulum) oscilación f; (in golf) swing m; Fam **to take a s. at sb** intentar darle un golpe a alguien; **to be in full s.** ir a toda marcha; Fam **everything went with a s.** todo fue sobre ruedas; Fam **to get into the s. of things** coger el ritmo

(b) (change) (in opinion, in mood) cambio m repentino (**in** de)

(c) (in playground) columpio m; Fam **it's swings and roundabouts** lo que se pierde aquí, se gana allá

**2** vt (pt & pp **swung** [swʌŋ]) (one's arms, racquet, axe) balancear; **to s. one's hips** menear las caderas; **to s. sth/sb onto one's**

**shoulder** echarse algo/a alguien al hombro; *Fam* **to s. a deal** cerrar un trato; *Fam* **to s. it so that...** *(arrange things)* arreglar las cosas para que...

**3** *vi* **(a)** *(move to and fro)* balancearse; *(on playground swing)* columpiarse; **to s. open** *(of door)* abrirse; **to s. into action** entrar en acción; *Fam* **he should s. for this** *(be hanged)* deberían colgarlo por esto; *Fam* **the party was really swinging** la fiesta estaba muy animada

**(b)** *(change direction)* girar, torcer; **to s. round** dar media vuelta

**swingeing** ['swɪndʒɪŋ] *adj* drástico(a)

**swipe** [swaɪp] **1** *n* *(with fist or stick)* **to take a s. at sb** dirigir un golpe a alguien; *Fig* **the programme takes a s. at the rich and famous** el programa dirige sus ataques contra los ricos y famosos

**2** *vt Fam (steal)* mangar, birlar

**3** *vi* **to s. at sb/sth** intentar dar un golpe a alguien/algo

**swirl** [swɜːl] **1** *n* *(of cream)* rizo *m*; *(of smoke)* voluta *f*; *(of leaves, dust)* remolino *m*

**2** *vt* revolver

**3** *vi* arremolinarse

**swish** [swɪʃ] **1** *n* *(sound) (of cane, whip)* silbido *m*; *(of dress, silk)* frufrú *m*, *(sonido m del) roce m*

**2** *adj Fam (elegant, smart)* distinguido(a), refinado(a)

**3** *vt* *(cane, whip)* hacer silbar; **to s. its tail** *(of animal)* menear *or* agitar la cola

**4** *vi* *(of dress, silk)* sonar al rozar; *(of cane, whip)* silbar

**Swiss** [swɪs] **1** *npl* **the S.** los suizos

**2** *adj* suizo(a); **S. chard** acelga *f*; **S. cheese plant** costilla *f* de hombre *m*; **s. roll** brazo *m* de gitano

**Switch**® [swɪtʃ] *n* **to pay by S.** pagar con tarjeta de (débito); **S. card** tarjeta *f* de débito

**switch** [swɪtʃ] **1** *n* **(a)** *(electrical)* interruptor *m* **(b)** *(in policy, opinion)* cambio *m*, viraje *m*; **to make a s.** hacer un cambio **(c)** *(stick)* vara *f*

**2** *vt* **(a)** *(change)* cambiar **(to** a); *(transfer)* trasladar; **to s. channels/jobs** cambiar de cadena/trabajo; **they switched their attention to something else** dirigieron su atención a otra cosa **(b)** *(exchange)* intercambiar

**3** *vi* *(change)* cambiar **(to** a); **to s. from gas to electricity** cambiar el gas por la electricidad, pasarse del gas a la electricidad

▶**switch off 1** *vt sep (appliance, heating)* apagar

**2** *vi* **(a)** *(of appliance, heating)* apagarse **(b)** *Fam (of person)* desconectar

▶**switch on 1** *vt sep (appliance, heating)* encender, *Am* prender

**2** *vi* *(of appliance, heating)* encenderse, *Am* prenderse

▶**switch over** *vi (change TV channel)* cambiar de cadena; **to s. over to gas** pasarse *or* cambiar al gas

**switchback** ['swɪtʃbæk] *n* carretera *f* en zigzag

**switchboard** ['swɪtʃbɔːd] *n* centralita *f*; **s. operator** telefonista *mf*

**Switzerland** ['swɪtsələnd] *n* Suiza

**swivel** ['swɪvəl] **1** *n* cabeza *f* giratoria; **s. chair** silla *f* giratoria

**2** *vi* *(pt & pp* **swivelled,** *US* **swiveled)** girar

**swizz** [swɪz] *n Fam* timo *m*

**swollen** ['swəʊlən] *pp of* **swell**

**swoon** [swuːn] **1** *n* desmayo *m*, desvanecimiento *m*

**2** *vi* desmayarse, desvanecerse

**swoop** [swuːp] **1** *n* *(of bird, plane)* (vuelo *m* en) picado *m*; *(of police)* redada *f*

**2** *vi* *(of bird, plane)* volar en picado; *(of police)* hacer una redada

**swop** [swɒp] **= swap**

**sword** [sɔːd] *n* espada *f*; **s. dance** danza *f* del sable

**swordfish** ['sɔːdfɪʃ] *n* pez *m* espada

**swore** [swɔː(r)] *pt of* **swear**

**sworn** [swɔːn] **1** *adj* **s. enemy** enemigo(a) *m,f* encarnizado(a)

**2** *pp of* **swear**

**swot** [swɒt] *Br Fam* **1** *n* *(studious pupil)* empollón(ona) *m,f*

**2** *vi* *(pt & pp* **swotted)** *(study hard)* empollar

▶**swot up on** *vt insep Br Fam (subject)* empollarse

**swum** [swʌm] *pp of* **swim**

**swung** [swʌŋ] *pt & pp of* **swing**

**sycamore** ['sɪkəmɔː(r)] *n* plátano *m* falso, sicomoro *m*

**sycophant** ['sɪkəfənt] *n* adulador(ora) *m,f*

**sycophantic** [sɪkə'fæntɪk] *adj* adulador(ora)

**Sydney** ['sɪdnɪ] *n* Sídney

**syllable** ['sɪləbəl] *n* sílaba *f*

**syllabus** ['sɪləbəs] *n* programa *m* de estudios, currículo *m*

**sylph-like** ['sɪlflaɪk] *adj Hum (woman)* delgada; *(figura)* de sílfide

**symbiotic** [sɪmb(a)ɪ'ɒtɪk] *adj* simbiótico(a)

**symbol** ['sɪmbəl] *n* símbolo *m*

**symbolic** [sɪm'bɒlɪk] *adj* simbólico(a)

**symbolism** ['sɪmbəlɪzəm] *n Art* simbolismo *m*

**symbolist** ['sɪmbəlɪst] *n & adj Art* simbolista *mf*

**symbolize** ['sɪmbəlaɪz] *vt* simbolizar

**symmetrical** [sɪ'metrɪkəl] *adj* simétrico(a)

**symmetry** ['sɪmɪtrɪ] *n* simetría *f*

**sympathetic** [sɪmpə'θetɪk] *adj (understanding)* comprensivo(a); *(compassionate)* compasivo(a); **to be s. to a proposal/cause** simpatizar con una propuesta/causa; **a s. audience** un público bien dispuesto

**sympathize** ['sɪmpəθaɪz] *vi* **(a)** *(show sympathy)* compadecerse (**with** de) **(b) to s. (with sth/sb)** *(understand)* comprender (algo/a alguien); *(agree)* estar de a favor (de algo/alguien)

**sympathizer** ['sɪmpəθaɪzə(r)] *n (political)* simpatizante *mf*

**sympathy** ['sɪmpəθɪ] *n* **(a)** *(pity, compassion)* compasión *f*; *Formal* **you have my deepest s.** le doy mi más sincero pésame **(b)** *(understanding)* comprensión *f*; *(support)* apoyo *m*, solidaridad *f*; **to feel s. for sb** simpatizar con alguien; *Ind* **s. strike** huelga *f* de solidaridad *or* apoyo

**symphony** ['sɪmfənɪ] *n Mus* sinfonía *f*; **s. orchestra** orquesta *f* sinfónica

**symposium** [sɪm'pəʊzɪəm] *(pl* **symposia** [sɪm'pəʊzɪə]*) n* simposio *m*

**symptom** ['sɪm(p)təm] *n also Fig* síntoma *m*

**symptomatic** [sɪm(p)tə'mætɪk] *adj* sintomático(a) *(of de)*

**synagogue** ['sɪnəgɒg] *n* sinagoga *f*

**sync** [sɪŋk] *n Fam* sincronización *f*; **to be in/out of s. with...** estar/no estar en sintonía con...

**synchronization** [sɪŋkrənaɪ'zeɪʃən] *n* sincronización *f*

**synchronize** ['sɪŋkrənaɪz] *vt* sincronizar

**syncopation** [sɪŋkə'peɪʃən] *n Mus* síncopa *f*

**syndicalism** ['sɪndɪkəlɪzəm] *n Pol* sindicalismo *m* (revolucionario)

**syndicalist** ['sɪndɪkəlɪst] *n Pol* sindicalista *mf* (revolucionario(a))

**syndicate 1** *n* ['sɪndɪkət] *Com* agrupación *f*; **crime s.** organización *f* criminal

**2** *vt* ['sɪndɪkeɪt] *Journ* = producir para difusión conjunta en diferentes medios; **syndicated**

**columnist** = columnista que publica simultáneamente en varios medios

**syndrome** ['sɪndrəʊm] *n Med & Fig* síndrome *m*

**synergy** ['sɪnədʒɪ] *n* sinergia *f*

**synod** ['sɪnəd] *n Rel* sínodo *m*

**synonym** ['sɪnənɪm] *n* sinónimo *m*

**synonymous** [sɪ'nɒnɪməs] *adj* sinónimo(a)

**synopsis** [sɪ'nɒpsɪs] *(pl* **synopses** [sɪ'nɒpsiːz]*) n* sinopsis *f inv*, resumen *m*

**syntax** ['sɪntæks] *n Ling* sintaxis *f inv*; *Comptr* **s. error** error *m* de sintaxis

**synth** [sɪnθ] *n Fam* sintetizador *m*

**synthesis** ['sɪnθɪsɪs] *(pl* **syntheses** ['sɪnθɪsiːz]*) n* síntesis *f inv*

**synthesize** ['sɪnθəsaɪz] *vt* sintetizar

**synthesizer** ['sɪnθəsaɪzə(r)] *n* sintetizador *m*

**synthetic** [sɪn'θetɪk] **1** *npl* **synthetics** fibras *fpl* sintéticas

**2** *adj* sintético(a)

**syphilis** ['sɪfɪlɪs] *n* sífilis *f inv*

**syphon** = **siphon**

**Syria** ['sɪrɪə] *n* Siria

**Syrian** ['sɪrɪən] *n & adj* sirio(a) *m,f*

**syringe** [sɪ'rɪndʒ] **1** *n* jeringuilla *f*

**2** *vt Med (ears)* destaponar

**syrup** ['sɪrəp] *n (of sugar)* almíbar *m*; *(medicinal)* jarabe *m*

**syrupy** ['sɪrəpɪ] *adj (smile, music)* almibarado(a)

**SYSOP** ['sɪsɒp] *n Comptr (abbr* **Systems Operator***)* operador *m* de sistemas

**system** ['sɪstəm] *n* **(a)** *(structure, method)* sistema *m*; **the S.** *(established order)* el sistema; *Fam* **it was a shock to the s.** fue todo un trauma; *Fam* **to get sb out of one's s.** quitarse a alguien de la cabeza **(b)** *Comptr* **systems analyst** analista *mf* de sistemas

**systematic** [sɪstə'mætɪk] *adj* sistemático(a)

**systematize** ['sɪstəmətaɪz] *vt* sistematizar

# T

**, t** [tiː] *n* (**a**) *(letter)* T, t *f* (**b**) *(idioms)* **that's
[y]ou to a T** *(of impersonation)* es clavado a ti; **it
[s]uits me to a T** me viene como anillo al dedo
[(abbr] **ton(s)**) tonelada(s) *f(pl)* *(Br 1.016 kilos,
[U]S 907 kilos)*

**[t]a** [taː] *exclam Br Fam* gracias

**[t]ab** [tæb] *n* (**a**) *(on garment)* etiqueta *f; Fam* **to
[k]eep tabs on sth/sb** vigilar de cerca algo/a
[al]guien (**b**) *(on typewriter, word processor)* tabula-
[d]or *m;* **t. (key)** tecla *f* de tabular, tabulador *m*
*(c)* *US Fam (bill)* cuenta *f* (**d**) *Fam (of drug)* pasti *f*,
[p]astilla *f*

**[t]abby** ['tæbɪ] *n* **t. (cat)** gato *m* atigrado

**[t]abernacle** ['tæbənækəl] *n (church)* taberná-
[cu]lo *m; (on altar)* sagrario *m*

**[t]able** ['teɪbəl] **1** *n* (**a**) *(furniture)* mesa *f;* **to lay
[or] set the t.** poner la mesa; **to clear the t.**
[re]coger la mesa; **at t.** a la mesa; **t. lamp** lám-
[pa]ra *f* de mesa; **t. linen** mantelería *f;* **t. man-
[n]ers** modales *mpl* (en la mesa); **t. mat**
[sal]vamanteles *m inv;* **t. salt** sal *f* de mesa; **t.
[te]nnis** ping-pong *m*, tenis *m* de mesa; **t. wine**
[vi]no *m* de mesa
(**b**) *(of facts, figures)* tabla *f;* **league t.** (tabla *f*
[d]e) clasificación *f* (de la liga); **t. of contents**
[ín]dice *m; Math* **twelve times t.** tabla *f* (de
[m]ultiplicar) del doce
(**c**) *(idioms)* **the offer is still on the t.** la
[of]erta está aún sobre la mesa; **to turn the ta-
[b]les on sb** cambiarle *or* volverle las tornas a
[al]guien
**[2]** *vt* **to t. a motion/proposal** *Br (present)*
[so]meter a discusión una moción/propuesta;
[U]S *(postpone)* posponer la discusión de una mo-
[ci]ón/propuesta

**[t]ablecloth** ['teɪbəlklɒθ] *n* mantel *m*

**[t]ablespoon** ['teɪbəlspuːn] *n (utensil)* cuchara
[d]e servir; **a t. of flour** una cucharada (grande)
[de] harina

**[t]ablet** ['tæblɪt] *n* (**a**) *(pill)* comprimido *m*, pas-
[til]la *f* (**b**) *(inscribed stone)* lápida *f* (**c**) *(bar) (of
[so]ap)* pastilla *f; (of chocolate)* tableta *f*

**[t]ableware** ['teɪbəlweə(r)] *n* servicio *m* de
[m]esa, vajilla *f*

**[t]abloid** ['tæblɔɪd] *n (newspaper)* diario *m* po-
[pu]lar *or* sensacionalista (de formato tabloide);

**the t. press** la prensa popular *or* sensacionalista

**taboo** [təˈbuː] **1** *n (pl* **taboos***)* tabú *m*
**2** *adj* tabú

**tabular** ['tæbjʊlə(r)] *adj* **in t. form** en forma
tabular

**tabulate** ['tæbjʊleɪt] *vt (arrange in table)* tabular

**tachometer** [tæˈkɒmɪtə(r)] *n Aut* tacómetro
*m*

**tacit** ['tæsɪt] *adj* tácito(a)

**tacitly** ['tæsɪtlɪ] *adv* tácitamente

**taciturn** ['tæsɪtɜːn] *adj* taciturno(a), retraí-
do(a)

**tack** [tæk] **1** *n* (**a**) *(small nail)* tachuela *f* (**b**)
*Naut* bordada *f; Fig* **to change t.** cambiar de
enfoque
**2** *vt* (**a**) *(fasten)* **to t. (down)** clavar; *Fig* **to t.
sth on** *(add)* añadir algo a posteriori (**b**) *(in
sewing)* **to t. up a hem** hilvanar un dobladillo
**3** *vi Naut* dar bordadas

**tackle** ['tækəl] **1** *n* (**a**) *(equipment)* equipo *m;*
**(fishing) t.** aparejos *mpl* de pesca (**b**) *(challenge) (in football)* entrada *f; (in rugby)* placaje *m*
**2** *vt* (**a**) *(deal with)* abordar; **to t. sb about sth**
*(confront)* abordar a alguien para tratar algo (**b**)
*(in football)* entrar a; *(in rugby)* hacer un placaje a

**tacky** ['tækɪ] *adj* (**a**) *(sticky)* pegajoso(a) (**b**)
*Fam (tasteless) (person, dress)* hortera; *(behaviour)*
cutre, impresentable

**tact** [tækt] *n* tacto *m*, discreción *f*

**tactful** ['tæktfʊl] *adj* discreto(a), diplomáti-
co(a)

**tactic** ['tæktɪk] *n* táctica *f*

**tactical** ['tæktɪkəl] *adj* táctico(a); *Pol* **t. voting** voto *m* útil

**tactician** [tækˈtɪʃən] *n* táctico(a) *m,f*

**tactile** ['tæktaɪl] *adj* táctil

**tactless** ['tæktlɪs] *adj* falto(a) de tacto, indis-
creto(a)

**tactlessly** ['tæktlɪslɪ] *adv* indiscretamente,
sin tacto alguno

**tad** [tæd] *n US Fam* **a t. short** un pelín corto

**tadpole** ['tædpəʊl] *n* renacuajo *m*

**Tadzhikistan** [taːdʒɪkɪˈstaːn] *n* Tayikistán

**taffeta** ['tæfɪtə] *n* tafetán *m*

**tag** [tæg] **1** *n* **(a)** *(label)* etiqueta *f*; *Gram* **t. question** cláusula *f* final interrogativa **(b)** *(game)* **to play t.** jugar a pillarse *or* al corre que te pillo

**2** *vt* (*pt & pp* **tagged**) *(label)* etiquetar

▸**tag along** *vi* pegarse; **to t. along with sb** pegarse a alguien

▸**tag on** *vt sep* añadir (a posteriori)

**Tagus** ['teɪgəs] *n* **the T.** el Tajo

**Tahiti** [tə'hiːtɪ] *n* Tahití

**Tahitian** [tɔː'hiːʃən] *n & adj* tahitiano(a) *m,f*

**tail** [teɪl] **1** *n* **(a)** *(of bird, fish, plane)* cola *f*; *(of mammal, reptile)* rabo *m*, cola *f*; *(of shirt)* faldón *m*; **tails** *(of coin)* cruz *f*; **tails, t. coat** frac *m* **(b)** *(idioms)* **with his t. between his legs** con el rabo entre las piernas; *Fam* **to put a t. on sb** ponerle a alguien un vigilante que le sigue a todas partes; *Fam* **to turn t.** salir por piernas; **t. end** *(of conversation, film)* final *m*

**2** *vt Fam (follow)* seguir a todas partes

▸**tail away, tail off** *vi (of attendance)* decrecer; *(of performance)* decaer; *(of voice)* desvanecerse

**tailback** ['teɪlbæk] *n Aut* caravana *f*

**tailboard** ['teɪlbɔːd], *US* **tailgate** ['teɪlgeɪt] *n Aut* puerta *f* trasera

**taillight** ['teɪllaɪt] *n US Aut* faro *m* trasero

**tailor** ['teɪlə(r)] **1** *n* sastre *m*; **t.'s dummy** maniquí *m*; **t.'s (shop)** sastrería *f*

**2** *(suit)* confeccionar; *Fig (speech, policy)* adaptar (**to** a)

**tailor-made** ['teɪləmeɪd] *adj (suit)* hecho(a) a medida; *Fig* **the job was t. for her** el trabajo parecía hecho a su medida

**tailplane** ['teɪlpleɪn] *n Av* plano *m* de cola

**tailspin** ['teɪlspɪn] *n Av* barrena *f*; *Fig* **to go into a t.** entrar en barrena

**tailwind** ['teɪlwɪnd] *n* viento *m* de cola

**taint** [teɪnt] **1** *n* impureza *f*, contaminación *f*; *Fig* tara *f*

**2** *vt (contaminate)* contaminar; *Fig* manchar

**Taiwan** [taɪ'wɑːn] *n* Taiwán

**Taiwanese** [taɪwə'niːz] *n & adj* taiwanés(esa) *m,f*

**Tajikistan** = **Tadzhikistan**

**take** [teɪk] **1** *vt* (*pt* **took** [tʊk], *pp* **taken** ['teɪkən]) **(a)** *(grasp)* tomar, coger, *Am* agarrar; **to t. hold of sth** agarrar algo; **to t. sb by the arm** tomar *o* coger a alguien del brazo; **to t. sb in one's arms** tomar *o* coger en brazos a alguien; **to t. the opportunity to do sth** aprovechar la oportunidad para hacer algo

**(b)** *(remove, steal)* tomar, coger; **to t. sth away from sb** quitarle algo a alguien; **to t. sth out of sth** sacar algo de algo

**(c)** *(tolerate) (heat, pressure)* soportar, aguantar; **she can't t. a joke** no sabe aguantar una broma; **I can't t. (it) any more** no lo aguanto más

**(d)** *(lead, carry)* llevar; **to t. sb home/to the station** llevar a alguien a casa/a la estación; **to t. sb to court** llevar a alguien a juicio; **to t. flowers to sb, to t. sb flowers** llevarle flores a alguien; **to t. the dog for a walk** sacar a pasear al perro; **her job takes her all over the world** su trabajo le hace viajar por todo el mundo; **if you can get the money we'll t. it from there** si consigues el dinero, entonces veremos

**(e)** *(get on) (bus, road)* tomar; **t. the first turning on the left** gira por la primera a la izquierda

**(f)** *(require) (effort, dedication, strength)* requerir; **it took four of us to carry him** hicimos falta cuatro para llevarlo; **it takes courage to..** hace falta valor para...; **how long does it t.?** ¿cuánto tiempo lleva?; **learning a language takes a long time** aprender un idioma lleva mucho tiempo; **it took me an hour to get here** tardé una hora en llegar; **that will t. some explaining** eso va a ser complicado de explicar

**(g)** *(adopt) (precautions, measures)* tomar; **to t. legal advice** consultar a un abogado; **to t. sth as an example** tomar algo como ejemplo

**(h)** *(record) (temperature, notes)* tomar; **to t. sb's details** tomar los datos de alguien

**(i)** *(capture) (town)* tomar; *(chess piece)* comer(se); **to t. power** hacerse con el poder; **to t. first prize** ganar el primer premio

**(j)** *(assume)* **I t. it that...** supongo que...

**(k)** *(accept)* aceptar; **will you t. a cheque?** ¿se puede pagar con cheque?; **I'll t. the red one** me quedo con el rojo; **does this machine t. pound coins?** ¿esta máquina acepta monedas de una libra?; **my car only takes diesel** mi coche sólo funciona con gasóleo; **this bus takes fifty passengers** en este autobús caben cincuenta pasajeros; **t. it or leave it!** ¡lo tomas o lo dejas!; **to t. sth well/badly** tomarse algo bien/mal; **to t. sth the wrong way** malentender algo; **you can t. it from me that...** créeme cuando te digo que...

**(l)** *(exam, subject, course)* hacer; **he takes them for English** *(teaches them)* les da inglés

**(m)** *(in phrases)* **to t. a bath** darse un baño; **to t. drugs** tomar drogas; **to t. fright** asustarse; **to be taken ill** ponerse enfermo(a); **to t. a look at sth** echar un vistazo a algo; **to t. a photograph of sb/sth** hacer *o* sacar una fotografía a alguien/algo; **to t. a seat** sentarse, tomar asiento; **to t. a walk** dar un paseo

**2** *vi (be successful) (of fire)* prender; *(of plant cutting)* arraigar; *(of innovation)* cuajar; *(of dye)* coger

**3** *n* **(a)** *(recording) (of film, music)* toma *f*

**(b)** *(money)* recaudación *f*; *Fam* **to be on the t.** engordar el bolsillo

▸**take after** *vt insep (resemble)* parecerse a

▶**take apart** vt (machine, engine) desmontar; (argument) destrozar

▶**take away 1** vt sep (remove) quitar; Math restar (**from** de); **the men are coming to t. away the rubbish tomorrow** los hombres vendrán a llevarse la basura mañana; **to t. sth away from sb** quitar algo a alguien; Br **to t. away** (food) para llevar
**2** vi **to t. away from the pleasure/value of sth** restar placer/valor a algo

▶**take back** vt sep (**a**) (return) devolver; **that takes me back to my childhood** eso me hace volver a la infancia (**b**) (accept again) (former employee) readmitir; (faulty goods) admitir (devolución de); **she's a fool to t. him back** es tonta por dejarle volver (**c**) (withdraw) retirar; **t. that back!** ¡retira eso!

▶**take down** vt sep (**a**) (remove) (from shelf) bajar; (poster) quitar (**b**) (lower) **to t. down one's trousers** bajarse los pantalones; Fam **to t. sb down a peg or two** bajarle los humos a alguien (**c**) (dismantle) (tent, scaffolding) desmontar; (wall, barricade) desmantelar (**d**) (record) anotar, apuntar; (notes) tomar

▶**take for** vt sep **I took him for somebody else** lo tomé por or confundí con otro; **what do you t. me for?** ¿por quién me tomas?

▶**take in** vt sep (**a**) (lead, carry) (person) conducir dentro; (harvest, washing) recoger (**b**) (orphan) recoger, adoptar; (lodgers) admitir (**c**) (garment) meter (**d**) (include) abarcar, cubrir; **the tour takes in all the major sights** el recorrido cubre todos los principales puntos de interés (**e**) (understand) asimilar; **to t. in the situation** hacerse cargo de la situación (**f**) (deceive) engañar, embaucar

▶**take off 1** vt sep (**a**) (remove) (clothes, make-up) quitarse; (lid) quitar; **t. your feet off the table!** ¡quita los pies de la mesa!; **he never took his eyes off us** no apartó la mirada de nosotros; **he took £10 off (the price)** rebajó 10 libras (del precio); **to t. sth off sb's hands** quitar algo de las manos a alguien; **to t. years off sb** (of clothes, diet) quitar a alguien años de encima (**b**) (lead) (person) llevar; **to t. oneself off** retirarse (**c**) (mimic) **to t. sb off** imitar a alguien (**d**) (not work) **to t. the day off** tomarse el día libre
**2** vi (**a**) (leave) (of plane) despegar; (of person) marcharse (**b**) Fam (succeed) empezar a cuajar; **it never took off** nunca cuajó

▶**take on** vt sep (**a**) (task, responsibility) aceptar; (problem, opponent) enfrentarse a; (fuel) repostar; (supplies) reponer (**b**) (hire) (worker) contratar (**c**) (acquire) tomar, adquirir

▶**take out** vt sep (**a**) (remove) sacar; **her job really takes it out of her** su trabajo la deja

totalmente agotada; **to t. it out on sb** pagarla or desahogarse con alguien (**b**) (person) sacar; **to t. sb out for a meal/to a restaurant** llevar a alguien a comer/a un restaurante (**c**) (obtain) (licence) sacarse; (insurance policy) contratar, suscribir; **to t. out a subscription** suscribirse

▶**take over 1** vt sep (**a**) (become responsible for) hacerse cargo de (**b**) (take control of) (place) tomar; (company) absorber, adquirir
**2** vi (**a**) (assume power) tomar posesión (**b**) (relieve) tomar el relevo (**from** de)

▶**take to** vt insep (**a**) (go to) **to t. to one's heels** darse a la fuga; **to t. to one's bed** meterse en la cama; **to t. to the hills** echarse al monte (**b**) (adopt habit) **to t. to doing sth** adquirir la costumbre de hacer algo, empezar a hacer algo; **to t. to drink** darse a la bebida (**c**) (like) **I took to them** me cayeron bien

▶**take up 1** vt sep (**a**) (carry) subir
(**b**) (lead) (person) llevar, subir
(**c**) (lift) (carpet, floorboards, paving stones) levantar
(**d**) (shorten) (skirt, hem) subir, acortar
(**e**) (accept) (challenge, offer, suggestion) aceptar; **to t. sb up on an offer** aceptar una oferta de alguien
(**f**) (discuss) (subject, problem) discutir (**with** con)
(**g**) (assume) (position) tomar; (post, duties) asumir
(**h**) (hobby, studies) **she's taken up fencing/psychology** ha empezado a practicar esgrima/estudiar psicología; **we t. up the story just after...** retomamos la historia justo después de...
(**i**) (occupy) (space, time, attention) ocupar
**2** vi **to t. up with sb** trabar amistad con alguien

▶**take upon** vt sep **she took it upon herself to tell him my secret** decidió por su cuenta contarle mi secreto

**takeaway** ['teɪkəweɪ] Br **1** n (food) comida f para llevar; (restaurant) establecimiento m de comida para llevar
**2** adj (food) para llevar

**take-home pay** ['teɪkhəʊm'peɪ] n salario m neto

**taken** ['teɪkən] **1** adj (**a**) (occupied) **is this seat t.?** ¿está ocupado este asiento? (**b**) (impressed) **I was very t. with him/it** me impresionó mucho
**2** pp of **take**

**takeoff** ['teɪkɒf] n (**a**) (imitation) imitación f; **to do a t. of sb** imitar a alguien (**b**) (of plane, economy) despegue m

**takeover** ['teɪkəʊvə(r)] n (**a**) Com (of company) absorción f, adquisición f; **t. bid** oferta f pública de adquisición (de acciones), OPA f (**b**) Pol ocupación f

**taker** ['teɪkə(r)] *n* there were no takers nadie aceptó la oferta

**taking** ['teɪkɪŋ] *n* it's yours for the t. está a tu disposición; *Com* **takings** recaudación *f*

**talc** [tælk] *n* talco *m*

**talcum powder** ['tælkəm'paʊdə(r)] *n* polvos *mpl* de talco

**tale** [teɪl] *n* (**a**) *(story)* historia *f*; *(legend)* cuento *m*; **she lived to tell the t.** vivió para contarlo (**b**) *(lie)* cuento *m*, patraña *f*; **to tell tales (about sb)** contar patrañas (sobre alguien)

**talent** ['tælənt] *n* (**a**) *(ability)* talento *m*, dotes *fpl*; *(person with ability)* talento *m*; *Mus & Sport* **t. scout** or **spotter** cazatalentos *mf inv* (**b**) *Br Fam (attractive people)* ganado *m*, titis *mfpl*

**talented** ['tæləntɪd] *adj* con talento

**talisman** ['tælɪzmən] *n* talismán *m*

**talk** [tɔːk] **1** *n* (**a**) *(conversation)* conversación *f*, charla *f*, *CAm, Méx* plática *f*; **to have a t. with sb** hablar con alguien; *Fam* **to be all t. (and no action)** hablar mucho (y no hacer nada); *TV & Rad* **t. show** programa *m* de entrevistas (**b**) **talks** *(negotiations)* conversaciones *fpl* (**c**) *(gossip)* habladurías *fpl*; *(speculation)* especulaciones *fpl*; **there is some t. of his returning** se dice que va a volver; **it's the t. of the town** es la comidilla local (**d**) *(lecture)* conferencia *f*, charla *f*

**2** *vt* (**a**) *(speak) (Spanish, German)* hablar; **to t. nonsense** decir tonterías; **to t. politics** hablar de política; **to t. (common) sense** hablar con sensatez; **to t. (some) sense into sb** hacer entrar en razón a alguien; **she can t. her way out of anything** sabe salir con palabras de cualquier situación (**b**) *(convince)* **to t. sb into/out of doing sth** persuadir a alguien para que haga/para que no haga algo

**3** *vi* (**a**) *(speak)* hablar (**to/about** con/de), *CAm, Méx* platicar (**to/about** con/de); **to t. to oneself** hablar solo; **to t. of** or **about doing sth** hablar de hacer algo; **talking of embarrassing situations,...** hablando de situaciones embarazosas,...; **to t. big** fanfarronear; *Fam* **now you're talking!** ¡así se habla!; *Fam* **YOU can t.!** ¡mira quién fue a hablar!; **to make a prisoner t.** hacer hablar a un prisionero; **what are you talking about?** ¡pero qué dices!; **I don't know what you're talking about** no sé de qué me hablas (**b**) *(gossip)* cotillear, murmurar (**c**) *(give lecture)* dar una conferencia (**on** sobre)

▸**talk back** *vi* responder, replicar

▸**talk down** *vi* **to t. down to sb** hablar con aires de superioridad a alguien

▸**talk over** *vt sep* hablar de, tratar de

**talkative** ['tɔːkətɪv] *adj* hablador(ora), locuaz

**talker** ['tɔːkə(r)] *n* hablador(ora) *m,f*

**talking** ['tɔːkɪŋ] *adj* **t. book** audiolibro *m*, = cinta grabada con la lectura de un libro; **t. point** tema *m* de conversación; *Fam* **t. shop** = sitio donde se habla mucho y se hace poco

**talking-to** ['tɔːkɪŋtuː] (*pl* **talking-tos**) *n Fam* rapapolvo *m*, sermón *m*; **to give sb a t.** echarle a alguien un buen rapapolvo or sermón

**tall** [tɔːl] **1** *adj* alto(a); **how t. are you?** ¿cuánto mides?; **I'm six foot t.** mido un metro ochenta; *Fig* **that's a t. order** eso es mucho pedir; *Fig* **a t. story** un cuento chino

**2** *adv* **to walk** or **stand t.** andar con la cabeza bien alta

**Tallin** ['tælɪn] *n* Tallin(n)

**tallow** ['tæləʊ] *n* sebo *m*

**tally** ['tælɪ] **1** *n* cuenta *f*; **to keep a t. of sth** llevar la cuenta de algo

**2** *vi (of figures, report)* encajar, concordar

**talon** ['tælən] *n* garra *f*

**tamarind** ['tæmərɪnd] *n* tamarindo *m*

**tambourine** [tæmbə'riːn] *n Mus* pandereta *f*

**tame** [teɪm] **1** *adj* (**a**) *(not timid or vicious)* manso(a); *(domesticated)* domesticado(a) (**b**) *(unadventurous)* soso(a)

**2** *vt (animal)* domesticar; *Fig (emotion)* dominar

**tamely** ['teɪmlɪ] *adv (accept, agree to)* dócilmente; **t. worded** pusilánime, blando(a)

**Tamil** ['tæmɪl] **1** *n* (**a**) *(person)* tamil *mf* (**b**) *(language)* tamil *m*

**2** *adj* tamil

▸**tamper with** ['tæmpə(r)] *vt insep (lock)* intentar forzar; *(documents, records)* manipular, falsear

**tampon** ['tæmpɒn] *n* tampón *m*

**tan¹** [tæn] *n Math (abbr* **tangent**) tangente *f*

**tan²** **1** *n (colour)* marrón *m* claro; *(from sun)* bronceado *m*, moreno *m*

**2** *adj (colour)* marrón claro

**3** *vt (pt & pp* **tanned**) *(leather)* curtir; *(of sun) (skin)* broncear, tostar; *Fam* **to t. sb, to t. sb's hide** dar una zurra a alguien

**4** *vi (of person, skin)* broncearse, ponerse moreno(a)

**tandem** ['tændəm] *n (bicycle)* tándem *m*; *Fig* **to do sth in t.** formar un tándem para hacer algo

**tang** [tæŋ] *n (taste)* sabor *m* fuerte; *(smell)* olor *m* penetrante

**tangent** ['tændʒənt] *n Math* tangente *f*; *Fig* **to go off at a t.** salirse por la tangente

**tangerine** [tændʒə'riːn] **1** *n (fruit, colour)* mandarina *f*

**2** *adj (colour)* naranja, anaranjado

**tangible** ['tændʒɪbəl] *adj* tangible, palpable; *Fin* **t. assets** (activo *m*) inmovilizado *m*

**tangibly** ['tændʒɪblɪ] *adv* claramente

**Tangier(s)** [tæn'dʒɪə(z)] *n* Tánger

**tangle** ['tæŋgəl] **1** n (of threads, hair) maraña f, lío m; also Fig **to be in a t.** estar hecho(a) un lío; **to get into a t.** enredarse; Fig hacerse un lío
**2** vt **to get tangled up (in sth)** quedarse enredado(a) (en algo); Fig verse involucrado(a) (en algo)
▸**tangle with** vt insep Fam (quarrel, fight with) buscarse un lío con

**tangled** ['tæŋgəld] adj enredado(a), enmarañado(a)

**tango** ['tæŋgəʊ] **1** n (pl **tangos**) (dance) tango m
**2** vi bailar el tango; Fam **it takes two to t.** tiene que haber sido cosa de dos

**tangy** ['tæŋɪ] adj (taste) ligeramente ácido(a); (smell) penetrante

**tank** [tæŋk] **1** n (a) (container) depósito m, cisterna f (b) Mil tanque m, carro m de combate (c) **t. top** (garment) chaleco m de lana
▸**tank along** vi Fam ir a toda pastilla
▸**tank up** vt sep Br very Fam **to get tanked up** cogerse un pedo or una bolinga

**tankard** ['tæŋkəd] n jarra f, bock m

**tanker** ['tæŋkə(r)] n (ship) (in general) buque m cisterna; (for oil) petrolero m; (lorry) camión m cisterna

**tanned** [tænd] adj moreno(a), bronceado(a); **to be t.** estar moreno(a) or bronceado(a,f

**tanner** ['tænə(r)] n curtidor(ora) m,f

**tannery** ['tænərɪ] n curtiduría f, tenería f

**tannin** ['tænɪn] n tanino m

**tannoy**® ['tænɔɪ] n (sistema m de) megafonía f; **over the t.** por megafonía

**tantalize** ['tæntəlaɪz] vt poner los dientes largos a (**with** con)

**tantalizing** ['tæntəlaɪzɪŋ] adj sugerente

**tantamount** ['tæntəmaʊnt] adj equivalente; **to be t.** equivaler a

**tantrum** ['tæntrəm] n rabieta f; **to throw a t.** coger una rabieta

**Tanzania** [tænzə'nɪə] n Tanzania

**Tanzanian** [tænzə'nɪən] n & adj tanzano(a) m,f

**tap¹** [tæp] **1** n (a) Br grifo m; **on t.** (of beer) de barril; Fig **to be on t.** (of person, thing) estar disponible; **t. water** agua f del grifo (b) **to put a t. on the phone** intervenir or pinchar el teléfono
**2** vt (pt & pp **tapped**) (tree) sangrar; (resources) aprovechar, explotar; (phone) intervenir, pinchar; Fam **to t. sb for money** sacar dinero a alguien

**tap²** [tæp] **1** n (a) (light blow) golpecito m; **to give sth a t.** darle un golpecito a algo; **to give sb a t. on the shoulder** darle un golpecito en el hombro a alguien (b) **t. dancing** claqué m
**2** vt (pt & pp **tapped**) dar un golpecito a; **I tapped him on the shoulder** le di un golpe-

cito en el hombro
**3** vi **to t. at** or **on the door** llamar suavemente a la puerta

**tape** [teɪp] **1** n (a) (ribbon) cinta f; (adhesive or Fam **sticky**) **t.** cinta adhesiva; Sport (**finishing**) **t.** (cinta de) meta f, **t.** (**measure**) cinta f métrica (b) (for recording, cassette) cinta (magnetofónica); **t. recorder** casete m; **t. recording** grabación f (magnetofónica)
**2** vt (a) (stick with tape) pegar con cinta adhesiva; Fig **I've got him/it taped** lo tengo pillado or controlado (b) (record) grabar

**taper** ['teɪpə(r)] **1** n (candle) candela f
**2** vi estrecharse; (to a point) acabar en punta
▸**taper off** vi (of object) estrecharse; (of production, numbers) disminuir

**tape-record** ['teɪprɪkɔːd] vt grabar (en cinta)

**tapestry** ['tæpɪstrɪ] n (cloth) tapiz m; (art) tapicería f

**tapeworm** ['teɪpwɜːm] n tenia f, solitaria f

**tapioca** [tæpɪ'əʊkə] n tapioca f

**tapping** ['tæpɪŋ] n (sound) golpeteo m

**tar** [tɑː(r)] **1** n (a) (substance) alquitrán m (b) Old-fashioned Fam (sailor) marinero m
**2** vt (pt & pp **tarred**) alquitranar; **to t. and feather sb** emplumar a alguien; Fig **we have all been tarred with the same brush** nos han metido a todos en el mismo saco

**tarantula** [tə'ræntjʊlə] n tarántula f

**tardily** ['tɑːdɪlɪ] adv (late) tardíamente; (slowly) lentamente

**tardy** ['tɑːdɪ] adj (late) tardío(a); (slow) lento(a)

**target** ['tɑːgɪt] **1** n (of bullet, missile, joke) blanco m, objetivo m; Fig (aim, goal) objetivo m, meta f; Fig **to set oneself a t.** trazarse una meta; **to be on t.** ir según lo previsto; **to be on t. to do sth** ir camino de hacer algo; TV & Rad **t. audience** audiencia f a la que está orientada la emisión; **t. language** (in translating) lengua f de destino or llegada; **t. market** mercado m objeto or objetivo; Sport **t. practice** prácticas fpl de tiro
**2** vt (a) (aim) **to t. sth at sb** (missile) apuntar algo hacia or a algo; Fig (campaign, TV programme, benefits) destinar algo a algo (b) (aim at) apuntar a, tener como objetivo

**tariff** ['tærɪf] n (tax) arancel m; (price list) tarifa f; **t. barrier** barrera f arancelaria

**tarmac**® ['tɑːmæk] **1** n asfalto m; Av (runway) pista f
**2** vt (pt & pp **tarmacked**) asfaltar

**tarnish** ['tɑːnɪʃ] **1** vt (metal, reputation) empañar
**2** vi (of metal) empañarse, deslucirse

**tarot** ['tærəʊ] n tarot m

**tarpaulin** [tɑː'pɔːlɪn] n lona f impermeable, hule m

**tarragon** ['tærəgən] n estragón m

**tart** [tɑːt] **1** n (**a**) (cake) (large) tarta f, pastel m; (small) pastelillo m (**b**) Fam Pej (promiscuous woman) zorra f; Old-fashioned Fam (prostitute) fulana f
**2** adj (in taste) agrio(a); (tone) áspero(a)
►**tart up** vt sep Fam (room, pub) remozar; **to t. oneself up** emperifollarse

**tartan** ['tɑːtən] n tartán m, tela f escocesa; **t. tie/jacket** corbata f/chaqueta f de tela escocesa

**Tartar** ['tɑːtə(r)] n tártaro(a) m,f

**tartar** ['tɑːtə(r)] n (on teeth) sarro m

**tartar(e) sauce** ['tɑːtə'sɔːs] n salsa f tártara

**tartly** ['tɑːtlɪ] adv ásperamente

**task** [tɑːsk] n tarea f; **to take sb to t. for (doing) sth** reprender a alguien por (haber hecho) algo

**taskforce** ['tɑːskfɔːs] n Mil destacamento m; Fig (committee) equipo m de trabajo

**taskmaster** ['tɑːskmɑːstə(r)] n **he is a hard t.** es muy exigente

**Tasmania** [tæz'meɪnɪə] n Tasmania

**Tasmanian** [tæz'meɪnɪən] n & adj tasmano(a) m,f

**Tasman Sea** ['tæzmən'siː] n **the T.** el Mar de Tasmania

**tassel** ['tæsəl] n borla f

**taste** [teɪst] **1** n (**a**) (flavour) sabor m, gusto m; (sense of) **t.** (sentido m del) gusto; Anat **t. bud** papila f gustativa
(**b**) (sample) **to have a t. of sth** probar algo; **a t. of things to come** una muestra de lo que vendrá; **to give sb a t. of his own medicine** pagar a alguien con su misma moneda
(**c**) (liking) afición f, gusto m; **to acquire or develop a t. for sth** aficionarse a algo; **add sugar to t.** añada azúcar a su gusto; **it's a matter of t.** es una cuestión de gustos; **violent films are not to my t.** las películas violentas no son de mi gusto
(**d**) (judgement) gusto m; **in bad or poor t.** de mal gusto
**2** vt (**a**) (detect flavour of) notar (un sabor a)
(**b**) (sample) probar; (wine) catar; Fig **to t. success/despair** probar el éxito/la desesperación
**3** vi saber, tener sabor (**of** a); **it tastes fine to me** a mí me sabe bien

**tasteful** ['teɪstfʊl] adj de buen gusto

**tastefully** ['teɪstfəlɪ] adv con buen gusto

**tasteless** ['teɪstlɪs] adj (**a**) (food) insípido(a) (**b**) (remark, clothes) de mal gusto

**taster** ['teɪstə(r)] n (**a**) (person) catador(ora) m,f (**b**) (foretaste) muestra f, anticipo m

**tasty** ['teɪstɪ] adj (delicious) sabroso(a), rico(a); Fam (good-looking) apetitoso(a)

**tat** [tæt] n Fam baratijas fpl

**ta-ta** ['tæ'tɑː] exclam Br Fam ¡chao!

**tatters** ['tætəz] npl **to be in t.** (clothes) estar hecho(a) jirones; Fig (ruined) haber quedado arruinado(a)

**tattered** ['tætəd] adj andrajoso(a)

**tattle** ['tætəl] **1** n habladurías fpl, chismes mpl
**2** vi chismorrear

**tattoo**[1] [tə'tuː] **1** (pl **tattoos**) n (**a**) (on drum) retreta f (**b**) (military show) exhibición f militar

**tattoo**[2] **1** n (pl **tattoos**) (design) tatuaje m
**2** vt tatuar

**tatty** ['tætɪ] adj Fam sobado(a), ajado(a)

**taught** [tɔːt] pt & pp of **teach**

**taunt** [tɔːnt] **1** n (words) pulla f
**2** vt mofarse de, hacer mofa de

**Taurus** ['tɔːrəs] n (sign of zodiac) tauro m; **to be (a) T.** ser tauro

**taut** [tɔːt] adj tenso(a)

**tauten** ['tɔːtən] **1** vt tensar
**2** vi tensarse

**tautness** ['tɔːtnɪs] n tensión f

**tautological** [tɔːtə'lɒdʒɪkəl] adj tautológico(a)

**tautology** [tɔː'tɒlədʒɪ] n tautología f

**tavern** ['tævən] n Literary taberna f

**tawdry** ['tɔːdrɪ] adj (conduct, motive) oscuro(a), sórdido(a); (decor, jewellery) de oropel

**tawny** ['tɔːnɪ] adj leonado(a); **t. owl** cárabo m

**tax** [tæks] **1** n impuesto m, tributo m; (taxation) impuestos mpl; **to pay t.** ser un/una contribuyente, pagar impuestos; **t. allowance** mínimo m exento, tramo m (de ingresos) libre de impuestos; **t. avoidance** elusión f fiscal; **t. bracket** banda f impositiva, tramo m impositivo; **t. collector** recaudador(ora) m,f de impuestos; **t. cut** reducción f fiscal; Br Aut **t. disc** pegatina f del impuesto de circulación; **t. evasion** fraude m or evasión f fiscal; **t. exile** (person) exiliado(a) m,f fiscal; **t. free** libre de impuestos; **t. haven** paraíso m fiscal; **t. inspector** inspector(ora) m,f de Hacienda; **t. incentive** incentivo m fiscal; **t. relief** desgravación f fiscal; **t. return** declaración f de la renta; **t. system** sistema m impositivo
**2** vt (**a**) Fin (goods, income) gravar; (people) cobrar impuestos a (**b**) (resources, patience, knowledge) poner a prueba (**c**) Formal (accuse) **he was taxed with having lied** se le imputó haber mentido

**taxable** ['tæksəbl] adj gravable, imponible

**taxation** [tæk'seɪʃən] n (system) fiscalidad f, sistema m fiscal or tributario; **an increase in t.** un aumento de los impuestos

**tax-deductible** [tæksdɪ'dʌktɪbəl] adj desgravable

**taxi** ['tæksɪ] **1** n taxi m; **t. driver** taxista mf; **t. rank** parada f de taxis
**2** vi (of aircraft) rodar

**taxidermist** ['tæksɪdɜ:mɪst] *n* taxidermista *mf*

**taxing** ['tæksɪŋ] *adj* difícil, arduo(a)

**taxonomy** [tæk'sɒnəmɪ] *n* taxonomía *f*

**taxpayer** ['tækspeɪə(r)] *n* contribuyente *mf*

**TB** [ti:'bi:] *n (tuberculosis)* tuberculosis *f inv*

**te** [ti:] *n Mus* si *m*

**tea** [ti:] *n* (a) *(plant, drink)* té *m; (herbal infusion)* infusión *f*, té *m*; **t. bag** bolsita *f* de té; **t. caddy** lata *f* de té; **t. cosy** cubretetera *m*; **t. leaves** *(dry)* hojas *fpl* de té; *(in bottom of cup)* posos *mpl* de té; **a t. party** una reunión para tomar el té; **t. service** *or* **set** servicio *m* de té; **t. strainer** colador *m (pequeño)*; **t. towel** trapo *m or* paño *m* de cocina; *(evening meal)* cena *f*; **to ask sb to t.** invitar a alguien a cenar; **(afternoon) tea** merienda *f*

**teach** [ti:tʃ] *(pt & pp* **taught** [tɔ:t]) **1** *vt* enseñar; **to t. sb sth, to t. sth to sb** enseñar algo a alguien; **to t. sb (how) to do sth** enseñarle a alguien a hacer algo; **he taught me Spanish at school** me daba clase de español en el colegio; **she taught herself to play the piano** aprendió (ella) sola a tocar el piano; *US* **to t. school** ser profesor(a); *Fig* **to t. sb a lesson** darle una lección a alguien; *Fam* **that'll t. him!** ¡así aprenderá!

**2** *vi* enseñar, dar clase(s)

**teacher** ['ti:tʃə(r)] *n (at primary school)* maestro(a) *m,f; (at secondary school)* profesor(ora) *m,f;* **French t.** profesor(ora) de francés; **t.'s pet** favorito(a) *m,f* del profesor; **t. training** estudios *mpl* de magisterio, formación *f* pedagógica; **t. training college** escuela *f* de magisterio

**teaching** ['ti:tʃɪŋ] *n* (a) *(profession, action)* enseñanza *f*, docencia *f*; **t. practice** prácticas *fpl* de enseñanza; **t. staff** profesorado *m*, personal *m* docente (b) *(doctrine)* enseñanza *f*

**teacup** ['ti:kʌp] *n* taza *f* de té

**teak** [ti:k] *n* teca *f*

**team** [ti:m] *n (of players, workers)* equipo *m; (of horses)* tiro *m; (of oxen)* yunta *f;* **a t. effort** una labor de equipo; **t. games** juegos *mpl* de equipo; **t. player** buen(a) trabajador(ora) *m,f* en equipo; **t. spirit** espíritu *m* de equipo

▶**team up** *vi* unirse **(with** a)

**team-mate** ['ti:mmeɪt] *n Sport* compañero(a) *m,f* de equipo

**teamwork** ['ti:mwɜ:k] *n* trabajo *m* en *or* de equipo

**teamster** ['ti:mstə(r)] *n US (lorry driver)* camionero(a) *m,f*

**teapot** ['ti:pɒt] *n* tetera *f*

**tear¹** [tɪə(r)] *n* lágrima *f;* **in tears** llorando; *Anat* **t. duct** conducto *m* lacrimal; **t. gas** gas *m* lacrimógeno

**tear²** [teə(r)] **1** *n* desgarrón *m; (of muscle)* desgarro *m*

**2** *vt (pt* **tore** [tɔ:(r)], *pp* **torn** [tɔ:n]) *(rip)* rasgar; *(snatch)* arrancar; **to t. sth in two** *or* **in half** romper algo en dos; *also Fig* **to t. sth to pieces** hacer trizas algo; *Fig* **to t. sb to pieces** hacer trizas a alguien; **she was torn between going and staying** tenía unas dudas tremendas sobre si irse o quedarse; *Fam* **that's torn it!** ¡estamos apañados!

**3** *vi* (a) *(of material)* rasgarse; *(of muscle)* desgarrarse (b) **to t. at sth** *(rip)* desgarrar algo (c) *(move quickly)* **to t. along/past/away** ir/pasar/alejarse muy deprisa

▶**tear apart** *vt sep (person)* destruir; *(party, country)* desmembrar

▶**tear away** *vt sep* (a) *(remove by tearing)* arrancar (b) **to t. oneself away from sth** despegarse de algo

▶**tear down** *vt sep (building, statue)* derribar; *(poster)* arrancar

▶**tear into** *vt insep* **to t. into sb** *(physically)* arrojarse sobre alguien; *(verbally)* arremeter contra alguien

▶**tear off** *vt sep (detach by tearing)* arrancar

**2** *vi (run away)* salir pitando

▶**tear out** *vt sep* arrancar; *Fig* **to t. one's hair out** tirarse de los pelos

▶**tear up** *vt sep (document, photo)* romper, rasgar; *(plant, floorboards)* arrancar

**tearaway** ['teərəweɪ] *n* gamberro(a) *m,f*, alborotador(ora) *m,f*

**teardrop** ['tɪədrɒp] *n* lágrima *f*

**tearful** ['tɪəful] *adj (person)* lloroso(a); *(goodbye, reunion)* lacrimoso(a)

**tearfully** ['tɪəfəlɪ] *adv* entre lágrimas, lacrimosamente

**tearing** ['teərɪŋ] *adj Fam* **to be in a t. hurry** tener muchísima prisa

**tearjerker** ['tɪədʒɜ:kə(r)] *n Fam (film, book)* **it's a real t.** es lacrimógeno a más no poder

**tearoom** ['ti:ru:m] *n* salón *m* de té

**tearstained** ['tɪəsteɪnd] *adj* **her face was t.** tenía un rastro de lágrimas en la cara

**tease** [ti:z] **1** *n (person)* guasón(ona) *m,f*, bromista *mf*

**2** *vt* tomar el pelo a *(about* por)

**3** *vi* bromear; **I was only teasing!** ¡sólo era una broma!

▶**tease out** *vt sep (information)* sonsacar, extraer

**teaser** ['ti:zə(r)] *n Fam (problem)* rompecabezas *m inv*

**teashop** ['ti:ʃɒp] *n* salón *m* de té

**teasing** ['ti:zɪŋ] *n* burlas *fpl*, pitorreo *m*

**teaspoon** ['ti:spu:n] *n* cucharilla *f;* **a t. of sugar** una cucharadita de azúcar

**teat** [ti:t] *n (of animal)* teta *f; (of feeding bottle)* tetina *f*, tetilla *f*

**teatime** ['ti:taɪm] *n* hora *f* del té

**technical** ['tɛknɪkəl] *adj* técnico(a); *Br Educ*
**t. college** escuela *f* de formación profesional;
*Sch* **t. drawing** dibujo *m* técnico; **t. hitch** fallo
*m* técnico

**technicality** [tɛknɪ'kælɪtɪ] *n* detalle *m* técnico

**technically** ['tɛknɪklɪ] *adv* técnicamente; **t.,
you are still married** en puridad *or* teóricamente seguís casados

**technician** [tɛk'nɪʃən] *n* técnico(a) *m,f*

**technique** [tɛk'niːk] *n* técnica *f*

**technocrat** ['tɛknəkræt] *n* tecnócrata *mf*

**technological** [tɛknə'lɒdʒɪkəl] *adj* tecnológico(a)

**technology** [tɛk'nɒlədʒɪ] *n* tecnología *f*

**tedious** ['tiːdɪəs] *adj* tedioso(a)

**tedium** ['tiːdɪəm] *n* tedio *m*

**tee** [tiː] *n* (*in golf*) *(peg)* tee *m*; *(area)* salida *f* (del hoyo), tee *m*

▸**tee off** *vi* (*in golf*) dar el primer golpe

**teem** [tiːm] *vi* **(a)** *(rain)* **it was teeming
(down)** llovía a cántaros **(b) to t. with** *(insects, ideas)* rebosar de

**teeming** ['tiːmɪŋ] *adj* (*streets*) atestado(a); *(crowds)* numeroso(a)

**teenage** ['tiːneɪdʒ] *adj* adolescente

**teenager** ['tiːneɪdʒə(r)] *n* adolescente *mf*

**teen idol** ['tiːn'aɪdəl] *n Fam* ídolo *m* juvenil

**teens** [tiːnz] *npl* adolescencia *f*; **to be in
one's t.** ser (un) adolescente

**teensy-weensy** ['tiːnzɪ'wiːnzɪ] *adj Fam* **a t.
bit of...** un poquitín de...

**teeny-bopper** ['tiːnɪbɒpə(r)] *n Fam* fan *f*
quinceañera

**teeny(-weeny)** ['tiːnɪ('wiːnɪ)] = **teensy-
weensy**

**teeshirt** ['tiːʃɜːt] *n* camiseta *f*

**teeter** ['tiːtə(r)] *vi* tambalearse; *Fig* **to t. on
the brink of** tambalearse al borde de

**teeth** [tiːθ] *pl of* **tooth**

**teethe** [tiːð] *vi* **to be teething** estar echando
los dientes

**teething** ['tiːðɪŋ] *n* dentición *f*; *Fig* **t. troubles** *(of project)* problemas *mpl* de partida

**teetotaller**, *US* **teetotaler** [tiː'təʊtələ(r)]
*n* abstemio(a) *m,f*

**TEFL** ['tɛfəl] *n* (*abbr* **Teaching of English
as a Foreign Language**) enseñanza *f* del
inglés como idioma extranjero

**Teh(e)ran** [teə'rɑːn] *n* Teherán

**tel** (*abbr* **telephone**) tel, teléfono *m*

**telecommunications** [tɛlɪkəmjuːnɪ-
'keɪʃənz] *n* telecomunicaciones *fpl*

**telecommute** ['tɛləkəmjuːt] *vi* teletrabajar,
trabajar desde casa por ordenador

**teleconference** [tɛlɪ'kɒnfərəns] *n* teleconferencia *f*

**telegenic** [tɛlɪ'dʒɛnɪk] *adj* telegénico(a)

**telegram** ['tɛlɪgræm] *n* telegrama *m*

**telegraph** ['tɛlɪgrɑːf] **1** *n* telégrafo *m*; **t. pole**
poste *m* telegráfico; **t. wire** tendido *m* telegráfico

**2** *vt* telegrafiar

**telegraphic** [tɛlɪ'græfɪk] *adj* telegráfico(a)

**telemarketing** [tɛlɪ'mɑːkɪtɪŋ] *n Com* telemarketing *m*, ventas *fpl* por teléfono

**telepathic** [tɛlɪ'pæθɪk] *adj* telepático(a)

**telepathy** [tɪ'lepəθɪ] *n* telepatía *f*

**telephone** ['tɛlɪfəʊn] **1** *n* teléfono *m*; **to be
on the t.** *(be subscriber)* tener teléfono; *(be speaking)* estar hablando por teléfono; **to speak to
sb on the t.** hablar con alguien por teléfono;
*Com* **t. banking** telebanca *f*, banca *f* telefónica;
**t. box** cabina *f* telefónica; **t. call** llamada *f* telefónica; **t. directory** *or* **book** guía *f* telefónica,
listín *m* de teléfonos; **t. number** número *m* de
teléfono

**2** *vt & vi* telefonear, llamar por teléfono

**telephonist** [tɪ'lefənɪst] *n Br* telefonista *mf*

**telephoto** [tɛlɪ'fəʊtəʊ] *adj* **t. lens** teleobjetivo

**teleprinter** ['tɛlɪprɪntə(r)] *n* teletipo *m*, tele-
impresor *m*

**telesales** [tɛlɪ'seɪlz] *npl Com* televentas *fpl*,
ventas *fpl* por teléfono

**telescope** ['tɛlɪskəʊp] **1** *n* telescopio *m*;
*Naut* catalejo *m*

**2** *vi* plegarse (como un telescopio)

**telescopic** [tɛlɪs'kɒpɪk] *adj* **(a)** *(relating to
vision)* telescópico(a); **t. sight** *(of rifle)* mira *f*
telescópica **(b)** *(expanding)* *(ladder)* extensible;
*(umbrella)* plegable

**teleshopping** ['tɛlɪʃɒpɪŋ] *n Com* telecompra *f*

**teletext** ['tɛlɪtɛkst] *n TV* teletexto *m*

**televise** ['tɛlɪvaɪz] *vt* televisar

**television** [tɛlɪ'vɪʒən] *n* televisión *f*; **on t.** en
*or* por (la) televisión; **to watch t.** ver la televisión; **it makes good t.** es muy televisivo; **t.
camera** cámara *f* de televisión; *Br* **t. licence** =
certificado de haber pagado el impuesto que
autoriza a ver la televisión, con el que se finan-
cian las cadenas públicas; **t. programme** programa *m* de televisión; **t. screen** pantalla *f* de
televisión; **t. set** televisor *m*

**teleworking** ['tɛlɪwɜːkɪŋ] *n* teletrabajo *m inv*

**telex** ['tɛlɛks] **1** *n* télex *m inv*

**2** *vt* *(message)* enviar por télex

**tell** [tɛl] (*pt & pp* **told** [təʊld]) **1** *vt* **(a)** *(say)*
decir; *(story, joke, secret)* contar; **to t. sb sth, to
t. sth to sb** contar algo a alguien; **to t. the
truth/a lie** decir la verdad/una mentira; **to t.
you the truth...** a decir verdad...; **can you t.
me the way to the station?** ¿me puede decir
cómo se va a la estación?; **we are told that...**

se dice que...; **I told you so!** ¡te lo dije!; **you're telling me!** ¡a mí me lo vas a contar!; **let me t. you, I was frightened!** te confieso que estaba asustado; **to t. the time** *(of clock)* indicar *or* dar la hora; **to t. sb the time** *(of person)* decir la hora a alguien; **his expression told us the answer** la expresión de su cara nos reveló la respuesta

**(b)** *(discern) (attitude, mood)* ver, saber; **we couldn't t. if he was angry or not** no se sabía si estaba enfadado o no; **you can t. she's lived abroad** se nota que ha vivido en el extranjero; **there's no telling what she'll do next** no hay manera de saber qué hará a continuación

**(c)** *(distinguish)* distinguir **(from** de); **to t. two people/things apart** distinguir entre dos personas/cosas; **to t. right from wrong** distinguir lo que está bien de lo que está mal; **I can't t. the difference** ne veo la diferencia

**(d)** *(order)* **to t. sb to do sth** mandar a alguien hacer algo, decir a alguien que haga algo; **do as you are told!** ¡haz lo que te dicen *or* mandan!; **I'm not asking you, I'm telling you!** no es una petición, ¡es una orden!; **she wouldn't be told** no hacía caso de lo que le decían

**(e)** *Pol (count)* escrutar; **all told** en total

**2** *vi* **(a)** *(say)* **please don't t.!** ¡no te chives!; **that would be telling!** ¡eso sería contar demasiado!

**(b)** *(discern)* **it's difficult** *or* **hard to t.** es difícil de saber; **it's too early to t.** es demasiado pronto para saberlo; **you never can t.** nunca se sabe

**(c)** *(have effect)* hacerse notar

▶**tell off** *vt sep Fam (scold)* **to t. sb off (for)** reñir *or* regañar a alguien (por)

▶**tell on** *vt insep Fam (inform)* chivarse de

**teller** ['telə(r)] *n* **(a)** *(of votes)* escrutador(ora) *m,f* **(b)** *Fin (in bank)* cajero(a) *m,f*

**telling** ['telɪŋ] **1** *n (of story)* narración *f*, relato *m*; **it loses nothing in the t.** no pierde nada al contarlo

**2** *adj (blow, contribution)* decisivo(a); *(argument)* contundente

**telling off** ['telɪŋ'ɒf] *n Fam* bronca *f*; **to give sb a t.** echar una bronca a alguien

**telltale** ['telteɪl] **1** *n (person)* chivato(a) *m,f*

**2** *adj (sign, odour)* revelador(ora)

**telly** ['telɪ] *n Br Fam* tele *f*; **on t.** en *or* por la tele; **t. addict** teleadicto(a) *m,f*

**temerity** [tɪ'merɪtɪ] *n* osadía *f*, atrevimiento *m*; **to have the t. to do sth** tener la osadía de hacer algo

**temp** [temp] *Fam* **1** *n* trabajador(ora) *m,f* temporal (administrativo(a)); **to be a t.** hacer trabajo temporal de administrativo

**2** *vi* hacer trabajo temporal de administrativo(a)

**temper** ['tempə(r)] **1** *n (character)* carácter *m*; *(mood)* humor *m*; *(bad mood)* mal humor; **to be in a good/(bad) t.** estar de buen/mal humor; **to keep one's t.** mantener la calma; **to lose one's t.** perder los estribos; **to have a short t.** tener mal genio; **to fly into a t.** ponerse hecho(a) una furia; *Fam* **t.,t.!** ¡calma, calma!; **t. tantrum** rabieta *f*

**2** *vt* **(a)** *(steel)* templar **(b)** *(action)* moderar, mitigar

**temperament** ['tempərəmənt] *n* temperamento *m*

**temperamental** [tempərə'mentəl] *adj (person)* temperamental; *Fig (machine)* caprichoso(a)

**temperance** ['tempərəns] *n* **(a)** *(moderation)* moderación *f*, sobriedad *f* **(b)** *(abstinence from alcohol)* abstinencia *f* (del alcohol); *Hist* **t. movement** liga *f* antialcohólica

**temperate** ['tempərət] *adj* **(a)** *Geog (climate, zone)* templado(a) **(b)** *(language, criticism)* moderado(a)

**temperature** ['tempərətʃə(r)] *n* temperatura *f*; **to take sb's t.** tomar la temperatura a alguien; **to have** *or* **to run a t.** tener fiebre

**tempered** ['tempəd] *adj (steel)* templado(a)

**tempest** ['tempɪst] *n Literary* tempestad *f*

**tempestuous** [tem'pestjʊəs] *adj* tempestuoso(a), tormentoso(a)

**template** ['templɪt] *n also Comptr* plantilla *f*

**temple¹** ['tempəl] *n (place of worship)* templo *m*

**temple²** ['tempəl] *n (side of head)* sien *f*

**tempo** ['tempəʊ] *(pl* **tempos**) *n Mus* tempo *m*

**temporal** ['tempərəl] *adj* **(a)** *(power)* temporal, terrenal **(b)** *Gram* temporal

**temporarily** [tempə'reərɪlɪ] *adv* temporalmente

**temporary** ['tempərərɪ] *adj (in general)* temporal; *(office, arrangements, repairs)* provisional; **t. job** trabajo *m* temporal

**tempt** [tem(p)t] *vt* tentar; **to t. sb to do sth** tentar a alguien a hacer algo; **I'm tempted to accept** me siento tentado de aceptar; **to t. fate** tentar (a) la suerte

**temptation** [tem(p)'teɪʃən] *n* tentación *f*

**tempting** [tem(p)'tɪŋ] *adj* tentador(ora)

**temptress** ['tem(p)trɪs] *n Literary* seductora *f*, mujer *f* fatal

**ten** [ten] **1** *n* **(a)** *(number)* diez *m* **(b)** *(idioms)* **they're t. a penny** los hay a patadas; **t. to one he'll find out** me apuesto el cuello a que lo descubrirá

**2** *adj* diez; **the T. Commandments** los Diez Mandamientos; *see also* **eight**

**tenable** ['tenəbəl] *adj* sostenible

**tenacious** [te'neɪʃəs] *adj* tenaz

**tenacity** [te'næsɪtɪ] *n* tenacidad *f*

**tenancy** ['tenənsɪ] n Law (right) arrendamiento m, alquiler m; (period) período m de alquiler; **t. agreement** contrato m de alquiler or arrendamiento

**tenant** ['tenənt] n (of house) inquilino(a) m,f; (of land) arrendatario(a) m,f

**tend¹** [tend] vt (look after) cuidar (de)

**tend²** vi tender (**towards** hacia); **to t. do do sth** soler hacer algo

▶**tend to** vt insep (look after) atender a

**tendency** ['tendənsɪ] n (trend) tendencia f; (leaning) inclinación f; **to have a t. to (do) sth** tener tendencia a (hacer) algo

**tendentious** [ten'denʃəs] adj Formal tendencioso(a)

**tender¹** ['tendə(r)] n Naut barcaza f; Rail ténder m

**tender²** adj (a) (gentle, affectionate) cariñoso(a), afectuoso(a) (b) (sore) dolorido(a) (c) (meat) tierno(a); Fig **at the t. age of...** a la tierna edad de...

**tender³** 1 n Com (bid) oferta f; **to make** or **put in a t.** hacer or presentar una oferta

2 vt (offer) (one's services, money) ofrecer; **to t. one's resignation** presentar la dimisión

3 vi Com **to t. for a contract** presentarse a una licitación de contrata

**tenderhearted** [tendə'hɑːtɪd] adj bondadoso(a)

**tenderly** ['tendəlɪ] adv (affectionately) cariñosamente, afectuosamente

**tenderness** ['tendənɪs] n (a) (affection) ternura f, cariño m (b) (pain) dolor m (c) (of meat) blandura f, terneza f

**tendon** ['tendən] n Anat tendón m

**tendril** ['tendrɪl] n Bot zarcillo m

**tenement** ['tenɪmənt] n bloque m de pisos (en área deprimida)

**tenet** ['tenet] n principio m, postulado m

**tenfold** ['tenfəʊld] 1 adj **a t. increase** un aumento por diez

2 adv diez veces

**tenner** ['tenə(r)] n Br Fam (ten-pound note) billete m de diez libras

**tennis** ['tenɪs] n tenis m; **to play t.** jugar al tenis; **t. ball** pelota f de tenis; **t. club** club m de tenis; **t. court** pista f or cancha f de tenis; Med **t. elbow** codo m de tenista; **t. player** tenista m,f; **t. racquet** or **racket** raqueta f de tenis; **t. shoe** zapatilla f de tenis

**tenor** ['tenə(r)] n (a) Mus tenor m; **t. sax(ophone)** saxo m tenor (b) (content, sense) tenor m

**tense¹** [tens] n Gram tiempo m; **in the present/future t.** en (tiempo) presente/futuro

**tense²** 1 adj tenso(a); **my neck was very t.** tenía el cuello muy tenso

2 vt tensar; **to t. oneself** ponerse tenso(a)

3 vi tensarse, ponerse tenso(a)

▶**tense up** vi ponerse tenso(a)

**tensely** ['tenslɪ] adv (nervously) tensamente

**tension** ['tenʃən] n tensión f

**tent** [tent] n tienda f de campaña, CSur carpa f; **t. peg** piqueta f, clavija f; **t. pole** mástil m (de tienda)

**tentacle** ['tentəkəl] n tentáculo m

**tentative** ['tentətɪv] adj (person) vacilante, titubeante; (arrangement, conclusions) provisional

**tentatively** ['tentətɪvlɪ] adv (hesitantly) con vacilación, con titubeo; (provisionally) provisionalmente

**tenterhooks** ['tentəhʊks] npl **to be on t.** estar sobre ascuas; **to keep sb on t.** tener a alguien sobre ascuas

**tenth** [tenθ] 1 n (a) (fraction) décimo m, décima parte f (b) (in series) décimo(a) m,f (c) (of month) diez m

2 adj décimo(a); see also **eighth**

**tenuous** ['tenjʊəs] adj (connection) tenue; (argument) flojo(a); (comparison) traído(a) por los pelos

**tenure** ['tenjə(r)] n (of land) arriendo m; (of office) ocupación f; Univ titularidad f; **to have t.** ser profesor(ora) numerario(a) or titular

**tepid** ['tepɪd] adj also Fig tibio(a); **to be t.** (of water) estar tibio(a)

**term** [tɜːm] 1 n (a) (word, expression) término m; **I told her in no uncertain terms** se lo dije en términos claros; **in terms of salary/pollution** en cuanto a salario/contaminación

(b) (relations) **I'm on good/bad terms (with her)** ahora me llevo bien/mal con ella; **to be on friendly terms with sb** llevarse bien con alguien; **not to be on speaking terms** no hablarse; **to come to terms with sth** llegar a aceptar algo

(c) Com **terms** (of contract) términos mpl, condiciones fpl; **terms of reference** (of commission) competencias fpl; **terms of payment** condiciones fpl de pago

(d) Sch & Univ (of three months) trimestre m; (of four months) cuatrimestre m; **t. of office** (of politician) mandato m; **a t. of imprisonment** un período de reclusión; **in the long/short t.** a largo/corto plazo; **her pregnancy has reached (full) t.** (ella) ha salido de cuentas; US Univ **t. paper** trabajo m de fin de trimestre

2 vt denominar, llamar

**terminal** ['tɜːmɪnəl] 1 n (a) Elec (of battery) polo m (b) (rail, bus, air) terminal f (c) Comptr terminal m

2 adj (phase, illness) terminal

**terminally** ['tɜːmɪnəlɪ] adv **to be t. ill** estar en la fase terminal de una enfermedad; **t. ill patient** enfermo(a) m,f terminal

**terminate** ['tɜːmɪneɪt] **1** vt **(a)** (contract) rescindir; (project) suspender **(b)** (pregnancy) interrumpir

**2** vi **(a)** (of contract) finalizar **(b)** (of bus, train) **the train terminates here** esta es la última parada del tren

**termination** [tɜːmɪ'neɪʃən] n (of contract) rescisión f; (of project) suspensión f; **t. (of pregnancy)** interrupción f (del embarazo)

**terminology** [tɜːmɪ'nɒlədʒɪ] n terminología f

**terminus** ['tɜːmɪnəs] n (of bus) última parada f, final m de trayecto

**termite** ['tɜːmaɪt] n termes m inv, termita f

**tern** [tɜːn] n charrán m común

**Terr** (abbr **Terrace**) = nombre que recibe una calle con casas adosadas

**terrace** ['terɪs] n **(a)** (outside cafe, hotel) terraza f **(b)** (on hillside) terraza f **(c)** Br **the terraces** (in football ground) las gradas **(d)** Br (of houses) hilera f de casas adosadas

**terraced** ['terɪst] adj (hillside) en terrazas; Br (house, row) adosado(a)

**terracotta** ['terə'kɒtə] n terracota f

**terrain** [tə'reɪn] n terreno m

**terrapin** ['terəpɪn] n tortuga f acuática

**terrestrial** [tɪ'restrɪəl] adj terrestre

**terrible** ['terɪbl] adj (shocking) horrible, terrible; (of poor quality) horroroso(a); **I'm t. at French** se me da fatal el francés

**terribly** ['terɪblɪ] adv **(a)** (badly) horriblemente **(b)** Fam (very) tremendamente

**terrier** ['terɪə(r)] n (dog) terrier m; Fig (persistent person) batallador(ora) m,f

**terrific** [tə'rɪfɪk] adj Fam (food, book, weather) estupendo(a); (amount, size, speed) tremendo(a)

**terrifically** [tə'rɪfɪklɪ] adv Fam (very) tremendamente; **it was t. hot** hacía un calor tremendo

**terrified** ['terɪfaɪd] adj aterrorizado(a), aterrado(a); **to be t. of** tener terror a

**terrify** ['terɪfaɪ] vt aterrar, aterrorizar

**terrifying** ['terɪfaɪɪŋ] adj aterrador(ora)

**territorial** [terɪ'tɔːrɪəl] adj territorial; Br **the T. Army** = cuerpo militar de reservistas voluntarios que reciben instrucción en su tiempo libre; **t. waters** aguas fpl territoriales

**territory** ['terɪtərɪ] n territorio m; Fig (area of activity) ámbito m

**terror** ['terə(r)] n (fear) terror m; **a reign of t.** un imperio del terror; Fam **that child is a t.** ese niño es un demonio or diablo

**terrorism** ['terərɪzəm] n terrorismo m

**terrorist** ['terərɪst] n & adj terrorista mf

**terrorize** ['terəraɪz] vt aterrorizar

**terror-stricken** ['terəstrɪkən], **terror-struck** ['terəstrʌk] adj aterrado(a); **to be t.** estar aterrado

**terse** [tɜːs] adj tajante, seco(a)

**terseness** ['tɜːsnɪs] n sequedad f

**tertiary** ['tɜːʃərɪ] adj Educ superior; **t. education** enseñanza f superior

**TESL** ['tesəl] n (abbr **Teaching of English as a Second Language**) enseñanza f del inglés como segunda lengua

**TESOL** ['tiːsəl] n (abbr **Teaching of English to Speakers of Other Languages**) enseñanza f del inglés a hablantes de otras lenguas

**TESSA** ['tesə] n Br Fin (abbr **tax-exempt special savings account**) = plan de ahorro que permite unos máximos anuales de inversión y de capitalización de intereses exentos de tributación fiscal

**test** [test] **1** n **(a)** (trial, check) prueba f; **to put sth/sb to the t.** poner algo/a alguien a prueba; **to pass the t.** superar la prueba; **to stand the t. of time** resistir la prueba del tiempo; **t. ban** suspensión f de pruebas nucleares; **t. case** resolución f judicial que sienta jurisprudencia; **t. drive** prueba f de carretera; **t. flight** vuelo m de prueba; **t. pilot** piloto mf de pruebas; **t. tube** probeta f; **t. tube baby** niño(a) m,f probeta

**(b)** (examination) examen m; **(driving) t.** examen m de conducir; **eye t.** revisión f de la vista; **blood t.** análisis m inv de sangre; **French t.** prueba f or control m de francés

**(c)** (in cricket) **t. (match)** encuentro m internacional de cinco días

**2** vt **(a)** (examine) (pupil) examinar; (sight, hearing) revisar; **to t. sb's knowledge** poner a prueba los conocimientos de alguien; **to t. sb for drugs/Aids** hacer a alguien la prueba antidoping/del sida

**(b)** (try out) (object, system) probar

**3** vi **to t. for Aids** hacerse la prueba del sida; **to t. positive/negative** (for drugs, Aids) dar positivo/negativo

▸**test out** vt sep (idea, scheme) poner a prueba

**testament** ['testəmənt] n **(a)** Law (will) testamento m **(b)** (tribute) testimonio m; **to be a t. to** dar testimonio de **(c)** Rel **the Old/New T.** el Antiguo/Nuevo Testamento

**test-bed** ['testbed] n banco m de pruebas

**test-drive** ['testdraɪv] vt Aut probar en carretera

**testicle** ['testɪkəl] n Anat testículo m

**testify** ['testɪfaɪ] Law **1** vt **to t. that...** testificar or atestiguar que...

**2** vi testificar, declarar (**for/against** a favor de/en contra de); Fig **to t. to sth** (be proof of) atestiguar algo

**testily** ['testɪlɪ] adv irritadamente

**testimonial** [testɪˈməʊnɪəl] n (**a**) *(character reference)* referencias *fpl* (**b**) *Sport* t. (**match**) partido m de homenaje

**testimony** [ˈtestɪmənɪ] n *Law* testimonio m; **to bear t. to sth** atestiguar algo

**testing** [ˈtestɪŋ] **1** *(of machine, bridge)* prueba f; **t. ground** campo m de pruebas
 **2** adj *(problem)* difícil, arduo(a)

**testis** [ˈtestɪs] ( pl **testes** [ˈtestiːz]) n *Anat* testículo m

**testosterone** [tesˈtɒstərəʊn] n *Biol* testosterona f

**testy** [ˈtestɪ] adj *(person, mood)* irritable; *(tone, manner)* susceptible; **to be t.** *(by nature)* ser irritable; *(temporarily)* estar irritable or irritado(a)

**tetanus** [ˈtetənəs] n *Med* tétanos m inv

**tetchy** [ˈtetʃɪ] adj *Fam* susceptible, irritable; **to be t.** estar susceptible

**tether** [ˈteðə(r)] **1** n *(for tying animal)* correa f, atadura f; *Fig* **to be at the end of one's t.** estar al borde de la desesperación
 **2** vt *(animal)* atar

**Texan** [ˈteksən] n & adj tejano(a) m,f

**Texas** [ˈteksəs] n Texas, Tejas

**text** [tekst] n texto m; *Comptr* **t. editor** editor m de textos

**textbook** [ˈtekstbʊk] n libro m de texto; *Fig* **a t. example** un ejemplo modélico or de libro

**textile** [ˈtekstaɪl] **1** n tejido m; **textiles** *(industry)* la industria textil
 **2** adj textil

**textual** [ˈtekstjʊəl] adj textual

**texture** [ˈtekstʃə(r)] n textura f

**Thai** [taɪ] **1** n (**a**) *(person)* tailandés(esa) m,f (**b**) *(language)* tailandés m
 **2** adj tailandés(esa)

**Thailand** [ˈtaɪlænd] n Tailandia

**Thames** [temz] n **the T.** el Támesis

**than** [ðæn] *unstressed* [ðən] conj *(in general)* que; *(with numbers, amounts)* de; **he's taller t. me** es más alto que yo; **he was taller t. I had expected** era más alto de lo que me esperaba; **she stands a better chance of winning t. she did last year** tiene más posibilidades de ganar (de las) que (tuvo) el año pasado; **he is more t. a friend** es más que un amigo; **more/less t. ten** más/menos de diez; **more t. once** más de una vez

**thank** [θæŋk] vt dar las gracias a; **I thanked everybody** se lo agradecí a todo el mundo; **to t. sb for sth** agradecer algo a alguien, dar las gracias a alguien por algo; **to t. sb for doing sth.** agradecer a alguien que haya hecho algo, dar gracias a alguien por haber hecho algo; **t. God!** ¡gracias a Dios!; **t. you** gracias; **t. you very much** muchas gracias; **no, t. you** no, gracias; **t. you for coming** gracias por venir; *Ironic* **I'll t. you to mind your own business!** te agradecería que te ocuparas de tus asuntos; *Ironic* **we have Michael to t. for this** esto se lo tenemos que agradecer a Michael

**thankful** [ˈθæŋkfʊl] adj agradecido(a); **to be t. that…** dar gracias de que…

**thankfully** [ˈθæŋkfʊlɪ] adv afortunadamente

**thankless** [ˈθæŋklɪs] adj ingrato(a)

**thanks** [θæŋks] npl gracias fpl; *Fam* **t.!** ¡gracias!; *Fam* **no t.** no, gracias; **t. for coming** gracias por venir; *Fam* **t. for nothing!** ¡gracias por nada!; **to give t. to sb for sth** darle a alguien las gracias por algo; **give him my t.** dale las gracias de mi parte; **t. to him/to his help** gracias a él/a su ayuda; **no t. to you/them!** a pesar de ti/ellos

**thanksgiving** [θæŋksˈgɪvɪŋ] n agradecimiento m; *US* **T. (Day)** día m de acción de gracias *(el cuarto jueves de noviembre)*

**thank you** [ˈθæŋkju] n agradecimiento m; **to say t. to sb** dar las gracias a alguien; **t. letter** carta f de agradecimiento

**that** [ðæt] **1** *demonstrative adj* ( pl **those** [ðəʊz]) *(masculine)* ese; *(further away)* aquel; *(feminine)* esa; *(further away)* aquella; **t. man standing in front of you** ese hombre (que está) delante de ti; **t. man right at the back** aquel hombre del fondo; **compare t. edition with these two** compara esa edición con estas dos; **t. one** *(masculine)* ése; *(further away)* aquél; *(feminine)* ésa; *(further away)* aquélla; **at t. time** en aquella época; **t. fool of a teacher** ese or aquel profesor tan tonto; **well, how's t. leg of yours?** a ver, ¿cómo va esa pierna?; **what about t. drink you owe me?** ¿qué pasa con esa copa que me debes?
 **2** *demonstrative pron* ( pl **those**) *(in near to middle distance)* *(indefinite)* eso; *(masculine)* ése; *(feminine)* ésa; *(further away)* *(indefinite)* aquello; *(masculine)* aquél; *(feminine)* aquélla; **give me t.** dame eso; **this is new and t.'s old** éste es nuevo y ése es viejo; **what's t.?** ¿qué es eso?; **who's t.?** *(pointing)* ¿quién es ése/ésa?; *(who are you?)* ¿quién es?; **who's t. at the back in the blue coat?** ¿quién es aquél del fondo con el abrigo azul?; **is t. all the luggage you're taking?** ¿es ése todo el equipaje que llevas?; **t.'s where he lives** ahí es donde vive; **all t. about my family** lo de or aquello de mi familia; **t. was two years ago** eso fue hace dos años; **t.'s strange!** ¡qué raro!, ¡es extraño!; **with t. she turned and left** con eso, dio media vuelta y se marchó; **what do you mean by t.?** ¿qué quieres decir con eso?; **it was a long journey and a tedious one at t.** fue un viaje largo y, encima, tedioso; **can you run as fast as t.?** ¿puedes correr así de deprisa?; **t.'s right!**, **t.'s it!** ¡eso es!; **t.'s all** eso es todo; **t.'s t.!** ¡ya está!; **t. will do** eso valdrá; **t.'s enough of t.!** ¡ya basta!

**3** *adv* (**a**) *(in comparisons)* así de; **t. high** así de alto; **can you run t. fast?** ¿puedes correr así de deprisa?; **t. many** tantos(as); **t. much** tanto
(**b**) *(so, very)* tan; **is she t. tall?** ¿tan alta es?; *Fam* **he's t. stupid** he... es tan estúpido que...

**4** *[unstressed ðət] relative pron*

> El pronombre relativo **that** puede omitirse salvo cuando es sujeto de la oración subordinada.

(**a**) que; **the letter t. came yesterday** la carta que llegó ayer; **the letter t. I sent you** la carta que te envié; **you're the only person t. can help me** eres la única persona que puede ayudarme
(**b**) *(with following preposition)* que; **the envelope t. I put it in** el sobre en que lo guardé; **the woman t. we're talking about** la mujer de quien *or* de la que estamos hablando; **the person t. I gave it to** la persona a quien *or* a la que se lo di
(**c**) *(when)* que; **the last time t. I saw him** la última vez que lo vi; **the day t. I left** el día (en) que me fui

**5** *[unstressed ðət] conj*

> **that** se puede omitir cuando introduce una oración subordinada.

(**a**) *(introducing subordinate clause)* que; **she said t. she would come** dijo que vendría; **I'll see to it t. everything is ready** me ocuparé de que todo esté listo
(**b**) *Literary (in exclamations)* **t. it should have come to this!** ¡que hayamos tenido que llegar a esto!; **oh t. it were possible!** ¡ojalá fuese posible!

**thatch** [θætʃ] **1** *n* (on roof) paja *f*; *Fam* (of hair) mata *f*
**2** *vt* (roof) cubrir con paja; **thatched cottage** casa *f* de campo con techo de paja; **thatched roof** techo *m* de paja

**thaw** [θɔ:] **1** *n* deshielo *m*; *Fig* **a t. in relations** una mejora de las relaciones
**2** *vt* fundir, derretir; *(food)* descongelar
**3** *vi* (of snow, ice) derretirse, fundirse; *(food)* descongelarse; *Fig (of person, manner)* relajarse
▸**thaw out** *vi* (of lake) deshelarse; (of food) descongelarse; (of person) (in front of fire) entrar en calor

**the** [before consonant sounds ðə, before vowel sounds ðɪ, stressed ðiː] *definite article* (**a**) *(singular)* (masculine) el; *(feminine)* la; *(plural)* (masculine) los; *(feminine)* las; **t. book** el libro; **t. table** la mesa; **t. books** los libros; **t. tables** las mesas; **to/from the airport** al/del aeropuerto; **t. good/beautiful** *(as concepts)* lo bueno/bello; **I'll see him in t. summer** lo veré en verano; **she's got t. measles/the flu** tiene (el) saram-

pión/(la) gripe; **t. best** el/la mejor; **t. longest** el/la más largo(a)
(**b**) *(specifying)* **t. reason I asked is...** el motivo de mi pregunta es...; **I was absent at t. time** yo no estaba en ese momento; **t. Europe of today** la Europa actual; **t. minute I saw her** en cuanto la vi; *Fam* **how's t. knee?** ¿qué tal esa rodilla?
(**c**) *(denoting class, group)* **t. poor/blind** los pobres/ciegos; **t. Wilsons** los Wilson
(**d**) *(with titles)* **Edward t. Eighth** Eduardo octavo; **Catherine t. Great** Catalina la Grande
(**e**) *(proportions, rates)* **to be paid by t. hour** cobrar por horas; **15 kilometres to t. litre** 15 kilómetros por *or* el litro
(**f**) *(in exclamations)* **t. arrogance/stupidity of it!** ¡qué arrogancia/estupidez!; **£200 for a shirt – t. man's mad!** ¡200 libras por una camisa! ¡ese tipo está loco!
(**g**) *[stressed ðiː]* **not THE Professor Branestawm?** ¿no será el famosísimo Profesor Branestawm?; **it's THE car for the nineties** es el coche de los noventa
(**h**) *(in comparisons)* **t. sooner t. better** cuanto antes, mejor; **t. less we argue, t. more work we'll get done** cuanto menos discutamos, más trabajaremos; **I was all t. more puzzled by his calmness** lo que más me extrañaba era su tranquilidad; **she felt all t. better for having told him** se sentía mucho mejor por habérselo dicho
(**i**) *(with dates)* **t. sixties** los sesenta; **t. eighteen hundreds** el siglo diecinueve

**theatre,** *US* **theater** [ˈθɪətə(r)] *n* teatro *m*; *Br Med* (operating) **t.** quirófano *m*; *Mil* **t. of war** escenario *m* de guerra; **t. company** compañía *f* de teatro

**theatre-goer,** *US* **theater-goer** [ˈθɪətəɡəʊə(r)] *n* aficionado(a) *m,f* al teatro

**theatrical** [θɪˈætrɪkəl] *adj also Fig* teatral; **t. company** compañía *f* teatral

**thee** [ðiː] *pron Literary or Rel* (plural) os; *(singular)* te; *(after preposition)* (plural) vos; *(singular)* ti

**theft** [θeft] *n* robo *m*; *(not as serious)* hurto *m*

**theftproof** [ˈθeftpruːf] *adj* (vehicle, door) a prueba de robo, antirrobo

**their** [ˈðeə(r)] *possessive adj* (**a**) *(singular)* su; *(plural)* sus; **we took t. car** *(not his or hers)* cogimos el coche de ellos
(**b**) *(for parts of body, clothes) (translated by definite article)* **t. eyes are blue** tienen los ojos azules; **they both forgot t. hats** los dos se olvidaron el sombrero
(**c**) *(indefinite use)* su; **somebody called but they didn't leave t. name** ha llamado alguien, pero no ha dejado su nombre; **someone's left t. umbrella** alguien se ha dejado el paraguas

**theirs** ['ðeəz] *possessive pron* (**a**) *(singular)* el suyo *m*, la suya *f*; *(plural)* los suyos *mpl*, las suyas *fpl*; **our house is big but t. is bigger** nuestra casa es grande, pero la suya es mayor

(**b**) *(used attributively) (singular)* suyo *m*, suya *f*; *(plural)* suyos *mpl*, suyas *pl*; **this book is t.** este libro es suyo; **a friend of t.** un amigo suyo

(**c**) *(indefinite use)* **if anyone hasn't got t. they can use mine** si alguien no tiene el suyo, puede usar el mío

**theism** ['θi:ɪzəm] *n Rel* teísmo *m*

**them** [ðem, *unstressed* ðəm] *pron* (**a**) *(direct object)* los *mpl*, las *fpl*; **I hate t.** los odio; **I can forgive their son but not THEM** puedo perdonar a su hijo, pero no a ellos

(**b**) *(indirect object)* les; **I gave t. the book** les di el libro; **I gave it to t.** se lo di

(**c**) *(after preposition)* ellos *mpl*, ellas *fpl*; **I'm thinking of t.** estoy pensando en ellos

(**d**) *(as complement of verb* to be*)* ellos *mpl*, ellas *fpl*; **it's t.!** ¡son ellos!; **it was t. who did it** fueron ellos los que lo hicieron

(**e**) *(indefinite use)* **if anyone comes, tell t. ...** si viene alguien, dile que. . .

**thematic** [θi:'mætɪk] *adj* temático(a)

**theme** [θi:m] *n* (**a**) *(of speech)* tema *m*, asunto *m*; **t. park** parque *m* temático (**b**) *(in literature, music)* tema *m*; *TV & Rad* **t. song** *or* **tune** sintonía *f*

**themselves** [ðəm'selvz, *stressed* ðem'selvz] *pron* (**a**) *(reflexive)* se; **they've hurt t.** se han hecho daño

(**b**) *(emphatic)* **they did all the work t.** hicieron todo el trabajo ellos mismos *or* ellos solos; **they told me t.** me lo dijeron ellos mismos

(**c**) *(after preposition)* **they were all by t.** estaban ellos solos; **they were talking about t.** estaban hablando de sí mismos; **they were fighting among t.** se estaban peleando entre ellos

**then** [ðen] **1** *adv* (**a**) *(at that time)* entonces; **it was better t.** era mejor entonces; **before t.** antes (de eso); **since/until t.** desde/hasta entonces; **by t.** para entonces; **t. and there** en aquel instante, al momento

(**b**) *(next)* luego; **what t.?** y luego, ¿qué?; **and t. there's the cost** y luego está el coste

(**c**) *(in that case)* entonces; **if you don't like it, t. choose another one** si no te gusta, elige otro

(**d**) *(therefore)* entonces; **you already knew, t.?** entonces, ¿ya lo sabías?

**2** *adj* **the t. President** el entonces presidente

**thence** [ðens] *adv Formal* (**a**) *(from there)* de allí, de ahí; **we went to Paris and t. to Rome** fuimos a París y de ahí a Roma (**b**) *(because of that)* de ahí

**theologian** [θi:ə'ləʊdʒ(ɪ)ən] *n* teólogo(a) *m,f*

**theological** [θi:ə'lɒdʒɪkəl] *adj* teológico(a)

**theology** [θi:'ɒlədʒɪ] *n* teología *f*

**theorem** ['θɪərəm] *n Math* teorema *m*

**theoretical** [θi:ə'retɪkəl] *adj* teórico(a)

**theoretically** [θi:ə'retɪklɪ] *adv (relating to theory)* en la teoría, teóricamente; *(hypothetically)* en teoría, teóricamente; **it's t. possible** en teoría es posible

**theoretician** [θi:ərɪ'tɪʃən] *n* teórico(a) *m,f*

**theorist** ['θi:ərɪst] *n* teórico(a) *m,f*

**theorize** ['θi:əraɪz] *vi* teorizar

**theory** ['θi:ərɪ] *n* teoría *f*; **in t.** en teoría

**therapeutic** [θerə'pju:tɪk] *adj also Fig* terapéutico(a)

**therapist** ['θerəpɪst] *n* terapeuta *mf*

**therapy** ['θerəpɪ] *n* terapia *f*

**there** [ðeə(r), *unstressed* ðə(r)] **1** *pron* **t. is, t. are** hay; **t. was, t. were** había/hubo; **t. will be** habrá; **there's a page missing** falta una página; **t. are** *or Fam* **there's two slices left** quedan dos lonchas; **t. isn't any** no hay; **t. are four of us** somos cuatro; **t. comes a time when. . .** llega un momento en que. . .

**2** *adv (referring to place)* ahí; *(more distant) (at precise point)* allí; *(more vaguely)* allá; **the keys aren't t.** las llaves no están ahí/allí; **who's t.?** *(after knock on door)* ¿quién es?; **up/down t.** ahí arriba/abajo; **I'm going t. tomorrow** voy para allá mañana; **we went to Paris and from t. to Rome** fuimos a París, y de allí a Roma; **somewhere near t.** por allí cerca; **put it over t.** ponlo ahí; **give me that book t.** dame ese libro de ahí; **do we have time to get t. and back?** ¿tenemos tiempo de ir (allí) y volver?; **t. and then** en aquel instante, al momento; **hey! you t.!** ¡oye, tú!; **t. they are!** ¡ahí están!; **t. she goes!** ¡va por ahí!; **t. you are!** *(when giving sb sth)* ¡ahí tienes!; *Fam* **he's not all t.** no está bien de la cabeza

(**b**) *(at that point)* **we'll stop t. for today** lo dejamos aquí por hoy; **t.'s the difficulty** ahí está la dificultad; *Fam* **t. you have me!, you've got me t.!** *(I don't know the answer)* ¡ahí me has pillado!

**3** *exclam* **t. now, that's done!** ¡hala, ya está!; **t. (you are), I told you so** ¿ves?, ya te lo dije; **t., t.! don't worry!** ¡venga, no te preocupes!

**thereabouts** ['ðeərə'baʊts] *adv* (**a**) *(with place)* (**or**) **t.** (o) por ahí (**b**) *(with number, quantity, distance)* (**or**) **t.** más o menos, (o) por ahí

**thereafter** [ðeər'ɑ:ftə(r)] *adv Formal* en lo sucesivo, a partir de ahí

**thereby** ['ðeəbaɪ] *adv Formal* así, de ese modo; **t. hangs a tale!** y el asunto tiene miga

**therefore** ['ðeəfɔ:(r)] *adv* por (lo) tanto, por consiguiente; **I think, t. I am** pienso, luego existo

**thermal** ['θɜːməl] **1** n Met corriente f de aire ascendente, (corriente f) térmica f

**2** adj térmico(a); **t. energy** energía f térmica; Comptr **t. paper** papel m térmico; Geol **t. springs** aguas fpl termales; **t. underwear** ropa f interior térmica

**thermodynamics** [θɜːməʊdaɪˈnæmɪks] n termodinámica f

**thermoelectric** [θɜːməʊɪˈlektrɪk] adj termoeléctrico(a)

**thermometer** [θəˈmɒmɪtə(r)] n termómetro m

**Thermos**® ['θɜːmɒs] n T. **(flask)** termo m

**thermostat** ['θɜːməstæt] n termostato m

**thesaurus** [θɪˈsɔːrəs] n diccionario m de sinónimos

**these** [ðiːz] **1** adj estos(as); **t. ones** éstos

**2** pron éstos(as); **t. are the ones I want** éstos son los que quiero

**thesis** ['θiːsɪs] (pl theses ['θiːsiːz]) n tesis f inv

**Thespian** ['θespɪən] n Literary actor m, actriz f

**they** [ðeɪ] pron **(a)** (personal use) ellos mpl, ellas fpl (usually omitted, except for contrast); **they're Scottish** son escoceses; **THEY haven't got it!** ¡ellos no lo tienen!; **t. alone know** sólo ellos lo saben

**(b)** (indefinite use) **nobody ever admits they've lied** la gente nunca reconoce que ha mentido; **t. say that…** dicen que…

**they'd** [ðeɪd] = **they had, they would**

**they'll** [ðeɪl] = **they will, they shall**

**they're** [ðeə(r)] = **they are**

**they've** [ðeɪv] = **they have**

**thick** [θɪk] **1** n in the **t. of the forest** en la espesura del bosque; **in the t. of it** or **of things** en primera línea; **through t. and thin** para lo bueno y para lo malo

**2** adj **(a)** (in size) grueso(a); **the wall is a metre t.** el muro tiene un metro de espesor

**(b)** (mist, smoke) denso(a); (forest) espeso(a); (beard) poblado(a), tupido(a); (accent) acusado(a), marcado(a); (sauce) espeso(a), denso(a); **a voice t. with emotion** una voz quebrada por la emoción; **the air was t. with smoke** un humo espeso invadía el aire; **the snow was t. on the ground** había una espesa capa de nieve; Fig **to be t. on the ground** (plentiful) ser abundante

**(c)** Fam (stupid) corto(a), lerdo(a); **to be as t. as two short planks** or **a brick** no tener dos dedos de frente

**(d)** (idioms) **to have a t. skin** tener mucha correa or mucho aguante (ante críticas o insultos); Fam **to give sb a t. ear** dar a alguien un coscorrón; Fam **they're as t. as thieves** están a partir un piñón; Fam **that's a bit t.!** ¡eso es un poco fuerte!

**3** adv **to cut the bread t.** cortar el pan en rebanadas gruesas; **to spread the butter t.** untar mucha mantequilla; Fam **to lay it on a bit t.** cargar las tintas; **to come t. and fast** llegar a raudales

**thicken** ['θɪkən] **1** vt (sauce) espesar

**2** vi (of fog, smoke, sauce) espesarse; Hum **the plot thickens** la cosa se complica

**thicket** ['θɪkɪt] n matorral m

**thickly** ['θɪklɪ] adv **(a) t. cut slices of cheese** lonchas de queso gruesas; **to spread butter t.** untar una gruesa capa de mantequilla **(b)** (to say sth) con la voz quebrada

**thickness** ['θɪknɪs] n (of wall, lips, layer) grosor m; (of forest, hair, beard) espesura f; (of sauce) consistencia f

**thickset** ['θɪk'set] adj (person) chaparro(a)

**thick-skinned** [θɪk'skɪnd] adj Fig **to be t.** tener mucha correa or mucho aguante (ante críticas o insultos)

**thief** [θiːf] (pl thieves [θiːvz]) n ladrón(ona) m, f

**thieve** [θiːv] vt & vi robar

**thieving** ['θiːvɪŋ] **1** n robo m

**2** adj ladrón(ona)

**thigh** [θaɪ] n muslo m

**thighbone** ['θaɪbəʊn] n fémur m

**thimble** ['θɪmbəl] n dedal m

**thin** [θɪn] **1** adj **(a)** (not thick) delgado(a), fino(a); (person, face, arm) delgado(a); (paper, slice, layer) fino(a); (blanket, clothing) ligero(a), fino(a); **to grow** or **become thinner** (person) adelgazar

**(b)** (sparse) (hair, beard) ralo(a), escaso(a); (crowd, vegetation) escaso(a), disperso(a); (fog, mist) ligero(a), tenue

**(c)** (soup) claro(a); (paint, sauce) aguado(a)

**(d)** (voice) atiplado(a)

**(e)** (idioms) **he had vanished into t. air** había desaparecido como por arte de magia; **they saw this demand as the t. end of the wedge** consideraron que esta demanda era sólo el principio (y luego pedirían más); **to have a t. skin** ser muy susceptible; **to have a t. time (of it)** estar en horas bajas; **to be t. on the ground** (scarce) ser escaso(a)

**2** adv **to slice sth t.** cortar algo en rodajas finas; **to spread sth t.** (butter, jam) untar una capa fina de algo; **our resources are spread very t.** los recursos que tenemos son insuficientes

**3** vt (pt & pp thinned) (paint) diluir, aclarar; (sauce) aclarar, aguar

**4** vi (of crowd) dispersarse; (fog, mist) despejarse; **his hair is thinning** está empezando a perder pelo

**thine** [ðaɪn] Literary & Rel **1** adj tu

**2** pron tuyo

**thing** [θɪŋ] n (a) (object) cosa f; Fam what's that t.? ¿qué es ese chisme?; my/your things (clothes) mi/tu ropa; (belongings) mis/tus cosas

(b) Fam (person) poor t.! ¡pobre!; you lucky t.! ¡vaya suerte que tienes!; you silly t.! ¡qué bobo(a) eres!

(c) (action, remark, fact) cosa f; things are going badly las cosas van mal; Fam how are things?, how's things? ¿qué tal van las cosas?, ¿cómo te va?; that was a silly t. to do/say hacer/decir eso fue una tontería; you take things too seriously te tomas las cosas demasiado en serio; for one t. para empezar; what with one t. and another entre unas cosas y otras; it's just one of those things son cosas que pasan; the t. is,... el caso es que...; it's the only t. we can do es lo único que podemos hacer; the important t. is that... lo importante es que...; that's quite another t. eso es algo completamente distinto; I don't know a t. about algebra no tengo ni idea de álgebra; to know a t. or two (about) saber bastante (de)

(d) (idioms) she has a t. about... (likes) le mola cantidad or le priva...; (dislikes) le tiene manía a...; she's got a t. about tidiness/punctuality es muy maniática con la limpieza/puntualidad; the latest t. in shoes lo último en zapatos; it's not the done t. esas cosas no se hacen

**thingummy** ['θɪŋəmɪ], **thingumajig** ['θɪŋəmɪdʒɪɡ], **thingumabob** ['θɪŋəmɪbɒb] n Fam (object) chisme m, cacharro m; (person) fulanito(a) m,f, mengano(a) m,f

**think** [θɪŋk] 1 vt (pt & pp thought [θɔːt]) (a) (have in mind) to t. that... pensar que...; to t. evil/kind thoughts tener pensamientos malévolos/benévolos; what are you thinking? ¿en qué estás pensando?; did you t. to bring any money? ¿se te ha ocurrido traer algo de dinero?

(b) (believe, have as opinion) creer, pensar; he thinks he knows everything se cree que lo sabe todo; who do you t. you are? ¿quién te has creído que eres?; anyone would t. she was asleep cualquiera hubiera creído que está dormida; who'd have thought it! ¡quién lo hubiera pensado!; all this is very sad, don't you t.? todo esto es muy triste, ¿no crees?; it is thought that... se cree que...; they were thought to be rich se les creía or consideraba ricos; I t. so creo que sí; I t. not no creo; I thought so, I thought as much ya me lo figuraba; I should t. so too! ¡menos mal!; I shouldn't t. so no creo; Fam that's what YOU t.! eso es lo que tú te crees

(c) (imagine) imaginarse; I (really) can't t. what/where/why... no se me ocurre qué/dónde/por qué...; t. what we could do

with all that money! ¡imagínate lo que podríamos hacer con todo ese dinero!; to t. that he's only twenty! ¡y pensar que sólo tiene veinte años!

2 vi pensar; to t. ahead planear con anticipación; to t. aloud pensar en voz alta; to t. (long and) hard pensárselo muy bien; Fam to t. big ser ambicioso(a); I did it without thinking lo hice sin darme cuenta; if you t. I'll help you do it, you can t. again! ¡vas listo si crees que te voy a ayudar!; it makes you t. da que pensar; to t. on one's feet improvisar, discurrir sobre la marcha

3 n to have a t. pensárselo; Fam you've got another t. coming! ¡estás muy equivocado(a)!

▸**think about** vt insep (a) (in general) pensar en; to t. about doing sth pensar en hacer algo; it's quite cheap when you t. about it si lo piensas bien, sale bastante barato; I'll t. about it me lo pensaré; that will give them something to t. about eso les hará reflexionar; I'd t. twice about that, if I were you yo, en tu lugar, me lo pensaría dos veces

(b) (take into account) tener en cuenta; I've got my family to t. about debo tener en cuenta a mi familia

(c) (have opinion about) opinar de, pensar de

▸**think back to** vt insep recordar

▸**think of** vt insep (a) (take into account) pensar en, tener en cuenta; I can't t. of everything! ¡no puedo ocuparme de or estar en todo!

(b) (have in mind) pensar en; to t. of doing sth pensar en hacer algo; what were you thinking of giving her? ¿qué estabas pensando regalarle?; come to t. of it, I DID see her that night ahora que caigo or que lo pienso, sí que la vi aquella noche; just t. of it – a holiday in the Caribbean! ¡imagínate unas vacaciones en el Caribe!

(c) (recall) recordar; I can't t. of the answer no se me ocurre cuál es la respuesta

(d) (have opinion about) opinar de, pensar de; to t. well/badly of sb tener buena/mala opinión de alguien; I don't t. much of the idea la idea no me parece muy buena

▸**think out** vt sep meditar

▸**think over** vt sep reflexionar sobre, pensar sobre; I'll t. it over me lo pensaré

▸**think through** vt sep pensar or meditar bien

▸**think up** vt sep idear; (excuse) inventar

**thinker** ['θɪŋkə(r)] n pensador(ora) m,f

**thinking** ['θɪŋkɪŋ] 1 n (a) (process of thought) pensamiento m; to do some t. pensar un poco

(b) (opinion) opinión f, parecer m; to my (way of) t. en mi opinión

2 adj the t. man's cover girl una belleza con cerebro

**think-tank** ['θɪŋktæŋk] *n* grupo *m* de expertos, equipo *m* de cerebros

**thinly** ['θɪnlɪ] *adv* **to spread sth t.** extender una capa fina de algo; **to slice sth t.** cortar algo en rodajas finas; **t. populated** escasamente poblado(a)

**thinner** ['θɪnə(r)] *n* disolvente *m*

**thinness** ['θɪnnɪs] *n (of person, face, arms)* delgadez *f*; *(of paper, slice, layer)* finura *f*; *(of blanket, clothing)* ligereza *f*; *(of liquid)* fluidez *f*

**third** [θɜ:d] **1** *n* **(a)** *(fraction)* tercio *m* **(b)** *(in series)* tercero(a) *m,f*; **Edward the T.** *(written)* Eduardo III; *(spoken)* Eduardo tercero **(c)** *(of month)* tres *m*; **the t. of May** el tres de mayo; **we're leaving on the t.** nos vamos el (día) tres **(d)** *Mus* tercera *f* **(e)** *Br Univ* **to get a t.** *(in degree)* = licenciarse con una media de aprobado raspado
**2** *adj* tercero(a); *(before masculine singular noun)* tercer; **the t. century** el siglo tercero *or* tres; **I was t. in the race** llegué el tercero en la carrera; *Med* **t. degree burns** quemaduras *fpl* de tercer grado; *Fam* **to give sb the t. degree** someter a alguien a un duro interrogatorio; *Law* **t. party** tercero *m*; **t. party cover** seguro *m* a terceros; **t. rate** *(mediocre)* de tercera (categoría); **the T. World** el Tercer Mundo

**thirdly** ['θɜ:dlɪ] *adv* en tercer lugar

**third-world** ['θɜ:d'wɜ:ld] *adj* del tercer mundo, tercermundista

**thirst** [θɜ:st] **1** *n* sed *f*; *Fig* **the t. for knowledge** la sed de conocimientos
**2** *vi Fig* **tener sed (for de)**

**thirsty** ['θɜ:stɪ] *adj* sediento(a) **(for de)**; **to be t.** tener sed; *Fam* **all this talking is t. work** tanto hablar da sed

**thirteen** [θɜ:'ti:n] *n & adj* trece *m; see also* **eight**

**thirteenth** [θɜ:'ti:nθ] **1** *n* **(a)** *(fraction)* treceavo *m*, treceava parte *f* **(b)** *(in series)* decimotercero(a) *m,f* **(c)** *(of month)* trece *m*
**2** *adj* decimotercero(a); *(before masculine singular noun)* decimotercer; *see also* **eleventh**

**thirtieth** ['θɜ:tɪɪθ] **1** *n* **(a)** *(in series)* trigésimo(a) *m,f* **(b)** *(of month)* treinta *m*; **(on) the t. of May** el treinta de mayo; **we're leaving on the t.** nos vamos el (día) treinta
**2** *adj* trigésimo(a)

**thirty** ['θɜ:tɪ] *n & adj* treinta *m; see also* **eighty**

**thirty first** ['θɜtɪ'fɜst] **1** *n* **(a)** *(in series)* trigésimo(a) *m,f* primero(a) **(b)** *(of month)* treinta y uno *m*
**2** *adj* trigésimo(a) primero(a); *(before masculine singular noun)* trigésimo primer

**thirty one** ['θɜtɪ'wʌn] **1** *n* treinta y uno *m*
**2** *adj* treinta y uno(a); *(before masculine noun)* treinta y un

**this** [ðɪs] **1** *demonstrative adj* ( *pl* **these** [ði:z]) este(a); **t. one** éste(a); **t. book** este libro; **t. question** esta pregunta; **I saw him t. morning** lo he visto esta mañana
**2** *demonstrative pron* ( *pl* **these**) éste(a); *(indefinite)* esto; **who's t.?** ¿quién es éste?; **what's t.?** ¿qué es esto?; **t. is Jason Wallace** *(introducing another person)* te presento a Jason Wallace; *(introducing self on telephone)* soy Jason Wallace; **t. is ridiculous!** ¡esto es ridículo!; **t. is what she told me** eso es lo que ella me dijo; **t. is where I live** aquí es donde vivo, vivo aquí; **listen to t.** escucha esto; **drink some of t.** toma un poco (de esto); **what's t. I hear about you resigning?** ¿qué es eso de que vas a dimitir?; **do it like t.** hazlo así; **in a case like t.** en un caso así; *Fam* **we talked about t. and that** hablamos de todo un poco
**3** *adv* **t. high/far** tan alto/lejos; *(gesturing with hands)* así de alto/lejos; **t. much is certain,...** esto es cierto,...

**thistle** ['θɪsəl] *n* cardo *m*

**thither** ['ðɪðə(r)] *adv* **to run hither and t.** correr de aquí para allá

**thong** [θɒŋ] *n* correa *f*

**thorax** ['θɔ:ræks] *n Anat* tórax *m inv*

**thorn** [θɔ:n] *n* espina *f*; *Fig* **to be a t. in sb's flesh** *or* **side** no dar tregua a alguien

**thorny** ['θɔ:nɪ] *adj also Fig* espinoso(a)

**thorough** ['θʌrə] *adj (search, person)* minucioso(a); *(knowledge)* profundo(a); **to do** *or* **make a t. job of it** hacerlo con mucho esmero; **a t. scoundrel** un perfecto canalla

**thoroughbred** ['θʌrəbred] *n & adj (horse)* purasangre *m*

**thoroughfare** ['θʌrəfeə(r)] *n* vía *f* (pública)

**thoroughgoing** ['θʌrəgəʊɪŋ] *adj (search, revision, inspection)* minucioso(a), concienzudo(a); *(knowledge)* profundo(a)

**thoroughly** ['θʌrəlɪ] *adv* **(a)** *(with thoroughness)* minuciosamente, concienzudamente **(b)** *(entirely)* completamente

**thoroughness** ['θʌrənɪs] *n* minuciosidad *f*

**those** [ðəʊz] *(plural of* **that)** **1** *adj* esos(as); *(further away)* aquellos(as); **t. ones** ésos(as); *(further away)* aquéllos(as)
**2** *pron* ésos(as); *(further away)* aquéllos(as); **t. of us who remember the war** aquéllos *or* los que recordamos la guerra; **t. of you who were present** los que estuvisteis presentes

**thou** [ðaʊ] *pron Literary & Rel* tú

**though** [ðəʊ] **1** *conj* aunque; **t. I say so myself** aunque no esté bien que yo lo diga; **strange t. it may seem** aunque parezca raro; **even t. you'll laugh at me** aunque te rías de mí; **as t.** como si
**2** *adv* sin embargo

**thought** [θɔ:t] **1** n **(a)** *(thinking)* pensamiento *m; (idea)* idea *f;* **that's** *or* **there's a t.!** ¡qué buena idea!; **it's quite a t.!** *(pleasant)* ¡sería genial!; *(unpleasant)* ¡sería horrible!; **what a kind t.!** ¡qué detalle tan amable!; **the mere t. of it** sólo (de) pensar en ello; **I didn't give it another t.** no me lo pensé dos veces; **what are your thoughts on the matter?** ¿qué es lo que piensas del asunto?

**(b)** *(reflection)* reflexión *f;* **after much t.** tras mucho reflexionar; **to give a great deal of t. to sth** reflexionar mucho sobre algo; **she was deep** *or* **lost in t.** estaba sumida en sus pensamientos

**(c)** *(intention)* **I had no t. of offending you** no tenía intención de ofenderte; **you must give up all thought(s) of seeing him** olvida la idea de verlo

**2** *pt & pp of* **think**

**thoughtful** ['θɔ:tful] *adj* **(a)** *(pensive) (person)* pensativo(a), meditabundo(a); *(book, writer)* ponderado(a), concienzudo(a) **(b)** *(considerate)* considerado(a), atento(a)

**thoughtfully** ['θɔ:tfəlɪ] *adv (considerately)* consideradamente

**thoughtless** ['θɔ:tlɪs] *adj* desconsiderado(a) **(of** con)

**thought-out** ['θɔ:t'aʊt] *adj* **well/poorly t.** *(plan, scheme)* bien/mal meditado(a)

**thought-provoking** ['θɔ:tprəvəʊkɪŋ] *adj* intelectualmente estimulante

**thousand** ['θaʊzənd] **1** n *a or* **one t.** mil; **three t.** tres mil; **thousands of people** millares *or* miles de personas; **in thousands** a millares; *Fam* **to have a t. and one things to do** tener mil cosas que hacer; **she's one in a t.** hay pocas como ella

**2** *adj* mil; **a t. years** mil años

**thousandth** ['θaʊzən(t)θ] **1** n **(a)** *(fraction)* milésima *f*, milésima parte *f* **(b)** *(in series)* milésimo(a) *m,f*

**2** *adj* milésimo(a)

**thrash** [θræʃ] *vt also Fig* dar una paliza a

▶**thrash about, thrash around 1** *vt sep* **to t. one's arms and legs about** agitar con violencia los brazos y las piernas

**2** *vi (move furiously)* agitarse *or* revolverse (con violencia)

▶**thrash out** *vt sep (solution)* alcanzar por fin; **they are still thrashing out an agreement** todavía están luchando por alcanzar un acuerdo

**thread** [θred] **1** n **(a)** *(of cotton, nylon)* hilo *m*; **a (piece of) t.** un hilo; *Fig* **to hang by a t.** pender de un hilo; **to lose the t. of the conversation** perder el hilo de la conversación **(b)** *(of screw, bolt)* rosca *f*

**2** *vt (needle)* enhebrar; *(beads)* ensartar; **to t.**

**one's way between the cars** avanzar sorteando los coches

**threadbare** ['θredbeə(r)] *adj (clothes, carpet)* raído(a); *Fig (argument, joke)* trillado(a)

**threat** [θret] n amenaza *f*

**threaten** ['θretən] **1** *vt* amenazar; **to t. to do sth** amenazar con hacer algo; **to t. sb with sth** amenazar a alguien con algo

**2** *vi* amenazar

**threatening** ['θretənɪŋ] *adj* amenazante, amenazador(ora)

**three** [θri:] n *& adj* tres *m; see also* **eight**

**three-cornered** [θri:'kɔ:nəd] *adj* triangular; **t. hat** sombrero *m* de tres picos

**three-course meal** ['θri:kɔ:s'mi:l] n comida *f* de tres platos

**three-dimensional** [θri:daɪ'menʃənəl] *adj* tridimensional

**threefold** ['θri:fəʊld] **1** *adj* triplicado(a), por tres

**2** *adv* tres veces; **to increase t.** triplicarse

**three-legged** [θri:'legɪd] *adj (stool)* de tres patas; **t. race** = carrera por parejas con un pie atado

**three-piece** ['θri:pi:s] *adj* **t. suit** terno *m*; **t. suite** tresillo *m*, sofá *m* y dos sillones

**three-point turn** ['θri:pɔɪnt'tɜ:n] n *Aut* cambio *m* de sentido con marcha atrás

**threescore** ['θri:skɔ:(r)] *adj Literary* sesenta; **t. (years) and ten** setenta (años)

**threesome** ['θri:səm] n trío *m*; **we went as a t.** fuimos los tres juntos

**three-wheeler** [θri:'wi:lə(r)] n *(car)* automóvil *m* de tres ruedas; *(tricycle)* triciclo *m*

**thresh** [θreʃ] *vt* trillar

**threshold** ['θreʃəʊld] n *also Fig* umbral *m*; **to cross the t.** franquear el umbral; **to be on the t. (of)** estar en el umbral *or* en puertas (de)

**threw** [θru:] *pt of* **throw**

**thrice** [θraɪs] *adv Literary* tres veces

**thrift** [θrɪft] n ahorro *m*, frugalidad *f*

**thriftless** ['θrɪftlɪs] *adj* derrochador(ora)

**thrifty** ['θrɪftɪ] *adj (person)* ahorrativo(a); *(meal)* frugal

**thrill** [θrɪl] **1** n *(excitement)* emoción *f; (trembling)* estremecimiento *m;* **he gets a t. out of ordering people about** disfruta dando órdenes a la gente

**2** *vt* encantar, entusiasmar; **he was thrilled with his present** estaba entusiasmado con su regalo; **I'm thrilled for you** me alegro muchísimo por ti

**3** *vi Literary* estremecerse

**thriller** ['θrɪlə(r)] n *(novel)* novela *f* de suspense; *(film)* película *f* de suspense

**thrilling** ['θrɪlɪŋ] *adj* apasionante, emocionante

**thrive** [θraɪv] (*pt* **thrived** *or* **throve** [θrəʊv]) *vi* (*of person, plant*) medrar; (*of business*) prosperar; **to t. on other people's misfortunes** aprovecharse de las desgracias ajenas; **some people t. on stress** algunas personas se crecen con el estrés

**thriving** ['θraɪvɪŋ] *adj* (*plant*) lozano(a); (*person*) mejor que nunca; (*business*) próspero(a), floreciente

**throat** [θrəʊt] *n* (**a**) garganta *f*; **to grab sb by the t.** agarrar a alguien por el cuello; **to clear one's t.** carraspear, aclararse la garganta (**b**) *Fam* (*idioms*) **to ram** *or* **shove sth down sb's t.** hacerle tragar algo a alguien; **there's no need to jump down my t.!** ¡no hay motivo para que me eches así los perros!; **they're always at each other's throats** siempre se están tirando los trastos (a la cabeza)

**throaty** ['θrəʊtɪ] *adj* (*cough, voice*) ronco(a)

**throb** [θrɒb] **1** *n* (*of heart*) palpitación *f*, latido *m*; (*of engine*) zumbido *m*

**2** *vi* (*pt & pp* **throbbed**) (*of heart*) palpitar, latir; (*of engine*) zumbar; (*of drums*) retumbar; **my head is throbbing** me late la cabeza de dolor

**throes** [θrəʊz] *npl* **the t. of death, death t.** la agonía de la muerte; **we're in the t. of moving house** estamos pasando la agonía de mudarnos de casa

**thrombosis** [θrɒm'bəʊsɪs] *n Med* trombosis *f inv*

**throne** [θrəʊn] *n* trono *m*

**throng** [θrɒŋ] **1** *n* muchedumbre *f*, gentío *m*

**2** *vt* atestar, abarrotar

**3** *vi* (*gather*) aglomerarse, apelotonarse; **to t. round sb** apiñarse en torno a alguien; **people thronged to the new cinemas** la gente acudió en masa a los nuevos cines

**throttle** ['θrɒtəl] **1** *n Aut* estrangulador *m*; **at full t.** a toda velocidad

**2** *vt* (*strangle*) estrangular

**through** [θruː] **1** *prep* (**a**) (*with place*) a través de; **to go t. a tunnel** atravesar un túnel, pasar a través de un túnel; **we went t. Belgium** atravesamos Bélgica; **to look t. a hole** mirar por un agujero; **she came in t. the window** entró por la ventana

(**b**) (*in the course of*) **all t. his life** durante toda su vida; **halfway t. a book/a film** a mitad de un libro o una película; *Fam* **he's been t. a lot** ha pasado mucho; **to get t. sth** (*finish*) terminar algo

(**c**) (*by means of*) por; **to send sth t. the post** mandar algo por correo; **I found out t. my brother** me enteré por mi hermano

(**d**) (*because of*) por; **t. ignorance/carelessness** por ignorancia/descuido

(**e**) *US* **Tuesday t. Thursday** desde el martes hasta el jueves inclusive

**2** *adv* (**a**) (*to other side*) **to go t.** (*of bullet, nail*) traspasar, pasar al otro lado; **to let sb t.** dejar pasar a alguien; **to get t. to the final** llegar *or* pasar a la final

(**b**) (*from start to finish*) **to sleep all night t.** dormir de un tirón; **to read a book right t.** leerse un libro de principio a fin; **t. and t.** de la cabeza a los pies

(**c**) (*in contact*) **to get t. to sb** (*on phone*) conseguir contactar *or* comunicar con alguien; *Fam* (*make oneself understood*) comunicarse con alguien; **I'll put you t. to him** (*on phone*) le pongo *or* paso con él

**3** *adj* (**a**) (*finished*) **to be t. with sth/sb** haber terminado con algo/alguien

(**b**) (*direct*) **t. ticket** billete *m* directo; **t. train** tren *m* directo

**throughout** [θruː'aʊt] **1** *prep* (*place*) por todo(a); (*time*) durante todo(a), a lo largo de todo(a); **t. the country** por todo el país; **t. her life** durante toda su vida

**2** *adv* (*place*) en su totalidad; (*time*) en todo momento

**throughput** ['θruːpʊt] *n Com* rendimiento *m*

**throve** [θrəʊv] *pt of* **thrive**

**throw** [θrəʊ] **1** *vt* (*pt* **threw** [θruː], *pp* **thrown** [θrəʊn]) (**a**) (*with hands*) (*in general*) tirar, *Am* aventar; (*ball, javelin*) lanzar; **the rioters began throwing stones** los alborotadores empezaron a arrojar piedras; **to t. sth at sb/sth** tirarle algo a alguien/algo; **to t. sth in sb's face** arrojar algo a alguien en la cara; *Fig* echar en cara algo a alguien; **to t. (sb) forwards/backwards** lanzar (a alguien) hacia delante/atrás; **to t. oneself into** (*river*) tirarse a; *Fig* (*undertaking, work*) entregarse a; **to t. oneself on sb's mercy** ponerse a merced de alguien; **she threw herself at him** prácticamente se echó en sus brazos; **to t. sb into confusion** sumir a alguien en la confusión; **to t. a switch** dar al interruptor; **to t. open the door** abrir la puerta de golpe; *Fam* **she tends to t. her weight about** tiende a abusar de su autoridad

(**b**) (*glance*) lanzar

(**c**) (*image, shadow*) proyectar; *Fig* **to t. light on sth** arrojar luz sobre algo

(**d**) (*have*) **to t. a fit** (*get angry*) ponerse hecho(a) una furia; *Fam* **to t. a party** dar una fiesta

(**e**) *Sport* (*in wrestling*) derribar; **the horse threw its rider** el caballo desmontó al jinete

(**f**) *Fam* (*disconcert*) desconcertar

**2** *n* (*of dice, darts*) tirada *f*; (*of ball, javelin, discus*) lanzamiento *m*; (*in wrestling*) derribo *m*

▸**throw away** *vt sep* (**a**) (*discard*) tirar, *Am* botar (**b**) (*opportunity, life, money*) desperdiciar

▶**throw in** vt sep (**a**) (into a place) echar, tirar; Fig **to t. in one's hand** or **one's cards** or **the towel** tirar la toalla; Fig **he threw in his lot with the rebels** unió su destino al de los rebeldes (**b**) (add) añadir; (include as extra) incluir (como extra)

▶**throw out** vt sep (**a**) (eject) (person) echar; (thing) tirar; (proposal) rechazar; **to t. sb out of work** echar a alguien del trabajo (**b**) (emit) (light, heat) despedir

▶**throw together** vt sep (assemble or gather hurriedly) juntar a la carrera; (make hurriedly) pergeñar; **chance had thrown us together** el azar quiso que nos conociéramos

▶**throw up** vt sep (**a**) (raise) **to t. up one's hands** (in horror, dismay) echarse las manos a la cabeza (**b**) (reveal) (facts, information) poner de manifiesto (**c**) (abandon) (career) abandonar
**2** vi Fam (vomit) devolver, echar la papilla

**throwaway** ['θrəʊweɪ] adj (disposable) desechable; **a t. line** or **remark** un comentario insustancial or pasajero

**throwback** ['θrəʊbæk] n Biol regresión f, salto m atrás; Fig retorno m

**throw-in** ['θrəʊɪn] n (in football) saque m de banda

**thrown** [θrəʊn] pp of **throw**

**thru** [θruː] prep & adv US Fam = **through**

**thrush**[1] [θrʌʃ] n (bird) tordo m, zorzal m

**thrush**[2] n (disease) candidiasis f inv

**thrust** [θrʌst] **1** n (**a**) (with knife) cuchillada f; (in fencing) estocada f (**b**) (of army) ofensiva f (**c**) (of argument) sentido m, objetivo m; **the main t. of his argument was that…** lo que pretendía demostrar con su argumento era que… (**c**) Av empuje m
**2** vt (pt & pp **thrust**) hundir (**into** en); **she thrust the letter into my hands** me echó la carta en las manos; **he was suddenly thrust into a position of responsibility** se vio de repente en un puesto de responsabilidad

▶**thrust aside** vt sep apartar, apartar

▶**thrust forward** vt sep (push forward) empujar (hacia delante); Fig **to t. oneself forward** (for job, to gain attention) hacerse notar

▶**thrust on** vt sep **fame was thrust upon him** la fama le cayó encima; **he thrust himself on them** tuvieron que cargar con él

▶**thrust out** vt sep (one's arm, leg) extender de golpe

▶**thrust upon** = **thrust on**

**thrusting** ['θrʌstɪŋ] adj agresivamente ambicioso(a)

**thruway** ['θruːweɪ] n US Aut autopista f

**thud** [θʌd] **1** n golpe m sordo
**2** vi (pt & pp **thudded**) hacer un ruido sordo

**thug** [θʌg] n matón m

**thumb** [θʌm] **1** n pulgar m; Fig **she's got him under her t.** lo tiene completamente dominado; Fam **he's all thumbs** es un manazas; Fam **to give sb/sth the thumbs up** dar el visto bueno a alguien/algo; Fam **to give sb/sth the thumbs down** no dar el visto bueno a alguien/algo
**2** vt **to t. one's nose at sb** hacerle burla a alguien; Fam **to t. a lift** or **ride** hacer dedo; **I thumbed a ride to Glasgow** fui a Glasgow a dedo; **a well thumbed book** un libro manoseado
**3** vi **to t. through sth** hojear algo

**thumbnail** ['θʌmneɪl] n uña f del pulgar; **t. sketch** reseña f, descripción f pasajera

**thumbprint** ['θʌmprɪnt] n huella f del pulgar

**thumbtack** ['θʌmtæk] n US chincheta f

**thump** [θʌmp] **1** n (blow) porrazo m; (sound) ruido m seco
**2** vt (hit) dar un porrazo a
**3** vi (**a**) (on table, door) golpear (**b**) (walk heavily) **I could hear him thumping around upstairs** lo oía dar fuertes pisadas en el piso de arriba (**c**) (of heart) **my heart was thumping** el corazón me latía con fuerza

**thumping** ['θʌmpɪŋ] Fam **1** adj enorme, tremendo(a)
**2** adv **a t. great book/house** un pedazo de libro/casa, un libro/una casa de aquí te espero

**thunder** ['θʌndə(r)] **1** n truenos mpl; **with a face like t.** con el rostro encendido por la ira
**2** vi (**a**) (during storm) tronar; (of guns, waves) retumbar; **to t. along** (of train, lorry) pasar con estrépito (**b**) (of speaker) tronar, vociferar

**thunderbolt** ['θʌndəbəʊlt] n rayo m; Fig (news) mazazo m

**thunderclap** ['θʌndəklæp] n trueno m

**thundercloud** ['θʌndəklaʊd] n nube f de tormenta

**thundering** ['θʌndərɪŋ] adj (very large) tremendo(a), enorme; **to be in a t. rage** estar hecho(a) una furia

**thunderous** ['θʌndərəs] adj (voice, applause) atronador(ora)

**thunderstorm** ['θʌndəstɔːm] n tormenta f

**thunderstruck** ['θʌndəstrʌk] adj pasmado(a), atónito(a)

**Thur** (abbr **Thursday**) jueves m inv

**Thursday** ['θɜːzdeɪ] n jueves m inv; see also **Saturday**

**thus** [ðʌs] adv Formal (**a**) (in this way) así, de este modo (**b**) (therefore) por consiguiente (**c**) **t. far** hasta el momento

**thwart** [θwɔːt] vt (person, plan) frustrar

**thy** [ðaɪ] adj Literary & Rel tu; **love t. neighbour** amarás al prójimo

**thyme** [taɪm] n tomillo m

**thyroid** ['θaɪərɔɪd] *Anat* **1** *n* (glándula *f*) tiroides *m inv*
**2** *adj* tiroideo(a)

**thyself** [ðaɪ'self] *pron Literary & Rel* tú mismo; **for t.** para ti mismo

**tiara** [tɪ'ɑ:rə] *n (jewellery)* diadema *f; (of Pope)* tiara *f*

**Tibet** [tɪ'bet] *n* (el) Tíbet

**Tibetan** [tɪ'betən] **1** *n* **(a)** *(person)* tibetano(a) *m,f* **(b)** *(language)* tibetano *m*
**2** *adj* tibetano(a)

**tibia** ['tɪbɪə] *n Anat* tibia *f*

**tic** [tɪk] *n Med* tic *m;* **a nervous t.** un tic nervioso

**tick¹** [tɪk] *n (parasite)* garrapata *f*

**tick²** *n Br Fam (credit)* **to buy sth on t.** comprar algo fiado

**tick³ 1** *n* **(a)** *(of clock)* tictac *m; Fam (moment)* momentín *m,* segundo *m; Fam* **I'll be with you in a t.!** ¡estoy contigo en un segundo! **(b)** *(mark)* marca *f,* señal *f* de visto bueno
**2** *vi (of clock)* hacer tictac; **the minutes are ticking by** *or* **away** los minutos pasan; *Fam* **I don't know what makes him t.** no sé qué es lo que le mueve

▸**tick off** *vt sep* **(a)** *(on list)* marcar con una señal de visto bueno **(b)** *Br Fam (reprimand)* echar una bronca a **(c)** *US Fam (irritate)* fastidiar

▸**tick over** *vi (of engine)* estar al ralentí; *(of business)* ir tirando

**ticket** ['tɪkɪt] **1** *n* **(a)** *(for train, plane, lottery)* billete *m, Am* boleto *m; (for theatre, cinema)* entrada *f; (parking)* **t.** multa *f* de aparcamiento; **I got a (parking) t.** me pusieron una multa de aparcamiento); **t. inspector** revisor(ora) *m,f;* **t. office** taquilla *f, Am* boletería *f;* **t. tout** reventa *mf;* **t. window** ventanilla *f*
**(b)** *(label) (price)* **t.** etiqueta *f* (de precio)
**(c)** *US Pol (list of candidates)* candidatura *f;* **she ran on an anti-corruption t.** se presentó bajo la bandera de la anticorrupción
**(d)** *Fam* **it was just the t.!** ¡era justo lo que necesitaba!
**2** *vt (goods)* etiquetar

**ticking** ['tɪkɪŋ] *n* **(a)** *(of clock)* tictac *m*
**(b)** *Tex* terliz *m,* cutí *m (para colchones)*

**ticking off** *n Br Fam (reprimand)* bronca *f,* rapapolvo *m;* **to give sb a t.** echar una bronca *or* un rapapolvo a alguien

**tickle** ['tɪkəl] **1** *n* cosquillas *fpl;* **to have a t. in one's throat** tener picor de garganta
**2** *vt* **(a)** hacer cosquillas a **(b)** *Fig (amuse)* divertir; **to t. sb's fancy** apetecer a alguien; **to be tickled pink** estar encantado(a)
**3** *vi* hacer cosquillas

**ticklish** ['tɪklɪʃ] *adj* **(a)** *(person)* **to be t.** tener cosquillas **(b)** *Fam (situation, problem)* delicado(a), peliagudo(a)

**tidal** ['taɪdəl] *adj* **the river is t. up to Stirling** la marea llega hasta Stirling; **t. energy** energía *f* mareomotriz; **t. wave** maremoto *m*

**tiddler** ['tɪdlə(r)] *n Br Fam (small fish)* pececillo *m; (child)* renacuajo(a) *m,f*

**tiddly** ['tɪdlɪ] *adj Br Fam* **(a)** *(small)* minúsculo(a) **(b)** *(drunk)* achispado(a)

**tiddlywinks** ['tɪdlɪwɪŋks] *n* (juego *m* de la) pulga *f*

**tide** [taɪd] *n* marea *f; Fig (of events)* rumbo *m,* curso *m;* **high/low t.** marea *f* alta/baja; *Fig* **to go against the t.** ir contra (la) corriente; *Fig* **the rising t. of discontent** la creciente ola de descontento; *Fig* **the t. has turned** se han vuelto las tornas

▸**tide over** *vt sep* **to t. sb over** *(of money)* sacar a alguien del apuro; **I lent him a fiver to t. him over till payday** le presté cinco libras para que llegara hasta el día de cobro

**tidemark** ['taɪdmɑ:k] *n (mark left by tide)* línea *f* de la marea; *Br Fam (in bath)* cerco *m* (de suciedad)

**tidings** ['taɪdɪŋz] *npl Literary* nuevas *fpl,* noticias *fpl*

**tidy** ['taɪdɪ] **1** *adj* **(a)** *(room, habits)* ordenado(a); *(appearance)* arreglado(a), aseado(a); *(mind)* metódico(a) **(b)** *Fam (considerable)* considerable
**2** *vt (room)* ordenar; *(garden, hair)* arreglar

▸**tidy up** *vi* recoger

**tie** [taɪ] **1** *n* **(a)** *(link)* lazo *m,* vínculo *m* **(b)** *(item of clothing)* corbata *f* **(c)** *Sport (draw)* empate *m; (match)* eliminatoria *f,* partido *m* de clasificación
**2** *vt (shoelace, piece of string)* atar; **to t. sth to sth** atar algo a algo; **to t. a knot** atar *or* hacer un nudo; *Fig* **to have one's hands tied** *(have no alternative)* tener las manos atadas; *Fig* **he was tied to his desk** estaba atado a su trabajo; *Fig* **she felt tied by a sense of duty** se sentía obligada por sentido del deber
**3** *vi (in race, contest)* empatar

▸**tie back** *vt sep (hair, curtains)* recoger

▸**tie down** *vt sep (immobilize)* atar; *Fig* **children t. you down** los hijos atan mucho; *Fig* **I don't want to be tied down to a specific date** no quiero comprometerme a una fecha concreta

▸**tie in** *vi (of facts, story)* encajar, concordar

▸**tie on** *vt* atar

▸**tie up** *vt sep* **(a)** *(animal, parcel)* atar; *(boat)* amarrar; *Fig (deal)* cerrar; **my capital is tied up in property** tengo mi capital invertido en bienes inmuebles **(b)** *Fig* **to be tied up** *(busy)* estar muy ocupado(a)

**tie-break(er)** ['taɪbreɪk(ər)] *n (in tennis)* tie-break *m,* muerte *f* súbita; *(in quiz, competition)* desempate *m*

**tie-in** ['taɪɪn] n (a) (link) relación f (**with** con) (b) **a film/TV t.** = un producto a veces promocional relacionado con una nueva película o programa televisivo

**tier** [tɪə(r)] n (of theatre) fila f; (of stadium) grada f; (of wedding cake) piso m; (administrative) nivel m

**TIFF** [tɪf] n Comptr (abbr **Tagged Image File Format**) TIFF

**tiff** [tɪf] n Fam riña f, desavenencia f

**tig** [tɪg] n (game) **to play t.** jugar a pillarse or al corre que te pillo

**tiger** ['taɪgə(r)] n tigre m

**tight** [taɪt] **1** adj (a) (clothes) ajustado(a), estrecho(a); (knot, screw) apretado(a); Fig (bend) cerrado(a); Fig (restrictions) severo(a); **to be a t. fit** (of clothes) quedar muy justo(a); **to keep a t. hold on sth** tener algo bien agarrado; **we're a bit t. for time** vamos un poco cortos or justos de tiempo; Fig **to be in a t. spot** or **corner** estar en un aprieto; Fig **to run a t. ship** llevar el timón con mano firme; **to work to a t. schedule** trabajar con un calendario estricto
(b) (race, finish) reñido(a); Fam **money's a bit t. at the moment** ahora ando un poco justo de dinero
(c) Fam (mean) agarrado(a), roñoso(a)
(d) Fam (drunk) mamado(a)
**2** adv (hold, squeeze) con fuerza; (seal, shut) bien; **hold t.!** ¡agárrate fuerte!; **sleep t.!** ¡que descanses!

**tighten** ['taɪtən] **1** vt (screw, knot) apretar; (rope) tensar; (restrictions, security) intensificar; (conditions, rules) endurecer; **to t. one's grip on** (rope, handle) asir con más fuerza; Fig **he tightened his grip on the organization** incrementó su control sobre la organización; Fig **to t. one's belt** apretarse el cinturón
**2** vi (of knot) apretarse; (of grip) intensificarse; (of rope) tensarse
▶**tighten up** vt sep (screw) apretar; (restrictions, security) intensificar

**tightfisted** [taɪt'fɪstɪd] adj Fam agarrado(a), rata

**tightknit** ['taɪt'nɪt] adj (community) muy integrado(a)

**tight-lipped** ['taɪtlɪpt] adj **to be t.** (about sth) (silent) no soltar prenda (sobre algo); (angry) estar enfurruñado(a) (por algo)

**tightly** ['taɪtlɪ] adv (hold, squeeze) con fuerza; (seal, close) bien

**tightness** ['taɪtnɪs] n (of link, clothing) estrechez f; (of regulations, security) rigidez f

**tightrope** ['taɪtrəʊp] n cuerda f floja; Fig **to be walking a t.** estar en la cuerda floja; **t. walker** funambulista mf

**tights** [taɪts] npl (garment) medias fpl, pantis mpl; (woollen) leotardos mpl

**tigress** ['taɪgrɪs] n tigresa f

**'til** [tɪl] = **until**

**tile** [taɪl] **1** n (on roof) teja f; (on floor) baldosa f; (on wall) azulejo m
**2** vt (put tiles on) (roof) tejar; (floor) embaldosar; (walls) alicatar

**tiled** [taɪld] adj (roof) de tejas; (floor) embaldosado(a); (wall) alicatado(a)

**till¹** [tɪl] vt (field) labrar

**till²** n (cash register) caja f (registradora); Fig **to be caught with one's hand** or **fingers in the t.** ser atrapado haciendo un desfalco

**till³** = **until**

**tiller** ['tɪlə(r)] n (on boat) caña f del timón

**tilt** [tɪlt] **1** n (a) (angle) inclinación f (b) (speed) **at full t.** a toda marcha
**2** vt also Fig inclinar; **to t. one's head** inclinar la cabeza
**3** vi (a) (incline) inclinarse; **to t. backwards/forwards** inclinarse hacia delante/hacia atrás (b) **to t. at windmills** arremeter contra molinos de viento
▶**tilt over** vi (fall) venirse abajo

**timber** ['tɪmbə(r)] n (wood) madera f (de construcción); **t.!** ¡árbol va!; **t. merchant** maderero m

**time** [taɪm] **1** n (a) (in general) tiempo m; **in t.** (eventually) con el tiempo; **in t. for sth/to do sth** a tiempo para algo/para hacer algo; **in good t.** (early) con tiempo; **she'll do it in her own good t.** lo hará a su ritmo; **all in good t.!** cada cosa a su (debido) tiempo, todo se andará; **he did it in his own t.** (out of working hours) lo hizo fuera de las horas de trabajo; (at his own pace) lo hizo a su aire or ritmo; **when I have the t.** cuando tenga tiempo; **now my t. is my own** ahora tengo todo el tiempo del mundo; **to take one's t.** (doing sth) tomarse (uno) su tiempo (para hacer algo); **you took your t.!** ¡has tardado mucho!; **it takes t.** lleva tiempo; **I've no t. for him** no me cae nada bien; **in no t. at all, in next to no t.** en un abrir y cerrar de ojos; **t. is getting on** no queda mucho tiempo; **t.'s up!** ¡se acabó el tiempo!; Fam **to do t.** (go to prison) pasar una temporada a la sombra; **if I had my t. over again** si pudiera vivir otra vez; **t. will tell** el tiempo lo dirá; Prov **t. is money** el tiempo es oro; **t. bomb** bomba f de relojería; Fig **to be sitting on a t. bomb** estar (sentado(a)) sobre un volcán; **t. frame** plazo m de tiempo; Fig **to be in a t. warp** seguir anclado(a) en el pasado
(b) (period) **in a short t.** dentro de poco; **in a long t.** desde hace (mucho) tiempo; **in three weeks' t.** dentro de tres semanas; **to take a long t. over sth/to do sth** tomarse mucho tiempo para algo/para hacer algo; **for some t.** durante bastante tiempo; **for the t. being** por ahora, por el momento; **to have a good t.**

pasárselo bien; **to give sb a hard t.** hacer pasar a alguien un mal rato

(**c**) *(age)* época *f*; **before my t.** antes de mi época; **to be ahead of one's t.** estar por delante de su tiempo, ser un adelantado de su tiempo; **she was a good singer in her t.** en sus tiempos fue una gran cantante; **to move with the times** ir con los tiempos; **she's seen a few things in her t.** ella ha visto unas cuantas cosas en su vida; **t. capsule** = recipiente que contiene objetos propios de una época y que se entierra para que futuras generaciones puedan conocer cómo se vivía entonces

(**d**) *(moment)* momento *m*; **I didn't know it at the t.** en aquel momento *or* entonces no lo sabía; **at that t.** en aquel momento *or* entonces; **at the present t.** en el momento presente; **at one t. it was different** hubo un tiempo en que era distinto; **at no t.** en ningún momento; **at the same t.** al mismo tiempo; **at all times** en todo momento; **this t. next year** el año que viene por estas fechas; **from that t. (onwards)** desde entonces (en adelante); **at that t. of (the) year** por aquellas fechas; **the t. for talking is past** la ocasión de hablar ya ha pasado; *Fam* **not before t.!** ¡ya era hora!; *Fam* **it's high t.!** ¡ya era hora!

(**e**) *(on clock)* hora *f*; **what's the t.?** ¿qué hora es?; **to pass the t. of day with sb** charlar un rato con alguien; **this t. tomorrow** mañana a estas horas; **on t.** a la hora en punto; **to be on t.** llegar a la hora; **I was just in t. to see it** llegué justo a tiempo para verlo; **it is t. we left** es hora de que nos vayamos; **t. difference** diferencia *f* horaria; **t. lag** lapso *m*; *Ind* **t. sheet** ficha *f* de horas trabajadas; **t. signal** señal *f* horaria; **t. switch** temporizador *m*

(**f**) *(occasion)* vez *f*; **at times** a veces; **every t.** siempre; **every t. she looks at me** cada vez que me mira; **from t. to t.** de vez en cuando; **t. and t. again, t. after t.** una y otra vez

(**g**) *(in multiplication)* **four times two is eight** cuatro por dos son ocho; **three times as big (as)** tres veces mayor (que)

(**h**) *Mus* tiempo *m*; **to keep t.** llevar el ritmo *or* compás

**2** *vt* (**a**) *(meeting, visit)* programar

(**b**) *(remark, action)* **well timed** oportuno(a); **badly timed** inoportuno(a)

(**c**) *(person, race)* cronometrar

**time-consuming** ['taɪmkənsjuːmɪŋ] *adj* **a t. task** una tarea que lleva mucho tiempo; **to be t.** llevar mucho tiempo

**time-honoured** ['taɪmɒnəd] *adj* ancestral

**timekeeping** ['taɪmkiːpɪŋ] *n* (**a**) *Ind (in factory)* control *m* de puntualidad (**b**) *(punctuality)* puntualidad *f*; **good/poor t.** mucha/poca puntualidad

**timely** ['taɪmlɪ] *adj* oportuno(a)

**time-out** ['taɪmaʊt] *n Sport* tiempo *m* muerto; *Fig* descanso *m*

**timepiece** ['taɪmpiːs] *n* reloj *m*

**timer** ['taɪmə(r)] *n (device)* temporizador *m*

**time-saving** ['taɪmseɪvɪŋ] *adj (device, method)* que ahorra tiempo

**timescale** ['taɪmskeɪl] *n* plazo *m* (de tiempo)

**time-share** ['taɪmʃeə(r)] *n* multipropiedad *f*, copropiedad *f*

**timespan** ['taɪmspæn] *n* plazo *m*

**timetable** ['taɪmteɪbəl] **1** *n (for buses, trains, school)* horario *m*; *(for event, project)* programa *m*; **to work to a t.** tener un horario de trabajo

**2** *vt* programar

**time-wasting** ['taɪmweɪstɪŋ] *n* pérdida *f* de tiempo

**timid** ['tɪmɪd] *adj* tímido(a)

**timidity** [tɪ'mɪdɪtɪ] *n* timidez *f*

**timidly** ['tɪmɪdlɪ] *adv* tímidamente

**timing** ['taɪmɪŋ] *n* (**a**) *(of announcement, election)* (elección *f* del) momento *m*, oportunidad *f*; **they questioned the t. of the election** la fecha de las elecciones fue polémica

(**b**) *(of remark, action)* **how's that for t.!** we've finished one day before the deadline ¡qué le parece! hemos terminado un día antes de la fecha límite; **her remarks were good/bad t.** sus comentarios vinieron en buen/mal momento

(**c**) *(of musician)* compás *m*, (sentido *m* del) ritmo *m*; **the comedian's t. was perfect** el humorista hizo un uso perfecto de las pausas y del ritmo

**timorous** ['tɪmərəs] *adj* timorato(a), temeroso(a)

**tin** [tɪn] *n* (**a**) *(metal)* estaño *m*; **t. mine** mina *f* de estaño; **t. plate** hojalata *f*; **t. soldier** soldadito *m* de plomo; **t. whistle** flautín *m* (**b**) *(mould)* molde *m*; **cake t.** molde *m* *(para bizcocho, plum-cake, etc)* (**c**) *(container)* lata *f*, *Am* tarro *m*; **t. opener** abrelatas *m inv*

**tinder** ['tɪndə(r)] *n* yesca *f*

**tinderbox** ['tɪndəbɒks] *n Fig* **the country is a t.** el país es un polvorín

**tinfoil** ['tɪnfɔɪl] *n* papel *m* (de) aluminio

**ting-a-ling** ['tɪŋəlɪŋ] *n & adv* tilín *m*

**tinge** [tɪndʒ] **1** *n (of colour, emotion)* matiz *m*

**2** *vt* **tinged with** *(colour)* con un matiz de; *(emotion)* teñido(a) de

**tingle** ['tɪŋgəl] **1** *n (physical sensation)* hormigueo *m*; *(of fear, excitement)* estremecimiento *m*

**2** *vi* **my hands are tingling** siento un hormigueo en las manos; **to t. with fear/excitement** estremecerse de miedo/emoción

**tingling** ['tɪŋglɪŋ] *n (of skin)* hormigueo *m*

**tinker** ['tɪŋkə(r)] **1** *n* quincallero(a) *m,f*, chamarilero(a) *m,f*

**2** *vi* enredar (**with** con)

**tinkle** ['tɪŋkəl] **1** *n (of bell)* tintineo *m*; *Br Fam* **I'll give you a t.** *(on phone)* te daré un toque *or* telefonazo
**2** *vi* tintinear

**tinned** [tɪnd] *adj Br (food)* de lata

**tinnitus** [tɪn'aɪtəs] *n Med* zumbido *m* de oídos

**tinny** ['tɪnɪ] *adj (sound)* metálico(a)

**tinsel** ['tɪnsəl] *n* espumillón *m*

**tint** [tɪnt] **1** *n (colour)* matiz *m*; *(in hair)* tinte *m*
**2** *vt (hair)* teñir

**tiny** ['taɪnɪ] *adj* diminuto(a), minúsculo(a); **a t. bit** un poquitín

**tip**[1] [tɪp] **1** *n (end)* punta *f*; **on the tips of one's toes** de puntillas; **to have sth on the t. of one's tongue** tener algo en la punta de la lengua; *Fig* **the t. of the iceberg** la punta del iceberg
**2** *vt (pt & pp tipped)* **tipped with steel** con la punta de acero

**tip**[2] **1** *n* **(a)** *(payment)* propina *f* **(b)** *(piece of advice)* consejo *m*
**2** *vt (pt & pp tipped)* **(a)** *(give money to)* dar (una) propina a **(b)** *(predict)* **to t. a winner** pronosticar quién será el ganador; **to t. sb for promotion** pronosticar que alguien será ascendido(a)

**tip**[3] **1** *n (for rubbish)* vertedero *m*; *Fam* **this room's a t.!** ¡esta habitación es una pocilga!
**2** *vt (pt & pp tipped)* **(a)** *(pour) (rubbish, liquid)* verter **(b) to t. the scales at 95 kg** pesar 95 kg; *Fig* **to t. the scales** *or* **balance (in sb's favour)** inclinar la balanza (a favor de alguien)

▸**tip off** *vt sep (warn)* avisar, prevenir

▸**tip out** *vt sep* vaciar

▸**tip over 1** *vt sep* volcar
**2** *vi* volcarse

▸**tip up 1** *vt sep* inclinar
**2** *vi* inclinarse

**tip-off** ['tɪpɒf] *n* soplo *m*

**Tippex®** ['tɪpeks] **1** *n* Tippex® *m* , corrector *m*
**2** *vt* **to t. sth out** borrar algo con Tippex®

**tipple** ['tɪpəl] *Fam* **1** *n (drink)* bebida *f* preferida; **what's your t.?** ¿qué bebes?
**2** *vi* beber, empinar el codo

**tipsy** ['tɪpsɪ] *adj* achispado(a); **to be t.** estar achispado(a)

**tiptoe** ['tɪptəʊ] **1** *n* **on t.** de puntillas
**2** *vi* caminar *or* andar de puntillas; **to t. in/out** entrar/salir de puntillas

**tiptop** ['tɪptɒp] *adj* inmejorable, perfecto(a); **in t. condition** en inmejorables condiciones

**tirade** [taɪ'reɪd] *n* invectiva *f*, diatriba *f*

**tire**[1] *US* = **tyre**

**tire**[2] ['taɪə(r)] **1** *vt* cansar, fatigar
**2** *vi* cansarse, fatigarse; **to t. of (doing) sth** cansarse de (hacer) algo

▸**tire out** *vt sep (exhaust)* agotar, fatigar

**tired** ['taɪəd] *adj* cansado(a), fatigado(a); **to be t.** estar cansado(a) *or* fatigado(a); **to be t. of (doing) sth** estar cansado(a) de (hacer) algo; *Fig* **a t. old cliché** un lugar común muy manido

**tireless** ['taɪəlɪs] *adj* incansable, infatigable

**tiresome** ['taɪəsəm] *adj* pesado(a)

**tiring** ['taɪərɪŋ] *adj* agotador(ora)

**tissue** ['tɪsjuː] *n* **(a)** *Biol* tejido *m* **(b)** *(paper handkerchief)* kleenex® *m inv*, pañuelo *m* de papel; *Fig* **a t. of lies** una sarta de mentiras; **t. paper** papel *m* de seda

**tit**[1] [tɪt] *n (bird)* herrerillo *m*, paro *m*

**tit**[2] *n* **t. for tat** donde las dan, las toman; **to give sb t. for tat** pagar a alguien con la misma moneda

**tit**[3] *n very Fam* **(a)** *(breast)* teta *f*; **to get on sb's tits** hincharle las pelotas a alguien **(b)** *(idiot)* gilipichis *mf inv*

**titanic** [taɪ'tænɪk] *adj (conflict, struggle)* titánico(a), descomunal

**titanium** [taɪ'teɪnɪəm] *n Chem* titanio *m*

**titbit** ['tɪtbɪt] *n (snack)* tentempié *m*, refrigerio *m*; *Fig* **a t. of gossip** un cotilleo; **a t. of information** una noticia

**titch** [tɪtʃ] *n Br Fam (small person)* renacuajo(a) *m,f*

**titchy** ['tɪtʃɪ] *adj Br Fam* diminuto(a), minúsculo(a)

**tit-for-tat** [tɪtfə'tæt] *adj Fam* como represalia

**titillate** ['tɪtɪleɪt] *vt* excitar

**titillation** [tɪtɪ'leɪʃən] *n* provocación *f*, excitación *f*

**title** ['taɪtl] **1** *n* **(a)** *(of book, chapter)* título *m*; **they publish ten titles a month** publican diez títulos al mes; **t. page** portada *f*; *Cin & Th* **t. rôle** papel *m* principal; *Mus* **t. track** *(of album)* canción *f* que da título al disco **(b)** *(of person)* título *m* **(c)** *Sport* título *m*; **t. fight** combate *m* por el título **(d)** *Law (to property)* título *m* de propiedad **(e)** *Cin & TV* **the titles** los títulos (de crédito)
**2** *vt* titular

**titled** ['taɪtld] *adj (person)* con título nobiliario

**titleholder** ['taɪtlhəʊldə(r)] *n Sport* campeón(ona) *m,f*

**titter** ['tɪtə(r)] **1** *n* risilla *f*
**2** *vi* reírse tontamente

**tittle-tattle** ['tɪtltætl] *Fam* **1** *n* habladurías *fpl*, chismes *mpl*
**2** *vi* chismorrear

**titular** ['tɪtjʊlə(r)] *adj* nominal

**tizzy** ['tɪzɪ] *n Fam* **to get into a t.** ponerse histérico(a)

**TNT** [ti:en'ti:] *n Chem (abbr* **trinitro-toluene**) TNT *m*, trinitrotolueno *m*

**to** [tu:, *unstressed* tə] **1** *prep* **(a)** *(towards)* a; **to go to France** ir a Francia; **to go to church/to school** ir a misa/al colegio; **to the front** hacia el frente; **to the left/right** a la izquierda/derecha

**(b)** *(until)* hasta; **to this day** hasta el día de hoy; **it's ten to (six)** son (las seis) menos diez; *Am* faltan diez para las seis; **to count (up) to ten** contar hasta diez; **a year to the day** hoy hace exactamente un año

**(c)** *(expressing indirect object)* a; **to give sth to sb** dar algo a alguien; **give it to me** dámelo; **to speak to sb** hablar con alguien

**(d)** *(with result)* **to my surprise/joy** para mi sorpresa/alegría; **to my horror, I discovered that…** cuál no sería mi horror al descubrir que…

**(e)** *(expressing a proportion)* a; **by six votes to four** por seis votos a cuatro; **there are 200 pesetas to the pound** la libra está a 200 pesetas

**2** *particle* **(a)** *(with the infinitive)* **to go** ir; **I have a lot to do** tengo mucho que hacer; **I have nothing to do** no tengo nada que hacer; **he came to help me** vino a ayudarme; **she's old enough to go to school** ya tiene edad para ir al colegio; **it's too hot to drink** está demasiado caliente para beberlo; **I want him to know** quiero que lo sepa

**(b)** *(representing verb)* **I want to** quiero hacerlo; **you ought to** deberías hacerlo; **I was told to** me dijeron que lo hiciera

**toad** [təʊd] *n (animal)* sapo *m*; *Fam Pej (person)* gusano *m*; *Br Culin* **t. in the hole** *(sausage in batter)* = salchichas rebozadas en harina, huevo y leche

**toadstool** ['təʊdstu:l] *n* seta *f* venenosa

**toady** ['təʊdɪ] *Fam* **1** *n* pelotillero(a) *m,f*, cobista *mf*
**2** *vi* **to t. to sb** hacer la pelota a alguien, dar coba a alguien

**toast** [təʊst] **1** *n* **(a)** *(toasted bread)* pan *m* tostado; **a slice** *or* **piece of t.** una tostada; **t. rack** portatostadas *m inv* **(b)** *(tribute)* brindis *m inv*; **to drink a t. to sb** hacer un brindis a la salud de alguien
**2** *vt* **(a)** *(bread)* tostar; **toasted cheese** tostada *f* de queso; **toasted sandwich** sándwich *m* (caliente) **(b)** *(tribute)* brindar a la salud de

**toaster** ['təʊstə(r)] *n* tostador *m*

**tobacco** [tə'bækəʊ] *n* tabaco *m*; **t. pouch** petaca *f*

**tobacconist** [tə'bækənɪst] *n* estanquero(a) *m,f*; *Br* **t.'s (shop)** estanco *m*

**toboggan** [tə'bɒgən] **1** *n* tobogán *m (trineo)*
**2** *vi* tirarse por el tobogán *(pista de nieve)*

**today** [tə'deɪ] *adv* hoy; **a week ago t.** hace (hoy) una semana; **t.'s date/paper** la fecha/el periódico de hoy

**toddle** ['tɒdəl] *vi (of infant)* dar los primeros pasos; *Fam* **he toddled off** se largó

**toddler** ['tɒdlə(r)] *n* niño(a) *m,f* pequeño(a) *(que aprende a caminar)*

**to-do** [tə'du:] *(pl* **to-dos***) n Fam* revuelo *m*

**toe** [təʊ] *n* **(a)** *(of foot)* dedo *m* del pie; *(of sock, shoe)* puntera *f*; **big t.** dedo *m* gordo del pie; **little t.** meñique *m* del pie **(b)** *(idioms)* **to be on one's toes** estar alerta; **to keep sb on his/her toes** no dar tregua a alguien

**toehold** ['təʊhəʊld] *n (in climbing)* punto *m* de apoyo; *Fig* **to gain a t. in the market** lograr introducirse en el mercado

**toenail** ['təʊneɪl] *n* uña *f* del pie; **t. clipper(s)** cortaúñas *m inv*

**toff** [tɒf] *n Br Old-fashioned Fam* pijo(a) *m,f*

**toffee** ['tɒfɪ] *n (small sweet)* (caramelo *m* de) tofe *m*; *(substance)* caramelo *m*; *Fam* **he can't sing for t.** no tiene ni idea de cantar; **t. apple** manzana *f* de caramelo

**tofu** ['təʊfu:] *n Culin* tofu *m*

**together** [tə'geðə(r)] **1** *adv* juntos(as); **t. with** junto(a) con; **all t.** todos juntos; **to go** *or* **belong t.** ir juntos(as); **to act t.** obrar al unísono; **to get t. again** *(of couple, partners)* volver a juntarse
**2** *adj US Fam* equilibrado(a)

**togetherness** [tə'geðənɪs] *n* unidad *f*, unión *f*

**toggle** ['tɒgəl] **1** *n (on coat)* botón *m* de trenca; *Comptr* **t. switch** = combinación de teclas que permite pasar de una aplicación a otra
**2** *vi Comptr* = abrir y cerrar una función o pantalla con la misma tecla; **you can t. between the two applications** puedes pasar de una aplicación a otra pulsando una tecla

**Togo** ['təʊgəʊ] *n* Togo

**Togolese** [təʊgəʊ'li:z] *n & adj* togolés(esa) *m,f*

**togs** [tɒgz] *npl Fam (clothes)* ropa *f*

**toil** [tɔɪl] **1** *n Literary* esfuerzo *m*
**2** *vi (work hard)* trabajar con afán; **to t. away at sth** esforzarse mucho en algo; **to t. up a hill** escalar penosamente una montaña

**toiler** ['tɔɪlə(r)] *n* trabajador(ora) *m,f* incansable

**toilet** ['tɔɪlɪt] *n* **(a)** *(room) (in house)* cuarto *m* de baño, retrete *m*; *(in public place)* servicio *m*, servicios *mpl*; *(object)* váter *m*, inodoro *m*; **to go to the t.** *(in house)* ir al baño; *(in public place)* ir al servicio; **t. paper** papel *m* higiénico; **t. roll** rollo *m* de papel higiénico; **t. seat** asiento *m* del váter **(b)** *Old-fashioned (washing and dressing)* aseo *m* personal; **t. bag** bolsa *f* de aseo; **t. soap** jabón *m* de tocador

**toiletries** ['tɔɪlɪtrɪz] *npl* artículos *mpl* de toca-dor

**token** ['təʊkən] **1** *n* (**a**) *(indication)* señal *f*, muestra *f*; **as a t. of respect** como señal *or* muestra de respeto; **by the same t.** de la misma manera (**b**) *(for vending machine)* ficha *f*; *(paper)* vale *m*

**2** *adj (resistance, effort)* simbólico(a); **I don't want to be the t. woman on the committee** no quiero estar en la comisión para cubrir el porcentaje femenino

**Tokyo** ['təʊkɪəʊ] *n* Tokio

**told** [təʊld] *pt & pp of* **tell**

**tolerable** ['tɒlərəbəl] *adj* (**a**) *(pain, discomfort)* soportable, tolerable (**b**) *(behaviour, effort)* aceptable

**tolerance** ['tɒlərəns] *n* tolerancia *f*; **to have a high/low t. for sth** ser muy/poco tolerante con algo

**tolerant** ['tɒlərənt] *adj* tolerante

**tolerate** ['tɒləreɪt] *vt* tolerar

**toleration** [tɒlə'reɪʃən] *n* tolerancia *f*

**toll¹** [təʊl] *n* (**a**) *(charge)* peaje *m*; **t. bridge** puente *m* de peaje; **t. road** carretera *f* de peaje (**b**) *(of dead, injured)* **the disease had taken its t.** la enfermedad había hecho estragos; **the death t. has risen to 100** el número de víctimas ha ascendido a 100

**toll²** **1** *vt (bell)* tañer

**2** *vi (of bell)* doblar; **to t. for the dead** tocar a muerto

**toll-free** [təʊl'fri:] *US* **1** *adj* **t. number** (número *m* de) teléfono *m* gratuito

**2** *adv (call)* gratuitamente

**Tom** [tɒm] *n Fam* **any T., Dick or Harry** cualquier mequetrefe

**tom** [tɒm] *n Fam* gato *m* (macho)

**tomahawk** ['tɒməhɔːk] *n* hacha *f* india

**tomato** [tə'mɑːtəʊ, *US* tə'meɪtəʊ] *(pl* **tomatoes)** *n* tomate *m*, *Méx* jitomate *m*; **t. juice** zumo *m* de tomate; **t. ketchup** (tomate) ketchup *m*, catchup *m*; **t. sauce** *(for pasta)* (salsa *f* de) tomate; *(ketchup)* (tomate) ketchup *m*, catchup *m*; **t. soup** crema *f* de tomate

**tomb** [tuːm] *n* tumba *f*

**tomboy** ['tɒmbɔɪ] *n* niña *f* poco femenina

**tombstone** ['tuːmstəʊn] *n* lápida *f*

**tomcat** ['tɒmkæt] *n* gato *m* (macho)

**tome** [təʊm] *n Formal* tomo *m*, volumen *m*

**tomfoolery** [tɒm'fuːlərɪ] *n Fam* tonterías *fpl*, niñerías *fpl*

**tomorrow** [tə'mɒrəʊ] **1** *n* mañana *m*; **the day after t.** pasado mañana; **t. is another day** mañana será otro día; *Fam* **she was eating like there was no t.** comía como si se fuese a acabar el mundo

**2** *adv* mañana; **t. morning/evening** mañana

por la mañana/tarde; *Fig* **what will the world be like t.?** ¿cómo será el mundo en el futuro?

**tom-tom** ['tɒmtɒm] *n Mus* tam-tam *m inv*

**ton** [tʌn] *n* (**a**) *(weight)* tonelada *f* (aproximada) *(Br 1.016 kilos, US 907 kilos)* (**b**) *(idioms)* *Fam* **this suitcase weighs a t.** esta maleta pesa un quintal *or* una tonelada; *Fam* **tons of…** *(lots of)* montones de…; *Fam* **he'll come down on you like a t. of bricks** te va a poner a caldo

**tone** [təʊn] *n (sound, colour)* tono *m*; *(on phone)* señal *f*, tono *m*; *(quality of sound)* timbre *m*; **t. of voice** tono *m* de voz; *Fig* **to raise/lower the t.** *(of place, occasion)* elevar/bajar el tono

▸**tone down** *vt sep (colour)* rebajar el tono de; *Fig (remarks)* bajar el tono de

▸**tone up** *vt sep (muscles)* tonificar, entonar

**tone-deaf** ['təʊn'def] *adj* **to be t.** tener mal oído

**Tonga** ['tɒŋgə] *n* Tonga

**Tongan** ['tɒŋgən] **1** *n* (**a**) *(person)* tongano(a) *m,f* (**b**) *(language)* tongano *m*

**2** *adj* de Tonga, tongano(a)

**tongs** [tɒŋz] *npl (for coal, heavy objects)* tenazas *fpl*; *(for food, smaller objects)* pinzas *fpl*; **a pair of t.** unas tenazas/pinzas; **(curling) t.** *(for hair)* tenacillas *fpl* de rizar

**tongue** [tʌŋ] *n* (**a**) *(in mouth, of land, flame)* lengua *f*; *(of shoe)* lengüeta *f*; *(language)* idioma *m*, lengua *f*; **to stick one's t. out** sacar la lengua; **t. twister** trabalenguas *m inv* (**b**) *(idioms)* **hold your t.!** ¡calla la boca!; **have you lost your t.?** ¿se te ha comido la lengua el gato?; **to say sth t.-in-cheek** decir algo en broma

**tongue-tied** ['tʌŋtaɪd] *adj* mudo(a); **to be t.** quedarse mudo(a)

**tonic** ['tɒnɪk] *n* tónico *m*, reconstituyente *m*; **t. (water)** *(agua f)* tónica *f*

**tonight** [tə'naɪt] *n & adv* esta noche

**tonnage** ['tʌnɪdʒ] *n Naut (of ship)* tonelaje *m*

**tonne** [tʌn] *n* tonelada *f* (métrica)

**tonsil** ['tɒnsəl] *n* amígdala *f*; **to have one's tonsils out** operarse de las amígdalas

**tonsillitis** [tɒnsɪ'laɪtɪs] *n Med* amigdalitis *f inv*

**too** [tuː] *adv* (**a**) *(excessively)* demasiado; **it's t. difficult** es demasiado difícil; **t. much** demasiado; **I know her all** *or* **only t. well** la conozco demasiado bien; **you're t. kind** es usted muy amable; **he's not t. well today** no se encuentra muy *or* demasiado bien hoy; **t. bad!** *(bad luck)* ¡qué se le va a hacer!; *(that's your problem)* ¡mala suerte!; **it's t. bad you weren't here earlier** es una pena que no te tuvieras aquí antes; *Fam* **t. right!** ¡desde luego!

(**b**) *(also)* también

(**c**) *(moreover)* además

**took** [tʊk] *pt of* **take**

**tool** [tu:l] *n* (**a**) *(implement)* herramienta *f*; **(set of) tools** herramienta *f*; **t. bag** bolsa *f* de herramientas; **t. box** caja *f* de herramientas; *Comptr* paleta *f* de herramientas; **t. kit** juego *m* de herramientas; **t. shed** cobertizo *m* para los aperos (**b**) *(means, instrument)* instrumento *m*

**toot** [tu:t] **1** *n* bocinazo *m*

   **2** *vt (horn, trumpet)* tocar

**tooth** [tu:θ] *(pl* **teeth** [ti:θ]*) n* (**a**) *(of person, saw)* diente *m*; *(molar)* muela *f*; *(of comb)* púa *f*; **(set of) teeth** dentadura *f*; **to cut a t.** echar un diente; **he had a t. out** le sacaron una muela; **t. decay** caries *f inv*

   (**b**) *(idioms)* **to lie through one's teeth** mentir como un/una bellaco(a); **in the teeth of opposition** haciendo frente a la oposición; **armed to the teeth** armado(a) hasta los dientes; **to fight t. and nail** luchar con uñas y dientes; *Fam* **to get one's teeth into sth** hincar el diente a algo; *Fam* **I'm fed up to the back teeth with him** estoy hasta la coronilla de él; *Fam* **long in the t.** entrado(a) en años

**toothache** ['tu:θeɪk] *n* dolor *m* de muelas

**toothbrush** ['tu:θbrʌʃ] *n* cepillo *m* de dientes

**toothless** ['tu:θlɪs] *adj* desdentado(a); *Fig* inoperante, ineficaz

**toothpaste** ['tu:θpeɪst] *n* dentífrico *m*, pasta *f* de dientes

**toothpick** ['tu:θpɪk] *n* palillo *m* (de dientes)

**toothy** ['tu:θɪ] *adj* **a t. grin** una sonrisa que enseña todos los dientes

**top**¹ [tɒp] *n (spinning top)* peonza *f*

**top**² [tɒp] **1** *n* (**a**) *(highest part)* parte *f* superior, parte *f* de arriba; *(of tree)* copa *f*; *(of mountain)* cima *f*; *(of bus)* piso *m* superior; *(of list)* cabeza *f*; **at the t. of the stairs** en lo alto de la escalera; **at the t. of the street** al final de la calle; **to be (at the) t. of the class** ser el primero/la primera de la clase; **from t. to bottom** de arriba abajo; **at the t. of one's voice** a grito pelado; *Mil* **to go over the t.** entrar en acción; *Fig* pasarse de la raya; *Fig* **over the t.** *(excessive)* exagerado(a); *Fig* **to make it to the t.** llegar a la cumbre

   (**b**) *(lid)* tapa *f*; *(of bottle)* tapón *m*; *(of pen)* capucha *f*

   (**c**) *(upper surface)* superficie *f*

   (**d**) *(garment) (T-shirt)* camiseta *f*; *(blouse)* blusa *f*

   (**e**) **on t.** encima; **on t. of** *(above)* encima de, sobre; *(in addition to)* además de; *Fig* **to be on t. of sth** tener algo bajo control; **you mustn't let things get on t. of you** no debes dejar que las cosas te agobien; *Fig* **to come out on t.** salir victorioso(a); **to be on t. of the world** estar en la gloria

   **2** *adj* (**a**) *(highest)* de más arriba, más alto(a); *(in pile)* de encima; **the t. people** *(in society)* la flor

y nata; *(in an organization)* los jefes; *Fam* **the t. brass** *(army officers)* los altos mandos; **t. coat** *(of paint)* última mano *f*; **t. deck** *(of bus)* piso *m* superior; *Fam Fig* **t. dog** mandamás *mf*; **to be on t. form** estar en plena forma; *Aut* **t. gear** *(fourth)* cuarta *f*, directa *f*; *(fifth)* quinta *f*, directa *f*; **t. hat** sombrero *m* de copa; **t. security prison** cárcel *f* de alta seguridad; **t. speed** velocidad *f* máxima; *Fig* **at t. speed** a toda velocidad

   (**b**) *(best, major)* mejor, más importante; **the t. ten** *(in general)* los diez mejores; *(in music charts)* el top diez, los diez primeros; **she came t. in history** fue la mejor en historia

   **3** *vt (pt & pp* **topped**) (**a**) *(place on top of)* cubrir (**with** de); **to t. it all** para colmo

   (**b**) *(exceed)* superar, sobrepasar

   (**c**) *(be at top of) (list, class)* encabezar; **to t. the bill** encabezar el cartel

   (**d**) *Fam* **to t. oneself** matarse, suicidarse

▸**top up** *vt sep (glass, petrol tank)* rellenar, llenar; *(sum of money)* complementar

**top-down** [tɒp'daʊn] *adj* **a t. management style** un estilo de dirección jerárquico

**top-heavy** [tɒp'hevɪ] *adj (structure)* sobrecargado(a) en la parte superior; *Fig (organization)* con demasiados altos cargos

**topic** ['tɒpɪk] *n* tema *m*, asunto *m*

**topical** ['tɒpɪkəl] *adj* actual, de actualidad

**topless** ['tɒplɪs] *adj (persona)* en topless; *(playa, bar)* de topless

**top-level** ['tɒplevəl] *adj* de alto nivel

**topmost** ['tɒpməʊst] *adj* superior, más alto(a); *(in pile)* de encima

**topography** [tɒ'pɒgrəfɪ] *n* topografía *f*

**topping** ['tɒpɪŋ] *n (for pizza)* ingrediente *m*; **cake with cream t.** pastel *m* con nata encima

**topple** ['tɒpəl] **1** *vt (person, structure, government)* derribar

   **2** *vi (of person, government)* derrumbarse

**top-secret** ['tɒpsɪ:krɪt] *adj* altamente confidencial

**topsoil** ['tɒpsɔɪl] *n* (capa *f* superficial del) suelo *m*

**topsy-turvy** [tɒpsɪ'tɜ:vɪ] *adj (untidy)* manga por hombro; *(confused)* enrevesado(a); **the whole world's turned t.** el mundo entero está patas arriba

**torch** [tɔ:tʃ] **1** *n* (**a**) *(burning stick)* antorcha *f*; *Fig* **to carry a t. for sb** estar enamorado(a) or prendado(a) de alguien (**b**) *Br (electric light)* linterna *f*

   **2** *vt* incendiar

**torchlight** ['tɔ:tʃlaɪt] *n* **by t.** con luz de linterna; **t. procession** procesión *f* de antorchas

**tore** [tɔ:(r)] *pt of* **tear**

**torment 1** *n* ['tɔ:ment] tormento *m*; **to be in t.** sufrir

**2** vt [tɔː'ment] *(cause extreme suffering)* atormentar; *(annoy)* hacer rabiar a

**tormentor** [tɔː'mentə(r)] *n* torturador(ora) *m,f*

**torn** [tɔːn] *pp of* **tear**

**tornado** [tɔː'neɪdəʊ] *(pl* **tornadoes)** *n* tornado *m*

**Toronto** [tə'rɒntəʊ] *n* Toronto

**torpedo** [tɔː'piːdəʊ] **1** *n (pl* **torpedoes)** *Naut* torpedo *m*; **t. boat** (barco *m*) torpedero *m*
**2** vt also Fig torpedear

**torpid** ['tɔːpɪd] *adj* aletargado(a)

**torpor** ['tɔːpə(r)] *n* letargo *m*

**torrent** ['tɒrənt] *n* torrente *m*; **it's raining in torrents** llueve torrencialmente; **a t. of abuse** un torrente de insultos

**torrential** [tɒ'renʃəl] *adj* torrencial

**torrid** ['tɒrɪd] *adj (weather)* tórrido(a); *(affair)* ardiente, apasionado(a)

**torso** ['tɔːsəʊ] *(pl* **torsos)** *n* torso *m*

**tortoise** ['tɔːtəs] *n* tortuga *f* (terrestre)

**tortoiseshell** ['tɔːtəʃel] *n* carey *m*; **t. (cat)** = gato con manchas negras y marrones

**tortuous** ['tɔːtjʊəs] *adj (path)* tortuoso(a); *(explanation)* enrevesado(a)

**torture** ['tɔːtʃə(r)] **1** *n* tortura *f*; *Fig* **it was sheer t.!** ¡fue una auténtica tortura!, ¡fue un tormento!; **t. chamber** cámara *f* de torturas
**2** vt torturar; *Fig* atormentar

**Tory** ['tɔːrɪ] *n & adj Br* conservador(ora) *m,f*

**tosh** [tɒʃ] *n Br Fam* chorradas *fpl*; **don't talk t.!** ¡no digas chorradas!

**toss** [tɒs] **1** *n* **(a)** *(of ball)* lanzamiento *m*; *(of head)* sacudida *f*; **to decide sth on the t. of a coin** decidir algo a cara o cruz; **to argue the t.** discutir inútilmente **(b)** *Br very Fam* **he couldn't give a t.** le importa un carajo
**2** vt *(ball)* lanzar; *(salad)* remover; **to t. sth to sb** echar algo a alguien; **to t. a coin** echar a cara o cruz; **to t. one's head** sacudir la cabeza; **to t. a pancake** dar la vuelta a una crepe lanzándola por el aire; **the ship was tossed by the sea** el mar sacudía *or* zarandeaba el barco
**3** vi **to t. (up) for sth** jugarse algo a cara o cruz; **to t. and turn in bed** dar vueltas en la cama

▸**toss about, toss around** vt sep *(ball)* lanzar; *(ship)* zarandear; *Fig (idea)* barajar

▸**toss off** vt sep **(a)** *Fam (write quickly)* escribir rápidamente **(b)** *Vulg (masturbate)* **to t. oneself off** hacerse una paja; **to t. sb off** hacerle una paja a alguien

▸**toss out** vt sep tirar

**toss-up** ['tɒsʌp] *n* **to have a t.** decidir a cara o cruz; *Fam* **it's a t. between the pub and the cinema** igual vamos al pub que vamos al cine; **it's a t. whether he'll say yes or no** lo mismo dice que sí o dice que no

**tot** [tɒt] *n* **(a)** *(child)* niño(a) *m,f* pequeño(a) **(b)** *(of whisky, rum)* dedal *m*, taponcito *m*

▸**tot up** *(pt & pp* **totted)** vt sep sumar

**total** ['təʊtəl] **1** *n* total *m*; **in t.** en total
**2** *adj* total; *Astron* **t. eclipse** eclipse *m* total; **t. failure** rotundo fracaso *m*
**3** vt *(pt & pp* **totalled,** *US* **totaled)** **(a)** *(amount to)* ascender a **(b)** *Aut very Fam (wreck)* jeringar, cargarse

**totalitarian** [təʊtælɪ'teərɪən] *adj* totalitario(a)

**totality** [təʊ'tælɪtɪ] *n* totalidad *f*, conjunto *m*

**totally** ['təʊtəlɪ] *adv* totalmente, completamente

**tote**[1] [təʊt] *n (in betting)* totalizador *m*

**tote**[2] *vt Fam (carry)* pasear, cargar con; *(gun)* portar

**totem pole** ['təʊtəm'pəʊl] *n* tótem *m*

**totter** ['tɒtə(r)] *vi (of person, government)* tambalearse; **to t. in/out** entrar/salir tambaleándose

**toucan** ['tuːkæn] *n* tucán *m*

**touch** [tʌtʃ] **1** *n* **(a)** *(act of touching)* toque *m*; *(lighter)* roce *m*; **I felt a t. on my arm** noté que me tocaban el brazo; **it was t. and go whether...** no era seguro si...; *Fam* **to be an easy** *or* **soft t.** *(financially)* ser desprendido(a), ser dadivoso(a)
**(b)** *(sense, feel)* tacto *m*; **hard/soft to the t.** duro(a)/blando(a) al tacto
**(c)** *(detail)* toque *m*; **there were some nice touches in the film** la película tenía algunos buenos detalles; *Fig* **he's lost his t.** ha perdido facultades
**(d)** *(small amount)* toque *m*, pizca *f*; **a t. (too) strong/short** un poquito fuerte/corto; **a t. of flu** una ligera gripe
**(e)** *(communication)* **to be/get in t. with sb** estar/ponerse en contacto con alguien; **to stay in/lose t. with sb** mantener/perder el contacto con alguien; **to lose t. with reality** desconectarse de la realidad
**(f)** *(in football, rugby)* **the ball has gone into t.** la pelota se ha ido fuera
**2** vt **(a)** *(physically)* tocar; *(affect)* afectar; **to t. bottom** *(of ship, economy)* tocar fondo; *Fam* **t. wood!** ¡toquemos madera!; **I never t. wine** nunca pruebo el vino; **the law can't t. her** la ley no puede tocarla; *Fig* **there's nothing to t. it** no tiene rival
**(b)** *(emotionally)* conmover

▸**touch down** vi *(of plane)* aterrizar

▸**touch on** vt insep tocar, mencionar

▸**touch up** vt sep **(a)** *(picture)* retocar **(b)** *Br Fam (molest)* manosear, sobar

**touchdown** ['tʌtʃdaʊn] *n* **(a)** *(of plane)* aterrizaje *m* **(b)** *(in American football)* ensayo

**touched** [tʌtʃt] *adj* (a) *(emotionally moved)* conmovido(a) (b) *Fam (mad)* tocado(a) del ala

**touching** ['tʌtʃɪŋ] *adj (moving)* conmovedor(ora)

**touchline** ['tʌtʃlaɪn] *n Sport* línea *f* de banda

**touch-sensitive screen** ['tʌtʃ'sensɪtɪv'skri:n] *n Comptr* pantalla *f* táctil

**touchstone** ['tʌtʃstəʊn] *n* piedra *f* de toque

**touchy** ['tʌtʃɪ] *adj (subject)* espinoso(a), peliagudo(a); *(person)* susceptible

**tough** [tʌf] **1** *n* matón *m*
**2** *adj* (a) *(material, person)* resistente, fuerte; *(meat, rule, policy)* duro(a); *Fam* **a t. guy** un tipo duro; **to get t. (with sb)** ponerse duro(a) (con alguien) (b) *(difficult)* difícil; *(unfair)* injusto(a); *Fam* **t. luck!** ¡mala suerte!
**3** *adv* **to act t.** hacerse el/la duro(a)

**toughen** ['tʌfən] *vt* endurecer; **toughened glass** vidrio *m* reforzado

**toughness** ['tʌfnɪs] *n* (a) *(of meat, task, skin, conditions)* dureza *f*; *(of material)* resistencia *f* (b) *(of person) (strength)* fortaleza *f*; *(hardness)* dureza *f*

**toupee** ['tu:peɪ] *n* bisoñé *m*

**tour** [tʊə(r)] **1** *n (of tourist)* recorrido *m*, viaje *m*; *(by pop group, theatre company)* gira *f*; **to go on a t.** *(of tourist)* hacer un recorrido turístico; **to go on t.** *(of pop group, theatre company)* irse de gira; *Mil* **t. of duty** período *m* de servicio en el extranjero; **t. of inspection** (recorrido *m* de) inspección *f*; **t. guide** *(person)* guía *mf* turístico(a); **t. operator** tour operador *m*, operador *m* turístico
**2** *vt (country, hospital)* recorrer; *(of pop group, theatre company)* ir de gira por
**3** *vi (of tourist)* hacer turismo; *(of pop group, theatre company)* estar de gira

**tour de force** ['tʊədə'fɔːs] *n* tour de force *m*, creación *f* magistral

**tourism** ['tʊərɪzm] *n* turismo *m*

**tourist** ['tʊərɪst] *n* turista *mf*; **t. attraction** atracción *f* turística; *Av* **t. class** clase *f* turista; **t. guide** *(person)* guía *mf* turístico(a); **t. (information) office** oficina *f* de turismo; *Fam* **t. trap** sitio *m* para turistas

**tournament** ['tʊənəmənt] *n* torneo *m*

**tourniquet** ['tʊənɪkeɪ] *n Med* torniquete *m*

**tousle** ['tʊəzəl] *vt* revolver; **tousled hair** pelo *m* revuelto

**tout** [taʊt] **1** *n* **(ticket) t.** reventa *mf*
**2** *vt (tickets)* revender; *(goods)* tratar de vender
**3** *vi* **to t. for custom** tratar de captar clientes

**tow** [təʊ] **1** *n* **to give sth/sb a t.** remolcar algo/a alguien; *Fam* **to have someone in t.** llevar a alguien detrás; **t. truck** grúa *f (automóvil)*
**2** *vt* remolcar, llevar a remolque; **the car was towed away** la grúa se llevó el coche

**toward** [tə'wɔːd] = **towards**

**towards** [tə'wɔːdz] *prep* hacia; **her feelings t. me** sus sentimientos por *or* hacia mí; **they behaved strangely t. us** se comportaron de un modo extraño con nosotros; **to contribute t. the cost of…** contribuir al coste de…; **15% of the budget will go t. improving safety** el 15% del presupuesto estará dedicado a mejoras en la seguridad; **this money can go t. your new bicycle** este dinero puede ser para tu bicicleta nueva

**towbar** ['təʊbɑː(r)] *n (on car)* barra *f* de remolque

**towel** ['taʊəl] **1** *n* toalla *f*; *Fig* **to throw in the t.** tirar la toalla; **t. rail** toallero *m*
**2** *vt (pt & pp* **towelled,** *US* **toweled) to t. oneself (dry)** secarse (con la toalla)

**towelling** ['taʊəlɪŋ] *n* toalla *f*; **t. bathrobe** albornoz *m*

**tower** ['taʊə(r)] **1** *n* torre *f*; *Fig* **she's a t. of strength** es un apoyo sólido como una roca; *Br* **t. block** torre *f*, bloque *m* alto *(edificio)*; *Comptr* **t. system** torre *f*
**2** *vi* **to t. above** *or* **over sth** elevarse por encima de algo; **to t. above** *or* **over sb** verse mucho más alto que alguien

**towering** ['taʊərɪŋ] *adj* colosal

**town** [taʊn] *n (big)* ciudad *f*; *(smaller)* pueblo *m*; **to go into t.** ir al centro (de la ciudad); **he's out of t.** está fuera (de la ciudad); *Fam Fig* **to go to t.** tirar la casa por la ventana; *(in explanation, description)* explayarse; **t. centre** centro *m* urbano; **t. clerk** secretario(a) *m,f* del ayuntamiento; **t. council** ayuntamiento *m*, cabildo *m*; **t. hall** ayuntamiento *m*; **t. planner** urbanista *mf*; **t. planning** urbanismo *m*

**townsfolk** ['taʊnzfəʊk] *npl* habitantes *mpl*, ciudadanos *mpl*

**township** ['taʊnʃɪp] *n* = en Sudáfrica, área urbana reservada para la población negra

**townspeople** ['taʊnzpiːpəl] *npl* habitantes *mpl*

**towrope** ['təʊrəʊp] *n* cuerda *f* para remolcar

**toxic** ['tɒksɪk] *adj Med* tóxico(a)

**toxin** ['tɒksɪn] *n Med* toxina *f*

**toy** [tɔɪ] **1** *n (pl* **toys)** juguete *m*; **t. soldier** soldadito *m* de juguete; **t. shop** juguetería *f*
**2** *vi* **to t. with sb** jugar con alguien; **to t. with an idea** darle vueltas a una idea; **to t. with sb's affections** jugar con los sentimientos de alguien

**toyboy** ['tɔɪbɔɪ] *n Fam* amiguito *m*, = amante muy joven

**TQM** [tiː kjuː'em] *n Com (abbr* **total quality management)** gestión *f* de calidad total

**trace** [treɪs] **1** *n* (a) *(sign)* rastro *m*, pista *f*; **without t.** sin dejar rastro (b) *(small amount)* rastro *m*, huella *f*; *Chem* **t. element** oligoelemento *m*

**2** vt **(a)** (draw) trazar; (with tracing paper) calcar **(b)** (track) (person) seguir la pista or el rastro a; Fig (development, history) trazar

**trachea** [trə'ki:ə] (pl **tracheae** [trə'ki:]) n Anat tráquea f

**tracheotomy** [trækɪ'ɒtəmɪ] n traqueotomía f; **to perform a t. (on sb)** hacer una traqueotomía (a alguien)

**track** [træk] **1** n (a) (single mark) huella f; (set of marks) rastro m; **tyre tracks** rodada f; **to be on the right/wrong t.** ir por (el) buen/mal camino; **to keep t. of sb** seguirle la pista a alguien; **to keep t. of** (movements, developments) estar al tanto de; **I've lost t. of her** le he perdido la pista; **I've lost t. of how much money I've spent** he perdido la cuenta del dinero que llevo gastado; Fam **to make tracks** pirarse, moverse; **to stop sb in his tracks** hacer que alguien se pare en seco

**(b)** (path) senda f, camino m; (for running) pista f; Sport **t. events** pruebas fpl en pista, carreras fpl de atletismo; **t. record** (previous performance) historial m, antecedentes mpl; **t. shoes** zapatillas fpl de deporte

**(c)** (on record, CD) corte m, canción f

**(d)** (of tank, tractor) oruga f

**(e)** (railway line) vía f

**2** vt rastrear

▶**track down** vt sep (locate) localizar

**tracked** [trækt] adj (vehicle) de oruga

**tracker dog** ['trækə'dɒg] n perro m rastreador

**tracksuit** ['træks(j)u:t] n chándal m; **t. top** chaqueta f de chándal; **t. trousers** or **bottoms** pantalones mpl de chándal

**tract¹** [trækt] n (a) (of land) tramo m (b) Anat **respiratory t.** vías fpl respiratorias; **digestive t.** aparato m digestivo

**tract²** n (pamphlet) panfleto m

**tractable** ['træktəbəl] adj (person, animal) dócil, manejable

**traction** ['trækʃən] n (force) tracción f; Med **to have one's legs in t.** tener la pierna en alto (por lesión); **t. engine** locomotora f de tracción

**tractor** ['træktə(r)] n (vehicle) tractor m; Comptr **t. feed** alimentación f automática de papel (por arrastre)

**trade** [treɪd] **1** n (**a**) (commerce) comercio m (in de); **t. association** asociación f gremial; **t. deficit** déficit m comercial; **t. discount** descuento m comercial; **t. embargo** embargo m comercial; **t. fair** feria f (de muestras); **t. gap** déficit m de la balanza comercial; **t. name** (of product) nombre m comercial; (of company) razón f social; **t. secret** secreto m de la casa; Geog **t. winds** vientos mpl alisios

**(b)** (swap) intercambio m; **to do a t.** hacer un intercambio

**(c)** (profession) oficio m; **he's a plumber by t.** su oficio es el de fontanero; **t. union** sindicato m; **t. unionist** sindicalista mf

**2** vt **to t. sth (for sth)** intercambiar algo (por algo); **to t. places with sb** cambiarse de sitio con alguien; **to t. insults/blows** intercambiar insultos/golpes

**3** vi comerciar

▶**trade in** vt sep entregar como parte del pago

▶**trade on** vt insep (exploit) aprovecharse de

**trade-in** ['treɪdɪn] n Com = artículo de segunda mano que se entrega como parte del pago

**trademark** ['treɪdmɑ:k] n Com marca f comercial or registrada; Fig sello m personal

**trade-off** ['treɪdɒf] n **a t. between speed and accuracy** un término medio or una solución a medio camino entre la velocidad y la precisión

**trader** ['treɪdə(r)] n comerciante mf

**tradesman** ['treɪdzmən] n pequeño comerciante m, tendero m; **tradesmen's entrance** entrada f de servicio

**trading** ['treɪdɪŋ] n **t. partner** socio(a) m,f comercial; **t. post** = establecimiento comercial en zonas remotas o de colonos; **t. stamp** cupón m, vale m

**tradition** [trə'dɪʃən] n tradición f

**traditional** [trə'dɪʃənəl] adj tradicional

**traditionalist** [trə'dɪʃənəlɪst] n & adj tradicionalista mf

**traffic** ['træfɪk] n **1** (**a**) (vehicles) tráfico m; **road/air t.** tráfico m rodado/aéreo; **t. calming measures** medidas fpl para reducir la velocidad del tráfico; **t. cone** cono m de señalización; Fam **t. cop** guardia mf de tráfico; **t. island** refugio m, isleta f; **t. jam** atasco m, embotellamiento m; Br **t. lights** semáforo m; Br **t. warden** = agente que pone multa por aparcamiento indebido (**b**) (trade) (in drugs, slaves) tráfico m (**in** de)

**2** vt traficar con

**3** vi traficar

**tragedy** ['trædʒɪdɪ] n tragedia f

**tragic** ['trædʒɪk] adj trágico(a)

**tragically** ['trædʒɪklɪ] adv trágicamente

**trail** [treɪl] **1** n (**a**) (of smoke, blood) rastro m; **to pick up the t.** encontrar el rastro; **to be on the t. of sb/sth** estar sobre la pista de alguien/algo (**b**) (path) camino m, senda f; **t. bike** moto f de trial or motocross

**2** vt (drag) arrastrar

**3** vi (**a**) (drag) arrastrar (**b**) (move slowly) avanzar con paso cansino; **to t. in and out** entrar y salir con desgana (**c**) (be losing) ir perdiendo

▶**trail away, trail off** vi ir debilitándose

**trailblazer** ['treɪlbleɪzə(r)] n innovador(ora) m,f, pionero(a) m,f

**trailer** ['treɪlə(r)] *n* (**a**) *(vehicle)* remolque *m*, tráiler *m*; *US (caravan)* caravana *f*, roulotte *f* (**b**) *Cin (for film)* avance *m*, tráiler *m*

**train** [treɪn] **1** *n* (**a**) *(means of transport)* tren *m*; **by t.** en tren (**b**) *(series)* concatenación *f*, serie *f*; **t. of thought** pensamientos *mpl* (**c**) *(retinue)* séquito *m* (**d**) *(of dress)* cola *f*
  **2** *vt* (**a**) *(person)* formar, adiestrar; *(animal, ear)* adiestrar, educar; *(in sport)* entrenar; **to t. sb for sth/to do sth** adiestrar a alguien para algo/para hacer algo (**b**) *(gun, telescope)* dirigir (**on** hacia)
  **3** *vi (of athlete, soldier)* entrenar(se); **to t. as a nurse/teacher** estudiar para (ser) enfermero(a)/maestro(a)

**trained** [treɪnd] *adj* experto(a); *Hum* **her husband is very well t.!** ¡qué marido tan apañado tiene!

**trainee** [treɪ'niː] *n* aprendiz(iza) *m,f*; *(at lawyer's, etc)* becario(a) *m,f (en prácticas)*

**trainer** ['treɪnə(r)] *n* (**a**) *(of athletes, football team, racehorses)* entrenador(ora) *m,f* (**b**) *Av* **t. (aircraft)** avión *m* de entrenamiento (**c**) *(shoe)* zapatilla *f* de deporte

**training** ['treɪnɪŋ] *n (for job)* formación *f*; *(in sport)* entrenamiento *m*; **to be in t.** estar entrenando; **to be out of t.** estar desentrenado(a); **t. course** cursillo *m* de formación; **t. officer** jefe(a) *m,f* de formación

**trainload** ['treɪnləʊd] *n* **a t. of...** un tren cargado de...

**traipse** [treɪps] *vi Fam* dar vueltas y vueltas, estar en danza; **to t. round the shops** patearse las tiendas

**trait** [treɪt] *n* rasgo *m*

**traitor** ['treɪtə(r)] *n* traidor(ora) *m,f*

**trajectory** [trə'dʒektərɪ] *n* trayectoria *f*

**tram** [træm] *n Br* tranvía *m*

**tramline** ['træmlaɪn] *n* carril *m* de tranvía; **tramlines** *(in tennis)* líneas *fpl* laterales

**tramp** [træmp] **1** *n* (**a**) *(vagabond)* vagabundo(a) *m,f* (**b**) *US very Fam (immoral woman)* fulana *f* (**c**) **t. (steamer)** carguero *m* (**d**) *(walk)* caminata *f*
  **2** *vt* **to t. the streets** recorrer a pie las calles
  **3** *vi* caminar con pasos pesados, marchar; **she tramped up the road** subió la carretera caminando con pasos pesados

**trample** ['træmpəl] **1** *vt* pisotear
  **2** *vi also Fig* **to t. on sth/sb** pisotear algo/a alguien

**trampoline** ['træmpə'liːn] *n* cama *f* elástica

**trance** [trɑːns] *n* trance *m*; **to go into a t.** entrar en trance

**tranquil** ['træŋkwɪl] *adj* tranquilo(a)

**tranquillity,** *US* **tranquility** [træŋ-'kwɪlɪtɪ] *n* tranquilidad *f*

**tranquillizer,** *US* **tranquilizer** ['træŋ-kwɪlaɪzə(r)] *n* tranquilizante *m*

**transaction** [træn'zækʃən] *n* transacción *f*

**transatlantic** [trænzət'læntɪk] *adj* transatlántico(a)

**transcend** [træn'send] *vt* ir más allá de, superar

**transcendental** [trænsen'dentəl] *adj* trascendental; **t. meditation** meditación *f* trascendental

**transcontinental** [trænzkɒntɪ'nentəl] *adj* transcontinental

**transcribe** [træns'kraɪb] *vt* transcribir

**transcript** ['trænskrɪpt] *n* transcripción *f*

**transcription** [træns'krɪpʃən] *n* transcripción *f*

**transfer 1** *n* ['trænsfɜː(r)] (**a**) *(move) (of employee, department, prisoners)* traslado *m*; *(of money, funds)* transferencia *f*; *(of footballer)* traspaso *m*; **t. of power** traspaso *m* de poderes; *Sport* **t. fee** (ficha *f* de) traspaso *m*; **t. lounge** *(in airport)* sala *f* de tránsito; **t. passengers** pasajeros *mpl* en tránsito; *Comptr* **t. speed** velocidad *f* de transmisión (**b**) *(sticker)* calcomanía *f*
  **2** *vt* [træns'fɜː(r)] *(employee, department, prisoners)* trasladar; *(funds)* transferir; *(footballer, power)* traspasar; *(attention, affection)* trasladar
  **3** *vi (within organization)* trasladarse; *(between planes, trains)* hacer transbordo

**transferable** [træns'fɜːrəbəl] *adj* transferible; **not t.** intransferible

**transfigure** [træns'fɪgə(r)] *vt* transfigurar

**transfix** [træns'fɪks] *vt (pierce)* atravesar; *Fig* **they were transfixed with fear** estaban paralizados por el miedo

**transform** [træns'fɔːm] *vt* transformar

**transformation** [trænsfə'meɪʃən] *n* transformación *f*

**transformer** [træns'fɔːmə(r)] *n Elec* transformador *m*

**transfusion** [træns'fjuːʒən] *n* **(blood) t.** transfusión *f* (de sangre)

**transgress** [trænz'gres] *Formal* **1** *vt (law)* transgredir, infringir
  **2** *vi (violate law)* infringir la ley; *(sin)* pecar

**transient** ['trænzɪənt] *adj* pasajero(a), transitorio(a)

**transistor** [træn'zɪstə(r)] *n Elec* transistor *m*

**transit** ['trænsɪt] *n* tránsito *m*; **in t.** en tránsito; **t. camp** campo *m* provisional; **t. visa** visado *m* de tránsito

**transition** [træn'zɪʃən] *n* transición *f*; **t. period** período *m* de transición

**transitional** [træn'zɪʃənəl] *adj* de transición

**transitive** ['trænzɪtɪv] *adj Gram* transitivo(a)

**transitory** ['trænsɪtərɪ] *adj* transitorio(a)

**translate** [træns'leɪt] **1** vt traducir (**from/into** de/a)

**2** vi (of person) traducir; (of word, expression) traducirse (**as** por); **this word doesn't t.** esta palabra no tiene traducción

**translation** [træns'leɪʃən] n traducción f

**translator** [træns'leɪtə(r)] n traductor(ora) m,f

**transliterate** [trænz'lɪtəreɪt] vt Ling transliterar

**translucent** [trænz'luːsənt] adj translúcido(a)

**transmission** [trænz'mɪʃən] n (action) transmisión f; TV & Rad (programme) programa m, emisión f; Aut **t. shaft** árbol m de transmisión

**transmit** [trænz'mɪt] vt transmitir

**transmitter** [trænz'mɪtə(r)] n (emitter) emisora f; (relay station) repetidor m

**transparent** [træns'pærənt] adj transparente; Fig **a t. lie** una mentira flagrante

**transpire** [træns'paɪə(r)] **1** vi (become apparent) **it transpired that...** se supo que...; **it/she transpired to be...** resultó ser...

**2** vi (happen) ocurrir, pasar

**transplant 1** n ['trænsplɑːnt] Med transplante m

**2** vt [træns'plɑːnt] (**a**) Med (organ) transplantar (**b**) (population) trasladar

**transport 1** n ['trænspɔːt] transporte m; **road/rail t.** transporte m por carretera/ferrocarril; Br **t. café** bar m de carretera; **t. costs** gastos mpl de transporte

**2** vt [træns'pɔːt] transportar

**transportation** [trænspɔː'teɪʃən] n transporte m; Hist (as punishment) deportación f

**transporter** [træns'pɔːtə(r)] n (vehicle) camión m para el transporte de vehículos

**transpose** [træns'pəʊz] vt (words) invertir; Typ transponer; (music) transportar

**transsexual** [træn(z)'seksjʊəl] n transexual mf

**Transvaal** ['trɑːnzvɑːl] n **the T.** la región de Transvaal

**transverse** ['trænzvɜːs] adj transversal

**transvestite** [trænz'vestaɪt] n (travesti mf, travestido(a) m,f

**trap** [træp] **1** n (**a**) (in hunting) & Fig trampa f; **to set a t.** tender or poner una trampa (**for** a); **to walk** or **fall straight into the t.** caer en la trampa (**b**) very Fam (mouth) **shut your t.!** ¡cierra el pico!

**2** vt (pt & pp **trapped**) (animal, person) atrapar; **to t. sb into saying/doing sth** engañar a alguien para que diga/haga algo

**trapdoor** ['træpdɔː(r)] n trampilla f

**trapeze** [trə'piːz] n trapecio m; **t. artist** trapecista mf

**trapper** ['træpə(r)] n (hunter) trampero m

**trappings** ['træpɪŋz] npl (of power, success) parafernalia f

**trash** [træʃ] **1** n (worthless objects) bazofia f, basura f; US (refuse) basura f; Fam **that book/film is a load of t.** ese libro/esa película es pura bazofia; US **t. can** cubo m de la basura

**2** vt Fam (vandalize) destrozar

**trashy** ['træʃɪ] adj Fam cutre

**trauma** ['trɔːmə] n Med traumatismo m; Psy trauma m

**traumatic** [trɔː'mætɪk] adj traumático(a)

**traumatize** ['trɔːmətaɪz] vt traumatizar

**travail** ['træveɪl] n Literary penalidad f, calamidad f

**travel** ['trævəl] **1** n viajes mpl; **on my travels** en mis viajes; **t. agency** agencia f de viajes; **t. agent** empleado(a) m,f de una agencia de viajes; **t. documents** documentación f para el viaje; **t. expenses** gastos mpl de viaje; **t. writer** autor(ora) m,f de libros de viajes

**2** vt (pt & pp **travelled**, US **traveled**) (road, country) viajar por

**3** vi (of person) viajar; (of vehicle) circular; (of sound, light, electricity) propagarse; **news travels fast round here** por aquí las noticias vuelan

**traveller**, US **traveler** ['trævələ(r)] n viajero(a) m,f; Br (**new age**) **t.** = persona que vive en una tienda o caravana sin lugar fijo de residencia y que lleva un estilo de vida contrario al de la sociedad convencional; Br **t.'s cheque** cheque m de viaje

**travelling**, US **traveling** ['trævəlɪŋ] **1** n viajes mpl; **t. bag** bolsa f de viaje; **t. companion** compañero(a) m,f de viaje; **t. expenses** gastos mpl de viaje

**2** adj (performer) ambulante; **t. salesman** viajante m (de comercio)

**travel-sick** ['trævəlsɪk] adj mareado(a); **to feel t.** estar mareado(a)

**traverse** ['trævəs] vt Literary atravesar, cruzar

**travesty** ['trævəstɪ] **1** n parodia f burda

**2** vt parodiar (burdamente)

**trawl** [trɔːl] **1** n (**a**) (net) red f de arrastre (**b**) Fig (search) rastreo m; **he had a t. through the records** hizo un rastreo de los archivos

**2** vt (**a**) (sea) hacer pesca de arrastre en (**b**) Fig (search through) rastrear

**3** vi (**a**) (fish) hacer pesca de arrastre (**b**) Fig **to t. through sth** rebuscar en or rastrear algo

**trawler** ['trɔːlə(r)] n (ship) barco m arrastrero

**tray** [treɪ] (pl **trays**) n bandeja f

**treacherous** ['tretʃərəs] adj (person, road) traicionero(a)

**treachery** ['tretʃərɪ] n traición f

**treacle** ['triːkəl] n melaza f

**tread** [tred] **1** *n* (**a**) *(sound of footstep)* pisadas *fpl*, pasos *mpl* (**b**) *(of tyre)* banda *f* de rodadura, dibujo *m* (**c**) *(of stair)* huella *f* (del peldaño)

**2** *vt* (*pt* **trod** [trɒd], *pp* **trodden** ['trɒdən]) *(ground, grapes)* pisar; *(path)* recorrer; **to t. sth underfoot** pisotear algo; **to t. sth into the carpet** ensuciar la moqueta con algo pegado al zapato; **to t. the boards** *(appear on stage)* pisar las tablas; **to t. water** flotar moviendo las piernas; *Fig* estar en un punto muerto

**3** *vi* andar; **to t. on sth** pisar algo; **to t. on sb's toes** pisar (el pie) a alguien; *Fig* meterse en los asuntos de alguien; *Fig* **to t. carefully** *or* **warily** andar con pies de plomo

**treadmill** ['tredmɪl] *n (in gym)* cinta *f* de carreras *or* de correr, tapiz *m* rodante; *Hist (in prison)* noria *f*; *Fig (routine)* rutina *f*

**treason** ['triːzən] *n* traición *f*

**treasonable** ['triːzənəbəl] *adj (offence, act)* del alta traición

**treasure** ['treʒə(r)] **1** *n also Fig* tesoro *m*; **t. hunt** juego *m* de las pistas

**2** *vt* apreciar mucho, tener en gran estima; **my most treasured possession** mi más preciado bien

**treasurer** ['treʒərə(r)] *n* tesorero(a) *m,f*

**treasure-trove** ['treʒətrəʊv] *n Law* tesoro *m* encontrado; *Fig* tesoro *m*

**treasury** ['treʒərɪ] *n* tesorería *f*; **the T.** *(government department)* ≃ (el Ministerio de Economía y) Hacienda *f*; *Fin* **t. bonds** bonos *mpl* del tesoro

**treat** [triːt] **1** *n (pleasure)* placer *m*; *(gift)* regalo *m*; **to give oneself a t.** darse un capricho; **it's my t.** *(I'm paying)* yo invito; **you've got a real t. in store** te aguarda una agradable sorpresa; *Fam* **it worked a t.** *(of plan)* funcionó a las mil maravillas

**2** *vt* (**a**) *(person, illness, metal)* tratar; **to t. sth as a joke** tomarse algo a broma; **you t. this place like a hotel!** ¡te comportas como si esto fuera un hotel! (**b**) *(give as a present)* **to t. sb to sth** invitar a alguien a algo; **I'll t. you** te invito; **to t. oneself to sth** darse el capricho de comprarse algo; *Ironic* **she treated us to one of her tantrums** nos deleitó con una de sus rabietas

**3** *vi Formal (negotiate)* negociar (**with** con)

**treatise** ['triːtɪz] *n* tratado *m*

**treatment** ['triːtmənt] *n (of prisoner)* trato *m*; *(of patient, machine, matter)* tratamiento *m*; **preferential t.** trato *m* de favor; *Fam* **to give sb the t.** *(beat up)* dar un buen repaso a alguien

**treaty** ['triːtɪ] *n (international)* tratado *m*; *(between individuals)* pacto *m*

**treble** ['trebəl] **1** *n Mus (person, voice)* soprano *m*, tiple *m*

**2** *adj (triple)* triple; *Mus* **t. clef** clave *f* de sol

**3** *vt (value, number)* triplicar

**4** *vi* triplicarse

**tree** [triː] *n* árbol *m*; *Fig* **to get to the top of the t.** llegar a lo más alto; *US Fam* **to be out of one's t.** *(be crazy)* estar como una cabra; **t. trunk** tronco *m* (de árbol)

**treetop** ['triːtɒp] *n* copa *f* de árbol

**trek** [trek] **1** *n (long walk)* caminata *f*; *(long journey)* largo camino *m*

**2** *vi* **to t. over the hills** recorrer las montañas; **to t. home** recorrer el largo camino hasta casa; *Fam* **to t. to the shops** darse una caminata hasta las tiendas

**trellis** ['trelɪs] *n* espaldar *m*, guía *f*

**tremble** ['trembəl] **1** *n* temblor *m*; **to be all of a t.** estar temblando como un flan

**2** *vi (vibrate)* temblar

**tremendous** [trɪ'mendəs] *adj (amount, size, noise)* tremendo(a); *(book, holiday, writer)* estupendo(a), extraordinario(a)

**tremendously** [trɪ'mendəslɪ] *adv (very)* enormemente, tremendamente

**tremor** ['tremə(r)] *n (of person)* temblor *m*; *(earthquake)* temblor de tierra

**tremulous** ['tremjʊləs] *adj* trémulo(a)

**trench** [tren(t)ʃ] *n (ditch)* zanja *f*; *Mil* trinchera *f*; **t. coat** trinchera; **t. warfare** guerra *f* de trincheras

**trenchant** ['tren(t)ʃənt] *adj* mordaz

**trend** [trend] *n* tendencia *f*; **to set/start a t.** establecer/iniciar una tendencia

**trendsetter** ['trendsetə(r)] *n* pionero(a) *m,f*

**trendy** ['trendɪ] *Br Fam* **1** *n Pej (person)* modernillo(a) *m,f*

**2** *adj (clothes, style)* de moda; *(person)* moderno(a)

**trepidation** [trepɪ'deɪʃən] *n Formal* inquietud *f*, miedo *m*

**trespass** ['trespəs] *vi Law* entrar sin autorización

**trespasser** ['trespəsə(r)] *n Law* intruso(a) *m,f*; **trespassers will be prosecuted** *(sign)* prohibido el paso (bajo sanción)

**tresses** ['tresɪz] *npl Literary (hair)* melena *f*, cabellera *f*

**trestle** ['tresəl] *n* caballete *m*; **t. table** mesa *f* de caballetes

**trial** ['traɪəl] *n* (**a**) *Law* juicio *m*; **to bring sb to t.** llevar a alguien a juicio; **to be on t.** estar siendo juzgado(a) (**b**) *(test)* ensayo *m*, prueba *f*; **on t.** a prueba; **t. and error** ensayo *m* y error, tanteo *m*; **by t. and error** probando hasta dar con la solución; **t. period** período *m* de prueba; **t. run** ensayo *m*; **t. separation** *(of married couple)* separación *f* de prueba (**c**) *(ordeal)* dura prueba *f*; **my boss is a real t.!** ¡aguantar a mi jefe es un verdadero calvario!

**triangle** ['traɪæŋgəl] *n* triángulo *m*

**triangular** [traɪˈæŋgjʊlə(r)] *adj* triangular

**tribal** [ˈtraɪbəl] *adj* tribal

**tribalism** [ˈtraɪbəlɪzəm] *n Pol* tribalismo *m*

**tribe** [traɪb] *n* tribu *f*

**tribesman** [ˈtraɪbzmən] *n* miembro *m* de una tribu

**tribulation** [trɪbjʊˈleɪʃən] *n Formal* tribulación *f*

**tribunal** [tr(a)ɪˈbjuːnəl] *n Law* tribunal *m*

**tributary** [ˈtrɪbjʊtərɪ] **1** *n (of river)* afluente *m*
**2** *adj* tributario(a)

**tribute** [ˈtrɪbjuːt] *n (homage)* tributo *m*; **to pay t.** to rendir tributo a

**trice** [traɪs] *n* **in a t.** en un santiamén

**triceps** [ˈtraɪseps] *n Anat* tríceps *m inv*

**trick** [trɪk] **1** *n* (**a**) *(ruse, deceitful behaviour, by magician)* truco *m*; *(practical joke)* broma *f*; **to play a t. on sb** gastar una broma a alguien; **to obtain sth by a t.** conseguir algo con engaños; **a nasty t.** una jugarreta; **t. photography** fotografía *f* trucada; **t. question** pregunta *f* con trampa
(**b**) *(in cardgame)* mano *f*, baza *f*; **to take** *or* **make a t.** ganar una mano
(**c**) *(idioms)* **he's been up to his old tricks again** ha vuelto a las andadas; **that should do the t.** esto debería servir; **she knows all the tricks** se las sabe todas; **the tricks of the trade** los trucos del oficio; **she doesn't miss a t.** no se le pasa una; *Fam* **how's tricks?** ¿cómo tu llevas?, ¿qué pasa?
**2** *vt (person)* engañar; **to t. sb into doing sth** engañar a alguien para que haga algo; **to t. sth out of sb** sacar algo a alguien con malas artes

**trickery** [ˈtrɪkərɪ] *n* engaños *mpl*, trampas *fpl*; **by t.** con malas artes

**trickle** [ˈtrɪkəl] **1** *n (of blood, water) (thin stream)* hilo *m*, reguero *m*; *(drops)* goteo *m*; *Fig (of complaints, letters)* goteo *m*; **t.-down theory** = teoría según la cual la riqueza de unos pocos termina por revertir en toda la sociedad
**2** *vt (liquid)* derramar un hilo de
**3** *vi (of liquid)* **water/blood trickled down** corría un hilo de agua/sangre; **to t. in/out** *(of people)* ir entrando/saliendo poco a poco; **news is beginning to t. through** la noticia está empezando a filtrarse

**tricky** [ˈtrɪkɪ] *adj (task, situation, subject)* delicado(a); *(question)* difícil; *Fam* **he's a t. customer** es un elemento de cuidado *or* un pájaro (de cuenta)

**tricycle** [ˈtraɪsɪkəl] *n* triciclo *m*

**trident** [ˈtraɪdənt] *n* tridente *m*

**tried-and-tested** [ˈtraɪdənˈtestɪd] *adj* probado(a)

**trier** [ˈtraɪə(r)] *n Fam* **to be a t.** tener mucho tesón

**trifle** [ˈtraɪfəl] *n* (**a**) *(insignificant thing)* nadería *f*; **a t. wide/short** un poquito ancho(a)/corto(a) (**b**) *Br Culin* = postre de frutas en gelatina y bizcocho cubiertas de crema y nata

▸**trifle with** *vt insep* jugar con; **a person not to be trifled with** una persona que hay que respetar

**trifling** [ˈtraɪflɪŋ] *adj* insignificante

**trigger** [ˈtrɪgə(r)] **1** *n (of gun)* gatillo *m*; *Fig (of change, decision)* factor *m* desencadenante, detonante *m*; *Fam* **to be t. happy** tener el gatillo demasiado ligero
**2** *vt (reaction)* desencadenar
▸**trigger off** *vt sep* desencadenar

**trigonometry** [trɪgəˈnɒmɪtrɪ] *n Math* trigonometría *f*

**trilby** [ˈtrɪlbɪ] *n Br* sombrero *m* flexible *or* de fieltro

**trill** [trɪl] **1** *n* trino *m*
**2** *vi* trinar

**trillion** [ˈtrɪljən] *n (million million)* billón *m*; *Fam* **I've got trillions of things to do!** ¡tengo millones de cosas que hacer!

**trilogy** [ˈtrɪlədʒɪ] *n* trilogía *f*

**trim** [trɪm] **1** *n* (**a**) *(of hair, hedge)* recorte *m* (**b**) **to be/keep in t.** *(keep fit)* estar/mantenerse en forma
**2** *adj (neat)* aseado(a); **to have a t. figure** *(of person)* tener buen tipo
**3** *vt (pt & pp* **trimmed***)* (**a**) *(cut) (hair, hedge, expenditure)* recortar; *(meat)* quitar la grasa a (**b**) *(decorate)* ribetear (**with** con)
▸**trim down** *vt sep (text, expenditure)* recortar; *(company)* racionalizar

**trimming** [ˈtrɪmɪŋ] *n (on clothes)* adorno *m*; *(on edge)* ribete *m*; *Culin* **turkey with all the trimmings** pavo *m* con la guarnición clásica *(patatas asadas, coles de bruselas, jugo de carne, etc)*

**Trinidad and Tobago** [ˈtrɪnɪdædəntəˈbeɪgəʊ] *n* Trinidad y Tobago

**Trinity** [ˈtrɪnɪtɪ] *n Rel* trinidad *f*

**trinket** [ˈtrɪŋkɪt] *n* baratija *f*, chuchería *f*

**trio** [ˈtriːəʊ] *n (pl* **trios***)* trío *m*

**trip** [trɪp] **1** *n* (**a**) *(journey)* viaje *m* (**b**) *very Fam (on drugs)* viaje *m*, flipe *m* (**c**) *(causing stumble)* zancadilla *f*; **t. wire** = cable tendido para hacer tropezar a quien pase
**2** *vt (pt & pp* **tripped***)* (**a**) *(cause to stumble)* poner la zancadilla a (**b**) *(switch)* hacer saltar
**3** *vi* (**a**) *(stumble)* tropezar (**b**) *(step lightly)* brincar, danzar; **to t. off the tongue** *(of word, name)* pronunciarse fácilmente (**c**) *Fam (on drugs)* **to be tripping** ir puesto(a), flipar
▸**trip over 1** *vt insep* tropezar con
**2** *vi* tropezar
▸**trip up 1** *vt sep (cause to fall)* poner la zancadilla a; *Fig (cause to make mistake)* confundir
**2** *vi (stumble)* tropezar

**tripe** [traɪp] *n Culin* callos *mpl*, *Andes, CSur* mondongo *m*; *Fam (nonsense)* tonterías *fpl*, bobadas *fpl*

**triple** ['trɪpəl] **1** *adj* triple; **t. jump** triple salto *m*

**2** *adv* **t. the amount** el triple

**3** *vt* triplicar, multiplicar por tres

**4** *vi* triplicarse, multiplicarse por tres

**triplet** ['trɪplɪt] *n* **(a)** *(child)* trillizo(a) *m,f* **(b)** *Mus* tresillo *m*

**triplicate** ['trɪplɪkət] *n* **in t.** por triplicado

**tripod** ['traɪpɒd] *n* trípode *m*

**Tripoli** ['trɪpəlɪ] *n* Trípoli *m*

**trite** [traɪt] *adj* manido(a)

**triumph** ['traɪəmf] **1** *n* triunfo *m*; **in t.** triunfalmente

**2** *vi* triunfar (**over** sobre)

**triumphant** [traɪ'ʌmfənt] *adj* triunfante

**triumvirate** [traɪ'ʌmvɪrɪt] *n* triunvirato *m*

**trivet** ['trɪvɪt] *n (on table)* salvamanteles *m inv* (de metal)

**trivia** ['trɪvɪə] *npl* trivialidades *fpl*; **t. quiz** concurso *m* de preguntas triviales

**trivial** ['trɪvɪəl] *adj* trivial

**trivialize** ['trɪvɪəlaɪz] *vt* trivializar

**trod** [trɒd] *pt of* **tread**

**trodden** ['trɒdən] *pp of* **tread**

**Trojan** ['trəʊdʒən] *Hist* **1** *n* troyano(a) *m,f*

**2** *adj* troyano(a); **T. Horse** caballo *m* de Troya; **the T. War** la guerra de Troya

**troll** [trəʊl] *n* troll *m*, trasgo *m*

**trolley** ['trɒlɪ] (*pl* **trolleys**) *n Br* carrito *m*; **t. car** *US* tranvía *m*; *Fam* **to be off one's t.** (mad) estar chalado(a)

**trollop** ['trɒləp] *n Old-fashioned or Hum (promiscuous woman)* fulana *f*

**trombone** [trɒm'bəʊn] *n Mus* trombón *m*

**trombonist** [trɒm'bəʊnɪst] *n Mus* trombonista *mf*

**troop** [tru:p] **1** *n* **(a) troops** *(soldiers)* tropas *fpl* **(b)** *(of people)* grupo *m*, batallón *m*

**2** *vi* **to t. in/out** entrar/salir con paso cansino

**trooper** ['tru:pə(r)] *n (soldier)* soldado *m (de caballería o división acorazada)*; *US (mounted policeman)* policía *mf* a caballo; *Fam* **to swear like a t.** jurar como un carretero

**trophy** ['trəʊfɪ] *n* trofeo *m*

**tropic** ['trɒpɪk] *n* trópico *m*; **the tropics** los trópicos

**tropical** ['trɒpɪkəl] *adj* tropical

**trot** [trɒt] **1** *n* trote *m*; **at a t.** al trote; *Fam* **on the t.** *(consecutively)* seguidos(as), uno(a) detrás de otro(a)

**2** *vi* (*pt & pp* **trotted**) *(of horse)* trotar; *(of person)* correr a paso lento

▸**trot out** *vt sep Fam (excuses, information)* salir con

**Trotskyism** ['trɒtskɪɪzəm] *n* trotskismo *m*

**Trotskyist** ['trɒtskɪɪst], **Trotskyite** ['trɒtskɪaɪt] *n & adj* trotskista *mf*

**trotter** ['trɒtə(r)] *n Culin (of pig)* pata *f*, manita *f*

**trouble** ['trʌbəl] **1** *n* **(a)** *(problem)* problema *m*; *(inconvenience)* molestia *f*; **to go to the t. of doing sth** tomarse la molestia de hacer algo; **what's** *or* **what seems to be the t.?** ¿cuál es el problema?; **the t. is that...** el problema es que...; **to have t. with sth/sb** tener problemas con algo/alguien; **to have t. doing sth** tener dificultades para hacer algo; **it has been nothing but t.** no ha traído nada más que problemas; **to be in t.** *(in difficulty)* tener problemas; *(in bad books of)* estar en un lío (**with** con); **to get into t.** meterse en líos; **to get sb out of t.** sacar a alguien de un apuro; **to keep out of t.** no meterse en líos; **to make t.** causar problemas; **it's more t. than it's worth** no da más que problemas; **her troubles are over** se han acabado sus problemas; **it's not worth the t.** no merece la pena; **(it's) no t.** no es molestia; *Fam* **man/woman t.** mal *m* de amores

**(b)** *(disorder, unrest)* conflicto *m*; **t. spot** punto *m* conflictivo

**2** *vt (worry)* preocupar, inquietar; *(inconvenience)* molestar

**3** *vi* **to t. to do sth** tomarse la molestia de hacer algo

**troubled** ['trʌbld] *adj (person, look)* preocupado(a), inquieto(a); *(period, region)* agitado(a)

**trouble-free** ['trʌbəlfri:] *adj (installation, operation)* sencillo(a), sin complicaciones; *(stay, holiday, period)* tranquilo(a)

**troublemaker** ['trʌbəlmeɪkə(r)] *n* alborotador(ora) *m,f*

**troubleshooter** ['trʌbəlʃu:tə(r)] *n (for organizational problems)* = experto contratado para localizar y resolver problemas financieros, estructurales, etc; *(for machines)* técnico(a) *m,f* (en averías)

**troublesome** ['trʌbəlsəm] *adj* problemático(a)

**trough** [trɒf] *n (a) (for food)* comedero *m*; *(for drink)* abrevadero *m* **(b)** *(of wave)* seno *m*; *(on graph)* depresión *f* **(c)** *(in weather front)* banda *f* de bajas presiones

**trounce** [traʊns] *vt* aplastar, arrollar

**troupe** [tru:p] *n (of actors, dancers)* compañía *f*

**trouser press** ['traʊzəpres] *n* prensa *f* para pantalones, percha *f* planchadora

**trousers** ['traʊzəz] *npl* **(a)** *Br* pantalones *mpl*; **a pair of t.** unos pantalones **(b)** *(idioms)* *Fam* **she's the one who wears the t.** ella es la que lleva los pantalones en casa; *Fam* **he was**

**caught with his t. down** lo pillaron en bragas

**trouser suit** ['trauzə'su:t] n traje m de chaqueta y pantalón (para mujer)

**trousseau** ['tru:səʊ] n ajuar m

**trout** [traʊt] (pl **trout**) n trucha f

**trowel** ['traʊəl] n (for gardening) pala f de jardinero, desplantador m; (for building) llana f, paleta f

**truancy** ['tru:ənsɪ] n Sch absentismo m escolar, novillos mpl

**truant** ['tru:ənt] n Sch niño(a) m,f que hace novillos; **to play t.** hacer novillos

**truce** [tru:s] n also Fig tregua f; **to call a t.** hacer una tregua

**truck** [trʌk] 1 n (a) (lorry) camión m; **t. driver** camionero(a) m,f; **t. stop** bar m de carretera (b) (rail wagon) vagón m de mercancías (c) Fam **I'll have no t. with him/it** no pienso tener nada que ver con él/ello

**2** vt (goods) transportar en camión

**3** vi US (drive a truck) conducir un camión

**trucker** ['trʌkə(r)] n US (lorry driver) camionero(a) m,f

**truculent** ['trʌkjʊlənt] adj agresivo(a), airado(a)

**trudge** [trʌdʒ] 1 n (long walk) caminata f

**2** vi caminar fatigosamente

**true** [tru:] 1 adj (a) (factually correct) cierto(a), verdadero(a); **it is t. that...** es cierto or verdad que...; **to come t.** (of wish) hacerse realidad, realizarse; **this also holds t. for...** esto también vale para...; **how t.!** ¡cuánta razón llevas!

(b) (real) (reason, feelings) verdadero(a); **t. north** norte m geográfico

(c) (faithful) leal, fiel; **to be t. to sb** ser leal a alguien; **she was t. to her principles** era fiel a sus principios; **t. to life** fiel a la realidad; **t. to form** or **type** como era de esperar; **t. love** amor m verdadero

(d) (accurate) exacto(a); **his aim was t.** acertó, dio en el blanco

**2** n **out of t.** torcido(a)

**truffle** ['trʌfəl] n (fungus, chocolate) trufa f

**truism** ['tru:ɪzəm] n perogrullada f

**truly** ['tru:lɪ] adv verdaderamente, realmente; **yours t.** (at end of letter) reciba un afectuoso saludo de; Fam (myself) este menda, un servidor

**trump** [trʌmp] 1 n (in cards) triunfo m, pinta f; **what's trumps?** ¿(en) qué pintan?; **spades are trumps** pintan picas; Fig **she played her t. card** jugó su mejor baza or el as que escondía en la manga; Fam Fig **she turned up trumps** dio la sorpresa

**2** vt (in cards) ganar arrastrando

▶**trump up** vt sep (charge, accusation) inventar

**trumpet** ['trʌmpɪt] 1 n trompeta f; Fig **to blow one's own t.** echarse flores

**2** vt (success, achievements) pregonar

**3** vi (of elephant) barritar

**trumpeter** ['trʌmpɪtə(r)] n trompetista mf

**truncate** [trʌŋ'keɪt] vt truncar

**truncheon** ['trʌn(t)ʃən] Br n porra f

**trundle** ['trʌndəl] 1 vt (push) empujar lentamente

**2** vi (of vehicle) rodar

**trunk** [trʌŋk] n (a) (of tree, body) tronco m; Br Tel **t. call** conferencia f, llamada f de larga distancia; Br Aut **t. road** carretera f troncal (b) (case) baúl m (c) US (of car) maletero m, CAm, Méx cajuela f, CSur baúl m (d) (of elephant) trompa f (e) **trunks** (swimming costume) bañador m (de hombre)

**truss** [trʌs] 1 n Med braguero m

**2** vt (tie up) atar

▶**truss up** vt sep atar

**trust** [trʌst] 1 n (a) (belief) confianza f; **he put his t. in them** depositó su confianza en ellos; **to take sth on t.** dar por cierto algo (b) Law **in t.** en fideicomiso; Fin **t. fund** fondo m en fideicomiso (c) Com (group of companies) trust m

**2** vt (a) (believe in) confiar en; **to t. sb to do sth** confiar en que alguien haga algo; **to t. sb with sth** confiar algo a alguien; Fam **t. him to say that!** ¡típico de él! (b) Formal **to t. (that)...** confiar en que...

**3** vi **to t. in sb/sth** tener confianza or confiar en alguien/algo; **to t. to luck** confiar en la suerte

**trusted** ['trʌstɪd] adj de confianza

**trustee** [trʌs'ti:] n Law (of fund, property) fideicomisario(a) m,f; (of charity) administrador(ora) m,f

**trusting** ['trʌstɪŋ] adj confiado(a)

**trustworthy** ['trʌstwɜ:ðɪ] adj (person) fiable, de confianza; (source) fidedigno(a), fiable

**trusty** ['trʌstɪ] adj fiel

**truth** [tru:θ] n verdad f; **to tell the t.** decir la verdad

**truthful** ['tru:θfʊl] adj (person) sincero(a); (story) veraz, verídico(a)

**try** [traɪ] 1 n (a) (attempt) intento m; **to give sth a t.** intentar algo; **to have a t. at doing sth** probar a hacer algo; **it's worth a t.** merece la pena intentarlo (b) (in rugby) ensayo m

**2** vt (a) (sample) probar; **I'll t. anything once** estoy dispuesto a probar todo una vez (b) (attempt) intentar; **to t. to do sth,** Fam **to t. and do sth** tratar de or intentar hacer algo; **have you tried the chemist's?** ¿has probado en la farmacia? (c) Law (case) ver; (person) juzgar (d) (test, person, patience) poner a prueba

**3** vi intentarlo; **he didn't really t.** no lo intentó de veras; **you must t. harder** debes esforzarte más; **just you t.!** ¡intégntalo y verás!

►**try on** *vt sep* (a) *(clothes)* probarse (b) *Fam* **the children tried it on with their teacher** los niños pusieron a prueba al profesor; **stop trying it on with me!** ¡conmigo eso no va a colar!
►**try out** *vt sep* *(method, machine)* ensayar, probar; **to t. sth out on sb** probar algo con alguien
**trying** ['traɪɪŋ] *adj* *(person, experience)* difícil; **these are t. times** corren tiempos duros
**tsar** [za:(r)] *n* zar *m*
**tsarist** ['za:rɪst] *n & adj* zarista *mf*
**tsetse** ['t(s)etsɪ] *n* **t.** (fly) mosca *f* tse-tsé
**T-shirt** ['ti:ʃɜ:t] *n* camiseta *f*
**tub** [tʌb] *n* (a) *(for washing clothes)* tina *f*; *(bath)* bañera *f* (b) *(for ice-cream)* tarrina *f* (c) *Fam (boat)* cascarón *m*
**tuba** ['tju:bə] *n Mus* tuba *f*
**tubby** ['tʌbɪ] *adj Fam (person)* rechoncho(a)
**tube** [tju:b] *n* (a) *(pipe, container)* tubo *m*; *Fam* **to go down the tubes** irse a pique (b) *Br Fam* **the t.** *(underground railway)* el metro (c) *US Fam (TV)* **the t.** la tele
**tuber** ['tju:bə(r)] *n Bot* tubérculo *m*
**tuberculosis** [tjʊbɜ:kjʊ'ləʊsɪs] *n* tuberculosis *f inv*
**tubing** ['tju:bɪŋ] *n (tubes)* tuberías *fpl*; **a piece of rubber/glass t.** un tubo de goma/vidrio
**tubular** ['tju:bjʊlə(r)] *adj* tubular; *Mus* **t. bells** campanas *fpl* tubulares
**TUC** [ti:ju:'si:] *n (abbr* **Trades Union Congress)** = confederación nacional de sindicatos británicos
**tuck** [tʌk] **1** *n* (a) *(in sewing)* pinza *f*, pliegue *m* (b) *Br Fam (food)* chucherías *fpl*, golosinas *fpl*; **t. shop** *(in school)* puesto *m* de golosinas *(en el colegio)*
**2** *vt* **to t. one's trousers into one's socks** remeterse los pantalones en los calcetines; **he tucked his briefcase under his arm** se encajó la cartera bajo el brazo; **to t. sb up in bed** arropar a alguien en la cama; **to t. sth into a drawer** guardar algo en un cajón
►**tuck in 1** *vt sep (sheets)* remeter; *(children in bed)* arropar
**2** *vi Fam (eat)* comer sin cortarse; **t. in!** ¡come, come!
►**tuck into** *vt insep Fam (meal)* comer con ganas
**Tudor** ['tju:də(r)] **1** *n Hist* **the Tudors** los Tudor
**2** *adj* Tudor
**Tue(s)** *(abbr* **Tuesday)** martes *m inv*
**Tuesday** ['tju:zdɪ] *n* martes *m inv; see also* **Saturday**
**tuft** [tʌft] *n (of hair)* mechón *m; (of grass)* mata *f*
**tug** [tʌg] **1** *n* (a) *(pull)* tirón *m*; **to give sth a t.** dar un tirón a algo; **t. of war** *(game)* = juego en el que dos equipos tiran de una soga; *Fig* lucha *f* a brazo partido (b) *Naut* remolcador *m*
**2** *vt (pt & pp* **tugged)** *(rope, handle)* tirar de;

*Naut* remolcar
**3** *vi* **to t. at sth** dar un tirón a algo
**tuition** [tjʊ'ɪʃən] *n* clases *fpl*
**tulip** ['tju:lɪp] *n* tulipán *m*
**tum** [tʌm] *n (in children's language)* tripa *f*, barriga *f*
**tumble** ['tʌmbəl] **1** *n (fall)* caída *f*, revolcón *m*; **to take a t.** *(of person)* caer, caerse; *Fig (of prices)* caer en picado
**2** *vi (of person)* caer, caerse; *Fig (of prices)* caer en picado
►**tumble down** *vi* desmoronarse
**tumbledown** ['tʌmbəldaʊn] *adj (house)* ruinoso(a), en ruinas
**tumble-drier** [tʌmbəl'draɪər] *n* secadora *f*
**tumbler** ['tʌmblə(r)] *n* vaso *m*
**tummy** ['tʌmɪ] *n Fam* tripa *f*, barriga *f*; **to have (a) t. ache** tener dolor de tripa
**tumour,** *US* **tumor** ['tju:mə(r)] *n Med* tumor *m*
**tumult** ['tju:mʌlt] *n* tumulto *m*
**tumultuous** [tjʊ'mʌltjʊəs] *adj* tumultuoso(a)
**tuna** ['tju:nə] *n* atún *m*
**tundra** ['tʌndrə] *n* tundra *f*
**tune** [tju:n] **1** *n* (a) melodía *f*; **I can't sing in t.** desafino al cantar; **to be out of t.** *(of instrument)* estar desafinado(a); *(of person)* desafinar (b) *(idioms)* **to be in t. with one's surroundings** estar a tono con el entorno; **to call the t.** llevar la batuta; **to change one's t.** cambiar de actitud; **to the t. of** por valor de
**2** *vt (musical instrument)* afinar; *(engine)* poner a punto; *(TV, radio)* sintonizar
►**tune in** *vi Rad & TV* **to t. in to sth** sintonizar (con) algo; **make sure you t. in next week** vuelva a sintonizarnos la próxima semana
**tuneful** ['tju:nfʊl] *adj* melodioso(a)
**tuneless** ['tju:nlɪs] *adj* sin melodía
**tuner** ['tju:nə(r)] *n Rad & TV* sintonizador *m*
**tungsten** ['tʌŋstən] *n Chem* tungsteno *m*; **t. steel** acero *m* de tungsteno
**tunic** ['tju:nɪk] *n* túnica *f*
**tuning fork** ['tju:nɪŋ'fɔ:k] *n Mus* diapasón *m*
**Tunis** ['tju:nɪs] *n* Túnez *(ciudad)*
**Tunisia** [tju:'nɪzɪə] *n* Túnez *(país)*
**Tunisian** [tju:'nɪzɪən] *n & adj* tunecino(a) *m,f*
**tunnel** ['tʌnəl] **1** *n* túnel *m*; *Fig* **t. vision** estrechez *f* de miras
**2** *vt (pt & pp* **tunnelled,** *US* **tunneled)** **to t. one's way out of prison** escapar de la cárcel haciendo un túnel
**3** *vi* abrir un túnel
**turban** ['tɜ:bən] *n* turbante *m*
**turbine** ['tɜ:baɪn] *n* turbina *f*
**turbo-charged** ['tɜ:bəʊtʃɑ:dʒd] *adj* turbo *inv*

**turbo-charger** ['tɜːbəʊtʃɑːdʒə(r)] n turbo m, turbocompresor m

**turbojet** ['tɜːbəʊdʒet] n (engine, plane) turborreactor m

**turboprop** ['tɜːbəʊprɒp] n (engine) turbopropulsor m, turbohélice f; (plane) avión m turbopropulsado

**turbot** ['tɜːbət] n rodaballo m

**turbulence** ['tɜːbjʊləns] n turbulencia f

**turbulent** ['tɜːbjʊlənt] adj turbulento(a)

**turd** [tɜːd] n very Fam (a) (excrement) cagada f, mierda f (b) (person) gilipollas mf inv

**tureen** [tjʊəˈriːn] n sopera f

**turf** [tɜːf] 1 n (surface) césped m; Fam (territory) territorio m; a piece of t. un tepe; t. accountant corredor m de apuestas

2 vt cubrir de césped

▶**turf out** vt sep Br Fam (eject) echar

**Turk** [tɜːk] n turco(a) m,f

**Turkey** ['tɜːkɪ] n Turquía

**turkey** ['tɜːkɪ] n (pl turkeys) n (a) (bird) pavo(a) m,f, Am guajolote m (b) Fam (bad play, film) fracaso m

**Turkish** ['tɜːkɪʃ] 1 n (language) turco m

2 adj turco(a); T. bath baño m turco; T. delight delicias fpl turcas, = dulce gelatinoso recubierto de azúcar en polvo

**Turkmenistan** [tɜːkmenɪˈstɑːn] n Turkmenistán

**turmeric** ['tɜːmərɪk] n cúrcuma f

**turmoil** ['tɜːmɔɪl] n (estado m de) confusión f or agitación f; the country is in (a) t. reina la confusión en el país; his mind was in t. tenía la mente trastornada

**turn** [tɜːn] 1 n (a) (of wheel, screw) vuelta f; the meat is done to a t. la carne está en su punto

(b) (change of direction) giro m; (in road) curva f; no right t. (on sign) prohibido girar a la derecha; Fig at every t. a cada paso; to take a t. for the better/worse cambiar a mejor/peor; events took an unexpected t. los acontecimientos tomaron un cariz or rumbo inesperado; at the t. of the year/century a principios de año/siglo; the t. of the tide el cambio de marea; Fig el punto de inflexión

(c) (in game, queue) turno m; it's my t. me toca a mí; to take turns (at doing sth) turnarse (para hacer algo); in t. a su vez

(d) Fam (fit) ataque m; Fig it gave me quite a t. me dio un buen susto

(e) Th número m

(f) (service) to do sb a good t. hacer un favor a alguien; one good t. deserves another amor con amor se paga

(g) t. of phrase (way of expressing oneself) modo m de expresión

2 vt (a) (cause to move) (wheel, handle) girar; (page) pasar; (key, omelette) dar la vuelta a; to t.

one's head/eyes volver la cabeza/la vista; Fam Fig without turning a hair sin pestañear; Fam Fig success has turned her head el éxito se le ha subido a la cabeza; the sight/story turned my stomach la visión/historia me revolvió las tripas

(b) (direct) to t. one's attention/one's thoughts to... centrar la atención/los pensamientos en...; to t. the conversation to... encauzar la conversación hacia...

(c) (go round) to t. the corner doblar or Am voltear la esquina; Fig superar la crisis; she's turned forty ha cumplido cuarenta años

(d) (change, convert) to t. sth into sth convertir algo en algo; to t. sth green/black poner or volver algo verde/negro; to t. sb against sb volver a alguien contra alguien

(e) (on lathe) tornear

3 vi (a) (rotate) (of wheel) girar; (of person) volverse; she turned to me se volvió hacia mí; Fig to t. to sb (for help/advice) acudir a alguien (en busca de ayuda/consejo); to t. to the right/the left torcer or doblar a la derecha/la izquierda; my thoughts often t. to this subject pienso en este asunto a menudo

(b) (change) her luck has turned ha cambiado su suerte; to t. against sb volverse contra alguien; to t. nasty (of person) ponerse agresivo(a); (of situation) ponerse feo(a); to t. red (sky, water) ponerse rojo(a), enrojecer; (person) ponerse colorado(a); to t. sour (of milk) cortarse, agriarse; Fig (of relationship) deteriorarse

▶**turn away** 1 vt sep (refuse entry) prohibir la entrada a; (reject) rechazar

2 vi (look away) desviar la mirada

▶**turn back** 1 vt sep to t. sb back hacer volver a alguien; to t. the clocks back atrasar los relojes; Fig retroceder en el tiempo, regresar al pasado

2 vi he turned back volvió sobre sus pasos; t. back to page 12 volvamos a la página 12

▶**turn down** vt sep (a) (volume, heat) bajar (b) (request, application, person) rechazar

▶**turn in** 1 vt sep (lost property) entregar; (person) entregar a la policía

2 vi Fam irse a dormir

▶**turn into** vt insep convertirse en

▶**turn off** vt sep (a) (water, gas) cerrar; (light, TV) apagar (b) Fam to t. sb off cortar el rollo a alguien

▶**turn on** 1 vt sep (a) (water, gas) abrir; (light, TV) encender (b) Fam to t. sb on (excite) entusiasmar a alguien; (sexually) poner cachondo(a) a alguien, excitar a alguien

2 vt insep (attack) volverse contra (b) (depend on) it all turns on... todo depende de...

▶**turn out** 1 vt sep (a) (eject) echar (b) (pocket, container) vaciar (c) (light) apagar; (gas) cerrar (d) (produce) producir; to be well turned out (of *person)* ir muy arreglado(a)

**2** *vi* **(a)** *(appear, attend)* acudir, presentarse **(b)** *(result)* salir; **to t. out well/badly** salir bien/mal; **he turned out to be a cousin of mine** resultó ser primo mío; **it turns out that...** resulta que...

►**turn over 1** *vt sep* **(a)** *(turn)* dar la vuelta a; **to t. sth over in one's mind** dar vueltas a algo; *Fig* **to t. over a new leaf** hacer borrón y cuenta nueva **(b)** *(hand in)* **to t. sth/sb over to sb** entregar algo/a alguien a alguien

**2** *vi* **(a)** *(of person)* darse la vuelta; *(of car)* volcarse **(b)** *(change TV channels)* cambiar de cadena

►**turn round 1** *vt sep* *(car, table)* dar la vuelta a; *(economy, situation, company)* enderezar

**2** *vi* *(of person)* darse la vuelta

►**turn up 1** *vt sep* *(trousers)* meter (de abajo); **to t. one's collar up** subirse el cuello **(b)** *(volume, heat)* subir

**2** *vi* *(of person, lost object)* aparecer; **something is sure to t. up** seguro que algo aparecerá

**turnabout** ['tɜːnəbaʊt] *n* *(in situation, opinion)* vuelco *m*, giro *m*

**turnaround** ['tɜːnəraʊnd] *n* **(a)** *(in situation, opinion)* vuelco *m*, giro *m* **(b)** *Com* **t. time** tiempo *m* de espera *(de pedidos)*

**turncoat** ['tɜːnkəʊt] *n* chaquetero(a) *m,f*

**turning** ['tɜːnɪŋ] *n* **(a)** *(off road)* *(in country)* giro *m*, desviación *f*; *(in town)* bocacalle *f* **(b)** **t. circle** *(of car)* (capacidad *f* de) giro *m*; *Fig* **t. point** punto *m* de inflexión

**turnip** ['tɜːnɪp] *n* nabo *m*

**turn-off** ['tɜːnɒf] *n* **(a)** *(on road)* salida *f*, desviación *f* **(b)** *Fam* **it's a t.** es un tostón; *(sexually)* es un corte de rollo

**turn-on** ['tɜːnɒn] *n* *Fam* **it's a t.** *(sexually)* te pone a cien

**turnout** ['tɜːnaʊt] *n* *(attendance)* concurrencia *f*, asistencia *f*; *(for election)* (índice *m* de) participación *f*

**turnover** ['tɜːnəʊvə(r)] *n* **(a)** *Com* volumen *m* de negocio, facturación *f* **(b)** *Culin* **apple t.** = especie de empanada de hojaldre rellena de compota de manzana

**turnpike** ['tɜːnpaɪk] *n* *US (road)* autopista *f* de peaje

**turnstile** ['tɜːnstaɪl] *n* torniquete *m* or torno *m* (de entrada)

**turntable** ['tɜːnteɪbəl] *n* *(for record)* plato *m*, giradiscos *m inv*

**turn(-)up** ['tɜːnʌp] *n* **(a)** *Br (on trousers)* vuelta *f* **(b)** *Fam* **what a t. for the books!** ¡eso sí que es una sorpresa!

**turpentine** ['tɜːpəntaɪn] *n* trementina *f*

**turquoise** ['tɜːkwɔɪz] **1** *n* *(colour)* (azul *m*) turquesa *m*; *(stone)* turquesa *f*

**2** *adj* turquesa

**turret** ['tʌrɪt] *n* *(on building)* torrecilla *f*; **(gun)** t. torreta *f*

**turtle** ['tɜːtəl] *n* *Br* tortuga *f* (marina); *US* tortuga *f*; **to turn t.** *(of ship)* volcar; **t. dove** tórtola *f*; **t. soup** sopa *f* de tortuga

**turtleneck** ['tɜːtəlnek] *n* cuello *m* alto; **t. sweater** jersey *m* de cuello alto

**Tuscan** ['tʌskən] *adj* toscano(a)

**Tuscany** ['tʌskənɪ] *n* (la) Toscana

**tusk** [tʌsk] *n* colmillo *m*

**tussle** ['tʌsəl] **1** *n* pelea *f*; **to have a t. with sb** tener una pelea con alguien

**2** *vi* **to t. (with sb for sth)** pelearse (con alguien por algo)

**tutor** ['tjuːtə(r)] **1** *n* tutor(ora) *m,f*; **private t.** profesor(ora) *m,f* particular

**2** *vt* **to t. sb in French** dar clases particulares de francés a alguien

**tutorial** [tjuːˈtɔːrɪəl] *n* *Br Univ* tutoría *f*

**tuxedo** [tʌkˈsiːdəʊ] *(pl* **tuxedos)** *n* esmoquin *m*

**Tuvalu** [tuːˈvɑːluː] *n* (las islas) Tuvalu

**TV** [tiːˈviː] *n* *(television)* televisión *f*; **TV dinner** = menú completo precocinado y congelado que sólo necesita calentarse en el mismo envase; **TV programme** programa *m* de televisión

**TVP** [tiːviːˈpiː] *n* *Culin* *(abbr* **textured vegetable protein)** proteína vegetal texturizada, = alimento proteínico a base de soja texturizada que se utiliza como sustituto de la carne

**twaddle** ['twɒdəl] *n* *Fam* tonterías *fpl*, sandeces *fpl*

**twang** [twæŋ] **1** *n* *(sound)* sonido *m* vibrante; **nasal t.** entonación *f* nasal

**2** *vi* *(of string)* producir un sonido vibrante

**tweak** [twiːk] *n* **to give sb's ear a t.** dar a alguien un tirón de orejas; *Fam* **to give sth a t.** *(statistics, text)* hacer un pequeño ajuste en algo

**2** *vt* *(nose, ear)* pellizcar

**twee** [twiː] *adj* *Br Fam Pej* cursi

**tweed** [twiːd] *n* *Tex* tweed *m*; **tweeds** *(suit)* traje *m* de tweed

**tweet** [twiːt] **1** *n* pío *m*, gorjeo *m*

**2** *vi* piar, gorjear

**tweezers** ['twiːzəz] *npl* pinzas *fpl*; **a pair of t.** unas pinzas

**twelfth** [twelfθ] **1** *n* **(a)** *(fraction)* doceavo *m*, doceava parte *f* **(b)** *(in series)* duodécimo(a) *m,f* **(c)** *(of month)* doce *m*

**2** *adj* duodécimo(a); **T. Night** noche *f* de Reyes; *see also* **eleventh**

**twelve** [twelv] *n & adj* doce *m*; *see also* **eight**

**twentieth** ['twentɪθ] **1** *n* **(a)** *(fraction)* veinteavo *m*, vigésima parte *f* **(b)** *(in series)* vigésimo(a) *m,f* **(c)** *(of month)* veinte *m*

**2** *adj* vigésimo(a); *see also* **eleventh**

**twenty** ['twentɪ] *n & adj* veinte *m*; *see also* **eighty**

**twenty first** ['twentɪ'fɜːst] **1** *n* **(a)** *(in series)* vigésimo(a) primero(a) **(b)** *(of month)* veintiuno *m*

**2** *adj* vigésimo(a) primero(a); *(before masculine singular noun)* vigésimo primer

**twenty one** ['twentɪ'wʌn] **1** *n* veintiuno *m*

**2** *adj* veintiuno(a); *(before masculine singular noun)* veintiún

**twerp** [twɜːp] *n Fam* gil *mf inv*, lerdo(a) *m,f*

**twice** [twaɪs] *adv* dos veces; **t. as big as…** el doble de grande que…; **t. as slow** el doble de lento(a); **it would cost t. as much** costaría el doble; **t. over** dos veces; **to think t. before doing sth** pensárselo dos veces antes de hacer algo; **he didn't have to be asked t.** no hubo que pedírselo dos veces

**twiddle** ['twɪdəl] **1** *vt (knob, dial)* dar vueltas a, girar; *Fig* **to t. one's thumbs** holgazanear

**2** *vi* **to t. with sth** juguetear *or* trastear con algo

**twig**¹ [twɪg] *n (small branch)* ramita *f*

**twig**² *(pt & pp* **twigged)** *Br Fam* **1** *vt (realize)* coscarse *or* percatarse de

**2** *vi (realize)* coscarse, percatarse; **to t. to sth** coscarse *or* percatarse de algo

**twilight** ['twaɪlaɪt] *n* crepúsculo *m*

**twin** [twɪn] **1** *n* gemelo(a) *m,f*; **t. brother** hermano *m* gemelo; **t. sister** hermana *f* gemela

**2** *adj (paired)* parejo(a); **t. beds** camas *fpl* gemelas; **t.-engine(d) aircraft** (avión *m*) bimotor *m*

**3** *vt (pt & pp* **twinned)** *(towns)* **Glasgow is twinned with…** Glasgow está hermanado con…

**twine** [twaɪn] **1** *n (string)* cordel *m*

**2** *vt* **to t. one's arms around sth/sb** rodear algo/a alguien con los brazos

**twinge** [twɪndʒ] *n (of pain)* punzada *f*; **a t. of conscience** un remordimiento (de conciencia)

**twinkle** ['twɪŋkəl] **1** *n (of stars, lights)* parpadeo *m*; *(of eyes)* brillo *m*

**2** *vi (of star, light)* parpadear; *(of eyes)* brillar

**twirl** [twɜːl] **1** *n (movement)* giro *m*, vuelta *f*

**2** *vt* hacer girar; **he twirled his moustache** se retorció el bigote

**3** *vi (of person)* girar sobre sí mismo(a)

**twist** [twɪst] **1** *n* **(a)** *(action)* **to give sth a t.** retorcer algo; **with a t. of the wrist** con un giro de muñeca **(b)** *(movement)* **twists and turns** *(of road)* vueltas *fpl* y revueltas; *Fig (of events)* avatares *mpl* **(c)** *(in story, plot)* giro *m* inesperado; *Br Fam* **to be round the t.** estar majareta **(d)** *(piece)* **a t. of lemon** un trozo de peladura de limón **(e)** *(dance)* twist *m*

**2** *vt (thread, rope)* retorcer; *(sb's words, meaning of text)* tergiversar; **to t. one's ankle** torcerse el tobillo; **to t. sb's arm** retorcerle el brazo a alguien; *Fig* presionar a alguien; *Fig* **to t. the knife in the wound** remover la herida

**3** *vi* **(a)** *(of smoke)* elevarse en espirales; *(of road)* torcer; **to t. and turn** *(of road)* serpentear **(b)** *(dance)* bailar el twist

▶**twist off 1** *vt sep (lid)* desenroscar

**2** *vi (of lid)* desenroscarse

**twisted** ['twɪstɪd] *adj also Fig* retorcido(a)

**twister** ['twɪstə(r)] *n* **(a)** *Br Fam (dishonest person)* embaucador(ora) *m,f* **(b)** *US (tornado)* tornado *m*

**twit** [twɪt] *n Fam* gil *mf inv*, memo(a) *m,f*

**twitch** [twɪtʃ] **1** *n* **(a)** *(pull)* tirón *m* **(b)** **to have a nervous t.** tener un tic nervioso

**2** *vt (pull)* dar un tirón a

**3** *vi (of face)* contraerse

**twitter** ['twɪtə(r)] **1** *n (of birds)* gorjeo *m*; *Fam* **to be in a t.** *(excited)* estar agitado(a)

**2** *vi (of bird)* gorjear; *Fig (of person)* parlotear

**two** [tuː] **1** *n (pl* **twos)** dos *m*; **to break/fold sth in t.** romper/doblar algo en dos; **to walk in twos, to walk t. by t.** caminar de dos en dos; *Fig* **to put t. and t. together** atar cabos; *Fam* **that makes t. of us** ya somos dos

**2** *adj* dos; *see also* **eight**

**two-bit** ['tuː'bɪt] *adj US Fam (insignificant)* de tres al cuarto

**two-dimensional** [tuːd(a)ɪ'menʃənəl] *adj* bidimensional; *Fig (character, film)* superficial, plano(a)

**two-faced** ['tuː'feɪst] *adj* falso(a), hipócrita

**twofold** ['tuː'fəʊld] *adj* doble; **a t. rise** una subida del doble, una duplicación

**two-legged** [tuː'legɪd] *adj* bípedo(a)

**twopence** ['tʌpəns] *n Br* moneda *f* de dos peniques; *Fam* **it isn't worth t.** no vale un pimiento

**two-piece** ['tuː'piːs] *adj* **t. suit** traje *m*; **t. swimsuit** biquini *m*

**two-pin** ['tuː'pɪn] *adj (plug, socket)* de dos clavijas

**twosome** ['tuː'səm] *n* dúo *m*

**two-time** ['tuː'taɪm] *vt Fam* **to t. sb** pegársela a alguien

**two-way** ['tuː'weɪ] *adj* **t. mirror** luna *f* de efecto espía *or* espejo; **t. radio** aparato *m* emisor y receptor de radio

**tycoon** [taɪ'kuːn] *n* magnate *m*

**type** [taɪp] **1** *n* **(a)** *(kind)* tipo *m*, clase *f*; *Fam* **he's not my t.** no es mi tipo **(b)** *Typ* tipo *m* (de imprenta); **in bold t.** en negrita

**2** *vt (with typewriter)* mecanografiar; *(with word processor)* escribir *or* introducir en el ordenador

**3** *vi* escribir a máquina

▶**type up** *vt sep* mecanografiar

**typecast** ['taɪpkɑːst] *(pt & pp* **typecast)** *vt* encasillar

**typeface** ['taɪpfeɪs] *n* tipo *m* de imprenta

**typescript** ['taɪpskrɪpt] *n* copia *f* mecanografiada

**typesetter** ['taɪpsetə(r)] *n (person)* tipógrafo(a) *m,f*

**typewriter** ['taɪpraɪtə(r)] *n* máquina *f* de escribir

**typhoid** ['taɪfɔɪd] *n Med* **t. (fever)** fiebre *f* tifoidea

**typhoon** [taɪ'fuːn] *n* tifón *m*

**typhus** ['taɪfəs] *n Med* tifus *m inv*

**typical** ['tɪpɪkəl] *adj* típico(a); **isn't that t. of him/her)!** ¡típico (de él/ella)!

**typify** ['tɪpɪfaɪ] *vt (exemplify)* tipificar; *(sum up)* caracterizar

**typing** ['taɪpɪŋ] *n (by typewriter)* mecanografía *f*; *(by word processor)* introducción *f* (de datos) en el ordenador; **t. error** error *m* mecanográfico; **t. paper** papel *m* para escribir a máquina; **t. pool** sección *f* de mecanografía; **t. speed** velocidad *f* de mecanografiado

**typist** ['taɪpɪst] *n* mecanógrafo(a) *m,f*

**typographic(al)** [taɪpə'græfɪkəl] *adj* tipográfico(a)

**typography** [taɪ'pɒgrəfɪ] *n* tipografía *f*

**tyrannical** [tɪ'rænɪkəl] *adj* tiránico(a)

**tyrannize** ['tɪrənaɪz] *vt* tiranizar

**tyranny** ['tɪrənɪ] *n* tiranía *f*

**tyrant** ['taɪrənt] *n* tirano(a) *m,f*

**tyre**, *US* **tire** ['taɪə(r)] *n* neumático *m*, rueda *f*, *Am* llanta *f*; **t. marks** rodada *f*; **t. pressure** presión *f* de los neumáticos *or* de las ruedas

**tzar, tzarist** = **tsar, tsarist**

# U

**U, u** [ju:] *n (letter)* U, u *f*; **U bend** sifón *m*; **U boat** submarino *m (alemán)*; **U turn** *(in car)* cambio *m* de sentido; *Fig* giro *m* radical *or* de 180 grados; **to do a U turn** *(in car)* cambiar de sentido

**UAE** [ju:eɪ'i:] *n (abbr* **United Arab Emirates)** EAU *mpl*, Emiratos *mpl* Árabes Unidos

**UB40** [ju:bi:'fɔ:tɪ] *n Br (abbr* **Unemployment Benefit form 40)** ≃ cartilla *f* de desempleado

**ubiquitous** [ju:'bɪkwɪtəs] *adj* ubicuo(a)

**udder** [ˈʌdə(r)] *n* ubre *f*

**UDA** [ju:di:'eɪ] *n Br (abbr* **Ulster Defence Association)** = organización paramilitar norirlandesa partidaria de la permanencia en el Reino Unido

**UDI** [ju:di:'aɪ] *n Pol (abbr* **Unilateral Declaration of Independence)** declaración *f* unilateral de independencia

**UEFA** [ju:'eɪfə] *n (abbr* **Union of European Football Associations)** UEFA *f*

**UFO** [ˈju:fəʊ] *(pl* **UFOs)** *n (abbr* **unidentified flying object)** OVNI *m*

**Uganda** [ju:'gændə] *n* Uganda

**Ugandan** [ju:'gændən] *n & adj* ugandés(esa) *m,f*

**ugh** [ʌx] *exclam* ¡puaj!

**ugly** [ˈʌglɪ] *adj* **(a)** *(in appearance)* feo(a); *Fig* **u. duckling** patito *m* feo **(b)** *(unpleasant)* desagradable

**UHF** [ju:eɪtʃ'ef] *n Rad (abbr* **ultrahigh frequency)** UHF *m or f*

**UHT** [ju:eɪtʃ'ti:] *adj (abbr* **ultra heat treated)** U. milk leche *f* uperisada *or* UHT

**UK** [ju:'keɪ] *n (abbr* **United Kingdom)** RU, Reino *m* Unido

**Ukraine** [ju:'kreɪn] *n* Ucrania

**Ukrainian** [ju:'kreɪnɪən] **1** *n* **(a)** *(person)* ucraniano(a) *m,f* **(b)** *(language)* ucraniano *m* **2** *adj* ucraniano(a)

**ukulele** [ju:kə'leɪlɪ] *n* ukelele *m*

**ulcer** [ˈʌlsə(r)] *n* úlcera *f*

**ulcerate** [ˈʌlsəreɪt] **1** *vt* ulcerar **2** *vi* ulcerarse

**ulna** [ˈʌlnə] *n Anat* cúbito *m*

**Ulster** [ˈʌlstə(r)] *n* el Ulster

**ulterior** [ʌl'tɪərɪə(r)] *adj* **u. motive** motivo *m* encubierto

**ultimate** [ˈʌltɪmət] **1** *n Fam* **the u. in hi-fi equipment** el no va más en alta fidelidad **2** *adj* **(a)** *(last) (responsibility, decision)* final, último(a) **(b)** *(supreme, best)* **the u. deterrent** la medida disuasoria definitiva; **the u. holiday** las vacaciones soñadas

**ultimately** [ˈʌltɪmətlɪ] *adv* **(a)** *(finally)* finalmente, en última instancia **(b)** *(basically)* básicamente

**ultimatum** [ʌltɪ'meɪtəm] *n* ultimátum *m*

**ultra-** [ˈʌltrə] *pref* ultra-

**ultramarine** [ʌltrəmə'ri:n] *n* azul *m* de ultramar

**ultramodern** [ʌltrə'mɒdən] *adj* ultramoderno(a)

**ultrasound** [ˈʌltrəsaʊnd] *n Med* ultrasonido *m*; **an u. scan** una ecografía

**ultraviolet** [ʌltrə'vaɪələt] *adj* ultravioleta

**umbilical cord** [ʌm'bɪlɪkəl'kɔ:d] *n* cordón *m* umbilical

**umbrage** [ˈʌmbrɪdʒ] *n* **to take u. (at sth)** sentirse ofendido(a) (por algo)

**umbrella** [ʌm'brelə] *n* paraguas *m inv*; *Fig* **under the u. of...** al amparo de..., bajo la protección de...; **u. organization** organización *f* aglutinante; **u. stand** paragüero *m*

**umpire** [ˈʌmpaɪə(r)] **1** *n (in tennis)* juez *mf* de silla; *(in cricket)* árbitro(a) *m,f* **2** *vt* arbitrar

**umpteen** [ʌmp'ti:n] *adj Fam* **to have u. things to do** tener montones de cosas que hacer

**umpteenth** [ʌmp'ti:nθ] *adj Fam* enésimo(a); **for the u. time** por enésima vez

**UN** [ju:'en] *n (abbr* **United Nations)** ONU *f*

**unabashed** [ʌnə'bæʃt] *adj* descarado(a); **to be u.** no sentir vergüenza

**unable** [ʌn'eɪbəl] *adj* **to be u. to do sth** *(owing to lack of skill, knowledge)* ser incapaz de hacer algo; *(owing to lack of time, money)* no poder hacer algo

**unabridged** [ʌnə'brɪdʒd] *adj* íntegro(a)

**unacceptable** [ʌnək'septəbəl] *adj* inaceptable

**unaccompanied** [ʌnə'kʌmpənɪd] **1** *adj (child)* no acompañado(a); *(violin, singer)* solo(a), sin acompañamiento

**2** *adv* to travel **u.** viajar solo(a); **to play/sing u.** tocar/cantar sin acompañamiento

**unaccomplished** [ʌnə'kʌmplɪʃt] *adj (unimpressive)* mediocre

**unaccountable** [ʌnə'kaʊntəbəl] *adj* **(a)** *(not answerable)* **to be u. (to sb)** no tener que rendir cuentas (a alguien) **(b)** *(puzzling)* inexplicable

**unaccustomed** [ʌnə'kʌstəmd] *adj* **(a)** to be **u. to sth** no estar acostumbrado(a) a algo **(b)** *(not usual)* inusual, desacostumbrado(a)

**unacknowledged** [ʌnək'nɒlɪdʒd] **1** *adj* no reconocido(a)

**2** *adv* to go **u.** *(of talent, achievement)* no ser reconocido(a)

**unadulterated** [ʌnə'dʌltəreɪtɪd] *adj* **(a)** *(food)* natural, no adulterado(a) **(b)** *(joy)* absoluto(a)

**unadventurous** [ʌnəd'ventʃərəs] *adj (person)* poco atrevido(a), convencional; *(decision, choice)* poco arriesgado(a)

**unaffected** [ʌnə'fektɪd] *adj* **(a)** *(sincere) (person, style, joy)* espontáneo(a) **(b)** *(not touched)* he was **u.** no se vio afectado

**unaffiliated** [ʌnə'fɪlɪeɪtɪd] *adj* no afiliado(a)

**unafraid** [ʌnə'freɪd] *adj* **to be u. of sth/sb** no temer algo/a alguien

**unaided** [ʌn'eɪdɪd] *adv* sin ayuda

**unaltered** [ʌn'ɔ:ltəd] *adj* **to remain u.** *(of weather, opinion)* permanecer igual

**unambiguous** [ʌnæm'bɪɡjʊəs] *adj* explícito(a), claro(a)

**unambitious** [ʌnæm'bɪʃəs] *adj (person, project)* poco ambicioso(a)

**unanimity** [ju:nə'nɪmɪtɪ] *n* unanimidad *f*

**unanimous** [jʊ'nænɪməs] *adj* unánime

**unanimously** [jʊ'nænɪməslɪ] *adv* unánimemente

**unannounced** [ʌnə'naʊnst] **1** *adj (arrival)* no anunciado(a)

**2** *adv* to arrive **u.** llegar sin previo aviso

**unanswerable** [ʌn'ɑ:nsərəbəl] *adj* incontestable

**unanswered** [ʌn'ɑ:nsəd] **1** *adj (question, letter)* no contestado(a)

**2** *adv* to go **u.** *(of question, letter)* quedar sin respuesta

**unappealing** [ʌnə'pi:lɪŋ] *adj* poco atractivo(a)

**unappetizing** [ʌn'æpɪtaɪzɪŋ] *adj* poco apetitoso(a)

**unappreciated** [ʌnə'pri:ʃɪeɪtɪd] *adj (effort, contribution)* no reconocido(a); **to feel u.** sentirse poco valorado(a)

**unapproachable** [ʌnə'prəʊtʃəbəl] *adj (person, manner)* inaccesible

**unarmed** [ʌn'ɑ:md] *adj* desarmado(a); **u. combat** combate *m* sin armas

**unashamed** [ʌnə'ʃeɪmd] *adj* descarado(a); **he was completely u. about it** no le dio ninguna vergüenza

**unassailable** [ʌnə'seɪləbəl] *adj (castle, position)* inexpugnable; *(argument, theory)* irrebatible

**unassuming** [ʌnə'sju:mɪŋ] *adj* modesto(a)

**unattached** [ʌnə'tætʃt] *adj* suelto(a); **to be u.** *(without partner)* no tener pareja

**unattainable** [ʌnə'teɪnəbəl] *adj* inalcanzable

**unattractive** [ʌnə'træktɪv] *adj* poco atractivo(a)

**unauthorized** [ʌn'ɔ:θəraɪzd] *adj* no autorizado(a)

**unavailable** [ʌnə'veɪləbəl] *adj* **to be u.** no estar disponible

**unavailing** [ʌnə'veɪlɪŋ] *adj (effort)* inútil, vano(a)

**unavoidable** [ʌnə'vɔɪdəbəl] *adj* inevitable

**unaware** [ʌnə'weə(r)] *adj* inconsciente; **to be u. of sth** no ser consciente de algo

**unawares** [ʌnə'weəz] *adv* **to catch sb u.** coger a alguien desprevenido(a)

**unbalanced** [ʌn'bælənst] *adj (person)* desequilibrado(a); *(report)* sesgado(a), parcial

**unbearable** [ʌn'beərəbəl] *adj* insoportable

**unbeatable** [ʌn'bi:təbəl] *adj (team, position)* invencible, imbatible; *(product, value, price)* insuperable

**unbeaten** [ʌn'bi:tən] *adj* invicto(a)

**unbecoming** [ʌnbɪ'kʌmɪŋ] *adj (behaviour)* impropio(a) **(to** de**)**; *(dress)* poco favorecedor(ora)

**unbeknown(st)** [ʌnbɪ'nəʊn(st)] *adv* **u. to me** sin mi conocimiento

**unbelievable** [ʌnbɪ'li:vəbəl] *adj* increíble

**unbending** [ʌn'bendɪŋ] *adj* inflexible

**unbias(s)ed** [ʌn'baɪəst] *adj* imparcial

**unblock** [ʌn'blɒk] *vt (sink, pipe)* desatascar; *(road)* desbloquear

**unborn** ['ʌnbɔ:n] *adj* **u. child** niño *m* (aún) no nacido

**unbounded** [ʌn'baʊndɪd] *adj* ilimitado(a)

**unbreakable** [ʌn'breɪkəbəl] *adj (plate, toy)* irrompible; *Fig (spirit, alliance)* inquebrantable

**unbridled** [ʌn'braɪdəld] *adj (passion, aggression)* desatado(a)

**unbroken** [ʌn'brəʊkən] *adj* **(a)** *(not broken)* intacto(a) **(b)** *(uninterrupted)* ininterrumpido(a)

**unburden** [ʌn'bɜːdən] *vt* **to u. oneself to sb** desahogarse con alguien

**unbusinesslike** [ʌn'bɪznɪslaɪk] *adj* poco profesional

**unbutton** [ʌn'bʌtən] *vt* desabrochar, desabotonar; **to u. one's shirt** desabrocharse la camisa

**uncalled-for** [ʌn'kɔːldfɔː(r)] *adj* **to be u.** *(of behaviour, remark)* estar fuera de lugar

**uncanny** [ʌn'kænɪ] *adj (coincidence, similarity, resemblance)* asombroso(a), extraño(a); *(knack, ability)* inexplicable

**uncaring** [ʌn'keərɪŋ] *adj* desafecto(a), indiferente; **an u. mother** una madre poco afectuosa

**unceasing** [ʌn'siːsɪŋ] *adj* constante, incesante

**uncertain** [ʌn'sɜːtən] *adj (future)* incierto(a); **to be u. about sth** no estar seguro(a) de algo; **it is u. if…** no se sabe si…; **in no u. terms** en términos bien claros

**uncertainty** [ʌn'sɜːtəntɪ] *n* (a) *(insecurity)* incertidumbre *f* (b) *(doubt)* duda *f*

**unchallenged** [ʌn'tʃælɪndʒd] **1** *adj (assumption, accusation)* no cuestionado(a)
**2** *adv* **to let sth pass u.** dejar pasar algo

**unchanged** [ʌn'tʃeɪndʒd] *adj* igual, sin cambios; **to remain u.** no haber cambiado

**unchanging** [ʌn'tʃeɪndʒɪŋ] *adj* inmutable

**uncharacteristic** [ʌnkærəktə'rɪstɪk] *adj* atípico(a), poco característico(a)

**uncharitable** [ʌn'tʃærɪtəbəl] *adj* cruel

**uncharted** [ʌn'tʃɑːtɪd] *adj* desconocido(a), inexplorado(a)

**unchecked** [ʌn'tʃekt] **1** *adj* (a) *(not restrained)* incontrolado(a) (b) *(not verified)* sin comprobar
**2** *adv* **to go u.** *(of corruption, epidemic)* avanzar sin freno

**uncivil** [ʌn'sɪv(ɪ)l] *adj* maleducado(a), descortés

**uncivilized** [ʌn'sɪvɪlaɪzd] *adj* poco civilizado(a), incivilizado(a); **at an u. hour** a una hora intempestiva

**unclaimed** [ʌn'kleɪmd] *adj (money, baggage)* no reclamado(a); **to go u.** *(of money, baggage)* no ser reclamado por nadie

**uncle** ['ʌŋkəl] *n* tío *m*; *US* **U. Sam** el Tío Sam

**unclean** [ʌn'kliːn] *adj* sucio(a)

**unclear** [ʌn'klɪə(r)] *adj* poco claro(a); **I'm still u. about what happened** todavía no tengo muy claro lo que pasó

**unclothed** [ʌn'kləʊðd] *adj* desvestido(a), desnudo(a)

**uncoil** [ʌn'kɔɪl] *vt* desenrollar

**uncombed** [ʌn'kəʊmd] *adj* despeinado(a)

**uncomfortable** [ʌn'kʌmfətəbəl] *adj* incómodo(a); **to be u.** *(physically)* estar incómodo(a); *(ill-at-ease)* sentirse incómodo(a); **there was an u. silence** se produjo un silencio embarazoso *or* incómodo

**uncommitted** [ʌnkə'mɪtɪd] *adj (voter)* indeciso(a); *(funds)* no comprometido(a)

**uncommon** [ʌn'kɒmən] *adj* inusual

**uncommunicative** [ʌnkə'mjuːnɪkətɪv] *adj* reservado(a), poco comunicativo(a)

**uncomplicated** [ʌn'kɒmplɪkeɪtɪd] *adj* sencillo(a)

**uncomplimentary** [ʌnkɒmplɪ'mentərɪ] *adj* poco elogioso(a)

**uncomprehending** [ʌnkɒmprɪ'hendɪŋ] *adj* **to be u. of sth** no entender algo; **with an u. look** con cara de no haber comprendido

**uncompromising** [ʌn'kɒmprəmaɪzɪŋ] *adj (person, opposition)* intransigente; *(honesty)* inquebrantable

**unconcealed** [ʌnkən'siːld] *adj* indisimulado(a), manifiesto(a)

**unconcerned** [ʌnkən'sɜːnd] **1** *adj* indiferente; **to be u. about sth** no preocuparse por algo
**2** *adv* **to watch/wait u.** mirar/esperar con indiferencia

**unconditional** [ʌnkən'dɪʃənəl] *adj* incondicional; **u. surrender** rendición *f* incondicional

**unconfirmed** [ʌnkən'fɜːmd] *adj* no confirmado(a)

**unconnected** [ʌnkə'nektɪd] *adj* inconexo(a), sin relación; **two u. facts** dos hechos independientes

**unconscious** [ʌn'kɒnʃəs] **1** *n Psy* **the u.** el inconsciente
**2** *adj* (a) *(not awake)* inconsciente; **to be u.** estar inconsciente (b) *(unintentional)* inintencionado(a); **to be u. of sth** no ser consciente de algo

**unconsciously** [ʌn'kɒnʃəslɪ] *adv* inconscientemente

**unconstitutional** [ʌnkɒnstɪ'tjuːʃənəl] *adj* inconstitucional, anticonstitucional

**uncontaminated** [ʌnkən'tæmɪneɪtɪd] *adj* sin contaminar

**uncontested** [ʌnkən'testɪd] *adj (right, superiority)* indisputado(a); *Pol* **u. seat** escaño *m* con un solo candidato

**uncontrollable** [ʌnkən'trəʊləbəl] *adj* incontrolable

**uncontroversial** [ʌnkɒntrə'vɜːʃəl] *adj* anodino(a), nada polémico(a)

**unconventional** [ʌnkən'venʃənəl] *adj* poco convencional

**unconvinced** [ʌnkən'vɪnst] *adj* **to be u.** no estar convencido(a); **I remain u.** sigo sin convencerme

**unconvincing** [ʌnkən'vɪnsɪŋ] *adj* poco convincente

**uncooked** [ʌn'kʊkt] *adj* crudo(a)

**uncool** [ʌn'ku:l] *adj Fam* poco enrollado(a)

**uncooperative** [ʌnkəʊ'ɒpərətɪv] *adj* **to be u.** no estar dispuesto(a) a cooperar

**uncoordinated** [ʌnkəʊ'ɔ:dɪneɪtɪd] *adj* (efforts) descoordinado(a); (person) falto(a) de coordinación, torpe

**uncork** [ʌn'kɔ:k] *vt* descorchar

**uncorroborated** [ʌnkə'rɒbəreɪtɪd] *adj* no confirmado(a)

**uncountable** [ʌn'kaʊntəbəl] *adj Gram* incontable

**uncouth** [ʌn'ku:θ] *adj* basto(a)

**uncover** [ʌn'kʌvə(r)] *vt* destapar; *Fig* (evidence, plot) descubrir

**uncritical** [ʌn'krɪtɪkəl] *adj* poco crítico(a); **to be u. of sb/sth** no ser crítico(a) con alguien/algo

**UNCTAD** ['ʌŋktæd] *n* (abbr **United Nations Conference on Trade and Development**) UNCTAD *f*

**unction** ['ʌŋkʃən] *n* (a) (of manner) untuosidad *f*, empalago *m* (b) *Rel* unción *f*; **extreme u.** extremaunción *f*

**unctuous** ['ʌŋktjʊəs] *adj Pej* untuoso(a), empalagoso(a)

**uncultivated** [ʌn'kʌltɪveɪtɪd] *adj* (a) (land) sin cultivar (b) (person) inculto(a)

**uncultured** [ʌn'kʌltʃəd] *adj* inculto(a)

**uncut** [ʌn'kʌt] *adj* (gem) en bruto; (text, film) íntegro(a)

**undamaged** [ʌn'dæmɪdʒd] *adj* intacto(a)

**undated** [ʌn'deɪtɪd] *adj* no fechado(a)

**undaunted** [ʌn'dɔ:ntɪd] *adj* imperturbable; **to be u. by sth** no amilanarse *or* arredrarse por algo

**undecided** [ʌndɪ'saɪdɪd] *adj* (a) (question, problem) sin resolver; **that's still u.** todavía está por decidir (b) (person) indeciso(a); **to be u. about sth** estar indeciso(a) sobre algo

**undefeated** [ʌndɪ'fi:tɪd] *adj* invicto(a)

**undefended** [ʌndɪ'fendɪd] *adj* indefenso(a)

**undemanding** [ʌndɪ'mɑ:ndɪŋ] *adj* (job) fácil, que exige poco esfuerzo; (person) poco exigente

**undemocratic** [ʌndemə'krætɪk] *adj* antidemocrático(a)

**undemonstrative** [ʌndɪ'mɒnstrətɪv] *adj* reservado(a)

**undeniable** [ʌndɪ'naɪəbəl] *adj* innegable

**undeniably** [ʌndɪ'naɪəblɪ] *adv* innegablemente

**under** ['ʌndə(r)] **1** *prep* (a) (beneath) debajo de, bajo; (with verbs of motion) bajo; **u. the table/the stairs** debajo de la mesa/las escaleras;

to **walk u. a ladder** pasar por debajo de una escalera; *Fam* **to be/feel u. the weather** (ill) estar/encontrarse pachucho(a)

(b) (less than) menos de; **in u. ten minutes** en menos de diez minutos; **he's u. thirty** tiene menos de treinta años; **children u. five** niños de menos de cinco años

(c) (having control of) **he has a hundred men u. him** tiene cien hombres a su cargo; **Spain u. Franco** la España de Franco

(d) (subject to) **to be u. orders to do sth** tener órdenes de hacer algo; **u. the terms of the agreement** según el acuerdo; **u. these conditions/circumstances** en estas condiciones/circunstancias

(e) (in the process of) **u. construction/observation** en construcción/observación; **the matter is u. investigation** se está investigando el asunto; **to get u. way** (of meeting, campaign) ponerse en marcha, arrancar; **to be u. way** (of meeting, campaign) estar en marcha

**2** *adv* (a) (underneath) debajo; (underwater) bajo el agua; **to go u.** (of company) hundirse

(b) (less) **for £5 or u.** por 5 libras o menos; **children of seven and u.** niños menores de ocho años

**underachiever** [ʌndərə'tʃi:və(r)] *n* persona *f* que rinde por debajo de sus posibilidades

**under-age** [ʌndər'eɪdʒ] *adj* **to be u.** ser menor de edad; **u. drinking** consumo *m* de alcohol por menores; **u. sex** relaciones *fpl* sexuales entre menores

**undercarriage** ['ʌndəkærɪdʒ] *n Av* tren *m* de aterrizaje

**undercharge** [ʌndə'tʃɑ:dʒ] *vt* cobrar de menos

**underclass** ['ʌndəklɑ:s] *n* clase *f* marginal

**underclothes** ['ʌndəkləʊðz] *npl* ropa *f* interior

**underclothing** ['ʌndəkləʊðɪŋ] *n* ropa *f* interior

**undercoat** ['ʌndəkəʊt] *n* primera mano *f* (de pintura)

**undercook** [ʌndə'kʊk] *vt* **to be undercooked** no estar lo suficientemente hecho(a)

**undercover** ['ʌndəkʌvə(r)] **1** *adj* (agent, investigation) secreto(a)

**2** *adv* **to work u.** trabajar en secreto

**undercurrent** ['ʌndəkʌrənt] *n* (in sea) corriente *f* submarina; *Fig* (of emotion, unrest) corriente *f* subyacente

**undercut** ['ʌndəkʌt] (pt & pp **undercut**) *vt Com* **to u. the competition** vender a precios más baratos que los de la competencia

**underdeveloped** [ʌndədɪ'veləpt] *adj* (economy, country) subdesarrollado(a)

**underdog** ['ʌndədɒg] *n* (a) (in contest) = competidor o equipo considerado probable perdedor; **England are the underdogs** Inglaterra tiene menos posibilidades de ganar **(b)** *(in society)* **the u.** los débiles y oprimidos

**underestimate 1** *n* [ˌʌndərˈestɪmɪt] infravaloración *f*

**2** *vt* [ˌʌndərˈestɪmeɪt] infravalorar, subestimar

**underexposed** [ˈʌndərɪksˈpəʊzd] *adj Phot* subexpuesto(a)

**underfed** [ˌʌndəˈfed] *adj* desnutrido(a), malnutrido(a)

**underfoot** [ˌʌndəˈfʊt] *adv* **it's wet u.** el suelo está mojado; **to trample sth u.** pisotear algo

**underfunding** [ˌʌndəˈfʌndɪŋ] *n* escasez *f* de fondos

**undergarment** [ˈʌndəgɑːmənt] *n* prenda *f* (de ropa) interior

**undergo** [ˌʌndəˈgəʊ] *(pt* **underwent** [ˌʌndəˈwent], *pp* **undergone** [ˌʌndəˈgɒn]*)* *vt* *(change)* experimentar; *(test)* ser sometido a; *(pain)* sufrir; **to u. treatment** *(of patient)* recibir tratamiento

**undergraduate** [ˌʌndəˈgrædjʊɪt] *n* estudiante *mf* universitario(a) *(sin licenciatura)*

**underground 1** [ˈʌndəgraʊnd] *n* **(a)** *Br (railway system)* metro *m* **(b)** *(resistance movement)* resistencia *f* (clandestina)

**2** *adj* **(a)** *(cables, passage)* subterráneo(a) **(b)** *(movement, newspaper)* clandestino(a)

**3** *adv (to work, live)* bajo tierra; *Fig* **to go u.** pasar a la clandestinidad

**undergrowth** [ˈʌndəgrəʊθ] *n* maleza *f*

**underhand** [ˈʌndəhænd] *adj* turbio(a), poco honrado(a)

**underlay** [ˈʌndəleɪ] *n (for carpet)* refuerzo *m (debajo de las moquetas)*

**underlie** [ˌʌndəˈlaɪ] *(pt* **underlay** [ˌʌndəˈleɪ], *pp* **underlain** [ˌʌndəˈleɪn]*)* *vt* subyacer tras *or* bajo

**underline** [ˌʌndəˈlaɪn] *vt also Fig* subrayar

**underlying** [ˌʌndəˈlaɪɪŋ] *adj* subyacente

**undermanning** [ˌʌndəˈmænɪŋ] *n Ind* insuficiencia *f* de personal

**undermentioned** [ˈʌndəmenʃənd] *adj Formal* abajo mencionado(a) *or* citado(a)

**undermine** [ˌʌndəˈmaɪn] *vt (weaken)* minar, socavar

**underneath** [ˌʌndəˈniːθ] **1** *n* parte *f* inferior *or* de abajo

**2** *prep* debajo de, bajo; *(with verbs of motion)* bajo; **he crawled u. the fence** se arrastró por debajo de la valla

**3** *adv* debajo

**undernourished** [ˌʌndəˈnʌrɪʃt] *adj* desnutrido(a)

**underpaid** [ˌʌndəˈpeɪd] *adj* mal pagado(a)

**underpants** [ˈʌndəpænts] *npl* calzoncillos *mpl*

**underpass** [ˈʌndəpɑːs] *n (for cars, pedestrians)* paso *m* subterráneo

**underperform** [ˌʌndəpəˈfɔːm] *vi Fin* rendir por debajo de sus posibilidades

**underpin** [ˌʌndəˈpɪn] *(pt & pp* **underpinned**) *vt (support)* sustentar

**underpopulated** [ˌʌndəˈpɒpjʊleɪtɪd] *adj* poco poblado(a)

**underprivileged** [ˌʌndəˈprɪvɪlɪdʒd] *adj* desfavorecido(a)

**underqualified** [ˌʌndəˈkwɒlɪfaɪd] *adj* **to be u.** no estar suficientemente cualificado(a)

**underrate** [ˌʌndəˈreɪt] *vt* subestimar, infravalorar

**underside** [ˈʌndəsaɪd] *n* parte *f* inferior

**undersized** [ˌʌndəˈsaɪzd] *adj* demasiado pequeño(a)

**underskirt** [ˈʌndəskɜːt] *n* enaguas *fpl*

**understaffed** [ˌʌndəˈstɑːft] *adj* **to be u.** no tener suficiente personal

**understand** [ˌʌndəˈstænd] *(pt & pp* **understood** [ˌʌndəˈstʊd]*)* **1** *vt* **(a)** *(comprehend)* entender, comprender; **they u. each other** se entienden mutuamente; **what I can't u. is why...** lo que no llego a entender es por qué...; **is that understood?** ¿entendido? **(b)** *(believe, assume)* **I u. that...** tengo entendido que...; **to give sb to u. that...** dar a entender a alguien que...; **are we to u. that ...?** ¿quiere eso decir que...?, ¿debemos entender (con eso) que...?; **it was understood that few of us would survive** se entendía *or* se daba por sabido que pocos sobreviviríamos

**2** *vi* entender, comprender

**understandable** [ˌʌndəˈstændəbəl] *adj* comprensible

**understandably** [ˌʌndəˈstændəblɪ] *adv* comprensiblemente

**understanding** [ˌʌndəˈstændɪŋ] **1** *n* **(a)** *(comprehension)* comprensión *f*; **it's beyond all u.** no tiene ninguna lógica, es incomprensible **(b)** *(sympathy)* comprensión *f* **(c)** *(agreement)* acuerdo *m*; **to come to** *or* **to reach an u.** llegar a un acuerdo; **on the u. that...** a condición de que...

**2** *adj* comprensivo(a)

**understatement** [ˌʌndəˈsteɪtmənt] *n* **that's an u.!** ¡eso es quedarse corto!

**understood** [ˌʌndəˈstʊd] *pt & pp of* **understand**

**understudy** [ˈʌndəstʌdɪ] *n Th* suplente *mf*, actor(triz) *m,f* suplente

**undertake** [ˌʌndəˈteɪk] *(pt* **undertook** [ˌʌndəˈtʊk], *pp* **undertaken** [ˌʌndəˈteɪkən]*)* *vt* emprender; **to u. to do sth** encargarse de hacer algo

**undertaker** [ˈʌndəteɪkə(r)] *n* encargado(a) *m,f* de una funeraria

**undertaking** [ˌʌndə'teɪkɪŋ] n (a) *(enterprise)* empresa f, proyecto m (b) *(promise)* compromiso m; **she gave me her u. that she would do it** me dijo que se comprometía a hacerlo

**undertone** ['ʌndətəʊn] n *(low voice)* voz f baja; Fig *(hint, suggestion)* tono m

**undertow** ['ʌndətəʊ] n resaca f

**undervalue** [ˌʌndə'væljuː] vt also Fig infravalorar

**underwater 1** adj ['ʌndəwɔːtə(r)] submarino(a)

**2** adv [ˌʌndə'wɔːtə(r)] **to swim u.** bucear

**underway** [ˌʌndə'weɪ] adj en marcha; **to get u.** ponerse en marcha

**underwear** ['ʌndəweə(r)] n ropa f interior

**underweight** [ˌʌndə'weɪt] adj **to be u.** *(of person)* estar muy flaco(a)

**underworld** ['ʌndəwɜːld] n (a) *(in mythology)* **the U.** el Hades (b) *(of criminals)* **the u.** el hampa

**underwrite** ['ʌndəraɪt] *(pt* **underwrote** [ˌʌndə'rəʊt], *pp* **underwritten** [ˌʌndə'rɪtn]) vt Fin asegurar; Fig *(pay for)* financiar

**underwriter** ['ʌndəraɪtə(r)] n Fin *(in insurance)* asegurador(ora) m,f

**undeserved** [ˌʌndɪ'zɜːvd] adj inmerecido(a)

**undeserving** [ˌʌndɪ'zɜːvɪŋ] adj indigno(a); **to be u. of sth** no merecer algo

**undesirable** [ˌʌndɪ'zaɪrəbəl] n & adj indeseable mf

**undetected** [ˌʌndɪ'tektɪd] **1** adj no detectado(a)

**2** adv **to go u.** no ser detectado(a)

**undetermined** [ˌʌndɪ'tɜːmɪnd] adj indeterminado(a); **to be u.** *(of cause)* no estar determinado(a)

**undeterred** [ˌʌndɪ'tɜːd] **1** adj **to be u. by sth** no desanimarse por algo

**2** adv **he carried on u.** siguió sin arredrarse

**undeveloped** [ˌʌndɪ'veləpt] adj no desarrollado(a); Phot *(film)* sin revelar; **u. land** tierra f sin explotar

**undigested** [ˌʌnda(ɪ)'dʒestɪd] adj also Fig no digerido(a)

**undignified** [ʌn'dɪgnɪfaɪd] adj poco digno(a), indecoroso(a)

**undiluted** [ˌʌndaɪ'luːtɪd] adj *(liquid)* no diluido(a); Fig *(pleasure)* puro(a), absoluto(a)

**undiminished** [ˌʌndɪ'mɪnɪʃt] adj no disminuido(a); **to remain u.** no haber disminuido

**undiplomatic** [ˌʌndɪplə'mætɪk] adj poco diplomático(a)

**undisciplined** [ʌn'dɪsɪplɪnd] adj indisciplinado(a)

**undisclosed** [ˌʌndɪs'kləʊzd] adj no revelado(a)

**undiscovered** [ˌʌndɪs'kʌvəd] **1** adj sin descubrir

**2** adv **to go/remain u.** estar/permanecer sin descubrir

**undiscriminating** [ˌʌndɪs'krɪmɪneɪtɪŋ] adj **to be u.** no hacer distinciones, no distinguir

**undisputed** [ˌʌndɪs'pjuːtɪd] adj indiscutible

**undistinguished** [ˌʌndɪs'tɪŋgwɪʃt] adj mediocre

**undisturbed** [ˌʌndɪs'tɜːbd] adj *(sleep)* tranquilo(a); **she left his papers u.** dejó sus papeles tal como estaban

**undivided** [ˌʌndɪ'vaɪdɪd] adj **he gave me his u. attention** me prestó toda su atención

**undo** [ʌn'duː] *(pt* **undid** [ʌn'dɪd], *pp* **undone** [ʌn'dʌn]) vt (a) *(mistake)* corregir; *(damage)* reparar; Comptr *(command)* deshacer (b) *(knot)* deshacer; *(button)* desabrochar; *(parcel, zip)* abrir; *(shoelaces)* desatar

**undoing** [ʌn'duːɪŋ] n perdición f

**undone** [ʌn'dʌn] adj (a) *(loose) (jacket, buttons)* desabrochado(a); *(laces)* desatado(a); **to come u.** *(jacket, buttons)* desabrocharse; *(laces)* desatarse (b) *(incomplete)* sin hacer; **to leave sth u.** dejar algo sin hacer

**undoubted** [ʌn'daʊtɪd] adj indudable

**undoubtedly** [ʌn'daʊtɪdlɪ] adv indudablemente

**undreamed-of** [ʌn'driːmdɒv], **undreamt-of** [ʌn'dremtɒv] adj inimaginable

**undress** [ʌn'dres] **1** n **in a state of u.** desvestido(a), desnudo(a)

**2** vt desvestir, desnudar; **to get undressed** desvestirse, desnudarse

**3** vi desvestirse, desnudarse

**undrinkable** [ʌn'drɪŋkəbəl] adj imbebible

**undue** [ʌn'djuː] adj excesivo(a)

**undulate** ['ʌndjʊleɪt] vi ondular

**undulation** [ˌʌndjʊ'leɪʃən] n ondulación f

**unduly** [ʌn'djuːlɪ] adv excesivamente

**undying** [ʌn'daɪɪŋ] adj eterno(a)

**unearned** [ʌn'ɜːnd] adj *(reward, punishment)* inmerecido(a); Fin **u. income** rendimientos mpl del capital, renta f no salarial

**unearth** [ʌn'ɜːθ] vt *(buried object)* desenterrar; Fig *(information, secret)* descubrir

**unearthly** [ʌn'ɜːθlɪ] adj (a) *(supernatural)* sobrenatural (b) Fam **at an u. hour** a una hora intempestiva; **an u. din** or **racket** un ruido espantoso; **for some u. reason** por algún motivo incomprensible

**unease** [ʌn'iːz] n inquietud f, desasosiego m

**uneasily** [ʌn'iːzɪlɪ] adv con inquietud

**uneasy** [ʌn'iːzɪ] adj *(person)* inquieto(a); *(sleep)* agitado(a); **to be u. (about sth)** estar inquieto(a) (por algo)

**uneconomic(al)** [ʌniːkəˈnɒmɪkəl] *adj* carente de rentabilidad, antieconómico(a)

**uneducated** [ʌnˈedjʊkeɪtɪd] *adj* inculto(a)

**unemotional** [ʌnɪˈməʊʃənəl] *adj (person)* frío(a), impasible

**unemployable** [ʌnɪmˈplɔɪəbəl] *adj* **to be u.** no ser apto(a) para trabajar

**unemployed** [ʌnɪmˈplɔɪd] **1** *npl* **the u.** los desempleados, los parados

**2** *adj (person)* desempleado(a), parado(a); **to be u.** estar en (el) paro

**unemployment** [ʌnɪmˈplɔɪmənt] *n* desempleo *m*, paro *m*; *Br* **u. benefit** subsidio *m* de desempleo; **u. stands at 10%** el índice o la tasa de desempleo se sitúa en el 10%

**unending** [ʌnˈendɪŋ] *adj* interminable

**unendurable** [ʌnɪnˈdjʊərəbəl] *adj* insoportable

**unenlightened** [ʌnɪnˈlaɪtənd] *adj (person, decision)* retrógrado(a)

**unenlightening** [ʌnɪnˈlaɪtnɪŋ] *adj* poco ilustrativo(a)

**unenterprising** [ʌnˈentəpraɪzɪŋ] *adj* poco emprendedor(ora)

**unenthusiastic** [ʌnɪnθ(j)uːzɪˈæstɪk] *adj (reaction, response)* tibio(a); *(person)* poco entusiasta

**unenviable** [ʌnˈenvɪəbəl] *adj* desagradable, nada envidiable

**unequal** [ʌnˈiːkwəl] *adj* desigual; **an u. struggle** una lucha desigual; **he was u. to the challenge** no estuvo a la altura de lo exigido

**unequalled** [ʌnˈiːkwəld] *adj* sin par

**unequivocal** [ʌnɪˈkwɪvəkəl] *adj* inequívoco(a)

**unerring** [ʌnˈɜːrɪŋ] *adj* infalible

**UNESCO** [juːˈneskəʊ] *n (abbr* **United Nations Educational, Scientific and Cultural Organization)** UNESCO *f*

**unethical** [ʌnˈeθɪkəl] *adj* poco ético(a)

**uneven** [ʌnˈiːvən] *adj (surface, road, breathing)* irregular; *(performance)* desigual

**uneventful** [ʌnɪˈventfʊl] *adj* sin incidentes

**unexceptionable** [ʌnɪkˈsepʃənəbəl] *adj* irreprochable

**unexceptional** [ʌnɪkˈsepʃənəl] *adj* mediocre; **to be u.** no tener nada de especial

**unexciting** [ʌnɪkˈsaɪtɪŋ] *adj* anodino(a), insulso(a)

**unexpected** [ʌnɪksˈpektɪd] *adj* inesperado(a)

**unexplained** [ʌnɪksˈpleɪnd] *adj* inexplicado(a)

**unexplored** [ʌnɪksˈplɔːd] *adj* inexplorado(a)

**unfailing** [ʌnˈfeɪlɪŋ] *adj (hope, courage)* firme, inconmovible; *(punctuality)* infalible; *(patience, good humour)* inagotable

**unfair** [ʌnˈfeə(r)] *adj* injusto(a); **to be u. to sb** ser injusto con alguien; *Com* **u. competition** competencia *f* desleal

**unfairly** [ʌnˈfeəlɪ] *adv* injustamente

**unfairness** [ʌnˈfeənɪs] *n* injusticia *f*

**unfaithful** [ʌnˈfeɪθfʊl] *adj* **to be u. (to sb)** ser infiel (a alguien)

**unfamiliar** [ʌnfəˈmɪlɪə(r)] *adj* extraño(a), desconocido(a); **to be u. with sth** no estar familiarizado(a) con algo; **I'm u. with that name** desconozco ese nombre

**unfashionable** [ʌnˈfæʃənəbəl] *adj* **to be u.** no estar de moda; **to become u.** pasar de moda

**unfasten** [ʌnˈfɑːsən] *vt (knot)* desatar, deshacer; *(door)* abrir; **to u. one's belt** desabrocharse el cinturón

**unfathomable** [ʌnˈfæðəməbəl] *adj* insondable

**unfavourable** [ʌnˈfeɪvərəbəl] *adj* desfavorable

**unfeeling** [ʌnˈfiːlɪŋ] *adj* insensible

**unfinished** [ʌnˈfɪnɪʃt] *adj* inacabado(a); **to leave sth u.** dejar algo sin terminar; **u. business** asuntos *mpl* pendientes

**unfit** [ʌnˈfɪt] *adj* **(a)** *(unsuitable)* inadecuado(a), inapropiado(a); **to be u. for sth** no ser apto(a) para algo **(b)** *(in poor physical condition)* bajo(a) de forma; *(injured)* lesionado(a)

**unflagging** [ʌnˈflægɪŋ] *adj* infatigable

**unflappable** [ʌnˈflæpəbəl] *adj* impasible, imperturbable

**unflattering** [ʌnˈflætərɪŋ] *adj* poco favorecedor(ora)

**unflinching** [ʌnˈflɪntʃɪŋ] *adj (resolve, courage)* a toda prueba; *(loyalty, support)* inquebrantable

**unfold** [ʌnˈfəʊld] **1** *vt* **(a)** *(newspaper, map)* desdoblar **(b)** *(story, proposal)* revelar

**2** *vi (of story, events)* desarrollarse

**unforced** [ʌnˈfɔːst] *adj (natural)* espontáneo(a); **u. error** error *m* no forzado

**unforeseeable** [ʌnfəˈsiːəbəl] *adj* imprevisible

**unforeseen** [ʌnfəˈsiːn] *adj* imprevisto(a)

**unforgettable** [ʌnfəˈgetəbəl] *adj* inolvidable

**unforgivable** [ʌnfəˈgɪvəbəl] *adj* imperdonable

**unforgiving** [ʌnfəˈgɪvɪŋ] *adj* implacable

**unforthcoming** [ʌnfɔːθˈkʌmɪŋ] *adj* reservado(a)

**unfortunate** [ʌnˈfɔːtjənɪt] *adj (person, choice, remark, mistake)* desafortunado(a); *(accident, event)* desgraciado(a)

**unfortunately** [ʌnfɔːtjənɪtlɪ] *adv* desgraciadamente

**unfounded** [ʌnˈfaʊndɪd] *adj* infundado(a)

**unfriendly** [ʌn'frendlɪ] *adj (person)* arisco(a), antipático(a); *(reception)* hostil

**unfulfilled** [ʌnfʊl'fɪld] *adj (promise)* incumplido(a); *(desire, ambition)* insatisfecho(a); *(potential)* desaprovechado(a); **to feel u.** sentirse insatisfecho(a)

**unfunny** [ʌn'fʌnɪ] *adj* **to be u.** no tener ninguna gracia

**unfurl** [ʌn'fɜːl] **1** *vt (flag, sails)* desplegar
**2** *vi* desplegarse

**unfurnished** [ʌn'fɜːnɪʃt] *adj* sin amueblar; **u. accommodation** vivienda *f* sin amueblar

**ungainly** [ʌn'ɡeɪnlɪ] *adj* desgarbado(a), torpe

**ungodly** [ʌn'ɡɒdlɪ] *adj* impío(a), blasfemo(a); *Fig* **at an u. hour** a una hora intempestiva

**ungovernable** [ʌn'ɡʌvənəbəl] *adj (people, country)* ingobernable; *(feelings)* incontrolable

**ungracious** [ʌn'ɡreɪʃəs] *adj* descortés

**ungrateful** [ʌn'ɡreɪtfʊl] *adj* desagradecido(a)

**ungrudging** [ʌn'ɡrʌdʒɪŋ] *adj* **to be u. in one's praise/support** no escatimar elogios/apoyo

**unguarded** [ʌn'ɡɑːdɪd] *adj* **(a)** *(place)* desprotegido(a) **(b)** *(remark)* imprudente; **in an u. moment** en un momento de despiste

**unhampered** [ʌn'hæmpəd] *adj* libre (by de)

**unhappily** [ʌn'hæpɪlɪ] *adv* **(a)** *(unfortunately)* desgraciadamente **(b)** *(sadly)* tristemente

**unhappiness** [ʌn'hæpɪnɪs] *n* infelicidad *f*, desdicha *f*

**unhappy** [ʌn'hæpɪ] *adj* **(a)** *(sad) (person, childhood, marriage)* infeliz; *(day, ending, face)* triste; **to be u.** *(person)* ser infeliz **(b)** *(worried)* **I'm u. about leaving the child alone** me preocupa dejar al niño solo **(c)** *(not pleased)* **to be u. with sth** estar descontento(a) *or* no estar contento(a) con algo **(d)** *(unfortunate) (choice, state of affairs)* desgraciado(a), desafortunado(a)

**unharmed** [ʌn'hɑːmd] *adj (person)* indemne, ileso(a); *(object)* intacto(a)

**UNHCR** [juːneɪtʃsiːˈɑː(r)] *n (abbr* **United Nations High Commission for Refugees)** ACNUR *m*

**unhealthy** [ʌn'helθɪ] *adj (ill)* enfermizo(a); *(unwholesome)* insano(a), malsano(a)

**unheard-of** [ʌn'hɜːdɒv] *adj* inaudito(a); **that was u. in my youth** eso era impensable cuando yo era joven

**unheeded** [ʌn'hiːdɪd] *adj* desoído(a), desatendido(a); **to go u.** ser ignorado(a), caer en saco roto

**unhelpful** [ʌn'helpfʊl] *adj (person)* poco servicial; *(criticism, advice)* poco constructivo(a)

**unhesitating** [ʌn'hezɪteɪtɪŋ] *adj (support)* decidido(a); *(reply)* inmediato(a)

**unhindered** [ʌn'hɪndəd] **1** *adj* **he was u. by any doubts** no tuvo ninguna duda
**2** *adv* **to work u.** trabajar sin estorbos

**unhinged** [ʌn'hɪndʒd] *adj (mad)* trastornado(a)

**unholy** [ʌn'həʊlɪ] *adj* profano(a); *(words)* blasfemo(a); *(thoughts)* impuro(a); *Fam* **an u. mess/noise** un desorden/ruido espantoso; **u. alliance** alianza *f* contra natura

**UNHRC** [juːeneɪtʃɑːˈsiː] *n (abbr* **United Nations Human Rights Commission)** UNHRC *f*

**unhurt** [ʌn'hɜːt] *adj* ileso(a); **to be u.** *(after accident)* salir ileso

**unhygienic** [ʌnhaɪ'dʒiːnɪk] *adj* antihigiénico(a)

**UNICEF** ['juːnɪsef] *n (abbr* **United Nations International Children's Emergency Fund)** UNICEF *m or f*

**unicorn** ['juːnɪkɔːn] *n* unicornio *m*

**unidentified** [ʌnaɪ'dentɪfaɪd] *adj* no identificado(a); **u. flying object** objeto *m* volador no identificado

**unification** [juːnɪfɪ'keɪʃən] *n* unificación *f*

**uniform** ['juːnɪfɔːm] **1** *n* uniforme *m*
**2** *adj (colour, size)* uniforme; *(temperature)* constante

**uniformity** [juːnɪ'fɔːmɪtɪ] *n* uniformidad *f*

**uniformly** ['juːnɪfɔːmlɪ] *adv* uniformemente

**unify** ['juːnɪfaɪ] **1** *vt* unificar
**2** *vi* unificarse

**unilateral** [juːnɪ'lætərəl] *adj* unilateral

**unimaginable** [ʌnɪ'mædʒɪnəbəl] *adj* inimaginable

**unimaginative** [ʌnɪ'mædʒɪnətɪv] *adj* **to be u.** *(of person)* tener poca imaginación; *(of book, meal, choice)* ser muy poco original, no tener originalidad

**unimpaired** [ʌnɪm'peəd] *adj* indemne; **her faculties remained u.** no había perdido facultades

**unimportant** [ʌnɪm'pɔːtənt] *adj* **to be u.** no importar

**unimpressed** [ʌnɪm'prest] *adj* **to be u. by sth** no quedar convencido(a) con algo

**uninformed** [ʌnɪn'fɔːmd] *adj* desinformado(a); **to be u. about sth** no estar informado(a) de algo

**uninhabitable** [ʌnɪn'hæbɪtəbəl] *adj* inhabitable

**uninhabited** [ʌnɪn'hæbɪtɪd] *adj* desierto(a)

**uninhibited** [ʌnɪn'hɪbɪtɪd] *adj* desinhibido(a)

**uninitiated** [ʌnɪ'nɪʃɪeɪtɪd] **1** *npl* **to the u.** para los profanos (en la materia)
**2** *adj* no iniciado(a), profano(a)

**uninspiring** [ʌnɪn'spaɪrɪŋ] *adj* anodino(a)

**unintelligible** [ˌʌnɪnˈtelɪdʒɪbəl] *adj* ininteligible

**unintended** [ˌʌnɪnˈtendɪd] *adj* no deseado(a)

**unintentional** [ˌʌnɪnˈtenʃənəl] *adj* inintencionado(a); **it was u.** fue sin querer

**uninterested** [ʌnˈɪntrestɪd] *adj* poco interesado(a); **he was completely u.** no le interesaba en absoluto

**uninteresting** [ʌnˈɪntrestɪŋ] *adj* sin interés, anodino(a)

**uninterrupted** [ˌʌnɪntəˈrʌptɪd] *adj* constante, ininterrumpido(a)

**uninvited** [ˌʌnɪnˈvaɪtɪd] **1** *adj (comment, advice)* no solicitado(a); **there were a few u. guests** algunos de los presentes no habían sido invitados

**2** *adv* **to arrive u.** llegar sin haber sido invitado(a)

**uninviting** [ˌʌnɪnˈvaɪtɪŋ] *adj (place)* inhóspito(a); *(food)* nada apetitoso(a); *(prospect)* desagradable

**union** [ˈjuːnjən] *n* **(a)** *(of countries)* unión *f*; **U. Jack** bandera *f* del Reino Unido **(b)** *(marriage)* enlace *m* **(c)** *Ind* sindicato *m*

**unionist** [ˈjuːnjənɪst] *n* **(a)** *(supporter of trade union)* sindicalista *mf* **(b)** *(in Northern Ireland)* unionista *mf (partidario de que Irlanda del Norte siga formando parte del Reino Unido)*

**unionize** [ˈjuːnjənaɪz] *vt* sindicar

**unique** [juːˈniːk] *adj* único(a); **to be u. to** ser exclusivo(a) de

**unisex** [ˈjuːnɪseks] *adj* unisex *inv*

**UNISON** [ˈjuːnɪsən] *n* = sindicato británico de funcionarios

**unison** [ˈjuːnɪsən] *n* **in u.** al unísono

**unit** [ˈjuːnɪt] *n (in general)* unidad *f*; *(in hospital)* unidad *f*, servicio *m*; *(in army)* sección *f*, unidad *f*; **(kitchen) u.** módulo *m* (de cocina); **u. of measurement** unidad de medida; *Com* **u. price** precio *m* por unidad; *Fin* **u. trust** sociedad *f* de inversión mobiliaria

**unitary** [ˈjuːnɪtərɪ] *adj* unitario(a)

**unite** [juːˈnaɪt] **1** *vt* unir

**2** *vi* unirse

**united** [juːˈnaɪtɪd] *adj* unido(a); **the U. Arab Emirates** los Emiratos Árabes Unidos; **the U. Kingdom (of Great Britain and Northern Ireland)** el Reino Unido (de Gran Bretaña e Irlanda del Norte); **the U. Nations** las Naciones Unidas; **the U. States (of America)** los Estados Unidos (de América)

**unity** [ˈjuːnɪtɪ] *n* unidad *f*

**univ** *(abbr* **university)** univ., universidad *f*

**universal** [juːnɪˈvɜːsəl] *adj* universal; **u. suffrage** sufragio *m* universal

**universally** [juːnɪˈvɜːsəlɪ] *adv* universalmente

**universe** [ˈjuːnɪvɜːs] *n* universo *m*

**university** [juːnɪˈvɜːsɪtɪ] *n* universidad *f*; **u. professor** catedrático(a) *m,f* de universidad; **u. student** estudiante *mf* universitario(a)

**UNIX** [ˈjuːnɪks] *n Comptr (abbr* **Uniplexed Information and Computing System)** UNIX *m*

**unjust** [ʌnˈdʒʌst] *adj* injusto(a)

**unjustifiable** [ʌndʒʌstɪˈfaɪəbəl] *adj* injustificable

**unjustified** [ʌnˈdʒʌstɪfaɪd] *adj* injustificado(a)

**unkempt** [ʌnˈkem(p)t] *adj (hair)* revuelto(a); *(beard, appearance)* descuidado(a)

**unkind** [ʌnˈkaɪnd] *adj (unpleasant)* antipático(a), desagradable; *(uncharitable)* cruel; **to be u. (to sb)** ser antipático(a) *or* desagradable (con alguien)

**unkindly** [ʌnˈkaɪndlɪ] *adv (harshly)* con dureza, duramente; **to behave u. towards sb** estar desagradable con alguien

**unknowingly** [ʌnˈnəʊɪŋlɪ] *adv* inconscientemente, inadvertidamente

**unknown** [ʌnˈnəʊn] **1** *n (person)* desconocido(a) *m,f*; **the u.** *(place, things)* lo desconocido

**2** *adj* desconocido(a); *Fig* **an u. quantity** una incógnita; **the U. Soldier** el soldado desconocido

**3** *adv* **u. to the rest of us** sin que lo supiéramos los demás

**unlace** [ʌnˈleɪs] *vt* desatar

**unladylike** [ʌnˈleɪdɪlaɪk] *adj* impropio(a) de una señora

**unlawful** [ʌnˈlɔːfʊl] *adj* ilegal, ilícito(a)

**unleaded** [ʌnˈledɪd] **1** *n* gasolina *f* sin plomo

**2** *adj* **u. petrol** gasolina *f* sin plomo

**unleash** [ʌnˈliːʃ] *vt (dogs)* soltar; *Fig (forces, criticism)* desencadenar

**unleavened** [ʌnˈlevənd] *adj* **u. bread** pan *m* ázimo

**unless** [ʌnˈles] *conj* a no ser que, a menos que; **u. I hear to the contrary** en tanto no se me indique lo contrario; **u. I'm mistaken** si no me equivoco

**unlike** [ʌnˈlaɪk] *prep* **to be u. sb/sth** no parecerse a alguien/algo; **he's not u. his sister** se parece bastante a su hermana; **u. his father,...** a diferencia de su padre,...; **it's u. him to do such a thing** no es propio de él hacer algo así

**unlikelihood** [ʌnˈlaɪklɪhʊd] *n* improbabilidad *f*

**unlikely** [ʌnˈlaɪklɪ] *adj* improbable; **it's u. to happen** no es probable que suceda; **he's u. to do it** no es probable que lo haga; **in the u. event of an accident** en el hipotético caso de un accidente

**unlimited** [ʌnˈlɪmɪtɪd] *adj* ilimitado(a), sin límites; **to be u.** no tener límite; **with u. mileage** *(of hired car)* sin límite de kilometraje

**unlisted** [ʌn'lɪstɪd] *adj* **(a)** *Fin* **u. company** compañía *f* que no se cotiza en bolsa; **u. securities** títulos *mpl* no cotizados **(b)** *US (phone number)* que no figura en la guía (telefónica)

**unlit** [ʌn'lɪt] *adj (fire, cigarette)* sin encender; *(place)* sin iluminar

**unload** [ʌn'ləʊd] **1** *vt (boat, gun, goods)* descargar; *Fig* **he always unloads his problems onto me** siempre me viene con sus problemas
**2** *vi (of lorry, ship)* descargar

**unlock** [ʌn'lɒk] *vt (door)* abrir; *Fig (mystery)* desvelar

**unlovable** [ʌn'lʌvəbəl] *adj* desagradable

**unloved** [ʌn'lʌvd] *adj* **to feel u.** no sentirse querido(a)

**unlovely** [ʌn'lʌvlɪ] *adj* poco atractivo(a), nada agraciado(a)

**unlucky** [ʌn'lʌkɪ] *adj (person)* sin suerte; *(coincidence)* desafortunado(a); *(day)* funesto(a), aciago(a); *(number, colour)* que da mala suerte; **to be u.** *(have bad luck)* tener mala suerte; *(bring bad luck)* traer *or* dar mala suerte; **I was u. enough to miss the train** tuve la mala suerte de perder el tren

**unmanageable** [ʌn'mænɪdʒəbəl] *adj (person)* rebelde, díscolo(a); *(situation)* ingobernable; *(hair)* rebelde

**unmanly** [ʌn'mænlɪ] *adj (effeminate)* poco viril; *(cowardly)* pusilánime

**unmanned** [ʌn'mænd] *adj (spacecraft)* no tripulado(a)

**unmarked** [ʌn'mɑːkt] *adj* **(a)** *(without scratches, cuts) (person)* incólume; *(object, surface)* inmaculado(a); **u. (police) car** coche *m* (de policía) camuflado **(b)** *(uncorrected)* sin corregir **(c)** *Sport* desmarcado(a)

**unmarried** [ʌn'mærɪd] *adj (person)* soltero(a); **an u. couple** una pareja no casada, una pareja de hecho

**unmask** [ʌn'mɑːsk] *vt (criminal)* desenmascarar; *(plot)* descubrir

**unmentionable** [ʌn'menʃənəbəl] *adj (subject)* vedado(a), innombrable

**unmistakable** [ʌnmɪs'teɪkəbəl] *adj* inconfundible

**unmitigated** [ʌn'mɪtɪgeɪtɪd] *adj (support, disaster)* completo(a), absoluto(a)

**unmoved** [ʌn'muːvd] **1** *adj* **she was u. by his appeal** su llamamiento no logró conmoverla
**2** *adv* **to watch/listen u.** observar/escuchar impertérrito(a)

**unnamed** [ʌn'neɪmd] *adj* no mencionado(a)

**unnatural** [ʌn'nætʃərəl] *adj* **(a)** *(abnormal)* anormal, antinatural; **it's u. to...** no es normal... **(b)** *(affected)* afectado(a)

**unnecessary** [ʌn'nesɪsərɪ] *adj* innecesario(a)

**unnerve** [ʌn'nɜːv] *vt* poner nervioso(a), desconcertar

**unnerving** [ʌn'nɜːvɪŋ] *adj* desconcertante

**unnoticed** [ʌn'nəʊtɪst] **1** *adj* inadvertido(a)
**2** *adv* **to pass** *or* **go u.** pasar desapercibido(a) *or* inadvertido(a)

**UNO** [ju:en'əʊ] *n (abbr* **United Nations Organization)** ONU *f*

**unobservant** [ʌnəb'zɜːvənt] *adj* **to be u.** ser poco observador(ora)

**unobserved** [ʌnəb'zɜːvd] *adv* **to do sth u.** hacer algo sin ser visto(a)

**unobstructed** [ʌnəb'strʌktɪd] *adj (exit, view)* despejado(a)

**unobtainable** [ʌnəb'teɪnəbəl] *adj* **to be u.** no poderse obtener, ser inasequible; *(on phone)* no estar disponible

**unobtrusive** [ʌnəb'truːsɪv] *adj* discreto(a)

**unoccupied** [ʌn'ɒkjʊpaɪd] *adj (seat)* libre; *(house, person)* desocupado(a)

**unofficial** [ʌnə'fɪʃəl] *adj* extraoficial; **to be u.** no ser oficial; **in an u. capacity** extraoficialmente, de forma oficiosa; *Ind* **u. strike** huelga *f* no apoyada por los sindicatos

**unopened** [ʌn'əʊpənd] *adj* sin abrir

**unopposed** [ʌnə'pəʊzd] **1** *adj* **to be u.** no tener oposición
**2** *adv* **to go u.** no encontrar oposición

**unorthodox** [ʌn'ɔːθədɒks] *adj* poco ortodoxo(a)

**unpack** [ʌn'pæk] **1** *vt (suitcase)* deshacer; *(box, contents)* desembalar
**2** *vi* deshacer el equipaje

**unpaid** [ʌn'peɪd] *adj* **(a)** *(work, volunteer)* no retribuido(a) **(b)** *(bill, debt)* impagado(a)

**unpalatable** [ʌn'pælətəbəl] *adj (food)* intragable; *Fig (truth)* desagradable, crudo(a)

**unparalleled** [ʌn'pærəleld] *adj (growth, decline)* sin precedentes; *(success)* sin igual; **a place of u. beauty** un lugar de una belleza incomparable

**unpardonable** [ʌn'pɑːdənəbəl] *adj* imperdonable

**unpatriotic** [ʌnpeɪtrɪ'ɒtɪk] *adj* antipatriótico(a)

**unperturbed** [ʌnpə'tɜːbd] **1** *adj* **to be u. by sth** no ser afectado(a) por algo
**2** *adv* **to remain u.** permanecer impasible

**unplanned** [ʌn'plænd] *adj* espontáneo(a); *(result, visit)* imprevisto(a); **an u. pregnancy** un embarazo no planeado

**unpleasant** [ʌn'plezənt] *adj* desagradable

**unpleasantness** [ʌn'plezəntnɪs] *n* **the u. of...** lo desagradable de...; **to cause u.** provocar mal ambiente

**unplug** [ʌn'plʌg] *(pt & pp* **unplugged)** *vt* desenchufar

**unplugged** [ʌnˈplʌgd] *adj Mus* desenchufado(a), acústico(a)

**unpolished** [ʌnˈpɒlɪʃt] *adj (shoes, surface)* deslustrado(a); *Fig (performance)* deslucido(a); *(style)* tosco(a)

**unpolluted** [ʌnpəˈluːtɪd] *adj* no contaminado(a), limpio(a)

**unpopular** [ʌnˈpɒpjʊlə(r)] *adj (politician, decision)* impopular; **he was u. with his colleagues** sus compañeros no le tenían mucho aprecio

**unpopularity** [ʌnpɒpjʊˈlærɪtɪ] *n* impopularidad *f*

**unprecedented** [ʌnˈpresɪdentɪd] *adj* sin precedente(s)

**unpredictable** [ʌnprɪˈdɪktəbəl] *adj* imprevisible, impredecible

**unprejudiced** [ʌnˈpredʒʊdɪst] *adj (view, person)* libre de prejuicios; **to be u.** no tener prejuicios

**unprepared** [ʌnprɪˈpeəd] *adj (speech)* improvisado(a); **to be u. for sth** *(of person)* no estar preparado(a) para algo

**unprepossessing** [ʌnpriːpəˈzesɪŋ] *adj* poco atractivo(a)

**unpresentable** [ʌnprɪˈzentəbəl] *adj* impresentable

**unpretentious** [ʌnprɪˈtenʃəs] *adj* modesto(a), sencillo(a)

**unprincipled** [ʌnˈprɪnsɪpəld] *adj* sin principios; **to be u.** no tener principios

**unprintable** [ʌnˈprɪntəbəl] *adj (offensive)* impublicable

**unproductive** [ʌnprəˈdʌktɪv] *adj (land, work)* improductivo(a); *(meeting, conversation, effort)* infructuoso(a)

**unprofessional** [ʌnprəˈfeʃənəl] *adj* poco profesional

**unprofitable** [ʌnˈprɒfɪtəbəl] *adj (company)* poco rentable; *(meeting)* infructuoso(a), poco productivo(a)

**unpromising** [ʌnˈprɒmɪsɪŋ] *adj* poco prometedor(ora)

**unpronounceable** [ʌnprəˈnaʊnsəbəl] *adj* impronunciable

**unprotected** [ʌnprəˈtektɪd] *adj* desprotegido(a)

**unprovoked** [ʌnprəˈvəʊkt] *adj* espontáneo(a), no provocado(a)

**unpublished** [ʌnˈpʌblɪʃt] *adj* inédito(a)

**unpunished** [ʌnˈpʌnɪʃt] **1** *adj* impune
**2** *adv* **to go u.** quedar impune

**unqualified** [ʌnˈkwɒlɪfaɪd] *adj* **(a)** *(doctor, teacher)* sin titulación; **I'm quite u. to talk about it** no estoy cualificado para hablar de ello **(b)** *(support, disaster)* completo(a), absoluto(a)

**unquestionable** [ʌnˈkwestʃənəbəl] *adj* incuestionable

**unquestioning** [ʌnˈkwestʃənɪŋ] *adj (trust, obedience)* ciego(a); *(support)* incondicional

**unravel** [ʌnˈrævəl] (*pt & pp* **unravelled,** *US* **unraveled**) **1** *vt (wool)* deshacer; *Fig (plot, mystery)* desentrañar
**2** *vi (wool)* deshacerse; *Fig (of plan)* desbaratarse; *Fig (of mystery)* desentrañarse

**unreadable** [ʌnˈriːdəbəl] *adj* ilegible

**unreal** [ʌnˈrɪəl] *adj* irreal

**unrealistic** [ʌnrɪəˈlɪstɪk] *adj* poco realista

**unreasonable** [ʌnˈriːzənəbəl] *adj (person)* poco razonable, irrazonable; *(demand)* absurdo(a), disparatado(a); *(price)* exorbitante, desorbitado(a)

**unrecognizable** [ʌnrekəgˈnaɪzəbl] *adj* irreconocible

**unrecognized** [ʌnˈrekəgnaɪzd] **1** *adj (talent, government)* no reconocido(a)
**2** *adv* **to go u.** *(of talent, famous person)* pasar desapercibido(a)

**unrecorded** [ʌnrɪˈkɔːdɪd] *adj* no registrado(a)

**unrefined** [ʌnrɪˈfaɪnd] *adj* **(a)** *(sugar, petrol)* sin refinar **(b)** *(person, taste)* poco refinado(a)

**unregistered** [ʌnˈredʒɪstəd] *adj (worker, immigrant)* sin papeles; *(voter)* no inscrito(a)

**unrelated** [ʌnrɪˈleɪtɪd] *adj* **(a)** *(events)* inconexo(a) **(b)** *(people)* no emparentado(a)

**unrelenting** [ʌnrɪˈlentɪŋ] *adj* implacable

**unreliable** [ʌnrɪˈlaɪəbəl] *adj* poco fiable

**unrelieved** [ʌnrɪˈliːvd] *adj (boredom, ugliness)* absoluto; *(pain)* sin alivio

**unremarkable** [ʌnrɪˈmɑːkəbəl] *adj* corriente

**unremitting** [ʌnrɪˈmɪtɪŋ] *adj* incesante, continuo(a)

**unrepentant** [ʌnrɪˈpentənt] *adj* impenitente; **to be u. about** no arrepentirse de

**unreported** [ʌnrɪˈpɔːtɪd] **1** *adj* **an u. incident/problem** un incidente/problema del que no se ha informado
**2** *adv* **many crimes go u.** muchos delitos no se denuncian

**unrepresentative** [ʌnreprɪˈzentətɪv] *adj* no representativo(a)

**unrepresented** [ʌnreprɪˈzentɪd] *adj* no representado(a), sin representación

**unrequited love** [ˈʌnrɪkwaɪtɪdˈlʌv] *n* amor *m* no correspondido

**unreserved** [ʌnrɪˈzɜːvd] *adj* **(a)** *(praise, support)* sin reservas **(b)** *(seat, table)* libre, no reservado(a)

**unresponsive** [ʌnrɪˈspɒnsɪv] *adj* indiferente **(to** ante); **the patient was u. to the**

**treatment** el paciente no respondió al tratamiento

**unrest** [ʌnˈrest] *n (unease)* malestar *m*; *(disturbances)* desórdenes *mpl*, disturbios *mpl*; *(in labour relations)* conflictividad *f*

**unrestricted** [ʌnrɪˈstrɪktɪd] *adj* ilimitado(a), absoluto(a)

**unrewarding** [ʌnrɪˈwɔːdɪŋ] *adj (financially)* poco rentable; *(intellectually)* ingrato(a), poco gratificante

**unripe** [ʌnˈraɪp] *adj* verde; **to be u.** estar verde

**unrivalled** [ʌnˈraɪvəld] *adj (person, brilliance, beauty)* incomparable; **to be u.** ser inigualable

**unroll** [ʌnˈrəʊl] *vt* desenrollar

**unromantic** [ʌnrəˈmæntɪk] *adj* poco romántico(a)

**unruffled** [ʌnˈrʌfəld] *adj* sereno(a), imperturbable

**unruly** [ʌnˈruːlɪ] *adj (hair)* rebelde; *(children, mob, behaviour)* revoltoso(a)

**unsaddle** [ʌnˈsædəl] *vt (horse)* desensillar

**unsafe** [ʌnˈseɪf] *adj* **(a)** *(dangerous)* peligroso(a) **(b)** *(at risk)* inseguro(a), en peligro

**unsaid** [ʌnˈsed] *adj* **to leave sth u.** no decir algo; **it's better left u.** mejor no decirlo

**unsalted** [ʌnˈsɔːltɪd] *adj* sin sal

**unsatisfactory** [ʌnsætɪsˈfæktərɪ] *adj* insatisfactorio(a)

**unsatisfying** [ʌnˈsætɪsfaɪɪŋ] *adj (explanation)* insatisfactorio(a); *(ending, meal)* decepcionante; *(experience)* poco gratificante

**unsavoury** [ʌnˈseɪvərɪ] *adj (person, reputation)* indeseable

**unscathed** [ʌnˈskeɪðd] *adj* ileso(a)

**unscheduled** [ʌnˈʃedjuːld] *adj* no programado(a), imprevisto(a)

**unscientific** [ʌnsaɪənˈtɪfɪk] *adj* poco científico(a)

**unscramble** [ʌnˈskræmbəl] *vt* descifrar

**unscrew** [ʌnˈskruː] **1** *vt* desatornillar **2** *vi* desatornillarse

**unscrupulous** [ʌnˈskruːpjʊləs] *adj* poco escrupuloso(a)

**unseat** [ʌnˈsiːt] *vt also Fig* derribar

**unseemly** [ʌnˈsiːmlɪ] *adj* indigno(a)

**unseen** [ʌnˈsiːn] *adj* invisible; **u. by the guards** sin ser visto por los guardias; *Sch* **u. translation** traducción *f* directa sin preparación

**unselfconscious** [ʌnselfˈkɒnʃəs] *adj* natural

**unselfish** [ʌnˈselfɪʃ] *adj* desinteresado(a), generoso(a)

**unsentimental** [ʌnsentɪˈmentəl] *adj* desapasionado(a)

**unsettle** [ʌnˈsetəl] *vt (make nervous)* desasosegar, intranquilizar

**unsettled** [ʌnˈsetəld] *adj* **(a)** *(restless)* inquieto(a) **(b)** *(unresolved)* sin resolver **(c)** *(unpaid)* sin pagar

**unshakeable** [ʌnˈʃeɪkəbəl] *adj (belief, determination)* inquebrantable

**unsightly** [ʌnˈsaɪtlɪ] *adj* feo(a), horrible

**unsigned** [ʌnˈsaɪnd] *adj (contract)* sin firmar; *(band)* sin contrato

**unskilful** [ʌnˈskɪlfʊl] *adj* torpe, desmañado(a)

**unskilled** [ʌnˈskɪld] *adj (worker)* no cualificado(a); **he is u. at such work** se le da mal ese tipo de trabajos

**unsociable** [ʌnˈsəʊʃəbəl] *adj* insociable

**unsold** [ʌnˈsəʊld] *adj* sin vender

**unsolicited** [ʌnsəˈlɪsɪtɪd] *adj* no solicitado(a); **the advice was u.** nadie había pedido ese consejo

**unsolved** [ʌnˈsɒlvd] *adj* sin resolver

**unsophisticated** [ʌnsəˈfɪstɪkeɪtɪd] *adj* sencillo(a), simple

**unsound** [ʌnˈsaʊnd] *adj* **(a)** *(health)* frágil; *Law* **to be of u. mind** no estar en plena posesión de las facultades mentales **(b)** *(decision, advice)* desacertado(a); *Fin (investment)* poco seguro(a)

**unsparing** [ʌnˈspeərɪŋ] *adj* **to be u. of one's time/in one's efforts** no escatimar tiempo/esfuerzo

**unspeakable** [ʌnˈspiːkəbəl] *adj (conditions, squalor)* inefable; *(pain)* indecible

**unspecified** [ʌnˈspesɪfaɪd] *adj* sin especificar

**unspoilt** [ʌnˈspɔɪlt] *adj* intacto(a)

**unspoken** [ʌnˈspəʊkən] *adj (fear)* oculto(a), no expresado(a); *(threat)* velado(a); *(agreement)* tácito(a)

**unsporting** [ʌnˈspɔːtɪŋ], **unsportsmanlike** [ʌnˈspɔːtsmənlaɪk] *adj* antideportivo(a)

**unstable** [ʌnˈsteɪbəl] *adj (structure, government)* inestable

**unsteady** [ʌnˈstedɪ] *adj (table, chair)* inestable, inseguro(a); *(hand, voice)* tembloroso(a); **he was u. on his feet** se tambaleaba

**unstinting** [ʌnˈstɪntɪŋ] *adj (praise, effort)* generoso(a), pródigo(a); **to be u. in one's praise (of sb/sth)** no escatimar elogios (a alguien/algo)

**unstressed** [ʌnˈstrest] *adj Ling* no acentuado(a), sin acento

**unsubstantiated** [ʌnsəbˈstænʃɪeɪtɪd] *adj (accusation, rumour)* no probado(a)

**unsuccessful** [ʌnsək'sesfʊl] *adj (person)* fracasado(a); *(attempt, project)* fallido(a); **to be u.** *(of person, project)* no tener éxito

**unsuccessfully** [ʌnsək'sesfəlɪ] *adv* sin éxito

**unsuitable** [ʌn's(j)uːtəbəl] *adj (person)* poco indicado(a) **(for** para), inadecuado(a) **(for** para); *(choice, time)* inoportuno(a) **(for** para), inconveniente **(for** para); **this film is u. for children** esta película no es tolerada *or* no está recomendada para niños

**unsuited** [ʌn'suːtɪd] *adj* **to be u. to sth** ser poco indicado(a) para algo

**unsupported** [ʌnsə'pɔːtɪd] *adj* **(a)** *(statement, charges)* infundado(a) **(b)** *(structure)* **to be u.** no tener apoyo

**unsure** [ʌn'ʃʊə(r)] *adj* inseguro(a); **to be u. of** *or* **about sth** tener dudas acerca de algo

**unsurpassed** [ʌnsə'pɑːst] *adj* sin igual, insuperable; **to be u.** ser insuperable

**unsuspected** [ʌnsəs'pektɪd] *adj* insospechado(a); **her treason was u. by her superiors** sus superiores nunca sospecharon su traición

**unsuspecting** [ʌnsəs'pektɪŋ] *adj* confiado(a)

**unsweetened** [ʌn'swiːtnd] *adj (without sugar)* sin azúcar; *(without sweeteners)* sin edulcorantes

**unswerving** [ʌn'swɜːvɪŋ] *adj* inquebrantable

**unsympathetic** [ʌnsɪmpə'θetɪk] *adj* poco comprensivo(a) **(to** con); **they are u. to such requests** suelen rechazar ese tipo de peticiones

**unsystematic** [ʌnsɪstə'mætɪk] *adj* poco sistemático(a)

**untainted** [ʌn'teɪntɪd] *adj* impoluto(a); **u. by corruption** sin mancha de corrupción

**untalented** [ʌn'tæləntɪd] *adj* sin talento

**untamed** [ʌn'teɪmd] *adj (animal)* salvaje

**untangle** [ʌn'tæŋgəl] *vt* desenredar, desenmarañar

**untapped** [ʌn'tæpt] *adj* sin explotar

**untenable** [ʌn'tenəbəl] *adj* insostenible

**untested** [ʌn'testɪd] *adj* **to be u.** no haber sido puesto(a) a prueba

**unthinkable** [ʌn'θɪŋkəbəl] *adj* impensable

**unthought-of** [ʌn'θɔːtɒv] *adj* **an u. possibility** una posibilidad en la que no se había pensado

**untidiness** [ʌn'taɪdɪnɪs] *n* desorden *m*

**untidy** [ʌn'taɪdɪ] *adj (person, place)* desordenado(a); **to be u.** *(of place)* estar desordenado(a)

**untie** [ʌn'taɪ] *vt* desatar; **to u. a knot** desatar *or* deshacer un nudo

**until** [ʌn'tɪl] **1** *prep* hasta; **u. ten o'clock** hasta las diez; **u. now** hasta ahora; **not u. tomorrow** hasta mañana, no

**2** *conj* hasta que; **u. she gets back** hasta que vuelva; **we waited u. the rain stopped** esperamos a que escampara; **he won't come u. he's invited** no vendrá mientras no lo invitemos

**untimely** [ʌn'taɪmlɪ] *adj* inoportuno(a); *(death)* prematuro(a)

**untiring** [ʌn'taɪərɪŋ] *adj* incansable

**untold** [ʌn'təʊld] *adj (wealth, beauty)* inconmensurable

**untouchable** [ʌn'tʌtʃəbəl] *n & adj* intocable *mf*

**untouched** [ʌn'tʌtʃt] *adj* intacto(a); **u. by human hand** no tocado(a) por la mano del hombre; **he left the meal u.** dejó la comida intacta

**untoward** [ʌntə'wɔːd] *adj (unlucky)* desafortunado(a); *(unusual)* inusual, fuera de lo común

**untrained** [ʌn'treɪnd] *adj (person)* sin preparación; *(animal)* sin adiestrar

**untranslatable** [ʌntræns'leɪtəbəl] *adj* intraducible

**untried** [ʌn'traɪd] *adj* **(a) to be u.** *(of system, person)* no haber sido puesto(a) a prueba **(b)** *Law (person, case)* pendiente de juicio

**untroubled** [ʌn'trʌbəld] *adj* tranquilo(a), despreocupado(a); **to be u. (by)** no estar afectado(a) (por)

**untrue** [ʌn'truː] *adj* **(a)** *(false)* falso(a) **(b)** *(unfaithful)* desleal **(to** a)

**untrustworthy** [ʌn'trʌstwɜːðɪ] *adj (person)* indigno(a) de confianza; *(information)* poco fiable

**untruth** [ʌn'truːθ] *n* falsedad *f*

**untruthful** [ʌn'truːθfʊl] *adj (person)* embustero(a), mentiroso(a); *(story, reply)* falso(a)

**unusable** [ʌn'juːzəbəl] *adj* inutilizable, inservible

**unused** [ʌn'juːzd] *adj* **(a)** *(not in use)* sin usar **(b)** *(never yet used)* sin estrenar **(c)** [ʌn'juːst] **to be u. to sth** no estar acostumbrado(a) a algo

**unusual** [ʌn'juːʒʊəl] *adj (not common)* inusual; *(strange)* extraño; **it's not u. for him to take two hours for lunch** no es nada raro que tarde dos horas en almorzar; **it's u. of her not to notice** es raro que no se dé cuenta

**unusually** [ʌn'juːʒʊəlɪ] *adv (abnormally)* insólitamente; *(very)* extraordinariamente

**unvaried** [ʌn'veərɪd] *adj* monótono(a), uniforme

**unvarnished** [ʌn'vɑːnɪʃt] *adj* sin barnizar; *Fig* **the u. truth** la verdad desnuda

**unveil** [ʌn'veɪl] *vt (statue, plaque)* descubrir; *Fig (product, plan)* revelar, desvelar

**unverifiable** [ʌn'verɪfaɪəbəl] *adj* inverificable

**unvoiced** [ʌn'vɔɪst] *adj* (a) *Ling* sordo(a) (b) *(unspoken)* no expresado(a); **an u. fear** un temor oculto

**unwaged** [ʌnweɪdʒd] **1** *npl* **the u.** los desempleados

**2** *adj (not earning money)* desempleado(a)

**unwanted** [ʌn'wɒntɪd] *adj (attentions, responsibility, baby)* no deseado(a); *(clothes, trinkets)* desechado(a)

**unwarranted** [ʌn'wɒrəntɪd] *adj* injustificado(a)

**unwary** [ʌn'weərɪ] *adj* incauto(a)

**unwavering** [ʌn'weɪvərɪŋ] *adj (loyalty, support)* inquebrantable; *(gaze)* fijo(a); *(concentration)* intenso(a)

**unwelcome** [ʌn'welkəm] *adj (visit, visitor)* inoportuno(a); *(news)* desagradable; **to make sb feel u.** hacer que alguien se sienta incómodo

**unwell** [ʌn'wel] *adj* indispuesto(a), enfermo(a); **to be u.** estar indispuesto(a) *or* enfermo(a)

**unwholesome** [ʌn'həʊlsəm] *adj (food, climate)* insalubre

**unwieldy** [ʌn'wiːldɪ] *adj (tool)* poco manejable; *(object)* aparatoso(a); *Fig (system)* aparatoso(a)

**unwilling** [ʌn'wɪlɪŋ] *adj* reacio(a); **to be u. to do sth** ser reacio(a) a hacer algo

**unwillingness** [ʌn'wɪlɪŋnɪs] *n* mala gana *f*

**unwind** [ʌn'waɪnd] *(pt & pp* **unwound** [ʌn'waʊnd]) **1** *vt* desenrollar

**2** *vi* (a) *(of string, wool)* desenrollarse (b) *Fam (relax)* relajarse, desconectar

**unwise** [ʌn'waɪz] *adj* imprudente

**unwitting** [ʌn'wɪtɪŋ] *adj* involuntario(a)

**unworkable** [ʌn'wɜːkəbəl] *adj* impracticable

**unworthy** [ʌn'wɜːðɪ] *adj* indigno(a) (**of** de)

**unwrap** [ʌn'ræp] *(pt & pp* **unwrapped**) *vt* desenvolver

**unwritten** [ʌn'rɪtən] *adj (language, law)* no escrito(a); *(agreement)* tácito(a), verbal

**unyielding** [ʌn'jiːldɪŋ] *adj* inflexible

**unzip** [ʌnzɪp] *(pt & pp* **unzipped**) *vt* abrir la cremallera de; **to u. one's trousers** bajarse la cremallera de los pantalones

**up** [ʌp] **1** *adv* (a) *(with motion)* hacia arriba; **to come/go up** subir; **to put one's hand up** levantar la mano; **to go up north** ir hacia el norte; **to go up to sb** acercarse a alguien; **to put a poster up** pegar un cartel; **up the Rovers!** ¡ánimo Rovers!, ¡aúpa Rovers!

(b) *(with position)* arriba; **up here/there** aquí/allí arriba; **up above** arriba; **further up** más arriba; **the sun was up** ya había salido el sol; **prices are up** los precios han subido

(c) *(ahead)* **to be one goal/five points up** ir ganando por *or* de un gol/cinco puntos

(d) *(in phrases with* to) **up to now** hasta ahora; **up to £100 a week** hasta 100 libras semanales; **up to the age of seven** hasta los siete años; **he's not up to the job** no está a la altura del puesto; **I don't feel up to it** no me siento en condiciones de hacerlo; **I'm sure he's up to something!** ¡estoy seguro de que prepara algo!; **what are the children up to?** ¿qué están tramando los niños?; **what have you been up to?** ¿qué has estado haciendo?; **it's up to you to do it** *(your responsibility)* te corresponde a ti hacerlo; **it's up to you whether you tell her** *(your decision)* depende de ti si se lo dices o no; **it's not up to much** *(not very good)* no es gran cosa

**2** *prep* (a) *(with motion)* **to go up the stairs** subir las escaleras; **to walk up the street** andar por la calle; **to climb up a hill** subir *or* escalar una colina; *Vulg* **up yours!** ¡vete a tomar por culo!

(b) *(with position)* **up a tree/ladder** en lo alto de un árbol/una escalera; **she lives up the street from me** vive en mi misma calle; **to be up against sth** enfrentarse a algo

**3** *adj* (a) *(out of bed)* **he isn't up** no está levantado; **I was up all night** pasé toda la noche levantado; **to be up and about** *(in morning)* estar levantado(a); *(after illness)* estar recuperado(a)

(b) *Fam (wrong)* **what's up?** ¿qué pasa?; **what's up with you/him?** ¿qué te/le pasa?; **something's up** algo pasa *or* ocurre

(c) *(finished)* **your time's up** se te ha terminado el tiempo; **the two weeks were nearly up** ya casi habían transcurrido las dos semanas

(d) *(idioms)* **to be up and running** *(of machine, project)* estar en marcha

**4** *n Fam* **life's ups and downs** los altibajos de la vida

**5** *vt* *(pt & pp* **upped**) *Fam (price)* subir

**6** *vi Fam* **to up and leave** *or* **go** coger y marcharse

**up-and-coming** ['ʌpənd'kʌmɪŋ] *adj* prometedor(ora)

**upbeat** [ʌp'biːt] *adj (optimistic)* optimista

**upbraid** [ʌp'breɪd] *vt* recriminar; **to u. sb for sth** recriminar algo a alguien

**upbringing** ['ʌpbrɪŋɪŋ] *n* crianza *f*, educación *f*

**update 1** *n* ['ʌpdeɪt] actualización *f*

**2** *vt* [ʌp'deɪt] actualizar; **to u. sb on sth** poner a alguien al corriente de algo

**upend** [ʌp'end] *vt (turn upside down)* poner boca abajo; *(knock over)* derribar

**up-front** [ʌp'frʌnt] **1** *adj Fam (frank)* claro(a), franco(a)

**2** *adv (to pay)* por adelantado

**upgrade 1** n ['ʌpgreɪd] *Comptr* actualización f

**2** vt [ʌp'greɪd] *(improve)* modernizar; *(promote)* ascender

**upheaval** [ʌp'hi:vəl] n trastorno m, conmoción f; **political u.** conmoción política; **emotional u.** trastornos mpl emocionales

**uphill** ['ʌphɪl] **1** adj *(road)* cuesta arriba; *Fig (struggle)* duro(a), arduo(a)

**2** adv cuesta arriba

**uphold** [ʌp'həʊld] *(pt & pp* **upheld** [ʌp'held]) vt *(opinion, principle)* defender; *(decision)* apoyar, corroborar; **to u. the law** hacer respetar la ley

**upholstered** [ʌp'həʊlstəd] adj tapizado(a)

**upholstery** [ʌp'həʊlstəri] n tapicería f

**upkeep** ['ʌpki:p] n mantenimiento m

**uplift 1** n ['ʌplɪft] subida f de ánimo; **to give sth/sb an u.** animar algo/a alguien

**2** [ʌp'lɪft] vt *(emotionally)* animar, levantar el espíritu a

**uplifting** [ʌp'lɪftɪŋ] adj estimulante

**up-market** ['ʌpmɑ:kɪt] adj de categoría

**upon** [ə'pɒn] prep en, sobre; **u. realizing what had happened...** al darse cuenta de lo ocurrido...; *Old-fashioned* **u. my word!** ¡caramba!

**upper** ['ʌpə(r)] **1** n *(of shoe)* empeine m; *Fam* **to be on one's uppers** estar sin un duro

**2** adj superior; *Typ* **u. case** mayúsculas fpl; **u. class** clase f alta; **to gain the u. hand** tomar la delantera; **the U. House** la cámara alta; **u. limit** límite m superior, tope m

**upper-class** ['ʌpə'klɑ:s] adj de clase alta

**upper-crust** [ʌpə'krʌst] adj *Fam (person, accent)* de clase alta

**uppermost** ['ʌpəməʊst] adj *(in position)* superior; *Fig* **it was u. in my mind** era una cuestión prioritaria para mí

**uppity** ['ʌpɪti] adj *Fam* creído(a), engreído(a); **to get u.** darse aires

**upright** ['ʌpraɪt] **1** n *(beam)* poste m, montante m

**2** adj **(a)** *(vertical)* vertical, derecho(a); **u. piano** piano m vertical **(b)** *(honest)* honrado(a)

**3** adv **to put/place sth u.** poner/colocar algo derecho

**uprising** [ʌp'raɪzɪŋ] n levantamiento m

**uproar** ['ʌprɔ:(r)] n *(noise)* alboroto m; *(protest)* escándalo m, polémica f; **the meeting was in an u.** se armó un gran alboroto en la reunión

**uproarious** [ʌp'rɔ:rɪəs] adj *(noisy)* escandaloso(a); *(funny)* divertidísimo(a)

**uproot** [ʌp'ru:t] vt desarraigar

**upset 1** n ['ʌpset] *(disturbance)* trastorno m; *(surprise)* resultado m inesperado; **to have a stomach u.** tener un trastorno gástrico

**2** vt [ʌp'set] *(pt & pp* **upset**) **(a)** *(liquid, container)* tirar, volcar **(b)** *(person)* disgustar; *(plans,*

*schedule)* trastornar, alterar; **the least thing upsets him** se disgusta por cualquier cosa

**3** adj [ʌp'set] *(unhappy)* disgustado(a); **to be u. about sth** estar disgustado por algo; **to have an u. stomach** tener un trastorno gástrico

**upsetting** [ʌp'setɪŋ] adj desagradable

**upshot** ['ʌpʃɒt] n resultado m

**upside down** ['ʌpsaɪd'daʊn] **1** adj al or del revés

**2** adv **to hang u.** *(of person, animal)* colgar cabeza abajo; **to turn sth u.** poner algo del revés; *Fig* poner algo patas arriba

**upstage** [ʌp'steɪdʒ] **1** adv *Th (move)* hacia el fondo de la escena; **to be** or **stand u. of sb** estar en segundo plano respecto a alguien

**2** vt *Th & Fig* dejar en segundo plano

**upstairs** [ʌp'steəz] **1** n the u. el piso de arriba

**2** adv arriba; **I ran u.** subí (al piso de) arriba corriendo

**3** adj **u. neighbours** vecinos mpl de arriba

**upstanding** [ʌp'stændɪŋ] adj *(honest)* honrado(a), recto(a)

**upstart** ['ʌpstɑ:t] n advenedizo(a) m,f

**upstream** ['ʌpstri:m] adv río arriba

**upsurge** ['ʌpsɜ:dʒ] n aumento m, incremento m

**upswing** ['ʌpswɪŋ] n *(improvement)* mejora f, alza f

**uptake** ['ʌpteɪk] n *Fam* **to be quick/slow on the u.** ser/no ser muy espabilado(a)

**uptight** [ʌp'taɪt] adj *Fam (nervous)* tenso(a); *(strait-laced)* estrecho(a)

**up-to-date** [ʌptə'deɪt] adj *(news, information)* reciente, actual; *(method, approach)* moderno(a); **to bring sb u. (on sth)** poner a alguien al día (sobre algo)

**upturn** ['ʌptɜ:n] n mejora f (**in** de)

**upturned** ['ʌptɜ:nd] adj *(bucket, box) (face down)* boca abajo; *(on its side)* volcado(a); *(nose)* respingón(ona)

**upward** ['ʌpwəd] **1** adj hacia arriba; **u. mobility** ascenso m en la escala social

**2** adv = **upwards**

**upwardly mobile** ['ʌpwədlɪ'məʊbaɪl] adj = que va ascendiendo en la escala social

**upwards** ['ʌpwədz] adv hacia arriba; **to look u.** mirar hacia arriba; **from £100 u.** a partir de 100 libras; **u. of** por encima de

**Urals** ['jʊərəlz] npl **the U.** los Urales

**uranium** [jʊ'reɪnɪəm] n *Chem* uranio m

**Uranus** [jʊ'reɪnəs] n *(planet)* Urano

**urban** ['ɜ:bən] adj urbano(a); **u. legend** or **myth** leyenda f popular; **u. renewal** remodelación f urbana; **u. sprawl** aglomeración f urbana

**urbane** [ɜ:'beɪn] adj cortés, comedido(a)

**rbanization** [ɜ:bənaɪ'zeɪʃən] *n (process)* uranización *f*

**rchin** ['ɜ:tʃɪn] *n (child)* pilluelo(a) *m,f*, golfio(a) *m,f*

**rethra** [ju'ri:θrə] *n Anat* uretra *f*

**rge** [ɜ:dʒ] **1** *n* impulso *m*, deseo *m* irresistible; **o have** *or* **feel an u.** **to do sth** sentir la necedad de hacer algo; **sexual urges** impulsos *pl* sexuales

**2** *vt* (a) *(encourage)* **to u.** **sb to do sth** instar a .guien a hacer algo (b) *(recommend)* rogar, pedir ncarecidamente (c) *(goad, incite)* **he urged his en into battle** incitó a sus hombres a entrar n batalla; **to u.** **a horse forward** espolear a n caballo

**urge on** *vt sep* alentar, animar; **to u.** **sb on to o sth** animar a alguien a hacer algo

**rgency** ['ɜ:dʒənsɪ] *n* urgencia *f*; **it's a mat-er of u.** es muy urgente

**rgent** ['ɜ:dʒənt] *adj* urgente; **to be in u. eed of sth** necesitar algo urgentemente; **this u.** es urgente

**rgently** ['ɜ:dʒəntlɪ] *adv* urgentemente

**rinal** [jə'raɪnəl] *n* urinario *m*

**rinary** ['jʊərɪnərɪ] *adj Anat* urinario(a)

**rinate** ['jʊərɪneɪt] *vi* orinar

**rine** ['jʊərɪn] *n* orina *f*

**rn** [ɜ:n] *n* urna *f*; **(tea) u.** = recipiente grande e metal con un grifo para el té

**rology** [jʊ'rɒlədʒɪ] *n Med* urología *f*

**Uruguay** ['jʊərəgwaɪ] *n* Uruguay

**ruguayan** [jʊərə'gwaɪən] *n & adj* uruuayo(a) *m,f*

**S** [ju:'es] **1** *n (abbr* **United States)** E.UU. *mpl*

**2** *adj* estadounidense

**s** *[stressed ʌs, unstressed əs] pron* (a) *(object)* nos; **he forgave our son but not US** perdonó a uestro hijo, pero a no nosotros; **she gave us e book** nos dio el libro; **she gave it to us** os lo dio

(b) *(after preposition)* nosotros

(c) *(as complement of verb to be)* nosotros; **it's s!** ¡somos nosotros!

**SA** [ju:es'eɪ] *n* (a) *(abbr* **United States f America)** EE.UU. *mpl* (b) *US (abbr* **nited States Army)** ejército *m* de los Es-dos Unidos

**sable** ['ju:zəbəl] *adj* utilizable; **it's no long-r u.** ya no sirve

**SAF** [ju:eser'ef] *n (abbr* **United States ir Force)** fuerzas *fpl* aéreas de los Estados nidos

**sage** ['ju:sɪdʒ] *n* (a) *(use) & Gram* uso *m* (b) *ustom)* uso *m*, costumbre *f*

**se 1** *n* [ju:s] (a) *(utilization)* uso *m*, utilización **to make (good) u. of sth** hacer (buen) uso algo; **to be in u.** estar en uso, usarse; **not to**

**be in u.**, **to be out of u.** *(method, site)* estar en desuso; **out of u.** *(sign)* no funciona; **directions** *or* **instructions for u.** instrucciones *fpl* de uso

(b) *(ability, permission to use)* **she has full u. of her faculties** está en plena posesión de sus facultades; **to have the u. of the bathroom** poder usar el cuarto de baño

(c) *(usefulness)* **to be of u.** ser útil; **can I be of any u. to you?** ¿te puedo ser útil en algo?; **it's not much u.** no sirve de mucho; *Fam* **he's no u.** es un inútil; **to have no u. for sth** no tener necesidad de algo; **it's no u. crying** llorar no sirve de nada; **it's no u., I can't do it!** ¡es inútil, no puedo hacerlo!; **what's the u. of worrying?** ¿de qué sirve preocuparse?

**2** *vt* [ju:z] (a) *(utilize)* usar, utilizar; **to u. force/diplomacy** hacer uso de la fuerza/la diplomacia; **he used every means at his disposal** empleó todos los medios a su alcance; **u. your head!** ¡piensa un poco!; *Fam* **I could u. some sleep** no me vendría mal dormir un poco

(b) *(exploit)* utilizar; **I feel I've been used** me siento utilizado

(c) *(consume) (drugs)* consumir; *(petrol, electricity)* funcionar con; **who has used all the coffee?** ¿quién ha gastado todo el café?

**3** *v aux* used to ['ju:stə]

---

As an auxiliary verb, always found in the form **used to**. Translated in Spanish either by a main verb in the imperfect or by the imperfect of **soler** plus an infinitive.

Como verbo auxiliar, aparece siempre en la forma **used to**. Se traduce al español por el verbo principal en pretérito imperfecto, o por el pretérito imperfecto de **soler** más infinitivo.

---

**we used to live abroad** antes vivíamos en el extranjero; **I used not to** *or* **didn't use to like him** antes no me caía bien; **I used to eat there a lot** solía comer allí muy a menudo; **things aren't what they used to be** las cosas ya no son lo que eran; **do you travel much? – I used to** ¿viajas mucho? – antes sí

▶**use up** *vt sep (food, fuel)* acabar; *(money, ideas)* agotar

**use-by date** ['ju:zbaɪdeɪt] *n Com* fecha *f* de caducidad

**used** [ju:zd] *adj* (a) *(second-hand)* usado(a); **a u. car** un coche usado *or* de segunda mano (b) [ju:st] *(accustomed)* **to be u. to (doing) sth** estar acostumbrado(a) a (hacer) algo; **to get u. to sth/sb** acostumbrarse a algo/alguien (c) *(exploited)* **to feel u.** sentirse utilizado(a) *or* manipulado(a)

**useful** ['ju:sfʊl] *adj* útil; **it will come in very u.** va a venir muy bien; **to make oneself u.** ayudar

**usefully** ['ju:sfəlı] *adv (profitably)* provechosamente

**usefulness** ['ju:sfʊlnıs] *n* utilidad *f*; **it has outlived its u.** ha dejado de ser útil

**useless** ['ju:slıs] *adj* (a) *(not useful)* inservible; **to be u.** *(system, method)* no servir para nada; **to be worse than u.** no servir de nada (b) *(incompetent)* **to be u. (at sth)** ser un/una inútil (para algo) (c) *(futile)* inútil

**user** ['ju:zə(r)] *n (of road, dictionary, computer)* usuario(a) *m,f*; *Fam (of drugs)* consumidor(ora) *m,f*

**user-friendly** [ju:zə'frendlı] *adj also Comptr* de fácil manejo

**usher** ['ʌʃə(r)] 1 *n (in court)* ujier *m*; *(in theatre, cinema)* acomodador *m*; *(at wedding)* = persona encargada de indicar a los invitados dónde deben sentarse

2 *vt* **to u. sb in** hacer pasar a alguien; **to u. sb out** acompañar a alguien afuera

**usherette** [ʌʃə'ret] *n Cin* acomodadora *f*

**USN** [ju:es'en] *n (abbr* **United States Navy)** armada *f* estadounidense

**USP** [ju:es'pi:] *n Com (abbr* **unique selling point** *or* **proposition)** rasgo *m* distintivo (del producto)

**USS** [ju:es'es] *n Naut (abbr* **United States Ship)** = título que precede a los nombres de buques de la marina estadounidense

**USSR** [ju:eses'ɑ:(r)] *n Formerly (abbr* **Union of Soviet Socialist Republics)** URSS *f*

**usual** ['ju:ʒʊəl] 1 *n Fam (in bar)* **the u.** lo de siempre

2 *adj* habitual, acostumbrado(a); **at the u. time** a la hora de siempre; **you're not your u.** cheery self today hoy no estás tan alegre como de costumbre; **it's not u. for him to be this late** no suele llegar tan tarde; **earlier/ later than u.** más pronto/tarde de lo normal; **as u.** como de costumbre

**usually** ['ju:ʒʊəlı] *adv* habitualmente, normalmente; **he was more than u. polite** estuvo más amable que de costumbre

**usurer** ['ju:ʒərə(r)] *n* usurero(a) *m,f*

**usurp** [ju:'zɜ:p] *vt* usurpar

**usurper** [ju:'zɜ:pə(r)] *n* usurpador(ora) *m,f*

**usury** ['ju:ʒʊrı] *n* usura *f*

**utensil** [ju:'tensəl] *n* utensilio *m*; **kitchen utensils** utensilios *mpl* de cocina

**uterus** ['ju:tərəs] *n Anat* útero *m*

**utilitarian** [ju:tılı'teərıən] 1 *n (in philosophy)* utilitarista *mf*

2 *adj* (a) *(approach)* pragmático(a); *(design)* funcional, práctico(a) (b) *(in philosophy)* utilitarista

**utility** [ju:'tılıtı] *n* (a) *(usefulness)* utilidad *f*; *Comptr* **u. program** utilidad *f*; **u. room** = cuarto utilizado para planchar, lavar, etc. (b) *(public)* **utilities** servicios *mpl* públicos (c) *US* **utilities** *(service charges)* servicio *m*

**utilize** ['ju:tılaız] *vt* utilizar

**utmost** ['ʌtməʊst] 1 *n* **to the u.** al máximo; **she did her u. to persuade them** hizo todo lo que pudo para convencerlos

2 *adj* (a) *(greatest)* sumo(a); **with the u. contempt** con el mayor desprecio; **it is of the u. importance that…** es de suma importancia que…; **with the u. ease** con suma facilidad (b) *(furthest)* **the u. ends of the earth** los últimos confines de la tierra

**utopia** [ju:'təʊpıə] *n* utopía *f*

**utopian** [ju:'təʊpıən] *n & adj* utópico(a) *m,f*

**utter¹** ['ʌtə(r)] *adj* total, completo(a); **it's u. madness** es una auténtica locura; **the film is u. rubbish** la película es una verdadera porquería

**utter²** *vt (cry)* lanzar, dar; *(word)* decir, pronunciar

**utterance** ['ʌtərəns] *n (act)* pronunciación *f*, mención *f*; *(words spoken)* expresión *f*; **to give utterance to sth** manifestar *or* expresar algo

**utterly** ['ʌtəlı] *adv* completamente, totalmente

**uttermost** ['ʌtəməʊst] = **utmost**

**UV** [ju:'vi:] *adj Phys (abbr* **ultra-violet)** ultravioleta; **UV rays** rayos *mpl* ultravioleta

**uvula** ['ju:vjələ] *n Anat* úvula *f*

**Uzbekistan** [ʊzbekı'stɑ:n] *n* Uzbekistán

# V

**V, v** [viː] *n* (**a**) *(letter)* V, v *f*; **V sign** *(for victory)* uve *f* de la victoria; *(as insult)* = gesto ofensivo que se forma mostrando el dorso de los dedos índice y corazón en forma de uve a la persona insultada (**b**) *(abbr* **very***)* muy (**c**) *(abbr* **versus***)* contra (**d**) *(abbr* **verse***) (pl* **vv***)* versículo *m*

**V** *Elec (abbr* **volt***)* V, voltio *m*; **240 V** 240 V

**VA** [viː'eɪ] *n US (abbr* **Veterans Administration***)* = organismo estadounidense que se ocupa de los veteranos de guerra

**vacancy** ['veɪkənsɪ] *n* (**a**) *(position, job)* (puesto *m*) vacante *f*; **to fill a v.** cubrir una vacante (**b**) *(at hotel)* habitación *f* libre; **no vacancies** *(sign)* completo

**vacant** ['veɪkənt] *adj* (**a**) *(seat, space)* libre; *(job)* vacante; **to be v.** *(of seat, space)* estar libre; **situations v.** *(in newspaper)* ofertas *fpl* de empleo (**b**) *(expression, look)* vacío(a), inexpresivo(a)

**vacantly** ['veɪkəntlɪ] *adv (absentmindedly)* distraídamente

**vacate** [və'keɪt] *vt (seat, flat)* dejar libre; *(one's post)* dejar vacante

**vacation** [və'keɪʃən] *n Br Univ & US* vacaciones *fpl*; *US* **to take a v.** tomarse unas vacaciones

**vaccinate** ['væksɪneɪt] *vt Med* vacunar

**vaccination** [væksɪ'neɪʃən] *n Med* vacunación *f*

**vaccine** ['væksiːn] *n Med* vacuna *f*

**vacillate** ['væsɪleɪt] *vi* vacilar, titubear (**between** entre)

**vacuous** ['vækjʊəs] *adj (remark, book, person)* vacuo(a), vacío(a); *(look, expression)* vacío(a), vago(a)

**vacuum** ['vækjʊm] **1** *n Phys* vacío *m*; **v. cleaner** aspiradora *f*, aspirador *m*; **v. flask** termo *m*
**2** *vt* pasar la aspiradora por

**vacuum-packed** [vækjʊm'pækt] *adj* envasado(a) al vacío

**vagabond** ['vægəbɒnd] *n* vagabundo(a) *m,f*

**vagary** ['veɪgərɪ] *n* **the vagaries of...** los avatares *or* caprichos de...

**vagina** [və'dʒaɪnə] *n* vagina *f*

**vagrancy** ['veɪgrənsɪ] *n Law* vagabundeo *m*

**vagrant** ['veɪgrənt] *n* mendigo(a) *m,f*, vagabundo(a) *m,f*

**vague** [veɪg] *adj (idea, feeling)* vago(a); *(shape, outline)* vago(a), borroso(a); **I haven't the vaguest idea** no tengo ni la más remota idea; **he was rather v. about it** no precisó mucho; **to bear a v. resemblance to sth/sb** parecerse *or* recordar vagamente a algo/alguien

**vaguely** ['veɪglɪ] *adv* vagamente

**vagueness** ['veɪgnɪs] *n* vaguedad *f*

**vain** [veɪn] **1** *n* **in v.** en vano
**2** *adj* (**a**) *(conceited)* vanidoso(a), vano(a) (**b**) *(hopeless)* vano(a)

**vale** [veɪl] *n Literary* valle *m*; *Fig* **v. of tears** valle de lágrimas

**Valencia** [və'lensɪə] *n* Valencia

**Valencian** [və'lensɪən] *n & adj* valenciano(a) *m,f*

**valency** ['veɪlənsɪ] *n Chem* valencia *f*

**valentine** ['væləntaɪn] *n* **v.** *(card)* = tarjeta para el día de los enamorados; **V.'s Day** día *m* de San Valentín, día *m* de los enamorados

**valet** ['væleɪ] *n* ayuda *m* de cámara

**valiant** ['vælɪənt] *adj Literary* valeroso(a)

**valiantly** ['vælɪəntlɪ] *adv* valerosamente

**valid** ['vælɪd] *adj* válido(a); **v. for six months** válido durante seis meses; **no longer v.** caducado(a)

**validate** ['vælɪdeɪt] *vt* validar

**validation** [vælɪ'deɪʃən] *n* validación *f*

**validity** [və'lɪdɪtɪ] *n* validez *f*

**valise** [væ'liːz] *n US (small suitcase)* maleta *f* de fin de semana

**valley** ['vælɪ] *(pl* **valleys***)* *n* valle *m*

**valour,** *US* **valor** ['vælə(r)] *n Literary* valor *m*

**valuable** ['væljʊəbəl] **1** *n* **valuables** objetos *mpl* de valor
**2** *adj* valioso(a)

**valuation** [væljʊ'eɪʃən] *n* (**a**) *(act)* tasación *f* (**b**) *(price)* valoración *f*

**value** ['væljuː] **1** *n* (**a**) *(worth)* valor *m*; **to be of v.** tener valor; **of great/little v.** muy/poco valioso(a); **of no v.** sin valor; **to be good/ poor v. (for money)** tener buena/mala relación calidad-precio; **to set a v. on sth** poner precio a algo; **to the v. of...** hasta un valor de...; **to make a v. judgment** hacer un juicio de valor **(b)** *(principle)* **values** valores *mpl*

**2** *vt* **(a)** *(evaluate)* valorar, tasar; **to get sth valued** pedir una valoración de algo **(b)** *(appreciate)* apreciar

**value-added tax** ['vælju:ædɪd'tæks] *n Fin* impuesto *m* sobre el valor añadido, IVA *m*

**valued** ['vælju:d] *adj (friend)* estimado(a), apreciado(a); *(contribution)* valioso(a)

**valueless** ['vælju:lɪs] *adj* sin valor

**valve** [vælv] *n Anat & Tech* válvula *f*; *Mus* pistón *m*

**vampire** ['væmpaɪə(r)] *n* vampiro *m*; **v. bat** vampiro *m*

**van¹** [væn] *n* **(a)** *Aut* camioneta *f*, furgoneta *f*; **v. driver** conductor(ora) *m,f* de camioneta **(b)** *Br Rail* furgón *m*

**van²** = **vanguard**

**Vancouver** [væn'ku:vər] *n* Vancouver

**vandal** ['vændəl] *n* vándalo *m*, gamberro(a) *m,f*

**vandalism** ['vændəlɪzəm] *n* vandalismo *m*, gamberrismo *m*

**vandalize** ['vændəlaɪz] *vt* destrozar

**vane** [veɪn] *n (for indicating wind direction)* veleta *f*

**vanguard** ['vænɡɑ:d] *n* vanguardia *f*; **to be in the v.** ir en vanguardia, estar a la vanguardia

**vanilla** [və'nɪlə] *n* vainilla *f*

**vanish** ['vænɪʃ] *vi* desaparecer; **to v. into thin air** esfumarse

**vanishing** ['vænɪʃɪŋ] *adj* **to do a v. act** *(disappear)* desaparecer; **v. point** punto *m* de fuga

**vanity** ['vænɪtɪ] *n* vanidad *f*; **v. case** bolsa *f* de aseo

**vanquish** ['væŋkwɪʃ] *vt Literary* vencer, derrotar

**vantage point** ['vɑ:ntɪdʒ'pɔɪnt] *n* atalaya *f*; *Fig* posición *f* aventajada

**Vanuatu** [vænu:'ætu:] *n* Vanuatu

**vapid** ['væpɪd] *adj* vacuo(a), insustancial

**vaporize** ['veɪpəraɪz] **1** *vt* evaporar

**2** *vi* evaporarse

**vapour** ['veɪpə(r)] *n* vapor *m*; **v. trail** *(from plane)* estela *f*

**variable** ['veərɪəbəl] **1** *n* variable *f*

**2** *adj* variable; *Ind* **v. costs** costes *mpl* variables

**variance** ['veərɪəns] *n* **to be at v. with sth/sb** discrepar de algo/alguien

**variant** ['veərɪənt] **1** *n* variante *f*

**2** *adj* alternativo(a); **v. spelling** variante *f* ortográfica

**variation** [veərɪ'eɪʃən] *n* variación *f*

**varicose vein** ['værɪkəʊs'veɪn] *n Med* variz *f*, vena *f* varicosa

**varied** ['veərɪd] *adj* variado(a)

**variegated** ['veərɪɡeɪtɪd] *adj* abigarrado(a), colorido(a)

**variety** [və'raɪətɪ] *n* **(a)** *(diversity)* variedad *f*; **a v. of reasons** diversos motivos; *Prov* **v. is the spice of life** en la variedad está el gusto **(b)** *(of plant)* variedad *f* **(c)** *Th* variedades *fpl*; **v. show** espectáculo *m* de variedades

**various** ['veərɪəs] *adj (different)* diversos(as), diferentes; *(several)* varios(as); **at v. times** en distintas ocasiones

**variously** ['veərɪəslɪ] *adv* **v. described as a hero or a bandit** descrito por unos como héroe y por otros como bandido

**varnish** ['vɑ:nɪʃ] **1** *n (for wood, oil painting)* barniz *m*; *(for nails)* esmalte *m* (de uñas)

**2** *vt (wood)* barnizar; **to v. one's nails** darse esmalte en las uñas

▸**varnish over** *vt sep Fig* maquillar

**vary** ['veərɪ] **1** *vt* variar

**2** *vi* variar **(in** de); **opinions v.** hay diversas opiniones

**varying** ['veərɪŋ] *adj* diverso(a), variado(a)

**vase** [vɑ:z] *n* jarrón *m*

**vasectomy** [və'sektəmɪ] *n Med* vasectomía *f*

**Vaseline®** ['væsəli:n] *n* vaselina® *f*

**vast** [vɑ:st] *adj (area)* vasto(a); *(majority, number)* inmenso(a)

**vastly** ['vɑ:stlɪ] *adv* enormemente

**VAT** [vi:eɪ'ti:] *n (abbr* **value added tax)** IVA *m*

**vat** [væt] *n (container)* tina *f*, cuba *f*

**Vatican** ['vætɪkən] *n* **the V.** el Vaticano; **V. City** Ciudad *f* del Vaticano

**vaudeville** ['vɔ:dəvɪl] *n Th* vodevil *m*

**vault¹** [vɔ:lt] *n* **(a)** *Archit* bóveda *f* **(b)** *(cellar)* sótano *m*; *(for burial)* cripta *f*; *(of bank)* cámara *f* acorazada

**vault²** *vt & vi* saltar

**vaulted** ['vɔ:ltɪd] *adj (ceiling)* abovedado(a)

**vaulting horse** ['vɔ:ltɪŋ'hɔ:s] *n* plinto *m*

**vaunt** [vɔ:nt] *vt* cacarear; **his much vaunted reputation as...** su cacareada reputación de...

**VC** [vi:'si:] *n* **(a)** *(abbr* **Vice-Chairman)** vicepresidente(a) *m,f* **(b)** *Br Mil (abbr* **Victoria Cross)** ≃ medalla *f* al mérito militar

**VCR** [vi:si:'ɑ:(r)] *n (abbr* **video cassette recorder)** *(aparato m de)* vídeo *m*

**VD** [vi:'di:] *n (abbr* **venereal disease)** enfermedad *f* venérea

**VDU** [vi:di:'ju:] *n Comptr (abbr* **visual display unit)** monitor *m*

**veal** [vi:l] *n (carne f de)* ternera *f*

**vector** ['vektə(r)] *n Math & Med* vector *m*

**veer** ['vɪə(r)] *vi* torcer, girar; **to v. to the left/ right** torcer a la izquierda/derecha; *Fig* **the**

**party has veered to the left** el partido ha dado un giro a la izquierda

▸**veer round** vi (of wind) cambiar de dirección

**veg** [vedʒ] n Br Fam verduras fpl; **meat and two v.** carne f con dos tipos de verdura

**vegan** ['viːgən] n vegetariano(a) m,f estricto(a) (que no come ningún producto de origen animal)

**vegetable** ['vedʒtəbəl] **1** n (a) (plant) hortaliza f; **vegetables** verdura f, verduras fpl; **eat up your vegetables** cómete la verdura; **v. garden** huerto m; **v. oil** aceite m vegetal **(b)** (brain-damaged person) vegetal m

**vegetarian** [vedʒɪ'teərɪən] n & adj vegetariano(a) m,f

**vegetate** ['vedʒɪteɪt] vi vegetar

**vegetation** [vedʒɪ'teɪʃən] n vegetación f

**vehemence** ['viːɪməns] n vehemencia f

**vehement** ['viːɪmənt] adj vehemente

**vehicle** ['viːɪkəl] n also Fig vehículo m

**vehicular** [vɪ'hɪkjʊlə(r)] adj de vehículos; **v. traffic** tráfico m de vehículos

**veil** [veɪl] **1** n velo m; Fig **a v. of smoke** una cortina de humo; Fig **to draw a v. over sth** correr un tupido velo sobre algo; Fig **under a v. of secrecy** rodeado(a) de un halo de secreto or misterio

**2** vt cubrir con un velo; Fig **veiled in secrecy** rodeado(a) de un halo secreto or misterio

**veiled** [veɪld] adj **(a)** (wearing veil) **to be v.** llevar velo **(b)** Fig (threat, reference) velado(a)

**vein** [veɪn] n **(a)** Anat vena f; (of leaf) nervio m **(b)** (in rock) filón m, veta f; (in wood, marble) veta f **(c)** (idioms) **in a lighter v.** en un tono más ligero; **in a similar v.** en la misma vena, en el mismo tono

**Velcro®** ['velkrəʊ] n velcro® m

**vellum** ['veləm] n pergamino m, vitela f; **v. (paper)** papel m pergamino

**velocity** [vɪ'lɒsɪti] n velocidad f

**velvet** ['velvɪt] n terciopelo m; **v. jacket** chaqueta f de terciopelo

**velveteen** [velvɪ'tiːn] n pana f lisa

**velvety** ['velvɪti] adj aterciopelado(a)

**venal** ['viːnəl] adj corrupto(a)

**vendetta** [ven'detə] n **to carry on a v. against sb** llevar a cabo una campaña para destruir a alguien

**vending machine** ['vendɪŋməˈʃiːn] n máquina f expendedora

**vendor** ['vendɔː(r)] n vendedor(ora) m,f

**veneer** [və'nɪə(r)] n laminado m, chapa f; Fig fachada f, pátina f

**venerable** ['venərəbəl] adj venerable

**venerate** ['venəreɪt] vt venerar

**veneration** [venə'reɪʃən] n veneración f

**venereal** [vɪ'nɪərɪəl] adj venéreo(a); **v. disease** enfermedad f venérea

**Venetian** [vɪ'niːʃən] **1** n veneciano(a) m,f

**2** adj veneciano(a); **V. blind** persiana f veneciana

**Venezuela** [vene'zweɪlə] n Venezuela

**Venezuelan** [vene'zweɪlən] n & adj venezolano(a) m,f

**vengeance** ['vendʒəns] n venganza f; **to take v. on sb** vengarse de alguien; Fig **the problem has returned with a v.** el problema se ha presentado de nuevo con agravantes

**vengeful** ['vendʒfʊl] adj vengativo(a)

**venial** ['viːnɪəl] adj (sin) venial; (error) leve

**Venice** ['venɪs] n Venecia

**venison** ['venɪsən] n (carne f de) venado m

**venom** ['venəm] n also Fig veneno m

**venomous** ['venəməs] adj venenoso(a); Fig (look, criticism) envenenado(a), ponzoñoso(a)

**vent** [vent] **1** n (orifice m de) ventilación f; Fig **she gave v. to her feelings** se desahogó, dio rienda suelta a sus sentimientos

**2** vt **she vented her anger on him** descargó su ira sobre él

**ventilate** ['ventɪleɪt] vt ventilar

**ventilation** [ventɪ'leɪʃən] n ventilación f

**ventilator** ['ventɪleɪtə(r)] n ventilador m

**ventriloquism** [ven'trɪləkwɪzəm] n ventriloquía f

**ventriloquist** [ven'trɪləkwɪst] n ventrílocuo(a) m,f; **v.'s dummy** muñeco m de ventrílocuo

**venture** ['ventʃə(r)] **1** n (undertaking) aventura f, iniciativa f; (in business) empresa f, operación f; Fin **v. capital** capital m de riesgo

**2** vt (stake) arriesgar; (comment) aventurar; **to v. to do sth** aventurarse a hacer algo; Prov **nothing ventured, nothing gained** el que no se arriesga no pasa la mar

**3** vi aventurarse

▸**venture on, venture upon** vt insep aventurarse en, meterse en

**venue** ['venjuː] n (for meeting) lugar m; (for concert) local m, sala f; (for football match) estadio m

**Venus** ['viːnəs] n (goddess) Venus f; (planet) Venus m

**veracity** [və'ræsɪti] n Formal veracidad f

**veranda(h)** [və'rændə] n porche m, galería f

**verb** [vɜːb] n verbo m

**verbal** ['vɜːbəl] adj verbal; **v. abuse** insultos mpl

**verbalize** ['vɜːbəlaɪz] vt expresar con palabras

**verbally** ['vɜːbəli] adv de palabra

**verbatim** [vɜː'beɪtɪm] **1** adj literal

**2** adv literalmente

**verbiage** ['vɜːbɪɪdʒ] n palabrería f, verborrea f

**verbose** [vɜː'bəʊs] *adj* verboso(a), prolijo(a)

**verbosity** [vɜː'bɒsɪtɪ] *n* verbosidad *f*, verborrea *f*

**verdict** ['vɜːdɪkt] *n Law & Fig* veredicto *m*; **to return a v. of guilty/not guilty** pronunciar un veredicto de culpabilidad/inocencia; **what's your v. on the play?** ¿qué te ha parecido la obra?

**verge** [vɜːdʒ] *n (edge)* borde *m*, margen *m*; *Fig* **on the v. of…** al borde de…; *Fig* **to be on the v. of doing sth** estar a punto de hacer algo

►**verge on** *vt insep* rayar en; **verging on…** rayano(a) *or* rayando en; **she was verging on hysteria** estaba a punto de la histeria

**verger** ['vɜːdʒə(r)] *n (in Church of England)* sacristán *m*

**verifiable** [verɪ'faɪəbəl] *adj* verificable

**verification** [verɪfɪ'keɪʃən] *n* verificación *f*

**verify** ['verɪfaɪ] *vt* verificar

**verisimilitude** [verɪsɪ'mɪlɪtjuːd] *n Formal* verosimilitud *f*

**veritable** ['verɪtəbəl] *adj Formal* verdadero(a)

**vermilion** [və'mɪljən] **1** *n* bermellón *m*
**2** *adj* bermejo(a)

**vermin** ['vɜːmɪn] *npl (insects)* bichos *mpl*, sabandijas *fpl*; *(bigger animals)* alimañas *fpl*; *Fig (people)* escoria *f*, gentuza *f*

**vermouth** ['vɜːməθ] *n* vermú *m*, vermut *m*

**vernacular** [və'nækjʊlə(r)] **1** *n Ling* lengua *f* vernácula; *(spoken language)* lenguaje *m* de la calle; **in the local v.** en el habla local
**2** *adj* vernáculo(a)

**verruca** [ve'ruːkə] *n Med* verruga *f (especialmente en las plantas de los pies)*

**versatile** ['vɜːsətaɪl] *adj (person)* polifacético(a), versátil; *(object)* polivalente, versátil

**versatility** [vɜːsə'tɪlɪtɪ] *n (of person)* carácter *m* polifacético, versatilidad *f*; *(of object)* polivalencia *f*

**verse** [vɜːs] *n (a) (poetry)* poesía *f*, verso *m (b) (stanza)* estrofa *f (c) (of Bible)* versículo *m*

**versed** [vɜːst] *adj* **to be v. in sth** estar versado(a) en algo

**version** ['vɜːʃən] *n* versión *f*; **the deluxe/economy v.** *(of car, computer)* el modelo de lujo/económico

**verso** ['vɜːsəʊ] *n Typ (of page)* verso *m*

**versus** ['vɜːsəs] *prep Law & Sport* contra

**vertebra** ['vɜːtɪbrə] *(pl* **vertebrae** ['vɜːtɪbriː]) *n Anat* vértebra *f*

**vertebral column** ['vɜːtɪbrəl'kɒləm] *n Anat (spine)* columna *f* vertebral

**vertebrate** ['vɜːtɪbrɪt] *n & adj* vertebrado(a) *m,f*

**vertex** ['vɜːteks] *(pl* **vertices** ['vɜːtɪsiːz]) *n Math* vértice *m*

**vertical** ['vɜːtɪkəl] *n & adj* vertical *f*

**vertically** ['vɜːtɪklɪ] *adv* verticalmente

**vertigo** ['vɜːtɪgəʊ] *n Med* vértigo *m*

**verve** [vɜːv] *n* nervio *m*, energía *f*

**very** ['verɪ] **1** *adv* **(a)** *(extremely)* muy; **v. good/little** muy bueno/poco; **v. much** mucho; **it isn't v. difficult** no es muy difícil; **are you hungry? – yes, v.** ¿tienes hambre? – sí, mucha; *Rad* **v. high frequency** frecuencia *f* muy alta
  **(b)** *(emphatic use)* **the v. first/best** el primero/el mejor de todos; **at the v. most** como muy mucho; **at the v. least/latest** como muy poco/muy tarde; **the v. same day** justo ese mismo día; **I v. nearly died** estuve en un tris de morir; **the v. next day** precisamente el día siguiente

**2** *adj (emphatic use)* **in this v. house** en esta misma casa; **this v. day** este mismo día; **those were his v. words** esas fueron sus palabras exactas; **at the v. beginning** al principio del todo; **the v. thought of it was enough to turn my stomach** sólo de pensarlo se me revolvía el estómago

**vessel** ['vesəl] *n* **(a)** *Naut* buque *m*, navío *m* **(b)** *(receptacle)* vasija *f*, recipiente *m* **(c)** *Anat* vaso *m*

**vest** [vest] *n Br (undershirt)* camiseta *f* (interior) *or* de tirantes; *US (waistcoat)* chaleco *m*

**vested** ['vestɪd] *adj* **to have a v. interest in sth/in doing sth** tener intereses creados en algo/en hacer algo

**vestibule** ['vestɪbjuːl] *n* vestíbulo *m*

**vestige** ['vestɪdʒ] *n* vestigio *m*

**vestments** ['vestmənts] *npl Rel* vestiduras *fpl* (sacerdotales)

**vestry** ['vestrɪ] *n Rel* sacristía *f*

**vet¹** [vet] *n* veterinario(a) *m,f*

**vet²** *(pt & pp* **vetted**) *vt (person)* someter a investigación; *(application)* investigar; *(speech, book, film)* inspeccionar, examinar

**vet³** *n US Mil Fam (veteran)* excombatiente *mf*, veterano(a) *m,f*

**veteran** ['vetərən] **1** *n Mil* excombatiente *mf*, veterano(a) *m,f*; *Fig* veterano(a) *m,f*
**2** *adj* veterano(a)

**veterinarian** [vetərɪ'neərɪən] *n US* veterinario(a) *m,f*

**veterinary** ['vetərɪnərɪ] *adj* veterinario(a); **v. medicine** veterinaria *f*; **v. surgeon** veterinario(a) *m,f*

**veto** ['viːtəʊ] **1** *n (pl* **vetoes**) veto *m*; **right** *or* **power of v.** derecho *m* de veto; **to impose a v. on sth** vetar algo
**2** *vt* vetar

**vetting** ['vetɪŋ] *n* investigación *f* (del historial) personal

**vex** [veks] *vt* molestar, disgustar

**vexation** [vek'seɪʃən] *n (annoyance)* disgusto *m*, molestia *f*; *(anger)* enfado *m*

**vexatious** [vek'seɪʃəs] *adj* molesto(a)

**vexed** [vekst] *adj* (a) *(angry)* disgustado(a) (b) **a v. question** una cuestión controvertida

**VHF** [viːeɪtʃ'ef] *adj Rad (abbr* **very high frequency)** VHF *f*

**VHS** [viːeɪtʃ'es] *n TV* VHS *m*

**via** ['vaɪə] *prep (travel)* vía; *(using)* a través de

**viability** [vaɪə'bɪlɪtɪ] *n* viabilidad *f*

**viable** ['vaɪəbəl] *adj* viable

**viaduct** ['vaɪədʌkt] *n* viaducto *m*

**vibes** [vaɪbz] *npl Fam* rollo *m*, vibraciones *fpl*; **good/bad v.** buen/mal rollo

**vibrant** ['vaɪbrənt] *adj (scene, city)* animado(a); *(colours)* vivo(a), brillante; *(personality)* pujante

**vibrate** [vaɪ'breɪt] *vi* vibrar

**vibration** [vaɪ'breɪʃən] *n* vibración *f*

**vibrator** [vaɪ'breɪtə(r)] *n* vibrador *m*

**vicar** ['vɪkə(r)] *n (in Church of England)* párroco *m*

**vicarage** ['vɪkərɪdʒ] *n (in Church of England)* casa *f* del párroco

**vicarious** [vɪ'keərɪəs] *adj* indirecto(a)

**vice¹** [vaɪs] *n (immorality)* vicio *m*; **the V. Squad** la brigada antivicio

**vice²** *n (for wood or metalwork)* torno *m* or tornillo *m* de banco

**vice-chairman** [vaɪs'tʃeəmən] *n* vicepresidente *m*

**vice-chairwoman** [vaɪs'tʃeəwʊmən] *n* vicepresidenta *f*

**vice-president** [vaɪs'prezɪdənt] *n* vicepresidente(a) *m,f*

**viceroy** ['vaɪsrɔɪ] *n (pl* **viceroys)** *n* virrey *m*

**vice versa** [vaɪs'vɜːsə] *adv* viceversa

**vicinity** [vɪ'sɪnɪtɪ] *n* cercanías *fpl*, inmediaciones *fpl*; **in the v.** en las cercanías; **a sum in the v. of £25,000** una cantidad que ronda las 25.000 libras

**vicious** ['vɪʃəs] *adj* (a) *(violent) (blow, kick, attack)* brutal; *(struggle, fight)* feroz; *(person)* cruel (b) *(malicious, cruel) (comment, criticism)* despiadado(a); *(gossip)* malintencionado(a); *(person)* cruel; **a v. circle** un círculo vicioso

**vicissitude** [vɪ'sɪsɪtjuːd] *n Formal* vicisitud *f*

**victim** ['vɪktɪm] *n* víctima *f*; **to be the v. of** ser víctima de; **to fall v. to sb's charms** caer rendido(a) ante los encantos de alguien

**victimization** [vɪktɪmaɪ'zeɪʃən] *n* persecución *f*, trato *m* injusto

**victimize** ['vɪktɪmaɪz] *vt* perseguir, tratar injustamente; **he was victimized at school** en la escuela se metían con él

**victor** ['vɪktə(r)] *n* vencedor(ora) *m,f*

**Victorian** [vɪk'tɔːrɪən] *n & adj* victoriano(a) *m,f*

**victorious** [vɪk'tɔːrɪəs] *adj* victorioso(a); **to be v. over sb** triunfar sobre alguien

**victory** ['vɪktərɪ] *n* victoria *f*; **v. celebrations** celebración *f* de la victoria

**victuals** ['vɪtəlz] *npl Old-fashioned (food)* vituallas *fpl*

**video** ['vɪdɪəʊ] 1 *n (pl* **videos)** *(medium)* vídeo *m*; *(cassette)* cinta *f* de vídeo; *(recorder)* (aparato *m* de) vídeo *m*; **to have sth on v.** tener algo (grabado) en vídeo; **v. camera** cámara *f* de vídeo; **v. cassette** cinta *f* de vídeo; **v. (cassette) recorder** (aparato *m* de) vídeo *m*; **v. game** videojuego *m*; **v. tape** cinta *f* de vídeo

2 *vt* (a) *(record)* grabar (en vídeo) (b) *(film)* hacer un vídeo de

**vie** [vaɪ] *(pt & pp* **vied** [vaɪd]*) vi* **to v. with sb (for sth/to do sth)** rivalizar con alguien (por algo/para hacer algo)

**Vienna** [vɪ'enə] *n* Viena

**Viennese** [vɪə'niːz] *n & adj* vienés(esa) *m,f*

**Vietnam** [vɪet'næm] *n* Vietnam; **the V. War** la guerra de Vietnam

**Vietnamese** [vɪetnə'miːz] 1 *n* (a) *(person)* vietnamita *mf* (b) *(language)* vietnamita *m*

2 *npl* **the V.** los vietnamitas

2 *adj* vietnamita

**view** [vjuː] 1 *n* (a) *(sight)* vista *f*; **in v.** a la vista; **in full v. of** delante de, a la vista de; **out of v.** fuera de la vista (b) *(scene, prospect)* vista *f*; **a room with a v.** una habitación con vistas; **to have a good v. of sth** tener una buena vista de algo; *Fig* **in v. of...** *(considering)* en vista de... (c) *(opinion)* opinión *f*; **in my v.** en mi opinión, a mi parecer (d) *(intention)* **with this in v.** teniendo esto en cuenta; **with a v. to doing sth** con vistas a hacer algo

2 *vt* (a) *(inspect, look at)* ver (b) *(consider)* ver, considerar; **she viewed it as a mistake** lo veía or consideraba un error; **to v. sth with horror/delight** contemplar algo con horror/placer

**viewer** ['vjuːə(r)] *n* (a) *TV* telespectador(ora) *m,f*, televidente *mf* (b) *Phot (for slides)* visor *m*

**viewfinder** ['vjuːfaɪndə(r)] *n Phot* visor *m*

**viewpoint** ['vjuːpɔɪnt] *n* punto *m* de vista

**vigil** ['vɪdʒɪl] *n* vigilia *f*; **to keep v.** observar vigilia

**vigilance** ['vɪdʒɪləns] *n* vigilancia *f*

**vigilant** ['vɪdʒɪlənt] *adj* alerta

**vigilante** [vɪdʒɪ'læntɪ] *n* miembro *m* de una patrulla de vecinos

**vignette** [vɪn'jet] *n Phot* viñeta *f*; *Fig (picture)* escena *f*; *(in writing)* retrato *m*, semblanza *f*

**vigorous** ['vɪgərəs] *adj* (a) *(strong and healthy)* vigoroso(a) (b) *(energetic)* enérgico(a); *(lifestyle)* dinámico(a); *(exercise)* intenso(a) **(c)** *(forceful)* fuerte

**vigour** ['vɪɡə(r)] *n (of person)* vigor *m; (of denial, criticism)* rotundidad *f*, fuerza *f*

**Viking** ['vaɪkɪŋ] *n & adj* vikingo(a) *m,f*

**vile** [vaɪl] *adj (despicable)* vil; *Fam (awful)* horroroso(a), espantoso(a)

**vilification** [vɪlɪfɪ'keɪʃən] *n* vilipendio *m*

**vilify** ['vɪlɪfaɪ] *vt* vilipendiar, denigrar

**villa** ['vɪlə] *n (in country)* villa *f; (in town)* chalé *m*

**village** ['vɪlɪdʒ] *n* pueblo *m; (smaller)* aldea *f;* **v. idiot** tonto(a) *m,f* del pueblo

**villager** ['vɪlɪdʒə(r)] *n* lugareño(a) *m,f*

**villain** ['vɪlən] *n (scoundrel)* canalla *mf*, villano(a) *m,f; Th & Cin* malo *m; Hum* **the v. of the piece** el malo de la película

**villainous** ['vɪlənəs] *adj* vil, infame

**villainy** ['vɪlənɪ] *n* villanía *f*, infamia *f*

**Vilnius** ['vɪlnɪəs] *n* Vilna, Vilnius

**vindicate** ['vɪndɪkeɪt] *vt (decision, action)* justificar; *(person)* dar la razón a

**vindication** [vɪndɪ'keɪʃən] *n (of decision, action)* justificación *f; (of person)* rehabilitación *f*

**vindictive** [vɪn'dɪktɪv] *adj* vengativo(a)

**vine** [vaɪn] *n (in vineyard)* vid *f; (decorative)* parra *f*

**vinegar** ['vɪnɪɡə(r)] *n* vinagre *m*

**vineyard** ['vɪnjəd] *n* viñedo *m*

**vintage** ['vɪntɪdʒ] *n (crop)* cosecha *f; Fig* **a v. year for comedy** un año excepcional en cuanto a comedias; **v. car** coche *m* antiguo *or* de época *(de entre 1919 y 1930);* **v. wine** vino *m* de gran reserva

**vinyl** ['vaɪnɪl] *n* vinilo *m*

**viola** [vɪ'əʊlə] *n* viola *f*

**violate** ['vaɪəleɪt] *vt (rule, law, agreement)* violar

**violation** [vaɪə'leɪʃən] *n (of rule, law, agreement)* violación *f*

**violence** ['vaɪələns] *n* violencia *f*

**violent** ['vaɪələnt] *adj* violento(a); **to take a v. dislike to sb** coger una enorme antipatía a alguien

**violently** ['vaɪələntlɪ] *adv* violentamente; **to be v. ill** vomitar muchísimo

**violet** ['vaɪələt] **1** *n (plant)* violeta *f; (colour)* violeta *m*

**2** *adj* **v.(-coloured)** (de color) violeta

**violin** [vaɪə'lɪn] *n* violín *m*

**violinist** ['vaɪə'lɪnɪst] *n* violinista *mf*

**VIP** [viː'aɪ'piː] *n (abbr* **very important person)** VIP *mf;* **V. lounge** sala *f* VIP; **to get V. treatment** recibir tratamiento de persona importante

**viper** ['vaɪpə(r)] *n* víbora *f*

**viral** ['vaɪrəl] *adj Med* vírico(a), viral

**virgin** ['vɜːdʒɪn] **1** *n* virgen *mf;* **the (Blessed) V.** la (Santísima) Virgen; **the V. Islands** las Islas

Vírgenes

**2** *adj* virgen

**Virginia** [vɜː'dʒɪnjə] *n* Virginia

**virginity** [və'dʒɪnɪtɪ] *n* virginidad *f*

**Virgo** ['vɜːɡəʊ] *n (sign of zodiac)* virgo *m;* **to be (a) V.** ser virgo

**virile** ['vɪraɪl] *adj* viril

**virility** [vɪ'rɪlɪtɪ] *n* virilidad *f*

**virology** [vaɪ'rɒlədʒɪ] *n Med* virología *f*

**virtual** ['vɜːtjʊəl] *adj* virtual; **the v. extinction of the wild variety** la práctica desaparición de la variedad silvestre; **it's a v. impossibility** es virtualmente imposible; **the organization was in a state of v. collapse** la organización se hallaba prácticamente al borde del hundimiento; *Comptr* **v. reality** realidad *f* virtual

**virtually** ['vɜːtjʊəlɪ] *adv* virtualmente, prácticamente

**virtue** ['vɜːtjuː] *n* virtud *f;* **by v. of** en virtud de; **to make a v. of necessity** hacer de la necesidad una virtud; **it has the added v. of being quicker** cuenta con la virtud añadida de ser más rápido(a)

**virtuoso** [vɜːtjʊ'əʊzəʊ] *(pl* **virtuosos** *or* **virtuosi** [vɜːtjʊ'əʊziː]) *n Mus* virtuoso(a) *m,f*

**virtuous** ['vɜːtjʊəs] *adj* virtuoso(a)

**virulent** ['vɪr(j)ʊlənt] *adj* virulento(a)

**virus** ['vaɪrəs] *n Med & Comptr* virus *m inv*

**visa** ['viːzə] *n* visado *m, Am* visa *f*

**vis-à-vis** ['viːzɑːˈviː] *prep (in comparison with)* en comparación con, frente a; *(in relation to)* en relación con, con relación *or* respecto a

**visceral** ['vɪsərəl] *adj* visceral

**viscount** ['vaɪkaʊnt] *n* vizconde *m*

**viscous** ['vɪskəs] *adj* viscoso(a)

**visibility** [vɪzɪ'bɪlɪtɪ] *n* visibilidad *f;* **v. was down to a few yards** no se veía más allá de unos pocos metros

**visible** ['vɪzɪbəl] *adj* visible

**visibly** ['vɪzɪblɪ] *adv* visiblemente

**vision** ['vɪʒən] *n* **(a)** *(eyesight)* visión *f*, vista *f;* **to have good/poor v.** estar bien/mal de la vista **(b)** *(plan)* concepto *m*, imagen *f;* **man/ woman of v.** hombre *m*/mujer *f* con visión de futuro **(c)** *(apparition)* visión *f*, aparición *f;* **to have** *or* **see visions** ver visiones; **I had visions of being left homeless** ya me veía en la calle

**visionary** ['vɪʒənərɪ] *n & adj* visionario(a) *m,f*

**visit** ['vɪzɪt] **1** *n* visita *f;* **to pay sb a v.** hacer una visita a alguien; **to be on a v.** estar de visita

**2** *vt* visitar

**3** *vi* **to be visiting** estar de visita

**visiting** ['vɪzɪtɪŋ] **1** *n* **v. card** tarjeta *f* de visita; **v. hours** horas *fpl* de visita; *Law* **v. rights** *(of divorced parent)* derecho *m* de visita (a los hijos)

**2** *adj (team)* visitante; **v. lecturer** profesor(ora) *m,f* invitado(a)

**visitor** ['vɪzɪtə(r)] *n (guest, in hospital)* visita *f; (tourist)* turista *mf*, visitante *mf*; **visitors' book** libro *m* de visitas

**visor** ['vaɪzə(r)] *n (of helmet, cap)* visera *f*

**vista** ['vɪstə] *n* vista *f*, panorama *m; Fig* horizonte *m*

**visual** ['vɪʒʊəl] *adj* visual; **the v. arts** las artes plásticas; **v. aids** medios *mpl* visuales; *Comptr* **v. display unit** monitor *m*

**visualize** ['vɪʒʊəlaɪz] *vt (imagine)* visualizar; *(foresee)* prever

**visually** ['vɪʒʊəlɪ] *adv* visualmente; **the v. handicapped** las personas con discapacidades visuales

**vital** ['vaɪtəl] *adj* **(a)** *(essential)* vital; **v. organ** órgano *m* vital; **v. statistics** *Hum (of woman)* medidas *fpl* **(b)** *(vigorous)* vital, lleno(a) de vida

**vitality** [vaɪ'tælɪtɪ] *n* vitalidad *f*

**vitally** ['vaɪtəlɪ] *adv* **supplies are v. needed** se necesitan suministros urgentemente; **v. important** de importancia vital

**vitamin** ['vɪtəmɪn, *US* 'vaɪtəmɪn] *n* vitamina *f*; **with added vitamins** enriquecido(a) con vitaminas

**vitreous** ['vɪtrɪəs] *adj* **v. enamel** esmalte *m* (vítreo); *Anat* **v. humour** humor *m* vítreo

**vitriol** ['vɪtrɪəl] *n (acid)* vitriolo *m; Fig (nasty remarks)* causticidad *f*

**vitriolic** [vɪtrɪ'ɒlɪk] *adj* cáustico(a), corrosivo(a)

**vituperative** [vɪ'tju:pərətɪv] *adj Formal* injurioso(a)

**viva** ['vaɪvə] *n Univ* **v. (voce)** examen *m* oral

**vivacious** [vɪ'veɪʃəs] *adj* vivaracho(a), vivaz

**vivacity** [vɪ'væsɪtɪ] *n* vivacidad *f*

**vivid** ['vɪvɪd] *adj (description, memory, impression)* vívido(a); *(imagination)* muy vivo(a); *(colours)* vivo(a)

**vividly** ['vɪvɪdlɪ] *adv (remember, describe)* vívidamente

**vivisection** [vɪvɪ'sekʃən] *n* vivisección *f*

**vixen** ['vɪksən] *n* zorra *f*

**viz** [vɪz] *adv (abbr* **videlicet)** a saber

**VOA** [vi:əʊ'eɪ] *n US (abbr* **Voice of America)** = cadena de radio exterior estadounidense

**vocabulary** [və'kæbjʊlərɪ] *n* vocabulario *m*

**vocal** ['vəʊkəl] **1** *n Mus* **vocals** voces *fpl*; **on vocals** como vocalista

**2 (a)** *adj (music)* vocal; *Anat* **v. cords** cuerdas *fpl* vocales **(b)** *(outspoken)* vehemente, explícito(a); **to be very v. in one's criticism** expresar las críticas muy a las claras

**vocalist** ['vəʊkəlɪst] *n Mus* vocalista *mf*

**vocation** [vəʊ'keɪʃən] *n* vocación *f*; **to have a v. (for sth)** tener vocación (para algo)

**vocational** [vəʊ'keɪʃənəl] *adj (course, qualification)* de formación profesional; **v. training** formación *f* profesional

**vocative** ['vɒkətɪv] *Gram* **1** *n* vocativo *m*

**2** *adj* vocativo(a)

**vociferous** [və'sɪfərəs] *adj* ruidoso(a), vehemente

**vociferously** [və'sɪfərəslɪ] *adv* ruidosamente, vehementemente

**vodka** ['vɒdkə] *n* vodka *m*

**vogue** [vəʊg] *n* **to be in v.** estar en boga

**voice** [vɔɪs] **1** *n* **(a)** *(of person)* voz *f*; **to raise/lower one's v.** levantar/bajar la voz; **at the top of one's v.** a voz en grito; **to lose one's v.** quedarse afónico(a); **v. box** laringe *f*

**(b)** *Gram* **active/passive v.** voz activa/pasiva

**(c)** *(idioms)* **the v. of reason** la voz de la razón; **with one v.** unánimemente; **to make one's v. heard** hacerse oír; **to give v. to one's feelings** expresar *or* manifestar los sentimientos; **these reforms would give small parties a v.** estas reformas darían voz a los partidos minoritarios

**2** *vt* **(a)** *(opinion, feelings)* expresar

**(b)** *Ling (consonant)* sonorizar

**voiced** [vɔɪst] *adj Ling* sonoro(a)

**voiceless** ['vɔɪslɪs] *adj Ling* sordo(a)

**voice-over** ['vɔɪsəʊvə(r)] *n Cin & TV* voz *f* en off

**void** [vɔɪd] **1** *n* vacío *m*

**2** *adj* **(a)** **v. of** carente de **(b)** *Law (deed, contract)* **(null and) v.** nulo(a) y sin valor

**volatile** ['vɒlətaɪl] *adj* **(a)** *(person)* temperamental; *(situation, economy, market)* inestable, muy cambiante **(b)** *Chem* volátil

**volcanic** [vɒl'kænɪk] *adj* volcánico(a)

**volcano** [vɒl'keɪnəʊ] *(pl* **volcanoes)** *n* volcán *m*

**vole** [vəʊl] *n* ratón *m* de campo

**volition** [və'lɪʃən] *n Formal* **of one's own v.** por propia voluntad

**volley** ['vɒlɪ] *(pl* **volleys)** *n* **(a)** *(of gunfire)* ráfaga *f; (of blows, stones)* lluvia *f; Fig (of insults)* torrente *m* **(b)** *(in tennis, football)* volea *f*

**volleyball** ['vɒlɪbɔ:l] *n* voleibol *m*, balonvolea *m*

**volt** [vəʊlt] *n Elec* voltio *m*

**voltage** ['vəʊltɪdʒ] *n Elec* voltaje *m*

**volte-face** ['vɒltfɑ:s] *n* viraje *m or* giro *m* radical

**voluble** ['vɒljʊbəl] *adj* locuaz

**volubly** ['vɒljʊblɪ] *adv* con locuacidad

**volume** ['vɒlju:m] *n* volumen *m; Fig* **to speak volumes** decir mucho; **to turn the v.**

**up/down** *(on TV, radio)* subir/bajar el volumen; **v. control** mando *m* del volumen

**voluminous** [vəˈljuːmɪnəs] *adj* voluminoso(a)

**voluntarily** [vɒlʌnˈteərɪlɪ] *adv* voluntariamente

**voluntary** [ˈvɒləntərɪ] *adj* voluntario(a); **v. redundancy** despido *m* voluntario; **to do v. work** trabajar como voluntario(a)

**volunteer** [vɒlənˈtɪə(r)] **1** *n* voluntario(a) *m,f*
  **2** *vt (information, advice)* ofrecer (voluntariamente); **to v. to do sth** ofrecerse a hacer algo
  **3** *vi* ofrecerse (voluntariamente)

**voluptuous** [vəˈlʌptjʊəs] *adj* voluptuoso(a)

**vomit** [ˈvɒmɪt] **1** *n* vómito *m*
  **2** *vt & vi* vomitar

**voodoo** [ˈvuːduː] *n* vudú *m*

**voracious** [vəˈreɪʃəs] *adj* voraz

**vortex** [ˈvɔːteks] *(pl* **vortices** [ˈvɔːtɪsiːz]) *n* torbellino *m*, remolino *m*; *Fig* vorágine *f*

**vote** [vəʊt] **1** *n (choice)* voto *m*; *(voting)* votación *f*; **to put sth to the v., to take a v. on sth** someter algo a votación; **to have the v.** tener derecho de voto; **they got 52% of the v.** obtuvieron un 52% de los votos; **v. of confidence** voto de confianza; **v. of no confidence** moción *f* de censura; **to propose a v. of thanks for sb** pedir el agradecimiento para alguien
  **2** *vt* **to v. Communist** votar a los comunistas; **to v. to do sth** votar hacer algo; **to v. a proposal down** rechazar una propuesta en votación; **to v. sb in** elegir a alguien (en votación); **I v. (that) we go** voto por ir; **they voted the holiday a success** coincidieron en que las vacaciones habían sido un éxito
  **3** *vi* votar **(for/against** por/en contra de); **to v. yes/no** votar a favor/en contra; **to v. on sth** someter algo a votación

**voter** [ˈvəʊtə(r)] *n* votante *mf*

**voting** [ˈvəʊtɪŋ] **1** *n* votación *f*; **v. booth** cabina *f* electoral
  **2** *adj (member)* con voto

**votive** [ˈvəʊtɪv] *adj Rel* votivo(a)

▶**vouch for** [vaʊtʃ] *vt insep (person)* responder de; *(quality, truth)* dar fe de

**voucher** [ˈvaʊtʃə(r)] *n* vale *m*, cupón *m*; **(gift) v.** vale *m* de regalo

**vow** [vaʊ] **1** *n Rel* voto *m*; *(promise)* promesa *f*; **to make a v. to do sth** prometer solemnemente hacer algo; **to take a v. of poverty/silence** hacer voto de pobreza/silencio
  **2** *vt* prometer solemnemente, jurar; **to v. to do sth** jurar hacer algo

**vowel** [ˈvaʊəl] *n* vocal *f*; **v. sound** sonido *m* vocálico

**voyage** [ˈvɔɪdʒ] *n* viaje *m (largo, marítimo o espacial)*

**voyager** [ˈvɔɪdʒə(r)] *n* viajero(a) *m,f*

**voyeur** [vɔɪˈjɜː(r)] *n* voyeur *mf*

**voyeuristic** [vɔɪjəˈrɪstɪk] *adj* voyeurista

**vs** *(abbr* **versus)** contra

**VSO** [viːesˈəʊ] *n Br (abbr* **Voluntary Service Overseas)** = agencia de voluntariado para la cooperación con países en vías de desarrollo

**VTOL** [viːtiːəʊˈel] *n Av (abbr* **vertical take-off and landing)** despegue *m* y aterrizaje verticales

**VTR** [viːtiːˈɑː(r)] *n TV (abbr* **video tape recorder)** (aparato *m* de) vídeo *m*

**vulgar** [ˈvʌlgə(r)] *adj (rude)* vulgar, grosero(a), *(in poor taste)* ordinario(a), chabacano(a); *(habit,* grosero(a); **don't be v.!** ¡no seas grosero!; *Math* **v. fraction** fracción *f*, quebrado *m*

**vulgarity** [vʌlˈgærɪtɪ] *n (rudeness)* vulgaridad *f*, grosería *f*; *(poor taste)* ordinariez *f*, chabacanería *f*

**vulnerability** [vʌlnərəˈbɪltɪ] *n* vulnerabilidad *f*

**vulnerable** [ˈvʌlnərəbəl] *adj* vulnerable

**vulture** [ˈvʌltʃə(r)] *n* buitre *m*

**vulva** [ˈvʌlvə] *n* vulva *f*

# W

**W, w** ['dʌbəlju:] n (**a**) (letter) W, w f (**b**) (abbr **west**) O, oeste m

**W** Elec (abbr **watts**) W, vatios m

**WAAF** [wæf] n Hist (abbr **Women's Auxiliary Air Force**) = sección femenina de las fuerzas aéreas británicas durante la Segunda Guerra Mundial

**wacky** ['wækɪ] adj Fam (person, behaviour, dress sense) estrafalario(a); (sense of humour, comedian) estrambótico(a)

**wad** [wɒd] n (of cotton) bolita f; (of paper) taco m; (of bank notes) fajo m

**wadding** ['wɒdɪŋ] n (for packing) relleno m

**waddle** ['wɒdəl] vi andar como un pato

**wade** [weɪd] vi (in water) caminar en el agua; **to w. across a stream** vadear un riachuelo; Fig **to w. in** entrometerse
▸**wade into** vt insep Fig (task) acometer; (person) arremeter contra

**wader** ['weɪdə(r)] n (**a**) (bird) (ave f) zancuda f (**b**) (boots) **waders** botas fpl altas de agua

**wafer** ['weɪfə(r)] n (biscuit) barquillo m; Rel hostia f

**wafer-thin** [weɪfə'θɪn] adj muy fino(a); Fig (majority) ajustado(a)

**waffle¹** ['wɒfəl] n (food) gofre m

**waffle²** Br Fam **1** n (wordiness) verborrea f, (in written text) paja f
**2** vi enrollarse

**waft** [wɒft] **1** vt llevar, hacer flotar
**2** vi flotar

**wag¹** [wæg] **1** n (action) meneo m; **with a w. of its tail** meneando la cola
**2** vt (pt & pp **wagged**) menear, agitar; **to w. one's finger at sb** advertir a alguien con el dedo
**3** vi menearse; Fam **tongues will w.** van a correr rumores

**wag²** n Fam (joker) bromista mf, guasón(ona) m,f

**wage** [weɪdʒ] **1** n (pay) **wage(s)** salario m, sueldo m; **daily w.** jornal m; **w. claim** reivindicación f salarial; **w. cut** recorte m salarial; **w. differential** diferencia f salarial; **w. earner** asalariado(a) m,f; **w. freeze** congelación f salarial; **w. packet** (envelope) sobre m de la paga; (money) salario m

**2** vt **to w. war (on)** librar una guerra (contra); **to w. a campaign against smoking** emprender una campaña contra el tabaco

**wager** ['weɪdʒə(r)] Formal **1** n apuesta f
**2** vt apostar, apostarse

**waggle** ['wægəl] **1** vt menear
**2** vi menearse

**wag(g)on** ['wægən] n (horse-drawn) carro m; Br Rail vagón m; Fig **to be on the w.** (of alcoholic) haber dejado de beber

**waif** [weɪf] n niño(a) m,f abandonado(a); **waifs and strays** niños mpl desamparados

**wail** [weɪl] **1** n (of person) quejido m, gemido m; (of siren) sonido m, aullido m
**2** vi (of person) gemir; (of siren) sonar, aullar

**waist** [weɪst] n cintura f

**waistband** ['weɪstbænd] n cinturilla f

**waistcoat** ['weɪskəʊt] n Br chaleco m

**waistline** ['weɪstlaɪn] n cintura f; **to watch one's w.** cuidar la línea

**wait** [weɪt] **1** n espera f; **we had a long w.** esperamos mucho; **it was worth the w.** mereció la pena esperar; **to lie in w. for sb** acechar a alguien

**2** vt **you must w. your turn** debes esperar tu turno

**3** vi (**a**) (in general) esperar; **to w. for sth/sb** esperar algo/a alguien; **to w. for sth to happen** esperar a que ocurra algo; **to keep sb waiting** tener a alguien esperando; **I can't w. to see her** estoy impaciente por verla; **repairs while you w.** (sign) arreglos en el acto; **we must w. and see** tendremos que esperar a ver (qué pasa) (**b**) (serve) **to w. at table** servir mesas
▸**wait about, wait around** vi esperar
▸**wait on** vt insep (serve) servir; **to w. on sb hand and foot** traérselo todo en bandeja a alguien
▸**wait up** vi **to w. up for sb** esperar a alguien levantado(a)

**waiter** ['weɪtə(r)] n camarero m, Am mesero m, CSur garzón m

**waiting** ['weɪtɪŋ] n espera f; **they are playing a w. game** están dejando que transcurra el tiempo a ver qué pasa; **w. list** lista f de espera; **w. room** sala f de espera

**waitress** ['weɪtrɪs] *n* camarera *f*, *Am* mesera *f*, *CSur* garzona *f*

**waive** [weɪv] *vt (rights, claim)* renunciar a; *(rule)* no aplicar

**wake¹** [weɪk] *n (of ship)* estela *f*; *Fig* **in the w. of sth** a raíz de algo; *Fig* **to follow in sb's w.** seguir los pasos de alguien

**wake²** *n (on night before funeral)* velatorio *m*

**wake³** (*pt* **woke** [wəʊk], *pp* **woken** ['wəʊkən]) **1** *vt* despertar

**2** *vi* despertarse

▸**wake up 1** *vt sep* despertar

**2** *vi* despertarse; *Fig* **to w. up to the truth** abrir los ojos a la realidad

**wakeful** ['weɪkfʊl] *adj* **(a)** *(sleepless)* desvelado(a); **to be w.** estar desvelado(a); **to have a w. night** pasar la noche en vela **(b)** *(vigilant)* alerta; **to be w.** estar alerta

**waken** ['weɪkən] *vt* despertar

**wakey** ['weɪkɪ] *exclam Fam* **w., w.!** ¡despierta ya!, ¡arriba!

**Wales** [weɪlz] *n* (País *m* de) Gales

**walk** [wɔːk] **1** *n* **(a)** *(short)* paseo *m*; *(long)* caminata *f*; **it's a ten-minute w. away** está a diez minutos de camino (de aquí); **to go for a w.** ir a dar un paseo **(b)** *(gait)* andares *mpl*, (manera *f* de) andar *m* **(c)** *(speed)* **at a w.** al paso, paseando **(d)** *(path)* paseo *m*, sendero *m* **(e)** *(profession, condition)* **people from all walks of life** gente de toda condición

**2** *vt* **to w. the dog** sacar *o* pasear al perro; **to w. sb home** acompañar a alguien a casa; **to w. the streets** caminar por las calles; *Euph (of prostitute)* hacer la calle

**3** *vi (move on foot)* andar, caminar; *(as opposed to riding, driving)* ir andando *or* caminando; *(for exercise, pleasure)* pasear, caminar; **to w. home** ir andando a casa

▸**walk away** *vi* irse (andando); *Fig* **to w. away from trouble** evitar los problemas; *Fig* **to w. away with a prize** salir premiado(a), llevarse un premio

▸**walk in** *vi* entrar

▸**walk into** *vt insep* **(a)** *(enter)* entrar en **(b)** *(collide with)* chocar con

▸**walk off** *vi* marcharse; **to w. off with sth** *(steal, win easily)* llevarse algo

▸**walk out** *vi* salir; *Ind (go on strike)* ponerse *or* declararse en huelga; **to w. out on sb** *(leave)* dejar *or* abandonar a alguien

▸**walk over** *vt insep Fam* **to w. all over sb** pisotear a alguien

**walkabout** ['wɔːkəbaʊt] *n (of politician)* paseo *m* entre la multitud

**walker** ['wɔːkə(r)] *n* caminante *mf*

**walkie-talkie** [wɔːkɪ'tɔːkɪ] *n Rad* walkie-talkie *m*

**walk-in cupboard** ['wɔːkɪn'kʌbəd] *n (for clothes)* armario *m* vestidor; *(for food)* despensa *f*

**walking** ['wɔːkɪŋ] **1** *n* **I like w.** me gusta caminar; **we do a lot of w.** andamos mucho; **w. frame** andador *m*; **w. shoes** botas *fpl (de senderismo)*; **w. stick** bastón *m*

**2** *adj* **at w. pace** al paso, paseando; *Fam* **she's a w. encyclopedia** es una enciclopedia ambulante *or* andante; **the w. wounded** los heridos que aún pueden andar

**Walkman®** ['wɔːkmən] *n* walkman® *m*

**walk-on part** ['wɔːkɒn'pɑːt] *n Cin & Th* papel *m* de figurante

**walkout** ['wɔːkaʊt] *n (strike)* huelga *f*; *(from meeting)* abandono *m* (en señal de protesta)

**walkover** ['wɔːkəʊvə(r)] *n Fam* **it was a w.** fue pan comido *or* un paseo

**walkway** ['wɔːkweɪ] *n (between buildings)* pasadizo *m*, pasaje *m*

**wall** [wɔːl] *n* **(a)** *(interior)* pared *f*; *(exterior, free-standing)* muro *m*; *(of garden, around building)* tapia *f*; *(of town, city)* muralla *f*; **the Great W. of China** la Gran Muralla china; **w. cupboard** alacena *f*; **w. hanging** tapiz *m* **(b)** *(idioms)* **a w. of silence** un muro de silencio; **to go to the w.** irse al traste; *Fam* **to drive sb up the w.** hacer que alguien se suba por las paredes

▸**wall in** *vt sep (surround with wall)* tapiar; *(enclose)* encerrar

▸**wall off** *vt sep* separar con un muro

▸**wall up** *vt sep* condenar, tapiar

**wallaby** ['wɒləbɪ] *n* wallaby *m*, valabí *m*

**wallet** ['wɒlɪt] *n* cartera *f*

**wallflower** ['wɔːlflaʊə(r)] *n (plant)* alhelí *m*; *Fig* **to be a w.** no tener con quien bailar

**Walloon** [wɒ'luːn] *n & adj* valón(ona) *m,f*

**wallop** ['wɒləp] *Fam* **1** *n* porrazo *m*, golpetazo *m*

**2** *vt* dar un porrazo *or* golpetazo a

**walloping** ['wɒləpɪŋ] *Fam* **1** *n* paliza *f*

**2** *adv (for emphasis)* **a w. great pay rise** una subida de sueldo de aquí te espero

**wallow** ['wɒləʊ] *vi* revolcarse; **to w. in self-pity** recrearse *or* regodearse en la autocompasión

**wallpaper** ['wɔːlpeɪpə(r)] **1** *n* papel *m* pintado

**2** *vt* empapelar

**wall-to-wall** ['wɔːltəwɔːl] *adj* **w. carpeting** enmoquetado *m*, moqueta *f*; *Fig* **w. coverage** cobertura *f* total

**wally** ['wɒlɪ] *n Br Fam (idiot)* idiota *mf*, chorra *mf*

**walnut** ['wɔːlnʌt] *n (fruit)* nuez *f*; *(tree, wood)* nogal *m*

**walrus** ['wɔːlrəs] *n* morsa *f*

**waltz** [wɔːls] **1** n vals m

**2** vi bailar el vals; Fam **she waltzed into the room** entró en la habitación como si tal cosa; Fam **to w. off with sth** largarse con algo

**WAN** ['dʌbəlju:'eɪ'en] n Comptr (abbr **wide area network**) red f de área extensa

**wan** [wɒn] adj macilento(a), pálido(a)

**wand** [wɒnd] n varita f

**wander** ['wɒndə(r)] **1** n vuelta f; **to go for a w.** ir a dar una vuelta

**2** vt (streets, world) vagar por

**3** vi (a) (roam, stray) vagar (**around** por); **she had wandered from the path** se había alejado del camino (b) (verbally, mentally) distraerse; **to w. from the subject** desviarse del tema, divagar; **my thoughts were wandering** mi mente empezaba a divagar

**wanderer** ['wɒndərə(r)] n trotamundos mf inv

**wandering** ['wɒndərɪŋ] adj (person, life) errante, errabundo(a); (tribe) nómada

**wane** [weɪn] **1** n **to be on the w.** (of moon) ir menguando; Fig (of popularity, enthusiasm, power) ir decayendo

**2** vi (of moon) menguar; (of popularity, enthusiasm, power) ir decayendo

**wangle** ['wæŋgəl] vt Fam agenciarse; **he wangled it so that…** se las apañó para que…; **could you w. me a ticket?** ¿podrías pillarme una entrada?

**wank** [wæŋk] Br Vulg **1** n **to have a w.** hacerse una paja

**2** vi hacerse una paja

**wanker** ['wæŋkə(r)] n Br Vulg gilipollas mf inv, soplapollas mf inv

**want** [wɒnt] **1** vt (a) (wish, desire) querer; **to w. to do sth** querer hacer algo; **to w. sb to do sth** querer que alguien haga algo; **she knows what she wants** sabe lo que quiere; **that's the last thing we w.!** ¡sólo nos faltaba eso!; **I know when I'm not wanted** sé perfectamente cuándo estoy de más; **what does he w. with me?** ¿qué quiere de mí?

(b) (need) necesitar; **the lawn wants cutting** hay que cortar el césped; **you w. to be careful with him** hay que tener cuidado con él

(c) (seek) **he's wanted by the police** lo busca la policía; **you're wanted on the phone** te llaman por teléfono; **wanted, a good cook** (advertisement) se necesita buen cocinero

**2** vi **he wants for nothing** no le falta de nada

**3** n (a) (need) necesidad f

(b) (lack) falta f, carencia f (**of** de); **for w. of anything better to do** a falta de algo mejor que hacer; **it wasn't for w. of trying** no será porque no lo intentamos

**wanting** ['wɒntɪŋ] adj **he is w. in intelligence** le falta inteligencia; **to be found w.** no dar la talla

**wanton** ['wɒntən] adj (a) (unjustified) injustificado(a), sin sentido; (cruelty) gratuito(a) (b) (unrestrained) descontrolado(a); (sexually) lascivo(a)

**war** [wɔː(r)] n guerra f; **to be at w. (with)** estar en guerra (con); **to go to w. (with/over)** entrar en guerra (con/por); Fig **a w. of words** una batalla dialéctica, un combate verbal; Fam Fig **you look as if you've been in the wars** parece que volvieras de la guerra; **w. criminal** criminal mf de guerra; **w. cry** grito m de guerra; **w. games** Mil maniobras fpl; (with model soldiers) juegos mpl de estrategia (militar); **w. memorial** monumento m a los caídos (en la guerra)

**warble** ['wɔːbəl] **1** n trino m

**2** vi trinar

**warbler** ['wɔːblə(r)] n curruca f

**ward** [wɔːd] n (a) (in hospital) sala f (b) (electoral division) distrito m electoral (c) Law **w. of court** pupilo(a) m,f bajo tutela

▸**ward off** vt sep (blow) rechazar, parar; (danger) ahuyentar, prevenir

**warden** ['wɔːdən] n (of park) guarda mf; (of institution, hostel) guardián(ana) m,f, vigilante mf

**warder** ['wɔːdə(r)] n Br (in prison) vigilante mf

**wardrobe** ['wɔːdrəʊb] n (a) (cupboard) armario m, ropero m (b) (clothes) guardarropa m; **to have a large w.** tener un amplio guardarropa (c) Th (costumes) vestuario m

**warehouse** ['weəhaʊs] n almacén m

**wares** [weəz] npl mercaderías fpl, mercancías fpl

**warfare** ['wɔːfeə(r)] n guerra f

**warhead** ['wɔːhed] n ojiva f

**warhorse** ['wɔːhɔːs] n Fig **an old w.** un veterano, un perro viejo

**warily** ['weərɪlɪ] adv cautelosamente

**wariness** ['weərɪnɪs] n cautela f, precaución f

**warlike** ['wɔːlaɪk] adj agresivo(a), belicoso(a)

**warlord** ['wɔːlɔːd] n señor m de la guerra

**warm** [wɔːm] **1** adj (iron, oven, bath) caliente; (water, soup) templado(a); (weather, welcome, colour) cálido(a); (garment) de abrigo; **it's w.** (of weather) hace calor; **to be w.** (of person) tener calor; Fig (in personality) ser cálido(a) or afectuoso(a); **to get w.** (of person) entrar en calor; (of room, water) calentarse; **you're getting warmer** (in guessing game) caliente, caliente

**2** vt calentar; **to w. oneself by the fire** calentarse al lado del fuego

**3** vi **to w. to sb** (take liking to) tomar afecto or cariño a alguien

▶**warm up 1** *vt sep (food)* calentar

**2** *vi (of dancer, athlete)* calentar, hacer calentamiento; *(of engine, radio)* calentarse

**warm-blooded** [wɔːmˈblʌdɪd] *adj* de sangre caliente

**warm-hearted** [wɔːmˈhɑːtɪd] *adj* cariñoso(a), amable

**warmly** [ˈwɔːmlɪ] *adv* **(a)** **w. dressed** abrigado(a) **(b)** *Fig (to applaud)* calurosamente; *(to thank)* de todo corazón

**warmonger** [ˈwɔːmʌŋgə(r)] *n* belicista *mf*

**warmth** [wɔːmθ] *n (heat)* calor *m*; *Fig (of welcome)* calidez *f*, calor *m*; *(of person's character)* calidez *f*, afectuosidad *f*; *(affection)* cariño *m*

**warm-up** [ˈwɔːmʌp] *n (of dancer, athlete)* calentamiento *m*

**warn** [wɔːn] *vt* **(a)** *(caution)* advertir; **to w. sb about sth** advertir a alguien de algo; **to w. sb against sth** prevenir a alguien contra algo; **he warned her not to go** le advirtió que no fuese; **you have been warned!** ¡quedas advertido! **(b)** *(alert, inform)* avisar, advertir; **she had been warned in advance** la habían avisado de antemano

**warning** [ˈwɔːnɪŋ] *n* **(a)** *(caution)* advertencia *f*, aviso *m*; **to give sb a w.** hacer una advertencia a alguien; *Fig* **w. sign** señal *f* de alarma **(b)** *(advance notice)* aviso *m*; **without w.** sin previo aviso

**warp** [wɔːp] **1** *vt* **(a)** *(wood, metal)* alabear, combar **(b)** *(person, mind)* corromper, pervertir

**2** *vi (of wood, metal)* alabearse, combarse

**warpath** [ˈwɔːpɑːθ] *n Fam* **to be on the w.** estar en pie de guerra

**warped** [wɔːpt] *adj* **(a)** *(wood, metal)* alabeado(a), combado(a) **(b)** *(person, mind)* degenerado(a), pervertido(a)

**warrant** [ˈwɒrənt] **1** *n Law* mandamiento *m* or orden *f* judicial; *Mil* **w. officer** ≃ subteniente *mf*

**2** *vt (justify)* justificar; *(deserve)* merecer

**warranty** [ˈwɒrəntɪ] *n Com* garantía *f*; **under w.** en garantía

**warren** [ˈwɒrən] *n (of rabbit)* red *f* de madrigueras; *Fig* laberinto *m*

**warring** [ˈwɔːrɪŋ] *adj* beligerante

**warrior** [ˈwɒrɪə(r)] *n* guerrero(a) *m,f*

**Warsaw** [ˈwɔːsɔː] *n* Varsovia; *Formerly* **W. Pact** Pacto *m* de Varsovia

**warship** [ˈwɔːʃɪp] *n* buque *m* de guerra

**wart** [wɔːt] *n* verruga *f*; **a biography of Margaret Thatcher, warts and all** una biografía de Margaret Thatcher que muestra lo bueno y lo menos bueno

**warthog** [ˈwɔːthɒg] *n* jabalí *m* verrugoso

**wartime** [ˈwɔːtaɪm] *n* tiempos *mpl* de guerra; **in w.** en tiempos de guerra

**wary** [ˈweərɪ] *adj* cauteloso(a), precavido(a); **to be w. of sth/sb** recelar de algo/alguien

**was** [wɒz] *pt of* **be**

**wash** [wɒʃ] **1** *n* **(a)** *(action)* lavado *m*; **to have a w.** lavarse; **to give sth a w.** lavar algo; **give the floor a good w.** friega bien el suelo; **your jeans are in the w.** *(are going to be washed)* tus vaqueros están para lavar; *(are being washed)* tus vaqueros están lavándose; *Fig* **it will all come out in the w.** *(be all right)* todo se arreglará **(b)** *(of ship)* estela *f*

**2** *vt* **(a)** *(clean)* lavar; *(floor)* fregar; **to w. oneself** lavarse; **to w. one's face/one's hands** lavarse la cara/las manos; **to w. the dishes** fregar *or* lavar los platos; *Fig* **to w. one's hands of sth** lavarse las manos en cuanto a algo **(b)** *(carry)* **the cargo was washed ashore** el mar arrastró el cargamento hasta la costa; **he was washed overboard** un golpe de mar lo tiró del barco

**3** *vi (wash oneself)* lavarse; *Fam* **that won't w.!** *(won't be believed)* ¡eso no va a colar!

▶**wash away** *vt sep* arrastrar

▶**wash down** *vt sep (food)* regar, rociar

▶**wash off** *vt sep* lavar, quitar lavando

▶**wash out** *vt sep* **(a)** *(cup, bottle)* enjuagar **(b)** **to be completely washed out** *(exhausted)* estar completamente agotado(a)

▶**wash up 1** *vt sep* **(a)** *Br (clean)* fregar, lavar **(b)** *(bring ashore) (of sea)* arrastrar hasta la playa

**2** *vi* **(a)** *Br (do dishes)* fregar *or* lavar los platos **(b)** *US (have a wash)* lavarse

**washbasin** [ˈwɒʃbeɪsən] *n* lavabo *m*

**washboard** [ˈwɒʃbɔːd] *n* tabla *f* de lavar

**washbowl** [ˈwɒʃbəʊl] *n (small)* palangana *f*; *(large)* barreño *m*

**washcloth** [ˈwɒʃklɒθ] *n US (face cloth)* toallita *f* (para la cara)

**washer** [ˈwɒʃə(r)] *n* **(a)** *Fam (for clothes)* lavadora *f* **(b)** *(for screw)* arandela *f*; *(rubber)* zapata *f*, junta *f*

**wash(-)hand basin** [ˈwɒʃhændˈbeɪsən] *n* lavabo *m*

**washing** [ˈwɒʃɪŋ] *n* **(a)** *(action)* **to do the w.** lavar la ropa; **w. machine** lavadora *f*; **w. powder** jabón *m or* detergente *m* (en polvo) **(b)** *(dirty clothes)* ropa *f* sucia; *(clean clothes)* ropa *f* limpia

**Washington DC** [ˈwɒʃɪŋtənˈdiːˈsiː] *n* Washington DC *(capital federal)*

**washing-up** [wɒʃɪŋˈʌp] *n Br* **to do the w.** fregar *or* lavar los platos; **w. bowl** barreño *m* para lavar los platos; **w. liquid** lavavajillas *m inv (detergente)*

**washout** [ˈwɒʃaʊt] *n Fam* fracaso *m*, desastre *m*

**washroom** [ˈwɒʃruːm] *n US* lavabo *m*, baño *m*

**wasn't** [wɒznt] = **was not**

**wasp** [wɒsp] *n* avispa *f*

**waspish** ['wɒspɪʃ] *adj* mordaz, hiriente

**wastage** ['weɪstɪdʒ] *n* desperdicio *m*, despilfarro *m*

**waste** [weɪst] **1** *n* (a) *(of money, time)* pérdida *f*, derroche *m*; *(of effort)* desperdicio *m*; **to go to w.** desperdiciarse (b) *(rubbish)* desechos *mpl*; *(radioactive, toxic)* residuos *mpl*; **household w.** basura *f*; **w. disposal unit** trituradora *f* de basuras (c) **wastes** *(desert)* erial *m*, desierto *m*
**2** *adj* *(heat, water)* residual; *(fuel)* de desecho
**3** *vt* *(squander)* *(money, energy)* malgastar, derrochar; *(time)* perder; *(opportunity, food)* desperdiciar; **she wasted no time (in) telling me** le faltó tiempo para decírmelo; *Prov* **w. not, want not** no malgastes y nada te faltará
▸**waste away** *vi* consumirse

**wasted** ['weɪstɪd] *adj* *(effort, opportunity)* desperdiciado(a), desaprovechado(a)

**wasteful** ['weɪstfʊl] *adj* **to be w.** *(of process, practice)* ser un despilfarro; *(of person)* ser despilfarrador(ora)

**wasteland** ['weɪstlænd] *n* yermo *m*, erial *m*

**wastepaper** [weɪst'peɪpə(r)] *n* papeles *mpl* viejos; **w. basket** papelera *f*

**waster** ['weɪstə(r)] *n Fam (idle person)* inútil *mf*

**wasting disease** ['weɪstɪŋdɪ'ziːz] *n* = enfermedad debilitante que consume los tejidos

**watch** [wɒtʃ] **1** *n* (a) *(timepiece)* reloj *m* (b) *(period of guard duty)* turno *m* de vigilancia; *(guard)* guardia *f*; **to be on w.** estar de guardia; **to keep a close w. on sth/sb** vigilar de cerca algo/a alguien
**2** *vt* (a) *(observe)* mirar, observar; *(film, match, programme)* ver; **to w. television** ver la televisión; **to w. sb doing sth** ver *or* observar a alguien hacer algo; **we are being watched** nos están observando (b) *(keep an eye on)* *(children, luggage)* vigilar (c) *(be careful of)* tener cuidado con, vigilar; **w. your language!** ¡cuidado con ese lenguaje!; *Fam* **w. it!** ¡ojo (con lo que haces)!, ¡cuidado!
**3** *vi* mirar, observar
▸**watch out** *vi* tener cuidado; **w. out!** ¡cuidado!; **to w. out for sth** estar al tanto por si aparece algo
▸**watch over** *vt insep* vigilar

**watchdog** ['wɒtʃdɒg] *n* perro *m* guardián; *Fig* organismo *m* regulador

**watchful** ['wɒtʃfʊl] *adj* vigilante, alerta

**watchmaker** ['wɒtʃmeɪkə(r)] *n* relojero(a) *m,f*

**watchman** ['wɒtʃmən] *n* vigilante *m*

**watchstrap** ['wɒtʃstræp] *n* correa *f* del reloj

**watchtower** ['wɒtʃtaʊə(r)] *n* atalaya *f*

**watchword** ['wɒtʃwɜːd] *n* consigna *f*

**water** ['wɔːtə(r)] **1** *n* (a) agua *f*; **to pass w.** *(urinate)* orinar; *Med* **w. on the brain** hidrocefalia *f*; **w. bed** cama *f* de agua; **w. biscuit** galleta *f* (cracker) sin sal; **w. bottle** cantimplora *f*; **w. chestnut** castaña *f* de agua; *Old-fashioned* **w. closet** retrete *m*; **w. heater** calentador *m* de agua; **w. level** nivel *m* del agua; **w. lily** nenúfar *m*; **w. meter** contador *m* del agua; **w. pistol** pistola *f* de agua; **w. polo** waterpolo *m*; **w. rat** rata *f* de agua; **w. skiing** esquí *m* acuático; **w. wings** manguitos *mpl*, flotadores *mpl*
(b) *(idioms)* **to spend money like w.** gastar dinero a manos llenas; **the argument doesn't hold w.** ese argumento no se tiene en pie; **to keep one's head above w.** mantenerse a flote; **that's all w. under the bridge now** todo eso es agua pasada
**2** *vt* (a) *(fields, plants)* regar
(b) *(horse)* dar de beber a
**3** *vi* *(of eyes)* llorar, empañarse; **my eyes are watering** me lloran los ojos; **it makes my mouth w.** me hace la boca agua
▸**water down** *vt sep (dilute)* aguar, diluir; *Fig (criticism, legislation)* atenuar, dulcificar

**waterborne** ['wɔːtəbɔːn] *adj (goods) (by sea)* transportado(a) por mar; *(by river)* transportado(a) por río; *(disease)* transmitido(a) por el agua

**watercourse** ['wɔːtəkɔːs] *n (river)* curso *m* de agua

**watercolour** ['wɔːtəkʌlə(r)] *n Art* acuarela *f*

**watercress** ['wɔːtəkres] *n* berros *mpl*

**waterfall** ['wɔːtəfɔːl] *n* cascada *f*, catarata *f*

**waterfowl** ['wɔːtəfaʊl] *n (pl* waterfowl*)* ave *f* acuática

**waterfront** ['wɔːtəfrʌnt] *n (promenade)* paseo *m* marítimo; **a w. development** = viviendas u oficinas frente al mar, a un río o a un lago

**watering can** ['wɔːtərɪŋkæn] *n* regadera *f*

**watering hole** ['wɔːtərɪŋhəʊl] *n (for animals)* bebedero *m*; *Fam (bar)* bar *m*

**waterline** ['wɔːtəlaɪn] *n* línea *f* de flotación

**waterlogged** ['wɔːtəlɒgd] *adj (shoes, clothes)* empapado(a); *(land)* anegado(a); *(pitch)* (totalmente) encharcado(a)

**watermark** ['wɔːtəmɑːk] *n (in paper)* filigrana *f*

**watermelon** ['wɔːtəmelən] *n* sandía *f*

**waterproof** ['wɔːtəpruːf] **1** *n* impermeable *m*
**2** *adj* impermeable
**3** *vt* impermeabilizar

**water-resistant** ['wɔːtərɪsɪstənt] *adj (watch)* sumergible; *(fabric)* impermeable

**watershed** ['wɔːtəʃed] *n Geog* línea *f* divisoria de aguas; *Fig* momento *m* decisivo *or* de inflexión

**waterside** ['wɔːtəsaɪd] *n* ribera *f*, orilla *f*

**water-ski** ['wɔːtəskiː] *vi* hacer esquí acuático

**watertight** ['wɔːtətart] *adj (seal)* hermético(a); *(compartment)* estanco(a); *Fig (argument, alibi)* irrefutable

**waterway** ['wɔːtəweɪ] *n* curso *m* de agua navegable

**waterworks** ['wɔːtəwɜːks] *n* (a) *(for treating water)* central *f* de abastecimiento de agua (b) *Br Euph (urinary system)* aparato *m* urinario (c) *Fam (tears)* **to turn on the w.** ponerse a llorar (a voluntad)

**watery** ['wɔːtərɪ] *adj (soup, beer)* aguado(a); *(eyes)* lloroso(a), acuoso(a); *(colour)* pálido(a), claro(a)

**watt** [wɒt] *n Elec* vatio *m*

**wattage** ['wɒtɪdʒ] *n Elec* potencia *f* en vatios

**wave** [weɪv] **1** *n* (a) *(of water)* ola *f*; *(of troops, crime)* oleada *f*; *(in hair) & Phys* onda *f*; *(of emotion)* arranque *m*; *Fig* **to make waves** alborotar, armar jaleo; **w. power** energía *f* de las olas (b) *(gesture)* saludo *m* (con la mano)

**2** *vt* (a) *(flag, stick)* agitar; **to w. one's arms about** agitar los brazos; **to w. goodbye to sb** decir adiós a alguien con la mano (b) **to have one's hair waved** ondularse el pelo

**3** *vi* (a) *(of person)* saludar (con la mano); **to w. to sb** saludar a alguien con la mano (b) *(of flag)* ondear

▸**wave aside** *vt insep (objection, criticism)* rechazar, desechar

**waveband** ['weɪvbænd] *n Rad* banda *f* de frecuencias

**wavelength** ['weɪvleŋθ] *n Rad* longitud *f* de onda; *Fig* **we're not on the same w.** no estamos en la misma onda

**waver** ['weɪvə(r)] *vi (of person)* vacilar, titubear; *(of voice)* temblar; *(of courage)* flaquear

**waverer** ['weɪvərə(r)] *n* indeciso(a) *m,f*

**wavy** ['weɪvɪ] *adj* ondulado(a)

**wax¹** [wæks] **1** *n (for candles, polishing)* cera *f*; *(in ear)* cera *f*, cerumen *m*

**2** *vt* (a) *(polish)* encerar (b) **to have one's legs waxed** hacerse la cera en las piernas

**wax²** *vi* (a) *(of moon)* crecer (b) *(become)* **to w. lyrical** ponerse lírico(a)

**waxed** [wækst] *adj (cloth, paper)* encerado(a)

**waxen** ['wæksən] *adj (complexion)* céreo(a)

**waxwork** ['wækswɜːk] *n* **w. (dummy)** figura *f* de cera; **waxworks** museo *m* de cera

**way** [weɪ] **1** *n* (a) *(route) also Fig* camino *m*; **to go the wrong w.** equivocarse de camino; **the w. to the station** el camino de la estación; **to ask the w.** preguntar cómo se va; **to show sb the w.** indicar el camino a alguien; **to lose one's w.** perderse; **to find one's w. to a place** llegar a un sitio; *Fig* **to find a w. out of a problem** encontrar la solución a un problema; **to know one's w. about** conocer la zona; **on the w.** en el camino; *Fam* **they've**

got a baby on the w. van a tener un bebé; *Fig* **she is well on the w. to success** va camino del éxito; **he was on his w. to Seville** iba camino de Sevilla; **I must be on my w.** debo irme ya; **out of the w.** retirado(a), apartado(a); *Fig* **he went out of his w. to help her** se esforzó por ayudarla; **the w. in** la entrada; **the w. out** la salida; **to make one's w. to a place** dirigirse a un lugar; **to make one's w. through the crowd** abrirse paso entre la multitud; *Fig* **to make one's w. in the world** abrirse camino en el mundo; *also Fig* **to make w. for sb/sth** dejar vía libre a alguien/algo; **to lead the w.** mostrar el camino; *Fig* marcar la pauta; **to stand in sb's w.** cerrar el paso a alguien; *Fig* interponerse en el camino de alguien; *also Fig* **to be in the w.** estar en medio; *also Fig* **to get in the w.** ponerse en medio; *also Fig* **to get out of the w.** quitarse de en medio; *also Fig* **to keep out of the w.** mantenerse alejado(a)

(b) *(distance)* **to go a part of/all the w.** hacer parte del/todo el camino; *Fig* **I'm with you all the w.** tienes todo mi apoyo; **to be a long w. from** estar muy lejos de; **we've still got a long w. to go** todavía nos queda mucho camino por delante; **to be a little/long w. off** *(in distance)* estar un poco/muy lejos; *(when guessing)* andar muy descaminado(a)

(c) *(direction)* dirección *f*; **which w....?** ¿en qué dirección...?; **this/that w.** por aquí/allí; *Fig* **to look the other w.** *(ignore sth)* hacer la vista gorda; *Fam* **down our w.** en mi tierra; **if the chance comes your w.** si se te presenta la ocasión; **the system works both ways** el sistema presenta inconvenientes, pero también ventajas; **we split the money three ways** dividimos el dinero en tres partes

(d) *(manner)* modo *m*, manera *f*; **in this w.** de esta manera; **this/that w.** así; **she prefers to do things (in) her own w.** prefiere hacer las cosas a su manera; **I don't like the w. things are going** no me gusta cómo van las cosas; **one w. or another** de un modo u otro; **to my w. of thinking** para mí, a mi parecer; **to find a w. of doing sth** hallar un modo de hacer algo; **to get into the w. of doing sth** acostumbrarse a hacer algo; **he has a w. with children** se le dan bien los niños; **he got his w.** se salió con la suya; **to get used to sb's ways** acostumbrarse a la manera de ser de alguien

(e) *(street)* calle *f*; **over** *or* **across the w.** enfrente

(f) *(respect)* sentido *m*; **in a w.** en cierto sentido; **in every w.** en todos los sentidos; **in no w.** de ningún modo

(g) *(state, condition)* **to be in a good/bad w.** *(business)* marchar bien/mal; **to be in a b. way**

*(person)* estar mal
**(h) by the w.,...** a propósito,..., por cierto,...; **by w. of an introduction/a warning** a modo de introducción/advertencia

**2** *adv Fam* mucho; **w. back in the 1920s** allá en los años 20; **we go w. back** nos conocemos desde hace mucho (tiempo); **w. ahead** mucho más adelante; **w. down south** muy al sur; **your guess was w. out** ibas muy desencaminado

**wayfarer** ['weɪfeərə(r)] *n* caminante *mf*
**waylay** [weɪ'leɪ] (*pt & pp* **waylaid** [weɪ'leɪd]) *vt (attack)* atracar, asaltar; *Fig (stop)* abordar, detener

**way-out** [weɪ'aʊt] *adj Fam* extravagante
**wayside** ['weɪsaɪd] *n* borde *m* de la carretera; *Fig* **to fall by the w.** irse a paseo
**wayward** ['weɪwəd] *adj* rebelde, desmandado(a)

**WBA** [dʌbəljuːbiː'eɪ] *n (abbr* **World Boxing Association)** Asociación *f* Mundial de Boxeo
**WBC** ['dʌbəljuːbiː'siː] *n (abbr* **World Boxing Council)** Consejo *m* Mundial de Boxeo
**WC** [dʌbəljuː'siː] *n (abbr* **water closet)** váter *m*, retrete *m*

**we** [wiː] *pron* nosotros(as) *(usually omitted, except for contrast)*; **we're Scottish** somos escoceses; **WE haven't got it!** ¡nosotros no lo tenemos!; **as we say in England** como decimos en Inglaterra; **we Spanish are...** (nosotros) los españoles somos...

**WEA** [dʌbəljuːiː'eɪ] *n Br (abbr* **Workers' Educational Association)** = asociación para la educación de adultos

**weak** [wiːk] *adj (person, currency, character, excuse)* débil; *(tea, coffee)* flojo(a); **to grow w.** debilitarse; **to have a w. heart** estar mal del corazón; **to be w. at physics** estar flojo en física; *Fig* **she went w. at the knees** le empezaron a temblar las piernas; *Fig* **w. spot** punto *m* débil
**weaken** ['wiːkən] **1** *vt* debilitar
**2** *vi* debilitarse
**weak-kneed** [wiːk'niːd] *adj Fig* débil de carácter, pusilánime
**weakling** ['wiːklɪŋ] *n* enclenque *mf*, canijo(a) *n,f*
**weakly** ['wiːklɪ] *adv* débilmente
**weakness** ['wiːknɪs] *n* debilidad *f*; *(weak point)* punto *m* débil, defecto *m*; **to have a w. for sth/sb** sentir *or* tener debilidad por algo/alguien
**weak-willed** [wiːk'wɪld] *adj* sin fuerza de voluntad
**weal** [wiːl] *n (mark on skin)* señal *f*, verdugón *m*
**wealth** [welθ] *n* riqueza *f*; *Fig* abundancia *f*, profusión *f*

**wealthy** ['welθɪ] **1** *npl* **the w.** los ricos
**2** *adj* rico(a), pudiente
**wean** [wiːn] *vt (baby)* destetar; *Fig* **to w. sb from a bad habit** quitar una mala costumbre a alguien
**weapon** ['wepən] *n* arma *f*
**wear** [weə(r)] **1** *n* **(a)** *(clothing)* ropa *f*; **evening/casual w.** ropa de noche/de sport *m (use)* uso *m*; **to get a lot of w. out of sth** aprovechar mucho algo; *Fam* **to be the worse for w.** estar para el arrastre; *Fam* **it was none the worse for w.** tampoco estaba tan mal; **w. and tear** deterioro *m*, desgaste *m*

**2** *vt (pt* **wore** [wɔː(r)]*, pp* **worn** [wɔːn]) **(a)** *(garment, glasses)* llevar; **what are you going to w.?** ¿qué te vas a poner?; **to w. black** ir de negro; **to w. one's hair long** llevar el pelo largo **(b)** *(erode)* desgastar; **to w. a hole in sth** terminar haciendo un agujero en algo **(c)** *Fam (accept)* **she won't w. it** por ahí no va a pasar
**3** *vi (of clothing)* **to w. thin** *(of clothes)* gastarse, desgastarse; **my patience is wearing thin** se me está acabando la paciencia; **that joke is wearing thin** esa broma ha dejado de tener gracia; **that excuse is wearing thin** esa excusa ya no sirve; **to w. well** *(of clothing, person, film)* envejecer bien
▸**wear away 1** *vt sep* gastar, desgastar
**2** *vi* desgastarse
▸**wear down 1** *vt sep* gastar, desgastar; *Fig* **to w. sb down** agotar *or* extenuar a alguien
**2** *vi* desgastarse
▸**wear off** *vi (of pain, effect)* pasar
▸**wear on** *vi (of time)* transcurrir, pasar
▸**wear out** *vt sep* gastar, desgastar; **to w. oneself out** agotarse
**wearily** ['wɪərɪlɪ] *adv (walk)* cansinamente; *(lean, sit down)* con aire de cansancio; *(sigh)* fatigosamente
**wearisome** ['wɪərɪsəm] *adj (boring)* tedioso(a); *(tiring)* fatigoso(a); *(annoying)* exasperante
**weary** ['wɪərɪ] **1** *adj* cansado(a); **to be w. of sth** estar hastiado(a) de algo; **to grow w. of sth** hartarse de algo
**2** *vt (tire)* fatigar, cansar; *(annoy)* hartar
**3** *vi* cansarse, hartarse **(of** de)
**weasel** ['wiːzəl] *n* comadreja *f*
**weather** ['weðə(r)] **1** *n* **(a)** tiempo *m*; **what's the w. like?** ¿qué (tal) tiempo hace?; **the w. is good/bad** hace buen/mal tiempo; **in this w.** con este tiempo; **w. permitting** si el tiempo lo permite; **w. forecast** pronóstico *m* meteorológico *or* del tiempo; **w. forecaster** meteorólogo(a) *n,f*; **w. map** *or* **chart** mapa *m* del tiempo **(b)** *(idioms)* **to make heavy w. of sth** hacer una montaña de algo; **to be under the w.** estar pocho(a)
**2** *vt (rock)* erosionar; *Fig* **to w. the storm**

capear el temporal

**3** vi (of rock) erosionarse

**weatherbeaten** ['weðəbi:tən] adj (person, face) curtido(a); (cliff, rock) erosionado(a)

**weathercock** ['weðəkɒk] n veleta f

**weatherman** ['weðəmæn] n hombre m del tiempo

**weatherproof** ['weðəpru:f] adj resistente (a las inclemencias del tiempo)

**weave** [wi:v] **1** n (pattern) tejido m

**2** vt (pt weaved or wove [wəʊv], pp weaved or woven ['wəʊvən]) tejer; Fig a skilfully woven plot una trama muy bien urdida

**3** vi tejer; Fig to w. through the traffic avanzar zigzagueando entre el tráfico

**weaver** ['wi:və(r)] n tejedor(ora) m,f

**weaving** ['wi:vɪŋ] n Tex tejeduría f

**web** [web] n **(a)** (of spider) telaraña f, tela f de araña; Fig (of lies, intrigue) trama f **(b)** (of duck, frog) membrana f interdigital **(c)** Comptr the W. la Web; **w. site** sitio m Web

**webbed** [webd] adj (foot) palmeado(a)

**webbing** ['webɪŋ] n (on chair, bed) cinchas fpl

**web-footed** [web'fʊtɪd] adj (bird) palmípedo(a); (animal) con membrana interdigital

**we'd** [wi:d] = we had, we would

**Wed** (abbr **Wednesday**) miércoles m inv

**wed** [wed] (pt & pp **wedded**) **1** vt casarse con; Fig to be wedded to (an idea, principle) aferrarse a; (one's work) entregarse en cuerpo y alma a

**2** vi desposarse, casarse

**wedding** ['wedɪŋ] n boda f; **w. breakfast** banquete m de bodas; **w. cake** tarta f or pastel m de boda; **w. day** día m de la boda; **w. dress** traje m de novia; **w. night** noche f de bodas; **w. ring** alianza f

**wedge** [wedʒ] **1** n (for door, wheel) cuña f, calzo m; (of cake) trozo m; Fig it has driven a w. between them los ha enemistado

**2** vt (insert) encajar; to w. a door open calzar una puerta para dejarla abierta

**wedlock** ['wedlɒk] n Law matrimonio m; to be born out of w. nacer fuera del matrimonio

**Wednesday** ['wenzdɪ] n miércoles m inv; see also **Saturday**

**wee¹** [wi:] adj Scot Fam pequeño(a); a w. bit un poquito

**wee²** Br Fam **1** n to do a w. (urinate) hacer pipí

**2** vi hacer pipí

**weed** [wi:d] **1** n **(a)** (plant) mala hierba f **(b)** Pej (weak person) canijo(a) m,f

**2** vt (garden) escardar

▸**weed out** vt sep Fig (people, applications) descartar; (mistakes) eliminar

**weedkiller** ['wi:dkɪlə(r)] n herbicida m

**weedy** ['wi:dɪ] adj Pej (person) enclenque

**week** [wi:k] n semana f; **next w.** la semana que viene; **last w.** la semana pasada; **every w.** todas las semanas; **once/twice a w.** una vez/dos veces a la semana; **within a w.** en el plazo de una semana; **in a w., in a w.'s time** dentro de una semana; **I haven't seen her for or in weeks** no la he visto desde hace semanas; **w. in w. out** semana tras semana; **tomorrow/Tuesday w.** de mañana/del martes en ocho días

**weekday** ['wi:kdeɪ] n día m entre semana, día m laborable; **weekdays only** sólo laborables

**weekend** [wi:k'end] n fin m de semana; Br **at** or US **on the w.** el fin de semana; **w. break** vacaciones fpl de fin de semana

**weekly** ['wi:klɪ] **1** adj semanal

**2** adv semanalmente

**3** n (newspaper) semanario m

**weep** [wi:p] **1** n to have a good w. desahogarse llorando

**2** vt (pt & pp **wept** [wept]) to w. tears of joy/anger llorar de alegría/rabia

**3** vi (of person) llorar

**weeping** ['wi:pɪŋ] **1** n llanto m

**2** adj lloroso(a); **w. willow** sauce m llorón

**weepy** ['wi:pɪ] Fam adj (book, film) lacrimógeno(a); (person) to be w. estar lloroso(a)

**wee(-)wee** ['wi:wi:] n Fam to do a w. (urinate) hacer pis or pipí

**weft** [weft] n Tex trama f

**weigh** [weɪ] **1** vt **(a)** (measure) pesar **(b)** (consider) sopesar; **he weighed his words carefully** midió bien sus palabras; **to w. one thing against another** sopesar una cosa frente a otra **(c)** Naut **to w. anchor** levar anclas

**2** vi pesar; **it weighs 2 kilos** pesa 2 kilos; **how much do you w.?** ¿cuánto pesas?; **it's weighing on my conscience** me pesa en la conciencia; **her experience weighed in her favour** su experiencia inclinó la balanza a su favor

▸**weigh down** vt sep cargar; Fig to be weighed down with grief estar abrumado(a) por la pena

▸**weigh in** vi (a) (of boxer, jockey) to w. in at... dar un peso de... **(b)** Fam (join in) meter baza

▸**weigh out** vt sep pesar

▸**weigh up** vt sep (situation, chances) sopesar

**weighbridge** ['weɪbrɪdʒ] n báscula f de puente

**weight** [weɪt] **1** n **(a)** (of person, object) peso m; **they're the same w.** pesan lo mismo; **to lose w.** adelgazar, perder peso; **to put on w.** engordar, ganar peso; **to have a w. problem** tener un problema de peso **(b)** (for scales, of clock) pesa f; **weights and measures** pesos mpl y medidas; **w. training** gimnasia f con pesas (c) *(load)* peso *m*, carga *f* (d) *(idioms)* **that's a w. off my mind** me he quitado un peso de encima; **to carry w.** influir, tener peso

**2** *vt Fig* **the system is weighted in his favour** el sistema se inclina a su favor

▸**weight down** *vt sep* sujetar *(con un peso)*

**weighting** ['weitiŋ] *n Fin* ponderación *f*; **London w.** *(in salary)* plus *m* salarial por residencia en Londres

**weightless** ['weitlis] *adj* ingrávido(a)

**weightlifter** ['weitliftə(r)] *n* levantador(ora) *m,f* de pesos

**weightlifting** ['weitliftiŋ] *n* halterofilia *f*, levantamiento *m* de pesos

**weighty** ['weiti] *adj (load, object)* pesado(a); *Fig (problem, matter)* grave; *(reason)* de peso

**weir** [wiə(r)] *n* presa *f*

**weird** [wiəd] *adj* extraño(a), raro(a)

**weirdo** ['wiədəu] *(pl* **weirdos** *) n Fam* bicho *m* raro

**welcome** ['welkəm] **1** *n* bienvenida *f*

**2** *adj (person)* bienvenido(a); *(news, change)* grato(a); **to make sb w.** ser hospitalario(a) con alguien; **I don't feel w. here** siento que no soy bienvenido(a) aquí; **you're always w.** siempre serás bienvenido; **w. home!** ¡bienvenido a casa!; **you're w. to borrow it** cógelo prestado cuando quieras

**3** *vt (person)* dar la bienvenida a; *(news, change)* acoger favorablemente; **we w. this change** este cambio nos parece muy positivo; **to w. the opportunity to do sth** alegrarse de tener la oportunidad de hacer algo

**welcoming** ['welkəmiŋ] *adj (person, attitude)* afable, hospitalario(a)

**weld** [weld] **1** *n* soldadura *f*

**2** *vt* soldar

**welder** ['weldə(r)] *n* soldador(ora) *m,f*

**welding** ['weldiŋ] *n* soldadura *f*

**welfare** ['welfeə(r)] *n* (a) bienestar *m*; *Br* the **W. State** el estado del bienestar; **w. work** trabajo *m* social (b) *US (social security)* **to be on w.** recibir un subsidio del Estado

**we'll** [wi:l] = **we will, we shall**

**well¹** [wel] *n (for water, oil)* pozo *m*; *(for lift, stairs)* hueco *m*

**well²** *(comparative* **better,** *superlative* **best)* **1** *adj* **to be w.** estar bien; **to get w.** ponerse bien; **how are you? – w., thank you** ¿cómo estás? – bien, gracias; **it is just as w.** menos mal; **that's all very w., but...** todo eso está muy bien, pero...

**2** *adv* (a) *(satisfactorily)* bien; **to speak w. of sb** hablar bien de alguien; **I did as w. as I could** lo hice lo mejor que pude; **to be doing w.** *(after operation)* irse recuperando; **w. done!** ¡bien hecho!; **you would do w. to say nothing** harías bien en no decir nada; **to come out**

of sth w. salir bien parado(a) de algo; **he apologized, as w. he might** se disculpó, y no era para menos; **very w.!** *(OK)* ¡vale!, ¡muy bien!

(b) *(for emphasis)* bien; **I know her w.** la conozco bien; **it is w. known that...** todo el mundo sabe que...; **it's w. worth trying** bien vale la pena intentarlo; **she's w. able to look after herself** es muy capaz de valerse por sí misma; **I can w. believe it** no me extraña nada; **I am w. aware of that** soy perfectamente consciente de eso; **w. before/after** mucho antes/después; **to leave w. alone** dejar las cosas como están

(c) *(also)* **as w.** también; **as w. as** *(in addition to)* además de

**3** *exclam* **w., who was it?** ¿y bien? ¿quién era?; **w., here we are (at last)!** bueno, ¡por fin hemos llegado!; **w., w.!** ¡vaya, vaya!; **w. I never!** ¡caramba!; **w., that's life!** en fin, ¡así es la vida!

▸**well up** *vi (of tears)* brotar

**well-adjusted** [welə'dʒʌstid] *adj (person)* equilibrado(a)

**well-advised** [weləd'vaizd] *adj* sensato(a), prudente; **you'd be w. to stay indoors today** hoy lo mejor sería no salir de casa

**well-appointed** [welə'pɔintid] *adj (house, room)* bien acondicionado(a)

**well-argued** [wel'ɑ:gju:d] *adj* bien argumentado(a)

**well-balanced** [wel'bælənst] *adj (person, diet)* equilibrado(a)

**well-behaved** [welbi'heivd] *adj* (bien) educado(a); **to be w.** portarse bien

**wellbeing** ['welbi:iŋ] *n* bienestar *m*

**well-built** [wel'bilt] *adj (building)* bien construido(a); *(person)* fornido(a)

**well-chosen** [wel'tʃəuzən] *adj* acertado(a)

**well-disposed** [weldis'pəuzd] *adj* **to be w. towards sb** tener buena disposición hacia alguien

**well-dressed** [wel'drest] *adj* elegante; **to be w.** ir bien vestido(a)

**well-earned** [wel'з:nd] *adj* (bien) merecido(a)

**well-fed** [wel'fed] *adj* bien alimentado(a)

**well-founded** [wel'faundid] *adj (suspicion, fear)* fundado(a)

**well-heeled** [wel'hi:ld] *adj Fam* adinerado(a)

**well-informed** [welin'fɔ:md] *adj* (bien) informado(a)

**wellington** ['weliŋtən] *n Br* **wellingtons, w. boots** botas *fpl* de agua

**well-intentioned** [welin'tenʃənd] *adj* bienintencionado(a)

**well-kept** [wel'kept] *adj (garden)* cuidado(a); *(secret)* bien guardado(a)

**well-known** [wel'nəʊn] *adj* conocido(a), famoso(a)

**well-loved** [wel'lʌvd] *adj* muy querido(a)

**well-made** [wel'meɪd] *adj* bien hecho(a)

**well-meaning** [wel'mi:nɪŋ] *adj* bienintencionado(a)

**well-nigh** ['welnaɪ] *adv* casi, prácticamente

**well-off** [wel'ɒf] *adj Br (wealthy)* acomodado(a), rico(a); *Fig* **you don't know when you're w.** no sabes lo afortunado que eres

**well-paid** [wel'peɪd] *adj* bien pagado(a)

**well-read** [wel'red] *adj* leído(a), = que ha leído mucho

**well-spoken** [wel'spəʊkən] *adj* bienhablado(a)

**well-timed** [wel'taɪmd] *adj* oportuno(a)

**well-to-do** [weltə'du:] *adj* acomodado(a), próspero(a)

**wellwisher** ['welwɪʃə(r)] *n* simpatizante *mf*, admirador(ora) *m,f*

**well-worn** [wel'wɔ:n] *adj (garment)* gastado(a); *(argument)* manido(a)

**well-written** [wel'rɪtən] *adj* bien escrito(a)

**Welsh** [welʃ] **1** *npl (people)* **the W.** los galeses

**2** *n (language)* galés *m*

**3** *adj* galés(esa); **W. dresser** aparador *m*

**welt** [welt] *n (mark on skin)* señal *f*, verdugón *m*

**welter** ['weltə(r)] *n* **a w. of...** un barullo de...

**welterweight** ['weltəweɪt] *n Sport* peso *m* wélter *m*

**wench** [wentʃ] *n Old-fashioned or Hum* moza *f*

**wend** [wend] *vt Literary* **they wended their way homewards** con paso cansino pusieron rumbo a casa

**went** [went] *pt of* **go**

**wept** [wept] *pt & pp of* **weep**

**were** [wɜ:(r)] *pt of* **be**

**we're** [wɪə(r)] = **we are**

**weren't** [wɜ:nt] = **were not**

**werewolf** ['wɪəwʊlf] *n* hombre *m* lobo

**west** [west] **1** *n* oeste *m*; **to the w. (of)** al oeste (de); **the W. of Spain** el oeste de España; **the W.** Occidente

**2** *adj (side, coast)* oeste, occidental; **W. Africa** África Occidental; **W. African** africano(a) *m,f* occidental; **the W. Bank** Cisjordania; **the W. Country** el suroeste de Inglaterra; **the W. End** *(of London)* = zona de Londres famosa por sus comercios y teatros; *Formerly* **W. Germany** Alemania Occidental; **W. Indian** antillano(a) *m,f*; **the W. Indies** las Antillas; **the W. Side** = el barrio oeste de Manhattan; **W. Virginia** Virginia Occidental; **w. wind** viento *m* de poniente *or* del oeste

**3** *adv* hacia el oeste, en dirección oeste; **to face w.** dar *or* mirar al oeste; *Fig* **to go w.** *(of TV, car)* romperse, estropearse

**westbound** ['westbaʊnd] *adj (train, traffic)* en dirección oeste; **the w. carriageway** el carril que va hacia el oeste

**westerly** ['westəlɪ] **1** *n (wind)* viento *m* de poniente *or* del oeste

**2** *adj (direction)* hacia el oeste; **the most w. point** el punto más occidental; **w. wind** viento *m* de poniente *or* del oeste

**western** ['westən] **1** *n (film)* película *f* del oeste, western *m*; *(novel)* novela *f* del oeste

**2** *adj* occidental; **w. Spain** la España occidental; **W. Europe** Europa occidental; **the W. Isles** *(of Scotland)* las Hébridas

**westernized** ['westənaɪzd] *adj* occidentalizado(a)

**Western Samoa** ['westənsə'məʊə] *n* Samoa Occidental

**Western Samoan** ['westənsə'məʊən] *n & adj* samoano(a) *m,f* occidental

**westward** ['westwəd] *adj & adv* hacia el oeste

**westwards** ['westwədz] *adv* hacia el oeste

**wet** [wet] **1** *adj* **(a)** *(damp)* húmedo(a); *(soaked)* mojado(a); *(weather)* lluvioso(a); **to be w.** *(damp)* estar húmedo(a); *(soaked)* estar mojado(a); *(of ink, paint)* estar fresco(a); **to get w.** mojarse; *Fig* **w. blanket** aguafiestas *mf inv*; **w. paint** *(sign)* recién pintado; **w. suit** traje *m* de submarinismo **(b)** *Br Fam (feeble)* soso(a)

**2** *vt (pt & pp* **wet** *or* **wetted)** *(dampen)* humedecer; *(soak)* mojar; **to w. the bed** mojar la cama, orinarse en la cama; **to w. oneself** mearse encima

**3** *n* **(a)** *(dampness)* humedad *f*; *(rain)* lluvia *f* **(b)** *Br Pol* conservador(ora) *m,f* moderado(a)

**WEU** [dʌbəlju:i:'u:] *n (abbr* **Western European Union)** UEO *f*

**we've** [wi:v] = **we have**

**whack** [wæk] *Fam* **1** *n* **(a)** *(blow)* porrazo *m* **(b)** *(share)* parte *f*

**2** *vt* **(a)** *(hit)* dar un porrazo a; **to w. sb on** *or* **over the head** dar un porrazo a alguien en la cabeza **(b)** *US very Fam (murder)* cepillarse, cargarse

**whacked** [wækt] *adj Fam (exhausted)* derrengado(a), molido(a)

**whacking** ['wækɪŋ] *Fam adv* **a w. great increase/fine** un incremento/una multa bestial

**whale** [weɪl] *n* ballena *f*; *Fam* **we had a w. of a time** nos lo pasamos bomba

**whaler** ['weɪlə(r)] *n (person, vessel)* ballenero *m*

**whaling** ['weɪlɪŋ] *n* caza *f* de ballenas

**wharf** [wɔ:f] *(pl* **wharves** [wɔ:vz]) *n* embarcadero *m*

**what** [wɒt] **1** adj (a) (in questions) qué; **w. sort do you want?** ¿qué tipo quieres?; **tell me w. books you want** dime qué libros quieres; **w. colour/size is it?** ¿de qué color/talla es?; **w. good is that?** ¿de qué sirve eso?

(b) (in relative constructions) **he took w. little I had left** cogió lo poco que me quedaba; **I'll give you w. money I have** te daré todo el dinero que tengo

**2** pron (a) (in questions) qué; **w. do you want?** ¿qué quieres?; **w. are you doing here?** ¿qué haces aquí?; **w.'s that?** ¿qué es eso?; **w.'s that to you?** ¿a ti qué te importa?; **w.'s to be done about this problem?** ¿qué podríamos hacer para resolver este problema?; **w. did I tell you?** ¿qué te dije?; **w. will people say?** ¿qué va a decir la gente?; **w.'s the Spanish for "dog"?** ¿cómo se dice "dog" en español?; **w.'s he/she/it like?** ¿cómo es?; **w. about the money I lent you?** ¿y el dinero que te presté?; **w. about a game of bridge?** ¿te apetece echar una partida de bridge?; **w. about me?** ¿y yo qué?; **if that doesn't work, w. then?** y si eso no funciona, ¿qué?; Fam **so w.?, w. of it?** ¿y qué?; Fam **d'you think I'm mad or w.?** ¿te crees que estoy loco o qué?; Fam **paper, pens, pencils, and w. not** or **w. have you** papel, bolígrafos, lápices y toda la pesca

(b) (relative) qué; **I don't know w. has happened** no sé qué ha pasado; **w. is most remarkable is that...** lo más sorprendente es que...; **w. I like is a good detective story** lo que más me gusta son las novelas policíacas; Fam **he knows w.'s w.** se conoce el percal, sabe cómo están las cosas; Fam **to give sb w. for** darle a alguien para el pelo

(c) **w. for?** (for what purpose) ¿para qué?; (why) ¿por qué?; **w.'s that for?** ¿para qué es eso?; **w. did he do that for?** ¿por qué hizo eso?; **tell me w. you're crying for** dime por qué lloras

(d) (in exclamations) **w. an idea!** ¡menuda idea!; **w. a fool he is!** ¡qué tonto es!; **w. a lot of people!** ¡cuánta gente!

**3** exclam **w.? you didn't check the dates?** ¿qué? ¿no lo comprobaste las fechas?; **w. next (I ask myself)!** ¡(me pregunto) con qué saldrán ahora!

**what-d'ye-call-her** ['wɒtjəkɔːlə(r)] n Fam (person) fulanita f, mengana f

**what-d'ye-call-him** ['wɒtjəkɔːlɪm] n Fam (person) fulanito m, mengano m

**what-d'ye-call-it** ['wɒtjəkɔːlɪt] n Fam (thing) chisme m, cosa se llame m

**whatever** [wɒt'evə(r)] **1** pron **w. it is, w. it may be** sea lo que sea; **w. happens** pase lo que pase; **do w. you like** haz lo que quieras; **w. you say** (expressing acquiescence) lo que tú digas; **give him w. he wants** dale lo que quiera; **w.**

**does that mean?** ¿y eso qué significa?

**2** adj (a) (no matter what) **I regret w. harm I may have done** pido disculpas por el daño que pueda haber ocasionado; **pay w. price they ask** paga el precio que sea (b) (emphatic) **for no reason w.** sin motivo alguno; **none/ nothing w.** absolutamente ninguno(a)/nada

**what's-her-name** ['wɒtsəneɪm], **what's-his-name** ['wɒtsɪzneɪm], **what's-its-name** ['wɒtsɪtsneɪm] n Fam = **what-d'ye-call-her/him/it**

**whatsit** ['wɒtsɪt] n Fam chisme m, chirimbolo m

**whatsoever** [wɒtsəʊ'evə(r)] adj **for no reason w.** sin motivo alguno; **none/nothing w.** absolutamente ninguno(a)/nada

**wheat** [wiːt] n trigo m; **w. germ** germen m de trigo

**wheaten** ['wiːtən] adj (loaf, roll) de trigo

**wheatfield** ['wiːtfiːld] n trigal m

**wheedle** ['wiːdəl] vt sep **to w. sth out of sb** sacar algo a alguien con halagos; **to w. sb into doing sth** hacerle zalamerías a ' alguien para que haga algo

**wheel** [wiːl] **1** n (a) (on car, trolley) rueda f; **the w. of fortune** la rueda de la fortuna (b) (for steering) volante m; **to be at** or **behind the w.** ir al volante

**2** vt (push) empujar, hacer rodar

**3** vi (turn) girar, dar vueltas

**wheelbarrow** ['wiːlbærəʊ] n carretilla f

**wheelbase** ['wiːlbeɪs] n Aut distancia f entre ejes, batalla f

**wheelchair** ['wiːltʃeə(r)] n silla f de ruedas

**-wheeled** [wiːld] suf **two/three/etc -w.** de dos/tres/etc ruedas

**wheeling** ['wiːlɪŋ] n **w. and dealing** tejemanejes mpl

**wheeze** [wiːz] **1** n (a) (noise) resuello m, resoplido m (b) Fam (trick) truco m, trampa f

**2** vi (breathe heavily) resollar, resoplar

**whelk** [welk] n bu(c)cino m

**whelp** [welp] n (dog) cachorro m; (person) mocoso(a) m,f

**when** [wen] **1** adv cuándo; **w. will you come?** ¿cuándo vienes?; **tell me w. it happened** dime cuándo ocurrió; **until w. can you stay?** ¿hasta cuándo te puedes quedar?; Fam **say w.!** (when pouring drink) ¡dime basta!

**2** conj (a) (with time) cuando; **I had just gone to bed w. the phone rang** acababa de acostarme cuando sonó el teléfono; **tell me w. you've finished** avísame cuando hayas terminado; **what's the good of talking w. you never listen?** ¿de qué sirve hablarte si nunca escuchas? (b) (whereas) cuando

**whence** [wens] adv Literary de dónde

**whenever** [wen'evə(r)] **1** *conj* **(a)** *(every time that)* cada vez que; **I go w. I can** voy siempre que puedo **(b)** *(no matter when)* **come w. you like** ven cuando quieras

**2** *adv* **(a)** *(referring to unspecified time)* cuando sea; **Sunday, Monday, or w.** el domingo, el lunes o cuando sea **(b)** *(in questions)* cuándo; **w. did you find the time to do all that?** ¿de dónde sacaste tiempo para hacer todo eso?

**where** [weə(r)] **1** *adv* **(a)** *(in questions)* dónde; **w. are you going?** ¿adónde *or* dónde vas?; **w. does he come from?** ¿de dónde es?; **w. am I?** ¿dónde estoy?; **tell me w. she is** dime dónde está; **w. did I go wrong?** ¿en qué *or* dónde me equivoqué?; **w. would we be if…?** ¿dónde estaríamos si…?

**2** *conj* donde; **I'll stay w. I am** me quedaré donde estoy; **go w. you like** ve a donde quieras; **that is w. you are mistaken** ahí es donde te equivocas; **the house w. I was born** la casa donde nací; **near w. I live** cerca de donde vivo; **they went to Paris, w. they stayed a week** fueron a París, donde permanecieron una semana; **w. there is disagreement, seek legal advice** en caso de disputa, pide asesoría jurídica

**whereabouts 1** *npl* ['weərəbauts] *(location)* **nobody knows her w., her w. are unknown** está en paradero desconocido

**2** *adv* [weərə'bauts] *(where)* dónde

**whereas** [weər'æz] *conj* **(a)** *(on the other hand)* mientras que **(b)** *Law* considerando que

**whereby** [weə'baɪ] *adv Formal* por el/la cual

**whereupon** [weərə'pɒn] *conj Literary* tras lo cual

**wherever** [weər'evə(r)] **1** *conj* **(a)** *(everywhere that)* allá donde, dondequiera que; **I see him w. I go** vaya donde vaya, siempre lo veo; **w. possible** *(allá)* donde sea posible **(b)** *(no matter where)* dondequiera que; **we'll go w. you want** iremos donde quieras

**2** *adv* **(a)** *(referring to unknown or unspecified place)* en cualquier parte; **at home, in the office, or w.** en casa, en la oficina o donde sea; **it's in Coatbridge, w. that is** está en Coatbridge, dondequiera que quede eso **(b)** *(in questions)* **w. can he be?** ¿dónde puede estar?

**wherewithal** ['weərwɪðɔːl] *n* **the w. (to do sth)** los medios (para hacer algo)

**whet** [wet] *(pt & pp* **whetted)** *vt (tool, blade)* afilar; *(appetite)* despertar, abrir

**whether** ['weðə(r)] *conj* **(a)** *(indirect question)* si; **I don't know w. it's true** no sé si es verdad **(b)** *(conditional)* **w. she comes or not we shall leave** nos iremos, venga ella o no; **w. or not this is true** sea eso verdad o no

**whew** [hjuː] *exclam* **(a)** *(relief, fatigue)* ¡uf! **(b)** *(astonishment)* ¡hala!

**whey** [weɪ] *n* suero *m*

**which** [wɪtʃ] **1** *adj* **(a)** *(in questions)* qué; **w. colour do you like best?** ¿qué color te gusta más?; **w. way do we go?** ¿hacia dónde vamos?; **w. one(s)?** ¿cuál(es)?

**(b)** *(in relative constructions)* **I was there for a week, during w. time…** estuve allí una semana, durante la cual…; **she came at noon, by w. time I had left** llegó a mediodía, para entonces yo ya me había marchado

**2** *pron* **(a)** *(in questions) (singular)* cuál; *(plural)* cuáles; **w. (one) have you chosen?** ¿cuál has escogido?; **w. of the two is prettier?** ¿cuál de las dos es más bonita?; **w. of you is going?** ¿cuál de vosotros va?; **I can never remember w. is w.** nunca me acuerdo de cuál es cuál

**(b)** *(relative) (singular)* que, el/la cual; *(plural)* que, los/las cuales; **the house w. is for sale** la casa que está en venta; **the house, w. has been empty for years** la casa, que lleva años vacía

**(c)** *(referring back to whole clause)* lo cual; **he's getting married, w. surprises me** se va a casar, lo cual *or* cosa que me sorprende; **she was back in London, w. annoyed me** estaba de vuelta en Londres, lo cual me molestó

**(d)** *(with prepositions)* **the house of w. I am speaking** la casa de la que estoy hablando; **the countries w. we are going to** los países a los que vamos a ir; **the town w. we live in** la ciudad en (la) que vivimos; **I was shocked by the anger with w. she said this** me sorprendió el enfado con (el) que dijo esto; **after w. he went out** tras lo cual, salió

**whichever** [wɪtʃ'evə(r)] **1** *adj* **take w. book you like best** coge el libro que prefieras; **w. way we do it there'll be problems** lo hagamos como lo hagamos habrá problemas

**2** *pron* cualquiera; **w. you choose, it will be a bargain** elijas el que elijas, será una ganga; **the 30th or the last Friday, w. comes first** el día 30 o el último viernes, lo que venga antes

**whiff** [wɪf] *n (smell)* olorcillo *m* (**of** a); **she caught a w. of it** le llegó el olorcillo; *Fig* **a w. of scandal** un tufillo a escándalo

**while** [waɪl] **1** *n* **(a)** *(time)* rato *m*; **after a w.** después de un rato; **for a w.** (durante) un rato; **in a w.** dentro de un rato; **a short *or* little w. ago** hace un rato; **a good w., quite a w.** un buen rato; **once in a w.** de vez en cuando **(b)** **it's not worth my w.** no me merece la pena; **I'll make it worth your w.** te recompensaré

**2** *conj* **(a)** *(during the time that)* mientras; **w. reading I fell asleep** me quedé dormido mientras leía; **it won't happen w. I'm in charge!** ¡esto no ocurrirá mientras yo esté al cargo! **(b)** *(although)* si bien; **w. I admit it's difficult,…** si bien admito que es difícil,… **(c)** *(whereas)* mientras que; **one wore white,**

**w. the other was all in black** uno iba de blanco, mientras que el otro vestía todo de negro

▶**while away** *vt sep (time)* matar, pasar

**whilst** [waɪlst] *conj Br* = **while**

**whim** [wɪm] *n* capricho *m*; **to do sth on a w.** hacer algo por capricho

**whimper** ['wɪmpə(r)] **1** *n* gimoteo *m*; *Fig* **without a w.** sin rechistar

**2** *vi* gemir, gimotear

**whimsical** ['wɪmzɪkəl] *adj (person, behaviour)* caprichoso(a); *(remark, story)* curioso(a), inusual

**whine** [waɪn] **1** *n (of person, animal)* gemido *m*; *(of machine)* chirrido *m*

**2** *vi (in pain)* gimotear; *(complain)* quejarse **(about** de)

**whinge** [wɪndʒ] *vi (complain)* quejarse

**whinny** ['wɪnɪ] **1** *n* relincho *m*

**2** *vi* relinchar

**whip** [wɪp] **1** *n* (**a**) *(for punishment)* látigo *m*; *(for horse)* fusta *f* (**b**) *Br Parl* = encargado de mantener la disciplina de un partido político en el parlamento

**2** *vt (pt & pp* **whipped)** (**a**) *(lash, hit)* azotar; *(horse)* fustigar; **whipped cream** nata *f* montada; *Fig* **he whipped the crowd into a frenzy** exaltó al gentío (**b**) *Fam (defeat)* dar una paliza a (**c**) *Fam (steal)* birlar, mangar

▶**whip off** *vt sep Fam (clothes)* quitarse

▶**whip out** *vt sep Fam* sacar rápidamente

▶**whip round** *Fam vi (turn quickly)* darse la vuelta rápidamente

▶**whip up** *vt sep* **to w. up one's audience** entusiasmar al público; **to w. up support (for sth)** recabar apoyo (para algo); *Fam* **I'll w. you up something to eat** te prepararé algo de comer

**whiplash** ['wɪplæʃ] *n* **w. (injury)** esguince *m* cervical *(lesión cervical por acción de la inercia)*

**whippersnapper** ['wɪpəsnæpə(r)] *n Fam* mocoso(a) *m,f*

**whippet** ['wɪpɪt] *n* lebrel *m*

**whipround** ['wɪpraʊnd] *n Fam* **to have a w. (for sb)** hacer una colecta (para alguien)

**whirl** [wɜːl] **1** *n* remolino *m*; **a w. of activity** un torbellino de actividad; **the social w.** el torbellino de la vida social; **my head's in a w.** tengo una gran confusión mental; *Fam* **let's give it a w.** probémoslo

**2** *vt* **to w. sth/sb around** hacer girar algo/a alguien

**3** *vi (dust, smoke, leaves)* arremolinarse; *(person)* girar vertiginosamente; **my head's whirling** me da vueltas la cabeza

▶**whirl along** *vi (of car, train)* avanzar rápidamente

▶**whirl round** *vi* volverse *or* darse la vuelta rápidamente

**whirlpool** ['wɜːlpuːl] *n* remolino *m*

**whirlwind** ['wɜːlwɪnd] *n* torbellino *m*; **w. romance** romance *m* arrebatado; **w. tour** visita *f* relámpago

**whirr** [wɜː(r)] **1** *n* zumbido *m*

**2** *vi* zumbar

**whisk** [wɪsk] **1** *n Culin* batidor *m* (manual)

**2** *vt* (**a**) *(eggs)* batir (**b**) *(move quickly)* **he was whisked into hospital** lo llevaron al hospital a toda prisa

**3** *vi (move quickly)* **she whisked past me** pasó zumbando a mi lado

▶**whisk away, whisk off** *vt sep* llevarse rápidamente

**whisker** ['wɪskə(r)] *n* **whiskers** *(of cat, mouse)* bigotes *mpl*; *(of man)* patillas *fpl*; *Fam* **to win by a w.** ganar por un pelo

**whisky,** *US* **whiskey** ['wɪskɪ] *n* whisky *m*

**whisper** ['wɪspə(r)] **1** *n* susurro *m*; **to speak in a w.** hablar en voz baja; **and remember, not a w. of it to anyone!** y recuerda, ¡ni una palabra a nadie!

**2** *vt* **to w. sth to sb** susurrar algo a alguien; **it is being whispered that...** se rumorea que...

**3** *vi* susurrar; **stop whispering at the back of the class!** ¡vale ya de cuchichear ahí atrás!

**whist** [wɪst] *n (cardgame)* whist *m*

**whistle** ['wɪsəl] **1** *n* (**a**) *(noise)* silbido *m* (**b**) *(musical instrument)* pífano *m*, flautín *m*; *(of referee, policeman)* silbato *m*, pito *m*

**2** *vt (tune)* silbar

**3** *vi* silbar; **the bullet whistled past his ear** la bala le pasó silbando junto al oído; *Fam* **he can w. for his money** puede esperar sentado su dinero

**whistle-stop tour** ['wɪsəlstɒp'tʊə(r)] *n* **a w. of Europe** un recorrido rápido por Europa

**Whit** [wɪt] *n* Pentecostés *m*; **W. Sunday** domingo *m* de Pentecostés

**whit** [wɪt] *n* **not a w.** ni pizca; **it won't make a w. of a difference** va a dar exactamente igual

**white** [waɪt] **1** *n* (**a**) *(colour, of eyes)* blanco *m* (**b**) *(person)* blanco(a) *m,f* (**c**) *(of egg)* clara *f*

**2** *adj* blanco(a); **to turn** *or* **go w.** ponerse blanco(a), empalidecer; **w. with fear** pálido(a) de miedo; **w. as a ghost** *or* **sheet** blanco(a) como la nieve; **w. chocolate** chocolate *m* blanco; **w. coffee** café *m* con leche; *Fig* **w. elephant** mamotreto *m* inútil; **w. fish** pescado *m* blanco; **w. flag** bandera *f* blanca; **w. flour** harina *f* (refinada); *US* **the W. House** la Casa Blanca; **w. lie** mentira *f* piadosa; **a w. man** un hombre blanco; **w. meat** carne *f* blanca; *Parl* **w. paper** libro *m* blanco; **w. sauce** (salsa *f*) bechamel *f*; **w. spirit** aguarrás *m*; **w. stick** bastón *m* de ciego; **w. tie** *(formal dress)* frac *m* y pajarita blanca; **w. wedding** boda *f* de blanco

**whitebait** ['waɪtbeɪt] *n* deep-fried w. pescaditos *mpl* fritos

**white-collar worker** ['waɪt'kɒlə-'wɜːkə(r)] *n* oficinista *mf*, administrativo(a) *m,f*

**white-haired** ['waɪt'heəd] *adj* canoso(a)

**Whitehall** ['waɪthɔːl] *n* = calle de Londres donde se encuentra la administración central británica

**white-hot** ['waɪt'hɒt] *adj* candente

**whiteness** ['waɪtnɪs] *n* blancura *f*

**whitewash** ['waɪtwɒʃ] **1** *n* cal *f*, lechada *f*; *Fig* encubrimiento *m*
  **2** *vt* encalar; *Fig* encubrir

**whither** ['wɪðə(r)] *adv Literary* adónde

**whiting** ['waɪtɪŋ] *n (fish)* pescadilla *f*

**whitish** ['waɪtɪʃ] *adj* blancuzco(a), blanquecino(a)

**Whitsun** ['wɪtsən] *n* Pentecostés *m*

**whittle** ['wɪtəl] *vt (carve)* tallar; *(sharpen)* sacar punta a, pelar; *Fig* **to w. sth down** ir reduciendo algo
  ▶**whittle away** *vt sep Fig* **his savings had been gradually whittled away** sus ahorros se habían visto mermados gradualmente

**whizz** [wɪz] **1** *n Fam (expert)* genio *m* (**at** de); **w. kid** joven *mf* prodigio
  **2** *vi (of bullet)* zumbar, silbar; *(of person, car)* ir corriendo, ir zumbando; **to w. past** pasar zumbando; **he whizzed through the work** hizo el trabajo a toda velocidad

**WHO** [dʌbəljuːeɪtʃ'əʊ] *n (abbr* **World Health Organization)** OMS *f*

**who** [huː] *pron* (**a**) *(in questions) (singular)* quién; *(plural)* quiénes; **w. is it?** ¿quién es?; **w. with?** ¿con quién?; **w. is it for?** ¿para quién es?; **w.'s speaking?** *(on phone)* ¿de parte de quién?; **w. did you say was there?** ¿quién has dicho que estaba allí?; **w. does he think he is?** ¿quién se cree que es?
  (**b**) *(relative)* que; **the people w. came yesterday** las personas que vinieron ayer; **those w. have already paid can leave** los que ya hayan pagado pueden marcharse; **Louise's father, w. is a doctor, was there** estuvo allí el padre de Louise, que es médico

**whodun(n)it** [huː'dʌnɪt] *n Fam (book)* novela *f* de suspense; *(film)* película *f* de suspense *(centrada en la resolución de un caso de asesinato)*

**whoever** [huː'evə(r)] *pron* (**a**) *(anyone that)* quienquiera; **w. finds it may keep it** quienquiera que *or* quien lo encuentre, puede quedarse con ello (**b**) *(no matter who)* **w. you are, speak!** habla, quienquiera que seas; **w. wrote that letter** el que escribió esa carta; *Fam* **ask Simon or Chris or w.** pregúntale a Simon, a Chris o a quien sea (**c**) *(in questions)* **w. can that be?** ¿quién puede ser?

**whole** [həʊl] **1** *n* totalidad *f*; **the w. of the village** todo el pueblo; **as a w.** en conjunto; **on the w.** en general
  **2** *adj* (**a**) *(entire, intact)* entero(a); **he swallowed it w.** se lo tragó entero; **to tell the w. truth** decir toda la verdad; **the w. world** todo el mundo; **to last a w. week** durar toda una semana; **w. milk** leche *f* entera (**b**) *Fam* **the w. lot of you** todos vosotros; **for a w. lot of reasons** por un montón de razones

**wholefood** ['həʊlfuːd] *n* alimentos *mpl* integrales; **w. restaurant** restaurante *m* macrobiótico

**wholehearted** [həʊl'hɑːtɪd] *adj (support, agreement)* incondicional, sin reservas

**wholemeal** ['həʊlmiːl] *adj* **w. bread** pan *m* integral; **w. flour** harina *f* integral

**wholesale** ['həʊlseɪl] **1** *n Com* compraventa *f* al por mayor, *Am* mayoreo *m*
  **2** *adj (price, dealer)* al por mayor; *Fig (rejection)* rotundo(a); *(slaughter)* indiscriminado(a)
  **3** *adv Com* al por mayor; *Fig (reject)* rotundamente

**wholesaler** ['həʊlseɪlə(r)] *n* mayorista *mf*

**wholesome** ['həʊlsəm] *adj* sano(a), saludable

**wholly** ['həʊllɪ] *adv* enteramente, completamente

**whom** [huːm]

> En la actualidad, sólo aparece en contextos formales. **Whom** se puede sustituir por **who** en todos los casos salvo cuando va después de preposición.

*pron* (**a**) *(in questions) (singular)* quién; *(plural)* quiénes; **w. did you see?** ¿a quién viste?; **to w. were you speaking?** ¿con quién estabas hablando?
  (**b**) *(relative)* que; **the woman w. you saw** la mujer que viste; **the man to w. you gave the money** el hombre al que diste el dinero; **somebody to w. he could talk** alguien con quien pudiera hablar; **the person of w. we were speaking** la persona de la que hablábamos; **the men, both of w. were quite young,...** los dos hombres, que eran bastante jóvenes,...

**whoop** [wuːp] **1** *n* grito *m*, alarido *m*
  **2** *vi (shout)* gritar

**whoopee** [wʊ'piː] **1** *n Fam* **to make w.** *(have fun)* pasarlo teta; *(have sex)* echar un quiqui
  **2** *exclam* ¡yupi!, ¡yuju!

**whooping cough** ['huːpɪŋ'kɒf] *n* tos *f* ferina

**whoops** [wʊps] *exclam* ¡huy!

**whopper** ['wɒpə(r)] *n Fam (huge thing)* enormidad *f*, pasada *f* (de grande); *(lie)* trola *f*, bola *f*

**whopping** ['wɒpɪŋ] *Fam adj* **w. (great)** enorme

**whore** [hɔ:(r)] n Fam puta f; **w. house** casa f de putas, burdel m

**whose** [hu:z] **1** possessive pron (in questions) (singular) de quién; (plural) de quiénes; **w. are these gloves?** ¿de quién son estos guantes?; **tell me w. they are** dime de quién son

**2** possessive adj (a) (in questions) (singular) de quién; (plural) de quiénes; **w. daughter are you?** ¿de quién eres hija?; **w. fault is it?** ¿de quién es la culpa?

**(b)** (relative) cuyo(a); **the pupil w. work I showed you** el alumno cuyo trabajo te enseñé; **the man to w. wife I gave the money** el hombre a cuya esposa entregué el dinero

**why** [waɪ] **1** adv **(a)** (in questions) por qué; **w. didn't you say so?** ¿por qué no lo dijiste?; **w. not?** ¿por qué no?; **w. get angry?** ¿para qué enfadarse?

**(b)** (in suggestions) por qué; **w. don't you phone him?** ¿por qué no lo llamas?; **w. don't I come with you?** ¿y si voy contigo?

**2** conj (relative) por qué; **I'll tell you w. I don't like her** te diré por qué no me gusta; **that is w. I didn't say anything** (es) por eso (por lo que) no dije nada; **the reason w...** la razón por la que...

**3** n **the whys and wherefores (of sth)** el cómo y por qué (de algo)

**4** exclam **w., it's David!** ¡vaya, si es David!

**WI** [dʌbəlju:'aɪ] n Br (abbr **Women's Institute**) = asociación de mujeres del medio rural que organiza diversas actividades

**wick** [wɪk] n **(a)** (of lamp, candle) pabilo m **(b)** Fam **she gets on my w.** me saca de mis casillas

**wicked** ['wɪkɪd] adj **(a)** (evil) perverso(a), malo(a); (dreadful) horroroso(a), horrible; **a w. sense of humour** un sentido del humor muy pícaro **(b)** Fam (excellent) genial

**wickedness** ['wɪkɪdnɪs] n maldad f, perversidad f

**wicker** ['wɪkə(r)] n mimbre m; **w. chairs** asientos mpl de mimbre

**wickerwork** ['wɪkəwɜ:k] n (baskets) cestería f

**wicket** ['wɪkɪt] n (in cricket) (stumps) palos mpl

**wicketkeeper** ['wɪkɪtki:pə(r)] n (in cricket) cátcher mf

**wide** [waɪd] **1** adj **(a)** (broad) ancho(a); **it's 4 metres w.** tiene 4 metros de ancho; **how w. is it?** ¿qué ancho tiene?, ¿cuánto mide de ancho?; **in the whole w. world** de todo el ancho mundo **(b)** (range, experience, gap) amplio(a), extenso(a)

**2** adv to open sth **w.** (eyes, mouth) abrir algo mucho; (door) abrir algo de par en par; **to be w. open to criticism** estar muy expuesto(a) a la crítica; **w. apart** muy separado(a); **to be w. awake** estar completamente despierto(a); **the**

shot went **w.** el tiro salió desviado; **his guess was w. of the mark** su conjetura estaba totalmente descaminada

**wide-angle** ['waɪdæŋgəl] adj Phot **w. lens** gran angular m

**wide-eyed** ['waɪdaɪd] adj con los ojos muy abiertos or como platos

**widely** ['waɪdlɪ] adv **(a)** (generally) en general; **she is w. expected to resign** en general se espera que dimita; **w. known** ampliamente conocido; **it is w. believed that...** existe la creencia generalizada de que... **(b)** (at a distance) **w. spaced** muy espaciado(a) **(c)** (a lot) **to travel w.** viajar mucho; **opinions differ w.** hay muchas y muy diversas opiniones

**widen** ['waɪdən] **1** vt (road, garment) ensanchar, ampliar; Fig (influence, limits) ampliar, extender

**2** vi (of river) ensancharse; (of gap) acrecentarse

▸**widen out** vi ensancharse

**wide-ranging** [waɪd'reɪndʒɪŋ] adj amplio(a), extenso(a)

**widespread** ['waɪdspred] adj extendido(a), generalizado(a)

**widow** ['wɪdəu] **1** n viuda f; **she was left a w. at the age of thirty** quedó viuda a los treinta (años); **w.'s pension** pensión f de viudedad

**2** vt **to be widowed** enviudar, quedarse viudo(a)

**widowed** ['wɪdəud] adj viudo(a)

**widower** ['wɪdəuə(r)] n viudo m

**width** [wɪdθ] n anchura f; (in swimming pool) ancho m

**wield** [wi:ld] vt **(a)** (sword) blandir, empuñar; (pen) manejar **(b)** (power, influence) ejercer

**wife** [waɪf] (pl **wives** [waɪvz]) n mujer f, esposa f; Fam **the w.** la parienta

**wifely** ['waɪflɪ] adj de esposa, conyugal

**wig** [wɪg] n peluca f

**wiggle** ['wɪgəl] **1** n meneo m

**2** vt menear

**3** vi menearse

**wiggly** ['wɪglɪ] adj Fam (line) ondulado(a)

**wigwam** ['wɪgwæm] n tipi m, tienda f india

**wild** [waɪld] **1** adj **(a)** (not domesticated) (plant) silvestre; (animal) salvaje; (countryside) agreste; **w. flowers** flores fpl silvestres; **a w. goose chase** una búsqueda inútil; Fam **w. horses wouldn't drag it out of me** no me lo sacan ni a tiros; Fig **to sow one's w. oats** darse la gran vida de joven; **the W. West** el salvaje oeste (americano)

**(b)** (unrestrained) (wind) furioso(a); (weather) desapacible, desabrido(a); (person, enthusiasm) descontrolado(a), desenfrenado(a); (promise, rumour) descabellado(a); **w. eyes** ojos mpl desorbitados; **to drive sb w.** poner a alguien fuera de sí

(c) *(random) (estimate)* descabellado(a); **it was just a w. guess** fue un intento de acertar al tuntún; **w. card** *Comptr* comodín *m*; *Sport* invitado(a) *m,f* por la organización; *Fig* incógnita *f*

(d) *Fam (enthusiastic)* **to be w. about sb/sth** estar loco(a) por alguien/algo; **I'm not w. about it** no me entusiasma mucho

**2** *adv* **to grow w.** *(of plant)* crecer silvestre; **to run w.** *(of children, criminals)* estar descontrolado(a); **the audience went w.** el público se desmelenó *or* enfervorizó

**3** *n* **in the w.** *(of animal)* en estado salvaje; **in the wilds of Alaska** en los remotos parajes de Alaska

**wildcat** ['waɪldkæt] *n* **(a)** gato *m* montés **(b)** *Ind* **w. strike** huelga *f* salvaje

**wilderness** ['wɪldənɪs] *n* desierto *m*, yermo *m*; *Fig* **his years in the w.** los años que pasó en el ostracismo

**wildfire** ['waɪldfaɪə(r)] *n* **to spread like w.** extenderse como un reguero de pólvora

**wildfowl** ['waɪldfaʊl] *(pl* **wildfowl)** *n* aves *fpl* de caza

**wildlife** ['waɪldlaɪf] *n* fauna *f*; *TV* **w. programme** programa *m* de animales

**wildly** ['waɪldlɪ] *adv* **(a)** *(behave)* descontroladamente; *(cheer, applaud)* enfervorizadamente, vehementemente; **to rush about w.** ir de aquí para allá como un/una loco(a) **(b)** *(at random)* al azar **(c)** *(for emphasis) (expensive, funny, enthusiastic)* enormemente, tremendamente; **w. inaccurate** disparatado(a); **w. exaggerated** exageradísimo(a)

**wildness** ['waɪldnɪs] *n* **(a)** *(of country, animal)* estado *m* salvaje **(b)** *(of wind, waves)* furia *f*, violencia *f*; *(of applause)* fervor *m*, vehemencia *f*; *(of ideas, words)* extravagancia *f*, excentricidad *f*

**wilful** ['wɪlfʊl] *adj* **(a)** *(stubborn)* obstinado(a), tozudo(a) **(b)** *(deliberate)* premeditado(a), deliberado(a); *Law* **w. murder** asesinato *m* premeditado

**wilfully** ['wɪlfʊlɪ] *adv* **(a)** *(stubbornly)* obstinadamente, tozudamente **(b)** *(deliberately)* deliberadamente

**will¹** [wɪl] **1** *n* **(a)** *(resolve, determination)* voluntad *f*; **at w.** a voluntad; **the w. to live** las ganas de vivir; **to show good w.** demostrar tener buena voluntad; **with the best w. in the world** con la mejor voluntad del mundo; **he imposed his w. on them** les impuso su voluntad; **this computer has a w. of its own** este ordenador hace lo que le da la gana; *Prov* **where there's a w. there's a way** quien la sigue, la consigue

(b) *Law* testamento *m*; **the last w. and testament of...** la última voluntad de...; **to make one's w.** hacer testamento

**2** *vt* **(a)** **he was willing her to win** deseaba vehementemente que ganara; **she was willing herself to do it** apeló a toda su fuerza de voluntad para hacerlo

(b) *(leave in one's will)* **to w. sth to sb** legar algo a alguien

**will²**

En el inglés hablado, y en el escrito en estilo coloquial, el verbo **will** se contrae de manera que **I/you/he** etc **will** se transforman en **I'll, you'll, he'll** etc. La forma negativa **will not** se transforma en **won't**.

*modal aux v* **(a)** *(expressing future tense)* **I'll do it tomorrow** lo haré mañana; **it won't take long** no llevará mucho tiempo; **persuading the parents w. be difficult** va a ser difícil convencer a los padres; **you'll write to me, won't you?** me escribirás, ¿verdad?; **you won't forget, w. you?** no te olvides, por favor; **w. you be there? - yes I w./no I won't** ¿vas a ir? - sí/no

(b) *(expressing wish, determination)* **I won't allow it!** ¡no lo permitiré!; **w. you help me?** ¿me ayudas?; **she won't let me see him** no me deja verlo; **won't you sit down?** ¿no se quiere sentar?; **be quiet for a minute, w. you?** estate callado un momento, ¿quieres?; **if she WILL insist on doing everything herself...** como insiste en hacerlo todo ella...; **WILL you go away!** ¡quieres hacer el favor de irte!; **it won't open** no se abre

(c) *(expressing general truth)* **the restaurant w. seat a hundred people** el restaurante puede albergar a cien personas; **these things w. happen** son cosas que pasan

(d) *(conjecture)* **you'll be tired** debes de estar cansado; **they'll be home by now** ya deben de haber llegado a casa

**willie** ['wɪlɪ] *n Fam (penis)* pilila *f*, pito *m*

**willies** ['wɪlɪz] *npl Fam* **to have the w.** tener canguelo; **this place gives me the w.** este lugar me da canguelo

**willing** ['wɪlɪŋ] *adj (assistant)* muy dispuesto(a); *(accomplice)* voluntario(a); **she was a w. participant** participó de muy buena gana; **to be w. to do sth** estar dispuesto(a) a hacer algo, hacer algo de buena gana; **God w.** si Dios quiere; **to show w.** mostrar buena disposición

**willingly** ['wɪlɪŋlɪ] *adv* de buena gana, gustosamente; **I would w. help** ayudaría gustoso

**willingness** ['wɪlɪŋnɪs] *n* buena disposición *f*

**will-o'-the-wisp** [wɪləðə'wɪsp] *n (light)* fuego *m* fatuo; *Fig (elusive aim)* quimera *f*

**willow** ['wɪləʊ] *n* **w. (tree)** sauce *m*

**willpower** ['wɪlpaʊə(r)] *n* fuerza *f* de voluntad

**willy** ['wɪlɪ] *n Fam (penis)* pilila *f*, pito *m*

**willy-nilly** ['wɪlɪ'nɪlɪ] *adv (like it or not)* a la fuerza, quieras o no; *(haphazardly)* a la buena de Dios

**wilt** [wɪlt] *vi (of plant)* marchitarse; *Fig (of person)* flaquear, resentirse

**wily** ['waɪlɪ] *adj* astuto(a), taimado(a)

**wimp** [wɪmp] *n Fam (physically)* debilucho(a) *m,f; (lacking character)* blandengue *mf*

**wimpish** ['wɪmpɪʃ] *adj Fam* blandengue

**win** [wɪn] **1** *n* victoria *f*, triunfo *m*

**2** *vt (pt & pp* **won** [wʌn]) *(battle, race, prize, election)* ganar; *(popularity, recognition)* obtener, ganar; *(confidence, love)* ganarse; *(parliamentary seat)* obtener, sacar; **to w. an argument** salir victorioso(a) en una discusión; **to w. money off** *or* **from sb** ganarle dinero a alguien; *Fam* **you can't w. them all, you w. some you lose some** a veces se gana y a veces se pierde

**3** *vi* ganar; *Fam* **you (just) can't w.** no hay forma de salir ganando; **OK, you w.!** vale, tú ganas

▸**win back** *vt sep* recuperar

▸**win out, win through** *vi (succeed)* triunfar

▸**win over, win round** *vt sep* convencer, ganarse (el apoyo de)

**wince** [wɪns] **1** *n (of pain)* mueca *f* de dolor; *(of embarrassment)* gesto *m* de bochorno

**2** *vi (with pain)* hacer una mueca de dolor; *(with embarrassment)* hacer un gesto de bochorno

**winch** [wɪntʃ] **1** *n* torno *m*, cabrestante *m*

**2** *vt* levantar con un torno *or* cabrestante

**wind¹** [wɪnd] **1** *n* (**a**) *(air current)* viento *m*; **to sail into** *or* **against the w.** navegar contra el viento; *Fig* **to sail close to the w.** lindar con lo prohibido; **w. energy** *or* **power** energía *f* eólica; **w. instrument** instrumento *m* de viento; **w. tunnel** túnel *m* aerodinámico (**b**) *(breath)* aliento *m*, resuello *m*; **let me get my w. back** deja que recupere el aliento (**c**) *(abdominal)* gases *mpl*, flatulencia *f*; **to break w.** soltar una ventosidad; **the baby's got w.** el bebé tiene gases (**d**) *(idioms) Fam* **to put the w. up sb** meter miedo a alguien; **to take the w. out of sb's sails** bajar la moral a alguien; **to get w. of sth** enterarse de algo

**2** *vt* **to w. sb** *(with punch)* dejar a alguien sin respiración

**wind²** [waɪnd] *(pt & pp* **wound** [waʊnd]) **1** *vt* (**a**) *(thread, string)* enrollar (**b**) *(handle)* dar vueltas a; *(clock, watch)* dar cuerda a; **to w. a tape on/back** pasar rápidamente/rebobinar una cinta

**2** *vi (of path, river)* serpentear, zigzaguear; **the road winds up/down the hill** la carretera sube/baja la colina haciendo eses

▸**wind down 1** *vt sep* (**a**) *(car window)* bajar, abrir (**b**) *(reduce) (production)* ir reduciendo; *(company)* ir reduciendo la actividad de

**2** *vi* (**a**) *(of party, meeting)* ir concluyendo (**b**) *Fam (of person)* relajarse

▸**wind round** *vt sep* **to w. sth round sth** enrollar algo alrededor de algo

▸**wind up 1** *vt sep* (**a**) *(car window)* subir, cerrar (**b**) *(bring to an end) (meeting, business)* concluir (**c**) *Fam (tease)* vacilar, tomar el pelo a; *(annoy)* mosquear

**2** *vi* (**a**) *(end speech, meeting)* concluir (**b**) *Fam (end up)* terminar

**windbag** ['wɪndbæg] *n Fam* charlatán(ana) *m,f*

**windbreak** ['wɪndbreɪk] *n* pantalla *f* contra el viento

**windcheater** ['wɪndtʃiːtə(r)] *n (jacket)* cazadora *f*

**windchill factor** ['wɪndtʃɪlfæktə(r)] *n* índice *m* de enfriamiento (del aire)

**winder** ['waɪndə(r)] *n (on watch)* cuerda *f; (on car door)* manivela *f*

**windfall** ['wɪndfɔːl] *n (of fruit)* fruta *f* caída; *Fig (of money)* dinero *m* caído del cielo; *Fin* **w. profits** *(of company)* beneficio *m* inesperado

**winding** ['waɪndɪŋ] *adj (path, stream)* serpenteante, zigzagueante; **w. staircase** escalera *f* de caracol

**windmill** ['wɪndmɪl] *n* molino *m* de viento

**window** ['wɪndəʊ] *n* (**a**) *(of house) & Comptr* ventana *f; (of vehicle)* ventana *f*, ventanilla *f; (of shop)* escaparate *m; (at bank, ticket office)* ventanilla *f;* **w. box** jardinera *f;* **w. cleaner** limpiacristales *mf inv;* **w. frame** marco *m* de ventana; **w. ledge** alféizar *m*, antepecho *m (cornisa exterior);* **w. seat** asiento *m* de ventana (**b**) *(idioms)* **to provide a w. on sth** dar una idea de algo; **w. of opportunity** período *m* favorable; *Fam* **that's my holiday out of the w.** ya me he quedado sin vacaciones

**window-dressing** ['wɪndəʊdresɪŋ] *n (in shop)* escaparatismo *m; Fig* presentación *f* engañosa de los hechos

**windowpane** ['wɪndəʊpeɪn] *n* cristal *m* (de ventana)

**window-shopping** ['wɪndəʊʃɒpɪŋ] *n* **to go w.** ir a ver escaparates

**windowsill** ['wɪndəʊsɪl] *n* alféizar *m*, antepecho *m*

**windpipe** ['wɪndpaɪp] *n* tráquea *f*

**windscreen** ['wɪndskriːn], *US* **windshield** ['wɪndʃiːld] *n* parabrisas *m inv;* **w. wiper** limpiaparabrisas *m inv*

**windsock** ['wɪndsɒk] *n Av* manga *f* (catavientos)

**windsurf** ['wɪndsɜːf] *vi* hacer windsurf, hacer tabla a vela

**windsurfing** ['wɪndsɜːfɪŋ] *n* **to go w.** ir a hacer windsurf *or* tabla a vela

**windswept** ['wɪndswept] *adj (hillside, scene)* azotado(a) por el viento; **w. hair** pelo *m* revuelto por el viento

**wind-up** ['waɪndʌp] *n Fam* vacilada *f*, tomadura *f* de pelo

**windward** ['wɪndwəd] *adj* de barlovento; **the W. Islands** las Islas de Barlovento

**windy**[1] ['wɪndɪ] *adj (day)* ventoso(a); *(place)* expuesto(a) al viento; **it's w.** hace viento

**windy**[2] ['waɪndɪ] *adj (road)* serpenteante, zigzagueante

**wine** [waɪn] **1** *n* vino *m*; **red/white w.** vino tinto/blanco; **w. bar** bar *m (de cierta elegancia, especializado en vinos y con una pequeña carta de comidas)*; **w. bottle** botella *f* de vino; **w. cellar** bodega *f*; **w. gum** ≃ gominola *f*; **w. list** carta *f* de vinos; **w. tasting** cata *f* de vinos; **w. vinegar** vinagre *m* de vino

**2** *vt* **to w. and dine sb** agasajar a alguien

**wineglass** ['waɪnglɑːs] *n* copa *f* de vino

**wing** [wɪŋ] **1** *n* **(a)** *(of bird, plane)* ala *f*; *Fig* **to take sb under one's w.** poner a alguien bajo la propia tutela, apadrinar a alguien; *Fig* **to spread** *or* **stretch one's wings** remontar el vuelo, echarse al ruedo; **w. nut** palomilla *f* **(b)** *(of car)* aleta *f*; **w. mirror** *(espejo m)* retrovisor *m* lateral **(c)** *(of building, hospital)* ala *f* **(d)** *(in football, rugby) (area)* banda *f*; *(player)* extremo *mf*, lateral *mf* **(e)** *(in theatre)* **the wings** los bastidores; **to be waiting in the wings** *(of actor)* esperar entre bastidores; *Fig* esperar su oportunidad **(f)** *Pol* **the left/right w.** la izquierda/derecha

**2** *vt* **(a)** *(injure) (bird)* herir en el ala; *(person)* herir en el brazo **(b)** *Fam (improvise)* **to w. it** improvisar **(c)** *(fly) (bird)* **to w. its way towards** volar hacia; *Fig* **my report should be winging its way towards you** mi informe ya está en camino

**winger** ['wɪŋə(r)] *n (in football, rugby)* extremo *mf*, lateral *mf*

**wingspan** ['wɪŋspæn] *n* envergadura *f* (de alas)

**wink** [wɪŋk] **1** *n* guiño *m*; **to give sb a w.** guiñarle un ojo a alguien; **to tip sb the w.** poner sobre aviso a alguien; *Fam* **I didn't sleep a w.** no pegué ojo

**2** *vi* guiñar, hacer un guiño; *(of star, light)* titilar

▸**wink at** *vt insep (person)* guiñar a, hacer un guiño a; *Fig (abuse, illegal practice)* hacer la vista gorda ante

**winkle** ['wɪŋkəl] *n (mollusc)* bígaro *m*

▸**winkle out** *vt sep Fam* **to w. sth out of sb** sacarle algo a alguien

**winner** ['wɪnə(r)] *n* vencedor(ora) *m,f*, ganador(ora) *m,f*; **this book will be a w.** este libro será un éxito; **to be on to a w.** tener un éxito entre manos

**winning** ['wɪnɪŋ] **1** *adj* **(a)** *(victorious) (team, person)* ganador(ora), vencedor(ora); *(goal)* de la victoria; *(ticket, number)* premiado(a); **w. post** meta *f*; **w. streak** racha *f* de suerte **(b)** *(attractive)* encantador(ora), atractivo(a)

**2** *npl* **winnings** ganancias *fpl*

**winnow** ['wɪnəʊ] *vt (grain)* aventar

**wino** ['waɪnəʊ] *(pl* **winos**) *n Fam (alcoholic)* borracho(a) *m,f*

**winsome** ['wɪnsəm] *adj* encantador(ora), atractivo(a)

**winter** ['wɪntə(r)] **1** *n* invierno *m*; **in (the) w.** en invierno; **w. break** vacaciones *fpl* de invierno; **w. clothing** ropa *f* de invierno

**2** *vi* pasar el invierno

**wintertime** ['wɪntətaɪm] *n* invierno *m*

**wint(e)ry** ['wɪntərɪ] *adj (weather)* invernal; *Fig (smile)* gélido(a), glacial

**wipe** [waɪp] **1** *n* **(a)** *(action)* **to give sth a w.** limpiar algo con un paño, pasar el paño a algo **(b)** *(moist tissue)* toallita *f* húmeda

**2** *vt* **(a)** *(table, plate)* pasar un paño por *or* a; **to w. one's nose** limpiarse la nariz; **he wiped his hands on the towel** se secó las manos con la toalla; **to w. one's shoes on the mat** limpiarse los zapatos en el felpudo; *Fam* **to w. the floor with sb** dar una paliza a alguien **(b)** *(recording tape)* borrar

▸**wipe away** *vt sep (tears)* enjugar; *(mark)* limpiar, quitar

▸**wipe off 1** *vt sep* limpiar; *Fam* **that'll w. the smile off his face!** ¡eso le borrará la sonrisa de la cara!

**2** *vi (of stain)* salir, quitarse

▸**wipe out** *vt sep* **(a)** *(erase) (memory)* borrar; *(debt)* saldar **(b)** *(destroy) (family, species)* hacer desaparecer

▸**wipe up** *vt sep* limpiar

**wiper** ['waɪpə(r)] *n Aut* limpiaparabrisas *m inv*

**wire** ['waɪə(r)] **1** *n* **(a)** *(in general)* alambre *m*; *(electrical)* cable *m*; **w. brush** cepillo *m* de púas metálicas; **w. fence** alambrada *f*; **w. mesh** malla *f* or tela *f* metálica; **w. wool** estropajo *m* de aluminio **(b)** *US (telegram)* telegrama *m* **(c)** *(idioms) Fam* **we got our wires crossed** tuvimos un cruce de cables y no nos entendimos; **the contest went right down to the w.** el desenlace del concurso no se decidió hasta el último momento

**2** *vt* **(a)** *(house)* cablear, tender el cableado de; **to w. sth to sth** *(connect electrically)* conectar algo a algo (con un cable); *(attach with wire)* sujetar algo a algo con un alambre **(b)** *(send telegram to)* mandar un telegrama a

**wirecutters** ['waɪəkʌtəz] *npl* cizallas *fpl*; **a pair of w.** unas cizallas

**wireless** ['waɪəlɪs] *n Old-fashioned* **w. (set)** radio *f*

**wiretapping** ['waɪətæpɪŋ] *n Tel* intervención *f* de la línea

**wiring** ['waɪərɪŋ] *n (electrical)* instalación *f* eléctrica

**wiry** ['waɪərɪ] *adj* (a) *(hair)* basto(a) y rizado(a) (b) *(person)* fibroso(a)

**wisdom** ['wɪzdəm] *n (knowledge)* sabiduría *f*; *(judgement)* sensatez *f*, cordura *f*; **w. tooth** muela *f* del juicio

**wise** [waɪz] *adj (knowledgeable)* sabio(a); *(sensible)* sensato(a), prudente; **a w. man** un sabio; *Fam Pej* **a w. guy** un sabelotodo; **the Three W. Men** los Reyes Magos; **it wouldn't be w. to do it** no sería aconsejable hacerlo; **to be w. after the event** verlo todo claro a posteriori; **to be none the wiser** no haber sacado nada en claro; *Fam* **to get w. to a fact** percatarse de un hecho; *Fam* **to get w. to sb** calar a alguien

▸**wise up** *Fam vi* **to w. up to sb** calar a alguien; **to w. up to the fact that...** aceptar el hecho de que...; **w. up!** ¡espabílate!

**-wise** [waɪz] *suff Fam (with reference to)* **health-/salary-w.** en cuanto a la salud/al salario

**wisecrack** ['waɪzkræk] *Fam* **1** *n* chiste *m*, salida *f* ingeniosa
**2** *vi* soltar un chiste *or* una salida ingeniosa

**wisely** ['waɪzlɪ] *adv (prudently)* sensatamente

**wish** [wɪʃ] **1** *n* (a) *(desire)* deseo *m*; **to make a w.** pedir un deseo; **to have no w. to do sth** no tener ningún deseo de hacer algo; **to do sth against sb's wishes** hacer algo en contra de los deseos de alguien (b) *(greeting)* **(with) best wishes** *(in letter, on card)* un saludo cordial *or* afectuoso; **they send you their best wishes** te envían saludos
**2** *vt* (a) *(want)* desear, querer; **to w. to do sth** desear hacer algo; **it is to be wished that...** sería deseable que...; **to w. sb well** desearle a alguien lo mejor; **to w. sb luck/a pleasant journey** desear a alguien suerte/un buen viaje (b) *(want something impossible, unlikely)* **I w. I had seen it!** ¡ojalá lo hubiera visto!; **I w. I hadn't left so early** ojalá no me hubiera marchado tan pronto; **w. you were here!** *(on postcard)* te echo de menos
**3** *vi* **to w. for sth** desear algo; **what more could you w. for?** ¿qué más se puede pedir *or* desear?; **as you w.** como quieras

**wishbone** ['wɪʃbəʊn] *n* espoleta *f (hueso de ave)*

**wishful** ['wɪʃfʊl] *adj* **that's just w. thinking** no son más que ilusiones

**wishy-washy** ['wɪʃɪwɒʃɪ] *adj Fam* vacilante

**wisp** [wɪsp] *n (of straw)* brizna *f*; *(of hair, wool)* mechón *m*; *(of smoke)* voluta *f*; *(of cloud)* jirón *m*

**wistful** ['wɪstfʊl] *adj* nostálgico(a)

**wit** [wɪt] *n* (a) *(intelligence, presence of mind)* inteligencia *f*, lucidez *f*; **he hasn't the w. to see it** no tiene la lucidez suficiente para verlo; **to have quick wits** tener rapidez mental; **to have lost one's wits** haber perdido la razón; **to have/keep one's wits about one** ser/ estar espabilado(a); **to be at one's w.'s end** estar al borde de la desesperación; **to live by one's wits** ser un pícaro; **to scare sb out of his wits** dar un susto de muerte a alguien (b) *(humour)* ingenio *m*, agudeza *f* (c) *(witty person)* ingenioso(a) *m,f*

**witch** [wɪtʃ] *n* bruja *f*; **w. doctor** hechicero *m*, curandero *m*

**witchcraft** ['wɪtʃkrɑːft] *n* brujería *f*

**witch-hunt** ['wɪtʃhʌnt] *n Pol* caza *f* de brujas

**with** [wɪð] *prep con*; **w. me** conmigo; **w. you** contigo; **w. himself/herself** consigo; **to travel/work w. sb** viajar/trabajar con alguien; **he is staying w. friends** se queda con *or* en casa de unos amigos; **a girl w. blue eyes** una chica de ojos azules; **I was left w. nobody to talk to** me quedé sin nadie con quien hablar; **this problem will always be w. us** siempre tendremos este problema; **she came in w. a suitcase** entró con una maleta en la mano; **I'm w. you** *(I support you)* estoy contigo; **I'm not w. you** *(I don't understand)* no te sigo; *Fam* **to be w. it** *(fashionable)* ser enrollado(a); **w. a smile** con una sonrisa, sonriendo

**withdraw** [wɪð'drɔː] ( *pt* **withdrew** [wɪð-'druː], *pp* **withdrawn** [wɪð'drɔːn]) **1** *vt* retirar; *(money)* sacar **(from** de**)**
**2** *vi* retirarse; **to w. in favour of sb** dejar paso a alguien; **she withdrew into herself** se encerró en sí misma

**withdrawal** [wɪð'drɔːəl] *n (of support, accusation)* retirada *f*; **to make a w.** *(from bank)* efectuar un reintegro; **w. symptoms** síndrome *m* de abstinencia

**withdrawn** [wɪð'drɔːn] *adj* retraído(a)

**wither** ['wɪðə(r)] *vi (of plant)* marchitarse; *(of limb)* atrofiarse

**withered** ['wɪðəd] *adj (plant)* marchito(a); *(limb)* atrofiado(a)

**withering** ['wɪðərɪŋ] *adj (look)* fulminante; *(tone)* mordaz

**withhold** [wɪð'həʊld] ( *pt & pp* **withheld** [wɪð'held]) *vt (consent, help)* negar **(from** a**)**; *(money)* retener **(from** a**)**; *(information, the truth)* ocultar **(from** a**)**

**within** [wɪð'ɪn] **1** *prep* (a) *(inside)* dentro de; **problems w. the party** problemas en el seno del partido
(b) *(not beyond)* **he lives w. a few kilometres of the city centre** vive a pocos kilómetros del centro; **w. a radius of ten miles** en un radio de diez millas; **w. limits** dentro de

un orden, hasta cierto punto; **w. reason** dentro de lo razonable; **w. sight** a la vista; *Fam* **to come w. an inch of doing sth** estar en un tris de hacer algo; **w. the law** dentro de la legalidad

(c) *(time)* en menos de; **w. an hour** en menos de una hora; **w. the next five years** *(during)* *(in future)* durante los próximos cinco años; *(in past)* durante los cinco años siguientes; *(before end of)* dentro de un plazo de cinco años; **they died w. a few days of each other** murieron con pocos días de diferencia

**2** *adv* **from w.** desde dentro

**without** [wɪð'aʊt] **1** *prep* sin; **w. any money/difficulty** sin dinero/dificultad; **a journey w. end** un viaje sin fin; **w. doing sth** sin hacer algo; **it goes w. saying that…** huelga decir que…; **to do** or **go w. sth** pasar sin algo

**2** *adv* **(a) she went w. so that her children would have enough to eat** ella se quedaba sin comer para que sus hijos tuvieran suficiente **(b)** *Formal* **from w.** desde fuera

**withstand** [wɪð'stænd] *(pt & pp* **withstood** [wɪð'stʊd]) *vt* soportar, aguantar

**witless** ['wɪtlɪs] *adj (person, remark)* necio(a), simple; **to scare sb w.** helar la sangre en las venas a alguien

**witness** ['wɪtnɪs] **1** *n* **(a)** *Law* testigo *mf*; **to call sb as w.** llamar a alguien a testificar; **w. for the defence/prosecution** testigo de descargo/de cargo; **w. box** estrado *m* del testigo **(b)** *(testimony)* **to bear w. (to sth)** dar testimonio (de algo)

**2** *vt (scene)* ser testigo de, presenciar; *Law* **to w. sb's signature** firmar en calidad de testigo de alguien

**3** *vi Law* **to w. to sth** dar testimonio de algo

**witter** ['wɪtə(r)] *vi Fam* **to w. (on)** parlotear

**witticism** ['wɪtɪsɪzəm] *n* ocurrencia *f*, agudeza *f*

**wittily** ['wɪtɪlɪ] *adv* ingeniosamente

**wittingly** ['wɪtɪŋlɪ] *adv (intentionally)* adrede, intencionadamente

**witty** ['wɪtɪ] *adj* ingenioso(a), agudo(a)

**wives** [waɪvz] *pl of* **wife**

**wizard** ['wɪzəd] *n* brujo *m*, mago *m*; *Fig* genio *m*

**wizened** ['wɪzənd] *adj* marchito(a), arrugado(a)

**wk** *(abbr* **week)** semana *f*

**wobble** ['wɒbəl] *vi (of chair, table)* tambalearse, cojear; *(of jelly)* temblar, agitarse

**wobbly** ['wɒblɪ] **1** *n Fam* **to throw a w.** ponerse hecho(a) un basilisco

**2** *adj (chair, table)* cojo(a); *(shelf, ladder)* tambaleante; **to be w. (on one's legs)** tambalearse, andar con paso inseguro

**woe** [wəʊ] *n Literary* infortunio *m*, desdicha *f*; **he gave me a tale of w.** me contó una sarta de desgracias

**woebegone** ['wəʊbɪgɒn] *adj (look, expression)* desconsolado(a)

**woeful** ['wəʊfʊl] *adj* **(a)** *(sad)* apesadumbrado(a), afligido(a) **(b)** *(terrible)* penoso(a), deplorable; **w. ignorance** una ignorancia supina

**wog** [wɒg] *n very Fam* moreno(a) *m,f*, = término ofensivo para referirse a una persona que no es de raza blanca, especialmente afrocaribeños

**wok** [wɒk] *n* wok *m*, = sartén china con forma de cuenco

**woke** [wəʊk] *pt of* **wake**[3]

**woken** ['wəʊkən] *pp of* **wake**[3]

**wolf** [wʊlf] *(pl* **wolves** [wʊlvz]) *n* **(a)** lobo *m*; **w. cub** lobezno *m*, lobato *m* **(b)** *(idioms)* **to earn enough to keep the w. from the door** ganar lo suficiente como para ir tirando; **to throw sb to the wolves** arrojar a alguien a las fieras; **a w. in sheep's clothing** un lobo con piel de cordero; **to cry w.** dar una falsa voz de alarma

▸**wolf down** *vt sep* tragar, engullir

**woman** ['wʊmən] *(pl* **women** ['wɪmɪn]) *n* mujer *f*; **don't be such an old w.!** *(said to man)* ¡no seas tan quejica!; **the women's movement** el movimiento feminista; **women's page** páginas *fpl* femeninas; **women's magazine** revista *f* femenina; *Euph* **women's problems** *(gynaecological)* problemas *mpl* femeninos; **w. driver** conductora *f*

**womanizer** ['wʊmənaɪzə(r)] *n* mujeriego *m*

**womanly** ['wʊmənlɪ] *adj* femenino(a)

**womb** [wuːm] *n* matriz *f*, útero *m*

**women** ['wɪmɪn] *pl of* **woman**

**womenfolk** ['wɪmɪnfəʊk] *n* mujeres *fpl*

**won** [wʌn] *pt & pp of* **win**

**wonder** ['wʌndə(r)] **1** *n* **(a)** *(miracle)* milagro *m*; **to work** or **do wonders** hacer milagros; **it's a w. (that) he hasn't lost it** es un milagro or es increíble que no lo haya perdido; **no w. the plan failed** no es de extrañar que el plan haya fracasado; **w. drug** panacea *f* **(b)** *(astonishment)* asombro *m*; **in w.** con asombro

**2** *vt* preguntarse; **one wonders whether…** me pregunto si…; **I was wondering if you were free tonight** se me ocurre que quizá no tengas nada que hacer esta noche

**3** *vi* **(a)** *(be curious)* tener curiosidad, pensar; **to w. about sth** preguntarse por algo; **I w. about her sometimes** hay veces que no la entiendo **(b)** *Literary (be amazed)* asombrarse (at de)

**wonderful** ['wʌndəfʊl] *adj* maravilloso(a)

**wonky** ['wɒŋkɪ] *adj Fam (wheel, floorboards)* flojo(a); *(table)* cojo(a)

**wont** [wəunt] *Formal* **1** *n* costumbre *f*; **as is his w.** como acostumbra

**2** *adj* **to be w. to do sth** ser dado(a) a hacer algo

**won't** [wəunt] = **will not**

**woo** [wu:] *vt* **(a)** *Literary (woman)* cortejar **(b)** *Fig (supporters, investors)* atraer

**wood** [wud] *n* **(a)** *(material)* madera *f*; *(for fire)* leña *f*; **made of w.** de madera; **w. carving** *(object)* talla *f* (en madera) **(b)** *(forest)* bosque *m*; **the woods** el bosque **(c)** *(idioms)* **she can't see the w. for the trees** los árboles no le dejan ver el bosque; **we're not out of the woods yet** todavía no hemos salido del túnel

**woodbine** ['wudbaın] *n (plant)* madreselva *f*

**woodcock** ['wudkɒk] *n* becada *f*, chocha *f*

**woodcut** ['wudkʌt] *n* grabado *m* en madera, xilografía *f*

**woodcutter** ['wudkʌtə(r)] *n* leñador(ora) *m,f*

**wooded** ['wudıd] *adj* cubierto(a) de árboles, boscoso(a)

**wooden** ['wudən] *adj (made of wood)* de madera; *Fig (unexpressive)* envarado(a), acartonado(a); **w. spoon** cuchara *f* de palo; *Fig* **to get the w. spoon** ser el farolillo rojo

**woodland** ['wudlənd] *n* bosque *m*

**woodlouse** ['wudlaus] *(pl* **woodlice** ['wudlaıs]) *n* cochinilla *f*

**woodpecker** ['wudpekə(r)] *n* pájaro *m* carpintero

**woodpile** ['wudpaıl] *n* montón *m* de leña

**woodshed** ['wudʃed] *n* leñera *f*

**woodwind** ['wudwınd] *n Mus (section of orchestra)* sección *f* de (instrumentos de) viento de madera; **w. instrument** instrumento *m* de viento de madera

**woodwork** ['wudwɜːk] *n* **(a)** *(craft)* carpintería *f* **(b)** *(of house, room)* madera *f*, carpintería *f*; *Fig* **to come** *or* **crawl out of the w.** salir de las sombras, surgir de la nada

**woodworm** ['wudwɜːm] *n* carcoma *f*

**woof** [wuf] *exclam (of dog)* ¡guau!

**wool** [wul] *n* lana *f*; *Fam* **to pull the w. over sb's eyes** dar el pego a alguien

**woollen** ['wulən] **1** *adj (dress)* de lana

**2** *npl* **woollens** prendas *fpl* de lana

**woolly** ['wulı] **1** *adj (jumper)* de lana; *Fig (idea, theory)* confuso(a)

**2** *npl Fam (garment)* **woolies** ropa *f* de lana

**wop** [wɒp] *n very Fam* = término despectivo para referirse a personas de origen italiano

**word** [wɜːd] **1** *n* **(a)** *(in general)* palabra *f*; **w. for w.** al pie de la letra; **in a w.** en una palabra; **in other words** en otras palabras; **not in so many words** no con esas palabras; **not a w.** ni una (sola) palabra; **she said it in her own words** lo dijo con sus propias palabras; **I can't**

put it into words no lo puedo expresar con palabras; **he's a man of few words** es hombre de pocas palabras; **I couldn't get a w. in (edgeways)** no pude meter baza; **the w. of God** la palabra de Dios; **I'll take your w. for it** daré por cierto lo que (me) dices; **to take sb at his w.** no poner en duda lo que alguien dice; **without a w.** sin mediar palabra; **it was too ridiculous for words** no se puede imaginar nada más ridículo; **my w.!** ¡Virgen Santa!; *Comptr* **w. processor** procesador *m* de textos

**(b)** *(remarks, conversation)* **to have a w. with sb** hablar con alguien; **to have words with sb** discutir con alguien; **to give sb the w.** dar un aviso a alguien; **you're putting words into my mouth** me estás atribuyendo cosas que no he dicho; **you've taken the words (right) out of my mouth** me has quitado la palabra de la boca; **to put in a good w. for sb** decir algo en favor de alguien; **he never has a good w. for anyone** nunca tiene buenas palabras para nadie; **a w. of warning** una advertencia; **a w. of advice** un consejo

**(c)** *(news)* **to receive w. from sb** tener noticias de alguien; **to send sb w. of sth** avisar a alguien de algo; **the w. is that…** se rumorea que…; **by w. of mouth** de palabra

**(d)** *(promise)* **w. of honour** palabra *f* de honor; **she gave me her w.** me dio su palabra; **I always keep my w.** yo siempre mantengo mi palabra; **he broke** *or* **went back on his w.** no cumplió con su palabra

**(e)** **words** *(lyrics)* letra *f*

**2** *vt* expresar; *(in writing)* redactar

**wording** ['wɜːdıŋ] *n* **to change the w. of sth** redactar algo de otra forma; **the w. was ambiguous** estaba redactado de forma ambigua

**word-processing** [wɜːd'prəusesıŋ] *n Comptr* tratamiento *m* de textos

**wordy** ['wɜːdı] *adj* verboso(a)

**wore** [wɔː(r)] *pt of* **wear**

**work** [wɜːk] **1** *n* **(a)** *(labour)* trabajo *m*; **to be at w. (on sth)** estar trabajando (en algo); **to get to w.** ponerse a trabajar; **w. in progress** *(sign)* trabajos en curso; *Comptr* **w. station** estación *f* de trabajo

**(b)** *(employment)* trabajo *m*, empleo *m*; **to look for w.** buscar empleo *or* trabajo; **to be out of w.** no tener trabajo, estar parado(a); **w. permit** permiso *m* de trabajo

**(c)** *(tasks)* trabajo *m*; **to have w. to do** tener trabajo (que hacer); **it will take a lot of w.** costará mucho trabajo; **to put a lot of w. into sth** poner mucho esfuerzo en algo; **let's get down to w.!** ¡manos a la obra!; **to have one's w. cut out** tenerlo bastante difícil; **to make quick** *or* **short w. of sth** despachar algo en seguida; **it's all in a day's w.** es el pan nuestro de cada día; **good** *or* **nice w.!** ¡buen trabajo!

**(d)** *(product, achievement)* obra *f*; **a w. of art** una obra de arte; **is this all your own w.?** ¿lo has hecho todo tú mismo?

**(e)** *Ind* **works council** comité *m* de empresa; **works outing** excursión *f* anual (de los trabajadores de una empresa)

**(f) works** *(construction)* obras *fpl*

**(g) works** *(mechanism)* mecanismo *m*

**(h)** *Fam* **the works** *(everything)* todo; **to give sb the works** *(beating)* dar una paliza a alguien; *(luxury treatment)* tratar a alguien a cuerpo de rey

**2** *vt* **(a) to w. sb hard** hacer trabajar mucho a alguien; **to w. oneself to death** matarse a trabajar; **to w. one's passage** pagarse el pasaje trabajando en el barco

**(b)** *(operate) (machine)* manejar, hacer funcionar

**(c)** *(bring about) (miracle, cure)* hacer, obrar; **to w. a change on sth/sb** operar un cambio en algo/alguien; **I'll w. it** *or* **things so that they pay in advance** lo arreglaré de forma que paguen por adelantado

**(d)** *(move)* **to w. one's hands free** lograr soltarse las manos; **to w. one's way through a book** ir avanzando en la lectura de un libro

**(e)** *(exploit) (mine, quarry)* explotar; *(land)* labrar

**3** *vi* **(a)** *(of person)* trabajar; **to w. for sb** trabajar para alguien; **her age works against her/in her favour** la edad juega en su contra/en su favor; *Ind* **to w. to rule** hacer huelga de celo

**(b)** *(function) (of machine, system)* funcionar

**(c)** *(have effect) (of medicine)* hacer efecto; *(of plan, method)* funcionar

▸ **work in** *vt sep* *(include)* añadir, incluir

▸ **work off** *vt sep* **he worked off 5 kilos** perdió 5 kilos haciendo ejercicio; **she worked off her anger** desahogó su enfado

▸ **work on 1** *vt insep* **to w. on sth** trabajar en algo

**2** *vi* *(continue to work)* seguir trabajando

▸ **work out 1** *vt sep* *(cost, total)* calcular; **to w. out the answer** dar con la solución; **to w. out how to do sth** dar con la manera de hacer algo; **I'm sure we can w. this thing out** estoy seguro de que lo podemos arreglar

**2** *vi* **(a)** *(of problem, situation)* **it all worked out in the end** al final todo salió bien; **to w. out well/badly (for sb)** salir bien/mal (a alguien) **(b)** *(total)* salir; **it works out at £150 a head** sale a 150 libras por cabeza **(c)** *(exercise)* hacer ejercicios

▸ **work up** *vt sep* **(a)** *(develop)* **to w. up enthusiasm/interest for sth** ir entusiasmándose con/interesándose por algo; **he had worked up an appetite** ya le había entrado el apetito **(b)** *(excite)* **to get worked up (about sth)** alterarse (por algo)

▸ **work up to** *vt insep* prepararse para

**workable** ['wɜːkəbəl] *adj* factible

**workaday** ['wɜːkədeɪ] *adj* corriente, de todos los días

**workaholic** [wɜːkə'hɒlɪk] *n Fam* **to be a w.** estar obsesionado(a) con el trabajo

**workbench** ['wɜːkbentʃ] *n* banco *m* de carpintero

**workday** ['wɜːkdeɪ] *n US* jornada *f* laboral

**worker** ['wɜːkə(r)] *n* trabajador(ora) *m,f*; **to be a fast/slow w.** trabajar rápido/lento; **w. bee** abeja *f* obrera; **w. participation** participación *f* (de los trabajadores) en la empresa

**workforce** ['wɜːkfɔːs] *n* *(working population)* población *f* activa; *(employees)* trabajadores *mpl*, mano *f* de obra

**workhouse** ['wɜːkhaʊs] *n Hist* = institución pública en la que los pobres trabajaban a cambio de comida y albergue

**working** ['wɜːkɪŋ] **1** *n* **(a)** *(operation) (of machine)* funcionamiento *m* **(b) workings** *(mechanism)* mecanismo *m*, maquinaria *f*

**2** *adj* *(person)* con trabajo, trabajador(ora); **to have a w. knowledge of French** tener un conocimiento básico de francés; **to be in w. order** funcionar bien; **w. agreement** acuerdo *m* tácito; **the w. class** la clase trabajadora *or* obrera; **w. clothes/conditions** ropa *f*/condiciones *fpl* de trabajo; **w. hours** horario *m* de trabajo; **w. life** vida *f* laboral; **w. lunch** almuerzo *m* de trabajo; **w. majority** mayoría *f* suficiente; **w. model** prototipo *m*; **w. party** comisión *f* de trabajo; **w. population** población *f* activa

**working-class** ['wɜːkɪŋ'klɑːs] *adj* de clase obrera

**workload** ['wɜːkləʊd] *n* cantidad *f* de trabajo

**workman** ['wɜːkmən] *n* obrero *m*

**workmanlike** ['wɜːkmənlaɪk] *adj* competente, profesional

**workmanship** ['wɜːkmənʃɪp] *n* confección *f*, factura *f*; **a fine piece of w.** un trabajo excelente

**work-out** ['wɜːkaʊt] *n* sesión *f* de ejercicios

**workplace** ['wɜːkpleɪs] *n* lugar *m* de trabajo

**workshop** ['wɜːkʃɒp] *n also Fig* taller *m*

**workshy** ['wɜːkʃaɪ] *adj* perezoso(a)

**worktop** ['wɜːktɒp] *n* *(in kitchen)* encimera *f*

**work-to-rule** [wɜːktə'ruːl] *n Ind* huelga *f* de celo

**world** [wɜːld] *n* **(a)** *(the earth)* mundo *m*; **the best/biggest in the w.** el mejor/más grande del mundo; **to go round the w.** dar la vuelta al mundo; **the w. over, all over the w.** en todas partes; **the W. Bank** el Banco Mundial; **w. champion** campeón(ona) *m,f* mundial; **the W. Cup** el Mundial (de fútbol), los Mundiales (de fútbol); **w. map** mapamundi *m*; **w.**

**music** música *f* étnica; **w. record** récord *m* mundial *or* del mundo; **W. Series** = final a siete partidos entre los dos campeones de las ligas de béisbol en Estados Unidos; **W. War One/Two** la Primera/Segunda Guerra Mundial

(b) *(sphere of activity)* mundo *m*; **the literary/ business w.** el mundo literario/de los negocios

(c) *(society)* **a man of the w.** un hombre de mundo; **to go up in the w.** prosperar; **to come down in the w.** venir a menos; **he's got the w. at his feet** tiene el mundo a sus pies

(d) *(for emphasis)* **that will do you the w. of good** te vendrá la mar de bien; **there's a w. of difference between the two parties** los dos partidos no tienen nada que ver (el uno con el otro); **she thinks the w. of him** lo quiere como a nada en el mundo; **they carried on for all the w. as if nothing had happened** siguieron tranquilamente como si nada hubiera pasado

(e) *(idioms)* **he's not long for this w.** le queda poco, está con un pie en la tumba; **to bring a child into the w.** traer un niño al mundo; **he wants to have the best of both worlds** él quiere tenerlo todo (y eso no es posible); **she lives in a w. of her own** vive en su propio mundo; *Fam* **it's out of this w.** es una maravilla; **not for (anything in) the w.** ni por todo el oro del mundo; **it's a small w.!** ¡el mundo es un pañuelo!; **what is the w. coming to?** ¿adónde vamos a ir a parar?

**world-beater** ['wɜːldbiːtə(r)] *n (sportsperson)* fuera de serie *mf*; *(product)* producto *m* fuera de serie

**world-famous** ['wɜːld'feɪməs] *adj* mundialmente famoso(a)

**worldly** ['wɜːldlɪ] *adj (pleasure)* mundano(a), terrenal; **w. goods** bienes *mpl* terrenales; **w. wisdom** gramática *f* parda

**worldly-wise** ['wɜːldlɪ'waɪz] *adj* **to be w.** tener mucha experiencia de *or* en la vida

**world-weary** ['wɜːldwɪərɪ] *adj* hastiado(a) (del mundo)

**worldwide** ['wɜːldwaɪd] **1** *adj* mundial; *Comptr* **the W. Web** la Web

**2** *adv* en todo el mundo

**worm** [wɜːm] **1** *n* gusano *m*; *(earthworm)* lombriz *f* (de tierra); *Med* **to have worms** tener lombrices; *Fig* **he's a w.** es un miserable *or* un gusano; *Fig* **the w. has turned!** ¡finalmente se enseña los dientes!

**2** *vt* (a) *(cat, dog)* administrar vermífugos a (b) **she wormed her way out of the situation** logró salir del paso; *Pej* **to w. oneself into sb's favour/confidence** ganarse el favor/la confianza de alguien; **to w. a secret out of sb** sonsacar un secreto a alguien

**worm-eaten** ['wɜːmiːtən] *adj (wood)* carcomido(a); *(fruit)* agusanado(a)

**worn** [wɔːn] *pp of* **wear**

**worried** ['wʌrɪd] *adj* preocupado(a); **to be w. (about)** estar preocupado(a) (por)

**worrier** ['wʌrɪə(r)] *n* **to be a w.** preocuparse por todo

**worry** ['wʌrɪ] **1** *n* preocupación *f*; **it's causing me a lot of w.** me tiene muy preocupado; **that's the least of my worries** eso es lo que menos me preocupa

**2** *vt (cause anxiety to)* preocupar; **it doesn't w. me** no me preocupa; **to w. oneself sick (about sth)** angustiarse (por algo)

**3** *vi* preocuparse **(about** de); **not to w.!** ¡no pasa nada!; **don't (you) w. about me** no te preocupes por mí; **there's** *or* **it's nothing to w. about** no hay de qué preocuparse

**worrying** ['wʌrɪɪŋ] *adj* preocupante

**worse** [wɜːs] **1** *adj (comparative of* **bad)** peor **(than** que); **there's nothing w. than...** no hay nada peor que...; **to get w.** empeorar; **it could have been w.** podría haber sido peor; **to make matters w.** empeorar las cosas; **to go from bad to w.** ir de mal en peor; **I'm none the w. for it** no me afectó en nada; **so much the w. for them!** ¡peor para ellos!; **she was the w. for drink** estaba bastante bebida; *Fam* **to be the w. for wear** *(of car, book, drunk person)* estar para el arrastre; **I can't go, w. luck!** ¡no puedo ir, qué fastidio!

**2** *adv (comparative of* **badly)** peor; **you could do (a lot) w. than accept their offer** harías bien en aceptar su oferta; **I don't think any w. of her for it** no tengo peor concepto de ella por eso; **he is w. off than before** las cosas le van peor que antes

**3** *n* **there was w. to come** lo peor no había llegado aún; **I've seen w.** he visto cosas peores; **a change for the w.** un cambio a peor

**worsen** ['wɜːsən] *vt & vi* empeorar

**Worship** ['wɜːʃɪp] *n* **His/Her W.** *(referring to judge)* Su Señoría; **His W. the Mayor** el excelentísimo señor alcalde

**worship** ['wɜːʃɪp] **1** *n (of deity)* adoración *f* **(of** de), culto *m* **(of** a); *(of person)* adoración *f* **(of** por); **place of w.** templo *m*

**2** *vt (pt & pp* **worshipped,** *US* **worshiped)** *(deity)* adorar, rendir culto a; *(person)* adorar; *(money)* rendir culto a

**worst** [wɜːst] **1** *adj (superlative of* **bad)** peor; **the w. book** el peor libro; **the w. film** la peor película; **his w. mistake** su error más grave; **the w. thing was...** lo peor fue...

**2** *adv (superlative of* **badly)** peor; **w. of all,...** y lo que es peor,...; **the elderly are the w. off**

los ancianos son los que peor están; **he came off w.** (él) llevó la peor parte, el fue quien salió peor

**3** *n* **he's the w. of them all** es el peor de todos; **the w. that could happen** lo peor que podría suceder; **the w. of it is that...** lo peor de todo es que...; **he's prepared for the w.** está preparado para lo peor; **at the w.,** if it comes to the w.** en el peor de los casos; **the w. is yet to come** lo peor está aún por llegar; **do your w.!** ¡aquí te espero!, ¡ven a por mí si puedes!; **the w. is over** ya ha pasado lo peor

**worst-case scenario** ['wɜːstkeɪsɪ-'nɑːrɪəʊ] (*pl* **worst-case scenarios**) *n* **this is a w.** esto es lo que ocurriría en el peor de los casos

**worsted** ['wʊstɪd] *n Tex* estameña *f*

**worth** [wɜːθ] **1** *n* valor *m*; **give me £20 w.** of **petrol** póngame 20 libras de gasolina; **to get one's money's w.** sacar partido al *or* del dinero

**2** *prep* (a) *(having a value of)* **to be w. a lot of money** valer mucho dinero; **how much is it w.?** ¿qué valor tiene?; **that's my opinion, for what it's w.** esa es mi opinión, si sirve de algo; **he's w. millions** está forrado; **he was pulling for all he was w.** tiraba con todas sus fuerzas (b) *(meriting)* **the museum is w. a visit** merece la pena visitar el museo; **this book is not w.** buying no merece la pena comprar este libro; **it is/isn't w. it** merece/ no merece la pena; **it's w. thinking about** es algo a tener en cuenta

**worthless** ['wɜːθlɪs] *adj* **to be w.** *(thing)* no valer nada, no tener ningún valor; **he's completely w.** es un perfecto inútil

**worthwhile** [wɜːθ'waɪl] *adj* **to be w.** merecer *or* valer la pena

**worthy** ['wɜːðɪ] **1** *n* **the town worthies** los notables *or* las fuerzas vivas de la ciudad

**2** *adj* *(person, life)* virtuoso(a); **to be w. of sth** merecer algo; **w. of respect** digno(a) de respeto

**would** [wʊd]

---

En el inglés hablado, y en el escrito en estilo coloquial, el verbo **would** se contrae de manera que **I/you/he** *etc* **would** se transforman en **I'd, you'd, he'd** *etc*. La forma negativa **would not** se transforma en **wouldn't**.

---

*modal aux v* (a) *(expressing conditional tense)* **she w. come if you invited her** si la invitases, vendría; **had he let go** *or* **if he had let go, he w. have fallen** si (se) hubiera soltado, se habría caído; **they w. never agree to such conditions** nunca aceptarían unas condiciones así; **w. you do it? – yes I w./no I wouldn't** ¿lo harías? – sí/no; **you wouldn't do it, w. you?** tú no lo harías, ¿verdad?

(b) *(expressing wish, determination)* **I wouldn't**

do it for anything** no lo haría por nada del mundo; **she wouldn't let me speak to him** no me dejaba hablar con él; **what w. you have me do?** ¿qué quieres que haga?; **the wound wouldn't heal** la herida no cicatrizaba; **w. you pass the mustard please?** ¿me pasas la mostaza, por favor?; **w. you like a drink?** ¿te apetece tomar algo?; **be quiet, w. you!** haz el favor de callarte, ¿quieres?

(c) *(for emphasis)* **you WOULD insist on going!** ¡pero tú tenías que insistir en ir!; **I forgot – you w.** se me olvidó – ¡hombre, cómo no!

(d) *(expressing past habit)* **she w. often return home exhausted** solía volver agotada a casa; **there w. always be some left over** siempre sobraba algo

(e) *(in reported speech)* **she told me she w. be there** me dijo que estaría allí; **I said I w. do it** dije que lo haría

(f) *(conjecture)* **w. that be my pen you're using?** ¿no será ese bolígrafo que estás usando el mío?; **that w. have been before your time** eso debe de haber sido antes de tu época; **I wouldn't know** no sé

**would-be** ['wʊdbiː] *adj* **a w. actor/politician** un aspirante a actor/político

**wouldn't** ['wʊdnt] = **would not**

**wound¹** [wuːnd] **1** *n* herida *f*

**2** *vt also Fig* herir

**wound²** [waʊnd] *pt & pp of* **wind²**

**wounded** ['wuːndɪd] **1** *npl* **the w.** los heridos

**2** *adj* herido(a); **to be w.** estar herido(a)

**wounding** ['wuːndɪŋ] *adj* hiriente

**wove** [wəʊv] *pt of* **weave**

**woven** ['wəʊvən] *pp of* **weave**

**wow** [waʊ] *Fam* **1** *vt* encandilar

**2** *exclam* ¡hala!

**WP** [dʌbəljuː'piː] *n Comptr* (a) *(abbr* **word processor***)* procesador *m* de textos (b) *(abbr* **word-processing***)* tratamiento *m* de textos

**WPC** [dʌbəljuːpiː'siː] *n* *(abbr* **woman police constable***)* agente *f* de policía

**wpm** [dʌbəljuːpiː'em] *(abbr* **words per minute***)* palabras *fpl* por minuto

**WRAC** [ræk] *n Br* *(abbr* **Women's Royal Army Corps***)* = sección femenina del ejército británico

**wrangle** ['ræŋgəl] **1** *n* disputa *f*

**2** *vi* pelear (**about** *or* **over** por), reñir (**about** *or* **over** por)

**wrap** [ræp] **1** *n* *(shawl)* chal *m*; *Fig* **to keep sth under wraps** mantener algo en secreto

**2** *vt* *(pt & pp* **wrapped***)* envolver (**in** con); **she wrapped the bandage round his head** le puso una venda alrededor de la cabeza; *Fig* **wrapped in mystery** rodeado(a) de misterio

▶**wrap up 1** *vt sep* (**a**) *(parcel, present)* envolver; *Fig* **to be wrapped up in sth** *(absorbed)* estar absorto(a) en algo (**b**) *Fam (bring to an end)* poner punto final a

**2** *vi (dress warmly)* abrigarse

**wrapper** ['ræpə(r)] *n* envoltorio *m*

**wrapping** ['ræpɪŋ] *n* envoltura *f*, envoltorio *m*; **w. paper** papel *m* de envolver

**wrath** [rɒθ] *n Literary* ira *f*

**wreak** [ri:k] *vt* **to w. havoc** causar estragos; **to w. vengeance on sb** vengarse de alguien

**wreath** [ri:θ] *n (of flowers)* corona *f* (de flores)

**wreathe** [ri:ð] *vt* coronar

**wreck** [rek] **1** *n (ship)* restos *mpl* del naufragio; *(car, train, plane)* restos *mpl* del accidente; *Fig* **to be a physical w.** estar destrozado(a) físicamente; *Fig* **to be a nervous w.** tener los nervios destrozados

**2** *vt (ship)* hundir; *(car, room, house)* destrozar; *Fig (plans, hopes, happiness)* dar al traste con; *Fig (marriage, career)* destruir, arruinar; **to w. one's health** destrozarse la salud

**wreckage** ['rekɪdʒ] *n (of ship)* restos *mpl* del naufragio; *(of car, train, plane)* restos *mpl* del accidente

**wrecker** ['rekə(r)] *n US (salvage vehicle)* grúa *f*

**wren** [ren] *n* chochín *m*

**wrench** [rentʃ] **1** *n* (**a**) *(pull)* tirón *m*; *(to ankle, shoulder)* torcedura *f*; *Fig* **it was a w. to leave me** partía el corazón tener que irme (**b**) *(spanner)* llave *f*; *(adjustable spanner)* llave *f* inglesa

**2** *vt* **to w. one's ankle/one's shoulder** torcerse un tobillo/un hombro; **to w. sth out of sb's hands** arrancarle algo a alguien de las manos

**wrest** [rest] *vt* **to w. sth from sb** arrebatar *or* arrancar algo a alguien

**wrestle** ['resəl] *vi* luchar; *Fig* **to w. with a problem** lidiar con un problema

**wrestler** ['reslə(r)] *n* luchador(ora) *m,f* (de lucha libre)

**wrestling** ['reslɪŋ] *n* lucha *f* libre; **w. match** combate *m* de lucha libre

**wretch** [retʃ] *n* miserable *mf*

**wretched** ['retʃɪd] *adj* (**a**) *(very bad)* horrible, inmundo(a) (**b**) *(unhappy)* abatido(a) (**c**) *(for emphasis)* **I can't find the w. umbrella!** ¡no encuentro el maldito paraguas!

**wriggle** ['rɪɡəl] **1** *vt* **to w. one's way out of a situation** lograr escurrir el bulto (de una situación)

**2** *vi* **to w. (about)** menearse; **to w. out of sth/of doing sth** escaquearse de algo/de hacer algo

**wring** [rɪŋ] *(pt & pp* **wrung** [rʌŋ]) *vt (clothes)* escurrir, estrujar; **to w. one's hands** retorcerse

las manos; *Fam* **I'd like to w. his neck** me gustaría retorcerle el pescuezo; *Fig* **to w. sth from sb** sacarle algo a alguien

**wringer** ['rɪŋə(r)] *n* escurridor *m* de rodillos; *Fam Fig* **to put sb through the w.** hacer pasar un mal trago a alguien

**wringing** ['rɪŋɪŋ] *adj* **to be w. (wet)** estar empapado(a)

**wrinkle** ['rɪŋkəl] **1** *n* arruga *f*

**2** *vi* arrugarse

**wrinkled** ['rɪŋkəld] *adj* arrugado(a)

**wrinkly** ['rɪŋklɪ] *adj* arrugado(a)

**wrist** [rɪst] *n* muñeca *f*

**wristwatch** ['rɪstwɒtʃ] *n* reloj *m* (de pulsera)

**writ** [rɪt] *n Law* mandato *m* judicial; **to serve a w. on sb** entregar un mandato judicial a alguien

**write** [raɪt] *(pt* **wrote** [rəʊt], *pp* **written** ['rɪtən]) **1** *vt (answer, name, letter)* escribir; *(cheque)* extender; *US* **to w. sb** escribir a alguien; **she had guilt written all over her face** su rostro era el vivo retrato de la culpabilidad

**2** *vi* escribir; *Br* **to w. to sb** escribir a alguien; **to w. for a newspaper** escribir *or* colaborar en un periódico; *Fam* **that's nothing to w. home about** eso no es nada del otro mundo

▶**write away for** *vt insep* **to w. away for sth** escribir pidiendo algo

▶**write back** *vi* responder, contestar *(por carta)*

▶**write down** *vt sep* escribir, anotar

▶**write in 1** *vt sep (name, answer)* escribir

**2** *vi (send letter)* escribir

▶**write off 1** *vt sep* (**a**) *(debt)* condonar (**b**) *Fam (car)* cargarse (**c**) *Fam (person)* descartar; **to w. sb off as a has-been** considerar que alguien está acabado

**2** *vi* **to w. off for sth** escribir pidiendo algo

▶**write out** *vt sep (instructions, recipe)* escribir, copiar; *(cheque)* extender

▶**write up** *vt sep (notes, thesis)* redactar; *(diary, journal)* poner al día

**write-off** ['raɪtɒf] *n* (**a**) *(of debt)* condonación *f* (**b**) *Fam (car)* siniestro *m* total

**write-protected** ['raɪtprə'tektɪd] *adj Comptr* protegido(a) contra escritura

**writer** ['raɪtə(r)] *n (by profession)* escritor(ora) *m,f*; *(of article, book)* autor(ora) *m,f*

**write-up** ['raɪtʌp] *n (of play)* crítica *f*

**writhe** [raɪð] *vi* retorcerse

**writing** ['raɪtɪŋ] *n* (**a**) *(action)* escritura *f*; *(profession)* literatura *f*; **w. desk** escritorio *m*; **w. paper** papel *m* de escribir (**b**) *(handwriting)* letra *f*, escritura *f* (**c**) *(thing written) (literature)* literatura *f*; *(written words)* escritura *f*; **in w.** por escrito; *Fig* **the w. is on the wall for him** tiene los días contados

**written** ['rɪtən] **1** *adj* escrito(a); **w. consent** consentimiento *m* por escrito; **w.**

**examination** examen *m* escrito

 **2** *pp of* **write**

**WRNS** [renz] *n Br* (*abbr* **Women's Royal Naval Service**) = sección femenina de la marina británica

**wrong** [rɒŋ] **1** *n* (*immoral actions*) mal *m*; **to know right from w.** distinguir el bien del mal; **he can do no w.** lo hace todo bien; **to do sb w.** agraviar a alguien; **to right a w.** deshacer un entuerto; *Prov* **two wrongs don't make a right** vengándose no se consigue nada; **to be in the w.** ser el/la culpable

 **2** *adj* (**a**) (*morally bad*) malo(a); **stealing is w.** robar está mal; **it was w. of you not to tell me** hiciste mal en no decírmelo

 (**b**) (*incorrect, mistaken*) erróneo(a), incorrecto(a); **to be w.** (*person*) estar equivocado(a); (*answer*) ser erróneo(a); **my watch is w.** mi reloj va mal; **you chose the w. moment** no escogiste el momento oportuno; **don't get the w. idea** no te equivoques; **I did/said the w. thing** hice/dije lo que no debía; **to drive on the w. side of the road** conducir por el lado contrario de la carretera; *Fig* **to catch sb on the w. foot** pillar a alguien desprevenido(a); *Fig* **to start** *or* **get off on the w. foot** empezar con mal pie; *Fig* **to go about it the w. way** hacerlo mal; *Fig* **to get on the w. side of sb** ponerse a mal con alguien; *Fig* **to back the w. horse** apostar por el perdedor; **you have the w. number** (*on phone*) se ha equivocado de número

 (**c**) (*amiss*) **what's w.?** ¿qué pasa?; **what's w. with you?** ¿qué te pasa?; **is anything w.?** ¿pasa algo?; *Fam* **to be w. in the head** estar chiflado(a); **there's something w. with our car** le pasa algo al coche

 **3** *adv* (**a**) (*morally*) mal; **he admitted he had done w.** admitió que había hecho mal

 (**b**) (*incorrectly*) mal; **to go w.** (*plan*) salir mal; (*make mistake*) equivocarse; **to guess w.** no acertar, equivocarse; **don't get me w., I like her** no me malentiendas, (ella) me cae bien

 **4** *vt* agraviar, tratar injustamente

**wrongdoer** ['rɒŋduː:ə(r)] *n* malhechor(ora) *m,f*

**wrongdoing** ['rɒŋduː:ɪŋ] *n* (*immoral actions*) desmanes *mpl*; (*crime*) delito *m*, delincuencia *f*

**wrongful** ['rɒŋfʊl] *adj* injusto(a); **w. dismissal** despido *m* improcedente

**wrong-headed** [rɒŋ'hedɪd] *adj* empecinado(a)

**wrongly** ['rɒŋlɪ] *adv* (**a**) (*unjustly*) injustamente (**b**) (*incorrectly*) erróneamente

**wrote** [rəʊt] *pt of* **write**

**wrought-iron** ['rɔːt'aɪən] *adj* de hierro forjado

**wrought-up** ['rɔːt'ʌp] *adj* **to be w.** (**about sth**) estar muy alterado(a) (por algo)

**wrung** [rʌŋ] *pt & pp of* **wring**

**wry** [raɪ] *adj* irónico(a)

**wt** (*abbr* **weight**) peso *m*

**WW** (*abbr* **World War**) **WWI/II** la Primera/Segunda Guerra Mundial

**WWF** [dʌbəlju:dʌbəlju:'ef] *n* (*abbr* **World Wildlife Fund, Worldwide Fund for Nature**) WWF *m*, Fondo *m* Mundial para la Naturaleza

**WWW** *n* (*abbr* **Worldwide Web**) WWW *f*

**WYSIWYG** ['wɪzɪwɪg], *n Comptr* (*abbr* **What You See Is What You Get**) WYSIWYG, = se imprime lo que ves

**X, x** [eks] *n (letter)* X, x *f*; **for x number of years** durante un número x de años, durante x años; *Formerly* **X (certificate) film** película *f* para mayores de 18 años

**xenon** ['zenɒn] *n Chem* xenón *m*

**xenophobia** [zenə'fəʊbɪə] *n* xenofobia *f*

**xenophobic** [zenə'fəʊbɪk] *adj* xenófobo(a)

**Xerox®** ['zɪərɒks] **1** *n* fotocopia *f*, xerocopia *f*
 **2** *vt* fotocopiar

**XL** (*abbr* **extra large**) XL, (talla *f*) muy grande

**Xmas** ['krɪsməs, 'eksməs] *n (abbr* **Christmas**) Navidad *f*

**X-ray** ['eksreɪ] **1** *n (pl* **X-rays**) *(radiation)* rayo *m* X; *(picture)* radiografía *f*; **X. examination** examen *m* por rayos X; **to have an X.** hacerse una radiografía
 **2** *vt* radiografiar

**xylophone** ['zaɪləfəʊn] *n* xilófono *m*

**Y, y** [waɪ] *n (letter)* Y, y *f*; **Y-fronts®** slip *m*, eslip *m*

**yacht** [jɒt] *n (sailing boat)* velero *m*; *(large private boat)* yate *m*; **y. club** club *m* náutico; **y. race** regata *f*

**yachting** ['jɒtɪŋ] *n (navegación f a)* vela *f*

**yachtsman** ['jɒtsmən] *n (in race)* tripulante *m*; *(round-the-world)* navegante *m*

**yak** [jæk] *n* yak *m*, yac *m*

**yam** [jæm] *n Br* ñame *m*; *US* boniato *m*

**Yank** [jæŋk], **Yankee** ['jæŋkɪ] *n Br Fam (person from the USA)* yanqui *mf*; *US Fam (person from north-eastern USA)* = estadounidense procedente del nordeste del país

**yank** [jæŋk] **1** *n Fam* **to give sth a y.** dar un tirón a algo
 **2** *vt Fam* **to y. the door open** abrir la puerta de un tirón; **to y. sth out** arrancar algo de un tirón

**yap** [jæp] *(pt & pp* **yapped)** *vi (of dog)* ladrar *(de forma aguda); Fam (of person)* chacharear, parlotear

**yard¹** [jɑːd] *n (measurement)* yarda *f* (0,914 m)

**yard²** *n* **(a)** *(of house, school)* patio *m*; *(of farm)* corral *m*; *US (garden)* jardín *m* **(b)** *(for working)* taller *m (al aire libre); (ship)* **y.** astillero *m* **(c)** *(for storage)* almacén *m*, depósito *m (al aire libre);* **(builder's) y.** almacén de materiales de construcción

**yardstick** ['jɑːdstɪk] *n (standard)* patrón *m* (de medida)

**yarn** [jɑːn] *n* **(a)** *Tex* hilo *m* **(b)** *Fam (story)* batallita *f*; **to spin a y.** contar batallitas

**yawn** [jɔːn] **1** *n* bostezo *m*; *Fam (boring thing)* pesadez *f*, latazo *m*
 **2** *vi* **(a)** *(of person)* bostezar **(b)** *(of chasm)* abrirse

**yds** (*abbr* **yards**) yardas *fpl*

**ye** [jiː] **1** *pron Literary* = **you**
 **2** *definite article Literary or Hum* = **the**

**yea** [jeɪ] **1** *n* **yeas and nays** votos *mpl* a favor y en contra
 **2** *adv Literary* = **yes**

**yeah** [jeə] *adv Fam* sí; **oh y.?** *(in disbelief, challenging)* ¿ah, sí?

**year** [jɪə(r)] *n* año *m*; *(at school, university)* curso *m*; **in the y. 1931** en el año 1931; **this y.** este año; **last y.** el año pasado; **next y.** el año que viene; **every y.** todos los años; **twice a y.** dos veces al año; **to earn £20,000 a y.** ganar 20.000 libras al año; **to be ten years old** tener diez años; **he got five years** *(prison sentence)* le cayeron cinco años; **for many years** durante muchos años; **y. in y. out** año tras año; **over the years** con el paso de los años; **years ago** hace años; **it's years since I saw him, I haven't seen him for** or **in years** hace años que no lo veo; **from his earliest years** desde temprana edad; **to be getting on in years** empezar a hacerse viejo(a)

**yearbook** ['jɪəbʊk] *n* anuario *m*

**yearlong** ['jɪəlɒŋ] *adj* **a y. wait** una espera de un año

**yearly** ['jɪəlɪ] **1** *adj* anual
**2** *adv* anualmente, cada año; **twice y.** dos veces al año

**yearn** [jɜːn] *vi* **to y. for sth/to do sth** anhelar algo/hacer algo

**yearning** ['jɜːnɪŋ] *n* anhelo *m*

**yeast** [jiːst] *n* levadura *f*

**yell** [jel] **1** *n* grito *m*; **to give a y.** dar un grito
**2** *vt & vi* gritar

**yellow** ['jeləʊ] **1** *n* amarillo *m*
**2** *adj* **(a)** *(in colour)* amarillo(a); **to turn** or **go y.** amarillear, ponerse amarillo(a); **y. card** *(in football)* tarjeta *f* amarilla; *Med* **y. fever** fiebre *f* amarilla; *Tel* **the Y. Pages®** las páginas amarillas; **the Y. River** el río Amarillo or Huango Ho **(b)** *Fam (cowardly)* cagueta, gallina
**3** *vi* amarillear, ponerse amarillo(a)

**yelp** [jelp] **1** *n* aullido *m*
**2** *vi* aullar

**Yemen** ['jemən] *n* Yemen

**Yemeni** ['jemənɪ] *n & adj* yemení *mf*

**yen**[1] [jen] *n (Japanese currency)* yen *m*

**yen**[2] *n* **to have a y. for sth/to do sth** tener muchas ganas de algo/de hacer algo

**Yerevan** [jerə'væn] *n* Ereván

**yes** [jes] **1** *n* sí *m*
**2** *adv* sí; **he said** *y.* dijo que sí; **didn't you hear me? – y., I did** ¿no me has oído? – sí; **y.?** *(to sb waiting to speak)* ¿sí?; *(answering phone)* ¿sí?, ¿diga?

**yes-man** ['jesmæn] *n* adulador(ora) *m,f*, cobista *mf*

**yesterday** ['jestədeɪ] **1** *n* ayer *m*
**2** *adv* ayer; **the day before y.** anteayer; **y. morning/evening** ayer por la mañana/por la tarde

**yet** [jet] **1** *adv* **(a)** *(still)* todavía, aún; **I haven't finished y.** todavía no he terminado; **don't go y.** no te vayas todavía; **I'll catch her y.!** ¡ya la atraparé!; **as y.** hasta ahora, por el momento; **not y.** todavía no; **y. again** una vez más; **y. more** aún más; **y. another mistake**

otro error más **(b)** *(in questions)* ya; **have they decided y.?** ¿han decidido ya?
**2** *conj* aunque, sin embargo; **small y. strong** pequeño aunque fuerte; **and y. I like him** y, sin embargo, me gusta

**yeti** ['jetɪ] *n* yeti *m*

**yew** [juː] *n* tejo *m*

**YHA** *(abbr* **Youth Hostels Association)** Asociación *f* de Albergues Juveniles

**Yiddish** ['jɪdɪʃ] *n & adj* yiddish *m*, yídish *m*

**yield** [jiːld] **1** *n (of field)* cosecha *f*; *(of mine, interest)* rendimiento *m*; *Fin (profit)* beneficio *m*
**2** *vt* **(a)** *(results, interest)* proporcionar; **to y. a profit** proporcionar beneficios **(b)** *(territory)* ceder; *(right)* conceder
**3** *vi (surrender)* rendirse *(to* a); **to y. to temptation** ceder a la tentación

**yippee** [jɪ'piː] *exclam* ¡yupi!, ¡viva!

**YMCA** [waɪemsiː'eɪ] *n (abbr* **Young Men's Christian Association)** ACJ *f*, Asociación *f* Cristiana de Jóvenes *(que regenta hostales económicos)*

**yob** [jɒb], **yobbo** ['jɒbəʊ] *n Fam* gamberro *m*

**yoga** ['jəʊgə] *n* yoga *m*

**yoghurt, yogurt** ['jɒgət] *n* yogur *m*

**yoke** [jəʊk] *n* **(a)** *(for oxen) & Fig* yugo *m* **(b)** *(for carrying)* balancín *m*
**2** *vt (oxen)* uncir (al yugo); *Fig* **to be yoked to…** estar uncido al yugo de…

**yokel** ['jəʊkəl] *n Pej* or *Hum* paleto(a) *m,f*

**yolk** [jəʊk] *n* yema *f* (de huevo)

**yonder** ['jɒndə(r)] *adv* **(over) y.** allá

**yonks** [jɒŋks] *npl Fam* **I haven't done that for y.** hace un montón de tiempo que no hago eso; **y. ago** hace la tira (de tiempo)

**you** [juː]

In Spanish, the formal form **usted** takes a third person singular verb and **ustedes** takes a third person plural verb. In many Latin American countries, **ustedes** is the standard form of the second person plural and is not considered formal.

*pron* **(a)** *(subject) (usually omitted in Spanish, except for contrast) (singular)* tú, *CSur* vos; *(plural)* vosotros(as); *(formal: singular)* usted; *(formal: plural)* ustedes; **y. seem angry** *(singular)* pareces enfadado; *(plural)* parecéis enfadados; *(formal: singular)* parece usted enfadado; *(formal: plural)* parecen ustedes enfadados; **have YOU got it?** *(singular)* ¿lo tienes tú?; *(plural)* ¿lo tenéis vosotros?; *(formal: singular)* ¿lo tiene usted?; *(formal: plural)* ¿lo tienen ustedes?
**(b)** *(direct object) (singular)* te; *(plural)* os; *(formal: singular)* lo *m*, la *f*; *(formal: plural)* los *mpl*, las *fpl*; **I can understand your son but not YOU** a tu hijo lo entiendo, pero a ti no
**(c)** *(indirect object) (singular)* te; *(plural)* os;

*(formal: singular)* le; *(formal: plural)* les; **I gave y. the book** te/os/le/les di el libro; **I told y.** *(singular)* te lo dije; *(plural)* os lo dije; *(formal: singular & plural)* se lo dije

(d) *(after preposition) (singular)* ti; *(plural)* vosotros(as); *(formal: singular)* usted; *(formal: plural)* ustedes; **I'm thinking of y.** *(singular)* pienso en ti; *(plural)* pienso en vosotros; *(formal: singular)* pienso en usted; *(formal: plural)* pienso en ustedes; **with y.** *(singular)* contigo

(e) *(impersonal)* **y. don't do that kind of thing** esas cosas no se hacen; **y. never know** nunca se sabe; **exercise is good for y.** es bueno hacer ejercicio; **y. have to be careful with him** hay que *or* uno tiene que tener cuidado con él

(f) *(as complement of verb* to be*)* **oh, it's y.!** ¡ah, eres tú!; **it was y. who did it** fuiste tú quien lo hiciste

(g) *(with interjections)* **poor old y.!** ¡pobrecito!; **y. idiot!** ¡idiota!; **don't y. forget!** ¡no te olvides!

(h) *(in apposition)* **y. men are all the same!** ¡todos los hombres sois iguales!

(i) *(with imperative)* **y. sit down here** tú siéntate aquí; **don't y. dare!** ¡ni se te ocurra!

**you'd** [ju:d] = **you had, you would**

**you-know-who** [ju:nəʊ'hu:] *n* **he was talking to y.** estaba hablando ya sabes con quién

**you'll** [ju:l] = **you will, you shall**

**young** [jʌŋ] **1** *npl* (a) *(people)* **the y.** los jóvenes (b) *(animals)* crías *fpl*

**2** *adj (person)* joven; *(appearance)* juvenil; **she's (two years) younger than me** es (dos años) menor que yo; **you're only y. once** sólo se es joven una vez en la vida; **y. man** (chico *m*) joven *m*; **y. woman** (chica *f*) joven *f*; **when I was a y. man** cuando era joven; **in his younger days** en su juventud; **the night is y.!** ¡la noche es joven!; **y. people** los jóvenes, la gente joven; **y. in spirit** *or* **at heart** joven de espíritu

**youngster** ['jʌŋstə(r)] *n* joven *mf*

**your** [jɔ:(r)] *possessive adj* (a) *(with singular possession)* tu; *(formal)* su; **y. house** tu/su casa; **y. books** tus/sus libros; **it wasn't YOUR idea!** ¡no fue idea tuya!

(b) *(with plural possession)* vuestro(a); *(formal)* su; **y. house** vuestra/su casa; **y. books** vuestros/sus libros; **it wasn't YOUR idea!** ¡no fue idea vuestra!

(c) *(for parts of body, clothes) (translated by definite article)* **did you hit y. head?** ¿te has dado un golpe en la cabeza?; **why did you put y. hand in y. pocket?** ¿por qué te has metido la mano en el bolsillo?

(d) *(impersonal)* **you should buy y. ticket first** hay que comprar el billete antes; **smok-** ing is bad for y. health el tabaco perjudica la salud; *Fam* **y. average Frenchman** el francés medio

**you're** [jɔ:(r)] = **you are**

**yours** [jɔ:z]

> In Spanish, the forms **tuyo(a)**, **suyo(a)** and **vuestro(a)** require a definite article in the singular and in the plural when they are the subject of the phrase.

*possessive pron* (a) *(of one person) (singular)* tuyo(a) *m,f*; *(plural)* tuyos(as) *m,fpl*; *(formal: singular)* suyo(a) *m,f*; *(formal: plural)* suyos(as) *m,fpl*; **my house is big but y. is bigger** mi casa es grande, pero la tuya/suya es mayor; **this book is y.** este libro es tuyo/suyo; **these books are y.** estos libros son tuyos/suyos; **a friend of y.?** un amigo tuyo/suyo; **where's that brother of y.?** ¿dónde anda ese hermano tuyo?; **y. (sincerely/faithfully)** atentamente

(b) *(of more than one person) (singular)* vuestro(a) *m,f*; *(plural)* vuestros(as) *m,fpl*; *(formal: singular)* suyo(a) *m,f*; *(formal: plural)* suyos(as) *m,fpl*; **this book is y.** este libro es vuestro/suyo; **these books are y.** estos libros son vuestros/suyos

**yourself** [jɔ:'self] *pron* (a) *(reflexive)* te; *(formal)* se; **have you hurt y.?** ¿te has hecho daño?; *(formal)* ¿se ha hecho daño?

(b) *(emphatic)* tú mismo *m*, tú misma *f*; *(formal)* usted mismo *m*, usted misma *f*; **did you do all the work y.?** ¿has hecho todo el trabajo tú solo?; *(formal)* ¿ha hecho todo el trabajo usted solo?; **you told me y.** me lo dijiste tú mismo; *(formal)* me lo dijo usted mismo; **you're not y. today** hoy no se te nota nada bien

(c) *(after preposition)* ti; *(formal)* usted; **did you do this by y.?** ¿lo has hecho tú solo?; *(formal)* ¿lo ha hecho usted solo?; **do you live by y.?** ¿vives solo?; **did you buy it for y.?** ¿te lo has comprado para ti?; *(formal)* ¿se lo ha comprado para usted?

**yourselves** [jɔ:'selvz] *pron* (a) *(reflexive)* os; *(formal)* se; **have you hurt y.?** ¿os habéis hecho daño?; *(formal)* ¿se han hecho daño?

(b) *(emphatic)* vosotros mismos *mpl*, vosotras mismas *fpl*; *(formal)* ustedes mismos *mpl*, ustedes mismas *fpl*; **did you do all the work y.?** ¿habéis hecho todo el trabajo vosotros solos?; *(formal)* ¿han hecho todo el trabajo ustedes solos?; **you told me y.** me lo dijisteis vosotros mismos; *(formal)* me lo dijeron ustedes mismos

(c) *(after preposition)* vosotros *mpl*, vosotras *fpl*; *(formal)* ustedes *mfpl*; **did you do this by y.?** ¿lo habéis hecho vosotros solos?; *(formal)* ¿lo han hecho ustedes solos?; **did you buy it for y.?** ¿os lo habéis comprado para vosotros?; *(formal)* ¿se lo han comprado para ustedes?;

**share the money among y.** repartíos el dinero

**youth** [ju:θ] *n* **(a)** *(period)* juventud *f*; **in his early y.** en su (primera) juventud **(b)** *(young man)* joven *m* **(c)** *(young people)* juventud *f*; **y. club** club *m* juvenil; **y. hostel** albergue *m* juvenil

**youthful** ['ju:θfʊl] *adj (person)* joven; *(looks, enthusiasm)* juvenil

**you've** [ju:v] = **you have**

**yowl** [jaʊl] **1** *n* aullido *m*, chillido *m*
**2** *vi* aullar, chillar

**yo-yo**® ['jəʊjəʊ] *(pl* **yo-yos**) *n* yoyó *m*

**yr** *(abbr* **year**) año *m*

**yuan** [ju:'æn] *n (Chinese currency)* yuan *m*

**yucca** ['jʌkə] *n* yuca *f*

**yuck** [jʌk] *exclam Fam* ¡puaj!, ¡aj!

**yucky** ['jʌkɪ] *adj Fam* asqueroso(a)

**Yugoslav** ['ju:gəʊslɑ:v] *n & adj* yugoslavo(a) *m,f*

**Yugoslavia** [ju:gəʊ'slɑ:vɪə] *n* Yugoslavia

**Yugoslavian** [ju:gəʊ'slɑ:vɪən] *adj* yugoslavo(a)

**yuletide** ['ju:ltaɪd] *n* Navidad *f*

**yummy** ['jʌmɪ] *adj Fam* rico(a)

**yuppie** ['jʌpɪ] *n* yupi *mf*; **a y. restaurant** un restaurante de yupis; *Fam* **y. flu** la gripe del yupi *(encefalomielitis miálgica)*

**YWCA** [waɪdʌbəlju:si:'eɪ] *n (abbr* **Young Women's Christian Association**) ACJ *f*, Asociación *f* Cristiana de Jóvenes *(que regenta hostales económicos)*

# Z

**Z, z** [zed, *US* zi:] *n (letter)* Z, z *f*

**Zaire** [zɑ:'ɪə(r)] *n Formerly* Zaire

**Zairean** [zɑ:'ɪərɪən] *n & adj* zaireño(a) *m,f*

**Zambia** ['zæmbɪə] *n* Zambia

**Zambian** ['zæmbɪən] *n & adj* zambiano(a) *m,f*

**zany** ['zeɪnɪ] *adj* estrafalario(a)

**zap** [zæp] *(pt & pp* **zapped**) *Fam vt* **(a)** *(destroy, disable)* fulminar **(b)** *Comptr (delete)* borrar

**zapper** ['zæpə(r)] *n Fam (TV remote control)* mando *m* a distancia, telemando *m*

**zeal** [zi:l] *n* celo *m*

**zealot** ['zelət] *n* fanático(a) *m,f*

**zealous** ['zeləs] *adj* celoso(a)

**zebra** ['zi:brə, 'zebrə] *n* cebra *f*; *Br Aut* **z. crossing** paso *m* de cebra

**zenith** ['zenɪθ] *n Astron & Fig* cenit *m*; **she was at the z. of her influence** su influencia estaba en el punto más alto

**zephyr** ['zefə(r)] *n* céfiro *m*

**zero** ['zɪərəʊ] **1** *n (pl* **zeros**) cero *m*; **22 degrees below z.** 22 grados bajo cero
**2** *adj Fam* nulo(a); **to have z. charm** no tener el más mínimo encanto
**3** *vi to* **z. in on sth** apuntar hacia algo

**zero-rated** ['zɪərəʊreɪtɪd] *adj Fin (for VAT)* con una tasa de IVA del 0%

**zest** [zest] *n* **(a)** *(enjoyment)* goce *m*, deleite *m* **(b)** *Culin (of orange, lemon)* piel *f*, cáscara *f*

**zigzag** ['zɪgzæg] **1** *n* zigzag *m*
**2** *vi (pt & pp* **zigzagged**) zigzaguear

**zilch** [zɪltʃ] *n Fam* nada de nada; **there's z. on TV** no hay nada de nada en la tele

**Zimbabwe** [zɪm'bɑ:bweɪ] *n* Zimbabue

**Zimbabwean** [zɪm'bɑ:bweɪən] *n & adj* zimbabuense *mf*, zimbabuo(a) *m,f*

**zinc** [zɪŋk] *n* cinc *m*, zinc *m*

**Zionism** ['zaɪənɪzəm] *n* sionismo *m*

**Zionist** ['zaɪənɪst] *n & adj* sionista *mf*

**zip** [zɪp] **1** *n* **(a)** *Br* **z. (fastener)** cremallera *f* **(b)** *Fam (vigour)* nervio *m*, brío *m* **(c)** *US* **z. code** código *m* postal
**2** *vi (pt & pp* **zipped**) **to z. past** *(of car, bullet)* pasar zumbando
▶**zip through** *vt insep Fam* **I zipped through the last chapters** me cepillé en un momento los últimos capítulos
▶**zip up 1** *vt sep (clothes)* cerrar la cremallera de
**2** *vi* cerrarse con cremallera

**zipper** ['zɪpə(r)] *n US* cremallera *f*

**zippy** ['zɪpɪ] *adj Fam* animado(a)

**zither** ['zɪðə(r)] *n Mus* cítara *f*

**zodiac** ['zəʊdɪæk] *n* zodiaco *m*, zodíaco *m*

**zombie** ['zombɪ] *n* zombi *mf*

**zone** [zəʊn] **1** *n* zona *f*
**2** *vt (town, area)* dividir en zonas

**zonked (out)** [zɒŋkt('aʊt)] *adj Fam* to be z. *(exhausted)* estar molido(a) *or* hecho(a) polvo; *(drugged)* estar colocado(a); *(drunk)* estar mamado(a) *or* pedo

**zoo** [zu:] (*pl* **zoos**) *n* zoo *m*, zoológico *m*

**zoological** [zʊə'lɒdʒɪkəl] *adj* zoológico(a); **z. garden(s)** parque *m* zoológico

**zoologist** [zʊ'ɒlədʒɪst] *n* zoólogo(a) *m,f*

**zoology** [zʊ'ɒlədʒɪ] *n* zoología *f*

**zoom** [zu:m] **1** *n* (a) *(noise)* zumbido *m* (b) *Phot* **z. lens** zoom *m*

  **2** *vi* to **z. along/past** ir/pasar zumbando *or* a toda velocidad

►**zoom in** *vi Cin TV* enfocar en primer plano

**zucchini** [zu:'ki:nɪ] (*pl* **zucchini** *or* **zucchinis**) *n US* calabacín *m*

**Zulu** ['zu:lu:] *n & adj* zulú *mf*